The
AMERICAN
EPHEMERIS
1950-2050
at Noon

Trans-Century Edition

Neil F. Michelsen
and
Rique Pottenger

The American Ephemeris, 1950-2050 at Noon
Trans-Century Edition

© 1982, 1988 by Neil F. Michelsen
© 1997, 2001, 2004, 2005, 2007, 2010, 2011 The Michelsen-Simms Family Trust

First Edition
First printing 2011

Compiled and programmed by Neil F. Michelsen and Rique Pottenger

Cover by Maria Kay Simms
The mandala used on the cover is Jupiter-Uranus, Figure 41, of the computer plotted orbital patterns of the two planets by Neil F. Michelsen for his book, *Tables of Planetary Phenomena*.

ISBN 978-1-934976-27-2

Library of Congress Control Number: 2011905035

Published by ACS Publications, an imprint of Starcrafts LLC
PO Box 466, Exeter, NH 03833
334-A Calef Highway, Epping, NH 03042
http://www.acspublications.com
http://www.starcraftspublishing.com
http://www.astrocom.com

Printed in the United States of America

Introduction to the *Trans-Century Edition* of *The American Ephemeris 1950-2050 at Noon*

by Maria Kay Simms,
with technical assistance from Rique Pottenger

This new *Trans-Century Edition* of *The American Ephemeris* is in response to multiple requests for one "century" ephemeris that would span the "most useful years" of both 20th and 21st centuries. Richard Tarnas, who was the first to suggest that we publish an ephemeris for 1950-2050, pointed out that when traveling, he would like to be able to tote just one ephemeris for quick and easy lookups of both birth positions and future transits for the majority of people he might meet. Then later, David Roell of Astrology Center of America, contacted me after he received customer requests for just one book spanning the years from mid 20th to mid 21st centuries. It was David who suggested the "Trans-Century" name for the edition, and so it shall be, in both midnight and noon versions.

Of course many of our younger colleagues may be thinking, "Why bother? We can do our quick lookups by computer. Yes, these days we all can—although I think I'm far from the only pre-1950 born elder who would bet that in a race—book vs. computer—we could flip to our target date in our book ephemeris faster than our challenger could log onto a computer and find the same information online, or within astrological software. And, even if that race proved to be only a matter of seconds in difference as to who "won," we who have the book will have definitely "gotcha" if the power is ever out or the batteries running your phone or laptop die. Books are always worth having, preserving and valuing through the ages.

A Brief History of Publication of *The American Ephemeris*

Since the 1976 first edition of *The American Ephemeris, 1931-1980*, *The American Ephemeris for the 20th Century, 1900 to 2000* has been published in successive Midnight and Noon editions, each with revisions according to the latest and most accurate orbital data available. Since 1988, files and algorithms from Jet Propulsion Laboratory export ephemeris files have been used. Specialty versions have included *The American Heliocentric Ephemeris* and *The American Sidereal Ephemeris*.

In 1982 Neil F. Michelsen published his first 21st century ephemeris. *The American Ephemeris for the 21st Century at Midnight*. This first edition included the entire century in a relatively small first printing, but at that time many users were simply not quite ready to look so very far into the future, and expressed to Neil their preference for a lighter and less costly option. In response, Neil programmed and published the popular 2000-2050 versions which have now been reprinted many times over two decades.

Neil was always adamant that subsequent printings of his ephemerides be updated when new data became available. Several years after his 1990 passing, in 1997, newer data called for an update, so ACS published Expanded Second Editions of the two 2000-2050 books with revisions by Rique Pottenger.

The New American Ephemeris

In 2005, I proposed (as Trustee of The Michelsen-Simms Family Trust) that a new revision of *The American Ephemeris for the 21st Century* needed to be done, and that it was time once again to expand it to the entire century. ACS declined to publish the new version, but provided a letter of permission for the Trust and Rique Pottenger to produce and publish a new full 21st century ephemeris using the Michelsen programming routines and the name "American Ephemeris" within its title. Subsequently, *The New American Ephemeris for the 21st Century, 2000-2100 at Midnight, Michelsen Memorial Edition,* compiled and programmed by Rique Pottenger, based on the earlier work of Neil F. Michelsen, was published in 2006 by Starcrafts Publishing, the imprint of Starcrafts LLC, a business that I had formed in New Hampshire. That volume is unique among the *American Ephemeris* series in that it includes a text section, partially in Neil's own writing and partially in the testimonials of others, that traces the early development of computer technology for astrologers, and Neil's contributions to it.

For this new full 21st century ephemeris, Pottenger obtained the most current Jet Propulsion Laboratory data, utilized programming refinements not available earlier and added various new features, the most of obvious of which were the inclusion of the two newly named "dwarf planets," Eris and Ceres, in response to the 2006 decisions of the International Astronomical Union in regard to the planets in our solar system.

Later in 2006 and in 2007, with Pottenger's continued work in providing updated files, Starcrafts Publishing received permission from ACS, Inc., to publish new editions of various other versions of the Michelsen ephemeris series, including the sidereal, heliocentric and midpoint ephemerides. Finally in 2008, the Michelsen-Simms Trust was able to regain full rights to the entire *American Ephemeris* series, and Starcrafts LLC acquired the asssets of the former Astro Communications Services, Inc. Now with the full right to use the original titles and imprint, we published the midnight and noon editions of the two 2000-2050 ephemerides as *The American Ephemeris* with the imprint ACS Publications, and with Neil F. Michelsen and Rique Pottenger as co-authors, and have done the same with this new Trans-Century Edition.

New Features in the Revised Editions of *The American Ephemeris* series

The Status and Positions of Pluto, Eris and Ceres

In 2006, the International Astronomical Union announced a redefinition of planet that is basically:

- a body that orbits around the Sun (or a star)
- has sufficient mass for its self-gravity to overcome rigid body forces so that it assumes an equilibrium (or to put it more simply, a nearly round shape)
- "has cleared the neighborhood" around its orbit

By that definition, IAU decided that Pluto could no longer be called a planet—and likely nothing else beyond Neptune would qualify either. Pluto occupies a region of the Universe called the Kuiper Belt that is apparently rife with icy rocks.

A new category of "dwarf planet" was created to include Pluto and a new planet beyond Pluto that when found to be larger than Pluto, was initially heralded as a new planet after discovery by astronomer Michael Brown of California Institute of Technology in July of 2005. The newcomer, at first nicknamed Xena by Brown, was on September 13, 2006, officially named for Eris, the Greek Goddess of Discord. Brown was quoted as saying the name was "too perfect to resist." It fit well the discord among astronomers that led to this decision (and reportedly still exists, particularly among some who were not present at the IAU meeting).

Then, during that 2006 IAU meeting, it was also decided to promote Ceres, the largest of the asteroids orbiting between Mars and Jupiter, to the new dwarf planet category. Ceres had briefly been thought a planet upon her discovery in 1801, until so many more bodies were also found orbiting nearby that the new category of asteroid was devised for them, thus the "asteroid belt."

We waited for IAU decisions in the summer of 2006, along with anxious school textbook publishers. We knew well that astrologers would never demote Pluto, no matter what the astronomers termed him to be, so we decided that the thing to do was to leave Pluto in his usual column of daily longitude positions, and to add Ceres in her own column between Mars and Jupiter. In order to avoid further expanding the book size or reducing the type size, Eris, orbiting so far beyond Pluto that her positions vary at most only a very few minutes from one month to the next, is listed with her monthly positions in the Astro Data box at lower right of each page.

Since 2006, more "dwarfs" have been discovered in the Kuiper Belt, and it is to be expected that more will be, perhaps many more. The astronomers have decided on a new term to define the subset of dwarf planets beyond Neptune. These are now called Plutoids, in honor of Pluto. We might also think of this as some sort of consolation prize—an apology for his demotion. But the page size of the ephemeris is limited, so it seems best at this time to include bodies such as Chiron and the asteroids that are in wide general use, rather than newly discovered Plutoids. When more decisive data and demand emerges, a Plutoid ephemeris is possible.

At the beginning of this publication year of 2011, news stories emerged questioning whether or not Eris is truly larger than Pluto. Sizes apparently can vary depending upon how much ice is present at a given time. Also it has been questioned whether Neptune, should also be demoted, since Pluto does, within its very lengthy orbit of our Sun, move inside the orbit of Neptune. So, by the IAU definition, Neptune, too, fails to clear its orbital "neighborhood. " So, we may not yet have heard the final verdict on the status of Pluto, Neptune, Eris and Ceres. In any case, it is clear that the choice of the Goddess of Discord for the name of the new planet that precipitated all this was quite apt.

Other New Features

Rique has rewritten the computer generating program to a great extent. The program is now Windows based, making it considerably easier to use. One advantage to this new version is that it enables checking for double ingresses that occur on the same day. One was found in December 2007. The Node crosses from Pisces to Aquarius, goes direct, and crosses back into Pisces on the same day. The old ephemeris generating program did not check for this detail, so the prior edition only shows the next ingress into Aquarius, which comes three days later.

Some station times will also be shown as slightly different from prior versions of the ephemeris, due to the new program's improvements in calculation.

A significantly more accurate formula has been obtained for the Galactic Center, so it too will show as slightly different from prior editions of this ephemeris.

Phenomena in the far left Astro Data column are sorted by time as well as date. In the previous ACS publication, they were not sorted by time, so if two events occurred on the same day, the later one might be higher in the column.

Planetary Ingress data includes R after the sign if the planet is retrograde when it ingresses.

General Information

This ephemeris, spanning one-half of the 20th and one-half of the 21st centuries, is based on UT (universal time) throughout. In prior volumes *The American Ephemeris for the 20th Century* is based on UT, while the *The American Ephemeris for the 21st Century* is based on ET (ephemeris time). A uniform measurement of time is required for the calculation of planetary positions because the Earth's rotation is too irregular to be used for this purpose, even though our clocks are synchronized to that rotation. Various disturbances such as tidal coupling with the Moon or earthquakes cause Earth to either speed up or slow down. Our clocks are adjusted to the changing speed of the Earth by the addition of a "leap second" such as was done on June 30, 1982. We are now adding leap seconds, rather than subtracting, since Earth's rotation is slowing slightly, causing the civil day to become very slightly longer.

The difference between ET and UT is called Delta T. In order to calculate the most accurate horoscopes, primarily for solar and lunar returns, the time of the chart must be adjusted by adding Delta T to the UT of the chart before interpolating to find the planetary positions. It is not feasible to predict so far in advance into the 21st century what the Delta T values will be, so this is why the 21st century ephemerides have previously been based on ET.

In deciding what to do with this first ephemeris that spans from the mid 20th century to the mid-21st century, Rique decided to use UT and to add a special algorithm that would compensate the Delta T for the 21st century positions. This will eliminate the need to include Delta T in the use of this ephemeris for calculating planetary positions for the 21st century dates.

Accuracy of Planetary Positions

Successive editions of the ephemeris differ slightly from earlier versions because of increased accuracy of data available from the Jet Propulsion Laboratory (JPL). Since 1984, JPL data has been used in *The Astronomical Almanac*, a joint publication of the US Naval Observatory and the Royal Greenwich Observatory. Differences are so small that they will show up mainly in the times of aspects, sign ingresses, 0 declinations and stations that appear in the phenomena section at the bottom of each page. The most dramatic changes are seen in a few void-of-course Moon times where an aspect time that previously started the void period shifts to just after the Moon enters a new sign, so that an earlier aspect becomes the determining time for the beginning of the void Moon.

Positions of Chiron are determined by numerical integration using elements from the *Soviet Asteroid Ephemeris*. The integration program is an adaptation of the A.P.A.E. Volume XXII procedure as implemented by Mark Pottenger.

All positions are apparent, meaning they are corrected for light time. For example, the light from the Sun takes 8-1/2 minutes to reach the Earth, and in that time the Sun moves about 20.5" (seconds of arc). So the Sun's apparent position is 20.5" less than the geometric one.

Finally, the planet positions are transformed to the ecliptic of date, which means that precession and nutation (the wobble of the Earth on its axis) are applied.

Eclipses

The solar and lunar eclipses were recalculated by using JPL data. Because of the accuracy of this data, it was justifiable to list the duration of the geocentric maximum of total and annular solar eclipses to the second of time. This edition identifies six different types of solar eclipses. Since the method of calculation is improved over editions published prior to 1997, solar eclipse times may be up to several minutes more accurate. See **Key to the Phenomena Section** for further explanation.

Additional Features

Sun and Moon positions are given to the nearest second of arc; all other positions to the nearest tenth of a minute. Because of its irregular movement, the True Node of Moon is listed daily. The Mean Node of Moon is listed once each month.

Direct/Retrograde indicators are given on the day that the planet goes direct or retrograde. Look in the far left Astro Data section at the bottom of the page for the exact ET time of the station. If the planet's station is marked D, those persons born prior to that time have the planet retrograde; after that time, direct.

Phenomena sections for each month give all lunar phases, solar and lunar eclipses, stations, ingresses, outer planet aspects, planetary crossings of the celestial equator and void-of-course Moon data. See **Key to the Phenomena Section** for details.

Key to the Phenomena Section

The phenomena data at the bottom of each page is listed in six sections, counting from left to right. Within sections 1, 2, 5 and 6, the first month is normally separated from the second month by a blank line, unless there are too many lines of phenomena, in which case, the blank line is removed, and users must look at the day numbers to see when one month ends and another starts (see Sep-Oct 2009). Also, overflow from the leftmost section appears in the bottom of the next to the leftmost section (see Jul-Aug 2010). All sections except Section 6 list the astrological events by day, hour and minute of occurrence, with the headings of these three columns shown as Dy Hr Mn. Illustrated examples of each section follow:

Section 1: Astro Data provides three types of information:

- **Stations** are indicated by a planet glyph followed by D or R, indicating whether the planet is direct or retrograde.

- Planets at 0° **Declination** are indicated by a planet glyph, a zero and N or S indicating whether the planet is moving North or South as it crosses the celestial equator.

- **Aspects** between the **Outer** planets, Jupiter through Pluto.

Astro Data			
		Dy	Hr Mn
☽ 0 S		2	16 : 38
☿ R		4	19 : 35
♃ D		6	7 : 19
☽ 0 N		15	23 : 56
♃ ∠ ♀		25	4 : 55
☿ D		29	0 : 40
☽ 0 S		29	23 : 11
♄ ⊼ ♅		1	4 : 23
☽ 0 N		12	7 : 12
☽ 0 S		26	5 : 23
♃ △ ♅		29	9 : 14
♄ ⚹ ♆		31	9 : 55

Section 1

Planet Ingresses		
	Dy	Hr Mn
☿ ♋	10	20 : 19
♀ ♋	19	2 : 35
♂ ♋	22	18 : 54
☉ ♌	22	23 : 19
☿ ♌	11	4 : 11
♀ ♌	11	20 : 40
☉ ♍	23	6 : 24
☿ ♍	27	19 : 32

Section 2

Section 2: Planetary Ingress Table

This table shows the day and time each planet enters a new sign of the zodiac.

Sections 3–4: Void ☽

Void of Course ☽ data for the first month is shown in Section 3, and the second month is shown in Section 4. The Void period starts with the last major aspect (☌⚹□△☍) to ☽ whose day, hour and minute are given, and ends when ☽ enters the next sign indicated by the sign glyph plus the day, hour and minute of entry. The Void period may begin in the preceding month. Ceres has not been added to the Void-of-Course data. Pluto remains, as before.

Section 3

Last Aspect Dy Hr Mn		☽ Ingress Dy Hr Mn
2 6:59	♇□♎	2 17:07
4 19:18	♇⚹♏	5 5:14
6 19:55	♂□♐	7 14:15
9 10:32	♇☌♑	9 19:26
11 20:59	☿☍♒	11 21:47
13 14:24	♇⚹♓	13 23:01
15 19:57	☿△♈	16 0:40
18 1:34	♀⚹♉	18 3:45
20 5:49	♂□♊	20 8:39
22 15:18	♂⚹♋	22 15:29
24 9:08	☿☌♌	25 0:26
27 0:33	♇△♍	27 11:37
29 13:07	♇□♎	30 0:28

Section 4

Last Aspect Dy Hr Mn		☽ Ingress Dy Hr Mn
1 1:55	♇⚹♏	1 13:09
3 9:09	☿△♐	3 23:14
5 19:23	♇☌♑	6 5:21
8 1:45	☿☍♒	8 7:48
9 23:00	♇⚹♓	10 8:11
12 7:07	♀△♈	12 8:23
14 0:15	♇△♉	14 10:01
16 1:52	☉□♊	16 14:08
18 12:31	☉⚹♋	18 21:04
20 7:07	♂⚹♌	21 6:34
23 6:20	♇△♍	23 18:09
25 19:09	♇□♎	26 7:02
28 8:03	♇⚹♏	28 19:57
30 20:43	♂⚹♐	31 7:01

☽ Phases & Eclipses Dy Hr Mn	
7 18:43	○ 15♓00
7 18:52	☍ P 0.184
14 11:16	☾ 21♊30
22 11:46	● 29♍20
22 11:41:16	☌ A 0.184
30 11:05	☽ 7♑09
7 3:14	○ 13♈43
14 0:27	☾ 20♊31
22 5:15	● 28♎40
29 21:26	☽ 6♒19

Section 5: Moon Phases and Eclipses

This box contains **Moon Phases** and **Eclipse** data. The day, hour, minute and zodiacal position of the Moon is given for each.

- ● New Moon
- ☽ FirstQuarter Moon
- ○ Full Moon
- ☾ Third Quarter Moon

Shown at left is the Section 5 data box showing Moon phases and Eclipses for both months on an ephemeris page. Note the extra symbols included in the upper month. An eclipse symbol following a phase symbol means an eclipse occurred on the day of that phase. The time and type of the eclipse are on the line below the Moon phase.

☍ indicates a **Lunar Eclipse**. The three types of lunar eclipses are indicated as follows:

A = an Appulse, a penumbral eclipse where Moon enters only the penumbra of Earth.

P = a Partial eclipse, where Moon enters the umbra without being totally immersed in it.

T = a Total eclipse, where Moon is entirely immersed within the umbra.

The time of greatest obscuration is given. This, in general, is not the exact time of the opposition in longitude. The magnitude of the lunar eclipse, which is the fraction of Moon's diameter obscured by the shadow of Earth at the greatest phase, is also given.

☌ = a **Solar Eclipse**. The six types are:

P = a **Partial** eclipse where Moon does not completely cover the solar disk.

T = a **Total** eclipse where Moon completely covers the solar disk, as seen from a shadow path on Earth's surface.

A = an **Annular** eclipse is "total," but Moon is too far from Earth for the apex of its shadow to reach Earth's surface. Thus Moon will not entirely hide Sun, and a narrow ring of light will surround the dark New Moon.

AT = an **Annular-Total** eclipse, total for part of the path, annular for the rest.

A non-C = a rare **Annular** eclipse where the central line does not touch Earth's surface.

T non-C = a rare **Total** eclipse where the central line does not touch Earth's surface.

The time of greatest eclipse is given to the second, which, in general, is not the exact time of conjunction in longitude. For perfect eclipses the magnitude is given; for total and annular ones, the duration in minutes and seconds is given.

Section 6: Monthly Positions

This box contains six items of Astro Data for each of the two months on the page, with a blank line separating the two months.

Beginning with the first line of the top month, a numbered identification of each line follows:

1. First day of the month for the phenomena given.

2. **The Julian Day** is the count of the number of days elapsed since December 31, 1899, at Greenwich Noon. January 1, 1900, is Julian Day 1; January 1, 1901, is Julian Day 366, etc. This information can be used to calculate the midpoint in time between two events. For the astronomical Julian Day number counted from January 1, 4713 BC, add 2,415,020 to the number given for noon on the first day of the month.

```
           Astro Data
1 January 2010
Julian Day # 40178
SVP 5⌓06'56"
GC   26✗58.7    ♀  7♏57.4
Eris 20♈55.4R   ⚹  4♈37.6
⚷    23♒08.6    ⚥  6♈38.3
☽ Mean ☊ 21♑36.5

1 February 2010
Julian Day # 40209
SVP 5⌓06'50"
GC   26✗58.8    ♀ 17♏24.5
Eris 20♈58.4    ⚹ 18♈36.0
⚷    25♒08.4    ⚥  3♍32.6R
☽ Mean ☊ 19♑58.0
```

Section 6

3. **SVP** (the **Synetic Vernal Point**) is the tropical 0° point in the sidereal zodiac, as defined by Cyril Fagan. The tropical and sidereal zodiacs coincided in AD 231 and have diverged at the rate of one degree every 71-1/2 years as the tropical zodiac's starting point continues its retrograde movement on the ecliptic because of the precession of the equinoxes. Tropical positions are converted to sidereal by adding the degree, minutes and seconds of the SVP to the tropical longitude and subtracting one sign.

4. The **monthly position** of the **Galactic Center** is given, using the longitude of Sagittarius A. As was explained earlier, the position will differ somewhat from prior editions due to a significantly more accurate formula for its calculation.

5. A **monthly position** for very slowly moving **Eris** is listed by her name. Next listed is **Chiron** ⚷ and the 3 major asteroids in general use by astrologers, **Pallas** ♀, **Vesta** ⚹, and **Juno** ⚥. Originally, **Ceres** ⚳ was listed here with the asteroids, but now that she is a "dwarf" planet, and fast moving, she has been moved into planetary order with a column showing her daily positions.

6. The mean position for Moon's North Node is given. Explanation follows:

The **Mean Lunar Node** (☽ Mean ☊) is so regular in its motion that it can be accurately calculated for any day in the month for noon from the position given in this section for the first day of the month.

☽ Mean ☊ Interpolation			
2	3.2'	17	50.8'
3	6.4'	18	54.0'
4	9.5'	19	57.2'
5	12.7'	20	1° 0.4'
6	15.9'	21	1° 3.5'
7	19.1'	22	1° 7.7'
8	22.2'	23	1° 9.9'
9	25.4'	23	1°13.1'
10	28.6'	25	1°16.2'
11	31.8'	26	1°19.4'
12	34.9'	27	1°22°6'
13	38.1'	28	1°25.8'
14	41.3'	29	1°29.9'
15	44.5'	30	1°32.1'
16	47.7'	31	1°35.3'

Mean Node Interpolation Table

Use the Mean Node Interpolation Table to correct the monthly positon given in Section 6 to be accurate for the current day.   Enter the table using the day of the month for which you want the mean Node. The minutes, or degrees and minutes, obtained must then be subtracted from the first of the month position.

Example: birthday of February 16, 2001: Moon's Mean Node position on that date (as given at the bottom right of the ephemeris page) is 14 ♋ 02.6. Entering the Mean ☊ Interpolation table at 16 gives 47.7'. So, 14° ♋ 2.6 –47.7' = 13° ♋14.9.

Key to the Glyphs

☉	Sun		●	New Moon
☽	Moon		☽	First Quarter Moon
☿	Mercury		○	Full Moon
♀	Venus		☾	Third Quarter Moon
♂	Mars			
⚳	Ceres		♂	Solar Eclipse
♃	Jupiter		☍	Lunar Eclipse
♄	Saturn			
♅	Uranus			
♆	Neptune			
♇	Pluto			
☊	Moon's Node			
	Eris			
⚷	Chiron			
⚴	Pallas			
⚵	Juno			
⚶	Vesta			

♈	Aries	♂	0° conjunction
♉	Taurus	⚺	30° semisextile
♊	Gemini	∠	45° semisquare
♋	Cancer		(or octile)
♌	Leo	✶	60° sextile
♍	Virgo	□	90° square
♎	Libra	△	120° trine
♏	Scorpio	⚼	135° sesquisquare
♐	Sagittarius		(or tri-octile)
♑	Capricorn	⚻	150° quincunx
♒	Aquarius	☍	180° opposition
♓	Pisces		

LONGITUDE — January 1950

Day	Sid.Time	☉	0 hr ☽	Noon ☽	True ☊	☿	♀	♂	⚳	♃	♄	♅	♆	♇
1 Su	18 42 16	10♑30 52	1♊24 56	7♊32 40	12♈28.8	29♑58.3	17♒09.1	2♎23.7	24♏52.9	6♒37.1	19♍26.1	2♋39.7	17♎16.3	17♌47.4
2 M	18 46 13	11 32 00	13 44 08	19 59 30	12R 17.4	0♒57.1	17 28.4	2 45.4	25 16.4	6 50.6	19R 25.8	2R 37.1	17 16.8	17R 46.3
3 Tu	18 50 09	12 33 09	26 18 54	2♋42 20	12 04.1	1 49.5	17 45.7	3 06.8	25 39.7	7 04.2	19 25.4	2 34.6	17 17.4	17 45.2
4 W	18 54 06	13 34 17	9♋09 47	15 41 06	11 50.1	2 34.9	18 00.8	3 27.9	26 03.0	7 17.9	19 24.9	2 32.1	17 17.9	17 44.1
5 Th	18 58 03	14 35 26	22 16 05	28 54 32	11 36.7	3 12.2	18 13.8	3 48.6	26 26.2	7 31.6	19 24.2	2 29.6	17 18.4	17 42.9
6 F	19 01 59	15 36 34	5♌36 08	12♌20 36	11 25.1	3 40.5	18 24.6	4 09.0	26 49.2	7 45.3	19 23.5	2 27.1	17 18.8	17 41.7
7 Sa	19 05 56	16 37 42	19 07 38	25 56 58	11 16.3	3 59.0	18 33.1	4 29.0	27 12.2	7 59.1	19 22.6	2 24.6	17 19.2	17 40.6
8 Su	19 09 52	17 38 50	2♍48 18	9♍41 27	11 10.5	4R 06.8	18 39.2	4 48.6	27 35.1	8 12.9	19 21.7	2 22.1	17 19.6	17 39.4
9 M	19 13 49	18 39 59	16 36 13	23 32 27	11 07.6	4 03.4	18 43.0	5 07.8	27 57.8	8 26.7	19 20.6	2 19.6	17 19.9	17 38.2
10 Tu	19 17 45	19 41 07	0♎30 04	7♎29 00	11 06.8	3 48.3	18R 44.4	5 26.6	28 20.5	8 40.6	19 19.4	2 17.2	17 20.2	17 36.9
11 W	19 21 42	20 42 15	14 29 11	21 30 36	11 06.8	3 21.4	18 43.3	5 45.1	28 43.0	8 54.5	19 18.1	2 14.8	17 20.5	17 35.7
12 Th	19 25 38	21 43 24	28 33 11	5♏36 51	11 06.2	2 42.8	18 39.8	6 03.1	29 05.5	9 08.5	19 16.7	2 12.4	17 20.7	17 34.4
13 F	19 29 35	22 44 32	12♏41 31	19 46 57	11 03.9	1 53.4	18 33.8	6 20.7	29 27.8	9 22.4	19 15.2	2 10.0	17 20.9	17 33.2
14 Sa	19 33 32	23 45 40	26 52 56	3♐59 08	10 58.8	0 54.3	18 25.2	6 37.9	29 50.0	9 36.5	19 13.6	2 07.6	17 21.1	17 31.9
15 Su	19 37 28	24 46 48	11♐05 08	18 10 27	10 50.9	29♑47.1	18 14.2	6 54.6	0♐12.1	9 50.5	19 11.9	2 05.3	17 21.2	17 30.6
16 M	19 41 25	25 47 56	25 14 33	2♑16 51	10 40.4	28 33.9	18 00.7	7 10.9	0 34.1	10 04.6	19 10.1	2 03.0	17 21.3	17 29.3
17 Tu	19 45 21	26 49 04	9♑16 45	16 13 38	10 28.3	27 16.9	17 44.7	7 26.7	0 56.0	10 18.7	19 08.2	2 00.7	17 21.4	17 28.0
18 W	19 49 18	27 50 11	23 06 57	29 56 11	10 15.8	25 58.6	17 26.3	7 42.1	1 17.7	10 32.8	19 06.2	1 58.5	17R 21.4	17 26.6
19 Th	19 53 14	28 51 17	6♒40 54	13♒20 47	10 04.3	24 41.4	17 05.5	7 56.9	1 39.4	10 46.9	19 04.0	1 56.2	17 21.4	17 25.3
20 F	19 57 11	29 52 23	19 55 35	26 25 12	9 54.8	23 27.4	16 42.5	8 11.3	2 00.8	11 01.1	19 01.8	1 54.0	17 21.4	17 24.0
21 Sa	20 01 07	0♒53 28	2♓49 40	9♓09 05	9 47.9	22 18.8	16 17.3	8 25.1	2 22.2	11 15.3	18 59.5	1 51.8	17 21.3	17 22.6
22 Su	20 05 04	1 54 31	15 23 42	21 33 50	9 43.8	21 16.9	15 50.0	8 38.5	2 43.4	11 29.5	18 57.1	1 49.7	17 21.2	17 21.2
23 M	20 09 01	2 55 34	27 39 54	3♈42 25	9D 42.1	20 22.8	15 20.9	8 51.3	3 04.5	11 43.7	18 54.6	1 47.6	17 21.0	17 19.8
24 Tu	20 12 57	3 56 36	9♈41 56	15 39 02	9 42.0	19 37.4	14 49.9	9 03.6	3 25.5	11 57.9	18 52.0	1 45.5	17 20.8	17 18.5
25 W	20 16 54	4 57 37	21 34 24	27 28 40	9R 42.6	19 01.0	14 17.4	9 15.3	3 46.3	12 12.2	18 49.3	1 43.4	17 20.6	17 17.1
26 Th	20 20 50	5 58 37	3♉22 33	9♉16 44	9 42.8	18 33.7	13 43.5	9 26.5	4 06.9	12 26.4	18 46.5	1 41.4	17 20.4	17 15.7
27 F	20 24 47	6 59 35	15 11 55	21 08 46	9 41.5	18 15.3	13 08.5	9 37.2	4 27.5	12 40.7	18 43.6	1 39.4	17 20.1	17 14.2
28 Sa	20 28 43	8 00 33	27 07 56	3♊10 01	9 38.2	18D 05.4	12 32.5	9 47.3	4 47.9	12 55.0	18 40.6	1 37.5	17 19.8	17 12.8
29 Su	20 32 40	9 01 29	9♊15 37	15 25 12	9 32.4	18 03.8	11 55.9	9 56.8	5 08.1	13 09.3	18 37.6	1 35.6	17 19.4	17 11.4
30 M	20 36 36	10 02 25	21 39 14	27 58 02	9 24.4	18 09.7	11 18.8	10 05.7	5 28.2	13 23.6	18 34.4	1 33.7	17 19.1	17 10.0
31 Tu	20 40 33	11 03 19	4♋21 52	10♋50 53	9 14.7	18 22.8	10 41.5	10 13.9	5 48.1	13 37.9	18 31.2	1 31.9	17 18.7	17 08.6

LONGITUDE — February 1950

Day	Sid.Time	☉	0 hr ☽	Noon ☽	True ☊	☿	♀	♂	⚳	♃	♄	♅	♆	♇
1 W	20 44 30	12♒04 12	17♋25 06	24♋04 28	9♈04.3	18♑42.5	10♒04.4	10♎21.6	6♐07.9	13♒52.2	18♍27.9	1♋30.1	17♎18.2	17♌07.1
2 Th	20 48 26	13 05 03	0♌48 47	7♌37 44	8R 54.2	19 08.3	9R 27.6	10 28.7	6 27.5	14 06.5	18R 24.5	1R 28.3	17R 17.7	17R 05.7
3 F	20 52 23	14 05 54	14 30 58	21 27 58	8 45.5	19 39.6	8 51.4	10 35.1	6 47.0	14 20.8	18 21.1	1 26.6	17 17.2	17 04.3
4 Sa	20 56 19	15 06 43	28 28 15	5♍31 12	8 38.9	20 15.9	8 16.1	10 40.9	7 06.3	14 35.1	18 17.5	1 24.9	17 16.7	17 02.8
5 Su	21 00 16	16 07 32	12♍36 16	19 42 51	8 34.9	20 56.9	7 41.9	10 46.0	7 25.5	14 49.4	18 13.9	1 23.3	17 16.1	17 01.4
6 M	21 04 12	17 08 19	26 50 27	3♎58 31	8D 33.3	21 42.1	7 09.0	10 50.5	7 44.5	15 03.7	18 10.2	1 21.7	17 15.5	17 00.0
7 Tu	21 08 09	18 09 05	11♎06 39	18 14 27	8 33.5	22 31.2	6 37.6	10 54.2	8 03.3	15 18.1	18 06.5	1 20.2	17 14.9	16 58.5
8 W	21 12 05	19 09 50	25 21 37	2♏27 52	8 34.6	23 23.9	6 08.0	10 57.3	8 21.9	15 32.4	18 02.6	1 18.7	17 14.2	16 57.1
9 Th	21 16 02	20 10 35	9♏33 00	16 36 52	8R 35.4	24 19.7	5 40.3	10 59.6	8 40.4	15 46.7	17 58.7	1 17.2	17 13.5	16 55.6
10 F	21 19 59	21 11 18	23 39 19	0♐40 13	8 35.1	25 18.5	5 14.5	11 01.3	8 58.7	16 01.0	17 54.8	1 15.8	17 12.8	16 54.2
11 Sa	21 23 55	22 12 01	7♐39 27	14 36 54	8 32.8	26 20.1	4 51.0	11R 02.2	9 16.8	16 15.3	17 50.8	1 14.4	17 12.0	16 52.8
12 Su	21 27 52	23 12 42	21 32 25	28 25 49	8 28.5	27 24.1	4 29.7	11 02.4	9 34.7	16 29.5	17 46.7	1 13.1	17 11.3	16 51.3
13 M	21 31 48	24 13 22	5♑16 57	12♑05 35	8 22.3	28 30.5	4 10.7	11 01.8	9 52.5	16 43.8	17 42.5	1 11.8	17 10.4	16 49.9
14 Tu	21 35 45	25 14 02	18 51 31	25 34 32	8 14.9	29 39.0	3 54.1	11 00.5	10 10.1	16 58.1	17 38.3	1 10.6	17 09.6	16 48.5
15 W	21 39 41	26 14 39	2♒14 23	8♒50 52	8 07.2	0♒49.6	3 40.0	10 58.4	10 27.4	17 12.3	17 34.1	1 09.4	17 08.7	16 47.1
16 Th	21 43 38	27 15 15	15 23 48	21 53 03	8 00.1	2 02.0	3 28.3	10 55.6	10 44.6	17 26.6	17 29.8	1 08.3	17 07.8	16 45.7
17 F	21 47 35	28 15 50	28 18 30	4♓40 06	7 54.2	3 16.1	3 19.1	10 51.9	11 01.5	17 40.8	17 25.4	1 07.2	17 06.9	16 44.3
18 Sa	21 51 31	29 16 23	10♓57 52	17 11 53	7 50.2	4 31.9	3 12.4	10 47.5	11 18.3	17 55.0	17 21.0	1 06.1	17 05.9	16 42.8
19 Su	21 55 28	0♓16 55	23 22 16	29 29 15	7D 48.1	5 49.3	3 08.1	10 42.3	11 34.9	18 09.2	17 16.6	1 05.2	17 04.9	16 41.4
20 M	21 59 24	1 17 24	5♈33 06	11♈34 09	7 47.7	7 08.1	3D 06.3	10 36.3	11 51.2	18 23.3	17 12.1	1 04.2	17 03.9	16 40.1
21 Tu	22 03 21	2 17 52	17 32 48	23 29 29	7 48.8	8 28.4	3 06.9	10 29.6	12 07.3	18 37.5	17 07.6	1 03.3	17 02.9	16 38.7
22 W	22 07 17	3 18 19	29 24 44	5♉19 03	7 50.5	9 50.0	3 09.9	10 22.1	12 23.2	18 51.6	17 03.0	1 02.5	17 01.8	16 37.3
23 Th	22 11 14	4 18 43	11♉13 01	17 07 16	7 52.3	11 12.9	3 15.2	10 13.7	12 38.9	19 05.7	16 58.4	1 01.7	17 00.7	16 35.9
24 F	22 15 10	5 19 05	23 02 23	28 59 01	7R 53.5	12 37.1	3 22.7	10 04.7	12 54.4	19 19.7	16 53.8	1 01.0	16 59.6	16 34.6
25 Sa	22 19 07	6 19 26	4♊57 50	10♊59 26	7 53.6	14 02.4	3 32.6	9 54.8	13 09.7	19 33.8	16 49.1	1 00.3	16 58.5	16 33.2
26 Su	22 23 03	7 19 45	17 04 27	23 13 29	7 52.3	15 29.0	3 44.5	9 44.2	13 24.7	19 47.8	16 44.5	0 59.7	16 57.3	16 31.9
27 M	22 27 00	8 20 01	29 27 04	5♋45 42	7 49.7	16 56.8	3 58.6	9 32.8	13 39.5	20 01.8	16 39.8	0 59.1	16 56.1	16 30.6
28 Tu	22 30 57	9 20 16	12♋09 49	18 39 44	7 46.0	18 25.7	4 14.8	9 20.6	13 54.0	20 15.7	16 35.0	0 58.6	16 54.9	16 29.3

Astro Data	Planet Ingress	Last Aspect	☽ Ingress	Last Aspect	☽ Ingress	☽ Phases & Eclipses	Astro Data
Dy Hr Mn	Dy Hr Mn	Dy Hr Mn	Dy Hr Mn	Dy Hr Mn	Dy Hr Mn	Dy Hr Mn	
☿R 8 16:55	☿ ♒ 1 12:39	2 10:56 ♄ □	♋ 3 6:56	1 2:04 ☿ ☍	♌ 1 22:34	4 7:48 ○ 13♋24	1 January 1950
☽0S 10 2:22	⚳ ♐ 14 22:48	4 18:48 ♄ ⚹	♌ 5 13:58	3 4:48 ♆ ⚹	♍ 4 2:37	11 10:31 ☾ 20♎38	Julian Day # 18263
♀R 10 13:35	☿ ♑R 15 7:35	6 22:51 ♀ ☍	♍ 7 19:06	5 14:12 ☿ △	♎ 6 5:19	18 8:00 ● 27♑40	SVP 5♓57'32"
♂0S 13 12:16	☉ ♒ 20 15:00	9 4:45 ♄ ☌	♎ 9 23:08	7 19:40 ☿ □	♏ 8 7:50	26 4:39 ☽ 5♉40	GC 26♐08.5 ⚴ 6♏03.5
♆R 18 19:19		11 10:31 ☉ □	♏ 12 2:28	10 2:08 ☿ ⚹	♐ 10 10:51		Eris 6♈20.2 ⚵ 2♎42.5
♆⚹♇ 22 12:53	☿ ♒ 14 19:12	13 17:23 ☉ ⚹	♐ 14 5:16	12 2:11 ☉ ⚹	♑ 12 14:45	2 22:16 ○ 13♌31	⚷ 15♐50.1 ⚶ 10♒59.8
☽0N 23 7:54	☉ ♓ 19 5:18	15 13:44 ♄ □	♑ 16 8:06	13 21:54 ♄ △	♒ 14 19:57	9 18:32 ☾ 20♏27	☽ Mean ☊ 12♈05.1
☿D 29 5:02		18 8:00 ☉ ☌	♒ 18 12:07	16 22:53 ☉ ☌	♓ 17 3:11	16 22:53 ● 27♒43	
☽0S 6 7:47		19 19:24 ♇ ☍	♓ 20 18:41	18 12:18 ♄ ☍	♈ 19 13:01	25 1:52 ☽ 5♊54	1 February 1950
♃⚼♅ 11 10:43		22 11:29 ☿ ⚹	♈ 23 4:37	21 1:58 ♃ ⚹	♉ 22 1:12		Julian Day # 18294
♂R 12 5:48		24 19:37 ☿ □	♉ 25 17:08	23 16:05 ♃ □	♊ 24 14:03		SVP 5♓57'26"
♃☍♇ 13 21:20		27 7:09 ♄ △	♊ 28 5:43	26 5:12 ♃ △	♋ 27 1:03		GC 26♐08.5 ⚴ 15♏19.7
♃△♆ 15 6:16		29 18:10 ♄ □	♋ 30 15:50				Eris 6♈28.4 ⚵ 4♎06.8R
♃⚻♄ 16 16:09	♀ D20 18:04						⚷ 18♐59.4 ⚶ 26♒29.0
☽0N 19 15:40	♄⊻⊻22 20:01						☽ Mean ☊ 10♈26.7

March 1950 — LONGITUDE

Day	Sid.Time	☉	0 hr ☽	Noon ☽	True ☊	☿	♀	♂	⚳	♃	♄	♅	♆	♇
1 W	22 34 53	10♓20 29	25♋15 42	1♌57 48	7♈41.8	19♒55.7	4♒32.9	9♎07.7	14♐08.4	20♒29.6	16♍30.3	0♋58.1	16♎53.7	16♌28.0
2 Th	22 38 50	11 20 39	8♌46 04	15 40 19	7R37.5	21 26.8	4 53.0	8R54.1	14 22.4	20 43.5	16R25.5	0R57.7	16R52.5	16R26.7
3 F	22 42 46	12 20 48	22 40 16	29 45 30	7 33.9	22 59.1	5 14.9	8 39.8	14 36.3	20 57.4	16 20.8	0 57.3	16 51.2	16 25.4
4 Sa	22 46 43	13 20 54	6♍55 27	14♍09 27	7 31.2	24 32.4	5 38.6	8 24.7	14 49.9	21 11.2	16 16.0	0 57.0	16 49.9	16 24.1
5 Su	22 50 39	14 20 59	21 26 45	28 46 30	7D29.9	26 06.9	6 04.1	8 09.0	15 03.2	21 25.0	16 11.2	0 56.8	16 48.6	16 22.9
6 M	22 54 36	15 21 02	6♎07 50	13♎29 55	7 29.8	27 42.4	6 31.2	7 52.6	15 16.3	21 38.7	16 06.4	0 56.6	16 47.2	16 21.6
7 Tu	22 58 32	16 21 03	20 51 52	28 12 55	7 30.6	29 19.1	7 00.0	7 35.5	15 29.1	21 52.4	16 01.6	0 56.4	16 45.9	16 20.4
8 W	23 02 29	17 21 03	5♏32 20	12♏49 29	7 31.9	0♓56.9	7 30.4	7 17.8	15 41.7	22 06.1	15 56.9	0 56.3	16 44.5	16 19.2
9 Th	23 06 26	18 21 01	20 03 49	27 14 55	7 33.2	2 35.8	8 02.2	6 59.4	15 54.0	22 19.7	15 52.1	0D56.3	16 43.1	16 18.0
10 F	23 10 22	19 20 58	4♐22 26	11♐26 07	7R34.0	4 15.8	8 35.5	6 40.5	16 06.0	22 33.3	15 47.3	0 56.3	16 41.7	16 16.8
11 Sa	23 14 19	20 20 53	18 25 48	25 21 25	7 34.1	5 57.0	9 10.2	6 21.0	16 17.8	22 46.8	15 42.5	0 56.3	16 40.3	16 15.7
12 Su	23 18 15	21 20 46	2♑12 55	9♑00 20	7 33.4	7 39.4	9 46.2	6 01.0	16 29.3	23 00.3	15 37.8	0 56.5	16 38.9	16 14.5
13 M	23 22 12	22 20 38	15 43 43	22 23 09	7 32.0	9 22.9	10 23.5	5 40.5	16 40.5	23 13.7	15 33.0	0 56.6	16 37.4	16 13.4
14 Tu	23 26 08	23 20 28	28 58 44	5♒30 35	7 30.1	11 07.5	11 02.0	5 19.5	16 51.4	23 27.1	15 28.3	0 56.8	16 35.9	16 12.3
15 W	23 30 05	24 20 16	11♒58 50	18 23 36	7 28.1	12 53.4	11 41.6	4 58.0	17 02.0	23 40.5	15 23.6	0 57.1	16 34.5	16 11.2
16 Th	23 34 01	25 20 03	24 45 00	1♓03 11	7 26.3	14 40.5	12 22.4	4 36.2	17 12.3	23 53.8	15 18.9	0 57.5	16 33.0	16 10.2
17 F	23 37 58	26 19 47	7♓18 15	13 30 23	7 25.0	16 28.8	13 04.3	4 14.0	17 22.3	24 07.0	15 14.2	0 57.8	16 31.4	16 09.1
18 Sa	23 41 55	27 19 29	19 39 42	25 46 22	7D24.1	18 18.3	13 47.2	3 51.5	17 32.0	24 20.2	15 09.6	0 58.3	16 29.9	16 08.1
19 Su	23 45 51	28 19 10	1♈50 34	7♈52 31	7 23.9	20 09.0	14 31.1	3 28.8	17 41.4	24 33.3	15 05.0	0 58.8	16 28.4	16 07.1
20 M	23 49 48	29 18 48	13 52 25	19 50 32	7 24.1	22 01.0	15 15.9	3 05.8	17 50.5	24 46.4	15 00.4	0 59.3	16 26.8	16 06.1
21 Tu	23 53 44	0♈18 25	25 47 09	1♉42 34	7 24.7	23 54.2	16 01.6	2 42.6	17 59.3	24 59.4	14 55.8	0 59.9	16 25.3	16 05.1
22 W	23 57 41	1 17 59	7♉37 09	13 31 16	7 25.4	25 48.6	16 48.2	2 19.3	18 07.8	25 12.3	14 51.3	1 00.6	16 23.7	16 04.1
23 Th	0 01 37	2 17 31	19 25 21	25 19 50	7 26.0	27 44.3	17 35.7	1 55.9	18 15.9	25 25.2	14 46.9	1 01.3	16 22.1	16 03.2
24 F	0 05 34	3 17 01	1♊15 12	7♊11 57	7 26.5	29 41.1	18 23.9	1 32.4	18 23.7	25 38.1	14 42.4	1 02.0	16 20.5	16 02.3
25 Sa	0 09 30	4 16 28	13 10 37	19 11 45	7 26.8	1♈39.1	19 13.0	1 09.0	18 31.2	25 50.8	14 38.1	1 02.9	16 18.9	16 01.4
26 Su	0 13 27	5 15 53	25 15 56	1♋23 42	7R27.0	3 38.1	20 02.8	0 45.6	18 38.4	26 03.5	14 33.7	1 03.7	16 17.3	16 00.6
27 M	0 17 24	6 15 16	7♋35 37	13 52 14	7 27.0	5 38.2	20 53.3	0 22.3	18 45.2	26 16.1	14 29.4	1 04.6	16 15.7	15 59.7
28 Tu	0 21 20	7 14 37	20 14 03	26 41 32	7D26.9	7 39.2	21 44.4	29♍59.1	18 51.7	26 28.7	14 25.2	1 05.6	16 14.1	15 58.9
29 W	0 25 17	8 13 55	3♌15 06	9♌55 03	7 26.9	9 41.1	22 36.3	29 36.1	18 57.9	26 41.2	14 21.0	1 06.6	16 12.4	15 58.1
30 Th	0 29 13	9 13 11	16 41 36	23 34 53	7 27.1	11 43.7	23 28.8	29 13.4	19 03.7	26 53.6	14 16.9	1 07.7	16 10.8	15 57.4
31 F	0 33 10	10 12 25	0♍34 49	7♍41 13	7 27.3	13 46.8	24 21.9	28 50.9	19 09.1	27 05.9	14 12.8	1 08.8	16 09.2	15 56.6

April 1950 — LONGITUDE

Day	Sid.Time	☉	0 hr ☽	Noon ☽	True ☊	☿	♀	♂	⚳	♃	♄	♅	♆	♇
1 Sa	0 37 06	11♈11 36	14♍53 45	22♍11 53	7♈27.5	15♈50.3	25♒15.6	28♍28.7	19♐14.2	27♒18.2	14♍08.8	1♋10.0	16♎07.5	15♌55.9
2 Su	0 41 03	12 10 45	29 34 56	7♎02 03	7R27.6	17 54.0	26 09.9	28R06.8	19 19.0	27 30.4	14R04.9	1 11.2	16R05.9	15R55.2
3 M	0 44 59	13 09 52	14♎32 17	22 04 33	7 27.5	19 57.6	27 04.7	27 45.4	19 23.3	27 42.5	14 01.0	1 12.5	16 04.2	15 54.5
4 Tu	0 48 56	14 08 58	29 37 44	7♏10 42	7 27.0	22 00.8	28 00.1	27 24.3	19 27.4	27 54.5	13 57.2	1 13.8	16 02.6	15 53.9
5 W	0 52 53	15 08 01	14♏42 17	22 11 28	7 26.3	24 03.4	28 56.0	27 03.7	19 31.0	28 06.5	13 53.4	1 15.2	16 00.9	15 53.2
6 Th	0 56 49	16 07 03	29 37 17	6♐58 53	7 25.3	26 05.0	29 52.4	26 43.6	19 34.4	28 18.4	13 49.8	1 16.6	15 59.3	15 52.6
7 F	1 00 46	17 06 02	14♐15 36	21 26 55	7 24.4	28 05.3	0♓49.3	26 24.0	19 37.3	28 30.2	13 46.2	1 18.1	15 57.7	15 52.1
8 Sa	1 04 42	18 05 00	28 32 29	5♑32 04	7D23.7	0♉03.9	1 46.6	26 04.9	19 39.8	28 41.9	13 42.6	1 19.6	15 56.0	15 51.5
9 Su	1 08 39	19 03 57	12♑25 37	19 13 11	7 23.5	2 00.4	2 44.4	25 46.5	19 42.0	28 53.5	13 39.2	1 21.2	15 54.4	15 51.0
10 M	1 12 35	20 02 51	25 54 55	2♒31 04	7 23.8	3 54.6	3 42.6	25 28.6	19 43.8	29 05.1	13 35.8	1 22.8	15 52.7	15 50.5
11 Tu	1 16 32	21 01 44	9♒01 57	15 27 55	7 24.6	5 45.9	4 41.2	25 11.3	19 45.3	29 16.5	13 32.5	1 24.5	15 51.1	15 50.0
12 W	1 20 28	22 00 35	21 49 19	28 06 34	7 25.8	7 34.2	5 40.3	24 54.7	19 46.3	29 27.9	13 29.2	1 26.2	15 49.4	15 49.6
13 Th	1 24 25	22 59 25	4♓20 03	10♓30 10	7 27.1	9 19.1	6 39.7	24 38.8	19 47.0	29 39.1	13 26.1	1 27.9	15 47.8	15 49.2
14 F	1 28 22	23 58 12	16 37 18	22 41 48	7 28.2	11 00.2	7 39.4	24 23.5	19R47.2	29 50.3	13 23.0	1 29.7	15 46.2	15 48.8
15 Sa	1 32 18	24 56 57	28 44 01	4♈44 16	7R28.7	12 37.4	8 39.6	24 09.0	19 47.1	0♓01.4	13 20.0	1 31.6	15 44.5	15 48.4
16 Su	1 36 15	25 55 41	10♈42 52	16 40 05	7 28.5	14 10.3	9 40.0	23 55.2	19 46.6	0 12.4	13 17.1	1 33.5	15 42.9	15 48.0
17 M	1 40 11	26 54 23	22 36 13	28 31 30	7 27.2	15 38.8	10 40.8	23 42.2	19 45.7	0 23.3	13 14.3	1 35.4	15 41.3	15 47.7
18 Tu	1 44 08	27 53 03	4♉26 13	10♉20 36	7 25.0	17 02.6	11 41.9	23 29.9	19 44.4	0 34.0	13 11.6	1 37.4	15 39.7	15 47.4
19 W	1 48 04	28 51 40	16 14 55	22 09 26	7 21.9	18 21.7	12 43.3	23 18.4	19 42.7	0 44.7	13 09.0	1 39.4	15 38.1	15 47.2
20 Th	1 52 01	29 50 16	28 04 25	4♊00 12	7 18.2	19 35.8	13 45.0	23 07.7	19 40.6	0 55.3	13 06.4	1 41.5	15 36.5	15 47.0
21 F	1 55 57	0♉48 50	9♊57 04	15 55 22	7 14.3	20 44.9	14 47.0	22 57.7	19 38.2	1 05.8	13 04.0	1 43.6	15 34.9	15 46.8
22 Sa	1 59 54	1 47 22	21 55 28	27 57 46	7 10.7	21 48.8	15 49.3	22 48.6	19 35.3	1 16.2	13 01.6	1 45.7	15 33.3	15 46.6
23 Su	2 03 51	2 45 52	4♋02 42	10♋10 41	7 07.9	22 47.4	16 51.8	22 40.2	19 32.1	1 26.4	12 59.4	1 47.9	15 31.8	15 46.4
24 M	2 07 47	3 44 19	16 22 11	22 37 40	7D06.2	23 40.7	17 54.6	22 32.7	19 28.5	1 36.6	12 57.2	1 50.2	15 30.2	15 46.3
25 Tu	2 11 44	4 42 44	28 57 38	5♌22 32	7 05.7	24 28.5	18 57.6	22 26.0	19 24.5	1 46.6	12 55.1	1 52.4	15 28.7	15 46.2
26 W	2 15 40	5 41 08	11♌52 50	18 28 56	7 06.3	25 10.8	20 00.9	22 20.0	19 20.1	1 56.5	12 53.2	1 54.8	15 27.1	15 46.2
27 Th	2 19 37	6 39 29	25 11 12	1♍59 56	7 07.6	25 47.6	21 04.4	22 14.9	19 15.3	2 06.3	12 51.3	1 57.1	15 25.6	15D46.1
28 F	2 23 33	7 37 48	8♍55 19	15 57 24	7 09.1	26 18.7	22 08.1	22 10.5	19 10.2	2 16.0	12 49.5	1 59.5	15 24.1	15 46.1
29 Sa	2 27 30	8 36 04	23 06 08	0♎21 15	7R10.1	26 44.3	23 12.0	22 06.9	19 04.7	2 25.6	12 47.8	2 01.9	15 22.6	15 46.1
30 Su	2 31 26	9 34 19	7♎42 20	15 08 47	7 10.0	27 04.3	24 16.2	22 04.1	18 58.8	2 35.1	12 46.3	2 04.4	15 21.1	15 46.2

Astro Data Dy Hr Mn	Planet Ingress Dy Hr Mn	Last Aspect Dy Hr Mn	☽ Ingress Dy Hr Mn	Last Aspect Dy Hr Mn	☽ Ingress Dy Hr Mn	☽ Phases & Eclipses Dy Hr Mn
♄⚻♇ 2 4:17	☿ ♓ 7 22:04	28 8:48 ♆ □	♌ 1 8:30	1 21:58 ♂ ☌	♎ 2 0:41	4 10:34 ○ 13♍17
♂0N 4 22:13	☉ ♈ 21 4:35	2 23:07 ☿ ☍	♍ 3 12:24	3 21:04 ♃ △	♏ 4 0:35	11 2:38 ☾ 19♐58
☽0S 5 16:08	☿ ♈ 24 15:52	4 15:28 ♄ ☌	♎ 5 14:00	5 23:37 ♀ □	♐ 6 0:37	18 15:20 ● 27♓28
♅D 9 19:25	♂ ♍R 28 11:05	7 14:02 ☿ △	♏ 7 14:55	8 1:04 ☿ △	♑ 8 2:29	18 15:31:31 ● A non-C
☽0N 18 22:55		9 3:38 ♃ □	♐ 9 16:37	9 23:29 ♂ △	♒ 10 7:24	26 20:10 ☽ 5♋36
☉0N 21 4:35	♀ ♓ 6 15:13	11 7:27 ♃ ✶	♑ 11 20:07	12 14:39 ♃ ☌	♓ 12 15:38	
♅∠♇ 24 15:53	☿ ♉ 8 11:13	13 11:55 ☉ ✶	♒ 14 1:52	14 15:18 ♂ ☍	♈ 15 2:32	2 20:49 ○ 12♎32
☿0N 26 7:21	♃ ♓ 15 8:58	15 22:08 ♃ ☌	♓ 16 9:59	17 8:25 ☉ ☌	♉ 17 15:00	2 20:44 ● T 1.033
☽0S 2 2:47	☉ ♉ 20 15:59	18 15:20 ☉ ☌	♈ 18 20:21	19 14:18 ♂ △	♊ 20 3:54	9 11:42 ☾ 19♑03
♆✶♇ 12 9:11		20 22:08 ♃ ✶	♉ 21 8:32	22 1:53 ♂ □	♋ 22 16:02	17 8:25 ● 26♈46
⚳R 14 16:22		23 17:50 ☿ ✶	♊ 23 21:28	24 14:09 ☿ ✶	♌ 25 1:57	25 10:40 ☽ 4♌39
☽0N 15 5:08		26 1:23 ♃ △	♋ 26 9:17	27 0:35 ☿ □	♍ 27 8:30	
♃⚼♆ 18 22:59		28 17:53 ♂ ✶	♌ 28 18:05	29 5:52 ☿ △	♎ 29 11:25	
♃△♅ 26 6:23		30 17:47 ♃ ☍	♍ 30 23:01			
♇D 28 8:40	☽0S29 13:27					

Astro Data

1 March 1950
Julian Day # 18322
SVP 5♓57'22"
GC 26♐08.6 ⚴ 19♏59.4
Eris 6♈43.6 ⚵ 29♍56.0R
⚷ 20♐56.4 ⚶ 10♓26.6
☽ Mean ☊ 8♈57.7

1 April 1950
Julian Day # 18353
SVP 5♓57'19"
GC 26♐08.7 ⚴ 18♏46.9R
Eris 7♈04.8 ⚵ 22♍35.9R
⚷ 21♐44.3 ⚶ 25♓34.3
☽ Mean ☊ 7♈19.2

LONGITUDE — May 1950

Day	Sid.Time	☉	0 hr ☽	Noon ☽	True ☊	☿	♀	♂	⚳	♃	♄	♅	♆	♇
1 M	2 35 23	10♉32 32	22♎39 47	0♏14 20	7♈08.5	27♉18.7	25♓20.6	22♍02.1	18♐52.6	2♓44.4	12♍44.8	2♋06.9	15♎19.7	15♌46.3
2 Tu	2 39 19	11 30 43	7♏51 18	15 29 28	7R05.3	27 27.7	26 25.1	22R00.9	18R46.0	2 53.6	12R43.4	2 09.5	15R18.2	15 46.4
3 W	2 43 16	12 28 53	23 07 28	0♐44 00	7 00.8	27R31.2	27 29.9	22D00.4	18 39.0	3 02.7	12 42.1	2 12.1	15 16.8	15 46.5
4 Th	2 47 13	13 27 01	8♐17 48	15 47 39	6 55.6	27 29.5	28 34.9	22 00.6	18 31.7	3 11.7	12 40.9	2 14.7	15 15.4	15 46.7
5 F	2 51 09	14 25 07	23 12 33	0♑31 37	6 50.4	27 22.8	29 40.1	22 01.6	18 24.1	3 20.6	12 39.9	2 17.3	15 14.0	15 46.8
6 Sa	2 55 06	15 23 12	7♑44 14	14 49 55	6 46.0	27 11.2	0♈45.4	22 03.3	18 16.1	3 29.3	12 38.9	2 20.0	15 12.6	15 47.1
7 Su	2 59 02	16 21 16	21 48 28	28 39 49	6 43.0	26 55.1	1 51.0	22 05.8	18 07.8	3 37.9	12 38.0	2 22.7	15 11.2	15 47.3
8 M	3 02 59	17 19 18	5♒24 04	12♒01 28	6D41.5	26 34.8	2 56.7	22 08.9	17 59.1	3 46.3	12 37.3	2 25.5	15 09.9	15 47.6
9 Tu	3 06 55	18 17 19	18 32 25	24 57 19	6 41.6	26 10.7	4 02.6	22 12.8	17 50.1	3 54.7	12 36.6	2 28.3	15 08.6	15 47.9
10 W	3 10 52	19 15 18	1♓16 44	7♓31 11	6 42.7	25 43.3	5 08.6	22 17.4	17 40.8	4 02.9	12 36.0	2 31.1	15 07.3	15 48.2
11 Th	3 14 49	20 13 16	13 41 14	19 47 30	6 44.1	25 13.2	6 14.8	22 22.7	17 31.2	4 10.9	12 35.6	2 33.9	15 06.0	15 48.5
12 F	3 18 45	21 11 13	25 50 30	1♈50 50	6R45.2	24 40.7	7 21.1	22 28.6	17 21.3	4 18.8	12 35.2	2 36.8	15 04.7	15 48.9
13 Sa	3 22 42	22 09 08	7♈48 59	13 45 27	6 45.0	24 06.6	8 27.6	22 35.2	17 11.1	4 26.6	12 35.0	2 39.7	15 03.5	15 49.3
14 Su	3 26 38	23 07 02	19 40 42	25 35 07	6 43.1	23 31.5	9 34.2	22 42.5	17 00.7	4 34.3	12D34.8	2 42.7	15 02.2	15 49.7
15 M	3 30 35	24 04 55	1♉29 07	7♉23 01	6 39.0	22 56.0	10 41.0	22 50.4	16 49.9	4 41.7	12 34.8	2 45.7	15 01.0	15 50.2
16 Tu	3 34 31	25 02 46	13 17 07	19 11 42	6 32.7	22 20.6	11 47.9	22 59.0	16 39.0	4 49.1	12 34.8	2 48.7	14 59.8	15 50.7
17 W	3 38 28	26 00 36	25 07 01	1♊03 15	6 24.6	21 46.1	12 54.9	23 08.2	16 27.7	4 56.3	12 35.0	2 51.7	14 58.7	15 51.2
18 Th	3 42 24	26 58 25	7♊00 39	12 59 24	6 15.3	21 12.9	14 02.0	23 18.0	16 16.3	5 03.3	12 35.3	2 54.7	14 57.5	15 51.7
19 F	3 46 21	27 56 12	18 59 40	25 01 40	6 05.6	20 41.7	15 09.3	23 28.5	16 04.6	5 10.2	12 35.7	2 57.8	14 56.4	15 52.3
20 Sa	3 50 18	28 53 58	1♋05 37	7♋11 43	5 56.4	20 13.0	16 16.7	23 39.5	15 52.7	5 17.0	12 36.1	3 00.9	14 55.3	15 52.9
21 Su	3 54 14	29 51 42	13 20 14	19 31 25	5 48.5	19 47.1	17 24.2	23 51.2	15 40.6	5 23.6	12 36.7	3 04.1	14 54.3	15 53.5
22 M	3 58 11	0♊49 24	25 45 33	2♌02 59	5 42.7	19 24.5	18 31.8	24 03.4	15 28.3	5 30.0	12 37.4	3 07.2	14 53.2	15 54.2
23 Tu	4 02 07	1 47 05	8♌24 03	14 49 07	5 39.1	19 05.6	19 39.5	24 16.2	15 15.9	5 36.3	12 38.2	3 10.4	14 52.2	15 54.9
24 W	4 06 04	2 44 45	21 18 33	27 52 44	5D37.7	18 50.5	20 47.3	24 29.5	15 03.3	5 42.4	12 39.1	3 13.6	14 51.2	15 55.6
25 Th	4 10 00	3 42 22	4♍32 02	11♍16 47	5 37.7	18 39.6	21 55.2	24 43.4	14 50.5	5 48.4	12 40.1	3 16.8	14 50.3	15 56.3
26 F	4 13 57	4 39 59	18 07 16	25 03 42	5R38.5	18 32.9	23 03.2	24 57.8	14 37.7	5 54.2	12 41.2	3 20.1	14 49.3	15 57.0
27 Sa	4 17 53	5 37 34	2♎06 11	9♎14 42	5 38.7	18D30.5	24 11.4	25 12.7	14 24.7	5 59.8	12 42.4	3 23.4	14 48.4	15 57.8
28 Su	4 21 50	6 35 07	16 29 05	23 49 01	5 37.4	18 32.7	25 19.6	25 28.2	14 11.6	6 05.3	12 43.8	3 26.7	14 47.5	15 58.6
29 M	4 25 47	7 32 39	1♏13 56	8♏43 09	5 34.0	18 39.3	26 27.9	25 44.1	13 58.5	6 10.6	12 45.2	3 30.0	14 46.7	15 59.4
30 Tu	4 29 43	8 30 10	16 15 43	23 50 34	5 28.0	18 50.5	27 36.3	26 00.5	13 45.3	6 15.8	12 46.7	3 33.3	14 45.8	16 00.3
31 W	4 33 40	9 27 39	1♐26 30	9♐02 12	5 20.0	19 06.1	28 44.8	26 17.4	13 32.0	6 20.8	12 48.3	3 36.6	14 45.0	16 01.2

LONGITUDE — June 1950

Day	Sid.Time	☉	0 hr ☽	Noon ☽	True ☊	☿	♀	♂	⚳	♃	♄	♅	♆	♇
1 Th	4 37 36	10♊25 08	16♐36 20	24♐07 37	5♈10.6	19♉26.1	29♈53.4	26♍34.8	13♐18.7	6♓25.6	12♍50.0	3♋40.0	14♎44.3	16♌02.1
2 F	4 41 33	11 22 36	1♑34 49	8♑56 54	5R01.1	19 50.5	1♉02.1	26 52.6	13R05.3	6 30.2	12 51.8	3 43.4	14R43.5	16 03.0
3 Sa	4 45 29	12 20 03	16 12 57	23 22 19	4 52.5	20 19.2	2 10.8	27 10.9	12 52.0	6 34.7	12 53.7	3 46.8	14 42.8	16 03.9
4 Su	4 49 26	13 17 29	0♒24 31	7♒19 20	4 45.8	20 52.1	3 19.7	27 29.6	12 38.6	6 39.0	12 55.7	3 50.2	14 42.1	16 04.9
5 M	4 53 22	14 14 54	14 06 42	20 46 46	4 41.4	21 29.1	4 28.6	27 48.8	12 25.3	6 43.1	12 57.9	3 53.7	14 41.4	16 05.9
6 Tu	4 57 19	15 12 19	27 19 50	3♓46 17	4D39.1	22 10.1	5 37.7	28 08.3	12 12.0	6 47.1	13 00.1	3 57.1	14 40.8	16 06.9
7 W	5 01 16	16 09 43	10♓06 39	16 21 31	4 38.6	22 55.0	6 46.8	28 28.3	11 58.7	6 50.8	13 02.4	4 00.6	14 40.2	16 07.9
8 Th	5 05 12	17 07 06	22 31 30	28 37 16	4R38.8	23 43.8	7 56.0	28 48.7	11 45.5	6 54.4	13 04.8	4 04.0	14 39.6	16 09.0
9 F	5 09 09	18 04 29	4♈39 28	10♈38 46	4 38.8	24 36.3	9 05.3	29 09.5	11 32.4	6 57.8	13 07.2	4 07.5	14 39.1	16 10.1
10 Sa	5 13 05	19 01 51	16 35 48	22 31 12	4 37.4	25 32.5	10 14.6	29 30.7	11 19.3	7 01.0	13 09.8	4 11.0	14 38.6	16 11.2
11 Su	5 17 02	19 59 13	28 25 33	4♉19 21	4 33.9	26 32.3	11 24.0	29 52.3	11 06.4	7 04.1	13 12.5	4 14.6	14 38.1	16 12.3
12 M	5 20 58	20 56 35	10♉13 09	16 07 21	4 27.8	27 35.5	12 33.5	0♎14.3	10 53.6	7 06.9	13 15.3	4 18.1	14 37.6	16 13.5
13 Tu	5 24 55	21 53 55	22 02 21	27 58 32	4 18.9	28 42.3	13 43.1	0 36.6	10 40.9	7 09.6	13 18.2	4 21.6	14 37.2	16 14.6
14 W	5 28 51	22 51 15	3♊56 09	9♊55 28	4 07.7	29 52.4	14 52.7	0 59.3	10 28.4	7 12.1	13 21.1	4 25.2	14 36.8	16 15.8
15 Th	5 32 48	23 48 35	15 56 40	21 59 57	3 54.9	1♊05.8	16 02.5	1 22.4	10 16.0	7 14.4	13 24.2	4 28.7	14 36.4	16 17.1
16 F	5 36 45	24 45 54	28 05 24	4♋13 10	3 41.5	2 22.6	17 12.2	1 45.9	10 03.8	7 16.5	13 27.4	4 32.3	14 36.1	16 18.3
17 Sa	5 40 41	25 43 13	10♋23 18	16 35 54	3 28.7	3 42.6	18 22.1	2 09.7	9 51.8	7 18.4	13 30.6	4 35.9	14 35.8	16 19.6
18 Su	5 44 38	26 40 30	22 51 02	29 08 47	3 17.6	5 05.8	19 32.0	2 33.8	9 40.0	7 20.2	13 33.9	4 39.4	14 35.6	16 20.8
19 M	5 48 34	27 37 48	5♌29 16	11♌52 37	3 09.0	6 32.2	20 41.9	2 58.2	9 28.4	7 21.7	13 37.3	4 43.0	14 35.3	16 22.1
20 Tu	5 52 31	28 35 04	18 18 58	24 48 30	3 03.2	8 01.7	21 51.9	3 23.0	9 17.0	7 23.1	13 40.9	4 46.6	14 35.1	16 23.5
21 W	5 56 27	29 32 20	1♍21 26	7♍57 59	3 00.1	9 34.4	23 02.0	3 48.2	9 05.9	7 24.2	13 44.4	4 50.2	14 34.9	16 24.8
22 Th	6 00 24	0♋29 34	14 38 23	21 22 54	2 59.0	11 10.2	24 12.1	4 13.6	8 55.0	7 25.2	13 48.1	4 53.8	14 34.8	16 26.1
23 F	6 04 21	1 26 49	28 11 44	5♎05 05	2 58.9	12 49.0	25 22.3	4 39.3	8 44.3	7 25.9	13 51.9	4 57.4	14 34.7	16 27.5
24 Sa	6 08 17	2 24 02	12♎03 06	19 05 51	2 58.5	14 30.9	26 32.6	5 05.4	8 34.0	7 26.5	13 55.7	5 01.0	14 34.6	16 28.9
25 Su	6 12 14	3 21 15	26 13 17	3♏25 15	2 56.6	16 15.7	27 42.9	5 31.7	8 23.9	7 26.9	13 59.7	5 04.6	14D34.6	16 30.3
26 M	6 16 10	4 18 28	10♏41 27	18 01 24	2 52.5	18 03.4	28 53.2	5 58.3	8 14.1	7R27.1	14 03.7	5 08.2	14 34.6	16 31.7
27 Tu	6 20 07	5 15 40	25 24 29	2♐49 55	2 45.6	19 54.0	0♊03.7	6 25.2	8 04.6	7 27.1	14 07.8	5 11.8	14 34.6	16 33.2
28 W	6 24 03	6 12 51	10♐16 37	17 44 03	2 36.4	21 47.2	1 14.2	6 52.4	7 55.4	7 26.9	14 12.0	5 15.4	14 34.6	16 34.6
29 Th	6 28 00	7 10 03	25 10 35	2♑35 17	2 25.6	23 43.1	2 24.7	7 19.9	7 46.4	7 26.5	14 16.2	5 19.0	14 34.7	16 36.1
30 F	6 31 56	8 07 14	9♑57 02	17 14 49	2 14.6	25 41.5	3 35.3	7 47.6	7 37.8	7 25.9	14 20.6	5 22.6	14 34.8	16 37.6

Astro Data

	Dy Hr Mn
♂ D	3 15:51
☿ R	3 16:07
♀0N	8 19:22
☽0N	12 10:38
♄ D	15 9:22
☽0S	26 22:04
☿ D	27 12:29
☽0N	8 16:18
♂0S	14 8:14
☽0S	23 4:02
♆ D	26 8:03
♃ R	27 0:14

Planet Ingress

	Dy Hr Mn
♀ ♈	5 19:19
☉ ♊	21 15:27
♀ ♉	1 14:19
♂ ♎	11 20:27
☿ ♊	14 14:33
☉ ♋	21 23:36
♀ ♊	27 10:45

Last Aspect / ☽ Ingress

Last Aspect Dy Hr Mn		☽ Ingress Dy Hr Mn
30 13:00 ♇ ✶	♏	1 11:37
3 6:55 ☿ ☍	♐	3 10:50
5 10:28 ♀ □	♑	5 11:08
7 9:00 ☿ △	♒	7 14:22
9 14:14 ☿ □	♓	9 21:34
11 22:18 ☿ ✶	♈	12 8:18
13 16:11 ♇ △	♉	14 20:59
17 0:54 ☉ ☌	♊	17 9:52
19 8:52 ♂ □	♋	19 21:50
21 20:29 ♂ ✶	♌	22 8:06
23 21:49 ♀ △	♍	24 15:51
26 11:50 ♂ ☌	♎	26 20:26
28 14:39 ♀ ☍	♏	28 22:01
30 15:29 ♂ ✶	♐	30 21:43

Last Aspect / ☽ Ingress

Last Aspect Dy Hr Mn		☽ Ingress Dy Hr Mn
1 16:01 ♂ □	♑	1 21:27
3 18:37 ♂ △	♒	3 23:18
5 13:21 ☿ □	♓	6 4:57
8 12:23 ♂ ☍	♈	8 14:44
10 4:18 ☉ ✶	♉	11 3:12
13 13:38 ☿ ☌	♊	13 16:05
15 15:53 ☉ ☌	♋	16 3:45
17 15:45 ♀ ✶	♌	18 13:37
20 19:29 ☉ ✶	♍	20 21:31
22 17:27 ☉ △	♎	23 3:09
24 7:33 ♇ ✶	♏	25 6:19
27 7:09 ♀ ☍	♐	27 7:26
28 19:30 ☿ ☍	♑	29 7:48

☽ Phases & Eclipses

Dy Hr Mn		
2 5:19	○	11♏15
8 22:32	☾	17♒45
17 0:54	●	25♉34
24 21:28	☽	3♍07
31 12:43	○	9♐29
7 11:35	☾	16♓09
15 15:53	●	23♊58
23 5:13	☽	1♎11
29 19:58	○	7♑29

Astro Data

1 May 1950
Julian Day # 18383
SVP 5♓57'15"
GC 26♐08.7 ⚴ 11♏07.0R
Eris 7♈24.8 ⚵ 18♍42.2R
⚷ 21♐03.7R ⚶ 9♈36.8
☽ Mean ☊ 5♈43.9

1 June 1950
Julian Day # 18414
SVP 5♓57'10"
GC 26♐08.8 ⚴ 3♏11.0R
Eris 7♈40.0 ⚵ 20♍10.8
⚷ 19♐15.1R ⚶ 23♈10.1
☽ Mean ☊ 4♈05.4

July 1950 LONGITUDE

Day	Sid.Time	☉	0 hr ☽	Noon ☽	True ☊	☿	♀	♂	⚳	♃	♄	♅	♆	♇
1 Sa	6 35 53	9♋04 25	24♑27 41	1♒34 56	2♈04.4	27♊42.1	4♊46.0	8♎15.6	7♐29.6	7♓25.2	14♍25.0	5♋26.2	14♎35.0	16♌39.1
2 Su	6 39 50	10 01 36	8♒35 57	15 30 21	1R56.1	29 44.8	5 56.7	8 43.9	7R21.6	7R24.2	14 29.5	5 29.8	14 35.2	16 40.7
3 M	6 43 46	10 58 47	22 17 56	28 58 41	1 50.3	1♋49.3	7 07.5	9 12.4	7 14.0	7 23.1	14 34.1	5 33.4	14 35.4	16 42.2
4 Tu	6 47 43	11 55 58	5♓32 44	12♓00 21	1 47.1	3 55.5	8 18.3	9 41.1	7 06.7	7 21.7	14 38.7	5 37.0	14 35.6	16 43.7
5 W	6 51 39	12 53 09	18 21 57	24 38 01	1D45.8	6 02.9	9 29.2	10 10.1	6 59.7	7 20.2	14 43.4	5 40.6	14 35.9	16 45.3
6 Th	6 55 36	13 50 21	0♈49 06	6♈55 51	1R45.7	8 11.5	10 40.1	10 39.4	6 53.1	7 18.4	14 48.2	5 44.2	14 36.2	16 46.9
7 F	6 59 32	14 47 33	12 58 54	18 58 55	1 45.7	10 20.8	11 51.1	11 08.8	6 46.8	7 16.5	14 53.1	5 47.8	14 36.6	16 48.5
8 Sa	7 03 29	15 44 46	24 56 36	0♉52 35	1 44.8	12 30.5	13 02.2	11 38.6	6 40.8	7 14.4	14 58.0	5 51.3	14 36.9	16 50.1
9 Su	7 07 25	16 41 58	6♉47 33	12 42 06	1 42.0	14 40.4	14 13.3	12 08.5	6 35.3	7 12.1	15 03.0	5 54.9	14 37.3	16 51.7
10 M	7 11 22	17 39 12	18 36 50	24 32 18	1 36.8	16 50.2	15 24.5	12 38.7	6 30.1	7 09.6	15 08.1	5 58.5	14 37.8	16 53.4
11 Tu	7 15 19	18 36 25	0♊28 59	6♊27 21	1 29.1	18 59.6	16 35.7	13 09.1	6 25.2	7 06.9	15 13.2	6 02.0	14 38.2	16 55.0
12 W	7 19 15	19 33 39	12 27 46	18 30 35	1 19.1	21 08.4	17 47.0	13 39.8	6 20.7	7 04.0	15 18.5	6 05.6	14 38.7	16 56.7
13 Th	7 23 12	20 30 54	24 36 03	0♋44 23	1 07.6	23 16.4	18 58.3	14 10.7	6 16.6	7 01.0	15 23.8	6 09.1	14 39.3	16 58.4
14 F	7 27 08	21 28 09	6♋55 44	13 10 11	0 55.4	25 23.3	20 09.7	14 41.7	6 12.8	6 57.7	15 29.1	6 12.6	14 39.9	17 00.1
15 Sa	7 31 05	22 25 24	19 27 47	25 48 31	0 43.8	27 29.1	21 21.2	15 13.1	6 09.4	6 54.3	15 34.5	6 16.1	14 40.4	17 01.7
16 Su	7 35 01	23 22 40	2♌12 22	8♌39 17	0 33.7	29 33.5	22 32.7	15 44.6	6 06.4	6 50.7	15 40.0	6 19.6	14 41.1	17 03.5
17 M	7 38 58	24 19 55	15 09 11	21 42 00	0 25.9	1♌36.6	23 44.2	16 16.3	6 03.8	6 46.9	15 45.6	6 23.1	14 41.7	17 05.2
18 Tu	7 42 54	25 17 11	28 17 40	4♍56 07	0 20.8	3 38.1	24 55.8	16 48.2	6 01.5	6 43.0	15 51.2	6 26.6	14 42.4	17 06.9
19 W	7 46 51	26 14 28	11♍37 21	18 21 20	0D18.3	5 38.0	26 07.4	17 20.4	5 59.6	6 38.8	15 56.8	6 30.0	14 43.2	17 08.6
20 Th	7 50 48	27 11 44	25 08 05	1♎57 37	0 17.7	7 36.2	27 19.1	17 52.7	5 58.0	6 34.5	16 02.6	6 33.4	14 43.9	17 10.4
21 F	7 54 44	28 09 01	8♎50 00	15 45 14	0R18.2	9 32.8	28 30.8	18 25.3	5 56.8	6 30.1	16 08.4	6 36.9	14 44.7	17 12.1
22 Sa	7 58 41	29 06 18	22 43 22	29 44 21	0 18.5	11 27.6	29 42.6	18 58.0	5 56.0	6 25.4	16 14.2	6 40.3	14 45.5	17 13.9
23 Su	8 02 37	0♌03 35	6♏48 10	13♏54 40	0 17.7	13 20.8	0♋54.4	19 30.9	5D55.6	6 20.6	16 20.1	6 43.7	14 46.3	17 15.7
24 M	8 06 34	1 00 53	21 03 38	28 14 47	0 15.0	15 12.1	2 06.3	20 04.0	5 55.5	6 15.7	16 26.1	6 47.0	14 47.2	17 17.5
25 Tu	8 10 30	1 58 11	5♐27 42	12♐41 53	0 10.0	17 01.8	3 18.2	20 37.3	5 55.8	6 10.5	16 32.1	6 50.4	14 48.1	17 19.2
26 W	8 14 27	2 55 29	19 56 44	27 11 34	0 03.0	18 49.7	4 30.1	21 10.8	5 56.4	6 05.3	16 38.2	6 53.7	14 49.1	17 21.0
27 Th	8 18 24	3 52 48	4♑25 38	11♑38 09	29♓54.7	20 35.9	5 42.2	21 44.4	5 57.5	5 59.9	16 44.3	6 57.1	14 50.0	17 22.8
28 F	8 22 20	4 50 08	18 48 19	25 55 24	29 46.0	22 20.3	6 54.2	22 18.2	5 58.8	5 54.3	16 50.5	7 00.4	14 51.0	17 24.6
29 Sa	8 26 17	5 47 28	2♒58 40	9♒57 31	29 38.0	24 03.0	8 06.3	22 52.2	6 00.5	5 48.6	16 56.7	7 03.6	14 52.1	17 26.5
30 Su	8 30 13	6 44 49	16 51 26	23 40 01	29 31.5	25 44.0	9 18.5	23 26.4	6 02.6	5 42.7	17 03.0	7 06.9	14 53.1	17 28.3
31 M	8 34 10	7 42 11	0♓23 02	7♓00 22	29 27.1	27 23.3	10 30.7	24 00.7	6 05.0	5 36.7	17 09.3	7 10.1	14 54.2	17 30.1

August 1950 LONGITUDE

Day	Sid.Time	☉	0 hr ☽	Noon ☽	True ☊	☿	♀	♂	⚳	♃	♄	♅	♆	♇
1 Tu	8 38 06	8♌39 34	13♓32 00	19♓58 05	29♓24.9	29♌00.9	11♋43.0	24♎35.2	6♐07.7	5♓30.6	17♍15.7	7♋13.3	14♎55.3	17♌31.9
2 W	8 42 03	9 36 57	26 18 52	2♈34 40	29D24.5	0♍36.9	12 55.3	25 09.8	6 10.8	5R24.4	17 22.1	7 16.5	14 56.4	17 33.7
3 Th	8 45 59	10 34 22	8♈45 57	14 53 10	29 25.3	2 11.1	14 07.7	25 44.6	6 14.2	5 18.0	17 28.6	7 19.7	14 57.6	17 35.6
4 F	8 49 56	11 31 48	20 56 54	26 57 42	29 26.6	3 43.6	15 20.1	26 19.6	6 18.0	5 11.5	17 35.1	7 22.8	14 58.8	17 37.4
5 Sa	8 53 52	12 29 16	2♉56 13	8♉53 05	29R27.4	5 14.4	16 32.6	26 54.7	6 22.0	5 04.9	17 41.7	7 25.9	15 00.0	17 39.3
6 Su	8 57 49	13 26 44	14 48 55	20 44 22	29 27.2	6 43.5	17 45.1	27 30.0	6 26.5	4 58.1	17 48.3	7 29.0	15 01.2	17 41.1
7 M	9 01 46	14 24 14	26 40 05	2♊36 38	29 25.3	8 10.9	18 57.7	28 05.5	6 31.2	4 51.3	17 54.9	7 32.1	15 02.5	17 42.9
8 Tu	9 05 42	15 21 46	8♊34 37	14 34 35	29 21.6	9 36.5	20 10.3	28 41.1	6 36.3	4 44.3	18 01.6	7 35.1	15 03.8	17 44.8
9 W	9 09 39	16 19 18	20 37 00	26 42 20	29 16.3	11 00.4	21 23.0	29 16.9	6 41.7	4 37.3	18 08.3	7 38.2	15 05.2	17 46.6
10 Th	9 13 35	17 16 52	2♋50 58	9♋03 13	29 09.7	12 22.5	22 35.7	29 52.8	6 47.4	4 30.2	18 15.1	7 41.1	15 06.5	17 48.5
11 F	9 17 32	18 14 28	15 19 19	21 39 28	29 02.6	13 42.7	23 48.5	0♏28.9	6 53.4	4 22.9	18 21.9	7 44.1	15 07.9	17 50.3
12 Sa	9 21 28	19 12 04	28 03 46	4♌32 13	28 55.7	15 01.1	25 01.3	1 05.1	6 59.7	4 15.6	18 28.8	7 47.0	15 09.3	17 52.2
13 Su	9 25 25	20 09 42	11♌04 47	17 41 22	28 49.8	16 17.6	26 14.2	1 41.5	7 06.4	4 08.2	18 35.6	7 49.9	15 10.7	17 54.0
14 M	9 29 22	21 07 21	24 21 47	1♍05 50	28 45.4	17 32.0	27 27.1	2 18.0	7 13.3	4 00.7	18 42.6	7 52.8	15 12.2	17 55.9
15 Tu	9 33 18	22 05 01	7♍53 13	14 43 42	28 42.8	18 44.4	28 40.0	2 54.7	7 20.5	3 53.2	18 49.5	7 55.6	15 13.7	17 57.7
16 W	9 37 15	23 02 42	21 36 57	28 32 42	28D42.0	19 54.7	29 53.0	3 31.5	7 28.1	3 45.6	18 56.5	7 58.4	15 15.2	17 59.6
17 Th	9 41 11	24 00 24	5♎30 36	12♎30 25	28 42.6	21 02.9	1♌06.1	4 08.5	7 35.9	3 37.9	19 03.5	8 01.2	15 16.7	18 01.4
18 F	9 45 08	24 58 08	19 31 51	26 34 39	28 44.0	22 08.7	2 19.2	4 45.6	7 44.0	3 30.2	19 10.5	8 03.9	15 18.3	18 03.2
19 Sa	9 49 04	25 55 52	3♏38 35	10♏43 24	28 45.3	23 12.1	3 32.3	5 22.8	7 52.4	3 22.5	19 17.6	8 06.6	15 19.8	18 05.1
20 Su	9 53 01	26 53 38	17 48 54	24 54 50	28R46.0	24 13.0	4 45.5	6 00.2	8 01.1	3 14.7	19 24.7	8 09.3	15 21.4	18 06.9
21 M	9 56 57	27 51 24	2♐00 57	9♐07 00	28 45.6	25 11.2	5 58.7	6 37.7	8 10.1	3 06.9	19 31.9	8 11.9	15 23.1	18 08.7
22 Tu	10 00 54	28 49 12	16 12 43	23 17 46	28 43.8	26 06.7	7 11.9	7 15.4	8 19.3	2 59.0	19 39.0	8 14.5	15 24.7	18 10.6
23 W	10 04 51	29 47 01	0♑21 49	7♑24 30	28 40.8	26 59.3	8 25.2	7 53.1	8 28.8	2 51.2	19 46.2	8 17.1	15 26.4	18 12.4
24 Th	10 08 47	0♍44 51	14 25 27	21 24 15	28 37.0	27 48.7	9 38.6	8 31.0	8 38.6	2 43.3	19 53.4	8 19.6	15 28.1	18 14.2
25 F	10 12 44	1 42 43	28 20 32	5♒13 53	28 32.9	28 34.9	10 52.0	9 09.1	8 48.7	2 35.4	20 00.7	8 22.1	15 29.8	18 16.0
26 Sa	10 16 40	2 40 36	12♒03 57	18 50 24	28 29.2	29 17.5	12 05.4	9 47.2	8 58.9	2 27.5	20 07.9	8 24.5	15 31.5	18 17.8
27 Su	10 20 37	3 38 30	25 32 58	2♓11 25	28 26.3	29 56.5	13 18.9	10 25.5	9 09.5	2 19.6	20 15.2	8 27.0	15 33.3	18 19.6
28 M	10 24 33	4 36 25	8♓45 36	15 15 25	28 24.5	0♎31.5	14 32.4	11 03.9	9 20.3	2 11.7	20 22.5	8 29.3	15 35.1	18 21.4
29 Tu	10 28 30	5 34 23	21 40 53	28 02 01	28D23.9	1 02.4	15 45.9	11 42.4	9 31.3	2 03.8	20 29.8	8 31.7	15 36.8	18 23.2
30 W	10 32 26	6 32 22	4♈19 00	10♈32 02	28 24.3	1 28.8	16 59.5	12 21.1	9 42.6	1 55.9	20 37.1	8 34.0	15 38.7	18 25.0
31 Th	10 36 23	7 30 22	16 41 22	22 47 22	28 25.5	1 50.5	18 13.2	12 59.8	9 54.1	1 48.1	20 44.5	8 36.2	15 40.5	18 26.7

Astro Data Dy Hr Mn	Planet Ingress Dy Hr Mn	Last Aspect Dy Hr Mn	☽ Ingress Dy Hr Mn	Last Aspect Dy Hr Mn	☽ Ingress Dy Hr Mn	☽ Phases & Eclipses Dy Hr Mn
♄⊻♆ 3 19:20	☿ ♋ 2 14:57	30 7:36 ♆ □	♒ 1 9:19	1 6:53 ♄ ☍	♈ 2 7:03	7 2:53 ☾ 14♈26
☽0N 5 22:59	☿ ♌ 16 17:08	2 14:04 ♇ ☍	♓ 3 13:51	4 10:40 ♂ ☍	♉ 4 18:06	15 5:05 ● 22♋09
☽0S 20 8:39	♀ ♋ 22 17:50	4 16:59 ♄ ☍	♈ 5 22:24	6 6:00 ♄ △	♊ 7 6:44	22 10:50 ☽ 29♎04
♃△♅ 20 15:19	☉ ♌ 23 10:30	7 7:38 ♇ △	♉ 8 10:13	9 17:18 ♂ △	♋ 9 18:27	29 4:18 ○ 5♒29
⚳ D 24 4:57	☊ ♓R 26 20:56	9 20:50 ☉ ⚹	♊ 10 23:02	11 16:28 ♀ ☌	♌ 12 3:36	
		12 10:24 ♀ ☌	♋ 13 10:34	13 16:48 ☉ ☌	♍ 14 10:03	5 19:56 ☾ 12♉48
☽0N 2 6:51	☿ ♍ 2 2:44	15 15:46 ☿ ☌	♌ 15 19:52	15 19:39 ☿ ☌	♎ 16 14:31	13 16:48 ● 20♌21
♄⊻♇ 4 23:48	♂ ♏ 10 16:48	17 16:05 ♀ ⚹	♍ 18 3:05	18 9:04 ☉ ⚹	♏ 18 17:49	20 15:35 ☽ 27♏02
☽0S 16 14:07	♀ ♌ 16 14:18	20 3:04 ♀ □	♎ 20 8:34	20 15:35 ☉ □	♐ 20 20:36	27 14:51 ○ 3♓45
☿0S 21 12:24	☉ ♍ 23 17:23	22 11:57 ♀ △	♏ 22 12:27	22 22:04 ☉ △	♑ 22 23:23	
☽0N 29 15:13	☿ ♎ 27 14:17	23 17:39 ♇ □	♐ 24 14:55	24 23:45 ☿ △	♒ 25 2:53	
		26 1:39 ♂ ⚹	♑ 26 16:39	26 11:02 ♇ ☍	♓ 27 8:02	
		28 5:38 ♂ □	♒ 28 18:55	28 21:38 ♄ ☍	♈ 29 15:44	
		30 16:12 ☿ ☍	♓ 30 23:19			

Astro Data

1 July 1950
Julian Day # 18444
SVP 5♓57'04"
GC 26♐08.9 ⚴ 1♏47.4
Eris 7♈46.0 ⚵ 25♍38.8
⚷ 17♐14.2R ⚶ 4♉54.2
☽ Mean ☊ 2♈30.1

1 August 1950
Julian Day # 18475
SVP 5♓56'58"
GC 26♐08.9 ⚴ 6♏34.8
Eris 7♈41.8R ⚵ 3♎50.6
⚷ 15♐50.3R ⚶ 14♉47.4
☽ Mean ☊ 0♈51.6

LONGITUDE — September 1950

Day	Sid.Time	☉	0 hr ☽	Noon ☽	True ☊	☿	♀	♂	⚳	♃	♄	♅	♆	♇
1 F	10 40 19	8♍28 25	28♈50 25	4♉50 57	28♓27.1	2♎07.2	19♌26.9	13♏38.7	10♐05.8	1♓40.3	20♍51.9	8♋38.4	15♎42.3	18♌28.5
2 Sa	10 44 16	9 26 30	10♉49 29	16 46 31	28 28.6	2 18.6	20 40.6	14 17.7	10 17.8	1R32.5	20 59.2	8 40.6	15 44.2	18 30.3
3 Su	10 48 13	10 24 36	22 42 37	28 38 20	28 29.7	2R24.5	21 54.4	14 56.9	10 30.0	1 24.8	21 06.6	8 42.7	15 46.1	18 32.0
4 M	10 52 09	11 22 44	4♊34 17	10♊31 02	28R30.1	2 24.5	23 08.2	15 36.1	10 42.5	1 17.1	21 14.1	8 44.8	15 48.0	18 33.7
5 Tu	10 56 06	12 20 55	16 29 13	22 29 23	28 29.8	2 18.5	24 22.1	16 15.5	10 55.1	1 09.5	21 21.5	8 46.9	15 49.9	18 35.5
6 W	11 00 02	13 19 07	28 32 07	4♋37 57	28 28.8	2 06.2	25 36.0	16 55.0	11 08.0	1 01.9	21 28.9	8 48.9	15 51.9	18 37.2
7 Th	11 03 59	14 17 22	10♋47 25	17 00 57	28 27.3	1 47.5	26 50.0	17 34.6	11 21.1	0 54.4	21 36.4	8 50.9	15 53.8	18 38.9
8 F	11 07 55	15 15 38	23 18 58	29 41 48	28 25.5	1 22.3	28 03.9	18 14.3	11 34.4	0 47.0	21 43.9	8 52.8	15 55.8	18 40.6
9 Sa	11 11 52	16 13 56	6♌09 42	12♌42 50	28 23.7	0 50.6	29 18.0	18 54.2	11 47.9	0 39.6	21 51.3	8 54.6	15 57.8	18 42.3
10 Su	11 15 48	17 12 17	19 21 17	26 05 02	28 22.3	0 12.7	0♍32.0	19 34.1	12 01.7	0 32.3	21 58.8	8 56.5	15 59.8	18 43.9
11 M	11 19 45	18 10 39	2♍53 56	9♍47 45	28 21.3	29♍28.7	1 46.1	20 14.2	12 15.6	0 25.1	22 06.3	8 58.3	16 01.8	18 45.6
12 Tu	11 23 42	19 09 03	16 46 08	23 48 41	28D20.9	28 39.3	3 00.3	20 54.4	12 29.7	0 18.0	22 13.8	9 00.0	16 03.8	18 47.2
13 W	11 27 38	20 07 29	0♎54 52	8♎04 07	28 21.0	27 45.0	4 14.5	21 34.7	12 44.1	0 11.0	22 21.3	9 01.7	16 05.9	18 48.9
14 Th	11 31 35	21 05 56	15 15 48	22 29 16	28 21.4	26 46.8	5 28.7	22 15.1	12 58.6	0 04.1	22 28.7	9 03.3	16 07.9	18 50.5
15 F	11 35 31	22 04 25	29 43 51	6♏58 54	28 21.9	25 45.8	6 42.9	22 55.6	13 13.3	29♒57.3	22 36.2	9 04.9	16 10.0	18 52.1
16 Sa	11 39 28	23 02 56	14♏13 46	21 27 55	28 22.5	24 43.1	7 57.2	23 36.2	13 28.3	29 50.6	22 43.7	9 06.5	16 12.1	18 53.7
17 Su	11 43 24	24 01 29	28 40 46	5♐51 52	28 22.8	23 40.2	9 11.5	24 16.9	13 43.4	29 44.0	22 51.2	9 08.0	16 14.2	18 55.3
18 M	11 47 21	25 00 04	13♐00 49	20 07 17	28R23.0	22 38.6	10 25.8	24 57.8	13 58.6	29 37.6	22 58.7	9 09.4	16 16.3	18 56.8
19 Tu	11 51 17	25 58 40	27 10 58	4♑11 40	28 23.0	21 39.9	11 40.2	25 38.7	14 14.1	29 31.3	23 06.2	9 10.8	16 18.4	18 58.4
20 W	11 55 14	26 57 17	11♑09 12	18 03 28	28 22.9	20 45.4	12 54.6	26 19.8	14 29.7	29 25.1	23 13.7	9 12.2	16 20.5	18 59.9
21 Th	11 59 11	27 55 56	24 54 22	1♒41 50	28D22.8	19 56.7	14 09.0	27 00.9	14 45.5	29 19.1	23 21.2	9 13.5	16 22.6	19 01.4
22 F	12 03 07	28 54 37	8♒25 52	15 06 25	28 22.8	19 15.1	15 23.5	27 42.2	15 01.5	29 13.2	23 28.7	9 14.7	16 24.8	19 02.9
23 Sa	12 07 04	29 53 20	21 43 31	28 17 09	28 22.9	18 41.5	16 38.0	28 23.5	15 17.7	29 07.4	23 36.1	9 16.0	16 26.9	19 04.4
24 Su	12 11 00	0♎52 04	4♓47 21	11♓14 10	28 23.1	18 16.9	17 52.5	29 04.9	15 34.0	29 01.8	23 43.6	9 17.1	16 29.1	19 05.9
25 M	12 14 57	1 50 50	17 37 38	23 57 49	28R23.2	18D01.8	19 07.0	29 46.5	15 50.4	28 56.3	23 51.0	9 18.2	16 31.3	19 07.3
26 Tu	12 18 53	2 49 38	0♈14 48	6♈28 41	28 23.2	17 56.8	20 21.6	0♐28.1	16 07.1	28 51.0	23 58.5	9 19.3	16 33.5	19 08.8
27 W	12 22 50	3 48 29	12 39 37	18 47 44	28 22.9	18 01.9	21 36.2	1 09.8	16 23.8	28 45.8	24 05.9	9 20.3	16 35.6	19 10.2
28 Th	12 26 46	4 47 21	24 53 13	0♉56 19	28 22.3	18 17.0	22 50.8	1 51.6	16 40.8	28 40.8	24 13.3	9 21.2	16 37.8	19 11.6
29 F	12 30 43	5 46 15	6♉57 17	12 56 24	28 21.3	18 42.1	24 05.5	2 33.6	16 57.9	28 36.0	24 20.7	9 22.1	16 40.0	19 12.9
30 Sa	12 34 40	6 45 12	18 54 00	24 50 28	28 20.2	19 16.6	25 20.2	3 15.6	17 15.1	28 31.3	24 28.1	9 23.0	16 42.2	19 14.3

LONGITUDE — October 1950

Day	Sid.Time	☉	0 hr ☽	Noon ☽	True ☊	☿	♀	♂	⚳	♃	♄	♅	♆	♇
1 Su	12 38 36	7♎44 11	0♊46 12	6♊41 39	28♓19.0	20♍00.1	26♍34.9	3♐57.7	17♐32.5	28♒26.8	24♍35.5	9♋23.8	16♎44.4	19♌15.6
2 M	12 42 33	8 43 12	12 37 17	18 33 37	28R18.0	20 51.9	27 49.6	4 39.9	17 50.0	28R22.5	24 42.9	9 24.5	16 46.7	19 16.9
3 Tu	12 46 29	9 42 15	24 31 10	0♋30 30	28D17.3	21 51.4	29 04.4	5 22.2	18 07.7	28 18.4	24 50.2	9 25.2	16 48.9	19 18.2
4 W	12 50 26	10 41 21	6♋32 11	12 36 46	28 17.1	22 57.9	0♎19.2	6 04.5	18 25.5	28 14.4	24 57.5	9 25.8	16 51.1	19 19.5
5 Th	12 54 22	11 40 29	18 44 50	24 56 58	28 17.5	24 10.6	1 34.0	6 47.0	18 43.5	28 10.6	25 04.8	9 26.4	16 53.3	19 20.8
6 F	12 58 19	12 39 39	1♌13 40	7♌35 26	28 18.4	25 28.8	2 48.9	7 29.6	19 01.6	28 07.0	25 12.1	9 27.0	16 55.6	19 22.0
7 Sa	13 02 15	13 38 52	14 02 44	20 35 55	28 19.6	26 51.9	4 03.7	8 12.3	19 19.8	28 03.6	25 19.4	9 27.5	16 57.8	19 23.2
8 Su	13 06 12	14 38 07	27 15 18	4♍01 03	28 20.8	28 19.0	5 18.6	8 55.0	19 38.1	28 00.3	25 26.6	9 27.9	17 00.0	19 24.4
9 M	13 10 09	15 37 24	10♍53 13	17 51 45	28R21.7	29 49.7	6 33.6	9 37.9	19 56.6	27 57.3	25 33.8	9 28.3	17 02.3	19 25.6
10 Tu	13 14 05	16 36 43	24 56 24	2♎06 48	28 21.9	1♎23.3	7 48.5	10 20.8	20 15.2	27 54.4	25 41.0	9 28.6	17 04.5	19 26.7
11 W	13 18 02	17 36 04	9♎22 23	16 42 27	28 21.2	2 59.4	9 03.5	11 03.8	20 34.0	27 51.8	25 48.2	9 28.8	17 06.7	19 27.9
12 Th	13 21 58	18 35 28	24 06 10	1♏32 36	28 19.4	4 37.4	10 18.5	11 46.9	20 52.8	27 49.3	25 55.3	9 29.1	17 09.0	19 29.0
13 F	13 25 55	19 34 53	9♏00 41	16 29 23	28 16.9	6 17.0	11 33.5	12 30.1	21 11.8	27 47.0	26 02.4	9 29.2	17 11.2	19 30.0
14 Sa	13 29 51	20 34 21	23 57 36	1♐24 18	28 13.9	7 57.8	12 48.5	13 13.4	21 30.9	27 45.0	26 09.5	9 29.3	17 13.4	19 31.1
15 Su	13 33 48	21 33 50	8♐48 33	16 09 30	28 11.0	9 39.5	14 03.5	13 56.8	21 50.2	27 43.1	26 16.5	9R29.4	17 15.7	19 32.1
16 M	13 37 44	22 33 21	23 26 27	0♑38 51	28 08.6	11 21.8	15 18.6	14 40.2	22 09.5	27 41.4	26 23.5	9 29.4	17 17.9	19 33.1
17 Tu	13 41 41	23 32 54	7♑46 17	14 48 30	28D07.3	13 04.5	16 33.6	15 23.8	22 29.0	27 39.9	26 30.5	9 29.3	17 20.1	19 34.1
18 W	13 45 38	24 32 28	21 45 22	28 36 54	28 07.1	14 47.5	17 48.7	16 07.4	22 48.5	27 38.7	26 37.4	9 29.2	17 22.4	19 35.1
19 Th	13 49 34	25 32 04	5♒23 11	12♒04 24	28 07.9	16 30.5	19 03.8	16 51.1	23 08.2	27 37.6	26 44.3	9 29.0	17 24.6	19 36.0
20 F	13 53 31	26 31 42	18 40 49	25 12 40	28 09.4	18 13.4	20 18.9	17 34.8	23 28.0	27 36.7	26 51.2	9 28.8	17 26.8	19 36.9
21 Sa	13 57 27	27 31 22	1♓40 18	8♓04 01	28 11.1	19 56.2	21 34.0	18 18.7	23 47.9	27 36.1	26 58.0	9 28.6	17 29.0	19 37.8
22 Su	14 01 24	28 31 03	14 24 09	20 40 59	28R12.3	21 38.7	22 49.2	19 02.6	24 07.8	27 35.6	27 04.8	9 28.2	17 31.2	19 38.7
23 M	14 05 20	29 30 46	26 54 49	3♈05 57	28 12.4	23 21.0	24 04.3	19 46.6	24 27.9	27D35.4	27 11.5	9 27.9	17 33.4	19 39.5
24 Tu	14 09 17	0♏30 31	9♈14 37	15 21 03	28 11.0	25 02.8	25 19.5	20 30.7	24 48.1	27 35.3	27 18.2	9 27.4	17 35.6	19 40.3
25 W	14 13 13	1 30 17	21 25 28	27 28 04	28 07.9	26 44.3	26 34.6	21 14.8	25 08.4	27 35.5	27 24.9	9 27.0	17 37.8	19 41.1
26 Th	14 17 10	2 30 06	3♉29 04	9♉28 38	28 03.2	28 25.3	27 49.8	21 59.0	25 28.8	27 35.8	27 31.5	9 26.4	17 40.0	19 41.8
27 F	14 21 07	3 29 57	15 26 57	21 24 14	27 57.1	0♏05.8	29 05.0	22 43.3	25 49.2	27 36.4	27 38.1	9 25.8	17 42.2	19 42.5
28 Sa	14 25 03	4 29 50	27 20 42	3♊16 34	27 50.1	1 45.9	0♏20.2	23 27.6	26 09.8	27 37.1	27 44.6	9 25.2	17 44.3	19 43.2
29 Su	14 29 00	5 29 45	9♊12 07	15 07 37	27 43.1	3 25.5	1 35.4	24 12.1	26 30.4	27 38.1	27 51.1	9 24.5	17 46.5	19 43.9
30 M	14 32 56	6 29 42	21 03 25	26 59 51	27 36.6	5 04.7	2 50.7	24 56.6	26 51.2	27 39.2	27 57.5	9 23.8	17 48.6	19 44.6
31 Tu	14 36 53	7 29 41	2♋57 19	8♋56 16	27 31.3	6 43.3	4 05.9	25 41.1	27 12.0	27 40.6	28 03.9	9 23.0	17 50.8	19 45.2

Astro Data	Planet Ingress	Last Aspect	☽ Ingress	Last Aspect	☽ Ingress	☽ Phases & Eclipses	Astro Data
Dy Hr Mn	Dy Hr Mn	Dy Hr Mn	Dy Hr Mn	Dy Hr Mn	Dy Hr Mn	Dy Hr Mn	1 September 1950
☿R 4 0:13	♀ ♍ 10 1:37	31 3:25 ♇ △	♉ 1 2:19	3 8:48 ♀ □	♋ 3 10:59	4 13:53 ☾ 11♊27	Julian Day # 18506
♃⚼♆ 7 13:29	☿ ♍R 10 19:16	2 20:48 ♀ □	♊ 3 14:45	5 12:15 ♄ ⚹	♌ 5 21:40	12 3:29 ● 18♍48	SVP 5♓56'54"
☽0S 12 21:58	♃ ♒R 15 2:23	5 16:10 ♀ ⚹	♋ 6 2:54	8 1:23 ♃ ☍	♍ 8 4:54	12 3:38:16 ● T 01'14"	GC 26♐09.0 ⚴ 15♏20.0
☿0N 18 0:58	☉ ♎ 23 14:44	7 20:51 ♄ ⚹	♌ 8 12:34	10 1:10 ♄ ☌	♎ 10 8:29	18 20:54 ☽ 25♐22	Eris 7♈28.4R ⚵ 13♎31.7
☉0S 23 14:44	♂ ♐ 25 19:48	9 23:46 ♂ □	♍ 10 18:55	12 6:01 ♃ △	♏ 12 9:31	26 4:21 ○ 2♈31	⚷ 15♐45.3 ⚶ 20♉57.4
☽0N 25 22:59		12 19:43 ☿ ☌	♎ 12 22:28	14 6:07 ♃ □	♐ 14 9:44	26 4:17 ● T 1.079	☽ Mean ☊ 29♓13.1
☿D 26 11:59	♀ ♎ 4 5:51	14 5:56 ♇ ⚹	♏ 15 0:27	16 7:04 ♃ ⚹	♑ 16 10:55		
	☿ ♎ 9 14:40	17 1:50 ♃ □	♐ 17 2:12	18 8:28 ♄ △	♒ 18 14:27	4 7:53 ☾ 10♋31	1 October 1950
♀0S 6 22:05	☉ ♏ 23 23:45	19 4:03 ♃ ⚹	♑ 19 4:49	20 16:26 ♃ ☌	♓ 20 20:53	11 13:34 ● 17♎40	Julian Day # 18536
☽0S 10 8:00	☿ ♏ 27 10:36	21 4:49 ☉ △	♒ 21 8:59	23 0:26 ♄ ☍	♈ 23 5:59	18 4:18 ☽ 24♑13	SVP 5♓56'51"
☿0S 12 10:43	♀ ♏ 28 5:33	23 13:32 ♃ ☌	♓ 23 15:09	25 12:15 ♃ ⚹	♉ 25 17:03	25 20:46 ○ 1♉52	GC 26♐09.1 ⚴ 25♏56.8
♅R 16 0:17		25 11:47 ♄ ☍	♈ 25 23:32	28 0:42 ♄ △	♊ 28 5:22		Eris 7♈10.3R ⚵ 23♎39.2
☽0N 23 5:22		28 7:33 ♃ ⚹	♉ 28 10:08	30 13:57 ♄ □	♋ 30 18:03		⚷ 17♐02.7 ⚶ 21♉23.4R
♃D 24 6:34		30 19:24 ♃ □	♊ 30 22:26				☽ Mean ☊ 27♓37.8
♃⚻♄ 27 5:05							

November 1950 — LONGITUDE

Day	Sid.Time	☉	0 hr ☽	Noon ☽	True ☊	☿	♀	♂	⚳	♃	♄	♅	♆	♇
1 W	14 40 49	8♏29 42	14♋57 11	21♋00 32	27♓27.7	8♏21.5	5♏21.2	26♐25.8	27♐32.9	27♒42.2	28♍10.2	9♋22.2	17♎52.9	19♌45.8
2 Th	14 44 46	9 29 45	27 06 53	3♌16 46	27D 26.0	9 59.2	6 36.5	27 10.5	27 53.9	27 43.9	28 16.5	9R 21.3	17 55.0	19 46.4
3 F	14 48 42	10 29 51	9♌30 45	15 49 26	27 25.9	11 36.5	7 51.7	27 55.3	28 15.0	27 45.9	28 22.7	9 20.3	17 57.1	19 46.9
4 Sa	14 52 39	11 29 58	22 13 20	28 43 01	27 26.9	13 13.4	9 07.0	28 40.1	28 36.2	27 48.0	28 28.9	9 19.3	17 59.2	19 47.4
5 Su	14 56 36	12 30 08	5♍18 56	12♍01 30	27 28.3	14 49.8	10 22.3	29 25.0	28 57.4	27 50.4	28 35.0	9 18.3	18 01.3	19 47.9
6 M	15 00 32	13 30 20	18 51 02	25 47 42	27R 29.0	16 25.8	11 37.7	0♑10.0	29 18.8	27 52.9	28 41.0	9 17.2	18 03.4	19 48.3
7 Tu	15 04 29	14 30 33	2♎51 31	10♎02 21	27 28.4	18 01.4	12 53.0	0 55.0	29 40.2	27 55.7	28 47.0	9 16.1	18 05.4	19 48.8
8 W	15 08 25	15 30 49	17 19 50	24 43 25	27 25.6	19 36.7	14 08.3	1 40.2	0♑01.6	27 58.6	28 53.0	9 14.9	18 07.5	19 49.1
9 Th	15 12 22	16 31 06	2♏12 18	9♏45 28	27 20.6	21 11.6	15 23.7	2 25.3	0 23.2	28 01.8	28 58.9	9 13.6	18 09.5	19 49.5
10 F	15 16 18	17 31 26	17 21 47	24 59 56	27 13.7	22 46.1	16 39.0	3 10.6	0 44.8	28 05.1	29 04.7	9 12.4	18 11.5	19 49.9
11 Sa	15 20 15	18 31 47	2♐38 30	10♐16 06	27 05.7	24 20.3	17 54.4	3 55.9	1 06.6	28 08.7	29 10.4	9 11.0	18 13.5	19 50.2
12 Su	15 24 11	19 32 10	17 51 21	25 23 00	26 57.6	25 54.2	19 09.7	4 41.3	1 28.3	28 12.4	29 16.1	9 09.7	18 15.5	19 50.4
13 M	15 28 08	20 32 34	2♑49 59	10♑11 22	26 50.5	27 27.8	20 25.1	5 26.7	1 50.2	28 16.3	29 21.8	9 08.2	18 17.5	19 50.7
14 Tu	15 32 05	21 33 00	17 26 30	24 34 54	26 45.2	29 01.2	21 40.5	6 12.2	2 12.1	28 20.4	29 27.3	9 06.8	18 19.4	19 50.9
15 W	15 36 01	22 33 26	1♒36 21	8♒30 47	26 42.2	0♐34.2	22 55.8	6 57.7	2 34.1	28 24.7	29 32.8	9 05.3	18 21.4	19 51.1
16 Th	15 39 58	23 33 55	15 18 20	21 59 16	26D 41.2	2 07.0	24 11.2	7 43.3	2 56.1	28 29.2	29 38.2	9 03.7	18 23.3	19 51.3
17 F	15 43 54	24 34 24	28 33 57	5♓02 49	26 41.6	3 39.5	25 26.6	8 29.0	3 18.2	28 33.9	29 43.6	9 02.1	18 25.2	19 51.4
18 Sa	15 47 51	25 34 55	11♓26 23	17 45 11	26R 42.4	5 11.8	26 42.0	9 14.7	3 40.4	28 38.7	29 48.8	9 00.5	18 27.1	19 51.5
19 Su	15 51 47	26 35 26	23 59 44	0♈10 35	26 42.6	6 43.8	27 57.4	10 00.4	4 02.6	28 43.7	29 54.1	8 58.8	18 28.9	19 51.6
20 M	15 55 44	27 36 00	6♈18 15	12 23 13	26 41.3	8 15.7	29 12.7	10 46.2	4 24.9	28 49.0	29 59.2	8 57.1	18 30.8	19 51.7
21 Tu	15 59 40	28 36 34	18 25 54	24 26 45	26 37.5	9 47.3	0♐28.1	11 32.1	4 47.2	28 54.3	0♎04.2	8 55.3	18 32.6	19R 51.7
22 W	16 03 37	29 37 10	0♉26 07	6♉24 19	26 30.9	11 18.6	1 43.5	12 18.0	5 09.6	28 59.9	0 09.2	8 53.5	18 34.4	19 51.7
23 Th	16 07 34	0♐37 47	12 21 38	18 18 19	26 21.6	12 49.7	2 58.9	13 04.0	5 32.1	29 05.6	0 14.1	8 51.7	18 36.2	19 51.6
24 F	16 11 30	1 38 26	24 14 36	0♊10 39	26 10.1	14 20.6	4 14.3	13 50.0	5 54.6	29 11.6	0 19.0	8 49.8	18 37.9	19 51.6
25 Sa	16 15 27	2 39 06	6♊06 39	12 02 46	25 57.1	15 51.2	5 29.7	14 36.0	6 17.1	29 17.6	0 23.7	8 47.9	18 39.7	19 51.5
26 Su	16 19 23	3 39 47	17 59 10	23 56 01	25 43.7	17 21.6	6 45.1	15 22.1	6 39.8	29 23.9	0 28.4	8 45.9	18 41.4	19 51.3
27 M	16 23 20	4 40 30	29 53 30	5♋51 51	25 31.0	18 51.7	8 00.5	16 08.2	7 02.4	29 30.3	0 33.0	8 44.0	18 43.1	19 51.2
28 Tu	16 27 16	5 41 14	11♋51 16	17 52 03	25 20.1	20 21.4	9 15.9	16 54.4	7 25.1	29 36.9	0 37.5	8 41.9	18 44.8	19 51.0
29 W	16 31 13	6 42 00	23 54 31	29 59 01	25 11.8	21 50.7	10 31.3	17 40.7	7 47.9	29 43.6	0 41.9	8 39.9	18 46.4	19 50.8
30 Th	16 35 09	7 42 47	6♌05 58	12♌15 46	25 06.3	23 19.7	11 46.7	18 26.9	8 10.7	29 50.6	0 46.3	8 37.8	18 48.0	19 50.6

December 1950 — LONGITUDE

Day	Sid.Time	☉	0 hr ☽	Noon ☽	True ☊	☿	♀	♂	⚳	♃	♄	♅	♆	♇
1 F	16 39 06	8♐43 35	18♌28 56	24♌45 57	25♓03.4	24♐48.2	13♐02.1	19♑13.3	8♑33.5	29♒57.6	0♎50.6	8♋35.7	18♎49.7	19♌50.3
2 Sa	16 43 03	9 44 25	1♍07 22	7♍33 42	25D 02.6	26 16.1	14 17.5	19 59.6	8 56.4	0♓04.9	0 54.7	8R 33.5	18 51.2	19R 50.0
3 Su	16 46 59	10 45 16	14 05 29	20 43 13	25R 02.7	27 43.4	15 32.9	20 46.0	9 19.4	0 12.2	0 58.8	8 31.4	18 52.8	19 49.7
4 M	16 50 56	11 46 09	27 27 20	4♎18 13	25 02.5	29 10.0	16 48.3	21 32.5	9 42.3	0 19.8	1 02.8	8 29.2	18 54.3	19 49.3
5 Tu	16 54 52	12 47 03	11♎16 06	18 21 05	25 00.7	0♑35.8	18 03.7	22 19.0	10 05.4	0 27.5	1 06.7	8 26.9	18 55.8	19 48.9
6 W	16 58 49	13 47 59	25 33 05	2♏51 51	24 56.5	2 00.6	19 19.2	23 05.5	10 28.4	0 35.3	1 10.6	8 24.7	18 57.3	19 48.5
7 Th	17 02 45	14 48 55	10♏16 50	17 47 17	24 49.4	3 24.2	20 34.6	23 52.1	10 51.5	0 43.3	1 14.3	8 22.4	18 58.7	19 48.1
8 F	17 06 42	15 49 53	25 22 15	3♐00 30	24 39.7	4 46.5	21 50.0	24 38.7	11 14.7	0 51.5	1 18.0	8 20.0	19 00.2	19 47.6
9 Sa	17 10 38	16 50 52	10♐40 41	18 21 20	24 28.3	6 07.2	23 05.5	25 25.3	11 37.9	0 59.8	1 21.5	8 17.7	19 01.6	19 47.2
10 Su	17 14 35	17 51 52	26 00 55	3♑37 57	24 16.5	7 26.1	24 20.9	26 12.0	12 01.1	1 08.3	1 25.0	8 15.3	19 02.9	19 46.6
11 M	17 18 32	18 52 53	11♑11 06	18 39 07	24 05.9	8 42.9	25 36.3	26 58.7	12 24.4	1 16.9	1 28.3	8 13.0	19 04.3	19 46.1
12 Tu	17 22 28	19 53 54	26 01 02	3♒16 05	23 57.4	9 57.3	26 51.8	27 45.5	12 47.6	1 25.6	1 31.6	8 10.6	19 05.6	19 45.5
13 W	17 26 25	20 54 56	10♒23 47	17 23 51	23 51.6	11 08.7	28 07.2	28 32.3	13 11.0	1 34.5	1 34.8	8 08.1	19 06.9	19 44.9
14 Th	17 30 21	21 55 59	24 16 15	1♓01 08	23 48.6	12 16.8	29 22.6	29 19.1	13 34.3	1 43.5	1 37.8	8 05.7	19 08.1	19 44.3
15 F	17 34 18	22 57 01	7♓38 48	14 09 42	23 47.5	13 21.0	0♑38.0	0♒05.9	13 57.7	1 52.6	1 40.8	8 03.2	19 09.3	19 43.7
16 Sa	17 38 14	23 58 05	20 34 21	26 53 21	23 47.4	14 20.8	1 53.4	0 52.8	14 21.1	2 01.9	1 43.7	8 00.7	19 10.5	19 43.0
17 Su	17 42 11	24 59 08	3♈07 19	9♈16 54	23 47.0	15 15.5	3 08.8	1 39.7	14 44.5	2 11.3	1 46.5	7 58.3	19 11.7	19 42.3
18 M	17 46 08	26 00 12	15 22 46	21 25 30	23 45.1	16 04.2	4 24.2	2 26.6	15 08.0	2 20.9	1 49.1	7 55.7	19 12.8	19 41.6
19 Tu	17 50 04	27 01 16	27 25 45	3♉24 03	23 40.7	16 46.3	5 39.6	3 13.5	15 31.5	2 30.6	1 51.7	7 53.2	19 13.9	19 40.8
20 W	17 54 01	28 02 21	9♉20 56	15 16 53	23 33.3	17 20.9	6 55.0	4 00.5	15 55.0	2 40.4	1 54.2	7 50.7	19 15.0	19 40.0
21 Th	17 57 57	29 03 26	21 12 18	27 07 35	23 23.0	17 47.1	8 10.4	4 47.5	16 18.5	2 50.3	1 56.5	7 48.1	19 16.1	19 39.2
22 F	18 01 54	0♑04 31	3♊03 02	8♊58 56	23 10.2	18 03.9	9 25.8	5 34.5	16 42.1	3 00.3	1 58.8	7 45.6	19 17.1	19 38.4
23 Sa	18 05 50	1 05 37	14 55 32	20 53 00	22 55.7	18R 10.5	10 41.2	6 21.5	17 05.6	3 10.5	2 01.0	7 43.0	19 18.1	19 37.6
24 Su	18 09 47	2 06 44	26 51 30	2♋51 11	22 40.8	18 06.2	11 56.5	7 08.5	17 29.2	3 20.8	2 03.0	7 40.5	19 19.0	19 36.7
25 M	18 13 43	3 07 50	8♋52 10	14 54 34	22 26.6	17 50.4	13 11.9	7 55.6	17 52.8	3 31.2	2 05.0	7 37.9	19 19.9	19 35.8
26 Tu	18 17 40	4 08 57	20 58 30	27 04 07	22 14.3	17 22.8	14 27.3	8 42.7	18 16.5	3 41.7	2 06.9	7 35.3	19 20.8	19 34.9
27 W	18 21 37	5 10 04	3♌11 33	9♌20 59	22 04.7	16 43.4	15 42.6	9 29.8	18 40.1	3 52.3	2 08.6	7 32.7	19 21.7	19 34.0
28 Th	18 25 33	6 11 12	15 32 39	21 46 47	21 58.1	15 52.9	16 58.0	10 16.9	19 03.8	4 03.1	2 10.2	7 30.1	19 22.5	19 33.0
29 F	18 29 30	7 12 20	28 03 40	4♍23 40	21 54.5	14 52.1	18 13.3	11 04.0	19 27.5	4 13.9	2 11.8	7 27.5	19 23.3	19 32.0
30 Sa	18 33 26	8 13 29	10♍47 07	17 14 24	21D 53.3	13 42.7	19 28.7	11 51.2	19 51.2	4 24.9	2 13.2	7 25.0	19 24.0	19 31.0
31 Su	18 37 23	9 14 38	23 45 57	0♎22 09	21R 53.3	12 26.7	20 44.0	12 38.3	20 14.9	4 35.9	2 14.5	7 22.4	19 24.8	19 30.0

Astro Data Dy Hr Mn	Planet Ingress Dy Hr Mn	Last Aspect Dy Hr Mn	☽ Ingress Dy Hr Mn	Last Aspect Dy Hr Mn	☽ Ingress Dy Hr Mn	☽ Phases & Eclipses Dy Hr Mn
☽0S 6 18:26	♂ ♑ 6 6:40	2 2:11 ♄ ⚹	♌ 2 5:38	1 12:05 ☿ △	♍ 1 21:53	3 1:00 ☾ 10♌02
☽0N 19 10:34	⚳ ♑ 8 10:10	4 11:54 ♂ △	♍ 4 14:21	4 1:57 ☿ □	♎ 4 4:29	9 23:25 ● 17♏00
♇ R 21 15:56	☿ ♐ 15 3:10	6 16:58 ♄ ☌	♎ 6 19:10	5 19:00 ♂ □	♏ 6 7:19	16 15:06 ☽ 23♒42
	♄ ♎ 20 15:50	8 17:15 ♃ △	♏ 8 20:29	7 22:09 ♂ ⚹	♐ 8 7:17	24 15:14 ○ 1♊47
☽0S 4 3:00	♀ ♐ 21 3:03	10 18:27 ♄ ⚹	♐ 10 19:51	9 20:05 ♀ ☌	♑ 10 6:16	
♃⚻♄ 13 13:10	☉ ♐ 22 21:03	12 18:17 ♄ □	♑ 12 19:25	12 2:21 ♂ ☌	♒ 12 6:34	2 16:22 ☾ 9♍55
☽0N 16 15:58		14 20:30 ☿ ⚹	♒ 14 21:14	14 8:45 ♀ ⚹	♓ 14 10:10	9 9:29 ● 16♐44
☿ R 23 14:49	♃ ♓ 1 19:57	16 23:56 ♃ ☌	♓ 17 2:38	16 5:56 ☉ □	♈ 16 17:58	16 5:56 ☽ 23♓43
♃⚼♆ 30 10:04	☿ ♑ 5 1:57	19 11:28 ♄ ☍	♈ 19 11:39	18 22:00 ☉ △	♉ 19 5:10	24 10:23 ○ 2♋03
☽0S 31 8:51	♀ ♑ 14 23:54	21 21:00 ♃ ⚹	♉ 21 23:08	20 20:52 ♇ □	♊ 21 17:49	
	♂ ♒ 15 8:59	24 9:59 ♃ □	♊ 24 11:38	23 9:28 ♇ ⚹	♋ 24 6:18	
	☉ ♑ 22 10:13	26 23:06 ♃ △	♋ 27 0:13	25 20:46 ♆ □	♌ 26 17:45	
		28 13:45 ♆ □	♌ 29 12:02	28 7:44 ♇ ☌	♍ 29 3:41	
				30 16:34 ♀ △	♎ 31 11:20	

Astro Data

1 November 1950
Julian Day # 18567
SVP 5♓56'47"
GC 26♐09.2 ⚴ 8♐07.0
Eris 6♈51.7R ⚵ 4♏23.2
⚷ 19♐32.8 ⚶ 15♉26.2R
☽ Mean ☊ 25♓59.3

1 December 1950
Julian Day # 18597
SVP 5♓56'42"
GC 26♐09.2 ⚴ 20♐25.0
Eris 6♈39.2R ⚵ 14♏34.7
⚷ 22♐41.2 ⚶ 8♉25.1R
☽ Mean ☊ 24♓24.0

LONGITUDE — January 1951

Day	Sid.Time	☉	0 hr ☽	Noon ☽	True ☊	☿	♀	♂	⚳	♃	♄	♅	♆	♇
1 M	18 41 19	10♑15 47	7♎03 23	13♎50 01	21♓53.5	11♑06.7	21♑59.3	13♒25.5	20♑38.6	4♓47.1	2♎15.7	7♋19.8	19♎25.4	19♌29.0
2 Tu	18 45 16	11 16 57	20 42 21	27 40 33	21R 52.4	9R 45.1	23 14.7	14 12.7	21 02.3	4 58.4	2 16.8	7R 17.2	19 26.1	19R 27.9
3 W	18 49 12	12 18 07	4♏44 42	11♏54 45	21 49.1	8 24.8	24 30.0	14 59.9	21 26.1	5 09.7	2 17.8	7 14.6	19 26.7	19 26.8
4 Th	18 53 09	13 19 17	19 10 25	26 31 17	21 43.3	7 08.1	25 45.3	15 47.1	21 49.9	5 21.2	2 18.7	7 12.0	19 27.3	19 25.7
5 F	18 57 06	14 20 28	3♐56 43	11♐25 50	21 34.9	5 57.4	27 00.6	16 34.4	22 13.6	5 32.8	2 19.5	7 09.5	19 27.9	19 24.6
6 Sa	19 01 02	15 21 39	18 57 39	26 30 59	21 24.9	4 54.3	28 15.9	17 21.6	22 37.4	5 44.5	2 20.2	7 06.9	19 28.4	19 23.5
7 Su	19 04 59	16 22 50	4♑04 33	11♑37 02	21 14.4	4 00.0	29 31.2	18 08.9	23 01.2	5 56.2	2 20.7	7 04.4	19 28.9	19 22.3
8 M	19 08 55	17 24 01	19 07 09	26 33 39	21 04.6	3 15.3	0♒46.5	18 56.1	23 25.0	6 08.1	2 21.2	7 01.8	19 29.4	19 21.2
9 Tu	19 12 52	18 25 11	3♒55 26	11♒11 37	20 56.7	2 40.6	2 01.8	19 43.4	23 48.8	6 20.0	2 21.5	6 59.3	19 29.8	19 20.0
10 W	19 16 48	19 26 21	18 21 28	25 24 28	20 51.3	2 15.9	3 17.1	20 30.7	24 12.6	6 32.1	2 21.8	6 56.8	19 30.2	19 18.8
11 Th	19 20 45	20 27 31	2♓20 20	9♓08 59	20D 48.6	2 00.9	4 32.4	21 17.9	24 36.4	6 44.2	2R 21.9	6 54.3	19 30.5	19 17.6
12 F	19 24 42	21 28 40	15 50 29	22 25 06	20 47.9	1D 55.2	5 47.6	22 05.2	25 00.2	6 56.4	2 21.9	6 51.8	19 30.8	19 16.3
13 Sa	19 28 38	22 29 48	28 53 12	5♈15 16	20 48.5	1 58.1	7 02.8	22 52.5	25 24.0	7 08.7	2 21.8	6 49.3	19 31.1	19 15.1
14 Su	19 32 35	23 30 55	11♈31 49	17 43 30	20R 49.4	2 09.2	8 18.1	23 39.8	25 47.8	7 21.1	2 21.6	6 46.8	19 31.3	19 13.8
15 M	19 36 31	24 32 02	23 50 56	29 54 46	20 49.4	2 27.6	9 33.3	24 27.1	26 11.6	7 33.5	2 21.2	6 44.4	19 31.6	19 12.5
16 Tu	19 40 28	25 33 09	5♉55 40	11♉54 16	20 47.6	2 52.9	10 48.5	25 14.3	26 35.4	7 46.0	2 20.8	6 42.0	19 31.7	19 11.2
17 W	19 44 24	26 34 14	17 51 11	23 47 01	20 43.7	3 24.2	12 03.6	26 01.6	26 59.2	7 58.7	2 20.3	6 39.6	19 31.9	19 09.9
18 Th	19 48 21	27 35 19	29 42 19	5♊37 35	20 37.4	4 01.2	13 18.8	26 48.9	27 23.0	8 11.3	2 19.6	6 37.2	19 32.0	19 08.6
19 F	19 52 17	28 36 23	11♊33 18	17 29 52	20 29.2	4 43.2	14 33.9	27 36.1	27 46.8	8 24.1	2 18.9	6 34.8	19 32.1	19 07.3
20 Sa	19 56 14	29 37 27	23 27 40	29 26 58	20 19.5	5 29.7	15 49.1	28 23.4	28 10.6	8 36.9	2 18.0	6 32.5	19R 32.1	19 05.9
21 Su	20 00 11	0♒38 29	5♋28 05	11♋31 11	20 09.4	6 20.3	17 04.2	29 10.6	28 34.4	8 49.8	2 17.1	6 30.2	19 32.1	19 04.6
22 M	20 04 07	1 39 31	17 36 28	23 44 03	19 59.7	7 14.6	18 19.3	29 57.9	28 58.2	9 02.8	2 16.0	6 27.9	19 32.1	19 03.2
23 Tu	20 08 04	2 40 32	29 54 02	6♌06 30	19 51.4	8 12.2	19 34.3	0♓45.1	29 21.9	9 15.8	2 14.8	6 25.7	19 32.0	19 01.9
24 W	20 12 00	3 41 32	12♌21 30	18 39 05	19 45.1	9 12.9	20 49.4	1 32.3	29 45.7	9 28.9	2 13.5	6 23.5	19 31.9	19 00.5
25 Th	20 15 57	4 42 32	24 59 18	1♍22 13	19 41.1	10 16.2	22 04.4	2 19.5	0♒09.4	9 42.1	2 12.1	6 21.3	19 31.8	18 59.1
26 F	20 19 53	5 43 30	7♍47 53	14 16 24	19D 39.3	11 22.1	23 19.5	3 06.7	0 33.1	9 55.3	2 10.6	6 19.1	19 31.6	18 57.7
27 Sa	20 23 50	6 44 28	20 47 53	27 22 27	19 39.4	12 30.2	24 34.5	3 53.9	0 56.8	10 08.6	2 09.1	6 16.9	19 31.4	18 56.3
28 Su	20 27 46	7 45 26	4♎00 15	10♎41 26	19 40.6	13 40.4	25 49.4	4 41.1	1 20.6	10 21.9	2 07.4	6 14.8	19 31.2	18 54.9
29 M	20 31 43	8 46 23	17 26 10	24 14 36	19 42.1	14 52.5	27 04.4	5 28.3	1 44.2	10 35.3	2 05.6	6 12.8	19 30.9	18 53.5
30 Tu	20 35 40	9 47 19	1♏06 50	8♏02 58	19R 42.9	16 06.3	28 19.3	6 15.4	2 07.9	10 48.8	2 03.7	6 10.7	19 30.6	18 52.0
31 W	20 39 36	10 48 14	15 03 00	22 06 54	19 42.3	17 21.7	29 34.3	7 02.6	2 31.6	11 02.3	2 01.7	6 08.7	19 30.3	18 50.6

LONGITUDE — February 1951

Day	Sid.Time	☉	0 hr ☽	Noon ☽	True ☊	☿	♀	♂	⚳	♃	♄	♅	♆	♇
1 Th	20 43 33	11♒49 09	29♏14 29	6♐25 31	19♓40.0	18♑38.7	0♓49.2	7♓49.7	2♒55.2	11♓15.8	1♎59.6	6♋06.7	19♎29.9	18♌49.2
2 F	20 47 29	12 50 03	13♐39 35	20 56 12	19R 36.1	19 57.1	2 04.1	8 36.8	3 18.9	11 29.5	1R 57.4	6R 04.8	19R 29.5	18R 47.7
3 Sa	20 51 26	13 50 57	28 14 45	5♑34 28	19 31.0	21 16.7	3 19.0	9 24.0	3 42.5	11 43.1	1 55.1	6 02.9	19 29.1	18 46.3
4 Su	20 55 22	14 51 49	12♑54 32	20 14 06	19 25.4	22 37.6	4 33.8	10 11.0	4 06.1	11 56.9	1 52.7	6 01.0	19 28.7	18 44.9
5 M	20 59 19	15 52 41	27 32 13	4♒48 00	19 20.2	23 59.7	5 48.6	10 58.1	4 29.7	12 10.6	1 50.2	5 59.2	19 28.2	18 43.4
6 Tu	21 03 15	16 53 31	12♒00 36	19 09 15	19 16.0	25 22.9	7 03.4	11 45.2	4 53.2	12 24.4	1 47.6	5 57.4	19 27.6	18 42.0
7 W	21 07 12	17 54 20	26 13 15	3♓12 04	19 13.4	26 47.2	8 18.2	12 32.2	5 16.7	12 38.3	1 45.0	5 55.7	19 27.1	18 40.5
8 Th	21 11 09	18 55 07	10♓05 18	16 52 40	19D 12.3	28 12.5	9 33.0	13 19.3	5 40.2	12 52.2	1 42.2	5 54.0	19 26.5	18 39.1
9 F	21 15 05	19 55 54	23 34 04	0♈09 31	19 12.7	29 38.8	10 47.7	14 06.3	6 03.7	13 06.1	1 39.4	5 52.3	19 25.9	18 37.6
10 Sa	21 19 02	20 56 38	6♈39 08	13 03 12	19 14.1	1♒06.1	12 02.4	14 53.2	6 27.2	13 20.1	1 36.4	5 50.7	19 25.2	18 36.2
11 Su	21 22 58	21 57 21	19 22 02	25 36 05	19 15.9	2 34.4	13 17.1	15 40.2	6 50.6	13 34.1	1 33.4	5 49.1	19 24.5	18 34.7
12 M	21 26 55	22 58 03	1♉45 50	7♉51 48	19 17.5	4 03.5	14 31.7	16 27.1	7 14.0	13 48.2	1 30.3	5 47.6	19 23.8	18 33.3
13 Tu	21 30 51	23 58 43	13 54 36	19 54 48	19R 18.3	5 33.6	15 46.3	17 14.0	7 37.4	14 02.3	1 27.1	5 46.1	19 23.1	18 31.8
14 W	21 34 48	24 59 21	25 53 02	1♊49 53	19 18.2	7 04.6	17 00.9	18 00.9	8 00.7	14 16.4	1 23.8	5 44.6	19 22.3	18 30.4
15 Th	21 38 44	25 59 58	7♊45 59	13 41 54	19 16.9	8 36.5	18 15.4	18 47.8	8 24.0	14 30.6	1 20.5	5 43.2	19 21.5	18 29.0
16 F	21 42 41	27 00 32	19 38 14	25 35 29	19 14.6	10 09.3	19 29.9	19 34.6	8 47.3	14 44.8	1 17.1	5 41.9	19 20.6	18 27.5
17 Sa	21 46 38	28 01 06	1♋34 12	7♋34 48	19 11.6	11 43.0	20 44.4	20 21.4	9 10.5	14 59.0	1 13.6	5 40.6	19 19.8	18 26.1
18 Su	21 50 34	29 01 37	13 37 44	19 43 22	19 08.2	13 17.6	21 58.8	21 08.2	9 33.7	15 13.2	1 10.0	5 39.3	19 18.9	18 24.7
19 M	21 54 31	0♓02 07	25 52 00	2♌03 54	19 05.0	14 53.1	23 13.2	21 54.9	9 56.9	15 27.5	1 06.4	5 38.1	19 18.0	18 23.3
20 Tu	21 58 27	1 02 35	8♌19 16	14 38 15	19 02.2	16 29.5	24 27.6	22 41.6	10 20.0	15 41.8	1 02.6	5 36.9	19 17.0	18 21.9
21 W	22 02 24	2 03 01	21 00 56	27 27 20	19 00.3	18 06.9	25 41.9	23 28.3	10 43.1	15 56.1	0 58.9	5 35.8	19 16.1	18 20.4
22 Th	22 06 20	3 03 26	3♍57 27	10♍31 13	18D 59.3	19 45.2	26 56.2	24 14.9	11 06.2	16 10.5	0 55.0	5 34.7	19 15.1	18 19.0
23 F	22 10 17	4 03 49	17 08 31	23 49 15	18 59.2	21 24.4	28 10.4	25 01.5	11 29.2	16 24.8	0 51.1	5 33.7	19 14.0	18 17.7
24 Sa	22 14 13	5 04 10	0♎33 13	7♎20 16	18 59.7	23 04.6	29 24.6	25 48.1	11 52.2	16 39.2	0 47.1	5 32.7	19 13.0	18 16.3
25 Su	22 18 10	6 04 30	14 10 13	21 02 50	19 00.7	24 45.8	0♈38.8	26 34.7	12 15.1	16 53.6	0 43.1	5 31.8	19 11.9	18 14.9
26 M	22 22 07	7 04 48	27 57 56	4♏55 18	19 01.8	26 28.0	1 52.9	27 21.2	12 38.0	17 08.1	0 39.0	5 30.9	19 10.8	18 13.5
27 Tu	22 26 03	8 05 05	11♏54 45	18 56 02	19 02.7	28 11.1	3 07.0	28 07.7	13 00.9	17 22.5	0 34.9	5 30.1	19 09.7	18 12.2
28 W	22 30 00	9 05 21	25 58 58	3♐03 17	19R 03.2	29 55.3	4 21.1	28 54.1	13 23.7	17 37.0	0 30.7	5 29.3	19 08.5	18 10.8

Astro Data

	Dy Hr Mn
♆✶♇	3 13:30
♄ R	12 1:17
♃△♅	12 4:27
☿ D	12 15:34
☽ 0N	12 23:09
♆ R	21 5:28
☽ 0S	27 13:32
☽ 0N	9 8:17
☽ 0S	23 19:36
♀0N	26 21:37

Planet Ingress

		Dy Hr Mn
♀	♒	7 21:10
☉	♒	20 20:52
♂	♓	22 13:05
⚳	♒	25 2:29
♀	♓	31 20:14
☿	♒	9 17:50
☉	♓	19 11:10
♀	♈	24 23:26
☿	♓	28 13:04

Last Aspect / ☽ Ingress

Last Aspect Dy Hr Mn		☽ Ingress Dy Hr Mn
2 3:38	♀ □	♏ 2 15:58
4 10:38	♀ ✶	♐ 4 17:38
6 0:49	♆ ✶	♑ 6 17:32
8 0:35	♆ □	♒ 8 17:35
10 3:09	♂ ☌	♓ 10 19:56
12 10:08	☉ ✶	♈ 13 2:05
15 0:26	♂ ✶	♉ 15 12:10
17 18:11	☉ △	♊ 18 0:36
20 9:44	♂ △	♋ 20 13:06
22 3:47	♆ □	♌ 23 0:12
24 16:34	♀ ☍	♍ 25 9:26
26 6:07	☿ △	♎ 27 16:46
29 17:27	♀ △	♏ 29 22:04

Last Aspect / ☽ Ingress

Last Aspect Dy Hr Mn		☽ Ingress Dy Hr Mn
31 6:28	♇ □	♐ 1 1:16
2 9:37	♆ ✶	♑ 3 2:52
4 16:20	☿ ☌	♒ 5 4:04
6 12:31	♆ △	♓ 7 6:29
9 10:57	☿ ✶	♈ 9 11:43
11 4:21	☉ ✶	♉ 11 20:33
13 20:55	☉ □	♊ 14 8:18
16 15:07	☉ △	♋ 16 20:51
18 16:55	♀ △	♌ 19 8:01
20 20:45	♆ ✶	♍ 21 16:43
23 20:33	♀ ☍	♎ 23 23:01
25 19:21	☿ △	♏ 26 3:31
28 5:57	☿ □	♐ 28 6:49

☽ Phases & Eclipses

Dy Hr Mn	
1 5:11	☾ 9♎58
7 20:10	● 16♑44
15 0:23	☽ 24♈02
23 4:47	○ 2♌22
30 15:14	☾ 9♏56
6 7:54	● 16♒43
13 20:55	☽ 24♉21
21 21:12	○ 2♍26
28 22:59	☾ 9♐33

Astro Data

1 January 1951
Julian Day # 18628
SVP 5♓56'36"
GC 26♐09.3 ⚳ 3♑08.3
Eris 6♈36.1 ⚵ 24♏20.9
⚷ 26♐09.8 ⚶ 6♉41.5
☽ Mean ☊ 22♓45.5

1 February 1951
Julian Day # 18659
SVP 5♓56'30"
GC 26♐09.4 ⚳ 15♑21.7
Eris 6♈44.0 ⚵ 2♐33.8
⚷ 29♐20.1 ⚶ 11♉20.3
☽ Mean ☊ 21♓07.1

March 1951

LONGITUDE

Day	Sid.Time	☉	0 hr ☽	Noon ☽	True ☊	☿	♀	♂	⚳	♃	♄	♅	♆	♇
1 Th	22 33 56	10♓05 35	10♐08 46	17♐15 08	19♓03.1	1♓40.6	5♈35.1	29♓40.6	13♒46.4	17♓51.4	0♎26.4	5♋28.6	19♎07.4	18♌09.5
2 F	22 37 53	11 05 48	24 22 07	1♑29 21	19R 02.7	3 26.8	6 49.1	0♈27.0	14 09.2	18 05.9	0R 22.2	5R 28.0	19R 06.2	18R 08.2
3 Sa	22 41 49	12 06 00	8♑36 32	15 43 16	19 02.0	5 14.2	8 03.0	1 13.3	14 31.9	18 20.4	0 17.8	5 27.4	19 05.0	18 06.9
4 Su	22 45 46	13 06 09	22 49 09	29 53 46	19 01.3	7 02.6	9 16.9	1 59.7	14 54.5	18 34.9	0 13.4	5 26.8	19 03.7	18 05.6
5 M	22 49 42	14 06 17	6♒56 40	13♒57 24	19 00.6	8 52.0	10 30.8	2 45.9	15 17.1	18 49.4	0 09.0	5 26.3	19 02.5	18 04.3
6 Tu	22 53 39	15 06 24	20 55 34	27 50 43	19 00.2	10 42.6	11 44.6	3 32.2	15 39.6	19 04.0	0 04.5	5 25.8	19 01.2	18 03.0
7 W	22 57 36	16 06 28	4♓42 28	11♓30 30	19D 00.0	12 34.2	12 58.4	4 18.4	16 02.1	19 18.5	0 00.0	5 25.4	18 59.9	18 01.8
8 Th	23 01 32	17 06 31	18 14 31	24 54 18	19 00.0	14 26.8	14 12.1	5 04.6	16 24.5	19 33.0	29♍55.5	5 25.1	18 58.5	18 00.5
9 F	23 05 29	18 06 32	1♈29 41	8♈00 36	19R 00.1	16 20.5	15 25.8	5 50.8	16 46.9	19 47.6	29 50.9	5 24.8	18 57.2	17 59.3
10 Sa	23 09 25	19 06 30	14 27 03	20 49 06	19 00.1	18 15.1	16 39.4	6 36.9	17 09.2	20 02.1	29 46.3	5 24.5	18 55.8	17 58.1
11 Su	23 13 22	20 06 27	27 06 53	3♉20 39	19 00.0	20 10.7	17 53.0	7 22.9	17 31.5	20 16.7	29 41.7	5 24.4	18 54.4	17 56.9
12 M	23 17 18	21 06 22	9♉30 41	15 37 20	18 59.8	22 07.3	19 06.5	8 09.0	17 53.7	20 31.2	29 37.1	5 24.2	18 53.0	17 55.7
13 Tu	23 21 15	22 06 14	21 41 00	27 42 08	18 59.5	24 04.6	20 20.0	8 54.9	18 15.8	20 45.7	29 32.4	5D 24.1	18 51.6	17 54.5
14 W	23 25 11	23 06 04	3♊41 15	9♊38 51	18 59.2	26 02.7	21 33.4	9 40.9	18 37.9	21 00.3	29 27.7	5 24.1	18 50.2	17 53.4
15 Th	23 29 08	24 05 52	15 35 31	21 31 48	18D 59.1	28 01.4	22 46.8	10 26.8	18 59.9	21 14.8	29 23.0	5 24.1	18 48.7	17 52.3
16 F	23 33 05	25 05 38	27 28 18	3♋25 37	18 59.2	0♈00.6	24 00.1	11 12.6	19 21.9	21 29.4	29 18.3	5 24.2	18 47.3	17 51.2
17 Sa	23 37 01	26 05 22	9♋24 18	15 24 58	18 59.5	2 00.1	25 13.4	11 58.5	19 43.8	21 43.9	29 13.6	5 24.4	18 45.8	17 50.1
18 Su	23 40 58	27 05 03	21 28 09	27 34 22	19 00.2	3 59.7	26 26.6	12 44.2	20 05.6	21 58.4	29 08.9	5 24.6	18 44.3	17 49.0
19 M	23 44 54	28 04 42	3♌44 07	9♌57 51	19 01.1	5 59.2	27 39.7	13 30.0	20 27.4	22 12.9	29 04.2	5 24.8	18 42.8	17 47.9
20 Tu	23 48 51	29 04 19	16 15 56	22 38 41	19 02.0	7 58.3	28 52.8	14 15.6	20 49.1	22 27.4	28 59.4	5 25.1	18 41.3	17 46.9
21 W	23 52 47	0♈03 54	29 06 21	5♍39 06	19 02.7	9 56.8	0♉05.8	15 01.3	21 10.7	22 41.9	28 54.7	5 25.5	18 39.8	17 45.9
22 Th	23 56 44	1 03 26	12♍16 58	18 59 56	19R 03.0	11 54.3	1 18.8	15 46.9	21 32.2	22 56.3	28 50.0	5 25.9	18 38.2	17 44.9
23 F	0 00 40	2 02 57	25 47 51	2♎40 29	19 02.7	13 50.4	2 31.7	16 32.4	21 53.7	23 10.8	28 45.2	5 26.3	18 36.6	17 43.9
24 Sa	0 04 37	3 02 25	9♎37 31	16 38 29	19 01.7	15 44.8	3 44.5	17 17.9	22 15.1	23 25.2	28 40.5	5 26.8	18 35.1	17 43.0
25 Su	0 08 33	4 01 51	23 42 55	0♏50 14	19 00.0	17 37.0	4 57.3	18 03.3	22 36.5	23 39.6	28 35.8	5 27.4	18 33.5	17 42.0
26 M	0 12 30	5 01 16	7♏59 49	15 11 02	18 58.0	19 26.7	6 10.0	18 48.8	22 57.8	23 54.0	28 31.1	5 28.0	18 31.9	17 41.1
27 Tu	0 16 27	6 00 39	22 23 14	29 35 47	18 55.8	21 13.3	7 22.6	19 34.1	23 19.0	24 08.4	28 26.5	5 28.7	18 30.3	17 40.2
28 W	0 20 23	7 00 00	6♐48 07	13♐59 40	18 54.1	22 56.6	8 35.2	20 19.4	23 40.1	24 22.8	28 21.8	5 29.4	18 28.7	17 39.4
29 Th	0 24 20	7 59 19	21 09 58	28 18 35	18D 53.0	24 36.0	9 47.8	21 04.7	24 01.1	24 37.1	28 17.2	5 30.2	18 27.1	17 38.5
30 F	0 28 16	8 58 37	5♑25 10	12♑29 27	18 52.8	26 11.3	11 00.2	21 50.0	24 22.1	24 51.5	28 12.5	5 31.0	18 25.5	17 37.7
31 Sa	0 32 13	9 57 53	19 31 13	26 30 18	18 53.4	27 41.9	12 12.6	22 35.1	24 43.0	25 05.8	28 08.0	5 31.9	18 23.9	17 36.9

April 1951

LONGITUDE

Day	Sid.Time	☉	0 hr ☽	Noon ☽	True ☊	☿	♀	♂	⚳	♃	♄	♅	♆	♇
1 Su	0 36 09	10♈57 07	3♒26 35	10♒19 58	18♓54.7	29♈07.6	13♉25.0	23♈20.3	25♒03.8	25♓20.0	28♍03.4	5♋32.8	18♎22.3	17♌36.2
2 M	0 40 06	11 56 19	17 10 24	23 57 51	18 56.2	0♉28.0	14 37.2	24 05.4	25 24.5	25 34.3	27R 58.9	5 33.8	18R 20.6	17R 35.4
3 Tu	0 44 02	12 55 29	0♓42 16	7♓23 38	18R 57.4	1 42.9	15 49.4	24 50.4	25 45.1	25 48.5	27 54.4	5 34.9	18 19.0	17 34.7
4 W	0 47 59	13 54 38	14 01 55	20 37 06	18 57.8	2 52.1	17 01.6	25 35.4	26 05.7	26 02.7	27 49.9	5 35.9	18 17.3	17 34.0
5 Th	0 51 56	14 53 44	27 09 08	3♈38 00	18 57.0	3 55.2	18 13.6	26 20.4	26 26.1	26 16.9	27 45.5	5 37.1	18 15.7	17 33.3
6 F	0 55 52	15 52 49	10♈03 41	16 26 12	18 54.8	4 52.1	19 25.6	27 05.3	26 46.5	26 31.0	27 41.1	5 38.3	18 14.0	17 32.6
7 Sa	0 59 49	16 51 51	22 45 31	29 01 43	18 51.2	5 42.7	20 37.6	27 50.2	27 06.7	26 45.1	27 36.7	5 39.5	18 12.4	17 32.0
8 Su	1 03 45	17 50 51	5♉14 52	11♉25 03	18 46.6	6 26.9	21 49.4	28 35.0	27 26.9	26 59.2	27 32.4	5 40.8	18 10.7	17 31.4
9 M	1 07 42	18 49 50	17 32 26	23 37 14	18 41.3	7 04.4	23 01.2	29 19.7	27 47.0	27 13.2	27 28.2	5 42.1	18 09.1	17 30.8
10 Tu	1 11 38	19 48 46	29 39 39	5♊40 00	18 36.0	7 35.4	24 12.9	0♉04.4	28 07.0	27 27.2	27 24.0	5 43.5	18 07.4	17 30.3
11 W	1 15 35	20 47 40	11♊38 38	17 35 55	18 31.3	7 59.7	25 24.5	0 49.1	28 26.9	27 41.2	27 19.8	5 45.0	18 05.8	17 29.8
12 Th	1 19 31	21 46 32	23 32 19	29 28 16	18 27.6	8 17.4	26 36.1	1 33.7	28 46.6	27 55.1	27 15.7	5 46.5	18 04.2	17 29.3
13 F	1 23 28	22 45 22	5♋24 19	11♋21 00	18 25.4	8 28.5	27 47.6	2 18.3	29 06.3	28 08.9	27 11.7	5 48.0	18 02.5	17 28.8
14 Sa	1 27 25	23 44 09	17 18 53	23 18 35	18D 24.6	8R 33.2	28 58.9	3 02.8	29 25.9	28 22.8	27 07.7	5 49.6	18 00.9	17 28.4
15 Su	1 31 21	24 42 54	29 20 41	5♌25 49	18 25.2	8 31.6	0♊10.2	3 47.3	29 45.4	28 36.6	27 03.8	5 51.2	17 59.2	17 27.9
16 M	1 35 18	25 41 37	11♌34 35	17 47 34	18 26.6	8 24.0	1 21.4	4 31.7	0♓04.7	28 50.3	26 59.9	5 52.9	17 57.6	17 27.6
17 Tu	1 39 14	26 40 17	24 05 20	0♍28 21	18 28.2	8 10.6	2 32.6	5 16.0	0 24.0	29 04.0	26 56.1	5 54.6	17 56.0	17 27.2
18 W	1 43 11	27 38 55	6♍57 06	13 31 54	18R 29.2	7 51.9	3 43.6	6 00.3	0 43.1	29 17.7	26 52.4	5 56.4	17 54.3	17 26.9
19 Th	1 47 07	28 37 32	20 13 02	27 00 36	18 29.0	7 28.2	4 54.5	6 44.6	1 02.1	29 31.3	26 48.7	5 58.2	17 52.7	17 26.5
20 F	1 51 04	29 36 05	3♎54 37	10♎54 53	18 27.0	7 00.1	6 05.4	7 28.8	1 21.1	29 44.8	26 45.1	6 00.1	17 51.1	17 26.3
21 Sa	1 55 00	0♉34 37	18 01 05	25 12 43	18 23.2	6 28.2	7 16.1	8 12.9	1 39.9	29 58.3	26 41.6	6 02.0	17 49.5	17 26.0
22 Su	1 58 57	1 33 08	2♏29 05	9♏49 25	18 17.7	5 53.1	8 26.7	8 57.0	1 58.5	0♈11.8	26 38.1	6 04.0	17 47.9	17 25.8
23 M	2 02 54	2 31 36	17 12 44	24 38 02	18 11.1	5 15.4	9 37.3	9 41.0	2 17.1	0 25.2	26 34.8	6 06.0	17 46.3	17 25.6
24 Tu	2 06 50	3 30 03	2♐04 15	9♐30 19	18 04.3	4 36.0	10 47.8	10 25.0	2 35.6	0 38.6	26 31.5	6 08.0	17 44.8	17 25.4
25 W	2 10 47	4 28 28	16 55 12	24 17 57	17 58.2	3 55.6	11 58.1	11 09.0	2 53.9	0 51.9	26 28.2	6 10.1	17 43.2	17 25.3
26 Th	2 14 43	5 26 51	1♑37 46	8♑53 57	17 53.7	3 14.9	13 08.4	11 52.9	3 12.1	1 05.1	26 25.1	6 12.2	17 41.6	17 25.2
27 F	2 18 40	6 25 13	16 05 59	23 13 29	17 51.0	2 34.6	14 18.5	12 36.7	3 30.2	1 18.3	26 22.0	6 14.4	17 40.1	17 25.1
28 Sa	2 22 36	7 23 33	0♒16 14	7♒14 06	17D 50.2	1 55.6	15 28.6	13 20.5	3 48.1	1 31.4	26 19.0	6 16.6	17 38.6	17 25.0
29 Su	2 26 33	8 21 52	14 07 08	20 55 26	17 50.7	1 18.3	16 38.6	14 04.3	4 05.9	1 44.5	26 16.1	6 18.8	17 37.0	17D 25.0
30 M	2 30 29	9 20 09	27 39 10	4♓18 34	17 51.8	0 43.5	17 48.4	14 48.0	4 23.6	1 57.5	26 13.3	6 21.1	17 35.5	17 25.0

Astro Data	Dy Hr Mn
♃⊼♇	2 15:27
♂0N	3 19:47
♃⊼♆	6 7:45
☽0N	8 17:45
♅D	14 10:41
☿0N	17 11:16
☉0N	21 10:26
☽0S	23 4:00
☽0N	5 1:43
♃☍♄	10 7:44
☿R	14 17:51
☽0S	19 13:46
♇D	30 5:20

Planet Ingress		Dy Hr Mn
♂	♈	1 22:03
♄	♍R	7 12:12
☿	♈	16 11:53
♀	♉	21 10:05
☉	♈	21 10:26
☿	♉	2 3:27
♂	♉	10 9:37
♀	♊	15 8:33
⚳	♓	16 6:08
☉	♉	20 21:48
♃	♈	21 14:57

Last Aspect Dy Hr Mn			☽ Ingress	Dy Hr Mn
1 15:09	♆	⚹	♑	2 9:29
3 17:40	♆	□	♒	4 12:11
5 20:44	♆	△	♓	6 15:45
8 21:05	♄	☍	♈	8 21:16
10 8:26	♆	☍	♉	11 5:33
13 15:39	♄	△	♊	13 16:36
16 3:45	♄	□	♋	16 5:06
18 15:04	♄	⚹	♌	18 16:44
21 0:47	♀	△	♍	21 1:39
23 5:13	♄	☌	♎	23 7:21
24 15:18	♆	☌	♏	25 10:36
27 10:05	♄	⚹	♐	27 12:40
29 11:58	♄	□	♑	29 14:51
31 14:48	♄	△	♒	31 18:02

Last Aspect Dy Hr Mn			☽ Ingress	Dy Hr Mn
2 12:14	♂	⚹	♓	2 22:44
5 1:11	♄	☍	♈	5 5:16
7 9:34	♂	☌	♉	7 13:52
9 19:36	♄	△	♊	10 0:41
12 8:48	♃	□	♋	12 13:04
15 0:31	♀	⚹	♌	15 1:18
17 4:17	☉	△	♍	17 11:07
19 16:28	♃	☍	♎	19 17:13
20 23:42	♆	☌	♏	21 19:55
23 15:08	♄	⚹	♐	23 20:40
25 15:32	♄	□	♑	25 21:19
27 17:19	♄	△	♒	27 23:32
29 6:10	♆	△	♓	30 4:13

☽ Phases & Eclipses Dy Hr Mn	
7 20:51	● 16♓29
7 20:53:10	● A 00'59"
15 17:40	☽ 24♊20
23 10:50	○ 2♎00
23 10:37	● A 0.642
30 5:35	☾ 8♑43
6 10:52	● 15♈50
14 12:56	☽ 23♋46
21 21:30	○ 0♏58
28 12:18	☾ 7♒24

Astro Data

1 March 1951
Julian Day # 18687
SVP 5♓56'26"
GC 26♐09.4 ⚴ 25♑29.0
Eris 6♈59.1 ⚵ 7♐43.2
⚷ 1♑29.7 ⚶ 19♉11.1
☽ Mean ☊ 19♓38.1

1 April 1951
Julian Day # 18718
SVP 5♓56'22"
GC 26♐09.5 ⚴ 4♒58.7
Eris 7♈20.3 ⚵ 9♐35.0R
⚷ 2♑42.6 ⚶ 0♊12.4
☽ Mean ☊ 17♓59.6

LONGITUDE — May 1951

Day	Sid.Time	☉	0 hr ☽	Noon ☽	True ☊	☿	♀	♂	⚳	♃	♄	♅	♆	♇
1 Tu	2 34 26	10♉18 24	10♓53 54	17♓25 25	17♓52.4	0♉11.6	18♊58.2	15♉31.6	4♓41.2	2♈10.4	26♍10.6	6♋23.5	17♎34.0	17♌25.0
2 W	2 38 23	11 16 38	23 53 23	0♈18 04	17R51.6	29♈43.1	20 07.8	16 15.2	4 58.6	2 23.3	26R07.9	6 25.8	17R32.5	17 25.0
3 Th	2 42 19	12 14 51	6♈39 42	12 58 29	17 48.7	29R18.5	21 17.4	16 58.7	5 15.9	2 36.1	26 05.3	6 28.2	17 31.1	17 25.1
4 F	2 46 16	13 13 02	19 14 38	25 28 16	17 43.3	28 58.0	22 26.8	17 42.2	5 33.0	2 48.9	26 02.9	6 30.7	17 29.6	17 25.2
5 Sa	2 50 12	14 11 11	1♉39 33	7♉48 37	17 35.5	28 41.8	23 36.1	18 25.7	5 50.0	3 01.5	26 00.5	6 33.2	17 28.2	17 25.4
6 Su	2 54 09	15 09 19	13 55 34	20 00 31	17 25.7	28 30.1	24 45.3	19 09.1	6 06.8	3 14.1	25 58.2	6 35.7	17 26.7	17 25.5
7 M	2 58 05	16 07 25	26 03 35	2♊04 55	17 14.7	28D23.1	25 54.4	19 52.4	6 23.5	3 26.7	25 56.0	6 38.3	17 25.3	17 25.7
8 Tu	3 02 02	17 05 29	8♊04 40	14 03 02	17 03.5	28 20.8	27 03.3	20 35.7	6 40.0	3 39.1	25 53.9	6 40.9	17 23.9	17 25.9
9 W	3 05 58	18 03 32	20 00 12	25 56 28	16 53.0	28 23.2	28 12.2	21 19.0	6 56.4	3 51.5	25 51.9	6 43.5	17 22.6	17 26.2
10 Th	3 09 55	19 01 32	1♋52 07	7♋47 31	16 44.1	28 30.3	29 20.9	22 02.1	7 12.6	4 03.8	25 50.0	6 46.2	17 21.2	17 26.5
11 F	3 13 52	19 59 31	13 43 04	19 39 11	16 37.5	28 41.9	0♋29.4	22 45.3	7 28.7	4 16.1	25 48.1	6 48.9	17 19.9	17 26.8
12 Sa	3 17 48	20 57 29	25 36 24	1♌35 13	16 33.3	28 58.2	1 37.9	23 28.4	7 44.6	4 28.2	25 46.4	6 51.6	17 18.6	17 27.1
13 Su	3 21 45	21 55 24	7♌36 13	13 40 00	16D31.4	29 18.9	2 46.2	24 11.4	8 00.3	4 40.3	25 44.8	6 54.4	17 17.3	17 27.5
14 M	3 25 41	22 53 18	19 47 11	25 58 24	16 31.1	29 43.9	3 54.3	24 54.4	8 15.8	4 52.3	25 43.3	6 57.2	17 16.0	17 27.8
15 Tu	3 29 38	23 51 09	2♍14 17	8♍35 26	16R31.5	0♉13.1	5 02.3	25 37.3	8 31.2	5 04.2	25 41.8	7 00.0	17 14.7	17 28.3
16 W	3 33 34	24 48 59	15 02 26	21 35 49	16 31.6	0 46.4	6 10.2	26 20.2	8 46.5	5 16.0	25 40.5	7 02.9	17 13.5	17 28.7
17 Th	3 37 31	25 46 48	28 16 00	5♎03 18	16 30.2	1 23.6	7 17.9	27 03.0	9 01.5	5 27.7	25 39.3	7 05.8	17 12.3	17 29.2
18 F	3 41 27	26 44 34	11♎57 55	18 59 50	16 26.7	2 04.7	8 25.4	27 45.7	9 16.4	5 39.4	25 38.1	7 08.7	17 11.1	17 29.7
19 Sa	3 45 24	27 42 19	26 08 55	3♏24 43	16 20.7	2 49.5	9 32.8	28 28.5	9 31.1	5 50.9	25 37.1	7 11.7	17 09.9	17 30.2
20 Su	3 49 21	28 40 03	10♏46 40	18 13 55	16 12.4	3 37.9	10 40.0	29 11.1	9 45.6	6 02.4	25 36.2	7 14.7	17 08.8	17 30.7
21 M	3 53 17	29 37 45	25 45 25	3♐19 58	16 02.5	4 29.8	11 47.1	29 53.7	9 59.9	6 13.8	25 35.4	7 17.7	17 07.7	17 31.3
22 Tu	3 57 14	0♊35 26	10♐56 16	18 32 56	15 52.2	5 25.0	12 54.0	0♊36.3	10 14.1	6 25.1	25 34.6	7 20.7	17 06.6	17 31.9
23 W	4 01 10	1 33 06	26 08 35	3♑41 55	15 42.7	6 23.5	14 00.7	1 18.8	10 28.0	6 36.3	25 34.0	7 23.8	17 05.5	17 32.5
24 Th	4 05 07	2 30 44	11♑11 46	18 37 08	15 35.1	7 25.1	15 07.2	2 01.3	10 41.8	6 47.4	25 33.5	7 26.9	17 04.4	17 33.2
25 F	4 09 03	3 28 22	25 57 13	3♒11 26	15 29.9	8 29.8	16 13.6	2 43.7	10 55.3	6 58.4	25 33.1	7 30.0	17 03.4	17 33.9
26 Sa	4 13 00	4 25 59	10♒19 24	17 20 56	15 27.2	9 37.6	17 19.8	3 26.0	11 08.7	7 09.3	25 32.8	7 33.2	17 02.4	17 34.6
27 Su	4 16 57	5 23 34	24 16 03	1♓04 53	15D26.3	10 48.2	18 25.8	4 08.4	11 21.9	7 20.1	25 32.5	7 36.3	17 01.4	17 35.3
28 M	4 20 53	6 21 09	7♓47 41	14 24 48	15R26.3	12 01.8	19 31.6	4 50.6	11 34.8	7 30.8	25D32.4	7 39.5	17 00.5	17 36.1
29 Tu	4 24 50	7 18 43	20 56 39	27 23 40	15 26.0	13 18.1	20 37.2	5 32.8	11 47.6	7 41.4	25 32.4	7 42.8	16 59.5	17 36.9
30 W	4 28 46	8 16 16	3♈46 18	10♈05 00	15 24.1	14 37.3	21 42.6	6 15.0	12 00.1	7 51.9	25 32.5	7 46.0	16 58.6	17 37.7
31 Th	4 32 43	9 13 48	16 20 13	22 32 20	15 19.9	15 59.1	22 47.8	6 57.1	12 12.4	8 02.3	25 32.7	7 49.3	16 57.8	17 38.5

LONGITUDE — June 1951

Day	Sid.Time	☉	0 hr ☽	Noon ☽	True ☊	☿	♀	♂	⚳	♃	♄	♅	♆	♇
1 F	4 36 39	10♊11 19	28♈41 45	4♉48 48	15♓12.8	17♉23.7	23♋52.8	7♊39.2	12♓24.6	8♈12.6	25♍33.0	7♋52.5	16♎56.9	17♌39.4
2 Sa	4 40 36	11 08 49	10♉53 46	16 56 56	15R02.9	18 50.9	24 57.6	8 21.2	12 36.4	8 22.7	25 33.4	7 55.9	16R56.1	17 40.2
3 Su	4 44 32	12 06 19	22 58 32	28 58 46	14 50.7	20 20.8	26 02.1	9 03.2	12 48.1	8 32.8	25 33.9	7 59.2	16 55.3	17 41.2
4 M	4 48 29	13 03 47	4♊57 49	10♊55 50	14 37.0	21 53.2	27 06.5	9 45.1	12 59.5	8 42.8	25 34.5	8 02.5	16 54.6	17 42.1
5 Tu	4 52 26	14 01 15	16 52 59	22 49 26	14 22.9	23 28.3	28 10.6	10 27.0	13 10.7	8 52.6	25 35.2	8 05.9	16 53.8	17 43.1
6 W	4 56 22	14 58 42	28 45 22	4♋40 58	14 09.7	25 06.0	29 14.5	11 08.9	13 21.7	9 02.3	25 36.0	8 09.3	16 53.1	17 44.0
7 Th	5 00 19	15 56 08	10♋36 26	16 32 03	13 58.2	26 46.3	0♌18.1	11 50.6	13 32.4	9 11.9	25 36.9	8 12.7	16 52.4	17 45.0
8 F	5 04 15	16 53 33	22 28 04	28 24 51	13 49.3	28 29.1	1 21.5	12 32.4	13 42.8	9 21.4	25 37.9	8 16.1	16 51.8	17 46.1
9 Sa	5 08 12	17 50 56	4♌22 45	10♌22 12	13 43.3	0♊14.5	2 24.6	13 14.1	13 53.1	9 30.7	25 39.0	8 19.5	16 51.2	17 47.1
10 Su	5 12 08	18 48 19	16 23 39	22 27 36	13 39.9	2 02.5	3 27.4	13 55.7	14 03.0	9 39.9	25 40.3	8 23.0	16 50.6	17 48.2
11 M	5 16 05	19 45 41	28 34 38	4♍45 17	13D38.6	3 52.9	4 30.0	14 37.3	14 12.8	9 49.0	25 41.6	8 26.5	16 50.0	17 49.3
12 Tu	5 20 01	20 43 01	11♍00 09	17 19 50	13R38.5	5 45.7	5 32.3	15 18.8	14 22.2	9 58.0	25 43.0	8 29.9	16 49.5	17 50.4
13 W	5 23 58	21 40 21	23 44 56	0♎16 00	13 38.3	7 41.0	6 34.2	16 00.3	14 31.4	10 06.9	25 44.5	8 33.4	16 49.0	17 51.6
14 Th	5 27 55	22 37 39	6♎53 33	13 38 00	13 37.0	9 38.5	7 35.9	16 41.7	14 40.4	10 15.6	25 46.1	8 36.9	16 48.5	17 52.7
15 F	5 31 51	23 34 57	20 29 40	27 28 45	13 33.7	11 38.3	8 37.2	17 23.1	14 49.0	10 24.2	25 47.8	8 40.4	16 48.1	17 53.9
16 Sa	5 35 48	24 32 14	4♏35 13	11♏48 54	13 28.0	13 40.2	9 38.3	18 04.5	14 57.4	10 32.6	25 49.6	8 44.0	16 47.7	17 55.1
17 Su	5 39 44	25 29 30	19 09 21	26 35 56	13 19.9	15 44.0	10 39.0	18 45.7	15 05.6	10 40.9	25 51.5	8 47.5	16 47.3	17 56.3
18 M	5 43 41	26 26 45	4♐07 43	11♐43 37	13 10.1	17 49.6	11 39.3	19 27.0	15 13.4	10 49.1	25 53.6	8 51.1	16 47.0	17 57.6
19 Tu	5 47 37	27 24 00	19 22 21	27 02 29	12 59.8	19 56.8	12 39.3	20 08.2	15 21.0	10 57.2	25 55.7	8 54.6	16 46.7	17 58.9
20 W	5 51 34	28 21 15	4♑42 34	12♑21 08	12 50.2	22 05.4	13 38.9	20 49.3	15 28.3	11 05.1	25 57.9	8 58.2	16 46.4	18 00.2
21 Th	5 55 30	29 18 29	19 56 49	27 28 22	12 42.4	24 15.1	14 38.1	21 30.4	15 35.4	11 12.9	26 00.2	9 01.8	16 46.1	18 01.5
22 F	5 59 27	0♋15 42	4♒54 44	12♒15 07	12 37.1	26 25.6	15 37.0	22 11.5	15 42.1	11 20.5	26 02.5	9 05.4	16 45.9	18 02.8
23 Sa	6 03 24	1 12 56	19 28 53	26 35 42	12 34.2	28 36.7	16 35.4	22 52.5	15 48.5	11 28.0	26 05.0	9 08.9	16 45.7	18 04.2
24 Su	6 07 20	2 10 09	3♓35 22	10♓27 56	12D33.3	0♋48.1	17 33.5	23 33.5	15 54.7	11 35.3	26 07.6	9 12.5	16 45.6	18 05.5
25 M	6 11 17	3 07 22	17 13 34	23 52 36	12R33.5	2 59.5	18 31.1	24 14.4	16 00.5	11 42.5	26 10.3	9 16.1	16 45.4	18 06.9
26 Tu	6 15 13	4 04 35	0♈25 24	6♈52 29	12 33.7	5 10.7	19 28.3	24 55.3	16 06.0	11 49.5	26 13.0	9 19.7	16 45.3	18 08.3
27 W	6 19 10	5 01 48	13 14 21	19 31 31	12 32.7	7 21.3	20 25.0	25 36.1	16 11.2	11 56.4	26 15.9	9 23.4	16 45.3	18 09.7
28 Th	6 23 06	5 59 01	25 44 33	1♉53 59	12 29.8	9 31.2	21 21.3	26 16.9	16 16.2	12 03.2	26 18.8	9 27.0	16D45.3	18 11.2
29 F	6 27 03	6 56 14	8♉00 18	14 04 01	12 24.4	11 40.1	22 17.1	26 57.7	16 20.8	12 09.7	26 21.9	9 30.6	16 45.3	18 12.6
30 Sa	6 30 59	7 53 28	20 05 33	26 05 20	12 16.5	13 47.8	23 12.4	27 38.4	16 25.0	12 16.2	26 25.0	9 34.2	16 45.3	18 14.1

Astro Data

	Dy Hr Mn
☽ 0N	2 7:33
♃□♇	2 15:16
♃ 0N	3 4:38
♆✶♇	7 6:22
☿ D	8 11:50
☽ 0S	16 23:02
♄ D	29 3:37
☽ 0N	29 12:18
♃□♅	29 16:25
☽ 0S	13 6:29
☽ 0N	25 17:50
♆ D	28 21:51

Planet Ingress

		Dy Hr Mn
☿	♈R	1 21:25
♀	♋	11 1:41
☿	♉	15 1:40
♂	♊	21 15:32
☉	♊	21 21:15
♀	♌	7 5:10
☿	♊	9 8:43
☉	♋	22 5:25
☿	♋	24 3:13

Last Aspect / ☽ Ingress

Last Aspect Dy Hr Mn			☽ Ingress	Dy Hr Mn
2 4:13	♄	☍	♈	2 11:26
4 18:37	☿	☌	♉	4 20:47
6 23:47	♄	△	♊	7 7:51
9 17:04	♀	☌	♋	9 20:13
12 6:37	☿	□	♌	12 8:49
14 19:30	☿	△	♍	14 19:44
16 21:02	♂	△	♎	17 3:05
18 9:27	♇	✶	♏	19 6:23
21 6:18	♂	☍	♐	21 6:44
22 23:06	♄	□	♑	23 6:07
24 23:21	♄	△	♒	25 6:41
26 12:24	♇	☍	♓	27 10:05
29 8:32	♄	☍	♈	29 16:53

Last Aspect / ☽ Ingress

Last Aspect Dy Hr Mn			☽ Ingress	Dy Hr Mn
31 12:33	♀	□	♉	1 2:33
3 5:32	♀	✶	♊	3 14:03
5 17:36	♄	□	♋	6 2:31
8 12:10	☿	✶	♌	8 15:12
10 4:10	☉	✶	♍	11 2:47
13 3:40	♄	☌	♎	13 11:31
15 4:50	☉	△	♏	15 16:17
17 10:49	♄	✶	♐	17 17:26
19 12:36	☉	☍	♑	19 16:38
21 9:39	♄	△	♒	21 16:04
23 16:05	☿	△	♓	23 17:49
25 16:12	♄	☍	♈	25 23:13
28 0:25	♂	✶	♉	28 8:17
30 12:40	♄	△	♊	30 19:51

☽ Phases & Eclipses

Dy Hr Mn		
6 1:36	●	14♉44
14 5:32	☽	22♌38
21 5:45	○	29♏23
27 20:17	☾	5♓43
4 16:40	●	13♊15
12 18:52	☽	20♍59
19 12:36	○	27♐25
26 6:21	☾	3♈51

Astro Data

1 May 1951
Julian Day # 18748
SVP 5♓56'19"
GC 26♐09.6 ⚵ 11♒27.2
Eris 7♈40.3 ⚴ 6♐33.4R
⚷ 2♑31.1R ⚶ 12♊11.1
☽ Mean ☊ 16♓24.3

1 June 1951
Julian Day # 18779
SVP 5♓56'14"
GC 26♐09.6 ⚵ 13♒49.6R
Eris 7♈55.6 ⚴ 29♏58.6R
⚷ 1♑05.6R ⚶ 25♊17.1
☽ Mean ☊ 14♓45.8

July 1951 — LONGITUDE

Day	Sid.Time	☉	0 hr ☽	Noon ☽	True ☊	☿	♀	♂	⚳	♃	♄	♅	♆	♇
1 Su	6 34 56	8♋50 41	2♊03 42	8♊01 01	12♓06.6	15♋54.2	24♌07.2	28♊19.0	16♓29.0	12♈22.4	26♍28.2	9♋37.8	16♎45.4	18♌15.6
2 M	6 38 53	9 47 54	13 57 34	19 53 36	11R55.4	17 59.1	25 01.5	28 59.7	16 32.6	12 28.5	26 31.5	9 41.4	16 45.5	18 17.1
3 Tu	6 42 49	10 45 08	25 49 22	1♋45 04	11 43.8	20 02.5	25 55.2	29 40.2	16 35.9	12 34.5	26 34.9	9 45.1	16 45.6	18 18.6
4 W	6 46 46	11 42 21	7♋40 54	13 37 03	11 32.8	22 04.1	26 48.4	0♋20.8	16 38.9	12 40.3	26 38.4	9 48.7	16 45.8	18 20.2
5 Th	6 50 42	12 39 35	19 33 44	25 31 08	11 23.4	24 03.9	27 41.0	1 01.3	16 41.5	12 45.9	26 41.9	9 52.3	16 46.0	18 21.7
6 F	6 54 39	13 36 48	1♌29 28	7♌28 58	11 16.2	26 01.9	28 32.9	1 41.7	16 43.8	12 51.3	26 45.6	9 55.9	16 46.2	18 23.3
7 Sa	6 58 35	14 34 01	13 29 54	19 32 33	11 11.5	27 58.0	29 24.3	2 22.1	16 45.7	12 56.6	26 49.3	9 59.6	16 46.5	18 24.9
8 Su	7 02 32	15 31 14	25 37 16	1♍44 23	11D09.2	29 52.2	0♍14.9	3 02.5	16 47.4	13 01.7	26 53.1	10 03.2	16 46.8	18 26.5
9 M	7 06 29	16 28 27	7♍54 20	14 07 31	11 08.7	1♌44.5	1 04.9	3 42.8	16 48.6	13 06.6	26 57.0	10 06.8	16 47.1	18 28.1
10 Tu	7 10 25	17 25 40	20 24 25	26 45 28	11 09.5	3 34.8	1 54.2	4 23.0	16 49.5	13 11.4	27 01.0	10 10.4	16 47.4	18 29.7
11 W	7 14 22	18 22 53	3♎11 11	9♎42 01	11R10.4	5 23.2	2 42.8	5 03.3	16 50.1	13 16.0	27 05.1	10 14.0	16 47.8	18 31.4
12 Th	7 18 18	19 20 05	16 18 24	23 00 44	11 10.6	7 09.7	3 30.5	5 43.4	16R50.3	13 20.4	27 09.2	10 17.6	16 48.2	18 33.0
13 F	7 22 15	20 17 18	29 49 20	6♏44 25	11 09.4	8 54.1	4 17.5	6 23.6	16 50.2	13 24.6	27 13.5	10 21.1	16 48.7	18 34.7
14 Sa	7 26 11	21 14 31	13♏46 04	20 54 15	11 06.2	10 36.7	5 03.7	7 03.7	16 49.7	13 28.7	27 17.8	10 24.7	16 49.2	18 36.4
15 Su	7 30 08	22 11 44	28 08 41	5♐28 58	11 01.2	12 17.2	5 49.0	7 43.7	16 48.9	13 32.6	27 22.1	10 28.3	16 49.7	18 38.1
16 M	7 34 04	23 08 57	12♐54 25	20 24 14	10 54.9	13 55.9	6 33.4	8 23.7	16 47.7	13 36.3	27 26.6	10 31.9	16 50.3	18 39.8
17 Tu	7 38 01	24 06 10	27 57 23	5♑32 41	10 48.0	15 32.5	7 16.9	9 03.7	16 46.2	13 39.8	27 31.1	10 35.4	16 50.8	18 41.5
18 W	7 41 58	25 03 23	13♑08 53	20 44 40	10 41.6	17 07.2	7 59.4	9 43.6	16 44.3	13 43.1	27 35.7	10 39.0	16 51.5	18 43.2
19 Th	7 45 54	26 00 37	28 18 43	5♒49 48	10 36.4	18 40.0	8 40.9	10 23.5	16 42.1	13 46.3	27 40.4	10 42.5	16 52.1	18 45.0
20 F	7 49 51	26 57 51	13♒16 47	20 38 44	10 32.9	20 10.8	9 21.4	11 03.3	16 39.5	13 49.3	27 45.2	10 46.0	16 52.8	18 46.7
21 Sa	7 53 47	27 55 06	27 54 52	5♓04 37	10D31.4	21 39.6	10 00.8	11 43.1	16 36.5	13 52.0	27 50.0	10 49.5	16 53.5	18 48.5
22 Su	7 57 44	28 52 22	12♓07 35	19 03 37	10 31.6	23 06.4	10 39.1	12 22.9	16 33.2	13 54.6	27 54.9	10 53.0	16 54.2	18 50.2
23 M	8 01 40	29 49 38	25 52 42	2♈34 58	10 32.7	24 31.1	11 16.3	13 02.6	16 29.5	13 57.0	27 59.9	10 56.5	16 55.0	18 52.0
24 Tu	8 05 37	0♌46 55	9♈10 41	15 40 14	10 34.1	25 53.9	11 52.2	13 42.3	16 25.5	13 59.3	28 04.9	10 59.9	16 55.8	18 53.8
25 W	8 09 33	1 44 13	22 04 02	28 22 37	10R35.0	27 14.5	12 27.0	14 21.9	16 21.1	14 01.3	28 10.0	11 03.4	16 56.6	18 55.5
26 Th	8 13 30	2 41 32	4♉36 31	10♉46 16	10 34.7	28 33.0	13 00.4	15 01.5	16 16.3	14 03.1	28 15.2	11 06.8	16 57.5	18 57.3
27 F	8 17 27	3 38 52	16 52 27	22 55 37	10 32.9	29 49.4	13 32.5	15 41.1	16 11.2	14 04.7	28 20.4	11 10.3	16 58.4	18 59.1
28 Sa	8 21 23	4 36 13	28 56 20	4♊55 05	10 29.5	1♍03.5	14 03.2	16 20.6	16 05.8	14 06.2	28 25.7	11 13.7	16 59.3	19 01.0
29 Su	8 25 20	5 33 35	10♊52 23	16 48 40	10 24.8	2 15.3	14 32.5	17 00.1	16 00.0	14 07.4	28 31.1	11 17.0	17 00.2	19 02.8
30 M	8 29 16	6 30 58	22 44 24	28 39 57	10 19.1	3 24.8	15 00.3	17 39.6	15 53.9	14 08.5	28 36.5	11 20.4	17 01.2	19 04.6
31 Tu	8 33 13	7 28 22	4♋35 40	10♋31 52	10 13.2	4 31.8	15 26.5	18 19.0	15 47.4	14 09.3	28 42.0	11 23.8	17 02.2	19 06.4

August 1951 — LONGITUDE

Day	Sid.Time	☉	0 hr ☽	Noon ☽	True ☊	☿	♀	♂	⚳	♃	♄	♅	♆	♇
1 W	8 37 09	8♌25 47	16♋28 51	22♋26 53	10♓07.6	5♍36.3	15♍51.2	18♋58.4	15♓40.5	14♈10.0	28♍47.6	11♋27.1	17♎03.3	19♌08.3
2 Th	8 41 06	9 23 13	28 26 11	4♌26 59	10R02.9	6 38.1	16 14.2	19 37.7	15R33.4	14 10.4	28 53.2	11 30.4	17 04.3	19 10.1
3 F	8 45 02	10 20 39	10♌29 29	16 33 51	9 59.4	7 37.2	16 35.4	20 17.0	15 25.9	14R10.7	28 58.9	11 33.7	17 05.4	19 12.0
4 Sa	8 48 59	11 18 07	22 40 18	28 49 01	9D57.5	8 33.5	16 54.9	20 56.3	15 18.0	14 10.8	29 04.6	11 37.0	17 06.5	19 13.8
5 Su	8 52 56	12 15 35	5♍00 11	11♍14 01	9 57.0	9 26.7	17 12.5	21 35.5	15 09.9	14 10.6	29 10.4	11 40.2	17 07.7	19 15.7
6 M	8 56 52	13 13 05	17 30 45	23 50 36	9 57.6	10 16.9	17 28.3	22 14.6	15 01.4	14 10.3	29 16.3	11 43.4	17 08.9	19 17.5
7 Tu	9 00 49	14 10 35	0♎13 48	6♎40 37	9 59.0	11 03.7	17 42.0	22 53.8	14 52.7	14 09.7	29 22.2	11 46.6	17 10.1	19 19.4
8 W	9 04 45	15 08 05	13 11 19	19 46 09	10 00.5	11 47.0	17 53.8	23 32.9	14 43.6	14 09.0	29 28.1	11 49.8	17 11.3	19 21.2
9 Th	9 08 42	16 05 37	26 25 21	3♏09 08	10 01.7	12 26.8	18 03.4	24 11.9	14 34.2	14 08.1	29 34.2	11 53.0	17 12.6	19 23.1
10 F	9 12 38	17 03 10	9♏57 41	16 51 06	10R02.2	13 02.7	18 10.9	24 51.0	14 24.6	14 06.9	29 40.2	11 56.1	17 13.9	19 24.9
11 Sa	9 16 35	18 00 43	23 49 26	0♐52 37	10 01.7	13 34.5	18 16.2	25 29.9	14 14.6	14 05.6	29 46.4	11 59.2	17 15.2	19 26.8
12 Su	9 20 31	18 58 17	8♐00 31	15 12 49	10 00.3	14 02.1	18R19.3	26 08.9	14 04.4	14 04.1	29 52.5	12 02.3	17 16.5	19 28.7
13 M	9 24 28	19 55 53	22 29 07	29 48 52	9 58.2	14 25.3	18 20.1	26 47.8	13 54.0	14 02.4	29 58.8	12 05.3	17 17.9	19 30.5
14 Tu	9 28 25	20 53 29	7♑11 23	14♑35 53	9 55.7	14 43.8	18 18.5	27 26.7	13 43.3	14 00.4	0♎05.0	12 08.3	17 19.3	19 32.4
15 W	9 32 21	21 51 06	22 01 29	29 27 14	9 53.4	14 57.4	18 14.5	28 05.5	13 32.3	13 58.3	0 11.4	12 11.3	17 20.7	19 34.3
16 Th	9 36 18	22 48 44	6♒52 08	14♒15 13	9 51.7	15 05.9	18 08.2	28 44.3	13 21.2	13 56.0	0 17.7	12 14.3	17 22.2	19 36.1
17 F	9 40 14	23 46 24	21 35 33	28 52 15	9D50.6	15R09.1	17 59.5	29 23.0	13 09.7	13 53.5	0 24.1	12 17.2	17 23.6	19 38.0
18 Sa	9 44 11	24 44 04	6♓04 34	13♓11 51	9 50.4	15 06.8	17 48.4	0♌01.7	12 58.1	13 50.8	0 30.6	12 20.1	17 25.1	19 39.9
19 Su	9 48 07	25 41 46	20 13 37	27 09 30	9 50.9	14 58.9	17 34.9	0 40.4	12 46.3	13 48.0	0 37.1	12 23.0	17 26.7	19 41.7
20 M	9 52 04	26 39 30	3♈59 17	10♈42 54	9 51.9	14 45.2	17 19.0	1 19.1	12 34.3	13 44.9	0 43.6	12 25.9	17 28.2	19 43.6
21 Tu	9 56 00	27 37 15	17 20 24	23 51 58	9 52.9	14 25.8	17 00.9	1 57.7	12 22.1	13 41.6	0 50.2	12 28.7	17 29.8	19 45.4
22 W	9 59 57	28 35 02	0♉17 52	6♉38 28	9 53.9	14 00.7	16 40.4	2 36.3	12 09.7	13 38.2	0 56.8	12 31.4	17 31.4	19 47.3
23 Th	10 03 54	29 32 51	12 54 10	19 05 28	9R54.5	13 30.0	16 17.9	3 14.8	11 57.2	13 34.5	1 03.5	12 34.2	17 33.0	19 49.1
24 F	10 07 50	0♍30 41	25 12 54	1♊16 58	9 54.7	12 53.9	15 53.2	3 53.3	11 44.5	13 30.7	1 10.2	12 36.9	17 34.6	19 51.0
25 Sa	10 11 47	1 28 33	7♊18 17	13 17 23	9 54.5	12 12.8	15 26.5	4 31.8	11 31.7	13 26.7	1 17.0	12 39.6	17 36.3	19 52.8
26 Su	10 15 43	2 26 27	19 14 51	25 11 15	9 53.9	11 27.2	14 58.0	5 10.2	11 18.8	13 22.6	1 23.8	12 42.2	17 37.9	19 54.6
27 M	10 19 40	3 24 23	1♋07 05	7♋02 55	9 53.2	10 37.7	14 27.7	5 48.6	11 05.7	13 18.2	1 30.6	12 44.8	17 39.6	19 56.5
28 Tu	10 23 36	4 22 20	12 59 13	18 56 26	9 52.4	9 45.0	13 55.9	6 27.0	10 52.6	13 13.7	1 37.4	12 47.4	17 41.4	19 58.3
29 W	10 27 33	5 20 20	24 55 01	0♌55 20	9 51.7	8 50.2	13 22.8	7 05.3	10 39.4	13 09.0	1 44.3	12 49.9	17 43.1	20 00.1
30 Th	10 31 29	6 18 21	6♌57 44	13 02 32	9 51.3	7 54.2	12 48.4	7 43.6	10 26.1	13 04.1	1 51.2	12 52.4	17 44.9	20 01.9
31 F	10 35 26	7 16 23	19 10 00	25 20 21	9 51.0	6 58.1	12 13.0	8 21.9	10 12.8	12 59.1	1 58.2	12 54.9	17 46.7	20 03.7

Astro Data Dy Hr Mn	Planet Ingress Dy Hr Mn	Last Aspect Dy Hr Mn	☽ Ingress Dy Hr Mn	Last Aspect Dy Hr Mn	☽ Ingress Dy Hr Mn	☽ Phases & Eclipses Dy Hr Mn	Astro Data
☽0S 10 12:05	♂ ♋ 3 23:42	3 7:32 ♂ ☌	♋ 3 8:27	2 0:49 ♄ ⚹	♌ 2 3:08	4 7:48 ● 11♋32	1 July 1951
⚳R 12 15:18	♀ ♍ 8 4:54	5 14:23 ♄ ⚹	♌ 5 21:00	3 17:12 ♇ ☌	♍ 4 14:18	12 4:56 ☽ 19♎03	Julian Day # 18809
☽0N 23 1:25	☿ ♌ 8 13:39	7 9:46 ♇ ☌	♍ 8 8:36	6 22:17 ♄ ☌	♎ 6 23:34	18 19:17 ○ 25♑21	SVP 5♓56'08"
	☉ ♌ 23 16:21	10 12:29 ♄ ☌	♎ 10 18:04	8 19:11 ♂ □	♏ 9 6:24	25 18:59 ☾ 2♉01	GC 26♐09.7 ⚴ 10♒35.7R
♃R 4 6:53	☿ ♍ 27 15:24	12 4:56 ☉ □	♏ 13 0:19	11 10:07 ♄ ⚹	♐ 11 10:31		Eris 8♈01.7 ⚵ 24♏52.3R
☽0S 6 17:05		14 22:39 ♄ ⚹	♐ 15 3:03	13 12:16 ♄ □	♑ 13 12:18	2 22:39 ● 9♌49	⚷ 29♐08.7R ⚶ 8♋18.1
♀0S 11 7:24	♄ ♎ 13 16:44	16 23:15 ♄ □	♑ 17 3:14	15 9:42 ♂ ☍	♒ 15 12:53	10 12:22 ☽ 17♏04	☽ Mean ☊ 13♓10.5
♀R 13 7:51	♂ ♌ 18 10:55	18 22:55 ♄ △	♒ 19 2:41	17 2:59 ☉ ☍	♓ 17 13:52	17 2:59 ○ 23♒25	
☿R 17 14:04	☉ ♍ 23 23:16	20 11:09 ☿ ☍	♓ 21 3:29	18 19:44 ♀ ☍	♈ 19 16:58	17 3:14 • A 0.119	1 August 1951
☽0N 19 10:52		23 6:40 ☉ △	♈ 23 7:21	21 19:33 ☉ △	♉ 21 23:26	24 10:20 ☾ 0♊27	Julian Day # 18840
		25 9:34 ☿ △	♉ 25 15:07	23 13:25 ♇ □	♊ 24 9:27		SVP 5♓56'03"
		27 22:53 ♄ △	♊ 28 2:08	26 1:19 ♇ ⚹	♋ 26 21:44		GC 26♐09.8 ⚴ 2♒53.9R
		30 11:53 ♄ □	♋ 30 14:42	28 9:29 ♆ □	♌ 29 10:10		Eris 7♈57.7R ⚵ 24♏16.9
				31 1:43 ♇ ☌	♍ 31 21:00		⚷ 27♐26.4R ⚶ 21♋50.0
							☽ Mean ☊ 11♓32.0

LONGITUDE — September 1951

Day	Sid.Time	☉	0 hr ☽	Noon ☽	True ☊	☿	♀	♂	⚳	♃	♄	♅	♆	♇
1 Sa	10 39 23	8♍14 27	1♍33 46	7♍50 24	9♓50.9	6♍03.2	11♍36.8	9♌00.1	9♓59.4	12♈53.8	2♎05.2	12♋57.3	17♎48.5	20♌05.5
2 Su	10 43 19	9 12 33	14 10 22	20 33 44	9R50.9	5R10.7	11R00.1	9 38.3	9R46.0	12R48.5	2 12.2	12 59.7	17 50.3	20 07.3
3 M	10 47 16	10 10 41	27 00 33	3♎30 50	9 51.0	4 21.7	10 23.1	10 16.5	9 32.6	12 43.0	2 19.2	13 02.0	17 52.1	20 09.1
4 Tu	10 51 12	11 08 50	10♎04 35	16 41 47	9 50.9	3 37.4	9 46.0	10 54.6	9 19.3	12 37.3	2 26.3	13 04.3	17 54.0	20 10.9
5 W	10 55 09	12 07 00	23 22 24	0♏06 22	9 50.7	2 58.9	9 09.1	11 32.6	9 05.9	12 31.4	2 33.4	13 06.6	17 55.9	20 12.6
6 Th	10 59 05	13 05 12	6♏53 36	13 44 03	9 50.4	2 27.1	8 32.5	12 10.7	8 52.6	12 25.5	2 40.5	13 08.8	17 57.8	20 14.4
7 F	11 03 02	14 03 26	20 37 35	27 34 06	9 50.1	2 02.8	7 56.6	12 48.7	8 39.3	12 19.4	2 47.7	13 11.0	17 59.7	20 16.1
8 Sa	11 06 58	15 01 41	4♐33 27	11♐35 27	9D49.9	1 46.7	7 21.5	13 26.6	8 26.2	12 13.1	2 54.8	13 13.1	18 01.6	20 17.8
9 Su	11 10 55	15 59 58	18 39 55	25 46 36	9 50.0	1D39.1	6 47.4	14 04.6	8 13.0	12 06.7	3 02.0	13 15.2	18 03.6	20 19.6
10 M	11 14 52	16 58 16	2♑55 12	10♑05 22	9 50.4	1 40.5	6 14.7	14 42.5	8 00.0	12 00.2	3 09.2	13 17.3	18 05.5	20 21.3
11 Tu	11 18 48	17 56 36	17 16 45	24 28 53	9 51.0	1 50.9	5 43.4	15 20.3	7 47.1	11 53.6	3 16.5	13 19.3	18 07.5	20 23.0
12 W	11 22 45	18 54 57	1♒41 18	8♒53 28	9 51.7	2 10.5	5 13.7	15 58.1	7 34.4	11 46.8	3 23.7	13 21.3	18 09.5	20 24.7
13 Th	11 26 41	19 53 20	16 04 50	23 14 49	9 52.4	2 39.1	4 45.9	16 35.9	7 21.7	11 39.9	3 31.0	13 23.2	18 11.5	20 26.3
14 F	11 30 38	20 51 45	0♓22 50	7♓28 19	9R52.7	3 16.4	4 20.0	17 13.6	7 09.2	11 32.9	3 38.3	13 25.1	18 13.5	20 28.0
15 Sa	11 34 34	21 50 11	14 30 44	21 29 32	9 52.5	4 02.1	3 56.2	17 51.3	6 56.9	11 25.9	3 45.6	13 26.9	18 15.6	20 29.6
16 Su	11 38 31	22 48 39	28 24 19	5♈14 41	9 51.6	4 55.9	3 34.5	18 29.0	6 44.7	11 18.7	3 52.9	13 28.7	18 17.6	20 31.3
17 M	11 42 27	23 47 09	12♈00 20	18 41 03	9 50.1	5 57.2	3 15.1	19 06.6	6 32.8	11 11.4	4 00.2	13 30.4	18 19.7	20 32.9
18 Tu	11 46 24	24 45 41	25 16 45	1♉47 24	9 48.2	7 05.5	2 58.1	19 44.2	6 21.0	11 04.0	4 07.6	13 32.1	18 21.7	20 34.5
19 W	11 50 21	25 44 16	8♉13 04	14 33 56	9 45.9	8 20.1	2 43.4	20 21.8	6 09.4	10 56.5	4 14.9	13 33.7	18 23.8	20 36.1
20 Th	11 54 17	26 42 52	20 50 13	27 02 16	9 43.8	9 40.5	2 31.1	20 59.3	5 58.1	10 49.0	4 22.3	13 35.3	18 25.9	20 37.7
21 F	11 58 14	27 41 31	3♊10 28	9♊15 17	9 42.1	11 06.0	2 21.3	21 36.8	5 46.9	10 41.4	4 29.7	13 36.9	18 28.0	20 39.2
22 Sa	12 02 10	28 40 12	15 17 10	21 16 42	9D41.1	12 36.0	2 14.0	22 14.3	5 36.0	10 33.7	4 37.0	13 38.4	18 30.2	20 40.8
23 Su	12 06 07	29 38 55	27 14 25	3♋10 56	9 40.9	14 10.0	2 09.1	22 51.7	5 25.4	10 25.9	4 44.4	13 39.8	18 32.3	20 42.3
24 M	12 10 03	0♎37 40	9♋06 49	15 02 42	9 41.6	15 47.2	2D06.6	23 29.1	5 15.0	10 18.1	4 51.8	13 41.3	18 34.4	20 43.8
25 Tu	12 14 00	1 36 28	20 59 09	26 56 47	9 42.9	17 27.3	2 06.5	24 06.5	5 04.9	10 10.2	4 59.2	13 42.6	18 36.6	20 45.3
26 W	12 17 56	2 35 18	2♌56 09	8♌57 48	9 44.6	19 09.6	2 08.7	24 43.8	4 55.1	10 02.3	5 06.7	13 43.9	18 38.8	20 46.8
27 Th	12 21 53	3 34 10	15 02 14	21 09 55	9 46.2	20 53.7	2 13.3	25 21.1	4 45.5	9 54.3	5 14.1	13 45.2	18 40.9	20 48.3
28 F	12 25 50	4 33 04	27 21 16	3♍36 36	9R47.1	22 39.3	2 20.2	25 58.3	4 36.3	9 46.3	5 21.5	13 46.4	18 43.1	20 49.7
29 Sa	12 29 46	5 32 00	9♍56 13	16 20 20	9 47.1	24 25.9	2 29.3	26 35.6	4 27.3	9 38.3	5 28.9	13 47.5	18 45.3	20 51.1
30 Su	12 33 43	6 30 59	22 49 03	29 22 24	9 45.8	26 13.3	2 40.5	27 12.7	4 18.7	9 30.3	5 36.3	13 48.6	18 47.5	20 52.5

LONGITUDE — October 1951

Day	Sid.Time	☉	0 hr ☽	Noon ☽	True ☊	☿	♀	♂	⚳	♃	♄	♅	♆	♇
1 M	12 37 39	7♎29 59	6♎00 21	12♎42 46	9♓43.2	28♍01.1	2♍53.8	27♌49.8	4♓10.4	9♈22.2	5♎43.7	13♋49.7	18♎49.7	20♌53.9
2 Tu	12 41 36	8 29 01	19 29 25	26 20 00	9R39.3	29 49.1	3 09.2	28 26.9	4R02.4	9R14.1	5 51.1	13 50.7	18 51.9	20 55.3
3 W	12 45 32	9 28 06	3♏14 10	10♏11 29	9 34.8	1♎37.2	3 26.6	29 04.0	3 54.7	9 06.1	5 58.6	13 51.6	18 54.1	20 56.6
4 Th	12 49 29	10 27 12	17 11 31	24 13 46	9 30.2	3 25.1	3 45.9	29 41.0	3 47.4	8 58.0	6 06.0	13 52.5	18 56.3	20 58.0
5 F	12 53 25	11 26 21	1♐17 47	8♐23 04	9 26.1	5 12.8	4 07.1	0♍18.0	3 40.4	8 49.9	6 13.4	13 53.4	18 58.5	20 59.3
6 Sa	12 57 22	12 25 31	15 29 10	22 35 42	9 23.2	7 00.1	4 30.1	0 54.9	3 33.8	8 41.9	6 20.8	13 54.2	19 00.7	21 00.6
7 Su	13 01 18	13 24 43	29 42 16	6♑48 33	9D21.8	8 46.9	4 54.8	1 31.8	3 27.6	8 33.9	6 28.2	13 54.9	19 03.0	21 01.8
8 M	13 05 15	14 23 56	13♑54 17	20 59 11	9 21.8	10 33.3	5 21.2	2 08.6	3 21.6	8 25.9	6 35.5	13 55.6	19 05.2	21 03.1
9 Tu	13 09 12	15 23 12	28 03 05	5♒05 46	9 22.8	12 19.0	5 49.3	2 45.4	3 16.1	8 17.9	6 42.9	13 56.2	19 07.4	21 04.3
10 W	13 13 08	16 22 29	12♒07 05	19 06 51	9 24.3	14 04.1	6 18.9	3 22.2	3 10.9	8 10.0	6 50.3	13 56.8	19 09.7	21 05.5
11 Th	13 17 05	17 21 47	26 04 54	3♓01 05	9R25.4	15 48.5	6 50.1	3 58.9	3 06.1	8 02.1	6 57.6	13 57.3	19 11.9	21 06.7
12 F	13 21 01	18 21 08	9♓55 10	16 46 59	9 25.3	17 32.3	7 22.7	4 35.6	3 01.6	7 54.3	7 04.9	13 57.8	19 14.1	21 07.9
13 Sa	13 24 58	19 20 30	23 36 17	0♈22 51	9 23.5	19 15.3	7 56.7	5 12.2	2 57.5	7 46.6	7 12.2	13 58.2	19 16.4	21 09.0
14 Su	13 28 54	20 19 54	7♈06 27	13 46 50	9 19.6	20 57.7	8 32.2	5 48.8	2 53.7	7 38.9	7 19.5	13 58.6	19 18.6	21 10.1
15 M	13 32 51	21 19 21	20 23 48	26 57 11	9 13.8	22 39.4	9 08.9	6 25.4	2 50.4	7 31.3	7 26.8	13 58.9	19 20.8	21 11.2
16 Tu	13 36 47	22 18 49	3♉26 48	9♉52 34	9 06.5	24 20.4	9 47.0	7 01.9	2 47.4	7 23.7	7 34.1	13 59.2	19 23.1	21 12.3
17 W	13 40 44	23 18 20	16 14 27	22 32 27	8 58.4	26 00.8	10 26.3	7 38.4	2 44.8	7 16.3	7 41.3	13 59.4	19 25.3	21 13.3
18 Th	13 44 41	24 17 53	28 46 40	4♊57 16	8 50.4	27 40.4	11 06.7	8 14.8	2 42.5	7 08.9	7 48.5	13 59.5	19 27.6	21 14.3
19 F	13 48 37	25 17 28	11♊04 28	17 08 35	8 43.2	29 19.4	11 48.3	8 51.2	2 40.6	7 01.6	7 55.7	13 59.6	19 29.8	21 15.3
20 Sa	13 52 34	26 17 05	23 09 58	29 09 03	8 37.6	0♏57.8	12 31.0	9 27.6	2 39.1	6 54.4	8 02.9	13R59.7	19 32.0	21 16.3
21 Su	13 56 30	27 16 45	5♋06 19	11♋02 18	8 33.9	2 35.6	13 14.8	10 03.9	2 38.0	6 47.3	8 10.1	13 59.7	19 34.2	21 17.2
22 M	14 00 27	28 16 26	16 57 33	22 52 43	8D32.2	4 12.7	13 59.6	10 40.1	2 37.2	6 40.4	8 17.2	13 59.6	19 36.5	21 18.1
23 Tu	14 04 23	29 16 10	28 48 24	4♌45 15	8 32.2	5 49.3	14 45.4	11 16.4	2D36.8	6 33.5	8 24.3	13 59.5	19 38.7	21 19.0
24 W	14 08 20	0♏15 56	10♌43 57	16 45 08	8 33.2	7 25.3	15 32.2	11 52.6	2 36.7	6 26.7	8 31.4	13 59.3	19 40.9	21 19.9
25 Th	14 12 16	1 15 45	22 49 27	28 57 32	8R34.3	9 00.7	16 19.8	12 28.7	2 37.1	6 20.1	8 38.5	13 59.1	19 43.1	21 20.7
26 F	14 16 13	2 15 35	5♍09 57	11♍27 13	8 34.7	10 35.6	17 08.3	13 04.8	2 37.7	6 13.6	8 45.5	13 58.8	19 45.3	21 21.5
27 Sa	14 20 10	3 15 28	17 49 49	24 18 05	8 33.3	12 10.0	17 57.7	13 40.8	2 38.8	6 07.3	8 52.5	13 58.5	19 47.5	21 22.3
28 Su	14 24 06	4 15 23	0♎52 18	7♎32 35	8 29.8	13 43.9	18 47.9	14 16.8	2 40.2	6 01.0	8 59.5	13 58.1	19 49.7	21 23.1
29 M	14 28 03	5 15 20	14 18 58	21 11 16	8 23.8	15 17.3	19 38.8	14 52.8	2 42.0	5 55.0	9 06.4	13 57.7	19 51.8	21 23.8
30 Tu	14 31 59	6 15 19	28 09 13	5♏12 21	8 15.7	16 50.2	20 30.5	15 28.7	2 44.1	5 49.0	9 13.3	13 57.2	19 54.0	21 24.5
31 W	14 35 56	7 15 20	12♏20 03	19 31 38	8 06.1	18 22.6	21 23.0	16 04.5	2 46.6	5 43.2	9 20.2	13 56.6	19 56.2	21 25.2

Astro Data

	Dy Hr Mn
♃□♅	1 1:09
☽0S	2 23:03
♀0N	5 0:05
☿D	9 20:23
☽0N	15 20:42
☉0S	23 20:38
♀D	25 0:58
♄0S	25 4:58
☽0S	30 6:47
♄∠♇	3 4:27
☿0S	4 19:01
☽0N	13 5:06
♃☍♄	15 19:12
♅R	20 20:55
⚳D	24 2:40

Planet Ingress

	Dy Hr Mn
☉ ♎	23 20:37
☿ ♎	2 14:25
♂ ♍	5 0:20
☿ ♏	19 21:52
☉ ♏	24 5:36
♃□♇	25 10:01
☽0S	27 15:49

Last Aspect / ☽ Ingress

Last Aspect Dy Hr Mn		☽ Ingress	Dy Hr Mn
1 21:44	♅ ⚹	♎	3 5:32
4 18:17	♇ ⚹	♏	5 11:49
6 23:21	♇ □	♐	7 16:11
9 2:47	♇ △	♑	9 19:06
11 1:23	♆ □	♒	11 21:11
13 7:17	♇ ☍	♓	13 23:21
15 12:38	☉ ☍	♈	16 2:47
17 15:23	♇ △	♉	18 8:41
20 11:19	☉ △	♊	20 17:47
23 4:13	☉ □	♋	23 5:34
24 19:09	♆ □	♌	25 18:08
27 20:34	♂ ☌	♍	28 5:05
30 5:20	☿ ☌	♎	30 13:08

Last Aspect / ☽ Ingress

Last Aspect Dy Hr Mn		☽ Ingress	Dy Hr Mn
2 15:52	♂ ⚹	♏	2 18:23
4 21:41	♂ □	♐	4 21:48
6 9:19	♇ △	♑	7 0:30
8 8:46	♆ □	♒	9 3:19
10 15:24	♇ ☍	♓	11 6:46
12 7:04	♅ △	♈	13 11:19
15 2:58	☿ ☍	♉	15 17:37
17 9:28	♇ □	♊	18 2:22
20 5:43	☉ △	♋	20 13:42
22 23:55	☉ □	♌	23 2:25
24 21:04	♇ ☌	♍	25 14:01
26 23:26	♀ ☌	♎	27 22:25
29 12:22	♇ ⚹	♏	30 3:09

☽ Phases & Eclipses

Dy Hr Mn		
1 12:50	●	8♍16
1 12:51:21	●	A 02'36"
8 18:16	☽	15♐17
15 12:38	○	21♓52
15 12:27	●	A 0.804
23 4:13	☾	29♊20
1 1:57	●	7♎05
8 0:00	☽	13♑54
15 0:51	○	20♈52
22 23:55	☾	28♋46
30 13:54	●	6♏20

Astro Data

1 September 1951
Julian Day # 18871
SVP 5♓55'58"
GC 26♐09.9 ⚴ 26♑29.0R
Eris 7♈44.5R ⚵ 28♏19.4
⚷ 26♐47.8 ⚶ 5♌11.0
☽ Mean ☊ 9♓53.5

1 October 1951
Julian Day # 18901
SVP 5♓55'55"
GC 26♐09.9 ⚴ 25♑23.6
Eris 7♈26.4R ⚵ 5♐21.7
⚷ 27♐28.5 ⚶ 17♌35.3
☽ Mean ☊ 8♓18.2

November 1951 LONGITUDE

Day	Sid.Time	☉	0 hr ☽	Noon ☽	True ☊	☿	♀	♂	⚳	♃	♄	♅	♆	♇
1 Th	14 39 52	8♏15 22	26♏46 16	4♐03 03	7♓56.3	19♏54.6	22♍16.1	16♍40.3	2♓49.5	5♈37.6	9♎27.0	13♋56.0	19♎58.3	21♌25.9
2 F	14 43 49	9 15 27	11♐21 05	18 39 29	7R47.3	21 26.1	23 09.9	17 16.1	2 52.7	5R32.2	9 33.8	13R55.4	20 00.5	21 26.5
3 Sa	14 47 45	10 15 33	25 57 23	3♑14 01	7 40.2	22 57.2	24 04.4	17 51.8	2 56.3	5 26.9	9 40.6	13 54.7	20 02.6	21 27.1
4 Su	14 51 42	11 15 41	10♑28 43	17 40 57	7 35.5	24 27.9	24 59.4	18 27.4	3 00.2	5 21.7	9 47.3	13 53.9	20 04.7	21 27.7
5 M	14 55 39	12 15 51	24 50 17	1♒56 25	7D33.2	25 58.1	25 55.1	19 03.0	3 04.4	5 16.8	9 53.9	13 53.1	20 06.9	21 28.2
6 Tu	14 59 35	13 16 01	8♒59 12	15 58 32	7 32.8	27 27.8	26 51.4	19 38.5	3 09.0	5 12.0	10 00.6	13 52.3	20 09.0	21 28.7
7 W	15 03 32	14 16 14	22 54 25	29 46 54	7R33.3	28 57.1	27 48.2	20 14.0	3 13.9	5 07.4	10 07.2	13 51.4	20 11.1	21 29.2
8 Th	15 07 28	15 16 27	6♓36 06	13♓22 08	7 33.3	0♐25.9	28 45.6	20 49.4	3 19.2	5 02.9	10 13.7	13 50.4	20 13.1	21 29.7
9 F	15 11 25	16 16 42	20 05 07	26 45 10	7 31.7	1 54.3	29 43.5	21 24.8	3 24.8	4 58.7	10 20.2	13 49.4	20 15.2	21 30.1
10 Sa	15 15 21	17 16 59	3♈22 24	9♈56 52	7 27.7	3 22.1	0♎41.9	22 00.1	3 30.7	4 54.6	10 26.6	13 48.3	20 17.2	21 30.5
11 Su	15 19 18	18 17 17	16 28 37	22 57 39	7 20.7	4 49.5	1 40.9	22 35.3	3 36.9	4 50.7	10 33.0	13 47.2	20 19.3	21 30.9
12 M	15 23 14	19 17 37	29 24 00	5♉47 36	7 10.8	6 16.3	2 40.3	23 10.5	3 43.5	4 47.1	10 39.4	13 46.1	20 21.3	21 31.2
13 Tu	15 27 11	20 17 58	12♉08 26	18 26 28	6 58.7	7 42.5	3 40.1	23 45.7	3 50.3	4 43.6	10 45.7	13 44.9	20 23.3	21 31.5
14 W	15 31 08	21 18 21	24 41 39	0♊54 01	6 45.2	9 08.1	4 40.5	24 20.8	3 57.5	4 40.3	10 51.9	13 43.6	20 25.3	21 31.8
15 Th	15 35 04	22 18 46	7♊03 35	13 10 25	6 31.6	10 32.9	5 41.3	24 55.8	4 04.9	4 37.1	10 58.1	13 42.3	20 27.3	21 32.0
16 F	15 39 01	23 19 13	19 14 38	25 16 26	6 19.0	11 57.1	6 42.5	25 30.8	4 12.7	4 34.2	11 04.3	13 41.0	20 29.2	21 32.3
17 Sa	15 42 57	24 19 41	1♋16 00	7♋13 40	6 08.5	13 20.3	7 44.1	26 05.7	4 20.8	4 31.5	11 10.4	13 39.6	20 31.2	21 32.5
18 Su	15 46 54	25 20 11	13 09 47	19 04 44	6 00.6	14 42.7	8 46.1	26 40.5	4 29.2	4 29.0	11 16.4	13 38.2	20 33.1	21 32.6
19 M	15 50 50	26 20 43	24 59 01	0♌53 09	5 55.5	16 04.0	9 48.5	27 15.3	4 37.8	4 26.7	11 22.4	13 36.7	20 35.0	21 32.8
20 Tu	15 54 47	27 21 16	6♌47 41	12 43 15	5 52.9	17 24.2	10 51.3	27 50.1	4 46.8	4 24.6	11 28.3	13 35.2	20 36.9	21 32.9
21 W	15 58 43	28 21 52	18 40 30	24 40 06	5 52.1	18 43.0	11 54.5	28 24.7	4 56.0	4 22.7	11 34.2	13 33.6	20 38.8	21 33.0
22 Th	16 02 40	29 22 29	0♍42 45	6♍49 08	5 52.1	20 00.4	12 58.0	28 59.3	5 05.5	4 21.0	11 40.0	13 32.0	20 40.6	21 33.0
23 F	16 06 37	0♐23 07	12 59 56	19 15 50	5 51.7	21 16.0	14 01.8	29 33.9	5 15.3	4 19.5	11 45.7	13 30.4	20 42.4	21R33.0
24 Sa	16 10 33	1 23 47	25 37 26	2♎05 17	5 49.6	22 29.7	15 06.0	0♎08.3	5 25.3	4 18.2	11 51.4	13 28.7	20 44.3	21 33.0
25 Su	16 14 30	2 24 29	8♎39 51	15 21 27	5 45.2	23 41.3	16 10.4	0 42.7	5 35.7	4 17.1	11 57.0	13 26.9	20 46.0	21 33.0
26 M	16 18 26	3 25 13	22 10 16	29 06 21	5 37.9	24 50.3	17 15.2	1 17.1	5 46.3	4 16.2	12 02.6	13 25.2	20 47.8	21 32.9
27 Tu	16 22 23	4 25 58	6♏09 31	13♏19 23	5 28.0	25 56.4	18 20.3	1 51.3	5 57.1	4 15.5	12 08.0	13 23.3	20 49.6	21 32.8
28 W	16 26 19	5 26 44	20 35 21	27 56 37	5 16.4	26 59.3	19 25.7	2 25.5	6 08.2	4 15.1	12 13.5	13 21.5	20 51.3	21 32.7
29 Th	16 30 16	6 27 32	5♐22 13	12♐51 01	5 04.2	27 58.4	20 31.3	2 59.6	6 19.6	4D14.8	12 18.8	13 19.6	20 53.0	21 32.6
30 F	16 34 13	7 28 22	20 21 47	27 53 16	4 52.8	28 53.3	21 37.2	3 33.7	6 31.3	4 14.8	12 24.1	13 17.7	20 54.7	21 32.4

December 1951 LONGITUDE

Day	Sid.Time	☉	0 hr ☽	Noon ☽	True ☊	☿	♀	♂	⚳	♃	♄	♅	♆	♇
1 Sa	16 38 09	8♐29 12	5♑24 12	12♑53 25	4♓43.6	29♐43.3	22♎43.4	4♎07.7	6♓43.1	4♈15.0	12♎29.3	13♋15.7	20♎56.4	21♌32.2
2 Su	16 42 06	9 30 03	20 19 52	27 42 41	4R37.1	0♑27.7	23 49.8	4 41.5	6 55.3	4 15.3	12 34.4	13R13.7	20 58.0	21R31.9
3 M	16 46 02	10 30 55	5♒01 07	12♒14 41	4 33.5	1 05.9	24 56.4	5 15.3	7 07.6	4 15.9	12 39.5	13 11.7	20 59.6	21 31.7
4 Tu	16 49 59	11 31 48	19 23 01	26 25 59	4D32.3	1 37.1	26 03.3	5 49.0	7 20.2	4 16.7	12 44.5	13 09.6	21 01.2	21 31.4
5 W	16 53 55	12 32 42	3♓23 34	10♓15 50	4R32.2	2 00.3	27 10.4	6 22.7	7 33.1	4 17.7	12 49.4	13 07.5	21 02.8	21 31.0
6 Th	16 57 52	13 33 36	17 03 01	23 45 22	4 31.9	2R14.9	28 17.7	6 56.2	7 46.2	4 19.0	12 54.2	13 05.4	21 04.3	21 30.7
7 F	17 01 48	14 34 31	0♈23 12	6♈56 49	4 30.2	2 19.9	29 25.3	7 29.7	7 59.4	4 20.4	12 59.0	13 03.2	21 05.8	21 30.3
8 Sa	17 05 45	15 35 27	13 26 34	19 52 47	4 26.0	2 14.6	0♏33.0	8 03.1	8 13.0	4 22.0	13 03.6	13 01.0	21 07.3	21 29.9
9 Su	17 09 42	16 36 23	26 15 43	2♉35 40	4 18.9	1 58.4	1 41.0	8 36.4	8 26.7	4 23.8	13 08.2	12 58.8	21 08.7	21 29.4
10 M	17 13 38	17 37 20	8♉52 51	15 07 28	4 08.8	1 30.8	2 49.1	9 09.6	8 40.6	4 25.9	13 12.8	12 56.5	21 10.2	21 29.0
11 Tu	17 17 35	18 38 18	21 19 41	27 29 39	3 56.4	0 51.7	3 57.5	9 42.7	8 54.8	4 28.1	13 17.2	12 54.3	21 11.6	21 28.5
12 W	17 21 31	19 39 17	3♊37 27	9♊43 12	3 42.6	0 01.5	5 06.0	10 15.7	9 09.1	4 30.6	13 21.5	12 52.0	21 13.0	21 28.0
13 Th	17 25 28	20 40 17	15 47 01	21 48 59	3 28.6	29♐01.0	6 14.7	10 48.7	9 23.7	4 33.2	13 25.8	12 49.6	21 14.3	21 27.4
14 F	17 29 24	21 41 17	27 49 13	3♋47 51	3 15.6	27 51.6	7 23.6	11 21.5	9 38.5	4 36.1	13 30.0	12 47.3	21 15.6	21 26.9
15 Sa	17 33 21	22 42 18	9♋45 02	15 41 00	3 04.5	26 35.2	8 32.7	11 54.3	9 53.5	4 39.1	13 34.1	12 44.9	21 16.9	21 26.3
16 Su	17 37 17	23 43 20	21 35 59	27 30 15	2 56.1	25 14.2	9 41.9	12 27.0	10 08.6	4 42.3	13 38.1	12 42.5	21 18.2	21 25.6
17 M	17 41 14	24 44 23	3♌24 10	9♌18 07	2 50.5	23 51.2	10 51.3	12 59.5	10 24.0	4 45.8	13 42.0	12 40.1	21 19.4	21 25.0
18 Tu	17 45 11	25 45 27	15 12 32	21 07 55	2D47.7	22 29.1	12 00.8	13 32.0	10 39.5	4 49.4	13 45.9	12 37.7	21 20.6	21 24.3
19 W	17 49 07	26 46 31	27 04 48	3♍03 45	2 47.0	21 10.6	13 10.6	14 04.4	10 55.2	4 53.2	13 49.6	12 35.2	21 21.8	21 23.6
20 Th	17 53 04	27 47 36	9♍05 24	15 10 23	2 47.4	19 58.2	14 20.4	14 36.6	11 11.1	4 57.2	13 53.3	12 32.7	21 23.0	21 22.9
21 F	17 57 00	28 48 42	21 19 22	27 33 01	2R47.9	18 53.7	15 30.4	15 08.8	11 27.2	5 01.4	13 56.9	12 30.2	21 24.1	21 22.1
22 Sa	18 00 57	29 49 49	3♎51 58	10♎16 50	2 47.3	17 58.7	16 40.6	15 40.9	11 43.5	5 05.8	14 00.3	12 27.7	21 25.2	21 21.3
23 Su	18 04 53	0♑50 56	16 48 12	23 26 32	2 44.9	17 14.0	17 50.8	16 12.8	11 59.9	5 10.4	14 03.7	12 25.2	21 26.2	21 20.5
24 M	18 08 50	1 52 04	0♏12 13	7♏05 29	2 40.1	16 40.1	19 01.2	16 44.6	12 16.5	5 15.2	14 07.0	12 22.7	21 27.3	21 19.7
25 Tu	18 12 46	2 53 13	14 06 23	21 14 46	2 33.0	16 16.9	20 11.8	17 16.4	12 33.3	5 20.2	14 10.2	12 20.1	21 28.3	21 18.8
26 W	18 16 43	3 54 23	28 30 17	5♐52 21	2 24.2	16D04.3	21 22.4	17 48.0	12 50.3	5 25.3	14 13.3	12 17.6	21 29.2	21 18.0
27 Th	18 20 40	4 55 33	13♐20 08	20 52 37	2 14.7	16 01.6	22 33.2	18 19.4	13 07.4	5 30.6	14 16.3	12 15.0	21 30.2	21 17.1
28 F	18 24 36	5 56 43	28 28 33	6♑06 38	2 05.8	16 08.3	23 44.1	18 50.8	13 24.7	5 36.1	14 19.2	12 12.5	21 31.1	21 16.2
29 Sa	18 28 33	6 57 54	13♑45 26	21 23 32	1 58.4	16 23.5	24 55.1	19 22.0	13 42.1	5 41.8	14 22.0	12 09.9	21 31.9	21 15.2
30 Su	18 32 29	7 59 05	28 59 36	6♒32 24	1 53.4	16 46.5	26 06.1	19 53.1	13 59.7	5 47.7	14 24.7	12 07.3	21 32.8	21 14.3
31 M	18 36 26	9 00 15	14♒00 53	21 24 10	1D50.9	17 16.6	27 17.3	20 24.1	14 17.4	5 53.7	14 27.3	12 04.7	21 33.6	21 13.3

Astro Data	Planet Ingress	Last Aspect	☽ Ingress	Last Aspect	☽ Ingress	☽ Phases & Eclipses	Astro Data
Dy Hr Mn	Dy Hr Mn	Dy Hr Mn	Dy Hr Mn	Dy Hr Mn	Dy Hr Mn	Dy Hr Mn	
☽0N 9 11:05	☿ ♐ 8 4:59	31 15:17 ♀ ✶	♐ 1 5:20	2 5:10 ♀ □	♒ 2 15:45	6 6:59 ☽ 13♒03	1 November 1951
♀0S 12 0:32	♀ ♎ 9 18:48	2 19:54 ♀ □	♑ 3 6:40	4 11:18 ♀ △	♓ 4 18:08	13 15:52 ○ 20♉28	Julian Day # 18932
♇ R 23 16:29	☉ ♐ 23 2:51	5 1:07 ♀ △	♒ 5 8:43	5 17:02 ♅ △	♈ 6 23:18	21 20:01 ☾ 28♌42	SVP 5♓55'52"
☽0S 24 0:41	♂ ♎ 24 6:11	7 10:22 ☿ □	♓ 7 12:23	8 15:02 ♇ △	♉ 9 7:04	29 1:00 ● 6♐00	GC 26♐10.0 ⚴ 29♑12.0
♃ D 30 4:08		9 17:48 ♀ ☍	♈ 9 17:53	11 0:18 ♇ □	♊ 11 16:54		Eris 7♈07.8R ⚵ 14♐43.3
♂0S 30 20:59	☿ ♑ 1 20:41	11 9:19 ♇ △	♉ 12 1:07	14 1:10 ☿ ☍	♋ 14 4:22	5 16:20 ☽ 12♓44	⚷ 29♐24.5 ⚶ 29♌17.5
	♀ ♏ 8 0:19	13 22:42 ♂ △	♊ 14 10:15	15 23:23 ♆ □	♌ 16 17:05	13 9:30 ○ 20♊34	☽ Mean ☊ 6♓39.7
☽0N 6 15:39	☿ ♐R 12 12:39	16 12:30 ♂ □	♋ 16 21:27	18 22:13 ☉ △	♍ 19 5:52	21 14:37 ☾ 28♍55	
☿ R 7 11:57	☉ ♑ 22 16:00	19 4:14 ♂ ✶	♌ 19 10:12	21 14:37 ☉ □	♎ 21 16:41	28 11:43 ● 5♑56	1 December 1951
♄□♅ 8 2:48		21 20:01 ☉ □	♍ 21 22:35	23 8:24 ♆ ☌	♏ 23 23:38		Julian Day # 18962
♆✶♇ 20 10:37		23 16:13 ☿ □	♎ 24 8:09	25 12:07 ♇ □	♐ 26 2:27		SVP 5♓55'46"
☽0S 21 7:59		26 3:59 ☿ ✶	♏ 26 13:32	27 12:59 ♆ ✶	♑ 28 2:24		GC 26♐10.1 ⚴ 6♒02.8
☿ D 27 6:37		28 1:34 ♇ □	♐ 28 15:20	29 18:02 ♀ ✶	♒ 30 1:36		Eris 6♈55.2R ⚵ 25♐01.8
		30 13:42 ☿ ☌	♑ 30 15:22				⚷ 2♑07.8 ⚶ 8♍32.6
							☽ Mean ☊ 5♓04.4

LONGITUDE — January 1952

Day	Sid.Time	☉	0 hr ☽	Noon ☽	True ☊	☿	♀	♂	⚳	♃	♄	♅	♆	♇
1 Tu	18 40 22	10♑01 26	28♒41 37	5♓52 46	1♓50.5	17♐53.0	28♏28.6	20♎54.9	14♓35.3	5♈59.9	14♎29.9	12♋02.1	21♎34.3	21♌12.3
2 W	18 44 19	11 02 36	12♓57 24	19 55 27	1 51.4	18 35.1	29 40.0	21 25.6	14 53.4	6 06.3	14 32.3	11R 59.5	21 35.1	21R 11.2
3 Th	18 48 16	12 03 46	26 46 58	3♈32 12	1R 52.4	19 22.3	0♐51.4	21 56.2	15 11.5	6 12.9	14 34.6	11 56.9	21 35.8	21 10.2
4 F	18 52 12	13 04 55	10♈11 27	16 45 04	1 52.7	20 14.0	2 03.0	22 26.6	15 29.9	6 19.6	14 36.8	11 54.3	21 36.4	21 09.1
5 Sa	18 56 09	14 06 05	23 13 29	29 37 09	1 51.3	21 09.7	3 14.6	22 56.8	15 48.3	6 26.5	14 38.9	11 51.7	21 37.1	21 08.0
6 Su	19 00 05	15 07 14	5♉56 30	12♉12 00	1 47.7	22 09.0	4 26.3	23 27.0	16 06.9	6 33.5	14 40.9	11 49.1	21 37.7	21 06.9
7 M	19 04 02	16 08 22	18 24 04	24 33 06	1 42.1	23 11.5	5 38.1	23 57.0	16 25.6	6 40.7	14 42.7	11 46.5	21 38.2	21 05.8
8 Tu	19 07 58	17 09 31	0♊39 29	6♊43 34	1 34.7	24 16.8	6 49.9	24 26.8	16 44.5	6 48.1	14 44.5	11 44.0	21 38.8	21 04.6
9 W	19 11 55	18 10 39	12 45 39	18 46 02	1 26.3	25 24.7	8 01.9	24 56.5	17 03.5	6 55.6	14 46.2	11 41.4	21 39.3	21 03.5
10 Th	19 15 51	19 11 47	24 44 57	0♋42 39	1 17.6	26 34.8	9 13.9	25 26.0	17 22.6	7 03.3	14 47.8	11 38.8	21 39.8	21 02.3
11 F	19 19 48	20 12 54	6♋39 21	12 35 14	1 09.6	27 47.0	10 26.0	25 55.4	17 41.9	7 11.2	14 49.3	11 36.3	21 40.2	21 01.1
12 Sa	19 23 45	21 14 01	18 30 32	24 25 27	1 02.8	29 01.0	11 38.2	26 24.6	18 01.2	7 19.1	14 50.6	11 33.7	21 40.6	20 59.9
13 Su	19 27 41	22 15 07	0♌20 10	6♌14 56	0 57.9	0♑16.7	12 50.4	26 53.6	18 20.7	7 27.3	14 51.9	11 31.2	21 41.0	20 58.7
14 M	19 31 38	23 16 14	12 10 00	18 05 38	0 55.0	1 33.9	14 02.7	27 22.5	18 40.3	7 35.6	14 53.1	11 28.6	21 41.3	20 57.4
15 Tu	19 35 34	24 17 20	24 02 09	29 59 52	0D 54.0	2 52.5	15 15.1	27 51.2	19 00.0	7 44.0	14 54.1	11 26.1	21 41.6	20 56.2
16 W	19 39 31	25 18 25	5♍59 11	12♍00 30	0 54.6	4 12.3	16 27.5	28 19.8	19 19.8	7 52.5	14 55.1	11 23.6	21 41.8	20 54.9
17 Th	19 43 27	26 19 31	18 04 16	24 10 57	0 56.1	5 33.4	17 40.0	28 48.1	19 39.7	8 01.3	14 55.9	11 21.1	21 42.1	20 53.6
18 F	19 47 24	27 20 36	0♎21 04	6♎35 07	0 57.9	6 55.4	18 52.6	29 16.3	19 59.8	8 10.1	14 56.6	11 18.6	21 42.3	20 52.3
19 Sa	19 51 20	28 21 40	12 53 38	19 17 09	0R 59.3	8 18.5	20 05.2	29 44.3	20 19.9	8 19.1	14 57.2	11 16.2	21 42.4	20 51.0
20 Su	19 55 17	29 22 45	25 46 09	2♏21 07	0 59.6	9 42.6	21 17.8	0♏12.1	20 40.2	8 28.2	14 57.7	11 13.7	21 42.5	20 49.6
21 M	19 59 14	0♒23 49	9♏02 26	15 50 24	0 58.6	11 07.5	22 30.6	0 39.7	21 00.6	8 37.5	14 58.1	11 11.3	21 42.6	20 48.3
22 Tu	20 03 10	1 24 53	22 45 15	29 47 00	0 56.2	12 33.3	23 43.4	1 07.1	21 21.0	8 46.9	14 58.4	11 08.9	21 42.7	20 47.0
23 W	20 07 07	2 25 56	6♐55 34	14♐10 40	0 52.7	13 59.9	24 56.2	1 34.3	21 41.6	8 56.4	14 58.6	11 06.5	21R 42.7	20 45.6
24 Th	20 11 03	3 26 59	21 31 49	28 58 18	0 48.6	15 27.3	26 09.1	2 01.3	22 02.3	9 06.1	14R 58.7	11 04.2	21 42.7	20 44.2
25 F	20 15 00	4 28 02	6♑29 15	14♑03 38	0 44.7	16 55.5	27 22.0	2 28.0	22 23.0	9 15.8	14 58.7	11 01.9	21 42.7	20 42.9
26 Sa	20 18 56	5 29 03	21 40 15	29 17 49	0 41.5	18 24.4	28 34.9	2 54.6	22 43.9	9 25.7	14 58.5	10 59.6	21 42.6	20 41.5
27 Su	20 22 53	6 30 04	6♒55 02	14♒30 35	0 39.5	19 54.0	29 47.9	3 20.9	23 04.8	9 35.8	14 58.3	10 57.3	21 42.5	20 40.1
28 M	20 26 49	7 31 04	22 03 16	29 31 59	0D 38.8	21 24.3	1♑01.0	3 47.0	23 25.9	9 45.9	14 57.9	10 55.0	21 42.3	20 38.7
29 Tu	20 30 46	8 32 03	6♓55 46	14♓13 51	0 39.2	22 55.3	2 14.1	4 12.8	23 47.0	9 56.2	14 57.5	10 52.8	21 42.1	20 37.3
30 W	20 34 43	9 33 00	21 25 40	28 30 50	0 40.4	24 27.1	3 27.2	4 38.4	24 08.2	10 06.6	14 56.9	10 50.6	21 41.9	20 35.8
31 Th	20 38 39	10 33 57	5♈29 08	12♈20 32	0 41.9	25 59.5	4 40.3	5 03.8	24 29.5	10 17.1	14 56.2	10 48.4	21 41.6	20 34.4

LONGITUDE — February 1952

Day	Sid.Time	☉	0 hr ☽	Noon ☽	True ☊	☿	♀	♂	⚳	♃	♄	♅	♆	♇
1 F	20 42 36	11♒34 52	19♈05 09	25♈43 13	0♓43.2	27♑32.6	5♑53.5	5♏28.9	24♓50.9	10♈27.7	14♎55.4	10♋46.3	21♎41.4	20♌33.0
2 Sa	20 46 32	12 35 46	2♉15 03	8♉41 03	0R 43.8	29 06.4	7 06.7	5 53.8	25 12.4	10 38.4	14R 54.6	10R 44.2	21R 41.0	20R 31.5
3 Su	20 50 29	13 36 38	15 01 42	21 17 30	0 43.7	0♒41.0	8 19.9	6 18.3	25 33.9	10 49.3	14 53.6	10 42.1	21 40.7	20 30.1
4 M	20 54 25	14 37 29	27 28 57	3♊36 36	0 42.7	2 16.2	9 33.1	6 42.7	25 55.6	11 00.2	14 52.5	10 40.1	21 40.3	20 28.6
5 Tu	20 58 22	15 38 19	9♊40 58	15 42 33	0 41.1	3 52.2	10 46.4	7 06.7	26 17.3	11 11.2	14 51.3	10 38.1	21 39.9	20 27.2
6 W	21 02 18	16 39 07	21 41 53	27 39 24	0 39.0	5 28.9	11 59.7	7 30.5	26 39.0	11 22.4	14 50.0	10 36.1	21 39.4	20 25.7
7 Th	21 06 15	17 39 54	3♋35 34	9♋30 46	0 36.9	7 06.4	13 13.1	7 54.0	27 00.9	11 33.6	14 48.6	10 34.2	21 39.0	20 24.3
8 F	21 10 12	18 40 40	15 25 26	21 19 52	0 34.9	8 44.7	14 26.4	8 17.2	27 22.8	11 45.0	14 47.0	10 32.3	21 38.4	20 22.8
9 Sa	21 14 08	19 41 24	27 14 26	3♌09 26	0 33.4	10 23.7	15 39.8	8 40.2	27 44.8	11 56.4	14 45.4	10 30.5	21 37.9	20 21.4
10 Su	21 18 05	20 42 06	9♌05 07	15 01 46	0 32.4	12 03.5	16 53.2	9 02.8	28 06.8	12 08.0	14 43.7	10 28.7	21 37.3	20 19.9
11 M	21 22 01	21 42 48	20 59 37	26 58 54	0D 32.0	13 44.2	18 06.7	9 25.1	28 28.9	12 19.6	14 41.9	10 26.9	21 36.7	20 18.5
12 Tu	21 25 58	22 43 28	2♍59 52	9♍02 43	0 32.1	15 25.6	19 20.2	9 47.1	28 51.1	12 31.3	14 40.0	10 25.1	21 36.1	20 17.0
13 W	21 29 54	23 44 06	15 07 42	21 15 03	0 32.5	17 07.9	20 33.6	10 08.8	29 13.4	12 43.1	14 38.0	10 23.4	21 35.4	20 15.5
14 Th	21 33 51	24 44 43	27 25 00	3♎37 49	0 33.1	18 51.1	21 47.2	10 30.2	29 35.7	12 55.1	14 35.9	10 21.8	21 34.7	20 14.1
15 F	21 37 47	25 45 20	9♎53 47	16 13 09	0 33.7	20 35.1	23 00.7	10 51.2	29 58.0	13 07.0	14 33.7	10 20.2	21 34.0	20 12.6
16 Sa	21 41 44	26 45 54	22 36 13	29 03 17	0 34.2	22 20.0	24 14.3	11 11.9	0♈20.5	13 19.1	14 31.4	10 18.6	21 33.2	20 11.2
17 Su	21 45 41	27 46 28	5♏34 37	12♏10 29	0 34.4	24 05.8	25 27.8	11 32.2	0 43.0	13 31.3	14 29.0	10 17.1	21 32.4	20 09.7
18 M	21 49 37	28 47 01	18 51 09	25 36 48	0R 34.5	25 52.5	26 41.4	11 52.2	1 05.5	13 43.5	14 26.5	10 15.6	21 31.6	20 08.3
19 Tu	21 53 34	29 47 32	2♐27 35	9♐23 37	0D 34.5	27 40.1	27 55.1	12 11.7	1 28.1	13 55.9	14 24.0	10 14.2	21 30.7	20 06.9
20 W	21 57 30	0♓48 02	16 24 52	23 31 13	0 34.5	29 28.6	29 08.7	12 31.0	1 50.8	14 08.3	14 21.3	10 12.8	21 29.9	20 05.4
21 Th	22 01 27	1 48 31	0♑42 28	7♑58 15	0 34.6	1♓18.0	0♒22.4	12 49.8	2 13.5	14 20.7	14 18.6	10 11.4	21 29.0	20 04.0
22 F	22 05 23	2 48 58	15 18 06	22 41 21	0 34.8	3 08.2	1 36.1	13 08.2	2 36.3	14 33.3	14 15.7	10 10.1	21 28.0	20 02.6
23 Sa	22 09 20	3 49 24	0♒07 17	7♒35 02	0 35.0	4 59.2	2 49.8	13 26.2	2 59.1	14 45.9	14 12.8	10 08.9	21 27.1	20 01.2
24 Su	22 13 16	4 49 49	15 03 39	22 32 07	0R 35.2	6 51.1	4 03.5	13 43.8	3 22.0	14 58.7	14 09.8	10 07.7	21 26.1	19 59.8
25 M	22 17 13	5 50 11	29 59 24	7♓24 29	0 35.2	8 43.7	5 17.2	14 01.0	3 44.9	15 11.4	14 06.7	10 06.5	21 25.1	19 58.4
26 Tu	22 21 10	6 50 33	14♓46 24	22 04 16	0 34.9	10 37.0	6 30.9	14 17.7	4 07.9	15 24.3	14 03.6	10 05.4	21 24.0	19 57.0
27 W	22 25 06	7 50 52	29 17 18	6♈24 53	0 34.2	12 30.8	7 44.6	14 34.0	4 30.9	15 37.2	14 00.3	10 04.4	21 23.0	19 55.6
28 Th	22 29 03	8 51 09	13♈26 30	20 21 50	0 33.3	14 25.2	8 58.4	14 49.8	4 54.0	15 50.2	13 57.0	10 03.3	21 21.9	19 54.2
29 F	22 32 59	9 51 24	27 10 42	3♉53 03	0 32.1	16 19.9	10 12.1	15 05.2	5 17.1	16 03.2	13 53.6	10 02.4	21 20.8	19 52.9

Astro Data

	Dy Hr Mn
☽ 0N	2 21:21
♃□♇	3 3:32
☽ 0S	17 13:43
♆ R	23 16:28
♄ R	24 17:55
☽ 0N	30 6:00
♃□♅	2 22:47
☽ 0S	13 19:11
♃☍♄	21 8:36
☽ 0N	26 16:46

Planet Ingress

		Dy Hr Mn
♀	♐	2 18:44
☿	♑	13 6:44
♂	♏	20 1:33
☉	♒	21 2:38
♀	♑	27 15:58
☿	♒	3 1:38
⚳	♈	15 14:06
☉	♓	19 16:57
☿	♓	20 18:55
♀	♒	21 4:42

Last Aspect / ☽ Ingress

Last Aspect Dy Hr Mn		☽ Ingress Dy Hr Mn
31 22:32 ♀ □	♓	1 2:10
2 9:33 ☿ □	♈	3 5:42
4 22:58 ♂ ☍	♉	5 12:43
7 5:15 ♇ □	♊	7 22:42
10 2:46 ☿ ☍	♋	10 10:34
12 16:12 ♂ □	♌	12 23:19
15 7:31 ♂ ⚹	♍	15 12:00
17 16:34 ☉ △	♎	17 23:19
20 6:09 ☉ □	♏	20 7:44
21 20:37 ♇ □	♐	22 12:22
24 7:04 ♀ ☌	♑	24 13:39
26 0:04 ♆ □	♒	26 13:06
27 23:27 ♆ △	♓	28 12:45
30 4:16 ☿ ⚹	♈	30 14:32

Last Aspect / ☽ Ingress

Last Aspect Dy Hr Mn		☽ Ingress Dy Hr Mn
1 15:47 ☿ □	♉	1 19:51
3 10:29 ♇ □	♊	4 4:55
5 23:56 ♆ △	♋	6 16:44
8 12:38 ♆ □	♌	9 5:36
11 1:15 ♆ ⚹	♍	11 18:02
13 10:30 ♀ △	♎	14 5:00
16 7:24 ☉ △	♏	16 13:45
18 18:01 ☉ □	♐	18 19:42
20 8:36 ♆ ⚹	♑	20 22:49
22 10:01 ♆ □	♒	22 23:48
24 10:14 ♆ △	♓	25 0:01
25 22:58 ♂ △	♈	27 1:11
28 13:45 ♆ ☍	♉	29 5:02

☽ Phases & Eclipses

Dy Hr Mn	
4 4:42	☽ 12♈46
12 4:55	○ 20♋56
20 6:09	☾ 29♎08
26 22:26	● 5♒56
2 20:01	☽ 12♉56
11 0:28	○ 21♌14
11 0:39	• P 0.083
18 18:01	☾ 29♏02
25 9:16	● 5♓43
25 9:11:05	• T 03'09"

Astro Data

1 January 1952
Julian Day # 18993
SVP 5♓55'40"
GC 26♐10.1 ⚴ 15♒01.9
Eris 6♈51.9 ⚵ 6♑22.5
⚷ 5♑20.7 ⚶ 14♍09.4
☽ Mean ☊ 3♓25.9

1 February 1952
Julian Day # 19024
SVP 5♓55'35"
GC 26♐10.2 ⚴ 25♒00.8
Eris 6♈59.7 ⚵ 17♑54.8
⚷ 8♑26.6 ⚶ 13♍18.8R
☽ Mean ☊ 1♓47.5

March 1952 — LONGITUDE

Day	Sid.Time	☉	0 hr ☽	Noon ☽	True ☊	☿	♀	♂	⚳	♃	♄	♅	♆	♇
1 Sa	22 36 56	10♓51 38	10♉29 00	16♉58 47	0♓31.0	18♓14.9	11♒25.9	15♏20.0	5♈40.2	16♈16.3	13♎50.1	10♋01.5	21♎19.6	19♌51.5
2 Su	22 40 52	11 51 49	23 22 42	29 41 09	0R 30.2	20 09.9	12 39.7	15 34.4	6 03.4	16 29.5	13R 46.6	10R 00.6	21R 18.5	19R 50.2
3 M	22 44 49	12 51 59	5♊54 38	12♊03 40	0D 29.9	22 04.7	13 53.4	15 48.3	6 26.6	16 42.7	13 43.0	9 59.8	21 17.3	19 48.8
4 Tu	22 48 45	13 52 06	18 08 48	24 10 38	0 30.2	23 59.0	15 07.2	16 01.8	6 49.9	16 56.0	13 39.3	9 59.1	21 16.1	19 47.5
5 W	22 52 42	14 52 11	0♋09 46	6♋06 47	0 31.0	25 52.6	16 21.0	16 14.7	7 13.2	17 09.3	13 35.5	9 58.4	21 14.8	19 46.2
6 Th	22 56 39	15 52 14	12 02 16	17 56 48	0 32.3	27 45.2	17 34.8	16 27.0	7 36.6	17 22.7	13 31.7	9 57.7	21 13.6	19 44.9
7 F	23 00 35	16 52 15	23 50 56	29 45 11	0 33.8	29 36.3	18 48.6	16 38.9	7 59.9	17 36.2	13 27.8	9 57.1	21 12.3	19 43.7
8 Sa	23 04 32	17 52 14	5♌40 03	11♌35 58	0 35.2	1♈25.6	20 02.4	16 50.2	8 23.3	17 49.7	13 23.9	9 56.6	21 11.0	19 42.4
9 Su	23 08 28	18 52 11	17 33 23	23 32 39	0R 36.0	3 12.7	21 16.2	17 00.9	8 46.8	18 03.2	13 19.9	9 56.1	21 09.7	19 41.1
10 M	23 12 25	19 52 05	29 34 07	5♍38 04	0 36.1	4 57.0	22 30.0	17 11.1	9 10.2	18 16.8	13 15.9	9 55.7	21 08.4	19 39.9
11 Tu	23 16 21	20 51 58	11♍44 44	17 54 21	0 35.1	6 38.0	23 43.8	17 20.8	9 33.7	18 30.5	13 11.8	9 55.3	21 07.0	19 38.7
12 W	23 20 18	21 51 49	24 07 03	0♎22 58	0 33.1	8 15.4	24 57.6	17 29.8	9 57.3	18 44.1	13 07.6	9 54.9	21 05.6	19 37.5
13 Th	23 24 14	22 51 37	6♎42 11	13 04 46	0 30.2	9 48.5	26 11.4	17 38.2	10 20.8	18 57.9	13 03.4	9 54.7	21 04.2	19 36.3
14 F	23 28 11	23 51 24	19 30 45	26 00 08	0 26.6	11 16.8	27 25.2	17 46.1	10 44.4	19 11.6	12 59.2	9 54.4	21 02.8	19 35.1
15 Sa	23 32 08	24 51 09	2♏32 55	9♏09 04	0 22.8	12 40.0	28 39.1	17 53.3	11 08.0	19 25.5	12 54.9	9 54.3	21 01.4	19 34.0
16 Su	23 36 04	25 50 53	15 48 33	22 31 22	0 19.4	13 57.4	29 52.9	17 59.8	11 31.7	19 39.3	12 50.6	9 54.1	21 00.0	19 32.8
17 M	23 40 01	26 50 35	29 17 27	6♐06 45	0 16.8	15 08.7	1♓06.8	18 05.8	11 55.4	19 53.2	12 46.2	9D 54.1	20 58.5	19 31.7
18 Tu	23 43 57	27 50 15	12♐59 14	19 54 50	0D 15.4	16 13.4	2 20.6	18 11.0	12 19.1	20 07.2	12 41.8	9 54.1	20 57.0	19 30.6
19 W	23 47 54	28 49 53	26 53 28	3♑55 02	0 15.2	17 11.3	3 34.5	18 15.6	12 42.8	20 21.1	12 37.3	9 54.1	20 55.6	19 29.6
20 Th	23 51 50	29 49 30	10♑59 24	18 06 23	0 16.1	18 01.9	4 48.4	18 19.6	13 06.5	20 35.1	12 32.9	9 54.2	20 54.1	19 28.5
21 F	23 55 47	0♈49 05	25 15 45	2♒27 12	0 17.6	18 45.1	6 02.2	18 22.8	13 30.3	20 49.2	12 28.4	9 54.4	20 52.6	19 27.5
22 Sa	23 59 43	1 48 38	9♒40 22	16 54 49	0R 18.9	19 20.7	7 16.1	18 25.3	13 54.1	21 03.3	12 23.8	9 54.6	20 51.0	19 26.4
23 Su	0 03 40	2 48 09	24 10 02	1♓25 25	0 19.5	19 48.5	8 30.0	18 27.1	14 17.9	21 17.4	12 19.3	9 54.8	20 49.5	19 25.4
24 M	0 07 37	3 47 39	8♓40 22	15 54 10	0 18.6	20 08.4	9 43.8	18R 28.2	14 41.7	21 31.5	12 14.7	9 55.1	20 47.9	19 24.5
25 Tu	0 11 33	4 47 06	23 06 07	0♈15 30	0 15.9	20 20.6	10 57.7	18 28.5	15 05.6	21 45.6	12 10.1	9 55.5	20 46.4	19 23.5
26 W	0 15 30	5 46 31	7♈21 39	14 23 55	0 11.6	20R 25.0	12 11.6	18 28.1	15 29.4	21 59.8	12 05.4	9 55.9	20 44.8	19 22.6
27 Th	0 19 26	6 45 55	21 21 44	28 14 38	0 06.0	20 21.9	13 25.4	18 27.0	15 53.3	22 14.1	12 00.8	9 56.4	20 43.2	19 21.7
28 F	0 23 23	7 45 16	5♉02 15	11♉44 20	29♒59.7	20 11.5	14 39.3	18 25.1	16 17.2	22 28.3	11 56.1	9 56.9	20 41.6	19 20.8
29 Sa	0 27 19	8 44 35	18 20 47	24 51 34	29 53.5	19 54.2	15 53.1	18 22.4	16 41.1	22 42.6	11 51.5	9 57.5	20 40.0	19 19.9
30 Su	0 31 16	9 43 52	1♊16 50	7♊36 47	29 48.1	19 30.4	17 07.0	18 19.0	17 05.0	22 56.8	11 46.8	9 58.1	20 38.4	19 19.1
31 M	0 35 12	10 43 06	13 51 46	20 02 10	29 44.2	19 00.9	18 20.9	18 14.9	17 29.0	23 11.1	11 42.1	9 58.8	20 36.8	19 18.2

April 1952 — LONGITUDE

Day	Sid.Time	☉	0 hr ☽	Noon ☽	True ☊	☿	♀	♂	⚳	♃	♄	♅	♆	♇
1 Tu	0 39 09	11♈42 19	26♊08 29	2♋11 16	29♒42.0	18♈26.2	19♓34.7	18♏09.9	17♈52.9	23♈25.5	11♎37.5	9♋59.6	20♎35.2	19♌17.4
2 W	0 43 06	12 41 29	8♋11 04	14 08 32	29D 41.4	17R 47.1	20 48.5	18R 04.2	18 16.9	23 39.8	11R 32.8	10 00.4	20R 33.6	19R 16.7
3 Th	0 47 02	13 40 36	20 04 18	25 59 00	29 42.2	17 04.5	22 02.4	17 57.8	18 40.9	23 54.2	11 28.1	10 01.2	20 31.9	19 15.9
4 F	0 50 59	14 39 42	1♌53 19	7♌47 52	29 43.6	16 19.2	23 16.2	17 50.6	19 04.8	24 08.5	11 23.5	10 02.1	20 30.3	19 15.2
5 Sa	0 54 55	15 38 45	13 43 17	19 40 11	29R 45.0	15 32.3	24 30.0	17 42.6	19 28.8	24 22.9	11 18.8	10 03.1	20 28.7	19 14.5
6 Su	0 58 52	16 37 45	25 39 08	1♍40 39	29 45.4	14 44.6	25 43.8	17 33.8	19 52.8	24 37.3	11 14.2	10 04.1	20 27.0	19 13.8
7 M	1 02 48	17 36 44	7♍45 12	13 53 14	29 44.3	13 57.1	26 57.7	17 24.3	20 16.8	24 51.7	11 09.5	10 05.1	20 25.4	19 13.2
8 Tu	1 06 45	18 35 40	20 05 04	26 21 00	29 41.1	13 10.6	28 11.5	17 14.1	20 40.8	25 06.1	11 04.9	10 06.2	20 23.7	19 12.5
9 W	1 10 41	19 34 34	2♎41 13	9♎05 50	29 35.7	12 26.1	29 25.3	17 03.1	21 04.8	25 20.5	11 00.3	10 07.4	20 22.1	19 11.9
10 Th	1 14 38	20 33 26	15 34 53	22 08 19	29 28.3	11 44.2	0♈39.1	16 51.3	21 28.8	25 35.0	10 55.7	10 08.6	20 20.4	19 11.4
11 F	1 18 34	21 32 16	28 46 00	5♏27 42	29 19.7	11 05.5	1 52.9	16 38.9	21 52.8	25 49.4	10 51.2	10 09.8	20 18.8	19 10.8
12 Sa	1 22 31	22 31 04	12♏13 09	19 02 02	29 10.7	10 30.8	3 06.7	16 25.7	22 16.8	26 03.8	10 46.6	10 11.1	20 17.1	19 10.3
13 Su	1 26 28	23 29 51	25 53 58	2♐48 34	29 02.2	10 00.3	4 20.5	16 11.8	22 40.8	26 18.3	10 42.1	10 12.5	20 15.5	19 09.8
14 M	1 30 24	24 28 36	9♐45 27	16 44 13	28 55.3	9 34.5	5 34.3	15 57.3	23 04.8	26 32.7	10 37.6	10 13.9	20 13.9	19 09.3
15 Tu	1 34 21	25 27 19	23 44 32	0♑46 04	28 50.5	9 13.6	6 48.1	15 42.0	23 28.9	26 47.2	10 33.2	10 15.4	20 12.2	19 08.9
16 W	1 38 17	26 26 00	7♑48 32	14 51 41	28D 48.0	8 57.8	8 01.9	15 26.1	23 52.9	27 01.6	10 28.8	10 16.9	20 10.6	19 08.5
17 Th	1 42 14	27 24 40	21 55 19	28 59 16	28 47.4	8 47.1	9 15.7	15 09.6	24 16.9	27 16.1	10 24.4	10 18.4	20 09.0	19 08.1
18 F	1 46 10	28 23 17	6♒03 22	13♒07 30	28 47.9	8D 41.6	10 29.5	14 52.4	24 40.9	27 30.5	10 20.1	10 20.0	20 07.3	19 07.7
19 Sa	1 50 07	29 21 54	20 11 30	27 15 13	28R 48.4	8 41.3	11 43.3	14 34.6	25 05.0	27 45.0	10 15.8	10 21.7	20 05.7	19 07.4
20 Su	1 54 03	0♉20 28	4♓18 28	11♓21 01	28 47.8	8 46.1	12 57.0	14 16.3	25 29.0	27 59.4	10 11.5	10 23.4	20 04.1	19 07.1
21 M	1 58 00	1 19 01	18 22 36	25 22 54	28 45.1	8 55.8	14 10.8	13 57.5	25 53.0	28 13.9	10 07.3	10 25.1	20 02.5	19 06.8
22 Tu	2 01 57	2 17 32	2♈21 33	9♈18 11	28 39.7	9 10.3	15 24.6	13 38.1	26 17.0	28 28.3	10 03.2	10 26.9	20 00.9	19 06.5
23 W	2 05 53	3 16 02	16 12 22	23 03 42	28 31.8	9 29.6	16 38.4	13 18.3	26 41.0	28 42.7	9 59.0	10 28.7	19 59.3	19 06.3
24 Th	2 09 50	4 14 29	29 51 44	6♉36 07	28 21.7	9 53.4	17 52.1	12 58.0	27 05.0	28 57.2	9 55.0	10 30.6	19 57.7	19 06.1
25 F	2 13 46	5 12 55	13♉16 31	19 52 37	28 10.3	10 21.5	19 05.9	12 37.4	27 29.0	29 11.6	9 51.0	10 32.5	19 56.1	19 05.9
26 Sa	2 17 43	6 11 19	26 24 16	2♊51 19	27 58.9	10 53.8	20 19.7	12 16.4	27 53.0	29 26.0	9 47.0	10 34.5	19 54.5	19 05.8
27 Su	2 21 39	7 09 41	9♊13 47	15 31 43	27 48.5	11 30.1	21 33.4	11 55.1	28 16.9	29 40.3	9 43.1	10 36.5	19 53.0	19 05.7
28 M	2 25 36	8 08 01	21 45 19	27 54 49	27 40.0	12 10.3	22 47.2	11 33.5	28 40.9	29 54.7	9 39.3	10 38.6	19 51.4	19 05.6
29 Tu	2 29 32	9 06 19	4♋00 35	10♋03 02	27 33.9	12 54.1	24 00.9	11 11.8	29 04.8	0♉09.1	9 35.6	10 40.7	19 49.9	19 05.5
30 W	2 33 29	10 04 35	16 02 40	22 00 01	27 30.2	13 41.5	25 14.6	10 49.8	29 28.8	0 23.4	9 31.9	10 42.8	19 48.3	19D 05.5

Astro Data

	Dy Hr Mn
☿0N	7 19:38
☽0S	12 1:39
♃△♇	16 1:38
♅D	18 4:11
☉0N	20 16:14
♃☍♆	21 17:12
☽0N	25 3:08
♂R	25 11:07
☿R	26 13:55
⚳0N	28 16:13
☽0S	8 9:18
♀0N	12 20:02
♄□♅	18 12:13
☿D	19 1:32
☽0N	21 11:04

Planet Ingress

		Dy Hr Mn
☿	♈	7 17:10
♀	♓	16 14:18
☉	♈	20 16:14
☊	♒R	28 10:45
♀	♈	9 23:17
☉	♉	20 3:37
♃	♉	28 20:50

♇ D30 23:20

Last Aspect / ☽ Ingress

Last Aspect Dy Hr Mn			☽ Ingress	Dy Hr Mn
1 17:22	♇	□	♊	2 12:36
4 11:32	☿	□	♋	4 23:40
7 11:39	☿	△	♌	7 12:30
9 7:14	♆	⚹	♍	10 0:51
11 18:14	☉	☍	♎	12 11:16
14 14:53	♀	△	♏	14 19:20
16 18:23	☉	△	♐	17 1:15
19 2:40	☉	□	♑	19 5:19
20 16:41	♆	□	♒	21 7:55
22 18:58	♃	⚹	♓	23 9:39
24 16:16	♂	△	♈	25 11:34
27 1:20	♃	☌	♉	27 15:05
29 1:49	♇	□	♊	29 21:36

Last Aspect / ☽ Ingress

Last Aspect Dy Hr Mn			☽ Ingress	Dy Hr Mn
31 18:18	♃	⚹	♋	1 7:39
3 7:41	♃	□	♌	3 20:10
5 21:39	♃	△	♍	6 8:40
8 15:53	♀	☍	♎	8 18:56
10 18:22	♃	☍	♏	11 2:13
12 12:14	♇	□	♐	13 7:08
15 5:05	♃	△	♑	15 10:41
17 9:07	☉	□	♒	17 13:43
19 15:51	☉	⚹	♓	19 16:40
20 16:53	♂	△	♈	21 19:56
23 22:09	♃	☌	♉	24 0:15
25 10:35	♇	□	♊	26 6:40
28 16:00	♃	⚹	♋	28 16:06

☽ Phases & Eclipses

Dy Hr Mn	
3 13:43	☽ 12♊56
11 18:14	○ 21♍08
19 2:40	☾ 28♐27
25 20:13	● 5♈07
2 8:48	☽ 12♋34
10 8:53	○ 20♎26
17 9:07	☾ 27♑18
24 7:27	● 4♉03

Astro Data

1 March 1952
Julian Day # 19053
SVP 5♓55'31"
GC 26♐10.3 ⚴ 4♓38.9
Eris 7♈15.2 ⚵ 28♑25.6
⚷ 10♑46.5 ⚶ 6♍47.2R
☽ Mean ☊ 0♓15.3

1 April 1952
Julian Day # 19084
SVP 5♓55'27"
GC 26♐10.3 ⚴ 14♓44.7
Eris 7♈36.4 ⚵ 8♒47.6
⚷ 12♑14.3 ⚶ 0♍31.5R
☽ Mean ☊ 28♒36.8

LONGITUDE May 1952

Day	Sid.Time	☉	0 hr ☽	Noon ☽	True ☊	☿	♀	♂	⚳	♃	♄	♅	♆	♇
1 Th	2 37 26	11♉02 49	27♋55 42	3♌50 20	27♒28.7	14♈32.2	26♈28.4	10♏27.7	29♈52.7	0♉37.7	9♎28.2	10♋45.0	19♎46.8	19♌05.5
2 F	2 41 22	12 01 00	9♌44 34	15 39 07	27R 28.6	15 26.2	27 42.1	10R 05.6	0♉16.6	0 52.0	9R 24.6	10 47.2	19R 45.3	19 05.5
3 Sa	2 45 19	12 59 10	21 34 38	27 31 49	27 28.7	16 23.4	28 55.8	9 43.4	0 40.5	1 06.3	9 21.1	10 49.5	19 43.8	19 05.6
4 Su	2 49 15	13 57 18	3♍31 21	9♍33 51	27 28.2	17 23.5	0♉09.5	9 21.2	1 04.4	1 20.6	9 17.7	10 51.8	19 42.4	19 05.7
5 M	2 53 12	14 55 24	15 39 57	21 50 11	27 26.0	18 26.5	1 23.2	8 59.0	1 28.3	1 34.8	9 14.4	10 54.2	19 40.9	19 05.8
6 Tu	2 57 08	15 53 28	28 05 05	4♎25 01	27 21.4	19 32.3	2 36.9	8 37.0	1 52.1	1 49.0	9 11.1	10 56.6	19 39.4	19 05.9
7 W	3 01 05	16 51 30	10♎50 19	17 21 13	27 14.2	20 40.8	3 50.6	8 15.1	2 15.9	2 03.2	9 07.9	10 59.0	19 38.0	19 06.1
8 Th	3 05 01	17 49 30	23 57 47	0♏39 58	27 04.6	21 51.9	5 04.2	7 53.4	2 39.7	2 17.4	9 04.7	11 01.4	19 36.6	19 06.3
9 F	3 08 58	18 47 29	7♏27 37	14 20 26	26 53.3	23 05.6	6 17.9	7 31.9	3 03.5	2 31.5	9 01.7	11 03.9	19 35.2	19 06.5
10 Sa	3 12 55	19 45 26	21 17 57	28 19 38	26 41.5	24 21.7	7 31.6	7 10.7	3 27.3	2 45.6	8 58.7	11 06.5	19 33.8	19 06.8
11 Su	3 16 51	20 43 22	5♐24 52	12♐32 56	26 30.3	25 40.3	8 45.3	6 49.8	3 51.1	2 59.7	8 55.8	11 09.1	19 32.5	19 07.1
12 M	3 20 48	21 41 16	19 43 06	26 54 38	26 20.9	27 01.3	9 58.9	6 29.2	4 14.8	3 13.7	8 53.0	11 11.7	19 31.1	19 07.4
13 Tu	3 24 44	22 39 09	4♑06 49	11♑19 01	26 14.0	28 24.5	11 12.6	6 09.0	4 38.5	3 27.8	8 50.3	11 14.3	19 29.8	19 07.7
14 W	3 28 41	23 37 01	18 30 37	25 41 08	26 09.9	29 50.1	12 26.3	5 49.2	5 02.2	3 41.7	8 47.6	11 17.0	19 28.5	19 08.1
15 Th	3 32 37	24 34 51	2♒50 11	9♒57 28	26 08.2	1♉18.0	13 39.9	5 29.9	5 25.9	3 55.7	8 45.1	11 19.7	19 27.2	19 08.5
16 F	3 36 34	25 32 41	17 02 45	24 05 53	26 07.9	2 48.1	14 53.6	5 11.1	5 49.6	4 09.6	8 42.6	11 22.5	19 26.0	19 08.9
17 Sa	3 40 31	26 30 29	1♓06 48	8♓05 27	26 07.7	4 20.5	16 07.3	4 52.8	6 13.2	4 23.5	8 40.2	11 25.3	19 24.7	19 09.3
18 Su	3 44 27	27 28 15	15 01 49	21 55 54	26 06.4	5 55.0	17 20.9	4 35.1	6 36.8	4 37.4	8 37.9	11 28.1	19 23.5	19 09.8
19 M	3 48 24	28 26 01	28 47 40	5♈37 05	26 03.0	7 31.8	18 34.6	4 17.9	7 00.4	4 51.2	8 35.7	11 30.9	19 22.3	19 10.3
20 Tu	3 52 20	29 23 46	12♈24 07	19 08 39	25 56.8	9 10.8	19 48.3	4 01.4	7 24.0	5 04.9	8 33.6	11 33.8	19 21.1	19 10.8
21 W	3 56 17	0♊21 29	25 50 35	2♉29 47	25 47.7	10 52.0	21 01.9	3 45.5	7 47.5	5 18.7	8 31.6	11 36.7	19 19.9	19 11.4
22 Th	4 00 13	1 19 12	9♉06 06	15 39 21	25 36.4	12 35.3	22 15.6	3 30.3	8 11.0	5 32.4	8 29.7	11 39.7	19 18.8	19 12.0
23 F	4 04 10	2 16 53	22 09 23	28 36 04	25 23.6	14 20.9	23 29.3	3 15.9	8 34.5	5 46.0	8 27.8	11 42.6	19 17.7	19 12.6
24 Sa	4 08 06	3 14 33	4♊59 18	11♊18 59	25 10.7	16 08.6	24 42.9	3 02.1	8 57.9	5 59.6	8 26.1	11 45.6	19 16.6	19 13.2
25 Su	4 12 03	4 12 12	17 35 07	23 47 45	24 58.7	17 58.6	25 56.6	2 49.1	9 21.3	6 13.2	8 24.4	11 48.7	19 15.5	19 13.9
26 M	4 16 00	5 09 49	29 56 58	6♋02 57	24 48.7	19 50.7	27 10.2	2 36.8	9 44.7	6 26.7	8 22.9	11 51.7	19 14.5	19 14.6
27 Tu	4 19 56	6 07 25	12♋05 56	18 06 15	24 41.2	21 44.9	28 23.9	2 25.3	10 08.1	6 40.1	8 21.5	11 54.8	19 13.5	19 15.3
28 W	4 23 53	7 05 00	24 04 14	0♌00 22	24 36.5	23 41.2	29 37.6	2 14.7	10 31.4	6 53.6	8 20.1	11 57.9	19 12.5	19 16.1
29 Th	4 27 49	8 02 34	5♌55 07	11 49 02	24 34.1	25 39.6	0♊51.2	2 04.8	10 54.6	7 06.9	8 18.8	12 01.1	19 11.5	19 16.8
30 F	4 31 46	9 00 06	17 42 42	23 36 45	24D 33.5	27 40.0	2 04.9	1 55.7	11 17.9	7 20.2	8 17.7	12 04.2	19 10.6	19 17.6
31 Sa	4 35 42	9 57 36	29 31 51	5♍28 40	24R 33.7	29 42.4	3 18.5	1 47.4	11 41.1	7 33.5	8 16.6	12 07.4	19 09.7	19 18.4

LONGITUDE June 1952

Day	Sid.Time	☉	0 hr ☽	Noon ☽	True ☊	☿	♀	♂	⚳	♃	♄	♅	♆	♇
1 Su	4 39 39	10♊55 06	11♍27 53	17♍30 11	24♒33.5	1♊46.5	4♊32.1	1♏40.0	12♉04.3	7♉46.7	8♎15.7	12♋10.6	19♎08.8	19♌19.3
2 M	4 43 35	11 52 34	23 36 14	29 46 41	24R 32.2	3 52.3	5 45.8	1R 33.4	12 27.4	7 59.8	8R 14.8	12 13.9	19R 07.9	19 20.2
3 Tu	4 47 32	12 50 00	6♎02 08	12♎23 07	24 28.8	5 59.7	6 59.4	1 27.6	12 50.5	8 12.9	8 14.0	12 17.1	19 07.1	19 21.0
4 W	4 51 29	13 47 26	18 50 05	25 23 23	24 23.0	8 08.4	8 13.1	1 22.6	13 13.5	8 25.9	8 13.4	12 20.4	19 06.3	19 22.0
5 Th	4 55 25	14 44 50	2♏03 16	8♏49 47	24 15.1	10 18.3	9 26.7	1 18.5	13 36.5	8 38.9	8 12.8	12 23.7	19 05.5	19 22.9
6 F	4 59 22	15 42 14	15 42 54	22 42 21	24 05.5	12 29.2	10 40.3	1 15.2	13 59.5	8 51.8	8 12.4	12 27.0	19 04.8	19 23.9
7 Sa	5 03 18	16 39 36	29 47 44	6♐58 27	23 55.2	14 40.7	11 54.0	1 12.6	14 22.4	9 04.6	8 12.0	12 30.3	19 04.1	19 24.9
8 Su	5 07 15	17 36 58	14♐13 47	21 32 52	23 45.5	16 52.6	13 07.6	1 11.0	14 45.3	9 17.4	8 11.8	12 33.7	19 03.4	19 25.9
9 M	5 11 11	18 34 19	28 54 44	6♑18 23	23 37.3	19 04.7	14 21.3	1D 10.1	15 08.1	9 30.1	8 11.6	12 37.1	19 02.7	19 26.9
10 Tu	5 15 08	19 31 39	13♑42 48	21 07 00	23 31.4	21 16.7	15 34.9	1 10.0	15 30.9	9 42.8	8D 11.5	12 40.5	19 02.1	19 28.0
11 W	5 19 04	20 28 59	28 30 04	5♒51 11	23 28.3	23 28.3	16 48.6	1 10.7	15 53.7	9 55.4	8 11.6	12 43.9	19 01.5	19 29.1
12 Th	5 23 01	21 26 18	13♒09 41	20 24 59	23D 26.9	25 39.2	18 02.2	1 12.2	16 16.4	10 07.9	8 11.7	12 47.3	19 00.9	19 30.2
13 F	5 26 58	22 23 36	27 36 41	4♓44 29	23 27.1	27 49.2	19 15.9	1 14.4	16 39.0	10 20.4	8 12.0	12 50.8	19 00.4	19 31.3
14 Sa	5 30 54	23 20 54	11♓48 12	18 47 46	23R 27.7	29 58.1	20 29.6	1 17.4	17 01.6	10 32.7	8 12.3	12 54.2	18 59.9	19 32.5
15 Su	5 34 51	24 18 12	25 43 11	2♈34 31	23 27.5	2♋05.6	21 43.2	1 21.2	17 24.2	10 45.0	8 12.8	12 57.7	18 59.4	19 33.7
16 M	5 38 47	25 15 30	9♈21 52	16 05 21	23 25.6	4 11.6	22 56.9	1 25.8	17 46.7	10 57.3	8 13.3	13 01.2	18 58.9	19 34.9
17 Tu	5 42 44	26 12 47	22 45 08	29 21 21	23 21.4	6 16.0	24 10.6	1 31.1	18 09.2	11 09.4	8 13.9	13 04.7	18 58.5	19 36.1
18 W	5 46 40	27 10 04	5♉54 07	12♉23 34	23 15.0	8 18.6	25 24.3	1 37.2	18 31.6	11 21.5	8 14.7	13 08.2	18 58.1	19 37.3
19 Th	5 50 37	28 07 21	18 49 49	25 12 56	23 06.7	10 19.2	26 38.0	1 43.9	18 53.9	11 33.5	8 15.5	13 11.8	18 57.7	19 38.6
20 F	5 54 33	29 04 37	1♊33 00	7♊50 05	22 57.2	12 17.9	27 51.7	1 51.5	19 16.2	11 45.4	8 16.5	13 15.3	18 57.4	19 39.9
21 Sa	5 58 30	0♋01 53	14 04 16	20 15 38	22 47.6	14 14.5	29 05.4	1 59.7	19 38.5	11 57.3	8 17.5	13 18.9	18 57.1	19 41.2
22 Su	6 02 27	0 59 09	26 24 15	2♋30 15	22 38.6	16 09.0	0♋19.1	2 08.6	20 00.6	12 09.0	8 18.7	13 22.4	18 56.9	19 42.5
23 M	6 06 23	1 56 24	8♋33 45	14 34 56	22 31.2	18 01.4	1 32.9	2 18.3	20 22.8	12 20.7	8 19.9	13 26.0	18 56.6	19 43.8
24 Tu	6 10 20	2 53 39	20 34 00	26 31 13	22 25.8	19 51.5	2 46.6	2 28.6	20 44.8	12 32.3	8 21.3	13 29.6	18 56.4	19 45.2
25 W	6 14 16	3 50 54	2♌26 51	8♌21 15	22 22.7	21 39.5	4 00.3	2 39.6	21 06.8	12 43.8	8 22.7	13 33.2	18 56.2	19 46.6
26 Th	6 18 13	4 48 08	14 14 50	20 07 59	22D 21.5	23 25.3	5 14.1	2 51.2	21 28.7	12 55.2	8 24.3	13 36.8	18 56.1	19 48.0
27 F	6 22 09	5 45 21	26 01 12	1♍55 01	22 21.9	25 08.9	6 27.8	3 03.6	21 50.6	13 06.5	8 25.9	13 40.4	18 56.0	19 49.4
28 Sa	6 26 06	6 42 34	7♍49 57	13 46 37	22 23.1	26 50.2	7 41.5	3 16.5	22 12.4	13 17.7	8 27.7	13 44.0	18 55.9	19 50.8
29 Su	6 30 02	7 39 47	19 45 37	25 47 34	22 24.5	28 29.3	8 55.3	3 30.1	22 34.1	13 28.9	8 29.5	13 47.6	18D 55.9	19 52.3
30 M	6 33 59	8 36 59	1♎53 07	8♎02 54	22R 25.1	0♌06.2	10 09.0	3 44.3	22 55.8	13 39.9	8 31.4	13 51.2	18 55.9	19 53.8

Astro Data

	Dy Hr Mn
☽0S	5 17:26
☽0N	18 16:25
♆✶♇	26 10:46
☽0S	2 1:09
♃⚻♄	3 14:00
♂D	10 2:45
♄D	10 13:19
☽0N	14 21:00
☽0S	29 7:58
♆D	30 9:23

Planet Ingress

	Dy Hr Mn
⚳ ♉	1 19:19
♀ ♉	4 8:55
☿ ♉	14 14:43
☉ ♊	21 3:04
♀ ♊	28 19:19
☿ ♊	31 15:26
☿ ♋	14 12:22
☉ ♋	21 11:13
♀ ♋	22 5:46
☿ ♌	30 10:27

Last Aspect / ☽ Ingress (May)

Last Aspect Dy Hr Mn		☽ Ingress Dy Hr Mn
30 19:19	♀ □	♌ 1 4:12
3 15:08	♀ △	♍ 3 16:57
4 21:23	☉ △	♎ 6 3:39
7 18:39	☿ ☍	♏ 8 10:49
9 20:16	☉ ☍	♐ 10 14:50
12 12:12	☿ △	♑ 12 17:09
14 8:17	☉ △	♒ 14 19:14
16 14:39	☉ □	♓ 16 22:05
18 22:25	☉ ✶	♈ 19 2:07
20 12:22	☿ ☌	♉ 21 7:29
23 1:28	♀ ☌	♊ 23 14:37
25 3:14	♆ △	♋ 26 0:06
28 11:09	♀ ✶	♌ 28 11:59
30 21:56	☿ □	♍ 31 0:57

Last Aspect / ☽ Ingress (June)

Last Aspect Dy Hr Mn		☽ Ingress Dy Hr Mn
1 1:22	♅ ✶	♎ 2 12:26
4 0:58	♇ ✶	♏ 4 20:19
6 6:20	♇ □	♐ 7 0:21
8 8:32	♇ △	♑ 9 1:46
10 8:38	♆ □	♒ 11 2:26
12 22:17	☿ △	♓ 13 4:00
14 20:28	☉ □	♈ 15 7:29
17 5:50	☉ ✶	♉ 17 13:11
19 1:30	♇ □	♊ 19 21:03
21 10:53	♇ ✶	♋ 22 7:04
23 20:44	♆ □	♌ 24 19:02
26 11:19	♇ ☌	♍ 27 8:06
29 18:09	☿ ✶	♎ 29 20:18

☽ Phases & Eclipses

Dy Hr Mn	
2 3:58	☽ 11♌42
9 20:16	○ 19♏07
16 14:39	☾ 25♒39
23 19:28	● 2♊35
31 21:46	☽ 10♍21
8 5:07	○ 17♐21
14 20:28	☾ 23♓41
22 8:45	● 0♋51
30 13:11	☽ 8♎40

Astro Data

1 May 1952
Julian Day # 19114
SVP 5♓55'23"
GC 26♐10.4 ⚴ 23♓48.9
Eris 7♈56.3 ⚵ 17♒11.9
⚷ 12♑23.9R ⚶ 1♍02.8
☽ Mean ☊ 27♒01.5

1 June 1952
Julian Day # 19145
SVP 5♓55'18"
GC 26♐10.5 ⚴ 1♈48.6
Eris 8♈11.4 ⚵ 22♒57.0
⚷ 11♑19.0R ⚶ 7♍52.9
☽ Mean ☊ 25♒23.0

July 1952 — LONGITUDE

Day	Sid.Time	☉	0 hr ☽	Noon ☽	True ☊	☿	♀	♂	⚳	♃	♄	♅	♆	♇
1 Tu	6 37 56	9♋34 11	14♎17 32	20♎37 34	22♒24.4	1♌40.8	11♋22.8	3♏59.1	23♉17.4	13♉50.8	8♎33.5	13♋54.9	18♎55.9	19♌55.3
2 W	6 41 52	10 31 22	27 03 34	3♏35 58	22R 22.1	3 13.2	12 36.5	4 14.5	23 38.9	14 01.7	8 35.6	13 58.5	18 55.9	19 56.8
3 Th	6 45 49	11 28 34	10♏15 08	17 01 18	22 18.2	4 43.3	13 50.3	4 30.5	24 00.4	14 12.4	8 37.8	14 02.1	18 56.0	19 58.3
4 F	6 49 45	12 25 45	23 54 33	0♐54 51	22 13.1	6 11.1	15 04.0	4 47.0	24 21.7	14 23.1	8 40.1	14 05.8	18 56.1	19 59.8
5 Sa	6 53 42	13 22 56	8♐01 55	15 15 20	22 07.4	7 36.5	16 17.8	5 04.1	24 43.0	14 33.6	8 42.5	14 09.4	18 56.3	20 01.4
6 Su	6 57 38	14 20 06	22 34 29	29 58 34	22 01.8	8 59.7	17 31.6	5 21.8	25 04.3	14 44.0	8 45.0	14 13.0	18 56.5	20 03.0
7 M	7 01 35	15 17 17	7♑26 38	14♑57 36	21 57.2	10 20.4	18 45.3	5 40.0	25 25.4	14 54.4	8 47.6	14 16.7	18 56.7	20 04.6
8 Tu	7 05 32	16 14 28	22 30 21	0♒03 40	21 54.1	11 38.8	19 59.1	5 58.7	25 46.5	15 04.6	8 50.3	14 20.3	18 56.9	20 06.2
9 W	7 09 28	17 11 39	7♒36 24	15 07 27	21D52.6	12 54.6	21 12.9	6 17.9	26 07.5	15 14.7	8 53.1	14 23.9	18 57.2	20 07.8
10 Th	7 13 25	18 08 50	22 35 48	0♓00 36	21 52.6	14 08.0	22 26.7	6 37.6	26 28.4	15 24.7	8 56.0	14 27.6	18 57.5	20 09.4
11 F	7 17 21	19 06 02	7♓21 07	14 36 48	21 53.7	15 18.7	23 40.5	6 57.8	26 49.2	15 34.6	8 58.9	14 31.2	18 57.9	20 11.0
12 Sa	7 21 18	20 03 14	21 47 13	28 52 07	21 55.1	16 26.8	24 54.3	7 18.5	27 10.0	15 44.4	9 02.0	14 34.8	18 58.2	20 12.7
13 Su	7 25 14	21 00 26	5♈51 23	12♈45 00	21R56.2	17 32.2	26 08.1	7 39.6	27 30.6	15 54.1	9 05.1	14 38.4	18 58.7	20 14.4
14 M	7 29 11	21 57 40	19 33 04	26 15 45	21 56.4	18 34.8	27 21.9	8 01.3	27 51.2	16 03.6	9 08.3	14 42.0	18 59.1	20 16.0
15 Tu	7 33 07	22 54 54	2♉53 16	9♉25 54	21 55.3	19 34.4	28 35.8	8 23.4	28 11.7	16 13.1	9 11.6	14 45.7	18 59.6	20 17.7
16 W	7 37 04	23 52 08	15 53 56	22 17 40	21 53.0	20 31.0	29 49.6	8 45.9	28 32.1	16 22.4	9 15.0	14 49.3	19 00.1	20 19.5
17 Th	7 41 01	24 49 24	28 37 27	4♊53 34	21 49.6	21 24.5	1♌03.4	9 08.9	28 52.4	16 31.6	9 18.5	14 52.9	19 00.6	20 21.2
18 F	7 44 57	25 46 40	11♊06 20	17 16 03	21 45.6	22 14.8	2 17.3	9 32.3	29 12.6	16 40.6	9 22.0	14 56.5	19 01.2	20 22.9
19 Sa	7 48 54	26 43 56	23 22 58	29 27 22	21 41.4	23 01.6	3 31.2	9 56.2	29 32.7	16 49.6	9 25.7	15 00.0	19 01.8	20 24.6
20 Su	7 52 50	27 41 13	5♋29 32	11♋29 40	21 37.5	23 44.9	4 45.0	10 20.5	29 52.7	16 58.4	9 29.4	15 03.6	19 02.4	20 26.4
21 M	7 56 47	28 38 31	17 28 03	23 24 55	21 34.5	24 24.6	5 58.9	10 45.2	0♊12.6	17 07.1	9 33.2	15 07.2	19 03.1	20 28.2
22 Tu	8 00 43	29 35 49	29 20 31	5♌15 06	21 32.4	25 00.4	7 12.8	11 10.3	0 32.5	17 15.6	9 37.1	15 10.7	19 03.7	20 29.9
23 W	8 04 40	0♌33 08	11♌08 57	17 02 20	21D31.5	25 32.2	8 26.7	11 35.8	0 52.2	17 24.1	9 41.1	15 14.3	19 04.5	20 31.7
24 Th	8 08 36	1 30 27	22 55 35	28 49 01	21 31.6	25 59.8	9 40.6	12 01.7	1 11.8	17 32.4	9 45.2	15 17.8	19 05.2	20 33.5
25 F	8 12 33	2 27 47	4♍43 00	10♍37 55	21 32.5	26 23.1	10 54.5	12 28.0	1 31.2	17 40.5	9 49.3	15 21.3	19 06.0	20 35.3
26 Sa	8 16 30	3 25 08	16 34 11	22 32 15	21 33.9	26 41.9	12 08.4	12 54.7	1 50.6	17 48.5	9 53.5	15 24.9	19 06.8	20 37.1
27 Su	8 20 26	4 22 28	28 32 35	4♎35 41	21 35.3	26 56.0	13 22.3	13 21.7	2 09.9	17 56.4	9 57.8	15 28.3	19 07.7	20 38.9
28 M	8 24 23	5 19 50	10♎42 03	16 52 12	21 36.5	27 05.3	14 36.2	13 49.1	2 29.0	18 04.1	10 02.2	15 31.8	19 08.5	20 40.7
29 Tu	8 28 19	6 17 12	23 06 40	29 25 57	21R37.2	27R09.6	15 50.1	14 16.9	2 48.0	18 11.7	10 06.6	15 35.3	19 09.4	20 42.6
30 W	8 32 16	7 14 34	5♏50 34	12♏20 58	21 37.2	27 08.8	17 04.0	14 45.0	3 07.0	18 19.1	10 11.2	15 38.7	19 10.4	20 44.4
31 Th	8 36 12	8 11 57	18 57 32	25 40 35	21 36.7	27 02.9	18 17.9	15 13.4	3 25.7	18 26.4	10 15.8	15 42.2	19 11.3	20 46.2

August 1952 — LONGITUDE

Day	Sid.Time	☉	0 hr ☽	Noon ☽	True ☊	☿	♀	♂	⚳	♃	♄	♅	♆	♇
1 F	8 40 09	9♌09 21	2♐30 22	9♐26 58	21♒35.6	26♌51.8	19♌31.8	15♏42.2	3♊44.4	18♉33.6	10♎20.4	15♋45.6	19♎12.3	20♌48.1
2 Sa	8 44 05	10 06 45	16 30 21	23 40 18	21R34.3	26R35.6	20 45.7	16 11.3	4 02.9	18 40.6	10 25.2	15 49.0	19 13.4	20 49.9
3 Su	8 48 02	11 04 10	0♑56 29	8♑18 20	21 33.0	26 14.2	21 59.7	16 40.7	4 21.4	18 47.4	10 30.0	15 52.4	19 14.4	20 51.8
4 M	8 51 59	12 01 36	15 45 08	23 16 00	21 32.0	25 47.9	23 13.6	17 10.5	4 39.7	18 54.1	10 34.9	15 55.7	19 15.5	20 53.7
5 Tu	8 55 55	12 59 02	0♒49 55	8♒25 44	21D31.4	25 16.8	24 27.5	17 40.5	4 57.8	19 00.6	10 39.8	15 59.1	19 16.6	20 55.5
6 W	8 59 52	13 56 30	16 02 16	23 38 18	21 31.3	24 41.4	25 41.4	18 10.9	5 15.8	19 07.0	10 44.8	16 02.4	19 17.8	20 57.4
7 Th	9 03 48	14 53 58	1♓12 38	8♓44 09	21 31.5	24 02.0	26 55.3	18 41.5	5 33.7	19 13.2	10 49.9	16 05.7	19 18.9	20 59.3
8 F	9 07 45	15 51 28	16 11 51	23 34 51	21 31.9	23 19.1	28 09.2	19 12.4	5 51.5	19 19.3	10 55.1	16 09.0	19 20.1	21 01.1
9 Sa	9 11 41	16 48 59	0♈52 26	8♈04 02	21 32.4	22 33.5	29 23.2	19 43.6	6 09.1	19 25.2	11 00.3	16 12.2	19 21.3	21 03.0
10 Su	9 15 38	17 46 31	15 09 19	22 08 02	21 32.7	21 45.8	0♍37.1	20 15.1	6 26.5	19 31.0	11 05.6	16 15.5	19 22.6	21 04.9
11 M	9 19 34	18 44 05	29 00 09	5♉45 43	21 33.0	20 56.9	1 51.0	20 46.9	6 43.9	19 36.5	11 10.9	16 18.7	19 23.9	21 06.8
12 Tu	9 23 31	19 41 40	12♉24 56	18 58 05	21R33.0	20 07.7	3 04.9	21 18.9	7 01.0	19 41.9	11 16.3	16 21.9	19 25.2	21 08.7
13 W	9 27 28	20 39 17	25 25 30	1♊47 37	21D33.0	19 19.0	4 18.9	21 51.2	7 18.0	19 47.2	11 21.8	16 25.0	19 26.5	21 10.5
14 Th	9 31 24	21 36 55	8♊04 52	14 17 44	21 33.0	18 31.8	5 32.8	22 23.8	7 34.9	19 52.3	11 27.3	16 28.2	19 27.8	21 12.4
15 F	9 35 21	22 34 35	20 26 40	26 32 11	21 33.1	17 47.1	6 46.8	22 56.6	7 51.6	19 57.2	11 32.9	16 31.3	19 29.2	21 14.3
16 Sa	9 39 17	23 32 17	2♋34 44	8♋34 46	21 33.2	17 05.9	8 00.7	23 29.7	8 08.2	20 01.9	11 38.6	16 34.4	19 30.6	21 16.2
17 Su	9 43 14	24 29 59	14 32 44	20 29 03	21 33.5	16 29.0	9 14.7	24 03.1	8 24.6	20 06.4	11 44.3	16 37.5	19 32.1	21 18.1
18 M	9 47 10	25 27 44	26 24 06	2♌18 16	21 33.8	15 57.1	10 28.6	24 36.7	8 40.8	20 10.8	11 50.1	16 40.5	19 33.5	21 20.0
19 Tu	9 51 07	26 25 29	8♌11 54	14 05 19	21R34.1	15 31.0	11 42.6	25 10.5	8 56.8	20 15.0	11 55.9	16 43.5	19 35.0	21 21.9
20 W	9 55 03	27 23 16	19 58 50	25 52 44	21 34.1	15 11.4	12 56.5	25 44.6	9 12.7	20 19.0	12 01.8	16 46.5	19 36.5	21 23.7
21 Th	9 59 00	28 21 05	1♍47 19	7♍42 51	21 33.8	14 58.7	14 10.5	26 18.9	9 28.4	20 22.8	12 07.7	16 49.4	19 38.1	21 25.6
22 F	10 02 57	29 18 55	13 39 37	19 37 53	21 33.2	14D53.4	15 24.4	26 53.5	9 43.9	20 26.5	12 13.7	16 52.3	19 39.6	21 27.5
23 Sa	10 06 53	0♍16 46	25 37 56	1♎40 02	21 32.1	14 55.7	16 38.4	27 28.3	9 59.2	20 29.9	12 19.7	16 55.2	19 41.2	21 29.3
24 Su	10 10 50	1 14 38	7♎44 30	13 51 39	21 30.9	15 05.8	17 52.3	28 03.3	10 14.3	20 33.2	12 25.8	16 58.1	19 42.8	21 31.2
25 M	10 14 46	2 12 32	20 01 46	26 15 13	21 29.5	15 23.9	19 06.2	28 38.6	10 29.3	20 36.3	12 32.0	17 00.9	19 44.4	21 33.1
26 Tu	10 18 43	3 10 27	2♏32 19	8♏53 26	21 28.2	15 50.0	20 20.2	29 14.0	10 44.0	20 39.2	12 38.1	17 03.7	19 46.1	21 34.9
27 W	10 22 39	4 08 24	15 18 54	21 49 04	21D27.4	16 23.9	21 34.1	29 49.7	10 58.6	20 41.9	12 44.4	17 06.4	19 47.7	21 36.8
28 Th	10 26 36	5 06 22	28 24 14	5♐04 41	21 27.1	17 05.7	22 48.0	0♐25.6	11 12.9	20 44.4	12 50.7	17 09.1	19 49.4	21 38.6
29 F	10 30 32	6 04 21	11♐50 41	18 42 22	21 27.4	17 55.0	24 01.9	1 01.7	11 27.1	20 46.7	12 57.0	17 11.8	19 51.1	21 40.5
30 Sa	10 34 29	7 02 21	25 39 52	2♑43 09	21 28.3	18 51.6	25 15.9	1 38.0	11 41.0	20 48.9	13 03.4	17 14.5	19 52.9	21 42.3
31 Su	10 38 26	8 00 23	9♑52 06	17 06 28	21 29.4	19 55.2	26 29.8	2 14.5	11 54.8	20 50.8	13 09.8	17 17.1	19 54.6	21 44.1

Astro Data

	Dy Hr Mn
♃⚹♅	2 1:20
☽0N	12 3:07
☽0S	26 13:59
☿R	29 20:31
☽0N	8 11:53
♃⚻♆	8 16:02
☿D	22 16:55
☽0S	22 19:46

Planet Ingress

	Dy Hr Mn
♀ ♌	16 15:23
⚳ ♊	20 20:44
☉ ♌	22 22:07
♀ ♍	9 23:58
☉ ♍	23 5:03
♂ ♐	27 18:53

Last Aspect / ☽ Ingress

Last Aspect Dy Hr Mn		☽ Ingress Dy Hr Mn
1 10:40 ♇ ⚹	♏	2 5:25
3 17:10 ♇ □	♐	4 10:27
5 19:51 ♇ △	♑	6 12:02
7 18:35 ♀ ☍	♒	8 11:54
9 20:03 ♇ ☍	♓	10 11:59
12 4:37 ♀ △	♈	12 13:56
14 14:11 ♀ □	♉	14 18:45
16 15:13 ☉ ⚹	♊	17 2:37
18 22:27 ♀ ⚹	♋	19 13:05
21 23:31 ☉ ☌	♌	22 1:20
24 6:02 ☿ ☌	♍	24 14:24
26 2:23 ♃ △	♎	27 2:54
29 7:41 ☿ ⚹	♏	29 13:04
31 14:24 ☿ □	♐	31 19:37

Last Aspect Dy Hr Mn		☽ Ingress Dy Hr Mn
2 16:44 ☿ △	♑	2 22:27
4 5:36 ♆ □	♒	4 22:41
6 15:32 ♀ ☍	♓	6 22:05
8 5:01 ♃ ⚹	♈	8 22:33
10 11:24 ☿ △	♉	11 1:46
12 16:32 ♂ ☍	♊	13 8:36
15 3:31 ☉ ⚹	♋	15 18:52
17 19:35 ♂ △	♌	18 7:19
20 15:20 ☉ ☌	♍	20 20:22
23 3:15 ♂ ☌	♎	23 8:42
25 2:55 ♇ ⚹	♏	25 19:10
27 11:37 ♇ □	♐	28 2:53
29 22:05 ♀ □	♑	30 7:24

☽ Phases & Eclipses

Dy Hr Mn	
7 12:33	○ 15♑19
14 3:42	☾ 21♈38
21 23:31	● 29♋06
30 1:51	☽ 6♏50
5 19:40	○ 13♒17
5 19:47	• P 0.532
12 13:27	☾ 19♉45
20 15:20	● 27♌31
20 15:13:05	• A 06'40"
28 12:03	☽ 5♐06

Astro Data

1 July 1952
Julian Day # 19175
SVP 5♓55'13"
GC 26♐10.6 ⚴ 7♈17.1
Eris 8♈17.4 ⚵ 23♒57.3R
⚷ 9♑31.6R ⚶ 18♍23.1
☽ Mean ☊ 23♒47.7

1 August 1952
Julian Day # 19206
SVP 5♓55'08"
GC 26♐10.6 ⚴ 9♈07.7R
Eris 8♈13.2R ⚵ 19♒10.8R
⚷ 7♑42.3R ⚶ 1♎39.8
☽ Mean ☊ 22♒09.2

LONGITUDE — September 1952

Day	Sid.Time	☉	0 hr ☽	Noon ☽	True ☊	☿	♀	♂	ʔ	♃	♄	♅	♆	♇
1 M	10 42 22	8♍58 26	24♑25 51	1♒49 41	21♒30.5	21♌05.5	27♍43.7	2♐51.2	12♊08.3	20♉52.5	13♎16.3	17♋19.7	19♎56.4	21♌45.9
2 Tu	10 46 19	9 56 31	9♒17 16	16 47 46	21R 31.1	22 21.9	28 57.6	3 28.1	12 21.6	20 54.1	13 22.8	17 22.2	19 58.2	21 47.8
3 W	10 50 15	10 54 37	24 20 12	1♓53 30	21 30.9	23 44.0	0♎11.4	4 05.2	12 34.7	20 55.5	13 29.3	17 24.7	20 00.0	21 49.6
4 Th	10 54 12	11 52 45	9♓26 33	16 58 12	21 29.7	25 11.4	1 25.3	4 42.4	12 47.5	20 56.6	13 35.9	17 27.2	20 01.9	21 51.4
5 F	10 58 08	12 50 54	24 27 18	1♈52 50	21 27.6	26 43.5	2 39.2	5 19.9	13 00.2	20 57.6	13 42.5	17 29.6	20 03.7	21 53.1
6 Sa	11 02 05	13 49 05	9♈13 50	16 29 28	21 24.7	28 19.9	3 53.0	5 57.5	13 12.6	20 58.3	13 49.2	17 32.0	20 05.6	21 54.9
7 Su	11 06 01	14 47 19	23 39 06	0♉42 14	21 21.5	29 59.9	5 06.9	6 35.3	13 24.7	20 58.9	13 55.9	17 34.3	20 07.5	21 56.7
8 M	11 09 58	15 45 34	7♉38 35	14 28 01	21 18.6	1♍43.0	6 20.7	7 13.2	13 36.7	20 59.3	14 02.6	17 36.7	20 09.4	21 58.4
9 Tu	11 13 55	16 43 51	21 10 32	27 46 19	21 16.3	3 28.8	7 34.6	7 51.4	13 48.4	20R 59.4	14 09.4	17 38.9	20 11.3	22 00.2
10 W	11 17 51	17 42 11	4♊15 39	10♊38 56	21D 15.0	5 16.8	8 48.4	8 29.7	13 59.8	20 59.4	14 16.2	17 41.2	20 13.2	22 01.9
11 Th	11 21 48	18 40 33	16 56 38	23 09 16	21 14.9	7 06.5	10 02.3	9 08.2	14 11.0	20 59.1	14 23.1	17 43.3	20 15.2	22 03.7
12 F	11 25 44	19 38 56	29 17 25	5♋21 39	21 15.8	8 57.6	11 16.1	9 46.8	14 21.9	20 58.7	14 29.9	17 45.5	20 17.2	22 05.4
13 Sa	11 29 41	20 37 22	11♋22 36	17 20 52	21 17.4	10 49.6	12 29.9	10 25.6	14 32.6	20 58.1	14 36.8	17 47.6	20 19.1	22 07.1
14 Su	11 33 37	21 35 50	23 17 03	29 11 42	21 19.1	12 42.3	13 43.8	11 04.6	14 43.0	20 57.2	14 43.8	17 49.7	20 21.2	22 08.8
15 M	11 37 34	22 34 20	5♌05 23	10♌58 37	21R 20.5	14 35.3	14 57.6	11 43.7	14 53.1	20 56.2	14 50.7	17 51.7	20 23.2	22 10.5
16 Tu	11 41 30	23 32 52	16 51 53	22 45 39	21 21.0	16 28.4	16 11.4	12 23.0	15 03.0	20 54.9	14 57.7	17 53.6	20 25.2	22 12.1
17 W	11 45 27	24 31 26	28 40 17	4♍36 11	21 20.1	18 21.4	17 25.2	13 02.5	15 12.5	20 53.5	15 04.7	17 55.6	20 27.2	22 13.8
18 Th	11 49 24	25 30 02	10♍33 39	16 33 00	21 17.5	20 14.1	18 39.0	13 42.1	15 21.8	20 51.8	15 11.8	17 57.5	20 29.3	22 15.4
19 F	11 53 20	26 28 40	22 34 26	28 38 13	21 13.3	22 06.4	19 52.8	14 21.9	15 30.8	20 49.9	15 18.9	17 59.3	20 31.4	22 17.0
20 Sa	11 57 17	27 27 20	4♎44 29	10♎53 25	21 07.6	23 58.2	21 06.6	15 01.8	15 39.5	20 47.9	15 26.0	18 01.1	20 33.5	22 18.6
21 Su	12 01 13	28 26 02	17 05 07	23 19 43	21 01.1	25 49.3	22 20.4	15 41.8	15 47.9	20 45.6	15 33.1	18 02.8	20 35.5	22 20.2
22 M	12 05 10	29 24 46	29 37 20	5♏58 02	20 54.4	27 39.7	23 34.1	16 22.1	15 56.0	20 43.2	15 40.2	18 04.5	20 37.7	22 21.8
23 Tu	12 09 06	0♎23 31	12♏21 56	18 49 07	20 48.2	29 29.3	24 47.9	17 02.4	16 03.8	20 40.5	15 47.4	18 06.2	20 39.8	22 23.4
24 W	12 13 03	1 22 19	25 19 43	1♐53 50	20 43.2	1♎18.1	26 01.6	17 42.9	16 11.3	20 37.7	15 54.5	18 07.8	20 41.9	22 24.9
25 Th	12 16 59	2 21 08	8♐31 35	15 13 06	20 40.0	3 06.0	27 15.4	18 23.5	16 18.5	20 34.6	16 01.7	18 09.3	20 44.0	22 26.4
26 F	12 20 56	3 19 59	21 58 31	28 47 57	20D 38.6	4 53.1	28 29.1	19 04.3	16 25.3	20 31.4	16 08.9	18 10.8	20 46.2	22 28.0
27 Sa	12 24 53	4 18 51	5♑41 28	12♑39 08	20 38.8	6 39.2	29 42.8	19 45.2	16 31.8	20 28.0	16 16.2	18 12.3	20 48.4	22 29.4
28 Su	12 28 49	5 17 46	19 40 59	26 46 54	20 39.9	8 24.5	0♏56.5	20 26.2	16 38.0	20 24.4	16 23.4	18 13.7	20 50.5	22 30.9
29 M	12 32 46	6 16 42	3♒56 47	11♒10 21	20R 41.0	10 08.9	2 10.2	21 07.4	16 43.9	20 20.6	16 30.7	18 15.0	20 52.7	22 32.4
30 Tu	12 36 42	7 15 40	18 27 16	25 47 02	20 41.2	11 52.3	3 23.9	21 48.7	16 49.4	20 16.6	16 37.9	18 16.3	20 54.9	22 33.8

LONGITUDE — October 1952

Day	Sid.Time	☉	0 hr ☽	Noon ☽	True ☊	☿	♀	♂	ʔ	♃	♄	♅	♆	♇
1 W	12 40 39	8♎14 39	3♓09 03	10♓32 34	20♒39.7	13♎34.9	4♏37.5	22♐30.1	16♊54.6	20♉12.4	16♎45.2	18♋17.6	20♎57.1	22♌35.2
2 Th	12 44 35	9 13 40	17 56 46	25 20 44	20R 35.9	15 16.6	5 51.1	23 11.6	16 59.5	20R 08.1	16 52.5	18 18.8	20 59.3	22 36.6
3 F	12 48 32	10 12 44	2♈43 30	10♈04 05	20 30.0	16 57.5	7 04.8	23 53.2	17 04.0	20 03.6	16 59.8	18 19.9	21 01.5	22 38.0
4 Sa	12 52 28	11 11 49	17 21 31	24 34 55	20 22.3	18 37.5	8 18.4	24 34.9	17 08.1	19 58.9	17 07.1	18 21.0	21 03.7	22 39.4
5 Su	12 56 25	12 10 56	1♉43 29	8♉46 33	20 13.8	20 16.7	9 32.0	25 16.8	17 12.0	19 54.0	17 14.4	18 22.1	21 05.9	22 40.7
6 M	13 00 21	13 10 06	15 43 36	22 34 17	20 05.5	21 55.1	10 45.6	25 58.8	17 15.4	19 49.0	17 21.8	18 23.1	21 08.1	22 42.1
7 Tu	13 04 18	14 09 18	29 18 25	5♊55 58	19 58.3	23 32.8	11 59.1	26 40.8	17 18.5	19 43.8	17 29.1	18 24.0	21 10.3	22 43.4
8 W	13 08 15	15 08 32	12♊27 04	18 51 58	19 52.8	25 09.6	13 12.7	27 23.0	17 21.2	19 38.4	17 36.4	18 24.9	21 12.5	22 44.6
9 Th	13 12 11	16 07 49	25 11 03	1♋24 46	19 49.5	26 45.7	14 26.2	28 05.3	17 23.5	19 32.9	17 43.8	18 25.8	21 14.8	22 45.9
10 F	13 16 08	17 07 08	7♋33 41	13 38 23	19D 48.2	28 21.1	15 39.8	28 47.8	17 25.5	19 27.2	17 51.1	18 26.6	21 17.0	22 47.1
11 Sa	13 20 04	18 06 29	19 39 31	25 37 45	19 48.4	29 55.7	16 53.3	29 30.3	17 27.1	19 21.3	17 58.4	18 27.3	21 19.2	22 48.4
12 Su	13 24 01	19 05 53	1♌33 46	7♌28 14	19 49.3	1♏29.7	18 06.8	0♑12.9	17 28.3	19 15.3	18 05.8	18 28.0	21 21.5	22 49.5
13 M	13 27 57	20 05 19	13 21 51	19 15 14	19R 49.8	3 02.9	19 20.3	0 55.6	17 29.1	19 09.2	18 13.1	18 28.6	21 23.7	22 50.7
14 Tu	13 31 54	21 04 47	25 09 01	1♍03 47	19 49.1	4 35.5	20 33.8	1 38.4	17R 29.6	19 02.9	18 20.5	18 29.2	21 26.0	22 51.9
15 W	13 35 50	22 04 17	7♍00 05	12 58 23	19 46.3	6 07.4	21 47.3	2 21.4	17 29.6	18 56.4	18 27.8	18 29.7	21 28.2	22 53.0
16 Th	13 39 47	23 03 49	18 59 08	25 02 41	19 41.0	7 38.7	23 00.8	3 04.4	17 29.3	18 49.9	18 35.1	18 30.2	21 30.4	22 54.1
17 F	13 43 44	24 03 24	1♎09 22	7♎19 24	19 33.0	9 09.2	24 14.2	3 47.5	17 28.5	18 43.2	18 42.4	18 30.6	21 32.7	22 55.2
18 Sa	13 47 40	25 03 01	13 32 56	19 50 06	19 22.8	10 39.2	25 27.7	4 30.8	17 27.4	18 36.3	18 49.8	18 31.0	21 34.9	22 56.2
19 Su	13 51 37	26 02 39	26 10 54	2♏35 19	19 11.1	12 08.4	26 41.1	5 14.1	17 25.8	18 29.4	18 57.1	18 31.3	21 37.1	22 57.2
20 M	13 55 33	27 02 20	9♏03 16	15 34 37	18 59.0	13 37.0	27 54.5	5 57.5	17 23.9	18 22.3	19 04.4	18 31.5	21 39.4	22 58.2
21 Tu	13 59 30	28 02 03	22 09 12	28 46 52	18 47.6	15 05.0	29 07.9	6 41.0	17 21.5	18 15.2	19 11.7	18 31.7	21 41.6	22 59.2
22 W	14 03 26	29 01 48	5♐27 25	12♐10 39	18 38.1	16 32.3	0♐21.3	7 24.6	17 18.8	18 07.9	19 18.9	18 31.9	21 43.8	23 00.2
23 Th	14 07 23	0♏01 34	18 56 27	25 44 38	18 31.1	17 58.8	1 34.7	8 08.3	17 15.6	18 00.5	19 26.2	18 32.0	21 46.1	23 01.1
24 F	14 11 19	1 01 22	2♑35 08	9♑27 49	18 27.0	19 24.7	2 48.0	8 52.1	17 12.1	17 53.0	19 33.5	18R 32.0	21 48.3	23 02.0
25 Sa	14 15 16	2 01 12	16 22 41	23 19 40	18D 25.3	20 49.8	4 01.3	9 36.0	17 08.2	17 45.5	19 40.7	18 32.0	21 50.5	23 02.9
26 Su	14 19 13	3 01 04	0♒18 45	7♒19 55	18R 25.1	22 14.1	5 14.7	10 19.9	17 03.8	17 37.9	19 47.9	18 31.9	21 52.7	23 03.7
27 M	14 23 09	4 00 57	14 23 06	21 28 14	18 25.2	23 37.6	6 27.9	11 03.9	16 59.1	17 30.1	19 55.1	18 31.8	21 54.9	23 04.6
28 Tu	14 27 06	5 00 51	28 35 11	5♓43 44	18 24.2	25 00.3	7 41.2	11 48.0	16 53.9	17 22.4	20 02.3	18 31.6	21 57.1	23 05.3
29 W	14 31 02	6 00 48	12♓53 36	20 04 24	18 21.2	26 22.0	8 54.4	12 32.2	16 48.4	17 14.5	20 09.5	18 31.4	21 59.3	23 06.1
30 Th	14 34 59	7 00 46	27 15 40	4♈26 51	18 15.3	27 42.7	10 07.6	13 16.4	16 42.5	17 06.6	20 16.6	18 31.1	22 01.5	23 06.9
31 F	14 38 55	8 00 45	11♈37 18	18 46 22	18 06.4	29 02.4	11 20.8	14 00.7	16 36.2	16 58.6	20 23.8	18 30.8	22 03.6	23 07.6

Astro Data

	Dy Hr Mn
☽0N	4 22:31
♀0S	5 9:55
♃ R	9 19:40
☽0S	19 1:58
☉0S	23 2:23
♃⚻♆	23 15:41
☿0S	25 12:10
☽0N	2 9:04
ʔ R	15 2:30
♄□♅	15 18:51
☽0S	16 8:53
♃⚻♄	17 13:14
♃✱♅	19 5:44
♅ R	24 16:47
☽0N	29 17:25

Planet Ingress

		Dy Hr Mn
♀	♎	3 8:17
☿	♍	7 12:02
☉	♎	23 2:24
☿	♎	23 18:45
♀	♏	27 17:36
☿	♏	11 13:05
♂	♑	12 4:45
♀	♐	22 5:02
☉	♏	23 11:22

Last Aspect / ☽ Ingress

Last Aspect Dy Hr Mn			☽ Ingress	Dy Hr Mn
1 4:45	♀	△	♒	1 9:03
2 21:44	☿	☍	♓	3 9:00
4 18:22	♃	✱	♈	5 8:57
7 10:38	☿	△	♉	7 10:48
9 1:28	♇	□	♊	9 16:06
11 9:52	♇	✱	♋	12 1:24
13 19:18	♃	✱	♌	14 13:38
16 10:52	♇	☌	♍	17 2:42
19 7:22	☉	☌	♎	19 14:41
21 10:06	♇	✱	♏	22 0:43
23 18:37	♇	□	♐	24 8:33
26 11:24	♀	✱	♑	26 14:06
28 1:56	♆	□	♒	28 17:24
30 6:44	♇	☍	♓	30 18:52

Last Aspect / ☽ Ingress

Last Aspect Dy Hr Mn			☽ Ingress	Dy Hr Mn
2 8:20	♂	□	♈	2 19:34
4 12:00	♂	△	♉	4 21:05
6 12:14	♇	□	♊	7 1:15
9 5:11	♂	☍	♋	9 9:16
11 3:18	♆	□	♌	11 20:50
13 19:19	♇	☌	♍	14 9:51
16 7:32	♀	✱	♎	16 21:44
18 22:42	☉	☌	♏	19 7:10
21 12:42	♀	☌	♐	21 14:12
23 7:12	♇	△	♑	23 19:28
25 9:26	♆	□	♒	25 23:28
27 16:02	☿	□	♓	28 2:23
29 23:36	☿	△	♈	30 4:34

☽ Phases & Eclipses

Dy Hr Mn		
4 3:19	○	11♓32
11 2:36	☾	18♊18
19 7:22	●	26♍17
26 20:31	☽	3♑41
3 12:15	○	10♈13
10 19:33	☾	17♋26
18 22:42	●	25♎30
26 4:04	☽	2♒41

Astro Data

1 September 1952
Julian Day # 19237
SVP 5♓55'03"
GC 26♐10.7 ⚳ 5♈31.2R
Eris 7♈59.9R ⚵ 11♒59.2R
⚷ 6♑41.8R ⚶ 16♎29.3
☽ Mean ☊ 20♒30.7

1 October 1952
Julian Day # 19267
SVP 5♓55'00"
GC 26♐10.8 ⚳ 27♓49.5R
Eris 7♈41.8R ⚵ 9♒15.7
⚷ 6♑54.6 ⚶ 1♏47.3
☽ Mean ☊ 18♒55.4

November 1952 — LONGITUDE

Day	Sid.Time	☉	0 hr ☽	Noon ☽	True ☊	☿	♀	♂	⚳	♃	♄	♅	♆	♇
1 Sa	14 42 52	9♏00 47	25♈53 18	2♉57 23	17♒55.3	0♐20.9	12♐34.0	14♑45.1	16♊29.5	16♉50.6	20♎30.9	18♋30.4	22♎05.8	23♌08.3
2 Su	14 46 48	10 00 50	9♉57 57	16 54 21	17R 42.8	1 38.2	13 47.1	15 29.5	16R 22.5	16R 42.6	20 37.9	18R 29.9	22 08.0	23 08.9
3 M	14 50 45	11 00 55	23 46 04	0♊32 38	17 30.3	2 54.1	15 00.2	16 14.0	16 15.0	16 34.5	20 45.0	18 29.4	22 10.1	23 09.5
4 Tu	14 54 42	12 01 03	7♊13 46	13 49 17	17 19.0	4 08.4	16 13.3	16 58.6	16 07.2	16 26.4	20 52.0	18 28.9	22 12.3	23 10.2
5 W	14 58 38	13 01 12	20 19 09	26 43 26	17 09.9	5 21.1	17 26.4	17 43.2	15 59.1	16 18.2	20 59.0	18 28.3	22 14.4	23 10.7
6 Th	15 02 35	14 01 23	3♋02 21	9♋16 13	17 03.5	6 31.9	18 39.4	18 27.9	15 50.5	16 10.1	21 06.0	18 27.6	22 16.5	23 11.3
7 F	15 06 31	15 01 36	15 25 28	21 30 35	16 59.7	7 40.6	19 52.4	19 12.7	15 41.7	16 01.9	21 12.9	18 26.9	22 18.6	23 11.8
8 Sa	15 10 28	16 01 52	27 32 09	3♌30 46	16 58.1	8 47.0	21 05.4	19 57.5	15 32.4	15 53.7	21 19.9	18 26.1	22 20.7	23 12.3
9 Su	15 14 24	17 02 09	9♌27 07	15 21 52	16 57.8	9 50.7	22 18.4	20 42.4	15 22.8	15 45.6	21 26.7	18 25.3	22 22.8	23 12.8
10 M	15 18 21	18 02 28	21 15 44	27 09 25	16 57.7	10 51.5	23 31.3	21 27.4	15 12.9	15 37.4	21 33.6	18 24.5	22 24.9	23 13.2
11 Tu	15 22 17	19 02 49	3♍03 37	8♍59 01	16 56.6	11 49.0	24 44.2	22 12.4	15 02.7	15 29.2	21 40.4	18 23.5	22 26.9	23 13.6
12 W	15 26 14	20 03 12	14 56 17	20 56 01	16 53.6	12 42.8	25 57.1	22 57.4	14 52.1	15 21.1	21 47.2	18 22.6	22 29.0	23 14.0
13 Th	15 30 11	21 03 37	26 58 47	3♎05 07	16 47.9	13 32.3	27 10.0	23 42.6	14 41.2	15 13.0	21 53.9	18 21.6	22 31.0	23 14.3
14 F	15 34 07	22 04 04	9♎15 25	15 30 04	16 39.3	14 17.2	28 22.8	24 27.7	14 30.1	15 04.9	22 00.6	18 20.5	22 33.0	23 14.6
15 Sa	15 38 04	23 04 32	21 49 18	28 13 18	16 28.3	14 56.7	29 35.6	25 13.0	14 18.6	14 56.9	22 07.3	18 19.4	22 35.0	23 14.9
16 Su	15 42 00	24 05 02	4♏42 08	11♏15 44	16 15.5	15 30.3	0♑48.4	25 58.3	14 06.9	14 48.9	22 13.9	18 18.2	22 37.0	23 15.2
17 M	15 45 57	25 05 34	17 53 58	24 36 35	16 02.2	15 57.3	2 01.1	26 43.6	13 54.9	14 41.0	22 20.5	18 17.0	22 39.0	23 15.4
18 Tu	15 49 53	26 06 08	1♐23 15	8♐13 33	15 49.6	16 16.9	3 13.8	27 29.0	13 42.7	14 33.1	22 27.0	18 15.7	22 40.9	23 15.6
19 W	15 53 50	27 06 43	15 07 02	22 03 14	15 39.0	16R 28.3	4 26.5	28 14.4	13 30.2	14 25.3	22 33.6	18 14.4	22 42.8	23 15.8
20 Th	15 57 46	28 07 20	29 01 40	6♑01 49	15 31.1	16 30.9	5 39.1	28 59.9	13 17.6	14 17.6	22 40.0	18 13.1	22 44.8	23 15.9
21 F	16 01 43	29 07 57	13♑03 17	20 05 39	15 26.3	16 23.9	6 51.7	29 45.5	13 04.7	14 09.9	22 46.4	18 11.7	22 46.7	23 16.0
22 Sa	16 05 40	0♐08 36	27 08 35	4♒11 48	15D 24.2	16 06.7	8 04.3	0♒31.0	12 51.6	14 02.4	22 52.8	18 10.2	22 48.5	23 16.1
23 Su	16 09 36	1 09 16	11♒15 06	18 18 18	15R 23.8	15 38.9	9 16.8	1 16.7	12 38.3	13 54.9	22 59.1	18 08.7	22 50.4	23 16.2
24 M	16 13 33	2 09 57	25 21 17	2♓23 58	15 24.0	15 00.3	10 29.2	2 02.3	12 24.9	13 47.5	23 05.4	18 07.2	22 52.2	23R 16.2
25 Tu	16 17 29	3 10 39	9♓26 14	16 28 02	15 23.3	14 11.1	11 41.6	2 48.0	12 11.3	13 40.2	23 11.6	18 05.6	22 54.1	23 16.2
26 W	16 21 26	4 11 22	23 29 13	0♈29 41	15 20.7	13 11.9	12 54.0	3 33.7	11 57.7	13 33.1	23 17.7	18 04.0	22 55.9	23 16.1
27 Th	16 25 22	5 12 07	7♈29 14	14 27 39	15 15.5	12 03.9	14 06.3	4 19.5	11 43.9	13 26.0	23 23.8	18 02.3	22 57.6	23 16.1
28 F	16 29 19	6 12 52	21 24 39	28 19 55	15 07.5	10 48.7	15 18.5	5 05.3	11 30.0	13 19.1	23 29.9	18 00.6	22 59.4	23 16.0
29 Sa	16 33 15	7 13 38	5♉13 05	12♉03 47	14 57.2	9 28.6	16 30.7	5 51.1	11 16.0	13 12.2	23 35.9	17 58.9	23 01.1	23 15.9
30 Su	16 37 12	8 14 25	18 51 36	25 36 12	14 45.6	8 06.1	17 42.8	6 36.9	11 01.9	13 05.5	23 41.8	17 57.1	23 02.8	23 15.7

December 1952 — LONGITUDE

Day	Sid.Time	☉	0 hr ☽	Noon ☽	True ☊	☿	♀	♂	⚳	♃	♄	♅	♆	♇
1 M	16 41 09	9♐15 14	2♊17 12	8♊54 17	14♒33.8	6♐44.0	18♑54.9	7♒22.8	10♊47.9	12♉59.0	23♎47.7	17♋55.2	23♎04.5	23♌15.5
2 Tu	16 45 05	10 16 03	15 27 15	21 55 53	14R 23.1	5R 25.0	20 06.9	8 08.7	10R 33.7	12R 52.5	23 53.5	17R 53.4	23 06.2	23R 15.3
3 W	16 49 02	11 16 54	28 20 07	4♋39 57	14 14.4	4 11.7	21 18.9	8 54.7	10 19.6	12 46.3	23 59.3	17 51.5	23 07.9	23 15.1
4 Th	16 52 58	12 17 46	10♋55 29	17 06 52	14 08.2	3 06.3	22 30.7	9 40.6	10 05.5	12 40.1	24 05.0	17 49.5	23 09.5	23 14.8
5 F	16 56 55	13 18 40	23 14 24	29 18 24	14 04.6	2 10.5	23 42.6	10 26.6	9 51.4	12 34.1	24 10.6	17 47.6	23 11.1	23 14.5
6 Sa	17 00 51	14 19 34	5♌19 18	11♌17 35	14D 03.4	1 25.4	24 54.3	11 12.6	9 37.3	12 28.3	24 16.2	17 45.6	23 12.6	23 14.2
7 Su	17 04 48	15 20 30	17 13 48	23 08 31	14 03.7	0 51.5	26 06.0	11 58.6	9 23.3	12 22.6	24 21.7	17 43.5	23 14.2	23 13.8
8 M	17 08 45	16 21 27	29 02 22	4♍56 01	14 04.6	0 29.1	27 17.6	12 44.7	9 09.4	12 17.1	24 27.2	17 41.4	23 15.7	23 13.4
9 Tu	17 12 41	17 22 25	10♍50 08	16 45 24	14R 05.2	0D 17.8	28 29.2	13 30.8	8 55.5	12 11.7	24 32.6	17 39.3	23 17.2	23 13.0
10 W	17 16 38	18 23 24	22 42 30	28 42 08	14 04.5	0 17.1	29 40.6	14 16.9	8 41.7	12 06.5	24 37.9	17 37.2	23 18.7	23 12.6
11 Th	17 20 34	19 24 24	4♎44 56	10♎51 31	14 01.9	0 26.4	0♒52.0	15 03.0	8 28.1	12 01.5	24 43.1	17 35.0	23 20.1	23 12.1
12 F	17 24 31	20 25 25	17 02 27	23 18 16	13 57.1	0 44.8	2 03.3	15 49.1	8 14.6	11 56.6	24 48.3	17 32.8	23 21.5	23 11.6
13 Sa	17 28 27	21 26 28	29 39 22	6♏06 05	13 50.1	1 11.6	3 14.6	16 35.3	8 01.2	11 51.9	24 53.4	17 30.5	23 22.9	23 11.1
14 Su	17 32 24	22 27 31	12♏38 39	19 17 09	13 41.7	1 45.8	4 25.7	17 21.4	7 48.1	11 47.4	24 58.5	17 28.3	23 24.3	23 10.6
15 M	17 36 20	23 28 35	26 01 34	2♐51 42	13 32.6	2 26.7	5 36.8	18 07.6	7 35.1	11 43.1	25 03.4	17 26.0	23 25.6	23 10.0
16 Tu	17 40 17	24 29 41	9♐47 16	16 47 49	13 23.9	3 13.5	6 47.8	18 53.8	7 22.3	11 39.0	25 08.3	17 23.7	23 26.9	23 09.4
17 W	17 44 14	25 30 47	23 52 47	1♑01 29	13 16.6	4 05.5	7 58.7	19 40.1	7 09.7	11 35.1	25 13.1	17 21.3	23 28.2	23 08.7
18 Th	17 48 10	26 31 53	8♑13 13	15 27 12	13 11.4	5 02.1	9 09.5	20 26.3	6 57.4	11 31.3	25 17.9	17 19.0	23 29.5	23 08.1
19 F	17 52 07	27 33 00	22 42 39	29 58 47	13D 08.5	6 02.8	10 20.2	21 12.6	6 45.3	11 27.8	25 22.5	17 16.6	23 30.7	23 07.4
20 Sa	17 56 03	28 34 07	7♒14 53	14♒30 18	13 07.7	7 07.0	11 30.8	21 58.8	6 33.5	11 24.4	25 27.1	17 14.2	23 31.9	23 06.7
21 Su	18 00 00	29 35 15	21 44 27	28 56 51	13 08.5	8 14.4	12 41.3	22 45.1	6 21.9	11 21.3	25 31.6	17 11.8	23 33.1	23 06.0
22 M	18 03 56	0♑36 22	6♓07 08	13♓14 58	13 09.9	9 24.4	13 51.6	23 31.3	6 10.7	11 18.3	25 36.0	17 09.3	23 34.2	23 05.2
23 Tu	18 07 53	1 37 30	20 20 08	27 22 30	13R 10.8	10 36.9	15 01.9	24 17.6	5 59.7	11 15.6	25 40.4	17 06.8	23 35.3	23 04.4
24 W	18 11 49	2 38 38	4♈21 56	11♈18 24	13 10.5	11 51.5	16 12.0	25 03.9	5 49.0	11 13.0	25 44.6	17 04.4	23 36.4	23 03.6
25 Th	18 15 46	3 39 45	18 11 51	25 02 16	13 08.5	13 07.9	17 22.0	25 50.2	5 38.7	11 10.7	25 48.8	17 01.9	23 37.4	23 02.8
26 F	18 19 43	4 40 53	1♉49 39	8♉33 58	13 04.6	14 26.0	18 31.9	26 36.4	5 28.7	11 08.6	25 52.9	16 59.3	23 38.4	23 01.9
27 Sa	18 23 39	5 42 01	15 15 13	21 53 22	12 59.2	15 45.5	19 41.6	27 22.7	5 19.0	11 06.6	25 56.9	16 56.8	23 39.4	23 01.0
28 Su	18 27 36	6 43 09	28 28 22	5♊00 11	12 52.9	17 06.3	20 51.2	28 09.0	5 09.7	11 04.9	26 00.8	16 54.3	23 40.3	23 00.1
29 M	18 31 32	7 44 17	11♊28 47	17 54 08	12 46.4	18 28.3	22 00.7	28 55.3	5 00.7	11 03.4	26 04.6	16 51.7	23 41.2	22 59.2
30 Tu	18 35 29	8 45 25	24 16 12	0♋35 00	12 40.5	19 51.3	23 10.0	29 41.5	4 52.1	11 02.1	26 08.3	16 49.2	23 42.1	22 58.3
31 W	18 39 25	9 46 34	6♋50 32	13 02 54	12 35.8	21 15.3	24 19.1	0♓27.8	4 43.9	11 01.0	26 12.0	16 46.6	23 43.0	22 57.3

Astro Data

	Dy Hr Mn
☽0S	12 16:19
☿R	20 6:43
♄☌♆	21 13:17
♇R	24 17:04
☽0N	25 22:56
♄✶♇	26 5:53
♆✶♇	7 7:24
☽0S	9 23:47
☿D	10 1:27
☽0N	23 3:31

Planet Ingress

	Dy Hr Mn
☿ ♐	1 5:34
♀ ♑	15 20:03
♂ ♒	21 19:40
☉ ♐	22 8:36
♀ ♒	10 18:30
☉ ♑	21 21:43
♂ ♓	30 21:35

Last Aspect / ☽ Ingress

Last Aspect Dy Hr Mn		☽ Ingress Dy Hr Mn
31 19:20	♇ △	♉ 1 6:58
2 22:55	♇ □	♊ 3 11:02
5 5:20	♇ ✶	♋ 5 18:12
7 13:36	♆ □	♌ 8 4:56
10 3:59	♇ ☌	♍ 10 17:47
12 23:05	♀ □	♎ 13 5:57
15 14:49	♀ ✶	♏ 15 15:18
17 15:59	♂ ✶	♐ 17 21:33
19 14:05	♇ △	♑ 20 1:40
22 4:34	☉ ✶	♒ 22 4:52
23 20:27	♇ ☍	♓ 24 7:55
25 14:46	♅ △	♈ 26 11:09
28 3:33	♄ ☍	♉ 28 14:54
30 7:49	♇ □	♊ 30 19:53

Last Aspect / ☽ Ingress

Last Aspect Dy Hr Mn		☽ Ingress Dy Hr Mn
2 15:41	♄ △	♋ 3 3:09
5 1:46	♄ □	♌ 5 13:23
7 14:30	♄ ✶	♍ 8 1:57
10 14:09	♀ △	♎ 10 14:35
12 14:52	♄ ☌	♏ 13 0:39
14 18:56	♇ □	♐ 15 7:00
17 2:12	♄ ✶	♑ 17 10:17
19 4:22	♄ □	♒ 19 12:02
21 13:09	☉ ✶	♓ 21 13:45
22 18:35	♅ ☍	♈ 23 16:30
25 13:29	♂ ✶	♉ 25 20:46
27 22:37	♂ □	♊ 28 2:48
30 10:11	♂ △	♋ 30 10:53

☽ Phases & Eclipses

Dy Hr Mn		
1 23:10	○	9♉29
9 15:43	☾	17♌11
17 12:56	●	25♏08
24 11:34	☽	2♓09
1 12:41	○	9♊17
9 13:22	☾	17♍26
17 2:02	●	25♐05
23 19:52	☽	1♈58
31 5:06	○	9♋29

Astro Data

1 November 1952
Julian Day # 19298
SVP 5♓54'56"
GC 26♐10.8 ⚴ 21♓16.2R
Eris 7♈23.3R ⚵ 13♒08.0
⚷ 8♑22.1 ⚶ 18♏13.2
☽ Mean ☊ 17♒16.9

1 December 1952
Julian Day # 19328
SVP 5♓54'51"
GC 26♐10.9 ⚴ 20♓38.3
Eris 7♈10.8R ⚵ 21♒55.3
⚷ 10♑42.6 ⚶ 4♐25.4
☽ Mean ☊ 15♒41.6

LONGITUDE — January 1953

Day	Sid.Time	☉	0 hr ☽	Noon ☽	True ☊	☿	♀	♂	⚳	♃	♄	♅	♆	♇
1 Th	18 43 22	10♑47 42	19♋12 10	25♋18 28	12♒32.7	22♐40.1	25♒28.1	1♓14.0	4♊36.0	11♉00.1	26♎15.6	16♋44.0	23♎43.8	22♌56.3
2 F	18 47 19	11 48 50	1♌22 02	7♌23 03	12D 31.2	24 05.7	26 36.9	2 00.3	4R 28.6	10R 59.4	26 19.0	16R 41.4	23 44.6	22R 55.3
3 Sa	18 51 15	12 49 59	13 21 51	19 18 45	12 31.3	25 32.0	27 45.6	2 46.5	4 21.5	10 58.9	26 22.4	16 38.8	23 45.3	22 54.2
4 Su	18 55 12	13 51 07	25 14 08	1♍08 25	12 32.5	26 59.0	28 54.0	3 32.8	4 14.7	10D 58.6	26 25.7	16 36.3	23 46.0	22 53.2
5 M	18 59 08	14 52 16	7♍02 06	12 55 42	12 34.4	28 26.6	0♓02.4	4 19.0	4 08.4	10 58.6	26 28.9	16 33.7	23 46.7	22 52.1
6 Tu	19 03 05	15 53 25	18 49 44	24 44 48	12 36.2	29 54.8	1 10.5	5 05.2	4 02.5	10 58.7	26 32.0	16 31.0	23 47.4	22 51.0
7 W	19 07 01	16 54 34	0♎41 30	6♎40 27	12R 37.6	1♑23.6	2 18.4	5 51.4	3 57.0	10 59.1	26 35.0	16 28.4	23 48.0	22 49.9
8 Th	19 10 58	17 55 43	12 42 17	18 47 36	12 38.0	2 52.9	3 26.2	6 37.6	3 51.9	10 59.6	26 37.9	16 25.8	23 48.6	22 48.8
9 F	19 14 54	18 56 52	24 57 02	1♏11 10	12 37.4	4 22.8	4 33.7	7 23.8	3 47.2	11 00.4	26 40.7	16 23.2	23 49.1	22 47.6
10 Sa	19 18 51	19 58 01	7♏30 32	13 55 37	12 35.7	5 53.1	5 41.1	8 10.0	3 42.9	11 01.3	26 43.4	16 20.6	23 49.6	22 46.4
11 Su	19 22 48	20 59 10	20 26 50	27 04 28	12 33.1	7 24.0	6 48.2	8 56.2	3 39.1	11 02.5	26 46.0	16 18.0	23 50.1	22 45.3
12 M	19 26 44	22 00 19	3♐48 44	10♐39 42	12 30.1	8 55.4	7 55.2	9 42.3	3 35.6	11 03.9	26 48.5	16 15.5	23 50.6	22 44.1
13 Tu	19 30 41	23 01 28	17 37 15	24 41 10	12 27.1	10 27.2	9 01.9	10 28.5	3 32.6	11 05.5	26 50.9	16 12.9	23 51.0	22 42.8
14 W	19 34 37	24 02 37	1♑51 02	9♑06 16	12 24.6	11 59.6	10 08.4	11 14.6	3 30.0	11 07.3	26 53.3	16 10.3	23 51.4	22 41.6
15 Th	19 38 34	25 03 45	16 26 08	23 49 49	12 22.9	13 32.4	11 14.6	12 00.7	3 27.8	11 09.3	26 55.5	16 07.7	23 51.7	22 40.3
16 F	19 42 30	26 04 53	1♒16 21	8♒44 41	12D 22.3	15 05.8	12 20.6	12 46.8	3 26.1	11 11.5	26 57.6	16 05.2	23 52.0	22 39.1
17 Sa	19 46 27	27 06 00	16 13 48	23 42 38	12 22.5	16 39.7	13 26.4	13 32.9	3 24.7	11 13.9	26 59.6	16 02.6	23 52.3	22 37.8
18 Su	19 50 23	28 07 06	1♓10 12	8♓35 34	12 23.3	18 14.1	14 31.9	14 19.0	3 23.8	11 16.5	27 01.5	16 00.1	23 52.5	22 36.5
19 M	19 54 20	29 08 12	15 57 57	23 16 38	12 24.4	19 49.0	15 37.1	15 05.1	3D 23.3	11 19.3	27 03.3	15 57.6	23 52.7	22 35.2
20 Tu	19 58 17	0♒09 16	0♈31 04	7♈40 50	12 25.4	21 24.5	16 42.0	15 51.1	3 23.2	11 22.3	27 05.0	15 55.1	23 52.9	22 33.9
21 W	20 02 13	1 10 20	14 45 40	21 45 25	12R 26.0	23 00.5	17 46.6	16 37.1	3 23.5	11 25.5	27 06.6	15 52.6	23 53.0	22 32.5
22 Th	20 06 10	2 11 23	28 39 53	5♉29 16	12 26.2	24 37.1	18 51.0	17 23.1	3 24.3	11 28.9	27 08.1	15 50.1	23 53.1	22 31.2
23 F	20 10 06	3 12 24	12♉13 37	18 53 06	12 25.8	26 14.3	19 55.0	18 09.0	3 25.4	11 32.5	27 09.5	15 47.6	23 53.2	22 29.8
24 Sa	20 14 03	4 13 25	25 27 55	1♊58 19	12 25.0	27 52.1	20 58.7	18 55.0	3 27.0	11 36.3	27 10.8	15 45.2	23R 53.3	22 28.4
25 Su	20 17 59	5 14 25	8♊24 35	14 46 57	12 24.1	29 30.5	22 02.0	19 40.9	3 29.0	11 40.2	27 11.9	15 42.8	23 53.3	22 27.1
26 M	20 21 56	6 15 23	21 05 42	27 21 07	12 23.2	1♒09.5	23 05.0	20 26.8	3 31.3	11 44.4	27 13.0	15 40.4	23 53.2	22 25.7
27 Tu	20 25 52	7 16 21	3♋33 26	9♋42 54	12 22.4	2 49.2	24 07.7	21 12.6	3 34.1	11 48.7	27 14.0	15 38.0	23 53.2	22 24.3
28 W	20 29 49	8 17 17	15 49 47	21 54 17	12 21.9	4 29.5	25 10.0	21 58.5	3 37.3	11 53.3	27 14.8	15 35.7	23 53.1	22 22.9
29 Th	20 33 46	9 18 13	27 56 39	3♌57 06	12D 21.7	6 10.5	26 11.8	22 44.3	3 40.8	11 58.0	27 15.6	15 33.4	23 52.9	22 21.5
30 F	20 37 42	10 19 07	9♌55 52	15 53 11	12 21.7	7 52.2	27 13.3	23 30.0	3 44.7	12 02.9	27 16.2	15 31.1	23 52.7	22 20.0
31 Sa	20 41 39	11 20 00	21 49 17	27 44 25	12 21.7	9 34.6	28 14.4	24 15.8	3 49.0	12 08.0	27 16.8	15 28.8	23 52.5	22 18.6

LONGITUDE — February 1953

Day	Sid.Time	☉	0 hr ☽	Noon ☽	True ☊	☿	♀	♂	⚳	♃	♄	♅	♆	♇
1 Su	20 45 35	12♒20 53	3♍38 53	9♍32 58	12♒21.8	11♒17.7	29♓15.0	25♓01.5	3♊53.7	12♉13.2	27♎17.2	15♋26.5	23♎52.3	22♌17.2
2 M	20 49 32	13 21 44	15 27 00	21 21 19	12R 21.7	13 01.5	0♈15.3	25 47.2	3 58.8	12 18.6	27 17.5	15R 24.3	23R 52.0	22R 15.7
3 Tu	20 53 28	14 22 35	27 16 18	3♎12 21	12 21.5	14 46.0	1 15.0	26 32.8	4 04.2	12 24.2	27 17.8	15 22.1	23 51.7	22 14.3
4 W	20 57 25	15 23 24	9♎09 54	15 09 26	12 21.2	16 31.2	2 14.3	27 18.4	4 10.0	12 30.0	27R 17.9	15 20.0	23 51.4	22 12.8
5 Th	21 01 21	16 24 13	21 11 26	27 16 23	12 20.8	18 17.1	3 13.1	28 04.0	4 16.2	12 35.9	27 17.9	15 17.8	23 51.0	22 11.4
6 F	21 05 18	17 25 00	3♏24 50	9♏37 18	12D 20.6	20 03.7	4 11.4	28 49.6	4 22.7	12 42.0	27 17.8	15 15.7	23 50.6	22 09.9
7 Sa	21 09 15	18 25 47	15 54 18	22 16 20	12 20.5	21 50.9	5 09.3	29 35.1	4 29.6	12 48.3	27 17.6	15 13.7	23 50.2	22 08.5
8 Su	21 13 11	19 26 33	28 43 55	5♐17 28	12 20.8	23 38.8	6 06.5	0♈20.6	4 36.8	12 54.8	27 17.3	15 11.6	23 49.7	22 07.0
9 M	21 17 08	20 27 18	11♐57 20	18 43 49	12 21.4	25 27.2	7 03.3	1 06.1	4 44.4	13 01.4	27 16.9	15 09.6	23 49.2	22 05.5
10 Tu	21 21 04	21 28 02	25 37 05	2♑37 12	12 22.2	27 16.1	7 59.4	1 51.5	4 52.3	13 08.2	27 16.4	15 07.7	23 48.7	22 04.1
11 W	21 25 01	22 28 44	9♑44 02	16 57 21	12 23.0	29 05.4	8 55.0	2 37.0	5 00.6	13 15.1	27 15.8	15 05.8	23 48.1	22 02.6
12 Th	21 28 57	23 29 26	24 16 39	1♒41 21	12R 23.6	0♓55.1	9 50.0	3 22.3	5 09.2	13 22.2	27 15.0	15 03.9	23 47.5	22 01.1
13 F	21 32 54	24 30 06	9♒10 37	16 43 30	12 23.7	2 45.0	10 44.3	4 07.7	5 18.1	13 29.4	27 14.2	15 02.0	23 46.9	21 59.7
14 Sa	21 36 50	25 30 45	24 18 52	1♓55 32	12 23.2	4 35.0	11 38.0	4 53.0	5 27.4	13 36.8	27 13.3	15 00.2	23 46.2	21 58.2
15 Su	21 40 47	26 31 22	9♓32 15	17 07 46	12 22.0	6 24.8	12 31.0	5 38.3	5 36.9	13 44.4	27 12.2	14 58.4	23 45.6	21 56.7
16 M	21 44 44	27 31 58	24 40 52	2♈10 26	12 20.1	8 14.3	13 23.3	6 23.5	5 46.8	13 52.1	27 11.1	14 56.7	23 44.8	21 55.3
17 Tu	21 48 40	28 32 31	9♈35 30	16 55 14	12 18.1	10 03.3	14 14.8	7 08.7	5 57.0	13 59.9	27 09.8	14 55.0	23 44.1	21 53.8
18 W	21 52 37	29 33 03	24 09 01	1♉16 24	12 16.1	11 51.5	15 05.6	7 53.9	6 07.5	14 07.9	27 08.5	14 53.4	23 43.3	21 52.3
19 Th	21 56 33	0♓33 34	8♉17 07	15 11 03	12 14.6	13 38.4	15 55.6	8 39.0	6 18.3	14 16.1	27 07.0	14 51.8	23 42.5	21 50.9
20 F	22 00 30	1 34 02	21 58 18	28 39 01	12D 14.0	15 23.8	16 44.8	9 24.1	6 29.5	14 24.4	27 05.5	14 50.2	23 41.7	21 49.5
21 Sa	22 04 26	2 34 29	5♊13 31	11♊42 09	12 14.2	17 07.3	17 33.1	10 09.1	6 40.9	14 32.8	27 03.8	14 48.7	23 40.8	21 48.0
22 Su	22 08 23	3 34 54	18 05 22	24 23 38	12 15.3	18 48.3	18 20.4	10 54.1	6 52.6	14 41.4	27 02.1	14 47.2	23 39.9	21 46.6
23 M	22 12 19	4 35 17	0♋37 27	6♋47 19	12 16.9	20 26.5	19 06.9	11 39.1	7 04.5	14 50.1	27 00.2	14 45.8	23 39.0	21 45.2
24 Tu	22 16 16	5 35 37	12 53 44	18 57 11	12 18.6	22 01.1	19 52.4	12 24.0	7 16.8	14 58.9	26 58.3	14 44.4	23 38.0	21 43.7
25 W	22 20 13	6 35 56	24 58 09	0♌57 03	12R 19.9	23 31.7	20 36.9	13 08.9	7 29.3	15 07.8	26 56.3	14 43.1	23 37.1	21 42.3
26 Th	22 24 09	7 36 13	6♌54 18	12 50 17	12 20.4	24 57.7	21 20.3	13 53.7	7 42.1	15 16.9	26 54.1	14 41.8	23 36.1	21 40.9
27 F	22 28 06	8 36 29	18 45 21	24 39 49	12 19.7	26 18.3	22 02.6	14 38.5	7 55.2	15 26.2	26 51.9	14 40.6	23 35.0	21 39.5
28 Sa	22 32 02	9 36 42	0♍34 00	6♍28 10	12 17.6	27 33.1	22 43.8	15 23.3	8 08.5	15 35.5	26 49.6	14 39.4	23 34.0	21 38.1

Astro Data

	Dy Hr Mn
♃ D	5 7:52
☽ 0S	6 6:54
☽ 0N	19 10:10
⚳ D	20 4:56
♆ R	25 0:57
♀ 0N	31 17:35
☽ 0S	2 13:36
♄ R	5 2:31
♂ 0N	9 11:53
☽ 0N	15 20:00
♃ ⚹ ♅	23 1:57
☿ 0N	28 6:51

Planet Ingress

	Dy Hr Mn
♀ ♓	5 11:10
☿ ♑	6 13:24
☉ ♒	20 8:21
☿ ♒	25 19:10
♀ ♈	2 5:54
♂ ♈	8 1:07
☿ ♓	11 23:57
☉ ♓	18 22:41

Last Aspect / ☽ Ingress

Last Aspect Dy Hr Mn		☽ Ingress	Dy Hr Mn
1 13:53	♄ □	♌	1 21:17
4 6:58	♀ ☍	♍	4 9:41
5 19:22	♅ ⚹	♎	6 22:36
9 3:18	♄ ☌	♏	9 9:44
11 4:13	♇ □	♐	11 17:14
13 15:39	♄ ⚹	♑	13 20:55
15 17:01	♄ □	♒	15 21:57
17 17:17	♄ △	♓	17 22:07
19 22:26	☉ ⚹	♈	19 23:08
21 21:18	♄ ☍	♉	22 2:20
24 3:20	☿ △	♊	24 8:21
26 11:44	♄ △	♋	26 17:07
28 22:37	♄ □	♌	29 4:06
31 11:04	♄ ⚹	♍	31 16:35

Last Aspect / ☽ Ingress

Last Aspect Dy Hr Mn		☽ Ingress	Dy Hr Mn
2 21:36	♂ ☍	♎	3 5:31
5 12:03	♄ ☌	♏	5 17:21
7 11:45	♇ □	♐	8 2:20
10 2:52	♄ ⚹	♑	10 7:32
12 4:50	♄ □	♒	12 9:17
14 4:36	♄ △	♓	14 8:58
15 8:36	♅ △	♈	16 8:30
18 8:52	☉ ⚹	♉	18 9:50
19 23:46	♇ □	♊	20 14:27
22 17:03	♄ △	♋	22 22:48
25 3:58	♄ □	♌	25 10:05
27 16:28	♄ ⚹	♍	27 22:51

☽ Phases & Eclipses

Dy Hr Mn	
8 10:09	☾ 17♎51
15 14:08	● 25♑09
22 5:43	☽ 1♉55
29 23:44	○ 9♌48
29 23:47	• T 1.331
7 4:09	☾ 18♏06
14 1:10	● 25♒03
14 0:59:00	• P 0.760
20 17:44	☽ 1♊49
28 18:59	○ 9♍54

Astro Data

1 January 1953
Julian Day # 19359
SVP 5♓54'45"
GC 26♐11.0 ⚴ 25♓41.0
Eris 7♈07.7 ⚵ 4♓26.9
⚷ 13♑39.1 ⚶ 21♐10.0
☽ Mean ☊ 14♒03.1

1 February 1953
Julian Day # 19390
SVP 5♓54'39"
GC 26♐11.0 ⚴ 4♈45.5
Eris 7♈15.6 ⚵ 19♓16.7
⚷ 16♑37.2 ⚶ 7♑33.2
☽ Mean ☊ 12♒24.7

March 1953

LONGITUDE

Day	Sid.Time	☉	0 hr ☽	Noon☽	True☊	☿	♀	♂	⚳	♃	♄	♅	♆	♇
1 Su	22 35 59	10♓36 54	12♍22 33	18♍17 25	12♒14.0	28♓41.5	23♈23.8	16♈08.0	8♊22.0	15♉45.0	26♎47.2	14♋38.2	23♎32.9	21♌36.7
2 M	22 39 55	11 37 03	24 13 00	0♎09 31	12R 09.3	29 42.7	24 02.6	16 52.6	8 35.9	15 54.5	26R 44.7	14R 37.1	23R 31.8	21R 35.4
3 Tu	22 43 52	12 37 11	6♎07 13	12 06 19	12 03.8	0♈36.4	24 40.1	17 37.3	8 49.9	16 04.3	26 42.1	14 36.1	23 30.7	21 34.0
4 W	22 47 48	13 37 18	18 07 07	24 09 50	11 58.1	1 22.1	25 16.3	18 21.8	9 04.2	16 14.1	26 39.5	14 35.1	23 29.5	21 32.7
5 Th	22 51 45	14 37 22	0♏14 49	6♏22 21	11 52.8	1 59.3	25 51.2	19 06.4	9 18.8	16 24.0	26 36.7	14 34.1	23 28.3	21 31.3
6 F	22 55 42	15 37 26	12 32 47	18 46 28	11 48.6	2 27.8	26 24.6	19 50.9	9 33.6	16 34.1	26 33.9	14 33.3	23 27.1	21 30.0
7 Sa	22 59 38	16 37 27	25 03 49	1♐25 12	11 45.8	2 47.3	26 56.6	20 35.3	9 48.6	16 44.2	26 30.9	14 32.4	23 25.9	21 28.7
8 Su	23 03 35	17 37 27	7♐51 03	14 21 45	11D 44.6	2R 57.7	27 27.0	21 19.7	10 03.8	16 54.5	26 27.9	14 31.6	23 24.7	21 27.4
9 M	23 07 31	18 37 26	20 57 41	27 39 13	11 44.9	2 59.1	27 55.9	22 04.1	10 19.3	17 04.9	26 24.9	14 30.9	23 23.4	21 26.1
10 Tu	23 11 28	19 37 22	4♑26 40	11♑20 14	11 46.1	2 51.7	28 23.1	22 48.4	10 35.0	17 15.4	26 21.7	14 30.2	23 22.1	21 24.8
11 W	23 15 24	20 37 18	18 20 05	25 26 14	11 47.6	2 35.7	28 48.7	23 32.7	10 50.9	17 26.0	26 18.5	14 29.6	23 20.8	21 23.6
12 Th	23 19 21	21 37 11	2♒38 31	9♒56 41	11R 48.4	2 11.6	29 12.5	24 17.0	11 07.1	17 36.7	26 15.1	14 29.0	23 19.5	21 22.4
13 F	23 23 17	22 37 03	17 20 14	24 48 30	11 47.7	1 40.1	29 34.4	25 01.2	11 23.4	17 47.5	26 11.8	14 28.4	23 18.2	21 21.1
14 Sa	23 27 14	23 36 52	2♓20 38	9♓55 37	11 45.2	1 02.0	29 54.5	25 45.3	11 40.0	17 58.4	26 08.3	14 28.0	23 16.8	21 19.9
15 Su	23 31 11	24 36 40	17 32 15	25 09 18	11 40.6	0 18.2	0♉12.7	26 29.4	11 56.7	18 09.4	26 04.8	14 27.5	23 15.4	21 18.7
16 M	23 35 07	25 36 26	2♈45 26	10♈19 19	11 34.4	29♓29.8	0 28.8	27 13.5	12 13.7	18 20.5	26 01.2	14 27.1	23 14.0	21 17.5
17 Tu	23 39 04	26 36 10	17 49 43	25 15 29	11 27.3	28 37.8	0 42.9	27 57.5	12 30.8	18 31.7	25 57.5	14 26.8	23 12.6	21 16.4
18 W	23 43 00	27 35 52	2♉35 41	9♉49 31	11 20.3	27 43.5	0 54.9	28 41.5	12 48.2	18 43.0	25 53.8	14 26.6	23 11.2	21 15.2
19 Th	23 46 57	28 35 31	16 56 26	23 56 05	11 14.3	26 48.1	1 04.6	29 25.4	13 05.7	18 54.4	25 50.0	14 26.3	23 09.7	21 14.1
20 F	23 50 53	29 35 09	0♊48 19	7♊33 10	11 10.0	25 52.9	1 12.1	0♉09.3	13 23.4	19 05.9	25 46.1	14 26.2	23 08.3	21 13.0
21 Sa	23 54 50	0♈34 44	14 10 52	20 41 44	11D 07.7	24 58.8	1 17.3	0 53.2	13 41.4	19 17.4	25 42.2	14 26.1	23 06.8	21 11.9
22 Su	23 58 46	1 34 17	27 06 13	3♋24 52	11 07.2	24 07.0	1R 20.1	1 37.0	13 59.4	19 29.1	25 38.3	14D 26.0	23 05.3	21 10.9
23 M	0 02 43	2 33 47	9♋38 15	15 47 00	11 07.9	23 18.4	1 20.5	2 20.7	14 17.7	19 40.8	25 34.2	14 26.0	23 03.8	21 09.8
24 Tu	0 06 40	3 33 15	21 51 45	27 53 08	11 09.1	22 33.7	1 18.4	3 04.4	14 36.2	19 52.6	25 30.2	14 26.1	23 02.3	21 08.8
25 W	0 10 36	4 32 41	3♌51 48	9♌48 21	11R 09.8	21 53.6	1 13.9	3 48.1	14 54.8	20 04.5	25 26.1	14 26.2	23 00.7	21 07.8
26 Th	0 14 33	5 32 05	15 43 22	21 37 22	11 09.1	21 18.5	1 06.8	4 31.7	15 13.5	20 16.5	25 21.9	14 26.4	22 59.2	21 06.8
27 F	0 18 29	6 31 26	27 30 53	3♍24 21	11 06.4	20 48.9	0 57.3	5 15.2	15 32.5	20 28.5	25 17.7	14 26.6	22 57.6	21 05.9
28 Sa	0 22 26	7 30 45	9♍18 11	15 12 44	11 01.3	20 25.0	0 45.2	5 58.7	15 51.6	20 40.6	25 13.4	14 26.9	22 56.1	21 04.9
29 Su	0 26 22	8 30 02	21 08 21	27 05 17	10 53.7	20 06.9	0 30.7	6 42.2	16 10.8	20 52.8	25 09.1	14 27.2	22 54.5	21 04.0
30 M	0 30 19	9 29 17	3♎03 46	9♎04 01	10 44.0	19 54.6	0 13.7	7 25.6	16 30.2	21 05.1	25 04.8	14 27.6	22 52.9	21 03.1
31 Tu	0 34 15	10 28 29	15 06 10	21 10 23	10 32.9	19D 48.1	29♈54.3	8 08.9	16 49.8	21 17.4	25 00.4	14 28.0	22 51.3	21 02.2

April 1953

LONGITUDE

Day	Sid.Time	☉	0 hr ☽	Noon☽	True☊	☿	♀	♂	⚳	♃	♄	♅	♆	♇
1 W	0 38 12	11♈27 40	27♎16 47	3♏25 29	10♒21.3	19♓47.2	29♈32.6	8♉52.2	17♊09.5	21♉29.8	24♎56.0	14♋28.5	22♎49.7	21♌01.4
2 Th	0 42 08	12 26 49	9♏36 35	15 50 13	10R 10.4	19 51.9	29R 08.7	9 35.5	17 29.3	21 42.3	24R 51.6	14 29.0	22R 48.1	21R 00.6
3 F	0 46 05	13 25 56	22 06 31	28 25 38	10 01.1	20 01.9	28 42.6	10 18.7	17 49.3	21 54.8	24 47.2	14 29.6	22 46.5	20 59.8
4 Sa	0 50 02	14 25 02	4♐47 44	11♐13 01	9 54.1	20 17.1	28 14.5	11 01.9	18 09.5	22 07.4	24 42.7	14 30.3	22 44.9	20 59.0
5 Su	0 53 58	15 24 05	17 41 42	24 14 04	9 49.7	20 37.2	27 44.5	11 45.0	18 29.7	22 20.1	24 38.2	14 31.0	22 43.3	20 58.2
6 M	0 57 55	16 23 07	0♑50 20	7♑30 47	9D 47.7	21 02.1	27 12.8	12 28.1	18 50.2	22 32.8	24 33.6	14 31.7	22 41.6	20 57.5
7 Tu	1 01 51	17 22 07	14 15 41	21 05 17	9 47.4	21 31.4	26 39.6	13 11.2	19 10.7	22 45.6	24 29.1	14 32.6	22 40.0	20 56.8
8 W	1 05 48	18 21 05	27 59 46	4♒59 16	9R 47.8	22 05.0	26 05.1	13 54.2	19 31.4	22 58.4	24 24.5	14 33.4	22 38.4	20 56.1
9 Th	1 09 44	19 20 02	12♒03 50	19 13 23	9 47.6	22 42.6	25 29.5	14 37.1	19 52.2	23 11.3	24 19.9	14 34.3	22 36.7	20 55.5
10 F	1 13 41	20 18 56	26 27 46	3♓46 34	9 45.6	23 24.1	24 52.9	15 20.0	20 13.2	23 24.3	24 15.3	14 35.3	22 35.1	20 54.9
11 Sa	1 17 37	21 17 49	11♓09 16	18 35 11	9 41.1	24 09.2	24 15.8	16 02.9	20 34.3	23 37.3	24 10.7	14 36.3	22 33.4	20 54.2
12 Su	1 21 34	22 16 40	26 03 27	3♈33 04	9 33.9	24 57.8	23 38.2	16 45.7	20 55.5	23 50.4	24 06.1	14 37.4	22 31.8	20 53.7
13 M	1 25 31	23 15 30	11♈02 55	18 31 49	9 24.4	25 49.6	23 00.4	17 28.4	21 16.8	24 03.5	24 01.5	14 38.5	22 30.1	20 53.1
14 Tu	1 29 27	24 14 17	25 58 35	3♉22 04	9 13.4	26 44.6	22 22.7	18 11.2	21 38.2	24 16.6	23 56.9	14 39.7	22 28.5	20 52.6
15 W	1 33 24	25 13 02	10♉41 12	17 55 04	9 02.4	27 42.6	21 45.3	18 53.8	21 59.8	24 29.9	23 52.3	14 40.9	22 26.8	20 52.1
16 Th	1 37 20	26 11 46	25 02 54	2♊04 09	8 52.4	28 43.4	21 08.5	19 36.5	22 21.5	24 43.1	23 47.6	14 42.1	22 25.2	20 51.6
17 F	1 41 17	27 10 27	8♊58 28	15 45 41	8 44.5	29 47.0	20 32.5	20 19.1	22 43.3	24 56.4	23 43.0	14 43.5	22 23.6	20 51.2
18 Sa	1 45 13	28 09 06	22 25 48	28 59 02	8 39.2	0♈53.1	19 57.5	21 01.6	23 05.2	25 09.8	23 38.4	14 44.8	22 21.9	20 50.8
19 Su	1 49 10	29 07 43	5♋25 42	11♋46 14	8 36.3	2 01.8	19 23.7	21 44.1	23 27.2	25 23.2	23 33.8	14 46.3	22 20.3	20 50.4
20 M	1 53 06	0♉06 17	18 01 11	24 11 08	8D 35.3	3 12.8	18 51.3	22 26.5	23 49.3	25 36.6	23 29.3	14 47.7	22 18.7	20 50.0
21 Tu	1 57 03	1 04 50	0♌16 45	6♌18 43	8R 35.2	4 26.2	18 20.6	23 08.9	24 11.6	25 50.1	23 24.7	14 49.3	22 17.0	20 49.7
22 W	2 01 00	2 03 20	12 17 42	18 14 24	8 35.0	5 41.9	17 51.6	23 51.3	24 33.9	26 03.6	23 20.2	14 50.8	22 15.4	20 49.4
23 Th	2 04 56	3 01 48	24 09 30	0♍03 38	8 33.5	6 59.7	17 24.6	24 33.6	24 56.3	26 17.2	23 15.6	14 52.4	22 13.8	20 49.1
24 F	2 08 53	4 00 14	5♍57 25	11 51 26	8 29.9	8 19.6	16 59.6	25 15.8	25 18.9	26 30.7	23 11.1	14 54.1	22 12.2	20 48.9
25 Sa	2 12 49	4 58 38	17 46 13	23 42 15	8 23.7	9 41.6	16 36.7	25 58.0	25 41.5	26 44.4	23 06.7	14 55.8	22 10.6	20 48.6
26 Su	2 16 46	5 56 59	29 39 57	5♎39 41	8 14.6	11 05.7	16 16.2	26 40.2	26 04.2	26 58.0	23 02.2	14 57.6	22 09.0	20 48.4
27 M	2 20 42	6 55 19	11♎41 46	17 46 26	8 03.2	12 31.8	15 57.9	27 22.3	26 27.0	27 11.7	22 57.8	14 59.4	22 07.4	20 48.3
28 Tu	2 24 39	7 53 37	23 53 52	0♏04 13	7 50.2	13 59.8	15 42.0	28 04.3	26 49.9	27 25.4	22 53.4	15 01.2	22 05.8	20 48.1
29 W	2 28 35	8 51 53	6♏17 32	12 33 52	7 36.6	15 29.7	15 28.6	28 46.4	27 12.9	27 39.1	22 49.1	15 03.1	22 04.3	20 48.0
30 Th	2 32 32	9 50 08	18 53 12	25 15 32	7 23.7	17 01.6	15 17.6	29 28.3	27 36.0	27 52.9	22 44.7	15 05.0	22 02.7	20 47.9

Astro Data (Dy Hr Mn)

☽0S 1 19:58
☿R 9 3:43
☽0N 15 7:23
☉0N 20 22:00
☿0S 22 19:23
♅D 22 21:22
♀R 23 3:52
☽0S 29 2:11
♃□♇ 30 8:26
☿D 1 3:35
♃⚻♆ 7 2:43
☽0N 11 17:40
♃⚻♄ 13 9:20
☿0N 23 0:09
☽0S 25 8:30

Planet Ingress (Dy Hr Mn)

☿ ♈ 2 19:21
♀ ♉ 14 18:58
☿ ♓R 15 21:16
♂ ♉ 20 6:54
☉ ♈ 20 22:01
♀ ♈R 31 5:17

☿ ♈ 17 16:48
☉ ♉ 20 9:25

Last Aspect Dy Hr Mn		☽ Ingress	Dy Hr Mn
2 11:01	☿ ☍	♎	2 11:41
4 16:55	♄ ☌	♏	4 23:31
6 17:12	♇ □	♐	7 9:20
9 12:31	♀ △	♑	9 16:10
11 17:48	♀ □	♒	11 19:37
13 19:47	♀ ⚹	♓	13 20:17
15 11:05	☉ ☌	♈	15 19:39
17 16:38	♂ ☌	♉	17 19:44
19 20:45	☉ ⚹	♊	19 22:35
21 21:19	♄ △	♋	22 5:29
24 7:16	♄ □	♌	24 16:14
26 19:35	♄ ⚹	♍	27 5:04
28 23:16	♃ △	♎	29 17:51

Last Aspect Dy Hr Mn		☽ Ingress	Dy Hr Mn
1 4:39	♀ ☍	♏	1 5:19
2 23:25	♃ ☍	♐	3 14:58
5 18:09	♀ △	♑	5 22:29
7 21:19	♀ □	♒	8 3:27
9 21:59	♀ ⚹	♓	10 5:49
11 21:27	☿ ☌	♈	12 6:19
13 20:48	♄ ☍	♉	14 6:31
16 5:48	☿ ⚹	♊	16 8:27
18 10:20	☉ ⚹	♋	18 13:53
20 14:51	♃ ⚹	♌	20 23:27
23 4:10	♃ □	♍	23 11:53
25 18:14	♃ △	♎	26 0:40
27 22:07	♄ ☌	♏	28 11:52
30 20:20	♂ ☍	♐	30 20:52

☽ Phases & Eclipses (Dy Hr Mn)

8 18:26 ☾ 17♐54
15 11:05 ● 24♓34
22 8:11 ☽ 1♋25
30 12:55 ○ 9♎32

7 4:58 ☾ 17♑05
13 20:09 ● 23♈35
21 0:41 ☽ 0♌37
29 4:20 ○ 8♏33

Astro Data

1 March 1953
Julian Day # 19418
SVP 5♓54'36"
GC 26♐11.1 ⚴ 15♈16.3
Eris 7♈30.6 ⚵ 4♈00.8
⚷ 18♑54.0 ⚶ 21♑41.4
☽ Mean ☊ 10♒55.7

1 April 1953
Julian Day # 19449
SVP 5♓54'33"
GC 26♐11.2 ⚴ 28♈42.8
Eris 7♈51.7 ⚵ 21♈20.1
⚷ 20♑33.9 ⚶ 6♒05.2
☽ Mean ☊ 9♒17.2

LONGITUDE — May 1953

Day	Sid.Time	☉	0 hr ☽	Noon☽	True☊	☿	♀	♂	⚳	♃	♄	♅	♆	♇
1 F	2 36 29	10♉48 21	1♐40 47	8♐08 55	7♒12.6	18♈35.5	15♈09.1	0♊10.3	27♊59.2	28♉06.7	22♎40.5	15♋07.0	22♎01.2	20♌47.9
2 Sa	2 40 25	11 46 32	14 39 53	21 13 39	7R 04.0	20 11.2	15R 03.0	0 52.1	28 22.5	28 20.5	22R 36.2	15 09.0	21R 59.6	20D 47.9
3 Su	2 44 22	12 44 42	27 50 12	4♑29 32	6 58.3	21 48.8	14 59.3	1 34.0	28 45.8	28 34.4	22 32.0	15 11.1	21 58.1	20 47.9
4 M	2 48 18	13 42 50	11♑11 43	17 56 48	6 55.4	23 28.3	14D 58.1	2 15.8	29 09.2	28 48.3	22 27.9	15 13.2	21 56.6	20 47.9
5 Tu	2 52 15	14 40 57	24 44 51	1♒35 59	6D 54.5	25 09.6	14 59.2	2 57.5	29 32.8	29 02.1	22 23.8	15 15.4	21 55.1	20 48.0
6 W	2 56 11	15 39 02	8♒30 16	15 27 48	6R 54.5	26 52.9	15 02.6	3 39.2	29 56.4	29 16.1	22 19.7	15 17.6	21 53.6	20 48.0
7 Th	3 00 08	16 37 06	22 28 35	29 32 37	6 54.1	28 38.1	15 08.4	4 20.9	0♋20.0	29 30.0	22 15.7	15 19.8	21 52.2	20 48.2
8 F	3 04 04	17 35 08	6♓39 48	13♓49 55	6 52.1	0♉25.2	15 16.3	5 02.5	0 43.8	29 44.0	22 11.8	15 22.1	21 50.7	20 48.3
9 Sa	3 08 01	18 33 10	21 02 41	28 17 41	6 47.7	2 14.2	15 26.5	5 44.1	1 07.6	29 57.9	22 07.9	15 24.4	21 49.3	20 48.5
10 Su	3 11 58	19 31 10	5♈34 20	12♈52 01	6 40.6	4 05.1	15 38.7	6 25.6	1 31.5	0♊11.9	22 04.0	15 26.8	21 47.9	20 48.7
11 M	3 15 54	20 29 08	20 09 56	27 27 16	6 31.2	5 57.9	15 53.0	7 07.1	1 55.5	0 25.9	22 00.2	15 29.2	21 46.5	20 48.9
12 Tu	3 19 51	21 27 05	4♉43 08	11♉56 37	6 20.4	7 52.5	16 09.3	7 48.6	2 19.6	0 39.9	21 56.5	15 31.6	21 45.1	20 49.2
13 W	3 23 47	22 25 01	19 06 52	26 13 06	6 09.3	9 49.1	16 27.5	8 30.0	2 43.7	0 54.0	21 52.9	15 34.1	21 43.7	20 49.4
14 Th	3 27 44	23 22 55	3♊14 36	10♊10 48	5 59.1	11 47.5	16 47.5	9 11.4	3 07.9	1 08.0	21 49.3	15 36.6	21 42.4	20 49.8
15 F	3 31 40	24 20 48	17 01 16	23 45 46	5 50.9	13 47.7	17 09.3	9 52.7	3 32.2	1 22.1	21 45.7	15 39.2	21 41.0	20 50.1
16 Sa	3 35 37	25 18 39	0♋24 08	6♋56 26	5 45.2	15 49.7	17 32.9	10 34.0	3 56.5	1 36.2	21 42.3	15 41.8	21 39.7	20 50.5
17 Su	3 39 33	26 16 29	13 22 48	19 43 33	5 41.9	17 53.4	17 58.1	11 15.3	4 20.9	1 50.2	21 38.9	15 44.4	21 38.4	20 50.9
18 M	3 43 30	27 14 17	25 59 04	2♌09 49	5D 40.8	19 58.6	18 24.9	11 56.5	4 45.4	2 04.3	21 35.6	15 47.1	21 37.1	20 51.3
19 Tu	3 47 27	28 12 03	8♌16 22	14 19 18	5 41.0	22 05.4	18 53.2	12 37.6	5 09.9	2 18.4	21 32.3	15 49.8	21 35.9	20 51.8
20 W	3 51 23	29 09 47	20 19 16	26 16 56	5R 41.4	24 13.4	19 23.0	13 18.7	5 34.5	2 32.5	21 29.2	15 52.5	21 34.7	20 52.2
21 Th	3 55 20	0♊07 30	2♍12 57	8♍08 01	5 41.1	26 22.7	19 54.3	13 59.8	5 59.2	2 46.6	21 26.1	15 55.2	21 33.4	20 52.8
22 F	3 59 16	1 05 11	14 02 46	19 57 52	5 39.2	28 32.9	20 26.9	14 40.8	6 23.9	3 00.7	21 23.0	15 58.0	21 32.3	20 53.3
23 Sa	4 03 13	2 02 51	25 53 54	1♎51 29	5 35.2	0♊43.9	21 00.8	15 21.8	6 48.7	3 14.7	21 20.1	16 00.9	21 31.1	20 53.9
24 Su	4 07 09	3 00 29	7♎51 07	13 53 16	5 28.8	2 55.4	21 36.1	16 02.8	7 13.5	3 28.8	21 17.2	16 03.7	21 29.9	20 54.4
25 M	4 11 06	3 58 06	19 58 23	26 06 48	5 20.4	5 07.2	22 12.5	16 43.7	7 38.4	3 42.9	21 14.4	16 06.6	21 28.8	20 55.1
26 Tu	4 15 02	4 55 41	2♏18 48	8♏34 34	5 10.5	7 19.0	22 50.2	17 24.5	8 03.4	3 57.0	21 11.7	16 09.6	21 27.7	20 55.7
27 W	4 18 59	5 53 16	14 54 16	21 17 57	5 00.0	9 30.6	23 29.0	18 05.3	8 28.4	4 11.1	21 09.1	16 12.5	21 26.6	20 56.4
28 Th	4 22 56	6 50 49	27 45 34	4♐17 04	4 50.1	11 41.6	24 08.9	18 46.1	8 53.4	4 25.2	21 06.6	16 15.5	21 25.6	20 57.1
29 F	4 26 52	7 48 20	10♐52 18	17 31 04	4 41.5	13 51.8	24 49.8	19 26.9	9 18.5	4 39.2	21 04.2	16 18.5	21 24.6	20 57.8
30 Sa	4 30 49	8 45 51	24 13 09	0♑58 19	4 35.1	16 00.9	25 31.8	20 07.6	9 43.7	4 53.3	21 01.8	16 21.5	21 23.6	20 58.6
31 Su	4 34 45	9 43 21	7♑46 17	14 36 49	4 31.1	18 08.7	26 14.7	20 48.2	10 08.9	5 07.3	20 59.5	16 24.6	21 22.6	20 59.3

LONGITUDE — June 1953

Day	Sid.Time	☉	0 hr ☽	Noon☽	True☊	☿	♀	♂	⚳	♃	♄	♅	♆	♇
1 M	4 38 42	10♊40 50	21♑29 40	28♑24 37	4♒29.4	20♊14.9	26♈58.6	21♊28.9	10♋34.1	5♊21.4	20♎57.3	16♋27.7	21♎21.7	21♌00.1
2 Tu	4 42 38	11 38 18	5♒21 28	12♒20 02	4D 29.5	22 19.5	27 43.4	22 09.4	10 59.5	5 35.4	20R 55.2	16 30.8	21R 20.7	21 01.0
3 W	4 46 35	12 35 46	19 20 10	26 21 45	4 30.4	24 22.1	28 29.1	22 50.0	11 24.8	5 49.5	20 53.2	16 34.0	21 19.8	21 01.8
4 Th	4 50 32	13 33 13	3♓24 37	10♓28 39	4R 31.1	26 22.7	29 15.6	23 30.5	11 50.2	6 03.5	20 51.3	16 37.2	21 19.0	21 02.7
5 F	4 54 28	14 30 39	17 33 41	24 39 32	4 30.7	28 21.2	0♉02.9	24 11.0	12 15.7	6 17.5	20 49.5	16 40.4	21 18.1	21 03.6
6 Sa	4 58 25	15 28 04	1♈45 58	8♈52 42	4 28.5	0♋17.3	0 50.9	24 51.4	12 41.2	6 31.5	20 47.8	16 43.6	21 17.3	21 04.5
7 Su	5 02 21	16 25 29	15 59 25	23 05 43	4 24.4	2 11.2	1 39.7	25 31.8	13 06.7	6 45.4	20 46.1	16 46.8	21 16.5	21 05.5
8 M	5 06 18	17 22 53	0♉11 11	7♉15 19	4 18.4	4 02.6	2 29.3	26 12.2	13 32.3	6 59.4	20 44.6	16 50.1	21 15.7	21 06.5
9 Tu	5 10 14	18 20 17	14 17 38	21 17 36	4 11.4	5 51.6	3 19.5	26 52.5	13 58.0	7 13.3	20 43.1	16 53.4	21 15.0	21 07.5
10 W	5 14 11	19 17 40	28 14 42	5♊08 27	4 04.1	7 38.1	4 10.3	27 32.8	14 23.7	7 27.2	20 41.8	16 56.7	21 14.3	21 08.5
11 Th	5 18 07	20 15 03	11♊58 24	18 44 12	3 57.4	9 22.1	5 01.8	28 13.1	14 49.4	7 41.1	20 40.5	17 00.0	21 13.6	21 09.6
12 F	5 22 04	21 12 25	25 25 32	2♋02 10	3 52.1	11 03.5	5 53.9	28 53.3	15 15.2	7 55.0	20 39.4	17 03.4	21 13.0	21 10.6
13 Sa	5 26 01	22 09 46	8♋34 01	15 01 02	3 48.5	12 42.3	6 46.6	29 33.5	15 41.0	8 08.9	20 38.3	17 06.8	21 12.4	21 11.7
14 Su	5 29 57	23 07 06	21 23 19	27 41 00	3D 46.9	14 18.6	7 39.9	0♋13.7	16 06.8	8 22.7	20 37.3	17 10.2	21 11.8	21 12.9
15 M	5 33 54	24 04 25	3♌54 22	10♌03 44	3 46.9	15 52.3	8 33.7	0 53.8	16 32.7	8 36.5	20 36.5	17 13.6	21 11.2	21 14.0
16 Tu	5 37 50	25 01 44	16 09 31	22 12 09	3 48.0	17 23.4	9 28.0	1 33.9	16 58.6	8 50.3	20 35.7	17 17.0	21 10.7	21 15.2
17 W	5 41 47	25 59 01	28 12 10	4♍10 07	3 49.6	18 51.8	10 22.8	2 14.0	17 24.6	9 04.0	20 35.0	17 20.5	21 10.2	21 16.4
18 Th	5 45 43	26 56 18	10♍06 34	16 02 09	3R 51.0	20 17.5	11 18.1	2 54.0	17 50.6	9 17.8	20 34.5	17 23.9	21 09.7	21 17.6
19 F	5 49 40	27 53 35	21 57 29	27 53 11	3 51.6	21 40.6	12 13.9	3 33.9	18 16.6	9 31.4	20 34.0	17 27.4	21 09.3	21 18.8
20 Sa	5 53 36	28 50 50	3♎49 52	9♎48 10	3 50.9	23 00.9	13 10.1	4 13.9	18 42.7	9 45.1	20 33.6	17 30.9	21 08.9	21 20.1
21 Su	5 57 33	29 48 05	15 48 39	21 51 53	3 48.8	24 18.4	14 06.7	4 53.8	19 08.8	9 58.7	20 33.3	17 34.4	21 08.5	21 21.3
22 M	6 01 30	0♋45 19	27 58 24	4♏08 39	3 45.3	25 33.1	15 03.8	5 33.7	19 34.9	10 12.3	20 33.2	17 37.9	21 08.2	21 22.6
23 Tu	6 05 26	1 42 32	10♏23 03	16 41 56	3 40.9	26 45.0	16 01.4	6 13.5	20 01.1	10 25.9	20D 33.1	17 41.4	21 07.9	21 23.9
24 W	6 09 23	2 39 45	23 05 34	29 34 08	3 36.0	27 53.8	16 59.3	6 53.3	20 27.3	10 39.4	20 33.1	17 45.0	21 07.6	21 25.3
25 Th	6 13 19	3 36 58	6♐07 42	12♐46 16	3 31.3	28 59.7	17 57.6	7 33.1	20 53.5	10 52.9	20 33.2	17 48.5	21 07.3	21 26.6
26 F	6 17 16	4 34 10	19 29 44	26 19 52	3 27.2	0♌02.5	18 56.3	8 12.8	21 19.8	11 06.3	20 33.5	17 52.1	21 07.1	21 28.0
27 Sa	6 21 12	5 31 22	3♑10 24	10♑06 58	3 24.4	1 02.2	19 55.3	8 52.5	21 46.0	11 19.7	20 33.8	17 55.7	21 06.9	21 29.4
28 Su	6 25 09	6 28 34	17 07 08	24 10 24	3D 22.9	1 58.5	20 54.7	9 32.2	22 12.3	11 33.1	20 34.2	17 59.3	21 06.8	21 30.8
29 M	6 29 05	7 25 45	1♒16 16	8♒24 11	3 22.7	2 51.5	21 54.5	10 11.8	22 38.7	11 46.4	20 34.8	18 02.9	21 06.7	21 32.3
30 Tu	6 33 02	8 22 57	15 33 37	22 44 03	3 23.5	3 41.0	22 54.6	10 51.4	23 05.1	11 59.7	20 35.4	18 06.5	21 06.6	21 33.7

Astro Data

	Dy Hr Mn
♇ D	2 20:21
♀ D	4 12:33
☽0N	9 1:11
♃∠♅	11 18:44
♄☌♆	17 17:28
☽0S	22 15:11
♄✶♇	31 13:29
♃⚼♄	3 17:41
☽0N	5 6:21
♃⚼♆	5 13:03
♆✶♇	13 21:03
☽0S	18 22:19
♄ D	23 17:26

Planet Ingress

	Dy Hr Mn
♂ ♊	1 6:08
⚳ ♋	6 15:42
☿ ♉	8 6:24
♃ ♊	9 15:33
☉ ♊	21 8:53
☿ ♊	23 3:58
♀ ♉	5 10:34
☿ ♋	6 8:23
♂ ♋	14 3:49
☉ ♋	21 17:00
☿ ♌	26 11:01

Last Aspect / ☽ Ingress

Last Aspect Dy Hr Mn		☽ Ingress Dy Hr Mn
2 14:30	♄ ✶	♑ 3 3:55
5 7:27	♃ △	♒ 5 9:12
7 11:55	♃ □	♓ 7 12:46
9 14:48	♃ ✶	♈ 9 14:49
11 3:04	♄ ☍	♉ 11 16:12
13 5:06	☉ ☌	♊ 13 18:27
15 8:26	♄ △	♋ 15 23:16
18 1:37	☉ ✶	♌ 18 7:47
20 18:20	☉ □	♍ 20 19:31
22 3:52	♅ ✶	♎ 23 8:16
25 3:59	♀ ☍	♏ 25 19:32
27 11:20	♇ □	♐ 28 4:08
30 1:48	♀ △	♑ 30 10:17

Last Aspect / ☽ Ingress

Last Aspect Dy Hr Mn		☽ Ingress Dy Hr Mn
1 9:23	♀ □	♒ 1 14:45
3 15:50	♀ ✶	♓ 3 18:12
5 19:14	☿ □	♈ 5 21:01
7 16:19	♂ ✶	♉ 7 23:41
9 11:43	♇ □	♊ 10 3:03
12 5:58	♂ ☌	♋ 12 8:17
13 23:39	♆ □	♌ 14 16:27
16 18:08	☉ ✶	♍ 17 3:37
19 12:01	☉ □	♎ 19 16:16
21 17:22	☿ □	♏ 22 3:57
24 8:37	☿ △	♐ 24 12:48
26 3:29	♇ △	♑ 26 18:29
28 6:48	♆ □	♒ 28 21:51

☽ Phases & Eclipses

Dy Hr Mn		
6 12:21	☾	15♒40
13 5:06	●	22♉08
20 18:20	☽	29♌25
28 17:03	○	7♐03
4 17:35	☾	13♓47
11 14:55	●	20♊22
19 12:01	☽	27♍54
27 3:29	○	5♑11

Astro Data

1 May 1953
Julian Day # 19479
SVP 5♓54'29"
GC 26♐11.2 ⚴ 13♉06.4
Eris 8♈11.7 ⚵ 8♉45.0
⚷ 21♑02.1R ⚶ 18♒00.3
☽ Mean ☊ 7♒41.9

1 June 1953
Julian Day # 19510
SVP 5♓54'24"
GC 26♐11.3 ⚴ 29♉09.2
Eris 8♈26.9 ⚵ 27♉04.5
⚷ 20♑17.8R ⚶ 26♒55.1
☽ Mean ☊ 6♒03.4

July 1953 — LONGITUDE

Day	Sid.Time	☉	0 hr ☽	Noon ☽	True ☊	☿	♀	♂	⚳	♃	♄	♅	♆	♇
1 W	6 36 59	9♋20 08	29♒54 58	7♓05 55	3♒24.9	4♌27.0	23♉55.0	11♋31.0	23♋31.5	12♊12.9	20♎36.1	18♋10.1	21♎06.5	21♌35.2
2 Th	6 40 55	10 17 20	14♓16 27	21 26 11	3 26.1	5 09.2	24 55.8	12 10.6	23 57.9	12 26.1	20 36.9	18 13.7	21D 06.5	21 36.7
3 F	6 44 52	11 14 32	28 34 46	5♈41 53	3R 26.9	5 47.6	25 56.8	12 50.1	24 24.3	12 39.3	20 37.8	18 17.3	21 06.5	21 38.2
4 Sa	6 48 48	12 11 44	12♈47 16	19 50 39	3 26.8	6 22.1	26 58.2	13 29.6	24 50.8	12 52.4	20 38.8	18 21.0	21 06.5	21 39.7
5 Su	6 52 45	13 08 57	26 51 49	3♉50 34	3 25.8	6 52.5	27 59.8	14 09.1	25 17.3	13 05.4	20 40.0	18 24.6	21 06.6	21 41.2
6 M	6 56 41	14 06 09	10♉46 42	17 40 02	3 24.0	7 18.7	29 01.7	14 48.5	25 43.8	13 18.4	20 41.2	18 28.2	21 06.7	21 42.8
7 Tu	7 00 38	15 03 23	24 30 25	1♊17 40	3 21.7	7 40.5	0♊03.9	15 27.9	26 10.4	13 31.4	20 42.5	18 31.9	21 06.8	21 44.4
8 W	7 04 34	16 00 36	8♊01 40	14 42 15	3 19.2	7 57.9	1 06.4	16 07.3	26 37.0	13 44.3	20 43.9	18 35.5	21 07.0	21 45.9
9 Th	7 08 31	16 57 50	21 19 21	27 52 51	3 17.0	8 10.8	2 09.1	16 46.7	27 03.6	13 57.1	20 45.4	18 39.2	21 07.2	21 47.6
10 F	7 12 28	17 55 04	4♋22 42	10♋48 51	3 15.4	8 18.9	3 12.0	17 26.0	27 30.2	14 09.9	20 47.0	18 42.8	21 07.4	21 49.2
11 Sa	7 16 24	18 52 19	17 11 21	23 30 13	3D 14.4	8R 22.4	4 15.2	18 05.3	27 56.8	14 22.7	20 48.7	18 46.5	21 07.7	21 50.8
12 Su	7 20 21	19 49 33	29 45 33	5♌57 30	3 14.2	8 21.1	5 18.6	18 44.6	28 23.5	14 35.3	20 50.5	18 50.1	21 08.0	21 52.5
13 M	7 24 17	20 46 48	12♌06 15	18 12 01	3 14.7	8 15.0	6 22.3	19 23.8	28 50.2	14 48.0	20 52.4	18 53.8	21 08.3	21 54.1
14 Tu	7 28 14	21 44 03	24 15 06	0♍15 49	3 15.5	8 04.2	7 26.2	20 03.0	29 16.9	15 00.5	20 54.4	18 57.4	21 08.7	21 55.8
15 W	7 32 10	22 41 18	6♍14 32	12 11 41	3 16.6	7 48.7	8 30.2	20 42.2	29 43.6	15 13.0	20 56.5	19 01.1	21 09.1	21 57.5
16 Th	7 36 07	23 38 33	18 07 41	24 03 02	3 17.6	7 28.7	9 34.5	21 21.4	0♌10.4	15 25.4	20 58.6	19 04.7	21 09.5	21 59.2
17 F	7 40 03	24 35 48	29 58 14	5♎53 51	3 18.3	7 04.3	10 39.0	22 00.5	0 37.1	15 37.8	21 00.9	19 08.4	21 09.9	22 00.9
18 Sa	7 44 00	25 33 03	11♎50 25	17 48 30	3R 18.7	6 36.0	11 43.7	22 39.6	1 03.9	15 50.1	21 03.3	19 12.0	21 10.4	22 02.6
19 Su	7 47 57	26 30 19	23 48 41	29 51 34	3 18.8	6 03.9	12 48.6	23 18.7	1 30.7	16 02.3	21 05.7	19 15.6	21 10.9	22 04.3
20 M	7 51 53	27 27 35	5♏57 41	12♏07 35	3 18.6	5 28.6	13 53.7	23 57.7	1 57.5	16 14.5	21 08.3	19 19.2	21 11.5	22 06.1
21 Tu	7 55 50	28 24 51	18 21 47	24 40 46	3 18.2	4 50.6	14 58.9	24 36.8	2 24.3	16 26.6	21 10.9	19 22.9	21 12.1	22 07.8
22 W	7 59 46	29 22 07	1♐04 57	7♐34 39	3 17.7	4 10.3	16 04.4	25 15.7	2 51.1	16 38.6	21 13.6	19 26.5	21 12.7	22 09.6
23 Th	8 03 43	0♌19 24	14 10 10	20 51 38	3 17.3	3 28.6	17 10.0	25 54.7	3 18.0	16 50.5	21 16.5	19 30.1	21 13.3	22 11.4
24 F	8 07 39	1 16 42	27 39 06	4♑32 31	3 17.1	2 46.0	18 15.8	26 33.7	3 44.8	17 02.4	21 19.4	19 33.7	21 14.0	22 13.2
25 Sa	8 11 36	2 13 59	11♑31 40	18 36 15	3 17.0	2 03.4	19 21.8	27 12.6	4 11.7	17 14.2	21 22.4	19 37.3	21 14.7	22 15.0
26 Su	8 15 33	3 11 18	25 45 46	2♒59 39	3 17.0	1 21.4	20 27.9	27 51.5	4 38.5	17 25.9	21 25.5	19 40.9	21 15.5	22 16.8
27 M	8 19 29	4 08 37	10♒17 13	17 37 40	3 16.9	0 40.9	21 34.2	28 30.3	5 05.4	17 37.6	21 28.6	19 44.4	21 16.2	22 18.6
28 Tu	8 23 26	5 05 57	25 00 09	2♓23 48	3 16.8	0 02.6	22 40.7	29 09.2	5 32.3	17 49.1	21 31.9	19 48.0	21 17.0	22 20.4
29 W	8 27 22	6 03 17	9♓47 41	17 10 57	3 16.6	29♋27.2	23 47.4	29 48.0	5 59.2	18 00.6	21 35.2	19 51.5	21 17.9	22 22.3
30 Th	8 31 19	7 00 39	24 32 47	1♈52 24	3 16.3	28 55.4	24 54.2	0♌26.8	6 26.1	18 12.0	21 38.6	19 55.1	21 18.7	22 24.1
31 F	8 35 15	7 58 01	9♈09 09	16 22 29	3 15.9	28 27.9	26 01.2	1 05.6	6 53.1	18 23.3	21 42.2	19 58.6	21 19.6	22 25.9

August 1953 — LONGITUDE

Day	Sid.Time	☉	0 hr ☽	Noon ☽	True ☊	☿	♀	♂	⚳	♃	♄	♅	♆	♇
1 Sa	8 39 12	8♌55 25	23♈31 58	0♉37 14	3♒15.7	28♋05.2	27♊08.3	1♌44.3	7♌20.0	18♊34.5	21♎45.7	20♋02.1	21♎20.5	22♌27.8
2 Su	8 43 08	9 52 50	7♉38 05	14 34 22	3D 15.6	27R 47.8	28 15.6	2 23.1	7 47.0	18 45.7	21 49.4	20 05.6	21 21.5	22 29.7
3 M	8 47 05	10 50 17	21 26 03	28 13 09	3 15.9	27 36.1	29 23.0	3 01.8	8 13.9	18 56.7	21 53.2	20 09.1	21 22.5	22 31.5
4 Tu	8 51 02	11 47 44	4♊55 46	11♊34 01	3 16.5	27D 30.5	0♋30.6	3 40.5	8 40.9	19 07.7	21 57.0	20 12.5	21 23.5	22 33.4
5 W	8 54 58	12 45 13	18 08 05	24 38 09	3 17.3	27 31.2	1 38.3	4 19.2	9 07.8	19 18.6	22 00.9	20 16.0	21 24.5	22 35.3
6 Th	8 58 55	13 42 43	1♋04 24	7♋27 03	3 18.2	27 38.5	2 46.2	4 57.8	9 34.8	19 29.3	22 05.0	20 19.4	21 25.6	22 37.1
7 F	9 02 51	14 40 14	13 46 20	20 02 25	3 18.9	27 52.4	3 54.2	5 36.5	10 01.8	19 40.0	22 09.0	20 22.8	21 26.7	22 39.0
8 Sa	9 06 48	15 37 47	26 15 32	2♌25 52	3R 19.3	28 13.2	5 02.3	6 15.1	10 28.8	19 50.6	22 13.2	20 26.2	21 27.8	22 40.9
9 Su	9 10 44	16 35 20	8♌33 38	14 39 01	3 19.0	28 40.7	6 10.5	6 53.7	10 55.8	20 01.1	22 17.4	20 29.6	21 29.0	22 42.8
10 M	9 14 41	17 32 54	20 42 13	26 43 29	3 18.0	29 15.0	7 18.9	7 32.3	11 22.8	20 11.5	22 21.7	20 33.0	21 30.1	22 44.7
11 Tu	9 18 37	18 30 30	2♍43 00	8♍41 03	3 16.3	29 56.1	8 27.4	8 10.8	11 49.8	20 21.8	22 26.1	20 36.3	21 31.4	22 46.6
12 W	9 22 34	19 28 07	14 37 51	20 33 43	3 14.0	0♌43.9	9 36.1	8 49.3	12 16.8	20 31.9	22 30.6	20 39.6	21 32.6	22 48.5
13 Th	9 26 31	20 25 44	26 28 58	2♎23 55	3 11.4	1 38.2	10 44.8	9 27.8	12 43.8	20 42.0	22 35.1	20 42.9	21 33.9	22 50.4
14 F	9 30 27	21 23 23	8♎18 57	14 14 28	3 08.7	2 38.9	11 53.7	10 06.3	13 10.8	20 52.0	22 39.7	20 46.2	21 35.1	22 52.3
15 Sa	9 34 24	22 21 03	20 10 55	26 08 45	3 06.4	3 45.8	13 02.7	10 44.8	13 37.8	21 01.8	22 44.4	20 49.4	21 36.5	22 54.2
16 Su	9 38 20	23 18 43	2♏08 27	8♏10 32	3 04.7	4 58.7	14 11.8	11 23.2	14 04.8	21 11.5	22 49.2	20 52.7	21 37.8	22 56.1
17 M	9 42 17	24 16 25	14 15 32	20 24 00	3D 04.0	6 17.3	15 21.0	12 01.7	14 31.7	21 21.2	22 54.0	20 55.9	21 39.2	22 58.0
18 Tu	9 46 13	25 14 08	26 36 29	2♐53 29	3 04.1	7 41.2	16 30.3	12 40.1	14 58.7	21 30.7	22 58.9	20 59.0	21 40.6	22 59.9
19 W	9 50 10	26 11 52	9♐15 33	15 43 10	3 05.1	9 10.2	17 39.7	13 18.5	15 25.7	21 40.1	23 03.9	21 02.2	21 42.0	23 01.8
20 Th	9 54 06	27 09 38	22 16 45	28 56 39	3 06.5	10 43.9	18 49.3	13 56.8	15 52.7	21 49.4	23 08.9	21 05.3	21 43.4	23 03.7
21 F	9 58 03	28 07 24	5♑43 10	12♑36 25	3 07.9	12 21.9	19 58.9	14 35.2	16 19.7	21 58.5	23 14.0	21 08.4	21 44.9	23 05.6
22 Sa	10 02 00	29 05 11	19 36 26	26 43 05	3R 08.8	14 03.7	21 08.7	15 13.5	16 46.6	22 07.6	23 19.2	21 11.5	21 46.4	23 07.5
23 Su	10 05 56	0♍03 00	3♒56 04	11♒14 53	3 08.8	15 49.0	22 18.6	15 51.8	17 13.6	22 16.5	23 24.4	21 14.5	21 47.9	23 09.4
24 M	10 09 53	1 00 50	18 38 52	26 07 10	3 07.4	17 37.3	23 28.6	16 30.1	17 40.6	22 25.3	23 29.7	21 17.5	21 49.5	23 11.3
25 Tu	10 13 49	1 58 42	3♓38 48	11♓12 38	3 04.7	19 28.2	24 38.6	17 08.4	18 07.5	22 34.0	23 35.0	21 20.5	21 51.1	23 13.2
26 W	10 17 46	2 56 35	18 47 28	26 22 04	3 01.0	21 21.1	25 48.8	17 46.6	18 34.4	22 42.5	23 40.4	21 23.5	21 52.6	23 15.1
27 Th	10 21 42	3 54 29	3♈55 11	11♈25 41	2 56.7	23 15.8	26 59.1	18 24.8	19 01.4	22 50.9	23 45.9	21 26.4	21 54.3	23 16.9
28 F	10 25 39	4 52 26	18 52 31	26 14 47	2 52.6	25 11.7	28 09.5	19 03.1	19 28.3	22 59.2	23 51.4	21 29.3	21 55.9	23 18.8
29 Sa	10 29 35	5 50 24	3♉31 46	10♉42 55	2 49.3	27 08.6	29 20.1	19 41.3	19 55.2	23 07.4	23 57.0	21 32.2	21 57.6	23 20.7
30 Su	10 33 32	6 48 24	17 47 54	24 46 30	2D 47.3	29 06.1	0♌30.7	20 19.5	20 22.1	23 15.4	24 02.7	21 35.0	21 59.2	23 22.5
31 M	10 37 28	7 46 26	1♊38 44	8♊24 43	2 46.6	1♍03.9	1 41.4	20 57.6	20 49.0	23 23.3	24 08.4	21 37.8	22 00.9	23 24.4

Astro Data

	Dy Hr Mn
☽ 0N	2 11:17
♆ D	2 22:13
☿ R	11 17:26
☽ 0S	16 5:41
♄☌♆	22 1:22
☽ 0N	29 18:06
☿ D	4 21:22
☽ 0S	12 12:50
♃⊻♅	13 15:15
♄✶♇	18 19:52
♃△♆	19 17:47
☽ 0N	26 3:31
♃✶♇	31 16:25

Planet Ingress

	Dy Hr Mn
♀ ♊	7 10:30
⚳ ♌	16 2:42
☉ ♌	23 3:52
☿ ♋R	28 13:40
♂ ♌	29 19:25
♀ ♋	4 1:08
☿ ♌	11 14:04
☉ ♍	23 10:45
♀ ♌	30 1:35
☿ ♍	30 22:59

Last Aspect / ☽ Ingress (July)

Last Aspect Dy Hr Mn		☽ Ingress	Dy Hr Mn
30 12:19	♀ □	♓	1 0:08
2 18:19	♀ ✶	♈	3 2:23
4 15:06	♇ △	♉	5 5:23
7 9:38	♀ ☌	♊	7 9:42
9 0:50	♇ ✶	♋	9 15:54
11 7:28	♆ □	♌	12 0:28
13 19:21	♇ ☌	♍	14 11:28
16 11:06	☉ ✶	♎	17 0:04
19 4:47	☉ □	♏	19 12:17
21 19:35	☉ △	♐	21 21:59
23 14:22	♇ △	♑	24 4:07
26 3:05	♂ ☍	♒	26 7:03
27 19:38	♇ ☍	♓	28 8:07
30 7:19	☿ △	♈	30 8:56

Last Aspect / ☽ Ingress (August)

Last Aspect Dy Hr Mn		☽ Ingress	Dy Hr Mn
1 7:48	☿ □	♉	1 10:57
3 10:55	☿ ✶	♊	3 15:10
5 8:12	♇ ✶	♋	5 21:59
8 3:32	☿ ☌	♌	8 7:16
10 4:02	♇ ☌	♍	10 18:33
12 12:12	♅ ✶	♎	13 7:08
15 5:28	♇ ✶	♏	15 19:43
17 20:08	☉ □	♐	18 6:30
20 8:34	☉ △	♑	20 13:53
22 6:15	♄ □	♒	22 17:29
24 7:46	♄ △	♓	24 18:12
26 11:03	♀ △	♈	26 17:46
28 15:25	♀ □	♉	28 18:10
30 20:48	☿ □	♊	30 21:07

☽ Phases & Eclipses

Dy Hr Mn	
3 22:03	☾ 11♈38
11 2:28	● 18♋30
11 2:43:38	◐ P 0.202
19 4:47	☽ 26♎13
26 12:21	○ 3♒12
26 12:21	◐ T 1.863
2 3:16	☾ 9♉32
9 16:10	● 16♌45
9 15:54:32	◐ P 0.373
17 20:08	☽ 24♏36
24 20:21	○ 1♓21
31 10:46	☾ 7♊43

Astro Data

1 July 1953
Julian Day # 19540
SVP 5♓54'18"
GC 26♐11.4 ⚴ 15♊37.2
Eris 8♈33.0 ⚵ 14♊47.1
⚷ 18♑43.0R ⚶ 0♓16.7
☽ Mean ☊ 4♒28.1

1 August 1953
Julian Day # 19571
SVP 5♓54'13"
GC 26♐11.5 ⚴ 3♋18.4
Eris 8♈29.0R ⚵ 2♋39.1
⚷ 16♑52.2R ⚶ 26♒38.9R
☽ Mean ☊ 2♒49.6

LONGITUDE — September 1953

Day	Sid.Time	☉	0 hr ☽	Noon☽	True☊	☿	♀	♂	⚳	♃	♄	♅	♆	♇
1 Tu	10 41 25	8♍44 30	15♊04 38	21♊38 51	2♒47.3	3♍01.8	2♌52.2	21♌35.8	21♌15.9	23♊31.1	24♎14.2	21♋40.6	22♎02.7	23♌26.3
2 W	10 45 22	9 42 36	28 07 42	4♋31 39	2 48.7	4 59.4	4 03.1	22 14.0	21 42.8	23 38.7	24 20.0	21 43.3	22 04.4	23 28.1
3 Th	10 49 18	10 40 44	10♋51 06	17 06 32	2 50.2	6 56.7	5 14.1	22 52.1	22 09.7	23 46.1	24 25.9	21 46.0	22 06.2	23 29.9
4 F	10 53 15	11 38 54	23 18 23	29 27 05	2R51.2	8 53.5	6 25.3	23 30.2	22 36.5	23 53.5	24 31.8	21 48.7	22 08.0	23 31.8
5 Sa	10 57 11	12 37 06	5♌33 02	11♌36 38	2 50.8	10 49.5	7 36.5	24 08.3	23 03.4	24 00.6	24 37.8	21 51.3	22 09.8	23 33.6
6 Su	11 01 08	13 35 20	17 38 13	23 38 07	2 48.7	12 44.8	8 47.7	24 46.4	23 30.2	24 07.7	24 43.8	21 53.9	22 11.6	23 35.4
7 M	11 05 04	14 33 35	29 36 37	5♍34 00	2 44.5	14 39.2	9 59.1	25 24.5	23 57.0	24 14.5	24 49.9	21 56.4	22 13.4	23 37.2
8 Tu	11 09 01	15 31 52	11♍30 30	17 26 21	2 38.4	16 32.6	11 10.6	26 02.5	24 23.8	24 21.3	24 56.0	21 58.9	22 15.3	23 39.0
9 W	11 12 57	16 30 11	23 21 47	29 16 58	2 30.8	18 25.1	12 22.1	26 40.6	24 50.5	24 27.8	25 02.2	22 01.4	22 17.2	23 40.8
10 Th	11 16 54	17 28 32	5♎12 10	11♎07 35	2 22.2	20 16.5	13 33.8	27 18.6	25 17.3	24 34.2	25 08.4	22 03.8	22 19.1	23 42.6
11 F	11 20 51	18 26 54	17 03 27	23 00 03	2 13.5	22 06.8	14 45.5	27 56.6	25 44.0	24 40.5	25 14.7	22 06.2	22 21.0	23 44.3
12 Sa	11 24 47	19 25 18	28 57 38	4♏56 33	2 05.5	23 56.0	15 57.3	28 34.6	26 10.7	24 46.6	25 21.0	22 08.6	22 22.9	23 46.1
13 Su	11 28 44	20 23 44	10♏57 08	16 59 46	1 58.9	25 44.2	17 09.1	29 12.6	26 37.4	24 52.5	25 27.4	22 10.9	22 24.9	23 47.8
14 M	11 32 40	21 22 11	23 04 52	29 12 54	1 54.3	27 31.3	18 21.1	29 50.5	27 04.1	24 58.3	25 33.8	22 13.2	22 26.8	23 49.6
15 Tu	11 36 37	22 20 40	5♐24 19	11♐39 39	1D51.8	29 17.3	19 33.1	0♍28.5	27 30.7	25 03.9	25 40.2	22 15.4	22 28.8	23 51.3
16 W	11 40 33	23 19 11	17 59 23	24 24 03	1 51.2	1♎02.2	20 45.3	1 06.4	27 57.3	25 09.4	25 46.7	22 17.6	22 30.8	23 53.0
17 Th	11 44 30	24 17 44	0♑54 09	7♑30 10	1 51.8	2 46.0	21 57.4	1 44.3	28 23.9	25 14.7	25 53.3	22 19.8	22 32.8	23 54.7
18 F	11 48 26	25 16 18	14 12 31	21 01 31	1R52.8	4 28.8	23 09.7	2 22.2	28 50.5	25 19.8	25 59.8	22 21.9	22 34.9	23 56.4
19 Sa	11 52 23	26 14 53	27 57 27	5♒00 23	1 53.1	6 10.6	24 22.1	3 00.1	29 17.0	25 24.7	26 06.4	22 23.9	22 36.9	23 58.0
20 Su	11 56 20	27 13 31	12♒10 17	19 26 54	1 51.8	7 51.3	25 34.5	3 38.0	29 43.5	25 29.5	26 13.1	22 26.0	22 39.0	23 59.7
21 M	12 00 16	28 12 09	26 49 47	4♓18 15	1 48.4	9 31.1	26 47.0	4 15.8	0♍10.0	25 34.1	26 19.8	22 27.9	22 41.0	24 01.3
22 Tu	12 04 13	29 10 50	11♓51 25	19 28 12	1 42.5	11 09.8	27 59.5	4 53.7	0 36.4	25 38.5	26 26.5	22 29.9	22 43.1	24 03.0
23 W	12 08 09	0♎09 33	27 07 19	4♈47 23	1 34.7	12 47.6	29 12.2	5 31.5	1 02.9	25 42.7	26 33.2	22 31.8	22 45.2	24 04.6
24 Th	12 12 06	1 08 17	12♈26 59	20 04 39	1 25.8	14 24.4	0♍24.9	6 09.3	1 29.2	25 46.8	26 40.0	22 33.6	22 47.3	24 06.2
25 F	12 16 02	2 07 04	27 39 03	5♉08 56	1 16.9	16 00.3	1 37.7	6 47.1	1 55.6	25 50.7	26 46.8	22 35.4	22 49.4	24 07.7
26 Sa	12 19 59	3 05 53	12♉33 16	19 51 14	1 09.2	17 35.3	2 50.5	7 24.9	2 21.9	25 54.4	26 53.6	22 37.1	22 51.5	24 09.3
27 Su	12 23 55	4 04 45	27 02 15	4♊05 56	1 03.4	19 09.3	4 03.5	8 02.6	2 48.2	25 57.9	27 00.5	22 38.8	22 53.7	24 10.8
28 M	12 27 52	5 03 38	11♊02 09	17 50 57	0 59.9	20 42.5	5 16.5	8 40.4	3 14.5	26 01.3	27 07.4	22 40.5	22 55.8	24 12.4
29 Tu	12 31 49	6 02 34	24 32 34	1♋07 20	0D58.6	22 14.8	6 29.5	9 18.2	3 40.7	26 04.5	27 14.4	22 42.1	22 58.0	24 13.9
30 W	12 35 45	7 01 32	7♋35 43	13 58 15	0 58.6	23 46.2	7 42.7	9 55.9	4 06.9	26 07.4	27 21.3	22 43.7	23 00.1	24 15.4

LONGITUDE — October 1953

Day	Sid.Time	☉	0 hr ☽	Noon☽	True☊	☿	♀	♂	⚳	♃	♄	♅	♆	♇
1 Th	12 39 42	8♎00 33	20♋15 30	26♋28 04	0♒59.1	25♎16.7	8♍55.9	10♍33.6	4♍33.0	26♊10.2	27♎28.3	22♋45.2	23♎02.3	24♌16.9
2 F	12 43 38	8 59 36	2♌36 35	8♌41 37	0R58.9	26 46.3	10 09.2	11 11.4	4 59.1	26 12.8	27 35.3	22 46.6	23 04.5	24 18.3
3 Sa	12 47 35	9 58 40	14 43 47	20 43 36	0 57.0	28 15.1	11 22.5	11 49.1	5 25.2	26 15.2	27 42.3	22 48.0	23 06.7	24 19.8
4 Su	12 51 31	10 57 48	26 41 36	2♍38 15	0 52.7	29 43.0	12 35.9	12 26.7	5 51.2	26 17.4	27 49.4	22 49.4	23 08.9	24 21.2
5 M	12 55 28	11 56 57	8♍33 57	14 29 06	0 45.5	1♏10.0	13 49.4	13 04.4	6 17.2	26 19.4	27 56.5	22 50.7	23 11.1	24 22.6
6 Tu	12 59 24	12 56 08	20 24 01	26 18 59	0 35.5	2 36.1	15 02.9	13 42.1	6 43.2	26 21.2	28 03.5	22 52.0	23 13.3	24 23.9
7 W	13 03 21	13 55 22	2♎14 16	8♎10 04	0 23.3	4 01.3	16 16.5	14 19.7	7 09.1	26 22.9	28 10.7	22 53.2	23 15.5	24 25.3
8 Th	13 07 18	14 54 38	14 06 35	20 03 58	0 09.6	5 25.5	17 30.1	14 57.4	7 34.9	26 24.3	28 17.8	22 54.3	23 17.7	24 26.6
9 F	13 11 14	15 53 56	26 02 24	2♏02 00	29♑55.7	6 48.8	18 43.8	15 35.0	8 00.7	26 25.5	28 24.9	22 55.4	23 19.9	24 27.9
10 Sa	13 15 11	16 53 15	8♏02 56	14 05 24	29 42.6	8 11.1	19 57.6	16 12.6	8 26.5	26 26.5	28 32.1	22 56.5	23 22.1	24 29.2
11 Su	13 19 07	17 52 37	20 09 33	26 15 38	29 31.5	9 32.3	21 11.4	16 50.2	8 52.1	26 27.3	28 39.3	22 57.5	23 24.4	24 30.5
12 M	13 23 04	18 52 01	2♐23 53	8♐34 36	29 23.0	10 52.4	22 25.2	17 27.8	9 17.8	26 28.0	28 46.5	22 58.4	23 26.6	24 31.8
13 Tu	13 27 00	19 51 26	14 48 07	21 04 47	29 17.5	12 11.3	23 39.1	18 05.3	9 43.4	26 28.4	28 53.7	22 59.3	23 28.8	24 33.0
14 W	13 30 57	20 50 54	27 25 01	3♑49 13	29 14.6	13 29.1	24 53.1	18 42.9	10 08.9	26R28.6	29 00.9	23 00.1	23 31.1	24 34.2
15 Th	13 34 53	21 50 23	10♑17 50	16 51 19	29 13.8	14 45.5	26 07.1	19 20.4	10 34.4	26 28.6	29 08.1	23 00.9	23 33.3	24 35.4
16 F	13 38 50	22 49 53	23 30 06	0♒14 34	29 13.7	16 00.6	27 21.1	19 58.0	10 59.8	26 28.5	29 15.4	23 01.7	23 35.6	24 36.5
17 Sa	13 42 47	23 49 26	7♒05 04	14 01 50	29 13.3	17 14.1	28 35.2	20 35.5	11 25.2	26 28.1	29 22.6	23 02.4	23 37.8	24 37.7
18 Su	13 46 43	24 49 00	21 05 01	28 14 34	29 11.2	18 26.0	29 49.3	21 12.9	11 50.5	26 27.5	29 29.9	23 03.0	23 40.0	24 38.8
19 M	13 50 40	25 48 36	5♓30 19	12♓51 52	29 06.5	19 36.2	1♎03.5	21 50.4	12 15.7	26 26.7	29 37.1	23 03.6	23 42.3	24 39.9
20 Tu	13 54 36	26 48 13	20 18 36	27 49 41	28 59.1	20 44.4	2 17.7	22 27.9	12 40.9	26 25.7	29 44.4	23 04.1	23 44.5	24 40.9
21 W	13 58 33	27 47 53	5♈24 06	13♈00 37	28 49.3	21 50.6	3 32.0	23 05.3	13 06.0	26 24.6	29 51.6	23 04.5	23 46.7	24 42.0
22 Th	14 02 29	28 47 34	20 37 56	28 14 37	28 38.0	22 54.5	4 46.3	23 42.7	13 31.0	26 23.2	29 58.9	23 04.9	23 49.0	24 43.0
23 F	14 06 26	29 47 18	5♉49 16	13♉20 33	28 26.5	23 55.8	6 00.7	24 20.2	13 56.0	26 21.6	0♏06.2	23 05.3	23 51.2	24 44.0
24 Sa	14 10 22	0♏47 03	20 47 14	28 08 18	28 16.2	24 54.3	7 15.1	24 57.6	14 20.9	26 19.8	0 13.4	23 05.6	23 53.4	24 44.9
25 Su	14 14 19	1 46 51	5♊22 55	12♊30 28	28 08.1	25 49.8	8 29.5	25 35.0	14 45.8	26 17.8	0 20.7	23 05.9	23 55.7	24 45.9
26 M	14 18 16	2 46 41	19 30 37	26 23 13	28 02.7	26 41.8	9 44.0	26 12.4	15 10.5	26 15.7	0 28.0	23 06.1	23 57.9	24 46.8
27 Tu	14 22 12	3 46 33	3♋08 18	9♋46 07	27 59.9	27 30.1	10 58.5	26 49.7	15 35.3	26 13.3	0 35.3	23 06.2	24 00.1	24 47.7
28 W	14 26 09	4 46 27	16 17 02	22 41 32	27D58.9	28 14.1	12 13.1	27 27.1	15 59.9	26 10.7	0 42.5	23 06.3	24 02.3	24 48.5
29 Th	14 30 05	5 46 23	29 00 09	5♌13 33	27R58.9	28 53.5	13 27.7	28 04.4	16 24.4	26 08.0	0 49.8	23R06.3	24 04.5	24 49.4
30 F	14 34 02	6 46 22	11♌22 22	17 27 17	27 58.6	29 27.6	14 42.4	28 41.8	16 48.9	26 05.0	0 57.0	23 06.3	24 06.7	24 50.2
31 Sa	14 37 58	7 46 23	23 28 57	29 28 01	27 56.8	29 56.0	15 57.0	29 19.1	17 13.3	26 01.8	1 04.3	23 06.2	24 08.9	24 51.0

Astro Data Dy Hr Mn	Planet Ingress Dy Hr Mn
☽0S 8 19:22	♂ ♍ 14 17:59
☿0S 17 3:07	☿ ♎ 15 21:45
☽0N 22 14:29	⚳ ♍ 21 2:56
☉0S 23 8:06	☉ ♎ 23 8:06
	♀ ♍ 24 3:48
☽0S 6 1:15	
♃ R 15 2:56	☿ ♏ 4 16:40
☽0N 20 0:52	☊ ♑R 9 4:29
♀0S 21 13:01	♀ ♎ 18 15:27
♅ R 29 14:19	♄ ♏ 22 15:36
	☉ ♏ 23 17:06
	☿ ♐ 31 15:49

Last Aspect Dy Hr Mn	☽ Ingress Dy Hr Mn	Last Aspect Dy Hr Mn	☽ Ingress Dy Hr Mn
1 16:49 ♄ △	♋ 2 3:30	1 13:58 ♄ □	♌ 1 18:53
4 2:18 ♄ □	♌ 4 13:05	4 5:16 ☿ ✶	♍ 4 6:40
6 14:25 ♂ ☌	♍ 7 0:47	6 12:05 ♃ □	♎ 6 19:28
9 2:08 ♃ □	♎ 9 13:27	9 4:41 ♄ ☌	♏ 9 7:56
11 22:31 ♂ ✶	♏ 12 2:05	11 8:33 ♇ □	♐ 11 19:19
14 13:17 ♂ □	♐ 14 13:32	14 2:55 ♄ ✶	♑ 14 4:51
16 14:35 ♄ ✶	♑ 16 22:21	16 10:14 ♄ □	♒ 16 11:34
18 20:42 ♄ □	♒ 19 3:30	18 14:06 ♄ △	♓ 18 14:55
20 23:06 ♄ △	♓ 21 5:06	20 9:47 ♃ □	♈ 20 15:27
23 4:16 ☉ ☍	♈ 23 4:30	22 14:46 ♄ ☍	♉ 22 14:47
24 22:31 ♄ ☍	♉ 25 3:45	24 6:34 ♂ △	♊ 24 15:04
26 19:11 ♇ □	♊ 27 5:01	26 11:47 ♃ ☌	♋ 26 18:24
29 4:50 ♄ △	♋ 29 9:56	28 23:08 ☿ △	♌ 29 1:55
		31 12:58 ☿ □	♍ 31 13:04

☽ Phases & Eclipses Dy Hr Mn	
8 7:48	● 15♍22
16 9:49	☽ 23♐14
23 4:16	○ 29♓51
29 21:51	☾ 6♋27
8 0:40	● 14♎27
15 21:44	☽ 22♑15
22 12:56	○ 28♈50
29 13:09	☾ 5♌49

Astro Data

1 September 1953
Julian Day # 19602
SVP 5♓54'09"
GC 26♐11.5 ⚴ 21♋10.1
Eris 8♈15.8R ✱ 19♋33.9
⚷ 15♑35.2R ⚵ 19♒20.9R
☽ Mean ☊ 1♒11.1

1 October 1953
Julian Day # 19632
SVP 5♓54'06"
GC 26♐11.6 ⚴ 7♌50.4
Eris 7♈57.8R ✱ 4♌22.6
⚷ 15♑23.6 ⚵ 16♒28.3
☽ Mean ☊ 29♑35.8

November 1953 LONGITUDE

Day	Sid.Time	☉	0 hr ☽	Noon☽	True☊	☿	♀	♂	⚳	♃	♄	♅	♆	♇
1 Su	14 41 55	8♏46 25	5♍25 09	11♍20 55	27♑52.7	0♐18.1	17♎11.8	29♍56.4	17♍37.6	25♊58.5	1♏11.5	23♋06.1	24♎11.1	24♌51.7
2 M	14 45 51	9 46 30	17 15 52	23 10 30	27R 45.7	0 33.2	18 26.5	0♎33.7	18 01.8	25R 54.9	1 18.7	23R 05.9	24 13.3	24 52.4
3 Tu	14 49 48	10 46 37	29 05 18	5♎00 39	27 35.9	0R 40.7	19 41.3	1 11.0	18 26.0	25 51.2	1 25.9	23 05.7	24 15.5	24 53.1
4 W	14 53 44	11 46 46	10♎56 54	16 54 21	27 23.8	0 39.9	20 56.1	1 48.2	18 50.0	25 47.3	1 33.1	23 05.4	24 17.6	24 53.8
5 Th	14 57 41	12 46 57	22 53 15	28 53 48	27 10.2	0 30.2	22 11.0	2 25.5	19 14.0	25 43.1	1 40.3	23 05.0	24 19.8	24 54.4
6 F	15 01 38	13 47 10	4♏56 08	11♏00 24	26 56.2	0 11.2	23 25.8	3 02.7	19 37.9	25 38.9	1 47.5	23 04.6	24 21.9	24 55.1
7 Sa	15 05 34	14 47 24	17 06 42	23 15 06	26 43.1	29♏42.4	24 40.7	3 39.9	20 01.7	25 34.4	1 54.7	23 04.2	24 24.1	24 55.6
8 Su	15 09 31	15 47 41	29 25 40	5♐38 29	26 31.8	29 03.7	25 55.7	4 17.1	20 25.4	25 29.7	2 01.8	23 03.6	24 26.2	24 56.2
9 M	15 13 27	16 47 59	11♐53 38	18 11 13	26 23.3	28 15.2	27 10.6	4 54.3	20 48.9	25 24.9	2 09.0	23 03.1	24 28.3	24 56.7
10 Tu	15 17 24	17 48 18	24 31 21	0♑54 12	26 17.7	27 17.5	28 25.6	5 31.5	21 12.4	25 19.9	2 16.1	23 02.5	24 30.4	24 57.2
11 W	15 21 20	18 48 40	7♑19 57	13 48 49	26D 14.9	26 11.6	29 40.6	6 08.6	21 35.8	25 14.7	2 23.2	23 01.8	24 32.5	24 57.7
12 Th	15 25 17	19 49 02	20 21 03	26 56 55	26 14.3	24 58.8	0♏55.6	6 45.7	21 59.1	25 09.4	2 30.2	23 01.1	24 34.6	24 58.1
13 F	15 29 14	20 49 26	3♒36 42	10♒20 41	26R 14.7	23 41.1	2 10.7	7 22.8	22 22.2	25 03.9	2 37.3	23 00.3	24 36.6	24 58.5
14 Sa	15 33 10	21 49 51	17 09 05	24 02 09	26 14.9	22 20.7	3 25.8	7 59.9	22 45.3	24 58.3	2 44.3	22 59.5	24 38.7	24 58.9
15 Su	15 37 07	22 50 18	1♓00 00	8♓02 43	26 13.9	21 00.4	4 40.8	8 37.0	23 08.2	24 52.5	2 51.3	22 58.6	24 40.7	24 59.3
16 M	15 41 03	23 50 46	15 10 12	22 22 16	26 10.7	19 42.6	5 55.9	9 14.0	23 31.1	24 46.5	2 58.2	22 57.7	24 42.7	24 59.6
17 Tu	15 45 00	24 51 15	29 38 35	6♈58 38	26 05.1	18 30.0	7 11.1	9 51.0	23 53.8	24 40.4	3 05.2	22 56.7	24 44.7	24 59.9
18 W	15 48 56	25 51 45	14♈21 42	21 47 00	25 57.3	17 24.8	8 26.2	10 28.1	24 16.4	24 34.1	3 12.1	22 55.7	24 46.7	25 00.1
19 Th	15 52 53	26 52 17	29 13 32	6♉40 14	25 48.0	16 28.9	9 41.4	11 05.0	24 38.9	24 27.8	3 19.0	22 54.6	24 48.7	25 00.4
20 F	15 56 49	27 52 50	14♉06 01	21 29 44	25 38.5	15 43.5	10 56.5	11 42.0	25 01.2	24 21.2	3 25.8	22 53.5	24 50.7	25 00.6
21 Sa	16 00 46	28 53 25	28 50 18	6♊06 44	25 29.9	15 09.5	12 11.7	12 19.0	25 23.5	24 14.6	3 32.7	22 52.3	24 52.6	25 00.8
22 Su	16 04 43	29 54 01	13♊18 11	20 23 57	25 23.1	14 47.2	13 26.9	12 55.9	25 45.6	24 07.8	3 39.5	22 51.1	24 54.5	25 00.9
23 M	16 08 39	0♐54 39	27 23 31	4♋16 32	25 18.7	14D 36.5	14 42.2	13 32.8	26 07.6	24 00.9	3 46.2	22 49.8	24 56.4	25 01.0
24 Tu	16 12 36	1 55 18	11♋02 51	17 42 29	25D 16.6	14 37.0	15 57.4	14 09.7	26 29.4	23 53.9	3 52.9	22 48.5	24 58.3	25 01.1
25 W	16 16 32	2 55 59	24 15 35	0♌42 28	25 16.4	14 47.9	17 12.7	14 46.6	26 51.2	23 46.8	3 59.6	22 47.1	25 00.2	25 01.2
26 Th	16 20 29	3 56 42	7♌03 31	13 19 14	25 17.4	15 08.7	18 28.0	15 23.5	27 12.7	23 39.5	4 06.3	22 45.7	25 02.0	25R 01.2
27 F	16 24 25	4 57 26	19 30 11	25 36 57	25R 18.6	15 38.2	19 43.3	16 00.3	27 34.2	23 32.2	4 12.9	22 44.2	25 03.9	25 01.2
28 Sa	16 28 22	5 58 11	1♍40 11	7♍40 31	25 19.0	16 15.8	20 58.6	16 37.1	27 55.5	23 24.8	4 19.5	22 42.7	25 05.7	25 01.2
29 Su	16 32 18	6 58 58	13 38 38	19 35 10	25 17.9	17 00.4	22 13.9	17 14.0	28 16.7	23 17.2	4 26.0	22 41.2	25 07.5	25 01.1
30 M	16 36 15	7 59 46	25 30 45	1♎25 59	25 14.9	17 51.4	23 29.3	17 50.7	28 37.7	23 09.6	4 32.5	22 39.6	25 09.2	25 01.0

December 1953 LONGITUDE

Day	Sid.Time	☉	0 hr ☽	Noon☽	True☊	☿	♀	♂	⚳	♃	♄	♅	♆	♇
1 Tu	16 40 12	9♐00 36	7♎21 26	13♎17 38	25♑09.8	18♏47.8	24♏44.6	18♎27.5	28♍58.5	23♊01.9	4♏38.9	22♋38.0	25♎11.0	25♌00.9
2 W	16 44 08	10 01 28	19 15 03	25 14 09	25R 02.8	19 49.0	26 00.0	19 04.2	29 19.2	22R 54.2	4 45.3	22R 36.3	25 12.7	25R 00.7
3 Th	16 48 05	11 02 20	1♏15 17	7♏18 47	24 54.7	20 54.4	27 15.4	19 41.0	29 39.8	22 46.3	4 51.7	22 34.6	25 14.4	25 00.5
4 F	16 52 01	12 03 14	13 24 54	19 33 52	24 46.1	22 03.5	28 30.8	20 17.6	0♎00.2	22 38.4	4 58.0	22 32.8	25 16.1	25 00.3
5 Sa	16 55 58	13 04 10	25 45 49	2♐00 51	24 38.1	23 15.6	29 46.2	20 54.3	0 20.4	22 30.5	5 04.3	22 31.0	25 17.7	25 00.1
6 Su	16 59 54	14 05 06	8♐19 02	14 40 21	24 31.3	24 30.5	1♐01.6	21 31.0	0 40.4	22 22.5	5 10.5	22 29.2	25 19.4	24 59.8
7 M	17 03 51	15 06 03	21 04 48	27 32 21	24 26.3	25 47.7	2 17.0	22 07.6	1 00.3	22 14.4	5 16.6	22 27.3	25 21.0	24 59.5
8 Tu	17 07 47	16 07 01	4♑02 54	10♑36 26	24 23.4	27 06.9	3 32.4	22 44.2	1 20.0	22 06.3	5 22.7	22 25.4	25 22.6	24 59.2
9 W	17 11 44	17 08 00	17 12 50	23 52 06	24D 22.4	28 27.9	4 47.9	23 20.7	1 39.5	21 58.2	5 28.8	22 23.4	25 24.1	24 58.8
10 Th	17 15 41	18 09 00	0♒34 08	7♒18 56	24 23.0	29 50.3	6 03.3	23 57.3	1 58.9	21 50.1	5 34.8	22 21.4	25 25.7	24 58.5
11 F	17 19 37	19 10 00	14 06 29	20 56 46	24 24.5	1♐14.0	7 18.8	24 33.8	2 18.0	21 41.9	5 40.8	22 19.4	25 27.2	24 58.0
12 Sa	17 23 34	20 11 01	27 49 46	4♓45 28	24 26.0	2 38.8	8 34.2	25 10.2	2 37.0	21 33.7	5 46.7	22 17.3	25 28.7	24 57.6
13 Su	17 27 30	21 12 03	11♓43 51	18 44 50	24R 26.8	4 04.6	9 49.7	25 46.7	2 55.8	21 25.6	5 52.5	22 15.2	25 30.1	24 57.1
14 M	17 31 27	22 13 04	25 48 19	2♈54 07	24 26.4	5 31.2	11 05.1	26 23.1	3 14.3	21 17.4	5 58.3	22 13.1	25 31.5	24 56.6
15 Tu	17 35 23	23 14 06	10♈02 00	17 11 40	24 24.4	6 58.5	12 20.6	26 59.5	3 32.7	21 09.2	6 04.0	22 10.9	25 32.9	24 56.1
16 W	17 39 20	24 15 09	24 22 42	1♉34 38	24 21.2	8 26.4	13 36.0	27 35.8	3 50.9	21 01.1	6 09.6	22 08.8	25 34.3	24 55.5
17 Th	17 43 16	25 16 12	8♉46 55	15 58 56	24 17.0	9 55.0	14 51.5	28 12.1	4 08.9	20 52.9	6 15.2	22 06.5	25 35.7	24 55.0
18 F	17 47 13	26 17 16	23 10 02	0♊19 30	24 12.5	11 24.0	16 06.9	28 48.4	4 26.7	20 44.8	6 20.8	22 04.3	25 37.0	24 54.4
19 Sa	17 51 10	27 18 20	7♊26 42	14 30 57	24 08.5	12 53.4	17 22.4	29 24.7	4 44.2	20 36.8	6 26.2	22 02.0	25 38.3	24 53.7
20 Su	17 55 06	28 19 24	21 31 38	28 28 13	24 05.4	14 23.3	18 37.9	0♏00.9	5 01.6	20 28.7	6 31.6	21 59.7	25 39.5	24 53.1
21 M	17 59 03	29 20 29	5♋20 15	12♋07 24	24D 03.6	15 53.5	19 53.3	0 37.2	5 18.7	20 20.8	6 37.0	21 57.4	25 40.8	24 52.4
22 Tu	18 02 59	0♑21 35	18 49 24	25 26 09	24 03.1	17 24.1	21 08.8	1 13.3	5 35.6	20 12.8	6 42.2	21 55.1	25 42.0	24 51.7
23 W	18 06 56	1 22 41	1♌57 36	8♌23 53	24 03.7	18 55.0	22 24.3	1 49.5	5 52.3	20 04.9	6 47.5	21 52.7	25 43.1	24 50.9
24 Th	18 10 52	2 23 47	14 45 09	21 01 42	24 05.2	20 26.2	23 39.8	2 25.6	6 08.7	19 57.1	6 52.6	21 50.3	25 44.3	24 50.2
25 F	18 14 49	3 24 54	27 13 53	3♍22 08	24 06.8	21 57.7	24 55.2	3 01.7	6 24.9	19 49.4	6 57.6	21 47.9	25 45.4	24 49.4
26 Sa	18 18 46	4 26 02	9♍26 55	15 28 46	24 08.4	23 29.6	26 10.7	3 37.7	6 40.9	19 41.7	7 02.6	21 45.4	25 46.5	24 48.6
27 Su	18 22 42	5 27 10	21 28 16	27 25 58	24R 09.4	25 01.7	27 26.2	4 13.7	6 56.6	19 34.1	7 07.6	21 43.0	25 47.5	24 47.7
28 M	18 26 39	6 28 18	3♎22 30	9♎18 28	24 09.6	26 34.0	28 41.7	4 49.7	7 12.1	19 26.6	7 12.4	21 40.5	25 48.6	24 46.9
29 Tu	18 30 35	7 29 28	15 14 28	21 11 07	24 08.9	28 06.7	29 57.2	5 25.7	7 27.3	19 19.1	7 17.2	21 38.0	25 49.5	24 46.0
30 W	18 34 32	8 30 37	27 08 58	3♏08 37	24 07.6	29 39.7	1♑12.7	6 01.6	7 42.3	19 11.8	7 21.9	21 35.5	25 50.5	24 45.1
31 Th	18 38 28	9 31 47	9♏10 34	15 15 17	24 05.7	1♑13.0	2 28.2	6 37.4	7 57.0	19 04.6	7 26.5	21 33.0	25 51.4	24 44.1

Astro Data Dy Hr Mn	Planet Ingress Dy Hr Mn	Last Aspect Dy Hr Mn	☽ Ingress Dy Hr Mn	Last Aspect Dy Hr Mn	☽ Ingress Dy Hr Mn	☽ Phases & Eclipses Dy Hr Mn
☽0S 2 6:58	♂ ♎ 1 14:19	2 17:32 ♃ □	♎ 3 1:51	2 11:57 ♆ ☌	♏ 2 21:30	6 17:58 ● 14♏02
☿R 3 21:50	☿ ♏R 6 22:19	5 5:42 ♃ △	♏ 5 14:12	5 7:13 ♀ ☌	♐ 5 8:09	14 7:52 ☽ 21♒39
♂0S 6 6:32	♀ ♏ 11 18:12	7 23:57 ☿ ☌	♐ 8 1:06	7 7:56 ♆ ✶	♑ 7 16:33	20 23:12 ○ 28♉21
♃✶♇ 14 9:25	☉ ♐ 22 14:22	10 6:51 ♀ ✶	♑ 10 10:18	9 21:10 ☿ ✶	♒ 9 22:59	28 8:16 ☾ 5♍49
☽0N 16 8:47		12 8:44 ☿ ✶	♒ 12 17:31	11 19:53 ♆ △	♓ 12 3:46	
♃△♆ 16 23:10	⚳ ♎ 4 11:49	14 13:38 ♇ ☍	♓ 14 22:17	13 17:57 ♅ △	♈ 14 7:06	6 10:48 ● 14♐02
☿D 23 22:57	♀ ♐ 5 16:24	16 15:57 ♃ □	♈ 17 0:35	16 5:05 ♂ ☍	♉ 16 9:22	13 16:30 ☽ 21♓23
♆✶♇ 26 0:50	☿ ♐ 10 14:48	18 17:12 ♇ △	♉ 19 1:15	18 2:55 ♇ □	♊ 18 11:27	20 11:44 ○ 28♊19
♇R 26 20:44	♂ ♏ 20 11:22	20 23:12 ☉ ☍	♊ 21 1:55	20 11:44 ☉ ☍	♋ 20 14:40	28 5:43 ☾ 6♎12
☽0S 29 13:18	☉ ♑ 22 3:31	22 19:54 ♇ ✶	♋ 23 4:31	22 12:29 ♆ □	♌ 22 20:23	
	♀ ♑ 29 12:53	25 1:21 ♆ □	♌ 25 10:40	24 21:07 ♆ ✶	♍ 25 5:24	
♃⚺♅ 5 9:58	☿ ♑ 30 17:14	27 10:55 ♆ □	♍ 27 20:41	27 12:01 ♀ □	♎ 27 17:11	
☽0N 13 14:10		29 19:25 ♃ □	♎ 30 9:06	30 4:00 ☿ ✶	♏ 30 5:43	
♃⚻♄ 15 21:06						
☽0S 26 20:50						

Astro Data

1 November 1953
Julian Day # 19663
SVP 5♓54'02"
GC 26♐11.7 ⚵ 23♌14.0
Eris 7♈39.2R ⚴ 17♌03.1
⚷ 16♑24.4 ⚶ 20♒20.1
☽ Mean ☊ 27♑57.3

1 December 1953
Julian Day # 19693
SVP 5♓53'58"
GC 26♐11.7 ⚵ 4♍36.8
Eris 7♈26.6R ⚴ 25♌10.3
⚷ 18♑22.4 ⚶ 28♒48.7
☽ Mean ☊ 26♑22.0

LONGITUDE January 1954

Day	Sid.Time	☉	0 hr ☽	Noon☽	True☊	☿	♀	♂	⚳	♃	♄	♅	♆	♇
1 F	18 42 25	10♑32 57	21♏23 14	27♏34 46	24♑03.5	2♑46.6	3♑43.7	7♏13.3	8♎11.4	18♊57.5	7♏31.0	21♋30.4	25♎52.3	24♌43.2
2 Sa	18 46 21	11 34 08	3♐50 14	10♐09 50	24R 01.6	4 20.5	4 59.2	7 49.1	8 25.5	18R 50.5	7 35.5	21R 27.9	25 53.2	24R 42.2
3 Su	18 50 18	12 35 19	16 33 48	23 02 11	23 59.9	5 54.8	6 14.7	8 24.8	8 39.4	18 43.6	7 39.9	21 25.3	25 54.0	24 41.2
4 M	18 54 15	13 36 30	29 35 02	6♑12 17	23 58.9	7 29.4	7 30.2	9 00.5	8 53.0	18 36.8	7 44.2	21 22.8	25 54.8	24 40.2
5 Tu	18 58 11	14 37 41	12♑53 48	19 39 23	23D 58.4	9 04.4	8 45.7	9 36.2	9 06.3	18 30.2	7 48.4	21 20.2	25 55.6	24 39.1
6 W	19 02 08	15 38 52	26 28 48	3♒21 41	23 58.5	10 39.7	10 01.2	10 11.8	9 19.3	18 23.7	7 52.5	21 17.6	25 56.3	24 38.1
7 Th	19 06 04	16 40 02	10♒17 44	17 16 31	23 59.0	12 15.4	11 16.7	10 47.4	9 32.0	18 17.3	7 56.6	21 15.0	25 57.0	24 37.0
8 F	19 10 01	17 41 12	24 17 39	1♓20 42	23 59.6	13 51.6	12 32.2	11 22.9	9 44.4	18 11.1	8 00.6	21 12.4	25 57.7	24 35.9
9 Sa	19 13 57	18 42 22	8♓25 16	15 30 57	24 00.2	15 28.1	13 47.7	11 58.3	9 56.5	18 05.0	8 04.4	21 09.8	25 58.3	24 34.8
10 Su	19 17 54	19 43 31	22 37 21	29 44 06	24 00.6	17 05.1	15 03.1	12 33.8	10 08.3	17 59.1	8 08.2	21 07.2	25 58.9	24 33.6
11 M	19 21 50	20 44 39	6♈50 53	13♈57 21	24R 00.8	18 42.5	16 18.6	13 09.1	10 19.8	17 53.3	8 11.9	21 04.6	25 59.5	24 32.5
12 Tu	19 25 47	21 45 47	21 03 13	28 08 13	24 00.8	20 20.4	17 34.1	13 44.5	10 31.0	17 47.7	8 15.6	21 02.0	26 00.0	24 31.3
13 W	19 29 44	22 46 54	5♉12 05	12♉14 35	24 00.7	21 58.8	18 49.5	14 19.7	10 41.8	17 42.2	8 19.1	20 59.4	26 00.5	24 30.1
14 Th	19 33 40	23 48 01	19 15 26	26 14 26	24D 00.6	23 37.6	20 05.0	14 54.9	10 52.3	17 37.0	8 22.5	20 56.8	26 00.9	24 28.9
15 F	19 37 37	24 49 07	3♊11 20	10♊05 53	24 00.7	25 17.0	21 20.4	15 30.1	11 02.5	17 31.8	8 25.9	20 54.2	26 01.4	24 27.6
16 Sa	19 41 33	25 50 12	16 57 54	23 47 07	24 00.8	26 56.8	22 35.9	16 05.2	11 12.3	17 26.9	8 29.1	20 51.6	26 01.8	24 26.4
17 Su	19 45 30	26 51 17	0♋33 20	7♋16 21	24 01.0	28 37.2	23 51.3	16 40.3	11 21.8	17 22.1	8 32.3	20 49.0	26 02.1	24 25.1
18 M	19 49 26	27 52 21	13 56 00	20 32 07	24R 01.2	0♒18.0	25 06.7	17 15.3	11 31.0	17 17.5	8 35.4	20 46.4	26 02.5	24 23.9
19 Tu	19 53 23	28 53 24	27 04 34	3♌33 17	24 01.1	1 59.4	26 22.1	17 50.3	11 39.8	17 13.1	8 38.3	20 43.8	26 02.7	24 22.6
20 W	19 57 19	29 54 27	9♌58 15	16 19 27	24 00.7	3 41.3	27 37.5	18 25.2	11 48.2	17 08.9	8 41.2	20 41.3	26 03.0	24 21.3
21 Th	20 01 16	0♒55 29	22 36 57	28 50 54	24 00.0	5 23.6	28 53.0	19 00.1	11 56.3	17 04.8	8 44.0	20 38.7	26 03.2	24 20.0
22 F	20 05 13	1 56 30	5♍01 26	11♍08 50	23 59.0	7 06.5	0♒08.4	19 34.9	12 04.0	17 01.0	8 46.7	20 36.1	26 03.4	24 18.6
23 Sa	20 09 09	2 57 31	17 13 21	23 15 20	23 57.7	8 49.8	1 23.8	20 09.6	12 11.3	16 57.3	8 49.3	20 33.6	26 03.6	24 17.3
24 Su	20 13 06	3 58 31	29 15 11	5♎13 19	23 56.4	10 33.5	2 39.1	20 44.3	12 18.3	16 53.8	8 51.8	20 31.1	26 03.7	24 15.9
25 M	20 17 02	4 59 31	11♎10 14	17 06 26	23 55.4	12 17.6	3 54.5	21 18.9	12 24.9	16 50.5	8 54.2	20 28.6	26 03.8	24 14.6
26 Tu	20 20 59	6 00 30	23 02 27	28 58 52	23D 54.7	14 01.9	5 09.9	21 53.5	12 31.1	16 47.4	8 56.5	20 26.1	26R 03.8	24 13.2
27 W	20 24 55	7 01 29	4♏56 16	10♏55 13	23 54.6	15 46.5	6 25.3	22 28.0	12 36.9	16 44.5	8 58.7	20 23.6	26 03.8	24 11.8
28 Th	20 28 52	8 02 27	16 56 21	23 00 15	23 55.1	17 31.3	7 40.7	23 02.4	12 42.3	16 41.7	9 00.8	20 21.2	26 03.8	24 10.4
29 F	20 32 48	9 03 24	29 07 28	5♐18 34	23 56.2	19 16.0	8 56.0	23 36.8	12 47.3	16 39.2	9 02.8	20 18.7	26 03.8	24 09.0
30 Sa	20 36 45	10 04 21	11♐34 04	17 54 24	23 57.6	21 00.6	10 11.4	24 11.1	12 51.9	16 36.9	9 04.7	20 16.3	26 03.7	24 07.6
31 Su	20 40 42	11 05 16	24 19 58	0♑51 05	23 59.0	22 45.0	11 26.7	24 45.3	12 56.1	16 34.8	9 06.5	20 13.9	26 03.6	24 06.1

LONGITUDE February 1954

Day	Sid.Time	☉	0 hr ☽	Noon☽	True☊	☿	♀	♂	⚳	♃	♄	♅	♆	♇
1 M	20 44 38	12♒06 12	7♑27 57	14♑10 41	23♑59.9	24♒28.8	12♒42.1	25♏19.5	12♎59.9	16♊32.9	9♏08.2	20♋11.5	26♎03.4	24♌04.7
2 Tu	20 48 35	13 07 06	20 59 17	27 53 35	24R 00.1	26 12.0	13 57.4	25 53.5	13 03.3	16R 31.2	9 09.8	20R 09.2	26R 03.2	24R 03.3
3 W	20 52 31	14 07 59	4♒53 19	11♒58 04	23 59.3	27 54.1	15 12.7	26 27.5	13 06.3	16 29.6	9 11.3	20 06.9	26 03.0	24 01.8
4 Th	20 56 28	15 08 51	19 07 18	26 20 21	23 57.4	29 34.9	16 28.0	27 01.5	13 08.8	16 28.3	9 12.7	20 04.6	26 02.7	24 00.4
5 F	21 00 24	16 09 41	3♓36 27	10♓54 48	23 54.6	1♓13.9	17 43.4	27 35.3	13 10.9	16 27.2	9 13.9	20 02.3	26 02.4	23 58.9
6 Sa	21 04 21	17 10 30	18 14 30	25 34 41	23 51.3	2 50.9	18 58.6	28 09.1	13 12.6	16 26.3	9 15.1	20 00.0	26 02.1	23 57.5
7 Su	21 08 17	18 11 18	2♈54 30	10♈13 09	23 48.0	4 25.2	20 13.9	28 42.7	13 13.8	16 25.6	9 16.2	19 57.8	26 01.8	23 56.0
8 M	21 12 14	19 12 05	17 29 54	24 44 08	23 45.3	5 56.4	21 29.2	29 16.3	13 14.6	16 25.1	9 17.2	19 55.6	26 01.4	23 54.5
9 Tu	21 16 11	20 12 49	1♉55 19	9♉03 05	23D 43.6	7 23.8	22 44.4	29 49.8	13R 15.0	16D 24.9	9 18.0	19 53.5	26 00.9	23 53.0
10 W	21 20 07	21 13 33	16 07 07	23 07 15	23 43.2	8 46.9	23 59.7	0♐23.3	13 15.0	16 24.8	9 18.8	19 51.3	26 00.5	23 51.6
11 Th	21 24 04	22 14 14	0♊03 23	6♊55 31	23 43.9	10 05.0	25 14.9	0 56.6	13 14.5	16 24.9	9 19.4	19 49.3	26 00.0	23 50.1
12 F	21 28 00	23 14 54	13 43 43	20 28 03	23 45.4	11 17.3	26 30.1	1 29.8	13 13.6	16 25.2	9 20.0	19 47.2	25 59.5	23 48.6
13 Sa	21 31 57	24 15 33	27 08 40	3♋45 43	23 47.0	12 23.1	27 45.3	2 03.0	13 12.3	16 25.8	9 20.4	19 45.2	25 58.9	23 47.2
14 Su	21 35 53	25 16 09	10♋19 21	16 49 44	23R 48.2	13 21.7	29 00.4	2 36.0	13 10.5	16 26.5	9 20.8	19 43.2	25 58.4	23 45.7
15 M	21 39 50	26 16 44	23 16 59	29 41 15	23 48.2	14 12.4	0♓15.6	3 09.0	13 08.3	16 27.4	9 21.0	19 41.2	25 57.7	23 44.2
16 Tu	21 43 46	27 17 17	6♌02 39	12♌21 17	23 46.7	14 54.5	1 30.7	3 41.9	13 05.6	16 28.5	9R 21.1	19 39.3	25 57.1	23 42.7
17 W	21 47 43	28 17 49	18 37 15	24 50 38	23 43.3	15 27.5	2 45.9	4 14.7	13 02.6	16 29.9	9 21.2	19 37.4	25 56.4	23 41.3
18 Th	21 51 40	29 18 19	1♍01 32	7♍10 04	23 38.2	15 50.9	4 01.0	4 47.3	12 59.1	16 31.4	9 21.1	19 35.6	25 55.7	23 39.8
19 F	21 55 36	0♓18 48	13 16 19	19 20 25	23 31.8	16R 04.2	5 16.1	5 19.9	12 55.1	16 33.1	9 20.9	19 33.8	25 55.0	23 38.3
20 Sa	21 59 33	1 19 15	25 22 34	1♎22 55	23 24.5	16 07.5	6 31.1	5 52.4	12 50.8	16 35.0	9 20.6	19 32.0	25 54.2	23 36.9
21 Su	22 03 29	2 19 41	7♎21 44	13 19 15	23 17.2	16 00.5	7 46.2	6 24.8	12 46.0	16 37.1	9 20.2	19 30.3	25 53.4	23 35.4
22 M	22 07 26	3 20 05	19 15 49	25 11 47	23 10.6	15 43.6	9 01.2	6 57.0	12 40.8	16 39.4	9 19.7	19 28.6	25 52.6	23 33.9
23 Tu	22 11 22	4 20 28	1♏07 33	7♏03 34	23 05.3	15 17.1	10 16.3	7 29.2	12 35.1	16 41.9	9 19.1	19 27.0	25 51.8	23 32.5
24 W	22 15 19	5 20 49	13 00 20	18 58 22	23 01.8	14 41.8	11 31.3	8 01.3	12 29.1	16 44.6	9 18.5	19 25.4	25 50.9	23 31.0
25 Th	22 19 15	6 21 09	24 58 15	1♐00 32	23D 00.1	13 58.6	12 46.3	8 33.2	12 22.6	16 47.5	9 17.7	19 23.8	25 50.0	23 29.6
26 F	22 23 12	7 21 28	7♐05 52	13 14 50	23 00.1	13 08.5	14 01.3	9 05.0	12 15.7	16 50.6	9 16.8	19 22.3	25 49.0	23 28.2
27 Sa	22 27 09	8 21 45	19 28 04	25 46 10	23 01.2	12 12.9	15 16.2	9 36.7	12 08.5	16 53.8	9 15.7	19 20.9	25 48.1	23 26.7
28 Su	22 31 05	9 22 01	2♑09 41	8♑39 10	23 02.6	11 13.3	16 31.2	10 08.3	12 00.8	16 57.3	9 14.6	19 19.4	25 47.1	23 25.3

Astro Data	Planet Ingress	Last Aspect	☽ Ingress	Last Aspect	☽ Ingress	☽ Phases & Eclipses	Astro Data
Dy Hr Mn	Dy Hr Mn	Dy Hr Mn	Dy Hr Mn	Dy Hr Mn	Dy Hr Mn	Dy Hr Mn	1 January 1954
☽0N 9 19:18	☿ ♒ 18 7:43	1 6:29 ♇ □	♐ 1 16:39	2 8:49 ♆ □	♒ 2 15:38	5 2:21 ● 14♑13	Julian Day # 19724
☽0S 23 5:13	☉ ♒ 20 14:11	3 17:16 ♆ ⚹	♑ 4 0:45	4 13:11 ♂ □	♓ 4 18:03	5 2:31:27 ◐ A 01'42"	SVP 5♓53'52"
♆R 27 10:50	♀ ♒ 22 9:20	5 23:02 ♆ □	♒ 6 6:09	6 16:23 ♂ △	♈ 6 19:14	12 0:22 ☽ 21♈16	GC 26♐11.8 ⚴ 9♍53.1
		8 2:50 ♆ △	♓ 8 9:43	8 14:09 ♆ ☍	♉ 8 20:47	19 2:37 ○ 28♋30	Eris 7♈23.3 ⚵ 26♌54.0R
☽0N 6 2:44	☿ ♓ 4 18:03	9 21:31 ♅ △	♈ 10 12:27	10 13:39 ♀ □	♊ 10 23:54	19 2:32 ◑ T 1.032	⚷ 21♑02.2 ⚶ 10♓24.8
⚳R 9 21:40	♂ ♐ 9 19:18	12 8:22 ♆ ☍	♉ 12 15:10	12 23:58 ♀ △	♋ 13 5:10	27 3:28 ☾ 6♏40	☽ Mean ☊ 24♑43.5
♃D 10 9:26	♀ ♓ 15 7:01	14 8:59 ♇ □	♊ 14 18:29	15 5:01 ♆ □	♌ 15 12:35		
♄R 17 6:16	☉ ♓ 19 4:32	16 15:58 ♆ △	♋ 16 23:01	17 19:17 ☉ ☍	♍ 17 22:00	3 15:55 ● 14♒18	1 February 1954
☽0S 19 13:18		19 2:37 ☉ ☍	♌ 19 5:24	19 12:26 ♅ ⚹	♎ 20 9:14	10 8:29 ☽ 21♉05	Julian Day # 19755
☿R 20 7:32		21 6:36 ♆ ⚹	♍ 21 14:14	22 13:23 ♆ ☌	♏ 22 21:43	17 19:17 ○ 28♌36	SVP 5♓53'46"
		23 6:39 ♅ ⚹	♎ 24 1:30	24 21:05 ♇ □	♐ 25 10:00	25 23:29 ☾ 6♐50	GC 26♐11.9 ⚴ 5♍33.6R
		26 6:07 ♆ ☌	♏ 26 14:03	27 12:04 ♆ ⚹	♑ 27 19:58		Eris 7♈31.1 ⚵ 21♌09.3R
		28 14:18 ♇ □	♐ 29 1:42				⚷ 23♑51.7 ⚶ 23♓34.9
		31 3:12 ♆ ⚹	♑ 31 10:27				☽ Mean ☊ 23♑05.0

March 1954

LONGITUDE

Day	Sid.Time	☉	0 hr ☽	Noon ☽	True ☊	☿	♀	♂	⚳	♃	♄	♅	♆	♇
1 M	22 35 02	10♓22 15	15♑15 01	21♑57 35	23♑03.3	10♓11.2	17♓46.1	10♐39.7	11♎52.7	17♊00.9	9♏13.4	19♋18.1	25♎46.1	23♌23.9
2 Tu	22 38 58	11 22 27	28 47 07	5♒43 40	23R 02.6	9R 08.1	19 01.1	11 11.0	11R 44.3	17 04.7	9R 12.1	19R 16.8	25R 45.0	23R 22.5
3 W	22 42 55	12 22 38	12♒47 09	19 57 16	22 59.8	8 05.5	20 16.0	11 42.2	11 35.5	17 08.7	9 10.7	19 15.5	25 44.0	23 21.1
4 Th	22 46 51	13 22 48	27 13 33	4♓35 18	22 54.7	7 04.8	21 30.9	12 13.2	11 26.3	17 12.9	9 09.2	19 14.2	25 42.9	23 19.8
5 F	22 50 48	14 22 55	12♓01 39	19 31 31	22 47.6	6 07.2	22 45.7	12 44.1	11 16.8	17 17.2	9 07.6	19 13.1	25 41.8	23 18.4
6 Sa	22 54 44	15 23 00	27 03 46	4♈37 06	22 39.4	5 13.9	24 00.6	13 14.8	11 06.9	17 21.8	9 05.9	19 11.9	25 40.6	23 17.0
7 Su	22 58 41	16 23 04	12♈10 16	19 41 58	22 31.0	4 25.6	25 15.4	13 45.4	10 56.7	17 26.5	9 04.1	19 10.8	25 39.4	23 15.7
8 M	23 02 38	17 23 05	27 11 05	4♉36 34	22 23.6	3 43.0	26 30.2	14 15.9	10 46.2	17 31.4	9 02.2	19 09.8	25 38.3	23 14.4
9 Tu	23 06 34	18 23 05	11♉57 33	19 13 23	22 18.0	3 06.6	27 45.0	14 46.2	10 35.3	17 36.4	9 00.2	19 08.8	25 37.0	23 13.0
10 W	23 10 31	19 23 02	26 23 34	3♊27 51	22 14.7	2 36.6	28 59.7	15 16.3	10 24.2	17 41.7	8 58.2	19 07.9	25 35.8	23 11.7
11 Th	23 14 27	20 22 57	10♊26 06	17 18 22	22D 13.5	2 13.3	0♈14.4	15 46.3	10 12.8	17 47.1	8 56.0	19 07.0	25 34.6	23 10.4
12 F	23 18 24	21 22 50	24 04 50	0♋45 45	22 13.8	1 56.5	1 29.1	16 16.1	10 01.1	17 52.6	8 53.7	19 06.2	25 33.3	23 09.2
13 Sa	23 22 20	22 22 41	7♋21 28	13 52 21	22R 14.5	1 46.2	2 43.8	16 45.7	9 49.2	17 58.4	8 51.4	19 05.4	25 32.0	23 07.9
14 Su	23 26 17	23 22 29	20 18 50	26 41 18	22 14.7	1D 42.3	3 58.5	17 15.2	9 37.0	18 04.2	8 48.9	19 04.7	25 30.7	23 06.7
15 M	23 30 13	24 22 15	3♌00 11	9♌15 52	22 13.2	1 44.6	5 13.1	17 44.5	9 24.6	18 10.3	8 46.4	19 04.0	25 29.4	23 05.4
16 Tu	23 34 10	25 21 59	15 28 41	21 38 59	22 09.3	1 52.7	6 27.7	18 13.6	9 12.1	18 16.5	8 43.8	19 03.4	25 28.0	23 04.2
17 W	23 38 07	26 21 41	27 47 02	3♍53 07	22 02.6	2 06.4	7 42.3	18 42.6	8 59.3	18 22.9	8 41.1	19 02.8	25 26.6	23 03.0
18 Th	23 42 03	27 21 21	9♍57 25	16 00 09	21 53.3	2 25.4	8 56.8	19 11.3	8 46.3	18 29.4	8 38.3	19 02.3	25 25.2	23 01.8
19 F	23 46 00	28 20 58	22 01 29	28 01 33	21 41.7	2 49.5	10 11.3	19 39.9	8 33.2	18 36.1	8 35.5	19 01.8	25 23.8	23 00.7
20 Sa	23 49 56	29 20 34	4♎00 31	9♎58 32	21 28.9	3 18.3	11 25.8	20 08.3	8 19.9	18 42.9	8 32.5	19 01.4	25 22.4	22 59.5
21 Su	23 53 53	0♈20 07	15 55 45	21 52 20	21 15.8	3 51.6	12 40.3	20 36.5	8 06.5	18 49.8	8 29.5	19 01.0	25 21.0	22 58.4
22 M	23 57 49	1 19 39	27 48 29	3♏44 27	21 03.5	4 29.0	13 54.7	21 04.5	7 53.0	18 57.0	8 26.4	19 00.7	25 19.5	22 57.3
23 Tu	0 01 46	2 19 09	9♏40 28	15 36 53	20 53.0	5 10.4	15 09.2	21 32.3	7 39.4	19 04.2	8 23.2	19 00.4	25 18.0	22 56.2
24 W	0 05 42	3 18 37	21 34 01	27 32 18	20 45.1	5 55.5	16 23.6	21 59.9	7 25.7	19 11.6	8 20.0	19 00.2	25 16.6	22 55.1
25 Th	0 09 39	4 18 03	3♐32 09	9♐34 05	20 39.9	6 44.1	17 37.9	22 27.3	7 12.0	19 19.2	8 16.7	19 00.1	25 15.1	22 54.1
26 F	0 13 35	5 17 28	15 38 37	21 46 20	20 37.3	7 36.0	18 52.3	22 54.4	6 58.2	19 26.9	8 13.3	19 00.0	25 13.5	22 53.1
27 Sa	0 17 32	6 16 50	27 57 49	4♑13 40	20D 36.5	8 31.0	20 06.6	23 21.4	6 44.4	19 34.7	8 09.8	19D 00.0	25 12.0	22 52.0
28 Su	0 21 29	7 16 11	10♑34 31	17 00 56	20R 36.6	9 29.0	21 20.9	23 48.0	6 30.6	19 42.7	8 06.3	19 00.0	25 10.5	22 51.1
29 M	0 25 25	8 15 31	23 33 29	0♒12 41	20 36.4	10 29.6	22 35.2	24 14.5	6 16.8	19 50.8	8 02.7	19 00.0	25 08.9	22 50.1
30 Tu	0 29 22	9 14 48	6♒58 54	13 52 28	20 34.7	11 33.0	23 49.4	24 40.7	6 03.1	19 59.0	7 59.0	19 00.2	25 07.4	22 49.1
31 W	0 33 18	10 14 04	20 53 28	28 01 53	20 30.6	12 38.8	25 03.6	25 06.7	5 49.3	20 07.4	7 55.3	19 00.3	25 05.8	22 48.2

April 1954

LONGITUDE

Day	Sid.Time	☉	0 hr ☽	Noon ☽	True ☊	☿	♀	♂	⚳	♃	♄	♅	♆	♇
1 Th	0 37 15	11♈13 17	5♓17 25	12♓39 37	20♑23.8	13♓47.0	26♈17.8	25♐32.3	5♎35.7	20♊15.8	7♏51.5	19♋00.6	25♎04.2	22♌47.3
2 F	0 41 11	12 12 29	20 07 43	27 40 45	20R 14.5	14 57.5	27 32.0	25 57.8	5R 22.1	20 24.5	7R 47.7	19 00.8	25R 02.6	22R 46.4
3 Sa	0 45 08	13 11 39	5♈17 32	12♈56 44	20 03.7	16 10.1	28 46.1	26 22.9	5 08.7	20 33.2	7 43.8	19 01.2	25 01.0	22 45.6
4 Su	0 49 04	14 10 47	20 36 53	28 16 29	19 52.4	17 24.8	0♉00.3	26 47.8	4 55.3	20 42.1	7 39.8	19 01.6	24 59.4	22 44.8
5 M	0 53 01	15 09 53	5♉54 06	13♉28 21	19 42.2	18 41.6	1 14.3	27 12.3	4 42.1	20 51.1	7 35.8	19 02.0	24 57.8	22 44.0
6 Tu	0 56 58	16 08 56	20 58 04	28 22 16	19 34.0	20 00.3	2 28.4	27 36.6	4 29.1	21 00.2	7 31.8	19 02.5	24 56.2	22 43.2
7 W	1 00 54	17 07 58	5♊40 10	12♊51 17	19 28.6	21 20.9	3 42.4	28 00.6	4 16.2	21 09.4	7 27.7	19 03.1	24 54.6	22 42.4
8 Th	1 04 51	18 06 57	19 55 18	26 52 09	19 25.7	22 43.3	4 56.4	28 24.3	4 03.6	21 18.8	7 23.6	19 03.7	24 53.0	22 41.7
9 F	1 08 47	19 05 54	3♋41 57	10♋24 57	19 24.8	24 07.5	6 10.4	28 47.7	3 51.1	21 28.2	7 19.4	19 04.4	24 51.3	22 41.0
10 Sa	1 12 44	20 04 49	17 01 30	23 32 04	19 24.7	25 33.5	7 24.3	29 10.7	3 38.9	21 37.8	7 15.1	19 05.1	24 49.7	22 40.3
11 Su	1 16 40	21 03 41	29 57 09	6♌17 18	19 24.2	27 01.2	8 38.2	29 33.5	3 26.9	21 47.5	7 10.9	19 05.8	24 48.1	22 39.7
12 M	1 20 37	22 02 31	12♌33 04	18 44 59	19 22.2	28 30.6	9 52.1	29 55.9	3 15.1	21 57.3	7 06.6	19 06.7	24 46.4	22 39.0
13 Tu	1 24 33	23 01 18	24 53 36	0♍59 24	19 17.8	0♈01.6	11 05.9	0♑17.9	3 03.6	22 07.1	7 02.3	19 07.5	24 44.8	22 38.4
14 W	1 28 30	24 00 04	7♍02 51	13 04 21	19 10.5	1 34.4	12 19.7	0 39.7	2 52.4	22 17.1	6 57.9	19 08.4	24 43.1	22 37.8
15 Th	1 32 27	24 58 47	19 04 18	25 03 01	19 00.4	3 08.7	13 33.4	1 01.0	2 41.4	22 27.2	6 53.5	19 09.4	24 41.5	22 37.3
16 F	1 36 23	25 57 28	1♎00 48	6♎57 54	18 48.0	4 44.8	14 47.1	1 22.0	2 30.8	22 37.4	6 49.1	19 10.4	24 39.8	22 36.8
17 Sa	1 40 20	26 56 07	12 54 32	18 50 54	18 34.2	6 22.4	16 00.8	1 42.7	2 20.4	22 47.7	6 44.6	19 11.5	24 38.2	22 36.3
18 Su	1 44 16	27 54 44	24 47 11	0♏43 32	18 20.1	8 01.7	17 14.5	2 03.0	2 10.4	22 58.1	6 40.2	19 12.7	24 36.6	22 35.8
19 M	1 48 13	28 53 20	6♏40 07	12 37 07	18 06.8	9 42.7	18 28.1	2 22.8	2 00.7	23 08.6	6 35.7	19 13.8	24 34.9	22 35.3
20 Tu	1 52 09	29 51 53	18 34 43	24 33 06	17 55.4	11 25.2	19 41.7	2 42.3	1 51.4	23 19.2	6 31.2	19 15.1	24 33.3	22 34.9
21 W	1 56 06	0♉50 25	0♐32 32	6♐33 16	17 46.5	13 09.5	20 55.3	3 01.4	1 42.3	23 29.9	6 26.6	19 16.3	24 31.7	22 34.5
22 Th	2 00 02	1 48 55	12 35 37	18 39 56	17 40.5	14 55.4	22 08.8	3 20.1	1 33.7	23 40.6	6 22.1	19 17.7	24 30.0	22 34.2
23 F	2 03 59	2 47 23	24 46 36	0♑56 04	17 37.3	16 42.9	23 22.3	3 38.3	1 25.4	23 51.5	6 17.6	19 19.1	24 28.4	22 33.8
24 Sa	2 07 56	3 45 50	7♑08 47	13 25 16	17D 36.2	18 32.2	24 35.8	3 56.1	1 17.4	24 02.4	6 13.0	19 20.5	24 26.8	22 33.5
25 Su	2 11 52	4 44 15	19 46 01	26 11 34	17R 36.3	20 23.1	25 49.2	4 13.5	1 09.8	24 13.5	6 08.5	19 22.0	24 25.2	22 33.3
26 M	2 15 49	5 42 38	2♒42 25	9♒19 05	17 36.4	22 15.7	27 02.6	4 30.4	1 02.6	24 24.6	6 03.9	19 23.5	24 23.6	22 33.0
27 Tu	2 19 45	6 41 00	16 01 58	22 51 27	17 35.4	24 10.0	28 16.0	4 46.8	0 55.8	24 35.8	5 59.3	19 25.1	24 22.0	22 32.8
28 W	2 23 42	7 39 21	29 47 44	6♓50 58	17 32.4	26 05.9	29 29.3	5 02.7	0 49.4	24 47.1	5 54.8	19 26.7	24 20.4	22 32.6
29 Th	2 27 38	8 37 39	14♓01 02	21 17 40	17 27.0	28 03.6	0♊42.6	5 18.1	0 43.4	24 58.4	5 50.2	19 28.4	24 18.8	22 32.4
30 F	2 31 35	9 35 57	28 40 24	6♈08 31	17 19.3	0♉02.8	1 55.9	5 33.1	0 37.7	25 09.9	5 45.7	19 30.1	24 17.2	22 32.3

Astro Data	Dy Hr Mn
☽0N	5 12:48
♀0N	13 15:15
☿D	14 15:07
☽0S	18 20:04
☉0N	21 3:54
♃⊻♅	22 23:57
♅D	27 17:31
☽0N	1 23:43
♃⊡♄	13 3:46
☽0S	15 1:34
♃✱♇	16 10:30
☿0N	17 3:43
♃△♆	26 10:03
☽0N	29 9:15

Planet Ingress		Dy Hr Mn
♀	♈	11 7:22
☉	♈	21 3:53
♀	♉	4 11:55
♂	♑	12 16:28
☿	♈	13 11:34
☉	♉	20 15:20
♀	♊	28 22:03
☿	♉	30 11:26

Last Aspect Dy Hr Mn			☽ Ingress	Dy Hr Mn
1 18:43	♆	□	♒	2 2:07
3 21:32	♆	△	♓	4 4:32
5 17:37	♀	☌	♈	6 4:40
7 21:32	♆	☍	♉	8 4:32
10 3:40	♀	✱	♊	10 6:06
12 2:39	♆	△	♋	12 10:37
14 9:47	♆	□	♌	14 18:17
16 19:27	♆	✱	♍	17 4:21
19 12:42	☉	☍	♎	19 15:57
21 19:01	♆	☌	♏	22 4:26
24 2:44	♇	□	♐	24 16:56
26 18:42	♆	✱	♑	27 3:55
29 2:54	♆	□	♒	29 11:37
31 7:06	♆	△	♓	31 15:16

Last Aspect Dy Hr Mn			☽ Ingress	Dy Hr Mn
2 9:12	♂	□	♈	2 15:40
4 9:37	♂	△	♉	4 14:43
6 2:50	♇	□	♊	6 14:40
8 14:46	♂	☍	♋	8 17:29
10 16:15	☿	△	♌	11 0:05
12 23:44	♆	✱	♍	13 10:03
15 6:43	♃	□	♎	15 21:58
18 5:48	☉	☍	♏	18 10:32
20 8:03	♇	□	♐	20 22:55
22 23:26	♆	✱	♑	23 10:11
25 11:14	♀	△	♒	25 19:02
27 22:16	♀	□	♓	28 0:21
29 18:05	♃	□	♈	30 2:08

☽ Phases & Eclipses Dy Hr Mn	
5 3:11	● 14♓01
11 17:52	☽ 20♊38
19 12:42	○ 28♍23
27 16:14	☾ 6♑27
3 12:25	● 13♈13
10 5:05	☽ 19♋48
18 5:48	○ 27♎40
26 4:57	☾ 5♒26

Astro Data

1 March 1954
Julian Day # 19783
SVP 5♓53'42"
GC 26♐11.9 ⚴ 26♌31.8R
Eris 7♈45.9 ⚵ 14♌35.0R
⚷ 26♑08.3 ⚶ 6♈08.5
☽ Mean ☊ 21♑36.1

1 April 1954
Julian Day # 19814
SVP 5♓53'39"
GC 26♐12.0 ⚴ 21♌20.5R
Eris 8♈06.9 ⚵ 12♌40.3
⚷ 27♑56.2 ⚶ 20♈18.0
☽ Mean ☊ 19♑57.6

LONGITUDE — May 1954

Day	Sid.Time	☉	0 hr ☽	Noon☽	True☊	☿	♀	♂	⚳	♃	♄	♅	♆	♇
1 Sa	2 35 31	10♉34 12	13♈41 03	21♈16 55	17♑10.0	2♉03.7	3♊09.1	5♑47.5	0♎32.5	25♊21.4	5♏41.1	19♋31.9	24♎15.6	22♌32.2
2 Su	2 39 28	11 32 26	28 54 47	6♉33 18	17R 00.2	4 06.1	4 22.3	6 01.3	0R 27.7	25 33.0	5R 36.6	19 33.7	24R 14.1	22R 32.1
3 M	2 43 25	12 30 39	14♉11 00	21 46 32	16 51.2	6 10.1	5 35.5	6 14.6	0 23.3	25 44.6	5 32.1	19 35.5	24 12.5	22 32.0
4 Tu	2 47 21	13 28 49	29 18 33	6♊45 56	16 44.0	8 15.4	6 48.6	6 27.4	0 19.3	25 56.4	5 27.5	19 37.4	24 11.0	22D 32.0
5 W	2 51 18	14 26 58	14♊07 42	21 23 07	16 39.2	10 22.0	8 01.7	6 39.6	0 15.7	26 08.2	5 23.1	19 39.4	24 09.5	22 32.0
6 Th	2 55 14	15 25 06	28 31 40	5♋33 03	16D 36.8	12 29.7	9 14.8	6 51.2	0 12.5	26 20.1	5 18.6	19 41.4	24 07.9	22 32.1
7 F	2 59 11	16 23 11	12♋27 10	19 14 07	16 36.3	14 38.5	10 27.8	7 02.3	0 09.7	26 32.0	5 14.2	19 43.4	24 06.5	22 32.1
8 Sa	3 03 07	17 21 14	25 54 07	2♌27 32	16 36.9	16 48.1	11 40.8	7 12.8	0 07.4	26 44.0	5 09.7	19 45.5	24 05.0	22 32.2
9 Su	3 07 04	18 19 15	8♌54 49	15 16 30	16R 37.5	18 58.3	12 53.8	7 22.6	0 05.5	26 56.1	5 05.4	19 47.6	24 03.5	22 32.3
10 M	3 11 00	19 17 14	21 33 08	27 45 17	16 37.2	21 08.8	14 06.7	7 31.9	0 03.9	27 08.2	5 01.0	19 49.8	24 02.0	22 32.5
11 Tu	3 14 57	20 15 12	3♍53 34	9♍58 33	16 35.0	23 19.5	15 19.6	7 40.5	0 02.8	27 20.4	4 56.7	19 52.0	24 00.6	22 32.7
12 W	3 18 54	21 13 08	16 00 48	22 00 51	16 30.8	25 30.0	16 32.4	7 48.5	0 02.1	27 32.7	4 52.4	19 54.3	23 59.2	22 32.9
13 Th	3 22 50	22 11 01	27 59 13	3♎56 21	16 24.3	27 40.1	17 45.2	7 55.8	0D 01.8	27 45.0	4 48.1	19 56.5	23 57.8	22 33.1
14 F	3 26 47	23 08 54	9♎52 41	15 48 36	16 15.9	29 49.5	18 57.9	8 02.5	0 02.0	27 57.4	4 43.9	19 58.9	23 56.4	22 33.4
15 Sa	3 30 43	24 06 44	21 44 26	27 40 30	16 06.4	1♊57.9	20 10.6	8 08.6	0 02.5	28 09.8	4 39.7	20 01.2	23 55.0	22 33.7
16 Su	3 34 40	25 04 33	3♏37 04	9♏34 22	15 56.6	4 05.0	21 23.3	8 13.9	0 03.4	28 22.3	4 35.6	20 03.7	23 53.6	22 34.0
17 M	3 38 36	26 02 21	15 32 37	21 31 59	15 47.4	6 10.6	22 35.9	8 18.6	0 04.7	28 34.8	4 31.5	20 06.1	23 52.3	22 34.3
18 Tu	3 42 33	27 00 07	27 32 40	3♐34 50	15 39.6	8 14.3	23 48.5	8 22.6	0 06.4	28 47.4	4 27.5	20 08.6	23 51.0	22 34.7
19 W	3 46 29	27 57 52	9♐38 39	15 44 18	15 33.7	10 16.1	25 01.0	8 25.9	0 08.5	29 00.0	4 23.5	20 11.1	23 49.7	22 35.1
20 Th	3 50 26	28 55 35	21 51 59	28 01 54	15 30.0	12 15.7	26 13.5	8 28.5	0 11.0	29 12.7	4 19.5	20 13.7	23 48.4	22 35.5
21 F	3 54 23	29 53 18	4♑14 17	10♑29 24	15D 28.4	14 12.9	27 26.0	8 30.4	0 13.9	29 25.4	4 15.6	20 16.3	23 47.1	22 36.0
22 Sa	3 58 19	0♊50 59	16 47 32	23 09 00	15 28.6	16 07.6	28 38.4	8 31.5	0 17.1	29 38.2	4 11.8	20 18.9	23 45.9	22 36.5
23 Su	4 02 16	1 48 39	29 34 06	6♒03 12	15 29.7	17 59.7	29 50.8	8R 31.9	0 20.8	29 51.0	4 08.0	20 21.6	23 44.7	22 37.0
24 M	4 06 12	2 46 18	12♒36 38	19 14 43	15 31.0	19 49.0	1♋03.1	8 31.6	0 24.8	0♋03.9	4 04.3	20 24.3	23 43.5	22 37.5
25 Tu	4 10 09	3 43 56	25 57 45	2♓45 59	15R 31.7	21 35.6	2 15.4	8 30.5	0 29.2	0 16.8	4 00.6	20 27.0	23 42.3	22 38.1
26 W	4 14 05	4 41 33	9♓39 36	16 38 41	15 31.1	23 19.2	3 27.6	8 28.6	0 33.9	0 29.8	3 57.0	20 29.8	23 41.1	22 38.7
27 Th	4 18 02	5 39 09	23 43 13	0♈53 02	15 28.8	25 00.0	4 39.8	8 26.0	0 39.0	0 42.8	3 53.5	20 32.6	23 40.0	22 39.3
28 F	4 21 58	6 36 44	8♈07 51	15 27 09	15 25.0	26 37.7	5 52.0	8 22.6	0 44.5	0 55.8	3 50.0	20 35.5	23 38.9	22 40.0
29 Sa	4 25 55	7 34 19	22 50 19	0♉16 33	15 20.0	28 12.5	7 04.1	8 18.4	0 50.3	1 08.8	3 46.6	20 38.3	23 37.8	22 40.7
30 Su	4 29 52	8 31 53	7♉44 55	15 14 23	15 14.6	29 44.2	8 16.2	8 13.5	0 56.5	1 21.9	3 43.2	20 41.2	23 36.7	22 41.4
31 M	4 33 48	9 29 25	22 43 50	0♊12 07	15 09.6	1♋12.9	9 28.3	8 07.8	1 03.0	1 35.1	3 40.0	20 44.2	23 35.7	22 42.1

LONGITUDE — June 1954

Day	Sid.Time	☉	0 hr ☽	Noon☽	True☊	☿	♀	♂	⚳	♃	♄	♅	♆	♇
1 Tu	4 37 45	10♊26 57	7♊38 09	15♊00 52	15♑05.7	2♋38.4	10♋40.2	8♑01.3	1♎09.9	1♋48.3	3♏36.8	20♋47.2	23♎34.7	22♌42.9
2 W	4 41 41	11 24 28	22 19 21	29 32 47	15R 03.2	4 00.8	11 52.2	7R 54.1	1 17.1	2 01.5	3R 33.6	20 50.2	23R 33.7	22 43.7
3 Th	4 45 38	12 21 57	6♋40 34	13♋42 13	15D 02.3	5 20.0	13 04.1	7 46.2	1 24.6	2 14.7	3 30.6	20 53.2	23 32.8	22 44.5
4 F	4 49 34	13 19 26	20 37 27	27 26 09	15 02.8	6 35.9	14 15.9	7 37.5	1 32.5	2 28.0	3 27.6	20 56.2	23 31.8	22 45.3
5 Sa	4 53 31	14 16 53	4♌08 20	10♌44 10	15 04.2	7 48.6	15 27.7	7 28.1	1 40.7	2 41.3	3 24.7	20 59.3	23 30.9	22 46.2
6 Su	4 57 27	15 14 19	17 13 56	23 37 59	15 05.7	8 58.0	16 39.5	7 18.1	1 49.3	2 54.6	3 21.9	21 02.4	23 30.0	22 47.1
7 M	5 01 24	16 11 44	29 56 47	6♍10 50	15R 07.0	10 03.9	17 51.2	7 07.3	1 58.1	3 07.9	3 19.2	21 05.6	23 29.2	22 48.0
8 Tu	5 05 21	17 09 08	12♍20 39	18 26 49	15 07.4	11 06.4	19 02.8	6 55.9	2 07.3	3 21.3	3 16.5	21 08.7	23 28.3	22 48.9
9 W	5 09 17	18 06 31	24 29 55	0♎30 30	15 06.7	12 05.3	20 14.4	6 43.8	2 16.7	3 34.7	3 13.9	21 11.9	23 27.5	22 49.9
10 Th	5 13 14	19 03 52	6♎29 09	12 26 25	15 04.8	13 00.6	21 25.9	6 31.1	2 26.5	3 48.1	3 11.4	21 15.1	23 26.8	22 50.9
11 F	5 17 10	20 01 13	18 22 50	24 18 54	15 01.9	13 52.3	22 37.4	6 17.8	2 36.6	4 01.6	3 09.0	21 18.4	23 26.0	22 51.9
12 Sa	5 21 07	20 58 33	0♏15 04	6♏11 48	14 58.3	14 40.1	23 48.8	6 03.9	2 46.9	4 15.0	3 06.7	21 21.6	23 25.3	22 52.9
13 Su	5 25 03	21 55 51	12 09 28	18 08 26	14 54.5	15 24.0	25 00.2	5 49.4	2 57.6	4 28.5	3 04.5	21 24.9	23 24.6	22 54.0
14 M	5 29 00	22 53 09	24 09 02	0♐11 31	14 50.9	16 04.0	26 11.5	5 34.4	3 08.5	4 42.0	3 02.3	21 28.2	23 24.0	22 55.1
15 Tu	5 32 56	23 50 27	6♐16 10	12 23 11	14 48.0	16 39.8	27 22.7	5 19.0	3 19.7	4 55.5	3 00.3	21 31.5	23 23.3	22 56.2
16 W	5 36 53	24 47 44	18 32 45	24 45 00	14 45.9	17 11.5	28 33.9	5 03.0	3 31.2	5 09.0	2 58.3	21 34.9	23 22.7	22 57.3
17 Th	5 40 50	25 45 00	1♑00 06	7♑18 09	14D 44.9	17 38.9	29 45.0	4 46.6	3 42.9	5 22.6	2 56.4	21 38.2	23 22.2	22 58.5
18 F	5 44 46	26 42 15	13 39 15	20 03 29	14 44.8	18 02.0	0♌56.0	4 29.8	3 54.9	5 36.1	2 54.6	21 41.6	23 21.6	22 59.7
19 Sa	5 48 43	27 39 31	26 30 57	3♒01 43	14 45.5	18 20.6	2 07.0	4 12.7	4 07.2	5 49.7	2 52.9	21 45.0	23 21.1	23 00.9
20 Su	5 52 39	28 36 45	9♒35 52	16 13 29	14 46.6	18 34.7	3 17.9	3 55.2	4 19.7	6 03.2	2 51.3	21 48.5	23 20.6	23 02.1
21 M	5 56 36	29 34 00	22 54 36	29 39 17	14 47.8	18 44.2	4 28.8	3 37.4	4 32.5	6 16.8	2 49.8	21 51.9	23 20.2	23 03.3
22 Tu	6 00 32	0♋31 14	6♓27 35	13♓19 30	14 48.8	18R 49.2	5 39.6	3 19.3	4 45.5	6 30.4	2 48.4	21 55.3	23 19.8	23 04.6
23 W	6 04 29	1 28 29	20 15 00	27 14 03	14R 49.3	18 49.6	6 50.3	3 01.0	4 58.8	6 44.0	2 47.1	21 58.8	23 19.4	23 05.9
24 Th	6 08 26	2 25 43	4♈16 30	11♈22 10	14 49.2	18 45.5	8 01.0	2 42.6	5 12.3	6 57.6	2 45.8	22 02.3	23 19.0	23 07.2
25 F	6 12 22	3 22 57	18 30 48	25 42 04	14 48.5	18 36.9	9 11.6	2 24.0	5 26.1	7 11.3	2 44.7	22 05.8	23 18.7	23 08.5
26 Sa	6 16 19	4 20 11	2♉55 32	10♉10 42	14 47.5	18 24.1	10 22.1	2 05.4	5 40.1	7 24.9	2 43.6	22 09.3	23 18.4	23 09.9
27 Su	6 20 15	5 17 26	17 27 00	24 43 47	14 46.4	18 07.0	11 32.6	1 46.7	5 54.3	7 38.5	2 42.7	22 12.9	23 18.1	23 11.2
28 M	6 24 12	6 14 40	2♊00 22	9♊16 01	14 45.4	17 46.1	12 43.0	1 28.0	6 08.7	7 52.1	2 41.8	22 16.4	23 17.9	23 12.6
29 Tu	6 28 08	7 11 54	16 30 01	23 41 38	14 44.7	17 21.5	13 53.3	1 09.4	6 23.4	8 05.8	2 41.1	22 20.0	23 17.7	23 14.0
30 W	6 32 05	8 09 09	0♋50 12	7♋55 05	14D 44.4	16 53.6	15 03.6	0 50.9	6 38.3	8 19.4	2 40.4	22 23.5	23 17.5	23 15.5

Astro Data (Dy Hr Mn)

	Dy Hr Mn
♇ D	4 17:45
☽0S	12 6:52
⚳ D	13 17:10
♂ R	23 12:47
☽0N	26 16:23
♃△♄	8 4:48
☽0S	8 13:15
☽0N	22 21:47
☿ R	23 2:08
♃∠♇	30 4:14

Planet Ingress

	Dy Hr Mn
☿ ♊	14 13:57
☉ ♊	21 14:47
♀ ♋	23 15:04
♃ ♋	24 4:43
☿ ♋	30 16:13
♀ ♌	17 17:04
☉ ♋	21 22:54

Last Aspect / ☽ Ingress

Last Aspect Dy Hr Mn		☽ Ingress	Dy Hr Mn
1 18:30	♃ ✶	♉	2 1:42
3 13:12	♇ □	♊	4 1:06
5 20:04	♃ ☌	♋	6 2:30
7 20:44	♆ □	♌	8 7:29
10 10:47	♃ ✶	♍	10 16:23
12 23:18	♃ □	♎	13 4:03
15 13:00	♃ △	♏	15 16:42
17 21:47	☉ ☍	♐	18 4:53
20 14:20	♃ ☍	♑	20 15:49
22 13:09	♆ □	♒	23 0:48
24 20:00	♆ △	♓	25 7:08
27 0:51	☿ □	♈	27 10:32
29 8:17	☿ ✶	♉	29 11:33
30 23:57	♇ □	♊	31 11:40

Last Aspect Dy Hr Mn		☽ Ingress	Dy Hr Mn
2 2:04	♆ △	♋	2 12:46
4 5:06	♆ □	♌	4 16:34
6 11:45	♆ ✶	♍	7 0:06
8 17:22	♅ ✶	♎	9 10:59
11 10:13	♆ ☌	♏	11 23:30
14 3:12	♀ △	♐	14 11:37
16 12:06	☉ ☍	♑	16 22:05
18 18:09	♆ □	♒	19 6:26
21 11:50	☉ △	♓	21 12:37
23 2:57	♅ △	♈	23 16:44
25 8:01	♆ ☍	♉	25 19:09
27 9:27	♇ □	♊	27 20:41
29 11:20	♆ △	♋	29 22:35

☽ Phases & Eclipses

Dy Hr Mn	
2 20:22	● 11♉53
9 18:17	☽ 18♌34
17 21:47	○ 26♏26
25 13:49	☾ 3♓48
1 4:03	● 10♊08
8 9:14	☽ 17♍03
16 12:06	○ 24♐48
23 19:46	☾ 1♈47
30 12:26	● 8♋10
30 12:32:05	✔ T 02'35"

Astro Data

1 May 1954
Julian Day # 19844
SVP 5♓53'36"
GC 26♐12.1 ⚴ 24♌00.3
Eris 8♈26.9 ✱ 16♌40.5
⚷ 28♑39.0 ⚶ 3♉55.4
☽ Mean ☊ 18♑22.2

1 June 1954
Julian Day # 19875
SVP 5♓53'31"
GC 26♐12.2 ⚴ 1♍52.6
Eris 8♈42.2 ✱ 24♌36.3
⚷ 28♑12.7R ⚶ 17♉38.3
☽ Mean ☊ 16♑43.7

July 1954 — LONGITUDE

Day	Sid.Time	☉	0 hr ☽	Noon ☽	True ☊	☿	♀	♂	⚳	♃	♄	♅	♆	♇
1 Th	6 36 01	9♋06 23	14♋55 46	21♋51 46	14♑44.4	16♋22.9	16♌13.8	0♑32.6	6♎53.4	8♋33.0	2♏39.9	22♋27.1	23♎17.4	23♌16.9
2 F	6 39 58	10 03 37	28 42 45	5♌28 30	14 44.6	15R49.8	17 23.9	0R14.4	7 08.7	8 46.6	2R39.4	22 30.7	23R17.3	23 18.4
3 Sa	6 43 55	11 00 50	12♌08 51	18 43 48	14 45.0	15 14.8	18 33.9	29♐56.6	7 24.3	9 00.3	2 39.1	22 34.3	23 17.2	23 19.9
4 Su	6 47 51	11 58 03	25 13 26	1♍37 55	14 45.3	14 38.4	19 43.9	29 39.0	7 40.0	9 13.9	2 38.8	22 37.9	23D17.2	23 21.4
5 M	6 51 48	12 55 17	7♍57 32	14 12 37	14 45.6	14 01.3	20 53.7	29 21.8	7 55.9	9 27.5	2 38.6	22 41.6	23 17.1	23 22.9
6 Tu	6 55 44	13 52 29	20 23 33	26 30 48	14R45.7	13 24.2	22 03.5	29 05.1	8 12.1	9 41.1	2D38.6	22 45.2	23 17.2	23 24.4
7 W	6 59 41	14 49 42	2♎34 53	8♎36 18	14D45.7	12 47.6	23 13.2	28 48.7	8 28.4	9 54.7	2 38.6	22 48.8	23 17.2	23 26.0
8 Th	7 03 37	15 46 55	14 35 37	20 33 25	14 45.7	12 12.2	24 22.8	28 32.8	8 44.9	10 08.3	2 38.7	22 52.4	23 17.3	23 27.5
9 F	7 07 34	16 44 07	26 30 15	2♏26 41	14 45.8	11 38.6	25 32.4	28 17.4	9 01.6	10 21.8	2 39.0	22 56.1	23 17.4	23 29.1
10 Sa	7 11 30	17 41 19	8♏23 17	14 20 37	14 46.0	11 07.4	26 41.8	28 02.6	9 18.5	10 35.4	2 39.3	22 59.7	23 17.6	23 30.7
11 Su	7 15 27	18 38 32	20 19 11	26 19 29	14 46.4	10 39.2	27 51.1	27 48.4	9 35.6	10 49.0	2 39.7	23 03.4	23 17.8	23 32.3
12 M	7 19 24	19 35 44	2♐21 59	8♐27 06	14 46.8	10 14.4	29 00.3	27 34.7	9 52.8	11 02.5	2 40.3	23 07.0	23 18.0	23 34.0
13 Tu	7 23 20	20 32 56	14 35 13	20 46 39	14 47.3	9 53.6	0♍09.5	27 21.7	10 10.2	11 16.0	2 40.9	23 10.7	23 18.2	23 35.6
14 W	7 27 17	21 30 09	27 01 41	3♑20 33	14R47.7	9 37.2	1 18.5	27 09.4	10 27.8	11 29.5	2 41.6	23 14.4	23 18.5	23 37.3
15 Th	7 31 13	22 27 22	9♑43 22	16 10 17	14 47.9	9 25.5	2 27.4	26 57.8	10 45.6	11 43.0	2 42.4	23 18.0	23 18.8	23 39.0
16 F	7 35 10	23 24 35	22 41 17	29 16 22	14 47.6	9D18.7	3 36.2	26 46.8	11 03.5	11 56.5	2 43.4	23 21.7	23 19.2	23 40.7
17 Sa	7 39 06	24 21 49	5♒55 27	12♒38 23	14 46.9	9 17.2	4 45.0	26 36.6	11 21.5	12 09.9	2 44.4	23 25.3	23 19.5	23 42.4
18 Su	7 43 03	25 19 02	19 24 59	26 15 01	14 45.8	9 21.1	5 53.6	26 27.1	11 39.8	12 23.3	2 45.5	23 29.0	23 19.9	23 44.1
19 M	7 46 59	26 16 17	3♓08 12	10♓04 14	14 44.5	9 30.5	7 02.1	26 18.4	11 58.2	12 36.7	2 46.7	23 32.7	23 20.4	23 45.8
20 Tu	7 50 56	27 13 32	17 02 50	24 03 38	14 43.1	9 45.6	8 10.4	26 10.4	12 16.7	12 50.1	2 48.0	23 36.3	23 20.8	23 47.5
21 W	7 54 53	28 10 48	1♈06 18	8♈10 30	14 42.0	10 06.5	9 18.7	26 03.2	12 35.4	13 03.5	2 49.4	23 40.0	23 21.4	23 49.3
22 Th	7 58 49	29 08 05	15 15 55	22 22 12	14D41.3	10 33.0	10 26.9	25 56.9	12 54.2	13 16.8	2 50.9	23 43.6	23 21.9	23 51.0
23 F	8 02 46	0♌05 22	29 29 02	6♉36 08	14 41.3	11 05.4	11 34.9	25 51.3	13 13.2	13 30.1	2 52.5	23 47.3	23 22.4	23 52.8
24 Sa	8 06 42	1 02 41	13♉43 09	20 49 49	14 41.9	11 43.4	12 42.8	25 46.5	13 32.3	13 43.4	2 54.2	23 50.9	23 23.0	23 54.6
25 Su	8 10 39	2 00 01	27 55 49	5♊00 51	14 43.0	12 27.2	13 50.7	25 42.6	13 51.6	13 56.7	2 56.0	23 54.6	23 23.7	23 56.4
26 M	8 14 35	2 57 21	12♊04 35	19 06 43	14 44.3	13 16.6	14 58.4	25 39.5	14 11.0	14 09.9	2 57.9	23 58.2	23 24.3	23 58.2
27 Tu	8 18 32	3 54 43	26 06 56	3♋04 53	14R45.2	14 11.6	16 05.9	25 37.3	14 30.5	14 23.1	2 59.8	24 01.8	23 25.0	24 00.0
28 W	8 22 28	4 52 05	10♋00 16	16 52 45	14 45.5	15 12.0	17 13.4	25 35.9	14 50.2	14 36.2	3 01.9	24 05.5	23 25.8	24 01.9
29 Th	8 26 25	5 49 28	23 42 02	0♌27 51	14 44.8	16 17.9	18 20.7	25D35.4	15 10.0	14 49.4	3 04.1	24 09.1	23 26.5	24 03.7
30 F	8 30 22	6 46 52	7♌09 57	13 48 08	14 43.1	17 29.1	19 27.8	25 35.7	15 30.0	15 02.5	3 06.3	24 12.7	23 27.3	24 05.5
31 Sa	8 34 18	7 44 17	20 22 16	26 52 13	14 40.3	18 45.4	20 34.9	25 36.8	15 50.0	15 15.5	3 08.7	24 16.3	23 28.1	24 07.4

August 1954 — LONGITUDE

Day	Sid.Time	☉	0 hr ☽	Noon ☽	True ☊	☿	♀	♂	⚳	♃	♄	♅	♆	♇
1 Su	8 38 15	8♌41 42	3♍18 00	9♍39 37	14♑36.7	20♋06.7	21♍41.8	25♐38.8	16♎10.2	15♋28.5	3♏11.1	24♋19.9	23♎29.0	24♌09.2
2 M	8 42 11	9 39 08	15 57 11	22 10 53	14R32.8	21 32.8	22 48.5	25 41.7	16 30.6	15 41.5	3 13.6	24 23.4	23 29.8	24 11.1
3 Tu	8 46 08	10 36 35	28 20 57	4♎27 41	14 29.1	23 03.6	23 55.1	25 45.4	16 51.0	15 54.5	3 16.3	24 27.0	23 30.7	24 13.0
4 W	8 50 04	11 34 02	10♎31 28	16 32 43	14 25.9	24 38.7	25 01.5	25 49.9	17 11.6	16 07.4	3 19.0	24 30.5	23 31.7	24 14.8
5 Th	8 54 01	12 31 31	22 31 53	28 29 30	14 23.8	26 17.9	26 07.8	25 55.3	17 32.2	16 20.2	3 21.8	24 34.1	23 32.6	24 16.7
6 F	8 57 57	13 29 00	4♏26 06	10♏22 15	14D22.9	28 01.0	27 13.9	26 01.4	17 53.0	16 33.0	3 24.7	24 37.6	23 33.6	24 18.6
7 Sa	9 01 54	14 26 29	16 18 32	22 15 35	14 23.1	29 47.7	28 19.9	26 08.4	18 13.9	16 45.8	3 27.7	24 41.1	23 34.7	24 20.5
8 Su	9 05 51	15 24 00	28 13 59	4♐14 21	14 24.3	1♌37.5	29 25.6	26 16.2	18 34.9	16 58.5	3 30.7	24 44.6	23 35.7	24 22.4
9 M	9 09 47	16 21 31	10♐17 15	16 23 17	14 25.9	3 30.1	0♎31.2	26 24.8	18 56.0	17 11.2	3 33.9	24 48.1	23 36.8	24 24.3
10 Tu	9 13 44	17 19 04	22 32 57	28 46 46	14 27.5	5 25.2	1 36.6	26 34.1	19 17.2	17 23.8	3 37.1	24 51.5	23 37.9	24 26.2
11 W	9 17 40	18 16 37	5♑05 08	11♑28 26	14R28.3	7 22.4	2 41.9	26 44.2	19 38.6	17 36.4	3 40.4	24 55.0	23 39.1	24 28.1
12 Th	9 21 37	19 14 11	17 56 57	24 30 50	14 27.9	9 21.2	3 46.9	26 55.0	20 00.0	17 48.9	3 43.9	24 58.4	23 40.2	24 30.0
13 F	9 25 33	20 11 46	1♒10 12	7♒55 00	14 26.0	11 21.4	4 51.7	27 06.6	20 21.5	18 01.4	3 47.4	25 01.8	23 41.4	24 32.0
14 Sa	9 29 30	21 09 23	14 45 03	21 40 07	14 22.4	13 22.5	5 56.3	27 18.9	20 43.1	18 13.8	3 50.9	25 05.2	23 42.7	24 33.9
15 Su	9 33 26	22 07 00	28 39 47	5♓43 32	14 17.4	15 24.2	7 00.7	27 31.9	21 04.8	18 26.1	3 54.6	25 08.6	23 43.9	24 35.8
16 M	9 37 23	23 04 39	12♓50 47	20 00 51	14 11.6	17 26.3	8 04.9	27 45.6	21 26.6	18 38.5	3 58.3	25 11.9	23 45.2	24 37.7
17 Tu	9 41 20	24 02 19	27 13 02	4♈26 35	14 05.7	19 28.4	9 08.9	28 00.0	21 48.5	18 50.7	4 02.1	25 15.3	23 46.5	24 39.6
18 W	9 45 16	25 00 01	11♈40 45	18 54 52	14 00.6	21 30.3	10 12.7	28 15.1	22 10.5	19 02.9	4 06.0	25 18.6	23 47.8	24 41.5
19 Th	9 49 13	25 57 44	26 08 16	3♉20 24	13 56.9	23 31.7	11 16.2	28 30.8	22 32.6	19 15.0	4 10.0	25 21.9	23 49.2	24 43.5
20 F	9 53 09	26 55 29	10♉30 46	17 38 59	13D55.0	25 32.6	12 19.5	28 47.1	22 54.7	19 27.1	4 14.1	25 25.1	23 50.6	24 45.4
21 Sa	9 57 06	27 53 16	24 44 45	1♊47 52	13 54.7	27 32.7	13 22.5	29 04.1	23 17.0	19 39.1	4 18.2	25 28.4	23 52.0	24 47.3
22 Su	10 01 02	28 51 05	8♊48 10	15 45 35	13 55.5	29 31.9	14 25.3	29 21.8	23 39.3	19 51.0	4 22.4	25 31.6	23 53.4	24 49.2
23 M	10 04 59	29 48 55	22 40 05	29 31 39	13 56.7	1♍30.1	15 27.9	29 40.0	24 01.8	20 02.9	4 26.7	25 34.8	23 54.9	24 51.1
24 Tu	10 08 55	0♍46 47	6♋20 18	13♋06 03	13R57.4	3 27.2	16 30.2	29 58.9	24 24.3	20 14.7	4 31.1	25 37.9	23 56.4	24 53.1
25 W	10 12 52	1 44 41	19 48 55	26 28 55	13 56.6	5 23.1	17 32.2	0♑18.4	24 46.9	20 26.5	4 35.5	25 41.1	23 57.9	24 55.0
26 Th	10 16 49	2 42 36	3♌06 00	9♌40 12	13 53.9	7 17.9	18 34.0	0 38.4	25 09.5	20 38.1	4 40.0	25 44.2	23 59.4	24 56.9
27 F	10 20 45	3 40 33	16 11 25	22 39 40	13 48.8	9 11.4	19 35.5	0 59.1	25 32.3	20 49.7	4 44.6	25 47.3	24 01.0	24 58.8
28 Sa	10 24 42	4 38 31	29 04 51	5♍26 58	13 41.5	11 03.7	20 36.7	1 20.3	25 55.1	21 01.3	4 49.2	25 50.3	24 02.5	25 00.7
29 Su	10 28 38	5 36 31	11♍45 59	18 01 53	13 32.6	12 54.7	21 37.6	1 42.0	26 18.0	21 12.7	4 54.0	25 53.4	24 04.1	25 02.6
30 M	10 32 35	6 34 33	24 14 44	0♎24 36	13 22.8	14 44.4	22 38.1	2 04.3	26 41.0	21 24.1	4 58.8	25 56.4	24 05.8	25 04.5
31 Tu	10 36 31	7 32 36	6♎31 37	12 35 56	13 13.1	16 32.9	23 38.4	2 27.2	27 04.0	21 35.4	5 03.6	25 59.3	24 07.4	25 06.4

Astro Data

	Dy Hr Mn
♆⚹♇	1 19:09
♆D	5 8:33
☽0S	5 21:10
♄D	6 15:53
♅□♆	15 17:36
☿D	17 6:50
☽0N	20 3:18
♅⚺♇	26 11:58
♂D	29 15:20
⚳0S	1 2:54
☽0S	2 5:56
♀0S	9 0:31
☽0N	16 10:31
☽0S	29 14:16

Planet Ingress

		Dy Hr Mn
♂	♐R	3 7:23
♀	♍	13 8:43
☉	♌	23 9:45
☿	♌	7 14:44
♀	♎	9 0:34
☿	♍	22 17:42
☉	♍	23 16:36
♂	♑	24 13:22

Last Aspect / ☽ Ingress

Last Aspect Dy Hr Mn		☽ Ingress	Dy Hr Mn
1 14:29	♆ □	♌	2 2:16
4 8:21	♂ △	♍	4 8:56
6 16:58	♂ □	♎	6 18:53
9 3:47	♂ ⚹	♏	9 7:04
11 15:22	♀ □	♐	11 19:19
14 0:26	♂ ☌	♑	14 5:40
16 1:11	♅ ☍	♒	16 13:19
18 12:21	♂ ⚹	♓	18 18:33
20 17:47	☉ △	♈	20 22:07
23 0:14	☉ □	♉	23 0:52
24 17:13	♇ □	♊	25 3:30
26 23:11	♂ ☍	♋	27 6:41
29 0:45	♅ ☌	♌	29 11:10
31 9:40	♂ △	♍	31 17:49

Last Aspect / ☽ Ingress

Last Aspect Dy Hr Mn		☽ Ingress	Dy Hr Mn
2 18:51	♂ □	♎	3 3:14
5 6:51	☿ □	♏	5 15:03
8 1:26	♀ ⚹	♐	8 3:32
10 7:42	♂ ☌	♑	10 14:20
12 12:50	♅ ☍	♒	12 21:54
14 21:51	♂ ⚹	♓	15 2:17
17 1:07	♂ □	♈	17 4:37
19 3:48	♂ △	♉	19 6:26
21 4:51	☉ □	♊	21 8:56
23 12:33	☉ ⚹	♋	23 12:50
25 10:33	♅ ☌	♌	25 18:22
27 16:20	♇ ☌	♍	28 1:44
30 3:15	♅ ⚹	♎	30 11:12

☽ Phases & Eclipses

Dy Hr Mn	
8 1:33	☽ 15♎22
16 0:29	○ 22♑57
16 0:20	☍ P 0.405
23 0:14	☾ 29♈37
29 22:20	● 6♌14
6 18:51	☽ 13♏45
14 11:03	○ 21♒07
21 4:51	☾ 27♉36
28 10:21	● 4♍35

Astro Data

1 July 1954
Julian Day # 19905
SVP 5♓53'25"
GC 26♐12.2 ⚴ 12♍10.8
Eris 8♈48.4 ⚵ 4♍16.6
⚷ 26♑51.3R ⚶ 0♊16.8
☽ Mean ☊ 15♑08.4

1 August 1954
Julian Day # 19936
SVP 5♓53'20"
GC 26♐12.3 ⚴ 24♍20.8
Eris 8♈44.6R ⚵ 15♍19.8
⚷ 25♑03.3R ⚶ 12♊17.2
☽ Mean ☊ 13♑30.0

LONGITUDE — September 1954

Day	Sid.Time	☉	0 hr ☽	Noon ☽	True ☊	☿	♀	♂	⚳	♃	♄	♅	♆	♇
1 W	10 40 28	8♍30 40	18♎37 49	24♎37 33	13♑04.3	18♍20.1	24♎38.3	2♑50.5	27♎27.2	21♋46.6	5♏08.6	26♋02.3	24♎09.1	25♌08.3
2 Th	10 44 24	9 28 46	0♏35 28	6♏31 59	12R 57.3	20 06.0	25 37.9	3 14.4	27 50.3	21 57.7	5 13.6	26 05.2	24 10.8	25 10.1
3 F	10 48 21	10 26 54	12 27 33	18 22 40	12 52.5	21 50.7	26 37.1	3 38.8	28 13.6	22 08.7	5 18.6	26 08.0	24 12.5	25 12.0
4 Sa	10 52 18	11 25 03	24 17 53	0♐13 47	12 49.8	23 34.2	27 35.9	4 03.7	28 36.9	22 19.7	5 23.8	26 10.9	24 14.2	25 13.9
5 Su	10 56 14	12 23 13	6♐10 59	12 10 08	12D 49.1	25 16.4	28 34.3	4 29.0	29 00.3	22 30.6	5 29.0	26 13.7	24 16.0	25 15.7
6 M	11 00 11	13 21 25	18 11 53	24 16 53	12 49.5	26 57.5	29 32.4	4 54.8	29 23.8	22 41.4	5 34.2	26 16.5	24 17.8	25 17.6
7 Tu	11 04 07	14 19 38	0♑25 47	6♑39 13	12R 50.2	28 37.3	0♏30.0	5 21.1	29 47.3	22 52.1	5 39.6	26 19.2	24 19.6	25 19.4
8 W	11 08 04	15 17 53	12 57 46	19 21 58	12 50.2	0♎16.0	1 27.2	5 47.8	0♏10.9	23 02.7	5 45.0	26 21.9	24 21.4	25 21.3
9 Th	11 12 00	16 16 10	25 52 17	2♒29 02	12 48.5	1 53.6	2 24.0	6 14.9	0 34.5	23 13.2	5 50.4	26 24.6	24 23.2	25 23.1
10 F	11 15 57	17 14 27	9♒12 29	16 02 43	12 44.5	3 30.0	3 20.3	6 42.5	0 58.2	23 23.6	5 55.9	26 27.2	24 25.1	25 24.9
11 Sa	11 19 53	18 12 47	22 59 38	0♓02 59	12 38.0	5 05.2	4 16.1	7 10.5	1 21.9	23 33.9	6 01.5	26 29.8	24 27.0	25 26.7
12 Su	11 23 50	19 11 08	7♓12 21	14 27 05	12 29.4	6 39.4	5 11.4	7 38.8	1 45.7	23 44.1	6 07.1	26 32.4	24 28.9	25 28.5
13 M	11 27 47	20 09 31	21 46 24	29 09 20	12 19.4	8 12.4	6 06.2	8 07.6	2 09.6	23 54.3	6 12.8	26 34.9	24 30.8	25 30.3
14 Tu	11 31 43	21 07 56	6♈34 51	14♈01 49	12 09.2	9 44.3	7 00.5	8 36.7	2 33.5	24 04.3	6 18.5	26 37.4	24 32.7	25 32.0
15 W	11 35 40	22 06 23	21 29 06	28 55 36	12 00.0	11 15.2	7 54.2	9 06.2	2 57.5	24 14.2	6 24.3	26 39.8	24 34.6	25 33.8
16 Th	11 39 36	23 04 52	6♉20 18	13♉42 17	11 52.9	12 44.9	8 47.3	9 36.1	3 21.5	24 24.0	6 30.1	26 42.2	24 36.6	25 35.6
17 F	11 43 33	24 03 23	21 00 49	28 15 19	11 48.2	14 13.5	9 39.9	10 06.3	3 45.6	24 33.8	6 36.0	26 44.6	24 38.6	25 37.3
18 Sa	11 47 29	25 01 57	5♊25 20	12♊30 38	11D 45.9	15 41.1	10 31.9	10 36.9	4 09.7	24 43.4	6 42.0	26 46.9	24 40.6	25 39.0
19 Su	11 51 26	26 00 33	19 31 05	26 26 42	11 45.4	17 07.5	11 23.2	11 07.8	4 33.9	24 52.9	6 48.0	26 49.2	24 42.6	25 40.7
20 M	11 55 22	26 59 11	3♋17 35	10♋03 54	11R 45.5	18 32.7	12 13.9	11 39.0	4 58.1	25 02.3	6 54.0	26 51.5	24 44.6	25 42.4
21 Tu	11 59 19	27 57 51	16 45 54	23 23 50	11 45.1	19 56.9	13 03.9	12 10.6	5 22.3	25 11.6	7 00.1	26 53.7	24 46.6	25 44.1
22 W	12 03 16	28 56 33	29 57 59	6♌28 36	11 43.0	21 19.8	13 53.2	12 42.5	5 46.7	25 20.7	7 06.2	26 55.8	24 48.7	25 45.8
23 Th	12 07 12	29 55 18	12♌55 56	19 20 13	11 38.3	22 41.5	14 41.8	13 14.7	6 11.0	25 29.8	7 12.4	26 58.0	24 50.7	25 47.5
24 F	12 11 09	0♎54 04	25 41 39	2♍00 23	11 30.6	24 02.0	15 29.6	13 47.3	6 35.4	25 38.7	7 18.7	27 00.0	24 52.8	25 49.1
25 Sa	12 15 05	1 52 53	8♍16 34	14 30 17	11 20.0	25 21.2	16 16.7	14 20.1	6 59.9	25 47.5	7 25.0	27 02.1	24 54.9	25 50.7
26 Su	12 19 02	2 51 44	20 41 40	26 50 45	11 07.3	26 39.1	17 02.9	14 53.2	7 24.4	25 56.2	7 31.3	27 04.0	24 57.0	25 52.3
27 M	12 22 58	3 50 37	2♎57 39	9♎02 25	10 53.3	27 55.6	17 48.3	15 26.7	7 48.9	26 04.8	7 37.7	27 06.0	24 59.1	25 53.9
28 Tu	12 26 55	4 49 31	15 05 09	21 05 59	10 39.2	29 10.5	18 32.7	16 00.4	8 13.5	26 13.2	7 44.1	27 07.9	25 01.2	25 55.5
29 W	12 30 51	5 48 28	27 05 04	3♏02 36	10 26.3	0♏24.0	19 16.3	16 34.4	8 38.1	26 21.5	7 50.5	27 09.7	25 03.3	25 57.1
30 Th	12 34 48	6 47 27	8♏58 48	14 53 59	10 15.4	1 35.8	19 58.9	17 08.6	9 02.8	26 29.7	7 57.0	27 11.5	25 05.5	25 58.6

LONGITUDE — October 1954

Day	Sid.Time	☉	0 hr ☽	Noon ☽	True ☊	☿	♀	♂	⚳	♃	♄	♅	♆	♇
1 F	12 38 44	7♎46 27	20♏48 28	26♏42 39	10♑07.3	2♏45.8	20♏40.5	17♑43.2	9♏27.5	26♋37.8	8♏03.5	27♋13.3	25♎07.6	26♌00.1
2 Sa	12 42 41	8 45 30	2♐36 59	8♐31 57	10R 02.1	3 54.0	21 21.0	18 18.0	9 52.2	26 45.7	8 10.1	27 15.0	25 09.8	26 01.6
3 Su	12 46 38	9 44 34	14 28 05	20 26 00	9 59.4	5 00.1	22 00.4	18 53.0	10 17.0	26 53.5	8 16.7	27 16.6	25 12.0	26 03.1
4 M	12 50 34	10 43 40	26 26 19	2♑29 40	9 58.5	6 04.1	22 38.7	19 28.3	10 41.8	27 01.1	8 23.4	27 18.2	25 14.1	26 04.6
5 Tu	12 54 31	11 42 48	8♑36 43	14 48 10	9 58.5	7 05.8	23 15.9	20 03.9	11 06.6	27 08.6	8 30.0	27 19.8	25 16.3	26 06.1
6 W	12 58 27	12 41 58	21 04 39	27 26 50	9 58.0	8 04.9	23 51.7	20 39.6	11 31.5	27 16.0	8 36.8	27 21.3	25 18.5	26 07.5
7 Th	13 02 24	13 41 09	3♒55 17	10♒30 31	9 56.1	9 01.2	24 26.3	21 15.6	11 56.4	27 23.2	8 43.5	27 22.8	25 20.7	26 08.9
8 F	13 06 20	14 40 22	17 12 57	24 02 51	9 51.8	9 54.6	24 59.6	21 51.8	12 21.3	27 30.3	8 50.3	27 24.2	25 22.9	26 10.3
9 Sa	13 10 17	15 39 37	1♓00 20	8♓05 19	9 44.9	10 44.7	25 31.4	22 28.2	12 46.3	27 37.2	8 57.1	27 25.5	25 25.1	26 11.7
10 Su	13 14 13	16 38 53	15 17 31	22 36 24	9 35.5	11 31.1	26 01.8	23 04.9	13 11.3	27 44.0	9 03.9	27 26.8	25 27.3	26 13.0
11 M	13 18 10	17 38 12	0♈01 13	7♈31 01	9 24.6	12 13.7	26 30.7	23 41.7	13 36.3	27 50.7	9 10.8	27 28.1	25 29.6	26 14.4
12 Tu	13 22 07	18 37 32	15 04 38	22 40 45	9 13.3	12 51.9	26 58.0	24 18.7	14 01.3	27 57.2	9 17.6	27 29.3	25 31.8	26 15.7
13 W	13 26 03	19 36 55	0♉17 59	7♉54 57	9 03.0	13 25.5	27 23.6	24 55.9	14 26.4	28 03.5	9 24.5	27 30.5	25 34.0	26 16.9
14 Th	13 30 00	20 36 20	15 30 17	23 02 44	8 54.8	13 53.8	27 47.6	25 33.3	14 51.5	28 09.7	9 31.5	27 31.6	25 36.2	26 18.2
15 F	13 33 56	21 35 47	0♊31 13	7♊54 51	8 49.3	14 16.5	28 09.9	26 10.9	15 16.6	28 15.7	9 38.4	27 32.6	25 38.5	26 19.5
16 Sa	13 37 53	22 35 16	15 12 56	22 25 02	8 46.4	14 33.1	28 30.3	26 48.6	15 41.7	28 21.6	9 45.4	27 33.6	25 40.7	26 20.7
17 Su	13 41 49	23 34 48	29 30 50	6♋30 18	8D 45.6	14R 42.9	28 48.9	27 26.5	16 06.9	28 27.3	9 52.4	27 34.6	25 43.0	26 21.9
18 M	13 45 46	24 34 22	13♋23 29	20 10 35	8R 45.7	14 45.5	29 05.6	28 04.6	16 32.1	28 32.9	9 59.5	27 35.5	25 45.2	26 23.1
19 Tu	13 49 42	25 33 58	26 51 53	3♌27 47	8 45.6	14 40.4	29 20.3	28 42.9	16 57.3	28 38.3	10 06.5	27 36.3	25 47.4	26 24.2
20 W	13 53 39	26 33 36	9♌58 39	16 24 55	8 43.9	14 27.1	29 32.9	29 21.3	17 22.5	28 43.5	10 13.6	27 37.1	25 49.7	26 25.3
21 Th	13 57 36	27 33 17	22 47 02	29 05 25	8 39.9	14 05.2	29 43.5	29 59.9	17 47.8	28 48.6	10 20.7	27 37.8	25 51.9	26 26.4
22 F	14 01 32	28 33 00	5♍20 27	11♍32 30	8 33.1	13 34.5	29 51.9	0♒38.7	18 13.0	28 53.5	10 27.8	27 38.5	25 54.2	26 27.5
23 Sa	14 05 29	29 32 45	17 41 55	23 48 59	8 23.5	12 54.9	29 58.1	1 17.6	18 38.3	28 58.2	10 34.9	27 39.1	25 56.4	26 28.6
24 Su	14 09 25	0♏32 32	29 53 57	5♎57 05	8 11.9	12 06.5	0♐02.0	1 56.6	19 03.6	29 02.7	10 42.0	27 39.7	25 58.6	26 29.6
25 M	14 13 22	1 32 22	11♎58 33	17 58 32	7 59.0	11 09.9	0R 03.6	2 35.8	19 29.0	29 07.1	10 49.1	27 40.2	26 00.9	26 30.6
26 Tu	14 17 18	2 32 13	23 57 13	29 54 44	7 46.1	10 06.0	0 02.9	3 15.2	19 54.3	29 11.3	10 56.3	27 40.7	26 03.1	26 31.6
27 W	14 21 15	3 32 06	5♏51 16	11♏46 58	7 34.1	8 56.0	29♏59.8	3 54.7	20 19.7	29 15.3	11 03.5	27 41.1	26 05.3	26 32.5
28 Th	14 25 11	4 32 02	17 42 02	23 36 41	7 24.1	7 41.6	29 54.3	4 34.3	20 45.1	29 19.2	11 10.6	27 41.5	26 07.6	26 33.4
29 F	14 29 08	5 31 59	29 31 08	5♐25 42	7 16.6	6 24.8	29 46.3	5 14.1	21 10.4	29 22.8	11 17.8	27 41.8	26 09.8	26 34.3
30 Sa	14 33 05	6 31 58	11♐20 40	17 16 26	7 11.9	5 07.9	29 35.9	5 54.0	21 35.8	29 26.3	11 25.0	27 42.0	26 12.0	26 35.2
31 Su	14 37 01	7 31 59	23 13 23	29 12 00	7D 09.7	3 53.3	29 23.1	6 34.0	22 01.3	29 29.6	11 32.2	27 42.2	26 14.2	26 36.0

Astro Data Dy Hr Mn	Planet Ingress Dy Hr Mn	Last Aspect Dy Hr Mn	☽ Ingress Dy Hr Mn	Last Aspect Dy Hr Mn	☽ Ingress Dy Hr Mn	☽ Phases & Eclipses Dy Hr Mn
☿0S 8 21:51	♀ ♏ 6 23:29	1 14:51 ♅ □	♏ 1 22:49	1 13:02 ♅ △	♐ 1 18:41	5 12:28 ☽ 12♐24
☽0N 12 19:50	⚳ ♏ 8 0:57	4 3:47 ♅ △	♐ 4 11:32	3 23:15 ♇ △	♑ 4 7:04	12 20:19 ○ 19♓31
♃□♆ 18 3:03	☿ ♎ 8 8:05	6 23:08 ♀ ⚹	♑ 6 23:10	6 11:50 ♅ ☍	♒ 6 16:45	19 11:11 ☾ 25♊59
☉0S 23 13:55	☉ ♎ 23 13:55	9 0:57 ♅ ☍	♒ 9 7:31	8 15:41 ♇ ☍	♓ 8 22:17	27 0:50 ● 3♎23
☽0S 25 21:08	☿ ♏ 29 4:06	11 4:10 ♇ ☍	♓ 11 11:55	10 20:23 ♃ △	♈ 10 23:58	
♃⊻♇ 25 22:47		13 7:49 ♅ △	♈ 13 13:22	12 20:22 ♃ □	♉ 12 23:32	5 5:31 ☽ 11♑27
	♂ ♒ 21 12:03	15 8:20 ♅ □	♉ 15 13:44	14 20:15 ♃ ⚹	♊ 14 23:10	12 5:10 ○ 18♈21
♃☌♅ 7 10:02	♀ ♐ 23 22:07	17 9:29 ♅ ⚹	♊ 17 14:55	16 18:38 ♇ ⚹	♋ 17 0:50	18 20:30 ☾ 24♋55
☽0N 10 6:14	☉ ♏ 23 22:56	19 11:11 ☉ □	♋ 19 18:13	19 4:21 ☉ △	♌ 19 5:41	26 17:47 ● 2♏47
♅R 18 8:25	♀ ♏R 27 10:42	21 21:00 ☉ ⚹	♌ 22 0:04	21 13:14 ♀ □	♍ 21 13:44	
☽0S 23 2:28		24 0:13 ♇ ☌	♍ 24 8:11	23 22:14 ♃ ⚹	♎ 24 0:12	
♀R 25 16:36		26 12:26 ♅ ⚹	♎ 26 18:11	26 10:32 ♃ □	♏ 26 12:11	
		29 0:07 ♅ □	♏ 29 5:52	29 0:39 ♀ ☌	♐ 29 0:59	
				31 6:47 ♇ △	♑ 31 13:36	

Astro Data

1 September 1954
Julian Day # 19967
SVP 5♓53'17"
GC 26♐12.4 ⚴ 7♎24.1
Eris 8♈31.5R ⚵ 26♍52.2
⚷ 23♑36.0R ⚶ 22♊31.8
☽ Mean ☊ 11♑51.5

1 October 1954
Julian Day # 19997
SVP 5♓53'14"
GC 26♐12.4 ⚴ 20♎30.8
Eris 8♈13.6R ⚵ 8♎06.7
⚷ 23♑05.3 ⚶ 29♊35.8
☽ Mean ☊ 10♑16.1

November 1954 LONGITUDE

Day	Sid.Time	☉	0 hr ☽	Noon☽	True☊	☿	♀	♂	⚳	♃	♄	♅	♆	♇
1 M	14 40 58	8♏32 01	5♑12 45	11♑16 12	7♑09.4	2♏43.3	29♏07.9	7♒14.2	22♏26.7	29♋32.7	11♏39.4	27♋42.3	26♎16.4	26♌36.9
2 Tu	14 44 54	9 32 05	17 22 54	23 33 27	7 10.2	1R40.1	28R50.4	7 54.5	22 52.1	29 35.6	11 46.6	27R42.4	26 18.6	26 37.6
3 W	14 48 51	10 32 11	29 48 28	6♒08 33	7R11.0	0 45.5	28 30.5	8 34.8	23 17.6	29 38.4	11 53.8	27 42.4	26 20.8	26 38.4
4 Th	14 52 47	11 32 18	12♒34 17	19 06 13	7 10.7	0 01.0	28 08.3	9 15.3	23 43.0	29 40.9	12 01.0	27 42.4	26 23.0	26 39.1
5 F	14 56 44	12 32 26	25 44 51	2♓30 33	7 08.8	29♎27.5	27 44.0	9 55.9	24 08.5	29 43.3	12 08.2	27 42.3	26 25.2	26 39.8
6 Sa	15 00 40	13 32 36	9♓23 37	16 24 09	7 04.7	29 05.6	27 17.7	10 36.6	24 33.9	29 45.5	12 15.4	27 42.2	26 27.3	26 40.5
7 Su	15 04 37	14 32 48	23 32 06	0♈47 10	6 58.5	28D55.3	26 49.4	11 17.4	24 59.4	29 47.4	12 22.7	27 42.0	26 29.5	26 41.2
8 M	15 08 34	15 33 01	8♈08 53	15 36 31	6 51.0	28 56.5	26 19.4	11 58.3	25 24.8	29 49.2	12 29.9	27 41.7	26 31.6	26 41.8
9 Tu	15 12 30	16 33 16	23 09 07	0♉45 32	6 42.9	29 08.5	25 47.8	12 39.3	25 50.3	29 50.8	12 37.1	27 41.4	26 33.8	26 42.4
10 W	15 16 27	17 33 32	8♉24 28	16 04 31	6 35.5	29 30.8	25 14.8	13 20.4	26 15.8	29 52.2	12 44.2	27 41.1	26 35.9	26 42.9
11 Th	15 20 23	18 33 50	23 44 15	1♊22 16	6 29.6	0♏02.4	24 40.7	14 01.6	26 41.3	29 53.4	12 51.4	27 40.7	26 38.0	26 43.5
12 F	15 24 20	19 34 10	8♊57 15	16 28 02	6 25.8	0 42.4	24 05.6	14 42.8	27 06.7	29 54.4	12 58.6	27 40.2	26 40.1	26 44.0
13 Sa	15 28 16	20 34 32	23 53 38	1♋13 17	6D24.2	1 30.1	23 29.7	15 24.1	27 32.2	29 55.3	13 05.8	27 39.7	26 42.2	26 44.5
14 Su	15 32 13	21 34 56	8♋26 26	15 32 44	6 24.4	2 24.5	22 53.4	16 05.5	27 57.7	29 55.9	13 13.0	27 39.1	26 44.3	26 44.9
15 M	15 36 09	22 35 22	22 32 02	29 24 21	6 25.6	3 24.8	22 16.9	16 47.0	28 23.2	29 56.3	13 20.1	27 38.5	26 46.4	26 45.3
16 Tu	15 40 06	23 35 49	6♌09 53	12♌48 53	6R26.9	4 30.2	21 40.4	17 28.6	28 48.7	29R56.5	13 27.3	27 37.8	26 48.4	26 45.7
17 W	15 44 03	24 36 18	19 21 45	25 48 55	6 27.4	5 40.1	21 04.2	18 10.2	29 14.2	29 56.6	13 34.4	27 37.1	26 50.5	26 46.1
18 Th	15 47 59	25 36 49	2♍10 53	8♍28 09	6 26.5	6 53.8	20 28.6	18 51.9	29 39.6	29 56.4	13 41.5	27 36.3	26 52.5	26 46.4
19 F	15 51 56	26 37 22	14 41 13	20 50 38	6 23.7	8 10.7	19 53.7	19 33.7	0♐05.1	29 56.0	13 48.6	27 35.5	26 54.5	26 46.7
20 Sa	15 55 52	27 37 57	26 56 51	3♎00 22	6 19.0	9 30.4	19 19.9	20 15.5	0 30.6	29 55.4	13 55.7	27 34.6	26 56.5	26 47.0
21 Su	15 59 49	28 38 33	9♎01 36	15 00 58	6 13.0	10 52.4	18 47.2	20 57.4	0 56.0	29 54.7	14 02.8	27 33.7	26 58.5	26 47.2
22 M	16 03 45	29 39 11	20 58 52	26 55 36	6 06.0	12 16.5	18 16.1	21 39.4	1 21.5	29 53.7	14 09.8	27 32.7	27 00.5	26 47.4
23 Tu	16 07 42	0♐39 51	2♏51 30	8♏46 50	5 58.9	13 42.1	17 46.5	22 21.5	1 47.0	29 52.5	14 16.8	27 31.6	27 02.4	26 47.6
24 W	16 11 38	1 40 32	14 41 53	20 36 52	5 52.3	15 09.2	17 18.7	23 03.6	2 12.4	29 51.1	14 23.9	27 30.5	27 04.3	26 47.8
25 Th	16 15 35	2 41 14	26 32 00	2♐27 31	5 47.0	16 37.4	16 52.8	23 45.8	2 37.9	29 49.6	14 30.8	27 29.4	27 06.3	26 47.9
26 F	16 19 32	3 41 58	8♐23 37	14 20 32	5 43.2	18 06.6	16 29.1	24 28.0	3 03.3	29 47.8	14 37.8	27 28.2	27 08.2	26 48.0
27 Sa	16 23 28	4 42 44	20 18 30	26 17 45	5D41.1	19 36.6	16 07.5	25 10.3	3 28.7	29 45.8	14 44.8	27 27.0	27 10.0	26 48.0
28 Su	16 27 25	5 43 30	2♑18 34	8♑21 15	5 40.7	21 07.2	15 48.1	25 52.6	3 54.1	29 43.6	14 51.7	27 25.7	27 11.9	26R48.1
29 M	16 31 21	6 44 18	14 26 06	20 33 29	5 41.6	22 38.3	15 31.1	26 35.0	4 19.5	29 41.3	14 58.6	27 24.4	27 13.7	26 48.1
30 Tu	16 35 18	7 45 06	26 43 46	2♒57 22	5 43.2	24 09.9	15 16.5	27 17.5	4 44.9	29 38.7	15 05.4	27 23.0	27 15.6	26 48.0

December 1954 LONGITUDE

Day	Sid.Time	☉	0 hr ☽	Noon☽	True☊	☿	♀	♂	⚳	♃	♄	♅	♆	♇
1 W	16 39 14	8♐45 56	9♒14 42	15♒36 11	5♑45.0	25♏41.9	15♏04.3	27♒59.9	5♐10.3	29♋36.0	15♏12.2	27♋21.6	27♎17.4	26♌48.0
2 Th	16 43 11	9 46 46	22 02 16	28 33 22	5R46.3	27 14.1	14R54.6	28 42.5	5 35.6	29R33.0	15 19.0	27R20.1	27 19.1	26R47.9
3 F	16 47 07	10 47 38	5♓09 52	11♓52 07	5 46.7	28 46.5	14 47.3	29 25.0	6 01.0	29 29.9	15 25.8	27 18.6	27 20.9	26 47.7
4 Sa	16 51 04	11 48 30	18 40 22	25 34 50	5 46.1	0♐19.2	14 42.6	0♓07.7	6 26.3	29 26.6	15 32.5	27 17.0	27 22.6	26 47.6
5 Su	16 55 01	12 49 23	2♈35 34	9♈42 30	5 44.3	1 51.9	14D40.3	0 50.3	6 51.6	29 23.0	15 39.2	27 15.4	27 24.3	26 47.4
6 M	16 58 57	13 50 16	16 55 23	24 13 50	5 41.7	3 24.8	14 40.4	1 33.0	7 16.9	29 19.3	15 45.9	27 13.8	27 26.0	26 47.2
7 Tu	17 02 54	14 51 11	1♉37 16	9♉04 55	5 38.8	4 57.8	14 43.0	2 15.7	7 42.1	29 15.5	15 52.5	27 12.1	27 27.7	26 47.0
8 W	17 06 50	15 52 06	16 35 53	24 09 05	5 36.1	6 30.9	14 47.9	2 58.4	8 07.4	29 11.4	15 59.1	27 10.3	27 29.3	26 46.7
9 Th	17 10 47	16 53 02	1♊43 23	9♊17 34	5 33.9	8 04.1	14 55.2	3 41.2	8 32.6	29 07.2	16 05.7	27 08.6	27 30.9	26 46.4
10 F	17 14 43	17 53 59	16 50 25	24 20 46	5D32.7	9 37.4	15 04.7	4 24.0	8 57.8	29 02.8	16 12.2	27 06.8	27 32.5	26 46.1
11 Sa	17 18 40	18 54 57	1♋47 33	9♋09 46	5 32.5	11 10.7	15 16.6	5 06.8	9 22.9	28 58.2	16 18.6	27 04.9	27 34.1	26 45.7
12 Su	17 22 37	19 55 56	16 26 39	23 37 32	5 33.1	12 44.1	15 30.6	5 49.7	9 48.1	28 53.4	16 25.1	27 03.0	27 35.7	26 45.3
13 M	17 26 33	20 56 56	0♌42 00	7♌39 44	5 34.2	14 17.6	15 46.7	6 32.6	10 13.2	28 48.5	16 31.5	27 01.1	27 37.2	26 44.9
14 Tu	17 30 30	21 57 57	14 30 40	21 14 49	5 35.4	15 51.2	16 04.9	7 15.4	10 38.3	28 43.4	16 37.8	26 59.1	27 38.7	26 44.5
15 W	17 34 26	22 58 59	27 52 21	4♍23 35	5 36.4	17 24.9	16 25.1	7 58.3	11 03.4	28 38.1	16 44.1	26 57.1	27 40.1	26 44.0
16 Th	17 38 23	24 00 01	10♍48 52	17 08 40	5R37.0	18 58.7	16 47.2	8 41.3	11 28.4	28 32.7	16 50.4	26 55.1	27 41.6	26 43.5
17 F	17 42 19	25 01 05	23 23 29	29 33 51	5 37.1	20 32.6	17 11.2	9 24.2	11 53.5	28 27.1	16 56.6	26 53.0	27 43.0	26 43.0
18 Sa	17 46 16	26 02 10	5♎40 20	11♎43 30	5 36.7	22 06.6	17 36.9	10 07.2	12 18.5	28 21.4	17 02.7	26 50.9	27 44.4	26 42.4
19 Su	17 50 12	27 03 15	17 43 54	23 42 06	5 35.8	23 40.8	18 04.4	10 50.2	12 43.4	28 15.5	17 08.8	26 48.8	27 45.7	26 41.8
20 M	17 54 09	28 04 22	29 38 38	5♏34 01	5 34.8	25 15.2	18 33.6	11 33.2	13 08.4	28 09.5	17 14.9	26 46.6	27 47.1	26 41.2
21 Tu	17 58 06	29 05 29	11♏28 43	17 23 12	5 33.7	26 49.7	19 04.4	12 16.2	13 33.3	28 03.3	17 20.9	26 44.4	27 48.4	26 40.6
22 W	18 02 02	0♑06 36	23 17 53	29 13 09	5 32.9	28 24.4	19 36.8	12 59.2	13 58.1	27 57.0	17 26.8	26 42.2	27 49.6	26 39.9
23 Th	18 05 59	1 07 45	5♐09 20	11♐06 47	5 32.3	29 59.4	20 10.6	13 42.3	14 23.0	27 50.6	17 32.7	26 39.9	27 50.9	26 39.2
24 F	18 09 55	2 08 54	17 05 45	23 06 31	5 32.0	1♑34.5	20 45.8	14 25.4	14 47.8	27 44.0	17 38.6	26 37.7	27 52.1	26 38.5
25 Sa	18 13 52	3 10 03	29 09 17	5♑14 16	5D31.9	3 09.9	21 22.4	15 08.4	15 12.5	27 37.3	17 44.3	26 35.3	27 53.3	26 37.8
26 Su	18 17 48	4 11 13	11♑21 39	17 31 37	5 31.9	4 45.5	22 00.4	15 51.5	15 37.3	27 30.5	17 50.1	26 33.0	27 54.5	26 37.0
27 M	18 21 45	5 12 23	23 44 18	29 59 52	5R32.0	6 21.4	22 39.6	16 34.6	16 02.0	27 23.5	17 55.7	26 30.7	27 55.6	26 36.2
28 Tu	18 25 41	6 13 33	6♒18 28	12♒40 15	5 32.0	7 57.6	23 20.0	17 17.8	16 26.6	27 16.5	18 01.3	26 28.3	27 56.7	26 35.4
29 W	18 29 38	7 14 43	19 05 21	25 33 56	5 31.8	9 34.0	24 01.5	18 00.9	16 51.2	27 09.3	18 06.9	26 25.9	27 57.7	26 34.6
30 Th	18 33 35	8 15 53	2♓06 08	8♓42 06	5 31.6	11 10.8	24 44.2	18 44.0	17 15.8	27 02.1	18 12.4	26 23.4	27 58.8	26 33.7
31 F	18 37 31	9 17 03	15 21 58	22 05 51	5 31.3	12 47.8	25 27.9	19 27.1	17 40.3	26 54.7	18 17.8	26 21.0	27 59.8	26 32.8

Astro Data

	Dy Hr Mn
♅ R	3 10:58
☽ 0N	6 15:53
☿ D	7 21:33
♆✶♇	14 20:48
♃ R	17 3:02
☽ 0S	19 7:30
♇ R	28 23:44
♅□♆	2 19:06
☽ 0N	3 23:25
♀ D	5 22:39
☽ 0S	16 14:08
♃□♆	23 10:57
♅⊻♇	23 22:40
☽ 0N	31 5:07

Planet Ingress

		Dy Hr Mn
☿	♎R	4 12:37
☿	♏	11 10:25
⚳	♐	19 7:11
☉	♐	22 20:14
☿	♐	4 7:02
♂	♓	4 7:41
☉	♑	22 9:24
☿	♑	23 12:10

Last Aspect / ☽ Ingress

Last Aspect Dy Hr Mn			☽ Ingress Dy Hr Mn
2 23:38	♃ ☍	♒	3 0:22
5 6:48	☿ △	♓	5 7:34
7 10:21	♃ △	♈	7 10:42
9 10:34	♃ □	♉	9 10:48
11 9:40	♃ ✶	♊	11 9:50
13 4:38	♇ ✶	♋	13 9:59
15 12:56	♃ ☌	♌	15 13:03
17 13:56	♆ ✶	♍	17 19:52
20 5:53	♃ ✶	♎	20 6:02
22 18:00	♃ □	♏	22 18:13
25 6:41	♃ △	♐	25 7:01
27 13:45	♆ ✶	♑	27 19:24
30 5:39	♃ ☍	♒	30 6:19

Last Aspect / ☽ Ingress

Last Aspect Dy Hr Mn			☽ Ingress Dy Hr Mn
2 12:18	♂ ☌	♓	2 14:38
4 18:36	♃ △	♈	4 19:35
6 20:15	♃ □	♉	6 21:23
8 19:57	♃ ✶	♊	8 21:16
10 17:09	♆ △	♋	10 21:06
12 20:52	♃ ☌	♌	12 22:48
14 23:36	♆ ✶	♍	15 3:54
17 9:51	♃ ✶	♎	17 12:51
19 21:07	♃ □	♏	20 0:43
22 9:27	♃ △	♐	22 13:35
24 21:28	♆ ✶	♑	25 1:40
27 8:02	♆ □	♒	27 12:00
29 16:25	♆ △	♓	29 20:09

☽ Phases & Eclipses

Dy Hr Mn	
3 20:55	☽ 10♒55
10 14:29	○ 17♉40
17 9:33	☾ 24♌30
25 12:30	● 2♐43
3 9:56	☽ 10♓42
10 0:57	○ 17♊26
17 2:21	☾ 24♍37
25 7:33	● 2♑59
25 7:36:11	● A 07'39"

Astro Data

1 November 1954
Julian Day # 20028
SVP 5♓53'10"
GC 26♐12.5 ⚴ 4♏15.2
Eris 7♈55.0R ⚵ 19♎25.8
⚷ 23♑43.1 ⚶ 2♋00.3R
☽ Mean ☊ 8♑37.6

1 December 1954
Julian Day # 20058
SVP 5♓53'05"
GC 26♐12.6 ⚴ 17♏25.4
Eris 7♈42.3R ⚵ 29♎39.3
⚷ 25♑20.8 ⚶ 27♊59.3R
☽ Mean ☊ 7♑02.3

LONGITUDE — January 1955

Day	Sid.Time	☉	0 hr ☽	Noon ☽	True ☊	☿	♀	♂	⚳	♃	♄	♅	♆	♇
1 Sa	18 41 28	10♑18 12	28♓53 52	5♈46 04	5♑31.1	14♑25.1	26♏12.7	20♓10.2	18♐04.8	26♋47.3	18♏23.1	26♋18.5	28♎00.7	26♌31.9
2 Su	18 45 24	11 19 22	12♈42 28	19 43 01	5D31.1	16 02.8	26 58.5	20 53.4	18 29.2	26R39.8	18 28.4	26R16.0	28 01.7	26R31.0
3 M	18 49 21	12 20 31	26 47 37	3♉56 03	5 31.5	17 40.7	27 45.2	21 36.5	18 53.6	26 32.2	18 33.6	26 13.5	28 02.6	26 30.0
4 Tu	18 53 17	13 21 40	11♉08 03	18 23 12	5 32.1	19 19.0	28 32.9	22 19.6	19 17.9	26 24.5	18 38.8	26 11.0	28 03.5	26 29.0
5 W	18 57 14	14 22 49	25 41 02	3♊00 56	5 32.9	20 57.6	29 21.4	23 02.7	19 42.2	26 16.8	18 43.8	26 08.5	28 04.3	26 28.0
6 Th	19 01 10	15 23 57	10♊22 15	17 44 11	5 33.6	22 36.4	0♐10.8	23 45.8	20 06.5	26 09.0	18 48.8	26 05.9	28 05.1	26 27.0
7 F	19 05 07	16 25 05	25 05 56	2♋26 38	5R34.0	24 15.5	1 01.0	24 28.9	20 30.7	26 01.2	18 53.8	26 03.4	28 05.9	26 25.9
8 Sa	19 09 04	17 26 13	9♋45 26	17 01 30	5 33.8	25 54.8	1 52.0	25 12.0	20 54.8	25 53.3	18 58.6	26 00.8	28 06.6	26 24.9
9 Su	19 13 00	18 27 21	24 14 01	1♌22 18	5 32.9	27 34.3	2 43.7	25 55.1	21 18.9	25 45.4	19 03.4	25 58.2	28 07.4	26 23.8
10 M	19 16 57	19 28 28	8♌25 43	15 23 48	5 31.4	29 14.0	3 36.2	26 38.2	21 42.9	25 37.4	19 08.2	25 55.7	28 08.0	26 22.7
11 Tu	19 20 53	20 29 36	22 16 09	29 20 03	5 29.3	0♒53.7	4 29.4	27 21.2	22 06.9	25 29.4	19 12.8	25 53.1	28 08.7	26 21.5
12 W	19 24 50	21 30 43	5♍42 55	12♍17 15	5 27.0	2 33.4	5 23.3	28 04.3	22 30.8	25 21.3	19 17.4	25 50.5	28 09.3	26 20.4
13 Th	19 28 46	22 31 50	18 45 44	25 08 35	5 24.9	4 13.1	6 17.8	28 47.3	22 54.7	25 13.3	19 21.9	25 47.9	28 09.9	26 19.2
14 F	19 32 43	23 32 57	1♎26 11	7♎38 57	5 23.3	5 52.5	7 13.0	29 30.3	23 18.5	25 05.2	19 26.3	25 45.3	28 10.4	26 18.0
15 Sa	19 36 39	24 34 03	13 47 21	19 51 58	5D22.4	7 31.5	8 08.8	0♈13.3	23 42.3	24 57.1	19 30.6	25 42.6	28 10.9	26 16.8
16 Su	19 40 36	25 35 10	25 53 21	1♏52 07	5 22.5	9 10.1	9 05.1	0 56.3	24 06.0	24 49.1	19 34.9	25 40.0	28 11.4	26 15.6
17 M	19 44 33	26 36 16	7♏48 52	13 44 15	5 23.4	10 47.9	10 02.0	1 39.3	24 29.6	24 41.0	19 39.0	25 37.4	28 11.8	26 14.4
18 Tu	19 48 29	27 37 22	19 38 51	25 33 17	5 25.0	12 24.8	10 59.4	2 22.3	24 53.2	24 32.9	19 43.1	25 34.8	28 12.2	26 13.1
19 W	19 52 26	28 38 28	1♐28 09	7♐23 58	5 26.8	14 00.5	11 57.4	3 05.3	25 16.7	24 24.9	19 47.1	25 32.2	28 12.6	26 11.9
20 Th	19 56 22	29 39 33	13 21 18	19 20 35	5 28.4	15 34.6	12 55.8	3 48.3	25 40.1	24 16.9	19 51.0	25 29.6	28 13.0	26 10.6
21 F	20 00 19	0♒40 38	25 22 17	1♑26 47	5R29.3	17 06.8	13 54.7	4 31.2	26 03.5	24 08.9	19 54.9	25 27.0	28 13.3	26 09.3
22 Sa	20 04 15	1 41 43	7♑34 23	13 45 24	5 29.1	18 36.6	14 54.1	5 14.2	26 26.8	24 00.9	19 58.6	25 24.4	28 13.5	26 08.0
23 Su	20 08 12	2 42 47	20 00 10	26 18 22	5 27.5	20 03.6	15 53.9	5 57.1	26 50.1	23 53.0	20 02.3	25 21.8	28 13.8	26 06.6
24 M	20 12 08	3 43 50	2♒40 35	9♒06 38	5 24.4	21 27.1	16 54.1	6 40.0	27 13.2	23 45.1	20 05.9	25 19.2	28 14.0	26 05.3
25 Tu	20 16 05	4 44 52	15 36 32	22 10 09	5 20.1	22 46.7	17 54.7	7 22.9	27 36.3	23 37.3	20 09.4	25 16.6	28 14.1	26 03.9
26 W	20 20 02	5 45 53	28 47 24	5♓28 04	5 15.1	24 01.6	18 55.8	8 05.8	27 59.4	23 29.5	20 12.8	25 14.1	28 14.3	26 02.6
27 Th	20 23 58	6 46 53	12♓11 59	18 58 56	5 09.9	25 11.0	19 57.1	8 48.6	28 22.3	23 21.8	20 16.1	25 11.5	28 14.4	26 01.2
28 F	20 27 55	7 47 52	25 48 40	2♈40 59	5 05.2	26 14.3	20 58.9	9 31.5	28 45.2	23 14.2	20 19.3	25 09.0	28 14.4	25 59.8
29 Sa	20 31 51	8 48 50	9♈35 38	16 32 25	5 01.8	27 10.5	22 01.0	10 14.3	29 08.0	23 06.7	20 22.4	25 06.5	28R14.5	25 58.4
30 Su	20 35 48	9 49 47	23 31 08	0♉31 37	4D59.9	27 58.8	23 03.4	10 57.1	29 30.7	22 59.2	20 25.4	25 03.9	28 14.5	25 57.0
31 M	20 39 44	10 50 42	7♉33 40	14 37 07	4 59.6	28 38.5	24 06.1	11 39.9	29 53.3	22 51.8	20 28.4	25 01.5	28 14.4	25 55.6

LONGITUDE — February 1955

Day	Sid.Time	☉	0 hr ☽	Noon ☽	True ☊	☿	♀	♂	⚳	♃	♄	♅	♆	♇
1 Tu	20 43 41	11♒51 37	21♉41 48	28♉47 31	5♑00.5	29♒08.8	25♐09.2	12♈22.6	0♑15.9	22♋44.6	20♏31.2	24♋59.0	28♎14.3	25♌54.2
2 W	20 47 37	12 52 29	5♊54 04	13♊01 13	5 02.0	29 29.0	26 12.6	13 05.3	0 38.3	22R37.4	20 34.0	24R56.5	28R14.2	25R52.7
3 Th	20 51 34	13 53 21	20 08 41	27 16 08	5R03.2	29R38.5	27 16.2	13 48.0	1 00.7	22 30.3	20 36.6	24 54.1	28 14.1	25 51.3
4 F	20 55 31	14 54 11	4♋23 12	11♋29 27	5 03.2	29 37.1	28 20.2	14 30.7	1 23.0	22 23.4	20 39.2	24 51.7	28 13.9	25 49.8
5 Sa	20 59 27	15 55 00	18 34 26	25 37 40	5 01.5	29 24.6	29 24.4	15 13.4	1 45.2	22 16.5	20 41.6	24 49.3	28 13.7	25 48.4
6 Su	21 03 24	16 55 47	2♌38 37	9♌36 46	4 57.6	29 01.1	0♑28.9	15 56.0	2 07.3	22 09.8	20 44.0	24 46.9	28 13.5	25 46.9
7 M	21 07 20	17 56 34	16 31 37	23 22 43	4 51.7	28 27.2	1 33.7	16 38.6	2 29.4	22 03.1	20 46.3	24 44.6	28 13.2	25 45.5
8 Tu	21 11 17	18 57 18	0♍09 39	6♍52 05	4 44.3	27 43.5	2 38.7	17 21.2	2 51.3	21 56.7	20 48.4	24 42.2	28 12.9	25 44.0
9 W	21 15 13	19 58 02	13 29 45	20 02 30	4 36.0	26 51.4	3 43.9	18 03.7	3 13.1	21 50.3	20 50.5	24 39.9	28 12.5	25 42.5
10 Th	21 19 10	20 58 44	26 30 17	2♎53 09	4 28.0	25 52.1	4 49.4	18 46.2	3 34.9	21 44.1	20 52.5	24 37.7	28 12.2	25 41.0
11 F	21 23 06	21 59 26	9♎11 14	15 24 46	4 20.9	24 47.5	5 55.1	19 28.7	3 56.5	21 38.0	20 54.4	24 35.4	28 11.8	25 39.6
12 Sa	21 27 03	23 00 06	21 34 06	27 39 38	4 15.5	23 39.2	7 01.1	20 11.2	4 18.1	21 32.0	20 56.1	24 33.2	28 11.3	25 38.1
13 Su	21 31 00	24 00 45	3♏41 51	9♏41 17	4 12.1	22 29.2	8 07.2	20 53.6	4 39.5	21 26.2	20 57.8	24 31.0	28 10.8	25 36.6
14 M	21 34 56	25 01 23	15 38 30	21 34 09	4D10.7	21 19.5	9 13.6	21 36.0	5 00.9	21 20.6	20 59.4	24 28.9	28 10.3	25 35.1
15 Tu	21 38 53	26 02 00	27 28 52	3♐23 19	4 10.9	20 11.7	10 20.1	22 18.4	5 22.2	21 15.0	21 00.8	24 26.7	28 09.8	25 33.6
16 W	21 42 49	27 02 36	9♐18 11	15 14 07	4 12.0	19 07.5	11 26.9	23 00.8	5 43.3	21 09.7	21 02.2	24 24.7	28 09.2	25 32.1
17 Th	21 46 46	28 03 10	21 11 47	27 11 50	4R13.0	18 08.2	12 33.8	23 43.1	6 04.4	21 04.5	21 03.5	24 22.6	28 08.6	25 30.6
18 F	21 50 42	29 03 43	3♑14 50	9♑21 22	4 13.1	17 14.7	13 40.9	24 25.4	6 25.3	20 59.5	21 04.7	24 20.6	28 08.0	25 29.2
19 Sa	21 54 39	0♓04 15	15 31 54	21 46 54	4 11.4	16 27.9	14 48.2	25 07.7	6 46.1	20 54.6	21 05.7	24 18.6	28 07.4	25 27.7
20 Su	21 58 35	1 04 46	28 06 41	4♒31 31	4 07.3	15 48.3	15 55.7	25 49.9	7 06.8	20 49.9	21 06.7	24 16.6	28 06.7	25 26.2
21 M	22 02 32	2 05 15	11♒01 33	17 36 49	4 00.7	15 16.1	17 03.3	26 32.2	7 27.4	20 45.4	21 07.5	24 14.7	28 05.9	25 24.7
22 Tu	22 06 29	3 05 42	24 17 14	1♓02 37	3 52.0	14 51.4	18 11.0	27 14.4	7 47.9	20 41.1	21 08.3	24 12.9	28 05.2	25 23.2
23 W	22 10 25	4 06 07	7♓52 38	14 46 53	3 41.8	14 34.3	19 19.0	27 56.5	8 08.3	20 36.9	21 08.9	24 11.0	28 04.4	25 21.8
24 Th	22 14 22	5 06 31	21 44 52	28 46 01	3 31.2	14D24.3	20 27.0	28 38.7	8 28.5	20 32.9	21 09.5	24 09.2	28 03.6	25 20.3
25 F	22 18 18	6 06 53	5♈49 44	12♈55 21	3 21.5	14 21.4	21 35.2	29 20.8	8 48.6	20 29.1	21 09.9	24 07.5	28 02.8	25 18.8
26 Sa	22 22 15	7 07 14	20 02 17	27 09 55	3 13.7	14 25.2	22 43.5	0♉02.9	9 08.6	20 25.5	21 10.2	24 05.7	28 01.9	25 17.4
27 Su	22 26 11	8 07 32	4♉17 45	11♉25 17	3 08.3	14 35.3	23 51.9	0 44.9	9 28.5	20 22.0	21 10.5	24 04.1	28 01.0	25 15.9
28 M	22 30 08	9 07 48	18 32 09	25 38 02	3 05.5	14 51.3	25 00.5	1 26.9	9 48.2	20 18.8	21R10.6	24 02.4	28 00.1	25 14.5

Astro Data

	Dy Hr Mn
♃⊻♇	3 19:56
♃☌♅	7 2:00
☽0S	12 23:06
♂0N	16 4:42
☽0N	27 10:59
♆R	29 19:18
☿R	3 20:57
☽0S	9 9:11
♃△♄	17 15:55
☽0N	23 18:37
☿D	25 10:17

Planet Ingress

	Dy Hr Mn
♀ ♐	6 6:48
☿ ♒	10 23:05
♂ ♈	15 4:33
☉ ♒	20 20:02
⚳ ♑	31 19:07
♀ ♑	6 1:15
☉ ♓	19 10:19
♂ ♉	26 10:22

Last Aspect / ☽ Ingress

Last Aspect Dy Hr Mn		☽ Ingress Dy Hr Mn
31 20:26	♃ △	♈ 1 1:56
3 2:06	♆ ☍	♉ 3 5:24
5 5:40	♀ ☍	♊ 5 7:04
7 4:53	♆ △	♋ 7 8:00
9 6:31	♆ □	♌ 9 9:41
11 10:24	♆ ⚹	♍ 11 13:43
13 19:21	♂ ☍	♎ 13 21:15
16 4:36	♆ ☌	♏ 16 8:15
18 16:36	☉ ⚹	♐ 18 21:01
21 5:38	♆ ⚹	♑ 21 9:09
23 15:38	♆ □	♒ 23 18:58
25 23:00	♆ △	♓ 26 2:11
27 22:53	♅ △	♈ 28 7:19
30 8:05	♆ ☍	♉ 30 11:06

Last Aspect / ☽ Ingress

Last Aspect Dy Hr Mn		☽ Ingress Dy Hr Mn
1 12:37	☿ □	♊ 1 14:02
3 16:01	♆ △	♋ 3 16:36
5 16:26	♆ □	♌ 5 19:28
7 20:33	♆ ⚹	♍ 7 23:43
9 20:33	♅ ⚹	♎ 10 6:33
12 13:03	♆ ☌	♏ 12 16:38
14 20:08	♇ □	♐ 15 5:07
17 13:53	♆ ⚹	♑ 17 17:34
20 0:01	♆ □	♒ 20 3:33
22 6:46	♆ △	♓ 22 10:09
24 4:08	♅ △	♈ 24 14:06
26 13:27	♆ ☍	♉ 26 16:46
28 11:20	♇ □	♊ 28 19:24

☽ Phases & Eclipses

Dy Hr Mn	
1 20:29	☽ 10♈40
8 12:44	○ 17♋28
8 12:33	• A 0.856
15 22:14	☾ 25♎00
24 1:07	● 3♒16
31 5:05	☽ 10♉33
7 1:43	○ 17♌31
14 19:40	☾ 25♏21
22 15:54	● 3♓16

Astro Data

1 January 1955
Julian Day # 20089
SVP 5♓53'00"
GC 26♐12.6 ⚴ 0♐27.8
Eris 7♈38.8 ⚵ 8♏48.6
⚷ 27♑44.6 ⚶ 20♊11.9R
☽ Mean ☊ 5♑23.8

1 February 1955
Julian Day # 20120
SVP 5♓52'55"
GC 26♐12.7 ⚴ 12♐16.8
Eris 7♈46.4 ⚵ 15♏31.3
⚷ 0♒24.8 ⚶ 16♊18.9R
☽ Mean ☊ 3♑45.4

March 1955 — LONGITUDE

Day	Sid.Time	☉	0 hr ☽	Noon ☽	True ☊	☿	♀	♂	⚳	♃	♄	♅	♆	♇
1 Tu	22 34 04	10♓08 03	2♊42 43	9♊46 00	3♑04.8	15♒12.8	26♑09.2	2♉08.9	10♑07.8	20♋15.7	21♏10.6	24♋00.8	27♎59.1	25♌13.1
2 W	22 38 01	11 08 15	16 47 48	23 48 02	3R 05.1	15 39.6	27 18.0	2 50.9	10 27.3	20R 12.9	21R 10.6	23R 59.3	27R 58.2	25R 11.6
3 Th	22 41 58	12 08 25	0♋46 39	7♋43 37	3 05.2	16 11.2	28 26.9	3 32.8	10 46.6	20 10.2	21 10.4	23 57.8	27 57.2	25 10.2
4 F	22 45 54	13 08 33	14 38 53	21 32 22	3 03.9	16 47.3	29 35.9	4 14.7	11 05.8	20 07.7	21 10.1	23 56.3	27 56.1	25 08.8
5 Sa	22 49 51	14 08 39	28 23 58	5♌13 34	3 00.1	17 27.5	0♒45.1	4 56.5	11 24.9	20 05.4	21 09.7	23 54.9	27 55.1	25 07.4
6 Su	22 53 47	15 08 43	12♌00 59	18 46 02	2 53.5	18 11.7	1 54.3	5 38.4	11 43.8	20 03.3	21 09.2	23 53.6	27 54.0	25 06.0
7 M	22 57 44	16 08 45	25 28 29	2♍08 05	2 44.0	18 59.5	3 03.7	6 20.1	12 02.6	20 01.4	21 08.6	23 52.3	27 52.9	25 04.7
8 Tu	23 01 40	17 08 44	8♍44 37	15 17 50	2 32.3	19 50.7	4 13.1	7 01.9	12 21.2	19 59.6	21 07.9	23 51.0	27 51.8	25 03.3
9 W	23 05 37	18 08 42	21 47 33	28 13 35	2 19.3	20 45.1	5 22.6	7 43.6	12 39.7	19 58.1	21 07.2	23 49.8	27 50.6	25 01.9
10 Th	23 09 33	19 08 38	4♎35 52	10♎54 19	2 06.3	21 42.3	6 32.3	8 25.3	12 58.1	19 56.8	21 06.3	23 48.6	27 49.4	25 00.6
11 F	23 13 30	20 08 33	17 08 59	23 19 58	1 54.3	22 42.4	7 42.0	9 06.9	13 16.2	19 55.6	21 05.3	23 47.5	27 48.2	24 59.3
12 Sa	23 17 27	21 08 25	29 27 27	5♏31 42	1 44.5	23 45.0	8 51.9	9 48.5	13 34.3	19 54.7	21 04.2	23 46.4	27 47.0	24 58.0
13 Su	23 21 23	22 08 16	11♏33 02	17 31 53	1 37.3	24 50.1	10 01.8	10 30.1	13 52.2	19 53.9	21 03.0	23 45.4	27 45.8	24 56.7
14 M	23 25 20	23 08 05	23 28 42	29 24 00	1 32.8	25 57.6	11 11.8	11 11.7	14 09.9	19 53.4	21 01.7	23 44.4	27 44.5	24 55.4
15 Tu	23 29 16	24 07 52	5♐18 24	11♐12 29	1 30.7	27 07.1	12 21.9	11 53.2	14 27.5	19 53.0	21 00.3	23 43.4	27 43.2	24 54.1
16 W	23 33 13	25 07 38	17 06 56	23 02 24	1 30.2	28 18.8	13 32.1	12 34.7	14 44.9	19D 52.8	20 58.9	23 42.6	27 41.9	24 52.9
17 Th	23 37 09	26 07 22	28 59 37	4♑59 15	1 30.2	29 32.5	14 42.3	13 16.1	15 02.1	19 52.9	20 57.3	23 41.7	27 40.6	24 51.6
18 F	23 41 06	27 07 04	11♑02 00	17 08 32	1 29.5	0♓48.0	15 52.6	13 57.5	15 19.2	19 53.1	20 55.6	23 41.0	27 39.3	24 50.4
19 Sa	23 45 02	28 06 44	23 19 30	29 35 29	1 27.2	2 05.4	17 03.0	14 38.9	15 36.1	19 53.5	20 53.9	23 40.2	27 37.9	24 49.2
20 Su	23 48 59	29 06 23	5♒56 58	12♒24 24	1 22.5	3 24.5	18 13.5	15 20.3	15 52.8	19 54.1	20 52.0	23 39.6	27 36.5	24 48.0
21 M	23 52 56	0♈06 00	18 58 05	25 38 12	1 14.9	4 45.2	19 24.0	16 01.6	16 09.3	19 54.9	20 50.0	23 39.0	27 35.1	24 46.8
22 Tu	23 56 52	1 05 35	2♓24 46	9♓17 40	1 04.9	6 07.6	20 34.7	16 42.9	16 25.7	19 55.9	20 48.0	23 38.4	27 33.7	24 45.7
23 W	0 00 49	2 05 08	16 16 36	23 21 06	0 53.2	7 31.6	21 45.3	17 24.2	16 41.9	19 57.1	20 45.9	23 37.9	27 32.3	24 44.5
24 Th	0 04 45	3 04 39	0♈30 32	7♈44 08	0 41.0	8 57.2	22 56.0	18 05.4	16 57.9	19 58.5	20 43.6	23 37.4	27 30.8	24 43.4
25 F	0 08 42	4 04 08	15 01 01	22 20 15	0 29.5	10 24.2	24 06.8	18 46.6	17 13.7	20 00.0	20 41.3	23 37.0	27 29.3	24 42.3
26 Sa	0 12 38	5 03 34	29 40 51	7♉01 51	0 20.1	11 52.8	25 17.6	19 27.8	17 29.3	20 01.8	20 38.9	23 36.6	27 27.9	24 41.2
27 Su	0 16 35	6 02 59	14♉22 19	21 41 26	0 13.4	13 22.8	26 28.5	20 08.9	17 44.7	20 03.7	20 36.4	23 36.3	27 26.4	24 40.2
28 M	0 20 31	7 02 22	28 58 29	6♊12 53	0 09.5	14 54.3	27 39.5	20 50.0	17 59.9	20 05.9	20 33.8	23 36.1	27 24.9	24 39.1
29 Tu	0 24 28	8 01 42	13♊24 12	20 32 07	0D 08.1	16 27.1	28 50.4	21 31.1	18 14.9	20 08.2	20 31.2	23 35.9	27 23.4	24 38.1
30 W	0 28 25	9 01 00	27 36 26	4♋37 04	0R 07.9	18 01.5	0♓01.5	22 12.1	18 29.8	20 10.7	20 28.4	23 35.8	27 21.8	24 37.1
31 Th	0 32 21	10 00 15	11♋34 01	18 27 20	0 07.8	19 37.2	1 12.6	22 53.1	18 44.4	20 13.4	20 25.6	23 35.7	27 20.3	24 36.2

April 1955 — LONGITUDE

Day	Sid.Time	☉	0 hr ☽	Noon ☽	True ☊	☿	♀	♂	⚳	♃	♄	♅	♆	♇
1 F	0 36 18	10♈59 28	25♋17 09	2♌03 33	0♑06.3	21♓14.3	2♓23.7	23♉34.1	18♑58.8	20♋16.3	20♏22.7	23♋35.7	27♎18.7	24♌35.2
2 Sa	0 40 14	11 58 39	8♌46 42	15 26 44	0R 02.7	22 52.9	3 34.8	24 15.0	19 12.9	20 19.3	20R 19.8	23D 35.7	27R 17.2	24R 34.3
3 Su	0 44 11	12 57 47	22 03 44	28 37 48	29♐56.2	24 32.9	4 46.0	24 55.9	19 26.9	20 22.6	20 16.7	23 35.8	27 15.6	24 33.4
4 M	0 48 07	13 56 53	5♍09 00	11♍37 22	29 46.9	26 14.3	5 57.3	25 36.7	19 40.7	20 26.0	20 13.6	23 35.9	27 14.0	24 32.5
5 Tu	0 52 04	14 55 57	18 02 54	24 25 37	29 35.4	27 57.1	7 08.6	26 17.6	19 54.2	20 29.5	20 10.4	23 36.1	27 12.4	24 31.7
6 W	0 56 00	15 54 59	0♎45 29	7♎02 30	29 22.7	29 41.4	8 19.9	26 58.3	20 07.5	20 33.3	20 07.1	23 36.3	27 10.8	24 30.8
7 Th	0 59 57	16 53 58	13 16 40	19 28 01	29 09.8	1♈27.2	9 31.3	27 39.1	20 20.6	20 37.2	20 03.8	23 36.6	27 09.2	24 30.0
8 F	1 03 53	17 52 56	25 36 35	1♏42 27	28 57.9	3 14.4	10 42.7	28 19.8	20 33.5	20 41.3	20 00.4	23 37.0	27 07.6	24 29.2
9 Sa	1 07 50	18 51 52	7♏45 46	13 46 43	28 48.0	5 03.1	11 54.2	29 00.5	20 46.1	20 45.6	19 56.9	23 37.4	27 06.0	24 28.5
10 Su	1 11 47	19 50 46	19 45 32	25 42 30	28 40.6	6 53.3	13 05.7	29 41.1	20 58.5	20 50.0	19 53.3	23 37.8	27 04.4	24 27.7
11 M	1 15 43	20 49 38	1♐37 59	7♐32 22	28 36.0	8 44.9	14 17.2	0♊21.8	21 10.6	20 54.6	19 49.7	23 38.3	27 02.7	24 27.0
12 Tu	1 19 40	21 48 28	13 26 08	19 19 47	28D 33.8	10 38.1	15 28.8	1 02.3	21 22.6	20 59.4	19 46.1	23 38.9	27 01.1	24 26.3
13 W	1 23 36	22 47 16	25 13 52	1♑08 59	28 33.4	12 32.8	16 40.4	1 42.9	21 34.2	21 04.3	19 42.4	23 39.5	26 59.5	24 25.7
14 Th	1 27 33	23 46 03	7♑05 46	13 04 51	28R 33.9	14 29.0	17 52.1	2 23.4	21 45.6	21 09.4	19 38.6	23 40.2	26 57.9	24 25.0
15 F	1 31 29	24 44 48	19 06 56	25 12 41	28 34.3	16 26.6	19 03.8	3 03.9	21 56.8	21 14.7	19 34.7	23 40.9	26 56.2	24 24.4
16 Sa	1 35 26	25 43 31	1♒22 45	7♒37 48	28 33.5	18 25.7	20 15.5	3 44.4	22 07.7	21 20.1	19 30.9	23 41.7	26 54.6	24 23.9
17 Su	1 39 22	26 42 13	13 58 25	20 25 09	28 30.9	20 26.2	21 27.3	4 24.8	22 18.3	21 25.6	19 26.9	23 42.5	26 52.9	24 23.3
18 M	1 43 19	27 40 53	26 58 27	3♓38 39	28 26.1	22 28.1	22 39.1	5 05.2	22 28.7	21 31.4	19 22.9	23 43.4	26 51.3	24 22.8
19 Tu	1 47 16	28 39 31	10♓25 58	17 20 26	28 19.1	24 31.3	23 50.9	5 45.6	22 38.8	21 37.2	19 18.9	23 44.3	26 49.6	24 22.3
20 W	1 51 12	29 38 07	24 21 56	1♈30 08	28 10.5	26 35.7	25 02.7	6 25.9	22 48.7	21 43.3	19 14.8	23 45.3	26 48.0	24 21.8
21 Th	1 55 09	0♉36 42	8♈44 31	16 04 20	28 01.4	28 41.3	26 14.6	7 06.2	22 58.2	21 49.4	19 10.7	23 46.3	26 46.4	24 21.3
22 F	1 59 05	1 35 14	23 28 44	0♉56 38	27 52.7	0♉47.8	27 26.5	7 46.5	23 07.5	21 55.8	19 06.5	23 47.4	26 44.7	24 20.9
23 Sa	2 03 02	2 33 45	8♉26 55	15 58 24	27 45.6	2 55.1	28 38.4	8 26.7	23 16.5	22 02.3	19 02.3	23 48.5	26 43.1	24 20.5
24 Su	2 06 58	3 32 14	23 29 51	1♊00 09	27 40.7	5 03.1	29 50.4	9 06.9	23 25.2	22 08.9	18 58.0	23 49.7	26 41.4	24 20.2
25 M	2 10 55	4 30 42	8♊28 15	15 53 14	27D 38.1	7 11.5	1♈02.3	9 47.1	23 33.6	22 15.6	18 53.8	23 51.0	26 39.8	24 19.8
26 Tu	2 14 51	5 29 07	23 14 20	0♋30 57	27 37.6	9 20.2	2 14.3	10 27.3	23 41.7	22 22.6	18 49.4	23 52.3	26 38.2	24 19.5
27 W	2 18 48	6 27 29	7♋42 40	14 49 12	27 38.4	11 28.7	3 26.3	11 07.4	23 49.5	22 29.6	18 45.1	23 53.6	26 36.6	24 19.3
28 Th	2 22 45	7 25 50	21 50 26	28 46 21	27R 39.3	13 37.0	4 38.3	11 47.5	23 57.1	22 36.8	18 40.7	23 55.0	26 35.0	24 19.0
29 F	2 26 41	8 24 09	5♌37 02	12♌22 39	27 39.5	15 44.6	5 50.4	12 27.6	24 04.3	22 44.1	18 36.3	23 56.5	26 33.4	24 18.8
30 Sa	2 30 38	9 22 25	19 03 25	25 39 37	27 38.2	17 51.2	7 02.4	13 07.6	24 11.2	22 51.6	18 31.9	23 58.0	26 31.8	24 18.6

Astro Data Dy Hr Mn	Planet Ingress Dy Hr Mn	Last Aspect Dy Hr Mn	☽ Ingress Dy Hr Mn	Last Aspect Dy Hr Mn	☽ Ingress Dy Hr Mn	☽ Phases & Eclipses Dy Hr Mn	Astro Data
♄R 1 6:19	♀ ♒ 4 20:22	2 19:09 ♆ △	♋ 2 22:40	1 3:36 ♆ □	♌ 1 8:20	1 12:40 ☽ 10♊10	1 March 1955
☽0S 8 18:13	☿ ♓ 17 20:49	4 23:10 ♆ □	♌ 5 2:48	3 9:30 ♆ ⚹	♍ 3 14:31	8 15:41 ○ 17♍18	Julian Day # 20148
♃D 16 20:38	☉ ♈ 21 9:35	7 4:20 ♆ ⚹	♍ 7 8:09	5 19:44 ☿ ☍	♎ 5 22:34	16 16:36 ☾ 25♐19	SVP 5♓52'51"
☉0N 21 9:34	♀ ♓ 30 11:30	9 3:48 ♅ ⚹	♎ 9 15:20	8 3:00 ♆ ☌	♏ 8 8:38	24 3:42 ● 2♈44	GC 26♐12.8 ⚵ 21♐03.8
☽0N 23 3:59		11 20:44 ♆ ☌	♏ 12 1:04	10 20:32 ♂ ☍	♐ 10 20:41	30 20:10 ☽ 9♋21	Eris 8♈01.1 ⚴ 18♏18.1
	☊ ♐R 2 23:08	14 4:17 ☿ □	♐ 14 13:13	13 3:36 ♆ ⚹	♑ 13 9:40		⚷ 2♒39.4 ⚶ 18♊38.8
♅D 1 12:50	☿ ♈ 6 16:14	16 23:51 ☿ ⚹	♑ 17 2:01	15 15:22 ♆ □	♒ 15 21:20	7 6:35 ○ 16♎41	☽ Mean ☊ 2♑16.4
♃△♄ 2 13:41	♂ ♊ 10 23:09	19 8:56 ☉ ⚹	♒ 19 12:47	18 0:26 ☉ ⚹	♓ 18 5:28	15 11:01 ☾ 24♑42	
☽0S 5 0:55	☉ ♉ 20 20:58	21 15:28 ♅ △	♓ 21 19:45	20 0:09 ♀ ☌	♈ 20 9:29	22 13:06 ● 1♉38	1 April 1955
☿0N 9 10:17	☿ ♉ 22 2:57	23 12:28 ♅ △	♈ 23 23:09	22 5:16 ♆ ☍	♉ 22 10:29	29 4:23 ☽ 8♌06	Julian Day # 20179
☽0N 19 13:43	♀ ♈ 24 15:13	25 20:24 ♆ ☍	♉ 26 0:31	24 9:59 ♀ ⚹	♊ 24 10:24		SVP 5♓52'48"
♀0N 27 16:45		27 20:34 ♀ □	♊ 28 1:42	26 5:36 ♆ △	♋ 26 11:09		GC 26♐12.9 ⚵ 27♐13.2
		30 3:24 ♀ △	♋ 30 4:05	28 8:12 ♆ △	♌ 28 14:08		Eris 8♈22.0 ⚴ 16♏29.8R
				30 13:35 ♆ ⚹	♍ 30 19:58		⚷ 4♒32.5 ⚶ 26♊04.0
							☽ Mean ☊ 0♑37.9

LONGITUDE — May 1955

Day	Sid.Time	☉	0 hr ☽	Noon ☽	True ☊	☿	♀	♂	⚳	♃	♄	♅	♆	♇
1 Su	2 34 34	10♉20 40	2♍11 30	8♍39 21	27♐34.8	19♉56.6	8♈14.5	13♊47.6	24♑17.8	22♋59.1	18♏27.5	23♋59.5	26♎30.2	24♌18.4
2 M	2 38 31	11 18 52	15 03 27	21 24 05	27R 29.5	22 00.5	9 26.6	14 27.6	24 24.1	23 06.9	18R 23.0	24 01.1	26R 28.6	24R 18.3
3 Tu	2 42 27	12 17 02	27 41 28	3♎55 51	27 22.6	24 02.5	10 38.7	15 07.5	24 30.0	23 14.7	18 18.6	24 02.7	26 27.0	24 18.2
4 W	2 46 24	13 15 11	10♎07 26	16 16 26	27 14.7	26 02.4	11 50.8	15 47.4	24 35.7	23 22.7	18 14.1	24 04.4	26 25.5	24 18.1
5 Th	2 50 20	14 13 17	22 23 02	28 27 23	27 06.6	27 59.9	13 03.0	16 27.3	24 41.0	23 30.8	18 09.6	24 06.1	26 23.9	24 18.0
6 F	2 54 17	15 11 22	4♏29 41	10♏30 07	26 59.3	29 54.9	14 15.2	17 07.1	24 46.0	23 39.0	18 05.1	24 07.9	26 22.4	24D 18.0
7 Sa	2 58 14	16 09 26	16 28 50	22 26 04	26 53.2	1♊47.0	15 27.4	17 46.9	24 50.7	23 47.3	18 00.6	24 09.7	26 20.9	24 18.0
8 Su	3 02 10	17 07 27	28 22 02	4♐16 59	26 48.9	3 36.2	16 39.6	18 26.7	24 55.1	23 55.8	17 56.1	24 11.6	26 19.3	24 18.1
9 M	3 06 07	18 05 28	10♐11 11	16 04 58	26D 46.5	5 22.3	17 51.8	19 06.5	24 59.1	24 04.3	17 51.6	24 13.5	26 17.8	24 18.1
10 Tu	3 10 03	19 03 26	21 58 41	27 52 42	26 45.9	7 05.1	19 04.1	19 46.2	25 02.8	24 13.0	17 47.0	24 15.5	26 16.4	24 18.2
11 W	3 14 00	20 01 24	3♑47 28	9♑43 26	26 46.6	8 44.5	20 16.3	20 25.9	25 06.1	24 21.8	17 42.5	24 17.5	26 14.9	24 18.3
12 Th	3 17 56	20 59 19	15 41 06	21 41 00	26 48.1	10 20.5	21 28.6	21 05.6	25 09.1	24 30.7	17 38.0	24 19.5	26 13.4	24 18.5
13 F	3 21 53	21 57 14	27 43 40	3♒49 42	26 49.8	11 52.9	22 40.9	21 45.2	25 11.8	24 39.8	17 33.5	24 21.6	26 12.0	24 18.7
14 Sa	3 25 49	22 55 07	9♒59 41	16 14 11	26R 50.9	13 21.8	23 53.3	22 24.8	25 14.1	24 48.9	17 29.0	24 23.7	26 10.5	24 18.9
15 Su	3 29 46	23 52 59	22 33 46	28 58 59	26 51.0	14 46.9	25 05.6	23 04.4	25 16.0	24 58.1	17 24.6	24 25.9	26 09.1	24 19.1
16 M	3 33 43	24 50 50	5♓30 18	12♓08 08	26 49.8	16 08.4	26 18.0	23 44.0	25 17.6	25 07.5	17 20.1	24 28.1	26 07.7	24 19.4
17 Tu	3 37 39	25 48 40	18 52 49	25 44 32	26 47.2	17 26.1	27 30.4	24 23.5	25 18.9	25 16.9	17 15.6	24 30.4	26 06.3	24 19.7
18 W	3 41 36	26 46 28	2♈43 20	9♈49 06	26 43.6	18 39.9	28 42.8	25 03.0	25 19.7	25 26.5	17 11.2	24 32.7	26 05.0	24 20.0
19 Th	3 45 32	27 44 15	17 01 33	24 20 10	26 39.6	19 49.9	29 55.2	25 42.5	25R 20.3	25 36.1	17 06.8	24 35.0	26 03.6	24 20.3
20 F	3 49 29	28 42 02	1♉44 18	9♉13 03	26 35.6	20 55.9	1♉07.6	26 22.0	25 20.4	25 45.9	17 02.4	24 37.4	26 02.3	24 20.7
21 Sa	3 53 25	29 39 47	16 45 26	24 20 17	26 32.4	21 57.9	2 20.1	27 01.4	25 20.2	25 55.8	16 58.1	24 39.8	26 01.0	24 21.1
22 Su	3 57 22	0♊37 30	1♊56 23	9♊32 29	26 30.4	22 55.9	3 32.6	27 40.9	25 19.6	26 05.7	16 53.7	24 42.3	25 59.7	24 21.6
23 M	4 01 18	1 35 13	17 07 22	24 39 51	26D 29.6	23 49.7	4 45.1	28 20.3	25 18.7	26 15.8	16 49.4	24 44.8	25 58.4	24 22.0
24 Tu	4 05 15	2 32 54	2♋08 55	9♋33 39	26 30.0	24 39.4	5 57.5	28 59.6	25 17.4	26 25.9	16 45.2	24 47.3	25 57.2	24 22.5
25 W	4 09 12	3 30 33	16 53 19	24 07 21	26 31.2	25 24.7	7 10.0	29 39.0	25 15.7	26 36.1	16 40.9	24 49.9	25 55.9	24 23.1
26 Th	4 13 08	4 28 11	1♌15 22	8♌17 07	26 32.6	26 05.7	8 22.6	0♋18.3	25 13.7	26 46.5	16 36.7	24 52.5	25 54.7	24 23.6
27 F	4 17 05	5 25 48	15 12 33	22 01 41	26 33.7	26 42.3	9 35.1	0 57.6	25 11.3	26 56.9	16 32.6	24 55.2	25 53.6	24 24.2
28 Sa	4 21 01	6 23 23	28 44 43	5♍21 51	26R 34.2	27 14.4	10 47.6	1 36.9	25 08.5	27 07.4	16 28.5	24 57.8	25 52.4	24 24.8
29 Su	4 24 58	7 20 56	11♍53 26	18 19 50	26 33.8	27 41.9	12 00.2	2 16.1	25 05.4	27 18.0	16 24.4	25 00.5	25 51.2	24 25.4
30 M	4 28 54	8 18 28	24 41 25	0♎58 37	26 32.6	28 04.9	13 12.7	2 55.3	25 01.9	27 28.6	16 20.3	25 03.3	25 50.1	24 26.1
31 Tu	4 32 51	9 15 59	7♎11 51	13 21 32	26 30.7	28 23.2	14 25.3	3 34.5	24 58.0	27 39.4	16 16.4	25 06.1	25 49.0	24 26.8

LONGITUDE — June 1955

Day	Sid.Time	☉	0 hr ☽	Noon ☽	True ☊	☿	♀	♂	⚳	♃	♄	♅	♆	♇
1 W	4 36 47	10♊13 29	19♎28 05	25♎31 53	26♐28.3	28♊36.8	15♉37.9	4♋13.7	24♑53.8	27♋50.2	16♏12.4	25♋08.9	25♎48.0	24♌27.5
2 Th	4 40 44	11 10 57	1♏33 20	7♏32 46	26R 26.0	28 45.8	16 50.5	4 52.8	24R 49.2	28 01.1	16R 08.6	25 11.8	25R 46.9	24 28.2
3 F	4 44 41	12 08 24	13 30 33	19 26 59	26 23.8	28R 50.1	18 03.1	5 31.9	24 44.3	28 12.1	16 04.7	25 14.6	25 45.9	24 29.0
4 Sa	4 48 37	13 05 50	25 22 23	1♐17 02	26 22.2	28 49.9	19 15.7	6 11.0	24 39.0	28 23.1	16 01.0	25 17.6	25 44.9	24 29.8
5 Su	4 52 34	14 03 15	7♐11 14	13 05 15	26 21.2	28 45.2	20 28.4	6 50.1	24 33.4	28 34.3	15 57.2	25 20.5	25 43.9	24 30.6
6 M	4 56 30	15 00 40	18 59 21	24 53 51	26D 20.8	28 36.2	21 41.1	7 29.1	24 27.4	28 45.5	15 53.6	25 23.5	25 43.0	24 31.5
7 Tu	5 00 27	15 58 03	0♑49 00	6♑45 07	26 21.0	28 23.0	22 53.7	8 08.1	24 21.1	28 56.7	15 50.0	25 26.5	25 42.1	24 32.3
8 W	5 04 23	16 55 26	12 42 30	18 41 29	26 21.6	28 05.8	24 06.5	8 47.1	24 14.4	29 08.1	15 46.4	25 29.5	25 41.2	24 33.2
9 Th	5 08 20	17 52 47	24 42 26	0♒45 41	26 22.4	27 45.1	25 19.2	9 26.1	24 07.4	29 19.5	15 43.0	25 32.6	25 40.3	24 34.2
10 F	5 12 16	18 50 09	6♒51 37	13 00 40	26 23.2	27 21.1	26 31.9	10 05.1	24 00.1	29 31.0	15 39.6	25 35.7	25 39.5	24 35.1
11 Sa	5 16 13	19 47 29	19 13 13	25 29 42	26 23.9	26 54.1	27 44.7	10 44.0	23 52.4	29 42.5	15 36.2	25 38.8	25 38.6	24 36.1
12 Su	5 20 10	20 44 49	1♓50 31	8♓16 07	26 24.3	26 24.7	28 57.4	11 23.0	23 44.4	29 54.1	15 32.9	25 41.9	25 37.9	24 37.1
13 M	5 24 06	21 42 09	14 46 51	21 23 06	26R 24.4	25 53.4	0♊10.2	12 01.9	23 36.1	0♌05.8	15 29.7	25 45.1	25 37.1	24 38.1
14 Tu	5 28 03	22 39 28	28 05 09	4♈53 14	26 24.3	25 20.6	1 23.0	12 40.7	23 27.5	0 17.5	15 26.6	25 48.3	25 36.4	24 39.1
15 W	5 31 59	23 36 47	11♈47 30	18 47 57	26 24.1	24 46.9	2 35.9	13 19.6	23 18.6	0 29.3	15 23.5	25 51.5	25 35.7	24 40.2
16 Th	5 35 56	24 34 06	25 54 32	3♉06 59	26 23.9	24 12.9	3 48.7	13 58.5	23 09.3	0 41.2	15 20.5	25 54.8	25 35.0	24 41.3
17 F	5 39 52	25 31 24	10♉24 54	17 47 44	26D 23.8	23 39.2	5 01.6	14 37.3	22 59.8	0 53.1	15 17.6	25 58.0	25 34.3	24 42.4
18 Sa	5 43 49	26 28 42	25 14 46	2♊45 09	26 23.8	23 06.4	6 14.5	15 16.1	22 50.0	1 05.1	15 14.8	26 01.3	25 33.7	24 43.6
19 Su	5 47 45	27 26 00	10♊17 53	17 51 54	26R 23.8	22 35.0	7 27.4	15 54.9	22 39.9	1 17.1	15 12.0	26 04.6	25 33.1	24 44.7
20 M	5 51 42	28 23 17	25 26 03	2♋59 11	26 23.8	22 05.5	8 40.3	16 33.7	22 29.6	1 29.2	15 09.3	26 08.0	25 32.6	24 45.9
21 Tu	5 55 39	29 20 34	10♋30 10	17 57 56	26 23.7	21 38.4	9 53.3	17 12.5	22 19.0	1 41.3	15 06.7	26 11.3	25 32.1	24 47.1
22 W	5 59 35	0♋17 50	25 21 32	2♌40 08	26 23.4	21 14.3	11 06.2	17 51.2	22 08.2	1 53.5	15 04.2	26 14.7	25 31.6	24 48.4
23 Th	6 03 32	1 15 06	9♌53 04	16 59 50	26 22.9	20 53.4	12 19.2	18 29.9	21 57.1	2 05.7	15 01.7	26 18.1	25 31.1	24 49.6
24 F	6 07 28	2 12 21	24 00 05	0♍53 40	26 22.4	20 36.3	13 32.2	19 08.7	21 45.8	2 18.0	14 59.4	26 21.5	25 30.7	24 50.9
25 Sa	6 11 25	3 09 35	7♍40 32	14 20 48	26 21.8	20 23.1	14 45.2	19 47.3	21 34.3	2 30.4	14 57.1	26 25.0	25 30.3	24 52.2
26 Su	6 15 21	4 06 49	20 54 43	27 22 35	26D 21.5	20 14.2	15 58.2	20 26.0	21 22.6	2 42.7	14 54.9	26 28.4	25 29.9	24 53.5
27 M	6 19 18	5 04 02	3♎44 50	10♎01 53	26 21.5	20D 09.7	17 11.2	21 04.7	21 10.6	2 55.1	14 52.8	26 31.9	25 29.6	24 54.9
28 Tu	6 23 15	6 01 15	16 14 16	22 22 30	26 21.8	20 09.9	18 24.3	21 43.3	20 58.6	3 07.6	14 50.8	26 35.4	25 29.2	24 56.2
29 W	6 27 11	6 58 27	28 27 07	4♏28 41	26 22.6	20 14.8	19 37.4	22 21.9	20 46.3	3 20.1	14 48.9	26 38.9	25 29.0	24 57.6
30 Th	6 31 08	7 55 39	10♏27 43	16 24 45	26 23.6	20 24.6	20 50.4	23 00.5	20 33.9	3 32.7	14 47.1	26 42.4	25 28.7	24 59.0

Astro Data

	Dy Hr Mn
☽0S	2 5:55
♇D	6 18:29
♃☌♅	10 20:38
♃⚺♇	11 2:26
♅⚺♇	11 23:19
☽0N	16 22:25
⚳R	20 10:11
♃□♆	21 23:11
☽0S	29 11:09
☿R	3 22:47
♅□♆	11 11:08
☽0N	13 5:30
☽0S	25 18:18
☿D	27 23:12

Planet Ingress

	Dy Hr Mn
☿ ♊	6 13:05
♀ ♉	19 13:35
☉ ♊	21 20:24
♂ ♋	26 0:50
♃ ♌	13 0:07
♀ ♊	13 8:38
☉ ♋	22 4:31

Last Aspect / ☽ Ingress

Last Aspect Dy Hr Mn		☽ Ingress Dy Hr Mn
2 16:59 ♅ ⚹	♎	3 4:26
5 7:56 ♆ ☌	♏	5 15:04
7 15:46 ♇ □	♐	8 3:19
10 8:45 ♆ ⚹	♑	10 16:19
12 21:00 ♅ ☍	♒	13 4:29
15 6:44 ♆ △	♓	15 13:53
17 12:08 ☉ ⚹	♈	17 19:21
19 14:48 ♆ ☍	♉	19 21:12
21 14:32 ♃ ⚹	♊	21 20:56
23 18:09 ♂ ☌	♋	23 20:33
25 16:12 ♃ ☌	♌	25 21:52
27 20:42 ☿ ⚹	♍	28 2:16
30 6:18 ☿ □	♎	30 10:08

Last Aspect / ☽ Ingress

Last Aspect Dy Hr Mn		☽ Ingress Dy Hr Mn
1 18:13 ☿ △	♏	1 20:54
4 6:01 ♃ △	♐	4 9:24
6 19:24 ☿ ☍	♑	6 22:21
9 9:07 ♃ ☍	♒	9 10:30
11 16:43 ♀ □	♓	11 20:32
13 19:52 ♅ △	♈	14 3:24
15 23:58 ♅ □	♉	16 6:50
18 1:12 ♅ ⚹	♊	18 7:37
20 4:12 ☉ ☌	♋	20 7:15
22 1:24 ☿ ☌	♌	22 7:36
24 2:37 ♆ ⚹	♍	24 10:26
26 10:18 ♅ ⚹	♎	26 16:55
28 20:21 ♅ □	♏	29 3:04

☽ Phases & Eclipses

Dy Hr Mn	
6 22:14	○ 15♏36
15 1:42	☾ 23♒28
21 20:59	● 0♊01
28 14:01	☽ 6♍28
5 14:08	○ 14♐08
5 14:23	• A 0.622
13 12:37	☾ 21♓44
20 4:12	● 28♊05
20 4:10:11	• T 07'08"
27 1:44	☽ 4♎40

Astro Data

1 May 1955
Julian Day # 20209
SVP 5♓52'45"
GC 26♐12.9 ⚴ 27♐34.1R
Eris 8♈41.9 ⚵ 10♏32.9R
⚷ 5♒26.7 ⚶ 6♋12.1
☽ Mean ☊ 29♐02.6

1 June 1955
Julian Day # 20240
SVP 5♓52'40"
GC 26♐13.0 ⚴ 21♐08.6R
Eris 8♈57.3 ⚵ 4♏27.3R
⚷ 5♒15.7R ⚶ 18♋27.5
☽ Mean ☊ 27♐24.1

July 1955

LONGITUDE

Day	Sid.Time	☉	0 hr ☽	Noon ☽	True ☊	☿	♀	♂	⚳	♃	♄	♅	♆	♇
1 F	6 35 04	8♋52 50	22♏20 16	28♏14 46	26♐24.8	20♊39.2	22♊03.5	23♋39.1	20♑21.4	3♌45.2	14♏45.3	26♋45.9	25♎28.5	25♌00.4
2 Sa	6 39 01	9 50 01	4♐08 42	10♐02 29	26 25.7	20 58.8	23 16.7	24 17.7	20R 08.7	3 57.9	14R 43.7	26 49.5	25R 28.3	25 01.9
3 Su	6 42 57	10 47 13	15 56 31	21 51 09	26R 26.3	21 23.3	24 29.8	24 56.3	19 56.0	4 10.5	14 42.1	26 53.0	25 28.2	25 03.3
4 M	6 46 54	11 44 24	27 46 43	3♑43 33	26 26.2	21 52.7	25 43.0	25 34.8	19 43.1	4 23.2	14 40.7	26 56.6	25 28.0	25 04.8
5 Tu	6 50 50	12 41 34	9♑41 55	15 42 05	26 25.3	22 27.0	26 56.2	26 13.3	19 30.1	4 35.9	14 39.3	27 00.2	25 28.0	25 06.3
6 W	6 54 47	13 38 45	21 44 16	27 48 43	26 23.7	23 06.1	28 09.4	26 51.8	19 17.1	4 48.7	14 38.0	27 03.8	25 27.9	25 07.8
7 Th	6 58 44	14 35 56	3♒55 39	10♒05 15	26 21.3	23 50.0	29 22.6	27 30.3	19 04.0	5 01.5	14 36.8	27 07.4	25D 27.9	25 09.4
8 F	7 02 40	15 33 07	16 17 42	22 33 14	26 18.6	24 38.7	0♋35.9	28 08.8	18 50.8	5 14.3	14 35.7	27 11.0	25 27.9	25 10.9
9 Sa	7 06 37	16 30 19	28 52 02	5♓14 16	26 15.7	25 32.1	1 49.1	28 47.3	18 37.6	5 27.2	14 34.7	27 14.6	25 27.9	25 12.5
10 Su	7 10 33	17 27 30	11♓40 09	18 09 53	26 13.2	26 30.2	3 02.4	29 25.8	18 24.4	5 40.0	14 33.8	27 18.2	25 28.0	25 14.1
11 M	7 14 30	18 24 43	24 43 39	1♈21 37	26 11.3	27 32.8	4 15.8	0♌04.2	18 11.2	5 53.0	14 33.0	27 21.9	25 28.1	25 15.7
12 Tu	7 18 26	19 21 55	8♈03 58	14 50 50	26D 10.5	28 39.9	5 29.1	0 42.6	17 58.0	6 05.9	14 32.3	27 25.5	25 28.2	25 17.3
13 W	7 22 23	20 19 08	21 42 20	28 38 29	26 10.6	29 51.5	6 42.5	1 21.1	17 44.8	6 18.9	14 31.7	27 29.2	25 28.4	25 18.9
14 Th	7 26 19	21 16 22	5♉39 19	12♉44 43	26 11.6	1♋07.6	7 55.9	1 59.5	17 31.6	6 31.8	14 31.2	27 32.8	25 28.6	25 20.6
15 F	7 30 16	22 13 37	19 54 31	27 08 27	26 12.9	2 27.9	9 09.3	2 37.9	17 18.5	6 44.9	14 30.8	27 36.5	25 28.8	25 22.2
16 Sa	7 34 13	23 10 52	4♊26 06	11♊46 58	26R 14.2	3 52.5	10 22.8	3 16.3	17 05.5	6 57.9	14 30.4	27 40.2	25 29.1	25 23.9
17 Su	7 38 09	24 08 08	19 10 25	26 35 41	26 14.7	5 21.2	11 36.2	3 54.7	16 52.5	7 11.0	14 30.2	27 43.8	25 29.4	25 25.6
18 M	7 42 06	25 05 24	4♋01 57	11♋28 18	26 14.0	6 53.9	12 49.7	4 33.1	16 39.6	7 24.0	14D 30.1	27 47.5	25 29.7	25 27.3
19 Tu	7 46 02	26 02 41	18 53 45	26 17 19	26 11.9	8 30.6	14 03.2	5 11.5	16 26.9	7 37.1	14 30.0	27 51.2	25 30.1	25 29.0
20 W	7 49 59	26 59 58	3♌38 03	10♌55 04	26 08.4	10 11.0	15 16.8	5 49.8	16 14.2	7 50.3	14 30.1	27 54.9	25 30.5	25 30.8
21 Th	7 53 55	27 57 15	18 07 32	25 14 46	26 04.0	11 55.0	16 30.4	6 28.2	16 01.7	8 03.4	14 30.3	27 58.5	25 30.9	25 32.5
22 F	7 57 52	28 54 33	2♍16 13	9♍11 29	25 59.1	13 42.4	17 43.9	7 06.6	15 49.3	8 16.5	14 30.5	28 02.2	25 31.3	25 34.3
23 Sa	8 01 48	29 51 52	16 00 21	22 42 42	25 54.5	15 33.0	18 57.5	7 44.9	15 37.1	8 29.7	14 30.9	28 05.9	25 31.8	25 36.0
24 Su	8 05 45	0♌49 10	29 18 36	5♎48 15	25 50.8	17 26.5	20 11.2	8 23.2	15 25.0	8 42.9	14 31.4	28 09.6	25 32.4	25 37.8
25 M	8 09 42	1 46 29	12♎11 56	18 30 04	25 48.4	19 22.7	21 24.8	9 01.5	15 13.2	8 56.0	14 31.9	28 13.2	25 32.9	25 39.6
26 Tu	8 13 38	2 43 48	24 43 07	0♏51 39	25D 47.5	21 21.2	22 38.5	9 39.8	15 01.5	9 09.2	14 32.6	28 16.9	25 33.5	25 41.4
27 W	8 17 35	3 41 08	6♏56 12	12 57 25	25 47.9	23 21.7	23 52.2	10 18.1	14 50.1	9 22.4	14 33.3	28 20.6	25 34.1	25 43.2
28 Th	8 21 31	4 38 28	18 55 55	24 52 20	25 49.2	25 23.9	25 05.9	10 56.4	14 38.8	9 35.6	14 34.2	28 24.2	25 34.8	25 45.0
29 F	8 25 28	5 35 49	0♐47 17	6♐41 23	25 50.8	27 27.4	26 19.6	11 34.7	14 27.8	9 48.8	14 35.1	28 27.9	25 35.4	25 46.9
30 Sa	8 29 24	6 33 11	12 35 14	18 29 22	25R 52.1	29 32.0	27 33.3	12 13.0	14 17.1	10 02.1	14 36.2	28 31.5	25 36.1	25 48.7
31 Su	8 33 21	7 30 33	24 24 19	0♑20 35	25 52.2	1♌37.3	28 47.1	12 51.2	14 06.5	10 15.3	14 37.3	28 35.2	25 36.9	25 50.6

August 1955

LONGITUDE

Day	Sid.Time	☉	0 hr ☽	Noon ☽	True ☊	☿	♀	♂	⚳	♃	♄	♅	♆	♇
1 M	8 37 17	8♌27 55	6♑18 35	12♑18 44	25♐50.8	3♌42.9	0♌00.9	13♌29.5	13♑56.3	10♌28.5	14♏38.5	28♋38.8	25♎37.7	25♌52.4
2 Tu	8 41 14	9 25 19	18 21 21	24 26 44	25R 47.4	5 48.6	1 14.7	14 07.7	13R 46.3	10 41.7	14 39.9	28 42.5	25 38.5	25 54.3
3 W	8 45 11	10 22 43	0♒35 07	6♒46 41	25 42.1	7 54.2	2 28.5	14 46.0	13 36.5	10 55.0	14 41.3	28 46.1	25 39.3	25 56.2
4 Th	8 49 07	11 20 08	13 01 34	19 19 49	25 35.2	9 59.3	3 42.4	15 24.2	13 27.1	11 08.2	14 42.8	28 49.7	25 40.2	25 58.0
5 F	8 53 04	12 17 34	25 41 30	2♓06 36	25 27.3	12 03.8	4 56.3	16 02.4	13 17.9	11 21.4	14 44.5	28 53.3	25 41.0	25 59.9
6 Sa	8 57 00	13 15 01	8♓35 06	15 06 55	25 19.2	14 07.5	6 10.2	16 40.7	13 09.0	11 34.6	14 46.2	28 56.9	25 42.0	26 01.8
7 Su	9 00 57	14 12 29	21 41 59	28 20 13	25 11.8	16 10.3	7 24.1	17 18.9	13 00.5	11 47.8	14 48.0	29 00.5	25 42.9	26 03.7
8 M	9 04 53	15 09 59	5♈01 33	11♈45 53	25 05.9	18 11.9	8 38.1	17 57.1	12 52.2	12 01.1	14 49.9	29 04.1	25 43.9	26 05.6
9 Tu	9 08 50	16 07 30	18 33 10	25 23 20	25 01.9	20 12.4	9 52.0	18 35.3	12 44.2	12 14.3	14 51.9	29 07.6	25 44.9	26 07.5
10 W	9 12 46	17 05 02	2♉16 21	9♉12 09	25D 00.0	22 11.6	11 06.0	19 13.5	12 36.6	12 27.5	14 53.9	29 11.2	25 45.9	26 09.4
11 Th	9 16 43	18 02 35	16 10 41	23 11 54	24 59.8	24 09.4	12 20.1	19 51.7	12 29.3	12 40.7	14 56.1	29 14.7	25 47.0	26 11.4
12 F	9 20 40	19 00 11	0♊15 44	7♊22 02	25 00.6	26 05.9	13 34.1	20 29.9	12 22.3	12 53.9	14 58.4	29 18.2	25 48.1	26 13.3
13 Sa	9 24 36	19 57 47	14 30 37	21 41 16	25R 01.3	28 01.0	14 48.2	21 08.1	12 15.7	13 07.1	15 00.8	29 21.8	25 49.2	26 15.2
14 Su	9 28 33	20 55 25	28 53 39	6♋07 21	25 00.8	29 54.7	16 02.3	21 46.4	12 09.3	13 20.2	15 03.2	29 25.3	25 50.4	26 17.2
15 M	9 32 29	21 53 05	13♋21 53	20 36 41	24 58.4	1♍46.9	17 16.4	22 24.6	12 03.4	13 33.4	15 05.8	29 28.7	25 51.6	26 19.1
16 Tu	9 36 26	22 50 46	27 51 05	5♌04 23	24 53.6	3 37.6	18 30.6	23 02.8	11 57.8	13 46.5	15 08.4	29 32.2	25 52.8	26 21.0
17 W	9 40 22	23 48 28	12♌15 51	19 24 43	24 46.3	5 27.0	19 44.7	23 41.0	11 52.5	13 59.7	15 11.1	29 35.6	25 54.0	26 23.0
18 Th	9 44 19	24 46 12	26 30 15	3♍31 48	24 37.2	7 14.8	20 58.9	24 19.2	11 47.6	14 12.8	15 13.9	29 39.1	25 55.3	26 24.9
19 F	9 48 15	25 43 57	10♍28 45	17 20 37	24 27.3	9 01.3	22 13.1	24 57.4	11 43.0	14 25.9	15 16.8	29 42.5	25 56.6	26 26.8
20 Sa	9 52 12	26 41 43	24 07 02	0♎47 46	24 17.5	10 46.3	23 27.4	25 35.5	11 38.8	14 39.0	15 19.8	29 45.8	25 57.9	26 28.8
21 Su	9 56 09	27 39 30	7♎22 41	13 51 50	24 08.9	12 29.9	24 41.6	26 13.7	11 35.0	14 52.0	15 22.9	29 49.2	25 59.3	26 30.7
22 M	10 00 05	28 37 19	20 15 22	26 33 33	24 02.3	14 12.1	25 55.8	26 51.9	11 31.5	15 05.1	15 26.1	29 52.5	26 00.6	26 32.7
23 Tu	10 04 02	29 35 08	2♏46 46	8♏55 27	23 58.1	15 52.9	27 10.1	27 30.1	11 28.4	15 18.1	15 29.3	29 55.9	26 02.0	26 34.6
24 W	10 07 58	0♍32 59	15 00 09	21 01 26	23D 56.0	17 32.4	28 24.4	28 08.3	11 25.6	15 31.1	15 32.7	29 59.2	26 03.4	26 36.5
25 Th	10 11 55	1 30 51	26 59 57	2♐56 21	23 55.5	19 10.5	29 38.7	28 46.5	11 23.2	15 44.0	15 36.1	0♌02.4	26 04.9	26 38.5
26 F	10 15 51	2 28 45	8♐51 18	14 45 29	23R 55.9	20 47.2	0♍53.1	29 24.7	11 21.2	15 57.0	15 39.6	0 05.7	26 06.4	26 40.4
27 Sa	10 19 48	3 26 40	20 39 35	26 34 16	23 56.1	22 22.6	2 07.4	0♍02.8	11 19.5	16 09.9	15 43.2	0 08.9	26 07.9	26 42.3
28 Su	10 23 44	4 24 36	2♑30 10	8♑27 53	23 55.1	23 56.7	3 21.7	0 41.0	11 18.2	16 22.8	15 46.8	0 12.1	26 09.4	26 44.3
29 M	10 27 41	5 22 33	14 28 00	20 31 01	23 52.1	25 29.4	4 36.1	1 19.2	11 17.3	16 35.6	15 50.6	0 15.3	26 11.0	26 46.2
30 Tu	10 31 38	6 20 32	26 37 24	2♒47 30	23 46.6	27 00.8	5 50.5	1 57.4	11 16.7	16 48.4	15 54.4	0 18.5	26 12.5	26 48.1
31 W	10 35 34	7 18 32	9♒01 40	15 20 05	23 38.5	28 30.9	7 04.9	2 35.5	11D 16.5	17 01.2	15 58.3	0 21.6	26 14.1	26 50.0

Astro Data Dy Hr Mn	Planet Ingress Dy Hr Mn	Last Aspect Dy Hr Mn	☽ Ingress Dy Hr Mn	Last Aspect Dy Hr Mn	☽ Ingress Dy Hr Mn	☽ Phases & Eclipses Dy Hr Mn
♆ D 7 19:39	♀ ♋ 8 0:15	1 8:58 ♅ △	♐ 1 15:34	2 20:23 ♅ ☍	♒ 2 22:52	5 5:29 ○ 12♑26
☽ 0N 10 11:30	♂ ♌ 11 9:22	3 19:20 ♆ ✶	♑ 4 4:29	5 0:33 ♇ ☍	♓ 5 8:04	12 20:31 ☾ 19♈42
♄ D 19 7:30	☿ ♋ 13 14:44	6 10:31 ♅ ☍	♒ 6 16:18	7 13:13 ♅ △	♈ 7 15:00	19 11:35 ● 26♋02
♆✶♇ 20 6:43	☉ ♌ 23 15:25	8 17:33 ♆ △	♓ 9 2:09	9 18:33 ♅ □	♉ 9 20:03	26 16:00 ☽ 2♏53
☽ 0S 23 3:32	☿ ♌ 30 17:22	11 4:45 ♅ △	♈ 11 9:33	11 22:19 ♅ ✶	♊ 11 23:33	
		13 14:18 ♅ ✶	♉ 13 14:20	14 0:08 ☿ ✶	♋ 14 1:50	3 19:30 ○ 10♒41
☽ 0N 6 17:33	♀ ♌ 1 11:43	15 12:46 ♅ ✶	♊ 15 16:43	16 2:46 ♅ ☌	♌ 16 3:34	11 2:33 ☾ 17♉40
☽ 0S 19 13:37	☿ ♍ 14 13:08	17 10:13 ♆ △	♋ 17 17:30	17 23:49 ♇ ☌	♍ 18 5:57	17 19:58 ● 24♌08
♃□♄ 24 16:02	☉ ♍ 23 22:19	19 14:34 ♅ ☌	♌ 19 18:03	20 10:08 ♅ ✶	♎ 20 10:34	25 8:52 ☽ 1♐23
⚳ D 31 15:38	♅ ♌ 24 18:04	21 12:30 ♇ ☌	♍ 21 20:06	22 18:25 ♀ □	♏ 22 18:37	
	♀ ♍ 25 18:52	23 21:50 ♅ ✶	♎ 24 1:16	25 4:34 ♀ □	♐ 25 6:03	
	♂ ♍ 27 10:13	26 6:55 ♅ □	♏ 26 10:19	27 12:16 ♇ △	♑ 27 18:57	
		28 19:12 ♅ △	♐ 28 22:24	29 23:11 ☿ △	♒ 30 6:35	
		31 2:53 ♇ △	♑ 31 11:18			

Astro Data

1 July 1955
Julian Day # 20270
SVP 5♓52'35"
GC 26♐13.1 ⚴ 12♐54.2R
Eris 9♈03.7 ✱ 2♏38.4
⚷ 4♒07.4R ⚵ 1♌22.0
☽ Mean ☊ 25♐48.8

1 August 1955
Julian Day # 20301
SVP 5♓52'30"
GC 26♐13.1 ⚴ 9♐26.0R
Eris 9♈00.0R ✱ 5♏28.8
⚷ 2♒25.0R ⚵ 15♌23.0
☽ Mean ☊ 24♐10.3

LONGITUDE — September 1955

Day	Sid.Time	☉	0 hr ☽	Noon ☽	True ☊	☿	♀	♂	⚳	♃	♄	♅	♆	♇
1 Th	10 39 31	8♍16 34	21♒42 54	28♒10 10	23♐28.2	29♍59.6	8♍19.3	3♍13.7	11♑16.6	17♌14.0	16♏02.3	0♌24.7	26♎15.7	26♌51.9
2 F	10 43 27	9 14 37	4♓41 50	11♓17 45	23R16.4	1♎27.0	9 33.8	3 51.9	11 17.1	17 26.7	16 06.4	0 27.7	26 17.4	26 53.9
3 Sa	10 47 24	10 12 42	17 57 43	24 41 27	23 04.3	2 53.1	10 48.2	4 30.1	11 17.9	17 39.4	16 10.5	0 30.8	26 19.0	26 55.8
4 Su	10 51 20	11 10 48	1♈28 37	8♈18 51	22 53.1	4 17.7	12 02.7	5 08.2	11 19.1	17 52.0	16 14.7	0 33.8	26 20.7	26 57.6
5 M	10 55 17	12 08 57	15 11 45	22 06 56	22 43.8	5 41.0	13 17.1	5 46.4	11 20.6	18 04.6	16 19.0	0 36.8	26 22.4	26 59.5
6 Tu	10 59 13	13 07 07	29 04 02	6♉02 41	22 37.2	7 02.8	14 31.6	6 24.6	11 22.5	18 17.2	16 23.4	0 39.7	26 24.1	27 01.4
7 W	11 03 10	14 05 20	13♉02 36	20 03 31	22 33.2	8 23.2	15 46.1	7 02.8	11 24.7	18 29.7	16 27.8	0 42.6	26 25.9	27 03.3
8 Th	11 07 06	15 03 34	27 05 14	4♊07 34	22D31.7	9 42.1	17 00.7	7 41.0	11 27.2	18 42.2	16 32.3	0 45.5	26 27.7	27 05.2
9 F	11 11 03	16 01 51	11♊10 24	18 13 37	22R31.4	10 59.4	18 15.2	8 19.2	11 30.1	18 54.7	16 36.9	0 48.4	26 29.5	27 07.0
10 Sa	11 15 00	17 00 10	25 17 07	2♋20 47	22 31.3	12 15.2	19 29.8	8 57.4	11 33.3	19 07.1	16 41.6	0 51.2	26 31.3	27 08.9
11 Su	11 18 56	17 58 30	9♋24 30	16 28 07	22 29.9	13 29.2	20 44.4	9 35.6	11 36.9	19 19.4	16 46.3	0 54.0	26 33.1	27 10.7
12 M	11 22 53	18 56 53	23 31 24	0♌34 06	22 26.3	14 41.6	21 59.0	10 13.8	11 40.8	19 31.8	16 51.1	0 56.8	26 34.9	27 12.6
13 Tu	11 26 49	19 55 18	7♌35 53	14 36 23	22 19.8	15 52.1	23 13.6	10 52.1	11 45.0	19 44.0	16 56.0	0 59.5	26 36.8	27 14.4
14 W	11 30 46	20 53 45	21 35 10	28 31 47	22 10.5	17 00.7	24 28.2	11 30.3	11 49.6	19 56.2	17 00.9	1 02.2	26 38.7	27 16.2
15 Th	11 34 42	21 52 14	5♍25 46	12♍16 38	21 59.0	18 07.2	25 42.8	12 08.5	11 54.4	20 08.4	17 05.9	1 04.8	26 40.6	27 18.0
16 F	11 38 39	22 50 45	19 03 57	25 47 18	21 46.3	19 11.7	26 57.5	12 46.8	11 59.6	20 20.5	17 11.0	1 07.4	26 42.5	27 19.8
17 Sa	11 42 35	23 49 18	2♎26 22	9♎00 52	21 33.7	20 13.8	28 12.1	13 25.0	12 05.2	20 32.6	17 16.1	1 10.0	26 44.4	27 21.6
18 Su	11 46 32	24 47 52	15 30 41	21 55 42	21 22.3	21 13.5	29 26.8	14 03.2	12 11.0	20 44.5	17 21.3	1 12.5	26 46.4	27 23.3
19 M	11 50 29	25 46 29	28 16 00	4♏31 42	21 13.1	22 10.6	0♎41.4	14 41.5	12 17.1	20 56.5	17 26.6	1 15.0	26 48.4	27 25.1
20 Tu	11 54 25	26 45 07	10♏43 03	16 50 21	21 06.7	23 04.8	1 56.1	15 19.7	12 23.6	21 08.4	17 31.9	1 17.5	26 50.4	27 26.8
21 W	11 58 22	27 43 47	22 54 03	28 54 37	21 02.9	23 56.1	3 10.8	15 58.0	12 30.3	21 20.2	17 37.3	1 19.9	26 52.4	27 28.6
22 Th	12 02 18	28 42 29	4♐52 36	10♐48 34	21D01.2	24 44.1	4 25.5	16 36.2	12 37.4	21 31.9	17 42.7	1 22.3	26 54.4	27 30.3
23 F	12 06 15	29 41 12	16 43 12	22 37 07	21R00.9	25 28.6	5 40.2	17 14.5	12 44.7	21 43.6	17 48.2	1 24.6	26 56.4	27 32.0
24 Sa	12 10 11	0♎39 57	28 31 02	4♑25 39	21 01.0	26 09.3	6 54.9	17 52.8	12 52.4	21 55.3	17 53.8	1 26.9	26 58.4	27 33.7
25 Su	12 14 08	1 38 44	10♑21 38	16 19 42	21 00.2	26 45.8	8 09.6	18 31.0	13 00.3	22 06.8	17 59.4	1 29.1	27 00.5	27 35.4
26 M	12 18 04	2 37 32	22 20 28	28 24 36	20 57.6	27 17.9	9 24.4	19 09.3	13 08.5	22 18.3	18 05.1	1 31.4	27 02.6	27 37.0
27 Tu	12 22 01	3 36 23	4♒32 40	10♒45 10	20 52.6	27 45.2	10 39.1	19 47.6	13 17.0	22 29.7	18 10.8	1 33.5	27 04.7	27 38.7
28 W	12 25 58	4 35 15	17 02 34	23 25 10	20 45.1	28 07.3	11 53.8	20 25.9	13 25.8	22 41.1	18 16.6	1 35.6	27 06.7	27 40.3
29 Th	12 29 54	5 34 08	29 53 16	6♓26 57	20 35.3	28 23.8	13 08.5	21 04.2	13 34.9	22 52.4	18 22.4	1 37.7	27 08.9	27 41.9
30 F	12 33 51	6 33 04	13♓06 14	19 51 00	20 24.0	28 34.2	14 23.3	21 42.5	13 44.2	23 03.6	18 28.3	1 39.7	27 11.0	27 43.5

LONGITUDE — October 1955

Day	Sid.Time	☉	0 hr ☽	Noon ☽	True ☊	☿	♀	♂	⚳	♃	♄	♅	♆	♇
1 Sa	12 37 47	7♎32 02	26♓40 59	3♈35 47	20♐12.2	28♎38.1	15♎38.0	22♍20.8	13♑53.8	23♌14.7	18♏34.3	1♌41.7	27♎13.1	27♌45.1
2 Su	12 41 44	8 31 01	10♈34 57	17 37 51	20R01.3	28R35.2	16 52.8	22 59.1	14 03.6	23 25.7	18 40.2	1 43.7	27 15.2	27 46.6
3 M	12 45 40	9 30 03	24 43 52	1♉52 18	19 52.2	28 25.0	18 07.5	23 37.4	14 13.7	23 36.7	18 46.3	1 45.6	27 17.4	27 48.2
4 Tu	12 49 37	10 29 07	9♉02 26	16 13 35	19 45.7	28 07.2	19 22.3	24 15.7	14 24.1	23 47.6	18 52.4	1 47.4	27 19.5	27 49.7
5 W	12 53 33	11 28 13	23 25 08	0♊36 29	19 42.0	27 41.6	20 37.0	24 54.1	14 34.7	23 58.4	18 58.5	1 49.2	27 21.7	27 51.2
6 Th	12 57 30	12 27 21	7♊47 08	14 56 41	19D40.6	27 08.1	21 51.8	25 32.4	14 45.5	24 09.2	19 04.7	1 51.0	27 23.9	27 52.7
7 F	13 01 27	13 26 32	22 04 48	29 11 14	19 40.8	26 26.7	23 06.6	26 10.8	14 56.6	24 19.8	19 10.9	1 52.7	27 26.1	27 54.2
8 Sa	13 05 23	14 25 46	6♋15 48	13♋18 22	19R41.2	25 37.8	24 21.4	26 49.1	15 08.0	24 30.4	19 17.2	1 54.4	27 28.2	27 55.6
9 Su	13 09 20	15 25 01	20 18 52	27 17 15	19 40.6	24 41.9	25 36.2	27 27.5	15 19.6	24 40.9	19 23.5	1 56.0	27 30.4	27 57.1
10 M	13 13 16	16 24 19	4♌13 26	11♌07 24	19 38.1	23 39.9	26 51.0	28 05.9	15 31.4	24 51.2	19 29.8	1 57.6	27 32.6	27 58.5
11 Tu	13 17 13	17 23 39	17 59 04	24 48 21	19 33.0	22 32.8	28 05.8	28 44.3	15 43.4	25 01.5	19 36.2	1 59.1	27 34.9	27 59.9
12 W	13 21 09	18 23 01	1♍35 08	8♍19 18	19 25.5	21 22.3	29 20.6	29 22.7	15 55.7	25 11.7	19 42.7	2 00.5	27 37.1	28 01.2
13 Th	13 25 06	19 22 26	15 00 40	21 39 05	19 16.0	20 10.1	0♏35.4	0♎01.1	16 08.2	25 21.8	19 49.2	2 01.9	27 39.3	28 02.6
14 F	13 29 02	20 21 53	28 14 24	4♎46 24	19 05.4	18 58.1	1 50.2	0 39.5	16 21.0	25 31.8	19 55.7	2 03.3	27 41.5	28 03.9
15 Sa	13 32 59	21 21 21	11♎14 59	17 40 01	18 54.8	17 48.4	3 05.0	1 17.9	16 33.9	25 41.8	20 02.2	2 04.6	27 43.7	28 05.2
16 Su	13 36 55	22 20 52	24 01 25	0♏19 10	18 45.2	16 43.0	4 19.9	1 56.4	16 47.1	25 51.6	20 08.8	2 05.9	27 46.0	28 06.5
17 M	13 40 52	23 20 25	6♏33 17	12 43 52	18 37.6	15 43.9	5 34.7	2 34.8	17 00.5	26 01.3	20 15.4	2 07.1	27 48.2	28 07.7
18 Tu	13 44 49	24 20 00	18 51 04	24 55 07	18 32.2	14 52.8	6 49.5	3 13.3	17 14.1	26 10.9	20 22.1	2 08.3	27 50.4	28 09.0
19 W	13 48 45	25 19 37	0♐56 18	6♐54 58	18D29.3	14 11.1	8 04.3	3 51.7	17 27.9	26 20.4	20 28.8	2 09.4	27 52.7	28 10.2
20 Th	13 52 42	26 19 16	12 51 32	18 46 29	18 28.5	13 39.7	9 19.2	4 30.2	17 41.9	26 29.8	20 35.5	2 10.4	27 54.9	28 11.4
21 F	13 56 38	27 18 56	24 40 19	0♑33 36	18 29.1	13 19.3	10 34.0	5 08.7	17 56.1	26 39.0	20 42.3	2 11.4	27 57.2	28 12.5
22 Sa	14 00 35	28 18 39	6♑26 56	12 20 57	18 30.4	13D10.2	11 48.8	5 47.2	18 10.5	26 48.2	20 49.0	2 12.4	27 59.4	28 13.7
23 Su	14 04 31	29 18 23	18 16 19	24 13 42	18R31.4	13 12.3	13 03.7	6 25.6	18 25.2	26 57.3	20 55.9	2 13.3	28 01.7	28 14.8
24 M	14 08 28	0♏18 08	0♒13 45	6♒17 08	18 31.3	13 25.4	14 18.5	7 04.1	18 39.9	27 06.2	21 02.7	2 14.1	28 03.9	28 15.9
25 Tu	14 12 24	1 17 56	12 24 31	18 36 30	18 29.5	13 48.8	15 33.3	7 42.6	18 54.9	27 15.0	21 09.6	2 14.9	28 06.1	28 17.0
26 W	14 16 21	2 17 44	24 53 38	1♓16 26	18 25.9	14 21.9	16 48.1	8 21.2	19 10.1	27 23.7	21 16.4	2 15.6	28 08.4	28 18.0
27 Th	14 20 18	3 17 35	7♓45 16	14 20 27	18 20.4	15 03.8	18 03.0	8 59.7	19 25.4	27 32.3	21 23.3	2 16.3	28 10.6	28 19.0
28 F	14 24 14	4 17 28	21 02 11	27 50 28	18 13.7	15 53.8	19 17.8	9 38.2	19 41.0	27 40.8	21 30.3	2 16.9	28 12.8	28 20.0
29 Sa	14 28 11	5 17 22	4♈45 12	11♈46 06	18 06.5	16 51.0	20 32.6	10 16.7	19 56.7	27 49.1	21 37.2	2 17.5	28 15.1	28 20.9
30 Su	14 32 07	6 17 18	18 52 43	26 04 28	17 59.6	17 54.5	21 47.4	10 55.3	20 12.5	27 57.3	21 44.2	2 18.0	28 17.3	28 21.9
31 M	14 36 04	7 17 15	3♉20 38	10♉40 20	17 54.0	19 03.5	23 02.2	11 33.9	20 28.6	28 05.4	21 51.2	2 18.5	28 19.5	28 22.8

Astro Data

	Dy Hr Mn
☿0S	1 2:14
☽0N	3 0:42
☽0S	15 22:46
♀0S	21 8:34
☉0S	23 19:41
☽0N	30 9:15
☿R	1 13:58
☽0S	13 5:44
♂0S	17 4:26
☿D	22 19:24
☽0N	27 18:34

Planet Ingress

	Dy Hr Mn
☿ ♎	1 12:06
♀ ♎	18 22:41
☉ ♎	23 19:41
♀ ♏	13 0:39
♂ ♎	13 11:20
☉ ♏	24 4:43

Last Aspect / ☽ Ingress (September)

Last Aspect Dy Hr Mn		☽ Ingress Dy Hr Mn
1 9:35	♇ ☍	♓ 1 15:23
2 20:43	♄ △	♈ 3 21:24
5 20:27	♇ △	♉ 6 1:36
7 23:58	♇ □	♊ 8 4:58
10 3:09	♇ ⚹	♋ 10 8:01
12 5:12	♆ □	♌ 12 11:02
14 9:49	♇ ☌	♍ 14 14:33
16 14:19	♀ ☌	♎ 16 19:35
18 22:21	♇ ⚹	♏ 19 3:18
21 9:26	☉ ⚹	♐ 21 14:11
23 22:01	♇ △	♑ 24 3:01
26 9:43	☿ □	♒ 26 15:07
28 20:57	☿ △	♓ 29 0:12

Last Aspect / ☽ Ingress (October)

Last Aspect Dy Hr Mn		☽ Ingress Dy Hr Mn
30 15:26	♂ ☍	♈ 1 5:46
3 6:17	☿ ☍	♉ 3 8:52
5 7:24	♇ □	♊ 5 10:59
7 9:49	♇ ⚹	♋ 7 13:23
9 12:23	♆ □	♌ 9 16:41
11 18:24	♀ ⚹	♍ 11 21:11
13 8:39	♄ ⚹	♎ 14 3:13
16 7:46	♇ ⚹	♏ 16 11:23
18 18:26	♇ □	♐ 18 22:07
21 7:12	♇ △	♑ 21 10:52
23 23:05	☉ □	♒ 23 23:33
26 6:25	♇ ☍	♓ 26 9:37
28 0:44	♄ △	♈ 28 15:46
30 15:48	♇ △	♉ 30 18:30

☽ Phases & Eclipses

Dy Hr Mn		
2 7:59	○	9♓05
9 7:59	☾	15♊52
16 6:19	●	22♍37
24 3:41	☽	0♑20
1 19:17	○	7♈50
8 14:04	☾	14♋31
15 19:32	●	21♎40
23 23:05	☽	29♑46
31 6:04	○	7♉02

Astro Data

1 September 1955
Julian Day # 20332
SVP 5♓52'26"
GC 26♐13.2 ⚵ 12♐19.6
Eris 8♈47.1R ⚶ 11♏48.8
⚷ 0♒51.8R ⚴ 29♌49.1
☽ Mean ☊ 22♐31.8

1 October 1955
Julian Day # 20362
SVP 5♓52'23"
GC 26♐13.3 ⚵ 19♐13.8
Eris 8♈29.3R ⚶ 20♏04.6
⚷ 0♒06.4R ⚴ 13♍57.7
☽ Mean ☊ 20♐56.4

November 1955

LONGITUDE

Day	Sid.Time	☉	0 hr ☽	Noon ☽	True ☊	☿	♀	♂	⚳	♃	♄	♅	♆	♇
1 Tu	14 40 00	8♏17 15	18♉02 40	25♉26 40	17♐50.3	20♎17.4	24♏17.0	12♎12.4	20♑44.8	28♌13.4	21♏58.2	2♌18.9	28♎21.7	28♌23.7
2 W	14 43 57	9 17 17	2♊51 21	10♊15 46	17D48.5	21 35.3	25 31.8	12 51.0	21 01.2	28 21.2	22 05.2	2 19.2	28 24.0	28 24.5
3 Th	14 47 53	10 17 21	17 39 03	25 00 24	17 48.4	22 56.8	26 46.6	13 29.6	21 17.7	28 28.9	22 12.3	2 19.5	28 26.2	28 25.4
4 F	14 51 50	11 17 27	2♋19 10	9♋34 46	17 49.6	24 21.2	28 01.4	14 08.2	21 34.4	28 36.5	22 19.4	2 19.8	28 28.4	28 26.2
5 Sa	14 55 47	12 17 35	16 46 46	23 54 51	17 51.0	25 48.0	29 16.3	14 46.9	21 51.2	28 44.0	22 26.4	2 20.0	28 30.6	28 26.9
6 Su	14 59 43	13 17 45	0♌58 49	7♌58 32	17R52.0	27 16.9	0♐31.1	15 25.5	22 08.2	28 51.3	22 33.5	2 20.1	28 32.8	28 27.7
7 M	15 03 40	14 17 57	14 53 58	21 45 08	17 51.9	28 47.5	1 45.9	16 04.1	22 25.4	28 58.4	22 40.6	2R20.2	28 34.9	28 28.4
8 Tu	15 07 36	15 18 11	28 32 08	5♍15 02	17 50.3	0♏19.5	3 00.7	16 42.8	22 42.7	29 05.4	22 47.7	2 20.2	28 37.1	28 29.1
9 W	15 11 33	16 18 28	11♍54 00	18 29 08	17 47.2	1 52.5	4 15.5	17 21.5	23 00.2	29 12.3	22 54.9	2 20.2	28 39.3	28 29.7
10 Th	15 15 29	17 18 46	25 00 35	1♎28 31	17 42.8	3 26.4	5 30.3	18 00.1	23 17.8	29 19.0	23 02.0	2 20.1	28 41.4	28 30.4
11 F	15 19 26	18 19 06	7♎53 01	14 14 15	17 37.8	5 00.9	6 45.1	18 38.8	23 35.5	29 25.6	23 09.1	2 19.9	28 43.6	28 31.0
12 Sa	15 23 22	19 19 28	20 32 19	26 47 21	17 32.7	6 36.0	7 59.9	19 17.5	23 53.4	29 32.0	23 16.3	2 19.7	28 45.7	28 31.5
13 Su	15 27 19	20 19 52	2♏59 28	9♏08 47	17 28.1	8 11.4	9 14.8	19 56.2	24 11.4	29 38.3	23 23.4	2 19.5	28 47.8	28 32.1
14 M	15 31 16	21 20 17	15 15 26	21 19 36	17 24.6	9 47.1	10 29.6	20 35.0	24 29.6	29 44.4	23 30.6	2 19.2	28 49.9	28 32.6
15 Tu	15 35 12	22 20 45	27 21 26	3♐21 09	17 22.4	11 23.0	11 44.4	21 13.7	24 47.9	29 50.4	23 37.8	2 18.8	28 52.0	28 33.1
16 W	15 39 09	23 21 14	9♐18 58	15 15 09	17D21.5	12 58.9	12 59.2	21 52.4	25 06.3	29 56.2	23 44.9	2 18.4	28 54.1	28 33.5
17 Th	15 43 05	24 21 44	21 10 00	27 03 51	17 21.9	14 34.9	14 14.0	22 31.2	25 24.9	0♍01.9	23 52.1	2 17.9	28 56.2	28 34.0
18 F	15 47 02	25 22 16	2♑57 06	8♑50 08	17 23.1	16 10.8	15 28.8	23 10.0	25 43.6	0 07.4	23 59.2	2 17.4	28 58.3	28 34.4
19 Sa	15 50 58	26 22 49	14 43 25	20 37 26	17 24.8	17 46.7	16 43.6	23 48.7	26 02.4	0 12.7	24 06.4	2 16.8	29 00.3	28 34.7
20 Su	15 54 55	27 23 23	26 32 43	2♒29 48	17 26.5	19 22.5	17 58.4	24 27.5	26 21.3	0 17.9	24 13.6	2 16.2	29 02.4	28 35.1
21 M	15 58 51	28 23 59	8♒29 15	14 31 41	17 27.8	20 58.2	19 13.2	25 06.3	26 40.4	0 22.9	24 20.7	2 15.5	29 04.4	28 35.4
22 Tu	16 02 48	29 24 36	20 37 40	26 47 49	17R28.4	22 33.7	20 27.9	25 45.1	26 59.6	0 27.7	24 27.9	2 14.8	29 06.4	28 35.7
23 W	16 06 45	0♐25 14	3♓02 43	9♓22 54	17 28.2	24 09.1	21 42.7	26 23.9	27 18.9	0 32.4	24 35.0	2 14.0	29 08.4	28 35.9
24 Th	16 10 41	1 25 53	15 48 53	22 21 07	17 27.1	25 44.4	22 57.5	27 02.7	27 38.3	0 36.9	24 42.1	2 13.1	29 10.3	28 36.1
25 F	16 14 38	2 26 33	28 59 56	5♈45 37	17 25.5	27 19.5	24 12.2	27 41.5	27 57.8	0 41.2	24 49.2	2 12.2	29 12.3	28 36.3
26 Sa	16 18 34	3 27 14	12♈38 17	19 37 55	17 23.7	28 54.5	25 26.9	28 20.4	28 17.4	0 45.3	24 56.4	2 11.3	29 14.2	28 36.4
27 Su	16 22 31	4 27 57	26 44 19	3♉57 08	17 21.9	0♐29.3	26 41.7	28 59.2	28 37.1	0 49.3	25 03.5	2 10.3	29 16.2	28 36.6
28 M	16 26 27	5 28 40	11♉15 50	18 39 41	17 20.5	2 04.1	27 56.4	29 38.1	28 57.0	0 53.1	25 10.6	2 09.2	29 18.1	28 36.7
29 Tu	16 30 24	6 29 25	26 07 50	3♊39 16	17D19.6	3 38.7	29 11.1	0♏16.9	29 16.9	0 56.8	25 17.6	2 08.2	29 19.9	28 36.7
30 W	16 34 20	7 30 11	11♊12 52	18 47 28	17 19.4	5 13.2	0♑25.8	0 55.8	29 36.9	1 00.2	25 24.7	2 07.0	29 21.8	28R36.8

December 1955

LONGITUDE

Day	Sid.Time	☉	0 hr ☽	Noon ☽	True ☊	☿	♀	♂	⚳	♃	♄	♅	♆	♇
1 Th	16 38 17	8♐30 59	26♊21 54	3♋54 59	17♐19.7	6♐47.6	1♑40.5	1♏34.7	29♑57.1	1♍03.5	25♏31.7	2♌05.8	29♎23.7	28♌36.8
2 F	16 42 14	9 31 47	11♋25 39	18 52 55	17 20.3	8 22.0	2 55.2	2 13.6	0♒17.3	1 06.6	25 38.8	2R04.6	29 25.5	28R36.7
3 Sa	16 46 10	10 32 37	26 15 56	3♌34 03	17 21.0	9 56.2	4 09.9	2 52.5	0 37.7	1 09.5	25 45.8	2 03.3	29 27.3	28 36.7
4 Su	16 50 07	11 33 29	10♌46 42	17 53 32	17 21.5	11 30.5	5 24.6	3 31.4	0 58.1	1 12.2	25 52.8	2 01.9	29 29.1	28 36.6
5 M	16 54 03	12 34 22	24 54 20	1♍49 03	17R21.9	13 04.7	6 39.3	4 10.4	1 18.6	1 14.7	25 59.8	2 00.6	29 30.9	28 36.5
6 Tu	16 58 00	13 35 16	8♍37 42	15 20 28	17 22.0	14 38.9	7 53.9	4 49.3	1 39.2	1 17.1	26 06.7	1 59.1	29 32.6	28 36.3
7 W	17 01 56	14 36 11	21 57 34	28 29 18	17 21.9	16 13.1	9 08.6	5 28.3	1 59.9	1 19.3	26 13.6	1 57.6	29 34.3	28 36.2
8 Th	17 05 53	15 37 08	4♎56 01	11♎18 05	17 21.7	17 47.3	10 23.2	6 07.3	2 20.7	1 21.2	26 20.6	1 56.1	29 36.0	28 35.9
9 F	17 09 50	16 38 05	17 35 54	23 49 51	17D21.6	19 21.6	11 37.9	6 46.2	2 41.6	1 23.0	26 27.4	1 54.5	29 37.7	28 35.7
10 Sa	17 13 46	17 39 04	0♏00 19	6♏07 41	17 21.5	20 55.9	12 52.5	7 25.2	3 02.6	1 24.6	26 34.3	1 52.9	29 39.3	28 35.4
11 Su	17 17 43	18 40 05	12 12 19	18 14 33	17 21.6	22 30.2	14 07.1	8 04.3	3 23.6	1 26.0	26 41.1	1 51.3	29 41.0	28 35.1
12 M	17 21 39	19 41 06	24 14 43	0♐13 08	17 21.8	24 04.7	15 21.7	8 43.3	3 44.7	1 27.2	26 47.9	1 49.6	29 42.6	28 34.8
13 Tu	17 25 36	20 42 08	6♐10 04	12 05 49	17R21.9	25 39.2	16 36.3	9 22.3	4 06.0	1 28.2	26 54.7	1 47.8	29 44.2	28 34.5
14 W	17 29 32	21 43 11	18 00 38	23 54 48	17 21.9	27 13.8	17 50.9	10 01.3	4 27.3	1 29.1	27 01.5	1 46.1	29 45.7	28 34.1
15 Th	17 33 29	22 44 15	29 48 33	5♑42 09	17 21.6	28 48.5	19 05.5	10 40.4	4 48.6	1 29.7	27 08.2	1 44.2	29 47.3	28 33.7
16 F	17 37 25	23 45 19	11♑35 54	17 30 02	17 21.0	0♑23.3	20 20.1	11 19.4	5 10.1	1 30.1	27 14.9	1 42.4	29 48.8	28 33.2
17 Sa	17 41 22	24 46 24	23 24 53	29 20 46	17 20.1	1 58.2	21 34.6	11 58.5	5 31.6	1R30.4	27 21.5	1 40.5	29 50.2	28 32.8
18 Su	17 45 19	25 47 29	5♒18 01	11♒16 59	17 18.9	3 33.2	22 49.1	12 37.6	5 53.2	1 30.4	27 28.1	1 38.5	29 51.7	28 32.3
19 M	17 49 15	26 48 35	17 18 05	23 21 43	17 17.6	5 08.3	24 03.6	13 16.6	6 14.9	1 30.2	27 34.7	1 36.6	29 53.1	28 31.7
20 Tu	17 53 12	27 49 41	29 28 20	5♓38 22	17 16.4	6 43.5	25 18.1	13 55.7	6 36.6	1 29.9	27 41.2	1 34.5	29 54.5	28 31.2
21 W	17 57 08	28 50 47	11♓52 19	18 10 37	17D15.7	8 18.8	26 32.6	14 34.8	6 58.4	1 29.3	27 47.7	1 32.5	29 55.9	28 30.6
22 Th	18 01 05	29 51 54	24 33 46	1♈02 13	17 15.4	9 54.1	27 47.1	15 13.9	7 20.3	1 28.6	27 54.2	1 30.4	29 57.2	28 30.0
23 F	18 05 01	0♑53 01	7♈36 22	14 16 37	17 15.8	11 29.4	29 01.5	15 53.0	7 42.2	1 27.6	28 00.6	1 28.3	29 58.5	28 29.3
24 Sa	18 08 58	1 54 07	21 03 14	27 56 27	17 16.7	13 04.8	0♒15.9	16 32.1	8 04.2	1 26.5	28 06.9	1 26.1	29 59.8	28 28.7
25 Su	18 12 54	2 55 14	4♉56 21	12♉02 54	17 17.9	14 40.1	1 30.3	17 11.2	8 26.3	1 25.2	28 13.3	1 24.0	0♏01.1	28 28.0
26 M	18 16 51	3 56 22	19 15 54	26 34 59	17 19.1	16 15.3	2 44.6	17 50.4	8 48.4	1 23.6	28 19.6	1 21.8	0 02.3	28 27.3
27 Tu	18 20 48	4 57 29	3♊59 36	11♊29 00	17R19.8	17 50.3	3 58.9	18 29.5	9 10.6	1 21.9	28 25.8	1 19.5	0 03.5	28 26.5
28 W	18 24 44	5 58 37	19 02 18	26 38 25	17 19.7	19 25.1	5 13.2	19 08.7	9 32.8	1 20.0	28 32.0	1 17.3	0 04.7	28 25.7
29 Th	18 28 41	6 59 44	4♋16 11	11♋54 18	17 18.5	20 59.5	6 27.5	19 47.8	9 55.1	1 17.9	28 38.1	1 15.0	0 05.8	28 25.0
30 F	18 32 37	8 00 52	19 31 30	27 06 28	17 16.4	22 33.4	7 41.8	20 27.0	10 17.4	1 15.6	28 44.2	1 12.7	0 06.9	28 24.1
31 Sa	18 36 34	9 02 00	4♌38 03	12♌05 07	17 13.5	24 06.8	8 56.0	21 06.2	10 39.8	1 13.1	28 50.3	1 10.3	0 08.0	28 23.3

Astro Data	Dy Hr Mn
♆✶♇	2 22:02
♃☌♇	2 23:26
♃✶♆	2 23:47
♅R	8 9:29
☽0S	9 10:51
☽0N	24 3:28
♇R	1 4:47
☽0S	6 16:10
♃R	18 4:30
☽0N	21 11:03
♃⚺♅	24 3:19
♄□♇	27 14:29

Planet Ingress		Dy Hr Mn
♀	♐	6 2:02
☿	♏	8 6:57
♃	♍	17 3:59
☉	♐	23 2:01
☿	♐	27 4:34
♂	♏	29 1:33
♀	♑	30 3:42
⚳	♒	1 15:28
☿	♑	16 6:06
☉	♑	22 15:11
♀	♒	24 6:52
♆	♏	24 15:22

Last Aspect Dy Hr Mn		☽ Ingress	Dy Hr Mn
1 16:47	♇ □	♊	1 19:23
3 17:45	♃ ✶	♋	3 20:11
5 21:58	♀ △	♌	5 22:20
8 2:03	☿ ✶	♍	8 2:36
9 20:13	♄ ✶	♎	10 9:15
12 17:21	♃ ✶	♏	12 18:12
15 4:54	♃ □	♐	15 5:17
17 15:50	♆ ✶	♑	17 17:59
20 5:01	♆ □	♒	20 6:58
22 17:29	☉ □	♓	22 18:10
24 18:58	☿ △	♈	25 1:47
27 4:13	♆ ☍	♉	27 5:27
29 3:58	♇ □	♊	29 6:11

Last Aspect Dy Hr Mn		☽ Ingress	Dy Hr Mn
1 4:48	♆ △	♋	1 5:46
3 5:13	♆ □	♌	3 6:07
5 7:58	♆ ✶	♍	5 8:50
7 7:47	♄ ✶	♎	7 14:48
9 23:17	♆ ☌	♏	9 23:59
12 8:42	♇ □	♐	12 11:34
14 23:56	♆ ✶	♑	15 0:23
17 13:00	♆ □	♒	17 13:19
20 0:50	♆ △	♓	20 1:02
22 9:39	☉ □	♈	22 10:05
24 15:33	♆ ☍	♉	24 15:33
26 15:02	♇ □	♊	26 17:33
28 14:49	♇ ✶	♋	28 17:17
30 14:36	♄ △	♌	30 16:36

☽ Phases & Eclipses Dy Hr Mn	
6 21:56	☾ 13♌43
14 12:02	● 21♏20
22 17:29	☽ 29♒38
29 16:50	○ 6♊42
29 16:59	● P 0.119
6 8:35	☾ 13♍27
14 7:07	● 21♐31
14 7:01:54	● A 12'09"
22 9:39	☽ 29♓46
29 3:44	○ 6♋39

Astro Data

1 November 1955
Julian Day # 20393
SVP 5♓52'20"
GC 26♐13.3 ⚴ 28♐48.2
Eris 8♈10.6R ⚵ 29♏57.0
⚷ 0♒24.8 ⚶ 28♍28.4
☽ Mean ☊ 19♐17.9

1 December 1955
Julian Day # 20423
SVP 5♓52'15"
GC 26♐13.4 ⚴ 9♑19.9
Eris 7♈57.8R ⚵ 10♐11.8
⚷ 1♒44.2 ⚶ 12♎00.5
☽ Mean ☊ 17♐42.6

LONGITUDE — January 1956

Day	Sid.Time	☉	0 hr ☽	Noon ☽	True ☊	☿	♀	♂	⚳	♃	♄	♅	♆	♇
1 Su	18 40 30	10♑03 08	19♌26 46	26♌42 16	17♐10.3	25♑39.3	10♒10.2	21♏45.3	11♒02.3	1♍10.5	28♏56.3	1♌07.9	0♏09.1	28♌22.4
2 M	18 44 27	11 04 17	3♍51 04	10♍52 50	17R 07.3	27 10.9	11 24.3	22 24.5	11 24.8	1R 07.6	29 02.2	1R 05.6	0 10.1	28R 21.5
3 Tu	18 48 23	12 05 26	17 47 23	24 34 46	17 05.1	28 41.2	12 38.5	23 03.8	11 47.3	1 04.6	29 08.1	1 03.1	0 11.1	28 20.6
4 W	18 52 20	13 06 35	1♎15 08	7♎48 48	17D 03.9	0♒10.0	13 52.6	23 43.0	12 09.9	1 01.3	29 13.9	1 00.7	0 12.0	28 19.7
5 Th	18 56 17	14 07 45	14 16 08	20 37 39	17 04.0	1 37.0	15 06.6	24 22.2	12 32.5	0 57.9	29 19.7	0 58.2	0 12.9	28 18.7
6 F	19 00 13	15 08 54	26 53 51	3♏05 18	17 05.1	3 01.8	16 20.7	25 01.4	12 55.2	0 54.3	29 25.4	0 55.8	0 13.8	28 17.7
7 Sa	19 04 10	16 10 04	9♏12 36	15 16 18	17 06.8	4 24.0	17 34.7	25 40.7	13 18.0	0 50.5	29 31.1	0 53.3	0 14.7	28 16.7
8 Su	19 08 06	17 11 14	21 17 00	27 15 15	17 08.7	5 43.0	18 48.7	26 19.9	13 40.8	0 46.6	29 36.7	0 50.8	0 15.5	28 15.7
9 M	19 12 03	18 12 24	3♐11 34	9♐06 27	17R 10.0	6 58.4	20 02.6	26 59.2	14 03.6	0 42.4	29 42.2	0 48.2	0 16.3	28 14.6
10 Tu	19 15 59	19 13 34	15 00 21	20 53 43	17 10.3	8 09.4	21 16.5	27 38.5	14 26.5	0 38.1	29 47.7	0 45.7	0 17.1	28 13.5
11 W	19 19 56	20 14 44	26 46 55	2♑40 18	17 08.9	9 15.3	22 30.4	28 17.8	14 49.4	0 33.6	29 53.1	0 43.2	0 17.8	28 12.4
12 Th	19 23 52	21 15 54	8♑34 11	14 28 51	17 05.9	10 15.5	23 44.2	28 57.0	15 12.3	0 29.0	29 58.5	0 40.6	0 18.5	28 11.3
13 F	19 27 49	22 17 03	20 24 33	26 21 30	17 01.0	11 09.0	24 58.0	29 36.3	15 35.3	0 24.2	0♐03.8	0 38.0	0 19.1	28 10.2
14 Sa	19 31 46	23 18 12	2♒19 54	8♒19 58	16 54.7	11 55.1	26 11.8	0♐15.6	15 58.4	0 19.2	0 09.0	0 35.4	0 19.8	28 09.0
15 Su	19 35 42	24 19 21	14 21 51	20 25 46	16 47.5	12 32.7	27 25.5	0 54.9	16 21.4	0 14.0	0 14.2	0 32.8	0 20.3	28 07.9
16 M	19 39 39	25 20 28	26 31 54	2♓40 26	16 40.1	13 01.0	28 39.1	1 34.2	16 44.5	0 08.7	0 19.3	0 30.2	0 20.9	28 06.7
17 Tu	19 43 35	26 21 36	8♓51 36	15 05 37	16 33.3	13 19.3	29 52.7	2 13.5	17 07.6	0 03.3	0 24.3	0 27.6	0 21.4	28 05.5
18 W	19 47 32	27 22 42	21 22 46	27 43 17	16 27.9	13R 26.7	1♓06.3	2 52.8	17 30.8	29♌57.7	0 29.2	0 25.0	0 21.9	28 04.2
19 Th	19 51 28	28 23 48	4♈07 30	10♈35 43	16 24.3	13 22.8	2 19.8	3 32.1	17 54.0	29 51.9	0 34.1	0 22.4	0 22.4	28 03.0
20 F	19 55 25	29 24 52	17 08 14	23 45 24	16D 22.6	13 07.3	3 33.3	4 11.4	18 17.2	29 46.0	0 38.9	0 19.8	0 22.8	28 01.7
21 Sa	19 59 21	0♒25 56	0♉27 30	7♉14 48	16 22.7	12 40.1	4 46.7	4 50.7	18 40.5	29 40.0	0 43.6	0 17.2	0 23.2	28 00.4
22 Su	20 03 18	1 26 59	14 07 33	21 05 52	16 23.8	12 01.6	6 00.0	5 30.1	19 03.7	29 33.8	0 48.3	0 14.5	0 23.5	27 59.1
23 M	20 07 15	2 28 01	28 09 50	5♊19 22	16R 25.0	11 12.8	7 13.3	6 09.4	19 27.0	29 27.5	0 52.9	0 11.9	0 23.8	27 57.8
24 Tu	20 11 11	3 29 02	12♊34 18	19 54 15	16 25.3	10 14.8	8 26.6	6 48.7	19 50.4	29 21.1	0 57.4	0 09.3	0 24.1	27 56.5
25 W	20 15 08	4 30 02	27 18 42	4♋46 55	16 23.9	9 09.1	9 39.7	7 28.1	20 13.7	29 14.6	1 01.8	0 06.7	0 24.4	27 55.2
26 Th	20 19 04	5 31 01	12♋18 04	19 51 05	16 20.3	7 57.9	10 52.8	8 07.4	20 37.1	29 07.9	1 06.2	0 04.1	0 24.6	27 53.8
27 F	20 23 01	6 31 59	27 24 49	4♌58 04	16 14.3	6 43.3	12 05.8	8 46.7	21 00.5	29 01.2	1 10.5	0 01.5	0 24.8	27 52.5
28 Sa	20 26 57	7 32 56	12♌29 33	19 58 04	16 06.6	5 27.5	13 18.8	9 26.1	21 23.9	28 54.3	1 14.7	29♋58.9	0 24.9	27 51.1
29 Su	20 30 54	8 33 52	27 22 27	4♍41 42	15 57.9	4 12.7	14 31.7	10 05.5	21 47.3	28 47.3	1 18.8	29 56.3	0 25.0	27 49.7
30 M	20 34 51	9 34 48	11♍54 58	19 01 36	15 49.4	3 01.1	15 44.5	10 44.8	22 10.8	28 40.2	1 22.8	29 53.8	0 25.1	27 48.3
31 Tu	20 38 47	10 35 42	26 01 10	2♎53 25	15 42.1	1 54.3	16 57.3	11 24.2	22 34.3	28 33.1	1 26.8	29 51.2	0R 25.2	27 46.9

LONGITUDE — February 1956

Day	Sid.Time	☉	0 hr ☽	Noon ☽	True ☊	☿	♀	♂	⚳	♃	♄	♅	♆	♇
1 W	20 42 44	11♒36 36	9♎38 18	16♎15 57	15♐36.8	0♒53.8	18♓10.0	12♐03.6	22♒57.7	28♌25.8	1♐30.6	29♋48.6	0♏25.2	27♌45.5
2 Th	20 46 40	12 37 29	22 46 40	29 10 51	15R 33.7	0R 00.6	19 22.6	12 42.9	23 21.2	28R 18.5	1 34.4	29R 46.1	0R 25.2	27R 44.1
3 F	20 50 37	13 38 21	5♏28 59	11♏41 42	15D 32.6	29♑15.4	20 35.1	13 22.3	23 44.8	28 11.0	1 38.1	29 43.6	0 25.1	27 42.6
4 Sa	20 54 33	14 39 13	17 49 35	23 53 20	15 32.9	28 38.7	21 47.6	14 01.7	24 08.3	28 03.5	1 41.7	29 41.1	0 25.0	27 41.2
5 Su	20 58 30	15 40 03	29 53 38	5♐51 09	15R 33.8	28 10.4	23 00.0	14 41.1	24 31.9	27 56.0	1 45.2	29 38.6	0 24.9	27 39.8
6 M	21 02 26	16 40 53	11♐46 34	17 40 32	15 34.1	27 50.6	24 12.3	15 20.5	24 55.4	27 48.3	1 48.7	29 36.1	0 24.7	27 38.3
7 Tu	21 06 23	17 41 42	23 33 40	29 26 33	15 32.9	27 39.0	25 24.5	15 59.9	25 19.0	27 40.7	1 52.0	29 33.6	0 24.5	27 36.8
8 W	21 10 20	18 42 29	5♑19 43	11♑13 38	15 29.5	27D 35.2	26 36.7	16 39.3	25 42.6	27 32.9	1 55.3	29 31.2	0 24.3	27 35.4
9 Th	21 14 16	19 43 16	17 08 46	23 05 28	15 23.3	27 38.7	27 48.8	17 18.7	26 06.2	27 25.1	1 58.5	29 28.8	0 24.0	27 33.9
10 F	21 18 13	20 44 01	29 04 05	5♒04 52	15 14.5	27 49.2	29 00.8	17 58.1	26 29.8	27 17.3	2 01.5	29 26.4	0 23.7	27 32.4
11 Sa	21 22 09	21 44 45	11♒08 02	17 13 45	15 03.3	28 06.1	0♈12.7	18 37.5	26 53.4	27 09.4	2 04.5	29 24.0	0 23.4	27 30.9
12 Su	21 26 06	22 45 28	23 22 08	29 33 15	14 50.6	28 29.0	1 24.5	19 16.9	27 17.0	27 01.6	2 07.4	29 21.7	0 23.1	27 29.4
13 M	21 30 02	23 46 09	5♓47 08	12♓03 50	14 37.5	28 57.4	2 36.2	19 56.3	27 40.7	26 53.7	2 10.2	29 19.3	0 22.7	27 27.9
14 Tu	21 33 59	24 46 49	18 23 20	24 45 39	14 25.3	29 30.9	3 47.8	20 35.7	28 04.3	26 45.7	2 12.9	29 17.0	0 22.2	27 26.4
15 W	21 37 55	25 47 27	1♈10 46	7♈38 44	14 15.0	0♒09.0	4 59.3	21 15.0	28 27.9	26 37.8	2 15.5	29 14.8	0 21.8	27 24.9
16 Th	21 41 52	26 48 04	14 09 34	20 43 21	14 07.3	0 51.4	6 10.7	21 54.4	28 51.6	26 29.9	2 18.0	29 12.5	0 21.3	27 23.4
17 F	21 45 48	27 48 39	27 20 11	4♉00 11	14 02.5	1 37.8	7 22.0	22 33.8	29 15.2	26 21.9	2 20.5	29 10.3	0 20.8	27 21.9
18 Sa	21 49 45	28 49 12	10♉43 29	17 30 15	14D 00.4	2 27.7	8 33.2	23 13.2	29 38.8	26 14.0	2 22.8	29 08.1	0 20.2	27 20.5
19 Su	21 53 42	29 49 43	24 20 38	1♊14 47	13R 59.9	3 21.0	9 44.3	23 52.5	0♓02.5	26 06.1	2 25.0	29 06.0	0 19.6	27 19.0
20 M	21 57 38	0♓50 13	8♊12 48	15 14 45	14 00.1	4 17.4	10 55.3	24 31.9	0 26.1	25 58.2	2 27.2	29 03.8	0 19.0	27 17.5
21 Tu	22 01 35	1 50 40	22 20 36	29 30 15	13 59.4	5 16.6	12 06.1	25 11.3	0 49.7	25 50.3	2 29.2	29 01.8	0 18.4	27 16.0
22 W	22 05 31	2 51 06	6♋43 26	13♋59 49	13 56.7	6 18.5	13 16.9	25 50.6	1 13.4	25 42.5	2 31.1	28 59.7	0 17.7	27 14.5
23 Th	22 09 28	3 51 30	21 18 53	28 39 57	13 51.2	7 22.8	14 27.5	26 30.0	1 37.0	25 34.7	2 33.0	28 57.7	0 17.0	27 13.0
24 F	22 13 24	4 51 52	6♌02 17	13♌24 57	13 42.9	8 29.5	15 37.9	27 09.4	2 00.6	25 27.0	2 34.7	28 55.7	0 16.2	27 11.5
25 Sa	22 17 21	5 52 12	20 47 00	28 07 23	13 32.2	9 38.2	16 48.3	27 48.7	2 24.2	25 19.3	2 36.3	28 53.8	0 15.5	27 10.0
26 Su	22 21 17	6 52 30	5♍25 07	12♍39 12	13 20.1	10 49.0	17 58.5	28 28.1	2 47.8	25 11.6	2 37.9	28 51.9	0 14.7	27 08.6
27 M	22 25 14	7 52 46	19 48 47	26 53 06	13 08.0	12 01.7	19 08.6	29 07.4	3 11.4	25 04.0	2 39.3	28 50.0	0 13.9	27 07.1
28 Tu	22 29 11	8 53 01	3♎51 32	10♎43 41	12 57.2	13 16.1	20 18.5	29 46.8	3 35.0	24 56.5	2 40.6	28 48.1	0 13.0	27 05.6
29 W	22 33 07	9 53 15	17 29 18	24 08 16	12 48.5	14 32.3	21 28.3	0♑26.1	3 58.6	24 49.0	2 41.9	28 46.4	0 12.1	27 04.2

Astro Data	Dy Hr Mn	Planet Ingress	Dy Hr Mn	Last Aspect Dy Hr Mn	☽ Ingress Dy Hr Mn	Last Aspect Dy Hr Mn	☽ Ingress Dy Hr Mn	☽ Phases & Eclipses Dy Hr Mn	
☽0S	2 23:57	☿ ♒	4 9:16	1 15:45 ♄ □	♍ 1 17:31	2 13:28 ☿ □	♏ 2 13:33	4 22:41	☾ 13♎34
♃⊻♅	5 3:58	♄ ♐	12 18:46	3 20:17 ☿ △	♎ 3 21:44	4 23:32 ♅ △	♐ 5 0:13	13 3:01	● 21♑54
♃⚹♆	14 9:31	♂ ♐	14 2:28	6 2:43 ♇ ⚹	♏ 6 6:00	7 8:26 ♃ △	♑ 7 13:08	20 22:58	☽ 29♈53
♃□♄	15 11:39	♀ ♓	17 14:22	8 16:48 ♄ ☌	♐ 8 17:32	10 0:47 ♅ ☍	♒ 10 1:52	27 14:40	○ 6♌39
♄⊻♆	16 20:43	♃ ♌R	18 2:04	11 2:55 ♇ △	♑ 11 6:33	12 8:01 ♇ ☍	♓ 12 12:52		
☽0N	17 17:30	☉ ♒	21 1:48	13 18:54 ♂ ⚹	♒ 13 19:19	14 21:20 ☿ ⚹	♈ 14 21:48	3 16:08	☾ 13♏49
♄△♅	17 22:34	♅ ♋R	28 1:57	16 3:17 ♀ ☌	♓ 16 6:47	17 3:20 ♅ □	♉ 17 4:48	11 21:38	● 22♒09
☿R	18 15:53			18 11:18 ☉ ⚹	♈ 18 16:17	19 9:21 ☉ □	♊ 19 9:50	19 9:21	☽ 29♉43
♅□♆	19 12:12	☿ ♑R	2 12:18	20 22:58 ☉ □	♉ 20 23:11	21 8:16 ♇ ⚹	♋ 21 12:50	26 1:42	○ 6♍27
☽0S	30 10:27	♀ ♈	11 7:46	23 2:15 ♃ □	♊ 23 3:06	23 12:29 ♅ ☌	♌ 23 14:10		
♆R	1 6:32	☿ ♒	15 6:34	25 3:11 ♃ ⚹	♋ 25 4:20	25 11:28 ♂ △	♍ 25 15:05		
♃☌♇	8 2:39	⚳ ♓	19 9:29	25 20:29 ♀ △	♌ 27 4:06	27 16:01 ♂ □	♎ 27 17:20		
☿D	8 12:10	☉ ♓	19 16:05	29 2:23 ♃ ☌	♍ 29 4:17	29 20:28 ♅ □	♏ 29 22:45		
♀0N	12 11:25	♂ ♑	28 20:05	31 6:41 ♅ ⚹	♎ 31 6:56				
☽0N	13 23:51	☽0S26 21:36							

Astro Data

1 January 1956
Julian Day # 20454
SVP 5♓52'10"
GC 26♐13.5 ⚴ 20♑45.6
Eris 7♈54.2 ⚵ 20♐57.8
⚷ 3♒52.8 ⚶ 24♎46.3
☽ Mean ☊ 16♐04.2

1 February 1956
Julian Day # 20485
SVP 5♓52'05"
GC 26♐13.6 ⚴ 2♒09.5
Eris 8♈01.5 ⚵ 1♑21.3
⚷ 6♒23.6 ⚶ 5♏04.4
☽ Mean ☊ 14♐25.7

March 1956

LONGITUDE

Day	Sid.Time	☉	0 hr ☽	Noon☽	True☊	☿	♀	♂	⚳	♃	♄	♅	♆	♇
1 Th	22 37 04	10♓53 26	0♏40 42	7♏06 48	12♐42.6	15♒50.1	22♈37.9	1♑05.4	4♓22.1	24♌41.7	2♐43.0	28♋44.6	0♏11.2	27♌02.7
2 F	22 41 00	11 53 37	13 26 57	19 41 36	12R39.3	17 09.5	23 47.5	1 44.8	4 45.7	24R34.4	2 44.1	28R42.9	0R10.3	27R01.3
3 Sa	22 44 57	12 53 45	25 51 18	1♐56 39	12D38.1	18 30.3	24 56.8	2 24.1	5 09.2	24 27.1	2 45.0	28 41.2	0 09.3	26 59.8
4 Su	22 48 53	13 53 53	7♐58 19	13 56 59	12R37.9	19 52.6	26 06.0	3 03.4	5 32.8	24 20.0	2 45.8	28 39.6	0 08.3	26 58.4
5 M	22 52 50	14 53 58	19 53 20	25 48 07	12 37.7	21 16.3	27 15.1	3 42.8	5 56.3	24 13.0	2 46.6	28 38.0	0 07.3	26 57.0
6 Tu	22 56 46	15 54 02	1♑41 59	7♑35 38	12 36.3	22 41.4	28 24.0	4 22.1	6 19.8	24 06.0	2 47.2	28 36.5	0 06.3	26 55.6
7 W	23 00 43	16 54 05	13 29 43	19 24 50	12 32.7	24 07.7	29 32.8	5 01.4	6 43.3	23 59.2	2 47.7	28 35.0	0 05.2	26 54.2
8 Th	23 04 40	17 54 05	25 21 32	1♒20 21	12 26.5	25 35.4	0♉41.3	5 40.7	7 06.8	23 52.5	2 48.2	28 33.5	0 04.1	26 52.8
9 F	23 08 36	18 54 04	7♒21 44	13 26 03	12 17.4	27 04.3	1 49.8	6 20.0	7 30.2	23 45.8	2 48.5	28 32.1	0 03.0	26 51.4
10 Sa	23 12 33	19 54 02	19 33 37	25 44 40	12 05.9	28 34.5	2 58.0	6 59.2	7 53.7	23 39.3	2 48.7	28 30.7	0 01.9	26 50.1
11 Su	23 16 29	20 53 57	1♓59 22	8♓17 47	11 52.7	0♓05.9	4 06.1	7 38.5	8 17.1	23 33.0	2R48.8	28 29.4	0 00.7	26 48.7
12 M	23 20 26	21 53 50	14 39 58	21 05 49	11 39.1	1 38.5	5 14.0	8 17.7	8 40.5	23 26.7	2 48.8	28 28.2	29♎59.5	26 47.4
13 Tu	23 24 22	22 53 42	27 35 15	4♈08 06	11 26.2	3 12.4	6 21.7	8 57.0	9 03.9	23 20.6	2 48.7	28 26.9	29 58.3	26 46.1
14 W	23 28 19	23 53 31	10♈44 11	17 23 16	11 15.3	4 47.5	7 29.2	9 36.2	9 27.2	23 14.6	2 48.6	28 25.8	29 57.1	26 44.7
15 Th	23 32 15	24 53 19	24 05 08	0♉49 35	11 07.1	6 23.8	8 36.5	10 15.4	9 50.6	23 08.7	2 48.3	28 24.6	29 55.8	26 43.5
16 F	23 36 12	25 53 04	7♉36 26	14 25 29	11 01.9	8 01.3	9 43.6	10 54.5	10 13.9	23 03.0	2 47.9	28 23.6	29 54.5	26 42.2
17 Sa	23 40 09	26 52 47	21 16 39	28 09 47	10D59.4	9 40.0	10 50.6	11 33.7	10 37.2	22 57.5	2 47.4	28 22.6	29 53.2	26 40.9
18 Su	23 44 05	27 52 28	5♊04 52	12♊01 50	10 58.9	11 19.9	11 57.3	12 12.9	11 00.4	22 52.1	2 46.8	28 21.6	29 51.9	26 39.7
19 M	23 48 02	28 52 06	19 00 39	26 01 18	10R59.1	13 01.1	13 03.7	12 52.0	11 23.6	22 46.8	2 46.1	28 20.7	29 50.6	26 38.4
20 Tu	23 51 58	29 51 43	3♋03 44	10♋07 51	10 58.8	14 43.6	14 10.0	13 31.1	11 46.8	22 41.7	2 45.3	28 19.8	29 49.2	26 37.2
21 W	23 55 55	0♈51 17	17 13 33	24 20 38	10 56.8	16 27.3	15 16.0	14 10.2	12 10.0	22 36.8	2 44.4	28 19.0	29 47.9	26 36.0
22 Th	23 59 51	1 50 48	1♌28 49	8♌37 45	10 52.3	18 12.2	16 21.8	14 49.2	12 33.1	22 32.0	2 43.4	28 18.2	29 46.5	26 34.8
23 F	0 03 48	2 50 17	15 46 59	22 56 00	10 45.2	19 58.5	17 27.3	15 28.3	12 56.2	22 27.3	2 42.4	28 17.5	29 45.1	26 33.7
24 Sa	0 07 44	3 49 44	0♍04 14	7♍11 02	10 35.8	21 46.0	18 32.6	16 07.3	13 19.3	22 22.9	2 41.2	28 16.8	29 43.6	26 32.5
25 Su	0 11 41	4 49 09	14 15 43	21 17 39	10 25.2	23 34.9	19 37.6	16 46.4	13 42.4	22 18.6	2 39.9	28 16.2	29 42.2	26 31.4
26 M	0 15 37	5 48 31	28 16 11	5♎10 45	10 14.5	25 25.0	20 42.3	17 25.3	14 05.4	22 14.5	2 38.5	28 15.7	29 40.7	26 30.3
27 Tu	0 19 34	6 47 52	12♎00 50	18 46 04	10 04.8	27 16.5	21 46.8	18 04.3	14 28.3	22 10.5	2 37.0	28 15.2	29 39.3	26 29.2
28 W	0 23 31	7 47 11	25 26 08	2♏00 54	9 56.9	29 09.3	22 51.0	18 43.3	14 51.3	22 06.7	2 35.5	28 14.7	29 37.8	26 28.2
29 Th	0 27 27	8 46 27	8♏30 18	14 54 26	9 51.6	1♈03.5	23 54.9	19 22.2	15 14.2	22 03.1	2 33.8	28 14.3	29 36.3	26 27.1
30 F	0 31 24	9 45 42	21 13 28	27 27 42	9 48.7	2 59.0	24 58.5	20 01.2	15 37.0	21 59.7	2 32.1	28 14.0	29 34.8	26 26.1
31 Sa	0 35 20	10 44 55	3♐37 31	9♐43 23	9D47.9	4 55.7	26 01.8	20 40.1	15 59.9	21 56.4	2 30.2	28 13.7	29 33.3	26 25.1

April 1956

LONGITUDE

Day	Sid.Time	☉	0 hr ☽	Noon☽	True☊	☿	♀	♂	⚳	♃	♄	♅	♆	♇
1 Su	0 39 17	11♈44 06	15♐45 50	21♐45 25	9♐48.4	6♈53.8	27♉04.8	21♑18.9	16♓22.7	21♌53.3	2♐28.3	28♋13.4	29♎31.7	26♌24.1
2 M	0 43 13	12 43 16	27 42 46	3♑38 33	9R49.3	8 53.1	28 07.5	21 57.8	16 45.4	21R50.4	2R26.3	28R13.2	29R30.2	26R23.2
3 Tu	0 47 10	13 42 24	9♑33 24	15 27 59	9 49.7	10 53.6	29 09.9	22 36.6	17 08.1	21 47.7	2 24.2	28 13.1	29 28.6	26 22.2
4 W	0 51 06	14 41 29	21 23 00	27 19 05	9 48.6	12 55.2	0♊11.9	23 15.4	17 30.8	21 45.2	2 22.0	28D13.0	29 27.1	26 21.3
5 Th	0 55 03	15 40 33	3♒16 52	9♒16 58	9 45.7	14 57.9	1 13.6	23 54.2	17 53.4	21 42.8	2 19.7	28 13.0	29 25.5	26 20.4
6 F	0 59 00	16 39 36	15 19 56	21 26 16	9 40.6	17 01.4	2 14.9	24 32.9	18 16.0	21 40.6	2 17.3	28 13.0	29 23.9	26 19.6
7 Sa	1 02 56	17 38 36	27 36 25	3♓50 46	9 33.5	19 05.8	3 15.9	25 11.6	18 38.6	21 38.7	2 14.8	28 13.1	29 22.3	26 18.7
8 Su	1 06 53	18 37 34	10♓09 35	16 33 05	9 25.1	21 10.8	4 16.5	25 50.3	19 01.1	21 36.9	2 12.3	28 13.2	29 20.7	26 17.9
9 M	1 10 49	19 36 31	23 01 22	29 34 27	9 16.1	23 16.3	5 16.7	26 28.9	19 23.5	21 35.2	2 09.7	28 13.4	29 19.1	26 17.1
10 Tu	1 14 46	20 35 26	6♈12 14	12♈54 34	9 07.6	25 22.0	6 16.5	27 07.5	19 45.9	21 33.8	2 07.0	28 13.7	29 17.5	26 16.4
11 W	1 18 42	21 34 19	19 41 09	26 31 40	9 00.4	27 27.7	7 15.9	27 46.0	20 08.3	21 32.6	2 04.2	28 14.0	29 15.9	26 15.6
12 Th	1 22 39	22 33 09	3♉25 42	10♉22 49	8 55.2	29 33.1	8 14.9	28 24.5	20 30.6	21 31.5	2 01.3	28 14.3	29 14.2	26 14.9
13 F	1 26 35	23 31 58	17 22 34	24 24 29	8 52.2	1♉37.9	9 13.5	29 02.9	20 52.8	21 30.7	1 58.4	28 14.7	29 12.6	26 14.2
14 Sa	1 30 32	24 30 45	1♊28 05	8♊32 57	8D51.3	3 41.9	10 11.5	29 41.4	21 15.0	21 30.0	1 55.3	28 15.2	29 11.0	26 13.6
15 Su	1 34 29	25 29 29	15 38 41	22 44 55	8 51.9	5 44.6	11 09.2	0♒19.7	21 37.1	21 29.5	1 52.2	28 15.7	29 09.4	26 12.9
16 M	1 38 25	26 28 11	29 51 20	6♋57 40	8 53.2	7 45.8	12 06.3	0 58.0	21 59.2	21 29.2	1 49.1	28 16.3	29 07.7	26 12.3
17 Tu	1 42 22	27 26 51	14♋03 39	21 09 06	8R54.2	9 45.1	13 02.9	1 36.3	22 21.3	21D29.1	1 45.8	28 16.9	29 06.1	26 11.7
18 W	1 46 18	28 25 29	28 13 47	5♌17 32	8 54.1	11 42.1	13 59.0	2 14.5	22 43.2	21 29.2	1 42.5	28 17.6	29 04.4	26 11.2
19 Th	1 50 15	29 24 04	12♌20 08	19 21 24	8 52.5	13 36.6	14 54.5	2 52.7	23 05.1	21 29.5	1 39.2	28 18.3	29 02.8	26 10.6
20 F	1 54 11	0♉22 37	26 21 07	3♍19 01	8 49.1	15 28.2	15 49.5	3 30.8	23 27.0	21 30.0	1 35.7	28 19.1	29 01.2	26 10.1
21 Sa	1 58 08	1 21 08	10♍14 52	17 08 23	8 44.3	17 16.7	16 43.9	4 08.9	23 48.8	21 30.6	1 32.2	28 19.9	28 59.5	26 09.7
22 Su	2 02 04	2 19 37	23 59 18	0♎47 20	8 38.6	19 01.9	17 37.7	4 46.9	24 10.5	21 31.4	1 28.7	28 20.8	28 57.9	26 09.2
23 M	2 06 01	3 18 04	7♎32 13	14 13 40	8 32.7	20 43.4	18 30.9	5 24.9	24 32.1	21 32.4	1 25.0	28 21.8	28 56.2	26 08.8
24 Tu	2 09 58	4 16 29	20 51 30	27 25 31	8 27.5	22 21.1	19 23.4	6 02.8	24 53.7	21 33.6	1 21.4	28 22.8	28 54.6	26 08.4
25 W	2 13 54	5 14 52	3♏55 36	10♏21 39	8 23.3	23 54.9	20 15.2	6 40.6	25 15.3	21 35.0	1 17.6	28 23.8	28 53.0	26 08.0
26 Th	2 17 51	6 13 13	16 43 41	23 01 44	8 20.7	25 24.5	21 06.4	7 18.4	25 36.7	21 36.6	1 13.8	28 24.9	28 51.4	26 07.7
27 F	2 21 47	7 11 32	29 15 56	5♐26 28	8D19.7	26 49.9	21 56.8	7 56.2	25 58.1	21 38.3	1 10.0	28 26.0	28 49.7	26 07.4
28 Sa	2 25 44	8 09 50	11♐33 37	17 37 40	8 20.0	28 10.9	22 46.5	8 33.9	26 19.5	21 40.2	1 06.1	28 27.2	28 48.1	26 07.1
29 Su	2 29 40	9 08 06	23 39 00	29 38 03	8 21.3	29 27.4	23 35.4	9 11.5	26 40.7	21 42.3	1 02.1	28 28.5	28 46.5	26 06.8
30 M	2 33 37	10 06 21	5♑35 17	11♑31 13	8 23.0	0♊39.3	24 23.6	9 49.0	27 01.9	21 44.6	0 58.2	28 29.8	28 44.9	26 06.6

Astro Data Dy Hr Mn	Planet Ingress Dy Hr Mn	Last Aspect Dy Hr Mn	☽ Ingress Dy Hr Mn	Last Aspect Dy Hr Mn	☽ Ingress Dy Hr Mn	☽ Phases & Eclipses Dy Hr Mn
♄R 12 3:29	♀ ♉ 7 21:31	3 5:35 ♅ △	♐ 3 8:09	2 3:38 ♆ ⚹	♑ 2 4:37	4 11:53 ☾ 13♐54
☽0N 12 7:02	☿ ♓ 11 10:27	5 15:16 ♀ △	♑ 5 20:32	4 16:17 ♆ □	♒ 4 17:24	12 13:37 ● 21♓58
⊙0N 20 15:20	♆ ♎R 12 1:53	8 6:26 ♅ ☍	♒ 8 9:19	7 3:26 ♆ △	♓ 7 4:37	19 17:14 ☽ 29♊05
☽0S 25 7:00	⊙ ♈ 20 15:20	10 18:12 ☿ ☌	♓ 10 20:11	9 9:32 ♅ △	♈ 9 12:47	26 13:11 ○ 5♎51
☿0N 30 23:26	☿ ♈ 28 22:41	13 1:36 ♅ △	♈ 13 4:26	11 16:46 ♆ ☍	♉ 11 18:03	
		15 10:25 ♆ ☍	♉ 15 10:32	13 20:16 ♂ △	♊ 13 21:30	3 8:06 ☾ 13♑33
♅D 5 11:22	♀ ♊ 4 7:23	17 12:22 ♅ ⚹	♊ 17 15:11	15 22:48 ♆ △	♋ 16 0:15	11 2:39 ● 21♈11
☽0N 8 15:09	☿ ♉ 12 17:10	19 18:31 ♆ △	♋ 19 18:47	18 1:27 ♆ □	♌ 18 3:00	17 23:28 ☽ 27♋55
♃D 17 12:59	♂ ♒ 14 23:40	21 21:09 ♆ □	♌ 21 21:31	20 4:36 ♆ ⚹	♍ 20 6:17	25 1:41 ○ 4♏50
☽0S 21 13:42	⊙ ♉ 20 2:43	23 23:27 ♆ ⚹	♍ 23 23:53	22 7:41 ♅ ⚹	♎ 22 10:36	
	☿ ♊ 29 22:41	25 24:00 ♅ ⚹	♎ 26 3:00	24 14:43 ♆ ☌	♏ 24 16:44	
		28 7:38 ♆ ☌	♏ 28 8:18	26 22:22 ♅ △	♐ 27 1:25	
		30 13:30 ♅ △	♐ 30 16:56	29 10:17 ♆ ⚹	♑ 29 12:44	

Astro Data

1 March 1956
Julian Day # 20514
SVP 5♓52'01"
GC 26♐13.6 ⚵ 12♒18.7
Eris 8♈16.7 ⚴ 10♑08.4
⚷ 8♒39.6 ⚶ 10♏40.6
☽ Mean ☊ 12♐53.5

1 April 1956
Julian Day # 20545
SVP 5♓51'58"
GC 26♐13.7 ⚵ 22♒03.4
Eris 8♈37.6 ⚴ 17♑39.5
⚷ 10♒34.5 ⚶ 9♏57.0R
☽ Mean ☊ 11♐15.0

LONGITUDE — May 1956

Day	Sid.Time	☉	0 hr ☽	Noon ☽	True ☊	☿	♀	♂	⚳	♃	♄	♅	♆	♇
1 Tu	2 37 33	11♉04 34	17♑26 24	23♑21 24	8♐24.7	1♊46.6	25♊10.9	10♒26.5	27♓23.1	21♌47.0	0♐54.1	28♋31.1	28♎43.3	26♌06.4
2 W	2 41 30	12 02 45	29 16 49	5♒13 15	8R25.7	2 49.2	25 57.3	11 04.0	27 44.1	21 49.7	0R50.0	28 32.5	28R41.7	26R06.3
3 Th	2 45 27	13 00 55	11♒11 20	17 11 39	8 25.9	3 47.0	26 42.9	11 41.3	28 05.1	21 52.5	0 45.9	28 34.0	28 40.1	26 06.1
4 F	2 49 23	13 59 03	23 14 50	29 21 24	8 24.9	4 40.0	27 27.6	12 18.6	28 26.0	21 55.4	0 41.8	28 35.5	28 38.6	26 06.0
5 Sa	2 53 20	14 57 11	5♓31 57	11♓46 56	8 22.9	5 28.0	28 11.3	12 55.8	28 46.8	21 58.6	0 37.6	28 37.0	28 37.0	26 05.9
6 Su	2 57 16	15 55 16	18 06 47	24 31 53	8 20.2	6 11.0	28 54.0	13 32.9	29 07.6	22 01.9	0 33.3	28 38.6	28 35.4	26 05.9
7 M	3 01 13	16 53 20	1♈02 30	7♈38 48	8 17.1	6 49.0	29 35.7	14 09.9	29 28.2	22 05.4	0 29.1	28 40.2	28 33.9	26D05.8
8 Tu	3 05 09	17 51 23	14 20 52	21 08 38	8 14.0	7 22.0	0♋16.3	14 46.8	29 48.8	22 09.0	0 24.8	28 41.9	28 32.4	26 05.8
9 W	3 09 06	18 49 24	28 01 56	5♉00 29	8 11.5	7 49.8	0 55.9	15 23.6	0♈09.3	22 12.8	0 20.4	28 43.7	28 30.8	26 05.9
10 Th	3 13 02	19 47 24	12♉03 52	19 11 34	8 09.8	8 12.5	1 34.3	16 00.3	0 29.7	22 16.8	0 16.1	28 45.4	28 29.3	26 05.9
11 F	3 16 59	20 45 22	26 22 58	3♊37 23	8D09.1	8 30.1	2 11.5	16 37.0	0 50.1	22 21.0	0 11.7	28 47.3	28 27.8	26 06.0
12 Sa	3 20 56	21 43 19	10♊54 05	18 12 18	8 09.2	8 42.6	2 47.4	17 13.5	1 10.3	22 25.3	0 07.3	28 49.2	28 26.4	26 06.2
13 Su	3 24 52	22 41 14	25 31 15	2♋50 12	8 10.0	8 50.1	3 22.1	17 49.9	1 30.4	22 29.8	0 02.9	28 51.1	28 24.9	26 06.3
14 M	3 28 49	23 39 08	10♋08 27	17 25 21	8 11.1	8R52.6	3 55.4	18 26.2	1 50.5	22 34.4	29♏58.5	28 53.0	28 23.4	26 06.5
15 Tu	3 32 45	24 36 59	24 40 19	1♌52 51	8 12.1	8 50.2	4 27.3	19 02.4	2 10.5	22 39.2	29 54.0	28 55.1	28 22.0	26 06.7
16 W	3 36 42	25 34 49	9♌02 34	16 09 06	8R12.8	8 43.2	4 57.8	19 38.5	2 30.3	22 44.2	29 49.6	28 57.1	28 20.6	26 07.0
17 Th	3 40 38	26 32 37	23 12 14	0♍11 44	8 12.9	8 31.6	5 26.8	20 14.5	2 50.1	22 49.3	29 45.1	28 59.2	28 19.2	26 07.2
18 F	3 44 35	27 30 23	7♍07 31	13 59 29	8 12.5	8 15.9	5 54.2	20 50.4	3 09.7	22 54.5	29 40.6	29 01.4	28 17.8	26 07.5
19 Sa	3 48 31	28 28 08	20 47 38	27 31 57	8 11.6	7 56.3	6 20.0	21 26.1	3 29.3	23 00.0	29 36.2	29 03.5	28 16.4	26 07.9
20 Su	3 52 28	29 25 50	4♎12 29	10♎49 16	8 10.6	7 33.1	6 44.1	22 01.7	3 48.8	23 05.5	29 31.7	29 05.8	28 15.1	26 08.2
21 M	3 56 25	0♊23 32	17 22 22	23 51 54	8 09.6	7 06.8	7 06.4	22 37.2	4 08.1	23 11.2	29 27.2	29 08.0	28 13.7	26 08.6
22 Tu	4 00 21	1 21 12	0♏17 55	6♏40 32	8 08.7	6 37.9	7 26.9	23 12.6	4 27.4	23 17.1	29 22.7	29 10.3	28 12.4	26 09.0
23 W	4 04 18	2 18 50	12 59 52	19 16 01	8 08.1	6 06.8	7 45.6	23 47.9	4 46.6	23 23.1	29 18.3	29 12.7	28 11.1	26 09.4
24 Th	4 08 14	3 16 27	25 29 08	1♐39 22	8D07.8	5 34.2	8 02.4	24 23.0	5 05.6	23 29.2	29 13.8	29 15.1	28 09.8	26 09.9
25 F	4 12 11	4 14 04	7♐46 52	13 51 51	8 07.8	5 00.6	8 17.1	24 57.9	5 24.5	23 35.5	29 09.4	29 17.5	28 08.6	26 10.4
26 Sa	4 16 07	5 11 38	19 54 31	25 55 08	8 08.0	4 26.5	8 29.8	25 32.8	5 43.4	23 41.9	29 04.9	29 20.0	28 07.3	26 10.9
27 Su	4 20 04	6 09 12	1♑53 57	7♑51 16	8 08.2	3 52.7	8 40.5	26 07.5	6 02.1	23 48.5	29 00.5	29 22.5	28 06.1	26 11.5
28 M	4 24 00	7 06 45	13 47 27	19 42 51	8 08.4	3 19.5	8 49.0	26 42.0	6 20.7	23 55.2	28 56.1	29 25.0	28 04.9	26 12.1
29 Tu	4 27 57	8 04 17	25 37 52	1♒32 56	8R08.4	2 47.8	8 55.2	27 16.4	6 39.2	24 02.0	28 51.7	29 27.6	28 03.7	26 12.7
30 W	4 31 54	9 01 48	7♒28 32	13 25 08	8 08.4	2 17.9	8 59.3	27 50.6	6 57.6	24 09.0	28 47.3	29 30.2	28 02.6	26 13.3
31 Th	4 35 50	9 59 18	19 23 16	25 23 27	8 08.3	1 50.3	9R01.0	28 24.7	7 15.8	24 16.1	28 43.0	29 32.9	28 01.5	26 14.0

LONGITUDE — June 1956

Day	Sid.Time	☉	0 hr ☽	Noon ☽	True ☊	☿	♀	♂	⚳	♃	♄	♅	♆	♇
1 F	4 39 47	10♊56 47	1♓26 14	7♓32 11	8♐08.2	1♊25.5	9♋00.4	28♒58.6	7♈33.9	24♌23.3	28♏38.6	29♋35.6	28♎00.4	26♌14.7
2 Sa	4 43 43	11 54 15	13 41 49	19 55 42	8D08.3	1R04.0	8R57.5	29 32.3	7 51.9	24 30.7	28R34.3	29 38.3	27R59.3	26 15.4
3 Su	4 47 40	12 51 43	26 14 20	2♈38 12	8 08.5	0 45.9	8 52.2	0♓05.8	8 09.8	24 38.1	28 30.0	29 41.0	27 58.2	26 16.1
4 M	4 51 36	13 49 10	9♈07 43	15 43 13	8 08.9	0 31.7	8 44.5	0 39.1	8 27.6	24 45.8	28 25.8	29 43.8	27 57.2	26 16.9
5 Tu	4 55 33	14 46 36	22 24 59	29 13 11	8 09.5	0 21.6	8 34.4	1 12.2	8 45.2	24 53.5	28 21.6	29 46.6	27 56.2	26 17.7
6 W	4 59 29	15 44 02	6♉07 51	13♉08 52	8 10.1	0D15.6	8 21.9	1 45.2	9 02.7	25 01.3	28 17.4	29 49.5	27 55.2	26 18.5
7 Th	5 03 26	16 41 27	20 16 00	27 28 51	8R10.5	0 14.1	8 07.0	2 17.9	9 20.0	25 09.3	28 13.3	29 52.4	27 54.2	26 19.4
8 F	5 07 23	17 38 52	4♊46 50	12♊09 15	8 10.6	0 16.9	7 49.8	2 50.4	9 37.2	25 17.4	28 09.2	29 55.3	27 53.3	26 20.3
9 Sa	5 11 19	18 36 15	19 35 15	27 03 53	8 10.3	0 24.3	7 30.3	3 22.6	9 54.3	25 25.6	28 05.1	29 58.3	27 52.4	26 21.2
10 Su	5 15 16	19 33 38	4♋34 05	12♋04 47	8 09.4	0 36.2	7 08.5	3 54.7	10 11.2	25 34.0	28 01.1	0♌01.3	27 51.5	26 22.1
11 M	5 19 12	20 31 00	19 34 54	27 03 23	8 08.1	0 52.6	6 44.6	4 26.5	10 28.0	25 42.4	27 57.1	0 04.3	27 50.7	26 23.1
12 Tu	5 23 09	21 28 21	4♌29 15	11♌51 40	8 06.6	1 13.5	6 18.6	4 58.1	10 44.6	25 51.0	27 53.2	0 07.3	27 49.8	26 24.1
13 W	5 27 05	22 25 41	19 09 52	26 23 17	8 05.2	1 38.9	5 50.6	5 29.4	11 01.1	25 59.7	27 49.3	0 10.4	27 49.0	26 25.1
14 Th	5 31 02	23 23 00	3♍31 28	10♍34 08	8D04.2	2 08.6	5 20.8	6 00.5	11 17.4	26 08.4	27 45.5	0 13.5	27 48.3	26 26.1
15 F	5 34 58	24 20 18	17 31 07	24 22 25	8 03.8	2 42.7	4 49.3	6 31.3	11 33.6	26 17.3	27 41.7	0 16.6	27 47.5	26 27.1
16 Sa	5 38 55	25 17 35	1♎08 07	7♎48 22	8 04.2	3 21.0	4 16.3	7 01.8	11 49.6	26 26.3	27 38.0	0 19.8	27 46.8	26 28.2
17 Su	5 42 52	26 14 51	14 23 26	20 53 36	8 05.2	4 03.5	3 41.9	7 32.1	12 05.4	26 35.4	27 34.4	0 23.0	27 46.1	26 29.3
18 M	5 46 48	27 12 07	27 19 11	3♏40 33	8 06.6	4 50.2	3 06.4	8 02.2	12 21.1	26 44.6	27 30.8	0 26.2	27 45.5	26 30.5
19 Tu	5 50 45	28 09 22	9♏58 02	16 12 02	8 08.0	5 40.9	2 30.1	8 31.9	12 36.6	26 53.9	27 27.2	0 29.4	27 44.8	26 31.6
20 W	5 54 41	29 06 36	22 22 51	28 30 51	8R09.0	6 35.5	1 53.0	9 01.4	12 52.0	27 03.3	27 23.8	0 32.7	27 44.2	26 32.8
21 Th	5 58 38	0♋03 49	4♐36 21	10♐39 38	8 09.2	7 34.1	1 15.6	9 30.5	13 07.2	27 12.8	27 20.4	0 35.9	27 43.7	26 34.0
22 F	6 02 34	1 01 03	16 41 00	22 40 44	8 08.5	8 36.5	0 37.9	9 59.4	13 22.2	27 22.4	27 17.0	0 39.3	27 43.1	26 35.2
23 Sa	6 06 31	1 58 15	28 39 04	4♑36 16	8 06.6	9 42.8	0 00.3	10 28.0	13 37.0	27 32.1	27 13.8	0 42.6	27 42.6	26 36.5
24 Su	6 10 27	2 55 28	10♑32 34	16 28 14	8 03.5	10 52.7	29♊22.9	10 56.2	13 51.7	27 41.9	27 10.5	0 45.9	27 42.1	26 37.7
25 M	6 14 24	3 52 40	22 23 29	28 18 37	7 59.6	12 06.4	28 46.2	11 24.1	14 06.1	27 51.7	27 07.4	0 49.3	27 41.7	26 39.0
26 Tu	6 18 21	4 49 52	4♒13 54	10♒09 38	7 55.1	13 23.7	28 10.2	11 51.7	14 20.4	28 01.7	27 04.3	0 52.7	27 41.3	26 40.3
27 W	6 22 17	5 47 04	16 06 07	22 03 42	7 50.6	14 44.6	27 35.1	12 18.9	14 34.5	28 11.7	27 01.3	0 56.1	27 40.9	26 41.7
28 Th	6 26 14	6 44 16	28 02 46	4♓03 43	7 46.6	16 09.1	27 01.3	12 45.8	14 48.5	28 21.9	26 58.4	0 59.5	27 40.5	26 43.0
29 F	6 30 10	7 41 27	10♓06 58	16 12 58	7 43.6	17 37.1	26 29.0	13 12.3	15 02.2	28 32.1	26 55.6	1 02.9	27 40.2	26 44.4
30 Sa	6 34 07	8 38 39	22 22 12	28 35 09	7D41.8	19 08.6	25 58.2	13 38.4	15 15.7	28 42.4	26 52.8	1 06.4	27 39.9	26 45.8

Astro Data	Dy Hr Mn
♅□♆	5 11:52
☽ 0N	5 23:42
♇ D	7 19:59
☿ R	14 12:12
☽ 0S	18 18:50
♄△♅	24 7:37
♀ R	31 18:04
☽ 0N	2 8:01
☿ D	7 8:33
♄⊻♆	13 14:23
☽ 0S	15 0:39
♃☌♇	16 17:45
♃□♄	22 2:03
♃⚹♆	24 12:39
☽ 0N	29 15:35

Planet Ingress		Dy Hr Mn
♀	♋	8 2:17
⚳	♈	9 1:05
♄	♏R	14 3:45
☉	♊	21 2:13
♂	♓	3 7:51
♅	♌	10 1:48
☉	♋	21 10:24
♀	♊R	23 12:10

Last Aspect Dy Hr Mn		☽ Ingress	Dy Hr Mn
1 22:51	♆ □	♒	2 1:27
4 10:36	♆ △	♓	4 13:15
6 20:32	♀ □	♈	6 22:05
9 1:11	♅ □	♉	9 3:24
11 3:59	♅ ⚹	♊	11 6:00
13 4:45	♆ △	♋	13 7:21
15 8:43	♄ △	♌	15 8:52
17 11:14	♄ □	♍	17 11:40
19 15:41	♄ ⚹	♎	19 16:25
21 21:51	♅ □	♏	21 23:26
24 7:18	♄ ☌	♐	24 8:46
26 16:24	♆ ⚹	♑	26 20:11
29 7:45	♅ ☍	♒	29 8:52
31 18:34	♄ □	♓	31 21:09

Last Aspect Dy Hr Mn		☽ Ingress	Dy Hr Mn
3 6:28	♅ △	♈	3 7:05
5 12:59	♅ □	♉	5 13:22
7 15:58	♅ ⚹	♊	7 16:09
9 13:18	♆ △	♋	9 16:42
11 13:26	♄ △	♌	11 16:45
13 14:23	♆ ⚹	♍	13 18:03
15 17:51	♄ ⚹	♎	15 21:58
18 0:50	♆ ☌	♏	18 5:03
20 9:49	♄ ☌	♐	20 14:55
22 22:07	♆ ⚹	♑	23 2:43
25 10:45	♆ □	♒	25 15:26
28 0:28	♃ ☍	♓	28 3:54
30 8:44	♄ △	♈	30 14:43

☽ Phases & Eclipses Dy Hr Mn	
3 2:55	☾ 12♒39
10 13:04	● 19♉50
17 5:15	☽ 26♌16
24 15:26	○ 3♐25
24 15:31	• P 0.965
1 19:13	☾ 11♓14
8 21:29	● 18♊02
8 21:20:09	• T 04'44"
15 11:56	☽ 24♍20
23 6:14	○ 1♑44

Astro Data

1 May 1956
Julian Day # 20575
SVP 5♓51'55"
GC 26♐13.8 ⚴ 29♒41.3
Eris 8♈57.5 ⚵ 21♑52.5
⚷ 11♒35.8 ⚶ 3♏21.7R
☽ Mean ☊ 9♐39.7

1 June 1956
Julian Day # 20606
SVP 5♓51'51"
GC 26♐13.8 ⚴ 4♓38.0
Eris 9♈12.7 ⚵ 21♑30.4R
⚷ 11♒35.8R ⚶ 28♎15.6R
☽ Mean ☊ 8♐01.2

July 1956

LONGITUDE

Day	Sid.Time	☉	0 hr ☽	Noon ☽	True ☊	☿	♀	♂	⚳	♃	♄	♅	♆	♇
1 Su	6 38 03	9♋35 51	4♈52 18	11♈14 10	7♐41.3	20♊43.5	25♊29.1	14♓04.1	15♈29.0	28♌52.8	26♏50.1	1♌09.9	27♎39.6	26♌47.2
2 M	6 42 00	10 33 04	17 41 14	24 13 55	7 42.0	22 21.8	25R01.9	14 29.4	15 42.2	29 03.3	26R47.5	1 13.4	27R39.4	26 48.6
3 Tu	6 45 56	11 30 16	0♉52 39	7♉37 44	7 43.3	24 03.4	24 36.8	14 54.4	15 55.1	29 13.8	26 44.9	1 16.9	27 39.2	26 50.1
4 W	6 49 53	12 27 29	14 29 27	21 27 54	7 44.7	25 48.2	24 13.8	15 18.8	16 07.8	29 24.4	26 42.5	1 20.4	27 39.0	26 51.5
5 Th	6 53 50	13 24 42	28 33 04	5♊44 48	7R45.5	27 36.1	23 53.0	15 42.9	16 20.3	29 35.2	26 40.1	1 24.0	27 38.9	26 53.0
6 F	6 57 46	14 21 56	13♊02 44	20 26 19	7 44.9	29 27.0	23 34.4	16 06.5	16 32.6	29 45.9	26 37.8	1 27.5	27 38.8	26 54.5
7 Sa	7 01 43	15 19 09	27 54 49	5♋27 19	7 42.7	1♋20.7	23 18.2	16 29.6	16 44.6	29 56.8	26 35.6	1 31.1	27 38.7	26 56.1
8 Su	7 05 39	16 16 23	13♋02 42	20 39 46	7 38.8	3 17.0	23 04.3	16 52.3	16 56.4	0♍07.7	26 33.5	1 34.7	27D38.7	26 57.6
9 M	7 09 36	17 13 37	28 17 12	5♌53 42	7 33.6	5 15.9	22 52.8	17 14.4	17 08.0	0 18.8	26 31.4	1 38.3	27 38.7	26 59.2
10 Tu	7 13 32	18 10 51	13♌27 57	20 58 45	7 27.8	7 16.9	22 43.7	17 36.1	17 19.4	0 29.8	26 29.5	1 41.9	27 38.7	27 00.8
11 W	7 17 29	19 08 05	28 25 02	5♍45 53	7 22.2	9 19.9	22 36.9	17 57.3	17 30.5	0 41.0	26 27.6	1 45.5	27 38.7	27 02.4
12 Th	7 21 26	20 05 18	13♍00 37	20 08 44	7 17.6	11 24.6	22 32.5	18 17.9	17 41.4	0 52.2	26 25.9	1 49.1	27 38.8	27 04.0
13 F	7 25 22	21 02 32	27 09 56	4♎04 07	7 14.5	13 30.7	22D30.4	18 38.0	17 52.1	1 03.5	26 24.2	1 52.8	27 39.0	27 05.6
14 Sa	7 29 19	21 59 46	10♎51 22	17 31 52	7D13.2	15 37.8	22 30.7	18 57.6	18 02.5	1 14.8	26 22.6	1 56.4	27 39.1	27 07.3
15 Su	7 33 15	22 57 00	24 05 58	0♏34 04	7 13.4	17 45.8	22 33.2	19 16.7	18 12.6	1 26.2	26 21.1	2 00.0	27 39.3	27 08.9
16 M	7 37 12	23 54 14	6♏56 39	13 14 15	7 14.5	19 54.2	22 38.0	19 35.1	18 22.5	1 37.7	26 19.7	2 03.7	27 39.5	27 10.6
17 Tu	7 41 08	24 51 28	19 27 24	25 36 38	7R15.7	22 02.8	22 45.0	19 53.1	18 32.2	1 49.2	26 18.4	2 07.4	27 39.8	27 12.3
18 W	7 45 05	25 48 43	1♐42 31	7♐45 33	7 16.2	24 11.3	22 54.1	20 10.4	18 41.6	2 00.8	26 17.2	2 11.0	27 40.0	27 14.0
19 Th	7 49 01	26 45 57	13 46 14	19 45 02	7 15.4	26 19.5	23 05.3	20 27.2	18 50.7	2 12.5	26 16.1	2 14.7	27 40.4	27 15.7
20 F	7 52 58	27 43 12	25 42 22	1♑38 38	7 12.5	28 27.0	23 18.6	20 43.3	18 59.5	2 24.2	26 15.0	2 18.4	27 40.7	27 17.5
21 Sa	7 56 55	28 40 28	7♑34 10	13 29 18	7 07.3	0♌33.8	23 33.8	20 58.8	19 08.1	2 35.9	26 14.1	2 22.1	27 41.1	27 19.2
22 Su	8 00 51	29 37 44	19 24 19	25 19 28	7 00.0	2 39.6	23 51.0	21 13.7	19 16.5	2 47.8	26 13.2	2 25.8	27 41.5	27 21.0
23 M	8 04 48	0♌35 00	1♒14 58	7♒11 03	6 50.9	4 44.3	24 10.0	21 28.0	19 24.5	2 59.6	26 12.5	2 29.4	27 41.9	27 22.7
24 Tu	8 08 44	1 32 17	13 07 54	19 05 44	6 40.8	6 47.7	24 30.8	21 41.6	19 32.3	3 11.5	26 11.9	2 33.1	27 42.4	27 24.5
25 W	8 12 41	2 29 35	25 04 44	1♓05 07	6 30.6	8 49.7	24 53.4	21 54.5	19 39.7	3 23.5	26 11.3	2 36.8	27 42.9	27 26.3
26 Th	8 16 37	3 26 54	7♓07 06	13 10 56	6 21.1	10 50.3	25 17.7	22 06.7	19 46.9	3 35.5	26 10.8	2 40.5	27 43.4	27 28.1
27 F	8 20 34	4 24 13	19 16 53	25 25 15	6 13.3	12 49.4	25 43.7	22 18.3	19 53.8	3 47.6	26 10.5	2 44.2	27 44.0	27 29.9
28 Sa	8 24 30	5 21 33	1♈36 23	7♈50 37	6 07.6	14 47.0	26 11.2	22 29.1	20 00.4	3 59.7	26 10.2	2 47.9	27 44.6	27 31.8
29 Su	8 28 27	6 18 55	14 08 22	20 30 02	6 04.3	16 42.9	26 40.2	22 39.2	20 06.7	4 11.9	26 10.0	2 51.6	27 45.2	27 33.6
30 M	8 32 23	7 16 17	26 56 02	3♉26 48	6D03.0	18 37.3	27 10.7	22 48.5	20 12.7	4 24.1	26D09.9	2 55.2	27 45.9	27 35.5
31 Tu	8 36 20	8 13 41	10♉02 47	16 44 20	6 03.2	20 30.0	27 42.6	22 57.1	20 18.4	4 36.3	26 10.0	2 58.9	27 46.6	27 37.3

August 1956

LONGITUDE

Day	Sid.Time	☉	0 hr ☽	Noon ☽	True ☊	☿	♀	♂	⚳	♃	♄	♅	♆	♇
1 W	8 40 17	9♌11 06	23♉31 49	0♊25 29	6♐03.7	22♌21.1	28♊15.9	23♓05.0	20♈23.8	4♍48.6	26♏10.1	3♌02.6	27♎47.3	27♌39.2
2 Th	8 44 13	10 08 32	7♊25 32	14 31 58	6R03.5	24 10.6	28 50.5	23 12.0	20 28.9	5 00.9	26 10.3	3 06.3	27 48.1	27 41.1
3 F	8 48 10	11 05 59	21 44 41	29 03 24	6 01.7	25 58.5	29 26.4	23 18.3	20 33.6	5 13.3	26 10.6	3 10.0	27 48.9	27 42.9
4 Sa	8 52 06	12 03 28	6♋27 34	13♋56 32	5 57.4	27 44.7	0♋03.4	23 23.7	20 38.0	5 25.7	26 11.0	3 13.6	27 49.7	27 44.8
5 Su	8 56 03	13 00 57	21 29 21	29 04 56	5 50.6	29 29.3	0 41.6	23 28.4	20 42.1	5 38.2	26 11.5	3 17.3	27 50.5	27 46.7
6 M	8 59 59	13 58 28	6♌42 03	14♌19 20	5 41.8	1♍12.4	1 21.0	23 32.2	20 45.8	5 50.7	26 12.2	3 20.9	27 51.4	27 48.7
7 Tu	9 03 56	14 56 00	21 55 25	29 28 56	5 31.9	2 53.8	2 01.4	23 35.2	20 49.2	6 03.2	26 12.9	3 24.6	27 52.3	27 50.6
8 W	9 07 53	15 53 32	6♍58 37	14♍23 21	5 22.1	4 33.7	2 42.8	23 37.4	20 52.3	6 15.7	26 13.7	3 28.2	27 53.2	27 52.5
9 Th	9 11 49	16 51 06	21 42 10	28 54 22	5 13.5	6 12.0	3 25.3	23 38.8	20 55.1	6 28.3	26 14.6	3 31.8	27 54.2	27 54.4
10 F	9 15 46	17 48 40	5♎59 27	12♎57 08	5 07.1	7 48.8	4 08.6	23R39.4	20 57.4	6 40.9	26 15.6	3 35.4	27 55.2	27 56.3
11 Sa	9 19 42	18 46 15	19 47 20	26 30 12	5 03.0	9 23.9	4 52.9	23 39.1	20 59.5	6 53.6	26 16.7	3 39.0	27 56.2	27 58.3
12 Su	9 23 39	19 43 51	3♏05 59	9♏35 06	5D01.2	10 57.5	5 38.1	23 38.0	21 01.2	7 06.2	26 17.8	3 42.6	27 57.3	28 00.2
13 M	9 27 35	20 41 29	15 58 02	22 15 23	5 00.8	12 29.6	6 24.2	23 36.1	21 02.5	7 19.0	26 19.1	3 46.2	27 58.4	28 02.2
14 Tu	9 31 32	21 39 07	28 27 44	4♐35 45	5R01.0	14 00.1	7 11.1	23 33.5	21 03.5	7 31.7	26 20.5	3 49.8	27 59.5	28 04.1
15 W	9 35 28	22 36 46	10♐40 04	16 41 20	5 00.5	15 29.0	7 58.8	23 30.0	21 04.2	7 44.4	26 22.0	3 53.3	28 00.6	28 06.0
16 Th	9 39 25	23 34 26	22 40 11	28 37 11	4 58.4	16 56.3	8 47.2	23 25.7	21R04.4	7 57.2	26 23.6	3 56.8	28 01.8	28 08.0
17 F	9 43 22	24 32 07	4♑32 54	10♑27 50	4 53.9	18 22.1	9 36.4	23 20.6	21 04.4	8 10.0	26 25.2	4 00.4	28 03.0	28 10.0
18 Sa	9 47 18	25 29 50	16 22 29	22 17 15	4 46.7	19 46.1	10 26.4	23 14.7	21 03.9	8 22.8	26 27.0	4 03.9	28 04.2	28 11.9
19 Su	9 51 15	26 27 33	28 12 29	4♒08 32	4 36.8	21 08.6	11 17.0	23 08.1	21 03.1	8 35.7	26 28.9	4 07.4	28 05.5	28 13.9
20 M	9 55 11	27 25 18	10♒05 39	16 04 04	4 24.6	22 29.3	12 08.3	23 00.8	21 02.0	8 48.5	26 30.8	4 10.8	28 06.8	28 15.8
21 Tu	9 59 08	28 23 04	22 04 00	28 05 34	4 11.2	23 48.4	13 00.2	22 52.6	21 00.5	9 01.4	26 32.8	4 14.3	28 08.1	28 17.8
22 W	10 03 04	29 20 52	4♓08 56	10♓14 13	3 57.5	25 05.6	13 52.8	22 43.8	20 58.6	9 14.3	26 35.0	4 17.7	28 09.4	28 19.7
23 Th	10 07 01	0♍18 41	16 21 29	22 30 53	3 44.7	26 21.0	14 46.0	22 34.3	20 56.3	9 27.2	26 37.2	4 21.1	28 10.8	28 21.7
24 F	10 10 57	1 16 31	28 42 31	4♈56 31	3 33.9	27 34.6	15 39.9	22 24.0	20 53.7	9 40.1	26 39.5	4 24.5	28 12.2	28 23.7
25 Sa	10 14 54	2 14 24	11♈13 02	17 32 16	3 25.7	28 46.2	16 34.2	22 13.1	20 50.7	9 53.0	26 41.9	4 27.9	28 13.6	28 25.6
26 Su	10 18 50	3 12 18	23 54 24	0♉19 42	3 20.4	29 55.7	17 29.2	22 01.6	20 47.3	10 06.0	26 44.4	4 31.3	28 15.0	28 27.6
27 M	10 22 47	4 10 13	6♉48 26	13 20 54	3 17.8	1♎03.2	18 24.6	21 49.5	20 43.6	10 18.9	26 47.0	4 34.6	28 16.5	28 29.5
28 Tu	10 26 44	5 08 11	19 57 24	26 38 16	3 17.0	2 08.4	19 20.7	21 36.7	20 39.5	10 31.9	26 49.7	4 37.9	28 18.0	28 31.5
29 W	10 30 40	6 06 11	3♊23 47	10♊14 13	3 16.9	3 11.3	20 17.2	21 23.5	20 35.0	10 44.9	26 52.5	4 41.2	28 19.5	28 33.4
30 Th	10 34 37	7 04 12	17 09 46	24 10 33	3 16.4	4 11.7	21 14.2	21 09.6	20 30.2	10 57.9	26 55.3	4 44.5	28 21.0	28 35.4
31 F	10 38 33	8 02 16	1♋16 36	8♋27 47	3 14.1	5 09.6	22 11.6	20 55.4	20 25.0	11 10.9	26 58.3	4 47.7	28 22.6	28 37.3

Astro Data	Planet Ingress	Last Aspect	☽ Ingress	Last Aspect	☽ Ingress	☽ Phases & Eclipses	Astro Data
Dy Hr Mn	Dy Hr Mn	Dy Hr Mn	Dy Hr Mn	Dy Hr Mn	Dy Hr Mn	Dy Hr Mn	
♄□♇ 2 5:08	☿ ♋ 6 19:02	2 20:51 ♃ △	♉ 2 22:26	1 7:11 ♇ □	♊ 1 11:16	1 8:41 ☾ 9♈28	1 July 1956
♆ D 9 6:10	♃ ♍ 7 19:01	5 1:36 ♃ □	♊ 5 2:26	3 12:39 ♀ ☌	♋ 3 13:32	8 4:38 ● 15♋59	Julian Day # 20636
☽0S 12 8:42	☿ ♌ 21 5:35	7 3:08 ♃ ✱	♋ 7 3:20	5 10:02 ♆ □	♌ 5 13:27	14 20:47 ☽ 22♎21	SVP 5♓51'46"
♀ D 13 21:20	☉ ♌ 22 21:20	8 22:59 ♆ △	♌ 9 2:42	7 9:26 ♆ ✱	♍ 7 12:50	22 21:29 ○ 0♒00	GC 26♐13.9 ⚴ 5♓11.2R
♃⚺♅ 19 18:41		10 22:45 ♆ ✱	♍ 11 2:34	9 7:32 ♄ ✱	♎ 9 13:50	30 19:31 ☾ 7♉34	Eris 9♈18.9 ⚵ 16♑14.3R
☽0N 26 22:20	♀ ♋ 4 9:49	12 22:43 ♄ ✱	♎ 13 4:54	11 14:40 ♇ ✱	♏ 11 18:20		⚷ 10♒38.3R ⚶ 0♏15.7
♄ D 30 18:36	☿ ♍ 5 19:06	15 6:34 ♆ ☌	♏ 15 10:56	13 23:12 ♇ □	♐ 14 3:00	6 11:25 ● 13♌57	☽ Mean ☊ 6♐25.9
	☉ ♍ 23 4:15	17 15:08 ♇ □	♐ 17 20:38	16 11:01 ♇ △	♑ 16 14:47	13 8:45 ☽ 20♏34	
☽0S 8 18:51	☿ ♎ 26 13:30	20 3:59 ♆ ✱	♑ 20 8:40	18 23:45 ♆ □	♒ 19 3:38	21 12:38 ○ 28♒25	1 August 1956
♆✱♇ 9 7:11		22 16:48 ♆ □	♒ 22 21:28	21 12:38 ☉ ☍	♓ 21 15:47	29 4:13 ☾ 5♊47	Julian Day # 20667
♂ R 10 16:18		25 5:16 ♆ △	♓ 25 9:50	23 20:16 ☿ ☍	♈ 24 2:30		SVP 5♓51'41"
⚳ R 16 19:01		27 13:28 ♄ △	♈ 27 20:54	26 8:31 ♇ △	♉ 26 11:23		GC 26♐14.0 ⚴ 0♓29.0R
☽0N 23 4:41		30 1:32 ♆ ☍	♉ 30 5:40	28 15:22 ♇ □	♊ 28 17:59		Eris 9♈15.1R ⚵ 9♑26.1R
☿0S 24 3:52				30 19:30 ♇ ✱	♋ 30 21:51		⚷ 9♒02.1R ⚶ 8♏22.4
							☽ Mean ☊ 4♐47.4

LONGITUDE — September 1956

Day	Sid.Time	☉	0 hr ☽	Noon ☽	True ☊	☿	♀	♂	⚳	♃	♄	♅	♆	♇
1 Sa	10 42 30	9♍00 21	15♋43 50	23♋04 17	3♐09.3	6♎04.7	23♋09.6	20♓40.6	20♈19.4	11♍23.9	27♏01.3	4♌50.9	28♎24.2	28♌39.2
2 Su	10 46 26	9 58 29	0♌28 30	7♌55 41	3R 01.9	6 56.9	24 07.9	20R 25.5	20R 13.5	11 36.9	27 04.4	4 54.1	28 25.8	28 41.2
3 M	10 50 23	10 56 38	15 24 53	22 54 58	2 52.2	7 45.9	25 06.7	20 10.0	20 07.2	11 49.9	27 07.6	4 57.3	28 27.4	28 43.1
4 Tu	10 54 19	11 54 48	0♍24 46	7♍53 05	2 41.1	8 31.7	26 05.9	19 54.2	20 00.6	12 02.9	27 10.9	5 00.4	28 29.0	28 45.0
5 W	10 58 16	12 53 01	15 18 41	22 40 28	2 30.0	9 13.9	27 05.5	19 38.1	19 53.6	12 15.9	27 14.3	5 03.5	28 30.7	28 46.9
6 Th	11 02 13	13 51 15	29 57 26	7♎08 45	2 20.2	9 52.4	28 05.5	19 21.8	19 46.2	12 28.9	27 17.7	5 06.6	28 32.4	28 48.9
7 F	11 06 09	14 49 31	14♎13 46	21 12 03	2 12.5	10 26.7	29 05.9	19 05.4	19 38.5	12 41.9	27 21.3	5 09.7	28 34.1	28 50.8
8 Sa	11 10 06	15 47 49	28 03 21	4♏47 37	2 07.4	10 56.8	0♌06.6	18 48.8	19 30.5	12 54.9	27 24.9	5 12.7	28 35.9	28 52.7
9 Su	11 14 02	16 46 08	11♏24 58	17 55 39	2 04.9	11 22.2	1 07.7	18 32.2	19 22.1	13 07.9	27 28.6	5 15.7	28 37.6	28 54.5
10 M	11 17 59	17 44 28	24 20 06	0♐38 46	2D 04.1	11 42.7	2 09.1	18 15.6	19 13.5	13 20.9	27 32.4	5 18.7	28 39.4	28 56.4
11 Tu	11 21 55	18 42 51	6♐52 14	13 01 07	2R 04.3	11 57.9	3 10.9	17 59.0	19 04.5	13 33.9	27 36.2	5 21.6	28 41.2	28 58.3
12 W	11 25 52	19 41 15	19 06 04	25 07 45	2 04.3	12 07.4	4 13.0	17 42.6	18 55.1	13 46.9	27 40.2	5 24.5	28 43.0	29 00.2
13 Th	11 29 48	20 39 40	1♑06 50	7♑03 59	2 03.0	12R 11.1	5 15.4	17 26.2	18 45.5	13 59.9	27 44.2	5 27.4	28 44.9	29 02.0
14 F	11 33 45	21 38 07	12 59 50	18 55 00	1 59.6	12 08.5	6 18.2	17 10.1	18 35.6	14 12.8	27 48.3	5 30.2	28 46.7	29 03.9
15 Sa	11 37 42	22 36 36	24 50 03	0♒45 30	1 53.8	11 59.3	7 21.2	16 54.1	18 25.4	14 25.8	27 52.5	5 33.0	28 48.6	29 05.7
16 Su	11 41 38	23 35 06	6♒41 50	12 39 30	1 45.4	11 43.4	8 24.6	16 38.5	18 15.0	14 38.7	27 56.7	5 35.8	28 50.5	29 07.5
17 M	11 45 35	24 33 38	18 38 50	24 40 11	1 34.9	11 20.5	9 28.2	16 23.2	18 04.2	14 51.6	28 01.1	5 38.5	28 52.4	29 09.3
18 Tu	11 49 31	25 32 12	0♓43 48	6♓49 52	1 23.2	10 50.6	10 32.1	16 08.2	17 53.2	15 04.5	28 05.5	5 41.2	28 54.3	29 11.1
19 W	11 53 28	26 30 47	12 58 33	19 09 56	1 11.2	10 13.8	11 36.3	15 53.6	17 42.0	15 17.4	28 09.9	5 43.8	28 56.3	29 12.9
20 Th	11 57 24	27 29 25	25 24 07	1♈41 05	0 59.9	9 30.4	12 40.8	15 39.5	17 30.5	15 30.3	28 14.5	5 46.4	28 58.3	29 14.7
21 F	12 01 21	28 28 04	8♈00 53	14 23 28	0 50.5	8 40.6	13 45.5	15 25.8	17 18.8	15 43.1	28 19.1	5 49.0	29 00.2	29 16.4
22 Sa	12 05 17	29 26 46	20 48 49	27 16 57	0 43.5	7 45.3	14 50.5	15 12.6	17 06.8	15 55.9	28 23.8	5 51.6	29 02.2	29 18.2
23 Su	12 09 14	0♎25 29	3♉47 51	10♉21 32	0 39.2	6 45.2	15 55.8	15 00.0	16 54.7	16 08.7	28 28.5	5 54.1	29 04.2	29 19.9
24 M	12 13 10	1 24 15	16 58 02	23 37 26	0D 37.3	5 41.5	17 01.3	14 47.9	16 42.3	16 21.5	28 33.4	5 56.5	29 06.3	29 21.7
25 Tu	12 17 07	2 23 04	0♊19 48	7♊05 14	0 37.2	4 35.5	18 07.1	14 36.4	16 29.8	16 34.3	28 38.3	5 59.0	29 08.3	29 23.4
26 W	12 21 04	3 21 54	13 53 50	20 45 44	0R 38.0	3 28.9	19 13.1	14 25.5	16 17.1	16 47.0	28 43.2	6 01.4	29 10.3	29 25.1
27 Th	12 25 00	4 20 47	27 40 59	4♋39 38	0 38.5	2 23.2	20 19.3	14 15.2	16 04.2	16 59.7	28 48.3	6 03.7	29 12.4	29 26.7
28 F	12 28 57	5 19 42	11♋41 41	18 47 03	0 37.6	1 20.1	21 25.8	14 05.6	15 51.2	17 12.4	28 53.3	6 06.0	29 14.5	29 28.4
29 Sa	12 32 53	6 18 39	25 55 32	3♌06 53	0 34.8	0 21.5	22 32.5	13 56.8	15 38.1	17 25.1	28 58.5	6 08.3	29 16.6	29 30.1
30 Su	12 36 50	7 17 39	10♌20 41	17 36 26	0 29.8	29♍28.8	23 39.4	13 48.6	15 24.8	17 37.7	29 03.7	6 10.5	29 18.7	29 31.7

LONGITUDE — October 1956

Day	Sid.Time	☉	0 hr ☽	Noon ☽	True ☊	☿	♀	♂	⚳	♃	♄	♅	♆	♇
1 M	12 40 46	8♎16 41	24♌53 30	2♍11 10	0♐22.9	28♍43.6	24♌46.5	13♓41.1	15♈11.4	17♍50.3	29♏09.0	6♌12.7	29♎20.8	29♌33.3
2 Tu	12 44 43	9 15 45	9♍28 36	16 44 58	0R 14.9	28R 06.9	25 53.8	13R 34.4	14R 58.0	18 02.9	29 14.4	6 14.8	29 22.9	29 34.9
3 W	12 48 39	10 14 51	23 59 24	1♎11 02	0 06.7	27 39.8	27 01.3	13 28.4	14 44.4	18 15.4	29 19.8	6 16.9	29 25.0	29 36.5
4 Th	12 52 36	11 13 59	8♎19 04	15 22 48	29♏59.3	27 22.9	28 09.0	13 23.3	14 30.8	18 27.9	29 25.2	6 18.9	29 27.2	29 38.0
5 F	12 56 33	12 13 10	22 21 37	29 15 03	29 53.7	27D 16.6	29 16.9	13 18.9	14 17.2	18 40.4	29 30.7	6 20.9	29 29.3	29 39.6
6 Sa	13 00 29	13 12 22	6♏02 48	12♏44 39	29 50.1	27 20.8	0♍25.0	13 15.3	14 03.5	18 52.8	29 36.3	6 22.9	29 31.5	29 41.1
7 Su	13 04 26	14 11 36	19 20 34	25 50 39	29D 48.7	27 35.6	1 33.2	13 12.5	13 49.9	19 05.1	29 42.0	6 24.8	29 33.7	29 42.6
8 M	13 08 22	15 10 52	2♐15 08	8♐34 18	29 49.0	28 00.5	2 41.7	13 10.6	13 36.2	19 17.5	29 47.7	6 26.6	29 35.9	29 44.1
9 Tu	13 12 19	16 10 10	14 48 34	20 58 26	29 50.2	28 35.0	3 50.3	13D 09.4	13 22.6	19 29.8	29 53.4	6 28.4	29 38.1	29 45.6
10 W	13 16 15	17 09 30	27 04 26	3♑07 09	29 51.7	29 18.5	4 59.0	13 09.1	13 08.9	19 42.0	29 59.2	6 30.2	29 40.2	29 47.0
11 Th	13 20 12	18 08 52	9♑07 11	15 05 11	29R 52.6	0♎10.3	6 08.0	13 09.6	12 55.4	19 54.2	0♐05.1	6 31.9	29 42.5	29 48.4
12 F	13 24 08	19 08 15	21 01 47	26 57 36	29 52.3	1 09.6	7 17.1	13 10.8	12 41.9	20 06.4	0 11.0	6 33.6	29 44.7	29 49.9
13 Sa	13 28 05	20 07 40	2♒53 18	8♒49 27	29 50.3	2 15.6	8 26.3	13 12.9	12 28.5	20 18.5	0 16.9	6 35.2	29 46.9	29 51.2
14 Su	13 32 02	21 07 07	14 46 39	20 45 25	29 46.6	3 27.6	9 35.7	13 15.8	12 15.2	20 30.5	0 23.0	6 36.8	29 49.1	29 52.6
15 M	13 35 58	22 06 35	26 46 15	2♓49 36	29 41.5	4 44.8	10 45.3	13 19.4	12 02.0	20 42.5	0 29.0	6 38.3	29 51.3	29 53.9
16 Tu	13 39 55	23 06 06	8♓55 51	15 05 20	29 35.3	6 06.5	11 55.0	13 23.8	11 48.9	20 54.5	0 35.1	6 39.8	29 53.5	29 55.3
17 W	13 43 51	24 05 38	21 18 19	27 35 00	29 28.9	7 32.0	13 04.9	13 29.0	11 35.9	21 06.3	0 41.3	6 41.2	29 55.8	29 56.5
18 Th	13 47 48	25 05 12	3♈55 30	10♈19 53	29 22.8	9 00.8	14 14.9	13 35.0	11 23.2	21 18.2	0 47.4	6 42.5	29 58.0	29 57.8
19 F	13 51 44	26 04 48	16 48 10	23 20 15	29 17.8	10 32.3	15 25.0	13 41.7	11 10.5	21 30.0	0 53.7	6 43.9	0♏00.2	29 59.1
20 Sa	13 55 41	27 04 26	29 56 02	6♉35 23	29 14.3	12 06.0	16 35.3	13 49.1	10 58.1	21 41.7	1 00.0	6 45.1	0 02.5	0♍00.3
21 Su	13 59 37	28 04 06	13♉18 04	20 03 54	29D 12.5	13 41.4	17 45.7	13 57.3	10 45.8	21 53.3	1 06.3	6 46.3	0 04.7	0 01.5
22 M	14 03 34	29 03 49	26 52 37	3♊44 00	29 12.2	15 18.3	18 56.3	14 06.1	10 33.8	22 04.9	1 12.6	6 47.5	0 07.0	0 02.7
23 Tu	14 07 31	0♏03 33	10♊37 49	17 33 49	29 13.1	16 56.4	20 07.0	14 15.7	10 22.0	22 16.5	1 19.0	6 48.6	0 09.2	0 03.8
24 W	14 11 27	1 03 20	24 31 47	1♋31 31	29 14.7	18 35.2	21 17.8	14 26.0	10 10.3	22 28.0	1 25.5	6 49.7	0 11.4	0 05.0
25 Th	14 15 24	2 03 09	8♋32 49	15 35 29	29 16.1	20 14.7	22 28.8	14 36.9	9 59.0	22 39.4	1 32.0	6 50.7	0 13.7	0 06.1
26 F	14 19 20	3 03 00	22 39 19	29 44 06	29R 16.9	21 54.5	23 39.9	14 48.5	9 47.9	22 50.7	1 38.5	6 51.6	0 15.9	0 07.2
27 Sa	14 23 17	4 02 54	6♌49 37	13♌55 38	29 16.6	23 34.7	24 51.1	15 00.7	9 37.0	23 02.0	1 45.0	6 52.5	0 18.2	0 08.2
28 Su	14 27 13	5 02 49	21 01 51	28 07 59	29 15.1	25 14.9	26 02.4	15 13.6	9 26.4	23 13.2	1 51.6	6 53.4	0 20.4	0 09.2
29 M	14 31 10	6 02 47	5♍13 40	12♍18 31	29 12.7	26 55.2	27 13.9	15 27.2	9 16.1	23 24.3	1 58.3	6 54.2	0 22.6	0 10.2
30 Tu	14 35 06	7 02 47	19 22 09	26 24 07	29 09.6	28 35.3	28 25.4	15 41.3	9 06.1	23 35.4	2 04.9	6 54.9	0 24.9	0 11.2
31 W	14 39 03	8 02 49	3♎23 58	10♎21 17	29 06.3	0♏15.3	29 37.1	15 56.1	8 56.4	23 46.4	2 11.6	6 55.6	0 27.1	0 12.2

Astro Data

	Dy Hr Mn
☽0S	5 5:41
♃∠♆	12 3:42
☿R	13 14:08
☽0N	19 11:19
⊙0S	23 1:35
☿0N	2 6:27
☽0S	2 15:17
♄⊻♆	5 2:03
☿D	5 14:21
♄□♇	7 15:42
♂D	10 10:06
☿0S	15 6:34
☽0N	16 18:49
♆✶♇	18 7:31
♃∠♅	20 19:55

Planet Ingress

	Dy Hr Mn
♀ ♌	8 9:23
☉ ♎	23 1:35
☿ ♍R	29 21:25
☊ ♏R	4 9:37
♀ ♍	6 3:12
♄ ♐	10 15:11
☿ ♎	11 7:30
♆ ♏	19 9:28
♇ ♍	20 6:12
☉ ♏	23 10:34
☿ ♏	31 8:19
♀ ♎	31 19:40
☽0S	29 22:30

Last Aspect / ☽ Ingress

Last Aspect Dy Hr Mn		☽ Ingress Dy Hr Mn
1 20:40 ♆ □	♌	1 23:14
3 21:18 ♇ ☌	♍	3 23:20
5 19:48 ♀ ✶	♎	6 0:04
8 2:58 ♀ □	♏	8 3:26
10 8:44 ♇ □	♐	10 10:46
12 19:47 ♇ △	♑	12 21:46
15 8:03 ♆ □	♒	15 10:28
17 20:55 ♇ ☍	♓	17 22:34
20 5:24 ♄ △	♈	20 8:47
22 15:44 ♇ △	♉	22 17:01
24 22:18 ♇ □	♊	24 23:25
27 3:01 ♇ ✶	♋	27 4:00
29 5:35 ♆ □	♌	29 6:49

Last Aspect / ☽ Ingress

Last Aspect Dy Hr Mn		☽ Ingress Dy Hr Mn
1 7:40 ♇ ☌	♍	1 8:24
3 8:53 ♄ ✶	♎	3 10:01
5 12:43 ♇ ✶	♏	5 13:19
7 19:15 ♄ ☌	♐	7 19:46
10 5:21 ♇ △	♑	10 5:48
12 17:39 ♆ □	♒	12 18:09
15 6:12 ♇ ☍	♓	15 6:25
16 23:25 ♃ ☍	♈	17 16:35
20 0:07 ♇ △	♉	20 0:07
21 15:16 ♃ △	♊	22 5:29
23 20:14 ♃ □	♋	24 9:23
26 0:46 ♀ ✶	♌	26 12:27
28 6:29 ☿ ✶	♍	28 15:09
30 15:47 ♀ ☌	♎	30 18:10

☽ Phases & Eclipses

Dy Hr Mn		
4 18:57	●	12♍12
12 0:13	☽	19♐13
20 3:19	○	27♓08
27 11:25	☾	4♋19
4 4:25	●	10♎55
11 18:44	☽	18♑26
19 17:25	○	26♈18
26 18:02	☾	3♌18

Astro Data

1 September 1956
Julian Day # 20698
SVP 5♓51'37"
GC 26♐14.0 ⚴ 22♒47.4R
Eris 9♈02.1R ⚵ 6♑48.2
⚷ 7♒27.0R ⚶ 20♏14.7
☽ Mean ☊ 3♐08.9

1 October 1956
Julian Day # 20728
SVP 5♓51'34"
GC 26♐14.1 ⚴ 17♒44.1R
Eris 8♈44.2R ⚵ 9♑45.4
⚷ 6♒32.1R ⚶ 3♐49.7
☽ Mean ☊ 1♐33.6

November 1956 LONGITUDE

Day	Sid.Time	☉	0 hr ☽	Noon ☽	True ☊	☿	♀	♂	⚳	♃	♄	♅	♆	♇
1 Th	14 43 00	9♏02 53	17♎15 38	24♎06 37	29♏03.5	1♏55.1	0♎48.9	16♓11.5	8♈46.9	23♍57.3	2♐18.3	6♌56.2	0♏29.3	0♍13.1
2 F	14 46 56	10 02 59	0♏53 53	7♏37 08	29R 01.5	3 34.6	2 00.7	16 27.5	8R 37.9	24 08.1	2 25.1	6 56.8	0 31.6	0 14.0
3 Sa	14 50 53	11 03 07	14 16 08	20 50 43	29D 00.4	5 13.8	3 12.7	16 44.0	8 29.1	24 18.8	2 31.9	6 57.3	0 33.8	0 14.8
4 Su	14 54 49	12 03 17	27 20 49	3♐46 25	29 00.2	6 52.7	4 24.8	17 01.2	8 20.7	24 29.5	2 38.7	6 57.7	0 36.0	0 15.7
5 M	14 58 46	13 03 28	10♐07 37	16 24 33	29 00.9	8 31.3	5 36.9	17 18.9	8 12.6	24 40.1	2 45.5	6 58.2	0 38.2	0 16.5
6 Tu	15 02 42	14 03 41	22 37 27	28 46 37	29 02.1	10 09.5	6 49.2	17 37.1	8 04.9	24 50.6	2 52.3	6 58.5	0 40.4	0 17.3
7 W	15 06 39	15 03 56	4♑52 25	10♑55 17	29 03.5	11 47.4	8 01.5	17 55.9	7 57.5	25 01.0	2 59.2	6 58.8	0 42.6	0 18.0
8 Th	15 10 35	16 04 12	16 55 39	22 54 03	29 04.7	13 24.8	9 14.0	18 15.2	7 50.5	25 11.3	3 06.1	6 59.0	0 44.8	0 18.8
9 F	15 14 32	17 04 30	28 51 01	4♒47 07	29 05.6	15 02.0	10 26.5	18 35.0	7 43.8	25 21.5	3 13.1	6 59.2	0 47.0	0 19.5
10 Sa	15 18 29	18 04 49	10♒42 57	16 39 05	29R 05.9	16 38.8	11 39.1	18 55.3	7 37.5	25 31.6	3 20.0	6 59.3	0 49.1	0 20.1
11 Su	15 22 25	19 05 10	22 36 08	28 34 43	29 05.8	18 15.2	12 51.7	19 16.1	7 31.6	25 41.7	3 27.0	6R 59.4	0 51.3	0 20.8
12 M	15 26 22	20 05 32	4♓35 22	10♓38 41	29 05.1	19 51.3	14 04.5	19 37.4	7 26.1	25 51.6	3 33.9	6 59.4	0 53.4	0 21.4
13 Tu	15 30 18	21 05 55	16 45 12	22 55 22	29 04.2	21 27.1	15 17.3	19 59.1	7 20.9	26 01.4	3 40.9	6 59.4	0 55.6	0 22.0
14 W	15 34 15	22 06 20	29 09 39	5♈28 26	29 03.2	23 02.6	16 30.2	20 21.3	7 16.2	26 11.2	3 48.0	6 59.3	0 57.7	0 22.5
15 Th	15 38 11	23 06 46	11♈52 01	18 20 37	29 02.4	24 37.8	17 43.2	20 43.9	7 11.8	26 20.8	3 55.0	6 59.2	0 59.8	0 23.0
16 F	15 42 08	24 07 14	24 54 23	1♉33 21	29 01.8	26 12.8	18 56.3	21 06.9	7 07.7	26 30.3	4 02.0	6 58.9	1 01.9	0 23.5
17 Sa	15 46 04	25 07 43	8♉17 29	15 06 36	29 01.4	27 47.4	20 09.4	21 30.3	7 04.1	26 39.8	4 09.1	6 58.7	1 04.0	0 24.0
18 Su	15 50 01	26 08 13	22 00 28	28 58 42	29D 01.3	29 21.9	21 22.6	21 54.1	7 00.9	26 49.1	4 16.1	6 58.4	1 06.1	0 24.4
19 M	15 53 58	27 08 45	6♊00 52	13♊06 27	29 01.4	0♐56.1	22 35.9	22 18.3	6 58.0	26 58.3	4 23.2	6 58.0	1 08.2	0 24.8
20 Tu	15 57 54	28 09 19	20 14 54	27 25 33	29R 01.5	2 30.1	23 49.2	22 42.9	6 55.5	27 07.4	4 30.3	6 57.6	1 10.2	0 25.2
21 W	16 01 51	29 09 55	4♋37 48	11♋51 00	29 01.5	4 03.9	25 02.6	23 07.8	6 53.5	27 16.4	4 37.4	6 57.1	1 12.3	0 25.6
22 Th	16 05 47	0♐10 32	19 04 30	26 17 44	29 01.5	5 37.6	26 16.1	23 33.1	6 51.8	27 25.3	4 44.5	6 56.6	1 14.3	0 25.9
23 F	16 09 44	1 11 11	3♌30 08	10♌41 13	29 01.3	7 11.1	27 29.6	23 58.8	6 50.5	27 34.1	4 51.6	6 56.0	1 16.3	0 26.2
24 Sa	16 13 40	2 11 51	17 50 33	24 57 46	29D 01.2	8 44.4	28 43.2	24 24.8	6 49.5	27 42.7	4 58.7	6 55.4	1 18.3	0 26.4
25 Su	16 17 37	3 12 33	2♍02 35	9♍04 45	29 01.2	10 17.6	29 56.9	24 51.1	6D 49.0	27 51.3	5 05.9	6 54.7	1 20.3	0 26.6
26 M	16 21 33	4 13 17	16 04 05	23 00 27	29 01.4	11 50.7	1♏10.6	25 17.8	6 48.8	27 59.7	5 13.0	6 53.9	1 22.3	0 26.8
27 Tu	16 25 30	5 14 02	29 53 45	6♎43 54	29 01.9	13 23.7	2 24.4	25 44.7	6 49.0	28 08.0	5 20.1	6 53.1	1 24.2	0 27.0
28 W	16 29 27	6 14 49	13♎30 52	20 14 37	29 02.6	14 56.5	3 38.2	26 12.0	6 49.6	28 16.2	5 27.2	6 52.3	1 26.1	0 27.1
29 Th	16 33 23	7 15 37	26 55 08	3♏32 23	29 03.3	16 29.3	4 52.1	26 39.6	6 50.6	28 24.2	5 34.3	6 51.4	1 28.0	0 27.2
30 F	16 37 20	8 16 26	10♏06 22	16 37 05	29R 03.9	18 01.9	6 06.0	27 07.5	6 52.0	28 32.1	5 41.5	6 50.4	1 29.9	0 27.3

December 1956 LONGITUDE

Day	Sid.Time	☉	0 hr ☽	Noon ☽	True ☊	☿	♀	♂	⚳	♃	♄	♅	♆	♇
1 Sa	16 41 16	9♐17 18	23♏04 33	29♏28 45	29♏04.2	19♐34.5	7♏20.0	27♓35.7	6♈53.7	28♍39.9	5♐48.6	6♌49.4	1♏31.8	0♍27.3
2 Su	16 45 13	10 18 10	5♐49 45	12♐07 35	29R 03.8	21 06.9	8 34.0	28 04.1	6 55.8	28 47.5	5 55.7	6R 48.4	1 33.7	0R 27.3
3 M	16 49 09	11 19 03	18 22 19	24 34 03	29 02.9	22 39.2	9 48.1	28 32.9	6 58.3	28 55.1	6 02.8	6 47.3	1 35.5	0 27.3
4 Tu	16 53 06	12 19 58	0♑42 55	6♑49 05	29 01.2	24 11.4	11 02.2	29 01.9	7 01.2	29 02.4	6 09.9	6 46.1	1 37.3	0 27.3
5 W	16 57 02	13 20 53	12 52 46	18 54 13	28 59.0	25 43.4	12 16.3	29 31.2	7 04.4	29 09.7	6 17.0	6 44.9	1 39.1	0 27.2
6 Th	17 00 59	14 21 49	24 53 42	0♒51 34	28 56.6	27 15.3	13 30.5	0♈00.7	7 08.0	29 16.8	6 24.1	6 43.7	1 40.9	0 27.1
7 F	17 04 56	15 22 46	6♒48 13	12 44 02	28 54.2	28 46.9	14 44.7	0 30.5	7 12.0	29 23.8	6 31.2	6 42.4	1 42.7	0 26.9
8 Sa	17 08 52	16 23 44	18 39 30	24 35 07	28 52.2	0♑18.3	15 59.0	1 00.6	7 16.3	29 30.6	6 38.2	6 41.0	1 44.4	0 26.7
9 Su	17 12 49	17 24 42	0♓31 23	6♓28 53	28D 50.9	1 49.4	17 13.3	1 30.8	7 20.9	29 37.2	6 45.3	6 39.6	1 46.1	0 26.5
10 M	17 16 45	18 25 41	12 28 10	18 29 51	28 50.4	3 20.1	18 27.6	2 01.3	7 26.0	29 43.8	6 52.3	6 38.2	1 47.8	0 26.3
11 Tu	17 20 42	19 26 40	24 34 30	0♈42 44	28 50.9	4 50.4	19 42.0	2 32.1	7 31.3	29 50.1	6 59.3	6 36.7	1 49.4	0 26.0
12 W	17 24 38	20 27 40	6♈55 07	13 12 12	28 52.1	6 20.2	20 56.4	3 03.0	7 37.0	29 56.4	7 06.3	6 35.1	1 51.1	0 25.7
13 Th	17 28 35	21 28 41	19 34 29	26 02 26	28 53.7	7 49.3	22 10.8	3 34.1	7 43.1	0♎02.4	7 13.3	6 33.6	1 52.7	0 25.4
14 F	17 32 31	22 29 42	2♉36 25	9♉16 43	28 55.2	9 17.7	23 25.2	4 05.5	7 49.4	0 08.4	7 20.3	6 31.9	1 54.3	0 25.1
15 Sa	17 36 28	23 30 44	16 03 29	22 56 46	28R 56.2	10 45.1	24 39.7	4 37.0	7 56.1	0 14.1	7 27.2	6 30.3	1 55.8	0 24.7
16 Su	17 40 25	24 31 46	29 56 27	7♊02 16	28 56.1	12 11.5	25 54.2	5 08.7	8 03.2	0 19.7	7 34.2	6 28.6	1 57.4	0 24.3
17 M	17 44 21	25 32 49	14♊13 45	21 30 19	28 54.6	13 36.5	27 08.7	5 40.6	8 10.5	0 25.2	7 41.1	6 26.8	1 58.9	0 23.8
18 Tu	17 48 18	26 33 52	28 51 11	6♋15 29	28 51.8	15 00.0	28 23.3	6 12.7	8 18.2	0 30.5	7 48.0	6 25.0	2 00.4	0 23.4
19 W	17 52 14	27 34 57	13♋42 11	21 10 14	28 47.9	16 21.7	29 37.9	6 44.9	8 26.1	0 35.6	7 54.8	6 23.2	2 01.9	0 22.9
20 Th	17 56 11	28 36 01	28 38 31	6♌05 57	28 43.5	17 41.3	0♐52.5	7 17.4	8 34.4	0 40.6	8 01.7	6 21.3	2 03.3	0 22.3
21 F	18 00 07	29 37 07	13♌31 32	20 54 19	28 39.2	18 58.3	2 07.2	7 49.9	8 43.0	0 45.4	8 08.5	6 19.4	2 04.7	0 21.8
22 Sa	18 04 04	0♑38 13	28 13 33	5♍28 33	28 35.8	20 12.3	3 21.8	8 22.7	8 51.9	0 50.1	8 15.2	6 17.5	2 06.1	0 21.2
23 Su	18 08 00	1 39 19	12♍38 51	19 44 08	28D 33.6	21 22.9	4 36.5	8 55.6	9 01.1	0 54.5	8 22.0	6 15.5	2 07.4	0 20.6
24 M	18 11 57	2 40 27	26 44 11	3♎38 59	28 33.0	22 29.4	5 51.2	9 28.6	9 10.6	0 58.8	8 28.7	6 13.5	2 08.8	0 19.9
25 Tu	18 15 54	3 41 35	10♎28 35	17 13 08	28 33.7	23 31.2	7 06.0	10 01.8	9 20.3	1 03.0	8 35.4	6 11.4	2 10.1	0 19.3
26 W	18 19 50	4 42 44	23 52 52	0♏28 02	28 35.2	24 27.6	8 20.7	10 35.2	9 30.4	1 06.9	8 42.1	6 09.3	2 11.3	0 18.6
27 Th	18 23 47	5 43 53	6♏58 58	13 25 57	28 36.9	25 17.9	9 35.5	11 08.6	9 40.7	1 10.7	8 48.7	6 07.2	2 12.6	0 17.9
28 F	18 27 43	6 45 03	19 49 19	26 09 22	28R 37.8	26 01.1	10 50.3	11 42.3	9 51.3	1 14.3	8 55.3	6 05.0	2 13.8	0 17.1
29 Sa	18 31 40	7 46 13	2♐26 22	8♐40 36	28 37.2	26 36.4	12 05.1	12 16.0	10 02.2	1 17.8	9 01.9	6 02.9	2 15.0	0 16.3
30 Su	18 35 36	8 47 23	14 52 18	21 01 40	28 34.8	27 02.8	13 20.0	12 49.9	10 13.4	1 21.0	9 08.4	6 00.6	2 16.1	0 15.5
31 M	18 39 33	9 48 34	27 08 53	3♑14 09	28 30.2	27 19.6	14 34.8	13 24.0	10 24.8	1 24.1	9 14.9	5 58.4	2 17.3	0 14.7

Astro Data	Planet Ingress	Last Aspect	☽ Ingress	Last Aspect	☽ Ingress	☽ Phases & Eclipses	Astro Data
Dy Hr Mn	Dy Hr Mn	Dy Hr Mn	Dy Hr Mn	Dy Hr Mn	Dy Hr Mn	Dy Hr Mn	1 November 1956
♀0S 3 21:14	☿ ♐ 18 21:42	31 6:04 ♅ ⚹	♏ 1 22:24	1 10:27 ♃ ⚹	♐ 1 12:59	2 16:44 ● 10♏15	Julian Day # 20759
♅R 12 6:51	☉ ♐ 22 7:50	3 18:28 ♃ ⚹	♐ 4 4:56	3 20:34 ♃ □	♑ 3 22:36	10 15:09 ☽ 18♒13	SVP 5♓51'32"
☽0N 13 3:12	♀ ♏ 25 13:01	6 4:12 ♃ □	♑ 6 14:24	6 10:13 ♂ ⚹	♒ 6 10:16	18 6:45 ○ 25♉55	GC 26♐14.2 ⚴ 17♒47.1
☽0S 26 4:00		8 16:41 ♃ △	♒ 9 2:19	7 17:52 ☉ ⚹	♓ 8 22:57	18 6:48 T 1.317	Eris 8♈25.6R ⚵ 17♑14.5
⚳D 26 10:11	♂ ♈ 6 11:24	10 15:09 ☉ □	♓ 11 14:51	11 10:17 ♃ ☍	♈ 11 10:37	25 1:13 ☾ 2♍45	⚷ 6♒36.2 ⚶ 19♐08.1
	☿ ♑ 8 7:11	13 18:04 ♃ ☍	♈ 14 1:36	13 2:50 ☉ △	♉ 13 19:15		☽ Mean ☊ 29♏55.0
♇R 2 7:16	♃ ♎ 13 2:17	15 10:44 ♀ ☍	♉ 16 9:12	15 15:15 ♀ ☍	♊ 16 0:06	2 8:13 ● 10♐09	
♂0N 8 8:45	♀ ♐ 19 19:07	18 12:45 ☿ ☍	♊ 18 13:45	17 19:06 ☉ ☍	♋ 18 1:52	2 8:00:04 P 0.805	1 December 1956
♄△♅ 8 19:56	☉ ♑ 21 20:59	20 11:29 ♃ □	♋ 20 16:18	19 3:30 ☿ ☍	♌ 20 2:11	10 11:51 ☽ 18♓25	Julian Day # 20789
☽0N 10 11:57		22 13:54 ♃ ⚹	♌ 22 18:10	20 15:08 ♄ △	♍ 22 2:56	17 19:06 ○ 25♊51	SVP 5♓51'27"
♃⚺♇ 17 6:21		24 18:58 ♀ ⚹	♍ 24 20:32	23 15:03 ☿ △	♎ 24 5:39	24 10:10 ☾ 2♎36	GC 26♐14.3 ⚴ 22♒13.5
☽0S 23 10:06		26 20:46 ♃ ☌	♎ 27 0:11	26 0:14 ☿ □	♏ 26 11:09		Eris 8♈13.0R ⚵ 27♑22.7
		28 1:19 ☿ ⚹	♏ 29 5:34	28 11:43 ☿ ⚹	♐ 28 19:20		⚷ 7♒41.1 ⚶ 4♑38.4
				29 19:20 ♀ ☌	♑ 31 5:37		☽ Mean ☊ 28♏19.7

LONGITUDE — January 1957

Day	Sid.Time	☉	0 hr ☽	Noon ☽	True ☊	☿	♀	♂	⚳	♃	♄	♅	♆	♇
1 Tu	18 43 29	10♑49 45	9♑17 36	15♑19 24	28♏23.5	27♑25.7	15♐49.7	13♈58.1	10♈36.5	1♎27.0	9♐21.3	5♌56.1	2♏18.3	0♍13.9
2 W	18 47 26	11 50 56	21 19 41	27 18 37	28R15.3	27R20.7	17 04.6	14 32.4	10 48.5	1 29.7	9 27.7	5R53.8	2 19.4	0R13.0
3 Th	18 51 23	12 52 07	3♒16 23	9♒13 11	28 06.1	27 03.9	18 19.5	15 06.8	11 00.7	1 32.2	9 34.1	5 51.5	2 20.4	0 12.1
4 F	18 55 19	13 53 17	15 09 14	21 04 47	27 57.0	26 35.2	19 34.4	15 41.3	11 13.2	1 34.6	9 40.4	5 49.1	2 21.4	0 11.2
5 Sa	18 59 16	14 54 27	27 00 09	2♓55 41	27 48.7	25 54.9	20 49.3	16 16.0	11 25.9	1 36.7	9 46.7	5 46.8	2 22.4	0 10.2
6 Su	19 03 12	15 55 37	8♓51 44	14 48 45	27 42.0	25 03.6	22 04.2	16 50.7	11 38.8	1 38.7	9 52.9	5 44.4	2 23.3	0 09.3
7 M	19 07 09	16 56 47	20 47 11	26 47 34	27 37.4	24 02.4	23 19.1	17 25.6	11 52.0	1 40.5	9 59.1	5 41.9	2 24.2	0 08.3
8 Tu	19 11 05	17 57 56	2♈50 25	8♈56 20	27D35.1	22 53.2	24 34.0	18 00.5	12 05.4	1 42.1	10 05.2	5 39.5	2 25.1	0 07.2
9 W	19 15 02	18 59 05	15 05 55	21 19 45	27 34.6	21 37.9	25 49.0	18 35.6	12 19.1	1 43.5	10 11.3	5 37.0	2 25.9	0 06.2
10 Th	19 18 58	20 00 13	27 38 27	4♉02 37	27 35.4	20 19.1	27 03.9	19 10.7	12 33.0	1 44.7	10 17.3	5 34.5	2 26.7	0 05.1
11 F	19 22 55	21 01 21	10♉32 47	17 09 28	27R36.4	18 59.1	28 18.9	19 46.0	12 47.1	1 45.7	10 23.3	5 32.0	2 27.5	0 04.1
12 Sa	19 26 52	22 02 28	23 53 04	0♊43 53	27 36.8	17 40.7	29 33.8	20 21.3	13 01.4	1 46.5	10 29.3	5 29.5	2 28.2	0 03.0
13 Su	19 30 48	23 03 35	7♊42 04	14 47 36	27 35.4	16 26.0	0♑48.8	20 56.7	13 16.0	1 47.2	10 35.1	5 27.0	2 29.0	0 01.8
14 M	19 34 45	24 04 41	22 00 16	29 19 39	27 31.7	15 17.1	2 03.8	21 32.2	13 30.7	1 47.6	10 41.0	5 24.4	2 29.6	0 00.7
15 Tu	19 38 41	25 05 46	6♋45 06	14♋15 42	27 25.6	14 15.5	3 18.7	22 07.8	13 45.7	1R47.9	10 46.7	5 21.9	2 30.3	29♌59.6
16 W	19 42 38	26 06 51	21 50 24	29 27 54	27 17.3	13 22.3	4 33.7	22 43.4	14 00.9	1 48.0	10 52.5	5 19.3	2 30.9	29 58.4
17 Th	19 46 34	27 07 55	7♌06 50	14♌45 46	27 07.9	12 38.3	5 48.7	23 19.2	14 16.2	1 47.9	10 58.1	5 16.7	2 31.5	29 57.2
18 F	19 50 31	28 08 59	22 23 16	29 57 57	26 58.5	12 03.8	7 03.7	23 54.9	14 31.8	1 47.6	11 03.7	5 14.2	2 32.0	29 56.0
19 Sa	19 54 28	29 10 02	7♍28 37	14♍54 14	26 50.2	11 38.8	8 18.7	24 30.8	14 47.5	1 47.0	11 09.3	5 11.6	2 32.5	29 54.7
20 Su	19 58 24	0♒11 05	22 13 59	29 27 16	26 44.1	11 22.9	9 33.7	25 06.7	15 03.5	1 46.4	11 14.8	5 09.0	2 33.0	29 53.5
21 M	20 02 21	1 12 07	6♎33 44	13♎33 13	26 40.4	11D15.9	10 48.7	25 42.7	15 19.6	1 45.5	11 20.2	5 06.3	2 33.4	29 52.2
22 Tu	20 06 17	2 13 09	20 25 45	27 11 32	26D39.0	11 17.3	12 03.7	26 18.8	15 36.0	1 44.4	11 25.5	5 03.7	2 33.8	29 50.9
23 W	20 10 14	3 14 11	3♏50 53	10♏24 12	26 39.0	11 26.4	13 18.7	26 54.9	15 52.5	1 43.1	11 30.8	5 01.1	2 34.2	29 49.6
24 Th	20 14 10	4 15 12	16 51 57	23 14 41	26R39.5	11 42.7	14 33.8	27 31.1	16 09.1	1 41.7	11 36.1	4 58.5	2 34.5	29 48.3
25 F	20 18 07	5 16 13	29 32 53	5♐47 07	26 39.1	12 05.6	15 48.8	28 07.4	16 26.0	1 40.0	11 41.2	4 55.9	2 34.8	29 47.0
26 Sa	20 22 03	6 17 13	11♐57 53	18 05 40	26 36.9	12 34.6	17 03.8	28 43.7	16 43.1	1 38.2	11 46.3	4 53.2	2 35.1	29 45.6
27 Su	20 26 00	7 18 13	24 10 55	0♑14 02	26 32.1	13 09.0	18 18.9	29 20.1	17 00.3	1 36.1	11 51.4	4 50.6	2 35.3	29 44.3
28 M	20 29 57	8 19 12	6♑15 23	12 15 18	26 24.2	13 48.4	19 33.9	29 56.5	17 17.6	1 33.9	11 56.3	4 48.0	2 35.5	29 42.9
29 Tu	20 33 53	9 20 10	18 14 04	24 11 54	26 13.4	14 32.3	20 48.9	0♉33.0	17 35.2	1 31.5	12 01.2	4 45.4	2 35.7	29 41.5
30 W	20 37 50	10 21 07	0♒09 02	6♒05 37	26 00.3	15 20.3	22 04.0	1 09.5	17 52.9	1 28.9	12 06.1	4 42.8	2 35.8	29 40.1
31 Th	20 41 46	11 22 03	12 01 51	17 57 52	25 45.8	16 12.1	23 19.0	1 46.1	18 10.8	1 26.1	12 10.8	4 40.2	2 35.9	29 38.7

LONGITUDE — February 1957

Day	Sid.Time	☉	0 hr ☽	Noon ☽	True ☊	☿	♀	♂	⚳	♃	♄	♅	♆	♇
1 F	20 45 43	12♒22 57	23♒53 50	29♒49 54	25♏31.2	17♑07.3	24♑34.1	2♉22.8	18♈28.8	1♎23.2	12♐15.5	4♌37.6	2♏35.9	29♌37.3
2 Sa	20 49 39	13 23 51	5♓46 15	11♓43 05	25R17.6	18 05.6	25 49.1	2 59.5	18 47.0	1R20.0	12 20.1	4R35.0	2R36.0	29R35.9
3 Su	20 53 36	14 24 44	17 40 38	23 39 11	25 06.0	19 06.6	27 04.1	3 36.2	19 05.3	1 16.7	12 24.6	4 32.4	2 36.0	29 34.4
4 M	20 57 32	15 25 35	29 39 01	5♈40 32	24 57.3	20 10.3	28 19.1	4 13.0	19 23.8	1 13.2	12 29.1	4 29.8	2 35.9	29 33.0
5 Tu	21 01 29	16 26 24	11♈44 06	17 50 12	24 51.6	21 16.4	29 34.1	4 49.9	19 42.4	1 09.5	12 33.4	4 27.3	2 35.8	29 31.5
6 W	21 05 25	17 27 13	23 59 18	0♉11 56	24 48.6	22 24.6	0♒49.2	5 26.8	20 01.2	1 05.6	12 37.7	4 24.7	2 35.7	29 30.1
7 Th	21 09 22	18 28 00	6♉28 40	12 50 04	24 47.7	23 34.8	2 04.2	6 03.7	20 20.1	1 01.6	12 41.9	4 22.2	2 35.6	29 28.6
8 F	21 13 19	19 28 45	19 16 42	25 49 07	24 47.6	24 46.9	3 19.2	6 40.6	20 39.2	0 57.4	12 46.1	4 19.7	2 35.4	29 27.1
9 Sa	21 17 15	20 29 29	2♊27 49	9♊13 16	24 47.2	26 00.8	4 34.2	7 17.6	20 58.3	0 53.1	12 50.1	4 17.2	2 35.2	29 25.7
10 Su	21 21 12	21 30 11	16 05 48	23 05 37	24 45.1	27 16.3	5 49.2	7 54.7	21 17.6	0 48.5	12 54.1	4 14.7	2 34.9	29 24.2
11 M	21 25 08	22 30 52	0♋12 47	7♋27 08	24 40.6	28 33.3	7 04.1	8 31.7	21 37.1	0 43.8	12 58.0	4 12.3	2 34.7	29 22.7
12 Tu	21 29 05	23 31 31	14 48 17	22 15 37	24 33.2	29 51.8	8 19.1	9 08.8	21 56.7	0 39.0	13 01.8	4 09.8	2 34.3	29 21.2
13 W	21 33 01	24 32 08	29 48 17	7♌25 11	24 23.4	1♒11.6	9 34.1	9 46.0	22 16.3	0 34.0	13 05.5	4 07.4	2 34.0	29 19.7
14 Th	21 36 58	25 32 44	15♌05 01	22 46 21	24 12.0	2 32.7	10 49.1	10 23.1	22 36.2	0 28.8	13 09.2	4 05.0	2 33.6	29 18.2
15 F	21 40 55	26 33 18	0♍27 39	8♍07 25	24 00.4	3 55.1	12 04.0	11 00.3	22 56.1	0 23.5	13 12.7	4 02.6	2 33.2	29 16.7
16 Sa	21 44 51	27 33 51	15 44 09	23 16 33	23 50.0	5 18.7	13 19.0	11 37.5	23 16.1	0 18.1	13 16.2	4 00.3	2 32.8	29 15.2
17 Su	21 48 48	28 34 23	0♎43 29	8♎04 03	23 41.9	6 43.5	14 33.9	12 14.7	23 36.3	0 12.5	13 19.6	3 58.0	2 32.3	29 13.7
18 M	21 52 44	29 34 53	15 17 35	22 23 42	23 36.5	8 09.4	15 48.9	12 51.9	23 56.6	0 06.8	13 22.9	3 55.7	2 31.8	29 12.2
19 Tu	21 56 41	0♓35 22	29 22 12	6♏13 08	23 33.7	9 36.4	17 03.8	13 29.2	24 17.0	0 00.9	13 26.1	3 53.4	2 31.2	29 10.7
20 W	22 00 37	1 35 49	12♏56 42	19 33 14	23D32.9	11 04.4	18 18.8	14 06.5	24 37.5	29♍54.9	13 29.2	3 51.2	2 30.7	29 09.2
21 Th	22 04 34	2 36 16	26 03 13	2♐27 11	23R32.9	12 33.5	19 33.7	14 43.8	24 58.1	29 48.8	13 32.3	3 49.0	2 30.1	29 07.7
22 F	22 08 30	3 36 41	8♐45 44	14 59 27	23 32.5	14 03.7	20 48.6	15 21.2	25 18.8	29 42.5	13 35.2	3 46.8	2 29.4	29 06.2
23 Sa	22 12 27	4 37 05	21 09 00	27 14 58	23 30.5	15 34.9	22 03.6	15 58.6	25 39.6	29 36.1	13 38.0	3 44.6	2 28.8	29 04.7
24 Su	22 16 23	5 37 27	3♑17 58	9♑18 32	23 26.1	17 07.1	23 18.5	16 36.0	26 00.5	29 29.6	13 40.8	3 42.5	2 28.1	29 03.2
25 M	22 20 20	6 37 48	15 17 13	21 14 30	23 18.7	18 40.4	24 33.4	17 13.4	26 21.6	29 23.0	13 43.5	3 40.4	2 27.4	29 01.7
26 Tu	22 24 17	7 38 07	27 10 47	3♒06 28	23 08.6	20 14.6	25 48.3	17 50.8	26 42.7	29 16.3	13 46.0	3 38.4	2 26.6	29 00.2
27 W	22 28 13	8 38 24	9♒01 53	14 57 20	22 56.1	21 49.9	27 03.2	18 28.3	27 03.9	29 09.5	13 48.5	3 36.3	2 25.8	28 58.7
28 Th	22 32 10	9 38 40	20 53 04	26 49 17	22 42.3	23 26.2	28 18.1	19 05.7	27 25.2	29 02.6	13 50.9	3 34.4	2 25.0	28 57.2

Astro Data Dy Hr Mn	Planet Ingress Dy Hr Mn	Last Aspect Dy Hr Mn	☽ Ingress Dy Hr Mn	Last Aspect Dy Hr Mn	☽ Ingress Dy Hr Mn	☽ Phases & Eclipses Dy Hr Mn
☿R 1 13:23	♀ ♑ 12 20:23	2 12:04 ☿ ☌	♒ 2 17:25	1 11:35 ♇ ☍	♓ 1 12:20	1 2:14 ● 10♑25
☽0N 6 20:11	♇ ♌R 15 2:45	4 8:35 ♀ ⚹	♓ 5 6:04	3 19:38 ♀ ⚹	♈ 4 0:42	9 7:06 ☽ 18♈47
♃R 16 9:22	☉ ♒ 20 7:39	7 6:58 ☿ ⚹	♈ 7 18:23	6 10:40 ♇ △	♉ 6 11:37	16 6:21 ○ 25♋52
☽0S 19 18:50	♂ ♉ 28 14:19	9 21:29 ♀ △	♉ 10 4:27	8 18:34 ♇ □	♊ 8 19:34	22 21:48 ☾ 2♏38
☿D 21 19:56		11 19:29 ☉ △	♊ 12 10:44	10 22:38 ♇ ⚹	♋ 10 23:39	30 21:25 ● 10♒45
⚳0N 26 7:36	♀ ♒ 5 20:16	13 22:41 ♂ ⚹	♋ 14 13:06	11 13:51 ♂ ⚹	♌ 13 0:19	
	☿ ♒ 12 14:30	16 6:21 ☉ ☍	♌ 16 12:50	14 22:11 ♇ ☌	♍ 14 23:17	7 23:23 ☽ 18♉57
♆R 2 15:51	☉ ♓ 18 21:58	18 11:57 ♇ ☌	♍ 18 12:03	15 20:03 ♄ □	♎ 16 22:50	14 16:38 ○ 25♌44
☽0N 3 3:26	♃ ♍R 19 15:37	19 6:51 ☿ △	♎ 20 12:55	18 23:41 ♇ ⚹	♏ 19 1:06	21 12:19 ☾ 2♐37
☽0S 16 5:59		22 16:46 ♇ ⚹	♏ 22 17:02	21 7:04 ♃ ⚹	♐ 21 7:23	
		25 0:28 ♇ □	♐ 25 0:52	23 16:37 ♃ □	♑ 23 17:27	
		27 11:01 ♇ △	♑ 27 11:32	26 4:18 ♃ △	♒ 26 5:42	
		29 4:24 ♀ ☌	♒ 29 23:42	28 16:18 ♇ ☍	♓ 28 18:25	

Astro Data

1 January 1957
Julian Day # 20820
SVP 5♓51'21"
GC 26♐14.3 ⚴ 29♒48.1
Eris 8♈09.5 ⚵ 9♒49.4
⚷ 9♒36.9 ⚶ 20♑58.3
☽ Mean ☊ 26♏41.2

1 February 1957
Julian Day # 20851
SVP 5♓51'17"
GC 26♐14.4 ⚴ 9♓11.6
Eris 8♈17.0 ⚵ 23♒35.8
⚷ 11♒58.7 ⚶ 7♒16.1
☽ Mean ☊ 25♏02.8

March 1957

LONGITUDE

Day	Sid.Time	☉	0 hr ☽	Noon ☽	True ☊	☿	♀	♂	⚳	♃	♄	♅	♆	♇
1 F	22 36 06	10♓38 55	2♓46 10	8♓43 53	22♏28.2	25♒03.6	29♒33.0	19♉43.2	27♈46.7	28♍55.6	13♐53.2	3♌32.4	2♏24.2	28♌55.7
2 Sa	22 40 03	11 39 07	14 42 35	20 42 24	22R15.1	26 41.9	0♓47.9	20 20.8	28 08.2	28R48.5	13 55.3	3R30.5	2R23.3	28R54.3
3 Su	22 43 59	12 39 17	26 43 30	2♈46 01	22 03.9	28 21.4	2 02.7	20 58.3	28 29.8	28 41.3	13 57.4	3 28.6	2 22.4	28 52.8
4 M	22 47 56	13 39 26	8♈50 09	14 56 06	21 55.4	0♓01.8	3 17.6	21 35.8	28 51.4	28 34.0	13 59.4	3 26.8	2 21.5	28 51.3
5 Tu	22 51 52	14 39 33	21 04 06	27 14 26	21 49.9	1 43.4	4 32.4	22 13.4	29 13.2	28 26.7	14 01.3	3 25.0	2 20.5	28 49.9
6 W	22 55 49	15 39 37	3♉27 24	9♉43 22	21D47.1	3 26.0	5 47.3	22 51.0	29 35.1	28 19.3	14 03.1	3 23.3	2 19.5	28 48.5
7 Th	22 59 46	16 39 40	16 02 42	22 25 50	21 46.4	5 09.7	7 02.1	23 28.6	29 57.0	28 11.8	14 04.8	3 21.5	2 18.5	28 47.0
8 F	23 03 42	17 39 41	28 53 11	5♊25 11	21R46.9	6 54.6	8 16.9	24 06.2	0♉19.0	28 04.3	14 06.4	3 19.9	2 17.5	28 45.6
9 Sa	23 07 39	18 39 39	12♊02 16	18 44 49	21 47.3	8 40.5	9 31.7	24 43.8	0 41.1	27 56.7	14 07.9	3 18.3	2 16.5	28 44.2
10 Su	23 11 35	19 39 35	25 33 10	2♋27 35	21 46.5	10 27.6	10 46.4	25 21.4	1 03.3	27 49.1	14 09.3	3 16.7	2 15.4	28 42.8
11 M	23 15 32	20 39 29	9♋28 11	16 34 59	21 43.8	12 15.9	12 01.2	25 59.1	1 25.5	27 41.5	14 10.6	3 15.1	2 14.3	28 41.4
12 Tu	23 19 28	21 39 21	23 47 49	1♌06 20	21 38.7	14 05.3	13 16.0	26 36.7	1 47.9	27 33.8	14 11.8	3 13.7	2 13.1	28 40.1
13 W	23 23 25	22 39 10	8♌29 59	15 58 00	21 31.5	15 55.8	14 30.7	27 14.4	2 10.2	27 26.1	14 12.9	3 12.2	2 12.0	28 38.7
14 Th	23 27 21	23 38 57	23 29 26	1♍03 10	21 22.9	17 47.5	15 45.4	27 52.0	2 32.7	27 18.3	14 13.9	3 10.8	2 10.8	28 37.4
15 F	23 31 18	24 38 42	8♍37 59	16 12 32	21 13.9	19 40.4	17 00.1	28 29.7	2 55.2	27 10.6	14 14.8	3 09.5	2 09.6	28 36.0
16 Sa	23 35 15	25 38 25	23 45 32	1♎15 41	21 05.7	21 34.4	18 14.8	29 07.3	3 17.8	27 02.8	14 15.6	3 08.1	2 08.4	28 34.7
17 Su	23 39 11	26 38 06	8♎41 49	16 02 55	20 59.3	23 29.5	19 29.5	29 45.0	3 40.5	26 55.0	14 16.4	3 06.9	2 07.2	28 33.4
18 M	23 43 08	27 37 46	23 18 09	0♏26 53	20 55.2	25 25.8	20 44.2	0♊22.7	4 03.2	26 47.2	14 17.0	3 05.7	2 05.9	28 32.1
19 Tu	23 47 04	28 37 23	7♏28 43	14 23 26	20D53.4	27 23.1	21 58.8	1 00.3	4 26.0	26 39.4	14 17.5	3 04.5	2 04.6	28 30.8
20 W	23 51 01	29 36 59	21 11 00	27 51 34	20 53.4	29 21.4	23 13.5	1 38.0	4 48.9	26 31.7	14 17.9	3 03.4	2 03.3	28 29.6
21 Th	23 54 57	0♈36 33	4♐25 24	10♐52 54	20 54.4	1♈20.6	24 28.1	2 15.7	5 11.8	26 23.9	14 18.2	3 02.3	2 02.0	28 28.4
22 F	23 58 54	1 36 05	17 14 34	23 30 55	20R55.5	3 20.7	25 42.7	2 53.4	5 34.8	26 16.2	14 18.4	3 01.3	2 00.6	28 27.1
23 Sa	0 02 50	2 35 35	29 42 33	5♑50 05	20 55.8	5 21.4	26 57.3	3 31.1	5 57.8	26 08.4	14R18.5	3 00.3	1 59.3	28 25.9
24 Su	0 06 47	3 35 04	11♑54 08	17 55 19	20 54.5	7 22.8	28 12.0	4 08.8	6 20.9	26 00.8	14 18.5	2 59.4	1 57.9	28 24.7
25 M	0 10 44	4 34 31	23 54 15	29 51 31	20 51.3	9 24.6	29 26.5	4 46.5	6 44.0	25 53.1	14 18.4	2 58.5	1 56.5	28 23.6
26 Tu	0 14 40	5 33 56	5♒47 38	11♒43 08	20 46.0	11 26.6	0♈41.1	5 24.2	7 07.3	25 45.5	14 18.2	2 57.7	1 55.1	28 22.4
27 W	0 18 37	6 33 19	17 38 30	23 34 08	20 39.1	13 28.6	1 55.7	6 01.9	7 30.5	25 37.9	14 17.9	2 57.0	1 53.7	28 21.3
28 Th	0 22 33	7 32 40	29 30 26	5♓27 44	20 31.1	15 30.4	3 10.2	6 39.6	7 53.9	25 30.4	14 17.5	2 56.2	1 52.2	28 20.2
29 F	0 26 30	8 32 00	11♓26 21	17 26 30	20 22.9	17 31.6	4 24.8	7 17.3	8 17.2	25 23.0	14 17.0	2 55.6	1 50.8	28 19.1
30 Sa	0 30 26	9 31 17	23 28 25	29 32 18	20 15.2	19 31.9	5 39.3	7 55.1	8 40.7	25 15.6	14 16.4	2 55.0	1 49.3	28 18.0
31 Su	0 34 23	10 30 32	5♈38 16	11♈46 29	20 08.7	21 31.0	6 53.8	8 32.8	9 04.1	25 08.3	14 15.7	2 54.4	1 47.8	28 16.9

April 1957

LONGITUDE

Day	Sid.Time	☉	0 hr ☽	Noon ☽	True ☊	☿	♀	♂	⚳	♃	♄	♅	♆	♇
1 M	0 38 19	11♈29 46	17♈57 03	24♈10 05	20♏04.0	23♈28.5	8♈08.3	9♊10.5	9♉27.7	25♍01.0	14♐14.9	2♌53.9	1♏46.3	28♌15.9
2 Tu	0 42 16	12 28 57	0♉25 42	6♉43 59	20R01.2	25 24.0	9 22.8	9 48.2	9 51.2	24R53.8	14R14.0	2R53.5	1R44.8	28R14.9
3 W	0 46 12	13 28 06	13 05 06	19 29 09	20D00.3	27 17.2	10 37.3	10 26.0	10 14.8	24 46.8	14 13.0	2 53.1	1 43.2	28 13.9
4 Th	0 50 09	14 27 13	25 56 19	2♊26 45	20 00.9	29 07.6	11 51.7	11 03.7	10 38.5	24 39.8	14 11.9	2 52.7	1 41.7	28 13.0
5 F	0 54 06	15 26 18	9♊00 39	15 38 11	20 02.3	0♉54.9	13 06.2	11 41.5	11 02.2	24 32.9	14 10.7	2 52.4	1 40.1	28 12.0
6 Sa	0 58 02	16 25 21	22 19 33	29 04 55	20 03.9	2 38.8	14 20.6	12 19.2	11 26.0	24 26.0	14 09.5	2 52.2	1 38.6	28 11.1
7 Su	1 01 59	17 24 21	5♋54 25	12♋48 11	20R04.8	4 18.8	15 35.0	12 56.9	11 49.8	24 19.3	14 08.1	2 52.0	1 37.0	28 10.2
8 M	1 05 55	18 23 19	19 46 14	26 48 32	20 04.6	5 54.6	16 49.3	13 34.7	12 13.6	24 12.7	14 06.6	2 51.9	1 35.4	28 09.3
9 Tu	1 09 52	19 22 14	3♌54 58	11♌05 18	20 03.0	7 26.0	18 03.7	14 12.4	12 37.5	24 06.3	14 05.0	2D51.8	1 33.9	28 08.5
10 W	1 13 48	20 21 07	18 19 10	25 36 05	20 00.2	8 52.7	19 18.0	14 50.1	13 01.4	23 59.9	14 03.4	2 51.8	1 32.3	28 07.7
11 Th	1 17 45	21 19 58	2♍55 28	10♍16 34	19 56.5	10 14.5	20 32.4	15 27.9	13 25.3	23 53.6	14 01.6	2 51.8	1 30.7	28 06.9
12 F	1 21 41	22 18 46	17 38 36	25 00 40	19 52.4	11 31.1	21 46.7	16 05.6	13 49.3	23 47.5	13 59.8	2 51.9	1 29.0	28 06.1
13 Sa	1 25 38	23 17 33	2♎21 52	9♎41 15	19 48.8	12 42.4	23 01.0	16 43.3	14 13.3	23 41.5	13 57.9	2 52.1	1 27.4	28 05.4
14 Su	1 29 35	24 16 17	16 57 56	24 11 05	19 46.0	13 48.2	24 15.2	17 21.0	14 37.4	23 35.6	13 55.9	2 52.3	1 25.8	28 04.6
15 M	1 33 31	25 15 00	1♏19 57	8♏23 57	19D44.4	14 48.4	25 29.5	17 58.7	15 01.4	23 29.9	13 53.8	2 52.5	1 24.2	28 03.9
16 Tu	1 37 28	26 13 40	15 22 34	22 15 27	19 44.0	15 42.9	26 43.7	18 36.4	15 25.6	23 24.3	13 51.6	2 52.8	1 22.6	28 03.3
17 W	1 41 24	27 12 19	29 02 24	5♐43 22	19 44.7	16 31.5	27 57.9	19 14.1	15 49.7	23 18.8	13 49.3	2 53.2	1 20.9	28 02.6
18 Th	1 45 21	28 10 56	12♐18 23	18 47 38	19 46.0	17 14.3	29 12.2	19 51.8	16 13.9	23 13.5	13 46.9	2 53.6	1 19.3	28 02.0
19 F	1 49 17	29 09 31	25 11 24	1♑30 02	19 47.6	17 51.0	0♉26.4	20 29.5	16 38.1	23 08.3	13 44.5	2 54.1	1 17.7	28 01.4
20 Sa	1 53 14	0♉08 05	7♑43 59	13 53 43	19 48.9	18 21.8	1 40.5	21 07.2	17 02.3	23 03.2	13 42.0	2 54.6	1 16.0	28 00.9
21 Su	1 57 10	1 06 37	19 59 47	26 02 44	19R49.6	18 46.6	2 54.7	21 44.9	17 26.6	22 58.3	13 39.4	2 55.2	1 14.4	28 00.3
22 M	2 01 07	2 05 07	2♒03 09	8♒01 37	19 49.6	19 05.4	4 08.9	22 22.6	17 50.9	22 53.6	13 36.7	2 55.8	1 12.8	27 59.8
23 Tu	2 05 04	3 03 36	13 58 44	19 55 03	19 48.8	19 18.2	5 23.0	23 00.3	18 15.2	22 49.0	13 33.9	2 56.5	1 11.1	27 59.3
24 W	2 09 00	4 02 03	25 51 09	1♓47 34	19 47.3	19R25.2	6 37.1	23 37.9	18 39.6	22 44.6	13 31.1	2 57.2	1 09.5	27 58.9
25 Th	2 12 57	5 00 28	7♓44 48	13 43 20	19 45.3	19 26.5	7 51.3	24 15.6	19 04.0	22 40.3	13 28.2	2 58.0	1 07.8	27 58.5
26 F	2 16 53	5 58 52	19 43 36	25 46 00	19 43.2	19 22.3	9 05.4	24 53.3	19 28.4	22 36.2	13 25.2	2 58.8	1 06.2	27 58.1
27 Sa	2 20 50	6 57 14	1♈50 54	7♈58 35	19 41.2	19 12.8	10 19.4	25 31.0	19 52.8	22 32.3	13 22.1	2 59.7	1 04.6	27 57.7
28 Su	2 24 46	7 55 34	14 09 19	20 23 18	19 39.7	18 58.2	11 33.5	26 08.7	20 17.3	22 28.5	13 19.0	3 00.7	1 02.9	27 57.3
29 M	2 28 43	8 53 53	26 40 42	3♉01 37	19 38.7	18 39.0	12 47.6	26 46.3	20 41.7	22 24.9	13 15.7	3 01.6	1 01.3	27 57.0
30 Tu	2 32 39	9 52 10	9♉26 07	15 54 14	19D38.2	18 15.6	14 01.6	27 24.0	21 06.3	22 21.5	13 12.5	3 02.7	0 59.7	27 56.7

Astro Data

	Dy Hr Mn
♃⚻♇	1 11:16
☽0N	2 9:52
☽0S	15 17:24
☉0N	20 21:16
☿0N	22 4:46
♄ R	24 0:45
♀0N	28 13:34
☽0N	29 16:14
♅ D	10 8:21
☽0S	12 2:57
☿ R	25 5:31
☽0N	25 23:17

Planet Ingress

		Dy Hr Mn
♀	♓	1 20:39
☿	♓	4 11:34
⚳	♉	7 15:17
♂	♊	17 21:34
☿	♈	20 19:48
☉	♈	20 21:16
♀	♈	25 22:46
☿	♉	4 23:37
♀	♉	19 3:28
☉	♉	20 8:41

Last Aspect / ☽ Ingress

Last Aspect Dy Hr Mn			☽ Ingress	Dy Hr Mn
3 3:59	♃	☍	♈	3 6:31
5 15:04	♇	△	♉	5 17:20
7 23:47	♇	□	♊	8 2:03
10 5:31	♇	⚹	♋	10 7:45
12 6:15	♃	⚹	♌	12 10:12
14 8:09	♇	☌	♍	14 10:20
16 8:25	♂	△	♎	16 9:59
18 8:47	♇	⚹	♏	18 11:15
20 15:27	☉	△	♐	20 15:53
22 21:32	♇	△	♑	23 0:34
25 11:04	♀	⚹	♒	25 12:17
27 21:39	♇	☍	♓	28 1:00
30 3:38	♃	☍	♈	30 12:55

Last Aspect / ☽ Ingress

Last Aspect Dy Hr Mn			☽ Ingress	Dy Hr Mn
1 19:51	♇	△	♉	1 23:11
4 4:13	♇	□	♊	4 7:30
6 10:25	♇	⚹	♋	6 13:37
8 7:37	♃	⚹	♌	8 17:24
10 16:09	♇	☌	♍	10 19:13
12 10:02	♃	☌	♎	12 20:08
14 18:31	♇	⚹	♏	14 21:45
16 22:14	♇	□	♐	17 1:43
19 7:09	☉	△	♑	19 9:08
21 5:56	♃	△	♒	21 19:53
24 4:18	♇	☍	♓	24 8:23
26 10:10	♂	□	♈	26 20:22
29 2:25	♇	△	♉	29 6:18

☽ Phases & Eclipses

Dy Hr Mn	
1 16:12	● 10♓49
9 11:50	☽ 18♊39
16 2:22	○ 25♍14
23 5:04	☾ 2♑18
31 9:19	● 10♈24
7 20:33	☽ 17♋45
14 12:09	○ 24♎17
21 23:01	☾ 1♒33
29 23:54	● 9♉23
30 0:04:54	● A non-C

Astro Data

1 March 1957
Julian Day # 20879
SVP 5♓51'13"
GC 26♐14.5 ⚵ 18♓32.3
Eris 8♈31.6 ⚴ 6♓47.9
⚷ 14♒06.5 ⚶ 21♒41.4
☽ Mean ☊ 23♏33.8

1 April 1957
Julian Day # 20910
SVP 5♓51'11"
GC 26♐14.5 ⚵ 29♓18.1
Eris 8♈52.5 ⚴ 21♓58.0
⚷ 16♒03.4 ⚶ 7♓01.4
☽ Mean ☊ 21♏55.3

LONGITUDE — May 1957

Day	Sid.Time	☉	0 hr ☽	Noon ☽	True ☊	☿	♀	♂	⚳	♃	♄	♅	♆	♇
1 W	2 36 36	10♉50 25	22♉25 56	29♉01 11	19♏38.3	17♉48.4	15♉15.7	28♊01.7	21♉30.8	22♍18.2	13♐09.1	3♌03.8	0♏58.1	27♌56.5
2 Th	2 40 32	11 48 38	5♊39 54	12♊22 00	19 38.8	17R 17.9	16 29.7	28 39.4	21 55.3	22R 15.2	13R 05.7	3 05.0	0R 56.5	27R 56.3
3 F	2 44 29	12 46 50	19 07 20	25 55 47	19 39.4	16 44.8	17 43.7	29 17.1	22 19.9	22 12.3	13 02.2	3 06.2	0 54.9	27 56.1
4 Sa	2 48 26	13 44 59	2♋47 11	9♋41 24	19 40.0	16 09.6	18 57.6	29 54.7	22 44.5	22 09.5	12 58.7	3 07.4	0 53.3	27 55.9
5 Su	2 52 22	14 43 07	16 38 14	23 37 30	19 40.5	15 33.0	20 11.6	0♋32.4	23 09.1	22 07.0	12 55.1	3 08.7	0 51.7	27 55.8
6 M	2 56 19	15 41 13	0♌39 00	7♌42 31	19R 40.7	14 55.7	21 25.6	1 10.1	23 33.7	22 04.6	12 51.4	3 10.1	0 50.1	27 55.6
7 Tu	3 00 15	16 39 16	14 47 47	21 54 33	19 40.7	14 18.3	22 39.5	1 47.7	23 58.3	22 02.4	12 47.7	3 11.5	0 48.6	27 55.6
8 W	3 04 12	17 37 18	29 02 30	6♍11 17	19 40.6	13 41.5	23 53.4	2 25.4	24 22.9	22 00.4	12 44.0	3 12.9	0 47.0	27 55.5
9 Th	3 08 08	18 35 17	13♍20 33	20 29 53	19 40.5	13 05.9	25 07.3	3 03.0	24 47.6	21 58.6	12 40.1	3 14.4	0 45.5	27D 55.5
10 F	3 12 05	19 33 15	27 38 51	4♎47 00	19D 40.5	12 32.1	26 21.2	3 40.6	25 12.2	21 56.9	12 36.3	3 16.0	0 43.9	27 55.5
11 Sa	3 16 01	20 31 11	11♎53 49	18 58 51	19 40.5	12 00.7	27 35.0	4 18.3	25 36.9	21 55.5	12 32.4	3 17.6	0 42.4	27 55.5
12 Su	3 19 58	21 29 06	26 01 37	3♏01 37	19 40.6	11 32.1	28 48.8	4 55.9	26 01.6	21 54.2	12 28.4	3 19.2	0 40.9	27 55.6
13 M	3 23 55	22 26 58	9♏58 27	16 51 41	19R 40.7	11 06.9	0♊02.7	5 33.5	26 26.3	21 53.1	12 24.4	3 20.9	0 39.4	27 55.7
14 Tu	3 27 51	23 24 50	23 40 59	0♐26 05	19 40.6	10 45.2	1 16.5	6 11.1	26 51.0	21 52.1	12 20.4	3 22.7	0 37.9	27 55.8
15 W	3 31 48	24 22 40	7♐06 45	13 42 50	19 40.3	10 27.5	2 30.3	6 48.8	27 15.7	21 51.4	12 16.3	3 24.4	0 36.4	27 56.0
16 Th	3 35 44	25 20 28	20 14 18	26 41 09	19 39.8	10 14.0	3 44.1	7 26.4	27 40.5	21 50.8	12 12.1	3 26.3	0 35.0	27 56.2
17 F	3 39 41	26 18 15	3♑03 29	9♑21 30	19 39.0	10 04.8	4 57.8	8 04.0	28 05.2	21 50.5	12 08.0	3 28.2	0 33.5	27 56.4
18 Sa	3 43 37	27 16 01	15 35 25	21 45 33	19 38.1	10D 00.0	6 11.6	8 41.6	28 30.0	21D 50.3	12 03.8	3 30.1	0 32.1	27 56.6
19 Su	3 47 34	28 13 46	27 52 18	3♒56 03	19 37.2	9 59.8	7 25.3	9 19.2	28 54.7	21 50.2	11 59.6	3 32.1	0 30.7	27 56.9
20 M	3 51 31	29 11 29	9♒57 18	15 56 33	19 36.5	10 04.2	8 39.1	9 56.8	29 19.5	21 50.4	11 55.3	3 34.1	0 29.3	27 57.2
21 Tu	3 55 27	0♊09 12	21 54 20	27 51 12	19D 36.2	10 13.1	9 52.8	10 34.4	29 44.3	21 50.8	11 51.0	3 36.1	0 27.9	27 57.5
22 W	3 59 24	1 06 53	3♓47 44	9♓44 31	19 36.4	10 26.5	11 06.5	11 12.0	0♊09.0	21 51.3	11 46.7	3 38.2	0 26.5	27 57.9
23 Th	4 03 20	2 04 34	15 42 08	21 41 09	19 37.0	10 44.4	12 20.2	11 49.6	0 33.8	21 52.0	11 42.4	3 40.4	0 25.2	27 58.2
24 F	4 07 17	3 02 13	27 42 07	3♈45 35	19 38.0	11 06.7	13 33.9	12 27.2	0 58.6	21 52.9	11 38.0	3 42.6	0 23.9	27 58.6
25 Sa	4 11 13	3 59 51	9♈52 03	16 01 58	19 39.3	11 33.2	14 47.6	13 04.8	1 23.4	21 53.9	11 33.6	3 44.8	0 22.6	27 59.1
26 Su	4 15 10	4 57 29	22 15 46	28 33 48	19 40.4	12 04.0	16 01.2	13 42.4	1 48.2	21 55.2	11 29.2	3 47.1	0 21.3	27 59.6
27 M	4 19 06	5 55 05	4♉56 21	11♉23 38	19R 41.2	12 38.8	17 14.9	14 20.0	2 13.0	21 56.6	11 24.8	3 49.4	0 20.0	28 00.1
28 Tu	4 23 03	6 52 40	17 55 46	24 32 49	19 41.3	13 17.6	18 28.5	14 57.6	2 37.8	21 58.2	11 20.4	3 51.7	0 18.8	28 00.6
29 W	4 26 59	7 50 15	1♊14 43	8♊01 20	19 40.5	14 00.3	19 42.1	15 35.2	3 02.6	22 00.0	11 16.0	3 54.1	0 17.5	28 01.1
30 Th	4 30 56	8 47 48	14 52 25	21 47 39	19 38.9	14 46.7	20 55.8	16 12.8	3 27.5	22 01.9	11 11.5	3 56.6	0 16.3	28 01.7
31 F	4 34 53	9 45 20	28 46 37	5♋48 53	19 36.5	15 36.7	22 09.4	16 50.4	3 52.3	22 04.1	11 07.1	3 59.0	0 15.1	28 02.4

LONGITUDE — June 1957

Day	Sid.Time	☉	0 hr ☽	Noon ☽	True ☊	☿	♀	♂	⚳	♃	♄	♅	♆	♇
1 Sa	4 38 49	10♊42 51	12♋53 53	20♋01 05	19♏33.7	16♉30.3	23♊23.0	17♋27.9	4♊17.1	22♍06.4	11♐02.6	4♌01.5	0♏14.0	28♌03.0
2 Su	4 42 46	11 40 21	27 09 54	4♌19 45	19R 31.0	17 27.4	24 36.5	18 05.5	4 41.9	22 08.8	10R 58.2	4 04.1	0R 12.8	28 03.7
3 M	4 46 42	12 37 49	11♌30 07	18 40 26	19 28.7	18 27.9	25 50.1	18 43.1	5 06.7	22 11.5	10 53.7	4 06.7	0 11.7	28 04.4
4 Tu	4 50 39	13 35 16	25 50 14	2♍59 07	19D 27.4	19 31.6	27 03.6	19 20.7	5 31.5	22 14.3	10 49.3	4 09.3	0 10.6	28 05.1
5 W	4 54 35	14 32 42	10♍06 41	17 12 38	19 27.0	20 38.6	28 17.2	19 58.3	5 56.3	22 17.3	10 44.8	4 12.0	0 09.6	28 05.8
6 Th	4 58 32	15 30 06	24 16 42	1♎18 41	19 27.7	21 48.8	29 30.7	20 35.9	6 21.1	22 20.5	10 40.4	4 14.7	0 08.5	28 06.6
7 F	5 02 29	16 27 30	8♎18 24	15 15 42	19 29.0	23 02.1	0♋44.2	21 13.5	6 45.8	22 23.8	10 36.0	4 17.4	0 07.5	28 07.4
8 Sa	5 06 25	17 24 52	22 10 28	29 02 35	19 30.5	24 18.4	1 57.6	21 51.0	7 10.6	22 27.3	10 31.6	4 20.2	0 06.5	28 08.3
9 Su	5 10 22	18 22 13	5♏51 58	12♏38 31	19R 31.5	25 37.8	3 11.1	22 28.6	7 35.4	22 30.9	10 27.2	4 23.0	0 05.5	28 09.1
10 M	5 14 18	19 19 34	19 22 07	26 02 41	19 31.5	27 00.2	4 24.6	23 06.2	8 00.1	22 34.7	10 22.8	4 25.8	0 04.6	28 10.0
11 Tu	5 18 15	20 16 53	2♐40 07	9♐14 21	19 30.1	28 25.5	5 38.0	23 43.8	8 24.9	22 38.7	10 18.5	4 28.7	0 03.7	28 10.9
12 W	5 22 11	21 14 12	15 45 17	22 12 51	19 27.2	29 53.8	6 51.4	24 21.3	8 49.6	22 42.9	10 14.2	4 31.6	0 02.8	28 11.9
13 Th	5 26 08	22 11 30	28 37 02	4♑57 49	19 22.8	1♊25.0	8 04.8	24 58.9	9 14.4	22 47.2	10 09.8	4 34.5	0 01.9	28 12.8
14 F	5 30 04	23 08 48	11♑15 14	17 29 21	19 17.4	2 59.1	9 18.2	25 36.5	9 39.1	22 51.6	10 05.6	4 37.5	0 01.1	28 13.8
15 Sa	5 34 01	24 06 05	23 40 18	29 48 15	19 11.5	4 36.0	10 31.6	26 14.1	10 03.8	22 56.2	10 01.3	4 40.4	0 00.3	28 14.8
16 Su	5 37 58	25 03 21	5♒53 25	11♒56 06	19 05.7	6 15.8	11 45.0	26 51.6	10 28.5	23 01.0	9 57.1	4 43.5	29♎59.5	28 15.9
17 M	5 41 54	26 00 37	17 56 36	23 55 20	19 00.7	7 58.5	12 58.3	27 29.2	10 53.2	23 05.9	9 52.9	4 46.5	29 58.7	28 16.9
18 Tu	5 45 51	26 57 53	29 52 43	5♓49 13	18 57.0	9 43.9	14 11.6	28 06.8	11 17.9	23 10.9	9 48.7	4 49.6	29 58.0	28 18.0
19 W	5 49 47	27 55 08	11♓45 21	17 41 41	18D 54.8	11 32.0	15 25.0	28 44.4	11 42.6	23 16.2	9 44.6	4 52.7	29 57.3	28 19.1
20 Th	5 53 44	28 52 24	23 38 47	29 37 15	18 54.2	13 22.9	16 38.3	29 21.9	12 07.2	23 21.5	9 40.5	4 55.8	29 56.6	28 20.3
21 F	5 57 40	29 49 39	5♈37 42	11♈40 45	18 54.8	15 16.3	17 51.6	29 59.5	12 31.9	23 27.0	9 36.5	4 59.0	29 56.0	28 21.4
22 Sa	6 01 37	0♋46 53	17 47 00	23 57 03	18 56.2	17 12.3	19 04.9	0♌37.1	12 56.5	23 32.7	9 32.5	5 02.2	29 55.4	28 22.6
23 Su	6 05 33	1 44 08	0♉11 28	6♉30 46	18R 57.5	19 10.7	20 18.2	1 14.7	13 21.1	23 38.5	9 28.5	5 05.4	29 54.8	28 23.8
24 M	6 09 30	2 41 23	12 55 25	19 25 47	18 58.1	21 11.3	21 31.4	1 52.3	13 45.8	23 44.4	9 24.6	5 08.6	29 54.2	28 25.0
25 Tu	6 13 27	3 38 38	26 02 10	2♊44 44	18 57.2	23 14.0	22 44.7	2 29.9	14 10.3	23 50.5	9 20.8	5 11.9	29 53.7	28 26.3
26 W	6 17 23	4 35 52	9♊33 31	16 28 25	18 54.5	25 18.6	23 57.9	3 07.5	14 34.9	23 56.8	9 16.9	5 15.2	29 53.2	28 27.6
27 Th	6 21 20	5 33 06	23 29 10	0♋35 22	18 49.7	27 24.8	25 11.2	3 45.1	14 59.5	24 03.1	9 13.2	5 18.5	29 52.7	28 28.9
28 F	6 25 16	6 30 21	7♋46 25	15 01 38	18 43.3	29 32.5	26 24.4	4 22.8	15 24.0	24 09.6	9 09.5	5 21.8	29 52.3	28 30.2
29 Sa	6 29 13	7 27 35	22 20 08	29 41 03	18 36.0	1♋41.4	27 37.6	5 00.4	15 48.5	24 16.3	9 05.8	5 25.2	29 51.9	28 31.5
30 Su	6 33 09	8 24 48	7♌03 22	14♌26 06	18 28.7	3 51.1	28 50.8	5 38.0	16 13.0	24 23.1	9 02.2	5 28.6	29 51.5	28 32.9

Astro Data

	Dy Hr Mn
☽0S	9 10:01
♇D	9 19:51
☿D	19 1:03
♃D	19 2:20
☽0N	23 7:19
☽0S	5 15:48
☽0N	19 15:57

Planet Ingress

	Dy Hr Mn
♂ ♋	4 15:22
♀ ♊	13 11:08
☉ ♊	21 8:10
⚳ ♊	22 3:15
♀ ♋	6 21:35
☿ ♊	12 13:40
♆ ♎R	15 20:07
♂ ♌	21 12:18
☉ ♋	21 16:21
☿ ♋	28 17:08

Last Aspect / ☽ Ingress

Last Aspect Dy Hr Mn		☽ Ingress Dy Hr Mn
1 10:03	♇ □	♊ 1 13:47
3 18:10	♂ ☌	♋ 3 19:08
5 9:25	♃ ⚹	♌ 5 22:54
7 22:07	♇ ☌	♍ 8 1:37
9 20:29	♀ △	♎ 10 3:57
12 3:15	♇ ⚹	♏ 12 6:48
14 7:32	♇ □	♐ 14 11:13
16 14:21	♇ △	♑ 16 18:13
18 23:44	☉ △	♒ 19 4:12
21 12:13	♇ ☍	♓ 21 16:20
23 12:22	♃ ☍	♈ 24 4:34
26 10:55	♇ △	♉ 26 14:43
28 18:14	♇ □	♊ 28 21:47
30 22:44	♇ ⚹	♋ 31 2:05

Last Aspect / ☽ Ingress

Last Aspect Dy Hr Mn		☽ Ingress Dy Hr Mn
1 15:31	♃ ⚹	♌ 2 4:45
4 3:46	♇ ☌	♍ 4 6:59
6 8:38	♀ □	♎ 6 9:45
8 10:25	♇ ⚹	♏ 8 13:41
10 15:50	♇ □	♐ 10 19:09
12 23:13	♇ △	♑ 13 2:36
15 4:38	♂ ☍	♒ 15 12:23
18 0:11	♆ △	♓ 18 0:15
20 11:28	♂ △	♈ 20 12:46
22 23:29	♆ ☍	♉ 22 23:38
25 4:18	♇ □	♊ 25 7:07
27 10:48	♆ △	♋ 27 11:01
29 12:18	♆ □	♌ 29 12:31

☽ Phases & Eclipses

Dy Hr Mn	
7 2:29	☽ 16♌16
13 22:34	○ 22♏52
13 22:31	• T 1.299
21 17:03	☾ 0♓21
29 11:39	● 7♊49
5 7:10	☽ 14♍21
12 10:02	○ 21♐10
20 10:22	☾ 28♓49
27 20:53	● 5♋54

Astro Data

1 May 1957
Julian Day # 20940
SVP 5♓51'08"
GC 26♐14.6 ⚴ 9♈43.6
Eris 9♈12.3 ⚵ 6♈58.6
⚷ 17♒11.9 ⚶ 20♓52.9
☽ Mean ☊ 20♏19.9

1 June 1957
Julian Day # 20971
SVP 5♓51'03"
GC 26♐14.7 ⚴ 20♈05.3
Eris 9♈27.7 ⚵ 22♈36.9
⚷ 17♒23.3R ⚶ 3♈40.4
☽ Mean ☊ 18♏41.4

July 1957

LONGITUDE

Day	Sid.Time	☉	0 hr ☽	Noon ☽	True ☊	☿	♀	♂	⚷	♃	♄	♅	♆	♇
1 M	6 37 06	9♋22 01	21♌48 19	29♌09 06	18♏22.4	6♋01.4	0♌04.0	6♌15.6	16♊37.5	24♍30.0	8♐58.7	5♌32.0	29♎51.2	28♌34.3
2 Tu	6 41 02	10 19 14	6♍27 41	13♍43 23	18R 17.7	8 12.1	1 17.1	6 53.3	17 01.9	24 37.0	8R 55.2	5 35.4	29R 50.9	28 35.7
3 W	6 44 59	11 16 27	20 55 39	28 04 07	18D 15.1	10 22.7	2 30.2	7 30.9	17 26.4	24 44.2	8 51.8	5 38.8	29 50.6	28 37.1
4 Th	6 48 56	12 13 39	5♎08 29	12♎08 39	18 14.3	12 33.1	3 43.4	8 08.5	17 50.8	24 51.5	8 48.5	5 42.3	29 50.4	28 38.6
5 F	6 52 52	13 10 51	19 04 32	25 56 13	18 14.8	14 43.0	4 56.4	8 46.2	18 15.1	24 58.9	8 45.2	5 45.8	29 50.1	28 40.0
6 Sa	6 56 49	14 08 03	2♏43 47	9♏27 24	18R 15.7	16 52.1	6 09.5	9 23.8	18 39.5	25 06.5	8 42.0	5 49.2	29 50.0	28 41.5
7 Su	7 00 45	15 05 14	16 07 15	22 43 32	18 15.8	19 00.3	7 22.6	10 01.5	19 03.8	25 14.1	8 38.9	5 52.7	29 49.8	28 43.0
8 M	7 04 42	16 02 25	29 16 27	5♐46 10	18 14.4	21 07.4	8 35.6	10 39.1	19 28.1	25 21.9	8 35.8	5 56.3	29 49.7	28 44.6
9 Tu	7 08 38	16 59 37	12♐12 51	18 36 38	18 10.7	23 13.2	9 48.6	11 16.8	19 52.4	25 29.8	8 32.8	5 59.8	29 49.6	28 46.1
10 W	7 12 35	17 56 48	24 57 40	1♑16 02	18 04.5	25 17.5	11 01.6	11 54.4	20 16.6	25 37.9	8 29.9	6 03.4	29 49.5	28 47.7
11 Th	7 16 31	18 54 00	7♑31 48	13 45 05	17 55.9	27 20.3	12 14.6	12 32.1	20 40.8	25 46.0	8 27.0	6 06.9	29D 49.5	28 49.2
12 F	7 20 28	19 51 11	19 55 55	26 04 23	17 45.5	29 21.5	13 27.5	13 09.8	21 05.0	25 54.3	8 24.2	6 10.5	29 49.5	28 50.8
13 Sa	7 24 25	20 48 23	2♒10 35	8♒14 39	17 34.1	1♌21.1	14 40.5	13 47.5	21 29.2	26 02.6	8 21.5	6 14.1	29 49.6	28 52.4
14 Su	7 28 21	21 45 36	14 16 42	20 16 55	17 22.8	3 18.8	15 53.4	14 25.1	21 53.3	26 11.1	8 18.9	6 17.7	29 49.6	28 54.1
15 M	7 32 18	22 42 49	26 15 32	2♓12 48	17 12.5	5 14.8	17 06.3	15 02.8	22 17.4	26 19.7	8 16.4	6 21.3	29 49.7	28 55.7
16 Tu	7 36 14	23 40 02	8♓09 03	14 04 38	17 04.1	7 09.1	18 19.1	15 40.5	22 41.4	26 28.4	8 13.9	6 24.9	29 49.9	28 57.4
17 W	7 40 11	24 37 16	19 59 59	25 55 32	16 58.0	9 01.5	19 32.0	16 18.2	23 05.4	26 37.2	8 11.5	6 28.6	29 50.0	28 59.0
18 Th	7 44 07	25 34 30	1♈51 50	7♈49 24	16 54.4	10 52.0	20 44.8	16 55.9	23 29.4	26 46.1	8 09.2	6 32.2	29 50.2	29 00.7
19 F	7 48 04	26 31 45	13 48 50	19 50 45	16D 52.8	12 40.8	21 57.6	17 33.7	23 53.4	26 55.1	8 07.0	6 35.9	29 50.5	29 02.4
20 Sa	7 52 00	27 29 01	25 55 47	2♉04 35	16 52.7	14 27.7	23 10.4	18 11.4	24 17.3	27 04.2	8 04.9	6 39.5	29 50.7	29 04.2
21 Su	7 55 57	28 26 18	8♉17 47	14 36 02	16R 53.0	16 12.9	24 23.2	18 49.1	24 41.2	27 13.5	8 02.8	6 43.2	29 51.0	29 05.9
22 M	7 59 54	29 23 36	20 59 55	27 29 57	16 52.6	17 56.2	25 35.9	19 26.9	25 05.0	27 22.8	8 00.9	6 46.9	29 51.4	29 07.6
23 Tu	8 03 50	0♌20 54	4♊06 35	10♊50 11	16 50.6	19 37.7	26 48.7	20 04.7	25 28.8	27 32.2	7 59.0	6 50.6	29 51.7	29 09.4
24 W	8 07 47	1 18 13	17 40 56	24 38 54	16 46.2	21 17.4	28 01.4	20 42.4	25 52.6	27 41.7	7 57.2	6 54.2	29 52.1	29 11.2
25 Th	8 11 43	2 15 34	1♋43 56	8♋55 41	16 39.3	22 55.3	29 14.1	21 20.2	26 16.3	27 51.3	7 55.5	6 57.9	29 52.5	29 13.0
26 F	8 15 40	3 12 55	16 13 36	23 36 55	16 30.2	24 31.4	0♍26.7	21 58.0	26 40.0	28 01.1	7 53.9	7 01.6	29 53.0	29 14.8
27 Sa	8 19 36	4 10 16	1♌04 39	8♌35 43	16 19.7	26 05.7	1 39.4	22 35.8	27 03.7	28 10.9	7 52.4	7 05.3	29 53.5	29 16.6
28 Su	8 23 33	5 07 39	16 08 49	23 42 42	16 09.2	27 38.2	2 52.0	23 13.7	27 27.2	28 20.8	7 51.0	7 09.0	29 54.0	29 18.4
29 M	8 27 29	6 05 02	1♍16 02	8♍47 34	15 59.7	29 08.9	4 04.6	23 51.5	27 50.8	28 30.7	7 49.6	7 12.7	29 54.6	29 20.3
30 Tu	8 31 26	7 02 25	16 16 11	23 40 54	15 52.3	0♍37.8	5 17.2	24 29.3	28 14.3	28 40.8	7 48.4	7 16.4	29 55.2	29 22.1
31 W	8 35 23	7 59 49	1♎00 55	8♎15 40	15 47.6	2 04.8	6 29.7	25 07.2	28 37.7	28 51.0	7 47.2	7 20.1	29 55.8	29 24.0

August 1957

LONGITUDE

Day	Sid.Time	☉	0 hr ☽	Noon ☽	True ☊	☿	♀	♂	⚷	♃	♄	♅	♆	♇
1 Th	8 39 19	8♌57 14	15♎24 45	22♎27 56	15♏45.2	3♍30.0	7♍42.2	25♌45.0	29♊01.1	29♍01.2	7♐46.2	7♌23.8	29♎56.4	29♌25.8
2 F	8 43 16	9 54 40	29 25 12	6♏16 38	15R 44.6	4 53.3	8 54.7	26 22.9	29 24.5	29 11.5	7R 45.2	7 27.5	29 57.1	29 27.7
3 Sa	8 47 12	10 52 06	13♏02 27	19 42 55	15 44.6	6 14.6	10 07.2	27 00.8	29 47.8	29 22.0	7 44.4	7 31.2	29 57.8	29 29.6
4 Su	8 51 09	11 49 32	26 18 24	2♐49 16	15 43.9	7 34.0	11 19.6	27 38.7	0♋11.0	29 32.5	7 43.6	7 34.9	29 58.5	29 31.5
5 M	8 55 05	12 47 00	9♐15 55	15 38 44	15 41.5	8 51.3	12 32.0	28 16.6	0 34.2	29 43.0	7 42.9	7 38.6	29 59.3	29 33.4
6 Tu	8 59 02	13 44 28	21 58 05	28 14 20	15 36.6	10 06.6	13 44.3	28 54.5	0 57.3	29 53.7	7 42.4	7 42.3	0♏00.1	29 35.3
7 W	9 02 58	14 41 57	4♑27 46	10♑38 41	15 28.8	11 19.8	14 56.7	29 32.4	1 20.4	0♎04.4	7 41.9	7 46.0	0 01.0	29 37.2
8 Th	9 06 55	15 39 27	16 47 20	22 53 55	15 18.3	12 30.8	16 09.0	0♍10.4	1 43.4	0 15.2	7 41.5	7 49.7	0 01.8	29 39.1
9 F	9 10 52	16 36 58	28 58 39	5♒01 39	15 05.7	13 39.5	17 21.2	0 48.3	2 06.4	0 26.1	7 41.2	7 53.4	0 02.7	29 41.1
10 Sa	9 14 48	17 34 30	11♒03 07	17 03 10	14 52.0	14 45.9	18 33.4	1 26.3	2 29.3	0 37.0	7 41.0	7 57.0	0 03.6	29 43.0
11 Su	9 18 45	18 32 03	23 01 56	28 59 35	14 38.3	15 49.8	19 45.6	2 04.2	2 52.1	0 48.0	7D 40.9	8 00.7	0 04.6	29 44.9
12 M	9 22 41	19 29 37	4♓56 18	10♓52 15	14 25.7	16 51.2	20 57.8	2 42.2	3 14.9	0 59.1	7 40.9	8 04.3	0 05.6	29 46.9
13 Tu	9 26 38	20 27 12	16 47 41	22 42 52	14 15.1	17 49.9	22 09.9	3 20.2	3 37.6	1 10.3	7 41.0	8 08.0	0 06.6	29 48.8
14 W	9 30 34	21 24 49	28 38 05	4♈33 43	14 07.2	18 45.7	23 22.0	3 58.2	4 00.2	1 21.5	7 41.2	8 11.6	0 07.6	29 50.8
15 Th	9 34 31	22 22 27	10♈30 10	16 27 51	14 02.0	19 38.7	24 34.0	4 36.2	4 22.8	1 32.8	7 41.5	8 15.2	0 08.7	29 52.8
16 F	9 38 27	23 20 07	22 27 17	28 29 00	13 59.4	20 28.5	25 46.0	5 14.3	4 45.3	1 44.1	7 41.9	8 18.9	0 09.8	29 54.7
17 Sa	9 42 24	24 17 48	4♉33 34	10♉41 36	13D 58.7	21 15.1	26 58.0	5 52.3	5 07.8	1 55.5	7 42.4	8 22.5	0 10.9	29 56.7
18 Su	9 46 21	25 15 31	16 53 41	23 10 29	13R 58.7	21 58.3	28 10.0	6 30.4	5 30.2	2 07.0	7 43.0	8 26.0	0 12.1	29 58.7
19 M	9 50 17	26 13 16	29 32 35	6♊00 35	13 58.4	22 37.8	29 21.9	7 08.5	5 52.5	2 18.5	7 43.6	8 29.6	0 13.3	0♍00.6
20 Tu	9 54 14	27 11 02	12♊35 01	19 16 21	13 56.8	23 13.4	0♎33.7	7 46.6	6 14.7	2 30.1	7 44.4	8 33.2	0 14.5	0 02.6
21 W	9 58 10	28 08 50	26 04 55	3♋00 56	13 53.0	23 45.0	1 45.6	8 24.7	6 36.9	2 41.8	7 45.3	8 36.7	0 15.7	0 04.6
22 Th	10 02 07	29 06 40	10♋04 26	17 15 15	13 46.6	24 12.2	2 57.4	9 02.9	6 59.0	2 53.5	7 46.3	8 40.3	0 17.0	0 06.6
23 F	10 06 03	0♍04 31	24 33 02	1♌57 07	13 38.1	24 34.9	4 09.2	9 41.1	7 21.0	3 05.3	7 47.3	8 43.8	0 18.3	0 08.5
24 Sa	10 10 00	1 02 24	9♌26 41	17 00 39	13 28.1	24 52.8	5 20.9	10 19.2	7 42.9	3 17.1	7 48.5	8 47.3	0 19.6	0 10.5
25 Su	10 13 56	2 00 18	24 37 48	2♍16 43	13 17.9	25 05.6	6 32.6	10 57.4	8 04.7	3 29.0	7 49.8	8 50.8	0 21.0	0 12.5
26 M	10 17 53	2 58 14	9♍56 00	17 34 11	13 08.6	25R 13.1	7 44.3	11 35.7	8 26.5	3 40.9	7 51.1	8 54.3	0 22.3	0 14.5
27 Tu	10 21 50	3 56 11	25 09 55	2♎41 58	13 01.4	25 15.0	8 55.9	12 13.9	8 48.1	3 52.9	7 52.6	8 57.7	0 23.7	0 16.5
28 W	10 25 46	4 54 10	10♎09 15	17 30 57	12 56.7	25 11.1	10 07.5	12 52.1	9 09.7	4 05.0	7 54.1	9 01.1	0 25.2	0 18.4
29 Th	10 29 43	5 52 10	24 46 25	1♏55 16	12D 54.4	25 01.3	11 19.0	13 30.4	9 31.2	4 17.0	7 55.8	9 04.6	0 26.6	0 20.4
30 F	10 33 39	6 50 12	8♏57 17	15 52 26	12 54.0	24 45.3	12 30.5	14 08.7	9 52.6	4 29.2	7 57.5	9 07.9	0 28.1	0 22.4
31 Sa	10 37 36	7 48 15	22 40 54	29 22 55	12R 54.5	24 23.2	13 42.0	14 47.0	10 13.9	4 41.3	7 59.3	9 11.3	0 29.6	0 24.3

Astro Data	Planet Ingress	Last Aspect	☽ Ingress	Last Aspect	☽ Ingress	☽ Phases & Eclipses	Astro Data
Dy Hr Mn	Dy Hr Mn	Dy Hr Mn	Dy Hr Mn	Dy Hr Mn	Dy Hr Mn	Dy Hr Mn	
☽0S 2 22:14	♀ ♌ 1 10:42	1 13:09 ♆ ⚹	♍ 1 13:23	2 0:55 ♆ ☌	♏ 2 1:01	4 12:09 ☽ 12♎14	1 July 1957
♆D 11 17:50	☿ ♌ 12 19:41	3 6:20 ♃ ☌	♎ 3 15:16	4 5:54 ♇ □	♐ 4 6:47	11 22:50 ○ 19♑20	Julian Day # 21001
☽0N 17 0:20	☉ ♌ 23 3:15	5 18:52 ♆ ☌	♏ 5 19:10	6 15:14 ♃ □	♑ 6 15:23	20 2:17 ☾ 27♈06	SVP 5♓50'58"
☽0S 30 6:39	♀ ♍ 26 3:10	7 23:00 ♇ □	♐ 8 1:20	7 21:18 ♀ △	♒ 9 2:01	27 4:28 ● 3♌52	GC 26♐14.7 ⚳ 29♈11.5
	☿ ♍ 30 1:44	10 9:15 ♆ ⚹	♑ 10 9:35	11 13:32 ♇ ☍	♓ 11 14:02		Eris 9♈34.0 ⚵ 7♉35.6
♃⚻♇ 4 9:18		12 19:22 ♆ □	♒ 12 19:43	13 10:46 ♀ ☍	♈ 14 2:46	2 18:55 ☽ 10♏11	⚷ 16♒37.1R ⚶ 13♈46.0
♄△♅ 6 12:14	⚷ ♋ 4 0:38	15 7:11 ♆ △	♓ 15 7:32	16 14:50 ♇ △	♉ 16 15:00	10 13:08 ○ 17♒37	☽ Mean ☊ 17♏06.1
♃⚻♆ 7 3:40	♆ ♏ 6 8:25	17 13:25 ♃ ☍	♈ 17 20:14	19 0:51 ♇ □	♊ 19 0:51	18 16:16 ☾ 25♉26	
♄D 11 23:57	♃ ♎ 7 2:11	20 7:40 ♆ ☍	♉ 20 7:58	21 2:58 ☉ ⚹	♋ 21 6:48	25 11:33 ● 1♍59	1 August 1957
☽0N 13 7:46	♂ ♍ 8 5:27	22 15:44 ☉ ⚹	♊ 22 16:34	22 23:45 ☿ ⚹	♌ 23 8:51		Julian Day # 21032
☿0S 20 5:31	♇ ♍ 19 4:23	24 20:52 ♆ △	♋ 24 21:05	23 22:54 ♅ ☌	♍ 25 8:26		SVP 5♓50'54"
♃0S 21 3:35	♀ ♎ 20 0:44	26 22:05 ♆ □	♌ 26 22:16	27 0:08 ☿ ☌	♎ 27 7:41		GC 26♐14.8 ⚳ 6♉43.9
♀0S 21 12:06	☉ ♍ 23 10:08	28 21:50 ♆ ⚹	♍ 28 21:59	27 22:54 ♀ ☌	♏ 29 8:45		Eris 9♈30.4R ⚵ 22♉25.0
☽0S 26 16:58		30 20:16 ♃ ☌	♎ 30 22:20	31 3:18 ☿ ⚹	♐ 31 13:07		⚷ 15♒08.3R ⚶ 20♈23.2
☿R 27 8:04							☽ Mean ☊ 15♏27.6

LONGITUDE — September 1957

Day	Sid.Time	☉	0 hr ☽	Noon ☽	True ☊	☿	♀	♂	⚳	♃	♄	♅	♆	♇
1 Su	10 41 32	8♍46 19	5♐58 52	12♐29 09	12♏54.6	23♍54.9	14♎53.4	15♍25.3	10♋35.1	4♎53.6	8♐01.3	9♌14.7	0♏31.1	0♍26.3
2 M	10 45 29	9 44 24	18 54 16	25 14 42	12R53.4	23R20.7	16 04.7	16 03.7	10 56.2	5 05.8	8 03.3	9 18.0	0 32.7	0 28.3
3 Tu	10 49 25	10 42 31	1♑30 56	7♑43 29	12 50.1	22 40.6	17 16.0	16 42.0	11 17.2	5 18.1	8 05.4	9 21.3	0 34.2	0 30.2
4 W	10 53 22	11 40 40	13 52 48	19 59 20	12 44.3	21 55.2	18 27.2	17 20.4	11 38.1	5 30.5	8 07.6	9 24.6	0 35.8	0 32.2
5 Th	10 57 19	12 38 50	26 03 30	2♒05 39	12 36.2	21 05.0	19 38.4	17 58.8	11 59.0	5 42.8	8 09.9	9 27.8	0 37.5	0 34.1
6 F	11 01 15	13 37 01	8♒06 08	14 05 14	12 26.3	20 10.8	20 49.6	18 37.2	12 19.7	5 55.3	8 12.3	9 31.1	0 39.1	0 36.1
7 Sa	11 05 12	14 35 14	20 03 15	26 00 23	12 15.3	19 13.4	22 00.7	19 15.6	12 40.3	6 07.7	8 14.8	9 34.3	0 40.8	0 38.0
8 Su	11 09 08	15 33 29	1♓56 54	7♓52 57	12 04.3	18 14.1	23 11.7	19 54.0	13 00.7	6 20.2	8 17.3	9 37.4	0 42.4	0 39.9
9 M	11 13 05	16 31 46	13 48 46	19 44 31	11 54.3	17 13.9	24 22.7	20 32.5	13 21.1	6 32.7	8 20.0	9 40.6	0 44.2	0 41.9
10 Tu	11 17 01	17 30 04	25 40 25	1♈36 40	11 45.9	16 14.2	25 33.6	21 11.0	13 41.4	6 45.3	8 22.7	9 43.7	0 45.9	0 43.8
11 W	11 20 58	18 28 24	7♈33 29	13 31 09	11 39.8	15 16.4	26 44.4	21 49.5	14 01.5	6 57.9	8 25.6	9 46.8	0 47.6	0 45.7
12 Th	11 24 54	19 26 46	19 29 56	25 30 10	11 36.1	14 22.0	27 55.3	22 28.0	14 21.6	7 10.5	8 28.5	9 49.9	0 49.4	0 47.6
13 F	11 28 51	20 25 10	1♉32 11	7♉36 23	11D34.7	13 32.1	29 06.0	23 06.5	14 41.5	7 23.1	8 31.5	9 52.9	0 51.2	0 49.5
14 Sa	11 32 47	21 23 36	13 43 13	19 53 08	11 34.9	12 48.2	0♏16.7	23 45.1	15 01.3	7 35.8	8 34.6	9 55.9	0 53.0	0 51.3
15 Su	11 36 44	22 22 05	26 06 37	2♊24 10	11 36.0	12 11.3	1 27.3	24 23.7	15 21.0	7 48.5	8 37.8	9 58.9	0 54.8	0 53.2
16 M	11 40 41	23 20 35	8♊46 18	15 13 33	11R37.1	11 42.4	2 37.9	25 02.3	15 40.5	8 01.2	8 41.0	10 01.8	0 56.7	0 55.1
17 Tu	11 44 37	24 19 08	21 46 21	28 25 11	11 37.3	11 22.1	3 48.4	25 41.0	15 59.9	8 14.0	8 44.4	10 04.7	0 58.6	0 56.9
18 W	11 48 34	25 17 43	5♋10 23	12♋02 14	11 35.9	11D11.1	4 58.9	26 19.6	16 19.2	8 26.8	8 47.8	10 07.6	1 00.4	0 58.8
19 Th	11 52 30	26 16 21	19 00 53	26 06 19	11 32.8	11 09.6	6 09.3	26 58.3	16 38.4	8 39.6	8 51.3	10 10.5	1 02.4	1 00.6
20 F	11 56 27	27 15 00	3♌18 22	10♌36 39	11 27.8	11 17.9	7 19.7	27 37.0	16 57.4	8 52.4	8 54.9	10 13.3	1 04.3	1 02.4
21 Sa	12 00 23	28 13 41	18 00 35	25 29 22	11 21.7	11 35.8	8 29.9	28 15.8	17 16.2	9 05.2	8 58.6	10 16.1	1 06.2	1 04.3
22 Su	12 04 20	29 12 25	3♍02 02	10♍37 25	11 15.3	12 03.3	9 40.2	28 54.5	17 35.0	9 18.1	9 02.4	10 18.8	1 08.2	1 06.0
23 M	12 08 16	0♎11 11	18 14 17	25 51 17	11 09.4	12 39.9	10 50.3	29 33.3	17 53.5	9 31.0	9 06.2	10 21.5	1 10.1	1 07.8
24 Tu	12 12 13	1 09 58	3♎27 05	11♎00 24	11 04.9	13 25.2	12 00.4	0♎12.1	18 12.0	9 43.9	9 10.2	10 24.2	1 12.1	1 09.6
25 W	12 16 10	2 08 48	18 30 05	25 55 04	11 02.2	14 18.8	13 10.4	0 50.9	18 30.2	9 56.8	9 14.2	10 26.8	1 14.1	1 11.4
26 Th	12 20 06	3 07 40	3♏14 32	10♏27 49	11D01.3	15 19.9	14 20.4	1 29.8	18 48.4	10 09.7	9 18.2	10 29.4	1 16.1	1 13.1
27 F	12 24 03	4 06 33	17 34 29	24 34 17	11 01.9	16 27.9	15 30.3	2 08.7	19 06.3	10 22.6	9 22.4	10 32.0	1 18.2	1 14.8
28 Sa	12 27 59	5 05 28	1♐27 08	8♐13 07	11 03.3	17 42.1	16 40.1	2 47.6	19 24.1	10 35.6	9 26.6	10 34.5	1 20.2	1 16.5
29 Su	12 31 56	6 04 25	14 52 28	21 25 31	11 04.7	19 02.0	17 49.8	3 26.5	19 41.7	10 48.6	9 31.0	10 37.0	1 22.3	1 18.2
30 M	12 35 52	7 03 24	27 52 39	4♑14 22	11R05.6	20 26.7	18 59.4	4 05.4	19 59.2	11 01.5	9 35.4	10 39.4	1 24.4	1 19.9

LONGITUDE — October 1957

Day	Sid.Time	☉	0 hr ☽	Noon ☽	True ☊	☿	♀	♂	⚳	♃	♄	♅	♆	♇
1 Tu	12 39 49	8♎02 24	10♑31 10	16♑43 34	11♏05.2	21♍55.6	20♏09.0	4♎44.4	20♋16.5	11♎14.5	9♐39.8	10♌41.8	1♏26.4	1♍21.6
2 W	12 43 45	9 01 27	22 52 09	28 57 26	11R03.4	23 28.2	21 18.4	5 23.4	20 33.6	11 27.5	9 44.3	10 44.1	1 28.5	1 23.2
3 Th	12 47 42	10 00 31	4♒59 58	11♒00 14	11 00.2	25 03.7	22 27.8	6 02.4	20 50.5	11 40.5	9 49.0	10 46.4	1 30.7	1 24.9
4 F	12 51 39	10 59 36	16 58 43	22 55 53	10 55.8	26 41.8	23 37.1	6 41.4	21 07.3	11 53.4	9 53.6	10 48.7	1 32.8	1 26.5
5 Sa	12 55 35	11 58 44	28 52 09	4♓47 53	10 50.8	28 21.9	24 46.3	7 20.5	21 23.8	12 06.4	9 58.4	10 50.9	1 34.9	1 28.1
6 Su	12 59 32	12 57 53	10♓43 27	16 39 10	10 45.7	0♎03.7	25 55.4	7 59.6	21 40.2	12 19.4	10 03.2	10 53.1	1 37.0	1 29.7
7 M	13 03 28	13 57 05	22 35 20	28 32 11	10 41.0	1 46.6	27 04.4	8 38.7	21 56.4	12 32.4	10 08.1	10 55.3	1 39.2	1 31.2
8 Tu	13 07 25	14 56 18	4♈30 00	10♈28 58	10 37.3	3 30.5	28 13.3	9 17.8	22 12.4	12 45.4	10 13.0	10 57.4	1 41.4	1 32.8
9 W	13 11 21	15 55 33	16 29 19	22 31 16	10 34.8	5 15.0	29 22.0	9 57.0	22 28.2	12 58.4	10 18.0	10 59.4	1 43.5	1 34.3
10 Th	13 15 18	16 54 51	28 35 00	4♉40 44	10D33.6	6 59.9	0♐30.7	10 36.2	22 43.8	13 11.4	10 23.1	11 01.4	1 45.7	1 35.8
11 F	13 19 14	17 54 10	10♉48 41	16 59 04	10 33.6	8 45.0	1 39.3	11 15.4	22 59.2	13 24.3	10 28.2	11 03.4	1 47.9	1 37.3
12 Sa	13 23 11	18 53 32	23 12 09	29 28 11	10 34.5	10 30.2	2 47.8	11 54.6	23 14.3	13 37.3	10 33.4	11 05.3	1 50.1	1 38.7
13 Su	13 27 07	19 52 56	5♊47 26	12♊10 10	10 36.0	12 15.2	3 56.1	12 33.9	23 29.3	13 50.3	10 38.7	11 07.1	1 52.3	1 40.2
14 M	13 31 04	20 52 22	18 36 43	25 07 21	10 37.5	14 00.0	5 04.3	13 13.2	23 44.1	14 03.2	10 44.0	11 09.0	1 54.5	1 41.6
15 Tu	13 35 01	21 51 51	1♋42 22	8♋22 01	10 38.6	15 44.5	6 12.4	13 52.5	23 58.6	14 16.2	10 49.4	11 10.7	1 56.7	1 43.0
16 W	13 38 57	22 51 22	15 06 31	21 56 05	10R39.1	17 28.6	7 20.4	14 31.9	24 12.9	14 29.1	10 54.9	11 12.5	1 58.9	1 44.4
17 Th	13 42 54	23 50 55	28 50 47	5♌50 41	10 38.7	19 12.3	8 28.3	15 11.3	24 27.0	14 42.0	11 00.4	11 14.1	2 01.1	1 45.8
18 F	13 46 50	24 50 31	12♌55 40	20 05 32	10 37.7	20 55.4	9 36.1	15 50.7	24 40.8	14 55.0	11 06.0	11 15.8	2 03.4	1 47.1
19 Sa	13 50 47	25 50 09	27 19 58	4♍38 29	10 36.0	22 38.1	10 43.7	16 30.1	24 54.4	15 07.9	11 11.6	11 17.3	2 05.6	1 48.4
20 Su	13 54 43	26 49 49	12♍00 27	19 25 09	10 34.3	24 20.2	11 51.2	17 09.6	25 07.7	15 20.7	11 17.3	11 18.9	2 07.8	1 49.7
21 M	13 58 40	27 49 31	26 51 43	4♎19 12	10 32.6	26 01.7	12 58.5	17 49.1	25 20.8	15 33.6	11 23.0	11 20.3	2 10.1	1 51.0
22 Tu	14 02 36	28 49 15	11♎46 34	19 12 49	10 31.5	27 42.7	14 05.7	18 28.6	25 33.7	15 46.4	11 28.8	11 21.8	2 12.3	1 52.2
23 W	14 06 33	29 49 02	26 36 56	3♏57 56	10D30.9	29 23.2	15 12.8	19 08.2	25 46.3	15 59.3	11 34.6	11 23.1	2 14.5	1 53.4
24 Th	14 10 30	0♏48 50	11♏14 59	18 27 18	10 30.9	1♏03.0	16 19.7	19 47.8	25 58.6	16 12.1	11 40.5	11 24.4	2 16.8	1 54.6
25 F	14 14 26	1 48 41	25 34 16	2♐35 26	10 31.4	2 42.3	17 26.5	20 27.4	26 10.6	16 24.9	11 46.5	11 25.7	2 19.0	1 55.8
26 Sa	14 18 23	2 48 33	9♐30 27	16 19 10	10 32.1	4 21.0	18 33.1	21 07.0	26 22.4	16 37.6	11 52.5	11 26.9	2 21.3	1 56.9
27 Su	14 22 19	3 48 27	23 01 33	29 37 42	10 32.9	5 59.2	19 39.5	21 46.7	26 33.9	16 50.3	11 58.5	11 28.1	2 23.5	1 58.1
28 M	14 26 16	4 48 22	6♑07 50	12♑32 17	10 33.4	7 36.9	20 45.7	22 26.4	26 45.1	17 03.0	12 04.6	11 29.2	2 25.8	1 59.2
29 Tu	14 30 12	5 48 20	18 51 25	25 05 43	10R33.8	9 14.0	21 51.8	23 06.1	26 56.1	17 15.7	12 10.8	11 30.3	2 28.0	2 00.2
30 W	14 34 09	6 48 18	1♒15 40	7♒21 51	10 33.9	10 50.7	22 57.7	23 45.9	27 06.7	17 28.4	12 17.0	11 31.3	2 30.3	2 01.3
31 Th	14 38 05	7 48 19	13 24 47	19 25 05	10 33.8	12 26.8	24 03.3	24 25.6	27 17.0	17 41.0	12 23.2	11 32.2	2 32.5	2 02.3

Astro Data (Dy Hr Mn)

Astro Data	Dy Hr Mn
☿0N	6 9:01
☽0N	9 14:10
☿D	19 3:35
♃✶♄	20 18:41
☽0S	23 3:59
☉0S	23 7:26
♂0S	27 6:08
♃✶♅	28 9:25
☽0N	6 20:13
☿0S	8 23:27
☽0S	20 13:57
♄△♅	20 20:59
♃∠♇	28 3:58

Planet Ingress (Dy Hr Mn)

Planet Ingress	Dy Hr Mn
♀ ♏	14 6:20
☉ ♎	23 7:26
♂ ♎	24 4:31
☿ ♎	6 11:09
♀ ♐	10 1:16
☉ ♏	23 16:24
☿ ♏	23 20:50

Last Aspect / ☽ Ingress (September)

Last Aspect Dy Hr Mn		☽ Ingress	Dy Hr Mn
2 8:33	☿ □	♑	2 21:05
4 15:34	☿ △	♒	5 7:50
7 3:03	♀ △	♓	7 20:04
9 13:43	♂ ☍	♈	10 8:45
12 17:20	♀ ☍	♉	12 20:57
14 19:52	♂ △	♊	15 7:26
17 6:50	♂ □	♋	17 14:50
19 13:31	♂ ✶	♌	19 18:31
20 11:22	♅ ☌	♍	21 19:11
23 18:06	♂ ☌	♎	23 18:33
24 11:02	♅ ✶	♏	25 18:40
26 20:53	☿ ✶	♐	27 21:27
29 7:05	☿ □	♑	30 3:59

Last Aspect / ☽ Ingress (October)

Last Aspect Dy Hr Mn		☽ Ingress	Dy Hr Mn
1 23:36	☿ △	♒	2 14:04
4 13:32	♀ □	♓	5 2:17
7 8:44	♀ △	♈	7 14:57
8 21:42	☉ ☍	♉	10 2:48
11 0:27	♅ □	♊	12 13:01
14 3:32	☉ △	♋	14 20:54
16 13:44	☉ □	♌	17 1:59
18 20:28	☉ ✶	♍	19 4:23
19 22:45	♄ □	♎	21 5:03
23 4:43	☉ ☌	♏	23 5:31
24 0:15	♅ □	♐	25 7:33
26 21:01	♂ ✶	♑	27 12:41
29 7:56	♂ □	♒	29 21:32

☽ Phases & Eclipses (Dy Hr Mn)

Dy Hr Mn	Phase	Position
1 4:35	☽	8♐28
9 4:55	○	16♓15
17 4:02	☾	24♊00
23 19:18	●	0♎29
30 17:49	☽	7♑18
8 21:42	○	15♈20
16 13:44	☾	22♋56
23 4:43	●	29♎31
23 4:53:28	●	T non-C
30 10:48	☽	6♒45

Astro Data

1 September 1957
Julian Day # 21063
SVP 5♓50'50"
GC 26♐14.9 ⚵ 10♉41.5
Eris 9♈17.5R ✵ 5♊36.4
⚷ 13♒32.5R ⚶ 21♈00.9R
☽ Mean ☊ 13♏49.1

1 October 1957
Julian Day # 21093
SVP 5♓50'48"
GC 26♐15.0 ⚵ 8♉41.3R
Eris 8♈59.7R ✵ 15♊03.1
⚷ 12♒29.0R ⚶ 15♈17.5R
☽ Mean ☊ 12♏13.8

November 1957 — LONGITUDE

Day	Sid.Time	☉	0 hr ☽	Noon ☽	True ☊	☿	♀	♂	⚳	♃	♄	♅	♆	♇
1 F	14 42 02	8♏48 21	25♒23 19	1♓20 02	10♏33.6	14♏02.5	25♐08.8	25♎05.4	27♋27.1	17♎53.5	12♐29.5	11♌33.1	2♏34.7	2♍03.3
2 Sa	14 45 59	9 48 24	7♓15 48	13 11 10	10D33.5	15 37.7	26 14.1	25 45.3	27 36.8	18 06.1	12 35.8	11 34.0	2 37.0	2 04.2
3 Su	14 49 55	10 48 30	19 06 37	25 02 38	10 33.5	17 12.5	27 19.1	26 25.1	27 46.3	18 18.6	12 42.1	11 34.8	2 39.2	2 05.2
4 M	14 53 52	11 48 37	0♈59 40	6♈58 07	10 33.6	18 46.9	28 23.9	27 05.0	27 55.4	18 31.1	12 48.5	11 35.5	2 41.4	2 06.1
5 Tu	14 57 48	12 48 45	12 58 21	19 00 42	10 33.8	20 20.9	29 28.4	27 44.9	28 04.2	18 43.5	12 54.9	11 36.2	2 43.6	2 07.0
6 W	15 01 45	13 48 55	25 05 27	1♉12 50	10R33.9	21 54.5	0♑32.8	28 24.9	28 12.7	18 55.9	13 01.4	11 36.8	2 45.8	2 07.8
7 Th	15 05 41	14 49 07	7♉23 03	13 36 18	10 34.0	23 27.7	1 36.8	29 04.9	28 20.8	19 08.2	13 07.9	11 37.4	2 48.0	2 08.6
8 F	15 09 38	15 49 21	19 52 41	26 12 19	10 33.8	25 00.5	2 40.6	29 44.9	28 28.6	19 20.5	13 14.4	11 37.9	2 50.3	2 09.4
9 Sa	15 13 34	16 49 37	2♊35 14	9♊01 31	10 33.3	26 33.1	3 44.2	0♏24.9	28 36.1	19 32.8	13 21.0	11 38.3	2 52.4	2 10.2
10 Su	15 17 31	17 49 54	15 31 10	22 04 12	10 32.5	28 05.2	4 47.4	1 05.0	28 43.3	19 45.0	13 27.6	11 38.7	2 54.6	2 10.9
11 M	15 21 28	18 50 14	28 40 34	5♋20 17	10 31.4	29 37.1	5 50.4	1 45.1	28 50.1	19 57.2	13 34.3	11 39.1	2 56.8	2 11.7
12 Tu	15 25 24	19 50 35	12♋03 18	18 49 34	10 30.4	1♐08.6	6 53.1	2 25.2	28 56.5	20 09.3	13 41.0	11 39.4	2 59.0	2 12.3
13 W	15 29 21	20 50 58	25 39 02	2♌31 38	10 29.5	2 39.8	7 55.5	3 05.4	29 02.6	20 21.4	13 47.7	11 39.6	3 01.2	2 13.0
14 Th	15 33 17	21 51 23	9♌27 17	16 25 53	10D29.0	4 10.7	8 57.5	3 45.6	29 08.3	20 33.4	13 54.4	11 39.8	3 03.3	2 13.6
15 F	15 37 14	22 51 50	23 27 17	0♍31 20	10 29.0	5 41.3	9 59.2	4 25.8	29 13.7	20 45.4	14 01.2	11 39.9	3 05.5	2 14.2
16 Sa	15 41 10	23 52 19	7♍37 48	14 46 25	10 29.6	7 11.5	11 00.6	5 06.1	29 18.7	20 57.3	14 07.9	11R40.0	3 07.6	2 14.8
17 Su	15 45 07	24 52 50	21 56 54	29 08 50	10 30.7	8 41.5	12 01.7	5 46.4	29 23.3	21 09.2	14 14.8	11 40.0	3 09.7	2 15.3
18 M	15 49 03	25 53 23	6♎21 48	13♎35 18	10 31.8	10 11.0	13 02.4	6 26.7	29 27.5	21 21.0	14 21.6	11 40.0	3 11.8	2 15.8
19 Tu	15 53 00	26 53 57	20 48 47	28 01 38	10R32.8	11 40.3	14 02.7	7 07.1	29 31.3	21 32.8	14 28.5	11 39.9	3 13.9	2 16.3
20 W	15 56 57	27 54 33	5♏13 15	12♏22 59	10 33.1	13 09.1	15 02.6	7 47.5	29 34.8	21 44.4	14 35.3	11 39.7	3 16.0	2 16.7
21 Th	16 00 53	28 55 10	19 30 11	26 34 16	10 32.5	14 37.5	16 02.1	8 27.9	29 37.8	21 56.1	14 42.3	11 39.5	3 18.1	2 17.1
22 F	16 04 50	29 55 50	3♐34 39	10♐30 49	10 30.8	16 05.4	17 01.2	9 08.4	29 40.5	22 07.6	14 49.2	11 39.3	3 20.2	2 17.5
23 Sa	16 08 46	0♐56 30	17 22 22	24 08 58	10 28.2	17 32.9	17 59.9	9 48.9	29 42.7	22 19.1	14 56.1	11 39.0	3 22.2	2 17.9
24 Su	16 12 43	1 57 12	0♑50 22	7♑26 27	10 24.9	18 59.7	18 58.1	10 29.4	29 44.5	22 30.6	15 03.1	11 38.6	3 24.3	2 18.2
25 M	16 16 39	2 57 55	13 57 13	20 22 45	10 21.4	20 25.9	19 55.8	11 10.0	29 46.0	22 41.9	15 10.1	11 38.2	3 26.3	2 18.5
26 Tu	16 20 36	3 58 39	26 43 15	2♒58 58	10 18.1	21 51.4	20 53.0	11 50.5	29 47.0	22 53.2	15 17.1	11 37.7	3 28.3	2 18.8
27 W	16 24 32	4 59 24	9♒10 18	15 17 39	10 15.6	23 16.1	21 49.7	12 31.1	29R47.6	23 04.4	15 24.1	11 37.1	3 30.3	2 19.0
28 Th	16 28 29	6 00 10	21 21 32	27 22 28	10D14.0	24 39.8	22 45.9	13 11.8	29 47.8	23 15.6	15 31.1	11 36.5	3 32.2	2 19.2
29 F	16 32 26	7 00 57	3♓21 02	9♓17 51	10 13.7	26 02.5	23 41.5	13 52.4	29 47.6	23 26.7	15 38.2	11 35.9	3 34.2	2 19.4
30 Sa	16 36 22	8 01 45	15 13 31	21 08 40	10 14.5	27 23.9	24 36.5	14 33.1	29 46.9	23 37.6	15 45.2	11 35.2	3 36.1	2 19.5

December 1957 — LONGITUDE

Day	Sid.Time	☉	0 hr ☽	Noon ☽	True ☊	☿	♀	♂	⚳	♃	♄	♅	♆	♇
1 Su	16 40 19	9♐02 34	27♓03 56	2♈59 56	10♏16.0	28♐43.9	25♑30.9	15♏13.9	29♋45.8	23♎48.6	15♐52.3	11♌34.5	3♏38.0	2♍19.6
2 M	16 44 15	10 03 24	8♈57 15	14 56 28	10 17.9	0♑02.2	26 24.6	15 54.6	29R44.4	23 59.4	15 59.3	11R33.6	3 39.9	2 19.7
3 Tu	16 48 12	11 04 15	20 58 08	27 02 44	10 19.5	1 18.7	27 17.7	16 35.4	29 42.4	24 10.1	16 06.4	11 32.8	3 41.8	2R19.7
4 W	16 52 08	12 05 06	3♉10 42	9♉22 26	10R20.2	2 32.9	28 10.2	17 16.2	29 40.1	24 20.8	16 13.5	11 31.9	3 43.7	2 19.7
5 Th	16 56 05	13 05 59	15 38 15	21 58 23	10 19.6	3 44.6	29 01.8	17 57.1	29 37.4	24 31.4	16 20.6	11 30.9	3 45.5	2 19.7
6 F	17 00 01	14 06 52	28 23 00	4♊52 10	10 17.3	4 53.5	29 52.8	18 38.0	29 34.2	24 41.9	16 27.7	11 29.9	3 47.4	2 19.7
7 Sa	17 03 58	15 07 47	11♊25 54	18 04 04	10 13.3	5 58.9	0♒42.9	19 18.9	29 30.6	24 52.3	16 34.8	11 28.9	3 49.2	2 19.6
8 Su	17 07 55	16 08 43	24 46 31	1♋32 57	10 07.9	7 00.5	1 32.3	19 59.8	29 26.6	25 02.6	16 41.9	11 27.7	3 51.0	2 19.5
9 M	17 11 51	17 09 39	8♋23 05	15 16 30	10 01.7	7 57.7	2 20.8	20 40.8	29 22.1	25 12.9	16 48.9	11 26.6	3 52.7	2 19.3
10 Tu	17 15 48	18 10 37	22 12 48	29 11 31	9 55.4	8 49.7	3 08.4	21 21.8	29 17.3	25 23.0	16 56.0	11 25.4	3 54.5	2 19.2
11 W	17 19 44	19 11 35	6♌12 13	13♌14 27	9 50.0	9 36.0	3 55.2	22 02.9	29 12.0	25 33.1	17 03.1	11 24.1	3 56.2	2 19.0
12 Th	17 23 41	20 12 35	20 17 48	27 21 53	9 46.0	10 15.7	4 41.0	22 44.0	29 06.3	25 43.0	17 10.2	11 22.8	3 57.9	2 18.7
13 F	17 27 37	21 13 36	4♍26 23	11♍30 59	9D43.8	10 48.0	5 25.8	23 25.1	29 00.1	25 52.9	17 17.3	11 21.5	3 59.6	2 18.5
14 Sa	17 31 34	22 14 38	18 35 27	25 39 33	9 43.4	11 12.0	6 09.5	24 06.3	28 53.6	26 02.6	17 24.4	11 20.1	4 01.2	2 18.2
15 Su	17 35 30	23 15 41	2♎43 09	9♎46 03	9 44.3	11R26.9	6 52.3	24 47.4	28 46.7	26 12.3	17 31.5	11 18.6	4 02.8	2 17.9
16 M	17 39 27	24 16 44	16 48 09	23 49 16	9 45.6	11 31.8	7 33.9	25 28.7	28 39.3	26 21.8	17 38.6	11 17.1	4 04.4	2 17.5
17 Tu	17 43 24	25 17 49	0♏49 15	7♏47 56	9R46.4	11 25.9	8 14.3	26 09.9	28 31.6	26 31.3	17 45.6	11 15.6	4 06.0	2 17.1
18 W	17 47 20	26 18 55	14 45 06	21 40 30	9 45.8	11 08.6	8 53.6	26 51.2	28 23.5	26 40.6	17 52.7	11 14.0	4 07.6	2 16.7
19 Th	17 51 17	27 20 01	28 33 53	5♐24 57	9 43.0	10 39.7	9 31.6	27 32.5	28 14.9	26 49.8	17 59.7	11 12.3	4 09.1	2 16.3
20 F	17 55 13	28 21 09	12♐13 24	18 58 53	9 37.7	9 59.1	10 08.4	28 13.9	28 06.0	26 58.9	18 06.8	11 10.7	4 10.6	2 15.8
21 Sa	17 59 10	29 22 16	25 41 08	2♑19 51	9 30.2	9 07.4	10 43.8	28 55.3	27 56.8	27 07.9	18 13.8	11 09.0	4 12.1	2 15.3
22 Su	18 03 06	0♑23 25	8♑54 46	15 25 43	9 21.0	8 05.6	11 17.7	29 36.7	27 47.1	27 16.8	18 20.8	11 07.2	4 13.5	2 14.8
23 M	18 07 03	1 24 33	21 52 33	28 15 12	9 11.0	6 55.1	11 50.2	0♐18.2	27 37.2	27 25.6	18 27.8	11 05.4	4 14.9	2 14.2
24 Tu	18 11 00	2 25 42	4♒33 42	10♒48 08	9 01.2	5 38.2	12 21.2	0 59.6	27 26.8	27 34.3	18 34.7	11 03.6	4 16.3	2 13.7
25 W	18 14 56	3 26 51	16 58 41	23 05 37	8 52.6	4 17.2	12 50.6	1 41.2	27 16.2	27 42.8	18 41.7	11 01.7	4 17.7	2 13.0
26 Th	18 18 53	4 28 00	29 09 16	5♓10 02	8 46.0	2 54.8	13 18.3	2 22.7	27 05.2	27 51.2	18 48.6	10 59.8	4 19.0	2 12.4
27 F	18 22 49	5 29 09	11♓08 26	17 04 57	8 41.6	1 33.8	13 44.3	3 04.3	26 53.9	27 59.5	18 55.5	10 57.8	4 20.3	2 11.7
28 Sa	18 26 46	6 30 18	23 00 11	28 54 45	8D39.5	0 16.8	14 08.5	3 45.9	26 42.4	28 07.6	19 02.4	10 55.8	4 21.6	2 11.0
29 Su	18 30 42	7 31 27	4♈49 17	10♈44 29	8 39.2	29♐06.1	14 30.8	4 27.5	26 30.5	28 15.7	19 09.3	10 53.8	4 22.9	2 10.3
30 M	18 34 39	8 32 36	16 41 00	22 39 33	8 39.9	28 03.3	14 51.3	5 09.2	26 18.4	28 23.6	19 16.2	10 51.7	4 24.1	2 09.6
31 Tu	18 38 35	9 33 44	28 40 47	4♉45 21	8R40.6	27 09.8	15 09.7	5 50.9	26 06.0	28 31.3	19 23.0	10 49.6	4 25.3	2 08.8

Astro Data	Dy Hr Mn
☽0N	3 2:59
☽0S	16 21:47
♅R	17 6:27
⚳R	28 10:53
☽0N	30 11:11
♇R	4 10:31
☽0S	14 4:02
☿R	16 11:05
☽0N	27 20:29
♄∠♆	31 21:52

Planet Ingress		Dy Hr Mn
♀	♑	5 23:46
♂	♏	8 21:04
☿	♐	11 18:00
☉	♐	22 13:39
☿	♑	2 11:19
♀	♒	6 15:26
☉	♑	22 2:49
♂	♐	23 1:29
☿	♐R	28 17:30

Last Aspect Dy Hr Mn		☽ Ingress	Dy Hr Mn
31 22:39	♂ △	♓	1 9:18
3 17:03	♀ □	♈	3 22:00
6 6:13	♂ ☍	♉	6 9:38
8 9:26	☿ ☍	♊	8 19:09
10 7:42	♃ △	♋	11 2:24
12 14:23	♃ □	♌	13 7:36
14 21:59	☉ □	♍	15 11:07
17 4:21	☉ ⚹	♎	17 13:25
19 1:04	♃ ☌	♏	19 15:17
21 16:19	☉ ☌	♐	21 17:52
23 8:42	♃ ⚹	♑	23 22:29
25 16:26	♃ □	♒	26 6:16
28 5:52	☿ ⚹	♓	28 17:16

Last Aspect Dy Hr Mn		☽ Ingress	Dy Hr Mn
1 2:17	☿ □	♈	1 5:56
3 12:32	♀ □	♉	3 17:48
6 2:08	♀ △	♊	6 3:00
8 0:20	♃ △	♋	8 9:16
10 5:23	♃ □	♌	10 13:23
12 9:10	♃ ⚹	♍	12 16:28
14 9:13	♂ ⚹	♎	14 19:23
16 16:24	♃ ☌	♏	16 22:35
18 21:29	♂ ☌	♐	19 2:30
21 6:12	☉ ☌	♑	21 7:47
23 10:25	♃ □	♒	23 15:19
25 21:15	♃ △	♓	26 1:41
27 15:46	♄ □	♈	28 14:13
30 23:33	♃ ☍	♉	31 2:37

☽ Phases & Eclipses Dy Hr Mn	
7 14:32	○ 14♉55
7 14:27	☍ T 1.030
14 21:59	☾ 22♌17
21 16:19	● 29♏06
29 6:58	☽ 6♓48
7 6:16	○ 14♊53
14 5:45	☾ 21♍59
21 6:12	● 29♐07
29 4:52	☽ 7♈13

Astro Data

1 November 1957
Julian Day # 21124
SVP 5♓50'45"
GC 26♐15.0 ⚵ 0♉06.2R
Eris 8♈41.1R ✱ 18♊22.8R
⚷ 12♒19.2 ⚶ 8♈13.6R
☽ Mean ☊ 10♏35.3

1 December 1957
Julian Day # 21154
SVP 5♓50'41"
GC 26♐15.1 ⚵ 22♈30.7R
Eris 8♈28.3R ✱ 13♊52.9R
⚷ 13♒09.6 ⚶ 6♈52.3
☽ Mean ☊ 9♏00.0

LONGITUDE — January 1958

Day	Sid.Time	☉	0 hr ☽	Noon☽	True☊	☿	♀	♂	?	♃	♄	♅	♆	♇
1 W	18 42 32	10♑34 53	10♉53 53	17♉06 56	8♏40.3	26♐26.3	15♒26.1	6♐32.6	25♋53.4	28♎39.0	19♐29.8	10♌47.5	4♏26.5	2♍08.0
2 Th	18 46 28	11 36 02	23 25 01	29 48 33	8R 38.1	25R 53.2	15 40.3	7 14.3	25R 40.6	28 46.5	19 36.5	10R 45.3	4 27.6	2R 07.2
3 F	18 50 25	12 37 10	6♊17 51	12♊53 07	8 33.3	25 30.4	15 52.3	7 56.1	25 27.5	28 53.9	19 43.3	10 43.1	4 28.7	2 06.3
4 Sa	18 54 22	13 38 18	19 34 27	26 21 45	8 26.0	25D 17.5	16 02.2	8 37.9	25 14.3	29 01.1	19 50.0	10 40.9	4 29.8	2 05.4
5 Su	18 58 18	14 39 26	3♋14 49	10♋13 17	8 16.3	25 14.2	16 09.6	9 19.8	25 00.9	29 08.2	19 56.7	10 38.6	4 30.8	2 04.5
6 M	19 02 15	15 40 34	17 16 36	24 24 10	8 05.3	25 19.8	16 14.8	10 01.7	24 47.3	29 15.2	20 03.3	10 36.4	4 31.8	2 03.6
7 Tu	19 06 11	16 41 42	1♌35 12	8♌48 52	7 54.1	25 33.6	16R 17.5	10 43.6	24 33.6	29 22.0	20 09.9	10 34.1	4 32.8	2 02.7
8 W	19 10 08	17 42 50	16 04 19	23 20 40	7 43.9	25 54.9	16 17.8	11 25.6	24 19.7	29 28.7	20 16.5	10 31.7	4 33.7	2 01.7
9 Th	19 14 04	18 43 57	0♍37 04	7♍52 45	7 35.9	26 23.0	16 15.6	12 07.6	24 05.8	29 35.2	20 23.1	10 29.4	4 34.7	2 00.7
10 F	19 18 01	19 45 05	15 07 04	22 19 24	7 30.5	26 57.3	16 10.9	12 49.6	23 51.7	29 41.6	20 29.6	10 27.0	4 35.5	1 59.7
11 Sa	19 21 58	20 46 12	29 29 20	6♎36 33	7 27.8	27 37.1	16 03.7	13 31.6	23 37.6	29 47.8	20 36.1	10 24.6	4 36.4	1 58.6
12 Su	19 25 54	21 47 20	13♎40 49	20 42 02	7D 27.1	28 21.9	15 54.0	14 13.7	23 23.4	29 53.9	20 42.5	10 22.1	4 37.2	1 57.6
13 M	19 29 51	22 48 28	27 40 09	4♏35 13	7R 27.2	29 11.2	15 41.8	14 55.9	23 09.2	29 59.8	20 48.9	10 19.7	4 38.0	1 56.5
14 Tu	19 33 47	23 49 35	11♏27 18	18 16 30	7 26.9	0♑04.5	15 27.1	15 38.0	22 54.9	0♏05.6	20 55.3	10 17.2	4 38.8	1 55.4
15 W	19 37 44	24 50 43	25 02 54	1♐46 36	7 24.8	1 01.3	15 10.0	16 20.2	22 40.7	0 11.2	21 01.6	10 14.7	4 39.5	1 54.3
16 Th	19 41 40	25 51 50	8♐27 39	15 06 07	7 20.0	2 01.4	14 50.5	17 02.4	22 26.4	0 16.6	21 07.8	10 12.2	4 40.2	1 53.1
17 F	19 45 37	26 52 57	21 42 00	28 15 15	7 12.1	3 04.4	14 28.8	17 44.7	22 12.2	0 21.9	21 14.1	10 09.7	4 40.8	1 51.9
18 Sa	19 49 33	27 54 03	4♑45 50	11♑13 40	7 01.2	4 10.0	14 04.7	18 27.0	21 58.1	0 27.1	21 20.3	10 07.2	4 41.4	1 50.8
19 Su	19 53 30	28 55 09	17 38 40	24 00 45	6 48.0	5 18.0	13 38.6	19 09.3	21 44.0	0 32.0	21 26.4	10 04.6	4 42.0	1 49.6
20 M	19 57 27	29 56 15	0♒19 49	6♒35 51	6 33.6	6 28.1	13 10.5	19 51.7	21 30.0	0 36.8	21 32.5	10 02.1	4 42.6	1 48.3
21 Tu	20 01 23	0♒57 19	12 48 49	18 58 44	6 19.3	7 40.1	12 40.6	20 34.0	21 16.2	0 41.5	21 38.5	9 59.5	4 43.1	1 47.1
22 W	20 05 20	1 58 23	25 05 42	1♓09 50	6 06.3	8 53.9	12 09.0	21 16.4	21 02.4	0 46.0	21 44.5	9 56.9	4 43.6	1 45.8
23 Th	20 09 16	2 59 26	7♓11 21	13 10 31	5 55.6	10 09.3	11 36.0	21 58.9	20 48.9	0 50.3	21 50.5	9 54.3	4 44.0	1 44.6
24 F	20 13 13	4 00 28	19 07 40	25 03 12	5 47.7	11 26.3	11 01.6	22 41.4	20 35.4	0 54.4	21 56.3	9 51.7	4 44.5	1 43.3
25 Sa	20 17 09	5 01 29	0♈57 34	6♈51 17	5 42.8	12 44.6	10 26.3	23 23.8	20 22.2	0 58.3	22 02.2	9 49.1	4 44.8	1 42.0
26 Su	20 21 06	6 02 29	12 44 55	18 39 05	5 40.4	14 04.1	9 50.1	24 06.4	20 09.2	1 02.1	22 08.0	9 46.4	4 45.2	1 40.6
27 M	20 25 02	7 03 28	24 34 25	0♉31 38	5 39.7	15 24.9	9 13.3	24 48.9	19 56.4	1 05.7	22 13.7	9 43.8	4 45.5	1 39.3
28 Tu	20 28 59	8 04 26	6♉31 23	12 34 25	5 39.7	16 46.8	8 36.2	25 31.5	19 43.8	1 09.2	22 19.3	9 41.2	4 45.8	1 37.9
29 W	20 32 56	9 05 22	18 41 24	24 53 02	5 39.0	18 09.8	7 59.1	26 14.1	19 31.4	1 12.4	22 25.0	9 38.6	4 46.0	1 36.6
30 Th	20 36 52	10 06 17	1♊09 58	7♊32 46	5 36.7	19 33.8	7 22.1	26 56.8	19 19.4	1 15.5	22 30.5	9 36.0	4 46.2	1 35.2
31 F	20 40 49	11 07 12	14 01 58	20 37 57	5 32.0	20 58.8	6 45.7	27 39.4	19 07.6	1 18.4	22 36.0	9 33.3	4 46.4	1 33.8

LONGITUDE — February 1958

Day	Sid.Time	☉	0 hr ☽	Noon☽	True☊	☿	♀	♂	?	♃	♄	♅	♆	♇
1 Sa	20 44 45	12♒08 04	27♊21 00	4♋11 13	5♏24.4	22♑24.7	6♒09.9	28♐22.1	18♋56.1	1♏21.1	22♐41.4	9♌30.7	4♏46.5	1♍32.4
2 Su	20 48 42	13 08 56	11♋08 33	18 12 45	5R 14.5	23 51.5	5R 35.1	29 04.9	18R 44.9	1 23.7	22 46.8	9R 28.1	4 46.7	1R 31.0
3 M	20 52 38	14 09 46	25 23 21	2♌39 41	5 02.9	25 19.2	5 01.5	29 47.6	18 34.0	1 26.0	22 52.1	9 25.5	4 46.7	1 29.6
4 Tu	20 56 35	15 10 35	10♌00 55	17 26 02	4 50.9	26 47.7	4 29.3	0♑30.4	18 23.4	1 28.2	22 57.3	9 22.9	4R 46.8	1 28.1
5 W	21 00 31	16 11 23	24 53 54	2♍23 21	4 40.0	28 17.1	3 58.6	1 13.2	18 13.2	1 30.2	23 02.5	9 20.3	4 46.8	1 26.7
6 Th	21 04 28	17 12 10	9♍53 08	17 22 07	4 31.1	29 47.4	3 29.8	1 56.1	18 03.3	1 32.0	23 07.6	9 17.7	4 46.7	1 25.2
7 F	21 08 25	18 12 56	24 49 12	2♎13 28	4 25.0	1♒18.4	3 02.9	2 39.0	17 53.8	1 33.6	23 12.7	9 15.1	4 46.7	1 23.8
8 Sa	21 12 21	19 13 40	9♎34 06	16 50 31	4 21.8	2 50.3	2 38.1	3 21.9	17 44.6	1 35.1	23 17.7	9 12.5	4 46.6	1 22.3
9 Su	21 16 18	20 14 24	24 02 15	1♏09 04	4D 20.8	4 23.0	2 15.6	4 04.9	17 35.8	1 36.3	23 22.6	9 09.9	4 46.4	1 20.8
10 M	21 20 14	21 15 07	8♏10 49	15 07 31	4R 21.0	5 56.5	1 55.3	4 47.8	17 27.3	1 37.4	23 27.4	9 07.4	4 46.3	1 19.3
11 Tu	21 24 11	22 15 49	21 59 17	28 46 18	4 20.9	7 30.8	1 37.4	5 30.9	17 19.3	1 38.3	23 32.2	9 04.8	4 46.1	1 17.9
12 W	21 28 07	23 16 29	5♐28 48	12♐07 03	4 19.4	9 06.0	1 21.9	6 13.9	17 11.7	1 39.0	23 36.9	9 02.3	4 45.9	1 16.4
13 Th	21 32 04	24 17 09	18 41 20	25 11 56	4 15.5	10 42.0	1 08.9	6 57.0	17 04.4	1 39.5	23 41.5	8 59.8	4 45.6	1 14.9
14 F	21 36 00	25 17 47	1♑39 05	8♑03 04	4 08.8	12 18.9	0 58.4	7 40.1	16 57.6	1 39.8	23 46.1	8 57.3	4 45.3	1 13.4
15 Sa	21 39 57	26 18 25	14 24 03	20 42 14	3 59.4	13 56.6	0 50.4	8 23.2	16 51.1	1R 39.9	23 50.5	8 54.8	4 45.0	1 11.9
16 Su	21 43 54	27 19 01	26 57 45	3♒10 45	3 47.9	15 35.2	0 44.8	9 06.4	16 45.1	1 39.8	23 54.9	8 52.3	4 44.6	1 10.3
17 M	21 47 50	28 19 35	9♒21 20	15 29 34	3 35.2	17 14.6	0D 41.7	9 49.6	16 39.5	1 39.6	23 59.3	8 49.9	4 44.2	1 08.8
18 Tu	21 51 47	29 20 08	21 35 35	27 39 27	3 22.5	18 55.0	0 41.1	10 32.8	16 34.4	1 39.1	24 03.5	8 47.5	4 43.8	1 07.3
19 W	21 55 43	0♓20 39	3♓41 17	9♓41 14	3 10.9	20 36.3	0 42.9	11 16.0	16 29.7	1 38.5	24 07.7	8 45.1	4 43.3	1 05.8
20 Th	21 59 40	1 21 09	15 39 25	21 36 05	3 01.3	22 18.5	0 47.0	11 59.3	16 25.4	1 37.6	24 11.8	8 42.7	4 42.8	1 04.3
21 F	22 03 36	2 21 37	27 31 26	3♈25 45	2 54.3	24 01.6	0 53.4	12 42.6	16 21.5	1 36.6	24 15.8	8 40.3	4 42.3	1 02.8
22 Sa	22 07 33	3 22 03	9♈19 24	15 12 44	2 50.0	25 45.7	1 02.1	13 25.9	16 18.1	1 35.4	24 19.7	8 38.0	4 41.7	1 01.2
23 Su	22 11 29	4 22 28	21 06 12	27 00 16	2D 48.2	27 30.7	1 13.0	14 09.2	16 15.1	1 34.0	24 23.5	8 35.7	4 41.1	0 59.7
24 M	22 15 26	5 22 51	2♉55 28	8♉52 23	2 48.2	29 16.7	1 26.1	14 52.6	16 12.5	1 32.4	24 27.3	8 33.5	4 40.5	0 58.2
25 Tu	22 19 22	6 23 11	14 51 36	20 53 45	2 49.1	1♓03.7	1 41.2	15 36.0	16 10.4	1 30.6	24 31.0	8 31.2	4 39.9	0 56.7
26 W	22 23 19	7 23 30	26 59 30	3♊09 30	2R 49.9	2 51.7	1 58.3	16 19.4	16 08.7	1 28.7	24 34.5	8 29.0	4 39.2	0 55.2
27 Th	22 27 16	8 23 47	9♊24 24	15 44 50	2 49.6	4 40.7	2 17.4	17 02.8	16 07.5	1 26.5	24 38.1	8 26.8	4 38.5	0 53.7
28 F	22 31 12	9 24 02	22 11 22	28 44 32	2 47.7	6 30.7	2 38.4	17 46.3	16 06.7	1 24.2	24 41.5	8 24.7	4 37.7	0 52.2

Astro Data

	Dy Hr Mn
☿ D	5 8:38
♀ R	8 2:46
☽ 0S	10 10:46
☽ 0N	24 5:39
♃⚹♇	4 11:32
♆ R	5 3:14
☽ 0S	6 19:41
♃ R	15 14:58
♄⚼♅	16 2:53
♀ D	18 6:17
☽ 0N	20 13:29

Planet Ingress

	Dy Hr Mn
♃ ♏	13 12:52
☿ ♑	14 10:03
☉ ♒	20 13:28
♂ ♑	3 18:57
☿ ♒	6 15:21
☉ ♓	19 3:48
☿ ♓	24 21:44

Last Aspect / ☽ Ingress

Last Aspect Dy Hr Mn		☽ Ingress Dy Hr Mn
1 8:42	♀ □	♊ 2 12:21
4 16:41	♃ △	♋ 4 18:22
6 20:11	♃ □	♌ 6 21:21
8 22:12	♃ ⚹	♍ 8 22:59
10 20:06	☿ □	♎ 11 0:52
13 3:58	♃ ☌	♏ 13 4:02
14 22:38	☉ ⚹	♐ 15 8:49
16 23:03	♄ ☌	♑ 17 15:13
19 22:08	☉ ☌	♒ 19 23:22
21 17:15	♄ ⚹	♓ 22 9:41
24 6:54	♂ □	♈ 24 22:03
26 23:45	♂ △	♉ 27 10:56
28 21:19	☿ △	♊ 29 21:47

Last Aspect / ☽ Ingress

Last Aspect Dy Hr Mn		☽ Ingress Dy Hr Mn
1 1:14	♂ ☍	♋ 1 4:41
2 22:31	☿ ☍	♌ 3 7:38
4 20:56	♄ △	♍ 5 8:11
6 21:19	♄ □	♎ 7 8:23
8 22:49	♄ ⚹	♏ 9 10:03
10 23:34	☉ □	♐ 11 14:11
13 10:10	☉ ⚹	♑ 13 20:55
14 11:14	♂ ☌	♒ 16 5:51
18 15:38	☉ ☌	♓ 18 16:39
20 17:17	♄ □	♈ 21 5:02
23 13:13	☿ ⚹	♉ 23 18:05
25 0:48	♂ △	♊ 26 5:52
28 4:34	♄ ☍	♋ 28 14:17

☽ Phases & Eclipses

Dy Hr Mn	
5 20:09	○ 15♋00
12 14:01	☾ 21♎52
19 22:08	● 29♑21
28 2:16	☽ 7♉40
4 8:05	○ 15♌01
10 23:34	☾ 21♏44
18 15:38	● 29♒29
26 20:52	☽ 7♊46

Astro Data

1 January 1958
Julian Day # 21185
SVP 5♓50'36"
GC 26♐15.2 ⚳ 22♈50.0
Eris 8♈24.6 ⚴ 8♊14.8R
⚷ 14♒52.5 ⚶ 11♈47.7
☽ Mean ☊ 7♏21.5

1 February 1958
Julian Day # 21216
SVP 5♓50'31"
GC 26♐15.2 ⚳ 0♉55.7
Eris 8♈32.0 ⚴ 9♊58.9
⚷ 17♒05.4 ⚶ 20♈55.0
☽ Mean ☊ 5♏43.0

March 1958

LONGITUDE

Day	Sid.Time	☉	0 hr ☽	Noon ☽	True ☊	☿	♀	♂	⚳	♃	♄	♅	♆	♇
1 Sa	22 35 09	10♓24 15	5♋24 46	12♋12 20	2♏43.6	8♓21.6	3♒01.2	18♑29.7	16♋06.3	1♏21.7	24♐44.8	8♌22.6	4♏37.0	0♍50.7
2 Su	22 39 05	11 24 26	19 07 25	26 09 58	2R 37.6	10 13.5	3 25.7	19 13.2	16D 06.4	1R 19.0	24 48.1	8R 20.5	4R 36.2	0R 49.2
3 M	22 43 02	12 24 34	3♌19 47	10♌36 24	2 30.1	12 06.4	3 52.0	19 56.8	16 06.9	1 16.1	24 51.2	8 18.4	4 35.4	0 47.7
4 Tu	22 46 58	13 24 41	17 59 11	25 27 14	2 22.2	14 00.1	4 19.9	20 40.3	16 07.8	1 13.1	24 54.3	8 16.4	4 34.5	0 46.2
5 W	22 50 55	14 24 46	2♍59 31	10♍34 50	2 14.8	15 54.7	4 49.4	21 23.9	16 09.2	1 09.8	24 57.3	8 14.4	4 33.6	0 44.8
6 Th	22 54 51	15 24 49	18 11 52	25 49 16	2 08.9	17 50.1	5 20.5	22 07.5	16 10.9	1 06.4	25 00.2	8 12.5	4 32.7	0 43.3
7 F	22 58 48	16 24 50	3♎25 44	10♎59 59	2 05.0	19 46.2	5 53.0	22 51.1	16 13.1	1 02.9	25 03.0	8 10.6	4 31.8	0 41.8
8 Sa	23 02 45	17 24 49	18 30 55	25 57 33	2D 03.3	21 42.9	6 26.9	23 34.8	16 15.7	0 59.1	25 05.7	8 08.7	4 30.8	0 40.4
9 Su	23 06 41	18 24 47	3♏19 08	10♏35 03	2 03.4	23 40.1	7 02.2	24 18.5	16 18.7	0 55.2	25 08.3	8 06.9	4 29.8	0 39.0
10 M	23 10 38	19 24 43	17 44 57	24 48 34	2 04.6	25 37.6	7 38.8	25 02.2	16 22.1	0 51.1	25 10.8	8 05.1	4 28.8	0 37.5
11 Tu	23 14 34	20 24 37	1♐45 54	8♐36 59	2R 05.9	27 35.3	8 16.7	25 45.9	16 25.9	0 46.9	25 13.2	8 03.3	4 27.7	0 36.1
12 W	23 18 31	21 24 30	15 22 02	22 01 19	2 06.4	29 33.0	8 55.8	26 29.7	16 30.1	0 42.5	25 15.6	8 01.6	4 26.7	0 34.7
13 Th	23 22 27	22 24 21	28 35 10	5♑03 58	2 05.6	1♈30.3	9 36.0	27 13.5	16 34.7	0 37.9	25 17.8	8 00.0	4 25.6	0 33.3
14 F	23 26 24	23 24 11	11♑28 06	17 47 58	2 03.0	3 27.0	10 17.3	27 57.3	16 39.7	0 33.2	25 20.0	7 58.4	4 24.5	0 31.9
15 Sa	23 30 20	24 23 59	24 03 59	0♒16 32	1 58.6	5 22.9	10 59.7	28 41.1	16 45.1	0 28.3	25 22.0	7 56.8	4 23.3	0 30.6
16 Su	23 34 17	25 23 45	6♒25 59	12 32 41	1 52.8	7 17.4	11 43.2	29 25.0	16 50.8	0 23.3	25 24.0	7 55.2	4 22.2	0 29.2
17 M	23 38 14	26 23 29	18 36 57	24 39 05	1 46.3	9 10.4	12 27.6	0♒08.8	16 57.0	0 18.1	25 25.8	7 53.7	4 21.0	0 27.9
18 Tu	23 42 10	27 23 11	0♓39 21	6♓38 00	1 39.7	11 01.2	13 12.9	0 52.7	17 03.5	0 12.8	25 27.6	7 52.3	4 19.8	0 26.5
19 W	23 46 07	28 22 52	12 35 17	18 31 26	1 33.6	12 49.6	13 59.1	1 36.6	17 10.4	0 07.3	25 29.3	7 50.9	4 18.5	0 25.2
20 Th	23 50 03	29 22 30	24 26 40	0♈21 12	1 28.8	14 35.1	14 46.2	2 20.5	17 17.6	0 01.7	25 30.8	7 49.5	4 17.3	0 23.9
21 F	23 54 00	0♈22 06	6♈15 17	12 09 10	1 25.4	16 17.1	15 34.1	3 04.4	17 25.3	29♎56.0	25 32.3	7 48.2	4 16.0	0 22.6
22 Sa	23 57 56	1 21 41	18 03 06	23 57 22	1D 23.7	17 55.3	16 22.8	3 48.4	17 33.3	29 50.1	25 33.7	7 47.0	4 14.7	0 21.4
23 Su	0 01 53	2 21 13	29 52 18	5♉48 15	1 23.5	19 29.1	17 12.3	4 32.4	17 41.6	29 44.1	25 34.9	7 45.8	4 13.4	0 20.1
24 M	0 05 49	3 20 43	11♉45 34	17 44 41	1 24.5	20 58.3	18 02.5	5 16.3	17 50.3	29 38.0	25 36.1	7 44.6	4 12.1	0 18.9
25 Tu	0 09 46	4 20 11	23 46 01	29 50 03	1 26.2	22 22.2	18 53.4	6 00.3	17 59.3	29 31.7	25 37.2	7 43.5	4 10.7	0 17.7
26 W	0 13 42	5 19 37	5♊57 17	12♊08 14	1 27.9	23 40.7	19 45.0	6 44.3	18 08.7	29 25.4	25 38.2	7 42.4	4 09.3	0 16.5
27 Th	0 17 39	6 19 00	18 23 23	24 43 18	1R 29.2	24 53.3	20 37.2	7 28.3	18 18.4	29 18.9	25 39.0	7 41.4	4 07.9	0 15.3
28 F	0 21 36	7 18 21	1♋08 27	7♋39 20	1 29.7	25 59.8	21 30.0	8 12.4	18 28.4	29 12.3	25 39.8	7 40.4	4 06.5	0 14.1
29 Sa	0 25 32	8 17 40	14 16 21	20 59 51	1 29.1	26 59.8	22 23.5	8 56.4	18 38.8	29 05.6	25 40.5	7 39.5	4 05.1	0 13.0
30 Su	0 29 29	9 16 57	27 50 06	4♌47 12	1 27.5	27 53.1	23 17.5	9 40.5	18 49.5	28 58.9	25 41.1	7 38.7	4 03.7	0 11.9
31 M	0 33 25	10 16 11	11♌51 10	19 01 48	1 25.2	28 39.6	24 12.1	10 24.5	19 00.5	28 52.0	25 41.6	7 37.8	4 02.2	0 10.8

April 1958

LONGITUDE

Day	Sid.Time	☉	0 hr ☽	Noon ☽	True ☊	☿	♀	♂	⚳	♃	♄	♅	♆	♇
1 Tu	0 37 22	11♈15 22	26♌18 44	3♍41 26	1♏22.5	29♈19.1	25♒07.2	11♒08.6	19♋11.7	28♎45.0	25♐41.9	7♌37.1	4♏00.8	0♍09.7
2 W	0 41 18	12 14 32	11♍09 08	18 40 56	1R 19.9	29 51.6	26 02.9	11 52.7	19 23.3	28R 38.0	25 42.2	7R 36.4	3R 59.3	0R 08.6
3 Th	0 45 15	13 13 39	26 15 46	3♎52 27	1 17.9	0♉16.8	26 59.0	12 36.8	19 35.2	28 30.9	25 42.4	7 35.7	3 57.8	0 07.6
4 F	0 49 11	14 12 44	11♎29 45	19 06 22	1D 16.7	0 35.0	27 55.7	13 20.9	19 47.4	28 23.7	25R 42.5	7 35.1	3 56.3	0 06.6
5 Sa	0 53 08	15 11 48	26 41 06	4♏12 46	1 16.5	0 46.0	28 52.8	14 05.1	19 59.9	28 16.4	25 42.5	7 34.6	3 54.8	0 05.6
6 Su	0 57 05	16 10 49	11♏40 21	19 02 57	1 17.0	0R 50.1	29 50.4	14 49.2	20 12.6	28 09.1	25 42.3	7 34.1	3 53.2	0 04.6
7 M	1 01 01	17 09 48	26 19 52	3♐30 34	1 18.0	0 47.5	0♓48.4	15 33.4	20 25.7	28 01.7	25 42.1	7 33.6	3 51.7	0 03.7
8 Tu	1 04 58	18 08 46	10♐34 42	17 32 05	1 19.1	0 38.3	1 46.8	16 17.6	20 39.0	27 54.3	25 41.8	7 33.2	3 50.1	0 02.7
9 W	1 08 54	19 07 42	24 22 40	1♑06 36	1 20.0	0 23.0	2 45.7	17 01.7	20 52.5	27 46.8	25 41.4	7 32.9	3 48.6	0 01.8
10 Th	1 12 51	20 06 37	7♑44 05	14 15 27	1R 20.5	0 01.9	3 44.9	17 45.9	21 06.4	27 39.3	25 40.9	7 32.6	3 47.0	0 01.0
11 F	1 16 47	21 05 29	20 41 04	27 01 24	1 20.5	29♈35.5	4 44.6	18 30.1	21 20.5	27 31.7	25 40.3	7 32.4	3 45.4	0 00.1
12 Sa	1 20 44	22 04 20	3♒16 55	9♒28 08	1 20.0	29 04.5	5 44.6	19 14.3	21 34.8	27 24.1	25 39.6	7 32.2	3 43.8	29♌59.3
13 Su	1 24 40	23 03 09	15 35 32	21 39 38	1 19.2	28 29.5	6 44.9	19 58.6	21 49.4	27 16.5	25 38.8	7 32.1	3 42.2	29 58.5
14 M	1 28 37	24 01 56	27 40 56	3♓39 55	1 18.3	27 51.3	7 45.6	20 42.8	22 04.3	27 08.8	25 37.9	7D 32.0	3 40.6	29 57.7
15 Tu	1 32 34	25 00 42	9♓37 02	15 32 43	1 17.3	27 10.5	8 46.6	21 27.0	22 19.4	27 01.2	25 36.9	7 32.0	3 39.0	29 56.9
16 W	1 36 30	25 59 25	21 27 23	27 21 25	1 16.5	26 28.0	9 47.9	22 11.2	22 34.8	26 53.5	25 35.8	7 32.0	3 37.4	29 56.2
17 Th	1 40 27	26 58 07	3♈15 10	9♈08 57	1 16.0	25 44.7	10 49.5	22 55.4	22 50.3	26 45.8	25 34.6	7 32.1	3 35.8	29 55.5
18 F	1 44 23	27 56 47	15 03 07	20 57 55	1D 15.7	25 01.3	11 51.4	23 39.7	23 06.2	26 38.1	25 33.3	7 32.2	3 34.1	29 54.8
19 Sa	1 48 20	28 55 25	26 53 40	2♉50 36	1 15.7	24 18.6	12 53.6	24 23.9	23 22.2	26 30.4	25 31.9	7 32.4	3 32.5	29 54.2
20 Su	1 52 16	29 54 01	8♉48 59	14 49 05	1 15.7	23 37.4	13 56.1	25 08.1	23 38.5	26 22.7	25 30.5	7 32.7	3 30.9	29 53.5
21 M	1 56 13	0♉52 35	20 51 09	26 55 27	1R 15.8	22 58.4	14 58.8	25 52.3	23 55.0	26 15.1	25 28.9	7 33.0	3 29.2	29 52.9
22 Tu	2 00 09	1 51 08	3♊02 14	9♊11 47	1 15.8	22 22.2	16 01.7	26 36.5	24 11.7	26 07.4	25 27.2	7 33.4	3 27.6	29 52.4
23 W	2 04 06	2 49 38	15 24 23	21 40 19	1 15.6	21 49.3	17 05.0	27 20.7	24 28.6	25 59.8	25 25.5	7 33.8	3 26.0	29 51.8
24 Th	2 08 03	3 48 06	27 59 55	4♋23 27	1 15.4	21 20.2	18 08.4	28 04.9	24 45.8	25 52.3	25 23.7	7 34.3	3 24.3	29 51.3
25 F	2 11 59	4 46 32	10♋51 15	17 23 34	1 15.2	20 55.2	19 12.1	28 49.1	25 03.1	25 44.7	25 21.7	7 34.8	3 22.7	29 50.8
26 Sa	2 15 56	5 44 56	24 00 42	0♌42 53	1D 15.0	20 34.6	20 16.0	29 33.3	25 20.7	25 37.2	25 19.7	7 35.4	3 21.1	29 50.4
27 Su	2 19 52	6 43 17	7♌30 18	14 23 05	1 15.0	20 18.7	21 20.1	0♓17.5	25 38.4	25 29.8	25 17.6	7 36.0	3 19.4	29 50.0
28 M	2 23 49	7 41 37	21 21 17	28 24 51	1 15.3	20 07.5	22 24.4	1 01.6	25 56.4	25 22.4	25 15.4	7 36.7	3 17.8	29 49.6
29 Tu	2 27 45	8 39 54	5♍33 39	12♍47 22	1 15.9	20D 01.2	23 28.9	1 45.8	26 14.5	25 15.0	25 13.2	7 37.4	3 16.2	29 49.2
30 W	2 31 42	9 38 10	20 05 37	27 27 51	1 16.5	19 59.8	24 33.6	2 29.9	26 32.8	25 07.8	25 10.8	7 38.2	3 14.5	29 48.8

Astro Data	Dy Hr Mn
⚳ D	1 20:21
☽ 0S	6 6:34
☿0N	13 9:18
♃✶♇	14 20:53
☽ 0N	19 19:50
☉0N	21 3:06
☽ 0S	2 17:45
♄ R	4 19:38
☿ R	6 14:25
♅ D	15 8:27
☽ 0N	16 1:40
♃✶♄	29 21:05
☽ 0S	30 3:33
☿ D	30 6:57

Planet Ingress	Dy Hr Mn
☿ ♈	12 17:31
♂ ♒	17 7:11
♃ ♎R	20 19:13
☉ ♈	21 3:06
☿ ♉	2 19:17
♀ ♓	6 16:00
☿ ♈R	10 13:51
♇ ♌R	11 14:59
☉ ♉	20 14:27
♂ ♓	27 2:31

Last Aspect Dy Hr Mn		☽ Ingress	Dy Hr Mn
1 23:31	♂ ☍	♌	2 18:27
4 11:07	♄ △	♍	4 19:15
6 10:42	♄ □	♎	6 18:35
8 10:36	♄ ✶	♏	8 18:34
10 13:38	☿ △	♐	10 20:56
12 17:55	♄ ☌	♑	13 2:36
15 8:43	♂ ☌	♒	15 11:28
17 13:33	♄ ✶	♓	17 22:41
20 9:50	☉ ☌	♈	20 11:17
22 23:50	♃ ☍	♉	23 0:16
24 12:38	♀ □	♊	25 12:20
27 20:32	♃ △	♋	27 21:53
30 2:04	♃ □	♌	30 3:46

Last Aspect Dy Hr Mn		☽ Ingress	Dy Hr Mn
1 4:36	☿ △	♍	1 6:01
2 23:07	♄ □	♎	3 5:54
5 2:55	♀ △	♏	5 5:16
6 4:45	♂ □	♐	7 6:07
9 6:06	♃ ✶	♑	9 10:00
11 16:43	☿ □	♒	11 17:41
14 4:34	♇ ☍	♓	14 4:38
16 8:25	♄ □	♈	16 17:23
19 6:05	♇ △	♉	19 6:16
21 17:49	♇ □	♊	21 18:03
24 3:30	♇ ✶	♋	24 3:46
26 2:59	♃ □	♌	26 10:44
28 14:23	♇ ☌	♍	28 14:41
30 8:18	♄ □	♎	30 16:06

☽ Phases & Eclipses Dy Hr Mn	
5 18:28	○ 14♍41
12 10:48	☾ 21♐21
20 9:50	● 29♓17
28 11:18	☽ 7♋17
4 3:45	○ 13♎52
4 4:00	• A 0.013
10 23:50	☾ 20♑36
19 3:23	● 28♈34
19 3:26:44	• A 07'07"
26 21:36	☽ 6♌08

Astro Data

1 March 1958
Julian Day # 21244
SVP 5♓50'27"
GC 26♐15.3 ⚴ 12♉35.3
Eris 8♈46.5 ⚵ 17♊23.9
⚷ 19♒09.5 ⚶ 1♉12.5
☽ Mean ☊ 4♏14.0

1 April 1958
Julian Day # 21275
SVP 5♓50'25"
GC 26♐15.4 ⚴ 28♉25.4
Eris 9♈07.2 ⚵ 29♊09.6
⚷ 21♒07.4 ⚶ 13♉49.6
☽ Mean ☊ 2♏35.5

LONGITUDE — May 1958

Day	Sid.Time	☉	0 hr ☽	Noon ☽	True ☊	☿	♀	♂	⚳	♃	♄	♅	♆	♇
1 Th	2 35 38	10♉36 23	4♎53 23	12♎21 24	1♏17.2	20♈03.3	25♓38.6	3♓14.1	26♋51.3	25♎00.6	25♐08.4	7♌39.0	3♏12.9	29♌48.5
2 F	2 39 35	11 34 34	19 51 01	27 21 13	1R17.5	20 11.5	26 43.7	3 58.2	27 10.0	24R53.4	25R05.9	7 39.9	3R11.3	29R48.2
3 Sa	2 43 31	12 32 44	4♏50 59	12♏19 14	1 17.4	20 24.5	27 48.9	4 42.3	27 28.9	24 46.4	25 03.3	7 40.9	3 09.7	29 48.0
4 Su	2 47 28	13 30 52	19 44 57	27 07 11	1 16.7	20 42.1	28 54.4	5 26.4	27 47.9	24 39.4	25 00.6	7 41.9	3 08.1	29 47.7
5 M	2 51 25	14 28 58	4♐25 03	11♐37 47	1 15.3	21 04.1	0♈00.0	6 10.5	28 07.1	24 32.5	24 57.8	7 42.9	3 06.5	29 47.5
6 Tu	2 55 21	15 27 03	18 44 49	25 45 40	1 13.6	21 30.5	1 05.9	6 54.6	28 26.4	24 25.7	24 55.0	7 44.0	3 04.9	29 47.4
7 W	2 59 18	16 25 07	2♑40 02	9♑27 49	1 11.7	22 01.2	2 11.8	7 38.7	28 46.0	24 19.0	24 52.1	7 45.2	3 03.3	29 47.2
8 Th	3 03 14	17 23 09	16 09 00	22 43 43	1 10.0	22 35.8	3 18.0	8 22.8	29 05.7	24 12.4	24 49.1	7 46.4	3 01.7	29 47.1
9 F	3 07 11	18 21 09	29 12 15	5♒34 56	1 08.8	23 14.4	4 24.3	9 06.8	29 25.5	24 05.9	24 46.1	7 47.7	3 00.1	29 47.0
10 Sa	3 11 07	19 19 08	11♒52 12	18 04 33	1D08.4	23 56.8	5 30.7	9 50.9	29 45.5	23 59.5	24 43.0	7 49.0	2 58.6	29 47.0
11 Su	3 15 04	20 17 06	24 12 32	0♓16 42	1 08.7	24 42.7	6 37.3	10 34.9	0♌05.7	23 53.3	24 39.8	7 50.3	2 57.0	29D46.9
12 M	3 19 01	21 15 03	6♓17 39	12 16 00	1 09.7	25 32.2	7 44.1	11 18.9	0 26.0	23 47.1	24 36.5	7 51.7	2 55.5	29 46.9
13 Tu	3 22 57	22 12 58	18 12 18	24 07 09	1 11.2	26 25.0	8 50.9	12 02.8	0 46.5	23 41.0	24 33.2	7 53.2	2 54.0	29 47.0
14 W	3 26 54	23 10 52	0♈01 08	5♈54 45	1 12.8	27 21.1	9 57.9	12 46.8	1 07.1	23 35.1	24 29.8	7 54.7	2 52.4	29 47.0
15 Th	3 30 50	24 08 45	11 48 31	17 42 55	1 14.2	28 20.4	11 05.1	13 30.7	1 27.9	23 29.3	24 26.3	7 56.2	2 50.9	29 47.1
16 F	3 34 47	25 06 36	23 38 23	29 35 18	1R14.8	29 22.6	12 12.3	14 14.6	1 48.8	23 23.6	24 22.8	7 57.8	2 49.4	29 47.3
17 Sa	3 38 43	26 04 26	5♉34 03	11♉34 56	1 14.4	0♉27.8	13 19.7	14 58.4	2 09.8	23 18.1	24 19.2	7 59.5	2 48.0	29 47.4
18 Su	3 42 40	27 02 15	17 38 14	23 44 10	1 12.7	1 35.9	14 27.2	15 42.2	2 31.0	23 12.7	24 15.6	8 01.2	2 46.5	29 47.6
19 M	3 46 36	28 00 02	29 52 58	6♊04 46	1 09.8	2 46.8	15 34.8	16 26.0	2 52.3	23 07.4	24 11.9	8 02.9	2 45.0	29 47.8
20 Tu	3 50 33	28 57 48	12♊19 43	18 37 54	1 05.9	4 00.3	16 42.5	17 09.8	3 13.8	23 02.3	24 08.2	8 04.7	2 43.6	29 48.0
21 W	3 54 29	29 55 33	24 59 24	1♋24 16	1 01.3	5 16.5	17 50.3	17 53.5	3 35.3	22 57.4	24 04.4	8 06.5	2 42.2	29 48.3
22 Th	3 58 26	0♊53 16	7♋52 34	14 24 18	0 56.7	6 35.4	18 58.3	18 37.2	3 57.0	22 52.5	24 00.5	8 08.4	2 40.8	29 48.6
23 F	4 02 23	1 50 58	20 59 31	27 38 14	0 52.6	7 56.7	20 06.3	19 20.8	4 18.9	22 47.9	23 56.6	8 10.4	2 39.4	29 48.9
24 Sa	4 06 19	2 48 38	4♌20 27	11♌06 11	0 49.5	9 20.6	21 14.4	20 04.4	4 40.8	22 43.4	23 52.7	8 12.3	2 38.0	29 49.3
25 Su	4 10 16	3 46 16	17 55 27	24 48 15	0D47.9	10 47.0	22 22.6	20 48.0	5 02.9	22 39.0	23 48.7	8 14.4	2 36.7	29 49.7
26 M	4 14 12	4 43 53	1♍44 31	8♍44 14	0 47.6	12 15.8	23 30.9	21 31.5	5 25.1	22 34.8	23 44.7	8 16.4	2 35.3	29 50.1
27 Tu	4 18 09	5 41 28	15 47 19	22 53 34	0 48.5	13 47.1	24 39.3	22 15.0	5 47.4	22 30.8	23 40.6	8 18.5	2 34.0	29 50.5
28 W	4 22 05	6 39 02	0♎02 51	7♎14 51	0 49.8	15 20.9	25 47.8	22 58.4	6 09.8	22 26.9	23 36.5	8 20.7	2 32.7	29 51.0
29 Th	4 26 02	7 36 35	14 29 14	21 45 33	0R51.0	16 57.0	26 56.4	23 41.8	6 32.4	22 23.2	23 32.3	8 22.9	2 31.5	29 51.5
30 F	4 29 58	8 34 06	29 03 17	6♏21 49	0 51.1	18 35.6	28 05.0	24 25.1	6 55.0	22 19.7	23 28.2	8 25.1	2 30.2	29 52.1
31 Sa	4 33 55	9 31 36	13♏40 28	20 58 29	0 49.7	20 16.6	29 13.8	25 08.4	7 17.7	22 16.3	23 23.9	8 27.4	2 29.0	29 52.6

LONGITUDE — June 1958

Day	Sid.Time	☉	0 hr ☽	Noon ☽	True ☊	☿	♀	♂	⚳	♃	♄	♅	♆	♇
1 Su	4 37 52	10♊29 05	28♏15 05	5♐29 29	0♏46.4	21♉59.9	0♉22.6	25♓51.7	7♌40.6	22♎13.1	23♐19.7	8♌29.7	2♏27.8	29♌53.2
2 M	4 41 48	11 26 33	12♐40 54	19 48 36	0R41.4	23 45.7	1 31.5	26 34.9	8 03.5	22R10.0	23R15.5	8 32.1	2R26.6	29 53.8
3 Tu	4 45 45	12 24 00	26 51 54	3♑50 16	0 35.1	25 33.8	2 40.5	27 18.0	8 26.6	22 07.2	23 11.2	8 34.5	2 25.4	29 54.5
4 W	4 49 41	13 21 26	10♑43 13	17 30 28	0 28.4	27 24.4	3 49.6	28 01.1	8 49.7	22 04.5	23 06.9	8 36.9	2 24.2	29 55.1
5 Th	4 53 38	14 18 51	24 11 48	0♒47 10	0 21.9	29 17.2	4 58.8	28 44.2	9 13.0	22 02.0	23 02.5	8 39.4	2 23.1	29 55.8
6 F	4 57 34	15 16 15	7♒16 38	13 40 26	0 16.4	1♊12.3	6 08.0	29 27.2	9 36.3	21 59.6	22 58.2	8 41.9	2 22.0	29 56.6
7 Sa	5 01 31	16 13 39	19 58 49	26 12 13	0 12.5	3 09.7	7 17.4	0♈10.1	9 59.8	21 57.4	22 53.8	8 44.4	2 20.9	29 57.3
8 Su	5 05 28	17 11 02	2♓21 05	8♓25 58	0D10.4	5 09.2	8 26.8	0 53.0	10 23.3	21 55.5	22 49.4	8 47.0	2 19.9	29 58.1
9 M	5 09 24	18 08 25	14 27 27	20 26 09	0 10.0	7 10.7	9 36.2	1 35.8	10 46.9	21 53.6	22 45.0	8 49.7	2 18.8	29 58.9
10 Tu	5 13 21	19 05 47	26 22 42	2♈17 46	0 10.7	9 14.2	10 45.8	2 18.6	11 10.6	21 52.0	22 40.6	8 52.3	2 17.8	29 59.8
11 W	5 17 17	20 03 08	8♈11 59	14 06 02	0 12.0	11 19.5	11 55.4	3 01.2	11 34.4	21 50.5	22 36.2	8 55.0	2 16.8	0♍00.6
12 Th	5 21 14	21 00 29	20 00 30	25 56 01	0R12.9	13 26.5	13 05.1	3 43.9	11 58.3	21 49.2	22 31.7	8 57.8	2 15.9	0 01.5
13 F	5 25 10	21 57 50	1♉53 08	7♉52 23	0 12.6	15 34.8	14 14.9	4 26.4	12 22.3	21 48.1	22 27.3	9 00.5	2 15.0	0 02.4
14 Sa	5 29 07	22 55 10	13 54 16	19 59 11	0 10.6	17 44.4	15 24.7	5 08.9	12 46.4	21 47.2	22 22.9	9 03.3	2 14.1	0 03.4
15 Su	5 33 03	23 52 30	26 07 29	2♊19 30	0 06.4	19 54.9	16 34.6	5 51.3	13 10.5	21 46.5	22 18.5	9 06.2	2 13.2	0 04.3
16 M	5 37 00	24 49 49	8♊35 24	14 55 23	29♎59.9	22 06.2	17 44.5	6 33.6	13 34.8	21 45.9	22 14.0	9 09.0	2 12.3	0 05.3
17 Tu	5 40 57	25 47 07	21 19 29	27 47 42	29 51.6	24 17.9	18 54.6	7 15.8	13 59.1	21 45.6	22 09.6	9 11.9	2 11.5	0 06.4
18 W	5 44 53	26 44 25	4♋19 57	10♋56 06	29 42.2	26 29.8	20 04.6	7 58.0	14 23.5	21D45.4	22 05.2	9 14.9	2 10.7	0 07.4
19 Th	5 48 50	27 41 43	17 35 57	24 19 16	29 32.5	28 41.5	21 14.8	8 40.0	14 48.0	21 45.3	22 00.8	9 17.9	2 09.9	0 08.5
20 F	5 52 46	28 39 00	1♌05 45	7♌55 08	29 23.8	0♋52.8	22 25.0	9 22.0	15 12.5	21 45.5	21 56.4	9 20.9	2 09.2	0 09.6
21 Sa	5 56 43	29 36 16	14 47 06	21 41 23	29 16.7	3 03.5	23 35.2	10 03.9	15 37.1	21 45.9	21 52.0	9 23.9	2 08.5	0 10.7
22 Su	6 00 39	0♋33 31	28 37 42	5♍35 49	29 12.0	5 13.4	24 45.5	10 45.7	16 01.8	21 46.4	21 47.7	9 26.9	2 07.8	0 11.8
23 M	6 04 36	1 30 46	12♍35 30	19 36 36	29D09.5	7 22.1	25 55.9	11 27.4	16 26.6	21 47.1	21 43.3	9 30.0	2 07.1	0 13.0
24 Tu	6 08 32	2 28 00	26 38 56	3♎42 21	29 09.0	9 29.5	27 06.3	12 09.0	16 51.4	21 48.0	21 39.0	9 33.1	2 06.5	0 14.2
25 W	6 12 29	3 25 13	10♎46 44	17 51 56	29R09.4	11 35.5	28 16.7	12 50.5	17 16.3	21 49.0	21 34.7	9 36.3	2 05.9	0 15.4
26 Th	6 16 26	4 22 26	24 57 48	2♏04 08	29 09.6	13 39.9	29 27.3	13 31.9	17 41.3	21 50.3	21 30.4	9 39.5	2 05.3	0 16.7
27 F	6 20 22	5 19 39	9♏10 42	16 17 12	29 08.5	15 42.5	0♊37.8	14 13.2	18 06.3	21 51.7	21 26.2	9 42.7	2 04.8	0 17.9
28 Sa	6 24 19	6 16 50	23 23 18	0♐28 36	29 05.3	17 43.4	1 48.5	14 54.4	18 31.4	21 53.3	21 22.0	9 45.9	2 04.3	0 19.2
29 Su	6 28 15	7 14 02	7♐32 39	14 34 58	28 59.4	19 42.3	2 59.1	15 35.5	18 56.6	21 55.1	21 17.8	9 49.1	2 03.8	0 20.5
30 M	6 32 12	8 11 13	21 35 00	28 32 14	28 51.0	21 39.3	4 09.9	16 16.5	19 21.8	21 57.0	21 13.7	9 52.4	2 03.4	0 21.9

Astro Data

	Dy Hr Mn
♀0N	8 12:22
♇ D	11 22:01
☽0N	13 8:22
☽0S	27 11:21
♄⚼♅	30 23:21
☽0N	9 16:37
♂0N	14 7:12
♃ D	19 1:44
♃✶♄	22 18:10
☽0S	23 17:51

Planet Ingress

		Dy Hr Mn
♀	♈	5 11:59
⚳	♌	11 5:14
☿	♉	17 1:53
☉	♊	21 13:51
♀	♉	1 4:07
☿	♊	5 20:59
♂	♈	7 6:21
♇	♍	10 18:50
☊	♎R	16 11:42
☿	♋	20 2:20
☉	♋	21 21:57
♀	♊	26 23:08

Last Aspect / ☽ Ingress (May)

Dy Hr Mn	Aspect	☽ Ingress	Dy Hr Mn
2 15:55	♇ ✶	♏	2 16:14
4 16:23	♇ □	♐	4 16:43
6 18:59	♇ △	♑	6 19:21
8 14:42	♃ □	♒	9 1:29
11 11:01	♇ ☍	♓	11 11:27
13 12:53	♄ □	♈	13 23:58
16 12:24	♇ △	♉	16 12:50
18 23:50	♇ □	♊	19 0:14
21 9:01	♇ ✶	♋	21 9:23
23 3:19	♃ □	♌	23 16:15
25 20:42	♇ ☌	♍	25 21:00
27 13:19	♄ □	♎	27 23:55
30 1:20	♇ ✶	♏	30 1:33

Last Aspect / ☽ Ingress (June)

Dy Hr Mn	Aspect	☽ Ingress	Dy Hr Mn
1 2:42	♇ □	♐	1 2:54
3 5:13	♇ △	♑	3 5:23
5 8:47	☿ △	♒	5 10:34
7 19:19	♇ ☍	♓	7 19:24
9 16:38	♄ □	♈	10 7:20
12 5:09	♄ △	♉	12 20:12
14 2:02	♀ ☌	♊	15 7:31
17 7:59	☉ ☌	♋	17 16:04
19 7:26	♃ □	♌	19 22:04
21 15:35	♀ □	♍	22 2:22
23 23:45	♀ △	♎	24 5:42
25 18:42	♃ ☌	♏	26 8:30
27 10:52	☿ △	♐	28 11:12
30 0:36	♃ ✶	♑	30 14:32

☽ Phases & Eclipses

Dy Hr Mn	
3 12:23	○ 12♏34
3 12:13	• P 0.009
10 14:38	☾ 19♒25
18 19:00	● 27♉19
26 4:38	☽ 4♍26
1 20:55	○ 10♐50
9 6:59	☾ 17♓56
17 7:59	● 25♊38
24 9:45	☽ 2♎23

Astro Data

1 May 1958
Julian Day # 21305
SVP 5♓50'22"
GC 26♐15.4 ⚴ 15♊25.5
Eris 9♈27.1 ✻ 12♋12.0
⚷ 22♒21.7 ⚶ 26♉38.6
☽ Mean ☊ 1♏00.2

1 June 1958
Julian Day # 21336
SVP 5♓50'18"
GC 26♐15.5 ⚴ 3♋45.1
Eris 9♈42.5 ✻ 26♋18.9
⚷ 22♒42.8R ⚶ 10♊06.3
☽ Mean ☊ 29♎21.7

July 1958 — LONGITUDE

Day	Sid.Time	☉	0 hr ☽	Noon ☽	True ☊	☿	♀	♂	⚳	♃	♄	♅	♆	♇
1 Tu	6 36 08	9♋08 24	5♑26 10	12♑16 18	28♎40.6	23♋34.4	5♊20.7	16♈57.4	19♌47.1	21♎59.2	21♐09.6	9♌55.7	2♏03.0	0♍23.2
2 W	6 40 05	10 05 35	19 02 14	25 43 38	28R29.4	25 27.4	6 31.5	17 38.1	20 12.4	22 01.4	21R05.5	9 59.0	2R02.6	0 24.6
3 Th	6 44 01	11 02 46	2♒20 13	8♒51 50	28 18.3	27 18.4	7 42.4	18 18.8	20 37.8	22 03.9	21 01.5	10 02.4	2 02.2	0 26.0
4 F	6 47 58	11 59 57	15 18 28	21 40 08	28 08.5	29 07.3	8 53.4	18 59.4	21 03.3	22 06.5	20 57.5	10 05.7	2 01.9	0 27.4
5 Sa	6 51 55	12 57 08	27 57 02	4♓09 25	28 00.7	0♌54.2	10 04.4	19 39.8	21 28.8	22 09.3	20 53.5	10 09.1	2 01.6	0 28.8
6 Su	6 55 51	13 54 20	10♓17 37	16 22 06	27 55.4	2 39.1	11 15.5	20 20.1	21 54.4	22 12.3	20 49.6	10 12.5	2 01.3	0 30.3
7 M	6 59 48	14 51 31	22 23 21	28 21 56	27 52.4	4 21.9	12 26.6	21 00.3	22 20.0	22 15.4	20 45.8	10 15.9	2 01.1	0 31.8
8 Tu	7 03 44	15 48 43	4♈18 27	10♈13 33	27D51.3	6 02.6	13 37.8	21 40.4	22 45.7	22 18.7	20 42.0	10 19.4	2 00.9	0 33.3
9 W	7 07 41	16 45 56	16 07 53	22 02 09	27R51.3	7 41.3	14 49.0	22 20.3	23 11.4	22 22.2	20 38.2	10 22.8	2 00.7	0 34.8
10 Th	7 11 37	17 43 08	27 57 01	3♉53 10	27 51.2	9 17.9	16 00.3	23 00.1	23 37.2	22 25.8	20 34.5	10 26.3	2 00.6	0 36.3
11 F	7 15 34	18 40 22	9♉51 17	15 51 59	27 50.2	10 52.4	17 11.6	23 39.8	24 03.0	22 29.6	20 30.9	10 29.8	2 00.5	0 37.9
12 Sa	7 19 30	19 37 35	21 55 53	28 03 30	27 47.1	12 24.9	18 23.0	24 19.3	24 28.9	22 33.6	20 27.3	10 33.3	2 00.4	0 39.4
13 Su	7 23 27	20 34 49	4♊15 20	10♊31 48	27 41.6	13 55.2	19 34.5	24 58.7	24 54.9	22 37.7	20 23.8	10 36.9	2D00.4	0 41.0
14 M	7 27 24	21 32 04	16 53 11	23 19 44	27 33.5	15 23.5	20 46.0	25 37.9	25 20.9	22 42.0	20 20.3	10 40.4	2 00.4	0 42.6
15 Tu	7 31 20	22 29 19	29 51 33	6♋28 37	27 23.2	16 49.7	21 57.5	26 16.9	25 46.9	22 46.5	20 16.9	10 44.0	2 00.4	0 44.3
16 W	7 35 17	23 26 35	13♋10 49	19 57 53	27 11.4	18 13.7	23 09.1	26 55.8	26 13.0	22 51.1	20 13.5	10 47.5	2 00.4	0 45.9
17 Th	7 39 13	24 23 51	26 49 29	3♌45 10	26 59.4	19 35.5	24 20.8	27 34.6	26 39.2	22 55.8	20 10.3	10 51.1	2 00.5	0 47.6
18 F	7 43 10	25 21 07	10♌44 24	17 46 36	26 48.3	20 55.0	25 32.5	28 13.2	27 05.3	23 00.7	20 07.0	10 54.7	2 00.7	0 49.2
19 Sa	7 47 06	26 18 24	24 51 09	1♍57 26	26 39.3	22 12.4	26 44.2	28 51.6	27 31.6	23 05.8	20 03.9	10 58.4	2 00.8	0 50.9
20 Su	7 51 03	27 15 40	9♍04 51	16 12 53	26 32.9	23 27.3	27 56.0	29 29.8	27 57.8	23 11.0	20 00.8	11 02.0	2 01.0	0 52.6
21 M	7 54 59	28 12 58	23 21 01	0♎28 49	26 29.2	24 39.9	29 07.8	0♉07.8	28 24.1	23 16.4	19 57.8	11 05.6	2 01.2	0 54.4
22 Tu	7 58 56	29 10 15	7♎35 59	14 42 13	26D27.8	25 50.1	0♋19.7	0 45.7	28 50.5	23 21.9	19 54.9	11 09.3	2 01.5	0 56.1
23 W	8 02 53	0♌07 32	21 47 19	28 51 08	26R27.6	26 57.7	1 31.6	1 23.4	29 16.9	23 27.6	19 52.0	11 12.9	2 01.7	0 57.9
24 Th	8 06 49	1 04 50	5♏53 34	12♏54 31	26 27.4	28 02.7	2 43.6	2 00.9	29 43.3	23 33.4	19 49.3	11 16.6	2 02.0	0 59.6
25 F	8 10 46	2 02 09	19 53 56	26 51 43	26 25.9	29 05.0	3 55.6	2 38.2	0♍09.8	23 39.3	19 46.6	11 20.3	2 02.4	1 01.4
26 Sa	8 14 42	2 59 27	3♐47 47	10♐42 00	26 22.1	0♍04.5	5 07.6	3 15.3	0 36.3	23 45.4	19 43.9	11 23.9	2 02.8	1 03.2
27 Su	8 18 39	3 56 47	17 34 13	24 24 14	26 15.5	1 01.1	6 19.7	3 52.3	1 02.8	23 51.7	19 41.4	11 27.6	2 03.2	1 05.0
28 M	8 22 35	4 54 06	1♑11 51	7♑56 48	26 06.4	1 54.6	7 31.9	4 29.0	1 29.4	23 58.0	19 38.9	11 31.3	2 03.6	1 06.8
29 Tu	8 26 32	5 51 27	14 38 51	21 17 45	25 55.1	2 44.9	8 44.1	5 05.6	1 56.0	24 04.6	19 36.5	11 35.0	2 04.1	1 08.6
30 W	8 30 28	6 48 47	27 53 14	4♒25 08	25 42.9	3 32.0	9 56.3	5 41.9	2 22.6	24 11.2	19 34.2	11 38.7	2 04.6	1 10.5
31 Th	8 34 25	7 46 09	10♒53 14	17 17 27	25 30.8	4 15.5	11 08.6	6 18.0	2 49.3	24 18.0	19 32.0	11 42.4	2 05.1	1 12.3

August 1958 — LONGITUDE

Day	Sid.Time	☉	0 hr ☽	Noon ☽	True ☊	☿	♀	♂	⚳	♃	♄	♅	♆	♇
1 F	8 38 22	8♌43 32	23♒37 43	29♒54 04	25♎19.9	4♍55.4	12♋21.0	6♉53.9	3♍16.0	24♎24.9	19♐29.9	11♌46.1	2♏05.7	1♍14.2
2 Sa	8 42 18	9 40 55	6♓06 34	12♓15 25	25R11.1	5 31.4	13 33.4	7 29.6	3 42.7	24 32.0	19R27.8	11 49.8	2 06.3	1 16.1
3 Su	8 46 15	10 38 20	18 20 51	24 23 11	25 04.8	6 03.5	14 45.8	8 05.1	4 09.5	24 39.1	19 25.9	11 53.5	2 06.9	1 17.9
4 M	8 50 11	11 35 45	0♈22 48	6♈20 10	25 01.1	6 31.4	15 58.3	8 40.3	4 36.3	24 46.5	19 24.0	11 57.3	2 07.6	1 19.8
5 Tu	8 54 08	12 33 12	12 15 48	18 10 14	24D59.6	6 54.9	17 10.8	9 15.3	5 03.1	24 53.9	19 22.2	12 01.0	2 08.3	1 21.7
6 W	8 58 04	13 30 40	24 04 05	29 58 00	24 59.5	7 13.9	18 23.4	9 50.1	5 30.0	25 01.5	19 20.5	12 04.7	2 09.0	1 23.6
7 Th	9 02 01	14 28 10	5♉52 36	11♉48 36	24R59.8	7 28.0	19 36.1	10 24.6	5 56.9	25 09.1	19 18.9	12 08.4	2 09.8	1 25.6
8 F	9 05 57	15 25 40	17 46 41	23 47 30	24 59.5	7 37.2	20 48.8	10 58.9	6 23.8	25 17.0	19 17.4	12 12.1	2 10.6	1 27.5
9 Sa	9 09 54	16 23 13	29 51 44	6♊00 01	24 57.7	7R41.4	22 01.5	11 32.9	6 50.7	25 24.9	19 15.9	12 15.8	2 11.4	1 29.4
10 Su	9 13 51	17 20 46	12♊12 56	18 31 01	24 53.8	7 40.2	23 14.3	12 06.6	7 17.7	25 32.9	19 14.6	12 19.5	2 12.2	1 31.4
11 M	9 17 47	18 18 21	24 54 42	1♋24 20	24 47.6	7 33.6	24 27.2	12 40.1	7 44.7	25 41.1	19 13.3	12 23.2	2 13.1	1 33.3
12 Tu	9 21 44	19 15 57	8♋00 10	14 42 18	24 39.2	7 21.6	25 40.1	13 13.3	8 11.7	25 49.4	19 12.2	12 26.9	2 14.0	1 35.3
13 W	9 25 40	20 13 35	21 30 41	28 25 07	24 29.5	7 04.1	26 53.0	13 46.2	8 38.8	25 57.8	19 11.1	12 30.6	2 15.0	1 37.2
14 Th	9 29 37	21 11 13	5♌25 16	12♌30 36	24 19.3	6 41.2	28 06.0	14 18.8	9 05.9	26 06.4	19 10.2	12 34.3	2 15.9	1 39.2
15 F	9 33 33	22 08 54	19 40 30	26 54 13	24 10.0	6 12.9	29 19.0	14 51.1	9 33.0	26 15.0	19 09.3	12 38.0	2 16.9	1 41.2
16 Sa	9 37 30	23 06 35	4♍10 53	11♍29 37	24 02.4	5 39.5	0♌32.1	15 23.1	10 00.1	26 23.8	19 08.5	12 41.7	2 18.0	1 43.1
17 Su	9 41 26	24 04 17	18 49 32	26 09 45	23 57.2	5 01.4	1 45.2	15 54.7	10 27.3	26 32.6	19 07.8	12 45.3	2 19.0	1 45.1
18 M	9 45 23	25 02 01	3♎29 25	10♎47 50	23D54.4	4 18.9	2 58.3	16 26.1	10 54.4	26 41.6	19 07.2	12 49.0	2 20.1	1 47.1
19 Tu	9 49 20	25 59 46	18 04 21	25 18 26	23 53.8	3 32.6	4 11.5	16 57.1	11 21.6	26 50.7	19 06.7	12 52.6	2 21.2	1 49.1
20 W	9 53 16	26 57 31	2♏29 41	9♏37 48	23 54.3	2 43.3	5 24.8	17 27.8	11 48.8	26 59.8	19 06.4	12 56.3	2 22.4	1 51.1
21 Th	9 57 13	27 55 18	16 42 34	23 43 53	23R55.0	1 51.7	6 38.0	17 58.2	12 16.0	27 09.1	19 06.1	12 59.9	2 23.5	1 53.1
22 F	10 01 09	28 53 06	0♐41 42	7♐36 00	23 54.7	0 58.8	7 51.3	18 28.2	12 43.3	27 18.5	19 05.9	13 03.5	2 24.7	1 55.1
23 Sa	10 05 06	29 50 56	14 26 49	21 14 13	23 52.7	0 05.6	9 04.7	18 57.8	13 10.5	27 28.0	19D05.8	13 07.1	2 26.0	1 57.1
24 Su	10 09 02	0♍48 46	27 58 15	4♑38 58	23 48.5	29♌13.1	10 18.1	19 27.1	13 37.8	27 37.6	19 05.8	13 10.7	2 27.2	1 59.1
25 M	10 12 59	1 46 38	11♑16 26	17 50 41	23 42.1	28 22.4	11 31.6	19 56.1	14 05.1	27 47.3	19 05.9	13 14.3	2 28.5	2 01.1
26 Tu	10 16 55	2 44 31	24 21 44	0♒49 36	23 34.2	27 34.7	12 45.0	20 24.6	14 32.4	27 57.1	19 06.1	13 17.9	2 29.8	2 03.1
27 W	10 20 52	3 42 25	7♒14 19	13 35 52	23 25.3	26 51.0	13 58.6	20 52.8	14 59.7	28 07.0	19 06.3	13 21.4	2 31.2	2 05.1
28 Th	10 24 49	4 40 21	19 54 18	26 09 37	23 16.5	26 12.2	15 12.1	21 20.6	15 27.0	28 16.9	19 06.7	13 24.9	2 32.5	2 07.1
29 F	10 28 45	5 38 18	2♓21 54	8♓31 13	23 08.7	25 39.4	16 25.7	21 48.0	15 54.3	28 27.0	19 07.2	13 28.5	2 33.9	2 09.1
30 Sa	10 32 42	6 36 16	14 37 41	20 41 28	23 02.5	25 13.3	17 39.4	22 15.0	16 21.7	28 37.1	19 07.8	13 32.0	2 35.3	2 11.1
31 Su	10 36 38	7 34 17	26 42 45	2♈41 48	22 58.3	24 54.5	18 53.1	22 41.6	16 49.0	28 47.4	19 08.5	13 35.4	2 36.8	2 13.0

Astro Data Dy Hr Mn	Planet Ingress Dy Hr Mn	Last Aspect Dy Hr Mn	☽ Ingress Dy Hr Mn	Last Aspect Dy Hr Mn	☽ Ingress Dy Hr Mn	☽ Phases & Eclipses Dy Hr Mn
☽0N 7 1:56	☿ ♌ 4 23:46	2 11:26 ☿ ☍	♒ 2 19:44	1 1:24 ♃ △	♓ 1 12:11	1 6:05 ○ 8♑54
♆D 14 5:52	♂ ♉ 21 7:03	4 12:50 ♃ △	♓ 5 3:57	3 2:10 ♄ □	♈ 3 23:14	9 0:21 ☾ 16♈18
☽0S 21 0:33	♀ ♋ 22 5:26	6 20:50 ♄ □	♈ 7 15:18	6 1:50 ♃ ☍	♉ 6 12:04	16 18:33 ● 23♋42
	☉ ♌ 23 8:50	9 12:41 ♃ ☍	♉ 10 4:09	8 5:24 ♀ ⚹	♊ 9 0:16	23 14:20 ☽ 0♏13
☽0N 3 11:08	⚳ ♍ 25 3:08	11 18:02 ☉ ⚹	♊ 12 15:46	11 1:20 ♃ △	♋ 11 9:25	30 16:47 ○ 7♒00
☿R 9 18:47	☿ ♍ 26 10:08	14 16:28 ♂ ⚹	♋ 15 0:15	13 9:05 ♀ ☌	♌ 13 14:43	
☽0S 17 8:41		17 0:47 ♂ □	♌ 17 5:31	15 10:54 ♃ ⚹	♍ 15 17:07	7 17:49 ☾ 14♉42
♄D 24 0:31	♀ ♌ 16 1:28	19 6:32 ♂ △	♍ 19 8:42	17 0:30 ♄ □	♎ 17 18:17	15 3:33 ● 21♌49
☽0N 30 19:07	☿ ♌R 23 14:31	21 9:31 ♀ □	♎ 21 11:11	19 14:35 ♃ ☌	♏ 19 19:50	21 19:45 ☽ 28♏14
	☉ ♍ 23 15:46	23 8:31 ☿ ⚹	♏ 23 13:57	21 19:45 ☉ □	♐ 21 22:48	29 5:53 ○ 5♓24
		25 16:08 ☿ □	♐ 25 17:25	24 2:50 ☿ △	♑ 24 3:38	
		27 11:02 ♃ ⚹	♑ 27 21:53	26 6:35 ♃ □	♒ 26 10:28	
		29 17:05 ♃ □	♒ 30 3:52	28 16:09 ♃ △	♓ 28 19:25	
				30 15:13 ♂ ⚹	♈ 31 6:35	

Astro Data

1 July 1958
Julian Day # 21366
SVP 5♓50'13"
GC 26♐15.6 ⚴ 21♋31.1
Eris 9♈49.0 ⚵ 10♌04.4
⚷ 22♒07.0R ⚶ 23♊04.1
☽ Mean ☊ 27♎46.4

1 August 1958
Julian Day # 21397
SVP 5♓50'08"
GC 26♐15.6 ⚴ 9♌23.6
Eris 9♈45.5R ⚵ 24♌05.7
⚷ 20♒45.9R ⚶ 6♋07.7
☽ Mean ☊ 26♎07.9

LONGITUDE — September 1958

Day	Sid.Time	☉	0 hr ☽	Noon ☽	True ☊	☿	♀	♂	⚳	♃	♄	♅	♆	♇
1 M	10 40 35	8♍32 19	8♈38 55	14♈34 25	22♎56.1	24♌43.5	20♌06.8	23♉07.8	17♍16.4	28♎57.7	19♐09.2	13♌38.9	2♏38.2	2♍15.0
2 Tu	10 44 31	9 30 23	20 28 44	26 22 17	22D 55.8	24D 40.8	21 20.6	23 33.5	17 43.8	29 08.1	19 10.1	13 42.3	2 39.7	2 17.0
3 W	10 48 28	10 28 29	2♉15 32	8♉09 03	22 56.7	24 46.6	22 34.4	23 58.8	18 11.2	29 18.6	19 11.1	13 45.8	2 41.2	2 19.0
4 Th	10 52 24	11 26 37	14 03 21	19 59 04	22 58.2	25 01.1	23 48.3	24 23.6	18 38.6	29 29.2	19 12.1	13 49.2	2 42.8	2 21.0
5 F	10 56 21	12 24 47	25 56 47	1♊57 08	22R 59.6	25 24.1	25 02.2	24 48.0	19 06.0	29 39.8	19 13.3	13 52.5	2 44.3	2 23.0
6 Sa	11 00 17	13 22 58	8♊00 46	14 08 19	23 00.1	25 55.8	26 16.1	25 11.9	19 33.4	29 50.6	19 14.5	13 55.9	2 45.9	2 24.9
7 Su	11 04 14	14 21 12	20 20 24	26 37 35	22 59.3	26 35.7	27 30.1	25 35.2	20 00.9	0♏01.4	19 15.9	13 59.3	2 47.5	2 26.9
8 M	11 08 11	15 19 28	3♋00 26	9♋29 24	22 56.9	27 23.8	28 44.1	25 58.1	20 28.3	0 12.3	19 17.3	14 02.6	2 49.1	2 28.9
9 Tu	11 12 07	16 17 46	16 04 51	22 47 04	22 53.1	28 19.5	29 58.2	26 20.5	20 55.8	0 23.3	19 18.9	14 05.9	2 50.8	2 30.8
10 W	11 16 04	17 16 06	29 36 10	6♌32 09	22 48.2	29 22.5	1♍12.3	26 42.3	21 23.2	0 34.4	19 20.5	14 09.1	2 52.5	2 32.8
11 Th	11 20 00	18 14 28	13♌34 50	20 43 51	22 42.8	0♍32.4	2 26.4	27 03.6	21 50.7	0 45.5	19 22.2	14 12.4	2 54.2	2 34.7
12 F	11 23 57	19 12 52	27 58 39	5♍18 33	22 37.8	1 48.5	3 40.6	27 24.4	22 18.1	0 56.7	19 24.1	14 15.6	2 55.9	2 36.7
13 Sa	11 27 53	20 11 18	12♍42 41	20 10 05	22 33.8	3 10.3	4 54.8	27 44.5	22 45.6	1 08.0	19 26.0	14 18.8	2 57.6	2 38.6
14 Su	11 31 50	21 09 45	27 39 40	5♎10 20	22 31.3	4 37.2	6 09.1	28 04.1	23 13.1	1 19.3	19 28.0	14 22.0	2 59.4	2 40.5
15 M	11 35 46	22 08 15	12♎40 59	20 10 33	22D 30.3	6 08.7	7 23.3	28 23.1	23 40.6	1 30.7	19 30.1	14 25.1	3 01.2	2 42.4
16 Tu	11 39 43	23 06 46	27 38 04	5♏02 38	22 30.7	7 44.2	8 37.6	28 41.5	24 08.0	1 42.2	19 32.3	14 28.2	3 03.0	2 44.3
17 W	11 43 40	24 05 19	12♏23 32	19 40 09	22 32.0	9 23.1	9 52.0	28 59.3	24 35.5	1 53.8	19 34.6	14 31.3	3 04.8	2 46.2
18 Th	11 47 36	25 03 54	26 52 03	3♐58 55	22 33.4	11 04.9	11 06.4	29 16.5	25 03.0	2 05.4	19 37.0	14 34.3	3 06.7	2 48.1
19 F	11 51 33	26 02 30	11♐00 33	17 56 54	22R 34.5	12 49.1	12 20.8	29 33.0	25 30.5	2 17.1	19 39.5	14 37.3	3 08.5	2 50.0
20 Sa	11 55 29	27 01 08	24 48 00	1♑33 56	22 34.6	14 35.1	13 35.2	29 48.9	25 57.9	2 28.8	19 42.0	14 40.3	3 10.4	2 51.8
21 Su	11 59 26	27 59 47	8♑14 53	14 51 04	22 33.6	16 22.7	14 49.6	0♊04.1	26 25.4	2 40.6	19 44.7	14 43.3	3 12.3	2 53.7
22 M	12 03 22	28 58 29	21 22 43	27 50 05	22 31.5	18 11.4	16 04.1	0 18.7	26 52.9	2 52.5	19 47.5	14 46.2	3 14.2	2 55.5
23 Tu	12 07 19	29 57 12	4♒13 28	10♒33 08	22 28.6	20 00.8	17 18.6	0 32.6	27 20.3	3 04.4	19 50.3	14 49.1	3 16.2	2 57.4
24 W	12 11 15	0♎55 56	16 49 20	23 02 19	22 25.2	21 50.7	18 33.2	0 45.7	27 47.8	3 16.3	19 53.2	14 52.0	3 18.1	2 59.2
25 Th	12 15 12	1 54 43	29 12 22	5♓19 42	22 21.8	23 40.9	19 47.7	0 58.2	28 15.2	3 28.4	19 56.2	14 54.8	3 20.1	3 01.0
26 F	12 19 09	2 53 31	11♓24 33	17 27 09	22 18.8	25 31.1	21 02.3	1 10.0	28 42.6	3 40.4	19 59.3	14 57.6	3 22.0	3 02.8
27 Sa	12 23 05	3 52 21	23 27 43	29 26 30	22 16.6	27 21.2	22 16.9	1 21.1	29 10.1	3 52.6	20 02.5	15 00.3	3 24.0	3 04.5
28 Su	12 27 02	4 51 13	5♈23 43	11♈19 37	22D 15.3	29 10.9	23 31.6	1 31.4	29 37.5	4 04.7	20 05.8	15 03.0	3 26.0	3 06.3
29 M	12 30 58	5 50 07	17 14 27	23 08 31	22 15.0	1♎00.3	24 46.3	1 40.9	0♎04.9	4 17.0	20 09.1	15 05.7	3 28.1	3 08.1
30 Tu	12 34 55	6 49 04	29 02 06	4♉55 33	22 15.4	2 49.1	26 01.0	1 49.7	0 32.3	4 29.2	20 12.6	15 08.3	3 30.1	3 09.8

LONGITUDE — October 1958

Day	Sid.Time	☉	0 hr ☽	Noon ☽	True ☊	☿	♀	♂	⚳	♃	♄	♅	♆	♇
1 W	12 38 51	7♎48 02	10♉49 12	16♉43 26	22♎16.4	4♎37.3	27♍15.7	1♊57.7	0♎59.7	4♏41.6	20♐16.1	15♌10.9	3♏32.2	3♍11.5
2 Th	12 42 48	8 47 03	22 38 40	28 35 21	22 17.7	6 24.9	28 30.5	2 04.8	1 27.1	4 53.9	20 19.7	15 13.5	3 34.2	3 13.2
3 F	12 46 44	9 46 06	4♊33 57	10♊34 58	22 18.9	8 11.8	29 45.3	2 11.2	1 54.5	5 06.3	20 23.4	15 16.0	3 36.3	3 14.9
4 Sa	12 50 41	10 45 11	16 38 54	22 46 17	22 19.9	9 57.9	1♎00.1	2 16.8	2 21.9	5 18.8	20 27.2	15 18.5	3 38.4	3 16.6
5 Su	12 54 37	11 44 19	28 57 39	5♋13 33	22R 20.4	11 43.3	2 14.9	2 21.5	2 49.2	5 31.3	20 31.0	15 21.0	3 40.5	3 18.2
6 M	12 58 34	12 43 29	11♋34 30	18 00 58	22 20.4	13 28.0	3 29.8	2 25.4	3 16.6	5 43.9	20 34.9	15 23.4	3 42.6	3 19.9
7 Tu	13 02 31	13 42 41	24 33 24	1♌12 10	22 20.0	15 11.8	4 44.6	2 28.4	3 43.9	5 56.4	20 38.9	15 25.7	3 44.8	3 21.5
8 W	13 06 27	14 41 55	7♌57 34	14 49 47	22 19.4	16 54.9	5 59.6	2 30.5	4 11.2	6 09.1	20 43.0	15 28.1	3 46.9	3 23.1
9 Th	13 10 24	15 41 12	21 48 51	28 54 40	22 18.6	18 37.2	7 14.5	2R 31.8	4 38.6	6 21.7	20 47.2	15 30.3	3 49.0	3 24.7
10 F	13 14 20	16 40 31	6♍06 59	13♍25 20	22 17.9	20 18.8	8 29.4	2 32.1	5 05.8	6 34.4	20 51.4	15 32.6	3 51.2	3 26.2
11 Sa	13 18 17	17 39 53	20 49 07	28 17 32	22 17.4	21 59.6	9 44.4	2 31.6	5 33.1	6 47.1	20 55.8	15 34.8	3 53.4	3 27.8
12 Su	13 22 13	18 39 16	5♎49 37	13♎24 19	22D 17.1	23 39.6	10 59.4	2 30.2	6 00.4	6 59.9	21 00.1	15 36.9	3 55.5	3 29.3
13 M	13 26 10	19 38 41	21 00 26	28 36 46	22 17.1	25 18.9	12 14.4	2 27.8	6 27.6	7 12.7	21 04.6	15 39.0	3 57.7	3 30.8
14 Tu	13 30 06	20 38 09	6♏12 06	13♏45 16	22 17.2	26 57.5	13 29.5	2 24.6	6 54.8	7 25.5	21 09.2	15 41.1	3 59.9	3 32.3
15 W	13 34 03	21 37 39	21 15 09	28 40 49	22R 17.3	28 35.4	14 44.5	2 20.4	7 22.0	7 38.4	21 13.8	15 43.1	4 02.1	3 33.7
16 Th	13 38 00	22 37 10	6♐01 27	13♐16 24	22 17.3	0♏12.7	15 59.6	2 15.4	7 49.2	7 51.3	21 18.4	15 45.1	4 04.3	3 35.2
17 F	13 41 56	23 36 43	20 25 12	27 27 34	22 17.2	1 49.2	17 14.7	2 09.5	8 16.4	8 04.2	21 23.2	15 47.0	4 06.5	3 36.6
18 Sa	13 45 53	24 36 18	4♑23 21	11♑12 33	22 17.1	3 25.2	18 29.7	2 02.6	8 43.5	8 17.1	21 28.0	15 48.9	4 08.7	3 38.0
19 Su	13 49 49	25 35 55	17 55 20	24 31 55	22D 17.1	5 00.4	19 44.9	1 54.9	9 10.6	8 30.1	21 32.9	15 50.7	4 11.0	3 39.4
20 M	13 53 46	26 35 33	1♒02 38	7♒27 52	22 17.1	6 35.1	21 00.0	1 46.4	9 37.7	8 43.1	21 37.9	15 52.5	4 13.2	3 40.7
21 Tu	13 57 42	27 35 13	13 48 03	20 03 38	22 17.5	8 09.2	22 15.1	1 36.9	10 04.7	8 56.1	21 42.9	15 54.2	4 15.4	3 42.1
22 W	14 01 39	28 34 55	26 15 05	2♓22 54	22 18.0	9 42.7	23 30.2	1 26.6	10 31.8	9 09.1	21 48.0	15 55.9	4 17.7	3 43.4
23 Th	14 05 35	29 34 38	8♓27 33	14 29 28	22 18.8	11 15.6	24 45.4	1 15.5	10 58.8	9 22.2	21 53.2	15 57.5	4 19.9	3 44.7
24 F	14 09 32	0♏34 23	20 29 06	26 26 52	22 19.6	12 47.9	26 00.5	1 03.5	11 25.7	9 35.2	21 58.4	15 59.1	4 22.1	3 45.9
25 Sa	14 13 29	1 34 10	2♈23 09	8♈18 19	22 20.2	14 19.7	27 15.7	0 50.8	11 52.7	9 48.3	22 03.6	16 00.6	4 24.4	3 47.1
26 Su	14 17 25	2 33 59	14 12 43	20 06 39	22R 20.6	15 51.0	28 30.9	0 37.2	12 19.6	10 01.4	22 09.0	16 02.1	4 26.6	3 48.4
27 M	14 21 22	3 33 50	26 00 26	1♉54 20	22 20.4	17 21.7	29 46.1	0 22.9	12 46.5	10 14.5	22 14.4	16 03.5	4 28.9	3 49.5
28 Tu	14 25 18	4 33 43	7♉48 38	13 43 36	22 19.6	18 51.9	1♏01.3	0 07.8	13 13.3	10 27.6	22 19.8	16 04.9	4 31.1	3 50.7
29 W	14 29 15	5 33 38	19 39 29	25 36 32	22 18.1	20 21.6	2 16.5	29♉52.0	13 40.1	10 40.7	22 25.4	16 06.2	4 33.3	3 51.8
30 Th	14 33 11	6 33 34	1♊35 02	7♊35 15	22 16.1	21 50.7	3 31.8	29 35.5	14 06.9	10 53.9	22 30.9	16 07.5	4 35.6	3 53.0
31 F	14 37 08	7 33 33	13 37 29	19 42 00	22 13.8	23 19.3	4 47.0	29 18.4	14 33.6	11 07.0	22 36.6	16 08.7	4 37.8	3 54.0

Astro Data	Dy Hr Mn
☿ D	2 7:41
☽ 0S	13 18:35
♃ ⚹ ♇	22 19:20
☉ 0S	23 13:10
♃ ☌ ♆	24 16:12
☽ 0N	27 1:37
☿ 0S	30 22:37
♃ ∠ ♄	5 11:10
♀ 0S	6 8:49
♂ R	10 9:46
☽ 0S	11 5:29
☽ 0N	24 7:30

Planet Ingress	Dy Hr Mn
♃ ♏	7 8:52
♀ ♍	9 12:35
☿ ♍	11 1:10
♂ ♊	21 5:26
☉ ♎	23 13:09
☿ ♎	28 22:45
⚳ ♎	29 7:42
♀ ♎	3 16:44
☿ ♏	16 8:52
☉ ♏	23 22:11
♀ ♏	27 16:26
♂ ♉R	29 0:01

Last Aspect Dy Hr Mn	☽ Ingress Dy Hr Mn
2 17:43 ♃ ☍	♉ 2 19:24
4 22:26 ☿ □	♊ 5 8:07
7 13:50 ♀ ⚹	♋ 7 18:22
9 18:27 ♂ ⚹	♌ 10 0:42
11 22:45 ♂ □	♍ 12 3:19
14 0:24 ♂ △	♎ 14 3:44
15 10:55 ♄ ⚹	♏ 16 3:49
18 3:53 ♂ ☍	♐ 18 5:16
20 3:18 ☉ □	♑ 20 9:13
22 14:18 ☉ △	♒ 22 16:03
24 5:53 ♄ ⚹	♓ 25 1:33
27 7:03 ☿ ☍	♈ 27 13:07
29 5:53 ♄ △	♉ 30 1:58

Last Aspect Dy Hr Mn	☽ Ingress Dy Hr Mn
2 11:49 ♀ △	♊ 2 14:50
4 7:27 ♄ ☍	♋ 5 2:00
6 2:13 ☿ □	♌ 7 9:51
8 22:11 ♄ △	♍ 9 13:49
11 0:07 ♄ □	♎ 11 14:44
13 6:10 ☿ ☌	♏ 13 14:11
14 15:05 ♅ □	♐ 15 14:09
17 4:55 ☉ ⚹	♑ 17 16:23
19 14:07 ☉ □	♒ 19 22:04
22 3:53 ☉ △	♓ 22 7:19
24 2:55 ♄ □	♈ 24 19:10
27 7:08 ♀ ☍	♉ 27 8:07
29 20:22 ♂ ☌	♊ 29 20:49

☽ Phases & Eclipses Dy Hr Mn	
6 10:24	☾ 13♊19
13 12:02	● 20♍11
20 3:18	☽ 26♐40
27 21:44	○ 4♈16
6 1:20	☾ 12♋17
12 20:52	● 19♎01
12 20:54:55	● T 05'11"
19 14:07	☽ 25♑41
27 15:41	○ 3♉43
27 15:27	● A 0.782

Astro Data

1 September 1958
Julian Day # 21428
SVP 5♓50'05"
GC 26♐15.7 ⚵ 26♌27.0
Eris 9♈32.8R ⚶ 7♍42.5
⚷ 19♒11.0R ⚴ 18♋29.2
☽ Mean ☊ 24♎29.4

1 October 1958
Julian Day # 21458
SVP 5♓50'03"
GC 26♐15.8 ⚵ 11♍58.1
Eris 9♈15.0R ⚶ 20♍17.2
⚷ 18♒01.2R ⚴ 29♋13.3
☽ Mean ☊ 22♎54.0

November 1958 LONGITUDE

Day	Sid.Time	☉	0 hr ☽	Noon ☽	True ☊	☿	♀	♂	⚳	♃	♄	♅	♆	♇
1 Sa	14 41 04	8♏33 34	25♊49 10	1♋59 17	22♎11.4	24♏47.3	6♏02.3	29♉00.6	15♎00.4	11♏20.2	22♐42.3	16♌09.9	4♏40.1	3♍55.1
2 Su	14 45 01	9 33 37	8♋12 43	14 29 50	22R 09.4	26 14.7	7 17.5	28R 42.2	15 27.0	11 33.3	22 48.0	16 11.0	4 42.3	3 56.1
3 M	14 48 58	10 33 42	20 51 00	27 16 36	22 07.9	27 41.6	8 32.8	28 23.3	15 53.7	11 46.5	22 53.8	16 12.0	4 44.6	3 57.1
4 Tu	14 52 54	11 33 50	3♌47 00	10♌22 33	22D 07.4	29 07.9	9 48.1	28 03.8	16 20.3	11 59.7	22 59.7	16 13.0	4 46.8	3 58.1
5 W	14 56 51	12 33 59	17 03 34	23 50 20	22 07.8	0♐33.5	11 03.4	27 43.9	16 46.8	12 12.9	23 05.6	16 14.0	4 49.0	3 59.1
6 Th	15 00 47	13 34 10	0♍43 01	7♍41 44	22 08.8	1 58.4	12 18.7	27 23.5	17 13.4	12 26.0	23 11.5	16 14.9	4 51.3	4 00.0
7 F	15 04 44	14 34 24	14 46 30	21 57 09	22 10.3	3 22.6	13 34.0	27 02.7	17 39.9	12 39.2	23 17.5	16 15.7	4 53.5	4 00.9
8 Sa	15 08 40	15 34 39	29 13 27	6♎34 55	22 11.5	4 46.0	14 49.4	26 41.6	18 06.3	12 52.4	23 23.6	16 16.5	4 55.7	4 01.8
9 Su	15 12 37	16 34 57	14♎00 58	21 30 48	22R 12.1	6 08.6	16 04.7	26 20.2	18 32.7	13 05.6	23 29.7	16 17.3	4 57.9	4 02.6
10 M	15 16 33	17 35 16	29 03 31	6♏38 02	22 11.5	7 30.2	17 20.1	25 58.5	18 59.1	13 18.8	23 35.8	16 18.0	5 00.1	4 03.4
11 Tu	15 20 30	18 35 37	14♏13 12	21 47 47	22 09.6	8 50.8	18 35.4	25 36.7	19 25.4	13 31.9	23 42.0	16 18.6	5 02.3	4 04.2
12 W	15 24 26	19 36 00	29 20 34	6♐50 22	22 06.4	10 10.2	19 50.8	25 14.7	19 51.6	13 45.1	23 48.2	16 19.2	5 04.5	4 04.9
13 Th	15 28 23	20 36 25	14♐16 05	21 36 45	22 02.2	11 28.4	21 06.1	24 52.6	20 17.8	13 58.2	23 54.5	16 19.7	5 06.7	4 05.7
14 F	15 32 20	21 36 51	28 51 35	5♑59 58	21 57.8	12 45.2	22 21.5	24 30.5	20 44.0	14 11.4	24 00.9	16 20.1	5 08.9	4 06.4
15 Sa	15 36 16	22 37 18	13♑01 27	19 55 49	21 53.8	14 00.4	23 36.9	24 08.5	21 10.1	14 24.5	24 07.2	16 20.5	5 11.0	4 07.0
16 Su	15 40 13	23 37 47	26 43 02	3♒23 11	21 50.7	15 13.7	24 52.3	23 46.5	21 36.1	14 37.6	24 13.6	16 20.9	5 13.2	4 07.7
17 M	15 44 09	24 38 17	9♒56 31	16 23 25	21D 49.0	16 25.1	26 07.6	23 24.7	22 02.1	14 50.8	24 20.1	16 21.2	5 15.4	4 08.3
18 Tu	15 48 06	25 38 48	22 44 20	28 59 48	21 48.7	17 34.1	27 23.0	23 03.0	22 28.1	15 03.8	24 26.5	16 21.4	5 17.5	4 08.8
19 W	15 52 02	26 39 21	5♓10 24	11♓16 44	21 49.7	18 40.6	28 38.4	22 41.6	22 54.0	15 16.9	24 33.1	16 21.6	5 19.6	4 09.4
20 Th	15 55 59	27 39 54	17 19 25	23 19 05	21 51.3	19 44.1	29 53.8	22 20.5	23 19.8	15 30.0	24 39.6	16 21.7	5 21.7	4 09.9
21 F	15 59 55	28 40 29	29 16 20	5♈11 47	21 53.1	20 44.3	1♐09.1	21 59.7	23 45.6	15 43.0	24 46.2	16R 21.8	5 23.8	4 10.4
22 Sa	16 03 52	29 41 06	11♈05 58	16 59 26	21R 54.2	21 40.7	2 24.5	21 39.3	24 11.3	15 56.0	24 52.8	16 21.8	5 25.9	4 10.8
23 Su	16 07 49	0♐41 43	22 52 39	28 46 07	21 54.1	22 32.8	3 39.9	21 19.3	24 36.9	16 09.0	24 59.4	16 21.7	5 28.0	4 11.3
24 M	16 11 45	1 42 22	4♉40 12	10♉35 17	21 52.1	23 20.0	4 55.3	20 59.8	25 02.5	16 22.0	25 06.1	16 21.6	5 30.1	4 11.7
25 Tu	16 15 42	2 43 02	16 31 41	22 29 42	21 48.2	24 01.7	6 10.7	20 40.7	25 28.0	16 34.9	25 12.8	16 21.5	5 32.1	4 12.0
26 W	16 19 38	3 43 43	28 29 32	4♊31 26	21 42.3	24 37.3	7 26.1	20 22.2	25 53.5	16 47.9	25 19.6	16 21.3	5 34.2	4 12.4
27 Th	16 23 35	4 44 26	10♊35 32	16 41 59	21 34.8	25 05.8	8 41.5	20 04.3	26 18.8	17 00.7	25 26.3	16 21.0	5 36.2	4 12.7
28 F	16 27 31	5 45 10	22 50 56	29 02 28	21 26.3	25 26.7	9 56.8	19 46.9	26 44.2	17 13.6	25 33.1	16 20.7	5 38.2	4 12.9
29 Sa	16 31 28	6 45 56	5♋16 41	11♋33 43	21 17.8	25R 39.0	11 12.2	19 30.2	27 09.4	17 26.5	25 39.9	16 20.3	5 40.2	4 13.2
30 Su	16 35 25	7 46 42	17 53 39	24 16 36	21 10.0	25 42.0	12 27.6	19 14.1	27 34.6	17 39.3	25 46.8	16 19.9	5 42.2	4 13.4

December 1958 LONGITUDE

Day	Sid.Time	☉	0 hr ☽	Noon ☽	True ☊	☿	♀	♂	⚳	♃	♄	♅	♆	♇
1 M	16 39 21	8♐47 31	0♌42 43	7♌12 08	21♎03.8	25♐34.8	13♐43.0	18♉58.7	27♎59.7	17♏52.0	25♐53.6	16♌19.4	5♏44.2	4♍13.6
2 Tu	16 43 18	9 48 20	13 45 02	20 21 36	20R 59.7	25R 17.0	14 58.4	18R 44.0	28 24.8	18 04.8	26 00.5	16R 18.9	5 46.1	4 13.7
3 W	16 47 14	10 49 11	27 02 01	3♍46 29	20D 57.8	24 48.1	16 13.8	18 30.1	28 49.7	18 17.5	26 07.4	16 18.3	5 48.0	4 13.8
4 Th	16 51 11	11 50 04	10♍35 10	17 28 15	20 57.6	24 08.0	17 29.2	18 16.8	29 14.6	18 30.2	26 14.4	16 17.6	5 50.0	4 13.9
5 F	16 55 07	12 50 58	24 25 49	1♎27 57	20 58.6	23 17.0	18 44.7	18 04.3	29 39.4	18 42.8	26 21.3	16 16.9	5 51.8	4 13.9
6 Sa	16 59 04	13 51 53	8♎34 35	15 45 35	20R 59.4	22 15.9	20 00.1	17 52.6	0♏04.2	18 55.4	26 28.3	16 16.2	5 53.7	4R 14.0
7 Su	17 03 00	14 52 49	23 00 43	0♏19 33	20 59.2	21 06.1	21 15.5	17 41.7	0 28.8	19 07.9	26 35.2	16 15.4	5 55.6	4 14.0
8 M	17 06 57	15 53 47	7♏41 33	15 06 02	20 56.8	19 49.5	22 30.9	17 31.6	0 53.4	19 20.4	26 42.2	16 14.5	5 57.4	4 13.9
9 Tu	17 10 54	16 54 46	22 32 09	29 58 58	20 52.0	18 28.3	23 46.3	17 22.3	1 17.9	19 32.9	26 49.2	16 13.6	5 59.2	4 13.8
10 W	17 14 50	17 55 46	7♐25 26	14♐50 29	20 44.6	17 05.3	25 01.7	17 13.8	1 42.3	19 45.3	26 56.3	16 12.6	6 01.0	4 13.7
11 Th	17 18 47	18 56 47	22 13 01	29 32 00	20 35.4	15 43.3	26 17.2	17 06.2	2 06.6	19 57.7	27 03.3	16 11.6	6 02.8	4 13.6
12 F	17 22 43	19 57 48	6♑46 28	13♑55 36	20 25.3	14 25.0	27 32.6	16 59.4	2 30.8	20 10.0	27 10.4	16 10.6	6 04.5	4 13.4
13 Sa	17 26 40	20 58 51	20 58 45	27 55 26	20 15.5	13 12.9	28 48.0	16 53.4	2 55.0	20 22.3	27 17.4	16 09.4	6 06.3	4 13.3
14 Su	17 30 36	21 59 53	4♒45 19	11♒28 19	20 07.2	12 09.0	0♑03.4	16 48.2	3 19.0	20 34.5	27 24.5	16 08.3	6 08.0	4 13.0
15 M	17 34 33	23 00 57	18 04 27	24 33 57	20 01.0	11 14.8	1 18.8	16 43.9	3 42.9	20 46.7	27 31.5	16 07.0	6 09.7	4 12.8
16 Tu	17 38 29	24 02 00	0♓57 09	7♓14 30	19 57.2	10 31.2	2 34.2	16 40.4	4 06.8	20 58.8	27 38.6	16 05.8	6 11.3	4 12.5
17 W	17 42 26	25 03 04	13 26 31	19 33 50	19D 55.7	9 58.6	3 49.6	16 37.8	4 30.5	21 10.9	27 45.7	16 04.5	6 13.0	4 12.2
18 Th	17 46 23	26 04 09	25 37 05	1♈36 58	19 55.6	9 37.1	5 05.0	16 35.9	4 54.1	21 22.9	27 52.8	16 03.1	6 14.6	4 11.8
19 F	17 50 19	27 05 14	7♈34 10	13 29 23	19R 56.2	9D 26.3	6 20.4	16D 34.9	5 17.7	21 34.8	27 59.9	16 01.7	6 16.2	4 11.4
20 Sa	17 54 16	28 06 19	19 23 19	25 16 37	19 56.2	9 25.7	7 35.8	16 34.7	5 41.1	21 46.7	28 07.0	16 00.2	6 17.7	4 11.0
21 Su	17 58 12	29 07 24	1♉09 56	7♉03 51	19 54.6	9 34.5	8 51.2	16 35.3	6 04.4	21 58.5	28 14.0	15 58.7	6 19.3	4 10.6
22 M	18 02 09	0♑08 30	12 58 57	18 55 42	19 50.7	9 52.1	10 06.5	16 36.6	6 27.6	22 10.2	28 21.1	15 57.2	6 20.8	4 10.1
23 Tu	18 06 05	1 09 36	24 54 34	0♊55 56	19 44.0	10 17.6	11 21.9	16 38.7	6 50.7	22 21.9	28 28.2	15 55.6	6 22.2	4 09.6
24 W	18 10 02	2 10 42	7♊00 07	13 07 21	19 34.5	10 50.3	12 37.2	16 41.6	7 13.7	22 33.5	28 35.3	15 53.9	6 23.7	4 09.1
25 Th	18 13 58	3 11 49	19 17 50	25 31 41	19 22.6	11 29.3	13 52.6	16 45.2	7 36.6	22 45.1	28 42.4	15 52.3	6 25.1	4 08.5
26 F	18 17 55	4 12 56	1♋48 56	8♋09 35	19 09.4	12 14.1	15 07.9	16 49.6	7 59.4	22 56.5	28 49.4	15 50.5	6 26.5	4 08.0
27 Sa	18 21 52	5 14 03	14 33 34	21 00 48	18 55.9	13 03.9	16 23.3	16 54.7	8 22.0	23 07.9	28 56.5	15 48.8	6 27.9	4 07.3
28 Su	18 25 48	6 15 10	27 31 09	4♌04 28	18 43.4	13 58.2	17 38.6	17 00.5	8 44.6	23 19.3	29 03.5	15 47.0	6 29.3	4 06.7
29 M	18 29 45	7 16 18	10♌40 36	17 19 26	18 33.1	14 56.4	18 54.0	17 06.9	9 07.0	23 30.5	29 10.6	15 45.1	6 30.6	4 06.0
30 Tu	18 33 41	8 17 26	24 00 49	0♍44 41	18 25.5	15 58.2	20 09.3	17 14.1	9 29.3	23 41.7	29 17.6	15 43.2	6 31.9	4 05.4
31 W	18 37 38	9 18 35	7♍30 58	14 19 38	18 21.0	17 03.1	21 24.6	17 21.9	9 51.4	23 52.8	29 24.6	15 41.3	6 33.2	4 04.6

Astro Data

	Dy Hr Mn
☽0S	7 15:53
⚳0S	8 11:31
☽0N	20 14:14
♅R	22 4:49
♃□♅	24 11:23
☿R	30 7:15
☽0S	5 0:32
♇R	6 15:43
☽0N	17 22:50
☿D	20 1:26
♂D	20 6:45

Planet Ingress

	Dy Hr Mn
☿ ♐	5 2:36
♀ ♐	20 13:59
☉ ♐	22 19:29
⚳ ♏	6 7:57
♀ ♑	14 10:55
☉ ♑	22 8:40

Last Aspect / ☽ Ingress

Last Aspect Dy Hr Mn		☽ Ingress Dy Hr Mn
31 17:46 ♄ ☍	♋	1 8:09
3 14:01 ♂ ⚹	♌	3 17:02
5 18:39 ♂ □	♍	5 22:45
7 20:13 ♂ △	♎	8 1:16
9 15:11 ♄ ⚹	♏	10 1:30
11 17:55 ♂ ☍	♐	12 1:03
13 15:49 ♄ ☌	♑	14 1:54
15 19:14 ♂ △	♒	16 5:53
18 8:33 ♀ □	♓	18 13:56
20 21:34 ☉ △	♈	21 1:28
23 4:14 ♄ △	♉	23 14:30
25 8:27 ♂ ☌	♊	26 3:00
28 5:11 ♄ ☍	♋	28 13:51
30 2:43 ♂ ⚹	♌	30 22:41

Last Aspect / ☽ Ingress

Last Aspect Dy Hr Mn		☽ Ingress Dy Hr Mn
2 22:15 ♄ △	♍	3 5:18
5 3:13 ♄ □	♎	5 9:31
7 5:50 ♄ ⚹	♏	7 11:28
8 18:57 ♃ ☌	♐	9 12:02
11 7:53 ♄ ☌	♑	11 12:46
12 22:46 ♃ ⚹	♒	13 15:38
15 17:35 ♄ ⚹	♓	15 22:12
18 4:26 ♄ □	♈	18 8:45
20 18:19 ☉ △	♉	20 21:38
22 18:37 ♃ ☍	♊	23 10:09
25 18:08 ♄ ☍	♋	25 20:33
27 15:59 ♃ △	♌	28 4:33
30 9:24 ♄ △	♍	30 10:41

☽ Phases & Eclipses

Dy Hr Mn	
4 14:19	☾ 11♌40
11 6:34	● 18♏22
18 4:59	☽ 25♒21
26 10:17	○ 3♊39
4 1:24	☾ 11♍23
10 17:23	● 18♐09
17 23:52	☽ 25♓33
26 3:54	○ 3♋52

Astro Data

1 November 1958
Julian Day # 21489
SVP 5♓50'00"
GC 26♐15.9 ⚴ 26♍44.6
Eris 8♈56.4R ⚵ 2♎20.8
⚷ 17♒39.6 ⚶ 8♌00.8
☽ Mean ☊ 21♎15.5

1 December 1958
Julian Day # 21519
SVP 5♓49'55"
GC 26♐15.9 ⚴ 9♎25.1
Eris 8♈43.6R ⚵ 12♎36.3
⚷ 18♒17.0 ⚶ 12♌35.1
☽ Mean ☊ 19♎40.2

LONGITUDE — January 1959

Day	Sid.Time	☉	0 hr ☽	Noon ☽	True ☊	☿	♀	♂	⚳	♃	♄	♅	♆	♇
1 Th	18 41 34	10♑19 44	21♍10 41	28♍04 08	18♎19.0	18♐10.7	22♑39.9	17♉30.4	10♏13.5	24♏03.8	29♐31.7	15♌39.4	6♏34.4	4♍03.9
2 F	18 45 31	11 20 53	5♎00 03	11♎58 26	18R 18.6	19 20.8	23 55.2	17 39.6	10 35.4	24 14.8	29 38.6	15R 37.4	6 35.6	4R 03.1
3 Sa	18 49 27	12 22 03	18 59 19	26 02 40	18 18.5	20 33.1	25 10.5	17 49.3	10 57.1	24 25.6	29 45.6	15 35.3	6 36.8	4 02.3
4 Su	18 53 24	13 23 13	3♏08 26	10♏16 26	18 17.4	21 47.3	26 25.8	17 59.7	11 18.8	24 36.4	29 52.6	15 33.2	6 37.9	4 01.5
5 M	18 57 21	14 24 23	17 26 27	24 38 07	18 13.9	23 03.2	27 41.1	18 10.7	11 40.3	24 47.1	29 59.6	15 31.1	6 39.0	4 00.6
6 Tu	19 01 17	15 25 34	1♐50 59	9♐04 30	18 07.5	24 20.7	28 56.4	18 22.3	12 01.6	24 57.7	0♑06.5	15 29.0	6 40.1	3 59.7
7 W	19 05 14	16 26 44	16 18 00	23 30 45	17 58.1	25 39.6	0♒11.7	18 34.6	12 22.8	25 08.2	0 13.4	15 26.8	6 41.2	3 58.8
8 Th	19 09 10	17 27 55	0♑41 58	7♑50 51	17 46.3	26 59.8	1 27.0	18 47.3	12 43.9	25 18.6	0 20.3	15 24.6	6 42.2	3 57.9
9 F	19 13 07	18 29 05	14 56 35	21 58 28	17 33.3	28 21.1	2 42.2	19 00.7	13 04.8	25 29.0	0 27.2	15 22.4	6 43.2	3 57.0
10 Sa	19 17 03	19 30 15	28 55 49	5♒48 05	17 20.5	29 43.4	3 57.5	19 14.6	13 25.6	25 39.2	0 34.0	15 20.1	6 44.2	3 56.0
11 Su	19 21 00	20 31 25	12♒34 52	19 15 52	17 09.1	1♑06.8	5 12.7	19 29.0	13 46.2	25 49.3	0 40.8	15 17.9	6 45.1	3 55.0
12 M	19 24 56	21 32 34	25 50 58	2♓20 12	17 00.1	2 31.0	6 28.0	19 44.0	14 06.6	25 59.4	0 47.6	15 15.5	6 46.0	3 54.0
13 Tu	19 28 53	22 33 43	8♓43 41	15 01 42	16 54.0	3 56.1	7 43.2	19 59.5	14 26.9	26 09.3	0 54.4	15 13.2	6 46.9	3 52.9
14 W	19 32 50	23 34 51	21 14 38	27 22 58	16 50.6	5 21.9	8 58.4	20 15.5	14 47.0	26 19.1	1 01.2	15 10.8	6 47.7	3 51.8
15 Th	19 36 46	24 35 58	3♈27 15	9♈28 04	16D 49.3	6 48.5	10 13.6	20 32.0	15 07.0	26 28.8	1 07.9	15 08.4	6 48.5	3 50.8
16 F	19 40 43	25 37 05	15 26 06	21 22 01	16R 49.2	8 15.8	11 28.7	20 48.9	15 26.8	26 38.4	1 14.5	15 06.0	6 49.2	3 49.6
17 Sa	19 44 39	26 38 11	27 16 31	3♉10 20	16 49.1	9 43.8	12 43.9	21 06.4	15 46.4	26 47.9	1 21.2	15 03.6	6 50.0	3 48.5
18 Su	19 48 36	27 39 16	9♉04 08	14 58 39	16 47.8	11 12.5	13 59.0	21 24.3	16 05.8	26 57.3	1 27.8	15 01.1	6 50.7	3 47.4
19 M	19 52 32	28 40 20	20 54 30	26 52 20	16 44.5	12 41.8	15 14.2	21 42.6	16 25.1	27 06.6	1 34.4	14 58.6	6 51.3	3 46.2
20 Tu	19 56 29	29 41 24	2♊52 45	8♊56 14	16 38.6	14 11.7	16 29.3	22 01.4	16 44.2	27 15.8	1 41.0	14 56.1	6 52.0	3 45.0
21 W	20 00 25	0♒42 26	15 03 16	21 14 13	16 29.9	15 42.2	17 44.3	22 20.6	17 03.1	27 24.9	1 47.5	14 53.6	6 52.6	3 43.8
22 Th	20 04 22	1 43 28	27 29 24	3♋49 01	16 18.9	17 13.4	18 59.4	22 40.2	17 21.8	27 33.8	1 53.9	14 51.1	6 53.1	3 42.6
23 F	20 08 19	2 44 29	10♋13 12	16 41 56	16 06.4	18 45.2	20 14.5	23 00.2	17 40.3	27 42.6	2 00.4	14 48.6	6 53.7	3 41.3
24 Sa	20 12 15	3 45 29	23 15 10	29 52 42	15 53.6	20 17.6	21 29.5	23 20.5	17 58.7	27 51.4	2 06.8	14 46.0	6 54.2	3 40.1
25 Su	20 16 12	4 46 28	6♌34 18	13♌19 39	15 41.6	21 50.6	22 44.5	23 41.3	18 16.8	27 59.9	2 13.2	14 43.4	6 54.6	3 38.8
26 M	20 20 08	5 47 27	20 08 23	27 00 03	15 31.7	23 24.2	23 59.5	24 02.4	18 34.8	28 08.4	2 19.5	14 40.9	6 55.1	3 37.5
27 Tu	20 24 05	6 48 25	3♍54 17	10♍50 38	15 24.4	24 58.5	25 14.5	24 23.9	18 52.5	28 16.8	2 25.7	14 38.3	6 55.5	3 36.2
28 W	20 28 01	7 49 22	17 48 43	24 48 11	15 20.2	26 33.4	26 29.4	24 45.7	19 10.1	28 25.0	2 32.0	14 35.7	6 55.8	3 34.8
29 Th	20 31 58	8 50 18	1♎48 42	8♎50 02	15D 18.4	28 08.9	27 44.3	25 07.9	19 27.4	28 33.1	2 38.2	14 33.1	6 56.2	3 33.5
30 F	20 35 54	9 51 13	15 51 56	22 54 16	15 18.4	29 45.2	28 59.2	25 30.4	19 44.6	28 41.0	2 44.3	14 30.5	6 56.5	3 32.1
31 Sa	20 39 51	10 52 08	29 56 54	6♏59 42	15R 18.9	1♒22.1	0♓14.1	25 53.2	20 01.5	28 48.9	2 50.4	14 27.8	6 56.7	3 30.8

LONGITUDE — February 1959

Day	Sid.Time	☉	0 hr ☽	Noon ☽	True ☊	☿	♀	♂	⚳	♃	♄	♅	♆	♇
1 Su	20 43 48	11♒53 02	14♏02 35	21♏05 27	15♎18.6	2♒59.7	1♓29.0	26♉16.4	20♏18.2	28♏56.6	2♑56.5	14♌25.2	6♏56.9	3♍29.4
2 M	20 47 44	12 53 56	28 08 10	5♐10 36	15R 16.5	4 38.0	2 43.9	26 39.8	20 34.7	29 04.1	3 02.5	14R 22.6	6 57.1	3R 28.0
3 Tu	20 51 41	13 54 49	12♐12 31	19 13 41	15 11.9	6 17.0	3 58.7	27 03.6	20 50.9	29 11.5	3 08.4	14 20.0	6 57.3	3 26.6
4 W	20 55 37	14 55 41	26 13 48	3♑12 30	15 04.7	7 56.7	5 13.5	27 27.6	21 07.0	29 18.8	3 14.3	14 17.3	6 57.4	3 25.1
5 Th	20 59 34	15 56 32	10♑09 25	17 04 07	14 55.5	9 37.2	6 28.3	27 52.0	21 22.7	29 26.0	3 20.2	14 14.7	6 57.5	3 23.7
6 F	21 03 30	16 57 22	23 56 10	0♒45 08	14 45.1	11 18.5	7 43.1	28 16.6	21 38.3	29 33.0	3 26.0	14 12.1	6 57.6	3 22.3
7 Sa	21 07 27	17 58 10	7♒30 37	14 12 16	14 34.8	13 00.5	8 57.8	28 41.5	21 53.6	29 39.8	3 31.7	14 09.4	6R 57.6	3 20.8
8 Su	21 11 23	18 58 58	20 49 47	27 22 55	14 25.6	14 43.4	10 12.5	29 06.7	22 08.7	29 46.6	3 37.4	14 06.8	6 57.6	3 19.3
9 M	21 15 20	19 59 44	3♓51 33	10♓15 37	14 18.3	16 27.0	11 27.2	29 32.2	22 23.5	29 53.1	3 43.0	14 04.2	6 57.5	3 17.9
10 Tu	21 19 17	21 00 29	16 35 10	22 50 20	14 13.4	18 11.4	12 41.9	29 57.9	22 38.1	29 59.5	3 48.6	14 01.6	6 57.4	3 16.4
11 W	21 23 13	22 01 12	29 01 20	5♈08 29	14D 10.9	19 56.6	13 56.5	0♊23.9	22 52.4	0♐05.8	3 54.1	13 59.0	6 57.3	3 14.9
12 Th	21 27 10	23 01 54	11♈12 10	17 12 49	14 10.5	21 42.7	15 11.1	0 50.1	23 06.4	0 11.9	3 59.6	13 56.4	6 57.2	3 13.4
13 F	21 31 06	24 02 34	23 10 58	29 07 11	14 11.4	23 29.5	16 25.6	1 16.5	23 20.2	0 17.9	4 04.9	13 53.8	6 57.0	3 11.9
14 Sa	21 35 03	25 03 12	5♉02 02	10♉56 11	14 12.7	25 17.2	17 40.2	1 43.2	23 33.7	0 23.7	4 10.3	13 51.2	6 56.8	3 10.4
15 Su	21 38 59	26 03 49	16 50 17	22 44 59	14R 13.6	27 05.6	18 54.7	2 10.1	23 46.9	0 29.3	4 15.5	13 48.7	6 56.5	3 08.9
16 M	21 42 56	27 04 24	28 40 58	4♊38 54	14 13.3	28 54.8	20 09.1	2 37.2	23 59.9	0 34.8	4 20.7	13 46.1	6 56.2	3 07.4
17 Tu	21 46 52	28 04 57	10♊39 26	16 43 10	14 11.2	0♓44.8	21 23.6	3 04.6	24 12.6	0 40.1	4 25.9	13 43.6	6 55.9	3 05.9
18 W	21 50 49	29 05 29	22 50 41	29 02 31	14 07.2	2 35.4	22 38.0	3 32.1	24 25.0	0 45.3	4 30.9	13 41.1	6 55.6	3 04.3
19 Th	21 54 46	0♓05 59	5♋19 07	11♋40 51	14 01.5	4 26.6	23 52.3	3 59.9	24 37.1	0 50.3	4 35.9	13 38.6	6 55.2	3 02.8
20 F	21 58 42	1 06 27	18 08 00	24 40 46	13 54.5	6 18.4	25 06.6	4 27.8	24 48.9	0 55.1	4 40.9	13 36.1	6 54.8	3 01.3
21 Sa	22 02 39	2 06 53	1♌19 11	8♌03 12	13 47.1	8 10.7	26 20.9	4 56.0	25 00.4	0 59.8	4 45.7	13 33.6	6 54.3	2 59.8
22 Su	22 06 35	3 07 18	14 52 37	21 47 09	13 40.1	10 03.3	27 35.1	5 24.3	25 11.7	1 04.3	4 50.5	13 31.2	6 53.8	2 58.2
23 M	22 10 32	4 07 40	28 46 21	5♍49 43	13 34.4	11 56.1	28 49.3	5 52.8	25 22.6	1 08.7	4 55.3	13 28.8	6 53.3	2 56.7
24 Tu	22 14 28	5 08 01	12♍56 37	20 06 25	13 30.4	13 48.9	0♈03.5	6 21.4	25 33.2	1 12.8	4 59.9	13 26.4	6 52.8	2 55.2
25 W	22 18 25	6 08 21	27 18 25	4♎31 54	13D 28.4	15 41.6	1 17.6	6 50.3	25 43.5	1 16.8	5 04.5	13 24.0	6 52.2	2 53.7
26 Th	22 22 21	7 08 39	11♎46 11	19 00 37	13 28.2	17 33.9	2 31.6	7 19.3	25 53.5	1 20.7	5 09.0	13 21.7	6 51.6	2 52.1
27 F	22 26 18	8 08 55	26 14 37	3♏27 39	13 29.3	19 25.5	3 45.7	7 48.5	26 03.2	1 24.3	5 13.4	13 19.3	6 51.0	2 50.6
28 Sa	22 30 15	9 09 10	10♏39 16	17 49 05	13 30.7	21 16.1	4 59.7	8 17.8	26 12.6	1 27.8	5 17.8	13 17.0	6 50.3	2 49.1

Astro Data

	Dy Hr Mn
☽0S	1 7:28
♄⚻♅	8 23:26
☽0N	14 8:55
☽0S	28 14:18
♄△♇	5 23:41
♆ R	7 13:35
☽0N	10 18:50
☽0S	24 22:38
♀0N	26 8:44

Planet Ingress

		Dy Hr Mn
♄	♑	5 13:33
♀	♒	7 8:16
☿	♑	10 16:48
☉	♒	20 19:19
☿	♒	30 15:41
♀	♓	31 7:28
♃	♐	10 13:46
♂	♊	10 13:57
☿	♓	17 2:15
☉	♓	19 9:38
♀	♈	24 10:53

Last Aspect / ☽ Ingress

Last Aspect Dy Hr Mn		☽ Ingress	Dy Hr Mn
1 14:33	♄ □	♎	1 15:21
3 18:21	♄ ✶	♏	3 18:42
5 17:34	♀ ✶	♐	5 20:56
7 15:57	☿ ☌	♑	7 22:50
9 18:07	♃ ✶	♒	10 1:52
12 0:06	♃ □	♓	12 7:39
14 9:53	♃ △	♈	14 17:09
16 21:27	☉ □	♉	17 5:33
19 15:56	☉ △	♊	19 18:16
21 4:28	♀ △	♋	22 4:47
24 8:19	♃ △	♌	24 12:13
26 14:00	♃ □	♍	26 17:13
28 18:15	♃ ✶	♎	28 20:54
30 23:22	♀ △	♏	31 0:05

Last Aspect / ☽ Ingress

Last Aspect Dy Hr Mn		☽ Ingress	Dy Hr Mn
2 1:30	♃ ☌	♐	2 3:11
3 3:39	♅ △	♑	4 6:29
6 9:51	♃ ✶	♒	6 10:40
8 16:27	♃ □	♓	8 16:50
9 14:30	♀ ☌	♈	11 1:55
13 0:47	☉ ✶	♉	13 13:47
15 22:23	☿ □	♊	16 2:39
18 12:06	☉ △	♋	18 13:51
20 12:52	♀ △	♌	20 21:38
21 21:40	♅ ☌	♍	23 2:06
23 23:52	☿ ☍	♎	25 4:29
26 2:40	♅ ✶	♏	27 6:14

☽ Phases & Eclipses

Dy Hr Mn		
2 10:50	☾	11♎18
9 5:34	●	18♑13
16 21:27	☽	26♈01
24 19:32	○	4♌05
31 19:06	☾	11♏10
7 19:22	●	18♒17
15 19:20	☽	26♉22
23 8:54	○	4♍00

Astro Data

1 January 1959
Julian Day # 21550
SVP 5♓49'50"
GC 26♐16.0 ⚴ 20♎00.6
Eris 8♈39.8 ⚵ 20♎52.0
⚷ 19♒48.0 ⚶ 10♌59.7R
☽ Mean ☊ 18♎01.7

1 February 1959
Julian Day # 21581
SVP 5♓49'46"
GC 26♐16.1 ⚴ 26♎28.9
Eris 8♈46.9 ⚵ 25♎22.1
⚷ 21♒52.4 ⚶ 3♌39.4R
☽ Mean ☊ 16♎23.2

March 1959 — LONGITUDE

Day	Sid.Time	☉	0 hr ☽	Noon ☽	True ☊	☿	♀	♂	⚳	♃	♄	♅	♆	♇
1 Su	22 34 11	10♓09 24	24♏56 47	2♐02 08	13♎31.9	23♓05.4	6♈13.6	8♊47.3	26♏21.6	1♐31.1	5♑22.1	13♌14.8	6♏49.6	2♍47.6
2 M	22 38 08	11 09 36	9♐04 57	16 05 04	13R 32.1	24 52.9	7 27.5	9 16.9	26 30.3	1 34.2	5 26.3	13R 12.5	6R 48.9	2R 46.1
3 Tu	22 42 04	12 09 47	23 02 24	29 56 51	13 30.8	26 38.3	8 41.4	9 46.7	26 38.7	1 37.2	5 30.4	13 10.3	6 48.1	2 44.6
4 W	22 46 01	13 09 56	6♑48 20	13♑36 48	13 28.1	28 21.0	9 55.2	10 16.7	26 46.7	1 40.0	5 34.4	13 08.1	6 47.3	2 43.1
5 Th	22 49 57	14 10 03	20 22 11	27 04 26	13 24.2	0♈00.5	11 09.0	10 46.8	26 54.3	1 42.6	5 38.4	13 06.0	6 46.5	2 41.6
6 F	22 53 54	15 10 09	3♒43 29	10♒19 15	13 19.6	1 36.4	12 22.8	11 17.0	27 01.7	1 45.0	5 42.3	13 03.9	6 45.7	2 40.1
7 Sa	22 57 50	16 10 13	16 51 42	23 20 48	13 15.0	3 08.0	13 36.5	11 47.4	27 08.6	1 47.2	5 46.1	13 01.8	6 44.8	2 38.6
8 Su	23 01 47	17 10 16	29 46 29	6♓08 46	13 10.9	4 34.8	14 50.1	12 17.9	27 15.2	1 49.2	5 49.8	12 59.7	6 43.9	2 37.1
9 M	23 05 44	18 10 16	12♓27 40	18 43 13	13 07.8	5 56.3	16 03.7	12 48.5	27 21.4	1 51.1	5 53.5	12 57.7	6 43.0	2 35.6
10 Tu	23 09 40	19 10 15	24 55 30	1♈04 39	13D 05.9	7 11.9	17 17.3	13 19.3	27 27.3	1 52.8	5 57.0	12 55.7	6 42.0	2 34.2
11 W	23 13 37	20 10 12	7♈10 50	13 14 16	13 05.3	8 21.2	18 30.8	13 50.2	27 32.8	1 54.2	6 00.5	12 53.8	6 41.0	2 32.7
12 Th	23 17 33	21 10 06	19 15 13	25 14 00	13 05.8	9 23.6	19 44.2	14 21.2	27 37.9	1 55.5	6 03.9	12 51.9	6 40.0	2 31.3
13 F	23 21 30	22 09 59	1♉10 59	7♉06 32	13 07.1	10 18.7	20 57.6	14 52.4	27 42.7	1 56.6	6 07.2	12 50.0	6 39.0	2 29.9
14 Sa	23 25 26	23 09 49	13 01 08	18 55 15	13 08.8	11 06.2	22 11.0	15 23.7	27 47.0	1 57.6	6 10.4	12 48.2	6 37.9	2 28.4
15 Su	23 29 23	24 09 37	24 49 24	0♊44 09	13 10.4	11 45.8	23 24.3	15 55.0	27 51.0	1 58.3	6 13.5	12 46.4	6 36.9	2 27.0
16 M	23 33 19	25 09 24	6♊40 03	12 37 42	13 11.6	12 17.2	24 37.5	16 26.5	27 54.6	1 58.9	6 16.5	12 44.7	6 35.8	2 25.7
17 Tu	23 37 16	26 09 07	18 37 42	24 40 39	13R 12.0	12 40.2	25 50.7	16 58.1	27 57.8	1 59.2	6 19.5	12 43.0	6 34.6	2 24.3
18 W	23 41 12	27 08 49	0♋47 10	6♋57 49	13 11.8	12 55.0	27 03.8	17 29.9	28 00.7	1R 59.4	6 22.3	12 41.3	6 33.5	2 22.9
19 Th	23 45 09	28 08 28	13 13 08	19 33 39	13 10.8	13R 01.3	28 16.8	18 01.7	28 03.1	1 59.4	6 25.1	12 39.7	6 32.3	2 21.6
20 F	23 49 06	29 08 05	25 59 47	2♌31 54	13 09.2	12 59.5	29 29.8	18 33.6	28 05.1	1 59.2	6 27.8	12 38.1	6 31.1	2 20.2
21 Sa	23 53 02	0♈07 40	9♌10 16	15 55 03	13 07.5	12 49.7	0♉42.8	19 05.6	28 06.8	1 58.8	6 30.3	12 36.6	6 29.9	2 18.9
22 Su	23 56 59	1 07 13	22 46 16	29 43 50	13 05.8	12 32.4	1 55.6	19 37.7	28 08.0	1 58.2	6 32.8	12 35.1	6 28.6	2 17.6
23 M	0 00 55	2 06 43	6♍47 27	13♍56 45	13 04.5	12 07.9	3 08.4	20 09.9	28 08.9	1 57.4	6 35.2	12 33.6	6 27.4	2 16.3
24 Tu	0 04 52	3 06 11	21 11 10	28 30 00	13D 03.7	11 37.1	4 21.2	20 42.2	28R 09.3	1 56.5	6 37.5	12 32.2	6 26.1	2 15.0
25 W	0 08 48	4 05 37	5♎52 27	13♎17 36	13 03.5	11 00.5	5 33.9	21 14.5	28 09.4	1 55.4	6 39.7	12 30.9	6 24.8	2 13.7
26 Th	0 12 45	5 05 01	20 44 30	28 12 08	13 03.7	10 19.0	6 46.5	21 47.0	28 09.0	1 54.0	6 41.8	12 29.6	6 23.5	2 12.5
27 F	0 16 41	6 04 24	5♏39 32	13♏05 45	13 04.2	9 33.6	7 59.0	22 19.5	28 08.2	1 52.5	6 43.9	12 28.3	6 22.1	2 11.3
28 Sa	0 20 38	7 03 44	20 29 53	27 51 10	13 04.8	8 45.4	9 11.5	22 52.1	28 07.1	1 50.8	6 45.8	12 27.1	6 20.8	2 10.1
29 Su	0 24 35	8 03 03	5♐08 56	12♐22 37	13 05.3	7 55.2	10 23.9	23 24.8	28 05.5	1 49.0	6 47.6	12 25.9	6 19.4	2 08.9
30 M	0 28 31	9 02 20	19 31 49	26 36 13	13 05.6	7 04.2	11 36.3	23 57.6	28 03.5	1 46.9	6 49.4	12 24.8	6 18.0	2 07.7
31 Tu	0 32 28	10 01 35	3♑35 39	10♑30 02	13R 05.6	6 13.5	12 48.5	24 30.4	28 01.1	1 44.7	6 51.0	12 23.8	6 16.6	2 06.6

April 1959 — LONGITUDE

Day	Sid.Time	☉	0 hr ☽	Noon ☽	True ☊	☿	♀	♂	⚳	♃	♄	♅	♆	♇
1 W	0 36 24	11♈00 49	17♑19 23	24♑03 46	13♎05.6	5♈23.9	14♉00.8	25♊03.4	27♏58.3	1♐42.2	6♑52.5	12♌22.8	6♏15.2	2♍05.4
2 Th	0 40 21	12 00 01	0♒43 22	7♒18 21	13R 05.5	4R 36.5	15 12.9	25 36.4	27R 55.1	1R 39.6	6 54.0	12R 21.8	6R 13.7	2R 04.3
3 F	0 44 17	12 59 10	13 48 57	20 15 25	13D 05.4	3 51.9	16 25.0	26 09.5	27 51.5	1 36.8	6 55.3	12 20.9	6 12.2	2 03.2
4 Sa	0 48 14	13 58 18	26 38 00	2♓56 58	13 05.5	3 11.0	17 37.0	26 42.6	27 47.5	1 33.9	6 56.6	12 20.0	6 10.8	2 02.2
5 Su	0 52 10	14 57 25	9♓12 34	15 25 03	13 05.6	2 34.2	18 48.9	27 15.9	27 43.0	1 30.7	6 57.7	12 19.2	6 09.3	2 01.1
6 M	0 56 07	15 56 29	21 34 41	27 41 41	13 05.8	2 02.1	20 00.8	27 49.2	27 38.2	1 27.4	6 58.8	12 18.4	6 07.8	2 00.1
7 Tu	1 00 03	16 55 31	3♈46 17	9♈48 45	13R 05.9	1 34.9	21 12.6	28 22.6	27 33.0	1 23.9	6 59.7	12 17.7	6 06.3	1 59.1
8 W	1 04 00	17 54 32	15 49 16	21 48 06	13 05.9	1 12.9	22 24.3	28 56.0	27 27.4	1 20.3	7 00.6	12 17.1	6 04.7	1 58.1
9 Th	1 07 57	18 53 30	27 45 29	3♉41 40	13 05.5	0 56.3	23 35.9	29 29.5	27 21.4	1 16.4	7 01.3	12 16.5	6 03.2	1 57.1
10 F	1 11 53	19 52 26	9♉36 56	15 31 32	13 04.9	0 45.1	24 47.5	0♋03.1	27 15.0	1 12.4	7 02.0	12 15.9	6 01.6	1 56.2
11 Sa	1 15 50	20 51 20	21 25 49	27 20 06	13 03.9	0D 39.3	25 59.0	0 36.8	27 08.2	1 08.3	7 02.6	12 15.4	6 00.1	1 55.3
12 Su	1 19 46	21 50 12	3♊14 45	9♊10 08	13 02.7	0 38.9	27 10.4	1 10.5	27 01.1	1 04.0	7 03.0	12 15.0	5 58.5	1 54.4
13 M	1 23 43	22 49 02	15 06 42	21 04 53	13 01.4	0 43.7	28 21.7	1 44.3	26 53.6	0 59.5	7 03.4	12 14.6	5 56.9	1 53.5
14 Tu	1 27 39	23 47 50	27 05 09	3♋08 00	13 00.3	0 53.7	29 32.9	2 18.1	26 45.7	0 54.8	7 03.6	12 14.2	5 55.4	1 52.7
15 W	1 31 36	24 46 35	9♋13 56	15 23 29	12D 59.6	1 08.6	0♊44.1	2 52.0	26 37.5	0 50.0	7 03.8	12 14.0	5 53.8	1 51.9
16 Th	1 35 32	25 45 19	21 37 10	27 55 31	12 59.5	1 28.2	1 55.1	3 25.9	26 29.0	0 45.1	7R 03.9	12 13.7	5 52.2	1 51.1
17 F	1 39 29	26 44 00	4♌19 00	10♌48 06	12 59.9	1 52.5	3 06.1	3 59.9	26 20.1	0 40.0	7 03.8	12 13.6	5 50.6	1 50.3
18 Sa	1 43 26	27 42 38	17 23 13	24 04 42	13 00.8	2 21.2	4 16.9	4 34.0	26 10.8	0 34.8	7 03.7	12 13.4	5 49.0	1 49.6
19 Su	1 47 22	28 41 15	0♍52 49	7♍47 40	13 01.9	2 54.0	5 27.7	5 08.1	26 01.3	0 29.4	7 03.5	12D 13.4	5 47.3	1 48.9
20 M	1 51 19	29 39 49	14 49 18	21 57 32	13 03.1	3 30.9	6 38.4	5 42.2	25 51.5	0 23.9	7 03.1	12 13.3	5 45.7	1 48.2
21 Tu	1 55 15	0♉38 21	29 12 05	6♎32 27	13R 03.8	4 11.6	7 49.0	6 16.4	25 41.3	0 18.3	7 02.7	12 13.4	5 44.1	1 47.6
22 W	1 59 12	1 36 51	13♎57 57	21 27 46	13 03.7	4 56.0	8 59.4	6 50.7	25 30.9	0 12.5	7 02.2	12 13.5	5 42.5	1 46.9
23 Th	2 03 08	2 35 19	29 00 53	6♏36 11	13 02.7	5 43.9	10 09.8	7 25.0	25 20.2	0 06.6	7 01.6	12 13.6	5 40.8	1 46.3
24 F	2 07 05	3 33 45	14♏12 28	21 48 28	13 00.7	6 35.1	11 20.1	7 59.3	25 09.2	0 00.5	7 00.9	12 13.8	5 39.2	1 45.7
25 Sa	2 11 01	4 32 10	29 22 59	6♐54 49	12 58.1	7 29.5	12 30.2	8 33.7	24 58.0	29♏54.4	7 00.0	12 14.1	5 37.6	1 45.2
26 Su	2 14 58	5 30 33	14♐22 53	21 46 17	12 55.2	8 27.0	13 40.3	9 08.1	24 46.5	29 48.1	6 59.1	12 14.4	5 35.9	1 44.7
27 M	2 18 55	6 28 55	29 04 14	6♑16 10	12 52.5	9 27.5	14 50.2	9 42.6	24 34.8	29 41.8	6 58.1	12 14.8	5 34.3	1 44.2
28 Tu	2 22 51	7 27 14	13♑21 41	20 20 35	12 50.5	10 30.7	16 00.1	10 17.1	24 22.9	29 35.3	6 57.0	12 15.2	5 32.7	1 43.7
29 W	2 26 48	8 25 33	27 12 48	3♒58 27	12D 49.6	11 36.7	17 09.8	10 51.7	24 10.7	29 28.7	6 55.9	12 15.6	5 31.0	1 43.3
30 Th	2 30 44	9 23 49	10♒37 44	17 10 57	12 49.7	12 45.3	18 19.5	11 26.3	23 58.4	29 22.0	6 54.6	12 16.2	5 29.4	1 42.9

Astro Data

	Dy Hr Mn
☿0N	5 0:12
☽0N	10 3:09
♃ R	18 22:09
☿ R	19 18:35
☉0N	21 8:55
♄⚹♆	21 9:10
☽0S	24 8:45
⚳ R	25 2:31
☽0N	6 9:39
☿0S	11 18:47
☿ D	12 1:52
♄ R	16 15:32
♅ D	20 6:57
☽0S	20 19:35
☿0N	23 2:59

Planet Ingress

		Dy Hr Mn
☿	♈	5 11:52
♀	♉	20 21:55
☉	♈	21 8:55
♂	♋	10 9:46
♀	♊	14 21:08
☉	♉	20 20:17
♃	♏R	24 14:10

Last Aspect / ☽ Ingress

Last Aspect Dy Hr Mn		☽ Ingress	Dy Hr Mn
28 18:39	☿ △	♐	1 8:33
3 5:25	☿ □	♑	3 12:05
4 11:09	☉ ⚹	♒	5 17:16
6 17:00	♅ ☍	♓	8 0:25
9 10:51	☉ ☌	♈	10 9:53
11 23:43	♀ ☌	♉	12 21:37
14 21:25	☉ ⚹	♊	15 10:31
17 15:10	☉ □	♋	17 22:28
20 5:53	♀ □	♌	20 7:22
21 17:49	♂ ⚹	♍	22 12:28
23 22:43	♂ □	♎	24 14:27
26 1:17	♂ △	♏	26 14:53
27 11:00	♅ □	♐	28 15:31
30 7:19	♂ ☍	♑	30 17:49

Last Aspect / ☽ Ingress

Last Aspect Dy Hr Mn		☽ Ingress	Dy Hr Mn
31 16:26	♀ △	♒	1 22:41
3 23:36	♂ △	♓	4 6:23
6 12:15	♂ □	♈	6 16:33
9 3:05	♂ ⚹	♉	9 4:32
11 8:57	♀ ☌	♊	11 17:25
13 15:47	☉ ⚹	♋	14 5:48
16 7:33	☉ □	♌	16 15:55
18 18:56	☉ △	♍	18 22:27
19 10:44	♄ △	♎	21 1:19
21 21:12	♅ ⚹	♏	23 1:34
25 0:54	♃ ☌	♐	25 0:59
25 21:44	♀ ☍	♑	27 1:32
29 4:04	♃ ⚹	♒	29 4:55

☽ Phases & Eclipses

Dy Hr Mn	
2 2:54	☾ 10♐47
9 10:51	● 18♓07
17 15:10	☽ 26♊17
24 20:02	○ 3♎26
24 20:11	P 0.264
31 11:06	☾ 9♑59
8 3:29	● 17♈34
8 3:23:36	A 07'25"
16 7:33	☽ 25♋34
23 5:13	○ 2♏19
29 20:38	☾ 8♒47

Astro Data

1 March 1959
Julian Day # 21609
SVP 5♓49'43"
GC 26♐16.1 ⚴ 26♎46.2R
Eris 9♈01.3 ⚵ 24♎51.3R
⚷ 23♒52.5 ⚶ 28♋07.3R
☽ Mean ☊ 14♎54.3

1 April 1959
Julian Day # 21640
SVP 5♓49'40"
GC 26♐16.2 ⚴ 19♎55.0R
Eris 9♈21.9 ⚵ 19♎15.0R
⚷ 25♒50.8 ⚶ 28♋28.5
☽ Mean ☊ 13♎15.7

LONGITUDE — May 1959

Day	Sid.Time	☉	0 hr ☽	Noon ☽	True ☊	☿	♀	♂	⚳	♃	♄	♅	♆	♇
1 F	2 34 41	10♉22 05	23♒38 31	0♓00 52	12♎50.8	13♈56.4	19♊29.0	12♋01.0	23♏45.8	29♏15.2	6♑53.2	12♌16.7	5♏27.8	1♍42.5
2 Sa	2 38 37	11 20 18	6♓18 27	12 31 46	12 52.4	15 10.0	20 38.4	12 35.7	23R33.1	29R08.4	6R51.7	12 17.4	5R26.1	1R42.1
3 Su	2 42 34	12 18 31	18 41 18	24 47 33	12 54.0	16 25.9	21 47.7	13 10.4	23 20.3	29 01.4	6 50.2	12 18.1	5 24.5	1 41.8
4 M	2 46 30	13 16 41	0♈50 58	6♈51 59	12R55.1	17 44.2	22 56.9	13 45.2	23 07.3	28 54.4	6 48.5	12 18.8	5 22.9	1 41.5
5 Tu	2 50 27	14 14 50	12 51 02	18 48 29	12 55.1	19 04.7	24 05.9	14 20.1	22 54.2	28 47.2	6 46.8	12 19.6	5 21.3	1 41.3
6 W	2 54 24	15 12 58	24 44 42	0♉40 01	12 53.6	20 27.4	25 14.9	14 54.9	22 41.0	28 40.0	6 44.9	12 20.4	5 19.6	1 41.0
7 Th	2 58 20	16 11 04	6♉34 42	12 29 04	12 50.5	21 52.3	26 23.7	15 29.9	22 27.7	28 32.8	6 43.0	12 21.3	5 18.0	1 40.8
8 F	3 02 17	17 09 08	18 23 22	24 17 50	12 45.8	23 19.4	27 32.4	16 04.8	22 14.3	28 25.5	6 41.0	12 22.3	5 16.4	1 40.6
9 Sa	3 06 13	18 07 11	0♊12 42	6♊08 14	12 39.9	24 48.6	28 40.9	16 39.8	22 00.9	28 18.1	6 38.9	12 23.3	5 14.9	1 40.5
10 Su	3 10 10	19 05 12	12 04 38	18 02 11	12 33.3	26 19.8	29 49.3	17 14.9	21 47.4	28 10.7	6 36.7	12 24.3	5 13.3	1 40.4
11 M	3 14 06	20 03 11	24 01 07	0♋01 44	12 26.6	27 53.2	0♋57.6	17 49.9	21 33.9	28 03.2	6 34.4	12 25.4	5 11.7	1 40.3
12 Tu	3 18 03	21 01 09	6♋04 20	12 09 15	12 20.6	29 28.6	2 05.8	18 25.1	21 20.4	27 55.7	6 32.1	12 26.6	5 10.1	1 40.2
13 W	3 21 59	21 59 05	18 16 50	24 27 28	12 15.9	1♉06.0	3 13.8	19 00.2	21 06.9	27 48.1	6 29.7	12 27.8	5 08.6	1D40.2
14 Th	3 25 56	22 56 59	0♌41 34	6♌59 31	12 12.9	2 45.5	4 21.6	19 35.4	20 53.4	27 40.6	6 27.1	12 29.0	5 07.0	1 40.2
15 F	3 29 53	23 54 51	13 21 48	19 48 49	12D11.5	4 27.1	5 29.3	20 10.6	20 40.0	27 33.0	6 24.5	12 30.4	5 05.5	1 40.2
16 Sa	3 33 49	24 52 42	26 21 01	2♍58 48	12 11.7	6 10.7	6 36.9	20 45.9	20 26.6	27 25.3	6 21.9	12 31.7	5 04.0	1 40.3
17 Su	3 37 46	25 50 31	9♍42 30	16 32 26	12 12.8	7 56.4	7 44.2	21 21.2	20 13.3	27 17.7	6 19.1	12 33.1	5 02.5	1 40.4
18 M	3 41 42	26 48 18	23 28 48	0♎31 41	12R14.0	9 44.1	8 51.4	21 56.5	20 00.1	27 10.1	6 16.3	12 34.6	5 01.0	1 40.5
19 Tu	3 45 39	27 46 03	7♎41 02	14 56 38	12 14.4	11 33.9	9 58.5	22 31.9	19 47.0	27 02.4	6 13.4	12 36.1	4 59.5	1 40.7
20 W	3 49 35	28 43 47	22 18 06	29 44 50	12 13.3	13 25.8	11 05.4	23 07.2	19 34.0	26 54.8	6 10.4	12 37.6	4 58.0	1 40.8
21 Th	3 53 32	29 41 29	7♏16 01	14♏50 43	12 10.1	15 19.6	12 12.1	23 42.7	19 21.2	26 47.2	6 07.4	12 39.2	4 56.6	1 41.1
22 F	3 57 28	0♊39 10	22 27 45	0♐05 53	12 04.8	17 15.5	13 18.6	24 18.1	19 08.4	26 39.6	6 04.3	12 40.9	4 55.1	1 41.3
23 Sa	4 01 25	1 36 50	7♐43 45	15 20 00	11 58.1	19 13.4	14 24.9	24 53.6	18 55.9	26 32.0	6 01.1	12 42.6	4 53.7	1 41.6
24 Su	4 05 22	2 34 28	22 53 19	0♑22 30	11 50.5	21 13.2	15 31.0	25 29.1	18 43.5	26 24.4	5 57.8	12 44.3	4 52.3	1 41.9
25 M	4 09 18	3 32 06	7♑46 29	15 04 24	11 43.3	23 14.9	16 37.0	26 04.6	18 31.3	26 16.8	5 54.5	12 46.1	4 50.9	1 42.2
26 Tu	4 13 15	4 29 42	22 15 35	29 19 36	11 37.2	25 18.4	17 42.7	26 40.2	18 19.3	26 09.3	5 51.2	12 48.0	4 49.5	1 42.6
27 W	4 17 11	5 27 17	6♒16 14	13♒05 26	11 33.0	27 23.5	18 48.3	27 15.8	18 07.6	26 01.8	5 47.7	12 49.9	4 48.2	1 42.9
28 Th	4 21 08	6 24 52	19 47 22	26 22 18	11D30.7	29 30.3	19 53.6	27 51.4	17 56.0	25 54.4	5 44.2	12 51.8	4 46.8	1 43.4
29 F	4 25 04	7 22 25	2♓50 40	9♓12 57	11 30.2	1♊38.4	20 58.8	28 27.1	17 44.7	25 47.0	5 40.6	12 53.8	4 45.5	1 43.8
30 Sa	4 29 01	8 19 58	15 29 42	21 41 33	11 30.8	3 47.8	22 03.7	29 02.8	17 33.6	25 39.7	5 37.0	12 55.8	4 44.2	1 44.3
31 Su	4 32 57	9 17 30	27 49 05	3♈52 58	11R31.7	5 58.3	23 08.4	29 38.5	17 22.7	25 32.4	5 33.3	12 57.8	4 42.9	1 44.8

LONGITUDE — June 1959

Day	Sid.Time	☉	0 hr ☽	Noon ☽	True ☊	☿	♀	♂	⚳	♃	♄	♅	♆	♇
1 M	4 36 54	10♊15 01	9♈53 47	15♈52 08	11♎31.8	8♊09.5	24♋12.9	0♌14.3	17♏12.2	25♏25.2	5♑29.6	12♌59.9	4♏41.6	1♍45.3
2 Tu	4 40 51	11 12 31	21 48 36	27 43 43	11R30.3	10 21.3	25 17.2	0 50.1	17R01.9	25R18.0	5R25.8	13 02.1	4R40.4	1 45.9
3 W	4 44 47	12 10 00	3♉37 57	9♉31 47	11 26.6	12 33.3	26 21.2	1 25.9	16 51.9	25 11.0	5 22.0	13 04.3	4 39.2	1 46.5
4 Th	4 48 44	13 07 29	15 25 35	21 19 43	11 20.4	14 45.4	27 25.0	2 01.7	16 42.2	25 04.0	5 18.1	13 06.5	4 37.9	1 47.1
5 F	4 52 40	14 04 56	27 14 31	3♊10 15	11 11.8	16 57.3	28 28.6	2 37.6	16 32.8	24 57.1	5 14.2	13 08.8	4 36.8	1 47.7
6 Sa	4 56 37	15 02 23	9♊07 09	15 05 26	11 01.1	19 08.6	29 31.8	3 13.5	16 23.7	24 50.3	5 10.2	13 11.1	4 35.6	1 48.4
7 Su	5 00 33	15 59 49	21 05 16	27 06 48	10 49.4	21 19.1	0♌34.9	3 49.5	16 15.0	24 43.5	5 06.2	13 13.5	4 34.5	1 49.1
8 M	5 04 30	16 57 14	3♋10 13	9♋15 37	10 37.5	23 28.6	1 37.6	4 25.5	16 06.5	24 36.9	5 02.1	13 15.9	4 33.4	1 49.8
9 Tu	5 08 26	17 54 39	15 23 12	21 33 06	10 26.4	25 36.9	2 40.1	5 01.5	15 58.5	24 30.4	4 58.0	13 18.3	4 32.3	1 50.6
10 W	5 12 23	18 52 02	27 45 29	4♌00 34	10 17.3	27 43.6	3 42.3	5 37.5	15 50.7	24 23.9	4 53.9	13 20.8	4 31.2	1 51.4
11 Th	5 16 20	19 49 24	10♌18 35	16 39 47	10 10.5	29 48.7	4 44.2	6 13.6	15 43.3	24 17.6	4 49.7	13 23.3	4 30.2	1 52.2
12 F	5 20 16	20 46 45	23 04 27	29 32 53	10 06.4	1♋52.1	5 45.8	6 49.7	15 36.3	24 11.4	4 45.5	13 25.9	4 29.1	1 53.0
13 Sa	5 24 13	21 44 05	6♍05 24	12♍42 21	10D04.7	3 53.4	6 47.1	7 25.8	15 29.6	24 05.3	4 41.3	13 28.5	4 28.1	1 53.9
14 Su	5 28 09	22 41 24	19 24 02	26 10 45	10 04.4	5 52.8	7 48.0	8 01.9	15 23.3	23 59.4	4 37.0	13 31.1	4 27.2	1 54.8
15 M	5 32 06	23 38 42	3♎02 46	10♎00 16	10R04.6	7 50.0	8 48.6	8 38.1	15 17.3	23 53.5	4 32.8	13 33.8	4 26.2	1 55.7
16 Tu	5 36 02	24 36 00	17 03 20	24 11 57	10 04.0	9 45.0	9 48.9	9 14.3	15 11.8	23 47.8	4 28.5	13 36.5	4 25.3	1 56.7
17 W	5 39 59	25 33 16	1♏25 56	8♏44 58	10 01.6	11 37.8	10 48.8	9 50.5	15 06.6	23 42.2	4 24.1	13 39.2	4 24.4	1 57.7
18 Th	5 43 55	26 30 32	16 08 30	23 35 51	9 56.7	13 28.3	11 48.3	10 26.8	15 01.7	23 36.8	4 19.8	13 42.0	4 23.5	1 58.7
19 F	5 47 52	27 27 47	1♐06 09	8♐38 19	9 49.2	15 16.5	12 47.4	11 03.1	14 57.3	23 31.5	4 15.4	13 44.8	4 22.7	1 59.7
20 Sa	5 51 49	28 25 01	16 11 13	23 43 35	9 39.6	17 02.4	13 46.2	11 39.4	14 53.2	23 26.3	4 11.1	13 47.7	4 21.9	2 00.7
21 Su	5 55 45	29 22 15	1♑14 10	8♑41 43	9 28.9	18 45.9	14 44.5	12 15.7	14 49.5	23 21.3	4 06.7	13 50.5	4 21.1	2 01.8
22 M	5 59 42	0♋19 29	16 05 07	23 23 20	9 18.3	20 27.0	15 42.4	12 52.0	14 46.2	23 16.5	4 02.3	13 53.4	4 20.4	2 02.9
23 Tu	6 03 38	1 16 42	0♒35 33	7♒41 09	9 09.1	22 05.8	16 39.9	13 28.4	14 43.2	23 11.7	3 57.9	13 56.4	4 19.6	2 04.1
24 W	6 07 35	2 13 55	14 39 43	21 31 02	9 02.0	23 42.3	17 36.9	14 04.8	14 40.6	23 07.2	3 53.5	13 59.4	4 18.9	2 05.2
25 Th	6 11 31	3 11 08	28 15 06	4♓52 04	8 57.5	25 16.3	18 33.5	14 41.3	14 38.4	23 02.7	3 49.0	14 02.4	4 18.3	2 06.4
26 F	6 15 28	4 08 21	11♓22 14	17 46 02	8 55.2	26 47.9	19 29.6	15 17.7	14 36.6	22 58.5	3 44.6	14 05.4	4 17.6	2 07.6
27 Sa	6 19 24	5 05 33	24 04 00	0♈16 42	8 54.5	28 17.2	20 25.2	15 54.2	14 35.2	22 54.4	3 40.2	14 08.5	4 17.0	2 08.8
28 Su	6 23 21	6 02 46	6♈24 46	12 28 54	8 54.5	29 43.9	21 20.3	16 30.7	14 34.1	22 50.4	3 35.8	14 11.5	4 16.4	2 10.1
29 M	6 27 18	6 59 59	18 29 45	24 27 59	8 53.9	1♌08.2	22 14.9	17 07.3	14 33.4	22 46.6	3 31.4	14 14.7	4 15.9	2 11.3
30 Tu	6 31 14	7 57 12	0♉24 16	6♉19 15	8 51.9	2 30.1	23 09.0	17 43.9	14D33.1	22 43.0	3 27.0	14 17.8	4 15.4	2 12.6

Astro Data

	Dy Hr Mn
☽ 0N	3 15:34
♇ D	13 21:51
☽ 0S	18 5:42
☽ 0N	30 22:28
☽ 0S	14 14:12
♄⚹♆	17 10:02
☽ 0N	27 7:04
⚳ D	30 20:26

Planet Ingress

	Dy Hr Mn
♀ ♋	10 15:45
☿ ♉	12 19:48
☉ ♊	21 19:42
☿ ♊	28 17:35
♂ ♌	1 2:26
♀ ♌	6 22:43
☿ ♋	11 14:11
☉ ♋	22 3:50
☿ ♌	28 16:31

Last Aspect Dy Hr Mn	☽ Ingress Dy Hr Mn
1 10:34 ♃ □	♓ 1 11:58
3 20:18 ♃ △	♈ 3 22:19
5 23:50 ♀ ⚹	♉ 6 10:39
8 20:17 ♃ ☍	♊ 8 23:34
11 7:05 ☿ ⚹	♋ 11 11:57
13 18:23 ♃ △	♌ 13 22:40
16 2:03 ♃ □	♍ 16 6:38
18 6:21 ♃ ⚹	♎ 18 11:06
20 0:53 ♂ □	♏ 20 12:24
22 6:38 ♃ ☌	♐ 22 11:51
23 7:51 ♅ △	♑ 24 11:24
26 7:16 ♂ ☍	♒ 26 13:09
28 11:09 ♃ □	♓ 28 18:42
31 3:10 ♂ △	♈ 31 4:18

Last Aspect Dy Hr Mn	☽ Ingress Dy Hr Mn
2 6:33 ♀ □	♉ 2 16:37
5 1:34 ♀ ⚹	♊ 5 5:35
6 21:55 ☿ ☌	♋ 7 17:44
9 17:40 ♃ △	♌ 10 4:19
12 2:09 ♃ □	♍ 12 12:50
14 8:10 ♃ ⚹	♎ 14 18:42
16 12:43 ☉ △	♏ 16 21:38
18 12:01 ♃ ☌	♐ 18 22:14
20 20:00 ☉ ☍	♑ 20 22:01
22 11:49 ♃ ⚹	♒ 22 23:00
24 14:49 ♃ □	♓ 25 3:09
27 7:37 ☿ △	♈ 27 11:28
29 7:10 ♀ △	♉ 29 23:11

☽ Phases & Eclipses

Dy Hr Mn	
7 20:11	● 16♉31
15 20:09	☽ 24♌14
22 12:56	○ 0♐41
29 8:14	☾ 7♓13
6 11:53	● 15♊02
14 5:22	☽ 22♍26
20 20:00	○ 28♐44
27 22:12	☾ 5♈30

Astro Data

1 May 1959
Julian Day # 21670
SVP 5♓49'37"
GC 26♐16.3 ⚴ 11♎20.1R
Eris 9♈41.8 ⚵ 12♎42.6R
⚷ 27♒09.8 ⚶ 4♌39.7
☽ Mean ☊ 11♎40.4

1 June 1959
Julian Day # 21701
SVP 5♓49'33"
GC 26♐16.3 ⚴ 8♎19.2
Eris 9♈57.3 ⚵ 9♎53.5R
⚷ 27♒39.5 ⚶ 14♌53.1
☽ Mean ☊ 10♎01.9

July 1959 — LONGITUDE

Day	Sid.Time	☉	0 hr ☽	Noon ☽	True ☊	☿	♀	♂	⚳	♃	♄	♅	♆	♇
1 W	6 35 11	8♋54 25	12♉13 30	18♉07 36	8♎47.6	3♌49.3	24♌02.5	18♌20.5	14♏33.1	22♏39.6	3♑22.6	14♌21.0	4♏14.9	2♍13.9
2 Th	6 39 07	9 51 38	24 02 04	29 57 20	8R 40.5	5 06.1	24 55.4	18 57.1	14 33.6	22R 36.3	3R 18.2	14 24.2	4R 14.4	2 15.3
3 F	6 43 04	10 48 51	5♊53 50	11♊51 55	8 30.8	6 20.1	25 47.7	19 33.8	14 34.4	22 33.2	3 13.8	14 27.4	4 14.0	2 16.6
4 Sa	6 47 00	11 46 05	17 51 52	23 53 57	8 18.9	7 31.5	26 39.5	20 10.5	14 35.5	22 30.2	3 09.5	14 30.7	4 13.6	2 18.0
5 Su	6 50 57	12 43 18	29 58 22	6♋05 14	8 05.8	8 40.1	27 30.5	20 47.2	14 37.1	22 27.5	3 05.1	14 34.0	4 13.2	2 19.4
6 M	6 54 53	13 40 32	12♋14 40	18 26 45	7 52.4	9 45.9	28 21.0	21 24.0	14 39.0	22 24.9	3 00.8	14 37.3	4 12.8	2 20.9
7 Tu	6 58 50	14 37 45	24 41 30	0♌58 58	7 40.0	10 48.8	29 10.7	22 00.8	14 41.2	22 22.5	2 56.5	14 40.6	4 12.5	2 22.3
8 W	7 02 47	15 34 58	7♌19 10	13 42 07	7 29.5	11 48.7	29 59.7	22 37.6	14 43.9	22 20.2	2 52.3	14 43.9	4 12.3	2 23.8
9 Th	7 06 43	16 32 12	20 07 50	26 36 24	7 21.8	12 45.5	0♍48.0	23 14.4	14 46.8	22 18.2	2 48.0	14 47.3	4 12.0	2 25.3
10 F	7 10 40	17 29 25	3♍07 52	9♍42 21	7 16.9	13 39.0	1 35.5	23 51.3	14 50.2	22 16.3	2 43.8	14 50.7	4 11.8	2 26.8
11 Sa	7 14 36	18 26 38	16 19 57	23 00 50	7 14.5	14 29.2	2 22.2	24 28.2	14 53.9	22 14.6	2 39.6	14 54.1	4 11.6	2 28.3
12 Su	7 18 33	19 23 51	29 45 09	6♎33 05	7 14.0	15 16.0	3 08.1	25 05.1	14 57.9	22 13.1	2 35.5	14 57.5	4 11.5	2 29.8
13 M	7 22 29	20 21 05	13♎24 46	20 20 20	7 14.1	15 59.1	3 53.1	25 42.1	15 02.3	22 11.7	2 31.4	15 01.0	4 11.3	2 31.4
14 Tu	7 26 26	21 18 18	27 19 52	4♏23 22	7 13.6	16 38.5	4 37.2	26 19.0	15 07.0	22 10.6	2 27.3	15 04.5	4 11.2	2 33.0
15 W	7 30 22	22 15 31	11♏30 45	18 41 49	7 11.4	17 14.1	5 20.4	26 56.0	15 12.0	22 09.6	2 23.3	15 08.0	4 11.2	2 34.6
16 Th	7 34 19	23 12 44	25 56 17	3♐13 39	7 06.8	17 45.6	6 02.6	27 33.1	15 17.4	22 08.8	2 19.3	15 11.5	4D 11.2	2 36.2
17 F	7 38 16	24 09 57	10♐33 21	17 54 38	6 59.8	18 12.9	6 43.8	28 10.1	15 23.1	22 08.2	2 15.3	15 15.0	4 11.2	2 37.9
18 Sa	7 42 12	25 07 11	25 16 41	2♑38 33	6 50.7	18 35.9	7 23.9	28 47.2	15 29.1	22 07.8	2 11.5	15 18.5	4 11.2	2 39.5
19 Su	7 46 09	26 04 25	9♑59 16	17 17 50	6 40.5	18 54.4	8 02.9	29 24.3	15 35.5	22D 07.5	2 07.6	15 22.1	4 11.3	2 41.2
20 M	7 50 05	27 01 39	24 33 16	1♒44 42	6 30.3	19 08.3	8 40.8	0♍01.5	15 42.1	22 07.5	2 03.8	15 25.6	4 11.4	2 42.9
21 Tu	7 54 02	27 58 54	8♒51 22	15 52 36	6 21.2	19 17.5	9 17.5	0 38.6	15 49.1	22 07.6	2 00.1	15 29.2	4 11.5	2 44.6
22 W	7 57 58	28 56 09	22 47 55	29 37 02	6 14.2	19R 21.8	9 53.0	1 15.8	15 56.4	22 07.9	1 56.4	15 32.8	4 11.7	2 46.3
23 Th	8 01 55	29 53 25	6♓19 46	12♓56 07	6 09.7	19 21.2	10 27.2	1 53.1	16 03.9	22 08.4	1 52.7	15 36.4	4 11.9	2 48.0
24 F	8 05 51	0♌50 42	19 26 16	25 50 28	6D 07.4	19 15.6	11 00.1	2 30.3	16 11.8	22 09.1	1 49.1	15 40.1	4 12.1	2 49.8
25 Sa	8 09 48	1 47 59	2♈09 08	8♈22 42	6 07.0	19 05.0	11 31.7	3 07.6	16 20.0	22 09.9	1 45.6	15 43.7	4 12.4	2 51.5
26 Su	8 13 45	2 45 18	14 31 45	20 36 51	6 07.5	18 49.5	12 01.8	3 44.9	16 28.4	22 10.9	1 42.1	15 47.3	4 12.7	2 53.3
27 M	8 17 41	3 42 37	26 38 39	2♉37 48	6R 08.0	18 29.1	12 30.5	4 22.2	16 37.2	22 12.1	1 38.7	15 51.0	4 13.0	2 55.1
28 Tu	8 21 38	4 39 58	8♉34 58	14 30 49	6 07.4	18 04.1	12 57.7	4 59.6	16 46.2	22 13.5	1 35.4	15 54.7	4 13.4	2 56.9
29 W	8 25 34	5 37 19	20 25 58	26 21 04	6 05.1	17 34.6	13 23.3	5 37.0	16 55.5	22 15.1	1 32.1	15 58.3	4 13.8	2 58.7
30 Th	8 29 31	6 34 42	2♊16 43	8♊13 27	6 00.7	17 01.1	13 47.3	6 14.5	17 05.1	22 16.8	1 28.9	16 02.0	4 14.2	3 00.6
31 F	8 33 27	7 32 06	14 11 47	20 12 12	5 54.0	16 23.8	14 09.6	6 52.0	17 15.0	22 18.7	1 25.7	16 05.7	4 14.7	3 02.4

August 1959 — LONGITUDE

Day	Sid.Time	☉	0 hr ☽	Noon ☽	True ☊	☿	♀	♂	⚳	♃	♄	♅	♆	♇
1 Sa	8 37 24	8♌29 30	26♊15 04	2♋20 45	5♎45.4	15♌43.4	14♍30.1	7♍29.5	17♏25.1	22♏20.8	1♑22.6	16♌09.4	4♏15.1	3♍04.3
2 Su	8 41 20	9 26 56	8♋29 32	14 41 37	5R 35.7	15R 00.5	14 48.9	8 07.0	17 35.5	22 23.1	1R 19.6	16 13.1	4 15.7	3 06.1
3 M	8 45 17	10 24 22	20 57 09	27 16 13	5 25.7	14 15.6	15 05.8	8 44.6	17 46.1	22 25.5	1 16.7	16 16.8	4 16.2	3 08.0
4 Tu	8 49 14	11 21 50	3♌38 51	10♌05 00	5 16.4	13 29.6	15 20.8	9 22.2	17 57.0	22 28.2	1 13.8	16 20.5	4 16.8	3 09.9
5 W	8 53 10	12 19 18	16 34 37	23 07 34	5 08.7	12 43.3	15 33.8	9 59.8	18 08.2	22 31.0	1 11.1	16 24.2	4 17.4	3 11.8
6 Th	8 57 07	13 16 48	29 43 44	6♍22 57	5 03.1	11 57.5	15 44.7	10 37.5	18 19.6	22 33.9	1 08.3	16 28.0	4 18.1	3 13.7
7 F	9 01 03	14 14 18	13♍05 04	19 49 56	5 00.0	11 13.0	15 53.6	11 15.2	18 31.3	22 37.1	1 05.7	16 31.7	4 18.8	3 15.6
8 Sa	9 05 00	15 11 49	26 37 25	3♎27 23	4D 58.9	10 30.9	16 00.3	11 52.9	18 43.2	22 40.4	1 03.2	16 35.4	4 19.5	3 17.6
9 Su	9 08 56	16 09 21	10♎19 45	17 14 24	4 59.4	9 51.8	16 04.8	12 30.7	18 55.4	22 43.9	1 00.7	16 39.1	4 20.2	3 19.5
10 M	9 12 53	17 06 54	24 11 15	1♏10 15	5 00.4	9 16.5	16R 07.0	13 08.5	19 07.8	22 47.6	0 58.3	16 42.9	4 21.0	3 21.5
11 Tu	9 16 49	18 04 28	8♏11 18	15 14 18	5R 01.2	8 45.9	16 06.9	13 46.3	19 20.4	22 51.4	0 56.0	16 46.6	4 21.8	3 23.4
12 W	9 20 46	19 02 02	22 19 06	29 25 31	5 00.7	8 20.6	16 04.5	14 24.1	19 33.2	22 55.4	0 53.8	16 50.3	4 22.6	3 25.4
13 Th	9 24 43	19 59 37	6♐33 19	13♐42 11	4 58.6	8 01.1	15 59.7	15 02.0	19 46.3	22 59.5	0 51.6	16 54.0	4 23.5	3 27.3
14 F	9 28 39	20 57 14	20 51 45	28 01 33	4 54.6	7 47.9	15 52.5	15 39.9	19 59.6	23 03.9	0 49.6	16 57.8	4 24.4	3 29.3
15 Sa	9 32 36	21 54 51	5♑11 05	12♑19 47	4 49.0	7D 41.4	15 43.0	16 17.9	20 13.1	23 08.4	0 47.6	17 01.5	4 25.3	3 31.3
16 Su	9 36 32	22 52 30	19 27 04	26 32 18	4 42.6	7 42.0	15 31.0	16 55.9	20 26.8	23 13.0	0 45.7	17 05.2	4 26.3	3 33.3
17 M	9 40 29	23 50 09	3♒34 53	10♒34 13	4 36.2	7 49.8	15 16.6	17 33.9	20 40.7	23 17.8	0 44.0	17 08.9	4 27.2	3 35.3
18 Tu	9 44 25	24 47 50	17 29 48	24 21 09	4 30.5	8 05.1	14 59.9	18 11.9	20 54.9	23 22.8	0 42.3	17 12.6	4 28.3	3 37.3
19 W	9 48 22	25 45 32	1♓07 53	7♓49 45	4 26.2	8 27.8	14 40.9	18 50.0	21 09.2	23 27.9	0 40.6	17 16.3	4 29.3	3 39.3
20 Th	9 52 18	26 43 15	14 26 35	20 58 17	4 23.6	8 58.0	14 19.6	19 28.1	21 23.7	23 33.2	0 39.1	17 20.0	4 30.4	3 41.3
21 F	9 56 15	27 41 00	27 24 56	3♈46 39	4D 22.8	9 35.6	13 56.1	20 06.2	21 38.5	23 38.6	0 37.7	17 23.7	4 31.5	3 43.3
22 Sa	10 00 12	28 38 46	10♈03 40	16 16 19	4 23.3	10 20.6	13 30.6	20 44.4	21 53.4	23 44.2	0 36.3	17 27.4	4 32.6	3 45.3
23 Su	10 04 08	29 36 34	22 25 00	28 30 09	4 24.8	11 12.6	13 03.2	21 22.6	22 08.5	23 49.9	0 35.1	17 31.0	4 33.8	3 47.3
24 M	10 08 05	0♍34 24	4♉32 17	10♉31 57	4 26.5	12 11.6	12 33.9	22 00.9	22 23.8	23 55.8	0 33.9	17 34.7	4 34.9	3 49.3
25 Tu	10 12 01	1 32 15	16 29 43	22 26 12	4R 27.8	13 17.2	12 03.0	22 39.1	22 39.3	24 01.8	0 32.9	17 38.3	4 36.2	3 51.3
26 W	10 15 58	2 30 09	28 22 01	4♊17 46	4 28.2	14 29.2	11 30.6	23 17.4	22 54.9	24 08.0	0 31.9	17 42.0	4 37.4	3 53.3
27 Th	10 19 54	3 28 04	10♊14 05	16 11 34	4 27.3	15 47.1	10 56.8	23 55.8	23 10.8	24 14.3	0 31.0	17 45.6	4 38.7	3 55.3
28 F	10 23 51	4 26 01	22 10 48	28 12 19	4 25.2	17 10.7	10 22.0	24 34.2	23 26.8	24 20.8	0 30.3	17 49.2	4 40.0	3 57.4
29 Sa	10 27 47	5 23 59	4♋16 39	10♋24 15	4 21.8	18 39.3	9 46.2	25 12.6	23 43.0	24 27.4	0 29.6	17 52.8	4 41.3	3 59.4
30 Su	10 31 44	6 22 00	16 35 33	22 50 52	4 17.7	20 12.7	9 09.8	25 51.1	23 59.3	24 34.1	0 29.0	17 56.4	4 42.6	4 01.4
31 M	10 35 41	7 20 02	29 10 30	5♌34 39	4 13.3	21 50.3	8 32.9	26 29.6	24 15.9	24 41.0	0 28.5	18 00.0	4 44.0	4 03.4

Astro Data	Dy Hr Mn
☽0S	11 21:10
♄△♇	13 11:49
♆ D	16 16:51
♃ D	20 8:00
☿ R	22 21:03
☽0N	24 16:54
♄□♅	3 11:36
☽0S	8 3:39
♀ R	10 23:16
♀0S	14 15:47
☿ D	15 22:06
☽0N	21 2:41
♀0N	28 18:02

Planet Ingress	Dy Hr Mn
♀ ♍	8 12:08
♂ ♍	20 11:03
☉ ♌	23 14:45
☉ ♍	23 21:44

Last Aspect Dy Hr Mn		☽ Ingress	Dy Hr Mn
2 0:59	♀ □	♊	2 12:05
4 17:52	♀ ✶	♋	5 0:03
6 19:37	♃ △	♌	7 10:08
9 5:28	♂ ☌	♍	9 18:15
11 10:37	♃ ✶	♎	12 0:26
13 21:38	♂ ✶	♏	14 4:33
16 2:15	♂ □	♐	16 6:42
18 5:26	♂ △	♑	18 7:42
20 3:33	☉ ☍	♒	20 9:05
21 22:50	♃ □	♓	22 12:41
24 5:03	♃ △	♈	24 19:53
26 8:33	☿ △	♉	27 6:43
29 3:40	♃ ☍	♊	29 19:23

Last Aspect Dy Hr Mn		☽ Ingress	Dy Hr Mn
31 4:47	☿ ✶	♋	1 7:24
3 2:47	♃ △	♌	3 17:09
5 10:53	♃ □	♍	6 0:29
7 16:57	♃ ✶	♎	8 5:56
9 10:59	♅ ✶	♏	10 10:00
12 0:58	♃ ☌	♐	12 12:58
13 23:18	☉ △	♑	14 15:18
16 6:20	♃ ✶	♒	16 17:53
18 12:51	☉ ☍	♓	18 21:59
20 16:49	♃ △	♈	21 4:51
23 14:23	☉ △	♉	23 14:58
25 15:15	♃ ☍	♊	26 3:18
28 4:22	♂ □	♋	28 15:33
30 18:01	♂ ✶	♌	31 1:33

☽ Phases & Eclipses Dy Hr Mn	
6 2:00	● 13♋17
13 12:01	☽ 20♎21
20 3:33	○ 26♑42
27 14:22	☾ 3♉48
4 14:34	● 11♌28
11 17:10	☽ 18♏17
18 12:51	○ 24♒50
26 8:03	☾ 2♊21

Astro Data

1 July 1959
Julian Day # 21731
SVP 5♓49'28"
GC 26♐16.4 ⚴ 11♎55.9
Eris 10♈04.0 ⚵ 12♎00.8
⚷ 27♒13.2R ⚶ 27♌01.7
☽ Mean ☊ 8♎26.6

1 August 1959
Julian Day # 21762
SVP 5♓49'24"
GC 26♐16.5 ⚴ 20♎05.1
Eris 10♈00.6R ⚵ 17♎54.0
⚷ 25♒59.8R ⚶ 11♍02.4
☽ Mean ☊ 6♎48.1

LONGITUDE — September 1959

Day	Sid.Time	☉	0 hr ☽	Noon☽	True☊	☿	♀	♂	⚳	♃	♄	♅	♆	♇
1 Tu	10 39 37	8♍18 06	12♌03 25	18♌36 52	4♎09.2	23♌31.6	7♍55.8	27♍08.1	24♏32.6	24♏48.1	0♑28.1	18♌03.6	4♏45.4	4♍05.4
2 W	10 43 34	9 16 12	25 14 55	1♍57 27	4R05.9	25 16.2	7R18.7	27 46.7	24 49.4	24 55.2	0R27.8	18 07.1	4 46.8	4 07.4
3 Th	10 47 30	10 14 19	8♍44 14	15 35 01	4 03.7	27 03.5	6 41.9	28 25.3	25 06.5	25 02.5	0 27.6	18 10.6	4 48.3	4 09.5
4 F	10 51 27	11 12 28	22 29 27	29 27 08	4D02.7	28 53.0	6 05.6	29 03.9	25 23.6	25 10.0	0D27.5	18 14.1	4 49.8	4 11.5
5 Sa	10 55 23	12 10 39	6♎27 40	13♎30 35	4 02.8	0♍44.5	5 29.9	29 42.6	25 41.0	25 17.6	0 27.5	18 17.6	4 51.3	4 13.5
6 Su	10 59 20	13 08 51	20 35 28	27 41 50	4 03.8	2 37.3	4 55.3	0♎21.3	25 58.5	25 25.3	0 27.6	18 21.1	4 52.8	4 15.5
7 M	11 03 16	14 07 05	4♏49 17	11♏57 23	4 05.1	4 31.2	4 21.7	1 00.1	26 16.1	25 33.1	0 27.8	18 24.6	4 54.4	4 17.5
8 Tu	11 07 13	15 05 21	19 05 45	26 14 01	4 06.3	6 25.8	3 49.5	1 38.9	26 33.9	25 41.1	0 28.1	18 28.0	4 55.9	4 19.5
9 W	11 11 09	16 03 38	3♐21 52	10♐28 58	4R07.0	8 20.9	3 18.8	2 17.7	26 51.8	25 49.2	0 28.5	18 31.4	4 57.5	4 21.4
10 Th	11 15 06	17 01 56	17 35 02	24 39 48	4 07.0	10 16.0	2 49.9	2 56.6	27 09.9	25 57.4	0 29.0	18 34.8	4 59.2	4 23.4
11 F	11 19 03	18 00 16	1♑43 01	8♑44 24	4 06.1	12 11.1	2 22.7	3 35.5	27 28.1	26 05.7	0 29.6	18 38.2	5 00.8	4 25.4
12 Sa	11 22 59	18 58 37	15 43 44	22 40 46	4 04.7	14 05.9	1 57.6	4 14.4	27 46.5	26 14.2	0 30.2	18 41.6	5 02.5	4 27.4
13 Su	11 26 56	19 57 00	29 35 17	6♒27 01	4 02.9	16 00.3	1 34.5	4 53.4	28 05.0	26 22.8	0 31.0	18 44.9	5 04.2	4 29.3
14 M	11 30 52	20 55 25	13♒15 47	20 01 21	4 01.0	17 54.1	1 13.6	5 32.4	28 23.6	26 31.5	0 31.9	18 48.2	5 05.9	4 31.3
15 Tu	11 34 49	21 53 51	26 43 34	3♓22 15	3 59.5	19 47.2	0 55.0	6 11.4	28 42.3	26 40.3	0 32.9	18 51.5	5 07.6	4 33.3
16 W	11 38 45	22 52 19	9♓57 17	16 28 34	3 58.5	21 39.5	0 38.7	6 50.5	29 01.2	26 49.2	0 33.9	18 54.7	5 09.4	4 35.2
17 Th	11 42 42	23 50 49	22 56 03	29 19 43	3D58.0	23 31.0	0 24.9	7 29.6	29 20.2	26 58.2	0 35.1	18 58.0	5 11.1	4 37.1
18 F	11 46 38	24 49 21	5♈39 37	11♈55 51	3 58.1	25 21.6	0 13.4	8 08.8	29 39.3	27 07.4	0 36.4	19 01.2	5 12.9	4 39.0
19 Sa	11 50 35	25 47 55	18 08 33	24 17 55	3 58.5	27 11.3	0 04.4	8 48.0	29 58.5	27 16.7	0 37.7	19 04.3	5 14.7	4 41.0
20 Su	11 54 32	26 46 31	0♉24 14	6♉27 45	3 59.2	29 00.0	29♌57.8	9 27.2	0♐17.9	27 26.0	0 39.2	19 07.5	5 16.6	4 42.9
21 M	11 58 28	27 45 09	12 28 52	18 27 57	3 59.9	0♎47.8	29 53.7	10 06.5	0 37.3	27 35.5	0 40.7	19 10.6	5 18.4	4 44.8
22 Tu	12 02 25	28 43 49	24 25 26	0♊21 48	4 00.6	2 34.6	29D52.0	10 45.8	0 56.9	27 45.1	0 42.4	19 13.7	5 20.3	4 46.6
23 W	12 06 21	29 42 31	6♊17 34	12 13 14	4 01.0	4 20.4	29 52.6	11 25.2	1 16.6	27 54.8	0 44.1	19 16.7	5 22.2	4 48.5
24 Th	12 10 18	0♎41 16	18 09 24	24 06 36	4R01.2	6 05.3	29 55.7	12 04.6	1 36.4	28 04.6	0 46.0	19 19.8	5 24.1	4 50.4
25 F	12 14 14	1 40 03	0♋05 26	6♋06 29	4 01.2	7 49.1	0♍01.0	12 44.0	1 56.4	28 14.5	0 47.9	19 22.8	5 26.0	4 52.2
26 Sa	12 18 11	2 38 53	12 10 19	18 17 30	4 01.1	9 32.1	0 08.6	13 23.5	2 16.4	28 24.5	0 49.9	19 25.7	5 28.0	4 54.1
27 Su	12 22 07	3 37 44	24 28 33	0♌43 58	4D01.1	11 14.1	0 18.4	14 03.0	2 36.5	28 34.6	0 52.1	19 28.7	5 29.9	4 55.9
28 M	12 26 04	4 36 38	7♌04 13	13 29 39	4 01.1	12 55.1	0 30.3	14 42.6	2 56.8	28 44.8	0 54.3	19 31.6	5 31.9	4 57.7
29 Tu	12 30 01	5 35 34	20 00 36	26 37 15	4 01.2	14 35.3	0 44.4	15 22.2	3 17.1	28 55.1	0 56.6	19 34.5	5 33.9	4 59.5
30 W	12 33 57	6 34 32	3♍19 45	10♍08 05	4 01.4	16 14.5	1 00.5	16 01.8	3 37.6	29 05.5	0 59.0	19 37.3	5 35.9	5 01.3

LONGITUDE — October 1959

Day	Sid.Time	☉	0 hr ☽	Noon☽	True☊	☿	♀	♂	⚳	♃	♄	♅	♆	♇
1 Th	12 37 54	7♎33 32	17♍02 07	24♍01 37	4♎01.6	17♎52.9	1♍18.5	16♎41.5	3♐58.1	29♏16.0	1♑01.5	19♌40.1	5♏37.9	5♍03.1
2 F	12 41 50	8 32 34	1♎06 12	8♎15 21	4R01.6	19 30.5	1 38.5	17 21.2	4 18.8	29 26.5	1 04.1	19 42.8	5 40.0	5 04.8
3 Sa	12 45 47	9 31 39	15 28 29	22 44 52	4 01.4	21 07.2	2 00.3	18 01.0	4 39.5	29 37.2	1 06.7	19 45.6	5 42.0	5 06.6
4 Su	12 49 43	10 30 45	0♏03 43	7♏24 12	4 00.9	22 43.0	2 23.9	18 40.8	5 00.4	29 47.9	1 09.5	19 48.3	5 44.1	5 08.3
5 M	12 53 40	11 29 54	14 45 29	22 06 41	4 00.1	24 18.1	2 49.2	19 20.7	5 21.3	29 58.8	1 12.4	19 50.9	5 46.1	5 10.0
6 Tu	12 57 36	12 29 04	29 27 01	6♐45 44	3 59.2	25 52.3	3 16.2	20 00.6	5 42.3	0♐09.7	1 15.3	19 53.5	5 48.2	5 11.7
7 W	13 01 33	13 28 16	14♐02 08	21 15 41	3 58.3	27 25.8	3 44.8	20 40.5	6 03.4	0 20.7	1 18.3	19 56.1	5 50.3	5 13.3
8 Th	13 05 29	14 27 30	28 25 53	5♑32 24	3D57.8	28 58.5	4 15.0	21 20.5	6 24.7	0 31.8	1 21.5	19 58.6	5 52.4	5 15.0
9 F	13 09 26	15 26 46	12♑34 56	19 33 21	3 57.7	0♏30.4	4 46.6	22 00.5	6 45.9	0 43.0	1 24.7	20 01.1	5 54.6	5 16.6
10 Sa	13 13 23	16 26 03	26 27 33	3♒17 32	3 58.2	2 01.6	5 19.7	22 40.6	7 07.3	0 54.3	1 28.0	20 03.6	5 56.7	5 18.3
11 Su	13 17 19	17 25 22	10♒03 21	16 45 05	3 59.1	3 32.0	5 54.2	23 20.7	7 28.8	1 05.6	1 31.3	20 06.0	5 58.8	5 19.9
12 M	13 21 16	18 24 43	23 22 51	29 56 49	4 00.3	5 01.7	6 30.0	24 00.8	7 50.3	1 17.0	1 34.8	20 08.4	6 01.0	5 21.4
13 Tu	13 25 12	19 24 05	6♓27 07	12♓53 57	4 01.5	6 30.6	7 07.1	24 41.0	8 11.9	1 28.5	1 38.4	20 10.7	6 03.2	5 23.0
14 W	13 29 09	20 23 30	19 17 26	25 37 46	4R02.3	7 58.7	7 45.5	25 21.2	8 33.6	1 40.1	1 42.0	20 13.0	6 05.3	5 24.6
15 Th	13 33 05	21 22 56	1♈55 05	8♈09 32	4 02.4	9 26.1	8 25.1	26 01.5	8 55.4	1 51.7	1 45.7	20 15.2	6 07.5	5 26.1
16 F	13 37 02	22 22 24	14 21 17	20 30 29	4 01.6	10 52.7	9 05.9	26 41.8	9 17.2	2 03.4	1 49.5	20 17.4	6 09.7	5 27.6
17 Sa	13 40 58	23 21 55	26 37 17	2♉41 51	3 59.8	12 18.5	9 47.8	27 22.1	9 39.1	2 15.1	1 53.4	20 19.6	6 11.9	5 29.1
18 Su	13 44 55	24 21 27	8♉44 22	14 45 03	3 57.1	13 43.5	10 30.8	28 02.5	10 01.1	2 27.0	1 57.3	20 21.7	6 14.1	5 30.5
19 M	13 48 52	25 21 02	20 44 07	26 41 48	3 53.7	15 07.7	11 14.8	28 42.9	10 23.1	2 38.9	2 01.3	20 23.8	6 16.3	5 32.0
20 Tu	13 52 48	26 20 39	2♊38 25	8♊34 16	3 49.9	16 31.0	11 59.9	29 23.4	10 45.3	2 50.9	2 05.5	20 25.8	6 18.5	5 33.4
21 W	13 56 45	27 20 18	14 29 43	20 25 09	3 46.2	17 53.3	12 45.9	0♏03.9	11 07.5	3 02.9	2 09.6	20 27.8	6 20.7	5 34.8
22 Th	14 00 41	28 19 59	26 21 00	2♋17 43	3 43.0	19 14.7	13 32.9	0 44.5	11 29.7	3 15.0	2 13.9	20 29.7	6 23.0	5 36.1
23 F	14 04 38	29 19 42	8♋15 47	14 15 45	3 40.9	20 35.1	14 20.7	1 25.1	11 52.0	3 27.2	2 18.2	20 31.6	6 25.2	5 37.5
24 Sa	14 08 34	0♏19 28	20 18 09	26 23 33	3D39.8	21 54.4	15 09.5	2 05.8	12 14.4	3 39.4	2 22.7	20 33.4	6 27.4	5 38.8
25 Su	14 12 31	1 19 16	2♌32 32	8♌45 39	3 40.0	23 12.5	15 59.0	2 46.5	12 36.9	3 51.7	2 27.2	20 35.2	6 29.7	5 40.1
26 M	14 16 27	2 19 06	15 03 29	21 26 33	3 41.1	24 29.4	16 49.4	3 27.2	12 59.4	4 04.0	2 31.7	20 36.9	6 31.9	5 41.4
27 Tu	14 20 24	3 18 59	27 55 21	4♍30 19	3 42.7	25 44.8	17 40.6	4 08.0	13 22.0	4 16.4	2 36.4	20 38.6	6 34.1	5 42.7
28 W	14 24 21	4 18 53	11♍11 47	18 00 01	3 44.2	26 58.9	18 32.5	4 48.9	13 44.6	4 28.8	2 41.1	20 40.2	6 36.4	5 43.9
29 Th	14 28 17	5 18 50	24 55 06	1♎57 00	3R45.0	28 11.2	19 25.1	5 29.8	14 07.3	4 41.3	2 45.8	20 41.8	6 38.6	5 45.1
30 F	14 32 14	6 18 49	9♎05 31	16 20 14	3 44.4	29 21.8	20 18.4	6 10.7	14 30.1	4 53.9	2 50.7	20 43.4	6 40.9	5 46.3
31 Sa	14 36 10	7 18 49	23 40 36	1♏05 50	3 42.2	0♐30.4	21 12.4	6 51.7	14 52.9	5 06.5	2 55.6	20 44.8	6 43.1	5 47.4

Astro Data	Dy Hr Mn
☽0S	4 11:04
♄ D	5 1:01
♂0S	8 11:59
☽0N	17 11:15
☿0S	22 14:00
♀ D	22 17:15
☉0S	23 19:08
☽0S	1 20:17
♃⚺♄	14 17:51
☽0N	14 18:15
☽0S	29 6:59

Planet Ingress		Dy Hr Mn
☿	♍	5 2:28
♂	♎	5 22:46
⚳	♐	19 13:51
♀	♌R	20 3:01
☿	♎	21 1:20
☉	♎	23 19:08
♀	♍	25 8:15
♃	♐	5 14:40
☿	♏	9 4:02
♂	♏	21 9:40
☉	♏	24 4:11
☿	♐	31 1:16

Last Aspect Dy Hr Mn		☽ Ingress Dy Hr Mn
1 23:18 ♃ □	♍	2 8:31
4 11:18 ♂ ☌	♎	4 12:56
5 20:09 ♅ ⚹	♏	6 15:53
8 11:04 ♃ ☌	♐	8 18:20
10 1:39 ♅ △	♑	10 21:04
12 18:14 ♃ ⚹	♒	13 0:43
14 23:46 ♃ □	♓	15 5:54
17 7:31 ♃ △	♈	17 13:16
19 1:46 ♅ △	♉	19 23:12
22 11:00 ♀ □	♊	22 11:16
24 23:45 ♀ ⚹	♋	24 23:49
27 7:49 ♃ △	♌	27 10:36
29 16:11 ♃ □	♍	29 18:04

Last Aspect Dy Hr Mn		☽ Ingress Dy Hr Mn
1 21:00 ♃ ⚹	♎	1 22:08
3 8:59 ☿ ☌	♏	3 23:54
5 8:18 ♅ □	♐	6 0:54
7 23:34 ☿ ⚹	♑	8 2:38
9 16:28 ♂ □	♒	10 6:12
12 0:34 ♂ △	♓	12 12:06
13 0:41 ♀ ☍	♈	14 20:20
17 0:51 ♂ ☍	♉	17 6:40
18 23:17 ♅ □	♊	19 18:40
22 3:17 ☉ △	♋	22 7:22
24 2:06 ☿ △	♌	24 19:03
26 18:17 ☿ □	♍	27 3:48
29 5:00 ☿ ⚹	♎	29 8:41
30 19:12 ♅ ⚹	♏	31 10:14

☽ Phases & Eclipses Dy Hr Mn		
3 1:56	●	9♍50
9 22:07	☽	16♐28
17 0:52	○	23♓24
17 1:03	•	A 0.987
25 2:22	☾	1♋16
2 12:31	●	8♎34
2 12:26:27	•	T 03'02"
9 4:22	☽	15♑08
16 15:59	○	22♈32
24 20:22	☾	0♌40
31 22:41	●	7♏46

Astro Data

1 September 1959
Julian Day # 21793
SVP 5♓49'20"
GC 26♐16.6 ⚵ 0♏51.0
Eris 9♈48.1R ✱ 26♎08.5
⚷ 24♒26.9R ⚶ 26♍02.7
☽ Mean ☊ 5♎09.6

1 October 1959
Julian Day # 21823
SVP 5♓49'18"
GC 26♐16.6 ⚵ 12♏41.7
Eris 9♈30.4R ✱ 5♏26.7
⚷ 23♒12.4R ⚶ 11♎12.5
☽ Mean ☊ 3♎34.2

November 1959 — LONGITUDE

Day	Sid.Time	☉	0 hr ☽	Noon ☽	True ☊	☿	♀	♂	⚳	♃	♄	♅	♆	♇
1 Su	14 40 07	8♏18 52	8♏34 59	16♏06 58	3♎38.4	1♐36.8	22♍07.1	7♏32.7	15♐15.8	5♐19.2	3♑00.6	20♌46.3	6♏45.4	5♍48.6
2 M	14 44 03	9 18 57	23 40 36	1♐14 37	3R33.3	2 40.8	23 02.3	8 13.8	15 38.7	5 31.9	3 05.6	20 47.7	6 47.6	5 49.7
3 Tu	14 48 00	10 19 03	8♐47 48	16 18 55	3 27.8	3 42.0	23 58.2	8 54.9	16 01.7	5 44.6	3 10.8	20 49.0	6 49.9	5 50.7
4 W	14 51 56	11 19 12	23 46 52	1♑10 43	3 22.5	4 40.2	24 54.6	9 36.0	16 24.7	5 57.4	3 16.0	20 50.3	6 52.1	5 51.8
5 Th	14 55 53	12 19 21	8♑29 40	15 43 06	3 18.4	5 35.1	25 51.6	10 17.2	16 47.8	6 10.3	3 21.2	20 51.5	6 54.3	5 52.8
6 F	14 59 50	13 19 33	22 50 38	29 52 00	3 15.8	6 26.1	26 49.1	10 58.5	17 10.9	6 23.1	3 26.5	20 52.7	6 56.6	5 53.8
7 Sa	15 03 46	14 19 45	6♒47 09	13♒36 10	3D14.9	7 12.8	27 47.1	11 39.8	17 34.1	6 36.1	3 31.9	20 53.8	6 58.8	5 54.8
8 Su	15 07 43	15 20 00	20 19 15	26 56 40	3 15.5	7 54.8	28 45.7	12 21.1	17 57.3	6 49.0	3 37.3	20 54.8	7 01.1	5 55.7
9 M	15 11 39	16 20 15	3♓28 48	9♓56 02	3 16.8	8 31.5	29 44.7	13 02.5	18 20.6	7 02.0	3 42.8	20 55.9	7 03.3	5 56.6
10 Tu	15 15 36	17 20 32	16 18 49	22 37 33	3R18.2	9 02.3	0♎44.2	13 43.9	18 43.9	7 15.1	3 48.4	20 56.8	7 05.5	5 57.5
11 W	15 19 32	18 20 51	28 52 41	5♈04 38	3 18.7	9 26.4	1 44.2	14 25.3	19 07.2	7 28.1	3 54.0	20 57.7	7 07.7	5 58.4
12 Th	15 23 29	19 21 11	11♈13 46	17 20 28	3 17.5	9 43.3	2 44.6	15 06.8	19 30.6	7 41.2	3 59.6	20 58.6	7 09.9	5 59.2
13 F	15 27 25	20 21 32	23 25 02	29 27 46	3 14.2	9R52.2	3 45.5	15 48.4	19 54.1	7 54.4	4 05.3	20 59.3	7 12.1	6 00.0
14 Sa	15 31 22	21 21 56	5♉28 55	11♉28 44	3 08.5	9 52.4	4 46.8	16 30.0	20 17.5	8 07.5	4 11.1	21 00.1	7 14.3	6 00.7
15 Su	15 35 19	22 22 20	17 27 25	23 25 10	3 00.6	9 43.3	5 48.4	17 11.6	20 41.0	8 20.7	4 16.9	21 00.8	7 16.5	6 01.5
16 M	15 39 15	23 22 47	29 22 10	5♊18 34	2 51.1	9 24.2	6 50.5	17 53.3	21 04.6	8 34.0	4 22.8	21 01.4	7 18.7	6 02.2
17 Tu	15 43 12	24 23 15	11♊14 36	17 10 25	2 40.6	8 54.9	7 53.0	18 35.0	21 28.2	8 47.2	4 28.7	21 02.0	7 20.9	6 02.9
18 W	15 47 08	25 23 45	23 06 15	29 02 21	2 30.2	8 15.1	8 55.8	19 16.8	21 51.8	9 00.5	4 34.7	21 02.5	7 23.0	6 03.5
19 Th	15 51 05	26 24 17	4♋58 59	10♋56 26	2 20.8	7 25.1	9 59.0	19 58.6	22 15.4	9 13.8	4 40.8	21 02.9	7 25.2	6 04.1
20 F	15 55 01	27 24 50	16 55 04	22 55 17	2 13.2	6 25.5	11 02.6	20 40.5	22 39.1	9 27.1	4 46.8	21 03.3	7 27.3	6 04.7
21 Sa	15 58 58	28 25 25	28 57 28	5♌02 08	2 07.9	5 17.4	12 06.5	21 22.4	23 02.9	9 40.5	4 53.0	21 03.7	7 29.5	6 05.3
22 Su	16 02 54	29 26 01	11♌09 45	17 20 53	2 04.9	4 02.5	13 10.7	22 04.4	23 26.6	9 53.9	4 59.1	21 04.0	7 31.6	6 05.8
23 M	16 06 51	0♐26 40	23 36 03	29 55 51	2D04.0	2 42.8	14 15.2	22 46.4	23 50.4	10 07.3	5 05.3	21 04.2	7 33.7	6 06.3
24 Tu	16 10 48	1 27 20	6♍20 50	12♍51 33	2 04.5	1 21.0	15 20.1	23 28.5	24 14.2	10 20.7	5 11.6	21 04.4	7 35.8	6 06.8
25 W	16 14 44	2 28 01	19 28 29	26 12 06	2R05.2	29♏59.6	16 25.2	24 10.6	24 38.1	10 34.1	5 17.9	21 04.5	7 37.9	6 07.2
26 Th	16 18 41	3 28 45	3♎02 44	10♎00 35	2 05.1	28 41.4	17 30.6	24 52.7	25 01.9	10 47.6	5 24.2	21R04.6	7 40.0	6 07.6
27 F	16 22 37	4 29 30	17 05 45	24 18 04	2 03.0	27 29.1	18 36.3	25 34.9	25 25.8	11 01.0	5 30.6	21 04.6	7 42.0	6 08.0
28 Sa	16 26 34	5 30 16	1♏37 14	9♏02 40	1 58.5	26 24.7	19 42.3	26 17.2	25 49.8	11 14.5	5 37.1	21 04.6	7 44.1	6 08.3
29 Su	16 30 30	6 31 04	16 33 34	24 08 55	1 51.3	25 29.9	20 48.5	26 59.5	26 13.7	11 28.0	5 43.5	21 04.5	7 46.1	6 08.6
30 M	16 34 27	7 31 53	1♐47 28	9♐27 51	1 42.0	24 45.9	21 55.0	27 41.8	26 37.7	11 41.5	5 50.0	21 04.3	7 48.1	6 08.9

December 1959 — LONGITUDE

Day	Sid.Time	☉	0 hr ☽	Noon ☽	True ☊	☿	♀	♂	⚳	♃	♄	♅	♆	♇
1 Tu	16 38 23	8♐32 44	17♐08 35	24♐48 11	1♎31.6	24♏13.3	23♎01.8	28♏24.2	27♐01.7	11♐55.0	5♑56.6	21♌04.1	7♏50.1	6♍09.2
2 W	16 42 20	9 33 36	2♑25 10	9♑58 14	1R21.4	23R52.3	24 08.7	29 06.6	27 25.7	12 08.5	6 03.1	21R03.8	7 52.1	6 09.4
3 Th	16 46 17	10 34 28	17 26 13	24 48 10	1 12.7	23D42.6	25 15.9	29 49.1	27 49.8	12 22.0	6 09.8	21 03.5	7 54.1	6 09.6
4 F	16 50 13	11 35 22	2♒03 22	9♒11 23	1 06.2	23 43.7	26 23.3	0♐31.6	28 13.8	12 35.6	6 16.4	21 03.1	7 56.1	6 09.7
5 Sa	16 54 10	12 36 16	16 11 58	23 05 06	1 02.4	23 54.9	27 30.9	1 14.2	28 37.9	12 49.1	6 23.1	21 02.7	7 58.0	6 09.9
6 Su	16 58 06	13 37 11	29 50 57	6♓29 49	1D00.8	24 15.4	28 38.7	1 56.8	29 02.0	13 02.6	6 29.8	21 02.2	7 59.9	6 10.0
7 M	17 02 03	14 38 07	13♓02 08	19 28 25	1R00.7	24 44.3	29 46.7	2 39.5	29 26.1	13 16.2	6 36.5	21 01.7	8 01.8	6 10.0
8 Tu	17 05 59	15 39 03	25 49 12	2♈05 07	1 00.9	25 20.8	0♏54.9	3 22.1	29 50.3	13 29.7	6 43.3	21 01.1	8 03.7	6R10.0
9 W	17 09 56	16 40 00	8♈16 44	14 24 41	1 00.2	26 04.1	2 03.3	4 04.9	0♑14.4	13 43.2	6 50.0	21 00.4	8 05.6	6 10.0
10 Th	17 13 52	17 40 58	20 29 30	26 31 46	0 57.4	26 53.3	3 11.8	4 47.7	0 38.6	13 56.8	6 56.8	20 59.7	8 07.4	6 10.0
11 F	17 17 49	18 41 56	2♉31 57	8♉30 32	0 52.0	27 47.8	4 20.6	5 30.5	1 02.7	14 10.3	7 03.7	20 58.9	8 09.2	6 09.9
12 Sa	17 21 46	19 42 55	14 27 56	20 24 29	0 43.5	28 46.9	5 29.5	6 13.4	1 26.9	14 23.8	7 10.5	20 58.1	8 11.0	6 09.8
13 Su	17 25 42	20 43 55	26 20 33	2♊16 22	0 32.1	29 50.0	6 38.6	6 56.3	1 51.1	14 37.3	7 17.4	20 57.3	8 12.8	6 09.7
14 M	17 29 39	21 44 56	8♊12 11	14 08 12	0 18.4	0♐56.6	7 47.9	7 39.2	2 15.3	14 50.8	7 24.3	20 56.3	8 14.6	6 09.5
15 Tu	17 33 35	22 45 57	20 04 35	26 01 30	0 03.5	2 06.3	8 57.3	8 22.2	2 39.5	15 04.3	7 31.2	20 55.4	8 16.3	6 09.4
16 W	17 37 32	23 46 59	1♋59 05	7♋57 29	29♍48.6	3 18.6	10 06.9	9 05.3	3 03.7	15 17.8	7 38.2	20 54.4	8 18.0	6 09.1
17 Th	17 41 28	24 48 02	13 56 51	19 57 20	29 34.8	4 33.3	11 16.6	9 48.4	3 27.9	15 31.2	7 45.1	20 53.3	8 19.7	6 08.9
18 F	17 45 25	25 49 05	25 59 09	2♌02 30	29 23.2	5 50.1	12 26.5	10 31.5	3 52.2	15 44.7	7 52.1	20 52.2	8 21.4	6 08.6
19 Sa	17 49 21	26 50 10	8♌07 40	14 14 55	29 14.5	7 08.6	13 36.6	11 14.7	4 16.4	15 58.1	7 59.1	20 51.0	8 23.0	6 08.3
20 Su	17 53 18	27 51 15	20 24 38	26 37 10	29 09.0	8 28.6	14 46.7	11 57.9	4 40.7	16 11.5	8 06.1	20 49.8	8 24.6	6 08.0
21 M	17 57 15	28 52 20	2♍52 57	9♍12 27	29 06.1	9 50.0	15 57.0	12 41.2	5 04.9	16 25.0	8 13.1	20 48.5	8 26.2	6 07.6
22 Tu	18 01 11	29 53 27	15 36 09	22 04 31	29 05.3	11 12.7	17 07.5	13 24.5	5 29.1	16 38.3	8 20.2	20 47.2	8 27.8	6 07.2
23 W	18 05 08	0♑54 34	28 38 05	5♎17 17	29 05.2	12 36.3	18 18.1	14 07.9	5 53.4	16 51.7	8 27.2	20 45.8	8 29.4	6 06.7
24 Th	18 09 04	1 55 42	12♎02 33	18 54 13	29 04.6	14 01.0	19 28.7	14 51.3	6 17.7	17 05.0	8 34.3	20 44.4	8 30.9	6 06.3
25 F	18 13 01	2 56 51	25 52 31	2♏57 33	29 02.3	15 26.4	20 39.6	15 34.8	6 41.9	17 18.4	8 41.3	20 42.9	8 32.4	6 05.8
26 Sa	18 16 57	3 58 00	10♏09 16	17 27 21	28 57.3	16 52.6	21 50.5	16 18.3	7 06.2	17 31.7	8 48.4	20 41.4	8 33.9	6 05.3
27 Su	18 20 54	4 59 10	24 51 20	2♐20 29	28 49.4	18 19.5	23 01.5	17 01.9	7 30.4	17 44.9	8 55.5	20 39.9	8 35.3	6 04.7
28 M	18 24 50	6 00 21	9♐53 52	17 30 18	28 39.2	19 47.0	24 12.7	17 45.5	7 54.7	17 58.2	9 02.6	20 38.3	8 36.7	6 04.1
29 Tu	18 28 47	7 01 32	25 08 30	2♑47 02	28 27.5	21 15.1	25 23.9	18 29.1	8 18.9	18 11.4	9 09.7	20 36.6	8 38.1	6 03.5
30 W	18 32 44	8 02 43	10♑24 25	17 59 15	28 15.9	22 43.7	26 35.3	19 12.8	8 43.2	18 24.6	9 16.7	20 34.9	8 39.5	6 02.9
31 Th	18 36 40	9 03 54	25 30 11	2♒56 04	28 05.6	24 12.8	27 46.7	19 56.5	9 07.4	18 37.7	9 23.8	20 33.2	8 40.8	6 02.2

Astro Data (Dy Hr Mn)	Planet Ingress (Dy Hr Mn)	Last Aspect (Dy Hr Mn)	☽ Ingress (Dy Hr Mn)	Last Aspect (Dy Hr Mn)	☽ Ingress (Dy Hr Mn)	☽ Phases & Eclipses (Dy Hr Mn)	Astro Data
♃□♇ 4 0:30	♀ ♎ 9 18:11	1 22:09 ♀ ⚹	♐ 2 10:02	1 9:00 ♀ ⚹	♑ 1 20:11	7 13:24 ☽ 14♒23	1 November 1959
♃⚺♆ 9 14:47	☉ ♐ 23 1:27	4 1:08 ♀ □	♑ 4 10:05	3 12:49 ♀ □	♒ 3 20:35	15 9:42 ○ 22♉17	Julian Day # 21854
☽0N 11 0:29	☿ ♏R 25 11:53	6 6:23 ♀ △	♒ 6 12:14	5 20:33 ♀ △	♓ 6 0:16	23 13:03 ☾ 0♍29	SVP 5♓49'15"
♀0S 12 2:51		8 1:03 ♅ ☍	♓ 8 17:35	7 22:25 ☿ △	♈ 8 7:59	30 8:46 ● 7♐24	GC 26♐16.7 ⚴ 25♏43.6
☿R 14 0:35	♂ ♐ 3 18:09	10 1:05 ☉ △	♈ 11 2:10	10 1:00 ♅ △	♉ 10 18:56		Eris 9♈11.8R ⚵ 15♏47.0
☽0S 25 17:44	♀ ♏ 7 16:41	12 19:11 ♅ △	♉ 13 13:04	13 6:34 ☿ ☍	♊ 13 7:24	7 2:12 ☽ 14♓13	⚷ 22♒40.9R ⚶ 27♎16.8
♅R 27 4:47	⚳ ♑ 8 21:41	15 9:42 ☉ ☍	♊ 16 1:16	15 4:49 ☉ ☍	♋ 15 20:00	15 4:49 ○ 22♊28	☽ Mean ☊ 1♎55.7
	☿ ♐ 13 15:42	17 19:49 ♅ ⚹	♋ 18 13:56	16 16:47 ♀ △	♌ 18 7:58	23 3:28 ☾ 0♎33	
♄⚻♅ 2 14:24	☊ ♍R 15 17:36	20 21:45 ☉ △	♌ 21 2:04	20 14:35 ☉ △	♍ 20 18:29	29 19:09 ● 7♑20	1 December 1959
♄△♇ 3 11:22	☉ ♑ 22 14:34	22 21:37 ♂ □	♍ 23 12:08	22 1:55 ♀ ⚹	♎ 23 2:29		Julian Day # 21884
☿D 3 21:27		25 18:05 ☿ ⚹	♎ 25 18:41	24 15:10 ♅ ⚹	♏ 25 7:01		SVP 5♓49'11"
☽0N 8 7:30		27 6:39 ♅ ⚹	♏ 27 21:21	26 19:45 ♀ ☌	♐ 27 8:16		GC 26♐16.8 ⚴ 8♐37.2
♇R 8 20:26		29 16:41 ♂ ☌	♐ 29 21:12	28 16:55 ♅ △	♑ 29 7:38		Eris 8♈58.8R ⚵ 25♏59.2
☽0S 23 2:54				31 2:56 ♀ ⚹	♒ 31 7:15		⚷ 23♒06.7 ⚶ 12♏57.4
♄⚹♆ 23 21:22							☽ Mean ☊ 0♎20.4

LONGITUDE — January 1960

Day	Sid.Time	☉	0 hr ☽	Noon ☽	True ☊	☿	♀	♂	⚳	♃	♄	♅	♆	♇
1 F	18 40 37	10♑05 05	10♒15 54	17♒28 57	27♍57.7	25♐42.4	28♏58.2	20♐40.3	9♑31.7	18♐50.9	9♑30.9	20♌31.4	8♏42.1	6♍01.5
2 Sa	18 44 33	11 06 16	24 34 45	1♓33 00	27R 52.7	27 12.4	0♐09.8	21 24.1	9 55.9	19 03.9	9 38.0	20R 29.6	8 43.4	6R 00.8
3 Su	18 48 30	12 07 26	8♓23 41	15 06 54	27D 50.2	28 42.8	1 21.5	22 07.9	10 20.1	19 17.0	9 45.1	20 27.8	8 44.6	6 00.1
4 M	18 52 26	13 08 37	21 42 59	28 12 21	27 49.7	0♑13.6	2 33.3	22 51.8	10 44.3	19 30.0	9 52.2	20 25.9	8 45.9	5 59.3
5 Tu	18 56 23	14 09 47	4♈35 30	10♈53 03	27R 49.9	1 44.9	3 45.1	23 35.8	11 08.5	19 43.0	9 59.3	20 23.9	8 47.0	5 58.5
6 W	19 00 19	15 10 56	17 05 38	23 13 53	27 49.6	3 16.6	4 57.0	24 19.7	11 32.7	19 55.9	10 06.3	20 22.0	8 48.2	5 57.6
7 Th	19 04 16	16 12 05	29 18 28	5♉20 02	27 47.8	4 48.6	6 09.0	25 03.7	11 56.9	20 08.8	10 13.4	20 20.0	8 49.3	5 56.8
8 F	19 08 13	17 13 14	11♉19 13	17 16 37	27 43.6	6 21.1	7 21.1	25 47.8	12 21.0	20 21.6	10 20.5	20 17.9	8 50.4	5 55.9
9 Sa	19 12 09	18 14 23	23 12 46	29 08 11	27 36.6	7 54.0	8 33.2	26 31.9	12 45.2	20 34.4	10 27.5	20 15.8	8 51.5	5 55.0
10 Su	19 16 06	19 15 31	5♊03 20	10♊58 37	27 27.0	9 27.3	9 45.4	27 16.0	13 09.3	20 47.1	10 34.6	20 13.7	8 52.5	5 54.1
11 M	19 20 02	20 16 39	16 54 24	22 51 00	27 15.3	11 01.0	10 57.7	28 00.2	13 33.4	20 59.8	10 41.6	20 11.6	8 53.5	5 53.1
12 Tu	19 23 59	21 17 46	28 48 40	4♋47 37	27 02.3	12 35.2	12 10.1	28 44.4	13 57.5	21 12.5	10 48.6	20 09.4	8 54.5	5 52.1
13 W	19 27 55	22 18 53	10♋48 02	16 50 03	26 49.3	14 09.8	13 22.5	29 28.6	14 21.6	21 25.1	10 55.6	20 07.2	8 55.4	5 51.1
14 Th	19 31 52	23 19 59	22 53 48	28 59 22	26 37.2	15 44.9	14 35.0	0♑12.9	14 45.6	21 37.6	11 02.6	20 05.0	8 56.4	5 50.1
15 F	19 35 48	24 21 05	5♌06 53	11♌16 24	26 27.1	17 20.4	15 47.5	0 57.3	15 09.7	21 50.1	11 09.6	20 02.7	8 57.2	5 49.1
16 Sa	19 39 45	25 22 11	17 28 03	23 41 58	26 19.6	18 56.5	17 00.1	1 41.7	15 33.7	22 02.6	11 16.6	20 00.4	8 58.1	5 48.0
17 Su	19 43 42	26 23 16	29 58 17	6♍17 11	26 14.9	20 33.1	18 12.7	2 26.1	15 57.7	22 15.0	11 23.5	19 58.1	8 58.9	5 46.9
18 M	19 47 38	27 24 21	12♍38 52	19 03 36	26D 12.9	22 10.1	19 25.4	3 10.5	16 21.7	22 27.3	11 30.4	19 55.7	8 59.7	5 45.8
19 Tu	19 51 35	28 25 26	25 31 38	2♎03 16	26 12.8	23 47.8	20 38.2	3 55.0	16 45.6	22 39.5	11 37.3	19 53.4	9 00.4	5 44.7
20 W	19 55 31	29 26 30	8♎38 48	15 18 33	26 13.6	25 25.9	21 51.0	4 39.6	17 09.5	22 51.7	11 44.2	19 51.0	9 01.1	5 43.5
21 Th	19 59 28	0♒27 34	22 02 49	28 51 50	26R 14.2	27 04.7	23 03.9	5 24.1	17 33.4	23 03.9	11 51.0	19 48.6	9 01.8	5 42.3
22 F	20 03 24	1 28 37	5♏45 50	12♏44 54	26 13.6	28 44.0	24 16.8	6 08.8	17 57.3	23 16.0	11 57.9	19 46.1	9 02.5	5 41.1
23 Sa	20 07 21	2 29 40	19 49 05	26 58 15	26 11.1	0♒23.9	25 29.8	6 53.4	18 21.2	23 28.0	12 04.7	19 43.7	9 03.1	5 39.9
24 Su	20 11 17	3 30 43	4♐12 08	11♐30 19	26 06.2	2 04.4	26 42.8	7 38.1	18 45.0	23 39.9	12 11.5	19 41.2	9 03.7	5 38.7
25 M	20 15 14	4 31 45	18 52 13	26 17 02	25 59.4	3 45.6	27 55.8	8 22.9	19 08.8	23 51.8	12 18.2	19 38.7	9 04.2	5 37.4
26 Tu	20 19 11	5 32 47	3♑43 54	11♑11 46	25 51.4	5 27.4	29 08.9	9 07.7	19 32.6	24 03.6	12 25.0	19 36.2	9 04.7	5 36.2
27 W	20 23 07	6 33 48	18 39 31	26 06 01	25 43.2	7 09.7	0♑22.1	9 52.5	19 56.3	24 15.3	12 31.7	19 33.6	9 05.2	5 34.9
28 Th	20 27 04	7 34 48	3♒30 07	10♒50 46	25 35.8	8 52.8	1 35.2	10 37.3	20 20.0	24 27.0	12 38.4	19 31.1	9 05.7	5 33.6
29 F	20 31 00	8 35 47	18 07 00	25 18 01	25 30.2	10 36.4	2 48.4	11 22.2	20 43.7	24 38.6	12 45.0	19 28.5	9 06.1	5 32.2
30 Sa	20 34 57	9 36 45	2♓23 10	9♓22 00	25 26.8	12 20.6	4 01.7	12 07.1	21 07.3	24 50.1	12 51.6	19 25.9	9 06.4	5 30.9
31 Su	20 38 53	10 37 42	16 14 13	22 59 43	25D 25.6	14 05.5	5 14.9	12 52.1	21 30.9	25 01.5	12 58.2	19 23.4	9 06.8	5 29.6

LONGITUDE — February 1960

Day	Sid.Time	☉	0 hr ☽	Noon ☽	True ☊	☿	♀	♂	⚳	♃	♄	♅	♆	♇
1 M	20 42 50	11♒38 38	29♓38 35	6♈11 01	25♍26.0	15♒50.9	6♑28.2	13♑37.1	21♑54.5	25♐12.9	13♑04.7	19♌20.8	9♏07.1	5♍28.2
2 Tu	20 46 46	12 39 32	12♈37 19	18 57 55	25 27.4	17 36.8	7 41.5	14 22.1	22 18.0	25 24.1	13 11.2	19R 18.2	9 07.4	5R 26.8
3 W	20 50 43	13 40 25	25 13 19	1♉24 05	25 28.9	19 23.3	8 54.9	15 07.1	22 41.5	25 35.3	13 17.7	19 15.5	9 07.6	5 25.4
4 Th	20 54 40	14 41 16	7♉30 49	13 34 07	25R 29.6	21 10.2	10 08.3	15 52.2	23 04.9	25 46.4	13 24.1	19 12.9	9 07.8	5 24.0
5 F	20 58 36	15 42 07	19 34 39	25 33 02	25 29.0	22 57.4	11 21.6	16 37.3	23 28.3	25 57.4	13 30.5	19 10.3	9 08.0	5 22.6
6 Sa	21 02 33	16 42 55	1♊29 53	7♊25 48	25 26.6	24 45.0	12 35.1	17 22.5	23 51.7	26 08.3	13 36.8	19 07.7	9 08.1	5 21.2
7 Su	21 06 29	17 43 43	13 21 22	19 17 06	25 22.6	26 32.7	13 48.5	18 07.7	24 15.0	26 19.1	13 43.1	19 05.0	9 08.2	5 19.7
8 M	21 10 26	18 44 29	25 13 32	1♋11 04	25 17.0	28 20.4	15 02.0	18 52.9	24 38.3	26 29.9	13 49.4	19 02.4	9 08.3	5 18.3
9 Tu	21 14 22	19 45 13	7♋10 10	13 11 08	25 10.6	0♓08.0	16 15.5	19 38.1	25 01.5	26 40.5	13 55.6	18 59.8	9R 08.3	5 16.8
10 W	21 18 19	20 45 56	19 14 18	25 19 56	25 04.0	1 55.3	17 29.0	20 23.4	25 24.7	26 51.1	14 01.7	18 57.1	9 08.3	5 15.3
11 Th	21 22 15	21 46 38	1♌28 12	7♌39 18	24 57.8	3 42.0	18 42.5	21 08.7	25 47.8	27 01.5	14 07.9	18 54.5	9 08.3	5 13.9
12 F	21 26 12	22 47 18	13 53 19	20 10 19	24 52.8	5 27.9	19 56.1	21 54.1	26 10.9	27 11.9	14 13.9	18 51.9	9 08.2	5 12.4
13 Sa	21 30 09	23 47 56	26 30 23	2♍53 30	24 49.3	7 12.7	21 09.7	22 39.4	26 33.9	27 22.1	14 19.9	18 49.3	9 08.1	5 10.9
14 Su	21 34 05	24 48 33	9♍19 41	15 48 55	24D 47.4	8 56.0	22 23.3	23 24.8	26 56.9	27 32.3	14 25.9	18 46.7	9 08.0	5 09.4
15 M	21 38 02	25 49 09	22 21 10	28 56 27	24 47.2	10 37.5	23 36.9	24 10.3	27 19.8	27 42.3	14 31.8	18 44.0	9 07.8	5 07.9
16 Tu	21 41 58	26 49 44	5♎34 43	12♎16 00	24 48.1	12 16.6	24 50.5	24 55.7	27 42.7	27 52.3	14 37.7	18 41.4	9 07.6	5 06.3
17 W	21 45 55	27 50 17	19 00 16	25 47 33	24 49.6	13 52.8	26 04.2	25 41.2	28 05.5	28 02.1	14 43.5	18 38.8	9 07.4	5 04.8
18 Th	21 49 51	28 50 49	2♏37 49	9♏31 06	24 51.2	15 25.6	27 17.9	26 26.8	28 28.3	28 11.8	14 49.3	18 36.3	9 07.1	5 03.3
19 F	21 53 48	29 51 20	16 27 20	23 26 29	24R 52.1	16 54.5	28 31.6	27 12.3	28 51.0	28 21.5	14 55.0	18 33.7	9 06.8	5 01.8
20 Sa	21 57 44	0♓51 50	0♐28 26	7♐33 04	24 52.1	18 18.8	29 45.3	27 57.9	29 13.7	28 31.0	15 00.7	18 31.1	9 06.5	5 00.2
21 Su	22 01 41	1 52 18	14 40 08	21 49 22	24 51.0	19 37.7	0♒59.0	28 43.5	29 36.3	28 40.4	15 06.3	18 28.6	9 06.1	4 58.7
22 M	22 05 38	2 52 45	29 00 24	6♑12 46	24 48.9	20 50.8	2 12.8	29 29.2	29 58.9	28 49.7	15 11.8	18 26.0	9 05.7	4 57.2
23 Tu	22 09 34	3 53 11	13♑25 58	20 39 25	24 46.1	21 57.3	3 26.6	0♒14.9	0♒21.3	28 58.8	15 17.3	18 23.5	9 05.3	4 55.6
24 W	22 13 31	4 53 35	27 52 27	5♒04 24	24 43.2	22 56.6	4 40.3	1 00.6	0 43.8	29 07.9	15 22.7	18 21.0	9 04.8	4 54.1
25 Th	22 17 27	5 53 58	12♒14 35	19 22 19	24 40.6	23 48.0	5 54.1	1 46.3	1 06.1	29 16.8	15 28.1	18 18.5	9 04.3	4 52.6
26 F	22 21 24	6 54 19	26 26 57	3♓27 53	24 38.8	24 31.1	7 07.9	2 32.1	1 28.4	29 25.6	15 33.4	18 16.1	9 03.8	4 51.0
27 Sa	22 25 20	7 54 38	10♓24 36	17 16 42	24D 37.8	25 05.4	8 21.7	3 17.8	1 50.7	29 34.3	15 38.7	18 13.6	9 03.2	4 49.5
28 Su	22 29 17	8 54 56	24 03 51	0♈45 49	24 37.8	25 30.4	9 35.6	4 03.6	2 12.8	29 42.9	15 43.8	18 11.2	9 02.6	4 47.9
29 M	22 33 13	9 55 11	7♈22 31	13 53 56	24 38.5	25 46.0	10 49.4	4 49.4	2 34.9	29 51.3	15 48.9	18 08.8	9 02.0	4 46.4

Astro Data

	Dy Hr Mn
☽0N	4 16:24
♃△♅	8 6:03
☽0S	19 10:02
♃∠♆	26 14:22
☽0N	1 2:51
♆R	10 0:07
☽0S	15 16:26
☿0N	27 6:41
☽0N	28 13:14

Planet Ingress

		Dy Hr Mn
♀	♐	2 8:43
☿	♑	4 8:24
♂	♑	14 4:59
☉	♒	21 1:10
☿	♒	23 6:16
♀	♑	27 4:46
☿	♓	9 10:13
☉	♓	19 15:26
♀	♒	20 16:47
⚳	♒	22 13:13
♂	♒	23 4:11

Last Aspect / ☽ Ingress

Last Aspect Dy Hr Mn		☽ Ingress Dy Hr Mn
2 3:36	☿ ⚹	♓ 2 9:19
4 1:31	♂ □	♈ 4 15:21
6 14:18	♂ △	♉ 7 1:22
8 18:05	♅ □	♊ 9 13:45
11 23:03	♂ ☍	♋ 12 2:23
13 23:51	☉ ☍	♌ 14 13:59
16 8:46	♃ △	♍ 17 0:03
19 4:47	☉ △	♎ 19 8:14
21 8:26	♅ □	♏ 21 13:59
22 23:53	♅ □	♐ 23 17:03
25 14:54	♀ ☌	♑ 25 18:00
26 13:59	♄ ☌	♒ 27 18:19
29 10:53	♃ ⚹	♓ 29 19:56

Last Aspect Dy Hr Mn		☽ Ingress Dy Hr Mn
31 15:42	♃ □	♈ 1 0:39
3 0:32	♃ △	♉ 3 9:16
5 5:52	☿ □	♊ 5 20:58
8 5:16	☿ △	♋ 8 9:37
10 1:38	♂ ☍	♌ 10 21:08
13 1:29	♃ △	♍ 13 6:35
15 9:44	♃ □	♎ 15 13:55
17 16:00	♃ ⚹	♏ 17 19:24
19 21:31	♀ ⚹	♐ 19 23:12
21 23:34	♃ ☌	♑ 22 1:39
23 14:19	☿ ⚹	♒ 24 3:32
26 5:00	♃ ⚹	♓ 26 6:04
28 10:05	♃ □	♈ 28 10:37

☽ Phases & Eclipses

Dy Hr Mn		
5 18:53	☽	14♈27
13 23:51	○	22♋49
21 15:01	☾	0♏35
28 6:15	●	7♒20
4 14:26	☽	14♉47
12 17:24	○	23♌01
19 23:47	☾	0♐21
26 18:24	●	7♓10

Astro Data

1 January 1960
Julian Day # 21915
SVP 5♓49'06"
GC 26♐16.8 ⚴ 21♐46.0
Eris 8♈54.8 ⚵ 6♐12.3
⚷ 24♒26.6 ⚶ 28♏56.1
☽ Mean ☊ 28♍41.9

1 February 1960
Julian Day # 21946
SVP 5♓49'01"
GC 26♐16.9 ⚴ 4♑12.2
Eris 9♈01.8 ⚵ 15♐26.3
⚷ 26♒22.9 ⚶ 14♐12.2
☽ Mean ☊ 27♍03.4

March 1960 LONGITUDE

Day	Sid.Time	☉	0 hr ☽	Noon ☽	True ☊	☿	♀	♂	⚳	♃	♄	♅	♆	♇
1 Tu	22 37 10	10♓55 25	20♈20 12	26♈41 30	24♍39.6	25♓52.0	12♒03.2	5♒35.3	2♒57.0	29♐59.6	15♑54.0	18♌06.4	9♏01.3	4♍44.9
2 W	22 41 07	11 55 36	2♉58 07	9♉10 26	24 40.9	25R 48.6	13 17.0	6 21.1	3 18.9	0♑07.8	15 58.9	18R 04.1	9R 00.6	4R 43.3
3 Th	22 45 03	12 55 46	15 18 52	21 23 53	24 41.9	25 35.8	14 30.9	7 07.0	3 40.8	0 15.8	16 03.9	18 01.8	8 59.9	4 41.8
4 F	22 49 00	13 55 54	27 26 00	3♊25 48	24R 42.7	25 14.0	15 44.7	7 52.9	4 02.6	0 23.7	16 08.7	17 59.5	8 59.2	4 40.3
5 Sa	22 52 56	14 55 59	9♊23 49	15 20 41	24 42.9	24 44.0	16 58.6	8 38.9	4 24.3	0 31.5	16 13.5	17 57.2	8 58.4	4 38.8
6 Su	22 56 53	15 56 03	21 16 58	27 13 15	24 42.6	24 06.4	18 12.4	9 24.8	4 46.0	0 39.1	16 18.2	17 55.0	8 57.6	4 37.3
7 M	23 00 49	16 56 04	3♋10 08	9♋08 11	24 42.0	23 22.2	19 26.3	10 10.7	5 07.5	0 46.6	16 22.8	17 52.8	8 56.8	4 35.8
8 Tu	23 04 46	17 56 03	15 07 55	21 09 51	24 41.2	22 32.4	20 40.1	10 56.7	5 29.0	0 54.0	16 27.3	17 50.6	8 55.9	4 34.3
9 W	23 08 42	18 56 00	27 14 27	3♌22 08	24 40.4	21 38.4	21 54.0	11 42.7	5 50.5	1 01.2	16 31.8	17 48.4	8 55.0	4 32.8
10 Th	23 12 39	19 55 55	9♌33 17	15 48 13	24 39.7	20 41.5	23 07.9	12 28.7	6 11.8	1 08.2	16 36.2	17 46.3	8 54.1	4 31.3
11 F	23 16 36	20 55 48	22 07 09	28 30 18	24 39.2	19 43.0	24 21.7	13 14.7	6 33.0	1 15.2	16 40.5	17 44.2	8 53.2	4 29.9
12 Sa	23 20 32	21 55 38	4♍57 46	11♍29 35	24D 39.0	18 44.2	25 35.6	14 00.8	6 54.2	1 21.9	16 44.8	17 42.2	8 52.2	4 28.4
13 Su	23 24 29	22 55 27	18 05 44	24 46 06	24 38.9	17 46.4	26 49.5	14 46.9	7 15.3	1 28.6	16 49.0	17 40.2	8 51.2	4 27.0
14 M	23 28 25	23 55 14	1♎30 31	8♎18 47	24R 38.9	16 50.8	28 03.4	15 32.9	7 36.3	1 35.0	16 53.1	17 38.2	8 50.2	4 25.5
15 Tu	23 32 22	24 54 58	15 10 35	22 05 37	24 38.9	15 58.4	29 17.2	16 19.0	7 57.2	1 41.4	16 57.1	17 36.2	8 49.2	4 24.1
16 W	23 36 18	25 54 41	29 03 30	6♏03 52	24 38.9	15 10.1	0♓31.1	17 05.1	8 18.0	1 47.6	17 01.0	17 34.3	8 48.1	4 22.7
17 Th	23 40 15	26 54 23	13♏06 20	20 10 28	24 38.7	14 26.7	1 45.0	17 51.3	8 38.7	1 53.6	17 04.9	17 32.5	8 47.0	4 21.3
18 F	23 44 11	27 54 02	27 15 52	4♐22 11	24 38.4	13 48.7	2 58.9	18 37.4	8 59.3	1 59.5	17 08.6	17 30.6	8 45.9	4 19.9
19 Sa	23 48 08	28 53 40	11♐29 01	18 36 01	24D 38.2	13 16.4	4 12.8	19 23.6	9 19.9	2 05.2	17 12.3	17 28.9	8 44.7	4 18.5
20 Su	23 52 04	29 53 16	25 42 52	2♑49 14	24 38.1	12 50.1	5 26.7	20 09.7	9 40.3	2 10.7	17 16.0	17 27.1	8 43.6	4 17.1
21 M	23 56 01	0♈52 51	9♑54 51	16 59 24	24 38.3	12 29.9	6 40.6	20 55.9	10 00.7	2 16.1	17 19.5	17 25.4	8 42.4	4 15.8
22 Tu	23 59 58	1 52 23	24 02 40	1♒04 21	24 38.8	12 15.9	7 54.6	21 42.1	10 20.9	2 21.4	17 22.9	17 23.7	8 41.2	4 14.4
23 W	0 03 54	2 51 54	8♒04 12	15 01 59	24 39.5	12D 08.0	9 08.5	22 28.3	10 41.1	2 26.4	17 26.3	17 22.1	8 39.9	4 13.1
24 Th	0 07 51	3 51 23	21 57 28	28 50 22	24 40.3	12 06.0	10 22.4	23 14.6	11 01.1	2 31.3	17 29.6	17 20.5	8 38.7	4 11.8
25 F	0 11 47	4 50 50	5♓40 29	12♓27 34	24R 40.9	12 09.8	11 36.3	24 00.8	11 21.0	2 36.1	17 32.8	17 19.0	8 37.4	4 10.5
26 Sa	0 15 44	5 50 15	19 11 25	25 51 50	24 41.1	12 19.2	12 50.2	24 47.0	11 40.9	2 40.6	17 35.9	17 17.5	8 36.1	4 09.2
27 Su	0 19 40	6 49 39	2♈28 41	9♈01 49	24 40.8	12 33.9	14 04.1	25 33.3	12 00.6	2 45.0	17 38.9	17 16.1	8 34.8	4 08.0
28 M	0 23 37	7 49 00	15 31 09	21 56 39	24 39.7	12 53.6	15 18.0	26 19.5	12 20.2	2 49.2	17 41.8	17 14.7	8 33.5	4 06.8
29 Tu	0 27 33	8 48 19	28 18 19	4♉36 14	24 38.0	13 18.2	16 31.9	27 05.8	12 39.7	2 53.3	17 44.6	17 13.3	8 32.1	4 05.5
30 W	0 31 30	9 47 36	10♉50 31	17 01 21	24 35.8	13 47.3	17 45.8	27 52.0	12 59.1	2 57.2	17 47.4	17 12.0	8 30.7	4 04.3
31 Th	0 35 27	10 46 50	23 08 59	29 13 43	24 33.4	14 20.8	18 59.7	28 38.3	13 18.3	3 00.9	17 50.0	17 10.7	8 29.4	4 03.1

April 1960 LONGITUDE

Day	Sid.Time	☉	0 hr ☽	Noon ☽	True ☊	☿	♀	♂	⚳	♃	♄	♅	♆	♇
1 F	0 39 23	11♈46 03	5♊15 53	11♊15 54	24♍31.1	14♓58.3	20♓13.6	29♒24.5	13♒37.5	3♑04.4	17♑52.6	17♌09.5	8♏27.9	4♍02.0
2 Sa	0 43 20	12 45 13	17 14 13	23 11 18	24R 29.2	15 39.8	21 27.5	0♓10.8	13 56.5	3 07.8	17 55.0	17R 08.4	8R 26.5	4R 00.8
3 Su	0 47 16	13 44 21	29 07 41	5♋03 56	24D 28.1	16 24.9	22 41.4	0 57.0	14 15.4	3 10.9	17 57.4	17 07.3	8 25.1	3 59.7
4 M	0 51 13	14 43 27	11♋00 36	16 58 16	24 27.8	17 13.4	23 55.2	1 43.3	14 34.2	3 13.9	17 59.7	17 06.2	8 23.6	3 58.6
5 Tu	0 55 09	15 42 30	22 57 33	28 59 02	24 28.4	18 05.2	25 09.1	2 29.6	14 52.8	3 16.7	18 01.9	17 05.2	8 22.2	3 57.5
6 W	0 59 06	16 41 31	5♌03 19	11♌10 56	24 29.7	19 00.2	26 23.0	3 15.8	15 11.4	3 19.4	18 04.0	17 04.2	8 20.7	3 56.5
7 Th	1 03 02	17 40 30	17 22 27	23 38 20	24 31.3	19 58.1	27 36.8	4 02.1	15 29.8	3 21.8	18 06.0	17 03.3	8 19.2	3 55.5
8 F	1 06 59	18 39 26	29 59 04	6♍24 58	24 32.8	20 58.8	28 50.7	4 48.3	15 48.0	3 24.1	18 07.9	17 02.5	8 17.7	3 54.4
9 Sa	1 10 56	19 38 20	12♍56 22	19 33 26	24R 33.7	22 02.1	0♈04.5	5 34.6	16 06.1	3 26.2	18 09.7	17 01.6	8 16.2	3 53.4
10 Su	1 14 52	20 37 12	26 16 16	3♎04 50	24 33.5	23 08.1	1 18.3	6 20.8	16 24.1	3 28.1	18 11.4	17 00.9	8 14.6	3 52.5
11 M	1 18 49	21 36 02	9♎58 57	16 58 20	24 32.1	24 16.5	2 32.2	7 07.1	16 42.0	3 29.8	18 13.0	17 00.2	8 13.1	3 51.5
12 Tu	1 22 45	22 34 50	24 02 34	1♏11 05	24 29.3	25 27.2	3 46.0	7 53.3	16 59.7	3 31.3	18 14.5	16 59.5	8 11.5	3 50.6
13 W	1 26 42	23 33 36	8♏23 14	15 38 17	24 25.5	26 40.2	4 59.8	8 39.5	17 17.3	3 32.7	18 16.0	16 58.9	8 10.0	3 49.7
14 Th	1 30 38	24 32 20	22 55 24	0♐13 45	24 21.2	27 55.4	6 13.6	9 25.8	17 34.7	3 33.9	18 17.3	16 58.4	8 08.4	3 48.8
15 F	1 34 35	25 31 03	7♐32 30	14 50 50	24 16.9	29 12.7	7 27.5	10 12.0	17 52.0	3 34.8	18 18.5	16 57.9	8 06.8	3 48.0
16 Sa	1 38 31	26 29 43	22 07 59	29 23 18	24 13.5	0♈32.1	8 41.3	10 58.2	18 09.2	3 35.6	18 19.7	16 57.4	8 05.2	3 47.2
17 Su	1 42 28	27 28 22	6♑36 11	13♑46 12	24 11.3	1 53.5	9 55.1	11 44.5	18 26.2	3 36.2	18 20.7	16 57.0	8 03.7	3 46.4
18 M	1 46 24	28 27 00	20 52 57	27 56 12	24D 10.5	3 16.8	11 08.9	12 30.7	18 43.0	3 36.7	18 21.7	16 56.7	8 02.1	3 45.6
19 Tu	1 50 21	29 25 36	4♒55 48	11♒51 41	24 11.1	4 42.0	12 22.7	13 16.9	18 59.7	3R 36.9	18 22.5	16 56.4	8 00.4	3 44.9
20 W	1 54 18	0♉24 10	18 43 49	25 32 16	24 12.4	6 09.2	13 36.6	14 03.1	19 16.3	3 36.9	18 23.3	16 56.2	7 58.8	3 44.2
21 Th	1 58 14	1 22 42	2♓17 07	8♓58 28	24 13.9	7 38.1	14 50.4	14 49.3	19 32.6	3 36.8	18 23.9	16 56.0	7 57.2	3 43.5
22 F	2 02 11	2 21 13	15 36 27	22 11 10	24R 14.7	9 08.9	16 04.2	15 35.4	19 48.8	3 36.4	18 24.5	16 55.9	7 55.6	3 42.8
23 Sa	2 06 07	3 19 42	28 42 43	5♈11 14	24 14.1	10 41.5	17 18.0	16 21.6	20 04.9	3 35.9	18 24.9	16D 55.8	7 54.0	3 42.2
24 Su	2 10 04	4 18 09	11♈36 46	17 59 25	24 11.7	12 15.9	18 31.8	17 07.7	20 20.7	3 35.2	18 25.3	16 55.8	7 52.3	3 41.5
25 M	2 14 00	5 16 34	24 19 14	0♉36 18	24 07.3	13 52.0	19 45.5	17 53.9	20 36.4	3 34.3	18 25.5	16 55.8	7 50.7	3 41.0
26 Tu	2 17 57	6 14 58	6♉50 39	13 02 22	24 01.1	15 29.9	20 59.3	18 40.0	20 52.0	3 33.2	18 25.7	16 55.9	7 49.1	3 40.4
27 W	2 21 53	7 13 20	19 11 32	25 18 16	23 53.5	17 09.7	22 13.1	19 26.1	21 07.3	3 31.9	18R 25.7	16 56.1	7 47.4	3 39.9
28 Th	2 25 50	8 11 40	1♊22 42	7♊25 00	23 45.2	18 51.1	23 26.9	20 12.1	21 22.5	3 30.4	18 25.7	16 56.3	7 45.8	3 39.4
29 F	2 29 47	9 09 58	13 25 24	19 24 09	23 37.0	20 34.4	24 40.7	20 58.2	21 37.5	3 28.8	18 25.6	16 56.5	7 44.1	3 38.9
30 Sa	2 33 43	10 08 14	25 21 32	1♋17 56	23 29.8	22 19.4	25 54.4	21 44.2	21 52.3	3 26.9	18 25.3	16 56.8	7 42.5	3 38.5

Astro Data

	Dy Hr Mn
☿R	1 15:11
☿0S	9 14:10
☽0S	13 23:53
☉0N	20 14:42
♄⚻♅	22 15:49
♃⚼♅	22 20:27
☿D	24 8:04
☽0N	26 22:06
☽0S	10 9:08
♀0N	12 7:07
♃R	20 4:55
☿0N	20 12:58
☽0N	23 5:11
♅D	24 7:46
♄R	27 14:06

Planet Ingress

	Dy Hr Mn
♃ ♑	1 13:10
♀ ♓	16 1:53
☉ ♈	20 14:43
♂ ♓	2 6:24
♀ ♈	9 10:32
☿ ♈	16 2:22
☉ ♉	20 2:06

Last Aspect / ☽ Ingress

Last Aspect Dy Hr Mn		☽ Ingress Dy Hr Mn
29 19:53	♅ △	♉ 1 18:18
3 20:08	☿ ⚹	♊ 4 5:08
6 6:03	☿ □	♋ 6 17:37
8 14:33	☿ △	♌ 9 5:25
11 3:24	♀ ☍	♍ 11 14:47
13 8:26	☉ ☍	♎ 13 21:19
16 1:35	♀ △	♏ 16 1:37
18 0:15	☉ △	♐ 18 4:37
20 6:40	☉ □	♑ 20 7:14
21 12:34	♄ ☌	♒ 22 10:10
24 1:39	♂ ☌	♓ 24 14:02
25 21:06	♄ ⚹	♈ 26 19:29
28 20:47	♂ ⚹	♉ 29 3:13
31 10:45	♂ □	♊ 31 13:32

Last Aspect / ☽ Ingress

Last Aspect Dy Hr Mn		☽ Ingress Dy Hr Mn
2 8:06	♀ □	♋ 3 1:46
5 3:30	♀ △	♌ 5 14:01
6 23:36	☉ △	♍ 8 0:02
9 16:50	☿ ☍	♎ 10 6:36
11 20:27	☉ ☍	♏ 12 10:01
14 7:51	☿ △	♐ 14 11:37
16 6:52	☉ △	♑ 16 13:01
18 12:57	☉ □	♒ 18 15:32
19 20:52	♅ ☍	♓ 20 19:55
22 5:06	♄ ⚹	♈ 23 2:23
24 13:08	♀ ☌	♉ 25 10:50
26 23:42	♂ ⚹	♊ 27 21:16
29 23:51	♀ ⚹	♋ 30 9:22

☽ Phases & Eclipses

Dy Hr Mn	
5 11:06	☽ 14♊54
13 8:26	○ 22♍47
13 8:28	☊ T 1.514
20 6:40	☾ 29♐40
27 7:37	● 6♈39
27 7:24:34	☋ P 0.706
4 7:05	☽ 14♋31
11 20:27	○ 21♎57
18 12:57	☾ 28♑29
25 21:44	● 5♉40

Astro Data

1 March 1960
Julian Day # 21975
SVP 5♓48'58"
GC 26♐17.0 ⚴ 14♑35.5
Eris 9♈16.6 ✱ 22♐23.4
⚷ 28♒23.2 ⚵ 27♐12.9
☽ Mean ☊ 25♍31.3

1 April 1960
Julian Day # 22006
SVP 5♓48'56"
GC 26♐17.0 ⚴ 23♑27.4
Eris 9♈37.3 ✱ 26♐49.7
⚷ 0♓20.5 ⚵ 8♑42.9
☽ Mean ☊ 23♍52.8

LONGITUDE — May 1960

Day	Sid.Time	☉	0 hr ☽	Noon ☽	True ☊	☿	♀	♂	⚳	♃	♄	♅	♆	♇
1 Su	2 37 40	11♉06 28	7♋13 45	13♋09 24	23♍24.2	24♈06.3	27♈08.2	22♓30.2	22♒06.9	3♑24.9	18♑25.0	16♌57.2	7♏40.9	3♍38.0
2 M	2 41 36	12 04 41	19 05 24	25 02 16	23R 20.5	25 54.9	28 21.9	23 16.2	22 21.3	3R 22.7	18R 24.6	16 57.6	7R 39.2	3R 37.7
3 Tu	2 45 33	13 02 51	1♌00 33	7♌00 52	23D 18.8	27 45.3	29 35.6	24 02.2	22 35.5	3 20.3	18 24.0	16 58.1	7 37.6	3 37.3
4 W	2 49 29	14 00 59	13 03 49	19 10 01	23 18.7	29 37.6	0♉49.4	24 48.1	22 49.6	3 17.7	18 23.4	16 58.6	7 36.0	3 37.0
5 Th	2 53 26	14 59 05	25 20 07	1♍34 42	23 19.6	1♉31.6	2 03.1	25 34.0	23 03.4	3 15.0	18 22.7	16 59.2	7 34.4	3 36.7
6 F	2 57 22	15 57 10	7♍54 23	14 19 41	23R 20.6	3 27.4	3 16.8	26 19.9	23 17.0	3 12.1	18 21.9	16 59.8	7 32.8	3 36.4
7 Sa	3 01 19	16 55 12	20 51 06	27 29 01	23 20.9	5 25.0	4 30.5	27 05.8	23 30.4	3 08.9	18 21.0	17 00.5	7 31.1	3 36.2
8 Su	3 05 16	17 53 12	4♎13 41	11♎05 17	23 19.4	7 24.3	5 44.2	27 51.6	23 43.7	3 05.7	18 20.0	17 01.2	7 29.5	3 36.0
9 M	3 09 12	18 51 11	18 03 47	25 09 00	23 15.9	9 25.3	6 57.9	28 37.4	23 56.7	3 02.2	18 18.9	17 02.0	7 27.9	3 35.8
10 Tu	3 13 09	19 49 08	2♏20 33	9♏37 51	23 10.0	11 28.0	8 11.6	29 23.2	24 09.5	2 58.6	18 17.7	17 02.9	7 26.3	3 35.6
11 W	3 17 05	20 47 03	17 00 07	24 26 25	23 02.4	13 32.3	9 25.3	0♈08.9	24 22.1	2 54.8	18 16.4	17 03.8	7 24.8	3 35.5
12 Th	3 21 02	21 44 57	1♐55 40	9♐26 41	22 53.6	15 38.0	10 39.0	0 54.7	24 34.4	2 50.9	18 15.0	17 04.7	7 23.2	3 35.4
13 F	3 24 58	22 42 50	16 58 14	24 29 06	22 45.0	17 45.2	11 52.7	1 40.4	24 46.6	2 46.7	18 13.5	17 05.7	7 21.6	3 35.3
14 Sa	3 28 55	23 40 41	1♑58 07	9♑24 15	22 37.4	19 53.5	13 06.4	2 26.0	24 58.5	2 42.5	18 12.0	17 06.8	7 20.1	3D 35.3
15 Su	3 32 51	24 38 31	16 46 35	24 04 24	22 31.9	22 02.9	14 20.0	3 11.7	25 10.2	2 38.0	18 10.3	17 07.9	7 18.5	3 35.3
16 M	3 36 48	25 36 20	1♒17 09	8♒24 29	22 28.6	24 13.2	15 33.7	3 57.3	25 21.7	2 33.4	18 08.6	17 09.0	7 17.0	3 35.3
17 Tu	3 40 45	26 34 07	15 26 12	22 22 17	22D 27.3	26 24.1	16 47.4	4 42.9	25 32.9	2 28.7	18 06.8	17 10.2	7 15.5	3 35.4
18 W	3 44 41	27 31 54	29 12 48	5♓57 59	22 27.4	28 35.4	18 01.1	5 28.4	25 43.9	2 23.8	18 04.8	17 11.5	7 13.9	3 35.5
19 Th	3 48 38	28 29 39	12♓38 04	19 13 23	22R 27.9	0♊46.9	19 14.8	6 13.9	25 54.6	2 18.7	18 02.8	17 12.8	7 12.4	3 35.6
20 F	3 52 34	29 27 23	25 44 18	2♈11 09	22 27.5	2 58.2	20 28.4	6 59.4	26 05.1	2 13.5	18 00.7	17 14.1	7 10.9	3 35.7
21 Sa	3 56 31	0♊25 06	8♈34 19	14 54 09	22 25.4	5 09.1	21 42.1	7 44.8	26 15.4	2 08.1	17 58.6	17 15.6	7 09.5	3 35.9
22 Su	4 00 27	1 22 48	21 10 56	27 24 58	22 20.7	7 19.4	22 55.8	8 30.2	26 25.4	2 02.7	17 56.3	17 17.0	7 08.0	3 36.1
23 M	4 04 24	2 20 29	3♉36 31	9♉45 48	22 13.2	9 28.7	24 09.5	9 15.6	26 35.1	1 57.0	17 54.0	17 18.5	7 06.5	3 36.4
24 Tu	4 08 20	3 18 09	15 53 00	21 58 18	22 03.2	11 36.8	25 23.2	10 00.9	26 44.6	1 51.3	17 51.5	17 20.1	7 05.1	3 36.6
25 W	4 12 17	4 15 48	28 01 50	4♊03 45	21 51.1	13 43.4	26 36.8	10 46.2	26 53.8	1 45.4	17 49.0	17 21.7	7 03.7	3 36.9
26 Th	4 16 14	5 13 25	10♊04 12	16 03 18	21 38.1	15 48.3	27 50.5	11 31.4	27 02.7	1 39.3	17 46.4	17 23.3	7 02.3	3 37.3
27 F	4 20 10	6 11 01	22 01 13	27 58 08	21 25.0	17 51.3	29 04.2	12 16.6	27 11.4	1 33.2	17 43.8	17 25.0	7 00.9	3 37.6
28 Sa	4 24 07	7 08 36	3♋54 16	9♋49 50	21 13.1	19 52.3	0♊17.9	13 01.7	27 19.8	1 26.9	17 41.0	17 26.8	6 59.5	3 38.0
29 Su	4 28 03	8 06 10	15 45 09	21 40 31	21 03.3	21 51.1	1 31.5	13 46.8	27 27.9	1 20.6	17 38.2	17 28.6	6 58.2	3 38.4
30 M	4 32 00	9 03 43	27 36 19	3♌32 58	20 56.0	23 47.6	2 45.2	14 31.8	27 35.7	1 14.1	17 35.3	17 30.4	6 56.9	3 38.9
31 Tu	4 35 56	10 01 14	9♌30 57	15 30 46	20 51.4	25 41.6	3 58.9	15 16.8	27 43.3	1 07.5	17 32.3	17 32.3	6 55.5	3 39.3

LONGITUDE — June 1960

Day	Sid.Time	☉	0 hr ☽	Noon ☽	True ☊	☿	♀	♂	⚳	♃	♄	♅	♆	♇
1 W	4 39 53	10♊58 43	21♌32 58	27♌38 09	20♍49.3	27♊33.1	5♊12.5	16♈01.8	27♒50.5	1♑00.8	17♑29.3	17♌34.2	6♏54.2	3♍39.9
2 Th	4 43 49	11 56 12	3♍46 55	9♍59 54	20R 48.7	29 22.0	6 26.2	16 46.7	27 57.5	0R 54.0	17R 26.2	17 36.2	6R 53.0	3 40.4
3 F	4 47 46	12 53 39	16 17 43	22 40 59	20 48.7	1♋08.3	7 39.8	17 31.5	28 04.2	0 47.1	17 23.0	17 38.2	6 51.7	3 40.9
4 Sa	4 51 43	13 51 05	29 10 16	5♎46 07	20 48.2	2 51.9	8 53.5	18 16.3	28 10.5	0 40.2	17 19.8	17 40.3	6 50.5	3 41.5
5 Su	4 55 39	14 48 30	12♎28 56	19 19 04	20 46.0	4 32.8	10 07.2	19 01.0	28 16.6	0 33.1	17 16.4	17 42.4	6 49.3	3 42.2
6 M	4 59 36	15 45 53	26 16 39	3♏21 42	20 41.5	6 10.9	11 20.8	19 45.7	28 22.4	0 26.0	17 13.1	17 44.5	6 48.1	3 42.8
7 Tu	5 03 32	16 43 16	10♏34 01	17 53 08	20 34.4	7 46.3	12 34.5	20 30.3	28 27.9	0 18.8	17 09.6	17 46.7	6 46.9	3 43.5
8 W	5 07 29	17 40 38	25 18 24	2♐48 56	20 25.1	9 18.9	13 48.1	21 14.9	28 33.0	0 11.6	17 06.1	17 49.0	6 45.8	3 44.2
9 Th	5 11 25	18 37 58	10♐23 35	18 01 06	20 14.5	10 48.7	15 01.8	21 59.4	28 37.9	0 04.3	17 02.6	17 51.3	6 44.6	3 44.9
10 F	5 15 22	19 35 18	25 40 05	3♑19 04	20 03.8	12 15.7	16 15.4	22 43.9	28 42.4	29♐56.9	16 59.0	17 53.6	6 43.5	3 45.7
11 Sa	5 19 18	20 32 38	10♑56 39	18 31 27	19 54.3	13 39.8	17 29.1	23 28.3	28 46.6	29 49.5	16 55.3	17 55.9	6 42.5	3 46.5
12 Su	5 23 15	21 29 56	26 02 17	3♒28 09	19 47.0	15 01.0	18 42.8	24 12.6	28 50.5	29 42.0	16 51.6	17 58.4	6 41.4	3 47.3
13 M	5 27 12	22 27 15	10♒48 13	18 01 57	19 42.3	16 19.3	19 56.4	24 56.9	28 54.1	29 34.5	16 47.8	18 00.8	6 40.4	3 48.1
14 Tu	5 31 08	23 24 32	25 09 00	2♓09 12	19 40.0	17 34.6	21 10.1	25 41.2	28 57.3	29 26.9	16 44.0	18 03.3	6 39.4	3 49.0
15 W	5 35 05	24 21 50	9♓02 35	15 49 22	19 39.3	18 46.9	22 23.8	26 25.4	29 00.2	29 19.3	16 40.1	18 05.8	6 38.4	3 49.9
16 Th	5 39 01	25 19 07	22 29 49	29 04 21	19 39.3	19 56.1	23 37.5	27 09.5	29 02.8	29 11.7	16 36.2	18 08.3	6 37.4	3 50.8
17 F	5 42 58	26 16 24	5♈33 25	11♈57 29	19 38.7	21 02.2	24 51.2	27 53.5	29 05.0	29 04.0	16 32.2	18 10.9	6 36.5	3 51.8
18 Sa	5 46 54	27 13 40	18 17 03	24 32 38	19 36.3	22 05.0	26 04.9	28 37.5	29 06.9	28 56.4	16 28.2	18 13.6	6 35.6	3 52.8
19 Su	5 50 51	28 10 57	0♉44 42	6♉53 43	19 31.5	23 04.5	27 18.6	29 21.5	29 08.4	28 48.7	16 24.1	18 16.2	6 34.7	3 53.8
20 M	5 54 47	29 08 13	13 00 06	19 04 13	19 23.9	24 00.7	28 32.3	0♉05.3	29 09.6	28 41.0	16 20.0	18 19.0	6 33.9	3 54.8
21 Tu	5 58 44	0♋05 29	25 06 26	1♊07 03	19 13.7	24 53.3	29 46.0	0 49.1	29 10.5	28 33.4	16 15.9	18 21.7	6 33.0	3 55.9
22 W	6 02 41	1 02 44	7♊06 21	13 04 32	19 01.4	25 42.4	0♋59.7	1 32.9	29R 11.0	28 25.7	16 11.7	18 24.5	6 32.2	3 57.0
23 Th	6 06 37	1 59 59	19 01 51	24 58 28	18 48.1	26 27.8	2 13.4	2 16.5	29 11.1	28 18.0	16 07.5	18 27.3	6 31.5	3 58.1
24 F	6 10 34	2 57 14	0♋54 35	6♋50 22	18 34.7	27 09.4	3 27.2	3 00.1	29 10.9	28 10.4	16 03.3	18 30.1	6 30.7	3 59.2
25 Sa	6 14 30	3 54 29	12 46 00	18 41 40	18 22.5	27 47.1	4 40.9	3 43.6	29 10.4	28 02.8	15 59.1	18 33.0	6 30.0	4 00.4
26 Su	6 18 27	4 51 43	24 37 35	0♌33 59	18 12.3	28 20.8	5 54.6	4 27.0	29 09.4	27 55.2	15 54.8	18 35.9	6 29.3	4 01.5
27 M	6 22 23	5 48 57	6♌31 09	12 29 22	18 04.7	28 50.3	7 08.4	5 10.4	29 08.2	27 47.6	15 50.5	18 38.9	6 28.7	4 02.8
28 Tu	6 26 20	6 46 11	18 29 01	24 30 27	17 59.9	29 15.6	8 22.1	5 53.7	29 06.5	27 40.1	15 46.2	18 41.9	6 28.0	4 04.0
29 W	6 30 16	7 43 24	0♍34 07	6♍40 30	17D 57.6	29 36.5	9 35.9	6 36.9	29 04.5	27 32.6	15 41.8	18 44.9	6 27.4	4 05.2
30 Th	6 34 13	8 40 36	12 50 05	19 03 25	17 57.0	29 52.9	10 49.6	7 20.0	29 02.2	27 25.2	15 37.4	18 47.9	6 26.9	4 06.5

Astro Data

	Dy Hr Mn
☽0S	7 19:34
♇D	15 0:50
♂0N	15 15:29
♃⚼♅	20 9:39
☽0N	20 11:31
♄⚻♅	31 12:13
☽0S	4 5:46
☽0N	16 18:32
⚳R	23 9:52

Planet Ingress

	Dy Hr Mn
♀ ♉	3 19:56
☿ ♉	4 16:45
♂ ♈	11 7:19
☿ ♊	19 3:27
☉ ♊	21 1:34
♀ ♊	28 6:11
☿ ♋	2 20:31
♃ ♐R	10 1:52
♂ ♉	20 9:05
☉ ♋	21 9:42
♀ ♋	21 16:34

Last Aspect / ☽ Ingress (May)

Last Aspect Dy Hr Mn		☽ Ingress	Dy Hr Mn
2 19:28	♀ □	♌	2 21:59
4 7:42	♅ ☌	♍	5 8:59
7 11:16	♂ ☍	♎	7 16:30
9 0:27	♄ □	♏	9 20:07
11 5:42	☉ ☍	♐	11 20:55
13 0:11	♅ △	♑	13 20:50
15 13:01	☉ △	♒	15 21:51
17 20:24	☿ □	♓	18 1:23
20 6:30	☉ ⚹	♈	20 7:55
21 17:51	♄ □	♉	22 17:00
24 19:31	♀ ☌	♊	25 3:55
26 14:41	♅ ⚹	♋	27 16:06
29 3:51	♄ ☍	♌	30 4:50

Last Aspect / ☽ Ingress (June)

Last Aspect Dy Hr Mn		☽ Ingress	Dy Hr Mn
1 11:48	☿ ⚹	♍	1 16:38
3 2:06	♄ △	♎	4 1:31
5 11:27	♂ ☍	♏	6 6:20
7 11:49	♅ □	♐	8 7:31
10 6:45	♃ ☌	♑	10 6:48
11 20:18	♂ □	♒	12 6:23
14 7:23	♃ ⚹	♓	14 8:17
16 12:13	♃ □	♈	16 13:42
18 20:25	♃ △	♉	18 22:33
20 22:36	☿ ⚹	♊	21 9:46
23 18:39	♃ ☍	♋	23 22:10
26 7:18	☿ ☌	♌	26 10:51
28 18:12	♃ △	♍	28 22:53

☽ Phases & Eclipses

Dy Hr Mn	
4 1:00	☽ 13♌34
11 5:42	○ 20♏32
17 19:54	☾ 26♒53
25 12:26	● 4♊17
2 16:01	☽ 12♍06
9 13:02	○ 18♐40
16 4:35	☾ 25♓01
24 3:27	● 2♋37

Astro Data

1 May 1960
Julian Day # 22036
SVP 5♓48'53"
GC 26♐17.1 ⚵ 28♑30.4
Eris 9♈57.1 ⚶ 26♐48.1R
⚷ 1♓42.1 ⚴ 15♑49.3
☽ Mean ☊ 22♍17.4

1 June 1960
Julian Day # 22067
SVP 5♓48'49"
GC 26♐17.2 ⚵ 28♑15.7R
Eris 10♈12.5 ⚶ 21♐53.1R
⚷ 2♓17.4 ⚴ 16♑39.1R
☽ Mean ☊ 20♍38.9

July 1960

LONGITUDE

Day	Sid.Time	☉	0 hr ☽	Noon ☽	True ☊	☿	♀	♂	⚳	♃	♄	♅	♆	♇
1 F	6 38 10	9♋37 49	25♍21 03	1♎43 32	17♍57.4	0♌04.8	12♋03.4	8♉03.0	28♒59.5	27♐17.8	15♑33.1	18♌51.0	6♏26.3	4♍07.8
2 Sa	6 42 06	10 35 01	8♎11 25	14 45 13	17R57.5	0 12.0	13 17.1	8 46.0	28R56.4	27R10.5	15R28.7	18 54.1	6R25.8	4 09.2
3 Su	6 46 03	11 32 12	21 25 23	28 12 20	17 56.3	0R14.6	14 30.9	9 28.9	28 53.0	27 03.3	15 24.3	18 57.2	6 25.3	4 10.5
4 M	6 49 59	12 29 23	5♏06 18	12♏07 26	17 53.1	0 12.5	15 44.7	10 11.7	28 49.2	26 56.1	15 19.9	19 00.3	6 24.9	4 11.9
5 Tu	6 53 56	13 26 35	19 15 41	26 30 48	17 47.7	0 05.8	16 58.4	10 54.4	28 45.1	26 49.0	15 15.4	19 03.5	6 24.5	4 13.3
6 W	6 57 52	14 23 45	3♐52 20	11♐19 37	17 40.3	29♋54.4	18 12.2	11 37.0	28 40.6	26 42.0	15 11.0	19 06.7	6 24.1	4 14.7
7 Th	7 01 49	15 20 56	18 51 42	26 27 31	17 31.6	29 38.6	19 26.0	12 19.6	28 35.8	26 35.0	15 06.6	19 10.0	6 23.7	4 16.1
8 F	7 05 45	16 18 07	4♑05 46	11♑45 04	17 22.7	29 18.6	20 39.8	13 02.0	28 30.6	26 28.2	15 02.2	19 13.2	6 23.4	4 17.6
9 Sa	7 09 42	17 15 18	19 24 01	27 01 11	17 14.8	28 54.5	21 53.5	13 44.4	28 25.1	26 21.4	14 57.8	19 16.5	6 23.1	4 19.1
10 Su	7 13 39	18 12 29	4♒35 15	12♒05 02	17 08.7	28 26.6	23 07.3	14 26.7	28 19.2	26 14.8	14 53.4	19 19.8	6 22.9	4 20.6
11 M	7 17 35	19 09 41	19 29 32	26 47 58	17 04.9	27 55.4	24 21.1	15 08.9	28 13.0	26 08.2	14 49.0	19 23.1	6 22.6	4 22.1
12 Tu	7 21 32	20 06 52	3♓59 45	11♓04 34	17D03.3	27 21.3	25 34.9	15 51.0	28 06.5	26 01.8	14 44.6	19 26.5	6 22.4	4 23.6
13 W	7 25 28	21 04 05	18 02 14	24 52 47	17 03.3	26 44.7	26 48.7	16 33.1	27 59.6	25 55.4	14 40.2	19 29.9	6 22.3	4 25.2
14 Th	7 29 25	22 01 18	1♈36 26	8♈13 28	17 04.2	26 06.4	28 02.5	17 15.0	27 52.4	25 49.2	14 35.8	19 33.3	6 22.1	4 26.7
15 F	7 33 21	22 58 31	14 44 18	21 09 24	17R04.8	25 26.8	29 16.4	17 56.9	27 44.9	25 43.1	14 31.4	19 36.7	6 22.0	4 28.3
16 Sa	7 37 18	23 55 45	27 29 17	3♉44 30	17 04.3	24 46.7	0♌30.2	18 38.6	27 37.0	25 37.1	14 27.1	19 40.1	6 21.9	4 30.0
17 Su	7 41 14	24 53 00	9♉55 37	16 03 09	17 02.0	24 06.7	1 44.0	19 20.3	27 28.8	25 31.2	14 22.8	19 43.6	6D21.9	4 31.6
18 M	7 45 11	25 50 15	22 07 40	28 09 39	16 57.6	23 27.6	2 57.9	20 01.8	27 20.4	25 25.5	14 18.5	19 47.0	6 21.9	4 33.2
19 Tu	7 49 08	26 47 32	4♊09 35	10♊07 55	16 51.2	22 50.0	4 11.7	20 43.3	27 11.6	25 19.9	14 14.2	19 50.5	6 21.9	4 34.9
20 W	7 53 04	27 44 49	16 05 02	22 01 20	16 43.1	22 14.7	5 25.6	21 24.7	27 02.5	25 14.4	14 10.0	19 54.1	6 22.0	4 36.6
21 Th	7 57 01	28 42 06	27 57 07	3♋52 43	16 34.3	21 42.2	6 39.5	22 05.9	26 53.1	25 09.1	14 05.8	19 57.6	6 22.1	4 38.3
22 F	8 00 57	29 39 24	9♋48 22	15 44 19	16 25.3	21 13.2	7 53.3	22 47.1	26 43.4	25 03.9	14 01.6	20 01.1	6 22.2	4 40.0
23 Sa	8 04 54	0♌36 43	21 40 49	27 38 02	16 17.1	20 48.3	9 07.2	23 28.1	26 33.4	24 58.9	13 57.4	20 04.7	6 22.3	4 41.7
24 Su	8 08 50	1 34 03	3♌36 12	9♌35 30	16 10.4	20 27.9	10 21.1	24 09.1	26 23.2	24 54.0	13 53.3	20 08.3	6 22.5	4 43.5
25 M	8 12 47	2 31 23	15 36 08	21 38 21	16 05.6	20 12.4	11 35.0	24 49.9	26 12.7	24 49.3	13 49.2	20 11.9	6 22.7	4 45.3
26 Tu	8 16 43	3 28 43	27 42 21	3♍48 25	16D02.9	20 02.3	12 48.9	25 30.6	26 02.0	24 44.7	13 45.2	20 15.5	6 23.0	4 47.0
27 W	8 20 40	4 26 04	9♍56 49	16 07 52	16 02.1	19D57.9	14 02.8	26 11.2	25 51.0	24 40.3	13 41.2	20 19.1	6 23.3	4 48.8
28 Th	8 24 37	5 23 26	22 21 55	28 39 19	16 02.8	19 59.3	15 16.6	26 51.7	25 39.8	24 36.0	13 37.2	20 22.7	6 23.6	4 50.6
29 F	8 28 33	6 20 48	5♎00 26	11♎25 40	16 04.1	20 06.7	16 30.5	27 32.1	25 28.4	24 31.9	13 33.3	20 26.4	6 23.9	4 52.5
30 Sa	8 32 30	7 18 11	17 55 25	24 30 03	16 05.5	20 20.4	17 44.4	28 12.4	25 16.8	24 28.0	13 29.4	20 30.0	6 24.3	4 54.3
31 Su	8 36 26	8 15 34	1♏09 56	7♏55 20	16R06.1	20 40.3	18 58.3	28 52.5	25 05.0	24 24.3	13 25.6	20 33.7	6 24.7	4 56.1

August 1960

LONGITUDE

Day	Sid.Time	☉	0 hr ☽	Noon ☽	True ☊	☿	♀	♂	⚳	♃	♄	♅	♆	♇
1 M	8 40 23	9♌12 58	14♏46 30	21♏43 33	16♍05.4	21♋06.5	20♌12.2	29♉32.5	24♒53.0	24♐20.7	13♑21.9	20♌37.4	6♏25.2	4♍58.0
2 Tu	8 44 19	10 10 23	28 46 31	5♐55 17	16R03.2	21 39.1	21 26.1	0♊12.4	24R40.8	24R17.3	13R18.2	20 41.0	6 25.6	4 59.9
3 W	8 48 16	11 07 48	13♐09 33	20 28 53	15 59.7	22 18.1	22 40.0	0 52.2	24 28.4	24 14.0	13 14.5	20 44.7	6 26.1	5 01.8
4 Th	8 52 12	12 05 14	27 52 38	5♑20 02	15 55.3	23 03.2	23 53.9	1 31.8	24 16.0	24 11.0	13 10.9	20 48.4	6 26.7	5 03.7
5 F	8 56 09	13 02 41	12♑50 08	20 21 51	15 50.6	23 54.6	25 07.8	2 11.4	24 03.3	24 08.1	13 07.4	20 52.1	6 27.2	5 05.6
6 Sa	9 00 06	14 00 08	27 54 03	5♒25 34	15 46.4	24 52.1	26 21.7	2 50.8	23 50.6	24 05.4	13 03.9	20 55.9	6 27.9	5 07.5
7 Su	9 04 02	14 57 37	12♒55 11	20 21 50	15 43.3	25 55.5	27 35.6	3 30.1	23 37.7	24 02.8	13 00.5	20 59.6	6 28.5	5 09.4
8 M	9 07 59	15 55 06	27 44 30	5♓02 18	15D41.5	27 04.7	28 49.5	4 09.2	23 24.8	24 00.5	12 57.2	21 03.3	6 29.1	5 11.3
9 Tu	9 11 55	16 52 37	12♓14 33	19 20 43	15 41.2	28 19.5	0♍03.4	4 48.3	23 11.7	23 58.3	12 53.9	21 07.0	6 29.8	5 13.3
10 W	9 15 52	17 50 09	26 20 26	3♈13 30	15 42.0	29 39.8	1 17.3	5 27.2	22 58.6	23 56.3	12 50.6	21 10.7	6 30.6	5 15.2
11 Th	9 19 48	18 47 42	9♈59 56	16 39 49	15 43.5	1♌05.1	2 31.2	6 06.0	22 45.4	23 54.5	12 47.5	21 14.5	6 31.3	5 17.2
12 F	9 23 45	19 45 17	23 13 24	29 41 01	15 45.0	2 35.4	3 45.1	6 44.6	22 32.2	23 52.9	12 44.4	21 18.2	6 32.1	5 19.2
13 Sa	9 27 41	20 42 53	6♉03 04	12♉20 03	15R46.0	4 10.2	4 59.0	7 23.1	22 19.0	23 51.4	12 41.4	21 21.9	6 32.9	5 21.1
14 Su	9 31 38	21 40 31	18 32 29	24 40 53	15 46.3	5 49.2	6 12.9	8 01.5	22 05.7	23 50.2	12 38.5	21 25.7	6 33.8	5 23.1
15 M	9 35 35	22 38 10	0♊45 50	6♊47 54	15 45.5	7 32.1	7 26.8	8 39.7	21 52.4	23 49.1	12 35.6	21 29.4	6 34.7	5 25.1
16 Tu	9 39 31	23 35 51	12 47 39	18 45 35	15 43.7	9 18.4	8 40.7	9 17.8	21 39.1	23 48.2	12 32.8	21 33.2	6 35.6	5 27.1
17 W	9 43 28	24 33 33	24 42 16	0♋38 10	15 41.1	11 07.8	9 54.7	9 55.7	21 25.9	23 47.5	12 30.1	21 36.9	6 36.5	5 29.1
18 Th	9 47 24	25 31 17	6♋33 46	12 29 29	15 38.0	12 59.9	11 08.6	10 33.5	21 12.7	23 47.0	12 27.4	21 40.6	6 37.5	5 31.1
19 F	9 51 21	26 29 03	18 25 43	24 22 51	15 34.8	14 54.1	12 22.5	11 11.1	20 59.5	23 46.7	12 24.9	21 44.4	6 38.5	5 33.1
20 Sa	9 55 17	27 26 49	0♌21 11	6♌21 02	15 32.0	16 50.2	13 36.4	11 48.6	20 46.4	23D46.6	12 22.4	21 48.1	6 39.5	5 35.2
21 Su	9 59 14	28 24 38	12 22 39	18 26 16	15 29.7	18 47.7	14 50.3	12 25.9	20 33.4	23 46.6	12 20.0	21 51.8	6 40.6	5 37.2
22 M	10 03 10	29 22 28	24 32 06	0♍40 20	15 28.3	20 46.2	16 04.2	13 03.1	20 20.5	23 46.9	12 17.7	21 55.5	6 41.6	5 39.2
23 Tu	10 07 07	0♍20 19	6♍51 07	13 04 39	15D27.8	22 45.5	17 18.1	13 40.1	20 07.7	23 47.3	12 15.5	21 59.2	6 42.8	5 41.2
24 W	10 11 04	1 18 12	19 21 02	25 40 25	15 28.0	24 45.1	18 32.0	14 16.9	19 55.0	23 47.9	12 13.3	22 02.9	6 43.9	5 43.3
25 Th	10 15 00	2 16 06	2♎02 58	8♎28 47	15 28.7	26 44.9	19 45.9	14 53.6	19 42.4	23 48.7	12 11.2	22 06.6	6 45.1	5 45.3
26 F	10 18 57	3 14 01	14 58 01	21 30 48	15 29.8	28 44.5	20 59.8	15 30.0	19 30.0	23 49.7	12 09.3	22 10.3	6 46.3	5 47.3
27 Sa	10 22 53	4 11 58	28 07 15	4♏47 31	15 30.8	0♍43.7	22 13.7	16 06.4	19 17.8	23 50.9	12 07.4	22 14.0	6 47.5	5 49.4
28 Su	10 26 50	5 09 56	11♏31 40	18 19 49	15 31.6	2 42.5	23 27.6	16 42.5	19 05.7	23 52.3	12 05.6	22 17.7	6 48.8	5 51.4
29 M	10 30 46	6 07 55	25 11 58	2♐08 10	15R31.9	4 40.5	24 41.5	17 18.5	18 53.9	23 53.9	12 03.9	22 21.3	6 50.1	5 53.4
30 Tu	10 34 43	7 05 56	9♐08 19	16 12 18	15 31.8	6 37.7	25 55.4	17 54.2	18 42.2	23 55.6	12 02.3	22 25.0	6 51.4	5 55.5
31 W	10 38 39	8 03 58	23 19 55	0♑30 51	15 31.4	8 34.1	27 09.3	18 29.8	18 30.7	23 57.6	12 00.8	22 28.6	6 52.7	5 57.5

Astro Data	Dy Hr Mn
☽0S	1 14:29
☿R	3 13:15
☽0N	14 3:05
♆D	18 6:55
☿D	27 18:25
☽0S	28 21:24
☽0N	10 12:56
♃D	20 16:40
☽0S	25 3:22

Planet Ingress	Dy Hr Mn
☿ ♌	1 1:13
☿ ♋R	6 1:23
♀ ♌	16 2:11
☉ ♌	22 20:37
♂ ♊	2 4:32
♀ ♍	9 10:54
☿ ♌	10 17:49
☉ ♍	23 3:34
☿ ♍	27 3:11

Last Aspect Dy Hr Mn		☽ Ingress Dy Hr Mn
1 3:46	♃ □	♎ 1 8:46
3 10:00	♃ ⚹	♏ 3 15:08
4 23:37	♅ □	♐ 5 17:42
7 12:12	♃ ☌	♑ 7 17:34
9 14:54	☿ ☍	♒ 9 16:43
11 10:55	♃ ⚹	♓ 11 17:19
13 15:46	♀ △	♈ 13 21:07
15 20:34	♃ △	♉ 16 4:48
18 6:58	☉ ⚹	♊ 18 15:40
20 18:28	♃ ☍	♋ 21 4:09
23 3:06	♂ ⚹	♌ 23 16:46
25 18:42	♂ □	♍ 26 4:31
28 8:24	♂ △	♎ 28 14:33
30 11:56	♃ ⚹	♏ 30 21:55

Last Aspect Dy Hr Mn		☽ Ingress Dy Hr Mn
2 1:57	♂ ☍	♐ 2 2:04
3 18:05	♃ ☌	♑ 4 3:25
5 18:01	☿ ☍	♒ 6 3:21
8 0:50	♀ ☍	♓ 8 3:42
10 5:05	☿ △	♈ 10 6:21
12 1:14	♃ △	♉ 12 12:36
14 5:37	☉ □	♊ 14 22:29
16 22:37	☉ ⚹	♋ 17 10:43
18 11:56	♄ ☍	♌ 19 23:18
22 9:15	☉ ☌	♍ 22 10:41
24 8:27	♃ □	♎ 24 20:09
26 16:13	♃ ⚹	♏ 27 3:24
28 21:51	♀ ⚹	♐ 29 8:19
31 5:52	♀ □	♑ 31 11:09

☽ Phases & Eclipses Dy Hr Mn	
2 3:48	☽ 10♎15
8 19:37	○ 16♑36
15 15:43	☾ 23♈07
23 18:31	● 0♌52
31 12:38	☽ 8♏17
7 2:41	○ 14♒35
14 5:37	☾ 21♉25
22 9:15	● 29♌16
29 19:22	☽ 6♐26

Astro Data

1 July 1960
Julian Day # 22097
SVP 5♓48'44"
GC 26♐17.3 ⚴ 22♑11.7R
Eris 10♈19.0 ⚵ 15♐21.1R
⚷ 1♓58.1R ⚶ 10♑57.7R
☽ Mean ☊ 19♍03.6

1 August 1960
Julian Day # 22128
SVP 5♓48'40"
GC 26♐17.3 ⚴ 14♑07.5R
Eris 10♈15.5R ⚵ 11♐49.6R
⚷ 0♓51.1R ⚶ 4♑59.2R
☽ Mean ☊ 17♍25.1

LONGITUDE — September 1960

Day	Sid.Time	☉	0 hr ☽	Noon ☽	True ☊	☿	♀	♂	⚳	♃	♄	♅	♆	♇
1 Th	10 42 36	9♍02 01	7♑44 44	15♑01 03	15♍30.8	10♍29.4	28♍23.1	19♊05.3	18♒19.5	23♐59.7	11♑59.3	22♌32.3	6♏54.1	5♍59.6
2 F	10 46 33	10 00 06	22 19 14	29 38 38	15R30.1	12 23.7	29 37.0	19 40.5	18R08.5	24 02.0	11R58.0	22 35.9	6 55.5	6 01.6
3 Sa	10 50 29	10 58 12	6♒58 30	14♒18 03	15 29.6	14 16.8	0♎50.8	20 15.5	17 57.7	24 04.5	11 56.8	22 39.5	6 56.9	6 03.6
4 Su	10 54 26	11 56 20	21 36 31	28 53 04	15 29.3	16 08.9	2 04.6	20 50.4	17 47.2	24 07.1	11 55.6	22 43.1	6 58.3	6 05.7
5 M	10 58 22	12 54 29	6♓06 56	13♓17 23	15D29.2	17 59.7	3 18.5	21 25.0	17 36.9	24 10.0	11 54.5	22 46.6	6 59.8	6 07.7
6 Tu	11 02 19	13 52 40	20 23 48	27 25 35	15 29.2	19 49.5	4 32.3	21 59.5	17 26.9	24 13.0	11 53.6	22 50.2	7 01.3	6 09.7
7 W	11 06 15	14 50 53	4♈22 19	11♈13 40	15R29.3	21 38.0	5 46.1	22 33.8	17 17.2	24 16.2	11 52.7	22 53.7	7 02.8	6 11.7
8 Th	11 10 12	15 49 08	17 59 25	24 39 29	15 29.3	23 25.4	6 59.9	23 07.8	17 07.8	24 19.5	11 51.9	22 57.3	7 04.3	6 13.7
9 F	11 14 08	16 47 25	1♉13 52	7♉42 44	15 29.2	25 11.6	8 13.7	23 41.7	16 58.6	24 23.1	11 51.3	23 00.8	7 05.9	6 15.8
10 Sa	11 18 05	17 45 43	14 06 16	20 24 49	15 29.0	26 56.7	9 27.5	24 15.3	16 49.8	24 26.8	11 50.7	23 04.3	7 07.5	6 17.8
11 Su	11 22 01	18 44 04	26 38 45	2♊48 31	15 28.8	28 40.7	10 41.2	24 48.8	16 41.2	24 30.7	11 50.2	23 07.7	7 09.1	6 19.8
12 M	11 25 58	19 42 27	8♊54 36	14 57 32	15D28.6	0♎23.5	11 55.0	25 22.0	16 33.0	24 34.8	11 49.8	23 11.2	7 10.7	6 21.8
13 Tu	11 29 55	20 40 53	20 57 54	26 56 15	15 28.7	2 05.2	13 08.8	25 55.0	16 25.1	24 39.0	11 49.5	23 14.6	7 12.4	6 23.8
14 W	11 33 51	21 39 20	2♋53 10	8♋49 14	15 29.0	3 45.9	14 22.6	26 27.7	16 17.5	24 43.4	11 49.3	23 18.0	7 14.1	6 25.8
15 Th	11 37 48	22 37 49	14 45 01	20 41 06	15 29.5	5 25.5	15 36.3	27 00.2	16 10.2	24 48.0	11D49.2	23 21.4	7 15.8	6 27.7
16 F	11 41 44	23 36 21	26 37 59	2♌36 12	15 30.3	7 04.0	16 50.1	27 32.5	16 03.3	24 52.8	11 49.2	23 24.8	7 17.5	6 29.7
17 Sa	11 45 41	24 34 55	8♌36 13	14 38 29	15 31.2	8 41.4	18 03.8	28 04.6	15 56.7	24 57.7	11 49.3	23 28.1	7 19.2	6 31.7
18 Su	11 49 37	25 33 30	20 43 23	26 51 16	15 32.0	10 17.9	19 17.6	28 36.4	15 50.4	25 02.8	11 49.5	23 31.4	7 21.0	6 33.6
19 M	11 53 34	26 32 08	3♍02 25	9♍17 06	15R32.5	11 53.3	20 31.3	29 07.9	15 44.5	25 08.0	11 49.8	23 34.7	7 22.8	6 35.6
20 Tu	11 57 30	27 30 48	15 35 29	21 57 42	15 32.5	13 27.8	21 45.0	29 39.2	15 39.0	25 13.4	11 50.2	23 38.0	7 24.6	6 37.5
21 W	12 01 27	28 29 30	28 23 48	4♎53 50	15 31.8	15 01.2	22 58.7	0♋10.2	15 33.8	25 19.0	11 50.7	23 41.2	7 26.4	6 39.4
22 Th	12 05 24	29 28 13	11♎27 44	18 05 25	15 30.5	16 33.7	24 12.4	0 40.9	15 28.9	25 24.7	11 51.3	23 44.5	7 28.3	6 41.3
23 F	12 09 20	0♎26 59	24 46 44	1♏31 32	15 28.7	18 05.2	25 26.1	1 11.4	15 24.5	25 30.6	11 52.0	23 47.6	7 30.1	6 43.3
24 Sa	12 13 17	1 25 46	8♏19 35	15 10 41	15 26.6	19 35.8	26 39.8	1 41.6	15 20.3	25 36.7	11 52.8	23 50.8	7 32.0	6 45.1
25 Su	12 17 13	2 24 36	22 04 34	29 00 59	15 24.5	21 05.3	27 53.5	2 11.5	15 16.6	25 42.9	11 53.7	23 53.9	7 33.9	6 47.0
26 M	12 21 10	3 23 27	5♐59 39	13♐00 20	15 22.8	22 33.9	29 07.2	2 41.1	15 13.2	25 49.3	11 54.7	23 57.0	7 35.8	6 48.9
27 Tu	12 25 06	4 22 19	20 02 44	27 06 37	15D21.9	24 01.5	0♏20.8	3 10.4	15 10.2	25 55.8	11 55.8	24 00.1	7 37.8	6 50.8
28 W	12 29 03	5 21 14	4♑11 43	11♑17 46	15 21.9	25 28.1	1 34.5	3 39.4	15 07.6	26 02.5	11 57.0	24 03.2	7 39.7	6 52.6
29 Th	12 32 59	6 20 10	18 24 30	25 31 38	15 22.7	26 53.7	2 48.1	4 08.1	15 05.3	26 09.3	11 58.3	24 06.2	7 41.7	6 54.4
30 F	12 36 56	7 19 08	2♒38 52	9♒45 55	15 24.0	28 18.3	4 01.7	4 36.6	15 03.4	26 16.2	11 59.7	24 09.1	7 43.7	6 56.3

LONGITUDE — October 1960

Day	Sid.Time	☉	0 hr ☽	Noon ☽	True ☊	☿	♀	♂	⚳	♃	♄	♅	♆	♇
1 Sa	12 40 53	8♎18 08	16♒52 25	23♒58 02	15♍25.3	29♎41.8	5♏15.3	5♋04.7	15♒01.9	26♐23.3	12♑01.2	24♌12.1	7♏45.7	6♍58.1
2 Su	12 44 49	9 17 09	1♓02 23	8♓05 03	15R26.3	1♏04.2	6 28.8	5 32.4	15R00.7	26 30.6	12 02.7	24 15.0	7 47.7	6 59.9
3 M	12 48 46	10 16 12	15 05 40	22 03 47	15 26.3	2 25.5	7 42.4	5 59.9	14 59.9	26 38.0	12 04.4	24 17.9	7 49.7	7 01.6
4 Tu	12 52 42	11 15 17	28 59 01	5♈50 58	15 25.0	3 45.7	8 55.9	6 27.0	14D59.4	26 45.5	12 06.2	24 20.7	7 51.8	7 03.4
5 W	12 56 39	12 14 25	12♈39 16	19 23 39	15 22.4	5 04.7	10 09.5	6 53.8	14 59.3	26 53.2	12 08.0	24 23.5	7 53.8	7 05.1
6 Th	13 00 35	13 13 34	26 03 49	2♉39 35	15 18.6	6 22.3	11 23.0	7 20.2	14 59.6	27 01.0	12 10.0	24 26.3	7 55.9	7 06.9
7 F	13 04 32	14 12 45	9♉10 52	15 37 35	15 14.0	7 38.7	12 36.5	7 46.3	15 00.2	27 09.0	12 12.1	24 29.0	7 58.0	7 08.6
8 Sa	13 08 28	15 11 59	21 59 49	28 17 40	15 09.0	8 53.6	13 50.0	8 12.1	15 01.2	27 17.0	12 14.2	24 31.7	8 00.1	7 10.3
9 Su	13 12 25	16 11 15	4♊31 21	10♊41 09	15 04.4	10 07.1	15 03.4	8 37.4	15 02.5	27 25.3	12 16.5	24 34.4	8 02.2	7 11.9
10 M	13 16 21	17 10 33	16 47 26	22 50 36	15 00.6	11 18.9	16 16.9	9 02.4	15 04.2	27 33.6	12 18.8	24 37.0	8 04.3	7 13.6
11 Tu	13 20 18	18 09 54	28 51 07	4♋49 31	14 58.2	12 29.0	17 30.4	9 27.0	15 06.3	27 42.1	12 21.2	24 39.6	8 06.4	7 15.3
12 W	13 24 15	19 09 17	10♋46 21	16 42 12	14D57.1	13 37.2	18 43.8	9 51.2	15 08.7	27 50.7	12 23.7	24 42.2	8 08.6	7 16.9
13 Th	13 28 11	20 08 42	22 37 43	28 33 29	14 57.5	14 43.3	19 57.2	10 15.0	15 11.4	27 59.4	12 26.4	24 44.7	8 10.7	7 18.5
14 F	13 32 08	21 08 09	4♌30 08	10♌28 20	14 58.8	15 47.3	21 10.6	10 38.4	15 14.5	28 08.3	12 29.1	24 47.1	8 12.9	7 20.1
15 Sa	13 36 04	22 07 39	16 28 40	22 31 44	15 00.5	16 48.9	22 24.0	11 01.4	15 17.9	28 17.3	12 31.9	24 49.6	8 15.0	7 21.6
16 Su	13 40 01	23 07 11	28 38 05	4♍48 15	15R01.9	17 47.8	23 37.4	11 24.0	15 21.7	28 26.4	12 34.7	24 51.9	8 17.2	7 23.2
17 M	13 43 57	24 06 45	11♍02 41	17 21 46	15 02.3	18 43.8	24 50.8	11 46.0	15 25.8	28 35.6	12 37.7	24 54.3	8 19.4	7 24.7
18 Tu	13 47 54	25 06 21	23 45 50	0♎15 04	15 01.2	19 36.7	26 04.1	12 07.7	15 30.2	28 44.9	12 40.8	24 56.6	8 21.6	7 26.2
19 W	13 51 50	26 06 00	6♎49 36	13 29 27	14 58.1	20 26.0	27 17.5	12 28.9	15 35.0	28 54.4	12 43.9	24 58.8	8 23.8	7 27.7
20 Th	13 55 47	27 05 41	20 14 29	27 04 28	14 53.1	21 11.4	28 30.8	12 49.6	15 40.0	29 04.0	12 47.2	25 01.0	8 26.0	7 29.1
21 F	13 59 44	28 05 23	3♏59 05	10♏57 52	14 46.6	21 52.5	29 44.1	13 09.8	15 45.5	29 13.7	12 50.5	25 03.2	8 28.2	7 30.6
22 Sa	14 03 40	29 05 08	18 00 16	25 05 42	14 39.3	22 29.0	0♐57.4	13 29.5	15 51.2	29 23.5	12 53.9	25 05.3	8 30.4	7 32.0
23 Su	14 07 37	0♏04 54	2♐13 30	9♐22 58	14 32.1	23 00.1	2 10.7	13 48.8	15 57.3	29 33.4	12 57.4	25 07.4	8 32.7	7 33.4
24 M	14 11 33	1 04 43	16 33 28	23 44 20	14 25.9	23 25.5	3 24.0	14 07.5	16 03.7	29 43.5	13 01.0	25 09.4	8 34.9	7 34.8
25 Tu	14 15 30	2 04 33	0♑54 59	8♑04 54	14 21.5	23 44.6	4 37.2	14 25.7	16 10.3	29 53.6	13 04.7	25 11.4	8 37.1	7 36.1
26 W	14 19 26	3 04 24	15 13 39	22 20 51	14D19.1	23 56.8	5 50.4	14 43.3	16 17.3	0♑03.8	13 08.4	25 13.3	8 39.4	7 37.4
27 Th	14 23 23	4 04 18	29 26 15	6♒29 37	14 18.6	24R01.5	7 03.6	15 00.5	16 24.6	0 14.2	13 12.3	25 15.2	8 41.6	7 38.7
28 F	14 27 19	5 04 13	13♒30 51	20 29 51	14 19.3	23 58.0	8 16.8	15 17.0	16 32.2	0 24.7	13 16.2	25 17.1	8 43.8	7 40.0
29 Sa	14 31 16	6 04 09	27 26 34	4♓20 57	14R20.4	23 45.9	9 29.9	15 33.1	16 40.1	0 35.2	13 20.2	25 18.8	8 46.1	7 41.2
30 Su	14 35 13	7 04 07	11♓13 00	18 02 41	14 20.7	23 24.7	10 43.0	15 48.5	16 48.3	0 45.9	13 24.2	25 20.6	8 48.3	7 42.5
31 M	14 39 09	8 04 07	24 49 57	1♈34 44	14 19.2	22 54.1	11 56.1	16 03.4	16 56.8	0 56.6	13 28.4	25 22.3	8 50.6	7 43.7

Astro Data

	Dy Hr Mn
♀0S	4 20:52
☽0N	6 23:06
☿0S	13 5:57
♄ D	15 22:48
☽0S	21 10:02
☉0S	23 0:59
☽0N	4 8:27
⚳ D	5 6:04
☽0S	18 18:37
☿ R	27 14:02
☽0N	31 16:17

Planet Ingress

		Dy Hr Mn
♀	♎	2 19:29
☿	♎	12 6:29
♂	♋	21 4:06
☉	♎	23 0:59
♀	♏	27 5:13
☿	♏	1 17:17
♀	♐	21 17:12
☉	♏	23 10:02
♃	♑	26 3:01

Last Aspect / ☽ Ingress

Dy Hr Mn				☽ Ingress Dy Hr Mn
2 11:57	♀	△	♒	2 12:35
4 4:07	♃	✱	♓	4 13:51
6 6:29	♃	□	♈	6 16:26
8 11:24	♃	△	♉	8 21:44
11 2:38	☿	△	♊	11 6:31
13 9:51	♂	☌	♋	13 18:10
15 16:17	☉	✱	♌	16 6:46
18 15:34	♂	✱	♍	18 18:07
21 2:55	♂	□	♎	21 2:58
23 1:14	♃	✱	♏	23 9:18
25 3:08	♅	□	♐	25 13:42
27 9:59	♃	☌	♑	27 16:54
29 14:34	☿	□	♒	29 19:32

Last Aspect / ☽ Ingress

Dy Hr Mn				☽ Ingress Dy Hr Mn
1 16:08	♃	✱	♓	1 22:14
3 19:59	♃	□	♈	4 1:46
6 1:37	♃	△	♉	6 7:09
8 4:47	♅	□	♊	8 15:16
10 21:32	♃	☍	♋	11 2:18
12 17:25	☉	□	♌	13 14:55
15 23:28	♃	△	♍	16 2:40
18 9:12	♃	□	♎	18 11:32
20 15:31	♃	✱	♏	20 17:06
22 11:59	♅	□	♐	22 20:16
24 22:07	♃	☌	♑	24 22:28
26 14:44	☿	✱	♒	27 0:57
28 20:17	♅	☍	♓	29 4:26
30 21:10	☿	△	♈	31 9:11

☽ Phases & Eclipses

Dy Hr Mn		
5 11:19	○	12♓53
5 11:21	•	T 1.424
12 22:19	☾	20♊08
20 23:12	●	27♍58
20 22:59:22	•	P 0.614
28 1:13	☽	4♑55
4 22:16	○	11♈41
12 17:25	☾	19♋23
20 12:02	●	27♎06
27 7:34	☽	3♒53

Astro Data

1 September 1960
Julian Day # 22159
SVP 5♓48'36"
GC 26♐17.4 ⚴ 10♑27.1R
Eris 10♈02.8R ⚵ 13♐32.3
⚷ 29♒20.7R ⚶ 5♑35.9
☽ Mean ☊ 15♍46.6

1 October 1960
Julian Day # 22189
SVP 5♓48'33"
GC 26♐17.5 ⚴ 12♑25.3
Eris 9♈45.1R ⚵ 19♐17.7
⚷ 28♒03.9R ⚶ 12♑15.1
☽ Mean ☊ 14♍11.3

November 1960 LONGITUDE

Day	Sid.Time	☉	0 hr ☽	Noon ☽	True ☊	☿	♀	♂	⚳	♃	♄	♅	♆	♇
1 Tu	14 43 06	9♏04 08	8♈16 58	14♈56 32	14♍15.4	22♏13.9	13♐09.2	16♋17.6	17♒05.6	1♑07.5	13♑32.6	25♌23.9	8♏52.8	7♍44.8
2 W	14 47 02	10 04 12	21 33 18	28 07 08	14R 09.0	21R 24.5	14 22.2	16 31.3	17 14.6	1 18.4	13 36.9	25 25.5	8 55.1	7 46.0
3 Th	14 50 59	11 04 17	4♉37 55	11♉05 29	14 00.2	20 26.3	15 35.3	16 44.3	17 23.9	1 29.4	13 41.3	25 27.0	8 57.3	7 47.1
4 F	14 54 55	12 04 24	17 29 46	23 50 40	13 49.7	19 20.4	16 48.2	16 56.8	17 33.5	1 40.6	13 45.8	25 28.5	8 59.6	7 48.2
5 Sa	14 58 52	13 04 32	0♊08 10	6♊22 16	13 38.5	18 08.0	18 01.2	17 08.6	17 43.4	1 51.8	13 50.3	25 30.0	9 01.8	7 49.3
6 Su	15 02 48	14 04 43	12 33 03	18 40 38	13 27.5	16 51.2	19 14.1	17 19.7	17 53.5	2 03.1	13 54.9	25 31.4	9 04.0	7 50.3
7 M	15 06 45	15 04 56	24 45 15	0♋47 10	13 17.8	15 32.1	20 27.0	17 30.1	18 03.9	2 14.5	13 59.6	25 32.7	9 06.3	7 51.3
8 Tu	15 10 42	16 05 11	6♋46 42	12 44 15	13 10.2	14 13.1	21 39.9	17 39.9	18 14.5	2 25.9	14 04.3	25 34.0	9 08.5	7 52.3
9 W	15 14 38	17 05 27	18 40 17	24 35 19	13 05.0	12 56.8	22 52.8	17 49.0	18 25.4	2 37.5	14 09.2	25 35.2	9 10.8	7 53.3
10 Th	15 18 35	18 05 46	0♌29 54	6♌24 38	13 02.3	11 45.8	24 05.6	17 57.4	18 36.6	2 49.1	14 14.0	25 36.4	9 13.0	7 54.2
11 F	15 22 31	19 06 06	12 20 10	18 17 09	13D 01.5	10 42.2	25 18.4	18 05.0	18 47.9	3 00.9	14 19.0	25 37.5	9 15.2	7 55.1
12 Sa	15 26 28	20 06 29	24 16 17	0♍18 13	13 01.8	9 47.7	26 31.1	18 11.9	18 59.6	3 12.7	14 24.0	25 38.6	9 17.4	7 56.0
13 Su	15 30 24	21 06 53	6♍23 40	12 33 16	13R 02.2	9 03.8	27 43.9	18 18.1	19 11.5	3 24.6	14 29.1	25 39.6	9 19.6	7 56.8
14 M	15 34 21	22 07 20	18 47 39	25 07 23	13 01.5	8 31.3	28 56.6	18 23.5	19 23.6	3 36.5	14 34.3	25 40.5	9 21.9	7 57.6
15 Tu	15 38 17	23 07 48	1♎32 59	8♎04 49	12 58.8	8 10.5	0♑09.2	18 28.1	19 35.9	3 48.6	14 39.5	25 41.4	9 24.1	7 58.4
16 W	15 42 14	24 08 18	14 43 12	21 28 17	12 53.6	8D 01.3	1 21.9	18 31.9	19 48.5	4 00.7	14 44.8	25 42.3	9 26.2	7 59.1
17 Th	15 46 11	25 08 49	28 20 02	5♏18 17	12 45.6	8 03.3	2 34.5	18 35.0	20 01.3	4 12.9	14 50.1	25 43.1	9 28.4	7 59.9
18 F	15 50 07	26 09 23	12♏22 40	19 32 38	12 35.4	8 16.1	3 47.0	18 37.2	20 14.4	4 25.1	14 55.6	25 43.8	9 30.6	8 00.6
19 Sa	15 54 04	27 09 58	26 47 28	4♐06 18	12 23.9	8 38.6	4 59.6	18 38.6	20 27.7	4 37.4	15 01.0	25 44.5	9 32.8	8 01.2
20 Su	15 58 00	28 10 35	11♐28 07	18 51 53	12 12.4	9 10.1	6 12.0	18R 39.2	20 41.1	4 49.8	15 06.6	25 45.1	9 34.9	8 01.9
21 M	16 01 57	29 11 13	26 16 30	3♑40 54	12 02.2	9 49.8	7 24.5	18 39.0	20 54.9	5 02.3	15 12.2	25 45.7	9 37.1	8 02.5
22 Tu	16 05 53	0♐11 52	11♑04 05	18 25 08	11 54.3	10 36.6	8 36.9	18 37.9	21 08.8	5 14.8	15 17.8	25 46.2	9 39.2	8 03.0
23 W	16 09 50	1 12 32	25 43 20	2♒58 03	11 49.2	11 29.7	9 49.3	18 36.0	21 22.9	5 27.4	15 23.5	25 46.7	9 41.4	8 03.6
24 Th	16 13 46	2 13 14	10♒08 51	17 15 27	11 46.8	12 28.5	11 01.6	18 33.2	21 37.2	5 40.1	15 29.3	25 47.1	9 43.5	8 04.1
25 F	16 17 43	3 13 56	24 17 41	1♓15 32	11 46.2	13 32.0	12 13.8	18 29.6	21 51.8	5 52.8	15 35.1	25 47.4	9 45.6	8 04.6
26 Sa	16 21 40	4 14 40	8♓09 04	14 58 25	11 46.2	14 39.8	13 26.0	18 25.1	22 06.5	6 05.5	15 41.0	25 47.7	9 47.7	8 05.0
27 Su	16 25 36	5 15 24	21 43 47	28 25 22	11 45.4	15 51.2	14 38.2	18 19.8	22 21.4	6 18.4	15 46.9	25 48.0	9 49.8	8 05.4
28 M	16 29 33	6 16 09	5♈03 26	11♈38 10	11 42.7	17 05.7	15 50.3	18 13.6	22 36.5	6 31.3	15 52.9	25 48.1	9 51.8	8 05.8
29 Tu	16 33 29	7 16 56	18 09 47	24 38 28	11 37.2	18 22.9	17 02.3	18 06.5	22 51.8	6 44.2	15 58.9	25 48.3	9 53.9	8 06.2
30 W	16 37 26	8 17 43	1♉04 21	7♉27 34	11 28.6	19 42.4	18 14.3	17 58.7	23 07.3	6 57.2	16 05.0	25R 48.3	9 55.9	8 06.5

December 1960 LONGITUDE

Day	Sid.Time	☉	0 hr ☽	Noon ☽	True ☊	☿	♀	♂	⚳	♃	♄	♅	♆	♇
1 Th	16 41 22	9♐18 32	13♉48 10	20♉06 14	11♍17.1	21♏03.8	19♑26.2	17♋49.9	23♒22.9	7♑10.2	16♑11.1	25♌48.3	9♏57.9	8♍06.8
2 F	16 45 19	10 19 22	26 21 47	2♊34 52	11R 03.5	22 26.9	20 38.0	17R 40.3	23 38.8	7 23.3	16 17.3	25R 48.3	10 00.0	8 07.0
3 Sa	16 49 15	11 20 13	8♊45 29	14 53 41	10 48.8	23 51.3	21 49.8	17 29.9	23 54.8	7 36.4	16 23.5	25 48.2	10 02.0	8 07.3
4 Su	16 53 12	12 21 05	20 59 30	27 03 04	10 34.4	25 17.0	23 01.5	17 18.6	24 11.0	7 49.6	16 29.7	25 48.0	10 03.9	8 07.5
5 M	16 57 09	13 21 58	3♋04 27	9♋03 51	10 21.3	26 43.8	24 13.1	17 06.5	24 27.4	8 02.8	16 36.0	25 47.8	10 05.9	8 07.6
6 Tu	17 01 05	14 22 52	15 01 29	20 57 36	10 10.6	28 11.3	25 24.7	16 53.6	24 43.9	8 16.1	16 42.4	25 47.6	10 07.8	8 07.8
7 W	17 05 02	15 23 47	26 52 33	2♌46 42	10 02.8	29 39.7	26 36.2	16 39.9	25 00.6	8 29.4	16 48.8	25 47.2	10 09.8	8 07.9
8 Th	17 08 58	16 24 44	8♌40 30	14 34 27	9 57.9	1♐08.6	27 47.6	16 25.3	25 17.4	8 42.8	16 55.2	25 46.9	10 11.7	8 07.9
9 F	17 12 55	17 25 41	20 29 04	26 24 59	9 55.6	2 38.1	28 58.9	16 10.0	25 34.4	8 56.2	17 01.6	25 46.4	10 13.6	8R 08.0
10 Sa	17 16 51	18 26 40	2♍22 47	8♍23 10	9 55.0	4 08.1	0♒10.2	15 54.0	25 51.6	9 09.6	17 08.1	25 45.9	10 15.4	8 08.0
11 Su	17 20 48	19 27 40	14 26 48	20 34 22	9 55.1	5 38.5	1 21.3	15 37.2	26 08.9	9 23.1	17 14.7	25 45.4	10 17.3	8 08.0
12 M	17 24 44	20 28 41	26 46 35	3♎04 05	9 54.5	7 09.2	2 32.4	15 19.7	26 26.4	9 36.6	17 21.3	25 44.8	10 19.1	8 07.9
13 Tu	17 28 41	21 29 43	9♎27 31	15 57 27	9 52.3	8 40.3	3 43.4	15 01.4	26 44.0	9 50.2	17 27.9	25 44.1	10 20.9	8 07.8
14 W	17 32 38	22 30 46	22 34 21	29 18 33	9 47.7	10 11.6	4 54.4	14 42.6	27 01.8	10 03.7	17 34.5	25 43.4	10 22.7	8 07.7
15 Th	17 36 34	23 31 50	6♏10 17	13♏09 33	9 40.3	11 43.1	6 05.2	14 23.1	27 19.7	10 17.4	17 41.2	25 42.7	10 24.5	8 07.5
16 F	17 40 31	24 32 56	20 16 12	27 29 48	9 30.6	13 14.9	7 15.9	14 03.0	27 37.8	10 31.0	17 47.9	25 41.8	10 26.2	8 07.4
17 Sa	17 44 27	25 34 02	4♐49 46	12♐15 13	9 19.4	14 46.9	8 26.6	13 42.3	27 56.0	10 44.7	17 54.6	25 41.0	10 28.0	8 07.1
18 Su	17 48 24	26 35 08	19 45 08	27 18 19	9 08.1	16 19.1	9 37.1	13 21.1	28 14.3	10 58.4	18 01.4	25 40.1	10 29.7	8 06.9
19 M	17 52 20	27 36 15	4♑53 25	12♑29 06	8 57.8	17 51.6	10 47.5	12 59.5	28 32.8	11 12.1	18 08.2	25 39.1	10 31.4	8 06.6
20 Tu	17 56 17	28 37 23	20 04 01	27 36 53	8 49.8	19 24.2	11 57.8	12 37.4	28 51.4	11 25.9	18 15.0	25 38.1	10 33.0	8 06.3
21 W	18 00 13	29 38 31	5♒06 35	12♒32 09	8 44.6	20 57.0	13 08.1	12 14.9	29 10.2	11 39.7	18 21.9	25 37.0	10 34.6	8 06.0
22 Th	18 04 10	0♑39 39	19 52 49	27 08 01	8D 42.1	22 30.0	14 18.1	11 52.1	29 29.0	11 53.5	18 28.7	25 35.9	10 36.3	8 05.6
23 F	18 08 07	1 40 48	4♓17 24	11♓20 46	8 41.7	24 03.2	15 28.1	11 29.0	29 48.0	12 07.3	18 35.6	25 34.7	10 37.8	8 05.2
24 Sa	18 12 03	2 41 56	18 18 06	25 09 32	8R 42.1	25 36.6	16 37.9	11 05.6	0♓07.1	12 21.1	18 42.5	25 33.4	10 39.4	8 04.8
25 Su	18 16 00	3 43 04	1♈55 17	8♈35 38	8 42.2	27 10.3	17 47.6	10 42.0	0 26.4	12 35.0	18 49.5	25 32.2	10 40.9	8 04.3
26 M	18 19 56	4 44 13	15 10 57	21 41 36	8 40.7	28 44.1	18 57.2	10 18.3	0 45.7	12 48.9	18 56.4	25 30.8	10 42.4	8 03.8
27 Tu	18 23 53	5 45 21	28 07 59	4♉30 29	8 36.9	0♑18.3	20 06.6	9 54.5	1 05.2	13 02.8	19 03.4	25 29.5	10 43.9	8 03.3
28 W	18 27 49	6 46 30	10♉49 28	17 05 17	8 30.4	1 52.7	21 15.9	9 30.6	1 24.8	13 16.7	19 10.4	25 28.0	10 45.4	8 02.8
29 Th	18 31 46	7 47 38	23 18 13	29 28 35	8 21.4	3 27.3	22 25.0	9 06.8	1 44.5	13 30.6	19 17.4	25 26.6	10 46.8	8 02.2
30 F	18 35 42	8 48 47	5♊36 36	11♊42 29	8 10.6	5 02.3	23 33.9	8 42.9	2 04.3	13 44.5	19 24.4	25 25.1	10 48.2	8 01.6
31 Sa	18 39 39	9 49 55	17 46 27	23 48 39	7 58.8	6 37.5	24 42.7	8 19.2	2 24.2	13 58.5	19 31.4	25 23.5	10 49.6	8 00.9

Astro Data

	Dy Hr Mn
☽0S	15 4:58
☿D	16 19:28
♂R	20 17:04
☽0N	27 23:00
♅R	1 4:21
♃△♇	5 20:46
♇R	10 4:38
☽0S	12 15:33
♃✶♆	16 2:23
♃⚼♅	17 5:52
☽0N	25 5:59

Planet Ingress

	Dy Hr Mn
♀ ♑	15 8:57
☉ ♐	22 7:18
☿ ♐	7 17:30
♀ ♒	10 8:34
☉ ♑	21 20:26
⚳ ♓	24 3:03
☿ ♑	27 7:21

Last Aspect / ☽ Ingress

Dy Hr Mn	Aspect	☽ Ingress	Dy Hr Mn
2 7:03	♅ △	♉	2 15:27
4 15:06	♅ □	♊	4 23:44
7 1:33	♅ ✶	♋	7 10:26
8 22:06	♂ ☌	♌	9 22:59
12 3:39	♀ △	♍	12 11:24
14 19:54	♀ □	♎	14 21:07
16 19:26	♅ ✶	♏	17 2:53
18 23:46	☉ ☌	♐	19 5:17
20 23:10	♅ △	♑	21 6:02
22 12:21	♂ ☍	♒	23 7:04
25 2:34	♅ ☍	♓	25 9:49
26 18:04	♂ △	♈	27 14:51
29 14:10	♅ △	♉	29 22:00

Last Aspect / ☽ Ingress

Dy Hr Mn	Aspect	☽ Ingress	Dy Hr Mn
1 22:56	♅ □	♊	2 7:01
4 9:31	♅ ✶	♋	4 17:52
7 4:45	☿ △	♌	7 6:21
9 10:42	♅ ☌	♍	9 19:13
11 9:38	☉ □	♎	12 6:10
14 5:39	♅ ✶	♏	14 13:13
16 9:02	♅ □	♐	16 16:07
18 10:47	☉ ☌	♑	18 16:16
19 21:01	♄ ☌	♒	20 15:49
22 9:27	♅ ☍	♓	22 16:47
24 12:54	☿ □	♈	24 20:34
27 2:58	☿ △	♉	27 3:30
29 4:10	♅ □	♊	29 13:01

☽ Phases & Eclipses

Dy Hr Mn	
3 11:58	○ 11♉04
11 13:47	☾ 19♌11
18 23:46	● 26♏39
25 15:42	☽ 3♓23
3 4:24	○ 11♊01
11 9:38	☾ 19♍22
18 10:47	● 26♐32
25 2:30	☽ 3♈19

Astro Data

1 November 1960
Julian Day # 22220
SVP 5♓48'31"
GC 26♐17.5 ⚴ 18♑32.6
Eris 9♈26.6R ⚵ 28♐06.8
⚷ 27♒25.6R ⚶ 23♑04.1
☽ Mean ☊ 12♍32.8

1 December 1960
Julian Day # 22250
SVP 5♓48'27"
GC 26♐17.6 ⚴ 26♑50.5
Eris 9♈13.8R ⚵ 8♑26.9
⚷ 27♒42.8 ⚶ 5♒43.7
☽ Mean ☊ 10♍57.4

LONGITUDE — January 1961

Day	Sid.Time	☉	0 hr ☽	Noon ☽	True ☊	☿	♀	♂	⚳	♃	♄	♅	♆	♇
1 Su	18 43 36	10♑51 04	29♊49 14	5♋48 21	7♍47.1	8♑13.1	25♒51.3	7♋55.6	2♓44.2	14♑12.4	19♑38.5	25♌21.9	10♏50.9	8♍00.3
2 M	18 47 32	11 52 13	11♋46 11	17 42 52	7R36.5	9 49.0	26 59.8	7R32.2	3 04.3	14 26.4	19 45.5	25R20.3	10 52.2	7R59.6
3 Tu	18 51 29	12 53 21	23 38 35	29 33 32	7 27.9	11 25.3	28 08.0	7 09.1	3 24.5	14 40.3	19 52.6	25 18.6	10 53.5	7 58.9
4 W	18 55 25	13 54 30	5♌27 58	11♌22 10	7 21.8	13 01.9	29 16.1	6 46.2	3 44.9	14 54.3	19 59.7	25 16.8	10 54.8	7 58.1
5 Th	18 59 22	14 55 39	17 16 25	23 11 05	7 18.2	14 38.9	0♓24.0	6 23.6	4 05.3	15 08.3	20 06.8	25 15.1	10 56.0	7 57.4
6 F	19 03 18	15 56 47	29 06 35	5♍03 20	7D17.0	16 16.3	1 31.7	6 01.4	4 25.8	15 22.2	20 13.9	25 13.2	10 57.2	7 56.6
7 Sa	19 07 15	16 57 56	11♍01 51	17 02 38	7 17.4	17 54.1	2 39.2	5 39.6	4 46.4	15 36.2	20 21.0	25 11.4	10 58.4	7 55.7
8 Su	19 11 11	17 59 05	23 06 16	29 13 20	7 18.6	19 32.4	3 46.4	5 18.2	5 07.1	15 50.2	20 28.1	25 09.5	10 59.5	7 54.9
9 M	19 15 08	19 00 14	5♎24 26	11♎40 12	7R19.8	21 11.0	4 53.5	4 57.3	5 27.9	16 04.1	20 35.2	25 07.5	11 00.6	7 54.0
10 Tu	19 19 05	20 01 22	18 01 13	24 28 04	7 19.9	22 50.1	6 00.4	4 37.0	5 48.8	16 18.1	20 42.3	25 05.6	11 01.7	7 53.1
11 W	19 23 01	21 02 31	1♏01 17	7♏41 18	7 18.5	24 29.6	7 07.0	4 17.1	6 09.7	16 32.1	20 49.3	25 03.6	11 02.8	7 52.2
12 Th	19 26 58	22 03 40	14 28 28	21 23 01	7 15.0	26 09.5	8 13.4	3 57.9	6 30.8	16 46.0	20 56.5	25 01.5	11 03.8	7 51.2
13 F	19 30 54	23 04 49	28 25 00	5♐34 17	7 09.8	27 49.9	9 19.6	3 39.3	6 51.9	17 00.0	21 03.6	24 59.4	11 04.8	7 50.2
14 Sa	19 34 51	24 05 58	12♐50 30	20 13 08	7 03.3	29 30.6	10 25.5	3 21.3	7 13.2	17 13.9	21 10.7	24 57.3	11 05.7	7 49.2
15 Su	19 38 47	25 07 06	27 41 21	5♑14 12	6 56.4	1♒11.8	11 31.2	3 04.0	7 34.5	17 27.8	21 17.8	24 55.2	11 06.6	7 48.2
16 M	19 42 44	26 08 15	12♑50 29	20 28 56	6 50.2	2 53.3	12 36.6	2 47.4	7 55.9	17 41.8	21 24.9	24 53.0	11 07.5	7 47.1
17 Tu	19 46 41	27 09 22	28 08 09	5♒46 44	6 45.4	4 35.2	13 41.7	2 31.5	8 17.3	17 55.7	21 32.0	24 50.8	11 08.4	7 46.1
18 W	19 50 37	28 10 29	13♒23 22	20 56 47	6 42.4	6 17.4	14 46.6	2 16.3	8 38.9	18 09.6	21 39.1	24 48.5	11 09.2	7 45.0
19 Th	19 54 34	29 11 35	28 25 56	5♓49 52	6D41.5	7 59.7	15 51.2	2 02.0	9 00.5	18 23.5	21 46.2	24 46.3	11 10.0	7 43.9
20 F	19 58 30	0♒12 41	13♓07 55	20 19 34	6 42.1	9 42.3	16 55.4	1 48.3	9 22.2	18 37.3	21 53.2	24 44.0	11 10.8	7 42.7
21 Sa	20 02 27	1 13 45	27 24 31	4♈22 39	6 43.5	11 24.9	17 59.4	1 35.5	9 44.0	18 51.2	22 00.3	24 41.6	11 11.5	7 41.6
22 Su	20 06 23	2 14 48	11♈14 01	17 58 48	6 45.0	13 07.4	19 03.0	1 23.5	10 05.8	19 05.0	22 07.3	24 39.3	11 12.2	7 40.4
23 M	20 10 20	3 15 51	24 37 15	1♉09 45	6R45.8	14 49.8	20 06.3	1 12.2	10 27.7	19 18.8	22 14.4	24 36.9	11 12.9	7 39.2
24 Tu	20 14 16	4 16 52	7♉36 44	13 58 39	6 45.3	16 31.9	21 09.3	1 01.8	10 49.6	19 32.6	22 21.4	24 34.5	11 13.5	7 37.9
25 W	20 18 13	5 17 52	20 15 58	26 29 12	6 43.4	18 13.4	22 11.8	0 52.2	11 11.7	19 46.3	22 28.4	24 32.1	11 14.1	7 36.7
26 Th	20 22 10	6 18 52	2♊38 48	8♊45 15	6 39.9	19 54.2	23 14.0	0 43.4	11 33.8	20 00.0	22 35.4	24 29.6	11 14.6	7 35.5
27 F	20 26 06	7 19 50	14 49 00	20 50 26	6 35.4	21 34.0	24 15.8	0 35.4	11 55.9	20 13.7	22 42.3	24 27.2	11 15.2	7 34.2
28 Sa	20 30 03	8 20 47	26 49 58	2♋47 57	6 30.2	23 12.4	25 17.3	0 28.3	12 18.1	20 27.4	22 49.3	24 24.7	11 15.7	7 32.9
29 Su	20 33 59	9 21 43	8♋44 43	14 40 35	6 25.1	24 49.2	26 18.3	0 21.9	12 40.4	20 41.0	22 56.2	24 22.2	11 16.1	7 31.6
30 M	20 37 56	10 22 38	20 35 47	26 30 38	6 20.4	26 23.9	27 18.8	0 16.4	13 02.7	20 54.7	23 03.1	24 19.7	11 16.5	7 30.3
31 Tu	20 41 52	11 23 31	2♌25 20	8♌20 09	6 16.8	27 56.1	28 18.9	0 11.6	13 25.1	21 08.2	23 10.0	24 17.1	11 16.9	7 28.9

LONGITUDE — February 1961

Day	Sid.Time	☉	0 hr ☽	Noon ☽	True ☊	☿	♀	♂	⚳	♃	♄	♅	♆	♇
1 W	20 45 49	12♒24 24	14♌15 19	20♌11 03	6♍14.4	29♒25.2	29♓18.6	0♋07.7	13♓47.5	21♑21.8	23♑16.9	24♌14.6	11♏17.3	7♍27.6
2 Th	20 49 45	13 25 16	26 07 36	2♍05 13	6D13.4	0♓50.6	0♈17.8	0R04.5	14 10.0	21 35.3	23 23.7	24R12.0	11 17.6	7R26.2
3 F	20 53 42	14 26 06	8♍04 11	14 04 48	6 13.6	2 11.7	1 16.5	0 02.1	14 32.6	21 48.8	23 30.5	24 09.5	11 17.9	7 24.8
4 Sa	20 57 39	15 26 56	20 07 21	26 12 12	6 14.6	3 27.9	2 14.7	0 00.5	14 55.2	22 02.2	23 37.3	24 06.9	11 18.2	7 23.4
5 Su	21 01 35	16 27 44	2♎19 43	8♎30 17	6 16.1	4 38.3	3 12.3	29♊59.7	15 17.8	22 15.6	23 44.0	24 04.3	11 18.4	7 22.0
6 M	21 05 32	17 28 32	14 44 18	21 02 12	6 17.7	5 42.3	4 09.5	29D59.6	15 40.5	22 29.0	23 50.8	24 01.7	11 18.6	7 20.6
7 Tu	21 09 28	18 29 18	27 24 24	3♏51 19	6 18.9	6 39.0	5 06.0	0♋00.3	16 03.2	22 42.3	23 57.5	23 59.1	11 18.7	7 19.1
8 W	21 13 25	19 30 04	10♏23 23	17 00 56	6R19.5	7 27.7	6 02.0	0 01.6	16 26.0	22 55.6	24 04.1	23 56.4	11 18.8	7 17.7
9 Th	21 17 21	20 30 49	23 44 18	0♐33 43	6 19.3	8 07.7	6 57.4	0 03.8	16 48.8	23 08.8	24 10.8	23 53.8	11 18.9	7 16.2
10 F	21 21 18	21 31 32	7♐29 19	14 31 10	6 18.3	8 38.3	7 52.2	0 06.6	17 11.7	23 22.0	24 17.4	23 51.2	11R19.0	7 14.7
11 Sa	21 25 14	22 32 15	21 39 07	28 52 56	6 16.8	8 59.0	8 46.3	0 10.2	17 34.6	23 35.1	24 24.0	23 48.5	11 19.0	7 13.3
12 Su	21 29 11	23 32 56	6♑12 09	13♑36 11	6 15.2	9R09.4	9 39.8	0 14.4	17 57.6	23 48.2	24 30.5	23 45.9	11 19.0	7 11.8
13 M	21 33 08	24 33 37	21 04 16	28 35 28	6 13.7	9 09.2	10 32.6	0 19.4	18 20.6	24 01.3	24 37.0	23 43.3	11 18.9	7 10.3
14 Tu	21 37 04	25 34 16	6♒08 43	13♒42 55	6 12.6	8 58.4	11 24.7	0 25.0	18 43.7	24 14.3	24 43.5	23 40.6	11 18.8	7 08.8
15 W	21 41 01	26 34 53	21 16 51	28 49 20	6D12.0	8 37.2	12 16.0	0 31.3	19 06.8	24 27.2	24 49.9	23 38.0	11 18.7	7 07.3
16 Th	21 44 57	27 35 30	6♓19 14	13♓45 29	6 12.0	8 06.2	13 06.6	0 38.2	19 29.9	24 40.1	24 56.3	23 35.4	11 18.5	7 05.7
17 F	21 48 54	28 36 04	21 07 09	28 23 28	6 12.4	7 26.1	13 56.3	0 45.8	19 53.0	24 52.9	25 02.6	23 32.8	11 18.3	7 04.2
18 Sa	21 52 50	29 36 37	5♈33 49	12♈37 45	6 13.1	6 37.9	14 45.2	0 54.0	20 16.2	25 05.7	25 08.9	23 30.1	11 18.1	7 02.7
19 Su	21 56 47	0♓37 08	19 35 00	26 25 28	6 13.7	5 43.0	15 33.3	1 02.9	20 39.5	25 18.4	25 15.2	23 27.5	11 17.9	7 01.2
20 M	22 00 43	1 37 37	3♉09 12	9♉46 22	6 14.1	4 42.7	16 20.5	1 12.3	21 02.7	25 31.0	25 21.4	23 24.9	11 17.6	6 59.6
21 Tu	22 04 40	2 38 04	16 17 15	22 42 14	6R14.4	3 38.8	17 06.7	1 22.4	21 26.0	25 43.6	25 27.5	23 22.3	11 17.2	6 58.1
22 W	22 08 36	3 38 29	29 01 45	5♊16 18	6 14.5	2 33.0	17 51.9	1 33.0	21 49.3	25 56.1	25 33.6	23 19.7	11 16.9	6 56.5
23 Th	22 12 33	4 38 53	11♊26 26	17 32 40	6 14.4	1 26.8	18 36.1	1 44.2	22 12.7	26 08.6	25 39.7	23 17.2	11 16.5	6 55.0
24 F	22 16 30	5 39 14	23 35 36	29 35 45	6D14.3	0 22.0	19 19.2	1 55.9	22 36.0	26 21.0	25 45.7	23 14.6	11 16.1	6 53.4
25 Sa	22 20 26	6 39 34	5♋33 42	11♋29 57	6 14.3	29♒20.0	20 01.3	2 08.2	22 59.4	26 33.3	25 51.7	23 12.1	11 15.6	6 51.9
26 Su	22 24 23	7 39 52	17 25 02	23 19 26	6 14.4	28 22.0	20 42.1	2 21.0	23 22.8	26 45.5	25 57.6	23 09.5	11 15.2	6 50.3
27 M	22 28 19	8 40 07	29 13 34	5♌07 53	6 14.7	27 29.0	21 21.8	2 34.3	23 46.3	26 57.7	26 03.5	23 07.0	11 14.6	6 48.8
28 Tu	22 32 16	9 40 21	11♌02 46	16 58 33	6 15.0	26 41.9	22 00.3	2 48.2	24 09.7	27 09.8	26 09.3	23 04.5	11 14.1	6 47.2

Astro Data	Dy Hr Mn
☽0S	9 0:31
☽0N	21 14:37
♄⚼♇	26 12:16
♀0N	31 11:18
☽0S	5 7:17
♃⚼♇	5 22:21
♂ D	6 2:51
♄⚻♅	7 16:04
♆ R	11 11:32
♃⚻♅	12 8:29
☿ R	12 23:35
☽0N	18 0:56
♃☌♄	19 0:02

Planet Ingress	Dy Hr Mn
♀ ♓	5 3:31
☿ ♒	14 18:58
☉ ♒	20 7:01
☿ ♓	1 21:39
♀ ♈	2 4:46
♂ ♊R	5 0:22
♂ ♋	7 5:26
☉ ♓	18 21:16
☿ ♒R	24 20:22

Last Aspect Dy Hr Mn		☽ Ingress Dy Hr Mn
31 15:09	♅ ⚹	♋ 1 0:22
2 16:11	♄ ☍	♌ 3 12:54
5 16:11	♅ ☌	♍ 6 1:48
7 18:37	♄ △	♎ 8 13:31
10 13:09	♅ ⚹	♏ 10 22:09
12 21:16	☿ ⚹	♐ 13 2:40
14 19:36	♅ △	♑ 15 3:41
16 21:30	☉ ☌	♒ 17 2:55
18 18:10	♅ ☍	♓ 19 2:32
20 14:39	♄ ⚹	♈ 21 4:26
23 0:02	♅ △	♉ 23 9:51
25 8:14	♅ □	♊ 25 18:50
27 19:29	♀ □	♋ 28 6:22
30 13:47	♀ △	♌ 30 19:05

Last Aspect Dy Hr Mn		☽ Ingress Dy Hr Mn
1 20:10	♅ ☌	♍ 2 7:48
4 6:52	♄ △	♎ 4 19:27
7 4:51	♂ △	♏ 7 4:51
9 0:41	♄ ⚹	♐ 9 11:01
11 3:37	♅ △	♑ 11 13:50
13 5:37	♄ ☌	♒ 13 14:14
15 8:10	☉ ☌	♓ 15 13:53
17 6:25	♄ ⚹	♈ 17 14:41
19 10:00	♃ □	♉ 19 18:21
21 17:49	♃ △	♊ 22 1:51
23 23:21	♅ ⚹	♋ 24 12:49
26 19:06	♃ ☍	♌ 27 1:34

☽ Phases & Eclipses Dy Hr Mn	
1 23:06	○ 11♋19
10 3:02	☾ 19♎39
16 21:30	● 26♑32
23 16:13	☽ 3♉27
31 18:47	○ 11♌41
8 16:49	☾ 19♏42
15 8:10	● 26♒25
15 8:19:15	● T 02'45"
22 8:34	☽ 3♊30

Astro Data

1 January 1961
Julian Day # 22281
SVP 5♓48'21"
GC 26♐17.7 ⚴ 6♒44.6
Eris 9♈10.0 ⚵ 20♑17.0
⚷ 28♒54.0 ⚶ 20♒03.0
☽ Mean ☊ 9♍19.0

1 February 1961
Julian Day # 22312
SVP 5♓48'16"
GC 26♐17.7 ⚴ 17♒12.4
Eris 9♈17.1 ⚵ 2♒45.6
⚷ 0♓43.4 ⚶ 4♓58.3
☽ Mean ☊ 7♍40.5

March 1961 — LONGITUDE

Day	Sid.Time	☉	0 hr ☽	Noon ☽	True ☊	☿	♀	♂	⚳	♃	♄	♅	♆	♇
1 W	22 36 12	10♓40 33	22♌55 35	28♌54 09	6♍15.2	26♒01.2	22♈37.5	3♋02.5	24♓33.2	27♑21.9	26♑15.1	23♌02.0	11♏13.5	6♍45.7
2 Th	22 40 09	11 40 43	4♍54 30	10♍56 52	6R15.2	25R27.3	23 13.3	3 17.3	24 56.7	27 33.8	26 20.8	22R59.6	11R12.9	6R44.2
3 F	22 44 05	12 40 51	17 01 30	23 08 34	6 14.9	25 00.3	23 47.7	3 32.5	25 20.3	27 45.7	26 26.4	22 57.1	11 12.3	6 42.6
4 Sa	22 48 02	13 40 58	29 18 16	5♎30 45	6 14.3	24 40.4	24 20.7	3 48.3	25 43.8	27 57.5	26 32.0	22 54.7	11 11.6	6 41.1
5 Su	22 51 59	14 41 02	11♎46 11	18 04 44	6 13.3	24 27.3	24 52.2	4 04.4	26 07.4	28 09.2	26 37.5	22 52.3	11 10.9	6 39.5
6 M	22 55 55	15 41 05	24 26 33	0♏51 48	6 12.0	24D21.0	25 22.1	4 21.0	26 31.0	28 20.9	26 43.0	22 49.9	11 10.2	6 38.0
7 Tu	22 59 52	16 41 06	7♏20 36	13 53 08	6 10.7	24 21.2	25 50.5	4 38.1	26 54.6	28 32.4	26 48.4	22 47.6	11 09.4	6 36.5
8 W	23 03 48	17 41 06	20 29 32	27 09 55	6 09.6	24 27.6	26 17.1	4 55.5	27 18.2	28 43.9	26 53.8	22 45.3	11 08.6	6 35.0
9 Th	23 07 45	18 41 04	3♐54 25	10♐43 07	6D08.9	24 39.9	26 42.1	5 13.4	27 41.8	28 55.3	26 59.1	22 43.0	11 07.8	6 33.5
10 F	23 11 41	19 41 01	17 36 05	24 33 19	6 08.9	24 57.7	27 05.2	5 31.6	28 05.5	29 06.6	27 04.3	22 40.7	11 07.0	6 32.0
11 Sa	23 15 38	20 40 56	1♑34 46	8♑40 18	6 09.4	25 20.8	27 26.6	5 50.3	28 29.2	29 17.8	27 09.5	22 38.4	11 06.1	6 30.5
12 Su	23 19 34	21 40 49	15 49 43	23 02 44	6 10.4	25 48.8	27 46.0	6 09.3	28 52.8	29 29.0	27 14.6	22 36.2	11 05.2	6 29.0
13 M	23 23 31	22 40 41	0♒18 56	7♒37 49	6 11.6	26 21.4	28 03.5	6 28.7	29 16.5	29 40.0	27 19.6	22 34.1	11 04.3	6 27.5
14 Tu	23 27 28	23 40 30	14 58 46	22 21 05	6R12.6	26 58.3	28 18.9	6 48.5	29 40.2	29 50.9	27 24.6	22 31.9	11 03.3	6 26.0
15 W	23 31 24	24 40 18	29 44 00	7♓06 39	6 13.0	27 39.3	28 32.3	7 08.6	0♈04.0	0♒01.8	27 29.5	22 29.8	11 02.3	6 24.5
16 Th	23 35 21	25 40 04	14♓28 11	21 47 42	6 12.4	28 24.0	28 43.5	7 29.1	0 27.7	0 12.5	27 34.3	22 27.7	11 01.3	6 23.1
17 F	23 39 17	26 39 49	29 04 21	6♈17 18	6 10.8	29 12.3	28 52.5	7 49.9	0 51.4	0 23.2	27 39.1	22 25.6	11 00.3	6 21.7
18 Sa	23 43 14	27 39 31	13♈25 52	20 29 24	6 08.2	0♓03.8	28 59.2	8 11.1	1 15.1	0 33.7	27 43.8	22 23.6	10 59.2	6 20.2
19 Su	23 47 10	28 39 10	27 27 25	4♉19 34	6 04.9	0 58.5	29 03.6	8 32.6	1 38.9	0 44.2	27 48.4	22 21.7	10 58.1	6 18.8
20 M	23 51 07	29 38 48	11♉05 37	17 45 30	6 01.5	1 56.1	29R05.6	8 54.4	2 02.6	0 54.5	27 52.9	22 19.7	10 57.0	6 17.4
21 Tu	23 55 03	0♈38 24	24 19 15	0♊47 04	5 58.3	2 56.5	29 05.2	9 16.5	2 26.4	1 04.8	27 57.4	22 17.8	10 55.9	6 16.0
22 W	23 59 00	1 37 57	7♊09 13	13 26 05	5 55.9	3 59.5	29 02.4	9 39.0	2 50.1	1 14.9	28 01.8	22 15.9	10 54.7	6 14.6
23 Th	0 02 56	2 37 28	19 38 06	25 45 48	5D54.6	5 04.9	28 57.1	10 01.7	3 13.9	1 24.9	28 06.1	22 14.1	10 53.6	6 13.3
24 F	0 06 53	3 36 57	1♋49 44	7♋50 29	5 54.4	6 12.7	28 49.2	10 24.7	3 37.7	1 34.8	28 10.4	22 12.3	10 52.4	6 11.9
25 Sa	0 10 50	4 36 23	13 48 42	19 44 58	5 55.4	7 22.7	28 38.9	10 48.0	4 01.4	1 44.6	28 14.5	22 10.6	10 51.1	6 10.6
26 Su	0 14 46	5 35 47	25 39 56	1♌34 13	5 57.0	8 34.8	28 26.1	11 11.6	4 25.2	1 54.3	28 18.6	22 08.9	10 49.9	6 09.3
27 M	0 18 43	6 35 09	7♌28 24	13 23 04	5 58.8	9 48.9	28 10.8	11 35.4	4 48.9	2 03.9	28 22.6	22 07.2	10 48.6	6 08.0
28 Tu	0 22 39	7 34 28	19 18 46	25 15 59	6R00.3	11 05.1	27 53.0	11 59.6	5 12.7	2 13.3	28 26.6	22 05.6	10 47.3	6 06.7
29 W	0 26 36	8 33 46	1♍15 14	7♍16 53	6 00.8	12 23.1	27 32.8	12 23.9	5 36.4	2 22.7	28 30.4	22 04.0	10 46.0	6 05.4
30 Th	0 30 32	9 33 01	13 21 20	19 28 53	5 59.9	13 42.9	27 10.4	12 48.5	6 00.2	2 31.9	28 34.2	22 02.5	10 44.7	6 04.2
31 F	0 34 29	10 32 13	25 39 48	1♎54 16	5 57.3	15 04.5	26 45.7	13 13.4	6 23.9	2 41.0	28 37.9	22 01.0	10 43.4	6 02.9

April 1961 — LONGITUDE

Day	Sid.Time	☉	0 hr ☽	Noon ☽	True ☊	☿	♀	♂	⚳	♃	♄	♅	♆	♇
1 Sa	0 38 25	11♈31 24	8♎12 25	14♎34 20	5♍53.1	16♓27.9	26♈18.9	13♋38.5	6♈47.6	2♒50.0	28♑41.5	21♌59.5	10♏42.0	6♍01.7
2 Su	0 42 22	12 30 33	21 00 02	27 29 29	5R47.5	17 52.9	25R50.1	14 03.8	7 11.4	2 58.8	28 45.0	21R58.2	10R40.6	6R00.5
3 M	0 46 19	13 29 40	4♏02 35	10♏39 14	5 41.2	19 19.6	25 19.4	14 29.3	7 35.1	3 07.5	28 48.4	21 56.8	10 39.2	5 59.4
4 Tu	0 50 15	14 28 45	17 19 16	24 02 30	5 34.8	20 47.9	24 47.2	14 55.1	7 58.8	3 16.1	28 51.8	21 55.5	10 37.8	5 58.2
5 W	0 54 12	15 27 48	0♐48 46	7♐37 51	5 29.2	22 17.8	24 13.4	15 21.1	8 22.5	3 24.6	28 55.0	21 54.2	10 36.4	5 57.1
6 Th	0 58 08	16 26 49	14 29 35	21 23 46	5 25.0	23 49.3	23 38.4	15 47.3	8 46.2	3 33.0	28 58.2	21 53.0	10 35.0	5 56.0
7 F	1 02 05	17 25 49	28 20 14	5♑18 50	5D22.5	25 22.3	23 02.4	16 13.7	9 09.9	3 41.2	29 01.3	21 51.9	10 33.5	5 54.9
8 Sa	1 06 01	18 24 46	12♑19 24	19 21 47	5 21.9	26 56.9	22 25.5	16 40.3	9 33.6	3 49.2	29 04.3	21 50.8	10 32.0	5 53.8
9 Su	1 09 58	19 23 43	26 25 51	3♒31 25	5 22.5	28 33.1	21 48.1	17 07.1	9 57.2	3 57.2	29 07.3	21 49.7	10 30.5	5 52.8
10 M	1 13 54	20 22 37	10♒38 19	17 46 19	5 23.8	0♈10.8	21 10.3	17 34.1	10 20.9	4 05.0	29 10.1	21 48.7	10 29.0	5 51.7
11 Tu	1 17 51	21 21 30	24 55 08	2♓04 27	5R24.6	1 50.0	20 32.5	18 01.3	10 44.5	4 12.6	29 12.8	21 47.7	10 27.5	5 50.7
12 W	1 21 48	22 20 21	9♓13 55	16 23 03	5 24.1	3 30.8	19 54.9	18 28.7	11 08.2	4 20.2	29 15.5	21 46.8	10 26.0	5 49.8
13 Th	1 25 44	23 19 10	23 31 24	0♈38 24	5 21.7	5 13.2	19 17.7	18 56.3	11 31.8	4 27.5	29 18.0	21 45.9	10 24.5	5 48.8
14 F	1 29 41	24 17 57	7♈43 30	14 46 07	5 16.9	6 57.0	18 41.1	19 24.0	11 55.4	4 34.8	29 20.5	21 45.1	10 22.9	5 47.9
15 Sa	1 33 37	25 16 42	21 45 41	28 41 38	5 10.1	8 42.5	18 05.5	19 52.0	12 19.0	4 41.9	29 22.9	21 44.4	10 21.3	5 47.0
16 Su	1 37 34	26 15 25	5♉33 29	12♉20 50	5 01.7	10 29.5	17 30.9	20 20.1	12 42.5	4 48.8	29 25.2	21 43.6	10 19.8	5 46.1
17 M	1 41 30	27 14 06	19 03 20	25 40 45	4 52.6	12 18.1	16 57.7	20 48.4	13 06.1	4 55.6	29 27.4	21 43.0	10 18.2	5 45.2
18 Tu	1 45 27	28 12 46	2♊12 59	8♊40 00	4 43.9	14 08.4	16 25.9	21 16.8	13 29.6	5 02.2	29 29.5	21 42.4	10 16.6	5 44.4
19 W	1 49 23	29 11 23	15 01 54	21 18 55	4 36.4	16 00.2	15 55.9	21 45.5	13 53.1	5 08.7	29 31.5	21 41.8	10 15.0	5 43.6
20 Th	1 53 20	0♉09 58	27 31 20	3♋39 32	4 30.8	17 53.5	15 27.7	22 14.2	14 16.6	5 15.0	29 33.4	21 41.3	10 13.4	5 42.8
21 F	1 57 17	1 08 30	9♋43 58	15 45 12	4 27.3	19 48.5	15 01.4	22 43.2	14 40.1	5 21.2	29 35.2	21 40.9	10 11.8	5 42.0
22 Sa	2 01 13	2 07 01	21 43 46	27 40 19	4D25.9	21 45.1	14 37.3	23 12.3	15 03.5	5 27.2	29 36.9	21 40.5	10 10.2	5 41.3
23 Su	2 05 10	3 05 30	3♌35 29	9♌29 55	4 26.0	23 43.3	14 15.3	23 41.5	15 26.9	5 33.1	29 38.5	21 40.2	10 08.6	5 40.6
24 M	2 09 06	4 03 56	15 24 19	21 19 20	4 26.8	25 43.0	13 55.6	24 10.9	15 50.3	5 38.8	29 40.0	21 39.9	10 07.0	5 39.9
25 Tu	2 13 03	5 02 20	27 15 38	3♍13 51	4R27.4	27 44.2	13 38.2	24 40.5	16 13.7	5 44.3	29 41.5	21 39.6	10 05.4	5 39.3
26 W	2 16 59	6 00 42	9♍14 35	15 18 24	4 26.8	29 46.8	13 23.2	25 10.1	16 37.0	5 49.7	29 42.8	21 39.5	10 03.7	5 38.7
27 Th	2 20 56	6 59 02	21 25 50	27 37 18	4 24.2	1♉50.9	13 10.7	25 39.9	17 00.3	5 54.9	29 44.0	21 39.3	10 02.1	5 38.1
28 F	2 24 52	7 57 20	3♎53 11	10♎13 45	4 19.2	3 56.2	13 00.5	26 09.9	17 23.6	6 00.0	29 45.2	21D39.3	10 00.5	5 37.5
29 Sa	2 28 49	8 55 36	16 39 14	23 09 42	4 11.8	6 02.7	12 52.9	26 40.0	17 46.9	6 04.8	29 46.2	21 39.3	9 58.8	5 37.0
30 Su	2 32 45	9 53 50	29 45 07	6♏25 24	4 02.4	8 10.3	12 47.6	27 10.1	18 10.1	6 09.5	29 47.2	21 39.3	9 57.2	5 36.5

Astro Data	Dy Hr Mn
☽0S	4 13:08
☿ D	6 23:16
☽0N	17 11:39
♀ R	20 20:13
☉0N	20 20:33
☽0S	31 19:53
☿0N	13 15:18
☽0N	13 21:13
♃⚻♇	24 16:25
☽0S	28 4:24
♅ D	29 7:50
⚳0N	29 22:57

Planet Ingress		Dy Hr Mn
⚳	♈	15 8:00
♃	♒	15 8:01
☿	♓	18 10:16
☉	♈	20 20:32
☿	♈	10 9:22
☉	♉	20 7:55
☿	♉	26 14:34

Last Aspect Dy Hr Mn			☽ Ingress	Dy Hr Mn
1 6:31	☿	☍	♍	1 14:12
3 21:09	♃	△	♎	4 1:21
6 7:14	♃	□	♏	6 10:24
8 14:50	♃	✶	♐	8 17:04
10 16:27	♀	△	♑	10 21:19
12 22:46	♃	☌	♒	12 23:29
14 21:51	♀	✶	♓	15 0:26
16 21:34	♄	✶	♈	17 1:32
19 2:45	♀	☌	♉	19 4:25
21 6:42	♄	△	♊	21 10:32
23 18:14	♀	✶	♋	23 20:22
26 5:45	♀	□	♌	26 8:48
28 17:07	♀	△	♍	28 21:30
31 5:41	♄	△	♎	31 8:21

Last Aspect Dy Hr Mn			☽ Ingress	Dy Hr Mn
2 14:19	♄	□	♏	2 16:36
4 20:35	♄	✶	♐	4 22:34
6 16:43	☿	□	♑	7 2:52
9 4:32	♄	☌	♒	9 6:03
10 18:47	♅	☍	♓	11 8:31
13 9:44	♄	✶	♈	13 10:55
15 13:12	♄	□	♉	15 14:16
17 18:56	♄	△	♊	17 19:55
20 4:34	☉	✶	♋	20 4:50
22 15:57	♄	☍	♌	22 16:43
24 22:42	☿	△	♍	25 5:31
27 16:04	♄	△	♎	27 16:34
30 0:03	♄	□	♏	30 0:27

☽ Phases & Eclipses Dy Hr Mn	
2 13:35	○ 11♍45
2 13:28	P 0.800
10 2:57	☾ 19♐18
16 18:51	● 25♓57
24 2:48	☽ 3♋14
1 5:47	○ 11♎16
8 10:16	☾ 18♑21
15 5:37	● 25♈01
22 21:49	☽ 2♌31
30 18:40	○ 10♏10

Astro Data

1 March 1961
Julian Day # 22340
SVP 5♓48'13"
GC 26♐17.8 ⚴ 26♒38.2
Eris 9♈31.4 ⚵ 14♒12.8
⚷ 2♓35.8 ⚶ 18♓34.9
☽ Mean ☊ 6♍11.5

1 April 1961
Julian Day # 22371
SVP 5♓48'11"
GC 26♐17.9 ⚴ 6♓32.6
Eris 9♈52.0 ⚵ 26♒42.7
⚷ 4♓32.6 ⚶ 3♈28.4
☽ Mean ☊ 4♍33.0

LONGITUDE — May 1961

Day	Sid.Time	☉	0 hr ☽	Noon ☽	True ☊	☿	♀	♂	⚳	♃	♄	♅	♆	♇
1 M	2 36 42	10♉52 03	13♏10 17	19♏59 28	3♍51.7	10♉18.7	12♈44.8	27♋40.5	18♈33.3	6♒14.1	29♑48.0	21♌39.4	9♏55.6	5♍36.0
2 Tu	2 40 39	11 50 14	26 52 32	3♐49 01	3R 40.9	12 27.9	12D 44.4	28 10.9	18 56.4	6 18.5	29 48.8	21 39.5	9R 53.9	5R 35.5
3 W	2 44 35	12 48 23	10♐48 23	17 50 05	3 31.1	14 37.5	12 46.3	28 41.5	19 19.6	6 22.7	29 49.4	21 39.7	9 52.3	5 35.1
4 Th	2 48 32	13 46 31	24 53 36	1♑58 22	3 23.3	16 47.4	12 50.6	29 12.2	19 42.7	6 26.7	29 50.0	21 40.0	9 50.7	5 34.7
5 F	2 52 28	14 44 37	9♑03 56	16 09 52	3 18.0	18 57.3	12 57.1	29 43.0	20 05.8	6 30.6	29 50.4	21 40.3	9 49.0	5 34.4
6 Sa	2 56 25	15 42 42	23 15 46	0♒21 21	3 15.2	21 06.8	13 05.8	0♌13.9	20 28.8	6 34.2	29 50.8	21 40.7	9 47.4	5 34.0
7 Su	3 00 21	16 40 45	7♒26 23	14 30 40	3D 14.4	23 15.8	13 16.8	0 44.9	20 51.8	6 37.7	29 51.1	21 41.1	9 45.8	5 33.7
8 M	3 04 18	17 38 48	21 34 05	28 36 30	3R 14.5	25 23.9	13 29.8	1 16.1	21 14.8	6 41.1	29 51.2	21 41.5	9 44.2	5 33.4
9 Tu	3 08 14	18 36 48	5♓37 50	12♓37 59	3 14.3	27 30.8	13 44.8	1 47.4	21 37.7	6 44.2	29R 51.3	21 42.1	9 42.6	5 33.2
10 W	3 12 11	19 34 48	19 36 52	26 34 20	3 12.6	29 36.3	14 01.8	2 18.7	22 00.6	6 47.2	29 51.3	21 42.6	9 40.9	5 33.0
11 Th	3 16 08	20 32 46	3♈30 14	10♈24 22	3 08.4	1♊40.1	14 20.7	2 50.2	22 23.5	6 49.9	29 51.1	21 43.2	9 39.3	5 32.8
12 F	3 20 04	21 30 43	17 16 29	24 06 20	3 01.4	3 41.9	14 41.4	3 21.8	22 46.3	6 52.5	29 50.9	21 43.9	9 37.7	5 32.6
13 Sa	3 24 01	22 28 38	0♉53 36	7♉37 59	2 51.6	5 41.5	15 03.9	3 53.5	23 09.1	6 55.0	29 50.6	21 44.7	9 36.2	5 32.5
14 Su	3 27 57	23 26 32	14 19 12	20 56 56	2 39.9	7 38.6	15 28.1	4 25.3	23 31.8	6 57.2	29 50.2	21 45.5	9 34.6	5 32.4
15 M	3 31 54	24 24 25	27 30 57	4♊01 03	2 27.2	9 33.3	15 54.0	4 57.2	23 54.5	6 59.2	29 49.7	21 46.3	9 33.0	5 32.3
16 Tu	3 35 50	25 22 16	10♊27 05	16 48 59	2 14.7	11 25.2	16 21.4	5 29.2	24 17.1	7 01.1	29 49.0	21 47.2	9 31.4	5D 32.3
17 W	3 39 47	26 20 05	23 06 46	29 20 31	2 03.5	13 14.2	16 50.4	6 01.4	24 39.7	7 02.7	29 48.3	21 48.1	9 29.9	5 32.3
18 Th	3 43 43	27 17 53	5♋30 24	11♋36 43	1 54.6	15 00.3	17 20.8	6 33.6	25 02.3	7 04.2	29 47.5	21 49.1	9 28.3	5 32.3
19 F	3 47 40	28 15 40	17 39 46	23 39 58	1 48.3	16 43.3	17 52.6	7 05.9	25 24.8	7 05.5	29 46.6	21 50.2	9 26.8	5 32.4
20 Sa	3 51 37	29 13 25	29 37 47	5♌33 47	1 44.6	18 23.2	18 25.8	7 38.3	25 47.3	7 06.6	29 45.6	21 51.3	9 25.3	5 32.5
21 Su	3 55 33	0♊11 08	11♌28 31	17 22 37	1 43.0	20 00.0	19 00.3	8 10.8	26 09.7	7 07.5	29 44.5	21 52.4	9 23.8	5 32.6
22 M	3 59 30	1 08 49	23 16 44	29 11 33	1 42.7	21 33.5	19 36.0	8 43.3	26 32.0	7 08.2	29 43.3	21 53.6	9 22.3	5 32.7
23 Tu	4 03 26	2 06 29	5♍07 45	11♍06 01	1 42.6	23 03.7	20 13.0	9 16.0	26 54.3	7 08.7	29 42.1	21 54.9	9 20.8	5 32.9
24 W	4 07 23	3 04 08	17 07 03	23 11 30	1 41.7	24 30.6	20 51.1	9 48.8	27 16.6	7 09.1	29 40.7	21 56.2	9 19.3	5 33.1
25 Th	4 11 19	4 01 45	29 20 00	5♎33 06	1 38.9	25 54.1	21 30.3	10 21.6	27 38.8	7R 09.2	29 39.2	21 57.6	9 17.9	5 33.3
26 F	4 15 16	4 59 20	11♎51 20	18 15 07	1 33.7	27 14.2	22 10.6	10 54.5	28 00.9	7 09.2	29 37.7	21 59.0	9 16.4	5 33.6
27 Sa	4 19 12	5 56 55	24 44 46	1♏20 29	1 26.0	28 30.9	22 51.9	11 27.5	28 23.0	7 08.9	29 36.0	22 00.4	9 15.0	5 33.9
28 Su	4 23 09	6 54 27	8♏02 21	14 50 16	1 16.0	29 44.1	23 34.3	12 00.6	28 45.1	7 08.5	29 34.3	22 01.9	9 13.6	5 34.2
29 M	4 27 06	7 51 59	21 44 02	28 43 16	1 04.7	0♋53.7	24 17.6	12 33.8	29 07.0	7 07.9	29 32.5	22 03.5	9 12.2	5 34.6
30 Tu	4 31 02	8 49 30	5♐47 26	12♐55 53	0 53.2	1 59.7	25 01.8	13 07.0	29 29.0	7 07.1	29 30.6	22 05.1	9 10.8	5 35.0
31 W	4 34 59	9 46 59	20 07 52	27 22 34	0 42.7	3 02.0	25 46.9	13 40.3	29 50.8	7 06.1	29 28.6	22 06.7	9 09.5	5 35.4

LONGITUDE — June 1961

Day	Sid.Time	☉	0 hr ☽	Noon ☽	True ☊	☿	♀	♂	⚳	♃	♄	♅	♆	♇
1 Th	4 38 55	10♊44 28	4♑39 05	11♑56 35	0♍34.2	4♋00.6	26♈32.9	14♌13.7	0♉12.6	7♒05.0	29♑26.5	22♌08.4	9♏08.1	5♍35.8
2 F	4 42 52	11 41 56	19 14 14	26 31 16	0R 28.3	4 55.4	27 19.7	14 47.2	0 34.4	7R 03.6	29R 24.3	22 10.2	9R 06.8	5 36.3
3 Sa	4 46 48	12 39 23	3♒47 01	11♒00 54	0 25.2	5 46.3	28 07.2	15 20.8	0 56.1	7 02.0	29 22.1	22 12.0	9 05.5	5 36.8
4 Su	4 50 45	13 36 49	18 12 29	25 21 25	0D 24.1	6 33.3	28 55.6	15 54.4	1 17.7	7 00.3	29 19.7	22 13.8	9 04.2	5 37.3
5 M	4 54 41	14 34 14	2♓27 29	9♓30 30	0R 24.1	7 16.1	29 44.7	16 28.1	1 39.2	6 58.4	29 17.3	22 15.7	9 03.0	5 37.9
6 Tu	4 58 38	15 31 39	16 30 26	23 27 14	0 24.0	7 54.9	0♉34.5	17 01.9	2 00.7	6 56.3	29 14.8	22 17.6	9 01.7	5 38.5
7 W	5 02 35	16 29 04	0♈20 58	7♈11 38	0 22.5	8 29.4	1 25.0	17 35.7	2 22.2	6 54.0	29 12.2	22 19.6	9 00.5	5 39.1
8 Th	5 06 31	17 26 27	13 59 19	20 44 02	0 18.8	8 59.7	2 16.1	18 09.6	2 43.5	6 51.5	29 09.6	22 21.6	8 59.3	5 39.8
9 F	5 10 28	18 23 51	27 25 50	4♉04 43	0 12.4	9 25.5	3 07.9	18 43.6	3 04.8	6 48.8	29 06.8	22 23.7	8 58.1	5 40.4
10 Sa	5 14 24	19 21 13	10♉40 40	17 13 40	0 03.5	9 46.9	4 00.2	19 17.7	3 26.0	6 45.9	29 04.0	22 25.8	8 56.9	5 41.1
11 Su	5 18 21	20 18 35	23 43 39	0♊10 35	29♌52.7	10 03.8	4 53.1	19 51.9	3 47.2	6 42.9	29 01.1	22 27.9	8 55.8	5 41.9
12 M	5 22 17	21 15 57	6♊34 23	12 55 01	29 40.9	10 16.2	5 46.6	20 26.1	4 08.2	6 39.7	28 58.2	22 30.1	8 54.7	5 42.6
13 Tu	5 26 14	22 13 18	19 12 29	25 26 45	29 29.3	10 24.0	6 40.7	21 00.4	4 29.2	6 36.3	28 55.1	22 32.4	8 53.6	5 43.4
14 W	5 30 10	23 10 38	1♋37 52	7♋45 57	29 18.9	10R 27.2	7 35.2	21 34.7	4 50.1	6 32.7	28 52.0	22 34.6	8 52.5	5 44.3
15 Th	5 34 07	24 07 58	13 51 06	19 53 33	29 10.5	10 25.9	8 30.3	22 09.2	5 11.0	6 29.0	28 48.9	22 37.0	8 51.5	5 45.1
16 F	5 38 04	25 05 16	25 53 30	1♌51 19	29 04.6	10 20.2	9 25.8	22 43.7	5 31.7	6 25.1	28 45.6	22 39.3	8 50.5	5 46.0
17 Sa	5 42 00	26 02 34	7♌47 19	13 41 58	29 01.2	10 10.1	10 21.8	23 18.2	5 52.4	6 21.0	28 42.3	22 41.7	8 49.5	5 46.9
18 Su	5 45 57	26 59 52	19 35 42	25 29 05	28D 59.9	9 55.8	11 18.2	23 52.9	6 13.0	6 16.7	28 38.9	22 44.2	8 48.5	5 47.8
19 M	5 49 53	27 57 08	1♍22 38	7♍16 59	29 00.1	9 37.6	12 15.1	24 27.6	6 33.5	6 12.3	28 35.5	22 46.7	8 47.6	5 48.8
20 Tu	5 53 50	28 54 24	13 12 46	19 10 37	29R 00.8	9 15.8	13 12.3	25 02.3	6 53.9	6 07.7	28 32.0	22 49.2	8 46.6	5 49.8
21 W	5 57 46	29 51 39	25 11 14	1♎15 15	29 01.2	8 50.5	14 10.0	25 37.2	7 14.2	6 03.0	28 28.4	22 51.7	8 45.8	5 50.8
22 Th	6 01 43	0♋48 53	7♎23 21	13 36 09	29 00.3	8 22.3	15 08.1	26 12.1	7 34.4	5 58.1	28 24.8	22 54.3	8 44.9	5 51.8
23 F	6 05 39	1 46 07	19 54 15	26 18 11	28 57.5	7 51.6	16 06.6	26 47.0	7 54.6	5 53.0	28 21.1	22 57.0	8 44.1	5 52.9
24 Sa	6 09 36	2 43 20	2♏48 23	9♏25 12	28 52.7	7 18.8	17 05.4	27 22.0	8 14.6	5 47.8	28 17.4	22 59.6	8 43.2	5 54.0
25 Su	6 13 33	3 40 33	16 08 52	22 59 26	28 46.0	6 44.5	18 04.6	27 57.1	8 34.6	5 42.5	28 13.6	23 02.3	8 42.5	5 55.1
26 M	6 17 29	4 37 45	29 56 49	7♐00 46	28 38.1	6 09.3	19 04.1	28 32.2	8 54.4	5 37.0	28 09.8	23 05.1	8 41.7	5 56.2
27 Tu	6 21 26	5 34 57	14♐10 48	21 26 18	28 29.8	5 33.8	20 04.0	29 07.4	9 14.2	5 31.4	28 05.9	23 07.9	8 41.0	5 57.4
28 W	6 25 22	6 32 08	28 46 29	6♑10 25	28 22.3	4 58.5	21 04.2	29 42.7	9 33.9	5 25.6	28 02.0	23 10.7	8 40.3	5 58.6
29 Th	6 29 19	7 29 19	13♑37 04	21 05 22	28 16.2	4 24.1	22 04.7	0♍18.0	9 53.4	5 19.7	27 58.0	23 13.5	8 39.6	5 59.8
30 F	6 33 15	8 26 31	28 34 12	6♒02 30	28 12.3	3 51.2	23 05.6	0 53.3	10 12.9	5 13.7	27 54.0	23 16.4	8 39.0	6 01.0

Astro Data

	Dy Hr Mn
♀ D	2 4:15
♄ R	9 16:21
☽ 0N	11 5:02
♇ D	17 4:24
☽ 0S	25 14:13
♃ R	25 18:35
☽ 0N	7 11:38
☿ R	14 17:07
☽ 0S	21 23:57
♃⚻♇	23 12:41

Planet Ingress

	Dy Hr Mn
♂ ♌	6 1:13
☿ ♊	10 16:34
☉ ♊	21 7:22
☿ ♋	28 17:23
⚳ ♉	31 22:05
♀ ♉	5 19:25
☊ ♌R	10 20:06
☉ ♋	21 15:30
♂ ♍	28 23:47

Last Aspect / ☽ Ingress

Last Aspect Dy Hr Mn		☽ Ingress	Dy Hr Mn
2 5:05	♄ ✱	♐	2 5:25
3 18:31	♅ △	♑	4 8:40
6 11:08	♄ ☌	♒	6 11:24
8 5:33	☿ □	♓	8 14:23
10 17:41	♄ ✱	♈	10 17:56
12 22:09	♄ □	♉	12 22:25
15 4:16	♄ △	♊	15 4:34
16 21:28	♅ ✱	♋	17 13:17
20 0:17	♄ ☍	♌	20 0:45
21 21:10	♅ ☌	♍	22 13:38
25 0:39	♄ △	♎	25 1:18
27 8:51	♄ □	♏	27 9:34
29 13:24	♄ ✱	♐	29 14:11
31 9:13	♀ △	♑	31 16:20

Last Aspect / ☽ Ingress

Last Aspect Dy Hr Mn		☽ Ingress	Dy Hr Mn
2 16:45	♄ ☌	♒	2 17:45
4 18:23	♀ ✱	♓	4 19:50
6 22:03	♄ ✱	♈	6 23:23
9 3:04	♄ □	♉	9 4:38
11 9:51	♄ △	♊	11 11:40
13 6:23	♅ ✱	♋	13 20:50
16 5:48	♄ ☍	♌	16 8:16
18 15:21	☉ ✱	♍	18 21:12
21 9:01	☉ □	♎	21 9:32
23 15:47	♄ □	♏	23 18:51
25 21:01	♄ ✱	♐	26 0:05
28 1:05	♂ △	♑	28 2:00
29 22:59	♄ ☌	♒	30 2:18

☽ Phases & Eclipses

Dy Hr Mn		
7 15:57	☾	16♒50
14 16:54	●	23♉38
22 16:18	☽	1♍19
30 4:37	○	8♐32
5 21:19	☾	14♓57
13 5:16	●	21♊57
21 9:01	☽	29♍45
28 12:37	○	6♑34

Astro Data

1 May 1961
Julian Day # 22401
SVP 5♓48'08"
GC 26♐18.0 ⚴ 15♓02.9
Eris 10♈11.9 ⚵ 8♓11.5
⚷ 5♓57.6 ⚶ 17♈26.1
☽ Mean ☊ 2♍57.6

1 June 1961
Julian Day # 22432
SVP 5♓48'04"
GC 26♐18.0 ⚴ 21♓55.6
Eris 10♈27.3 ⚵ 18♓45.5
⚷ 6♓39.6 ⚶ 1♉06.2
☽ Mean ☊ 1♍19.1

July 1961 — LONGITUDE

Day	Sid.Time	☉	0 hr ☽	Noon ☽	True ☊	☿	♀	♂	⚳	♃	♄	♅	♆	♇
1 Sa	6 37 12	9♋23 42	13♒29 17	20♒53 40	28♌10.5	3♋20.3	24♉06.7	1♍28.8	10♉32.3	5♒07.6	27♑50.0	23♌19.3	8♏38.4	6♍02.3
2 Su	6 41 09	10 20 53	28 14 52	5♓32 19	28D 10.5	2R 52.0	25 08.2	2 04.3	10 51.5	5R 01.3	27R 45.9	23 22.3	8R 37.8	6 03.6
3 M	6 45 05	11 18 05	12♓45 30	19 54 08	28 11.5	2 26.9	26 09.9	2 39.8	11 10.7	4 54.9	27 41.8	23 25.3	8 37.2	6 04.9
4 Tu	6 49 02	12 15 16	26 57 59	3♈56 59	28R 12.5	2 05.2	27 11.9	3 15.4	11 29.7	4 48.4	27 37.6	23 28.3	8 36.7	6 06.2
5 W	6 52 58	13 12 28	10♈51 08	17 40 32	28 12.7	1 47.5	28 14.2	3 51.1	11 48.6	4 41.8	27 33.4	23 31.3	8 36.2	6 07.6
6 Th	6 56 55	14 09 41	24 25 17	1♉05 36	28 11.3	1 34.1	29 16.8	4 26.8	12 07.5	4 35.1	27 29.2	23 34.4	8 35.7	6 08.9
7 F	7 00 51	15 06 53	7♉41 39	14 13 40	28 08.1	1 25.3	0♊19.6	5 02.6	12 26.2	4 28.2	27 24.9	23 37.5	8 35.3	6 10.3
8 Sa	7 04 48	16 04 06	20 41 52	27 06 26	28 03.2	1D 21.2	1 22.6	5 38.4	12 44.7	4 21.3	27 20.6	23 40.6	8 34.9	6 11.8
9 Su	7 08 44	17 01 20	3♊27 35	9♊45 29	27 56.8	1 22.1	2 25.9	6 14.3	13 03.2	4 14.3	27 16.3	23 43.7	8 34.5	6 13.2
10 M	7 12 41	17 58 34	16 00 20	22 12 18	27 49.8	1 28.2	3 29.4	6 50.3	13 21.6	4 07.2	27 12.0	23 46.9	8 34.2	6 14.7
11 Tu	7 16 38	18 55 48	28 21 32	4♋28 11	27 42.9	1 39.5	4 33.1	7 26.3	13 39.8	4 00.0	27 07.6	23 50.1	8 33.9	6 16.2
12 W	7 20 34	19 53 02	10♋32 26	16 34 27	27 36.7	1 56.1	5 37.1	8 02.4	13 57.9	3 52.7	27 03.2	23 53.4	8 33.6	6 17.7
13 Th	7 24 31	20 50 17	22 34 25	28 32 33	27 31.9	2 18.0	6 41.3	8 38.5	14 15.8	3 45.4	26 58.8	23 56.6	8 33.4	6 19.2
14 F	7 28 27	21 47 32	4♌29 05	10♌24 17	27 28.7	2 45.3	7 45.6	9 14.7	14 33.6	3 38.0	26 54.4	23 59.9	8 33.1	6 20.8
15 Sa	7 32 24	22 44 47	16 18 26	22 11 53	27D 27.3	3 17.9	8 50.2	9 51.0	14 51.3	3 30.5	26 50.0	24 03.2	8 33.0	6 22.3
16 Su	7 36 20	23 42 02	28 04 58	3♍58 08	27 27.3	3 55.8	9 55.0	10 27.3	15 08.9	3 23.0	26 45.6	24 06.6	8 32.8	6 23.9
17 M	7 40 17	24 39 18	9♍51 48	15 46 27	27 28.5	4 39.0	10 59.9	11 03.7	15 26.3	3 15.4	26 41.2	24 09.9	8 32.7	6 25.5
18 Tu	7 44 13	25 36 34	21 42 36	27 40 47	27 30.1	5 27.5	12 05.1	11 40.1	15 43.6	3 07.8	26 36.7	24 13.3	8 32.6	6 27.2
19 W	7 48 10	26 33 49	3♎41 34	9♎45 33	27 31.7	6 21.1	13 10.4	12 16.6	16 00.7	3 00.2	26 32.3	24 16.7	8 32.5	6 28.8
20 Th	7 52 07	27 31 06	15 53 18	22 05 26	27R 32.7	7 19.9	14 15.9	12 53.1	16 17.7	2 52.5	26 27.9	24 20.1	8D 32.5	6 30.5
21 F	7 56 03	28 28 22	28 22 30	4♏45 04	27 32.6	8 23.7	15 21.6	13 29.7	16 34.5	2 44.8	26 23.4	24 23.6	8 32.5	6 32.1
22 Sa	8 00 00	29 25 39	11♏13 37	17 48 34	27 31.4	9 32.5	16 27.5	14 06.3	16 51.2	2 37.0	26 19.0	24 27.1	8 32.6	6 33.8
23 Su	8 03 56	0♌22 56	24 30 16	1♐18 56	27 29.0	10 46.2	17 33.5	14 43.0	17 07.7	2 29.3	26 14.6	24 30.5	8 32.6	6 35.6
24 M	8 07 53	1 20 13	8♐14 40	15 17 22	27 25.9	12 04.7	18 39.7	15 19.8	17 24.1	2 21.5	26 10.2	24 34.0	8 32.7	6 37.3
25 Tu	8 11 49	2 17 31	22 26 49	29 42 35	27 22.4	13 27.8	19 46.0	15 56.6	17 40.3	2 13.7	26 05.8	24 37.6	8 32.9	6 39.0
26 W	8 15 46	3 14 50	7♑04 03	14♑30 25	27 19.2	14 55.4	20 52.5	16 33.4	17 56.4	2 06.0	26 01.4	24 41.1	8 33.0	6 40.8
27 Th	8 19 42	4 12 08	22 00 44	29 33 57	27 16.8	16 27.5	21 59.2	17 10.3	18 12.3	1 58.2	25 57.0	24 44.7	8 33.2	6 42.6
28 F	8 23 39	5 09 28	7♒08 54	14♒44 22	27D 15.3	18 03.7	23 06.0	17 47.3	18 28.0	1 50.5	25 52.7	24 48.2	8 33.5	6 44.4
29 Sa	8 27 36	6 06 49	22 19 09	29 52 06	27 15.0	19 43.8	24 13.0	18 24.3	18 43.5	1 42.7	25 48.3	24 51.8	8 33.7	6 46.2
30 Su	8 31 32	7 04 10	7♓22 11	14♓48 26	27 15.6	21 27.7	25 20.2	19 01.4	18 58.9	1 35.0	25 44.0	24 55.4	8 34.0	6 48.0
31 M	8 35 29	8 01 32	22 10 06	29 26 33	27 16.7	23 15.1	26 27.4	19 38.5	19 14.1	1 27.3	25 39.7	24 59.0	8 34.4	6 49.8

August 1961 — LONGITUDE

Day	Sid.Time	☉	0 hr ☽	Noon ☽	True ☊	☿	♀	♂	⚳	♃	♄	♅	♆	♇
1 Tu	8 39 25	8♌58 55	6♈37 19	13♈42 06	27♌17.9	25♋05.7	27♊34.9	20♍15.6	19♉29.2	1♒19.7	25♑35.5	25♌02.6	8♏34.7	6♍51.7
2 W	8 43 22	9 56 20	20 40 46	27 33 17	27 18.9	26 59.1	28 42.5	20 52.9	19 44.0	1R 12.0	25R 31.2	25 06.3	8 35.1	6 53.5
3 Th	8 47 18	10 53 46	4♉19 45	11♉00 21	27R 19.2	28 55.0	29 50.2	21 30.2	19 58.7	1 04.5	25 27.0	25 09.9	8 35.5	6 55.4
4 F	8 51 15	11 51 13	17 35 21	24 05 03	27 18.9	0♌53.1	0♋58.1	22 07.5	20 13.2	0 56.9	25 22.8	25 13.6	8 36.0	6 57.3
5 Sa	8 55 11	12 48 41	0♊29 49	6♊50 01	27 17.8	2 53.0	2 06.1	22 44.9	20 27.5	0 49.5	25 18.7	25 17.3	8 36.5	6 59.2
6 Su	8 59 08	13 46 10	13 06 03	19 18 19	27 16.3	4 54.4	3 14.2	23 22.3	20 41.5	0 42.0	25 14.6	25 20.9	8 37.0	7 01.1
7 M	9 03 05	14 43 41	25 27 11	1♋33 02	27 14.5	6 56.8	4 22.5	23 59.8	20 55.4	0 34.7	25 10.6	25 24.6	8 37.6	7 03.0
8 Tu	9 07 01	15 41 13	7♋36 15	13 37 10	27 12.8	9 00.0	5 30.9	24 37.4	21 09.1	0 27.4	25 06.5	25 28.3	8 38.2	7 05.0
9 W	9 10 58	16 38 46	19 36 06	25 33 24	27 11.3	11 03.7	6 39.4	25 15.0	21 22.6	0 20.2	25 02.6	25 32.0	8 38.8	7 06.9
10 Th	9 14 54	17 36 21	1♌29 20	7♌24 13	27 10.3	13 07.4	7 48.0	25 52.7	21 35.9	0 13.1	24 58.6	25 35.8	8 39.4	7 08.9
11 F	9 18 51	18 33 56	13 18 19	19 11 56	27D 09.7	15 11.1	8 56.8	26 30.4	21 48.9	0 06.1	24 54.7	25 39.5	8 40.1	7 10.8
12 Sa	9 22 47	19 31 33	25 05 20	0♍58 49	27 09.7	17 14.3	10 05.7	27 08.2	22 01.8	29♑59.1	24 50.9	25 43.2	8 40.8	7 12.8
13 Su	9 26 44	20 29 11	6♍52 40	12 47 11	27 09.9	19 17.1	11 14.7	27 46.0	22 14.4	29 52.3	24 47.1	25 46.9	8 41.6	7 14.8
14 M	9 30 40	21 26 50	18 42 43	24 39 35	27 10.4	21 19.0	12 23.8	28 23.9	22 26.8	29 45.5	24 43.4	25 50.7	8 42.3	7 16.8
15 Tu	9 34 37	22 24 30	0♎38 10	6♎38 50	27 11.0	23 20.1	13 33.0	29 01.9	22 39.0	29 38.9	24 39.7	25 54.4	8 43.1	7 18.8
16 W	9 38 33	23 22 11	12 41 59	18 48 03	27 11.5	25 20.1	14 42.4	29 39.9	22 50.9	29 32.3	24 36.1	25 58.2	8 44.0	7 20.8
17 Th	9 42 30	24 19 53	24 57 28	1♏10 42	27 11.8	27 19.1	15 51.8	0♎17.9	23 02.6	29 25.9	24 32.5	26 01.9	8 44.8	7 22.8
18 F	9 46 27	25 17 36	7♏28 10	13 50 20	27 11.9	29 16.8	17 01.3	0 56.0	23 14.1	29 19.6	24 29.0	26 05.6	8 45.7	7 24.8
19 Sa	9 50 23	26 15 20	20 17 38	26 50 27	27 12.0	1♍13.3	18 11.0	1 34.2	23 25.3	29 13.5	24 25.6	26 09.4	8 46.6	7 26.8
20 Su	9 54 20	27 13 06	3♐29 08	10♐13 59	27 12.0	3 08.6	19 20.8	2 12.4	23 36.2	29 07.4	24 22.2	26 13.1	8 47.6	7 28.8
21 M	9 58 16	28 10 52	17 05 11	24 02 51	27 12.0	5 02.5	20 30.6	2 50.7	23 47.0	29 01.5	24 18.9	26 16.9	8 48.6	7 30.9
22 Tu	10 02 13	29 08 40	1♑06 55	8♑17 15	27 12.2	6 55.0	21 40.6	3 29.0	23 57.4	28 55.7	24 15.7	26 20.6	8 49.6	7 32.9
23 W	10 06 09	0♍06 29	15 33 30	22 55 10	27 12.4	8 46.2	22 50.7	4 07.4	24 07.6	28 50.1	24 12.5	26 24.4	8 50.7	7 34.9
24 Th	10 10 06	1 04 19	0♒21 36	7♒51 59	27 12.7	10 36.1	24 00.8	4 45.8	24 17.6	28 44.6	24 09.4	26 28.1	8 51.7	7 37.0
25 F	10 14 03	2 02 11	15 25 19	23 00 33	27R 12.8	12 24.6	25 11.1	5 24.3	24 27.3	28 39.3	24 06.4	26 31.9	8 52.8	7 39.0
26 Sa	10 17 59	3 00 03	0♓36 31	8♓12 02	27 12.7	14 11.8	26 21.5	6 02.8	24 36.7	28 34.1	24 03.5	26 35.6	8 54.0	7 41.1
27 Su	10 21 56	3 57 58	15 45 52	23 16 56	27 12.4	15 57.6	27 32.0	6 41.4	24 45.9	28 29.0	24 00.6	26 39.3	8 55.1	7 43.1
28 M	10 25 52	4 55 54	0♈44 08	8♈06 35	27 11.7	17 42.2	28 42.5	7 20.0	24 54.7	28 24.1	23 57.8	26 43.0	8 56.3	7 45.2
29 Tu	10 29 49	5 53 52	15 23 31	22 34 20	27 10.7	19 25.4	29 53.2	7 58.7	25 03.3	28 19.4	23 55.1	26 46.7	8 57.5	7 47.2
30 W	10 33 45	6 51 51	29 38 37	6♉36 07	27 09.7	21 07.3	1♌04.0	8 37.4	25 11.6	28 14.8	23 52.4	26 50.4	8 58.8	7 49.3
31 Th	10 37 42	7 49 53	13♉26 46	20 10 37	27 08.8	22 48.0	2 14.9	9 16.2	25 19.6	28 10.4	23 49.8	26 54.1	9 00.0	7 51.4

Astro Data

	Dy Hr Mn
☽0N	4 18:20
☿D	8 19:37
☽0S	19 8:16
♆D	20 18:48
☽0N	1 2:17
♄⊼♅	5 16:29
☽0S	15 14:47
♂0S	19 2:44
☽0N	28 11:53

Planet Ingress

		Dy Hr Mn
♀	♊	7 4:32
☉	♌	23 2:24
♀	♋	3 15:28
☿	♌	4 1:15
♃	♑R	12 8:54
♂	♎	17 0:41
☿	♍	18 20:52
☉	♍	23 9:19
♀	♌	29 14:18

Last Aspect / ☽ Ingress (July)

Last Aspect Dy Hr Mn			☽ Ingress	Dy Hr Mn
1 17:38	♀	□	♓	2 2:52
4 1:11	♄	⚹	♈	4 5:12
6 5:32	♄	□	♉	6 10:01
8 12:27	♄	△	♊	8 17:27
10 15:05	♅	⚹	♋	11 3:13
13 8:52	♄	☍	♌	13 14:56
15 15:48	♅	☌	♍	16 3:55
18 9:52	♄	△	♎	18 16:39
20 23:13	☉	□	♏	21 3:05
23 3:08	♄	⚹	♐	23 9:42
25 3:35	♅	△	♑	25 12:29
27 6:17	♄	☌	♒	27 12:41
29 4:00	♅	☍	♓	29 12:13
31 6:39	♀	□	♈	31 12:56

Last Aspect / ☽ Ingress (August)

Last Aspect Dy Hr Mn			☽ Ingress	Dy Hr Mn
2 14:13	♀	⚹	♉	2 16:19
4 14:24	♄	△	♊	4 23:04
6 23:51	♅	⚹	♋	7 8:56
9 11:21	♂	⚹	♌	9 20:59
12 1:14	♅	☌	♍	12 10:00
14 22:09	♃	△	♎	14 22:44
17 8:40	♃	□	♏	17 9:44
19 16:17	♃	⚹	♐	19 17:44
21 19:33	☉	△	♑	21 22:07
23 21:29	♃	☌	♒	23 23:25
25 17:35	♅	☍	♓	25 23:02
27 20:19	♃	⚹	♈	27 22:49
29 21:42	♃	□	♉	30 0:37

☽ Phases & Eclipses

Dy Hr Mn	
5 3:32	☾ 12♈52
12 19:11	● 20♋10
20 23:13	☽ 27♎58
27 19:50	○ 4♒31
3 11:47	☾ 10♉53
11 10:36	● 18♌31
11 10:46:14	● A 06'35"
19 10:51	☽ 26♏13
26 3:13	○ 2♓39
26 3:08	● P 0.986

Astro Data

1 July 1961
Julian Day # 22462
SVP 5♓47'59"
GC 26♐18.1 ⚴ 25♓37.2
Eris 10♈33.9 ⚵ 26♓40.3
⚷ 6♓28.4R ⚶ 13♉12.8
☽ Mean ☊ 29♌43.8

1 August 1961
Julian Day # 22493
SVP 5♓47'54"
GC 26♐18.2 ⚴ 24♓51.5R
Eris 10♈30.6R ⚵ 0♈35.4
⚷ 5♓28.6R ⚶ 23♉55.6
☽ Mean ☊ 28♌05.4

LONGITUDE — September 1961

Day	Sid.Time	☉	0 hr ☽	Noon ☽	True ☊	☿	♀	♂	⚳	♃	♄	♅	♆	♇
1 F	10 41 38	8♍47 56	26♉47 51	3♊18 48	27♌08.3	24♍27.4	3♌25.9	9♎55.0	25♉27.4	28♑06.2	23♑47.3	26♌57.8	9♏01.3	7♍53.4
2 Sa	10 45 35	9 46 02	9♊43 49	16 03 21	27D08.4	26 05.6	4 36.9	10 34.0	25 34.8	28R02.1	23R44.9	27 01.5	9 02.7	7 55.5
3 Su	10 49 31	10 44 09	22 17 56	28 28 04	27 08.9	27 42.6	5 48.1	11 12.9	25 41.9	27 58.2	23 42.6	27 05.2	9 04.0	7 57.5
4 M	10 53 28	11 42 18	4♋34 17	10♋37 09	27 10.0	29 18.3	6 59.4	11 51.9	25 48.7	27 54.5	23 40.4	27 08.9	9 05.4	7 59.6
5 Tu	10 57 25	12 40 30	16 37 11	22 34 56	27 11.4	0♎52.9	8 10.7	12 31.0	25 55.2	27 50.9	23 38.2	27 12.5	9 06.8	8 01.6
6 W	11 01 21	13 38 43	28 30 54	4♌25 32	27 12.7	2 26.2	9 22.1	13 10.2	26 01.4	27 47.5	23 36.1	27 16.2	9 08.2	8 03.7
7 Th	11 05 18	14 36 58	10♌19 20	16 12 40	27R13.7	3 58.3	10 33.7	13 49.3	26 07.3	27 44.3	23 34.2	27 19.8	9 09.7	8 05.8
8 F	11 09 14	15 35 15	22 05 58	27 59 35	27 14.1	5 29.3	11 45.3	14 28.6	26 12.8	27 41.3	23 32.3	27 23.4	9 11.2	8 07.8
9 Sa	11 13 11	16 33 34	3♍53 50	9♍49 03	27 13.5	6 59.0	12 57.0	15 07.9	26 18.0	27 38.5	23 30.5	27 27.0	9 12.7	8 09.8
10 Su	11 17 07	17 31 54	15 45 28	21 43 23	27 12.0	8 27.6	14 08.7	15 47.3	26 22.9	27 35.9	23 28.8	27 30.6	9 14.2	8 11.9
11 M	11 21 04	18 30 16	27 43 01	3♎44 37	27 09.4	9 54.9	15 20.6	16 26.7	26 27.4	27 33.4	23 27.1	27 34.2	9 15.8	8 13.9
12 Tu	11 25 00	19 28 41	9♎48 22	15 54 31	27 06.1	11 21.1	16 32.5	17 06.1	26 31.6	27 31.2	23 25.6	27 37.7	9 17.3	8 15.9
13 W	11 28 57	20 27 06	22 03 16	28 14 51	27 02.3	12 45.9	17 44.5	17 45.7	26 35.4	27 29.1	23 24.2	27 41.3	9 18.9	8 18.0
14 Th	11 32 54	21 25 34	4♏29 27	10♏47 21	26 58.6	14 09.6	18 56.6	18 25.2	26 38.9	27 27.2	23 22.8	27 44.8	9 20.6	8 20.0
15 F	11 36 50	22 24 03	17 08 45	23 33 55	26 55.4	15 31.9	20 08.8	19 04.9	26 42.1	27 25.5	23 21.6	27 48.3	9 22.2	8 22.0
16 Sa	11 40 47	23 22 34	0♐03 06	6♐36 33	26 53.2	16 52.9	21 21.0	19 44.6	26 44.9	27 24.0	23 20.4	27 51.8	9 23.9	8 24.0
17 Su	11 44 43	24 21 07	13 14 30	19 57 10	26D52.2	18 12.6	22 33.3	20 24.3	26 47.3	27 22.7	23 19.4	27 55.2	9 25.6	8 26.0
18 M	11 48 40	25 19 41	26 44 45	3♑37 23	26 52.4	19 30.8	23 45.7	21 04.1	26 49.4	27 21.6	23 18.4	27 58.7	9 27.3	8 28.0
19 Tu	11 52 36	26 18 17	10♑35 09	17 38 04	26 53.5	20 47.6	24 58.2	21 44.0	26 51.1	27 20.7	23 17.6	28 02.1	9 29.0	8 30.0
20 W	11 56 33	27 16 54	24 46 02	1♒58 50	26 54.9	22 02.9	26 10.7	22 23.9	26 52.4	27 20.0	23 16.8	28 05.5	9 30.8	8 32.0
21 Th	12 00 29	28 15 34	9♒16 09	16 37 29	26R56.1	23 16.5	27 23.3	23 03.8	26 53.4	27 19.5	23 16.1	28 08.9	9 32.6	8 33.9
22 F	12 04 26	29 14 14	24 02 15	1♓29 41	26 56.3	24 28.5	28 36.0	23 43.8	26 54.0	27 19.2	23 15.6	28 12.2	9 34.4	8 35.9
23 Sa	12 08 23	0♎12 57	8♓58 55	16 28 56	26 55.1	25 38.7	29 48.7	24 23.9	26R54.2	27D19.1	23 15.1	28 15.5	9 36.2	8 37.8
24 Su	12 12 19	1 11 41	23 58 43	1♈27 10	26 52.2	26 47.0	1♍01.6	25 04.0	26 54.1	27 19.1	23 14.7	28 18.8	9 38.0	8 39.8
25 M	12 16 16	2 10 28	8♈53 11	16 15 44	26 47.8	27 53.3	2 14.4	25 44.2	26 53.6	27 19.4	23 14.4	28 22.1	9 39.9	8 41.7
26 Tu	12 20 12	3 09 16	23 33 53	0♉46 47	26 42.4	28 57.5	3 27.4	26 24.4	26 52.7	27 19.9	23 14.2	28 25.4	9 41.7	8 43.6
27 W	12 24 09	4 08 07	7♉53 48	14 54 24	26 36.7	29 59.3	4 40.4	27 04.7	26 51.4	27 20.5	23D14.2	28 28.6	9 43.6	8 45.5
28 Th	12 28 05	5 07 00	21 48 17	28 35 17	26 31.4	0♏58.7	5 53.5	27 45.0	26 49.7	27 21.4	23 14.2	28 31.8	9 45.5	8 47.4
29 F	12 32 02	6 05 55	5♊15 26	11♊48 52	26 27.3	1 55.5	7 06.7	28 25.4	26 47.7	27 22.4	23 14.3	28 35.0	9 47.5	8 49.3
30 Sa	12 35 58	7 04 53	18 15 53	24 36 53	26 24.7	2 49.3	8 19.9	29 05.9	26 45.3	27 23.6	23 14.5	28 38.1	9 49.4	8 51.2

LONGITUDE — October 1961

Day	Sid.Time	☉	0 hr ☽	Noon ☽	True ☊	☿	♀	♂	⚳	♃	♄	♅	♆	♇
1 Su	12 39 55	8♎03 52	0♋52 22	7♋02 52	26♌23.8	3♏40.0	9♍33.2	29♎46.4	26♉42.4	27♑25.1	23♑14.8	28♌41.2	9♏51.4	8♍53.0
2 M	12 43 51	9 02 55	13 09 00	19 11 23	26D24.3	4 27.4	10 46.6	0♏27.0	26R39.2	27 26.7	23 15.3	28 44.3	9 53.4	8 54.9
3 Tu	12 47 48	10 01 59	25 10 40	1♌07 30	26 25.7	5 11.0	12 00.0	1 07.6	26 35.6	27 28.5	23 15.8	28 47.4	9 55.3	8 56.7
4 W	12 51 45	11 01 06	7♌02 32	12 56 23	26 27.2	5 50.6	13 13.5	1 48.3	26 31.7	27 30.5	23 16.4	28 50.4	9 57.4	8 58.5
5 Th	12 55 41	12 00 14	18 49 39	24 42 54	26R28.0	6 25.8	14 27.0	2 29.1	26 27.3	27 32.7	23 17.1	28 53.4	9 59.4	9 00.3
6 F	12 59 38	12 59 26	0♍36 40	6♍31 25	26 27.4	6 56.1	15 40.6	3 09.9	26 22.5	27 35.1	23 17.9	28 56.3	10 01.4	9 02.1
7 Sa	13 03 34	13 58 39	12 27 37	18 25 39	26 24.8	7 21.3	16 54.3	3 50.7	26 17.4	27 37.7	23 18.8	28 59.3	10 03.5	9 03.9
8 Su	13 07 31	14 57 54	24 25 50	0♎28 28	26 20.0	7 40.8	18 08.0	4 31.7	26 11.8	27 40.5	23 19.8	29 02.1	10 05.5	9 05.6
9 M	13 11 27	15 57 12	6♎33 46	12 41 56	26 13.0	7 54.2	19 21.8	5 12.6	26 05.9	27 43.5	23 20.9	29 05.0	10 07.6	9 07.4
10 Tu	13 15 24	16 56 31	18 53 05	25 07 19	26 04.4	8R00.9	20 35.6	5 53.7	25 59.6	27 46.6	23 22.2	29 07.8	10 09.7	9 09.1
11 W	13 19 20	17 55 53	1♏24 39	7♏45 09	25 54.8	8 00.4	21 49.5	6 34.8	25 52.9	27 50.0	23 23.5	29 10.6	10 11.8	9 10.8
12 Th	13 23 17	18 55 16	14 08 46	20 35 31	25 45.2	7 52.4	23 03.4	7 15.9	25 45.9	27 53.5	23 24.9	29 13.3	10 13.9	9 12.4
13 F	13 27 14	19 54 42	27 05 22	3♐38 16	25 36.6	7 36.5	24 17.4	7 57.1	25 38.5	27 57.2	23 26.4	29 16.1	10 16.0	9 14.1
14 Sa	13 31 10	20 54 09	10♐14 15	16 53 16	25 29.8	7 12.2	25 31.4	8 38.4	25 30.7	28 01.1	23 28.0	29 18.7	10 18.2	9 15.8
15 Su	13 35 07	21 53 39	23 35 22	0♑20 34	25 25.3	6 39.4	26 45.5	9 19.7	25 22.6	28 05.2	23 29.7	29 21.4	10 20.3	9 17.4
16 M	13 39 03	22 53 10	7♑08 56	14 00 29	25D23.2	5 58.2	27 59.6	10 01.1	25 14.2	28 09.5	23 31.5	29 24.0	10 22.5	9 19.0
17 Tu	13 43 00	23 52 42	20 55 17	27 53 22	25 22.9	5 08.8	29 13.7	10 42.5	25 05.4	28 13.9	23 33.4	29 26.5	10 24.7	9 20.6
18 W	13 46 56	24 52 17	4♒54 44	11♒59 21	25R23.6	4 11.7	0♎27.9	11 24.0	24 56.2	28 18.5	23 35.4	29 29.0	10 26.8	9 22.1
19 Th	13 50 53	25 51 53	19 07 05	26 17 45	25 24.0	3 07.8	1 42.2	12 05.5	24 46.7	28 23.3	23 37.5	29 31.5	10 29.0	9 23.7
20 F	13 54 49	26 51 30	3♓31 04	10♓46 38	25 23.0	1 58.5	2 56.5	12 47.1	24 37.0	28 28.3	23 39.7	29 33.9	10 31.2	9 25.2
21 Sa	13 58 46	27 51 10	18 03 56	25 22 22	25 19.8	0 45.3	4 10.8	13 28.8	24 26.9	28 33.5	23 42.0	29 36.3	10 33.4	9 26.7
22 Su	14 02 43	28 50 51	2♈41 11	9♈59 35	25 13.9	29♎30.1	5 25.1	14 10.5	24 16.5	28 38.8	23 44.3	29 38.7	10 35.6	9 28.2
23 M	14 06 39	29 50 34	17 16 43	24 31 42	25 05.5	28 15.2	6 39.5	14 52.2	24 05.8	28 44.3	23 46.8	29 41.0	10 37.8	9 29.6
24 Tu	14 10 36	0♏50 19	1♉43 39	8♉51 44	24 55.3	27 02.7	7 54.0	15 34.0	23 54.8	28 49.9	23 49.4	29 43.2	10 40.0	9 31.1
25 W	14 14 32	1 50 06	15 55 14	22 53 32	24 44.2	25 55.0	9 08.5	16 15.9	23 43.5	28 55.7	23 52.0	29 45.4	10 42.3	9 32.5
26 Th	14 18 29	2 49 56	29 46 07	6♊32 40	24 33.7	24 54.1	10 23.0	16 57.8	23 32.0	29 01.7	23 54.8	29 47.6	10 44.5	9 33.9
27 F	14 22 25	3 49 47	13♊12 59	19 47 04	24 24.6	24 01.7	11 37.6	17 39.8	23 20.2	29 07.9	23 57.6	29 49.7	10 46.7	9 35.3
28 Sa	14 26 22	4 49 41	26 15 00	2♋37 03	24 17.8	23 19.3	12 52.2	18 21.9	23 08.2	29 14.2	24 00.5	29 51.8	10 48.9	9 36.6
29 Su	14 30 18	5 49 36	8♋53 35	15 05 03	24 13.5	22 47.7	14 06.8	19 04.0	22 55.9	29 20.7	24 03.6	29 53.9	10 51.2	9 37.9
30 M	14 34 15	6 49 34	21 11 59	27 14 59	24D11.5	22 27.6	15 21.5	19 46.1	22 43.5	29 27.3	24 06.7	29 55.9	10 53.4	9 39.2
31 Tu	14 38 12	7 49 34	3♌14 43	9♌11 51	24 11.1	22D19.0	16 36.2	20 28.3	22 30.8	29 34.1	24 09.9	29 57.8	10 55.7	9 40.5

Astro Data Dy Hr Mn	Planet Ingress Dy Hr Mn	Last Aspect Dy Hr Mn	☽ Ingress Dy Hr Mn	Last Aspect Dy Hr Mn	☽ Ingress Dy Hr Mn	☽ Phases & Eclipses Dy Hr Mn	Astro Data
☿0S 5 3:51	☿ ♎ 4 22:32	1 2:26 ♃ △	♊ 1 5:52	3 4:36 ♃ ☍	♌ 3 9:43	1 23:05 ☾ 9♊15	1 September 1961
♃⊼♅ 11 8:59	☉ ♎ 23 6:42	3 10:18 ☿ □	♋ 3 15:00	5 20:32 ♅ ☌	♍ 5 22:45	10 2:50 ● 17♍10	Julian Day # 22524
☽0S 11 20:21	♀ ♍ 23 15:43	5 22:36 ♃ ☍	♌ 6 3:01	8 6:26 ♃ △	♎ 8 11:04	17 20:23 ☽ 24♐42	SVP 5♓47'51"
♄□♇ 15 8:48	☿ ♏ 27 12:16	8 10:46 ♅ ☌	♍ 8 16:05	10 19:41 ♅ ⚹	♏ 10 21:19	24 11:33 ○ 1♈11	GC 26♐18.2 ⚴ 18♓54.0R
☉0S 23 6:42		10 23:43 ♃ △	♎ 11 4:33	13 3:58 ♅ □	♐ 13 5:21		Eris 10♈18.1R ⚵ 28♓02.3R
⚳R 23 15:02	♂ ♏ 1 20:02	13 10:55 ♅ ⚹	♏ 13 15:23	15 10:15 ♅ △	♑ 15 11:24	1 14:10 ☾ 8♋09	⚷ 4♓01.5R ⚶ 1♊39.2
♃D 23 15:27	♀ ♎ 18 2:58	15 19:54 ♅ □	♐ 15 23:54	17 14:31 ♀ △	♒ 17 15:37	9 18:52 ● 16♎14	☽ Mean ☊ 26♌26.8
☽0N 24 22:27	☿ ♎R 22 2:29	18 2:07 ♅ △	♑ 18 5:42	19 17:23 ♅ ☍	♓ 19 18:10	17 4:34 ☽ 23♑34	
♄D 27 19:32	☉ ♏ 23 15:47	20 4:17 ♃ ☌	♒ 20 8:43	21 17:15 ♃ ⚹	♈ 21 19:36	23 21:30 ○ 0♉14	1 October 1961
		22 6:56 ♀ ☍	♓ 22 9:36	23 20:36 ♅ △	♉ 23 21:07	31 8:58 ☾ 7♌42	Julian Day # 22554
☽0S 9 2:37		24 5:21 ♃ ⚹	♈ 24 9:40	26 0:01 ♅ □	♊ 26 0:24		SVP 5♓47'49"
☿R 10 22:42		26 8:43 ☿ ☍	♉ 26 10:42	28 6:47 ♅ ⚹	♋ 28 7:03		GC 26♐18.3 ⚴ 11♓24.0R
♀0S 21 0:21		28 11:54 ♅ □	♊ 28 14:31	30 16:27 ♃ ☍	♌ 30 17:30		Eris 10♈00.5R ⚵ 21♓06.3R
☽0N 22 8:42		30 21:04 ♂ △	♋ 30 22:19				⚷ 2♓42.2R ⚶ 4♊28.9R
☿D 31 18:02							☽ Mean ☊ 24♌51.5

November 1961 — LONGITUDE

Day	Sid.Time	☉	0 hr ☽	Noon ☽	True ☊	☿	♀	♂	⚳	♃	♄	♅	♆	♇
1 W	14 42 08	8♏49 36	15♌07 05	21♌01 07	24♌11.3	22♎21.8	17♎51.0	21♏10.6	22♉17.9	29♑41.1	24♑13.1	29♌59.7	10♏57.9	9♍41.7
2 Th	14 46 05	9 49 40	26 54 38	2♍48 19	24R 11.1	22 35.5	19 05.8	21 52.9	22R 04.9	29 48.2	24 16.5	0♍01.5	11 00.2	9 42.9
3 F	14 50 01	10 49 47	8♍42 50	14 38 48	24 09.3	22 59.4	20 20.6	22 35.3	21 51.6	29 55.4	24 20.0	0 03.3	11 02.4	9 44.1
4 Sa	14 53 58	11 49 55	20 36 47	26 37 18	24 05.1	23 32.7	21 35.5	23 17.8	21 38.3	0♒02.9	24 23.5	0 05.1	11 04.7	9 45.3
5 Su	14 57 54	12 50 05	2♎40 48	8♎47 42	23 58.1	24 14.6	22 50.3	24 00.3	21 24.7	0 10.4	24 27.1	0 06.8	11 06.9	9 46.4
6 M	15 01 51	13 50 18	14 58 18	21 12 50	23 48.4	25 04.3	24 05.2	24 42.8	21 11.1	0 18.1	24 30.9	0 08.4	11 09.2	9 47.5
7 Tu	15 05 47	14 50 32	27 31 27	3♏54 13	23 36.4	26 00.7	25 20.2	25 25.5	20 57.4	0 26.0	24 34.7	0 10.0	11 11.4	9 48.6
8 W	15 09 44	15 50 48	10♏21 06	16 52 00	23 23.0	27 03.1	26 35.1	26 08.1	20 43.6	0 34.0	24 38.5	0 11.6	11 13.6	9 49.7
9 Th	15 13 40	16 51 06	23 26 46	0♐05 08	23 09.6	28 10.7	27 50.1	26 50.9	20 29.7	0 42.2	24 42.5	0 13.1	11 15.9	9 50.7
10 F	15 17 37	17 51 26	6♐46 52	13 31 37	22 57.4	29 22.8	29 05.2	27 33.7	20 15.7	0 50.5	24 46.5	0 14.5	11 18.1	9 51.7
11 Sa	15 21 34	18 51 47	20 19 05	27 08 57	22 47.5	0♏38.8	0♏20.2	28 16.5	20 01.7	0 58.9	24 50.7	0 15.9	11 20.4	9 52.7
12 Su	15 25 30	19 52 10	4♑00 56	10♑54 45	22 40.5	1 58.0	1 35.3	28 59.4	19 47.7	1 07.5	24 54.9	0 17.2	11 22.6	9 53.6
13 M	15 29 27	20 52 34	17 50 11	24 47 04	22 36.5	3 20.0	2 50.3	29 42.4	19 33.7	1 16.2	24 59.2	0 18.5	11 24.8	9 54.6
14 Tu	15 33 23	21 52 59	1♒45 14	8♒44 36	22D 34.9	4 44.4	4 05.4	0♐25.4	19 19.7	1 25.0	25 03.5	0 19.7	11 27.1	9 55.4
15 W	15 37 20	22 53 26	15 45 06	22 46 40	22R 34.6	6 10.7	5 20.5	1 08.4	19 05.8	1 34.0	25 08.0	0 20.9	11 29.3	9 56.3
16 Th	15 41 16	23 53 54	29 49 14	6♓52 45	22 34.4	7 38.6	6 35.7	1 51.6	18 51.8	1 43.1	25 12.5	0 22.0	11 31.5	9 57.1
17 F	15 45 13	24 54 23	13♓57 06	21 02 08	22 32.8	9 07.8	7 50.8	2 34.7	18 38.0	1 52.4	25 17.1	0 23.1	11 33.7	9 57.9
18 Sa	15 49 09	25 54 54	28 07 36	5♈13 14	22 28.8	10 38.1	9 06.0	3 17.9	18 24.2	2 01.7	25 21.7	0 24.1	11 35.9	9 58.7
19 Su	15 53 06	26 55 25	12♈18 40	19 23 28	22 21.8	12 09.3	10 21.2	4 01.2	18 10.5	2 11.2	25 26.5	0 25.1	11 38.1	9 59.4
20 M	15 57 03	27 55 59	26 27 07	3♉29 05	22 12.0	13 41.2	11 36.4	4 44.5	17 57.0	2 20.8	25 31.3	0 26.0	11 40.2	10 00.1
21 Tu	16 00 59	28 56 33	10♉28 47	17 25 38	22 00.0	15 13.7	12 51.6	5 27.9	17 43.5	2 30.6	25 36.1	0 26.8	11 42.4	10 00.8
22 W	16 04 56	29 57 09	24 19 05	1♊08 38	21 47.1	16 46.6	14 06.8	6 11.4	17 30.2	2 40.4	25 41.1	0 27.6	11 44.6	10 01.5
23 Th	16 08 52	0♐57 46	7♊53 48	14 34 16	21 34.5	18 19.9	15 22.1	6 54.8	17 17.1	2 50.4	25 46.1	0 28.4	11 46.7	10 02.1
24 F	16 12 49	1 58 25	21 09 46	27 40 10	21 23.4	19 53.5	16 37.3	7 38.4	17 04.1	3 00.5	25 51.2	0 29.1	11 48.9	10 02.7
25 Sa	16 16 45	2 59 06	4♋05 26	10♋25 40	21 14.8	21 27.2	17 52.6	8 22.0	16 51.3	3 10.7	25 56.3	0 29.7	11 51.0	10 03.2
26 Su	16 20 42	3 59 48	16 44 52	22 51 55	21 08.9	23 01.1	19 07.9	9 05.6	16 38.8	3 21.0	26 01.6	0 30.3	11 53.1	10 03.8
27 M	16 24 39	5 00 31	28 58 39	5♌01 42	21 05.7	24 35.1	20 23.2	9 49.3	16 26.4	3 31.4	26 06.8	0 30.8	11 55.3	10 04.3
28 Tu	16 28 35	6 01 16	11♌01 38	16 59 01	21D 04.5	26 09.1	21 38.5	10 33.1	16 14.2	3 42.0	26 12.2	0 31.3	11 57.4	10 04.7
29 W	16 32 32	7 02 02	22 54 30	28 48 46	21R 04.6	27 43.2	22 53.9	11 16.9	16 02.3	3 52.6	26 17.6	0 31.7	11 59.4	10 05.2
30 Th	16 36 28	8 02 50	4♍42 29	10♍36 22	21 04.7	29 17.2	24 09.2	12 00.8	15 50.6	4 03.4	26 23.1	0 32.0	12 01.5	10 05.6

December 1961 — LONGITUDE

Day	Sid.Time	☉	0 hr ☽	Noon ☽	True ☊	☿	♀	♂	⚳	♃	♄	♅	♆	♇
1 F	16 40 25	9♐03 40	16♍31 07	22♍27 26	21♌03.8	0♐51.3	25♏24.6	12♐44.7	15♉39.2	4♒14.3	26♑28.6	0♍32.3	12♏03.6	10♍05.9
2 Sa	16 44 21	10 04 30	28 25 58	4♎27 22	21R 01.0	2 25.4	26 40.0	13 28.7	15R 28.1	4 25.2	26 34.2	0 32.5	12 05.6	10 06.3
3 Su	16 48 18	11 05 22	10♎32 13	16 41 04	20 55.6	3 59.5	27 55.4	14 12.7	15 17.2	4 36.3	26 39.8	0 32.7	12 07.7	10 06.6
4 M	16 52 14	12 06 16	22 54 21	29 12 29	20 47.7	5 33.5	29 10.8	14 56.8	15 06.7	4 47.5	26 45.5	0 32.8	12 09.7	10 06.8
5 Tu	16 56 11	13 07 11	5♏35 43	12♏04 14	20 37.5	7 07.5	0♐26.2	15 41.0	14 56.5	4 58.7	26 51.3	0R 32.9	12 11.7	10 07.1
6 W	17 00 07	14 08 07	18 38 05	25 17 14	20 26.0	8 41.6	1 41.6	16 25.2	14 46.5	5 10.1	26 57.1	0 32.9	12 13.7	10 07.3
7 Th	17 04 04	15 09 04	2♐01 29	8♐50 32	20 14.3	10 15.6	2 57.0	17 09.4	14 36.9	5 21.6	27 03.0	0 32.9	12 15.6	10 07.5
8 F	17 08 01	16 10 02	15 44 00	22 41 22	20 03.5	11 49.6	4 12.5	17 53.7	14 27.7	5 33.1	27 08.9	0 32.8	12 17.6	10 07.6
9 Sa	17 11 57	17 11 01	29 42 05	6♑45 32	19 54.8	13 23.7	5 27.9	18 38.1	14 18.8	5 44.8	27 14.9	0 32.6	12 19.5	10 07.7
10 Su	17 15 54	18 12 01	13♑51 07	20 58 12	19 48.8	14 57.8	6 43.4	19 22.5	14 10.2	5 56.5	27 20.9	0 32.4	12 21.4	10 07.8
11 M	17 19 50	19 13 02	28 06 12	5♒14 37	19 45.5	16 31.9	7 58.8	20 06.9	14 02.1	6 08.4	27 27.0	0 32.1	12 23.3	10R 07.9
12 Tu	17 23 47	20 14 03	12♒22 56	19 30 48	19D 44.6	18 06.1	9 14.3	20 51.4	13 54.2	6 20.3	27 33.1	0 31.8	12 25.2	10 07.9
13 W	17 27 43	21 15 04	26 37 51	3♓43 52	19 45.1	19 40.4	10 29.8	21 36.0	13 46.8	6 32.3	27 39.3	0 31.4	12 27.1	10 07.9
14 Th	17 31 40	22 16 07	10♓48 39	17 52 03	19R 45.8	21 14.7	11 45.2	22 20.5	13 39.7	6 44.4	27 45.5	0 31.0	12 28.9	10 07.8
15 F	17 35 37	23 17 09	24 53 57	1♈54 16	19 45.5	22 49.1	13 00.7	23 05.2	13 33.0	6 56.5	27 51.8	0 30.5	12 30.7	10 07.7
16 Sa	17 39 33	24 18 12	8♈52 56	15 49 50	19 43.4	24 23.7	14 16.2	23 49.9	13 26.8	7 08.8	27 58.1	0 29.9	12 32.5	10 07.6
17 Su	17 43 30	25 19 15	22 44 52	29 37 54	19 38.8	25 58.4	15 31.6	24 34.6	13 20.9	7 21.1	28 04.5	0 29.3	12 34.3	10 07.5
18 M	17 47 26	26 20 19	6♉28 47	13♉17 20	19 32.0	27 33.2	16 47.1	25 19.4	13 15.3	7 33.5	28 10.9	0 28.7	12 36.1	10 07.3
19 Tu	17 51 23	27 21 23	20 03 20	26 46 34	19 23.4	29 08.2	18 02.6	26 04.2	13 10.2	7 46.0	28 17.3	0 28.0	12 37.8	10 07.1
20 W	17 55 19	28 22 27	3♊26 47	10♊03 47	19 14.0	0♑43.4	19 18.0	26 49.1	13 05.5	7 58.5	28 23.8	0 27.2	12 39.5	10 06.8
21 Th	17 59 16	29 23 32	16 37 21	23 07 19	19 04.7	2 18.7	20 33.5	27 34.0	13 01.2	8 11.1	28 30.3	0 26.4	12 41.2	10 06.6
22 F	18 03 12	0♑24 38	29 33 33	5♋55 57	18 56.5	3 54.3	21 49.0	28 19.0	12 57.3	8 23.8	28 36.8	0 25.5	12 42.9	10 06.3
23 Sa	18 07 09	1 25 44	12♋14 32	18 29 18	18 50.2	5 30.1	23 04.5	29 04.0	12 53.8	8 36.6	28 43.4	0 24.6	12 44.5	10 06.0
24 Su	18 11 06	2 26 50	24 40 24	0♌48 00	18 46.1	7 06.0	24 20.0	29 49.0	12 50.8	8 49.4	28 50.1	0 23.6	12 46.1	10 05.6
25 M	18 15 02	3 27 57	6♌52 22	12 53 48	18D 44.3	8 42.2	25 35.4	0♑34.1	12 48.1	9 02.3	28 56.7	0 22.6	12 47.7	10 05.2
26 Tu	18 18 59	4 29 04	18 52 42	24 49 29	18 44.3	10 18.7	26 50.9	1 19.3	12 45.8	9 15.3	29 03.4	0 21.5	12 49.3	10 04.8
27 W	18 22 55	5 30 12	0♍44 41	6♍38 49	18 45.5	11 55.3	28 06.4	2 04.5	12 43.9	9 28.3	29 10.1	0 20.4	12 50.8	10 04.3
28 Th	18 26 52	6 31 20	12 32 28	18 26 14	18 47.2	13 32.2	29 21.9	2 49.8	12 42.4	9 41.3	29 16.9	0 19.2	12 52.4	10 03.8
29 F	18 30 48	7 32 29	24 20 47	0♎16 45	18R 48.5	15 09.3	0♑37.4	3 35.0	12 41.4	9 54.5	29 23.7	0 18.0	12 53.8	10 03.3
30 Sa	18 34 45	8 33 38	6♎14 48	12 15 35	18 48.7	16 46.6	1 52.9	4 20.4	12 40.7	10 07.7	29 30.5	0 16.7	12 55.3	10 02.8
31 Su	18 38 41	9 34 47	18 19 46	24 27 57	18 47.4	18 24.0	3 08.4	5 05.8	12D 40.4	10 20.9	29 37.3	0 15.4	12 56.7	10 02.2

Astro Data

	Dy Hr Mn
♃⊼♅	4 21:11
☽0S	5 10:42
♄⊡♇	12 2:58
☽0N	18 17:20
☽0S	2 20:22
♅ R	6 4:28
♇ R	12 11:54
☽0N	16 0:11
♃⊼♇	30 3:27
☽0S	30 6:07
⚳ D	31 15:28

Planet Ingress

	Dy Hr Mn
♅ ♍	1 16:01
♃ ♒	4 2:49
☿ ♏	10 23:53
♀ ♏	11 5:33
♂ ♐	13 21:50
☉ ♐	22 13:08
☿ ♐	30 22:54
♀ ♐	5 3:40
☿ ♑	20 1:04
☉ ♑	22 2:19
♂ ♑	24 17:50
♀ ♑	29 0:07

Last Aspect / ☽ Ingress

Last Aspect Dy Hr Mn		☽ Ingress Dy Hr Mn
1 14:46 ☿ ⚹	♍	2 6:17
4 7:32 ♄ △	♎	4 18:42
6 19:55 ☿ ☌	♏	7 4:40
9 5:50 ♂ ☌	♐	9 11:51
10 5:29 ♇ □	♑	11 16:59
13 20:56 ♂ ⚹	♒	13 20:59
15 12:12 ☉ □	♓	16 0:18
17 19:14 ♄ ⚹	♈	18 3:10
19 22:20 ♄ □	♉	20 6:03
22 9:44 ☉ ☍	♊	22 9:59
23 3:49 ♇ □	♋	24 16:20
26 18:14 ♄ ☍	♌	27 2:01
29 9:26 ☿ □	♍	29 14:25

Last Aspect / ☽ Ingress

Last Aspect Dy Hr Mn		☽ Ingress Dy Hr Mn
1 20:09 ♄ △	♎	2 3:08
4 7:19 ♄ □	♏	4 13:30
6 15:00 ♄ ⚹	♐	6 20:25
8 3:17 ♂ ☌	♑	9 0:31
10 22:48 ♄ ☌	♒	11 3:11
12 14:23 ♂ ⚹	♓	13 5:41
15 5:01 ♄ ⚹	♈	15 8:44
17 9:16 ♄ □	♉	17 12:39
19 14:44 ♄ △	♊	19 17:47
22 0:42 ☉ ☍	♋	22 0:50
24 8:06 ♄ ☍	♌	24 10:26
26 16:35 ♀ △	♍	26 22:29
29 10:12 ♄ △	♎	29 11:26
31 22:04 ♄ □	♏	31 22:42

☽ Phases & Eclipses

Dy Hr Mn	
8 9:58	● 15♏46
15 12:12	☽ 22♒54
22 9:44	○ 29♉51
30 6:18	☾ 7♍48
7 23:52	● 15♐39
14 20:05	☽ 22♓37
22 0:42	○ 29♊56
30 3:57	☾ 8♎13

Astro Data

1 November 1961
Julian Day # 22585
SVP 5♓47'46"
GC 26♐18.4 ⚵ 7♓23.8R
Eris 9♈42.0R ⚶ 17♓23.7
⚷ 1♓56.6R ⚴ 0♊51.2R
☽ Mean ☊ 23♌13.0

1 December 1961
Julian Day # 22615
SVP 5♓47'41"
GC 26♐18.4 ⚵ 8♓58.9
Eris 9♈29.0R ⚶ 21♓20.5
⚷ 2♓04.3 ⚴ 23♉21.1R
☽ Mean ☊ 21♌37.7

LONGITUDE — January 1962

Day	Sid.Time	☉	0 hr ☽	Noon ☽	True ☊	☿	♀	♂	⚳	♃	♄	♅	♆	♇
1 M	18 42 38	10♑35 57	0♏40 44	6♏58 37	18♌44.3	20♑01.6	4♑23.9	5♑51.2	12♉40.6	10♒34.3	29♑44.2	0♍14.0	12♏58.2	10♍01.6
2 Tu	18 46 35	11 37 08	13 22 04	19 51 26	18R39.7	21 39.3	5 39.4	6 36.7	12 41.1	10 47.6	29 51.1	0R12.6	12 59.5	10R01.0
3 W	18 50 31	12 38 18	26 26 59	3♐08 50	18 34.0	23 17.1	6 54.9	7 22.2	12 42.1	11 01.1	29 58.0	0 11.1	13 00.9	10 00.3
4 Th	18 54 28	13 39 29	9♐57 00	16 51 19	18 28.0	24 54.9	8 10.4	8 07.8	12 43.4	11 14.5	0♒04.9	0 09.6	13 02.2	9 59.6
5 F	18 58 24	14 40 40	23 51 30	0♑57 04	18 22.4	26 32.6	9 25.9	8 53.4	12 45.2	11 28.1	0 11.9	0 08.0	13 03.5	9 58.9
6 Sa	19 02 21	15 41 51	8♑07 28	15 21 59	18 17.9	28 10.1	10 41.4	9 39.0	12 47.3	11 41.6	0 18.9	0 06.4	13 04.8	9 58.2
7 Su	19 06 17	16 43 02	22 39 48	0♒00 03	18 15.1	29 47.4	11 56.9	10 24.7	12 49.8	11 55.2	0 25.9	0 04.8	13 06.1	9 57.4
8 M	19 10 14	17 44 12	7♒21 50	14 44 14	18D13.9	1♒24.2	13 12.4	11 10.4	12 52.7	12 08.9	0 32.9	0 03.1	13 07.3	9 56.6
9 Tu	19 14 10	18 45 23	22 06 24	29 27 31	18 14.2	3 00.5	14 27.9	11 56.2	12 56.0	12 22.6	0 39.9	0 01.3	13 08.4	9 55.8
10 W	19 18 07	19 46 32	6♓46 52	14♓03 48	18 15.5	4 36.0	15 43.4	12 42.0	12 59.7	12 36.4	0 47.0	29♌59.5	13 09.6	9 54.9
11 Th	19 22 04	20 47 41	21 17 50	28 28 31	18 17.1	6 10.5	16 58.9	13 27.9	13 03.8	12 50.2	0 54.0	29 57.7	13 10.7	9 54.0
12 F	19 26 00	21 48 50	5♈35 34	12♈38 47	18R18.2	7 43.7	18 14.3	14 13.7	13 08.2	13 04.0	1 01.1	29 55.9	13 11.8	9 53.1
13 Sa	19 29 57	22 49 57	19 38 00	26 33 12	18 18.5	9 15.4	19 29.8	14 59.6	13 13.0	13 17.9	1 08.2	29 54.0	13 12.9	9 52.2
14 Su	19 33 53	23 51 05	3♉24 22	10♉11 33	18 17.5	10 45.2	20 45.3	15 45.6	13 18.2	13 31.8	1 15.3	29 52.0	13 13.9	9 51.2
15 M	19 37 50	24 52 11	16 54 48	23 34 15	18 15.4	12 12.6	22 00.7	16 31.6	13 23.7	13 45.7	1 22.4	29 50.0	13 14.9	9 50.3
16 Tu	19 41 46	25 53 17	0♊09 58	6♊42 05	18 12.4	13 37.2	23 16.1	17 17.6	13 29.6	13 59.7	1 29.5	29 48.0	13 15.9	9 49.3
17 W	19 45 43	26 54 22	13 10 42	19 35 57	18 08.9	14 58.5	24 31.6	18 03.6	13 35.8	14 13.7	1 36.6	29 46.0	13 16.8	9 48.2
18 Th	19 49 39	27 55 26	25 57 55	2♋16 43	18 05.5	16 15.9	25 47.0	18 49.7	13 42.4	14 27.7	1 43.8	29 43.9	13 17.7	9 47.2
19 F	19 53 36	28 56 30	8♋32 27	14 45 15	18 02.6	17 28.6	27 02.4	19 35.9	13 49.4	14 41.8	1 50.9	29 41.8	13 18.6	9 46.1
20 Sa	19 57 33	29 57 33	20 55 14	27 02 32	18 00.5	18 36.0	28 17.9	20 22.0	13 56.6	14 55.8	1 58.0	29 39.6	13 19.4	9 45.0
21 Su	20 01 29	0♒58 35	3♌07 20	9♌09 47	17D59.3	19 37.2	29 33.3	21 08.2	14 04.2	15 10.0	2 05.2	29 37.5	13 20.2	9 43.9
22 M	20 05 26	1 59 36	15 10 06	21 08 32	17 59.1	20 31.4	0♒48.7	21 54.4	14 12.2	15 24.1	2 12.3	29 35.2	13 21.0	9 42.8
23 Tu	20 09 22	3 00 37	27 05 21	3♍00 51	17 59.7	21 17.9	2 04.1	22 40.7	14 20.4	15 38.3	2 19.4	29 33.0	13 21.7	9 41.6
24 W	20 13 19	4 01 38	8♍55 23	14 49 20	18 00.8	21 55.6	3 19.5	23 27.0	14 29.0	15 52.4	2 26.6	29 30.7	13 22.4	9 40.4
25 Th	20 17 15	5 02 37	20 43 06	26 37 09	18 02.1	22 23.9	4 34.8	24 13.3	14 37.9	16 06.7	2 33.7	29 28.4	13 23.1	9 39.2
26 F	20 21 12	6 03 36	2♎31 58	8♎28 03	18 03.4	22 41.9	5 50.2	24 59.7	14 47.1	16 20.9	2 40.9	29 26.1	13 23.8	9 38.0
27 Sa	20 25 08	7 04 35	14 25 58	20 26 16	18 04.3	22R49.1	7 05.6	25 46.0	14 56.6	16 35.1	2 48.0	29 23.7	13 24.4	9 36.7
28 Su	20 29 05	8 05 32	26 29 32	2♏36 20	18R04.8	22 45.1	8 21.0	26 32.5	15 06.5	16 49.4	2 55.1	29 21.4	13 24.9	9 35.5
29 M	20 33 02	9 06 29	8♏47 16	15 02 52	18 04.8	22 29.7	9 36.3	27 18.9	15 16.6	17 03.7	3 02.2	29 19.0	13 25.5	9 34.2
30 Tu	20 36 58	10 07 26	21 23 42	27 50 14	18 04.4	22 03.1	10 51.7	28 05.4	15 27.0	17 18.0	3 09.3	29 16.5	13 26.0	9 32.9
31 W	20 40 55	11 08 22	4♐22 54	11♐02 02	18 03.7	21 25.7	12 07.0	28 51.9	15 37.7	17 32.3	3 16.5	29 14.1	13 26.5	9 31.6

LONGITUDE — February 1962

Day	Sid.Time	☉	0 hr ☽	Noon ☽	True ☊	☿	♀	♂	⚳	♃	♄	♅	♆	♇
1 Th	20 44 51	12♒09 17	17♐47 51	24♐40 30	18♌03.0	20♒38.5	13♒22.4	29♑38.5	15♉48.7	17♒46.6	3♒23.6	29♌11.6	13♏26.9	9♍30.3
2 F	20 48 48	13 10 11	1♑39 55	8♑45 56	18R02.3	19R42.6	14 37.7	0♒25.0	16 00.0	18 00.9	3 30.6	29R09.1	13 27.3	9R28.9
3 Sa	20 52 44	14 11 04	15 58 11	23 16 09	18 01.9	18 39.7	15 53.0	1 11.6	16 11.6	18 15.3	3 37.7	29 06.6	13 27.7	9 27.5
4 Su	20 56 41	15 11 57	0♒39 08	8♒06 16	18D01.7	17 31.5	17 08.3	1 58.3	16 23.5	18 29.6	3 44.8	29 04.1	13 28.0	9 26.2
5 M	21 00 37	16 12 48	15 36 35	23 09 01	18 01.7	16 20.1	18 23.6	2 44.9	16 35.6	18 44.0	3 51.8	29 01.6	13 28.3	9 24.8
6 Tu	21 04 34	17 13 38	0♓42 23	8♓15 34	18R01.7	15 07.4	19 38.9	3 31.6	16 48.0	18 58.3	3 58.9	28 59.0	13 28.6	9 23.4
7 W	21 08 31	18 14 26	15 47 25	23 16 53	18 01.7	13 55.7	20 54.2	4 18.3	17 00.6	19 12.7	4 05.9	28 56.5	13 28.8	9 21.9
8 Th	21 12 27	19 15 13	0♈42 59	8♈04 55	18 01.7	12 46.6	22 09.5	5 05.0	17 13.6	19 27.1	4 12.9	28 53.9	13 29.0	9 20.5
9 F	21 16 24	20 15 59	15 21 59	22 33 41	18 01.5	11 41.7	23 24.7	5 51.7	17 26.7	19 41.4	4 19.8	28 51.3	13 29.2	9 19.1
10 Sa	21 20 20	21 16 43	29 39 39	6♉39 41	18 01.3	10 42.5	24 40.0	6 38.5	17 40.2	19 55.8	4 26.8	28 48.7	13 29.3	9 17.6
11 Su	21 24 17	22 17 25	13♉33 43	20 21 47	18D01.2	9 50.0	25 55.2	7 25.2	17 53.8	20 10.2	4 33.7	28 46.1	13 29.4	9 16.1
12 M	21 28 13	23 18 06	27 04 03	3♊40 45	18 01.2	9 04.7	27 10.4	8 12.0	18 07.7	20 24.5	4 40.6	28 43.5	13 29.5	9 14.7
13 Tu	21 32 10	24 18 45	10♊12 11	16 38 42	18 01.6	8 27.2	28 25.6	8 58.9	18 21.9	20 38.9	4 47.5	28 40.8	13R29.5	9 13.2
14 W	21 36 06	25 19 22	23 00 39	29 18 26	18 02.3	7 57.6	29 40.8	9 45.7	18 36.3	20 53.2	4 54.4	28 38.2	13 29.5	9 11.7
15 Th	21 40 03	26 19 58	5♋32 27	11♋43 04	18 03.1	7 35.9	0♓55.9	10 32.5	18 50.9	21 07.6	5 01.2	28 35.6	13 29.5	9 10.2
16 F	21 44 00	27 20 32	17 50 39	23 55 35	18 04.0	7 22.0	2 11.1	11 19.4	19 05.7	21 21.9	5 08.0	28 33.0	13 29.4	9 08.7
17 Sa	21 47 56	28 21 04	29 58 11	5♌58 47	18 04.7	7D15.5	3 26.2	12 06.3	19 20.8	21 36.2	5 14.8	28 30.3	13 29.3	9 07.2
18 Su	21 51 53	29 21 35	11♌57 41	17 55 10	18R05.0	7 16.2	4 41.3	12 53.2	19 36.1	21 50.5	5 21.5	28 27.7	13 29.1	9 05.6
19 M	21 55 49	0♓22 04	23 51 29	29 46 56	18 04.7	7 23.6	5 56.4	13 40.1	19 51.6	22 04.8	5 28.3	28 25.1	13 29.0	9 04.1
20 Tu	21 59 46	1 22 31	5♍41 44	11♍36 10	18 03.7	7 37.4	7 11.4	14 27.0	20 07.3	22 19.1	5 34.9	28 22.4	13 28.7	9 02.6
21 W	22 03 42	2 22 57	17 30 28	23 24 55	18 01.9	7 57.1	8 26.5	15 14.0	20 23.2	22 33.4	5 41.6	28 19.8	13 28.5	9 01.0
22 Th	22 07 39	3 23 22	29 19 47	5♎15 22	17 59.6	8 22.2	9 41.5	16 00.9	20 39.3	22 47.6	5 48.2	28 17.2	13 28.2	8 59.5
23 F	22 11 35	4 23 44	11♎11 58	17 09 56	17 57.0	8 52.5	10 56.6	16 47.9	20 55.6	23 01.9	5 54.8	28 14.6	13 27.9	8 57.9
24 Sa	22 15 32	5 24 06	23 09 38	29 11 26	17 54.4	9 27.5	12 11.6	17 34.9	21 12.1	23 16.1	6 01.4	28 11.9	13 27.6	8 56.4
25 Su	22 19 29	6 24 26	5♏15 46	11♏23 04	17 52.1	10 06.9	13 26.6	18 21.9	21 28.8	23 30.3	6 07.9	28 09.3	13 27.2	8 54.8
26 M	22 23 25	7 24 44	17 33 46	23 48 21	17 50.6	10 50.3	14 41.5	19 08.9	21 45.7	23 44.5	6 14.3	28 06.7	13 26.8	8 53.2
27 Tu	22 27 22	8 25 01	0♐07 18	6♐31 05	17D49.9	11 37.5	15 56.5	19 55.9	22 02.8	23 58.6	6 20.8	28 04.2	13 26.4	8 51.7
28 W	22 31 18	9 25 17	13 00 08	19 34 53	17 50.2	12 28.1	17 11.4	20 42.9	22 20.1	24 12.7	6 27.2	28 01.6	13 25.9	8 50.1

Astro Data (Dy Hr Mn)

	Dy Hr Mn
♄⚻♅	5 1:09
☽0N	12 6:38
♃□♆	13 2:40
☽0S	26 14:22
☿R	27 15:32
☽0N	8 14:35
♆R	13 20:07
☿D	17 21:36
☽0S	22 20:46

Planet Ingress (Dy Hr Mn)

		Dy Hr Mn
♄	♒	3 19:01
☿	♒	7 15:08
♅	♌R	10 5:53
☉	♒	20 12:58
♀	♒	21 20:31
♂	♒	1 23:06
♀	♓	14 18:09
☉	♓	19 3:15

Last Aspect / ☽ Ingress (January)

Last Aspect Dy Hr Mn		☽ Ingress Dy Hr Mn
3 6:16	♄ ⚹	♐ 3 6:23
4 2:06	♃ ⚹	♑ 5 10:24
7 11:37	☿ ☌	♒ 7 12:00
8 9:22	♆ □	♓ 9 12:53
10 22:11	☉ ⚹	♈ 11 14:34
13 17:50	♅ △	♉ 13 18:01
15 23:22	♅ □	♊ 15 23:42
18 7:10	♅ ⚹	♋ 18 7:39
20 14:45	♀ ☍	♌ 20 17:50
23 5:00	♅ ☌	♍ 23 5:53
25 6:47	♂ △	♎ 25 18:52
28 5:39	♅ ⚹	♏ 28 6:54
30 14:39	♅ □	♐ 30 15:59

Last Aspect / ☽ Ingress (February)

Last Aspect Dy Hr Mn		☽ Ingress Dy Hr Mn
1 19:45	♅ △	♑ 1 21:10
2 19:50	♆ ⚹	♒ 3 22:57
5 21:18	♅ ☍	♓ 5 22:53
6 20:19	♆ △	♈ 7 22:50
9 22:36	♅ △	♉ 10 0:35
12 3:01	♅ □	♊ 12 5:18
14 12:48	♀ △	♋ 14 13:20
15 15:28	♆ △	♌ 17 0:04
19 9:15	♅ ☌	♍ 19 12:27
20 15:49	♅ ⚹	♎ 22 1:22
24 10:02	♅ ⚹	♏ 24 13:36
26 20:10	♅ □	♐ 26 23:46

☽ Phases & Eclipses (Dy Hr Mn)

Dy Hr Mn	
6 12:35	● 15♑43
13 5:01	☽ 22♈32
20 18:16	○ 0♌13
28 23:36	☾ 8♏35
5 0:10	● 15♒43
5 0:12:04	● T 04'08"
11 15:43	☽ 22♉27
19 13:18	○ 0♍25
19 13:03	● A 0.612
27 15:50	☾ 8♐35

Astro Data

1 January 1962
Julian Day # 22646
SVP 5♓47'36"
GC 26♐18.5 ⚴ 15♓05.1
Eris 9♈25.1 ⚵ 1♈38.1
⚷ 3♓06.0 ⚶ 18♉54.8R
☽ Mean ☊ 19♌59.2

1 February 1962
Julian Day # 22677
SVP 5♓47'31"
GC 26♐18.6 ⚴ 24♓10.5
Eris 9♈32.0 ⚵ 15♈49.8
⚷ 4♓48.1 ⚶ 21♉12.2
☽ Mean ☊ 18♌20.7

March 1962

LONGITUDE

Day	Sid.Time	☉	0 hr ☽	Noon ☽	True ☊	☿	♀	♂	⚳	♃	♄	♅	♆	♇
1 Th	22 35 15	10♓25 31	26♐15 42	3♑02 54	17♌51.3	13♒22.0	18♓26.4	21♒30.0	22♉37.5	24♒26.9	6♒33.5	27♌59.0	13♏25.4	8♍48.6
2 F	22 39 11	11 25 44	9♑56 40	16 57 07	17 52.8	14 18.9	19 41.3	22 17.1	22 55.2	24 40.9	6 39.9	27R 56.5	13R 24.9	8R 47.0
3 Sa	22 43 08	12 25 55	24 04 11	1♒17 41	17 54.2	15 18.5	20 56.2	23 04.1	23 13.0	24 55.0	6 46.1	27 53.9	13 24.3	8 45.5
4 Su	22 47 04	13 26 05	8♒37 13	16 02 13	17R 54.8	16 20.8	22 11.0	23 51.2	23 31.0	25 09.0	6 52.4	27 51.4	13 23.7	8 43.9
5 M	22 51 01	14 26 13	23 31 57	1♓05 27	17 54.3	17 25.5	23 25.9	24 38.3	23 49.1	25 23.0	6 58.5	27 48.9	13 23.1	8 42.3
6 Tu	22 54 58	15 26 19	8♓41 38	16 19 18	17 52.5	18 32.5	24 40.7	25 25.4	24 07.4	25 37.0	7 04.7	27 46.4	13 22.4	8 40.8
7 W	22 58 54	16 26 23	23 57 09	1♈33 52	17 49.2	19 41.7	25 55.5	26 12.4	24 25.9	25 50.9	7 10.8	27 44.0	13 21.7	8 39.2
8 Th	23 02 51	17 26 25	9♈08 10	16 38 51	17 45.1	20 52.9	27 10.3	26 59.5	24 44.6	26 04.8	7 16.8	27 41.5	13 21.0	8 37.7
9 F	23 06 47	18 26 25	24 04 51	1♉25 17	17 40.6	22 06.0	28 25.1	27 46.6	25 03.4	26 18.7	7 22.8	27 39.1	13 20.3	8 36.2
10 Sa	23 10 44	19 26 23	8♉39 25	15 46 47	17 36.5	23 21.0	29 39.8	28 33.7	25 22.3	26 32.5	7 28.7	27 36.7	13 19.5	8 34.6
11 Su	23 14 40	20 26 19	22 47 03	29 40 08	17 33.4	24 37.8	0♈54.6	29 20.8	25 41.4	26 46.3	7 34.6	27 34.3	13 18.7	8 33.1
12 M	23 18 37	21 26 12	6♊26 05	13♊05 08	17D 31.6	25 56.2	2 09.3	0♓07.9	26 00.7	27 00.0	7 40.4	27 32.0	13 17.8	8 31.6
13 Tu	23 22 33	22 26 04	19 37 35	26 03 52	17 31.4	27 16.3	3 23.9	0 55.0	26 20.1	27 13.8	7 46.2	27 29.7	13 17.0	8 30.1
14 W	23 26 30	23 25 53	2♋24 29	8♋39 59	17 32.3	28 37.9	4 38.6	1 42.1	26 39.7	27 27.4	7 51.9	27 27.4	13 16.1	8 28.6
15 Th	23 30 26	24 25 40	14 50 55	20 57 53	17 34.0	0♓01.0	5 53.2	2 29.2	26 59.4	27 41.0	7 57.6	27 25.1	13 15.2	8 27.1
16 F	23 34 23	25 25 25	27 01 26	3♌02 09	17 35.6	1 25.6	7 07.8	3 16.2	27 19.2	27 54.6	8 03.2	27 22.9	13 14.2	8 25.6
17 Sa	23 38 20	26 25 07	9♌00 34	14 57 11	17R 36.5	2 51.7	8 22.3	4 03.3	27 39.2	28 08.1	8 08.8	27 20.7	13 13.3	8 24.1
18 Su	23 42 16	27 24 47	20 52 29	26 46 53	17 36.1	4 19.2	9 36.9	4 50.4	27 59.3	28 21.6	8 14.2	27 18.5	13 12.3	8 22.7
19 M	23 46 13	28 24 26	2♍40 49	8♍34 38	17 33.8	5 48.0	10 51.4	5 37.4	28 19.5	28 35.0	8 19.7	27 16.3	13 11.3	8 21.2
20 Tu	23 50 09	29 24 02	14 28 38	20 23 08	17 29.4	7 18.3	12 05.9	6 24.5	28 39.8	28 48.4	8 25.0	27 14.2	13 10.2	8 19.8
21 W	23 54 06	0♈23 36	26 18 23	2♎14 37	17 23.2	8 49.9	13 20.3	7 11.5	29 00.3	29 01.7	8 30.3	27 12.1	13 09.1	8 18.4
22 Th	23 58 02	1 23 07	8♎12 03	14 10 52	17 15.4	10 22.8	14 34.7	7 58.6	29 20.9	29 15.0	8 35.6	27 10.1	13 08.0	8 16.9
23 F	0 01 59	2 22 37	20 11 16	26 13 25	17 06.7	11 57.1	15 49.1	8 45.6	29 41.7	29 28.2	8 40.8	27 08.1	13 06.9	8 15.5
24 Sa	0 05 55	3 22 05	2♏17 32	8♏23 48	16 58.0	13 32.7	17 03.5	9 32.7	0♊02.5	29 41.4	8 45.9	27 06.1	13 05.8	8 14.1
25 Su	0 09 52	4 21 32	14 32 26	20 43 41	16 50.2	15 09.7	18 17.8	10 19.7	0 23.5	29 54.5	8 50.9	27 04.1	13 04.6	8 12.8
26 M	0 13 49	5 20 56	26 57 47	3♐15 03	16 43.9	16 48.0	19 32.2	11 06.7	0 44.5	0♓07.5	8 55.9	27 02.2	13 03.4	8 11.4
27 Tu	0 17 45	6 20 19	9♐35 46	16 00 15	16 39.7	18 27.6	20 46.5	11 53.7	1 05.7	0 20.5	9 00.8	27 00.4	13 02.2	8 10.1
28 W	0 21 42	7 19 40	22 28 53	29 01 59	16D 37.6	20 08.6	22 00.7	12 40.7	1 27.0	0 33.5	9 05.7	26 58.5	13 01.0	8 08.7
29 Th	0 25 38	8 18 59	5♑39 54	12♑22 58	16 37.3	21 50.9	23 15.0	13 27.7	1 48.5	0 46.3	9 10.5	26 56.8	12 59.7	8 07.4
30 F	0 29 35	9 18 16	19 11 27	26 05 36	16 38.1	23 34.6	24 29.2	14 14.7	2 10.0	0 59.1	9 15.2	26 55.0	12 58.4	8 06.1
31 Sa	0 33 31	10 17 32	3♒05 33	10♒11 20	16R 38.9	25 19.7	25 43.4	15 01.7	2 31.6	1 11.9	9 19.8	26 53.3	12 57.2	8 04.8

April 1962

LONGITUDE

Day	Sid.Time	☉	0 hr ☽	Noon ☽	True ☊	☿	♀	♂	⚳	♃	♄	♅	♆	♇
1 Su	0 37 28	11♈16 46	17♒22 51	24♒39 50	16♌38.8	27♓06.2	26♈57.6	15♓48.6	2♊53.4	1♓24.6	9♒24.4	26♌51.6	12♏55.8	8♍03.6
2 M	0 41 24	12 15 58	2♓01 53	9♓28 23	16R 36.8	28 54.0	28 11.7	16 35.6	3 15.2	1 37.2	9 28.9	26R 50.0	12R 54.5	8R 02.3
3 Tu	0 45 21	13 15 08	16 58 30	24 31 18	16 32.4	0♈43.3	29 25.8	17 22.5	3 37.2	1 49.7	9 33.3	26 48.4	12 53.1	8 01.1
4 W	0 49 18	14 14 16	2♈05 39	9♈40 18	16 25.6	2 34.0	0♉39.9	18 09.4	3 59.2	2 02.2	9 37.6	26 46.9	12 51.8	7 59.9
5 Th	0 53 14	15 13 22	17 14 00	24 45 26	16 17.0	4 26.1	1 53.9	18 56.3	4 21.3	2 14.6	9 41.9	26 45.4	12 50.4	7 58.7
6 F	0 57 11	16 12 26	2♉13 24	9♉36 44	16 07.6	6 19.6	3 08.0	19 43.2	4 43.6	2 26.9	9 46.1	26 44.0	12 49.0	7 57.6
7 Sa	1 01 07	17 11 28	16 54 31	24 05 58	15 58.6	8 14.5	4 22.0	20 30.0	5 05.9	2 39.1	9 50.2	26 42.6	12 47.6	7 56.4
8 Su	1 05 04	18 10 28	1♊10 31	8♊07 49	15 50.9	10 10.9	5 35.9	21 16.8	5 28.4	2 51.3	9 54.2	26 41.2	12 46.1	7 55.3
9 M	1 09 00	19 09 25	14 57 45	21 40 19	15 45.4	12 08.7	6 49.9	22 03.7	5 50.9	3 03.4	9 58.2	26 39.9	12 44.7	7 54.2
10 Tu	1 12 57	20 08 21	28 15 46	4♋44 26	15 42.2	14 07.8	8 03.8	22 50.4	6 13.5	3 15.4	10 02.0	26 38.6	12 43.2	7 53.1
11 W	1 16 53	21 07 13	11♋06 48	17 23 23	15D 41.0	16 08.2	9 17.6	23 37.2	6 36.2	3 27.3	10 05.8	26 37.4	12 41.7	7 52.0
12 Th	1 20 50	22 06 04	23 34 50	29 41 46	15 41.1	18 09.9	10 31.4	24 23.9	6 58.9	3 39.1	10 09.5	26 36.3	12 40.2	7 51.0
13 F	1 24 47	23 04 53	5♌44 51	11♌44 47	15R 41.6	20 12.9	11 45.2	25 10.6	7 21.8	3 50.9	10 13.1	26 35.2	12 38.7	7 50.0
14 Sa	1 28 43	24 03 39	17 42 13	23 37 47	15 41.4	22 16.9	12 59.0	25 57.3	7 44.7	4 02.6	10 16.7	26 34.1	12 37.2	7 49.0
15 Su	1 32 40	25 02 22	29 32 07	5♍25 47	15 39.4	24 21.9	14 12.7	26 44.0	8 07.8	4 14.2	10 20.1	26 33.1	12 35.7	7 48.0
16 M	1 36 36	26 01 04	11♍19 18	17 13 12	15 35.2	26 27.8	15 26.4	27 30.6	8 30.9	4 25.6	10 23.5	26 32.1	12 34.1	7 47.1
17 Tu	1 40 33	26 59 44	23 07 52	29 03 44	15 28.2	28 34.4	16 40.1	28 17.2	8 54.0	4 37.1	10 26.8	26 31.2	12 32.6	7 46.2
18 W	1 44 29	27 58 21	5♎01 06	11♎00 16	15 18.5	0♉41.6	17 53.7	29 03.8	9 17.3	4 48.4	10 30.0	26 30.3	12 31.0	7 45.3
19 Th	1 48 26	28 56 56	17 01 28	23 04 52	15 06.8	2 49.0	19 07.3	29 50.4	9 40.6	4 59.6	10 33.1	26 29.5	12 29.4	7 44.4
20 F	1 52 22	29 55 30	29 10 37	5♏18 49	14 53.9	4 56.4	20 20.8	0♈36.9	10 04.0	5 10.7	10 36.1	26 28.8	12 27.9	7 43.6
21 Sa	1 56 19	0♉54 02	11♏29 33	17 42 53	14 40.8	7 03.7	21 34.3	1 23.4	10 27.5	5 21.7	10 39.1	26 28.1	12 26.3	7 42.8
22 Su	2 00 15	1 52 31	23 58 51	0♐17 30	14 28.7	9 10.4	22 47.8	2 09.9	10 51.0	5 32.7	10 41.9	26 27.4	12 24.7	7 42.0
23 M	2 04 12	2 51 00	6♐38 53	13 03 04	14 18.7	11 16.3	24 01.3	2 56.3	11 14.6	5 43.5	10 44.7	26 26.8	12 23.1	7 41.2
24 Tu	2 08 09	3 49 26	19 30 09	26 00 14	14 11.4	13 21.1	25 14.7	3 42.7	11 38.3	5 54.2	10 47.4	26 26.2	12 21.5	7 40.5
25 W	2 12 05	4 47 51	2♑33 28	9♑10 00	14 06.9	15 24.4	26 28.1	4 29.1	12 02.0	6 04.9	10 50.0	26 25.7	12 19.9	7 39.8
26 Th	2 16 02	5 46 14	15 50 02	22 33 46	14 04.9	17 26.0	27 41.4	5 15.5	12 25.8	6 15.4	10 52.5	26 25.3	12 18.2	7 39.1
27 F	2 19 58	6 44 36	29 21 23	6♒13 04	14 04.4	19 25.5	28 54.7	6 01.8	12 49.7	6 25.8	10 54.9	26 24.9	12 16.6	7 38.4
28 Sa	2 23 55	7 42 56	13♒08 59	20 09 13	14 04.4	21 22.7	0♊08.0	6 48.1	13 13.6	6 36.2	10 57.2	26 24.6	12 15.0	7 37.8
29 Su	2 27 51	8 41 14	27 13 47	4♓22 35	14 03.5	23 17.2	1 21.2	7 34.3	13 37.6	6 46.4	10 59.4	26 24.3	12 13.4	7 37.2
30 M	2 31 48	9 39 32	11♓35 27	18 52 00	14 00.5	25 08.9	2 34.5	8 20.6	14 01.7	6 56.5	11 01.5	26 24.0	12 11.7	7 36.6

Astro Data	Dy Hr Mn
☽0N	8 0:38
♀0N	13 2:09
♃☍♅	14 11:57
♄⚻♇	19 17:27
☉0N	21 2:29
☽0S	22 2:28
☽0N	4 11:38
☿0N	5 13:00
☽0S	18 8:56
♂0N	22 23:20

Planet Ingress		Dy Hr Mn
♀	♈	10 18:28
♂	♓	12 7:58
☿	♓	15 11:43
☉	♈	21 2:30
⚳	♊	24 9:08
♃	♓	25 22:07
☿	♈	3 2:32
♀	♉	3 23:05
☿	♉	18 4:10
♂	♈	19 16:58
☉	♉	20 13:51
♀	♊	28 9:23

Last Aspect Dy Hr Mn			☽ Ingress	Dy Hr Mn
1 3:05	♅	△	♑	1 6:38
2 17:05	♀	⚹	♒	3 9:52
5 6:49	♅	☍	♓	5 10:16
7 2:19	♀	☌	♈	7 9:32
9 5:50	♅	△	♉	9 9:40
11 11:24	♂	□	♊	11 12:35
13 14:41	♅	⚹	♋	13 19:25
15 19:28	☉	△	♌	16 5:56
18 15:16	♃	☍	♍	18 18:33
19 21:22	♆	⚹	♎	21 7:28
23 18:33	♃	△	♏	23 19:29
26 0:10	♅	□	♐	26 5:49
28 8:15	♅	△	♑	28 13:46
30 8:57	♀	□	♒	30 18:43

Last Aspect Dy Hr Mn			☽ Ingress	Dy Hr Mn
1 16:06	♀	⚹	♓	1 20:42
3 0:01	♂	☌	♈	3 20:41
5 15:12	♅	△	♉	5 20:25
7 16:24	♅	□	♊	7 22:00
9 21:03	♅	⚹	♋	10 3:12
12 0:54	♂	△	♌	12 12:36
14 17:57	♅	☌	♍	15 0:57
17 10:19	♂	☍	♎	17 13:54
20 0:33	☉	☍	♏	20 1:37
22 4:43	♅	□	♐	22 11:27
24 12:48	♅	△	♑	24 19:20
26 21:58	♀	△	♒	27 1:08
28 22:37	♅	☍	♓	29 4:40

☽ Phases & Eclipses Dy Hr Mn		
6 10:31	●	15♓23
13 4:39	☽	22♊08
21 7:55	○	0♎13
29 4:11	☾	8♑00
4 19:45	●	14♈33
11 19:50	☽	21♋26
20 0:33	○	29♎28
27 12:59	☾	6♒47

Astro Data

1 March 1962
Julian Day # 22705
SVP 5♓47'28"
GC 26♐18.6 ⚴ 4♈02.3
Eris 9♈46.2 ⚵ 0♉36.1
⚷ 6♓36.6 ⚶ 27♉43.1
☽ Mean ☊ 16♌51.7

1 April 1962
Julian Day # 22736
SVP 5♓47'25"
GC 26♐18.7 ⚴ 16♈10.1
Eris 10♈06.8 ⚵ 18♉06.6
⚷ 8♓32.8 ⚶ 7♊53.4
☽ Mean ☊ 15♌13.2

LONGITUDE — May 1962

Day	Sid.Time	☉	0 hr ☽	Noon ☽	True ☊	☿	♀	♂	⚳	♃	♄	♅	♆	♇
1 Tu	2 35 44	10♉37 47	26♓11 46	3♈34 05	13♌54.9	26♉57.5	3♊47.6	9♈06.8	14♊25.8	7♓06.5	11♒03.5	26♌23.8	12♏10.1	7♍36.1
2 W	2 39 41	11 36 01	10♈58 10	18 23 06	13R46.5	28 42.9	5 00.8	9 52.9	14 50.0	7 16.3	11 05.5	26R23.7	12R08.5	7R35.5
3 Th	2 43 38	12 34 13	25 47 52	3♉11 25	13 36.0	0♊24.8	6 13.9	10 39.0	15 14.2	7 26.1	11 07.3	26D23.6	12 06.8	7 35.1
4 F	2 47 34	13 32 24	10♉32 39	17 50 32	13 24.4	2 03.2	7 27.0	11 25.1	15 38.6	7 35.8	11 09.0	26 23.6	12 05.2	7 34.6
5 Sa	2 51 31	14 30 33	25 04 08	2♊12 37	13 13.0	3 37.9	8 40.0	12 11.1	16 02.9	7 45.3	11 10.7	26 23.7	12 03.6	7 34.2
6 Su	2 55 27	15 28 40	9♊15 18	16 11 43	13 03.1	5 08.8	9 53.0	12 57.2	16 27.3	7 54.7	11 12.2	26 23.7	12 01.9	7 33.8
7 M	2 59 24	16 26 46	23 01 32	29 44 37	12 55.4	6 35.8	11 06.0	13 43.1	16 51.8	8 04.0	11 13.7	26 23.9	12 00.3	7 33.4
8 Tu	3 03 20	17 24 50	6♋21 02	12♋50 56	12 50.4	7 58.8	12 18.9	14 29.0	17 16.3	8 13.1	11 15.1	26 24.1	11 58.7	7 33.0
9 W	3 07 17	18 22 51	19 14 40	25 32 40	12 47.8	9 17.8	13 31.8	15 14.9	17 40.9	8 22.2	11 16.3	26 24.3	11 57.1	7 32.7
10 Th	3 11 13	19 20 51	1♌45 27	7♌53 36	12D47.0	10 32.7	14 44.7	16 00.7	18 05.5	8 31.1	11 17.5	26 24.6	11 55.4	7 32.5
11 F	3 15 10	20 18 49	13 57 46	19 58 37	12R46.9	11 43.4	15 57.5	16 46.5	18 30.2	8 39.8	11 18.6	26 25.0	11 53.8	7 32.2
12 Sa	3 19 07	21 16 45	25 56 49	1♍53 04	12 46.6	12 49.9	17 10.3	17 32.3	18 54.9	8 48.5	11 19.5	26 25.4	11 52.2	7 32.0
13 Su	3 23 03	22 14 40	7♍48 03	13 42 25	12 44.9	13 52.1	18 23.0	18 18.0	19 19.7	8 57.0	11 20.4	26 25.9	11 50.6	7 31.8
14 M	3 27 00	23 12 32	19 36 48	25 31 46	12 41.1	14 50.0	19 35.7	19 03.6	19 44.5	9 05.4	11 21.2	26 26.4	11 49.0	7 31.6
15 Tu	3 30 56	24 10 23	1♎27 54	7♎25 40	12 34.6	15 43.4	20 48.3	19 49.2	20 09.3	9 13.6	11 21.8	26 27.0	11 47.4	7 31.5
16 W	3 34 53	25 08 12	13 25 32	19 27 51	12 25.7	16 32.3	22 00.9	20 34.8	20 34.2	9 21.7	11 22.4	26 27.6	11 45.8	7 31.4
17 Th	3 38 49	26 06 00	25 32 58	1♏41 06	12 14.6	17 16.7	23 13.4	21 20.3	20 59.1	9 29.7	11 22.9	26 28.3	11 44.2	7 31.3
18 F	3 42 46	27 03 46	7♏52 28	14 07 09	12 02.3	17 56.4	24 25.9	22 05.8	21 24.1	9 37.6	11 23.3	26 29.0	11 42.7	7D31.3
19 Sa	3 46 42	28 01 31	20 25 15	26 46 43	11 49.8	18 31.5	25 38.4	22 51.2	21 49.1	9 45.3	11 23.6	26 29.8	11 41.1	7 31.2
20 Su	3 50 39	28 59 14	3♐11 33	9♐39 39	11 38.2	19 01.9	26 50.8	23 36.6	22 14.2	9 52.8	11 23.8	26 30.6	11 39.6	7 31.3
21 M	3 54 36	29 56 56	16 10 54	22 45 11	11 28.7	19 27.5	28 03.2	24 21.9	22 39.3	10 00.2	11R23.9	26 31.5	11 38.0	7 31.3
22 Tu	3 58 32	0♊54 37	29 22 21	6♑02 17	11 21.7	19 48.3	29 15.5	25 07.2	23 04.4	10 07.5	11 23.9	26 32.5	11 36.5	7 31.4
23 W	4 02 29	1 52 17	12♑44 54	19 30 04	11 17.5	20 04.3	0♋27.8	25 52.4	23 29.6	10 14.6	11 23.8	26 33.5	11 35.0	7 31.5
24 Th	4 06 25	2 49 55	26 17 45	3♒07 54	11D15.7	20 15.6	1 40.0	26 37.6	23 54.8	10 21.6	11 23.6	26 34.5	11 33.5	7 31.6
25 F	4 10 22	3 47 33	10♒00 31	16 55 34	11 15.5	20R22.0	2 52.2	27 22.8	24 20.1	10 28.4	11 23.3	26 35.6	11 32.0	7 31.8
26 Sa	4 14 18	4 45 10	23 53 04	0♓52 59	11R15.9	20 23.8	4 04.4	28 07.9	24 45.4	10 35.1	11 22.9	26 36.8	11 30.5	7 32.0
27 Su	4 18 15	5 42 45	7♓55 18	14 59 55	11 15.7	20 21.0	5 16.5	28 52.9	25 10.7	10 41.6	11 22.4	26 37.9	11 29.1	7 32.2
28 M	4 22 11	6 40 20	22 06 41	29 15 23	11 13.7	20 13.7	6 28.6	29 37.9	25 36.1	10 48.0	11 21.8	26 39.2	11 27.6	7 32.5
29 Tu	4 26 08	7 37 54	6♈25 42	13♈37 16	11 09.5	20 02.2	7 40.6	0♉22.9	26 01.5	10 54.2	11 21.1	26 40.5	11 26.2	7 32.8
30 W	4 30 05	8 35 27	20 49 33	28 02 00	11 02.9	19 46.6	8 52.6	1 07.8	26 26.9	11 00.2	11 20.3	26 41.8	11 24.8	7 33.1
31 Th	4 34 01	9 33 00	5♉13 57	12♉24 42	10 54.4	19 27.3	10 04.5	1 52.6	26 52.4	11 06.1	11 19.5	26 43.2	11 23.4	7 33.5

LONGITUDE — June 1962

Day	Sid.Time	☉	0 hr ☽	Noon ☽	True ☊	☿	♀	♂	⚳	♃	♄	♅	♆	♇
1 F	4 37 58	10♊30 31	19♉33 32	26♉39 42	10♌44.9	19♊04.6	11♋16.4	2♉37.4	27♊17.9	11♓11.8	11♒18.5	26♌44.7	11♏22.0	7♍33.8
2 Sa	4 41 54	11 28 02	3♊42 31	10♊41 21	10R35.5	18R38.8	12 28.2	3 22.1	27 43.4	11 17.4	11R17.4	26 46.2	11R20.6	7 34.3
3 Su	4 45 51	12 25 31	17 35 38	24 24 58	10 27.3	18 10.5	13 40.0	4 06.8	28 09.0	11 22.8	11 16.3	26 47.8	11 19.3	7 34.7
4 M	4 49 47	13 23 00	1♋08 59	7♋47 32	10 20.9	17 40.1	14 51.7	4 51.4	28 34.6	11 28.0	11 15.0	26 49.4	11 17.9	7 35.2
5 Tu	4 53 44	14 20 27	14 20 31	20 48 00	10 16.8	17 08.1	16 03.4	5 36.0	29 00.2	11 33.0	11 13.7	26 51.0	11 16.6	7 35.7
6 W	4 57 40	15 17 54	27 10 11	3♌27 20	10D15.0	16 35.0	17 15.1	6 20.5	29 25.9	11 37.9	11 12.2	26 52.7	11 15.3	7 36.2
7 Th	5 01 37	16 15 19	9♌39 49	15 48 06	10 14.9	16 01.5	18 26.6	7 05.0	29 51.6	11 42.6	11 10.7	26 54.4	11 14.1	7 36.8
8 F	5 05 34	17 12 43	21 52 41	27 54 08	10 15.8	15 28.1	19 38.2	7 49.3	0♋17.3	11 47.2	11 09.1	26 56.2	11 12.8	7 37.4
9 Sa	5 09 30	18 10 06	3♍53 05	9♍50 08	10R16.8	14 55.4	20 49.6	8 33.7	0 43.0	11 51.5	11 07.3	26 58.1	11 11.6	7 38.0
10 Su	5 13 27	19 07 28	15 45 57	21 41 11	10 17.1	14 23.9	22 01.0	9 17.9	1 08.8	11 55.7	11 05.5	26 59.9	11 10.4	7 38.6
11 M	5 17 23	20 04 49	27 36 28	3♎32 27	10 16.0	13 54.1	23 12.4	10 02.1	1 34.5	11 59.7	11 03.6	27 01.9	11 09.2	7 39.3
12 Tu	5 21 20	21 02 09	9♎29 43	15 28 53	10 13.0	13 26.7	24 23.7	10 46.3	2 00.3	12 03.6	11 01.7	27 03.8	11 08.0	7 40.0
13 W	5 25 16	21 59 28	21 30 28	27 34 57	10 08.1	13 01.9	25 34.9	11 30.4	2 26.2	12 07.2	10 59.6	27 05.9	11 06.8	7 40.8
14 Th	5 29 13	22 56 46	3♏42 46	9♏54 18	10 01.6	12 40.4	26 46.1	12 14.4	2 52.0	12 10.7	10 57.4	27 07.9	11 05.7	7 41.5
15 F	5 33 09	23 54 03	16 09 50	22 29 35	9 54.0	12 22.3	27 57.2	12 58.3	3 17.9	12 14.0	10 55.2	27 10.0	11 04.6	7 42.3
16 Sa	5 37 06	24 51 20	28 53 42	5♐22 13	9 46.2	12 08.0	29 08.2	13 42.2	3 43.8	12 17.1	10 52.9	27 12.2	11 03.5	7 43.1
17 Su	5 41 03	25 48 36	11♐55 07	18 32 19	9 39.0	11 57.9	0♌19.2	14 26.1	4 09.7	12 20.0	10 50.5	27 14.4	11 02.5	7 44.0
18 M	5 44 59	26 45 51	25 13 36	1♑58 44	9 33.1	11D52.0	1 30.1	15 09.9	4 35.6	12 22.8	10 48.0	27 16.6	11 01.5	7 44.9
19 Tu	5 48 56	27 43 06	8♑47 27	15 39 25	9 29.1	11 50.5	2 40.9	15 53.6	5 01.6	12 25.4	10 45.4	27 18.9	11 00.5	7 45.8
20 W	5 52 52	28 40 21	22 34 15	29 31 37	9D27.0	11 53.6	3 51.7	16 37.3	5 27.5	12 27.7	10 42.8	27 21.2	10 59.5	7 46.7
21 Th	5 56 49	29 37 35	6♒31 09	13♒32 30	9 26.6	12 01.3	5 02.4	17 20.9	5 53.5	12 29.9	10 40.1	27 23.6	10 58.5	7 47.7
22 F	6 00 45	0♋34 49	20 35 19	27 39 19	9 27.5	12 13.8	6 13.0	18 04.4	6 19.5	12 31.9	10 37.3	27 26.0	10 57.6	7 48.7
23 Sa	6 04 42	1 32 02	4♓44 12	11♓49 42	9 28.9	12 30.9	7 23.6	18 47.9	6 45.5	12 33.7	10 34.4	27 28.4	10 56.7	7 49.7
24 Su	6 08 38	2 29 16	18 55 35	26 01 37	9R29.9	12 52.8	8 34.1	19 31.3	7 11.6	12 35.4	10 31.4	27 30.9	10 55.8	7 50.7
25 M	6 12 35	3 26 30	3♈07 34	10♈13 11	9 29.8	13 19.3	9 44.5	20 14.6	7 37.6	12 36.8	10 28.4	27 33.4	10 54.9	7 51.8
26 Tu	6 16 32	4 23 43	17 18 14	24 22 27	9 28.4	13 50.4	10 54.9	20 57.9	8 03.7	12 38.0	10 25.3	27 36.0	10 54.1	7 52.9
27 W	6 20 28	5 20 57	1♉25 33	8♉27 12	9 25.4	14 26.2	12 05.2	21 41.1	8 29.8	12 39.1	10 22.2	27 38.6	10 53.3	7 54.0
28 Th	6 24 25	6 18 11	15 27 05	22 24 52	9 21.3	15 06.5	13 15.4	22 24.3	8 55.9	12 39.9	10 18.9	27 41.2	10 52.6	7 55.1
29 F	6 28 21	7 15 24	29 20 11	6♊12 42	9 16.5	15 51.3	14 25.5	23 07.4	9 22.0	12 40.6	10 15.6	27 43.9	10 51.8	7 56.3
30 Sa	6 32 18	8 12 38	13♊02 04	19 47 58	9 11.7	16 40.6	15 35.6	23 50.4	9 48.2	12 41.1	10 12.2	27 46.6	10 51.1	7 57.5

Astro Data

	Dy Hr Mn
☽ 0N	1 21:51
♅ D	4 8:56
♃☍♇	4 9:13
☽ 0S	15 16:49
♇ D	19 9:38
♄ R	21 23:22
☿ R	26 9:09
☽ 0N	29 6:07
♃⚺♄	2 12:10
♃△♆	2 23:30
☽ 0S	12 1:43
☿ D	19 7:45
☽ 0N	25 12:36

Planet Ingress

	Dy Hr Mn
☿ ♊	3 6:05
☉ ♊	21 13:17
♀ ♋	23 2:46
♂ ♉	28 23:47
⚳ ♋	7 19:52
♀ ♌	17 5:31
☉ ♋	21 21:24

Last Aspect / ☽ Ingress

Last Aspect Dy Hr Mn		☽ Ingress	Dy Hr Mn
30 23:45	☿ ✶	♈	1 6:12
3 0:58	♅ △	♉	3 6:49
5 2:13	♅ □	♊	5 8:16
7 6:00	♅ ✶	♋	7 12:28
8 21:15	☉ ✶	♌	9 20:35
12 0:57	♅ ☌	♍	12 8:11
14 6:53	☉ △	♎	14 21:03
17 1:48	♅ ✶	♏	17 8:43
19 14:32	☉ ☍	♐	19 18:02
21 22:35	♀ ☍	♑	22 1:08
23 23:55	♂ □	♒	24 6:31
26 7:01	♂ ✶	♓	26 10:29
27 20:58	☿ □	♈	28 13:15
30 9:46	♅ △	♉	30 15:17

Last Aspect / ☽ Ingress

Last Aspect Dy Hr Mn		☽ Ingress	Dy Hr Mn
1 12:09	♅ □	♊	1 17:40
3 16:14	♅ ✶	♋	3 21:56
5 2:17	♀ ☌	♌	6 5:23
8 10:04	♅ ☌	♍	8 16:12
10 12:45	♀ ✶	♎	11 4:51
13 11:03	♅ ✶	♏	13 16:45
15 23:17	♀ △	♐	16 2:03
18 3:38	♅ △	♑	18 8:30
19 12:26	♂ △	♒	20 12:49
22 11:37	♅ ☍	♓	22 15:59
24 0:25	♂ ✶	♈	24 18:43
26 17:30	♅ △	♉	26 21:34
28 21:10	♅ □	♊	29 1:09

☽ Phases & Eclipses

Dy Hr Mn	
4 4:25	● 13♉14
11 12:44	☽ 20♌21
19 14:32	○ 28♏08
26 19:05	☾ 5♓02
2 13:27	● 11♊31
10 6:21	☽ 18♍54
18 2:02	○ 26♐22
24 23:42	☾ 2♈57

Astro Data

1 May 1962
Julian Day # 22766
SVP 5♓47'23"
GC 26♐18.8 ⚴ 28♈45.8
Eris 10♈26.6 ⚵ 5♊31.2
⚷ 10♓00.7 ⚶ 19♊26.3
☽ Mean ☊ 13♌37.9

1 June 1962
Julian Day # 22797
SVP 5♓47'18"
GC 26♐18.9 ⚴ 12♉26.3
Eris 10♈42.1 ⚵ 23♊28.0
⚷ 10♓48.7 ⚶ 2♋21.4
☽ Mean ☊ 11♌59.4

July 1962

LONGITUDE

Day	Sid.Time	☉	0 hr ☽	Noon ☽	True ☊	☿	♀	♂	⚳	♃	♄	♅	♆	♇
1 Su	6 36 14	9♋09 52	26♊30 08	3♋08 21	9♌07.5	17♊34.1	16♌45.6	24♉33.4	10♋14.3	12♓41.3	10♒08.8	27♌49.3	10♏50.4	7♍58.7
2 M	6 40 11	10 07 06	9♋42 26	16 12 18	9R 04.4	18 32.0	17 55.5	25 16.2	10 40.5	12R 41.4	10R 05.3	27 52.1	10R 49.8	8 00.0
3 Tu	6 44 08	11 04 19	22 37 53	28 59 15	9D 02.7	19 34.2	19 05.3	25 59.1	11 06.7	12 41.3	10 01.8	27 54.9	10 49.1	8 01.2
4 W	6 48 04	12 01 33	5♌16 30	11♌29 49	9 02.3	20 40.5	20 15.1	26 41.8	11 32.9	12 41.0	9 58.1	27 57.8	10 48.5	8 02.5
5 Th	6 52 01	12 58 46	17 39 27	23 45 43	9 03.0	21 51.0	21 24.7	27 24.5	11 59.1	12 40.4	9 54.5	28 00.7	10 48.0	8 03.9
6 F	6 55 57	13 55 59	29 48 58	5♍49 39	9 04.5	23 05.5	22 34.3	28 07.1	12 25.3	12 39.7	9 50.7	28 03.6	10 47.4	8 05.2
7 Sa	6 59 54	14 53 12	11♍48 13	17 45 11	9 06.1	24 24.1	23 43.8	28 49.6	12 51.5	12 38.8	9 47.0	28 06.5	10 46.9	8 06.6
8 Su	7 03 50	15 50 25	23 41 06	29 36 31	9 07.6	25 46.7	24 53.2	29 32.0	13 17.7	12 37.7	9 43.1	28 09.5	10 46.4	8 07.9
9 M	7 07 47	16 47 37	5♎32 02	11♎28 15	9R 08.4	27 13.1	26 02.5	0♊14.4	13 43.9	12 36.4	9 39.2	28 12.5	10 46.0	8 09.4
10 Tu	7 11 43	17 44 50	17 25 46	23 25 11	9 08.4	28 43.4	27 11.7	0 56.7	14 10.1	12 34.9	9 35.3	28 15.5	10 45.6	8 10.8
11 W	7 15 40	18 42 02	29 27 04	5♏31 59	9 07.5	0♋17.5	28 20.8	1 38.9	14 36.4	12 33.3	9 31.3	28 18.6	10 45.2	8 12.2
12 Th	7 19 37	19 39 15	11♏40 28	17 53 01	9 05.7	1 55.2	29 29.8	2 21.1	15 02.6	12 31.4	9 27.3	28 21.7	10 44.8	8 13.7
13 F	7 23 33	20 36 27	24 10 02	0♐31 54	9 03.4	3 36.5	0♍38.7	3 03.2	15 28.9	12 29.3	9 23.2	28 24.8	10 44.5	8 15.2
14 Sa	7 27 30	21 33 40	6♐58 55	13 31 15	9 01.0	5 21.2	1 47.4	3 45.2	15 55.1	12 27.1	9 19.1	28 28.0	10 44.2	8 16.7
15 Su	7 31 26	22 30 53	20 09 03	26 52 18	8 58.7	7 09.2	2 56.1	4 27.1	16 21.4	12 24.7	9 15.0	28 31.2	10 44.0	8 18.3
16 M	7 35 23	23 28 06	3♑40 53	10♑34 36	8 56.9	9 00.3	4 04.7	5 09.0	16 47.6	12 22.0	9 10.8	28 34.4	10 43.7	8 19.8
17 Tu	7 39 19	24 25 19	17 33 07	24 36 02	8 55.8	10 54.2	5 13.1	5 50.8	17 13.9	12 19.2	9 06.6	28 37.6	10 43.5	8 21.4
18 W	7 43 16	25 22 33	1♒42 49	8♒52 54	8D 55.4	12 50.8	6 21.4	6 32.5	17 40.2	12 16.2	9 02.4	28 40.9	10 43.4	8 23.0
19 Th	7 47 12	26 19 47	16 05 37	23 20 20	8 55.7	14 49.8	7 29.7	7 14.1	18 06.4	12 13.1	8 58.1	28 44.2	10 43.2	8 24.6
20 F	7 51 09	27 17 01	0♓36 19	7♓52 54	8 56.4	16 50.9	8 37.8	7 55.7	18 32.7	12 09.7	8 53.8	28 47.5	10 43.1	8 26.3
21 Sa	7 55 06	28 14 17	15 09 24	22 25 13	8 57.3	18 53.7	9 45.7	8 37.2	18 59.0	12 06.2	8 49.5	28 50.8	10 43.0	8 27.9
22 Su	7 59 02	29 11 33	29 39 47	6♈52 33	8 58.1	20 58.1	10 53.6	9 18.6	19 25.2	12 02.4	8 45.1	28 54.2	10D 43.0	8 29.6
23 M	8 02 59	0♌08 50	14♈03 07	21 11 05	8R 58.5	23 03.6	12 01.3	9 59.9	19 51.5	11 58.6	8 40.7	28 57.6	10 43.0	8 31.3
24 Tu	8 06 55	1 06 08	28 16 09	5♉18 05	8 58.6	25 09.9	13 08.9	10 41.2	20 17.8	11 54.5	8 36.4	29 01.0	10 43.0	8 33.0
25 W	8 10 52	2 03 27	12♉16 42	19 11 52	8 58.3	27 16.8	14 16.4	11 22.4	20 44.0	11 50.2	8 31.9	29 04.4	10 43.1	8 34.7
26 Th	8 14 48	3 00 47	26 03 29	2♊51 29	8 57.8	29 23.8	15 23.7	12 03.5	21 10.3	11 45.8	8 27.5	29 07.9	10 43.1	8 36.5
27 F	8 18 45	3 58 08	9♊35 52	16 16 37	8 57.2	1♌30.8	16 30.9	12 44.5	21 36.6	11 41.2	8 23.1	29 11.3	10 43.3	8 38.2
28 Sa	8 22 41	4 55 30	22 53 44	29 27 16	8 56.7	3 37.5	17 38.0	13 25.4	22 02.8	11 36.5	8 18.6	29 14.8	10 43.4	8 40.0
29 Su	8 26 38	5 52 52	5♋57 15	12♋23 45	8 56.3	5 43.7	18 45.0	14 06.3	22 29.1	11 31.6	8 14.2	29 18.3	10 43.6	8 41.8
30 M	8 30 35	6 50 16	18 46 49	25 06 33	8 56.1	7 49.1	19 51.8	14 47.1	22 55.4	11 26.5	8 09.7	29 21.9	10 43.8	8 43.6
31 Tu	8 34 31	7 47 41	1♌23 02	7♌36 24	8D 56.1	9 53.5	20 58.4	15 27.8	23 21.6	11 21.2	8 05.3	29 25.4	10 44.1	8 45.4

August 1962

LONGITUDE

Day	Sid.Time	☉	0 hr ☽	Noon ☽	True ☊	☿	♀	♂	⚳	♃	♄	♅	♆	♇
1 W	8 38 28	8♌45 06	13♌46 48	19♌54 23	8♌56.1	11♌56.9	22♍04.9	16♊08.4	23♋47.9	11♓15.9	8♒00.8	29♌29.0	10♏44.4	8♍47.2
2 Th	8 42 24	9 42 32	25 59 22	2♍01 59	8R 56.1	13 59.1	23 11.3	16 48.9	24 14.1	11R 10.3	7R 56.3	29 32.5	10 44.7	8 49.1
3 F	8 46 21	10 39 59	8♍02 28	14 01 09	8 55.9	16 00.0	24 17.4	17 29.3	24 40.3	11 04.6	7 51.9	29 36.1	10 45.0	8 51.0
4 Sa	8 50 17	11 37 26	19 58 21	25 54 26	8 55.7	17 59.6	25 23.5	18 09.7	25 06.6	10 58.8	7 47.4	29 39.7	10 45.4	8 52.8
5 Su	8 54 14	12 34 55	1♎49 47	7♎44 52	8 55.3	19 57.7	26 29.3	18 50.0	25 32.8	10 52.8	7 43.0	29 43.4	10 45.8	8 54.7
6 M	8 58 10	13 32 24	13 40 09	19 36 06	8 54.8	21 54.3	27 35.0	19 30.1	25 59.0	10 46.7	7 38.6	29 47.0	10 46.2	8 56.6
7 Tu	9 02 07	14 29 54	25 33 15	1♏32 08	8 54.4	23 49.5	28 40.5	20 10.2	26 25.2	10 40.5	7 34.1	29 50.6	10 46.7	8 58.5
8 W	9 06 04	15 27 25	7♏33 19	13 37 21	8D 54.3	25 43.1	29 45.8	20 50.2	26 51.3	10 34.1	7 29.7	29 54.3	10 47.2	9 00.5
9 Th	9 10 00	16 24 56	19 44 47	25 56 12	8 54.4	27 35.2	0♎50.9	21 30.1	27 17.5	10 27.6	7 25.3	29 58.0	10 47.8	9 02.4
10 F	9 13 57	17 22 29	2♐12 05	8♐32 58	8 54.8	29 25.8	1 55.9	22 09.9	27 43.7	10 21.0	7 21.0	0♍01.6	10 48.3	9 04.4
11 Sa	9 17 53	18 20 02	14 59 16	21 31 23	8 55.6	1♍14.9	3 00.6	22 49.6	28 09.8	10 14.3	7 16.6	0 05.3	10 48.9	9 06.3
12 Su	9 21 50	19 17 36	28 09 37	4♑54 09	8 56.5	3 02.4	4 05.1	23 29.3	28 35.9	10 07.5	7 12.3	0 09.0	10 49.6	9 08.3
13 M	9 25 46	20 15 12	11♑45 06	18 42 24	8 57.3	4 48.5	5 09.4	24 08.8	29 02.0	10 00.5	7 08.0	0 12.7	10 50.2	9 10.3
14 Tu	9 29 43	21 12 48	25 45 53	2♒55 12	8R 57.8	6 33.0	6 13.5	24 48.3	29 28.1	9 53.5	7 03.8	0 16.5	10 50.9	9 12.3
15 W	9 33 39	22 10 25	10♒09 51	17 29 13	8 57.7	8 16.0	7 17.3	25 27.6	29 54.2	9 46.4	6 59.5	0 20.2	10 51.7	9 14.2
16 Th	9 37 36	23 08 04	24 52 29	2♓18 46	8 57.0	9 57.6	8 21.0	26 06.9	0♌20.3	9 39.2	6 55.3	0 23.9	10 52.4	9 16.3
17 F	9 41 33	24 05 44	9♓47 04	17 16 21	8 55.6	11 37.7	9 24.3	26 46.1	0 46.3	9 31.9	6 51.2	0 27.6	10 53.2	9 18.3
18 Sa	9 45 29	25 03 25	24 45 32	2♈13 35	8 53.7	13 16.4	10 27.5	27 25.2	1 12.4	9 24.5	6 47.0	0 31.4	10 54.0	9 20.3
19 Su	9 49 26	26 01 08	9♈39 31	17 02 27	8 51.7	14 53.6	11 30.4	28 04.2	1 38.4	9 17.0	6 43.0	0 35.1	10 54.9	9 22.3
20 M	9 53 22	26 58 52	24 21 37	1♉36 24	8 49.9	16 29.4	12 33.0	28 43.1	2 04.4	9 09.5	6 38.9	0 38.9	10 55.8	9 24.3
21 Tu	9 57 19	27 56 38	8♉46 19	15 51 01	8D 48.7	18 03.7	13 35.4	29 21.9	2 30.3	9 01.9	6 34.9	0 42.6	10 56.7	9 26.4
22 W	10 01 15	28 54 26	22 50 20	29 44 10	8 48.3	19 36.7	14 37.5	0♋00.6	2 56.3	8 54.3	6 30.9	0 46.4	10 57.6	9 28.4
23 Th	10 05 12	29 52 16	6♊32 36	13♊15 44	8 48.8	21 08.2	15 39.4	0 39.2	3 22.2	8 46.5	6 27.0	0 50.1	10 58.6	9 30.5
24 F	10 09 08	0♍50 08	19 53 47	26 27 01	8 50.0	22 38.3	16 40.9	1 17.7	3 48.1	8 38.8	6 23.2	0 53.9	10 59.6	9 32.5
25 Sa	10 13 05	1 48 01	2♋55 43	9♋20 12	8 51.5	24 07.0	17 42.2	1 56.2	4 14.0	8 31.0	6 19.4	0 57.6	11 00.6	9 34.6
26 Su	10 17 02	2 45 56	15 40 48	21 57 51	8 52.9	25 34.2	18 43.2	2 34.5	4 39.9	8 23.2	6 15.6	1 01.4	11 01.7	9 36.7
27 M	10 20 58	3 43 52	28 11 39	4♌22 31	8R 53.8	27 00.0	19 43.9	3 12.7	5 05.8	8 15.3	6 11.9	1 05.1	11 02.8	9 38.7
28 Tu	10 24 55	4 41 50	10♌30 43	16 36 33	8 53.6	28 24.3	20 44.2	3 50.8	5 31.6	8 07.4	6 08.2	1 08.9	11 03.9	9 40.8
29 W	10 28 51	5 39 50	22 40 15	28 42 04	8 52.1	29 47.0	21 44.3	4 28.8	5 57.4	7 59.5	6 04.6	1 12.6	11 05.0	9 42.9
30 Th	10 32 48	6 37 52	4♍42 13	10♍40 56	8 49.3	1♎08.3	22 44.0	5 06.7	6 23.1	7 51.6	6 01.1	1 16.4	11 06.2	9 44.9
31 F	10 36 44	7 35 55	16 38 27	22 34 58	8 45.2	2 28.0	23 43.3	5 44.5	6 48.8	7 43.6	5 57.6	1 20.1	11 07.4	9 47.0

Astro Data	Dy Hr Mn	Planet Ingress	Dy Hr Mn	Last Aspect Dy Hr Mn	☽ Ingress Dy Hr Mn	Last Aspect Dy Hr Mn	☽ Ingress Dy Hr Mn	☽ Phases & Eclipses Dy Hr Mn	
♃ R	2 8:58	♂ ♊	9 3:50	1 2:21 ♅ ⚹	♋ 1 6:19	2 7:01 ♅ ☌	♍ 2 7:57	1 23:52	● 9♋38
☽ 0S	9 10:33	☿ ♋	11 7:36	3 5:59 ♂ ⚹	♌ 3 13:55	4 10:51 ♀ ☌	♎ 4 20:17	9 23:39	☽ 17♎15
☽ 0N	22 18:37	♀ ♍	12 22:32	5 20:27 ♅ ☌	♍ 6 0:22	7 8:36 ♅ ⚹	♏ 7 8:56	17 11:40	○ 24♑25
♆ D	23 8:11	☉ ♌	23 8:18	8 11:50 ♂ △	♎ 8 12:48	9 19:46 ♅ □	♐ 9 19:48	17 11:54	• A 0.392
♄⚻♇	25 1:13	☿ ♌	26 18:50	11 0:07 ☿ △	♏ 11 1:05	11 14:30 ♂ ☍	♑ 12 3:18	24 4:18	☾ 0♉48
				13 8:00 ♅ □	♐ 13 11:00	12 22:24 ♆ ⚹	♒ 14 7:07	31 12:24	● 7♌49
☽ 0S	5 18:17	♀ ♎	8 17:13	15 14:56 ♅ △	♑ 15 17:32	16 1:33 ♂ △	♓ 16 8:17	31 12:24:58	• A 03'33"
♃△♆	6 13:41	♅ ♍	10 1:19	17 11:40 ☉ ☍	♒ 17 21:07	18 3:55 ♂ □	♈ 18 8:25		
♀0S	8 15:08	☿ ♍	10 19:29	19 20:57 ♅ ☍	♓ 19 23:00	20 6:59 ♂ ⚹	♉ 20 9:20	8 15:55	☽ 15♏37
♃☍♇	18 22:41	⚳ ♌	15 17:19	21 22:19 ☉ △	♈ 22 0:34	22 10:26 ☉ □	♊ 22 12:28	15 20:09	○ 22♒30
☽ 0N	19 1:51	♂ ♋	22 11:37	24 1:14 ♅ △	♉ 24 2:57	24 4:06 ☿ □	♋ 24 18:34	15 19:57	• A 0.596
☿0S	28 15:00	☉ ♍	23 15:12	26 5:23 ♅ □	♊ 26 6:57	26 19:50 ☿ ⚹	♌ 27 3:30	22 10:26	☾ 28♉51
		☿ ♎	29 15:48	28 11:37 ♅ ⚹	♋ 28 13:00	28 20:54 ♀ ⚹	♍ 29 14:36	30 3:09	● 6♍16
				30 1:05 ♀ ⚹	♌ 30 21:21				

Astro Data

1 July 1962
Julian Day # 22827
SVP 5♓47'13"
GC 26♐18.9 ⚴ 26♉10.2
Eris 10♈48.9 ⚵ 10♋26.0
⚷ 10♓45.0R ⚶ 15♋23.2
☽ Mean ☊ 10♌24.1

1 August 1962
Julian Day # 22858
SVP 5♓47'08"
GC 26♐19.0 ⚴ 10♊41.0
Eris 10♈45.8R ⚵ 27♋16.0
⚷ 9♓52.3R ⚶ 29♋06.4
☽ Mean ☊ 8♌45.6

LONGITUDE — September 1962

Day	Sid.Time	☉	0 hr ☽	Noon ☽	True ☊	☿	♀	♂	⚳	♃	♄	♅	♆	♇
1 Sa	10 40 41	8♍33 59	28♍30 44	4♎26 01	8♌40.1	3♎46.0	24♎42.3	6♋22.2	7♌14.5	7♓35.7	5♒54.2	1♍23.9	11♏08.6	9♍49.1
2 Su	10 44 37	9 32 05	10♎21 03	16 16 09	8R 34.6	5 02.4	25 40.9	6 59.7	7 40.2	7R 27.8	5R 50.9	1 27.6	11 09.9	9 51.2
3 M	10 48 34	10 30 13	22 11 38	28 07 52	8 29.3	6 17.1	26 39.1	7 37.2	8 05.8	7 19.8	5 47.6	1 31.3	11 11.2	9 53.3
4 Tu	10 52 30	11 28 22	4♏05 12	10♏04 06	8 24.7	7 29.9	27 36.9	8 14.5	8 31.4	7 11.9	5 44.4	1 35.1	11 12.5	9 55.3
5 W	10 56 27	12 26 33	16 04 58	22 08 18	8 21.4	8 40.9	28 34.3	8 51.7	8 57.0	7 04.1	5 41.3	1 38.8	11 13.8	9 57.4
6 Th	11 00 24	13 24 45	28 14 37	4♐24 25	8D 19.5	9 50.0	29 31.3	9 28.8	9 22.5	6 56.2	5 38.3	1 42.5	11 15.2	9 59.5
7 F	11 04 20	14 22 58	10♐38 14	16 56 38	8 19.1	10 56.9	0♏27.8	10 05.8	9 48.0	6 48.4	5 35.3	1 46.2	11 16.6	10 01.6
8 Sa	11 08 17	15 21 14	23 20 07	29 49 13	8 19.9	12 01.7	1 23.8	10 42.7	10 13.5	6 40.7	5 32.4	1 49.8	11 18.0	10 03.6
9 Su	11 12 13	16 19 30	6♑24 21	13♑05 56	8 21.4	13 04.2	2 19.4	11 19.5	10 38.9	6 32.9	5 29.5	1 53.5	11 19.5	10 05.7
10 M	11 16 10	17 17 48	19 54 16	26 49 34	8R 22.7	14 04.3	3 14.4	11 56.1	11 04.3	6 25.3	5 26.8	1 57.2	11 20.9	10 07.8
11 Tu	11 20 06	18 16 08	3♒51 50	11♒01 01	8 23.1	15 01.7	4 08.9	12 32.6	11 29.6	6 17.7	5 24.1	2 00.8	11 22.4	10 09.8
12 W	11 24 03	19 14 29	18 16 46	25 38 38	8 21.9	15 56.4	5 02.9	13 09.0	11 54.9	6 10.1	5 21.5	2 04.5	11 23.9	10 11.9
13 Th	11 27 59	20 12 52	3♓05 53	10♓37 39	8 18.9	16 48.2	5 56.3	13 45.3	12 20.2	6 02.7	5 19.0	2 08.1	11 25.5	10 14.0
14 F	11 31 56	21 11 17	18 12 49	25 50 11	8 14.1	17 36.7	6 49.1	14 21.4	12 45.4	5 55.3	5 16.6	2 11.7	11 27.1	10 16.0
15 Sa	11 35 53	22 09 44	3♈28 26	11♈06 10	8 07.9	18 21.9	7 41.4	14 57.5	13 10.5	5 48.0	5 14.3	2 15.3	11 28.6	10 18.1
16 Su	11 39 49	23 08 12	18 42 04	26 14 51	8 01.2	19 03.4	8 33.0	15 33.4	13 35.6	5 40.7	5 12.0	2 18.9	11 30.3	10 20.1
17 M	11 43 46	24 06 43	3♉43 23	11♉06 43	7 54.9	19 41.0	9 23.9	16 09.2	14 00.7	5 33.6	5 09.8	2 22.4	11 31.9	10 22.1
18 Tu	11 47 42	25 05 16	18 24 04	25 34 55	7 49.9	20 14.3	10 14.2	16 44.8	14 25.8	5 26.5	5 07.7	2 26.0	11 33.6	10 24.2
19 W	11 51 39	26 03 51	2♊38 54	9♊35 53	7 46.7	20 43.1	11 03.8	17 20.3	14 50.7	5 19.6	5 05.7	2 29.5	11 35.2	10 26.2
20 Th	11 55 35	27 02 28	16 25 55	23 09 11	7D 45.4	21 06.9	11 52.7	17 55.7	15 15.7	5 12.8	5 03.8	2 33.0	11 36.9	10 28.2
21 F	11 59 32	28 01 08	29 46 00	6♋16 45	7 45.6	21 25.5	12 40.8	18 31.0	15 40.6	5 06.0	5 02.0	2 36.5	11 38.7	10 30.2
22 Sa	12 03 28	28 59 50	12♋41 55	19 02 00	7 46.6	21 38.5	13 28.2	19 06.1	16 05.4	4 59.4	5 00.3	2 40.0	11 40.4	10 32.2
23 Su	12 07 25	29 58 34	25 17 33	1♌29 05	7R 47.6	21R 45.4	14 14.7	19 41.1	16 30.2	4 52.9	4 58.7	2 43.5	11 42.2	10 34.2
24 M	12 11 22	0♎57 20	7♌37 08	13 42 13	7 47.6	21 45.9	15 00.4	20 15.9	16 54.9	4 46.6	4 57.1	2 46.9	11 44.0	10 36.2
25 Tu	12 15 18	1 56 08	19 44 47	25 45 17	7 45.8	21 39.6	15 45.3	20 50.6	17 19.5	4 40.3	4 55.7	2 50.3	11 45.8	10 38.2
26 W	12 19 15	2 54 59	1♍44 08	7♍41 42	7 41.6	21 26.3	16 29.2	21 25.2	17 44.2	4 34.2	4 54.3	2 53.7	11 47.6	10 40.1
27 Th	12 23 11	3 53 51	13 38 17	19 34 10	7 34.9	21 05.6	17 12.2	21 59.6	18 08.7	4 28.2	4 53.1	2 57.1	11 49.5	10 42.1
28 F	12 27 08	4 52 46	25 29 39	1♎24 55	7 25.9	20 37.5	17 54.2	22 33.8	18 33.2	4 22.4	4 51.9	3 00.4	11 51.3	10 44.0
29 Sa	12 31 04	5 51 43	7♎20 12	13 15 42	7 15.1	20 01.8	18 35.3	23 07.9	18 57.6	4 16.7	4 50.8	3 03.7	11 53.2	10 45.9
30 Su	12 35 01	6 50 41	19 11 34	25 08 01	7 03.4	19 18.8	19 15.2	23 41.9	19 21.9	4 11.2	4 49.9	3 07.0	11 55.1	10 47.9

LONGITUDE — October 1962

Day	Sid.Time	☉	0 hr ☽	Noon ☽	True ☊	☿	♀	♂	⚳	♃	♄	♅	♆	♇
1 M	12 38 57	7♎49 42	1♏05 15	7♏03 27	6♌51.8	18♎28.8	19♏54.0	24♋15.6	19♌46.2	4♓05.8	4♒49.0	3♍10.3	11♏57.0	10♍49.8
2 Tu	12 42 54	8 48 44	13 02 53	19 03 47	6R 41.3	17R 32.5	20 31.7	24 49.3	20 10.4	4R 00.6	4R 48.2	3 13.5	11 59.0	10 51.7
3 W	12 46 50	9 47 49	25 06 28	1♐11 16	6 32.9	16 30.8	21 08.2	25 22.7	20 34.6	3 55.6	4 47.6	3 16.7	12 00.9	10 53.5
4 Th	12 50 47	10 46 55	7♐18 32	13 28 42	6 26.9	15 24.7	21 43.4	25 56.0	20 58.7	3 50.7	4 47.0	3 19.9	12 02.9	10 55.4
5 F	12 54 44	11 46 03	19 42 11	25 59 27	6 23.5	14 15.8	22 17.3	26 29.1	21 22.7	3 46.0	4 46.5	3 23.0	12 04.9	10 57.3
6 Sa	12 58 40	12 45 13	2♑21 01	8♑47 22	6D 22.3	13 05.7	22 49.9	27 02.1	21 46.6	3 41.5	4 46.2	3 26.2	12 06.9	10 59.1
7 Su	13 02 37	13 44 24	15 18 59	21 56 22	6 22.4	11 56.4	23 21.0	27 34.8	22 10.4	3 37.1	4 45.9	3 29.3	12 08.9	11 00.9
8 M	13 06 33	14 43 38	28 39 54	5♒29 58	6R 22.8	10 49.6	23 50.7	28 07.4	22 34.2	3 32.9	4 45.7	3 32.3	12 10.9	11 02.7
9 Tu	13 10 30	15 42 53	12♒26 49	19 30 34	6 22.2	9 47.4	24 18.8	28 39.9	22 57.9	3 28.9	4D 45.7	3 35.4	12 13.0	11 04.5
10 W	13 14 26	16 42 10	26 41 10	3♓58 23	6 19.6	8 51.5	24 45.3	29 12.1	23 21.5	3 25.1	4 45.7	3 38.4	12 15.1	11 06.3
11 Th	13 18 23	17 41 28	11♓21 47	18 50 41	6 14.4	8 03.5	25 10.1	29 44.2	23 45.0	3 21.4	4 45.8	3 41.3	12 17.1	11 08.0
12 F	13 22 19	18 40 48	26 24 12	4♈01 13	6 06.6	7 24.6	25 33.3	0♌16.0	24 08.5	3 18.0	4 46.1	3 44.3	12 19.2	11 09.8
13 Sa	13 26 16	19 40 11	11♈40 27	19 20 30	5 56.7	6 55.9	25 54.6	0 47.7	24 31.8	3 14.7	4 46.4	3 47.2	12 21.3	11 11.5
14 Su	13 30 13	20 39 35	26 59 53	4♉37 09	5 46.0	6 37.9	26 14.2	1 19.2	24 55.1	3 11.6	4 46.8	3 50.0	12 23.4	11 13.2
15 M	13 34 09	21 39 02	12♉10 55	19 39 57	5 35.5	6D 31.0	26 31.8	1 50.6	25 18.3	3 08.7	4 47.4	3 52.8	12 25.5	11 14.9
16 Tu	13 38 06	22 38 30	27 03 12	4♊19 50	5 26.7	6 35.1	26 47.4	2 21.7	25 41.4	3 06.0	4 48.0	3 55.6	12 27.7	11 16.5
17 W	13 42 02	23 38 02	11♊29 17	18 31 12	5 20.2	6 49.9	27 01.1	2 52.6	26 04.4	3 03.5	4 48.7	3 58.4	12 29.8	11 18.2
18 Th	13 45 59	24 37 35	25 25 28	2♋12 10	5 16.3	7 15.0	27 12.6	3 23.3	26 27.3	3 01.2	4 49.6	4 01.1	12 32.0	11 19.8
19 F	13 49 55	25 37 11	8♋51 32	15 23 59	5D 14.6	7 49.7	27 22.1	3 53.9	26 50.1	2 59.1	4 50.5	4 03.8	12 34.1	11 21.4
20 Sa	13 53 52	26 36 48	21 49 59	28 10 06	5R 14.3	8 33.3	27 29.3	4 24.2	27 12.8	2 57.2	4 51.5	4 06.4	12 36.3	11 23.0
21 Su	13 57 48	27 36 29	4♌24 58	10♌35 13	5 14.3	9 25.0	27 34.3	4 54.2	27 35.4	2 55.5	4 52.7	4 09.0	12 38.5	11 24.6
22 M	14 01 45	28 36 11	16 41 31	22 44 29	5 13.3	10 24.0	27R 37.1	5 24.1	27 57.9	2 53.9	4 53.9	4 11.6	12 40.7	11 26.1
23 Tu	14 05 42	29 35 56	28 44 45	4♍42 54	5 10.4	11 29.4	27 37.5	5 53.7	28 20.3	2 52.6	4 55.2	4 14.1	12 42.9	11 27.7
24 W	14 09 38	0♏35 42	10♍39 29	16 35 00	5 04.7	12 40.4	27 35.5	6 23.2	28 42.6	2 51.5	4 56.7	4 16.6	12 45.1	11 29.2
25 Th	14 13 35	1 35 31	22 29 56	28 24 39	4 56.0	13 56.3	27 31.2	6 52.3	29 04.8	2 50.6	4 58.2	4 19.1	12 47.3	11 30.6
26 F	14 17 31	2 35 22	4♎19 32	10♎14 52	4 44.6	15 16.4	27 24.5	7 21.3	29 26.8	2 49.9	4 59.9	4 21.5	12 49.5	11 32.1
27 Sa	14 21 28	3 35 15	16 10 56	22 07 56	4 30.9	16 40.0	27 15.3	7 49.9	29 48.8	2 49.4	5 01.6	4 23.8	12 51.7	11 33.5
28 Su	14 25 24	4 35 10	28 06 04	4♏05 28	4 16.2	18 06.7	27 03.7	8 18.4	0♍10.6	2D 49.1	5 03.4	4 26.1	12 53.9	11 35.0
29 M	14 29 21	5 35 07	10♏06 17	16 08 37	4 01.5	19 35.8	26 49.8	8 46.5	0 32.3	2 49.0	5 05.3	4 28.4	12 56.2	11 36.3
30 Tu	14 33 17	6 35 06	22 12 36	28 18 21	3 48.1	21 07.0	26 33.4	9 14.5	0 53.8	2 49.1	5 07.4	4 30.6	12 58.4	11 37.7
31 W	14 37 14	7 35 07	4♐26 01	10♐35 45	3 37.0	22 39.9	26 14.8	9 42.1	1 15.3	2 49.5	5 09.5	4 32.8	13 00.6	11 39.0

Astro Data	Dy Hr Mn
☽0S	2 0:41
☽0N	15 11:13
♃⚺♄	22 7:39
☉0S	23 12:35
☿R	24 1:52
☽0S	29 6:26
♃☍♅	8 13:55
♄D	9 16:25
☽0N	12 22:14
☿D	15 15:05
♀R	23 4:14
☽0S	26 12:43
♃D	29 10:31

Planet Ingress		Dy Hr Mn
♀	♏	7 0:11
☉	♎	23 12:35
♂	♌	11 23:54
☉	♏	23 21:40
⚳	♍	28 0:21

Last Aspect Dy Hr Mn		☽ Ingress	Dy Hr Mn
30 12:51	♆ ⚹	♎	1 3:01
3 8:45	♀ ☌	♏	3 15:46
4 15:03	☉ ⚹	♐	6 3:26
7 6:44	☉ □	♑	8 12:20
9 18:09	☉ △	♒	10 17:26
11 19:06	☿ △	♓	12 19:02
14 4:11	☉ ☍	♈	14 18:33
16 0:02	☿ ☍	♉	16 18:00
18 11:07	☉ △	♊	18 19:29
20 19:36	☉ □	♋	21 0:26
23 8:49	☉ ⚹	♌	23 9:07
25 3:55	☿ ⚹	♍	25 20:31
27 17:09	♂ ⚹	♎	28 9:08
30 8:57	♂ □	♏	30 21:49

Last Aspect Dy Hr Mn		☽ Ingress	Dy Hr Mn
2 23:59	♂ △	♐	3 9:40
4 15:26	☿ ⚹	♑	5 19:35
7 22:30	♂ ☍	♒	8 2:22
9 20:19	♀ □	♓	10 5:29
11 22:19	♀ △	♈	12 5:41
13 12:33	☉ ☍	♉	14 4:43
15 23:21	♀ ☍	♊	16 4:50
17 21:33	☉ △	♋	18 8:05
20 10:42	♀ △	♌	20 15:30
23 0:47	☉ ⚹	♍	23 2:31
25 10:12	♀ ⚹	♎	25 15:14
26 23:30	☿ ☌	♏	28 3:49
30 8:39	♀ ☌	♐	30 15:19

☽ Phases & Eclipses Dy Hr Mn	
7 6:44	☽ 14♐10
14 4:11	○ 20♓52
20 19:36	☾ 27♊21
28 19:39	● 5♎12
6 19:54	☽ 13♑05
13 12:33	○ 19♈42
20 8:47	☾ 26♋29
28 13:05	● 4♏38

Astro Data

1 September 1962
Julian Day # 22889
SVP 5♓47'05"
GC 26♐19.1 ⚴ 25♊07.3
Eris 10♈33.4R ⚵ 13♌08.2
⚷ 8♓28.7R ⚶ 12♌50.3
☽ Mean ☊ 7♌07.1

1 October 1962
Julian Day # 22919
SVP 5♓47'03"
GC 26♐19.1 ⚴ 8♋08.9
Eris 10♈15.9R ⚵ 27♌16.6
⚷ 7♓07.9R ⚶ 25♌51.4
☽ Mean ☊ 5♌31.7

November 1962 — LONGITUDE

Day	Sid.Time	☉	0 hr ☽	Noon ☽	True ☊	☿	♀	♂	⚳	♃	♄	♅	♆	♇
1 Th	14 41 11	8♏35 09	16♐47 44	23♐02 12	3♌28.8	24♎14.1	25♏53.8	10♌09.5	1♍36.6	2♓50.0	5♒11.7	4♍34.9	13♏02.9	11♍40.4
2 F	14 45 07	9 35 13	29 19 26	5♑39 42	3R 23.7	25 49.3	25R 30.7	10 36.6	1 57.8	2 50.7	5 14.1	4 37.0	13 05.1	11 41.6
3 Sa	14 49 04	10 35 19	12♑03 20	18 30 43	3 21.3	27 25.4	25 05.5	11 03.5	2 18.8	2 51.7	5 16.5	4 39.1	13 07.4	11 42.9
4 Su	14 53 00	11 35 27	25 02 14	1♒38 15	3 20.7	29 02.0	24 38.3	11 30.0	2 39.7	2 52.8	5 19.0	4 41.1	13 09.6	11 44.2
5 M	14 56 57	12 35 35	8♒19 10	15 05 19	3 20.8	0♏39.1	24 09.3	11 56.3	3 00.5	2 54.1	5 21.6	4 43.0	13 11.9	11 45.4
6 Tu	15 00 53	13 35 46	21 57 00	28 54 25	3 20.1	2 16.5	23 38.6	12 22.2	3 21.1	2 55.7	5 24.3	4 44.9	13 14.1	11 46.6
7 W	15 04 50	14 35 58	5♓57 41	13♓06 45	3 17.5	3 54.1	23 06.3	12 47.9	3 41.6	2 57.4	5 27.1	4 46.7	13 16.4	11 47.7
8 Th	15 08 46	15 36 11	20 21 25	27 41 18	3 12.4	5 31.7	22 32.8	13 13.2	4 01.9	2 59.4	5 30.0	4 48.5	13 18.6	11 48.8
9 F	15 12 43	16 36 25	5♈05 49	12♈34 11	3 04.6	7 09.4	21 58.2	13 38.3	4 22.1	3 01.5	5 32.9	4 50.3	13 20.9	11 49.9
10 Sa	15 16 40	17 36 42	20 05 25	27 38 23	2 54.7	8 46.9	21 22.7	14 03.0	4 42.1	3 03.9	5 36.0	4 52.0	13 23.1	11 51.0
11 Su	15 20 36	18 37 00	5♉11 51	12♉44 30	2 43.6	10 24.4	20 46.6	14 27.4	5 02.0	3 06.4	5 39.2	4 53.6	13 25.4	11 52.1
12 M	15 24 33	19 37 19	20 15 02	27 42 11	2 32.7	12 01.7	20 10.1	14 51.5	5 21.7	3 09.2	5 42.4	4 55.2	13 27.6	11 53.1
13 Tu	15 28 29	20 37 41	5♊04 51	12♊22 02	2 23.2	13 38.8	19 33.5	15 15.2	5 41.2	3 12.1	5 45.7	4 56.8	13 29.8	11 54.1
14 W	15 32 26	21 38 04	19 33 00	26 37 10	2 16.1	15 15.8	18 57.0	15 38.7	6 00.6	3 15.2	5 49.2	4 58.3	13 32.1	11 55.0
15 Th	15 36 22	22 38 29	3♋34 11	10♋23 56	2 11.7	16 52.5	18 21.0	16 01.7	6 19.8	3 18.6	5 52.7	4 59.7	13 34.3	11 56.0
16 F	15 40 19	23 38 56	17 06 28	23 41 58	2D 09.7	18 29.0	17 45.6	16 24.4	6 38.8	3 22.1	5 56.3	5 01.1	13 36.5	11 56.9
17 Sa	15 44 15	24 39 24	0♌10 50	6♌33 30	2 09.5	20 05.2	17 11.0	16 46.7	6 57.7	3 25.8	6 00.0	5 02.5	13 38.7	11 57.8
18 Su	15 48 12	25 39 55	12 50 30	19 02 29	2R 10.0	21 41.3	16 37.6	17 08.7	7 16.4	3 29.7	6 03.7	5 03.8	13 41.0	11 58.6
19 M	15 52 09	26 40 27	25 10 04	1♍13 55	2 10.0	23 17.1	16 05.6	17 30.3	7 34.8	3 33.8	6 07.6	5 05.0	13 43.2	11 59.4
20 Tu	15 56 05	27 41 01	7♍14 43	13 13 07	2 08.6	24 52.7	15 35.1	17 51.4	7 53.1	3 38.1	6 11.5	5 06.2	13 45.4	12 00.2
21 W	16 00 02	28 41 37	19 09 46	25 05 16	2 05.0	26 28.0	15 06.2	18 12.2	8 11.2	3 42.5	6 15.5	5 07.3	13 47.6	12 01.0
22 Th	16 03 58	29 42 14	1♎00 13	6♎55 07	1 58.9	28 03.2	14 39.3	18 32.6	8 29.2	3 47.2	6 19.6	5 08.4	13 49.7	12 01.7
23 F	16 07 55	0♐42 53	12 50 29	18 46 44	1 50.2	29 38.2	14 14.3	18 52.5	8 46.9	3 52.0	6 23.8	5 09.4	13 51.9	12 02.4
24 Sa	16 11 51	1 43 34	24 44 15	0♏43 21	1 39.7	1♐13.0	13 51.5	19 12.0	9 04.4	3 57.0	6 28.1	5 10.4	13 54.1	12 03.1
25 Su	16 15 48	2 44 16	6♏44 20	12 47 23	1 28.0	2 47.6	13 30.9	19 31.1	9 21.7	4 02.2	6 32.4	5 11.3	13 56.3	12 03.7
26 M	16 19 44	3 45 00	18 52 41	25 00 22	1 16.3	4 22.2	13 12.7	19 49.7	9 38.7	4 07.6	6 36.8	5 12.1	13 58.4	12 04.3
27 Tu	16 23 41	4 45 45	1♐10 31	7♐23 12	1 05.6	5 56.5	12 56.8	20 07.8	9 55.6	4 13.1	6 41.3	5 12.9	14 00.5	12 04.9
28 W	16 27 38	5 46 31	13 38 26	19 56 16	0 56.9	7 30.8	12 43.3	20 25.5	10 12.3	4 18.9	6 45.9	5 13.7	14 02.7	12 05.4
29 Th	16 31 34	6 47 19	26 16 42	2♑39 48	0 50.7	9 04.9	12 32.3	20 42.7	10 28.7	4 24.8	6 50.5	5 14.4	14 04.8	12 05.9
30 F	16 35 31	7 48 07	9♑05 35	15 34 08	0 47.1	10 39.0	12 23.8	20 59.4	10 44.9	4 30.9	6 55.3	5 15.0	14 06.9	12 06.4

December 1962 — LONGITUDE

Day	Sid.Time	☉	0 hr ☽	Noon ☽	True ☊	☿	♀	♂	⚳	♃	♄	♅	♆	♇
1 Sa	16 39 27	8♐48 57	22♑05 31	28♑39 53	0♌45.8	12♐13.0	12♏17.7	21♌15.6	11♍00.8	4♓37.1	7♒00.1	5♍15.6	14♏09.0	12♍06.9
2 Su	16 43 24	9 49 48	5♒17 20	11♒58 03	0D 46.3	13 46.9	12D 14.1	21 31.3	11 16.5	4 43.5	7 04.9	5 16.1	14 11.1	12 07.3
3 M	16 47 20	10 50 39	18 42 11	25 29 53	0 47.4	15 20.8	12 12.9	21 46.5	11 32.0	4 50.1	7 09.9	5 16.6	14 13.1	12 07.7
4 Tu	16 51 17	11 51 32	2♓21 20	9♓16 36	0R 48.2	16 54.7	12 14.2	22 01.2	11 47.2	4 56.9	7 14.9	5 17.0	14 15.2	12 08.0
5 W	16 55 13	12 52 25	16 15 45	23 18 46	0 47.7	18 28.5	12 17.8	22 15.3	12 02.2	5 03.8	7 20.0	5 17.3	14 17.2	12 08.3
6 Th	16 59 10	13 53 19	0♈25 33	7♈35 52	0 45.3	20 02.3	12 23.8	22 28.9	12 16.9	5 10.9	7 25.1	5 17.6	14 19.3	12 08.6
7 F	17 03 07	14 54 13	14 49 22	22 05 34	0 40.9	21 36.1	12 32.1	22 41.9	12 31.4	5 18.1	7 30.3	5 17.8	14 21.3	12 08.9
8 Sa	17 07 03	15 55 08	29 23 54	6♉43 37	0 34.7	23 10.0	12 42.7	22 54.3	12 45.5	5 25.5	7 35.6	5 18.0	14 23.3	12 09.1
9 Su	17 11 00	16 56 04	14♉03 55	21 23 54	0 27.7	24 43.8	12 55.5	23 06.2	12 59.5	5 33.1	7 40.9	5 18.1	14 25.2	12 09.3
10 M	17 14 56	17 57 01	28 42 37	5♊59 10	0 20.6	26 17.7	13 10.4	23 17.5	13 13.1	5 40.8	7 46.3	5R 18.2	14 27.2	12 09.4
11 Tu	17 18 53	18 57 59	13♊12 39	20 22 14	0 14.5	27 51.5	13 27.4	23 28.2	13 26.5	5 48.7	7 51.8	5 18.2	14 29.1	12 09.6
12 W	17 22 49	19 58 58	27 27 12	4♋26 58	0 10.0	29 25.4	13 46.4	23 38.2	13 39.6	5 56.7	7 57.3	5 18.2	14 31.1	12 09.7
13 Th	17 26 46	20 59 57	11♋21 05	18 09 16	0D 07.5	0♑59.3	14 07.4	23 47.7	13 52.4	6 04.8	8 02.9	5 18.1	14 33.0	12 09.7
14 F	17 30 42	22 00 58	24 51 23	1♌27 24	0 06.8	2 33.2	14 30.3	23 56.5	14 05.0	6 13.1	8 08.6	5 17.9	14 34.9	12R 09.7
15 Sa	17 34 39	23 01 59	7♌57 29	14 21 52	0 07.6	4 07.0	14 55.0	24 04.7	14 17.2	6 21.6	8 14.3	5 17.7	14 36.7	12 09.7
16 Su	17 38 36	24 03 01	20 40 53	26 55 00	0 09.2	5 40.8	15 21.6	24 12.1	14 29.1	6 30.2	8 20.1	5 17.4	14 38.6	12 09.7
17 M	17 42 32	25 04 04	3♍04 43	9♍10 34	0 10.9	7 14.4	15 49.8	24 19.0	14 40.7	6 38.9	8 25.9	5 17.1	14 40.4	12 09.6
18 Tu	17 46 29	26 05 08	15 13 09	21 13 05	0R 12.0	8 48.0	16 19.7	24 25.1	14 52.0	6 47.8	8 31.8	5 16.7	14 42.2	12 09.5
19 W	17 50 25	27 06 13	27 11 01	3♎07 33	0 11.9	10 21.4	16 51.1	24 30.5	15 03.0	6 56.8	8 37.7	5 16.3	14 44.0	12 09.4
20 Th	17 54 22	28 07 19	9♎03 20	14 58 57	0 10.4	11 54.5	17 24.1	24 35.2	15 13.7	7 05.9	8 43.7	5 15.8	14 45.8	12 09.2
21 F	17 58 18	29 08 25	20 55 01	26 52 04	0 07.4	13 27.2	17 58.6	24 39.2	15 24.0	7 15.2	8 49.7	5 15.3	14 47.5	12 09.0
22 Sa	18 02 15	0♑09 32	2♏50 37	8♏51 09	0 03.2	14 59.6	18 34.5	24 42.5	15 34.0	7 24.6	8 55.8	5 14.6	14 49.2	12 08.8
23 Su	18 06 11	1 10 40	14 54 05	20 59 47	29♋58.2	16 31.4	19 11.7	24 45.0	15 43.7	7 34.2	9 02.0	5 14.0	14 50.9	12 08.5
24 M	18 10 08	2 11 49	27 08 33	3♐20 39	29 53.0	18 02.5	19 50.2	24 46.7	15 53.0	7 43.9	9 08.2	5 13.3	14 52.6	12 08.3
25 Tu	18 14 05	3 12 58	9♐36 16	15 55 31	29 48.3	19 32.8	20 30.0	24R 47.7	16 01.9	7 53.7	9 14.4	5 12.5	14 54.2	12 07.9
26 W	18 18 01	4 14 07	22 18 28	28 45 08	29 44.6	21 02.0	21 11.0	24 47.9	16 10.5	8 03.6	9 20.7	5 11.7	14 55.9	12 07.6
27 Th	18 21 58	5 15 17	5♑15 28	11♑49 23	29 42.1	22 29.9	21 53.1	24 47.3	16 18.8	8 13.7	9 27.0	5 10.8	14 57.5	12 07.2
28 F	18 25 54	6 16 28	18 26 45	25 07 24	29D 41.1	23 56.3	22 36.3	24 45.9	16 26.7	8 23.8	9 33.4	5 09.9	14 59.1	12 06.8
29 Sa	18 29 51	7 17 38	1♒51 11	8♒37 53	29 41.2	25 20.9	23 20.5	24 43.8	16 34.2	8 34.1	9 39.8	5 08.9	15 00.6	12 06.3
30 Su	18 33 47	8 18 48	15 27 20	22 19 20	29 42.3	26 43.2	24 05.8	24 40.8	16 41.3	8 44.6	9 46.3	5 07.9	15 02.1	12 05.9
31 M	18 37 44	9 19 58	29 13 41	6♓10 13	29 43.8	28 02.9	24 52.1	24 37.0	16 48.1	8 55.1	9 52.8	5 06.8	15 03.7	12 05.4

Astro Data

	Dy Hr Mn
☽0N	9 9:11
☽0S	22 20:17
♀ D	3 11:26
☽0N	6 18:07
♃☍♅	7 11:01
♅ R	11 5:12
♇ R	14 21:46
☽0S	20 4:55
♂ R	26 6:11

Planet Ingress

	Dy Hr Mn
☿ ♏	5 2:20
☉ ♐	22 19:02
☿ ♐	23 17:31
☿ ♑	12 20:51
☉ ♑	22 8:15
☊ ♋R	23 3:32

Last Aspect / ☽ Ingress

Last Aspect Dy Hr Mn		☽ Ingress Dy Hr Mn
1 14:37	☿ ⚹	♑ 2 1:17
4 6:38	☿ □	♒ 4 9:02
6 3:16	♀ □	♓ 6 13:52
8 3:55	♀ △	♈ 8 15:45
9 13:45	♂ △	♉ 10 15:45
12 0:21	♀ ☍	♊ 12 15:43
13 16:56	♂ ⚹	♋ 14 17:49
16 11:54	☉ △	♌ 16 23:40
19 2:09	☉ □	♍ 19 9:33
21 20:00	☉ ⚹	♎ 21 21:58
23 12:12	♂ ⚹	♏ 24 10:33
26 1:36	♂ □	♐ 26 21:43
28 12:57	♂ △	♑ 29 7:00

Last Aspect / ☽ Ingress

Last Aspect Dy Hr Mn		☽ Ingress Dy Hr Mn
30 9:18	♆ ⚹	♒ 1 14:26
3 5:19	♂ ☍	♓ 3 19:53
5 2:45	☿ □	♈ 5 23:17
7 13:01	♂ △	♉ 8 0:59
9 14:50	♂ □	♊ 10 2:07
12 2:17	☿ ☍	♋ 12 4:21
13 5:36	♆ △	♌ 14 9:20
16 6:42	♂ ☌	♍ 16 17:59
18 22:42	☉ □	♎ 19 5:41
21 17:00	☉ ⚹	♏ 21 18:18
23 19:22	♂ □	♐ 24 5:33
26 4:39	♂ △	♑ 26 14:19
28 9:37	☿ ☌	♒ 28 20:42
30 16:05	♂ ☍	♓ 31 1:20

☽ Phases & Eclipses

Dy Hr Mn	
5 7:15	☽ 12♒24
11 22:03	○ 19♉02
19 2:09	☾ 26♌16
27 6:29	● 4♐32
4 16:48	☽ 12♓04
11 9:27	○ 18♊52
18 22:42	☾ 26♍32
26 22:59	● 4♑42

Astro Data

1 November 1962
Julian Day # 22950
SVP 5♓47'00"
GC 26♐19.2 ⚴ 18♋35.4
Eris 9♈57.3R ⚵ 10♍08.3
⚷ 6♓15.9R ⚶ 8♍34.2
☽ Mean ☊ 3♌53.2

1 December 1962
Julian Day # 22980
SVP 5♓46'55"
GC 26♐19.3 ⚴ 21♋58.7R
Eris 9♈44.3R ⚵ 20♍04.3
⚷ 6♓15.1 ⚶ 19♍24.3
☽ Mean ☊ 2♌17.9

LONGITUDE — January 1963

Day	Sid.Time	☉	0 hr ☽	Noon☽	True☊	☿	♀	♂	⚳	♃	♄	♅	♆	♇
1 Tu	18 41 40	10♑21 08	13♓08 44	20♓09 04	29♋45.1	29♑19.5	25♏39.2	24♌32.4	16♍54.4	9♓05.7	9♒59.3	5♍05.7	15♏05.1	12♍04.8
2 W	18 45 37	11 22 18	27 11 03	4♈14 28	29R46.0	0♒32.4	26 27.3	24R27.0	17 00.4	9 16.5	10 05.9	5R04.5	15 06.6	12R04.2
3 Th	18 49 34	12 23 27	11♈19 07	18 24 47	29 46.0	1 41.1	27 16.2	24 20.8	17 06.0	9 27.3	10 12.5	5 03.3	15 08.0	12 03.6
4 F	18 53 30	13 24 36	25 31 11	2♉38 01	29 45.2	2 44.7	28 06.0	24 13.7	17 11.2	9 38.3	10 19.2	5 02.0	15 09.4	12 03.0
5 Sa	18 57 27	14 25 45	9♉44 58	16 51 40	29 43.7	3 42.7	28 56.6	24 05.9	17 16.0	9 49.4	10 25.8	5 00.6	15 10.8	12 02.4
6 Su	19 01 23	15 26 54	23 57 40	1♊02 34	29 41.8	4 34.1	29 47.9	23 57.2	17 20.4	10 00.6	10 32.6	4 59.3	15 12.1	12 01.7
7 M	19 05 20	16 28 02	8♊05 54	15 07 11	29 39.9	5 18.1	0♐40.0	23 47.7	17 24.3	10 11.9	10 39.3	4 57.8	15 13.4	12 01.0
8 Tu	19 09 16	17 29 10	22 05 58	29 01 48	29 38.3	5 53.7	1 32.8	23 37.5	17 27.9	10 23.2	10 46.1	4 56.4	15 14.7	12 00.2
9 W	19 13 13	18 30 18	5♋54 16	12♋43 00	29 37.3	6 20.2	2 26.3	23 26.4	17 31.1	10 34.7	10 52.9	4 54.9	15 15.9	11 59.5
10 Th	19 17 10	19 31 25	19 27 41	26 08 05	29D36.9	6R36.5	3 20.5	23 14.5	17 33.8	10 46.3	10 59.8	4 53.3	15 17.2	11 58.7
11 F	19 21 06	20 32 33	2♌44 01	9♌15 24	29 37.0	6 42.1	4 15.3	23 01.9	17 36.2	10 58.0	11 06.6	4 51.7	15 18.4	11 57.8
12 Sa	19 25 03	21 33 39	15 42 13	22 04 33	29 37.5	6 36.2	5 10.8	22 48.5	17 38.1	11 09.7	11 13.5	4 50.0	15 19.5	11 57.0
13 Su	19 28 59	22 34 46	28 22 33	4♍36 27	29 38.2	6 18.5	6 06.8	22 34.3	17 39.5	11 21.6	11 20.4	4 48.3	15 20.7	11 56.1
14 M	19 32 56	23 35 53	10♍46 32	16 53 10	29 39.0	5 49.1	7 03.4	22 19.3	17 40.6	11 33.5	11 27.4	4 46.6	15 21.8	11 55.2
15 Tu	19 36 52	24 36 59	22 56 46	28 57 47	29 39.6	5 08.3	8 00.5	22 03.6	17R41.2	11 45.6	11 34.4	4 44.8	15 22.8	11 54.3
16 W	19 40 49	25 38 05	4♎56 44	10♎54 10	29 40.0	4 16.9	8 58.2	21 47.2	17 41.3	11 57.7	11 41.3	4 43.0	15 23.9	11 53.3
17 Th	19 44 45	26 39 11	16 50 37	22 46 42	29R40.1	3 16.2	9 56.4	21 30.1	17 41.0	12 09.9	11 48.4	4 41.1	15 24.9	11 52.3
18 F	19 48 42	27 40 16	28 42 59	4♏40 05	29 40.1	2 08.0	10 55.1	21 12.3	17 40.3	12 22.2	11 55.4	4 39.2	15 25.9	11 51.3
19 Sa	19 52 38	28 41 22	10♏38 35	16 39 04	29D40.0	0 54.3	11 54.2	20 53.8	17 39.2	12 34.6	12 02.4	4 37.3	15 26.8	11 50.3
20 Su	19 56 35	29 42 27	22 42 05	28 48 10	29 40.0	29♑37.4	12 53.8	20 34.7	17 37.6	12 47.0	12 09.5	4 35.3	15 27.7	11 49.3
21 M	20 00 32	0♒43 31	4♐57 49	11♐11 27	29 40.1	28 19.7	13 53.9	20 15.0	17 35.5	12 59.6	12 16.6	4 33.3	15 28.6	11 48.2
22 Tu	20 04 28	1 44 36	17 29 28	23 52 10	29 40.3	27 03.6	14 54.3	19 54.7	17 33.0	13 12.2	12 23.7	4 31.3	15 29.5	11 47.1
23 W	20 08 25	2 45 39	0♑19 46	6♑52 27	29 40.5	25 51.1	15 55.2	19 33.9	17 30.1	13 24.9	12 30.8	4 29.2	15 30.3	11 46.0
24 Th	20 12 21	3 46 42	13 30 14	20 13 06	29R40.8	24 44.2	16 56.4	19 12.6	17 26.7	13 37.6	12 38.0	4 27.1	15 31.1	11 44.8
25 F	20 16 18	4 47 45	27 00 53	3♒53 20	29 40.8	23 44.2	17 58.1	18 50.9	17 22.9	13 50.5	12 45.1	4 24.9	15 31.8	11 43.7
26 Sa	20 20 14	5 48 46	10♒50 08	17 50 50	29 40.6	22 52.0	19 00.0	18 28.6	17 18.6	14 03.4	12 52.2	4 22.7	15 32.6	11 42.5
27 Su	20 24 11	6 49 47	24 54 56	2♓01 53	29 40.0	22 08.5	20 02.3	18 06.1	17 13.9	14 16.4	12 59.4	4 20.5	15 33.3	11 41.3
28 M	20 28 08	7 50 46	9♓11 05	16 21 53	29 39.0	21 33.8	21 05.0	17 43.1	17 08.8	14 29.4	13 06.6	4 18.3	15 33.9	11 40.1
29 Tu	20 32 04	8 51 45	23 33 41	0♈45 52	29 38.0	21 08.1	22 07.9	17 19.9	17 03.2	14 42.5	13 13.8	4 16.0	15 34.5	11 38.8
30 W	20 36 01	9 52 42	7♈57 51	15 09 06	29 36.9	20 51.0	23 11.2	16 56.4	16 57.2	14 55.7	13 20.9	4 13.7	15 35.1	11 37.5
31 Th	20 39 57	10 53 38	22 19 09	29 27 35	29D36.2	20D42.4	24 14.8	16 32.8	16 50.8	15 08.9	13 28.1	4 11.3	15 35.7	11 36.3

LONGITUDE — February 1963

Day	Sid.Time	☉	0 hr ☽	Noon☽	True☊	☿	♀	♂	⚳	♃	♄	♅	♆	♇
1 F	20 43 54	11♒54 32	6♉34 04	13♉38 18	29♋36.0	20♑41.8	25♐18.6	16♌08.9	16♍44.0	15♓22.2	13♒35.3	4♍09.0	15♏36.2	11♍35.0
2 Sa	20 47 50	12 55 26	20 40 05	27 39 14	29 36.4	20 48.6	26 22.7	15R45.0	16R36.7	15 35.6	13 42.5	4R06.6	15 36.7	11R33.6
3 Su	20 51 47	13 56 18	4♊35 37	11♊29 08	29 37.3	21 02.4	27 27.1	15 21.0	16 29.1	15 49.0	13 49.7	4 04.2	15 37.1	11 32.3
4 M	20 55 43	14 57 08	18 19 43	25 07 20	29 38.6	21 22.6	28 31.8	14 57.0	16 21.1	16 02.4	13 56.9	4 01.8	15 37.5	11 31.0
5 Tu	20 59 40	15 57 57	1♋51 55	8♋33 27	29 39.8	21 48.8	29 36.7	14 33.0	16 12.7	16 15.9	14 04.1	3 59.3	15 37.9	11 29.6
6 W	21 03 37	16 58 45	15 11 53	21 47 12	29R40.6	22 20.4	0♑41.9	14 09.1	16 03.9	16 29.5	14 11.3	3 56.9	15 38.3	11 28.2
7 Th	21 07 33	17 59 32	28 19 22	4♌48 21	29 40.7	22 56.9	1 47.3	13 45.3	15 54.7	16 43.1	14 18.4	3 54.4	15 38.6	11 26.8
8 F	21 11 30	19 00 17	11♌14 10	17 36 47	29 39.8	23 38.0	2 52.9	13 21.6	15 45.2	16 56.8	14 25.6	3 51.9	15 38.9	11 25.4
9 Sa	21 15 26	20 01 01	23 56 14	0♍12 33	29 37.8	24 23.3	3 58.7	12 58.2	15 35.4	17 10.5	14 32.8	3 49.4	15 39.1	11 24.0
10 Su	21 19 23	21 01 43	6♍25 50	12 36 10	29 34.8	25 12.4	5 04.8	12 35.0	15 25.1	17 24.3	14 39.9	3 46.8	15 39.3	11 22.5
11 M	21 23 19	22 02 25	18 43 43	24 48 40	29 31.1	26 05.0	6 11.1	12 12.1	15 14.6	17 38.1	14 47.1	3 44.3	15 39.5	11 21.1
12 Tu	21 27 16	23 03 05	0♎51 15	6♎51 46	29 27.0	27 00.9	7 17.6	11 49.6	15 03.7	17 52.0	14 54.3	3 41.7	15 39.7	11 19.6
13 W	21 31 12	24 03 44	12 50 32	18 47 56	29 23.2	27 59.6	8 24.3	11 27.4	14 52.6	18 05.8	15 01.4	3 39.1	15 39.8	11 18.1
14 Th	21 35 09	25 04 21	24 44 24	0♏40 23	29 20.0	29 01.1	9 31.1	11 05.6	14 41.1	18 19.8	15 08.5	3 36.6	15 39.8	11 16.7
15 F	21 39 05	26 04 58	6♏36 23	12 32 58	29 17.8	0♒05.0	10 38.2	10 44.2	14 29.4	18 33.8	15 15.6	3 34.0	15R39.9	11 15.2
16 Sa	21 43 02	27 05 33	18 30 40	24 30 04	29D16.9	1 11.3	11 45.4	10 23.4	14 17.3	18 47.8	15 22.7	3 31.3	15 39.9	11 13.7
17 Su	21 46 59	28 06 07	0♐31 48	6♐36 26	29 17.2	2 19.8	12 52.9	10 03.0	14 05.1	19 01.8	15 29.8	3 28.7	15 39.9	11 12.2
18 M	21 50 55	29 06 40	12 44 37	18 56 53	29 18.4	3 30.3	14 00.4	9 43.2	13 52.6	19 15.9	15 36.9	3 26.1	15 39.8	11 10.6
19 Tu	21 54 52	0♓07 12	25 13 50	1♑35 58	29 20.1	4 42.6	15 08.2	9 24.0	13 39.8	19 30.1	15 44.0	3 23.5	15 39.7	11 09.1
20 W	21 58 48	1 07 43	8♑03 43	14 37 29	29 21.7	5 56.7	16 16.1	9 05.4	13 26.9	19 44.2	15 51.0	3 20.9	15 39.6	11 07.6
21 Th	22 02 45	2 08 12	21 17 31	28 04 00	29R22.5	7 12.5	17 24.1	8 47.4	13 13.8	19 58.4	15 58.0	3 18.2	15 39.4	11 06.0
22 F	22 06 41	3 08 39	4♒56 56	11♒56 11	29 21.8	8 29.9	18 32.3	8 30.0	13 00.5	20 12.6	16 05.0	3 15.6	15 39.2	11 04.5
23 Sa	22 10 38	4 09 05	19 01 28	26 12 18	29 19.5	9 48.8	19 40.6	8 13.4	12 47.0	20 26.9	16 12.0	3 13.0	15 39.0	11 02.9
24 Su	22 14 34	5 09 30	3♓28 04	10♓47 59	29 15.5	11 09.1	20 49.1	7 57.4	12 33.4	20 41.2	16 18.9	3 10.3	15 38.8	11 01.4
25 M	22 18 31	6 09 52	18 11 09	25 36 32	29 10.2	12 30.8	21 57.7	7 42.2	12 19.7	20 55.5	16 25.9	3 07.7	15 38.5	10 59.8
26 Tu	22 22 28	7 10 13	3♈03 04	10♈29 41	29 04.2	13 53.9	23 06.4	7 27.7	12 05.9	21 09.8	16 32.8	3 05.1	15 38.1	10 58.3
27 W	22 26 24	8 10 32	17 55 20	25 19 02	28 58.6	15 18.2	24 15.2	7 14.0	11 52.1	21 24.2	16 39.6	3 02.4	15 37.8	10 56.7
28 Th	22 30 21	9 10 49	2♉39 55	9♉57 15	28 54.0	16 43.7	25 24.1	7 01.0	11 38.1	21 38.5	16 46.5	2 59.8	15 37.4	10 55.1

Astro Data

	Dy Hr Mn
☽0N	3 0:33
☿R	11 11:47
♃⚺♄	13 6:25
♃☍♇	16 4:00
⚳R	16 8:57
☽0S	16 13:38
♄⚻♇	17 23:56
☽0N	30 6:13
☿D	1 1:57
♃△♆	2 14:04
☽0S	12 21:29
♆R	16 6:05
♄□♆	18 21:48
☽0N	26 13:34

Planet Ingress

	Dy Hr Mn
☿ ♒	2 1:10
♀ ♐	6 17:35
☿ ♑R	20 4:59
☉ ♒	20 18:54
♀ ♑	5 20:36
☿ ♒	15 10:08
☉ ♓	19 9:09

Last Aspect / ☽ Ingress

Last Aspect Dy Hr Mn		☽ Ingress Dy Hr Mn
1 21:57	♀ △	♈ 2 4:48
3 21:56	♂ △	♉ 4 7:34
6 9:45	♀ ☍	♊ 6 10:14
8 2:45	♂ ⚹	♋ 8 13:41
9 23:08	☉ ☍	♌ 10 19:01
12 13:22	♂ ☌	♍ 13 3:07
15 2:31	☉ △	♎ 15 14:05
17 20:34	☉ □	♏ 18 2:35
20 13:56	☉ ⚹	♐ 20 14:20
22 4:46	♂ △	♑ 22 23:23
24 19:25	☿ ☌	♒ 25 5:14
26 14:07	♀ ⚹	♓ 27 8:35
28 20:29	♀ □	♈ 29 10:44
31 2:32	♀ △	♉ 31 12:55

Last Aspect / ☽ Ingress

Last Aspect Dy Hr Mn		☽ Ingress Dy Hr Mn
2 0:07	☿ △	♊ 2 16:03
4 18:35	♀ ☍	♋ 4 20:40
6 13:03	☿ ☍	♌ 7 3:06
8 14:52	☉ ☍	♍ 9 11:36
11 14:44	☿ △	♎ 11 22:18
14 8:20	☿ □	♏ 14 10:38
16 17:38	☉ □	♐ 16 22:57
19 8:59	☉ ⚹	♑ 19 9:00
20 21:23	♃ ⚹	♒ 21 15:23
22 19:06	♄ ☌	♓ 23 18:17
25 5:37	♀ ⚹	♈ 25 19:05
27 10:07	♀ □	♉ 27 19:38

☽ Phases & Eclipses

Dy Hr Mn	
3 1:02	☽ 11♈55
9 23:08	○ 18♋59
9 23:19	◐ A 1.018
17 20:34	☾ 27♎01
25 13:42	● 4♒52
25 13:36:36	◐ A 00'25"
1 8:50	☽ 11♉46
8 14:52	○ 19♌08
16 17:38	☾ 27♏20
24 2:06	● 4♓45

Astro Data

1 January 1963
Julian Day # 23011
SVP 5♓46'50"
GC 26♐19.4 ⚴ 15♋11.1R
Eris 9♈40.2 ⚵ 26♍17.3
⚷ 7♓07.9 ⚶ 27♍41.5
☽ Mean ☊ 0♌39.4

1 February 1963
Julian Day # 23042
SVP 5♓46'45"
GC 26♐19.4 ⚴ 6♋55.2R
Eris 9♈47.0 ⚵ 26♍28.0R
⚷ 8♓42.9 ⚶ 0♎43.6R
☽ Mean ☊ 29♋01.0

March 1963

LONGITUDE

Day	Sid.Time	☉	0 hr ☽	Noon ☽	True ☊	☿	♀	♂	⚳	♃	♄	♅	♆	♇
1 F	22 34 17	10♓11 04	17♉10 27	24♉19 05	28♋51.0	18♒10.5	26♑33.1	6♌48.8	11♍24.2	21♓52.9	16♒53.3	2♍57.2	15♏36.9	10♍53.5
2 Sa	22 38 14	11 11 17	1♊22 54	8♊21 44	28D49.9	19 38.4	27 42.3	6R37.4	11R10.2	22 07.3	17 00.1	2R54.6	15R36.5	10R52.0
3 Su	22 42 10	12 11 28	15 15 35	22 04 33	28 50.2	21 07.6	28 51.5	6 26.8	10 56.2	22 21.8	17 06.9	2 52.0	15 36.0	10 50.4
4 M	22 46 07	13 11 37	28 48 47	5♋28 31	28 51.5	22 37.9	0♒00.9	6 17.0	10 42.2	22 36.2	17 13.6	2 49.4	15 35.5	10 48.8
5 Tu	22 50 03	14 11 43	12♋04 00	18 35 33	28R52.8	24 09.3	1 10.4	6 07.9	10 28.3	22 50.7	17 20.3	2 46.9	15 34.9	10 47.3
6 W	22 54 00	15 11 48	25 03 25	1♌27 54	28 53.2	25 41.9	2 19.9	5 59.7	10 14.4	23 05.1	17 27.0	2 44.3	15 34.3	10 45.7
7 Th	22 57 57	16 11 50	7♌49 15	14 07 43	28 51.9	27 15.6	3 29.5	5 52.3	10 00.6	23 19.6	17 33.6	2 41.7	15 33.7	10 44.2
8 F	23 01 53	17 11 51	20 23 32	26 36 51	28 48.4	28 50.4	4 39.3	5 45.6	9 46.9	23 34.1	17 40.2	2 39.2	15 33.1	10 42.6
9 Sa	23 05 50	18 11 49	2♍47 53	8♍56 45	28 42.5	0♓26.4	5 49.1	5 39.7	9 33.3	23 48.6	17 46.7	2 36.7	15 32.4	10 41.0
10 Su	23 09 46	19 11 45	15 03 35	21 08 32	28 34.5	2 03.5	6 59.0	5 34.6	9 19.8	24 03.1	17 53.2	2 34.2	15 31.7	10 39.5
11 M	23 13 43	20 11 40	27 11 41	3♎13 13	28 24.8	3 41.7	8 09.0	5 30.3	9 06.5	24 17.6	17 59.7	2 31.7	15 31.0	10 37.9
12 Tu	23 17 39	21 11 32	9♎13 14	15 11 56	28 14.3	5 21.1	9 19.1	5 26.8	8 53.3	24 32.2	18 06.1	2 29.3	15 30.2	10 36.4
13 W	23 21 36	22 11 23	21 09 31	27 06 13	28 04.0	7 01.7	10 29.3	5 24.0	8 40.4	24 46.7	18 12.5	2 26.8	15 29.4	10 34.9
14 Th	23 25 32	23 11 12	3♏02 18	8♏58 05	27 54.8	8 43.4	11 39.6	5 22.0	8 27.6	25 01.2	18 18.9	2 24.4	15 28.6	10 33.3
15 F	23 29 29	24 10 59	14 53 56	20 50 16	27 47.4	10 26.3	12 49.9	5 20.7	8 15.0	25 15.8	18 25.2	2 22.0	15 27.8	10 31.8
16 Sa	23 33 26	25 10 45	26 47 32	2♐46 14	27 42.3	12 10.4	14 00.3	5D20.2	8 02.6	25 30.3	18 31.5	2 19.6	15 26.9	10 30.3
17 Su	23 37 22	26 10 29	8♐46 54	14 50 07	27 39.5	13 55.8	15 10.8	5 20.4	7 50.5	25 44.8	18 37.7	2 17.3	15 26.0	10 28.8
18 M	23 41 19	27 10 11	20 56 28	27 06 35	27D38.8	15 42.3	16 21.4	5 21.3	7 38.6	25 59.4	18 43.9	2 15.0	15 25.0	10 27.3
19 Tu	23 45 15	28 09 51	3♑21 05	9♑40 35	27 39.2	17 30.1	17 32.0	5 22.9	7 27.0	26 13.9	18 50.0	2 12.7	15 24.1	10 25.8
20 W	23 49 12	29 09 30	16 05 41	22 36 54	27R39.9	19 19.1	18 42.7	5 25.3	7 15.7	26 28.5	18 56.1	2 10.4	15 23.1	10 24.3
21 Th	23 53 08	0♈09 07	29 14 44	5♒59 33	27 39.7	21 09.4	19 53.4	5 28.3	7 04.7	26 43.0	19 02.1	2 08.2	15 22.1	10 22.9
22 F	23 57 05	1 08 42	12♒51 36	19 50 59	27 37.6	23 00.9	21 04.2	5 32.1	6 54.0	26 57.5	19 08.1	2 06.0	15 21.1	10 21.4
23 Sa	0 01 01	2 08 16	26 57 37	4♓11 12	27 33.2	24 53.7	22 15.1	5 36.5	6 43.6	27 12.0	19 14.0	2 03.8	15 20.0	10 20.0
24 Su	0 04 58	3 07 47	11♓31 14	18 56 59	27 26.1	26 47.8	23 26.1	5 41.6	6 33.5	27 26.5	19 19.9	2 01.6	15 18.9	10 18.5
25 M	0 08 55	4 07 16	26 27 28	4♈01 34	27 17.0	28 43.1	24 37.0	5 47.3	6 23.8	27 41.0	19 25.7	1 59.5	15 17.8	10 17.1
26 Tu	0 12 51	5 06 44	11♈38 00	19 15 21	27 06.8	0♈39.6	25 48.1	5 53.7	6 14.4	27 55.5	19 31.5	1 57.4	15 16.7	10 15.7
27 W	0 16 48	6 06 09	26 52 14	4♉27 17	26 56.8	2 37.3	26 59.1	6 00.8	6 05.4	28 10.0	19 37.2	1 55.4	15 15.5	10 14.3
28 Th	0 20 44	7 05 32	11♉59 13	19 26 56	26 48.1	4 36.2	28 10.3	6 08.4	5 56.8	28 24.5	19 42.8	1 53.3	15 14.3	10 13.0
29 F	0 24 41	8 04 53	26 49 31	4♊06 17	26 41.7	6 36.1	29 21.4	6 16.7	5 48.6	28 38.9	19 48.4	1 51.4	15 13.1	10 11.6
30 Sa	0 28 37	9 04 12	11♊16 44	18 20 36	26 37.9	8 37.1	0♓32.7	6 25.6	5 40.7	28 53.3	19 53.9	1 49.4	15 11.9	10 10.3
31 Su	0 32 34	10 03 28	25 17 50	2♋08 30	26D36.3	10 39.0	1 43.9	6 35.1	5 33.3	29 07.7	19 59.4	1 47.5	15 10.7	10 08.9

April 1963

LONGITUDE

Day	Sid.Time	☉	0 hr ☽	Noon ☽	True ☊	☿	♀	♂	⚳	♃	♄	♅	♆	♇
1 M	0 36 30	11♈02 42	8♋52 51	15♋31 12	26♋36.2	12♈41.7	2♓55.2	6♌45.2	5♍26.2	29♓22.1	20♒04.8	1♍45.7	15♏09.4	10♍07.6
2 Tu	0 40 27	12 01 53	22 03 58	28 31 37	26R36.3	14 45.1	4 06.6	6 55.8	5R19.6	29 36.5	20 10.2	1R43.8	15R08.1	10R06.3
3 W	0 44 23	13 01 03	4♌54 36	11♌13 26	26 35.5	16 48.9	5 17.9	7 07.0	5 13.3	29 50.9	20 15.5	1 42.1	15 06.8	10 05.1
4 Th	0 48 20	14 00 09	17 28 34	23 40 29	26 32.8	18 53.1	6 29.4	7 18.7	5 07.5	0♈05.2	20 20.7	1 40.3	15 05.5	10 03.8
5 F	0 52 17	14 59 14	29 49 36	5♍56 18	26 27.3	20 57.3	7 40.8	7 30.9	5 02.1	0 19.5	20 25.8	1 38.6	15 04.1	10 02.6
6 Sa	0 56 13	15 58 16	12♍00 56	18 03 47	26 18.9	23 01.4	8 52.3	7 43.7	4 57.1	0 33.7	20 30.9	1 36.9	15 02.8	10 01.4
7 Su	1 00 10	16 57 16	24 05 09	0♎05 16	26 07.8	25 05.0	10 03.8	7 57.0	4 52.5	0 48.0	20 35.9	1 35.3	15 01.4	10 00.2
8 M	1 04 06	17 56 15	6♎04 18	12 02 28	25 54.6	27 07.8	11 15.4	8 10.7	4 48.4	1 02.2	20 40.9	1 33.7	15 00.0	9 59.0
9 Tu	1 08 03	18 55 11	17 59 55	23 56 48	25 40.4	29 09.4	12 27.0	8 25.0	4 44.7	1 16.4	20 45.8	1 32.2	14 58.6	9 57.8
10 W	1 11 59	19 54 05	29 53 17	5♏49 31	25 26.2	1♉09.7	13 38.7	8 39.7	4 41.4	1 30.6	20 50.6	1 30.7	14 57.1	9 56.7
11 Th	1 15 56	20 52 57	11♏45 42	17 42 02	25 13.3	3 08.1	14 50.3	8 54.9	4 38.5	1 44.7	20 55.3	1 29.3	14 55.7	9 55.6
12 F	1 19 52	21 51 47	23 38 47	29 36 11	25 02.6	5 04.3	16 02.1	9 10.5	4 36.1	1 58.8	21 00.0	1 27.9	14 54.2	9 54.5
13 Sa	1 23 49	22 50 35	5♐34 36	11♐34 23	24 54.6	6 58.1	17 13.8	9 26.6	4 34.0	2 12.9	21 04.6	1 26.5	14 52.8	9 53.4
14 Su	1 27 46	23 49 22	17 35 56	23 39 43	24 49.5	8 48.9	18 25.6	9 43.1	4 32.5	2 26.9	21 09.2	1 25.2	14 51.3	9 52.4
15 M	1 31 42	24 48 07	29 46 14	5♑56 02	24 47.0	10 36.6	19 37.4	10 00.1	4 31.3	2 40.9	21 13.6	1 23.9	14 49.8	9 51.3
16 Tu	1 35 39	25 46 50	12♑09 39	18 27 40	24 46.3	12 20.9	20 49.3	10 17.4	4 30.5	2 54.9	21 18.0	1 22.7	14 48.3	9 50.3
17 W	1 39 35	26 45 32	24 50 41	1♒19 16	24 46.2	14 01.3	22 01.1	10 35.2	4D30.2	3 08.8	21 22.3	1 21.6	14 46.8	9 49.4
18 Th	1 43 32	27 44 12	7♒53 57	14 35 13	24 45.6	15 37.8	23 13.0	10 53.3	4 30.3	3 22.7	21 26.6	1 20.5	14 45.2	9 48.4
19 F	1 47 28	28 42 50	21 23 26	28 18 53	24 43.4	17 10.1	24 25.0	11 11.9	4 30.9	3 36.5	21 30.7	1 19.4	14 43.7	9 47.5
20 Sa	1 51 25	29 41 26	5♓21 40	12♓31 43	24 38.7	18 38.0	25 37.0	11 30.9	4 31.8	3 50.3	21 34.8	1 18.4	14 42.1	9 46.6
21 Su	1 55 21	0♉40 01	19 48 45	27 12 16	24 31.4	20 01.3	26 48.9	11 50.2	4 33.2	4 04.1	21 38.8	1 17.4	14 40.5	9 45.7
22 M	1 59 18	1 38 34	4♈41 29	12♈15 25	24 21.8	21 20.0	28 01.0	12 09.9	4 34.9	4 17.8	21 42.7	1 16.5	14 39.0	9 44.8
23 Tu	2 03 15	2 37 05	19 52 53	27 32 31	24 11.0	22 33.8	29 13.0	12 29.9	4 37.1	4 31.5	21 46.6	1 15.6	14 37.4	9 44.0
24 W	2 07 11	3 35 35	5♉12 52	12♉52 26	24 00.1	23 42.6	0♈25.1	12 50.3	4 39.7	4 45.1	21 50.3	1 14.8	14 35.8	9 43.2
25 Th	2 11 08	4 34 02	20 29 46	28 03 31	23 50.6	24 46.4	1 37.1	13 11.1	4 42.7	4 58.7	21 54.0	1 14.0	14 34.2	9 42.4
26 F	2 15 04	5 32 28	5♊32 31	12♊55 48	23 43.3	25 45.0	2 49.2	13 32.2	4 46.1	5 12.2	21 57.6	1 13.3	14 32.6	9 41.7
27 Sa	2 19 01	6 30 51	20 12 37	27 22 29	23 38.7	26 38.5	4 01.3	13 53.7	4 49.9	5 25.7	22 01.1	1 12.7	14 31.0	9 41.0
28 Su	2 22 57	7 29 13	4♋25 06	11♋20 26	23D36.6	27 26.6	5 13.5	14 15.4	4 54.2	5 39.1	22 04.5	1 12.1	14 29.4	9 40.3
29 M	2 26 54	8 27 32	18 08 34	24 49 48	23 36.1	28 09.4	6 25.6	14 37.5	4 58.8	5 52.5	22 07.8	1 11.5	14 27.7	9 39.6
30 Tu	2 30 50	9 25 50	1♌24 30	7♌53 07	23R36.3	28 46.8	7 37.8	14 59.9	5 03.7	6 05.8	22 11.1	1 11.0	14 26.1	9 39.0

Astro Data	Dy Hr Mn
☽0S	12 4:13
♂D	16 17:21
☉0N	21 8:20
☽0N	25 23:26
☿0N	27 22:00
♃☌♆	4 12:28
☽0S	8 10:23
♃⚻♅	10 12:14
♃0N	14 16:03
⚳D	17 18:03
☽0N	22 10:34
♀0N	27 5:01

Planet Ingress		Dy Hr Mn
♀	♒	4 11:41
☿	♓	9 5:26
☉	♈	21 8:20
☿	♈	26 3:52
♀	♓	30 1:00
♃	♈	4 3:19
☿	♉	9 22:03
☉	♉	20 19:36
♀	♈	24 3:39

Last Aspect Dy Hr Mn			☽ Ingress	Dy Hr Mn
1 16:07	♀	△	♊	1 21:39
3 12:31	♃	□	♋	4 2:08
5 20:02	♃	△	♌	6 9:15
8 16:57	☿	☍	♍	8 18:34
10 17:53	♃	☍	♎	11 5:35
12 17:54	♄	△	♏	13 17:51
15 21:06	♃	△	♐	16 6:27
18 12:08	☉	□	♑	18 17:35
21 0:48	☉	⚹	♒	21 1:21
22 14:16	♀	☌	♓	23 5:04
25 2:22	☿	☌	♈	25 5:38
26 23:11	♀	⚹	♉	27 4:57
29 3:28	♀	□	♊	29 5:13
31 6:36	♃	□	♋	31 8:13

Last Aspect Dy Hr Mn			☽ Ingress	Dy Hr Mn
2 14:04	♃	△	♌	2 14:45
4 5:30	♄	☍	♍	5 0:20
6 6:01	♆	⚹	♎	7 11:49
9 5:32	♄	△	♏	10 0:14
11 18:33	♄	□	♐	12 12:48
14 12:21	☉	△	♑	15 0:27
17 2:52	☉	□	♒	17 9:34
19 12:44	☉	⚹	♓	19 14:53
21 11:19	♀	☌	♈	21 16:30
23 2:56	♄	⚹	♉	23 15:51
25 6:24	☿	☌	♊	25 15:06
27 2:58	♄	△	♋	27 16:27
29 18:22	☿	⚹	♌	29 21:25

☽ Phases & Eclipses Dy Hr Mn		
2 17:17	☽	11♊25
10 7:49	○	19♍01
18 12:08	☾	27♐10
25 12:10	●	4♈08
1 3:15	☽	10♋41
9 0:57	○	18♎28
17 2:52	☾	26♑23
23 20:29	●	2♉58
30 15:08	☽	9♌33

Astro Data

1 March 1963
Julian Day # 23070
SVP 5♓46'42"
GC 26♐19.5 ⚴ 7♋43.5
Eris 10♈01.0 ⚵ 21♍12.7R
⚷ 10♓27.7 ⚶ 27♍15.1R
☽ Mean ☊ 27♋32.0

1 April 1963
Julian Day # 23101
SVP 5♓46'39"
GC 26♐19.6 ⚴ 15♋58.6
Eris 10♈21.5 ⚵ 14♍04.9R
⚷ 12♓23.0 ⚶ 19♍37.6R
☽ Mean ☊ 25♋53.5

LONGITUDE — May 1963

Day	Sid.Time	☉	0 hr ☽	Noon ☽	True ☊	☿	♀	♂	⚳	♃	♄	♅	♆	♇
1 W	2 34 47	10♉24 05	14♌16 13	20♌34 19	23♋35.9	29♉18.7	8♈50.0	15♌22.6	5♍09.1	6♈19.0	22♒14.3	1♍10.6	14♏24.5	9♍38.3
2 Th	2 38 44	11 22 18	26 48 00	2♍57 52	23R33.9	29 45.2	10 02.2	15 45.6	5 14.8	6 32.2	22 17.3	1R10.2	14R22.9	9R37.8
3 F	2 42 40	12 20 29	9♍04 26	15 08 15	23 29.5	0♊06.2	11 14.4	16 08.9	5 20.9	6 45.3	22 20.3	1 09.8	14 21.2	9 37.2
4 Sa	2 46 37	13 18 38	21 09 48	27 09 33	23 22.5	0 21.7	12 26.6	16 32.5	5 27.4	6 58.4	22 23.2	1 09.5	14 19.6	9 36.7
5 Su	2 50 33	14 16 45	3♎07 54	9♎05 14	23 13.1	0 31.9	13 38.9	16 56.3	5 34.3	7 11.4	22 26.0	1 09.3	14 18.0	9 36.2
6 M	2 54 30	15 14 51	15 01 52	20 58 06	23 01.7	0R36.8	14 51.1	17 20.4	5 41.4	7 24.4	22 28.7	1 09.1	14 16.3	9 35.7
7 Tu	2 58 26	16 12 54	26 54 10	2♏50 19	22 49.3	0 36.4	16 03.4	17 44.8	5 49.0	7 37.3	22 31.4	1 09.0	14 14.7	9 35.3
8 W	3 02 23	17 10 56	8♏46 43	14 43 35	22 37.0	0 31.1	17 15.7	18 09.4	5 56.9	7 50.1	22 33.9	1D08.9	14 13.1	9 34.9
9 Th	3 06 19	18 08 56	20 41 05	26 39 22	22 25.7	0 21.0	18 28.0	18 34.3	6 05.1	8 02.8	22 36.4	1 08.9	14 11.4	9 34.5
10 F	3 10 16	19 06 55	2♐38 38	8♐39 04	22 16.4	0 06.3	19 40.3	18 59.4	6 13.7	8 15.5	22 38.7	1 08.9	14 09.8	9 34.1
11 Sa	3 14 13	20 04 52	14 40 54	20 44 21	22 09.6	29♉47.5	20 52.7	19 24.8	6 22.6	8 28.1	22 41.0	1 09.0	14 08.2	9 33.8
12 Su	3 18 09	21 02 48	26 49 42	2♑57 16	22 05.4	29 24.8	22 05.1	19 50.4	6 31.8	8 40.7	22 43.2	1 09.1	14 06.6	9 33.5
13 M	3 22 06	22 00 43	9♑07 24	15 20 27	22D03.5	28 58.7	23 17.5	20 16.3	6 41.4	8 53.2	22 45.2	1 09.3	14 04.9	9 33.3
14 Tu	3 26 02	22 58 36	21 36 51	27 57 01	22 03.4	28 29.7	24 29.9	20 42.4	6 51.2	9 05.6	22 47.2	1 09.6	14 03.3	9 33.0
15 W	3 29 59	23 56 28	4♒21 25	10♒50 30	22 04.2	27 58.3	25 42.3	21 08.7	7 01.4	9 17.9	22 49.1	1 09.9	14 01.7	9 32.8
16 Th	3 33 55	24 54 18	17 24 42	24 04 26	22R04.7	27 25.2	26 54.7	21 35.2	7 11.9	9 30.2	22 50.9	1 10.2	14 00.1	9 32.6
17 F	3 37 52	25 52 08	0♓50 03	7♓41 49	22 04.1	26 50.8	28 07.2	22 01.9	7 22.7	9 42.3	22 52.6	1 10.6	13 58.5	9 32.5
18 Sa	3 41 48	26 49 56	14 39 56	21 44 25	22 01.6	26 15.8	29 19.7	22 28.9	7 33.8	9 54.4	22 54.2	1 11.1	13 56.9	9 32.4
19 Su	3 45 45	27 47 43	28 55 08	6♈11 47	21 57.0	25 40.8	0♉32.2	22 56.1	7 45.1	10 06.5	22 55.7	1 11.6	13 55.4	9 32.3
20 M	3 49 42	28 45 29	13♈33 51	21 00 38	21 50.6	25 06.4	1 44.7	23 23.5	7 56.8	10 18.4	22 57.2	1 12.2	13 53.8	9 32.3
21 Tu	3 53 38	29 43 14	28 31 14	6♉04 35	21 43.0	24 33.3	2 57.2	23 51.1	8 08.8	10 30.3	22 58.5	1 12.8	13 52.2	9D32.2
22 W	3 57 35	0♊40 58	13♉39 28	21 14 36	21 35.3	24 01.9	4 09.7	24 18.8	8 21.0	10 42.0	22 59.7	1 13.4	13 50.7	9 32.3
23 Th	4 01 31	1 38 40	28 48 40	6♊20 24	21 28.5	23 32.8	5 22.3	24 46.8	8 33.5	10 53.7	23 00.8	1 14.2	13 49.1	9 32.3
24 F	4 05 28	2 36 22	13♊48 36	21 12 13	21 23.4	23 06.4	6 34.9	25 15.0	8 46.4	11 05.3	23 01.8	1 15.0	13 47.6	9 32.4
25 Sa	4 09 24	3 34 02	28 30 22	5♋42 23	21 20.3	22 43.1	7 47.4	25 43.4	8 59.4	11 16.8	23 02.8	1 15.8	13 46.1	9 32.5
26 Su	4 13 21	4 31 40	12♋47 46	19 46 15	21D19.3	22 23.3	9 00.0	26 12.0	9 12.8	11 28.2	23 03.6	1 16.7	13 44.6	9 32.6
27 M	4 17 17	5 29 17	26 37 44	3♌22 18	21 19.8	22 07.3	10 12.6	26 40.8	9 26.4	11 39.5	23 04.3	1 17.6	13 43.1	9 32.8
28 Tu	4 21 14	6 26 53	10♌00 10	16 31 39	21 21.0	21 55.3	11 25.2	27 09.7	9 40.2	11 50.8	23 04.9	1 18.6	13 41.6	9 33.0
29 W	4 25 11	7 24 27	22 57 12	29 17 17	21R22.1	21 47.5	12 37.8	27 38.8	9 54.3	12 01.9	23 05.5	1 19.7	13 40.1	9 33.2
30 Th	4 29 07	8 21 59	5♍32 28	11♍43 18	21 22.4	21D44.0	13 50.5	28 08.1	10 08.7	12 12.9	23 05.9	1 20.8	13 38.7	9 33.5
31 F	4 33 04	9 19 31	17 50 22	23 54 15	21 21.1	21 45.0	15 03.1	28 37.5	10 23.3	12 23.8	23 06.2	1 21.9	13 37.2	9 33.7

LONGITUDE — June 1963

Day	Sid.Time	☉	0 hr ☽	Noon ☽	True ☊	☿	♀	♂	⚳	♃	♄	♅	♆	♇
1 Sa	4 37 00	10♊17 01	29♍55 32	5♎54 45	21♋18.2	21♉50.4	16♉15.8	29♌07.2	10♍38.1	12♈34.7	23♒06.5	1♍23.1	13♏35.8	9♍34.1
2 Su	4 40 57	11 14 29	11♎52 26	17 49 04	21R13.5	22 00.3	17 28.4	29 36.9	10 53.1	12 45.4	23R06.6	1 24.3	13R34.4	9 34.4
3 M	4 44 53	12 11 57	23 45 06	29 40 58	21 07.6	22 14.7	18 41.1	0♍06.9	11 08.4	12 56.0	23 06.6	1 25.6	13 33.0	9 34.8
4 Tu	4 48 50	13 09 23	5♏37 02	11♏33 39	21 00.8	22 33.6	19 53.8	0 37.0	11 23.9	13 06.6	23 06.6	1 27.0	13 31.6	9 35.2
5 W	4 52 46	14 06 48	17 31 07	23 29 43	20 54.1	22 56.8	21 06.5	1 07.2	11 39.7	13 17.0	23 06.4	1 28.4	13 30.3	9 35.6
6 Th	4 56 43	15 04 12	29 29 40	5♐31 11	20 47.9	23 24.4	22 19.2	1 37.6	11 55.6	13 27.3	23 06.2	1 29.8	13 28.9	9 36.1
7 F	5 00 40	16 01 36	11♐34 28	17 39 41	20 43.0	23 56.2	23 32.0	2 08.2	12 11.8	13 37.5	23 05.8	1 31.3	13 27.6	9 36.6
8 Sa	5 04 36	16 58 58	23 47 01	29 56 36	20 39.6	24 32.2	24 44.7	2 38.9	12 28.1	13 47.6	23 05.4	1 32.9	13 26.3	9 37.1
9 Su	5 08 33	17 56 20	6♑08 37	12♑23 14	20D37.8	25 12.2	25 57.5	3 09.7	12 44.7	13 57.6	23 04.8	1 34.5	13 25.0	9 37.7
10 M	5 12 29	18 53 41	18 40 38	25 01 00	20 37.6	25 56.3	27 10.3	3 40.7	13 01.5	14 07.4	23 04.2	1 36.1	13 23.8	9 38.3
11 Tu	5 16 26	19 51 01	1♒24 32	7♒51 27	20 38.5	26 44.2	28 23.1	4 11.8	13 18.4	14 17.2	23 03.5	1 37.8	13 22.5	9 38.9
12 W	5 20 22	20 48 21	14 21 59	20 56 21	20 40.0	27 36.0	29 35.9	4 43.1	13 35.6	14 26.8	23 02.6	1 39.5	13 21.3	9 39.6
13 Th	5 24 19	21 45 41	27 34 47	4♓17 30	20 41.5	28 31.6	0♊48.7	5 14.5	13 52.9	14 36.3	23 01.7	1 41.3	13 20.1	9 40.2
14 F	5 28 15	22 42 59	11♓04 38	17 56 21	20R42.3	29 30.8	2 01.6	5 46.0	14 10.5	14 45.7	23 00.7	1 43.2	13 18.9	9 40.9
15 Sa	5 32 12	23 40 18	24 52 43	1♈53 41	20 42.2	0♊33.6	3 14.5	6 17.7	14 28.2	14 55.0	22 59.6	1 45.0	13 17.8	9 41.7
16 Su	5 36 09	24 37 36	8♈59 11	16 08 59	20 40.9	1 39.9	4 27.4	6 49.5	14 46.1	15 04.2	22 58.4	1 46.9	13 16.6	9 42.4
17 M	5 40 05	25 34 54	23 22 44	0♉39 58	20 38.6	2 49.7	5 40.3	7 21.5	15 04.2	15 13.2	22 57.0	1 48.9	13 15.5	9 43.2
18 Tu	5 44 02	26 32 11	8♉00 05	15 22 22	20 35.6	4 03.0	6 53.2	7 53.5	15 22.4	15 22.1	22 55.6	1 50.9	13 14.4	9 44.1
19 W	5 47 58	27 29 29	22 46 00	0♊10 05	20 32.5	5 19.6	8 06.2	8 25.8	15 40.9	15 30.9	22 54.2	1 53.0	13 13.3	9 44.9
20 Th	5 51 55	28 26 46	7♊33 41	14 55 50	20 29.7	6 39.6	9 19.1	8 58.1	15 59.5	15 39.5	22 52.6	1 55.1	13 12.3	9 45.8
21 F	5 55 51	29 24 03	22 15 35	29 32 06	20 27.7	8 02.9	10 32.1	9 30.6	16 18.2	15 48.0	22 50.9	1 57.2	13 11.3	9 46.7
22 Sa	5 59 48	0♋21 19	6♋44 33	13♋52 17	20D26.8	9 29.5	11 45.1	10 03.2	16 37.2	15 56.4	22 49.1	1 59.4	13 10.3	9 47.6
23 Su	6 03 44	1 18 35	20 54 46	27 51 34	20 26.8	10 59.3	12 58.1	10 35.9	16 56.3	16 04.6	22 47.3	2 01.7	13 09.3	9 48.6
24 M	6 07 41	2 15 50	4♌42 27	11♌27 17	20 27.6	12 32.3	14 11.2	11 08.7	17 15.5	16 12.7	22 45.3	2 03.9	13 08.4	9 49.6
25 Tu	6 11 38	3 13 04	18 06 05	24 38 59	20 28.8	14 08.5	15 24.2	11 41.7	17 35.0	16 20.7	22 43.3	2 06.3	13 07.5	9 50.6
26 W	6 15 34	4 10 19	1♍06 13	7♍28 07	20 30.2	15 47.8	16 37.3	12 14.7	17 54.5	16 28.5	22 41.2	2 08.6	13 06.6	9 51.6
27 Th	6 19 31	5 07 32	13 45 05	19 57 34	20 31.2	17 30.2	17 50.4	12 47.9	18 14.2	16 36.1	22 38.9	2 11.0	13 05.7	9 52.7
28 F	6 23 27	6 04 45	26 06 06	2♎11 11	20R31.7	19 15.6	19 03.5	13 21.2	18 34.1	16 43.7	22 36.6	2 13.5	13 04.9	9 53.8
29 Sa	6 27 24	7 01 57	8♎13 24	14 13 19	20 31.6	21 04.0	20 16.6	13 54.7	18 54.1	16 51.1	22 34.3	2 15.9	13 04.1	9 54.9
30 Su	6 31 20	7 59 09	20 11 29	26 08 30	20 30.9	22 55.2	21 29.7	14 28.2	19 14.2	16 58.3	22 31.8	2 18.5	13 03.3	9 56.1

Astro Data Dy Hr Mn	Planet Ingress Dy Hr Mn	Last Aspect Dy Hr Mn	☽ Ingress Dy Hr Mn	Last Aspect Dy Hr Mn	☽ Ingress Dy Hr Mn	☽ Phases & Eclipses Dy Hr Mn	Astro Data
☽0S 5 16:48	☿ ♊ 3 4:17	2 5:31 ☿ □	♍ 2 6:13	31 7:43 ☿ △	♎ 1 0:09	8 17:23 ○ 17♏24	1 May 1963
♃∠♄ 6 22:15	☿ ♉R 10 20:39	3 10:27 ♆ ⚹	♎ 4 17:42	2 22:42 ♄ △	♏ 3 12:39	16 13:36 ☾ 24♒58	Julian Day # 23131
☿R 6 22:30	♀ ♉ 19 1:21	6 15:04 ♄ △	♏ 7 6:16	5 11:13 ♄ □	♐ 6 1:01	23 4:00 ● 1♊19	SVP 5♓46'35"
♅D 9 10:16	☉ ♊ 21 18:58	9 3:50 ♄ □	♐ 9 18:42	7 22:39 ♄ ⚹	♑ 8 12:07	30 4:55 ☽ 8♍05	GC 26♐19.6 ⚵ 27♋32.9
♃⚻♇ 16 16:49		11 15:51 ♄ ⚹	♑ 12 6:13	10 16:29 ♀ △	♒ 10 21:22		Eris 10♈41.4 ⚴ 11♍34.1
☽0N 19 20:57	♂ ♍ 3 6:30	14 12:59 ☿ △	♒ 14 15:51	13 0:55 ☿ □	♓ 13 4:21	7 8:31 ○ 15♐53	⚷ 13♓53.3 ⚶ 16♍22.3
♇D 21 15:41	♀ ♊ 12 19:57	16 17:43 ☿ □	♓ 16 22:32	14 20:53 ☉ □	♈ 15 8:46	14 20:53 ☾ 23♓04	☽ Mean ☊ 24♋18.1
☿D 30 18:52	☿ ♊ 14 23:21	18 21:08 ☉ ⚹	♈ 19 1:48	17 3:03 ☉ ⚹	♉ 17 10:54	21 11:46 ● 29♊23	
	☉ ♋ 22 3:04	20 15:56 ♂ △	♉ 21 2:21	19 0:14 ♄ □	♊ 19 11:44	28 20:24 ☽ 6♎25	1 June 1963
☽0S 1 23:57		22 17:01 ♂ □	♊ 23 1:53	21 11:46 ☉ ☌	♋ 21 12:46		Julian Day # 23162
♄R 3 9:39		24 18:51 ♂ ⚹	♋ 25 2:29	22 15:33 ♃ □	♌ 23 15:44		SVP 5♓46'31"
♃⚻♆ 6 15:26		26 16:28 ☿ ⚹	♌ 27 5:58	25 8:27 ♄ ☍	♍ 25 21:56		GC 26♐19.7 ⚵ 11♌03.2
☽0N 16 5:08		29 8:45 ♂ ☌	♍ 29 13:22	27 7:26 ♀ □	♎ 28 7:41		Eris 10♈57.0 ⚴ 14♍27.0
☽0S 29 7:50				30 4:44 ♄ △	♏ 30 19:48		⚷ 14♓46.9 ⚶ 20♍15.5
							☽ Mean ☊ 22♋39.6

July 1963

LONGITUDE

Day	Sid.Time	☉	0 hr ☽	Noon ☽	True ☊	☿	♀	♂	⚳	♃	♄	♅	♆	♇
1 M	6 35 17	8♋56 21	2♏04 52	8♏01 09	20♋29.8	24♊49.1	22♊42.9	15♍01.8	19♍34.5	17♈05.4	22♒29.3	2♍21.0	13♏02.5	9♍57.3
2 Tu	6 39 13	9 53 32	13 57 49	19 55 23	20R 28.4	26 45.6	23 56.0	15 35.6	19 54.9	17 12.3	22R 26.6	2 23.6	13R 01.8	9 58.5
3 W	6 43 10	10 50 44	25 54 15	1♐54 49	20 27.0	28 44.6	25 09.2	16 09.4	20 15.5	17 19.1	22 23.9	2 26.2	13 01.1	9 59.7
4 Th	6 47 07	11 47 54	7♐57 29	14 02 32	20 25.8	0♋45.7	26 22.4	16 43.4	20 36.2	17 25.7	22 21.1	2 28.9	13 00.4	10 00.9
5 F	6 51 03	12 45 05	20 10 15	26 20 53	20 24.9	2 48.9	27 35.6	17 17.4	20 57.0	17 32.2	22 18.3	2 31.6	12 59.8	10 02.2
6 Sa	6 55 00	13 42 16	2♑34 37	8♑51 37	20D 24.4	4 53.8	28 48.9	17 51.6	21 17.9	17 38.5	22 15.4	2 34.4	12 59.2	10 03.5
7 Su	6 58 56	14 39 27	15 11 59	21 35 47	20 24.3	7 00.3	0♋02.1	18 25.8	21 38.9	17 44.7	22 12.4	2 37.1	12 58.6	10 04.8
8 M	7 02 53	15 36 38	28 03 06	4♒33 54	20 24.4	9 07.9	1 15.4	19 00.2	22 00.1	17 50.7	22 09.3	2 40.0	12 58.0	10 06.2
9 Tu	7 06 49	16 33 49	11♒08 13	17 45 59	20 24.7	11 16.5	2 28.7	19 34.7	22 21.4	17 56.5	22 06.1	2 42.8	12 57.5	10 07.6
10 W	7 10 46	17 31 00	24 27 09	1♓11 39	20 25.1	13 25.7	3 42.1	20 09.2	22 42.8	18 02.2	22 02.9	2 45.7	12 57.0	10 08.9
11 Th	7 14 43	18 28 11	7♓59 24	14 50 17	20 25.3	15 35.2	4 55.4	20 43.9	23 04.3	18 07.7	21 59.6	2 48.6	12 56.6	10 10.4
12 F	7 18 39	19 25 23	21 44 10	28 40 56	20 25.4	17 44.8	6 08.8	21 18.7	23 25.9	18 13.0	21 56.3	2 51.5	12 56.1	10 11.8
13 Sa	7 22 36	20 22 36	5♈40 25	12♈42 24	20 25.5	19 54.1	7 22.2	21 53.5	23 47.7	18 18.2	21 52.8	2 54.5	12 55.7	10 13.3
14 Su	7 26 32	21 19 49	19 46 41	26 53 01	20 25.5	22 03.0	8 35.6	22 28.5	24 09.5	18 23.2	21 49.3	2 57.5	12 55.4	10 14.7
15 M	7 30 29	22 17 03	4♉01 05	11♉10 34	20 25.5	24 11.1	9 49.1	23 03.5	24 31.5	18 28.0	21 45.8	3 00.6	12 55.0	10 16.2
16 Tu	7 34 25	23 14 17	18 21 06	25 32 14	20 25.7	26 18.4	11 02.5	23 38.7	24 53.5	18 32.7	21 42.2	3 03.6	12 54.7	10 17.8
17 W	7 38 22	24 11 32	2♊43 31	9♊54 28	20 26.0	28 24.5	12 16.0	24 13.9	25 15.7	18 37.2	21 38.5	3 06.7	12 54.4	10 19.3
18 Th	7 42 18	25 08 48	17 04 33	24 13 14	20 26.4	0♌29.5	13 29.6	24 49.3	25 38.0	18 41.5	21 34.8	3 09.9	12 54.2	10 20.9
19 F	7 46 15	26 06 05	1♋19 58	8♋24 13	20R 26.7	2 33.0	14 43.1	25 24.8	26 00.4	18 45.6	21 31.0	3 13.0	12 54.0	10 22.5
20 Sa	7 50 12	27 03 22	15 25 28	22 23 16	20 26.8	4 35.2	15 56.7	26 00.3	26 22.8	18 49.6	21 27.2	3 16.2	12 53.8	10 24.1
21 Su	7 54 08	28 00 39	29 17 10	6♌06 50	20 26.6	6 35.7	17 10.3	26 35.9	26 45.4	18 53.3	21 23.3	3 19.4	12 53.6	10 25.7
22 M	7 58 05	28 57 57	12♌51 59	19 32 25	20 26.0	8 34.7	18 23.9	27 11.7	27 08.1	18 56.9	21 19.3	3 22.7	12 53.5	10 27.4
23 Tu	8 02 01	29 55 15	26 08 00	2♍38 44	20 24.9	10 32.1	19 37.5	27 47.5	27 30.8	19 00.3	21 15.3	3 26.0	12 53.4	10 29.0
24 W	8 05 58	0♌52 34	9♍04 40	15 25 56	20 23.6	12 27.7	20 51.2	28 23.4	27 53.7	19 03.5	21 11.3	3 29.2	12 53.4	10 30.7
25 Th	8 09 54	1 49 53	21 42 47	27 55 30	20 22.2	14 21.7	22 04.8	28 59.4	28 16.6	19 06.5	21 07.2	3 32.6	12D 53.3	10 32.4
26 F	8 13 51	2 47 13	4♎04 27	10♎10 02	20 20.9	16 14.0	23 18.5	29 35.5	28 39.6	19 09.4	21 03.1	3 35.9	12 53.3	10 34.1
27 Sa	8 17 47	3 44 32	16 12 45	22 13 04	20 20.0	18 04.5	24 32.2	0♎11.7	29 02.8	19 12.0	20 59.0	3 39.3	12 53.4	10 35.9
28 Su	8 21 44	4 41 53	28 11 34	4♏08 46	20D 19.7	19 53.4	25 46.0	0 48.0	29 26.0	19 14.5	20 54.8	3 42.6	12 53.5	10 37.6
29 M	8 25 41	5 39 14	10♏05 17	16 01 40	20 20.0	21 40.5	26 59.7	1 24.3	29 49.2	19 16.8	20 50.5	3 46.1	12 53.6	10 39.4
30 Tu	8 29 37	6 36 35	21 58 32	27 56 26	20 20.9	23 26.0	28 13.5	2 00.8	0♎12.6	19 18.8	20 46.3	3 49.5	12 53.7	10 41.2
31 W	8 33 34	7 33 57	3♐55 57	9♐57 36	20 22.2	25 09.7	29 27.3	2 37.3	0 36.0	19 20.7	20 42.0	3 52.9	12 53.9	10 43.0

August 1963

LONGITUDE

Day	Sid.Time	☉	0 hr ☽	Noon ☽	True ☊	☿	♀	♂	⚳	♃	♄	♅	♆	♇
1 Th	8 37 30	8♌31 20	16♐01 55	22♐09 21	20♋23.6	26♌51.8	0♌41.1	3♎13.9	0♎59.5	19♈22.4	20♒37.7	3♍56.4	12♏54.1	10♍44.8
2 F	8 41 27	9 28 43	28 20 19	4♑35 13	20 24.8	28 32.2	1 54.9	3 50.6	1 23.1	19 23.9	20R 33.3	3 59.9	12 54.3	10 46.6
3 Sa	8 45 23	10 26 07	10♑54 20	17 17 54	20R 25.4	0♍10.9	3 08.8	4 27.4	1 46.8	19 25.2	20 28.9	4 03.4	12 54.6	10 48.5
4 Su	8 49 20	11 23 32	23 46 05	0♒18 58	20 25.2	1 47.9	4 22.7	5 04.3	2 10.5	19 26.3	20 24.5	4 06.9	12 54.9	10 50.4
5 M	8 53 16	12 20 58	6♒56 33	13 38 42	20 23.9	3 23.3	5 36.6	5 41.2	2 34.3	19 27.3	20 20.1	4 10.5	12 55.2	10 52.2
6 Tu	8 57 13	13 18 25	20 25 17	27 16 00	20 21.6	4 57.0	6 50.5	6 18.3	2 58.2	19 28.0	20 15.7	4 14.1	12 55.6	10 54.1
7 W	9 01 10	14 15 53	4♓10 32	11♓08 28	20 18.5	6 29.1	8 04.4	6 55.4	3 22.1	19 28.5	20 11.3	4 17.6	12 56.0	10 56.0
8 Th	9 05 06	15 13 21	18 09 22	25 12 45	20 15.0	7 59.5	9 18.4	7 32.6	3 46.1	19 28.8	20 06.8	4 21.2	12 56.4	10 57.9
9 F	9 09 03	16 10 52	2♈18 05	9♈24 52	20 11.7	9 28.2	10 32.4	8 09.8	4 10.2	19R 28.9	20 02.3	4 24.8	12 56.8	10 59.9
10 Sa	9 12 59	17 08 23	16 32 37	23 40 51	20 09.1	10 55.2	11 46.4	8 47.2	4 34.4	19 28.9	19 57.8	4 28.5	12 57.3	11 01.8
11 Su	9 16 56	18 05 56	0♉49 07	7♉57 02	20D 07.6	12 20.5	13 00.4	9 24.6	4 58.6	19 28.6	19 53.3	4 32.1	12 57.8	11 03.8
12 M	9 20 52	19 03 30	15 04 16	22 10 29	20 07.3	13 44.1	14 14.5	10 02.1	5 22.8	19 28.1	19 48.8	4 35.7	12 58.4	11 05.7
13 Tu	9 24 49	20 01 06	29 15 27	6♊18 55	20 08.0	15 05.9	15 28.5	10 39.8	5 47.2	19 27.5	19 44.4	4 39.4	12 59.0	11 07.7
14 W	9 28 45	20 58 44	13♊20 41	20 20 36	20 09.4	16 25.9	16 42.7	11 17.4	6 11.6	19 26.6	19 39.9	4 43.1	12 59.6	11 09.7
15 Th	9 32 42	21 56 23	27 18 28	4♋14 09	20 10.8	17 44.1	17 56.8	11 55.2	6 36.0	19 25.5	19 35.4	4 46.8	13 00.3	11 11.7
16 F	9 36 39	22 54 03	11♋07 29	17 58 18	20R 11.6	19 00.3	19 10.9	12 33.1	7 00.6	19 24.3	19 30.9	4 50.5	13 00.9	11 13.7
17 Sa	9 40 35	23 51 45	24 46 26	1♌31 42	20 11.1	20 14.7	20 25.1	13 11.0	7 25.1	19 22.8	19 26.4	4 54.2	13 01.7	11 15.7
18 Su	9 44 32	24 49 28	8♌13 55	14 52 57	20 08.9	21 27.0	21 39.3	13 49.0	7 49.8	19 21.2	19 21.9	4 57.9	13 02.4	11 17.7
19 M	9 48 28	25 47 13	21 28 36	28 00 46	20 05.1	22 37.2	22 53.5	14 27.1	8 14.5	19 19.3	19 17.5	5 01.6	13 03.2	11 19.8
20 Tu	9 52 25	26 44 59	4♍29 19	10♍54 13	19 59.7	23 45.3	24 07.8	15 05.3	8 39.2	19 17.2	19 13.0	5 05.3	13 04.0	11 21.8
21 W	9 56 21	27 42 46	17 15 24	23 32 56	19 53.3	24 51.1	25 22.0	15 43.6	9 04.0	19 15.0	19 08.6	5 09.1	13 04.8	11 23.8
22 Th	10 00 18	28 40 35	29 46 54	5♎57 26	19 46.6	25 54.5	26 36.3	16 21.9	9 28.9	19 12.5	19 04.2	5 12.8	13 05.7	11 25.9
23 F	10 04 14	29 38 24	12♎04 46	18 09 11	19 40.2	26 55.5	27 50.6	17 00.4	9 53.8	19 09.9	18 59.8	5 16.6	13 06.6	11 27.9
24 Sa	10 08 11	0♍36 15	24 10 59	0♏10 34	19 34.8	27 53.8	29 04.9	17 38.9	10 18.7	19 07.0	18 55.4	5 20.3	13 07.5	11 30.0
25 Su	10 12 07	1 34 08	6♏08 24	12 04 58	19 31.0	28 49.3	0♍19.2	18 17.4	10 43.7	19 04.0	18 51.1	5 24.1	13 08.5	11 32.1
26 M	10 16 04	2 32 01	18 00 48	23 56 28	19D 29.0	29 42.0	1 33.5	18 56.1	11 08.8	19 00.8	18 46.8	5 27.8	13 09.4	11 34.2
27 Tu	10 20 01	3 29 56	29 52 34	5♐49 43	19 28.6	0♎31.5	2 47.9	19 34.8	11 33.9	18 57.4	18 42.5	5 31.6	13 10.5	11 36.2
28 W	10 23 57	4 27 52	11♐48 32	17 49 41	19 29.4	1 17.8	4 02.2	20 13.6	11 59.0	18 53.8	18 38.2	5 35.4	13 11.5	11 38.3
29 Th	10 27 54	5 25 50	23 53 47	0♑01 26	19 30.7	2 00.6	5 16.6	20 52.5	12 24.2	18 50.0	18 34.0	5 39.1	13 12.6	11 40.4
30 F	10 31 50	6 23 49	6♑13 12	12 29 39	19R 31.9	2 39.7	6 31.0	21 31.5	12 49.4	18 46.1	18 29.9	5 42.9	13 13.7	11 42.5
31 Sa	10 35 47	7 21 49	18 51 14	25 18 21	19 31.9	3 14.8	7 45.4	22 10.5	13 14.7	18 41.9	18 25.7	5 46.6	13 14.8	11 44.6

Astro Data (Dy Hr Mn)	Planet Ingress (Dy Hr Mn)	Last Aspect (Dy Hr Mn)	☽ Ingress (Dy Hr Mn)	Last Aspect (Dy Hr Mn)	☽ Ingress (Dy Hr Mn)	☽ Phases & Eclipses (Dy Hr Mn)
♃⚼♅ 5 8:19	☿ ♋ 4 3:00	2 17:03 ♄ □	♐ 3 8:11	1 22:35 ☿ △	♑ 2 3:12	6 21:55 ○ 14♑06
☽0N 13 11:06	♀ ♋ 7 11:18	5 14:40 ♀ ☍	♑ 5 19:03	3 15:57 ♃ □	♒ 4 11:25	6 22:02 • P 0.706
♆D 25 19:14	☿ ♌ 18 6:19	7 5:48 ♂ △	♒ 8 3:36	5 23:47 ♄ ☌	♓ 6 16:46	14 1:57 ☾ 20♈56
☽0S 26 15:55	☉ ♌ 23 13:59	9 19:46 ♄ ☌	♓ 10 9:53	7 15:04 ♆ △	♈ 8 20:07	20 20:43 ● 27♋24
♂0S 28 19:43	♂ ♎ 27 4:14	11 22:42 ♂ ☍	♈ 12 14:16	10 5:47 ♄ ✶	♉ 10 22:37	20 20:35:37 • T 01'40"
	⚳ ♎ 29 23:05	14 3:30 ♄ ✶	♉ 14 17:15	12 8:02 ♄ □	♊ 13 1:16	28 13:13 ☽ 4♏45
♃R 9 15:26	♀ ♌ 31 22:38	16 13:30 ☿ ✶	♊ 16 19:27	14 13:10 ☉ ✶	♋ 15 4:39	
☽0N 9 16:25		18 13:03 ♂ □	♋ 18 21:45	16 14:31 ♃ □	♌ 17 9:17	5 9:31 ○ 12♒15
♃⚼♅ 10 14:41	☿ ♍ 3 9:20	20 20:43 ☉ ☌	♌ 21 1:15	19 7:35 ☉ ☌	♍ 19 15:40	12 6:21 ☾ 18♉50
♃✶♄ 18 18:56	☉ ♍ 23 20:58	22 15:13 ♄ ☍	♍ 23 7:06	21 14:44 ♀ ☌	♎ 22 0:25	19 7:35 ● 25♌37
☿0S 22 10:11	♀ ♍ 25 5:49	25 14:11 ♂ ☌	♎ 25 16:02	24 9:33 ♀ ✶	♏ 24 11:39	27 6:54 ☽ 3♐18
☽0S 22 23:39	☿ ♎ 26 20:33	27 17:11 ♀ □	♏ 28 3:38	26 1:37 ♄ □	♐ 27 0:15	
		30 12:38 ♀ △	♐ 30 16:08	28 17:01 ♂ ✶	♑ 29 11:57	
				31 5:53 ♂ □	♒ 31 20:37	

Astro Data

1 July 1963
Julian Day # 23192
SVP 5♓46'26"
GC 26♐19.8 ⚴ 24♌43.1
Eris 11♈03.9 ⚵ 20♒53.1
⚷ 14♓50.1R ⚶ 29♍08.0
☽ Mean ☊ 21♋04.3

1 August 1963
Julian Day # 23223
SVP 5♓46'21"
GC 26♐19.8 ⚴ 9♍03.1
Eris 11♈01.0R ⚵ 29♒44.9
⚷ 14♓04.2R ⚶ 11♎29.9
☽ Mean ☊ 19♋25.9

LONGITUDE — September 1963

Day	Sid.Time	☉	0 hr ☽	Noon ☽	True☊	☿	♀	♂	⚳	♃	♄	♅	♆	♇
1 Su	10 39 43	8♍19 51	1♒51 18	8♒30 18	19♋30.2	3♎45.8	8♍59.8	22♎49.6	13♎40.0	18♈37.6	18♒21.6	5♍50.4	13♏16.0	11♍46.7
2 M	10 43 40	9 17 54	15 15 23	22 06 29	19R 26.5	4 12.2	10 14.2	23 28.8	14 05.3	18R 33.1	18R 17.6	5 54.2	13 17.2	11 48.8
3 Tu	10 47 36	10 15 58	29 03 23	6♓05 43	19 20.6	4 33.9	11 28.7	24 08.0	14 30.7	18 28.5	18 13.6	5 57.9	13 18.4	11 50.9
4 W	10 51 33	11 14 05	13♓12 56	20 24 23	19 13.2	4 50.6	12 43.1	24 47.4	14 56.1	18 23.6	18 09.6	6 01.7	13 19.6	11 53.0
5 Th	10 55 30	12 12 13	27 39 18	4♈56 49	19 04.9	5 01.9	13 57.6	25 26.8	15 21.6	18 18.6	18 05.7	6 05.4	13 20.9	11 55.1
6 F	10 59 26	13 10 22	12♈16 01	19 35 59	18 56.9	5R 07.6	15 12.1	26 06.2	15 47.1	18 13.5	18 01.9	6 09.2	13 22.2	11 57.2
7 Sa	11 03 23	14 08 34	26 55 48	4♉14 37	18 50.1	5 07.4	16 26.6	26 45.8	16 12.6	18 08.2	17 58.0	6 12.9	13 23.5	11 59.3
8 Su	11 07 19	15 06 48	11♉31 43	18 46 26	18 45.2	5 01.0	17 41.1	27 25.4	16 38.2	18 02.7	17 54.3	6 16.6	13 24.9	12 01.4
9 M	11 11 16	16 05 04	25 58 15	3♊06 47	18D 42.5	4 48.2	18 55.7	28 05.1	17 03.8	17 57.1	17 50.6	6 20.4	13 26.3	12 03.5
10 Tu	11 15 12	17 03 22	10♊11 46	17 13 03	18 41.8	4 28.9	20 10.2	28 44.9	17 29.4	17 51.3	17 47.0	6 24.1	13 27.7	12 05.6
11 W	11 19 09	18 01 42	24 10 34	1♋04 21	18 42.2	4 03.0	21 24.8	29 24.8	17 55.1	17 45.3	17 43.4	6 27.8	13 29.1	12 07.7
12 Th	11 23 05	19 00 05	7♋54 29	14 41 03	18R 42.9	3 30.5	22 39.4	0♏04.7	18 20.8	17 39.3	17 39.9	6 31.5	13 30.6	12 09.7
13 F	11 27 02	19 58 29	21 24 13	28 04 08	18 42.5	2 51.6	23 54.0	0 44.7	18 46.6	17 33.0	17 36.4	6 35.2	13 32.1	12 11.8
14 Sa	11 30 59	20 56 56	4♌40 54	11♌14 40	18 40.3	2 06.6	25 08.6	1 24.8	19 12.4	17 26.7	17 33.1	6 38.9	13 33.6	12 13.9
15 Su	11 34 55	21 55 24	17 45 31	24 13 31	18 35.5	1 16.0	26 23.2	2 04.9	19 38.2	17 20.2	17 29.7	6 42.6	13 35.1	12 16.0
16 M	11 38 52	22 53 55	0♍38 44	7♍01 12	18 28.0	0 20.6	27 37.8	2 45.2	20 04.0	17 13.6	17 26.5	6 46.2	13 36.7	12 18.1
17 Tu	11 42 48	23 52 27	13 20 55	19 37 54	18 18.0	29♍21.2	28 52.5	3 25.5	20 29.8	17 06.8	17 23.3	6 49.9	13 38.2	12 20.1
18 W	11 46 45	24 51 02	25 52 10	2♎03 46	18 06.2	28 19.0	0♎07.1	4 05.9	20 55.7	16 59.9	17 20.2	6 53.5	13 39.8	12 22.2
19 Th	11 50 41	25 49 38	8♎12 43	14 19 07	17 53.7	27 15.3	1 21.8	4 46.3	21 21.7	16 53.0	17 17.2	6 57.1	13 41.5	12 24.3
20 F	11 54 38	26 48 16	20 23 05	26 24 47	17 41.6	26 11.6	2 36.5	5 26.9	21 47.6	16 45.9	17 14.3	7 00.7	13 43.1	12 26.3
21 Sa	11 58 34	27 46 56	2♏24 26	8♏22 17	17 30.9	25 09.3	3 51.1	6 07.5	22 13.6	16 38.7	17 11.4	7 04.3	13 44.8	12 28.4
22 Su	12 02 31	28 45 38	14 18 41	20 14 00	17 22.4	24 10.1	5 05.8	6 48.2	22 39.5	16 31.4	17 08.6	7 07.9	13 46.5	12 30.4
23 M	12 06 28	29 44 21	26 08 40	2♐03 11	17 16.4	23 15.6	6 20.5	7 28.9	23 05.6	16 24.0	17 05.9	7 11.5	13 48.2	12 32.4
24 Tu	12 10 24	0♎43 07	7♐58 04	13 53 55	17 13.1	22 27.1	7 35.2	8 09.7	23 31.6	16 16.5	17 03.3	7 15.0	13 49.9	12 34.5
25 W	12 14 21	1 41 54	19 51 19	25 50 57	17D 11.8	21 46.0	8 49.9	8 50.6	23 57.7	16 09.0	17 00.7	7 18.5	13 51.7	12 36.5
26 Th	12 18 17	2 40 43	1♑53 27	7♑59 31	17R 11.7	21 13.3	10 04.6	9 31.6	24 23.7	16 01.4	16 58.2	7 22.0	13 53.5	12 38.5
27 F	12 22 14	3 39 33	14 09 49	20 24 59	17 11.8	20 49.8	11 19.3	10 12.7	24 49.8	15 53.7	16 55.9	7 25.5	13 55.3	12 40.5
28 Sa	12 26 10	4 38 25	26 45 40	3♒12 24	17 10.9	20D 36.2	12 34.1	10 53.8	25 15.9	15 45.9	16 53.6	7 29.0	13 57.1	12 42.5
29 Su	12 30 07	5 37 19	9♒45 41	16 25 53	17 08.1	20 32.7	13 48.8	11 34.9	25 42.1	15 38.1	16 51.4	7 32.4	13 59.0	12 44.4
30 M	12 34 03	6 36 15	23 13 14	0♓07 50	17 02.7	20 39.6	15 03.5	12 16.2	26 08.2	15 30.2	16 49.3	7 35.8	14 00.8	12 46.4

LONGITUDE — October 1963

Day	Sid.Time	☉	0 hr ☽	Noon ☽	True☊	☿	♀	♂	⚳	♃	♄	♅	♆	♇
1 Tu	12 38 00	7♎35 13	7♓09 34	14♓18 08	16♋54.7	20♍56.5	16♎18.2	12♏57.5	26♎34.4	15♈22.3	16♒47.3	7♍39.2	14♏02.7	12♍48.4
2 W	12 41 56	8 34 12	21 33 03	28 53 33	16R 44.6	21 23.4	17 33.0	13 38.9	27 00.5	15R 14.3	16R 45.3	7 42.6	14 04.6	12 50.3
3 Th	12 45 53	9 33 13	6♈18 45	13♈47 34	16 33.3	21 59.7	18 47.7	14 20.3	27 26.7	15 06.3	16 43.5	7 46.0	14 06.5	12 52.2
4 F	12 49 50	10 32 17	21 18 47	28 51 08	16 22.1	22 44.9	20 02.4	15 01.8	27 52.9	14 58.3	16 41.7	7 49.3	14 08.4	12 54.1
5 Sa	12 53 46	11 31 23	6♉23 22	13♉54 13	16 12.4	23 38.2	21 17.2	15 43.4	28 19.1	14 50.3	16 40.1	7 52.6	14 10.4	12 56.0
6 Su	12 57 43	12 30 30	21 22 35	28 47 28	16 05.0	24 39.1	22 31.9	16 25.1	28 45.4	14 42.2	16 38.5	7 55.8	14 12.3	12 57.9
7 M	13 01 39	13 29 41	6♊08 06	13♊23 51	16 00.4	25 46.8	23 46.7	17 06.8	29 11.6	14 34.1	16 37.1	7 59.1	14 14.3	12 59.8
8 Tu	13 05 36	14 28 53	20 34 19	27 39 15	15 58.3	27 00.5	25 01.4	17 48.6	29 37.9	14 26.1	16 35.7	8 02.3	14 16.3	13 01.7
9 W	13 09 32	15 28 08	4♋38 35	11♋32 22	15 57.8	28 19.5	26 16.2	18 30.5	0♏04.1	14 18.0	16 34.4	8 05.5	14 18.3	13 03.5
10 Th	13 13 29	16 27 26	18 20 46	25 04 03	15 57.7	29 43.0	27 31.0	19 12.5	0 30.4	14 09.9	16 33.2	8 08.7	14 20.4	13 05.3
11 F	13 17 25	17 26 45	1♌42 32	8♌16 32	15 56.7	1♎10.6	28 45.8	19 54.5	0 56.7	14 01.8	16 32.2	8 11.8	14 22.4	13 07.1
12 Sa	13 21 22	18 26 07	14 46 25	21 12 31	15 53.8	2 41.4	0♏00.5	20 36.6	1 23.0	13 53.8	16 31.2	8 14.9	14 24.5	13 08.9
13 Su	13 25 19	19 25 31	27 35 11	3♍54 43	15 48.0	4 15.0	1 15.3	21 18.7	1 49.3	13 45.8	16 30.3	8 18.0	14 26.5	13 10.7
14 M	13 29 15	20 24 58	10♍11 22	16 25 24	15 39.2	5 50.9	2 30.1	22 01.0	2 15.6	13 37.8	16 29.5	8 21.0	14 28.6	13 12.5
15 Tu	13 33 12	21 24 26	22 37 00	28 46 21	15 27.6	7 28.6	3 44.9	22 43.3	2 42.0	13 29.8	16 28.8	8 24.0	14 30.7	13 14.2
16 W	13 37 08	22 23 57	4♎53 35	10♎58 51	15 14.1	9 07.8	4 59.7	23 25.7	3 08.3	13 21.9	16 28.3	8 27.0	14 32.8	13 16.0
17 Th	13 41 05	23 23 29	17 02 14	23 03 53	14 59.7	10 48.0	6 14.5	24 08.1	3 34.6	13 14.1	16 27.8	8 30.0	14 34.9	13 17.7
18 F	13 45 01	24 23 04	29 03 53	5♏02 24	14 45.6	12 29.1	7 29.3	24 50.6	4 01.0	13 06.3	16 27.4	8 32.9	14 37.0	13 19.4
19 Sa	13 48 58	25 22 41	10♏59 33	16 55 34	14 32.9	14 10.8	8 44.1	25 33.2	4 27.3	12 58.5	16 27.1	8 35.7	14 39.2	13 21.0
20 Su	13 52 54	26 22 20	22 50 39	28 45 05	14 22.7	15 52.9	9 58.9	26 15.8	4 53.7	12 50.9	16 26.9	8 38.6	14 41.3	13 22.7
21 M	13 56 51	27 22 00	4♐39 10	10♐33 17	14 15.3	17 35.1	11 13.7	26 58.6	5 20.0	12 43.3	16D 26.9	8 41.4	14 43.5	13 24.3
22 Tu	14 00 48	28 21 43	16 27 51	22 23 19	14 10.7	19 17.4	12 28.5	27 41.3	5 46.4	12 35.8	16 26.9	8 44.1	14 45.7	13 25.9
23 W	14 04 44	29 21 27	28 20 13	4♑19 06	14D 08.7	20 59.6	13 43.4	28 24.2	6 12.7	12 28.3	16 27.0	8 46.9	14 47.9	13 27.5
24 Th	14 08 41	0♏21 13	10♑20 34	16 25 15	14 08.4	22 41.7	14 58.2	29 07.1	6 39.1	12 21.0	16 27.3	8 49.6	14 50.0	13 29.1
25 F	14 12 37	1 21 01	22 33 47	28 46 51	14R 08.6	24 23.5	16 13.0	29 50.1	7 05.4	12 13.8	16 27.6	8 52.2	14 52.2	13 30.6
26 Sa	14 16 34	2 20 50	5♒05 06	11♒29 08	14 08.3	26 05.0	17 27.8	0♐33.1	7 31.8	12 06.7	16 28.1	8 54.8	14 54.4	13 32.2
27 Su	14 20 30	3 20 41	17 59 34	24 36 53	14 06.4	27 46.2	18 42.6	1 16.3	7 58.1	11 59.7	16 28.6	8 57.4	14 56.6	13 33.7
28 M	14 24 27	4 20 34	1♓21 30	8♓13 41	14 02.2	29 26.9	19 57.3	1 59.4	8 24.4	11 52.8	16 29.3	8 59.9	14 58.9	13 35.1
29 Tu	14 28 23	5 20 28	15 13 32	22 20 58	13 55.5	1♏07.3	21 12.1	2 42.7	8 50.8	11 46.0	16 30.0	9 02.4	15 01.1	13 36.6
30 W	14 32 20	6 20 24	29 35 41	6♈57 09	13 46.7	2 47.2	22 26.9	3 26.0	9 17.1	11 39.3	16 30.9	9 04.9	15 03.3	13 38.0
31 Th	14 36 17	7 20 22	14♈24 34	21 56 57	13 36.7	4 26.7	23 41.7	4 09.3	9 43.4	11 32.8	16 31.8	9 07.3	15 05.5	13 39.4

Astro Data

	Dy Hr Mn
⚳0S	5 13:12
☽0N	5 23:11
☿R	6 23:10
♃⚹♄	12 6:14
☽0S	19 6:43
♀0S	20 19:25
☿0N	22 6:27
☉0S	23 18:24
☿D	29 8:03
☽0N	3 8:30
♃⚻♆	9 11:09
☿0S	13 16:55
☽0S	16 13:14
♃⚻♇	17 2:54
♄D	21 16:22

Planet Ingress

		Dy Hr Mn
♂	♏	12 9:11
☿	♍R	16 20:29
♀	♎	18 9:43
☉	♎	23 18:24
⚳	♏	9 8:13
☿	♎	10 16:44
♀	♏	12 11:50
☉	♏	24 3:29
♂	♐	25 17:31
☿	♏	28 19:54

☽0N30 19:43

Last Aspect / ☽ Ingress

Last Aspect Dy Hr Mn		☽ Ingress	Dy Hr Mn
2 14:30	♂△	♓	3 1:37
4 0:10	♆△	♈	5 3:52
6 23:09	♂☍	♉	7 5:02
8 10:34	♄□	♊	9 6:45
11 8:57	♂△	♋	11 10:08
13 3:43	♀⚹	♌	13 15:30
14 23:34	♄☍	♍	15 22:47
18 7:48	♀☌	♎	18 8:00
19 17:50	♄△	♏	20 19:10
23 6:53	☉⚹	♐	23 7:50
25 4:15	☿□	♑	25 20:15
27 12:46	☿△	♒	28 6:03
29 12:45	♄☌	♓	30 11:47

Last Aspect / ☽ Ingress

Last Aspect Dy Hr Mn		☽ Ingress	Dy Hr Mn
1 23:19	☿☍	♈	2 13:48
3 20:42	♀☍	♉	4 13:50
6 4:47	☿△	♊	6 13:58
8 10:47	☿□	♋	8 16:01
10 16:52	♀□	♌	10 20:54
12 10:49	♂□	♍	13 4:34
14 23:29	♂⚹	♎	15 14:24
17 12:43	☉☌	♏	18 1:53
20 6:37	♂☌	♐	20 14:32
23 1:09	☉⚹	♑	23 3:21
25 14:08	♂⚹	♒	25 14:20
27 18:27	☿△	♓	27 21:36
29 9:54	♀△	♈	30 0:40

☽ Phases & Eclipses

Dy Hr Mn	
3 19:33	○ 10♓34
10 11:42	☾ 17♊03
17 20:51	● 24♍14
26 0:38	☽ 2♑13
3 4:44	○ 9♈15
9 19:27	☾ 15♋47
17 12:43	● 23♎25
25 17:20	☽ 1♒34

Astro Data

1 September 1963
Julian Day # 23254
SVP 5♓46'17"
GC 26♐19.9 ⚵ 23♍25.1
Eris 10♈48.7R ⚶ 9♎52.0
⚷ 12♓44.5R ⚴ 25♎49.8
☽ Mean ☊ 17♋47.4

1 October 1963
Julian Day # 23284
SVP 5♓46'15"
GC 26♐20.0 ⚵ 7♎14.0
Eris 10♈31.3R ⚶ 20♎15.4
⚷ 11♓22.8R ⚴ 10♏52.0
☽ Mean ☊ 16♋12.0

November 1963 — LONGITUDE

Day	Sid.Time	☉	0 hr ☽	Noon ☽	True ☊	☿	♀	♂	⚳	♃	♄	♅	♆	♇
1 F	14 40 13	8♏20 21	29♈33 06	7♉11 41	13♋26.6	6♏05.7	24♏56.5	4♐52.7	10♏09.7	11♈26.4	16♒32.9	9♍09.6	15♏07.8	13♍40.8
2 Sa	14 44 10	9 20 23	14♉51 15	22 30 22	13R 17.8	7 44.3	26 11.3	5 36.2	10 36.0	11R 20.1	16 34.0	9 11.9	15 10.0	13 42.2
3 Su	14 48 06	10 20 26	0♊07 37	7♊41 45	13 11.1	9 22.4	27 26.0	6 19.8	11 02.3	11 14.0	16 35.3	9 14.2	15 12.2	13 43.5
4 M	14 52 03	11 20 32	15 11 37	22 36 17	13 07.0	11 00.1	28 40.8	7 03.4	11 28.6	11 08.1	16 36.6	9 16.5	15 14.5	13 44.8
5 Tu	14 55 59	12 20 39	29 55 04	7♋07 28	13D 05.3	12 37.4	29 55.6	7 47.1	11 54.8	11 02.2	16 38.1	9 18.6	15 16.7	13 46.1
6 W	14 59 56	13 20 49	14♋13 12	21 12 11	13 05.4	14 14.3	1♐10.4	8 30.8	12 21.1	10 56.6	16 39.7	9 20.8	15 19.0	13 47.4
7 Th	15 03 52	14 21 00	28 04 30	4♌50 21	13R 06.1	15 50.8	2 25.1	9 14.6	12 47.4	10 51.1	16 41.3	9 22.9	15 21.2	13 48.6
8 F	15 07 49	15 21 14	11♌30 02	18 03 58	13 06.4	17 26.8	3 39.9	9 58.5	13 13.6	10 45.7	16 43.1	9 24.9	15 23.5	13 49.8
9 Sa	15 11 46	16 21 30	24 32 33	0♍56 16	13 05.2	19 02.6	4 54.7	10 42.5	13 39.9	10 40.5	16 44.9	9 26.9	15 25.7	13 51.0
10 Su	15 15 42	17 21 48	7♍15 35	13 30 59	13 01.8	20 37.9	6 09.5	11 26.5	14 06.1	10 35.5	16 46.9	9 28.9	15 28.0	13 52.2
11 M	15 19 39	18 22 07	19 42 55	25 51 47	12 56.0	22 12.9	7 24.2	12 10.5	14 32.3	10 30.7	16 49.0	9 30.8	15 30.2	13 53.3
12 Tu	15 23 35	19 22 29	1♎58 00	8♎01 56	12 48.0	23 47.6	8 39.0	12 54.6	14 58.5	10 26.0	16 51.1	9 32.7	15 32.5	13 54.4
13 W	15 27 32	20 22 52	14 03 54	20 04 12	12 38.3	25 22.0	9 53.8	13 38.8	15 24.7	10 21.5	16 53.4	9 34.5	15 34.7	13 55.5
14 Th	15 31 28	21 23 17	26 03 05	2♏00 47	12 27.8	26 56.1	11 08.6	14 23.1	15 50.8	10 17.2	16 55.7	9 36.2	15 37.0	13 56.5
15 F	15 35 25	22 23 44	7♏57 31	13 53 29	12 17.6	28 29.9	12 23.3	15 07.4	16 17.0	10 13.0	16 58.2	9 37.9	15 39.2	13 57.5
16 Sa	15 39 21	23 24 13	19 48 53	25 43 53	12 08.4	0♐03.4	13 38.1	15 51.8	16 43.1	10 09.1	17 00.7	9 39.6	15 41.4	13 58.5
17 Su	15 43 18	24 24 43	1♐38 42	7♐33 33	12 01.0	1 36.7	14 52.9	16 36.2	17 09.2	10 05.4	17 03.4	9 41.2	15 43.7	13 59.5
18 M	15 47 15	25 25 15	13 28 39	19 24 15	11 56.0	3 09.8	16 07.6	17 20.7	17 35.3	10 01.8	17 06.1	9 42.7	15 45.9	14 00.4
19 Tu	15 51 11	26 25 48	25 20 41	1♑18 14	11D 53.2	4 42.6	17 22.4	18 05.3	18 01.4	9 58.4	17 08.9	9 44.2	15 48.1	14 01.3
20 W	15 55 08	27 26 23	7♑17 18	13 18 15	11 52.6	6 15.3	18 37.1	18 49.9	18 27.4	9 55.3	17 11.9	9 45.7	15 50.3	14 02.2
21 Th	15 59 04	28 26 59	19 21 34	25 27 41	11 53.4	7 47.7	19 51.9	19 34.5	18 53.4	9 52.3	17 14.9	9 47.1	15 52.6	14 03.0
22 F	16 03 01	29 27 36	1♒37 09	7♒50 27	11 54.9	9 19.9	21 06.6	20 19.3	19 19.4	9 49.6	17 18.0	9 48.4	15 54.8	14 03.8
23 Sa	16 06 57	0♐28 15	14 08 10	20 30 49	11R 56.2	10 51.9	22 21.4	21 04.1	19 45.4	9 47.0	17 21.2	9 49.7	15 57.0	14 04.6
24 Su	16 10 54	1 28 54	26 58 56	3♓33 00	11 56.7	12 23.7	23 36.1	21 48.9	20 11.3	9 44.6	17 24.5	9 51.0	15 59.2	14 05.3
25 M	16 14 50	2 29 34	10♓13 27	17 00 38	11 55.6	13 55.3	24 50.8	22 33.8	20 37.2	9 42.5	17 27.9	9 52.2	16 01.3	14 06.0
26 Tu	16 18 47	3 30 16	23 54 46	0♈55 58	11 52.8	15 26.7	26 05.5	23 18.7	21 03.1	9 40.5	17 31.3	9 53.3	16 03.5	14 06.7
27 W	16 22 44	4 30 58	8♈04 08	15 19 01	11 48.5	16 57.9	27 20.2	24 03.7	21 29.0	9 38.8	17 34.9	9 54.4	16 05.7	14 07.4
28 Th	16 26 40	5 31 42	22 40 09	0♉06 50	11 43.2	18 28.9	28 34.9	24 48.8	21 54.8	9 37.2	17 38.6	9 55.4	16 07.8	14 08.0
29 F	16 30 37	6 32 27	7♉38 12	15 13 11	11 37.7	19 59.6	29 49.6	25 33.9	22 20.6	9 35.9	17 42.3	9 56.3	16 10.0	14 08.6
30 Sa	16 34 33	7 33 13	22 50 33	0♊28 59	11 32.8	21 30.0	1♑04.2	26 19.0	22 46.4	9 34.8	17 46.1	9 57.3	16 12.1	14 09.1

December 1963 — LONGITUDE

Day	Sid.Time	☉	0 hr ☽	Noon ☽	True ☊	☿	♀	♂	⚳	♃	♄	♅	♆	♇
1 Su	16 38 30	8♐34 00	8♊07 09	15♊43 41	11♋29.3	23♐00.2	2♑18.9	27♐04.2	23♏12.1	9♈33.9	17♒50.0	9♍58.1	16♏14.2	14♍09.7
2 M	16 42 26	9 34 48	23 17 20	0♋46 57	11D 27.3	24 30.0	3 33.5	27 49.5	23 37.8	9R 33.1	17 54.0	9 58.9	16 16.3	14 10.2
3 Tu	16 46 23	10 35 38	8♋11 34	15 30 22	11 27.0	25 59.4	4 48.2	28 34.8	24 03.5	9 32.6	17 58.1	9 59.7	16 18.4	14 10.6
4 W	16 50 19	11 36 29	22 42 48	29 48 26	11 27.9	27 28.3	6 02.8	29 20.2	24 29.1	9D 32.3	18 02.2	10 00.4	16 20.5	14 11.1
5 Th	16 54 16	12 37 21	6♌47 06	13♌38 46	11 29.5	28 56.7	7 17.4	0♑05.6	24 54.7	9 32.3	18 06.5	10 01.0	16 22.6	14 11.5
6 F	16 58 13	13 38 15	20 23 34	27 01 43	11 31.0	0♑24.5	8 32.1	0 51.1	25 20.3	9 32.4	18 10.8	10 01.6	16 24.7	14 11.8
7 Sa	17 02 09	14 39 09	3♍33 36	9♍59 38	11R 31.9	1 51.6	9 46.7	1 36.6	25 45.8	9 32.7	18 15.2	10 02.1	16 26.7	14 12.2
8 Su	17 06 06	15 40 05	16 20 17	22 36 04	11 31.8	3 17.8	11 01.2	2 22.1	26 11.3	9 33.2	18 19.7	10 02.6	16 28.7	14 12.5
9 M	17 10 02	16 41 03	28 47 32	4♎55 12	11 30.5	4 43.0	12 15.8	3 07.8	26 36.7	9 34.0	18 24.2	10 03.0	16 30.7	14 12.7
10 Tu	17 13 59	17 42 01	10♎59 38	17 01 19	11 28.0	6 07.1	13 30.4	3 53.4	27 02.2	9 34.9	18 28.8	10 03.3	16 32.7	14 13.0
11 W	17 17 55	18 43 01	23 00 46	28 58 27	11 24.6	7 29.8	14 45.0	4 39.2	27 27.5	9 36.1	18 33.5	10 03.6	16 34.7	14 13.2
12 Th	17 21 52	19 44 01	4♏54 48	10♏50 14	11 20.8	8 50.9	15 59.5	5 24.9	27 52.9	9 37.5	18 38.3	10 03.9	16 36.7	14 13.3
13 F	17 25 48	20 45 03	16 45 07	22 39 48	11 17.0	10 10.2	17 14.1	6 10.8	28 18.1	9 39.0	18 43.2	10 04.0	16 38.6	14 13.5
14 Sa	17 29 45	21 46 06	28 34 34	4♐29 45	11 13.7	11 27.2	18 28.6	6 56.6	28 43.4	9 40.8	18 48.1	10 04.2	16 40.6	14 13.6
15 Su	17 33 42	22 47 09	10♐25 35	16 22 18	11 11.2	12 41.7	19 43.1	7 42.6	29 08.6	9 42.8	18 53.1	10R 04.2	16 42.5	14 13.7
16 M	17 37 38	23 48 13	22 20 09	28 19 22	11 09.7	13 53.2	20 57.6	8 28.5	29 33.7	9 45.0	18 58.2	10 04.2	16 44.4	14R 13.7
17 Tu	17 41 35	24 49 18	4♑20 08	10♑22 41	11D 09.2	15 01.2	22 12.1	9 14.5	29 58.8	9 47.4	19 03.3	10 04.2	16 46.3	14 13.7
18 W	17 45 31	25 50 24	16 27 15	22 34 03	11 09.5	16 05.2	23 26.6	10 00.6	0♐23.9	9 50.0	19 08.5	10 04.1	16 48.1	14 13.7
19 Th	17 49 28	26 51 30	28 43 21	4♒55 25	11 10.5	17 04.6	24 41.1	10 46.7	0 48.9	9 52.8	19 13.8	10 03.9	16 50.0	14 13.6
20 F	17 53 24	27 52 36	11♒10 30	17 28 56	11 11.7	17 58.6	25 55.5	11 32.8	1 13.8	9 55.8	19 19.2	10 03.7	16 51.8	14 13.5
21 Sa	17 57 21	28 53 43	23 51 00	0♓17 01	11 12.9	18 46.5	27 09.9	12 19.0	1 38.7	9 59.0	19 24.6	10 03.5	16 53.6	14 13.4
22 Su	18 01 17	29 54 50	6♓47 17	13 22 08	11 13.9	19 27.5	28 24.3	13 05.3	2 03.6	10 02.4	19 30.0	10 03.1	16 55.3	14 13.3
23 M	18 05 14	0♑55 57	20 01 48	26 46 33	11R 14.3	20 00.7	29 38.7	13 51.5	2 28.3	10 06.0	19 35.6	10 02.7	16 57.1	14 13.1
24 Tu	18 09 11	1 57 04	3♈36 33	10♈31 56	11 14.2	20 25.2	0♒53.0	14 37.8	2 53.1	10 09.8	19 41.2	10 02.3	16 58.8	14 12.9
25 W	18 13 07	2 58 11	17 32 41	24 38 43	11 13.7	20R 40.0	2 07.3	15 24.2	3 17.7	10 13.7	19 46.8	10 01.8	17 00.5	14 12.6
26 Th	18 17 04	3 59 18	1♉49 49	9♉05 38	11 12.9	20 44.4	3 21.6	16 10.5	3 42.3	10 17.9	19 52.5	10 01.3	17 02.2	14 12.3
27 F	18 21 00	5 00 25	16 25 41	23 49 17	11 12.2	20 37.6	4 35.9	16 56.9	4 06.9	10 22.3	19 58.3	10 00.7	17 03.9	14 12.0
28 Sa	18 24 57	6 01 33	1♊15 42	8♊44 01	11 11.5	20 19.2	5 50.1	17 43.4	4 31.4	10 26.8	20 04.2	10 00.0	17 05.5	14 11.7
29 Su	18 28 53	7 02 40	16 13 16	23 42 24	11 11.1	19 48.9	7 04.3	18 29.9	4 55.8	10 31.6	20 10.1	9 59.3	17 07.1	14 11.3
30 M	18 32 50	8 03 48	1♋10 21	8♋36 05	11D 11.0	19 06.9	8 18.5	19 16.4	5 20.1	10 36.5	20 16.0	9 58.5	17 08.7	14 10.9
31 Tu	18 36 47	9 04 56	15 58 37	23 17 03	11 11.1	18 14.0	9 32.7	20 03.0	5 44.4	10 41.6	20 22.0	9 57.7	17 10.3	14 10.5

Astro Data

	Dy Hr Mn
☽0S	12 19:36
♃⚻♅	22 18:44
☽0N	27 6:39
♃ D	5 10:11
☽0S	10 2:24
♅ R	16 5:12
♇ R	17 7:07
♃⚻♅	22 16:37
☽0N	24 15:05
☿ R	26 9:39

Planet Ingress

	Dy Hr Mn
♀ ♐	5 13:25
☿ ♐	16 11:07
☉ ♐	23 0:49
♀ ♑	29 15:21
♂ ♑	5 9:03
☿ ♑	6 5:17
⚳ ♐	17 13:07
☉ ♑	22 14:02
♀ ♒	23 18:53

Last Aspect / ☽ Ingress

Last Aspect Dy Hr Mn		☽ Ingress Dy Hr Mn
31 3:23 ♄ ⚹	♉	1 0:42
2 18:18 ♀ ☍	♊	2 23:48
4 2:16 ♄ △	♋	5 0:08
6 1:51 ♆ △	♌	7 3:24
8 10:42 ☿ □	♍	9 10:14
11 3:49 ☿ ⚹	♎	11 20:07
13 5:37 ♄ △	♏	14 7:57
16 6:50 ☉ ☌	♐	16 20:40
18 7:33 ♂ ☌	♑	19 9:23
21 18:22 ☉ ⚹	♒	21 20:51
23 15:48 ♀ ⚹	♓	24 5:32
26 2:56 ♀ □	♈	26 10:25
28 9:19 ♀ △	♉	28 11:49
29 15:56 ♄ □	♊	30 11:14

Last Aspect / ☽ Ingress

Last Aspect Dy Hr Mn		☽ Ingress Dy Hr Mn
2 7:00 ♂ ☍	♋	2 10:44
3 13:20 ♆ △	♌	4 12:20
5 19:57 ♄ ☍	♍	6 17:26
8 0:14 ♆ ⚹	♎	9 2:21
10 14:56 ♄ △	♏	11 14:04
13 3:56 ♄ □	♐	14 2:53
16 2:06 ☉ ☌	♑	16 15:21
18 13:54 ♀ ☌	♒	19 2:29
21 9:12 ☉ ⚹	♓	21 11:28
23 17:34 ♀ ⚹	♈	23 17:41
25 5:12 ☿ □	♉	25 20:57
27 6:53 ☿ △	♊	27 21:58
29 6:17 ♄ △	♋	29 22:07
31 6:22 ♂ ☍	♌	31 23:09

☽ Phases & Eclipses

Dy Hr Mn	
1 13:55	○ 8♉25
8 6:37	☾ 15♌08
16 6:50	● 23♏11
24 7:56	☽ 1♓19
30 23:54	○ 8♊03
7 21:34	☾ 15♍03
16 2:06	● 23♐23
23 19:54	☽ 1♈16
30 11:04	○ 8♋01
30 11:07	☍ T 1.335

Astro Data

1 November 1963
Julian Day # 23315
SVP 5♓46'12"
GC 26♐20.0 ⚴ 21♎15.4
Eris 10♈12.7R ⚵ 1♏08.5
⚷ 10♓25.4R ⚶ 27♏09.0
☽ Mean ☊ 14♋33.5

1 December 1963
Julian Day # 23345
SVP 5♓46'07"
GC 26♐20.1 ⚴ 4♏19.5
Eris 9♈59.6R ⚵ 11♏22.2
⚷ 10♓16.7 ⚶ 13♐17.7
☽ Mean ☊ 12♋58.2

LONGITUDE — January 1964

Day	Sid.Time	☉	0 hr ☽	Noon ☽	True ☊	☿	♀	♂	⚳	♃	♄	♅	♆	♇
1 W	18 40 43	10♑06 04	0♌30 36	7♌38 39	11♋11.2	17♑11.2	10♒46.8	20♑49.6	6♐08.7	10♈46.9	20♒28.1	9♍56.8	17♏11.8	14♍10.0
2 Th	18 44 40	11 07 12	14 40 41	21 36 23	11R 11.2	16R 00.3	12 00.9	21 36.2	6 32.8	10 52.3	20 34.2	9R 55.9	17 13.3	14R 09.5
3 F	18 48 36	12 08 21	28 25 36	5♍08 17	11 11.2	14 43.4	13 14.9	22 22.9	6 56.9	10 58.0	20 40.3	9 54.9	17 14.8	14 09.0
4 Sa	18 52 33	13 09 30	11♍44 34	18 14 39	11 11.0	13 23.1	14 28.9	23 09.6	7 21.0	11 03.8	20 46.5	9 53.9	17 16.3	14 08.4
5 Su	18 56 29	14 10 38	24 38 52	0♎57 38	11 10.8	12 01.9	15 42.9	23 56.3	7 44.9	11 09.8	20 52.8	9 52.8	17 17.7	14 07.8
6 M	19 00 26	15 11 47	7♎11 26	13 20 47	11D 10.7	10 42.5	16 56.9	24 43.0	8 08.8	11 15.9	20 59.1	9 51.7	17 19.1	14 07.2
7 Tu	19 04 22	16 12 57	19 26 14	25 28 23	11 10.8	9 27.4	18 10.8	25 29.8	8 32.6	11 22.3	21 05.4	9 50.5	17 20.5	14 06.5
8 W	19 08 19	17 14 06	1♏27 49	7♏25 07	11 11.2	8 18.5	19 24.7	26 16.7	8 56.4	11 28.8	21 11.8	9 49.3	17 21.9	14 05.9
9 Th	19 12 16	18 15 15	13 20 53	19 15 40	11 11.8	7 17.4	20 38.5	27 03.5	9 20.0	11 35.4	21 18.3	9 48.0	17 23.2	14 05.2
10 F	19 16 12	19 16 25	25 10 01	1♐04 28	11 12.7	6 25.3	21 52.3	27 50.4	9 43.6	11 42.3	21 24.7	9 46.7	17 24.5	14 04.4
11 Sa	19 20 09	20 17 34	6♐59 28	12 55 29	11 13.6	5 42.8	23 06.1	28 37.4	10 07.2	11 49.3	21 31.3	9 45.3	17 25.7	14 03.7
12 Su	19 24 05	21 18 44	18 52 55	24 52 09	11 14.5	5 10.2	24 19.9	29 24.3	10 30.6	11 56.4	21 37.8	9 43.9	17 27.0	14 02.9
13 M	19 28 02	22 19 53	0♑53 31	6♑57 16	11R 14.9	4 47.4	25 33.6	0♒11.3	10 53.9	12 03.8	21 44.5	9 42.4	17 28.2	14 02.0
14 Tu	19 31 58	23 21 02	13 03 40	19 12 55	11 14.8	4D 34.1	26 47.2	0 58.3	11 17.2	12 11.2	21 51.1	9 40.9	17 29.4	14 01.2
15 W	19 35 55	24 22 10	25 25 10	1♒40 34	11 14.0	4 29.9	28 00.8	1 45.4	11 40.4	12 18.9	21 57.8	9 39.3	17 30.5	14 00.3
16 Th	19 39 51	25 23 18	7♒59 11	14 21 06	11 12.5	4 34.1	29 14.4	2 32.4	12 03.5	12 26.7	22 04.5	9 37.7	17 31.6	13 59.4
17 F	19 43 48	26 24 26	20 46 21	27 14 58	11 10.5	4 46.2	0♓27.9	3 19.5	12 26.5	12 34.6	22 11.3	9 36.1	17 32.7	13 58.5
18 Sa	19 47 45	27 25 32	3♓46 55	10♓22 15	11 08.0	5 05.6	1 41.4	4 06.6	12 49.4	12 42.7	22 18.0	9 34.4	17 33.8	13 57.6
19 Su	19 51 41	28 26 38	17 00 54	23 42 53	11 05.7	5 31.5	2 54.8	4 53.7	13 12.2	12 51.0	22 24.9	9 32.6	17 34.8	13 56.6
20 M	19 55 38	29 27 43	0♈28 10	7♈16 43	11 03.7	6 03.4	4 08.1	5 40.9	13 34.9	12 59.3	22 31.7	9 30.8	17 35.8	13 55.6
21 Tu	19 59 34	0♒28 47	14 08 29	21 03 26	11D 02.6	6 40.8	5 21.4	6 28.1	13 57.5	13 07.9	22 38.6	9 29.0	17 36.7	13 54.5
22 W	20 03 31	1 29 51	28 01 28	5♉02 30	11 02.4	7 23.1	6 34.7	7 15.2	14 20.1	13 16.6	22 45.5	9 27.1	17 37.7	13 53.5
23 Th	20 07 27	2 30 53	12♉06 24	19 12 58	11 03.1	8 09.8	7 47.8	8 02.4	14 42.5	13 25.4	22 52.4	9 25.2	17 38.6	13 52.4
24 F	20 11 24	3 31 54	26 21 57	3♊33 05	11 04.4	9 00.5	9 00.9	8 49.7	15 04.8	13 34.3	22 59.4	9 23.3	17 39.4	13 51.3
25 Sa	20 15 20	4 32 54	10♊45 58	18 00 10	11 05.8	9 54.8	10 14.0	9 36.9	15 27.0	13 43.4	23 06.4	9 21.3	17 40.3	13 50.2
26 Su	20 19 17	5 33 53	25 15 10	2♋30 23	11R 06.9	10 52.4	11 27.0	10 24.1	15 49.2	13 52.6	23 13.4	9 19.3	17 41.1	13 49.1
27 M	20 23 14	6 34 51	9♋45 12	16 58 56	11 07.0	11 53.0	12 39.9	11 11.4	16 11.2	14 02.0	23 20.4	9 17.3	17 41.8	13 47.9
28 Tu	20 27 10	7 35 49	24 10 53	1♌20 21	11 05.8	12 56.3	13 52.7	11 58.7	16 33.1	14 11.5	23 27.5	9 15.2	17 42.6	13 46.7
29 W	20 31 07	8 36 45	8♌26 41	15 29 14	11 03.1	14 02.0	15 05.5	12 46.0	16 54.9	14 21.1	23 34.6	9 13.1	17 43.3	13 45.5
30 Th	20 35 03	9 37 40	22 27 26	29 20 50	10 59.1	15 10.0	16 18.2	13 33.3	17 16.6	14 30.8	23 41.7	9 10.9	17 43.9	13 44.3
31 F	20 39 00	10 38 34	6♍09 03	12♍51 50	10 54.3	16 20.1	17 30.8	14 20.6	17 38.2	14 40.7	23 48.8	9 08.7	17 44.6	13 43.0

LONGITUDE — February 1964

Day	Sid.Time	☉	0 hr ☽	Noon ☽	True ☊	☿	♀	♂	⚳	♃	♄	♅	♆	♇
1 Sa	20 42 56	11♒39 28	19♍29 03	26♍00 40	10♋49.2	17♑32.0	18♓43.3	15♒07.9	17♐59.7	14♈50.7	23♒55.9	9♍06.5	17♏45.2	13♍41.8
2 Su	20 46 53	12 40 20	2♎26 48	8♎47 39	10R 44.6	18 45.7	19 55.8	15 55.3	18 21.0	15 00.7	24 03.0	9R 04.3	17 45.7	13R 40.5
3 M	20 50 49	13 41 12	15 03 30	21 14 45	10 40.9	20 01.1	21 08.2	16 42.7	18 42.3	15 11.0	24 10.2	9 02.0	17 46.3	13 39.2
4 Tu	20 54 46	14 42 03	27 21 51	3♏25 21	10 38.6	21 17.9	22 20.5	17 30.0	19 03.4	15 21.3	24 17.4	8 59.7	17 46.8	13 37.9
5 W	20 58 43	15 42 53	9♏25 46	15 23 45	10D 37.8	22 36.2	23 32.7	18 17.4	19 24.4	15 31.7	24 24.6	8 57.4	17 47.2	13 36.5
6 Th	21 02 39	16 43 42	21 19 55	27 14 54	10 38.4	23 55.8	24 44.9	19 04.8	19 45.3	15 42.3	24 31.8	8 55.0	17 47.7	13 35.2
7 F	21 06 36	17 44 30	3♐09 21	9♐03 55	10 39.9	25 16.7	25 56.9	19 52.2	20 06.1	15 53.0	24 39.0	8 52.7	17 48.1	13 33.8
8 Sa	21 10 32	18 45 17	14 59 13	20 55 53	10 41.7	26 38.8	27 08.9	20 39.6	20 26.7	16 03.8	24 46.2	8 50.3	17 48.4	13 32.4
9 Su	21 14 29	19 46 04	26 54 28	2♑55 31	10R 43.0	28 02.0	28 20.8	21 27.0	20 47.2	16 14.7	24 53.4	8 47.8	17 48.8	13 31.0
10 M	21 18 25	20 46 49	8♑59 32	15 06 56	10 43.2	29 26.3	29 32.6	22 14.5	21 07.6	16 25.7	25 00.7	8 45.4	17 49.1	13 29.6
11 Tu	21 22 22	21 47 33	21 18 05	27 33 19	10 41.7	0♒51.7	0♈44.3	23 01.9	21 27.8	16 36.8	25 07.9	8 42.9	17 49.3	13 28.2
12 W	21 26 18	22 48 16	3♒52 49	10♒16 44	10 38.1	2 18.1	1 56.0	23 49.3	21 47.9	16 48.0	25 15.2	8 40.4	17 49.6	13 26.7
13 Th	21 30 15	23 48 57	16 45 08	23 17 58	10 32.6	3 45.5	3 07.5	24 36.8	22 07.9	16 59.3	25 22.4	8 37.9	17 49.8	13 25.3
14 F	21 34 12	24 49 37	29 55 07	6♓36 24	10 25.4	5 13.9	4 18.9	25 24.2	22 27.7	17 10.7	25 29.7	8 35.4	17 49.9	13 23.8
15 Sa	21 38 08	25 50 16	13♓21 31	20 10 11	10 17.4	6 43.2	5 30.2	26 11.6	22 47.3	17 22.2	25 36.9	8 32.9	17 50.0	13 22.3
16 Su	21 42 05	26 50 53	27 01 59	3♈56 33	10 09.5	8 13.5	6 41.4	26 59.1	23 06.9	17 33.8	25 44.2	8 30.3	17 50.1	13 20.8
17 M	21 46 01	27 51 28	10♈53 28	17 52 20	10 02.6	9 44.8	7 52.5	27 46.5	23 26.2	17 45.4	25 51.4	8 27.8	17 50.2	13 19.3
18 Tu	21 49 58	28 52 01	24 52 44	1♉54 21	9 57.4	11 16.9	9 03.5	28 33.9	23 45.5	17 57.2	25 58.7	8 25.2	17R 50.2	13 17.8
19 W	21 53 54	29 52 33	8♉56 51	15 59 57	9 54.5	12 50.0	10 14.4	29 21.4	24 04.5	18 09.1	26 05.9	8 22.6	17 50.2	13 16.3
20 Th	21 57 51	0♓53 03	23 03 27	0♊07 08	9D 53.5	14 24.0	11 25.1	0♓08.8	24 23.5	18 21.0	26 13.2	8 20.0	17 50.1	13 14.8
21 F	22 01 47	1 53 31	7♊10 50	14 14 25	9 54.0	15 59.0	12 35.8	0 56.2	24 42.2	18 33.1	26 20.4	8 17.4	17 50.1	13 13.2
22 Sa	22 05 44	2 53 57	21 17 45	28 20 40	9R 55.0	17 34.9	13 46.3	1 43.6	25 00.8	18 45.2	26 27.6	8 14.8	17 50.0	13 11.7
23 Su	22 09 41	3 54 21	5♋23 02	12♋24 38	9 55.4	19 11.7	14 56.6	2 31.0	25 19.3	18 57.4	26 34.8	8 12.2	17 49.8	13 10.2
24 M	22 13 37	4 54 44	19 25 15	26 24 37	9 54.2	20 49.5	16 06.9	3 18.4	25 37.5	19 09.7	26 42.0	8 09.5	17 49.6	13 08.6
25 Tu	22 17 34	5 55 04	3♌22 26	10♌18 20	9 50.6	22 28.3	17 17.0	4 05.8	25 55.6	19 22.0	26 49.2	8 06.9	17 49.4	13 07.0
26 W	22 21 30	6 55 23	17 11 58	24 02 57	9 44.3	24 08.1	18 26.9	4 53.2	26 13.6	19 34.5	26 56.4	8 04.3	17 49.2	13 05.5
27 Th	22 25 27	7 55 39	0♍50 52	7♍35 23	9 35.7	25 48.8	19 36.7	5 40.6	26 31.3	19 47.0	27 03.6	8 01.7	17 48.9	13 03.9
28 F	22 29 23	8 55 54	14 16 08	20 52 51	9 25.4	27 30.5	20 46.4	6 27.9	26 48.9	19 59.6	27 10.8	7 59.0	17 48.6	13 02.3
29 Sa	22 33 20	9 56 08	27 25 18	3♎53 21	9 14.3	29 13.3	21 55.9	7 15.3	27 06.3	20 12.2	27 17.9	7 56.4	17 48.2	13 00.8

Astro Data	Dy Hr Mn
☽0S	6 10:02
☿D	15 11:42
☽0N	20 20:43
♃⊼♇	26 3:45
☽0S	2 18:23
♀0N	11 23:59
☽0N	17 1:48
♃⊼♆	17 21:42
♆R	18 14:29

Planet Ingress	Dy Hr Mn
♂ ♒	13 6:13
♀ ♓	17 2:54
☉ ♒	21 0:41
♀ ♈	10 21:09
☿ ♒	10 21:30
☉ ♓	19 14:57
♂ ♓	20 7:33
☿ ♓	29 22:50

Last Aspect Dy Hr Mn		☽ Ingress Dy Hr Mn	
2 10:11	♄ ☍	♍	3 2:48
4 21:48	♂ △	♎	5 10:10
7 12:03	♂ □	♏	7 21:04
10 4:58	♂ ✶	♐	10 9:49
12 10:48	♀ ✶	♑	12 22:14
14 20:43	☉ ☌	♒	15 8:48
17 2:33	♄ ☌	♓	17 17:04
19 21:06	☉ ✶	♈	19 23:10
21 14:46	♄ ✶	♉	22 3:23
23 18:12	♄ □	♊	24 6:05
25 20:31	♄ △	♋	26 7:51
27 13:11	♆ △	♌	28 9:45
30 2:04	♄ ☍	♍	30 13:09

Last Aspect Dy Hr Mn		☽ Ingress Dy Hr Mn	
31 21:16	♀ ☍	♎	1 19:25
3 17:47	♄ △	♏	4 5:12
6 6:26	♄ □	♐	6 17:35
9 1:52	♀ □	♑	9 6:11
10 17:16	♆ ✶	♒	11 16:39
13 15:48	♄ ☌	♓	14 0:09
15 7:54	♆ △	♈	16 5:10
18 6:25	☉ ✶	♉	18 8:45
20 5:19	♄ □	♊	20 11:48
22 8:46	♄ △	♋	22 14:49
23 23:22	♃ □	♌	24 18:11
26 17:08	♄ ☍	♍	26 22:30
28 6:25	♆ ✶	♎	29 4:46

☽ Phases & Eclipses Dy Hr Mn	
6 15:58	☾ 15♎22
14 20:43	● 23♑43
14 20:29:31	● P 0.559
22 5:29	☽ 1♉13
28 23:23	○ 8♌05
5 12:42	☾ 15♏45
13 13:01	● 23♒52
20 13:24	☽ 0♊57
27 12:39	○ 7♍57

Astro Data

1 January 1964
Julian Day # 23376
SVP 5♓46'01"
GC 26♐20.2 ⚴ 16♏50.7
Eris 9♈55.3 ⚵ 21♏03.1
⚷ 11♓01.1 ⚶ 0♑03.5
☽ Mean ☊ 11♋19.7

1 February 1964
Julian Day # 23407
SVP 5♓45'56"
GC 26♐20.3 ⚴ 27♏33.2
Eris 10♈01.9 ⚵ 29♏00.7
⚷ 12♓29.4 ⚶ 16♑34.2
☽ Mean ☊ 9♋41.2

March 1964

LONGITUDE

Day	Sid.Time	☉	0 hr ☽	Noon ☽	True ☊	☿	♀	♂	⚳	♃	♄	♅	♆	♇
1 Su	22 37 16	10♓56 19	10♎16 56	16♎36 06	9♋03.6	0♓57.1	23♈05.3	8♓02.6	27♐23.6	20♈24.9	27♒25.0	7♍53.8	17♏47.8	12♍59.2
2 M	22 41 13	11 56 29	22 50 58	29 01 44	8R 54.4	2 41.9	24 14.5	8 50.0	27 40.6	20 37.7	27 32.1	7R 51.1	17R 47.4	12R 57.6
3 Tu	22 45 10	12 56 38	5♏08 43	11♏12 17	8 47.2	4 27.8	25 23.6	9 37.3	27 57.5	20 50.6	27 39.2	7 48.5	17 47.0	12 56.0
4 W	22 49 06	13 56 44	17 12 53	23 11 03	8 42.5	6 14.8	26 32.5	10 24.6	28 14.2	21 03.5	27 46.3	7 45.9	17 46.5	12 54.5
5 Th	22 53 03	14 56 50	29 07 19	5♐02 20	8D 40.2	8 02.9	27 41.2	11 11.9	28 30.7	21 16.5	27 53.4	7 43.3	17 46.0	12 52.9
6 F	22 56 59	15 56 53	10♐56 43	16 51 08	8 39.6	9 52.1	28 49.8	11 59.2	28 47.0	21 29.5	28 00.4	7 40.7	17 45.5	12 51.3
7 Sa	23 00 56	16 56 56	22 46 18	28 42 52	8R 40.0	11 42.3	29 58.2	12 46.5	29 03.1	21 42.7	28 07.4	7 38.1	17 44.9	12 49.7
8 Su	23 04 52	17 56 56	4♑41 33	10♑43 00	8 40.2	13 33.7	1♉06.4	13 33.7	29 19.0	21 55.8	28 14.4	7 35.5	17 44.3	12 48.2
9 M	23 08 49	18 56 55	16 47 51	22 56 43	8 39.3	15 26.1	2 14.5	14 21.0	29 34.7	22 09.1	28 21.4	7 33.0	17 43.7	12 46.6
10 Tu	23 12 45	19 56 52	29 10 06	5♒28 30	8 36.2	17 19.6	3 22.4	15 08.2	29 50.2	22 22.4	28 28.3	7 30.4	17 43.0	12 45.0
11 W	23 16 42	20 56 48	11♒52 16	18 21 41	8 30.6	19 14.1	4 30.1	15 55.4	0♑05.5	22 35.7	28 35.2	7 27.9	17 42.3	12 43.5
12 Th	23 20 39	21 56 41	24 56 54	1♓37 56	8 22.2	21 09.7	5 37.6	16 42.6	0 20.6	22 49.1	28 42.1	7 25.3	17 41.6	12 41.9
13 F	23 24 35	22 56 33	8♓24 39	15 16 49	8 11.7	23 06.2	6 44.9	17 29.8	0 35.4	23 02.6	28 48.9	7 22.8	17 40.9	12 40.3
14 Sa	23 28 32	23 56 23	22 14 00	29 15 42	7 59.8	25 03.6	7 52.0	18 16.9	0 50.0	23 16.1	28 55.8	7 20.3	17 40.1	12 38.8
15 Su	23 32 28	24 56 11	6♈21 15	13♈29 57	7 47.9	27 01.8	8 58.9	19 04.1	1 04.4	23 29.6	29 02.6	7 17.8	17 39.3	12 37.2
16 M	23 36 25	25 55 56	20 41 01	27 53 39	7 37.3	29 00.8	10 05.6	19 51.2	1 18.6	23 43.2	29 09.3	7 15.4	17 38.4	12 35.7
17 Tu	23 40 21	26 55 40	5♉07 05	12♉20 34	7 29.0	1♈00.3	11 12.0	20 38.3	1 32.6	23 56.8	29 16.0	7 12.9	17 37.6	12 34.2
18 W	23 44 18	27 55 21	19 33 26	26 45 09	7 23.5	3 00.3	12 18.3	21 25.3	1 46.3	24 10.5	29 22.7	7 10.5	17 36.7	12 32.7
19 Th	23 48 14	28 55 01	3♊55 12	11♊03 16	7 20.6	5 00.5	13 24.3	22 12.4	1 59.7	24 24.3	29 29.4	7 08.1	17 35.8	12 31.2
20 F	23 52 11	29 54 37	18 09 05	25 12 28	7 19.8	7 00.7	14 30.1	22 59.4	2 13.0	24 38.0	29 36.0	7 05.7	17 34.8	12 29.7
21 Sa	23 56 07	0♈54 12	2♋13 20	9♋11 40	7 19.8	9 00.8	15 35.6	23 46.4	2 26.0	24 51.8	29 42.6	7 03.4	17 33.8	12 28.2
22 Su	0 00 04	1 53 44	16 07 28	23 00 46	7 19.2	11 00.4	16 40.9	24 33.3	2 38.7	25 05.7	29 49.1	7 01.1	17 32.8	12 26.7
23 M	0 04 01	2 53 14	29 51 37	6♌40 01	7 16.9	12 59.2	17 45.9	25 20.2	2 51.2	25 19.6	29 55.6	6 58.8	17 31.8	12 25.2
24 Tu	0 07 57	3 52 42	13♌26 00	20 09 31	7 12.0	14 56.9	18 50.6	26 07.1	3 03.5	25 33.5	0♓02.1	6 56.5	17 30.8	12 23.8
25 W	0 11 54	4 52 07	26 50 33	3♍28 59	7 04.0	16 53.1	19 55.1	26 54.0	3 15.4	25 47.5	0 08.5	6 54.3	17 29.7	12 22.4
26 Th	0 15 50	5 51 30	10♍04 44	16 37 40	6 53.3	18 47.4	20 59.3	27 40.8	3 27.2	26 01.4	0 14.9	6 52.1	17 28.6	12 20.9
27 F	0 19 47	6 50 51	23 07 38	29 34 32	6 40.5	20 39.4	22 03.2	28 27.6	3 38.6	26 15.5	0 21.2	6 49.9	17 27.5	12 19.5
28 Sa	0 23 43	7 50 10	5♎58 13	12♎18 36	6 26.9	22 28.7	23 06.8	29 14.4	3 49.8	26 29.5	0 27.5	6 47.8	17 26.3	12 18.1
29 Su	0 27 40	8 49 27	18 35 39	24 49 22	6 13.5	24 14.9	24 10.0	0♈01.2	4 00.8	26 43.6	0 33.7	6 45.6	17 25.2	12 16.7
30 M	0 31 36	9 48 42	0♏59 47	7♏07 01	6 01.6	25 57.6	25 13.0	0 47.9	4 11.4	26 57.7	0 39.9	6 43.6	17 24.0	12 15.4
31 Tu	0 35 33	10 47 55	13 11 17	19 12 48	5 52.0	27 36.4	26 15.6	1 34.6	4 21.8	27 11.8	0 46.0	6 41.5	17 22.8	12 14.0

April 1964

LONGITUDE

Day	Sid.Time	☉	0 hr ☽	Noon ☽	True ☊	☿	♀	♂	⚳	♃	♄	♅	♆	♇
1 W	0 39 30	11♈47 06	25♏11 54	1♐08 59	5♋45.1	29♈10.9	27♉18.0	2♈21.2	4♑31.9	27♈26.0	0♓52.1	6♍39.5	17♏21.5	12♍12.7
2 Th	0 43 26	12 46 15	7♐04 29	12 58 54	5R 41.1	0♉40.8	28 19.9	3 07.8	4 41.7	27 40.2	0 58.1	6R 37.5	17R 20.3	12R 11.3
3 F	0 47 23	13 45 23	18 52 48	24 46 46	5D 39.3	2 05.7	29 21.5	3 54.4	4 51.3	27 54.4	1 04.1	6 35.6	17 19.0	12 10.0
4 Sa	0 51 19	14 44 29	0♑41 27	6♑37 31	5R 38.9	3 25.4	0♊22.8	4 41.0	5 00.5	28 08.6	1 10.1	6 33.7	17 17.7	12 08.8
5 Su	0 55 16	15 43 33	12 35 38	18 36 31	5 39.0	4 39.6	1 23.7	5 27.5	5 09.4	28 22.8	1 16.0	6 31.8	17 16.4	12 07.5
6 M	0 59 12	16 42 35	24 40 50	0♒49 17	5 38.3	5 48.1	2 24.2	6 14.0	5 18.1	28 37.1	1 21.8	6 30.0	17 15.1	12 06.2
7 Tu	1 03 09	17 41 35	7♒02 30	13 21 04	5 35.8	6 50.7	3 24.3	7 00.5	5 26.4	28 51.4	1 27.6	6 28.2	17 13.7	12 05.0
8 W	1 07 05	18 40 34	19 45 31	26 16 17	5 31.0	7 47.2	4 24.1	7 46.9	5 34.5	29 05.7	1 33.3	6 26.4	17 12.3	12 03.8
9 Th	1 11 02	19 39 31	2♓53 40	9♓37 52	5 23.6	8 37.5	5 23.4	8 33.3	5 42.2	29 20.0	1 38.9	6 24.7	17 10.9	12 02.6
10 F	1 14 59	20 38 26	16 28 53	23 26 36	5 14.1	9 21.6	6 22.3	9 19.6	5 49.6	29 34.4	1 44.5	6 23.1	17 09.5	12 01.4
11 Sa	1 18 55	21 37 19	0♈30 38	7♈40 30	5 03.1	9 59.2	7 20.7	10 06.0	5 56.6	29 48.7	1 50.1	6 21.4	17 08.1	12 00.3
12 Su	1 22 52	22 36 10	14 55 30	22 14 47	4 52.0	10 30.3	8 18.7	10 52.2	6 03.4	0♉03.1	1 55.6	6 19.9	17 06.7	11 59.1
13 M	1 26 48	23 34 59	29 37 22	7♉02 12	4 42.0	10 55.1	9 16.2	11 38.5	6 09.8	0 17.4	2 01.0	6 18.3	17 05.2	11 58.0
14 Tu	1 30 45	24 33 46	14♉28 11	21 54 15	4 34.1	11 13.3	10 13.2	12 24.7	6 15.9	0 31.8	2 06.3	6 16.8	17 03.7	11 57.0
15 W	1 34 41	25 32 31	29 19 23	6♊42 40	4 28.8	11 25.2	11 09.7	13 10.8	6 21.7	0 46.2	2 11.6	6 15.4	17 02.3	11 55.9
16 Th	1 38 38	26 31 14	14♊03 18	21 20 37	4D 26.2	11R 30.8	12 05.7	13 56.9	6 27.1	1 00.6	2 16.9	6 14.0	17 00.8	11 54.9
17 F	1 42 34	27 29 55	28 34 08	5♋43 31	4 25.7	11 30.3	13 01.2	14 43.0	6 32.2	1 15.0	2 22.0	6 12.6	16 59.3	11 53.9
18 Sa	1 46 31	28 28 34	12♋48 31	19 49 04	4R 26.0	11 23.8	13 56.0	15 29.0	6 36.9	1 29.4	2 27.1	6 11.3	16 57.8	11 52.9
19 Su	1 50 28	29 27 10	26 45 10	3♌36 54	4 26.1	11 11.7	14 50.3	16 15.0	6 41.4	1 43.8	2 32.2	6 10.1	16 56.2	11 51.9
20 M	1 54 24	0♉25 44	10♌24 24	17 07 50	4 24.9	10 54.3	15 44.0	17 01.0	6 45.4	1 58.2	2 37.1	6 08.9	16 54.7	11 51.0
21 Tu	1 58 21	1 24 16	23 47 25	0♍23 20	4 21.4	10 32.1	16 37.1	17 46.9	6 49.1	2 12.6	2 42.0	6 07.7	16 53.1	11 50.0
22 W	2 02 17	2 22 45	6♍55 45	13 24 53	4 15.5	10 05.4	17 29.4	18 32.7	6 52.5	2 27.0	2 46.8	6 06.6	16 51.6	11 49.2
23 Th	2 06 14	3 21 13	19 50 50	26 13 47	4 07.2	9 34.9	18 21.2	19 18.5	6 55.5	2 41.4	2 51.6	6 05.5	16 50.0	11 48.3
24 F	2 10 10	4 19 38	2♎33 49	8♎51 02	3 57.2	9 01.2	19 12.2	20 04.3	6 58.1	2 55.8	2 56.3	6 04.5	16 48.4	11 47.4
25 Sa	2 14 07	5 18 01	15 05 30	21 17 20	3 46.3	8 24.8	20 02.4	20 50.0	7 00.4	3 10.2	3 00.9	6 03.5	16 46.8	11 46.6
26 Su	2 18 03	6 16 23	27 26 35	3♏33 21	3 35.7	7 46.6	20 52.0	21 35.6	7 02.3	3 24.6	3 05.4	6 02.6	16 45.2	11 45.8
27 M	2 22 00	7 14 43	9♏37 45	15 39 55	3 26.2	7 07.2	21 40.7	22 21.3	7 03.9	3 39.0	3 09.9	6 01.7	16 43.6	11 45.1
28 Tu	2 25 56	8 13 00	21 40 01	27 38 15	3 18.7	6 27.4	22 28.6	23 06.8	7 05.1	3 53.4	3 14.2	6 00.9	16 42.0	11 44.3
29 W	2 29 53	9 11 17	3♐34 53	9♐30 11	3 13.4	5 47.9	23 15.7	23 52.4	7 05.9	4 07.7	3 18.5	6 00.1	16 40.4	11 43.6
30 Th	2 33 50	10 09 31	15 24 30	21 18 14	3 10.5	5 09.3	24 02.0	24 37.8	7R 06.4	4 22.1	3 22.8	5 59.4	16 38.8	11 43.0

Astro Data	Dy Hr Mn
☽0S	1 2:50
♃□♅	11 0:09
☽0N	15 8:54
☿0N	18 2:08
☉0N	20 14:10
☽0S	28 10:38
♃□♇	31 15:23
♂0N	1 1:53
☽0N	11 18:34
☿R	16 21:51
♃⚹♄	24 13:05
☽0S	24 17:27

Planet Ingress		Dy Hr Mn
♀	♉	7 12:38
⚳	♑	11 3:20
☿	♈	16 23:54
☉	♈	20 14:10
♄	♓	24 4:18
♂	♈	29 11:24
☿	♉	2 0:57
♀	♊	4 3:03
♃	♉	12 6:52
☉	♉	20 1:27

Last Aspect Dy Hr Mn			☽ Ingress	Dy Hr Mn
2 9:04	♄	△	♏	2 13:54
4 21:22	♄	□	♐	5 1:47
7 10:48	♄	⚹	♑	7 14:35
9 10:26	♃	□	♒	10 1:35
12 6:43	♄	☌	♓	12 9:05
14 3:41	☿	☌	♈	14 13:15
16 14:07	♄	⚹	♉	16 15:30
18 16:26	♄	□	♊	18 17:26
20 19:34	♄	△	♋	20 20:11
22 15:42	♃	□	♌	23 0:15
24 21:52	♃	△	♍	25 5:42
27 9:47	♂	☍	♎	27 12:48
29 15:46	♃	☍	♏	29 22:03

Last Aspect Dy Hr Mn			☽ Ingress	Dy Hr Mn
1 3:29	♀	☍	♐	1 9:41
3 18:29	♃	△	♑	3 22:36
6 7:38	♃	□	♒	6 10:24
8 17:14	♃	⚹	♓	8 18:47
10 1:12	♆	△	♈	10 23:08
12 12:37	☉	☌	♉	13 0:37
14 4:12	♆	☍	♊	15 1:06
16 21:13	☉	⚹	♋	17 2:23
19 4:09	☉	□	♌	19 5:40
20 11:47	♂	△	♍	21 11:17
22 20:08	♀	□	♎	23 19:08
25 11:03	♂	☍	♏	26 5:01
27 14:07	♆	☌	♐	28 16:46

☽ Phases & Eclipses Dy Hr Mn		
6 10:00	☾	15♐52
14 2:14	●	23♓32
20 20:39	☽	0♋16
28 2:48	○	7♎27
5 5:45	☾	15♑28
12 12:37	●	22♈38
19 4:09	☽	29♋08
26 17:50	○	6♏31

Astro Data

1 March 1964
Julian Day # 23436
SVP 5♓45'53"
GC 26♐20.3 ⚴ 4♐42.2
Eris 10♈16.5 ⚵ 3♐51.4
⚷ 14♓14.3 ⚶ 1♒27.5
☽ Mean ☊ 8♋09.1

1 April 1964
Julian Day # 23467
SVP 5♓45'50"
GC 26♐20.4 ⚴ 7♐12.6R
Eris 10♈36.9 ⚵ 4♐50.9R
⚷ 16♓08.3 ⚶ 16♒21.0
☽ Mean ☊ 6♋30.6

LONGITUDE May 1964

Day	Sid.Time	☉	0 hr ☽	Noon☽	True☊	☿	♀	♂	⚳	♃	♄	♅	♆	♇
1 F	2 37 46	11♉07 44	27♐11 48	3♑05 40	3♋09.7	4♉32.4	24♊47.3	25♈23.3	7♑06.5	4♉36.4	3♓26.9	5♍58.8	16♏37.2	11♍42.3
2 Sa	2 41 43	12 05 56	9♑00 23	14 56 30	3D 10.3	3R 57.8	25 31.7	26 08.7	7R 06.2	4 50.8	3 31.0	5R 58.2	16R 35.6	11R 41.7
3 Su	2 45 39	13 04 06	20 54 36	26 55 18	3 11.5	3 25.9	26 15.1	26 54.0	7 05.5	5 05.1	3 35.0	5 57.6	16 33.9	11 41.1
4 M	2 49 36	14 02 15	2♒59 14	9♒07 03	3R 12.4	2 57.2	26 57.5	27 39.3	7 04.5	5 19.4	3 38.9	5 57.1	16 32.3	11 40.5
5 Tu	2 53 32	15 00 22	15 19 23	21 36 51	3 12.3	2 32.3	27 38.9	28 24.6	7 03.1	5 33.7	3 42.8	5 56.6	16 30.7	11 40.0
6 W	2 57 29	15 58 27	28 00 01	4♓29 24	3 10.6	2 11.3	28 19.2	29 09.8	7 01.3	5 48.0	3 46.5	5 56.2	16 29.0	11 39.5
7 Th	3 01 25	16 56 31	11♓05 25	17 48 25	3 07.0	1 54.5	28 58.4	29 55.0	6 59.1	6 02.2	3 50.2	5 55.9	16 27.4	11 39.0
8 F	3 05 22	17 54 34	24 38 35	1♈35 56	3 01.7	1 42.2	29 36.4	0♉40.1	6 56.6	6 16.5	3 53.8	5 55.6	16 25.8	11 38.5
9 Sa	3 09 19	18 52 36	8♈40 21	15 51 29	2 55.3	1 34.4	0♋13.3	1 25.1	6 53.6	6 30.7	3 57.3	5 55.3	16 24.1	11 38.1
10 Su	3 13 15	19 50 36	23 08 47	0♉31 33	2 48.7	1D 31.3	0 48.8	2 10.2	6 50.3	6 44.9	4 00.7	5 55.1	16 22.5	11 37.7
11 M	3 17 12	20 48 34	7♉58 52	15 29 40	2 42.6	1 32.8	1 23.1	2 55.1	6 46.7	6 59.1	4 04.0	5 55.0	16 20.9	11 37.4
12 Tu	3 21 08	21 46 32	23 02 47	0♊37 01	2 37.9	1 39.0	1 56.0	3 40.0	6 42.6	7 13.2	4 07.3	5D 54.9	16 19.2	11 37.0
13 W	3 25 05	22 44 27	8♊11 07	15 43 55	2 35.0	1 49.8	2 27.6	4 24.9	6 38.2	7 27.3	4 10.4	5 54.9	16 17.6	11 36.7
14 Th	3 29 01	23 42 21	23 14 17	0♋41 17	2D 33.9	2 05.1	2 57.6	5 09.7	6 33.4	7 41.4	4 13.5	5 54.9	16 16.0	11 36.5
15 F	3 32 58	24 40 14	8♋04 05	15 22 03	2 34.4	2 24.9	3 26.2	5 54.5	6 28.2	7 55.5	4 16.5	5 55.0	16 14.4	11 36.2
16 Sa	3 36 55	25 38 04	22 34 41	29 41 41	2 35.7	2 49.0	3 53.1	6 39.2	6 22.7	8 09.6	4 19.4	5 55.1	16 12.8	11 36.0
17 Su	3 40 51	26 35 53	6♌42 54	13♌38 17	2 37.0	3 17.3	4 18.4	7 23.8	6 16.8	8 23.6	4 22.2	5 55.3	16 11.2	11 35.8
18 M	3 44 48	27 33 40	20 27 55	27 11 59	2R 37.6	3 49.7	4 42.1	8 08.4	6 10.6	8 37.6	4 24.9	5 55.6	16 09.6	11 35.7
19 Tu	3 48 44	28 31 25	3♍50 42	10♍24 23	2 36.9	4 26.2	5 03.9	8 52.9	6 04.0	8 51.5	4 27.5	5 55.9	16 08.0	11 35.6
20 W	3 52 41	29 29 09	16 53 20	23 17 53	2 34.8	5 06.5	5 23.9	9 37.4	5 57.1	9 05.4	4 30.0	5 56.2	16 06.4	11 35.5
21 Th	3 56 37	0♊26 51	29 38 22	5♎55 09	2 31.3	5 50.5	5 42.1	10 21.8	5 49.8	9 19.3	4 32.5	5 56.6	16 04.8	11 35.4
22 F	4 00 34	1 24 32	12♎08 33	18 18 52	2 26.7	6 38.2	5 58.3	11 06.2	5 42.2	9 33.1	4 34.8	5 57.1	16 03.3	11D 35.4
23 Sa	4 04 30	2 22 11	24 26 24	0♏31 27	2 21.6	7 29.4	6 12.5	11 50.5	5 34.3	9 47.0	4 37.1	5 57.6	16 01.7	11 35.4
24 Su	4 08 27	3 19 48	6♏34 16	12 35 06	2 16.5	8 24.0	6 24.6	12 34.8	5 26.0	10 00.7	4 39.2	5 58.2	16 00.2	11 35.4
25 M	4 12 23	4 17 25	18 34 12	24 31 49	2 12.1	9 21.9	6 34.6	13 19.0	5 17.5	10 14.5	4 41.3	5 58.8	15 58.6	11 35.5
26 Tu	4 16 20	5 15 00	0♐28 11	6♐23 31	2 08.7	10 23.1	6 42.5	14 03.1	5 08.6	10 28.1	4 43.3	5 59.4	15 57.1	11 35.6
27 W	4 20 17	6 12 34	12 18 06	18 12 11	2 06.6	11 27.4	6 48.1	14 47.2	4 59.4	10 41.8	4 45.2	6 00.2	15 55.6	11 35.7
28 Th	4 24 13	7 10 07	24 06 02	29 59 60	2D 05.8	12 34.7	6R 51.4	15 31.3	4 49.9	10 55.4	4 46.9	6 00.9	15 54.1	11 35.9
29 F	4 28 10	8 07 39	5♑54 23	11♑49 32	2 06.1	13 45.1	6 52.4	16 15.2	4 40.2	11 09.0	4 48.6	6 01.8	15 52.6	11 36.1
30 Sa	4 32 06	9 05 09	17 45 52	23 43 47	2 07.3	14 58.3	6 51.1	16 59.2	4 30.1	11 22.5	4 50.2	6 02.6	15 51.1	11 36.3
31 Su	4 36 03	10 02 39	29 43 44	5♒46 11	2 08.8	16 14.5	6 47.4	17 43.1	4 19.8	11 36.0	4 51.7	6 03.6	15 49.7	11 36.5

LONGITUDE June 1964

Day	Sid.Time	☉	0 hr ☽	Noon☽	True☊	☿	♀	♂	⚳	♃	♄	♅	♆	♇
1 M	4 39 59	11♊00 09	11♒51 37	18♒00 34	2♋10.4	17♉33.5	6♋41.3	18♉26.9	4♑09.2	11♉49.4	4♓53.1	6♍04.6	15♏48.2	11♍36.8
2 Tu	4 43 56	11 57 37	24 13 31	0♓31 01	2R 11.5	18 55.3	6R 32.8	19 10.7	3R 58.4	12 02.8	4 54.4	6 05.6	15R 46.8	11 37.1
3 W	4 47 53	12 55 04	6♓53 33	13 21 36	2 11.9	20 19.9	6 21.9	19 54.4	3 47.3	12 16.1	4 55.6	6 06.7	15 45.4	11 37.5
4 Th	4 51 49	13 52 31	19 55 34	26 35 51	2 11.4	21 47.2	6 08.6	20 38.1	3 36.0	12 29.4	4 56.7	6 07.8	15 44.0	11 37.9
5 F	4 55 46	14 49 58	3♈22 41	10♈16 16	2 10.2	23 17.2	5 52.9	21 21.7	3 24.5	12 42.6	4 57.7	6 09.0	15 42.6	11 38.3
6 Sa	4 59 42	15 47 23	17 16 37	24 23 36	2 08.5	24 49.9	5 34.9	22 05.2	3 12.8	12 55.8	4 58.6	6 10.2	15 41.2	11 38.7
7 Su	5 03 39	16 44 48	1♉36 57	8♉56 11	2 06.5	26 25.3	5 14.6	22 48.7	3 00.8	13 08.9	4 59.4	6 11.5	15 39.9	11 39.2
8 M	5 07 35	17 42 13	16 20 40	23 49 34	2 04.8	28 03.3	4 52.1	23 32.2	2 48.7	13 22.0	5 00.1	6 12.9	15 38.6	11 39.7
9 Tu	5 11 32	18 39 36	1♊21 57	8♊56 41	2 03.5	29 44.0	4 27.5	24 15.5	2 36.4	13 35.0	5 00.8	6 14.3	15 37.2	11 40.2
10 W	5 15 28	19 36 59	16 32 37	24 08 31	2D 02.8	1♊27.4	4 00.8	24 58.9	2 23.9	13 47.9	5 01.3	6 15.7	15 35.9	11 40.7
11 Th	5 19 25	20 34 22	1♋43 12	9♋15 29	2 02.8	3 13.3	3 32.3	25 42.2	2 11.3	14 00.8	5 01.7	6 17.2	15 34.7	11 41.3
12 F	5 23 22	21 31 43	16 44 21	24 08 50	2 03.3	5 01.8	3 02.0	26 25.4	1 58.6	14 13.6	5 02.0	6 18.8	15 33.4	11 41.9
13 Sa	5 27 18	22 29 04	1♌28 11	8♌41 46	2 04.1	6 52.8	2 30.0	27 08.5	1 45.8	14 26.4	5 02.2	6 20.3	15 32.2	11 42.6
14 Su	5 31 15	23 26 24	15 49 11	22 50 08	2 04.8	8 46.4	1 56.6	27 51.6	1 32.8	14 39.1	5R 02.3	6 22.0	15 31.0	11 43.3
15 M	5 35 11	24 23 42	29 44 32	6♍32 22	2 05.4	10 42.3	1 22.0	28 34.6	1 19.8	14 51.7	5 02.3	6 23.7	15 29.8	11 44.0
16 Tu	5 39 08	25 21 00	13♍13 49	19 49 08	2R 05.7	12 40.5	0 46.2	29 17.6	1 06.6	15 04.3	5 02.3	6 25.4	15 28.6	11 44.7
17 W	5 43 04	26 18 17	26 18 37	2♎42 41	2 05.7	14 41.0	0 09.7	0♊00.5	0 53.5	15 16.8	5 02.1	6 27.2	15 27.5	11 45.5
18 Th	5 47 01	27 15 33	9♎01 44	15 16 16	2 05.5	16 43.5	29♊32.5	0 43.4	0 40.2	15 29.2	5 01.8	6 29.0	15 26.3	11 46.3
19 F	5 50 57	28 12 48	21 26 44	27 33 37	2 05.1	18 47.9	28 55.0	1 26.2	0 27.0	15 41.5	5 01.4	6 30.9	15 25.2	11 47.1
20 Sa	5 54 54	29 10 03	3♏37 24	9♏38 33	2 04.7	20 54.0	28 17.3	2 08.9	0 13.7	15 53.8	5 00.9	6 32.8	15 24.2	11 47.9
21 Su	5 58 51	0♋07 17	15 37 29	21 34 40	2 04.4	23 01.7	27 39.8	2 51.6	0 00.5	16 06.0	5 00.4	6 34.8	15 23.1	11 48.8
22 M	6 02 47	1 04 30	27 30 29	3♐25 19	2 04.2	25 10.6	27 02.6	3 34.2	29♐47.2	16 18.1	4 59.7	6 36.8	15 22.1	11 49.7
23 Tu	6 06 44	2 01 43	9♐19 32	15 13 28	2D 04.2	27 20.5	26 26.0	4 16.7	29 34.0	16 30.2	4 58.9	6 38.8	15 21.1	11 50.7
24 W	6 10 40	2 58 56	21 07 26	27 01 44	2R 04.2	29 31.1	25 50.3	4 59.2	29 20.8	16 42.2	4 58.1	6 40.9	15 20.1	11 51.6
25 Th	6 14 37	3 56 08	2♑56 41	8♑52 32	2 04.2	1♋42.2	25 15.6	5 41.7	29 07.6	16 54.0	4 57.1	6 43.1	15 19.1	11 52.6
26 F	6 18 33	4 53 20	14 49 34	20 48 04	2 04.1	3 53.5	24 42.2	6 24.0	28 54.6	17 05.9	4 56.0	6 45.3	15 18.2	11 53.6
27 Sa	6 22 30	5 50 32	26 48 18	2♒50 33	2 03.8	6 04.6	24 10.2	7 06.4	28 41.6	17 17.6	4 54.9	6 47.5	15 17.3	11 54.7
28 Su	6 26 26	6 47 43	8♒55 06	15 02 14	2 03.3	8 15.4	23 39.9	7 48.6	28 28.7	17 29.3	4 53.6	6 49.8	15 16.4	11 55.8
29 M	6 30 23	7 44 55	21 12 17	27 25 31	2 02.6	10 25.6	23 11.4	8 30.8	28 15.9	17 40.8	4 52.3	6 52.1	15 15.6	11 56.9
30 Tu	6 34 20	8 42 07	3♓42 18	10♓02 56	2 01.9	12 34.9	22 44.8	9 13.0	28 03.2	17 52.3	4 50.9	6 54.4	15 14.8	11 58.0

Astro Data	Dy Hr Mn
⚳ R	1 5:47
♃△♅	7 1:34
☽ 0N	9 5:20
☿ D	10 16:09
♅ D	13 11:26
☽ 0S	21 23:39
♇ D	22 21:29
♀ R	29 10:29
♃△♇	31 13:04
☽ 0N	5 15:08
♄ R	15 3:25
☽ 0S	18 5:58
♃☍♆	18 6:58

Planet Ingress		Dy Hr Mn
♂	♉	7 14:41
♀	♋	9 3:16
☉	♊	21 0:50
☿	♊	9 15:45
♂	♊	17 11:43
♀	♊R	17 18:17
☉	♋	21 8:57
⚳	♐R	21 12:49
☿	♋	24 17:17

Last Aspect Dy Hr Mn		☽ Ingress	Dy Hr Mn
30 19:14	♂ △	♑	1 5:42
3 11:57	♂ □	♒	3 18:06
6 1:33	♂ ⚹	♓	6 3:43
8 8:25	♀ □	♈	8 9:16
8 8:25	♀ □	♉	10 11:09
11 21:02	☉ ☌	♊	12 11:01
13 5:27	♇ □	♋	14 10:53
16 4:38	☉ ⚹	♌	16 12:31
18 12:42	☉ □	♍	18 17:02
21 0:40	☉ △	♎	21 0:41
21 11:34	♀ □	♏	23 10:58
24 18:50	♆ ☌	♐	25 23:03
26 22:34	♇ □	♑	28 12:00
29 21:32	♂ △	♒	31 0:32

Last Aspect Dy Hr Mn		☽ Ingress	Dy Hr Mn
1 12:54	♂ □	♓	2 11:01
4 2:17	☿ ⚹	♈	4 18:03
5 20:24	☉ ⚹	♉	6 21:20
8 19:34	☿ ☌	♊	8 21:50
10 4:22	☉ ☌	♋	10 21:16
12 15:54	♂ ⚹	♌	12 21:35
14 21:11	♂ □	♍	15 0:27
17 6:37	♂ △	♎	17 6:54
19 14:33	♀ △	♏	19 16:49
21 0:46	♃ ☍	♐	22 5:03
24 9:42	♀ ☍	♑	24 18:02
26 4:27	♃ △	♒	27 6:22
29 4:08	♀ △	♓	29 16:56

☽ Phases & Eclipses Dy Hr Mn	
4 22:20	☾ 14♒27
11 21:02	● 21♉10
18 12:42	☽ 27♌35
26 9:29	○ 5♐09
3 11:07	☾ 12♓53
10 4:22	● 19♊19
10 4:33:33	● P 0.755
16 23:02	☽ 25♍47
25 1:08	○ 3♑30
25 1:06	● T 1.556

Astro Data

1 May 1964
Julian Day # 23497
SVP 5♓45'47"
GC 26♐20.5 ⚴ 2♐43.9R
Eris 10♈56.7 ⚵ 0♐57.9R
⚷ 17♓39.8 ⚶ 29♒10.5
☽ Mean ☊ 4♋55.2

1 June 1964
Julian Day # 23528
SVP 5♓45'42"
GC 26♐20.5 ⚴ 23♏46.9R
Eris 11♈12.2 ⚵ 24♏14.1R
⚷ 18♓36.9 ⚶ 9♓49.2
☽ Mean ☊ 3♋16.8

July 1964 — LONGITUDE

Day	Sid.Time	☉	0 hr ☽	Noon ☽	True ☊	☿	♀	♂	⚳	♃	♄	♅	♆	♇
1 W	6 38 16	9♋39 18	16♓27 45	22♓57 05	2♋01.3	14♋43.1	22♊20.2	9♊55.1	27♐50.7	18♉03.7	4♓49.3	6♍56.8	15♏14.0	11♍59.1
2 Th	6 42 13	10 36 30	29 31 12	6♈10 24	2D 01.0	16 50.1	21R 57.8	10 37.1	27R 38.3	18 15.0	4R 47.7	6 59.2	15R 13.2	12 00.3
3 F	6 46 09	11 33 42	12♈54 53	19 44 52	2 01.1	18 55.7	21 37.7	11 19.1	27 26.0	18 26.2	4 46.0	7 01.7	15 12.4	12 01.5
4 Sa	6 50 06	12 30 55	26 40 25	3♉41 33	2 01.5	20 59.8	21 19.9	12 01.0	27 14.0	18 37.3	4 44.2	7 04.2	15 11.7	12 02.7
5 Su	6 54 02	13 28 07	10♉48 10	18 00 03	2 02.3	23 02.2	21 04.4	12 42.8	27 02.1	18 48.4	4 42.3	7 06.8	15 11.0	12 04.0
6 M	6 57 59	14 25 20	25 16 50	2♊38 03	2 03.3	25 03.0	20 51.2	13 24.6	26 50.4	18 59.3	4 40.3	7 09.4	15 10.4	12 05.3
7 Tu	7 01 55	15 22 34	10♊03 03	17 31 04	2R 04.0	27 01.9	20 40.5	14 06.4	26 38.9	19 10.1	4 38.2	7 12.0	15 09.8	12 06.6
8 W	7 05 52	16 19 48	25 01 11	2♋32 27	2 04.3	28 59.1	20 32.2	14 48.1	26 27.7	19 20.9	4 36.1	7 14.7	15 09.2	12 07.9
9 Th	7 09 49	17 17 02	10♋03 47	17 34 07	2 03.9	0♌54.3	20 26.2	15 29.7	26 16.6	19 31.5	4 33.8	7 17.4	15 08.6	12 09.3
10 F	7 13 45	18 14 16	25 02 20	2♌27 27	2 02.8	2 47.7	20 22.6	16 11.2	26 05.9	19 42.0	4 31.5	7 20.1	15 08.1	12 10.6
11 Sa	7 17 42	19 11 30	9♌48 30	17 04 39	2 00.9	4 39.2	20D 21.4	16 52.7	25 55.3	19 52.5	4 29.1	7 22.9	15 07.6	12 12.0
12 Su	7 21 38	20 08 44	24 15 15	1♍19 44	1 58.6	6 28.8	20 22.4	17 34.2	25 45.1	20 02.8	4 26.6	7 25.7	15 07.1	12 13.5
13 M	7 25 35	21 05 58	8♍17 45	15 09 07	1 56.2	8 16.4	20 25.7	18 15.5	25 35.1	20 13.0	4 24.0	7 28.6	15 06.6	12 14.9
14 Tu	7 29 31	22 03 12	21 53 46	28 31 50	1 54.2	10 02.1	20 31.3	18 56.8	25 25.3	20 23.1	4 21.3	7 31.5	15 06.2	12 16.4
15 W	7 33 28	23 00 27	5♎03 30	11♎29 08	1D 52.9	11 46.0	20 39.0	19 38.1	25 15.9	20 33.1	4 18.6	7 34.4	15 05.8	12 17.9
16 Th	7 37 24	23 57 41	17 49 06	24 03 56	1 52.4	13 27.9	20 48.8	20 19.3	25 06.8	20 43.0	4 15.7	7 37.3	15 05.5	12 19.4
17 F	7 41 21	24 54 55	0♏14 07	6♏20 15	1 52.9	15 07.8	21 00.7	21 00.4	24 57.9	20 52.7	4 12.8	7 40.3	15 05.1	12 20.9
18 Sa	7 45 18	25 52 10	12 22 54	18 22 39	1 54.1	16 45.9	21 14.6	21 41.4	24 49.4	21 02.4	4 09.8	7 43.3	15 04.8	12 22.5
19 Su	7 49 14	26 49 25	24 20 05	0♐15 48	1 55.7	18 22.1	21 30.4	22 22.4	24 41.2	21 11.9	4 06.8	7 46.3	15 04.6	12 24.0
20 M	7 53 11	27 46 40	6♐10 20	12 04 12	1 57.4	19 56.3	21 48.2	23 03.4	24 33.3	21 21.4	4 03.6	7 49.4	15 04.4	12 25.6
21 Tu	7 57 07	28 43 56	17 57 56	23 52 00	1R 58.5	21 28.7	22 07.8	23 44.2	24 25.8	21 30.7	4 00.4	7 52.5	15 04.2	12 27.3
22 W	8 01 04	29 41 12	29 46 48	5♑42 45	1 58.7	22 59.0	22 29.2	24 25.0	24 18.5	21 39.8	3 57.2	7 55.6	15 04.0	12 28.9
23 Th	8 05 00	0♌38 28	11♑40 12	17 39 28	1 57.7	24 27.5	22 52.3	25 05.8	24 11.6	21 48.9	3 53.8	7 58.8	15 03.9	12 30.6
24 F	8 08 57	1 35 45	23 40 51	29 44 33	1 55.2	25 54.0	23 17.1	25 46.5	24 05.1	21 57.8	3 50.4	8 02.0	15 03.8	12 32.2
25 Sa	8 12 54	2 33 03	5♒50 49	11♒59 48	1 51.4	27 18.5	23 43.5	26 27.1	23 58.9	22 06.6	3 47.0	8 05.2	15 03.7	12 33.9
26 Su	8 16 50	3 30 21	18 11 39	24 26 31	1 46.6	28 40.9	24 11.4	27 07.7	23 53.0	22 15.3	3 43.4	8 08.4	15D 03.6	12 35.6
27 M	8 20 47	4 27 40	0♓44 29	7♓05 39	1 41.3	0♍01.4	24 40.9	27 48.2	23 47.5	22 23.9	3 39.8	8 11.7	15 03.6	12 37.4
28 Tu	8 24 43	5 25 00	13 30 06	19 57 56	1 36.0	1 19.7	25 11.8	28 28.6	23 42.3	22 32.3	3 36.2	8 15.0	15 03.7	12 39.1
29 W	8 28 40	6 22 21	26 29 11	3♈03 58	1 31.5	2 35.9	25 44.1	29 09.0	23 37.4	22 40.5	3 32.4	8 18.3	15 03.7	12 40.9
30 Th	8 32 36	7 19 43	9♈42 21	16 24 24	1 28.2	3 49.8	26 17.8	29 49.3	23 33.0	22 48.7	3 28.7	8 21.7	15 03.8	12 42.7
31 F	8 36 33	8 17 06	23 10 11	29 59 47	1D 26.5	5 01.6	26 52.8	0♋29.6	23 28.9	22 56.7	3 24.8	8 25.0	15 03.9	12 44.5

August 1964 — LONGITUDE

Day	Sid.Time	☉	0 hr ☽	Noon ☽	True ☊	☿	♀	♂	⚳	♃	♄	♅	♆	♇
1 Sa	8 40 29	9♌14 30	6♉53 14	13♉50 32	1♋26.3	6♍11.0	27♊29.0	1♋09.8	23♐25.1	23♉04.6	3♓20.9	8♍28.4	15♏04.1	12♍46.3
2 Su	8 44 26	10 11 56	20 51 40	27 56 33	1 27.2	7 18.0	28 06.4	1 49.9	23R 21.7	23 12.3	3R 17.0	8 31.8	15 04.3	12 48.1
3 M	8 48 22	11 09 22	5♊05 02	12♊16 52	1 28.5	8 22.5	28 44.9	2 30.0	23 18.7	23 19.9	3 13.0	8 35.2	15 04.5	12 50.0
4 Tu	8 52 19	12 06 50	19 31 45	26 49 13	1R 29.4	9 24.3	29 24.6	3 10.0	23 16.0	23 27.4	3 09.0	8 38.7	15 04.7	12 51.8
5 W	8 56 16	13 04 19	4♋08 46	11♋29 43	1 29.1	10 23.5	0♋05.4	3 50.0	23 13.7	23 34.7	3 04.9	8 42.2	15 05.0	12 53.7
6 Th	9 00 12	14 01 50	18 51 22	26 12 53	1 27.1	11 19.9	0 47.1	4 29.9	23 11.7	23 41.8	3 00.8	8 45.7	15 05.3	12 55.6
7 F	9 04 09	14 59 21	3♌33 25	10♌52 03	1 23.0	12 13.3	1 29.9	5 09.7	23 10.2	23 48.8	2 56.6	8 49.2	15 05.7	12 57.5
8 Sa	9 08 05	15 56 54	18 07 55	25 20 11	1 17.1	13 03.5	2 13.6	5 49.4	23 08.9	23 55.7	2 52.4	8 52.7	15 06.0	12 59.4
9 Su	9 12 02	16 54 27	2♍28 05	9♍30 57	1 10.0	13 50.5	2 58.2	6 29.1	23 08.1	24 02.4	2 48.1	8 56.3	15 06.5	13 01.3
10 M	9 15 58	17 52 01	16 28 15	23 19 37	1 02.6	14 34.1	3 43.6	7 08.8	23D 07.6	24 08.9	2 43.8	8 59.8	15 06.9	13 03.3
11 Tu	9 19 55	18 49 37	0♎04 48	6♎43 43	0 55.7	15 14.0	4 30.0	7 48.3	23 07.5	24 15.3	2 39.5	9 03.4	15 07.4	13 05.2
12 W	9 23 51	19 47 13	13 16 24	19 43 03	0 50.2	15 50.1	5 17.1	8 27.8	23 07.7	24 21.5	2 35.2	9 07.0	15 07.9	13 07.2
13 Th	9 27 48	20 44 50	26 03 59	2♏19 34	0 46.4	16 22.2	6 05.0	9 07.2	23 08.3	24 27.5	2 30.8	9 10.6	15 08.4	13 09.2
14 F	9 31 45	21 42 29	8♏30 19	14 36 45	0D 44.6	16 50.0	6 53.7	9 46.6	23 09.2	24 33.4	2 26.4	9 14.3	15 09.0	13 11.2
15 Sa	9 35 41	22 40 08	20 39 30	26 39 10	0 44.4	17 13.4	7 43.1	10 25.9	23 10.5	24 39.2	2 22.0	9 17.9	15 09.6	13 13.2
16 Su	9 39 38	23 37 48	2♐36 25	8♐31 55	0 45.2	17 32.1	8 33.2	11 05.1	23 12.1	24 44.7	2 17.5	9 21.6	15 10.2	13 15.2
17 M	9 43 34	24 35 29	14 26 19	20 20 15	0R 46.3	17 45.9	9 24.0	11 44.3	23 14.1	24 50.2	2 13.0	9 25.2	15 10.9	13 17.2
18 Tu	9 47 31	25 33 12	26 14 22	2♑09 15	0 46.8	17 54.5	10 15.5	12 23.4	23 16.5	24 55.4	2 08.6	9 28.9	15 11.6	13 19.2
19 W	9 51 27	26 30 56	8♑05 27	14 03 31	0 45.7	17R 57.7	11 07.6	13 02.4	23 19.1	25 00.5	2 04.1	9 32.6	15 12.3	13 21.3
20 Th	9 55 24	27 28 40	20 03 53	26 06 58	0 42.7	17 55.4	12 00.4	13 41.4	23 22.1	25 05.3	1 59.6	9 36.3	15 13.1	13 23.3
21 F	9 59 21	28 26 26	2♒13 08	8♒22 39	0 37.2	17 47.5	12 53.7	14 20.3	23 25.5	25 10.1	1 55.0	9 40.0	15 13.9	13 25.4
22 Sa	10 03 17	29 24 14	14 35 44	20 52 33	0 29.5	17 33.7	13 47.6	14 59.1	23 29.2	25 14.6	1 50.5	9 43.7	15 14.7	13 27.5
23 Su	10 07 14	0♍22 02	27 13 10	3♓37 35	0 20.1	17 14.0	14 42.1	15 37.9	23 33.2	25 19.0	1 46.0	9 47.5	15 15.6	13 29.5
24 M	10 11 10	1 19 53	10♓05 45	16 37 35	0 09.7	16 48.5	15 37.1	16 16.6	23 37.5	25 23.2	1 41.4	9 51.2	15 16.4	13 31.6
25 Tu	10 15 07	2 17 44	23 12 54	29 51 33	29♊59.3	16 17.2	16 32.7	16 55.2	23 42.2	25 27.2	1 36.9	9 54.9	15 17.3	13 33.7
26 W	10 19 03	3 15 38	6♈33 18	13♈17 57	29 50.1	15 40.5	17 28.8	17 33.7	23 47.1	25 31.0	1 32.4	9 58.7	15 18.3	13 35.8
27 Th	10 23 00	4 13 33	20 05 17	26 55 06	29 42.9	14 58.7	18 25.4	18 12.2	23 52.4	25 34.7	1 27.8	10 02.4	15 19.3	13 37.8
28 F	10 26 56	5 11 30	3♉47 13	10♉41 28	29 38.2	14 12.2	19 22.5	18 50.7	23 58.0	25 38.2	1 23.3	10 06.2	15 20.3	13 39.9
29 Sa	10 30 53	6 09 28	17 37 44	24 35 54	29D 35.8	13 21.7	20 20.0	19 29.0	24 04.0	25 41.4	1 18.8	10 09.9	15 21.3	13 42.0
30 Su	10 34 49	7 07 29	1♊35 54	8♊37 37	29 35.3	12 28.0	21 18.0	20 07.3	24 10.2	25 44.5	1 14.3	10 13.7	15 22.4	13 44.2
31 M	10 38 46	8 05 32	15 40 59	22 45 54	29R 35.6	11 32.1	22 16.5	20 45.6	24 16.7	25 47.4	1 09.8	10 17.5	15 23.4	13 46.3

Astro Data

	Dy Hr Mn
☽ 0N	2 22:37
♀ D	11 13:00
☽ 0S	15 13:06
♆ D	27 7:02
☽ 0N	30 3:56
⚳ D	11 9:03
☽ 0S	11 21:12
☿ R	19 14:14
☽ 0N	26 8:53

Planet Ingress

	Dy Hr Mn
☿ ♌	9 0:38
☉ ♌	22 19:53
☿ ♍	27 11:35
♂ ♋	30 18:23
♀ ♋	5 8:53
☉ ♍	23 2:51
☊ ♊R	25 10:22

Last Aspect / ☽ Ingress

Last Aspect Dy Hr Mn		☽ Ingress Dy Hr Mn
1 10:54	♀ □	♈ 2 0:52
3 15:12	♀ ⚹	♉ 4 5:42
5 21:39	☿ ⚹	♊ 6 7:43
7 17:00	♀ ☌	♋ 8 7:57
9 15:10	♃ ⚹	♌ 10 8:01
11 17:28	♀ ⚹	♍ 12 9:44
13 23:23	☉ ⚹	♎ 14 14:41
16 11:47	☉ □	♏ 16 23:32
19 4:25	☉ △	♐ 19 11:28
21 11:43	♂ ☍	♑ 22 0:27
23 20:24	♃ △	♒ 24 12:30
26 21:03	☿ ☍	♓ 26 22:36
29 4:29	♂ □	♈ 29 6:25
31 6:17	♀ ⚹	♉ 31 12:00

Last Aspect / ☽ Ingress

Last Aspect Dy Hr Mn		☽ Ingress Dy Hr Mn
2 3:55	♃ ☌	♊ 2 15:28
4 16:27	♀ ☌	♋ 4 17:13
6 7:52	♃ ⚹	♌ 6 18:11
8 9:38	♃ □	♍ 8 19:50
10 13:28	♃ △	♎ 10 23:51
12 12:09	☉ ⚹	♏ 13 7:31
15 7:57	♃ ☍	♐ 15 18:44
17 21:25	☉ △	♑ 18 7:38
20 9:57	♃ △	♒ 20 19:39
22 20:19	♃ □	♓ 23 5:13
25 4:01	♃ ⚹	♈ 25 12:15
26 19:57	♀ □	♉ 27 17:24
29 13:53	♃ ☌	♊ 29 21:16

☽ Phases & Eclipses

Dy Hr Mn	
2 20:31	☾ 10♈57
9 11:31	● 17♋16
9 11:17:16	• P 0.322
16 11:47	☽ 23♎57
24 15:58	○ 1♒45
1 3:29	☾ 8♉54
7 19:17	● 15♌17
15 3:19	☽ 22♏19
23 5:25	○ 0♓06
30 9:15	☾ 7♊01

Astro Data

1 July 1964
Julian Day # 23558
SVP 5♓45'37"
GC 26♐20.6 ⚴ 18♏39.5R
Eris 11♈19.0 ⚵ 19♏51.5R
⚷ 18♓45.1R ⚶ 16♓03.0
☽ Mean ☊ 1♋41.5

1 August 1964
Julian Day # 23589
SVP 5♓45'32"
GC 26♐20.7 ⚴ 20♏12.9
Eris 11♈15.9R ⚵ 20♏11.2
⚷ 18♓04.3R ⚶ 16♓06.8R
☽ Mean ☊ 0♋03.0

LONGITUDE — September 1964

Day	Sid.Time	☉	0 hr ☽	Noon ☽	True ☊	☿	♀	♂	⚳	♃	♄	♅	♆	♇
1 Tu	10 42 43	9♍03 37	29♊52 13	6♋59 45	29♊35.6	10♍35.0	23♋15.3	21♋23.7	24♐23.5	25♉50.2	1♓05.3	10♍21.3	15♏24.6	13♍48.4
2 W	10 46 39	10 01 43	14♋08 15	21 17 23	29R 33.9	9R 38.0	24 14.6	22 01.8	24 30.7	25 52.7	1R 00.8	10 25.0	15 25.7	13 50.5
3 Th	10 50 36	10 59 52	28 26 46	5♌35 55	29 29.9	8 42.1	25 14.3	22 39.9	24 38.1	25 55.0	0 56.4	10 28.8	15 26.9	13 52.6
4 F	10 54 32	11 58 02	12♌44 18	19 51 20	29 23.0	7 48.8	26 14.4	23 17.8	24 45.8	25 57.2	0 52.0	10 32.6	15 28.1	13 54.7
5 Sa	10 58 29	12 56 15	26 56 22	3♍58 47	29 13.6	6 59.2	27 14.8	23 55.7	24 53.8	25 59.1	0 47.6	10 36.3	15 29.3	13 56.9
6 Su	11 02 25	13 54 29	10♍57 56	17 53 14	29 02.4	6 14.5	28 15.6	24 33.5	25 02.1	26 00.9	0 43.2	10 40.1	15 30.6	13 59.0
7 M	11 06 22	14 52 44	24 44 12	1♎30 22	28 50.5	5 35.8	29 16.8	25 11.2	25 10.6	26 02.4	0 38.8	10 43.9	15 31.9	14 01.1
8 Tu	11 10 18	15 51 02	8♎11 26	14 47 11	28 39.1	5 04.1	0♌18.3	25 48.9	25 19.5	26 03.8	0 34.5	10 47.6	15 33.2	14 03.2
9 W	11 14 15	16 49 20	21 17 32	27 42 32	28 29.3	4 40.1	1 20.1	26 26.4	25 28.6	26 04.9	0 30.3	10 51.4	15 34.5	14 05.3
10 Th	11 18 12	17 47 41	4♏02 20	10♏17 11	28 21.8	4 24.5	2 22.2	27 03.9	25 38.0	26 05.9	0 26.0	10 55.2	15 35.9	14 07.5
11 F	11 22 08	18 46 03	16 27 29	22 33 39	28 17.0	4D 17.7	3 24.7	27 41.3	25 47.6	26 06.6	0 21.8	10 58.9	15 37.3	14 09.6
12 Sa	11 26 05	19 44 27	28 36 13	4♐35 45	28 14.5	4 20.1	4 27.5	28 18.7	25 57.5	26 07.2	0 17.7	11 02.6	15 38.7	14 11.7
13 Su	11 30 01	20 42 53	10♐32 54	16 28 19	28 13.7	4 31.8	5 30.6	28 55.9	26 07.7	26 07.6	0 13.5	11 06.4	15 40.2	14 13.8
14 M	11 33 58	21 41 20	22 22 40	28 16 40	28 13.7	4 52.7	6 33.9	29 33.1	26 18.1	26R 07.7	0 09.5	11 10.1	15 41.7	14 15.9
15 Tu	11 37 54	22 39 49	4♑11 00	10♑06 20	28 13.3	5 22.7	7 37.6	0♌10.2	26 28.8	26 07.7	0 05.5	11 13.8	15 43.2	14 18.0
16 W	11 41 51	23 38 19	16 03 22	22 02 42	28 11.6	6 01.5	8 41.5	0 47.3	26 39.8	26 07.4	0 01.5	11 17.5	15 44.7	14 20.1
17 Th	11 45 47	24 36 51	28 04 56	4♒10 36	28 07.6	6 48.7	9 45.7	1 24.2	26 50.9	26 07.0	29♒57.6	11 21.3	15 46.2	14 22.2
18 F	11 49 44	25 35 25	10♒20 11	16 34 05	28 01.0	7 43.9	10 50.2	2 01.1	27 02.3	26 06.3	29 53.7	11 24.9	15 47.8	14 24.3
19 Sa	11 53 41	26 34 01	22 52 35	29 15 56	27 51.8	8 46.5	11 55.0	2 37.9	27 14.0	26 05.5	29 49.9	11 28.6	15 49.4	14 26.4
20 Su	11 57 37	27 32 38	5♓44 14	12♓17 28	27 40.4	9 56.0	13 00.0	3 14.6	27 25.9	26 04.5	29 46.1	11 32.3	15 51.0	14 28.5
21 M	12 01 34	28 31 17	18 55 34	25 38 17	27 27.9	11 11.7	14 05.2	3 51.2	27 38.0	26 03.2	29 42.4	11 35.9	15 52.7	14 30.6
22 Tu	12 05 30	29 29 58	2♈25 21	9♈16 20	27 15.4	12 33.0	15 10.7	4 27.8	27 50.3	26 01.8	29 38.8	11 39.6	15 54.3	14 32.6
23 W	12 09 27	0♎28 41	16 10 48	23 08 15	27 04.2	13 59.3	16 16.4	5 04.3	28 02.8	26 00.1	29 35.2	11 43.2	15 56.0	14 34.7
24 Th	12 13 23	1 27 26	0♉08 09	7♉09 57	26 55.2	15 29.9	17 22.4	5 40.6	28 15.6	25 58.3	29 31.7	11 46.8	15 57.7	14 36.7
25 F	12 17 20	2 26 14	14 13 11	21 17 22	26 49.1	17 04.2	18 28.6	6 17.0	28 28.6	25 56.2	29 28.3	11 50.4	15 59.4	14 38.8
26 Sa	12 21 16	3 25 03	28 22 05	5♊26 59	26 45.8	18 41.6	19 35.1	6 53.2	28 41.8	25 54.0	29 24.9	11 54.0	16 01.2	14 40.8
27 Su	12 25 13	4 23 55	12♊31 48	19 36 18	26D 44.6	20 21.6	20 41.8	7 29.3	28 55.2	25 51.5	29 21.6	11 57.6	16 03.0	14 42.8
28 M	12 29 10	5 22 50	26 40 19	3♋43 43	26R 44.6	22 03.8	21 48.6	8 05.4	29 08.8	25 48.9	29 18.4	12 01.1	16 04.8	14 44.9
29 Tu	12 33 06	6 21 46	10♋46 24	17 48 17	26 44.3	23 47.6	22 55.7	8 41.4	29 22.6	25 46.1	29 15.2	12 04.7	16 06.6	14 46.9
30 W	12 37 03	7 20 46	24 49 17	1♌49 16	26 42.5	25 32.8	24 03.0	9 17.3	29 36.6	25 43.1	29 12.2	12 08.2	16 08.4	14 48.9

LONGITUDE — October 1964

Day	Sid.Time	☉	0 hr ☽	Noon ☽	True ☊	☿	♀	♂	⚳	♃	♄	♅	♆	♇
1 Th	12 40 59	8♎19 47	8♌48 07	15♌45 38	26♊38.2	27♍18.8	25♌10.5	9♌53.1	29♐50.9	25♉39.8	29♒09.1	12♍11.7	16♏10.3	14♍50.9
2 F	12 44 56	9 18 50	22 41 37	29 35 48	26R 31.1	29 05.6	26 18.2	10 28.8	0♑05.3	25R 36.4	29R 06.2	12 15.2	16 12.1	14 52.8
3 Sa	12 48 52	10 17 56	6♍27 51	13♍17 29	26 21.4	0♎52.7	27 26.1	11 04.4	0 19.9	25 32.8	29 03.4	12 18.6	16 14.0	14 54.8
4 Su	12 52 49	11 17 04	20 04 20	26 48 03	26 09.7	2 40.0	28 34.2	11 39.9	0 34.7	25 29.0	29 00.6	12 22.0	16 15.9	14 56.8
5 M	12 56 45	12 16 14	3♎28 20	10♎04 52	25 57.3	4 27.3	29 42.4	12 15.3	0 49.7	25 25.0	28 57.9	12 25.4	16 17.8	14 58.7
6 Tu	13 00 42	13 15 26	16 37 26	23 05 50	25 45.3	6 14.5	0♍50.9	12 50.7	1 04.8	25 20.9	28 55.3	12 28.8	16 19.8	15 00.6
7 W	13 04 38	14 14 40	29 29 59	5♏49 51	25 34.8	8 01.3	1 59.5	13 25.9	1 20.2	25 16.5	28 52.8	12 32.2	16 21.7	15 02.5
8 Th	13 08 35	15 13 56	12♏05 31	18 17 07	25 26.7	9 47.8	3 08.2	14 01.0	1 35.7	25 12.0	28 50.4	12 35.5	16 23.7	15 04.4
9 F	13 12 32	16 13 14	24 24 54	0♐29 10	25 21.2	11 33.9	4 17.1	14 36.1	1 51.4	25 07.3	28 48.0	12 38.8	16 25.7	15 06.3
10 Sa	13 16 28	17 12 34	6♐30 20	12 28 50	25 18.3	13 19.4	5 26.2	15 11.0	2 07.3	25 02.4	28 45.8	12 42.1	16 27.7	15 08.2
11 Su	13 20 25	18 11 56	18 25 13	24 20 02	25D 17.5	15 04.3	6 35.5	15 45.8	2 23.3	24 57.3	28 43.6	12 45.4	16 29.7	15 10.0
12 M	13 24 21	19 11 19	0♑13 53	6♑07 27	25 17.8	16 48.6	7 44.9	16 20.6	2 39.6	24 52.1	28 41.6	12 48.6	16 31.8	15 11.9
13 Tu	13 28 18	20 10 44	12 01 23	17 56 22	25R 18.3	18 32.3	8 54.4	16 55.2	2 55.9	24 46.7	28 39.6	12 51.8	16 33.8	15 13.7
14 W	13 32 14	21 10 11	23 53 06	29 52 15	25 17.9	20 15.4	10 04.1	17 29.7	3 12.5	24 41.2	28 37.7	12 55.0	16 35.9	15 15.5
15 Th	13 36 11	22 09 40	5♒54 30	12♒00 30	25 15.8	21 57.8	11 14.0	18 04.1	3 29.2	24 35.5	28 35.9	12 58.1	16 38.0	15 17.3
16 F	13 40 07	23 09 11	18 10 48	24 25 59	25 11.4	23 39.5	12 23.9	18 38.4	3 46.0	24 29.6	28 34.2	13 01.2	16 40.1	15 19.1
17 Sa	13 44 04	24 08 43	0♓46 28	7♓12 38	25 04.8	25 20.5	13 34.1	19 12.6	4 03.0	24 23.6	28 32.6	13 04.3	16 42.2	15 20.8
18 Su	13 48 01	25 08 17	13 44 44	20 22 54	24 56.2	27 01.0	14 44.3	19 46.7	4 20.2	24 17.5	28 31.1	13 07.4	16 44.3	15 22.6
19 M	13 51 57	26 07 53	27 07 07	3♈57 16	24 46.4	28 40.7	15 54.7	20 20.6	4 37.5	24 11.2	28 29.7	13 10.4	16 46.4	15 24.3
20 Tu	13 55 54	27 07 31	10♈53 01	17 53 58	24 36.6	0♏19.8	17 05.2	20 54.5	4 54.9	24 04.8	28 28.4	13 13.4	16 48.5	15 26.0
21 W	13 59 50	28 07 11	24 59 33	2♉09 04	24 27.7	1 58.4	18 15.9	21 28.3	5 12.5	23 58.2	28 27.2	13 16.3	16 50.7	15 27.6
22 Th	14 03 47	29 06 53	9♉21 47	16 36 53	24 20.7	3 36.3	19 26.7	22 01.9	5 30.2	23 51.5	28 26.1	13 19.2	16 52.8	15 29.3
23 F	14 07 43	0♏06 37	23 53 32	1♊10 55	24 16.1	5 13.6	20 37.6	22 35.4	5 48.1	23 44.7	28 25.1	13 22.1	16 55.0	15 30.9
24 Sa	14 11 40	1 06 23	8♊28 17	15 44 55	24D 14.0	6 50.3	21 48.7	23 08.8	6 06.1	23 37.8	28 24.2	13 24.9	16 57.2	15 32.5
25 Su	14 15 36	2 06 11	23 00 11	0♋13 36	24 13.8	8 26.5	22 59.8	23 42.1	6 24.2	23 30.7	28 23.4	13 27.8	16 59.4	15 34.1
26 M	14 19 33	3 06 02	7♋24 45	14 33 17	24 14.7	10 02.2	24 11.1	24 15.3	6 42.5	23 23.6	28 22.7	13 30.5	17 01.6	15 35.7
27 Tu	14 23 30	4 05 55	21 39 00	28 41 44	24R 15.6	11 37.4	25 22.5	24 48.3	7 00.9	23 16.3	28 22.1	13 33.3	17 03.8	15 37.3
28 W	14 27 26	5 05 50	5♌41 24	12♌37 58	24 15.5	13 12.0	26 34.1	25 21.3	7 19.4	23 08.9	28 21.6	13 36.0	17 06.0	15 38.8
29 Th	14 31 23	6 05 47	19 31 24	26 21 43	24 13.5	14 46.2	27 45.7	25 54.0	7 38.0	23 01.5	28 21.2	13 38.6	17 08.2	15 40.3
30 F	14 35 19	7 05 47	3♍08 56	9♍53 03	24 09.5	16 19.8	28 57.4	26 26.7	7 56.8	22 53.9	28 20.9	13 41.3	17 10.4	15 41.8
31 Sa	14 39 16	8 05 48	16 34 05	23 12 01	24 03.4	17 53.1	0♎09.3	26 59.2	8 15.7	22 46.3	28 20.7	13 43.8	17 12.6	15 43.2

Astro Data	Planet Ingress	Last Aspect	☽ Ingress	Last Aspect	☽ Ingress	☽ Phases & Eclipses	Astro Data
Dy Hr Mn	Dy Hr Mn	Dy Hr Mn	Dy Hr Mn	Dy Hr Mn	Dy Hr Mn	Dy Hr Mn	
☽0S 8 5:50	♀ ♌ 8 4:53	30 20:43 ♇ □	♋ 1 0:13	2 11:09 ♄ ☍	♍ 2 12:42	6 4:34 ● 13♍36	1 September 1964
☿D 11 17:50	♂ ♌ 15 5:22	2 19:43 ♃ ⚹	♌ 3 2:36	4 9:39 ♃ △	♎ 4 17:44	13 21:24 ☽ 21♐06	Julian Day # 23620
♃R 14 19:01	♄ ♒R 16 21:04	4 22:21 ♃ □	♍ 5 5:12	6 22:53 ♄ △	♏ 7 0:57	21 17:31 ○ 28♓45	SVP 5♓45'28"
☽0N 22 15:32	⊙ ♎ 23 0:17	7 7:43 ♀ ⚹	♎ 7 9:19	9 8:40 ♄ □	♐ 9 11:02	28 15:01 ☾ 5♋30	GC 26♐20.7 ⚴ 26♏53.5
⊙0S 23 0:16		9 9:30 ♂ □	♏ 9 16:19	11 20:55 ♄ ⚹	♑ 11 23:32		Eris 11♈03.5R ⚵ 24♏52.7
	⚳ ♑ 2 3:15	11 22:44 ♂ △	♐ 12 2:47	14 1:42 ♃ △	♒ 14 12:15	5 16:20 ● 12♎27	⚷ 16♓47.9R ⚶ 9♓43.3R
☿0S 5 6:46	☿ ♎ 3 0:12	13 21:24 ⊙ □	♑ 14 15:30	16 19:50 ♄ ☌	♓ 16 22:33	13 16:56 ☽ 20♑23	☽ Mean ☊ 28♊24.5
☽0S 5 14:11	♀ ♍ 5 18:10	16 20:07 ♃ △	♒ 17 3:47	18 18:56 ♃ ⚹	♈ 19 5:05	21 4:45 ○ 27♈49	
☽0N 20 0:46	☿ ♏ 20 7:11	19 13:03 ♄ ☌	♓ 19 13:22	21 5:49 ♄ ⚹	♉ 21 8:24	27 21:59 ☾ 4♌31	1 October 1964
	⊙ ♏ 23 9:21	21 17:31 ⊙ ☍	♈ 21 19:44	23 7:27 ♄ □	♊ 23 10:03		Julian Day # 23650
	♀ ♎ 31 8:54	23 23:01 ♄ ⚹	♉ 23 23:46	25 8:57 ♄ △	♋ 25 11:37		SVP 5♓45'25"
		26 1:49 ♄ □	♊ 26 2:46	27 5:49 ♀ ⚹	♌ 27 14:14		GC 26♐20.8 ⚴ 6♐12.3
		28 4:30 ♄ △	♋ 28 5:39	29 15:31 ♄ ☍	♍ 29 18:25		Eris 10♈46.1R ⚵ 2♐16.5
		30 1:34 ♃ ⚹	♌ 30 8:52				⚷ 15♓26.2R ⚶ 3♓38.1R
							☽ Mean ☊ 26♊49.1

November 1964 — LONGITUDE

Day	Sid.Time	☉	0 hr ☽	Noon ☽	True ☊	☿	♀	♂	⚳	♃	♄	♅	♆	♇
1 Su	14 43 12	9♏05 52	29♍46 49	6♎18 28	23♊55.9	19♏25.9	1♎21.2	27♌31.6	8♑34.7	22♉38.5	28♒20.6	13♍46.4	17♏14.8	15♍44.7
2 M	14 47 09	10 05 57	12♎46 56	19 12 10	23R 47.7	20 58.2	2 33.3	28 03.9	8 53.9	22R 30.7	28D 20.6	13 48.9	17 17.1	15 46.1
3 Tu	14 51 05	11 06 05	25 34 10	1♏52 54	23 39.8	22 30.2	3 45.4	28 36.0	9 13.1	22 22.9	28 20.7	13 51.3	17 19.3	15 47.5
4 W	14 55 02	12 06 15	8♏08 24	14 20 43	23 32.9	24 01.7	4 57.7	29 07.9	9 32.5	22 15.0	28 21.0	13 53.7	17 21.6	15 48.8
5 Th	14 58 59	13 06 26	20 29 55	26 36 09	23 27.7	25 32.8	6 10.0	29 39.8	9 52.0	22 07.0	28 21.3	13 56.1	17 23.8	15 50.2
6 F	15 02 55	14 06 39	2♐39 35	8♐40 27	23 24.5	27 03.5	7 22.4	0♍11.4	10 11.6	21 59.0	28 21.7	13 58.4	17 26.1	15 51.5
7 Sa	15 06 52	15 06 54	14 39 02	20 35 39	23D 23.3	28 33.8	8 34.9	0 42.9	10 31.3	21 50.9	28 22.3	14 00.7	17 28.3	15 52.8
8 Su	15 10 48	16 07 10	26 30 41	2♑24 35	23 23.6	0♐03.6	9 47.5	1 14.3	10 51.1	21 42.8	28 22.9	14 03.0	17 30.6	15 54.0
9 M	15 14 45	17 07 28	8♑17 48	14 13 07	23 25.1	1 33.1	11 00.2	1 45.5	11 11.0	21 34.7	28 23.7	14 05.1	17 32.8	15 55.2
10 Tu	15 18 41	18 07 48	20 04 20	25 58 48	23 26.9	3 02.1	12 12.9	2 16.6	11 31.0	21 26.5	28 24.5	14 07.3	17 35.1	15 56.5
11 W	15 22 38	19 08 09	1♒54 53	7♒53 11	23 28.4	4 30.7	13 25.7	2 47.4	11 51.1	21 18.3	28 25.5	14 09.4	17 37.3	15 57.6
12 Th	15 26 34	20 08 31	13 54 23	19 59 06	23R 29.0	5 58.8	14 38.6	3 18.2	12 11.3	21 10.2	28 26.5	14 11.4	17 39.6	15 58.8
13 F	15 30 31	21 08 55	26 07 58	2♓21 36	23 28.3	7 26.4	15 51.6	3 48.7	12 31.6	21 02.0	28 27.7	14 13.5	17 41.8	15 59.9
14 Sa	15 34 28	22 09 20	8♓40 32	15 05 18	23 26.2	8 53.5	17 04.6	4 19.1	12 52.0	20 53.8	28 29.0	14 15.4	17 44.1	16 01.0
15 Su	15 38 24	23 09 46	21 36 17	28 13 51	23 22.8	10 20.0	18 17.8	4 49.3	13 12.5	20 45.6	28 30.3	14 17.3	17 46.3	16 02.0
16 M	15 42 21	24 10 14	4♈58 10	11♈49 19	23 18.6	11 45.9	19 30.9	5 19.4	13 33.1	20 37.5	28 31.8	14 19.2	17 48.5	16 03.1
17 Tu	15 46 17	25 10 43	18 47 12	25 51 35	23 14.2	13 11.2	20 44.2	5 49.2	13 53.7	20 29.4	28 33.4	14 21.0	17 50.8	16 04.1
18 W	15 50 14	26 11 14	3♉02 01	10♉17 56	23 10.1	14 35.6	21 57.5	6 18.9	14 14.5	20 21.3	28 35.1	14 22.7	17 53.0	16 05.1
19 Th	15 54 10	27 11 46	17 38 33	25 03 01	23 07.0	15 59.3	23 10.9	6 48.4	14 35.3	20 13.2	28 36.8	14 24.5	17 55.2	16 06.0
20 F	15 58 07	28 12 19	2♊30 19	9♊59 25	23D 05.2	17 22.1	24 24.3	7 17.7	14 56.3	20 05.2	28 38.7	14 26.1	17 57.5	16 06.9
21 Sa	16 02 03	29 12 54	17 29 15	24 58 43	23 04.7	18 43.8	25 37.8	7 46.9	15 17.3	19 57.2	28 40.7	14 27.7	17 59.7	16 07.8
22 Su	16 06 00	0♐13 31	2♋26 51	9♋52 41	23 05.4	20 04.3	26 51.4	8 15.8	15 38.4	19 49.3	28 42.8	14 29.3	18 01.9	16 08.7
23 M	16 09 57	1 14 09	17 15 27	24 34 26	23 06.7	21 23.5	28 05.1	8 44.6	15 59.5	19 41.4	28 45.0	14 30.8	18 04.1	16 09.5
24 Tu	16 13 53	2 14 49	1♌49 07	8♌59 05	23 08.1	22 41.2	29 18.8	9 13.1	16 20.8	19 33.6	28 47.2	14 32.3	18 06.3	16 10.3
25 W	16 17 50	3 15 31	16 04 04	23 03 55	23R 09.1	23 57.2	0♏32.5	9 41.5	16 42.1	19 25.9	28 49.6	14 33.7	18 08.5	16 11.1
26 Th	16 21 46	4 16 14	29 58 35	6♍48 07	23 09.4	25 11.2	1 46.3	10 09.6	17 03.5	19 18.2	28 52.1	14 35.0	18 10.7	16 11.8
27 F	16 25 43	5 16 59	13♍32 38	20 12 19	23 08.7	26 22.9	3 00.2	10 37.5	17 25.0	19 10.7	28 54.7	14 36.3	18 12.9	16 12.5
28 Sa	16 29 39	6 17 45	26 47 21	3♎18 00	23 07.3	27 32.1	4 14.1	11 05.2	17 46.5	19 03.2	28 57.3	14 37.6	18 15.0	16 13.2
29 Su	16 33 36	7 18 33	9♎44 31	16 07 09	23 05.2	28 38.3	5 28.1	11 32.7	18 08.1	18 55.8	29 00.1	14 38.8	18 17.2	16 13.8
30 M	16 37 32	8 19 22	22 26 10	28 41 50	23 02.9	29 41.1	6 42.1	11 59.9	18 29.8	18 48.5	29 02.9	14 39.9	18 19.4	16 14.4

December 1964 — LONGITUDE

Day	Sid.Time	☉	0 hr ☽	Noon ☽	True ☊	☿	♀	♂	⚳	♃	♄	♅	♆	♇
1 Tu	16 41 29	9♐20 13	4♏54 22	11♏04 01	23♊00.6	0♑40.1	7♏56.2	12♍26.9	18♑51.6	18♉41.3	29♒05.9	14♍41.0	18♏21.5	16♍15.0
2 W	16 45 26	10 21 05	17 11 01	23 15 36	22R 58.8	1 34.6	9 10.3	12 53.7	19 13.4	18R 34.2	29 08.9	14 42.0	18 23.6	16 15.6
3 Th	16 49 22	11 21 58	29 17 57	5♐18 18	22 57.6	2 24.1	10 24.5	13 20.2	19 35.3	18 27.2	29 12.1	14 43.0	18 25.7	16 16.1
4 F	16 53 19	12 22 52	11♐16 53	17 13 55	22D 57.0	3 07.9	11 38.7	13 46.5	19 57.3	18 20.4	29 15.3	14 43.9	18 27.8	16 16.6
5 Sa	16 57 15	13 23 48	23 09 38	29 04 18	22 57.0	3 45.2	12 52.9	14 12.5	20 19.3	18 13.7	29 18.7	14 44.7	18 29.9	16 17.0
6 Su	17 01 12	14 24 44	4♑58 13	10♑51 39	22 57.4	4 15.1	14 07.2	14 38.3	20 41.4	18 07.1	29 22.1	14 45.5	18 32.0	16 17.4
7 M	17 05 08	15 25 41	16 44 58	22 38 30	22 58.2	4 37.0	15 21.5	15 03.8	21 03.5	18 00.7	29 25.6	14 46.3	18 34.1	16 17.8
8 Tu	17 09 05	16 26 40	28 32 40	4♒27 52	22 59.0	4R 49.8	16 35.8	15 29.0	21 25.7	17 54.4	29 29.2	14 47.0	18 36.1	16 18.2
9 W	17 13 01	17 27 38	10♒24 34	16 23 15	22 59.7	4 52.9	17 50.2	15 53.9	21 48.0	17 48.2	29 32.9	14 47.6	18 38.2	16 18.5
10 Th	17 16 58	18 28 38	22 24 25	28 28 35	23 00.2	4 45.3	19 04.6	16 18.6	22 10.3	17 42.2	29 36.7	14 48.2	18 40.2	16 18.8
11 F	17 20 55	19 29 38	4♓36 19	10♓48 08	23R 00.4	4 26.6	20 19.0	16 43.0	22 32.7	17 36.4	29 40.5	14 48.7	18 42.2	16 19.0
12 Sa	17 24 51	20 30 38	17 04 36	23 26 13	23 00.5	3 56.4	21 33.5	17 07.1	22 55.1	17 30.7	29 44.5	14 49.2	18 44.2	16 19.2
13 Su	17 28 48	21 31 39	29 53 28	6♈26 50	23 00.4	3 14.7	22 48.0	17 30.8	23 17.6	17 25.1	29 48.5	14 49.6	18 46.2	16 19.4
14 M	17 32 44	22 32 40	13♈06 39	19 53 12	23D 00.3	2 21.9	24 02.5	17 54.3	23 40.1	17 19.8	29 52.7	14 49.9	18 48.1	16 19.6
15 Tu	17 36 41	23 33 42	26 46 39	3♉47 03	23 00.3	1 19.2	25 17.0	18 17.5	24 02.7	17 14.6	29 56.9	14 50.2	18 50.1	16 19.7
16 W	17 40 37	24 34 45	10♉54 16	18 08 01	23 00.5	0 07.9	26 31.6	18 40.4	24 25.3	17 09.5	0♓01.1	14 50.5	18 52.0	16 19.8
17 Th	17 44 34	25 35 48	25 27 48	2♊53 00	23 00.7	28♐50.1	27 46.2	19 02.9	24 48.0	17 04.7	0 05.5	14 50.7	18 53.9	16 19.8
18 F	17 48 31	26 36 51	10♊22 47	17 56 08	23R 00.8	27 28.4	29 00.8	19 25.1	25 10.7	17 00.0	0 10.0	14 50.8	18 55.8	16R 19.9
19 Sa	17 52 27	27 37 55	25 31 57	3♋09 02	23 00.7	26 05.5	0♐15.4	19 47.0	25 33.4	16 55.5	0 14.5	14R 50.9	18 57.6	16 19.8
20 Su	17 56 24	28 39 00	10♋46 08	18 22 00	23 00.4	24 44.2	1 30.1	20 08.6	25 56.2	16 51.2	0 19.1	14 50.9	18 59.5	16 19.8
21 M	18 00 20	29 40 05	25 55 26	3♌25 21	22 59.8	23 27.0	2 44.8	20 29.7	26 19.1	16 47.1	0 23.8	14 50.8	19 01.3	16 19.7
22 Tu	18 04 17	0♑41 11	10♌50 45	18 10 52	22 58.9	22 16.4	3 59.5	20 50.6	26 42.0	16 43.1	0 28.5	14 50.7	19 03.1	16 19.6
23 W	18 08 13	1 42 17	25 25 04	2♍32 54	22 58.0	21 14.1	5 14.3	21 11.1	27 04.9	16 39.4	0 33.4	14 50.6	19 04.9	16 19.5
24 Th	18 12 10	2 43 24	9♍34 05	16 28 33	22 57.2	20 21.5	6 29.0	21 31.2	27 27.8	16 35.8	0 38.3	14 50.4	19 06.7	16 19.3
25 F	18 16 06	3 44 31	23 16 21	29 57 37	22D 56.8	19 39.2	7 43.8	21 50.9	27 50.8	16 32.5	0 43.3	14 50.1	19 08.4	16 19.1
26 Sa	18 20 03	4 45 40	6♎32 40	13♎01 51	22 56.9	19 07.7	8 58.6	22 10.2	28 13.9	16 29.3	0 48.3	14 49.8	19 10.1	16 18.9
27 Su	18 24 00	5 46 48	19 25 35	25 44 20	22 57.6	18 46.8	10 13.5	22 29.1	28 36.9	16 26.3	0 53.4	14 49.4	19 11.8	16 18.6
28 M	18 27 56	6 47 58	1♏58 34	8♏08 47	22 58.7	18D 36.1	11 28.3	22 47.6	29 00.0	16 23.5	0 58.6	14 49.0	19 13.5	16 18.3
29 Tu	18 31 53	7 49 07	14 15 29	20 19 08	23 00.1	18 35.2	12 43.2	23 05.7	29 23.2	16 21.0	1 03.9	14 48.5	19 15.1	16 18.0
30 W	18 35 49	8 50 18	26 20 12	2♐19 07	23 01.5	18 43.4	13 58.1	23 23.3	29 46.4	16 18.6	1 09.2	14 47.9	19 16.8	16 17.6
31 Th	18 39 46	9 51 28	8♐16 18	14 12 06	23R 02.4	18 59.9	15 13.0	23 40.6	0♒09.6	16 16.4	1 14.6	14 47.3	19 18.4	16 17.2

Astro Data

	Dy Hr Mn
♄ D	1 20:44
☽ 0S	1 21:27
♀ 0S	3 10:20
☽ 0N	16 11:32
☽ 0S	29 3:33
♃☍♆	3 16:01
☿ R	9 7:04
☽ 0N	13 21:28
♇ R	18 18:38
♅ R	20 6:45
☽ 0S	26 9:29
☿ D	29 2:14
♃△♇	31 1:16

Planet Ingress

	Dy Hr Mn
♂ ♍	6 3:20
☿ ♐	8 11:02
☉ ♐	22 6:39
♀ ♏	25 1:25
☿ ♑	30 19:30
♄ ♓	16 5:39
☿ ♐R	16 14:31
♀ ♐	19 7:02
☉ ♑	21 19:50
⚳ ♒	31 2:07

Last Aspect / ☽ Ingress

Last Aspect Dy Hr Mn		☽ Ingress Dy Hr Mn
31 11:14 ♃ △	♎	1 0:24
3 5:28 ♂ ⚹	♏	3 8:25
5 18:20 ♂ □	♐	5 18:43
8 3:48 ♄ ⚹	♑	8 7:06
10 2:53 ♃ △	♒	10 20:08
13 4:30 ♄ ☌	♓	13 7:28
15 2:05 ☉ △	♈	15 15:10
17 16:32 ♄ ⚹	♉	17 18:57
19 17:45 ♄ □	♊	19 19:58
21 17:57 ♄ △	♋	21 20:04
23 18:20 ♀ □	♌	23 20:59
25 22:01 ♄ ☍	♍	26 0:02
28 0:21 ☿ □	♎	28 5:54
30 14:04 ☿ ⚹	♏	30 14:31

Last Aspect / ☽ Ingress

Last Aspect Dy Hr Mn		☽ Ingress Dy Hr Mn
2 23:45 ♄ □	♐	3 1:24
5 12:29 ♄ ⚹	♑	5 13:53
7 3:41 ♆ ⚹	♒	8 2:57
10 14:15 ♄ ☌	♓	10 15:00
12 8:06 ♀ △	♈	13 0:12
15 5:25 ♄ ⚹	♉	15 5:33
17 2:59 ♀ ☍	♊	17 7:21
19 2:41 ☉ ☍	♋	19 7:02
20 14:53 ♂ ⚹	♌	21 6:31
22 18:17 ☿ △	♍	23 7:41
24 21:07 ♂ ☌	♎	25 12:04
26 23:06 ☿ ⚹	♏	27 20:11
29 17:40 ♂ ⚹	♐	30 7:20

☽ Phases & Eclipses

Dy Hr Mn	
4 7:16	● 11♏54
12 12:20	☽ 20♒09
19 15:43	○ 27♉21
26 7:10	☾ 4♍04
4 1:18	● 11♐56
4 1:31:21	● P 0.752
12 6:01	☽ 20♓15
19 2:41	○ 27♊14
19 2:37	● T 1.175
25 19:27	☾ 4♎03

Astro Data

1 November 1964
Julian Day # 23681
SVP 5♓45'21"
GC 26♐20.9 ⚵ 17♐26.6
Eris 10♈27.6R ⚴ 11♐47.9
⚷ 14♓25.2R ⚶ 3♓40.9
☽ Mean ☊ 25♊10.6

1 December 1964
Julian Day # 23711
SVP 5♓45'17"
GC 26♐21.0 ⚵ 29♐05.3
Eris 10♈14.6R ⚴ 22♐06.7
⚷ 14♓10.9 ⚶ 9♓38.8
☽ Mean ☊ 23♊35.3

LONGITUDE — January 1965

Day	Sid.Time	☉	0 hr ☽	Noon ☽	True ☊	☿	♀	♂	⚳	♃	♄	♅	♆	♇
1 F	18 43 42	10♑52 39	20♐06 54	26♐01 01	23♊02.6	19♐23.9	16♐27.9	23♍57.3	0♒32.8	16♉14.5	1♓20.1	14♍46.7	19♏19.9	16♍16.8
2 Sa	18 47 39	11 53 50	1♑54 45	7♑48 23	23R 01.9	19 54.9	17 42.8	24 13.6	0 56.1	16R 12.7	1 25.6	14R 46.0	19 21.5	16R 16.3
3 Su	18 51 35	12 55 01	13 42 10	19 36 22	23 00.1	20 31.9	18 57.7	24 29.4	1 19.4	16 11.2	1 31.2	14 45.2	19 23.0	16 15.8
4 M	18 55 32	13 56 11	25 31 14	1♒26 59	22 57.2	21 14.5	20 12.7	24 44.8	1 42.7	16 09.9	1 36.9	14 44.4	19 24.5	16 15.3
5 Tu	18 59 29	14 57 22	7♒23 53	13 22 11	22 53.5	22 02.1	21 27.6	24 59.6	2 06.0	16 08.7	1 42.6	14 43.5	19 26.0	16 14.8
6 W	19 03 25	15 58 32	19 22 08	25 24 02	22 49.5	22 54.0	22 42.6	25 14.0	2 29.4	16 07.8	1 48.4	14 42.6	19 27.4	16 14.2
7 Th	19 07 22	16 59 42	1♓28 12	7♓34 56	22 45.5	23 49.8	23 57.6	25 27.8	2 52.8	16 07.1	1 54.3	14 41.6	19 28.8	16 13.6
8 F	19 11 18	18 00 52	13 44 36	19 57 34	22 42.1	24 49.2	25 12.5	25 41.2	3 16.2	16 06.6	2 00.2	14 40.6	19 30.2	16 12.9
9 Sa	19 15 15	19 02 01	26 14 13	2♈34 57	22 39.7	25 51.6	26 27.5	25 54.0	3 39.7	16D 06.3	2 06.1	14 39.5	19 31.6	16 12.2
10 Su	19 19 11	20 03 10	9♈00 11	15 30 18	22D 38.6	26 56.9	27 42.5	26 06.2	4 03.1	16 06.2	2 12.1	14 38.3	19 32.9	16 11.5
11 M	19 23 08	21 04 18	22 05 42	28 46 44	22 38.7	28 04.6	28 57.5	26 17.9	4 26.6	16 06.3	2 18.2	14 37.2	19 34.2	16 10.8
12 Tu	19 27 04	22 05 25	5♉33 41	12♉26 47	22 39.9	29 14.6	0♑12.5	26 29.1	4 50.1	16 06.7	2 24.3	14 35.9	19 35.5	16 10.1
13 W	19 31 01	23 06 32	19 26 11	26 31 53	22 41.5	0♑26.6	1 27.5	26 39.7	5 13.6	16 07.2	2 30.5	14 34.6	19 36.7	16 09.3
14 Th	19 34 58	24 07 38	3♊43 45	11♊01 31	22R 42.8	1 40.5	2 42.5	26 49.7	5 37.1	16 08.0	2 36.7	14 33.3	19 38.0	16 08.5
15 F	19 38 54	25 08 43	18 24 41	25 52 39	22 43.2	2 56.0	3 57.5	26 59.1	6 00.6	16 08.9	2 43.0	14 31.9	19 39.2	16 07.6
16 Sa	19 42 51	26 09 48	3♋24 33	10♋59 23	22 42.0	4 13.0	5 12.5	27 07.9	6 24.2	16 10.1	2 49.3	14 30.5	19 40.3	16 06.8
17 Su	19 46 47	27 10 53	18 36 02	26 13 15	22 39.1	5 31.4	6 27.5	27 16.1	6 47.7	16 11.5	2 55.7	14 29.1	19 41.5	16 05.9
18 M	19 50 44	28 11 56	3♌49 43	11♌24 08	22 34.6	6 51.0	7 42.5	27 23.7	7 11.3	16 13.0	3 02.1	14 27.5	19 42.6	16 04.9
19 Tu	19 54 40	29 13 00	18 55 16	26 21 58	22 29.0	8 11.9	8 57.6	27 30.7	7 34.9	16 14.8	3 08.6	14 26.0	19 43.6	16 04.0
20 W	19 58 37	0♒14 02	3♍43 14	10♍58 18	22 23.1	9 33.8	10 12.6	27 37.0	7 58.5	16 16.8	3 15.1	14 24.4	19 44.7	16 03.0
21 Th	20 02 34	1 15 04	18 06 33	25 07 35	22 17.7	10 56.8	11 27.6	27 42.6	8 22.1	16 18.9	3 21.6	14 22.7	19 45.7	16 02.0
22 F	20 06 30	2 16 06	2♎01 12	8♎47 27	22 13.6	12 20.7	12 42.7	27 47.6	8 45.7	16 21.3	3 28.2	14 21.0	19 46.6	16 01.0
23 Sa	20 10 27	3 17 07	15 26 27	21 58 31	22D 11.1	13 45.6	13 57.7	27 51.9	9 09.3	16 23.9	3 34.8	14 19.3	19 47.6	16 00.0
24 Su	20 14 23	4 18 08	28 24 06	4♏43 41	22 10.4	15 11.3	15 12.8	27 55.5	9 33.0	16 26.6	3 41.5	14 17.5	19 48.5	15 58.9
25 M	20 18 20	5 19 08	10♏57 50	17 07 12	22 11.0	16 37.9	16 27.8	27 58.4	9 56.6	16 29.6	3 48.2	14 15.7	19 49.4	15 57.8
26 Tu	20 22 16	6 20 08	23 12 22	29 14 01	22 12.5	18 05.3	17 42.9	28 00.6	10 20.2	16 32.8	3 54.9	14 13.8	19 50.2	15 56.7
27 W	20 26 13	7 21 07	5♐12 47	11♐09 16	22R 14.0	19 33.4	18 58.0	28 02.0	10 43.9	16 36.1	4 01.7	14 11.9	19 51.0	15 55.5
28 Th	20 30 09	8 22 05	17 04 03	22 57 44	22 14.6	21 02.4	20 13.0	28R 02.7	11 07.5	16 39.7	4 08.5	14 10.0	19 51.8	15 54.4
29 F	20 34 06	9 23 03	28 50 47	4♑43 43	22 13.6	22 32.1	21 28.1	28 02.7	11 31.2	16 43.4	4 15.4	14 08.0	19 52.6	15 53.2
30 Sa	20 38 03	10 24 00	10♑36 56	16 30 51	22 10.4	24 02.5	22 43.1	28 01.9	11 54.8	16 47.3	4 22.3	14 06.0	19 53.3	15 52.0
31 Su	20 41 59	11 24 56	22 25 46	28 22 00	22 04.8	25 33.7	23 58.2	28 00.3	12 18.5	16 51.4	4 29.2	14 04.0	19 54.0	15 50.8

LONGITUDE — February 1965

Day	Sid.Time	☉	0 hr ☽	Noon ☽	True ☊	☿	♀	♂	⚳	♃	♄	♅	♆	♇
1 M	20 45 56	12♒25 51	4♒19 49	10♒19 23	21♊57.0	27♑05.6	25♑13.3	27♍58.0	12♒42.1	16♉55.8	4♓36.2	14♍01.9	19♏54.6	15♍49.5
2 Tu	20 49 52	13 26 44	16 20 55	22 24 33	21R 47.4	28 38.2	26 28.3	27R 54.9	13 05.8	17 00.2	4 43.1	13R 59.8	19 55.2	15R 48.2
3 W	20 53 49	14 27 37	28 30 25	4♓38 37	21 36.9	0♒11.6	27 43.4	27 51.0	13 29.4	17 04.9	4 50.1	13 57.6	19 55.8	15 47.0
4 Th	20 57 45	15 28 29	10♓49 17	17 02 31	21 26.4	1 45.7	28 58.4	27 46.3	13 53.1	17 09.8	4 57.2	13 55.4	19 56.3	15 45.7
5 F	21 01 42	16 29 19	23 18 25	29 37 09	21 17.1	3 20.5	0♒13.5	27 40.8	14 16.7	17 14.8	5 04.2	13 53.2	19 56.9	15 44.3
6 Sa	21 05 38	17 30 07	5♈58 51	12♈23 41	21 09.6	4 56.1	1 28.5	27 34.6	14 40.3	17 20.0	5 11.3	13 51.0	19 57.3	15 43.0
7 Su	21 09 35	18 30 54	18 51 53	25 23 38	21 04.5	6 32.5	2 43.5	27 27.5	15 03.9	17 25.4	5 18.4	13 48.7	19 57.8	15 41.6
8 M	21 13 31	19 31 40	1♉59 13	8♉38 51	21D 01.9	8 09.6	3 58.6	27 19.7	15 27.5	17 31.0	5 25.5	13 46.4	19 58.2	15 40.3
9 Tu	21 17 28	20 32 24	15 22 47	22 11 16	21 01.3	9 47.5	5 13.6	27 11.1	15 51.1	17 36.7	5 32.7	13 44.1	19 58.6	15 38.9
10 W	21 21 25	21 33 07	29 04 30	6♊02 37	21 01.9	11 26.2	6 28.6	27 01.7	16 14.7	17 42.6	5 39.8	13 41.7	19 58.9	15 37.5
11 Th	21 25 21	22 33 48	13♊05 41	20 13 40	21R 02.4	13 05.8	7 43.6	26 51.5	16 38.3	17 48.7	5 47.0	13 39.4	19 59.2	15 36.0
12 F	21 29 18	23 34 27	27 26 25	4♋43 38	21 01.7	14 46.1	8 58.6	26 40.6	17 01.9	17 54.9	5 54.2	13 37.0	19 59.5	15 34.6
13 Sa	21 33 14	24 35 05	12♋04 52	19 29 29	20 58.7	16 27.3	10 13.6	26 28.9	17 25.4	18 01.3	6 01.4	13 34.5	19 59.7	15 33.2
14 Su	21 37 11	25 35 41	26 56 41	4♌25 33	20 53.1	18 09.3	11 28.6	26 16.4	17 48.9	18 07.9	6 08.7	13 32.1	20 00.0	15 31.7
15 M	21 41 07	26 36 16	11♌55 01	19 23 58	20 44.9	19 52.3	12 43.6	26 03.2	18 12.5	18 14.6	6 15.9	13 29.6	20 00.1	15 30.2
16 Tu	21 45 04	27 36 49	26 51 11	4♍15 33	20 34.7	21 36.1	13 58.6	25 49.3	18 36.0	18 21.5	6 23.2	13 27.2	20 00.3	15 28.8
17 W	21 49 01	28 37 20	11♍35 57	18 51 26	20 23.8	23 20.8	15 13.5	25 34.6	18 59.5	18 28.6	6 30.4	13 24.7	20 00.4	15 27.3
18 Th	21 52 57	29 37 50	26 01 09	3♎04 29	20 13.4	25 06.4	16 28.5	25 19.2	19 22.9	18 35.8	6 37.7	13 22.1	20 00.4	15 25.8
19 F	21 56 54	0♓38 18	10♎01 00	16 50 26	20 04.5	26 52.9	17 43.4	25 03.1	19 46.4	18 43.1	6 45.0	13 19.6	20R 00.5	15 24.2
20 Sa	22 00 50	1 38 45	23 32 44	0♏08 02	19 58.0	28 40.4	18 58.4	24 46.3	20 09.8	18 50.6	6 52.3	13 17.1	20 00.5	15 22.7
21 Su	22 04 47	2 39 11	6♏36 36	12 58 49	19 54.0	0♓28.7	20 13.3	24 28.9	20 33.2	18 58.2	6 59.6	13 14.5	20 00.4	15 21.2
22 M	22 08 43	3 39 36	19 15 11	25 26 18	19D 52.3	2 18.0	21 28.3	24 10.8	20 56.6	19 06.0	7 06.9	13 11.9	20 00.4	15 19.6
23 Tu	22 12 40	4 39 59	1♐32 48	7♐35 21	19 52.0	4 08.2	22 43.2	23 52.1	21 20.0	19 14.0	7 14.2	13 09.4	20 00.3	15 18.1
24 W	22 16 36	5 40 21	13 34 39	19 31 24	19R 52.2	5 59.2	23 58.2	23 32.9	21 43.3	19 22.1	7 21.5	13 06.8	20 00.2	15 16.5
25 Th	22 20 33	6 40 41	25 26 19	1♑20 03	19 51.7	7 51.1	25 13.1	23 13.0	22 06.7	19 30.3	7 28.9	13 04.2	20 00.0	15 15.0
26 F	22 24 29	7 41 00	7♑13 16	13 06 34	19 49.4	9 43.8	26 28.0	22 52.7	22 30.0	19 38.7	7 36.2	13 01.6	19 59.8	15 13.4
27 Sa	22 28 26	8 41 18	19 00 32	24 55 41	19 44.6	11 37.3	27 42.9	22 31.8	22 53.2	19 47.2	7 43.5	12 58.9	19 59.6	15 11.8
28 Su	22 32 23	9 41 34	0♒52 28	6♒51 18	19 36.9	13 31.4	28 57.8	22 10.5	23 16.5	19 55.8	7 50.8	12 56.3	19 59.3	15 10.3

Astro Data

Astro Data	Dy Hr Mn
☽ 0N	10 4:42
♃ D	10 9:33
♃△♇	14 18:44
☽ 0S	22 16:41
♂ R	28 22:38
☽ 0N	6 9:39
☽ 0S	19 1:40
♆ R	20 1:23
♃☍♆	28 21:19

Planet Ingress

Planet Ingress	Dy Hr Mn
♀ ♑	12 8:00
☿ ♑	13 3:12
☉ ♒	20 6:29
☿ ♒	3 9:02
♀ ♒	5 7:41
☉ ♓	18 20:48
☿ ♓	21 5:40

Last Aspect / ☽ Ingress (January)

Last Aspect Dy Hr Mn		☽ Ingress Dy Hr Mn
1 7:42	♂ □	♑ 1 20:06
3 22:08	♂ △	♒ 4 9:04
6 6:38	☿ ⚹	♓ 6 21:06
8 23:09	♀ □	♈ 9 7:08
11 12:21	♀ △	♉ 11 14:10
13 12:13	♂ △	♊ 13 17:48
15 13:47	♂ □	♋ 15 18:35
17 13:40	♂ ⚹	♌ 17 17:57
19 1:17	♆ □	♍ 19 17:55
21 16:30	♂ ☌	♎ 21 20:28
22 19:47	♀ □	♏ 24 3:01
26 9:33	♂ ⚹	♐ 26 13:32
28 22:22	♂ □	♑ 29 2:21
31 11:16	♂ △	♒ 31 15:18

Last Aspect / ☽ Ingress (February)

Last Aspect Dy Hr Mn		☽ Ingress Dy Hr Mn
2 7:05	♆ □	♓ 3 2:56
5 8:21	♂ ☍	♈ 5 12:43
6 22:17	☉ ⚹	♉ 7 20:24
9 20:38	♂ △	♊ 10 1:36
11 22:54	♂ □	♋ 12 4:14
13 23:06	♂ ⚹	♌ 14 4:54
16 0:27	☉ ☍	♍ 16 5:05
17 23:03	♂ ☌	♎ 18 6:45
20 8:54	☿ △	♏ 20 11:45
22 9:36	♂ ⚹	♐ 22 20:57
24 22:05	♀ ⚹	♑ 25 9:17
27 7:17	♂ △	♒ 27 22:14

☽ Phases & Eclipses

Dy Hr Mn		
2 21:07	●	12♑17
10 20:59	☽	20♈26
17 13:37	○	27♋15
24 11:07	☾	4♏16
1 16:36	●	12♒37
9 8:53	☽	20♉25
16 0:27	○	27♌08
23 5:39	☾	4♐24

Astro Data

1 January 1965
Julian Day # 23742
SVP 5♓45'11"
GC 26♐21.0 ⚵ 11♑18.9
Eris 10♈10.5 ⚶ 3♑19.6
⚷ 14♓49.1 ⚴ 19♓39.4
☽ Mean ☊ 21♊56.9

1 February 1965
Julian Day # 23773
SVP 5♓45'06"
GC 26♐21.1 ⚵ 23♑12.6
Eris 10♈17.3 ⚶ 14♑35.7
⚷ 16♓12.2 ⚴ 1♈51.0
☽ Mean ☊ 20♊18.4

March 1965 — LONGITUDE

Day	Sid.Time	☉	0 hr ☽	Noon ☽	True☊	☿	♀	♂	⚳	♃	♄	♅	♆	♇
1 M	22 36 19	10♓41 48	12♒52 32	18♒56 26	19♊26.5	15♓26.2	0♓12.7	21♍48.7	23♒39.7	20♉04.6	7♓58.2	12♍53.7	19♏59.0	15♍08.7
2 Tu	22 40 16	11 42 00	25 03 14	1♓13 03	19R13.8	17 21.3	1 27.6	21R26.5	24 02.9	20 13.5	8 05.5	12R51.1	19R58.7	15R07.1
3 W	22 44 12	12 42 11	7♓26 00	13 42 07	18 59.8	19 16.9	2 42.5	21 04.0	24 26.1	20 22.5	8 12.8	12 48.4	19 58.3	15 05.5
4 Th	22 48 09	13 42 20	20 01 24	26 23 47	18 45.8	21 12.6	3 57.4	20 41.2	24 49.2	20 31.7	8 20.1	12 45.8	19 57.9	15 03.9
5 F	22 52 05	14 42 27	2♈49 12	9♈17 34	18 33.1	23 08.2	5 12.2	20 18.2	25 12.3	20 40.9	8 27.4	12 43.2	19 57.5	15 02.3
6 Sa	22 56 02	15 42 32	15 48 47	22 22 47	18 22.6	25 03.6	6 27.1	19 54.9	25 35.4	20 50.4	8 34.7	12 40.5	19 57.0	15 00.8
7 Su	22 59 58	16 42 35	28 59 29	5♉38 52	18 15.1	26 58.5	7 41.9	19 31.4	25 58.4	20 59.9	8 42.0	12 37.9	19 56.5	14 59.2
8 M	23 03 55	17 42 35	12♉20 54	19 05 37	18 10.7	28 52.5	8 56.7	19 07.9	26 21.4	21 09.5	8 49.2	12 35.3	19 56.0	14 57.6
9 Tu	23 07 52	18 42 34	25 53 04	2♊43 18	18 08.7	0♈45.4	10 11.5	18 44.2	26 44.4	21 19.3	8 56.5	12 32.7	19 55.4	14 56.0
10 W	23 11 48	19 42 31	9♊36 25	16 32 29	18 08.4	2 36.7	11 26.3	18 20.5	27 07.3	21 29.2	9 03.7	12 30.1	19 54.9	14 54.4
11 Th	23 15 45	20 42 25	23 31 33	0♋33 39	18 08.2	4 26.0	12 41.1	17 56.9	27 30.2	21 39.2	9 11.0	12 27.5	19 54.2	14 52.8
12 F	23 19 41	21 42 18	7♋38 43	14 46 39	18 07.0	6 12.9	13 55.9	17 33.3	27 53.0	21 49.3	9 18.2	12 24.9	19 53.6	14 51.3
13 Sa	23 23 38	22 42 07	21 57 12	29 10 04	18 03.6	7 56.9	15 10.6	17 09.8	28 15.8	21 59.5	9 25.4	12 22.3	19 52.9	14 49.7
14 Su	23 27 34	23 41 55	6♌24 46	13♌40 46	17 57.3	9 37.6	16 25.3	16 46.4	28 38.6	22 09.9	9 32.6	12 19.8	19 52.2	14 48.1
15 M	23 31 31	24 41 41	20 57 23	28 13 50	17 48.3	11 14.3	17 40.1	16 23.3	29 01.3	22 20.3	9 39.8	12 17.2	19 51.5	14 46.6
16 Tu	23 35 27	25 41 24	5♍29 16	12♍42 51	17 37.3	12 46.7	18 54.8	16 00.3	29 24.0	22 30.9	9 46.9	12 14.7	19 50.7	14 45.0
17 W	23 39 24	26 41 05	19 53 42	27 00 58	17 25.2	14 14.3	20 09.4	15 37.7	29 46.6	22 41.5	9 54.0	12 12.2	19 49.9	14 43.4
18 Th	23 43 21	27 40 44	4♎03 56	11♎01 57	17 13.5	15 36.5	21 24.1	15 15.3	0♓09.2	22 52.2	10 01.1	12 09.6	19 49.1	14 41.9
19 F	23 47 17	28 40 21	17 54 31	24 41 15	17 03.2	16 53.0	22 38.8	14 53.3	0 31.7	23 03.1	10 08.2	12 07.2	19 48.2	14 40.4
20 Sa	23 51 14	29 39 57	1♏21 56	7♏56 33	16 55.4	18 03.3	23 53.4	14 31.7	0 54.2	23 14.0	10 15.3	12 04.7	19 47.4	14 38.8
21 Su	23 55 10	0♈39 30	14 25 09	20 47 58	16 50.2	19 07.1	25 08.1	14 10.5	1 16.6	23 25.0	10 22.3	12 02.2	19 46.5	14 37.3
22 M	23 59 07	1 39 02	27 05 20	3♐17 41	16 47.6	20 04.1	26 22.7	13 49.7	1 39.0	23 36.1	10 29.3	11 59.8	19 45.5	14 35.8
23 Tu	0 03 03	2 38 32	9♐25 31	15 29 26	16D46.9	20 53.9	27 37.3	13 29.5	2 01.4	23 47.4	10 36.3	11 57.4	19 44.6	14 34.3
24 W	0 07 00	3 38 01	21 30 04	27 28 04	16R47.1	21 36.4	28 51.9	13 09.7	2 23.7	23 58.7	10 43.3	11 55.0	19 43.6	14 32.8
25 Th	0 10 56	4 37 27	3♑24 06	9♑18 54	16 47.1	22 11.4	0♈06.5	12 50.5	2 45.9	24 10.1	10 50.2	11 52.6	19 42.6	14 31.4
26 F	0 14 53	5 36 52	15 13 07	21 07 28	16 45.9	22 38.8	1 21.1	12 31.9	3 08.1	24 21.6	10 57.1	11 50.3	19 41.5	14 29.9
27 Sa	0 18 50	6 36 15	27 02 33	2♒59 02	16 42.6	22 58.6	2 35.7	12 13.9	3 30.3	24 33.1	11 04.0	11 48.0	19 40.5	14 28.4
28 Su	0 22 46	7 35 36	8♒57 28	14 58 24	16 36.9	23 10.7	3 50.2	11 56.6	3 52.4	24 44.8	11 10.8	11 45.7	19 39.4	14 27.0
29 M	0 26 43	8 34 56	21 02 17	27 09 32	16 28.7	23R15.3	5 04.8	11 39.9	4 14.4	24 56.5	11 17.6	11 43.4	19 38.3	14 25.6
30 Tu	0 30 39	9 34 13	3♓20 28	9♓35 21	16 18.4	23 12.5	6 19.3	11 23.8	4 36.4	25 08.3	11 24.4	11 41.2	19 37.1	14 24.2
31 W	0 34 36	10 33 29	15 54 20	22 17 31	16 06.8	23 02.7	7 33.8	11 08.5	4 58.3	25 20.2	11 31.1	11 38.9	19 36.0	14 22.8

April 1965 — LONGITUDE

Day	Sid.Time	☉	0 hr ☽	Noon ☽	True☊	☿	♀	♂	⚳	♃	♄	♅	♆	♇
1 Th	0 38 32	11♈32 42	28♓44 54	5♈16 23	15♊55.2	22♈46.2	8♈48.3	10♍53.9	5♓20.1	25♉32.2	11♓37.8	11♍36.8	19♏34.8	14♍21.4
2 F	0 42 29	12 31 54	11♈51 49	18 31 00	15R44.5	22R23.4	10 02.8	10R40.0	5 41.9	25 44.2	11 44.5	11R34.6	19R33.6	14R20.0
3 Sa	0 46 25	13 31 03	25 13 40	1♉59 30	15 35.8	21 54.9	11 17.3	10 26.9	6 03.6	25 56.4	11 51.1	11 32.5	19 32.4	14 18.6
4 Su	0 50 22	14 30 11	8♉48 13	15 39 29	15 29.7	21 21.4	12 31.7	10 14.6	6 25.3	26 08.6	11 57.7	11 30.4	19 31.1	14 17.3
5 M	0 54 18	15 29 16	22 32 59	29 28 26	15 26.3	20 43.5	13 46.2	10 03.0	6 46.9	26 20.8	12 04.2	11 28.4	19 29.9	14 16.0
6 Tu	0 58 15	16 28 19	6♊25 35	13♊24 14	15D25.1	20 02.2	15 00.6	9 52.2	7 08.4	26 33.2	12 10.7	11 26.4	19 28.6	14 14.7
7 W	1 02 12	17 27 20	20 24 10	27 25 14	15 25.5	19 18.3	16 15.0	9 42.2	7 29.9	26 45.6	12 17.2	11 24.4	19 27.3	14 13.4
8 Th	1 06 08	18 26 18	4♋27 19	11♋30 17	15R26.3	18 32.6	17 29.4	9 32.9	7 51.3	26 58.0	12 23.6	11 22.4	19 25.9	14 12.2
9 F	1 10 05	19 25 14	18 34 01	25 38 22	15 26.2	17 46.0	18 43.8	9 24.5	8 12.6	27 10.6	12 30.0	11 20.5	19 24.6	14 10.9
10 Sa	1 14 01	20 24 08	2♌43 11	9♌48 15	15 24.6	16 59.6	19 58.1	9 16.9	8 33.8	27 23.2	12 36.3	11 18.7	19 23.2	14 09.7
11 Su	1 17 58	21 23 00	16 53 20	23 58 06	15 20.7	16 14.1	21 12.4	9 10.0	8 55.0	27 35.8	12 42.6	11 16.9	19 21.9	14 08.5
12 M	1 21 54	22 21 49	1♍02 13	8♍05 16	15 14.7	15 30.3	22 26.8	9 04.0	9 16.1	27 48.5	12 48.8	11 15.1	19 20.5	14 07.3
13 Tu	1 25 51	23 20 36	15 06 47	22 06 17	15 07.0	14 49.0	23 41.0	8 58.7	9 37.1	28 01.3	12 55.0	11 13.3	19 19.0	14 06.1
14 W	1 29 47	24 19 20	29 03 18	5♎57 20	14 58.5	14 10.9	24 55.3	8 54.2	9 58.0	28 14.1	13 01.1	11 11.6	19 17.6	14 05.0
15 Th	1 33 44	25 18 03	12♎47 56	19 34 41	14 50.2	13 36.4	26 09.6	8 50.5	10 18.9	28 27.0	13 07.2	11 10.0	19 16.2	14 03.9
16 F	1 37 41	26 16 44	26 17 15	2♏55 21	14 42.9	13 06.1	27 23.8	8 47.6	10 39.7	28 39.9	13 13.2	11 08.3	19 14.7	14 02.8
17 Sa	1 41 37	27 15 22	9♏28 48	15 57 31	14 37.4	12 40.3	28 38.0	8 45.4	11 00.4	28 52.9	13 19.2	11 06.7	19 13.2	14 01.7
18 Su	1 45 34	28 13 59	22 21 31	28 40 54	14 34.0	12 19.2	29 52.2	8 43.9	11 21.0	29 06.0	13 25.1	11 05.2	19 11.8	14 00.7
19 M	1 49 30	29 12 35	4♐55 51	11♐06 40	14D32.7	12 03.1	1♉06.4	8D43.3	11 41.5	29 19.1	13 31.0	11 03.7	19 10.3	13 59.6
20 Tu	1 53 27	0♉11 08	17 13 41	23 17 21	14 33.0	11 52.1	2 20.6	8 43.3	12 02.0	29 32.2	13 36.8	11 02.3	19 08.7	13 58.6
21 W	1 57 23	1 09 40	29 18 08	5♑16 35	14 34.3	11D46.1	3 34.8	8 44.1	12 22.4	29 45.4	13 42.5	11 00.9	19 07.2	13 57.7
22 Th	2 01 20	2 08 10	11♑13 15	17 08 46	14 35.8	11 45.3	4 48.9	8 45.6	12 42.6	29 58.6	13 48.2	10 59.5	19 05.7	13 56.7
23 F	2 05 16	3 06 39	23 03 44	28 58 48	14R36.8	11 49.5	6 03.1	8 47.9	13 02.8	0♊11.9	13 53.9	10 58.2	19 04.1	13 55.8
24 Sa	2 09 13	4 05 06	4♒54 37	10♒51 49	14 36.6	11 58.6	7 17.2	8 50.8	13 22.9	0 25.2	13 59.5	10 56.9	19 02.6	13 54.9
25 Su	2 13 10	5 03 31	16 51 01	22 52 49	14 34.9	12 12.5	8 31.3	8 54.5	13 42.9	0 38.5	14 05.0	10 55.7	19 01.0	13 54.0
26 M	2 17 06	6 01 55	28 57 47	5♓06 26	14 31.5	12 31.1	9 45.4	8 58.8	14 02.9	0 51.9	14 10.4	10 54.6	18 59.5	13 53.1
27 Tu	2 21 03	7 00 17	11♓19 14	17 36 34	14 26.7	12 54.3	10 59.5	9 03.8	14 22.7	1 05.4	14 15.8	10 53.4	18 57.9	13 52.3
28 W	2 24 59	7 58 37	23 58 45	0♈26 00	14 21.0	13 21.8	12 13.6	9 09.5	14 42.4	1 18.9	14 21.2	10 52.4	18 56.3	13 51.5
29 Th	2 28 56	8 56 56	6♈58 26	13 36 07	14 15.0	13 53.5	13 27.6	9 15.9	15 02.0	1 32.4	14 26.4	10 51.3	18 54.7	13 50.7
30 F	2 32 52	9 55 13	20 18 55	27 06 41	14 09.5	14 29.2	14 41.6	9 22.9	15 21.6	1 45.9	14 31.6	10 50.4	18 53.1	13 50.0

Astro Data

	Dy Hr Mn
☽0N	5 14:44
☿0N	9 9:03
☽0S	18 11:25
☉0N	20 20:04
♀0N	28 0:32
☿R	29 14:53
♄☍♅	1 9:07
☽0N	1 21:49
☽0S	14 20:18
♂D	19 21:56
☿D	22 4:00
♄☍♇	23 18:58
☽0N	29 6:55

Planet Ingress

		Dy Hr Mn
♀	♓	1 7:55
☿	♈	9 2:19
⚳	♓	18 2:15
☉	♈	20 20:05
♀	♈	25 9:54
♀	♉	18 14:31
☉	♉	20 7:26
♃	♊	22 14:32

Last Aspect / ☽ Ingress

Last Aspect Dy Hr Mn		☽ Ingress Dy Hr Mn
1 14:16	♃ □	♓ 2 9:38
4 1:34	♂ ☍	♈ 4 18:45
4 1:34	♂ ☍	♉ 7 1:49
8 15:42	♃ ☌	♊ 9 7:14
10 17:52	☉ □	♋ 11 11:03
13 0:27	☉ △	♌ 13 13:23
15 2:10	♃ □	♍ 15 14:55
17 11:24	☉ ☍	♎ 17 17:04
18 20:48	☿ ☍	♏ 19 21:32
21 21:10	♀ △	♐ 22 5:37
24 15:09	♀ □	♑ 24 17:07
26 18:40	♃ △	♒ 27 5:59
29 7:36	♃ □	♓ 29 17:32

Last Aspect / ☽ Ingress

Last Aspect Dy Hr Mn		☽ Ingress Dy Hr Mn
31 17:46	♃ ⚹	♈ 1 2:19
2 18:43	☿ ☌	♉ 3 8:29
5 6:30	♃ ☌	♊ 5 12:55
6 22:49	☿ ⚹	♋ 7 16:24
9 14:39	♃ ⚹	♌ 9 19:24
11 18:15	♃ □	♍ 11 22:14
13 22:22	♃ △	♎ 14 1:38
16 0:58	♀ ☍	♏ 16 6:42
18 12:49	♃ ☍	♐ 18 14:31
19 17:38	♇ □	♑ 21 1:24
22 15:57	♆ ⚹	♒ 23 14:04
25 4:20	♆ □	♓ 26 2:02
27 14:34	♆ △	♈ 28 11:12
29 12:33	☿ ☌	♉ 30 17:04

☽ Phases & Eclipses

Dy Hr Mn	
3 9:56	● 12♓37
10 17:52	☽ 19♊57
17 11:24	○ 26♍40
25 1:37	☾ 4♑12
2 0:21	● 12♈03
9 0:40	☽ 18♋57
15 23:02	○ 25♎45
23 21:07	☾ 3♒29

Astro Data

1 March 1965
Julian Day # 23801
SVP 5♓45'02"
GC 26♐21.2 ⚴ 3♒12.6
Eris 10♈31.3 ⚵ 24♑21.6
⚷ 17♓50.1 ⚶ 13♈50.9
☽ Mean ☊ 18♊49.4

1 April 1965
Julian Day # 23832
SVP 5♓44'59"
GC 26♐21.2 ⚴ 12♒50.5
Eris 10♈51.7 ⚵ 4♒06.1
⚷ 19♓43.1 ⚶ 27♈37.3
☽ Mean ☊ 17♊10.9

LONGITUDE — May 1965

Day	Sid.Time	☉	0 hr ☽	Noon☽	True☊	☿	♀	♂	⚳	♃	♄	♅	♆	♇
1 Sa	2 36 49	10♉53 28	3♉59 07	10♉55 49	14♊05.1	15♈08.8	15♉55.7	9♍30.5	15♓41.0	1♊59.5	14♓36.7	10♍49.4	18♏51.5	13♍49.3
2 Su	2 40 45	11 51 42	17 56 21	25 00 10	14R 02.2	15 52.1	17 09.7	9 38.8	16 00.3	2 13.1	14 41.8	10R 48.6	18R 49.8	13R 48.6
3 M	2 44 42	12 49 54	2♊06 45	9♊15 28	14D 01.0	16 39.0	18 23.7	9 47.7	16 19.5	2 26.8	14 46.8	10 47.7	18 48.2	13 47.9
4 Tu	2 48 39	13 48 05	16 25 45	23 37 01	14 01.2	17 29.3	19 37.7	9 57.2	16 38.6	2 40.4	14 51.7	10 47.0	18 46.6	13 47.3
5 W	2 52 35	14 46 13	0♋48 43	8♋00 22	14 02.3	18 22.8	20 51.6	10 07.3	16 57.6	2 54.1	14 56.6	10 46.3	18 45.0	13 46.7
6 Th	2 56 32	15 44 19	15 11 29	22 21 40	14 03.8	19 19.5	22 05.6	10 18.1	17 16.4	3 07.9	15 01.4	10 45.6	18 43.4	13 46.1
7 F	3 00 28	16 42 24	29 30 33	6♌37 51	14R 04.9	20 19.3	23 19.5	10 29.3	17 35.2	3 21.6	15 06.1	10 45.0	18 41.7	13 45.5
8 Sa	3 04 25	17 40 26	13♌43 18	20 46 39	14 05.2	21 21.9	24 33.4	10 41.2	17 53.8	3 35.4	15 10.7	10 44.4	18 40.1	13 45.0
9 Su	3 08 21	18 38 27	27 47 43	4♍46 20	14 04.3	22 27.4	25 47.3	10 53.6	18 12.4	3 49.2	15 15.3	10 43.9	18 38.5	13 44.5
10 M	3 12 18	19 36 25	11♍42 20	18 35 33	14 02.4	23 35.7	27 01.2	11 06.5	18 30.8	4 03.0	15 19.8	10 43.4	18 36.8	13 44.1
11 Tu	3 16 14	20 34 22	25 25 52	2♎13 09	13 59.5	24 46.6	28 15.0	11 20.0	18 49.0	4 16.9	15 24.2	10 43.0	18 35.2	13 43.6
12 W	3 20 11	21 32 17	8♎57 16	15 38 06	13 56.2	26 00.1	29 28.8	11 34.0	19 07.2	4 30.7	15 28.5	10 42.7	18 33.6	13 43.2
13 Th	3 24 08	22 30 10	22 15 32	28 49 31	13 53.0	27 16.1	0♊42.7	11 48.5	19 25.2	4 44.6	15 32.8	10 42.4	18 31.9	13 42.9
14 F	3 28 04	23 28 02	5♏19 57	11♏46 48	13 50.3	28 34.6	1 56.5	12 03.5	19 43.1	4 58.5	15 37.0	10 42.1	18 30.3	13 42.5
15 Sa	3 32 01	24 25 52	18 10 04	24 29 46	13 48.3	29 55.5	3 10.2	12 19.0	20 00.9	5 12.4	15 41.1	10 41.9	18 28.7	13 42.2
16 Su	3 35 57	25 23 40	0♐45 59	6♐58 50	13D 47.4	1♉18.8	4 24.0	12 34.9	20 18.6	5 26.3	15 45.1	10 41.8	18 27.1	13 41.9
17 M	3 39 54	26 21 28	13 08 27	19 15 04	13 47.3	2 44.4	5 37.8	12 51.3	20 36.1	5 40.3	15 49.0	10 41.7	18 25.5	13 41.7
18 Tu	3 43 50	27 19 14	25 18 55	1♑20 19	13 48.0	4 12.4	6 51.5	13 08.2	20 53.5	5 54.2	15 52.9	10D 41.7	18 23.9	13 41.5
19 W	3 47 47	28 16 59	7♑19 36	13 17 09	13 49.2	5 42.6	8 05.3	13 25.5	21 10.7	6 08.2	15 56.7	10 41.7	18 22.3	13 41.3
20 Th	3 51 43	29 14 42	19 13 24	25 08 49	13 50.5	7 15.2	9 19.0	13 43.3	21 27.8	6 22.2	16 00.4	10 41.8	18 20.7	13 41.1
21 F	3 55 40	0♊12 25	1♒03 53	6♒59 09	13 51.8	8 50.0	10 32.7	14 01.5	21 44.8	6 36.2	16 04.0	10 41.9	18 19.1	13 41.0
22 Sa	3 59 37	1 10 06	12 55 09	18 52 28	13 52.6	10 27.1	11 46.4	14 20.1	22 01.6	6 50.2	16 07.5	10 42.1	18 17.5	13 40.9
23 Su	4 03 33	2 07 46	24 51 40	0♓53 19	13R 52.9	12 06.4	13 00.0	14 39.1	22 18.3	7 04.2	16 11.0	10 42.3	18 15.9	13 40.8
24 M	4 07 30	3 05 26	6♓58 02	13 06 21	13 52.7	13 48.0	14 13.7	14 58.5	22 34.9	7 18.2	16 14.4	10 42.6	18 14.3	13D 40.8
25 Tu	4 11 26	4 03 04	19 18 49	25 35 55	13 52.1	15 31.8	15 27.4	15 18.4	22 51.2	7 32.2	16 17.6	10 42.9	18 12.8	13 40.8
26 W	4 15 23	5 00 41	1♈58 08	8♈25 49	13 51.2	17 17.9	16 41.0	15 38.6	23 07.5	7 46.2	16 20.8	10 43.3	18 11.2	13 40.8
27 Th	4 19 19	5 58 18	14 59 17	21 38 44	13 50.2	19 06.2	17 54.6	15 59.2	23 23.5	8 00.2	16 23.9	10 43.8	18 09.7	13 40.8
28 F	4 23 16	6 55 53	28 24 17	5♉15 55	13 49.3	20 56.8	19 08.3	16 20.2	23 39.4	8 14.3	16 26.9	10 44.3	18 08.1	13 40.9
29 Sa	4 27 12	7 53 27	12♉13 27	19 16 38	13 48.7	22 49.5	20 21.9	16 41.5	23 55.2	8 28.3	16 29.8	10 44.8	18 06.6	13 41.1
30 Su	4 31 09	8 51 01	26 25 01	3♊38 03	13D 48.4	24 44.4	21 35.5	17 03.3	24 10.8	8 42.3	16 32.7	10 45.5	18 05.1	13 41.2
31 M	4 35 06	9 48 34	10♊55 04	18 15 18	13 48.3	26 41.4	22 49.1	17 25.4	24 26.2	8 56.3	16 35.4	10 46.1	18 03.6	13 41.4

LONGITUDE — June 1965

Day	Sid.Time	☉	0 hr ☽	Noon☽	True☊	☿	♀	♂	⚳	♃	♄	♅	♆	♇
1 Tu	4 39 02	10♊46 05	25♊37 55	3♋01 59	13♊48.4	28♉40.6	24♊02.6	17♍47.8	24♓41.4	9♊10.3	16♓38.1	10♍46.8	18♏02.1	13♍41.6
2 W	4 42 59	11 43 36	10♋26 37	17 50 54	13 48.6	0♊41.7	25 16.2	18 10.6	24 56.5	9 24.4	16 40.6	10 47.6	18R 00.7	13 41.9
3 Th	4 46 55	12 41 05	25 13 58	2♌35 03	13 48.8	2 44.7	26 29.7	18 33.7	25 11.4	9 38.4	16 43.1	10 48.4	17 59.2	13 42.1
4 F	4 50 52	13 38 33	9♌53 25	17 08 29	13R 48.9	4 49.6	27 43.3	18 57.2	25 26.1	9 52.4	16 45.4	10 49.3	17 57.8	13 42.4
5 Sa	4 54 48	14 35 59	24 19 45	1♍26 51	13D 48.8	6 56.0	28 56.8	19 20.9	25 40.6	10 06.4	16 47.7	10 50.2	17 56.4	13 42.8
6 Su	4 58 45	15 33 25	8♍29 30	15 27 32	13 48.8	9 04.0	0♋10.3	19 45.0	25 55.0	10 20.3	16 49.9	10 51.2	17 55.0	13 43.1
7 M	5 02 42	16 30 49	22 20 54	29 09 34	13 48.9	11 13.2	1 23.7	20 09.4	26 09.2	10 34.3	16 52.0	10 52.2	17 53.6	13 43.5
8 Tu	5 06 38	17 28 12	5♎53 37	12♎33 11	13 49.1	13 23.5	2 37.2	20 34.1	26 23.1	10 48.3	16 54.0	10 53.3	17 52.2	13 44.0
9 W	5 10 35	18 25 34	19 08 25	25 39 30	13 49.5	15 34.6	3 50.6	20 59.1	26 36.9	11 02.2	16 55.9	10 54.5	17 50.8	13 44.4
10 Th	5 14 31	19 22 54	2♏06 39	8♏30 04	13 50.0	17 46.3	5 04.1	21 24.4	26 50.5	11 16.1	16 57.6	10 55.6	17 49.5	13 44.9
11 F	5 18 28	20 20 14	14 50 00	21 06 38	13 50.5	19 58.3	6 17.5	21 50.0	27 03.9	11 30.0	16 59.3	10 56.9	17 48.2	13 45.4
12 Sa	5 22 24	21 17 34	27 20 13	3♐30 57	13R 51.0	22 10.4	7 30.9	22 15.8	27 17.1	11 43.9	17 01.0	10 58.2	17 46.9	13 46.0
13 Su	5 26 21	22 14 52	9♐39 03	15 44 44	13 51.1	24 22.2	8 44.3	22 42.0	27 30.1	11 57.8	17 02.5	10 59.5	17 45.6	13 46.6
14 M	5 30 17	23 12 10	21 48 14	27 49 45	13 50.8	26 33.4	9 57.6	23 08.4	27 42.8	12 11.7	17 03.9	11 00.9	17 44.3	13 47.2
15 Tu	5 34 14	24 09 27	3♑49 32	9♑47 48	13 50.0	28 44.0	11 11.0	23 35.0	27 55.4	12 25.5	17 05.2	11 02.3	17 43.1	13 47.8
16 W	5 38 11	25 06 44	15 44 51	21 40 55	13 48.7	0♋53.5	12 24.3	24 01.9	28 07.8	12 39.4	17 06.4	11 03.8	17 41.9	13 48.5
17 Th	5 42 07	26 04 00	27 36 21	3♒31 27	13 47.1	3 01.7	13 37.6	24 29.1	28 19.9	12 53.2	17 07.5	11 05.3	17 40.7	13 49.2
18 F	5 46 04	27 01 16	9♒26 34	15 22 07	13 45.2	5 08.6	14 50.9	24 56.5	28 31.9	13 06.9	17 08.5	11 06.9	17 39.5	13 50.0
19 Sa	5 50 00	27 58 31	21 18 28	27 16 06	13 43.4	7 13.9	16 04.2	25 24.1	28 43.6	13 20.7	17 09.5	11 08.5	17 38.3	13 50.7
20 Su	5 53 57	28 55 46	3♓15 27	9♓17 02	13 41.9	9 17.5	17 17.5	25 52.0	28 55.1	13 34.4	17 10.3	11 10.2	17 37.2	13 51.5
21 M	5 57 53	29 53 01	15 21 20	21 28 53	13D 41.0	11 19.3	18 30.8	26 20.2	29 06.3	13 48.1	17 11.0	11 11.9	17 36.1	13 52.3
22 Tu	6 01 50	0♋50 16	27 40 13	3♈55 50	13 40.8	13 19.1	19 44.0	26 48.6	29 17.3	14 01.8	17 11.6	11 13.7	17 35.0	13 53.2
23 W	6 05 46	1 47 30	10♈16 16	16 42 00	13 41.4	15 17.0	20 57.3	27 17.2	29 28.1	14 15.5	17 12.1	11 15.5	17 33.9	13 54.0
24 Th	6 09 43	2 44 45	23 13 27	29 51 00	13 42.5	17 12.8	22 10.5	27 46.0	29 38.6	14 29.1	17 12.6	11 17.4	17 32.9	13 54.9
25 F	6 13 40	3 41 59	6♉34 57	13♉25 30	13 43.8	19 06.5	23 23.7	28 15.1	29 48.9	14 42.7	17 12.9	11 19.3	17 31.9	13 55.9
26 Sa	6 17 36	4 39 14	20 22 42	27 26 30	13 45.0	20 58.1	24 36.9	28 44.3	29 59.0	14 56.3	17 13.1	11 21.3	17 30.9	13 56.8
27 Su	6 21 33	5 36 28	4♊36 41	11♊52 49	13R 45.6	22 47.6	25 50.1	29 13.8	0♈08.8	15 09.8	17R 13.2	11 23.3	17 29.9	13 57.8
28 M	6 25 29	6 33 43	19 14 21	26 40 32	13 45.2	24 34.9	27 03.3	29 43.6	0 18.3	15 23.3	17 13.3	11 25.3	17 29.0	13 58.9
29 Tu	6 29 26	7 30 57	4♋10 26	11♋43 02	13 43.7	26 20.0	28 16.4	0♎13.5	0 27.6	15 36.8	17 13.2	11 27.4	17 28.0	13 59.9
30 W	6 33 22	8 28 11	19 17 11	26 51 40	13 41.1	28 03.0	29 29.6	0 43.7	0 36.6	15 50.2	17 13.0	11 29.6	17 27.2	14 01.0

Astro Data	Planet Ingress	Last Aspect	☽ Ingress	Last Aspect	☽ Ingress	☽ Phases & Eclipses	Astro Data
Dy Hr Mn	Dy Hr Mn	Dy Hr Mn	Dy Hr Mn	Dy Hr Mn	Dy Hr Mn	Dy Hr Mn	1 May 1965
☽0S 12 3:25	♀ ♊ 12 22:08	2 1:32 ♆ ☍	♊ 2 20:26	31 20:06 ♀ ☌	♋ 1 7:05	1 11:56 ● 10♉53	Julian Day # 23862
♅ D 18 14:32	☿ ♉ 15 13:19	4 1:07 ☿ ⚹	♋ 4 22:39	2 12:33 ♂ ⚹	♌ 3 7:46	8 6:20 ☽ 17♌27	SVP 5♓44'56"
♇ D 25 5:21	☉ ♊ 21 6:50	6 11:31 ♀ ⚹	♌ 7 0:50	5 7:22 ♀ ⚹	♍ 5 9:33	15 11:52 ○ 24♏26	GC 26♐21.3 ⚵ 19♒52.6
☽0N 26 16:36		8 19:04 ♀ □	♍ 9 3:47	6 19:41 ♂ ☌	♎ 7 13:29	23 14:40 ☾ 2♓14	Eris 11♈11.5 ⚶ 11♒35.7
	☿ ♊ 2 3:47	11 4:16 ♀ △	♎ 11 8:04	8 21:39 ☉ △	♏ 9 20:04	30 21:12 ● 9♊13	⚷ 21♓16.6 ⚴ 11♉03.1
☽0S 8 9:06	♀ ♋ 6 8:39	13 8:50 ☿ ☍	♏ 13 14:10	11 13:26 ♂ ⚹	♐ 12 5:10	30 21:16:55 ● T 05'15"	☽ Mean ☊ 15♊35.6
♃□♅ 8 21:29	☿ ♋ 16 2:04	15 11:52 ☉ ☍	♐ 15 22:32	14 8:54 ☿ ☍	♑ 14 16:20		
♃□♇ 21 19:49	☉ ♋ 21 14:56	17 5:13 ♄ □	♑ 18 9:20	16 16:57 ♂ △	♒ 17 4:51	6 12:11 ☽ 15♍34	1 June 1965
☽0N 23 1:10	⚳ ♈ 26 14:28	20 21:03 ☉ △	♒ 20 21:50	19 13:33 ☉ △	♓ 19 17:29	14 1:59 ○ 22♐48	Julian Day # 23893
♄ R 28 5:32	♂ ♎ 29 1:12	22 10:50 ♆ □	♓ 23 10:14	21 21:48 ♂ ☍	♈ 22 4:29	14 1:49 ◑ P 0.177	SVP 5♓44'51"
♂0S 30 13:14	♀ ♌ 30 21:59	24 21:55 ♆ △	♈ 25 20:19	23 20:39 ♀ □	♉ 24 12:16	22 5:36 ☾ 0♈35	GC 26♐21.4 ⚵ 23♒28.6
		27 4:36 ♀ ⚹	♉ 28 2:48	26 14:16 ♂ △	♊ 26 16:18	29 4:52 ● 7♋14	Eris 11♈27.1 ⚶ 15♒56.7
		29 18:54 ☿ ☌	♊ 30 5:58	28 17:04 ♂ □	♋ 28 17:20		⚷ 22♓18.4 ⚴ 24♉44.0
				30 16:32 ♀ ☌	♌ 30 16:59		☽ Mean ☊ 13♊57.1

July 1965 — LONGITUDE

Day	Sid.Time	☉	0 hr ☽	Noon ☽	True ☊	☿	♀	♂	⚳	♃	♄	♅	♆	♇
1 Th	6 37 19	9♋25 25	4♌25 16	11♌56 50	13♊37.8	29♋43.8	0♌42.7	1♎14.0	0♈45.4	16♊03.6	17♓12.7	11♍31.7	17♏26.3	14♍02.1
2 F	6 41 15	10 22 38	19 25 16	26 49 35	13R 34.3	1♌22.4	1 55.8	1 44.6	0 53.8	16 16.9	17R 12.3	11 34.0	17R 25.5	14 03.2
3 Sa	6 45 12	11 19 52	4♍09 01	11♍22 54	13 31.3	2 58.8	3 08.9	2 15.3	1 02.0	16 30.2	17 11.9	11 36.2	17 24.7	14 04.4
4 Su	6 49 09	12 17 04	18 30 47	25 32 25	13 29.1	4 33.0	4 22.0	2 46.3	1 09.9	16 43.5	17 11.3	11 38.5	17 23.9	14 05.5
5 M	6 53 05	13 14 17	2♎27 39	9♎16 33	13D 28.1	6 05.0	5 35.0	3 17.4	1 17.6	16 56.7	17 10.6	11 40.9	17 23.1	14 06.8
6 Tu	6 57 02	14 11 29	15 59 16	22 36 03	13 28.3	7 34.7	6 48.0	3 48.8	1 24.9	17 09.9	17 09.8	11 43.3	17 22.4	14 08.0
7 W	7 00 58	15 08 41	29 07 15	5♏33 15	13 29.4	9 02.2	8 01.0	4 20.3	1 32.0	17 23.0	17 09.0	11 45.7	17 21.7	14 09.2
8 Th	7 04 55	16 05 53	11♏54 29	18 11 23	13 31.0	10 27.5	9 14.0	4 52.0	1 38.8	17 36.1	17 08.0	11 48.2	17 21.0	14 10.5
9 F	7 08 51	17 03 05	24 24 27	0♐34 05	13 32.5	11 50.4	10 27.0	5 23.8	1 45.3	17 49.1	17 06.9	11 50.7	17 20.4	14 11.8
10 Sa	7 12 48	18 00 16	6♐40 44	12 44 49	13R 33.2	13 11.0	11 39.9	5 55.9	1 51.5	18 02.1	17 05.8	11 53.2	17 19.8	14 13.2
11 Su	7 16 44	18 57 28	18 46 43	24 46 47	13 32.5	14 29.2	12 52.8	6 28.1	1 57.4	18 15.0	17 04.5	11 55.8	17 19.2	14 14.5
12 M	7 20 41	19 54 40	0♑45 22	6♑42 45	13 30.2	15 45.0	14 05.7	7 00.5	2 02.9	18 27.9	17 03.1	11 58.5	17 18.6	14 15.9
13 Tu	7 24 38	20 51 53	12 39 13	18 35 03	13 26.2	16 58.4	15 18.6	7 33.1	2 08.2	18 40.8	17 01.7	12 01.1	17 18.1	14 17.3
14 W	7 28 34	21 49 05	24 30 28	0♒25 42	13 20.6	18 09.1	16 31.5	8 05.8	2 13.2	18 53.5	17 00.2	12 03.8	17 17.6	14 18.7
15 Th	7 32 31	22 46 18	6♒21 01	12 16 36	13 13.8	19 17.3	17 44.3	8 38.7	2 17.9	19 06.3	16 58.5	12 06.6	17 17.2	14 20.2
16 F	7 36 27	23 43 31	18 12 44	24 09 38	13 06.4	20 22.7	18 57.1	9 11.8	2 22.2	19 18.9	16 56.8	12 09.3	17 16.7	14 21.7
17 Sa	7 40 24	24 40 45	0♓07 36	6♓06 54	12 59.3	21 25.4	20 09.9	9 45.0	2 26.2	19 31.6	16 55.0	12 12.1	17 16.3	14 23.2
18 Su	7 44 20	25 37 59	12 07 52	18 10 50	12 53.0	22 25.2	21 22.6	10 18.4	2 29.9	19 44.1	16 53.1	12 15.0	17 16.0	14 24.7
19 M	7 48 17	26 35 14	24 16 11	0♈24 20	12 48.1	23 22.0	22 35.4	10 51.9	2 33.3	19 56.6	16 51.0	12 17.9	17 15.6	14 26.2
20 Tu	7 52 13	27 32 29	6♈35 43	12 50 46	12 45.1	24 15.7	23 48.1	11 25.6	2 36.3	20 09.0	16 48.9	12 20.8	17 15.3	14 27.8
21 W	7 56 10	28 29 46	19 09 58	25 33 47	12D 44.0	25 06.2	25 00.8	11 59.4	2 39.0	20 21.4	16 46.8	12 23.7	17 15.0	14 29.4
22 Th	8 00 07	29 27 03	2♉02 42	8♉37 09	12 44.3	25 53.3	26 13.5	12 33.4	2 41.4	20 33.7	16 44.5	12 26.7	17 14.8	14 31.0
23 F	8 04 03	0♌24 21	15 17 33	22 04 14	12 45.3	26 36.9	27 26.1	13 07.6	2 43.4	20 45.9	16 42.1	12 29.7	17 14.6	14 32.6
24 Sa	8 08 00	1 21 40	28 57 28	5♊57 24	12R 46.3	27 16.9	28 38.7	13 41.9	2 45.1	20 58.1	16 39.7	12 32.7	17 14.4	14 34.2
25 Su	8 11 56	2 19 00	13♊04 01	20 17 11	12 46.2	27 53.0	29 51.4	14 16.3	2 46.4	21 10.2	16 37.2	12 35.8	17 14.2	14 35.9
26 M	8 15 53	3 16 21	27 36 32	5♋01 33	12 44.4	28 25.2	1♍03.9	14 50.9	2 47.4	21 22.3	16 34.5	12 38.9	17 14.1	14 37.6
27 Tu	8 19 49	4 13 43	12♋31 27	20 05 17	12 40.4	28 53.2	2 16.5	15 25.7	2 48.0	21 34.2	16 31.8	12 42.0	17 14.0	14 39.3
28 W	8 23 46	5 11 05	27 41 56	5♌20 08	12 34.3	29 16.9	3 29.1	16 00.6	2R 48.3	21 46.1	16 29.1	12 45.2	17 14.0	14 41.0
29 Th	8 27 43	6 08 28	12♌58 30	20 35 41	12 26.8	29 36.0	4 41.6	16 35.6	2 48.2	21 57.9	16 26.2	12 48.4	17D 13.9	14 42.8
30 F	8 31 39	7 05 52	28 10 18	5♍41 06	12 18.7	29 50.5	5 54.1	17 10.8	2 47.7	22 09.7	16 23.3	12 51.6	17 13.9	14 44.5
31 Sa	8 35 36	8 03 17	13♍07 00	20 27 04	12 11.1	0♍00.2	7 06.5	17 46.2	2 46.9	22 21.4	16 20.2	12 54.8	17 14.0	14 46.3

August 1965 — LONGITUDE

Day	Sid.Time	☉	0 hr ☽	Noon ☽	True ☊	☿	♀	♂	⚳	♃	♄	♅	♆	♇
1 Su	8 39 32	9♌00 42	27♍40 37	4♎47 08	12♊05.0	0♍04.8	8♍18.9	18♎21.6	2♈45.8	22♊32.9	16♓17.1	12♍58.1	17♏14.1	14♍48.1
2 M	8 43 29	9 58 08	11♎46 23	18 38 18	12R 00.9	0R 04.4	9 31.3	18 57.2	2R 44.3	22 44.4	16R 14.0	13 01.4	17 14.2	14 49.9
3 Tu	8 47 25	10 55 34	25 22 59	2♏00 42	11D 58.9	29♌58.7	10 43.7	19 33.0	2 42.4	22 55.9	16 10.7	13 04.7	17 14.3	14 51.7
4 W	8 51 22	11 53 01	8♏31 52	14 56 56	11 58.6	29 47.8	11 56.0	20 08.8	2 40.1	23 07.2	16 07.4	13 08.1	17 14.5	14 53.6
5 Th	8 55 18	12 50 29	21 16 26	27 30 58	11 59.2	29 31.6	13 08.3	20 44.8	2 37.5	23 18.4	16 04.0	13 11.4	17 14.7	14 55.4
6 F	8 59 15	13 47 57	3♐41 07	9♐47 30	11R 59.7	29 10.3	14 20.6	21 21.0	2 34.6	23 29.6	16 00.6	13 14.8	17 14.9	14 57.3
7 Sa	9 03 12	14 45 26	15 50 42	21 51 18	11 59.3	28 43.8	15 32.8	21 57.2	2 31.2	23 40.7	15 57.1	13 18.2	17 15.2	14 59.2
8 Su	9 07 08	15 42 57	27 49 50	3♑46 48	11 56.9	28 12.5	16 45.0	22 33.6	2 27.5	23 51.7	15 53.5	13 21.7	17 15.5	15 01.1
9 M	9 11 05	16 40 28	9♑42 39	15 37 50	11 52.1	27 36.7	17 57.2	23 10.1	2 23.5	24 02.6	15 49.8	13 25.1	17 15.8	15 03.0
10 Tu	9 15 01	17 38 00	21 32 42	27 27 36	11 44.8	26 56.8	19 09.3	23 46.7	2 19.1	24 13.4	15 46.1	13 28.6	17 16.2	15 05.0
11 W	9 18 58	18 35 33	3♒22 48	9♒18 35	11 35.0	26 13.4	20 21.4	24 23.5	2 14.3	24 24.1	15 42.4	13 32.1	17 16.6	15 06.9
12 Th	9 22 54	19 33 07	15 15 09	21 12 42	11 23.4	25 27.0	21 33.4	25 00.4	2 09.2	24 34.7	15 38.5	13 35.6	17 17.0	15 08.9
13 F	9 26 51	20 30 42	27 11 25	3♓11 27	11 10.9	24 38.4	22 45.4	25 37.3	2 03.8	24 45.2	15 34.7	13 39.1	17 17.5	15 10.8
14 Sa	9 30 47	21 28 19	9♓12 58	15 16 08	10 58.6	23 48.5	23 57.4	26 14.5	1 58.0	24 55.6	15 30.7	13 42.7	17 18.0	15 12.8
15 Su	9 34 44	22 25 56	21 21 07	27 28 06	10 47.5	22 58.2	25 09.3	26 51.7	1 51.8	25 06.0	15 26.7	13 46.3	17 18.5	15 14.8
16 M	9 38 40	23 23 36	3♈37 18	9♈48 58	10 38.5	22 08.4	26 21.2	27 29.0	1 45.3	25 16.2	15 22.7	13 49.8	17 19.0	15 16.8
17 Tu	9 42 37	24 21 16	16 03 23	22 20 50	10 32.0	21 20.1	27 33.1	28 06.5	1 38.4	25 26.3	15 18.6	13 53.4	17 19.6	15 18.8
18 W	9 46 34	25 18 59	28 41 40	5♉06 16	10 28.3	20 34.4	28 44.9	28 44.1	1 31.2	25 36.3	15 14.5	13 57.0	17 20.2	15 20.8
19 Th	9 50 30	26 16 42	11♉34 59	18 08 15	10D 26.8	19 52.2	29 56.7	29 21.8	1 23.7	25 46.2	15 10.3	14 00.7	17 20.9	15 22.9
20 F	9 54 27	27 14 28	24 46 25	1♊29 52	10R 26.6	19 14.3	1♎08.4	29 59.6	1 15.8	25 56.0	15 06.1	14 04.3	17 21.6	15 24.9
21 Sa	9 58 23	28 12 16	8♊18 55	15 13 49	10 26.6	18 41.7	2 20.2	0♏37.5	1 07.6	26 05.7	15 01.8	14 08.0	17 22.3	15 27.0
22 Su	10 02 20	29 10 05	22 14 42	29 21 38	10 25.6	18 15.1	3 31.8	1 15.6	0 59.1	26 15.3	14 57.5	14 11.7	17 23.0	15 29.0
23 M	10 06 16	0♍07 56	6♋34 27	13♋52 51	10 22.6	17 55.1	4 43.5	1 53.7	0 50.3	26 24.7	14 53.2	14 15.3	17 23.8	15 31.1
24 Tu	10 10 13	1 05 48	21 16 22	28 44 16	10 16.9	17 42.2	5 55.1	2 32.0	0 41.2	26 34.1	14 48.8	14 19.0	17 24.6	15 33.2
25 W	10 14 10	2 03 42	6♌15 40	13♌49 29	10 08.6	17D 36.9	7 06.6	3 10.4	0 31.7	26 43.3	14 44.4	14 22.7	17 25.5	15 35.3
26 Th	10 18 06	3 01 38	21 24 30	28 59 24	9 58.3	17 39.4	8 18.2	3 48.9	0 22.0	26 52.4	14 40.0	14 26.5	17 26.3	15 37.4
27 F	10 22 03	3 59 35	6♍32 51	14♍03 33	9 47.1	17 50.0	9 29.6	4 27.5	0 12.0	27 01.4	14 35.5	14 30.2	17 27.2	15 39.5
28 Sa	10 25 59	4 57 34	21 30 14	28 51 52	9 36.4	18 08.6	10 41.1	5 06.3	0 01.7	27 10.3	14 31.0	14 33.9	17 28.2	15 41.6
29 Su	10 29 56	5 55 34	6♎07 32	13♎16 33	9 27.4	18 35.5	11 52.5	5 45.1	29♓51.1	27 19.0	14 26.5	14 37.7	17 29.1	15 43.7
30 M	10 33 52	6 53 35	20 18 29	27 13 03	9 20.8	19 10.4	13 03.8	6 24.0	29 40.2	27 27.6	14 22.0	14 41.4	17 30.1	15 45.8
31 Tu	10 37 49	7 51 38	4♏00 15	10♏40 13	9 16.7	19 53.1	14 15.1	7 03.1	29 29.2	27 36.1	14 17.5	14 45.2	17 31.1	15 47.9

Astro Data	Dy Hr Mn
☽0S	5 14:43
♃□♄	6 11:55
♃⚻♆	7 9:42
☽0N	20 7:41
⚳R	28 18:13
♆D	29 17:40
☽0S	1 21:41
☿R	1 21:56
☽0N	16 12:42
♄☍♇	17 11:11
♀0S	20 23:56
☿D	25 16:25
♄☍♅	28 3:36
☽0S	29 6:33

Planet Ingress	Dy Hr Mn
☿ ♌	1 15:55
☉ ♌	23 1:48
♀ ♍	25 14:51
☿ ♍	31 11:24
☿ ♌R	3 8:09
♀ ♎	19 13:06
♂ ♏	20 12:16
☉ ♍	23 8:43
⚳ ♓R	28 15:47

Last Aspect Dy Hr Mn		☽ Ingress Dy Hr Mn
1 20:48 ♆ □	♍	2 17:11
3 22:07 ♆ ⚹	♎	4 19:43
6 1:57 ♃ △	♏	7 1:38
8 10:23 ♆ ☌	♐	9 10:53
10 22:43 ♃ ☍	♑	11 22:29
13 17:01 ☉ ☍	♒	14 11:08
16 3:37 ☿ ☍	♓	16 23:45
19 3:55 ☉ △	♈	19 11:13
21 17:53 ☉ □	♉	21 20:14
23 22:16 ♀ □	♊	24 1:48
26 0:56 ☿ ⚹	♋	26 3:53
27 7:29 ♆ △	♌	28 3:37
30 2:31 ☿ ☌	♍	30 2:55

Last Aspect Dy Hr Mn		☽ Ingress Dy Hr Mn
31 15:11 ♃ □	♎	1 3:54
3 8:20 ☿ ⚹	♏	3 8:20
5 15:48 ☿ □	♐	5 16:49
8 1:15 ☿ △	♑	8 4:22
10 4:08 ♂ □	♒	10 17:09
12 20:02 ♂ △	♓	13 5:37
15 7:18 ♃ □	♈	15 16:57
17 23:28 ♂ ☍	♉	18 2:27
20 3:50 ☉ □	♊	20 9:20
22 11:39 ☉ ⚹	♋	22 13:04
23 17:44 ♆ △	♌	24 14:01
26 8:37 ♃ ⚹	♍	26 13:36
28 9:12 ♃ □	♎	28 13:52
30 12:26 ♃ △	♏	30 16:54

☽ Phases & Eclipses Dy Hr Mn	
5 19:36	☽ 13♎32
13 17:01	○ 21♑04
21 17:53	☾ 28♈44
28 11:45	● 5♌10
4 5:47	☽ 11♏38
12 8:22	○ 19♒24
20 3:50	☾ 26♉55
26 18:50	● 3♍18

Astro Data

1 July 1965
Julian Day # 23923
SVP 5♓44'45"
GC 26♐21.4 ⚵ 21♒57.9R
Eris 11♈33.9 ⚶ 15♒11.9R
⚷ 22♓32.7R ⚴ 7♊31.1
☽ Mean ☊ 12♊21.8

1 August 1965
Julian Day # 23954
SVP 5♓44'40"
GC 26♐21.5 ⚵ 15♒20.5R
Eris 11♈31.0R ⚶ 9♒09.0R
⚷ 21♓58.4R ⚴ 19♊55.1
☽ Mean ☊ 10♊43.3

LONGITUDE — September 1965

Day	Sid.Time	☉	0 hr ☽	Noon ☽	True ☊	☿	♀	♂	⚳	♃	♄	♅	♆	♇
1 W	10 41 45	8♍49 43	17♏13 14	23♏39 43	9♊14.9	20♌43.6	15♎26.3	7♏42.3	29♓17.9	27♊44.5	14♓12.9	14♍48.9	17♏32.2	15♍50.1
2 Th	10 45 42	9 47 49	0♐00 12	6♐15 16	9R 14.5	21 41.3	16 37.5	8 21.5	29R 06.3	27 52.7	14R 08.3	14 52.7	17 33.2	15 52.2
3 F	10 49 38	10 45 56	12 25 32	18 31 41	9 14.5	22 46.1	17 48.7	9 00.9	28 54.6	28 00.8	14 03.8	14 56.4	17 34.4	15 54.3
4 Sa	10 53 35	11 44 04	24 34 23	0♑34 16	9 13.5	23 57.5	18 59.8	9 40.4	28 42.6	28 08.7	13 59.2	15 00.2	17 35.5	15 56.5
5 Su	10 57 32	12 42 14	6♑31 59	12 28 11	9 10.8	25 15.0	20 10.8	10 19.9	28 30.5	28 16.6	13 54.6	15 04.0	17 36.7	15 58.6
6 M	11 01 28	13 40 26	18 23 24	24 18 12	9 05.6	26 38.1	21 21.8	10 59.6	28 18.1	28 24.2	13 50.0	15 07.8	17 37.9	16 00.7
7 Tu	11 05 25	14 38 39	0♒13 03	6♒08 24	8 57.5	28 06.4	22 32.7	11 39.4	28 05.6	28 31.8	13 45.4	15 11.6	17 39.1	16 02.9
8 W	11 09 21	15 36 54	12 04 39	18 02 06	8 46.9	29 39.2	23 43.6	12 19.2	27 53.0	28 39.2	13 40.8	15 15.3	17 40.3	16 05.0
9 Th	11 13 18	16 35 10	24 01 04	0♓01 45	8 34.3	1♍16.1	24 54.4	12 59.2	27 40.2	28 46.4	13 36.2	15 19.1	17 41.6	16 07.2
10 F	11 17 14	17 33 28	6♓04 22	12 09 01	8 20.7	2 56.5	26 05.1	13 39.3	27 27.2	28 53.5	13 31.7	15 22.9	17 42.9	16 09.3
11 Sa	11 21 11	18 31 48	18 15 51	24 24 57	8 07.3	4 39.9	27 15.8	14 19.4	27 14.2	29 00.5	13 27.1	15 26.6	17 44.2	16 11.4
12 Su	11 25 07	19 30 09	0♈36 21	6♈50 08	7 55.1	6 25.7	28 26.4	14 59.7	27 01.0	29 07.3	13 22.5	15 30.4	17 45.6	16 13.6
13 M	11 29 04	20 28 33	13 06 22	19 25 06	7 45.2	8 13.6	29 37.0	15 40.0	26 47.8	29 14.0	13 18.0	15 34.2	17 47.0	16 15.7
14 Tu	11 33 01	21 26 58	25 46 26	2♉10 29	7 38.0	10 03.0	0♏47.5	16 20.5	26 34.4	29 20.5	13 13.5	15 37.9	17 48.4	16 17.9
15 W	11 36 57	22 25 26	8♉37 22	15 07 16	7 33.7	11 53.7	1 57.9	17 01.0	26 21.0	29 26.8	13 08.9	15 41.7	17 49.8	16 20.0
16 Th	11 40 54	23 23 56	21 40 23	28 16 56	7D 31.9	13 45.2	3 08.3	17 41.7	26 07.6	29 33.0	13 04.5	15 45.5	17 51.3	16 22.1
17 F	11 44 50	24 22 28	4♊57 08	11♊41 15	7 31.7	15 37.3	4 18.6	18 22.4	25 54.1	29 39.1	13 00.0	15 49.2	17 52.8	16 24.2
18 Sa	11 48 47	25 21 02	18 29 29	25 22 03	7R 31.9	17 29.6	5 28.9	19 03.2	25 40.6	29 45.0	12 55.6	15 53.0	17 54.3	16 26.4
19 Su	11 52 43	26 19 39	2♋19 04	9♋20 37	7 31.3	19 22.0	6 39.0	19 44.2	25 27.1	29 50.7	12 51.1	15 56.7	17 55.8	16 28.5
20 M	11 56 40	27 18 17	16 26 40	23 37 04	7 28.8	21 14.2	7 49.2	20 25.2	25 13.6	29 56.2	12 46.8	16 00.4	17 57.4	16 30.6
21 Tu	12 00 36	28 16 58	0♌51 32	8♌09 36	7 24.0	23 06.1	8 59.2	21 06.3	25 00.1	0♋01.6	12 42.4	16 04.2	17 59.0	16 32.7
22 W	12 04 33	29 15 42	15 30 40	22 54 00	7 16.6	24 57.5	10 09.2	21 47.5	24 46.7	0 06.9	12 38.1	16 07.9	18 00.6	16 34.8
23 Th	12 08 30	0♎14 27	0♍18 43	7♍43 48	7 07.3	26 48.4	11 19.1	22 28.8	24 33.3	0 11.9	12 33.8	16 11.6	18 02.2	16 36.9
24 F	12 12 26	1 13 14	15 08 12	22 30 49	6 57.1	28 38.6	12 29.0	23 10.3	24 20.0	0 16.8	12 29.6	16 15.3	18 03.9	16 39.0
25 Sa	12 16 23	2 12 03	29 50 38	7♎06 37	6 47.1	0♎28.1	13 38.7	23 51.7	24 06.7	0 21.5	12 25.4	16 18.9	18 05.5	16 41.1
26 Su	12 20 19	3 10 55	14♎17 55	21 23 48	6 38.7	2 16.9	14 48.4	24 33.3	23 53.6	0 26.0	12 21.2	16 22.6	18 07.2	16 43.2
27 M	12 24 16	4 09 48	28 23 42	5♏17 14	6 32.4	4 04.8	15 58.1	25 15.0	23 40.6	0 30.4	12 17.1	16 26.3	18 09.0	16 45.3
28 Tu	12 28 12	5 08 43	12♏04 11	18 44 33	6 28.6	5 51.9	17 07.6	25 56.8	23 27.7	0 34.6	12 13.1	16 29.9	18 10.7	16 47.3
29 W	12 32 09	6 07 40	25 18 26	1♐46 05	6D 27.1	7 38.2	18 17.1	26 38.6	23 14.9	0 38.5	12 09.1	16 33.5	18 12.5	16 49.4
30 Th	12 36 05	7 06 39	8♐07 53	14 24 18	6 27.3	9 23.6	19 26.4	27 20.6	23 02.3	0 42.4	12 05.1	16 37.1	18 14.3	16 51.4

LONGITUDE — October 1965

Day	Sid.Time	☉	0 hr ☽	Noon ☽	True ☊	☿	♀	♂	⚳	♃	♄	♅	♆	♇
1 F	12 40 02	8♎05 39	20♐35 52	26♐43 11	6♊28.1	11♎08.1	20♏35.7	28♏02.6	22♓49.9	0♋46.0	12♓01.2	16♍40.7	18♏16.1	16♍53.5
2 Sa	12 43 59	9 04 41	2♑46 53	8♑47 37	6R 28.6	12 51.7	21 44.9	28 44.7	22R 37.6	0 49.5	11R 57.4	16 44.3	18 17.9	16 55.5
3 Su	12 47 55	10 03 45	14 46 03	20 42 49	6 27.9	14 34.5	22 54.0	29 26.9	22 25.6	0 52.7	11 53.6	16 47.9	18 19.7	16 57.5
4 M	12 51 52	11 02 51	26 38 35	2♒33 57	6 25.2	16 16.5	24 03.0	0♐09.2	22 13.7	0 55.8	11 49.9	16 51.4	18 21.6	16 59.5
5 Tu	12 55 48	12 01 59	8♒29 30	14 25 48	6 20.4	17 57.6	25 11.9	0 51.6	22 02.1	0 58.7	11 46.3	16 54.9	18 23.5	17 01.5
6 W	12 59 45	13 01 08	20 23 20	26 22 33	6 13.5	19 37.9	26 20.7	1 34.0	21 50.7	1 01.4	11 42.7	16 58.4	18 25.4	17 03.5
7 Th	13 03 41	14 00 19	2♓23 51	8♓27 35	6 04.9	21 17.3	27 29.4	2 16.6	21 39.6	1 03.9	11 39.2	17 01.9	18 27.3	17 05.4
8 F	13 07 38	14 59 32	14 34 00	20 43 22	5 55.4	22 56.0	28 38.0	2 59.2	21 28.6	1 06.2	11 35.7	17 05.3	18 29.2	17 07.4
9 Sa	13 11 34	15 58 47	26 55 47	3♈11 24	5 45.8	24 34.0	29 46.4	3 41.9	21 18.0	1 08.4	11 32.3	17 08.8	18 31.2	17 09.3
10 Su	13 15 31	16 58 04	9♈30 15	15 52 20	5 37.3	26 11.1	0♐54.8	4 24.6	21 07.6	1 10.3	11 29.0	17 12.2	18 33.1	17 11.2
11 M	13 19 27	17 57 23	22 17 37	28 46 03	5 30.4	27 47.6	2 03.0	5 07.5	20 57.5	1 12.1	11 25.8	17 15.6	18 35.1	17 13.1
12 Tu	13 23 24	18 56 44	5♉17 33	11♉52 01	5 25.7	29 23.3	3 11.1	5 50.4	20 47.7	1 13.6	11 22.6	17 19.0	18 37.1	17 15.0
13 W	13 27 21	19 56 08	18 29 21	25 09 29	5D 23.3	0♏58.3	4 19.1	6 33.4	20 38.1	1 15.0	11 19.6	17 22.3	18 39.1	17 16.9
14 Th	13 31 17	20 55 33	1♊52 21	8♊37 52	5 22.8	2 32.7	5 26.9	7 16.5	20 28.9	1 16.1	11 16.6	17 25.6	18 41.2	17 18.8
15 F	13 35 14	21 55 01	15 26 00	22 16 44	5 23.7	4 06.3	6 34.7	7 59.7	20 20.0	1 17.1	11 13.6	17 28.9	18 43.2	17 20.6
16 Sa	13 39 10	22 54 32	29 10 03	6♋05 54	5 25.1	5 39.3	7 42.3	8 42.9	20 11.4	1 17.9	11 10.8	17 32.2	18 45.3	17 22.4
17 Su	13 43 07	23 54 04	13♋04 17	20 05 07	5R 26.0	7 11.7	8 49.8	9 26.3	20 03.2	1 18.4	11 08.1	17 35.4	18 47.4	17 24.3
18 M	13 47 03	24 53 39	27 08 18	4♌13 42	5 25.6	8 43.4	9 57.1	10 09.7	19 55.2	1 18.8	11 05.4	17 38.6	18 49.4	17 26.1
19 Tu	13 51 00	25 53 16	11♌21 06	18 30 12	5 23.6	10 14.5	11 04.3	10 53.2	19 47.6	1R 19.0	11 02.8	17 41.8	18 51.5	17 27.8
20 W	13 54 56	26 52 56	25 40 38	2♍51 58	5 19.9	11 45.0	12 11.3	11 36.7	19 40.3	1 18.9	11 00.3	17 45.0	18 53.7	17 29.6
21 Th	13 58 53	27 52 37	10♍03 39	17 15 06	5 14.8	13 14.9	13 18.2	12 20.4	19 33.4	1 18.7	10 57.9	17 48.1	18 55.8	17 31.3
22 F	14 02 50	28 52 21	24 25 40	1♎34 40	5 09.0	14 44.1	14 25.0	13 04.1	19 26.9	1 18.2	10 55.6	17 51.2	18 57.9	17 33.1
23 Sa	14 06 46	29 52 07	8♎41 27	15 45 19	5 03.3	16 12.7	15 31.6	13 47.9	19 20.7	1 17.6	10 53.3	17 54.2	19 00.0	17 34.8
24 Su	14 10 43	0♏51 55	22 45 41	29 41 59	4 58.5	17 40.7	16 38.0	14 31.8	19 14.8	1 16.8	10 51.2	17 57.3	19 02.2	17 36.4
25 M	14 14 39	1 51 45	6♏33 46	13♏20 39	4 55.1	19 08.0	17 44.2	15 15.7	19 09.3	1 15.7	10 49.1	18 00.2	19 04.4	17 38.1
26 Tu	14 18 36	2 51 37	20 02 25	26 38 54	4D 53.3	20 34.6	18 50.3	15 59.7	19 04.2	1 14.4	10 47.2	18 03.2	19 06.5	17 39.7
27 W	14 22 32	3 51 31	3♐10 06	9♐36 06	4 53.1	22 00.6	19 56.2	16 43.8	18 59.5	1 13.0	10 45.4	18 06.1	19 08.7	17 41.4
28 Th	14 26 29	4 51 26	15 57 05	22 13 20	4 54.1	23 25.9	21 01.9	17 28.0	18 55.2	1 11.3	10 43.6	18 09.0	19 10.9	17 43.0
29 F	14 30 25	5 51 24	28 25 14	4♑33 11	4 55.8	24 50.4	22 07.5	18 12.2	18 51.2	1 09.5	10 41.9	18 11.9	19 13.1	17 44.5
30 Sa	14 34 22	6 51 23	10♑37 41	16 39 17	4 57.6	26 14.1	23 12.8	18 56.5	18 47.6	1 07.4	10 40.4	18 14.7	19 15.3	17 46.1
31 Su	14 38 19	7 51 23	22 38 33	28 36 04	4R 58.9	27 37.0	24 17.9	19 40.9	18 44.4	1 05.2	10 38.9	18 17.5	19 17.5	17 47.6

Astro Data

	Dy Hr Mn
☽0N	12 17:49
⊙0S	23 6:06
☽0S	25 16:32
☿0S	27 1:04
♅☌♇	9 20:17
☽0N	10 0:36
♃ R	19 19:32
☽0S	23 2:01

Planet Ingress

	Dy Hr Mn
☿ ♍	8 17:14
♀ ♏	13 19:50
♃ ♋	21 4:40
⊙ ♎	23 6:06
☿ ♎	25 5:49
♂ ♐	4 6:46
♀ ♐	9 16:46
☿ ♏	12 21:15
⊙ ♏	23 15:10

Last Aspect / ☽ Ingress

Last Aspect Dy Hr Mn		☽ Ingress Dy Hr Mn
1 6:06	☿ □	♐ 1 24:00
4 7:05	♃ ☍	♑ 4 10:51
6 5:22	♀ □	♒ 6 23:34
9 9:28	♃ △	♓ 9 11:57
11 21:00	♃ □	♈ 11 22:50
14 6:39	♃ ⚹	♉ 14 7:56
16 2:26	⊙ △	♊ 16 15:06
18 19:38	♃ ☌	♋ 18 20:01
20 18:34	⊙ ⚹	♌ 20 22:35
22 10:07	♂ □	♍ 22 23:30
24 23:28	♀ ☌	♎ 25 0:15
25 3:18	⊙ ☌	♏ 27 2:47
29 1:56	♂ ☌	♐ 29 8:42

Last Aspect / ☽ Ingress

Last Aspect Dy Hr Mn		☽ Ingress Dy Hr Mn
30 16:45	♇ □	♑ 1 18:29
3 16:54	♀ ⚹	♒ 4 6:48
6 11:56	♀ □	♓ 6 19:14
9 4:48	♀ △	♈ 9 5:54
11 9:57	☿ ☍	♉ 11 14:16
13 0:16	♆ ☍	♊ 13 20:40
15 11:19	⊙ △	♋ 16 1:27
17 19:00	⊙ □	♌ 18 4:51
20 1:16	⊙ ⚹	♍ 20 7:13
21 14:49	♆ ⚹	♎ 22 9:21
23 11:35	♆ ⚹	♏ 24 12:31
25 23:38	☿ ☌	♐ 26 18:09
28 9:30	♀ ☌	♑ 29 3:05
31 9:45	☿ ⚹	♒ 31 14:49

☽ Phases & Eclipses

Dy Hr Mn	
2 19:27	☽ 10♐06
10 23:32	○ 18♓01
18 11:58	☾ 25♊21
25 3:18	● 1♎51
2 12:37	☽ 9♑06
10 14:14	○ 17♈04
17 19:00	☾ 24♋11
24 14:11	● 0♏57

Astro Data

1 September 1965
Julian Day # 23985
SVP 5♓44'36"
GC 26♐21.6 ⚵ 7♒58.3R
Eris 11♈18.8R ⚴ 2♒36.0R
⚷ 20♓46.0R ⚶ 0♋55.8
☽Mean ☊ 9♊04.8

1 October 1965
Julian Day # 24015
SVP 5♓44'33"
GC 26♐21.7 ⚵ 5♒02.4R
Eris 11♈01.4R ⚴ 1♒24.8
⚷ 19♓24.4R ⚶ 9♋19.6
☽Mean ☊ 7♊29.5

November 1965 LONGITUDE

Day	Sid.Time	☉	0 hr ☽	Noon☽	True☊	☿	♀	♂	⚳	♃	♄	♅	♆	♇
1 M	14 42 15	8♏51 25	4♒32 27	10♒28 19	4♊59.2	28♏58.9	25♐22.7	20♐25.3	18♓41.6	1♋02.7	10♓37.6	18♍20.2	19♏19.8	17♍49.1
2 Tu	14 46 12	9 51 29	16 24 18	22 20 59	4R58.5	0♐19.9	26 27.4	21 09.9	18R39.1	1R00.1	10R36.3	18 22.9	19 22.0	17 50.6
3 W	14 50 08	10 51 35	28 18 58	4♓18 48	4 56.6	1 39.9	27 31.8	21 54.4	18 37.0	0 57.2	10 35.2	18 25.6	19 24.2	17 52.1
4 Th	14 54 05	11 51 42	10♓21 00	16 26 04	4 53.7	2 58.7	28 35.9	22 39.1	18 35.3	0 54.2	10 34.1	18 28.2	19 26.4	17 53.5
5 F	14 58 01	12 51 50	22 34 26	28 46 27	4 50.3	4 16.3	29 39.8	23 23.8	18 34.0	0 51.0	10 33.1	18 30.8	19 28.7	17 54.9
6 Sa	15 01 58	13 52 00	5♈02 26	11♈22 38	4 46.8	5 32.4	0♑43.5	24 08.5	18 33.1	0 47.6	10 32.3	18 33.3	19 30.9	17 56.3
7 Su	15 05 54	14 52 12	17 47 13	24 16 14	4 43.7	6 47.1	1 46.8	24 53.3	18D32.5	0 44.0	10 31.5	18 35.8	19 33.2	17 57.6
8 M	15 09 51	15 52 25	0♉49 44	7♉27 37	4 41.3	8 00.0	2 49.9	25 38.2	18 32.3	0 40.2	10 30.9	18 38.3	19 35.4	17 59.0
9 Tu	15 13 48	16 52 41	14 09 44	20 55 54	4 39.8	9 11.1	3 52.7	26 23.2	18 32.5	0 36.2	10 30.4	18 40.7	19 37.6	18 00.3
10 W	15 17 44	17 52 58	27 45 48	4♊39 09	4D39.3	10 20.0	4 55.1	27 08.2	18 33.1	0 32.0	10 29.9	18 43.1	19 39.9	18 01.6
11 Th	15 21 41	18 53 16	11♊35 34	18 34 41	4 39.7	11 26.6	5 57.3	27 53.3	18 34.0	0 27.7	10 29.6	18 45.4	19 42.1	18 02.8
12 F	15 25 37	19 53 37	25 36 04	2♋39 19	4 40.7	12 30.5	6 59.1	28 38.4	18 35.3	0 23.2	10 29.4	18 47.7	19 44.4	18 04.1
13 Sa	15 29 34	20 54 00	9♋44 02	16 49 50	4 41.9	13 31.3	8 00.6	29 23.6	18 37.0	0 18.5	10D29.3	18 50.0	19 46.7	18 05.3
14 Su	15 33 30	21 54 24	23 56 20	1♌03 11	4 42.9	14 28.8	9 01.8	0♑08.8	18 39.0	0 13.6	10 29.2	18 52.2	19 48.9	18 06.4
15 M	15 37 27	22 54 51	8♌10 04	15 16 39	4R43.5	15 22.4	10 02.6	0 54.2	18 41.4	0 08.6	10 29.3	18 54.3	19 51.2	18 07.6
16 Tu	15 41 23	23 55 19	22 22 41	29 27 52	4 43.5	16 11.8	11 03.0	1 39.5	18 44.1	0 03.4	10 29.5	18 56.4	19 53.4	18 08.7
17 W	15 45 20	24 55 49	6♍31 56	13♍34 38	4 43.0	16 56.2	12 03.0	2 25.0	18 47.2	29♊58.0	10 29.8	18 58.5	19 55.7	18 09.8
18 Th	15 49 17	25 56 21	20 35 43	27 34 57	4 42.2	17 35.2	13 02.7	3 10.4	18 50.7	29 52.5	10 30.2	19 00.5	19 57.9	18 10.8
19 F	15 53 13	26 56 55	4♎32 03	11♎26 47	4 41.2	18 08.0	14 01.9	3 56.0	18 54.5	29 46.8	10 30.7	19 02.5	20 00.1	18 11.9
20 Sa	15 57 10	27 57 30	18 18 54	25 08 10	4 40.3	18 34.0	15 00.7	4 41.6	18 58.6	29 40.9	10 31.4	19 04.4	20 02.4	18 12.9
21 Su	16 01 06	28 58 07	1♏54 22	8♏37 15	4 39.6	18 52.4	15 59.1	5 27.3	19 03.2	29 34.9	10 32.1	19 06.2	20 04.6	18 13.8
22 M	16 05 03	29 58 46	15 16 40	21 52 27	4D39.2	19R02.4	16 57.0	6 13.0	19 08.0	29 28.8	10 32.9	19 08.1	20 06.8	18 14.8
23 Tu	16 08 59	0♐59 26	28 24 29	4♐52 41	4 39.1	19 03.3	17 54.4	6 58.8	19 13.2	29 22.5	10 33.9	19 09.8	20 09.1	18 15.7
24 W	16 12 56	2 00 08	11♐17 03	17 37 34	4 39.2	18 54.3	18 51.3	7 44.6	19 18.7	29 16.0	10 34.9	19 11.5	20 11.3	18 16.6
25 Th	16 16 52	3 00 51	23 54 22	0♑07 33	4 39.3	18 34.9	19 47.7	8 30.5	19 24.6	29 09.5	10 36.1	19 13.2	20 13.5	18 17.4
26 F	16 20 49	4 01 35	6♑17 20	12 23 58	4R39.4	18 04.7	20 43.6	9 16.4	19 30.8	29 02.8	10 37.3	19 14.8	20 15.7	18 18.2
27 Sa	16 24 46	5 02 21	18 27 45	24 29 02	4 39.5	17 23.7	21 38.9	10 02.4	19 37.3	28 56.0	10 38.7	19 16.4	20 17.9	18 19.0
28 Su	16 28 42	6 03 07	0♒28 15	6♒25 50	4 39.4	16 32.0	22 33.6	10 48.4	19 44.1	28 49.0	10 40.1	19 17.9	20 20.1	18 19.8
29 M	16 32 39	7 03 55	12 22 16	18 18 05	4 39.2	15 30.5	23 27.7	11 34.5	19 51.3	28 42.0	10 41.7	19 19.4	20 22.3	18 20.5
30 Tu	16 36 35	8 04 43	24 13 50	0♓10 04	4D39.0	14 20.4	24 21.1	12 20.6	19 58.8	28 34.8	10 43.4	19 20.8	20 24.5	18 21.2

December 1965 LONGITUDE

Day	Sid.Time	☉	0 hr ☽	Noon☽	True☊	☿	♀	♂	⚳	♃	♄	♅	♆	♇
1 W	16 40 32	9♐05 32	6♓07 23	12♓06 23	4♊39.0	13♐03.7	25♑13.9	13♑06.8	20♓06.6	28♊27.5	10♓45.2	19♍22.1	20♏26.6	18♍21.9
2 Th	16 44 28	10 06 22	18 07 38	24 11 45	4 39.2	11R42.6	26 05.9	13 53.0	20 14.6	28R20.2	10 47.0	19 23.4	20 28.8	18 22.5
3 F	16 48 25	11 07 13	0♈19 17	6♈30 46	4 39.6	10 19.8	26 57.3	14 39.3	20 23.0	28 12.7	10 49.0	19 24.7	20 30.9	18 23.1
4 Sa	16 52 22	12 08 05	12 46 41	19 07 29	4 40.3	8 58.0	27 47.9	15 25.6	20 31.7	28 05.2	10 51.1	19 25.8	20 33.1	18 23.6
5 Su	16 56 18	13 08 58	25 33 32	2♉05 08	4 41.2	7 40.1	28 37.7	16 11.9	20 40.7	27 57.5	10 53.3	19 27.0	20 35.2	18 24.2
6 M	17 00 15	14 09 51	8♉42 29	15 25 40	4 41.9	6 28.5	29 26.6	16 58.3	20 50.0	27 49.8	10 55.6	19 28.1	20 37.3	18 24.7
7 Tu	17 04 11	15 10 46	22 14 39	29 09 17	4R42.4	5 25.3	0♒14.7	17 44.7	20 59.5	27 42.1	10 58.0	19 29.1	20 39.4	18 25.1
8 W	17 08 08	16 11 41	6♊09 18	13♊14 17	4 42.3	4 31.9	1 01.9	18 31.2	21 09.4	27 34.2	11 00.4	19 30.1	20 41.5	18 25.6
9 Th	17 12 04	17 12 38	20 23 40	27 36 51	4 41.6	3 49.3	1 48.2	19 17.7	21 19.5	27 26.3	11 03.0	19 31.0	20 43.5	18 26.0
10 F	17 16 01	18 13 35	4♋53 04	12♋11 31	4 40.3	3 18.0	2 33.5	20 04.2	21 29.9	27 18.4	11 05.7	19 31.9	20 45.6	18 26.4
11 Sa	17 19 57	19 14 33	19 31 21	26 51 43	4 38.4	2 58.0	3 17.8	20 50.8	21 40.5	27 10.4	11 08.5	19 32.7	20 47.6	18 26.7
12 Su	17 23 54	20 15 33	4♌11 46	11♌30 43	4 36.5	2D49.0	4 01.1	21 37.4	21 51.4	27 02.3	11 11.4	19 33.4	20 49.7	18 27.0
13 M	17 27 51	21 16 33	18 47 51	26 02 31	4 34.7	2 50.4	4 43.3	22 24.1	22 02.6	26 54.3	11 14.3	19 34.1	20 51.7	18 27.3
14 Tu	17 31 47	22 17 34	3♍14 13	10♍22 31	4D33.5	3 01.4	5 24.3	23 10.8	22 14.0	26 46.2	11 17.4	19 34.8	20 53.7	18 27.5
15 W	17 35 44	23 18 37	17 27 08	24 27 51	4 33.1	3 21.3	6 04.2	23 57.5	22 25.7	26 38.0	11 20.6	19 35.3	20 55.7	18 27.7
16 Th	17 39 40	24 19 40	1♎24 32	8♎17 11	4 33.6	3 49.3	6 42.8	24 44.2	22 37.7	26 29.9	11 23.8	19 35.9	20 57.6	18 27.9
17 F	17 43 37	25 20 44	15 05 48	21 50 29	4 34.9	4 24.5	7 20.2	25 31.0	22 49.9	26 21.7	11 27.2	19 36.3	20 59.6	18 28.0
18 Sa	17 47 33	26 21 50	28 31 21	5♏08 31	4 36.4	5 06.2	7 56.3	26 17.9	23 02.3	26 13.5	11 30.6	19 36.7	21 01.5	18 28.1
19 Su	17 51 30	27 22 56	11♏42 08	18 12 22	4 37.9	5 53.5	8 30.9	27 04.7	23 15.0	26 05.4	11 34.2	19 37.1	21 03.4	18 28.2
20 M	17 55 26	28 24 03	24 39 21	1♐03 14	4R38.7	6 46.0	9 04.2	27 51.6	23 27.9	25 57.2	11 37.8	19 37.4	21 05.3	18R28.2
21 Tu	17 59 23	29 25 10	7♐24 08	13 42 10	4 38.4	7 42.8	9 36.0	28 38.6	23 41.0	25 49.1	11 41.5	19 37.6	21 07.2	18 28.3
22 W	18 03 20	0♑26 18	19 57 27	26 10 06	4 36.8	8 43.7	10 06.2	29 25.5	23 54.4	25 40.9	11 45.3	19 37.8	21 09.0	18 28.2
23 Th	18 07 16	1 27 27	2♑20 13	8♑27 56	4 33.7	9 47.9	10 34.8	0♒12.5	24 08.0	25 32.9	11 49.2	19 38.0	21 10.9	18 28.2
24 F	18 11 13	2 28 36	14 33 22	20 36 41	4 29.3	10 55.2	11 01.7	0 59.5	24 21.9	25 24.8	11 53.2	19R38.0	21 12.7	18 28.1
25 Sa	18 15 09	3 29 45	26 38 03	2♒37 40	4 24.0	12 05.1	11 26.9	1 46.6	24 35.9	25 16.8	11 57.3	19 38.0	21 14.5	18 28.0
26 Su	18 19 06	4 30 54	8♒35 47	14 32 42	4 18.3	13 17.4	11 50.3	2 33.7	24 50.2	25 08.8	12 01.4	19 38.0	21 16.3	18 27.8
27 M	18 23 02	5 32 04	20 28 46	26 24 11	4 13.0	14 31.8	12 11.8	3 20.8	25 04.7	25 00.9	12 05.7	19 37.9	21 18.0	18 27.6
28 Tu	18 26 59	6 33 13	2♓19 32	8♓15 12	4 08.4	15 48.0	12 31.4	4 07.9	25 19.4	24 53.0	12 10.0	19 37.7	21 19.7	18 27.4
29 W	18 30 55	7 34 23	14 11 40	20 09 28	4 05.2	17 05.8	12 48.9	4 55.0	25 34.2	24 45.2	12 14.4	19 37.5	21 21.4	18 27.1
30 Th	18 34 52	8 35 32	26 09 09	2♈11 17	4D03.6	18 25.1	13 04.4	5 42.2	25 49.3	24 37.5	12 18.9	19 37.3	21 23.1	18 26.8
31 F	18 38 49	9 36 41	8♈16 29	14 25 21	4 03.5	19 45.6	13 17.7	6 29.3	26 04.6	24 29.8	12 23.4	19 36.9	21 24.8	18 26.5

Astro Data Dy Hr Mn	Planet Ingress Dy Hr Mn	Last Aspect Dy Hr Mn	☽ Ingress Dy Hr Mn	Last Aspect Dy Hr Mn	☽ Ingress Dy Hr Mn	☽ Phases & Eclipses Dy Hr Mn
☽0N 6 9:19	☿ ♐ 2 6:04	2 21:05 ♀ ⚹	♓ 3 3:23	2 20:03 ♃ □	♈ 2 23:22	1 8:26 ☽ 8♒42
⚳D 8 11:56	♀ ♑ 5 19:36	5 13:52 ♀ □	♈ 5 14:21	5 5:14 ♀ □	♉ 5 8:11	9 4:15 ○ 16♉33
♄D 14 3:17	♂ ♑ 14 7:19	7 13:12 ♂ △	♉ 7 22:29	6 21:11 ♆ ☍	♊ 7 13:27	16 1:54 ☾ 23♌30
☽0S 19 9:30	♃ ♊R 17 3:08	9 9:41 ♆ ☍	♊ 10 3:54	9 11:43 ♃ ☌	♋ 9 15:57	23 4:10 ● 0♐40
☿R 23 2:14	☉ ♐ 22 12:29	12 4:47 ♂ ☍	♋ 12 7:29	11 2:03 ♆ △	♌ 11 17:08	23 4:14:15 ● A 04'02"
		13 19:24 ☉ △	♌ 14 10:13	13 13:25 ♃ ⚹	♍ 13 18:35	
☽0N 3 18:44	♀ ♒ 7 4:37	16 1:54 ☉ □	♍ 16 12:54	15 15:42 ♃ □	♎ 15 21:33	1 5:24 ☽ 8♓49
☿D 12 20:41	☉ ♑ 22 1:40	18 15:55 ♃ □	♎ 18 16:10	17 20:02 ♃ △	♏ 18 2:40	8 17:21 ○ 16♊25
☽0S 16 14:57	♂ ♒ 23 5:36	20 19:59 ♃ △	♏ 20 20:37	20 5:37 ♂ ⚹	♐ 20 10:01	8 17:10 ● A 0.882
♇R 21 5:06		22 8:47 ♆ ☌	♐ 23 2:56	22 11:04 ♃ ☍	♑ 22 19:27	15 9:52 ☾ 23♍13
♅R 25 6:06		25 10:09 ♃ ☍	♑ 25 11:45	24 13:12 ♆ ⚹	♒ 25 6:44	22 21:03 ● 0♑49
☽0N 31 2:59		27 5:52 ♀ ☌	♒ 27 23:03	27 9:13 ♃ △	♓ 27 19:17	31 1:46 ☽ 9♈11
		30 8:50 ♃ △	♓ 30 11:40	29 21:07 ♃ □	♈ 30 7:40	

Astro Data

1 November 1965
Julian Day # 24046
SVP 5♓44'29"
GC 26♐21.7 ⚴ 7♒15.2
Eris 10♈42.9R ⚵ 6♒22.7
⚷ 18♓19.2R ⚶ 13♋58.7
☽ Mean ☊ 5♊51.0

1 December 1965
Julian Day # 24076
SVP 5♓44'25"
GC 26♐21.8 ⚴ 13♒05.0
Eris 10♈29.8R ⚵ 15♒35.0
⚷ 17♓58.2 ⚶ 12♋31.9R
☽ Mean ☊ 4♊15.7

LONGITUDE — January 1966

Day	Sid.Time	☉	0 hr ☽	Noon ☽	True ☊	☿	♀	♂	⚳	♃	♄	♅	♆	♇
1 Sa	18 42 45	10♑37 50	20♈38 29	26♈56 28	4♊04.6	21♐07.3	13♒28.8	7♒16.5	26♓20.1	24♊22.3	12♓28.1	19♍36.6	21♏26.4	18♍26.1
2 Su	18 46 42	11 38 59	3♉19 51	9♉49 10	4 06.2	22 30.1	13 37.6	8 03.8	26 35.8	24R 14.8	12 32.8	19R 36.1	21 28.0	18R 25.8
3 M	18 50 38	12 40 08	16 24 50	23 07 13	4R 07.6	23 53.8	13 44.1	8 51.0	26 51.7	24 07.4	12 37.6	19 35.6	21 29.6	18 25.3
4 Tu	18 54 35	13 41 16	29 56 31	6♊52 50	4 08.0	25 18.4	13 48.2	9 38.2	27 07.7	24 00.1	12 42.5	19 35.1	21 31.2	18 24.9
5 W	18 58 31	14 42 24	13♊56 05	21 06 01	4 06.8	26 43.7	13R 49.9	10 25.5	27 24.0	23 53.0	12 47.4	19 34.5	21 32.7	18 24.4
6 Th	19 02 28	15 43 32	28 22 10	5♋43 52	4 03.6	28 09.8	13 49.1	11 12.8	27 40.4	23 45.9	12 52.5	19 33.8	21 34.2	18 23.9
7 F	19 06 25	16 44 40	13♋10 18	20 40 26	3 58.4	29 36.6	13 45.8	12 00.1	27 56.9	23 39.0	12 57.6	19 33.1	21 35.7	18 23.4
8 Sa	19 10 21	17 45 48	28 13 06	5♌47 04	3 51.8	1♑04.1	13 40.0	12 47.4	28 13.7	23 32.1	13 02.7	19 32.4	21 37.1	18 22.8
9 Su	19 14 18	18 46 56	13♌21 02	20 53 44	3 44.7	2 32.2	13 31.7	13 34.7	28 30.6	23 25.4	13 08.0	19 31.5	21 38.6	18 22.2
10 M	19 18 14	19 48 03	28 24 00	5♍50 44	3 37.9	4 00.8	13 20.8	14 22.0	28 47.7	23 18.8	13 13.3	19 30.7	21 40.0	18 21.6
11 Tu	19 22 11	20 49 10	13♍13 03	20 30 14	3 32.6	5 30.0	13 07.4	15 09.3	29 05.0	23 12.4	13 18.7	19 29.8	21 41.4	18 20.9
12 W	19 26 07	21 50 17	27 41 44	4♎47 15	3 29.1	6 59.8	12 51.6	15 56.7	29 22.4	23 06.0	13 24.1	19 28.8	21 42.7	18 20.2
13 Th	19 30 04	22 51 25	11♎46 36	18 39 50	3D 27.6	8 30.2	12 33.4	16 44.0	29 39.9	22 59.9	13 29.6	19 27.7	21 44.0	18 19.5
14 F	19 34 00	23 52 32	25 27 03	2♏08 32	3 27.8	10 01.0	12 12.8	17 31.4	29 57.7	22 53.8	13 35.2	19 26.7	21 45.3	18 18.7
15 Sa	19 37 57	24 53 39	8♏44 35	15 15 37	3 28.9	11 32.4	11 49.9	18 18.8	0♈15.5	22 48.0	13 40.9	19 25.5	21 46.6	18 18.0
16 Su	19 41 54	25 54 46	21 42 02	28 04 16	3R 29.9	13 04.3	11 24.9	19 06.1	0 33.6	22 42.2	13 46.6	19 24.4	21 47.8	18 17.2
17 M	19 45 50	26 55 52	4♐22 44	10♐37 50	3 29.7	14 36.8	10 57.9	19 53.5	0 51.8	22 36.6	13 52.3	19 23.1	21 49.0	18 16.3
18 Tu	19 49 47	27 56 59	16 49 59	22 59 31	3 27.6	16 09.8	10 28.9	20 40.9	1 10.1	22 31.2	13 58.2	19 21.9	21 50.2	18 15.5
19 W	19 53 43	28 58 04	29 06 45	5♑11 58	3 22.9	17 43.3	9 58.2	21 28.4	1 28.6	22 26.0	14 04.1	19 20.5	21 51.3	18 14.6
20 Th	19 57 40	29 59 10	11♑15 25	17 17 19	3 15.5	19 17.4	9 26.0	22 15.8	1 47.2	22 20.9	14 10.0	19 19.2	21 52.4	18 13.7
21 F	20 01 36	1♒00 15	23 17 51	29 17 11	3 05.7	20 52.0	8 52.4	23 03.2	2 05.9	22 16.0	14 16.0	19 17.7	21 53.5	18 12.7
22 Sa	20 05 33	2 01 19	5♒15 29	11♒12 55	2 54.1	22 27.2	8 17.6	23 50.6	2 24.8	22 11.3	14 22.1	19 16.3	21 54.6	18 11.8
23 Su	20 09 29	3 02 22	17 09 36	23 05 44	2 41.7	24 03.0	7 41.9	24 38.0	2 43.8	22 06.7	14 28.2	19 14.8	21 55.6	18 10.8
24 M	20 13 26	4 03 24	29 01 31	4♓57 08	2 29.5	25 39.4	7 05.5	25 25.4	3 03.0	22 02.3	14 34.4	19 13.2	21 56.6	18 09.7
25 Tu	20 17 23	5 04 26	10♓52 52	16 49 00	2 18.6	27 16.4	6 28.7	26 12.8	3 22.3	21 58.1	14 40.6	19 11.6	21 57.5	18 08.7
26 W	20 21 19	6 05 26	22 45 51	28 43 50	2 09.8	28 53.9	5 51.6	27 00.2	3 41.7	21 54.1	14 46.9	19 09.9	21 58.4	18 07.6
27 Th	20 25 16	7 06 25	4♈43 20	10♈44 51	2 03.7	0♒32.2	5 14.7	27 47.6	4 01.2	21 50.3	14 53.3	19 08.2	21 59.3	18 06.5
28 F	20 29 12	8 07 24	16 48 53	22 55 59	2 00.2	2 11.0	4 38.0	28 35.0	4 20.9	21 46.7	14 59.6	19 06.5	22 00.2	18 05.4
29 Sa	20 33 09	9 08 21	29 06 44	5♉21 44	1D 59.0	3 50.6	4 02.0	29 22.4	4 40.6	21 43.2	15 06.1	19 04.7	22 01.0	18 04.3
30 Su	20 37 05	10 09 16	11♉41 34	18 06 51	1 59.1	5 30.8	3 26.7	0♓09.8	5 00.5	21 40.0	15 12.5	19 02.9	22 01.8	18 03.1
31 M	20 41 02	11 10 11	24 38 10	1♊16 00	1R 59.5	7 11.7	2 52.5	0 57.2	5 20.5	21 36.9	15 19.1	19 01.0	22 02.6	18 01.9

LONGITUDE — February 1966

Day	Sid.Time	☉	0 hr ☽	Noon ☽	True ☊	☿	♀	♂	⚳	♃	♄	♅	♆	♇
1 Tu	20 44 58	12♒11 04	8♊00 48	14♊52 54	1♊58.8	8♒53.3	2♒19.6	1♓44.6	5♈40.6	21♊34.1	15♓25.6	18♍59.1	22♏03.3	18♍00.7
2 W	20 48 55	13 11 56	21 52 28	28 59 32	1R 56.2	10 35.6	1R 48.2	2 31.9	6 00.9	21R 31.4	15 32.3	18R 57.2	22 04.0	17R 59.5
3 Th	20 52 52	14 12 47	6♋13 55	13♋35 09	1 50.9	12 18.6	1 18.4	3 19.3	6 21.2	21 28.9	15 38.9	18 55.2	22 04.7	17 58.3
4 F	20 56 48	15 13 36	21 02 37	28 35 23	1 42.9	14 02.4	0 50.5	4 06.6	6 41.6	21 26.7	15 45.6	18 53.2	22 05.3	17 57.0
5 Sa	21 00 45	16 14 24	6♌12 20	13♌52 09	1 32.7	15 46.9	0 24.5	4 53.9	7 02.1	21 24.6	15 52.3	18 51.2	22 05.9	17 55.7
6 Su	21 04 41	17 15 11	21 33 22	29 14 29	1 21.6	17 32.1	0 00.7	5 41.2	7 22.8	21 22.7	15 59.1	18 49.1	22 06.4	17 54.4
7 M	21 08 38	18 15 57	6♍53 58	14♍30 23	1 10.8	19 18.1	29♑39.2	6 28.5	7 43.5	21 21.1	16 05.9	18 47.0	22 07.0	17 53.1
8 Tu	21 12 34	19 16 41	22 02 29	29 29 09	1 01.6	21 04.8	29 19.9	7 15.8	8 04.3	21 19.6	16 12.8	18 44.9	22 07.5	17 51.8
9 W	21 16 31	20 17 25	6♎49 32	14♎03 02	0 54.8	22 52.1	29 03.1	8 03.1	8 25.3	21 18.3	16 19.6	18 42.7	22 07.9	17 50.4
10 Th	21 20 27	21 18 07	21 09 16	28 08 06	0 50.8	24 40.2	28 48.8	8 50.3	8 46.3	21 17.3	16 26.5	18 40.5	22 08.4	17 49.0
11 F	21 24 24	22 18 48	4♏59 35	11♏43 57	0D 49.1	26 28.8	28 36.9	9 37.6	9 07.4	21 16.4	16 33.5	18 38.2	22 08.7	17 47.6
12 Sa	21 28 21	23 19 29	18 21 32	24 52 49	0R 48.8	28 18.1	28 27.5	10 24.8	9 28.6	21 15.7	16 40.5	18 36.0	22 09.1	17 46.2
13 Su	21 32 17	24 20 08	1♐18 17	7♐38 32	0 48.7	0♓07.8	28 20.6	11 12.0	9 49.9	21 15.3	16 47.5	18 33.7	22 09.4	17 44.8
14 M	21 36 14	25 20 46	13 54 08	20 05 40	0 47.6	1 58.0	28 16.3	11 59.2	10 11.3	21D 15.0	16 54.5	18 31.4	22 09.7	17 43.4
15 Tu	21 40 10	26 21 23	26 13 42	2♑18 48	0 44.4	3 48.5	28D 14.4	12 46.4	10 32.8	21 14.9	17 01.6	18 29.0	22 10.0	17 41.9
16 W	21 44 07	27 21 59	8♑21 26	14 22 04	0 38.3	5 39.2	28 14.9	13 33.6	10 54.3	21 15.1	17 08.7	18 26.7	22 10.2	17 40.5
17 Th	21 48 03	28 22 33	20 21 09	26 19 01	0 29.1	7 29.9	28 17.8	14 20.7	11 16.0	21 15.4	17 15.8	18 24.3	22 10.4	17 39.0
18 F	21 52 00	29 23 06	2♒16 00	8♒12 24	0 17.0	9 20.4	28 23.1	15 07.9	11 37.7	21 16.0	17 23.0	18 21.8	22 10.5	17 37.5
19 Sa	21 55 56	0♓23 38	14 08 25	20 04 18	0 02.9	11 10.6	28 30.7	15 55.0	11 59.5	21 16.7	17 30.1	18 19.4	22 10.7	17 36.0
20 Su	21 59 53	1 24 07	26 00 11	1♓56 16	29♉47.7	13 00.1	28 40.5	16 42.0	12 21.4	21 17.7	17 37.3	18 16.9	22 10.8	17 34.5
21 M	22 03 50	2 24 36	7♓52 42	13 49 36	29 32.7	14 48.7	28 52.5	17 29.1	12 43.3	21 18.8	17 44.5	18 14.5	22R 10.8	17 33.0
22 Tu	22 07 46	3 25 02	19 47 09	25 45 32	29 19.2	16 36.0	29 06.6	18 16.1	13 05.3	21 20.2	17 51.8	18 12.0	22 10.8	17 31.4
23 W	22 11 43	4 25 27	1♈44 56	7♈45 35	29 08.0	18 21.7	29 22.7	19 03.1	13 27.5	21 21.7	17 59.0	18 09.4	22 10.8	17 29.9
24 Th	22 15 39	5 25 50	13 47 46	19 51 47	28 59.7	20 05.2	29 40.9	19 50.1	13 49.6	21 23.4	18 06.3	18 06.9	22 10.7	17 28.4
25 F	22 19 36	6 26 11	25 57 59	2♉06 47	28 54.6	21 46.2	0♒01.0	20 37.1	14 11.9	21 25.4	18 13.6	18 04.4	22 10.7	17 26.8
26 Sa	22 23 32	7 26 31	8♉18 37	14 33 57	28 52.1	23 24.1	0 22.9	21 24.0	14 34.2	21 27.5	18 20.9	18 01.8	22 10.5	17 25.2
27 Su	22 27 29	8 26 48	20 53 17	27 17 10	28 51.5	24 58.3	0 46.6	22 10.9	14 56.6	21 29.8	18 28.2	17 59.3	22 10.4	17 23.7
28 M	22 31 25	9 27 03	3♊46 06	10♊20 35	28 51.6	26 28.3	1 12.0	22 57.8	15 19.0	21 32.4	18 35.6	17 56.7	22 10.2	17 22.1

Astro Data	Planet Ingress	Last Aspect	☽ Ingress	Last Aspect	☽ Ingress	☽ Phases & Eclipses	Astro Data
Dy Hr Mn	Dy Hr Mn	Dy Hr Mn	Dy Hr Mn	Dy Hr Mn	Dy Hr Mn	Dy Hr Mn	1 January 1966
♀R 5 16:21	☿ ♑ 7 18:26	1 7:10 ♃ ⚹	♉ 1 17:46	1 23:26 ♃ ☌	♋ 2 13:41	7 5:16 ○ 16♋28	Julian Day # 24107
☽0S 12 20:18	⚳ ♈ 14 15:09	3 9:06 ♆ ☍	♊ 4 0:06	4 1:40 ♆ △	♌ 4 14:14	13 20:00 ☾ 23♎12	SVP 5♓44'19"
♃⚻♆ 25 14:57	☉ ♒ 20 12:20	5 22:19 ☿ ☍	♋ 6 2:40	6 0:51 ♆ □	♍ 6 13:11	21 15:46 ● 1♒10	GC 26♐21.9 ⚴ 21♒26.7
☽0N 27 9:13	☿ ♒ 27 4:10	7 13:28 ♆ △	♌ 8 2:50	8 11:45 ♀ △	♎ 8 12:50	29 19:48 ☽ 9♉28	Eris 10♈25.6 ⚵ 28♒05.6
	♂ ♓ 30 7:01	9 16:00 ♃ ⚹	♍ 10 2:34	10 13:10 ♀ □	♏ 10 15:15		⚷ 18♓28.8 ⚶ 5♋21.6R
☽0S 9 3:52		11 16:28 ♃ □	♎ 12 3:53	12 19:26 ☿ □	♐ 12 21:33	5 15:58 ○ 16♌24	☽ Mean ☊ 2♊37.2
♃ D 15 6:57	♀ ♑R 6 12:46	13 20:00 ☉ □	♏ 14 8:08	14 23:12 ☉ ⚹	♑ 15 7:26	12 8:53 ☾ 23♏12	
♀ D 15 18:41	☿ ♓ 13 10:17	16 7:34 ☉ ⚹	♐ 16 15:39	17 16:01 ♀ ☌	♒ 17 19:26	20 10:49 ● 1♓21	1 February 1966
♄☍♇ 20 4:11	☉ ♓ 19 2:38	18 11:05 ♃ ☍	♑ 19 1:45	19 16:16 ♆ □	♓ 20 8:05	28 10:15 ☽ 9♊23	Julian Day # 24138
♆R 22 10:42	☊ ♉R 19 16:40	20 21:10 ♆ ⚹	♒ 21 13:26	22 18:52 ♀ ⚹	♈ 22 20:30		SVP 5♓44'14"
☽0N 23 14:19	♀ ♒ 25 10:55	23 15:20 ♂ ☌	♓ 24 1:58	25 7:48 ♀ □	♉ 25 7:53		GC 26♐21.9 ⚴ 1♓07.5
♄☍♅ 24 13:30		26 12:24 ☿ ⚹	♈ 26 14:33	27 7:05 ☿ ⚹	♊ 27 17:03		Eris 10♈32.1 ⚵ 12♓37.9
		28 23:44 ♂ ⚹	♉ 29 1:43				⚷ 19♓45.7 ⚶ 29♊12.4R
		30 19:14 ♆ ☍	♊ 31 9:43				☽ Mean ☊ 0♊58.7

March 1966

LONGITUDE

Day	Sid.Time	☉	0 hr ☽	Noon ☽	True ☊	☿	♀	♂	⚳	♃	♄	♅	♆	♇
1 Tu	22 35 22	10♓27 17	17♊01 07	23♊48 04	28♉51.0	27♓53.5	1♒39.1	23♓44.6	15♈41.5	21♊35.1	18♓42.9	17♍54.1	22♏10.0	17♍20.5
2 W	22 39 19	11 27 28	0♋41 46	7♋42 24	28R 48.7	29 13.3	2 07.9	24 31.5	16 04.1	21 38.0	18 50.3	17R 51.5	22R 09.7	17R 18.9
3 Th	22 43 15	12 27 37	14 49 59	22 04 21	28 44.0	0♈27.1	2 38.1	25 18.2	16 26.7	21 41.1	18 57.6	17 48.9	22 09.5	17 17.4
4 F	22 47 12	13 27 45	29 25 08	6♌51 42	28 36.6	1 34.3	3 09.9	26 05.0	16 49.4	21 44.3	19 05.0	17 46.3	22 09.1	17 15.8
5 Sa	22 51 08	14 27 50	14♌23 14	21 58 40	28 27.0	2 34.3	3 43.1	26 51.7	17 12.1	21 47.8	19 12.4	17 43.7	22 08.8	17 14.2
6 Su	22 55 05	15 27 53	29 36 45	7♍16 06	28 16.3	3 26.8	4 17.7	27 38.4	17 34.9	21 51.4	19 19.7	17 41.1	22 08.4	17 12.6
7 M	22 59 01	16 27 54	14♍55 16	22 32 47	28 05.8	4 11.3	4 53.6	28 25.0	17 57.8	21 55.3	19 27.1	17 38.4	22 08.0	17 11.0
8 Tu	23 02 58	17 27 53	0♎07 15	7♎37 24	27 56.6	4 47.3	5 30.8	29 11.6	18 20.7	21 59.2	19 34.5	17 35.8	22 07.5	17 09.4
9 W	23 06 54	18 27 50	15 02 10	22 20 39	27 49.7	5 14.7	6 09.3	29 58.2	18 43.6	22 03.4	19 41.9	17 33.2	22 07.1	17 07.8
10 Th	23 10 51	19 27 46	29 32 14	6♏36 30	27 45.5	5 33.3	6 48.9	0♈44.8	19 06.6	22 07.8	19 49.3	17 30.6	22 06.6	17 06.2
11 F	23 14 48	20 27 40	13♏33 17	20 22 36	27D 43.8	5R 43.0	7 29.7	1 31.3	19 29.7	22 12.3	19 56.7	17 27.9	22 06.0	17 04.6
12 Sa	23 18 44	21 27 33	27 04 39	3♐39 45	27 43.7	5 43.8	8 11.6	2 17.8	19 52.8	22 17.0	20 04.1	17 25.3	22 05.4	17 03.0
13 Su	23 22 41	22 27 23	10♐08 22	16 31 00	27R 44.2	5 36.0	8 54.5	3 04.2	20 16.0	22 21.9	20 11.5	17 22.7	22 04.8	17 01.4
14 M	23 26 37	23 27 13	22 48 15	29 00 44	27 44.1	5 19.9	9 38.4	3 50.6	20 39.2	22 26.9	20 18.9	17 20.1	22 04.2	16 59.8
15 Tu	23 30 34	24 27 00	5♑09 04	11♑13 52	27 42.6	4 56.0	10 23.3	4 37.0	21 02.5	22 32.1	20 26.3	17 17.5	22 03.6	16 58.2
16 W	23 34 30	25 26 46	17 15 46	23 15 19	27 38.8	4 24.9	11 09.1	5 23.3	21 25.8	22 37.5	20 33.7	17 14.9	22 02.9	16 56.7
17 Th	23 38 27	26 26 30	29 13 06	5♒09 36	27 32.5	3 47.4	11 55.8	6 09.7	21 49.1	22 43.1	20 41.1	17 12.3	22 02.1	16 55.1
18 F	23 42 23	27 26 12	11♒05 18	17 00 36	27 23.7	3 04.4	12 43.4	6 55.9	22 12.5	22 48.8	20 48.4	17 09.8	22 01.4	16 53.5
19 Sa	23 46 20	28 25 53	22 55 54	28 51 31	27 13.2	2 16.9	13 31.7	7 42.2	22 35.9	22 54.7	20 55.8	17 07.2	22 00.6	16 52.0
20 Su	23 50 17	29 25 31	4♓47 43	10♓44 47	27 01.8	1 26.0	14 20.9	8 28.3	22 59.4	23 00.7	21 03.2	17 04.6	21 59.8	16 50.4
21 M	23 54 13	0♈25 08	16 42 54	22 42 15	26 50.4	0 32.8	15 10.8	9 14.5	23 22.9	23 06.9	21 10.5	17 02.1	21 59.0	16 48.9
22 Tu	23 58 10	1 24 42	28 43 00	4♈45 17	26 40.1	29♓38.6	16 01.4	10 00.6	23 46.5	23 13.2	21 17.8	16 59.6	21 58.1	16 47.3
23 W	0 02 06	2 24 14	10♈49 16	16 55 04	26 31.7	28 44.5	16 52.7	10 46.7	24 10.1	23 19.7	21 25.2	16 57.1	21 57.2	16 45.8
24 Th	0 06 03	3 23 45	23 02 51	29 12 46	26 25.7	27 51.6	17 44.7	11 32.7	24 33.7	23 26.4	21 32.5	16 54.6	21 56.3	16 44.3
25 F	0 09 59	4 23 13	5♉25 01	11♉39 49	26 22.2	27 00.8	18 37.3	12 18.7	24 57.4	23 33.2	21 39.8	16 52.1	21 55.3	16 42.7
26 Sa	0 13 56	5 22 39	17 57 25	24 18 05	26D 21.0	26 13.1	19 30.5	13 04.7	25 21.0	23 40.1	21 47.0	16 49.6	21 54.4	16 41.2
27 Su	0 17 52	6 22 03	0♊42 07	7♊09 50	26 21.4	25 29.2	20 24.3	13 50.6	25 44.8	23 47.2	21 54.3	16 47.2	21 53.4	16 39.8
28 M	0 21 49	7 21 25	13 41 34	20 17 40	26 22.6	24 49.8	21 18.7	14 36.4	26 08.5	23 54.5	22 01.5	16 44.8	21 52.3	16 38.3
29 Tu	0 25 45	8 20 44	26 58 27	3♋44 11	26R 23.5	24 15.3	22 13.6	15 22.2	26 32.3	24 01.9	22 08.7	16 42.4	21 51.3	16 36.8
30 W	0 29 42	9 20 01	10♋35 07	17 31 24	26 23.3	23 46.1	23 09.0	16 08.0	26 56.2	24 09.4	22 16.0	16 40.1	21 50.2	16 35.4
31 Th	0 33 39	10 19 16	24 33 06	1♌40 09	26 21.3	23 22.4	24 05.0	16 53.7	27 20.0	24 17.1	22 23.1	16 37.7	21 49.1	16 33.9

April 1966

LONGITUDE

Day	Sid.Time	☉	0 hr ☽	Noon ☽	True ☊	☿	♀	♂	⚳	♃	♄	♅	♆	♇
1 F	0 37 35	11♈18 28	8♌52 21	16♌09 18	26♉17.5	23♓04.4	25♒01.4	17♈39.4	27♈43.9	24♊24.9	22♓30.3	16♍35.4	21♏48.0	16♍32.5
2 Sa	0 41 32	12 17 38	23 30 29	0♍55 11	26R 12.0	22R 52.1	25 58.4	18 25.1	28 07.8	24 32.8	22 37.4	16R 33.1	21R 46.8	16R 31.1
3 Su	0 45 28	13 16 46	8♍22 33	15 51 34	26 05.6	22D 45.5	26 55.7	19 10.6	28 31.7	24 40.9	22 44.5	16 30.9	21 45.7	16 29.7
4 M	0 49 25	14 15 51	23 21 08	0♎50 08	25 59.1	22 44.5	27 53.5	19 56.2	28 55.7	24 49.1	22 51.6	16 28.6	21 44.5	16 28.3
5 Tu	0 53 21	15 14 54	8♎17 24	15 41 49	25 53.5	22 48.9	28 51.8	20 41.7	29 19.6	24 57.5	22 58.6	16 26.4	21 43.3	16 27.0
6 W	0 57 18	16 13 55	23 02 22	0♏18 11	25 49.4	22 58.7	29 50.5	21 27.1	29 43.6	25 05.9	23 05.7	16 24.2	21 42.0	16 25.6
7 Th	1 01 14	17 12 55	7♏28 30	14 32 47	25D 47.1	23 13.5	0♓49.5	22 12.5	0♉07.6	25 14.5	23 12.7	16 22.1	21 40.8	16 24.3
8 F	1 05 11	18 11 52	21 30 39	28 21 54	25 46.6	23 33.3	1 49.0	22 57.9	0 31.7	25 23.2	23 19.6	16 20.0	21 39.5	16 23.0
9 Sa	1 09 08	19 10 48	5♐06 28	11♐44 30	25 47.4	23 57.7	2 48.8	23 43.2	0 55.7	25 32.0	23 26.6	16 17.9	21 38.2	16 21.7
10 Su	1 13 04	20 09 42	18 16 13	24 41 57	25 49.0	24 26.7	3 49.0	24 28.4	1 19.8	25 41.0	23 33.5	16 15.9	21 36.9	16 20.4
11 M	1 17 01	21 08 34	1♑02 10	7♑17 20	25 50.5	24 59.9	4 49.5	25 13.6	1 43.9	25 50.0	23 40.3	16 13.8	21 35.6	16 19.1
12 Tu	1 20 57	22 07 25	13 28 01	19 34 48	25R 51.3	25 37.1	5 50.4	25 58.8	2 08.1	25 59.2	23 47.2	16 11.9	21 34.2	16 17.9
13 W	1 24 54	23 06 14	25 38 15	1♒39 01	25 51.0	26 18.2	6 51.6	26 43.9	2 32.2	26 08.5	23 54.0	16 09.9	21 32.8	16 16.7
14 Th	1 28 50	24 05 01	7♒37 39	13 34 46	25 49.2	27 02.9	7 53.1	27 29.0	2 56.4	26 17.9	24 00.7	16 08.0	21 31.5	16 15.5
15 F	1 32 47	25 03 46	19 30 55	25 26 38	25 46.0	27 51.2	8 55.0	28 14.0	3 20.6	26 27.5	24 07.5	16 06.2	21 30.0	16 14.3
16 Sa	1 36 43	26 02 30	1♓22 25	7♓18 43	25 41.8	28 42.7	9 57.1	28 59.0	3 44.8	26 37.1	24 14.2	16 04.3	21 28.6	16 13.2
17 Su	1 40 40	27 01 11	13 15 59	19 14 34	25 36.9	29 37.5	10 59.4	29 44.0	4 09.0	26 46.8	24 20.8	16 02.5	21 27.2	16 12.0
18 M	1 44 37	27 59 51	25 14 50	1♈17 04	25 31.9	0♈35.2	12 02.1	0♉28.8	4 33.2	26 56.7	24 27.4	16 00.8	21 25.7	16 10.9
19 Tu	1 48 33	28 58 29	7♈21 31	13 28 23	25 27.5	1 35.8	13 05.0	1 13.7	4 57.4	27 06.6	24 34.0	15 59.1	21 24.3	16 09.8
20 W	1 52 30	29 57 05	19 37 52	25 50 05	25 23.9	2 39.1	14 08.2	1 58.5	5 21.7	27 16.7	24 40.5	15 57.4	21 22.8	16 08.7
21 Th	1 56 26	0♉55 40	2♉05 10	8♉23 11	25 21.6	3 45.1	15 11.6	2 43.2	5 45.9	27 26.8	24 47.0	15 55.8	21 21.3	16 07.7
22 F	2 00 23	1 54 12	14 44 14	21 08 22	25D 20.6	4 53.6	16 15.2	3 27.9	6 10.2	27 37.1	24 53.4	15 54.2	21 19.8	16 06.7
23 Sa	2 04 19	2 52 43	27 35 38	4♊06 05	25 20.8	6 04.6	17 19.1	4 12.5	6 34.5	27 47.5	24 59.8	15 52.7	21 18.3	16 05.7
24 Su	2 08 16	3 51 11	10♊39 47	17 16 45	25 21.8	7 17.9	18 23.1	4 57.1	6 58.8	27 57.9	25 06.2	15 51.2	21 16.7	16 04.7
25 M	2 12 12	4 49 38	23 57 03	0♋40 44	25 23.2	8 33.5	19 27.4	5 41.6	7 23.1	28 08.4	25 12.4	15 49.7	21 15.2	16 03.8
26 Tu	2 16 09	5 48 02	7♋27 50	14 18 22	25 24.6	9 51.3	20 31.9	6 26.1	7 47.4	28 19.1	25 18.7	15 48.3	21 13.7	16 02.9
27 W	2 20 06	6 46 25	21 12 20	28 09 42	25R 25.4	11 11.3	21 36.6	7 10.6	8 11.7	28 29.8	25 24.9	15 47.0	21 12.1	16 02.0
28 Th	2 24 02	7 44 45	5♌10 23	12♌14 15	25 25.6	12 33.4	22 41.5	7 54.9	8 36.0	28 40.6	25 31.0	15 45.7	21 10.5	16 01.1
29 F	2 27 59	8 43 03	19 21 04	26 30 35	25 24.9	13 57.5	23 46.5	8 39.2	9 00.4	28 51.5	25 37.1	15 44.4	21 09.0	16 00.3
30 Sa	2 31 55	9 41 19	3♍42 25	10♍56 08	25 23.6	15 23.7	24 51.7	9 23.5	9 24.7	29 02.5	25 43.2	15 43.2	21 07.4	15 59.5

Astro Data	Dy Hr Mn
☿0N	1 12:30
⚳0N	2 0:22
☽0S	8 13:57
♃⚻♆	10 6:04
♂0N	11 15:08
☿ R	12 2:17
☉0N	21 1:53
☽0N	22 19:54
♄△♆	27 9:17
☿0S	27 19:26
☿ D	4 4:24
♅☌♇	4 20:31
☽0S	5 0:46
☽0N	19 2:50
☿0N	23 16:40

Planet Ingress		Dy Hr Mn
☿	♈	3 2:57
♂	♈	9 12:55
☉	♈	21 1:53
☿	♓R	22 2:34
♀	♓	6 15:53
⚳	♉	7 4:22
♂	♉	17 20:35
☿	♈	17 21:31
☉	♉	20 13:12

Last Aspect Dy Hr Mn			☽ Ingress	Dy Hr Mn
1 19:55	☿	□	♋	1 22:48
3 17:36	♂	△	♌	4 0:57
5 12:16	♆	□	♍	6 0:36
7 21:48	♂	☍	♎	7 23:48
9 11:32	♃	△	♏	10 0:47
11 15:04	♆	☌	♐	12 5:18
14 0:19	☉	□	♑	14 13:55
16 16:48	☉	⚹	♒	17 1:35
18 23:51	♃	△	♓	19 14:19
21 12:50	♃	□	♈	22 2:33
24 0:40	♃	⚹	♉	24 13:32
26 15:24	☿	⚹	♊	26 22:41
28 19:49	☿	□	♋	29 5:23
30 22:22	☿	△	♌	31 9:12

Last Aspect Dy Hr Mn			☽ Ingress	Dy Hr Mn
2 3:27	♀	☍	♍	2 10:31
4 2:16	♃	□	♎	4 10:40
6 11:11	♀	△	♏	6 11:30
8 3:20	☿	△	♐	8 14:54
10 13:52	♃	☍	♑	10 22:02
13 1:32	♂	□	♒	13 8:42
15 18:02	♂	⚹	♓	15 21:13
18 3:16	♃	□	♈	18 9:27
20 14:49	♃	⚹	♉	20 20:00
22 19:03	♄	⚹	♊	23 4:27
25 7:25	♃	☌	♋	25 10:48
27 7:14	♄	△	♌	27 15:09
29 15:58	♃	⚹	♍	29 17:50

☽ Phases & Eclipses Dy Hr Mn		
7 1:45	○	16♍02
14 0:19	☾	22♐58
22 4:46	●	1♈07
29 20:43	☽	8♋42
5 11:13	○	15♎13
12 17:28	☾	22♑21
20 20:35	●	0♉18
28 3:49	☽	7♌25

Astro Data

1 March 1966
Julian Day # 24166
SVP 5♓44'10"
GC 26♐22.0 ⚵ 10♓23.1
Eris 10♈46.0 ✱ 26♓57.9
⚷ 21♓20.2 ⚶ 29♊16.6
☽ Mean ☊ 29♉29.8

1 April 1966
Julian Day # 24197
SVP 5♓44'06"
GC 26♐22.1 ⚵ 20♓41.3
Eris 11♈06.4 ✱ 13♈45.9
⚷ 23♓12.1 ⚶ 5♋04.4
☽ Mean ☊ 27♉51.2

LONGITUDE — May 1966

Day	Sid.Time	☉	0 hr ☽	Noon ☽	True ☊	☿	♀	♂	⚳	♃	♄	♅	♆	♇
1 Su	2 35 52	10♉39 33	18♍11 11	25♍27 00	25♉21.8	16♈51.9	25♓57.2	10♉07.7	9♉49.0	29♊13.6	25♓49.1	15♍42.0	21♏05.8	15♍58.7
2 M	2 39 48	11 37 44	2♎42 53	9♎58 10	25R 20.0	18 22.1	27 02.7	10 51.9	10 13.3	29 24.7	25 55.1	15R 40.9	21R 04.2	15R 57.9
3 Tu	2 43 45	12 35 54	17 12 06	24 23 59	25 18.5	19 54.2	28 08.5	11 36.0	10 37.7	29 35.9	26 00.9	15 39.8	21 02.6	15 57.2
4 W	2 47 41	13 34 02	1♏33 07	8♏38 52	25 17.5	21 28.3	29 14.4	12 20.0	11 02.0	29 47.3	26 06.8	15 38.8	21 01.0	15 56.5
5 Th	2 51 38	14 32 09	15 40 37	22 37 55	25D 17.2	23 04.3	0♈20.5	13 04.1	11 26.3	29 58.6	26 12.5	15 37.8	20 59.3	15 55.8
6 F	2 55 35	15 30 14	29 30 22	6♐17 40	25 17.3	24 42.3	1 26.8	13 48.0	11 50.7	0♋10.1	26 18.2	15 36.9	20 57.7	15 55.1
7 Sa	2 59 31	16 28 17	12♐59 40	19 36 17	25 17.9	26 22.1	2 33.2	14 31.9	12 15.0	0 21.6	26 23.9	15 36.0	20 56.1	15 54.5
8 Su	3 03 28	17 26 19	26 07 34	2♑33 39	25 18.6	28 04.0	3 39.7	15 15.8	12 39.3	0 33.2	26 29.4	15 35.2	20 54.5	15 53.9
9 M	3 07 24	18 24 19	8♑54 46	15 11 14	25 19.3	29 47.7	4 46.4	15 59.6	13 03.7	0 44.9	26 35.0	15 34.4	20 52.9	15 53.4
10 Tu	3 11 21	19 22 19	21 23 26	27 31 47	25 19.9	1♉33.4	5 53.2	16 43.3	13 28.0	0 56.7	26 40.4	15 33.7	20 51.2	15 52.8
11 W	3 15 17	20 20 16	3♒36 47	9♒38 58	25R 20.3	3 21.1	7 00.2	17 27.0	13 52.3	1 08.5	26 45.8	15 33.0	20 49.6	15 52.3
12 Th	3 19 14	21 18 13	15 38 51	21 37 00	25 20.4	5 10.7	8 07.3	18 10.7	14 16.6	1 20.4	26 51.1	15 32.4	20 48.0	15 51.9
13 F	3 23 10	22 16 08	27 34 02	3♓30 29	25 20.3	7 02.2	9 14.6	18 54.3	14 41.0	1 32.3	26 56.4	15 31.8	20 46.3	15 51.4
14 Sa	3 27 07	23 14 02	9♓26 57	15 23 58	25 20.1	8 55.7	10 21.9	19 37.8	15 05.3	1 44.3	27 01.6	15 31.3	20 44.7	15 51.0
15 Su	3 31 04	24 11 54	21 22 06	27 21 51	25 20.0	10 51.0	11 29.4	20 21.3	15 29.6	1 56.4	27 06.7	15 30.8	20 43.1	15 50.6
16 M	3 35 00	25 09 45	3♈23 41	9♈28 05	25D 19.9	12 48.3	12 37.0	21 04.7	15 53.9	2 08.5	27 11.8	15 30.4	20 41.5	15 50.3
17 Tu	3 38 57	26 07 35	15 35 24	21 46 01	25 19.9	14 47.5	13 44.7	21 48.1	16 18.2	2 20.7	27 16.8	15 30.0	20 39.8	15 49.9
18 W	3 42 53	27 05 24	28 00 13	4♉18 15	25 20.1	16 48.5	14 52.5	22 31.5	16 42.5	2 33.0	27 21.7	15 29.7	20 38.2	15 49.6
19 Th	3 46 50	28 03 12	10♉40 17	17 06 27	25R 20.2	18 51.2	16 00.4	23 14.8	17 06.8	2 45.3	27 26.6	15 29.5	20 36.6	15 49.4
20 F	3 50 46	29 00 58	23 36 46	0♊11 14	25 20.2	20 55.6	17 08.5	23 58.0	17 31.0	2 57.7	27 31.3	15 29.3	20 35.0	15 49.1
21 Sa	3 54 43	29 58 43	6♊49 47	13 32 17	25 20.0	23 01.6	18 16.6	24 41.2	17 55.3	3 10.1	27 36.0	15 29.1	20 33.4	15 48.9
22 Su	3 58 39	0♊56 27	20 18 32	27 08 18	25 19.6	25 09.0	19 24.8	25 24.3	18 19.6	3 22.6	27 40.7	15 29.0	20 31.8	15 48.8
23 M	4 02 36	1 54 09	4♋01 19	10♋57 17	25 18.9	27 17.7	20 33.1	26 07.4	18 43.8	3 35.1	27 45.2	15D 29.0	20 30.2	15 48.6
24 Tu	4 06 33	2 51 49	17 55 51	24 56 42	25 18.1	29 27.5	21 41.5	26 50.4	19 08.0	3 47.7	27 49.7	15 29.0	20 28.6	15 48.5
25 W	4 10 29	3 49 29	1♌59 27	9♌03 46	25 17.3	1♊38.2	22 50.0	27 33.4	19 32.2	4 00.3	27 54.1	15 29.1	20 27.0	15 48.5
26 Th	4 14 26	4 47 06	16 09 17	23 15 40	25D 16.7	3 49.6	23 58.6	28 16.3	19 56.4	4 13.0	27 58.4	15 29.2	20 25.4	15D 48.4
27 F	4 18 22	5 44 42	0♍22 35	7♍29 43	25 16.6	6 01.3	25 07.3	28 59.2	20 20.6	4 25.7	28 02.7	15 29.4	20 23.9	15 48.4
28 Sa	4 22 19	6 42 17	14 36 44	21 43 19	25 16.9	8 13.3	26 16.0	29 42.0	20 44.8	4 38.5	28 06.8	15 29.6	20 22.3	15 48.4
29 Su	4 26 15	7 39 50	28 49 11	5♎54 02	25 17.6	10 25.1	27 24.8	0♊24.7	21 08.9	4 51.3	28 10.9	15 29.9	20 20.8	15 48.5
30 M	4 30 12	8 37 22	12♎57 32	19 59 25	25 18.6	12 36.6	28 33.7	1 07.4	21 33.0	5 04.1	28 14.9	15 30.2	20 19.2	15 48.5
31 Tu	4 34 08	9 34 52	26 59 20	3♏57 02	25 19.6	14 47.3	29 42.7	1 50.0	21 57.1	5 17.0	28 18.8	15 30.6	20 17.7	15 48.7

LONGITUDE — June 1966

Day	Sid.Time	☉	0 hr ☽	Noon ☽	True ☊	☿	♀	♂	⚳	♃	♄	♅	♆	♇
1 W	4 38 05	10♊32 21	10♏52 10	17♏44 29	25♉20.3	16♊57.2	0♉51.8	2♊32.6	22♉21.2	5♋29.9	28♓22.7	15♍31.1	20♏16.2	15♍48.8
2 Th	4 42 02	11 29 50	24 33 41	1♐19 32	25R 20.3	19 05.9	2 00.9	3 15.2	22 45.3	5 42.9	28 26.4	15 31.6	20R 14.7	15 49.0
3 F	4 45 58	12 27 17	8♐01 47	14 40 15	25 19.5	21 13.2	3 10.2	3 57.7	23 09.3	5 55.9	28 30.1	15 32.1	20 13.2	15 49.2
4 Sa	4 49 55	13 24 43	21 14 48	27 45 20	25 17.9	23 18.8	4 19.5	4 40.1	23 33.4	6 08.9	28 33.7	15 32.7	20 11.8	15 49.4
5 Su	4 53 51	14 22 08	4♑11 49	10♑34 16	25 15.4	25 22.7	5 28.8	5 22.5	23 57.4	6 22.0	28 37.2	15 33.4	20 10.3	15 49.7
6 M	4 57 48	15 19 33	16 52 46	23 07 29	25 12.5	27 24.7	6 38.3	6 04.8	24 21.4	6 35.1	28 40.6	15 34.1	20 08.9	15 50.0
7 Tu	5 01 44	16 16 57	29 18 36	5♒26 23	25 09.4	29 24.5	7 47.8	6 47.1	24 45.4	6 48.2	28 44.0	15 34.8	20 07.4	15 50.3
8 W	5 05 41	17 14 20	11♒31 12	17 33 25	25 06.6	1♋22.2	8 57.4	7 29.3	25 09.3	7 01.4	28 47.2	15 35.7	20 06.0	15 50.7
9 Th	5 09 38	18 11 42	23 33 28	29 31 49	25 04.4	3 17.7	10 07.1	8 11.5	25 33.2	7 14.6	28 50.4	15 36.5	20 04.6	15 51.1
10 F	5 13 34	19 09 04	5♓28 59	11♓25 31	25D 03.1	5 10.8	11 16.8	8 53.6	25 57.1	7 27.8	28 53.5	15 37.4	20 03.2	15 51.5
11 Sa	5 17 31	20 06 25	17 21 59	23 18 58	25 02.9	7 01.5	12 26.6	9 35.7	26 21.0	7 41.1	28 56.4	15 38.4	20 01.9	15 51.9
12 Su	5 21 27	21 03 46	29 17 04	5♈16 52	25 03.6	8 49.8	13 36.5	10 17.8	26 44.8	7 54.4	28 59.3	15 39.4	20 00.5	15 52.4
13 M	5 25 24	22 01 07	11♈18 58	17 23 56	25 05.1	10 35.7	14 46.5	10 59.7	27 08.7	8 07.7	29 02.1	15 40.5	19 59.2	15 52.9
14 Tu	5 29 20	22 58 27	23 32 19	29 44 38	25 06.7	12 19.1	15 56.5	11 41.7	27 32.5	8 21.0	29 04.8	15 41.6	19 57.9	15 53.5
15 W	5 33 17	23 55 46	6♉01 20	12♉22 48	25R 08.1	14 00.0	17 06.5	12 23.6	27 56.2	8 34.4	29 07.4	15 42.8	19 56.6	15 54.1
16 Th	5 37 13	24 53 05	18 49 24	25 21 19	25 08.6	15 38.3	18 16.7	13 05.4	28 20.0	8 47.7	29 09.9	15 44.0	19 55.3	15 54.7
17 F	5 41 10	25 50 24	1♊58 44	8♊41 40	25 07.9	17 14.2	19 26.8	13 47.2	28 43.7	9 01.1	29 12.4	15 45.3	19 54.1	15 55.3
18 Sa	5 45 07	26 47 43	15 30 01	22 23 36	25 05.8	18 47.5	20 37.1	14 28.9	29 07.3	9 14.6	29 14.7	15 46.6	19 52.8	15 56.0
19 Su	5 49 03	27 45 01	29 22 03	6♋24 55	25 02.2	20 18.2	21 47.4	15 10.6	29 31.0	9 28.0	29 16.9	15 48.0	19 51.6	15 56.7
20 M	5 53 00	28 42 18	13♋31 41	20 41 40	24 57.6	21 46.4	22 57.8	15 52.2	29 54.6	9 41.4	29 19.1	15 49.4	19 50.4	15 57.4
21 Tu	5 56 56	29 39 35	27 54 10	5♌08 27	24 52.6	23 12.0	24 08.2	16 33.8	0♊18.2	9 54.9	29 21.1	15 50.9	19 49.3	15 58.2
22 W	6 00 53	0♋36 51	12♌23 43	19 39 15	24 47.8	24 34.9	25 18.6	17 15.3	0 41.7	10 08.4	29 23.1	15 52.4	19 48.1	15 59.0
23 Th	6 04 49	1 34 06	26 54 20	4♍08 18	24 44.0	25 55.1	26 29.1	17 56.8	1 05.2	10 21.9	29 24.9	15 54.0	19 47.0	15 59.8
24 F	6 08 46	2 31 21	11♍20 38	18 30 49	24 41.6	27 12.6	27 39.7	18 38.2	1 28.7	10 35.4	29 26.7	15 55.6	19 45.9	16 00.6
25 Sa	6 12 42	3 28 35	25 38 30	2♎43 24	24D 40.8	28 27.4	28 50.3	19 19.6	1 52.1	10 48.9	29 28.3	15 57.3	19 44.8	16 01.5
26 Su	6 16 39	4 25 49	9♎45 18	16 44 05	24 41.3	29 39.3	0♊01.0	20 00.9	2 15.5	11 02.4	29 29.9	15 59.0	19 43.8	16 02.4
27 M	6 20 36	5 23 02	23 39 41	0♏32 06	24 42.6	0♌48.3	1 11.7	20 42.2	2 38.8	11 16.0	29 31.3	16 00.8	19 42.7	16 03.3
28 Tu	6 24 32	6 20 14	7♏21 19	14 07 23	24R 43.8	1 54.4	2 22.5	21 23.4	3 02.1	11 29.5	29 32.7	16 02.6	19 41.7	16 04.3
29 W	6 28 29	7 17 26	20 50 21	27 30 15	24 44.2	2 57.5	3 33.3	22 04.6	3 25.4	11 43.0	29 34.0	16 04.5	19 40.8	16 05.3
30 Th	6 32 25	8 14 38	4♐07 07	10♐40 59	24 43.0	3 57.4	4 44.2	22 45.7	3 48.6	11 56.6	29 35.1	16 06.4	19 39.8	16 06.3

Astro Data

	Dy Hr Mn
☽0S	2 10:09
♀0N	8 5:15
☽0N	16 10:51
♅ D	23 16:37
♇ D	27 11:12
☽0S	29 17:02
♃□♆	31 13:11
☽0N	12 18:58
☽0S	25 22:07
♅☌♇	30 9:58

Planet Ingress

		Dy Hr Mn
♀	♈	5 4:33
♃	♋	5 14:52
☿	♉	9 14:48
☉	♊	21 12:32
☿	♊	24 17:59
♂	♊	28 22:07
♀	♉	31 18:00
☿	♋	7 19:11
⚳	♊	20 17:30
☉	♋	21 20:33
♀	♊	26 11:40
☿	♌	26 19:05

Last Aspect / ☽ Ingress

Last Aspect Dy Hr Mn		☽ Ingress Dy Hr Mn
1 18:19	♃ □	♎ 1 19:31
3 20:50	♃ △	♏ 3 21:23
5 18:16	♄ △	♐ 6 0:52
8 2:19	☿ △	♑ 8 7:12
10 10:18	♄ ✶	♒ 10 16:52
12 11:19	☉ □	♓ 13 4:55
15 11:30	♄ ☌	♈ 15 17:15
16 18:49	♀ ☌	♉ 18 3:49
20 9:42	☉ ☌	♊ 20 11:40
22 12:57	♄ □	♋ 22 17:00
24 16:57	♄ △	♌ 24 20:37
26 20:54	♂ □	♍ 26 23:22
28 22:51	♄ ☍	♎ 29 2:00
31 4:02	♀ ☍	♏ 31 5:11

Last Aspect / ☽ Ingress

Last Aspect Dy Hr Mn		☽ Ingress Dy Hr Mn
2 6:51	♄ △	♐ 2 9:38
4 13:30	♄ □	♑ 4 16:10
6 22:49	♄ ✶	♒ 7 1:21
8 17:04	♆ □	♓ 9 12:57
11 23:21	♄ ☌	♈ 12 1:26
13 21:48	☉ ✶	♉ 14 12:30
16 18:57	♄ ✶	♊ 16 20:26
18 23:49	♄ □	♋ 19 1:05
21 2:23	♄ △	♌ 21 3:29
22 22:11	♀ □	♍ 23 5:08
25 6:28	♄ ☍	♎ 25 7:23
26 17:58	♂ △	♏ 27 11:04
29 15:44	♄ △	♐ 29 16:31

☽ Phases & Eclipses

Dy Hr Mn		
4 21:00	○	13♏56
4 21:11	•	A 0.916
12 11:19	☾	21♒17
20 9:42	●	28♉55
20 9:38:24	●	A 00'04"
27 8:50	☽	5♍37
3 7:40	○	12♐17
11 4:58	☾	19♓50
18 20:09	●	27♊07
25 13:22	☽	3♎32

Astro Data

1 May 1966
Julian Day # 24227
SVP 5♓44'03"
GC 26♐22.1 ⚴ 0♈15.3
Eris 11♈26.2 ⚵ 0♉39.9
⚷ 24♓47.3 ⚶ 14♋21.6
☽ Mean ☊ 26♉15.9

1 June 1966
Julian Day # 24258
SVP 5♓43'58"
GC 26♐22.2 ⚴ 9♈10.0
Eris 11♈41.8 ⚵ 18♉31.0
⚷ 25♓53.5 ⚶ 26♋11.7
☽ Mean ☊ 24♉37.4

July 1966 — LONGITUDE

Day	Sid.Time	☉	0 hr ☽	Noon ☽	True ☊	☿	♀	♂	⚳	♃	♄	♅	♆	♇
1 F	6 36 22	9♋11 49	17♐11 52	23♐39 46	24♉39.8	4♌54.1	5♊55.1	23♊26.8	4♊11.8	12♋10.1	29♓36.2	16♍08.3	19♏38.9	16♍07.4
2 Sa	6 40 18	10 09 01	0♑04 41	6♑26 37	24R 34.6	5 47.4	7 06.1	24 07.8	4 34.9	12 23.7	29 37.1	16 10.3	19R 38.0	16 08.4
3 Su	6 44 15	11 06 12	12 45 35	19 01 36	24 27.6	6 37.4	8 17.1	24 48.8	4 58.0	12 37.3	29 38.0	16 12.4	19 37.1	16 09.5
4 M	6 48 11	12 03 23	25 14 44	1♒25 02	24 19.3	7 23.8	9 28.2	25 29.7	5 21.0	12 50.8	29 38.8	16 14.5	19 36.3	16 10.7
5 Tu	6 52 08	13 00 34	7♒32 38	13 37 41	24 10.5	8 06.6	10 39.3	26 10.5	5 44.0	13 04.4	29 39.4	16 16.6	19 35.4	16 11.8
6 W	6 56 05	13 57 46	19 40 24	25 41 01	24 02.2	8 45.5	11 50.5	26 51.4	6 07.0	13 17.9	29 40.0	16 18.8	19 34.6	16 13.0
7 Th	7 00 01	14 54 57	1♓39 51	7♓37 15	23 55.0	9 20.5	13 01.7	27 32.2	6 29.9	13 31.5	29 40.4	16 21.0	19 33.9	16 14.2
8 F	7 03 58	15 52 09	13 33 38	19 29 27	23 49.5	9 51.5	14 13.0	28 12.9	6 52.7	13 45.0	29 40.8	16 23.2	19 33.1	16 15.4
9 Sa	7 07 54	16 49 21	25 25 11	1♈21 24	23 46.1	10 18.3	15 24.4	28 53.6	7 15.5	13 58.6	29 41.1	16 25.5	19 32.4	16 16.7
10 Su	7 11 51	17 46 34	7♈18 40	13 17 35	23D 44.7	10 40.7	16 35.8	29 34.2	7 38.2	14 12.1	29 41.2	16 27.9	19 31.7	16 18.0
11 M	7 15 47	18 43 47	19 18 46	25 22 52	23 44.8	10 58.7	17 47.2	0♋14.8	8 00.9	14 25.7	29R 41.3	16 30.3	19 31.1	16 19.3
12 Tu	7 19 44	19 41 00	1♉30 31	7♉42 20	23 45.6	11 12.2	18 58.7	0 55.3	8 23.6	14 39.2	29 41.2	16 32.7	19 30.4	16 20.6
13 W	7 23 40	20 38 14	13 58 55	20 20 49	23R 46.3	11 21.0	20 10.3	1 35.9	8 46.2	14 52.7	29 41.1	16 35.2	19 29.8	16 22.0
14 Th	7 27 37	21 35 29	26 48 33	3♊22 29	23 46.0	11R 25.0	21 21.9	2 16.3	9 08.7	15 06.2	29 40.8	16 37.7	19 29.3	16 23.4
15 F	7 31 34	22 32 44	10♊02 58	16 50 08	23 43.8	11 24.3	22 33.5	2 56.7	9 31.2	15 19.7	29 40.5	16 40.2	19 28.7	16 24.8
16 Sa	7 35 30	23 30 00	23 44 02	0♋44 31	23 39.3	11 18.7	23 45.2	3 37.1	9 53.6	15 33.2	29 40.0	16 42.8	19 28.2	16 26.2
17 Su	7 39 27	24 27 16	7♋51 16	15 03 47	23 32.5	11 08.3	24 57.0	4 17.4	10 15.9	15 46.7	29 39.5	16 45.4	19 27.8	16 27.7
18 M	7 43 23	25 24 33	22 21 20	29 43 06	23 23.9	10 53.2	26 08.8	4 57.7	10 38.2	16 00.1	29 38.8	16 48.1	19 27.3	16 29.1
19 Tu	7 47 20	26 21 50	7♌08 05	14♌35 10	23 14.6	10 33.5	27 20.6	5 37.9	11 00.4	16 13.6	29 38.1	16 50.8	19 26.9	16 30.7
20 W	7 51 16	27 19 07	22 03 14	29 31 08	23 05.6	10 09.3	28 32.5	6 18.1	11 22.6	16 27.0	29 37.2	16 53.5	19 26.5	16 32.2
21 Th	7 55 13	28 16 25	6♍57 45	14♍22 07	22 57.9	9 41.0	29 44.4	6 58.2	11 44.7	16 40.4	29 36.3	16 56.3	19 26.2	16 33.7
22 F	7 59 09	29 13 43	21 43 22	29 00 46	22 52.5	9 08.9	0♋56.4	7 38.3	12 06.7	16 53.8	29 35.2	16 59.1	19 25.8	16 35.3
23 Sa	8 03 06	0♌11 01	6♎13 47	13♎22 02	22 49.3	8 33.4	2 08.4	8 18.3	12 28.7	17 07.2	29 34.1	17 01.9	19 25.5	16 36.9
24 Su	8 07 03	1 08 19	20 25 19	27 23 32	22D 48.3	7 55.0	3 20.5	8 58.3	12 50.5	17 20.5	29 32.8	17 04.8	19 25.3	16 38.5
25 M	8 10 59	2 05 38	4♏16 45	11♏05 05	22R 48.4	7 14.2	4 32.6	9 38.2	13 12.3	17 33.8	29 31.5	17 07.7	19 25.1	16 40.1
26 Tu	8 14 56	3 02 57	17 48 45	24 28 01	22 48.6	6 31.8	5 44.7	10 18.1	13 34.1	17 47.1	29 30.0	17 10.6	19 24.9	16 41.8
27 W	8 18 52	4 00 17	1♐03 09	7♐34 27	22 47.8	5 48.4	6 56.9	10 57.9	13 55.7	18 00.4	29 28.5	17 13.6	19 24.7	16 43.5
28 Th	8 22 49	4 57 37	14 02 12	20 26 40	22 44.9	5 04.8	8 09.2	11 37.7	14 17.3	18 13.6	29 26.9	17 16.6	19 24.6	16 45.1
29 F	8 26 45	5 54 58	26 48 07	3♑06 45	22 39.4	4 21.8	9 21.5	12 17.5	14 38.8	18 26.8	29 25.2	17 19.7	19 24.5	16 46.9
30 Sa	8 30 42	6 52 19	9♑22 46	15 36 20	22 31.1	3 40.1	10 33.8	12 57.2	15 00.2	18 40.0	29 23.3	17 22.7	19 24.4	16 48.6
31 Su	8 34 39	7 49 41	21 47 34	27 56 37	22 20.4	3 00.6	11 46.2	13 36.8	15 21.6	18 53.2	29 21.4	17 25.8	19D 24.4	16 50.3

August 1966 — LONGITUDE

Day	Sid.Time	☉	0 hr ☽	Noon ☽	True ☊	☿	♀	♂	⚳	♃	♄	♅	♆	♇
1 M	8 38 35	8♌47 04	4♒03 33	10♒08 30	22♉07.9	2♌24.0	12♋58.6	14♋16.4	15♊42.8	19♋06.3	29♓19.4	17♍28.9	19♏24.3	16♍52.1
2 Tu	8 42 32	9 44 28	16 11 35	22 12 54	21R 54.6	1R 51.0	14 11.1	14 56.0	16 04.0	19 19.4	29R 17.3	17 32.1	19 24.4	16 53.9
3 W	8 46 28	10 41 52	28 12 36	4♓10 52	21 41.8	1 22.2	15 23.6	15 35.5	16 25.1	19 32.4	29 15.1	17 35.3	19 24.4	16 55.7
4 Th	8 50 25	11 39 18	10♓07 55	16 03 59	21 30.4	0 58.4	16 36.2	16 15.0	16 46.1	19 45.4	29 12.9	17 38.5	19 24.5	16 57.5
5 F	8 54 21	12 36 45	21 59 23	27 54 27	21 21.2	0 40.0	17 48.8	16 54.4	17 07.1	19 58.4	29 10.5	17 41.7	19 24.6	16 59.4
6 Sa	8 58 18	13 34 12	3♈49 35	9♈45 14	21 14.7	0 27.4	19 01.4	17 33.8	17 27.9	20 11.4	29 08.1	17 45.0	19 24.8	17 01.2
7 Su	9 02 14	14 31 41	15 41 53	21 40 04	21 10.8	0D 21.0	20 14.2	18 13.1	17 48.6	20 24.3	29 05.5	17 48.3	19 25.0	17 03.1
8 M	9 06 11	15 29 12	27 40 23	3♉43 24	21 09.1	0 21.1	21 26.9	18 52.4	18 09.3	20 37.2	29 02.9	17 51.6	19 25.2	17 05.0
9 Tu	9 10 07	16 26 43	9♉49 48	16 00 12	21 08.8	0 27.9	22 39.7	19 31.7	18 29.8	20 50.0	29 00.2	17 54.9	19 25.4	17 06.9
10 W	9 14 04	17 24 16	22 15 15	28 35 36	21 08.7	0 41.5	23 52.6	20 10.9	18 50.3	21 02.8	28 57.4	17 58.3	19 25.7	17 08.8
11 Th	9 18 01	18 21 51	5♊01 50	11♊34 29	21 07.8	1 02.2	25 05.5	20 50.1	19 10.7	21 15.5	28 54.5	18 01.7	19 26.0	17 10.7
12 F	9 21 57	19 19 27	18 14 01	25 00 46	21 04.9	1 29.8	26 18.5	21 29.2	19 30.9	21 28.2	28 51.6	18 05.1	19 26.4	17 12.7
13 Sa	9 25 54	20 17 04	1♋54 56	8♋56 33	20 59.6	2 04.4	27 31.5	22 08.3	19 51.1	21 40.9	28 48.5	18 08.5	19 26.8	17 14.6
14 Su	9 29 50	21 14 43	16 05 26	23 21 12	20 51.8	2 45.9	28 44.5	22 47.3	20 11.1	21 53.5	28 45.4	18 12.0	19 27.2	17 16.6
15 M	9 33 47	22 12 24	0♌43 13	8♌10 39	20 41.8	3 34.2	29 57.6	23 26.3	20 31.1	22 06.1	28 42.2	18 15.5	19 27.6	17 18.6
16 Tu	9 37 43	23 10 05	15 42 26	23 17 22	20 30.8	4 29.2	1♌10.7	24 05.3	20 50.9	22 18.6	28 39.0	18 19.0	19 28.1	17 20.6
17 W	9 41 40	24 07 48	0♍54 06	8♍31 13	20 20.1	5 30.7	2 23.9	24 44.2	21 10.6	22 31.0	28 35.6	18 22.5	19 28.6	17 22.6
18 Th	9 45 37	25 05 32	16 07 22	23 41 13	20 10.8	6 38.4	3 37.1	25 23.1	21 30.2	22 43.4	28 32.2	18 26.0	19 29.2	17 24.6
19 F	9 49 33	26 03 17	1♎11 35	8♎37 28	20 03.9	7 52.2	4 50.4	26 01.9	21 49.7	22 55.8	28 28.7	18 29.6	19 29.7	17 26.6
20 Sa	9 53 30	27 01 03	15 58 05	23 12 50	19 59.7	9 11.7	6 03.7	26 40.6	22 09.1	23 08.1	28 25.2	18 33.1	19 30.3	17 28.7
21 Su	9 57 26	27 58 50	0♏21 21	7♏23 27	19D 57.8	10 36.5	7 17.0	27 19.4	22 28.3	23 20.3	28 21.5	18 36.7	19 31.0	17 30.7
22 M	10 01 23	28 56 38	14 19 09	21 08 34	19R 57.5	12 06.4	8 30.4	27 58.0	22 47.4	23 32.5	28 17.9	18 40.3	19 31.6	17 32.8
23 Tu	10 05 19	29 54 28	27 51 57	4♐29 41	19 57.5	13 40.9	9 43.8	28 36.7	23 06.4	23 44.6	28 14.1	18 44.0	19 32.3	17 34.9
24 W	10 09 16	0♍52 19	11♐02 07	17 29 43	19 56.6	15 19.6	10 57.3	29 15.3	23 25.3	23 56.6	28 10.3	18 47.6	19 33.1	17 36.9
25 Th	10 13 12	1 50 11	23 52 54	0♑12 08	19 53.7	17 02.0	12 10.8	29 53.8	23 44.0	24 08.6	28 06.5	18 51.2	19 33.8	17 39.0
26 F	10 17 09	2 48 04	6♑27 50	12 40 24	19 48.3	18 47.8	13 24.3	0♌32.3	24 02.6	24 20.6	28 02.5	18 54.9	19 34.6	17 41.1
27 Sa	10 21 06	3 45 59	18 50 13	24 57 37	19 40.2	20 36.4	14 37.9	1 10.7	24 21.1	24 32.4	27 58.6	18 58.6	19 35.5	17 43.2
28 Su	10 25 02	4 43 55	1♒02 52	7♒06 16	19 29.5	22 27.3	15 51.5	1 49.1	24 39.4	24 44.2	27 54.5	19 02.3	19 36.3	17 45.3
29 M	10 28 59	5 41 52	13 08 02	19 08 23	19 17.1	24 20.3	17 05.2	2 27.5	24 57.6	24 55.9	27 50.4	19 06.0	19 37.2	17 47.5
30 Tu	10 32 55	6 39 51	25 07 29	1♓05 31	19 04.0	26 14.8	18 18.9	3 05.8	25 15.7	25 07.6	27 46.3	19 09.7	19 38.1	17 49.6
31 W	10 36 52	7 37 51	7♓02 39	12 59 02	18 51.2	28 10.4	19 32.6	3 44.1	25 33.6	25 19.2	27 42.1	19 13.4	19 39.1	17 51.7

Astro Data	Planet Ingress	Last Aspect	☽ Ingress	Last Aspect	☽ Ingress	☽ Phases & Eclipses	Astro Data
Dy Hr Mn	Dy Hr Mn	Dy Hr Mn	Dy Hr Mn	Dy Hr Mn	Dy Hr Mn	Dy Hr Mn	1 July 1966
☽0N 10 2:16	♂ ♋ 11 3:15	1 23:07 ♄ □	♑ 1 23:51	2 6:24 ♆ □	♓ 3 3:36	2 19:36 ○ 10♑27	Julian Day # 24288
♄R 11 13:03	♀ ♋ 21 17:11	4 8:33 ♄ ✶	♒ 4 9:14	5 14:34 ♄ ☌	♈ 5 16:15	10 21:43 ☾ 18♈10	SVP 5♓43'53"
☿R 14 20:15	☉ ♌ 23 7:23	6 14:29 ♂ △	♓ 6 20:39	7 9:25 ♃ □	♉ 8 4:38	18 4:30 ● 25♋07	GC 26♐22.3 ⚴ 16♈05.0
♃✶♇ 20 22:27		9 8:37 ♄ ☌	♈ 9 9:16	10 12:41 ♄ ✶	♊ 10 14:38	24 19:00 ☽ 1♏25	Eris 11♈48.9 ⚵ 5♊52.5
♃✶♅ 23 0:02	♀ ♌ 15 12:47	10 21:43 ☉ □	♉ 11 21:03	12 18:41 ♄ □	♋ 12 20:41		⚷ 26♓13.8R ⚶ 8♌58.5
☽0S 23 3:23	☉ ♍ 23 14:18	14 5:16 ♄ ✶	♊ 14 5:51	14 21:35 ♀ ☌	♌ 14 22:50	1 9:05 ○ 8♒40	☽ Mean ☊ 23♉02.1
	♂ ♌ 25 15:52	16 10:10 ♄ □	♋ 16 10:44	16 11:48 ☉ ☌	♍ 16 22:35	9 12:55 ☾ 16♉29	
♆D 1 4:30		18 11:53 ♄ △	♌ 18 12:27	18 19:43 ♄ ☍	♎ 18 22:05	16 11:48 ● 23♌10	1 August 1966
♃△♆ 2 21:13		20 10:18 ♀ ✶	♍ 20 12:46	20 18:50 ☉ ✶	♏ 20 23:24	23 3:02 ☽ 29♏33	Julian Day # 24319
☽0N 6 8:26		22 12:57 ♄ ☍	♎ 22 13:38	23 3:02 ☉ □	♐ 23 3:51	31 0:14 ○ 7♓09	SVP 5♓43'47"
☿D 7 23:43		23 18:28 ♃ □	♏ 24 16:32	25 8:02 ♄ □	♑ 25 11:37		GC 26♐22.4 ⚴ 20♈09.8
☽0S 19 10:43		26 21:09 ♄ △	♐ 26 22:04	27 17:54 ♄ ✶	♒ 27 21:56		Eris 11♈46.1R ⚵ 23♊30.0
		29 4:59 ♀ ☍	♑ 29 6:04	30 0:24 ☿ ☍	♓ 30 9:48		⚷ 25♓45.8R ⚶ 23♌03.2
		31 14:46 ♄ ✶	♒ 31 16:02				☽ Mean ☊ 21♉23.7

LONGITUDE — September 1966

Day	Sid.Time	☉	0 hr ☽	Noon☽	True☊	☿	♀	♂	⚳	♃	♄	♅	♆	♇
1 Th	10 40 48	8♍35 53	18♓54 52	24♓50 20	18♉39.7	0♍06.9	20♌46.4	4♌22.3	25♊51.3	25♋30.7	27♓37.9	19♍17.1	19♏40.0	17♍53.8
2 F	10 44 45	9 33 57	0♈45 40	6♈41 07	18R 30.5	2 03.8	22 00.2	5 00.5	26 08.9	25 42.1	27R 33.6	19 20.8	19 41.1	17 56.0
3 Sa	10 48 41	10 32 02	12 36 58	18 33 32	18 24.0	4 01.0	23 14.1	5 38.6	26 26.4	25 53.5	27 29.3	19 24.6	19 42.1	17 58.1
4 Su	10 52 38	11 30 10	24 31 14	0♉30 26	18 20.1	5 58.1	24 28.0	6 16.7	26 43.7	26 04.8	27 25.0	19 28.3	19 43.1	18 00.3
5 M	10 56 34	12 28 19	6♉31 38	12 35 19	18D 18.5	7 55.0	25 41.9	6 54.8	27 00.8	26 16.0	27 20.6	19 32.1	19 44.2	18 02.4
6 Tu	11 00 31	13 26 30	18 42 01	24 52 19	18 18.5	9 51.4	26 55.9	7 32.8	27 17.8	26 27.1	27 16.2	19 35.8	19 45.4	18 04.6
7 W	11 04 28	14 24 43	1♊06 46	7♊26 00	18R 19.1	11 47.2	28 09.9	8 10.8	27 34.6	26 38.2	27 11.7	19 39.6	19 46.5	18 06.7
8 Th	11 08 24	15 22 59	13 50 33	20 21 00	18 19.2	13 42.4	29 24.0	8 48.7	27 51.3	26 49.2	27 07.2	19 43.4	19 47.7	18 08.9
9 F	11 12 21	16 21 16	26 57 50	3♋41 29	18 17.8	15 36.7	0♍38.1	9 26.6	28 07.7	27 00.0	27 02.7	19 47.2	19 48.9	18 11.1
10 Sa	11 16 17	17 19 36	10♋32 16	17 30 20	18 14.3	17 30.2	1 52.2	10 04.4	28 24.0	27 10.8	26 58.2	19 50.9	19 50.1	18 13.2
11 Su	11 20 14	18 17 57	24 35 43	1♌48 12	18 08.6	19 22.7	3 06.4	10 42.2	28 40.2	27 21.6	26 53.6	19 54.7	19 51.4	18 15.4
12 M	11 24 10	19 16 21	9♌07 25	16 32 41	18 01.0	21 14.2	4 20.6	11 20.0	28 56.1	27 32.2	26 49.1	19 58.5	19 52.7	18 17.6
13 Tu	11 28 07	20 14 47	24 03 11	1♍37 49	17 52.4	23 04.7	5 34.8	11 57.7	29 11.8	27 42.7	26 44.5	20 02.3	19 54.0	18 19.7
14 W	11 32 03	21 13 14	9♍15 21	16 54 26	17 43.8	24 54.2	6 49.1	12 35.3	29 27.4	27 53.1	26 39.9	20 06.1	19 55.4	18 21.9
15 Th	11 36 00	22 11 44	24 33 39	2♎11 34	17 36.3	26 42.6	8 03.4	13 13.0	29 42.8	28 03.5	26 35.2	20 09.9	19 56.7	18 24.0
16 F	11 39 57	23 10 15	9♎46 50	17 18 15	17 30.9	28 29.9	9 17.8	13 50.5	29 57.9	28 13.7	26 30.6	20 13.6	19 58.1	18 26.2
17 Sa	11 43 53	24 08 48	24 44 47	2♏05 34	17 27.7	0♎16.2	10 32.1	14 28.0	0♋12.9	28 23.9	26 25.9	20 17.4	19 59.6	18 28.4
18 Su	11 47 50	25 07 22	9♏20 01	16 27 42	17D 26.8	2 01.5	11 46.5	15 05.5	0 27.6	28 33.9	26 21.3	20 21.2	20 01.0	18 30.5
19 M	11 51 46	26 05 59	23 28 25	0♐22 10	17 27.3	3 45.6	13 01.0	15 42.9	0 42.2	28 43.8	26 16.6	20 25.0	20 02.5	18 32.7
20 Tu	11 55 43	27 04 37	7♐09 04	13 49 24	17 28.3	5 28.8	14 15.4	16 20.3	0 56.5	28 53.7	26 12.0	20 28.7	20 04.0	18 34.8
21 W	11 59 39	28 03 17	20 23 31	26 51 51	17R 29.0	7 10.9	15 29.9	16 57.6	1 10.6	29 03.4	26 07.3	20 32.5	20 05.5	18 37.0
22 Th	12 03 36	29 01 58	3♑14 54	9♑33 09	17 28.3	8 52.1	16 44.4	17 34.9	1 24.5	29 13.0	26 02.7	20 36.3	20 07.1	18 39.1
23 F	12 07 32	0♎00 41	15 47 09	21 57 25	17 25.9	10 32.2	17 59.0	18 12.1	1 38.2	29 22.6	25 58.1	20 40.0	20 08.7	18 41.2
24 Sa	12 11 29	0 59 26	28 04 26	4♒08 42	17 21.3	12 11.4	19 13.5	18 49.3	1 51.7	29 32.0	25 53.4	20 43.7	20 10.3	18 43.4
25 Su	12 15 26	1 58 13	10♒10 40	16 10 45	17 15.0	13 49.6	20 28.1	19 26.4	2 04.9	29 41.3	25 48.8	20 47.5	20 11.9	18 45.5
26 M	12 19 22	2 57 01	22 09 20	28 06 46	17 07.2	15 26.9	21 42.7	20 03.5	2 17.9	29 50.4	25 44.2	20 51.2	20 13.5	18 47.6
27 Tu	12 23 19	3 55 51	4♓03 22	9♓59 26	16 58.9	17 03.3	22 57.4	20 40.5	2 30.6	29 59.5	25 39.6	20 54.9	20 15.2	18 49.7
28 W	12 27 15	4 54 43	15 55 12	21 50 55	16 50.8	18 38.8	24 12.0	21 17.5	2 43.1	0♌08.5	25 35.1	20 58.6	20 16.9	18 51.8
29 Th	12 31 12	5 53 37	27 46 48	3♈43 04	16 43.6	20 13.4	25 26.7	21 54.4	2 55.4	0 17.3	25 30.5	21 02.3	20 18.6	18 53.9
30 F	12 35 08	6 52 33	9♈39 55	15 37 35	16 37.9	21 47.1	26 41.5	22 31.3	3 07.4	0 26.0	25 26.0	21 06.0	20 20.3	18 56.0

LONGITUDE — October 1966

Day	Sid.Time	☉	0 hr ☽	Noon☽	True☊	☿	♀	♂	⚳	♃	♄	♅	♆	♇
1 Sa	12 39 05	7♎51 31	21♈36 15	27♈36 11	16♉34.2	23♎19.9	27♍56.2	23♌08.1	3♋19.2	0♌34.6	25♓21.5	21♍09.7	20♏22.1	18♍58.0
2 Su	12 43 01	8 50 31	3♉37 37	9♉40 51	16D 32.4	24 51.9	29 11.0	23 44.9	3 30.7	0 43.0	25R 17.0	21 13.3	20 23.9	19 00.1
3 M	12 46 58	9 49 33	15 46 10	21 53 55	16 32.3	26 23.1	0♎25.8	24 21.6	3 41.9	0 51.4	25 12.6	21 17.0	20 25.7	19 02.2
4 Tu	12 50 55	10 48 38	28 04 28	4♊18 11	16 33.4	27 53.4	1 40.6	24 58.3	3 52.9	0 59.6	25 08.2	21 20.6	20 27.5	19 04.2
5 W	12 54 51	11 47 44	10♊35 30	16 56 50	16 35.0	29 22.8	2 55.4	25 35.0	4 03.6	1 07.7	25 03.9	21 24.2	20 29.3	19 06.3
6 Th	12 58 48	12 46 54	23 22 36	29 53 14	16 36.4	0♏51.4	4 10.3	26 11.5	4 14.0	1 15.7	24 59.5	21 27.8	20 31.2	19 08.3
7 F	13 02 44	13 46 05	6♋29 08	13♋10 38	16R 37.1	2 19.2	5 25.2	26 48.1	4 24.1	1 23.5	24 55.2	21 31.4	20 33.0	19 10.3
8 Sa	13 06 41	14 45 19	19 58 02	26 51 31	16 36.5	3 46.1	6 40.1	27 24.6	4 34.0	1 31.2	24 51.0	21 35.0	20 34.9	19 12.3
9 Su	13 10 37	15 44 35	3♌51 11	10♌57 00	16 34.5	5 12.1	7 55.1	28 01.0	4 43.5	1 38.7	24 46.8	21 38.5	20 36.8	19 14.3
10 M	13 14 34	16 43 54	18 08 44	25 26 02	16 31.3	6 37.3	9 10.0	28 37.4	4 52.8	1 46.1	24 42.7	21 42.0	20 38.8	19 16.3
11 Tu	13 18 30	17 43 14	2♍48 20	10♍14 55	16 27.3	8 01.5	10 25.0	29 13.7	5 01.7	1 53.4	24 38.6	21 45.6	20 40.7	19 18.2
12 W	13 22 27	18 42 37	17 44 52	25 17 09	16 23.2	9 24.8	11 40.0	29 50.0	5 10.4	2 00.5	24 34.5	21 49.0	20 42.7	19 20.2
13 Th	13 26 24	19 42 02	2♎50 37	10♎24 05	16 19.7	10 47.1	12 55.0	0♍26.2	5 18.7	2 07.5	24 30.5	21 52.5	20 44.7	19 22.1
14 F	13 30 20	20 41 30	17 56 19	25 26 09	16 17.3	12 08.4	14 10.0	1 02.4	5 26.7	2 14.3	24 26.6	21 56.0	20 46.7	19 24.0
15 Sa	13 34 17	21 40 59	2♏52 29	10♏14 22	16D 16.1	13 28.7	15 25.1	1 38.5	5 34.4	2 21.0	24 22.7	21 59.4	20 48.7	19 25.9
16 Su	13 38 13	22 40 30	17 30 59	24 41 42	16 16.2	14 47.7	16 40.2	2 14.5	5 41.8	2 27.6	24 18.9	22 02.8	20 50.7	19 27.8
17 M	13 42 10	23 40 03	1♐46 04	8♐43 48	16 17.2	16 05.6	17 55.3	2 50.5	5 48.8	2 33.9	24 15.2	22 06.1	20 52.7	19 29.7
18 Tu	13 46 06	24 39 38	15 34 48	22 19 05	16 18.7	17 22.3	19 10.4	3 26.5	5 55.5	2 40.2	24 11.5	22 09.5	20 54.8	19 31.6
19 W	13 50 03	25 39 15	28 56 52	5♑28 25	16 20.2	18 37.5	20 25.5	4 02.3	6 01.9	2 46.2	24 07.9	22 12.8	20 56.9	19 33.4
20 Th	13 53 59	26 38 53	11♑54 06	18 14 23	16R 21.1	19 51.2	21 40.6	4 38.1	6 07.9	2 52.2	24 04.3	22 16.1	20 58.9	19 35.2
21 F	13 57 56	27 38 33	24 29 45	0♒40 44	16 21.3	21 03.4	22 55.7	5 13.9	6 13.6	2 57.9	24 00.8	22 19.4	21 01.0	19 37.0
22 Sa	14 01 53	28 38 15	6♒47 55	12 51 49	16 20.6	22 13.7	24 10.9	5 49.6	6 18.9	3 03.5	23 57.4	22 22.6	21 03.2	19 38.8
23 Su	14 05 49	29 37 59	18 53 01	24 52 02	16 19.2	23 22.2	25 26.0	6 25.2	6 23.8	3 08.9	23 54.1	22 25.9	21 05.3	19 40.6
24 M	14 09 46	0♏37 44	0♓49 26	6♓45 40	16 17.1	24 28.6	26 41.2	7 00.7	6 28.4	3 14.2	23 50.9	22 29.0	21 07.4	19 42.3
25 Tu	14 13 42	1 37 31	12 41 15	18 36 36	16 14.8	25 32.6	27 56.4	7 36.2	6 32.7	3 19.3	23 47.7	22 32.2	21 09.5	19 44.0
26 W	14 17 39	2 37 20	24 32 07	0♈28 12	16 12.6	26 34.1	29 11.6	8 11.7	6 36.5	3 24.2	23 44.6	22 35.3	21 11.7	19 45.8
27 Th	14 21 35	3 37 10	6♈25 09	12 23 19	16 10.6	27 32.7	0♏26.7	8 47.0	6 40.0	3 29.0	23 41.6	22 38.4	21 13.8	19 47.4
28 F	14 25 32	4 37 02	18 22 56	24 24 17	16 09.3	28 28.3	1 42.0	9 22.4	6 43.2	3 33.6	23 38.6	22 41.5	21 16.0	19 49.1
29 Sa	14 29 28	5 36 57	0♉27 34	6♉33 00	16D 08.5	29 20.3	2 57.2	9 57.6	6 45.9	3 38.0	23 35.8	22 44.5	21 18.2	19 50.7
30 Su	14 33 25	6 36 53	12 40 45	18 51 00	16 08.3	0♐08.4	4 12.4	10 32.8	6 48.3	3 42.3	23 33.0	22 47.5	21 20.4	19 52.4
31 M	14 37 21	7 36 51	25 03 55	1♊19 39	16 08.7	0 52.3	5 27.6	11 07.9	6 50.2	3 46.4	23 30.3	22 50.5	21 22.6	19 54.0

Astro Data Dy Hr Mn	Planet Ingress Dy Hr Mn	Last Aspect Dy Hr Mn	☽ Ingress Dy Hr Mn	Last Aspect Dy Hr Mn	☽ Ingress Dy Hr Mn	☽ Phases & Eclipses Dy Hr Mn	Astro Data
☽0N 2 13:57	☿ ♍ 1 10:35	1 17:38 ♄ ☌	♈ 1 22:27	1 2:35 ♂ △	♉ 1 16:47	8 2:07 ☾ 14♊59	1 September 1966
♃△♄ 9 16:13	♀ ♍ 8 23:40	4 2:59 ♃ □	♉ 4 10:59	3 18:25 ♄ ✶	♊ 4 3:43	14 19:13 ● 21♍31	Julian Day # 24350
♅✶♆ 10 4:28	⚳ ♋ 16 15:19	6 16:36 ♄ ✶	♊ 6 21:52	6 4:52 ♂ ✶	♋ 6 12:12	21 14:25 ☽ 28♐09	SVP 5♓43'43"
☽0S 15 20:32	☿ ♎ 17 8:19	9 0:13 ♄ □	♋ 9 5:26	8 8:32 ♄ △	♌ 8 17:25	29 16:47 ○ 6♈05	GC 26♐22.4 ⚴ 19♈12.5R
☿0S 18 15:53	☉ ♎ 23 11:43	11 4:32 ♃ ☌	♌ 11 9:01	10 17:26 ♂ ☌	♍ 10 19:27		Eris 11♈34.0R ⚵ 10♋14.2
☉0S 23 11:43	♃ ♌ 27 13:19	12 17:21 ♆ □	♍ 13 9:26	12 10:53 ♄ ☍	♎ 12 19:29	7 13:08 ☾ 13♋49	⚷ 24♓37.7R ⚶ 7♍42.7
☽0N 29 19:44		15 5:25 ♃ ✶	♎ 15 8:33	14 3:52 ☉ ☌	♏ 14 19:21	14 3:52 ● 20♎21	☽ Mean ☊ 19♉45.2
	♀ ♎ 3 3:44	17 5:52 ♃ □	♏ 17 8:34	16 11:22 ♄ △	♐ 16 20:59	21 5:34 ☽ 27♑23	
♀0S 5 19:39	☿ ♏ 5 22:03	19 9:06 ♃ △	♐ 19 11:21	18 16:34 ☉ ✶	♑ 19 1:55	29 10:00 ○ 5♉32	1 October 1966
☽0S 13 7:32	♂ ♍ 12 18:37	21 14:25 ☉ □	♑ 21 17:52	21 5:34 ☉ □	♒ 21 10:41	29 10:12 • A 0.952	Julian Day # 24380
☽0N 27 2:25	☉ ♏ 23 20:51	24 2:45 ♃ ☍	♒ 24 3:48	23 13:16 ♀ △	♓ 23 22:20		SVP 5♓43'40"
	♀ ♏ 27 3:28	25 20:05 ♆ □	♓ 26 15:48	26 3:23 ☿ △	♈ 26 11:03		GC 26♐22.5 ⚴ 12♈37.4R
	☿ ♐ 30 7:38	28 19:31 ♄ ☌	♈ 29 4:29	26 17:58 ♃ △	♉ 28 23:05		Eris 11♈16.7R ⚵ 24♋46.8
				30 21:03 ♄ ✶	♊ 31 9:28		⚷ 23♓16.5R ⚶ 22♍13.5
							☽ Mean ☊ 18♉09.8

November 1966 — LONGITUDE

Day	Sid.Time	☉	0 hr ☽	Noon☽	True☊	☿	♀	♂	⚳	♃	♄	♅	♆	♇
1 Tu	14 41 18	8♏36 51	7♊38 21	14♊00 10	16♉09.3	1♐31.3	6♏42.9	11♍43.0	6♋51.8	3♌50.3	23♓27.8	22♍53.4	21♏24.8	19♍55.5
2 W	14 45 15	9 36 54	20 25 18	26 53 51	16 10.0	2 05.0	7 58.1	12 17.9	6 53.0	3 54.0	23R 25.3	22 56.3	21 27.0	19 57.1
3 Th	14 49 11	10 36 58	3♋26 02	10♋01 58	16 10.6	2 32.9	9 13.4	12 52.9	6 53.8	3 57.5	23 22.9	22 59.2	21 29.2	19 58.6
4 F	14 53 08	11 37 05	16 41 48	23 25 40	16 11.1	2 54.1	10 28.7	13 27.7	6R54.2	4 00.9	23 20.5	23 02.0	21 31.4	20 00.1
5 Sa	14 57 04	12 37 13	0♌13 41	7♌05 53	16R11.2	3 08.2	11 44.0	14 02.5	6 54.2	4 04.1	23 18.3	23 04.8	21 33.7	20 01.6
6 Su	15 01 01	13 37 24	14 02 18	21 02 53	16 11.2	3R14.5	12 59.3	14 37.2	6 53.8	4 07.1	23 16.2	23 07.5	21 35.9	20 03.1
7 M	15 04 57	14 37 37	28 07 30	5♍15 57	16 11.1	3 12.3	14 14.6	15 11.9	6 53.0	4 09.9	23 14.1	23 10.2	21 38.1	20 04.5
8 Tu	15 08 54	15 37 51	12♍27 55	19 43 00	16D11.0	3 00.9	15 29.9	15 46.4	6 51.7	4 12.5	23 12.2	23 12.9	21 40.4	20 05.9
9 W	15 12 50	16 38 08	27 00 41	4♎20 22	16 11.0	2 40.0	16 45.2	16 20.9	6 50.1	4 14.9	23 10.4	23 15.5	21 42.6	20 07.3
10 Th	15 16 47	17 38 27	11♎41 20	19 02 49	16 11.1	2 09.1	18 00.6	16 55.3	6 48.0	4 17.2	23 08.6	23 18.1	21 44.9	20 08.7
11 F	15 20 44	18 38 47	26 24 01	3♏44 02	16R11.3	1 28.2	19 15.9	17 29.7	6 45.5	4 19.2	23 07.0	23 20.7	21 47.1	20 10.0
12 Sa	15 24 40	19 39 10	11♏02 04	18 17 16	16 11.3	0 37.5	20 31.3	18 03.9	6 42.6	4 21.1	23 05.4	23 23.2	21 49.4	20 11.3
13 Su	15 28 37	20 39 34	25 28 53	2♐36 13	16 11.2	29♏37.6	21 46.6	18 38.1	6 39.3	4 22.7	23 04.0	23 25.7	21 51.6	20 12.6
14 M	15 32 33	21 40 00	9♐38 43	16 35 54	16 10.7	28 29.7	23 02.0	19 12.2	6 35.6	4 24.2	23 02.7	23 28.1	21 53.9	20 13.9
15 Tu	15 36 30	22 40 27	23 27 26	0♑13 07	16 10.0	27 15.2	24 17.4	19 46.2	6 31.4	4 25.5	23 01.4	23 30.5	21 56.1	20 15.1
16 W	15 40 26	23 40 56	6♑52 52	13 26 45	16 09.1	25 56.3	25 32.7	20 20.1	6 26.9	4 26.5	23 00.3	23 32.8	21 58.4	20 16.3
17 Th	15 44 23	24 41 26	19 54 54	26 17 36	16 08.1	24 35.3	26 48.1	20 54.0	6 21.9	4 27.4	22 59.3	23 35.1	22 00.6	20 17.4
18 F	15 48 20	25 41 57	2♒35 10	8♒48 04	16 07.3	23 15.0	28 03.5	21 27.7	6 16.5	4 28.1	22 58.4	23 37.3	22 02.9	20 18.6
19 Sa	15 52 16	26 42 30	14 56 45	21 01 45	16D06.8	21 57.9	29 18.8	22 01.4	6 10.8	4 28.6	22 57.5	23 39.5	22 05.1	20 19.7
20 Su	15 56 13	27 43 04	27 03 38	3♓02 59	16 06.8	20 46.7	0♐34.2	22 34.9	6 04.6	4R28.9	22 56.8	23 41.7	22 07.4	20 20.8
21 M	16 00 09	28 43 39	9♓00 24	14 56 29	16 07.3	19 43.3	1 49.6	23 08.4	5 58.0	4 28.9	22 56.2	23 43.8	22 09.6	20 21.8
22 Tu	16 04 06	29 44 15	20 51 49	26 47 00	16 08.4	18 49.6	3 05.0	23 41.8	5 51.1	4 28.8	22 55.7	23 45.9	22 11.9	20 22.9
23 W	16 08 02	0♐44 53	2♈42 36	8♈39 08	16 09.8	18 06.8	4 20.3	24 15.1	5 43.7	4 28.5	22 55.3	23 47.9	22 14.1	20 23.8
24 Th	16 11 59	1 45 31	14 37 08	20 37 01	16 11.2	17 35.4	5 35.7	24 48.3	5 36.0	4 28.0	22 55.1	23 49.8	22 16.3	20 24.8
25 F	16 15 55	2 46 11	26 39 15	2♉44 12	16 12.3	17 15.7	6 51.1	25 21.4	5 27.9	4 27.3	22 54.9	23 51.8	22 18.6	20 25.7
26 Sa	16 19 52	3 46 52	8♉52 11	15 03 29	16R12.8	17D07.5	8 06.5	25 54.4	5 19.4	4 26.4	22D54.8	23 53.6	22 20.8	20 26.6
27 Su	16 23 49	4 47 34	21 18 17	27 36 47	16 12.4	17 10.2	9 21.8	26 27.3	5 10.5	4 25.3	22 54.8	23 55.5	22 23.0	20 27.5
28 M	16 27 45	5 48 18	3♊59 02	10♊25 07	16 11.0	17 23.2	10 37.2	27 00.1	5 01.3	4 24.0	22 55.0	23 57.2	22 25.2	20 28.4
29 Tu	16 31 42	6 49 03	16 54 59	23 28 35	16 08.6	17 45.7	11 52.6	27 32.8	4 51.8	4 22.5	22 55.2	23 58.9	22 27.4	20 29.2
30 W	16 35 38	7 49 49	0♋05 48	6♋46 29	16 05.4	18 16.7	13 08.0	28 05.4	4 41.9	4 20.8	22 55.6	24 00.6	22 29.6	20 30.0

December 1966 — LONGITUDE

Day	Sid.Time	☉	0 hr ☽	Noon☽	True☊	☿	♀	♂	⚳	♃	♄	♅	♆	♇
1 Th	16 39 35	8♐50 37	13♋30 28	20♋17 32	16♉01.9	18♏55.5	14♐23.4	28♍38.0	4♋31.6	4♌18.9	22♓56.1	24♍02.2	22♏31.8	20♍30.7
2 F	16 43 31	9 51 26	27 07 29	4♌00 04	15R58.6	19 41.1	15 38.7	29 10.4	4R21.1	4R16.8	22 56.6	24 03.8	22 34.0	20 31.4
3 Sa	16 47 28	10 52 17	10♌55 04	17 52 17	15 56.0	20 32.7	16 54.1	29 42.7	4 10.2	4 14.6	22 57.3	24 05.3	22 36.1	20 32.1
4 Su	16 51 24	11 53 08	24 51 28	1♍52 26	15D54.4	21 29.6	18 09.5	0♎14.9	3 59.0	4 12.1	22 58.1	24 06.8	22 38.3	20 32.8
5 M	16 55 21	12 54 01	8♍54 58	15 58 53	15 54.1	22 31.1	19 24.9	0 46.9	3 47.5	4 09.4	22 59.0	24 08.2	22 40.5	20 33.4
6 Tu	16 59 18	13 54 56	23 03 58	0♎09 59	15 54.9	23 36.7	20 40.3	1 18.9	3 35.8	4 06.6	23 00.0	24 09.6	22 42.6	20 34.0
7 W	17 03 14	14 55 52	7♎16 44	14 23 55	15 56.3	24 45.8	21 55.7	1 50.7	3 23.7	4 03.5	23 01.1	24 10.9	22 44.7	20 34.5
8 Th	17 07 11	15 56 49	21 31 15	28 38 23	15 57.8	25 57.9	23 11.1	2 22.5	3 11.4	4 00.3	23 02.3	24 12.1	22 46.8	20 35.0
9 F	17 11 07	16 57 47	5♏44 59	12♏50 36	15R58.7	27 12.6	24 26.5	2 54.1	2 58.9	3 56.8	23 03.7	24 13.3	22 48.9	20 35.5
10 Sa	17 15 04	17 58 46	19 54 49	26 57 09	15 58.2	28 29.6	25 41.9	3 25.5	2 46.1	3 53.2	23 05.1	24 14.4	22 51.0	20 36.0
11 Su	17 19 00	18 59 47	3♐57 06	10♐54 13	15 56.1	29 48.5	26 57.3	3 56.9	2 33.1	3 49.4	23 06.6	24 15.5	22 53.1	20 36.4
12 M	17 22 57	20 00 48	17 48 02	24 38 06	15 52.2	1♐09.1	28 12.7	4 28.1	2 19.9	3 45.4	23 08.3	24 16.6	22 55.2	20 36.8
13 Tu	17 26 53	21 01 51	1♑24 04	8♑05 37	15 46.8	2 31.2	29 28.1	4 59.2	2 06.6	3 41.2	23 10.0	24 17.5	22 57.2	20 37.2
14 W	17 30 50	22 02 54	14 42 31	21 14 38	15 40.4	3 54.6	0♑43.5	5 30.1	1 53.1	3 36.9	23 11.9	24 18.5	22 59.3	20 37.5
15 Th	17 34 47	23 03 57	27 41 55	4♒04 25	15 33.7	5 19.0	1 58.9	6 00.9	1 39.4	3 32.4	23 13.8	24 19.3	23 01.3	20 37.8
16 F	17 38 43	24 05 01	10♒22 16	16 35 43	15 27.6	6 44.4	3 14.3	6 31.6	1 25.6	3 27.7	23 15.9	24 20.1	23 03.3	20 38.0
17 Sa	17 42 40	25 06 05	22 45 04	28 50 44	15 22.6	8 10.6	4 29.7	7 02.1	1 11.6	3 22.8	23 18.1	24 20.9	23 05.3	20 38.2
18 Su	17 46 36	26 07 10	4♓53 09	10♓52 51	15 19.4	9 37.6	5 45.1	7 32.5	0 57.6	3 17.8	23 20.3	24 21.6	23 07.3	20 38.4
19 M	17 50 33	27 08 15	16 50 25	22 46 25	15D17.9	11 05.2	7 00.5	8 02.7	0 43.5	3 12.6	23 22.7	24 22.2	23 09.2	20 38.6
20 Tu	17 54 29	28 09 21	28 41 30	4♈36 18	15 18.0	12 33.4	8 15.8	8 32.8	0 29.3	3 07.2	23 25.2	24 22.8	23 11.1	20 38.7
21 W	17 58 26	29 10 26	10♈31 30	16 27 44	15 19.2	14 02.1	9 31.2	9 02.7	0 15.1	3 01.7	23 27.8	24 23.3	23 13.1	20 38.8
22 Th	18 02 22	0♑11 32	22 25 40	28 25 54	15 20.8	15 31.2	10 46.6	9 32.5	0 00.9	2 56.0	23 30.4	24 23.8	23 15.0	20 38.9
23 F	18 06 19	1 12 38	4♉29 03	10♉35 39	15R21.9	17 00.8	12 01.9	10 02.1	29♊46.7	2 50.2	23 33.2	24 24.2	23 16.8	20R38.9
24 Sa	18 10 16	2 13 44	16 46 14	23 01 12	15 21.7	18 30.8	13 17.3	10 31.6	29 32.4	2 44.2	23 36.1	24 24.6	23 18.7	20 38.9
25 Su	18 14 12	3 14 51	29 20 56	5♊45 42	15 19.5	20 01.2	14 32.6	11 00.8	29 18.2	2 38.1	23 39.0	24 24.9	23 20.5	20 38.8
26 M	18 18 09	4 15 58	12♊15 39	18 50 52	15 15.1	21 31.9	15 47.9	11 30.0	29 04.1	2 31.9	23 42.1	24 25.1	23 22.4	20 38.7
27 Tu	18 22 05	5 17 05	25 31 17	2♋16 45	15 08.5	23 02.9	17 03.3	11 58.9	28 50.0	2 25.5	23 45.3	24 25.3	23 24.2	20 38.6
28 W	18 26 02	6 18 12	9♋06 56	16 01 30	15 00.3	24 34.3	18 18.6	12 27.7	28 36.0	2 19.0	23 48.5	24 25.4	23 26.0	20 38.5
29 Th	18 29 58	7 19 20	22 59 54	0♌01 37	14 51.1	26 06.0	19 33.9	12 56.3	28 22.1	2 12.4	23 51.9	24R25.5	23 27.7	20 38.3
30 F	18 33 55	8 20 28	7♌06 01	14 12 27	14 42.3	27 38.0	20 49.2	13 24.7	28 08.3	2 05.7	23 55.3	24 25.5	23 29.5	20 38.1
31 Sa	18 37 52	9 21 36	21 20 17	28 28 53	14 34.7	29 10.4	22 04.5	13 53.0	27 54.6	1 58.8	23 58.9	24 25.5	23 31.2	20 37.9

Astro Data	Dy Hr Mn
⚳ R	4 23:32
☿ R	6 17:56
♄☍♅	8 8:21
☽ 0S	9 17:24
♃ R	21 10:22
☽ 0N	23 9:56
♄ D	26 15:33
☿ D	26 17:50
☽ 0S	7 0:26
♂ 0S	12 6:03
☽ 0N	20 17:37
♇ R	23 15:37
♅ R	30 7:30

Planet Ingress	Dy Hr Mn
☿ ♏R	13 3:26
♀ ♐	20 1:06
☉ ♐	22 18:14
♂ ♎	4 0:55
☿ ♐	11 15:27
♀ ♑	13 22:09
☉ ♑	22 7:28
⚳ ♊R	22 13:31

Last Aspect Dy Hr Mn		☽ Ingress	Dy Hr Mn
2 5:36	♄ □	♋	2 17:43
4 11:51	♄ △	♌	4 23:36
6 12:56	♆ □	♍	7 3:10
8 17:47	♅ ☌	♎	9 4:54
9 11:51	♃ ⚹	♏	11 5:53
13 7:19	☿ ☌	♐	13 7:36
15 0:03	♅ □	♑	15 11:37
17 13:04	♀ ⚹	♒	17 19:03
20 0:20	☉ □	♓	20 5:53
22 5:52	♅ ☍	♈	22 18:31
23 3:34	♃ △	♉	25 6:37
27 9:42	♂ △	♊	27 16:31
29 19:42	♂ □	♋	29 23:50

Last Aspect Dy Hr Mn		☽ Ingress	Dy Hr Mn
2 3:14	♂ ⚹	♌	2 5:02
3 20:09	♆ □	♍	4 8:48
6 1:50	♅ ☌	♎	6 11:43
8 1:55	♀ ⚹	♏	8 14:18
10 14:54	☿ ☌	♐	10 17:13
12 18:59	♀ ☌	♑	12 21:30
14 17:41	♅ △	♒	15 4:19
17 3:57	☉ ⚹	♓	17 14:17
19 21:41	☉ □	♈	20 2:39
21 6:24	☿ △	♉	22 15:07
24 14:39	♅ △	♊	25 1:14
26 22:02	♅ □	♋	27 7:58
29 2:27	♅ ⚹	♌	29 11:57
31 13:18	☿ △	♍	31 14:33

☽ Phases & Eclipses Dy Hr Mn	
5 22:18	☾ 13♌03
12 14:26	● 19♏45
12 14:22:50	● T 01'58"
20 0:20	☽ 27♒14
28 2:40	○ 5♊25
5 6:22	☾ 12♍40
12 3:13	● 19♐38
19 21:41	☽ 27♓33
27 17:43	○ 5♋32

Astro Data

1 November 1966
Julian Day # 24411
SVP 5♓43'36"
GC 26♐22.6 ⚴ 4♈13.8R
Eris 10♈58.2R ⚵ 6♌45.8
⚷ 22♓07.6R ⚶ 7♎18.2
☽ Mean ☊ 16♉31.3

1 December 1966
Julian Day # 24441
SVP 5♓43'31"
GC 26♐22.6 ⚴ 1♈10.4
Eris 10♈45.0R ⚵ 13♌20.4
⚷ 21♓40.3R ⚶ 21♎38.6
☽ Mean ☊ 14♉56.0

LONGITUDE — January 1967

Day	Sid.Time	☉	0 hr ☽	Noon ☽	True ☊	☿	♀	♂	⚳	♃	♄	♅	♆	♇
1 Su	18 41 48	10♑22 45	5♍37 41	12♍46 09	14♉29.1	0♑43.0	23♑19.8	14♎21.1	27♊41.1	1♌51.8	24♓02.5	24♍25.4	23♏32.9	20♍37.6
2 M	18 45 45	11 23 53	19 53 53	27 00 31	14R 26.0	2 16.0	24 35.1	14 48.9	27R 27.7	1R 44.7	24 06.2	24R 25.2	23 34.5	20R 37.3
3 Tu	18 49 41	12 25 02	4♎05 46	11♎09 27	14D 25.0	3 49.4	25 50.4	15 16.6	27 14.6	1 37.5	24 10.0	24 25.0	23 36.2	20 36.9
4 W	18 53 38	13 26 12	18 11 25	25 11 36	14 25.4	5 23.1	27 05.6	15 44.1	27 01.6	1 30.3	24 13.9	24 24.8	23 37.8	20 36.6
5 Th	18 57 34	14 27 22	2♏09 56	9♏06 24	14R 26.1	6 57.1	28 20.9	16 11.3	26 48.8	1 22.9	24 17.9	24 24.4	23 39.4	20 36.2
6 F	19 01 31	15 28 32	16 00 58	22 53 34	14 25.9	8 31.5	29 36.2	16 38.4	26 36.3	1 15.4	24 22.0	24 24.1	23 41.0	20 35.7
7 Sa	19 05 27	16 29 42	29 44 10	6♐32 39	14 23.7	10 06.3	0♒51.4	17 05.2	26 24.0	1 07.9	24 26.2	24 23.6	23 42.5	20 35.3
8 Su	19 09 24	17 30 52	13♐18 55	20 02 48	14 18.8	11 41.5	2 06.7	17 31.8	26 11.9	1 00.3	24 30.4	24 23.1	23 44.0	20 34.8
9 M	19 13 21	18 32 03	26 44 07	3♑22 40	14 11.0	13 17.1	3 21.9	17 58.2	26 00.2	0 52.6	24 34.7	24 22.6	23 45.5	20 34.2
10 Tu	19 17 17	19 33 13	9♑58 14	16 30 38	14 00.6	14 53.1	4 37.2	18 24.4	25 48.7	0 44.8	24 39.2	24 22.0	23 47.0	20 33.7
11 W	19 21 14	20 34 23	22 59 40	29 25 10	13 48.4	16 29.6	5 52.4	18 50.3	25 37.5	0 37.0	24 43.7	24 21.3	23 48.4	20 33.1
12 Th	19 25 10	21 35 32	5♒47 04	12♒05 17	13 35.6	18 06.5	7 07.6	19 16.0	25 26.6	0 29.1	24 48.3	24 20.6	23 49.8	20 32.5
13 F	19 29 07	22 36 41	18 19 51	24 30 49	13 23.3	19 43.9	8 22.8	19 41.4	25 16.1	0 21.2	24 52.9	24 19.9	23 51.2	20 31.8
14 Sa	19 33 03	23 37 50	0♓38 23	6♓42 45	13 12.6	21 21.7	9 38.0	20 06.6	25 05.8	0 13.3	24 57.7	24 19.1	23 52.6	20 31.1
15 Su	19 37 00	24 38 57	12 44 15	18 43 15	13 04.3	23 00.1	10 53.2	20 31.5	24 56.0	0 05.3	25 02.5	24 18.2	23 53.9	20 30.4
16 M	19 40 56	25 40 04	24 40 12	0♈35 35	12 58.7	24 38.9	12 08.3	20 56.2	24 46.4	29♋57.3	25 07.4	24 17.3	23 55.2	20 29.7
17 Tu	19 44 53	26 41 11	6♈30 00	12 24 00	12 55.7	26 18.3	13 23.5	21 20.5	24 37.3	29 49.2	25 12.4	24 16.3	23 56.5	20 28.9
18 W	19 48 50	27 42 16	18 18 17	24 13 29	12D 54.7	27 58.2	14 38.6	21 44.7	24 28.5	29 41.2	25 17.4	24 15.3	23 57.7	20 28.1
19 Th	19 52 46	28 43 21	0♉10 18	6♉09 26	12R 54.7	29 38.6	15 53.7	22 08.5	24 20.1	29 33.1	25 22.6	24 14.2	23 58.9	20 27.3
20 F	19 56 43	29 44 25	12 11 36	18 17 28	12 54.7	1♒19.6	17 08.8	22 32.1	24 12.1	29 25.1	25 27.8	24 13.1	24 00.1	20 26.4
21 Sa	20 00 39	0♒45 28	24 27 42	0♊42 53	12 53.5	3 01.1	18 23.8	22 55.3	24 04.5	29 17.0	25 33.0	24 11.9	24 01.3	20 25.6
22 Su	20 04 36	1 46 30	7♊03 36	13 30 17	12 50.1	4 43.2	19 38.9	23 18.3	23 57.2	29 09.0	25 38.4	24 10.6	24 02.4	20 24.6
23 M	20 08 32	2 47 32	20 03 17	26 42 50	12 44.0	6 25.8	20 53.9	23 41.0	23 50.4	29 01.0	25 43.8	24 09.4	24 03.5	20 23.7
24 Tu	20 12 29	3 48 32	3♋29 01	10♋21 46	12 35.2	8 08.8	22 08.9	24 03.4	23 44.0	28 52.9	25 49.3	24 08.1	24 04.6	20 22.8
25 W	20 16 25	4 49 31	17 20 47	24 25 40	12 24.1	9 52.4	23 23.9	24 25.4	23 38.0	28 45.0	25 54.8	24 06.7	24 05.6	20 21.8
26 Th	20 20 22	5 50 30	1♌35 47	8♌50 22	12 11.9	11 36.5	24 38.9	24 47.2	23 32.4	28 37.0	26 00.5	24 05.3	24 06.6	20 20.8
27 F	20 24 19	6 51 28	16 08 33	23 29 19	11 59.8	13 21.0	25 53.8	25 08.6	23 27.2	28 29.1	26 06.1	24 03.8	24 07.6	20 19.7
28 Sa	20 28 15	7 52 25	0♍51 39	8♍14 29	11 49.1	15 05.8	27 08.7	25 29.7	23 22.5	28 21.3	26 11.9	24 02.3	24 08.5	20 18.7
29 Su	20 32 12	8 53 21	15 36 51	22 57 50	11 41.0	16 51.0	28 23.6	25 50.4	23 18.2	28 13.4	26 17.7	24 00.7	24 09.4	20 17.6
30 M	20 36 08	9 54 16	0♎16 38	7♎32 36	11 35.7	18 36.3	29 38.5	26 10.8	23 14.2	28 05.7	26 23.6	23 59.1	24 10.3	20 16.5
31 Tu	20 40 05	10 55 10	14 45 14	21 54 09	11 33.2	20 21.8	0♓53.4	26 30.8	23 10.8	27 58.0	26 29.5	23 57.5	24 11.1	20 15.3

LONGITUDE — February 1967

Day	Sid.Time	☉	0 hr ☽	Noon ☽	True ☊	☿	♀	♂	⚳	♃	♄	♅	♆	♇
1 W	20 44 01	11♒56 04	28♎59 09	6♏00 08	11♉32.5	22♒07.3	2♓08.2	26♎50.5	23♊07.7	27♋50.4	26♓35.5	23♍55.8	24♏11.9	20♍14.2
2 Th	20 47 58	12 56 58	12♏57 05	19 50 06	11R 32.5	23 52.7	3 23.0	27 09.8	23R 05.1	27R 42.8	26 41.5	23R 54.1	24 12.7	20R 13.0
3 F	20 51 54	13 57 50	26 39 19	3♐24 54	11 31.6	25 37.7	4 37.8	27 28.7	23 02.9	27 35.3	26 47.6	23 52.3	24 13.4	20 11.8
4 Sa	20 55 51	14 58 42	10♐07 02	16 45 55	11 28.8	27 22.2	5 52.6	27 47.2	23 01.1	27 27.9	26 53.8	23 50.5	24 14.2	20 10.6
5 Su	20 59 48	15 59 33	23 21 42	29 54 31	11 23.1	29 05.9	7 07.3	28 05.3	22 59.8	27 20.6	27 00.0	23 48.6	24 14.8	20 09.3
6 M	21 03 44	17 00 22	6♑24 30	12♑51 44	11 14.3	0♓48.5	8 22.1	28 23.0	22 58.8	27 13.4	27 06.3	23 46.7	24 15.5	20 08.1
7 Tu	21 07 41	18 01 11	19 16 15	25 38 05	11 02.7	2 29.6	9 36.8	28 40.2	22D 58.4	27 06.3	27 12.6	23 44.8	24 16.1	20 06.8
8 W	21 11 37	19 01 59	1♒57 15	8♒13 44	10 49.1	4 08.9	10 51.4	28 57.0	22 58.3	26 59.3	27 19.0	23 42.8	24 16.7	20 05.5
9 Th	21 15 34	20 02 45	14 27 33	20 38 41	10 34.6	5 46.0	12 06.1	29 13.4	22 58.7	26 52.4	27 25.4	23 40.8	24 17.2	20 04.2
10 F	21 19 30	21 03 30	26 47 11	2♓53 07	10 20.7	7 20.2	13 20.7	29 29.4	22 59.4	26 45.6	27 31.9	23 38.8	24 17.7	20 02.8
11 Sa	21 23 27	22 04 14	8♓56 34	14 57 41	10 08.3	8 51.2	14 35.3	29 44.8	23 00.7	26 38.9	27 38.4	23 36.7	24 18.2	20 01.5
12 Su	21 27 23	23 04 56	20 56 40	26 53 47	9 58.3	10 18.2	15 49.8	29 59.8	23 02.3	26 32.4	27 45.0	23 34.6	24 18.6	20 00.1
13 M	21 31 20	24 05 37	2♈49 21	8♈43 43	9 51.4	11 40.7	17 04.4	0♏14.3	23 04.3	26 25.9	27 51.6	23 32.5	24 19.0	19 58.7
14 Tu	21 35 17	25 06 16	14 37 19	20 30 39	9 47.2	12 57.9	18 18.9	0 28.3	23 06.8	26 19.7	27 58.3	23 30.3	24 19.4	19 57.3
15 W	21 39 13	26 06 53	26 24 14	2♉18 40	9D 45.5	14 09.2	19 33.3	0 41.8	23 09.7	26 13.5	28 05.0	23 28.1	24 19.7	19 55.9
16 Th	21 43 10	27 07 29	8♉14 34	14 12 34	9 45.4	15 13.8	20 47.7	0 54.8	23 12.9	26 07.5	28 11.7	23 25.8	24 20.0	19 54.4
17 F	21 47 06	28 08 03	20 13 22	26 17 40	9R 45.6	16 11.1	22 02.1	1 07.3	23 16.6	26 01.7	28 18.5	23 23.6	24 20.3	19 53.0
18 Sa	21 51 03	29 08 35	2♊26 08	8♊39 28	9 45.2	17 00.3	23 16.5	1 19.3	23 20.7	25 56.0	28 25.3	23 21.3	24 20.5	19 51.5
19 Su	21 54 59	0♓09 05	14 58 18	21 23 13	9 43.2	17 40.9	24 30.8	1 30.7	23 25.2	25 50.4	28 32.2	23 19.0	24 20.8	19 50.0
20 M	21 58 56	1 09 34	27 54 46	4♋33 19	9 38.8	18 12.3	25 45.0	1 41.6	23 30.0	25 45.0	28 39.1	23 16.6	24 20.9	19 48.5
21 Tu	22 02 52	2 10 01	11♋19 10	18 12 27	9 31.9	18 34.2	26 59.3	1 51.9	23 35.3	25 39.8	28 46.0	23 14.3	24 21.1	19 47.0
22 W	22 06 49	3 10 26	25 13 05	2♌20 50	9 23.0	18R 46.1	28 13.5	2 01.6	23 40.9	25 34.7	28 53.0	23 11.9	24 21.2	19 45.5
23 Th	22 10 46	4 10 49	9♌35 12	16 55 31	9 12.8	18 47.9	29 27.6	2 10.8	23 46.9	25 29.8	29 00.0	23 09.5	24 21.2	19 44.0
24 F	22 14 42	5 11 10	24 20 53	1♍50 14	9 02.5	18 39.8	0♈41.7	2 19.3	23 53.3	25 25.0	29 07.1	23 07.0	24R 21.3	19 42.5
25 Sa	22 18 39	6 11 29	9♍22 24	16 56 06	8 53.4	18 21.9	1 55.8	2 27.3	24 00.0	25 20.4	29 14.1	23 04.6	24 21.3	19 40.9
26 Su	22 22 35	7 11 47	24 30 02	2♎02 58	8 46.5	17 54.8	3 09.8	2 34.7	24 07.1	25 16.0	29 21.2	23 02.1	24 21.2	19 39.4
27 M	22 26 32	8 12 04	9♎33 44	17 01 17	8 42.1	17 19.1	4 23.7	2 41.4	24 14.6	25 11.8	29 28.3	22 59.6	24 21.1	19 37.8
28 Tu	22 30 28	9 12 18	24 24 48	1♏43 35	8D 40.3	16 35.7	5 37.7	2 47.5	24 22.4	25 07.7	29 35.5	22 57.1	24 21.0	19 36.2

Astro Data (Dy Hr Mn)

☽0S 3 5:12
♄☍♅ 6 22:53
☽0N 17 0:48
♅⚹♆ 25 22:52
☽0S 30 10:33

♃△♄ 7 0:41
⚳D 8 3:20
☽0N 13 7:20
☿R 23 4:24
♆R 24 22:07
♀0N 25 20:00
☽0S 26 18:48

Planet Ingress (Dy Hr Mn)

☿ ♑ 1 0:52
♀ ♒ 6 19:36
♃ ♋R 16 3:50
☿ ♒ 19 17:05
☉ ♒ 20 18:08
♀ ♓ 30 18:53

☿ ♓ 6 0:38
♂ ♏ 12 12:20
☉ ♓ 19 8:24
♀ ♈ 23 22:30

Last Aspect / ☽ Ingress (January)

Last Aspect Dy Hr Mn			☽ Ingress	Dy Hr Mn
2 7:38	♅	☌	♎	2 17:04
4 15:35	♀	□	♏	4 20:16
6 14:38	♅	⚹	♐	7 0:28
8 20:02	♄	□	♑	9 5:53
11 3:11	♄	⚹	♒	11 13:05
13 10:43	♆	□	♓	13 22:45
16 10:43	♃	△	♈	16 10:48
18 22:54	♃	□	♉	18 23:39
21 9:18	♃	⚹	♊	21 10:38
23 10:14	♄	□	♋	23 17:51
25 19:11	♃	☌	♌	25 21:20
27 16:17	♀	☍	♍	27 22:36
29 20:33	♃	⚹	♎	29 23:33

Last Aspect / ☽ Ingress (February)

Last Aspect Dy Hr Mn			☽ Ingress	Dy Hr Mn
31 22:10	♃	□	♏	1 1:44
3 1:45	♃	△	♐	3 5:55
5 10:17	☿	⚹	♑	5 12:10
7 17:53	♂	□	♒	7 20:17
10 5:10	♂	△	♓	10 6:19
12 13:45	♄	☌	♈	12 18:17
14 23:45	♃	□	♉	15 7:19
17 15:59	♄	⚹	♊	17 19:16
20 1:15	♄	□	♋	20 3:48
22 6:09	♄	△	♌	22 8:04
24 0:01	♆	□	♍	24 9:04
26 7:41	♄	☍	♎	26 8:44
28 1:13	♃	□	♏	28 9:09

☽ Phases & Eclipses (Dy Hr Mn)

3 14:19 ☾ 12♎31
10 18:06 ● 19♑49
18 19:41 ☽ 28♈02
26 6:40 ○ 5♌37

1 23:03 ☾ 12♏24
9 10:44 ● 20♒00
17 15:56 ☽ 28♉18
24 17:43 ○ 5♍26

Astro Data

1 January 1967
Julian Day # 24472
SVP 5♓43'25"
GC 26♐22.7 ⚴ 4♈54.2
Eris 10♈40.6 ⚵ 12♌24.3R
⚷ 22♓03.8 ⚶ 5♏39.8
☽ Mean ☊ 13♉17.6

1 February 1967
Julian Day # 24503
SVP 5♓43'20"
GC 26♐22.8 ⚴ 13♈50.2
Eris 10♈47.0 ⚵ 5♌08.5R
⚷ 23♓14.7 ⚶ 17♏59.3
☽ Mean ☊ 11♉39.1

March 1967

LONGITUDE

Day	Sid.Time	☉	0 hr ☽	Noon ☽	True ☊	☿	♀	♂	⚳	♃	♄	♅	♆	♇
1 W	22 34 25	10♓12 32	8♏57 08	16♏05 10	8♉40.2	15♓45.9	6♈51.5	2♏52.9	24♊30.5	25♋03.8	29♓42.7	22♍54.6	24♏20.9	19♍34.7
2 Th	22 38 21	11 12 44	23 07 31	0♐04 11	8R41.0	14R50.8	8 05.4	2 57.7	24 39.0	25R00.1	29 49.9	22R52.1	24R20.7	19R33.1
3 F	22 42 18	12 12 54	6♐55 17	13 41 00	8 41.4	13 51.9	9 19.2	3 01.8	24 47.9	24 56.6	29 57.1	22 49.5	24 20.5	19 31.5
4 Sa	22 46 15	13 13 03	20 21 37	26 57 24	8 40.4	12 50.7	10 33.0	3 05.2	24 57.0	24 53.2	0♈04.4	22 47.0	24 20.3	19 29.9
5 Su	22 50 11	14 13 11	3♑28 43	9♑55 53	8 37.3	11 48.6	11 46.7	3 07.9	25 06.5	24 50.1	0 11.7	22 44.4	24 20.0	19 28.3
6 M	22 54 08	15 13 16	16 19 15	22 39 06	8 31.8	10 47.2	13 00.3	3 09.9	25 16.4	24 47.1	0 19.0	22 41.8	24 19.7	19 26.7
7 Tu	22 58 04	16 13 21	28 55 44	5♒09 26	8 24.1	9 47.7	14 14.0	3 11.1	25 26.5	24 44.3	0 26.3	22 39.2	24 19.4	19 25.1
8 W	23 02 01	17 13 23	11♒20 26	17 28 57	8 14.8	8 51.3	15 27.5	3R11.7	25 37.0	24 41.7	0 33.6	22 36.6	24 19.0	19 23.5
9 Th	23 05 57	18 13 24	23 35 11	29 39 17	8 04.9	7 59.1	16 41.1	3 11.5	25 47.8	24 39.3	0 41.0	22 34.0	24 18.6	19 21.9
10 F	23 09 54	19 13 22	5♓41 27	11♓41 49	7 55.2	7 11.9	17 54.5	3 10.6	25 58.9	24 37.1	0 48.4	22 31.4	24 18.2	19 20.3
11 Sa	23 13 50	20 13 19	17 40 35	23 37 53	7 46.6	6 30.2	19 08.0	3 08.9	26 10.3	24 35.0	0 55.7	22 28.8	24 17.7	19 18.7
12 Su	23 17 47	21 13 14	29 33 56	5♈28 57	7 39.9	5 54.6	20 21.3	3 06.4	26 22.0	24 33.2	1 03.1	22 26.2	24 17.2	19 17.1
13 M	23 21 44	22 13 07	11♈23 10	17 16 53	7 35.3	5 25.4	21 34.6	3 03.2	26 33.9	24 31.6	1 10.6	22 23.5	24 16.7	19 15.5
14 Tu	23 25 40	23 12 58	23 10 23	29 04 02	7D33.0	5 02.6	22 47.9	2 59.2	26 46.2	24 30.1	1 18.0	22 20.9	24 16.2	19 13.9
15 W	23 29 37	24 12 47	4♉58 15	10♉53 27	7 32.6	4 46.2	24 01.1	2 54.5	26 58.8	24 28.9	1 25.4	22 18.3	24 15.6	19 12.3
16 Th	23 33 33	25 12 33	16 50 07	22 48 47	7 33.6	4 36.3	25 14.3	2 49.0	27 11.6	24 27.8	1 32.9	22 15.7	24 14.9	19 10.7
17 F	23 37 30	26 12 18	28 49 59	4♊54 18	7 35.2	4D32.6	26 27.4	2 42.7	27 24.8	24 27.0	1 40.3	22 13.1	24 14.3	19 09.1
18 Sa	23 41 26	27 12 00	11♊02 21	17 14 42	7R36.6	4 35.0	27 40.4	2 35.6	27 38.2	24 26.3	1 47.8	22 10.5	24 13.6	19 07.5
19 Su	23 45 23	28 11 40	23 31 58	29 54 44	7 37.0	4 43.2	28 53.4	2 27.8	27 51.8	24 25.9	1 55.3	22 07.9	24 12.9	19 05.9
20 M	23 49 19	29 11 18	6♋23 33	12♋58 51	7 36.0	4 56.9	0♉06.3	2 19.2	28 05.7	24D25.6	2 02.7	22 05.3	24 12.2	19 04.3
21 Tu	23 53 16	0♈10 53	19 41 04	26 30 27	7 33.4	5 15.8	1 19.1	2 09.8	28 19.9	24 25.5	2 10.2	22 02.7	24 11.4	19 02.8
22 W	23 57 13	1 10 26	3♌27 09	10♌31 08	7 29.3	5 39.8	2 31.9	1 59.7	28 34.4	24 25.6	2 17.7	22 00.1	24 10.6	19 01.2
23 Th	0 01 09	2 09 57	17 42 10	24 59 50	7 24.3	6 08.4	3 44.6	1 48.9	28 49.0	24 25.9	2 25.2	21 57.5	24 09.8	18 59.7
24 F	0 05 06	3 09 26	2♍23 30	9♍52 21	7 19.1	6 41.5	4 57.3	1 37.2	29 04.0	24 26.4	2 32.7	21 55.0	24 08.9	18 58.1
25 Sa	0 09 02	4 08 52	17 25 22	25 01 22	7 14.4	7 18.8	6 09.8	1 24.9	29 19.1	24 27.1	2 40.1	21 52.4	24 08.1	18 56.6
26 Su	0 12 59	5 08 16	2♎39 06	10♎17 14	7 10.9	8 00.0	7 22.3	1 11.8	29 34.5	24 28.0	2 47.6	21 49.9	24 07.1	18 55.0
27 M	0 16 55	6 07 38	17 54 27	25 29 31	7D09.0	8 44.9	8 34.8	0 58.0	29 50.1	24 29.1	2 55.1	21 47.4	24 06.2	18 53.5
28 Tu	0 20 52	7 06 59	3♏01 16	10♏28 43	7 08.6	9 33.3	9 47.1	0 43.5	0♋06.0	24 30.3	3 02.5	21 44.9	24 05.3	18 52.0
29 W	0 24 48	8 06 17	17 51 03	25 07 36	7 09.4	10 25.0	10 59.4	0 28.3	0 22.0	24 31.8	3 10.0	21 42.4	24 04.3	18 50.5
30 Th	0 28 45	9 05 34	2♐17 57	9♐21 48	7 10.8	11 19.8	12 11.7	0 12.4	0 38.3	24 33.4	3 17.5	21 39.9	24 03.3	18 49.0
31 F	0 32 42	10 04 49	16 19 05	23 09 48	7 12.3	12 17.5	13 23.8	29♎55.9	0 54.9	24 35.3	3 24.9	21 37.5	24 02.2	18 47.5

April 1967

LONGITUDE

Day	Sid.Time	☉	0 hr ☽	Noon ☽	True ☊	☿	♀	♂	⚳	♃	♄	♅	♆	♇
1 Sa	0 36 38	11♈04 02	29♐54 08	6♑32 21	7♉13.1	13♓18.1	14♉35.9	29♎38.8	1♋11.6	24♋37.3	3♈32.4	21♍35.0	24♏01.2	18♍46.1
2 Su	0 40 35	12 03 14	13♑04 45	19 31 46	7R13.0	14 21.3	15 47.9	29R21.0	1 28.5	24 39.5	3 39.8	21R32.6	24R00.1	18R44.6
3 M	0 44 31	13 02 24	25 53 47	2♒11 16	7 11.7	15 27.0	16 59.9	29 02.6	1 45.6	24 41.8	3 47.2	21 30.3	23 59.0	18 43.2
4 Tu	0 48 28	14 01 32	8♒24 40	14 34 25	7 09.4	16 35.1	18 11.7	28 43.7	2 03.0	24 44.4	3 54.6	21 27.9	23 57.8	18 41.7
5 W	0 52 24	15 00 38	20 40 58	26 44 43	7 06.2	17 45.6	19 23.5	28 24.2	2 20.5	24 47.1	4 02.1	21 25.6	23 56.7	18 40.3
6 Th	0 56 21	15 59 42	2♓46 05	8♓45 26	7 02.7	18 58.2	20 35.3	28 04.2	2 38.3	24 50.1	4 09.4	21 23.2	23 55.5	18 38.9
7 F	1 00 17	16 58 44	14 43 07	20 39 27	6 59.2	20 13.0	21 46.9	27 43.8	2 56.2	24 53.2	4 16.8	21 20.9	23 54.3	18 37.6
8 Sa	1 04 14	17 57 44	26 34 45	2♈29 18	6 56.2	21 29.8	22 58.5	27 22.9	3 14.3	24 56.4	4 24.2	21 18.7	23 53.1	18 36.2
9 Su	1 08 11	18 56 43	8♈23 24	14 17 17	6 54.0	22 48.5	24 10.0	27 01.6	3 32.6	24 59.9	4 31.5	21 16.4	23 51.8	18 34.8
10 M	1 12 07	19 55 39	20 11 13	26 05 29	6D52.8	24 09.2	25 21.4	26 40.0	3 51.1	25 03.5	4 38.8	21 14.2	23 50.6	18 33.5
11 Tu	1 16 04	20 54 34	2♉00 20	7♉56 03	6 52.4	25 31.8	26 32.7	26 18.1	4 09.8	25 07.3	4 46.1	21 12.1	23 49.3	18 32.2
12 W	1 20 00	21 53 26	13 52 55	19 51 15	6 52.8	26 56.2	27 44.0	25 55.9	4 28.6	25 11.3	4 53.4	21 09.9	23 48.0	18 30.9
13 Th	1 23 57	22 52 16	25 51 22	1♊53 38	6 53.8	28 22.3	28 55.1	25 33.5	4 47.7	25 15.5	5 00.7	21 07.8	23 46.6	18 29.6
14 F	1 27 53	23 51 05	7♊58 24	14 06 05	6 55.0	29 50.3	0♊06.2	25 10.9	5 06.9	25 19.8	5 07.9	21 05.7	23 45.3	18 28.4
15 Sa	1 31 50	24 49 51	20 17 04	26 31 48	6 56.2	1♈19.9	1 17.2	24 48.2	5 26.2	25 24.3	5 15.1	21 03.7	23 43.9	18 27.2
16 Su	1 35 46	25 48 34	2♋50 42	9♋14 11	6 57.0	2 51.3	2 28.1	24 25.4	5 45.8	25 28.9	5 22.3	21 01.7	23 42.6	18 25.9
17 M	1 39 43	26 47 16	15 42 40	22 16 33	6R57.5	4 24.3	3 38.9	24 02.5	6 05.4	25 33.7	5 29.5	20 59.7	23 41.2	18 24.8
18 Tu	1 43 40	27 45 55	28 56 09	5♌41 45	6 57.4	5 59.1	4 49.6	23 39.7	6 25.3	25 38.7	5 36.6	20 57.8	23 39.7	18 23.6
19 W	1 47 36	28 44 32	12♌33 33	19 31 38	6 56.9	7 35.5	6 00.1	23 16.9	6 45.3	25 43.9	5 43.7	20 55.9	23 38.3	18 22.4
20 Th	1 51 33	29 43 07	26 35 58	3♍46 22	6 56.2	9 13.5	7 10.6	22 54.2	7 05.4	25 49.1	5 50.8	20 54.0	23 36.9	18 21.3
21 F	1 55 29	0♉41 40	11♍02 30	18 23 52	6 55.5	10 53.3	8 21.0	22 31.6	7 25.7	25 54.6	5 57.8	20 52.2	23 35.4	18 20.2
22 Sa	1 59 26	1 40 10	25 49 48	3♎19 29	6 54.9	12 34.7	9 31.3	22 09.2	7 46.2	26 00.2	6 04.9	20 50.4	23 33.9	18 19.1
23 Su	2 03 22	2 38 38	10♎51 58	18 26 09	6 54.5	14 17.8	10 41.5	21 47.1	8 06.8	26 06.0	6 11.8	20 48.6	23 32.5	18 18.1
24 M	2 07 19	3 37 05	26 00 55	3♏35 04	6D54.4	16 02.6	11 51.5	21 25.2	8 27.5	26 11.9	6 18.8	20 46.9	23 31.0	18 17.0
25 Tu	2 11 15	4 35 29	11♏07 28	18 36 59	6 54.4	17 49.0	13 01.5	21 03.6	8 48.3	26 17.9	6 25.7	20 45.3	23 29.5	18 16.0
26 W	2 15 12	5 33 52	26 02 37	3♐23 29	6 54.5	19 37.2	14 11.4	20 42.4	9 09.3	26 24.1	6 32.6	20 43.6	23 27.9	18 15.1
27 Th	2 19 08	6 32 13	10♐38 50	17 48 06	6R54.6	21 27.1	15 21.1	20 21.5	9 30.5	26 30.5	6 39.4	20 42.1	23 26.4	18 14.1
28 F	2 23 05	7 30 33	24 50 54	1♑47 00	6 54.6	23 18.7	16 30.7	20 01.1	9 51.7	26 37.0	6 46.3	20 40.5	23 24.9	18 13.2
29 Sa	2 27 02	8 28 51	8♑36 19	15 18 56	6 54.5	25 12.0	17 40.2	19 41.1	10 13.1	26 43.6	6 53.0	20 39.0	23 23.3	18 12.3
30 Su	2 30 58	9 27 08	21 55 02	28 24 54	6D54.4	27 07.1	18 49.6	19 21.6	10 34.7	26 50.4	6 59.8	20 37.6	23 21.8	18 11.4

Astro Data

	Dy Hr Mn
♂ R	8 17:44
☽ 0N	12 13:28
☿ D	17 14:27
☉0N	21 7:36
♃ D	21 9:16
☽ 0S	26 5:36
☽ 0N	8 19:35
♄0N	12 13:49
☿0N	18 11:13
☽ 0S	22 16:40

Planet Ingress

	Dy Hr Mn
♄ ♈	3 21:32
♀ ♉	20 9:56
☉ ♈	21 7:37
⚳ ♋	28 3:00
♂ ♎R	31 6:10
♀ ♊	14 9:54
☿ ♈	14 14:38
☉ ♉	20 18:55

Last Aspect / ☽ Ingress

Last Aspect Dy Hr Mn		☽ Ingress Dy Hr Mn
2 11:35 ♄ △	♐	2 11:53
4 4:25 ♅ □	♑	4 17:35
6 16:03 ♃ ☍	♒	7 2:03
9 1:26 ♆ □	♓	9 12:41
11 13:55 ♃ △	♈	12 0:53
14 2:44 ♃ □	♉	14 13:54
16 17:13 ☉ ⚹	♊	17 2:19
19 9:53 ♀ ⚹	♋	19 12:10
21 8:22 ♃ ☌	♌	21 18:04
23 10:38 ♆ □	♍	23 20:08
25 11:06 ♃ ⚹	♎	25 19:50
27 10:24 ♃ □	♏	27 19:10
29 11:01 ♃ △	♐	29 20:08

Last Aspect / ☽ Ingress

Last Aspect Dy Hr Mn		☽ Ingress Dy Hr Mn
31 23:48 ♂ ⚹	♑	1 0:11
3 6:08 ♂ □	♒	3 7:49
5 15:12 ♂ △	♓	5 18:29
7 20:36 ♃ △	♈	8 6:57
10 13:08 ♂ ☍	♉	10 19:56
13 5:27 ♀ ☌	♊	13 8:15
15 8:47 ♂ △	♋	15 18:37
17 20:48 ☉ □	♌	18 1:54
20 4:45 ☉ △	♍	20 5:43
22 0:12 ♃ ⚹	♎	22 6:41
24 0:13 ♃ □	♏	24 6:19
26 0:30 ♃ △	♐	26 6:27
27 19:08 ☿ △	♑	28 8:54
30 9:10 ☿ □	♒	30 14:57

☽ Phases & Eclipses

Dy Hr Mn	
3 9:10	☾ 12♐06
11 4:30	● 19♓55
19 8:31	☽ 28♊03
26 3:21	○ 4♎47
1 20:58	☾ 11♑26
9 22:20	● 19♈22
17 20:48	☽ 27♋09
24 12:03	○ 3♏37
24 12:06	☍ T 1.336

Astro Data

1 March 1967
Julian Day # 24531
SVP 5♓43'16"
GC 26♐22.8 ⚴ 24♈54.0
Eris 11♈00.7 ✱ 0♌24.3R
⚷ 24♓45.7 ⚵ 26♏25.3
☽ Mean ☊ 10♉10.1

1 April 1967
Julian Day # 24562
SVP 5♓43'12"
GC 26♐22.9 ⚴ 9♉27.0
Eris 11♈21.0 ✱ 1♌46.2
⚷ 26♓36.4 ⚵ 0♐37.2
☽ Mean ☊ 8♉31.6

LONGITUDE

Day	Sid.Time	☉	0 hr ☽	Noon ☽	True ☊	☿	♀	♂	⚳	♃	♄	♅	♆	♇
1 M	2 34 55	10♉25 23	4♒48 57	11♒07 36	6♉54.3	29♈03.8	19♊58.9	19♎02.6	10♋56.3	26♋57.3	7♈06.5	20♍36.2	23♏20.2	18♍10.5
2 Tu	2 38 51	11 23 36	17 21 21	23 30 44	6 54.4	1♉02.2	21 08.1	18R 44.2	11 18.1	27 04.4	7 13.1	20R 34.8	23R 18.6	18R 09.7
3 W	2 42 48	12 21 48	29 36 18	5♓38 35	6 54.8	3 02.3	22 17.1	18 26.3	11 40.0	27 11.6	7 19.7	20 33.5	23 17.0	18 08.9
4 Th	2 46 44	13 19 58	11♓38 09	17 35 31	6 55.3	5 03.9	23 26.0	18 09.1	12 02.0	27 18.9	7 26.3	20 32.2	23 15.4	18 08.1
5 F	2 50 41	14 18 07	23 31 13	29 25 45	6 56.1	7 07.1	24 34.8	17 52.5	12 24.1	27 26.4	7 32.8	20 31.0	23 13.8	18 07.4
6 Sa	2 54 37	15 16 15	5♈19 34	11♈13 07	6 56.9	9 11.8	25 43.5	17 36.5	12 46.4	27 34.0	7 39.3	20 29.8	23 12.2	18 06.6
7 Su	2 58 34	16 14 21	17 06 48	23 01 01	6 57.5	11 17.9	26 52.0	17 21.3	13 08.7	27 41.7	7 45.7	20 28.7	23 10.6	18 06.0
8 M	3 02 31	17 12 25	28 56 07	4♉52 24	6R 57.8	13 25.2	28 00.4	17 06.7	13 31.2	27 49.5	7 52.1	20 27.6	23 09.0	18 05.3
9 Tu	3 06 27	18 10 28	10♉50 10	16 49 42	6 57.7	15 33.7	29 08.7	16 52.9	13 53.8	27 57.5	7 58.4	20 26.6	23 07.4	18 04.7
10 W	3 10 24	19 08 29	22 51 14	28 55 00	6 56.9	17 43.0	0♋16.8	16 39.9	14 16.5	28 05.6	8 04.7	20 25.6	23 05.7	18 04.0
11 Th	3 14 20	20 06 29	5♊01 12	11♊10 04	6 55.5	19 53.1	1 24.8	16 27.6	14 39.3	28 13.9	8 10.9	20 24.7	23 04.1	18 03.5
12 F	3 18 17	21 04 27	17 21 46	23 36 30	6 53.6	22 03.8	2 32.6	16 16.0	15 02.2	28 22.2	8 17.1	20 23.8	23 02.5	18 02.9
13 Sa	3 22 13	22 02 23	29 54 26	6♋15 47	6 51.5	24 14.7	3 40.3	16 05.3	15 25.2	28 30.7	8 23.3	20 22.9	23 00.9	18 02.4
14 Su	3 26 10	23 00 18	12♋40 44	19 09 26	6 49.5	26 25.6	4 47.8	15 55.4	15 48.3	28 39.3	8 29.3	20 22.2	22 59.2	18 01.9
15 M	3 30 07	23 58 11	25 42 06	2♌18 52	6 47.8	28 36.2	5 55.2	15 46.2	16 11.5	28 48.0	8 35.4	20 21.4	22 57.6	18 01.5
16 Tu	3 34 03	24 56 02	8♌59 56	15 45 24	6D 46.8	0♊46.3	7 02.4	15 37.9	16 34.8	28 56.8	8 41.3	20 20.8	22 56.0	18 01.0
17 W	3 38 00	25 53 51	22 35 23	29 29 56	6 46.6	2 55.5	8 09.4	15 30.4	16 58.2	29 05.7	8 47.2	20 20.1	22 54.3	18 00.6
18 Th	3 41 56	26 51 39	6♍29 04	13♍32 41	6 47.2	5 03.6	9 16.3	15 23.7	17 21.7	29 14.7	8 53.1	20 19.6	22 52.7	18 00.3
19 F	3 45 53	27 49 25	20 40 40	27 52 45	6 48.4	7 10.3	10 23.0	15 17.8	17 45.3	29 23.9	8 58.9	20 19.0	22 51.1	17 59.9
20 Sa	3 49 49	28 47 09	5♎08 35	12♎27 42	6 49.7	9 15.4	11 29.4	15 12.7	18 08.9	29 33.1	9 04.6	20 18.6	22 49.5	17 59.6
21 Su	3 53 46	29 44 52	19 49 31	27 13 22	6R 50.6	11 18.6	12 35.8	15 08.5	18 32.7	29 42.5	9 10.3	20 18.1	22 47.9	17 59.4
22 M	3 57 42	0♊42 33	4♏38 28	12♏03 56	6 50.8	13 19.8	13 41.9	15 05.0	18 56.5	29 51.9	9 15.9	20 17.8	22 46.2	17 59.1
23 Tu	4 01 39	1 40 12	19 28 53	26 52 21	6 49.8	15 18.8	14 47.8	15 02.3	19 20.4	0♌01.5	9 21.4	20 17.5	22 44.6	17 58.9
24 W	4 05 36	2 37 51	4♐13 24	11♐31 09	6 47.5	17 15.3	15 53.5	15 00.5	19 44.4	0 11.1	9 26.9	20 17.2	22 43.0	17 58.7
25 Th	4 09 32	3 35 28	18 44 46	25 53 33	6 44.2	19 09.3	16 59.0	14D 59.4	20 08.5	0 20.9	9 32.3	20 17.0	22 41.4	17 58.6
26 F	4 13 29	4 33 05	2♑56 54	9♑54 21	6 40.3	21 00.7	18 04.3	14 59.1	20 32.7	0 30.7	9 37.7	20 16.9	22 39.9	17 58.5
27 Sa	4 17 25	5 30 40	16 45 36	23 30 29	6 36.2	22 49.5	19 09.4	14 59.5	20 56.9	0 40.7	9 43.0	20 16.8	22 38.3	17 58.4
28 Su	4 21 22	6 28 14	0♒08 59	6♒41 13	6 32.6	24 35.4	20 14.3	15 00.8	21 21.3	0 50.7	9 48.2	20D 16.7	22 36.7	17 58.3
29 M	4 25 18	7 25 47	13 07 26	19 27 58	6 29.9	26 18.5	21 18.9	15 02.8	21 45.6	1 00.8	9 53.3	20 16.7	22 35.1	17D 58.3
30 Tu	4 29 15	8 23 20	25 43 14	1♓53 44	6D 28.5	27 58.7	22 23.4	15 05.5	22 10.1	1 11.0	9 58.4	20 16.8	22 33.6	17 58.3
31 W	4 33 11	9 20 51	8♓00 02	14 02 41	6 28.4	29 36.0	23 27.6	15 09.0	22 34.7	1 21.3	10 03.4	20 16.9	22 32.0	17 58.3

LONGITUDE

Day	Sid.Time	☉	0 hr ☽	Noon ☽	True ☊	☿	♀	♂	⚳	♃	♄	♅	♆	♇
1 Th	4 37 08	10♊18 22	20♓02 20	25♓59 35	6♉29.3	1♋10.4	24♋31.5	15♎13.2	22♋59.3	1♌31.7	10♈08.4	20♍17.0	22♏30.5	17♍58.4
2 F	4 41 05	11 15 52	1♈55 04	7♈49 25	6 30.9	2 41.7	25 35.2	15 18.2	23 24.0	1 42.2	10 13.3	20 17.3	22R 29.0	17 58.5
3 Sa	4 45 01	12 13 21	13 43 12	19 37 02	6 32.6	4 10.1	26 38.7	15 23.8	23 48.7	1 52.8	10 18.1	20 17.5	22 27.4	17 58.6
4 Su	4 48 58	13 10 49	25 31 28	1♉27 00	6R 33.7	5 35.4	27 41.9	15 30.2	24 13.6	2 03.4	10 22.8	20 17.9	22 25.9	17 58.8
5 M	4 52 54	14 08 17	7♉24 06	13 23 13	6 33.5	6 57.7	28 44.8	15 37.3	24 38.5	2 14.2	10 27.4	20 18.2	22 24.4	17 59.0
6 Tu	4 56 51	15 05 44	19 24 44	25 28 58	6 31.8	8 16.8	29 47.5	15 45.0	25 03.4	2 25.0	10 32.0	20 18.7	22 23.0	17 59.2
7 W	5 00 47	16 03 10	1♊36 13	7♊46 41	6 28.3	9 32.8	0♌49.9	15 53.5	25 28.5	2 35.9	10 36.5	20 19.2	22 21.5	17 59.5
8 Th	5 04 44	17 00 35	14 00 32	20 17 53	6 23.0	10 45.6	1 52.0	16 02.6	25 53.6	2 46.8	10 40.9	20 19.7	22 20.1	17 59.7
9 F	5 08 40	17 58 00	26 38 49	3♋03 19	6 16.5	11 55.2	2 53.8	16 12.4	26 18.8	2 57.9	10 45.3	20 20.3	22 18.6	18 00.1
10 Sa	5 12 37	18 55 23	9♋31 23	16 02 57	6 09.3	13 01.4	3 55.3	16 22.9	26 44.0	3 09.0	10 49.5	20 20.9	22 17.2	18 00.4
11 Su	5 16 34	19 52 46	22 37 55	29 16 13	6 02.2	14 04.2	4 56.5	16 33.9	27 09.3	3 20.2	10 53.7	20 21.6	22 15.8	18 00.8
12 M	5 20 30	20 50 08	5♌57 42	12♌42 17	5 56.2	15 03.5	5 57.3	16 45.7	27 34.6	3 31.4	10 57.8	20 22.4	22 14.4	18 01.2
13 Tu	5 24 27	21 47 29	19 29 49	26 20 13	5 51.7	15 59.3	6 57.9	16 58.0	28 00.0	3 42.8	11 01.8	20 23.2	22 13.0	18 01.7
14 W	5 28 23	22 44 48	3♍13 23	10♍09 13	5D 49.2	16 51.5	7 58.0	17 10.9	28 25.5	3 54.2	11 05.8	20 24.1	22 11.7	18 02.2
15 Th	5 32 20	23 42 07	17 07 37	24 08 30	5 48.5	17 39.9	8 57.8	17 24.5	28 51.0	4 05.6	11 09.6	20 25.0	22 10.3	18 02.7
16 F	5 36 16	24 39 25	1♎11 44	8♎17 12	5 49.0	18 24.5	9 57.3	17 38.6	29 16.6	4 17.2	11 13.4	20 25.9	22 09.0	18 03.2
17 Sa	5 40 13	25 36 42	15 24 43	22 34 04	5R 50.1	19 05.2	10 56.3	17 53.3	29 42.2	4 28.8	11 17.1	20 26.9	22 07.7	18 03.8
18 Su	5 44 09	26 33 58	29 44 58	6♏57 05	5 50.6	19 41.9	11 54.9	18 08.5	0♌07.9	4 40.4	11 20.7	20 28.0	22 06.4	18 04.4
19 M	5 48 06	27 31 13	14♏09 58	21 23 08	5 49.6	20 14.4	12 53.2	18 24.3	0 33.6	4 52.1	11 24.2	20 29.1	22 05.2	18 05.0
20 Tu	5 52 03	28 28 28	28 36 01	5♐48 00	5 46.5	20 42.7	13 50.9	18 40.6	0 59.4	5 03.9	11 27.6	20 30.3	22 03.9	18 05.7
21 W	5 55 59	29 25 42	12♐58 26	20 06 36	5 41.1	21 06.6	14 48.3	18 57.5	1 25.3	5 15.7	11 31.0	20 31.5	22 02.7	18 06.4
22 Th	5 59 56	0♋22 56	27 11 51	4♑13 32	5 33.7	21 26.1	15 45.2	19 14.8	1 51.1	5 27.6	11 34.2	20 32.8	22 01.5	18 07.1
23 F	6 03 52	1 20 10	11♑11 03	18 03 54	5 24.9	21 41.2	16 41.6	19 32.7	2 17.1	5 39.6	11 37.4	20 34.1	22 00.4	18 07.8
24 Sa	6 07 49	2 17 23	24 51 41	1♒34 06	5 15.7	21 51.7	17 37.6	19 51.1	2 43.0	5 51.6	11 40.4	20 35.5	21 59.2	18 08.6
25 Su	6 11 45	3 14 35	8♒10 59	14 42 17	5 07.1	21R 57.6	18 33.0	20 09.9	3 09.1	6 03.6	11 43.4	20 36.9	21 58.1	18 09.4
26 M	6 15 42	4 11 48	21 08 04	27 28 32	4 59.9	21 58.9	19 28.0	20 29.2	3 35.1	6 15.7	11 46.3	20 38.4	21 57.0	18 10.3
27 Tu	6 19 39	5 09 01	3♓43 58	9♓54 46	4 54.7	21 55.6	20 22.4	20 49.0	4 01.2	6 27.9	11 49.1	20 39.9	21 55.9	18 11.2
28 W	6 23 35	6 06 13	16 01 24	22 04 23	4 51.6	21 47.8	21 16.2	21 09.2	4 27.4	6 40.1	11 51.8	20 41.4	21 54.8	18 12.1
29 Th	6 27 32	7 03 26	28 04 19	4♈01 48	4D 50.5	21 35.7	22 09.5	21 29.9	4 53.6	6 52.3	11 54.4	20 43.1	21 53.8	18 13.0
30 F	6 31 28	8 00 38	9♈57 31	15 52 07	4 50.7	21 19.3	23 02.2	21 51.0	5 19.8	7 04.6	11 56.9	20 44.7	21 52.7	18 13.9

Astro Data

	Dy Hr Mn
☽ 0N	6 1:54
♄⚼♆	10 15:06
☽ 0S	20 1:45
♂ D	26 9:29
♅ D	28 21:36
♇ D	29 20:30
☽ 0N	2 8:32
♃∠♇	9 16:55
☽ 0S	16 8:02
♃∠♅	22 23:40
☿ R	26 6:50
☽ 0N	29 15:28

Planet Ingress

	Dy Hr Mn
☿ ♉	1 23:26
♀ ♋	10 6:05
☿ ♊	16 3:27
☉ ♊	21 18:18
♃ ♌	23 8:21
☿ ♋	31 18:02
♀ ♌	6 16:48
⚳ ♌	18 4:37
☉ ♋	22 2:23

Last Aspect / ☽ Ingress (May)

Last Aspect Dy Hr Mn		☽ Ingress Dy Hr Mn
2 11:36	♆ □	♓ 3 0:47
5 7:55	♃ △	♈ 5 13:10
7 21:36	♃ □	♉ 8 2:09
10 10:21	♃ ✶	♊ 10 14:08
12 5:51	♅ □	♋ 13 0:11
15 5:34	♃ ☌	♌ 15 7:49
17 5:18	☉ □	♍ 17 12:52
19 14:33	♃ ✶	♎ 19 15:31
21 16:04	♃ □	♏ 21 16:30
23 5:18	♆ ☌	♐ 23 17:06
25 2:34	♅ □	♑ 25 18:58
27 10:27	♆ ✶	♒ 27 23:44
30 3:12	☿ △	♓ 30 8:18

Last Aspect / ☽ Ingress (June)

Last Aspect Dy Hr Mn		☽ Ingress Dy Hr Mn
1 8:45	♀ △	♈ 1 20:07
4 3:40	♀ □	♉ 4 9:04
6 5:54	♆ ☍	♊ 6 20:52
8 12:03	♅ □	♋ 9 6:18
10 23:21	♆ △	♌ 11 13:19
13 4:48	♆ □	♍ 13 18:24
15 11:12	☉ □	♎ 15 21:58
17 17:27	☉ △	♏ 18 0:25
19 13:10	♆ ☌	♐ 20 2:20
21 12:42	♅ □	♑ 22 4:46
23 18:56	♆ ✶	♒ 24 9:11
26 1:33	♆ □	♓ 26 16:49
28 11:41	♆ △	♈ 29 3:53

☽ Phases & Eclipses

Dy Hr Mn	
1 10:33	☾ 10♒22
9 14:55	● 18♉18
9 14:42:09	• P 0.720
17 5:18	☽ 25♌38
23 20:22	○ 2♐00
31 1:52	☾ 8♓57
8 5:13	● 16♊44
15 11:12	☽ 23♍40
22 4:57	○ 0♑06
29 18:39	☾ 7♈19

Astro Data

1 May 1967
Julian Day # 24592
SVP 5♓43'08"
GC 26♐23.0 ⚴ 25♉13.2
Eris 11♈40.8 ⚵ 8♌12.6
⚷ 28♓13.3 ⚶ 27♏38.8R
☽ Mean ☊ 6♉56.3

1 June 1967
Julian Day # 24623
SVP 5♓43'04"
GC 26♐23.1 ⚴ 12♊47.3
Eris 11♈56.5 ⚵ 17♌48.3
⚷ 29♓23.7 ⚶ 20♏31.2R
☽ Mean ☊ 5♉17.8

July 1967 LONGITUDE

Day	Sid.Time	☉	0 hr ☽	Noon ☽	True ☊	☿	♀	♂	⚳	♃	♄	♅	♆	♇
1 Sa	6 35 25	8♋57 51	21♈46 16	27♈40 40	4♉51.3	20♋58.8	23♌54.3	22♎12.6	5♌46.1	7♌17.0	11♈59.3	20♍46.4	21♏51.8	18♍14.9
2 Su	6 39 21	9 55 04	3♉35 56	9♉32 43	4R 51.4	20R 34.7	24 45.8	22 34.6	6 12.5	7 29.4	12 01.7	20 48.2	21R 50.8	18 15.9
3 M	6 43 18	10 52 17	15 31 37	21 33 11	4 50.0	20 07.1	25 36.6	22 57.0	6 38.8	7 41.8	12 03.9	20 50.0	21 49.8	18 17.0
4 Tu	6 47 14	11 49 30	27 37 55	3♊46 17	4 46.5	19 36.5	26 26.8	23 19.8	7 05.3	7 54.3	12 06.0	20 51.8	21 48.9	18 18.0
5 W	6 51 11	12 46 44	9♊58 37	16 15 15	4 40.4	19 03.3	27 16.2	23 43.1	7 31.7	8 06.8	12 08.1	20 53.7	21 48.0	18 19.1
6 Th	6 55 08	13 43 57	22 36 21	29 02 04	4 32.0	18 28.0	28 05.0	24 06.7	7 58.2	8 19.3	12 10.0	20 55.7	21 47.2	18 20.3
7 F	6 59 04	14 41 11	5♋32 23	12♋07 15	4 21.7	17 51.3	28 53.0	24 30.7	8 24.7	8 31.9	12 11.9	20 57.7	21 46.3	18 21.4
8 Sa	7 03 01	15 38 25	18 46 29	25 29 51	4 10.4	17 13.7	29 40.2	24 55.1	8 51.3	8 44.6	12 13.6	20 59.7	21 45.5	18 22.6
9 Su	7 06 57	16 35 39	2♌17 00	9♌07 36	3 59.2	16 35.8	0♍26.6	25 19.9	9 17.9	8 57.3	12 15.2	21 01.8	21 44.8	18 23.8
10 M	7 10 54	17 32 53	16 01 12	22 57 22	3 49.4	15 58.4	1 12.2	25 45.1	9 44.6	9 10.0	12 16.8	21 03.9	21 44.0	18 25.1
11 Tu	7 14 50	18 30 07	29 55 42	6♍55 45	3 41.7	15 21.9	1 56.9	26 10.6	10 11.2	9 22.7	12 18.2	21 06.1	21 43.3	18 26.3
12 W	7 18 47	19 27 20	13♍57 08	20 59 31	3 36.7	14 47.2	2 40.7	26 36.5	10 37.9	9 35.5	12 19.6	21 08.3	21 42.6	18 27.6
13 Th	7 22 43	20 24 34	28 02 37	5♎06 11	3 34.2	14 14.8	3 23.5	27 02.7	11 04.7	9 48.3	12 20.8	21 10.5	21 41.9	18 28.9
14 F	7 26 40	21 21 48	12♎10 01	19 13 57	3D 33.5	13 45.3	4 05.4	27 29.3	11 31.4	10 01.1	12 21.9	21 12.8	21 41.3	18 30.3
15 Sa	7 30 37	22 19 01	26 17 51	3♏21 37	3R 33.6	13 19.2	4 46.2	27 56.2	11 58.2	10 13.9	12 23.0	21 15.2	21 40.7	18 31.6
16 Su	7 34 33	23 16 15	10♏25 07	17 28 12	3 33.1	12 57.0	5 26.0	28 23.4	12 25.1	10 26.8	12 23.9	21 17.5	21 40.1	18 33.0
17 M	7 38 30	24 13 29	24 30 43	1♐32 28	3 30.9	12 39.2	6 04.6	28 51.0	12 51.9	10 39.7	12 24.7	21 20.0	21 39.5	18 34.4
18 Tu	7 42 26	25 10 43	8♐33 11	15 32 35	3 26.2	12 26.1	6 42.1	29 18.9	13 18.8	10 52.7	12 25.5	21 22.4	21 39.0	18 35.9
19 W	7 46 23	26 07 58	22 30 18	29 25 59	3 18.8	12 18.1	7 18.4	29 47.1	13 45.7	11 05.6	12 26.1	21 24.9	21 38.5	18 37.3
20 Th	7 50 19	27 05 12	6♑19 12	13♑09 34	3 08.8	12D 15.3	7 53.5	0♏15.5	14 12.7	11 18.6	12 26.6	21 27.5	21 38.1	18 38.8
21 F	7 54 16	28 02 27	19 56 40	26 40 08	2 57.0	12 18.1	8 27.2	0 44.3	14 39.6	11 31.6	12 27.1	21 30.0	21 37.6	18 40.3
22 Sa	7 58 12	28 59 43	3♒19 37	9♒54 51	2 44.6	12 26.6	8 59.7	1 13.4	15 06.6	11 44.6	12 27.4	21 32.7	21 37.2	18 41.8
23 Su	8 02 09	29 56 59	16 25 40	22 51 57	2 32.8	12 40.8	9 30.7	1 42.7	15 33.6	11 57.6	12 27.6	21 35.3	21 36.9	18 43.4
24 M	8 06 06	0♌54 16	29 13 40	5♓30 56	2 22.6	13 00.9	10 00.3	2 12.4	16 00.7	12 10.7	12R 27.7	21 38.0	21 36.5	18 45.0
25 Tu	8 10 02	1 51 33	11♓43 53	17 52 49	2 14.7	13 26.8	10 28.4	2 42.3	16 27.7	12 23.8	12 27.7	21 40.7	21 36.2	18 46.6
26 W	8 13 59	2 48 51	23 58 05	0♈00 04	2 09.4	13 58.7	10 55.0	3 12.5	16 54.8	12 36.9	12 27.7	21 43.5	21 35.9	18 48.2
27 Th	8 17 55	3 46 11	5♈59 18	11 56 18	2 06.5	14 36.5	11 20.0	3 42.9	17 21.9	12 50.0	12 27.5	21 46.3	21 35.7	18 49.8
28 F	8 21 52	4 43 31	17 51 41	23 46 04	2D 05.5	15 20.1	11 43.3	4 13.6	17 49.1	13 03.1	12 27.2	21 49.1	21 35.5	18 51.5
29 Sa	8 25 48	5 40 52	29 40 08	5♉34 33	2R 05.4	16 09.5	12 04.9	4 44.6	18 16.2	13 16.2	12 26.8	21 52.0	21 35.3	18 53.1
30 Su	8 29 45	6 38 14	11♉30 00	17 27 10	2 05.1	17 04.6	12 24.7	5 15.8	18 43.4	13 29.3	12 26.3	21 54.9	21 35.1	18 54.8
31 M	8 33 41	7 35 38	23 26 45	29 29 23	2 03.7	18 05.4	12 42.8	5 47.3	19 10.6	13 42.5	12 25.7	21 57.8	21 35.0	18 56.6

August 1967 LONGITUDE

Day	Sid.Time	☉	0 hr ☽	Noon ☽	True ☊	☿	♀	♂	⚳	♃	♄	♅	♆	♇
1 Tu	8 37 38	8♌33 02	5♊35 41	11♊46 12	2♉00.2	19♋11.7	12♍58.9	6♏19.0	19♌37.8	13♌55.7	12♈25.0	22♍00.8	21♏34.9	18♍58.3
2 W	8 41 35	9 30 28	18 01 27	24 21 49	1R 54.2	20 23.3	13 13.1	6 51.0	20 05.1	14 08.8	12R 24.2	22 03.8	21R 34.9	19 00.1
3 Th	8 45 31	10 27 54	0♋47 39	7♋19 09	1 45.7	21 40.3	13 25.3	7 23.3	20 32.3	14 22.0	12 23.3	22 06.8	21D 34.9	19 01.8
4 F	8 49 28	11 25 22	13 56 23	20 39 19	1 35.2	23 02.3	13 35.4	7 55.7	20 59.6	14 35.2	12 22.3	22 09.9	21 34.9	19 03.6
5 Sa	8 53 24	12 22 51	27 27 47	4♌21 27	1 23.6	24 29.1	13 43.5	8 28.4	21 26.9	14 48.4	12 21.2	22 13.0	21 34.9	19 05.4
6 Su	8 57 21	13 20 21	11♌19 52	18 22 29	1 12.1	26 00.6	13 49.3	9 01.4	21 54.3	15 01.6	12 20.0	22 16.1	21 35.0	19 07.3
7 M	9 01 17	14 17 52	25 28 39	2♍37 41	1 01.8	27 36.5	13 53.0	9 34.6	22 21.6	15 14.8	12 18.7	22 19.3	21 35.1	19 09.1
8 Tu	9 05 14	15 15 23	9♍48 48	17 01 17	0 53.8	29 16.5	13R 54.4	10 08.0	22 48.9	15 28.0	12 17.3	22 22.4	21 35.2	19 11.0
9 W	9 09 10	16 12 56	24 14 26	1♎27 33	0 48.6	1♌00.3	13 53.5	10 41.6	23 16.3	15 41.2	12 15.8	22 25.6	21 35.4	19 12.9
10 Th	9 13 07	17 10 29	8♎40 05	15 51 30	0 45.9	2 47.5	13 50.2	11 15.5	23 43.7	15 54.4	12 14.2	22 28.9	21 35.6	19 14.8
11 F	9 17 04	18 08 03	23 01 26	0♏09 32	0D 45.3	4 37.9	13 44.6	11 49.5	24 11.1	16 07.5	12 12.5	22 32.1	21 35.9	19 16.7
12 Sa	9 21 00	19 05 38	7♏15 36	14 19 27	0R 45.5	6 30.9	13 36.5	12 23.8	24 38.5	16 20.7	12 10.7	22 35.4	21 36.1	19 18.6
13 Su	9 24 57	20 03 14	21 20 59	28 20 08	0 45.3	8 26.2	13 26.1	12 58.3	25 05.9	16 33.9	12 08.8	22 38.7	21 36.4	19 20.5
14 M	9 28 53	21 00 51	5♐16 53	12♐11 11	0 43.6	10 23.5	13 13.3	13 33.0	25 33.3	16 47.1	12 06.9	22 42.1	21 36.8	19 22.5
15 Tu	9 32 50	21 58 29	19 03 00	25 52 19	0 39.6	12 22.3	12 58.1	14 07.8	26 00.7	17 00.2	12 04.8	22 45.5	21 37.1	19 24.5
16 W	9 36 46	22 56 08	2♑39 03	9♑23 06	0 33.1	14 22.3	12 40.5	14 42.9	26 28.2	17 13.4	12 02.6	22 48.8	21 37.5	19 26.5
17 Th	9 40 43	23 53 48	16 04 23	22 42 46	0 24.2	16 23.1	12 20.7	15 18.2	26 55.6	17 26.5	12 00.4	22 52.3	21 38.0	19 28.5
18 F	9 44 39	24 51 29	29 18 06	5♒50 16	0 13.6	18 24.4	11 58.6	15 53.7	27 23.1	17 39.7	11 58.0	22 55.7	21 38.4	19 30.5
19 Sa	9 48 36	25 49 11	12♒19 08	18 44 35	0 02.5	20 25.9	11 34.4	16 29.3	27 50.6	17 52.8	11 55.6	22 59.1	21 38.9	19 32.5
20 Su	9 52 33	26 46 55	25 06 33	1♓24 59	29♈51.8	22 27.3	11 08.1	17 05.1	28 18.0	18 05.9	11 53.1	23 02.6	21 39.5	19 34.5
21 M	9 56 29	27 44 40	7♓39 55	13 51 23	29 42.5	24 28.5	10 40.0	17 41.2	28 45.5	18 19.0	11 50.4	23 06.1	21 40.0	19 36.6
22 Tu	10 00 26	28 42 26	19 59 33	26 04 35	29 35.3	26 29.1	10 10.0	18 17.4	29 13.0	18 32.1	11 47.7	23 09.6	21 40.6	19 38.6
23 W	10 04 22	29 40 14	2♈06 44	8♈06 19	29 30.6	28 29.1	9 38.4	18 53.7	29 40.5	18 45.1	11 45.0	23 13.1	21 41.2	19 40.7
24 Th	10 08 19	0♍38 03	14 03 44	19 59 23	29D 28.3	0♍28.3	9 05.4	19 30.3	0♍08.0	18 58.2	11 42.1	23 16.7	21 41.9	19 42.8
25 F	10 12 15	1 35 54	25 53 47	1♉47 27	29 27.8	2 26.5	8 31.2	20 07.0	0 35.5	19 11.2	11 39.1	23 20.3	21 42.6	19 44.8
26 Sa	10 16 12	2 33 47	7♉40 57	13 34 55	29 28.5	4 23.8	7 55.9	20 43.9	1 03.0	19 24.2	11 36.1	23 23.8	21 43.3	19 46.9
27 Su	10 20 08	3 31 42	19 29 59	25 26 48	29R 29.4	6 19.9	7 19.8	21 20.9	1 30.5	19 37.2	11 33.0	23 27.5	21 44.0	19 49.0
28 M	10 24 05	4 29 39	1♊26 02	7♊28 21	29 29.6	8 14.9	6 43.0	21 58.2	1 58.1	19 50.2	11 29.8	23 31.1	21 44.8	19 51.2
29 Tu	10 28 02	5 27 37	13 34 25	19 44 52	29 28.5	10 08.7	6 06.0	22 35.6	2 25.6	20 03.1	11 26.5	23 34.7	21 45.6	19 53.3
30 W	10 31 58	6 25 37	26 00 16	2♋21 09	29 25.4	12 01.3	5 28.8	23 13.1	2 53.1	20 16.0	11 23.2	23 38.4	21 46.4	19 55.4
31 Th	10 35 55	7 23 40	8♋47 58	15 21 05	29 20.2	13 52.7	4 51.7	23 50.9	3 20.7	20 28.9	11 19.8	23 42.0	21 47.3	19 57.5

Astro Data	Dy Hr Mn
☽0S	13 12:41
☿ D	20 12:01
♅✶♆	24 0:24
♄ R	25 4:08
♃△♄	25 19:16
☽0N	26 22:34
♆ D	3 15:20
♀ R	8 14:29
☽0S	9 18:01
☽0N	23 5:36
♃⊻♇	28 14:11

Planet Ingress		Dy Hr Mn
♀	♍	8 22:11
♂	♏	19 22:56
☉	♌	23 13:16
☿	♌	8 22:09
☊	♈R	19 17:23
☉	♍	23 20:12
⚳	♍	24 5:01
☿	♍	24 6:17

Last Aspect Dy Hr Mn		☽ Ingress	Dy Hr Mn
1 3:44	♀ △	♉	1 16:43
3 20:37	♀ □	♊	4 4:39
6 10:07	♀ ✶	♋	6 13:47
8 10:56	♂ □	♌	8 19:58
10 16:58	♂ ✶	♍	11 0:07
12 13:13	♆ ✶	♎	13 3:20
15 2:29	♂ ☌	♏	15 6:17
16 22:36	☉ △	♐	17 9:22
19 12:38	♂ ✶	♑	19 12:59
21 14:39	☉ ☍	♒	21 17:59
23 9:40	♆ □	♓	24 1:28
25 19:30	♅ ☍	♈	26 12:00
27 17:44	☿ □	♉	29 0:40
30 20:59	♅ △	♊	31 13:00

Last Aspect Dy Hr Mn		☽ Ingress	Dy Hr Mn
2 7:39	♅ □	♋	2 22:32
4 16:42	☿ ☌	♌	5 4:26
6 17:26	♆ □	♍	7 7:36
8 20:56	♅ ☌	♎	9 9:34
10 14:22	☉ ✶	♏	11 11:44
13 2:11	♅ ✶	♐	13 14:52
15 6:29	♅ □	♑	15 19:18
17 12:17	♅ △	♒	18 1:17
20 2:27	☉ ☍	♓	20 9:18
22 6:13	♅ ☍	♈	22 19:47
24 9:54	♃ △	♉	25 8:21
27 7:58	♅ △	♊	27 21:08
29 19:24	♅ □	♋	30 7:34

☽ Phases & Eclipses Dy Hr Mn	
7 17:00	● 14♋53
14 15:53	☽ 21♎31
21 14:39	○ 28♑09
29 12:14	☾ 5♉41
6 2:48	● 12♌58
12 20:44	☽ 19♏27
20 2:27	○ 26♒24
28 5:35	☾ 4♊14

Astro Data

1 July 1967
Julian Day # 24653
SVP 5♓42'58"
GC 26♐23.1 ⚴ 0♋34.2
Eris 12♈03.7 ⚵ 28♌32.8
⚷ 29♓49.7 ⚶ 17♏48.1
☽Mean ☊ 3♉42.5

1 August 1967
Julian Day # 24684
SVP 5♓42'53"
GC 26♐23.2 ⚴ 19♋12.4
Eris 12♈01.1R ⚵ 10♍21.4
⚷ 29♓27.8R ⚶ 22♏11.3
☽Mean ☊ 2♉04.0

LONGITUDE — September 1967

Day	Sid.Time	☉	0 hr ☽	Noon☽	True☊	☿	♀	♂	⚳	♃	♄	♅	♆	♇
1 F	10 39 51	8♍21 44	22♋00 43	28♋46 59	29♈13.4	15♍42.8	4♍15.0	24♏28.8	3♍48.2	20♌41.8	11♈16.3	23♍45.7	21♏48.2	19♍59.7
2 Sa	10 43 48	9 19 49	5♌39 49	12♌39 01	29R 05.6	17 31.7	3R 38.9	25 06.8	4 15.7	20 54.6	11R 12.7	23 49.4	21 49.2	20 01.8
3 Su	10 47 44	10 17 57	19 44 10	26 54 46	28 57.6	19 19.3	3 03.6	25 45.0	4 43.3	21 07.5	11 09.1	23 53.1	21 50.1	20 04.0
4 M	10 51 41	11 16 06	4♍10 04	11♍29 17	28 50.6	21 05.7	2 29.3	26 23.4	5 10.8	21 20.2	11 05.4	23 56.8	21 51.1	20 06.2
5 Tu	10 55 37	12 14 17	18 51 29	26 15 40	28 45.2	22 50.9	1 56.3	27 01.9	5 38.3	21 33.0	11 01.6	24 00.5	21 52.1	20 08.3
6 W	10 59 34	13 12 30	3♎40 51	11♎06 02	28 41.9	24 34.9	1 24.7	27 40.6	6 05.8	21 45.7	10 57.8	24 04.2	21 53.2	20 10.5
7 Th	11 03 31	14 10 44	18 30 18	25 52 49	28D 40.7	26 17.7	0 54.6	28 19.4	6 33.4	21 58.3	10 53.9	24 08.0	21 54.3	20 12.6
8 F	11 07 27	15 09 00	3♏12 51	10♏29 47	28 41.1	27 59.3	0 26.4	28 58.4	7 00.9	22 11.0	10 49.9	24 11.7	21 55.4	20 14.8
9 Sa	11 11 24	16 07 17	17 43 10	24 52 37	28 42.3	29 39.7	29♌60.0	29 37.5	7 28.4	22 23.6	10 45.9	24 15.5	21 56.5	20 17.0
10 Su	11 15 20	17 05 36	1♐57 55	8♐58 56	28R 43.4	1♎19.0	29 35.6	0♐16.8	7 55.9	22 36.1	10 41.9	24 19.2	21 57.7	20 19.2
11 M	11 19 17	18 03 56	15 55 36	22 47 56	28 43.5	2 57.1	29 13.3	0 56.2	8 23.4	22 48.7	10 37.7	24 23.0	21 58.9	20 21.4
12 Tu	11 23 13	19 02 18	29 36 02	6♑19 59	28 42.1	4 34.2	28 53.3	1 35.8	8 50.9	23 01.1	10 33.6	24 26.8	22 00.1	20 23.5
13 W	11 27 10	20 00 42	12♑59 55	19 36 00	28 39.0	6 10.1	28 35.5	2 15.5	9 18.3	23 13.6	10 29.4	24 30.6	22 01.4	20 25.7
14 Th	11 31 06	20 59 07	26 08 21	2♒37 07	28 34.3	7 44.9	28 20.1	2 55.3	9 45.8	23 26.0	10 25.1	24 34.3	22 02.7	20 27.9
15 F	11 35 03	21 57 33	9♒02 27	15 24 29	28 28.5	9 18.7	28 07.1	3 35.2	10 13.3	23 38.3	10 20.8	24 38.1	22 04.0	20 30.1
16 Sa	11 39 00	22 56 02	21 43 20	27 59 07	28 22.2	10 51.3	27 56.4	4 15.3	10 40.7	23 50.6	10 16.4	24 41.9	22 05.3	20 32.3
17 Su	11 42 56	23 54 32	4♓11 59	10♓22 01	28 16.1	12 22.9	27 48.2	4 55.5	11 08.1	24 02.8	10 12.0	24 45.7	22 06.7	20 34.5
18 M	11 46 53	24 53 04	16 29 23	22 34 13	28 11.0	13 53.5	27 42.5	5 35.8	11 35.5	24 15.0	10 07.6	24 49.5	22 08.0	20 36.6
19 Tu	11 50 49	25 51 37	28 36 41	4♈37 00	28 07.2	15 22.9	27D 39.1	6 16.3	12 03.0	24 27.2	10 03.1	24 53.2	22 09.5	20 38.8
20 W	11 54 46	26 50 13	10♈35 22	16 32 03	28D 05.0	16 51.3	27 38.2	6 56.9	12 30.3	24 39.3	9 58.6	24 57.0	22 10.9	20 41.0
21 Th	11 58 42	27 48 51	22 27 20	28 21 33	28 04.3	18 18.6	27 39.6	7 37.6	12 57.7	24 51.3	9 54.1	25 00.8	22 12.4	20 43.2
22 F	12 02 39	28 47 31	4♉15 04	10♉08 18	28 04.9	19 44.8	27 43.3	8 18.4	13 25.1	25 03.3	9 49.6	25 04.6	22 13.9	20 45.3
23 Sa	12 06 35	29 46 13	16 01 40	21 55 41	28 06.4	21 09.9	27 49.4	8 59.4	13 52.5	25 15.2	9 45.0	25 08.4	22 15.4	20 47.5
24 Su	12 10 32	0♎44 57	27 50 50	3♊47 41	28 08.2	22 33.9	27 57.7	9 40.4	14 19.8	25 27.1	9 40.4	25 12.1	22 16.9	20 49.7
25 M	12 14 29	1 43 44	9♊46 47	15 48 43	28 09.7	23 56.8	28 08.2	10 21.6	14 47.1	25 38.9	9 35.7	25 15.9	22 18.5	20 51.8
26 Tu	12 18 25	2 42 32	21 54 06	28 03 32	28R 10.6	25 18.5	28 20.8	11 02.9	15 14.4	25 50.6	9 31.1	25 19.7	22 20.1	20 54.0
27 W	12 22 22	3 41 24	4♋17 35	10♋36 49	28 10.5	26 38.9	28 35.6	11 44.3	15 41.7	26 02.3	9 26.4	25 23.5	22 21.7	20 56.1
28 Th	12 26 18	4 40 17	17 01 45	23 32 51	28 09.4	27 58.1	28 52.3	12 25.9	16 09.0	26 14.0	9 21.7	25 27.2	22 23.3	20 58.3
29 F	12 30 15	5 39 13	0♌10 29	6♌54 55	28 07.2	29 16.0	29 11.0	13 07.5	16 36.2	26 25.5	9 17.0	25 31.0	22 25.0	21 00.4
30 Sa	12 34 11	6 38 10	13 46 18	20 44 38	28 04.5	0♏32.4	29 31.6	13 49.3	17 03.5	26 37.0	9 12.3	25 34.7	22 26.7	21 02.5

LONGITUDE — October 1967

Day	Sid.Time	☉	0 hr ☽	Noon☽	True☊	☿	♀	♂	⚳	♃	♄	♅	♆	♇
1 Su	12 38 08	7♎37 11	27♌49 46	5♍01 21	28♈01.6	1♏47.5	29♌54.0	14♐31.2	17♍30.7	26♌48.4	9♈07.6	25♍38.4	22♏28.4	21♍04.6
2 M	12 42 04	8 36 13	12♍18 52	19 41 37	27R 59.0	3 01.0	0♍18.2	15 13.1	17 57.9	26 59.8	9R 02.9	25 42.2	22 30.1	21 06.7
3 Tu	12 46 01	9 35 17	27 08 46	4♎39 18	27 57.1	4 12.9	0 44.1	15 55.2	18 25.0	27 11.1	8 58.2	25 45.9	22 31.8	21 08.8
4 W	12 49 58	10 34 23	12♎12 09	19 46 07	27D 56.1	5 23.0	1 11.6	16 37.5	18 52.2	27 22.3	8 53.5	25 49.6	22 33.6	21 10.9
5 Th	12 53 54	11 33 32	27 20 04	4♏52 50	27 56.1	6 31.3	1 40.8	17 19.8	19 19.3	27 33.4	8 48.8	25 53.3	22 35.4	21 13.0
6 F	12 57 51	12 32 42	12♏23 21	19 50 38	27 56.7	7 37.6	2 11.4	18 02.2	19 46.4	27 44.5	8 44.1	25 56.9	22 37.2	21 15.1
7 Sa	13 01 47	13 31 55	27 13 52	4♐32 20	27 57.8	8 41.7	2 43.6	18 44.7	20 13.4	27 55.5	8 39.4	26 00.6	22 39.0	21 17.1
8 Su	13 05 44	14 31 09	11♐45 32	18 53 04	27 58.9	9 43.5	3 17.1	19 27.4	20 40.5	28 06.4	8 34.7	26 04.3	22 40.9	21 19.2
9 M	13 09 40	15 30 25	25 54 44	2♑50 26	27 59.7	10 42.8	3 52.1	20 10.1	21 07.5	28 17.2	8 30.0	26 07.9	22 42.8	21 21.2
10 Tu	13 13 37	16 29 42	9♑40 12	16 24 11	27R 59.9	11 39.3	4 28.3	20 52.9	21 34.4	28 27.9	8 25.4	26 11.5	22 44.6	21 23.3
11 W	13 17 33	17 29 02	23 02 34	29 35 38	27 59.7	12 32.7	5 05.8	21 35.9	22 01.4	28 38.6	8 20.7	26 15.1	22 46.5	21 25.3
12 Th	13 21 30	18 28 23	6♒03 43	12♒27 09	27 58.9	13 22.8	5 44.6	22 18.9	22 28.3	28 49.1	8 16.1	26 18.7	22 48.5	21 27.3
13 F	13 25 27	19 27 46	18 46 18	25 01 33	27 57.9	14 09.3	6 24.5	23 02.0	22 55.1	28 59.6	8 11.6	26 22.3	22 50.4	21 29.3
14 Sa	13 29 23	20 27 10	1♓13 15	7♓21 46	27 56.9	14 51.8	7 05.6	23 45.2	23 22.0	29 10.0	8 07.0	26 25.8	22 52.4	21 31.2
15 Su	13 33 20	21 26 37	13 27 28	19 30 40	27 55.9	15 29.9	7 47.8	24 28.5	23 48.8	29 20.3	8 02.5	26 29.4	22 54.3	21 33.2
16 M	13 37 16	22 26 05	25 31 42	1♈30 50	27 55.1	16 03.2	8 31.1	25 11.9	24 15.5	29 30.4	7 58.0	26 32.9	22 56.3	21 35.1
17 Tu	13 41 13	23 25 35	7♈28 24	13 24 40	27 54.7	16 31.3	9 15.4	25 55.3	24 42.2	29 40.6	7 53.5	26 36.4	22 58.3	21 37.1
18 W	13 45 09	24 25 07	19 19 53	25 14 20	27D 54.5	16 53.5	10 00.7	26 38.9	25 08.9	29 50.6	7 49.1	26 39.8	23 00.4	21 39.0
19 Th	13 49 06	25 24 41	1♉08 18	7♉02 02	27 54.6	17 09.4	10 46.9	27 22.5	25 35.6	0♍00.5	7 44.7	26 43.3	23 02.4	21 40.9
20 F	13 53 02	26 24 18	12 55 49	18 49 57	27 54.7	17R 18.5	11 34.1	28 06.2	26 02.2	0 10.3	7 40.4	26 46.7	23 04.4	21 42.8
21 Sa	13 56 59	27 23 56	24 44 45	0♊40 33	27R 54.8	17 20.2	12 22.2	28 50.0	26 28.7	0 20.0	7 36.1	26 50.1	23 06.5	21 44.6
22 Su	14 00 55	28 23 37	6♊37 41	12 36 33	27 54.8	17 13.9	13 11.1	29 33.9	26 55.3	0 29.6	7 31.8	26 53.5	23 08.6	21 46.5
23 M	14 04 52	29 23 20	18 37 31	24 41 02	27 54.7	16 59.2	14 00.9	0♑17.9	27 21.7	0 39.1	7 27.6	26 56.8	23 10.7	21 48.3
24 Tu	14 08 49	0♏23 05	0♋47 32	6♋57 28	27 54.5	16 35.8	14 51.4	1 01.9	27 48.2	0 48.5	7 23.5	27 00.2	23 12.8	21 50.1
25 W	14 12 45	1 22 52	13 11 18	19 29 30	27D 54.3	16 03.3	15 42.8	1 46.1	28 14.6	0 57.8	7 19.4	27 03.5	23 14.9	21 51.9
26 Th	14 16 42	2 22 42	25 52 33	2♌20 52	27 54.2	15 21.8	16 34.9	2 30.3	28 40.9	1 07.0	7 15.3	27 06.8	23 17.0	21 53.7
27 F	14 20 38	3 22 34	8♌54 53	15 34 56	27 54.3	14 31.5	17 27.7	3 14.6	29 07.2	1 16.1	7 11.3	27 10.0	23 19.2	21 55.4
28 Sa	14 24 35	4 22 28	22 21 18	29 14 12	27 54.7	13 33.0	18 21.1	3 58.9	29 33.5	1 25.0	7 07.4	27 13.2	23 21.3	21 57.2
29 Su	14 28 31	5 22 24	6♍13 41	13♍19 42	27 55.3	12 27.2	19 15.3	4 43.4	29 59.7	1 33.9	7 03.5	27 16.4	23 23.5	21 58.9
30 M	14 32 28	6 22 22	20 32 03	27 50 20	27 56.0	11 15.6	20 10.1	5 27.9	0♎25.8	1 42.6	6 59.7	27 19.6	23 25.6	22 00.6
31 Tu	14 36 24	7 22 22	5♎14 02	12♎42 24	27 56.6	9 59.9	21 05.5	6 12.5	0 51.9	1 51.2	6 56.0	27 22.7	23 27.8	22 02.3

Astro Data	Planet Ingress	Last Aspect	☽ Ingress	Last Aspect	☽ Ingress	☽ Phases & Eclipses	Astro Data
Dy Hr Mn	Dy Hr Mn	Dy Hr Mn	Dy Hr Mn	Dy Hr Mn	Dy Hr Mn	Dy Hr Mn	
☽0S 6 1:51	♀ ♌R 9 11:58	1 4:01 ♂ △	♌ 1 14:08	1 3:14 ♀ ☌	♍ 1 3:38	4 11:37 ● 11♍15	1 September 1967
♃□♆ 7 3:32	☿ ♎ 9 16:53	3 9:58 ♂ □	♍ 3 17:07	2 21:43 ♅ ☌	♎ 3 4:34	11 3:06 ☽ 17♐42	Julian Day # 24715
☿0S 10 9:39	♂ ♐ 10 1:44	5 13:18 ♂ ✶	♎ 5 18:03	5 0:13 ♃ ✶	♏ 5 4:14	18 16:59 ○ 25♓05	SVP 5♓42'48"
☽0N 19 12:20	☉ ♎ 23 17:38	7 5:33 ♃ ✶	♏ 7 18:44	7 1:00 ♃ □	♐ 7 4:32	26 21:44 ☾ 3♋06	GC 26♐23.3 ⚴ 7♌28.8
♀D 20 9:34	☿ ♏ 30 1:46	9 20:25 ♂ ☌	♐ 9 20:40	9 3:59 ♃ △	♑ 9 7:04		Eris 11♈49.2R ⚵ 22♍25.2
♃⊼♄ 21 16:06		11 23:03 ♀ △	♑ 12 0:43	11 5:50 ♅ △	♒ 11 12:45	3 20:24 ● 9♎56	⚷ 28♓24.1R ⚶ 1♐48.2
♃⊻♅ 22 15:52	♀ ♍ 1 18:07	13 21:03 ♅ △	♒ 14 7:08	13 19:47 ♃ ☍	♓ 13 21:38	10 12:11 ☽ 16♑30	☽ Mean ☊ 0♉25.6
☉0S 23 17:39	♃ ♍ 19 10:51	16 11:55 ♀ ☍	♓ 16 15:53	16 1:59 ♅ ☍	♈ 16 8:58	18 10:11 ○ 24♈21	
	♂ ♑ 23 2:14	18 16:59 ☉ ☍	♈ 19 2:46	18 21:30 ♃ △	♉ 18 21:41	18 10:15 • T 1.143	1 October 1967
☽0S 3 12:13	☉ ♏ 24 2:44	21 10:34 ♀ △	♉ 21 15:20	21 4:12 ♅ △	♊ 21 10:38	26 12:04 ☾ 2♌23	Julian Day # 24745
♄⊼♆ 16 18:07	⚳ ♎ 29 12:18	24 0:05 ♀ □	♊ 24 4:21	23 22:04 ☉ △	♋ 23 22:27		SVP 5♓42'45"
☽0N 16 18:38		26 12:34 ♀ ✶	♋ 26 15:45	26 2:16 ♅ ✶	♌ 26 7:40		GC 26♐23.3 ⚴ 24♌11.3
☿R 21 5:15		28 20:54 ☿ □	♌ 28 23:41	28 1:44 ♆ □	♍ 28 13:19		Eris 11♈31.9R ⚵ 4♎00.1
☽0S 30 23:19				30 11:09 ♅ ☌	♎ 30 15:31		⚷ 27♓03.7R ⚶ 14♐03.2
							☽ Mean ☊ 28♈50.2

November 1967 LONGITUDE

Day	Sid.Time	☉	0 hr ☽	Noon ☽	True ☊	☿	♀	♂	⚳	♃	♄	♅	♆	♇
1 W	14 40 21	8♏22 25	20♎14 33	27♎49 27	27♈56.9	8♏42.3	22♍01.5	6♑57.1	1♎18.0	1♍59.7	6♈52.3	27♍25.8	23♏30.0	22♍03.9
2 Th	14 44 18	9 22 29	5♏25 56	13♏02 48	27R56.6	7R25.1	22 58.1	7 41.9	1 43.9	2 08.0	6R48.7	27 28.9	23 32.2	22 05.5
3 F	14 48 14	10 22 36	20 38 47	28 12 40	27 55.7	6 10.8	23 55.2	8 26.7	2 09.9	2 16.3	6 45.2	27 31.9	23 34.4	22 07.1
4 Sa	14 52 11	11 22 44	5♐43 18	13♐09 38	27 54.2	5 01.6	24 52.9	9 11.6	2 35.7	2 24.4	6 41.8	27 34.9	23 36.6	22 08.7
5 Su	14 56 07	12 22 54	20 30 46	27 46 01	27 52.3	3 59.9	25 51.1	9 56.5	3 01.5	2 32.4	6 38.4	27 37.9	23 38.8	22 10.3
6 M	15 00 04	13 23 05	4♑54 48	11♑56 48	27 50.5	3 07.2	26 49.7	10 41.5	3 27.3	2 40.2	6 35.1	27 40.8	23 41.0	22 11.8
7 Tu	15 04 00	14 23 18	18 51 50	25 39 55	27 49.0	2 24.9	27 48.9	11 26.6	3 53.0	2 47.9	6 31.9	27 43.7	23 43.3	22 13.3
8 W	15 07 57	15 23 32	2♒21 09	8♒55 49	27D48.2	1 53.9	28 48.5	12 11.7	4 18.6	2 55.5	6 28.8	27 46.6	23 45.5	22 14.8
9 Th	15 11 54	16 23 48	15 24 17	21 46 59	27 48.1	1 34.6	29 48.6	12 56.9	4 44.1	3 02.9	6 25.7	27 49.4	23 47.7	22 16.3
10 F	15 15 50	17 24 05	28 04 25	4♓17 05	27 48.9	1D26.9	0♎49.1	13 42.2	5 09.6	3 10.2	6 22.7	27 52.2	23 50.0	22 17.7
11 Sa	15 19 47	18 24 24	10♓25 34	16 30 25	27 50.3	1 30.4	1 50.0	14 27.5	5 35.0	3 17.4	6 19.9	27 55.0	23 52.2	22 19.1
12 Su	15 23 43	19 24 44	22 32 10	28 31 22	27 52.0	1 44.7	2 51.4	15 12.9	6 00.3	3 24.4	6 17.1	27 57.7	23 54.5	22 20.5
13 M	15 27 40	20 25 05	4♈28 31	10♈24 07	27 53.6	2 08.9	3 53.1	15 58.3	6 25.6	3 31.3	6 14.4	28 00.4	23 56.7	22 21.9
14 Tu	15 31 36	21 25 28	16 18 37	22 12 27	27R54.6	2 42.2	4 55.3	16 43.8	6 50.8	3 38.1	6 11.7	28 03.0	23 59.0	22 23.2
15 W	15 35 33	22 25 53	28 06 00	3♉59 37	27 54.5	3 23.7	5 57.8	17 29.3	7 15.9	3 44.6	6 09.2	28 05.6	24 01.2	22 24.5
16 Th	15 39 29	23 26 19	9♉53 37	15 48 20	27 53.2	4 12.6	7 00.7	18 14.9	7 40.9	3 51.1	6 06.8	28 08.1	24 03.5	22 25.8
17 F	15 43 26	24 26 47	21 44 00	27 40 52	27 50.5	5 07.9	8 03.9	19 00.5	8 05.9	3 57.4	6 04.5	28 10.6	24 05.7	22 27.0
18 Sa	15 47 22	25 27 16	3♊39 10	9♊39 07	27 46.6	6 08.8	9 07.5	19 46.2	8 30.8	4 03.5	6 02.2	28 13.1	24 08.0	22 28.2
19 Su	15 51 19	26 27 47	15 40 55	21 44 47	27 41.7	7 14.7	10 11.5	20 31.9	8 55.6	4 09.5	6 00.1	28 15.5	24 10.2	22 29.4
20 M	15 55 16	27 28 20	27 50 53	3♋59 28	27 36.3	8 24.8	11 15.7	21 17.7	9 20.3	4 15.4	5 58.0	28 17.9	24 12.5	22 30.6
21 Tu	15 59 12	28 28 54	10♋10 44	16 24 57	27 31.1	9 38.6	12 20.3	22 03.5	9 45.0	4 21.0	5 56.1	28 20.3	24 14.7	22 31.7
22 W	16 03 09	29 29 30	22 42 20	29 03 10	27 26.8	10 55.4	13 25.2	22 49.4	10 09.5	4 26.6	5 54.2	28 22.6	24 17.0	22 32.9
23 Th	16 07 05	0♐30 08	5♌27 43	11♌56 19	27 23.6	12 15.0	14 30.4	23 35.3	10 34.0	4 31.9	5 52.5	28 24.8	24 19.2	22 33.9
24 F	16 11 02	1 30 47	18 29 13	25 06 44	27D22.1	13 36.7	15 35.8	24 21.3	10 58.4	4 37.1	5 50.8	28 27.0	24 21.5	22 35.0
25 Sa	16 14 58	2 31 28	1♍49 08	8♍36 40	27 22.0	15 00.4	16 41.6	25 07.3	11 22.7	4 42.1	5 49.3	28 29.2	24 23.7	22 36.0
26 Su	16 18 55	3 32 10	15 29 30	22 27 46	27 23.1	16 25.7	17 47.6	25 53.3	11 46.9	4 47.0	5 47.8	28 31.3	24 26.0	22 37.0
27 M	16 22 52	4 32 54	29 31 30	6♎40 37	27 24.6	17 52.4	18 53.9	26 39.4	12 11.0	4 51.7	5 46.5	28 33.4	24 28.2	22 37.9
28 Tu	16 26 48	5 33 40	13♎54 55	21 14 03	27R25.7	19 20.1	20 00.4	27 25.6	12 35.0	4 56.2	5 45.3	28 35.4	24 30.4	22 38.9
29 W	16 30 45	6 34 28	28 37 28	6♏04 31	27 25.5	20 48.8	21 07.2	28 11.7	12 58.9	5 00.6	5 44.1	28 37.4	24 32.6	22 39.8
30 Th	16 34 41	7 35 16	13♏34 22	21 06 00	27 23.5	22 18.3	22 14.2	28 57.9	13 22.7	5 04.8	5 43.1	28 39.3	24 34.8	22 40.6

December 1967 LONGITUDE

Day	Sid.Time	☉	0 hr ☽	Noon ☽	True ☊	☿	♀	♂	⚳	♃	♄	♅	♆	♇
1 F	16 38 38	8♐36 06	28♏38 22	6♐10 17	27♈19.5	23♏48.5	23♎21.4	29♑44.2	13♎46.4	5♍08.8	5♈42.2	28♍41.2	24♏37.1	22♍41.5
2 Sa	16 42 34	9 36 58	13♐40 33	21 07 59	27R13.6	25 19.2	24 28.9	0♒30.5	14 10.0	5 12.6	5R41.4	28 43.0	24 39.3	22 42.3
3 Su	16 46 31	10 37 50	28 31 31	5♑50 08	27 06.6	26 50.3	25 36.5	1 16.8	14 33.4	5 16.3	5 40.7	28 44.8	24 41.4	22 43.1
4 M	16 50 27	11 38 44	13♑03 00	20 09 30	26 59.3	28 21.8	26 44.4	2 03.2	14 56.8	5 19.8	5 40.1	28 46.5	24 43.6	22 43.8
5 Tu	16 54 24	12 39 38	27 09 09	4♒01 41	26 52.7	29 53.5	27 52.5	2 49.6	15 20.1	5 23.0	5 39.6	28 48.2	24 45.8	22 44.5
6 W	16 58 21	13 40 33	10♒47 03	17 25 19	26 47.6	1♐25.6	29 00.7	3 36.0	15 43.2	5 26.2	5 39.2	28 49.8	24 48.0	22 45.2
7 Th	17 02 17	14 41 29	23 56 44	0♓21 42	26 44.4	2 57.8	0♏09.1	4 22.4	16 06.2	5 29.1	5 39.0	28 51.3	24 50.1	22 45.8
8 F	17 06 14	15 42 26	6♓40 40	12 54 11	26D43.2	4 30.2	1 17.8	5 08.9	16 29.1	5 31.8	5D38.8	28 52.9	24 52.3	22 46.4
9 Sa	17 10 10	16 43 23	19 02 52	25 07 22	26 43.5	6 02.8	2 26.6	5 55.4	16 51.9	5 34.4	5 38.8	28 54.3	24 54.4	22 47.0
10 Su	17 14 07	17 44 21	1♈08 20	7♈06 28	26 44.7	7 35.5	3 35.5	6 41.9	17 14.6	5 36.8	5 38.8	28 55.7	24 56.5	22 47.5
11 M	17 18 03	18 45 19	13 02 23	18 56 46	26R45.9	9 08.3	4 44.7	7 28.5	17 37.1	5 38.9	5 39.0	28 57.1	24 58.6	22 48.0
12 Tu	17 22 00	19 46 18	24 50 13	0♉43 20	26 46.1	10 41.2	5 54.0	8 15.1	17 59.5	5 40.9	5 39.3	28 58.4	25 00.7	22 48.5
13 W	17 25 56	20 47 18	6♉36 38	12 30 38	26 44.5	12 14.3	7 03.4	9 01.7	18 21.8	5 42.8	5 39.7	28 59.6	25 02.8	22 49.0
14 Th	17 29 53	21 48 18	18 25 47	24 22 28	26 40.6	13 47.4	8 13.0	9 48.3	18 43.9	5 44.4	5 40.2	29 00.8	25 04.9	22 49.4
15 F	17 33 50	22 49 19	0♊21 02	6♊21 47	26 34.1	15 20.7	9 22.8	10 34.9	19 05.9	5 45.8	5 40.8	29 02.0	25 06.9	22 49.8
16 Sa	17 37 46	23 50 21	12 24 55	18 30 39	26 25.3	16 54.0	10 32.7	11 21.5	19 27.8	5 47.1	5 41.5	29 03.1	25 09.0	22 50.1
17 Su	17 41 43	24 51 23	24 39 06	0♋50 21	26 14.6	18 27.5	11 42.8	12 08.2	19 49.5	5 48.1	5 42.3	29 04.1	25 11.0	22 50.4
18 M	17 45 39	25 52 26	7♋04 29	13 21 30	26 03.1	20 01.1	12 53.0	12 54.9	20 11.1	5 49.0	5 43.3	29 05.1	25 13.0	22 50.7
19 Tu	17 49 36	26 53 30	19 41 25	26 04 13	25 51.7	21 34.9	14 03.3	13 41.6	20 32.5	5 49.6	5 44.3	29 06.0	25 15.0	22 50.9
20 W	17 53 32	27 54 35	2♌29 54	8♌58 29	25 41.6	23 08.8	15 13.7	14 28.3	20 53.8	5 50.1	5 45.5	29 06.9	25 17.0	22 51.1
21 Th	17 57 29	28 55 40	15 29 58	22 04 24	25 33.7	24 42.9	16 24.3	15 15.0	21 15.0	5R50.4	5 46.7	29 07.7	25 19.0	22 51.3
22 F	18 01 25	29 56 46	28 41 50	5♍22 21	25 28.4	26 17.1	17 35.1	16 01.7	21 36.0	5 50.5	5 48.1	29 08.4	25 20.9	22 51.5
23 Sa	18 05 22	0♑57 52	12♍06 04	18 53 05	25D25.7	27 51.6	18 45.9	16 48.5	21 56.8	5 50.4	5 49.6	29 09.1	25 22.8	22 51.6
24 Su	18 09 19	1 58 59	25 43 33	2♎37 34	25 25.0	29 26.2	19 56.8	17 35.2	22 17.5	5 50.0	5 51.2	29 09.8	25 24.7	22 51.6
25 M	18 13 15	3 00 07	9♎35 14	16 36 35	25R25.4	1♑01.1	21 07.9	18 22.0	22 38.0	5 49.5	5 52.9	29 10.4	25 26.6	22R51.7
26 Tu	18 17 12	4 01 16	23 41 37	0♏50 14	25 25.5	2 36.2	22 19.1	19 08.8	22 58.4	5 48.8	5 54.7	29 10.9	25 28.5	22 51.7
27 W	18 21 08	5 02 25	8♏02 13	15 17 14	25 24.0	4 11.6	23 30.4	19 55.6	23 18.5	5 47.9	5 56.6	29 11.4	25 30.4	22 51.7
28 Th	18 25 05	6 03 35	22 34 51	29 54 28	25 20.0	5 47.3	24 41.8	20 42.4	23 38.6	5 46.8	5 58.6	29 11.8	25 32.2	22 51.6
29 F	18 29 01	7 04 46	7♐15 21	14♐36 40	25 13.1	7 23.2	25 53.2	21 29.2	23 58.4	5 45.6	6 00.7	29 12.1	25 34.0	22 51.5
30 Sa	18 32 58	8 05 56	21 57 31	29 16 55	25 03.4	8 59.4	27 04.8	22 16.0	24 18.1	5 44.1	6 02.9	29 12.4	25 35.8	22 51.4
31 Su	18 36 55	9 07 07	6♑33 53	13♑47 28	24 51.9	10 36.0	28 16.5	23 02.8	24 37.5	5 42.4	6 05.2	29 12.7	25 37.6	22 51.2

Astro Data Dy Hr Mn	Planet Ingress Dy Hr Mn
☿ D 10 16:17	♀ ♎ 9 16:32
♀0S 12 3:36	☉ ♐ 23 0:04
☽0N 13 0:37	
♄0S 18 9:03	♂ ♒ 1 20:12
☽0S 27 8:37	☿ ♐ 5 13:41
	♀ ♏ 7 8:48
♄ D 9 10:27	☉ ♑ 22 13:16
☽0N 10 6:46	☿ ♑ 24 20:33
♃⊼♄ 11 12:46	
♄0N 20 0:59	
♃ R 22 10:02	
♃⊼♄ 23 22:13	
☽0S 24 14:48	
♇ R 26 4:48	
⚳0S 29 11:11	

Last Aspect Dy Hr Mn	☽ Ingress Dy Hr Mn	Last Aspect Dy Hr Mn	☽ Ingress Dy Hr Mn
31 2:47 ♄ ☍	♏ 1 15:26	1 1:12 ♂ ⚹	♐ 1 2:10
3 10:55 ♅ ⚹	♐ 3 14:51	3 0:20 ♅ □	♑ 3 2:25
5 11:47 ♅ □	♑ 5 15:44	5 3:51 ☿ ⚹	♒ 5 4:57
7 16:09 ♀ △	♒ 7 19:45	7 1:37 ♆ □	♓ 7 11:19
9 15:50 ♆ □	♓ 10 3:42	9 19:33 ♅ ☍	♈ 9 21:43
12 10:52 ♅ ☍	♈ 12 14:58	11 11:34 ☉ △	♉ 12 10:32
14 0:05 ♂ □	♉ 15 3:52	14 21:20 ♅ △	♊ 14 23:18
17 13:00 ♅ △	♊ 17 16:40	17 8:34 ♅ □	♋ 17 10:23
20 0:51 ♅ □	♋ 20 4:13	19 17:40 ♅ ⚹	♌ 19 19:21
22 12:54 ☉ △	♌ 22 13:47	22 1:27 ☉ △	♍ 22 2:21
24 10:38 ♆ □	♍ 24 20:46	24 5:59 ♅ ☌	♎ 24 7:27
26 22:20 ♅ ☌	♎ 27 0:48	25 15:10 ♂ △	♏ 26 10:36
28 22:37 ♂ □	♏ 29 2:13	28 10:50 ♅ ⚹	♐ 28 12:09
		30 11:53 ♅ □	♑ 30 13:11

☽ Phases & Eclipses Dy Hr Mn	
2 5:48	● 9♏07
2 5:38:17	● T non-C
9 1:00	☽ 15♒56
17 4:53	○ 24♉09
25 0:23	☾ 2♍02
1 16:10	● 8♐47
8 17:57	☽ 15♓58
16 23:21	○ 24♊19
24 10:48	☾ 1♎56
31 3:38	● 8♑46

Astro Data

1 November 1967
Julian Day # 24776
SVP 5♓42'42"
GC 26♐23.4 ⚴ 9♍44.3
Eris 11♈13.4R ⚵ 15♎31.8
⚷ 25♓51.7R ⚶ 28♐28.4
☽ Mean ☊ 27♈11.7

1 December 1967
Julian Day # 24806
SVP 5♓42'37"
GC 26♐23.5 ⚴ 22♍13.6
Eris 11♈00.1R ⚵ 25♎48.8
⚷ 25♓18.5R ⚶ 13♑23.9
☽ Mean ☊ 25♈36.4

LONGITUDE — January 1968

Day	Sid.Time	☉	0 hr ☽	Noon ☽	True ☊	☿	♀	♂	⚳	♃	♄	♅	♆	♇
1 M	18 40 51	10♑08 18	20♑56 48	28♑01 06	24♈39.7	12♑12.8	29♏28.2	23♒49.7	24♎56.8	5♍40.5	6♈07.7	29♍12.9	25♏39.3	22♍51.0
2 Tu	18 44 48	11 09 29	4♒59 45	11♒52 17	24R 28.2	13 50.0	0♐40.0	24 36.5	25 15.9	5R 38.5	6 10.2	29 13.0	25 41.0	22R 50.8
3 W	18 48 44	12 10 40	18 38 24	25 17 59	24 18.5	15 27.5	1 51.9	25 23.3	25 34.8	5 36.2	6 12.8	29R 13.1	25 42.7	22 50.6
4 Th	18 52 41	13 11 51	1♓51 04	8♓17 51	24 11.3	17 05.4	3 03.9	26 10.2	25 53.5	5 33.7	6 15.6	29 13.1	25 44.4	22 50.3
5 F	18 56 37	14 13 01	14 38 39	20 53 53	24 06.8	18 43.5	4 16.0	26 57.0	26 12.0	5 31.1	6 18.4	29 13.1	25 46.1	22 49.9
6 Sa	19 00 34	15 14 11	27 04 05	3♈09 50	24 04.7	20 22.1	5 28.1	27 43.8	26 30.3	5 28.3	6 21.3	29 13.0	25 47.7	22 49.6
7 Su	19 04 30	16 15 20	9♈11 48	15 10 38	24 04.3	22 00.9	6 40.3	28 30.6	26 48.4	5 25.3	6 24.4	29 12.8	25 49.3	22 49.2
8 M	19 08 27	17 16 29	21 07 05	27 01 49	24 04.3	23 40.1	7 52.5	29 17.4	27 06.3	5 22.1	6 27.5	29 12.6	25 50.9	22 48.8
9 Tu	19 12 24	18 17 38	2♉55 34	8♉49 01	24 03.6	25 19.6	9 04.8	0♓04.2	27 24.0	5 18.7	6 30.7	29 12.3	25 52.4	22 48.3
10 W	19 16 20	19 18 46	14 42 50	20 37 39	24 01.2	26 59.3	10 17.2	0 51.0	27 41.4	5 15.1	6 34.0	29 12.0	25 54.0	22 47.8
11 Th	19 20 17	20 19 54	26 34 03	2♊32 34	23 56.2	28 39.4	11 29.7	1 37.8	27 58.7	5 11.4	6 37.5	29 11.6	25 55.5	22 47.3
12 F	19 24 13	21 21 01	8♊33 41	14 37 49	23 48.3	0♒19.6	12 42.2	2 24.6	28 15.7	5 07.5	6 41.0	29 11.2	25 57.0	22 46.8
13 Sa	19 28 10	22 22 08	20 45 17	26 56 23	23 37.7	1 59.9	13 54.8	3 11.4	28 32.5	5 03.4	6 44.6	29 10.7	25 58.4	22 46.2
14 Su	19 32 06	23 23 15	3♋11 15	9♋30 01	23 24.9	3 40.4	15 07.4	3 58.2	28 49.1	4 59.1	6 48.3	29 10.2	25 59.8	22 45.6
15 M	19 36 03	24 24 21	15 52 42	22 19 14	23 10.9	5 20.8	16 20.1	4 44.9	29 05.4	4 54.7	6 52.1	29 09.6	26 01.2	22 44.9
16 Tu	19 39 59	25 25 26	28 49 30	5♌23 19	22 57.1	7 01.2	17 32.8	5 31.6	29 21.5	4 50.1	6 56.0	29 08.9	26 02.6	22 44.3
17 W	19 43 56	26 26 31	12♌00 28	18 40 43	22 44.7	8 41.3	18 45.6	6 18.4	29 37.3	4 45.3	6 59.9	29 08.2	26 03.9	22 43.6
18 Th	19 47 53	27 27 36	25 23 45	2♍09 22	22 34.7	10 21.0	19 58.5	7 05.1	29 52.9	4 40.4	7 04.0	29 07.5	26 05.3	22 42.8
19 F	19 51 49	28 28 40	8♍57 16	15 47 15	22 27.8	12 00.2	21 11.4	7 51.8	0♏08.3	4 35.3	7 08.1	29 06.6	26 06.5	22 42.1
20 Sa	19 55 46	29 29 43	22 39 09	29 32 48	22 23.8	13 38.6	22 24.3	8 38.4	0 23.4	4 30.0	7 12.4	29 05.8	26 07.8	22 41.3
21 Su	19 59 42	0♒30 47	6♎28 07	13♎25 01	22D 22.4	15 16.0	23 37.3	9 25.1	0 38.2	4 24.6	7 16.7	29 04.9	26 09.0	22 40.5
22 M	20 03 39	1 31 49	20 23 27	27 23 25	22R 22.2	16 52.1	24 50.4	10 11.7	0 52.8	4 19.1	7 21.1	29 03.9	26 10.2	22 39.6
23 Tu	20 07 35	2 32 52	4♏24 52	11♏27 45	22 22.1	18 26.6	26 03.4	10 58.4	1 07.1	4 13.4	7 25.6	29 02.9	26 11.4	22 38.7
24 W	20 11 32	3 33 54	18 32 00	25 37 27	22 20.5	19 59.0	27 16.6	11 45.0	1 21.2	4 07.5	7 30.2	29 01.8	26 12.5	22 37.8
25 Th	20 15 28	4 34 56	2♐43 55	9♐51 07	22 16.6	21 28.9	28 29.8	12 31.6	1 35.0	4 01.6	7 34.8	29 00.7	26 13.6	22 36.9
26 F	20 19 25	5 35 58	16 58 40	24 06 07	22 09.7	22 55.8	29 43.0	13 18.2	1 48.4	3 55.4	7 39.6	28 59.5	26 14.7	22 36.0
27 Sa	20 23 22	6 36 58	1♑12 57	8♑18 36	22 00.2	24 19.1	0♑56.2	14 04.8	2 01.6	3 49.2	7 44.4	28 58.3	26 15.8	22 35.0
28 Su	20 27 18	7 37 58	15 22 24	22 23 43	21 48.6	25 38.3	2 09.5	14 51.3	2 14.5	3 42.8	7 49.3	28 57.0	26 16.8	22 34.0
29 M	20 31 15	8 38 57	29 21 56	6♒16 27	21 36.2	26 52.5	3 22.8	15 37.8	2 27.2	3 36.3	7 54.3	28 55.7	26 17.8	22 33.0
30 Tu	20 35 11	9 39 56	13♒06 44	19 52 21	21 24.3	28 01.0	4 36.2	16 24.3	2 39.5	3 29.7	7 59.3	28 54.3	26 18.7	22 31.9
31 W	20 39 08	10 40 53	26 32 58	3♓08 22	21 14.1	29 03.1	5 49.6	17 10.8	2 51.5	3 22.9	8 04.5	28 52.9	26 19.6	22 30.8

LONGITUDE — February 1968

Day	Sid.Time	☉	0 hr ☽	Noon ☽	True ☊	☿	♀	♂	⚳	♃	♄	♅	♆	♇
1 Th	20 43 04	11♒41 48	9♓38 27	16♓03 15	21♈06.3	29♒58.0	7♑03.0	17♓57.3	3♏03.1	3♍16.1	8♈09.7	28♍51.4	26♏20.5	22♍29.7
2 F	20 47 01	12 42 43	22 22 54	28 37 40	21R 01.3	0♓44.8	8 16.4	18 43.7	3 14.5	3R 09.1	8 14.9	28R 49.9	26 21.4	22R 28.6
3 Sa	20 50 57	13 43 36	4♈47 54	10♈54 03	20D 58.9	1 22.8	9 29.9	19 30.1	3 25.6	3 02.1	8 20.3	28 48.4	26 22.2	22 27.4
4 Su	20 54 54	14 44 28	16 56 36	22 56 08	20 58.4	1 51.2	10 43.3	20 16.5	3 36.3	2 55.0	8 25.7	28 46.8	26 23.0	22 26.2
5 M	20 58 51	15 45 19	28 53 17	4♉48 42	20 58.9	2 09.4	11 56.8	21 02.9	3 46.7	2 47.7	8 31.2	28 45.1	26 23.7	22 25.1
6 Tu	21 02 47	16 46 08	10♉43 02	16 37 01	20R 59.3	2R 16.9	13 10.4	21 49.2	3 56.8	2 40.4	8 36.8	28 43.4	26 24.4	22 23.8
7 W	21 06 44	17 46 56	22 31 18	28 26 36	20 58.6	2 13.6	14 23.9	22 35.5	4 06.5	2 33.0	8 42.4	28 41.7	26 25.1	22 22.6
8 Th	21 10 40	18 47 42	4♊23 35	10♊22 52	20 56.0	1 59.3	15 37.5	23 21.8	4 16.0	2 25.6	8 48.1	28 39.9	26 25.8	22 21.3
9 F	21 14 37	19 48 27	16 25 03	22 30 42	20 51.0	1 34.2	16 51.1	24 08.0	4 25.0	2 18.0	8 53.8	28 38.1	26 26.4	22 20.0
10 Sa	21 18 33	20 49 11	28 40 18	4♋54 14	20 43.7	0 59.0	18 04.7	24 54.2	4 33.7	2 10.4	8 59.7	28 36.3	26 27.0	22 18.8
11 Su	21 22 30	21 49 52	11♋12 51	17 36 23	20 34.5	0 14.4	19 18.3	25 40.4	4 42.1	2 02.8	9 05.6	28 34.4	26 27.6	22 17.4
12 M	21 26 27	22 50 33	24 04 57	0♌38 35	20 24.2	29♒21.6	20 31.9	26 26.5	4 50.1	1 55.1	9 11.5	28 32.5	26 28.1	22 16.1
13 Tu	21 30 23	23 51 12	7♌17 10	14 00 33	20 13.8	28 22.2	21 45.6	27 12.6	4 57.8	1 47.3	9 17.5	28 30.5	26 28.6	22 14.7
14 W	21 34 20	24 51 49	20 48 25	27 40 24	20 04.4	27 17.7	22 59.3	27 58.7	5 05.1	1 39.6	9 23.6	28 28.5	26 29.0	22 13.4
15 Th	21 38 16	25 52 25	4♍36 02	11♍34 50	19 57.0	26 10.0	24 13.0	28 44.7	5 12.0	1 31.7	9 29.7	28 26.5	26 29.5	22 12.0
16 F	21 42 13	26 52 59	18 36 15	25 39 45	19 52.1	25 00.9	25 26.7	29 30.7	5 18.5	1 23.9	9 35.9	28 24.4	26 29.8	22 10.6
17 Sa	21 46 09	27 53 32	2♎44 48	9♎50 54	19D 49.6	23 52.2	26 40.4	0♈16.7	5 24.7	1 16.0	9 42.1	28 22.3	26 30.2	22 09.1
18 Su	21 50 06	28 54 04	16 57 37	24 04 32	19 49.3	22 45.7	27 54.2	1 02.6	5 30.5	1 08.1	9 48.4	28 20.2	26 30.5	22 07.7
19 M	21 54 02	29 54 34	1♏11 18	8♏17 39	19 50.1	21 42.9	29 08.0	1 48.5	5 35.9	1 00.2	9 54.8	28 18.0	26 30.8	22 06.3
20 Tu	21 57 59	0♓55 04	15 23 20	22 28 09	19R 51.2	20 44.9	0♒21.8	2 34.4	5 40.9	0 52.3	10 01.2	28 15.8	26 31.0	22 04.8
21 W	22 01 55	1 55 32	29 31 57	6♐34 35	19 51.3	19 52.7	1 35.6	3 20.2	5 45.6	0 44.4	10 07.6	28 13.6	26 31.3	22 03.3
22 Th	22 05 52	2 55 59	13♐35 55	20 35 49	19 49.8	19 07.2	2 49.4	4 06.0	5 49.8	0 36.5	10 14.1	28 11.3	26 31.5	22 01.8
23 F	22 09 49	3 56 24	27 34 06	4♑30 38	19 46.3	18 28.8	4 03.3	4 51.7	5 53.6	0 28.6	10 20.7	28 09.0	26 31.6	22 00.3
24 Sa	22 13 45	4 56 48	11♑25 11	18 17 32	19 40.8	17 57.6	5 17.1	5 37.5	5 57.0	0 20.7	10 27.3	28 06.7	26 31.7	21 58.8
25 Su	22 17 42	5 57 11	25 07 28	1♒54 42	19 33.8	17 33.9	6 31.0	6 23.2	6 00.0	0 12.9	10 33.9	28 04.4	26 31.8	21 57.3
26 M	22 21 38	6 57 32	8♒39 00	15 20 05	19 26.2	17 17.5	7 44.8	7 08.8	6 02.6	0 05.1	10 40.6	28 02.0	26R 31.9	21 55.7
27 Tu	22 25 35	7 57 51	21 57 45	28 31 46	19 18.8	17D 08.2	8 58.7	7 54.4	6 04.8	29♌57.3	10 47.4	27 59.6	26 31.9	21 54.2
28 W	22 29 31	8 58 09	5♓01 59	11♓28 18	19 12.4	17 05.8	10 12.6	8 40.0	6 06.6	29 49.5	10 54.2	27 57.2	26 31.8	21 52.6
29 Th	22 33 28	9 58 25	17 50 39	24 09 03	19 07.7	17 10.0	11 26.5	9 25.5	6 07.9	29 41.8	11 01.0	27 54.8	26 31.8	21 51.1

Astro Data	Dy Hr Mn
♅ R	4 6:14
☽ 0N	6 13:41
☽ 0S	20 19:15
☽ 0N	2 21:30
☿ R	6 16:41
☽ 0S	17 1:02
♂ 0N	18 18:25
♆ R	27 8:55
☿ D	28 8:36

Planet Ingress	Dy Hr Mn
♀ ♐	1 22:37
♂ ♓	9 9:49
☿ ♒	12 7:19
⚳ ♏	18 22:59
☉ ♒	20 23:54
♀ ♑	26 17:35
☿ ♓	1 12:57
☿ ♒R	11 18:54
♂ ♈	17 3:18
☉ ♓	19 14:09
♀ ♒	20 4:55
♃ ♌R	27 3:33

Last Aspect Dy Hr Mn		☽ Ingress	Dy Hr Mn
1 14:43	♀ ⚹	♒	1 15:23
3 12:45	♆ □	♓	3 20:35
6 4:13	♅ ☍	♈	6 5:45
8 16:55	♂ ⚹	♉	8 18:02
11 5:17	♅ △	♊	11 6:54
13 16:19	♅ □	♋	13 17:54
16 0:36	♅ ⚹	♌	16 2:09
18 1:13	♆ □	♍	18 8:11
20 11:54	☉ △	♎	20 12:47
22 7:13	♀ ⚹	♏	22 16:28
24 17:45	♅ ⚹	♐	24 19:23
26 20:14	♅ □	♑	26 21:57
28 23:16	♅ △	♒	29 1:06
31 3:56	☿ ☌	♓	31 6:16

Last Aspect Dy Hr Mn		☽ Ingress	Dy Hr Mn
2 12:24	♅ ☍	♈	2 14:39
3 18:07	☉ ⚹	♉	5 2:15
7 12:30	♅ △	♊	7 15:09
9 23:54	♅ □	♋	10 2:34
12 8:11	♅ ⚹	♌	12 10:50
14 11:23	☿ ☍	♍	14 16:02
16 18:54	♂ ☍	♎	16 19:21
18 20:46	☉ △	♏	18 22:00
20 21:49	♅ ⚹	♐	21 0:48
23 1:02	♅ □	♑	23 4:12
25 5:13	♅ △	♒	25 8:37
27 14:36	♃ ☍	♓	27 14:42
29 19:12	♅ ☍	♈	29 23:14

☽ Phases & Eclipses Dy Hr Mn	
7 14:23	☽ 16♈21
15 16:11	○ 24♋35
22 19:38	☾ 1♏51
29 16:29	● 8♒50
6 12:20	☽ 16♉47
14 6:43	○ 24♌38
21 3:28	☾ 1♐34
28 6:56	● 8♓45

Astro Data

1 January 1968
Julian Day # 24837
SVP 5♓42'30"
GC 26♐23.5 ⚴ 0♎57.0
Eris 10♈55.5 ⚵ 4♏50.8
⚷ 25♓35.0 ⚶ 29♑19.0
☽ Mean ☊ 23♈58.0

1 February 1968
Julian Day # 24868
SVP 5♓42'24"
GC 26♐23.6 ⚴ 2♎55.0R
Eris 11♈01.7 ⚵ 11♏10.9
⚷ 26♓40.1 ⚶ 15♒20.7
☽ Mean ☊ 22♈19.5

March 1968 — LONGITUDE

Day	Sid.Time	☉	0 hr ☽	Noon ☽	True ☊	☿	♀	♂	⚳	♃	♄	♅	♆	♇
1 F	22 37 24	10♓58 39	0♈23 35	6♈34 25	19♈05.0	17♒20.3	12♒40.4	10♈11.0	6♏08.9	29♌34.1	11♈07.8	27♍52.3	26♏31.7	21♍49.5
2 Sa	22 41 21	11 58 51	12 41 45	18 45 52	19D 04.1	17 36.5	13 54.3	10 56.5	6R 09.4	29R 26.5	11 14.7	27R 49.9	26R 31.6	21R 47.9
3 Su	22 45 18	12 59 01	24 47 09	0♉46 00	19 04.8	17 58.3	15 08.2	11 41.9	6 09.4	29 19.0	11 21.7	27 47.4	26 31.4	21 46.3
4 M	22 49 14	13 59 09	6♉42 52	12 38 16	19 06.3	18 25.1	16 22.1	12 27.3	6 09.1	29 11.5	11 28.7	27 44.9	26 31.2	21 44.7
5 Tu	22 53 11	14 59 15	18 32 44	24 26 53	19 08.2	18 56.7	17 36.0	13 12.6	6 08.3	29 04.2	11 35.7	27 42.4	26 31.0	21 43.1
6 W	22 57 07	15 59 20	0♊21 19	6♊16 39	19R 09.6	19 32.8	18 50.0	13 57.9	6 07.1	28 56.8	11 42.7	27 39.8	26 30.7	21 41.5
7 Th	23 01 04	16 59 21	12 13 32	18 12 35	19 10.0	20 13.0	20 03.9	14 43.1	6 05.5	28 49.6	11 49.8	27 37.3	26 30.5	21 39.9
8 F	23 05 00	17 59 21	24 14 27	0♋19 45	19 09.2	20 57.2	21 17.8	15 28.3	6 03.5	28 42.5	11 56.9	27 34.7	26 30.1	21 38.3
9 Sa	23 08 57	18 59 19	6♋29 03	12 42 52	19 07.0	21 44.9	22 31.7	16 13.5	6 01.0	28 35.4	12 04.1	27 32.2	26 29.8	21 36.7
10 Su	23 12 53	19 59 14	19 01 43	25 25 58	19 03.6	22 36.0	23 45.6	16 58.6	5 58.1	28 28.5	12 11.3	27 29.6	26 29.4	21 35.1
11 M	23 16 50	20 59 08	1♌55 56	8♌31 51	18 59.4	23 30.2	24 59.6	17 43.6	5 54.8	28 21.7	12 18.5	27 27.0	26 29.0	21 33.5
12 Tu	23 20 47	21 58 59	15 13 48	22 01 44	18 55.1	24 27.4	26 13.5	18 28.7	5 51.1	28 14.9	12 25.7	27 24.4	26 28.5	21 31.9
13 W	23 24 43	22 58 48	28 55 31	5♍54 50	18 51.1	25 27.4	27 27.4	19 13.6	5 47.0	28 08.3	12 33.0	27 21.8	26 28.1	21 30.3
14 Th	23 28 40	23 58 35	12♍59 15	20 08 14	18 48.1	26 30.0	28 41.4	19 58.5	5 42.4	28 01.8	12 40.3	27 19.2	26 27.5	21 28.6
15 F	23 32 36	24 58 19	27 21 07	4♎37 10	18D 46.2	27 35.0	29 55.3	20 43.4	5 37.5	27 55.4	12 47.6	27 16.6	26 27.0	21 27.0
16 Sa	23 36 33	25 58 02	11♎55 34	19 15 31	18 45.7	28 42.3	1♓09.2	21 28.2	5 32.1	27 49.1	12 54.9	27 14.0	26 26.4	21 25.4
17 Su	23 40 29	26 57 43	26 36 11	3♏56 45	18 46.2	29 51.9	2 23.2	22 13.0	5 26.3	27 43.0	13 02.2	27 11.4	26 25.8	21 23.8
18 M	23 44 26	27 57 23	11♏16 28	18 34 40	18 47.4	1♓03.5	3 37.1	22 57.8	5 20.1	27 37.0	13 09.6	27 08.8	26 25.2	21 22.2
19 Tu	23 48 22	28 57 00	25 50 44	3♐04 10	18 48.7	2 17.2	4 51.1	23 42.4	5 13.6	27 31.1	13 17.0	27 06.2	26 24.5	21 20.6
20 W	23 52 19	29 56 36	10♐14 32	17 21 32	18R 49.8	3 32.8	6 05.0	24 27.1	5 06.6	27 25.4	13 24.4	27 03.6	26 23.8	21 19.0
21 Th	23 56 16	0♈56 11	24 24 55	1♑24 31	18 50.2	4 50.2	7 19.0	25 11.7	4 59.3	27 19.8	13 31.9	27 00.9	26 23.1	21 17.4
22 F	0 00 12	1 55 43	8♑20 14	15 12 02	18 49.7	6 09.4	8 32.9	25 56.3	4 51.5	27 14.4	13 39.3	26 58.3	26 22.4	21 15.9
23 Sa	0 04 09	2 55 14	21 59 54	28 43 54	18 48.5	7 30.3	9 46.9	26 40.8	4 43.4	27 09.1	13 46.8	26 55.8	26 21.6	21 14.3
24 Su	0 08 05	3 54 43	5♒24 03	12♒00 28	18 46.7	8 52.8	11 00.9	27 25.2	4 35.0	27 03.9	13 54.3	26 53.2	26 20.8	21 12.7
25 M	0 12 02	4 54 10	18 33 12	25 02 23	18 44.7	10 17.0	12 14.8	28 09.7	4 26.1	26 58.9	14 01.8	26 50.6	26 19.9	21 11.1
26 Tu	0 15 58	5 53 35	1♓28 05	7♓50 25	18 42.8	11 42.7	13 28.8	28 54.0	4 16.9	26 54.1	14 09.3	26 48.0	26 19.1	21 09.6
27 W	0 19 55	6 52 59	14 09 29	20 25 24	18 41.2	13 10.0	14 42.7	29 38.4	4 07.4	26 49.4	14 16.8	26 45.4	26 18.2	21 08.0
28 Th	0 23 51	7 52 20	26 38 19	2♈48 21	18 40.2	14 38.8	15 56.7	0♉22.7	3 57.6	26 44.9	14 24.3	26 42.9	26 17.2	21 06.5
29 F	0 27 48	8 51 39	8♈55 39	15 00 25	18D 39.7	16 09.1	17 10.6	1 06.9	3 47.4	26 40.5	14 31.9	26 40.3	26 16.3	21 05.0
30 Sa	0 31 45	9 50 56	21 02 50	27 03 08	18 39.8	17 40.9	18 24.6	1 51.1	3 36.9	26 36.3	14 39.4	26 37.8	26 15.3	21 03.4
31 Su	0 35 41	10 50 11	3♉01 35	8♉58 27	18 40.3	19 14.1	19 38.5	2 35.2	3 26.1	26 32.3	14 46.9	26 35.3	26 14.3	21 01.9

April 1968 — LONGITUDE

Day	Sid.Time	☉	0 hr ☽	Noon ☽	True ☊	☿	♀	♂	⚳	♃	♄	♅	♆	♇
1 M	0 39 38	11♈49 24	14♉54 06	20♉48 51	18♈41.0	20♓48.8	20♓52.4	3♉19.3	3♏15.1	26♌28.5	14♈54.5	26♍32.8	26♏13.3	21♍00.5
2 Tu	0 43 34	12 48 35	26 43 07	2♊37 20	18 41.7	22 25.0	22 06.4	4 03.4	3R 03.7	26R 24.8	15 02.1	26R 30.3	26R 12.2	20R 59.0
3 W	0 47 31	13 47 44	8♊31 57	14 27 27	18 42.3	24 02.6	23 20.3	4 47.3	2 52.1	26 21.4	15 09.6	26 27.8	26 11.2	20 57.5
4 Th	0 51 27	14 46 50	20 24 22	26 23 14	18 42.7	25 41.6	24 34.2	5 31.3	2 40.3	26 18.0	15 17.2	26 25.4	26 10.1	20 56.1
5 F	0 55 24	15 45 54	2♋24 36	8♋29 03	18R 42.9	27 22.1	25 48.1	6 15.2	2 28.2	26 14.9	15 24.7	26 23.0	26 09.0	20 54.6
6 Sa	0 59 20	16 44 56	14 37 07	20 49 23	18 42.9	29 04.1	27 02.0	6 59.0	2 16.0	26 12.0	15 32.3	26 20.6	26 07.8	20 53.2
7 Su	1 03 17	17 43 55	27 06 23	3♌28 37	18 42.9	0♈47.5	28 15.9	7 42.8	2 03.5	26 09.2	15 39.9	26 18.2	26 06.6	20 51.8
8 M	1 07 14	18 42 52	9♌56 32	16 30 31	18D 42.8	2 32.4	29 29.8	8 26.6	1 50.8	26 06.6	15 47.4	26 15.8	26 05.4	20 50.4
9 Tu	1 11 10	19 41 47	23 10 52	29 57 47	18 42.9	4 18.8	0♈43.7	9 10.3	1 38.0	26 04.2	15 55.0	26 13.5	26 04.2	20 49.0
10 W	1 15 07	20 40 39	6♍51 21	13♍51 29	18 43.0	6 06.6	1 57.6	9 53.9	1 25.0	26 02.0	16 02.5	26 11.2	26 03.0	20 47.7
11 Th	1 19 03	21 39 30	20 58 00	28 10 30	18 43.2	7 56.0	3 11.4	10 37.5	1 11.9	26 00.0	16 10.1	26 08.9	26 01.7	20 46.3
12 F	1 23 00	22 38 18	5♎28 27	12♎51 09	18R 43.4	9 46.9	4 25.3	11 21.0	0 58.6	25 58.1	16 17.6	26 06.6	26 00.5	20 45.0
13 Sa	1 26 56	23 37 04	20 17 46	27 47 20	18 43.4	11 39.3	5 39.1	12 04.5	0 45.3	25 56.4	16 25.1	26 04.4	25 59.2	20 43.7
14 Su	1 30 53	24 35 48	5♏18 48	12♏51 03	18 43.1	13 33.3	6 53.0	12 47.9	0 31.8	25 55.0	16 32.6	26 02.2	25 57.9	20 42.4
15 M	1 34 49	25 34 30	20 22 58	27 53 27	18 42.4	15 28.7	8 06.9	13 31.3	0 18.3	25 53.7	16 40.2	26 00.0	25 56.5	20 41.1
16 Tu	1 38 46	26 33 11	5♐21 30	12♐46 11	18 41.6	17 25.7	9 20.7	14 14.7	0 04.7	25 52.6	16 47.7	25 57.9	25 55.2	20 39.9
17 W	1 42 43	27 31 50	20 06 42	27 22 24	18 40.7	19 24.2	10 34.6	14 58.0	29♎51.1	25 51.6	16 55.1	25 55.8	25 53.8	20 38.7
18 Th	1 46 39	28 30 27	4♑32 49	11♑37 36	18 40.0	21 24.1	11 48.4	15 41.2	29 37.5	25 50.9	17 02.6	25 53.7	25 52.4	20 37.5
19 F	1 50 36	29 29 02	18 36 34	25 29 38	18D 39.6	23 25.5	13 02.2	16 24.4	29 23.8	25 50.3	17 10.1	25 51.7	25 51.0	20 36.3
20 Sa	1 54 32	0♉27 36	2♒16 53	8♒58 28	18 39.7	25 28.2	14 16.1	17 07.6	29 10.2	25 50.0	17 17.5	25 49.7	25 49.6	20 35.1
21 Su	1 58 29	1 26 09	15 34 37	22 05 38	18 40.3	27 32.2	15 29.9	17 50.7	28 56.6	25D 49.8	17 25.0	25 47.7	25 48.2	20 34.0
22 M	2 02 25	2 24 39	28 31 51	4♓53 37	18 41.4	29 37.4	16 43.8	18 33.7	28 43.0	25 49.8	17 32.4	25 45.7	25 46.7	20 32.9
23 Tu	2 06 22	3 23 08	11♓11 18	17 25 18	18 42.6	1♉43.7	17 57.6	19 16.7	28 29.4	25 50.0	17 39.8	25 43.8	25 45.3	20 31.8
24 W	2 10 18	4 21 35	23 35 59	29 43 41	18 43.8	3 50.9	19 11.4	19 59.7	28 16.0	25 50.4	17 47.1	25 42.0	25 43.8	20 30.7
25 Th	2 14 15	5 20 01	5♈48 46	11♈51 33	18R 44.5	5 58.9	20 25.2	20 42.6	28 02.6	25 50.9	17 54.5	25 40.1	25 42.3	20 29.6
26 F	2 18 12	6 18 24	17 52 21	23 51 26	18 44.6	8 07.5	21 39.0	21 25.5	27 49.4	25 51.7	18 01.8	25 38.3	25 40.8	20 28.6
27 Sa	2 22 08	7 16 46	29 49 06	5♉45 35	18 43.7	10 16.4	22 52.8	22 08.3	27 36.3	25 52.6	18 09.1	25 36.6	25 39.3	20 27.6
28 Su	2 26 05	8 15 06	11♉41 11	17 36 07	18 41.9	12 25.4	24 06.6	22 51.1	27 23.3	25 53.7	18 16.4	25 34.9	25 37.7	20 26.6
29 M	2 30 01	9 13 25	23 30 39	29 25 04	18 39.1	14 34.2	25 20.4	23 33.8	27 10.5	25 55.0	18 23.6	25 33.2	25 36.2	20 25.7
30 Tu	2 33 58	10 11 41	5♊19 36	11♊14 35	18 35.7	16 42.5	26 34.2	24 16.4	26 57.9	25 56.5	18 30.9	25 31.6	25 34.7	20 24.8

Astro Data Dy Hr Mn	Planet Ingress Dy Hr Mn	Last Aspect Dy Hr Mn	☽ Ingress Dy Hr Mn	Last Aspect Dy Hr Mn	☽ Ingress Dy Hr Mn	☽ Phases & Eclipses Dy Hr Mn
☽0N 1 5:34	♀ ♓ 15 13:32	3 9:07 ♃ △	♉ 3 10:27	1 23:37 ♅ △	♊ 2 6:40	7 9:20 ☽ 16♊53
⚳R 3 4:24	☿ ♓ 17 14:45	5 21:18 ♃ □	♊ 5 23:17	4 12:04 ♅ □	♋ 4 19:13	14 18:52 ○ 24♍16
♄☌♆ 4 20:31	☉ ♈ 20 13:22	8 8:51 ♃ ✶	♋ 8 11:21	7 1:08 ♀ △	♌ 7 5:28	21 11:07 ☾ 0♑54
☽0S 15 9:44	♂ ♉ 27 23:43	10 15:49 ♅ ✶	♌ 10 20:27	9 5:09 ♃ ☌	♍ 9 12:04	28 22:48 ● 8♈19
♃☌♄ 16 1:49		12 22:45 ♃ ☌	♍ 13 1:51	11 8:39 ♅ ☌	♎ 11 15:01	28 22:59:51 ● P 0.899
☉0N 20 13:23	☿ ♈ 7 1:01	14 23:55 ♅ ☌	♎ 15 4:23	13 9:03 ♃ ✶	♏ 13 15:32	
⚳0N 27 5:41	♀ ♈ 8 21:48	17 4:45 ☿ △	♏ 17 5:33	15 8:59 ♅ ✶	♐ 15 15:23	6 3:27 ☽ 16♋24
☽0N 28 12:52	⚳ ♎R 16 20:21	19 4:39 ☉ △	♐ 19 6:53	17 12:17 ☉ △	♑ 17 16:23	13 4:52 ○ 23♎20
♃⚺♅ 29 14:46	☉ ♉ 20 0:41	21 5:02 ♃ △	♑ 21 9:34	19 19:35 ☉ □	♒ 19 19:57	13 4:47 ● T 1.111
♃□♆ 9 11:32	☿ ♉ 22 16:18	23 8:47 ♅ △	♒ 23 14:16	22 0:06 ☿ ✶	♓ 22 2:46	19 19:35 ☾ 29♑48
☿0N 9 22:13		25 18:10 ♂ ✶	♓ 25 21:15	24 4:11 ♆ △	♈ 24 12:32	27 15:21 ● 7♉25
♀0N 11 18:11		28 0:11 ♅ ☍	♈ 28 6:32	26 16:02 ♃ △	♉ 27 0:22	
☽0S 11 20:23	♅✶✶20 13:49	30 11:07 ♃ △	♉ 30 17:55	29 4:52 ♃ □	♊ 29 13:11	
♃□♆ 20 4:22	♃ D21 23:26					
♃⚺♅ 20 7:35	☽0N24 18:57					

Astro Data

1 March 1968
Julian Day # 24897
SVP 5♓42'21"
GC 26♐23.7 ⚴ 27♍02.8R
Eris 11♈15.9 ⚵ 13♏20.6R
⚷ 28♓11.1 ⚶ 0♓08.6
☽ Mean ☊ 20♈47.3

1 April 1968
Julian Day # 24928
SVP 5♓42'17"
GC 26♐23.8 ⚴ 17♍36.4R
Eris 11♈36.2 ⚵ 10♏30.2R
⚷ 0♈00.7 ⚶ 15♓27.2
☽ Mean ☊ 19♈08.8

LONGITUDE — May 1968

Day	Sid.Time	☉	0 hr ☽	Noon ☽	True ☊	☿	♀	♂	⚳	♃	♄	♅	♆	♇
1 W	2 37 54	11♉09 56	17♊10 17	23♊07 04	18♈32.0	18♉50.2	27♈48.0	24♉59.1	26♎45.4	25♌58.2	18♈38.1	25♍30.0	25♏33.1	20♍23.9
2 Th	2 41 51	12 08 09	29 05 17	5♋05 19	18R 28.5	20 56.7	29 01.8	25 41.7	26R 33.2	26 00.0	18 45.3	25R 28.5	25R 31.5	20R 23.0
3 F	2 45 47	13 06 20	11♋07 33	17 12 28	18 25.5	23 01.9	0♉15.5	26 24.2	26 21.2	26 02.0	18 52.4	25 27.0	25 30.0	20 22.1
4 Sa	2 49 44	14 04 28	23 20 29	29 32 06	18 23.5	25 05.4	1 29.3	27 06.7	26 09.4	26 04.2	18 59.5	25 25.5	25 28.4	20 21.3
5 Su	2 53 41	15 02 35	5♌47 46	12♌08 01	18D 22.6	27 07.0	2 43.1	27 49.1	25 57.9	26 06.6	19 06.6	25 24.1	25 26.8	20 20.5
6 M	2 57 37	16 00 40	18 33 18	25 04 04	18 22.9	29 06.4	3 56.8	28 31.5	25 46.6	26 09.2	19 13.7	25 22.7	25 25.2	20 19.8
7 Tu	3 01 34	16 58 43	1♍40 44	8♍23 40	18 24.0	1♊03.4	5 10.5	29 13.8	25 35.6	26 11.9	19 20.7	25 21.4	25 23.6	20 19.0
8 W	3 05 30	17 56 44	15 13 08	22 09 18	18 25.5	2 57.7	6 24.3	29 56.1	25 24.8	26 14.8	19 27.6	25 20.1	25 22.0	20 18.3
9 Th	3 09 27	18 54 43	29 12 12	6♎21 45	18R 26.8	4 49.3	7 38.0	0♊38.3	25 14.4	26 17.9	19 34.6	25 18.9	25 20.4	20 17.7
10 F	3 13 23	19 52 40	13♎37 39	20 59 27	18 27.1	6 37.8	8 51.7	1 20.5	25 04.2	26 21.1	19 41.5	25 17.7	25 18.8	20 17.0
11 Sa	3 17 20	20 50 36	28 26 30	5♏57 58	18 26.2	8 23.2	10 05.4	2 02.6	24 54.4	26 24.5	19 48.4	25 16.6	25 17.1	20 16.4
12 Su	3 21 16	21 48 30	13♏32 49	21 09 55	18 23.6	10 05.5	11 19.1	2 44.7	24 44.9	26 28.1	19 55.2	25 15.5	25 15.5	20 15.8
13 M	3 25 13	22 46 22	28 47 58	6♐25 41	18 19.7	11 44.3	12 32.8	3 26.7	24 35.7	26 31.9	20 02.0	25 14.5	25 13.9	20 15.2
14 Tu	3 29 10	23 44 13	14♐01 43	21 34 50	18 14.8	13 19.8	13 46.5	4 08.7	24 26.8	26 35.8	20 08.7	25 13.5	25 12.3	20 14.7
15 W	3 33 06	24 42 03	29 03 53	6♑27 51	18 09.7	14 51.9	15 00.2	4 50.6	24 18.3	26 39.9	20 15.5	25 12.6	25 10.7	20 14.2
16 Th	3 37 03	25 39 52	13♑45 57	20 57 33	18 05.1	16 20.3	16 13.9	5 32.5	24 10.1	26 44.1	20 22.1	25 11.7	25 09.0	20 13.7
17 F	3 40 59	26 37 39	28 02 16	4♒59 52	18 01.7	17 45.3	17 27.6	6 14.4	24 02.3	26 48.5	20 28.8	25 10.9	25 07.4	20 13.3
18 Sa	3 44 56	27 35 25	11♒50 21	18 33 51	17D 59.8	19 06.5	18 41.3	6 56.2	23 54.8	26 53.1	20 35.3	25 10.1	25 05.8	20 12.9
19 Su	3 48 52	28 33 10	25 10 38	1♓41 05	17 59.4	20 24.1	19 55.0	7 38.0	23 47.7	26 57.8	20 41.9	25 09.3	25 04.1	20 12.5
20 M	3 52 49	29 30 54	8♓05 37	14 24 48	18 00.3	21 38.0	21 08.7	8 19.7	23 40.9	27 02.6	20 48.4	25 08.6	25 02.5	20 12.1
21 Tu	3 56 45	0♊28 37	20 39 08	26 49 11	18 01.7	22 48.0	22 22.4	9 01.3	23 34.6	27 07.7	20 54.8	25 08.0	25 00.9	20 11.8
22 W	4 00 42	1 26 19	2♈55 33	8♈58 44	18R 03.0	23 54.3	23 36.1	9 43.0	23 28.6	27 12.8	21 01.2	25 07.4	24 59.3	20 11.5
23 Th	4 04 39	2 23 59	14 59 17	20 57 43	18 03.3	24 56.6	24 49.8	10 24.6	23 23.0	27 18.2	21 07.5	25 06.9	24 57.7	20 11.3
24 F	4 08 35	3 21 39	26 54 29	2♉50 02	18 02.0	25 54.9	26 03.5	11 06.1	23 17.7	27 23.6	21 13.8	25 06.4	24 56.1	20 11.0
25 Sa	4 12 32	4 19 18	8♉44 44	14 38 59	17 58.7	26 49.2	27 17.2	11 47.6	23 12.9	27 29.3	21 20.1	25 06.0	24 54.5	20 10.8
26 Su	4 16 28	5 16 55	20 33 04	26 27 17	17 53.3	27 39.4	28 30.8	12 29.1	23 08.5	27 35.0	21 26.3	25 05.6	24 52.9	20 10.7
27 M	4 20 25	6 14 31	2♊21 55	8♊17 11	17 45.9	28 25.5	29 44.5	13 10.5	23 04.4	27 41.0	21 32.4	25 05.3	24 51.3	20 10.5
28 Tu	4 24 21	7 12 07	14 13 18	20 10 29	17 37.0	29 07.2	0♊58.2	13 51.8	23 00.8	27 47.0	21 38.5	25 05.0	24 49.7	20 10.4
29 W	4 28 18	8 09 41	26 08 56	2♋08 50	17 27.5	29 44.7	2 11.9	14 33.2	22 57.5	27 53.3	21 44.5	25 04.8	24 48.1	20 10.4
30 Th	4 32 14	9 07 13	8♋10 25	14 13 54	17 18.2	0♋17.7	3 25.6	15 14.4	22 54.6	27 59.6	21 50.5	25 04.6	24 46.5	20D 10.3
31 F	4 36 11	10 04 45	20 19 32	26 27 33	17 10.0	0 46.3	4 39.3	15 55.7	22 52.2	28 06.1	21 56.4	25 04.5	24 45.0	20 10.3

LONGITUDE — June 1968

Day	Sid.Time	☉	0 hr ☽	Noon ☽	True ☊	☿	♀	♂	⚳	♃	♄	♅	♆	♇
1 Sa	4 40 08	11♊02 15	2♌38 17	8♌52 02	17♈03.6	1♋10.3	5♊53.0	16♊36.9	22♎50.1	28♌12.7	22♈02.2	25♍04.5	24♏43.4	20♍10.4
2 Su	4 44 04	11 59 44	15 09 09	21 30 00	16R 59.4	1 29.8	7 06.6	17 18.0	22R 48.4	28 19.5	22 08.0	25D 04.5	24R 41.9	20 10.4
3 M	4 48 01	12 57 12	27 54 59	4♍24 29	16D 57.3	1 44.6	8 20.3	17 59.1	22 47.2	28 26.4	22 13.7	25 04.5	24 40.4	20 10.5
4 Tu	4 51 57	13 54 39	10♍58 53	17 38 36	16 57.0	1 54.8	9 34.0	18 40.2	22 46.3	28 33.4	22 19.4	25 04.6	24 38.8	20 10.6
5 W	4 55 54	14 52 04	24 23 56	1♎15 10	16 57.7	2R 00.4	10 47.7	19 21.2	22D 45.8	28 40.6	22 25.0	25 04.8	24 37.3	20 10.8
6 Th	4 59 50	15 49 28	8♎12 32	15 16 06	16R 58.2	2 01.4	12 01.3	20 02.1	22 45.7	28 47.9	22 30.5	25 05.0	24 35.8	20 10.9
7 F	5 03 47	16 46 51	22 25 50	29 41 32	16 57.7	1 57.9	13 15.0	20 43.1	22 46.0	28 55.3	22 36.0	25 05.3	24 34.3	20 11.2
8 Sa	5 07 43	17 44 12	7♏02 48	14♏29 04	16 55.1	1 50.0	14 28.7	21 23.9	22 46.7	29 02.9	22 41.4	25 05.6	24 32.9	20 11.4
9 Su	5 11 40	18 41 33	21 59 34	29 33 19	16 50.1	1 37.9	15 42.3	22 04.8	22 47.7	29 10.5	22 46.7	25 06.0	24 31.4	20 11.7
10 M	5 15 37	19 38 54	7♐09 11	14♐45 56	16 42.8	1 21.8	16 56.0	22 45.6	22 49.2	29 18.3	22 52.0	25 06.4	24 30.0	20 12.0
11 Tu	5 19 33	20 36 13	22 22 13	29 56 41	16 33.9	1 02.0	18 09.7	23 26.3	22 51.0	29 26.2	22 57.2	25 06.9	24 28.6	20 12.4
12 W	5 23 30	21 33 32	7♑28 03	14♑55 05	16 24.5	0 38.7	19 23.3	24 07.0	22 53.2	29 34.3	23 02.3	25 07.4	24 27.1	20 12.7
13 Th	5 27 26	22 30 50	22 16 47	29 32 17	16 15.7	0 12.4	20 37.0	24 47.7	22 55.8	29 42.4	23 07.4	25 08.0	24 25.8	20 13.1
14 F	5 31 23	23 28 07	6♒40 57	13♒42 22	16 08.4	29♊43.5	21 50.7	25 28.3	22 58.7	29 50.7	23 12.4	25 08.6	24 24.4	20 13.6
15 Sa	5 35 19	24 25 24	20 36 20	27 22 51	16 03.3	29 12.4	23 04.4	26 08.9	23 02.0	29 59.0	23 17.3	25 09.3	24 23.0	20 14.0
16 Su	5 39 16	25 22 41	4♓02 06	10♓34 23	16 00.4	28 39.8	24 18.1	26 49.5	23 05.6	0♍07.5	23 22.2	25 10.1	24 21.7	20 14.5
17 M	5 43 13	26 19 58	17 00 09	23 19 56	15D 59.5	28 06.0	25 31.8	27 30.0	23 09.6	0 16.1	23 26.9	25 10.8	24 20.3	20 15.1
18 Tu	5 47 09	27 17 14	29 34 18	5♈43 54	15R 59.6	27 31.7	26 45.5	28 10.5	23 14.0	0 24.8	23 31.6	25 11.7	24 19.0	20 15.6
19 W	5 51 06	28 14 30	11♈49 24	17 51 25	15 59.8	26 57.6	27 59.2	28 50.9	23 18.7	0 33.6	23 36.3	25 12.6	24 17.7	20 16.2
20 Th	5 55 02	29 11 45	23 50 38	29 47 40	15 59.0	26 24.1	29 12.9	29 31.3	23 23.7	0 42.6	23 40.8	25 13.5	24 16.5	20 16.8
21 F	5 58 59	0♋09 01	5♉43 07	11♉37 33	15 56.2	25 51.8	0♋26.6	0♋11.7	23 29.1	0 51.6	23 45.3	25 14.5	24 15.2	20 17.5
22 Sa	6 02 55	1 06 16	17 31 28	23 25 21	15 51.0	25 21.3	1 40.3	0 52.0	23 34.9	1 00.7	23 49.7	25 15.6	24 14.0	20 18.2
23 Su	6 06 52	2 03 31	29 19 38	5♊14 40	15 43.0	24 53.2	2 54.1	1 32.3	23 40.9	1 10.0	23 54.0	25 16.7	24 12.8	20 18.9
24 M	6 10 48	3 00 46	11♊10 48	17 08 18	15 32.5	24 27.8	4 07.8	2 12.6	23 47.4	1 19.3	23 58.2	25 17.9	24 11.6	20 19.6
25 Tu	6 14 45	3 58 01	23 07 24	29 08 17	15 20.2	24 05.7	5 21.5	2 52.8	23 54.1	1 28.7	24 02.3	25 19.1	24 10.4	20 20.4
26 W	6 18 42	4 55 16	5♋11 07	11♋16 02	15 06.9	23 47.2	6 35.3	3 33.0	24 01.2	1 38.3	24 06.4	25 20.3	24 09.3	20 21.2
27 Th	6 22 38	5 52 30	17 23 07	23 32 30	14 53.8	23 32.6	7 49.0	4 13.1	24 08.5	1 47.9	24 10.4	25 21.6	24 08.2	20 22.1
28 F	6 26 35	6 49 44	29 44 15	5♌58 29	14 42.1	23 22.3	9 02.8	4 53.2	24 16.2	1 57.6	24 14.3	25 23.0	24 07.1	20 22.9
29 Sa	6 30 31	7 46 57	12♌15 19	18 34 52	14 32.6	23D 16.4	10 16.5	5 33.3	24 24.3	2 07.5	24 18.1	25 24.4	24 06.0	20 23.8
30 Su	6 34 28	8 44 10	24 57 18	1♍22 48	14 25.8	23 15.2	11 30.3	6 13.3	24 32.6	2 17.4	24 21.8	25 25.9	24 04.9	20 24.8

Astro Data (Dy Hr Mn)

Astro Data	Dy Hr Mn
☽0S	9 6:41
♅⚹♆	12 11:52
♄⚻♇	15 7:48
☽0N	22 0:20
♇ D	31 4:01
♅ D	2 0:37
☽0S	5 14:49
⚳0S	6 0:14
☿ R	6 5:16
⚳ D	6 5:53
☽0N	18 6:04
♄⚻♆	27 1:26
☿ D	30 6:09

Planet Ingress (Dy Hr Mn)

Planet Ingress	Dy Hr Mn
♀ ♉	3 6:56
☿ ♊	6 22:56
♂ ♊	8 14:14
☉ ♊	21 0:06
♀ ♊	27 17:02
☿ ♋	29 22:44
☿ ♊R	13 22:32
♃ ♍	15 14:44
♀ ♋	21 3:20
♂ ♋	21 5:03
☉ ♋	21 8:13

Last Aspect / ☽ Ingress (May)

Last Aspect Dy Hr Mn		☽ Ingress Dy Hr Mn
1 22:30	♀ ⚹	♋ 2 1:50
4 7:02	♂ ⚹	♌ 4 12:54
6 20:38	☿ □	♍ 6 20:58
8 17:29	♆ ⚹	♎ 9 1:21
10 20:41	♃ ⚹	♏ 11 2:30
12 20:22	♃ □	♐ 13 1:53
14 20:04	♃ △	♑ 15 1:31
16 20:32	☉ △	♒ 17 3:22
19 5:44	☉ □	♓ 19 8:53
21 8:43	♅ ☍	♈ 21 18:14
24 0:54	♃ △	♉ 24 6:15
26 16:40	♀ ☌	♊ 26 19:12
29 6:57	☿ ☌	♋ 29 7:43
31 9:18	♅ ⚹	♌ 31 18:53

Last Aspect / ☽ Ingress (June)

Last Aspect Dy Hr Mn		☽ Ingress Dy Hr Mn
3 0:52	♃ ☌	♍ 3 3:52
5 1:12	♅ ☌	♎ 5 9:49
7 10:43	♃ ⚹	♏ 7 12:30
9 11:24	♃ □	♐ 9 12:42
11 11:11	♃ △	♑ 11 12:05
13 4:42	♅ △	♒ 13 12:46
15 15:09	☿ △	♓ 15 16:42
17 20:45	☿ □	♈ 18 0:50
20 11:25	♂ ⚹	♉ 20 12:25
22 15:44	♅ △	♊ 23 1:22
25 4:22	♅ □	♋ 25 13:43
27 15:32	♅ ⚹	♌ 28 0:30
29 22:50	♄ △	♍ 30 9:26

☽ Phases & Eclipses

Dy Hr Mn	
5 17:54	☽ 15♌17
12 13:05	○ 21♏51
19 5:44	☾ 28♒18
27 7:30	● 6♊04
4 4:47	☽ 13♍37
10 20:13	○ 19♐59
17 18:14	☾ 26♓35
25 22:24	● 4♋23

Astro Data

1 May 1968
Julian Day # 24958
SVP 5♓42'14"
GC 26♐23.8 ⚴ 13♍57.6
Eris 11♈55.9 ⚵ 4♏05.5R
⚷ 1♈38.5 ⚶ 29♓27.9
☽ Mean ☊ 17♈33.5

1 June 1968
Julian Day # 24989
SVP 5♓42'08"
GC 26♐23.9 ⚴ 17♍19.7
Eris 12♈11.6 ⚵ 28♎37.3R
⚷ 2♈51.7 ⚶ 12♈41.6
☽ Mean ☊ 15♈55.0

July 1968

LONGITUDE

Day	Sid.Time	☉	0 hr ☽	Noon ☽	True ☊	☿	♀	♂	⚳	♃	♄	♅	♆	♇
1 M	6 38 24	9♋41 23	7♍51 36	14♍23 55	14♈21.8	23♊18.8	12♋44.0	6♋53.3	24♎41.2	2♍27.4	24♈25.5	25♍27.4	24♏03.9	20♍25.7
2 Tu	6 42 21	10 38 36	21 00 01	27 40 10	14R20.2	23 27.3	13 57.8	7 33.2	24 50.1	2 37.5	24 29.0	25 28.9	24R02.9	20 26.7
3 W	6 46 17	11 35 48	4♎24 38	11♎13 40	14 19.9	23 40.7	15 11.6	8 13.1	24 59.4	2 47.6	24 32.5	25 30.5	24 01.9	20 27.7
4 Th	6 50 14	12 32 59	18 07 29	25 06 12	14 19.7	23 59.1	16 25.3	8 53.0	25 08.9	2 57.9	24 35.8	25 32.2	24 01.0	20 28.7
5 F	6 54 11	13 30 11	2♏09 53	9♏18 28	14 18.5	24 22.6	17 39.1	9 32.9	25 18.7	3 08.2	24 39.1	25 33.9	24 00.0	20 29.8
6 Sa	6 58 07	14 27 22	16 31 47	23 49 28	14 15.2	24 51.0	18 52.9	10 12.7	25 28.7	3 18.6	24 42.3	25 35.6	23 59.1	20 30.9
7 Su	7 02 04	15 24 33	1♐11 01	8♐35 46	14 09.3	25 24.5	20 06.6	10 52.4	25 39.1	3 29.2	24 45.4	25 37.4	23 58.3	20 32.0
8 M	7 06 00	16 21 45	16 02 50	23 31 16	14 00.8	26 02.9	21 20.4	11 32.2	25 49.7	3 39.7	24 48.4	25 39.3	23 57.4	20 33.2
9 Tu	7 09 57	17 18 56	0♑59 59	8♑27 47	13 50.5	26 46.3	22 34.2	12 11.9	26 00.6	3 50.4	24 51.3	25 41.2	23 56.6	20 34.4
10 W	7 13 53	18 16 07	15 53 32	23 16 06	13 39.4	27 34.5	23 48.0	12 51.5	26 11.8	4 01.1	24 54.2	25 43.1	23 55.8	20 35.6
11 Th	7 17 50	19 13 18	0♒34 27	7♒47 40	13 28.8	28 27.6	25 01.8	13 31.1	26 23.2	4 11.9	24 56.9	25 45.1	23 55.1	20 36.8
12 F	7 21 46	20 10 30	14 55 00	21 55 56	13 19.9	29 25.4	26 15.6	14 10.7	26 34.8	4 22.8	24 59.5	25 47.1	23 54.3	20 38.1
13 Sa	7 25 43	21 07 42	28 50 05	5♓37 17	13 13.3	0♋28.0	27 29.4	14 50.3	26 46.8	4 33.8	25 02.1	25 49.2	23 53.6	20 39.4
14 Su	7 29 40	22 04 55	12♓17 34	18 51 06	13 09.2	1 35.1	28 43.2	15 29.8	26 58.9	4 44.8	25 04.5	25 51.3	23 52.9	20 40.7
15 M	7 33 36	23 02 08	25 18 11	1♈39 15	13D07.4	2 46.9	29 57.0	16 09.3	27 11.3	4 55.9	25 06.9	25 53.4	23 52.3	20 42.0
16 Tu	7 37 33	23 59 22	7♈54 49	14 05 29	13R07.0	4 03.2	1♌10.8	16 48.8	27 24.0	5 07.1	25 09.1	25 55.6	23 51.6	20 43.4
17 W	7 41 29	24 56 36	20 11 51	26 14 36	13 07.1	5 23.9	2 24.6	17 28.2	27 36.8	5 18.3	25 11.3	25 57.9	23 51.0	20 44.7
18 Th	7 45 26	25 53 51	2♉14 23	8♉11 54	13 06.5	6 48.9	3 38.4	18 07.6	27 49.9	5 29.6	25 13.3	26 00.2	23 50.5	20 46.2
19 F	7 49 22	26 51 07	14 07 48	20 02 44	13 04.4	8 18.1	4 52.3	18 47.0	28 03.3	5 41.0	25 15.3	26 02.5	23 49.9	20 47.6
20 Sa	7 53 19	27 48 24	25 57 18	1♊52 03	12 59.9	9 51.5	6 06.1	19 26.4	28 16.9	5 52.4	25 17.2	26 04.9	23 49.4	20 49.0
21 Su	7 57 15	28 45 41	7♊47 33	13 44 15	12 52.8	11 28.8	7 20.0	20 05.7	28 30.7	6 03.9	25 18.9	26 07.3	23 49.0	20 50.5
22 M	8 01 12	29 42 59	19 42 36	25 42 56	12 43.4	13 09.9	8 33.8	20 45.0	28 44.7	6 15.4	25 20.6	26 09.7	23 48.5	20 52.0
23 Tu	8 05 09	0♌40 18	1♋45 34	7♋50 46	12 32.0	14 54.6	9 47.7	21 24.2	28 58.9	6 27.0	25 22.1	26 12.2	23 48.1	20 53.6
24 W	8 09 05	1 37 38	13 58 43	20 09 32	12 19.8	16 42.7	11 01.6	22 03.4	29 13.3	6 38.7	25 23.6	26 14.8	23 47.7	20 55.1
25 Th	8 13 02	2 34 58	26 23 19	2♌40 07	12 07.7	18 33.9	12 15.5	22 42.6	29 28.0	6 50.4	25 24.9	26 17.3	23 47.4	20 56.7
26 F	8 16 58	3 32 19	8♌59 55	15 22 43	11 56.8	20 28.0	13 29.3	23 21.8	29 42.8	7 02.2	25 26.2	26 19.9	23 47.0	20 58.3
27 Sa	8 20 55	4 29 41	21 48 28	28 17 07	11 48.0	22 24.6	14 43.2	24 00.9	29 57.9	7 14.1	25 27.3	26 22.6	23 46.8	20 59.9
28 Su	8 24 51	5 27 03	4♍48 38	11♍22 58	11 41.9	24 23.4	15 57.1	24 40.0	0♏13.2	7 25.9	25 28.4	26 25.3	23 46.5	21 01.6
29 M	8 28 48	6 24 26	18 00 08	24 40 08	11 38.4	26 24.2	17 11.0	25 19.1	0 28.6	7 37.9	25 29.3	26 28.0	23 46.3	21 03.2
30 Tu	8 32 44	7 21 49	1♎22 59	8♎08 45	11D37.2	28 26.5	18 24.9	25 58.1	0 44.3	7 49.9	25 30.2	26 30.7	23 46.1	21 04.9
31 W	8 36 41	8 19 13	14 57 29	21 49 16	11 37.4	0♌30.1	19 38.7	26 37.1	1 00.1	8 01.9	25 30.9	26 33.5	23 45.9	21 06.6

August 1968

LONGITUDE

Day	Sid.Time	☉	0 hr ☽	Noon ☽	True ☊	☿	♀	♂	⚳	♃	♄	♅	♆	♇
1 Th	8 40 38	9♌16 37	28♎44 10	5♏42 12	11♈37.9	2♌34.5	20♌52.6	27♋16.1	1♏16.1	8♍14.0	25♈31.5	26♍36.4	23♏45.8	21♍08.4
2 F	8 44 34	10 14 02	12♏43 23	19 47 39	11R37.6	4 39.5	22 06.5	27 55.1	1 32.3	8 26.1	25 32.0	26 39.2	23R45.7	21 10.1
3 Sa	8 48 31	11 11 28	26 54 52	4♐04 48	11 35.6	6 44.7	23 20.4	28 34.0	1 48.7	8 38.3	25 32.5	26 42.1	23 45.6	21 11.9
4 Su	8 52 27	12 08 54	11♐17 08	18 31 25	11 31.3	8 49.9	24 34.3	29 12.9	2 05.3	8 50.5	25 32.8	26 45.0	23D45.6	21 13.7
5 M	8 56 24	13 06 22	25 47 06	3♑03 32	11 24.8	10 54.8	25 48.2	29 51.7	2 22.0	9 02.8	25 33.0	26 48.0	23 45.6	21 15.5
6 Tu	9 00 20	14 03 50	10♑19 59	17 35 38	11 16.8	12 59.2	27 02.0	0♌30.5	2 38.9	9 15.1	25R33.1	26 51.0	23 45.6	21 17.3
7 W	9 04 17	15 01 19	24 49 41	2♒01 16	11 08.0	15 02.9	28 15.9	1 09.3	2 55.9	9 27.4	25 33.1	26 54.0	23 45.7	21 19.1
8 Th	9 08 14	15 58 48	9♒09 36	16 13 58	10 59.5	17 05.8	29 29.8	1 48.1	3 13.1	9 39.8	25 33.0	26 57.1	23 45.7	21 21.0
9 F	9 12 10	16 56 19	23 13 43	0♓08 20	10 52.4	19 07.6	0♍43.7	2 26.9	3 30.5	9 52.2	25 32.8	27 00.2	23 45.9	21 22.9
10 Sa	9 16 07	17 53 51	6♓57 28	13 40 51	10 47.2	21 08.3	1 57.5	3 05.6	3 48.1	10 04.7	25 32.5	27 03.3	23 46.0	21 24.7
11 Su	9 20 03	18 51 24	20 18 23	26 50 06	10 44.2	23 07.8	3 11.4	3 44.3	4 05.7	10 17.1	25 32.1	27 06.4	23 46.2	21 26.6
12 M	9 24 00	19 48 59	3♈16 11	9♈36 52	10D43.2	25 06.1	4 25.3	4 22.9	4 23.6	10 29.7	25 31.6	27 09.6	23 46.4	21 28.6
13 Tu	9 27 56	20 46 35	15 52 32	22 03 39	10 43.7	27 03.0	5 39.2	5 01.6	4 41.6	10 42.2	25 31.0	27 12.8	23 46.7	21 30.5
14 W	9 31 53	21 44 12	28 10 42	4♉14 15	10 44.9	28 58.5	6 53.0	5 40.2	4 59.7	10 54.8	25 30.3	27 16.0	23 47.0	21 32.4
15 Th	9 35 49	22 41 51	10♉14 55	16 13 20	10R45.9	0♍52.7	8 06.9	6 18.8	5 18.0	11 07.4	25 29.5	27 19.3	23 47.3	21 34.4
16 F	9 39 46	23 39 31	22 10 07	28 05 55	10 46.0	2 45.4	9 20.8	6 57.3	5 36.4	11 20.1	25 28.5	27 22.6	23 47.6	21 36.4
17 Sa	9 43 43	24 37 14	4♊01 23	9♊57 08	10 44.6	4 36.7	10 34.7	7 35.9	5 55.0	11 32.7	25 27.5	27 25.9	23 48.0	21 38.4
18 Su	9 47 39	25 34 57	15 53 45	21 51 48	10 41.4	6 26.6	11 48.6	8 14.4	6 13.7	11 45.4	25 26.4	27 29.2	23 48.4	21 40.4
19 M	9 51 36	26 32 43	27 51 49	3♋54 17	10 36.3	8 15.1	13 02.4	8 52.9	6 32.5	11 58.2	25 25.2	27 32.6	23 48.9	21 42.4
20 Tu	9 55 32	27 30 30	9♋59 37	16 08 10	10 29.9	10 02.1	14 16.3	9 31.4	6 51.5	12 10.9	25 23.8	27 36.0	23 49.4	21 44.5
21 W	9 59 29	28 28 18	22 20 15	28 36 05	10 22.6	11 47.8	15 30.2	10 09.8	7 10.6	12 23.7	25 22.4	27 39.4	23 49.9	21 46.5
22 Th	10 03 25	29 26 08	4♌55 51	11♌19 36	10 15.3	13 32.1	16 44.1	10 48.2	7 29.9	12 36.5	25 20.9	27 42.8	23 50.4	21 48.6
23 F	10 07 22	0♍24 00	17 47 22	24 19 07	10 08.8	15 15.0	17 58.0	11 26.6	7 49.2	12 49.4	25 19.2	27 46.3	23 51.0	21 50.6
24 Sa	10 11 18	1 21 53	0♍54 42	7♍34 00	10 03.7	16 56.5	19 11.8	12 05.0	8 08.7	13 02.2	25 17.5	27 49.8	23 51.6	21 52.7
25 Su	10 15 15	2 19 47	14 16 46	21 02 49	10 00.4	18 36.7	20 25.7	12 43.4	8 28.3	13 15.1	25 15.7	27 53.2	23 52.2	21 54.8
26 M	10 19 11	3 17 43	27 51 51	4♎43 38	9D58.9	20 15.6	21 39.6	13 21.7	8 48.1	13 27.9	25 13.8	27 56.8	23 52.9	21 56.9
27 Tu	10 23 08	4 15 40	11♎37 53	18 34 21	9 59.1	21 53.1	22 53.4	14 00.0	9 07.9	13 40.8	25 11.7	28 00.3	23 53.6	21 59.0
28 W	10 27 05	5 13 39	25 32 48	2♏33 00	10 00.2	23 29.4	24 07.3	14 38.2	9 27.9	13 53.7	25 09.6	28 03.8	23 54.3	22 01.1
29 Th	10 31 01	6 11 38	9♏34 43	16 37 46	10 01.7	25 04.3	25 21.1	15 16.5	9 48.0	14 06.7	25 07.4	28 07.4	23 55.1	22 03.3
30 F	10 34 58	7 09 40	23 41 56	0♐47 00	10R02.7	26 37.9	26 35.0	15 54.7	10 08.2	14 19.6	25 05.1	28 11.0	23 55.9	22 05.4
31 Sa	10 38 54	8 07 42	7♐52 46	14 58 59	10 02.6	28 10.2	27 48.8	16 32.9	10 28.5	14 32.6	25 02.7	28 14.6	23 56.7	22 07.5

Astro Data

	Dy Hr Mn
☽0S	2 20:27
☽0N	15 13:04
☽0S	30 1:03
♆D	5 1:17
♄R	7 2:22
☽0N	11 21:18
♃□♄	12 15:35
☽0S	26 6:45

Planet Ingress

		Dy Hr Mn
☿	♋	13 1:30
♀	♌	15 12:59
☉	♌	22 19:07
⚳	♏	27 15:19
☿	♌	31 6:11
♂	♌	5 17:07
♀	♍	8 21:49
☿	♍	15 0:53
☉	♍	23 2:03

Last Aspect / ☽ Ingress

Last Aspect Dy Hr Mn		☽ Ingress	Dy Hr Mn
2 8:04	♅ ☌	♎	2 16:10
4 11:08	♄ ☍	♏	4 20:20
6 14:54	♅ ✶	♐	6 22:05
8 16:15	☿ ☍	♑	8 22:24
10 16:01	♅ △	♒	10 23:03
12 17:19	♄ ✶	♓	13 2:03
15 8:25	♀ △	♈	15 8:51
17 9:53	♄ ☌	♉	17 19:30
20 3:02	☉ ✶	♊	20 8:13
22 12:54	♅ □	♋	22 20:31
24 23:46	♅ ✶	♌	25 6:55
27 6:46	♄ △	♍	27 15:10
29 15:40	☿ ✶	♎	29 21:32

Last Aspect / ☽ Ingress

Last Aspect Dy Hr Mn		☽ Ingress	Dy Hr Mn
31 20:45	♂ □	♏	1 2:11
3 2:20	♂ △	♐	3 5:11
5 1:38	♅ □	♑	5 6:57
7 3:25	♅ △	♒	7 8:37
9 4:01	♄ ✶	♓	9 11:45
11 12:30	♅ ☍	♈	11 17:53
13 23:37	☿ △	♉	14 3:36
16 10:32	♅ △	♊	16 15:51
18 23:18	♅ □	♋	19 4:15
21 10:11	♅ ✶	♌	21 14:40
23 13:50	♄ △	♍	23 22:21
26 0:06	♅ ☌	♎	26 3:45
27 23:22	♄ ☍	♏	28 7:38
30 7:35	♅ ✶	♐	30 10:40

☽ Phases & Eclipses

Dy Hr Mn	
3 12:42	☽ 11♎37
10 3:18	○ 17♑55
17 9:11	☾ 24♈50
25 11:49	● 2♌35
1 18:34	☽ 9♏32
8 11:32	○ 15♒58
16 2:13	☾ 23♉16
23 23:57	● 0♍53
30 23:34	☽ 7♐38

Astro Data

1 July 1968
Julian Day # 25019
SVP 5♓42'02"
GC 26♐24.0 ⚵ 25♍04.7
Eris 12♈18.6 ⚴ 27♎49.9
⚷ 3♈21.8 ⚶ 23♈39.5
☽ Mean ☊ 14♈19.7

1 August 1968
Julian Day # 25050
SVP 5♓41'57"
GC 26♐24.0 ⚵ 5♎44.0
Eris 12♈15.8R ⚴ 1♏31.8
⚷ 3♈04.4R ⚶ 1♉57.6
☽ Mean ☊ 12♈41.3

LONGITUDE — September 1968

Day	Sid.Time	☉	0 hr ☽	Noon ☽	True ☊	☿	♀	♂	⚳	♃	♄	♅	♆	♇
1 Su	10 42 51	9♍05 47	22♐05 23	29♐11 40	10♈01.2	29♍41.3	29♍02.6	17♌11.0	10♏48.9	14♍45.5	25♈00.2	28♍18.2	23♏57.6	22♍09.7
2 M	10 46 47	10 03 52	6♑17 31	13♑22 33	9R58.5	1♎11.0	0♎16.4	17 49.2	11 09.5	14 58.5	24R57.6	28 21.9	23 58.5	22 11.9
3 Tu	10 50 44	11 01 59	20 26 22	27 28 34	9 54.8	2 39.5	1 30.2	18 27.3	11 30.1	15 11.5	24 55.0	28 25.5	23 59.4	22 14.0
4 W	10 54 41	12 00 07	4♒28 41	11♒26 19	9 50.7	4 06.6	2 44.0	19 05.4	11 50.8	15 24.4	24 52.2	28 29.2	24 00.4	22 16.2
5 Th	10 58 37	12 58 17	18 21 01	25 12 24	9 46.6	5 32.4	3 57.8	19 43.5	12 11.6	15 37.4	24 49.4	28 32.8	24 01.3	22 18.4
6 F	11 02 34	13 56 28	2♓00 06	8♓43 49	9 43.3	6 56.8	5 11.6	20 21.5	12 32.6	15 50.4	24 46.4	28 36.5	24 02.4	22 20.6
7 Sa	11 06 30	14 54 41	15 23 18	21 58 24	9 41.1	8 19.9	6 25.4	20 59.5	12 53.6	16 03.4	24 43.4	28 40.2	24 03.4	22 22.7
8 Su	11 10 27	15 52 56	28 29 01	4♈55 08	9D40.0	9 41.6	7 39.1	21 37.5	13 14.7	16 16.4	24 40.3	28 43.9	24 04.5	22 24.9
9 M	11 14 23	16 51 13	11♈16 49	17 34 14	9 40.1	11 01.8	8 52.9	22 15.5	13 35.9	16 29.4	24 37.2	28 47.7	24 05.6	22 27.1
10 Tu	11 18 20	17 49 31	23 47 35	29 57 10	9 41.2	12 20.6	10 06.6	22 53.4	13 57.2	16 42.4	24 33.9	28 51.4	24 06.7	22 29.3
11 W	11 22 16	18 47 52	6♉03 21	12♉06 31	9 42.7	13 37.8	11 20.3	23 31.4	14 18.6	16 55.4	24 30.6	28 55.1	24 07.8	22 31.5
12 Th	11 26 13	19 46 15	18 07 09	24 05 44	9 44.3	14 53.5	12 34.1	24 09.3	14 40.0	17 08.4	24 27.2	28 58.9	24 09.0	22 33.7
13 F	11 30 09	20 44 40	0♊02 49	5♊58 57	9 45.5	16 07.5	13 47.8	24 47.2	15 01.6	17 21.4	24 23.7	29 02.6	24 10.2	22 35.9
14 Sa	11 34 06	21 43 07	11 54 44	17 50 45	9R46.2	17 19.9	15 01.5	25 25.0	15 23.3	17 34.4	24 20.1	29 06.4	24 11.5	22 38.1
15 Su	11 38 03	22 41 36	23 47 36	29 45 53	9 46.1	18 30.4	16 15.2	26 02.9	15 45.0	17 47.3	24 16.5	29 10.1	24 12.7	22 40.3
16 M	11 41 59	23 40 07	5♋46 10	11♋49 02	9 45.2	19 39.0	17 28.9	26 40.7	16 06.8	18 00.3	24 12.8	29 13.9	24 14.0	22 42.5
17 Tu	11 45 56	24 38 41	17 55 00	24 04 34	9 43.7	20 45.6	18 42.6	27 18.5	16 28.7	18 13.3	24 09.0	29 17.7	24 15.4	22 44.7
18 W	11 49 52	25 37 17	0♌18 12	6♌36 15	9 41.9	21 50.1	19 56.3	27 56.3	16 50.7	18 26.2	24 05.2	29 21.5	24 16.7	22 46.9
19 Th	11 53 49	26 35 54	12 59 04	19 26 52	9 39.9	22 52.3	21 09.9	28 34.1	17 12.8	18 39.2	24 01.3	29 25.3	24 18.1	22 49.1
20 F	11 57 45	27 34 34	25 59 49	2♍37 57	9 38.3	23 52.0	22 23.6	29 11.8	17 34.9	18 52.1	23 57.3	29 29.1	24 19.5	22 51.3
21 Sa	12 01 42	28 33 16	9♍21 14	16 09 33	9 37.0	24 49.2	23 37.3	29 49.6	17 57.1	19 05.0	23 53.3	29 32.8	24 20.9	22 53.5
22 Su	12 05 38	29 32 00	23 02 37	0♎00 07	9D36.4	25 43.6	24 50.9	0♍27.3	18 19.4	19 18.0	23 49.2	29 36.6	24 22.4	22 55.7
23 M	12 09 35	0♎30 46	7♎01 38	14 06 39	9 36.3	26 34.9	26 04.6	1 04.9	18 41.8	19 30.8	23 45.1	29 40.4	24 23.9	22 57.9
24 Tu	12 13 32	1 29 34	21 14 38	28 24 58	9 36.6	27 23.0	27 18.2	1 42.6	19 04.2	19 43.7	23 40.9	29 44.2	24 25.4	23 00.1
25 W	12 17 28	2 28 23	5♏37 02	12♏50 12	9 37.2	28 07.5	28 31.8	2 20.2	19 26.8	19 56.6	23 36.7	29 48.0	24 26.9	23 02.3
26 Th	12 21 25	3 27 15	20 03 52	27 17 25	9 37.8	28 48.2	29 45.4	2 57.8	19 49.3	20 09.4	23 32.4	29 51.8	24 28.4	23 04.5
27 F	12 25 21	4 26 08	4♐30 21	11♐42 07	9 38.3	29 24.7	0♏59.0	3 35.4	20 12.0	20 22.2	23 28.0	29 55.6	24 30.0	23 06.6
28 Sa	12 29 18	5 25 03	18 52 19	26 00 33	9R38.5	29 56.7	2 12.6	4 12.9	20 34.7	20 35.0	23 23.6	29 59.3	24 31.6	23 08.8
29 Su	12 33 14	6 24 00	3♑06 30	10♑09 54	9 38.6	0♏23.9	3 26.1	4 50.5	20 57.5	20 47.8	23 19.2	0♎03.1	24 33.3	23 11.0
30 M	12 37 11	7 22 59	17 10 31	24 08 12	9 38.5	0 45.7	4 39.7	5 28.0	21 20.3	21 00.5	23 14.8	0 06.9	24 34.9	23 13.1

LONGITUDE — October 1968

Day	Sid.Time	☉	0 hr ☽	Noon ☽	True ☊	☿	♀	♂	⚳	♃	♄	♅	♆	♇
1 Tu	12 41 07	8♎21 59	1♒02 48	7♒54 13	9♈38.3	1♏01.8	5♏53.2	6♍05.5	21♏43.2	21♍13.2	23♈10.2	0♎10.7	24♏36.6	23♍15.3
2 W	12 45 04	9 21 01	14 42 22	21 27 13	9D38.3	1R11.8	7 06.7	6 42.9	22 06.2	21 25.9	23R05.7	0 14.4	24 38.3	23 17.4
3 Th	12 49 01	10 20 05	28 08 41	4♓46 47	9 38.3	1 15.1	8 20.2	7 20.4	22 29.2	21 38.6	23 01.1	0 18.2	24 40.0	23 19.6
4 F	12 52 57	11 19 10	11♓21 28	17 52 44	9 38.4	1 11.4	9 33.7	7 57.8	22 52.3	21 51.2	22 56.5	0 21.9	24 41.7	23 21.7
5 Sa	12 56 54	12 18 17	24 20 36	0♈45 06	9R38.5	1 00.3	10 47.2	8 35.2	23 15.4	22 03.8	22 51.9	0 25.6	24 43.5	23 23.8
6 Su	13 00 50	13 17 27	7♈06 15	13 24 09	9 38.5	0 41.5	12 00.6	9 12.5	23 38.6	22 16.3	22 47.2	0 29.4	24 45.3	23 25.9
7 M	13 04 47	14 16 38	19 38 52	25 50 31	9 38.4	0 14.7	13 14.0	9 49.9	24 01.8	22 28.9	22 42.6	0 33.1	24 47.1	23 28.0
8 Tu	13 08 43	15 15 52	1♉59 16	8♉05 18	9 37.9	29♎39.8	14 27.5	10 27.2	24 25.1	22 41.4	22 37.9	0 36.8	24 48.9	23 30.1
9 W	13 12 40	16 15 07	14 08 51	20 10 10	9 37.1	28 56.9	15 40.9	11 04.5	24 48.5	22 53.8	22 33.1	0 40.5	24 50.7	23 32.1
10 Th	13 16 36	17 14 25	26 09 33	2♊07 22	9 36.1	28 06.4	16 54.2	11 41.8	25 11.9	23 06.2	22 28.4	0 44.2	24 52.6	23 34.2
11 F	13 20 33	18 13 46	8♊03 58	13 59 49	9 35.0	27 08.8	18 07.6	12 19.0	25 35.3	23 18.6	22 23.7	0 47.8	24 54.5	23 36.3
12 Sa	13 24 30	19 13 08	19 55 20	25 51 01	9 33.9	26 05.2	19 21.0	12 56.3	25 58.8	23 30.9	22 18.9	0 51.5	24 56.4	23 38.3
13 Su	13 28 26	20 12 33	1♋47 23	7♋44 59	9 33.1	24 56.7	20 34.3	13 33.5	26 22.4	23 43.2	22 14.1	0 55.1	24 58.3	23 40.3
14 M	13 32 23	21 12 00	13 44 22	19 46 07	9D32.8	23 44.9	21 47.6	14 10.7	26 46.0	23 55.5	22 09.4	0 58.7	25 00.2	23 42.3
15 Tu	13 36 19	22 11 30	25 50 48	1♌59 01	9 33.0	22 31.8	23 01.0	14 47.9	27 09.6	24 07.7	22 04.6	1 02.4	25 02.2	23 44.3
16 W	13 40 16	23 11 01	8♌11 17	14 28 10	9 33.7	21 19.3	24 14.3	15 25.0	27 33.3	24 19.9	21 59.8	1 05.9	25 04.2	23 46.3
17 Th	13 44 12	24 10 35	20 50 08	27 17 38	9 34.9	20 09.5	25 27.5	16 02.2	27 57.1	24 32.0	21 55.0	1 09.5	25 06.1	23 48.3
18 F	13 48 09	25 10 11	3♍51 02	10♍30 35	9 36.2	19 04.6	26 40.8	16 39.3	28 20.9	24 44.0	21 50.3	1 13.1	25 08.1	23 50.3
19 Sa	13 52 05	26 09 50	17 16 28	24 08 42	9 37.2	18 06.4	27 54.1	17 16.4	28 44.7	24 56.1	21 45.5	1 16.6	25 10.1	23 52.2
20 Su	13 56 02	27 09 30	1♎07 13	8♎11 45	9R37.7	17 16.7	29 07.3	17 53.4	29 08.5	25 08.0	21 40.8	1 20.1	25 12.2	23 54.1
21 M	13 59 59	28 09 13	15 21 54	22 37 06	9 37.3	16 36.8	0♐20.5	18 30.4	29 32.5	25 19.9	21 36.0	1 23.6	25 14.2	23 56.0
22 Tu	14 03 55	29 08 57	29 56 38	7♏19 41	9 35.9	16 07.5	1 33.7	19 07.5	29 56.4	25 31.8	21 31.3	1 27.1	25 16.3	23 57.9
23 W	14 07 52	0♏08 44	14♏45 16	22 12 24	9 33.7	15 49.3	2 46.9	19 44.4	0♐20.4	25 43.6	21 26.6	1 30.6	25 18.4	23 59.8
24 Th	14 11 48	1 08 33	29 40 01	7♐07 05	9 30.8	15D42.6	4 00.1	20 21.4	0 44.4	25 55.3	21 21.9	1 34.0	25 20.4	24 01.7
25 F	14 15 45	2 08 23	14♐32 35	21 55 38	9 27.8	15 47.1	5 13.2	20 58.3	1 08.5	26 07.0	21 17.3	1 37.4	25 22.5	24 03.5
26 Sa	14 19 41	3 08 15	29 15 24	6♑31 15	9 25.2	16 02.4	6 26.4	21 35.2	1 32.6	26 18.6	21 12.6	1 40.8	25 24.7	24 05.3
27 Su	14 23 38	4 08 09	13♑42 38	20 49 11	9 23.5	16 27.9	7 39.5	22 12.1	1 56.7	26 30.2	21 08.0	1 44.2	25 26.8	24 07.1
28 M	14 27 34	5 08 05	27 50 40	4♒46 59	9D22.9	17 02.9	8 52.6	22 48.9	2 20.9	26 41.6	21 03.5	1 47.5	25 28.9	24 08.9
29 Tu	14 31 31	6 08 02	11♒38 08	18 24 13	9 23.4	17 46.5	10 05.6	23 25.7	2 45.1	26 53.1	20 58.9	1 50.8	25 31.1	24 10.7
30 W	14 35 28	7 08 00	25 05 26	1♓41 59	9 24.7	18 37.9	11 18.6	24 02.5	3 09.3	27 04.4	20 54.5	1 54.1	25 33.2	24 12.4
31 Th	14 39 24	8 08 00	8♓14 08	14 42 13	9 26.4	19 36.2	12 31.6	24 39.3	3 33.6	27 15.7	20 50.0	1 57.3	25 35.4	24 14.1

Astro Data

	Dy Hr Mn
☿0S	1 11:56
♀0S	4 7:44
☽0N	8 5:57
♄⊼♆	16 6:08
☽0S	22 14:53
☉0S	22 23:27
♄⊼♇	30 17:52
☿R	3 11:40
☽0N	5 13:46
♃⊼♄	8 7:07
♃☌♇	13 5:12
☽0S	20 0:57
♃⚹♆	20 22:06
☿D	24 14:18
♅0S	25 17:13

Planet Ingress

		Dy Hr Mn
☿	♎	1 16:59
♀	♎	2 6:39
♂	♍	21 18:39
☉	♎	22 23:26
♀	♏	26 16:45
☿	♏	28 14:40
♅	♎	28 16:09
☿	♎R	7 22:46
♀	♐	21 5:16
⚳	♐	22 15:36
☉	♏	23 8:30

Last Aspect / ☽ Ingress

Last Aspect Dy Hr Mn			☽ Ingress Dy Hr Mn
1 12:56	☿ □	♑	1 13:22
3 13:38	♅ △	♒	3 16:19
5 11:20	♄ ⚹	♓	5 20:27
8 0:24	♅ ☍	♈	8 2:49
10 1:33	♄ ☌	♉	10 12:06
12 21:54	♅ △	♊	12 23:54
15 10:48	♅ □	♋	15 12:28
17 22:07	♅ ⚹	♌	17 23:25
20 5:30	♂ ☌	♍	20 7:15
22 11:19	♅ ☌	♎	22 12:00
24 10:11	☿ ☌	♏	24 14:39
26 16:18	♅ ⚹	♐	26 16:30
28 7:37	♄ △	♑	28 18:44
30 12:46	♆ ⚹	♒	30 22:11

Last Aspect / ☽ Ingress

Last Aspect Dy Hr Mn			☽ Ingress Dy Hr Mn
2 17:43	♆ □	♓	3 3:21
5 0:41	♆ △	♈	5 10:35
7 5:57	♄ ☌	♉	7 20:07
9 21:23	♆ ☍	♊	10 7:43
12 12:26	♆ △	♋	12 20:23
14 22:22	♆ △	♌	15 8:08
17 8:15	♀ □	♍	17 16:58
19 19:06	♀ ⚹	♎	19 22:05
21 21:44	☉ ☌	♏	22 0:05
23 17:44	♃ ⚹	♐	24 0:32
25 18:56	♃ □	♑	26 1:13
27 21:50	♃ △	♒	28 3:43
30 0:48	♆ □	♓	30 8:54

☽ Phases & Eclipses

Dy Hr Mn	
6 22:07	○ 14♓21
14 20:31	☾ 22♊04
22 11:08	● 29♍30
22 11:18:06	◐ T 00'40"
29 5:07	☽ 6♑07
6 11:46	○ 13♈17
6 11:42	◑ T 1.169
14 15:05	☾ 21♋20
21 21:44	● 28♎33
28 12:40	☽ 5♒10

Astro Data

1 September 1968
Julian Day # 25081
SVP 5♓41'53"
GC 26♐24.1 ⚴ 17♎56.9
Eris 12♈03.7R ⚵ 8♏25.0
⚷ 2♈04.2R ⚶ 5♉17.9
☽ Mean ☊ 11♈02.8

1 October 1968
Julian Day # 25111
SVP 5♓41'49"
GC 26♐24.2 ⚴ 0♏38.0
Eris 11♈46.5R ⚵ 16♏59.1
⚷ 0♈44.7R ⚶ 2♉04.0R
☽ Mean ☊ 9♈27.4

November 1968 LONGITUDE

Day	Sid.Time	☉	0 hr ☽	Noon ☽	True ☊	☿	♀	♂	⚳	♃	♄	♅	♆	♇
1 F	14 43 21	9♏08 02	21♓06 29	27♓27 15	9♈27.9	20♎40.6	13♐44.6	25♍16.0	3♐57.8	27♍26.9	20♈45.6	2♎00.5	25♏37.6	24♍15.8
2 Sa	14 47 17	10 08 05	3♈44 48	9♈59 24	9R 28.4	21 50.3	14 57.5	25 52.7	4 22.1	27 38.0	20R 41.2	2 03.7	25 39.7	24 17.5
3 Su	14 51 14	11 08 10	16 11 19	22 20 45	9 27.6	23 04.5	16 10.4	26 29.4	4 46.5	27 49.1	20 36.9	2 06.9	25 41.9	24 19.1
4 M	14 55 10	12 08 17	28 27 56	4♉33 04	9 25.1	24 22.7	17 23.3	27 06.0	5 10.8	28 00.1	20 32.6	2 10.0	25 44.1	24 20.8
5 Tu	14 59 07	13 08 26	10♉36 20	16 37 54	9 20.9	25 44.2	18 36.2	27 42.7	5 35.2	28 11.0	20 28.4	2 13.1	25 46.3	24 22.4
6 W	15 03 03	14 08 36	22 37 57	28 36 41	9 15.2	27 08.5	19 49.0	28 19.3	5 59.6	28 21.8	20 24.2	2 16.2	25 48.5	24 24.0
7 Th	15 07 00	15 08 49	4♊34 16	10♊30 57	9 08.5	28 35.1	21 01.8	28 55.8	6 24.1	28 32.6	20 20.1	2 19.2	25 50.8	24 25.5
8 F	15 10 57	16 09 03	16 26 58	22 22 34	9 01.4	0♏03.7	22 14.5	29 32.4	6 48.5	28 43.2	20 16.1	2 22.3	25 53.0	24 27.1
9 Sa	15 14 53	17 09 19	28 18 03	4♋13 46	8 54.7	1 33.9	23 27.3	0♎08.9	7 13.0	28 53.8	20 12.1	2 25.2	25 55.2	24 28.6
10 Su	15 18 50	18 09 37	10♋10 05	16 07 26	8 48.9	3 05.4	24 40.0	0 45.4	7 37.5	29 04.3	20 08.2	2 28.2	25 57.5	24 30.1
11 M	15 22 46	19 09 57	22 06 14	28 07 00	8 44.8	4 37.9	25 52.6	1 21.8	8 02.0	29 14.8	20 04.3	2 31.1	25 59.7	24 31.5
12 Tu	15 26 43	20 10 19	4♌10 15	10♌16 31	8D 42.4	6 11.2	27 05.2	1 58.3	8 26.6	29 25.1	20 00.5	2 33.9	26 02.0	24 33.0
13 W	15 30 39	21 10 43	16 26 22	22 40 24	8 41.8	7 45.2	28 17.8	2 34.7	8 51.1	29 35.3	19 56.8	2 36.8	26 04.2	24 34.4
14 Th	15 34 36	22 11 09	28 59 11	5♍23 17	8 42.5	9 19.7	29 30.4	3 11.0	9 15.7	29 45.5	19 53.1	2 39.6	26 06.4	24 35.8
15 F	15 38 32	23 11 37	11♍53 14	18 29 29	8 43.9	10 54.5	0♑42.9	3 47.4	9 40.3	29 55.5	19 49.5	2 42.3	26 08.7	24 37.1
16 Sa	15 42 29	24 12 06	25 12 28	2♎02 26	8R 45.0	12 29.6	1 55.4	4 23.7	10 04.9	0♎05.5	19 46.0	2 45.0	26 11.0	24 38.5
17 Su	15 46 26	25 12 37	8♎59 35	16 03 55	8 45.0	14 04.9	3 07.9	4 59.9	10 29.6	0 15.4	19 42.6	2 47.7	26 13.2	24 39.8
18 M	15 50 22	26 13 10	23 15 14	0♏33 09	8 43.0	15 40.2	4 20.3	5 36.2	10 54.2	0 25.1	19 39.2	2 50.4	26 15.5	24 41.0
19 Tu	15 54 19	27 13 45	7♏57 04	15 26 10	8 38.8	17 15.7	5 32.7	6 12.4	11 18.9	0 34.8	19 35.9	2 53.0	26 17.7	24 42.3
20 W	15 58 15	28 14 22	22 59 26	0♐35 41	8 32.5	18 51.1	6 45.0	6 48.6	11 43.5	0 44.3	19 32.7	2 55.5	26 20.0	24 43.5
21 Th	16 02 12	29 15 00	8♐13 34	15 51 43	8 24.7	20 26.5	7 57.3	7 24.7	12 08.2	0 53.8	19 29.6	2 58.0	26 22.2	24 44.7
22 F	16 06 08	0♐15 39	23 28 44	1♑03 16	8 16.5	22 01.8	9 09.6	8 00.8	12 32.9	1 03.1	19 26.6	3 00.5	26 24.5	24 45.9
23 Sa	16 10 05	1 16 20	8♑34 05	16 00 09	8 08.9	23 37.0	10 21.8	8 36.9	12 57.6	1 12.4	19 23.7	3 02.9	26 26.7	24 47.0
24 Su	16 14 01	2 17 01	23 20 35	0♒34 46	8 02.9	25 12.2	11 33.9	9 12.9	13 22.4	1 21.5	19 20.8	3 05.3	26 29.0	24 48.1
25 M	16 17 58	3 17 44	7♒42 16	14 42 53	7 59.0	26 47.2	12 46.0	9 48.9	13 47.1	1 30.5	19 18.1	3 07.7	26 31.2	24 49.2
26 Tu	16 21 55	4 18 28	21 36 35	28 23 32	7D 57.3	28 22.1	13 58.1	10 24.8	14 11.8	1 39.4	19 15.4	3 10.0	26 33.5	24 50.2
27 W	16 25 51	5 19 12	5♓03 59	11♓38 19	7 57.3	29 56.9	15 10.0	11 00.7	14 36.5	1 48.2	19 12.8	3 12.2	26 35.7	24 51.2
28 Th	16 29 48	6 19 58	18 07 00	24 30 30	7 58.2	1♐31.6	16 22.0	11 36.5	15 01.3	1 56.9	19 10.4	3 14.4	26 38.0	24 52.2
29 F	16 33 44	7 20 45	0♈49 22	7♈04 06	7R 58.7	3 06.2	17 33.8	12 12.4	15 26.0	2 05.4	19 08.0	3 16.6	26 40.2	24 53.2
30 Sa	16 37 41	8 21 32	13 15 15	19 23 16	7 58.0	4 40.7	18 45.6	12 48.1	15 50.7	2 13.8	19 05.7	3 18.7	26 42.4	24 54.1

December 1968 LONGITUDE

Day	Sid.Time	☉	0 hr ☽	Noon ☽	True ☊	☿	♀	♂	⚳	♃	♄	♅	♆	♇
1 Su	16 41 37	9♐22 21	25♈28 39	1♉31 49	7♈55.1	6♐15.1	19♑57.3	13♎23.9	16♐15.5	2♎22.1	19♈03.5	3♎20.8	26♏44.6	24♍55.0
2 M	16 45 34	10 23 10	7♉33 09	13 32 59	7R 49.5	7 49.5	21 09.0	13 59.6	16 40.2	2 30.3	19R 01.4	3 22.8	26 46.8	24 55.8
3 Tu	16 49 30	11 24 01	19 31 38	25 29 21	7 41.1	9 23.8	22 20.6	14 35.2	17 05.0	2 38.4	18 59.4	3 24.8	26 49.0	24 56.7
4 W	16 53 27	12 24 53	1♊26 23	7♊22 56	7 30.2	10 58.1	23 32.1	15 10.9	17 29.7	2 46.3	18 57.6	3 26.7	26 51.2	24 57.5
5 Th	16 57 24	13 25 45	13 19 10	19 15 16	7 17.6	12 32.3	24 43.5	15 46.4	17 54.4	2 54.1	18 55.8	3 28.5	26 53.4	24 58.2
6 F	17 01 20	14 26 39	25 11 23	1♋07 41	7 04.1	14 06.5	25 54.9	16 22.0	18 19.2	3 01.8	18 54.1	3 30.4	26 55.6	24 59.0
7 Sa	17 05 17	15 27 34	7♋04 21	13 01 34	6 51.0	15 40.7	27 06.1	16 57.5	18 43.9	3 09.3	18 52.5	3 32.2	26 57.8	24 59.7
8 Su	17 09 13	16 28 30	18 59 34	24 58 36	6 39.4	17 15.0	28 17.3	17 32.9	19 08.7	3 16.7	18 51.1	3 33.9	26 59.9	25 00.3
9 M	17 13 10	17 29 27	0♌58 57	7♌00 59	6 30.0	18 49.2	29 28.4	18 08.3	19 33.4	3 24.0	18 49.7	3 35.6	27 02.1	25 01.0
10 Tu	17 17 06	18 30 26	13 05 02	19 11 33	6 23.5	20 23.6	0♒39.5	18 43.7	19 58.1	3 31.1	18 48.4	3 37.2	27 04.2	25 01.6
11 W	17 21 03	19 31 25	25 21 00	1♍33 52	6 19.8	21 58.0	1 50.4	19 19.0	20 22.8	3 38.1	18 47.3	3 38.7	27 06.4	25 02.1
12 Th	17 25 00	20 32 25	7♍50 40	14 11 59	6D 18.3	23 32.4	3 01.2	19 54.3	20 47.5	3 44.9	18 46.2	3 40.3	27 08.5	25 02.7
13 F	17 28 56	21 33 26	20 38 19	27 10 15	6R 18.2	25 07.0	4 12.0	20 29.5	21 12.2	3 51.6	18 45.3	3 41.7	27 10.6	25 03.2
14 Sa	17 32 53	22 34 29	3♎48 16	10♎32 49	6 18.3	26 41.7	5 22.6	21 04.7	21 36.9	3 58.2	18 44.5	3 43.1	27 12.7	25 03.6
15 Su	17 36 49	23 35 32	17 24 14	24 22 48	6 17.2	28 16.5	6 33.2	21 39.8	22 01.6	4 04.6	18 43.7	3 44.5	27 14.7	25 04.1
16 M	17 40 46	24 36 36	1♏28 33	8♏41 25	6 13.9	29 51.4	7 43.7	22 14.9	22 26.3	4 10.8	18 43.1	3 45.8	27 16.8	25 04.5
17 Tu	17 44 42	25 37 42	16 01 03	23 26 56	6 07.9	1♑26.4	8 54.0	22 49.9	22 51.0	4 16.9	18 42.6	3 47.1	27 18.8	25 04.8
18 W	17 48 39	26 38 48	0♐58 15	8♐33 58	5 59.0	3 01.6	10 04.3	23 24.9	23 15.6	4 22.9	18 42.2	3 48.3	27 20.9	25 05.2
19 Th	17 52 35	27 39 55	16 12 52	23 53 33	5 48.1	4 36.9	11 14.4	23 59.8	23 40.3	4 28.7	18 42.0	3 49.4	27 22.9	25 05.5
20 F	17 56 32	28 41 03	1♑34 31	9♑14 14	5 36.3	6 12.4	12 24.4	24 34.6	24 04.9	4 34.3	18D 41.8	3 50.5	27 24.9	25 05.7
21 Sa	18 00 29	29 42 11	16 51 14	24 24 09	5 25.1	7 48.0	13 34.3	25 09.4	24 29.5	4 39.8	18 41.7	3 51.5	27 26.9	25 06.0
22 Su	18 04 25	0♑43 19	1♒51 48	9♒13 14	5 15.7	9 23.7	14 44.1	25 44.2	24 54.1	4 45.1	18 41.8	3 52.5	27 28.9	25 06.2
23 M	18 08 22	1 44 27	16 27 43	23 34 49	5 08.9	10 59.5	15 53.7	26 18.9	25 18.7	4 50.3	18 42.0	3 53.4	27 30.8	25 06.3
24 Tu	18 12 18	2 45 36	0♓34 16	7♓26 05	5 04.9	12 35.4	17 03.2	26 53.5	25 43.3	4 55.3	18 42.2	3 54.3	27 32.8	25 06.4
25 W	18 16 15	3 46 44	14 10 26	20 47 38	5 03.3	14 11.3	18 12.6	27 28.0	26 07.8	5 00.1	18 42.6	3 55.1	27 34.7	25 06.5
26 Th	18 20 11	4 47 53	27 18 09	3♈42 30	5 03.0	15 47.2	19 21.8	28 02.5	26 32.3	5 04.8	18 43.1	3 55.9	27 36.6	25 06.6
27 F	18 24 08	5 49 01	10♈01 18	16 15 09	5 02.8	17 23.2	20 30.9	28 36.9	26 56.8	5 09.2	18 43.7	3 56.6	27 38.5	25R 06.6
28 Sa	18 28 04	6 50 10	22 24 44	28 30 38	5 01.5	18 59.0	21 39.8	29 11.3	27 21.3	5 13.6	18 44.5	3 57.2	27 40.3	25 06.6
29 Su	18 32 01	7 51 18	4♉33 30	10♉33 55	4 58.1	20 34.6	22 48.5	29 45.6	27 45.7	5 17.7	18 45.3	3 57.8	27 42.2	25 06.6
30 M	18 35 58	8 52 27	16 32 25	22 29 32	4 51.8	22 10.1	23 57.1	0♏19.8	28 10.2	5 21.7	18 46.2	3 58.3	27 44.0	25 06.5
31 Tu	18 39 54	9 53 35	28 25 41	4♊21 17	4 42.4	23 45.1	25 05.5	0 53.9	28 34.6	5 25.5	18 47.3	3 58.8	27 45.8	25 06.4

Astro Data

	Dy Hr Mn
☽0N	1 19:59
♂0S	14 11:43
☽0S	16 11:03
☽0N	29 1:02
♃0S	4 6:56
♃☌♅	11 14:59
☽0S	13 19:04
♄ D	21 11:38
☽0N	26 6:38
♇ R	27 17:05

Planet Ingress

	Dy Hr Mn
☿ ♏	8 11:00
♂ ♎	9 6:10
♀ ♑	14 21:48
♃ ♎	15 22:44
☉ ♐	22 5:49
☿ ♐	27 12:47
♀ ♒	9 22:40
☿ ♑	16 14:11
☉ ♑	21 19:00
♂ ♏	29 22:07

Last Aspect / ☽ Ingress

Last Aspect Dy Hr Mn		☽ Ingress Dy Hr Mn
1 11:59 ♃ ☍	♈	1 16:51
3 13:36 ☿ ☍	♉	4 3:01
6 11:30 ♃ △	♊	6 14:48
9 3:18 ♂ □	♋	9 3:26
11 14:17 ♃ ⚹	♌	11 15:45
13 23:49 ♀ △	♍	14 1:55
16 1:42 ♆ ⚹	♎	16 8:26
17 18:05 ♄ ☍	♏	18 11:06
20 8:01 ☉ ☌	♐	20 11:04
22 2:01 ♇ □	♑	22 10:19
24 5:10 ♆ ⚹	♒	24 11:02
26 11:57 ☿ □	♓	26 14:52
28 16:02 ♆ △	♈	28 22:26

Last Aspect / ☽ Ingress

Last Aspect Dy Hr Mn		☽ Ingress Dy Hr Mn
30 11:26 ♄ ☌	♉	1 8:58
3 14:41 ♆ ☍	♊	3 21:06
5 23:34 ♇ □	♋	6 9:43
8 19:21 ♀ ☍	♌	8 22:02
11 3:23 ♆ □	♍	11 8:59
13 12:01 ♆ ⚹	♎	13 17:08
15 19:26 ☿ ⚹	♏	15 21:31
17 18:12 ♆ ☌	♐	17 22:28
19 18:19 ☉ ☌	♑	19 21:32
21 16:54 ♆ ⚹	♒	21 20:59
23 18:45 ♆ □	♓	23 23:01
26 0:33 ♆ △	♈	26 5:02
28 13:24 ♂ ☍	♉	28 14:57
30 22:37 ♆ ☍	♊	31 3:11

☽ Phases & Eclipses

Dy Hr Mn	
5 4:25	○ 12♉49
13 8:53	☾ 21♌03
20 8:01	● 28♏04
26 23:30	☽ 4♓48
4 23:07	○ 12♊53
13 0:49	☾ 21♍05
19 18:19	● 27♐56
26 14:14	☽ 4♈54

Astro Data

1 November 1968
Julian Day # 25142
SVP 5♓41'45"
GC 26♐24.2 ⚵ 14♏11.5
Eris 11♈28.0R ⚴ 27♏00.3
⚷ 29♓30.6R ⚶ 24♈25.8R
☽ Mean ☊ 7♈48.9

1 December 1968
Julian Day # 25172
SVP 5♓41'41"
GC 26♐24.3 ⚵ 27♏22.5
Eris 11♈14.8R ⚴ 7♐15.4
⚷ 28♓53.3R ⚶ 20♈06.9R
☽ Mean ☊ 6♈13.6

LONGITUDE — January 1969

Day	Sid.Time	☉	0 hr ☽	Noon ☽	True ☊	☿	♀	♂	⚳	♃	♄	♅	♆	♇
1 W	18 43 51	10♑54 44	10♊16 42	16♊12 15	4♈30.3	25♑19.7	26♒13.7	1♏28.0	28♐58.9	5♎29.1	18♈48.5	3♎59.2	27♏47.6	25♍06.2
2 Th	18 47 47	11 55 52	22 08 10	28 04 40	4R16.3	26 53.6	27 21.7	2 02.1	29 23.3	5 32.6	18 49.7	3 59.6	27 49.3	25R06.1
3 F	18 51 44	12 57 01	4♋01 58	10♋00 12	4 01.3	28 26.8	28 29.5	2 36.0	29 47.6	5 35.9	18 51.1	3 59.9	27 51.0	25 05.9
4 Sa	18 55 40	13 58 09	15 59 30	22 00 01	3 46.7	29 58.8	29 37.2	3 09.9	0♑11.9	5 39.0	18 52.6	4 00.1	27 52.8	25 05.6
5 Su	18 59 37	14 59 17	28 01 50	4♌05 08	3 33.5	1♒29.6	0♓44.6	3 43.7	0 36.2	5 41.9	18 54.2	4 00.3	27 54.4	25 05.3
6 M	19 03 33	16 00 25	10♌10 01	16 16 42	3 22.9	2 58.9	1 51.8	4 17.5	1 00.4	5 44.6	18 55.9	4 00.4	27 56.1	25 05.0
7 Tu	19 07 30	17 01 33	22 25 21	28 36 13	3 15.2	4 26.2	2 58.8	4 51.1	1 24.6	5 47.2	18 57.7	4R00.5	27 57.7	25 04.7
8 W	19 11 27	18 02 42	4♍49 35	11♍05 46	3 10.6	5 51.2	4 05.6	5 24.7	1 48.8	5 49.6	18 59.7	4 00.5	27 59.4	25 04.3
9 Th	19 15 23	19 03 50	17 25 07	23 48 01	3D08.6	7 13.4	5 12.2	5 58.2	2 12.9	5 51.8	19 01.7	4 00.5	28 01.0	25 03.9
10 F	19 19 20	20 04 58	0♎14 54	6♎46 11	3 08.3	8 32.3	6 18.5	6 31.7	2 37.0	5 53.8	19 03.8	4 00.4	28 02.5	25 03.5
11 Sa	19 23 16	21 06 06	13 22 16	20 03 35	3R08.6	9 47.3	7 24.5	7 05.0	3 01.1	5 55.6	19 06.0	4 00.2	28 04.1	25 03.0
12 Su	19 27 13	22 07 14	26 50 29	3♏43 15	3 08.1	10 57.8	8 30.4	7 38.3	3 25.1	5 57.2	19 08.4	4 00.0	28 05.6	25 02.5
13 M	19 31 09	23 08 22	10♏42 05	17 47 02	3 05.7	12 03.1	9 35.9	8 11.5	3 49.1	5 58.7	19 10.8	3 59.8	28 07.1	25 02.0
14 Tu	19 35 06	24 09 30	24 58 01	2♐14 45	3 00.8	13 02.3	10 41.3	8 44.6	4 13.1	5 59.9	19 13.4	3 59.4	28 08.5	25 01.4
15 W	19 39 03	25 10 38	9♐36 46	17 03 23	2 53.4	13 54.6	11 46.3	9 17.6	4 37.0	6 01.0	19 16.0	3 59.1	28 10.0	25 00.8
16 Th	19 42 59	26 11 46	24 33 42	2♑06 39	2 43.9	14 39.1	12 51.1	9 50.5	5 00.9	6 01.9	19 18.8	3 58.6	28 11.4	25 00.2
17 F	19 46 56	27 12 53	9♑41 02	17 15 32	2 33.4	15 15.0	13 55.5	10 23.4	5 24.7	6 02.5	19 21.7	3 58.2	28 12.8	24 59.5
18 Sa	19 50 52	28 14 00	24 48 48	2♒19 31	2 23.2	15 41.4	14 59.7	10 56.1	5 48.5	6 03.0	19 24.6	3 57.6	28 14.1	24 58.8
19 Su	19 54 49	29 15 06	9♒46 27	17 08 32	2 14.6	15R57.5	16 03.6	11 28.7	6 12.3	6 03.3	19 27.7	3 57.0	28 15.4	24 58.1
20 M	19 58 45	0♒16 12	24 24 51	1♓34 42	2 08.3	16 02.6	17 07.1	12 01.2	6 36.0	6R03.4	19 30.9	3 56.4	28 16.7	24 57.4
21 Tu	20 02 42	1 17 16	8♓37 36	15 33 18	2 04.6	15 56.4	18 10.3	12 33.7	6 59.6	6 03.3	19 34.1	3 55.7	28 18.0	24 56.6
22 W	20 06 38	2 18 20	22 21 44	29 03 00	2D03.3	15 38.5	19 13.2	13 06.0	7 23.3	6 03.0	19 37.5	3 54.9	28 19.2	24 55.8
23 Th	20 10 35	3 19 22	5♈37 22	12♈05 15	2 03.6	15 09.1	20 15.7	13 38.2	7 46.8	6 02.6	19 40.9	3 54.1	28 20.5	24 55.0
24 F	20 14 32	4 20 24	18 27 06	24 43 31	2R04.5	14 28.8	21 17.8	14 10.3	8 10.3	6 01.9	19 44.5	3 53.2	28 21.6	24 54.1
25 Sa	20 18 28	5 21 24	0♉55 05	7♉02 27	2 04.9	13 38.3	22 19.5	14 42.3	8 33.8	6 01.0	19 48.1	3 52.3	28 22.8	24 53.2
26 Su	20 22 25	6 22 24	13 06 16	19 07 11	2 03.8	12 39.1	23 20.8	15 14.2	8 57.2	6 00.0	19 51.9	3 51.3	28 23.9	24 52.3
27 M	20 26 21	7 23 22	25 05 49	1♊02 48	2 00.6	11 32.9	24 21.7	15 45.9	9 20.5	5 58.7	19 55.7	3 50.3	28 25.0	24 51.3
28 Tu	20 30 18	8 24 19	6♊58 42	12 54 02	1 55.1	10 21.5	25 22.2	16 17.6	9 43.8	5 57.3	19 59.6	3 49.2	28 26.0	24 50.4
29 W	20 34 14	9 25 15	18 49 20	24 45 02	1 47.5	9 07.2	26 22.2	16 49.1	10 07.1	5 55.7	20 03.6	3 48.1	28 27.1	24 49.4
30 Th	20 38 11	10 26 10	0♋41 31	6♋39 08	1 38.2	7 52.2	27 21.8	17 20.5	10 30.3	5 53.9	20 07.7	3 46.9	28 28.1	24 48.3
31 F	20 42 07	11 27 04	12 38 12	18 38 58	1 28.1	6 38.7	28 20.9	17 51.8	10 53.4	5 51.9	20 11.9	3 45.7	28 29.0	24 47.3

LONGITUDE — February 1969

Day	Sid.Time	☉	0 hr ☽	Noon ☽	True ☊	☿	♀	♂	⚳	♃	♄	♅	♆	♇
1 Sa	20 46 04	12♒27 56	24♋41 37	0♌46 20	1♈18.2	5♒28.5	29♓19.4	18♏23.0	11♑16.5	5♎49.7	20♈16.2	3♎44.5	28♏30.0	24♍46.2
2 Su	20 50 01	13 28 48	6♌53 15	13 02 27	1R09.3	4R23.3	0♈17.5	18 54.1	11 39.5	5R47.3	20 20.6	3R43.1	28 30.9	24R45.1
3 M	20 53 57	14 29 38	19 14 02	25 28 04	1 02.2	3 24.4	1 15.0	19 25.0	12 02.4	5 44.8	20 25.0	3 41.8	28 31.7	24 44.0
4 Tu	20 57 54	15 30 27	1♍44 37	8♍03 45	0 57.3	2 32.9	2 12.0	19 55.8	12 25.3	5 42.1	20 29.5	3 40.4	28 32.6	24 42.9
5 W	21 01 50	16 31 15	14 25 34	20 50 08	0D54.8	1 49.3	3 08.4	20 26.5	12 48.1	5 39.1	20 34.2	3 38.9	28 33.4	24 41.7
6 Th	21 05 47	17 32 02	27 17 36	3♎48 05	0 54.3	1 14.1	4 04.2	20 57.0	13 10.9	5 36.0	20 38.9	3 37.4	28 34.1	24 40.5
7 F	21 09 43	18 32 48	10♎21 45	16 58 46	0 55.2	0 47.1	4 59.4	21 27.4	13 33.6	5 32.8	20 43.6	3 35.8	28 34.9	24 39.3
8 Sa	21 13 40	19 33 33	23 39 20	0♏23 37	0 56.7	0 28.5	5 54.0	21 57.6	13 56.2	5 29.3	20 48.5	3 34.2	28 35.6	24 38.0
9 Su	21 17 36	20 34 17	7♏11 46	14 03 57	0R57.8	0D17.8	6 47.9	22 27.8	14 18.8	5 25.7	20 53.4	3 32.6	28 36.2	24 36.8
10 M	21 21 33	21 35 00	21 00 14	28 00 39	0 57.8	0 14.9	7 41.2	22 57.7	14 41.3	5 21.8	20 58.5	3 30.9	28 36.9	24 35.5
11 Tu	21 25 30	22 35 43	5♐05 08	12♐13 30	0 56.2	0 19.1	8 33.7	23 27.5	15 03.7	5 17.9	21 03.6	3 29.2	28 37.5	24 34.2
12 W	21 29 26	23 36 24	19 25 29	26 40 40	0 52.9	0 30.2	9 25.6	23 57.2	15 26.1	5 13.7	21 08.7	3 27.4	28 38.1	24 32.9
13 Th	21 33 23	24 37 04	3♑58 30	11♑18 20	0 48.1	0 47.6	10 16.7	24 26.7	15 48.4	5 09.4	21 14.0	3 25.6	28 38.6	24 31.6
14 F	21 37 19	25 37 43	18 39 23	26 00 48	0 42.7	1 10.8	11 07.0	24 56.0	16 10.6	5 04.9	21 19.3	3 23.8	28 39.1	24 30.2
15 Sa	21 41 16	26 38 20	3♒21 38	10♒40 59	0 37.2	1 39.4	11 56.5	25 25.1	16 32.7	5 00.3	21 24.7	3 21.9	28 39.6	24 28.8
16 Su	21 45 12	27 38 56	17 57 53	25 11 28	0 32.6	2 13.1	12 45.1	25 54.1	16 54.7	4 55.5	21 30.2	3 20.0	28 40.0	24 27.4
17 M	21 49 09	28 39 30	2♓20 58	9♓25 41	0 29.4	2 51.3	13 32.9	26 22.9	17 16.7	4 50.5	21 35.7	3 18.0	28 40.4	24 26.0
18 Tu	21 53 05	29 40 03	16 25 05	23 18 46	0D27.8	3 33.8	14 19.8	26 51.5	17 38.6	4 45.4	21 41.3	3 16.0	28 40.8	24 24.6
19 W	21 57 02	0♓40 34	0♈06 29	6♈48 07	0 27.8	4 20.1	15 05.7	27 19.9	18 00.4	4 40.1	21 47.0	3 14.0	28 41.1	24 23.2
20 Th	22 00 59	1 41 04	13 23 44	19 53 27	0 28.9	5 10.1	15 50.6	27 48.2	18 22.1	4 34.7	21 52.8	3 11.9	28 41.4	24 21.7
21 F	22 04 55	2 41 31	26 17 34	2♉36 26	0 30.6	6 03.4	16 34.5	28 16.2	18 43.8	4 29.1	21 58.6	3 09.8	28 41.7	24 20.2
22 Sa	22 08 52	3 41 57	8♉50 30	15 00 15	0 32.3	6 59.7	17 17.3	28 44.1	19 05.3	4 23.4	22 04.4	3 07.7	28 41.9	24 18.8
23 Su	22 12 48	4 42 21	21 06 14	27 09 02	0R33.4	7 58.9	17 59.0	29 11.7	19 26.8	4 17.6	22 10.4	3 05.5	28 42.1	24 17.3
24 M	22 16 45	5 42 43	3♊09 16	9♊07 31	0 33.6	9 00.7	18 39.6	29 39.2	19 48.1	4 11.6	22 16.4	3 03.3	28 42.3	24 15.8
25 Tu	22 20 41	6 43 03	15 04 24	21 00 31	0 32.6	10 05.0	19 18.9	0♐06.4	20 09.4	4 05.5	22 22.4	3 01.1	28 42.4	24 14.2
26 W	22 24 38	7 43 21	26 56 27	2♋52 46	0 30.6	11 11.6	19 57.0	0 33.4	20 30.6	3 59.3	22 28.6	2 58.9	28 42.5	24 12.7
27 Th	22 28 34	8 43 37	8♋49 59	14 48 35	0 27.8	12 20.3	20 33.8	1 00.2	20 51.7	3 52.9	22 34.7	2 56.6	28 42.6	24 11.2
28 F	22 32 31	9 43 51	20 49 03	26 51 45	0 24.5	13 31.0	21 09.2	1 26.8	21 12.7	3 46.5	22 41.0	2 54.3	28R42.6	24 09.6

Astro Data

	Dy Hr Mn
♅ R	8 7:28
☽ 0S	10 0:31
☿ R	20 10:56
♃ R	20 12:29
☽ 0N	22 14:22
♀ 0N	31 5:32
☽ 0S	6 5:17
☿ D	10 9:38
☽ 0N	18 23:57
♆ R	28 20:20

Planet Ingress

	Dy Hr Mn
⚳ ♑	4 0:14
☿ ♒	4 12:18
♀ ♓	4 20:07
☉ ♒	20 5:38
♀ ♈	2 4:45
☉ ♓	18 19:55
♂ ♐	25 6:21

Last Aspect / ☽ Ingress (January)

Last Aspect Dy Hr Mn		☽ Ingress Dy Hr Mn
2 10:24 ♀ △	♋	2 15:53
4 23:44 ♆ △	♌	5 3:55
7 10:45 ♆ □	♍	7 14:42
9 19:53 ♆ ⚹	♎	9 23:32
11 14:00 ☉ □	♏	12 5:32
14 5:14 ♆ ☌	♐	14 8:19
16 0:43 ♇ □	♑	16 8:39
18 5:27 ♆ ⚹	♒	18 8:17
20 6:27 ♆ □	♓	20 9:20
22 10:41 ♆ △	♈	22 13:43
24 2:24 ♄ ☌	♉	24 22:13
27 6:41 ♆ ☍	♊	27 9:53
29 15:34 ♀ □	♋	29 22:36

Last Aspect / ☽ Ingress (February)

Last Aspect Dy Hr Mn		☽ Ingress Dy Hr Mn
1 8:54 ♀ △	♌	1 10:29
3 17:52 ♆ □	♍	3 20:40
6 2:21 ♆ ⚹	♎	6 5:00
7 18:47 ♄ ☍	♏	8 11:18
10 13:02 ♆ ☌	♐	10 15:23
12 8:29 ♇ □	♑	12 17:28
14 16:19 ♆ ⚹	♒	14 18:30
16 17:49 ♆ □	♓	16 20:03
18 21:28 ♆ △	♈	18 23:48
20 15:44 ♄ ☌	♉	21 7:02
23 16:14 ♂ ☍	♊	23 17:41
25 18:31 ♇ □	♋	26 6:11
28 15:39 ♆ △	♌	28 18:12

☽ Phases & Eclipses

Dy Hr Mn	
3 18:28	○ 13♋13
11 14:00	☾ 21♎11
18 4:59	● 27♑56
25 8:23	☽ 5♉12
2 12:56	○ 13♌31
10 0:08	☾ 21♏05
16 16:25	● 27♒50
24 4:30	☽ 5♊24

Astro Data

1 January 1969
Julian Day # 25203
SVP 5♓41'34"
GC 26♐24.4 ⚵ 10♐37.3
Eris 11♈10.4 ✱ 17♐53.9
⚷ 29♓04.9 ⚶ 22♈20.9
☽ Mean ☊ 4♈35.2

1 February 1969
Julian Day # 25234
SVP 5♓41'28"
GC 26♐24.5 ⚵ 22♐54.2
Eris 11♈16.8 ✱ 28♐00.6
⚷ 0♈05.6 ⚶ 29♈46.9
☽ Mean ☊ 2♈56.7

March 1969 — LONGITUDE

Day	Sid.Time	☉	0 hr ☽	Noon☽	True☊	☿	♀	♂	⚳	♃	♄	♅	♆	♇
1 Sa	22 36 28	10♓44 03	2♌57 03	9♌05 16	0♈21.1	14♒43.7	21♈43.2	1♐53.2	21♑33.6	3♎39.9	22♈47.3	2♎52.0	28♏42.6	24♍08.1
2 Su	22 40 24	11 44 14	15 16 39	21 31 22	0R 18.1	15 58.2	22 15.8	2 19.3	21 54.3	3R 33.2	22 53.6	2R 49.6	28R 42.6	24R 06.5
3 M	22 44 21	12 44 22	27 49 35	4♍11 23	0 15.8	17 14.4	22 46.8	2 45.3	22 15.0	3 26.4	23 00.0	2 47.2	28 42.5	24 04.9
4 Tu	22 48 17	13 44 28	10♍36 48	17 05 49	0D 14.5	18 32.2	23 16.2	3 10.9	22 35.6	3 19.6	23 06.5	2 44.8	28 42.4	24 03.3
5 W	22 52 14	14 44 33	23 38 24	0♎14 27	0 14.1	19 51.6	23 44.0	3 36.3	22 56.1	3 12.6	23 13.0	2 42.4	28 42.2	24 01.7
6 Th	22 56 10	15 44 35	6♎53 53	13 36 34	0 14.4	21 12.6	24 10.1	4 01.5	23 16.5	3 05.5	23 19.5	2 40.0	28 42.1	24 00.1
7 F	23 00 07	16 44 36	20 22 20	27 11 02	0 15.3	22 35.0	24 34.5	4 26.4	23 36.8	2 58.4	23 26.1	2 37.5	28 41.9	23 58.5
8 Sa	23 04 03	17 44 36	4♏02 30	10♏56 34	0 16.4	23 58.8	24 57.0	4 51.1	23 56.9	2 51.2	23 32.8	2 35.0	28 41.6	23 56.9
9 Su	23 08 00	18 44 33	17 53 03	24 51 46	0 17.4	25 24.0	25 17.7	5 15.5	24 17.0	2 43.9	23 39.5	2 32.5	28 41.3	23 55.3
10 M	23 11 57	19 44 30	1♐52 32	8♐55 09	0R 18.0	26 50.5	25 36.4	5 39.6	24 37.0	2 36.5	23 46.2	2 30.0	28 41.0	23 53.7
11 Tu	23 15 53	20 44 24	15 59 24	23 05 02	0 18.2	28 18.4	25 53.2	6 03.4	24 56.8	2 29.1	23 53.0	2 27.5	28 40.7	23 52.1
12 W	23 19 50	21 44 17	0♑11 47	7♑19 20	0 17.9	29 47.6	26 07.9	6 27.0	25 16.5	2 21.6	23 59.9	2 25.0	28 40.3	23 50.5
13 Th	23 23 46	22 44 09	14 27 23	21 35 31	0 17.3	1♓18.0	26 20.5	6 50.2	25 36.1	2 14.1	24 06.8	2 22.4	28 39.9	23 48.9
14 F	23 27 43	23 43 58	28 43 22	5♒50 29	0 16.5	2 49.8	26 30.9	7 13.2	25 55.6	2 06.5	24 13.7	2 19.9	28 39.5	23 47.2
15 Sa	23 31 39	24 43 46	12♒56 24	20 00 39	0 15.8	4 22.7	26 39.0	7 35.8	26 15.0	1 58.8	24 20.6	2 17.3	28 39.0	23 45.6
16 Su	23 35 36	25 43 32	27 02 45	4♓02 15	0 15.2	5 57.0	26 44.9	7 58.1	26 34.2	1 51.2	24 27.6	2 14.7	28 38.5	23 44.0
17 M	23 39 32	26 43 16	10♓58 41	17 51 39	0D 14.9	7 32.4	26R 48.5	8 20.0	26 53.3	1 43.5	24 34.7	2 12.1	28 38.0	23 42.4
18 Tu	23 43 29	27 42 59	24 40 48	1♈25 50	0 14.9	9 09.1	26 49.7	8 41.6	27 12.3	1 35.7	24 41.8	2 09.5	28 37.5	23 40.7
19 W	23 47 26	28 42 39	8♈06 30	14 42 40	0 14.9	10 47.1	26 48.5	9 02.9	27 31.1	1 28.0	24 48.9	2 06.9	28 36.9	23 39.1
20 Th	23 51 22	29 42 17	21 14 14	27 41 13	0R 15.0	12 26.3	26 44.8	9 23.8	27 49.9	1 20.2	24 56.0	2 04.3	28 36.2	23 37.5
21 F	23 55 19	0♈41 53	4♉03 42	10♉21 50	0 15.0	14 06.8	26 38.6	9 44.4	28 08.4	1 12.4	25 03.2	2 01.7	28 35.6	23 35.9
22 Sa	23 59 15	1 41 26	16 35 52	22 46 07	0 14.9	15 48.6	26 29.9	10 04.6	28 26.9	1 04.6	25 10.4	1 59.1	28 34.9	23 34.3
23 Su	0 03 12	2 40 58	28 52 55	4♊56 41	0 14.6	17 31.6	26 18.8	10 24.4	28 45.2	0 56.9	25 17.6	1 56.5	28 34.2	23 32.7
24 M	0 07 08	3 40 27	10♊57 55	16 57 06	0 14.4	19 15.9	26 05.1	10 43.8	29 03.3	0 49.1	25 24.9	1 53.9	28 33.5	23 31.1
25 Tu	0 11 05	4 39 54	22 54 46	28 51 29	0D 14.2	21 01.5	25 49.0	11 02.8	29 21.4	0 41.4	25 32.2	1 51.3	28 32.7	23 29.5
26 W	0 15 01	5 39 19	4♋47 50	10♋44 24	0 14.2	22 48.4	25 30.5	11 21.5	29 39.2	0 33.6	25 39.5	1 48.7	28 31.9	23 27.9
27 Th	0 18 58	6 38 41	16 41 45	22 40 30	0 14.5	24 36.7	25 09.5	11 39.7	29 56.9	0 25.9	25 46.9	1 46.1	28 31.1	23 26.4
28 F	0 22 54	7 38 01	28 41 11	4♌44 22	0 15.0	26 26.3	24 46.3	11 57.5	0♒14.5	0 18.3	25 54.3	1 43.5	28 30.2	23 24.8
29 Sa	0 26 51	8 37 19	10♌50 34	17 00 14	0 15.8	28 17.2	24 20.9	12 14.9	0 31.9	0 10.6	26 01.7	1 40.9	28 29.3	23 23.2
30 Su	0 30 48	9 36 35	23 13 49	29 31 40	0 16.7	0♈09.5	23 53.4	12 31.9	0 49.2	0 03.0	26 09.1	1 38.3	28 28.4	23 21.7
31 M	0 34 44	10 35 48	5♍54 06	12♍21 21	0 17.5	2 03.1	23 24.0	12 48.4	1 06.3	29♍55.5	26 16.5	1 35.8	28 27.5	23 20.1

April 1969 — LONGITUDE

Day	Sid.Time	☉	0 hr ☽	Noon☽	True☊	☿	♀	♂	⚳	♃	♄	♅	♆	♇
1 Tu	0 38 41	11♈34 59	18♍53 32	25♍30 44	0♈18.0	3♈58.1	22♈52.8	13♐04.4	1♒23.3	29♍48.0	26♈24.0	1♎33.2	28♏26.5	23♍18.6
2 W	0 42 37	12 34 08	2♎12 53	8♎59 52	0R 17.9	5 54.4	22R 19.9	13 20.0	1 40.0	29R 40.5	26 31.5	1R 30.7	28R 25.5	23R 17.1
3 Th	0 46 34	13 33 14	15 51 26	22 47 16	0 17.1	7 52.1	21 45.7	13 35.1	1 56.7	29 33.2	26 39.0	1 28.1	28 24.5	23 15.6
4 F	0 50 30	14 32 19	29 46 58	6♏50 02	0 15.7	9 51.0	21 10.2	13 49.8	2 13.1	29 25.8	26 46.5	1 25.6	28 23.5	23 14.1
5 Sa	0 54 27	15 31 22	13♏55 57	21 04 08	0 13.8	11 51.2	20 33.8	14 03.9	2 29.4	29 18.6	26 54.0	1 23.1	28 22.4	23 12.6
6 Su	0 58 23	16 30 24	28 13 58	5♐24 52	0 11.8	13 52.5	19 56.6	14 17.6	2 45.6	29 11.4	27 01.5	1 20.6	28 21.3	23 11.1
7 M	1 02 20	17 29 23	12♐36 14	19 47 31	0 09.9	15 55.0	19 19.0	14 30.7	3 01.5	29 04.3	27 09.1	1 18.1	28 20.2	23 09.7
8 Tu	1 06 17	18 28 21	26 58 11	4♑07 49	0 08.6	17 58.4	18 41.1	14 43.3	3 17.3	28 57.3	27 16.7	1 15.7	28 19.1	23 08.3
9 W	1 10 13	19 27 17	11♑15 59	18 22 22	0D 08.1	20 02.8	18 03.3	14 55.3	3 32.9	28 50.4	27 24.3	1 13.2	28 17.9	23 06.8
10 Th	1 14 10	20 26 11	25 26 40	2♒28 41	0 08.4	22 07.9	17 25.7	15 06.8	3 48.3	28 43.6	27 31.9	1 10.8	28 16.8	23 05.4
11 F	1 18 06	21 25 04	9♒28 14	16 25 11	0 09.5	24 13.6	16 48.7	15 17.7	4 03.5	28 36.9	27 39.5	1 08.4	28 15.6	23 04.0
12 Sa	1 22 03	22 23 54	23 19 26	0♓10 52	0 10.9	26 19.7	16 12.4	15 28.0	4 18.6	28 30.3	27 47.1	1 06.0	28 14.3	23 02.7
13 Su	1 25 59	23 22 43	6♓59 26	13 45 04	0 12.3	28 25.9	15 37.1	15 37.8	4 33.4	28 23.8	27 54.7	1 03.7	28 13.1	23 01.3
14 M	1 29 56	24 21 30	20 27 42	27 07 16	0R 13.0	0♉32.0	15 03.0	15 46.9	4 48.1	28 17.4	28 02.3	1 01.3	28 11.8	23 00.0
15 Tu	1 33 52	25 20 16	3♈43 42	10♈16 58	0 12.7	2 37.7	14 30.4	15 55.4	5 02.6	28 11.1	28 10.0	0 59.0	28 10.6	22 58.6
16 W	1 37 49	26 18 59	16 47 00	23 13 47	0 11.0	4 42.7	13 59.3	16 03.2	5 16.8	28 04.9	28 17.6	0 56.7	28 09.2	22 57.3
17 Th	1 41 46	27 17 40	29 37 15	5♉57 27	0 08.0	6 46.7	13 29.9	16 10.5	5 30.9	27 58.9	28 25.3	0 54.5	28 07.9	22 56.0
18 F	1 45 42	28 16 20	12♉14 24	18 28 11	0 03.9	8 49.3	13 02.5	16 17.1	5 44.7	27 53.0	28 32.9	0 52.2	28 06.6	22 54.8
19 Sa	1 49 39	29 14 58	24 38 54	0♊46 42	29♓58.9	10 50.3	12 37.0	16 23.0	5 58.3	27 47.2	28 40.5	0 50.0	28 05.2	22 53.5
20 Su	1 53 35	0♉13 33	6♊51 48	12 54 28	29 53.7	12 49.2	12 13.8	16 28.2	6 11.8	27 41.6	28 48.2	0 47.9	28 03.8	22 52.3
21 M	1 57 32	1 12 06	18 55 00	24 53 45	29 48.9	14 45.9	11 52.7	16 32.8	6 25.0	27 36.1	28 55.8	0 45.7	28 02.5	22 51.1
22 Tu	2 01 28	2 10 38	0♋51 08	6♋47 36	29 45.0	16 39.9	11 33.9	16 36.7	6 38.0	27 30.7	29 03.5	0 43.6	28 01.0	22 49.9
23 W	2 05 25	3 09 07	12 43 37	18 39 44	29 42.4	18 30.9	11 17.5	16 39.9	6 50.7	27 25.5	29 11.1	0 41.5	27 59.6	22 48.8
24 Th	2 09 21	4 07 34	24 36 30	0♌34 31	29D 41.3	20 18.8	11 03.5	16 42.4	7 03.3	27 20.4	29 18.7	0 39.5	27 58.2	22 47.6
25 F	2 13 18	5 05 59	6♌34 21	12 36 38	29 41.5	22 03.4	10 51.9	16 44.2	7 15.6	27 15.5	29 26.3	0 37.5	27 56.7	22 46.5
26 Sa	2 17 15	6 04 22	18 41 59	24 50 59	29 42.7	23 44.3	10 42.7	16R 45.2	7 27.7	27 10.7	29 33.9	0 35.5	27 55.3	22 45.4
27 Su	2 21 11	7 02 42	1♍04 12	7♍22 12	29 44.3	25 21.4	10 36.0	16 45.6	7 39.5	27 06.1	29 41.5	0 33.6	27 53.8	22 44.4
28 M	2 25 08	8 01 01	13 45 28	20 14 24	29R 45.6	26 54.6	10 31.7	16 45.2	7 51.2	27 01.7	29 49.1	0 31.7	27 52.3	22 43.3
29 Tu	2 29 04	8 59 17	26 49 21	3♎30 33	29 45.9	28 23.7	10D 29.8	16 44.1	8 02.5	26 57.4	29 56.7	0 29.8	27 50.8	22 42.3
30 W	2 33 01	9 57 32	10♎18 04	17 11 54	29 44.6	29 48.7	10 30.2	16 42.2	8 13.7	26 53.3	0♉04.3	0 28.0	27 49.2	22 41.3

Astro Data

	Dy Hr Mn
♃0N	2 7:26
☽0S	5 11:38
♄⚻♇	11 9:19
♃☌♅	11 19:40
☽0N	18 9:32
♀R	18 11:49
☉0N	20 19:08
♅0N	26 23:21
☿0N	1 13:27
☽0S	1 20:09
☽0N	14 17:17
♄⚻♆	15 13:33
♃⚻♄	15 13:55
♃⚹♆	15 14:34
♂R	27 11:24

Planet Ingress

	Dy Hr Mn
☿ ♓	12 15:19
☉ ♈	20 19:08
⚳ ♒	27 16:09
☿ ♈	30 9:59
♃ ♍R	30 21:36
☿ ♉	14 5:55
☊ ♓R	19 6:53
☉ ♉	20 6:27
♄ ♉	29 22:23
☿ ♊	30 15:18
☽0S29 5:39	
♀ D29 19:20	

Last Aspect / ☽ Ingress (March)

Last Aspect Dy Hr Mn		☽ Ingress Dy Hr Mn
3 1:40	♆ □	♍ 3 4:07
5 9:13	♆ ⚹	♎ 5 11:34
7 7:17	♀ ☍	♏ 7 16:56
9 18:33	♆ ☌	♐ 9 20:48
11 21:50	☿ ⚹	♑ 11 23:40
13 23:54	♆ ⚹	♒ 14 2:09
16 2:44	♆ □	♓ 16 5:04
18 7:00	♆ △	♈ 18 9:27
20 10:15	♀ ☌	♉ 20 16:20
22 23:24	♆ ☍	♊ 23 2:12
25 6:00	♀ ⚹	♋ 25 14:18
27 23:39	♆ △	♌ 28 2:37
30 10:00	♆ □	♍ 30 12:54

Last Aspect / ☽ Ingress (April)

Last Aspect Dy Hr Mn		☽ Ingress Dy Hr Mn
1 19:37	♃ ☌	♎ 1 20:03
3 18:42	♄ ☍	♏ 4 0:22
6 1:41	♃ ⚹	♐ 6 2:57
8 3:24	♃ □	♑ 8 5:04
10 5:39	♃ △	♒ 10 7:46
12 8:36	♆ □	♓ 12 11:41
14 14:06	♃ ☍	♈ 14 17:13
16 21:36	♄ ☌	♉ 17 0:43
19 6:44	♆ ☍	♊ 19 10:28
21 20:13	♄ ⚹	♋ 21 22:17
24 9:26	♄ □	♌ 24 10:51
26 21:12	♄ △	♍ 26 21:57
29 1:52	♆ ⚹	♎ 29 5:44

☽ Phases & Eclipses

Dy Hr Mn	
4 5:17	○ 13♍28
11 7:44	☾ 20♐34
18 4:51	● 27♓25
18 4:54:18	● A 00'26"
26 0:48	☽ 5♋12
2 18:45	○ 12♎51
2 18:32	● A 0.703
9 13:58	☾ 19♑32
16 18:16	● 26♈34
24 19:45	☽ 4♌26

Astro Data

1 March 1969
Julian Day # 25262
SVP 5♓41'25"
GC 26♐24.5 ⚴ 2♑28.8
Eris 11♈30.5 ⚵ 6♑05.2
⚷ 1♈30.5 ⚶ 9♉09.5
☽ Mean ☊ 1♈27.7

1 April 1969
Julian Day # 25293
SVP 5♓41'21"
GC 26♐24.6 ⚴ 10♑14.2
Eris 11♈50.7 ⚵ 12♑56.3
⚷ 3♈19.0 ⚶ 21♉10.5
☽ Mean ☊ 29♓49.2

LONGITUDE

May 1969

Day	Sid.Time	☉	0 hr ☽	Noon ☽	True ☊	☿	♀	♂	⚳	♃	♄	♅	♆	♇
1 Th	2 36 57	10♉55 44	24♎11 50	1♏17 32	29♓41.5	1♊09.3	10♈33.0	16♐39.6	8♒24.5	26♍49.3	0♉11.8	0♎26.2	27♏47.7	22♍40.4
2 F	2 40 54	11 53 55	8♏28 29	15 43 59	29R 36.6	2 25.6	10 38.1	16R 36.3	8 35.2	26R 45.5	0 19.4	0R 24.4	27R 46.2	22R 39.4
3 Sa	2 44 50	12 52 05	23 03 16	0♐25 23	29 30.4	3 37.4	10 45.4	16 32.2	8 45.6	26 41.9	0 26.9	0 22.7	27 44.6	22 38.5
4 Su	2 48 47	13 50 12	7♐49 21	15 14 07	29 23.7	4 44.7	10 55.0	16 27.3	8 55.7	26 38.4	0 34.4	0 21.1	27 43.1	22 37.6
5 M	2 52 44	14 48 19	22 38 42	0♑02 06	29 17.4	5 47.4	11 06.7	16 21.7	9 05.6	26 35.1	0 41.9	0 19.4	27 41.5	22 36.8
6 Tu	2 56 40	15 46 23	7♑23 25	14 41 53	29 12.4	6 45.4	11 20.4	16 15.3	9 15.2	26 32.0	0 49.4	0 17.8	27 39.9	22 35.9
7 W	3 00 37	16 44 27	21 56 52	29 07 53	29 09.1	7 38.6	11 36.2	16 08.2	9 24.6	26 29.1	0 56.9	0 16.3	27 38.3	22 35.1
8 Th	3 04 33	17 42 29	6♒14 33	13♒16 42	29D 07.8	8 27.1	11 53.9	16 00.2	9 33.6	26 26.3	1 04.3	0 14.8	27 36.8	22 34.3
9 F	3 08 30	18 40 29	20 14 13	27 07 07	29 07.9	9 10.7	12 13.5	15 51.6	9 42.4	26 23.7	1 11.8	0 13.3	27 35.2	22 33.6
10 Sa	3 12 26	19 38 29	3♓55 31	10♓39 34	29 08.9	9 49.4	12 35.0	15 42.1	9 51.0	26 21.3	1 19.2	0 11.9	27 33.6	22 32.9
11 Su	3 16 23	20 36 26	17 19 28	23 55 28	29R 09.8	10 23.2	12 58.2	15 32.0	9 59.2	26 19.0	1 26.5	0 10.6	27 31.9	22 32.2
12 M	3 20 19	21 34 23	0♈27 48	6♈56 42	29 09.6	10 51.9	13 23.0	15 21.0	10 07.2	26 16.9	1 33.9	0 09.2	27 30.3	22 31.5
13 Tu	3 24 16	22 32 18	13 22 22	19 45 03	29 07.6	11 15.7	13 49.5	15 09.4	10 14.8	26 15.0	1 41.2	0 07.9	27 28.7	22 30.9
14 W	3 28 13	23 30 12	26 04 53	2♉22 03	29 03.2	11 34.4	14 17.6	14 57.1	10 22.2	26 13.3	1 48.5	0 06.7	27 27.1	22 30.3
15 Th	3 32 09	24 28 05	8♉36 40	14 48 53	28 56.3	11 48.1	14 47.2	14 44.0	10 29.3	26 11.8	1 55.8	0 05.5	27 25.5	22 29.7
16 F	3 36 06	25 25 56	20 58 46	27 06 27	28 47.3	11 56.9	15 18.2	14 30.3	10 36.0	26 10.5	2 03.1	0 04.4	27 23.8	22 29.1
17 Sa	3 40 02	26 23 46	3♊12 01	9♊15 36	28 36.8	12R 00.7	15 50.7	14 16.0	10 42.5	26 09.3	2 10.3	0 03.3	27 22.2	22 28.6
18 Su	3 43 59	27 21 34	15 17 19	21 17 22	28 25.7	11 59.7	16 24.4	14 01.0	10 48.7	26 08.3	2 17.5	0 02.3	27 20.6	22 28.1
19 M	3 47 55	28 19 21	27 15 54	3♋13 12	28 15.1	11 54.1	16 59.5	13 45.4	10 54.5	26 07.5	2 24.6	0 01.3	27 19.0	22 27.7
20 Tu	3 51 52	29 17 07	9♋09 30	15 05 10	28 05.9	11 44.0	17 35.7	13 29.2	11 00.1	26 06.9	2 31.8	0 00.3	27 17.3	22 27.2
21 W	3 55 48	0♊14 50	21 00 32	26 56 02	27 58.6	11 29.7	18 13.2	13 12.5	11 05.3	26 06.5	2 38.9	29♍59.4	27 15.7	22 26.8
22 Th	3 59 45	1 12 33	2♌52 09	8♌49 22	27 53.8	11 11.4	18 51.8	12 55.3	11 10.2	26D 06.3	2 45.9	29 58.6	27 14.1	22 26.5
23 F	4 03 42	2 10 13	14 48 15	20 49 23	27 51.3	10 49.5	19 31.5	12 37.6	11 14.8	26 06.2	2 52.9	29 57.8	27 12.5	22 26.1
24 Sa	4 07 38	3 07 52	26 53 22	3♍00 50	27D 50.6	10 24.4	20 12.2	12 19.4	11 19.0	26 06.3	2 59.9	29 57.1	27 10.8	22 25.8
25 Su	4 11 35	4 05 30	9♍12 25	15 28 45	27R 51.0	9 56.5	20 54.0	12 00.9	11 23.0	26 06.6	3 06.9	29 56.4	27 09.2	22 25.5
26 M	4 15 31	5 03 06	21 50 27	28 18 04	27 51.3	9 26.3	21 36.7	11 42.0	11 26.6	26 07.1	3 13.8	29 55.7	27 07.6	22 25.3
27 Tu	4 19 28	6 00 41	4♎52 07	11♎32 59	27 50.6	8 54.4	22 20.4	11 22.7	11 29.8	26 07.8	3 20.6	29 55.1	27 06.0	22 25.1
28 W	4 23 24	6 58 14	18 20 59	25 16 14	27 47.9	8 21.2	23 05.0	11 03.2	11 32.8	26 08.6	3 27.4	29 54.6	27 04.4	22 24.9
29 Th	4 27 21	7 55 46	2♏18 45	9♏28 16	27 42.7	7 47.5	23 50.4	10 43.4	11 35.4	26 09.6	3 34.2	29 54.1	27 02.8	22 24.8
30 F	4 31 17	8 53 16	16 44 23	24 06 27	27 35.2	7 13.7	24 36.7	10 23.4	11 37.7	26 10.8	3 41.0	29 53.7	27 01.2	22 24.6
31 Sa	4 35 14	9 50 46	1♐33 34	9♐04 43	27 25.8	6 40.5	25 23.8	10 03.2	11 39.6	26 12.2	3 47.7	29 53.3	26 59.7	22 24.6

LONGITUDE

June 1969

Day	Sid.Time	☉	0 hr ☽	Noon ☽	True ☊	☿	♀	♂	⚳	♃	♄	♅	♆	♇
1 Su	4 39 11	10♊48 15	16♐38 40	24♐14 07	27♓15.6	6♊08.4	26♈11.7	9♐42.9	11♒41.2	26♍13.7	3♉54.3	29♍53.0	26♏58.1	22♍24.5
2 M	4 43 07	11 45 42	1♑49 43	9♑24 07	27R 05.8	5R 38.0	27 00.3	9R 22.5	11 42.4	26 15.5	4 00.9	29R 52.7	26R 56.5	22D 24.5
3 Tu	4 47 04	12 43 09	16 56 05	24 24 30	26 57.5	5 09.8	27 49.7	9 02.1	11 43.3	26 17.4	4 07.5	29 52.5	26 55.0	22 24.5
4 W	4 51 00	13 40 35	1♒48 24	9♒07 04	26 51.5	4 44.2	28 39.8	8 41.7	11 43.8	26 19.5	4 14.0	29 52.3	26 53.4	22 24.6
5 Th	4 54 57	14 38 01	16 19 56	23 26 42	26 48.1	4 21.6	29 30.5	8 21.3	11R 44.0	26 21.7	4 20.5	29 52.2	26 51.9	22 24.6
6 F	4 58 53	15 35 25	0♓27 13	7♓21 29	26D 46.7	4 02.5	0♉21.9	8 01.0	11 43.8	26 24.1	4 26.9	29D 52.1	26 50.4	22 24.7
7 Sa	5 02 50	16 32 49	14 09 41	20 52 04	26R 46.6	3 47.1	1 13.9	7 40.8	11 43.3	26 26.7	4 33.3	29 52.1	26 48.9	22 24.9
8 Su	5 06 47	17 30 13	27 28 58	4♈00 47	26 46.5	3 35.7	2 06.5	7 20.8	11 42.4	26 29.5	4 39.6	29 52.2	26 47.4	22 25.0
9 M	5 10 43	18 27 36	10♈27 58	16 50 54	26 45.3	3 28.4	2 59.7	7 01.0	11 41.2	26 32.4	4 45.8	29 52.3	26 45.9	22 25.2
10 Tu	5 14 40	19 24 58	23 10 04	29 25 49	26 41.9	3D 25.5	3 53.4	6 41.5	11 39.6	26 35.5	4 52.0	29 52.4	26 44.4	22 25.5
11 W	5 18 36	20 22 20	5♉38 34	11♉48 39	26 35.9	3 27.0	4 47.7	6 22.4	11 37.6	26 38.8	4 58.2	29 52.6	26 42.9	22 25.7
12 Th	5 22 33	21 19 41	17 56 23	24 02 03	26 26.9	3 33.1	5 42.5	6 03.6	11 35.3	26 42.2	5 04.3	29 52.9	26 41.5	22 26.0
13 F	5 26 29	22 17 02	0♊05 51	6♊08 02	26 15.5	3 43.7	6 37.8	5 45.2	11 32.6	26 45.8	5 10.3	29 53.2	26 40.0	22 26.4
14 Sa	5 30 26	23 14 22	12 08 46	18 08 14	26 02.2	3 58.8	7 33.5	5 27.2	11 29.5	26 49.5	5 16.3	29 53.5	26 38.6	22 26.7
15 Su	5 34 22	24 11 42	24 06 34	0♋03 56	25 48.2	4 18.5	8 29.7	5 09.7	11 26.1	26 53.5	5 22.2	29 53.9	26 37.2	22 27.1
16 M	5 38 19	25 09 01	6♋00 29	11 56 26	25 34.7	4 42.7	9 26.4	4 52.8	11 22.3	26 57.6	5 28.1	29 54.4	26 35.8	22 27.6
17 Tu	5 42 16	26 06 19	17 51 56	23 47 16	25 22.6	5 11.4	10 23.4	4 36.4	11 18.2	27 01.8	5 33.9	29 54.9	26 34.5	22 28.0
18 W	5 46 12	27 03 37	29 42 40	5♌38 26	25 12.9	5 44.5	11 20.9	4 20.7	11 13.7	27 06.2	5 39.7	29 55.5	26 33.1	22 28.5
19 Th	5 50 09	28 00 54	11♌34 57	17 32 36	25 05.9	6 21.9	12 18.8	4 05.5	11 08.9	27 10.8	5 45.3	29 56.1	26 31.8	22 29.0
20 F	5 54 05	28 58 10	23 31 50	29 33 07	25 01.7	7 03.6	13 17.1	3 51.0	11 03.7	27 15.5	5 50.9	29 56.8	26 30.5	22 29.6
21 Sa	5 58 02	29 55 26	5♍37 00	11♍44 03	24 59.9	7 49.5	14 15.7	3 37.2	10 58.2	27 20.4	5 56.5	29 57.5	26 29.2	22 30.2
22 Su	6 01 58	0♋52 40	17 54 50	24 09 58	24 59.5	8 39.5	15 14.7	3 24.1	10 52.3	27 25.4	6 02.0	29 58.3	26 27.9	22 30.8
23 M	6 05 55	1 49 54	0♎30 04	6♎55 43	24 59.4	9 33.6	16 14.1	3 11.7	10 46.1	27 30.6	6 07.4	29 59.2	26 26.6	22 31.4
24 Tu	6 09 51	2 47 08	13 27 29	20 05 51	24 58.6	10 31.7	17 13.7	3 00.1	10 39.5	27 35.9	6 12.7	0♎00.1	26 25.4	22 32.1
25 W	6 13 48	3 44 21	26 51 16	3♏43 59	24 56.0	11 33.8	18 13.8	2 49.3	10 32.6	27 41.4	6 18.0	0 01.0	26 24.2	22 32.8
26 Th	6 17 45	4 41 33	10♏44 09	17 51 45	24 51.1	12 39.7	19 14.1	2 39.2	10 25.4	27 47.0	6 23.2	0 02.0	26 23.0	22 33.5
27 F	6 21 41	5 38 45	25 06 32	2♐28 00	24 43.7	13 49.5	20 14.8	2 29.9	10 17.8	27 52.8	6 28.3	0 03.0	26 21.8	22 34.3
28 Sa	6 25 38	6 35 57	9♐55 27	17 27 57	24 34.3	15 03.1	21 15.7	2 21.5	10 10.0	27 58.7	6 33.4	0 04.1	26 20.6	22 35.1
29 Su	6 29 34	7 33 08	25 04 19	2♑43 17	24 24.0	16 20.5	22 17.0	2 13.8	10 01.8	28 04.7	6 38.4	0 05.3	26 19.5	22 35.9
30 M	6 33 31	8 30 20	10♑23 23	18 03 09	24 14.0	17 41.5	23 18.5	2 07.0	9 53.4	28 10.9	6 43.3	0 06.5	26 18.4	22 36.8

Astro Data	Dy Hr Mn
♄⚻♅	3 1:05
☽0N	11 22:53
☿R	17 19:07
♃D	23 8:20
☽0S	26 14:27
♇D	2 14:00
⚳R	5 12:26
♅D	7 6:34
☽0N	8 3:37
☿D	10 15:48
♃⚹♆	12 8:35
☽0S	22 21:28

Planet Ingress	Dy Hr Mn
♅ ♍R	20 20:51
☉ ♊	21 5:50
♀ ♉	6 1:48
☉ ♋	21 13:55
♅ ♎	24 10:36

Last Aspect Dy Hr Mn		☽ Ingress Dy Hr Mn
30 11:09	♂ ⚹	♏ 1 9:50
3 7:39	♆ ☌	♐ 3 11:19
5 6:25	♃ □	♑ 5 11:57
7 9:30	♆ ⚹	♒ 7 13:28
9 12:49	♆ □	♓ 9 17:04
11 18:36	♆ △	♈ 11 23:09
13 3:29	♂ △	♉ 14 7:28
16 12:34	♆ ☍	♊ 16 17:41
18 21:43	♃ □	♋ 19 5:30
21 18:11	♅ ⚹	♌ 21 18:12
24 0:36	♆ □	♍ 24 6:07
26 14:59	♅ ☌	♎ 26 15:07
28 8:01	♀ ☍	♏ 28 20:05
30 21:20	♅ ⚹	♐ 30 21:30

Last Aspect Dy Hr Mn		☽ Ingress Dy Hr Mn
1 20:55	♅ □	♑ 1 21:07
3 20:51	♅ △	♒ 3 21:03
5 23:03	♀ ⚹	♓ 5 23:13
8 4:22	♅ ☍	♈ 8 4:36
9 15:18	☉ ⚹	♉ 10 13:06
12 23:34	♅ △	♊ 12 23:48
15 11:40	♅ □	♋ 15 11:52
18 0:25	♅ ⚹	♌ 18 0:35
20 10:45	☉ ⚹	♍ 20 12:53
22 23:01	♅ ☌	♎ 22 23:03
23 17:14	☿ △	♏ 25 5:31
27 4:29	♃ ⚹	♐ 27 8:00
29 4:40	♃ □	♑ 29 7:44

☽ Phases & Eclipses Dy Hr Mn	
2 5:13	○ 11♏37
8 20:12	☾ 18♒02
16 8:26	● 25♉17
24 12:15	☽ 3♍08
31 13:18	○ 9♐54
7 3:39	☾ 16♓13
14 23:09	● 23♊41
23 1:44	☽ 1♎25
29 20:04	○ 7♑52

Astro Data

1 May 1969
Julian Day # 25323
SVP 5♓41'18"
GC 26♐24.7 ⚴ 13♑10.6
Eris 12♈10.4 ⚵ 16♑11.7
⚷ 4♈58.2 ⚶ 3♊40.6
☽ Mean ☊ 28♓13.9

1 June 1969
Julian Day # 25354
SVP 5♓41'12"
GC 26♐24.7 ⚴ 9♑41.1R
Eris 12♈26.1 ⚵ 14♑37.1R
⚷ 6♈15.4 ⚶ 17♊00.6
☽ Mean ☊ 26♓35.4

July 1969

LONGITUDE

Day	Sid.Time	☉	0 hr ☽	Noon☽	True☊	☿	♀	♂	⚳	♃	♄	♅	♆	♇
1 Tu	6 37 27	9♋27 31	25♑41 10	3♒16 04	24♓05.5	19♊06.2	24♉20.3	2♐00.9	9♒44.6	28♍17.2	6♉48.1	0♎07.7	26♏17.3	22♍37.7
2 W	6 41 24	10 24 42	10♒46 39	18 11 57	23R 59.2	20 34.5	25 22.5	1R 55.7	9R 35.5	28 23.7	6 52.9	0 09.0	26R 16.3	22 38.6
3 Th	6 45 21	11 21 53	25 31 11	2♓43 47	23 55.5	22 06.4	26 24.8	1 51.4	9 26.1	28 30.3	6 57.6	0 10.4	26 15.2	22 39.6
4 F	6 49 17	12 19 04	9♓49 26	16 48 02	23D 54.0	23 41.8	27 27.5	1 47.8	9 16.5	28 37.0	7 02.2	0 11.8	26 14.2	22 40.5
5 Sa	6 53 14	13 16 16	23 39 37	0♈24 24	23 53.9	25 20.6	28 30.3	1 45.1	9 06.6	28 43.9	7 06.8	0 13.2	26 13.2	22 41.5
6 Su	6 57 10	14 13 28	7♈02 43	13 34 59	23R 54.2	27 02.7	29 33.5	1 43.2	8 56.4	28 50.9	7 11.2	0 14.7	26 12.3	22 42.6
7 M	7 01 07	15 10 40	20 01 40	26 23 16	23 53.7	28 48.1	0♊36.8	1D 42.2	8 45.9	28 58.0	7 15.6	0 16.3	26 11.3	22 43.6
8 Tu	7 05 03	16 07 53	2♉40 20	8♉53 22	23 51.4	0♋36.7	1 40.4	1 41.9	8 35.2	29 05.2	7 19.9	0 17.9	26 10.4	22 44.7
9 W	7 09 00	17 05 06	15 02 55	21 09 26	23 46.7	2 28.2	2 44.3	1 42.6	8 24.3	29 12.6	7 24.1	0 19.5	26 09.5	22 45.8
10 Th	7 12 56	18 02 19	27 13 23	3♊15 13	23 39.6	4 22.6	3 48.3	1 44.0	8 13.1	29 20.1	7 28.2	0 21.2	26 08.7	22 47.0
11 F	7 16 53	18 59 33	9♊15 17	15 13 57	23 30.1	6 19.5	4 52.6	1 46.3	8 01.7	29 27.8	7 32.3	0 22.9	26 07.8	22 48.2
12 Sa	7 20 50	19 56 47	21 11 31	27 08 16	23 19.1	8 18.9	5 57.0	1 49.4	7 50.1	29 35.5	7 36.2	0 24.7	26 07.0	22 49.4
13 Su	7 24 46	20 54 02	3♋04 26	9♋00 15	23 07.3	10 20.4	7 01.7	1 53.3	7 38.3	29 43.4	7 40.1	0 26.5	26 06.2	22 50.6
14 M	7 28 43	21 51 17	14 55 54	20 51 36	22 55.9	12 23.7	8 06.5	1 58.0	7 26.3	29 51.4	7 43.9	0 28.4	26 05.5	22 51.9
15 Tu	7 32 39	22 48 32	26 47 32	2♌43 53	22 45.8	14 28.7	9 11.6	2 03.6	7 14.1	29 59.5	7 47.6	0 30.3	26 04.8	22 53.1
16 W	7 36 36	23 45 48	8♌40 53	14 38 44	22 37.7	16 34.9	10 16.8	2 09.9	7 01.8	0♎07.7	7 51.2	0 32.3	26 04.1	22 54.5
17 Th	7 40 32	24 43 04	20 37 43	26 38 05	22 32.1	18 42.1	11 22.2	2 17.0	6 49.4	0 16.1	7 54.8	0 34.3	26 03.4	22 55.8
18 F	7 44 29	25 40 20	2♍40 10	8♍44 20	22 28.9	20 49.9	12 27.8	2 24.9	6 36.7	0 24.5	7 58.2	0 36.4	26 02.8	22 57.1
19 Sa	7 48 25	26 37 36	14 50 57	21 00 27	22D 27.9	22 58.1	13 33.5	2 33.6	6 24.0	0 33.1	8 01.5	0 38.5	26 02.1	22 58.5
20 Su	7 52 22	27 34 52	27 13 17	3♎29 56	22 28.3	25 06.3	14 39.5	2 43.0	6 11.2	0 41.8	8 04.8	0 40.6	26 01.6	22 59.9
21 M	7 56 19	28 32 09	9♎50 55	16 16 41	22R 29.3	27 14.4	15 45.5	2 53.1	5 58.2	0 50.5	8 07.9	0 42.8	26 01.0	23 01.4
22 Tu	8 00 15	29 29 26	22 47 45	29 24 33	22 29.8	29 21.9	16 51.8	3 04.0	5 45.2	0 59.4	8 11.0	0 45.1	26 00.5	23 02.8
23 W	8 04 12	0♌26 44	6♏07 30	12♏56 53	22 29.0	1♌28.8	17 58.2	3 15.6	5 32.2	1 08.4	8 14.0	0 47.3	26 00.0	23 04.3
24 Th	8 08 08	1 24 02	19 52 55	26 55 41	22 26.5	3 34.8	19 04.7	3 28.0	5 19.0	1 17.5	8 16.9	0 49.7	25 59.5	23 05.8
25 F	8 12 05	2 21 20	4♐05 05	11♐20 50	22 22.0	5 39.8	20 11.4	3 41.0	5 05.9	1 26.7	8 19.6	0 52.0	25 59.1	23 07.4
26 Sa	8 16 01	3 18 38	18 42 26	26 09 13	22 15.9	7 43.6	21 18.3	3 54.7	4 52.7	1 36.0	8 22.3	0 54.4	25 58.7	23 08.9
27 Su	8 19 58	4 15 58	3♑40 17	11♑14 34	22 09.0	9 46.1	22 25.3	4 09.0	4 39.4	1 45.4	8 24.9	0 56.9	25 58.4	23 10.5
28 M	8 23 54	5 13 17	18 50 51	26 27 50	22 02.1	11 47.3	23 32.5	4 24.0	4 26.2	1 54.9	8 27.4	0 59.4	25 58.0	23 12.1
29 Tu	8 27 51	6 10 38	4♒04 11	11♒38 34	21 56.3	13 46.9	24 39.8	4 39.7	4 13.0	2 04.5	8 29.8	1 01.9	25 57.7	23 13.7
30 W	8 31 48	7 07 59	19 09 45	26 36 39	21 52.1	15 45.1	25 47.2	4 55.9	3 59.9	2 14.2	8 32.1	1 04.5	25 57.4	23 15.4
31 Th	8 35 44	8 05 21	3♓58 18	11♓13 59	21D 49.9	17 41.7	26 54.8	5 12.8	3 46.7	2 24.0	8 34.3	1 07.0	25 57.2	23 17.1

August 1969

LONGITUDE

Day	Sid.Time	☉	0 hr ☽	Noon☽	True☊	☿	♀	♂	⚳	♃	♄	♅	♆	♇
1 F	8 39 41	9♌02 44	18♓23 10	25♓25 30	21♓49.5	19♌36.7	28♊02.6	5♐30.3	3♒33.7	2♎33.8	8♉36.4	1♎09.7	25♏57.0	23♍18.7
2 Sa	8 43 37	10 00 08	2♈20 51	9♈09 14	21 50.4	21 30.2	29 10.4	5 48.4	3R 20.7	2 43.8	8 38.4	1 12.4	25R 56.8	23 20.4
3 Su	8 47 34	10 57 33	15 50 50	22 25 55	21 51.8	23 22.0	0♋18.4	6 07.0	3 07.7	2 53.8	8 40.3	1 15.1	25 56.7	23 22.2
4 M	8 51 30	11 55 00	28 54 53	5♉18 12	21R 52.8	25 12.3	1 26.6	6 26.3	2 54.9	3 04.0	8 42.1	1 17.8	25 56.5	23 23.9
5 Tu	8 55 27	12 52 28	11♉36 21	17 49 54	21 52.9	27 00.9	2 34.9	6 46.0	2 42.2	3 14.2	8 43.8	1 20.6	25 56.4	23 25.7
6 W	8 59 23	13 49 57	23 59 24	0♊05 25	21 51.5	28 48.0	3 43.3	7 06.4	2 29.5	3 24.5	8 45.4	1 23.4	25 56.4	23 27.5
7 Th	9 03 20	14 47 27	6♊08 28	12 09 06	21 48.5	0♍33.5	4 51.8	7 27.3	2 17.1	3 34.9	8 46.9	1 26.3	25D 56.4	23 29.3
8 F	9 07 17	15 44 59	18 07 50	24 05 07	21 44.0	2 17.4	6 00.4	7 48.7	2 04.7	3 45.4	8 48.3	1 29.2	25 56.4	23 31.1
9 Sa	9 11 13	16 42 32	0♋01 25	5♋57 07	21 38.4	3 59.7	7 09.2	8 10.7	1 52.6	3 55.9	8 49.6	1 32.1	25 56.4	23 33.0
10 Su	9 15 10	17 40 06	11 52 37	17 48 14	21 32.3	5 40.5	8 18.1	8 33.1	1 40.6	4 06.5	8 50.8	1 35.0	25 56.5	23 34.8
11 M	9 19 06	18 37 42	23 44 17	29 41 02	21 26.3	7 19.8	9 27.1	8 56.1	1 28.7	4 17.3	8 51.9	1 38.0	25 56.6	23 36.7
12 Tu	9 23 03	19 35 18	5♌38 45	11♌37 39	21 21.1	8 57.5	10 36.3	9 19.6	1 17.1	4 28.0	8 52.9	1 41.1	25 56.8	23 38.6
13 W	9 26 59	20 32 56	17 37 57	23 39 51	21 17.0	10 33.7	11 45.5	9 43.5	1 05.7	4 38.9	8 53.7	1 44.1	25 56.9	23 40.5
14 Th	9 30 56	21 30 35	29 43 33	5♍49 15	21 14.5	12 08.4	12 54.8	10 08.0	0 54.5	4 49.8	8 54.5	1 47.2	25 57.1	23 42.5
15 F	9 34 52	22 28 16	11♍57 09	18 07 28	21D 13.5	13 41.5	14 04.3	10 32.9	0 43.5	5 00.9	8 55.2	1 50.3	25 57.4	23 44.4
16 Sa	9 38 49	23 25 57	24 20 26	0♎36 17	21 13.8	15 13.2	15 13.8	10 58.3	0 32.8	5 11.9	8 55.7	1 53.4	25 57.6	23 46.4
17 Su	9 42 46	24 23 39	6♎55 17	13 17 42	21 14.9	16 43.3	16 23.5	11 24.1	0 22.3	5 23.1	8 56.2	1 56.6	25 57.9	23 48.3
18 M	9 46 42	25 21 23	19 43 48	26 13 54	21 16.5	18 11.8	17 33.3	11 50.4	0 12.1	5 34.3	8 56.5	1 59.8	25 58.3	23 50.3
19 Tu	9 50 39	26 19 08	2♏48 15	9♏27 08	21 17.9	19 38.8	18 43.1	12 17.0	0 02.1	5 45.6	8 56.7	2 03.0	25 58.6	23 52.3
20 W	9 54 35	27 16 54	16 10 47	22 59 24	21R 18.7	21 04.3	19 53.1	12 44.2	29♑52.5	5 56.9	8R 56.9	2 06.3	25 59.0	23 54.4
21 Th	9 58 32	28 14 41	29 53 05	6♐51 53	21 18.5	22 28.1	21 03.1	13 11.7	29 43.1	6 08.4	8 56.9	2 09.6	25 59.5	23 56.4
22 F	10 02 28	29 12 29	13♐55 45	21 04 31	21 17.3	23 50.3	22 13.3	13 39.6	29 34.0	6 19.8	8 56.8	2 12.9	26 00.0	23 58.4
23 Sa	10 06 25	0♍10 18	28 17 51	5♑35 21	21 15.3	25 10.9	23 23.6	14 08.0	29 25.2	6 31.4	8 56.6	2 16.2	26 00.5	24 00.5
24 Su	10 10 21	1 08 09	12♑56 24	20 20 17	21 12.8	26 29.7	24 33.9	14 36.7	29 16.7	6 43.0	8 56.3	2 19.6	26 01.0	24 02.6
25 M	10 14 18	2 06 01	27 46 11	5♒13 10	21 10.3	27 46.9	25 44.4	15 05.8	29 08.5	6 54.6	8 55.9	2 23.0	26 01.5	24 04.7
26 Tu	10 18 15	3 03 54	12♒40 14	20 06 21	21 08.2	29 02.2	26 54.9	15 35.2	29 00.7	7 06.3	8 55.4	2 26.4	26 02.1	24 06.8
27 W	10 22 11	4 01 48	27 30 32	4♓51 47	21 06.8	0♎15.6	28 05.6	16 05.0	28 53.1	7 18.1	8 54.8	2 29.8	26 02.8	24 08.9
28 Th	10 26 08	4 59 44	12♓09 16	19 22 10	21D 06.3	1 27.2	29 16.3	16 35.1	28 45.9	7 29.9	8 54.1	2 33.2	26 03.4	24 11.0
29 F	10 30 04	5 57 42	26 29 53	3♈31 54	21 06.6	2 36.7	0♌27.2	17 05.6	28 39.0	7 41.8	8 53.3	2 36.7	26 04.1	24 13.1
30 Sa	10 34 01	6 55 41	10♈27 53	17 17 40	21 07.4	3 44.1	1 38.1	17 36.5	28 32.4	7 53.7	8 52.4	2 40.2	26 04.8	24 15.2
31 Su	10 37 57	7 53 42	24 01 09	0♉38 28	21 08.5	4 49.3	2 49.2	18 07.6	28 26.2	8 05.7	8 51.3	2 43.7	26 05.6	24 17.4

Astro Data Dy Hr Mn	Planet Ingress Dy Hr Mn	Last Aspect Dy Hr Mn	☽ Ingress Dy Hr Mn	Last Aspect Dy Hr Mn	☽ Ingress Dy Hr Mn	☽ Phases & Eclipses Dy Hr Mn	Astro Data
☽0N 5 9:26	♀ ♊ 6 22:04	1 4:03 ♃ △	♒ 1 6:49	1 16:55 ♀ □	♈ 1 19:54	6 13:17 ☾ 14♈17	1 July 1969
♂D 8 6:07	☿ ♋ 8 3:58	3 1:14 ♆ □	♓ 3 7:26	3 14:00 ☿ △	♉ 4 2:02	14 14:11 ● 21♋57	Julian Day # 25384
♄□♇ 17 23:49	♃ ♎ 15 13:30	5 8:59 ♃ ☍	♈ 5 11:16	6 9:01 ☿ □	♊ 6 11:49	22 12:09 ☽ 29♎30	SVP 5♓41'06"
☽0S 20 2:52	☿ ♌ 22 19:11	7 17:21 ☿ ⚹	♉ 7 18:53	8 10:51 ♇ □	♋ 8 23:57	29 2:45 ○ 5♒49	GC 26♐24.8 ⚴ 1♑34.6R
♃☌♅ 20 7:57	☉ ♌ 23 0:48	10 4:07 ♃ △	♊ 10 5:31	11 4:27 ♆ △	♌ 11 12:38		Eris 12♈33.3 ⚵ 8♑39.4R
		12 17:01 ♃ □	♋ 12 17:47	13 16:32 ♆ □	♍ 14 0:32		⚷ 6♈50.9 ⚶ 0♋00.9
☽0N 1 17:28	♀ ♋ 3 5:30	15 6:24 ♃ ⚹	♌ 15 6:29	16 3:07 ♆ ⚹	♎ 16 10:51	5 1:38 ☾ 12♉28	☽ Mean ☊ 25♓00.2
♃0S 2 12:39	☿ ♍ 7 4:21	17 10:51 ♆ □	♍ 17 18:42	18 10:16 ☉ ⚹	♏ 18 18:54	13 5:16 ● 20♌17	
♆D 7 14:55	⚳ ♑R 19 17:16	19 23:45 ☉ ⚹	♎ 20 5:20	20 20:03 ☉ □	♐ 21 0:12	20 20:03 ☽ 27♏36	1 August 1969
♅0S 11 1:31	☉ ♍ 23 7:43	22 12:09 ☉ □	♏ 22 13:04	23 2:28 ☉ △	♑ 23 2:49	27 10:32 ○ 3♓58	Julian Day # 25415
☽0S 16 7:56	☿ ♎ 27 6:50	24 10:25 ♆ ☌	♐ 24 17:10	24 22:54 ☿ △	♒ 25 3:36	27 10:48 A 0.013	SVP 5♓41'01"
♄R 21 5:44	♀ ♌ 29 2:48	26 7:10 ♇ □	♑ 26 18:09	26 21:37 ♆ □	♓ 27 4:03		GC 26♐24.9 ⚴ 25♐11.4R
♄□♇ 21 17:43		28 11:13 ♆ ⚹	♒ 28 17:34	28 23:16 ♆ △	♈ 29 5:57		Eris 12♈30.7R ⚵ 2♑23.0R
☿0S 25 8:41		30 10:57 ♆ □	♓ 30 17:30	30 12:35 ♂ △	♉ 31 10:50		⚷ 6♈39.7R ⚶ 13♋17.9
☽0N 29 3:18							☽ Mean ☊ 23♓21.7

LONGITUDE — September 1969

Day	Sid.Time	☉	0 hr ☽	Noon ☽	True ☊	☿	♀	♂	⚳	♃	♄	♅	♆	♇
1 M	10 41 54	8♍51 45	7♉09 46	13♉35 22	21♓09.6	5♎52.3	4♌00.3	18♐39.1	28♑20.4	8♎17.7	8♉50.2	2♎47.2	26♏06.4	24♍19.5
2 Tu	10 45 50	9 49 51	19 55 39	26 11 02	21 10.4	6 52.7	5 11.5	19 10.9	28R 14.8	8 29.8	8R 49.0	2 50.8	26 07.2	24 21.7
3 W	10 49 47	10 47 58	2♊22 02	8♊29 10	21R 10.7	7 50.6	6 22.8	19 43.0	28 09.6	8 41.9	8 47.7	2 54.4	26 08.0	24 23.8
4 Th	10 53 44	11 46 07	14 32 59	20 34 04	21 10.6	8 45.8	7 34.2	20 15.4	28 04.8	8 54.1	8 46.2	2 57.9	26 08.9	24 26.0
5 F	10 57 40	12 44 18	26 32 58	2♋30 15	21 10.1	9 38.0	8 45.7	20 48.1	28 00.3	9 06.3	8 44.7	3 01.5	26 09.8	24 28.2
6 Sa	11 01 37	13 42 31	8♋26 29	14 22 11	21 09.3	10 27.2	9 57.3	21 21.1	27 56.2	9 18.6	8 43.0	3 05.2	26 10.7	24 30.4
7 Su	11 05 33	14 40 46	20 17 52	26 14 00	21 08.4	11 13.0	11 09.0	21 54.4	27 52.4	9 30.9	8 41.3	3 08.8	26 11.7	24 32.6
8 M	11 09 30	15 39 03	2♌11 03	8♌09 24	21 07.6	11 55.3	12 20.7	22 28.0	27 49.0	9 43.2	8 39.5	3 12.4	26 12.7	24 34.8
9 Tu	11 13 26	16 37 21	14 09 27	20 11 31	21 06.9	12 33.7	13 32.5	23 01.8	27 46.0	9 55.6	8 37.5	3 16.1	26 13.7	24 37.0
10 W	11 17 23	17 35 42	26 15 55	2♍22 53	21 06.5	13 08.1	14 44.4	23 36.0	27 43.3	10 08.0	8 35.5	3 19.8	26 14.8	24 39.2
11 Th	11 21 19	18 34 05	8♍32 38	14 45 22	21D 06.4	13 38.2	15 56.4	24 10.4	27 41.0	10 20.5	8 33.3	3 23.5	26 15.9	24 41.4
12 F	11 25 16	19 32 29	21 01 13	27 20 17	21 06.4	14 03.5	17 08.5	24 45.1	27 39.0	10 33.0	8 31.1	3 27.2	26 17.0	24 43.6
13 Sa	11 29 13	20 30 55	3♎42 41	10♎08 27	21R 06.4	14 23.9	18 20.6	25 20.0	27 37.4	10 45.5	8 28.8	3 30.9	26 18.1	24 45.8
14 Su	11 33 09	21 29 23	16 37 37	23 10 14	21 06.4	14 38.9	19 32.9	25 55.2	27 36.2	10 58.1	8 26.3	3 34.6	26 19.3	24 48.0
15 M	11 37 06	22 27 53	29 46 16	6♏25 44	21 06.3	14 48.3	20 45.2	26 30.7	27 35.3	11 10.7	8 23.8	3 38.3	26 20.5	24 50.3
16 Tu	11 41 02	23 26 24	13♏08 36	19 54 49	21 06.1	14R 51.6	21 57.5	27 06.4	27D 34.8	11 23.4	8 21.2	3 42.1	26 21.7	24 52.5
17 W	11 44 59	24 24 57	26 44 21	3♐37 06	21 05.9	14 48.5	23 10.0	27 42.3	27 34.7	11 36.0	8 18.5	3 45.8	26 23.0	24 54.7
18 Th	11 48 55	25 23 32	10♐33 01	17 31 57	21D 05.7	14 38.8	24 22.5	28 18.5	27 34.9	11 48.7	8 15.7	3 49.6	26 24.3	24 56.9
19 F	11 52 52	26 22 09	24 33 46	1♑38 15	21 05.7	14 22.2	25 35.0	28 54.9	27 35.5	12 01.4	8 12.8	3 53.3	26 25.6	24 59.2
20 Sa	11 56 48	27 20 47	8♑45 11	15 54 16	21 05.9	13 58.6	26 47.7	29 31.5	27 36.4	12 14.2	8 09.9	3 57.1	26 26.9	25 01.4
21 Su	12 00 45	28 19 26	23 05 10	0♒17 27	21 06.4	13 27.8	28 00.4	0♑08.3	27 37.7	12 26.9	8 06.8	4 00.9	26 28.3	25 03.6
22 M	12 04 42	29 18 08	7♒30 41	14 44 21	21 07.1	12 49.9	29 13.2	0 45.4	27 39.3	12 39.7	8 03.7	4 04.6	26 29.7	25 05.8
23 Tu	12 08 38	0♎16 51	21 57 52	29 10 40	21 07.8	12 05.2	0♍26.0	1 22.6	27 41.3	12 52.5	8 00.5	4 08.4	26 31.1	25 08.0
24 W	12 12 35	1 15 36	6♓22 07	13♓31 36	21R 08.2	11 14.2	1 38.9	2 00.1	27 43.6	13 05.4	7 57.2	4 12.2	26 32.5	25 10.3
25 Th	12 16 31	2 14 22	20 38 29	27 42 13	21 08.2	10 17.6	2 51.9	2 37.7	27 46.3	13 18.2	7 53.8	4 16.0	26 34.0	25 12.5
26 F	12 20 28	3 13 11	4♈42 15	11♈38 07	21 07.7	9 16.2	4 05.0	3 15.5	27 49.3	13 31.1	7 50.3	4 19.8	26 35.5	25 14.7
27 Sa	12 24 24	4 12 01	18 29 25	25 15 52	21 06.4	8 11.2	5 18.1	3 53.6	27 52.6	13 44.0	7 46.8	4 23.6	26 37.0	25 16.9
28 Su	12 28 21	5 10 54	1♉57 13	8♉33 24	21 04.6	7 04.2	6 31.3	4 31.8	27 56.3	13 56.9	7 43.2	4 27.3	26 38.6	25 19.1
29 M	12 32 17	6 09 49	15 04 23	21 30 16	21 02.5	5 56.6	7 44.5	5 10.1	28 00.3	14 09.8	7 39.5	4 31.1	26 40.1	25 21.3
30 Tu	12 36 14	7 08 47	27 51 14	4♊07 32	21 00.4	4 50.3	8 57.8	5 48.7	28 04.6	14 22.8	7 35.8	4 34.9	26 41.7	25 23.5

LONGITUDE — October 1969

Day	Sid.Time	☉	0 hr ☽	Noon ☽	True ☊	☿	♀	♂	⚳	♃	♄	♅	♆	♇
1 W	12 40 10	8♎07 46	10♊19 32	16♊27 37	20♓58.6	3♎46.9	10♍11.2	6♑27.4	28♑09.3	14♎35.7	7♉32.0	4♎38.7	26♏43.3	25♍25.7
2 Th	12 44 07	9 06 48	22 32 17	28 34 00	20D 57.4	2R 48.3	11 24.6	7 06.4	28 14.2	14 48.7	7R 28.1	4 42.5	26 45.0	25 27.8
3 F	12 48 04	10 05 52	4♋33 21	10♋30 54	20 57.0	1 56.1	12 38.2	7 45.4	28 19.5	15 01.7	7 24.1	4 46.3	26 46.6	25 30.0
4 Sa	12 52 00	11 04 59	16 27 14	22 22 58	20 57.5	1 11.7	13 51.7	8 24.7	28 25.1	15 14.6	7 20.1	4 50.1	26 48.3	25 32.2
5 Su	12 55 57	12 04 07	28 18 42	4♌15 02	20 58.6	0 36.3	15 05.3	9 04.1	28 31.1	15 27.6	7 16.0	4 53.8	26 50.0	25 34.3
6 M	12 59 53	13 03 18	10♌12 33	16 11 48	21 00.2	0 10.7	16 19.0	9 43.7	28 37.3	15 40.6	7 11.9	4 57.6	26 51.8	25 36.5
7 Tu	13 03 50	14 02 32	22 13 19	28 17 37	21 01.9	29♍55.5	17 32.8	10 23.4	28 43.8	15 53.6	7 07.7	5 01.4	26 53.5	25 38.6
8 W	13 07 46	15 01 47	4♍25 07	10♍36 13	21R 03.1	29D 51.1	18 46.6	11 03.3	28 50.7	16 06.6	7 03.4	5 05.1	26 55.3	25 40.8
9 Th	13 11 43	16 01 05	16 51 15	23 10 29	21 03.5	29 57.4	20 00.4	11 43.3	28 57.8	16 19.7	6 59.1	5 08.9	26 57.1	25 42.9
10 F	13 15 39	17 00 24	29 34 07	6♎02 14	21 02.6	0♎14.2	21 14.3	12 23.5	29 05.3	16 32.7	6 54.8	5 12.6	26 58.9	25 45.0
11 Sa	13 19 36	17 59 46	12♎34 53	19 11 59	21 00.4	0 41.1	22 28.2	13 03.9	29 13.0	16 45.7	6 50.4	5 16.3	27 00.7	25 47.1
12 Su	13 23 33	18 59 10	25 53 25	2♏38 59	20 57.0	1 17.5	23 42.2	13 44.3	29 21.0	16 58.7	6 45.9	5 20.0	27 02.6	25 49.2
13 M	13 27 29	19 58 36	9♏28 21	16 21 13	20 52.7	2 02.8	24 56.3	14 25.0	29 29.4	17 11.7	6 41.4	5 23.7	27 04.5	25 51.2
14 Tu	13 31 26	20 58 04	23 17 11	0♐15 48	20 48.0	2 56.1	26 10.4	15 05.7	29 38.0	17 24.7	6 36.9	5 27.4	27 06.4	25 53.3
15 W	13 35 22	21 57 34	7♐16 40	14 19 19	20 43.7	3 56.7	27 24.5	15 46.6	29 46.8	17 37.7	6 32.3	5 31.1	27 08.3	25 55.4
16 Th	13 39 19	22 57 05	21 23 19	28 28 16	20 40.3	5 03.9	28 38.7	16 27.7	29 56.0	17 50.7	6 27.7	5 34.8	27 10.2	25 57.4
17 F	13 43 15	23 56 39	5♑33 47	12♑39 32	20D 38.3	6 16.7	29 52.9	17 08.8	0♒05.4	18 03.7	6 23.1	5 38.5	27 12.1	25 59.4
18 Sa	13 47 12	24 56 14	19 45 14	26 50 36	20 37.9	7 34.5	1♎07.2	17 50.1	0 15.1	18 16.7	6 18.4	5 42.1	27 14.1	26 01.5
19 Su	13 51 08	25 55 50	3♒55 24	10♒59 26	20 38.6	8 56.6	2 21.5	18 31.5	0 25.1	18 29.7	6 13.7	5 45.7	27 16.1	26 03.4
20 M	13 55 05	26 55 29	18 02 31	25 04 28	20 40.0	10 22.4	3 35.8	19 13.0	0 35.3	18 42.7	6 09.0	5 49.3	27 18.1	26 05.4
21 Tu	13 59 02	27 55 09	2♓05 06	9♓04 12	20R 41.4	11 51.2	4 50.2	19 54.7	0 45.8	18 55.6	6 04.3	5 52.9	27 20.1	26 07.4
22 W	14 02 58	28 54 50	16 01 34	22 57 00	20 41.8	13 22.5	6 04.6	20 36.4	0 56.5	19 08.5	5 59.5	5 56.5	27 22.1	26 09.3
23 Th	14 06 55	29 54 34	29 50 13	6♈40 58	20 40.7	14 55.9	7 19.1	21 18.2	1 07.5	19 21.5	5 54.7	6 00.1	27 24.2	26 11.3
24 F	14 10 51	0♏54 19	13♈28 59	20 13 59	20 37.6	16 31.0	8 33.6	22 00.2	1 18.7	19 34.4	5 49.9	6 03.6	27 26.2	26 13.2
25 Sa	14 14 48	1 54 06	26 55 43	3♉33 56	20 32.4	18 07.5	9 48.1	22 42.2	1 30.2	19 47.2	5 45.1	6 07.1	27 28.3	26 15.1
26 Su	14 18 44	2 53 56	10♉08 25	16 39 02	20 25.6	19 44.9	11 02.7	23 24.4	1 41.9	20 00.1	5 40.3	6 10.6	27 30.4	26 17.0
27 M	14 22 41	3 53 47	23 05 39	29 28 13	20 17.8	21 23.2	12 17.3	24 06.6	1 53.9	20 13.0	5 35.5	6 14.1	27 32.5	26 18.8
28 Tu	14 26 37	4 53 41	5♊46 46	12♊01 24	20 09.7	23 02.0	13 32.0	24 48.9	2 06.0	20 25.8	5 30.6	6 17.6	27 34.6	26 20.7
29 W	14 30 34	5 53 36	18 12 17	24 19 40	20 02.2	24 41.2	14 46.7	25 31.4	2 18.4	20 38.6	5 25.8	6 21.0	27 36.7	26 22.5
30 Th	14 34 31	6 53 34	0♋23 52	6♋25 16	19 56.0	26 20.6	16 01.4	26 13.9	2 31.1	20 51.4	5 21.0	6 24.4	27 38.8	26 24.3
31 F	14 38 27	7 53 34	12 24 19	18 21 31	19 51.7	28 00.2	17 16.1	26 56.5	2 43.9	21 04.1	5 16.1	6 27.8	27 41.0	26 26.1

Astro Data

	Dy Hr Mn
♃⚻♄	3 22:08
☽0S	12 14:05
♃∠♆	16 8:33
☿R	16 12:41
⚳D	17 9:29
☉0S	23 5:07
☽0N	25 13:16
☿0N	7 0:26
☿D	8 9:53
☽0S	9 21:54
☿0S	15 16:14
♀0S	20 11:28
♄⚻♅	22 20:35
☽0N	22 21:29

Planet Ingress

		Dy Hr Mn
♂	♑	21 6:35
♀	♍	23 3:26
☉	♎	23 5:07
☿	♍R	7 2:57
☿	♎	9 16:56
⚳	♒	16 22:15
♀	♎	17 14:17
☉	♏	23 14:11

Last Aspect / ☽ Ingress (September)

Last Aspect Dy Hr Mn			☽ Ingress	Dy Hr Mn
2 11:53	♆	☍	♊	2 19:23
4 19:46	♇	□	♋	5 6:57
7 11:55	♆	△	♌	7 19:36
9 23:57	♆	□	♍	10 7:20
12 10:00	♆	⚹	♎	12 17:01
14 17:15	♂	⚹	♏	15 0:25
16 23:21	♆	☌	♐	17 5:42
19 7:11	♂	☌	♑	19 9:14
21 8:29	☉	△	♒	21 11:31
23 7:34	♆	□	♓	23 13:22
25 10:04	♆	△	♈	25 15:55
26 15:20	♃	☍	♉	27 20:29
29 21:46	♆	☍	♊	30 4:05

Last Aspect / ☽ Ingress (October)

Last Aspect Dy Hr Mn			☽ Ingress	Dy Hr Mn
2 5:48	♇	□	♋	2 14:52
4 20:58	♆	△	♌	5 3:25
7 9:14	♆	□	♍	7 15:21
9 19:07	♆	⚹	♎	10 0:48
11 9:39	☉	☌	♏	12 7:19
14 6:34	♆	☌	♐	14 11:33
16 12:19	♀	□	♑	16 14:35
18 12:40	♆	⚹	♒	18 17:21
20 15:49	♆	□	♓	20 20:26
22 19:43	♆	△	♈	23 0:17
24 15:20	♂	□	♉	25 5:32
27 8:21	♆	☍	♊	27 13:00
29 16:03	♇	□	♋	29 23:13

☽ Phases & Eclipses

Dy Hr Mn		
3 16:58	☾	11♊00
11 19:56	●	18♍53
11 19:58:19	●	A 03'11"
19 2:24	☽	25♐59
25 20:21	○	2♈35
25 20:10	○	A 0.901
3 11:05	☾	10♋04
11 9:39	●	17♎54
18 8:32	☽	24♑48
25 8:44	○	1♉46

Astro Data

1 September 1969
Julian Day # 25446
SVP 5♓40'57"
GC 26♐24.9 ⚵ 25♐01.1
Eris 12♈18.8R ⚴ 0♑51.1
⚷ 5♈44.0R ⚶ 26♋07.0
☽ Mean ☊ 21♓43.2

1 October 1969
Julian Day # 25476
SVP 5♓40'54"
GC 26♐25.0 ⚵ 29♐48.8
Eris 12♈01.6R ⚴ 4♑34.6
⚷ 4♈25.9R ⚶ 7♌37.6
☽ Mean ☊ 20♓07.8

November 1969 — LONGITUDE

Day	Sid.Time	☉	0 hr ☽	Noon ☽	True ☊	☿	♀	♂	⚳	♃	♄	♅	♆	♇
1 Sa	14 42 24	8♏53 36	24♋17 24	0♌12 34	19♓49.4	29♎39.7	18♎30.9	27♑39.2	2♒57.0	21♎16.9	5♉11.3	6♎31.1	27♏43.1	26♍27.9
2 Su	14 46 20	9 53 39	6♌07 38	12 03 15	19D48.9	1♏19.2	19 45.8	28 21.9	3 10.3	21 29.6	5R06.5	6 34.5	27 45.3	26 29.6
3 M	14 50 17	10 53 46	18 00 03	23 58 44	19 49.7	2 58.5	21 00.6	29 04.8	3 23.8	21 42.2	5 01.7	6 37.8	27 47.4	26 31.4
4 Tu	14 54 13	11 53 54	29 59 56	6♍04 17	19 50.9	4 37.6	22 15.5	29 47.7	3 37.5	21 54.9	4 56.9	6 41.1	27 49.6	26 33.1
5 W	14 58 10	12 54 04	12♍12 25	18 24 53	19R51.6	6 16.5	23 30.4	0♒30.8	3 51.4	22 07.5	4 52.2	6 44.3	27 51.8	26 34.7
6 Th	15 02 06	13 54 16	24 42 11	1♎04 47	19 51.0	7 55.1	24 45.4	1 13.9	4 05.5	22 20.1	4 47.4	6 47.6	27 54.0	26 36.4
7 F	15 06 03	14 54 30	7♎33 01	14 07 07	19 48.2	9 33.4	26 00.3	1 57.1	4 19.8	22 32.6	4 42.7	6 50.8	27 56.2	26 38.0
8 Sa	15 10 00	15 54 46	20 47 11	27 33 14	19 43.0	11 11.4	27 15.3	2 40.3	4 34.3	22 45.1	4 38.0	6 53.9	27 58.4	26 39.6
9 Su	15 13 56	16 55 04	4♏25 03	11♏22 22	19 35.5	12 49.1	28 30.4	3 23.6	4 49.0	22 57.6	4 33.3	6 57.1	28 00.6	26 41.2
10 M	15 17 53	17 55 24	18 24 41	25 31 26	19 26.3	14 26.5	29 45.4	4 07.1	5 03.9	23 10.0	4 28.6	7 00.2	28 02.9	26 42.8
11 Tu	15 21 49	18 55 46	2♐41 53	9♐55 14	19 16.3	16 03.5	1♏00.5	4 50.5	5 19.0	23 22.4	4 24.0	7 03.2	28 05.1	26 44.3
12 W	15 25 46	19 56 09	17 10 39	24 27 13	19 06.8	17 40.2	2 15.6	5 34.1	5 34.3	23 34.7	4 19.5	7 06.3	28 07.3	26 45.9
13 Th	15 29 42	20 56 34	1♑44 07	9♑00 32	18 58.8	19 16.6	3 30.7	6 17.7	5 49.8	23 47.0	4 14.9	7 09.3	28 09.6	26 47.4
14 F	15 33 39	21 57 00	16 15 44	23 29 07	18 53.2	20 52.7	4 45.8	7 01.4	6 05.4	23 59.3	4 10.4	7 12.3	28 11.8	26 48.8
15 Sa	15 37 35	22 57 27	0♒40 10	7♒48 31	18 50.0	22 28.5	6 01.0	7 45.1	6 21.3	24 11.5	4 06.0	7 15.2	28 14.1	26 50.3
16 Su	15 41 32	23 57 56	14 53 53	21 56 08	18D49.0	24 04.1	7 16.1	8 28.9	6 37.3	24 23.7	4 01.6	7 18.1	28 16.3	26 51.7
17 M	15 45 29	24 58 25	28 55 10	5♓51 00	18R49.3	25 39.3	8 31.3	9 12.7	6 53.4	24 35.8	3 57.2	7 21.0	28 18.6	26 53.1
18 Tu	15 49 25	25 58 56	12♓43 41	19 33 18	18 49.6	27 14.3	9 46.5	9 56.6	7 09.7	24 47.8	3 52.9	7 23.8	28 20.8	26 54.4
19 W	15 53 22	26 59 29	26 19 58	3♈03 46	18 48.8	28 49.1	11 01.7	10 40.6	7 26.2	24 59.8	3 48.7	7 26.6	28 23.1	26 55.7
20 Th	15 57 18	28 00 02	9♈44 47	16 23 05	18 45.7	0♐23.6	12 16.9	11 24.6	7 42.9	25 11.8	3 44.5	7 29.4	28 25.3	26 57.0
21 F	16 01 15	29 00 37	22 58 44	29 31 41	18 39.8	1 57.9	13 32.2	12 08.6	7 59.7	25 23.7	3 40.4	7 32.1	28 27.6	26 58.3
22 Sa	16 05 11	0♐01 13	6♉01 58	12♉29 31	18 30.9	3 32.1	14 47.4	12 52.7	8 16.7	25 35.5	3 36.3	7 34.8	28 29.9	26 59.6
23 Su	16 09 08	1 01 51	18 54 16	25 16 11	18 19.5	5 06.0	16 02.7	13 36.8	8 33.8	25 47.3	3 32.3	7 37.4	28 32.1	27 00.8
24 M	16 13 04	2 02 29	1♊35 11	7♊51 15	18 06.3	6 39.8	17 18.0	14 21.0	8 51.1	25 59.0	3 28.4	7 40.0	28 34.4	27 02.0
25 Tu	16 17 01	3 03 10	14 04 21	20 14 32	17 52.6	8 13.5	18 33.3	15 05.2	9 08.5	26 10.6	3 24.5	7 42.5	28 36.6	27 03.1
26 W	16 20 58	4 03 52	26 21 51	2♋26 26	17 39.6	9 47.0	19 48.6	15 49.4	9 26.1	26 22.2	3 20.7	7 45.1	28 38.9	27 04.3
27 Th	16 24 54	5 04 35	8♋28 28	14 28 12	17 28.2	11 20.5	21 03.9	16 33.7	9 43.8	26 33.8	3 16.9	7 47.5	28 41.1	27 05.4
28 F	16 28 51	6 05 19	20 25 57	26 22 04	17 19.4	12 53.8	22 19.3	17 18.0	10 01.6	26 45.2	3 13.3	7 50.0	28 43.4	27 06.4
29 Sa	16 32 47	7 06 06	2♌17 00	8♌11 13	17 13.3	14 27.0	23 34.6	18 02.3	10 19.6	26 56.6	3 09.7	7 52.4	28 45.6	27 07.5
30 Su	16 36 44	8 06 53	14 05 17	19 59 46	17 10.0	16 00.2	24 50.0	18 46.7	10 37.8	27 08.0	3 06.2	7 54.7	28 47.8	27 08.5

December 1969 — LONGITUDE

Day	Sid.Time	☉	0 hr ☽	Noon ☽	True ☊	☿	♀	♂	⚳	♃	♄	♅	♆	♇
1 M	16 40 40	9♐07 42	25♌55 18	1♍52 33	17♓08.7	17♐33.2	26♏05.4	19♒31.1	10♒56.0	27♎19.2	3♉02.7	7♎57.0	28♏50.1	27♍09.5
2 Tu	16 44 37	10 08 32	7♍52 11	13 54 55	17R08.6	19 06.2	27 20.8	20 15.5	11 14.4	27 30.4	2R59.4	7 59.3	28 52.3	27 10.4
3 W	16 48 34	11 09 24	20 01 27	26 12 27	17 08.4	20 39.1	28 36.2	21 00.0	11 33.0	27 41.5	2 56.1	8 01.5	28 54.5	27 11.3
4 Th	16 52 30	12 10 17	2♎28 35	8♎50 27	17 07.0	22 12.0	29 51.6	21 44.5	11 51.6	27 52.5	2 52.9	8 03.6	28 56.7	27 12.2
5 F	16 56 27	13 11 11	15 18 36	21 53 26	17 03.4	23 44.8	1♐07.0	22 29.0	12 10.4	28 03.5	2 49.8	8 05.7	28 58.9	27 13.1
6 Sa	17 00 23	14 12 07	28 35 17	5♏24 19	16 57.1	25 17.5	2 22.4	23 13.6	12 29.3	28 14.4	2 46.8	8 07.8	29 01.1	27 13.9
7 Su	17 04 20	15 13 04	12♏20 31	19 23 41	16 48.0	26 50.0	3 37.9	23 58.2	12 48.4	28 25.2	2 43.9	8 09.8	29 03.3	27 14.7
8 M	17 08 16	16 14 02	26 33 24	3♐49 03	16 36.8	28 22.5	4 53.3	24 42.8	13 07.5	28 35.9	2 41.1	8 11.8	29 05.5	27 15.4
9 Tu	17 12 13	17 15 01	11♐09 50	18 34 45	16 24.5	29 54.8	6 08.8	25 27.4	13 26.8	28 46.5	2 38.3	8 13.7	29 07.7	27 16.2
10 W	17 16 09	18 16 02	26 02 41	3♑32 26	16 12.6	1♑26.9	7 24.3	26 12.0	13 46.2	28 57.1	2 35.7	8 15.6	29 09.9	27 16.9
11 Th	17 20 06	19 17 02	11♑02 45	18 32 25	16 02.4	2 58.8	8 39.7	26 56.7	14 05.7	29 07.5	2 33.1	8 17.4	29 12.0	27 17.5
12 F	17 24 03	20 18 04	26 00 19	3♒25 27	15 54.8	4 30.5	9 55.2	27 41.4	14 25.3	29 17.9	2 30.7	8 19.2	29 14.2	27 18.1
13 Sa	17 27 59	21 19 06	10♒46 59	18 04 13	15 50.1	6 01.7	11 10.7	28 26.1	14 45.0	29 28.1	2 28.3	8 20.9	29 16.3	27 18.7
14 Su	17 31 56	22 20 09	25 16 43	2♓24 09	15D48.1	7 32.6	12 26.2	29 10.8	15 04.9	29 38.3	2 26.1	8 22.6	29 18.4	27 19.3
15 M	17 35 52	23 21 11	9♓26 24	16 23 26	15R47.7	9 02.9	13 41.6	29 55.6	15 24.8	29 48.4	2 23.9	8 24.2	29 20.5	27 19.8
16 Tu	17 39 49	24 22 15	23 15 23	0♈02 27	15 47.7	10 32.5	14 57.1	0♓40.3	15 44.9	29 58.4	2 21.9	8 25.8	29 22.6	27 20.3
17 W	17 43 45	25 23 18	6♈44 52	13 22 57	15 46.6	12 01.4	16 12.6	1 25.1	16 05.0	0♏08.3	2 19.9	8 27.3	29 24.7	27 20.7
18 Th	17 47 42	26 24 22	19 57 00	26 27 18	15 43.4	13 29.4	17 28.1	2 09.8	16 25.2	0 18.0	2 18.1	8 28.8	29 26.8	27 21.2
19 F	17 51 38	27 25 26	2♉54 11	9♉17 53	15 37.4	14 56.3	18 43.6	2 54.6	16 45.6	0 27.7	2 16.4	8 30.2	29 28.8	27 21.6
20 Sa	17 55 35	28 26 31	15 38 39	21 56 41	15 28.3	16 21.8	19 59.0	3 39.4	17 06.0	0 37.3	2 14.7	8 31.5	29 30.9	27 21.9
21 Su	17 59 32	29 27 36	28 12 09	4♊25 11	15 16.7	17 45.7	21 14.5	4 24.1	17 26.5	0 46.8	2 13.2	8 32.8	29 32.9	27 22.2
22 M	18 03 28	0♑28 41	10♊35 55	16 44 26	15 03.2	19 07.7	22 30.0	5 08.9	17 47.1	0 56.1	2 11.8	8 34.1	29 34.9	27 22.5
23 Tu	18 07 25	1 29 47	22 50 50	28 55 11	14 49.1	20 27.5	23 45.5	5 53.7	18 07.9	1 05.4	2 10.5	8 35.3	29 36.9	27 22.8
24 W	18 11 21	2 30 54	4♋57 35	10♋58 09	14 35.6	21 44.7	25 01.0	6 38.5	18 28.6	1 14.6	2 09.3	8 36.4	29 38.9	27 23.0
25 Th	18 15 18	3 32 00	16 57 01	22 54 22	14 23.8	22 58.7	26 16.5	7 23.2	18 49.5	1 23.6	2 08.2	8 37.5	29 40.9	27 23.2
26 F	18 19 14	4 33 07	28 50 23	4♌45 20	14 14.4	24 09.1	27 32.0	8 08.0	19 10.5	1 32.5	2 07.2	8 38.5	29 42.8	27 23.3
27 Sa	18 23 11	5 34 15	10♌39 33	16 33 21	14 07.9	25 15.3	28 47.5	8 52.8	19 31.5	1 41.3	2 06.3	8 39.5	29 44.7	27 23.4
28 Su	18 27 08	6 35 22	22 27 09	28 21 25	14 04.2	26 16.6	0♑03.0	9 37.5	19 52.7	1 50.0	2 05.6	8 40.4	29 46.6	27 23.5
29 M	18 31 04	7 36 30	4♍16 40	10♍13 26	14D02.8	27 12.2	1 18.5	10 22.3	20 13.9	1 58.6	2 04.9	8 41.3	29 48.5	27R23.6
30 Tu	18 35 01	8 37 39	16 12 19	22 13 57	14 03.0	28 01.5	2 33.9	11 07.0	20 35.1	2 07.1	2 04.4	8 42.1	29 50.4	27 23.6
31 W	18 38 57	9 38 48	28 19 00	4♎28 06	14R03.6	28 43.4	3 49.4	11 51.8	20 56.5	2 15.4	2 03.9	8 42.9	29 52.2	27 23.6

Astro Data

	Dy Hr Mn
☽0S	6 6:44
☽0N	19 3:10
♃⚺♇	30 13:14
☽0S	3 15:08
♃⚺♆	12 1:11
☽0N	16 7:42
♃☍♄	30 4:44
♇R	30 8:07
☽0S	30 22:00

Planet Ingress

	Dy Hr Mn
☿ ♏	1 16:53
♂ ♒	4 18:51
♀ ♏	10 16:40
☿ ♐	20 6:00
☉ ♐	22 11:31
♀ ♐	4 14:41
☿ ♑	9 13:21
♂ ♓	15 14:22
♃ ♏	16 15:55
☉ ♑	22 0:44
♀ ♑	28 11:04

Last Aspect / ☽ Ingress (November)

Last Aspect Dy Hr Mn		☽ Ingress Dy Hr Mn
1 10:43 ☿ □	♌	1 11:35
3 19:38 ♆ □	♍	4 0:00
6 6:01 ♆ ⚹	♎	6 9:59
8 11:25 ♀ ☌	♏	8 16:18
10 16:15 ♆ ☌	♐	10 19:30
12 15:49 ♇ □	♑	12 21:08
14 19:53 ♆ ⚹	♒	14 22:53
16 22:55 ♆ □	♓	17 1:52
19 3:38 ♆ △	♈	19 6:32
21 4:18 ♃ ☍	♉	21 12:52
23 18:13 ♆ ☍	♊	23 20:59
26 1:23 ♇ □	♋	26 7:10
28 16:47 ♆ △	♌	28 19:22

Last Aspect / ☽ Ingress (December)

Last Aspect Dy Hr Mn		☽ Ingress Dy Hr Mn
1 5:52 ♆ □	♍	1 8:14
3 17:12 ♆ ⚹	♎	3 19:17
5 23:13 ♃ ☌	♏	6 2:30
8 4:11 ♆ ☌	♐	8 5:43
10 4:34 ♃ ⚹	♑	10 6:20
12 5:14 ♃ □	♒	12 6:27
14 7:16 ♃ △	♓	14 7:56
16 10:49 ♆ △	♈	16 11:56
18 11:54 ☉ △	♉	18 18:35
21 2:34 ♆ ☍	♊	21 3:28
23 8:57 ♇ □	♋	23 14:08
26 1:45 ♆ △	♌	26 2:21
28 14:53 ♆ □	♍	28 15:20
31 3:01 ♆ ⚹	♎	31 3:18

☽ Phases & Eclipses

Dy Hr Mn		
2 7:14	☾	9♌42
9 22:11	●	17♏21
16 15:45	☽	24♒07
23 23:54	○	1♊32
2 3:50	☾	9♍48
9 9:42	●	17♐09
16 1:09	☽	23♓55
23 17:35	○	1♋44
31 22:52	☾	10♎06

Astro Data

1 November 1969
Julian Day # 25507
SVP 5♓40'49"
GC 26♐25.1 ⚴ 7♑55.7
Eris 11♈43.1R ⚵ 12♑25.7
⚷ 3♈09.3R ⚶ 17♌46.8
☽ Mean ☊ 18♓29.3

1 December 1969
Julian Day # 25537
SVP 5♓40'44"
GC 26♐25.1 ⚴ 17♑29.8
Eris 11♈29.8R ⚵ 22♑36.8
⚷ 2♈26.6R ⚶ 24♌32.1
☽ Mean ☊ 16♓54.0

LONGITUDE — January 1970

Day	Sid.Time	☉	0 hr ☽	Noon ☽	True ☊	☿	♀	♂	⚳	♃	♄	♅	♆	♇
1 Th	18 42 54	10♑39 57	10♎41 56	17♎01 10	14♓03.5	29♑17.0	5♑04.9	12♓36.5	21♒18.0	2♏23.6	2♉03.6	8♎43.6	29♏54.1	27♍23.5
2 F	18 46 50	11 41 07	23 26 24	29 58 11	14R 01.7	29 41.6	6 20.4	13 21.3	21 39.5	2 31.7	2R 03.4	8 44.2	29 55.9	27R 23.4
3 Sa	18 50 47	12 42 17	6♏36 59	13♏23 10	13 57.8	29R 56.2	7 35.9	14 06.0	22 01.1	2 39.6	2D 03.3	8 44.8	29 57.7	27 23.3
4 Su	18 54 43	13 43 27	20 16 56	27 18 19	13 51.4	29 60.0	8 51.5	14 50.8	22 22.7	2 47.4	2 03.3	8 45.3	29 59.4	27 23.1
5 M	18 58 40	14 44 38	4♐27 09	11♐43 01	13 43.1	29 52.4	10 07.0	15 35.5	22 44.5	2 55.1	2 03.4	8 45.8	0♐01.2	27 22.9
6 Tu	19 02 37	15 45 49	19 05 20	26 33 13	13 33.7	29 33.0	11 22.5	16 20.2	23 06.3	3 02.7	2 03.7	8 46.2	0 02.9	27 22.7
7 W	19 06 33	16 46 59	4♑05 37	11♑41 20	13 24.4	29 01.8	12 38.0	17 04.9	23 28.1	3 10.1	2 04.0	8 46.6	0 04.6	27 22.5
8 Th	19 10 30	17 48 10	19 19 01	26 57 16	13 16.3	28 19.0	13 53.5	17 49.6	23 50.1	3 17.4	2 04.5	8 46.9	0 06.3	27 22.2
9 F	19 14 26	18 49 20	4♒34 41	12♒09 57	13 10.4	27 25.6	15 09.0	18 34.3	24 12.1	3 24.5	2 05.1	8 47.1	0 07.9	27 21.9
10 Sa	19 18 23	19 50 30	19 41 53	27 09 27	13 07.0	26 22.8	16 24.4	19 19.0	24 34.1	3 31.5	2 05.7	8 47.3	0 09.5	27 21.5
11 Su	19 22 19	20 51 39	4♓31 51	11♓48 27	13D 05.9	25 12.4	17 39.9	20 03.6	24 56.3	3 38.4	2 06.6	8 47.5	0 11.2	27 21.1
12 M	19 26 16	21 52 48	18 58 50	26 02 47	13 06.4	23 56.6	18 55.4	20 48.3	25 18.4	3 45.1	2 07.5	8R 47.5	0 12.7	27 20.7
13 Tu	19 30 12	22 53 56	3♈00 15	9♈51 22	13 07.5	22 37.8	20 10.9	21 32.9	25 40.7	3 51.7	2 08.5	8 47.5	0 14.3	27 20.2
14 W	19 34 09	23 55 03	16 36 18	23 15 23	13R 08.1	21 18.5	21 26.3	22 17.5	26 03.0	3 58.1	2 09.6	8 47.5	0 15.8	27 19.7
15 Th	19 38 06	24 56 10	29 48 58	6♉17 29	13 07.4	20 01.2	22 41.8	23 02.1	26 25.3	4 04.3	2 10.9	8 47.4	0 17.3	27 19.2
16 F	19 42 02	25 57 16	12♉41 20	19 00 58	13 04.6	18 48.1	23 57.2	23 46.7	26 47.7	4 10.5	2 12.2	8 47.2	0 18.8	27 18.7
17 Sa	19 45 59	26 58 21	25 16 49	1♊29 17	12 59.7	17 41.0	25 12.7	24 31.3	27 10.2	4 16.4	2 13.7	8 47.0	0 20.2	27 18.1
18 Su	19 49 55	27 59 25	7♊38 45	13 45 35	12 52.9	16 41.4	26 28.1	25 15.8	27 32.7	4 22.2	2 15.3	8 46.8	0 21.6	27 17.5
19 M	19 53 52	29 00 29	19 50 06	25 52 35	12 44.8	15 50.3	27 43.5	26 00.3	27 55.2	4 27.9	2 17.0	8 46.5	0 23.0	27 16.8
20 Tu	19 57 48	0♒01 32	1♋53 20	7♋52 33	12 36.1	15 08.3	28 58.9	26 44.8	28 17.8	4 33.4	2 18.8	8 46.1	0 24.4	27 16.2
21 W	20 01 45	1 02 34	13 50 30	19 47 22	12 27.8	14 35.6	0♒14.4	27 29.2	28 40.5	4 38.7	2 20.7	8 45.7	0 25.7	27 15.4
22 Th	20 05 41	2 03 36	25 43 21	1♌38 39	12 20.5	14 12.2	1 29.8	28 13.7	29 03.2	4 43.9	2 22.7	8 45.2	0 27.0	27 14.7
23 F	20 09 38	3 04 36	7♌33 29	13 28 04	12 14.9	13 57.8	2 45.1	28 58.1	29 25.9	4 48.9	2 24.8	8 44.6	0 28.3	27 14.0
24 Sa	20 13 35	4 05 36	19 22 37	25 17 25	12 11.3	13D 52.1	4 00.5	29 42.5	29 48.7	4 53.8	2 27.0	8 44.0	0 29.6	27 13.2
25 Su	20 17 31	5 06 35	1♍12 45	7♍08 55	12D 09.7	13 54.5	5 15.9	0♈26.8	0♓11.5	4 58.5	2 29.4	8 43.4	0 30.8	27 12.3
26 M	20 21 28	6 07 34	13 06 18	19 05 17	12 09.8	14 04.5	6 31.3	1 11.1	0 34.4	5 03.0	2 31.8	8 42.7	0 32.0	27 11.5
27 Tu	20 25 24	7 08 31	25 06 16	1♎09 46	12 11.1	14 21.5	7 46.7	1 55.4	0 57.3	5 07.3	2 34.3	8 41.9	0 33.1	27 10.6
28 W	20 29 21	8 09 28	7♎16 13	13 26 11	12 12.9	14 45.0	9 02.0	2 39.7	1 20.2	5 11.5	2 37.0	8 41.1	0 34.3	27 09.7
29 Th	20 33 17	9 10 25	19 40 10	25 58 42	12 14.5	15 14.3	10 17.4	3 24.0	1 43.2	5 15.5	2 39.7	8 40.3	0 35.4	27 08.8
30 F	20 37 14	10 11 21	2♏22 21	8♏51 35	12R 15.2	15 49.1	11 32.7	4 08.2	2 06.2	5 19.4	2 42.6	8 39.3	0 36.4	27 07.8
31 Sa	20 41 10	11 12 16	15 26 53	22 08 38	12 14.7	16 28.7	12 48.0	4 52.4	2 29.2	5 23.0	2 45.5	8 38.4	0 37.5	27 06.8

LONGITUDE — February 1970

Day	Sid.Time	☉	0 hr ☽	Noon ☽	True ☊	☿	♀	♂	⚳	♃	♄	♅	♆	♇
1 Su	20 45 07	12♒13 10	28♏57 09	5♐52 36	12♓12.7	17♑12.8	14♒03.4	5♈36.6	2♓52.3	5♏26.5	2♉48.6	8♎37.4	0♐38.5	27♍05.8
2 M	20 49 04	13 14 04	12♐55 02	20 04 20	12R 09.6	18 00.9	15 18.7	6 20.7	3 15.5	5 29.9	2 51.7	8R 36.3	0 39.5	27R 04.8
3 Tu	20 53 00	14 14 57	27 20 09	4♑41 59	12 05.7	18 52.7	16 34.0	7 04.8	3 38.6	5 33.0	2 55.0	8 35.2	0 40.4	27 03.7
4 W	20 56 57	15 15 49	12♑09 08	19 40 41	12 01.6	19 47.9	17 49.3	7 48.9	4 01.8	5 36.0	2 58.3	8 34.0	0 41.3	27 02.6
5 Th	21 00 53	16 16 40	27 15 32	4♒52 30	11 58.1	20 46.1	19 04.6	8 33.0	4 25.0	5 38.7	3 01.8	8 32.8	0 42.2	27 01.5
6 F	21 04 50	17 17 30	12♒30 18	20 07 37	11 55.6	21 47.2	20 19.9	9 17.0	4 48.3	5 41.3	3 05.3	8 31.5	0 43.1	27 00.3
7 Sa	21 08 46	18 18 18	27 43 08	5♓15 40	11D 54.4	22 50.8	21 35.2	10 01.0	5 11.6	5 43.7	3 09.0	8 30.2	0 43.9	26 59.2
8 Su	21 12 43	19 19 05	12♓44 08	20 07 35	11 54.4	23 56.7	22 50.5	10 45.0	5 34.9	5 46.0	3 12.7	8 28.8	0 44.7	26 58.0
9 M	21 16 39	20 19 51	27 25 17	4♈36 42	11 55.4	25 04.9	24 05.7	11 29.0	5 58.2	5 48.0	3 16.5	8 27.4	0 45.4	26 56.8
10 Tu	21 20 36	21 20 35	11♈41 27	18 39 21	11 56.9	26 15.1	25 20.9	12 12.9	6 21.5	5 49.9	3 20.5	8 26.0	0 46.1	26 55.5
11 W	21 24 33	22 21 17	25 30 23	2♉14 40	11 58.2	27 27.1	26 36.2	12 56.8	6 44.9	5 51.5	3 24.5	8 24.5	0 46.8	26 54.3
12 Th	21 28 29	23 21 58	8♉52 27	15 24 05	11R 59.1	28 40.9	27 51.4	13 40.6	7 08.3	5 53.0	3 28.6	8 22.9	0 47.5	26 53.0
13 F	21 32 26	24 22 38	21 49 56	28 10 30	11 59.3	29 56.4	29 06.5	14 24.4	7 31.7	5 54.3	3 32.8	8 21.3	0 48.1	26 51.7
14 Sa	21 36 22	25 23 15	4♊26 16	10♊37 44	11 58.6	1♒13.4	0♓21.7	15 08.2	7 55.2	5 55.4	3 37.1	8 19.7	0 48.7	26 50.4
15 Su	21 40 19	26 23 51	16 45 27	22 49 54	11 57.1	2 31.8	1 36.9	15 51.9	8 18.6	5 56.4	3 41.4	8 18.0	0 49.2	26 49.1
16 M	21 44 15	27 24 25	28 51 35	4♋51 01	11 55.2	3 51.7	2 52.0	16 35.6	8 42.1	5 57.1	3 45.9	8 16.3	0 49.8	26 47.7
17 Tu	21 48 12	28 24 58	10♋48 38	16 44 52	11 53.0	5 12.9	4 07.1	17 19.3	9 05.6	5 57.7	3 50.4	8 14.5	0 50.2	26 46.4
18 W	21 52 09	29 25 29	22 40 07	28 34 46	11 50.9	6 35.3	5 22.2	18 02.9	9 29.1	5 58.0	3 55.1	8 12.7	0 50.7	26 45.0
19 Th	21 56 05	0♓25 58	4♌29 09	10♌23 36	11 49.2	7 59.0	6 37.3	18 46.5	9 52.6	5R 58.2	3 59.8	8 10.9	0 51.1	26 43.6
20 F	22 00 02	1 26 25	16 18 23	22 13 49	11 48.0	9 23.8	7 52.4	19 30.1	10 16.1	5 58.2	4 04.6	8 09.0	0 51.5	26 42.1
21 Sa	22 03 58	2 26 51	28 10 07	4♍07 34	11D 47.4	10 49.8	9 07.4	20 13.6	10 39.7	5 58.0	4 09.4	8 07.1	0 51.8	26 40.7
22 Su	22 07 55	3 27 15	10♍06 23	16 06 49	11 47.3	12 17.0	10 22.4	20 57.1	11 03.2	5 57.6	4 14.4	8 05.1	0 52.2	26 39.3
23 M	22 11 51	4 27 37	22 09 06	28 13 29	11 47.7	13 45.2	11 37.5	21 40.5	11 26.8	5 57.0	4 19.4	8 03.2	0 52.4	26 37.8
24 Tu	22 15 48	5 27 58	4♎20 12	10♎29 31	11 48.2	15 14.5	12 52.4	22 23.9	11 50.4	5 56.2	4 24.5	8 01.1	0 52.7	26 36.3
25 W	22 19 44	6 28 18	16 41 44	22 57 07	11 48.9	16 44.9	14 07.4	23 07.3	12 14.0	5 55.3	4 29.7	7 59.1	0 52.9	26 34.8
26 Th	22 23 41	7 28 36	29 15 58	5♏38 36	11 49.4	18 16.4	15 22.4	23 50.6	12 37.5	5 54.1	4 35.0	7 57.0	0 53.1	26 33.3
27 F	22 27 37	8 28 52	12♏05 18	18 36 24	11 49.8	19 48.9	16 37.3	24 33.9	13 01.2	5 52.8	4 40.3	7 54.8	0 53.2	26 31.8
28 Sa	22 31 34	9 29 07	25 12 09	1♐52 50	11R 49.9	21 22.4	17 52.3	25 17.1	13 24.8	5 51.3	4 45.7	7 52.7	0 53.3	26 30.2

Astro Data

	Dy Hr Mn
♄ D	3 21:06
☿ R	4 8:09
☽ 0N	12 13:51
♅ R	13 6:09
☿ D	24 16:38
♂ 0N	26 1:42
☽ 0S	27 3:37
☽ 0N	8 23:05
♃ R	19 21:58
☽ 0S	23 9:14

Planet Ingress

		Dy Hr Mn
☿	♒	4 4:24
☿	♊R	4 11:54
♆	♐	4 19:55
☉	♒	20 11:24
♀	♒	21 7:26
♂	♈	24 21:29
⚳	♓	24 23:55
☿	♒	13 13:08
♀	♓	14 5:04
☉	♓	19 1:42

Last Aspect / ☽ Ingress

Last Aspect Dy Hr Mn			☽ Ingress	Dy Hr Mn
2 11:29	☿	□	♏	2 12:03
4 16:32	♆	☌	♐	4 16:33
6 13:19	♇	□	♑	6 17:30
8 14:02	☿	☌	♒	8 16:47
9 6:39	♅	△	♓	10 16:37
12 14:14	♇	☍	♈	12 18:48
14 13:18	☉	□	♉	15 0:20
17 3:54	♇	△	♊	17 9:07
19 14:48	♇	□	♋	19 20:13
22 4:37	♂	△	♌	22 8:40
23 2:25	♅	✶	♍	24 21:33
27 4:07	♇	☌	♎	27 9:42
28 14:38	☿	□	♏	29 19:34

Last Aspect / ☽ Ingress

Last Aspect Dy Hr Mn			☽ Ingress	Dy Hr Mn
31 20:46	♇	✶	♐	1 1:50
2 23:34	♇	□	♑	3 4:22
4 23:39	♇	△	♒	5 4:19
6 12:21	♀	☌	♓	7 3:37
8 23:14	♇	☍	♈	9 4:17
11 2:36	☿	□	♉	11 7:59
13 13:59	♀	□	♊	13 15:29
15 19:55	♇	□	♋	16 2:17
18 8:17	♇	✶	♌	18 14:53
20 6:07	♂	△	♍	21 3:42
23 8:52	♇	☌	♎	23 15:30
25 12:21	♂	☍	♏	26 1:23
28 2:22	♇	✶	♐	28 8:38

☽ Phases & Eclipses

Dy Hr Mn	
7 20:35	● 17♑09
14 13:18	☽ 23♈58
22 12:55	○ 2♌06
30 14:38	☾ 10♏18
6 7:13	● 17♒05
13 4:10	☽ 24♉03
21 8:19	○ 2♍18
21 8:30	P 0.046

Astro Data

1 January 1970
Julian Day # 25568
SVP 5♓40'39"
GC 26♐25.2 ⚴ 28♑14.9
Eris 11♈25.2 ⚵ 4♒53.0
⚷ 2♈31.7 ⚶ 26♌05.6R
☽ Mean ☊ 15♓15.6

1 February 1970
Julian Day # 25599
SVP 5♓40'33"
GC 26♐25.3 ⚴ 9♒12.8
Eris 11♈31.4 ⚵ 18♒18.5
⚷ 3♈26.7 ⚶ 20♌45.5R
☽ Mean ☊ 13♓37.1

March 1970 — LONGITUDE

Day	Sid.Time	☉	0 hr ☽	Noon ☽	True ☊	☿	♀	♂	⚳	♃	♄	♅	♆	♇
1 Su	22 35 31	10♓29 21	8♐38 39	15♐29 46	11♓49.9	22♒57.1	19♓07.2	26♈00.3	13♓48.4	5♏49.6	4♉51.2	7♎50.5	0♐53.4	26♍28.7
2 M	22 39 27	11 29 33	22 26 15	29 28 07	11D 49.9	24 32.7	20 22.1	26 43.5	14 12.0	5R 47.7	4 56.7	7R 48.3	0R 53.5	26R 27.2
3 Tu	22 43 24	12 29 44	6♑35 14	13♑47 21	11 49.9	26 09.4	21 36.9	27 26.7	14 35.7	5 45.6	5 02.4	7 46.1	0 53.5	26 25.6
4 W	22 47 20	13 29 53	21 04 06	28 24 57	11 50.1	27 47.2	22 51.8	28 09.8	14 59.3	5 43.3	5 08.1	7 43.8	0 53.4	26 24.0
5 Th	22 51 17	14 30 01	5♒49 17	13♒16 17	11 50.3	29 26.1	24 06.6	28 52.8	15 22.9	5 40.9	5 13.8	7 41.5	0 53.4	26 22.4
6 F	22 55 13	15 30 06	20 45 04	28 14 40	11R 50.5	1♓06.0	25 21.5	29 35.9	15 46.6	5 38.2	5 19.7	7 39.2	0 53.3	26 20.9
7 Sa	22 59 10	16 30 10	5♓44 01	13♓12 06	11 50.5	2 47.0	26 36.3	0♉18.9	16 10.2	5 35.4	5 25.5	7 36.8	0 53.2	26 19.3
8 Su	23 03 06	17 30 13	20 37 51	28 00 17	11 50.4	4 29.2	27 51.0	1 01.8	16 33.9	5 32.4	5 31.5	7 34.4	0 53.0	26 17.7
9 M	23 07 03	18 30 13	5♈18 32	12♈31 50	11 49.9	6 12.4	29 05.8	1 44.7	16 57.5	5 29.2	5 37.5	7 32.0	0 52.8	26 16.0
10 Tu	23 11 00	19 30 11	19 39 32	26 41 11	11 49.0	7 56.8	0♈20.5	2 27.6	17 21.1	5 25.9	5 43.6	7 29.6	0 52.6	26 14.4
11 W	23 14 56	20 30 07	3♉36 27	10♉25 10	11 48.0	9 42.3	1 35.2	3 10.4	17 44.8	5 22.4	5 49.7	7 27.2	0 52.3	26 12.8
12 Th	23 18 53	21 30 01	17 07 20	23 43 04	11 46.9	11 29.0	2 49.9	3 53.2	18 08.4	5 18.7	5 55.9	7 24.7	0 52.0	26 11.2
13 F	23 22 49	22 29 53	0♊12 36	6♊36 17	11 46.0	13 16.8	4 04.5	4 36.0	18 32.0	5 14.8	6 02.2	7 22.3	0 51.7	26 09.6
14 Sa	23 26 46	23 29 42	12 54 31	19 07 47	11D 45.6	15 05.8	5 19.2	5 18.7	18 55.6	5 10.8	6 08.5	7 19.8	0 51.4	26 07.9
15 Su	23 30 42	24 29 30	25 16 38	1♋21 37	11 45.6	16 56.0	6 33.8	6 01.4	19 19.2	5 06.6	6 14.9	7 17.3	0 51.0	26 06.3
16 M	23 34 39	25 29 15	7♋23 19	13 22 20	11 46.3	18 47.3	7 48.4	6 44.0	19 42.8	5 02.2	6 21.3	7 14.7	0 50.6	26 04.7
17 Tu	23 38 35	26 28 58	19 19 15	25 14 40	11 47.4	20 39.9	9 02.9	7 26.6	20 06.4	4 57.7	6 27.8	7 12.2	0 50.1	26 03.0
18 W	23 42 32	27 28 38	1♌09 07	7♌03 09	11 48.9	22 33.6	10 17.4	8 09.2	20 30.0	4 53.0	6 34.4	7 09.7	0 49.6	26 01.4
19 Th	23 46 29	28 28 17	12 57 18	18 52 01	11 50.3	24 28.5	11 31.9	8 51.7	20 53.5	4 48.2	6 40.9	7 07.1	0 49.1	25 59.8
20 F	23 50 25	29 27 53	24 47 45	0♍44 55	11R 51.3	26 24.5	12 46.4	9 34.1	21 17.1	4 43.2	6 47.6	7 04.6	0 48.6	25 58.2
21 Sa	23 54 22	0♈27 27	6♍43 53	12 44 57	11 51.7	28 21.7	14 00.8	10 16.6	21 40.6	4 38.1	6 54.3	7 02.0	0 48.0	25 56.5
22 Su	23 58 18	1 26 59	18 48 26	24 54 32	11 51.1	0♈19.8	15 15.2	10 58.9	22 04.2	4 32.8	7 01.0	6 59.4	0 47.4	25 54.9
23 M	0 02 15	2 26 29	1♎03 30	7♎15 28	11 49.5	2 19.0	16 29.6	11 41.3	22 27.7	4 27.4	7 07.8	6 56.8	0 46.7	25 53.3
24 Tu	0 06 11	3 25 56	13 30 34	19 48 54	11 46.9	4 19.1	17 43.9	12 23.6	22 51.2	4 21.9	7 14.6	6 54.2	0 46.1	25 51.7
25 W	0 10 08	4 25 22	26 10 33	2♏35 34	11 43.5	6 20.0	18 58.2	13 05.8	23 14.7	4 16.2	7 21.4	6 51.6	0 45.4	25 50.1
26 Th	0 14 04	5 24 46	9♏03 58	15 35 45	11 39.9	8 21.6	20 12.5	13 48.0	23 38.1	4 10.4	7 28.3	6 49.0	0 44.7	25 48.4
27 F	0 18 01	6 24 09	22 10 58	28 49 36	11 36.3	10 23.7	21 26.8	14 30.2	24 01.6	4 04.4	7 35.3	6 46.4	0 43.9	25 46.8
28 Sa	0 21 58	7 23 29	5♐31 37	12♐17 03	11 33.4	12 26.2	22 41.0	15 12.3	24 25.0	3 58.4	7 42.3	6 43.8	0 43.1	25 45.3
29 Su	0 25 54	8 22 48	19 05 51	25 58 00	11D 31.6	14 28.8	23 55.3	15 54.4	24 48.4	3 52.2	7 49.3	6 41.2	0 42.3	25 43.7
30 M	0 29 51	9 22 05	2♑53 28	9♑52 11	11 31.1	16 31.4	25 09.4	16 36.5	25 11.8	3 45.9	7 56.4	6 38.6	0 41.5	25 42.1
31 Tu	0 33 47	10 21 20	16 54 03	23 58 55	11 31.6	18 33.5	26 23.6	17 18.5	25 35.2	3 39.4	8 03.5	6 36.0	0 40.6	25 40.5

April 1970 — LONGITUDE

Day	Sid.Time	☉	0 hr ☽	Noon ☽	True ☊	☿	♀	♂	⚳	♃	♄	♅	♆	♇
1 W	0 37 44	11♈20 34	1♒06 38	8♒16 55	11♓33.0	20♈35.0	27♈37.7	18♉00.5	25♓58.6	3♏32.9	8♉10.6	6♎33.5	0♐39.7	25♍39.0
2 Th	0 41 40	12 19 46	15 29 27	22 43 52	11 34.4	22 35.5	28 51.8	18 42.4	26 21.9	3R 26.3	8 17.8	6R 30.9	0R 38.8	25R 37.4
3 F	0 45 37	13 18 56	29 59 40	7♓16 19	11R 35.3	24 34.6	0♉05.9	19 24.3	26 45.2	3 19.5	8 25.0	6 28.3	0 37.9	25 35.9
4 Sa	0 49 33	14 18 04	14♓33 10	21 49 33	11 35.0	26 32.0	1 20.0	20 06.2	27 08.5	3 12.7	8 32.3	6 25.7	0 36.9	25 34.3
5 Su	0 53 30	15 17 10	29 04 45	6♈18 00	11 33.1	28 27.3	2 34.0	20 48.0	27 31.8	3 05.8	8 39.6	6 23.1	0 35.9	25 32.8
6 M	0 57 27	16 16 14	13♈28 34	20 35 45	11 29.4	0♉20.2	3 48.0	21 29.8	27 55.0	2 58.8	8 46.9	6 20.6	0 34.8	25 31.3
7 Tu	1 01 23	17 15 16	27 38 53	4♉37 24	11 24.3	2 10.2	5 01.9	22 11.5	28 18.2	2 51.7	8 54.2	6 18.0	0 33.8	25 29.8
8 W	1 05 20	18 14 16	11♉30 50	18 18 49	11 18.3	3 57.0	6 15.9	22 53.2	28 41.4	2 44.5	9 01.6	6 15.5	0 32.7	25 28.3
9 Th	1 09 16	19 13 14	25 01 08	1♊37 40	11 12.2	5 40.2	7 29.8	23 34.9	29 04.6	2 37.3	9 09.0	6 13.0	0 31.6	25 26.8
10 F	1 13 13	20 12 10	8♊08 27	14 33 36	11 06.7	7 19.5	8 43.6	24 16.5	29 27.7	2 30.0	9 16.4	6 10.5	0 30.5	25 25.4
11 Sa	1 17 09	21 11 03	20 53 24	27 08 11	11 02.4	8 54.7	9 57.5	24 58.1	29 50.8	2 22.6	9 23.9	6 08.0	0 29.4	25 24.0
12 Su	1 21 06	22 09 54	3♋18 23	9♋24 29	10 59.7	10 25.4	11 11.3	25 39.6	0♈13.8	2 15.2	9 31.3	6 05.5	0 28.2	25 22.5
13 M	1 25 02	23 08 43	15 27 03	21 26 40	10D 58.7	11 51.5	12 25.0	26 21.1	0 36.9	2 07.7	9 38.8	6 03.1	0 27.0	25 21.1
14 Tu	1 28 59	24 07 30	27 23 59	3♌19 37	10 59.1	13 12.7	13 38.8	27 02.6	0 59.9	2 00.2	9 46.3	6 00.6	0 25.8	25 19.7
15 W	1 32 56	25 06 14	9♌14 14	15 08 29	11 00.4	14 28.8	14 52.5	27 44.0	1 22.8	1 52.7	9 53.9	5 58.2	0 24.6	25 18.4
16 Th	1 36 52	26 04 57	21 02 59	26 58 22	11 01.9	15 39.7	16 06.1	28 25.4	1 45.7	1 45.1	10 01.4	5 55.8	0 23.3	25 17.0
17 F	1 40 49	27 03 37	2♍55 13	8♍54 06	11R 02.7	16 45.2	17 19.7	29 06.7	2 08.6	1 37.5	10 09.0	5 53.4	0 22.0	25 15.7
18 Sa	1 44 45	28 02 14	14 55 31	20 59 55	11 02.2	17 45.2	18 33.3	29 48.0	2 31.4	1 29.8	10 16.6	5 51.1	0 20.7	25 14.4
19 Su	1 48 42	29 00 50	27 07 42	3♎19 13	10 59.8	18 39.6	19 46.8	0♊29.3	2 54.2	1 22.2	10 24.2	5 48.7	0 19.4	25 13.0
20 M	1 52 38	29 59 24	9♎34 44	15 54 24	10 55.2	19 28.3	21 00.3	1 10.5	3 17.0	1 14.5	10 31.8	5 46.4	0 18.1	25 11.8
21 Tu	1 56 35	0♉57 55	22 18 21	28 46 35	10 48.5	20 11.3	22 13.8	1 51.6	3 39.7	1 06.8	10 39.4	5 44.2	0 16.7	25 10.5
22 W	2 00 31	1 56 25	5♏19 04	11♏55 40	10 40.4	20 48.5	23 27.3	2 32.8	4 02.4	0 59.2	10 47.0	5 41.9	0 15.4	25 09.3
23 Th	2 04 28	2 54 53	18 36 11	25 20 21	10 31.5	21 19.8	24 40.7	3 13.9	4 25.1	0 51.5	10 54.7	5 39.7	0 14.0	25 08.0
24 F	2 08 24	3 53 19	2♐07 53	8♐58 25	10 22.8	21 45.2	25 54.0	3 54.9	4 47.7	0 43.8	11 02.4	5 37.5	0 12.6	25 06.9
25 Sa	2 12 21	4 51 44	15 51 39	22 47 12	10 15.4	22 04.8	27 07.3	4 35.9	5 10.2	0 36.2	11 10.0	5 35.3	0 11.2	25 05.7
26 Su	2 16 18	5 50 07	29 44 44	6♑43 57	10 09.9	22 18.6	28 20.6	5 16.9	5 32.8	0 28.6	11 17.7	5 33.2	0 09.7	25 04.5
27 M	2 20 14	6 48 29	13♑44 33	20 46 17	10 06.6	22R 26.7	29 33.9	5 57.9	5 55.2	0 21.0	11 25.4	5 31.1	0 08.3	25 03.4
28 Tu	2 24 11	7 46 48	27 48 57	4♒52 22	10D 05.4	22 29.2	0♊47.1	6 38.8	6 17.7	0 13.4	11 33.1	5 29.0	0 06.8	25 02.3
29 W	2 28 07	8 45 07	11♒56 22	19 00 48	10 05.7	22 26.3	2 00.3	7 19.6	6 40.0	0 05.9	11 40.8	5 27.0	0 05.4	25 01.2
30 Th	2 32 04	9 43 24	26 05 31	3♓10 21	10R 06.4	22 18.1	3 13.5	8 00.5	7 02.4	29♎58.4	11 48.5	5 24.9	0 03.9	25 00.2

Astro Data

	Dy Hr Mn
♆ R	3 9:00
☽ 0N	8 10:05
♃☍♄	8 14:26
♀0N	12 12:52
☉0N	21 0:56
♄⚻♅	22 7:57
☽ 0S	22 15:48
☿0N	23 19:37
☽ 0N	4 20:16
♄□♇	18 6:03
☽ 0S	18 23:18
☿ R	28 10:51
♃⚺♆	29 13:58

Planet Ingress

		Dy Hr Mn
☿	♓	5 20:10
♂	♉	7 1:28
♀	♈	10 5:25
☉	♈	21 0:56
☿	♈	22 7:59
♀	♉	3 10:05
☿	♉	6 7:40
⚳	♈	11 21:36
♂	♊	18 18:59
☉	♉	20 12:15
♀	♊	27 20:33
♃	♎R	30 6:43

Last Aspect / ☽ Ingress

Last Aspect Dy Hr Mn			☽ Ingress	Dy Hr Mn
2 7:05	♂	△	♑	2 12:54
4 11:34	♂	□	♒	4 14:34
6 14:17	♂	⚹	♓	6 14:49
8 11:44	♀	☌	♈	8 15:16
9 3:42	♅	☍	♉	10 17:43
12 16:32	♇	△	♊	12 23:37
15 1:39	♇	□	♋	15 9:18
17 14:45	☉	△	♌	17 21:40
18 19:21	♀	△	♍	20 10:30
22 13:58	♇	☌	♎	22 21:56
24 7:37	♀	☍	♏	25 7:10
27 6:31	♇	⚹	♐	27 14:07
29 11:35	♇	□	♑	29 19:00
31 16:27	♀	□	♒	31 22:08

Last Aspect / ☽ Ingress

Last Aspect Dy Hr Mn			☽ Ingress	Dy Hr Mn
2 23:04	♀	⚹	♓	3 0:01
4 18:11	♇	☍	♈	5 1:32
6 4:09	☉	☌	♉	7 4:02
9 0:48	♇	△	♊	9 9:02
11 8:39	♇	□	♋	11 17:33
13 22:30	♂	⚹	♌	14 5:16
16 15:07	♂	□	♍	16 18:07
18 20:18	♇	☌	♎	19 5:35
19 16:47	♅	☌	♏	21 14:15
23 11:38	♇	⚹	♐	23 20:15
25 15:59	♇	□	♑	26 0:26
27 19:18	♇	△	♒	28 3:43
29 17:46	☿	□	♓	30 6:37

☽ Phases & Eclipses

Dy Hr Mn		
1 2:33	☾	10♐06
7 17:42	●	16♓44
7 17:37:49	●	T 03'28"
14 21:16	☽	23♊53
23 1:52	○	2♎01
30 11:04	☾	9♑20
6 4:09	●	15♈57
13 15:44	☽	23♋18
21 16:21	○	1♏09
28 17:18	☾	8♒00

Astro Data

1 March 1970
Julian Day # 25627
SVP 5♓40'29"
GC 26♐25.4 ⚴ 18♒50.0
Eris 11♈45.0 ⚵ 1♓03.4
⚷ 4♈48.4 ⚶ 13♌48.8R
☽ Mean ☊ 12♓08.1

1 April 1970
Julian Day # 25658
SVP 5♓40'25"
GC 26♐25.4 ⚴ 28♒39.0
Eris 12♈05.1 ⚵ 15♓33.9
⚷ 6♈35.6 ⚶ 11♌10.3
☽ Mean ☊ 10♓29.6

LONGITUDE — May 1970

Day	Sid.Time	☉	0 hr ☽	Noon ☽	True☊	☿	♀	♂	⚳	♃	♄	♅	♆	♇
1 F	2 36 00	10♉41 39	10♓15 08	17♓19 39	10♓06.3	22♉05.0	4♊26.6	8♊41.3	7♈24.7	29♎50.9	11♉56.2	5♎23.0	0♐02.4	24♍59.1
2 Sa	2 39 57	11 39 53	24 23 36	1♈26 42	10R 04.5	21R 47.2	5 39.7	9 22.0	7 46.9	29R 43.5	12 03.9	5R 21.0	0R 00.9	24R 58.1
3 Su	2 43 53	12 38 05	8♈28 35	15 28 51	10 00.2	21 25.2	6 52.7	10 02.8	8 09.1	29 36.1	12 11.6	5 19.1	29♏59.3	24 57.1
4 M	2 47 50	13 36 16	22 27 02	29 22 43	9 53.3	20 59.4	8 05.8	10 43.5	8 31.2	29 28.8	12 19.3	5 17.2	29 57.8	24 56.2
5 Tu	2 51 47	14 34 25	6♉15 25	13♉04 43	9 44.0	20 30.3	9 18.7	11 24.1	8 53.3	29 21.6	12 27.0	5 15.4	29 56.2	24 55.2
6 W	2 55 43	15 32 32	19 50 10	26 31 28	9 33.2	19 58.4	10 31.7	12 04.8	9 15.3	29 14.4	12 34.7	5 13.6	29 54.7	24 54.3
7 Th	2 59 40	16 30 38	3♊08 18	9♊40 30	9 21.9	19 24.4	11 44.6	12 45.3	9 37.3	29 07.4	12 42.4	5 11.9	29 53.1	24 53.4
8 F	3 03 36	17 28 42	16 07 57	22 30 40	9 11.3	18 48.8	12 57.5	13 25.9	9 59.2	29 00.4	12 50.1	5 10.2	29 51.6	24 52.6
9 Sa	3 07 33	18 26 45	28 48 44	5♋02 21	9 02.3	18 12.4	14 10.3	14 06.4	10 21.0	28 53.5	12 57.8	5 08.5	29 50.0	24 51.8
10 Su	3 11 29	19 24 45	11♋11 49	17 17 30	8 55.5	17 35.7	15 23.1	14 46.9	10 42.8	28 46.6	13 05.5	5 06.9	29 48.4	24 51.0
11 M	3 15 26	20 22 44	23 19 50	29 19 21	8 51.3	16 59.4	16 35.8	15 27.4	11 04.5	28 39.9	13 13.2	5 05.3	29 46.8	24 50.2
12 Tu	3 19 23	21 20 41	5♌16 36	11♌12 12	8D 49.2	16 24.1	17 48.5	16 07.8	11 26.2	28 33.3	13 20.9	5 03.7	29 45.2	24 49.5
13 W	3 23 19	22 18 36	17 06 48	23 01 03	8 48.8	15 50.4	19 01.2	16 48.1	11 47.8	28 26.8	13 28.5	5 02.2	29 43.6	24 48.7
14 Th	3 27 16	23 16 29	28 55 39	4♍51 16	8R 49.0	15 18.9	20 13.8	17 28.5	12 09.3	28 20.3	13 36.2	5 00.8	29 42.0	24 48.1
15 F	3 31 12	24 14 20	10♍48 36	16 48 18	8 48.8	14 50.1	21 26.4	18 08.8	12 30.8	28 14.0	13 43.8	4 59.3	29 40.4	24 47.4
16 Sa	3 35 09	25 12 10	22 51 00	28 57 17	8 47.2	14 24.4	22 38.9	18 49.0	12 52.2	28 07.8	13 51.4	4 58.0	29 38.8	24 46.8
17 Su	3 39 05	26 09 58	5♎07 42	11♎22 42	8 43.5	14 02.2	23 51.3	19 29.3	13 13.5	28 01.8	13 59.0	4 56.6	29 37.1	24 46.2
18 M	3 43 02	27 07 44	17 42 41	24 07 56	8 37.2	13 43.7	25 03.8	20 09.5	13 34.7	27 55.8	14 06.6	4 55.4	29 35.5	24 45.6
19 Tu	3 46 58	28 05 29	0♏38 38	7♏14 52	8 28.3	13 29.3	26 16.2	20 49.6	13 55.9	27 50.0	14 14.2	4 54.1	29 33.9	24 45.1
20 W	3 50 55	29 03 12	13 56 33	20 43 29	8 17.5	13 19.2	27 28.5	21 29.7	14 17.0	27 44.3	14 21.7	4 52.9	29 32.3	24 44.6
21 Th	3 54 52	0♊00 54	27 35 24	4♐31 49	8 05.8	13D 13.4	28 40.8	22 09.8	14 38.1	27 38.7	14 29.3	4 51.8	29 30.6	24 44.1
22 F	3 58 48	0 58 35	11♐32 14	18 36 02	7 54.3	13 12.2	29 53.0	22 49.9	14 59.0	27 33.3	14 36.8	4 50.7	29 29.0	24 43.6
23 Sa	4 02 45	1 56 15	25 42 33	2♑51 05	7 44.2	13 15.4	1♋05.2	23 29.9	15 19.9	27 28.0	14 44.3	4 49.7	29 27.4	24 43.2
24 Su	4 06 41	2 53 54	10♑00 57	17 11 29	7 36.4	13 23.2	2 17.4	24 09.9	15 40.8	27 22.8	14 51.7	4 48.7	29 25.8	24 42.8
25 M	4 10 38	3 51 31	24 22 07	1♒32 17	7 31.4	13 35.5	3 29.5	24 49.9	16 01.5	27 17.8	14 59.2	4 47.7	29 24.2	24 42.5
26 Tu	4 14 34	4 49 08	8♒41 33	15 49 35	7 28.9	13 52.3	4 41.5	25 29.8	16 22.2	27 13.0	15 06.6	4 46.8	29 22.5	24 42.2
27 W	4 18 31	5 46 43	22 56 05	0♓00 51	7 28.2	14 13.5	5 53.5	26 09.7	16 42.7	27 08.2	15 14.0	4 46.0	29 20.9	24 41.9
28 Th	4 22 27	6 44 18	7♓03 47	14 04 46	7 28.1	14 38.9	7 05.5	26 49.6	17 03.2	27 03.7	15 21.4	4 45.2	29 19.3	24 41.6
29 F	4 26 24	7 41 51	21 03 46	28 00 44	7 27.4	15 08.7	8 17.4	27 29.4	17 23.7	26 59.3	15 28.8	4 44.4	29 17.7	24 41.4
30 Sa	4 30 21	8 39 24	4♈55 39	11♈48 27	7 24.9	15 42.5	9 29.3	28 09.3	17 44.0	26 55.0	15 36.1	4 43.7	29 16.1	24 41.2
31 Su	4 34 17	9 36 56	18 39 03	25 27 23	7 19.7	16 20.4	10 41.1	28 49.0	18 04.2	26 50.9	15 43.4	4 43.1	29 14.5	24 41.0

LONGITUDE — June 1970

Day	Sid.Time	☉	0 hr ☽	Noon ☽	True☊	☿	♀	♂	⚳	♃	♄	♅	♆	♇
1 M	4 38 14	10♊34 28	2♉13 18	8♉56 39	7♓11.6	17♉02.2	11♋52.9	29♊28.8	18♈24.4	26♎47.0	15♉50.6	4♎42.5	29♏12.9	24♍40.9
2 Tu	4 42 10	11 31 58	15 37 14	22 14 52	7R 01.1	17 47.8	13 04.6	0♋08.5	18 44.5	26R 43.2	15 57.9	4R 41.9	29R 11.3	24R 40.8
3 W	4 46 07	12 29 28	28 49 22	5♊20 32	6 48.8	18 37.1	14 16.3	0 48.2	19 04.4	26 39.6	16 05.1	4 41.4	29 09.8	24 40.7
4 Th	4 50 03	13 26 56	11♊48 13	18 12 18	6 35.9	19 30.1	15 27.9	1 27.9	19 24.3	26 36.2	16 12.3	4 41.0	29 08.2	24D 40.7
5 F	4 54 00	14 24 24	24 32 42	0♋49 23	6 23.6	20 26.6	16 39.5	2 07.6	19 44.1	26 32.9	16 19.4	4 40.6	29 06.6	24 40.7
6 Sa	4 57 56	15 21 51	7♋02 26	13 11 57	6 12.9	21 26.5	17 51.0	2 47.2	20 03.8	26 29.8	16 26.5	4 40.3	29 05.1	24 40.7
7 Su	5 01 53	16 19 17	19 18 07	25 21 13	6 04.7	22 29.8	19 02.4	3 26.8	20 23.4	26 26.9	16 33.6	4 40.0	29 03.5	24 40.8
8 M	5 05 50	17 16 41	1♌21 34	7♌19 34	5 59.1	23 36.5	20 13.8	4 06.3	20 42.8	26 24.1	16 40.6	4 39.7	29 02.0	24 40.9
9 Tu	5 09 46	18 14 05	13 15 41	19 10 25	5 56.0	24 46.3	21 25.2	4 45.9	21 02.2	26 21.6	16 47.6	4 39.6	29 00.5	24 41.0
10 W	5 13 43	19 11 27	25 04 21	0♍58 05	5D 55.0	25 59.4	22 36.5	5 25.4	21 21.5	26 19.2	16 54.5	4 39.4	28 59.0	24 41.1
11 Th	5 17 39	20 08 49	6♍52 15	12 47 31	5R 55.0	27 15.6	23 47.7	6 04.8	21 40.6	26 16.9	17 01.4	4D 39.4	28 57.5	24 41.3
12 F	5 21 36	21 06 09	18 44 34	24 44 05	5 55.0	28 34.9	24 58.9	6 44.3	21 59.7	26 14.9	17 08.3	4 39.3	28 56.0	24 41.5
13 Sa	5 25 32	22 03 29	0♎46 45	6♎53 14	5 54.1	29 57.3	26 09.9	7 23.7	22 18.6	26 13.0	17 15.1	4 39.4	28 54.5	24 41.8
14 Su	5 29 29	23 00 47	13 04 09	19 20 06	5 51.3	1♊22.8	27 21.0	8 03.1	22 37.5	26 11.3	17 21.9	4 39.5	28 53.1	24 42.1
15 M	5 33 25	23 58 05	25 41 35	2♏09 01	5 46.3	2 51.2	28 31.9	8 42.4	22 56.2	26 09.8	17 28.6	4 39.6	28 51.6	24 42.4
16 Tu	5 37 22	24 55 22	8♏42 44	15 22 55	5 38.9	4 22.6	29 42.8	9 21.8	23 14.8	26 08.5	17 35.3	4 39.8	28 50.2	24 42.7
17 W	5 41 19	25 52 38	22 09 38	29 02 46	5 29.6	5 57.0	0♌53.7	10 01.1	23 33.3	26 07.4	17 42.0	4 40.0	28 48.8	24 43.1
18 Th	5 45 15	26 49 53	6♐02 03	13♐07 02	5 19.4	7 34.4	2 04.4	10 40.4	23 51.7	26 06.4	17 48.6	4 40.3	28 47.4	24 43.5
19 F	5 49 12	27 47 08	20 17 08	27 31 37	5 09.2	9 14.6	3 15.1	11 19.6	24 09.9	26 05.6	17 55.1	4 40.7	28 46.0	24 44.0
20 Sa	5 53 08	28 44 23	4♑49 37	12♑10 12	5 00.3	10 57.8	4 25.7	11 58.8	24 28.1	26 05.0	18 01.6	4 41.1	28 44.7	24 44.5
21 Su	5 57 05	29 41 37	19 32 25	26 55 15	4 53.4	12 43.7	5 36.2	12 38.0	24 46.1	26 04.6	18 08.1	4 41.6	28 43.3	24 45.0
22 M	6 01 01	0♋38 50	4♒17 49	11♒39 14	4 49.2	14 32.5	6 46.7	13 17.2	25 03.9	26D 04.3	18 14.5	4 42.1	28 42.0	24 45.5
23 Tu	6 04 58	1 36 04	18 58 45	26 15 44	4D 47.3	16 24.0	7 57.1	13 56.4	25 21.7	26 04.2	18 20.8	4 42.6	28 40.7	24 46.1
24 W	6 08 55	2 33 17	3♓29 41	10♓40 12	4 47.1	18 18.1	9 07.4	14 35.5	25 39.3	26 04.4	18 27.1	4 43.2	28 39.4	24 46.7
25 Th	6 12 51	3 30 30	17 47 03	24 50 03	4R 47.7	20 14.7	10 17.7	15 14.6	25 56.8	26 04.6	18 33.3	4 43.9	28 38.2	24 47.3
26 F	6 16 48	4 27 44	1♈49 09	8♈44 21	4 47.8	22 13.7	11 27.8	15 53.7	26 14.2	26 05.1	18 39.5	4 44.6	28 36.9	24 48.0
27 Sa	6 20 44	5 24 57	15 35 42	22 23 17	4 46.5	24 14.9	12 37.9	16 32.8	26 31.4	26 05.7	18 45.6	4 45.4	28 35.7	24 48.7
28 Su	6 24 41	6 22 10	29 07 13	5♉47 37	4 43.1	26 18.1	13 48.0	17 11.8	26 48.4	26 06.6	18 51.7	4 46.2	28 34.5	24 49.4
29 M	6 28 37	7 19 24	12♉24 35	18 58 13	4 37.4	28 23.2	14 57.9	17 50.8	27 05.4	26 07.6	18 57.7	4 47.1	28 33.3	24 50.2
30 Tu	6 32 34	8 16 37	25 28 36	1♊55 49	4 29.5	0♋29.8	16 07.8	18 29.9	27 22.2	26 08.8	19 03.7	4 48.0	28 32.1	24 51.0

Astro Data

	Dy Hr Mn
☽0N	2 3:50
☽0S	16 7:06
☿D	22 6:46
☽0N	29 8:57
♇D	5 2:24
⚳0N	11 8:25
♅D	12 9:40
☽0S	12 14:28
♃D	23 9:44
☽0N	25 13:37

Planet Ingress

	Dy Hr Mn
♆ ♏R	3 1:31
☉ ♊	21 11:37
♀ ♋	22 14:19
♂ ♋	2 6:50
☿ ♊	13 12:46
♀ ♌	16 17:49
☉ ♋	21 19:43
☿ ♋	30 6:22

Last Aspect / ☽ Ingress

Last Aspect Dy Hr Mn		☽ Ingress Dy Hr Mn
2 0:59	♇ ☍	♈ 2 9:32
4 12:11	♃ ☍	♉ 4 13:05
6 18:07	♆ ☍	♊ 6 18:17
9 0:16	♃ △	♋ 9 2:17
11 12:55	♆ △	♌ 11 13:22
14 1:35	♆ □	♍ 14 2:10
16 13:21	♆ ⚹	♎ 16 14:02
18 18:58	♃ ☌	♏ 18 22:49
21 3:38	☉ ☍	♐ 21 4:11
23 3:01	♃ ⚹	♑ 23 7:13
25 8:26	♆ ⚹	♒ 25 9:25
27 10:52	♆ □	♓ 27 11:59
29 14:13	♆ △	♈ 29 15:27
31 18:16	♂ ⚹	♉ 31 20:03

Last Aspect / ☽ Ingress

Last Aspect Dy Hr Mn		☽ Ingress Dy Hr Mn
3 0:39	♆ ☍	♊ 3 2:10
5 3:51	♃ △	♋ 5 10:25
7 19:23	♆ △	♌ 7 21:17
10 7:58	♆ □	♍ 10 10:02
12 20:37	☿ △	♎ 12 22:28
15 4:37	♀ □	♏ 15 8:02
17 11:36	♆ ☌	♐ 17 13:39
19 12:27	☉ ☍	♑ 19 16:04
21 14:56	♆ ⚹	♒ 21 17:00
23 16:00	♆ □	♓ 23 18:11
25 18:31	♆ △	♈ 25 20:52
27 18:36	♃ ☍	♉ 28 1:35
30 5:41	♆ ☍	♊ 30 8:24

☽ Phases & Eclipses

Dy Hr Mn	
5 14:51	● 14♉41
13 10:26	☽ 22♌15
21 3:38	○ 29♏41
27 22:32	☾ 6♓12
4 2:21	● 13♊04
12 4:06	☽ 20♍47
19 12:27	○ 27♐48
26 4:01	☾ 4♈09

Astro Data

1 May 1970
Julian Day # 25688
SVP 5♓40'22"
GC 26♐25.5 ⚴ 6♓41.6
Eris 12♈24.9 ⚵ 29♓45.4
⚷ 8♈16.3 ⚶ 15♌16.7
☽ Mean ☊ 8♓54.3

1 June 1970
Julian Day # 25719
SVP 5♓40'17"
GC 26♐25.6 ⚴ 12♓33.9
Eris 12♈40.7 ⚵ 14♈18.2
⚷ 9♈37.3 ⚶ 24♌19.8
☽ Mean ☊ 7♓15.8

July 1970

LONGITUDE

Day	Sid.Time	☉	0 hr ☽	Noon ☽	True☊	☿	♀	♂	⚳	♃	♄	♅	♆	♇
1 W	6 36 30	9♋13 51	8♊19 54	14♊40 54	4♓20.3	2♋37.8	17♌17.6	19♋08.8	27♈38.8	26♎10.1	19♉09.6	4♎49.0	28♏31.0	24♍51.8
2 Th	6 40 27	10 11 05	20 58 53	27 13 53	4R 10.5	4 46.9	18 27.3	19 47.8	27 55.3	26 11.7	19 15.4	4 50.0	28R 29.9	24 52.6
3 F	6 44 24	11 08 18	3♋25 58	9♋35 13	4 01.1	6 56.6	19 36.9	20 26.8	28 11.6	26 13.4	19 21.2	4 51.1	28 28.8	24 53.5
4 Sa	6 48 20	12 05 32	15 41 43	21 45 38	3 53.1	9 06.9	20 46.4	21 05.7	28 27.8	26 15.3	19 26.9	4 52.3	28 27.7	24 54.4
5 Su	6 52 17	13 02 45	27 47 07	3♌46 25	3 46.9	11 17.3	21 55.9	21 44.6	28 43.8	26 17.3	19 32.5	4 53.5	28 26.6	24 55.4
6 M	6 56 13	13 59 59	9♌43 46	15 39 28	3 43.0	13 27.7	23 05.2	22 23.5	28 59.7	26 19.6	19 38.1	4 54.7	28 25.6	24 56.3
7 Tu	7 00 10	14 57 12	21 33 55	27 27 29	3D 41.1	15 37.6	24 14.5	23 02.3	29 15.3	26 22.0	19 43.6	4 56.0	28 24.6	24 57.3
8 W	7 04 06	15 54 25	3♍20 38	9♍13 52	3 41.1	17 47.0	25 23.6	23 41.2	29 30.9	26 24.6	19 49.0	4 57.3	28 23.6	24 58.4
9 Th	7 08 03	16 51 38	15 07 42	21 02 43	3 42.1	19 55.5	26 32.7	24 20.0	29 46.2	26 27.3	19 54.4	4 58.7	28 22.7	24 59.4
10 F	7 11 59	17 48 51	26 59 31	2♎58 44	3 43.5	22 03.0	27 41.6	24 58.8	0♉01.4	26 30.2	19 59.6	5 00.1	28 21.7	25 00.5
11 Sa	7 15 56	18 46 04	9♎00 58	15 06 54	3R 44.3	24 09.3	28 50.5	25 37.6	0 16.4	26 33.3	20 04.9	5 01.6	28 20.8	25 01.6
12 Su	7 19 53	19 43 16	21 17 09	27 32 19	3 44.1	26 14.2	29 59.2	26 16.3	0 31.2	26 36.6	20 10.0	5 03.2	28 20.0	25 02.8
13 M	7 23 49	20 40 29	3♏52 59	10♏19 40	3 42.2	28 17.7	1♍07.9	26 55.1	0 45.8	26 40.0	20 15.1	5 04.8	28 19.1	25 03.9
14 Tu	7 27 46	21 37 42	16 52 47	23 32 41	3 38.7	0♌19.7	2 16.4	27 33.8	1 00.3	26 43.6	20 20.1	5 06.4	28 18.3	25 05.1
15 W	7 31 42	22 34 55	0♐19 34	7♐13 29	3 33.7	2 20.0	3 24.8	28 12.5	1 14.5	26 47.4	20 25.0	5 08.1	28 17.5	25 06.4
16 Th	7 35 39	23 32 08	14 14 21	21 21 52	3 28.0	4 18.6	4 33.1	28 51.2	1 28.6	26 51.3	20 29.9	5 09.8	28 16.8	25 07.6
17 F	7 39 35	24 29 22	28 35 35	5♑54 49	3 22.1	6 15.5	5 41.2	29 29.9	1 42.5	26 55.4	20 34.7	5 11.6	28 16.0	25 08.9
18 Sa	7 43 32	25 26 35	13♑18 48	20 46 31	3 16.9	8 10.7	6 49.3	0♌08.5	1 56.2	26 59.7	20 39.4	5 13.4	28 15.3	25 10.2
19 Su	7 47 28	26 23 49	28 16 56	5♒48 53	3 13.1	10 04.0	7 57.2	0 47.1	2 09.7	27 04.1	20 44.0	5 15.3	28 14.6	25 11.5
20 M	7 51 25	27 21 04	13♒21 14	20 52 51	3D 11.0	11 55.6	9 05.0	1 25.8	2 22.9	27 08.6	20 48.5	5 17.2	28 14.0	25 12.9
21 Tu	7 55 22	28 18 19	28 22 40	5♓49 44	3 10.5	13 45.3	10 12.6	2 04.4	2 36.0	27 13.3	20 53.0	5 19.1	28 13.4	25 14.3
22 W	7 59 18	29 15 35	13♓13 12	20 32 26	3 11.3	15 33.3	11 20.2	2 42.9	2 48.9	27 18.2	20 57.4	5 21.1	28 12.8	25 15.7
23 Th	8 03 15	0♌12 51	27 46 52	4♈56 10	3 12.7	17 19.5	12 27.6	3 21.5	3 01.6	27 23.2	21 01.7	5 23.2	28 12.2	25 17.1
24 F	8 07 11	1 10 09	12♈00 05	18 58 31	3R 13.9	19 03.9	13 34.8	4 00.1	3 14.0	27 28.4	21 05.9	5 25.3	28 11.7	25 18.6
25 Sa	8 11 08	2 07 27	25 51 29	2♉39 04	3 14.4	20 46.6	14 41.9	4 38.6	3 26.2	27 33.7	21 10.0	5 27.4	28 11.2	25 20.1
26 Su	8 15 04	3 04 46	9♉21 26	15 58 48	3 13.7	22 27.4	15 48.9	5 17.1	3 38.2	27 39.2	21 14.1	5 29.6	28 10.7	25 21.6
27 M	8 19 01	4 02 07	22 31 26	28 59 37	3 11.7	24 06.5	16 55.8	5 55.6	3 50.0	27 44.8	21 18.0	5 31.8	28 10.2	25 23.1
28 Tu	8 22 57	4 59 28	5♊23 37	11♊43 44	3 08.5	25 43.9	18 02.5	6 34.2	4 01.5	27 50.6	21 21.9	5 34.1	28 09.8	25 24.7
29 W	8 26 54	5 56 51	18 00 17	24 13 31	3 04.5	27 19.4	19 09.0	7 12.7	4 12.8	27 56.5	21 25.7	5 36.4	28 09.4	25 26.2
30 Th	8 30 51	6 54 14	0♋23 42	6♋31 07	3 00.1	28 53.3	20 15.4	7 51.1	4 23.9	28 02.6	21 29.4	5 38.8	28 09.1	25 27.8
31 F	8 34 47	7 51 38	12 36 00	18 38 35	2 56.0	0♍25.3	21 21.7	8 29.6	4 34.7	28 08.8	21 33.0	5 41.2	28 08.8	25 29.5

August 1970

LONGITUDE

Day	Sid.Time	☉	0 hr ☽	Noon ☽	True☊	☿	♀	♂	⚳	♃	♄	♅	♆	♇
1 Sa	8 38 44	8♌49 04	24♋39 07	0♌37 49	2♓52.5	1♍55.6	22♍27.7	9♌08.1	4♉45.3	28♎15.1	21♉36.5	5♎43.6	28♏08.5	25♍31.1
2 Su	8 42 40	9 46 30	6♌34 57	12 30 44	2R 50.0	3 24.1	23 33.7	9 46.5	4 55.6	28 21.6	21 39.9	5 46.1	28R 08.2	25 32.8
3 M	8 46 37	10 43 57	18 25 25	24 19 18	2D 48.6	4 50.8	24 39.4	10 24.9	5 05.7	28 28.2	21 43.3	5 48.6	28 08.0	25 34.5
4 Tu	8 50 33	11 41 24	0♍12 41	6♍05 51	2 48.4	6 15.6	25 45.0	11 03.3	5 15.5	28 35.0	21 46.5	5 51.1	28 07.8	25 36.2
5 W	8 54 30	12 38 53	11 59 10	17 53 00	2 49.1	7 38.6	26 50.4	11 41.8	5 25.1	28 41.9	21 49.7	5 53.7	28 07.6	25 37.9
6 Th	8 58 26	13 36 22	23 47 46	29 43 53	2 50.4	8 59.7	27 55.6	12 20.1	5 34.3	28 48.9	21 52.7	5 56.3	28 07.5	25 39.7
7 F	9 02 23	14 33 52	5♎41 50	11♎42 04	2 51.9	10 18.9	29 00.6	12 58.5	5 43.3	28 56.1	21 55.7	5 59.0	28 07.4	25 41.5
8 Sa	9 06 20	15 31 23	17 45 07	23 51 31	2 53.2	11 36.1	0♎05.4	13 36.9	5 52.1	29 03.4	21 58.5	6 01.7	28 07.3	25 43.2
9 Su	9 10 16	16 28 55	0♏01 47	6♏16 28	2R 54.1	12 51.3	1 10.0	14 15.2	6 00.5	29 10.8	22 01.3	6 04.5	28D 07.3	25 45.1
10 M	9 14 13	17 26 28	12 36 04	19 01 06	2 54.4	14 04.4	2 14.5	14 53.6	6 08.7	29 18.3	22 04.0	6 07.2	28 07.3	25 46.9
11 Tu	9 18 09	18 24 02	25 32 01	2♐09 13	2 53.9	15 15.3	3 18.6	15 31.9	6 16.6	29 26.0	22 06.5	6 10.1	28 07.3	25 48.7
12 W	9 22 06	19 21 36	8♐53 00	15 43 34	2 52.9	16 24.0	4 22.6	16 10.2	6 24.2	29 33.8	22 09.0	6 12.9	28 07.4	25 50.6
13 Th	9 26 02	20 19 12	22 41 01	29 45 17	2 51.6	17 30.4	5 26.4	16 48.5	6 31.5	29 41.7	22 11.4	6 15.8	28 07.5	25 52.5
14 F	9 29 59	21 16 48	6♑56 07	14♑13 09	2 50.1	18 34.3	6 29.9	17 26.8	6 38.5	29 49.8	22 13.6	6 18.7	28 07.6	25 54.4
15 Sa	9 33 56	22 14 26	21 35 46	29 03 13	2 48.9	19 35.7	7 33.1	18 05.1	6 45.2	29 58.0	22 15.8	6 21.7	28 07.8	25 56.3
16 Su	9 37 52	23 12 05	6♒34 37	14♒08 53	2 48.1	20 34.5	8 36.2	18 43.4	6 51.6	0♏06.2	22 17.9	6 24.6	28 08.0	25 58.3
17 M	9 41 49	24 09 44	21 44 52	29 21 23	2D 47.8	21 30.4	9 38.9	19 21.7	6 57.8	0 14.6	22 19.8	6 27.7	28 08.2	26 00.2
18 Tu	9 45 45	25 07 25	6♓57 13	14♓31 10	2 47.9	22 23.5	10 41.4	19 59.9	7 03.6	0 23.1	22 21.7	6 30.7	28 08.4	26 02.2
19 W	9 49 42	26 05 08	22 02 09	29 29 10	2 48.3	23 13.4	11 43.6	20 38.2	7 09.0	0 31.8	22 23.5	6 33.8	28 08.7	26 04.2
20 Th	9 53 38	27 02 52	6♈51 23	14♈08 07	2 48.8	24 00.2	12 45.6	21 16.4	7 14.2	0 40.5	22 25.1	6 36.9	28 09.0	26 06.2
21 F	9 57 35	28 00 37	21 18 51	28 23 14	2 49.3	24 43.4	13 47.2	21 54.6	7 19.0	0 49.3	22 26.7	6 40.0	28 09.4	26 08.2
22 Sa	10 01 31	28 58 25	5♉21 06	12♉12 25	2 49.6	25 23.0	14 48.6	22 32.9	7 23.6	0 58.3	22 28.1	6 43.2	28 09.8	26 10.2
23 Su	10 05 28	29 56 14	18 57 15	25 35 50	2R 49.7	25 58.8	15 49.7	23 11.1	7 27.7	1 07.4	22 29.5	6 46.4	28 10.2	26 12.3
24 M	10 09 24	0♍54 05	2♊08 26	8♊35 26	2 49.7	26 30.5	16 50.5	23 49.3	7 31.6	1 16.5	22 30.7	6 49.6	28 10.6	26 14.3
25 Tu	10 13 21	1 51 57	14 57 13	21 14 15	2D 49.6	26 57.8	17 50.9	24 27.5	7 35.1	1 25.8	22 31.9	6 52.8	28 11.1	26 16.4
26 W	10 17 18	2 49 52	27 26 58	3♋35 51	2 49.6	27 20.6	18 51.1	25 05.7	7 38.3	1 35.2	22 32.9	6 56.1	28 11.6	26 18.5
27 Th	10 21 14	3 47 48	9♋41 22	15 43 59	2 49.7	27 38.5	19 50.9	25 43.9	7 41.1	1 44.7	22 33.9	6 59.4	28 12.2	26 20.6
28 F	10 25 11	4 45 46	21 44 07	27 42 13	2 49.8	27 51.3	20 50.4	26 22.1	7 43.5	1 54.2	22 34.7	7 02.7	28 12.8	26 22.7
29 Sa	10 29 07	5 43 46	3♌38 40	9♌33 50	2 50.1	27R 58.7	21 49.5	27 00.3	7 45.7	2 03.9	22 35.4	7 06.1	28 13.4	26 24.8
30 Su	10 33 04	6 41 47	15 28 06	21 21 47	2R 50.3	28 00.5	22 48.2	27 38.5	7 47.4	2 13.7	22 36.0	7 09.5	28 14.0	26 26.9
31 M	10 37 00	7 39 50	27 15 13	3♍08 41	2 50.4	27 56.4	23 46.6	28 16.7	7 48.8	2 23.6	22 36.5	7 12.9	28 14.7	26 29.0

Astro Data Dy Hr Mn	Planet Ingress Dy Hr Mn	Last Aspect Dy Hr Mn	☽ Ingress Dy Hr Mn	Last Aspect Dy Hr Mn	☽ Ingress Dy Hr Mn	☽ Phases & Eclipses Dy Hr Mn	Astro Data
☽0S 9 21:06	⚳ ♉ 10 9:50	2 10:00 ♃ △	♋ 2 17:21	1 7:11 ♃ □	♌ 1 10:44	3 15:18 ● 11♋16	1 July 1970
♄♇♅ 10 15:10	♀ ♍ 12 12:16	5 1:20 ♆ △	♌ 5 4:26	3 20:32 ♃ ⚹	♍ 3 23:34	11 19:43 ☽ 19♎04	Julian Day # 25749
☽0N 22 20:06	☿ ♌ 14 8:06	7 13:56 ♆ □	♍ 7 17:11	6 8:45 ♆ ⚹	♎ 6 12:32	18 19:58 ○ 25♑46	SVP 5♓40'11"
♃⚺♆ 31 12:01	♂ ♌ 18 6:43	10 2:46 ♆ ⚹	♎ 10 6:02	8 22:13 ♃ ☌	♏ 8 23:57	25 11:00 ☾ 2♉05	GC 26♐25.6 ⚵ 14♓36.7R
	☉ ♌ 23 6:37	12 10:13 ♃ ☌	♏ 12 16:41	11 4:43 ♆ ☌	♐ 11 8:07		Eris 12♈48.0 ⚶ 27♈53.9
☽0S 6 3:06	☿ ♍ 31 5:21	14 20:26 ♆ ☌	♐ 14 23:26	13 11:54 ♃ ⚹	♑ 13 12:25	2 5:58 ● 9♌32	⚷ 10♈18.3 ⚴ 5♍55.4
♀0S 8 5:44		16 21:10 ♃ ⚹	♑ 17 2:19	15 13:28 ♃ □	♒ 15 13:31	10 8:50 ☽ 17♏19	☽ Mean ☊ 5♓40.5
♆ D 10 2:20	♀ ♎ 8 9:59	18 23:57 ♆ ⚹	♒ 19 2:44	17 10:04 ♆ □	♓ 17 13:01	17 3:15 ○ 23♒49	
☽0N 19 5:16	♃ ♏ 15 17:58	20 23:46 ♆ □	♓ 21 2:36	19 9:50 ♆ △	♈ 19 12:50	17 3:23 • P 0.408	1 August 1970
☿0S 20 12:14	☉ ♍ 23 13:34	23 3:30 ☉ △	♈ 23 3:42	21 11:19 ☉ △	♉ 21 14:46	23 20:34 ☾ 0♊17	Julian Day # 25780
☿ R 30 7:27		25 2:56 ♃ ☍	♉ 25 7:18	23 16:42 ♆ ☍	♊ 23 20:03	31 22:01 ● 8♍04	SVP 5♓40'05"
		27 10:28 ♆ ☍	♊ 27 13:53	25 23:26 ☿ □	♋ 26 4:58	31 21:54:49 • A 06'48"	GC 26♐25.7 ⚵ 11♓39.0R
		29 19:17 ♃ △	♋ 29 23:14	28 13:02 ♆ △	♌ 28 16:38		Eris 12♈45.5R ⚶ 10♉45.4
				31 2:01 ♆ □	♍ 31 5:36		⚷ 10♈13.1R ⚴ 19♍42.8
							☽ Mean ☊ 4♓02.1

LONGITUDE — September 1970

Day	Sid.Time	☉	0 hr ☽	Noon ☽	True ☊	☿	♀	♂	⚳	♃	♄	♅	♆	♇
1 Tu	10 40 57	8♍37 54	9♍02 29	14♍56 53	2♓50.3	27♍46.3	24♎44.5	28♌54.9	7♉49.8	2♏33.6	22♉36.9	7♎16.3	28♏15.4	26♍31.2
2 W	10 44 53	9 36 00	20 52 11	26 48 38	2R49.8	27R30.0	25 42.1	29 33.0	7 50.5	2 43.6	22 37.1	7 19.7	28 16.1	26 33.4
3 Th	10 48 50	10 34 08	2♎46 32	8♎46 10	2 49.0	27 07.4	26 39.2	0♍11.2	7R50.8	2 53.8	22 37.3	7 23.2	28 16.9	26 35.5
4 F	10 52 47	11 32 17	14 47 50	20 51 50	2 47.8	26 38.5	27 35.9	0 49.4	7 50.7	3 04.0	22R37.4	7 26.7	28 17.7	26 37.7
5 Sa	10 56 43	12 30 28	26 58 30	3♏08 10	2 46.6	26 03.5	28 32.2	1 27.5	7 50.3	3 14.4	22 37.3	7 30.2	28 18.5	26 39.9
6 Su	11 00 40	13 28 41	9♏21 12	15 37 56	2 45.3	25 22.7	29 27.9	2 05.7	7 49.5	3 24.8	22 37.2	7 33.7	28 19.4	26 42.1
7 M	11 04 36	14 26 55	21 58 46	28 24 02	2 44.4	24 36.4	0♏23.2	2 43.8	7 48.3	3 35.3	22 36.9	7 37.3	28 20.3	26 44.3
8 Tu	11 08 33	15 25 10	4♐54 07	11♐29 21	2D43.9	23 45.2	1 18.0	3 21.9	7 46.8	3 45.9	22 36.6	7 40.8	28 21.2	26 46.5
9 W	11 12 29	16 23 27	18 10 00	24 56 21	2 44.0	22 49.9	2 12.2	4 00.1	7 44.8	3 56.6	22 36.1	7 44.4	28 22.1	26 48.7
10 Th	11 16 26	17 21 46	1♑48 33	8♑46 43	2 44.7	21 51.5	3 05.9	4 38.2	7 42.5	4 07.3	22 35.5	7 48.0	28 23.1	26 50.9
11 F	11 20 22	18 20 06	15 50 48	23 00 42	2 45.8	20 51.0	3 59.0	5 16.3	7 39.9	4 18.2	22 34.8	7 51.6	28 24.1	26 53.1
12 Sa	11 24 19	19 18 28	0♒16 06	7♒36 36	2 46.9	19 49.8	4 51.6	5 54.4	7 36.8	4 29.1	22 34.0	7 55.3	28 25.2	26 55.3
13 Su	11 28 16	20 16 51	15 01 36	22 30 21	2R47.7	18 49.3	5 43.5	6 32.5	7 33.4	4 40.1	22 33.1	7 58.9	28 26.3	26 57.6
14 M	11 32 12	21 15 16	0♓01 58	7♓35 27	2 47.9	17 50.8	6 34.7	7 10.6	7 29.6	4 51.1	22 32.1	8 02.6	28 27.4	26 59.8
15 Tu	11 36 09	22 13 42	15 09 40	22 43 30	2 47.1	16 55.8	7 25.3	7 48.7	7 25.4	5 02.3	22 31.0	8 06.2	28 28.5	27 02.0
16 W	11 40 05	23 12 10	0♈15 44	7♈45 16	2 45.3	16 05.8	8 15.2	8 26.8	7 20.9	5 13.5	22 29.8	8 09.9	28 29.6	27 04.2
17 Th	11 44 02	24 10 41	15 11 01	22 32 02	2 42.7	15 21.9	9 04.4	9 04.9	7 16.0	5 24.8	22 28.5	8 13.6	28 30.8	27 06.5
18 F	11 47 58	25 09 13	29 47 32	6♉56 53	2 39.7	14 45.3	9 52.9	9 43.0	7 10.7	5 36.1	22 27.0	8 17.3	28 32.0	27 08.7
19 Sa	11 51 55	26 07 48	13♉59 36	20 55 26	2 36.7	14 16.9	10 40.5	10 21.1	7 05.0	5 47.6	22 25.5	8 21.0	28 33.3	27 11.0
20 Su	11 55 51	27 06 25	27 44 17	4♊26 12	2 34.2	13 57.6	11 27.4	10 59.2	6 59.0	5 59.1	22 23.9	8 24.8	28 34.6	27 13.2
21 M	11 59 48	28 05 04	11♊01 22	17 30 06	2D32.6	13D47.7	12 13.5	11 37.3	6 52.6	6 10.6	22 22.2	8 28.5	28 35.9	27 15.4
22 Tu	12 03 45	29 03 46	23 52 49	0♋10 00	2 32.1	13 47.6	12 58.7	12 15.4	6 45.8	6 22.2	22 20.3	8 32.3	28 37.2	27 17.7
23 W	12 07 41	0♎02 29	6♋22 11	12 29 56	2 32.8	13 57.3	13 43.1	12 53.5	6 38.7	6 33.9	22 18.4	8 36.0	28 38.5	27 19.9
24 Th	12 11 38	1 01 15	18 33 52	24 34 34	2 34.2	14 16.9	14 26.5	13 31.6	6 31.3	6 45.7	22 16.4	8 39.8	28 39.9	27 22.2
25 F	12 15 34	2 00 03	0♌32 39	6♌28 41	2 36.0	14 46.0	15 08.9	14 09.7	6 23.4	6 57.5	22 14.2	8 43.5	28 41.3	27 24.4
26 Sa	12 19 31	2 58 54	12 23 14	18 16 51	2 37.6	15 24.3	15 50.3	14 47.7	6 15.3	7 09.4	22 12.0	8 47.3	28 42.8	27 26.7
27 Su	12 23 27	3 57 46	24 10 02	0♍03 15	2R38.4	16 11.2	16 30.7	15 25.8	6 06.8	7 21.3	22 09.7	8 51.1	28 44.2	27 28.9
28 M	12 27 24	4 56 40	5♍56 56	11 51 27	2 38.0	17 06.2	17 10.1	16 03.9	5 57.9	7 33.3	22 07.2	8 54.9	28 45.7	27 31.1
29 Tu	12 31 20	5 55 37	17 47 12	23 44 27	2 36.0	18 08.7	17 48.3	16 42.0	5 48.8	7 45.4	22 04.7	8 58.6	28 47.2	27 33.3
30 W	12 35 17	6 54 36	29 43 29	5♎44 33	2 32.3	19 18.0	18 25.3	17 20.1	5 39.3	7 57.5	22 02.1	9 02.4	28 48.8	27 35.6

LONGITUDE — October 1970

Day	Sid.Time	☉	0 hr ☽	Noon ☽	True ☊	☿	♀	♂	⚳	♃	♄	♅	♆	♇
1 Th	12 39 14	7♎53 36	11♎47 51	17♎53 34	2♓27.1	20♍33.2	19♏01.1	17♍58.2	5♉29.5	8♏09.6	21♉59.4	9♎06.2	28♏50.3	27♍37.8
2 F	12 43 10	8 52 39	24 01 50	0♏12 48	2R20.8	21 53.9	19 35.6	18 36.3	5R19.4	8 21.8	21R56.6	9 10.0	28 51.9	27 40.0
3 Sa	12 47 07	9 51 44	6♏26 36	12 43 20	2 14.1	23 19.2	20 08.9	19 14.4	5 09.0	8 34.1	21 53.7	9 13.8	28 53.5	27 42.2
4 Su	12 51 03	10 50 51	19 03 07	25 26 06	2 07.7	24 48.6	20 40.7	19 52.5	4 58.3	8 46.4	21 50.7	9 17.6	28 55.1	27 44.4
5 M	12 55 00	11 49 59	1♐52 23	8♐22 06	2 02.2	26 21.4	21 11.1	20 30.5	4 47.3	8 58.7	21 47.6	9 21.4	28 56.8	27 46.6
6 Tu	12 58 56	12 49 09	14 55 26	21 32 29	1 58.4	27 57.0	21 40.0	21 08.6	4 36.1	9 11.2	21 44.4	9 25.2	28 58.5	27 48.8
7 W	13 02 53	13 48 22	28 13 27	4♑58 28	1D56.4	29 34.9	22 07.3	21 46.7	4 24.6	9 23.6	21 41.2	9 29.0	29 00.2	27 51.0
8 Th	13 06 49	14 47 36	11♑47 41	18 41 12	1 56.1	1♎14.8	22 33.1	22 24.8	4 12.9	9 36.1	21 37.9	9 32.7	29 01.9	27 53.2
9 F	13 10 46	15 46 51	25 39 05	2♒41 22	1 57.0	2 56.1	22 57.1	23 02.8	4 00.9	9 48.6	21 34.5	9 36.5	29 03.6	27 55.3
10 Sa	13 14 43	16 46 08	9♒47 58	16 58 43	1 58.2	4 38.6	23 19.4	23 40.9	3 48.8	10 01.2	21 31.0	9 40.3	29 05.4	27 57.5
11 Su	13 18 39	17 45 27	24 13 23	1♓31 32	1R58.9	6 21.9	23 39.9	24 19.0	3 36.4	10 13.8	21 27.4	9 44.1	29 07.2	27 59.6
12 M	13 22 36	18 44 48	8♓52 41	16 16 10	1 58.1	8 05.8	23 58.5	24 57.1	3 23.8	10 26.5	21 23.8	9 47.8	29 09.0	28 01.8
13 Tu	13 26 32	19 44 11	23 41 13	1♈06 55	1 55.1	9 50.0	24 15.2	25 35.1	3 11.1	10 39.2	21 20.1	9 51.6	29 10.8	28 03.9
14 W	13 30 29	20 43 35	8♈32 20	15 56 26	1 50.0	11 34.3	24 29.9	26 13.2	2 58.2	10 51.9	21 16.3	9 55.3	29 12.7	28 06.0
15 Th	13 34 25	21 43 02	23 18 12	0♉36 39	1 42.9	13 18.7	24 42.5	26 51.3	2 45.1	11 04.6	21 12.4	9 59.0	29 14.5	28 08.1
16 F	13 38 22	22 42 31	7♉50 52	15 00 02	1 34.6	15 03.0	24 53.0	27 29.3	2 31.9	11 17.4	21 08.5	10 02.8	29 16.4	28 10.2
17 Sa	13 42 18	23 42 01	22 03 30	29 00 47	1 26.2	16 47.0	25 01.3	28 07.4	2 18.6	11 30.3	21 04.5	10 06.5	29 18.3	28 12.3
18 Su	13 46 15	24 41 35	5♊51 31	12♊35 33	1 18.5	18 30.7	25 07.4	28 45.5	2 05.1	11 43.1	21 00.5	10 10.2	29 20.2	28 14.3
19 M	13 50 12	25 41 10	19 12 53	25 43 41	1 12.5	20 14.0	25 11.3	29 23.6	1 51.6	11 56.0	20 56.3	10 13.9	29 22.2	28 16.4
20 Tu	13 54 08	26 40 48	2♋08 14	8♋26 56	1 08.5	21 56.9	25R12.8	0♎01.7	1 37.9	12 08.9	20 52.2	10 17.6	29 24.1	28 18.4
21 W	13 58 05	27 40 28	14 40 15	20 48 47	1D06.6	23 39.3	25 12.1	0 39.8	1 24.2	12 21.9	20 47.9	10 21.3	29 26.1	28 20.4
22 Th	14 02 01	28 40 10	26 53 07	2♌53 56	1 06.4	25 21.3	25 08.9	1 17.9	1 10.4	12 34.8	20 43.6	10 24.9	29 28.1	28 22.4
23 F	14 05 58	29 39 54	8♌51 53	14 47 41	1 07.1	27 02.7	25 03.3	1 55.9	0 56.6	12 47.8	20 39.3	10 28.6	29 30.1	28 24.4
24 Sa	14 09 54	0♏39 41	20 41 58	26 35 26	1R07.9	28 43.6	24 55.4	2 34.0	0 42.8	13 00.9	20 34.9	10 32.2	29 32.1	28 26.4
25 Su	14 13 51	1 39 29	2♍28 43	8♍22 25	1 07.7	0♏23.9	24 45.0	3 12.1	0 29.0	13 13.9	20 30.5	10 35.8	29 34.2	28 28.4
26 M	14 17 47	2 39 20	14 17 07	20 13 19	1 05.7	2 03.7	24 32.2	3 50.2	0 15.2	13 27.0	20 26.0	10 39.4	29 36.2	28 30.3
27 Tu	14 21 44	3 39 13	26 11 30	2♎12 06	1 01.2	3 43.0	24 17.1	4 28.3	0 01.4	13 40.1	20 21.4	10 43.0	29 38.3	28 32.2
28 W	14 25 40	4 39 08	8♎15 26	14 21 48	0 54.0	5 21.8	23 59.6	5 06.4	29♈47.6	13 53.2	20 16.8	10 46.5	29 40.3	28 34.2
29 Th	14 29 37	5 39 06	20 31 25	26 44 26	0 44.4	7 00.0	23 39.8	5 44.5	29 33.9	14 06.3	20 12.2	10 50.1	29 42.4	28 36.0
30 F	14 33 34	6 39 05	3♏00 57	9♏20 58	0 33.0	8 37.8	23 17.8	6 22.6	29 20.3	14 19.4	20 07.6	10 53.6	29 44.5	28 37.9
31 Sa	14 37 30	7 39 06	15 44 29	22 11 23	0 20.8	10 15.0	22 53.7	7 00.7	29 06.7	14 32.6	20 02.9	10 57.1	29 46.7	28 39.8

Astro Data Dy Hr Mn	Planet Ingress Dy Hr Mn	Last Aspect Dy Hr Mn	☽ Ingress Dy Hr Mn	Last Aspect Dy Hr Mn	☽ Ingress Dy Hr Mn	☽ Phases & Eclipses Dy Hr Mn	Astro Data
☽0S 2 8:59	♂ ♍ 3 4:57	2 14:56 ♆ ⚹	♎ 2 18:25	30 18:35 ♅ ☌	♏ 2 11:35	8 19:38 ☽ 15♐44	1 September 1970
⚳R 3 19:37	♀ ♏ 7 1:54	5 2:19 ♀ ☌	♏ 5 5:54	4 18:31 ♆ ☌	♐ 4 20:31	15 11:09 ○ 22♓12	Julian Day # 25811
♄R 4 13:57	☉ ♎ 23 10:59	7 11:53 ♆ ☌	♐ 7 14:58	7 1:06 ☿ □	♑ 7 3:10	22 9:42 ☾ 28♊58	SVP 5♓40'01"
♄□♅ 7 9:50		9 15:18 ♇ □	♑ 9 20:51	9 5:49 ☿ ⚹	♒ 9 7:26	30 14:31 ● 7♎01	GC 26♐25.8 ⚴ 4♓24.4R
☿0N 11 2:50	☿ ♎ 7 18:04	11 20:56 ♆ ⚹	♒ 11 23:34	11 8:03 ♆ □	♓ 11 9:30		Eris 12♈33.7R ⚵ 21♉02.6
☽0N 15 16:09	♂ ♎ 20 10:57	13 21:28 ♆ □	♓ 13 23:57	13 8:52 ♆ △	♈ 13 10:12	8 4:43 ☽ 14♑30	⚷ 9♈22.2R ⚶ 4♎42.3
☿D 22 0:15	☉ ♏ 23 20:04	15 21:10 ♆ △	♈ 15 23:35	14 20:21 ☉ ☍	♉ 15 11:00	14 20:21 ○ 21♈04	☽ Mean ☊ 2♓23.6
☉0S 23 10:59	☿ ♏ 25 6:16	16 12:40 ♅ ☍	♉ 18 0:21	17 12:31 ♆ ☍	♊ 17 13:43	22 2:47 ☾ 28♋17	
☽0S 29 15:13	⚳ ♈R 27 14:22	20 1:28 ♆ ☍	♊ 20 4:02	19 19:12 ♂ □	♋ 19 19:59	30 6:28 ● 6♏25	1 October 1970
♃⚺♅ 8 2:46		22 9:42 ☉ □	♋ 22 11:41	22 5:07 ♆ △	♌ 22 6:12		Julian Day # 25841
☿0S 10 8:57		24 20:14 ♆ △	♌ 24 22:54	24 18:01 ♆ □	♍ 24 18:57		SVP 5♓39'58"
☽0N 13 2:35		27 9:19 ♆ □	♍ 27 11:53	27 6:53 ♆ ⚹	♎ 27 7:37		GC 26♐25.8 ⚴ 27♒58.6R
♀R 20 15:57		29 22:09 ♆ ⚹	♎ 30 0:33	28 4:56 ♅ ☌	♏ 29 18:15		Eris 12♈16.6R ⚵ 26♉11.2
♂0S 24 11:44	♃∠∠26 19:13						⚷ 8♈05.7R ⚶ 19♎58.8
⚳0S 25 5:23	☽0S26 22:00						☽ Mean ☊ 0♓48.2

November 1970 LONGITUDE

Day	Sid.Time	☉	0 hr ☽	Noon ☽	True ☊	☿	♀	♂	⚳	♃	♄	♅	♆	♇
1 Su	14 41 27	8♏39 09	28♏41 36	5♐14 57	0♓08.9	11♏51.8	22♏27.5	7♎38.9	28♈53.3	14♏45.7	19♉58.1	11♎00.6	29♏48.8	28♍41.6
2 M	14 45 23	9 39 14	11♐51 19	18 30 31	29♒58.5	13 28.1	21R59.5	8 17.0	28R40.0	14 58.9	19R53.4	11 04.0	29 50.9	28 43.4
3 Tu	14 49 20	10 39 20	25 12 26	1♑56 55	29R50.5	15 03.9	21 29.7	8 55.1	28 26.9	15 12.1	19 48.6	11 07.5	29 53.1	28 45.2
4 W	14 53 16	11 39 28	8♑43 54	15 33 17	29 45.3	16 39.3	20 58.3	9 33.2	28 13.9	15 25.3	19 43.8	11 10.9	29 55.2	28 47.0
5 Th	14 57 13	12 39 38	22 25 02	29 19 09	29 42.7	18 14.3	20 25.5	10 11.3	28 01.0	15 38.5	19 39.0	11 14.3	29 57.4	28 48.8
6 F	15 01 10	13 39 49	6♒15 36	13♒14 24	29D42.1	19 48.9	19 51.5	10 49.4	27 48.3	15 51.7	19 34.2	11 17.6	29 59.6	28 50.5
7 Sa	15 05 06	14 40 01	20 15 33	27 19 00	29R42.2	21 23.1	19 16.5	11 27.5	27 35.9	16 04.9	19 29.3	11 21.0	0♐01.8	28 52.2
8 Su	15 09 03	15 40 15	4♓24 39	11♓32 23	29 41.8	22 57.0	18 40.8	12 05.6	27 23.6	16 18.2	19 24.5	11 24.3	0 04.0	28 53.9
9 M	15 12 59	16 40 30	18 41 57	25 53 02	29 39.7	24 30.5	18 04.5	12 43.7	27 11.6	16 31.4	19 19.6	11 27.5	0 06.2	28 55.5
10 Tu	15 16 56	17 40 47	3♈05 14	10♈18 01	29 34.8	26 03.6	17 27.9	13 21.8	26 59.8	16 44.6	19 14.7	11 30.8	0 08.4	28 57.2
11 W	15 20 52	18 41 05	17 30 48	24 42 53	29 27.1	27 36.5	16 51.4	13 59.9	26 48.2	16 57.8	19 09.8	11 34.0	0 10.6	28 58.8
12 Th	15 24 49	19 41 25	1♉53 32	9♉01 59	29 16.6	29 09.0	16 15.0	14 38.0	26 36.9	17 11.0	19 04.9	11 37.2	0 12.8	29 00.4
13 F	15 28 45	20 41 47	16 07 29	23 09 19	29 04.5	0♐41.2	15 39.2	15 16.1	26 25.9	17 24.3	19 00.1	11 40.4	0 15.0	29 02.0
14 Sa	15 32 42	21 42 10	0♊06 49	6♊59 27	28 51.8	2 13.1	15 04.1	15 54.2	26 15.1	17 37.5	18 55.2	11 43.5	0 17.3	29 03.5
15 Su	15 36 39	22 42 35	13 46 45	20 28 27	28 40.0	3 44.7	14 30.0	16 32.3	26 04.7	17 50.7	18 50.3	11 46.6	0 19.5	29 05.0
16 M	15 40 35	23 43 02	27 04 21	3♋34 27	28 30.0	5 16.0	13 57.1	17 10.4	25 54.5	18 03.9	18 45.5	11 49.7	0 21.8	29 06.5
17 Tu	15 44 32	24 43 31	9♋58 51	16 17 48	28 22.7	6 47.1	13 25.6	17 48.5	25 44.6	18 17.1	18 40.6	11 52.7	0 24.0	29 08.0
18 W	15 48 28	25 44 01	22 31 37	28 40 46	28 18.0	8 17.8	12 55.8	18 26.6	25 35.1	18 30.3	18 35.8	11 55.8	0 26.3	29 09.4
19 Th	15 52 25	26 44 33	4♌45 45	10♌47 10	28 15.8	9 48.3	12 27.7	19 04.7	25 25.9	18 43.5	18 31.0	11 58.7	0 28.5	29 10.8
20 F	15 56 21	27 45 07	16 45 39	22 41 52	28 15.2	11 18.5	12 01.6	19 42.8	25 17.0	18 56.6	18 26.2	12 01.7	0 30.8	29 12.2
21 Sa	16 00 18	28 45 43	28 36 31	4♍30 19	28 15.2	12 48.3	11 37.6	20 21.0	25 08.4	19 09.8	18 21.4	12 04.6	0 33.0	29 13.6
22 Su	16 04 14	29 46 20	10♍23 57	16 18 09	28 14.5	14 17.8	11 15.7	20 59.1	25 00.2	19 22.9	18 16.7	12 07.4	0 35.3	29 14.9
23 M	16 08 11	0♐46 59	22 13 33	28 10 50	28 12.1	15 47.0	10 56.1	21 37.2	24 52.3	19 36.0	18 11.9	12 10.3	0 37.5	29 16.2
24 Tu	16 12 08	1 47 39	4♎10 35	10♎13 21	28 07.3	17 15.7	10 38.9	22 15.3	24 44.8	19 49.2	18 07.2	12 13.1	0 39.8	29 17.5
25 W	16 16 04	2 48 22	16 19 37	22 29 48	27 59.6	18 44.0	10 24.1	22 53.5	24 37.7	20 02.2	18 02.6	12 15.8	0 42.1	29 18.7
26 Th	16 20 01	3 49 05	28 44 15	5♏03 12	27 49.2	20 11.9	10 11.8	23 31.6	24 30.9	20 15.3	17 58.0	12 18.5	0 44.3	29 20.0
27 F	16 23 57	4 49 51	11♏26 47	17 55 03	27 36.8	21 39.1	10 01.9	24 09.7	24 24.5	20 28.4	17 53.4	12 21.2	0 46.6	29 21.1
28 Sa	16 27 54	5 50 37	24 27 57	1♐05 18	27 23.4	23 05.8	9 54.5	24 47.8	24 18.5	20 41.4	17 48.9	12 23.8	0 48.8	29 22.3
29 Su	16 31 50	6 51 25	7♐46 53	14 32 21	27 10.2	24 31.7	9 49.6	25 26.0	24 12.9	20 54.4	17 44.4	12 26.4	0 51.1	29 23.4
30 M	16 35 47	7 52 15	21 21 20	28 13 24	26 58.6	25 56.8	9D47.1	26 04.1	24 07.6	21 07.4	17 40.0	12 29.0	0 53.3	29 24.5

December 1970 LONGITUDE

Day	Sid.Time	☉	0 hr ☽	Noon ☽	True ☊	☿	♀	♂	⚳	♃	♄	♅	♆	♇
1 Tu	16 39 43	8♐53 05	5♑08 05	12♑04 57	26♒49.6	27♐21.0	9♏47.1	26♎42.2	24♈02.8	21♏20.4	17♉35.6	12♎31.5	0♐55.6	29♍25.6
2 W	16 43 40	9 53 57	19 03 34	26 03 31	26R43.6	28 44.1	9 49.5	27 20.3	23R58.3	21 33.3	17R31.2	12 34.0	0 57.8	29 26.6
3 Th	16 47 37	10 54 49	3♒04 29	10♒06 09	26 40.4	0♑06.0	9 54.3	27 58.4	23 54.3	21 46.2	17 27.0	12 36.4	1 00.1	29 27.6
4 F	16 51 33	11 55 42	17 08 16	24 10 41	26D39.5	1 26.4	10 01.4	28 36.5	23 50.6	21 59.0	17 22.7	12 38.8	1 02.3	29 28.6
5 Sa	16 55 30	12 56 36	1♓13 14	8♓15 49	26R39.7	2 45.1	10 10.7	29 14.6	23 47.4	22 11.9	17 18.6	12 41.2	1 04.5	29 29.6
6 Su	16 59 26	13 57 30	15 18 21	22 20 46	26 39.5	4 01.9	10 22.3	29 52.7	23 44.5	22 24.7	17 14.5	12 43.4	1 06.7	29 30.5
7 M	17 03 23	14 58 25	29 22 57	6♈24 47	26 37.7	5 16.4	10 36.0	0♏30.8	23 42.0	22 37.4	17 10.4	12 45.7	1 08.9	29 31.3
8 Tu	17 07 19	15 59 21	13♈26 07	20 26 43	26 33.5	6 28.3	10 51.9	1 08.9	23 40.0	22 50.1	17 06.5	12 47.9	1 11.1	29 32.2
9 W	17 11 16	17 00 18	27 26 21	4♉24 41	26 26.5	7 37.2	11 09.8	1 47.0	23 38.3	23 02.8	17 02.6	12 50.1	1 13.3	29 33.0
10 Th	17 15 12	18 01 15	11♉21 20	18 15 56	26 16.9	8 42.6	11 29.7	2 25.1	23 37.0	23 15.5	16 58.7	12 52.2	1 15.5	29 33.8
11 F	17 19 09	19 02 13	25 08 04	1♊57 16	26 05.7	9 44.0	11 51.5	3 03.2	23 36.2	23 28.1	16 55.0	12 54.2	1 17.7	29 34.5
12 Sa	17 23 06	20 03 12	8♊43 10	15 25 21	25 53.9	10 40.7	12 15.2	3 41.3	23D35.7	23 40.6	16 51.3	12 56.3	1 19.9	29 35.3
13 Su	17 27 02	21 04 12	22 03 32	28 37 26	25 42.7	11 32.2	12 40.7	4 19.4	23 35.6	23 53.1	16 47.7	12 58.2	1 22.0	29 35.9
14 M	17 30 59	22 05 12	5♋06 52	11♋31 47	25 33.2	12 17.7	13 07.9	4 57.5	23 35.9	24 05.6	16 44.2	13 00.2	1 24.2	29 36.6
15 Tu	17 34 55	23 06 14	17 52 10	24 08 06	25 26.1	12 56.4	13 36.9	5 35.6	23 36.6	24 18.0	16 40.8	13 02.0	1 26.3	29 37.2
16 W	17 38 52	24 07 16	0♌19 49	6♌27 35	25 21.6	13 27.3	14 07.4	6 13.7	23 37.7	24 30.4	16 37.4	13 03.8	1 28.5	29 37.8
17 Th	17 42 48	25 08 19	12 31 46	18 32 47	25D19.6	13 49.7	14 39.5	6 51.7	23 39.2	24 42.7	16 34.1	13 05.6	1 30.6	29 38.3
18 F	17 46 45	26 09 23	24 31 09	0♍27 26	25 19.5	14R02.7	15 13.2	7 29.8	23 41.0	24 55.0	16 30.9	13 07.3	1 32.7	29 38.9
19 Sa	17 50 42	27 10 27	6♍22 12	12 16 08	25 20.3	14 05.3	15 48.2	8 07.9	23 43.3	25 07.2	16 27.8	13 09.0	1 34.8	29 39.3
20 Su	17 54 38	28 11 33	18 09 51	24 04 04	25R21.1	13 57.0	16 24.7	8 46.0	23 45.9	25 19.4	16 24.8	13 10.6	1 36.8	29 39.8
21 M	17 58 35	29 12 39	29 59 27	5♎56 41	25 21.0	13 37.1	17 02.5	9 24.1	23 48.8	25 31.5	16 21.9	13 12.2	1 38.9	29 40.2
22 Tu	18 02 31	0♑13 46	11♎56 27	17 59 24	25 19.0	13 05.5	17 41.6	10 02.1	23 52.2	25 43.6	16 19.1	13 13.7	1 40.9	29 40.6
23 W	18 06 28	1 14 54	24 06 07	0♏17 10	25 14.9	12 22.3	18 21.9	10 40.2	23 55.9	25 55.6	16 16.3	13 15.2	1 43.0	29 40.9
24 Th	18 10 24	2 16 02	6♏33 03	12 54 09	25 08.6	11 28.1	19 03.4	11 18.3	24 00.0	26 07.5	16 13.7	13 16.6	1 45.0	29 41.2
25 F	18 14 21	3 17 11	19 20 47	25 53 10	25 00.5	10 24.1	19 46.0	11 56.3	24 04.5	26 19.4	16 11.2	13 17.9	1 47.0	29 41.5
26 Sa	18 18 17	4 18 21	2♐31 22	9♐15 19	24 51.4	9 12.1	20 29.7	12 34.4	24 09.3	26 31.2	16 08.7	13 19.2	1 49.0	29 41.7
27 Su	18 22 14	5 19 31	16 04 52	22 59 39	24 42.4	7 54.1	21 14.5	13 12.4	24 14.4	26 43.0	16 06.4	13 20.5	1 51.0	29 41.9
28 M	18 26 11	6 20 41	29 59 15	7♑03 07	24 34.4	6 32.7	22 00.3	13 50.5	24 20.0	26 54.7	16 04.1	13 21.7	1 52.9	29 42.1
29 Tu	18 30 07	7 21 52	14♑10 36	21 20 59	24 28.3	5 10.7	22 47.0	14 28.5	24 25.9	27 06.3	16 02.0	13 22.8	1 54.8	29 42.3
30 W	18 34 04	8 23 03	28 33 32	5♒47 30	24 24.5	3 50.8	23 34.6	15 06.5	24 32.1	27 17.8	16 00.0	13 23.9	1 56.8	29 42.4
31 Th	18 38 00	9 24 14	13♒02 10	20 16 51	24D23.0	2 35.4	24 23.1	15 44.6	24 38.6	27 29.3	15 58.0	13 25.0	1 58.7	29 42.4

Astro Data

	Dy Hr Mn
☽0N	9 10:32
♃☍♄	18 19:20
☽0S	23 5:09
⚳0N	29 16:35
♀D	1 0:03
☽0N	6 15:43
⚳D	13 5:01
☿R	19 5:58
☽0S	20 12:24

Planet Ingress

		Dy Hr Mn
☊	♒R	2 8:14
♆	♐	6 16:32
☿	♐	13 1:16
☉	♐	22 17:25
☿	♑	3 10:14
♂	♏	6 16:34
☉	♑	22 6:36

Last Aspect / ☽ Ingress

Last Aspect Dy Hr Mn		☽ Ingress Dy Hr Mn
1 2:02	♆ ☌	♐ 1 2:24
3 6:19	♇ □	♑ 3 8:32
5 13:06	♆ ⚹	♒ 5 13:11
7 0:39	☿ □	♓ 7 16:33
9 17:05	♇ ☍	♈ 9 18:52
10 17:20	♂ ☍	♉ 11 20:50
13 22:09	♇ △	♊ 13 23:48
16 3:43	♇ □	♋ 16 5:23
18 12:56	♇ ⚹	♌ 18 14:36
20 23:13	☉ □	♍ 21 2:50
23 14:11	♇ ☌	♎ 23 15:39
25 12:48	♂ ☌	♏ 26 2:25
28 8:54	♇ ⚹	♐ 28 10:02
30 14:04	♇ □	♑ 30 15:05

Last Aspect / ☽ Ingress

Last Aspect Dy Hr Mn		☽ Ingress Dy Hr Mn
2 17:48	♇ △	♒ 2 18:45
4 19:54	♂ △	♓ 4 21:55
7 0:14	♇ ☍	♈ 7 1:03
8 3:46	☉ △	♉ 9 4:24
11 7:48	♇ △	♊ 11 8:33
13 13:48	♇ □	♋ 13 14:32
15 22:38	♇ ⚹	♌ 15 23:21
18 2:29	☉ △	♍ 18 11:04
20 23:21	♇ ☌	♎ 21 0:01
22 2:44	☿ □	♏ 23 11:27
25 18:54	♇ ⚹	♐ 25 19:28
27 23:31	♇ □	♑ 28 0:01
30 1:54	♇ △	♒ 30 2:24

☽ Phases & Eclipses

Dy Hr Mn	
6 12:47	☽ 13♒42
13 7:28	○ 20♉30
20 23:13	☾ 28♌13
28 21:14	● 6♐14
5 20:36	☽ 13♓18
12 21:03	○ 20♊26
20 21:09	☾ 28♍35
28 10:43	● 6♑17

Astro Data

1 November 1970
Julian Day # 25872
SVP 5♓39'54"
GC 26♐25.9 ⚵ 26♒12.1
Eris 11♈58.1R ⚶ 23♉54.3R
⚷ 6♈47.0R ⚴ 6♏15.8
☽ Mean ☊ 29♒09.7

1 December 1970
Julian Day # 25902
SVP 5♓39'49"
GC 26♐26.0 ⚵ 29♒24.3
Eris 11♈44.8R ⚶ 17♉37.9R
⚷ 5♈59.3R ⚴ 22♏14.2
☽ Mean ☊ 27♒34.4

LONGITUDE — January 1971

Day	Sid.Time	☉	0 hr ☽	Noon☽	True☊	☿	♀	♂	⚳	♃	♄	♅	♆	♇
1 F	18 41 57	10♑25 24	27♒30 55	4♓43 51	24♒23.3	1♑26.5	25♏12.5	16♏22.6	24♈45.6	27♏40.7	15♉56.2	13♎25.9	2♐00.5	29♍42.5
2 Sa	18 45 53	11 26 34	11♓55 13	19 04 37	24 24.6	0R 26.0	26 02.7	17 00.6	24 52.8	27 52.0	15R 54.5	13 26.8	2 02.4	29R 42.5
3 Su	18 49 50	12 27 44	26 11 48	3♈16 33	24R 25.8	29♐34.8	26 53.6	17 38.6	25 00.4	28 03.2	15 52.9	13 27.7	2 04.2	29 42.4
4 M	18 53 46	13 28 54	10♈18 42	17 18 10	24 26.0	28 53.6	27 45.4	18 16.5	25 08.3	28 14.4	15 51.4	13 28.5	2 06.0	29 42.4
5 Tu	18 57 43	14 30 03	24 14 51	1♉08 44	24 24.7	28 22.6	28 37.8	18 54.5	25 16.5	28 25.5	15 50.0	13 29.3	2 07.8	29 42.3
6 W	19 01 40	15 31 12	7♉59 46	14 47 55	24 21.5	28 01.8	29 30.9	19 32.5	25 25.0	28 36.5	15 48.7	13 30.0	2 09.6	29 42.1
7 Th	19 05 36	16 32 21	21 33 07	28 15 20	24 16.6	27D50.8	0♐24.8	20 10.4	25 33.8	28 47.4	15 47.5	13 30.6	2 11.4	29 41.9
8 F	19 09 33	17 33 30	4♊54 31	11♊30 36	24 10.6	27 49.1	1 19.2	20 48.4	25 43.0	28 58.2	15 46.4	13 31.2	2 13.1	29 41.7
9 Sa	19 13 29	18 34 38	18 03 30	24 33 09	24 04.1	27 56.0	2 14.3	21 26.3	25 52.4	29 09.0	15 45.5	13 31.7	2 14.8	29 41.5
10 Su	19 17 26	19 35 45	0♋59 30	7♋22 31	23 57.9	28 10.9	3 10.0	22 04.2	26 02.2	29 19.6	15 44.7	13 32.2	2 16.5	29 41.2
11 M	19 21 22	20 36 53	13 42 12	19 58 32	23 52.7	28 33.1	4 06.3	22 42.1	26 12.2	29 30.2	15 43.9	13 32.6	2 18.2	29 40.9
12 Tu	19 25 19	21 38 00	26 11 35	2♌21 27	23 49.1	29 01.9	5 03.2	23 20.0	26 22.6	29 40.7	15 43.3	13 32.9	2 19.8	29 40.6
13 W	19 29 15	22 39 06	8♌28 16	14 32 16	23D47.1	29 36.7	6 00.5	23 58.0	26 33.2	29 51.1	15 42.8	13 33.2	2 21.4	29 40.2
14 Th	19 33 12	23 40 13	20 33 39	26 32 44	23 46.7	0♑16.9	6 58.5	24 35.8	26 44.1	0♐01.4	15 42.4	13 33.5	2 23.0	29 39.8
15 F	19 37 09	24 41 19	2♍29 51	8♍25 25	23 47.5	1 02.0	7 56.9	25 13.7	26 55.2	0 11.6	15 42.1	13 33.7	2 24.5	29 39.4
16 Sa	19 41 05	25 42 24	14 19 53	20 13 42	23 49.2	1 51.4	8 55.8	25 51.6	27 06.7	0 21.6	15 41.9	13 33.8	2 26.1	29 38.9
17 Su	19 45 02	26 43 30	26 07 25	2♎01 35	23 51.1	2 44.8	9 55.2	26 29.5	27 18.4	0 31.6	15D41.9	13R33.9	2 27.6	29 38.4
18 M	19 48 58	27 44 35	7♎56 48	13 53 39	23 52.7	3 41.6	10 55.0	27 07.3	27 30.3	0 41.5	15 41.9	13 33.9	2 29.1	29 37.9
19 Tu	19 52 55	28 45 40	19 52 47	25 54 48	23R53.5	4 41.7	11 55.2	27 45.2	27 42.6	0 51.3	15 42.1	13 33.9	2 30.5	29 37.3
20 W	19 56 51	29 46 44	2♏00 20	8♏10 00	23 53.2	5 44.6	12 55.9	28 23.0	27 55.1	1 01.0	15 42.4	13 33.8	2 32.0	29 36.7
21 Th	20 00 48	0♒47 49	14 24 22	20 43 57	23 51.8	6 50.1	13 57.0	29 00.8	28 07.8	1 10.6	15 42.8	13 33.6	2 33.4	29 36.1
22 F	20 04 44	1 48 52	27 09 15	3♐40 38	23 49.5	7 57.9	14 58.4	29 38.6	28 20.8	1 20.1	15 43.3	13 33.4	2 34.8	29 35.4
23 Sa	20 08 41	2 49 56	10♐18 23	17 02 43	23 46.6	9 07.9	16 00.3	0♐16.4	28 34.1	1 29.5	15 43.9	13 33.1	2 36.1	29 34.7
24 Su	20 12 38	3 50 59	23 53 37	0♑51 02	23 43.5	10 19.8	17 02.5	0 54.2	28 47.5	1 38.7	15 44.6	13 32.8	2 37.4	29 34.0
25 M	20 16 34	4 52 01	7♑54 40	15 04 07	23 40.8	11 33.5	18 05.0	1 32.0	29 01.3	1 47.9	15 45.5	13 32.5	2 38.7	29 33.2
26 Tu	20 20 31	5 53 03	22 18 48	29 37 59	23 38.8	12 48.8	19 07.8	2 09.7	29 15.2	1 56.9	15 46.4	13 32.0	2 40.0	29 32.5
27 W	20 24 27	6 54 04	7♒00 50	14♒26 25	23D37.7	14 05.6	20 11.0	2 47.5	29 29.4	2 05.8	15 47.5	13 31.5	2 41.2	29 31.7
28 Th	20 28 24	7 55 03	21 53 44	29 21 45	23 37.6	15 23.8	21 14.5	3 25.2	29 43.8	2 14.6	15 48.7	13 31.0	2 42.4	29 30.8
29 F	20 32 20	8 56 02	6♓49 27	14♓15 53	23 38.2	16 43.3	22 18.2	4 02.9	29 58.5	2 23.2	15 50.0	13 30.4	2 43.6	29 29.9
30 Sa	20 36 17	9 57 00	21 40 10	29 01 31	23 39.3	18 04.0	23 22.3	4 40.5	0♉13.4	2 31.8	15 51.4	13 29.7	2 44.7	29 29.1
31 Su	20 40 14	10 57 56	6♈19 17	13♈32 55	23 40.4	19 25.9	24 26.6	5 18.2	0 28.4	2 40.2	15 52.9	13 29.0	2 45.9	29 28.1

LONGITUDE — February 1971

Day	Sid.Time	☉	0 hr ☽	Noon☽	True☊	☿	♀	♂	⚳	♃	♄	♅	♆	♇
1 M	20 44 10	11♒58 51	20♈42 03	27♈46 22	23♒41.2	20♑48.8	25♐31.2	5♐55.8	0♉43.7	2♐48.5	15♉54.5	13♎28.3	2♐46.9	29♍27.2
2 Tu	20 48 07	12 59 44	4♉45 44	11♉40 05	23R41.5	22 12.8	26 36.0	6 33.4	0 59.2	2 56.6	15 56.3	13R 27.5	2 48.0	29R 26.2
3 W	20 52 03	14 00 37	18 29 27	25 13 56	23 41.3	23 37.8	27 41.1	7 11.0	1 14.9	3 04.7	15 58.1	13 26.6	2 49.0	29 25.2
4 Th	20 56 00	15 01 28	1♊53 40	8♊28 53	23 40.6	25 03.8	28 46.4	7 48.5	1 30.8	3 12.6	16 00.1	13 25.7	2 50.0	29 24.2
5 F	20 59 56	16 02 17	14 59 47	21 26 27	23 39.7	26 30.6	29 51.9	8 26.1	1 46.9	3 20.3	16 02.2	13 24.7	2 51.0	29 23.1
6 Sa	21 03 53	17 03 05	27 49 37	4♋09 02	23 38.8	27 58.4	0♑57.7	9 03.6	2 03.2	3 28.0	16 04.3	13 23.7	2 51.9	29 22.0
7 Su	21 07 49	18 03 52	10♋25 08	16 38 09	23 38.0	29 27.1	2 03.7	9 41.1	2 19.7	3 35.5	16 06.6	13 22.6	2 52.8	29 20.9
8 M	21 11 46	19 04 37	22 48 18	28 55 50	23 37.4	0♒56.6	3 09.9	10 18.6	2 36.4	3 42.8	16 09.0	13 21.5	2 53.6	29 19.8
9 Tu	21 15 43	20 05 21	5♌00 56	11♌03 52	23 37.0	2 27.0	4 16.3	10 56.1	2 53.3	3 50.1	16 11.5	13 20.4	2 54.5	29 18.6
10 W	21 19 39	21 06 04	17 04 48	23 04 00	23D36.9	3 58.2	5 22.9	11 33.5	3 10.3	3 57.1	16 14.1	13 19.1	2 55.3	29 17.4
11 Th	21 23 36	22 06 45	29 01 40	4♍58 03	23 37.0	5 30.3	6 29.7	12 10.9	3 27.5	4 04.1	16 16.8	13 17.9	2 56.0	29 16.2
12 F	21 27 32	23 07 25	10♍53 26	16 48 04	23R37.1	7 03.3	7 36.7	12 48.3	3 44.9	4 10.9	16 19.6	13 16.6	2 56.8	29 15.0
13 Sa	21 31 29	24 08 03	22 42 16	28 36 22	23 37.0	8 37.1	8 43.9	13 25.7	4 02.4	4 17.5	16 22.5	13 15.2	2 57.5	29 13.8
14 Su	21 35 25	25 08 40	4♎30 43	10♎25 43	23 36.9	10 11.7	9 51.3	14 03.1	4 20.1	4 24.0	16 25.5	13 13.8	2 58.1	29 12.5
15 M	21 39 22	26 09 16	16 21 47	22 19 21	23 36.6	11 47.3	10 58.8	14 40.4	4 38.0	4 30.4	16 28.6	13 12.3	2 58.8	29 11.2
16 Tu	21 43 18	27 09 51	28 18 55	4♏20 57	23 36.3	13 23.6	12 06.5	15 17.7	4 56.1	4 36.6	16 31.8	13 10.8	2 59.4	29 09.9
17 W	21 47 15	28 10 25	10♏25 59	16 34 32	23 36.0	15 00.9	13 14.3	15 55.0	5 14.3	4 42.6	16 35.1	13 09.3	2 59.9	29 08.6
18 Th	21 51 11	29 10 57	22 47 09	29 04 21	23D35.9	16 39.1	14 22.3	16 32.2	5 32.7	4 48.5	16 38.5	13 07.7	3 00.5	29 07.2
19 F	21 55 08	0♓11 28	5♐26 39	11♐54 31	23 36.0	18 18.1	15 30.5	17 09.5	5 51.2	4 54.3	16 42.0	13 06.1	3 01.0	29 05.9
20 Sa	21 59 05	1 11 58	18 28 24	25 08 38	23 36.5	19 58.1	16 38.8	17 46.7	6 09.9	4 59.8	16 45.6	13 04.4	3 01.4	29 04.5
21 Su	22 03 01	2 12 27	1♑55 30	8♑49 10	23 37.2	21 39.0	17 47.3	18 23.8	6 28.7	5 05.3	16 49.3	13 02.7	3 01.9	29 03.1
22 M	22 06 58	3 12 54	15 49 39	22 56 49	23 38.1	23 20.8	18 55.8	19 01.0	6 47.7	5 10.5	16 53.1	13 01.0	3 02.3	29 01.7
23 Tu	22 10 54	4 13 20	0♒10 21	7♒29 55	23 38.8	25 03.6	20 04.5	19 38.1	7 06.8	5 15.6	16 57.0	12 59.2	3 02.6	29 00.2
24 W	22 14 51	5 13 44	14 54 43	22 23 58	23R39.1	26 47.4	21 13.4	20 15.1	7 26.0	5 20.6	17 00.9	12 57.3	3 03.0	28 58.8
25 Th	22 18 47	6 14 07	29 56 43	7♓31 49	23 38.8	28 32.2	22 22.3	20 52.2	7 45.4	5 25.3	17 05.0	12 55.4	3 03.3	28 57.3
26 F	22 22 44	7 14 28	15♓08 06	22 44 18	23 37.8	0♓17.9	23 31.4	21 29.2	8 05.0	5 29.9	17 09.2	12 53.5	3 03.5	28 55.8
27 Sa	22 26 40	8 14 47	0♈19 12	7♈51 36	23 36.2	2 04.7	24 40.5	22 06.1	8 24.7	5 34.4	17 13.4	12 51.6	3 03.7	28 54.3
28 Su	22 30 37	9 15 04	15 20 25	22 44 42	23 34.3	3 52.4	25 49.8	22 43.0	8 44.5	5 38.6	17 17.7	12 49.6	3 03.9	28 52.8

Astro Data

	Dy Hr Mn
♇ R	1 22:00
☽ 0N	2 20:24
♃∠♅	5 20:49
☿ D	8 4:36
♃✳♇	12 11:47
☽ 0S	16 19:29
♄ D	17 13:01
♅ R	18 6:54
☽ 0N	30 3:32
♃☌♆	1 6:49
☽ 0S	13 2:17
☽ 0N	26 13:45

Planet Ingress

		Dy Hr Mn
☿	♐R	2 23:36
♀	♐	7 1:00
☿	♑	14 2:16
♃	♐	14 8:49
☉	♒	20 17:13
♂	♐	23 1:34
⚳	♉	29 14:27
♀	♑	5 14:57
☿	♒	7 20:51
☉	♓	19 7:27
☿	♓	26 7:57

Last Aspect / ☽ Ingress (January)

Last Aspect Dy Hr Mn			☽ Ingress	Dy Hr Mn
1 0:07	♃	□	♓	1 4:08
3 6:03	☿	□	♈	3 6:26
5 7:20	☿	△	♉	5 10:00
7 14:36	♇	△	♊	7 15:08
9 21:34	♇	□	♋	9 22:09
12 6:46	♇	✳	♌	12 7:24
14 7:52	♂	□	♍	14 18:57
17 7:09	♇	☌	♎	17 7:53
19 18:08	☉	□	♏	19 20:04
22 4:31	♇	✳	♐	22 5:16
24 9:48	♇	□	♑	24 10:33
26 11:51	♇	△	♒	26 12:36
27 21:57	♀	✳	♓	28 13:01
30 12:45	♇	☍	♈	30 13:36

Last Aspect / ☽ Ingress (February)

Last Aspect Dy Hr Mn			☽ Ingress	Dy Hr Mn
1 7:51	♀	△	♉	1 15:49
3 19:31	♇	△	♊	3 20:34
6 2:56	♇	□	♋	6 4:07
8 12:47	♇	✳	♌	8 14:06
10 7:41	☉	☍	♍	11 1:58
13 13:16	♇	☌	♎	13 14:50
15 20:23	☉	△	♏	16 3:22
18 12:14	☉	□	♐	18 13:45
20 18:58	♇	□	♑	20 20:37
22 22:05	♇	△	♒	22 23:43
24 19:54	☿	☌	♓	25 0:05
26 21:47	♇	☍	♈	26 23:30
28 17:28	♀	□	♉	28 23:54

☽ Phases & Eclipses

Dy Hr Mn		
4 4:55	☽	13♈11
11 13:20	○	20♋40
19 18:08	☾	29♎01
26 22:55	●	6♒21
2 14:31	☽	13♉06
10 7:41	○	20♌55
10 7:45	•	T 1.308
18 12:14	☾	29♏12
25 9:49	●	6♓09
25 9:37:26	•	P 0.787

Astro Data

1 January 1971
Julian Day # 25933
SVP 5♓39'43"
GC 26♐26.1 ⚴ 6♓18.7
Eris 11♈40.0 ⚵ 16♉40.8
⚷ 5♈58.0 ⚶ 8♐38.2
☽ Mean ☊ 25♒56.0

1 February 1971
Julian Day # 25964
SVP 5♓39'38"
GC 26♐26.1 ⚴ 15♓30.5
Eris 11♈46.1 ⚵ 23♉43.8
⚷ 6♈47.4 ⚶ 24♐31.2
☽ Mean ☊ 24♒17.5

March 1971 LONGITUDE

Day	Sid.Time	☉	0 hr ☽	Noon ☽	True ☊	☿	♀	♂	⚳	♃	♄	♅	♆	♇
1 M	22 34 34	10♓15 19	0♉03 40	7♉16 42	23♒32.2	5♓41.2	26♑59.2	23♐19.9	9♉04.4	5♐42.7	17♉22.2	12♎47.6	3♐04.1	28♍51.3
2 Tu	22 38 30	11 15 32	14 23 23	21 23 29	23R 30.6	7 31.0	28 08.6	23 56.7	9 24.5	5 46.6	17 26.7	12R 45.5	3 04.2	28R 49.7
3 W	22 42 27	12 15 43	28 16 55	5♊03 44	23D 29.7	9 21.8	29 18.2	24 33.5	9 44.7	5 50.4	17 31.3	12 43.4	3 04.3	28 48.2
4 Th	22 46 23	13 15 52	11♊44 09	18 18 28	23 29.6	11 13.6	0♒27.9	25 10.3	10 05.0	5 53.9	17 36.0	12 41.3	3 04.4	28 46.6
5 F	22 50 20	14 15 59	24 47 01	1♋10 15	23 30.4	13 06.4	1 37.6	25 47.0	10 25.4	5 57.3	17 40.7	12 39.2	3R 04.4	28 45.1
6 Sa	22 54 16	15 16 04	7♋28 39	13 42 40	23 31.8	15 00.1	2 47.5	26 23.6	10 46.0	6 00.6	17 45.6	12 37.0	3 04.4	28 43.5
7 Su	22 58 13	16 16 07	19 52 48	25 59 32	23 33.5	16 54.8	3 57.4	27 00.3	11 06.6	6 03.6	17 50.5	12 34.8	3 04.3	28 41.9
8 M	23 02 10	17 16 07	2♌03 21	8♌04 42	23 35.0	18 50.3	5 07.4	27 36.9	11 27.4	6 06.5	17 55.5	12 32.5	3 04.3	28 40.3
9 Tu	23 06 06	18 16 06	14 03 58	20 01 36	23R 35.8	20 46.5	6 17.5	28 13.4	11 48.3	6 09.1	18 00.6	12 30.3	3 04.2	28 38.7
10 W	23 10 03	19 16 02	25 57 56	1♍53 18	23 35.6	22 43.5	7 27.7	28 49.9	12 09.3	6 11.6	18 05.7	12 28.0	3 04.0	28 37.1
11 Th	23 13 59	20 15 57	7♍48 02	13 42 24	23 34.0	24 41.1	8 37.9	29 26.3	12 30.3	6 14.0	18 11.0	12 25.6	3 03.8	28 35.5
12 F	23 17 56	21 15 49	19 36 41	25 31 08	23 30.9	26 39.1	9 48.3	0♑02.8	12 51.5	6 16.1	18 16.3	12 23.3	3 03.6	28 33.9
13 Sa	23 21 52	22 15 40	1♎25 59	7♎21 29	23 26.7	28 37.3	10 58.7	0 39.1	13 12.8	6 18.0	18 21.7	12 20.9	3 03.4	28 32.3
14 Su	23 25 49	23 15 28	13 17 51	19 15 20	23 21.4	0♈35.7	12 09.1	1 15.4	13 34.2	6 19.8	18 27.1	12 18.5	3 03.1	28 30.6
15 M	23 29 45	24 15 15	25 14 12	1♏14 42	23 15.8	2 33.9	13 19.7	1 51.7	13 55.7	6 21.4	18 32.7	12 16.1	3 02.8	28 29.0
16 Tu	23 33 42	25 15 00	7♏17 08	13 21 48	23 10.4	4 31.8	14 30.3	2 27.9	14 17.3	6 22.8	18 38.3	12 13.7	3 02.5	28 27.4
17 W	23 37 38	26 14 43	19 29 03	25 39 13	23 05.9	6 28.9	15 41.0	3 04.1	14 39.0	6 24.0	18 43.9	12 11.3	3 02.1	28 25.7
18 Th	23 41 35	27 14 25	1♐52 43	8♐09 56	23 02.6	8 25.0	16 51.8	3 40.2	15 00.8	6 25.1	18 49.7	12 08.8	3 01.7	28 24.1
19 F	23 45 32	28 14 05	14 31 16	20 57 10	23D 00.9	10 19.7	18 02.6	4 16.2	15 22.7	6 25.9	18 55.5	12 06.3	3 01.2	28 22.5
20 Sa	23 49 28	29 13 43	27 28 02	4♑04 16	23 00.8	12 12.7	19 13.5	4 52.2	15 44.7	6 26.6	19 01.3	12 03.8	3 00.8	28 20.8
21 Su	23 53 25	0♈13 19	10♑46 13	17 34 11	23 01.7	14 03.4	20 24.5	5 28.2	16 06.8	6 27.0	19 07.3	12 01.3	3 00.3	28 19.2
22 M	23 57 21	1 12 54	24 28 24	1♒29 00	23 03.2	15 51.5	21 35.5	6 04.1	16 28.9	6R 27.3	19 13.3	11 58.8	2 59.8	28 17.6
23 Tu	0 01 18	2 12 27	8♒35 58	15 49 08	23R 04.3	17 36.6	22 46.6	6 39.9	16 51.1	6 27.4	19 19.4	11 56.3	2 59.2	28 15.9
24 W	0 05 14	3 11 58	23 08 12	0♓32 39	23 04.3	19 18.1	23 57.7	7 15.6	17 13.5	6 27.3	19 25.5	11 53.7	2 58.6	28 14.3
25 Th	0 09 11	4 11 27	8♓01 46	15 34 40	23 02.5	20 55.6	25 08.8	7 51.3	17 35.9	6 27.0	19 31.7	11 51.2	2 58.0	28 12.6
26 F	0 13 07	5 10 54	23 10 17	0♈47 26	22 58.7	22 28.7	26 20.1	8 26.9	17 58.4	6 26.5	19 37.9	11 48.6	2 57.3	28 11.0
27 Sa	0 17 04	6 10 19	8♈24 49	16 01 05	22 53.1	23 57.1	27 31.3	9 02.4	18 20.9	6 25.9	19 44.2	11 46.0	2 56.6	28 09.4
28 Su	0 21 01	7 09 42	23 34 55	1♉05 07	22 46.4	25 20.3	28 42.6	9 37.9	18 43.6	6 25.0	19 50.6	11 43.4	2 55.9	28 07.8
29 M	0 24 57	8 09 03	8♉30 32	15 50 14	22 39.4	26 37.9	29 54.0	10 13.3	19 06.3	6 24.0	19 57.0	11 40.8	2 55.2	28 06.2
30 Tu	0 28 54	9 08 22	23 03 29	0♊09 45	22 33.1	27 49.8	1♓05.4	10 48.6	19 29.1	6 22.8	20 03.5	11 38.2	2 54.4	28 04.5
31 W	0 32 50	10 07 39	7♊08 44	14 00 18	22 28.3	28 55.5	2 16.8	11 23.8	19 52.0	6 21.3	20 10.0	11 35.7	2 53.6	28 03.0

April 1971 LONGITUDE

Day	Sid.Time	☉	0 hr ☽	Noon ☽	True ☊	☿	♀	♂	⚳	♃	♄	♅	♆	♇
1 Th	0 36 47	11♈06 53	20♊44 33	27♊21 40	22♒25.4	29♈54.9	3♓28.2	11♑59.0	20♉15.0	6♐19.7	20♉16.6	11♎33.1	2♐52.8	28♍01.4
2 F	0 40 43	12 06 05	3♋52 03	10♋16 08	22D 24.3	0♉47.8	4 39.7	12 34.0	20 38.0	6R 18.0	20 23.2	11R 30.5	2R 51.9	27R 59.8
3 Sa	0 44 40	13 05 15	16 34 27	22 47 37	22 24.7	1 33.9	5 51.3	13 09.0	21 01.1	6 16.0	20 29.9	11 27.9	2 51.1	27 58.2
4 Su	0 48 36	14 04 22	28 56 14	5♌00 57	22 25.9	2 13.2	7 02.9	13 43.9	21 24.2	6 13.8	20 36.6	11 25.3	2 50.2	27 56.6
5 M	0 52 33	15 03 27	11♌02 22	17 01 07	22R 26.8	2 45.6	8 14.5	14 18.7	21 47.4	6 11.5	20 43.4	11 22.7	2 49.2	27 55.1
6 Tu	0 56 30	16 02 29	22 57 48	28 52 58	22 26.7	3 11.0	9 26.1	14 53.4	22 10.7	6 09.0	20 50.2	11 20.1	2 48.3	27 53.5
7 W	1 00 26	17 01 30	4♍47 09	10♍40 49	22 24.8	3 29.5	10 37.8	15 28.1	22 34.1	6 06.3	20 57.1	11 17.5	2 47.3	27 52.0
8 Th	1 04 23	18 00 28	16 34 25	22 28 21	22 20.6	3 41.0	11 49.5	16 02.6	22 57.5	6 03.4	21 04.0	11 15.0	2 46.3	27 50.5
9 F	1 08 19	18 59 24	28 22 57	4♎18 31	22 13.8	3R 45.8	13 01.2	16 37.1	23 20.9	6 00.4	21 11.0	11 12.4	2 45.2	27 49.0
10 Sa	1 12 16	19 58 18	10♎15 19	16 13 36	22 04.9	3 43.9	14 13.0	17 11.4	23 44.4	5 57.2	21 18.0	11 09.8	2 44.1	27 47.5
11 Su	1 16 12	20 57 09	22 13 31	28 15 16	21 54.3	3 35.7	15 24.8	17 45.7	24 08.0	5 53.8	21 25.0	11 07.3	2 43.1	27 46.0
12 M	1 20 09	21 55 59	4♏18 59	10♏24 47	21 42.9	3 21.5	16 36.6	18 19.8	24 31.7	5 50.2	21 32.1	11 04.7	2 42.0	27 44.5
13 Tu	1 24 05	22 54 47	16 32 50	22 43 13	21 31.8	3 01.6	17 48.5	18 53.9	24 55.4	5 46.5	21 39.2	11 02.2	2 40.8	27 43.1
14 W	1 28 02	23 53 34	28 56 07	5♐11 40	21 22.0	2 36.5	19 00.4	19 27.9	25 19.1	5 42.6	21 46.3	10 59.7	2 39.7	27 41.6
15 Th	1 31 59	24 52 18	11♐30 03	17 51 28	21 14.3	2 06.9	20 12.3	20 01.7	25 42.9	5 38.5	21 53.5	10 57.2	2 38.5	27 40.2
16 F	1 35 55	25 51 01	24 16 10	0♑44 22	21 09.0	1 33.2	21 24.3	20 35.5	26 06.8	5 34.3	22 00.8	10 54.7	2 37.3	27 38.8
17 Sa	1 39 52	26 49 42	7♑16 22	13 52 26	21 06.3	0 56.3	22 36.3	21 09.1	26 30.7	5 29.9	22 08.0	10 52.3	2 36.1	27 37.4
18 Su	1 43 48	27 48 22	20 32 53	27 17 58	21D 05.5	0 16.8	23 48.3	21 42.6	26 54.7	5 25.4	22 15.3	10 49.8	2 34.8	27 36.0
19 M	1 47 45	28 46 59	4♒07 57	11♒03 02	21R 05.8	29♈35.5	25 00.4	22 16.0	27 18.7	5 20.7	22 22.6	10 47.4	2 33.6	27 34.7
20 Tu	1 51 41	29 45 35	18 03 21	25 08 54	21 06.0	28 53.3	26 12.4	22 49.3	27 42.7	5 15.8	22 30.0	10 45.0	2 32.3	27 33.3
21 W	1 55 38	0♉44 10	2♓19 38	9♓35 17	21 04.8	28 10.8	27 24.5	23 22.4	28 06.9	5 10.8	22 37.4	10 42.6	2 31.0	27 32.0
22 Th	1 59 34	1 42 42	16 55 28	24 19 36	21 01.3	27 29.0	28 36.6	23 55.4	28 31.0	5 05.6	22 44.8	10 40.2	2 29.7	27 30.7
23 F	2 03 31	2 41 13	1♈46 57	9♈16 35	20 55.2	26 48.4	29 48.8	24 28.3	28 55.2	5 00.3	22 52.2	10 37.8	2 28.3	27 29.4
24 Sa	2 07 28	3 39 43	16 47 28	24 18 25	20 46.5	26 09.9	1♈00.9	25 01.0	29 19.5	4 54.9	22 59.7	10 35.5	2 27.0	27 28.2
25 Su	2 11 24	4 38 10	1♉48 14	9♉15 42	20 36.1	25 34.0	2 13.1	25 33.6	29 43.8	4 49.3	23 07.2	10 33.2	2 25.6	27 26.9
26 M	2 15 21	5 36 36	16 39 40	23 59 03	20 25.1	25 01.2	3 25.3	26 06.0	0♊08.1	4 43.6	23 14.7	10 30.9	2 24.2	27 25.7
27 Tu	2 19 17	6 34 59	1♊12 57	8♊20 39	20 14.8	24 32.1	4 37.5	26 38.2	0 32.5	4 37.8	23 22.2	10 28.7	2 22.8	27 24.5
28 W	2 23 14	7 33 21	15 21 38	22 15 32	20 06.3	24 06.9	5 49.8	27 10.3	0 56.9	4 31.8	23 29.8	10 26.4	2 21.4	27 23.4
29 Th	2 27 10	8 31 41	29 02 16	5♋41 52	20 00.2	23 46.0	7 02.0	27 42.3	1 21.4	4 25.7	23 37.4	10 24.2	2 19.9	27 22.2
30 F	2 31 07	9 29 59	12♋14 34	18 40 43	19 56.6	23 29.7	8 14.3	28 14.1	1 45.9	4 19.5	23 45.0	10 22.1	2 18.5	27 21.1

Astro Data

	Dy Hr Mn
♆ R	5 18:08
☽ 0S	12 8:41
☿ 0N	14 23:45
☉ 0N	21 6:38
♃ R	23 11:33
☽ 0N	26 1:05
☽ 0S	8 14:45
☿ R	9 17:11
☽ 0N	22 10:58
♀ 0N	26 16:54

Planet Ingress

	Dy Hr Mn
♀ ♒	4 2:24
♂ ♑	12 10:11
☿ ♈	14 4:46
☉ ♈	21 6:38
♀ ♓	29 14:02
☿ ♉	1 14:11
☿ ♈R	18 21:52
☉ ♉	20 17:54
♀ ♈	23 15:44
⚳ ♊	26 4:00

Last Aspect / ☽ Ingress

Last Aspect Dy Hr Mn		☽ Ingress Dy Hr Mn
3 0:56 ♇ △	♊	3 3:01
5 7:27 ♇ □	♋	5 9:47
7 17:20 ♇ ⚹	♌	7 19:55
10 5:28 ♂ △	♍	10 8:10
12 18:10 ♇ ☌	♎	12 21:06
13 22:03 ♅ ☌	♏	15 9:31
17 17:21 ♇ ⚹	♐	17 20:23
20 2:30 ☉ □	♑	20 4:37
22 6:34 ♇ △	♒	22 9:29
24 0:25 ♀ ☌	♓	24 11:07
26 7:54 ♇ ☍	♈	26 10:45
28 7:52 ♀ ⚹	♉	28 10:15
30 8:28 ♇ △	♊	30 11:43

Last Aspect / ☽ Ingress

Last Aspect Dy Hr Mn		☽ Ingress Dy Hr Mn
1 13:13 ♇ □	♋	1 16:51
3 22:05 ♇ ⚹	♌	4 2:05
5 19:33 ♄ □	♍	6 14:16
8 22:53 ♇ ☌	♎	9 3:17
10 20:10 ☉ ☍	♏	11 15:28
13 21:38 ♇ ⚹	♐	14 2:03
16 6:17 ♇ □	♑	16 10:38
18 12:58 ☉ □	♒	18 16:46
20 17:58 ☿ ⚹	♓	20 20:08
22 19:30 ♀ ☌	♈	22 21:08
24 14:51 ☿ ☌	♉	24 21:06
26 17:41 ♇ △	♊	26 21:58
28 21:03 ♇ □	♋	29 1:43

☽ Phases & Eclipses

Dy Hr Mn	
4 2:01	☽ 12♊51
12 2:34	○ 20♍52
20 2:30	☾ 28♐50
26 19:23	● 5♈29
2 15:46	☽ 12♋15
10 20:10	○ 20♎18
18 12:58	☾ 27♑51
25 4:02	● 4♉19

Astro Data

1 March 1971
Julian Day # 25992
SVP 5♓39'34"
GC 26♐26.2 ⚴ 25♓00.0
Eris 11♈59.5 ⚵ 4♊24.8
⚷ 8♈05.7 ⚶ 7♑57.7
☽ Mean ☊ 22♒48.5

1 April 1971
Julian Day # 26023
SVP 5♓39'30"
GC 26♐26.3 ⚴ 6♈15.4
Eris 12♈19.6 ⚵ 18♊34.8
⚷ 9♈51.7 ⚶ 21♑05.9
☽ Mean ☊ 21♒10.0

LONGITUDE — May 1971

Day	Sid.Time	☉	0 hr ☽	Noon ☽	True ☊	☿	♀	♂	⚳	♃	♄	♅	♆	♇
1 Sa	2 35 03	10♉28 14	25♋00 47	1♌15 19	19♒55.2	23♈18.0	9♈26.6	28♑45.7	2♊10.5	4♐13.2	23♉52.6	10♎19.9	2♐17.0	27♍20.0
2 Su	2 39 00	11 26 28	7♌24 56	13 30 17	19R 54.9	23D 11.1	10 38.9	29 17.1	2 35.0	4R 06.7	24 00.2	10R 17.8	2R 15.5	27R 18.9
3 M	2 42 57	12 24 39	19 32 03	25 30 56	19 54.9	23 09.0	11 51.2	29 48.4	2 59.7	4 00.2	24 07.9	10 15.8	2 14.0	27 17.9
4 Tu	2 46 53	13 22 49	1♍27 35	7♍22 41	19 53.9	23 11.8	13 03.5	0♒19.5	3 24.3	3 53.6	24 15.5	10 13.7	2 12.5	27 16.8
5 W	2 50 50	14 20 56	13 16 51	19 10 43	19 51.1	23 19.2	14 15.8	0 50.4	3 49.0	3 46.8	24 23.2	10 11.7	2 11.0	27 15.8
6 Th	2 54 46	15 19 02	25 04 48	0♎59 39	19 45.7	23 31.4	15 28.2	1 21.1	4 13.7	3 40.0	24 30.9	10 09.7	2 09.5	27 14.9
7 F	2 58 43	16 17 06	6♎55 42	12 53 22	19 37.6	23 48.2	16 40.5	1 51.6	4 38.4	3 33.1	24 38.6	10 07.8	2 07.9	27 13.9
8 Sa	3 02 39	17 15 08	18 53 00	24 54 52	19 27.0	24 09.4	17 52.9	2 22.0	5 03.2	3 26.1	24 46.3	10 05.9	2 06.4	27 13.0
9 Su	3 06 36	18 13 08	0♏59 12	7♏06 12	19 14.4	24 35.0	19 05.3	2 52.1	5 28.0	3 19.0	24 54.0	10 04.0	2 04.8	27 12.1
10 M	3 10 32	19 11 07	13 15 58	19 28 35	19 00.9	25 04.8	20 17.7	3 22.1	5 52.9	3 11.9	25 01.8	10 02.2	2 03.2	27 11.2
11 Tu	3 14 29	20 09 04	25 44 05	2♐02 29	18 47.7	25 38.6	21 30.1	3 51.8	6 17.7	3 04.7	25 09.5	10 00.4	2 01.7	27 10.4
12 W	3 18 26	21 06 59	8♐23 45	14 47 53	18 35.9	26 16.5	22 42.6	4 21.3	6 42.6	2 57.4	25 17.3	9 58.6	2 00.1	27 09.5
13 Th	3 22 22	22 04 53	21 14 50	27 44 37	18 26.4	26 58.1	23 55.0	4 50.6	7 07.6	2 50.1	25 25.0	9 56.9	1 58.5	27 08.8
14 F	3 26 19	23 02 46	4♑17 13	10♑52 39	18 19.7	27 43.4	25 07.5	5 19.7	7 32.5	2 42.7	25 32.8	9 55.3	1 56.9	27 08.0
15 Sa	3 30 15	24 00 38	17 30 59	24 12 18	18 15.9	28 32.2	26 20.0	5 48.5	7 57.5	2 35.3	25 40.5	9 53.6	1 55.3	27 07.3
16 Su	3 34 12	24 58 28	0♒56 40	7♒44 14	18D 14.4	29 24.4	27 32.5	6 17.1	8 22.5	2 27.8	25 48.3	9 52.0	1 53.7	27 06.6
17 M	3 38 08	25 56 17	14 35 06	21 29 23	18R 14.2	0♉19.9	28 45.0	6 45.4	8 47.5	2 20.3	25 56.1	9 50.5	1 52.1	27 05.9
18 Tu	3 42 05	26 54 05	28 27 09	5♓28 28	18 14.1	1 18.7	29 57.6	7 13.5	9 12.6	2 12.7	26 03.8	9 49.0	1 50.5	27 05.2
19 W	3 46 01	27 51 52	12♓33 17	19 41 28	18 12.8	2 20.5	1♉10.1	7 41.4	9 37.7	2 05.1	26 11.6	9 47.5	1 48.9	27 04.6
20 Th	3 49 58	28 49 38	26 52 50	4♈07 00	18 09.3	3 25.3	2 22.7	8 08.9	10 02.8	1 57.5	26 19.3	9 46.1	1 47.2	27 04.0
21 F	3 53 55	29 47 22	11♈23 32	18 41 49	18 03.2	4 33.0	3 35.3	8 36.2	10 27.9	1 49.9	26 27.1	9 44.7	1 45.6	27 03.5
22 Sa	3 57 51	0♊45 06	26 01 09	3♉20 41	17 54.6	5 43.6	4 47.9	9 03.1	10 53.1	1 42.2	26 34.8	9 43.4	1 44.0	27 02.9
23 Su	4 01 48	1 42 48	10♉39 33	17 56 48	17 44.2	6 56.9	6 00.5	9 29.8	11 18.3	1 34.6	26 42.6	9 42.1	1 42.4	27 02.4
24 M	4 05 44	2 40 29	25 11 32	2♊22 49	17 33.1	8 13.0	7 13.2	9 56.2	11 43.5	1 26.9	26 50.3	9 40.8	1 40.7	27 02.0
25 Tu	4 09 41	3 38 09	9♊29 52	16 32 00	17 22.5	9 31.7	8 25.8	10 22.2	12 08.7	1 19.3	26 58.1	9 39.7	1 39.1	27 01.6
26 W	4 13 37	4 35 48	23 28 37	0♋19 20	17 13.6	10 53.0	9 38.5	10 47.9	12 33.9	1 11.7	27 05.8	9 38.5	1 37.5	27 01.2
27 Th	4 17 34	5 33 26	7♋03 54	13 42 13	17 07.1	12 16.9	10 51.1	11 13.3	12 59.2	1 04.0	27 13.5	9 37.4	1 35.9	27 00.8
28 F	4 21 30	6 31 02	20 14 22	26 40 31	17 03.1	13 43.3	12 03.8	11 38.4	13 24.5	0 56.4	27 21.2	9 36.4	1 34.3	27 00.4
29 Sa	4 25 27	7 28 36	3♌01 01	9♌16 15	17D 01.4	15 12.3	13 16.5	12 03.1	13 49.8	0 48.9	27 28.9	9 35.4	1 32.6	27 00.1
30 Su	4 29 24	8 26 09	15 26 45	21 33 04	17 01.2	16 43.8	14 29.2	12 27.5	14 15.1	0 41.3	27 36.6	9 34.4	1 31.0	26 59.9
31 M	4 33 20	9 23 41	27 35 49	3♍35 38	17R 01.6	18 17.8	15 41.9	12 51.5	14 40.4	0 33.8	27 44.3	9 33.5	1 29.4	26 59.6

LONGITUDE — June 1971

Day	Sid.Time	☉	0 hr ☽	Noon ☽	True ☊	☿	♀	♂	⚳	♃	♄	♅	♆	♇
1 Tu	4 37 17	10♊21 12	9♍33 13	15♍29 12	17♒01.6	19♉54.2	16♉54.6	13♒15.1	15♊05.7	0♐26.4	27♉51.9	9♎32.6	1♐27.8	26♍59.4
2 W	4 41 13	11 18 41	21 24 17	27 19 06	17R 00.2	21 33.2	18 07.3	13 38.4	15 31.1	0R 19.0	27 59.6	9R 31.8	1R 26.2	26R 59.2
3 Th	4 45 10	12 16 08	3♎14 17	9♎10 26	16 56.8	23 14.6	19 20.0	14 01.3	15 56.4	0 11.6	28 07.2	9 31.1	1 24.6	26 59.1
4 F	4 49 06	13 13 35	15 08 07	21 07 50	16 51.1	24 58.4	20 32.8	14 23.7	16 21.8	0 04.3	28 14.8	9 30.4	1 23.0	26 58.9
5 Sa	4 53 03	14 11 00	27 10 01	3♏15 06	16 43.2	26 44.7	21 45.6	14 45.8	16 47.2	29♏57.1	28 22.4	9 29.7	1 21.5	26 58.9
6 Su	4 56 59	15 08 25	9♏23 23	15 35 09	16 33.5	28 33.4	22 58.3	15 07.5	17 12.6	29 49.9	28 29.9	9 29.1	1 19.9	26 58.8
7 M	5 00 56	16 05 48	21 50 34	28 09 45	16 23.0	0♊24.5	24 11.1	15 28.8	17 38.0	29 42.8	28 37.5	9 28.6	1 18.3	26D 58.8
8 Tu	5 04 53	17 03 11	4♐32 45	10♐59 32	16 12.7	2 18.0	25 23.9	15 49.6	18 03.4	29 35.8	28 45.0	9 28.1	1 16.8	26 58.8
9 W	5 08 49	18 00 33	17 30 03	24 04 08	16 03.5	4 13.8	26 36.7	16 10.0	18 28.8	29 28.8	28 52.5	9 27.6	1 15.2	26 58.8
10 Th	5 12 46	18 57 53	0♑41 38	7♑22 21	15 56.2	6 11.8	27 49.6	16 30.0	18 54.2	29 22.0	29 00.0	9 27.2	1 13.7	26 58.9
11 F	5 16 42	19 55 14	14 06 03	20 52 33	15 51.2	8 12.0	29 02.4	16 49.5	19 19.7	29 15.2	29 07.4	9 26.9	1 12.2	26 59.0
12 Sa	5 20 39	20 52 33	27 41 36	4♒33 02	15D 48.8	10 14.2	0♊15.3	17 08.5	19 45.1	29 08.5	29 14.8	9 26.6	1 10.7	26 59.2
13 Su	5 24 35	21 49 52	11♒26 39	18 22 18	15 48.2	12 18.3	1 28.2	17 27.0	20 10.6	29 01.9	29 22.2	9 26.4	1 09.2	26 59.3
14 M	5 28 32	22 47 11	25 19 52	2♓19 13	15 48.9	14 24.2	2 41.1	17 45.0	20 36.1	28 55.5	29 29.6	9 26.2	1 07.7	26 59.5
15 Tu	5 32 28	23 44 29	9♓20 15	16 22 50	15R 49.8	16 31.6	3 54.0	18 02.5	21 01.5	28 49.1	29 36.9	9 26.0	1 06.2	26 59.8
16 W	5 36 25	24 41 47	23 26 51	0♈32 09	15 49.8	18 40.4	5 07.0	18 19.4	21 27.0	28 42.8	29 44.2	9 25.9	1 04.8	27 00.0
17 Th	5 40 22	25 39 04	7♈38 32	14 45 45	15 48.3	20 50.3	6 19.9	18 35.9	21 52.5	28 36.7	29 51.5	9D 25.9	1 03.3	27 00.3
18 F	5 44 18	26 36 21	21 53 29	29 01 24	15 44.8	23 01.1	7 32.9	18 51.7	22 18.0	28 30.6	29 58.8	9 25.9	1 01.9	27 00.7
19 Sa	5 48 15	27 33 38	6♉09 02	13♉15 57	15 39.3	25 12.4	8 45.9	19 07.0	22 43.5	28 24.7	0♊06.0	9 26.0	1 00.5	27 01.0
20 Su	5 52 11	28 30 55	20 21 35	27 25 23	15 32.5	27 24.1	9 58.9	19 21.7	23 09.0	28 18.9	0 13.1	9 26.1	0 59.1	27 01.4
21 M	5 56 08	29 28 12	4♊26 49	11♊25 18	15 25.1	29 35.8	11 11.9	19 35.8	23 34.5	28 13.3	0 20.3	9 26.3	0 57.7	27 01.9
22 Tu	6 00 04	0♋25 28	18 20 19	25 11 26	15 18.0	1♋47.3	12 25.0	19 49.3	24 00.0	28 07.8	0 27.4	9 26.5	0 56.3	27 02.3
23 W	6 04 01	1 22 44	1♋58 13	8♋40 23	15 12.1	3 58.3	13 38.1	20 02.2	24 25.6	28 02.4	0 34.5	9 26.8	0 54.9	27 02.8
24 Th	6 07 58	2 19 59	15 17 43	21 50 06	15 07.9	6 08.5	14 51.1	20 14.4	24 51.1	27 57.1	0 41.5	9 27.2	0 53.6	27 03.4
25 F	6 11 54	3 17 14	28 17 31	4♌40 04	15D 05.6	8 17.8	16 04.2	20 26.0	25 16.6	27 52.0	0 48.5	9 27.6	0 52.3	27 03.9
26 Sa	6 15 51	4 14 29	10♌57 57	17 11 25	15 05.1	10 25.8	17 17.3	20 37.0	25 42.1	27 47.1	0 55.4	9 28.0	0 51.0	27 04.5
27 Su	6 19 47	5 11 43	23 20 50	29 26 37	15 05.9	12 32.5	18 30.5	20 47.3	26 07.6	27 42.3	1 02.3	9 28.5	0 49.7	27 05.1
28 M	6 23 44	6 08 56	5♍29 16	11♍29 17	15 07.4	14 37.7	19 43.6	20 56.9	26 33.1	27 37.6	1 09.2	9 29.1	0 48.5	27 05.8
29 Tu	6 27 40	7 06 09	17 27 14	23 23 45	15 08.9	16 41.3	20 56.8	21 05.8	26 58.6	27 33.1	1 16.0	9 29.7	0 47.2	27 06.5
30 W	6 31 37	8 03 21	29 19 24	5♎14 50	15R 09.7	18 43.1	22 09.9	21 14.1	27 24.1	27 28.8	1 22.8	9 30.3	0 46.0	27 07.2

Astro Data

	Dy Hr Mn
☿ D	3 10:25
☽ 0S	5 20:51
♄⚼♅	10 13:02
☽ 0N	19 18:01
♃☌♆	22 4:57
♄△♇	25 22:15
☽ 0S	2 3:23
♇ D	7 15:16
♃☍♄	12 1:14
☽ 0N	15 22:58
♅ D	17 14:51
♄☍♆	25 23:04
☽ 0S	29 10:31

Planet Ingress

		Dy Hr Mn
♂	♒	3 20:57
☿	♉	17 3:32
♀	♉	18 12:48
☉	♊	21 17:15
♃	♏R	5 2:12
☿	♊	7 6:45
♀	♊	12 6:58
♄	♊	18 16:09
☿	♋	21 16:25
☉	♋	22 1:20

Last Aspect / ☽ Ingress

Last Aspect Dy Hr Mn		☽ Ingress	Dy Hr Mn
1 6:58	♂ ☍	♌	1 9:34
3 9:11	♄ □	♍	3 21:03
6 4:25	♇ ☌	♎	6 9:59
8 10:27	☿ ☍	♏	8 22:03
11 2:45	♇ ⚹	♐	11 8:08
13 10:54	♇ □	♑	13 16:09
15 20:15	☿ □	♒	15 22:19
18 1:42	♀ ⚹	♓	18 2:39
20 2:37	☉ ⚹	♈	20 5:11
20 21:19	♅ ☍	♉	22 6:31
24 3:04	♇ △	♊	24 8:01
26 6:11	♇ □	♋	26 11:26
28 13:17	♄ ⚹	♌	28 18:16
31 0:09	♄ □	♍	31 4:48

Last Aspect / ☽ Ingress

Last Aspect Dy Hr Mn		☽ Ingress	Dy Hr Mn
2 13:23	♄ △	♎	2 17:26
3 22:05	♂ △	♏	5 5:36
7 14:54	♃ ☌	♐	7 15:28
9 17:17	♇ □	♑	9 22:45
12 3:46	♀ △	♒	12 4:03
14 7:07	♄ □	♓	14 8:01
16 10:38	♄ ⚹	♈	16 11:06
18 7:38	☉ ⚹	♉	18 13:39
20 13:31	♃ ☍	♊	20 16:24
22 15:16	♇ □	♋	22 20:30
24 23:17	♃ △	♌	25 3:12
27 8:35	♃ □	♍	27 13:06
29 20:22	♃ ⚹	♎	30 1:22

☽ Phases & Eclipses

Dy Hr Mn	
2 7:34	☽ 11♌16
10 11:24	○ 19♏10
17 20:15	☾ 26♒16
24 12:32	● 2♊42
1 0:42	☽ 9♍54
9 0:04	○ 17♐32
16 1:24	☾ 24♓16
22 21:57	● 0♋49
30 18:11	☽ 8♎18

Astro Data

1 May 1971
Julian Day # 26053
SVP 5♓39'26"
GC 26♐26.3 ⚴ 17♈31.1
Eris 12♈39.3 ⚵ 3♋15.1
⚷ 11♈33.7 ⚶ 0♒54.4
☽ Mean ☊ 19♒34.7

1 June 1971
Julian Day # 26084
SVP 5♓39'21"
GC 26♐26.4 ⚴ 29♈13.2
Eris 12♈55.2 ⚵ 18♋37.9
⚷ 12♈58.5 ⚶ 6♒04.0
☽ Mean ☊ 17♒56.2

July 1971 — LONGITUDE

Day	Sid.Time	☉	0 hr ☽	Noon ☽	True ☊	☿	♀	♂	⚳	♃	♄	♅	♆	♇
1 Th	6 35 33	9♋00 33	11♎10 41	17♎07 33	15♒09.4	20♋43.2	23♊23.1	21♒21.6	27♊49.6	27♏24.6	1♊29.5	9♎31.1	0♐44.8	27♍07.9
2 F	6 39 30	9 57 45	23 06 03	29 06 45	15R 07.6	22 41.3	24 36.3	21 28.5	28 15.1	27R 20.6	1 36.2	9 31.8	0R 43.6	27 08.7
3 Sa	6 43 27	10 54 57	5♏10 12	11♏16 55	15 04.4	24 37.5	25 49.6	21 34.7	28 40.6	27 16.7	1 42.8	9 32.6	0 42.5	27 09.5
4 Su	6 47 23	11 52 08	17 27 19	23 41 49	15 00.1	26 31.7	27 02.8	21 40.1	29 06.1	27 13.0	1 49.4	9 33.5	0 41.3	27 10.4
5 M	6 51 20	12 49 19	0♐00 44	6♐24 17	14 55.1	28 24.0	28 16.1	21 44.8	29 31.5	27 09.5	1 56.0	9 34.4	0 40.2	27 11.2
6 Tu	6 55 16	13 46 30	12 52 38	19 25 50	14 50.1	0♌14.2	29 29.4	21 48.8	29 57.0	27 06.2	2 02.4	9 35.4	0 39.2	27 12.1
7 W	6 59 13	14 43 40	26 03 53	2♑46 39	14 45.6	2 02.4	0♋42.7	21 52.0	0♋22.5	27 03.0	2 08.9	9 36.4	0 38.1	27 13.1
8 Th	7 03 09	15 40 51	9♑33 55	16 25 25	14 42.2	3 48.6	1 56.0	21 54.5	0 47.9	27 00.0	2 15.2	9 37.5	0 37.1	27 14.0
9 F	7 07 06	16 38 02	23 20 47	0♒19 37	14 40.1	5 32.8	3 09.3	21 56.2	1 13.3	26 57.1	2 21.6	9 38.6	0 36.1	27 15.0
10 Sa	7 11 02	17 35 13	7♒21 27	14 25 49	14D 39.5	7 14.9	4 22.7	21R 57.2	1 38.8	26 54.4	2 27.8	9 39.8	0 35.1	27 16.0
11 Su	7 14 59	18 32 24	21 32 12	28 40 06	14 40.0	8 55.1	5 36.1	21 57.4	2 04.2	26 51.9	2 34.1	9 41.0	0 34.1	27 17.1
12 M	7 18 56	19 29 36	5♓49 04	12♓58 37	14 41.2	10 33.2	6 49.5	21 56.9	2 29.6	26 49.6	2 40.2	9 42.3	0 33.2	27 18.2
13 Tu	7 22 52	20 26 48	20 08 20	27 17 49	14 42.6	12 09.3	8 02.9	21 55.5	2 55.0	26 47.5	2 46.3	9 43.6	0 32.2	27 19.3
14 W	7 26 49	21 24 01	4♈26 43	11♈34 41	14R 43.6	13 43.3	9 16.3	21 53.4	3 20.4	26 45.5	2 52.3	9 45.0	0 31.4	27 20.4
15 Th	7 30 45	22 21 14	18 41 26	25 46 41	14 43.8	15 15.4	10 29.8	21 50.5	3 45.8	26 43.7	2 58.3	9 46.4	0 30.5	27 21.6
16 F	7 34 42	23 18 28	2♉50 11	9♉51 42	14 43.1	16 45.3	11 43.3	21 46.8	4 11.2	26 42.1	3 04.2	9 47.9	0 29.7	27 22.8
17 Sa	7 38 38	24 15 43	16 51 00	23 47 53	14 41.4	18 13.2	12 56.8	21 42.4	4 36.5	26 40.7	3 10.1	9 49.4	0 28.9	27 24.0
18 Su	7 42 35	25 12 58	0♊42 07	7♊33 31	14 39.1	19 39.1	14 10.4	21 37.2	5 01.9	26 39.4	3 15.9	9 51.0	0 28.1	27 25.2
19 M	7 46 31	26 10 14	14 21 53	21 07 02	14 36.5	21 02.8	15 24.0	21 31.3	5 27.2	26 38.4	3 21.6	9 52.6	0 27.3	27 26.5
20 Tu	7 50 28	27 07 31	27 48 48	4♋27 04	14 34.1	22 24.4	16 37.6	21 24.6	5 52.5	26 37.5	3 27.3	9 54.3	0 26.6	27 27.8
21 W	7 54 25	28 04 49	11♋01 41	17 32 35	14 32.1	23 43.8	17 51.2	21 17.1	6 17.8	26 36.8	3 32.9	9 56.0	0 25.9	27 29.1
22 Th	7 58 21	29 02 06	23 59 43	0♌23 05	14 30.9	25 00.9	19 04.8	21 09.0	6 43.1	26 36.3	3 38.4	9 57.8	0 25.2	27 30.5
23 F	8 02 18	29 59 25	6♌42 43	12 58 44	14D 30.4	26 15.8	20 18.5	21 00.2	7 08.4	26 36.0	3 43.9	9 59.6	0 24.6	27 31.9
24 Sa	8 06 14	0♌56 44	19 11 15	25 20 27	14 30.6	27 28.3	21 32.2	20 50.7	7 33.6	26D 35.8	3 49.3	10 01.4	0 24.0	27 33.3
25 Su	8 10 11	1 54 03	1♍26 36	7♍29 59	14 31.4	28 38.5	22 45.9	20 40.6	7 58.8	26 35.9	3 54.6	10 03.3	0 23.4	27 34.7
26 M	8 14 07	2 51 23	13 30 56	19 29 50	14 32.5	29 46.1	23 59.6	20 29.8	8 24.0	26 36.1	3 59.8	10 05.3	0 22.9	27 36.2
27 Tu	8 18 04	3 48 43	25 27 07	1♎23 15	14 33.6	0♍51.1	25 13.3	20 18.5	8 49.2	26 36.5	4 05.0	10 07.3	0 22.3	27 37.6
28 W	8 22 00	4 46 04	7♎18 44	13 14 04	14 34.5	1 53.5	26 27.1	20 06.6	9 14.4	26 37.1	4 10.1	10 09.3	0 21.9	27 39.1
29 Th	8 25 57	5 43 25	19 09 49	25 06 33	14R 35.0	2 53.1	27 40.9	19 54.1	9 39.5	26 37.8	4 15.1	10 11.4	0 21.4	27 40.7
30 F	8 29 54	6 40 47	1♏04 50	7♏05 16	14 35.2	3 49.8	28 54.7	19 41.2	10 04.6	26 38.8	4 20.1	10 13.5	0 21.0	27 42.2
31 Sa	8 33 50	7 38 09	13 08 24	19 14 49	14 35.0	4 43.5	0♌08.5	19 27.8	10 29.7	26 39.9	4 24.9	10 15.7	0 20.6	27 43.8

August 1971 — LONGITUDE

Day	Sid.Time	☉	0 hr ☽	Noon ☽	True ☊	☿	♀	♂	⚳	♃	♄	♅	♆	♇
1 Su	8 37 47	8♌35 32	25♏25 02	1♐39 34	14♒34.6	5♍34.1	1♌22.3	19♒14.0	10♋54.8	26♏41.2	4♊29.7	10♎17.9	0♐20.2	27♍45.4
2 M	8 41 43	9 32 55	7♐58 53	14 23 22	14R 34.1	6 21.3	2 36.2	18R 59.8	11 19.8	26 42.7	4 34.4	10 20.2	0R 19.9	27 47.0
3 Tu	8 45 40	10 30 20	20 53 21	27 29 04	14 33.5	7 05.1	3 50.0	18 45.2	11 44.8	26 44.4	4 39.1	10 22.5	0 19.6	27 48.7
4 W	8 49 36	11 27 45	4♑10 39	10♑58 08	14 33.1	7 45.2	5 03.9	18 30.4	12 09.8	26 46.3	4 43.6	10 24.8	0 19.3	27 50.4
5 Th	8 53 33	12 25 11	17 51 26	24 50 20	14 32.9	8 21.6	6 17.9	18 15.3	12 34.7	26 48.3	4 48.1	10 27.2	0 19.1	27 52.1
6 F	8 57 30	13 22 37	1♒54 28	9♒03 23	14D 32.8	8 53.9	7 31.8	17 59.9	12 59.6	26 50.5	4 52.5	10 29.6	0 18.8	27 53.8
7 Sa	9 01 26	14 20 05	16 16 30	23 33 07	14R 32.8	9 22.1	8 45.7	17 44.3	13 24.5	26 52.9	4 56.8	10 32.1	0 18.7	27 55.5
8 Su	9 05 23	15 17 33	0♓52 29	8♓13 44	14 32.8	9 45.8	9 59.7	17 28.6	13 49.4	26 55.5	5 01.0	10 34.6	0 18.5	27 57.3
9 M	9 09 19	16 15 03	15 36 03	22 58 34	14 32.7	10 05.0	11 13.7	17 12.8	14 14.2	26 58.2	5 05.2	10 37.2	0 18.4	27 59.0
10 Tu	9 13 16	17 12 34	0♈20 26	7♈40 52	14 32.5	10 19.4	12 27.7	16 56.9	14 39.0	27 01.1	5 09.2	10 39.7	0 18.3	28 00.8
11 W	9 17 12	18 10 06	14 59 10	22 14 42	14 32.2	10 28.8	13 41.8	16 41.0	15 03.8	27 04.2	5 13.2	10 42.4	0 18.3	28 02.6
12 Th	9 21 09	19 07 40	29 26 58	6♉35 31	14D 31.9	10R 33.1	14 55.9	16 25.1	15 28.5	27 07.4	5 17.1	10 45.0	0D 18.2	28 04.5
13 F	9 25 05	20 05 16	13♉40 03	20 40 22	14 31.8	10 32.0	16 09.9	16 09.3	15 53.2	27 10.9	5 20.9	10 47.7	0 18.2	28 06.3
14 Sa	9 29 02	21 02 52	27 36 19	4♊27 53	14 32.0	10 25.5	17 24.1	15 53.5	16 17.9	27 14.4	5 24.6	10 50.4	0 18.3	28 08.2
15 Su	9 32 58	22 00 31	11♊15 03	17 57 55	14 32.5	10 13.4	18 38.2	15 38.0	16 42.5	27 18.2	5 28.2	10 53.2	0 18.4	28 10.1
16 M	9 36 55	22 58 11	24 36 35	1♋11 11	14 33.2	9 55.7	19 52.4	15 22.6	17 07.1	27 22.1	5 31.7	10 56.0	0 18.5	28 12.0
17 Tu	9 40 52	23 55 52	7♋41 55	14 08 55	14 34.0	9 32.6	21 06.5	15 07.5	17 31.6	27 26.2	5 35.1	10 58.9	0 18.6	28 13.9
18 W	9 44 48	24 53 35	20 32 23	26 52 30	14 34.8	9 03.9	22 20.7	14 52.7	17 56.2	27 30.5	5 38.5	11 01.7	0 18.8	28 15.9
19 Th	9 48 45	25 51 20	3♌09 26	9♌23 23	14R 35.2	8 30.1	23 35.0	14 38.3	18 20.6	27 34.9	5 41.7	11 04.6	0 19.0	28 17.9
20 F	9 52 41	26 49 06	15 34 32	21 43 02	14 35.2	7 51.4	24 49.2	14 24.2	18 45.0	27 39.5	5 44.9	11 07.6	0 19.2	28 19.8
21 Sa	9 56 38	27 46 53	27 49 06	3♍52 55	14 34.5	7 08.2	26 03.5	14 10.6	19 09.4	27 44.3	5 47.9	11 10.6	0 19.5	28 21.8
22 Su	10 00 34	28 44 41	9♍54 42	15 54 40	14 33.1	6 21.1	27 17.7	13 57.4	19 33.8	27 49.2	5 50.9	11 13.6	0 19.8	28 23.8
23 M	10 04 31	29 42 31	21 53 03	27 50 08	14 31.0	5 30.9	28 32.0	13 44.8	19 58.1	27 54.2	5 53.7	11 16.6	0 20.2	28 25.9
24 Tu	10 08 27	0♍40 22	3♎46 12	9♎41 35	14 28.6	4 38.4	29 46.3	13 32.7	20 22.3	27 59.5	5 56.5	11 19.7	0 20.5	28 27.9
25 W	10 12 24	1 38 14	15 36 37	21 31 42	14 26.0	3 44.5	1♍00.6	13 21.2	20 46.5	28 04.8	5 59.1	11 22.8	0 20.9	28 29.9
26 Th	10 16 21	2 36 08	27 27 15	3♏23 43	14 23.7	2 50.2	2 15.0	13 10.3	21 10.6	28 10.4	6 01.7	11 25.9	0 21.4	28 32.0
27 F	10 20 17	3 34 03	9♏21 35	15 21 20	14 21.9	1 56.7	3 29.3	13 00.0	21 34.7	28 16.1	6 04.1	11 29.1	0 21.8	28 34.1
28 Sa	10 24 14	4 32 00	21 23 30	27 28 39	14D 20.9	1 05.2	4 43.7	12 50.4	21 58.7	28 21.9	6 06.5	11 32.2	0 22.3	28 36.2
29 Su	10 28 10	5 29 58	3♐37 18	9♐50 02	14 20.8	0 16.6	5 58.1	12 41.5	22 22.7	28 27.9	6 08.7	11 35.5	0 22.9	28 38.3
30 M	10 32 07	6 27 57	16 07 22	22 29 49	14 21.5	29♌32.2	7 12.5	12 33.4	22 46.6	28 34.1	6 10.9	11 38.7	0 23.4	28 40.4
31 Tu	10 36 03	7 25 57	28 57 52	5♑31 57	14 22.8	28 53.0	8 26.9	12 25.9	23 10.5	28 40.4	6 12.9	11 42.0	0 24.0	28 42.5

Astro Data	Planet Ingress	Last Aspect	☽ Ingress	Last Aspect	☽ Ingress	☽ Phases & Eclipses	Astro Data
Dy Hr Mn	Dy Hr Mn	Dy Hr Mn	Dy Hr Mn	Dy Hr Mn	Dy Hr Mn	Dy Hr Mn	
♃✶♇ 5 2:31	☿ ♌ 6 8:53	2 2:00 ♀ △	♏ 2 13:46	1 4:30 ♇ ✶	♐ 1 8:49	8 10:37 ○ 15♑38	1 July 1971
♂ R 11 6:30	⚳ ♋ 6 14:50	4 18:40 ♃ ☌	♐ 4 23:59	3 12:35 ♇ □	♑ 3 16:32	15 5:47 ☾ 22♈06	Julian Day # 26114
☽ 0N 13 4:02	♀ ♋ 6 22:02	7 2:04 ♇ □	♑ 7 7:03	5 17:10 ♇ △	♒ 5 20:47	22 9:15 ● 28♋56	SVP 5♓39'16"
♃ D 24 19:09	☉ ♌ 23 12:15	9 6:43 ♇ △	♒ 9 11:26	7 17:29 ♃ □	♓ 7 22:34	22 9:31:08 • P 0.069	GC 26♐26.5 ⚴ 10♉16.8
☽ 0S 26 18:00	☿ ♍ 26 17:03	11 8:59 ♃ □	♓ 11 14:14	9 20:10 ♇ ☍	♈ 9 23:27	30 11:07 ☽ 6♏39	Eris 13♈02.6 ⚵ 3♌20.1
	♀ ♌ 31 9:15	13 12:02 ♇ ☍	♈ 13 16:32	11 4:46 ☉ △	♉ 12 0:55		⚷ 13♈44.8 ⚶ 4♒14.0R
☽ 0N 9 11:10		15 5:47 ☉ □	♉ 15 19:10	14 0:54 ♇ △	♊ 14 4:10	6 19:42 ○ 13♒41	☽ Mean ☊ 16♒20.9
♆ D 12 15:14	☉ ♍ 23 19:15	17 18:16 ♇ △	♊ 17 22:47	16 6:31 ♇ □	♋ 16 9:50	6 19:43 • T 1.728	
☿ R 12 19:14	♀ ♍ 24 16:25	19 23:21 ♇ □	♋ 20 3:56	18 14:39 ♇ ✶	♌ 18 17:57	13 10:55 ☾ 20♉03	1 August 1971
☽ 0S 23 1:14	☿ ♌R 29 20:41	22 9:15 ☉ ☌	♌ 22 11:16	20 23:46 ♃ □	♍ 21 4:19	20 22:53 ● 27♌15	Julian Day # 26145
		24 16:38 ☿ ☌	♍ 24 21:09	23 13:12 ♇ ☌	♎ 23 16:22	20 22:38:50 • P 0.508	SVP 5♓39'11"
		27 4:23 ♇ ☌	♎ 27 9:12	24 19:41 ♂ △	♏ 26 5:09	29 2:56 ☽ 5♐08	GC 26♐26.5 ⚴ 20♉54.6
		29 17:46 ♀ □	♏ 29 21:50	28 14:13 ♇ ✶	♐ 28 16:56		Eris 13♈00.3R ⚵ 18♌07.0
				31 0:25 ☿ △	♑ 31 1:54		⚷ 13♈45.8R ⚶ 27♑12.7R
							☽ Mean ☊ 14♒42.5

LONGITUDE — September 1971

Day	Sid.Time	☉	0 hr ☽	Noon ☽	True ☊	☿	♀	♂	⚳	♃	♄	♅	♆	♇
1 W	10 40 00	8♍23 59	12♑12 23	18♑59 26	14♒24.3	28♌19.8	9♍41.3	12♒19.2	23♋34.3	28♏46.8	6♊14.9	11♎45.3	0♐24.6	28♍44.7
2 Th	10 43 56	9 22 02	25 53 14	2♒53 45	14R 25.5	27R 53.6	10 55.7	12R 13.2	23 58.1	28 53.4	6 16.7	11 48.6	0 25.3	28 46.8
3 F	10 47 53	10 20 07	10♒00 50	17 14 09	14 25.8	27 34.8	12 10.2	12 08.1	24 21.8	29 00.1	6 18.4	11 52.0	0 26.0	28 49.0
4 Sa	10 51 50	11 18 13	24 33 11	1♓57 13	14 24.9	27D 24.2	13 24.6	12 03.6	24 45.4	29 07.0	6 20.1	11 55.3	0 26.7	28 51.1
5 Su	10 55 46	12 16 21	9♓25 25	16 56 44	14 22.7	27 22.1	14 39.1	12 00.0	25 09.0	29 14.0	6 21.6	11 58.7	0 27.5	28 53.3
6 M	10 59 43	13 14 30	24 30 04	2♈04 12	14 19.4	27 28.6	15 53.6	11 57.2	25 32.5	29 21.1	6 23.0	12 02.1	0 28.3	28 55.5
7 Tu	11 03 39	14 12 41	9♈37 55	17 10 01	14 15.3	27 43.9	17 08.1	11 55.1	25 55.9	29 28.4	6 24.3	12 05.6	0 29.1	28 57.7
8 W	11 07 36	15 10 55	24 39 23	2♉05 01	14 11.1	28 08.1	18 22.6	11 53.9	26 19.3	29 35.8	6 25.5	12 09.0	0 29.9	28 59.9
9 Th	11 11 32	16 09 10	9♉26 04	16 41 50	14 07.6	28 40.9	19 37.1	11D 53.4	26 42.6	29 43.3	6 26.6	12 12.5	0 30.8	29 02.1
10 F	11 15 29	17 07 28	23 51 50	0♊55 45	14 05.1	29 22.1	20 51.6	11 53.8	27 05.9	29 51.0	6 27.6	12 16.0	0 31.7	29 04.3
11 Sa	11 19 25	18 05 47	7♊53 25	14 44 52	14D 04.0	0♍11.5	22 06.2	11 54.9	27 29.1	29 58.8	6 28.5	12 19.5	0 32.6	29 06.5
12 Su	11 23 22	19 04 09	21 30 13	28 09 41	14 04.3	1 08.5	23 20.8	11 56.8	27 52.2	0♐06.8	6 29.3	12 23.1	0 33.6	29 08.8
13 M	11 27 19	20 02 33	4♋43 36	11♋12 20	14 05.5	2 12.8	24 35.4	11 59.6	28 15.2	0 14.8	6 30.0	12 26.6	0 34.6	29 11.0
14 Tu	11 31 15	21 00 59	17 36 18	23 55 56	14 07.1	3 23.9	25 49.9	12 03.1	28 38.2	0 23.0	6 30.5	12 30.2	0 35.6	29 13.2
15 W	11 35 12	21 59 27	0♌11 39	6♌23 53	14R 08.4	4 41.0	27 04.6	12 07.4	29 01.0	0 31.4	6 31.0	12 33.8	0 36.7	29 15.5
16 Th	11 39 08	22 57 57	12 33 03	18 39 31	14 08.5	6 03.8	28 19.2	12 12.5	29 23.8	0 39.8	6 31.3	12 37.4	0 37.8	29 17.7
17 F	11 43 05	23 56 29	24 43 39	0♍45 48	14 07.1	7 31.5	29 33.8	12 18.5	29 46.6	0 48.4	6 31.6	12 41.0	0 38.9	29 20.0
18 Sa	11 47 01	24 55 03	6♍46 14	12 45 15	14 03.6	9 03.7	0♎48.4	12 25.1	0♌09.2	0 57.0	6R 31.7	12 44.7	0 40.0	29 22.2
19 Su	11 50 58	25 53 39	18 43 05	24 39 58	13 58.2	10 39.6	2 03.1	12 32.6	0 31.7	1 05.8	6 31.7	12 48.3	0 41.2	29 24.5
20 M	11 54 54	26 52 17	0♎36 07	6♎31 45	13 51.0	12 18.8	3 17.7	12 40.9	0 54.2	1 14.8	6 31.6	12 52.0	0 42.4	29 26.8
21 Tu	11 58 51	27 50 57	12 27 05	18 22 19	13 42.7	14 00.6	4 32.4	12 49.9	1 16.6	1 23.8	6 31.4	12 55.7	0 43.7	29 29.0
22 W	12 02 48	28 49 39	24 17 41	0♏13 26	13 34.0	15 44.7	5 47.1	12 59.6	1 38.8	1 32.9	6 31.1	12 59.4	0 44.9	29 31.3
23 Th	12 06 44	29 48 23	6♏09 50	12 07 12	13 25.7	17 30.6	7 01.8	13 10.1	2 01.0	1 42.2	6 30.6	13 03.1	0 46.2	29 33.5
24 F	12 10 41	0♎47 08	18 05 51	24 06 09	13 18.7	19 17.7	8 16.4	13 21.3	2 23.1	1 51.6	6 30.1	13 06.8	0 47.5	29 35.8
25 Sa	12 14 37	1 45 55	0♐08 31	6♐13 23	13 13.4	21 05.9	9 31.1	13 33.3	2 45.1	2 01.1	6 29.5	13 10.5	0 48.9	29 38.1
26 Su	12 18 34	2 44 45	12 21 12	18 32 31	13 10.3	22 54.8	10 45.8	13 46.0	3 07.0	2 10.7	6 28.7	13 14.3	0 50.2	29 40.3
27 M	12 22 30	3 43 35	24 47 48	1♑07 36	13D 09.1	24 44.1	12 00.5	13 59.3	3 28.8	2 20.4	6 27.9	13 18.0	0 51.6	29 42.6
28 Tu	12 26 27	4 42 28	7♑32 28	14 02 53	13 09.4	26 33.6	13 15.2	14 13.3	3 50.5	2 30.2	6 26.9	13 21.8	0 53.1	29 44.8
29 W	12 30 23	5 41 22	20 39 20	27 22 14	13 10.4	28 23.0	14 29.9	14 28.0	4 12.1	2 40.1	6 25.8	13 25.5	0 54.5	29 47.1
30 Th	12 34 20	6 40 18	4♒11 56	11♒08 40	13R 11.1	0♎12.2	15 44.6	14 43.4	4 33.5	2 50.1	6 24.6	13 29.3	0 56.0	29 49.3

LONGITUDE — October 1971

Day	Sid.Time	☉	0 hr ☽	Noon ☽	True ☊	☿	♀	♂	⚳	♃	♄	♅	♆	♇
1 F	12 38 17	7♎39 16	18♒12 28	25♒23 18	13♒10.5	2♎01.2	16♎59.4	14♒59.4	4♌54.9	3♐00.2	6♊23.3	13♎33.1	0♐57.5	29♍51.6
2 Sa	12 42 13	8 38 15	2♓40 52	10♓04 39	13R 07.9	3 49.6	18 14.1	15 16.0	5 16.2	3 10.4	6R 21.9	13 36.8	0 59.0	29 53.8
3 Su	12 46 10	9 37 17	17 33 58	25 07 52	13 02.9	5 37.6	19 28.8	15 33.2	5 37.3	3 20.7	6 20.4	13 40.6	1 00.5	29 56.1
4 M	12 50 06	10 36 20	2♈45 13	10♈24 42	12 55.7	7 25.0	20 43.5	15 51.0	5 58.3	3 31.1	6 18.8	13 44.4	1 02.1	29 58.3
5 Tu	12 54 03	11 35 25	18 04 57	25 44 29	12 47.0	9 11.7	21 58.2	16 09.4	6 19.2	3 41.6	6 17.1	13 48.2	1 03.7	0♎00.5
6 W	12 57 59	12 34 33	3♉21 52	10♉55 46	12 38.0	10 57.8	23 12.9	16 28.4	6 40.0	3 52.1	6 15.3	13 52.0	1 05.3	0 02.8
7 Th	13 01 56	13 33 43	18 24 59	25 48 31	12 29.7	12 43.1	24 27.7	16 47.9	7 00.7	4 02.8	6 13.4	13 55.7	1 07.0	0 05.0
8 F	13 05 52	14 32 55	3♊05 35	10♊15 39	12 23.2	14 27.7	25 42.4	17 07.9	7 21.3	4 13.6	6 11.4	13 59.5	1 08.6	0 07.2
9 Sa	13 09 49	15 32 09	17 18 22	24 13 40	12 19.0	16 11.6	26 57.1	17 28.5	7 41.7	4 24.4	6 09.3	14 03.3	1 10.3	0 09.4
10 Su	13 13 46	16 31 26	1♋01 36	7♋42 26	12D 17.0	17 54.7	28 11.9	17 49.6	8 02.0	4 35.4	6 07.1	14 07.1	1 12.1	0 11.6
11 M	13 17 42	17 30 45	14 16 33	20 44 23	12 16.6	19 37.1	29 26.6	18 11.2	8 22.1	4 46.4	6 04.7	14 10.9	1 13.8	0 13.8
12 Tu	13 21 39	18 30 06	27 06 30	3♌23 28	12R 17.1	21 18.8	0♏41.4	18 33.3	8 42.1	4 57.5	6 02.3	14 14.7	1 15.5	0 16.0
13 W	13 25 35	19 29 30	9♌35 52	15 44 20	12 17.3	22 59.7	1 56.2	18 55.9	9 02.0	5 08.7	5 59.8	14 18.5	1 17.3	0 18.1
14 Th	13 29 32	20 28 56	21 49 26	27 51 44	12 16.1	24 39.9	3 10.9	19 19.0	9 21.8	5 20.0	5 57.2	14 22.2	1 19.1	0 20.3
15 F	13 33 28	21 28 24	3♍51 45	9♍50 00	12 12.6	26 19.4	4 25.7	19 42.5	9 41.4	5 31.3	5 54.5	14 26.0	1 20.9	0 22.4
16 Sa	13 37 25	22 27 55	15 46 54	21 42 53	12 06.3	27 58.2	5 40.5	20 06.5	10 00.8	5 42.7	5 51.7	14 29.8	1 22.8	0 24.6
17 Su	13 41 21	23 27 27	27 38 17	3♎33 24	11 57.2	29 36.3	6 55.2	20 31.0	10 20.1	5 54.2	5 48.8	14 33.5	1 24.6	0 26.7
18 M	13 45 18	24 27 02	9♎28 31	15 23 53	11 45.6	1♏13.8	8 10.0	20 55.9	10 39.2	6 05.8	5 45.8	14 37.3	1 26.5	0 28.8
19 Tu	13 49 14	25 26 38	21 19 40	27 16 04	11 32.2	2 50.6	9 24.8	21 21.2	10 58.2	6 17.5	5 42.7	14 41.0	1 28.4	0 30.9
20 W	13 53 11	26 26 17	3♏13 15	9♏11 21	11 18.1	4 26.8	10 39.6	21 47.0	11 17.0	6 29.2	5 39.6	14 44.8	1 30.3	0 33.0
21 Th	13 57 08	27 25 58	15 10 33	21 11 00	11 04.5	6 02.4	11 54.3	22 13.1	11 35.7	6 41.0	5 36.3	14 48.5	1 32.2	0 35.1
22 F	14 01 04	28 25 41	27 12 53	3♐16 25	10 52.5	7 37.4	13 09.1	22 39.7	11 54.1	6 52.9	5 33.0	14 52.2	1 34.2	0 37.1
23 Sa	14 05 01	29 25 25	9♐21 50	15 29 25	10 43.0	9 11.8	14 23.9	23 06.6	12 12.4	7 04.8	5 29.6	14 55.9	1 36.2	0 39.2
24 Su	14 08 57	0♏25 12	21 39 28	27 52 21	10 36.4	10 45.7	15 38.7	23 34.0	12 30.6	7 16.8	5 26.1	14 59.6	1 38.2	0 41.2
25 M	14 12 54	1 25 00	4♑08 28	10♑28 13	10 32.7	12 19.0	16 53.5	24 01.7	12 48.5	7 28.9	5 22.5	15 03.3	1 40.2	0 43.3
26 Tu	14 16 50	2 24 50	16 52 04	23 20 29	10D 31.2	13 51.7	18 08.2	24 29.7	13 06.3	7 41.0	5 18.9	15 07.0	1 42.2	0 45.3
27 W	14 20 47	3 24 41	29 53 55	6♒32 50	10R 31.0	15 24.0	19 23.0	24 58.1	13 23.9	7 53.2	5 15.1	15 10.6	1 44.2	0 47.3
28 Th	14 24 43	4 24 34	13♒17 37	20 08 38	10 30.9	16 55.7	20 37.8	25 26.9	13 41.3	8 05.5	5 11.3	15 14.3	1 46.2	0 49.2
29 F	14 28 40	5 24 29	27 06 06	4♓10 09	10 29.5	18 26.9	21 52.5	25 56.0	13 58.5	8 17.8	5 07.4	15 17.9	1 48.3	0 51.2
30 Sa	14 32 37	6 24 25	11♓20 44	18 37 39	10 25.8	19 57.6	23 07.3	26 25.4	14 15.5	8 30.2	5 03.5	15 21.5	1 50.4	0 53.1
31 Su	14 36 33	7 24 23	26 00 25	3♈28 26	10 19.3	21 27.8	24 22.1	26 55.1	14 32.3	8 42.6	4 59.5	15 25.1	1 52.5	0 55.0

Astro Data Dy Hr Mn	Planet Ingress Dy Hr Mn	Last Aspect Dy Hr Mn	☽ Ingress Dy Hr Mn	Last Aspect Dy Hr Mn	☽ Ingress Dy Hr Mn	☽ Phases & Eclipses Dy Hr Mn
♃⚹♇ 1 0:08	☿ ♍ 11 6:45	2 5:07 ♃ ⚹	♒ 2 7:04	30 20:35 ♀ △	♓ 1 19:37	5 4:02 ○ 11♓57
☿D 5 6:01	♃ ♐ 11 15:33	4 7:23 ♃ □	♓ 4 8:51	3 19:35 ♇ ☍	♈ 3 19:40	11 18:23 ☾ 18♊21
☽0N 5 20:52	♀ ♎ 17 20:25	6 7:39 ♃ △	♈ 6 8:43	5 5:34 ♀ ☍	♉ 5 18:42	19 14:42 ● 26♍00
♂D 9 13:51	⚳ ♌ 18 2:15	8 5:24 ☿ △	♉ 8 8:37	6 21:04 ♂ □	♊ 7 18:53	27 17:17 ☽ 3♑57
♃☌♆ 16 5:28	☉ ♎ 23 16:45	10 10:08 ♃ ☍	♊ 10 10:25	9 17:16 ♀ △	♋ 9 22:10	
♄R 19 2:17	☿ ♎ 30 9:19	12 13:48 ♇ □	♋ 12 15:21	11 9:35 ☿ □	♌ 12 5:30	4 12:19 ○ 10♈37
☽0S 19 7:45		14 22:09 ♇ ⚹	♌ 14 23:38	14 4:37 ☿ ⚹	♍ 14 16:16	11 5:29 ☾ 17♋15
♀0S 20 5:56	♇ ♎ 5 6:14	16 0:05 ♅ ⚹	♍ 17 10:29	15 4:08 ♄ □	♎ 17 4:47	19 7:59 ● 25♎17
☉0S 23 16:44	♀ ♏ 11 22:43	19 21:37 ♇ ☌	♎ 19 22:47	19 7:59 ☉ ☌	♏ 19 17:31	27 5:54 ☽ 3♒09
	☿ ♏ 17 17:49	21 0:55 ♅ ☌	♏ 22 11:33	21 14:09 ♂ □	♐ 22 5:31	
☿0S 2 10:59	☉ ♏ 24 1:53	24 22:57 ♇ ⚹	♐ 24 23:43	24 3:23 ♂ ⚹	♑ 24 16:05	
☽0N 3 7:51		27 9:19 ♇ □	♑ 27 9:53	26 1:20 ♀ ⚹	♒ 27 0:11	
☽0S 16 13:28		29 16:17 ♇ △	♒ 29 16:39	28 21:30 ♂ ☌	♓ 29 4:57	
♃☍♄ 17 2:59				30 20:00 ♀ △	♈ 31 6:26	
☽0N 30 17:53						

Astro Data

1 September 1971
Julian Day # 26176
SVP 5♓39'06"
GC 26♐26.6 ⚴ 29♉41.0
Eris 12♈48.7R ⚵ 2♍18.6
⚷ 12♈59.9R ⚶ 23♑03.5R
☽ Mean ☊ 13♒04.0

1 October 1971
Julian Day # 26206
SVP 5♓39'03"
GC 26♐26.7 ⚴ 4♊23.4
Eris 12♈31.6R ⚵ 15♍17.3
⚷ 11♈45.4R ⚶ 25♑46.6
☽ Mean ☊ 11♒28.6

November 1971 — LONGITUDE

Day	Sid.Time	☉	0 hr ☽	Noon ☽	True ☊	☿	♀	♂	⚳	♃	♄	♅	♆	♇
1 M	14 40 30	8♏24 23	11♈00 46	18♈36 23	10♒10.2	22♏57.5	25♏36.8	27♒25.1	14♌48.9	8♐55.1	4♊55.4	15♎28.7	1♐54.6	0♎56.9
2 Tu	14 44 26	9 24 24	26 13 59	3♉52 13	9R59.2	24 26.7	26 51.6	27 55.4	15 05.3	9 07.6	4R51.3	15 32.2	1 56.7	0 58.8
3 W	14 48 23	10 24 27	11♉29 38	19 04 49	9 47.6	25 55.3	28 06.3	28 26.0	15 21.5	9 20.2	4 47.1	15 35.8	1 58.8	1 00.7
4 Th	14 52 19	11 24 33	26 36 25	4♊03 12	9 36.6	27 23.5	29 21.1	28 56.8	15 37.5	9 32.8	4 42.8	15 39.3	2 00.9	1 02.5
5 F	14 56 16	12 24 40	11♊24 11	18 38 33	9 27.6	28 51.1	0♐35.8	29 27.9	15 53.3	9 45.5	4 38.5	15 42.8	2 03.1	1 04.3
6 Sa	15 00 12	13 24 50	25 45 44	2♋45 25	9 21.2	0♐18.2	1 50.5	29 59.3	16 08.9	9 58.2	4 34.1	15 46.3	2 05.2	1 06.1
7 Su	15 04 09	14 25 01	9♋37 29	16 22 01	9 17.6	1 44.6	3 05.3	0♓31.0	16 24.2	10 11.0	4 29.7	15 49.7	2 07.4	1 07.9
8 M	15 08 06	15 25 14	22 59 18	29 29 42	9D16.1	3 10.5	4 20.0	1 02.8	16 39.3	10 23.9	4 25.2	15 53.1	2 09.6	1 09.7
9 Tu	15 12 02	16 25 30	5♌53 44	12♌11 58	9R15.9	4 35.7	5 34.8	1 35.0	16 54.1	10 36.7	4 20.7	15 56.6	2 11.8	1 11.4
10 W	15 15 59	17 25 47	18 25 03	24 33 37	9 15.8	6 00.1	6 49.5	2 07.3	17 08.8	10 49.7	4 16.1	15 59.9	2 13.9	1 13.1
11 Th	15 19 55	18 26 06	0♍38 21	6♍39 55	9 14.6	7 23.8	8 04.2	2 39.9	17 23.1	11 02.6	4 11.5	16 03.3	2 16.1	1 14.8
12 F	15 23 52	19 26 28	12 38 58	18 36 06	9 11.3	8 46.7	9 19.0	3 12.7	17 37.2	11 15.6	4 06.9	16 06.6	2 18.4	1 16.5
13 Sa	15 27 48	20 26 51	24 31 54	0♎26 54	9 05.2	10 08.6	10 33.7	3 45.8	17 51.1	11 28.7	4 02.2	16 09.9	2 20.6	1 18.1
14 Su	15 31 45	21 27 16	6♎21 36	12 16 26	8 56.2	11 29.6	11 48.5	4 19.0	18 04.7	11 41.7	3 57.4	16 13.2	2 22.8	1 19.8
15 M	15 35 41	22 27 43	18 11 47	24 07 58	8 44.7	12 49.3	13 03.2	4 52.5	18 18.1	11 54.8	3 52.7	16 16.5	2 25.0	1 21.4
16 Tu	15 39 38	23 28 12	0♏05 17	6♏03 58	8 31.3	14 07.9	14 17.9	5 26.2	18 31.1	12 08.0	3 47.9	16 19.7	2 27.3	1 22.9
17 W	15 43 35	24 28 42	12 04 11	18 06 05	8 17.1	15 24.9	15 32.7	6 00.1	18 43.9	12 21.2	3 43.1	16 22.9	2 29.5	1 24.5
18 Th	15 47 31	25 29 14	24 09 49	0♐15 27	8 03.4	16 40.4	16 47.4	6 34.2	18 56.4	12 34.4	3 38.2	16 26.1	2 31.7	1 26.0
19 F	15 51 28	26 29 48	6♐23 05	12 32 48	7 51.3	17 54.1	18 02.1	7 08.4	19 08.7	12 47.7	3 33.4	16 29.2	2 34.0	1 27.5
20 Sa	15 55 24	27 30 23	18 44 41	24 58 50	7 41.6	19 05.7	19 16.8	7 42.9	19 20.6	13 00.9	3 28.5	16 32.3	2 36.2	1 29.0
21 Su	15 59 21	28 30 59	1♑15 23	7♑34 28	7 34.9	20 15.0	20 31.5	8 17.6	19 32.3	13 14.3	3 23.6	16 35.4	2 38.5	1 30.4
22 M	16 03 17	29 31 37	13 56 17	20 21 04	7 31.1	21 21.6	21 46.3	8 52.4	19 43.6	13 27.6	3 18.7	16 38.4	2 40.7	1 31.8
23 Tu	16 07 14	0♐32 16	26 49 02	3♒20 29	7D29.7	22 25.2	23 01.0	9 27.4	19 54.7	13 41.0	3 13.8	16 41.4	2 43.0	1 33.2
24 W	16 11 11	1 32 56	9♒55 43	16 35 01	7 29.9	23 25.4	24 15.6	10 02.5	20 05.4	13 54.3	3 08.9	16 44.4	2 45.3	1 34.6
25 Th	16 15 07	2 33 37	23 18 43	0♓07 03	7R30.3	24 21.7	25 30.3	10 37.9	20 15.8	14 07.7	3 03.9	16 47.3	2 47.5	1 35.9
26 F	16 19 04	3 34 19	7♓00 15	13 58 28	7 29.9	25 13.5	26 45.0	11 13.3	20 26.0	14 21.2	2 59.0	16 50.2	2 49.8	1 37.2
27 Sa	16 23 00	4 35 02	21 01 45	28 10 02	7 27.6	26 00.3	27 59.7	11 49.0	20 35.7	14 34.6	2 54.1	16 53.1	2 52.0	1 38.5
28 Su	16 26 57	5 35 47	5♈23 05	12♈40 33	7 22.8	26 41.4	29 14.3	12 24.7	20 45.2	14 48.1	2 49.2	16 55.9	2 54.3	1 39.7
29 M	16 30 53	6 36 32	20 01 52	27 26 18	7 15.7	27 16.1	0♑29.0	13 00.6	20 54.3	15 01.6	2 44.3	16 58.7	2 56.6	1 40.9
30 Tu	16 34 50	7 37 18	4♉52 59	12♉20 54	7 06.8	27 43.6	1 43.6	13 36.7	21 03.1	15 15.1	2 39.4	17 01.5	2 58.8	1 42.1

December 1971 — LONGITUDE

Day	Sid.Time	☉	0 hr ☽	Noon ☽	True ☊	☿	♀	♂	⚳	♃	♄	♅	♆	♇
1 W	16 38 46	8♐38 05	19♉48 56	27♉15 57	6♒57.2	28♐03.1	2♑58.2	14♓12.8	21♌11.6	15♐28.6	2♊34.5	17♎04.2	3♐01.1	1♎43.3
2 Th	16 42 43	9 38 54	4♊40 46	12♊02 17	6R48.1	28R13.8	4 12.8	14 49.1	21 19.7	15 42.1	2R29.6	17 06.9	3 03.3	1 44.4
3 F	16 46 40	10 39 44	19 19 31	26 31 35	6 40.6	28 14.8	5 27.4	15 25.5	21 27.5	15 55.6	2 24.7	17 09.5	3 05.6	1 45.5
4 Sa	16 50 36	11 40 35	3♋37 49	10♋37 41	6 35.2	28 05.5	6 42.0	16 02.1	21 34.9	16 09.2	2 19.9	17 12.1	3 07.8	1 46.6
5 Su	16 54 33	12 41 27	17 30 54	24 17 17	6D32.3	27 45.3	7 56.6	16 38.7	21 41.9	16 22.8	2 15.1	17 14.6	3 10.0	1 47.6
6 M	16 58 29	13 42 21	0♌56 55	7♌29 57	6 31.6	27 13.8	9 11.2	17 15.5	21 48.6	16 36.3	2 10.3	17 17.2	3 12.3	1 48.6
7 Tu	17 02 26	14 43 15	13 56 43	20 17 38	6 32.3	26 31.0	10 25.7	17 52.3	21 54.9	16 49.9	2 05.6	17 19.6	3 14.5	1 49.6
8 W	17 06 22	15 44 11	26 33 13	2♍44 02	6 33.5	25 37.5	11 40.3	18 29.3	22 00.8	17 03.5	2 00.9	17 22.1	3 16.7	1 50.5
9 Th	17 10 19	16 45 08	8♍50 41	14 53 50	6R34.3	24 34.1	12 54.8	19 06.3	22 06.4	17 17.1	1 56.2	17 24.4	3 18.9	1 51.4
10 F	17 14 15	17 46 07	20 54 07	26 52 11	6 33.7	23 22.4	14 09.3	19 43.5	22 11.6	17 30.6	1 51.5	17 26.8	3 21.1	1 52.3
11 Sa	17 18 12	18 47 06	2♎48 41	8♎44 15	6 31.3	22 04.3	15 23.8	20 20.8	22 16.3	17 44.2	1 46.9	17 29.1	3 23.3	1 53.1
12 Su	17 22 09	19 48 07	14 39 27	20 34 52	6 26.8	20 42.4	16 38.3	20 58.2	22 20.7	17 57.8	1 42.3	17 31.3	3 25.5	1 53.9
13 M	17 26 05	20 49 08	26 31 00	2♏28 20	6 20.4	19 19.3	17 52.8	21 35.6	22 24.7	18 11.4	1 37.8	17 33.5	3 27.7	1 54.7
14 Tu	17 30 02	21 50 11	8♏27 16	14 28 10	6 12.5	17 58.0	19 07.3	22 13.2	22 28.2	18 25.0	1 33.3	17 35.7	3 29.9	1 55.5
15 W	17 33 58	22 51 15	20 31 21	26 37 08	6 03.9	16 41.0	20 21.8	22 50.8	22 31.4	18 38.6	1 28.9	17 37.8	3 32.1	1 56.2
16 Th	17 37 55	23 52 19	2♐45 30	8♐56 49	5 55.5	15 30.8	21 36.2	23 28.6	22 34.1	18 52.2	1 24.5	17 39.8	3 34.2	1 56.8
17 F	17 41 51	24 53 25	15 11 05	21 28 23	5 48.1	14 29.1	22 50.7	24 06.4	22 36.5	19 05.8	1 20.2	17 41.9	3 36.4	1 57.5
18 Sa	17 45 48	25 54 31	27 48 44	4♑12 06	5 42.3	13 37.4	24 05.1	24 44.3	22 38.4	19 19.3	1 16.0	17 43.8	3 38.5	1 58.1
19 Su	17 49 44	26 55 37	10♑38 27	17 07 47	5 38.6	12 56.3	25 19.5	25 22.3	22 39.8	19 32.9	1 11.8	17 45.8	3 40.6	1 58.7
20 M	17 53 41	27 56 44	23 40 02	0♒15 10	5D37.0	12 26.2	26 33.9	26 00.4	22 40.9	19 46.4	1 07.7	17 47.6	3 42.7	1 59.2
21 Tu	17 57 38	28 57 51	6♒53 09	13 33 59	5 37.1	12 07.0	27 48.3	26 38.5	22R41.5	20 00.0	1 03.6	17 49.4	3 44.8	1 59.7
22 W	18 01 34	29 58 59	20 17 40	27 04 12	5 38.4	11D58.4	29 02.6	27 16.7	22 41.7	20 13.5	0 59.6	17 51.2	3 46.9	2 00.2
23 Th	18 05 31	1♑00 07	3♓53 37	10♓45 55	5 40.0	11 59.6	0♒16.9	27 55.0	22 41.5	20 27.0	0 55.7	17 52.9	3 49.0	2 00.6
24 F	18 09 27	2 01 15	17 41 08	24 39 14	5R41.2	12 10.1	1 31.2	28 33.4	22 40.8	20 40.5	0 51.8	17 54.6	3 51.0	2 01.0
25 Sa	18 13 24	3 02 23	1♈40 10	8♈43 49	5 41.2	12 29.1	2 45.5	29 11.8	22 39.7	20 54.0	0 48.0	17 56.2	3 53.1	2 01.4
26 Su	18 17 20	4 03 31	15 50 01	22 58 31	5 39.8	12 55.7	3 59.7	29 50.3	22 38.1	21 07.4	0 44.3	17 57.8	3 55.1	2 01.7
27 M	18 21 17	5 04 39	0♉09 00	7♉21 01	5 37.0	13 29.2	5 13.9	0♈28.8	22 36.2	21 20.8	0 40.7	17 59.3	3 57.1	2 02.0
28 Tu	18 25 13	6 05 47	14 34 06	21 47 37	5 33.1	14 08.9	6 28.1	1 07.4	22 33.8	21 34.2	0 37.2	18 00.7	3 59.1	2 02.3
29 W	18 29 10	7 06 55	29 00 58	6♊13 25	5 28.7	14 54.2	7 42.2	1 46.0	22 30.9	21 47.6	0 33.7	18 02.1	4 01.1	2 02.5
30 Th	18 33 07	8 08 03	13♊24 16	20 32 47	5 24.4	15 44.3	8 56.3	2 24.7	22 27.6	22 01.0	0 30.3	18 03.5	4 03.0	2 02.7
31 F	18 37 03	9 09 11	27 38 17	4♋40 09	5 21.0	16 38.8	10 10.4	3 03.4	22 23.9	22 14.3	0 27.1	18 04.8	4 05.0	2 02.9

Astro Data	Dy Hr Mn
☽0S	12 19:00
☽0N	27 1:16
♄☍♆	27 18:50
☿R	3 2:31
♄⯓♅	5 13:32
☽0S	10 1:21
♃⚹♅	10 3:44
♄△♇	10 8:37
⚳R	22 10:41
☿D	22 20:48
☽0N	24 6:20
♂0N	27 16:45

Planet Ingress	Dy Hr Mn
♀ ♐	5 0:30
☿ ♐	6 6:59
♂ ♓	6 12:31
☉ ♐	22 23:14
♀ ♑	29 2:41
☉ ♑	22 12:24
♀ ♒	23 6:32
♂ ♈	26 18:04

Last Aspect Dy Hr Mn		☽ Ingress Dy Hr Mn
2 2:20	♂ ⚹	♉ 2 5:55
4 3:43	♀ ☍	♊ 4 5:27
6 7:02	♂ △	♋ 6 7:15
7 11:02	♅ □	♌ 8 12:56
9 20:51	☉ □	♍ 10 22:44
12 13:51	☉ ⚹	♎ 13 11:05
14 20:02	♅ ☌	♏ 15 23:49
18 1:46	☉ ☌	♐ 18 11:30
19 23:49	♀ ☌	♑ 20 21:36
22 5:02	♅ □	♒ 23 5:52
25 3:04	♀ ⚹	♓ 25 11:48
27 11:41	♀ □	♈ 27 15:04
29 11:43	☿ △	♉ 29 16:08

Last Aspect Dy Hr Mn		☽ Ingress Dy Hr Mn
30 14:07	♂ ⚹	♊ 1 16:25
3 14:53	☿ ☍	♋ 3 17:51
4 23:29	♅ □	♌ 5 22:17
7 23:10	☿ △	♍ 8 6:40
10 5:37	☿ □	♎ 10 18:19
12 12:14	☿ ⚹	♏ 13 7:01
15 4:11	♂ △	♐ 15 18:37
17 19:03	☉ ☌	♑ 18 4:07
20 4:36	♀ ☌	♒ 20 11:32
21 23:40	♃ ⚹	♓ 22 17:10
24 19:00	♂ ☌	♈ 24 21:09
26 8:51	♃ △	♉ 26 23:45
27 8:08	♀ □	♊ 29 1:38
30 14:31	♃ ☍	♋ 31 4:01

☽ Phases & Eclipses Dy Hr Mn	
2 21:19	○ 9♉48
9 20:51	☾ 16♌48
18 1:46	● 25♏03
25 16:37	☽ 2♓45
2 7:48	○ 9♊28
9 16:02	☾ 16♍55
17 19:03	● 25♐11
25 1:35	☽ 2♈36
31 20:20	○ 9♋30

Astro Data

1 November 1971
Julian Day # 26237
SVP 5♓39'00"
GC 26♐26.8 ⚴ 1♊56.9R
Eris 12♈13.1R ⚵ 27♍35.3
⚷ 10♈24.8R ⚶ 4♒00.8
☽ Mean ☊ 9♒50.1

1 December 1971
Julian Day # 26267
SVP 5♓38'55"
GC 26♐26.8 ⚴ 22♉36.8R
Eris 11♈59.7R ⚵ 7♎52.3
⚷ 9♈32.3R ⚶ 15♒08.3
☽ Mean ☊ 8♒14.8

LONGITUDE — January 1972

Day	Sid.Time	☉	0 hr ☽	Noon ☽	True ☊	☿	♀	♂	⚳	♃	♄	♅	♆	♇
1 Sa	18 41 00	10♑10 20	11♋37 49	18♋30 49	5♒18.7	17♐37.2	11♒24.5	3♈42.2	22♌19.8	22♐27.6	0♊23.9	18♎06.0	4♐06.9	2♎03.0
2 Su	18 44 56	11 11 28	25 18 48	2♌01 31	5D 17.7	18 39.0	12 38.5	4 21.0	22R 15.2	22 40.9	0R 20.7	18 07.2	4 08.8	2 03.1
3 M	18 48 53	12 12 37	8♌38 52	15 10 49	5 18.0	19 43.8	13 52.5	4 59.9	22 10.2	22 54.2	0 17.7	18 08.4	4 10.7	2 03.2
4 Tu	18 52 49	13 13 46	21 37 30	27 59 05	5 19.2	20 51.3	15 06.4	5 38.8	22 04.8	23 07.4	0 14.8	18 09.4	4 12.6	2R 03.2
5 W	18 56 46	14 14 54	4♍15 52	10♍28 14	5 20.8	22 01.2	16 20.3	6 17.7	21 58.9	23 20.6	0 12.0	18 10.5	4 14.4	2 03.2
6 Th	19 00 43	15 16 03	16 36 38	22 41 31	5 22.5	23 13.3	17 34.2	6 56.7	21 52.7	23 33.7	0 09.2	18 11.4	4 16.2	2 03.1
7 F	19 04 39	16 17 13	28 43 28	4♎43 01	5 23.7	24 27.3	18 48.0	7 35.7	21 46.0	23 46.8	0 06.6	18 12.4	4 18.0	2 03.0
8 Sa	19 08 36	17 18 22	10♎40 46	16 37 20	5R 24.1	25 43.0	20 01.8	8 14.8	21 38.9	23 59.9	0 04.0	18 13.2	4 19.8	2 02.9
9 Su	19 12 32	18 19 31	22 33 19	28 29 20	5 23.8	27 00.2	21 15.6	8 53.9	21 31.3	24 12.9	0 01.6	18 14.0	4 21.6	2 02.8
10 M	19 16 29	19 20 41	4♏25 58	10♏23 48	5 22.6	28 18.9	22 29.3	9 33.0	21 23.4	24 25.9	29♉59.2	18 14.8	4 23.3	2 02.6
11 Tu	19 20 25	20 21 50	16 23 23	22 25 13	5 20.8	29 38.8	23 43.0	10 12.2	21 15.1	24 38.9	29 56.9	18 15.5	4 25.0	2 02.4
12 W	19 24 22	21 22 59	28 29 46	4♐37 29	5 18.7	0♑59.9	24 56.6	10 51.4	21 06.4	24 51.8	29 54.8	18 16.1	4 26.7	2 02.1
13 Th	19 28 18	22 24 09	10♐48 42	17 03 45	5 16.6	2 22.1	26 10.2	11 30.6	20 57.3	25 04.7	29 52.8	18 16.7	4 28.4	2 01.8
14 F	19 32 15	23 25 18	23 22 51	29 46 10	5 14.9	3 45.3	27 23.8	12 09.9	20 47.9	25 17.5	29 50.8	18 17.2	4 30.1	2 01.5
15 Sa	19 36 12	24 26 27	6♑13 49	12♑45 48	5 13.6	5 09.4	28 37.3	12 49.1	20 38.1	25 30.3	29 49.0	18 17.7	4 31.7	2 01.2
16 Su	19 40 08	25 27 35	19 22 04	26 02 30	5D 12.9	6 34.3	29 50.7	13 28.5	20 27.9	25 43.1	29 47.3	18 18.1	4 33.3	2 00.8
17 M	19 44 05	26 28 43	2♒46 54	9♒35 02	5 12.8	8 00.1	1♓04.2	14 07.8	20 17.4	25 55.7	29 45.7	18 18.5	4 34.9	2 00.4
18 Tu	19 48 01	27 29 50	16 26 36	23 21 17	5 13.2	9 26.6	2 17.5	14 47.2	20 06.5	26 08.4	29 44.2	18 18.7	4 36.4	1 59.9
19 W	19 51 58	28 30 57	0♓18 43	7♓18 31	5 13.7	10 53.9	3 30.8	15 26.6	19 55.4	26 20.9	29 42.8	18 19.0	4 37.9	1 59.4
20 Th	19 55 54	29 32 03	14 20 19	21 23 43	5 14.4	12 21.9	4 44.1	16 06.0	19 43.9	26 33.5	29 41.5	18 19.2	4 39.4	1 58.9
21 F	19 59 51	0♒33 07	28 28 22	5♈33 54	5 14.9	13 50.5	5 57.3	16 45.5	19 32.2	26 45.9	29 40.3	18 19.3	4 40.9	1 58.3
22 Sa	20 03 47	1 34 11	12♈39 58	19 46 15	5R 15.1	15 19.8	7 10.4	17 24.9	19 20.2	26 58.3	29 39.2	18R 19.4	4 42.3	1 57.8
23 Su	20 07 44	2 35 14	26 52 26	3♉58 16	5 15.2	16 49.8	8 23.4	18 04.4	19 07.9	27 10.7	29 38.3	18 19.4	4 43.7	1 57.1
24 M	20 11 41	3 36 16	11♉03 26	18 07 40	5 15.1	18 20.5	9 36.4	18 43.9	18 55.4	27 23.0	29 37.4	18 19.3	4 45.1	1 56.5
25 Tu	20 15 37	4 37 17	25 10 44	2♊12 21	5D 15.1	19 51.7	10 49.4	19 23.4	18 42.6	27 35.2	29 36.7	18 19.2	4 46.5	1 55.8
26 W	20 19 34	5 38 17	9♊12 16	16 10 13	5 15.1	21 23.7	12 02.2	20 02.9	18 29.7	27 47.3	29 36.1	18 19.1	4 47.8	1 55.1
27 Th	20 23 30	6 39 16	23 05 56	29 59 10	5 15.2	22 56.2	13 15.0	20 42.5	18 16.6	27 59.4	29 35.6	18 18.9	4 49.1	1 54.4
28 F	20 27 27	7 40 13	6♋49 39	13♋37 09	5 15.3	24 29.5	14 27.7	21 22.0	18 03.2	28 11.5	29 35.2	18 18.6	4 50.4	1 53.6
29 Sa	20 31 23	8 41 10	20 21 26	27 02 18	5R 15.5	26 03.3	15 40.4	22 01.6	17 49.7	28 23.4	29 34.9	18 18.3	4 51.6	1 52.8
30 Su	20 35 20	9 42 05	3♌39 34	10♌13 07	5 15.5	27 37.9	16 52.9	22 41.1	17 36.1	28 35.3	29D 34.8	18 17.9	4 52.9	1 52.0
31 M	20 39 16	10 43 00	16 42 49	23 08 40	5 15.3	29 13.1	18 05.4	23 20.7	17 22.3	28 47.1	29 34.7	18 17.5	4 54.1	1 51.1

LONGITUDE — February 1972

Day	Sid.Time	☉	0 hr ☽	Noon ☽	True ☊	☿	♀	♂	⚳	♃	♄	♅	♆	♇
1 Tu	20 43 13	11♒43 53	29♌30 39	5♍48 51	5♒14.7	0♒48.9	19♓17.8	24♈00.3	17♌08.5	28♐58.9	29♉34.8	18♎17.0	4♐55.2	1♎50.3
2 W	20 47 10	12 44 46	12♍03 22	18 14 24	5R 13.8	2 25.5	20 30.1	24 39.8	16R 54.5	29 10.5	29 35.0	18R 16.5	4 56.3	1R 49.3
3 Th	20 51 06	13 45 38	24 22 11	0♎27 02	5 12.6	4 02.8	21 42.3	25 19.4	16 40.5	29 22.1	29 35.3	18 15.9	4 57.4	1 48.4
4 F	20 55 03	14 46 28	6♎29 16	12 29 19	5 11.3	5 40.8	22 54.5	25 59.0	16 26.4	29 33.6	29 35.7	18 15.2	4 58.5	1 47.4
5 Sa	20 58 59	15 47 18	18 27 37	24 24 40	5 10.2	7 19.6	24 06.6	26 38.6	16 12.2	29 45.1	29 36.2	18 14.5	4 59.5	1 46.4
6 Su	21 02 56	16 48 07	0♏20 57	6♏17 03	5D 09.4	8 59.0	25 18.5	27 18.2	15 58.1	29 56.4	29 36.8	18 13.8	5 00.5	1 45.4
7 M	21 06 52	17 48 55	12 13 32	18 10 59	5 09.1	10 39.3	26 30.4	27 57.8	15 43.9	0♑07.7	29 37.6	18 12.9	5 01.5	1 44.4
8 Tu	21 10 49	18 49 42	24 10 00	0♐11 11	5 09.4	12 20.4	27 42.2	28 37.4	15 29.8	0 18.9	29 38.4	18 12.1	5 02.4	1 43.3
9 W	21 14 45	19 50 28	6♐15 06	12 22 20	5 10.3	14 02.2	28 53.9	29 17.0	15 15.7	0 30.0	29 39.4	18 11.2	5 03.4	1 42.2
10 Th	21 18 42	20 51 13	18 33 25	24 48 51	5 11.6	15 44.9	0♈05.6	29 56.6	15 01.6	0 41.0	29 40.5	18 10.2	5 04.2	1 41.1
11 F	21 22 39	21 51 57	1♑09 05	7♑34 29	5 13.0	17 28.3	1 17.1	0♉36.2	14 47.7	0 51.9	29 41.7	18 09.2	5 05.1	1 39.9
12 Sa	21 26 35	22 52 40	14 05 21	20 41 53	5 14.2	19 12.6	2 28.5	1 15.8	14 33.8	1 02.8	29 43.0	18 08.1	5 05.9	1 38.8
13 Su	21 30 32	23 53 22	27 24 10	4♒12 12	5R 14.7	20 57.8	3 39.8	1 55.4	14 20.1	1 13.5	29 44.4	18 07.0	5 06.7	1 37.6
14 M	21 34 28	24 54 02	11♒05 49	18 04 44	5 14.3	22 43.7	4 51.0	2 35.1	14 06.4	1 24.2	29 45.9	18 05.9	5 07.4	1 36.4
15 Tu	21 38 25	25 54 41	25 08 33	2♓16 43	5 12.7	24 30.6	6 02.1	3 14.7	13 53.0	1 34.7	29 47.6	18 04.6	5 08.1	1 35.1
16 W	21 42 21	26 55 18	9♓28 35	16 43 27	5 10.3	26 18.2	7 13.1	3 54.3	13 39.7	1 45.2	29 49.3	18 03.4	5 08.8	1 33.9
17 Th	21 46 18	27 55 54	24 00 29	1♈18 51	5 07.1	28 06.7	8 24.0	4 33.9	13 26.6	1 55.5	29 51.2	18 02.1	5 09.5	1 32.6
18 F	21 50 14	28 56 28	8♈37 43	15 56 16	5 03.7	29 56.0	9 34.8	5 13.6	13 13.7	2 05.8	29 53.2	18 00.7	5 10.1	1 31.3
19 Sa	21 54 11	29 57 00	23 13 44	0♉29 25	5 00.8	1♓46.0	10 45.4	5 53.2	13 01.0	2 16.0	29 55.2	17 59.3	5 10.6	1 29.9
20 Su	21 58 08	0♓57 30	7♉42 44	14 53 12	4 58.7	3 36.8	11 55.9	6 32.8	12 48.5	2 26.0	29 57.4	17 57.8	5 11.2	1 28.6
21 M	22 02 04	1 57 59	22 00 26	29 04 08	4D 57.8	5 28.3	13 06.3	7 12.4	12 36.4	2 35.9	29 59.7	17 56.3	5 11.7	1 27.2
22 Tu	22 06 01	2 58 26	6♊04 10	13♊00 24	4 58.1	7 20.4	14 16.6	7 52.0	12 24.4	2 45.8	0♊02.1	17 54.8	5 12.2	1 25.8
23 W	22 09 57	3 58 50	19 52 51	26 41 31	4 59.4	9 13.1	15 26.7	8 31.6	12 12.8	2 55.5	0 04.6	17 53.2	5 12.6	1 24.4
24 Th	22 13 54	4 59 13	3♋26 31	10♋07 57	5 01.0	11 06.2	16 36.7	9 11.2	12 01.5	3 05.1	0 07.2	17 51.6	5 13.1	1 23.0
25 F	22 17 50	5 59 34	16 45 55	23 20 34	5R 02.4	12 59.6	17 46.5	9 50.8	11 50.5	3 14.6	0 10.0	17 49.9	5 13.4	1 21.6
26 Sa	22 21 47	6 59 53	29 52 01	6♌20 23	5 02.9	14 53.2	18 56.2	10 30.4	11 39.8	3 24.0	0 12.8	17 48.2	5 13.8	1 20.2
27 Su	22 25 43	8 00 10	12♌45 46	19 08 16	5 02.0	16 46.8	20 05.8	11 09.9	11 29.4	3 33.3	0 15.7	17 46.5	5 14.1	1 18.7
28 M	22 29 40	9 00 25	25 27 58	1♍44 55	4 59.3	18 40.1	21 15.1	11 49.5	11 19.3	3 42.4	0 18.7	17 44.7	5 14.4	1 17.2
29 Tu	22 33 37	10 00 39	7♍59 14	14 10 58	4 54.9	20 33.0	22 24.4	12 29.0	11 09.7	3 51.5	0 21.8	17 42.8	5 14.6	1 15.7

Astro Data Dy Hr Mn	Planet Ingress Dy Hr Mn	Last Aspect Dy Hr Mn	☽ Ingress Dy Hr Mn	Last Aspect Dy Hr Mn	☽ Ingress Dy Hr Mn	☽ Phases & Eclipses Dy Hr Mn
♇ R 4 14:44	♄ ♉R 10 3:43	1 11:17 ♅ □	♌ 2 8:22	1 0:08 ♄ □	♍ 1 0:56	8 13:31 ☾ 17♎22
☽ 0S 6 9:07	☿ ♑ 11 18:18	4 2:39 ♃ △	♍ 4 15:50	3 10:18 ♄ △	♎ 3 11:06	16 10:52 ● 25♑25
☽ 0N 20 11:38	♀ ♓ 16 15:01	6 13:45 ♃ □	♎ 7 2:33	5 22:58 ♃ ✱	♏ 5 23:18	16 11:02:37 ● A 01'53"
♅ R 23 5:26	☉ ♒ 20 22:59	9 8:38 ☿ ✱	♏ 9 15:03	8 10:55 ♄ ☍	♐ 8 11:38	23 9:29 ☽ 2♉29
♄ D 31 10:22	☿ ♒ 31 23:46	12 2:49 ♄ ☍	♐ 12 2:57	10 3:45 ☉ ✱	♑ 10 21:50	30 10:58 ○ 9♌39
		14 7:05 ♀ ✱	♑ 14 12:26	13 4:08 ♄ △	♒ 13 4:36	30 10:53 ● T 1.050
☽ 0S 2 17:46	♃ ♑ 6 19:37	16 18:40 ♄ △	♒ 16 19:04	15 7:49 ♄ □	♓ 15 8:11	
♃⚻♄ 4 16:28	♀ ♈ 10 10:08	18 22:59 ♄ □	♓ 18 23:28	17 9:36 ♄ ✱	♈ 17 9:51	7 11:11 ☾ 17♏47
♀0N 11 12:10	♂ ♉ 10 14:04	21 2:03 ♄ ✱	♈ 21 2:35	19 11:02 ☉ ✱	♉ 19 11:11	15 0:29 ● 25♒26
♃□♇ 15 12:47	☿ ♓ 18 12:53	23 0:21 ♃ △	♉ 23 5:17	21 13:35 ♄ ☌	♊ 21 13:35	21 17:20 ☽ 2♊11
☽ 0N 16 19:27	☉ ♓ 19 13:11	25 7:34 ♄ ☌	♊ 25 8:14	22 20:32 ♅ △	♋ 23 17:52	29 3:12 ○ 9♍39
	♄ ♊ 21 14:52	27 8:28 ♃ ☍	♋ 27 12:01	25 1:58 ♅ □	♌ 26 0:15	
		29 16:36 ♄ ✱	♌ 29 17:21	27 14:00 ♀ △	♍ 28 8:39	

Astro Data

1 January 1972
Julian Day # 26298
SVP 5♓38'48"
GC 26♐26.9 ⚵ 16♉43.6R
Eris 11♈54.8 ⚴ 15♎51.8
⚷ 9♈24.7 ⚶ 28♒27.2
☽ Mean ☊ 6♒36.4

1 February 1972
Julian Day # 26329
SVP 5♓38'43"
GC 26♐27.0 ⚵ 21♉17.4
Eris 12♈00.7 ⚴ 19♎40.3
⚷ 10♈08.5 ⚶ 12♓43.3
☽ Mean ☊ 4♒57.9

March 1972 — LONGITUDE

Day	Sid.Time	☉	0 hr ☽	Noon ☽	True ☊	☿	♀	♂	⚳	♃	♄	♅	♆	♇
1 W	22 37 33	11♓00 50	20♍20 13	26♍27 06	4♒49.0	22♓25.1	23♈33.4	13♉08.5	11♌00.3	4♑00.4	0♊25.1	17♎41.0	5♐14.8	1♎14.2
2 Th	22 41 30	12 01 00	2♎31 44	8♎34 18	4R42.0	24 16.0	24 42.3	13 48.0	10R51.4	4 09.2	0 28.4	17R39.1	5 15.0	1R12.7
3 F	22 45 26	13 01 08	14 35 00	20 34 03	4 34.8	26 05.5	25 51.1	14 27.5	10 42.8	4 17.9	0 31.8	17 37.1	5 15.1	1 11.1
4 Sa	22 49 23	14 01 15	26 31 46	2♏28 27	4 27.9	27 53.2	26 59.6	15 07.0	10 34.6	4 26.4	0 35.3	17 35.1	5 15.2	1 09.6
5 Su	22 53 19	15 01 20	8♏24 30	14 20 19	4 22.2	29 38.4	28 08.0	15 46.5	10 26.8	4 34.8	0 38.9	17 33.1	5 15.3	1 08.0
6 M	22 57 16	16 01 23	20 16 23	26 13 11	4 18.2	1♈20.9	29 16.2	16 26.0	10 19.4	4 43.1	0 42.6	17 31.1	5R15.3	1 06.5
7 Tu	23 01 12	17 01 25	2♐11 16	8♐11 13	4D16.0	3 00.1	0♉24.3	17 05.4	10 12.4	4 51.3	0 46.4	17 29.0	5 15.3	1 04.9
8 W	23 05 09	18 01 25	14 13 36	20 19 04	4 15.5	4 35.4	1 32.1	17 44.9	10 05.8	4 59.3	0 50.3	17 26.9	5 15.3	1 03.3
9 Th	23 09 06	19 01 24	26 28 13	2♑41 40	4 16.3	6 06.3	2 39.8	18 24.3	9 59.6	5 07.2	0 54.3	17 24.7	5 15.3	1 01.7
10 F	23 13 02	20 01 20	9♑00 00	15 23 48	4 17.7	7 32.3	3 47.3	19 03.8	9 53.8	5 15.0	0 58.4	17 22.6	5 15.2	1 00.1
11 Sa	23 16 59	21 01 16	21 53 32	28 29 39	4R18.8	8 52.9	4 54.6	19 43.2	9 48.5	5 22.6	1 02.5	17 20.4	5 15.0	0 58.5
12 Su	23 20 55	22 01 09	5♒12 28	12♒02 11	4 18.6	10 07.5	6 01.7	20 22.6	9 43.6	5 30.1	1 06.8	17 18.1	5 14.9	0 56.9
13 M	23 24 52	23 01 01	18 58 50	26 02 19	4 16.6	11 15.7	7 08.5	21 02.0	9 39.1	5 37.5	1 11.1	17 15.9	5 14.7	0 55.3
14 Tu	23 28 48	24 00 51	3♓12 18	10♓28 18	4 12.4	12 17.1	8 15.2	21 41.4	9 35.1	5 44.7	1 15.6	17 13.6	5 14.5	0 53.6
15 W	23 32 45	25 00 38	17 49 37	25 15 20	4 06.0	13 11.2	9 21.7	22 20.8	9 31.5	5 51.7	1 20.1	17 11.3	5 14.2	0 52.0
16 Th	23 36 41	26 00 24	2♈44 24	10♈15 41	3 58.2	13 57.8	10 27.9	23 00.1	9 28.3	5 58.6	1 24.7	17 08.9	5 13.9	0 50.4
17 F	23 40 38	27 00 08	17 47 56	25 19 53	3 49.8	14 36.5	11 33.9	23 39.5	9 25.6	6 05.4	1 29.4	17 06.6	5 13.6	0 48.7
18 Sa	23 44 35	27 59 50	2♉50 19	10♉18 08	3 42.0	15 07.2	12 39.6	24 18.8	9 23.3	6 12.0	1 34.2	17 04.2	5 13.2	0 47.1
19 Su	23 48 31	28 59 29	17 42 21	25 02 08	3 35.8	15 29.8	13 45.1	24 58.2	9 21.5	6 18.5	1 39.0	17 01.8	5 12.8	0 45.4
20 M	23 52 28	29 59 07	2♊16 53	9♊26 08	3 31.7	15 44.2	14 50.4	25 37.5	9 20.1	6 24.8	1 44.0	16 59.4	5 12.4	0 43.8
21 Tu	23 56 24	0♈58 42	16 29 38	23 27 19	3D29.9	15R50.4	15 55.4	26 16.8	9 19.1	6 30.9	1 49.0	16 56.9	5 12.0	0 42.1
22 W	0 00 21	1 58 15	0♋19 12	7♋05 29	3 29.7	15 48.6	17 00.1	26 56.1	9D18.6	6 36.9	1 54.1	16 54.5	5 11.5	0 40.5
23 Th	0 04 17	2 57 45	13 46 25	20 22 20	3 30.4	15 39.2	18 04.6	27 35.3	9 18.5	6 42.8	1 59.3	16 52.0	5 11.0	0 38.8
24 F	0 08 14	3 57 13	26 53 35	3♌20 34	3R30.9	15 22.3	19 08.8	28 14.6	9 18.8	6 48.5	2 04.5	16 49.5	5 10.4	0 37.2
25 Sa	0 12 10	4 56 39	9♌43 41	16 03 18	3 30.1	14 58.6	20 12.6	28 53.8	9 19.6	6 54.0	2 09.8	16 47.0	5 09.8	0 35.6
26 Su	0 16 07	5 56 02	22 19 46	28 33 25	3 27.2	14 28.5	21 16.2	29 33.1	9 20.8	6 59.4	2 15.2	16 44.5	5 09.2	0 33.9
27 M	0 20 04	6 55 23	4♍44 34	10♍53 28	3 21.6	13 53.0	22 19.5	0♊12.2	9 22.4	7 04.6	2 20.7	16 41.9	5 08.6	0 32.3
28 Tu	0 24 00	7 54 42	17 00 20	23 05 23	3 13.2	13 12.6	23 22.4	0 51.4	9 24.4	7 09.6	2 26.2	16 39.4	5 07.9	0 30.6
29 W	0 27 57	8 53 59	29 08 47	5♎10 42	3 02.5	12 28.4	24 25.0	1 30.6	9 26.9	7 14.5	2 31.9	16 36.9	5 07.2	0 29.0
30 Th	0 31 53	9 53 13	11♎11 15	17 10 37	2 50.2	11 41.4	25 27.3	2 09.7	9 29.7	7 19.2	2 37.5	16 34.3	5 06.5	0 27.4
31 F	0 35 50	10 52 26	23 08 54	29 06 18	2 37.2	10 52.4	26 29.2	2 48.9	9 33.0	7 23.7	2 43.3	16 31.7	5 05.7	0 25.8

April 1972 — LONGITUDE

Day	Sid.Time	☉	0 hr ☽	Noon ☽	True ☊	☿	♀	♂	⚳	♃	♄	♅	♆	♇
1 Sa	0 39 46	11♈51 37	5♏02 58	10♏59 08	2♒24.7	10♈02.6	27♉30.7	3♊28.0	9♌36.7	7♑28.1	2♊49.1	16♎29.2	5♐04.9	0♎24.2
2 Su	0 43 43	12 50 46	16 55 02	22 50 57	2R13.7	9R12.9	28 31.9	4 07.1	9 40.8	7 32.3	2 55.0	16R26.6	5R04.1	0R22.5
3 M	0 47 39	13 49 53	28 47 13	4♐44 12	2 05.0	8 24.3	29 32.8	4 46.1	9 45.2	7 36.3	3 00.9	16 24.0	5 03.3	0 21.0
4 Tu	0 51 36	14 48 58	10♐42 21	16 42 06	1 59.0	7 37.7	0♊33.2	5 25.2	9 50.1	7 40.2	3 07.0	16 21.4	5 02.4	0 19.4
5 W	0 55 32	15 48 02	22 43 58	28 48 31	1 55.7	6 53.9	1 33.2	6 04.3	9 55.4	7 43.9	3 13.0	16 18.8	5 01.5	0 17.8
6 Th	0 59 29	16 47 03	4♑56 19	11♑07 59	1D54.4	6 13.5	2 32.9	6 43.3	10 01.0	7 47.4	3 19.2	16 16.2	5 00.6	0 16.2
7 F	1 03 26	17 46 03	17 24 07	23 45 21	1R54.4	5 37.1	3 32.1	7 22.3	10 07.0	7 50.7	3 25.4	16 13.7	4 59.7	0 14.7
8 Sa	1 07 22	18 45 02	0♒12 16	6♒45 24	1 54.4	5 05.2	4 30.8	8 01.3	10 13.4	7 53.9	3 31.6	16 11.1	4 58.7	0 13.1
9 Su	1 11 19	19 43 58	13 25 15	20 12 13	1 53.3	4 38.2	5 29.1	8 40.3	10 20.2	7 56.9	3 37.9	16 08.5	4 57.7	0 11.6
10 M	1 15 15	20 42 53	27 06 31	4♓08 18	1 50.2	4 16.2	6 27.0	9 19.3	10 27.3	7 59.7	3 44.3	16 05.9	4 56.7	0 10.0
11 Tu	1 19 12	21 41 45	11♓17 26	18 33 38	1 44.4	3 59.5	7 24.4	9 58.2	10 34.8	8 02.3	3 50.7	16 03.3	4 55.6	0 08.5
12 W	1 23 08	22 40 36	25 56 22	3♈24 50	1 36.0	3 48.1	8 21.3	10 37.2	10 42.7	8 04.7	3 57.2	16 00.8	4 54.5	0 07.0
13 Th	1 27 05	23 39 25	10♈58 03	18 34 48	1 25.6	3D42.1	9 17.7	11 16.1	10 50.9	8 07.0	4 03.8	15 58.2	4 53.4	0 05.5
14 F	1 31 01	24 38 13	26 13 44	3♉53 23	1 14.5	3 41.3	10 13.5	11 55.0	10 59.5	8 09.0	4 10.4	15 55.6	4 52.3	0 04.1
15 Sa	1 34 58	25 36 58	11♉32 18	19 09 01	1 03.8	3 45.7	11 08.8	12 33.9	11 08.4	8 10.9	4 17.0	15 53.1	4 51.2	0 02.6
16 Su	1 38 55	26 35 41	26 42 15	4♊10 52	0 55.0	3 55.2	12 03.6	13 12.8	11 17.7	8 12.6	4 23.7	15 50.6	4 50.0	0 01.2
17 M	1 42 51	27 34 22	11♊33 54	18 50 39	0 48.6	4 09.6	12 57.7	13 51.7	11 27.3	8 14.1	4 30.4	15 48.0	4 48.8	29♍59.8
18 Tu	1 46 48	28 33 01	26 00 41	3♋03 42	0 44.9	4 28.8	13 51.3	14 30.5	11 37.2	8 15.4	4 37.2	15 45.5	4 47.6	29 58.3
19 W	1 50 44	29 31 38	9♋59 42	16 48 47	0 43.4	4 52.6	14 44.2	15 09.4	11 47.4	8 16.5	4 44.1	15 43.0	4 46.4	29 57.0
20 Th	1 54 41	0♉30 12	23 31 13	0♌07 23	0 43.2	5 20.7	15 36.5	15 48.2	11 58.0	8 17.5	4 51.0	15 40.6	4 45.1	29 55.6
21 F	1 58 37	1 28 44	6♌37 43	13 02 45	0 43.0	5 53.1	16 28.0	16 27.0	12 08.9	8 18.2	4 57.9	15 38.1	4 43.8	29 54.2
22 Sa	2 02 34	2 27 14	19 22 59	25 38 57	0 41.6	6 29.4	17 18.9	17 05.8	12 20.1	8 18.8	5 04.9	15 35.6	4 42.5	29 52.9
23 Su	2 06 30	3 25 41	1♍51 12	8♍00 13	0 38.1	7 09.7	18 09.0	17 44.6	12 31.6	8 19.2	5 11.9	15 33.2	4 41.2	29 51.6
24 M	2 10 27	4 24 07	14 06 29	20 10 25	0 31.9	7 53.6	18 58.4	18 23.3	12 43.4	8R19.4	5 18.9	15 30.8	4 39.9	29 50.3
25 Tu	2 14 24	5 22 30	26 12 25	2♎12 52	0 22.7	8 41.0	19 46.9	19 02.0	12 55.5	8 19.4	5 26.0	15 28.4	4 38.6	29 49.0
26 W	2 18 20	6 20 52	8♎12 02	14 10 12	0 11.1	9 31.8	20 34.7	19 40.7	13 07.8	8 19.2	5 33.1	15 26.0	4 37.2	29 47.8
27 Th	2 22 17	7 19 12	20 07 37	26 04 29	29♑57.7	10 25.8	21 21.5	20 19.4	13 20.5	8 18.8	5 40.3	15 23.7	4 35.8	29 46.5
28 F	2 26 13	8 17 29	2♏00 59	7♏57 18	29 43.7	11 22.9	22 07.6	20 58.1	13 33.4	8 18.3	5 47.5	15 21.4	4 34.4	29 45.3
29 Sa	2 30 10	9 15 45	13 53 34	19 50 00	29 30.0	12 23.0	22 52.6	21 36.8	13 46.7	8 17.5	5 54.7	15 19.1	4 33.0	29 44.1
30 Su	2 34 06	10 14 00	25 46 44	1♐44 00	29 18.0	13 26.0	23 36.8	22 15.4	14 00.1	8 16.6	6 02.0	15 16.8	4 31.6	29 42.9

Astro Data

	Dy Hr Mn
☽0S	1 1:53
☿0N	5 11:44
♆R	7 5:19
♃⚺♆	10 12:31
♄△♇	10 19:16
☽0N	15 5:38
☉0N	20 12:21
☿R	21 18:39
♄⚼♅	22 13:09
⚳D	23 5:05
☽0S	28 8:27
☽0N	11 16:14
☿D	14 3:28
♄☍♆	19 18:47
☽0S	24 13:41

Planet Ingress

	Dy Hr Mn
☿ ♈	5 16:59
♀ ♉	7 3:25
☉ ♈	20 12:21
♂ ♊	27 4:30
♀ ♊	3 22:48
♇ ♍R	17 7:50
☉ ♉	19 23:37
☊ ♑R	27 8:04
♃ R	25 0:18

Last Aspect / ☽ Ingress (March)

Last Aspect Dy Hr Mn		☽ Ingress Dy Hr Mn
1 2:39	☿ ☍	♎ 1 19:00
3 23:46	♀ ☍	♏ 4 7:00
5 15:05	♂ ☍	♐ 6 19:36
8 7:05	☉ □	♑ 9 6:49
10 21:17	☉ ⚹	♒ 11 14:43
13 3:06	♂ □	♓ 13 18:39
15 11:35	☉ ☌	♈ 15 19:37
16 22:56	♅ ☍	♉ 17 19:27
19 19:01	☉ ⚹	♊ 19 20:12
21 0:49	♅ △	♋ 21 23:26
24 2:00	♂ ⚹	♌ 24 5:46
26 14:02	♂ □	♍ 26 14:48
28 12:37	♀ △	♎ 29 1:42
30 10:47	♅ ☌	♏ 31 13:48

Last Aspect / ☽ Ingress (April)

Last Aspect Dy Hr Mn		☽ Ingress Dy Hr Mn
3 0:34	♀ ☍	♐ 3 2:27
4 11:19	♅ ⚹	♑ 5 14:20
6 23:44	☉ □	♒ 7 23:37
9 11:06	☉ ⚹	♓ 10 4:58
10 21:08	♂ □	♈ 12 6:32
13 20:31	☉ ☌	♉ 14 5:54
14 18:42	♃ △	♊ 16 5:16
18 6:44	♇ □	♋ 18 6:46
20 11:38	♇ ⚹	♌ 20 11:46
21 18:56	♀ ⚹	♍ 22 20:24
25 7:13	♇ ☌	♎ 25 7:34
27 1:49	♀ △	♏ 27 19:56
30 7:57	♇ ⚹	♐ 30 8:31

☽ Phases & Eclipses

Dy Hr Mn		
8 7:05	☾	17♐49
15 11:35	●	25♓00
22 2:12	☽	1♋34
29 20:05	○	9♎14
6 23:44	☾	17♑16
13 20:31	●	24♈00
20 12:45	☽	0♌32
28 12:44	○	8♏19

Astro Data

1 March 1972
Julian Day # 26358
SVP 5♓38'39"
GC 26♐27.0 ⚴ 2♊14.6
Eris 12♈14.6 ⚵ 18♎03.3R
⚷ 11♈26.5 ⚶ 26♓25.3
☽ Mean ☊ 3♒25.7

1 April 1972
Julian Day # 26389
SVP 5♓38'36"
GC 26♐27.1 ⚴ 17♊35.2
Eris 12♈34.6 ⚵ 11♎35.8R
⚷ 13♈11.6 ⚶ 11♈03.2
☽ Mean ☊ 1♒47.2

LONGITUDE — May 1972

Day	Sid.Time	☉	0 hr ☽	Noon ☽	True ☊	☿	♀	♂	⚳	♃	♄	♅	♆	♇
1 M	2 38 03	11♉12 12	7♐42 00	13♐41 00	29♑08.3	14♈31.7	24♊19.9	22♊54.0	14♌13.9	8♑15.5	6♊09.3	15♎14.6	4♐30.1	29♍41.8
2 Tu	2 41 59	12 10 23	19 41 17	25 43 11	29R 01.4	15 40.0	25 02.1	23 32.7	14 27.9	8R 14.2	6 16.7	15R 12.3	4R 28.7	29R 40.7
3 W	2 45 56	13 08 33	1♑47 06	7♑53 25	28 57.3	16 50.9	25 43.1	24 11.3	14 42.2	8 12.7	6 24.0	15 10.1	4 27.2	29 39.6
4 Th	2 49 53	14 06 41	14 02 36	20 15 10	28D 55.6	18 04.3	26 23.1	24 49.8	14 56.7	8 11.0	6 31.4	15 08.0	4 25.7	29 38.5
5 F	2 53 49	15 04 48	26 31 36	2♒52 26	28 55.3	19 20.1	27 02.0	25 28.4	15 11.4	8 09.1	6 38.9	15 05.8	4 24.2	29 37.5
6 Sa	2 57 46	16 02 53	9♒18 15	15 49 31	28R 55.6	20 38.3	27 39.6	26 07.0	15 26.5	8 07.1	6 46.3	15 03.7	4 22.7	29 36.4
7 Su	3 01 42	17 00 56	22 26 46	29 10 24	28 55.0	21 58.8	28 16.1	26 45.5	15 41.7	8 04.8	6 53.8	15 01.7	4 21.2	29 35.4
8 M	3 05 39	17 58 59	6♓00 46	12♓58 04	28 52.8	23 21.5	28 51.2	27 24.0	15 57.2	8 02.4	7 01.3	14 59.6	4 19.6	29 34.5
9 Tu	3 09 35	18 57 00	20 02 25	27 13 39	28 48.2	24 46.5	29 25.1	28 02.5	16 12.9	7 59.8	7 08.9	14 57.6	4 18.1	29 33.5
10 W	3 13 32	19 54 59	4♈31 30	11♈55 24	28 41.2	26 13.7	29 57.6	28 41.0	16 28.8	7 57.1	7 16.4	14 55.6	4 16.5	29 32.6
11 Th	3 17 28	20 52 58	19 24 35	26 58 05	28 32.4	27 43.0	0♋28.6	29 19.5	16 45.0	7 54.1	7 24.0	14 53.7	4 15.0	29 31.7
12 F	3 21 25	21 50 55	4♉34 42	12♉13 09	28 22.6	29 14.4	0 58.2	29 58.0	17 01.4	7 51.0	7 31.6	14 51.8	4 13.4	29 30.8
13 Sa	3 25 22	22 48 50	19 51 59	27 29 47	28 13.2	0♉48.0	1 26.3	0♋36.5	17 18.0	7 47.6	7 39.2	14 49.9	4 11.8	29 30.0
14 Su	3 29 18	23 46 44	5♊05 10	12♊36 50	28 05.3	2 23.7	1 52.8	1 14.9	17 34.9	7 44.2	7 46.9	14 48.1	4 10.2	29 29.2
15 M	3 33 15	24 44 37	20 03 41	27 24 47	27 59.6	4 01.5	2 17.6	1 53.4	17 51.9	7 40.5	7 54.5	14 46.3	4 08.6	29 28.4
16 Tu	3 37 11	25 42 28	4♋39 26	11♋47 10	27 56.4	5 41.4	2 40.7	2 31.8	18 09.2	7 36.7	8 02.2	14 44.5	4 07.0	29 27.7
17 W	3 41 08	26 40 17	18 47 44	25 41 03	27D 55.3	7 23.5	3 02.1	3 10.2	18 26.6	7 32.7	8 09.9	14 42.8	4 05.4	29 26.9
18 Th	3 45 04	27 38 04	2♌27 15	9♌06 36	27 55.7	9 07.6	3 21.6	3 48.6	18 44.3	7 28.5	8 17.6	14 41.1	4 03.8	29 26.3
19 F	3 49 01	28 35 50	15 39 28	22 06 19	27R 56.4	10 53.8	3 39.2	4 27.0	19 02.1	7 24.2	8 25.3	14 39.5	4 02.2	29 25.6
20 Sa	3 52 57	29 33 34	28 27 39	4♍44 03	27 56.4	12 42.1	3 54.8	5 05.4	19 20.1	7 19.7	8 33.1	14 37.9	4 00.6	29 24.9
21 Su	3 56 54	0♊31 16	10♍56 05	17 04 20	27 54.9	14 32.5	4 08.4	5 43.7	19 38.4	7 15.1	8 40.8	14 36.4	3 59.0	29 24.3
22 M	4 00 51	1 28 57	23 09 22	29 11 44	27 51.2	16 24.9	4 20.0	6 22.1	19 56.8	7 10.3	8 48.6	14 34.8	3 57.4	29 23.8
23 Tu	4 04 47	2 26 36	5♎11 56	11♎10 28	27 45.4	18 19.5	4 29.4	7 00.4	20 15.3	7 05.4	8 56.3	14 33.4	3 55.7	29 23.2
24 W	4 08 44	3 24 14	17 07 47	23 04 16	27 37.5	20 16.1	4 36.6	7 38.7	20 34.1	7 00.3	9 04.1	14 32.0	3 54.1	29 22.7
25 Th	4 12 40	4 21 51	29 00 18	4♏56 12	27 28.2	22 14.6	4 41.5	8 17.0	20 53.0	6 55.0	9 11.9	14 30.6	3 52.5	29 22.2
26 F	4 16 37	5 19 26	10♏52 15	16 48 43	27 18.3	24 15.2	4R 44.2	8 55.3	21 12.1	6 49.6	9 19.6	14 29.2	3 50.9	29 21.8
27 Sa	4 20 33	6 17 00	22 45 49	28 43 46	27 08.7	26 17.6	4 44.5	9 33.6	21 31.4	6 44.1	9 27.4	14 28.0	3 49.2	29 21.3
28 Su	4 24 30	7 14 32	4♐42 45	10♐42 56	27 00.2	28 21.8	4 42.4	10 11.8	21 50.8	6 38.5	9 35.2	14 26.7	3 47.6	29 20.9
29 M	4 28 26	8 12 04	16 44 31	22 47 40	26 53.6	0♊27.6	4 38.0	10 50.1	22 10.4	6 32.7	9 43.0	14 25.5	3 46.0	29 20.6
30 Tu	4 32 23	9 09 35	28 52 36	4♑59 31	26 49.1	2 35.0	4 31.1	11 28.3	22 30.2	6 26.8	9 50.8	14 24.4	3 44.4	29 20.3
31 W	4 36 20	10 07 04	11♑08 39	17 20 16	26D 46.8	4 43.7	4 21.8	12 06.5	22 50.1	6 20.8	9 58.6	14 23.3	3 42.8	29 20.0

LONGITUDE — June 1972

Day	Sid.Time	☉	0 hr ☽	Noon ☽	True ☊	☿	♀	♂	⚳	♃	♄	♅	♆	♇
1 Th	4 40 16	11♊04 33	23♑34 38	29♑52 06	26♑46.4	6♊53.5	4♋10.1	12♋44.7	23♌10.1	6♑14.6	10♊06.4	14♎22.2	3♐41.2	29♍19.7
2 F	4 44 13	12 02 01	6♒12 59	12♒37 38	26 47.2	9 04.3	3R 56.0	13 22.9	23 30.3	6R 08.3	10 14.2	14R 21.2	3R 39.6	29R 19.5
3 Sa	4 48 09	12 59 28	19 06 24	25 39 41	26 48.6	11 15.8	3 39.5	14 01.1	23 50.7	6 01.9	10 22.0	14 20.2	3 38.0	29 19.3
4 Su	4 52 06	13 56 55	2♓17 48	9♓01 04	26R 49.5	13 27.8	3 20.7	14 39.3	24 11.2	5 55.4	10 29.8	14 19.3	3 36.4	29 19.1
5 M	4 56 02	14 54 20	15 49 44	22 43 59	26 49.4	15 39.9	2 59.7	15 17.5	24 31.8	5 48.8	10 37.6	14 18.5	3 34.8	29 18.9
6 Tu	4 59 59	15 51 45	29 43 55	6♈49 28	26 47.6	17 51.9	2 36.4	15 55.7	24 52.6	5 42.1	10 45.4	14 17.6	3 33.2	29 18.8
7 W	5 03 55	16 49 10	14♈00 27	21 16 32	26 44.2	20 03.6	2 11.1	16 33.8	25 13.5	5 35.3	10 53.1	14 16.9	3 31.6	29 18.8
8 Th	5 07 52	17 46 34	28 37 12	6♉01 46	26 39.5	22 14.6	1 43.8	17 12.0	25 34.6	5 28.4	11 00.9	14 16.2	3 30.1	29D 18.7
9 F	5 11 49	18 43 57	13♉29 23	20 59 04	26 34.1	24 24.7	1 14.6	17 50.1	25 55.8	5 21.4	11 08.7	14 15.5	3 28.5	29 18.7
10 Sa	5 15 45	19 41 20	28 29 44	6♊00 14	26 28.8	26 33.7	0 43.7	18 28.3	26 17.1	5 14.3	11 16.4	14 14.9	3 27.0	29 18.7
11 Su	5 19 42	20 38 43	13♊29 24	20 56 06	26 24.3	28 41.4	0 11.3	19 06.4	26 38.5	5 07.2	11 24.2	14 14.3	3 25.4	29 18.8
12 M	5 23 38	21 36 04	28 19 18	5♋38 04	26 21.2	0♋47.5	29♊37.5	19 44.5	27 00.1	5 00.0	11 31.9	14 13.8	3 23.9	29 18.9
13 Tu	5 27 35	22 33 25	12♋51 37	19 59 20	26D 19.8	2 51.9	29 02.5	20 22.7	27 21.8	4 52.7	11 39.6	14 13.4	3 22.4	29 19.0
14 W	5 31 31	23 30 45	27 00 48	3♌55 45	26 19.9	4 54.5	28 26.6	21 00.8	27 43.7	4 45.3	11 47.3	14 13.0	3 20.9	29 19.2
15 Th	5 35 28	24 28 04	10♌44 05	17 25 52	26 21.0	6 55.1	27 49.9	21 38.9	28 05.6	4 37.9	11 55.0	14 12.6	3 19.4	29 19.4
16 F	5 39 25	25 25 22	24 01 16	0♍30 37	26 22.5	8 53.7	27 12.6	22 17.0	28 27.7	4 30.5	12 02.7	14 12.3	3 17.9	29 19.6
17 Sa	5 43 21	26 22 39	6♍54 17	13 12 44	26 23.9	10 50.1	26 35.1	22 55.0	28 49.8	4 23.0	12 10.4	14 12.1	3 16.4	29 19.8
18 Su	5 47 18	27 19 56	19 26 28	25 36 02	26R 24.6	12 44.4	25 57.5	23 33.1	29 12.1	4 15.4	12 18.0	14 11.9	3 15.0	29 20.1
19 M	5 51 14	28 17 11	1♎42 01	7♎44 57	26 24.2	14 36.5	25 20.1	24 11.2	29 34.5	4 07.8	12 25.6	14 11.7	3 13.5	29 20.4
20 Tu	5 55 11	29 14 26	13 45 27	19 44 02	26 22.5	16 26.3	24 43.1	24 49.2	29 57.0	4 00.2	12 33.2	14 11.6	3 12.1	29 20.8
21 W	5 59 07	0♋11 41	25 41 16	1♏37 39	26 19.8	18 13.8	24 06.8	25 27.3	0♍19.6	3 52.6	12 40.8	14D 11.6	3 10.7	29 21.2
22 Th	6 03 04	1 08 54	7♏33 41	13 29 49	26 16.3	19 59.0	23 31.4	26 05.3	0 42.4	3 45.0	12 48.3	14 11.6	3 09.3	29 21.6
23 F	6 07 00	2 06 07	19 26 27	25 23 58	26 12.3	21 42.0	22 57.1	26 43.4	1 05.2	3 37.3	12 55.9	14 11.7	3 07.9	29 22.0
24 Sa	6 10 57	3 03 20	1♐22 44	7♐23 03	26 08.5	23 22.6	22 24.1	27 21.4	1 28.1	3 29.6	13 03.4	14 11.8	3 06.6	29 22.5
25 Su	6 14 54	4 00 32	13 25 10	19 29 20	26 05.1	25 00.9	21 52.6	27 59.4	1 51.1	3 21.9	13 10.9	14 12.0	3 05.2	29 23.0
26 M	6 18 50	4 57 44	25 35 46	1♑44 39	26 02.7	26 36.9	21 22.8	28 37.4	2 14.2	3 14.3	13 18.3	14 12.2	3 03.9	29 23.6
27 Tu	6 22 47	5 54 56	7♑56 07	14 10 21	26D 01.2	28 10.5	20 54.8	29 15.4	2 37.4	3 06.6	13 25.7	14 12.5	3 02.6	29 24.2
28 W	6 26 43	6 52 07	20 27 26	26 47 31	26 00.8	29 41.8	20 28.8	29 53.4	3 00.7	2 58.9	13 33.1	14 12.8	3 01.3	29 24.8
29 Th	6 30 40	7 49 19	3♒10 41	9♒37 05	26 01.3	1♌10.7	20 04.9	0♌31.4	3 24.1	2 51.3	13 40.5	14 13.2	3 00.0	29 25.4
30 F	6 34 36	8 46 30	16 06 47	22 39 55	26 02.3	2 37.2	19 43.2	1 09.4	3 47.6	2 43.7	13 47.9	14 13.6	2 58.8	29 26.1

Astro Data

	Dy Hr Mn
☽0N	9 1:14
♃⊼♄	14 6:12
☽0S	21 18:56
♀R	27 3:14
☽0N	5 7:52
♇D	9 5:43
☽0S	18 1:30
♅D	21 17:28
♃⊻♆	28 3:05

Planet Ingress

	Dy Hr Mn
♀ ♋	10 13:51
♂ ♋	12 13:14
☿ ♉	12 23:45
☉ ♊	20 23:00
☿ ♊	29 6:46
♀ ♊R	11 20:08
☿ ♋	12 2:56
⚳ ♍	20 15:09
☉ ♋	21 7:06
♂ ♌	28 16:09
☿ ♌	28 16:52

Last Aspect / ☽ Ingress

Last Aspect Dy Hr Mn		☽ Ingress Dy Hr Mn
2 19:50	♇ □	♑ 2 20:29
5 5:53	♇ △	♒ 5 6:35
7 10:19	♀ △	♓ 7 13:28
9 15:51	♇ ☍	♈ 9 16:35
11 15:53	♂ ⚹	♉ 11 16:47
13 15:10	♇ △	♊ 13 15:57
15 15:24	♇ □	♋ 15 16:16
17 18:39	♇ ⚹	♌ 17 19:38
20 1:16	☉ □	♍ 20 2:56
22 12:24	♇ ☌	♎ 22 13:36
23 18:48	♅ ☌	♏ 25 2:01
27 13:15	♇ ⚹	♐ 27 14:33
30 0:55	♇ □	♑ 30 2:13

Last Aspect / ☽ Ingress

Last Aspect Dy Hr Mn		☽ Ingress Dy Hr Mn
1 10:58	♇ △	♒ 1 12:15
2 15:12	♅ △	♓ 3 19:52
5 23:17	♇ ☍	♈ 6 0:27
7 9:39	☿ ⚹	♉ 8 2:15
10 1:18	♇ △	♊ 10 2:24
12 2:43	☿ ☌	♋ 12 2:45
14 3:59	♇ ⚹	♌ 14 5:10
16 6:09	♀ ⚹	♍ 16 11:03
18 19:20	♇ ☌	♎ 18 20:39
20 22:50	♂ □	♏ 21 8:43
23 19:58	♇ ⚹	♐ 23 21:14
26 7:25	♇ □	♑ 26 8:36
28 16:56	♇ △	♒ 28 18:02

☽ Phases & Eclipses

Dy Hr Mn	
6 12:26	☾ 16♒04
13 4:08	● 22♉30
20 1:16	☽ 29♌08
28 4:28	○ 6♐56
4 21:22	☾ 14♓19
11 11:30	● 20♊38
18 15:41	☽ 27♍29
26 18:46	○ 5♑14

Astro Data

1 May 1972
Julian Day # 26419
SVP 5♓38'33"
GC 26♐27.2 ⚵ 3♋55.9
Eris 12♈54.3 ⚶ 5♎34.3R
⚷ 14♈54.6 ⚴ 24♈55.0
☽ Mean ☊ 0♒11.9

1 June 1972
Julian Day # 26450
SVP 5♓38'27"
GC 26♐27.2 ⚵ 21♋09.2
Eris 13♈10.1 ⚶ 4♎03.6
⚷ 16♈22.2 ⚴ 8♉39.2
☽ Mean ☊ 28♑33.4

July 1972

LONGITUDE

Day	Sid.Time	☉	0 hr ☽	Noon ☽	True ☊	☿	♀	♂	⚳	♃	♄	♅	♆	♇
1 Sa	6 38 33	9♋43 41	29♒16 34	5♓56 50	26♑03.6	4♌01.3	19♊23.7	1♌47.4	4♍11.1	2♑36.1	13♊55.2	14♎14.1	2♐57.6	29♍26.8
2 Su	6 42 29	10 40 53	12♓40 49	19 28 34	26 04.7	5 22.9	19R 06.5	2 25.4	4 34.8	2R 28.6	14 02.4	14 14.7	2R 56.4	29 27.5
3 M	6 46 26	11 38 04	26 20 07	3♈15 28	26R 05.4	6 42.1	18 51.7	3 03.4	4 58.5	2 21.0	14 09.7	14 15.3	2 55.2	29 28.3
4 Tu	6 50 23	12 35 16	10♈14 34	17 17 19	26 05.4	7 58.7	18 39.3	3 41.4	5 22.3	2 13.6	14 16.9	14 15.9	2 54.0	29 29.1
5 W	6 54 19	13 32 29	24 23 30	1♉32 52	26 04.9	9 12.7	18 29.3	4 19.4	5 46.2	2 06.1	14 24.1	14 16.6	2 52.9	29 29.9
6 Th	6 58 16	14 29 41	8♉45 04	15 59 39	26 04.0	10 24.1	18 21.8	4 57.3	6 10.2	1 58.8	14 31.2	14 17.3	2 51.7	29 30.7
7 F	7 02 12	15 26 54	23 16 05	0♊33 44	26 02.8	11 32.8	18 16.6	5 35.3	6 34.3	1 51.5	14 38.3	14 18.2	2 50.6	29 31.6
8 Sa	7 06 09	16 24 08	7♊51 57	15 09 58	26 01.6	12 38.7	18D 13.8	6 13.3	6 58.4	1 44.2	14 45.4	14 19.0	2 49.6	29 32.6
9 Su	7 10 05	17 21 21	22 27 02	29 42 24	26 00.7	13 41.7	18 13.3	6 51.3	7 22.6	1 37.0	14 52.4	14 19.9	2 48.5	29 33.5
10 M	7 14 02	18 18 35	6♋55 17	14♋04 59	26D 00.2	14 41.8	18 15.1	7 29.3	7 46.9	1 29.9	14 59.4	14 20.9	2 47.5	29 34.5
11 Tu	7 17 58	19 15 50	21 10 52	28 12 23	26 00.1	15 38.8	18 19.2	8 07.3	8 11.3	1 22.9	15 06.3	14 21.9	2 46.5	29 35.5
12 W	7 21 55	20 13 04	5♌09 05	12♌00 35	26 00.3	16 32.6	18 25.5	8 45.3	8 35.8	1 16.0	15 13.2	14 23.0	2 45.5	29 36.5
13 Th	7 25 52	21 10 18	18 46 42	25 27 18	26 00.7	17 23.2	18 33.9	9 23.2	9 00.3	1 09.1	15 20.1	14 24.1	2 44.6	29 37.6
14 F	7 29 48	22 07 33	2♍02 22	8♍32 02	26 01.1	18 10.3	18 44.5	10 01.2	9 24.9	1 02.4	15 26.9	14 25.2	2 43.6	29 38.7
15 Sa	7 33 45	23 04 47	14 56 28	21 15 58	26 01.4	18 53.8	18 57.0	10 39.2	9 49.5	0 55.7	15 33.6	14 26.5	2 42.7	29 39.8
16 Su	7 37 41	24 02 02	27 30 53	3♎41 39	26 01.7	19 33.7	19 11.6	11 17.2	10 14.2	0 49.2	15 40.4	14 27.7	2 41.9	29 41.0
17 M	7 41 38	24 59 17	9♎48 44	15 52 38	26 01.8	20 09.7	19 28.1	11 55.1	10 39.0	0 42.7	15 47.0	14 29.0	2 41.0	29 42.2
18 Tu	7 45 34	25 56 32	21 53 54	27 53 05	26 01.8	20 41.6	19 46.5	12 33.1	11 03.9	0 36.4	15 53.6	14 30.4	2 40.2	29 43.4
19 W	7 49 31	26 53 47	3♏50 45	9♏47 29	26 01.8	21 09.5	20 06.7	13 11.1	11 28.8	0 30.2	16 00.2	14 31.8	2 39.4	29 44.6
20 Th	7 53 27	27 51 03	15 43 51	21 40 24	26 01.9	21 33.0	20 28.6	13 49.1	11 53.8	0 24.1	16 06.7	14 33.3	2 38.6	29 45.9
21 F	7 57 24	28 48 19	27 37 40	3♐36 10	26 02.1	21 52.0	20 52.3	14 27.0	12 18.8	0 18.2	16 13.2	14 34.8	2 37.9	29 47.2
22 Sa	8 01 21	29 45 35	9♐36 22	15 38 44	26 02.5	22 06.4	21 17.6	15 05.0	12 43.9	0 12.3	16 19.6	14 36.4	2 37.2	29 48.5
23 Su	8 05 17	0♌42 51	21 43 41	27 51 32	26 02.9	22 16.1	21 44.5	15 43.0	13 09.1	0 06.6	16 25.9	14 38.0	2 36.5	29 49.9
24 M	8 09 14	1 40 09	4♑02 39	10♑17 16	26 03.3	22R 20.8	22 12.9	16 20.9	13 34.3	0 01.1	16 32.2	14 39.6	2 35.9	29 51.2
25 Tu	8 13 10	2 37 26	16 35 35	22 57 46	26R 03.5	22 20.6	22 42.8	16 58.9	13 59.5	29♐55.6	16 38.5	14 41.3	2 35.2	29 52.6
26 W	8 17 07	3 34 44	29 23 53	5♒54 00	26 03.5	22 15.4	23 14.1	17 36.9	14 24.8	29 50.4	16 44.6	14 43.1	2 34.7	29 54.1
27 Th	8 21 03	4 32 03	12♒28 05	19 06 02	26 03.0	22 05.1	23 46.8	18 14.9	14 50.2	29 45.2	16 50.8	14 44.9	2 34.1	29 55.5
28 F	8 25 00	5 29 23	25 47 46	2♓33 05	26 02.1	21 49.7	24 20.8	18 52.9	15 15.6	29 40.2	16 56.8	14 46.7	2 33.6	29 57.0
29 Sa	8 28 57	6 26 43	9♓21 47	16 13 38	26 00.9	21 29.5	24 56.2	19 30.8	15 41.1	29 35.4	17 02.8	14 48.6	2 33.0	29 58.5
30 Su	8 32 53	7 24 05	23 08 23	0♈05 43	25 59.6	21 04.4	25 32.7	20 08.8	16 06.6	29 30.7	17 08.8	14 50.6	2 32.6	0♎00.0
31 M	8 36 50	8 21 27	7♈05 22	14 07 02	25 58.4	20 34.8	26 10.4	20 46.8	16 32.2	29 26.1	17 14.7	14 52.6	2 32.1	0 01.6

August 1972

LONGITUDE

Day	Sid.Time	☉	0 hr ☽	Noon ☽	True ☊	☿	♀	♂	⚳	♃	♄	♅	♆	♇
1 Tu	8 40 46	9♌18 51	21♈10 24	28♈15 10	25♑57.6	20♌01.0	26♊49.3	21♌24.8	16♍57.8	29♐21.8	17♊20.5	14♎54.6	2♐31.7	0♎03.1
2 W	8 44 43	10 16 16	5♉21 03	12♉27 43	25D 57.4	19R 23.3	27 29.3	22 02.8	17 23.5	29R 17.5	17 26.2	14 56.7	2R 31.3	0 04.7
3 Th	8 48 39	11 13 42	19 34 53	26 42 14	25 57.8	18 42.3	28 10.4	22 40.8	17 49.2	29 13.5	17 31.9	14 58.8	2 31.0	0 06.4
4 F	8 52 36	12 11 09	3♊49 28	10♊56 16	25 58.7	17 58.7	28 52.4	23 18.8	18 15.0	29 09.6	17 37.5	15 00.9	2 30.6	0 08.0
5 Sa	8 56 32	13 08 38	18 02 16	25 07 10	25 59.9	17 13.0	29 35.5	23 56.9	18 40.8	29 05.9	17 43.1	15 03.1	2 30.4	0 09.7
6 Su	9 00 29	14 06 08	2♋10 36	9♋12 11	26 01.0	16 26.1	0♋19.5	24 34.9	19 06.6	29 02.3	17 48.6	15 05.4	2 30.1	0 11.4
7 M	9 04 26	15 03 39	16 11 34	23 08 24	26R 01.6	15 38.8	1 04.4	25 13.0	19 32.5	28 58.9	17 54.0	15 07.7	2 29.9	0 13.1
8 Tu	9 08 22	16 01 12	0♌02 18	6♌52 56	26 01.3	14 51.9	1 50.1	25 51.0	19 58.5	28 55.7	17 59.3	15 10.0	2 29.7	0 14.8
9 W	9 12 19	16 58 45	13 40 01	20 23 17	26 00.0	14 06.3	2 36.7	26 29.1	20 24.5	28 52.7	18 04.6	15 12.4	2 29.5	0 16.6
10 Th	9 16 15	17 56 19	27 02 29	3♍37 29	25 57.6	13 23.0	3 24.1	27 07.1	20 50.5	28 49.9	18 09.8	15 14.8	2 29.4	0 18.4
11 F	9 20 12	18 53 55	10♍08 10	16 34 31	25 54.4	12 42.9	4 12.3	27 45.2	21 16.6	28 47.2	18 14.9	15 17.3	2 29.3	0 20.2
12 Sa	9 24 08	19 51 31	22 56 35	29 14 28	25 50.7	12 06.6	5 01.2	28 23.2	21 42.7	28 44.7	18 20.0	15 19.8	2 29.2	0 22.0
13 Su	9 28 05	20 49 09	5♎28 22	11♎38 33	25 47.0	11 35.1	5 50.8	29 01.3	22 08.8	28 42.4	18 24.9	15 22.3	2D 29.2	0 23.8
14 M	9 32 01	21 46 47	17 45 20	23 49 06	25 43.7	11 08.9	6 41.1	29 39.4	22 35.0	28 40.3	18 29.8	15 24.9	2 29.2	0 25.7
15 Tu	9 35 58	22 44 27	29 50 17	5♏49 23	25 41.4	10 48.7	7 32.2	0♍17.5	23 01.2	28 38.3	18 34.6	15 27.5	2 29.2	0 27.6
16 W	9 39 54	23 42 07	11♏46 55	17 43 27	25D 40.1	10 35.0	8 23.8	0 55.6	23 27.5	28 36.6	18 39.3	15 30.1	2 29.3	0 29.5
17 Th	9 43 51	24 39 49	23 39 32	29 35 48	25 40.1	10D 28.3	9 16.1	1 33.7	23 53.8	28 35.0	18 44.0	15 32.8	2 29.4	0 31.4
18 F	9 47 48	25 37 32	5♐32 51	11♐31 16	25 41.0	10 28.7	10 09.0	2 11.8	24 20.1	28 33.6	18 48.6	15 35.5	2 29.5	0 33.3
19 Sa	9 51 44	26 35 15	17 31 41	23 34 39	25 42.6	10 36.5	11 02.5	2 49.9	24 46.5	28 32.5	18 53.1	15 38.3	2 29.6	0 35.3
20 Su	9 55 41	27 33 00	29 40 45	5♑50 30	25 44.3	10 52.0	11 56.5	3 28.0	25 12.8	28 31.5	18 57.5	15 41.1	2 29.8	0 37.2
21 M	9 59 37	28 30 47	12♑04 21	18 22 43	25R 45.4	11 15.1	12 51.1	4 06.2	25 39.2	28 30.6	19 01.8	15 43.9	2 30.1	0 39.2
22 Tu	10 03 34	29 28 34	24 45 58	1♒14 19	25 45.5	11 45.9	13 46.3	4 44.3	26 05.7	28 30.0	19 06.0	15 46.8	2 30.3	0 41.2
23 W	10 07 30	0♍26 23	7♒47 57	14 26 56	25 44.1	12 24.2	14 42.0	5 22.5	26 32.2	28 29.6	19 10.2	15 49.7	2 30.6	0 43.2
24 Th	10 11 27	1 24 13	21 11 12	28 00 34	25 41.1	13 09.9	15 38.1	6 00.6	26 58.7	28D 29.3	19 14.2	15 52.6	2 30.9	0 45.2
25 F	10 15 24	2 22 04	4♓54 46	11♓53 25	25 36.6	14 02.9	16 34.8	6 38.8	27 25.2	28 29.3	19 18.2	15 55.6	2 31.3	0 47.3
26 Sa	10 19 20	3 19 57	18 55 59	26 01 55	25 31.0	15 02.8	17 32.0	7 17.0	27 51.7	28 29.4	19 22.1	15 58.6	2 31.7	0 49.3
27 Su	10 23 17	4 17 52	3♈10 33	10♈21 14	25 25.2	16 09.5	18 29.6	7 55.1	28 18.3	28 29.7	19 25.9	16 01.6	2 32.1	0 51.4
28 M	10 27 13	5 15 48	17 33 14	24 45 52	25 19.8	17 22.5	19 27.6	8 33.3	28 44.9	28 30.2	19 29.6	16 04.7	2 32.5	0 53.5
29 Tu	10 31 10	6 13 46	1♉58 30	9♉10 32	25 15.6	18 41.4	20 26.2	9 11.6	29 11.5	28 30.9	19 33.2	16 07.8	2 33.0	0 55.6
30 W	10 35 06	7 11 46	16 21 27	23 30 47	25 13.0	20 05.9	21 25.1	9 49.8	29 38.2	28 31.8	19 36.7	16 10.9	2 33.5	0 57.7
31 Th	10 39 03	8 09 48	0♊38 11	7♊43 24	25D 12.2	21 35.4	22 24.4	10 28.0	0♎04.9	28 32.8	19 40.1	16 14.1	2 34.1	0 59.8

Astro Data	Dy Hr Mn
☽0N	2 13:05
♄△♅	4 8:22
♀D	9 4:55
☽0S	15 9:43
☿R	24 23:03
♃□♇	25 22:42
☽0N	29 18:42
☽0S	11 18:42
♆D	14 3:08
☿D	17 22:39
♃D	25 8:01
☽0N	26 2:10

Planet Ingress		Dy Hr Mn
☉	♌	22 18:03
♃	♐R	24 16:42
♇	♎	30 11:39
♀	♋	6 1:26
♂	♍	15 0:59
☉	♍	23 1:03
⚳	♎	31 7:38

Last Aspect Dy Hr Mn			☽ Ingress	Dy Hr Mn
30 6:45	♀	△	♓	1 1:18
3 5:27	♇	☍	♈	3 6:22
4 14:17	♀	✶	♉	5 9:25
7 10:18	♇	△	♊	7 11:05
9 11:45	♇	□	♋	9 12:29
11 14:23	♇	✶	♌	11 15:05
12 23:29	♀	✶	♍	13 20:16
16 4:11	♇	☌	♎	16 4:49
18 7:46	☉	□	♏	18 16:15
21 4:20	♇	✶	♐	21 4:46
23 15:51	♇	□	♑	23 16:10
26 0:55	♇	△	♒	26 1:07
28 6:56	♃	✶	♓	28 7:29
30 11:00	♃	□	♈	30 11:50

Last Aspect Dy Hr Mn			☽ Ingress	Dy Hr Mn
1 13:52	♃	△	♉	1 14:57
3 4:54	♂	□	♊	3 17:33
5 20:01	♀	☌	♋	5 20:18
6 22:08	♅	□	♌	7 23:56
10 3:17	♃	△	♍	10 5:23
12 11:03	♃	□	♎	12 13:27
15 0:17	♂	✶	♏	15 0:19
17 1:09	☉	□	♐	17 12:49
19 21:45	♃	☌	♑	20 0:38
21 6:58	♅	□	♒	22 9:43
24 12:50	♃	✶	♓	24 15:28
26 16:08	♃	□	♈	26 18:40
28 18:14	♃	△	♉	28 20:43
30 8:13	♀	✶	♊	30 22:56

☽ Phases & Eclipses Dy Hr Mn		
4 3:25	☾	12♈15
10 19:39	●	18♋37
10 19:45:53	•	T 02'36"
18 7:46	☽	25♎46
26 7:24	○	3♒24
26 7:16	•	P 0.543
2 8:02	☾	10♉07
9 5:26	●	16♌43
17 1:09	☽	24♏14
24 18:22	○	1♓40
31 12:48	☾	8♊12

Astro Data

1 July 1972
Julian Day # 26480
SVP 5♓38'22"
GC 26♐27.3 ⚴ 7♌33.5
Eris 13♈17.3 ⚵ 7♎17.9
⚷ 17♈12.6 ⚶ 21♉03.0
☽ Mean ☊ 26♑58.1

1 August 1972
Julian Day # 26511
SVP 5♓38'17"
GC 26♐27.4 ⚴ 23♌58.9
Eris 13♈14.9R ⚵ 13♎58.4
⚷ 17♈18.2R ⚶ 2♊24.8
☽ Mean ☊ 25♑19.6

LONGITUDE September 1972

Day	Sid.Time	☉	0 hr ☽	Noon ☽	True ☊	☿	♀	♂	⚳	♃	♄	♅	♆	♇
1 F	10 42 59	9♍07 53	14♊46 12	21♊46 27	25♑12.8	23♌09.5	23♋24.2	11♍06.3	0♎31.6	28♐34.1	19♊43.4	16♎17.2	2♐34.7	1♎02.0
2 Sa	10 46 56	10 05 59	28 44 05	5♋39 02	25 14.0	24 47.7	24 24.3	11 44.5	0 58.3	28 35.5	19 46.7	16 20.5	2 35.3	1 04.1
3 Su	10 50 53	11 04 07	12♋31 16	19 20 48	25R15.0	26 29.5	25 24.8	12 22.8	1 25.0	28 37.2	19 49.8	16 23.7	2 35.9	1 06.3
4 M	10 54 49	12 02 17	26 07 35	2♌51 37	25 14.8	28 14.4	26 25.7	13 01.1	1 51.8	28 39.0	19 52.9	16 27.0	2 36.6	1 08.5
5 Tu	10 58 46	13 00 29	9♌32 51	16 11 15	25 12.9	0♍01.8	27 26.9	13 39.4	2 18.6	28 41.0	19 55.8	16 30.2	2 37.3	1 10.6
6 W	11 02 42	13 58 42	22 46 45	29 19 16	25 08.6	1 51.4	28 28.5	14 17.7	2 45.4	28 43.2	19 58.7	16 33.6	2 38.0	1 12.8
7 Th	11 06 39	14 56 58	5♍48 44	12♍15 05	25 02.1	3 42.7	29 30.4	14 56.1	3 12.2	28 45.5	20 01.4	16 36.9	2 38.8	1 15.0
8 F	11 10 35	15 55 15	18 38 14	24 58 09	24 53.8	5 35.2	0♌32.6	15 34.4	3 39.1	28 48.1	20 04.0	16 40.3	2 39.6	1 17.2
9 Sa	11 14 32	16 53 34	1♎14 51	7♎28 21	24 44.3	7 28.7	1 35.1	16 12.8	4 05.9	28 50.8	20 06.6	16 43.7	2 40.4	1 19.4
10 Su	11 18 28	17 51 54	13 38 43	19 46 07	24 34.5	9 22.8	2 37.9	16 51.2	4 32.8	28 53.7	20 09.0	16 47.1	2 41.3	1 21.7
11 M	11 22 25	18 50 17	25 50 43	1♏52 46	24 25.4	11 17.2	3 41.1	17 29.5	4 59.7	28 56.8	20 11.4	16 50.5	2 42.2	1 23.9
12 Tu	11 26 21	19 48 41	7♏52 35	13 50 31	24 17.9	13 11.6	4 44.5	18 07.9	5 26.6	29 00.1	20 13.6	16 54.0	2 43.1	1 26.1
13 W	11 30 18	20 47 06	19 47 01	25 42 32	24 12.4	15 05.9	5 48.2	18 46.4	5 53.6	29 03.6	20 15.7	16 57.4	2 44.1	1 28.4
14 Th	11 34 15	21 45 34	1♐37 36	7♐32 47	24 09.1	16 59.9	6 52.1	19 24.8	6 20.5	29 07.2	20 17.8	17 00.9	2 45.1	1 30.6
15 F	11 38 11	22 44 03	13 28 41	19 25 55	24D07.9	18 53.4	7 56.4	20 03.2	6 47.4	29 11.0	20 19.7	17 04.5	2 46.1	1 32.9
16 Sa	11 42 08	23 42 33	25 25 09	1♑27 02	24 08.1	20 46.3	9 00.9	20 41.7	7 14.4	29 15.0	20 21.5	17 08.0	2 47.1	1 35.1
17 Su	11 46 04	24 41 06	7♑32 14	13 41 23	24R08.9	22 38.6	10 05.6	21 20.1	7 41.4	29 19.2	20 23.2	17 11.6	2 48.2	1 37.4
18 M	11 50 01	25 39 40	19 55 06	26 13 59	24 09.2	24 30.0	11 10.6	21 58.6	8 08.3	29 23.5	20 24.8	17 15.1	2 49.3	1 39.7
19 Tu	11 53 57	26 38 15	2♒38 32	9♒09 11	24 08.1	26 20.6	12 15.9	22 37.1	8 35.3	29 28.0	20 26.3	17 18.7	2 50.4	1 41.9
20 W	11 57 54	27 36 53	15 46 15	22 29 57	24 04.9	28 10.3	13 21.4	23 15.6	9 02.3	29 32.7	20 27.7	17 22.3	2 51.6	1 44.2
21 Th	12 01 50	28 35 32	29 20 19	6♓17 16	23 59.2	29 59.1	14 27.1	23 54.2	9 29.3	29 37.5	20 29.0	17 25.9	2 52.8	1 46.5
22 F	12 05 47	29 34 12	13♓20 30	20 29 33	23 51.2	1♎47.0	15 33.1	24 32.7	9 56.3	29 42.5	20 30.2	17 29.6	2 54.0	1 48.8
23 Sa	12 09 44	0♎32 55	27 43 46	5♈02 21	23 41.5	3 33.9	16 39.3	25 11.2	10 23.3	29 47.7	20 31.2	17 33.2	2 55.3	1 51.0
24 Su	12 13 40	1 31 40	12♈24 21	19 48 43	23 31.2	5 19.9	17 45.7	25 49.8	10 50.4	29 53.0	20 32.2	17 36.9	2 56.5	1 53.3
25 M	12 17 37	2 30 27	27 14 23	4♉40 14	23 21.5	7 05.0	18 52.3	26 28.4	11 17.4	29 58.5	20 33.0	17 40.6	2 57.8	1 55.6
26 Tu	12 21 33	3 29 16	12♉05 12	19 28 20	23 13.5	8 49.1	19 59.2	27 07.0	11 44.4	0♑04.2	20 33.8	17 44.3	2 59.2	1 57.9
27 W	12 25 30	4 28 07	26 48 47	4♊05 52	23 07.9	10 32.2	21 06.3	27 45.6	12 11.5	0 10.0	20 34.4	17 48.0	3 00.5	2 00.1
28 Th	12 29 26	5 27 01	11♊19 01	18 27 52	23 04.8	12 14.5	22 13.5	28 24.3	12 38.5	0 16.0	20 34.9	17 51.7	3 01.9	2 02.4
29 F	12 33 23	6 25 57	25 32 11	2♋31 53	23D03.7	13 55.8	23 21.0	29 03.0	13 05.5	0 22.1	20 35.3	17 55.4	3 03.3	2 04.7
30 Sa	12 37 19	7 24 55	9♋26 59	16 17 35	23R03.8	15 36.3	24 28.7	29 41.6	13 32.6	0 28.4	20 35.6	17 59.1	3 04.8	2 07.0

LONGITUDE October 1972

Day	Sid.Time	☉	0 hr ☽	Noon ☽	True ☊	☿	♀	♂	⚳	♃	♄	♅	♆	♇
1 Su	12 41 16	8♎23 56	23♋03 51	29♋46 02	23♑03.8	17♎15.9	25♌36.6	0♎20.3	13♎59.7	0♑34.8	20♊35.8	18♎02.9	3♐06.2	2♎09.3
2 M	12 45 13	9 22 59	6♌24 21	12♌59 03	23R02.4	18 54.6	26 44.6	0 59.1	14 26.7	0 41.4	20R35.9	18 06.6	3 07.7	2 11.5
3 Tu	12 49 09	10 22 04	19 30 23	25 58 33	22 58.6	20 32.5	27 52.9	1 37.8	14 53.8	0 48.2	20 35.9	18 10.4	3 09.2	2 13.8
4 W	12 53 06	11 21 11	2♍23 46	8♍46 10	22 51.9	22 09.6	29 01.3	2 16.6	15 20.8	0 55.1	20 35.7	18 14.1	3 10.8	2 16.1
5 Th	12 57 02	12 20 21	15 05 54	21 23 04	22 42.3	23 45.9	0♍09.9	2 55.4	15 47.9	1 02.1	20 35.5	18 17.9	3 12.3	2 18.3
6 F	13 00 59	13 19 33	27 37 44	3♎49 59	22 30.1	25 21.3	1 18.6	3 34.2	16 14.9	1 09.3	20 35.1	18 21.7	3 13.9	2 20.6
7 Sa	13 04 55	14 18 46	9♎59 52	16 07 27	22 16.4	26 56.0	2 27.5	4 13.0	16 42.0	1 16.7	20 34.6	18 25.4	3 15.5	2 22.8
8 Su	13 08 52	15 18 02	22 12 48	28 16 00	22 02.1	28 30.0	3 36.6	4 51.8	17 09.0	1 24.2	20 34.0	18 29.2	3 17.2	2 25.0
9 M	13 12 48	16 17 20	4♏17 11	10♏16 30	21 48.7	0♏03.2	4 45.8	5 30.7	17 36.1	1 31.8	20 33.3	18 33.0	3 18.8	2 27.3
10 Tu	13 16 45	17 16 40	16 14 09	22 10 24	21 37.0	1 35.6	5 55.2	6 09.6	18 03.1	1 39.6	20 32.5	18 36.8	3 20.5	2 29.5
11 W	13 20 41	18 16 02	28 05 33	3♐59 57	21 27.9	3 07.4	7 04.8	6 48.5	18 30.1	1 47.5	20 31.6	18 40.6	3 22.2	2 31.7
12 Th	13 24 38	19 15 26	9♐54 02	15 48 13	21 21.7	4 38.4	8 14.4	7 27.4	18 57.2	1 55.5	20 30.5	18 44.4	3 23.9	2 33.9
13 F	13 28 35	20 14 51	21 43 04	27 39 07	21 18.2	6 08.7	9 24.3	8 06.3	19 24.2	2 03.7	20 29.4	18 48.2	3 25.7	2 36.1
14 Sa	13 32 31	21 14 18	3♑36 59	9♑37 18	21D16.8	7 38.2	10 34.2	8 45.3	19 51.2	2 12.0	20 28.2	18 51.9	3 27.4	2 38.3
15 Su	13 36 28	22 13 47	15 40 44	21 47 57	21R16.7	9 07.1	11 44.3	9 24.2	20 18.2	2 20.5	20 26.8	18 55.7	3 29.2	2 40.5
16 M	13 40 24	23 13 18	27 59 39	4♒16 29	21 16.5	10 35.2	12 54.6	10 03.2	20 45.2	2 29.0	20 25.3	18 59.5	3 31.0	2 42.7
17 Tu	13 44 21	24 12 51	10♒39 05	17 08 02	21 15.1	12 02.6	14 05.0	10 42.2	21 12.1	2 37.7	20 23.8	19 03.3	3 32.9	2 44.9
18 W	13 48 17	25 12 25	23 43 50	0♓26 52	21 11.6	13 29.2	15 15.5	11 21.2	21 39.1	2 46.6	20 22.1	19 07.1	3 34.7	2 47.0
19 Th	13 52 14	26 12 01	7♓17 23	14 15 27	21 05.5	14 55.0	16 26.1	12 00.3	22 06.1	2 55.5	20 20.3	19 10.8	3 36.6	2 49.1
20 F	13 56 10	27 11 39	21 20 58	28 33 36	20 56.8	16 20.1	17 36.8	12 39.3	22 33.0	3 04.6	20 18.4	19 14.6	3 38.5	2 51.3
21 Sa	14 00 07	28 11 18	5♈52 48	13♈17 45	20 46.2	17 44.4	18 47.7	13 18.4	22 59.9	3 13.8	20 16.4	19 18.3	3 40.4	2 53.4
22 Su	14 04 04	29 11 00	20 47 29	28 20 48	20 34.8	19 07.8	19 58.7	13 57.5	23 26.8	3 23.1	20 14.3	19 22.1	3 42.3	2 55.5
23 M	14 08 00	0♏10 44	5♉56 25	13♉32 57	20 23.8	20 30.3	21 09.9	14 36.7	23 53.7	3 32.6	20 12.2	19 25.8	3 44.3	2 57.6
24 Tu	14 11 57	1 10 29	21 09 01	28 43 18	20 14.6	21 51.8	22 21.1	15 15.8	24 20.6	3 42.1	20 09.9	19 29.6	3 46.2	2 59.6
25 W	14 15 53	2 10 17	6♊14 35	13♊41 51	20 08.0	23 12.4	23 32.5	15 55.0	24 47.5	3 51.8	20 07.5	19 33.3	3 48.2	3 01.7
26 Th	14 19 50	3 10 07	21 04 15	28 21 08	20 04.2	24 31.9	24 44.0	16 34.2	25 14.3	4 01.6	20 05.0	19 37.0	3 50.2	3 03.7
27 F	14 23 46	4 10 00	5♋32 06	12♋36 54	20D02.7	25 50.2	25 55.6	17 13.4	25 41.1	4 11.5	20 02.4	19 40.7	3 52.2	3 05.8
28 Sa	14 27 43	5 09 54	19 35 30	26 27 59	20R02.6	27 07.3	27 07.3	17 52.7	26 07.9	4 21.5	19 59.7	19 44.4	3 54.2	3 07.8
29 Su	14 31 40	6 09 51	3♌14 33	9♌55 30	20 02.7	28 23.0	28 19.1	18 31.9	26 34.7	4 31.6	19 56.9	19 48.1	3 56.3	3 09.8
30 M	14 35 36	7 09 50	16 31 13	23 02 04	20 01.7	29 37.3	29 31.0	19 11.2	27 01.5	4 41.8	19 54.1	19 51.7	3 58.3	3 11.8
31 Tu	14 39 33	8 09 51	29 28 29	5♍50 52	19 58.5	0♐49.9	0♎43.0	19 50.5	27 28.3	4 52.1	19 51.1	19 55.4	4 00.4	3 13.7

Astro Data Dy Hr Mn	Planet Ingress Dy Hr Mn	Last Aspect Dy Hr Mn	☽ Ingress Dy Hr Mn	Last Aspect Dy Hr Mn	☽ Ingress Dy Hr Mn	☽ Phases & Eclipses Dy Hr Mn
☽0S 8 3:03	☿ ♍ 5 11:36	1 23:44 ♃ ☍	♋ 2 2:11	30 15:00 ♅ □	♌ 1 12:25	7 17:28 ● 15♍10
☽0N 22 11:34	♀ ♌ 7 23:27	3 23:36 ♀ ☌	♌ 4 6:54	3 15:54 ♀ ☌	♍ 3 19:31	15 19:13 ☽ 23♐02
☉0S 22 22:33	☿ ♎ 21 12:11	6 10:53 ♃ △	♍ 6 13:15	5 10:29 ♄ □	♎ 6 4:35	23 4:07 ○ 0♈14
☿0S 23 2:48	☉ ♎ 22 22:33	8 19:20 ♃ □	♎ 8 21:36	8 12:32 ☿ ☌	♏ 8 15:27	29 19:16 ☾ 6♋44
	♃ ♑ 25 18:20	11 6:08 ♃ ⚹	♏ 11 8:15	8 23:47 ♀ ⚹	♐ 11 3:52	
♄ R 2 16:25	♂ ♎ 30 23:23	13 1:08 ☉ ⚹	♐ 13 20:42	12 21:32 ♄ ☍	♑ 13 16:44	7 8:08 ● 14♎09
♅∠♆ 2 23:40		16 7:37 ♃ ☌	♑ 16 9:07	15 12:55 ☉ □	♒ 16 3:51	15 12:55 ☽ 22♑16
♂0S 4 6:34	♀ ♍ 5 8:33	18 10:50 ☉ △	♒ 18 19:04	18 1:54 ☉ △	♓ 18 11:12	22 13:25 ○ 29♈15
☽0S 5 9:43	☿ ♏ 9 11:11	21 0:26 ♃ ⚹	♓ 21 1:09	19 22:17 ♄ □	♈ 20 14:22	29 4:41 ☾ 5♌52
⚳0S 6 6:46	☉ ♏ 23 7:41	23 3:21 ♃ □	♈ 23 3:44	22 13:25 ☉ ☍	♉ 22 14:37	
♃□♇ 18 13:32	☿ ♐ 30 19:27	25 4:22 ♃ △	♉ 25 4:27	24 1:03 ♀ △	♊ 24 14:02	
☽0N 19 21:45	♀ ♎ 30 21:40	27 1:04 ♂ △	♊ 27 5:14	26 5:29 ♀ □	♋ 26 14:44	
♃⚺♆ 25 0:50		29 5:43 ♂ □	♋ 29 7:39	28 13:16 ☿ △	♌ 28 18:14	
♄△♅ 30 20:26				30 6:14 ♄ ⚹	♍ 31 0:59	

Astro Data

1 September 1972
Julian Day # 26542
SVP 5♓38'13"
GC 26♐27.5 ⚳ 9♍46.9
Eris 13♈03.1R ⚵ 22♎42.7
⚷ 16♈36.2R ⚶ 11♊22.5
☽ Mean ☊ 23♑41.2

1 October 1972
Julian Day # 26572
SVP 5♓38'09"
GC 26♐27.5 ⚳ 24♍25.5
Eris 12♈46.0R ⚵ 2♏17.9
⚷ 15♈23.3R ⚶ 16♊13.9
☽ Mean ☊ 22♑05.8

November 1972 LONGITUDE

Day	Sid.Time	☉	0 hr ☽	Noon☽	True☊	☿	♀	♂	⚳	♃	♄	♅	♆	♇
1 W	14 43 29	9♏09 54	12♍09 38	18♍25 08	19♑52.6	2♐00.7	1♎55.2	20♎29.9	27♎55.0	5♑02.6	19♊48.0	19♎59.0	4♐02.5	3♎15.7
2 Th	14 47 26	10 09 59	24 37 43	0♎47 42	19R 43.9	3 09.5	3 07.4	21 09.2	28 21.7	5 13.1	19R 44.9	20 02.7	4 04.6	3 17.6
3 F	14 51 22	11 10 06	6♎55 20	13 00 53	19 32.8	4 16.1	4 19.7	21 48.6	28 48.4	5 23.8	19 41.6	20 06.3	4 06.7	3 19.5
4 Sa	14 55 19	12 10 15	19 04 32	25 06 28	19 20.1	5 20.2	5 32.1	22 28.0	29 15.1	5 34.5	19 38.3	20 09.9	4 08.8	3 21.4
5 Su	14 59 15	13 10 26	1♏06 52	7♏05 52	19 06.9	6 21.6	6 44.6	23 07.5	29 41.7	5 45.3	19 34.9	20 13.4	4 10.9	3 23.3
6 M	15 03 12	14 10 39	13 03 38	19 00 18	18 54.4	7 19.8	7 57.1	23 46.9	0♏08.3	5 56.3	19 31.4	20 17.0	4 13.0	3 25.1
7 Tu	15 07 08	15 10 54	24 56 03	0♐51 04	18 43.5	8 14.6	9 09.8	24 26.4	0 34.9	6 07.3	19 27.8	20 20.5	4 15.2	3 27.0
8 W	15 11 05	16 11 11	6♐45 35	12 39 51	18 35.1	9 05.6	10 22.5	25 05.9	1 01.5	6 18.4	19 24.2	20 24.0	4 17.4	3 28.8
9 Th	15 15 02	17 11 29	18 34 09	24 28 50	18 29.3	9 52.1	11 35.4	25 45.4	1 28.0	6 29.7	19 20.5	20 27.5	4 19.5	3 30.6
10 F	15 18 58	18 11 49	0♑24 17	6♑20 55	18 26.3	10 33.8	12 48.2	26 25.0	1 54.5	6 41.0	19 16.7	20 31.0	4 21.7	3 32.3
11 Sa	15 22 55	19 12 10	12 19 13	18 19 43	18D 25.4	11 10.0	14 01.2	27 04.5	2 20.9	6 52.4	19 12.8	20 34.5	4 23.9	3 34.1
12 Su	15 26 51	20 12 33	24 22 56	0♒29 30	18 26.0	11 40.0	15 14.2	27 44.1	2 47.4	7 03.9	19 08.8	20 37.9	4 26.1	3 35.8
13 M	15 30 48	21 12 57	6♒40 00	12 55 03	18R 26.9	12 03.3	16 27.3	28 23.7	3 13.8	7 15.4	19 04.8	20 41.3	4 28.3	3 37.5
14 Tu	15 34 44	22 13 22	19 15 17	25 41 17	18 27.1	12 19.1	17 40.5	29 03.4	3 40.1	7 27.1	19 00.7	20 44.7	4 30.5	3 39.2
15 W	15 38 41	23 13 49	2♓13 36	8♓52 43	18 25.8	12R 26.7	18 53.8	29 43.0	4 06.5	7 38.8	18 56.6	20 48.0	4 32.8	3 40.8
16 Th	15 42 37	24 14 17	15 39 01	22 32 45	18 22.4	12 25.3	20 07.1	0♏22.7	4 32.7	7 50.6	18 52.3	20 51.4	4 35.0	3 42.4
17 F	15 46 34	25 14 46	29 34 02	6♈42 44	18 16.8	12 14.3	21 20.4	1 02.4	4 59.0	8 02.5	18 48.1	20 54.7	4 37.2	3 44.0
18 Sa	15 50 31	26 15 17	13♈58 35	21 21 02	18 09.6	11 53.1	22 33.9	1 42.1	5 25.2	8 14.5	18 43.7	20 57.9	4 39.4	3 45.6
19 Su	15 54 27	27 15 49	28 49 19	6♉22 27	18 01.5	11 21.5	23 47.3	2 21.8	5 51.4	8 26.6	18 39.3	21 01.2	4 41.7	3 47.1
20 M	15 58 24	28 16 22	13♉59 17	21 38 28	17 53.6	10 39.3	25 00.9	3 01.6	6 17.5	8 38.7	18 34.9	21 04.4	4 43.9	3 48.7
21 Tu	16 02 20	29 16 57	29 18 36	6♊58 15	17 47.0	9 46.9	26 14.5	3 41.4	6 43.6	8 50.9	18 30.4	21 07.6	4 46.2	3 50.2
22 W	16 06 17	0♐17 34	14♊36 00	22 10 36	17 42.4	8 45.0	27 28.2	4 21.2	7 09.6	9 03.1	18 25.9	21 10.8	4 48.4	3 51.6
23 Th	16 10 13	1 18 12	29 40 52	7♋05 52	17D 40.0	7 34.9	28 41.9	5 01.1	7 35.7	9 15.5	18 21.3	21 13.9	4 50.7	3 53.1
24 F	16 14 10	2 18 52	14♋24 53	21 37 21	17 39.6	6 18.3	29 55.7	5 40.9	8 01.6	9 27.9	18 16.7	21 17.0	4 53.0	3 54.5
25 Sa	16 18 07	3 19 33	28 43 00	5♌41 41	17 40.5	4 57.6	1♏09.6	6 20.8	8 27.5	9 40.4	18 12.0	21 20.1	4 55.2	3 55.9
26 Su	16 22 03	4 20 16	12♌33 27	19 18 29	17 41.9	3 35.3	2 23.5	7 00.7	8 53.4	9 52.9	18 07.3	21 23.1	4 57.5	3 57.3
27 M	16 26 00	5 21 00	25 57 06	2♍29 40	17R 42.8	2 14.2	3 37.4	7 40.7	9 19.3	10 05.5	18 02.6	21 26.1	4 59.7	3 58.6
28 Tu	16 29 56	6 21 46	8♍56 38	15 18 28	17 42.4	0 57.0	4 51.5	8 20.7	9 45.0	10 18.2	17 57.8	21 29.1	5 02.0	3 59.9
29 W	16 33 53	7 22 33	21 35 42	27 48 49	17 40.2	29♏46.3	6 05.5	9 00.7	10 10.8	10 30.9	17 53.0	21 32.0	5 04.3	4 01.2
30 Th	16 37 49	8 23 22	3♎58 19	10♎04 41	17 36.1	28 43.9	7 19.6	9 40.7	10 36.5	10 43.7	17 48.1	21 34.9	5 06.5	4 02.4

December 1972 LONGITUDE

Day	Sid.Time	☉	0 hr ☽	Noon☽	True☊	☿	♀	♂	⚳	♃	♄	♅	♆	♇
1 F	16 41 46	9♐24 13	16♎08 22	22♎09 48	17♑30.4	27♏51.5	8♏33.8	10♏20.7	11♏02.1	10♑56.5	17♊43.3	21♎37.8	5♐08.8	4♎03.6
2 Sa	16 45 42	10 25 04	28 09 21	4♏07 25	17R 23.6	27R 10.1	9 48.0	11 00.8	11 27.7	11 09.4	17R 38.4	21 40.6	5 11.0	4 04.8
3 Su	16 49 39	11 25 57	10♏04 17	16 00 16	17 16.4	26 40.2	11 02.2	11 40.9	11 53.2	11 22.4	17 33.5	21 43.4	5 13.3	4 06.0
4 M	16 53 36	12 26 52	21 55 39	27 50 39	17 09.5	26 21.7	12 16.5	12 21.0	12 18.7	11 35.4	17 28.6	21 46.1	5 15.5	4 07.1
5 Tu	16 57 32	13 27 47	3♐45 31	9♐40 28	17 03.7	26D 14.4	13 30.8	13 01.2	12 44.1	11 48.5	17 23.6	21 48.8	5 17.8	4 08.2
6 W	17 01 29	14 28 44	15 35 43	21 31 29	16 59.3	26 17.6	14 45.1	13 41.4	13 09.5	12 01.6	17 18.7	21 51.5	5 20.0	4 09.2
7 Th	17 05 25	15 29 41	27 27 59	3♑25 29	16 56.6	26 30.7	15 59.5	14 21.6	13 34.8	12 14.8	17 13.7	21 54.1	5 22.3	4 10.3
8 F	17 09 22	16 30 40	9♑24 13	15 24 29	16D 55.6	26 52.8	17 13.9	15 01.8	14 00.0	12 28.0	17 08.8	21 56.7	5 24.5	4 11.3
9 Sa	17 13 18	17 31 39	21 26 34	27 30 51	16 56.1	27 23.1	18 28.4	15 42.1	14 25.2	12 41.3	17 03.8	21 59.3	5 26.7	4 12.2
10 Su	17 17 15	18 32 39	3♒37 40	9♒47 26	16 57.6	28 00.7	19 42.8	16 22.3	14 50.3	12 54.6	16 58.9	22 01.8	5 28.9	4 13.2
11 M	17 21 11	19 33 39	16 00 34	22 17 29	16 59.3	28 44.8	20 57.4	17 02.6	15 15.4	13 07.9	16 53.9	22 04.2	5 31.1	4 14.1
12 Tu	17 25 08	20 34 40	28 38 40	5♓04 33	17 00.9	29 34.7	22 11.9	17 42.9	15 40.4	13 21.3	16 49.0	22 06.7	5 33.4	4 14.9
13 W	17 29 05	21 35 42	11♓35 33	18 12 06	17R 01.7	0♐29.6	23 26.4	18 23.3	16 05.3	13 34.8	16 44.0	22 09.0	5 35.5	4 15.8
14 Th	17 33 01	22 36 44	24 54 31	1♈43 06	17 01.4	1 28.9	24 41.0	19 03.6	16 30.1	13 48.2	16 39.1	22 11.4	5 37.7	4 16.6
15 F	17 36 58	23 37 46	8♈38 01	15 39 20	17 00.0	2 32.1	25 55.6	19 44.0	16 54.9	14 01.7	16 34.2	22 13.7	5 39.9	4 17.3
16 Sa	17 40 54	24 38 49	22 46 57	0♉00 38	16 57.7	3 38.8	27 10.3	20 24.4	17 19.6	14 15.3	16 29.3	22 15.9	5 42.1	4 18.1
17 Su	17 44 51	25 39 53	7♉19 57	14 44 17	16 54.8	4 48.4	28 24.9	21 04.8	17 44.2	14 28.9	16 24.5	22 18.1	5 44.2	4 18.8
18 M	17 48 47	26 40 56	22 12 52	29 44 43	16 51.9	6 00.6	29 39.6	21 45.3	18 08.8	14 42.5	16 19.6	22 20.2	5 46.4	4 19.5
19 Tu	17 52 44	27 42 01	7♊18 47	14♊53 52	16 49.5	7 15.1	0♐54.3	22 25.8	18 33.3	14 56.1	16 14.8	22 22.4	5 48.5	4 20.1
20 W	17 56 40	28 43 05	22 28 45	0♋02 11	16 48.0	8 31.5	2 09.0	23 06.3	18 57.7	15 09.8	16 10.0	22 24.4	5 50.7	4 20.7
21 Th	18 00 37	29 44 11	7♋32 59	15 00 06	16D 47.4	9 49.7	3 23.8	23 46.8	19 22.0	15 23.5	16 05.3	22 26.4	5 52.8	4 21.3
22 F	18 04 34	0♑45 17	22 22 32	29 39 31	16 47.7	11 09.5	4 38.5	24 27.4	19 46.3	15 37.3	16 00.6	22 28.4	5 54.9	4 21.8
23 Sa	18 08 30	1 46 23	6♌50 26	13♌54 49	16 48.6	12 30.6	5 53.3	25 08.0	20 10.5	15 51.1	15 55.9	22 30.3	5 57.0	4 22.3
24 Su	18 12 27	2 47 30	20 52 26	27 43 12	16 49.9	13 52.9	7 08.1	25 48.6	20 34.6	16 04.8	15 51.3	22 32.2	5 59.0	4 22.8
25 M	18 16 23	3 48 37	4♍27 09	11♍04 29	16 51.0	15 16.2	8 23.0	26 29.2	20 58.6	16 18.7	15 46.7	22 34.0	6 01.1	4 23.2
26 Tu	18 20 20	4 49 45	17 35 30	24 00 36	16R 51.8	16 40.5	9 37.8	27 09.9	21 22.5	16 32.5	15 42.1	22 35.7	6 03.1	4 23.6
27 W	18 24 16	5 50 54	0♎20 13	6♎34 53	16 52.0	18 05.7	10 52.7	27 50.6	21 46.4	16 46.4	15 37.6	22 37.4	6 05.2	4 23.9
28 Th	18 28 13	6 52 03	12 45 08	18 51 30	16 51.7	19 31.6	12 07.6	28 31.3	22 10.1	17 00.3	15 33.2	22 39.1	6 07.2	4 24.3
29 F	18 32 09	7 53 13	24 54 35	0♏54 55	16 51.0	20 58.2	13 22.5	29 12.1	22 33.8	17 14.2	15 28.8	22 40.7	6 09.2	4 24.6
30 Sa	18 36 06	8 54 23	6♏53 03	12 49 31	16 50.0	22 25.4	14 37.4	29 52.9	22 57.4	17 28.1	15 24.4	22 42.3	6 11.2	4 24.8
31 Su	18 40 03	9 55 33	18 44 50	24 39 26	16 48.9	23 53.3	15 52.4	0♐33.7	23 20.9	17 42.0	15 20.2	22 43.8	6 13.1	4 25.0

Astro Data Dy Hr Mn	Planet Ingress Dy Hr Mn	Last Aspect Dy Hr Mn	☽ Ingress Dy Hr Mn	Last Aspect Dy Hr Mn	☽ Ingress Dy Hr Mn	☽ Phases & Eclipses Dy Hr Mn
☽0S 1 14:47	⚳ ♏ 6 4:30	1 14:39 ♄ □	♎ 2 10:27	1 10:56 ♅ ☌	♏ 2 3:42	6 1:21 ● 13♏44
♀0S 2 22:55	♂ ♏ 15 22:17	4 6:26 ♂ ☌	♏ 4 21:46	4 9:03 ☿ ☌	♐ 4 16:22	14 5:01 ☽ 21♒56
☿R 15 20:27	☉ ♐ 22 5:03	6 1:21 ☉ ☌	♐ 7 10:16	6 12:41 ♅ ⚹	♑ 7 5:06	20 23:07 ○ 28♉44
☽0N 16 6:51	♀ ♏ 24 13:23	9 14:44 ♂ ⚹	♑ 9 23:11	9 11:44 ☿ ⚹	♒ 9 16:53	27 17:45 ☾ 5♍36
☽0S 28 19:49	☿ ♏R 29 7:08	12 6:18 ♂ □	♒ 12 11:02	12 1:01 ☿ □	♓ 12 2:33	
		14 18:32 ♂ △	♓ 14 19:56	13 22:21 ♀ △	♈ 14 8:59	5 20:24 ● 13♐49
☿D 5 16:23	☿ ♐ 12 23:20	16 15:08 ☉ △	♈ 17 0:44	16 2:26 ☉ △	♉ 16 11:59	13 18:36 ☽ 21♓52
☽0N 13 13:47	♀ ♐ 18 18:34	18 14:08 ♀ ☍	♉ 19 1:53	18 11:51 ♀ ☍	♊ 18 12:24	20 9:45 ○ 28♊37
♃⚻♄ 23 18:20	☉ ♑ 21 18:13	20 23:07 ☉ ☍	♊ 21 1:05	20 9:45 ☉ ☍	♋ 20 11:57	27 10:27 ☾ 5♎47
☽0S 26 2:50	♂ ♐ 30 16:12	22 21:12 ♀ △	♋ 23 0:31	22 3:00 ♂ △	♌ 22 12:34	
		24 11:26 ♅ □	♌ 25 2:12	24 8:27 ♂ □	♍ 24 16:03	
		26 15:45 ♅ ⚹	♍ 27 7:24	26 18:18 ♂ ⚹	♎ 26 23:21	
		29 15:29 ☿ ⚹	♎ 29 16:15	28 19:32 ♅ ☌	♏ 29 10:10	
				30 21:36 ♃ ⚹	♐ 31 22:51	

Astro Data

1 November 1972
Julian Day # 26603
SVP 5♓38'06"
GC 26♐27.6 ⚴ 8♎46.3
Eris 12♈27.6R ⚵ 12♏46.7
⚷ 14♈01.5R ⚶ 15♊12.9R
☽ Mean ☊ 20♑27.3

1 December 1972
Julian Day # 26633
SVP 5♓38'02"
GC 26♐27.7 ⚴ 21♎36.8
Eris 12♈14.3R ⚵ 22♏59.5
⚷ 13♈05.4R ⚶ 8♊31.7R
☽ Mean ☊ 18♑52.0

LONGITUDE — January 1973

Day	Sid.Time	☉	0 hr ☽	Noon ☽	True☊	☿	♀	♂	⚳	♃	♄	♅	♆	♇
1 M	18 43 59	10♑56 44	0♐33 48	6♐28 18	16♑48.0	25♐21.7	17♐07.3	1♐14.5	23♏44.3	17♑56.0	15♊15.9	22♎45.2	6♐15.1	4♎25.2
2 Tu	18 47 56	11 57 55	12 23 21	18 19 16	16R47.3	26 50.6	18 22.3	1 55.3	24 07.6	18 10.0	15R11.8	22 46.6	6 17.0	4 25.4
3 W	18 51 52	12 59 06	24 16 22	0♑14 55	16 46.8	28 20.0	19 37.3	2 36.2	24 30.8	18 23.9	15 07.7	22 48.0	6 18.9	4 25.5
4 Th	18 55 49	14 00 17	6♑15 11	12 17 24	16D46.7	29 49.9	20 52.2	3 17.1	24 53.9	18 37.9	15 03.7	22 49.3	6 20.8	4 25.6
5 F	18 59 45	15 01 28	18 21 44	24 28 25	16 46.7	1♑20.3	22 07.2	3 58.0	25 16.9	18 51.9	14 59.7	22 50.5	6 22.7	4R25.6
6 Sa	19 03 42	16 02 39	0♒37 37	6♒49 29	16R46.8	2 51.1	23 22.2	4 39.0	25 39.7	19 06.0	14 55.8	22 51.7	6 24.6	4 25.6
7 Su	19 07 39	17 03 50	13 04 12	19 21 56	16 46.8	4 22.3	24 37.3	5 20.0	26 02.5	19 20.0	14 52.0	22 52.8	6 26.4	4 25.6
8 M	19 11 35	18 05 00	25 42 50	2♓07 06	16 46.7	5 54.0	25 52.3	6 01.0	26 25.2	19 34.0	14 48.3	22 53.9	6 28.2	4 25.5
9 Tu	19 15 32	19 06 10	8♓34 52	15 06 20	16 46.5	7 26.1	27 07.3	6 42.0	26 47.8	19 48.0	14 44.7	22 54.9	6 30.0	4 25.4
10 W	19 19 28	20 07 19	21 41 38	28 20 58	16 46.2	8 58.6	28 22.3	7 23.0	27 10.2	20 02.0	14 41.1	22 55.9	6 31.8	4 25.3
11 Th	19 23 25	21 08 28	5♈04 27	11♈52 12	16D46.0	10 31.6	29 37.4	8 04.1	27 32.6	20 16.1	14 37.6	22 56.8	6 33.5	4 25.1
12 F	19 27 21	22 09 36	18 44 18	25 40 47	16 45.9	12 05.0	0♑52.4	8 45.1	27 54.8	20 30.1	14 34.2	22 57.7	6 35.2	4 24.9
13 Sa	19 31 18	23 10 44	2♉41 35	9♉46 37	16 46.1	13 38.9	2 07.4	9 26.2	28 16.9	20 44.1	14 30.9	22 58.5	6 36.9	4 24.7
14 Su	19 35 14	24 11 51	16 55 40	24 08 26	16 46.7	15 13.3	3 22.5	10 07.4	28 38.9	20 58.1	14 27.7	22 59.2	6 38.6	4 24.4
15 M	19 39 11	25 12 57	1♊24 31	8♊43 24	16 47.4	16 48.2	4 37.5	10 48.5	29 00.7	21 12.2	14 24.5	22 59.9	6 40.3	4 24.1
16 Tu	19 43 08	26 14 03	16 04 27	23 26 57	16 48.2	18 23.5	5 52.6	11 29.7	29 22.5	21 26.2	14 21.5	23 00.5	6 41.9	4 23.8
17 W	19 47 04	27 15 08	0♋50 08	8♋13 07	16R48.7	19 59.4	7 07.6	12 10.9	29 44.1	21 40.2	14 18.5	23 01.1	6 43.5	4 23.5
18 Th	19 51 01	28 16 12	15 35 01	22 54 57	16 48.7	21 35.7	8 22.7	12 52.1	0♐05.6	21 54.2	14 15.7	23 01.6	6 45.1	4 23.1
19 F	19 54 57	29 17 15	0♌12 03	7♌25 30	16 48.1	23 12.6	9 37.7	13 33.4	0 27.0	22 08.2	14 12.9	23 02.1	6 46.7	4 22.6
20 Sa	19 58 54	0♒18 18	14 34 35	21 38 40	16 46.8	24 50.1	10 52.8	14 14.7	0 48.2	22 22.2	14 10.3	23 02.5	6 48.2	4 22.2
21 Su	20 02 50	1 19 20	28 37 16	5♍30 02	16 44.9	26 28.1	12 07.8	14 56.0	1 09.3	22 36.1	14 07.7	23 02.8	6 49.7	4 21.7
22 M	20 06 47	2 20 22	12♍16 44	18 57 16	16 42.7	28 06.8	13 22.9	15 37.3	1 30.3	22 50.1	14 05.2	23 03.1	6 51.2	4 21.1
23 Tu	20 10 43	3 21 23	25 31 42	2♎00 12	16 40.5	29 46.0	14 38.0	16 18.7	1 51.1	23 04.0	14 02.8	23 03.4	6 52.6	4 20.6
24 W	20 14 40	4 22 24	8♎23 01	14 40 31	16 38.7	1♒25.8	15 53.1	17 00.0	2 11.8	23 17.9	14 00.6	23 03.5	6 54.1	4 20.0
25 Th	20 18 37	5 23 24	20 53 10	27 01 27	16D37.6	3 06.3	17 08.1	17 41.4	2 32.3	23 31.8	13 58.4	23 03.7	6 55.5	4 19.3
26 F	20 22 33	6 24 24	3♏05 55	9♏07 10	16 37.4	4 47.4	18 23.2	18 22.9	2 52.7	23 45.7	13 56.4	23R03.7	6 56.8	4 18.7
27 Sa	20 26 30	7 25 23	15 05 47	21 02 24	16 38.0	6 29.1	19 38.3	19 04.3	3 13.0	23 59.6	13 54.4	23 03.8	6 58.2	4 18.0
28 Su	20 30 26	8 26 21	26 57 39	2♐52 07	16 39.4	8 11.5	20 53.4	19 45.8	3 33.1	24 13.4	13 52.5	23 03.7	6 59.5	4 17.3
29 M	20 34 23	9 27 19	8♐46 24	14 41 06	16 41.2	9 54.6	22 08.5	20 27.3	3 53.1	24 27.3	13 50.8	23 03.6	7 00.8	4 16.5
30 Tu	20 38 19	10 28 16	20 36 45	26 33 51	16 42.9	11 38.3	23 23.6	21 08.9	4 12.9	24 41.1	13 49.2	23 03.5	7 02.0	4 15.7
31 W	20 42 16	11 29 12	2♑32 52	8♑34 15	16R44.1	13 22.6	24 38.7	21 50.4	4 32.5	24 54.8	13 47.6	23 03.2	7 03.3	4 14.9

LONGITUDE — February 1973

Day	Sid.Time	☉	0 hr ☽	Noon ☽	True☊	☿	♀	♂	⚳	♃	♄	♅	♆	♇
1 Th	20 46 12	12♒30 08	14♑38 21	20♑45 29	16♑44.3	15♒07.6	25♑53.8	22♐32.0	4♐52.0	25♑08.6	13♊46.2	23♎03.0	7♐04.5	4♎14.1
2 F	20 50 09	13 31 02	26 55 56	3♒09 53	16R43.2	16 53.2	27 08.8	23 13.6	5 11.3	25 22.3	13R44.9	23R02.7	7 05.6	4R13.2
3 Sa	20 54 06	14 31 55	9♒27 30	15 48 51	16 40.6	18 39.4	28 23.9	23 55.2	5 30.5	25 36.0	13 43.7	23 02.3	7 06.8	4 12.3
4 Su	20 58 02	15 32 47	22 13 58	28 42 49	16 36.7	20 26.2	29 39.0	24 36.9	5 49.5	25 49.7	13 42.6	23 01.8	7 07.9	4 11.4
5 M	21 01 59	16 33 38	5♓15 20	11♓51 24	16 31.9	22 13.5	0♒54.1	25 18.5	6 08.3	26 03.3	13 41.7	23 01.4	7 09.0	4 10.4
6 Tu	21 05 55	17 34 28	18 30 53	25 13 36	16 26.7	24 01.2	2 09.1	26 00.2	6 26.9	26 16.9	13 40.8	23 00.8	7 10.0	4 09.5
7 W	21 09 52	18 35 16	1♈59 22	8♈47 59	16 21.8	25 49.3	3 24.2	26 41.9	6 45.4	26 30.4	13 40.1	23 00.2	7 11.0	4 08.4
8 Th	21 13 48	19 36 02	15 39 15	22 33 00	16 17.8	27 37.6	4 39.3	27 23.6	7 03.6	26 44.0	13 39.4	22 59.6	7 12.0	4 07.4
9 F	21 17 45	20 36 47	29 29 01	6♉27 10	16 15.3	29 26.1	5 54.3	28 05.4	7 21.7	26 57.4	13 38.9	22 58.8	7 13.0	4 06.3
10 Sa	21 21 41	21 37 31	13♉27 16	20 29 10	16D14.5	1♓14.6	7 09.4	28 47.1	7 39.7	27 10.9	13 38.5	22 58.1	7 13.9	4 05.3
11 Su	21 25 38	22 38 12	27 32 41	4♊37 41	16 15.0	3 02.9	8 24.4	29 28.9	7 57.4	27 24.3	13 38.2	22 57.3	7 14.8	4 04.1
12 M	21 29 35	23 38 53	11♊43 57	18 51 17	16 16.3	4 50.9	9 39.4	0♑10.7	8 14.9	27 37.6	13 38.0	22 56.4	7 15.6	4 03.0
13 Tu	21 33 31	24 39 31	25 59 24	3♋08 01	16R17.7	6 38.2	10 54.4	0 52.6	8 32.2	27 50.9	13D38.0	22 55.5	7 16.5	4 01.8
14 W	21 37 28	25 40 08	10♋16 45	17 25 13	16 18.3	8 24.7	12 09.4	1 34.4	8 49.4	28 04.2	13 38.0	22 54.5	7 17.3	4 00.7
15 Th	21 41 24	26 40 43	24 32 57	1♌39 26	16 17.3	10 09.9	13 24.5	2 16.3	9 06.3	28 17.4	13 38.2	22 53.5	7 18.0	3 59.5
16 F	21 45 21	27 41 16	8♌44 09	15 46 32	16 14.3	11 53.5	14 39.4	2 58.2	9 23.1	28 30.6	13 38.5	22 52.5	7 18.7	3 58.2
17 Sa	21 49 17	28 41 48	22 46 02	29 42 08	16 09.1	13 35.0	15 54.4	3 40.1	9 39.6	28 43.7	13 38.9	22 51.4	7 19.4	3 57.0
18 Su	21 53 14	29 42 19	6♍34 21	13♍22 15	16 02.3	15 14.1	17 09.4	4 22.0	9 55.9	28 56.8	13 39.4	22 50.2	7 20.1	3 55.7
19 M	21 57 10	0♓42 47	20 05 29	26 43 48	15 54.3	16 50.1	18 24.4	5 04.0	10 12.1	29 09.8	13 40.0	22 49.0	7 20.7	3 54.4
20 Tu	22 01 07	1 43 15	3♎17 04	9♎45 13	15 46.2	18 22.6	19 39.4	5 46.0	10 28.0	29 22.8	13 40.7	22 47.7	7 21.3	3 53.1
21 W	22 05 04	2 43 40	16 08 20	22 26 34	15 38.8	19 50.9	20 54.3	6 28.0	10 43.6	29 35.7	13 41.6	22 46.4	7 21.9	3 51.7
22 Th	22 09 00	3 44 05	28 40 10	4♏49 30	15 32.9	21 14.4	22 09.3	7 10.0	10 59.1	29 48.5	13 42.5	22 45.0	7 22.4	3 50.4
23 F	22 12 57	4 44 28	10♏55 00	16 57 08	15 28.9	22 32.5	23 24.2	7 52.0	11 14.4	0♒01.3	13 43.6	22 43.6	7 22.9	3 49.0
24 Sa	22 16 53	5 44 50	22 56 28	28 53 37	15D26.9	23 44.5	24 39.2	8 34.1	11 29.4	0 14.1	13 44.7	22 42.2	7 23.4	3 47.6
25 Su	22 20 50	6 45 10	4♐49 11	10♐43 50	15 26.7	24 49.8	25 54.1	9 16.2	11 44.1	0 26.8	13 46.0	22 40.7	7 23.8	3 46.2
26 M	22 24 46	7 45 29	16 38 14	22 33 03	15 27.6	25 47.7	27 09.1	9 58.3	11 58.7	0 39.4	13 47.4	22 39.2	7 24.2	3 44.8
27 Tu	22 28 43	8 45 46	28 28 57	4♑26 36	15R28.8	26 37.8	28 24.0	10 40.5	12 13.0	0 52.0	13 49.0	22 37.6	7 24.5	3 43.3
28 W	22 32 39	9 46 02	10♑26 36	16 29 33	15 29.3	27 19.5	29 38.9	11 22.6	12 27.1	1 04.4	13 50.6	22 36.0	7 24.9	3 41.9

Astro Data	Dy Hr Mn	Planet Ingress	Dy Hr Mn	Last Aspect Dy Hr Mn	☽ Ingress Dy Hr Mn	Last Aspect Dy Hr Mn	☽ Ingress Dy Hr Mn	☽ Phases & Eclipses Dy Hr Mn	
♇ R	6 6:56	☿ ♑	4 14:41	3 7:37 ☿ ☌	♑ 3 11:30	1 23:07 ♀ ☌	♒ 2 5:55	4 15:42	● 14♑10
☽ 0N	9 19:17	♀ ♑	11 19:15	5 8:48 ♅ □	♒ 5 22:47	4 4:00 ♂ ⚹	♓ 4 14:22	4 15:45:37	● A 07'49"
♃∠♆	17 18:27	⚳ ♐	18 5:45	7 23:01 ♀ ⚹	♓ 8 8:03	6 13:55 ♃ ⚹	♈ 6 20:29	12 5:27	☽ 21♈53
☽ 0S	22 12:20	☉ ♒	20 4:48	10 12:03 ♀ □	♈ 10 14:57	8 22:06 ☿ ⚹	♉ 9 0:53	18 21:28	○ 28♋40
♃□♅	23 10:53	☿ ♒	23 15:23	12 7:19 ♅ ☍	♉ 12 19:24	10 23:34 ♃ △	♊ 11 4:10	18 21:17	● A 0.866
♅ R	27 5:30			14 12:06 ☉ △	♊ 14 21:41	12 20:41 ☉ △	♋ 13 6:44	26 6:05	☾ 6♏09
		♀ ♒	4 18:43	16 11:17 ♅ △	♋ 16 22:39	15 6:13 ♃ ☍	♌ 15 9:12		
☽ 0N	6 1:18	☿ ♓	9 19:30	18 21:28 ☉ ☍	♌ 18 23:40	17 10:07 ☉ ☍	♍ 17 12:31	3 9:23	● 14♒25
♄ D	13 12:49	♂ ♑	12 5:51	20 14:24 ♅ ⚹	♍ 21 2:23	19 16:31 ♃ △	♎ 19 17:58	10 14:05	☽ 21♉43
♃⚼♄	17 2:49	☉ ♓	18 19:01	23 7:13 ☿ △	♎ 23 8:16	22 2:02 ♃ □	♏ 22 2:35	17 10:07	○ 28♌37
☽ 0S	18 22:36	♃ ♒	23 9:28	25 5:01 ♃ □	♏ 25 17:52	24 2:27 ♀ □	♐ 24 14:14	25 3:10	☾ 6♐23
☿0N	26 19:10	♀ ♓	28 18:45	27 18:06 ♃ ⚹	♐ 28 6:10	26 22:24 ♀ ⚹	♑ 27 3:04		
				30 4:56 ♅ ⚹	♑ 30 18:54				

Astro Data

1 January 1973
Julian Day # 26664
SVP 5♓37'56"
GC 26♐27.7 ⚴ 3♏12.8
Eris 12♈09.6 ⚵ 3♐04.9
⚷ 12♈53.2 ⚶ 1♊58.6R
☽ Mean ☊ 17♑13.5

1 February 1973
Julian Day # 26695
SVP 5♓37'50"
GC 26♐27.8 ⚴ 11♏59.0
Eris 12♈15.6 ⚵ 12♐00.6
⚷ 13♈32.9 ⚶ 1♊41.7
☽ Mean ☊ 15♑35.1

March 1973 LONGITUDE

Day	Sid.Time	☉	0 hr ☽	Noon ☽	True ☊	☿	♀	♂	⚳	♃	♄	♅	♆	♇
1 Th	22 36 36	10♓46 17	22♑35 59	28♑46 22	15♑28.3	27♓52.4	0♓53.8	12♑04.8	12♐40.9	1♒16.9	13♊52.3	22♎34.3	7♐25.2	3♎40.4
2 F	22 40 33	11 46 29	5♒01 09	11♒20 37	15R 25.1	28 16.2	2 08.7	12 47.0	12 54.4	1 29.2	13 54.1	22R 32.6	7 25.4	3R 38.9
3 Sa	22 44 29	12 46 40	17 45 01	24 14 30	15 19.4	28 30.6	3 23.6	13 29.2	13 07.7	1 41.5	13 56.1	22 30.8	7 25.6	3 37.4
4 Su	22 48 26	13 46 50	0♓49 04	7♓28 38	15 11.3	28R 35.7	4 38.5	14 11.4	13 20.8	1 53.7	13 58.2	22 29.1	7 25.8	3 35.9
5 M	22 52 22	14 46 57	14 13 01	21 01 54	15 01.6	28 31.4	5 53.4	14 53.7	13 33.6	2 05.9	14 00.3	22 27.2	7 26.0	3 34.3
6 Tu	22 56 19	15 47 03	27 54 53	4♈51 30	14 51.1	28 18.1	7 08.3	15 35.9	13 46.1	2 18.0	14 02.6	22 25.4	7 26.1	3 32.8
7 W	23 00 15	16 47 06	11♈51 11	18 53 23	14 41.0	27 56.1	8 23.1	16 18.2	13 58.3	2 29.9	14 05.0	22 23.5	7 26.2	3 31.2
8 Th	23 04 12	17 47 08	25 57 30	3♉02 58	14 32.4	27 26.0	9 37.9	17 00.5	14 10.3	2 41.9	14 07.5	22 21.5	7 26.2	3 29.6
9 F	23 08 08	18 47 07	10♉09 15	17 15 50	14 26.1	26 48.7	10 52.8	17 42.8	14 22.0	2 53.7	14 10.0	22 19.5	7R 26.3	3 28.1
10 Sa	23 12 05	19 47 04	24 22 18	1♊28 19	14 22.5	26 05.0	12 07.6	18 25.1	14 33.4	3 05.5	14 12.7	22 17.5	7 26.3	3 26.5
11 Su	23 16 02	20 47 00	8♊33 35	15 37 54	14D 21.1	25 16.0	13 22.4	19 07.4	14 44.5	3 17.1	14 15.5	22 15.5	7 26.2	3 24.9
12 M	23 19 58	21 46 53	22 41 06	29 43 05	14 21.1	24 22.9	14 37.2	19 49.8	14 55.3	3 28.7	14 18.4	22 13.4	7 26.1	3 23.3
13 Tu	23 23 55	22 46 43	6♋43 46	13♋43 05	14R 21.5	23 27.0	15 51.9	20 32.1	15 05.9	3 40.2	14 21.4	22 11.3	7 26.0	3 21.7
14 W	23 27 51	23 46 32	20 40 58	27 37 20	14 20.8	22 29.6	17 06.7	21 14.5	15 16.1	3 51.6	14 24.6	22 09.2	7 25.9	3 20.0
15 Th	23 31 48	24 46 18	4♌32 05	11♌25 05	14 18.1	21 32.0	18 21.4	21 56.9	15 26.0	4 03.0	14 27.8	22 07.0	7 25.7	3 18.4
16 F	23 35 44	25 46 01	18 16 09	25 05 04	14 12.6	20 35.4	19 36.1	22 39.3	15 35.7	4 14.2	14 31.1	22 04.8	7 25.5	3 16.8
17 Sa	23 39 41	26 45 43	1♍51 36	8♍35 30	14 04.2	19 40.9	20 50.8	23 21.7	15 45.0	4 25.4	14 34.4	22 02.6	7 25.2	3 15.1
18 Su	23 43 37	27 45 23	15 16 28	21 54 15	13 53.4	18 49.5	22 05.5	24 04.1	15 54.1	4 36.4	14 37.9	22 00.3	7 25.0	3 13.5
19 M	23 47 34	28 45 00	28 28 36	4♎59 17	13 40.9	18 02.2	23 20.2	24 46.5	16 02.8	4 47.4	14 41.5	21 58.0	7 24.6	3 11.9
20 Tu	23 51 30	29 44 35	11♎26 10	17 49 07	13 28.0	17 19.6	24 34.8	25 29.0	16 11.2	4 58.3	14 45.2	21 55.7	7 24.3	3 10.2
21 W	23 55 27	0♈44 09	24 08 06	0♏23 10	13 15.8	16 42.2	25 49.5	26 11.5	16 19.2	5 09.0	14 49.0	21 53.4	7 23.9	3 08.6
22 Th	23 59 24	1 43 41	6♏34 26	12 42 07	13 05.3	16 10.4	27 04.1	26 54.0	16 27.0	5 19.7	14 52.9	21 51.0	7 23.5	3 06.9
23 F	0 03 20	2 43 11	18 46 28	24 47 51	12 57.3	15 44.5	28 18.7	27 36.5	16 34.4	5 30.3	14 56.8	21 48.7	7 23.1	3 05.2
24 Sa	0 07 17	3 42 39	0♐46 43	6♐43 31	12 52.1	15 24.6	29 33.4	28 19.0	16 41.5	5 40.8	15 00.9	21 46.3	7 22.6	3 03.6
25 Su	0 11 13	4 42 05	12 38 50	18 33 14	12 49.3	15 10.7	0♈48.0	29 01.5	16 48.3	5 51.1	15 05.0	21 43.9	7 22.1	3 01.9
26 M	0 15 10	5 41 30	24 27 22	0♑21 52	12D 48.4	15D 02.9	2 02.5	29 44.1	16 54.7	6 01.4	15 09.2	21 41.4	7 21.6	3 00.3
27 Tu	0 19 06	6 40 53	6♑17 28	12 14 49	12R 48.4	15 00.9	3 17.1	0♒26.6	17 00.7	6 11.6	15 13.6	21 39.0	7 21.0	2 58.6
28 W	0 23 03	7 40 14	18 14 39	24 17 37	12 48.1	15 04.6	4 31.7	1 09.2	17 06.5	6 21.6	15 18.0	21 36.5	7 20.4	2 57.0
29 Th	0 26 59	8 39 33	0♒24 25	6♒35 37	12 46.4	15 13.8	5 46.2	1 51.8	17 11.8	6 31.6	15 22.5	21 34.0	7 19.8	2 55.3
30 F	0 30 56	9 38 50	12 51 50	19 13 31	12 42.5	15 28.2	7 00.8	2 34.4	17 16.8	6 41.4	15 27.1	21 31.5	7 19.1	2 53.7
31 Sa	0 34 53	10 38 06	25 41 04	2♓14 46	12 36.0	15 47.8	8 15.3	3 17.0	17 21.5	6 51.1	15 31.7	21 29.0	7 18.5	2 52.0

April 1973 LONGITUDE

Day	Sid.Time	☉	0 hr ☽	Noon ☽	True ☊	☿	♀	♂	⚳	♃	♄	♅	♆	♇
1 Su	0 38 49	11♈37 19	8♓54 47	15♓41 07	12♑26.8	16♓12.1	9♈29.8	3♒59.5	17♐25.8	7♒00.7	15♊36.5	21♎26.5	7♐17.7	2♎50.4
2 M	0 42 46	12 36 31	22 33 35	29 31 54	12R 15.6	16 40.9	10 44.3	4 42.1	17 29.7	7 10.2	15 41.3	21R 24.0	7R 17.0	2R 48.8
3 Tu	0 46 42	13 35 41	6♈35 35	13♈44 00	12 03.4	17 14.1	11 58.8	5 24.8	17 33.2	7 19.6	15 46.2	21 21.4	7 16.2	2 47.2
4 W	0 50 39	14 34 48	20 56 23	28 11 54	11 51.5	17 51.4	13 13.2	6 07.4	17 36.4	7 28.8	15 51.2	21 18.9	7 15.4	2 45.5
5 Th	0 54 35	15 33 54	5♉29 38	12♉48 38	11 41.3	18 32.6	14 27.7	6 50.0	17 39.2	7 38.0	15 56.3	21 16.3	7 14.6	2 43.9
6 F	0 58 32	16 32 57	20 07 59	27 26 50	11 33.6	19 17.4	15 42.1	7 32.6	17 41.6	7 47.0	16 01.4	21 13.7	7 13.7	2 42.3
7 Sa	1 02 28	17 31 59	4♊44 25	12♊00 03	11 28.8	20 05.7	16 56.5	8 15.2	17 43.6	7 55.9	16 06.6	21 11.2	7 12.9	2 40.7
8 Su	1 06 25	18 30 58	19 13 13	26 23 30	11 26.5	20 57.3	18 10.9	8 57.8	17 45.3	8 04.6	16 12.0	21 08.6	7 11.9	2 39.2
9 M	1 10 22	19 29 54	3♋30 37	10♋34 23	11 26.0	21 52.1	19 25.3	9 40.4	17 46.6	8 13.2	16 17.3	21 06.0	7 11.0	2 37.6
10 Tu	1 14 18	20 28 49	17 34 45	24 31 41	11 26.0	22 49.7	20 39.6	10 23.0	17 47.5	8 21.7	16 22.8	21 03.4	7 10.1	2 36.0
11 W	1 18 15	21 27 41	1♌25 15	8♌15 31	11 25.2	23 50.3	21 53.9	11 05.6	17R 48.0	8 30.1	16 28.3	21 00.9	7 09.1	2 34.5
12 Th	1 22 11	22 26 30	15 02 37	21 46 38	11 22.5	24 53.5	23 08.3	11 48.2	17 48.1	8 38.3	16 33.9	20 58.3	7 08.0	2 32.9
13 F	1 26 08	23 25 18	28 27 40	5♍05 47	11 17.0	25 59.3	24 22.6	12 30.8	17 47.8	8 46.4	16 39.6	20 55.7	7 07.0	2 31.4
14 Sa	1 30 04	24 24 03	11♍41 02	18 13 27	11 08.8	27 07.6	25 36.8	13 13.5	17 47.2	8 54.4	16 45.3	20 53.1	7 05.9	2 29.9
15 Su	1 34 01	25 22 45	24 43 01	1♎09 43	10 58.1	28 18.2	26 51.1	13 56.1	17 46.2	9 02.2	16 51.1	20 50.6	7 04.9	2 28.4
16 M	1 37 57	26 21 26	7♎33 32	13 54 25	10 45.7	29 31.2	28 05.3	14 38.7	17 44.7	9 09.9	16 56.9	20 48.0	7 03.7	2 26.9
17 Tu	1 41 54	27 20 05	20 12 21	26 27 18	10 32.9	0♈46.3	29 19.5	15 21.3	17 42.9	9 17.4	17 02.9	20 45.4	7 02.6	2 25.4
18 W	1 45 51	28 18 42	2♏39 18	8♏48 24	10 20.7	2 03.6	0♉33.7	16 03.9	17 40.7	9 24.8	17 08.8	20 42.9	7 01.5	2 24.0
19 Th	1 49 47	29 17 17	14 54 42	20 58 19	10 10.2	3 23.0	1 47.9	16 46.5	17 38.2	9 32.1	17 14.9	20 40.3	7 00.3	2 22.5
20 F	1 53 44	0♉15 50	26 59 28	2♐58 25	10 02.0	4 44.5	3 02.1	17 29.1	17 35.2	9 39.2	17 21.0	20 37.8	6 59.1	2 21.1
21 Sa	1 57 40	1 14 22	8♐55 27	14 50 58	9 56.5	6 07.9	4 16.3	18 11.7	17 31.8	9 46.2	17 27.2	20 35.3	6 57.9	2 19.7
22 Su	2 01 37	2 12 52	20 45 22	26 39 09	9 53.6	7 33.2	5 30.4	18 54.3	17 28.1	9 53.0	17 33.4	20 32.7	6 56.6	2 18.3
23 M	2 05 33	3 11 20	2♑32 50	8♑26 59	9D 52.7	9 00.5	6 44.5	19 36.9	17 23.9	9 59.7	17 39.7	20 30.2	6 55.4	2 16.9
24 Tu	2 09 30	4 09 46	14 22 13	20 19 10	9 53.0	10 29.7	7 58.7	20 19.4	17 19.4	10 06.2	17 46.1	20 27.8	6 54.1	2 15.6
25 W	2 13 26	5 08 11	26 18 30	2♒20 54	9R 53.5	12 00.7	9 12.8	21 02.0	17 14.5	10 12.5	17 52.5	20 25.3	6 52.8	2 14.3
26 Th	2 17 23	6 06 34	8♒27 02	14 37 33	9 53.2	13 33.5	10 26.8	21 44.6	17 09.3	10 18.8	17 58.9	20 22.8	6 51.4	2 12.9
27 F	2 21 20	7 04 56	20 53 06	27 14 16	9 51.2	15 08.2	11 40.9	22 27.1	17 03.6	10 24.8	18 05.5	20 20.4	6 50.1	2 11.6
28 Sa	2 25 16	8 03 16	3♓41 34	10♓15 26	9 47.0	16 44.7	12 55.0	23 09.7	16 57.6	10 30.7	18 12.0	20 18.0	6 48.7	2 10.4
29 Su	2 29 13	9 01 35	16 56 10	23 43 56	9 40.7	18 23.0	14 09.0	23 52.2	16 51.2	10 36.4	18 18.6	20 15.5	6 47.4	2 09.1
30 M	2 33 09	9 59 52	0♈38 45	7♈40 27	9 32.5	20 03.2	15 23.0	24 34.7	16 44.4	10 42.0	18 25.3	20 13.2	6 46.0	2 07.9

Astro Data Dy Hr Mn	Planet Ingress Dy Hr Mn	Last Aspect Dy Hr Mn	☽ Ingress Dy Hr Mn	Last Aspect Dy Hr Mn	☽ Ingress Dy Hr Mn	☽ Phases & Eclipses Dy Hr Mn
☿R 4 12:58	☉ ♈ 20 18:12	1 10:11 ☿ ⚹	♒ 1 14:22	1 12:56 ☿ ☌	♈ 2 12:48	5 0:07 ● 14♓17
☽0N 5 9:06	♀ ♈ 24 20:34	3 8:50 ♅ △	♓ 3 22:31	4 0:39 ♅ ☍	♉ 4 14:58	11 21:26 ☽ 21♊11
♅∠♆ 6 2:57	♂ ♒ 26 20:59	6 0:53 ☿ ☌	♈ 6 3:37	5 21:53 ☿ ⚹	♊ 6 16:12	18 23:33 ○ 28♍14
♆R 9 14:32		7 17:56 ♅ ☍	♉ 8 6:51	8 3:14 ♅ △	♋ 8 18:04	26 23:46 ☾ 6♑11
♃△♇ 12 2:05	☿ ♈ 16 21:17	10 3:21 ☿ ⚹	♊ 10 9:31	10 8:50 ☿ △	♌ 10 21:31	
☿0S 14 21:03	♀ ♉ 18 1:05	12 3:26 ☿ □	♋ 12 12:29	12 14:41 ♀ △	♍ 13 2:47	3 11:45 ● 13♈35
☽0S 18 7:25	☉ ♉ 20 5:30	14 4:50 ☉ △	♌ 14 16:07	15 6:07 ☿ ☍	♎ 15 9:50	10 4:28 ☽ 20♋10
☉0N 20 18:13		16 6:43 ♅ ⚹	♍ 16 20:42	17 18:10 ♀ ☍	♏ 17 18:51	17 13:51 ○ 27♎25
☿D 27 8:18		18 23:33 ☉ ☍	♎ 19 2:48	19 3:10 ♂ □	♐ 20 6:02	25 17:59 ☾ 5♒23
♀0N 27 11:02		21 3:27 ♂ □	♏ 21 11:15	21 23:37 ♅ ⚹	♑ 22 18:49	
☽0N 1 18:18		23 19:52 ♀ △	♐ 23 22:26	24 12:17 ♅ □	♒ 25 7:21	
♃⚹♆ 3 4:00		25 18:26 ♅ ⚹	♑ 26 11:16	27 2:26 ♂ ☌	♓ 27 17:10	
⚳R 12 7:48		28 6:42 ♅ □	♒ 28 23:12	29 2:22 ♄ □	♈ 29 22:53	
☽0S 14 13:44		30 16:17 ♅ △	♓ 31 7:55			
☿0N 21 14:34	☽0N29 3:33					

Astro Data

1 March 1973
Julian Day # 26723
SVP 5♓37'47"
GC 26♐27.9 ⚴ 15♏50.6
Eris 12♈29.0 ⚵ 18♐16.6
⚷ 14♈45.3 ⚶ 6♊38.5
☽ Mean ☊ 14♑06.1

1 April 1973
Julian Day # 26754
SVP 5♓37'44"
GC 26♐27.9 ⚴ 13♏23.8R
Eris 12♈49.0 ⚵ 21♐59.8
⚷ 16♈29.1 ⚶ 15♊48.3
☽ Mean ☊ 12♑27.6

LONGITUDE — May 1973

Day	Sid.Time	☉	0 hr ☽	Noon ☽	True ☊	☿	♀	♂	⚳	♃	♄	♅	♆	♇
1 Tu	2 37 06	10♉58 07	14♈48 41	22♈02 53	9♑23.4	21♈45.1	16♉37.1	25♒17.1	16♐37.3	10♒47.4	18♊32.0	20♎10.8	6♐44.6	2♎06.7
2 W	2 41 02	11 56 21	29 22 20	6♉46 06	9R 14.4	23 28.9	17 51.1	25 59.6	16R 29.8	10 52.7	18 38.8	20R 08.4	6R 43.1	2R 05.5
3 Th	2 44 59	12 54 33	14♉13 10	21 42 24	9 06.6	25 14.5	19 05.0	26 42.0	16 22.0	10 57.7	18 45.6	20 06.1	6 41.7	2 04.3
4 F	2 48 55	13 52 43	29 12 40	6♊42 46	9 00.8	27 01.9	20 19.0	27 24.5	16 13.9	11 02.7	18 52.5	20 03.8	6 40.3	2 03.2
5 Sa	2 52 52	14 50 52	14♊11 39	21 38 17	8 57.4	28 51.2	21 33.0	28 06.8	16 05.4	11 07.4	18 59.4	20 01.6	6 38.8	2 02.1
6 Su	2 56 49	15 48 58	29 01 50	6♋21 35	8D 56.2	0♉42.3	22 46.9	28 49.2	15 56.5	11 12.0	19 06.4	19 59.3	6 37.3	2 01.0
7 M	3 00 45	16 47 03	13♋36 58	20 47 36	8 56.6	2 35.2	24 00.8	29 31.5	15 47.4	11 16.4	19 13.4	19 57.1	6 35.8	1 59.9
8 Tu	3 04 42	17 45 06	27 53 14	4♌53 46	8 57.5	4 30.0	25 14.7	0♓13.8	15 38.0	11 20.6	19 20.4	19 54.9	6 34.3	1 58.9
9 W	3 08 38	18 43 07	11♌49 12	18 39 37	8R 58.1	6 26.5	26 28.6	0 56.1	15 28.2	11 24.6	19 27.5	19 52.7	6 32.8	1 57.8
10 Th	3 12 35	19 41 06	25 25 10	2♍06 04	8 57.3	8 24.9	27 42.5	1 38.3	15 18.2	11 28.5	19 34.6	19 50.6	6 31.3	1 56.8
11 F	3 16 31	20 39 03	8♍42 33	15 14 53	8 54.6	10 25.0	28 56.3	2 20.6	15 07.9	11 32.2	19 41.8	19 48.5	6 29.7	1 55.9
12 Sa	3 20 28	21 36 58	21 43 18	28 08 04	8 49.9	12 26.8	0♊10.1	3 02.7	14 57.3	11 35.7	19 49.0	19 46.4	6 28.2	1 54.9
13 Su	3 24 24	22 34 51	4♎29 24	10♎47 32	8 43.4	14 30.3	1 23.9	3 44.9	14 46.5	11 39.1	19 56.2	19 44.4	6 26.6	1 54.0
14 M	3 28 21	23 32 43	17 02 40	23 15 00	8 35.7	16 35.3	2 37.7	4 27.0	14 35.4	11 42.2	20 03.4	19 42.4	6 25.0	1 53.1
15 Tu	3 32 18	24 30 33	29 24 41	5♏31 55	8 27.6	18 41.8	3 51.5	5 09.1	14 24.1	11 45.2	20 10.7	19 40.4	6 23.5	1 52.3
16 W	3 36 14	25 28 22	11♏36 50	17 39 36	8 19.8	20 49.5	5 05.3	5 51.1	14 12.5	11 48.0	20 18.1	19 38.5	6 21.9	1 51.4
17 Th	3 40 11	26 26 09	23 40 24	29 39 25	8 13.2	22 58.5	6 19.0	6 33.2	14 00.8	11 50.6	20 25.4	19 36.6	6 20.3	1 50.6
18 F	3 44 07	27 23 55	5♐36 51	11♐32 56	8 08.3	25 08.5	7 32.7	7 15.1	13 48.8	11 53.1	20 32.8	19 34.7	6 18.7	1 49.9
19 Sa	3 48 04	28 21 39	17 27 55	23 22 07	8 05.2	27 19.2	8 46.4	7 57.1	13 36.6	11 55.3	20 40.2	19 32.9	6 17.1	1 49.1
20 Su	3 52 00	29 19 22	29 15 51	5♑09 28	8D 04.0	29 30.4	10 00.1	8 39.0	13 24.3	11 57.4	20 47.7	19 31.1	6 15.5	1 48.4
21 M	3 55 57	0♊17 04	11♑03 24	16 58 05	8 04.4	1♊42.0	11 13.8	9 20.9	13 11.8	11 59.3	20 55.2	19 29.3	6 13.9	1 47.7
22 Tu	3 59 53	1 14 45	22 53 59	28 51 39	8 05.7	3 53.6	12 27.5	10 02.7	12 59.1	12 01.0	21 02.7	19 27.6	6 12.3	1 47.1
23 W	4 03 50	2 12 25	4♒51 35	10♒54 23	8 07.4	6 04.9	13 41.2	10 44.5	12 46.3	12 02.5	21 10.2	19 25.9	6 10.7	1 46.4
24 Th	4 07 47	3 10 04	17 00 38	23 10 55	8R 08.7	8 15.7	14 54.8	11 26.2	12 33.4	12 03.8	21 17.7	19 24.3	6 09.1	1 45.8
25 F	4 11 43	4 07 41	29 25 49	5♓45 54	8 09.1	10 25.8	16 08.4	12 07.9	12 20.4	12 05.0	21 25.3	19 22.7	6 07.4	1 45.3
26 Sa	4 15 40	5 05 18	12♓11 43	18 43 43	8 08.3	12 34.7	17 22.0	12 49.5	12 07.3	12 05.9	21 32.9	19 21.1	6 05.8	1 44.7
27 Su	4 19 36	6 02 54	25 22 19	2♈07 48	8 06.1	14 42.3	18 35.7	13 31.0	11 54.0	12 06.7	21 40.5	19 19.6	6 04.2	1 44.2
28 M	4 23 33	7 00 29	9♈00 20	15 59 56	8 02.7	16 48.4	19 49.2	14 12.5	11 40.8	12 07.2	21 48.2	19 18.1	6 02.6	1 43.7
29 Tu	4 27 29	7 58 03	23 06 28	0♉19 35	7 58.6	18 52.8	21 02.8	14 54.0	11 27.4	12 07.6	21 55.8	19 16.7	6 00.9	1 43.3
30 W	4 31 26	8 55 36	7♉38 46	15 03 18	7 54.4	20 55.2	22 16.4	15 35.4	11 14.1	12R 07.8	22 03.5	19 15.3	5 59.3	1 42.9
31 Th	4 35 22	9 53 09	22 32 17	0♊04 41	7 50.8	22 55.5	23 30.0	16 16.7	11 00.7	12 07.7	22 11.2	19 14.0	5 57.7	1 42.5

LONGITUDE — June 1973

Day	Sid.Time	☉	0 hr ☽	Noon ☽	True ☊	☿	♀	♂	⚳	♃	♄	♅	♆	♇
1 F	4 39 19	10♊50 40	7♊39 21	15♊15 03	7♑48.3	24♊53.5	24♊43.5	16♓57.9	10♐47.3	12♒07.5	22♊18.9	19♎12.7	5♐56.1	1♎42.2
2 Sa	4 43 16	11 48 11	22 50 34	0♋24 42	7D 47.0	26 49.3	25 57.0	17 39.1	10R 33.9	12R 07.1	22 26.7	19R 11.5	5R 54.5	1R 41.8
3 Su	4 47 12	12 45 40	7♋56 18	15 24 23	7 47.0	28 42.6	27 10.6	18 20.2	10 20.6	12 06.5	22 34.4	19 10.3	5 52.8	1 41.6
4 M	4 51 09	13 43 08	22 48 05	0♌06 43	7 47.9	0♋33.5	28 24.1	19 01.2	10 07.3	12 05.8	22 42.1	19 09.1	5 51.2	1 41.3
5 Tu	4 55 05	14 40 35	7♌19 44	14 26 47	7 49.3	2 21.7	29 37.6	19 42.1	9 54.0	12 04.8	22 49.9	19 08.0	5 49.6	1 41.1
6 W	4 59 02	15 38 01	21 27 40	28 22 19	7 50.6	4 07.4	0♋51.0	20 23.0	9 40.8	12 03.6	22 57.7	19 06.9	5 48.0	1 40.9
7 Th	5 02 58	16 35 25	5♍10 50	11♍53 21	7R 51.3	5 50.5	2 04.5	21 03.7	9 27.7	12 02.3	23 05.5	19 05.9	5 46.4	1 40.7
8 F	5 06 55	17 32 48	18 30 07	25 01 28	7 51.2	7 30.9	3 17.9	21 44.4	9 14.8	12 00.7	23 13.2	19 05.0	5 44.9	1 40.6
9 Sa	5 10 51	18 30 10	1♎27 44	7♎49 19	7 50.2	9 08.6	4 31.3	22 25.0	9 01.9	11 59.0	23 21.0	19 04.0	5 43.3	1 40.5
10 Su	5 14 48	19 27 31	14 06 37	20 20 01	7 48.4	10 43.6	5 44.7	23 05.5	8 49.2	11 57.1	23 28.8	19 03.2	5 41.7	1 40.4
11 M	5 18 45	20 24 52	26 29 56	2♏36 46	7 46.0	12 15.9	6 58.1	23 45.9	8 36.6	11 55.0	23 36.6	19 02.4	5 40.2	1D 40.4
12 Tu	5 22 41	21 22 11	8♏40 52	14 42 37	7 43.5	13 45.4	8 11.5	24 26.3	8 24.1	11 52.7	23 44.5	19 01.6	5 38.6	1 40.4
13 W	5 26 38	22 19 29	20 42 20	26 40 22	7 41.2	15 12.2	9 24.8	25 06.5	8 11.9	11 50.2	23 52.3	19 00.9	5 37.1	1 40.5
14 Th	5 30 34	23 16 47	2♐37 01	8♐32 34	7 39.2	16 36.2	10 38.2	25 46.7	7 59.8	11 47.6	24 00.1	19 00.2	5 35.5	1 40.5
15 F	5 34 31	24 14 04	14 27 19	20 21 33	7 37.9	17 57.3	11 51.5	26 26.7	7 47.9	11 44.7	24 07.9	18 59.6	5 34.0	1 40.6
16 Sa	5 38 27	25 11 20	26 15 31	2♑09 31	7D 37.3	19 15.5	13 04.8	27 06.7	7 36.2	11 41.7	24 15.7	18 59.0	5 32.5	1 40.8
17 Su	5 42 24	26 08 36	8♑03 50	13 58 46	7 37.3	20 30.9	14 18.0	27 46.5	7 24.7	11 38.5	24 23.5	18 58.5	5 31.0	1 40.9
18 M	5 46 20	27 05 52	19 54 36	25 51 41	7 37.9	21 43.2	15 31.3	28 26.2	7 13.5	11 35.1	24 31.3	18 58.0	5 29.5	1 41.1
19 Tu	5 50 17	28 03 07	1♒50 20	7♒50 57	7 38.7	22 52.6	16 44.6	29 05.9	7 02.5	11 31.6	24 39.1	18 57.6	5 28.0	1 41.4
20 W	5 54 14	29 00 21	13 53 53	19 59 33	7 39.6	23 58.8	17 57.8	29 45.4	6 51.7	11 27.9	24 46.9	18 57.3	5 26.6	1 41.6
21 Th	5 58 10	29 57 35	26 08 23	2♓20 47	7 40.3	25 01.9	19 11.0	0♈24.8	6 41.2	11 24.0	24 54.7	18 57.0	5 25.1	1 41.9
22 F	6 02 07	0♋54 50	8♓37 12	14 58 05	7 40.9	26 01.7	20 24.2	1 04.1	6 31.0	11 19.9	25 02.5	18 56.7	5 23.7	1 42.3
23 Sa	6 06 03	1 52 04	21 23 51	27 54 53	7R 41.1	26 58.3	21 37.4	1 43.2	6 21.0	11 15.7	25 10.3	18 56.5	5 22.3	1 42.6
24 Su	6 10 00	2 49 17	4♈31 34	11♈14 11	7 41.1	27 51.3	22 50.6	2 22.2	6 11.4	11 11.3	25 18.1	18 56.3	5 20.9	1 43.0
25 M	6 13 56	3 46 31	18 02 58	24 58 03	7 40.9	28 40.9	24 03.8	3 01.1	6 02.0	11 06.7	25 25.9	18 56.2	5 19.5	1 43.5
26 Tu	6 17 53	4 43 45	1♉59 26	9♉07 00	7 40.6	29 26.8	25 16.9	3 39.9	5 52.9	11 02.0	25 33.6	18D 56.2	5 18.1	1 43.9
27 W	6 21 49	5 40 59	16 20 29	23 39 28	7 40.3	0♌09.0	26 30.1	4 18.5	5 44.1	10 57.1	25 41.4	18 56.2	5 16.8	1 44.4
28 Th	6 25 46	6 38 13	1♊03 20	8♊31 21	7 40.2	0 47.3	27 43.2	4 57.0	5 35.7	10 52.1	25 49.1	18 56.2	5 15.4	1 45.0
29 F	6 29 43	7 35 28	16 02 36	23 36 05	7 40.2	1 21.6	28 56.3	5 35.3	5 27.5	10 46.9	25 56.8	18 56.4	5 14.1	1 45.5
30 Sa	6 33 39	8 32 42	1♋10 42	8♋45 15	7 40.2	1 51.8	0♌09.4	6 13.4	5 19.7	10 41.5	26 04.6	18 56.5	5 12.8	1 46.1

Astro Data

	Dy Hr Mn
☽ 0S	11 18:32
♄△♅	12 5:28
☽ 0N	26 11:41
♃ R	30 22:10
☽ 0S	7 23:54
♇ D	11 20:11
☽ 0N	22 18:21
♅ D	26 22:01
♃⚼♄	28 17:30

Planet Ingress

	Dy Hr Mn
☿ ♉	6 2:55
♂ ♓	8 4:09
♀ ♊	12 8:42
☿ ♊	20 17:24
☉ ♊	21 4:54
☿ ♋	4 4:42
♀ ♋	5 19:20
♂ ♈	20 20:54
☉ ♋	21 13:01
☿ ♌	27 6:42
♀ ♌	30 8:55

Last Aspect / ☽ Ingress

Last Aspect Dy Hr Mn		☽ Ingress	Dy Hr Mn
1 17:35	♂ ✶	♉	2 1:01
3 20:23	♂ □	♊	4 1:16
6 1:23	☿ ✶	♋	6 1:35
7 17:57	♀ ✶	♌	8 3:36
10 3:18	♀ □	♍	10 8:13
11 22:49	☉ △	♎	12 15:31
14 5:45	♄ △	♏	15 1:09
17 4:58	☉ ☍	♐	17 12:41
19 6:27	♄ ☍	♑	20 1:30
21 17:06	♅ □	♒	22 14:17
24 8:19	♄ △	♓	25 1:05
26 17:10	♄ □	♈	27 8:14
28 21:54	♄ ✶	♉	29 11:28
30 12:54	♂ ✶	♊	31 11:53

Last Aspect / ☽ Ingress

Last Aspect Dy Hr Mn		☽ Ingress	Dy Hr Mn
2 5:29	☿ ☌	♋	2 11:21
3 18:05	♅ □	♌	4 11:49
6 2:30	♄ ✶	♍	6 14:51
8 8:38	♄ □	♎	8 21:16
10 18:11	♄ △	♏	11 6:52
13 8:40	♂ △	♐	13 18:43
16 1:07	♂ □	♑	16 7:37
18 17:29	♂ ✶	♒	18 20:19
21 7:01	☉ △	♓	21 7:29
23 10:09	☿ △	♈	23 15:48
25 18:45	☿ □	♉	25 20:37
27 17:02	♀ ✶	♊	27 22:18
29 15:45	♄ ☌	♋	29 22:08

☽ Phases & Eclipses

Dy Hr Mn	
2 20:55	● 12♉18
9 12:07	☽ 18♌43
17 4:58	○ 26♏09
25 8:40	☾ 4♓00
1 4:34	● 10♊33
7 21:11	☽ 16♍57
15 20:35	○ 24♐35
15 20:50	• A 0.468
23 19:45	☾ 2♈11
30 11:39	● 8♋32
30 11:37:57	• T 07'04"

Astro Data

1 May 1973
Julian Day # 26784
SVP 5♓37'40"
GC 26♐28.0 ⚴ 5♏04.9R
Eris 13♈08.7 ✱ 21♐03.8R
⚷ 18♈13.5 ⚶ 26♊50.1
☽ Mean ☊ 10♑52.2

1 June 1973
Julian Day # 26815
SVP 5♓37'36"
GC 26♐28.1 ⚴ 27♎56.3R
Eris 13♈24.5 ✱ 15♐28.7R
⚷ 19♈44.9 ⚶ 9♋31.0
☽ Mean ☊ 9♑13.8

July 1973 — LONGITUDE

Day	Sid.Time	☉	0 hr ☽	Noon ☽	True ☊	☿	♀	♂	⚳	♃	♄	♅	♆	♇
1 Su	6 37 36	9♋29 55	16♋18 37	23♋49 37	7♑40.1	2♌17.8	1♌22.5	6♈51.4	5♐12.2	10♒36.0	26♊12.2	18♎56.7	5♐11.5	1♎46.7
2 M	6 41 32	10 27 09	1♌17 15	8♌40 32	7R40.0	2 39.5	2 35.5	7 29.2	5R05.1	10R30.4	26 19.9	18 57.0	5R10.3	1 47.4
3 Tu	6 45 29	11 24 22	15 58 41	23 11 03	7 39.6	2 56.7	3 48.6	8 06.9	4 58.3	10 24.6	26 27.6	18 57.3	5 09.1	1 48.1
4 W	6 49 25	12 21 35	0♍17 11	7♍16 45	7 39.2	3 09.3	5 01.6	8 44.4	4 51.9	10 18.7	26 35.2	18 57.7	5 07.8	1 48.8
5 Th	6 53 22	13 18 48	14 09 36	20 55 47	7 38.7	3 17.3	6 14.6	9 21.7	4 45.8	10 12.7	26 42.8	18 58.1	5 06.6	1 49.6
6 F	6 57 19	14 16 01	27 35 23	4♎08 42	7D38.3	3R20.7	7 27.6	9 58.8	4 40.1	10 06.5	26 50.4	18 58.6	5 05.5	1 50.3
7 Sa	7 01 15	15 13 13	10♎36 01	16 57 47	7 38.2	3 19.3	8 40.5	10 35.7	4 34.8	10 00.3	26 58.0	18 59.2	5 04.3	1 51.2
8 Su	7 05 12	16 10 25	23 14 27	29 26 32	7 38.5	3 13.2	9 53.4	11 12.5	4 29.8	9 53.9	27 05.5	18 59.7	5 03.2	1 52.0
9 M	7 09 08	17 07 37	5♏34 32	11♏39 00	7 39.1	3 02.5	11 06.3	11 49.0	4 25.1	9 47.3	27 13.1	19 00.4	5 02.1	1 52.9
10 Tu	7 13 05	18 04 49	17 40 28	23 39 27	7 40.0	2 47.2	12 19.2	12 25.4	4 20.9	9 40.7	27 20.6	19 01.1	5 01.0	1 53.8
11 W	7 17 01	19 02 01	29 36 28	5♐32 00	7 41.1	2 27.6	13 32.1	13 01.6	4 17.0	9 34.0	27 28.0	19 01.8	4 59.9	1 54.7
12 Th	7 20 58	19 59 13	11♐26 31	17 20 27	7 42.1	2 03.8	14 44.9	13 37.6	4 13.4	9 27.2	27 35.5	19 02.6	4 58.9	1 55.7
13 F	7 24 54	20 56 25	23 14 12	29 08 10	7R42.8	1 36.1	15 57.7	14 13.3	4 10.3	9 20.2	27 42.9	19 03.5	4 57.9	1 56.7
14 Sa	7 28 51	21 53 37	5♑02 41	10♑58 06	7 42.9	1 04.9	17 10.5	14 48.9	4 07.5	9 13.2	27 50.3	19 04.4	4 56.9	1 57.7
15 Su	7 32 48	22 50 50	16 54 41	22 52 43	7 42.3	0 30.6	18 23.3	15 24.2	4 05.1	9 06.1	27 57.7	19 05.3	4 55.9	1 58.8
16 M	7 36 44	23 48 03	28 52 29	4♒54 12	7 41.0	29♋53.8	19 36.0	15 59.3	4 03.0	8 58.9	28 05.0	19 06.3	4 55.0	1 59.9
17 Tu	7 40 41	24 45 16	10♒58 06	17 04 25	7 39.0	29 14.9	20 48.7	16 34.2	4 01.3	8 51.7	28 12.3	19 07.4	4 54.1	2 01.0
18 W	7 44 37	25 42 30	23 13 22	29 25 08	7 36.4	28 34.7	22 01.4	17 08.8	4 00.0	8 44.3	28 19.5	19 08.5	4 53.2	2 02.1
19 Th	7 48 34	26 39 45	5♓39 58	11♓58 03	7 33.7	27 53.8	23 14.1	17 43.3	3 59.0	8 36.9	28 26.8	19 09.6	4 52.3	2 03.3
20 F	7 52 30	27 37 00	18 19 38	24 44 55	7 31.1	27 12.8	24 26.7	18 17.4	3 58.4	8 29.5	28 34.0	19 10.8	4 51.5	2 04.5
21 Sa	7 56 27	28 34 15	1♈14 07	7♈47 28	7 29.1	26 32.6	25 39.3	18 51.3	3D58.2	8 21.9	28 41.1	19 12.1	4 50.7	2 05.7
22 Su	8 00 23	29 31 32	14 25 10	21 07 24	7D27.9	25 53.8	26 51.9	19 25.0	3 58.3	8 14.4	28 48.2	19 13.4	4 49.9	2 07.0
23 M	8 04 20	0♌28 49	27 54 20	4♉46 04	7 27.8	25 17.2	28 04.5	19 58.3	3 58.8	8 06.7	28 55.3	19 14.7	4 49.1	2 08.3
24 Tu	8 08 17	1 26 08	11♉42 40	18 44 08	7 28.5	24 43.5	29 17.0	20 31.4	3 59.6	7 59.1	29 02.4	19 16.1	4 48.4	2 09.6
25 W	8 12 13	2 23 27	25 50 22	3♊01 11	7 29.8	24 13.2	0♍29.6	21 04.3	4 00.8	7 51.4	29 09.4	19 17.6	4 47.7	2 10.9
26 Th	8 16 10	3 20 48	10♊16 17	17 35 13	7 31.1	23 46.9	1 42.1	21 36.8	4 02.3	7 43.6	29 16.3	19 19.1	4 47.0	2 12.3
27 F	8 20 06	4 18 09	24 57 27	2♋22 18	7R32.0	23 25.3	2 54.5	22 09.0	4 04.3	7 35.9	29 23.2	19 20.6	4 46.4	2 13.7
28 Sa	8 24 03	5 15 32	9♋48 58	17 16 35	7 31.8	23 08.7	4 07.0	22 40.9	4 06.5	7 28.1	29 30.1	19 22.2	4 45.8	2 15.1
29 Su	8 27 59	6 12 55	24 44 11	2♌10 44	7 30.2	22 57.5	5 19.4	23 12.5	4 09.1	7 20.3	29 36.9	19 23.9	4 45.2	2 16.6
30 M	8 31 56	7 10 18	9♌35 15	16 56 44	7 27.3	22D52.1	6 31.8	23 43.7	4 12.1	7 12.5	29 43.7	19 25.6	4 44.7	2 18.0
31 Tu	8 35 52	8 07 43	24 14 17	1♍27 05	7 23.2	22 52.7	7 44.2	24 14.6	4 15.4	7 04.7	29 50.5	19 27.3	4 44.2	2 19.5

August 1973 — LONGITUDE

Day	Sid.Time	☉	0 hr ☽	Noon ☽	True ☊	☿	♀	♂	⚳	♃	♄	♅	♆	♇
1 W	8 39 49	9♌05 08	8♍34 28	15♍35 52	7♑18.6	22♋59.4	8♍56.5	24♈45.2	4♐19.0	6♒56.9	29♊57.1	19♎29.1	4♐43.7	2♎21.1
2 Th	8 43 46	10 02 34	22 30 57	29 19 29	7R14.0	23 12.6	10 08.8	25 15.4	4 23.0	6R49.1	0♋03.8	19 31.0	4R43.2	2 22.6
3 F	8 47 42	11 00 01	6♎01 25	12♎36 50	7 10.1	23 32.1	11 21.1	25 45.3	4 27.3	6 41.4	0 10.3	19 32.8	4 42.8	2 24.2
4 Sa	8 51 39	11 57 28	19 05 58	25 29 07	7 07.4	23 58.2	12 33.3	26 14.8	4 31.9	6 33.6	0 16.9	19 34.8	4 42.4	2 25.8
5 Su	8 55 35	12 54 56	1♏46 45	7♏59 19	7D06.1	24 30.7	13 45.5	26 43.9	4 36.9	6 25.9	0 23.4	19 36.8	4 42.0	2 27.4
6 M	8 59 32	13 52 25	14 07 24	20 11 35	7 06.2	25 09.7	14 57.7	27 12.7	4 42.2	6 18.2	0 29.8	19 38.8	4 41.7	2 29.0
7 Tu	9 03 28	14 49 54	26 12 29	2♐10 43	7 07.3	25 55.2	16 09.8	27 41.0	4 47.8	6 10.6	0 36.1	19 40.8	4 41.4	2 30.7
8 W	9 07 25	15 47 25	8♐06 56	14 01 44	7 08.9	26 47.0	17 21.9	28 09.0	4 53.7	6 03.0	0 42.5	19 43.0	4 41.1	2 32.4
9 Th	9 11 21	16 44 56	19 55 44	25 49 29	7R10.3	27 45.0	18 34.0	28 36.6	4 59.9	5 55.5	0 48.7	19 45.1	4 40.8	2 34.1
10 F	9 15 18	17 42 28	1♑43 33	7♑38 26	7 10.9	28 49.0	19 46.0	29 03.8	5 06.5	5 48.0	0 54.9	19 47.3	4 40.6	2 35.8
11 Sa	9 19 15	18 40 01	13 34 36	19 32 29	7 10.1	29 58.9	20 58.0	29 30.5	5 13.3	5 40.6	1 01.1	19 49.5	4 40.5	2 37.6
12 Su	9 23 11	19 37 35	25 32 26	1♒34 47	7 07.4	1♌14.6	22 09.9	29 56.8	5 20.5	5 33.2	1 07.1	19 51.8	4 40.3	2 39.4
13 M	9 27 08	20 35 10	7♒39 49	13 47 45	7 02.7	2 35.6	23 21.8	0♉22.7	5 27.9	5 25.9	1 13.2	19 54.1	4 40.2	2 41.2
14 Tu	9 31 04	21 32 47	19 58 45	26 12 56	6 56.4	4 01.8	24 33.7	0 48.1	5 35.7	5 18.7	1 19.1	19 56.5	4 40.1	2 43.0
15 W	9 35 01	22 30 24	2♓30 24	8♓51 10	6 48.8	5 32.9	25 45.5	1 13.1	5 43.7	5 11.6	1 25.0	19 58.9	4 40.1	2 44.8
16 Th	9 38 57	23 28 03	15 15 16	21 42 40	6 40.7	7 08.5	26 57.2	1 37.5	5 52.0	5 04.5	1 30.8	20 01.4	4D40.0	2 46.7
17 F	9 42 54	24 25 43	28 13 20	4♈47 14	6 33.0	8 48.2	28 09.0	2 01.5	6 00.6	4 57.6	1 36.6	20 03.8	4 40.0	2 48.6
18 Sa	9 46 50	25 23 25	11♈24 18	18 04 30	6 26.5	10 31.7	29 20.7	2 25.0	6 09.4	4 50.7	1 42.3	20 06.4	4 40.1	2 50.5
19 Su	9 50 47	26 21 08	24 47 48	1♉34 08	6 21.9	12 18.5	0♎32.3	2 48.0	6 18.6	4 43.9	1 47.9	20 08.9	4 40.2	2 52.4
20 M	9 54 44	27 18 53	8♉23 32	15 15 57	6D19.3	14 08.3	1 43.9	3 10.5	6 28.0	4 37.3	1 53.5	20 11.5	4 40.3	2 54.3
21 Tu	9 58 40	28 16 40	22 11 22	29 09 46	6 18.7	16 00.5	2 55.5	3 32.4	6 37.6	4 30.7	1 59.0	20 14.2	4 40.4	2 56.3
22 W	10 02 37	29 14 29	6♊11 07	13♊15 20	6 19.2	17 54.9	4 07.1	3 53.8	6 47.6	4 24.3	2 04.4	20 16.9	4 40.6	2 58.2
23 Th	10 06 33	0♍12 19	20 22 16	27 31 46	6R20.1	19 50.9	5 18.6	4 14.6	6 57.8	4 18.0	2 09.7	20 19.6	4 40.8	3 00.2
24 F	10 10 30	1 10 11	4♋43 32	11♋57 14	6 20.2	21 48.2	6 30.0	4 34.9	7 08.2	4 11.8	2 15.0	20 22.3	4 41.0	3 02.2
25 Sa	10 14 26	2 08 05	19 12 26	26 28 33	6 18.6	23 46.4	7 41.4	4 54.5	7 18.9	4 05.7	2 20.2	20 25.1	4 41.3	3 04.2
26 Su	10 18 23	3 06 00	3♌45 00	11♌01 03	6 14.7	25 45.2	8 52.8	5 13.5	7 29.9	3 59.8	2 25.3	20 27.9	4 41.6	3 06.3
27 M	10 22 19	4 03 57	18 15 57	25 28 55	6 08.3	27 44.2	10 04.1	5 31.9	7 41.1	3 54.0	2 30.4	20 30.8	4 42.0	3 08.3
28 Tu	10 26 16	5 01 56	2♍39 08	9♍45 52	5 59.8	29 43.3	11 15.4	5 49.7	7 52.5	3 48.3	2 35.4	20 33.7	4 42.3	3 10.4
29 W	10 30 13	5 59 56	16 48 24	23 46 08	5 50.2	1♍42.2	12 26.6	6 06.8	8 04.2	3 42.8	2 40.3	20 36.6	4 42.7	3 12.5
30 Th	10 34 09	6 57 57	0♎38 35	7♎25 23	5 40.3	3 40.7	13 37.8	6 23.2	8 16.1	3 37.5	2 45.1	20 39.6	4 43.2	3 14.6
31 F	10 38 06	7 56 00	14 06 18	20 41 16	5 31.3	5 38.5	14 49.0	6 39.0	8 28.3	3 32.2	2 49.8	20 42.6	4 43.6	3 16.7

Astro Data

	Dy Hr Mn
♂0N	1 2:19
☽0S	5 7:26
☿R	6 17:00
☽0N	20 0:12
⚳D	21 16:04
☿D	30 21:48
☽0S	1 17:03
♅∠♆	7 17:14
☽0N	16 6:19
♆D	16 16:05
♃⚹♆	20 1:20
♀0S	20 11:28
☽0S	29 3:17

Planet Ingress

	Dy Hr Mn
☿ ♋R	16 8:03
☉ ♌	22 23:56
♀ ♍	25 2:13
♄ ♋	1 22:20
☿ ♌	11 12:21
♂ ♉	12 14:56
♀ ♎	19 1:10
☉ ♍	23 6:53
☿ ♍	28 15:22

Last Aspect / ☽ Ingress (July)

Last Aspect Dy Hr Mn		☽ Ingress Dy Hr Mn
1 4:12	♅ □	♌ 1 21:55
3 17:34	♄ ⚹	♍ 3 23:31
5 22:31	♄ □	♎ 6 4:23
8 7:23	♄ △	♏ 8 13:05
9 23:51	☉ △	♐ 11 0:48
13 9:05	♄ ☍	♑ 13 13:45
15 11:56	☉ ☍	♒ 16 2:15
18 9:52	♄ △	♓ 18 13:07
20 19:09	♄ □	♈ 20 21:43
23 1:42	♄ ⚹	♉ 23 3:41
24 21:46	☿ ⚹	♊ 25 6:58
27 7:08	♄ ☌	♋ 27 8:10
28 21:18	☿ ☌	♌ 29 8:29
31 9:17	♄ ⚹	♍ 31 9:34

Last Aspect / ☽ Ingress (August)

Last Aspect Dy Hr Mn		☽ Ingress Dy Hr Mn
2 1:01	☿ ⚹	♎ 2 13:12
4 13:30	♂ ☍	♏ 4 20:35
6 22:33	☿ △	♐ 7 7:37
9 17:54	♂ △	♑ 9 20:30
12 8:39	♂ □	♒ 12 8:52
14 2:16	☉ ☍	♓ 14 19:14
16 22:39	♀ ☍	♈ 17 3:16
19 2:03	☉ △	♉ 19 9:14
21 10:22	☉ □	♊ 21 13:26
22 23:53	♅ △	♋ 23 16:08
25 1:58	♅ □	♌ 25 17:49
27 16:22	☿ ☌	♍ 27 19:33
28 5:12	♂ △	♎ 29 22:52

☽ Phases & Eclipses

Dy Hr Mn	
7 8:26	☽ 15♎05
15 11:56	○ 22♑51
15 11:39	☍ A 0.104
23 3:58	☾ 0♉10
29 18:59	● 6♌30
5 22:27	☽ 13♏20
14 2:16	○ 21♒09
21 10:22	☾ 28♉13
28 3:25	● 4♍41

Astro Data

1 July 1973
Julian Day # 26845
SVP 5♓37'30"
GC 26♐28.1 ⚴ 27♎41.7
Eris 13♈31.9 ⚵ 9♐12.0R
⚷ 20♈40.7 ⚶ 22♋31.0
☽ Mean ☊ 7♑38.5

1 August 1973
Julian Day # 26876
SVP 5♓37'25"
GC 26♐28.2 ⚴ 3♏19.2
Eris 13♈29.6R ⚵ 6♐32.5
⚷ 20♈52.7R ⚶ 6♌22.7
☽ Mean ☊ 6♑00.0

LONGITUDE — September 1973

Day	Sid.Time	☉	0 hr ☽	Noon ☽	True ☊	☿	♀	♂	⚳	♃	♄	♅	♆	♇
1 Sa	10 42 02	8♍54 05	27♎10 20	3♏33 41	5♑24.1	7♍35.7	16♎00.0	6♉54.1	8♐40.7	3♒27.2	2♋54.5	20♎45.6	4♐44.1	3♎18.8
2 Su	10 45 59	9 52 11	9♏51 37	16 04 31	5R 19.2	9 32.0	17 11.1	7 08.5	8 53.3	3R 22.3	2 59.0	20 48.6	4 44.7	3 20.9
3 M	10 49 55	10 50 18	22 12 54	28 17 17	5 16.5	11 27.4	18 22.1	7 22.2	9 06.1	3 17.5	3 03.5	20 51.7	4 45.2	3 23.1
4 Tu	10 53 52	11 48 27	4♐18 17	10♐16 32	5D 15.6	13 21.8	19 33.0	7 35.2	9 19.2	3 13.0	3 07.9	20 54.9	4 45.8	3 25.2
5 W	10 57 48	12 46 37	16 12 43	22 07 30	5 15.9	15 15.2	20 43.9	7 47.5	9 32.5	3 08.6	3 12.2	20 58.0	4 46.5	3 27.4
6 Th	11 01 45	13 44 49	28 01 35	3♑55 37	5R 16.3	17 07.4	21 54.7	7 59.0	9 45.9	3 04.3	3 16.5	21 01.2	4 47.1	3 29.6
7 F	11 05 42	14 43 02	9♑50 17	15 46 11	5 15.8	18 58.6	23 05.4	8 09.8	9 59.6	3 00.2	3 20.6	21 04.4	4 47.8	3 31.8
8 Sa	11 09 38	15 41 17	21 43 56	27 44 03	5 13.5	20 48.6	24 16.1	8 19.8	10 13.5	2 56.3	3 24.7	21 07.6	4 48.5	3 34.0
9 Su	11 13 35	16 39 33	3♒47 04	9♒53 22	5 08.8	22 37.4	25 26.7	8 29.0	10 27.6	2 52.6	3 28.6	21 10.9	4 49.3	3 36.2
10 M	11 17 31	17 37 51	16 03 21	22 17 17	5 01.4	24 25.2	26 37.3	8 37.4	10 41.9	2 49.1	3 32.5	21 14.2	4 50.1	3 38.4
11 Tu	11 21 28	18 36 11	28 35 22	4♓57 43	4 51.7	26 11.8	27 47.8	8 45.1	10 56.4	2 45.7	3 36.3	21 17.5	4 50.9	3 40.6
12 W	11 25 24	19 34 32	11♓24 21	17 55 14	4 40.2	27 57.2	28 58.2	8 51.9	11 11.0	2 42.5	3 40.0	21 20.8	4 51.7	3 42.9
13 Th	11 29 21	20 32 55	24 30 12	1♈09 04	4 28.0	29 41.6	0♏08.6	8 57.9	11 25.9	2 39.5	3 43.6	21 24.2	4 52.6	3 45.1
14 F	11 33 17	21 31 20	7♈51 33	14 37 20	4 16.2	1♎24.8	1 18.8	9 03.1	11 40.9	2 36.7	3 47.1	21 27.5	4 53.5	3 47.3
15 Sa	11 37 14	22 29 48	21 26 05	28 17 27	4 06.1	3 07.0	2 29.1	9 07.5	11 56.2	2 34.1	3 50.5	21 30.9	4 54.5	3 49.6
16 Su	11 41 10	23 28 17	5♉11 05	12♉06 39	3 58.3	4 48.0	3 39.2	9 11.0	12 11.6	2 31.6	3 53.8	21 34.4	4 55.4	3 51.9
17 M	11 45 07	24 26 48	19 03 51	26 02 27	3 53.4	6 28.1	4 49.3	9 13.6	12 27.1	2 29.4	3 57.0	21 37.8	4 56.4	3 54.1
18 Tu	11 49 04	25 25 22	3♊02 13	10♊02 59	3 51.1	8 07.1	5 59.3	9 15.3	12 42.9	2 27.3	4 00.1	21 41.3	4 57.5	3 56.4
19 W	11 53 00	26 23 58	17 04 37	24 07 01	3 50.5	9 45.0	7 09.3	9R 16.2	12 58.8	2 25.5	4 03.2	21 44.8	4 58.5	3 58.7
20 Th	11 56 57	27 22 36	1♋10 05	8♋13 44	3 50.5	11 22.0	8 19.2	9 16.2	13 14.9	2 23.8	4 06.1	21 48.3	4 59.6	4 01.0
21 F	12 00 53	28 21 16	15 17 50	22 22 16	3 49.7	12 58.0	9 29.0	9 15.2	13 31.2	2 22.3	4 08.9	21 51.8	5 00.7	4 03.2
22 Sa	12 04 50	29 19 59	29 26 50	6♌31 17	3 47.0	14 33.0	10 38.7	9 13.4	13 47.6	2 21.0	4 11.7	21 55.4	5 01.9	4 05.5
23 Su	12 08 46	0♎18 43	13♌35 20	20 38 36	3 41.6	16 07.1	11 48.4	9 10.7	14 04.2	2 19.9	4 14.3	21 58.9	5 03.1	4 07.8
24 M	12 12 43	1 17 30	27 40 39	4♍41 02	3 33.2	17 40.2	12 58.0	9 07.1	14 21.0	2 19.0	4 16.8	22 02.5	5 04.3	4 10.1
25 Tu	12 16 39	2 16 19	11♍39 14	18 34 43	3 22.3	19 12.3	14 07.5	9 02.5	14 37.9	2 18.3	4 19.2	22 06.1	5 05.5	4 12.4
26 W	12 20 36	3 15 10	25 27 00	2♎15 35	3 09.8	20 43.5	15 16.9	8 57.1	14 54.9	2 17.8	4 21.5	22 09.7	5 06.8	4 14.7
27 Th	12 24 33	4 14 03	9♎00 04	15 40 05	2 57.0	22 13.8	16 26.3	8 50.8	15 12.2	2 17.5	4 23.7	22 13.4	5 08.1	4 17.0
28 F	12 28 29	5 12 58	22 15 22	28 45 47	2 45.1	23 43.2	17 35.6	8 43.6	15 29.5	2D 17.4	4 25.8	22 17.0	5 09.4	4 19.3
29 Sa	12 32 26	6 11 55	5♏11 15	11♏31 51	2 35.1	25 11.6	18 44.7	8 35.5	15 47.0	2 17.5	4 27.8	22 20.7	5 10.7	4 21.6
30 Su	12 36 22	7 10 54	17 47 44	23 59 09	2 27.6	26 39.0	19 53.8	8 26.6	16 04.7	2 17.7	4 29.7	22 24.4	5 12.1	4 23.9

LONGITUDE — October 1973

Day	Sid.Time	☉	0 hr ☽	Noon ☽	True ☊	☿	♀	♂	⚳	♃	♄	♅	♆	♇
1 M	12 40 19	8♎09 54	0♐06 29	6♐10 08	2♑23.0	28♎05.5	21♏02.8	8♉16.9	16♐22.5	2♒18.2	4♋31.5	22♎28.0	5♐13.5	4♎26.2
2 Tu	12 44 15	9 08 57	12 10 37	18 08 30	2R 20.7	29 31.0	22 11.7	8R 06.3	16 40.4	2 18.9	4 33.2	22 31.7	5 14.9	4 28.5
3 W	12 48 12	10 08 01	24 04 24	29 58 58	2 20.1	0♏55.5	23 20.5	7 55.0	16 58.5	2 19.8	4 34.8	22 35.5	5 16.4	4 30.8
4 Th	12 52 08	11 07 07	5♑52 52	11♑46 49	2 20.1	2 19.0	24 29.2	7 42.8	17 16.7	2 20.9	4 36.2	22 39.2	5 17.9	4 33.1
5 F	12 56 05	12 06 15	17 41 28	23 37 34	2 19.7	3 41.5	25 37.8	7 29.9	17 35.1	2 22.1	4 37.6	22 42.9	5 19.4	4 35.4
6 Sa	13 00 02	13 05 24	29 35 45	5♒36 42	2 17.7	5 02.8	26 46.3	7 16.3	17 53.6	2 23.6	4 38.8	22 46.6	5 20.9	4 37.6
7 Su	13 03 58	14 04 36	11♒41 00	17 49 14	2 13.5	6 23.1	27 54.6	7 02.0	18 12.2	2 25.3	4 40.0	22 50.4	5 22.5	4 39.9
8 M	13 07 55	15 03 49	24 01 53	0♓19 22	2 06.7	7 42.1	29 02.9	6 47.1	18 30.9	2 27.1	4 41.0	22 54.1	5 24.0	4 42.2
9 Tu	13 11 51	16 03 04	6♓42 00	13 10 00	1 57.4	8 59.9	0♐11.0	6 31.5	18 49.7	2 29.2	4 41.9	22 57.9	5 25.6	4 44.4
10 W	13 15 48	17 02 20	19 43 28	26 22 24	1 46.3	10 16.4	1 19.0	6 15.3	19 08.7	2 31.4	4 42.7	23 01.6	5 27.3	4 46.7
11 Th	13 19 44	18 01 39	3♈06 37	9♈55 53	1 34.3	11 31.4	2 26.8	5 58.5	19 27.8	2 33.9	4 43.4	23 05.4	5 28.9	4 49.0
12 F	13 23 41	19 01 00	16 49 47	23 47 50	1 22.7	12 45.0	3 34.6	5 41.2	19 47.0	2 36.5	4 44.0	23 09.2	5 30.6	4 51.2
13 Sa	13 27 37	20 00 23	0♉49 29	7♉54 04	1 12.7	13 57.0	4 42.2	5 23.4	20 06.3	2 39.3	4 44.4	23 13.0	5 32.3	4 53.4
14 Su	13 31 34	20 59 48	15 00 58	22 09 29	1 05.1	15 07.2	5 49.6	5 05.1	20 25.7	2 42.3	4 44.8	23 16.7	5 34.0	4 55.7
15 M	13 35 31	21 59 15	29 19 00	6♊28 56	1 00.3	16 15.6	6 57.0	4 46.5	20 45.3	2 45.5	4 45.0	23 20.5	5 35.7	4 57.9
16 Tu	13 39 27	22 58 45	13♊38 44	20 47 58	0D 58.1	17 21.9	8 04.2	4 27.4	21 04.9	2 48.9	4R 45.2	23 24.3	5 37.5	5 00.1
17 W	13 43 24	23 58 16	27 56 15	5♋03 18	0 57.8	18 26.0	9 11.2	4 08.1	21 24.7	2 52.5	4 45.2	23 28.1	5 39.3	5 02.3
18 Th	13 47 20	24 57 51	12♋08 54	19 12 53	0R 58.3	19 27.7	10 18.1	3 48.4	21 44.6	2 56.2	4 45.1	23 31.9	5 41.1	5 04.5
19 F	13 51 17	25 57 27	26 15 09	3♌15 36	0 58.2	20 26.7	11 24.8	3 28.6	22 04.5	3 00.1	4 44.9	23 35.6	5 42.9	5 06.7
20 Sa	13 55 13	26 57 06	10♌14 11	17 10 49	0 56.4	21 22.8	12 31.4	3 08.5	22 24.6	3 04.2	4 44.6	23 39.4	5 44.7	5 08.9
21 Su	13 59 10	27 56 47	24 05 27	0♍57 58	0 52.3	22 15.7	13 37.8	2 48.3	22 44.8	3 08.5	4 44.2	23 43.2	5 46.6	5 11.1
22 M	14 03 06	28 56 30	7♍48 16	14 36 11	0 45.5	23 04.9	14 44.1	2 28.1	23 05.0	3 13.0	4 43.7	23 47.0	5 48.5	5 13.2
23 Tu	14 07 03	29 56 15	21 21 33	28 04 11	0 36.6	23 50.3	15 50.1	2 07.8	23 25.4	3 17.7	4 43.0	23 50.7	5 50.4	5 15.3
24 W	14 10 59	0♏56 03	4♎43 52	11♎20 24	0 26.1	24 31.2	16 56.0	1 47.5	23 45.9	3 22.5	4 42.2	23 54.5	5 52.3	5 17.5
25 Th	14 14 56	1 55 52	17 53 35	24 23 15	0 15.3	25 07.3	18 01.8	1 27.4	24 06.5	3 27.5	4 41.4	23 58.3	5 54.2	5 19.6
26 F	14 18 53	2 55 44	0♏49 16	7♏11 32	0 05.2	25 38.1	19 07.3	1 07.4	24 27.1	3 32.7	4 40.4	24 02.0	5 56.2	5 21.7
27 Sa	14 22 49	3 55 38	13 30 02	19 44 46	29♐56.7	26 02.9	20 12.6	0 47.5	24 47.9	3 38.1	4 39.3	24 05.8	5 58.1	5 23.8
28 Su	14 26 46	4 55 33	25 55 51	2♐03 27	29 50.5	26 21.3	21 17.8	0 28.0	25 08.7	3 43.6	4 38.1	24 09.5	6 00.1	5 25.8
29 M	14 30 42	5 55 31	8♐07 48	14 09 12	29 46.8	26R 32.5	22 22.7	0 08.7	25 29.6	3 49.3	4 36.8	24 13.2	6 02.1	5 27.9
30 Tu	14 34 39	6 55 30	20 08 02	26 04 42	29D 45.3	26 36.1	23 27.4	29♈49.7	25 50.7	3 55.2	4 35.4	24 17.0	6 04.2	5 29.9
31 W	14 38 35	7 55 30	1♑59 43	7♑53 37	29 45.5	26 31.3	24 31.8	29 31.2	26 11.8	4 01.2	4 33.8	24 20.7	6 06.2	5 32.0

Astro Data

	Dy Hr Mn
♃△♇	2 16:39
♃⚻♄	5 1:47
☽0N	12 13:32
♄□♇	14 17:26
☿0S	14 18:13
♂ R	19 23:20
☉0S	23 4:21
☽0S	25 12:16
♃ D	28 13:26
♄□♇	7 12:48
☽0N	9 21:58
♄ R	17 5:50
☽0S	22 18:51
☿ R	30 10:29

Planet Ingress

	Dy Hr Mn
♀ ♏	13 9:05
☿ ♎	13 16:16
☉ ♎	23 4:21
☿ ♏	2 20:12
♀ ♐	9 8:08
☉ ♏	23 13:30
☊ ♐R	27 2:02
♂ ♈R	29 22:56

Last Aspect / ☽ Ingress

Last Aspect Dy Hr Mn		☽ Ingress Dy Hr Mn
31 12:02 ♅ ☌	♏	1 5:17
1 23:01 ☉ ⚹	♐	3 15:24
5 9:38 ♅ ⚹	♑	6 4:01
8 4:20 ♀ □	♒	8 16:30
10 21:07 ♀ △	♓	11 2:40
13 8:59 ☿ ☍	♈	13 9:56
15 0:06 ♅ ☍	♉	15 14:59
17 9:03 ☉ △	♊	17 18:48
19 16:11 ☉ □	♋	19 22:01
21 22:54 ☉ ⚹	♌	22 0:56
23 14:17 ♅ ⚹	♍	24 3:58
25 3:34 ♀ ⚹	♎	26 8:00
28 1:30 ☿ ☌	♏	28 14:18
30 3:15 ♀ ☌	♐	30 23:47

Last Aspect / ☽ Ingress

Last Aspect Dy Hr Mn		☽ Ingress Dy Hr Mn
2 20:55 ♅ ⚹	♑	3 12:02
5 16:28 ♀ ⚹	♒	6 0:49
8 9:20 ♀ □	♓	8 11:23
9 3:26 ☿ △	♈	10 18:29
12 10:53 ♅ ☍	♉	12 22:36
13 23:07 ☿ ☍	♊	15 1:09
16 16:24 ♅ △	♋	17 3:28
18 22:33 ☉ □	♌	19 6:25
21 6:19 ☉ ⚹	♍	21 10:19
23 3:59 ☿ ⚹	♎	23 15:28
25 11:13 ♅ ☌	♏	25 22:28
28 0:34 ☿ ☌	♐	28 7:57
30 19:24 ♂ △	♑	30 19:57

☽ Phases & Eclipses

Dy Hr Mn	
4 15:22	☽ 11♐57
12 15:16	○ 19♓42
19 16:11	☾ 26♊34
26 13:54	● 3♎20
4 10:32	☽ 11♑04
12 3:09	○ 18♈39
18 22:33	☾ 25♋24
26 3:17	● 2♏34

Astro Data

1 September 1973
Julian Day # 26907
SVP 5♓37'21"
GC 26♐28.3 ⚴ 12♏35.2
Eris 13♈18.0R ⚵ 9♐00.4
⚷ 20♈16.1R ⚶ 20♌25.6
☽ Mean ☊ 4♑21.5

1 October 1973
Julian Day # 26937
SVP 5♓37'18"
GC 26♐28.4 ⚴ 23♏30.9
Eris 13♈01.0R ⚵ 15♐11.4
⚷ 19♈05.8R ⚶ 3♍57.1
☽ Mean ☊ 2♑46.1

November 1973 — LONGITUDE

Day	Sid.Time	☉	0 hr ☽	Noon ☽	True☊	☿	♀	♂	⚳	♃	♄	♅	♆	♇
1 Th	14 42 32	8♏55 33	13♑46 57	19♑40 22	29♐46.7	26♏17.7	25♐36.1	29♈13.1	26♐32.9	4♒07.5	4♋32.2	24♎24.4	6♐08.2	5♎34.0
2 F	14 46 28	9 55 37	25 34 29	1♒29 58	29R47.9	25R54.7	26 40.1	28R55.4	26 54.2	4 13.8	4R30.4	24 28.1	6 10.3	5 36.0
3 Sa	14 50 25	10 55 42	7♒27 30	13 27 45	29 48.2	25 22.2	27 43.8	28 38.3	27 15.6	4 20.4	4 28.6	24 31.7	6 12.4	5 37.9
4 Su	14 54 22	11 55 50	19 31 22	25 39 00	29 47.0	24 40.0	28 47.2	28 21.7	27 37.0	4 27.1	4 26.6	24 35.4	6 14.5	5 39.9
5 M	14 58 18	12 55 58	1♓51 16	8♓08 41	29 43.9	23 48.5	29 50.4	28 05.7	27 58.5	4 33.9	4 24.6	24 39.0	6 16.6	5 41.8
6 Tu	15 02 15	13 56 08	14 31 44	21 00 48	29 38.9	22 48.2	0♑53.3	27 50.3	28 20.0	4 40.9	4 22.4	24 42.7	6 18.7	5 43.7
7 W	15 06 11	14 56 20	27 36 10	4♈17 59	29 32.4	21 40.3	1 55.9	27 35.6	28 41.7	4 48.1	4 20.2	24 46.3	6 20.8	5 45.6
8 Th	15 10 08	15 56 33	11♈06 15	18 00 50	29 25.1	20 26.4	2 58.2	27 21.5	29 03.4	4 55.4	4 17.8	24 49.9	6 22.9	5 47.5
9 F	15 14 04	16 56 48	25 01 27	2♉07 37	29 17.8	19 08.3	4 00.1	27 08.1	29 25.2	5 02.9	4 15.3	24 53.5	6 25.1	5 49.4
10 Sa	15 18 01	17 57 05	9♉18 44	16 34 05	29 11.6	17 48.5	5 01.7	26 55.4	29 47.0	5 10.5	4 12.8	24 57.0	6 27.3	5 51.2
11 Su	15 21 57	18 57 23	23 52 49	1♊14 02	29 07.1	16 29.4	6 03.0	26 43.5	0♑08.9	5 18.3	4 10.1	25 00.6	6 29.4	5 53.0
12 M	15 25 54	19 57 44	8♊36 48	16 00 10	29D04.5	15 13.7	7 03.9	26 32.3	0 30.9	5 26.2	4 07.4	25 04.1	6 31.6	5 54.8
13 Tu	15 29 51	20 58 06	23 23 14	0♋45 10	29 03.8	14 03.9	8 04.5	26 21.8	0 53.0	5 34.3	4 04.5	25 07.6	6 33.8	5 56.6
14 W	15 33 47	21 58 30	8♋05 13	15 22 44	29 04.6	13 02.0	9 04.6	26 12.1	1 15.1	5 42.5	4 01.6	25 11.1	6 36.0	5 58.3
15 Th	15 37 44	22 58 55	22 37 14	29 48 16	29 06.1	12 09.7	10 04.4	26 03.2	1 37.2	5 50.8	3 58.5	25 14.6	6 38.2	6 00.1
16 F	15 41 40	23 59 23	6♌55 34	13♌58 56	29R07.4	11 28.2	11 03.8	25 55.1	1 59.5	5 59.3	3 55.4	25 18.0	6 40.4	6 01.8
17 Sa	15 45 37	24 59 53	20 58 14	27 53 27	29 07.7	10 58.3	12 02.7	25 47.8	2 21.8	6 07.9	3 52.2	25 21.5	6 42.6	6 03.4
18 Su	15 49 33	26 00 24	4♍44 37	11♍31 46	29 06.6	10 40.0	13 01.2	25 41.2	2 44.1	6 16.7	3 48.9	25 24.9	6 44.8	6 05.1
19 M	15 53 30	27 00 57	18 15 00	24 54 25	29 04.0	10D33.4	13 59.3	25 35.5	3 06.5	6 25.6	3 45.5	25 28.2	6 47.1	6 06.7
20 Tu	15 57 26	28 01 32	1♎30 09	8♎02 18	29 00.0	10 37.8	14 56.9	25 30.6	3 29.0	6 34.6	3 42.0	25 31.6	6 49.3	6 08.3
21 W	16 01 23	29 02 08	14 30 58	20 56 17	28 55.1	10 52.6	15 54.0	25 26.5	3 51.5	6 43.8	3 38.5	25 34.9	6 51.6	6 09.9
22 Th	16 05 20	0♐02 47	27 18 20	3♏37 13	28 49.9	11 17.0	16 50.6	25 23.3	4 14.1	6 53.1	3 34.8	25 38.2	6 53.8	6 11.5
23 F	16 09 16	1 03 27	9♏53 03	16 05 55	28 45.0	11 50.1	17 46.7	25 20.8	4 36.8	7 02.5	3 31.1	25 41.5	6 56.0	6 13.0
24 Sa	16 13 13	2 04 08	22 15 56	28 23 13	28 41.1	12 31.0	18 42.2	25 19.2	4 59.5	7 12.0	3 27.3	25 44.7	6 58.3	6 14.5
25 Su	16 17 09	3 04 51	4♐27 56	10♐30 15	28 38.3	13 18.8	19 37.1	25D18.4	5 22.2	7 21.7	3 23.5	25 48.0	7 00.6	6 16.0
26 M	16 21 06	4 05 35	16 30 22	22 28 30	28D37.0	14 12.8	20 31.5	25 18.4	5 45.0	7 31.5	3 19.5	25 51.1	7 02.8	6 17.4
27 Tu	16 25 02	5 06 20	28 24 56	4♑19 58	28 37.0	15 12.1	21 25.2	25 19.2	6 07.8	7 41.4	3 15.5	25 54.3	7 05.1	6 18.8
28 W	16 28 59	6 07 07	10♑13 57	16 07 17	28 38.0	16 16.0	22 18.3	25 20.8	6 30.7	7 51.5	3 11.4	25 57.4	7 07.3	6 20.2
29 Th	16 32 56	7 07 54	22 00 22	27 53 41	28 39.6	17 24.0	23 10.7	25 23.2	6 53.6	8 01.6	3 07.3	26 00.5	7 09.6	6 21.6
30 F	16 36 52	8 08 43	3♒47 44	9♒43 02	28 41.4	18 35.5	24 02.4	25 26.3	7 16.6	8 11.9	3 03.1	26 03.6	7 11.9	6 22.9

December 1973 — LONGITUDE

Day	Sid.Time	☉	0 hr ☽	Noon ☽	True☊	☿	♀	♂	⚳	♃	♄	♅	♆	♇
1 Sa	16 40 49	9♐09 32	15♒40 10	21♒39 41	28♐42.8	19♏49.9	24♑53.4	25♈30.2	7♑39.6	8♒22.3	2♋58.8	26♎06.6	7♐14.1	6♎24.2
2 Su	16 44 45	10 10 23	27 42 13	3♓48 20	28R43.7	21 06.9	25 43.6	25 34.9	8 02.7	8 32.8	2R54.5	26 09.6	7 16.4	6 25.5
3 M	16 48 42	11 11 14	9♓58 39	16 13 45	28 43.7	22 26.2	26 33.0	25 40.4	8 25.8	8 43.4	2 50.1	26 12.6	7 18.6	6 26.7
4 Tu	16 52 38	12 12 06	22 34 11	29 00 27	28 43.0	23 47.3	27 21.6	25 46.5	8 48.9	8 54.1	2 45.6	26 15.5	7 20.9	6 27.9
5 W	16 56 35	13 12 59	5♈32 59	12♈12 07	28 41.5	25 10.0	28 09.3	25 53.4	9 12.1	9 04.9	2 41.1	26 18.4	7 23.1	6 29.1
6 Th	17 00 31	14 13 53	18 58 06	25 51 02	28 39.7	26 34.1	28 56.1	26 01.0	9 35.3	9 15.8	2 36.6	26 21.2	7 25.4	6 30.3
7 F	17 04 28	15 14 47	2♉50 54	9♉57 28	28 37.8	27 59.4	29 41.9	26 09.3	9 58.5	9 26.8	2 32.0	26 24.0	7 27.6	6 31.4
8 Sa	17 08 25	16 15 43	17 10 22	24 29 02	28 36.2	29 25.6	0♒26.7	26 18.3	10 21.8	9 38.0	2 27.4	26 26.8	7 29.9	6 32.5
9 Su	17 12 21	17 16 39	1♊52 45	9♊20 39	28 35.1	0♐52.8	1 10.6	26 27.9	10 45.1	9 49.2	2 22.7	26 29.6	7 32.1	6 33.5
10 M	17 16 18	18 17 36	16 51 41	24 24 47	28D34.6	2 20.7	1 53.3	26 38.2	11 08.5	10 00.5	2 18.0	26 32.3	7 34.4	6 34.6
11 Tu	17 20 14	19 18 34	1♋58 46	9♋32 29	28 34.7	3 49.2	2 35.0	26 49.1	11 31.9	10 12.0	2 13.2	26 34.9	7 36.6	6 35.6
12 W	17 24 11	20 19 33	17 04 47	24 34 36	28 35.3	5 18.3	3 15.4	27 00.6	11 55.3	10 23.5	2 08.5	26 37.6	7 38.8	6 36.5
13 Th	17 28 07	21 20 33	2♌01 01	9♌23 13	28 35.9	6 47.9	3 54.7	27 12.8	12 18.7	10 35.1	2 03.6	26 40.1	7 41.0	6 37.5
14 F	17 32 04	22 21 34	16 40 30	23 52 25	28 36.6	8 17.9	4 32.7	27 25.5	12 42.2	10 46.8	1 58.8	26 42.7	7 43.2	6 38.4
15 Sa	17 36 00	23 22 36	0♍58 35	7♍58 50	28 37.0	9 48.2	5 09.5	27 38.8	13 05.7	10 58.6	1 53.9	26 45.2	7 45.4	6 39.2
16 Su	17 39 57	24 23 39	14 53 06	21 41 25	28R37.2	11 18.9	5 44.8	27 52.7	13 29.2	11 10.4	1 49.0	26 47.6	7 47.6	6 40.1
17 M	17 43 54	25 24 42	28 23 58	5♎00 58	28 37.1	12 49.9	6 18.8	28 07.1	13 52.7	11 22.4	1 44.1	26 50.0	7 49.8	6 40.9
18 Tu	17 47 50	26 25 47	11♎32 43	17 59 33	28 37.0	14 21.2	6 51.3	28 22.1	14 16.3	11 34.5	1 39.2	26 52.4	7 52.0	6 41.6
19 W	17 51 47	27 26 53	24 21 49	0♏39 55	28 36.8	15 52.8	7 22.3	28 37.6	14 39.9	11 46.6	1 34.3	26 54.7	7 54.2	6 42.4
20 Th	17 55 43	28 27 59	6♏54 12	13 05 04	28D36.7	17 24.6	7 51.8	28 53.7	15 03.5	11 58.8	1 29.3	26 57.0	7 56.3	6 43.0
21 F	17 59 40	29 29 06	19 12 51	25 17 55	28 36.8	18 56.6	8 19.6	29 10.2	15 27.2	12 11.1	1 24.4	26 59.3	7 58.4	6 43.7
22 Sa	18 03 36	0♑30 14	1♐20 35	7♐21 10	28 36.9	20 28.8	8 45.7	29 27.3	15 50.8	12 23.5	1 19.4	27 01.5	8 00.6	6 44.3
23 Su	18 07 33	1 31 23	13 19 58	19 17 16	28R37.1	22 01.3	9 10.0	29 44.9	16 14.5	12 35.9	1 14.4	27 03.6	8 02.7	6 44.9
24 M	18 11 29	2 32 32	25 13 18	1♑08 22	28 37.1	23 34.0	9 32.5	0♉02.9	16 38.2	12 48.5	1 09.5	27 05.7	8 04.8	6 45.5
25 Tu	18 15 26	3 33 41	7♑02 43	12 56 35	28 37.0	25 07.0	9 53.1	0 21.5	17 02.0	13 01.1	1 04.5	27 07.7	8 06.9	6 46.0
26 W	18 19 23	4 34 51	18 50 15	24 43 59	28 36.5	26 40.2	10 11.8	0 40.4	17 25.7	13 13.8	0 59.5	27 09.8	8 09.0	6 46.5
27 Th	18 23 19	5 36 00	0♒38 04	6♒32 48	28 35.6	28 13.6	10 28.4	0 59.9	17 49.5	13 26.5	0 54.6	27 11.7	8 11.1	6 47.0
28 F	18 27 16	6 37 10	12 28 32	18 25 36	28 34.5	29 47.3	10 42.9	1 19.8	18 13.2	13 39.3	0 49.6	27 13.6	8 13.1	6 47.4
29 Sa	18 31 12	7 38 20	24 24 23	0♓25 17	28 33.2	1♑21.3	10 55.2	1 40.1	18 37.0	13 52.2	0 44.7	27 15.5	8 15.2	6 47.8
30 Su	18 35 09	8 39 30	6♓28 43	12 35 10	28 32.0	2 55.5	11 05.3	2 00.8	19 00.8	14 05.2	0 39.8	27 17.3	8 17.2	6 48.1
31 M	18 39 05	9 40 40	18 45 04	24 58 55	28 31.1	4 30.1	11 13.2	2 21.9	19 24.6	14 18.2	0 34.9	27 19.0	8 19.2	6 48.4

Astro Data	Dy Hr Mn
♃⚻♄	4 10:50
☽0N	6 6:53
♃△♇	16 20:35
☽0S	18 23:42
☿D	19 14:14
♃⚹♆	22 14:30
♂D	26 0:06
☽0N	3 15:12
☽0S	16 5:14
☽0N	30 22:20

Planet Ingress	Dy Hr Mn
♀ ♑	5 15:39
⚳ ♑	11 2:14
☉ ♐	22 10:54
♀ ♒	7 21:37
☿ ♐	8 21:29
☉ ♑	22 0:08
♂ ♉	24 8:09
☿ ♑	28 15:14

Last Aspect Dy Hr Mn		☽ Ingress Dy Hr Mn
2 6:55	♂ □	♒ 2 8:58
4 18:39	♀ ⚹	♓ 4 20:26
6 15:02	☿ △	♈ 7 4:19
9 3:43	♂ ☌	♉ 9 8:25
10 14:27	☉ ☍	♊ 11 9:59
13 4:56	♂ ⚹	♋ 13 10:46
15 5:47	♂ □	♌ 15 12:20
17 8:23	♂ △	♍ 17 15:41
19 16:08	☉ ⚹	♎ 19 21:15
21 20:47	♅ ☌	♏ 22 5:06
23 15:31	♀ ⚹	♐ 24 15:11
26 18:51	♅ ⚹	♑ 27 3:13
29 8:09	♅ □	♒ 29 16:17

Last Aspect Dy Hr Mn		☽ Ingress Dy Hr Mn
1 20:53	♅ △	♓ 2 4:32
4 8:45	♀ ⚹	♈ 4 13:50
6 17:37	♀ □	♉ 6 19:08
8 20:54	☿ ☍	♊ 8 20:58
10 15:34	♂ ⚹	♋ 10 20:52
12 15:58	♂ □	♌ 12 20:44
14 18:04	♂ △	♍ 14 22:20
16 17:13	☉ □	♎ 17 2:53
19 8:01	♂ ☍	♏ 19 10:44
20 9:49	♃ □	♐ 21 21:20
24 3:46	♅ ⚹	♑ 24 9:41
26 16:57	♅ □	♒ 26 22:43
29 5:41	♅ △	♓ 29 11:10
30 3:36	☉ ⚹	♈ 31 21:34

☽ Phases & Eclipses Dy Hr Mn	
3 6:29	☽ 10♒42
10 14:27	○ 18♉03
17 6:34	☾ 24♌46
24 19:55	● 2♐24
3 1:29	☽ 10♓45
10 1:35	○ 17♊51
10 1:44	☍ P 0.101
16 17:13	☾ 24♍37
24 15:07	● 2♑40
24 15:02:00	☌ A 12'02"

Astro Data

1 November 1973
Julian Day # 26968
SVP 5♓37'15"
GC 26♐28.4 ⚵ 5♐54.4
Eris 12♈42.6R ⚴ 24♐11.8
⚷ 17♈42.6R ⚶ 17♍29.5
☽ Mean ☊ 1♑07.6

1 December 1973
Julian Day # 26998
SVP 5♓37'10"
GC 26♐28.5 ⚵ 18♐21.5
Eris 12♈29.2R ⚴ 4♑32.3
⚷ 16♈42.0R ⚶ 29♍35.7
☽ Mean ☊ 29♐32.3

LONGITUDE — January 1974

Day	Sid.Time	☉	0 hr ☽	Noon ☽	True ☊	☿	♀	♂	⚳	♃	♄	♅	♆	♇
1 Tu	18 43 02	10♑41 49	1♈17 12	7♈40 23	28♐30.6	6♑04.9	11♒18.6	2♉43.4	19♑48.4	14♒31.2	0♋30.1	27♎20.7	8♐21.2	6♎48.7
2 W	18 46 58	11 42 58	14 08 56	20 43 17	28D30.8	7 40.1	11R21.7	3 05.3	20 12.3	14 44.4	0R25.3	27 22.4	8 23.1	6 49.0
3 Th	18 50 55	12 44 07	27 23 47	4♉10 45	28 31.5	9 15.6	11 22.3	3 27.6	20 36.1	14 57.6	0 20.5	27 24.0	8 25.1	6 49.2
4 F	18 54 52	13 45 16	11♉04 23	18 04 45	28 32.7	10 51.4	11 20.5	3 50.3	20 59.9	15 10.8	0 15.7	27 25.5	8 27.0	6 49.3
5 Sa	18 58 48	14 46 25	25 11 49	2♊25 22	28 33.9	12 27.7	11 16.1	4 13.3	21 23.8	15 24.1	0 11.0	27 27.0	8 29.0	6 49.5
6 Su	19 02 45	15 47 33	9♊45 00	17 10 09	28R34.8	14 04.3	11 09.2	4 36.6	21 47.6	15 37.5	0 06.3	27 28.5	8 30.9	6 49.6
7 M	19 06 41	16 48 41	24 40 04	2♋13 47	28 35.1	15 41.3	10 59.8	5 00.3	22 11.5	15 50.9	0 01.6	27 29.9	8 32.7	6 49.7
8 Tu	19 10 38	17 49 49	9♋50 15	17 28 14	28 34.3	17 18.7	10 47.8	5 24.3	22 35.3	16 04.4	29♊57.0	27 31.2	8 34.6	6R49.7
9 W	19 14 34	18 50 57	25 06 29	2♌43 40	28 32.5	18 56.5	10 33.3	5 48.6	22 59.2	16 17.9	29 52.5	27 32.5	8 36.4	6 49.7
10 Th	19 18 31	19 52 04	10♌18 31	17 49 50	28 29.9	20 34.8	10 16.4	6 13.2	23 23.0	16 31.5	29 47.9	27 33.7	8 38.3	6 49.7
11 F	19 22 28	20 53 11	25 16 34	2♍37 49	28 26.7	22 13.5	9 57.0	6 38.1	23 46.9	16 45.1	29 43.5	27 34.9	8 40.1	6 49.6
12 Sa	19 26 24	21 54 18	9♍52 50	17 01 08	28 23.6	23 52.7	9 35.4	7 03.3	24 10.8	16 58.7	29 39.1	27 36.0	8 41.8	6 49.5
13 Su	19 30 21	22 55 25	24 02 23	0♎56 27	28 21.1	25 32.3	9 11.5	7 28.8	24 34.6	17 12.4	29 34.7	27 37.1	8 43.6	6 49.4
14 M	19 34 17	23 56 32	7♎43 22	14 23 20	28D19.5	27 12.4	8 45.5	7 54.6	24 58.5	17 26.2	29 30.4	27 38.1	8 45.3	6 49.2
15 Tu	19 38 14	24 57 39	20 56 39	27 23 43	28 19.2	28 53.0	8 17.5	8 20.6	25 22.4	17 40.0	29 26.2	27 39.1	8 47.0	6 49.0
16 W	19 42 10	25 58 45	3♏45 02	10♏01 06	28 20.0	0♒34.0	7 47.7	8 46.9	25 46.2	17 53.8	29 22.0	27 40.0	8 48.7	6 48.7
17 Th	19 46 07	26 59 52	16 12 31	22 19 49	28 21.5	2 15.4	7 16.2	9 13.5	26 10.1	18 07.7	29 17.9	27 40.8	8 50.4	6 48.4
18 F	19 50 03	28 00 58	28 23 35	4♐24 24	28 23.4	3 57.3	6 43.3	9 40.3	26 33.9	18 21.6	29 13.8	27 41.6	8 52.1	6 48.1
19 Sa	19 54 00	29 02 04	10♐22 47	16 19 16	28 25.0	5 39.5	6 09.1	10 07.3	26 57.8	18 35.5	29 09.9	27 42.4	8 53.7	6 47.8
20 Su	19 57 57	0♒03 09	22 14 19	28 08 23	28R25.6	7 22.1	5 33.9	10 34.7	27 21.6	18 49.5	29 06.0	27 43.0	8 55.3	6 47.4
21 M	20 01 53	1 04 14	4♑01 53	9♑55 11	28 24.9	9 05.0	4 57.9	11 02.2	27 45.4	19 03.5	29 02.1	27 43.7	8 56.8	6 47.0
22 Tu	20 05 50	2 05 18	15 48 38	21 42 30	28 22.4	10 48.1	4 21.3	11 30.0	28 09.3	19 17.6	28 58.4	27 44.2	8 58.4	6 46.6
23 W	20 09 46	3 06 22	27 37 06	3♒32 38	28 18.2	12 31.4	3 44.4	11 58.0	28 33.1	19 31.7	28 54.7	27 44.8	8 59.9	6 46.1
24 Th	20 13 43	4 07 25	9♒29 22	15 27 28	28 12.3	14 14.8	3 07.5	12 26.2	28 56.9	19 45.8	28 51.1	27 45.2	9 01.4	6 45.6
25 F	20 17 39	5 08 27	21 27 09	27 28 36	28 05.4	15 58.1	2 30.8	12 54.7	29 20.7	19 59.9	28 47.6	27 45.6	9 02.9	6 45.0
26 Sa	20 21 36	6 09 28	3♓32 01	9♓37 37	27 58.0	17 41.2	1 54.5	13 23.3	29 44.4	20 14.1	28 44.2	27 45.9	9 04.3	6 44.4
27 Su	20 25 32	7 10 28	15 45 34	21 56 09	27 50.9	19 23.9	1 18.9	13 52.2	0♒08.2	20 28.2	28 40.8	27 46.2	9 05.7	6 43.8
28 M	20 29 29	8 11 26	28 09 36	4♈26 12	27 44.9	21 06.1	0 44.2	14 21.2	0 31.9	20 42.4	28 37.6	27 46.5	9 07.1	6 43.2
29 Tu	20 33 26	9 12 24	10♈46 14	17 10 02	27 40.7	22 47.5	0 10.7	14 50.5	0 55.6	20 56.7	28 34.4	27 46.6	9 08.4	6 42.5
30 W	20 37 22	10 13 21	23 37 55	0♉10 14	27D38.3	24 27.8	29♑38.5	15 19.9	1 19.3	21 10.9	28 31.3	27 46.8	9 09.8	6 41.8
31 Th	20 41 19	11 14 16	6♉47 20	13 29 30	27 37.8	26 06.6	29 07.9	15 49.5	1 43.0	21 25.2	28 28.4	27R46.8	9 11.1	6 41.1

LONGITUDE — February 1974

Day	Sid.Time	☉	0 hr ☽	Noon ☽	True ☊	☿	♀	♂	⚳	♃	♄	♅	♆	♇
1 F	20 45 15	12♒15 10	20♉17 02	27♉10 10	27♐38.6	27♒43.7	28♑39.1	16♉19.3	2♒06.7	21♒39.5	28♊25.5	27♎46.8	9♐12.3	6♎40.3
2 Sa	20 49 12	13 16 03	4♊09 02	11♊13 42	27 39.9	29 18.6	28R12.1	16 49.3	2 30.3	21 53.8	28R22.7	27R46.8	9 13.6	6R39.5
3 Su	20 53 08	14 16 54	18 24 05	25 39 58	27R40.7	0♓50.7	27 47.2	17 19.4	2 54.0	22 08.1	28 20.0	27 46.7	9 14.8	6 38.7
4 M	20 57 05	15 17 44	3♋00 57	10♋26 29	27 40.1	2 19.6	27 24.5	17 49.7	3 17.6	22 22.4	28 17.4	27 46.5	9 16.0	6 37.8
5 Tu	21 01 01	16 18 33	17 55 49	25 28 02	27 37.3	3 44.7	27 04.0	18 20.1	3 41.1	22 36.8	28 14.9	27 46.3	9 17.1	6 37.0
6 W	21 04 58	17 19 20	3♌02 04	10♌36 43	27 32.2	5 05.2	26 45.9	18 50.7	4 04.7	22 51.1	28 12.5	27 46.0	9 18.2	6 36.1
7 Th	21 08 55	18 20 06	18 10 45	25 42 51	27 25.1	6 20.6	26 30.2	19 21.5	4 28.2	23 05.5	28 10.3	27 45.7	9 19.3	6 35.1
8 F	21 12 51	19 20 51	3♍11 48	10♍36 28	27 16.7	7 30.0	26 17.0	19 52.3	4 51.7	23 19.9	28 08.1	27 45.3	9 20.4	6 34.1
9 Sa	21 16 48	20 21 34	17 55 49	25 09 02	27 08.1	8 32.7	26 06.3	20 23.3	5 15.2	23 34.2	28 06.0	27 44.9	9 21.4	6 33.1
10 Su	21 20 44	21 22 17	2♎15 30	9♎14 48	27 00.4	9 28.0	25 58.0	20 54.5	5 38.7	23 48.6	28 04.0	27 44.4	9 22.4	6 32.1
11 M	21 24 41	22 22 58	16 06 42	22 51 13	26 54.4	10 15.2	25 52.3	21 25.8	6 02.1	24 03.0	28 02.1	27 43.8	9 23.4	6 31.1
12 Tu	21 28 37	23 23 38	29 28 28	5♏58 48	26 50.5	10 53.5	25D49.1	21 57.2	6 25.5	24 17.4	28 00.3	27 43.3	9 24.3	6 30.0
13 W	21 32 34	24 24 17	12♏22 37	18 40 27	26D48.8	11 22.3	25 48.3	22 28.7	6 48.8	24 31.8	27 58.7	27 42.6	9 25.2	6 28.9
14 Th	21 36 30	25 24 55	24 52 53	1♐00 34	26 48.8	11 41.2	25 50.0	23 00.4	7 12.2	24 46.2	27 57.1	27 41.9	9 26.1	6 27.8
15 F	21 40 27	26 25 32	7♐04 09	13 04 21	26 49.6	11R49.8	25 54.0	23 32.2	7 35.5	25 00.6	27 55.7	27 41.1	9 26.9	6 26.6
16 Sa	21 44 24	27 26 08	19 01 50	24 57 14	26R50.2	11 47.9	26 00.4	24 04.1	7 58.7	25 15.0	27 54.3	27 40.3	9 27.7	6 25.4
17 Su	21 48 20	28 26 43	0♑51 14	6♑44 24	26 49.7	11 35.7	26 09.1	24 36.2	8 22.0	25 29.4	27 53.1	27 39.5	9 28.5	6 24.3
18 M	21 52 17	29 27 16	12 37 19	18 30 29	26 47.1	11 13.3	26 20.0	25 08.3	8 45.2	25 43.8	27 52.0	27 38.6	9 29.3	6 23.0
19 Tu	21 56 13	0♓27 48	24 24 24	0♒19 28	26 41.9	10 41.3	26 33.1	25 40.6	9 08.3	25 58.1	27 51.0	27 37.6	9 30.0	6 21.8
20 W	22 00 10	1 28 18	6♒16 02	12 14 26	26 33.9	10 00.6	26 48.2	26 13.0	9 31.5	26 12.5	27 50.1	27 36.6	9 30.6	6 20.5
21 Th	22 04 06	2 28 47	18 14 55	24 17 41	26 23.5	9 12.2	27 05.4	26 45.5	9 54.6	26 26.9	27 49.3	27 35.5	9 31.3	6 19.2
22 F	22 08 03	3 29 14	0♓22 53	6♓30 38	26 11.3	8 17.3	27 24.6	27 18.1	10 17.6	26 41.3	27 48.6	27 34.4	9 31.9	6 17.9
23 Sa	22 11 59	4 29 39	12 41 01	18 54 05	25 58.3	7 17.5	27 45.6	27 50.7	10 40.6	26 55.6	27 48.1	27 33.2	9 32.5	6 16.6
24 Su	22 15 56	5 30 03	25 09 52	1♈28 24	25 45.7	6 14.3	28 08.5	28 23.5	11 03.6	27 09.9	27 47.6	27 32.0	9 33.0	6 15.2
25 M	22 19 52	6 30 25	7♈49 41	14 13 47	25 34.6	5 09.4	28 33.1	28 56.4	11 26.5	27 24.3	27 47.3	27 30.8	9 33.5	6 13.9
26 Tu	22 23 49	7 30 45	20 40 43	27 10 36	25 25.9	4 04.4	28 59.4	29 29.4	11 49.4	27 38.6	27 47.1	27 29.4	9 34.0	6 12.5
27 W	22 27 46	8 31 03	3♉43 30	10♉19 33	25 20.2	3 00.9	29 27.4	0♊02.5	12 12.2	27 52.8	27D47.0	27 28.1	9 34.4	6 11.1
28 Th	22 31 42	9 31 20	16 58 55	23 41 46	25 17.1	2 00.1	29 56.9	0 35.7	12 35.0	28 07.1	27 47.0	27 26.7	9 34.8	6 09.6

Astro Data (Dy Hr Mn)

Astro Data	Dy Hr Mn
♀R	3 6:06
♃⊡♄	4 18:29
♇R	9 0:52
☽0S	12 13:37
☽0N	27 4:38
♅R	1 2:57
♃⊡♇	1 13:20
☽0S	9 0:31
♀D	13 7:28
☿R	15 19:47
☽0N	23 11:01
♃△♅	25 22:00
♃△♄	27 2:13
♄D	27 21:14

Planet Ingress (Dy Hr Mn)

Planet Ingress	Dy Hr Mn
♄ ♊R	7 20:26
☿ ♒	16 3:56
☉ ♒	20 10:46
⚳ ♒	27 3:44
♀ ♑R	29 19:51
☿ ♓	2 22:42
☉ ♓	19 0:59
♂ ♊	27 10:11
♀ ♒	28 14:25

Last Aspect / ☽ Ingress (January)

Last Aspect Dy Hr Mn		☽ Ingress	Dy Hr Mn
2 23:59	♅ ☍	♉	3 4:38
4 6:59	♃ □	♊	5 8:00
7 4:29	♅ △	♋	7 8:28
9 3:49	♅ □	♌	9 7:42
11 7:16	♄ ⚹	♍	11 7:41
13 9:38	♄ □	♎	13 10:21
15 15:49	♄ △	♏	15 16:54
17 22:05	☉ ⚹	♐	18 3:12
20 13:57	♄ ☍	♑	20 15:47
23 0:15	♅ □	♒	23 4:50
25 14:36	♄ △	♓	25 17:00
28 0:57	♄ □	♈	28 3:32
30 11:04	♀ □	♉	30 11:41

Last Aspect / ☽ Ingress (February)

Last Aspect Dy Hr Mn		☽ Ingress	Dy Hr Mn
1 14:29	♀ △	♊	1 16:53
3 16:21	♄ ☌	♋	3 19:06
5 15:39	♅ □	♌	5 19:11
7 15:55	♄ ⚹	♍	7 18:52
9 16:57	♄ □	♎	9 20:10
11 21:21	♄ △	♏	12 0:58
14 1:49	♀ ⚹	♐	14 10:01
16 17:59	♄ ☍	♑	16 22:16
19 6:33	♅ □	♒	19 11:21
21 18:57	♄ △	♓	21 23:15
24 5:53	♂ ⚹	♈	24 9:12
26 15:27	♀ □	♉	26 17:11
28 19:59	♃ □	♊	28 23:10

☽ Phases & Eclipses (Dy Hr Mn)

Dy Hr Mn	Phase
1 18:06	☽ 10♈57
8 12:36	○ 17♋51
15 7:04	☾ 24♎45
23 11:02	● 3♒04
31 7:39	☽ 11♉03
6 23:24	○ 17♌48
14 0:04	☾ 24♏55
22 5:34	● 3♓13

Astro Data

1 January 1974
Julian Day # 27029
SVP 5♓37'05"
GC 26♐28.6 ⚴ 1♑11.3
Eris 12♈24.3 ⚵ 16♑14.2
⚷ 16♈23.5 ⚶ 10♎01.3
☽ Mean ☊ 27♐53.9

1 February 1974
Julian Day # 27060
SVP 5♓37'00"
GC 26♐28.6 ⚴ 13♑28.1
Eris 12♈30.1 ⚵ 28♑26.7
⚷ 16♈57.4 ⚶ 16♎29.8
☽ Mean ☊ 26♐15.4

March 1974 — LONGITUDE

Day	Sid.Time	☉	0 hr ☽	Noon☽	True☊	☿	♀	♂	⚳	♃	♄	♅	♆	♇
1 F	22 35 39	10♓31 34	0♊28 16	7♊18 37	25♐16.2	1♓03.4	0♒28.0	1♊08.9	12♒57.7	28♒21.4	27♊47.1	27♎25.2	9♐35.2	6♎08.2
2 Sa	22 39 35	11 31 46	14 12 57	21 11 23	25R 16.3	0R 11.7	1 00.5	1 42.3	13 20.4	28 35.6	27 47.4	27R 23.7	9 35.5	6R 06.7
3 Su	22 43 32	12 31 56	28 14 00	5♋20 43	25 16.1	29♒25.7	1 34.4	2 15.7	13 43.0	28 49.8	27 47.7	27 22.2	9 35.9	6 05.3
4 M	22 47 28	13 32 04	12♋31 27	19 45 53	25 14.2	28 46.0	2 09.7	2 49.2	14 05.6	29 04.0	27 48.2	27 20.6	9 36.1	6 03.8
5 Tu	22 51 25	14 32 10	27 03 39	4♌24 11	25 09.9	28 13.0	2 46.3	3 22.8	14 28.1	29 18.2	27 48.8	27 19.0	9 36.4	6 02.3
6 W	22 55 22	15 32 14	11♌46 48	19 10 38	25 02.7	27 46.8	3 24.1	3 56.4	14 50.6	29 32.3	27 49.5	27 17.4	9 36.6	6 00.8
7 Th	22 59 18	16 32 16	26 34 45	3♍58 08	24 52.9	27 27.5	4 03.2	4 30.2	15 13.0	29 46.4	27 50.3	27 15.7	9 36.7	5 59.2
8 F	23 03 15	17 32 15	11♍19 44	18 38 30	24 41.3	27 14.9	4 43.4	5 03.9	15 35.4	0♓00.5	27 51.2	27 13.9	9 36.9	5 57.7
9 Sa	23 07 11	18 32 13	25 53 26	3♎03 39	24 29.2	27D 09.0	5 24.7	5 37.8	15 57.7	0 14.5	27 52.2	27 12.1	9 37.0	5 56.1
10 Su	23 11 08	19 32 09	10♎08 25	17 07 08	24 18.0	27 09.4	6 07.1	6 11.7	16 19.9	0 28.5	27 53.4	27 10.3	9 37.0	5 54.6
11 M	23 15 04	20 32 03	23 59 24	0♏44 59	24 08.6	27 16.0	6 50.5	6 45.7	16 42.1	0 42.5	27 54.6	27 08.4	9R 37.1	5 53.0
12 Tu	23 19 01	21 31 56	7♏23 51	13 56 06	24 01.9	27 28.4	7 34.9	7 19.7	17 04.3	0 56.5	27 56.0	27 06.5	9 37.1	5 51.4
13 W	23 22 57	22 31 47	20 21 59	26 41 53	23 57.8	27 46.2	8 20.3	7 53.8	17 26.3	1 10.4	27 57.4	27 04.6	9 37.0	5 49.8
14 Th	23 26 54	23 31 36	2♐56 17	9♐05 45	23 56.0	28 09.3	9 06.6	8 28.0	17 48.3	1 24.3	27 59.0	27 02.6	9 37.0	5 48.2
15 F	23 30 50	24 31 23	15 10 54	21 12 25	23 55.6	28 37.2	9 53.7	9 02.2	18 10.3	1 38.2	28 00.7	27 00.6	9 36.9	5 46.6
16 Sa	23 34 47	25 31 09	27 10 58	3♑07 17	23 55.5	29 09.7	10 41.7	9 36.5	18 32.2	1 52.0	28 02.5	26 58.6	9 36.8	5 44.9
17 Su	23 38 44	26 30 53	9♑02 02	14 55 55	23 54.6	29 46.5	11 30.5	10 10.9	18 54.0	2 05.7	28 04.4	26 56.5	9 36.6	5 43.3
18 M	23 42 40	27 30 36	20 49 36	26 43 43	23 51.8	0♓27.4	12 20.1	10 45.3	19 15.8	2 19.5	28 06.4	26 54.4	9 36.4	5 41.7
19 Tu	23 46 37	28 30 16	2♒38 52	8♒35 35	23 46.5	1 11.9	13 10.4	11 19.8	19 37.5	2 33.2	28 08.5	26 52.3	9 36.2	5 40.0
20 W	23 50 33	29 29 55	14 34 22	20 35 38	23 38.4	2 00.1	14 01.4	11 54.3	19 59.1	2 46.8	28 10.7	26 50.1	9 35.9	5 38.4
21 Th	23 54 30	0♈29 32	26 39 45	2♓47 01	23 27.6	2 51.5	14 53.1	12 28.9	20 20.6	3 00.4	28 13.1	26 47.9	9 35.6	5 36.7
22 F	23 58 26	1 29 07	8♓57 38	15 11 46	23 14.9	3 46.1	15 45.5	13 03.5	20 42.1	3 14.0	28 15.5	26 45.7	9 35.3	5 35.1
23 Sa	0 02 23	2 28 39	21 29 30	27 50 49	23 01.3	4 43.6	16 38.5	13 38.2	21 03.5	3 27.5	28 18.0	26 43.5	9 34.9	5 33.4
24 Su	0 06 19	3 28 10	4♈15 41	10♈43 59	22 48.1	5 43.9	17 32.1	14 12.9	21 24.8	3 41.0	28 20.7	26 41.2	9 34.5	5 31.8
25 M	0 10 16	4 27 39	17 15 36	23 50 20	22 36.4	6 46.8	18 26.2	14 47.7	21 46.1	3 54.4	28 23.4	26 38.9	9 34.1	5 30.1
26 Tu	0 14 13	5 27 06	0♉28 02	7♉08 30	22 27.2	7 52.2	19 21.0	15 22.5	22 07.3	4 07.7	28 26.3	26 36.6	9 33.6	5 28.4
27 W	0 18 09	6 26 31	13 51 33	20 37 03	22 20.9	8 59.9	20 16.2	15 57.4	22 28.3	4 21.0	28 29.2	26 34.2	9 33.1	5 26.8
28 Th	0 22 06	7 25 53	27 24 53	4♊14 57	22 17.5	10 09.9	21 12.0	16 32.3	22 49.4	4 34.3	28 32.3	26 31.8	9 32.6	5 25.1
29 F	0 26 02	8 25 13	11♊07 12	18 01 34	22D 16.4	11 22.1	22 08.3	17 07.3	23 10.3	4 47.5	28 35.4	26 29.5	9 32.1	5 23.4
30 Sa	0 29 59	9 24 31	24 58 05	1♋56 43	22R 16.5	12 36.3	23 05.0	17 42.3	23 31.1	5 00.6	28 38.7	26 27.1	9 31.5	5 21.8
31 Su	0 33 55	10 23 47	8♋57 27	16 00 14	22 16.5	13 52.5	24 02.2	18 17.4	23 51.9	5 13.7	28 42.0	26 24.6	9 30.9	5 20.1

April 1974 — LONGITUDE

Day	Sid.Time	☉	0 hr ☽	Noon☽	True☊	☿	♀	♂	⚳	♃	♄	♅	♆	♇
1 M	0 37 52	11♈23 00	23♋04 59	0♌11 34	22♐15.2	15♓10.6	24♒59.9	18♊52.5	24♒12.6	5♓26.7	28♊45.5	26♎22.2	9♐30.2	5♎18.5
2 Tu	0 41 48	12 22 11	7♌19 45	14 29 13	22R 11.7	16 30.5	25 58.0	19 27.6	24 33.1	5 39.7	28 49.0	26R 19.7	9R 29.6	5R 16.8
3 W	0 45 45	13 21 19	21 39 35	28 50 23	22 05.6	17 52.3	26 56.4	20 02.8	24 53.6	5 52.6	28 52.6	26 17.2	9 28.9	5 15.2
4 Th	0 49 42	14 20 25	6♍01 00	13♍10 50	21 57.0	19 15.8	27 55.4	20 38.0	25 14.0	6 05.4	28 56.4	26 14.8	9 28.1	5 13.5
5 F	0 53 38	15 19 29	20 19 11	27 25 21	21 46.8	20 41.0	28 54.6	21 13.2	25 34.3	6 18.2	29 00.2	26 12.3	9 27.4	5 11.9
6 Sa	0 57 35	16 18 30	4♎28 37	11♎28 21	21 36.1	22 07.9	29 54.3	21 48.5	25 54.5	6 30.9	29 04.1	26 09.7	9 26.6	5 10.3
7 Su	1 01 31	17 17 30	18 23 57	25 14 54	21 26.0	23 36.4	0♓54.4	22 23.8	26 14.7	6 43.5	29 08.1	26 07.2	9 25.8	5 08.7
8 M	1 05 28	18 16 28	2♏00 49	8♏41 24	21 17.5	25 06.6	1 54.7	22 59.1	26 34.7	6 56.1	29 12.2	26 04.7	9 24.9	5 07.0
9 Tu	1 09 24	19 15 23	15 16 32	21 46 31	21 11.4	26 38.4	2 55.5	23 34.5	26 54.6	7 08.6	29 16.4	26 02.1	9 24.1	5 05.4
10 W	1 13 21	20 14 17	28 10 27	4♐29 33	21 07.7	28 11.7	3 56.6	24 09.9	27 14.4	7 21.0	29 20.6	25 59.6	9 23.2	5 03.8
11 Th	1 17 17	21 13 10	10♐43 47	16 53 35	21D 06.3	29 46.7	4 58.0	24 45.3	27 34.2	7 33.3	29 25.0	25 57.0	9 22.2	5 02.3
12 F	1 21 14	22 12 00	22 59 24	29 01 48	21 06.4	1♈23.2	5 59.7	25 20.7	27 53.8	7 45.6	29 29.4	25 54.5	9 21.3	5 00.7
13 Sa	1 25 11	23 10 49	5♑01 22	10♑58 43	21 07.3	3 01.4	7 01.7	25 56.2	28 13.3	7 57.8	29 33.9	25 51.9	9 20.3	4 59.1
14 Su	1 29 07	24 09 36	16 54 31	22 49 26	21R 07.9	4 41.1	8 03.9	26 31.8	28 32.7	8 09.9	29 38.6	25 49.3	9 19.3	4 57.6
15 M	1 33 04	25 08 21	28 44 08	4♒39 16	21 07.4	6 22.3	9 06.5	27 07.3	28 52.0	8 22.0	29 43.2	25 46.8	9 18.3	4 56.0
16 Tu	1 37 00	26 07 04	10♒35 30	16 33 26	21 05.0	8 05.2	10 09.3	27 42.9	29 11.2	8 33.9	29 48.0	25 44.2	9 17.2	4 54.5
17 W	1 40 57	27 05 46	22 33 41	28 36 45	21 00.5	9 49.7	11 12.4	28 18.5	29 30.3	8 45.8	29 52.9	25 41.6	9 16.2	4 53.0
18 Th	1 44 53	28 04 26	4♓43 09	10♓53 18	20 54.0	11 35.7	12 15.8	28 54.1	29 49.3	8 57.6	29 57.8	25 39.0	9 15.1	4 51.5
19 F	1 48 50	29 03 04	17 07 32	23 26 08	20 45.8	13 23.4	13 19.4	29 29.8	0♓08.1	9 09.3	0♋02.8	25 36.5	9 13.9	4 50.0
20 Sa	1 52 46	0♉01 40	29 49 16	6♈17 03	20 36.9	15 12.7	14 23.2	0♋05.5	0 26.9	9 20.9	0 07.9	25 33.9	9 12.8	4 48.5
21 Su	1 56 43	1 00 15	12♈49 28	19 26 24	20 28.0	17 03.6	15 27.2	0 41.2	0 45.5	9 32.5	0 13.1	25 31.3	9 11.6	4 47.0
22 M	2 00 39	1 58 48	26 07 43	2♉53 07	20 20.2	18 56.1	16 31.5	1 17.0	1 04.0	9 43.9	0 18.3	25 28.8	9 10.4	4 45.6
23 Tu	2 04 36	2 57 19	9♉42 18	16 34 54	20 14.2	20 50.3	17 35.9	1 52.8	1 22.4	9 55.3	0 23.6	25 26.2	9 09.2	4 44.2
24 W	2 08 33	3 55 48	23 30 30	0♊28 41	20 10.4	22 46.1	18 40.6	2 28.6	1 40.6	10 06.5	0 29.0	25 23.7	9 08.0	4 42.8
25 Th	2 12 29	4 54 15	7♊29 01	14 31 05	20D 08.8	24 43.5	19 45.4	3 04.4	1 58.7	10 17.7	0 34.5	25 21.2	9 06.7	4 41.4
26 F	2 16 26	5 52 40	21 34 31	28 38 57	20 08.9	26 42.5	20 50.5	3 40.3	2 16.7	10 28.8	0 40.0	25 18.6	9 05.5	4 40.0
27 Sa	2 20 22	6 51 03	5♋44 03	12♋49 34	20 10.0	28 43.0	21 55.7	4 16.2	2 34.5	10 39.8	0 45.7	25 16.1	9 04.2	4 38.7
28 Su	2 24 19	7 49 24	19 55 13	27 00 48	20R 11.2	0♉45.1	23 01.1	4 52.1	2 52.3	10 50.6	0 51.3	25 13.6	9 02.9	4 37.3
29 M	2 28 15	8 47 42	4♌06 06	11♌10 55	20 11.6	2 48.6	24 06.6	5 28.0	3 09.8	11 01.4	0 57.1	25 11.1	9 01.5	4 36.0
30 Tu	2 32 12	9 45 59	18 15 03	25 18 16	20 10.5	4 53.4	25 12.4	6 04.0	3 27.3	11 12.1	1 02.9	25 08.7	9 00.2	4 34.7

Astro Data

	Dy Hr Mn
☽0S	8 11:37
☿D	9 22:17
♆R	12 1:20
☉0N	21 0:06
☽0N	22 18:06
♃⚻♇	31 22:28
☽0S	4 20:34
☿0N	15 1:01
☽0N	19 1:54
♃□♆	19 20:40
♃⚼♅	25 18:03

Planet Ingress

	Dy Hr Mn
☿ ♒R	2 17:49
♃ ♓	8 11:11
☿ ♓	17 20:11
☉ ♈	21 0:07
♀ ♓	6 14:17
☿ ♈	11 15:20
♄ ♋	18 22:34
⚳ ♓	19 1:37
♂ ♋	20 8:18
☉ ♉	20 11:19
☿ ♉	28 3:10

Last Aspect / ☽ Ingress

Last Aspect Dy Hr Mn		☽ Ingress Dy Hr Mn
3 2:31 ☿ △	♋	3 3:00
5 0:26 ♅ □	♌	5 4:49
7 5:04 ♃ ☍	♍	7 5:33
9 3:17 ♄ □	♎	9 6:52
11 6:56 ♄ △	♏	11 10:40
13 14:07 ☿ □	♐	13 18:20
16 3:36 ☿ ⚹	♑	16 5:41
18 13:44 ☉ ⚹	♒	18 18:38
21 3:02 ♄ △	♓	21 6:33
23 12:51 ♄ □	♈	23 16:02
25 20:17 ♄ ⚹	♉	25 23:09
27 11:20 ♀ □	♊	28 4:33
30 6:18 ♄ ☌	♋	30 8:40

Last Aspect / ☽ Ingress

Last Aspect Dy Hr Mn		☽ Ingress Dy Hr Mn
1 5:34 ♅ □	♌	1 11:41
3 12:04 ♄ ⚹	♍	3 13:56
5 14:42 ♄ □	♎	5 16:22
7 18:55 ♄ △	♏	7 20:25
9 22:22 ☿ △	♐	10 3:27
12 12:55 ♄ ☍	♑	12 13:56
14 18:04 ♅ □	♒	15 2:34
17 14:31 ♄ △	♓	17 14:44
19 23:57 ♂ □	♈	20 0:20
21 22:53 ♅ ☍	♉	22 6:53
23 13:55 ♀ ⚹	♊	24 11:11
26 8:10 ☿ ⚹	♋	26 14:17
28 8:59 ♅ □	♌	28 17:03
30 11:44 ♅ ⚹	♍	30 20:00

☽ Phases & Eclipses

Dy Hr Mn	
1 18:03	☽ 10♊47
8 10:03	○ 17♍27
15 19:15	☾ 24♐49
23 21:24	● 2♈52
31 1:44	☽ 9♋58
6 21:00	○ 16♎41
14 14:57	☾ 24♑17
22 10:16	● 1♉55
29 7:39	☽ 8♌37

Astro Data

1 March 1974
Julian Day # 27088
SVP 5♓36'56"
GC 26♐28.7 ⚴ 23♑35.3
Eris 12♈43.4 ⚵ 9♒31.7
⚷ 18♈06.3 ⚶ 16♎48.5R
☽ Mean ☊ 24♐46.4

1 April 1974
Julian Day # 27119
SVP 5♓36'53"
GC 26♐28.8 ⚴ 2♒59.0
Eris 13♈03.3 ⚵ 21♒26.4
⚷ 19♈48.8 ⚶ 10♎38.4R
☽ Mean ☊ 23♐07.9

LONGITUDE — May 1974

Day	Sid.Time	☉	0 hr ☽	Noon☽	True☊	☿	♀	♂	⚳	♃	♄	♅	♆	♇
1 W	2 36 08	10♉44 13	2♍20 23	9♍21 06	20♐07.7	6♉59.5	26♓18.3	6♋39.9	3♓44.6	11♓22.6	1♋08.8	25♎06.2	8♐58.8	4♎33.4
2 Th	2 40 05	11 42 25	16 20 11	23 17 19	20R 03.3	9 06.8	27 24.3	7 15.9	4 01.7	11 33.1	1 14.7	25R 03.8	8R 57.4	4R 32.2
3 F	2 44 02	12 40 36	0♎12 11	7♎04 29	19 57.8	11 15.1	28 30.5	7 51.9	4 18.7	11 43.4	1 20.7	25 01.4	8 56.0	4 31.0
4 Sa	2 47 58	13 38 44	13 53 52	20 40 04	19 51.9	13 24.1	29 36.9	8 27.9	4 35.6	11 53.7	1 26.8	24 59.0	8 54.6	4 29.8
5 Su	2 51 55	14 36 51	27 22 46	4♏01 44	19 46.3	15 33.8	0♈43.4	9 04.0	4 52.3	12 03.8	1 32.9	24 56.6	8 53.2	4 28.6
6 M	2 55 51	15 34 56	10♏36 47	17 07 46	19 41.7	17 43.9	1 50.0	9 40.0	5 08.8	12 13.8	1 39.1	24 54.2	8 51.7	4 27.4
7 Tu	2 59 48	16 32 59	23 34 36	29 57 17	19 38.5	19 54.1	2 56.8	10 16.1	5 25.3	12 23.8	1 45.3	24 51.9	8 50.3	4 26.3
8 W	3 03 44	17 31 01	6♐15 52	12♐30 30	19D 36.9	22 04.1	4 03.7	10 52.2	5 41.5	12 33.6	1 51.6	24 49.6	8 48.8	4 25.2
9 Th	3 07 41	18 29 01	18 41 22	24 48 46	19 36.8	24 13.8	5 10.8	11 28.3	5 57.6	12 43.3	1 58.0	24 47.3	8 47.3	4 24.1
10 F	3 11 37	19 27 00	0♑53 01	6♑54 30	19 37.8	26 22.7	6 18.0	12 04.5	6 13.6	12 52.8	2 04.4	24 45.0	8 45.8	4 23.0
11 Sa	3 15 34	20 24 58	12 53 41	18 51 02	19 39.5	28 30.6	7 25.3	12 40.6	6 29.3	13 02.3	2 10.8	24 42.8	8 44.3	4 22.0
12 Su	3 19 31	21 22 54	24 47 04	0♒42 23	19 41.2	0♊37.3	8 32.8	13 16.8	6 44.9	13 11.6	2 17.4	24 40.6	8 42.8	4 21.0
13 M	3 23 27	22 20 48	6♒37 32	12 33 08	19R 42.5	2 42.4	9 40.4	13 53.0	7 00.4	13 20.8	2 23.9	24 38.4	8 41.3	4 20.0
14 Tu	3 27 24	23 18 42	18 29 47	24 28 06	19 42.9	4 45.6	10 48.0	14 29.2	7 15.6	13 29.9	2 30.6	24 36.2	8 39.7	4 19.0
15 W	3 31 20	24 16 34	0♓28 41	6♓32 08	19 42.3	6 46.9	11 55.8	15 05.4	7 30.7	13 38.9	2 37.2	24 34.1	8 38.2	4 18.1
16 Th	3 35 17	25 14 25	12 39 00	18 49 49	19 40.5	8 45.9	13 03.8	15 41.7	7 45.7	13 47.7	2 43.9	24 32.0	8 36.6	4 17.2
17 F	3 39 13	26 12 15	25 05 04	1♈25 08	19 37.9	10 42.4	14 11.8	16 18.0	8 00.4	13 56.4	2 50.7	24 29.9	8 35.0	4 16.3
18 Sa	3 43 10	27 10 03	7♈50 22	14 21 01	19 34.7	12 36.4	15 19.9	16 54.2	8 14.9	14 05.0	2 57.5	24 27.9	8 33.4	4 15.4
19 Su	3 47 06	28 07 51	20 57 15	27 39 07	19 31.5	14 27.6	16 28.1	17 30.6	8 29.3	14 13.4	3 04.4	24 25.9	8 31.9	4 14.6
20 M	3 51 03	29 05 37	4♉26 31	11♉19 17	19 28.6	16 16.0	17 36.4	18 06.9	8 43.5	14 21.7	3 11.3	24 23.9	8 30.3	4 13.8
21 Tu	3 55 00	0♊03 22	18 17 08	25 19 38	19 26.6	18 01.5	18 44.9	18 43.2	8 57.5	14 29.9	3 18.3	24 21.9	8 28.7	4 13.0
22 W	3 58 56	1 01 06	2♊26 17	9♊36 29	19D 25.4	19 44.0	19 53.4	19 19.6	9 11.3	14 37.9	3 25.3	24 20.0	8 27.1	4 12.3
23 Th	4 02 53	1 58 48	16 49 35	24 04 52	19 25.3	21 23.4	21 01.9	19 56.0	9 24.9	14 45.8	3 32.3	24 18.2	8 25.5	4 11.6
24 F	4 06 49	2 56 29	1♋21 36	8♋39 05	19 25.9	22 59.7	22 10.6	20 32.4	9 38.2	14 53.5	3 39.4	24 16.3	8 23.8	4 10.9
25 Sa	4 10 46	3 54 09	15 56 35	23 13 28	19 26.9	24 32.9	23 19.4	21 08.8	9 51.4	15 01.1	3 46.5	24 14.6	8 22.2	4 10.3
26 Su	4 14 42	4 51 47	0♌29 07	7♌43 00	19 28.0	26 02.8	24 28.2	21 45.3	10 04.4	15 08.6	3 53.7	24 12.8	8 20.6	4 09.6
27 M	4 18 39	5 49 23	14 54 38	22 03 38	19 28.8	27 29.5	25 37.1	22 21.7	10 17.2	15 15.9	4 00.8	24 11.1	8 19.0	4 09.0
28 Tu	4 22 35	6 46 58	29 09 41	6♍12 33	19R 29.2	28 52.9	26 46.1	22 58.2	10 29.7	15 23.1	4 08.1	24 09.4	8 17.4	4 08.5
29 W	4 26 32	7 44 32	13♍12 01	20 07 58	19 28.9	0♋13.0	27 55.2	23 34.7	10 42.0	15 30.1	4 15.3	24 07.8	8 15.7	4 08.0
30 Th	4 30 29	8 42 04	27 00 19	3♎49 00	19 28.1	1 29.7	29 04.3	24 11.2	10 54.2	15 37.0	4 22.6	24 06.2	8 14.1	4 07.5
31 F	4 34 25	9 39 34	10♎34 01	17 15 21	19 27.1	2 42.9	0♉13.5	24 47.7	11 06.0	15 43.7	4 30.0	24 04.6	8 12.5	4 07.0

LONGITUDE — June 1974

Day	Sid.Time	☉	0 hr ☽	Noon☽	True☊	☿	♀	♂	⚳	♃	♄	♅	♆	♇
1 Sa	4 38 22	10♊37 04	23♎53 02	0♏27 07	19♐25.9	3♋52.7	1♉22.8	25♋24.2	11♓17.7	15♓50.2	4♋37.3	24♎03.1	8♐10.9	4♎06.6
2 Su	4 42 18	11 34 32	6♏57 38	13 24 39	19R 24.9	4 59.0	2 32.2	26 00.7	11 29.2	15 56.6	4 44.7	24R 01.6	8R 09.2	4R 06.1
3 M	4 46 15	12 31 59	19 48 15	26 08 31	19 24.1	6 01.7	3 41.6	26 37.3	11 40.4	16 02.9	4 52.1	24 00.2	8 07.6	4 05.8
4 Tu	4 50 11	13 29 25	2♐25 33	8♐39 28	19D 23.7	7 00.7	4 51.1	27 13.9	11 51.3	16 09.0	4 59.6	23 58.8	8 06.0	4 05.4
5 W	4 54 08	14 26 51	14 50 25	20 58 33	19 23.6	7 56.0	6 00.7	27 50.5	12 02.1	16 14.9	5 07.0	23 57.5	8 04.4	4 05.1
6 Th	4 58 04	15 24 15	27 04 04	3♑07 12	19 23.7	8 47.5	7 10.3	28 27.1	12 12.6	16 20.7	5 14.5	23 56.2	8 02.8	4 04.9
7 F	5 02 01	16 21 38	9♑08 11	15 07 17	19 24.0	9 35.1	8 20.0	29 03.7	12 22.8	16 26.3	5 22.1	23 54.9	8 01.2	4 04.6
8 Sa	5 05 58	17 19 01	21 04 51	27 01 13	19 24.3	10 18.7	9 29.8	29 40.3	12 32.8	16 31.7	5 29.6	23 53.7	7 59.6	4 04.4
9 Su	5 09 54	18 16 23	2♒56 45	8♒51 54	19 24.5	10 58.2	10 39.7	0♌16.9	12 42.6	16 37.0	5 37.2	23 52.6	7 58.0	4 04.2
10 M	5 13 51	19 13 44	14 47 05	20 42 48	19R 24.5	11 33.6	11 49.6	0 53.6	12 52.1	16 42.1	5 44.8	23 51.5	7 56.4	4 04.1
11 Tu	5 17 47	20 11 05	26 39 32	2♓37 49	19 24.5	12 04.7	12 59.6	1 30.3	13 01.3	16 47.1	5 52.4	23 50.4	7 54.8	4 04.0
12 W	5 21 44	21 08 26	8♓38 12	14 41 14	19D 24.5	12 31.5	14 09.6	2 07.0	13 10.3	16 51.9	6 00.0	23 49.4	7 53.3	4 03.9
13 Th	5 25 40	22 05 45	20 47 27	26 57 26	19 24.5	12 53.9	15 19.7	2 43.7	13 19.0	16 56.5	6 07.7	23 48.4	7 51.7	4 03.8
14 F	5 29 37	23 03 05	3♈11 41	9♈30 44	19 24.6	13 11.8	16 29.9	3 20.4	13 27.5	17 00.9	6 15.3	23 47.5	7 50.1	4D 03.8
15 Sa	5 33 33	24 00 24	15 55 02	22 25 00	19 24.9	13 25.2	17 40.1	3 57.2	13 35.6	17 05.1	6 23.0	23 46.6	7 48.6	4 03.8
16 Su	5 37 30	24 57 43	29 00 57	5♉43 08	19 25.4	13 34.0	18 50.4	4 33.9	13 43.5	17 09.2	6 30.7	23 45.8	7 47.0	4 03.9
17 M	5 41 27	25 55 01	12♉31 42	19 26 39	19 26.0	13R 38.3	20 00.7	5 10.7	13 51.1	17 13.1	6 38.4	23 45.0	7 45.5	4 04.0
18 Tu	5 45 23	26 52 19	26 27 51	3♊35 03	19 26.4	13 38.1	21 11.1	5 47.5	13 58.5	17 16.8	6 46.2	23 44.3	7 44.0	4 04.1
19 W	5 49 20	27 49 37	10♊47 48	18 05 31	19R 26.7	13 33.3	22 21.6	6 24.4	14 05.5	17 20.4	6 53.9	23 43.6	7 42.5	4 04.2
20 Th	5 53 16	28 46 54	25 27 30	2♋52 52	19 26.5	13 24.2	23 32.1	7 01.2	14 12.2	17 23.7	7 01.7	23 43.0	7 41.0	4 04.4
21 F	5 57 13	29 44 11	10♋20 42	17 49 57	19 25.8	13 10.9	24 42.7	7 38.1	14 18.7	17 26.9	7 09.4	23 42.4	7 39.5	4 04.6
22 Sa	6 01 09	0♋41 27	25 19 33	2♌48 29	19 24.7	12 53.5	25 53.3	8 14.9	14 24.8	17 29.9	7 17.2	23 41.9	7 38.0	4 04.9
23 Su	6 05 06	1 38 43	10♌15 42	17 40 18	19 23.4	12 32.3	27 04.0	8 51.8	14 30.6	17 32.7	7 25.0	23 41.4	7 36.6	4 05.2
24 M	6 09 03	2 35 58	25 01 27	2♍18 28	19 22.0	12 07.6	28 14.7	9 28.8	14 36.2	17 35.3	7 32.8	23 41.0	7 35.2	4 05.5
25 Tu	6 12 59	3 33 12	9♍30 47	16 37 59	19 20.9	11 39.8	29 25.4	10 05.7	14 41.4	17 37.7	7 40.6	23 40.6	7 33.7	4 05.8
26 W	6 16 56	4 30 26	23 39 50	0♎36 11	19D 20.4	11 09.4	0♊36.2	10 42.6	14 46.3	17 40.0	7 48.4	23 40.3	7 32.3	4 06.2
27 Th	6 20 52	5 27 39	7♎27 01	14 12 25	19 20.5	10 36.7	1 47.1	11 19.6	14 50.9	17 42.0	7 56.2	23 40.1	7 30.9	4 06.6
28 F	6 24 49	6 24 52	20 52 34	27 27 40	19 21.3	10 02.3	2 58.0	11 56.6	14 55.2	17 43.9	8 04.0	23 39.8	7 29.5	4 07.0
29 Sa	6 28 45	7 22 04	3♏58 02	10♏23 57	19 22.6	9 26.8	4 08.9	12 33.5	14 59.1	17 45.5	8 11.8	23 39.7	7 28.2	4 07.5
30 Su	6 32 42	8 19 16	16 45 46	23 03 47	19 24.0	8 50.7	5 19.9	13 10.5	15 02.8	17 47.0	8 19.6	23 39.6	7 26.8	4 08.0

Astro Data	Planet Ingress	Last Aspect	☽ Ingress	Last Aspect	☽ Ingress	☽ Phases & Eclipses	Astro Data
Dy Hr Mn	Dy Hr Mn	Dy Hr Mn	Dy Hr Mn	Dy Hr Mn	Dy Hr Mn	Dy Hr Mn	1 May 1974
☽0S 2 2:48	♀ ♈ 4 20:21	2 19:45 ♀ ☍	♎ 2 23:39	1 2:19 ♂ □	♏ 1 11:10	6 8:55 ○ 15♏27	Julian Day # 27149
♀0N 7 21:16	☿ ♊ 12 4:55	4 19:41 ♅ ☌	♏ 5 4:43	3 12:58 ♂ △	♐ 3 19:21	14 9:29 ☾ 23♒13	SVP 5♓36'50"
☽0N 16 10:00	☉ ♊ 21 10:36	6 13:20 ☿ ☍	♐ 7 12:05	5 17:51 ♅ ⚹	♑ 6 5:48	21 20:34 ● 0♊24	GC 26♐28.8 ⚵ 9♒12.7
♄□♇ 28 13:16	☿ ♋ 29 8:03	9 11:57 ♅ ⚹	♑ 9 22:15	8 17:40 ♂ ☍	♒ 8 18:02	28 13:03 ☽ 6♍49	Eris 13♈23.1 ⚶ 2♓05.2
☽0S 29 7:48	♀ ♉ 31 7:19	11 23:49 ♅ □	♒ 12 10:34	10 18:21 ♅ △	♓ 11 6:43		⚷ 21♈34.4 ⚴ 4♎23.5R
		14 12:16 ♅ △	♓ 14 23:03	13 1:45 ☉ □	♈ 13 17:52	4 22:10 ○ 13♐54	☽ Mean ☊ 21♐32.6
☽0N 12 17:53	♂ ♌ 9 0:54	17 1:19 ☉ ⚹	♈ 17 9:20	15 15:08 ☉ ⚹	♉ 16 1:46	4 22:16 ☍ P 0.827	
♇ D 14 13:17	☉ ♋ 21 18:38	19 6:16 ♅ ☍	♉ 19 16:10	17 13:04 ♀ ☌	♊ 18 5:59	13 1:45 ☾ 21♓41	1 June 1974
☿ R 17 22:38	♀ ♊ 25 23:44	21 0:14 ♂ ⚹	♊ 21 19:54	20 4:56 ☉ ☌	♋ 20 7:21	20 4:56 ● 28♊30	Julian Day # 27180
♄⚻♆ 24 18:07		23 12:22 ♅ △	♋ 23 21:46	21 23:57 ♀ ⚹	♌ 22 7:30	20 4:47:20 ● T 05'09"	SVP 5♓36'45"
☽0S 25 13:51		25 13:41 ♅ □	♌ 25 23:12	24 4:42 ♀ □	♍ 24 8:11	26 19:20 ☽ 4♎48	GC 26♐28.9 ⚵ 11♒06.5R
		27 22:11 ☿ ⚹	♍ 28 1:25	25 13:42 ♃ ☍	♎ 26 10:57		Eris 13♈39.0 ⚶ 11♓21.7
		29 18:17 ♂ ⚹	♎ 30 5:16	28 5:04 ♅ ☌	♏ 28 16:40		⚷ 23♈09.7 ⚴ 4♎37.4
							☽ Mean ☊ 19♐54.1

July 1974 LONGITUDE

Day	Sid.Time	☉	0 hr ☽	Noon ☽	True ☊	☿	♀	♂	⚳	♃	♄	♅	♆	♇
1 M	6 36 38	9♋16 27	29♏18 22	5♐29 50	19♐25.1	8♋14.8	6♊31.0	13♌47.6	15♓06.1	17♓48.3	8♋27.4	23♎39.5	7♐25.5	4♎08.6
2 Tu	6 40 35	10 13 38	11♐38 30	17 44 38	19R 25.7	7R 39.5	7 42.1	14 24.6	15 09.0	17 49.4	8 35.2	23D 39.5	7R 24.2	4 09.2
3 W	6 44 32	11 10 49	23 48 33	29 50 31	19 25.3	7 05.6	8 53.2	15 01.7	15 11.7	17 50.3	8 43.1	23 39.6	7 22.9	4 09.8
4 Th	6 48 28	12 08 00	5♑50 46	11♑49 34	19 23.8	6 33.6	10 04.4	15 38.7	15 14.0	17 51.0	8 50.9	23 39.7	7 21.7	4 10.4
5 F	6 52 25	13 05 11	17 47 09	23 43 45	19 21.2	6 04.0	11 15.6	16 15.8	15 16.0	17 51.6	8 58.7	23 39.8	7 20.4	4 11.1
6 Sa	6 56 21	14 02 22	29 39 38	5♒35 03	19 17.7	5 37.5	12 26.9	16 52.9	15 17.6	17 51.9	9 06.5	23 40.0	7 19.2	4 11.8
7 Su	7 00 18	14 59 33	11♒30 15	17 25 33	19 13.5	5 14.4	13 38.3	17 30.0	15 18.9	17R 52.0	9 14.2	23 40.3	7 18.0	4 12.5
8 M	7 04 14	15 56 45	23 21 14	29 17 38	19 09.1	4 55.3	14 49.7	18 07.2	15 19.9	17 52.0	9 22.0	23 40.6	7 16.8	4 13.3
9 Tu	7 08 11	16 53 56	5♓15 08	11♓14 06	19 05.1	4 40.4	16 01.1	18 44.3	15 20.5	17 51.7	9 29.8	23 41.0	7 15.6	4 14.1
10 W	7 12 07	17 51 08	17 14 58	23 18 10	19 01.8	4 30.1	17 12.6	19 21.5	15R 20.7	17 51.2	9 37.6	23 41.4	7 14.5	4 14.9
11 Th	7 16 04	18 48 20	29 24 10	5♈33 27	18 59.7	4D 24.6	18 24.2	19 58.7	15 20.6	17 50.6	9 45.3	23 41.9	7 13.4	4 15.8
12 F	7 20 01	19 45 33	11♈46 33	18 03 56	18D 58.9	4 24.2	19 35.8	20 35.9	15 20.2	17 49.7	9 53.1	23 42.4	7 12.3	4 16.7
13 Sa	7 23 57	20 42 47	24 26 08	0♉53 37	18 59.3	4 29.0	20 47.4	21 13.2	15 19.4	17 48.7	10 00.8	23 43.0	7 11.2	4 17.6
14 Su	7 27 54	21 40 01	7♉26 50	14 06 12	19 00.5	4 39.1	21 59.1	21 50.4	15 18.2	17 47.5	10 08.5	23 43.6	7 10.1	4 18.5
15 M	7 31 50	22 37 15	20 52 00	27 44 29	19 02.0	4 54.7	23 10.9	22 27.7	15 16.7	17 46.0	10 16.2	23 44.3	7 09.1	4 19.5
16 Tu	7 35 47	23 34 30	4♊43 45	11♊49 45	19R 03.0	5 15.7	24 22.7	23 05.0	15 14.8	17 44.4	10 23.9	23 45.0	7 08.1	4 20.5
17 W	7 39 43	24 31 46	19 02 17	26 20 57	19 03.0	5 42.2	25 34.5	23 42.3	15 12.6	17 42.6	10 31.6	23 45.8	7 07.1	4 21.6
18 Th	7 43 40	25 29 03	3♋45 10	11♋14 10	19 01.4	6 14.2	26 46.4	24 19.7	15 10.0	17 40.6	10 39.2	23 46.6	7 06.2	4 22.7
19 F	7 47 36	26 26 20	18 46 58	26 22 28	18 58.2	6 51.6	27 58.3	24 57.1	15 07.0	17 38.4	10 46.9	23 47.5	7 05.2	4 23.8
20 Sa	7 51 33	27 23 37	3♌59 26	11♌36 33	18 53.5	7 34.5	29 10.3	25 34.5	15 03.7	17 36.0	10 54.5	23 48.5	7 04.3	4 24.9
21 Su	7 55 30	28 20 54	19 12 30	26 46 02	18 47.9	8 22.8	0♋22.3	26 11.9	15 00.0	17 33.4	11 02.1	23 49.5	7 03.5	4 26.1
22 M	7 59 26	29 18 12	4♍15 56	11♍41 12	18 42.2	9 16.4	1 34.4	26 49.3	14 56.0	17 30.6	11 09.7	23 50.5	7 02.6	4 27.3
23 Tu	8 03 23	0♌15 31	19 00 58	26 14 35	18 37.3	10 15.2	2 46.5	27 26.8	14 51.6	17 27.7	11 17.2	23 51.6	7 01.8	4 28.5
24 W	8 07 19	1 12 49	3♎21 35	10♎21 44	18 33.8	11 19.2	3 58.6	28 04.2	14 46.8	17 24.5	11 24.7	23 52.7	7 01.0	4 29.7
25 Th	8 11 16	2 10 08	17 14 57	24 01 20	18D 32.0	12 28.3	5 10.8	28 41.7	14 41.7	17 21.2	11 32.2	23 53.9	7 00.2	4 31.0
26 F	8 15 12	3 07 28	0♏41 07	7♏14 38	18 31.8	13 42.4	6 23.1	29 19.2	14 36.3	17 17.7	11 39.7	23 55.2	6 59.5	4 32.3
27 Sa	8 19 09	4 04 47	13 42 18	20 04 37	18 32.7	15 01.4	7 35.3	29 56.8	14 30.5	17 14.0	11 47.1	23 56.5	6 58.8	4 33.6
28 Su	8 23 05	5 02 08	26 22 04	2♐35 12	18 34.0	16 25.2	8 47.7	0♍34.3	14 24.3	17 10.1	11 54.6	23 57.8	6 58.1	4 35.0
29 M	8 27 02	5 59 29	8♐44 33	14 50 37	18R 34.9	17 53.5	10 00.0	1 11.9	14 17.9	17 06.1	12 02.0	23 59.2	6 57.5	4 36.4
30 Tu	8 30 59	6 56 50	20 53 56	26 54 56	18 34.6	19 26.2	11 12.4	1 49.5	14 11.1	17 01.9	12 09.3	24 00.7	6 56.8	4 37.8
31 W	8 34 55	7 54 12	2♑54 05	8♑51 47	18 32.4	21 03.1	12 24.9	2 27.1	14 03.9	16 57.5	12 16.6	24 02.2	6 56.2	4 39.3

August 1974 LONGITUDE

Day	Sid.Time	☉	0 hr ☽	Noon ☽	True ☊	☿	♀	♂	⚳	♃	♄	♅	♆	♇
1 Th	8 38 52	8♌51 35	14♑48 24	20♑44 15	18♐28.0	22♋44.0	13♋37.4	3♍04.7	13♓56.4	16♓52.9	12♋23.9	24♎03.7	6♐55.7	4♎40.7
2 F	8 42 48	9 48 58	26 39 39	2♒34 52	18R 21.5	24 28.5	14 49.9	3 42.4	13R 48.7	16R 48.2	12 31.2	24 05.3	6R 55.1	4 42.2
3 Sa	8 46 45	10 46 22	8♒30 08	14 25 40	18 13.0	26 16.5	16 02.5	4 20.1	13 40.5	16 43.3	12 38.4	24 06.9	6 54.6	4 43.7
4 Su	8 50 41	11 43 48	20 21 41	26 18 23	18 03.2	28 07.6	17 15.2	4 57.8	13 32.1	16 38.3	12 45.6	24 08.6	6 54.2	4 45.3
5 M	8 54 38	12 41 14	2♓15 58	8♓14 38	17 53.0	0♌01.5	18 27.8	5 35.5	13 23.4	16 33.1	12 52.8	24 10.4	6 53.7	4 46.8
6 Tu	8 58 34	13 38 41	14 14 37	20 16 09	17 43.3	1 57.7	19 40.6	6 13.2	13 14.3	16 27.7	12 59.9	24 12.1	6 53.3	4 48.4
7 W	9 02 31	14 36 10	26 19 31	2♈24 59	17 34.9	3 56.0	20 53.4	6 51.0	13 05.0	16 22.2	13 06.9	24 14.0	6 52.9	4 50.0
8 Th	9 06 28	15 33 39	8♈32 53	14 43 35	17 28.6	5 56.0	22 06.2	7 28.8	12 55.4	16 16.6	13 14.0	24 15.8	6 52.6	4 51.7
9 F	9 10 24	16 31 10	20 57 28	27 14 56	17 24.5	7 57.2	23 19.0	8 06.6	12 45.5	16 10.8	13 21.0	24 17.7	6 52.2	4 53.3
10 Sa	9 14 21	17 28 42	3♉36 26	10♉02 25	17D 22.7	9 59.5	24 32.0	8 44.5	12 35.3	16 04.8	13 27.9	24 19.7	6 51.9	4 55.0
11 Su	9 18 17	18 26 16	16 33 20	23 09 37	17 22.5	12 02.3	25 44.9	9 22.3	12 24.9	15 58.7	13 34.8	24 21.7	6 51.7	4 56.7
12 M	9 22 14	19 23 52	29 51 39	6♊39 47	17R 23.1	14 05.5	26 57.9	10 00.2	12 14.2	15 52.5	13 41.7	24 23.8	6 51.5	4 58.5
13 Tu	9 26 10	20 21 28	13♊34 18	20 35 20	17 23.3	16 08.6	28 11.0	10 38.2	12 03.3	15 46.2	13 48.5	24 25.9	6 51.3	5 00.2
14 W	9 30 07	21 19 07	27 42 53	4♋56 50	17 22.1	18 11.6	29 24.1	11 16.1	11 52.1	15 39.7	13 55.3	24 28.0	6 51.1	5 02.0
15 Th	9 34 03	22 16 47	12♋16 48	19 42 16	17 18.8	20 14.1	0♌37.3	11 54.1	11 40.7	15 33.1	14 02.1	24 30.2	6 51.0	5 03.8
16 F	9 38 00	23 14 28	27 12 28	4♌46 25	17 12.9	22 16.0	1 50.5	12 32.1	11 29.0	15 26.4	14 08.7	24 32.4	6 50.9	5 05.6
17 Sa	9 41 57	24 12 10	12♌23 00	20 00 54	17 04.7	24 17.1	3 03.7	13 10.1	11 17.2	15 19.6	14 15.4	24 34.7	6 50.8	5 07.5
18 Su	9 45 53	25 09 54	27 38 45	5♍15 09	16 55.1	26 17.3	4 17.0	13 48.2	11 05.2	15 12.6	14 22.0	24 37.0	6D 50.8	5 09.3
19 M	9 49 50	26 07 39	12♍48 45	20 18 15	16 45.1	28 16.4	5 30.3	14 26.3	10 53.0	15 05.6	14 28.5	24 39.4	6 50.8	5 11.2
20 Tu	9 53 46	27 05 25	27 42 36	5♎00 51	16 36.1	0♍14.4	6 43.6	15 04.4	10 40.6	14 58.5	14 35.0	24 41.8	6 50.8	5 13.1
21 W	9 57 43	28 03 12	12♎12 21	19 16 37	16 28.9	2 11.2	7 57.0	15 42.5	10 28.1	14 51.2	14 41.4	24 44.2	6 50.8	5 15.0
22 Th	10 01 39	29 01 01	26 13 27	3♏02 48	16 24.1	4 06.8	9 10.5	16 20.7	10 15.4	14 43.9	14 47.7	24 46.7	6 50.8	5 16.9
23 F	10 05 36	29 58 51	9♏44 49	16 19 50	16 21.6	6 01.1	10 24.0	16 58.9	10 02.6	14 36.5	14 54.0	24 49.2	6 51.1	5 18.9
24 Sa	10 09 32	0♍56 42	22 48 15	29 10 36	16D 20.9	7 54.0	11 37.5	17 37.1	9 49.7	14 29.1	15 00.3	24 51.8	6 51.2	5 20.9
25 Su	10 13 29	1 54 34	5♐27 27	11♐39 26	16R 21.1	9 45.7	12 51.0	18 15.3	9 36.7	14 21.5	15 06.5	24 54.4	6 51.4	5 22.9
26 M	10 17 26	2 52 28	17 47 11	23 51 20	16 20.9	11 36.0	14 04.6	18 53.6	9 23.6	14 13.9	15 12.6	24 57.0	6 51.6	5 24.9
27 Tu	10 21 22	3 50 22	29 52 32	5♑51 23	16 19.4	13 25.1	15 18.2	19 31.9	9 10.4	14 06.3	15 18.7	24 59.7	6 51.9	5 26.9
28 W	10 25 19	4 48 18	11♑48 27	17 44 17	16 15.8	15 12.8	16 31.9	20 10.2	8 57.2	13 58.5	15 24.7	25 02.4	6 52.2	5 28.9
29 Th	10 29 15	5 46 16	23 39 21	29 34 08	16 09.4	16 59.1	17 45.6	20 48.6	8 43.9	13 50.8	15 30.6	25 05.1	6 52.5	5 31.0
30 F	10 33 12	6 44 14	5♒28 59	11♒24 18	16 00.2	18 44.2	18 59.3	21 26.9	8 30.6	13 43.0	15 36.5	25 07.9	6 52.9	5 33.1
31 Sa	10 37 08	7 42 15	17 20 20	23 17 22	15 48.6	20 28.0	20 13.1	22 05.3	8 17.2	13 35.1	15 42.3	25 10.7	6 53.3	5 35.1

Astro Data

	Dy Hr Mn
♅ D	2 0:16
♃ R	7 16:13
☽ 0N	10 1:11
⚳ R	10 17:22
☿ D	12 1:55
☽ 0S	22 22:16
☽ 0N	6 7:49
♆ D	19 3:37
☽ 0S	19 8:44
♃△♄	22 5:19

Planet Ingress

	Dy Hr Mn
♀ ♋	21 4:34
☉ ♌	23 5:30
♂ ♍	27 14:04
☿ ♌	5 11:42
♀ ♌	14 23:47
☿ ♍	20 9:04
☉ ♍	23 12:29

Last Aspect / ☽ Ingress

Last Aspect Dy Hr Mn		☽ Ingress Dy Hr Mn
30 1:55	♃ △	♐ 1 1:20
2 23:42	♅ ⚹	♑ 3 12:19
5 11:52	♅ □	♒ 6 0:41
8 0:39	♅ △	♓ 8 13:25
10 1:13	♃ ☌	♈ 11 1:10
12 22:39	♅ ☍	♉ 13 10:21
15 2:25	☉ ⚹	♊ 15 15:54
17 10:37	♀ ☌	♋ 17 17:56
19 12:06	☉ ☌	♌ 19 17:43
21 11:03	♂ ☌	♍ 21 17:10
22 21:29	♃ ☍	♎ 23 18:19
25 20:49	♂ ⚹	♏ 25 22:45
27 6:39	♃ △	♐ 28 7:00
30 6:11	♅ ⚹	♑ 30 18:11

Last Aspect / ☽ Ingress

Last Aspect Dy Hr Mn		☽ Ingress Dy Hr Mn
1 18:45	♅ □	♒ 2 6:46
4 7:38	♅ △	♓ 4 19:26
6 10:41	♀ △	♈ 7 7:15
9 6:22	♅ ☍	♉ 9 17:13
11 17:07	♀ ⚹	♊ 12 0:15
13 18:31	♅ △	♋ 14 3:49
15 19:42	♅ □	♌ 16 4:26
17 19:44	☿ ☌	♍ 18 3:42
19 3:42	♃ ☍	♎ 20 3:45
22 4:21	☉ ⚹	♏ 22 6:37
23 13:16	♂ ⚹	♐ 24 13:34
26 14:11	♅ ⚹	♑ 27 0:15
29 2:52	♅ □	♒ 29 12:53

☽ Phases & Eclipses

Dy Hr Mn	
4 12:40	○ 12♑10
12 15:28	☾ 19♈54
19 12:06	● 26♋27
26 3:51	☽ 2♏48
3 3:57	○ 10♒27
11 2:46	☾ 18♉04
17 19:02	● 24♌29
24 15:38	☽ 1♐05

Astro Data

1 July 1974
Julian Day # 27210
SVP 5♓36'40"
GC 26♐29.0 ⚵ 7♒17.2R
Eris 13♈46.5 ⚴ 17♓21.6
⚷ 24♈11.0 ⚶ 11♎13.4
☽ Mean ☊ 18♐18.8

1 August 1974
Julian Day # 27241
SVP 5♓36'35"
GC 26♐29.1 ⚵ 29♑21.7R
Eris 13♈44.4R ⚴ 18♓25.8R
⚷ 24♈29.6R ⚶ 22♎15.2
☽ Mean ☊ 16♐40.3

LONGITUDE September 1974

Day	Sid.Time	☉	0 hr ☽	Noon ☽	True ☊	☿	♀	♂	⚳	♃	♄	♅	♆	♇
1 Su	10 41 05	8♍40 16	29♒15 37	5♓15 15	15♐35.4	22♍10.6	21♌26.9	22♍43.8	8♓03.9	13♓27.3	15♋48.1	25♎13.6	6♐53.7	5♎37.2
2 M	10 45 01	9 38 20	11♓16 26	17 19 17	15R 21.5	23 51.9	22 40.8	23 22.2	7R 50.6	13R 19.4	15 53.8	25 16.5	6 54.1	5 39.3
3 Tu	10 48 58	10 36 25	23 23 56	29 30 30	15 08.2	25 31.9	23 54.7	24 00.7	7 37.2	13 11.4	15 59.4	25 19.4	6 54.6	5 41.5
4 W	10 52 55	11 34 32	5♈39 05	11♈49 51	14 56.6	27 10.7	25 08.6	24 39.2	7 24.0	13 03.5	16 04.9	25 22.3	6 55.1	5 43.6
5 Th	10 56 51	12 32 40	18 02 56	24 18 32	14 47.4	28 48.3	26 22.6	25 17.8	7 10.7	12 55.6	16 10.4	25 25.3	6 55.7	5 45.8
6 F	11 00 48	13 30 51	0♉36 51	6♉58 07	14 41.1	0♎24.8	27 36.6	25 56.3	6 57.6	12 47.6	16 15.8	25 28.3	6 56.3	5 47.9
7 Sa	11 04 44	14 29 03	13 22 38	19 50 42	14 37.5	2 00.0	28 50.7	26 34.9	6 44.5	12 39.7	16 21.2	25 31.4	6 56.9	5 50.1
8 Su	11 08 41	15 27 18	26 22 39	2♊58 48	14D 36.2	3 34.1	0♍04.8	27 13.6	6 31.5	12 31.7	16 26.4	25 34.5	6 57.5	5 52.3
9 M	11 12 37	16 25 35	9♊39 31	16 25 06	14R 36.0	5 07.0	1 18.9	27 52.3	6 18.6	12 23.8	16 31.6	25 37.6	6 58.2	5 54.5
10 Tu	11 16 34	17 23 54	23 15 49	0♋11 55	14 35.7	6 38.8	2 33.1	28 31.0	6 05.8	12 15.9	16 36.7	25 40.7	6 58.9	5 56.7
11 W	11 20 30	18 22 15	7♋13 28	14 20 30	14 34.2	8 09.3	3 47.3	29 09.7	5 53.2	12 08.0	16 41.8	25 43.9	6 59.6	5 58.9
12 Th	11 24 27	19 20 38	21 32 52	28 50 15	14 30.3	9 38.8	5 01.5	29 48.5	5 40.7	12 00.2	16 46.7	25 47.1	7 00.4	6 01.1
13 F	11 28 24	20 19 03	6♌12 09	13♌37 54	14 23.8	11 07.0	6 15.8	0♎27.3	5 28.4	11 52.4	16 51.6	25 50.3	7 01.2	6 03.4
14 Sa	11 32 20	21 17 30	21 06 38	28 37 19	14 14.7	12 34.1	7 30.1	1 06.1	5 16.2	11 44.7	16 56.4	25 53.6	7 02.1	6 05.6
15 Su	11 36 17	22 15 59	6♍08 48	13♍39 51	14 03.9	14 00.0	8 44.4	1 45.0	5 04.2	11 36.9	17 01.1	25 56.8	7 02.9	6 07.9
16 M	11 40 13	23 14 30	21 09 12	28 35 39	13 52.6	15 24.7	9 58.8	2 23.9	4 52.4	11 29.3	17 05.7	26 00.1	7 03.8	6 10.1
17 Tu	11 44 10	24 13 03	5♎58 02	13♎15 24	13 42.1	16 48.2	11 13.2	3 02.8	4 40.9	11 21.7	17 10.3	26 03.5	7 04.7	6 12.4
18 W	11 48 06	25 11 38	20 26 53	27 31 54	13 33.6	18 10.4	12 27.6	3 41.8	4 29.5	11 14.2	17 14.8	26 06.8	7 05.7	6 14.7
19 Th	11 52 03	26 10 14	4♏30 00	11♏21 01	13 27.6	19 31.4	13 42.1	4 20.8	4 18.4	11 06.8	17 19.1	26 10.2	7 06.7	6 17.0
20 F	11 55 59	27 08 53	18 04 54	24 41 48	13 24.2	20 51.0	14 56.6	4 59.8	4 07.5	10 59.4	17 23.4	26 13.6	7 07.7	6 19.2
21 Sa	11 59 56	28 07 32	1♐12 03	7♐36 02	13D 22.9	22 09.2	16 11.1	5 38.8	3 56.9	10 52.1	17 27.6	26 17.0	7 08.8	6 21.5
22 Su	12 03 52	29 06 14	13 54 17	20 07 22	13R 22.9	23 25.9	17 25.6	6 17.9	3 46.6	10 45.0	17 31.8	26 20.5	7 09.8	6 23.8
23 M	12 07 49	0♎04 57	26 15 55	2♑20 36	13 23.0	24 41.2	18 40.2	6 57.0	3 36.5	10 37.9	17 35.8	26 23.9	7 10.9	6 26.1
24 Tu	12 11 46	1 03 43	8♑22 05	14 21 02	13 22.2	25 54.9	19 54.8	7 36.2	3 26.7	10 30.9	17 39.7	26 27.4	7 12.1	6 28.4
25 W	12 15 42	2 02 29	20 18 05	26 13 54	13 19.5	27 06.9	21 09.4	8 15.4	3 17.2	10 24.0	17 43.6	26 30.9	7 13.2	6 30.7
26 Th	12 19 39	3 01 18	2♒09 03	8♒04 06	13 14.4	28 17.2	22 24.0	8 54.6	3 07.9	10 17.3	17 47.3	26 34.5	7 14.4	6 33.1
27 F	12 23 35	4 00 08	13 59 33	19 55 53	13 06.6	29 25.6	23 38.7	9 33.8	2 59.0	10 10.6	17 51.0	26 38.0	7 15.7	6 35.4
28 Sa	12 27 32	4 59 00	25 53 29	1♓52 42	12 56.6	0♏32.0	24 53.4	10 13.1	2 50.4	10 04.1	17 54.5	26 41.6	7 16.9	6 37.7
29 Su	12 31 28	5 57 54	7♓53 51	13 57 10	12 44.9	1 36.3	26 08.1	10 52.4	2 42.1	9 57.7	17 58.0	26 45.1	7 18.2	6 40.0
30 M	12 35 25	6 56 49	20 02 50	26 10 59	12 32.6	2 38.3	27 22.8	11 31.8	2 34.2	9 51.4	18 01.4	26 48.7	7 19.5	6 42.3

LONGITUDE October 1974

Day	Sid.Time	☉	0 hr ☽	Noon ☽	True ☊	☿	♀	♂	⚳	♃	♄	♅	♆	♇
1 Tu	12 39 21	7♎55 47	2♈21 43	8♈35 06	12♐20.8	3♏37.8	28♍37.6	12♎11.2	2♓26.6	9♓45.3	18♋04.7	26♎52.3	7♐20.8	6♎44.6
2 W	12 43 18	8 54 47	14 51 10	21 09 56	12R 10.5	4 34.6	29 52.4	12 50.6	2R 19.3	9R 39.3	18 07.8	26 56.0	7 22.2	6 46.9
3 Th	12 47 15	9 53 48	27 31 23	3♉55 33	12 02.4	5 28.5	1♎07.2	13 30.0	2 12.3	9 33.5	18 10.9	26 59.6	7 23.6	6 49.2
4 F	12 51 11	10 52 52	10♉22 25	16 52 02	11 57.1	6 19.3	2 22.0	14 09.5	2 05.7	9 27.8	18 13.9	27 03.3	7 25.0	6 51.5
5 Sa	12 55 08	11 51 59	23 24 27	29 59 45	11D 54.3	7 06.6	3 36.9	14 49.0	1 59.4	9 22.2	18 16.8	27 06.9	7 26.4	6 53.9
6 Su	12 59 04	12 51 07	6♊38 01	13♊19 22	11 53.7	7 50.2	4 51.7	15 28.6	1 53.5	9 16.8	18 19.6	27 10.6	7 27.9	6 56.2
7 M	13 03 01	13 50 18	20 03 57	26 51 54	11 54.3	8 29.7	6 06.6	16 08.2	1 47.9	9 11.6	18 22.3	27 14.3	7 29.4	6 58.5
8 Tu	13 06 57	14 49 31	3♋43 20	10♋38 22	11R 54.9	9 04.7	7 21.6	16 47.8	1 42.7	9 06.5	18 24.9	27 18.0	7 30.9	7 00.8
9 W	13 10 54	15 48 47	17 37 03	24 39 24	11 54.7	9 34.8	8 36.5	17 27.5	1 37.9	9 01.6	18 27.3	27 21.7	7 32.4	7 03.1
10 Th	13 14 50	16 48 05	1♌45 18	8♌54 34	11 52.6	9 59.7	9 51.5	18 07.2	1 33.4	8 56.8	18 29.7	27 25.4	7 34.0	7 05.4
11 F	13 18 47	17 47 25	16 06 55	23 21 55	11 48.3	10 18.7	11 06.5	18 46.9	1 29.3	8 52.2	18 32.0	27 29.2	7 35.6	7 07.6
12 Sa	13 22 44	18 46 47	0♍39 00	7♍57 31	11 41.9	10 31.4	12 21.5	19 26.7	1 25.5	8 47.8	18 34.2	27 32.9	7 37.2	7 09.9
13 Su	13 26 40	19 46 12	15 16 41	22 35 39	11 34.1	10R 37.4	13 36.5	20 06.6	1 22.1	8 43.6	18 36.2	27 36.6	7 38.9	7 12.2
14 M	13 30 37	20 45 39	29 53 31	7♎09 21	11 25.7	10 36.1	14 51.5	20 46.4	1 19.1	8 39.5	18 38.2	27 40.4	7 40.5	7 14.5
15 Tu	13 34 33	21 45 08	14♎22 16	21 31 27	11 17.9	10 27.0	16 06.6	21 26.3	1 16.5	8 35.7	18 40.0	27 44.2	7 42.2	7 16.7
16 W	13 38 30	22 44 39	28 36 10	5♏35 49	11 11.5	10 09.7	17 21.7	22 06.2	1 14.2	8 32.0	18 41.7	27 47.9	7 43.9	7 19.0
17 Th	13 42 26	23 44 12	12♏29 55	19 18 09	11 07.1	9 44.0	18 36.8	22 46.2	1 12.3	8 28.5	18 43.4	27 51.7	7 45.6	7 21.2
18 F	13 46 23	24 43 47	26 00 22	2♐36 31	11D 05.0	9 09.7	19 51.9	23 26.2	1 10.8	8 25.2	18 44.9	27 55.5	7 47.4	7 23.5
19 Sa	13 50 19	25 43 23	9♐06 45	15 31 16	11 04.7	8 26.8	21 07.0	24 06.3	1 09.6	8 22.1	18 46.3	27 59.2	7 49.2	7 25.7
20 Su	13 54 16	26 43 02	21 50 25	28 04 38	11 05.7	7 35.5	22 22.1	24 46.3	1 08.9	8 19.1	18 47.6	28 03.0	7 51.0	7 27.9
21 M	13 58 13	27 42 42	4♑14 26	10♑20 21	11 07.2	6 36.7	23 37.3	25 26.5	1D 08.5	8 16.4	18 48.8	28 06.8	7 52.8	7 30.1
22 Tu	14 02 09	28 42 24	16 22 58	22 22 56	11R 08.4	5 31.1	24 52.4	26 06.6	1 08.4	8 13.9	18 49.8	28 10.6	7 54.6	7 32.3
23 W	14 06 06	29 42 08	28 20 53	4♒17 27	11 08.5	4 20.3	26 07.6	26 46.8	1 08.8	8 11.6	18 50.8	28 14.3	7 56.5	7 34.5
24 Th	14 10 02	0♏41 53	10♒13 16	16 08 57	11 07.0	3 05.9	27 22.7	27 27.0	1 09.5	8 09.4	18 51.7	28 18.1	7 58.3	7 36.7
25 F	14 13 59	1 41 40	22 05 06	28 02 17	11 03.8	1 49.9	28 37.9	28 07.3	1 10.6	8 07.5	18 52.4	28 21.9	8 00.2	7 38.9
26 Sa	14 17 55	2 41 29	4♓01 01	10♓01 48	10 58.9	0 34.7	29 53.1	28 47.6	1 12.0	8 05.8	18 53.0	28 25.7	8 02.1	7 41.0
27 Su	14 21 52	3 41 20	16 05 02	22 11 06	10 52.9	29♎22.5	1♏08.3	29 27.9	1 13.8	8 04.2	18 53.5	28 29.4	8 04.1	7 43.1
28 M	14 25 48	4 41 12	28 20 19	4♈32 56	10 46.3	28 15.5	2 23.5	0♏08.3	1 15.9	8 02.9	18 53.9	28 33.2	8 06.0	7 45.3
29 Tu	14 29 45	5 41 06	10♈49 08	17 09 02	10 39.9	27 15.9	3 38.7	0 48.7	1 18.4	8 01.8	18 54.2	28 36.9	8 08.0	7 47.4
30 W	14 33 41	6 41 02	23 32 41	0♉00 05	10 34.3	26 25.2	4 53.9	1 29.1	1 21.3	8 00.9	18 54.4	28 40.7	8 10.0	7 49.5
31 Th	14 37 38	7 41 00	6♉31 11	13 05 51	10 30.1	25 44.8	6 09.2	2 09.6	1 24.5	8 00.1	18R 54.5	28 44.4	8 12.0	7 51.6

Astro Data	Planet Ingress	Last Aspect	☽ Ingress	Last Aspect	☽ Ingress	☽ Phases & Eclipses	Astro Data
Dy Hr Mn	Dy Hr Mn	Dy Hr Mn	Dy Hr Mn	Dy Hr Mn	Dy Hr Mn	Dy Hr Mn	1 September 1974
☽0N 2 14:06	☿ ♎ 6 5:48	31 15:49 ♅ △	♓ 1 1:29	2 22:56 ♅ ☍	♉ 3 4:39	1 19:25 ○ 8♓58	Julian Day # 27272
☿0S 6 14:44	♀ ♍ 8 10:28	3 2:58 ☿ ☍	♈ 3 12:58	4 14:31 ♄ ⚹	♊ 5 12:00	9 12:01 ☾ 16♊26	SVP 5♓36'31"
♂0S 15 13:04	♂ ♎ 12 19:08	5 16:22 ♀ △	♉ 5 22:50	7 12:40 ♅ △	♋ 7 17:30	16 2:45 ● 22♍52	GC 26♐29.1 ⚴ 23♑23.9R
☽0S 15 19:32	☉ ♎ 23 9:58	8 6:12 ♀ □	♊ 8 6:36	9 16:36 ♅ □	♌ 9 21:03	23 7:08 ☽ 29♐53	Eris 13♈32.9R ⚵ 13♓10.5R
♃⚼♅ 19 4:22	☿ ♏ 28 0:20	10 8:58 ♂ □	♋ 10 11:40	11 18:49 ♅ ⚹	♍ 11 22:56		⚷ 23♈58.8R ⚶ 5♏49.3
☉0S 23 9:59		12 13:40 ♂ ⚹	♌ 12 13:54	13 5:26 ♄ ⚹	♎ 14 0:11	1 10:38 ○ 7♈52	☽ Mean ☊ 15♐01.8
☽0N 29 20:38	♀ ♎ 2 14:27	14 7:38 ♅ ⚹	♍ 14 14:12	15 22:34 ♅ ☌	♏ 16 2:23	8 19:46 ☾ 15♋09	
	☉ ♏ 23 19:11	16 2:45 ☉ ☌	♎ 16 14:17	17 10:58 ♄ △	♐ 18 7:14	15 12:25 ● 21♎46	1 October 1974
♀0S 5 6:12	♀ ♏ 26 14:12	18 9:34 ♅ ☌	♏ 18 16:14	20 11:57 ♅ ⚹	♑ 20 15:44	23 1:53 ☽ 29♑17	Julian Day # 27302
☽0S 13 4:47	☿ ♎R 26 23:21	20 16:52 ☉ ⚹	♐ 20 21:46	23 1:53 ☉ □	♒ 23 3:20	31 1:19 ○ 7♉14	SVP 5♓36'29"
☿ R 13 19:48	♂ ♏ 28 7:05	23 7:08 ☉ □	♑ 23 7:22	25 13:20 ♀ △	♓ 25 15:57		GC 26♐29.2 ⚴ 22♑55.7
⚳ D 22 1:56		25 13:59 ☿ □	♒ 25 19:38	27 5:32 ♄ △	♈ 28 3:13		Eris 13♈16.0R ⚵ 6♓28.9R
☽0N 27 3:52		28 1:33 ♅ △	♓ 28 8:14	30 9:32 ♅ ☍	♉ 30 12:00		⚷ 22♈51.3R ⚶ 20♏24.7
♃□♆ 27 13:10		30 14:36 ♀ ☍	♈ 30 19:25				☽ Mean ☊ 13♐26.5
♄ R 31 14:56							

November 1974 — LONGITUDE

Day	Sid.Time	☉	0 hr ☽	Noon ☽	True ☊	☿	♀	♂	⚳	♃	♄	♅	♆	♇
1 F	14 41 35	8♏41 00	19♉43 57	26♉25 19	10♐27.7	25♎15.6	7♏24.4	2♏50.2	1♓28.0	7♓59.6	18♋54.4	28♎48.2	8♐14.0	7♎53.6
2 Sa	14 45 31	9 41 01	3♊09 46	9♊57 04	10D 26.9	24R57.9	8 39.7	3 30.7	1 31.9	7R59.3	18R54.3	28 51.9	8 16.0	7 55.7
3 Su	14 49 28	10 41 05	16 47 02	23 39 27	10 27.4	24D51.8	9 54.9	4 11.3	1 36.1	7D59.2	18 54.0	28 55.6	8 18.0	7 57.7
4 M	14 53 24	11 41 11	0♋34 08	7♋30 54	10 28.8	24 57.0	11 10.2	4 52.0	1 40.7	7 59.3	18 53.7	28 59.4	8 20.1	7 59.7
5 Tu	14 57 21	12 41 19	14 29 35	21 29 59	10 30.4	25 12.9	12 25.5	5 32.7	1 45.6	7 59.6	18 53.2	29 03.1	8 22.2	8 01.7
6 W	15 01 17	13 41 29	28 31 57	5♌35 18	10R31.5	25 38.8	13 40.8	6 13.4	1 50.8	8 00.1	18 52.6	29 06.8	8 24.3	8 03.7
7 Th	15 05 14	14 41 41	12♌39 51	19 45 22	10 31.6	26 13.9	14 56.1	6 54.2	1 56.3	8 00.8	18 51.8	29 10.4	8 26.4	8 05.7
8 F	15 09 10	15 41 55	26 51 37	3♍58 18	10 30.5	26 57.3	16 11.4	7 35.0	2 02.2	8 01.8	18 51.0	29 14.1	8 28.5	8 07.6
9 Sa	15 13 07	16 42 11	11♍05 06	18 11 40	10 28.4	27 48.2	17 26.7	8 15.8	2 08.4	8 02.9	18 50.1	29 17.8	8 30.6	8 09.5
10 Su	15 17 04	17 42 29	25 17 34	2♎22 21	10 25.4	28 45.6	18 42.0	8 56.7	2 14.9	8 04.2	18 49.0	29 21.4	8 32.7	8 11.4
11 M	15 21 00	18 42 49	9♎25 35	16 26 47	10 22.1	29 48.7	19 57.3	9 37.7	2 21.7	8 05.7	18 47.9	29 25.0	8 34.9	8 13.3
12 Tu	15 24 57	19 43 11	23 25 27	0♏21 08	10 19.1	0♏56.9	21 12.7	10 18.6	2 28.8	8 07.4	18 46.6	29 28.6	8 37.0	8 15.2
13 W	15 28 53	20 43 35	7♏13 25	14 01 55	10 16.7	2 09.3	22 28.0	10 59.7	2 36.3	8 09.4	18 45.2	29 32.2	8 39.2	8 17.0
14 Th	15 32 50	21 44 01	20 46 19	27 26 21	10D 15.2	3 25.4	23 43.4	11 40.7	2 44.0	8 11.5	18 43.7	29 35.8	8 41.4	8 18.9
15 F	15 36 46	22 44 28	4♐01 53	10♐32 48	10 14.7	4 44.6	24 58.7	12 21.8	2 52.1	8 13.9	18 42.1	29 39.4	8 43.5	8 20.7
16 Sa	15 40 43	23 44 57	16 59 06	23 20 53	10 15.2	6 06.5	26 14.1	13 03.0	3 00.4	8 16.4	18 40.4	29 42.9	8 45.7	8 22.4
17 Su	15 44 39	24 45 27	29 38 17	5♑51 35	10 16.2	7 30.6	27 29.5	13 44.1	3 09.1	8 19.1	18 38.6	29 46.5	8 47.9	8 24.2
18 M	15 48 36	25 45 58	12♑01 04	18 07 07	10 17.6	8 56.5	28 44.8	14 25.4	3 18.0	8 22.1	18 36.7	29 50.0	8 50.2	8 25.9
19 Tu	15 52 33	26 46 31	24 10 09	0♒10 40	10 19.0	10 24.0	0♐00.2	15 06.6	3 27.2	8 25.2	18 34.6	29 53.5	8 52.4	8 27.6
20 W	15 56 29	27 47 05	6♒09 10	12 06 13	10 20.0	11 52.8	1 15.6	15 47.9	3 36.7	8 28.5	18 32.5	29 56.9	8 54.6	8 29.3
21 Th	16 00 26	28 47 40	18 02 23	23 58 16	10R 20.5	13 22.7	2 30.9	16 29.2	3 46.5	8 32.1	18 30.3	0♏00.4	8 56.8	8 31.0
22 F	16 04 22	29 48 17	29 54 27	5♓51 33	10 20.5	14 53.4	3 46.3	17 10.6	3 56.6	8 35.8	18 27.9	0 03.8	8 59.1	8 32.6
23 Sa	16 08 19	0♐48 54	11♓50 08	17 50 49	10 19.9	16 24.8	5 01.6	17 52.0	4 06.9	8 39.7	18 25.5	0 07.2	9 01.3	8 34.2
24 Su	16 12 15	1 49 33	23 54 08	0♈00 36	10 19.1	17 56.7	6 17.0	18 33.5	4 17.5	8 43.8	18 23.0	0 10.5	9 03.5	8 35.8
25 M	16 16 12	2 50 13	6♈10 43	12 24 53	10 18.1	19 29.1	7 32.4	19 15.0	4 28.3	8 48.1	18 20.3	0 13.9	9 05.8	8 37.3
26 Tu	16 20 08	3 50 54	18 43 02	25 06 47	10 17.1	21 01.9	8 47.7	19 56.5	4 39.4	8 52.5	18 17.6	0 17.2	9 08.0	8 38.9
27 W	16 24 05	4 51 36	1♉35 02	8♉08 20	10 16.4	22 34.9	10 03.1	20 38.1	4 50.8	8 57.2	18 14.8	0 20.5	9 10.3	8 40.4
28 Th	16 28 02	5 52 19	14 46 44	21 30 10	10 15.9	24 08.1	11 18.5	21 19.7	5 02.4	9 02.0	18 11.9	0 23.7	9 12.6	8 41.8
29 F	16 31 58	6 53 04	28 18 28	5♊11 22	10D 15.7	25 41.5	12 33.8	22 01.3	5 14.2	9 07.0	18 08.8	0 27.0	9 14.8	8 43.3
30 Sa	16 35 55	7 53 50	12♊08 32	19 09 32	10 15.7	27 15.0	13 49.2	22 43.0	5 26.3	9 12.2	18 05.7	0 30.2	9 17.1	8 44.7

December 1974 — LONGITUDE

Day	Sid.Time	☉	0 hr ☽	Noon ☽	True ☊	☿	♀	♂	⚳	♃	♄	♅	♆	♇
1 Su	16 39 51	8♐54 37	26♊13 53	3♋21 00	10♐15.8	28♏48.6	15♐04.6	23♏24.7	5♓38.6	9♓17.6	18♋02.6	0♏33.4	9♐19.3	8♎46.1
2 M	16 43 48	9 55 26	10♋30 19	17 41 12	10R 15.9	0♐22.3	16 19.9	24 06.5	5 51.2	9 23.2	17R59.3	0 36.5	9 21.6	8 47.5
3 Tu	16 47 44	10 56 16	24 53 05	2♌05 20	10 15.9	1 56.0	17 35.3	24 48.3	6 04.0	9 28.9	17 55.9	0 39.6	9 23.9	8 48.8
4 W	16 51 41	11 57 07	9♌17 25	16 28 47	10 15.8	3 29.7	18 50.7	25 30.2	6 17.0	9 34.8	17 52.5	0 42.7	9 26.1	8 50.1
5 Th	16 55 38	12 57 59	23 39 01	0♍47 41	10D 15.7	5 03.5	20 06.1	26 12.1	6 30.3	9 40.9	17 48.9	0 45.8	9 28.4	8 51.4
6 F	16 59 34	13 58 53	7♍54 25	14 58 58	10 15.6	6 37.2	21 21.4	26 54.1	6 43.7	9 47.2	17 45.3	0 48.8	9 30.6	8 52.6
7 Sa	17 03 31	14 59 48	22 01 05	29 00 34	10 15.7	8 11.0	22 36.8	27 36.0	6 57.4	9 53.6	17 41.6	0 51.8	9 32.9	8 53.8
8 Su	17 07 27	16 00 45	5♎57 17	12♎51 07	10 16.1	9 44.8	23 52.2	28 18.1	7 11.3	10 00.2	17 37.8	0 54.7	9 35.1	8 55.0
9 M	17 11 24	17 01 42	19 41 58	26 29 47	10 16.7	11 18.7	25 07.6	29 00.2	7 25.4	10 06.9	17 34.0	0 57.6	9 37.4	8 56.2
10 Tu	17 15 20	18 02 41	3♏14 29	9♏56 03	10 17.5	12 52.5	26 23.0	29 42.3	7 39.8	10 13.8	17 30.1	1 00.5	9 39.6	8 57.3
11 W	17 19 17	19 03 41	16 34 24	23 09 32	10 18.1	14 26.5	27 38.4	0♐24.4	7 54.3	10 20.9	17 26.1	1 03.4	9 41.9	8 58.4
12 Th	17 23 13	20 04 42	29 41 24	6♐09 59	10R 18.5	16 00.4	28 53.7	1 06.6	8 09.0	10 28.2	17 22.0	1 06.2	9 44.1	8 59.4
13 F	17 27 10	21 05 44	12♐35 17	18 57 19	10 18.4	17 34.5	0♑09.1	1 48.9	8 24.0	10 35.6	17 17.9	1 08.9	9 46.4	9 00.5
14 Sa	17 31 07	22 06 47	25 16 05	1♑31 41	10 17.7	19 08.6	1 24.5	2 31.2	8 39.1	10 43.1	17 13.7	1 11.7	9 48.6	9 01.4
15 Su	17 35 03	23 07 50	7♑44 11	13 53 44	10 16.3	20 42.8	2 39.9	3 13.5	8 54.4	10 50.9	17 09.4	1 14.4	9 50.8	9 02.4
16 M	17 39 00	24 08 54	20 00 28	26 04 38	10 14.3	22 17.1	3 55.3	3 55.9	9 10.0	10 58.7	17 05.1	1 17.0	9 53.0	9 03.3
17 Tu	17 42 56	25 09 59	2♒06 28	8♒06 16	10 11.9	23 51.6	5 10.6	4 38.3	9 25.7	11 06.7	17 00.7	1 19.6	9 55.2	9 04.2
18 W	17 46 53	26 11 04	14 04 22	20 01 11	10 09.5	25 26.1	6 26.0	5 20.7	9 41.5	11 14.9	16 56.3	1 22.2	9 57.4	9 05.1
19 Th	17 50 49	27 12 09	25 57 09	1♓52 42	10 07.3	27 00.9	7 41.4	6 03.2	9 57.6	11 23.2	16 51.8	1 24.7	9 59.6	9 05.9
20 F	17 54 46	28 13 15	7♓48 22	13 44 41	10 05.7	28 35.7	8 56.7	6 45.7	10 13.9	11 31.7	16 47.3	1 27.2	10 01.8	9 06.7
21 Sa	17 58 42	29 14 21	19 42 13	25 41 33	10D 05.0	0♑10.8	10 12.1	7 28.3	10 30.3	11 40.3	16 42.7	1 29.7	10 03.9	9 07.5
22 Su	18 02 39	0♑15 27	1♈43 16	7♈47 58	10 05.2	1 46.1	11 27.4	8 10.9	10 46.9	11 49.1	16 38.1	1 32.1	10 06.1	9 08.2
23 M	18 06 36	1 16 33	13 56 15	20 08 41	10 06.1	3 21.5	12 42.8	8 53.5	11 03.6	11 58.0	16 33.4	1 34.4	10 08.2	9 08.9
24 Tu	18 10 32	2 17 40	26 25 49	2♉48 10	10 07.7	4 57.2	13 58.1	9 36.2	11 20.5	12 07.0	16 28.7	1 36.8	10 10.4	9 09.5
25 W	18 14 29	3 18 46	9♉16 08	15 50 07	10 09.3	6 33.1	15 13.4	10 18.9	11 37.6	12 16.2	16 24.0	1 39.0	10 12.5	9 10.2
26 Th	18 18 25	4 19 53	22 30 22	29 17 01	10R 10.5	8 09.3	16 28.7	11 01.7	11 54.9	12 25.4	16 19.2	1 41.3	10 14.6	9 10.7
27 F	18 22 22	5 21 00	6♊10 07	13♊09 31	10 10.9	9 45.7	17 44.1	11 44.5	12 12.3	12 34.9	16 14.4	1 43.4	10 16.7	9 11.3
28 Sa	18 26 18	6 22 07	20 14 55	27 25 53	10 09.9	11 22.3	18 59.4	12 27.3	12 29.8	12 44.4	16 09.6	1 45.6	10 18.8	9 11.8
29 Su	18 30 15	7 23 15	4♋41 48	12♋01 54	10 07.6	12 59.2	20 14.7	13 10.2	12 47.5	12 54.1	16 04.7	1 47.7	10 20.9	9 12.3
30 M	18 34 11	8 24 22	19 25 17	26 50 59	10 04.0	14 36.4	21 29.9	13 53.1	13 05.4	13 03.9	15 59.8	1 49.7	10 22.9	9 12.8
31 Tu	18 38 08	9 25 30	4♌17 55	11♌45 03	9 59.7	16 13.8	22 45.2	14 36.1	13 23.3	13 13.9	15 54.9	1 51.7	10 25.0	9 13.2

Astro Data	Planet Ingress	Last Aspect	☽ Ingress	Last Aspect	☽ Ingress	☽ Phases & Eclipses	Astro Data
Dy Hr Mn	Dy Hr Mn	Dy Hr Mn	Dy Hr Mn	Dy Hr Mn	Dy Hr Mn	Dy Hr Mn	
♃ D 3 12:13	☿ ♏ 11 16:05	31 22:31 ♄ ⚹	♊ 1 18:23	30 1:59 ♀ ☍	♋ 1 6:22	7 2:47 ☾ 14♌19	1 November 1974
☿ D 3 12:51	♀ ♐ 19 11:56	3 21:12 ♅ △	♋ 3 23:01	2 23:15 ♂ △	♌ 3 8:31	14 0:53 ● 21♏16	Julian Day # 27333
♃⚻♇ 4 6:43	♅ ♏ 21 9:32	6 0:56 ♅ □	♌ 6 2:30	5 3:53 ♂ □	♍ 5 10:40	21 22:39 ☽ 29♒15	SVP 5♓36'25"
☽0S 9 11:31	☉ ♐ 22 16:38	8 3:58 ♅ ⚹	♍ 8 5:18	7 9:27 ♂ ⚹	♎ 7 13:42	29 15:10 ○ 7♊01	GC 26♐29.3 ⚴ 27♑13.4
♃⚻♇ 20 22:21		9 13:05 ♄ ⚹	♎ 10 7:58	9 9:20 ♀ ⚹	♏ 9 18:13	29 15:13 ☍ T 1.289	Eris 12♈57.5R ⚵ 5♓22.7
☽0N 23 11:54	☿ ♐ 2 6:17	12 10:28 ♅ ☌	♏ 12 11:23	11 1:37 ♄ △	♐ 12 0:34		⚷ 21♈27.2R ⚶ 6♐24.1
	♂ ♐ 10 22:05	14 4:36 ♀ ☌	♐ 14 16:39	13 16:25 ☉ ☌	♑ 14 9:04	6 10:10 ☾ 13♍54	☽ Mean ☊ 11♐47.9
♃□♆ 2 0:34	♀ ♑ 13 9:06	17 0:12 ♅ ⚹	♑ 17 0:42	15 18:21 ♄ ☍	♒ 16 19:48	13 16:25 ● 21♐17	
☽0S 6 16:46	☿ ♑ 21 9:16	19 11:37 ♀ ⚹	♒ 19 11:39	19 1:38 ☉ ⚹	♓ 19 8:12	13 16:12:29 ☌ P 0.827	1 December 1974
☽0N 20 20:18	☉ ♑ 22 5:56	21 22:39 ☉ □	♓ 22 0:11	21 19:43 ☉ □	♈ 21 20:35	21 19:43 ☽ 29♓34	Julian Day # 27363
		23 13:09 ♄ △	♈ 24 11:59	23 5:07 ♄ □	♉ 24 6:45	29 3:51 ○ 7♋02	SVP 5♓36'21"
		25 23:14 ♄ □	♉ 26 21:05	25 13:01 ♄ ⚹	♊ 26 13:15		GC 26♐29.3 ⚴ 4♒22.6
		28 17:16 ☿ ☍	♊ 29 2:58	27 11:00 ♃ □	♋ 28 16:15		Eris 12♈44.0R ⚵ 11♓20.8
				30 2:34 ♀ ☍	♌ 30 17:05		⚷ 20♈22.1R ⚶ 22♐22.0
							☽ Mean ☊ 10♐12.6

LONGITUDE — January 1975

Day	Sid.Time	☉	0 hr ☽	Noon ☽	True ☊	☿	♀	♂	⚷	♃	♄	♅	♆	♇
1 W	18 42 05	10♑26 38	19♌11 18	26♌35 42	9✗55.3	17♏51.5	24♑00.5	15✗19.1	13♓41.5	13♓23.9	15♋50.0	1♏53.6	10✗27.0	9♎13.6
2 Th	18 46 01	11 27 47	3♍57 22	11♍15 32	9R51.5	19 29.3	25 15.8	16 02.1	13 59.8	13 34.1	15R45.1	1 55.5	10 29.0	9 13.9
3 F	18 49 58	12 28 55	18 29 36	25 39 06	9 48.8	21 07.4	26 31.0	16 45.2	14 18.2	13 44.4	15 40.1	1 57.4	10 31.0	9 14.2
4 Sa	18 53 54	13 30 04	2♎43 44	9♎43 20	9D 47.6	22 45.6	27 46.3	17 28.3	14 36.7	13 54.8	15 35.2	1 59.2	10 33.0	9 14.5
5 Su	18 57 51	14 31 13	16 37 51	23 27 22	9 47.9	24 24.0	29 01.5	18 11.5	14 55.4	14 05.3	15 30.2	2 00.9	10 35.0	9 14.7
6 M	19 01 47	15 32 23	0♏12 00	6♏51 59	9 49.2	26 02.4	0♒16.8	18 54.7	15 14.2	14 16.0	15 25.2	2 02.6	10 36.9	9 14.9
7 Tu	19 05 44	16 33 33	13 27 34	19 59 03	9 50.8	27 40.8	1 32.0	19 38.0	15 33.2	14 26.7	15 20.3	2 04.3	10 38.8	9 15.1
8 W	19 09 40	17 34 43	26 26 43	2✗50 50	9R52.1	29 19.2	2 47.2	20 21.3	15 52.2	14 37.6	15 15.3	2 05.8	10 40.7	9 15.2
9 Th	19 13 37	18 35 53	9✗11 43	15 29 36	9 52.1	0♒57.4	4 02.4	21 04.6	16 11.4	14 48.6	15 10.4	2 07.4	10 42.6	9 15.3
10 F	19 17 34	19 37 02	21 44 44	27 57 19	9 50.4	2 35.3	5 17.6	21 48.0	16 30.8	14 59.7	15 05.4	2 08.9	10 44.5	9 15.4
11 Sa	19 21 30	20 38 12	4♑07 33	10♑15 36	9 46.5	4 12.8	6 32.8	22 31.4	16 50.2	15 10.9	15 00.5	2 10.3	10 46.4	9R15.4
12 Su	19 25 27	21 39 22	16 21 38	22 25 46	9 40.6	5 49.7	7 48.0	23 14.8	17 09.8	15 22.2	14 55.6	2 11.7	10 48.2	9 15.4
13 M	19 29 23	22 40 31	28 28 49	4♒28 57	9 32.9	7 25.8	9 03.2	23 58.3	17 29.5	15 33.6	14 50.7	2 13.0	10 50.0	9 15.3
14 Tu	19 33 20	23 41 39	10♒28 18	16 26 23	9 24.0	9 00.8	10 18.4	24 41.8	17 49.3	15 45.1	14 45.8	2 14.3	10 51.8	9 15.3
15 W	19 37 16	24 42 47	22 23 24	28 19 35	9 14.8	10 34.5	11 33.5	25 25.4	18 09.2	15 56.6	14 40.9	2 15.5	10 53.6	9 15.1
16 Th	19 41 13	25 43 55	4♓15 13	10♓10 36	9 06.2	12 06.6	12 48.6	26 09.0	18 29.2	16 08.3	14 36.1	2 16.7	10 55.3	9 15.0
17 F	19 45 09	26 45 01	16 06 05	22 02 04	8 58.9	13 36.6	14 03.8	26 52.6	18 49.3	16 20.1	14 31.3	2 17.8	10 57.0	9 14.8
18 Sa	19 49 06	27 46 07	27 59 00	3♈57 22	8 53.6	15 04.2	15 19.0	27 36.3	19 09.5	16 32.0	14 26.5	2 18.9	10 58.7	9 14.6
19 Su	19 53 03	28 47 13	9♈57 40	16 00 30	8 50.5	16 28.8	16 33.9	28 20.0	19 29.9	16 43.9	14 21.8	2 19.9	11 00.4	9 14.3
20 M	19 56 59	29 48 17	22 06 25	28 16 03	8D 49.9	17 49.9	17 49.0	29 03.8	19 50.3	16 56.0	14 17.1	2 20.8	11 02.1	9 14.0
21 Tu	20 00 56	0♒49 21	4♉30 00	10♉48 52	8 49.9	19 06.9	19 04.0	29 47.5	0♑11.4	17 08.1	14 12.4	2 21.7	11 03.7	9 13.7
22 W	20 04 52	1 50 23	17 13 16	23 43 43	8 50.9	20 19.0	20 19.1	0♑31.4	20 31.5	17 20.3	14 07.8	2 22.6	11 05.3	9 13.4
23 Th	20 08 49	2 51 25	0♊16 44	7♊14 42	8R51.7	21 25.5	21 34.1	1 15.2	20 52.2	17 32.6	14 03.3	2 23.3	11 06.9	9 13.0
24 F	20 12 45	3 52 26	13 55 53	20 54 27	8 51.0	22 25.6	22 49.1	1 59.1	21 13.0	17 45.0	13 58.7	2 24.1	11 08.4	9 12.5
25 Sa	20 16 42	4 53 25	28 00 19	5♋13 16	8 48.2	23 18.5	24 04.0	2 43.0	21 33.9	17 57.5	13 54.3	2 24.8	11 09.9	9 12.1
26 Su	20 20 39	5 54 24	12♋32 50	19 58 20	8 43.0	24 03.4	25 19.0	3 27.0	21 54.9	18 10.0	13 49.9	2 25.4	11 11.4	9 11.6
27 M	20 24 35	6 55 22	27 28 52	5♌03 19	8 35.4	24 39.3	26 33.9	4 11.0	22 16.0	18 22.7	13 45.5	2 25.9	11 12.9	9 11.1
28 Tu	20 28 32	7 56 19	12♌40 25	20 18 47	8 26.3	25 05.6	27 48.8	4 55.0	22 37.2	18 35.3	13 41.2	2 26.4	11 14.4	9 10.5
29 W	20 32 28	8 57 15	27 57 00	5♍33 38	8 16.7	25R21.4	29 03.6	5 39.1	22 58.4	18 48.1	13 37.0	2 26.9	11 15.8	9 09.9
30 Th	20 36 25	9 58 10	13♍07 23	20 37 03	8 08.0	25 26.5	0♓18.5	6 23.2	23 19.8	19 00.9	13 32.8	2 27.3	11 17.2	9 09.3
31 F	20 40 21	10 59 04	28 01 40	5♎20 25	8 01.0	25 20.3	1 33.3	7 07.3	23 41.2	19 13.8	13 28.7	2 27.6	11 18.5	9 08.7

LONGITUDE — February 1975

Day	Sid.Time	☉	0 hr ☽	Noon ☽	True ☊	☿	♀	♂	⚷	♃	♄	♅	♆	♇
1 Sa	20 44 18	11♒59 58	12♎32 47	19♎38 25	7✗56.5	25♒02.8	2♓48.1	7♑51.5	24♑02.7	19♓26.8	13♋24.6	2♏27.9	11✗19.9	9♎08.0
2 Su	20 48 14	13 00 51	26 37 12	3♏29 10	7D 54.3	24R34.3	4 02.9	8 35.8	24 24.2	19 39.8	13R20.6	2 28.1	11 21.2	9R07.3
3 M	20 52 11	14 01 43	10♏15 32	16 53 08	7 53.9	23 55.3	5 17.6	9 20.0	24 45.9	19 52.9	13 16.7	2 28.3	11 22.5	9 06.5
4 Tu	20 56 07	15 02 34	23 26 51	29 54 40	7R54.4	23 06.8	6 32.4	10 04.3	25 07.6	20 06.1	13 12.9	2 28.4	11 23.7	9 05.7
5 W	21 00 04	16 03 25	6✗17 34	12✗36 06	7 54.5	22 10.1	7 47.1	10 48.7	25 29.4	20 19.3	13 09.1	2R28.5	11 25.0	9 04.9
6 Th	21 04 01	17 04 14	18 50 40	25 02 00	7 53.0	21 06.8	9 01.7	11 33.0	25 51.3	20 32.6	13 05.4	2 28.5	11 26.2	9 04.1
7 F	21 07 57	18 05 03	1♑10 20	7♑16 10	7 49.2	19 58.7	10 16.4	12 17.4	26 13.2	20 46.0	13 01.8	2 28.4	11 27.3	9 03.2
8 Sa	21 11 54	19 05 51	13 19 53	19 21 50	7 42.4	18 47.8	11 31.0	13 01.9	26 35.3	20 59.4	12 58.3	2 28.3	11 28.5	9 02.3
9 Su	21 15 50	20 06 37	25 21 34	1♒21 34	7 32.6	17 36.0	12 45.6	13 46.3	26 57.3	21 12.9	12 54.8	2 28.2	11 29.6	9 01.4
10 M	21 19 47	21 07 22	7♒19 51	13 17 20	7 20.3	16 25.4	14 00.2	14 30.8	27 19.5	21 26.4	12 51.5	2 27.9	11 30.6	9 00.5
11 Tu	21 23 43	22 08 06	19 14 13	25 10 37	7 06.3	15 17.7	15 14.8	15 15.4	27 41.7	21 40.0	12 48.2	2 27.7	11 31.7	8 59.5
12 W	21 27 40	23 08 49	1♓06 43	7♓02 40	6 51.7	14 14.4	16 29.3	15 59.9	28 04.0	21 53.6	12 45.0	2 27.3	11 32.7	8 58.5
13 Th	21 31 36	24 09 30	12 58 38	18 54 47	6 37.6	13 16.7	17 43.8	16 44.5	28 26.3	22 07.3	12 41.9	2 26.9	11 33.7	8 57.4
14 F	21 35 33	25 10 09	24 51 09	0♈48 37	6 25.4	12 25.7	18 58.2	17 29.2	28 48.7	22 21.0	12 38.9	2 26.5	11 34.6	8 56.4
15 Sa	21 39 30	26 10 47	6♈46 49	12 46 19	6 15.7	11 41.9	20 12.6	18 13.8	29 11.2	22 34.8	12 36.0	2 26.0	11 35.5	8 55.3
16 Su	21 43 26	27 11 24	18 47 30	24 50 46	6 08.9	11 05.7	21 27.0	18 58.5	29 33.7	22 48.6	12 33.2	2 25.5	11 36.4	8 54.2
17 M	21 47 23	28 11 58	0♉56 36	7♉05 02	6 04.7	10 37.3	22 41.3	19 43.2	29 56.3	23 02.4	12 30.5	2 24.8	11 37.3	8 53.0
18 Tu	21 51 19	29 12 31	13 18 05	19 34 49	6D 03.6	10 16.7	23 55.6	20 27.9	0♒18.9	23 16.3	12 27.9	2 24.2	11 38.1	8 51.9
19 W	21 55 16	0♓13 02	25 56 21	2♊23 11	6R03.4	10 03.7	25 09.8	21 12.7	0 41.6	23 30.3	12 25.4	2 23.5	11 38.9	8 50.7
20 Th	21 59 12	1 13 32	8♊56 01	15 35 15	6 03.2	9D 58.0	26 24.1	21 57.5	1 04.3	23 44.3	12 23.0	2 22.7	11 39.6	8 49.5
21 F	22 03 09	2 13 59	22 21 19	29 14 34	6 01.9	9 59.2	27 38.3	22 42.3	1 27.1	23 58.3	12 20.6	2 21.9	11 40.3	8 48.2
22 Sa	22 07 05	3 14 25	6♋15 11	13♋23 13	5 58.3	10 07.1	28 52.4	23 27.2	1 49.9	24 12.3	12 18.4	2 21.1	11 41.0	8 47.0
23 Su	22 11 02	4 14 48	20 38 26	28 00 26	5 52.0	10 21.2	0♈06.5	24 12.1	2 12.8	24 26.4	12 16.3	2 20.1	11 41.7	8 45.7
24 M	22 14 59	5 15 10	5♌28 34	13♌01 54	5 43.1	10 41.2	1 20.6	24 57.0	2 35.7	24 40.6	12 14.3	2 19.2	11 42.3	8 44.4
25 Tu	22 18 55	6 15 30	20 39 20	28 19 31	5 32.2	11 06.5	2 34.6	25 41.9	2 58.6	24 54.7	12 12.4	2 18.2	11 42.9	8 43.1
26 W	22 22 52	7 15 48	6♍01 00	13♍42 16	5 20.6	11 36.6	3 48.6	26 26.9	3 21.7	25 08.9	12 10.6	2 17.1	11 43.4	8 41.7
27 Th	22 26 48	8 16 05	21 21 46	28 58 06	5 09.7	12 11.9	5 02.5	27 11.9	3 44.8	25 23.1	12 08.9	2 16.0	11 44.0	8 40.4
28 F	22 30 45	9 16 19	6♎29 56	13♎56 11	5 00.7	12 51.3	6 16.3	27 56.9	4 07.8	25 37.3	12 07.3	2 14.8	11 44.5	8 39.0

Astro Data

	Dy Hr Mn
☽ 0S	2 23:10
4△♄	10 20:34
♇ R	11 17:39
☽ ON	17 4:18
4☐⚷	22 16:38
☽ 0S	30 8:26
☿ R	30 10:47
⚷ R	6 1:48
☽ ON	13 11:23
☿ D	20 19:28
♀ON	25 7:04
☽ 0S	26 19:47

Planet Ingress

	Dy Hr Mn
♀ ♒	6 6:39
♀ ♒	8 21:58
☉ ♒	20 16:36
☿ ♑	21 18:49
♀ ♓	30 6:05
♃ ♈	17 15:56
☉ ♓	19 6:50
♀ ♈	23 9:53

Last Aspect / ☽ Ingress

Last Aspect Dy Hr Mn	☽ Ingress Dy Hr Mn
31 16:50 ♂ △	♍ 1 17:32
3 13:36 ♀ △	♎ 3 19:21
5 22:55 ♀ ☐	♏ 5 23:39
8 4:24 ☿ ✶	✗ 8 6:39
9 23:22 ♂ ♂	♑ 10 15:58
12 10:20 ☉ ☐	♒ 13 3:03
15 5:45 ♂ ✶	♓ 15 15:23
17 22:24 ♂ ☐	♈ 18 4:03
20 15:14 ♀ ☐	♉ 20 15:21
22 5:07 ♀ ☐	♊ 22 23:23
24 15:34 ♀ △	♋ 25 3:20
26 9:03 ♀ △	♌ 27 4:00
29 0:50 ♀ ♂	♍ 29 3:14
30 9:23 4 ♂	♎ 31 3:13

Last Aspect Dy Hr Mn	☽ Ingress Dy Hr Mn
1 21:00 ♀ △	♏ 2 5:53
4 0:09 ♀ ☐	✗ 4 12:10
6 5:00 ♀ ✶	♑ 6 21:42
8 15:18 4 ✶	♒ 9 9:16
11 5:17 ☉ ♂	♓ 11 21:45
13 18:36 4 ☐	♈ 14 10:22
16 17:03 ☉ ✶	♉ 16 22:09
18 21:06 ♀ ✶	♊ 19 7:35
21 8:57 ♀ △	♋ 21 13:44
23 6:07 4 △	♌ 23 15:13
24 9:54 ♀ △	♍ 25 14:37
27 9:03 ♂ △	♎ 27 13:38

☽ Phases & Eclipses

Dy Hr Mn	
4 19:04	☾ 13♎48
12 10:20	● 21♑35
20 15:14	☽ 29♈57
27 15:09	○ 7♌03
3 6:23	☾ 13♏47
11 5:17	● 21♒51
19 7:38	☽ 0♊02
26 1:15	○ 6♍49

Astro Data

1 January 1975
Julian Day # 27394
SVP 5♓36'15"
GC 26✗29.4 — ♀ 13♒33.0
Eris 12♈39.0 — ⚵ 22♓41.5
⚷ 19♈57.2 — ⚸ 9♑01.7
☽ Mean Ω 8✗34.2

1 February 1975
Julian Day # 27425
SVP 5♓36'10"
GC 26✗29.5 — ♀ 23♒37.6
Eris 12♈44.7 — ⚵ 7♉19.1
⚷ 20♈25.1 — ⚸ 25♑31.8
☽ Mean Ω 6✗55.7

March 1975 — LONGITUDE

Day	Sid.Time	☉	0 hr ☽	Noon ☽	True ☊	☿	♀	♂	⚳	♃	♄	♅	♆	♇
1 Sa	22 34 41	10♓16 33	21♎16 01	28♎28 47	4♐54.3	13♒34.7	7♈30.1	28♑42.0	4♈31.0	25♓51.6	12♋05.8	2♏13.6	11♐44.9	8♎37.6
2 Su	22 38 38	11 16 45	5♏34 08	12♏31 55	4R50.7	14 21.8	8 43.9	29 27.1	4 54.2	26 05.9	12R04.5	2R12.3	11 45.3	8R36.2
3 M	22 42 34	12 16 55	19 22 12	26 05 12	4D49.3	15 12.4	9 57.7	0♒12.2	5 17.4	26 20.2	12 03.2	2 11.0	11 45.7	8 34.7
4 Tu	22 46 31	13 17 04	2♐41 19	9♐10 58	4R49.2	16 06.2	11 11.3	0 57.3	5 40.6	26 34.6	12 02.0	2 09.7	11 46.1	8 33.3
5 W	22 50 28	14 17 11	15 34 44	21 53 10	4 49.1	17 03.0	12 25.0	1 42.5	6 03.9	26 48.9	12 01.0	2 08.3	11 46.4	8 31.8
6 Th	22 54 24	15 17 17	28 06 55	4♑16 33	4 47.7	18 02.6	13 38.6	2 27.7	6 27.2	27 03.3	12 00.1	2 06.8	11 46.7	8 30.3
7 F	22 58 21	16 17 21	10♑22 42	16 25 56	4 44.2	19 04.8	14 52.1	3 12.9	6 50.6	27 17.7	11 59.2	2 05.4	11 46.9	8 28.8
8 Sa	23 02 17	17 17 24	22 26 48	28 25 47	4 37.9	20 09.5	16 05.6	3 58.1	7 14.0	27 32.2	11 58.5	2 03.8	11 47.2	8 27.3
9 Su	23 06 14	18 17 25	4♒23 21	10♒19 54	4 28.7	21 16.5	17 19.1	4 43.4	7 37.4	27 46.6	11 57.9	2 02.3	11 47.3	8 25.8
10 M	23 10 10	19 17 24	16 15 49	22 11 25	4 17.0	22 25.6	18 32.5	5 28.7	8 00.9	28 01.1	11 57.4	2 00.6	11 47.5	8 24.2
11 Tu	23 14 07	20 17 21	28 06 58	4♓02 42	4 03.6	23 36.8	19 45.8	6 14.0	8 24.4	28 15.5	11 57.1	1 59.0	11 47.6	8 22.7
12 W	23 18 03	21 17 16	9♓58 49	15 55 31	3 49.6	24 50.0	20 59.1	6 59.3	8 47.9	28 30.0	11 56.8	1 57.3	11 47.7	8 21.1
13 Th	23 22 00	22 17 10	21 52 57	27 51 15	3 36.0	26 05.0	22 12.3	7 44.7	9 11.5	28 44.5	11D56.6	1 55.5	11R47.7	8 19.5
14 F	23 25 57	23 17 01	3♈50 35	9♈51 07	3 24.2	27 21.9	23 25.5	8 30.0	9 35.0	28 59.0	11 56.6	1 53.7	11 47.8	8 17.9
15 Sa	23 29 53	24 16 50	15 53 01	21 56 29	3 14.7	28 40.4	24 38.7	9 15.4	9 58.6	29 13.5	11 56.7	1 51.9	11 47.7	8 16.3
16 Su	23 33 50	25 16 38	28 01 44	4♉09 03	3 08.2	0♓00.6	25 51.7	10 00.8	10 22.3	29 28.0	11 56.9	1 50.1	11 47.7	8 14.7
17 M	23 37 46	26 16 23	10♉18 43	16 31 06	3 04.5	1 22.3	27 04.7	10 46.2	10 45.9	29 42.6	11 57.2	1 48.2	11 47.6	8 13.1
18 Tu	23 41 43	27 16 06	22 46 33	29 05 29	3D03.2	2 45.7	28 17.7	11 31.7	11 09.6	29 57.1	11 57.6	1 46.2	11 47.5	8 11.5
19 W	23 45 39	28 15 47	5♊28 20	11♊55 34	3 03.3	4 10.5	29 30.6	12 17.1	11 33.3	0♈11.6	11 58.1	1 44.3	11 47.3	8 09.9
20 Th	23 49 36	29 15 26	18 27 37	25 04 55	3R03.8	5 36.8	0♉43.4	13 02.6	11 57.0	0 26.2	11 58.7	1 42.3	11 47.1	8 08.2
21 F	23 53 32	0♈15 02	1♋47 53	8♋36 50	3 03.6	7 04.5	1 56.1	13 48.1	12 20.8	0 40.7	11 59.5	1 40.2	11 46.9	8 06.6
22 Sa	23 57 29	1 14 36	15 32 00	22 33 32	3 01.6	8 33.7	3 08.8	14 33.6	12 44.5	0 55.2	12 00.3	1 38.2	11 46.7	8 04.9
23 Su	0 01 26	2 14 08	29 41 24	6♌55 25	2 57.4	10 04.2	4 21.4	15 19.1	13 08.3	1 09.8	12 01.3	1 36.1	11 46.4	8 03.3
24 M	0 05 22	3 13 37	14♌15 10	21 40 04	2 50.9	11 36.1	5 34.0	16 04.6	13 32.1	1 24.3	12 02.4	1 33.9	11 46.1	8 01.6
25 Tu	0 09 19	4 13 04	29 09 19	6♍41 54	2 42.8	13 09.4	6 46.5	16 50.2	13 55.9	1 38.8	12 03.6	1 31.8	11 45.7	8 00.0
26 W	0 13 15	5 12 29	14♍16 41	21 52 23	2 33.8	14 44.1	7 58.9	17 35.7	14 19.7	1 53.3	12 04.9	1 29.6	11 45.4	7 58.3
27 Th	0 17 12	6 11 51	29 27 39	7♎01 09	2 25.3	16 20.1	9 11.2	18 21.3	14 43.5	2 07.9	12 06.3	1 27.4	11 44.9	7 56.6
28 F	0 21 08	7 11 12	14♎31 36	21 57 51	2 18.2	17 57.5	10 23.4	19 06.9	15 07.4	2 22.4	12 07.8	1 25.1	11 44.5	7 55.0
29 Sa	0 25 05	8 10 31	29 18 54	6♏33 57	2 13.3	19 36.3	11 35.6	19 52.5	15 31.2	2 36.9	12 09.4	1 22.9	11 44.0	7 53.3
30 Su	0 29 01	9 09 48	13♏42 23	20 43 50	2D10.7	21 16.4	12 47.7	20 38.1	15 55.1	2 51.3	12 11.2	1 20.6	11 43.5	7 51.6
31 M	0 32 58	10 09 03	27 38 07	4♐25 14	2 10.1	22 57.9	13 59.8	21 23.7	16 19.0	3 05.8	12 13.0	1 18.3	11 43.0	7 49.9

April 1975 — LONGITUDE

Day	Sid.Time	☉	0 hr ☽	Noon ☽	True ☊	☿	♀	♂	⚳	♃	♄	♅	♆	♇
1 Tu	0 36 54	11♈08 16	11♐05 22	17♐38 48	2♐10.9	24♓40.8	15♉11.7	22♒09.3	16♈42.9	3♈20.3	12♋14.9	1♏15.9	11♐42.4	7♎48.3
2 W	0 40 51	12 07 28	24 05 57	0♑27 19	2 12.0	26 25.1	16 23.6	22 55.0	17 06.8	3 34.7	12 17.0	1R13.6	11R41.8	7R46.6
3 Th	0 44 48	13 06 38	6♑43 26	12 54 54	2R12.6	28 10.8	17 35.4	23 40.6	17 30.7	3 49.2	12 19.1	1 11.2	11 41.2	7 45.0
4 F	0 48 44	14 05 46	19 02 20	25 06 21	2 11.9	29 57.9	18 47.2	24 26.3	17 54.6	4 03.6	12 21.4	1 08.8	11 40.6	7 43.3
5 Sa	0 52 41	15 04 52	1♒07 33	7♒06 32	2 09.3	1♈46.5	19 58.8	25 12.0	18 18.6	4 18.0	12 23.8	1 06.4	11 39.9	7 41.6
6 Su	0 56 37	16 03 56	13 03 51	19 00 02	2 04.6	3 36.5	21 10.4	25 57.7	18 42.5	4 32.4	12 26.2	1 04.0	11 39.1	7 40.0
7 M	1 00 34	17 02 59	24 55 35	0♓50 58	1 58.2	5 27.9	22 21.9	26 43.4	19 06.4	4 46.8	12 28.8	1 01.5	11 38.4	7 38.3
8 Tu	1 04 30	18 01 59	6♓46 35	12 42 48	1 50.4	7 20.8	23 33.3	27 29.1	19 30.4	5 01.1	12 31.5	0 59.0	11 37.6	7 36.7
9 W	1 08 27	19 00 58	18 39 56	24 38 17	1 42.1	9 15.1	24 44.7	28 14.8	19 54.4	5 15.4	12 34.3	0 56.5	11 36.8	7 35.1
10 Th	1 12 23	19 59 55	0♈38 04	6♈39 32	1 34.1	11 10.9	25 55.9	29 00.5	20 18.3	5 29.7	12 37.1	0 54.0	11 36.0	7 33.4
11 F	1 16 20	20 58 50	12 42 50	18 48 08	1 27.1	13 08.1	27 07.1	29 46.2	20 42.3	5 44.0	12 40.1	0 51.5	11 35.1	7 31.8
12 Sa	1 20 17	21 57 43	24 55 34	1♉05 16	1 21.7	15 06.7	28 18.2	0♓31.9	21 06.2	5 58.3	12 43.2	0 49.0	11 34.2	7 30.2
13 Su	1 24 13	22 56 34	7♉17 22	13 31 59	1 18.2	17 06.7	29 29.2	1 17.6	21 30.2	6 12.5	12 46.4	0 46.5	11 33.3	7 28.6
14 M	1 28 10	23 55 22	19 49 16	26 09 22	1D16.7	19 08.0	0♊40.1	2 03.3	21 54.2	6 26.7	12 49.6	0 44.0	11 32.4	7 27.0
15 Tu	1 32 06	24 54 09	2♊32 27	8♊58 42	1 16.8	21 10.6	1 50.9	2 49.0	22 18.1	6 40.8	12 53.0	0 41.4	11 31.4	7 25.4
16 W	1 36 03	25 52 54	15 28 19	22 01 30	1 18.0	23 14.4	3 01.6	3 34.7	22 42.1	6 55.0	12 56.5	0 38.9	11 30.4	7 23.9
17 Th	1 39 59	26 51 36	28 38 29	5♋19 28	1 19.6	25 19.3	4 12.2	4 20.4	23 06.1	7 09.1	13 00.0	0 36.3	11 29.4	7 22.3
18 F	1 43 56	27 50 17	12♋04 38	18 54 10	1R20.8	27 25.1	5 22.8	5 06.1	23 30.0	7 23.2	13 03.7	0 33.7	11 28.4	7 20.8
19 Sa	1 47 52	28 48 55	25 48 09	2♌46 40	1 21.0	29 31.7	6 33.2	5 51.8	23 54.0	7 37.2	13 07.4	0 31.2	11 27.3	7 19.2
20 Su	1 51 49	29 47 30	9♌49 39	16 56 57	1 19.9	1♉39.0	7 43.5	6 37.5	24 17.9	7 51.2	13 11.3	0 28.6	11 26.2	7 17.7
21 M	1 55 46	0♉46 04	24 08 21	1♍23 25	1 17.5	3 46.7	8 53.7	7 23.1	24 41.8	8 05.1	13 15.2	0 26.1	11 25.1	7 16.2
22 Tu	1 59 42	1 44 35	8♍41 40	16 02 26	1 13.9	5 54.6	10 03.8	8 08.8	25 05.8	8 19.1	13 19.2	0 23.5	11 24.0	7 14.7
23 W	2 03 39	2 43 04	23 24 58	0♎48 24	1 09.9	8 02.4	11 13.8	8 54.5	25 29.7	8 32.9	13 23.3	0 20.9	11 22.8	7 13.3
24 Th	2 07 35	3 41 31	8♎11 50	15 34 17	1 06.0	10 09.9	12 23.6	9 40.1	25 53.6	8 46.8	13 27.5	0 18.4	11 21.6	7 11.8
25 F	2 11 32	4 39 56	22 54 48	0♏12 28	1 02.8	12 16.8	13 33.4	10 25.8	26 17.5	9 00.6	13 31.8	0 15.8	11 20.4	7 10.4
26 Sa	2 15 28	5 38 19	7♏26 27	14 35 59	1 00.8	14 22.7	14 43.0	11 11.4	26 41.4	9 14.3	13 36.1	0 13.2	11 19.2	7 08.9
27 Su	2 19 25	6 36 40	21 40 28	28 39 25	1D00.0	16 27.3	15 52.5	11 57.0	27 05.3	9 28.0	13 40.6	0 10.7	11 18.0	7 07.5
28 M	2 23 21	7 35 00	5♐32 31	12♐19 34	1 00.3	18 30.4	17 01.9	12 42.7	27 29.1	9 41.7	13 45.1	0 08.2	11 16.7	7 06.1
29 Tu	2 27 18	8 33 18	19 00 31	25 35 28	1 01.5	20 31.7	18 11.2	13 28.3	27 53.0	9 55.3	13 49.7	0 05.6	11 15.4	7 04.8
30 W	2 31 15	9 31 35	2♑04 35	8♑28 11	1 03.0	22 30.7	19 20.3	14 13.9	28 16.8	10 08.9	13 54.4	0 03.1	11 14.1	7 03.4

Astro Data	Dy Hr Mn
☽ 0N	12 17:40
♄ D	14 8:32
♆ R	14 10:02
☉0N	21 5:57
♃⚻♅	25 1:53
☽ 0S	26 6:54
♃0N	28 22:42
⚳0N	31 19:12
☿0N	7 1:51
☽ 0N	8 23:47
♃☍♇	18 8:20
☽ 0S	22 15:52

Planet Ingress		Dy Hr Mn
♂	♒	3 5:32
☿	♓	16 11:50
♃	♈	18 16:47
♀	♉	19 21:42
☉	♈	21 5:57
☿	♈	4 12:28
♂	♓	11 19:15
♀	♊	13 22:26
☿	♉	19 17:20
☉	♉	20 17:07

Last Aspect Dy Hr Mn		☽ Ingress Dy Hr Mn
1 12:24 ♂ □	♏	1 14:33
3 12:28 ♃ △	♐	3 19:05
5 21:40 ♃ □	♑	6 3:39
8 10:10 ♃ ⚹	♒	8 15:09
10 12:32 ☿ ☌	♓	11 3:49
13 13:49 ♃ ☌	♈	13 16:18
16 2:53 ☿ ⚹	♉	16 3:52
18 13:39 ♃ ⚹	♊	18 13:43
20 20:05 ☉ □	♋	20 20:48
21 17:53 ♄ ☌	♌	23 0:31
24 2:28 ♂ ☍	♍	25 1:21
25 23:25 ☿ ☍	♎	27 0:51
28 7:08 ♂ △	♏	29 1:08
30 13:04 ☿ △	♐	31 4:10

Last Aspect Dy Hr Mn		☽ Ingress Dy Hr Mn
2 3:09 ☿ □	♑	2 11:08
3 22:09 ♀ △	♒	4 21:45
7 3:04 ♂ ☌	♓	7 10:17
9 12:14 ♀ ⚹	♈	9 22:44
11 16:39 ☉ ☌	♉	12 9:53
13 10:32 ♄ ⚹	♊	14 19:14
16 19:34 ☉ ⚹	♋	17 2:27
19 5:26 ☿ □	♌	19 7:14
20 2:44 ♆ △	♍	21 9:42
22 7:32 ♄ ⚹	♎	23 10:41
24 8:32 ♄ □	♏	25 11:39
26 11:34 ☿ ☍	♐	27 14:20
28 21:14 ♀ ☍	♑	29 20:08

☽ Phases & Eclipses Dy Hr Mn	
4 20:20	☾ 13♐38
12 23:47	● 21♓47
20 20:05	☽ 29♊35
27 10:36	○ 6♎08
3 12:25	☾ 13♑08
11 16:39	● 21♈10
19 4:41	☽ 28♋31
25 19:55	○ 4♏59

Astro Data

1 March 1975
Julian Day # 27453
SVP 5♓36'07"
GC 26♐29.5 ⚳ 2♓57.0
Eris 12♈57.8 ⚵ 22♈15.4
⚷ 21♈30.4 ⚶ 10♒00.9
☽ Mean ☊ 5♐26.7

1 April 1975
Julian Day # 27484
SVP 5♓36'04"
GC 26♐29.6 ⚳ 13♓00.6
Eris 13♈17.6 ⚵ 9♉54.3
⚷ 23♈11.4 ⚶ 25♒14.1
☽ Mean ☊ 3♐48.2

LONGITUDE — May 1975

Day	Sid.Time	☉	0 hr ☽	Noon ☽	True ☊	☿	♀	♂	⚳	♃	♄	♅	♆	♇
1 Th	2 35 11	10♉29 50	14♑46 40	21♑00 26	1♐04.4	24♉27.4	20♊29.4	14♓59.5	28♈40.7	10♈22.4	13♋59.2	0♏00.6	11♐12.8	7♎02.1
2 F	2 39 08	11 28 03	27 10 01	3♒15 57	1R 05.4	26 21.3	21 38.3	15 45.1	29 04.5	10 35.9	14 04.0	29♎58.1	11R 11.5	7R 00.8
3 Sa	2 43 04	12 26 15	9♒18 47	15 19 07	1 05.6	28 12.4	22 47.0	16 30.6	29 28.3	10 49.3	14 09.0	29R 55.6	11 10.1	6 59.5
4 Su	2 47 01	13 24 25	21 17 31	27 14 35	1 04.9	0♊00.4	23 55.7	17 16.2	29 52.1	11 02.7	14 14.0	29 53.1	11 08.7	6 58.2
5 M	2 50 57	14 22 34	3♓10 52	9♓06 55	1 03.6	1 45.1	25 04.2	18 01.7	0♉15.9	11 16.0	14 19.1	29 50.7	11 07.3	6 57.0
6 Tu	2 54 54	15 20 42	15 03 16	21 00 26	1 01.6	3 26.4	26 12.6	18 47.3	0 39.6	11 29.3	14 24.2	29 48.2	11 05.9	6 55.7
7 W	2 58 50	16 18 48	26 58 51	2♈58 57	0 59.4	5 04.3	27 20.8	19 32.8	1 03.4	11 42.5	14 29.5	29 45.8	11 04.5	6 54.5
8 Th	3 02 47	17 16 52	9♈01 06	15 05 40	0 57.3	6 38.4	28 28.9	20 18.3	1 27.1	11 55.6	14 34.8	29 43.4	11 03.1	6 53.3
9 F	3 06 43	18 14 55	21 12 56	27 23 08	0 55.5	8 08.9	29 36.9	21 03.7	1 50.8	12 08.7	14 40.2	29 41.0	11 01.6	6 52.2
10 Sa	3 10 40	19 12 57	3♉36 29	9♉53 07	0 54.2	9 35.5	0♋44.7	21 49.2	2 14.5	12 21.7	14 45.6	29 38.6	11 00.1	6 51.0
11 Su	3 14 37	20 10 57	16 13 10	22 36 42	0D 53.6	10 58.3	1 52.3	22 34.6	2 38.2	12 34.7	14 51.2	29 36.2	10 58.7	6 49.9
12 M	3 18 33	21 08 55	29 03 44	5♊34 17	0 53.5	12 17.2	2 59.8	23 20.0	3 01.8	12 47.6	14 56.8	29 33.9	10 57.2	6 48.8
13 Tu	3 22 30	22 06 52	12♊08 20	18 45 49	0 53.9	13 32.0	4 07.2	24 05.3	3 25.5	13 00.5	15 02.4	29 31.6	10 55.7	6 47.8
14 W	3 26 26	23 04 48	25 26 40	2♋10 47	0 54.5	14 42.8	5 14.4	24 50.7	3 49.1	13 13.2	15 08.2	29 29.3	10 54.2	6 46.8
15 Th	3 30 23	24 02 41	8♋58 05	15 48 27	0 55.2	15 49.5	6 21.4	25 36.0	4 12.6	13 25.9	15 14.0	29 27.0	10 52.6	6 45.7
16 F	3 34 19	25 00 33	22 41 44	29 37 49	0 55.8	16 51.9	7 28.2	26 21.2	4 36.2	13 38.6	15 19.8	29 24.8	10 51.1	6 44.8
17 Sa	3 38 16	25 58 23	6♌36 31	13♌37 40	0R 56.1	17 50.2	8 34.9	27 06.5	4 59.7	13 51.1	15 25.7	29 22.6	10 49.5	6 43.8
18 Su	3 42 13	26 56 12	20 41 03	27 46 25	0 56.2	18 44.1	9 41.4	27 51.7	5 23.2	14 03.6	15 31.7	29 20.4	10 48.0	6 42.9
19 M	3 46 09	27 53 58	4♍53 32	12♍02 03	0 56.1	19 33.6	10 47.7	28 36.8	5 46.7	14 16.0	15 37.8	29 18.3	10 46.4	6 42.0
20 Tu	3 50 06	28 51 43	19 11 38	26 21 54	0 55.9	20 18.7	11 53.7	29 22.0	6 10.1	14 28.3	15 43.9	29 16.1	10 44.8	6 41.1
21 W	3 54 02	29 49 26	3♎32 23	10♎42 38	0 55.8	20 59.3	12 59.6	0♈07.1	6 33.5	14 40.6	15 50.1	29 14.0	10 43.3	6 40.2
22 Th	3 57 59	0♊47 08	17 52 09	25 00 24	0D 55.7	21 35.3	14 05.3	0 52.2	6 56.9	14 52.8	15 56.3	29 12.0	10 41.7	6 39.4
23 F	4 01 55	1 44 48	2♏06 53	9♏11 04	0 55.8	22 06.6	15 10.8	1 37.2	7 20.2	15 04.9	16 02.6	29 09.9	10 40.1	6 38.6
24 Sa	4 05 52	2 42 27	16 12 27	23 10 33	0R 55.8	22 33.3	16 16.1	2 22.2	7 43.5	15 16.9	16 08.9	29 07.9	10 38.5	6 37.9
25 Su	4 09 48	3 40 04	0♐04 57	6♐55 18	0 55.8	22 55.3	17 21.2	3 07.2	8 06.8	15 28.9	16 15.3	29 06.0	10 36.9	6 37.1
26 M	4 13 45	4 37 40	13 41 17	20 22 43	0 55.7	23 12.5	18 26.0	3 52.1	8 30.0	15 40.7	16 21.8	29 04.0	10 35.3	6 36.4
27 Tu	4 17 42	5 35 16	26 59 25	3♑31 21	0 55.3	23 25.0	19 30.6	4 37.0	8 53.3	15 52.5	16 28.3	29 02.1	10 33.6	6 35.8
28 W	4 21 38	6 32 50	9♑58 34	16 21 09	0 54.7	23 32.7	20 35.0	5 21.9	9 16.4	16 04.2	16 34.8	29 00.3	10 32.0	6 35.1
29 Th	4 25 35	7 30 23	22 39 18	28 53 18	0 53.9	23R 35.8	21 39.1	6 06.7	9 39.6	16 15.8	16 41.4	28 58.4	10 30.4	6 34.5
30 F	4 29 31	8 27 55	5♒03 27	11♒10 10	0 53.1	23 34.3	22 43.0	6 51.5	10 02.7	16 27.3	16 48.1	28 56.6	10 28.8	6 33.9
31 Sa	4 33 28	9 25 26	17 13 53	23 15 04	0 52.4	23 28.3	23 46.6	7 36.2	10 25.8	16 38.8	16 54.8	28 54.9	10 27.2	6 33.4

LONGITUDE — June 1975

Day	Sid.Time	☉	0 hr ☽	Noon ☽	True ☊	☿	♀	♂	⚳	♃	♄	♅	♆	♇
1 Su	4 37 24	10♊22 57	29♒14 14	5♓11 58	0♐52.0	23♊18.0	24♋50.0	8♈20.9	10♉48.8	16♈50.1	17♋01.5	28♎53.2	10♐25.5	6♎32.9
2 M	4 41 21	11 20 26	11♓08 47	17 05 18	0D 52.0	23R 03.7	25 53.1	9 05.6	11 11.8	17 01.4	17 08.3	28R 51.5	10R 23.9	6R 32.4
3 Tu	4 45 17	12 17 55	23 02 04	28 59 41	0 52.5	22 45.5	26 56.0	9 50.2	11 34.8	17 12.5	17 15.1	28 49.9	10 22.3	6 31.9
4 W	4 49 14	13 15 23	4♈58 42	10♈59 40	0 53.4	22 23.7	27 58.5	10 34.7	11 57.7	17 23.6	17 22.0	28 48.3	10 20.7	6 31.5
5 Th	4 53 11	14 12 51	17 03 07	23 09 33	0 54.6	21 58.9	29 00.8	11 19.2	12 20.5	17 34.5	17 28.9	28 46.7	10 19.1	6 31.1
6 F	4 57 07	15 10 17	29 19 23	5♉33 02	0 55.7	21 31.3	0♌02.8	12 03.7	12 43.4	17 45.4	17 35.9	28 45.2	10 17.4	6 30.7
7 Sa	5 01 04	16 07 43	11♉50 50	18 13 04	0R 56.6	21 01.5	1 04.5	12 48.1	13 06.2	17 56.1	17 42.9	28 43.7	10 15.8	6 30.4
8 Su	5 05 00	17 05 09	24 39 55	1♊11 30	0 57.0	20 29.9	2 05.9	13 32.4	13 28.9	18 06.8	17 50.0	28 42.3	10 14.2	6 30.1
9 M	5 08 57	18 02 33	7♊47 51	14 28 56	0 56.6	19 57.0	3 07.0	14 16.7	13 51.6	18 17.4	17 57.1	28 40.9	10 12.6	6 29.8
10 Tu	5 12 53	18 59 57	21 14 34	28 04 33	0 55.3	19 23.6	4 07.8	15 01.0	14 14.3	18 27.8	18 04.2	28 39.5	10 11.0	6 29.6
11 W	5 16 50	19 57 20	4♋58 34	11♋56 14	0 53.2	18 50.0	5 08.2	15 45.1	14 36.9	18 38.1	18 11.4	28 38.3	10 09.4	6 29.4
12 Th	5 20 46	20 54 42	18 57 06	26 00 41	0 50.6	18 16.9	6 08.2	16 29.3	14 59.4	18 48.4	18 18.6	28 37.0	10 07.8	6 29.2
13 F	5 24 43	21 52 03	3♌06 28	10♌13 54	0 47.9	17 44.9	7 07.9	17 13.3	15 21.9	18 58.5	18 25.8	28 35.8	10 06.2	6 29.1
14 Sa	5 28 40	22 49 24	17 22 28	24 31 40	0 45.5	17 14.4	8 07.3	17 57.3	15 44.4	19 08.5	18 33.1	28 34.6	10 04.6	6 29.0
15 Su	5 32 36	23 46 43	1♍40 59	8♍49 59	0 43.9	16 46.1	9 06.2	18 41.2	16 06.7	19 18.4	18 40.4	28 33.5	10 03.1	6 28.9
16 M	5 36 33	24 44 01	15 58 17	23 05 31	0D 43.3	16 20.3	10 04.7	19 25.1	16 29.1	19 28.2	18 47.7	28 32.5	10 01.5	6D 28.9
17 Tu	5 40 29	25 41 18	0♎11 23	7♎15 37	0 43.6	15 57.6	11 02.8	20 08.8	16 51.4	19 37.8	18 55.1	28 31.4	10 00.0	6 28.9
18 W	5 44 26	26 38 35	14 18 00	21 18 21	0 44.8	15 38.3	12 00.5	20 52.6	17 13.6	19 47.3	19 02.5	28 30.5	9 58.4	6 28.9
19 Th	5 48 22	27 35 51	28 16 30	5♏12 17	0 46.2	15 22.7	12 57.7	21 36.2	17 35.7	19 56.8	19 09.9	28 29.5	9 56.9	6 29.0
20 F	5 52 19	28 33 06	12♏05 33	18 56 12	0R 47.4	15 11.1	13 54.5	22 19.8	17 57.9	20 06.1	19 17.3	28 28.7	9 55.4	6 29.1
21 Sa	5 56 15	29 30 20	25 44 04	2♐29 02	0 47.8	15 03.8	14 50.8	23 03.3	18 19.9	20 15.2	19 24.8	28 27.8	9 53.8	6 29.2
22 Su	6 00 12	0♋27 34	9♐10 57	15 49 43	0 47.0	15D 00.9	15 46.6	23 46.8	18 41.9	20 24.3	19 32.3	28 27.1	9 52.3	6 29.3
23 M	6 04 09	1 24 47	22 25 11	28 57 16	0 44.7	15 02.5	16 41.9	24 30.1	19 03.8	20 33.2	19 39.8	28 26.3	9 50.9	6 29.5
24 Tu	6 08 05	2 22 00	5♑25 52	11♑50 58	0 40.9	15 08.9	17 36.7	25 13.4	19 25.7	20 42.0	19 47.4	28 25.7	9 49.4	6 29.8
25 W	6 12 02	3 19 13	18 12 32	24 30 35	0 36.0	15 20.0	18 30.9	25 56.7	19 47.5	20 50.7	19 54.9	28 25.0	9 47.9	6 30.0
26 Th	6 15 58	4 16 25	0♒45 13	6♒56 33	0 30.4	15 35.8	19 24.6	26 39.8	20 09.2	20 59.2	20 02.5	28 24.5	9 46.5	6 30.3
27 F	6 19 55	5 13 37	13 04 46	19 10 07	0 24.7	15 56.4	20 17.6	27 22.9	20 30.9	21 07.6	20 10.1	28 23.9	9 45.1	6 30.6
28 Sa	6 23 51	6 10 49	25 12 54	1♓13 27	0 19.6	16 21.8	21 10.1	28 05.9	20 52.5	21 15.9	20 17.7	28 23.4	9 43.6	6 31.0
29 Su	6 27 48	7 08 01	7♓12 11	13 09 32	0 15.5	16 51.9	22 02.0	28 48.8	21 14.1	21 24.0	20 25.4	28 23.0	9 42.2	6 31.4
30 M	6 31 44	8 05 13	19 06 01	25 02 09	0 13.0	17 26.7	22 53.2	29 31.7	21 35.5	21 32.0	20 33.0	28 22.6	9 40.8	6 31.8

Astro Data	Planet Ingress	Last Aspect	☽ Ingress	Last Aspect	☽ Ingress	☽ Phases & Eclipses	Astro Data
Dy Hr Mn	Dy Hr Mn	Dy Hr Mn	Dy Hr Mn	Dy Hr Mn	Dy Hr Mn	Dy Hr Mn	1 May 1975
♃△♆ 4 21:51	♅ ♎R 1 17:46	2 5:31 ♅ □	♒ 2 5:34	31 23:19 ♅ △	♓ 1 1:32	3 5:44 ☾ 12♒11	Julian Day # 27514
☽0N 6 6:34	☿ ♊ 4 11:55	4 17:19 ♅ △	♓ 4 17:34	3 7:27 ♀ △	♈ 3 14:01	11 7:05 ● 19♉59	SVP 5♓36'01"
☽0S 19 22:26	⚳ ♉ 4 19:58	6 23:33 ♀ □	♈ 7 6:03	6 0:26 ♀ □	♉ 6 1:19	11 7:16:44 ● P 0.864	GC 26♐29.7 ⚴ 21♓58.8
♂0N 26 9:01	♀ ♋ 9 20:11	9 16:44 ♀ ⚹	♉ 9 17:03	7 11:03 ♄ ⚹	♊ 8 9:49	18 10:29 ☽ 26♌53	Eris 13♈37.4 ⚵ 27♉30.6
☿R 29 16:01	♂ ♈ 21 8:14	11 11:56 ♂ ⚹	♊ 12 1:44	10 13:01 ♅ △	♋ 10 15:21	25 5:51 ○ 3♐25	⚷ 24♈58.3 ⚶ 8♓42.1
	☉ ♊ 21 16:24	14 7:14 ♅ △	♋ 14 8:08	12 16:24 ♅ □	♌ 12 18:45	25 5:48 ● T 1.426	☽ Mean ☊ 2♐12.9
☽0N 2 14:24		16 11:38 ♅ □	♌ 16 12:38	14 18:47 ♅ ⚹	♍ 14 21:11		
♃□♄ 4 3:02	♀ ♌ 6 10:54	18 14:38 ♅ ⚹	♍ 18 15:45	16 14:58 ☉ □	♎ 16 23:41	1 23:22 ☾ 10♓50	1 June 1975
☽0S 16 4:03	☉ ♋ 22 0:26	20 17:18 ♂ ☍	♎ 20 18:05	19 0:23 ♅ ☌	♏ 19 2:59	9 18:49 ● 18♊19	Julian Day # 27545
♇D 17 4:03		22 19:03 ♅ ☌	♏ 22 20:25	20 12:38 ♄ △	♐ 21 7:34	16 14:58 ☽ 24♍51	SVP 5♓35'57"
☿D 22 15:19		23 23:48 ♄ △	♐ 24 23:51	23 11:03 ♅ ⚹	♑ 23 13:56	23 16:54 ○ 1♑36	GC 26♐29.8 ⚴ 29♓47.0
☽0N 29 22:53		27 3:46 ♅ ⚹	♑ 27 5:31	25 19:29 ♅ □	♒ 25 22:33		Eris 13♈53.4 ⚵ 15♊45.7
		29 12:10 ♅ □	♒ 29 14:09	28 6:20 ♅ △	♓ 28 9:33		⚷ 26♈37.4 ⚶ 20♓35.4
				30 2:50 ♄ △	♈ 30 22:02		☽ Mean ☊ 0♐34.4

July 1975 LONGITUDE

Day	Sid.Time	☉	0 hr ☽	Noon☽	True☊	☿	♀	♂	⚳	♃	♄	♅	♆	♇
1 Tu	6 35 41	9♋02 26	0♈58 29	6♈55 37	0♐12.0	18♊06.2	23♌43.8	0♉14.5	21♉56.9	21♈39.9	20♋40.7	28♎22.3	9♐39.5	6♎32.3
2 W	6 39 38	9 59 38	12 54 10	18 54 44	0D 12.3	18 50.3	24 33.7	0 57.1	22 18.3	21 47.6	20 48.4	28R 22.0	9R 38.1	6 32.8
3 Th	6 43 34	10 56 50	24 57 56	1♉04 23	0 13.6	19 38.9	25 22.9	1 39.7	22 39.5	21 55.2	20 56.1	28 21.8	9 36.8	6 33.3
4 F	6 47 31	11 54 03	7♉14 40	13 29 20	0 15.1	20 32.0	26 11.3	2 22.2	23 00.7	22 02.6	21 03.8	28 21.7	9 35.5	6 33.8
5 Sa	6 51 27	12 51 16	19 48 53	26 13 45	0R 16.0	21 29.5	26 59.0	3 04.7	23 21.8	22 09.9	21 11.6	28 21.5	9 34.2	6 34.4
6 Su	6 55 24	13 48 29	2♊44 18	9♊20 47	0 15.7	22 31.4	27 45.9	3 47.0	23 42.8	22 17.0	21 19.3	28D 21.5	9 32.9	6 35.1
7 M	6 59 20	14 45 43	16 03 22	22 52 02	0 13.6	23 37.7	28 32.0	4 29.2	24 03.8	22 24.0	21 27.1	28 21.5	9 31.6	6 35.7
8 Tu	7 03 17	15 42 57	29 46 40	6♋46 59	0 09.6	24 48.1	29 17.3	5 11.4	24 24.7	22 30.8	21 34.8	28 21.5	9 30.4	6 36.4
9 W	7 07 13	16 40 11	13♋52 32	21 02 46	0 03.8	26 02.8	0♍01.6	5 53.4	24 45.4	22 37.5	21 42.6	28 21.6	9 29.2	6 37.1
10 Th	7 11 10	17 37 24	28 16 57	5♌34 16	29♏56.8	27 21.6	0 45.1	6 35.3	25 06.1	22 44.0	21 50.4	28 21.8	9 28.0	6 37.9
11 F	7 15 07	18 34 38	12♌53 49	20 14 40	29 49.5	28 44.5	1 27.6	7 17.1	25 26.7	22 50.4	21 58.1	28 22.0	9 26.8	6 38.7
12 Sa	7 19 03	19 31 52	27 35 53	4♍56 32	29 42.8	0♋11.3	2 09.1	7 58.9	25 47.3	22 56.6	22 05.9	28 22.2	9 25.6	6 39.5
13 Su	7 23 00	20 29 06	12♍15 47	19 32 55	29 37.6	1 42.1	2 49.5	8 40.5	26 07.7	23 02.6	22 13.7	28 22.5	9 24.5	6 40.3
14 M	7 26 56	21 26 20	26 47 17	3♎58 25	29 34.3	3 16.7	3 28.9	9 22.0	26 28.0	23 08.5	22 21.5	28 22.9	9 23.4	6 41.2
15 Tu	7 30 53	22 23 34	11♎05 57	18 09 37	29D 33.0	4 55.1	4 07.2	10 03.4	26 48.2	23 14.2	22 29.3	28 23.3	9 22.3	6 42.1
16 W	7 34 49	23 20 48	25 09 18	2♏04 59	29 33.1	6 37.0	4 44.3	10 44.7	27 08.4	23 19.7	22 37.0	28 23.8	9 21.2	6 43.0
17 Th	7 38 46	24 18 02	8♏56 42	15 44 32	29 34.0	8 22.4	5 20.2	11 25.8	27 28.4	23 25.1	22 44.8	28 24.3	9 20.2	6 44.0
18 F	7 42 42	25 15 16	22 28 38	29 09 10	29R 34.6	10 11.0	5 54.8	12 06.9	27 48.4	23 30.3	22 52.6	28 24.8	9 19.2	6 45.0
19 Sa	7 46 39	26 12 30	5♐46 17	12♐20 09	29 33.8	12 02.7	6 28.1	12 47.9	28 08.2	23 35.3	23 00.4	28 25.5	9 18.2	6 46.0
20 Su	7 50 36	27 09 45	18 50 55	25 18 42	29 31.0	13 57.2	7 00.1	13 28.7	28 28.0	23 40.2	23 08.2	28 26.1	9 17.2	6 47.1
21 M	7 54 32	28 07 00	1♑43 37	8♑05 45	29 25.7	15 54.3	7 30.7	14 09.4	28 47.6	23 44.9	23 15.9	28 26.9	9 16.3	6 48.2
22 Tu	7 58 29	29 04 15	14 25 11	20 41 57	29 18.0	17 53.7	7 59.7	14 50.0	29 07.2	23 49.4	23 23.7	28 27.6	9 15.4	6 49.3
23 W	8 02 25	0♌01 31	26 56 07	3♒07 44	29 08.2	19 55.1	8 27.3	15 30.5	29 26.6	23 53.8	23 31.5	28 28.5	9 14.5	6 50.5
24 Th	8 06 22	0 58 48	9♒16 53	15 23 38	28 57.2	21 58.2	8 53.3	16 10.9	29 45.9	23 57.9	23 39.2	28 29.4	9 13.6	6 51.7
25 F	8 10 18	1 56 05	21 28 07	27 30 28	28 45.9	24 02.6	9 17.7	16 51.1	0♊05.1	24 01.9	23 46.9	28 30.3	9 12.8	6 52.9
26 Sa	8 14 15	2 53 22	3♓30 53	9♓29 36	28 35.3	26 08.1	9 40.3	17 31.3	0 24.2	24 05.7	23 54.7	28 31.3	9 12.0	6 54.1
27 Su	8 18 11	3 50 41	15 26 54	21 23 07	28 26.4	28 14.2	10 01.3	18 11.3	0 43.2	24 09.4	24 02.4	28 32.3	9 11.2	6 55.4
28 M	8 22 08	4 48 01	27 18 39	3♈13 54	28 19.6	0♌20.7	10 20.4	18 51.1	1 02.1	24 12.8	24 10.1	28 33.4	9 10.5	6 56.7
29 Tu	8 26 05	5 45 21	9♈09 24	15 05 39	28 15.3	2 27.3	10 37.7	19 30.9	1 20.8	24 16.1	24 17.8	28 34.5	9 09.7	6 58.0
30 W	8 30 01	6 42 43	21 03 13	27 02 42	28D 13.2	4 33.7	10 53.1	20 10.5	1 39.5	24 19.2	24 25.5	28 35.7	9 09.0	6 59.3
31 Th	8 33 58	7 40 05	3♉04 45	9♉10 00	28 12.7	6 39.8	11 06.5	20 49.9	1 58.0	24 22.0	24 33.1	28 36.9	9 08.4	7 00.7

August 1975 LONGITUDE

Day	Sid.Time	☉	0 hr ☽	Noon☽	True☊	☿	♀	♂	⚳	♃	♄	♅	♆	♇
1 F	8 37 54	8♌37 29	15♉19 06	21♉32 42	28♏13.0	8♌45.1	11♍17.9	21♉29.3	2♊16.4	24♈24.7	24♋40.8	28♎38.2	9♐07.7	7♎02.1
2 Sa	8 41 51	9 34 54	27 51 25	4♊15 50	28R 13.0	10 49.7	11 27.2	22 08.4	2 34.6	24 27.3	24 48.4	28 39.6	9R 07.1	7 03.5
3 Su	8 45 47	10 32 20	10♊46 27	17 23 44	28 11.7	12 53.3	11 34.4	22 47.5	2 52.8	24 29.6	24 56.0	28 40.9	9 06.5	7 05.0
4 M	8 49 44	11 29 47	24 07 57	0♋59 19	28 08.1	14 55.8	11 39.4	23 26.4	3 10.7	24 31.7	25 03.6	28 42.4	9 06.0	7 06.5
5 Tu	8 53 40	12 27 15	7♋57 48	15 03 15	28 02.0	16 57.1	11R 42.2	24 05.1	3 28.6	24 33.6	25 11.2	28 43.9	9 05.5	7 08.0
6 W	8 57 37	13 24 45	22 15 16	29 33 15	27 53.6	18 57.0	11 42.7	24 43.7	3 46.3	24 35.4	25 18.7	28 45.4	9 05.0	7 09.5
7 Th	9 01 34	14 22 15	6♌56 26	14♌23 48	27 43.4	20 55.6	11 40.9	25 22.1	4 03.9	24 36.9	25 26.3	28 47.0	9 04.5	7 11.1
8 F	9 05 30	15 19 47	21 54 13	29 26 28	27 32.7	22 52.8	11 36.8	26 00.4	4 21.3	24 38.3	25 33.8	28 48.6	9 04.1	7 12.7
9 Sa	9 09 27	16 17 19	6♍59 16	14♍31 20	27 22.7	24 48.5	11 30.3	26 38.5	4 38.6	24 39.4	25 41.2	28 50.3	9 03.7	7 14.3
10 Su	9 13 23	17 14 52	22 01 29	29 28 38	27 14.5	26 42.7	11 21.4	27 16.4	4 55.7	24 40.4	25 48.7	28 52.0	9 03.3	7 15.9
11 M	9 17 20	18 12 27	6♎51 52	14♎10 26	27 08.8	28 35.5	11 10.1	27 54.2	5 12.7	24 41.1	25 56.1	28 53.8	9 03.0	7 17.6
12 Tu	9 21 16	19 10 02	21 23 49	28 31 40	27 05.7	0♍26.7	10 56.4	28 31.8	5 29.5	24 41.7	26 03.5	28 55.6	9 02.7	7 19.2
13 W	9 25 13	20 07 38	5♏33 47	12♏30 11	27D 04.6	2 16.5	10 40.4	29 09.2	5 46.2	24 42.1	26 10.9	28 57.5	9 02.4	7 21.0
14 Th	9 29 09	21 05 15	19 20 58	26 06 20	27R 04.5	4 04.7	10 22.1	29 46.4	6 02.7	24R 42.2	26 18.2	28 59.4	9 02.1	7 22.7
15 F	9 33 06	22 02 53	2♐46 35	9♐22 02	27 04.2	5 51.5	10 01.5	0♊23.5	6 19.0	24 42.2	26 25.5	29 01.4	9 01.9	7 24.4
16 Sa	9 37 03	23 00 32	15 53 04	22 20 03	27 02.5	7 36.8	9 38.6	1 00.4	6 35.2	24 41.9	26 32.8	29 03.4	9 01.8	7 26.2
17 Su	9 40 59	23 58 12	28 43 20	5♑03 16	26 58.5	9 20.6	9 13.7	1 37.1	6 51.2	24 41.5	26 40.0	29 05.4	9 01.6	7 28.0
18 M	9 44 56	24 55 53	11♑20 11	17 34 20	26 51.6	11 02.9	8 46.8	2 13.6	7 07.0	24 40.9	26 47.2	29 07.5	9 01.5	7 29.8
19 Tu	9 48 52	25 53 35	23 46 00	29 55 23	26 42.0	12 43.8	8 17.9	2 49.9	7 22.7	24 40.0	26 54.4	29 09.6	9 01.4	7 31.7
20 W	9 52 49	26 51 18	6♒02 40	12♒08 02	26 29.9	14 23.3	7 47.4	3 26.1	7 38.2	24 39.0	27 01.5	29 11.8	9 01.4	7 33.5
21 Th	9 56 45	27 49 03	18 11 37	24 13 33	26 16.4	16 01.4	7 15.2	4 02.0	7 53.5	24 37.8	27 08.6	29 14.0	9D 01.3	7 35.4
22 F	10 00 42	28 46 49	0♓13 58	6♓13 00	26 02.5	17 38.1	6 41.7	4 37.8	8 08.6	24 36.4	27 15.6	29 16.3	9 01.4	7 37.3
23 Sa	10 04 38	29 44 36	12 10 49	18 07 35	25 49.3	19 13.3	6 07.0	5 13.3	8 23.5	24 34.7	27 22.6	29 18.6	9 01.4	7 39.2
24 Su	10 08 35	0♍42 25	24 03 30	29 58 48	25 38.0	20 47.2	5 31.3	5 48.6	8 38.2	24 32.9	27 29.6	29 20.9	9 01.5	7 41.1
25 M	10 12 32	1 40 15	5♈53 48	11♈48 48	25 29.1	22 19.7	4 54.9	6 23.8	8 52.8	24 30.9	27 36.5	29 23.3	9 01.6	7 43.1
26 Tu	10 16 28	2 38 08	17 44 10	23 40 21	25 23.0	23 50.8	4 17.9	6 58.7	9 07.1	24 28.7	27 43.4	29 25.8	9 01.7	7 45.1
27 W	10 20 25	3 36 02	29 37 48	5♉37 03	25 19.6	25 20.5	3 40.7	7 33.4	9 21.3	24 26.3	27 50.3	29 28.2	9 01.9	7 47.0
28 Th	10 24 21	4 33 57	11♉38 38	17 43 10	25D 18.4	26 48.8	3 03.4	8 07.9	9 35.3	24 23.7	27 57.1	29 30.7	9 02.1	7 49.1
29 F	10 28 18	5 31 55	23 51 14	0♊03 30	25R 18.2	28 15.7	2 26.4	8 42.2	9 49.0	24 20.9	28 03.8	29 33.3	9 02.4	7 51.1
30 Sa	10 32 14	6 29 54	6♊20 35	12 43 07	25 18.2	29 41.2	1 49.8	9 16.2	10 02.5	24 17.9	28 10.5	29 35.9	9 02.6	7 53.1
31 Su	10 36 11	7 27 56	19 11 40	25 46 47	25 17.1	1♎05.2	1 13.8	9 50.0	10 15.9	24 14.7	28 17.2	29 38.5	9 02.9	7 55.2

Astro Data

	Dy Hr Mn
♅D	7 3:58
☽0S	13 10:41
☽0N	27 7:09
♃⚼♆	27 22:23
♄⚼♆	28 13:02
♃□♄	29 2:51
♀R	6 5:21
☽0S	9 19:25
♃R	14 19:32
♆D	21 14:53
☽0N	23 14:27
☿0S	29 23:02

Planet Ingress

	Dy Hr Mn
♂ ♉	1 3:53
♀ ♍	9 11:06
☊ ♏R	10 1:19
☿ ♋	12 8:56
☉ ♌	23 11:22
⚳ ♊	25 5:35
☿ ♌	28 8:05
☿ ♍	12 6:12
♂ ♊	14 20:47
☉ ♍	23 18:24
☿ ♎	30 17:20

Last Aspect / ☽ Ingress

Last Aspect Dy Hr Mn		☽ Ingress Dy Hr Mn
3 6:42	♅ ☍	♉ 3 9:54
5 13:29	♀ □	♊ 5 18:58
7 22:25	♀ ⚹	♋ 8 0:23
10 0:08	♅ □	♌ 10 2:50
12 3:22	☿ ⚹	♍ 12 3:55
13 16:28	♄ ⚹	♎ 14 5:21
16 5:36	♅ ☌	♏ 16 8:23
18 4:26	☉ △	♐ 18 13:32
20 17:50	♅ ⚹	♑ 20 20:46
23 5:28	☉ ☍	♒ 23 5:56
25 13:59	♅ △	♓ 25 16:58
28 4:53	☿ △	♈ 28 5:27
30 15:06	♅ ☍	♉ 30 17:53

Last Aspect / ☽ Ingress

Last Aspect Dy Hr Mn		☽ Ingress Dy Hr Mn
1 18:02	♄ ⚹	♊ 2 4:02
4 8:01	♅ △	♋ 4 10:17
6 10:42	♅ □	♌ 6 12:44
8 11:00	♅ ⚹	♍ 8 12:53
10 8:17	♂ △	♎ 10 12:51
12 12:41	♅ ☌	♏ 12 14:30
14 18:54	♂ ☍	♐ 14 18:59
17 0:40	♅ ⚹	♑ 17 2:25
19 10:30	♅ □	♒ 19 12:09
21 22:02	♅ △	♓ 21 23:32
24 6:55	♄ △	♈ 24 12:02
26 23:38	♅ ☍	♉ 27 0:45
29 8:07	♄ ⚹	♊ 29 11:53
31 18:58	♅ △	♋ 31 19:35

☽ Phases & Eclipses

Dy Hr Mn		
1 16:37	☾	9♈13
9 4:10	●	16♋21
15 19:47	☽	22♎42
23 5:28	○	29♑46
31 8:48	☾	7♉32
7 11:57	●	14♌22
14 2:24	☽	20♏42
21 19:48	○	28♒08
29 23:20	☾	5♊59

Astro Data

1 July 1975
Julian Day # 27575
SVP 5♓35'52"
GC 26♐29.8 ⚴ 4♈57.2
Eris 14♈01.0 ✱ 3♋06.3
⚷ 27♈44.5 ⚵ 28♓58.7
☽ Mean ☊ 28♏59.1

1 August 1975
Julian Day # 27606
SVP 5♓35'47"
GC 26♐29.9 ⚴ 6♈20.7R
Eris 13♈59.1R ✱ 20♋21.9
⚷ 28♈09.9 ⚵ 2♈29.2
☽ Mean ☊ 27♏20.6

LONGITUDE — September 1975

Day	Sid.Time	☉	0 hr ☽	Noon ☽	True ☊	☿	♀	♂	⚳	♃	♄	♅	♆	♇
1 M	10 40 07	8♍25 59	2♋28 54	9♋18 20	25♏14.0	2♎27.8	0♍38.8	10♊23.6	10♊28.9	24♈11.4	28♋23.8	29♎41.2	9♐03.3	7♎57.3
2 Tu	10 44 04	9 24 04	16 15 17	23 19 44	25R 08.4	3 48.8	0R 04.9	10 56.9	10 41.8	24R 07.8	28 30.3	29 43.9	9 03.6	7 59.3
3 W	10 48 01	10 22 12	0♌31 29	7♌50 07	25 00.4	5 08.3	29♌32.4	11 30.0	10 54.5	24 04.1	28 36.8	29 46.6	9 04.1	8 01.4
4 Th	10 51 57	11 20 20	15 14 57	22 45 06	24 50.7	6 26.3	29 01.3	12 02.8	11 06.9	24 00.1	28 43.3	29 49.4	9 04.5	8 03.6
5 F	10 55 54	12 18 31	0♍19 28	7♍56 46	24 40.2	7 42.5	28 31.9	12 35.3	11 19.1	23 56.0	28 49.7	29 52.2	9 05.0	8 05.7
6 Sa	10 59 50	13 16 43	15 35 37	23 14 34	24 30.4	8 57.1	28 04.3	13 07.6	11 31.0	23 51.7	28 56.0	29 55.0	9 05.5	8 07.8
7 Su	11 03 47	14 14 58	0♎52 13	8♎27 12	24 22.2	10 09.9	27 38.6	13 39.6	11 42.7	23 47.3	29 02.3	29 57.9	9 06.0	8 10.0
8 M	11 07 43	15 13 13	15 58 20	23 24 37	24 16.5	11 20.9	27 15.0	14 11.3	11 54.1	23 42.6	29 08.5	0♏00.8	9 06.6	8 12.2
9 Tu	11 11 40	16 11 31	0♏45 13	7♏59 35	24 13.4	12 30.0	26 53.6	14 42.8	12 05.3	23 37.8	29 14.6	0 03.8	9 07.2	8 14.4
10 W	11 15 36	17 09 49	15 07 21	22 08 22	24D 12.5	13 36.9	26 34.4	15 13.9	12 16.2	23 32.8	29 20.7	0 06.7	9 07.8	8 16.5
11 Th	11 19 33	18 08 10	29 02 37	5♐50 18	24R 12.7	14 41.8	26 17.5	15 44.8	12 26.9	23 27.7	29 26.8	0 09.8	9 08.4	8 18.8
12 F	11 23 30	19 06 32	12♐31 40	19 07 07	24 13.1	15 44.4	26 02.9	16 15.3	12 37.3	23 22.4	29 32.8	0 12.8	9 09.1	8 21.0
13 Sa	11 27 26	20 04 55	25 37 04	2♑01 58	24 12.4	16 44.5	25 50.7	16 45.6	12 47.4	23 16.9	29 38.7	0 15.9	9 09.9	8 23.2
14 Su	11 31 23	21 03 21	8♑22 19	14 38 37	24 09.7	17 42.0	25 41.0	17 15.6	12 57.3	23 11.3	29 44.5	0 19.0	9 10.6	8 25.4
15 M	11 35 19	22 01 47	20 51 18	27 00 51	24 04.7	18 36.8	25 33.6	17 45.2	13 06.9	23 05.5	29 50.3	0 22.1	9 11.4	8 27.7
16 Tu	11 39 16	23 00 16	3♒07 40	9♒12 09	23 57.2	19 28.6	25 28.6	18 14.5	13 16.2	22 59.6	29 56.0	0 25.3	9 12.2	8 29.9
17 W	11 43 12	23 58 46	15 14 37	21 15 25	23 47.6	20 17.3	25D 26.1	18 43.5	13 25.2	22 53.5	0♌01.7	0 28.5	9 13.1	8 32.2
18 Th	11 47 09	24 57 17	27 14 49	3♓13 04	23 36.7	21 02.5	25 25.9	19 12.2	13 34.0	22 47.3	0 07.2	0 31.7	9 14.0	8 34.5
19 F	11 51 05	25 55 51	9♓10 24	15 07 00	23 25.4	21 44.1	25 28.1	19 40.5	13 42.4	22 40.9	0 12.7	0 34.9	9 14.9	8 36.7
20 Sa	11 55 02	26 54 26	21 03 04	26 58 48	23 14.8	22 21.6	25 32.6	20 08.5	13 50.6	22 34.5	0 18.2	0 38.2	9 15.8	8 39.0
21 Su	11 58 58	27 53 04	2♈54 23	8♈50 01	23 05.7	22 54.9	25 39.3	20 36.2	13 58.4	22 27.9	0 23.5	0 41.5	9 16.8	8 41.3
22 M	12 02 55	28 51 43	14 45 56	20 42 20	22 58.6	23 23.6	25 48.3	21 03.4	14 06.0	22 21.1	0 28.8	0 44.8	9 17.8	8 43.6
23 Tu	12 06 52	29 50 25	26 39 32	2♉37 48	22 54.1	23 47.3	25 59.5	21 30.4	14 13.2	22 14.3	0 34.0	0 48.1	9 18.8	8 45.9
24 W	12 10 48	0♎49 08	8♉37 30	14 39 00	22D 51.8	24 05.6	26 12.7	21 56.9	14 20.1	22 07.3	0 39.2	0 51.5	9 19.9	8 48.2
25 Th	12 14 45	1 47 54	20 42 42	26 49 05	22 51.5	24 18.2	26 28.1	22 23.1	14 26.7	22 00.2	0 44.2	0 54.9	9 21.0	8 50.5
26 F	12 18 41	2 46 42	2♊58 36	9♊11 47	22 52.4	24R 24.7	26 45.4	22 48.8	14 33.0	21 53.1	0 49.2	0 58.3	9 22.1	8 52.9
27 Sa	12 22 38	3 45 32	15 29 10	21 51 15	22R 53.6	24 24.6	27 04.7	23 14.2	14 39.0	21 45.8	0 54.1	1 01.8	9 23.3	8 55.2
28 Su	12 26 34	4 44 25	28 18 35	4♋51 38	22 54.2	24 17.6	27 25.8	23 39.2	14 44.6	21 38.4	0 59.0	1 05.2	9 24.4	8 57.5
29 M	12 30 31	5 43 20	11♋30 52	18 16 38	22 53.4	24 03.4	27 48.8	24 03.7	14 49.9	21 30.9	1 03.7	1 08.7	9 25.7	8 59.8
30 Tu	12 34 27	6 42 17	25 09 11	2♌08 41	22 50.8	23 41.7	28 13.5	24 27.8	14 54.8	21 23.4	1 08.4	1 12.2	9 26.9	9 02.2

LONGITUDE — October 1975

Day	Sid.Time	☉	0 hr ☽	Noon ☽	True ☊	☿	♀	♂	⚳	♃	♄	♅	♆	♇
1 W	12 38 24	7♎41 17	9♌15 05	16♌28 11	22♏46.3	23♎12.4	28♌40.0	24♊51.5	14♊59.4	21♈15.8	1♌13.0	1♏15.7	9♐28.2	9♎04.5
2 Th	12 42 21	8 40 19	23 47 33	1♍12 34	22R 40.4	22R 35.5	29 08.0	25 14.7	15 03.7	21R 08.1	1 17.5	1 19.3	9 29.5	9 06.8
3 F	12 46 17	9 39 22	8♍42 25	16 16 03	22 33.9	21 51.1	29 37.7	25 37.5	15 07.6	21 00.3	1 21.9	1 22.8	9 30.8	9 09.1
4 Sa	12 50 14	10 38 29	23 52 18	1♎29 52	22 27.5	20 59.7	0♍08.8	25 59.8	15 11.1	20 52.4	1 26.2	1 26.4	9 32.1	9 11.5
5 Su	12 54 10	11 37 37	9♎07 24	16 43 33	22 22.3	20 01.9	0 41.4	26 21.6	15 14.2	20 44.6	1 30.5	1 30.0	9 33.5	9 13.8
6 M	12 58 07	12 36 47	24 17 03	1♏46 42	22 18.9	18 58.7	1 15.4	26 42.9	15 17.0	20 36.6	1 34.6	1 33.6	9 34.9	9 16.1
7 Tu	13 02 03	13 35 59	9♏11 31	16 30 40	22D 17.3	17 51.3	1 50.8	27 03.7	15 19.5	20 28.6	1 38.7	1 37.2	9 36.3	9 18.5
8 W	13 06 00	14 35 13	23 43 32	0♐49 43	22 17.5	16 41.3	2 27.5	27 24.0	15 21.5	20 20.6	1 42.7	1 40.9	9 37.8	9 20.8
9 Th	13 09 56	15 34 29	7♐48 59	14 41 17	22 18.7	15 30.4	3 05.4	27 43.8	15 23.2	20 12.6	1 46.5	1 44.5	9 39.3	9 23.1
10 F	13 13 53	16 33 47	21 26 45	28 05 36	22 20.2	14 20.6	3 44.5	28 03.0	15 24.5	20 04.5	1 50.3	1 48.2	9 40.8	9 25.4
11 Sa	13 17 50	17 33 07	4♑38 11	11♑04 55	22R 21.3	13 13.8	4 24.8	28 21.7	15 25.4	19 56.4	1 54.0	1 51.8	9 42.3	9 27.7
12 Su	13 21 46	18 32 28	17 26 18	23 42 50	22 21.4	12 11.9	5 06.2	28 39.9	15R 26.0	19 48.3	1 57.6	1 55.5	9 43.9	9 30.1
13 M	13 25 43	19 31 51	29 55 03	6♒03 30	22 20.0	11 16.8	5 48.8	28 57.5	15 26.1	19 40.2	2 01.1	1 59.2	9 45.5	9 32.4
14 Tu	13 29 39	20 31 16	12♒08 42	18 11 11	22 17.1	10 30.0	6 32.3	29 14.5	15 25.9	19 32.1	2 04.5	2 02.9	9 47.1	9 34.7
15 W	13 33 36	21 30 42	24 11 26	0♓09 55	22 13.0	9 52.8	7 16.9	29 31.0	15 25.2	19 24.0	2 07.8	2 06.7	9 48.7	9 37.0
16 Th	13 37 32	22 30 11	6♓07 06	12 03 21	22 08.0	9 25.9	8 02.4	29 46.8	15 24.2	19 15.9	2 11.1	2 10.4	9 50.3	9 39.2
17 F	13 41 29	23 29 41	17 59 02	23 54 31	22 02.7	9D 10.0	8 48.9	0♋02.0	15 22.8	19 07.9	2 14.2	2 14.1	9 52.0	9 41.5
18 Sa	13 45 25	24 29 13	29 50 06	5♈46 03	21 57.7	9 05.2	9 36.3	0 16.7	15 21.0	18 59.8	2 17.2	2 17.8	9 53.7	9 43.8
19 Su	13 49 22	25 28 47	11♈42 38	17 40 04	21 53.5	9 11.5	10 24.5	0 30.7	15 18.8	18 51.8	2 20.1	2 21.6	9 55.4	9 46.1
20 M	13 53 18	26 28 23	23 38 36	29 38 26	21 50.5	9 28.5	11 13.7	0 44.0	15 16.2	18 43.9	2 22.9	2 25.3	9 57.2	9 48.3
21 Tu	13 57 15	27 28 01	5♉39 46	11♉42 49	21D 48.8	9 55.7	12 03.6	0 56.7	15 13.3	18 36.0	2 25.6	2 29.1	9 58.9	9 50.6
22 W	14 01 12	28 27 41	17 47 49	23 54 59	21 48.4	10 32.3	12 54.3	1 08.8	15 09.9	18 28.1	2 28.2	2 32.9	10 00.7	9 52.8
23 Th	14 05 08	29 27 24	0♊04 34	6♊16 50	21 49.1	11 17.5	13 45.8	1 20.1	15 06.1	18 20.3	2 30.7	2 36.6	10 02.5	9 55.0
24 F	14 09 05	0♏27 08	12 32 03	18 50 31	21 50.4	12 10.7	14 38.0	1 30.8	15 01.9	18 12.5	2 33.2	2 40.4	10 04.4	9 57.3
25 Sa	14 13 01	1 26 55	25 12 33	1♋38 27	21 52.0	13 10.8	15 31.0	1 40.7	14 57.4	18 04.9	2 35.5	2 44.2	10 06.2	9 59.5
26 Su	14 16 58	2 26 44	8♋08 33	14 43 08	21 53.3	14 17.1	16 24.6	1 49.9	14 52.4	17 57.2	2 37.7	2 47.9	10 08.1	10 01.7
27 M	14 20 54	3 26 35	21 22 31	28 06 55	21R 54.1	15 28.8	17 18.9	1 58.4	14 47.0	17 49.7	2 39.7	2 51.7	10 10.0	10 03.9
28 Tu	14 24 51	4 26 28	4♌56 32	11♌51 29	21 54.0	16 45.2	18 13.8	2 06.2	14 41.3	17 42.3	2 41.7	2 55.5	10 11.9	10 06.0
29 W	14 28 47	5 26 24	18 51 48	25 57 23	21 53.1	18 05.6	19 09.4	2 13.1	14 35.2	17 34.9	2 43.6	2 59.2	10 13.8	10 08.2
30 Th	14 32 44	6 26 21	3♍08 02	10♍23 23	21 51.6	19 29.3	20 05.5	2 19.3	14 28.6	17 27.6	2 45.4	3 03.0	10 15.7	10 10.4
31 F	14 36 41	7 26 21	17 42 56	25 06 04	21 49.8	20 55.9	21 02.2	2 24.7	14 21.7	17 20.5	2 47.0	3 06.8	10 17.7	10 12.5

Astro Data Dy Hr Mn	Planet Ingress Dy Hr Mn	Last Aspect Dy Hr Mn	☽ Ingress Dy Hr Mn	Last Aspect Dy Hr Mn	☽ Ingress Dy Hr Mn	☽ Phases & Eclipses Dy Hr Mn	Astro Data
♃♇♆ 3 12:03	♀ ♌R 2 15:34	2 22:43 ♅ □	♌ 2 23:08	2 8:33 ♀ ☌	♍ 2 10:03	5 19:19 ● 12♍36	1 September 1975
☽0S 6 5:56	♅ ♏ 8 5:16	4 23:15 ♅ ✶	♍ 4 23:29	4 3:08 ♂ □	♎ 4 9:39	12 11:59 ☽ 19♐06	Julian Day # 27637
♀D 18 1:46	♄ ♌ 17 4:57	6 21:01 ♄ ✶	♎ 6 22:38	6 3:41 ♂ △	♏ 6 9:09	20 11:50 ○ 26♓54	SVP 5♓35'43"
☽0N 19 20:40	☉ ♎ 23 15:55	8 21:25 ♄ □	♏ 8 22:46	6 11:41 ♄ □	♐ 8 10:35	28 11:46 ☾ 4♋44	GC 26♐30.0 ⚳ 2♈17.2R
☉0S 23 15:56		11 0:37 ♄ △	♐ 11 1:41	10 11:55 ♂ ☍	♑ 10 15:29		Eris 13♈47.7R ⚴ 6♌37.6
☿R 26 23:46	♀ ♍ 4 5:19	13 0:36 ♀ △	♑ 13 8:11	12 4:35 ♃ □	♒ 13 0:10	5 3:23 ● 11♎16	⚷ 27♈45.1R ⚵ 28♓59.5R
	♂ ♋ 17 8:44	15 17:35 ♄ ☍	♒ 15 17:51	15 10:40 ♂ △	♓ 15 11:40	12 1:15 ☽ 18♑06	☽ Mean ☊ 25♏42.1
☽0S 3 16:47	☉ ♏ 24 1:06	17 20:21 ♀ ☍	♓ 18 5:32	16 7:30 ♆ □	♈ 18 0:20	20 5:06 ○ 26♈11	
♄□♅ 4 18:04		20 11:50 ☉ ☍	♈ 20 18:07	20 5:06 ☉ ☍	♉ 20 12:43	27 22:07 ☾ 3♌52	1 October 1975
⚳R 13 9:26		22 22:26 ♀ △	♉ 23 6:43	21 12:44 ♀ △	♊ 22 23:51		Julian Day # 27667
☽0N 17 2:29		25 11:18 ♀ □	♊ 25 18:13	24 10:49 ♃ ✶	♋ 25 8:57		SVP 5♓35'41"
♄□♅ 17 14:05		27 21:59 ♀ ✶	♋ 28 3:07	26 17:48 ♃ □	♌ 27 15:20		GC 26♐30.0 ⚳ 24♓33.0R
☿D 18 10:15		29 21:52 ☿ □	♌ 30 8:20	28 21:56 ♃ △	♍ 29 18:47		Eris 13♈30.9R ⚴ 21♌02.4
☽0S 31 2:15				31 4:57 ♀ ☌	♎ 31 19:55		⚷ 26♈41.0R ⚵ 21♓41.7R
							☽ Mean ☊ 24♏06.7

November 1975 LONGITUDE

Day	Sid.Time	☉	0 hr ☽	Noon ☽	True ☊	☿	♀	♂	⚳	♃	♄	♅	♆	♇
1 Sa	14 40 37	8♏26 23	2♎31 58	9♎59 45	21♏48.0	22♎24.8	21♍59.5	2♋29.3	14♊14.4	17♈13.4	2♌48.6	3♏10.5	10♐19.6	10♎14.6
2 Su	14 44 34	9 26 27	17 28 26	24 56 58	21R46.7	23 55.7	22 57.3	2 33.1	14R06.7	17R06.5	2 50.0	3 14.3	10 21.6	10 16.7
3 M	14 48 30	10 26 33	2♏24 17	9♏49 22	21D45.8	25 28.2	23 55.6	2 36.1	13 58.7	16 59.7	2 51.3	3 18.0	10 23.6	10 18.8
4 Tu	14 52 27	11 26 41	17 11 13	24 28 58	21 45.7	27 01.9	24 54.4	2 38.2	13 50.3	16 53.0	2 52.6	3 21.8	10 25.7	10 20.9
5 W	14 56 23	12 26 51	1♐41 51	8♐49 14	21 46.0	28 36.6	25 53.7	2 39.5	13 41.5	16 46.4	2 53.7	3 25.5	10 27.7	10 23.0
6 Th	15 00 20	13 27 03	15 50 41	22 45 51	21 46.7	0♏12.1	26 53.4	2R39.9	13 32.4	16 40.0	2 54.7	3 29.3	10 29.8	10 25.0
7 F	15 04 16	14 27 16	29 34 38	6♑16 59	21 47.4	1 48.2	27 53.6	2 39.5	13 23.0	16 33.7	2 55.5	3 33.0	10 31.8	10 27.0
8 Sa	15 08 13	15 27 30	12♑53 02	19 23 02	21 48.1	3 24.7	28 54.2	2 38.2	13 13.2	16 27.5	2 56.3	3 36.7	10 33.9	10 29.0
9 Su	15 12 10	16 27 46	25 47 17	2♒06 13	21 48.6	5 01.5	29 55.2	2 36.0	13 03.1	16 21.5	2 57.0	3 40.4	10 36.0	10 31.0
10 M	15 16 06	17 28 04	8♒20 18	14 30 03	21R48.8	6 38.4	0♎56.7	2 33.0	12 52.7	16 15.7	2 57.5	3 44.1	10 38.1	10 33.0
11 Tu	15 20 03	18 28 23	20 36 01	26 38 47	21 48.7	8 15.4	1 58.5	2 29.1	12 41.9	16 10.0	2 57.9	3 47.8	10 40.2	10 34.9
12 W	15 23 59	19 28 43	2♓38 54	8♓36 57	21 48.6	9 52.4	3 00.7	2 24.3	12 30.9	16 04.4	2 58.3	3 51.5	10 42.4	10 36.9
13 Th	15 27 56	20 29 05	14 33 31	20 29 08	21 48.4	11 29.4	4 03.3	2 18.7	12 19.6	15 59.0	2 58.5	3 55.1	10 44.5	10 38.8
14 F	15 31 52	21 29 28	26 24 19	2♈19 35	21D48.3	13 06.3	5 06.2	2 12.2	12 08.0	15 53.8	2R58.5	3 58.8	10 46.7	10 40.7
15 Sa	15 35 49	22 29 52	8♈15 24	14 12 12	21 48.3	14 43.1	6 09.5	2 04.8	11 56.2	15 48.8	2 58.5	4 02.4	10 48.8	10 42.5
16 Su	15 39 45	23 30 18	20 10 21	26 10 14	21 48.4	16 19.7	7 13.2	1 56.5	11 44.1	15 43.9	2 58.4	4 06.0	10 51.0	10 44.4
17 M	15 43 42	24 30 46	2♉12 10	8♉16 25	21 48.6	17 56.1	8 17.1	1 47.4	11 31.8	15 39.2	2 58.1	4 09.6	10 53.2	10 46.2
18 Tu	15 47 39	25 31 15	14 23 14	20 32 48	21R48.7	19 32.3	9 21.4	1 37.4	11 19.2	15 34.7	2 57.8	4 13.2	10 55.4	10 48.0
19 W	15 51 35	26 31 46	26 45 17	3♊00 50	21 48.6	21 08.4	10 26.0	1 26.6	11 06.5	15 30.4	2 57.3	4 16.8	10 57.6	10 49.8
20 Th	15 55 32	27 32 18	9♊19 33	15 41 29	21 48.2	22 44.2	11 31.0	1 14.9	10 53.5	15 26.2	2 56.7	4 20.4	10 59.8	10 51.6
21 F	15 59 28	28 32 52	22 06 44	28 35 17	21 47.5	24 19.8	12 36.2	1 02.4	10 40.4	15 22.3	2 56.1	4 23.9	11 02.0	10 53.3
22 Sa	16 03 25	29 33 27	5♋07 13	11♋42 29	21 46.6	25 55.3	13 41.7	0 49.1	10 27.1	15 18.5	2 55.2	4 27.4	11 04.2	10 55.0
23 Su	16 07 21	0♐34 04	18 21 08	25 03 08	21 45.5	27 30.6	14 47.4	0 35.0	10 13.6	15 14.9	2 54.3	4 30.9	11 06.4	10 56.7
24 M	16 11 18	1 34 43	1♌48 28	8♌37 08	21 44.5	29 05.6	15 53.5	0 20.1	10 00.0	15 11.5	2 53.3	4 34.4	11 08.7	10 58.4
25 Tu	16 15 14	2 35 23	15 29 04	22 24 12	21D43.9	0♐40.6	16 59.8	0 04.4	9 46.3	15 08.3	2 52.2	4 37.8	11 10.9	11 00.0
26 W	16 19 11	3 36 05	29 22 29	6♍23 46	21 43.7	2 15.3	18 06.4	29♊47.9	9 32.4	15 05.3	2 50.9	4 41.3	11 13.1	11 01.6
27 Th	16 23 08	4 36 49	13♍27 55	20 34 42	21 44.1	3 50.0	19 13.2	29 30.8	9 18.5	15 02.5	2 49.6	4 44.7	11 15.4	11 03.2
28 F	16 27 04	5 37 34	27 43 52	4♎55 05	21 45.0	5 24.5	20 20.2	29 12.9	9 04.5	14 59.9	2 48.1	4 48.1	11 17.6	11 04.8
29 Sa	16 31 01	6 38 21	12♎07 57	19 22 01	21 46.2	6 58.9	21 27.5	28 54.3	8 50.4	14 57.5	2 46.5	4 51.4	11 19.9	11 06.3
30 Su	16 34 57	7 39 09	26 36 45	3♏51 33	21 47.3	8 33.2	22 35.0	28 35.2	8 36.3	14 55.3	2 44.8	4 54.7	11 22.2	11 07.8

December 1975 LONGITUDE

Day	Sid.Time	☉	0 hr ☽	Noon ☽	True ☊	☿	♀	♂	⚳	♃	♄	♅	♆	♇
1 M	16 38 54	8♐39 59	11♏05 49	18♏18 52	21♏47.8	10♐07.4	23♎42.7	28♊15.4	8♊22.1	14♈53.3	2♌43.0	4♏58.1	11♐24.4	11♎09.3
2 Tu	16 42 50	9 40 50	25 30 00	2♐38 35	21R47.6	11 41.5	24 50.6	27R55.0	8R08.0	14R51.6	2R41.1	5 01.3	11 26.7	11 10.7
3 W	16 46 47	10 41 42	9♐43 57	16 45 30	21 46.3	13 15.6	25 58.7	27 34.2	7 53.8	14 50.0	2 39.1	5 04.6	11 28.9	11 12.1
4 Th	16 50 43	11 42 35	23 42 44	0♑35 12	21 44.1	14 49.7	27 07.1	27 12.8	7 39.7	14 48.6	2 37.0	5 07.8	11 31.2	11 13.5
5 F	16 54 40	12 43 30	7♑22 33	14 04 35	21 41.0	16 23.7	28 15.6	26 51.0	7 25.7	14 47.4	2 34.8	5 11.0	11 33.5	11 14.9
6 Sa	16 58 37	13 44 25	20 41 09	27 12 16	21 37.5	17 57.8	29 24.2	26 28.9	7 11.7	14 46.5	2 32.5	5 14.2	11 35.7	11 16.2
7 Su	17 02 33	14 45 21	3♒38 02	9♒58 40	21 34.1	19 31.8	0♏33.1	26 06.4	6 57.8	14 45.8	2 30.1	5 17.3	11 38.0	11 17.5
8 M	17 06 30	15 46 18	16 14 26	22 25 44	21 31.3	21 05.8	1 42.1	25 43.6	6 44.0	14 45.2	2 27.6	5 20.4	11 40.3	11 18.8
9 Tu	17 10 26	16 47 15	28 33 02	4♓36 48	21 29.4	22 39.9	2 51.3	25 20.5	6 30.3	14 44.9	2 25.0	5 23.5	11 42.5	11 20.0
10 W	17 14 23	17 48 13	10♓37 36	16 36 02	21D28.7	24 14.0	4 00.6	24 57.3	6 16.7	14D44.8	2 22.2	5 26.6	11 44.8	11 21.3
11 Th	17 18 19	18 49 12	22 32 42	28 28 13	21 29.1	25 48.1	5 10.1	24 33.9	6 03.3	14 44.9	2 19.4	5 29.6	11 47.0	11 22.4
12 F	17 22 16	19 50 11	4♈23 13	10♈18 20	21 30.5	27 22.3	6 19.8	24 10.5	5 50.1	14 45.2	2 16.5	5 32.5	11 49.3	11 23.6
13 Sa	17 26 12	20 51 11	16 14 11	22 11 20	21 32.3	28 56.5	7 29.6	23 47.0	5 37.0	14 45.7	2 13.5	5 35.5	11 51.5	11 24.7
14 Su	17 30 09	21 52 11	28 10 23	4♉11 50	21 34.1	0♑30.8	8 39.5	23 23.5	5 24.2	14 46.5	2 10.5	5 38.4	11 53.7	11 25.8
15 M	17 34 06	22 53 13	10♉16 11	16 23 52	21R35.2	2 05.1	9 49.6	23 00.1	5 11.5	14 47.4	2 07.3	5 41.3	11 56.0	11 26.8
16 Tu	17 38 02	23 54 14	22 35 14	28 50 36	21 35.1	3 39.4	10 59.8	22 36.8	4 59.1	14 48.5	2 04.0	5 44.1	11 58.2	11 27.9
17 W	17 41 59	24 55 16	5♊10 12	11♊34 11	21 33.4	5 13.8	12 10.2	22 13.7	4 46.9	14 49.9	2 00.7	5 46.9	12 00.4	11 28.9
18 Th	17 45 55	25 56 19	18 02 37	24 35 29	21 29.9	6 48.1	13 20.6	21 50.7	4 34.9	14 51.4	1 57.2	5 49.6	12 02.6	11 29.8
19 F	17 49 52	26 57 23	1♋12 40	7♋54 01	21 24.9	8 22.4	14 31.3	21 28.1	4 23.3	14 53.2	1 53.7	5 52.4	12 04.9	11 30.7
20 Sa	17 53 48	27 58 27	14 39 17	21 28 08	21 18.9	9 56.7	15 42.0	21 05.7	4 11.9	14 55.2	1 50.1	5 55.1	12 07.1	11 31.6
21 Su	17 57 45	28 59 31	28 20 13	5♌15 09	21 12.5	11 30.8	16 52.8	20 43.6	4 00.7	14 57.3	1 46.5	5 57.7	12 09.2	11 32.5
22 M	18 01 42	0♑00 37	12♌12 31	19 11 54	21 06.6	13 04.7	18 03.8	20 22.0	3 49.9	14 59.7	1 42.7	6 00.3	12 11.4	11 33.3
23 Tu	18 05 38	1 01 43	26 12 53	3♍15 06	21 02.0	14 38.4	19 14.9	20 00.7	3 39.4	15 02.3	1 38.9	6 02.9	12 13.6	11 34.1
24 W	18 09 35	2 02 49	10♍18 13	17 21 54	20 59.1	16 11.7	20 26.1	19 39.9	3 29.2	15 05.0	1 35.0	6 05.4	12 15.8	11 34.9
25 Th	18 13 31	3 03 57	24 25 55	1♎30 01	20D58.1	17 44.7	21 37.4	19 19.6	3 19.3	15 08.0	1 31.0	6 07.9	12 17.9	11 35.6
26 F	18 17 28	4 05 05	8♎34 00	15 37 43	20 58.6	19 17.0	22 48.8	18 59.9	3 09.7	15 11.2	1 27.0	6 10.3	12 20.1	11 36.3
27 Sa	18 21 24	5 06 13	22 41 01	29 43 43	20 59.8	20 48.7	24 00.3	18 40.7	3 00.5	15 14.5	1 22.9	6 12.7	12 22.2	11 36.9
28 Su	18 25 21	6 07 23	6♏45 40	13♏46 42	21R01.0	22 19.5	25 12.0	18 22.1	2 51.7	15 18.1	1 18.7	6 15.0	12 24.3	11 37.5
29 M	18 29 17	7 08 32	20 46 34	27 45 04	21 01.0	23 49.2	26 23.7	18 04.2	2 43.2	15 21.8	1 14.4	6 17.3	12 26.4	11 38.1
30 Tu	18 33 14	8 09 43	4♐41 54	11♐36 45	20 59.0	25 17.6	27 35.4	17 46.9	2 35.1	15 25.8	1 10.1	6 19.6	12 28.5	11 38.7
31 W	18 37 11	9 10 53	18 29 18	25 19 12	20 54.7	26 44.4	28 47.3	17 30.3	2 27.4	15 29.9	1 05.8	6 21.8	12 30.6	11 39.2

Astro Data Dy Hr Mn	Planet Ingress Dy Hr Mn	Last Aspect Dy Hr Mn	☽ Ingress Dy Hr Mn	Last Aspect Dy Hr Mn	☽ Ingress Dy Hr Mn	☽ Phases & Eclipses Dy Hr Mn
♂R 6 12:01	☿ ♏ 6 8:58	2 10:10 ☿ ☌	♏ 2 20:07	30 13:45 ♅ ☌	♐ 2 7:33	3 13:05 ● 10♏29
♀0S 12 2:56	♀ ♎ 9 13:52	4 12:45 ♀ ⚹	♐ 4 21:10	4 6:15 ♂ ☍	♑ 4 10:58	3 13:15:06 ◐ P 0.959
☽0N 13 9:06	☉ ♐ 22 22:31	6 19:49 ♀ □	♑ 7 0:45	6 16:29 ♀ □	♒ 6 17:12	10 18:21 ☽ 17♒44
♄R 14 19:25	☿ ♐ 25 1:44	9 7:28 ♀ △	♒ 9 7:59	8 18:15 ♂ △	♓ 9 2:52	18 22:28 ○ 25♉58
☽0S 27 9:29	♂ ♊R 25 18:30	10 18:21 ☉ □	♓ 11 18:42	11 5:46 ☿ □	♈ 11 15:06	18 22:23 ◑ T 1.064
		13 12:00 ☉ △	♈ 14 7:17	14 3:34 ☿ △	♉ 14 3:39	26 6:52 ☾ 3♍23
♃D 10 12:39	♀ ♏ 7 0:29	15 15:13 ♃ ☌	♉ 16 19:38	14 21:46 ♀ ☍	♊ 16 14:12	
☽0N 10 17:15	☿ ♑ 14 4:10	18 22:28 ☉ ☍	♊ 19 6:14	18 14:39 ☉ ☍	♋ 18 21:49	3 0:50 ● 10♐13
☽0S 24 15:30	☉ ♑ 22 11:46	20 11:32 ♃ ⚹	♋ 21 14:36	20 0:53 ♀ △	♌ 21 2:54	10 14:39 ☽ 17♓55
		23 16:58 ☿ △	♌ 23 20:48	22 13:57 ♂ ⚹	♍ 23 6:28	18 14:39 ○ 26♊03
		26 0:57 ♂ ⚹	♍ 26 1:04	24 17:42 ♀ ⚹	♎ 25 9:27	25 14:52 ☾ 3♎11
		28 2:41 ♂ □	♎ 28 3:48	26 18:58 ☿ □	♏ 27 12:28	
		30 3:27 ♂ △	♏ 30 5:37	29 9:27 ♀ ☌	♐ 29 15:53	
				30 22:33 ♂ ☍	♑ 31 20:16	

Astro Data

1 November 1975
Julian Day # 27698
SVP 5♓35'38"
GC 26♐30.1 ⚳ 18♓25.5R
Eris 13♈12.4R ⚴ 3♍58.3
⚷ 25♈16.1R ⚶ 17♓53.6R
☽ Mean ☊ 22♏28.2

1 December 1975
Julian Day # 27728
SVP 5♓35'34"
GC 26♐30.2 ⚳ 18♓10.8
Eris 12♈58.8R ⚴ 13♍36.8
⚷ 24♈06.7R ⚶ 20♓47.0
☽ Mean ☊ 20♏52.9

LONGITUDE — January 1976

Day	Sid.Time	☉	0 hr ☽	Noon☽	True☊	☿	♀	♂	⚳	♃	♄	♅	♆	♇
1 Th	18 41 07	10♑12 04	2♑06 06	8♑49 39	20♏48.0	28♑09.3	29♏59.3	17♊14.4	2♊20.0	15♈34.3	1♌01.4	6♏24.0	12♐32.6	11♎39.7
2 F	18 45 04	11 13 15	15 29 34	22 05 33	20R39.4	29 31.9	1♐11.3	16R59.3	2R13.1	15 38.8	0R56.9	6 26.1	12 34.7	11 40.1
3 Sa	18 49 00	12 14 26	28 37 25	5♒05 02	20 29.6	0♒51.6	2 23.4	16 44.9	2 06.5	15 43.5	0 52.4	6 28.2	12 36.7	11 40.5
4 Su	18 52 57	13 15 36	11♒28 19	17 47 18	20 19.6	2 08.2	3 35.6	16 31.3	2 00.4	15 48.4	0 47.9	6 30.2	12 38.8	11 40.9
5 M	18 56 53	14 16 47	24 02 06	0♓12 54	20 10.6	3 20.9	4 47.8	16 18.5	1 54.6	15 53.5	0 43.2	6 32.2	12 40.8	11 41.2
6 Tu	19 00 50	15 17 57	6♓20 00	12 23 44	20 03.2	4 29.1	6 00.1	16 06.5	1 49.3	15 58.7	0 38.6	6 34.1	12 42.7	11 41.5
7 W	19 04 46	16 19 07	18 24 33	24 22 55	19 58.1	5 32.1	7 12.5	15 55.3	1 44.3	16 04.2	0 33.9	6 36.0	12 44.7	11 41.8
8 Th	19 08 43	17 20 16	0♈19 24	6♈14 35	19 55.3	6 29.2	8 24.9	15 44.9	1 39.8	16 09.8	0 29.2	6 37.8	12 46.7	11 42.0
9 F	19 12 40	18 21 25	12 09 06	18 03 36	19D54.5	7 19.4	9 37.4	15 35.3	1 35.7	16 15.6	0 24.4	6 39.6	12 48.6	11 42.2
10 Sa	19 16 36	19 22 34	23 58 46	29 55 16	19 55.0	8 02.0	10 50.0	15 26.5	1 32.0	16 21.6	0 19.6	6 41.4	12 50.5	11 42.4
11 Su	19 20 33	20 23 42	5♉53 49	11♉55 04	19R55.8	8 35.9	12 02.6	15 18.6	1 28.7	16 27.7	0 14.8	6 43.0	12 52.4	11 42.5
12 M	19 24 29	21 24 49	17 59 39	24 08 10	19 56.0	9 00.4	13 15.3	15 11.5	1 25.9	16 34.0	0 10.0	6 44.7	12 54.3	11 42.6
13 Tu	19 28 26	22 25 56	0♊21 12	6♊39 13	19 54.5	9R14.6	14 28.0	15 05.3	1 23.4	16 40.5	0 05.1	6 46.3	12 56.2	11R42.6
14 W	19 32 22	23 27 03	13 02 37	19 31 43	19 50.6	9 17.7	15 40.8	14 59.8	1 21.4	16 47.2	0 00.3	6 47.8	12 58.0	11 42.6
15 Th	19 36 19	24 28 09	26 06 41	2♋47 34	19 44.2	9 09.4	16 53.6	14 55.2	1 19.8	16 54.0	29♋55.4	6 49.3	12 59.8	11 42.6
16 F	19 40 15	25 29 14	9♋34 17	16 26 37	19 35.2	8 49.2	18 06.5	14 51.3	1 18.6	17 00.9	29 50.5	6 50.7	13 01.6	11 42.6
17 Sa	19 44 12	26 30 19	23 24 11	0♌26 28	19 24.5	8 17.4	19 19.4	14 48.3	1 17.8	17 08.1	29 45.5	6 52.1	13 03.4	11 42.5
18 Su	19 48 09	27 31 23	7♌32 49	14 42 31	19 13.2	7 34.5	20 32.4	14 46.1	1D17.5	17 15.4	29 40.6	6 53.4	13 05.1	11 42.3
19 M	19 52 05	28 32 27	21 54 46	29 08 43	19 02.5	6 41.3	21 45.4	14 44.6	1 17.5	17 22.8	29 35.7	6 54.6	13 06.9	11 42.2
20 Tu	19 56 02	29 33 30	6♍23 33	13♍38 28	18 53.5	5 39.2	22 58.5	14D43.9	1 18.0	17 30.4	29 30.7	6 55.9	13 08.6	11 42.0
21 W	19 59 58	0♒34 33	20 52 45	28 05 45	18 47.1	4 30.1	24 11.6	14 44.0	1 18.8	17 38.2	29 25.8	6 57.0	13 10.3	11 41.8
22 Th	20 03 55	1 35 35	5♎16 57	12♎25 57	18 43.4	3 16.1	25 24.8	14 44.8	1 20.1	17 46.1	29 20.8	6 58.1	13 11.9	11 41.5
23 F	20 07 51	2 36 37	19 32 27	26 36 14	18D42.1	1 59.5	26 38.0	14 46.4	1 21.8	17 54.2	29 15.9	6 59.2	13 13.6	11 41.2
24 Sa	20 11 48	3 37 39	3♏37 13	10♏35 22	18R42.0	0 42.5	27 51.3	14 48.8	1 23.8	18 02.4	29 11.0	7 00.2	13 15.2	11 40.9
25 Su	20 15 44	4 38 40	17 30 43	24 23 18	18 42.0	29♑27.6	29 04.6	14 51.8	1 26.3	18 10.7	29 06.1	7 01.1	13 16.8	11 40.5
26 M	20 19 41	5 39 41	1♐13 13	8♐00 31	18 40.7	28 16.7	0♑17.9	14 55.6	1 29.1	18 19.2	29 01.2	7 02.0	13 18.3	11 40.1
27 Tu	20 23 38	6 40 41	14 45 16	21 27 31	18 37.1	27 11.5	1 31.3	15 00.1	1 32.4	18 27.9	28 56.3	7 02.8	13 19.9	11 39.7
28 W	20 27 34	7 41 41	28 07 14	4♑44 24	18 30.4	26 13.3	2 44.7	15 05.2	1 36.0	18 36.6	28 51.4	7 03.6	13 21.4	11 39.2
29 Th	20 31 31	8 42 40	11♑18 58	17 50 50	18 20.6	25 23.0	3 58.1	15 11.1	1 40.1	18 45.6	28 46.6	7 04.3	13 22.9	11 38.7
30 F	20 35 27	9 43 38	24 19 54	0♒46 02	18 08.2	24 41.2	5 11.6	15 17.6	1 44.5	18 54.6	28 41.8	7 05.0	13 24.3	11 38.2
31 Sa	20 39 24	10 44 35	7♒09 09	13 29 10	17 54.2	24 08.2	6 25.0	15 24.8	1 49.3	19 03.8	28 37.0	7 05.6	13 25.8	11 37.6

LONGITUDE — February 1976

Day	Sid.Time	☉	0 hr ☽	Noon☽	True☊	☿	♀	♂	⚳	♃	♄	♅	♆	♇
1 Su	20 43 20	11♒45 31	19♒45 59	25♒59 37	17♏39.9	23♑43.9	7♑38.6	15♊32.7	1♊54.4	19♈13.1	28♋32.2	7♏06.2	13♐27.2	11♎37.0
2 M	20 47 17	12 46 25	2♓10 04	8♓17 27	17R26.4	23R28.2	8 52.1	15 41.2	2 00.0	19 22.6	28R27.5	7 06.7	13 28.5	11R36.4
3 Tu	20 51 13	13 47 19	14 21 54	20 23 38	17 14.9	23D20.8	10 05.6	15 50.3	2 05.9	19 32.2	28 22.8	7 07.1	13 29.9	11 35.7
4 W	20 55 10	14 48 11	26 22 56	2♈20 10	17 06.1	23 21.1	11 19.2	16 00.1	2 12.1	19 41.9	28 18.2	7 07.5	13 31.2	11 35.0
5 Th	20 59 07	15 49 02	8♈15 43	14 10 06	17 00.2	23 28.7	12 32.8	16 10.4	2 18.8	19 51.7	28 13.6	7 07.8	13 32.5	11 34.3
6 F	21 03 03	16 49 52	20 03 50	25 57 29	16 57.1	23 43.1	13 46.4	16 21.3	2 25.7	20 01.7	28 09.0	7 08.1	13 33.8	11 33.5
7 Sa	21 07 00	17 50 40	1♉51 42	7♉47 07	16 56.0	24 03.9	15 00.1	16 32.8	2 33.1	20 11.7	28 04.5	7 08.3	13 35.0	11 32.7
8 Su	21 10 56	18 51 27	13 44 26	19 44 21	16 55.9	24 30.4	16 13.7	16 44.9	2 40.7	20 21.9	28 00.1	7 08.5	13 36.2	11 31.9
9 M	21 14 53	19 52 12	25 47 35	1♊54 49	16 55.6	25 02.3	17 27.4	16 57.5	2 48.7	20 32.2	27 55.6	7 08.6	13 37.4	11 31.1
10 Tu	21 18 49	20 52 56	8♊06 43	14 23 57	16 53.9	25 39.0	18 41.1	17 10.7	2 57.1	20 42.7	27 51.3	7R08.6	13 38.5	11 30.2
11 W	21 22 46	21 53 38	20 47 03	27 16 31	16 50.1	26 20.3	19 54.8	17 24.3	3 05.8	20 53.2	27 47.0	7 08.6	13 39.6	11 29.3
12 Th	21 26 42	22 54 18	3♋52 44	10♋35 55	16 43.5	27 05.6	21 08.6	17 38.5	3 14.8	21 03.8	27 42.8	7 08.6	13 40.7	11 28.3
13 F	21 30 39	23 54 57	17 26 12	24 23 27	16 34.3	27 54.7	22 22.3	17 53.2	3 24.1	21 14.6	27 38.6	7 08.4	13 41.8	11 27.4
14 Sa	21 34 36	24 55 35	1♌27 25	8♌37 36	16 23.2	28 47.3	23 36.1	18 08.4	3 33.7	21 25.4	27 34.5	7 08.3	13 42.8	11 26.4
15 Su	21 38 32	25 56 11	15 53 19	23 13 45	16 11.2	29 43.1	24 49.8	18 24.0	3 43.7	21 36.4	27 30.4	7 08.0	13 43.8	11 25.4
16 M	21 42 29	26 56 45	0♍37 52	8♍04 35	15 59.7	0♒41.8	26 03.6	18 40.1	3 53.9	21 47.5	27 26.5	7 07.8	13 44.8	11 24.3
17 Tu	21 46 25	27 57 18	15 32 44	23 01 08	15 50.0	1 43.1	27 17.5	18 56.6	4 04.5	21 58.6	27 22.6	7 07.4	13 45.7	11 23.2
18 W	21 50 22	28 57 49	0♎28 40	7♎54 20	15 42.9	2 47.0	28 31.3	19 13.6	4 15.3	22 09.9	27 18.7	7 07.0	13 46.6	11 22.2
19 Th	21 54 18	29 58 19	15 17 12	22 36 34	15 38.6	3 53.3	29 45.1	19 31.0	4 26.5	22 21.2	27 15.0	7 06.6	13 47.4	11 21.0
20 F	21 58 15	0♓58 48	29 51 51	7♏02 38	15D36.9	5 01.6	0♒59.0	19 48.9	4 37.9	22 32.7	27 11.3	7 06.1	13 48.3	11 19.9
21 Sa	22 02 11	1 59 16	14♏08 41	21 09 54	15R36.8	6 12.0	2 12.9	20 07.1	4 49.6	22 44.3	27 07.7	7 05.5	13 49.1	11 18.7
22 Su	22 06 08	2 59 42	28 06 18	4♐57 58	15 36.9	7 24.4	3 26.7	20 25.7	5 01.6	22 55.9	27 04.1	7 04.9	13 49.8	11 17.5
23 M	22 10 05	4 00 08	11♐45 06	18 27 55	15 36.1	8 38.5	4 40.7	20 44.8	5 13.9	23 07.6	27 00.7	7 04.3	13 50.6	11 16.3
24 Tu	22 14 01	5 00 31	25 06 40	1♑41 36	15 33.2	9 54.3	5 54.6	21 04.2	5 26.5	23 19.5	26 57.3	7 03.6	13 51.3	11 15.0
25 W	22 17 58	6 00 54	8♑12 57	14 40 59	15 27.6	11 11.6	7 08.5	21 24.0	5 39.3	23 31.4	26 54.1	7 02.8	13 52.0	11 13.8
26 Th	22 21 54	7 01 15	21 05 52	27 27 48	15 19.2	12 30.6	8 22.4	21 44.1	5 52.3	23 43.4	26 50.9	7 02.0	13 52.6	11 12.5
27 F	22 25 51	8 01 34	3♒46 55	10♒03 22	15 08.4	13 51.0	9 36.4	22 04.6	6 05.7	23 55.4	26 47.8	7 01.1	13 53.2	11 11.2
28 Sa	22 29 47	9 01 52	16 17 14	22 28 36	14 56.1	15 12.7	10 50.3	22 25.5	6 19.3	24 07.6	26 44.8	7 00.2	13 53.8	11 09.8
29 Su	22 33 44	10 02 08	28 37 33	4♓44 11	14 43.4	16 35.9	12 04.3	22 46.7	6 33.1	24 19.8	26 41.8	6 59.3	13 54.3	11 08.5

Astro Data (Dy Hr Mn)

	Dy Hr Mn
☽ 0N	7 2:34
☿ R	14 6:41
♇ R	14 11:41
⚳ D	18 21:22
♂ D	20 21:27
☽ 0S	20 22:29
♄□♆	2 7:56
☽ 0N	3 11:40
☿ D	3 22:57
♅ R	10 22:11
☽ 0S	17 7:46

Planet Ingress

		Dy Hr Mn
♀	♐	1 12:14
☿	♒	2 20:22
♄	♋R	14 13:16
☉	♒	20 22:25
☿	♑R	25 1:30
♀	♑	26 6:09
☿	♒	15 19:03
☉	♓	19 12:40
♀	♒	19 16:50

Last Aspect / ☽ Ingress (January)

Last Aspect Dy Hr Mn		☽ Ingress Dy Hr Mn
2 0:13	♃ □	♒ 3 2:33
4 9:38	♂ △	♓ 5 11:35
6 19:17	♂ □	♈ 7 23:21
9 12:40	☉ □	♉ 10 12:10
12 6:13	☉ △	♊ 12 23:19
14 6:54	♃ ⚹	♋ 15 7:00
17 10:51	♄ ☌	♌ 17 11:15
18 22:37	♀ △	♍ 19 13:25
21 14:13	♄ ⚹	♎ 21 15:10
23 16:31	♄ □	♏ 23 17:48
25 20:13	♄ △	♐ 25 21:51
27 6:34	♃ △	♑ 28 3:24
30 8:09	♄ ☍	♒ 30 10:34

Last Aspect / ☽ Ingress (February)

Last Aspect Dy Hr Mn		☽ Ingress Dy Hr Mn
31 22:47	♃ ⚹	♓ 1 19:47
4 3:55	♄ △	♈ 4 7:17
6 16:26	♄ □	♉ 6 20:13
9 4:15	♄ ⚹	♊ 9 8:16
11 1:13	☉ △	♋ 11 16:59
13 18:23	☿ ☍	♌ 13 21:32
15 16:43	☉ ☍	♍ 15 22:59
17 19:29	♀ △	♎ 17 23:14
19 19:38	♄ □	♏ 20 0:14
21 22:16	♄ △	♐ 22 3:18
23 20:32	♃ △	♑ 24 8:54
26 10:50	♄ ☍	♒ 26 16:48
28 15:16	♃ ⚹	♓ 29 2:42

☽ Phases & Eclipses

Dy Hr Mn	
1 14:40	● 10♑19
9 12:40	☽ 18♈23
17 4:47	○ 26♋12
23 23:04	☾ 3♏05
31 6:20	● 10♒30
8 10:05	☽ 18♉47
15 16:43	○ 26♌08
22 8:16	☾ 2♐50
29 23:25	● 10♓31

Astro Data

1 January 1976
Julian Day # 27759
SVP 5♓35'28"
GC 26♐30.2 ⚴ 23♓22.2
Eris 12♈53.6 ⚵ 18♍56.0
⚷ 23♈35.3R ⚶ 28♓48.1
☽ Mean ☊ 19♏14.4

1 February 1976
Julian Day # 27790
SVP 5♓35'23"
GC 26♐30.3 ⚴ 2♈22.6
Eris 12♈59.1 ⚵ 17♍35.1R
⚷ 23♈57.1 ⚶ 9♈48.2
☽ Mean ☊ 17♏35.9

March 1976 LONGITUDE

Day	Sid.Time	☉	0 hr ☽	Noon ☽	True ☊	☿	♀	♂	⚳	♃	♄	♅	♆	♇
1 M	22 37 40	11♓02 22	10♓48 33	16♓50 48	14♏31.4	18♒00.3	13♒18.3	23♊08.3	6♊47.2	24♈32.2	26♋39.0	6♏58.2	13♐54.8	11♎07.1
2 Tu	22 41 37	12 02 34	22 51 02	28 49 27	14R 21.1	19 26.0	14 32.2	23 30.1	7 01.6	24 44.6	26R 36.3	6R 57.2	13 55.3	11R 05.7
3 W	22 45 34	13 02 45	4♈46 14	10♈41 38	14 13.2	20 53.0	15 46.2	23 52.3	7 16.2	24 57.0	26 33.6	6 56.1	13 55.7	11 04.3
4 Th	22 49 30	14 02 53	16 35 58	22 29 34	14 08.0	22 21.2	17 00.2	24 14.9	7 31.0	25 09.6	26 31.1	6 54.9	13 56.1	11 02.9
5 F	22 53 27	15 03 00	28 22 51	4♉16 16	14D 05.5	23 50.6	18 14.1	24 37.7	7 46.0	25 22.2	26 28.7	6 53.7	13 56.5	11 01.4
6 Sa	22 57 23	16 03 05	10♉10 18	16 05 30	14 04.9	25 21.2	19 28.1	25 00.8	8 01.3	25 34.9	26 26.3	6 52.4	13 56.8	11 00.0
7 Su	23 01 20	17 03 07	22 02 28	28 01 47	14 05.6	26 52.9	20 42.1	25 24.2	8 16.8	25 47.6	26 24.1	6 51.1	13 57.1	10 58.5
8 M	23 05 16	18 03 07	4♊04 07	10♊10 07	14R 06.5	28 25.8	21 56.1	25 47.9	8 32.5	26 00.5	26 22.0	6 49.8	13 57.4	10 57.0
9 Tu	23 09 13	19 03 06	16 20 26	22 35 45	14 06.7	29 59.9	23 10.1	26 11.8	8 48.5	26 13.4	26 19.9	6 48.4	13 57.6	10 55.5
10 W	23 13 09	20 03 02	28 56 39	5♋23 44	14 05.4	1♓35.1	24 24.0	26 36.1	9 04.6	26 26.3	26 18.0	6 46.9	13 57.8	10 54.0
11 Th	23 17 06	21 02 56	11♋57 28	18 38 18	14 02.1	3 11.5	25 38.0	27 00.5	9 21.0	26 39.3	26 16.2	6 45.4	13 58.0	10 52.4
12 F	23 21 03	22 02 47	25 26 28	2♌22 06	13 56.6	4 49.0	26 52.0	27 25.3	9 37.5	26 52.4	26 14.4	6 43.9	13 58.1	10 50.9
13 Sa	23 24 59	23 02 37	9♌25 08	16 35 19	13 49.6	6 27.8	28 06.0	27 50.3	9 54.3	27 05.5	26 12.8	6 42.3	13 58.2	10 49.3
14 Su	23 28 56	24 02 24	23 52 11	1♍15 02	13 41.7	8 07.7	29 20.0	28 15.5	10 11.3	27 18.7	26 11.3	6 40.7	13 58.3	10 47.7
15 M	23 32 52	25 02 09	8♍42 59	16 14 58	13 34.0	9 48.8	0♓33.9	28 40.9	10 28.4	27 32.0	26 09.9	6 39.0	13R 58.3	10 46.2
16 Tu	23 36 49	26 01 52	23 49 47	1♎26 08	13 27.4	11 31.0	1 47.9	29 06.6	10 45.7	27 45.3	26 08.6	6 37.4	13 58.3	10 44.6
17 W	23 40 45	27 01 33	9♎02 42	16 38 11	13 22.8	13 14.6	3 01.9	29 32.5	11 03.3	27 58.6	26 07.4	6 35.6	13 58.3	10 42.9
18 Th	23 44 42	28 01 12	24 11 22	1♏41 11	13D 20.3	14 59.3	4 15.9	29 58.6	11 21.0	28 12.0	26 06.4	6 33.8	13 58.2	10 41.3
19 F	23 48 38	29 00 50	9♏06 44	16 27 14	13 19.8	16 45.3	5 29.9	0♋25.0	11 38.9	28 25.5	26 05.4	6 32.0	13 58.1	10 39.7
20 Sa	23 52 35	0♈00 26	23 42 11	0♐51 12	13 20.6	18 32.5	6 43.9	0 51.5	11 56.9	28 39.0	26 04.5	6 30.2	13 57.9	10 38.1
21 Su	23 56 31	1 00 00	7♐54 05	14 50 50	13 22.0	20 21.0	7 57.9	1 18.3	12 15.2	28 52.5	26 03.8	6 28.3	13 57.8	10 36.4
22 M	0 00 28	1 59 32	21 41 29	28 26 16	13R 22.9	22 10.8	9 11.9	1 45.2	12 33.6	29 06.1	26 03.1	6 26.4	13 57.6	10 34.8
23 Tu	0 04 25	2 59 03	5♑05 26	11♑39 19	13 22.6	24 01.8	10 25.9	2 12.3	12 52.2	29 19.7	26 02.6	6 24.4	13 57.3	10 33.1
24 W	0 08 21	3 58 32	18 08 16	24 32 40	13 20.6	25 54.1	11 39.9	2 39.7	13 10.9	29 33.4	26 02.2	6 22.4	13 57.1	10 31.5
25 Th	0 12 18	4 57 59	0♒52 54	7♒09 21	13 16.8	27 47.8	12 53.9	3 07.2	13 29.8	29 47.1	26 01.9	6 20.4	13 56.8	10 29.8
26 F	0 16 14	5 57 24	13 22 22	19 32 19	13 11.4	29 42.7	14 07.9	3 34.9	13 48.9	0♉00.9	26 01.7	6 18.3	13 56.4	10 28.2
27 Sa	0 20 11	6 56 47	25 39 31	1♓44 16	13 05.1	1♈38.8	15 21.9	4 02.8	14 08.1	0 14.7	26D 01.6	6 16.2	13 56.1	10 26.5
28 Su	0 24 07	7 56 09	7♓46 51	13 47 31	12 58.4	3 36.2	16 35.9	4 30.9	14 27.5	0 28.6	26 01.6	6 14.1	13 55.7	10 24.8
29 M	0 28 04	8 55 28	19 46 30	25 44 03	12 52.1	5 34.8	17 49.9	4 59.1	14 47.1	0 42.4	26 01.7	6 12.0	13 55.3	10 23.1
30 Tu	0 32 00	9 54 46	1♈40 23	7♈35 43	12 46.7	7 34.5	19 03.8	5 27.5	15 06.8	0 56.3	26 02.0	6 09.8	13 54.8	10 21.5
31 W	0 35 57	10 54 01	13 30 17	19 24 19	12 42.8	9 35.4	20 17.8	5 56.1	15 26.6	1 10.3	26 02.3	6 07.6	13 54.3	10 19.8

April 1976 LONGITUDE

Day	Sid.Time	☉	0 hr ☽	Noon ☽	True ☊	☿	♀	♂	⚳	♃	♄	♅	♆	♇
1 Th	0 39 54	11♈53 15	25♈18 05	1♉11 51	12♏40.6	11♈37.2	21♓31.8	6♋24.8	15♊46.6	1♉24.3	26♋02.8	6♏05.3	13♐53.8	10♎18.1
2 F	0 43 50	12 52 26	7♉05 55	13 00 37	12D 39.9	13 39.9	22 45.8	6 53.7	16 06.7	1 38.3	26 03.3	6R 03.1	13R 53.2	10R 16.4
3 Sa	0 47 47	13 51 35	18 56 18	24 53 23	12 40.5	15 43.4	23 59.7	7 22.8	16 27.0	1 52.3	26 04.0	6 00.8	13 52.6	10 14.8
4 Su	0 51 43	14 50 42	0♊52 17	6♊53 27	12 42.0	17 47.5	25 13.7	7 52.0	16 47.4	2 06.4	26 04.8	5 58.5	13 52.0	10 13.1
5 M	0 55 40	15 49 47	12 57 23	19 04 35	12 43.8	19 52.1	26 27.6	8 21.4	17 07.9	2 20.5	26 05.7	5 56.1	13 51.4	10 11.4
6 Tu	0 59 36	16 48 50	25 15 35	1♋30 54	12 45.3	21 56.8	27 41.6	8 50.9	17 28.6	2 34.6	26 06.8	5 53.8	13 50.7	10 09.8
7 W	1 03 33	17 47 50	7♋51 04	14 16 37	12R 46.0	24 01.6	28 55.5	9 20.5	17 49.4	2 48.8	26 07.9	5 51.4	13 50.0	10 08.1
8 Th	1 07 29	18 46 48	20 47 59	27 25 35	12 45.8	26 06.0	0♈09.4	9 50.3	18 10.3	3 02.9	26 09.1	5 49.0	13 49.3	10 06.5
9 F	1 11 26	19 45 43	4♌09 47	11♌00 48	12 44.5	28 09.9	1 23.4	10 20.2	18 31.4	3 17.1	26 10.5	5 46.6	13 48.5	10 04.8
10 Sa	1 15 23	20 44 36	17 58 45	25 03 35	12 42.4	0♉12.8	2 37.3	10 50.3	18 52.6	3 31.3	26 11.9	5 44.2	13 47.7	10 03.2
11 Su	1 19 19	21 43 27	2♍15 05	9♍32 51	12 39.7	2 14.5	3 51.2	11 20.4	19 13.9	3 45.5	26 13.5	5 41.7	13 46.9	10 01.5
12 M	1 23 16	22 42 16	16 56 18	24 24 41	12 37.0	4 14.6	5 05.1	11 50.7	19 35.3	3 59.8	26 15.1	5 39.3	13 46.1	9 59.9
13 Tu	1 27 12	23 41 03	1♎57 01	9♎32 14	12 34.7	6 12.8	6 19.0	12 21.2	19 56.8	4 14.0	26 16.9	5 36.8	13 45.2	9 58.3
14 W	1 31 09	24 39 47	17 09 08	24 46 28	12 33.2	8 08.7	7 32.9	12 51.7	20 18.4	4 28.3	26 18.8	5 34.3	13 44.3	9 56.7
15 Th	1 35 05	25 38 30	2♏22 58	9♏57 24	12D 32.6	10 02.0	8 46.7	13 22.3	20 40.2	4 42.6	26 20.7	5 31.8	13 43.4	9 55.1
16 F	1 39 02	26 37 10	17 28 39	24 55 41	12 32.8	11 52.3	10 00.6	13 53.1	21 02.0	4 56.9	26 22.8	5 29.3	13 42.4	9 53.5
17 Sa	1 42 58	27 35 49	2♐17 40	9♐33 55	12 33.7	13 39.4	11 14.5	14 24.0	21 24.0	5 11.2	26 25.0	5 26.8	13 41.4	9 51.9
18 Su	1 46 55	28 34 26	16 43 55	23 47 22	12 34.8	15 22.9	12 28.4	14 55.0	21 46.1	5 25.5	26 27.3	5 24.3	13 40.4	9 50.3
19 M	1 50 51	29 33 02	0♑44 06	7♑34 06	12 35.8	17 02.8	13 42.2	15 26.1	22 08.3	5 39.8	26 29.7	5 21.8	13 39.4	9 48.8
20 Tu	1 54 48	0♉31 36	14 17 31	20 54 33	12R 36.5	18 38.6	14 56.1	15 57.3	22 30.5	5 54.2	26 32.2	5 19.2	13 38.4	9 47.2
21 W	1 58 45	1 30 08	27 25 33	3♒50 55	12 36.7	20 10.3	16 10.0	16 28.6	22 52.9	6 08.5	26 34.8	5 16.7	13 37.3	9 45.7
22 Th	2 02 41	2 28 39	10♒11 04	16 26 29	12 36.3	21 37.6	17 23.8	17 00.0	23 15.4	6 22.9	26 37.5	5 14.1	13 36.2	9 44.2
23 F	2 06 38	3 27 08	22 37 39	28 45 05	12 35.5	23 00.4	18 37.7	17 31.5	23 38.0	6 37.2	26 40.3	5 11.6	13 35.1	9 42.7
24 Sa	2 10 34	4 25 35	4♓49 15	10♓50 39	12 34.5	24 18.6	19 51.5	18 03.1	24 00.7	6 51.6	26 43.1	5 09.0	13 33.9	9 41.2
25 Su	2 14 31	5 24 01	16 49 45	22 46 59	12 33.5	25 32.1	21 05.4	18 34.9	24 23.4	7 06.0	26 46.1	5 06.4	13 32.7	9 39.7
26 M	2 18 27	6 22 24	28 42 46	4♈37 30	12 32.6	26 40.7	22 19.2	19 06.7	24 46.3	7 20.3	26 49.2	5 03.9	13 31.6	9 38.2
27 Tu	2 22 24	7 20 47	10♈31 34	16 25 17	12 31.9	27 44.5	23 33.0	19 38.6	25 09.3	7 34.7	26 52.4	5 01.3	13 30.3	9 36.8
28 W	2 26 20	8 19 07	22 19 00	28 13 00	12 31.5	28 43.2	24 46.9	20 10.6	25 32.3	7 49.0	26 55.7	4 58.8	13 29.1	9 35.4
29 Th	2 30 17	9 17 26	4♉07 36	10♉03 03	12D 31.3	29 36.8	26 00.7	20 42.7	25 55.4	8 03.4	26 59.0	4 56.2	13 27.8	9 34.0
30 F	2 34 14	10 15 43	15 59 38	21 57 37	12 31.4	0♊25.2	27 14.5	21 14.9	26 18.7	8 17.8	27 02.5	4 53.7	13 26.6	9 32.6

Astro Data	Planet Ingress	Last Aspect	☽ Ingress	Last Aspect	☽ Ingress	☽ Phases & Eclipses	Astro Data
Dy Hr Mn	Dy Hr Mn	Dy Hr Mn	Dy Hr Mn	Dy Hr Mn	Dy Hr Mn	Dy Hr Mn	
☽0N 1 19:18	☿ ♓ 9 12:02	2 7:33 ♄ △	♈ 2 14:22	1 1:31 ♄ □	♉ 1 9:34	9 4:38 ☽ 18♊45	1 March 1976
♃□♄ 9 22:34	♀ ♓ 15 0:59	4 20:11 ♄ □	♉ 5 3:18	3 14:22 ♄ ⚹	♊ 3 22:15	16 2:53 ○ 25♍39	Julian Day # 27819
☽0S 15 18:41	♂ ♋ 18 13:15	7 9:22 ☿ □	♊ 7 15:56	6 3:53 ♀ □	♋ 6 9:06	22 18:54 ☾ 2♑17	SVP 5♓35'20"
♆ R 15 20:40	☉ ♈ 20 11:50	9 19:03 ♂ ☌	♋ 10 1:59	8 9:42 ♄ ☌	♌ 8 16:36	30 17:08 ● 10♈07	GC 26♐30.4 ⚴ 13♈05.3
☉0N 20 11:50	♃ ♉ 26 10:25	12 2:21 ♃ □	♌ 12 7:55	10 4:10 ☉ △	♍ 10 20:16		Eris 13♈12.7 ⚵ 11♍05.5R
♃⚻♆ 21 21:12	☿ ♈ 26 15:36	14 8:37 ♀ ☍	♍ 14 9:59	12 14:57 ♄ ⚹	♎ 12 20:54	7 19:02 ☽ 18♋05	⚷ 25♈01.4 ⚶ 21♈33.6
♄ D 27 19:58		16 8:14 ♂ □	♎ 16 9:44	14 14:26 ♄ □	♏ 14 20:14	14 11:49 ○ 24♎39	☽ Mean ☊ 16♏03.8
☿0N 28 12:23	♀ ♈ 8 8:56	18 9:10 ♂ △	♏ 18 9:17	16 14:22 ♄ △	♐ 16 20:15	21 7:14 ☾ 1♒19	
☽0N 29 1:20	☿ ♉ 10 9:29	20 10:28 ☉ △	♐ 20 10:34	18 20:52 ☉ △	♑ 18 22:43	29 10:19 ● 9♉13	1 April 1976
	☉ ♉ 19 23:03	22 13:13 ♃ △	♑ 22 14:48	20 22:23 ♄ ☍	♒ 21 4:47	29 10:23:30 ● A 06'41"	Julian Day # 27850
♀0N 11 5:08	☿ ♊ 29 23:11	24 21:39 ♃ □	♒ 24 22:19	22 23:20 ☿ □	♓ 23 14:28		SVP 5♓35'17"
☽0S 12 5:27		26 1:06 ♆ ⚹	♓ 27 8:34	25 20:06 ♄ △	♈ 26 2:37		GC 26♐30.5 ⚴ 26♈14.2
♃☍♅ 18 10:16		29 12:36 ♄ △	♈ 29 20:37	28 9:22 ♄ □	♉ 28 15:37		Eris 13♈32.6 ⚵ 4♍50.2R
☽0N 25 6:57							⚷ 26♈41.5 ⚶ 4♉54.1
							☽ Mean ☊ 14♏25.3

LONGITUDE — May 1976

Day	Sid.Time	☉	0 hr ☽	Noon ☽	True ☊	☿	♀	♂	⚳	♃	♄	♅	♆	♇
1 Sa	2 38 10	11♉13 58	27♉57 15	3♊58 49	12♏31.5	1♊08.5	28♈28.3	21♋47.2	26♊42.0	8♉32.1	27♋06.1	4♏51.1	13♐25.3	9♎31.2
2 Su	2 42 07	12 12 12	10♊02 34	16 08 49	12R31.6	1 46.5	29 42.1	22 19.6	27 05.4	8 46.5	27 09.7	4R48.6	13R24.0	9R29.8
3 M	2 46 03	13 10 23	22 17 51	28 29 57	12 31.5	2 19.2	0♉55.9	22 52.0	27 28.9	9 00.8	27 13.5	4 46.1	13 22.6	9 28.5
4 Tu	2 50 00	14 08 33	4♋45 28	11♋04 41	12 31.4	2 46.5	2 09.7	23 24.6	27 52.4	9 15.1	27 17.3	4 43.6	13 21.3	9 27.2
5 W	2 53 56	15 06 41	17 27 57	23 55 34	12 31.2	3 08.5	3 23.5	23 57.2	28 16.1	9 29.5	27 21.3	4 41.1	13 19.9	9 25.9
6 Th	2 57 53	16 04 47	0♌27 52	7♌05 07	12D31.1	3 25.2	4 37.3	24 29.9	28 39.8	9 43.8	27 25.3	4 38.6	13 18.5	9 24.6
7 F	3 01 49	17 02 50	13 47 34	20 35 25	12 31.0	3 36.6	5 51.0	25 02.7	29 03.6	9 58.1	27 29.4	4 36.1	13 17.1	9 23.4
8 Sa	3 05 46	18 00 52	27 28 47	4♍27 44	12 31.2	3R42.8	7 04.8	25 35.6	29 27.4	10 12.3	27 33.6	4 33.6	13 15.7	9 22.2
9 Su	3 09 43	18 58 52	11♍32 11	18 41 59	12 31.6	3 43.9	8 18.5	26 08.6	29 51.3	10 26.6	27 37.8	4 31.2	13 14.3	9 21.0
10 M	3 13 39	19 56 50	25 56 49	3♎16 14	12 32.2	3 40.0	9 32.3	26 41.6	0♋15.3	10 40.8	27 42.2	4 28.7	13 12.8	9 19.8
11 Tu	3 17 36	20 54 46	10♎39 40	18 06 24	12 32.9	3 31.3	10 46.0	27 14.7	0 39.4	10 55.1	27 46.6	4 26.3	13 11.4	9 18.6
12 W	3 21 32	21 52 41	25 35 35	3♏06 16	12R33.3	3 18.1	11 59.7	27 47.8	1 03.6	11 09.3	27 51.1	4 23.9	13 09.9	9 17.5
13 Th	3 25 29	22 50 34	10♏37 25	18 07 59	12 33.4	3 00.7	13 13.5	28 21.0	1 27.8	11 23.5	27 55.7	4 21.5	13 08.4	9 16.4
14 F	3 29 25	23 48 25	25 36 53	3♐03 04	12 32.9	2 39.4	14 27.2	28 54.3	1 52.0	11 37.7	28 00.4	4 19.1	13 06.9	9 15.3
15 Sa	3 33 22	24 46 15	10♐25 34	17 43 33	12 31.8	2 14.6	15 40.9	29 27.7	2 16.4	11 51.8	28 05.2	4 16.8	13 05.4	9 14.3
16 Su	3 37 18	25 44 04	24 56 14	2♑03 04	12 30.3	1 46.8	16 54.6	0♌01.2	2 40.8	12 06.0	28 10.0	4 14.5	13 03.9	9 13.2
17 M	3 41 15	26 41 51	9♑03 36	15 57 35	12 28.6	1 16.4	18 08.3	0 34.7	3 05.3	12 20.1	28 15.0	4 12.2	13 02.4	9 12.2
18 Tu	3 45 12	27 39 37	22 44 54	29 25 35	12 26.9	0 44.2	19 22.1	1 08.2	3 29.8	12 34.2	28 20.0	4 09.9	13 00.8	9 11.2
19 W	3 49 08	28 37 22	5♒59 49	12♒27 50	12 25.6	0 10.5	20 35.8	1 41.9	3 54.4	12 48.2	28 25.0	4 07.6	12 59.3	9 10.3
20 Th	3 53 05	29 35 06	18 50 03	25 06 53	12D25.0	29♉36.0	21 49.5	2 15.6	4 19.0	13 02.2	28 30.2	4 05.4	12 57.7	9 09.4
21 F	3 57 01	0♊32 49	1♓18 52	7♓26 31	12 25.0	29 01.4	23 03.2	2 49.3	4 43.7	13 16.3	28 35.4	4 03.2	12 56.1	9 08.5
22 Sa	4 00 58	1 30 31	13 30 25	19 31 10	12 25.9	28 27.2	24 16.9	3 23.2	5 08.5	13 30.2	28 40.7	4 01.0	12 54.5	9 07.6
23 Su	4 04 54	2 28 11	25 29 20	1♈25 31	12 27.2	27 54.0	25 30.6	3 57.0	5 33.3	13 44.2	28 46.0	3 58.9	12 53.0	9 06.8
24 M	4 08 51	3 25 51	7♈20 17	13 14 10	12 28.8	27 22.4	26 44.3	4 31.0	5 58.2	13 58.1	28 51.5	3 56.7	12 51.4	9 05.9
25 Tu	4 12 47	4 23 30	19 07 42	25 01 23	12 30.3	26 52.8	27 58.0	5 05.0	6 23.2	14 12.0	28 57.0	3 54.6	12 49.8	9 05.2
26 W	4 16 44	5 21 07	0♉55 40	6♉50 59	12R31.2	26 25.8	29 11.7	5 39.1	6 48.2	14 25.8	29 02.5	3 52.6	12 48.2	9 04.4
27 Th	4 20 41	6 18 44	12 47 42	18 46 10	12 31.1	26 01.8	0♊25.4	6 13.3	7 13.2	14 39.7	29 08.2	3 50.5	12 46.6	9 03.7
28 F	4 24 37	7 16 19	24 46 41	0♊49 33	12 29.9	25 41.2	1 39.1	6 47.5	7 38.3	14 53.4	29 13.9	3 48.5	12 44.9	9 03.0
29 Sa	4 28 34	8 13 54	6♊54 58	13 03 08	12 27.5	25 24.2	2 52.8	7 21.8	8 03.5	15 07.2	29 19.6	3 46.6	12 43.3	9 02.3
30 Su	4 32 30	9 11 27	19 14 14	25 28 23	12 24.0	25 11.2	4 06.5	7 56.1	8 28.7	15 20.9	29 25.5	3 44.6	12 41.7	9 01.7
31 M	4 36 27	10 08 59	1♋45 43	8♋06 19	12 19.7	25 02.3	5 20.2	8 30.5	8 54.0	15 34.6	29 31.4	3 42.7	12 40.1	9 01.1

LONGITUDE — June 1976

Day	Sid.Time	☉	0 hr ☽	Noon ☽	True ☊	☿	♀	♂	⚳	♃	♄	♅	♆	♇
1 Tu	4 40 23	11♊06 30	14♋30 16	20♋57 38	12♏15.2	24♉57.7	6♊33.9	9♌04.9	9♋19.3	15♉48.2	29♋37.3	3♏40.9	12♐38.5	9♎00.5
2 W	4 44 20	12 04 00	27 28 28	4♌02 50	12R11.0	24D57.4	7 47.6	9 39.5	9 44.6	16 01.8	29 43.4	3R39.1	12R36.8	8R59.9
3 Th	4 48 16	13 01 28	10♌40 47	17 22 22	12 07.6	25 01.6	9 01.3	10 14.0	10 10.0	16 15.3	29 49.4	3 37.3	12 35.2	8 59.4
4 F	4 52 13	13 58 56	24 07 36	0♍56 33	12 05.6	25 10.3	10 15.0	10 48.6	10 35.5	16 28.8	29 55.6	3 35.5	12 33.6	8 59.0
5 Sa	4 56 10	14 56 22	7♍49 13	14 45 36	12D04.9	25 23.5	11 28.7	11 23.3	11 01.0	16 42.2	0♌01.8	3 33.8	12 32.0	8 58.5
6 Su	5 00 06	15 53 46	21 45 38	28 49 15	12 05.4	25 41.2	12 42.4	11 58.0	11 26.5	16 55.6	0 08.0	3 32.1	12 30.4	8 58.1
7 M	5 04 03	16 51 10	5♎56 17	13♎06 33	12 06.7	26 03.2	13 56.1	12 32.8	11 52.1	17 09.0	0 14.3	3 30.5	12 28.7	8 57.7
8 Tu	5 07 59	17 48 32	20 19 44	27 35 27	12R08.0	26 29.7	15 09.8	13 07.6	12 17.7	17 22.2	0 20.7	3 28.9	12 27.1	8 57.3
9 W	5 11 56	18 45 54	4♏53 13	12♏12 29	12 08.6	27 00.4	16 23.4	13 42.5	12 43.3	17 35.5	0 27.1	3 27.3	12 25.5	8 57.0
10 Th	5 15 52	19 43 14	19 32 35	26 52 46	12 07.8	27 35.4	17 37.1	14 17.4	13 09.0	17 48.7	0 33.6	3 25.8	12 23.9	8 56.7
11 F	5 19 49	20 40 34	4♐12 15	11♐30 13	12 05.3	28 14.5	18 50.8	14 52.4	13 34.8	18 01.8	0 40.1	3 24.4	12 22.3	8 56.5
12 Sa	5 23 45	21 37 53	18 45 50	25 58 17	12 01.0	28 57.7	20 04.5	15 27.4	14 00.5	18 14.9	0 46.7	3 22.9	12 20.7	8 56.2
13 Su	5 27 42	22 35 11	3♑06 49	10♑10 45	11 55.3	29 44.8	21 18.2	16 02.5	14 26.4	18 27.9	0 53.3	3 21.5	12 19.1	8 56.1
14 M	5 31 39	23 32 29	17 09 33	24 02 45	11 48.8	0♊35.9	22 31.9	16 37.6	14 52.2	18 40.9	0 59.9	3 20.2	12 17.5	8 55.9
15 Tu	5 35 35	24 29 46	0♒50 03	7♒31 18	11 42.3	1 30.8	23 45.6	17 12.8	15 18.1	18 53.8	1 06.6	3 18.9	12 15.9	8 55.8
16 W	5 39 32	25 27 02	14 06 28	20 35 39	11 36.6	2 29.5	24 59.2	17 48.0	15 44.0	19 06.7	1 13.4	3 17.7	12 14.4	8 55.7
17 Th	5 43 28	26 24 19	26 59 04	3♓17 04	11 32.3	3 31.8	26 12.9	18 23.3	16 10.0	19 19.5	1 20.2	3 16.4	12 12.8	8 55.6
18 F	5 47 25	27 21 35	9♓30 04	15 38 33	11 29.8	4 37.8	27 26.7	18 58.6	16 36.0	19 32.2	1 27.0	3 15.3	12 11.2	8D55.6
19 Sa	5 51 21	28 18 50	21 43 04	27 44 13	11D29.0	5 47.3	28 40.4	19 34.0	17 02.0	19 44.9	1 33.9	3 14.2	12 09.7	8 55.6
20 Su	5 55 18	29 16 06	3♈42 38	9♈38 58	11 29.5	7 00.4	29 54.1	20 09.4	17 28.0	19 57.5	1 40.8	3 13.1	12 08.1	8 55.6
21 M	5 59 14	0♋13 21	15 33 51	21 27 57	11 30.7	8 17.0	1♋07.8	20 44.9	17 54.1	20 10.0	1 47.8	3 12.1	12 06.6	8 55.7
22 Tu	6 03 11	1 10 36	27 21 54	3♉16 19	11R31.8	9 37.0	2 21.5	21 20.4	18 20.3	20 22.5	1 54.8	3 11.1	12 05.1	8 55.8
23 W	6 07 08	2 07 51	9♉11 47	15 08 52	11 32.1	11 00.4	3 35.2	21 56.0	18 46.4	20 34.9	2 01.9	3 10.2	12 03.6	8 55.9
24 Th	6 11 04	3 05 06	21 08 03	27 09 50	11 30.7	12 27.2	4 49.0	22 31.6	19 12.6	20 47.2	2 09.0	3 09.3	12 02.1	8 56.1
25 F	6 15 01	4 02 21	3♊14 35	9♊22 39	11 27.2	13 57.3	6 02.7	23 07.2	19 38.8	20 59.5	2 16.1	3 08.5	12 00.6	8 56.3
26 Sa	6 18 57	4 59 35	15 34 18	21 49 45	11 21.5	15 30.6	7 16.5	23 43.0	20 05.1	21 11.7	2 23.2	3 07.7	11 59.1	8 56.6
27 Su	6 22 54	5 56 50	28 09 08	4♋32 31	11 13.9	17 07.3	8 30.2	24 18.7	20 31.4	21 23.8	2 30.4	3 06.9	11 57.7	8 56.8
28 M	6 26 50	6 54 04	10♋59 52	17 31 07	11 04.8	18 47.1	9 44.0	24 54.5	20 57.7	21 35.8	2 37.7	3 06.3	11 56.2	8 57.1
29 Tu	6 30 47	7 51 18	24 06 09	0♌44 46	10 55.2	20 30.1	10 57.7	25 30.4	21 24.0	21 47.8	2 44.9	3 05.6	11 54.8	8 57.5
30 W	6 34 44	8 48 31	7♌26 46	14 11 53	10 46.1	22 16.1	12 11.5	26 06.3	21 50.4	21 59.7	2 52.2	3 05.1	11 53.4	8 57.8

Astro Data

	Dy Hr Mn
♃⊼♇	5 6:33
☿R	9 5:03
☽0S	9 14:36
♄□♆	15 12:48
♃⊼♆	20 5:00
☽0N	22 13:37
☿D	2 1:19
☽0S	5 21:51
♇D	18 21:43
☽0N	18 21:59

Planet Ingress

	Dy Hr Mn
♀ ♉	2 17:49
⚳ ♋	9 20:40
♂ ♌	16 11:10
☿ ♉R	19 19:21
☉ ♊	20 22:21
♀ ♊	27 3:43
♄ ♌	5 5:09
☿ ♊	13 19:20
♀ ♋	20 13:56
☉ ♋	21 6:24

Last Aspect / ☽ Ingress

Last Aspect Dy Hr Mn		☽ Ingress Dy Hr Mn
30 22:14	♄ ⚹	♊ 1 4:05
2 6:37	♆ ☍	♋ 3 14:53
5 18:21	♄ ☌	♌ 5 23:09
7 5:17	☉ □	♍ 8 4:21
10 2:51	♄ ⚹	♎ 10 6:39
12 3:34	♄ □	♏ 12 7:03
14 5:02	♂ △	♐ 14 7:04
15 4:23	♆ ☌	♑ 16 8:31
18 10:01	♄ ☍	♒ 18 13:02
20 21:22	☉ □	♓ 20 21:27
23 6:35	♄ △	♈ 23 9:07
25 20:03	♄ □	♉ 25 22:07
28 8:49	♄ ⚹	♊ 28 10:22
29 11:21	♆ ☍	♋ 30 20:39

Last Aspect / ☽ Ingress

Last Aspect Dy Hr Mn		☽ Ingress Dy Hr Mn
2 4:03	♄ ☌	♌ 2 4:37
4 1:43	☿ □	♍ 4 10:21
6 6:34	☿ △	♎ 6 14:00
7 18:40	☉ △	♏ 8 15:58
10 13:13	☿ ☍	♐ 10 17:07
12 4:15	☉ ☍	♑ 12 18:45
14 2:29	♃ △	♒ 14 22:31
16 21:51	☉ △	♓ 17 5:43
19 14:05	♀ □	♈ 19 16:32
21 10:28	♂ △	♉ 22 5:21
24 2:18	♂ □	♊ 24 17:37
26 15:46	♂ ⚹	♋ 27 3:29
28 19:34	♃ ⚹	♌ 29 10:39

☽ Phases & Eclipses

Dy Hr Mn	
7 5:17	☽ 16♌47
13 20:04	○ 23♏10
13 19:54	P 0.122
20 21:22	☾ 29♒58
29 1:47	● 7♊49
5 12:20	☽ 14♍57
12 4:15	○ 21♐19
19 13:15	☾ 28♓22
27 14:50	● 6♋04

Astro Data

1 May 1976
Julian Day # 27880
SVP 5♓35'14"
GC 26♐30.5 ⚴ 10♉14.0
Eris 13♈52.2 ⚵ 4♍11.6
⚷ 28♈29.7 ⚶ 18♉06.3
☽ Mean ☊ 12♏49.9

1 June 1976
Julian Day # 27911
SVP 5♓35'10"
GC 26♐30.6 ⚴ 25♉46.9
Eris 14♈08.1 ⚵ 8♍40.8
⚷ 0♉12.1 ⚶ 1♊42.8
☽ Mean ☊ 11♏11.4

July 1976

LONGITUDE

Day	Sid.Time	☉	0 hr ☽	Noon ☽	True ☊	☿	♀	♂	⚳	♃	♄	♅	♆	♇
1 Th	6 38 40	9♋45 45	20♌59 54	27♌50 32	10♏38.5	24♊05.1	13♋25.3	26♌42.3	22♋16.8	22♉11.5	2♌59.5	3♏04.5	11♐52.0	8♎58.3
2 F	6 42 37	10 42 58	4♍43 33	11♍38 44	10R33.0	25 56.9	14 39.0	27 18.3	22 43.2	22 23.2	3 06.9	3R04.0	11R50.6	8 58.7
3 Sa	6 46 33	11 40 10	18 35 53	25 34 48	10 29.8	27 51.5	15 52.8	27 54.3	23 09.6	22 34.8	3 14.3	3 03.6	11 49.3	8 59.2
4 Su	6 50 30	12 37 22	2♎35 22	9♎37 25	10D28.7	29 48.7	17 06.5	28 30.4	23 36.1	22 46.3	3 21.7	3 03.2	11 47.9	8 59.7
5 M	6 54 26	13 34 34	16 40 51	23 45 31	10 28.9	1♋48.2	18 20.3	29 06.5	24 02.6	22 57.8	3 29.1	3 02.9	11 46.6	9 00.2
6 Tu	6 58 23	14 31 46	0♏51 18	7♏57 59	10R29.4	3 49.9	19 34.1	29 42.7	24 29.1	23 09.2	3 36.6	3 02.6	11 45.3	9 00.8
7 W	7 02 19	15 28 57	15 05 24	22 13 15	10 28.9	5 53.5	20 47.9	0♍18.9	24 55.6	23 20.4	3 44.0	3 02.4	11 44.0	9 01.4
8 Th	7 06 16	16 26 09	29 21 12	6♐28 53	10 26.5	7 58.8	22 01.6	0 55.2	25 22.1	23 31.6	3 51.5	3 02.2	11 42.7	9 02.0
9 F	7 10 13	17 23 20	13♐35 50	20 41 33	10 21.7	10 05.5	23 15.4	1 31.5	25 48.7	23 42.7	3 59.1	3 02.1	11 41.5	9 02.7
10 Sa	7 14 09	18 20 32	27 45 29	4♑47 04	10 14.2	12 13.2	24 29.2	2 07.9	26 15.3	23 53.7	4 06.6	3D02.1	11 40.3	9 03.4
11 Su	7 18 06	19 17 43	11♑45 44	18 40 56	10 04.5	14 21.8	25 43.0	2 44.3	26 41.9	24 04.7	4 14.2	3 02.0	11 39.1	9 04.1
12 M	7 22 02	20 14 55	25 32 10	2♒19 01	9 53.6	16 30.9	26 56.8	3 20.7	27 08.5	24 15.5	4 21.7	3 02.1	11 37.9	9 04.9
13 Tu	7 25 59	21 12 07	9♒01 06	15 38 12	9 42.5	18 40.1	28 10.5	3 57.2	27 35.1	24 26.2	4 29.3	3 02.2	11 36.7	9 05.7
14 W	7 29 55	22 09 19	22 10 09	28 36 57	9 32.3	20 49.3	29 24.3	4 33.7	28 01.8	24 36.8	4 37.0	3 02.3	11 35.6	9 06.5
15 Th	7 33 52	23 06 32	4♓58 40	11♓15 30	9 23.9	22 58.1	0♌38.1	5 10.3	28 28.4	24 47.3	4 44.6	3 02.5	11 34.4	9 07.4
16 F	7 37 48	24 03 45	17 27 44	23 35 46	9 17.9	25 06.3	1 51.9	5 46.9	28 55.1	24 57.7	4 52.2	3 02.8	11 33.3	9 08.3
17 Sa	7 41 45	25 00 59	29 40 01	5♈41 03	9 14.3	27 13.8	3 05.8	6 23.5	29 21.8	25 08.0	4 59.9	3 03.0	11 32.3	9 09.2
18 Su	7 45 42	25 58 14	11♈39 26	17 35 46	9D12.8	29 20.3	4 19.6	7 00.2	29 48.6	25 18.2	5 07.6	3 03.4	11 31.2	9 10.1
19 M	7 49 38	26 55 29	23 30 44	29 25 00	9R12.6	1♌25.6	5 33.4	7 37.0	0♌15.3	25 28.3	5 15.2	3 03.8	11 30.2	9 11.1
20 Tu	7 53 35	27 52 45	5♉19 14	11♉14 09	9 12.6	3 29.6	6 47.2	8 13.8	0 42.0	25 38.3	5 22.9	3 04.3	11 29.2	9 12.1
21 W	7 57 31	28 50 02	17 10 23	23 08 38	9 12.0	5 32.3	8 01.0	8 50.6	1 08.8	25 48.2	5 30.6	3 04.8	11 28.2	9 13.2
22 Th	8 01 28	29 47 20	29 09 29	5♊13 31	9 09.6	7 33.5	9 14.9	9 27.5	1 35.6	25 58.0	5 38.3	3 05.3	11 27.2	9 14.2
23 F	8 05 24	0♌44 38	11♊21 17	17 33 13	9 04.9	9 33.2	10 28.7	10 04.4	2 02.4	26 07.6	5 46.1	3 05.9	11 26.3	9 15.4
24 Sa	8 09 21	1 41 57	23 49 43	0♋11 03	8 57.6	11 31.2	11 42.6	10 41.4	2 29.2	26 17.1	5 53.8	3 06.6	11 25.4	9 16.5
25 Su	8 13 17	2 39 18	6♋37 25	13 08 54	8 47.9	13 27.7	12 56.4	11 18.4	2 56.0	26 26.6	6 01.5	3 07.3	11 24.5	9 17.7
26 M	8 17 14	3 36 39	19 45 29	26 27 00	8 36.4	15 22.5	14 10.3	11 55.5	3 22.9	26 35.9	6 09.3	3 08.1	11 23.7	9 18.9
27 Tu	8 21 11	4 34 00	3♌13 12	10♌03 45	8 24.2	17 15.6	15 24.2	12 32.6	3 49.7	26 45.0	6 17.0	3 08.9	11 22.9	9 20.1
28 W	8 25 07	5 31 22	16 58 12	23 56 01	8 12.6	19 07.0	16 38.0	13 09.8	4 16.6	26 54.1	6 24.8	3 09.8	11 22.1	9 21.3
29 Th	8 29 04	6 28 45	0♍56 42	7♍59 38	8 02.6	20 56.7	17 51.9	13 47.0	4 43.4	27 03.0	6 32.5	3 10.7	11 21.3	9 22.6
30 F	8 33 00	7 26 09	15 04 16	22 10 03	7 55.2	22 44.8	19 05.8	14 24.2	5 10.3	27 11.8	6 40.2	3 11.7	11 20.6	9 23.9
31 Sa	8 36 57	8 23 33	29 16 30	6♎23 10	7 50.6	24 31.2	20 19.6	15 01.5	5 37.2	27 20.4	6 48.0	3 12.7	11 19.9	9 25.3

August 1976

LONGITUDE

Day	Sid.Time	☉	0 hr ☽	Noon ☽	True ☊	☿	♀	♂	⚳	♃	♄	♅	♆	♇
1 Su	8 40 53	9♌20 57	13♎29 42	20♎35 47	7♏48.5	26♌15.9	21♌33.5	15♍38.9	6♌04.0	27♉29.0	6♌55.7	3♏13.8	11♐19.2	9♎26.6
2 M	8 44 50	10 18 23	27 41 11	4♏45 43	7R48.0	27 59.0	22 47.3	16 16.2	6 30.9	27 37.4	7 03.4	3 14.9	11R18.5	9 28.0
3 Tu	8 48 46	11 15 48	11♏49 16	18 51 43	7 48.0	29 40.4	24 01.2	16 53.7	6 57.8	27 45.6	7 11.2	3 16.1	11 17.9	9 29.4
4 W	8 52 43	12 13 15	25 52 59	2♐52 58	7 47.0	1♍20.2	25 15.1	17 31.1	7 24.7	27 53.8	7 18.9	3 17.3	11 17.3	9 30.9
5 Th	8 56 40	13 10 42	9♐51 34	16 48 40	7 44.1	2 58.3	26 28.9	18 08.6	7 51.6	28 01.8	7 26.6	3 18.6	11 16.7	9 32.4
6 F	9 00 36	14 08 10	23 44 05	0♑37 37	7 38.5	4 34.8	27 42.8	18 46.2	8 18.5	28 09.6	7 34.3	3 20.0	11 16.2	9 33.9
7 Sa	9 04 33	15 05 39	7♑29 03	14 18 06	7 30.2	6 09.7	28 56.6	19 23.8	8 45.4	28 17.4	7 42.0	3 21.3	11 15.7	9 35.4
8 Su	9 08 29	16 03 09	21 04 30	27 47 56	7 19.5	7 43.0	0♍10.5	20 01.4	9 12.3	28 24.9	7 49.7	3 22.8	11 15.2	9 36.9
9 M	9 12 26	17 00 40	4♒28 07	11♒04 48	7 07.5	9 14.6	1 24.3	20 39.1	9 39.2	28 32.4	7 57.4	3 24.2	11 14.8	9 38.5
10 Tu	9 16 22	17 58 11	17 37 44	24 06 43	6 55.1	10 44.6	2 38.2	21 16.8	10 06.1	28 39.6	8 05.1	3 25.8	11 14.4	9 40.1
11 W	9 20 19	18 55 44	0♓31 41	6♓52 33	6 43.7	12 12.9	3 52.0	21 54.6	10 33.0	28 46.8	8 12.7	3 27.3	11 14.0	9 41.7
12 Th	9 24 15	19 53 18	13 09 20	19 22 09	6 34.1	13 39.6	5 05.9	22 32.4	10 59.9	28 53.8	8 20.4	3 29.0	11 13.6	9 43.4
13 F	9 28 12	20 50 53	25 31 11	1♈36 43	6 27.0	15 04.6	6 19.7	23 10.2	11 26.8	29 00.6	8 28.0	3 30.6	11 13.3	9 45.1
14 Sa	9 32 08	21 48 30	7♈39 05	13 38 41	6 22.5	16 27.9	7 33.5	23 48.1	11 53.7	29 07.3	8 35.6	3 32.3	11 13.0	9 46.8
15 Su	9 36 05	22 46 08	19 36 01	25 31 35	6D20.3	17 49.4	8 47.4	24 26.1	12 20.7	29 13.8	8 43.2	3 34.1	11 12.7	9 48.5
16 M	9 40 02	23 43 48	1♉26 00	7♉19 51	6 19.9	19 09.2	10 01.2	25 04.1	12 47.6	29 20.2	8 50.8	3 35.9	11 12.5	9 50.2
17 Tu	9 43 58	24 41 30	13 13 47	19 08 30	6R20.1	20 27.2	11 15.1	25 42.1	13 14.5	29 26.4	8 58.4	3 37.8	11 12.3	9 52.0
18 W	9 47 55	25 39 12	25 04 39	1♊02 56	6 20.1	21 43.3	12 28.9	26 20.2	13 41.4	29 32.5	9 05.9	3 39.7	11 12.2	9 53.8
19 Th	9 51 51	26 36 57	7♊04 01	13 08 35	6 18.8	22 57.5	13 42.7	26 58.3	14 08.3	29 38.4	9 13.4	3 41.6	11 12.0	9 55.6
20 F	9 55 48	27 34 43	19 17 13	25 30 31	6 15.5	24 09.8	14 56.6	27 36.5	14 35.2	29 44.1	9 20.9	3 43.6	11 11.9	9 57.4
21 Sa	9 59 44	28 32 31	1♋48 58	8♋13 01	6 09.9	25 19.9	16 10.4	28 14.8	15 02.1	29 49.7	9 28.4	3 45.7	11 11.9	9 59.3
22 Su	10 03 41	29 30 21	14 42 57	21 18 59	6 01.9	26 27.9	17 24.2	28 53.0	15 29.0	29 55.1	9 35.9	3 47.7	11D11.8	10 01.2
23 M	10 07 37	0♍28 12	28 01 12	4♌49 32	5 52.4	27 33.7	18 38.1	29 31.4	15 55.8	0♊00.3	9 43.3	3 49.9	11 11.8	10 03.1
24 Tu	10 11 34	1 26 04	11♌43 43	18 43 26	5 42.0	28 37.2	19 51.9	0♎09.7	16 22.7	0 05.4	9 50.7	3 52.0	11 11.8	10 05.0
25 W	10 15 31	2 23 59	25 48 07	2♍57 09	5 32.1	29 38.1	21 05.7	0 48.2	16 49.6	0 10.3	9 58.1	3 54.3	11 11.9	10 06.9
26 Th	10 19 27	3 21 54	10♍09 47	17 25 11	5 23.6	0♎36.5	22 19.6	1 26.6	17 16.4	0 15.0	10 05.4	3 56.5	11 12.0	10 08.9
27 F	10 23 24	4 19 51	24 42 31	2♎00 54	5 17.4	1 32.2	23 33.4	2 05.1	17 43.3	0 19.5	10 12.8	3 58.8	11 12.1	10 10.8
28 Sa	10 27 20	5 17 50	9♎19 31	16 37 35	5 13.7	2 24.9	24 47.2	2 43.7	18 10.1	0 23.9	10 20.0	4 01.1	11 12.3	10 12.8
29 Su	10 31 17	6 15 50	23 54 25	1♏09 27	5D12.3	3 14.6	26 01.0	3 22.3	18 36.9	0 28.1	10 27.3	4 03.5	11 12.5	10 14.8
30 M	10 35 13	7 13 51	8♏22 12	15 32 17	5 12.6	4 01.0	27 14.8	4 01.0	19 03.7	0 32.1	10 34.5	4 06.0	11 12.7	10 16.8
31 Tu	10 39 10	8 11 54	22 39 27	29 43 30	5R13.3	4 43.9	28 28.6	4 39.7	19 30.5	0 35.9	10 41.7	4 08.4	11 13.0	10 18.9

Astro Data	Dy Hr Mn
♄□♅	2 3:14
☽0S	3 4:09
♅D	11 6:05
♃⚼♇	11 10:44
☽0N	16 7:27
☽0S	30 10:58
☽0N	12 16:40
☿0S	22 10:27
♆D	23 2:04
♂0S	26 12:23
☽0S	26 19:22
♄⚹♇	27 3:20

Planet Ingress		Dy Hr Mn
☿	♋	4 14:18
♂	♍	6 23:27
♀	♌	14 23:36
☿	♌	18 19:35
⚳	♌	18 22:16
☉	♌	22 17:18
☿	♍	3 16:41
♀	♍	8 8:36
☉	♍	23 0:18
♃	♊	23 10:24
♂	♎	24 5:55
☿	♎	25 20:52

Last Aspect Dy Hr Mn			☽ Ingress	Dy Hr Mn
1 9:55	♂	☌	♍	1 15:46
3 16:32	☿	□	♎	3 19:34
5 21:27	♂	⚹	♏	5 22:33
7 13:55	♃	☍	♐	8 1:05
8 20:48	♆	☌	♑	10 3:49
12 1:32	♀	☍	♒	12 7:53
14 4:26	♃	□	♓	14 14:36
16 15:36	☿	△	♈	17 0:40
19 6:29	☉	□	♉	19 13:11
22 0:20	☉	⚹	♊	22 1:40
23 0:11	♆	☍	♋	24 11:39
26 12:16	♃	⚹	♌	26 18:19
28 17:09	♃	□	♍	28 22:23
30 20:35	♃	△	♎	31 1:13

Last Aspect Dy Hr Mn			☽ Ingress	Dy Hr Mn
1 22:55	☿	⚹	♏	2 3:55
4 3:22	♃	☍	♐	4 7:03
6 6:25	♀	△	♑	6 10:54
8 13:07	♃	△	♒	8 15:57
10 20:34	♃	□	♓	10 23:00
13 6:49	♃	⚹	♈	13 8:49
15 5:55	☉	△	♉	15 21:05
18 8:57	♃	☌	♊	18 9:54
20 16:17	☉	⚹	♋	20 20:34
23 3:28	♃	⚹	♌	23 3:31
23 23:05	♆	△	♍	25 7:04
26 20:50	♀	☌	♎	27 8:42
28 3:05	♆	⚹	♏	29 10:05
31 9:40	♀	⚹	♐	31 12:28

☽ Phases & Eclipses Dy Hr Mn	
4 17:28	☽ 12♎50
11 13:09	○ 19♑20
19 6:29	☾ 26♈42
27 1:39	● 4♌09
2 22:06	☽ 10♏43
9 23:43	○ 17♒29
18 0:13	☾ 25♉11
25 11:01	● 2♍22

Astro Data

1 July 1976
Julian Day # 27941
SVP 5♓35'05"
GC 26♐30.7 ⚵ 11♊42.8
Eris 14♈15.6 ⚶ 16♍09.4
⚷ 1♉23.8 ⚴ 14♊35.5
☽ Mean ☊ 9♏36.1

1 August 1976
Julian Day # 27972
SVP 5♓35'00"
GC 26♐30.7 ⚵ 28♊51.4
Eris 14♈13.5R ⚶ 25♍42.8
⚷ 1♉54.7 ⚴ 27♊17.7
☽ Mean ☊ 7♏57.6

LONGITUDE September 1976

Day	Sid.Time	☉	0 hr ☽	Noon ☽	True ☊	☿	♀	♂	⚳	♃	♄	♅	♆	♇
1 W	10 43 06	9♍09 58	6♐44 20	13♐41 55	5♏13.4	5♎23.1	29♍42.4	5♎18.4	19♌57.3	0♊39.5	10♌48.8	4♏10.9	11♐13.3	10♎21.0
2 Th	10 47 03	10 08 03	20 36 13	27 27 17	5R12.0	5 58.3	0♎56.1	5 57.2	20 24.1	0 43.0	10 56.0	4 13.5	11 13.6	10 23.0
3 F	10 51 00	11 06 10	4♑15 07	10♑59 46	5 08.5	6 29.3	2 09.9	6 36.0	20 50.8	0 46.3	11 03.0	4 16.1	11 13.9	10 25.1
4 Sa	10 54 56	12 04 18	17 41 15	24 19 35	5 02.8	6 55.8	3 23.6	7 14.9	21 17.6	0 49.4	11 10.1	4 18.7	11 14.3	10 27.2
5 Su	10 58 53	13 02 28	0♒54 48	7♒26 51	4 55.1	7 17.5	4 37.4	7 53.8	21 44.3	0 52.2	11 17.1	4 21.3	11 14.8	10 29.4
6 M	11 02 49	14 00 39	13 55 44	20 21 27	4 46.3	7 34.2	5 51.1	8 32.8	22 11.0	0 55.0	11 24.0	4 24.0	11 15.2	10 31.5
7 Tu	11 06 46	14 58 52	26 43 57	3♓03 16	4 37.3	7 45.4	7 04.8	9 11.8	22 37.6	0 57.5	11 30.9	4 26.8	11 15.7	10 33.6
8 W	11 10 42	15 57 06	9♓19 23	15 32 21	4 28.9	7R50.9	8 18.5	9 50.9	23 04.3	0 59.8	11 37.8	4 29.5	11 16.2	10 35.8
9 Th	11 14 39	16 55 22	21 42 16	27 49 13	4 22.0	7 50.4	9 32.2	10 30.0	23 30.9	1 01.9	11 44.6	4 32.3	11 16.8	10 38.0
10 F	11 18 35	17 53 40	3♈53 23	9♈54 58	4 17.0	7 43.6	10 45.9	11 09.2	23 57.6	1 03.9	11 51.4	4 35.1	11 17.3	10 40.2
11 Sa	11 22 32	18 52 00	15 54 13	21 51 27	4 14.1	7 30.3	11 59.6	11 48.4	24 24.2	1 05.6	11 58.1	4 38.0	11 18.0	10 42.4
12 Su	11 26 29	19 50 22	27 47 03	3♉41 23	4D13.2	7 10.4	13 13.2	12 27.6	24 50.7	1 07.2	12 04.8	4 40.9	11 18.6	10 44.6
13 M	11 30 25	20 48 46	9♉34 56	15 28 12	4 13.8	6 43.7	14 26.9	13 06.9	25 17.3	1 08.5	12 11.5	4 43.9	11 19.3	10 46.8
14 Tu	11 34 22	21 47 13	21 21 44	27 16 05	4 15.2	6 10.3	15 40.5	13 46.3	25 43.8	1 09.7	12 18.1	4 46.8	11 20.0	10 49.0
15 W	11 38 18	22 45 41	3♊11 52	9♊09 42	4 16.7	5 30.4	16 54.2	14 25.7	26 10.3	1 10.6	12 24.6	4 49.8	11 20.7	10 51.3
16 Th	11 42 15	23 44 12	15 10 15	21 14 08	4R17.6	4 44.3	18 07.8	15 05.1	26 36.8	1 11.4	12 31.1	4 52.9	11 21.5	10 53.5
17 F	11 46 11	24 42 44	27 22 00	3♋34 27	4 17.2	3 52.5	19 21.4	15 44.6	27 03.3	1 12.0	12 37.5	4 55.9	11 22.3	10 55.8
18 Sa	11 50 08	25 41 19	9♋52 05	16 15 24	4 15.2	2 55.8	20 35.0	16 24.2	27 29.7	1 12.3	12 43.9	4 59.0	11 23.1	10 58.1
19 Su	11 54 04	26 39 56	22 44 52	29 20 50	4 11.7	1 55.2	21 48.7	17 03.8	27 56.1	1R12.5	12 50.3	5 02.2	11 24.0	11 00.3
20 M	11 58 01	27 38 35	6♌03 33	12♌53 06	4 06.9	0 51.9	23 02.3	17 43.5	28 22.5	1 12.4	12 56.5	5 05.3	11 24.9	11 02.6
21 Tu	12 01 58	28 37 17	19 49 27	26 52 24	4 01.4	29♍47.1	24 15.8	18 23.2	28 48.9	1 12.2	13 02.8	5 08.5	11 25.8	11 04.9
22 W	12 05 54	29 36 00	4♍01 32	11♍16 19	3 56.0	28 42.5	25 29.4	19 02.9	29 15.2	1 11.7	13 08.9	5 11.7	11 26.8	11 07.2
23 Th	12 09 51	0♎34 46	18 36 00	25 59 45	3 51.5	27 39.7	26 43.0	19 42.7	29 41.5	1 11.1	13 15.0	5 14.9	11 27.8	11 09.5
24 F	12 13 47	1 33 33	3♎26 33	10♎55 22	3 48.3	26 40.2	27 56.6	20 22.6	0♍07.7	1 10.2	13 21.0	5 18.2	11 28.8	11 11.8
25 Sa	12 17 44	2 32 23	18 25 06	25 54 42	3D46.7	25 45.6	29 10.1	21 02.5	0 33.9	1 09.2	13 27.0	5 21.5	11 29.9	11 14.2
26 Su	12 21 40	3 31 14	3♏23 07	10♏49 25	3 46.7	24 57.5	0♏23.6	21 42.5	1 00.1	1 07.9	13 32.9	5 24.8	11 30.9	11 16.5
27 M	12 25 37	4 30 07	18 12 46	25 32 28	3 47.7	24 17.1	1 37.2	22 22.5	1 26.2	1 06.4	13 38.8	5 28.2	11 32.1	11 18.8
28 Tu	12 29 33	5 29 02	2♐47 58	9♐58 50	3 49.2	23 45.4	2 50.7	23 02.5	1 52.3	1 04.8	13 44.5	5 31.5	11 33.2	11 21.1
29 W	12 33 30	6 27 59	17 04 48	24 05 41	3R50.4	23 23.2	4 04.2	23 42.7	2 18.4	1 02.9	13 50.3	5 34.9	11 34.4	11 23.5
30 Th	12 37 26	7 26 58	1♑01 26	7♑52 06	3 50.9	23D11.1	5 17.7	24 22.8	2 44.4	1 00.8	13 55.9	5 38.3	11 35.6	11 25.8

LONGITUDE October 1976

Day	Sid.Time	☉	0 hr ☽	Noon ☽	True ☊	☿	♀	♂	⚳	♃	♄	♅	♆	♇
1 F	12 41 23	8♎25 58	14♑37 46	21♑18 37	3♏50.3	23♍09.4	6♏31.1	25♎03.0	3♍10.4	0♊58.6	14♌01.5	5♏41.8	11♐36.8	11♎28.2
2 Sa	12 45 20	9 25 00	27 54 51	4♒26 40	3R48.5	23 18.1	7 44.6	25 43.3	3 36.3	0R56.1	14 07.0	5 45.2	11 38.1	11 30.5
3 Su	12 49 16	10 24 03	10♒54 21	17 18 07	3 45.7	23 36.9	8 58.0	26 23.6	4 02.2	0 53.5	14 12.4	5 48.7	11 39.3	11 32.9
4 M	12 53 13	11 23 09	23 38 14	29 54 57	3 42.3	24 05.7	10 11.4	27 03.9	4 28.1	0 50.6	14 17.8	5 52.2	11 40.6	11 35.2
5 Tu	12 57 09	12 22 16	6♓08 29	12♓19 04	3 38.8	24 43.8	11 24.8	27 44.3	4 53.9	0 47.6	14 23.1	5 55.7	11 42.0	11 37.5
6 W	13 01 06	13 21 25	18 26 57	24 32 19	3 35.5	25 30.6	12 38.2	28 24.8	5 19.6	0 44.3	14 28.3	5 59.2	11 43.3	11 39.9
7 Th	13 05 02	14 20 36	0♈35 23	6♈36 22	3 32.9	26 25.5	13 51.5	29 05.3	5 45.3	0 40.9	14 33.4	6 02.8	11 44.7	11 42.2
8 F	13 08 59	15 19 49	12 35 30	18 33 00	3 31.3	27 27.7	15 04.9	29 45.8	6 11.0	0 37.3	14 38.5	6 06.3	11 46.1	11 44.6
9 Sa	13 12 55	16 19 05	24 29 07	0♉24 06	3D30.6	28 36.5	16 18.2	0♏26.4	6 36.6	0 33.5	14 43.5	6 09.9	11 47.6	11 46.9
10 Su	13 16 52	17 18 22	6♉18 14	12 11 50	3 30.8	29 51.0	17 31.5	1 07.1	7 02.1	0 29.5	14 48.4	6 13.5	11 49.1	11 49.2
11 M	13 20 49	18 17 42	18 05 14	23 58 48	3 31.6	1♎10.7	18 44.8	1 47.8	7 27.6	0 25.3	14 53.2	6 17.1	11 50.6	11 51.6
12 Tu	13 24 45	19 17 03	29 52 56	5♊48 03	3 32.9	2 34.7	19 58.0	2 28.5	7 53.1	0 21.0	14 57.9	6 20.8	11 52.1	11 53.9
13 W	13 28 42	20 16 27	11♊44 36	17 43 06	3 34.2	4 02.5	21 11.3	3 09.3	8 18.5	0 16.4	15 02.6	6 24.4	11 53.6	11 56.2
14 Th	13 32 38	21 15 54	23 44 01	29 47 54	3 35.3	5 33.4	22 24.5	3 50.2	8 43.8	0 11.7	15 07.2	6 28.1	11 55.2	11 58.6
15 F	13 36 35	22 15 22	5♋55 17	12♋06 44	3R36.0	7 06.9	23 37.8	4 31.1	9 09.1	0 06.9	15 11.7	6 31.7	11 56.8	12 00.9
16 Sa	13 40 31	23 14 53	18 22 46	24 43 55	3 36.2	8 42.5	24 51.0	5 12.1	9 34.3	0 01.8	15 16.1	6 35.4	11 58.4	12 03.2
17 Su	13 44 28	24 14 26	1♌10 41	7♌43 29	3 36.0	10 19.9	26 04.2	5 53.1	9 59.5	29♉56.6	15 20.4	6 39.1	12 00.1	12 05.5
18 M	13 48 24	25 14 02	14 22 42	21 08 37	3 35.3	11 58.6	27 17.3	6 34.2	10 24.6	29 51.2	15 24.7	6 42.8	12 01.7	12 07.8
19 Tu	13 52 21	26 13 39	28 01 23	5♍01 02	3 34.5	13 38.3	28 30.5	7 15.3	10 49.6	29 45.6	15 28.8	6 46.5	12 03.4	12 10.1
20 W	13 56 18	27 13 19	12♍07 28	19 20 21	3 33.6	15 18.8	29 43.6	7 56.5	11 14.6	29 39.9	15 32.9	6 50.2	12 05.1	12 12.4
21 Th	14 00 14	28 13 02	26 39 15	4♎03 30	3 33.0	16 59.9	0♐56.8	8 37.7	11 39.5	29 34.1	15 36.9	6 54.0	12 06.9	12 14.7
22 F	14 04 11	29 12 46	11♎32 17	19 04 38	3D32.7	18 41.2	2 09.9	9 19.0	12 04.3	29 28.0	15 40.7	6 57.7	12 08.6	12 17.0
23 Sa	14 08 07	0♏12 32	26 39 27	4♏15 33	3 32.6	20 22.8	3 23.0	10 00.3	12 29.1	29 21.9	15 44.5	7 01.4	12 10.4	12 19.2
24 Su	14 12 04	1 12 21	11♏51 43	19 26 44	3 32.6	22 04.3	4 36.0	10 41.7	12 53.8	29 15.6	15 48.2	7 05.2	12 12.2	12 21.5
25 M	14 16 00	2 12 11	26 59 27	4♐28 47	3 32.8	23 45.8	5 49.1	11 23.2	13 18.4	29 09.1	15 51.8	7 08.9	12 14.0	12 23.7
26 Tu	14 19 57	3 12 03	11♐53 49	19 13 45	3R32.9	25 27.2	7 02.1	12 04.7	13 42.9	29 02.5	15 55.3	7 12.7	12 15.8	12 26.0
27 W	14 23 53	4 11 57	26 27 59	3♑36 03	3 32.8	27 08.3	8 15.1	12 46.2	14 07.4	28 55.8	15 58.7	7 16.4	12 17.7	12 28.2
28 Th	14 27 50	5 11 52	10♑37 43	17 32 50	3 32.8	28 49.1	9 28.1	13 27.8	14 31.7	28 49.0	16 02.1	7 20.2	12 19.6	12 30.4
29 F	14 31 47	6 11 49	24 21 27	1♒03 43	3D32.7	0♏29.6	10 41.0	14 09.5	14 56.0	28 42.0	16 05.3	7 24.0	12 21.5	12 32.6
30 Sa	14 35 43	7 11 48	7♒39 53	14 10 16	3 32.7	2 09.7	11 54.0	14 51.2	15 20.2	28 35.0	16 08.4	7 27.7	12 23.4	12 34.8
31 Su	14 39 40	8 11 48	20 35 15	26 55 17	3 32.9	3 49.5	13 06.9	15 32.9	15 44.4	28 27.8	16 11.4	7 31.5	12 25.3	12 37.0

Astro Data

	Dy Hr Mn
♀0S	3 18:35
♄△♆	5 3:32
☿R	8 22:04
☽0N	9 0:30
♃R	19 18:39
⊙0S	22 21:48
☽0S	23 5:24
☿0N	25 11:40
☿D	1 3:58
☽0N	6 6:46
♆⚹♇	10 6:49
☿0S	13 20:32
☽0S	20 16:04

Planet Ingress

		Dy Hr Mn
♀	♎	1 17:44
☿	♍R	21 7:15
⊙	♎	22 21:48
⚳	♍	24 4:57
♀	♏	26 4:17
♂	♏	8 20:23
☿	♎	10 14:47
♃	♉R	16 20:24
♀	♐	20 17:22
⊙	♏	23 6:58
☿	♏	29 4:55

Last Aspect / ☽ Ingress (September)

Last Aspect Dy Hr Mn		☽ Ingress	Dy Hr Mn
1 7:43	♆ ☌	♑	2 16:29
3 12:12	⊙ △	♒	4 22:20
5 19:09	♄ ☍	♓	7 6:11
8 12:52	⊙ ☍	♈	9 16:18
10 15:55	♄ △	♉	12 4:30
13 23:52	⊙ △	♊	14 17:32
16 17:20	⊙ □	♋	17 5:07
19 6:46	⊙ ⚹	♌	19 13:11
21 7:09	♀ ⚹	♍	21 17:16
23 14:31	☿ ☌	♎	23 18:28
25 17:41	♀ ☌	♏	25 18:34
27 10:01	☿ ⚹	♐	27 19:21
29 11:18	♂ ⚹	♑	29 22:13

Last Aspect / ☽ Ingress (October)

Last Aspect Dy Hr Mn		☽ Ingress	Dy Hr Mn
1 19:09	♂ □	♒	2 3:49
4 6:14	♂ △	♓	4 12:10
6 14:04	☿ ☍	♈	6 22:50
8 4:55	⊙ ☍	♉	9 11:11
11 0:07	♀ ☍	♊	12 0:14
13 17:34	⊙ △	♋	14 12:24
16 21:49	♃ ⚹	♌	16 21:49
19 3:04	♃ □	♍	19 3:25
21 4:47	♃ △	♎	21 5:26
23 5:10	⊙ ☌	♏	23 5:17
25 3:31	♃ ☍	♐	25 4:49
26 23:41	☿ ⚹	♑	27 5:55
29 7:47	♃ △	♒	29 10:05
31 14:55	♃ □	♓	31 17:53

☽ Phases & Eclipses

Dy Hr Mn		
1 3:35	☽	8♐50
8 12:52	○	15♓59
16 17:20	☾	23♊57
23 19:55	●	0♎54
30 11:12	☽	7♑25
8 4:55	○	15♈02
16 8:59	☾	23♋07
23 5:10	●	29♎55
23 5:12:58	●	T 04'47"
29 22:05	☽	6♒37

Astro Data

1 September 1976
Julian Day # 28003
SVP 5♓34'57"
GC 26♐30.8 ⚴ 16♋14.4
Eris 14♈02.0R ⚵ 6♎16.4
⚷ 1♉34.8R ⚶ 8♋55.4
☽ Mean ☊ 6♏19.1

1 October 1976
Julian Day # 28033
SVP 5♓34'54"
GC 26♐30.9 ⚴ 2♌31.1
Eris 13♈45.1R ⚵ 16♎55.3
⚷ 0♉33.3R ⚶ 18♋23.6
☽ Mean ☊ 4♏43.8

November 1976 — LONGITUDE

Day	Sid.Time	☉	0 hr ☽	Noon ☽	True ☊	☿	♀	♂	⚳	♃	♄	♅	♆	♇
1 M	14 43 36	9♏11 50	3♓10 48	9♓22 16	3♏33.4	5♏28.8	14♐19.7	16♏14.7	16♍08.4	28♉20.5	16♌14.3	7♏35.3	12♐27.3	12♎39.1
2 Tu	14 47 33	10 11 54	15 30 10	21 34 56	3 34.1	7 07.7	15 32.5	16 56.6	16 32.3	28R 13.1	16 17.1	7 39.0	12 29.3	12 41.3
3 W	14 51 29	11 11 59	27 37 02	3♈36 52	3 34.8	8 46.2	16 45.3	17 38.5	16 56.2	28 05.6	16 19.8	7 42.8	12 31.2	12 43.4
4 Th	14 55 26	12 12 05	9♈34 50	15 31 18	3 35.6	10 24.3	17 58.1	18 20.4	17 20.0	27 58.1	16 22.4	7 46.5	12 33.2	12 45.5
5 F	14 59 22	13 12 14	21 26 39	27 21 11	3R 36.0	12 01.9	19 10.9	19 02.4	17 43.6	27 50.4	16 24.9	7 50.3	12 35.3	12 47.6
6 Sa	15 03 19	14 12 24	3♉15 13	9♉09 03	3 36.0	13 39.2	20 23.6	19 44.5	18 07.2	27 42.7	16 27.3	7 54.0	12 37.3	12 49.7
7 Su	15 07 15	15 12 36	15 02 56	20 57 09	3 35.4	15 16.1	21 36.2	20 26.6	18 30.7	27 34.9	16 29.6	7 57.8	12 39.3	12 51.8
8 M	15 11 12	16 12 50	26 51 58	2♊47 38	3 34.2	16 52.5	22 48.9	21 08.7	18 54.1	27 27.1	16 31.8	8 01.5	12 41.4	12 53.8
9 Tu	15 15 09	17 13 06	8♊44 25	14 42 35	3 32.4	18 28.7	24 01.5	21 50.9	19 17.3	27 19.1	16 33.9	8 05.2	12 43.5	12 55.8
10 W	15 19 05	18 13 23	20 42 26	26 44 14	3 30.2	20 04.4	25 14.0	22 33.2	19 40.5	27 11.2	16 35.9	8 09.0	12 45.6	12 57.9
11 Th	15 23 02	19 13 43	2♋48 19	8♋55 02	3 27.8	21 39.9	26 26.6	23 15.5	20 03.6	27 03.2	16 37.8	8 12.7	12 47.7	12 59.9
12 F	15 26 58	20 14 04	15 04 43	21 17 44	3 25.6	23 15.0	27 39.1	23 57.9	20 26.6	26 55.1	16 39.5	8 16.4	12 49.8	13 01.8
13 Sa	15 30 55	21 14 27	27 34 30	3♌55 22	3 24.0	24 49.8	28 51.5	24 40.3	20 49.4	26 47.0	16 41.2	8 20.1	12 51.9	13 03.8
14 Su	15 34 51	22 14 52	10♌20 45	16 51 02	3D 23.1	26 24.3	0♑03.9	25 22.8	21 12.2	26 38.9	16 42.7	8 23.8	12 54.0	13 05.7
15 M	15 38 48	23 15 19	23 26 36	0♍07 44	3 23.1	27 58.5	1 16.3	26 05.3	21 34.8	26 30.7	16 44.2	8 27.5	12 56.2	13 07.6
16 Tu	15 42 44	24 15 48	6♍54 45	13 47 49	3 24.0	29 32.5	2 28.6	26 47.9	21 57.3	26 22.5	16 45.5	8 31.1	12 58.3	13 09.5
17 W	15 46 41	25 16 19	20 47 04	27 52 28	3 25.4	1♐06.3	3 40.9	27 30.5	22 19.7	26 14.3	16 46.7	8 34.8	13 00.5	13 11.4
18 Th	15 50 38	26 16 52	5♎03 53	12♎21 01	3 26.8	2 39.8	4 53.2	28 13.2	22 41.9	26 06.2	16 47.8	8 38.4	13 02.7	13 13.3
19 F	15 54 34	27 17 26	19 43 24	27 10 24	3R 27.7	4 13.1	6 05.4	28 56.0	23 04.1	25 58.0	16 48.8	8 42.0	13 04.9	13 15.1
20 Sa	15 58 31	28 18 02	4♏41 11	12♏14 49	3 27.6	5 46.2	7 17.6	29 38.8	23 26.1	25 49.8	16 49.7	8 45.7	13 07.1	13 16.9
21 Su	16 02 27	29 18 40	19 50 10	27 26 03	3 26.1	7 19.1	8 29.7	0♐21.6	23 48.0	25 41.6	16 50.4	8 49.3	13 09.3	13 18.7
22 M	16 06 24	0♐19 19	5♐01 15	12♐34 29	3 23.4	8 51.8	9 41.8	1 04.5	24 09.7	25 33.5	16 51.1	8 52.8	13 11.5	13 20.5
23 Tu	16 10 20	1 19 59	20 04 35	27 30 26	3 19.5	10 24.4	10 53.9	1 47.5	24 31.3	25 25.4	16 51.6	8 56.4	13 13.7	13 22.2
24 W	16 14 17	2 20 41	4♑51 06	12♑05 47	3 15.2	11 56.8	12 05.9	2 30.5	24 52.8	25 17.3	16 52.1	9 00.0	13 15.9	13 23.9
25 Th	16 18 13	3 21 24	19 13 54	26 15 02	3 10.9	13 29.0	13 17.8	3 13.5	25 14.1	25 09.3	16 52.4	9 03.5	13 18.2	13 25.6
26 F	16 22 10	4 22 08	3♒08 59	9♒55 45	3 07.5	15 01.1	14 29.7	3 56.7	25 35.3	25 01.3	16 52.6	9 07.0	13 20.4	13 27.3
27 Sa	16 26 07	5 22 53	16 35 26	23 08 19	3 05.3	16 33.0	15 41.5	4 39.8	25 56.3	24 53.3	16R 52.7	9 10.5	13 22.7	13 28.9
28 Su	16 30 03	6 23 39	29 34 48	5♓55 20	3D 04.5	18 04.7	16 53.2	5 23.0	26 17.2	24 45.5	16 52.7	9 13.9	13 24.9	13 30.5
29 M	16 34 00	7 24 26	12♓10 28	18 20 47	3 05.1	19 36.2	18 04.9	6 06.3	26 37.9	24 37.7	16 52.5	9 17.4	13 27.2	13 32.1
30 Tu	16 37 56	8 25 14	24 26 54	0♈29 25	3 06.6	21 07.6	19 16.5	6 49.6	26 58.4	24 29.9	16 52.3	9 20.8	13 29.4	13 33.7

December 1976 — LONGITUDE

Day	Sid.Time	☉	0 hr ☽	Noon ☽	True ☊	☿	♀	♂	⚳	♃	♄	♅	♆	♇
1 W	16 41 53	9♐26 03	6♈28 59	12♈26 10	3♏08.4	22♐38.7	20♑28.0	7♐32.9	27♍18.8	24♉22.3	16♌51.9	9♏24.2	13♐31.7	13♎35.2
2 Th	16 45 49	10 26 52	18 21 35	24 15 45	3R 09.9	24 09.5	21 39.5	8 16.3	27 39.1	24R 14.7	16R 51.4	9 27.6	13 33.9	13 36.7
3 F	16 49 46	11 27 43	0♉09 13	6♉02 27	3 10.2	25 40.1	22 50.9	8 59.8	27 59.2	24 07.2	16 50.9	9 30.9	13 36.2	13 38.2
4 Sa	16 53 42	12 28 35	11 55 53	17 49 54	3 08.9	27 10.3	24 02.2	9 43.3	28 19.1	23 59.9	16 50.2	9 34.2	13 38.4	13 39.7
5 Su	16 57 39	13 29 27	23 44 53	29 41 08	3 05.7	28 40.2	25 13.4	10 26.8	28 38.8	23 52.6	16 49.3	9 37.5	13 40.7	13 41.1
6 M	17 01 36	14 30 21	5♊38 53	11♊38 25	3 00.4	0♑09.6	26 24.5	11 10.4	28 58.4	23 45.4	16 48.4	9 40.8	13 43.0	13 42.5
7 Tu	17 05 32	15 31 16	17 39 54	23 43 30	2 53.3	1 38.5	27 35.6	11 54.1	29 17.7	23 38.3	16 47.4	9 44.0	13 45.2	13 43.8
8 W	17 09 29	16 32 11	29 49 23	5♋57 39	2 45.0	3 06.8	28 46.5	12 37.8	29 36.9	23 31.4	16 46.3	9 47.3	13 47.5	13 45.2
9 Th	17 13 25	17 33 08	12♋08 27	18 21 52	2 36.4	4 34.4	29 57.4	13 21.5	29 56.0	23 24.6	16 45.0	9 50.4	13 49.8	13 46.5
10 F	17 17 22	18 34 06	24 38 03	0♌57 07	2 28.2	6 01.1	1♒08.2	14 05.3	0♎14.8	23 17.9	16 43.7	9 53.6	13 52.0	13 47.8
11 Sa	17 21 18	19 35 05	7♌19 12	13 44 28	2 21.3	7 26.8	2 18.9	14 49.1	0 33.4	23 11.3	16 42.2	9 56.7	13 54.3	13 49.0
12 Su	17 25 15	20 36 04	20 13 06	26 45 17	2 16.4	8 51.4	3 29.4	15 33.0	0 51.9	23 04.8	16 40.6	9 59.8	13 56.5	13 50.2
13 M	17 29 12	21 37 05	3♍21 15	10♍01 13	2D 13.7	10 14.5	4 39.9	16 17.0	1 10.1	22 58.5	16 38.9	10 02.9	13 58.8	13 51.4
14 Tu	17 33 08	22 38 07	16 45 22	23 33 57	2 12.9	11 36.0	5 50.3	17 01.0	1 28.2	22 52.4	16 37.2	10 05.9	14 01.0	13 52.5
15 W	17 37 05	23 39 10	0♎27 06	7♎24 57	2 13.6	12 55.5	7 00.6	17 45.0	1 46.0	22 46.4	16 35.3	10 08.9	14 03.3	13 53.7
16 Th	17 41 01	24 40 14	14 27 34	21 34 53	2R 14.6	14 12.8	8 10.7	18 29.1	2 03.6	22 40.5	16 33.3	10 11.9	14 05.5	13 54.7
17 F	17 44 58	25 41 19	28 46 47	6♏02 57	2 14.9	15 27.4	9 20.8	19 13.3	2 21.0	22 34.8	16 31.2	10 14.8	14 07.7	13 55.8
18 Sa	17 48 54	26 42 24	13♏22 59	20 46 17	2 13.4	16 38.9	10 30.7	19 57.5	2 38.2	22 29.3	16 29.0	10 17.7	14 10.0	13 56.8
19 Su	17 52 51	27 43 31	28 12 07	5♐39 37	2 09.6	17 46.8	11 40.6	20 41.7	2 55.2	22 23.9	16 26.7	10 20.6	14 12.2	13 57.8
20 M	17 56 47	28 44 38	13♐07 46	20 35 30	2 03.1	18 50.5	12 50.3	21 26.0	3 11.9	22 18.7	16 24.2	10 23.4	14 14.4	13 58.8
21 Tu	18 00 44	29 45 46	28 01 42	5♑25 14	1 54.5	19 49.4	13 59.8	22 10.4	3 28.4	22 13.7	16 21.7	10 26.2	14 16.6	13 59.7
22 W	18 04 41	0♑46 55	12♑45 02	20 00 09	1 44.6	20 42.7	15 09.3	22 54.8	3 44.7	22 08.8	16 19.1	10 28.9	14 18.8	14 00.6
23 Th	18 08 37	1 48 03	27 09 46	4♒13 12	1 34.6	21 29.7	16 18.6	23 39.2	4 00.7	22 04.1	16 16.4	10 31.6	14 21.0	14 01.4
24 F	18 12 34	2 49 12	11♒10 01	17 59 55	1 25.7	22 09.5	17 27.7	24 23.7	4 16.5	21 59.6	16 13.6	10 34.3	14 23.2	14 02.3
25 Sa	18 16 30	3 50 21	24 42 48	1♓18 46	1 18.7	22 41.2	18 36.7	25 08.2	4 32.0	21 55.3	16 10.7	10 36.9	14 25.3	14 03.0
26 Su	18 20 27	4 51 30	7♓48 02	14 10 57	1 14.1	23 03.9	19 45.6	25 52.8	4 47.3	21 51.2	16 07.8	10 39.5	14 27.5	14 03.8
27 M	18 24 23	5 52 39	20 28 01	26 39 47	1D 11.9	23R 16.6	20 54.3	26 37.4	5 02.3	21 47.3	16 04.7	10 42.1	14 29.6	14 04.5
28 Tu	18 28 20	6 53 48	2♈46 51	8♈49 53	1 11.4	23 18.7	22 02.8	27 22.1	5 17.0	21 43.5	16 01.5	10 44.6	14 31.8	14 05.2
29 W	18 32 16	7 54 56	14 49 35	20 46 38	1R 11.9	23 09.5	23 11.1	28 06.8	5 31.5	21 40.0	15 58.3	10 47.0	14 33.9	14 05.8
30 Th	18 36 13	8 56 05	26 41 45	2♉35 36	1 12.2	22 48.4	24 19.3	28 51.5	5 45.7	21 36.6	15 54.9	10 49.5	14 36.0	14 06.4
31 F	18 40 10	9 57 14	8♉28 51	14 22 08	1 11.3	22 15.5	25 27.3	29 36.3	5 59.6	21 33.5	15 51.5	10 51.8	14 38.1	14 07.0

Astro Data	Dy Hr Mn
☽ 0N	2 12:26
♃□♇	5 18:58
☽ 0S	17 1:53
♄ R	27 18:46
☽ 0N	29 19:15
♆✶♇	5 22:20
☽ 0S	14 9:52
☽ 0N	27 4:11
☿ R	28 4:32

Planet Ingress	Dy Hr Mn
♀ ♑	14 10:42
☿ ♐	16 19:02
♂ ♐	20 23:53
☉ ♐	22 4:22
☿ ♑	6 9:25
♀ ♒	9 12:53
⚳ ♎	9 17:07
☉ ♑	21 17:35

Last Aspect Dy Hr Mn		☽ Ingress Dy Hr Mn
3 1:04	♃ ✶	♈ 3 4:46
4 17:31	♀ △	♉ 5 17:23
8 1:18	♃ ☌	♊ 8 6:21
10 8:41	♀ ☍	♋ 10 18:28
12 22:38	♃ ✶	♌ 13 4:36
15 7:39	☿ □	♍ 15 11:46
17 11:21	♂ ✶	♎ 17 15:34
18 19:16	♄ ✶	♏ 19 16:32
21 15:11	☉ ☌	♐ 21 16:03
22 18:50	♄ △	♑ 23 16:03
25 10:08	♃ △	♒ 25 18:30
27 15:13	♃ □	♓ 28 0:47
30 0:13	♃ ✶	♈ 30 11:01

Last Aspect Dy Hr Mn		☽ Ingress Dy Hr Mn
2 11:45	☿ △	♉ 2 23:41
5 1:59	♀ △	♊ 5 12:38
6 22:17	♄ ✶	♋ 8 0:21
9 21:35	♃ ✶	♌ 10 10:12
12 5:19	♃ □	♍ 12 17:55
14 10:48	♃ △	♎ 14 23:13
16 17:33	☉ ✶	♏ 17 2:01
18 14:46	♃ ☍	♐ 19 2:54
21 2:08	☉ ☌	♑ 21 3:12
22 15:34	♃ △	♒ 23 4:48
25 0:06	♂ ✶	♓ 25 9:36
27 11:55	♂ □	♈ 27 18:32
30 3:53	♂ △	♉ 30 6:43

☽ Phases & Eclipses Dy Hr Mn	
6 23:15	○ 14♉41
6 23:01	☍ A 0.838
14 22:39	☾ 22♌42
21 15:11	● 29♏27
28 12:59	☽ 6♓26
6 18:15	○ 14♊46
14 10:14	☾ 22♍34
21 2:08	● 29♐21
28 7:48	☽ 6♈43

Astro Data

1 November 1976
Julian Day # 28064
SVP 5♓34'51"
GC 26♐30.9 ⚴ 17♌26.4
Eris 13♈26.7R ⚵ 27♎55.7
⚷ 29♈08.0R ⚶ 24♋56.5
☽ Mean ☊ 3♏05.3

1 December 1976
Julian Day # 28094
SVP 5♓34'47"
GC 26♐31.0 ⚴ 27♌56.8
Eris 13♈13.2R ⚵ 8♏08.7
⚷ 27♈55.1R ⚶ 26♋05.8R
☽ Mean ☊ 1♏30.0

LONGITUDE — January 1977

Day	Sid.Time	☉	0 hr ☽	Noon ☽	True ☊	☿	♀	♂	⚳	♃	♄	♅	♆	♇
1 Sa	18 44 06	10♑58 22	20♉16 00	26♉11 02	1♏08.2	21♑31.1	26♒35.0	0♑21.1	6♎13.3	21♉30.5	15♌48.0	10♏54.2	14♐40.2	14♎07.6
2 Su	18 48 03	11 59 31	2♊07 41	8♊06 25	1R 02.4	20R 35.9	27 42.6	1 06.0	6 26.6	21R 27.7	15R 44.4	10 56.5	14 42.3	14 08.1
3 M	18 51 59	13 00 39	14 07 33	20 11 26	0 53.8	19 31.3	28 50.0	1 50.9	6 39.7	21 25.2	15 40.8	10 58.7	14 44.3	14 08.5
4 Tu	18 55 56	14 01 47	26 18 16	2♋28 14	0 42.6	18 19.1	29 57.2	2 35.9	6 52.5	21 22.8	15 37.0	11 00.9	14 46.4	14 09.0
5 W	18 59 52	15 02 56	8♋41 26	14 57 55	0 29.7	17 01.5	1♓04.1	3 20.9	7 05.0	21 20.7	15 33.2	11 03.1	14 48.4	14 09.4
6 Th	19 03 49	16 04 04	21 17 41	27 40 41	0 16.1	15 41.1	2 10.8	4 05.9	7 17.2	21 18.7	15 29.3	11 05.2	14 50.4	14 09.7
7 F	19 07 45	17 05 11	4♌06 48	10♌35 58	0 03.1	14 20.5	3 17.3	4 51.0	7 29.1	21 17.0	15 25.4	11 07.2	14 52.4	14 10.1
8 Sa	19 11 42	18 06 19	17 08 03	23 42 55	29♎51.8	13 02.3	4 23.5	5 36.1	7 40.6	21 15.4	15 21.4	11 09.3	14 54.4	14 10.4
9 Su	19 15 39	19 07 27	0♍20 28	7♍00 38	29 43.1	11 48.7	5 29.5	6 21.3	7 51.9	21 14.1	15 17.3	11 11.2	14 56.3	14 10.6
10 M	19 19 35	20 08 35	13 43 21	20 28 36	29 37.4	10 41.7	6 35.3	7 06.5	8 02.8	21 13.0	15 13.1	11 13.1	14 58.3	14 10.8
11 Tu	19 23 32	21 09 42	27 16 22	4♎06 43	29 34.6	9 42.7	7 40.7	7 51.8	8 13.4	21 12.0	15 08.9	11 15.0	15 00.2	14 11.0
12 W	19 27 28	22 10 50	10♎59 40	17 55 18	29 33.7	8 52.7	8 46.0	8 37.1	8 23.7	21 11.3	15 04.6	11 16.8	15 02.1	14 11.2
13 Th	19 31 25	23 11 57	24 53 40	1♏54 48	29 33.7	8 12.3	9 50.9	9 22.4	8 33.6	21 10.8	15 00.3	11 18.6	15 04.0	14 11.3
14 F	19 35 21	24 13 05	8♏58 39	16 05 08	29 33.1	7 41.6	10 55.6	10 07.8	8 43.2	21D 10.5	14 55.9	11 20.3	15 05.8	14 11.4
15 Sa	19 39 18	25 14 12	23 14 07	0♐25 17	29 30.6	7 20.6	11 59.9	10 53.2	8 52.4	21 10.4	14 51.5	11 22.0	15 07.7	14R 11.4
16 Su	19 43 14	26 15 20	7♐38 17	14 52 36	29 25.4	7D 08.9	13 04.0	11 38.7	9 01.3	21 10.5	14 47.0	11 23.6	15 09.5	14 11.4
17 M	19 47 11	27 16 27	22 07 39	29 22 42	29 17.1	7 06.0	14 07.7	12 24.2	9 09.8	21 10.8	14 42.5	11 25.2	15 11.3	14 11.4
18 Tu	19 51 08	28 17 33	6♑36 59	13♑49 41	29 06.2	7 11.5	15 11.2	13 09.7	9 18.0	21 11.4	14 37.9	11 26.7	15 13.1	14 11.4
19 W	19 55 04	29 18 40	20 59 55	28 06 54	28 53.6	7 24.5	16 14.2	13 55.3	9 25.8	21 12.1	14 33.3	11 28.2	15 14.9	14 11.3
20 Th	19 59 01	0♒19 45	5♒09 51	12♒08 06	28 40.6	7 44.7	17 17.0	14 40.9	9 33.2	21 13.0	14 28.6	11 29.6	15 16.6	14 11.1
21 F	20 02 57	1 20 50	19 01 06	25 48 26	28 28.7	8 11.2	18 19.4	15 26.6	9 40.2	21 14.2	14 23.9	11 31.0	15 18.3	14 11.0
22 Sa	20 06 54	2 21 53	2♓29 51	9♓05 14	28 18.8	8 43.6	19 21.4	16 12.3	9 46.8	21 15.5	14 19.2	11 32.3	15 20.0	14 10.7
23 Su	20 10 50	3 22 56	15 34 37	21 58 10	28 11.8	9 21.3	20 23.0	16 58.0	9 53.1	21 17.1	14 14.5	11 33.5	15 21.7	14 10.5
24 M	20 14 47	4 23 58	28 16 11	4♈29 05	28 07.5	10 03.9	21 24.2	17 43.7	9 59.0	21 18.9	14 09.7	11 34.7	15 23.3	14 10.2
25 Tu	20 18 43	5 24 59	10♈37 21	16 41 33	28D 05.6	10 50.7	22 25.0	18 29.5	10 04.4	21 20.8	14 04.9	11 35.9	15 25.0	14 09.9
26 W	20 22 40	6 25 59	22 42 19	28 40 18	28R 05.3	11 41.5	23 25.4	19 15.4	10 09.5	21 23.0	14 00.0	11 37.0	15 26.6	14 09.6
27 Th	20 26 37	7 26 57	4♉36 11	10♉30 42	28 05.3	12 35.9	24 25.3	20 01.2	10 14.2	21 25.4	13 55.2	11 38.0	15 28.1	14 09.2
28 F	20 30 33	8 27 55	16 24 31	22 18 23	28 04.5	13 33.5	25 24.8	20 47.1	10 18.4	21 27.9	13 50.3	11 39.0	15 29.7	14 08.8
29 Sa	20 34 30	9 28 51	28 12 56	4♊08 51	28 02.0	14 34.0	26 23.7	21 33.0	10 22.3	21 30.7	13 45.4	11 39.9	15 31.2	14 08.3
30 Su	20 38 26	10 29 46	10♊06 43	16 07 08	27 56.9	15 37.2	27 22.2	22 19.0	10 25.8	21 33.6	13 40.5	11 40.8	15 32.7	14 07.9
31 M	20 42 23	11 30 40	22 10 34	28 17 29	27 49.2	16 42.9	28 20.1	23 04.9	10 28.8	21 36.8	13 35.7	11 41.6	15 34.2	14 07.4

LONGITUDE — February 1977

Day	Sid.Time	☉	0 hr ☽	Noon ☽	True ☊	☿	♀	♂	⚳	♃	♄	♅	♆	♇
1 Tu	20 46 19	12♒31 33	4♋28 14	10♋43 06	27♎38.9	17♑50.8	29♓17.5	23♑50.9	10♎31.4	21♉40.1	13♌30.7	11♏42.4	15♐35.6	14♎06.8
2 W	20 50 16	13 32 24	17 02 16	23 25 51	27R 26.7	19 00.7	0♈14.4	24 37.0	10 33.6	21 43.7	13R 25.8	11 43.1	15 37.0	14R 06.2
3 Th	20 54 12	14 33 15	29 53 51	6♌26 11	27 13.8	20 12.5	1 10.6	25 23.1	10 35.4	21 47.4	13 20.9	11 43.7	15 38.4	14 05.6
4 F	20 58 09	15 34 04	13♌02 40	19 43 05	27 01.4	21 26.1	2 06.3	26 09.2	10 36.7	21 51.3	13 16.0	11 44.3	15 39.8	14 05.0
5 Sa	21 02 06	16 34 52	26 27 06	3♍14 24	26 50.6	22 41.4	3 01.3	26 55.3	10 37.6	21 55.4	13 11.1	11 44.9	15 41.1	14 04.3
6 Su	21 06 02	17 35 38	10♍04 35	16 57 16	26 42.3	23 58.1	3 55.7	27 41.4	10R 38.1	21 59.7	13 06.3	11 45.4	15 42.4	14 03.6
7 M	21 09 59	18 36 24	23 52 06	0♎48 43	26 36.9	25 16.3	4 49.5	28 27.6	10 38.1	22 04.2	13 01.4	11 45.8	15 43.7	14 02.9
8 Tu	21 13 55	19 37 09	7♎46 49	14 46 06	26D 34.3	26 35.9	5 42.5	29 13.9	10 37.8	22 08.8	12 56.5	11 46.2	15 44.9	14 02.1
9 W	21 17 52	20 37 52	21 46 22	28 47 26	26 33.8	27 56.7	6 34.8	0♒00.1	10 36.9	22 13.6	12 51.7	11 46.5	15 46.2	14 01.3
10 Th	21 21 48	21 38 35	5♏49 09	12♏51 26	26R 34.2	29 18.8	7 26.4	0 46.4	10 35.7	22 18.6	12 46.8	11 46.8	15 47.3	14 00.5
11 F	21 25 45	22 39 16	19 54 09	26 57 13	26 34.4	0♒42.1	8 17.2	1 32.7	10 34.0	22 23.8	12 42.0	11 47.0	15 48.5	13 59.6
12 Sa	21 29 41	23 39 57	4♐00 31	11♐03 55	26 33.0	2 06.4	9 07.3	2 19.0	10 31.8	22 29.2	12 37.3	11 47.1	15 49.6	13 58.7
13 Su	21 33 38	24 40 37	18 07 15	25 10 16	26 29.4	3 31.9	9 56.5	3 05.4	10 29.3	22 34.7	12 32.5	11 47.2	15 50.7	13 57.8
14 M	21 37 35	25 41 15	2♑12 41	9♑14 09	26 23.2	4 58.4	10 44.8	3 51.8	10 26.2	22 40.4	12 27.8	11R 47.3	15 51.8	13 56.9
15 Tu	21 41 31	26 41 52	16 14 18	23 12 40	26 14.7	6 25.9	11 32.3	4 38.2	10 22.8	22 46.3	12 23.1	11 47.3	15 52.8	13 55.9
16 W	21 45 28	27 42 28	0♒08 48	7♒02 15	26 04.8	7 54.5	12 18.9	5 24.6	10 18.9	22 52.3	12 18.4	11 47.2	15 53.9	13 54.9
17 Th	21 49 24	28 43 02	13 52 32	20 39 13	25 54.4	9 24.0	13 04.5	6 11.1	10 14.5	22 58.5	12 13.8	11 47.1	15 54.8	13 53.9
18 F	21 53 21	29 43 35	27 21 57	4♓00 25	25 44.7	10 54.5	13 49.1	6 57.6	10 09.8	23 04.9	12 09.3	11 46.9	15 55.8	13 52.8
19 Sa	21 57 17	0♓44 06	10♓34 21	17 03 40	25 36.8	12 26.0	14 32.6	7 44.1	10 04.6	23 11.5	12 04.7	11 46.7	15 56.7	13 51.7
20 Su	22 01 14	1 44 36	23 28 17	29 48 15	25 31.1	13 58.5	15 15.1	8 30.6	9 59.0	23 18.1	12 00.2	11 46.4	15 57.6	13 50.6
21 M	22 05 10	2 45 04	6♈03 45	12♈15 01	25 27.8	15 31.9	15 56.5	9 17.1	9 52.9	23 25.0	11 55.8	11 46.0	15 58.4	13 49.5
22 Tu	22 09 07	3 45 30	18 22 21	24 26 10	25D 26.8	17 06.2	16 36.7	10 03.7	9 46.5	23 32.0	11 51.4	11 45.6	15 59.2	13 48.3
23 W	22 13 04	4 45 54	0♉26 57	6♉25 13	25 27.3	18 41.5	17 15.6	10 50.3	9 39.6	23 39.2	11 47.1	11 45.2	16 00.0	13 47.1
24 Th	22 17 00	5 46 17	12 21 32	18 16 31	25 28.6	20 17.8	17 53.3	11 36.9	9 32.4	23 46.5	11 42.8	11 44.7	16 00.7	13 45.9
25 F	22 20 57	6 46 37	24 10 48	0♊05 03	25R 29.7	21 55.1	18 29.7	12 23.5	9 24.7	23 54.0	11 38.6	11 44.1	16 01.5	13 44.7
26 Sa	22 24 53	7 46 55	5♊59 56	11 56 06	25 29.9	23 33.4	19 04.7	13 10.1	9 16.7	24 01.6	11 34.5	11 43.5	16 02.1	13 43.5
27 Su	22 28 50	8 47 12	17 54 15	23 54 59	25 28.4	25 12.6	19 38.3	13 56.7	9 08.3	24 09.4	11 30.4	11 42.9	16 02.8	13 42.2
28 M	22 32 46	9 47 27	29 58 54	6♋06 35	25 25.0	26 52.9	20 10.4	14 43.4	8 59.5	24 17.3	11 26.4	11 42.2	16 03.4	13 40.9

Astro Data	Dy Hr Mn
☽ 0S	10 16:32
♄△♆	12 21:54
♃ D	15 10:56
♇ R	16 7:05
☿ D	17 8:00
☽ 0N	23 14:35
♄✶♇	24 9:01
♀0N	31 0:16
☽ 0S	6 23:33
⚳ R	7 2:43
♅ R	14 19:50
☽ 0N	20 0:33
♄□♅	24 0:04

Planet Ingress		Dy Hr Mn
♂	♑	1 0:42
♀	♓	4 13:01
☊	♎R	7 18:05
☉	♒	20 4:14
♀	♈	2 5:54
♂	♒	9 11:57
☿	♒	10 23:55
☉	♓	18 18:30

Last Aspect Dy Hr Mn		☽ Ingress	Dy Hr Mn
1 12:54	♀ □	♊	1 19:43
4 6:37	♀ △	♋	4 7:12
6 0:04	♃ ✶	♌	6 16:20
8 7:32	♃ □	♍	8 23:23
10 13:18	♃ △	♎	11 4:48
12 19:55	☉ □	♏	13 8:44
15 2:41	☉ ✶	♐	15 11:18
16 12:28	♆ ☌	♑	17 13:02
19 14:11	☉ ☌	♒	19 15:12
21 3:53	♃ □	♓	21 19:30
23 10:42	♃ ✶	♈	24 3:19
25 15:49	♂ □	♉	26 14:41
28 18:53	♀ ✶	♊	29 3:37
31 12:06	♀ □	♋	31 15:20

Last Aspect Dy Hr Mn		☽ Ingress	Dy Hr Mn
2 14:21	♂ ☍	♌	3 0:11
4 15:50	♃ □	♍	5 6:17
7 7:42	♂ △	♎	7 10:36
9 10:24	☿ □	♏	9 14:04
11 4:12	♃ ☍	♐	11 17:11
13 11:06	☉ ✶	♑	13 20:14
15 11:14	♃ △	♒	15 23:45
18 3:37	☉ ☌	♓	18 4:45
19 23:34	♃ ✶	♈	20 12:22
21 19:39	♀ ☌	♉	22 23:06
24 23:18	♃ ☌	♊	25 11:50
27 14:59	☿ △	♋	28 0:02

☽ Phases & Eclipses Dy Hr Mn		
5 12:10	○	15♋03
12 19:55	☾	22♎31
19 14:11	●	29♑24
27 5:11	☽	7♉10
4 3:56	○	15♌14
11 4:07	☾	22♏19
18 3:37	●	29♒22
26 2:50	☽	7♊24

Astro Data

1 January 1977
Julian Day # 28125
SVP 5♓34'42"
GC 26♐31.1 ⚴ 1♍19.6R
Eris 13♈08.2 ⚵ 17♏38.9
⚷ 27♈18.7R ⚶ 20♋42.0R
☽ Mean ☊ 29♎51.5

1 February 1977
Julian Day # 28156
SVP 5♓34'37"
GC 26♐31.2 ⚴ 24♌40.6R
Eris 13♈13.9 ⚵ 25♏12.3
⚷ 27♈35.9 ⚶ 13♋08.1R
☽ Mean ☊ 28♎13.0

March 1977

LONGITUDE

Day	Sid.Time	☉	0 hr ☽	Noon ☽	True ☊	☿	♀	♂	⚳	♃	♄	♅	♆	♇
1 Tu	22 36 43	10♓47 39	12♋18 32	18♋35 10	25♎19.8	28♒34.2	20♈41.0	15♒30.1	8♎50.3	24♉25.3	11♌22.4	11♏41.4	16♐04.0	13♎39.6
2 W	22 40 39	11 47 49	24 56 52	1♌23 52	25R13.1	0♓16.5	21 09.9	16 16.7	8R40.8	24 33.5	11R18.5	11R40.6	16 04.5	13R38.2
3 Th	22 44 36	12 47 58	7♌56 20	14 34 19	25 05.7	1 59.9	21 37.2	17 03.4	8 31.0	24 41.8	11 14.7	11 39.7	16 05.1	13 36.9
4 F	22 48 33	13 48 04	21 17 44	28 06 23	24 58.4	3 44.3	22 02.8	17 50.1	8 20.8	24 50.3	11 11.0	11 38.8	16 05.5	13 35.5
5 Sa	22 52 29	14 48 09	4♍59 57	11♍58 03	24 52.1	5 29.8	22 26.5	18 36.9	8 10.4	24 58.9	11 07.3	11 37.8	16 06.0	13 34.1
6 Su	22 56 26	15 48 12	19 00 09	26 05 41	24 47.5	7 16.4	22 48.5	19 23.6	7 59.6	25 07.6	11 03.7	11 36.8	16 06.4	13 32.7
7 M	23 00 22	16 48 12	3♎14 00	10♎24 28	24D44.8	9 04.1	23 08.5	20 10.3	7 48.5	25 16.5	11 00.2	11 35.7	16 06.8	13 31.2
8 Tu	23 04 19	17 48 11	17 36 25	24 49 12	24 43.9	10 53.0	23 26.5	20 57.1	7 37.1	25 25.5	10 56.8	11 34.6	16 07.1	13 29.8
9 W	23 08 15	18 48 09	2♏02 13	9♏14 56	24 44.6	12 42.9	23 42.6	21 43.9	7 25.4	25 34.6	10 53.4	11 33.5	16 07.4	13 28.3
10 Th	23 12 12	19 48 05	16 26 49	23 37 30	24 46.0	14 33.9	23 56.5	22 30.6	7 13.5	25 43.8	10 50.2	11 32.2	16 07.7	13 26.8
11 F	23 16 08	20 47 59	0♐46 35	7♐53 47	24R47.3	16 26.1	24 08.3	23 17.4	7 01.4	25 53.2	10 47.0	11 31.0	16 08.0	13 25.3
12 Sa	23 20 05	21 47 52	14 58 53	22 01 41	24 47.9	18 19.4	24 17.9	24 04.2	6 49.0	26 02.7	10 43.9	11 29.7	16 08.2	13 23.8
13 Su	23 24 01	22 47 43	29 02 02	5♑59 47	24 47.2	20 13.7	24 25.2	24 51.0	6 36.4	26 12.3	10 40.9	11 28.3	16 08.4	13 22.3
14 M	23 27 58	23 47 32	12♑54 52	19 47 08	24 45.0	22 09.2	24 30.3	25 37.9	6 23.6	26 22.0	10 38.0	11 26.9	16 08.5	13 20.7
15 Tu	23 31 55	24 47 19	26 36 32	3♒22 57	24 41.5	24 05.6	24R33.3	26 24.7	6 10.6	26 31.8	10 35.1	11 25.5	16 08.6	13 19.2
16 W	23 35 51	25 47 05	10♒06 18	16 46 29	24 37.1	26 03.0	24 33.3	27 11.5	5 57.4	26 41.8	10 32.4	11 24.0	16 08.7	13 17.6
17 Th	23 39 48	26 46 49	23 23 24	29 56 59	24 32.4	28 01.3	24 31.2	27 58.4	5 44.1	26 51.8	10 29.8	11 22.5	16R08.8	13 16.0
18 F	23 43 44	27 46 31	6♓27 10	12♓53 52	24 28.1	0♈00.3	24 26.6	28 45.2	5 30.7	27 02.0	10 27.2	11 20.9	16 08.8	13 14.4
19 Sa	23 47 41	28 46 12	19 17 06	25 36 50	24 24.6	2 00.1	24 19.5	29 32.0	5 17.1	27 12.3	10 24.8	11 19.3	16 08.8	13 12.8
20 Su	23 51 37	29 45 50	1♈53 07	8♈06 04	24 22.2	4 00.4	24 10.0	0♓18.9	5 03.5	27 22.7	10 22.4	11 17.6	16 08.7	13 11.2
21 M	23 55 34	0♈45 26	14 15 46	20 22 25	24D21.2	6 01.1	23 57.9	1 05.7	4 49.8	27 33.2	10 20.2	11 15.9	16 08.6	13 09.6
22 Tu	23 59 30	1 45 00	26 26 15	2♉27 31	24 21.4	8 02.0	23 43.4	1 52.6	4 36.0	27 43.8	10 18.0	11 14.2	16 08.5	13 07.9
23 W	0 03 27	2 44 32	8♉26 34	14 23 46	24 22.5	10 02.9	23 26.5	2 39.4	4 22.2	27 54.4	10 16.0	11 12.4	16 08.3	13 06.3
24 Th	0 07 24	3 44 02	20 19 31	26 14 18	24 24.1	12 03.4	23 07.1	3 26.3	4 08.3	28 05.2	10 14.0	11 10.6	16 08.1	13 04.6
25 F	0 11 20	4 43 29	2♊08 35	8♊02 55	24 25.7	14 03.4	22 45.4	4 13.1	3 54.5	28 16.1	10 12.2	11 08.8	16 07.9	13 03.0
26 Sa	0 15 17	5 42 54	13 57 51	19 53 59	24 27.1	16 02.5	22 21.5	4 59.9	3 40.7	28 27.1	10 10.5	11 06.9	16 07.7	13 01.3
27 Su	0 19 13	6 42 17	25 51 52	1♋52 09	24R27.8	18 00.3	21 55.4	5 46.7	3 26.9	28 38.2	10 08.8	11 05.0	16 07.4	12 59.7
28 M	0 23 10	7 41 38	7♋55 25	14 02 15	24 27.7	19 56.5	21 27.2	6 33.6	3 13.2	28 49.4	10 07.3	11 03.0	16 07.1	12 58.0
29 Tu	0 27 06	8 40 56	20 13 14	26 28 54	24 26.9	21 50.7	20 57.2	7 20.4	2 59.6	29 00.6	10 05.9	11 01.0	16 06.7	12 56.3
30 W	0 31 03	9 40 12	2♌49 44	9♌16 10	24 25.5	23 42.5	20 25.4	8 07.2	2 46.0	29 12.0	10 04.6	10 59.0	16 06.3	12 54.7
31 Th	0 34 59	10 39 26	15 48 31	22 27 04	24 23.8	25 31.4	19 52.1	8 54.0	2 32.6	29 23.4	10 03.3	10 57.0	16 05.9	12 53.0

April 1977

LONGITUDE

Day	Sid.Time	☉	0 hr ☽	Noon ☽	True ☊	☿	♀	♂	⚳	♃	♄	♅	♆	♇
1 F	0 38 56	11♈38 38	29♌11 56	6♍03 07	24♎22.0	27♈17.1	19♈17.4	9♓40.8	2♎19.2	29♉34.9	10♌02.2	10♏54.9	16♐05.5	12♎51.3
2 Sa	0 42 53	12 37 47	13♍00 30	20 03 48	24R20.5	28 59.2	18R41.6	10 27.5	2R06.0	29 46.5	10R01.2	10R52.7	16R05.0	12R49.6
3 Su	0 46 49	13 36 54	27 12 37	4♎26 23	24 19.4	0♉37.3	18 04.9	11 14.3	1 53.0	29 58.2	10 00.3	10 50.6	16 04.5	12 47.9
4 M	0 50 46	14 35 59	11♎44 24	19 05 53	24D19.0	2 11.0	17 27.5	12 01.1	1 40.2	0♊09.9	9 59.6	10 48.4	16 03.9	12 46.3
5 Tu	0 54 42	15 35 02	26 29 56	3♏55 38	24 19.0	3 40.2	16 49.7	12 47.8	1 27.5	0 21.8	9 58.9	10 46.2	16 03.4	12 44.6
6 W	0 58 39	16 34 03	11♏22 00	18 48 06	24 19.5	5 04.3	16 11.8	13 34.6	1 15.0	0 33.7	9 58.3	10 44.0	16 02.8	12 42.9
7 Th	1 02 35	17 33 02	26 13 02	3♐35 55	24 20.1	6 23.3	15 33.9	14 21.3	1 02.8	0 45.7	9 57.9	10 41.8	16 02.2	12 41.2
8 F	1 06 32	18 31 59	10♐56 03	18 12 47	24 20.6	7 36.9	14 56.5	15 08.1	0 50.8	0 57.7	9 57.5	10 39.5	16 01.5	12 39.6
9 Sa	1 10 28	19 30 55	25 25 35	2♑34 03	24 21.0	8 44.8	14 19.6	15 54.8	0 39.0	1 09.9	9 57.3	10 37.2	16 00.8	12 37.9
10 Su	1 14 25	20 29 49	9♑37 54	16 36 59	24R21.2	9 47.0	13 43.6	16 41.5	0 27.5	1 22.1	9D57.1	10 34.9	16 00.1	12 36.2
11 M	1 18 21	21 28 42	23 31 11	0♒20 32	24 21.2	10 43.2	13 08.7	17 28.2	0 16.2	1 34.3	9 57.1	10 32.5	15 59.3	12 34.6
12 Tu	1 22 18	22 27 32	7♒05 07	13 45 02	24 21.1	11 33.3	12 35.0	18 14.9	0 05.3	1 46.7	9 57.2	10 30.2	15 58.6	12 32.9
13 W	1 26 15	23 26 21	20 20 29	26 51 39	24D20.9	12 17.3	12 02.9	19 01.6	29♍54.6	1 59.1	9 57.4	10 27.8	15 57.8	12 31.3
14 Th	1 30 11	24 25 08	3♓18 46	9♓42 04	24 20.9	12 55.0	11 32.4	19 48.2	29 44.3	2 11.6	9 57.7	10 25.4	15 56.9	12 29.6
15 F	1 34 08	25 23 53	16 01 47	22 18 10	24 21.0	13 26.5	11 03.8	20 34.8	29 34.2	2 24.1	9 58.1	10 23.0	15 56.1	12 28.0
16 Sa	1 38 04	26 22 37	28 31 25	4♈41 47	24 21.1	13 51.6	10 37.1	21 21.5	29 24.5	2 36.7	9 58.6	10 20.5	15 55.2	12 26.4
17 Su	1 42 01	27 21 19	10♈49 29	16 54 45	24R21.2	14 10.5	10 12.5	22 08.1	29 15.1	2 49.3	9 59.2	10 18.1	15 54.3	12 24.8
18 M	1 45 57	28 19 58	22 57 48	28 58 50	24 21.2	14 23.2	9 50.1	22 54.6	29 06.1	3 02.0	10 00.0	10 15.6	15 53.3	12 23.2
19 Tu	1 49 54	29 18 36	4♉58 07	10♉55 52	24 21.0	14R29.7	9 29.9	23 41.2	28 57.4	3 14.8	10 00.8	10 13.1	15 52.4	12 21.6
20 W	1 53 50	0♉17 12	16 52 21	22 47 50	24 20.5	14 30.2	9 12.1	24 27.7	28 49.1	3 27.6	10 01.8	10 10.6	15 51.4	12 20.0
21 Th	1 57 47	1 15 46	28 42 38	4♊37 02	24 19.7	14 25.0	8 56.7	25 14.2	28 41.2	3 40.5	10 02.8	10 08.1	15 50.4	12 18.4
22 F	2 01 44	2 14 18	10♊31 24	16 26 07	24 18.6	14 14.2	8 43.6	26 00.7	28 33.7	3 53.5	10 04.0	10 05.6	15 49.3	12 16.9
23 Sa	2 05 40	3 12 48	22 21 34	28 18 12	24 17.5	13 58.2	8 33.0	26 47.2	28 26.5	4 06.4	10 05.3	10 03.1	15 48.3	12 15.3
24 Su	2 09 37	4 11 15	4♋16 27	10♋16 50	24 16.4	13 37.4	8 24.8	27 33.6	28 19.7	4 19.5	10 06.6	10 00.6	15 47.2	12 13.8
25 M	2 13 33	5 09 41	16 19 50	22 25 58	24 15.6	13 12.2	8 19.1	28 20.0	28 13.4	4 32.6	10 08.1	9 58.0	15 46.1	12 12.3
26 Tu	2 17 30	6 08 05	28 35 46	4♌49 46	24D15.3	12 43.1	8D15.7	29 06.4	28 07.4	4 45.7	10 09.7	9 55.5	15 44.9	12 10.8
27 W	2 21 26	7 06 26	11♌08 29	17 32 25	24 15.5	12 10.8	8 14.8	29 52.7	28 01.8	4 58.9	10 11.4	9 53.0	15 43.8	12 09.3
28 Th	2 25 23	8 04 45	24 02 01	0♍37 41	24 16.3	11 35.7	8 16.1	0♈39.1	27 56.7	5 12.1	10 13.2	9 50.4	15 42.6	12 07.8
29 F	2 29 19	9 03 02	7♍19 44	14 08 25	24 17.4	10 58.7	8 19.8	1 25.3	27 51.9	5 25.3	10 15.1	9 47.9	15 41.4	12 06.3
30 Sa	2 33 16	10 01 18	21 03 51	28 06 00	24 18.5	10 20.4	8 25.8	2 11.6	27 47.6	5 38.6	10 17.1	9 45.3	15 40.1	12 04.9

Astro Data	Dy Hr Mn
☽0S	6 8:10
♀R	16 3:01
♆R	18 7:35
☽0N	19 8:37
☿0N	19 16:57
☉0N	20 17:42
♃⊡♇	24 10:51
☽0S	2 18:15
♄D	11 5:41
☽0N	15 14:48
☿R	20 2:08
♄□♅	22 22:25
♀D	27 9:49
☽0S	30 4:40

Planet Ingress		Dy Hr Mn
☿	♓	2 8:09
☿	♈	18 11:56
♂	♓	20 2:19
☉	♈	20 17:42
☿	♉	3 2:46
♃	♊	3 15:42
⚳	♍R	12 23:48
☉	♉	20 4:57
♂	♈	27 15:46

Last Aspect Dy Hr Mn			☽ Ingress	Dy Hr Mn
1 23:08	♃	✶	♌	2 9:25
4 6:12	♃	□	♍	4 15:19
6 10:21	♃	△	♎	6 18:34
8 9:40	♀	☍	♏	8 20:37
10 15:34	♃	☍	♐	10 22:42
12 15:55	♀	△	♑	13 1:40
14 23:43	♃	△	♒	15 6:00
17 8:09	♂	☌	♓	17 12:06
19 18:33	☉	☌	♈	19 20:23
21 18:58	♀	☌	♉	22 7:05
24 15:49	♃	☌	♊	24 19:39
26 16:47	♀	✶	♋	27 8:16
29 16:52	♃	✶	♌	29 18:40

Last Aspect Dy Hr Mn			☽ Ingress	Dy Hr Mn
1 0:31	♃	□	♍	1 1:25
3 4:30	♃	△	♎	3 4:39
4 9:26	♀	☍	♏	5 5:40
6 3:06	♂	△	♐	7 6:08
8 12:34	☉	△	♑	9 7:40
10 19:15	☉	□	♒	11 11:24
13 5:10	☉	✶	♓	13 17:49
15 8:29	♂	☌	♈	16 2:52
18 10:35	☉	☌	♉	18 14:02
20 15:37	♂	✶	♊	21 2:37
23 8:44	♂	□	♋	23 15:25
26 0:15	♂	△	♌	26 2:43
27 8:38	♆	△	♍	28 10:52
29 14:42	♆	□	♎	30 15:13

☽ Phases & Eclipses Dy Hr Mn	
5 17:13	○ 15♍01
12 11:35	☾ 21♐47
19 18:33	● 29♓02
27 22:27	☽ 7♋08
4 4:09	○ 14♎17
4 4:18	• P 0.193
10 19:15	☾ 20♑48
18 10:35	● 28♈17
18 10:30:42	• A 07'04"
26 14:42	☽ 6♌15

Astro Data

1 March 1977
Julian Day # 28184
SVP 5♓34'34"
GC 26♐31.2 ⚴ 16♌01.8R
Eris 13♈27.0 ✱ 29♏18.6
⚷ 28♈34.6 ⚶ 10♋46.5
☽ Mean ☊ 26♎44.0

1 April 1977
Julian Day # 28215
SVP 5♓34'32"
GC 26♐31.3 ⚴ 13♌30.9
Eris 13♈46.8 ✱ 29♏28.3R
⚷ 0♉13.0 ⚶ 14♋35.4
☽ Mean ☊ 25♎05.5

LONGITUDE — May 1977

Day	Sid.Time	☉	0 hr ☽	Noon☽	True☊	☿	♀	♂	⚳	♃	♄	♅	♆	♇
1 Su	2 37 13	10♉59 31	5♎14 42	12♎29 37	24♎19.4	9♉41.5	8♈34.0	2♈57.8	27♍43.7	5♊51.9	10♌19.3	9♏42.8	15♐38.9	12♎03.5
2 M	2 41 09	11 57 42	19 50 13	27 15 49	24R 19.6	9R 02.7	8 44.3	3 44.0	27R 40.1	6 05.3	10 21.5	9R 40.2	15R 37.6	12R 02.1
3 Tu	2 45 06	12 55 51	4♏45 33	12♏18 25	24 19.0	8 24.7	8 56.8	4 30.2	27 37.0	6 18.7	10 23.8	9 37.7	15 36.4	12 00.7
4 W	2 49 02	13 53 59	19 53 18	27 28 58	24 17.4	7 48.1	9 11.3	5 16.4	27 34.4	6 32.2	10 26.2	9 35.2	15 35.1	11 59.3
5 Th	2 52 59	14 52 06	5♐04 14	12♐37 50	24 15.1	7 13.6	9 27.8	6 02.5	27 32.1	6 45.7	10 28.7	9 32.6	15 33.7	11 58.0
6 F	2 56 55	15 50 10	20 08 40	27 35 41	24 12.3	6 41.6	9 46.2	6 48.5	27 30.2	6 59.2	10 31.3	9 30.1	15 32.4	11 56.6
7 Sa	3 00 52	16 48 14	4♑58 00	12♑14 53	24 09.6	6 12.8	10 06.5	7 34.6	27 28.8	7 12.7	10 34.0	9 27.6	15 31.0	11 55.3
8 Su	3 04 48	17 46 16	19 25 48	26 30 23	24 07.5	5 47.5	10 28.6	8 20.6	27 27.7	7 26.3	10 36.8	9 25.1	15 29.7	11 54.0
9 M	3 08 45	18 44 16	3♒28 27	10♒19 58	24D 06.2	5 26.0	10 52.5	9 06.6	27 27.1	7 39.9	10 39.7	9 22.6	15 28.3	11 52.8
10 Tu	3 12 42	19 42 15	17 05 03	23 43 55	24 06.0	5 08.6	11 18.0	9 52.5	27D 26.8	7 53.5	10 42.7	9 20.1	15 26.9	11 51.5
11 W	3 16 38	20 40 13	0♓16 53	6♓44 19	24 06.8	4 55.5	11 45.1	10 38.5	27 27.0	8 07.2	10 45.8	9 17.6	15 25.4	11 50.3
12 Th	3 20 35	21 38 10	13 06 40	19 24 23	24 08.3	4 47.0	12 13.8	11 24.3	27 27.6	8 20.9	10 49.0	9 15.1	15 24.0	11 49.1
13 F	3 24 31	22 36 05	25 37 56	1♈47 48	24 10.0	4D 42.9	12 44.0	12 10.2	27 28.6	8 34.6	10 52.3	9 12.6	15 22.5	11 47.9
14 Sa	3 28 28	23 33 59	7♈54 26	13 58 16	24R 11.3	4 43.5	13 15.6	12 56.0	27 30.0	8 48.3	10 55.7	9 10.2	15 21.1	11 46.8
15 Su	3 32 24	24 31 52	19 59 44	25 59 14	24 11.7	4 48.8	13 48.6	13 41.7	27 31.7	9 02.1	10 59.2	9 07.8	15 19.6	11 45.6
16 M	3 36 21	25 29 43	1♉57 08	7♉53 45	24 10.8	4 58.6	14 22.9	14 27.5	27 33.9	9 15.9	11 02.7	9 05.3	15 18.1	11 44.5
17 Tu	3 40 17	26 27 34	13 49 24	19 44 24	24 08.3	5 12.9	14 58.5	15 13.1	27 36.5	9 29.7	11 06.4	9 02.9	15 16.6	11 43.4
18 W	3 44 14	27 25 22	25 38 59	1♊33 25	24 04.2	5 31.7	15 35.3	15 58.8	27 39.5	9 43.5	11 10.1	9 00.6	15 15.1	11 42.4
19 Th	3 48 11	28 23 10	7♊27 57	13 22 49	23 58.8	5 54.9	16 13.3	16 44.4	27 42.8	9 57.4	11 13.9	8 58.2	15 13.6	11 41.4
20 F	3 52 07	29 20 56	19 18 16	25 14 32	23 52.5	6 22.3	16 52.4	17 29.9	27 46.6	10 11.2	11 17.9	8 55.9	15 12.0	11 40.4
21 Sa	3 56 04	0♊18 40	1♋11 53	7♋10 36	23 46.0	6 53.9	17 32.5	18 15.4	27 50.7	10 25.1	11 21.9	8 53.5	15 10.5	11 39.4
22 Su	4 00 00	1 16 23	13 10 58	19 13 19	23 39.9	7 29.5	18 13.8	19 00.9	27 55.2	10 39.0	11 26.0	8 51.2	15 08.9	11 38.4
23 M	4 03 57	2 14 05	25 18 00	1♌25 23	23 34.8	8 09.0	18 56.0	19 46.3	28 00.1	10 52.9	11 30.2	8 49.0	15 07.3	11 37.5
24 Tu	4 07 53	3 11 45	7♌35 53	13 49 54	23 31.3	8 52.3	19 39.1	20 31.7	28 05.3	11 06.8	11 34.4	8 46.7	15 05.8	11 36.6
25 W	4 11 50	4 09 23	20 07 55	26 30 20	23D 29.5	9 39.2	20 23.2	21 17.0	28 10.9	11 20.7	11 38.8	8 44.5	15 04.2	11 35.8
26 Th	4 15 46	5 07 00	2♍57 38	9♍30 15	23 29.3	10 29.8	21 08.2	22 02.2	28 16.9	11 34.6	11 43.2	8 42.3	15 02.6	11 34.9
27 F	4 19 43	6 04 35	16 08 34	22 52 58	23 30.2	11 23.7	21 54.0	22 47.4	28 23.2	11 48.6	11 47.7	8 40.1	15 01.0	11 34.1
28 Sa	4 23 40	7 02 09	29 43 43	6♎41 00	23 31.5	12 21.1	22 40.6	23 32.6	28 29.8	12 02.5	11 52.3	8 38.0	14 59.4	11 33.3
29 Su	4 27 36	7 59 42	13♎44 53	20 55 18	23R 32.3	13 21.7	23 28.1	24 17.7	28 36.9	12 16.5	11 57.0	8 35.9	14 57.8	11 32.6
30 M	4 31 33	8 57 13	28 12 00	5♏34 31	23 31.8	14 25.6	24 16.3	25 02.8	28 44.2	12 30.4	12 01.7	8 33.8	14 56.2	11 31.9
31 Tu	4 35 29	9 54 43	13♏02 14	20 34 19	23 29.4	15 32.5	25 05.2	25 47.8	28 51.9	12 44.4	12 06.5	8 31.7	14 54.6	11 31.2

LONGITUDE — June 1977

Day	Sid.Time	☉	0 hr ☽	Noon☽	True☊	☿	♀	♂	⚳	♃	♄	♅	♆	♇
1 W	4 39 26	10♊52 12	28♏09 44	5♐47 19	23♎24.9	16♉42.6	25♈54.8	26♈32.7	28♍59.9	12♊58.3	12♌11.4	8♏29.7	14♐53.0	11♎30.5
2 Th	4 43 22	11 49 40	13♐25 46	21 03 43	23R 18.8	17 55.6	26 45.2	27 17.6	29 08.2	13 12.3	12 16.4	8R 27.7	14R 51.3	11R 29.9
3 F	4 47 19	12 47 07	28 39 48	6♑12 45	23 11.6	19 11.6	27 36.2	28 02.5	29 16.9	13 26.2	12 21.4	8 25.7	14 49.7	11 29.3
4 Sa	4 51 15	13 44 33	13♑41 21	21 04 36	23 04.3	20 30.4	28 27.8	28 47.3	29 25.8	13 40.2	12 26.6	8 23.8	14 48.1	11 28.7
5 Su	4 55 12	14 41 59	28 21 39	5♒31 54	22 57.9	21 52.2	29 20.0	29 32.1	29 35.1	13 54.1	12 31.8	8 21.9	14 46.5	11 28.2
6 M	4 59 09	15 39 23	12♒34 57	19 30 37	22 53.1	23 16.8	0♉12.9	0♉16.8	29 44.7	14 08.1	12 37.0	8 20.1	14 44.9	11 27.7
7 Tu	5 03 05	16 36 47	26 18 54	2♓59 59	22 50.3	24 44.2	1 06.3	1 01.4	29 54.6	14 22.0	12 42.4	8 18.2	14 43.2	11 27.2
8 W	5 07 02	17 34 11	9♓34 11	16 01 55	22D 49.3	26 14.3	2 00.3	1 46.0	0♎04.8	14 36.0	12 47.8	8 16.5	14 41.6	11 26.8
9 Th	5 10 58	18 31 33	22 23 41	28 40 03	22 49.7	27 47.3	2 54.8	2 30.6	0 15.2	14 49.9	12 53.2	8 14.7	14 40.0	11 26.3
10 F	5 14 55	19 28 56	4♈51 38	10♈59 02	22R 50.6	29 23.0	3 49.8	3 15.0	0 26.0	15 03.8	12 58.8	8 13.0	14 38.4	11 26.0
11 Sa	5 18 51	20 26 18	17 02 51	23 03 43	22 51.1	1♊01.4	4 45.3	3 59.5	0 37.0	15 17.8	13 04.4	8 11.3	14 36.8	11 25.6
12 Su	5 22 48	21 23 39	29 02 11	4♉58 49	22 50.3	2 42.5	5 41.2	4 43.8	0 48.4	15 31.7	13 10.0	8 09.7	14 35.1	11 25.3
13 M	5 26 44	22 21 00	10♉54 08	16 48 34	22 47.4	4 26.4	6 37.6	5 28.2	1 00.0	15 45.6	13 15.8	8 08.1	14 33.5	11 25.0
14 Tu	5 30 41	23 18 20	22 42 35	28 36 32	22 42.1	6 12.8	7 34.5	6 12.4	1 11.9	15 59.5	13 21.6	8 06.5	14 31.9	11 24.8
15 W	5 34 38	24 15 40	4♊30 47	10♊25 38	22 34.3	8 01.9	8 31.8	6 56.6	1 24.0	16 13.4	13 27.4	8 05.0	14 30.3	11 24.5
16 Th	5 38 34	25 12 59	16 21 19	22 18 05	22 24.3	9 53.6	9 29.5	7 40.7	1 36.4	16 27.2	13 33.3	8 03.5	14 28.7	11 24.4
17 F	5 42 31	26 10 18	28 16 07	4♋15 37	22 13.0	11 47.8	10 27.6	8 24.8	1 49.1	16 41.1	13 39.3	8 02.1	14 27.2	11 24.2
18 Sa	5 46 27	27 07 36	10♋16 44	16 19 37	22 01.1	13 44.4	11 26.0	9 08.8	2 02.0	16 54.9	13 45.4	8 00.7	14 25.6	11 24.1
19 Su	5 50 24	28 04 54	22 24 27	28 31 22	21 49.8	15 43.3	12 24.8	9 52.7	2 15.2	17 08.7	13 51.5	7 59.4	14 24.0	11 24.0
20 M	5 54 20	29 02 11	4♌40 35	10♌52 16	21 40.0	17 44.4	13 24.0	10 36.6	2 28.7	17 22.5	13 57.6	7 58.1	14 22.4	11 24.0
21 Tu	5 58 17	29 59 27	17 06 41	23 24 04	21 32.5	19 47.6	14 23.6	11 20.4	2 42.3	17 36.3	14 03.8	7 56.8	14 20.9	11D 23.9
22 W	6 02 13	0♋56 43	29 44 43	6♍08 56	21 27.6	21 52.5	15 23.4	12 04.1	2 56.2	17 50.0	14 10.1	7 55.6	14 19.3	11 24.0
23 Th	6 06 10	1 53 58	12♍37 04	19 09 26	21 25.2	23 59.2	16 23.6	12 47.8	3 10.4	18 03.8	14 16.4	7 54.5	14 17.8	11 24.0
24 F	6 10 07	2 51 12	25 46 25	2♎28 21	21D 24.5	26 07.2	17 24.1	13 31.4	3 24.8	18 17.5	14 22.8	7 53.4	14 16.3	11 24.1
25 Sa	6 14 03	3 48 26	9♎15 32	16 08 14	21R 24.7	28 16.4	18 24.9	14 14.9	3 39.4	18 31.1	14 29.2	7 52.3	14 14.8	11 24.2
26 Su	6 18 00	4 45 39	23 06 37	0♏10 46	21 24.6	0♋26.5	19 26.0	14 58.3	3 54.2	18 44.8	14 35.7	7 51.3	14 13.3	11 24.3
27 M	6 21 56	5 42 51	7♏20 38	14 36 01	21 22.9	2 37.2	20 27.3	15 41.7	4 09.3	18 58.4	14 42.2	7 50.3	14 11.8	11 24.5
28 Tu	6 25 53	6 40 03	21 56 31	29 21 36	21 19.0	4 48.2	21 29.0	16 25.1	4 24.5	19 12.0	14 48.8	7 49.4	14 10.3	11 24.7
29 W	6 29 49	7 37 15	6♐50 28	14♐22 12	21 12.4	6 59.3	22 30.9	17 08.3	4 40.0	19 25.6	14 55.4	7 48.5	14 08.9	11 25.0
30 Th	6 33 46	8 34 27	21 55 41	29 29 43	21 03.5	9 10.1	23 33.1	17 51.5	4 55.7	19 39.1	15 02.1	7 47.7	14 07.4	11 25.3

Astro Data

	Dy Hr Mn
♂0N	1 6:24
⚳D	10 13:40
☽0N	12 20:36
☿D	13 20:52
♃⚻♅	15 20:22
♄✶♇	24 22:11
♃△♇	26 12:28
♃✶♄	27 9:46
☽0S	27 14:10
♃☍♆	8 20:41
☽0N	9 3:41
♇D	21 13:21
♄△♆	23 16:13
☽0S	23 22:07

Planet Ingress

	Dy Hr Mn
☉ ♊	21 4:14
♂ ♉	6 3:00
♀ ♉	6 6:10
⚳ ♎	8 0:52
☿ ♊	10 21:07
☉ ♋	21 12:14
☿ ♋	26 7:07

Last Aspect / ☽ Ingress

Last Aspect Dy Hr Mn	☽ Ingress Dy Hr Mn	Last Aspect Dy Hr Mn	☽ Ingress Dy Hr Mn
1 17:10 ♆ ✶	♏ 2 16:24	31 3:21 ☿ ☍	♐ 1 2:54
3 13:03 ☉ ☍	♐ 4 15:59	2 22:21 ♂ △	♑ 3 2:07
5 16:40 ♆ ☌	♑ 6 15:54	5 1:24 ♂ □	♒ 5 2:44
7 20:09 ☉ △	♒ 8 18:00	6 19:24 ☿ □	♓ 7 6:35
10 4:08 ☉ □	♓ 10 23:29	9 10:04 ☿ ✶	♈ 9 14:34
12 16:39 ☉ ✶	♈ 13 8:29	11 6:18 ☉ ✶	♉ 12 1:56
14 14:44 ♆ △	♉ 15 20:04	13 4:44 ♄ □	♊ 14 14:50
18 2:51 ☉ ☌	♊ 18 8:50	16 18:23 ☉ ☌	♋ 17 3:28
19 19:16 ☿ ✶	♋ 20 21:35	18 2:14 ♀ □	♌ 19 14:53
22 11:34 ♂ □	♌ 23 9:13	21 3:47 ☿ ✶	♍ 22 0:29
25 1:33 ♂ △	♍ 25 18:31	23 22:27 ☿ □	♎ 24 7:35
26 22:00 ♆ □	♎ 28 0:28	25 16:11 ♃ △	♏ 26 11:42
29 17:53 ♂ ☍	♏ 30 2:57	27 22:18 ♀ ☍	♐ 28 13:02
		29 20:09 ♃ ☍	♑ 30 12:48

☽ Phases & Eclipses

Dy Hr Mn	
3 13:03	○ 12♏58
10 4:08	☾ 19♒23
18 2:51	● 27♉03
26 3:20	☽ 4♍46
1 20:31	○ 11♐13
8 15:07	☾ 17♓42
16 18:23	● 25♊28
24 12:44	☽ 2♎53

Astro Data

1 May 1977
Julian Day # 28245
SVP 5♓34'29"
GC 26♐31.4 ⚴ 18♌18.0
Eris 14♈06.4 ⚵ 24♏51.6R
⚷ 2♉02.4 ⚶ 22♋47.9
☽ Mean ☊ 23♎30.2

1 June 1977
Julian Day # 28276
SVP 5♓34'25"
GC 26♐31.4 ⚴ 27♌29.9
Eris 14♈22.4 ⚵ 18♏09.2R
⚷ 3♉48.9 ⚶ 4♌04.8
☽ Mean ☊ 21♎51.7

July 1977 — LONGITUDE

Day	Sid.Time	☉	0 hr ☽	Noon ☽	True ☊	☿	♀	♂	⚳	♃	♄	♅	♆	♇
1 F	6 37 42	9♋31 38	7♑03 00	14♑34 15	20♎53.1	11♋20.4	24♉35.6	18♉34.6	5♎11.5	19♊52.6	15♌08.8	7♏46.9	14♐06.0	11♎25.6
2 Sa	6 41 39	10 28 49	22 02 13	29 25 46	20R 42.5	13 30.0	25 38.3	19 17.6	5 27.6	20 06.1	15 15.5	7R 46.2	14R 04.6	11 26.0
3 Su	6 45 36	11 26 00	6♒43 54	13♒55 50	20 32.8	15 38.7	26 41.3	20 00.6	5 43.9	20 19.5	15 22.3	7 45.5	14 03.2	11 26.3
4 M	6 49 32	12 23 12	21 00 58	27 58 57	20 25.0	17 46.2	27 44.5	20 43.5	6 00.4	20 32.9	15 29.2	7 44.8	14 01.8	11 26.8
5 Tu	6 53 29	13 20 23	4♓49 36	11♓32 56	20 19.7	19 52.5	28 47.9	21 26.3	6 17.0	20 46.3	15 36.1	7 44.3	14 00.4	11 27.2
6 W	6 57 25	14 17 35	18 09 11	24 38 39	20 16.8	21 57.2	29 51.6	22 09.1	6 33.8	20 59.6	15 43.0	7 43.7	13 59.1	11 27.7
7 Th	7 01 22	15 14 47	1♈01 48	7♈19 11	20D 15.7	24 00.5	0♊55.5	22 51.8	6 50.9	21 12.9	15 49.9	7 43.2	13 57.7	11 28.2
8 F	7 05 18	16 11 59	13 31 23	19 39 03	20R 15.6	26 02.1	1 59.6	23 34.4	7 08.0	21 26.1	15 56.9	7 42.8	13 56.4	11 28.7
9 Sa	7 09 15	17 09 12	25 42 52	1♉43 30	20 15.3	28 01.9	3 04.0	24 16.9	7 25.4	21 39.4	16 04.0	7 42.4	13 55.1	11 29.3
10 Su	7 13 11	18 06 25	7♉41 37	13 37 50	20 13.9	0♌00.0	4 08.5	24 59.4	7 43.0	21 52.5	16 11.0	7 42.1	13 53.8	11 29.9
11 M	7 17 08	19 03 39	19 32 49	25 27 06	20 10.3	1 56.3	5 13.3	25 41.8	8 00.7	22 05.7	16 18.1	7 41.8	13 52.6	11 30.6
12 Tu	7 21 05	20 00 53	1♊21 16	7♊15 46	20 04.1	3 50.7	6 18.2	26 24.1	8 18.6	22 18.7	16 25.3	7 41.6	13 51.3	11 31.3
13 W	7 25 01	20 58 08	13 11 04	19 07 33	19 55.1	5 43.3	7 23.3	27 06.3	8 36.7	22 31.8	16 32.5	7 41.4	13 50.1	11 32.0
14 Th	7 28 58	21 55 23	25 05 32	1♋05 20	19 43.8	7 34.0	8 28.6	27 48.5	8 54.9	22 44.8	16 39.7	7 41.3	13 48.9	11 32.7
15 F	7 32 54	22 52 38	7♋07 08	13 11 09	19 30.8	9 22.8	9 34.1	28 30.5	9 13.3	22 57.7	16 46.9	7D 41.2	13 47.7	11 33.5
16 Sa	7 36 51	23 49 54	19 17 31	25 26 18	19 17.3	11 09.7	10 39.8	29 12.5	9 31.8	23 10.6	16 54.2	7 41.2	13 46.6	11 34.3
17 Su	7 40 47	24 47 10	1♌37 37	7♌51 30	19 04.4	12 54.7	11 45.6	29 54.4	9 50.5	23 23.4	17 01.5	7 41.2	13 45.4	11 35.2
18 M	7 44 44	25 44 27	14 07 59	20 27 07	18 53.1	14 37.9	12 51.6	0♊36.2	10 09.4	23 36.2	17 08.8	7 41.3	13 44.3	11 36.0
19 Tu	7 48 40	26 41 44	26 48 57	3♍13 33	18 44.3	16 19.2	13 57.7	1 17.9	10 28.4	23 49.0	17 16.2	7 41.4	13 43.2	11 36.9
20 W	7 52 37	27 39 01	9♍41 00	16 11 24	18 38.4	17 58.6	15 04.0	1 59.6	10 47.5	24 01.6	17 23.5	7 41.6	13 42.2	11 37.9
21 Th	7 56 34	28 36 18	22 44 53	29 21 39	18 35.2	19 36.2	16 10.5	2 41.1	11 06.8	24 14.3	17 30.9	7 41.9	13 41.1	11 38.8
22 F	8 00 30	29 33 36	6♎01 50	12♎45 40	18D 34.1	21 11.8	17 17.1	3 22.6	11 26.2	24 26.8	17 38.4	7 42.2	13 40.1	11 39.8
23 Sa	8 04 27	0♌30 54	19 33 20	26 24 59	18R 34.1	22 45.6	18 23.9	4 04.0	11 45.8	24 39.3	17 45.8	7 42.5	13 39.1	11 40.9
24 Su	8 08 23	1 28 12	3♏20 47	10♏20 49	18 33.9	24 17.6	19 30.8	4 45.2	12 05.5	24 51.7	17 53.3	7 42.9	13 38.1	11 41.9
25 M	8 12 20	2 25 30	17 25 04	24 33 28	18 32.4	25 47.6	20 37.8	5 26.4	12 25.3	25 04.1	18 00.8	7 43.4	13 37.2	11 43.0
26 Tu	8 16 16	3 22 49	1♐45 46	9♐01 38	18 28.7	27 15.7	21 45.0	6 07.5	12 45.3	25 16.4	18 08.3	7 43.9	13 36.3	11 44.1
27 W	8 20 13	4 20 09	16 20 33	23 41 53	18 22.5	28 41.9	22 52.3	6 48.6	13 05.4	25 28.7	18 15.8	7 44.4	13 35.4	11 45.3
28 Th	8 24 09	5 17 29	1♑04 51	8♑28 32	18 13.9	0♍06.1	23 59.8	7 29.5	13 25.6	25 40.9	18 23.3	7 45.0	13 34.5	11 46.5
29 F	8 28 06	6 14 49	15 51 58	23 14 06	18 03.9	1 28.3	25 07.4	8 10.3	13 46.0	25 53.0	18 30.9	7 45.7	13 33.7	11 47.7
30 Sa	8 32 03	7 12 11	0♒33 54	7♒50 24	17 53.5	2 48.5	26 15.2	8 51.1	14 06.4	26 05.0	18 38.5	7 46.4	13 32.9	11 48.9
31 Su	8 35 59	8 09 33	15 02 40	22 09 56	17 43.9	4 06.7	27 23.1	9 31.7	14 27.0	26 17.0	18 46.1	7 47.2	13 32.1	11 50.2

August 1977 — LONGITUDE

Day	Sid.Time	☉	0 hr ☽	Noon ☽	True ☊	☿	♀	♂	⚳	♃	♄	♅	♆	♇
1 M	8 39 56	9♌06 56	29♒11 33	6♓07 05	17♎36.1	5♍22.7	28♊31.1	10♊12.3	14♎47.7	26♊28.9	18♌53.7	7♏48.0	13♐31.4	11♎51.5
2 Tu	8 43 52	10 04 19	12♓56 13	19 38 50	17R 30.7	6 36.6	29 39.2	10 52.8	15 08.5	26 40.8	19 01.3	7 48.9	13R 30.6	11 52.8
3 W	8 47 49	11 01 44	26 14 59	2♈44 50	17 27.7	7 48.3	0♋47.5	11 33.2	15 29.4	26 52.5	19 08.9	7 49.8	13 30.0	11 54.1
4 Th	8 51 45	11 59 10	9♈08 42	15 27 00	17D 26.8	8 57.6	1 55.9	12 13.4	15 50.4	27 04.2	19 16.5	7 50.8	13 29.3	11 55.5
5 F	8 55 42	12 56 38	21 40 14	27 48 57	17 27.0	10 04.6	3 04.4	12 53.6	16 11.6	27 15.8	19 24.2	7 51.8	13 28.6	11 56.9
6 Sa	8 59 38	13 54 06	3♉53 46	9♉55 20	17R 27.6	11 09.1	4 13.1	13 33.7	16 32.8	27 27.3	19 31.8	7 52.8	13 28.0	11 58.4
7 Su	9 03 35	14 51 36	15 54 18	21 51 21	17 27.4	12 11.0	5 21.9	14 13.7	16 54.2	27 38.8	19 39.5	7 54.0	13 27.4	11 59.8
8 M	9 07 32	15 49 07	27 47 07	3♊42 15	17 25.6	13 10.3	6 30.8	14 53.6	17 15.6	27 50.2	19 47.1	7 55.1	13 26.9	12 01.3
9 Tu	9 11 28	16 46 40	9♊37 22	15 33 02	17 21.8	14 06.7	7 39.8	15 33.4	17 37.2	28 01.5	19 54.8	7 56.4	13 26.4	12 02.8
10 W	9 15 25	17 44 14	21 29 48	27 28 09	17 15.6	15 00.2	8 48.9	16 13.1	17 58.9	28 12.7	20 02.5	7 57.6	13 25.9	12 04.4
11 Th	9 19 21	18 41 49	3♋28 32	9♋31 20	17 07.4	15 50.6	9 58.1	16 52.7	18 20.6	28 23.8	20 10.2	7 59.0	13 25.4	12 05.9
12 F	9 23 18	19 39 26	15 36 52	21 45 23	16 57.7	16 37.8	11 07.5	17 32.2	18 42.5	28 34.8	20 17.9	8 00.3	13 25.0	12 07.5
13 Sa	9 27 14	20 37 03	27 57 05	4♌12 07	16 47.4	17 21.5	12 16.9	18 11.6	19 04.4	28 45.8	20 25.5	8 01.8	13 24.6	12 09.2
14 Su	9 31 11	21 34 42	10♌30 32	16 52 21	16 37.5	18 01.6	13 26.5	18 50.9	19 26.5	28 56.6	20 33.2	8 03.2	13 24.2	12 10.8
15 M	9 35 07	22 32 23	23 17 34	29 46 06	16 29.0	18 37.9	14 36.2	19 30.1	19 48.6	29 07.4	20 40.9	8 04.7	13 23.9	12 12.5
16 Tu	9 39 04	23 30 04	6♍17 50	12♍52 42	16 22.5	19 10.2	15 45.9	20 09.1	20 10.9	29 18.0	20 48.6	8 06.3	13 23.6	12 14.2
17 W	9 43 01	24 27 47	19 30 32	26 11 14	16 18.4	19 38.2	16 55.8	20 48.1	20 33.2	29 28.6	20 56.3	8 07.9	13 23.3	12 15.9
18 Th	9 46 57	25 25 31	2♎54 41	9♎40 48	16D 16.6	20 01.8	18 05.8	21 26.9	20 55.6	29 39.1	21 03.9	8 09.6	13 23.1	12 17.6
19 F	9 50 54	26 23 16	16 29 28	23 20 39	16 16.6	20 20.7	19 15.8	22 05.6	21 18.1	29 49.4	21 11.6	8 11.3	13 22.8	12 19.4
20 Sa	9 54 50	27 21 02	0♏14 17	7♏10 20	16 17.6	20 34.6	20 26.0	22 44.2	21 40.7	29 59.7	21 19.3	8 13.1	13 22.7	12 21.1
21 Su	9 58 47	28 18 49	14 08 45	21 09 27	16R 18.5	20 43.3	21 36.3	23 22.7	22 03.3	0♋09.9	21 26.9	8 14.9	13 22.5	12 23.0
22 M	10 02 43	29 16 37	28 12 22	5♐17 22	16 18.6	20R 46.6	22 46.6	24 01.0	22 26.1	0 19.9	21 34.5	8 16.7	13 22.4	12 24.8
23 Tu	10 06 40	0♍14 27	12♐24 14	19 32 45	16 17.0	20 44.3	23 57.1	24 39.3	22 48.9	0 29.9	21 42.2	8 18.6	13 22.3	12 26.6
24 W	10 10 36	1 12 18	26 42 33	3♑53 14	16 13.5	20 36.2	25 07.6	25 17.4	23 11.8	0 39.7	21 49.8	8 20.6	13 22.3	12 28.5
25 Th	10 14 33	2 10 09	11♑04 20	18 15 17	16 08.3	20 22.3	26 18.2	25 55.4	23 34.8	0 49.5	21 57.4	8 22.6	13D 22.3	12 30.4
26 F	10 18 30	3 08 03	25 25 28	2♒34 15	16 02.0	20 02.3	27 28.9	26 33.3	23 57.8	0 59.1	22 05.0	8 24.6	13 22.3	12 32.3
27 Sa	10 22 26	4 05 57	9♒40 58	16 44 58	15 55.3	19 36.4	28 39.8	27 11.1	24 20.9	1 08.6	22 12.6	8 26.7	13 22.3	12 34.2
28 Su	10 26 23	5 03 53	23 45 38	0♓42 25	15 49.2	19 04.6	29 50.7	27 48.7	24 44.1	1 18.0	22 20.1	8 28.8	13 22.4	12 36.2
29 M	10 30 19	6 01 50	7♓34 49	14 22 28	15 44.3	18 27.3	1♌01.7	28 26.2	25 07.4	1 27.3	22 27.7	8 31.0	13 22.5	12 38.2
30 Tu	10 34 16	6 59 49	21 05 04	27 42 29	15 41.0	17 44.6	2 12.8	29 03.6	25 30.7	1 36.5	22 35.2	8 33.2	13 22.7	12 40.1
31 W	10 38 12	7 57 50	4♈14 39	10♈41 37	15D 39.6	16 57.2	3 23.9	29 40.9	25 54.1	1 45.5	22 42.7	8 35.4	13 22.8	12 42.2

Astro Data Dy Hr Mn	Planet Ingress Dy Hr Mn	Last Aspect Dy Hr Mn	☽ Ingress Dy Hr Mn	Last Aspect Dy Hr Mn	☽ Ingress Dy Hr Mn	☽ Phases & Eclipses Dy Hr Mn	Astro Data
☽0N 6 12:42	♀ ♊ 6 15:09	2 5:22 ♀ △	♒ 2 12:56	31 21:41 ♀ △	♓ 1 1:23	1 3:24 ○ 9♑11	1 July 1977
♃□♅ 14 5:36	☿ ♌ 10 12:00	4 11:33 ♀ □	♓ 4 15:31	3 0:59 ♃ □	♈ 3 6:54	8 4:39 ☾ 15♈54	Julian Day # 28306
♅ D 16 8:41	♂ ♊ 17 15:13	6 7:06 ♂ ✶	♈ 6 22:03	5 10:54 ♃ ✶	♉ 5 16:18	16 8:36 ● 23♋42	SVP 5♓34'20"
☽0S 21 4:50	☉ ♌ 22 23:04	9 3:09 ☿ □	♉ 9 8:33	7 7:31 ♄ □	♊ 8 4:29	23 19:38 ☽ 0♏49	GC 26♐31.5 ⚶ 8♍33.1
	☿ ♍ 28 10:15	11 12:32 ♂ ☌	♊ 11 21:15	10 13:31 ♃ ☌	♋ 10 17:04	30 10:52 ○ 7♒09	Eris 14♈30.0 ✱ 14♏30.9R
☽0N 2 22:52		13 18:59 ♃ ☌	♋ 14 9:50	12 1:19 ☿ ✶	♌ 13 3:57		⚷ 5♉06.6 ⚵ 16♌39.2
⚳0S 4 10:51	♀ ♋ 2 19:19	16 19:45 ♂ ✶	♌ 16 20:51	15 10:48 ♃ ✶	♍ 15 12:26	6 20:40 ☾ 14♉15	☽ Mean ☊ 20♎16.4
☽0S 17 11:25	♃ ♋ 20 12:43	18 18:03 ♃ ✶	♍ 19 5:58	17 17:57 ♃ □	♎ 17 18:49	14 21:31 ● 21♌58	
☿0S 22 3:56	☉ ♍ 23 6:00	21 10:32 ☉ ✶	♎ 21 13:09	19 23:25 ♃ △	♏ 19 23:35	22 1:04 ☽ 28♏50	1 August 1977
☿ R 22 14:19	♀ ♌ 28 15:09	23 8:53 ♃ △	♏ 23 18:13	22 1:04 ☉ □	♐ 22 3:03	28 20:10 ○ 5♓24	Julian Day # 28337
♆ D 25 12:07		25 14:18 ☿ □	♐ 25 21:04	23 20:58 ♂ ☍	♑ 24 5:30		SVP 5♓34'15"
☿0N 27 14:27		27 20:59 ☿ △	♑ 27 22:15	26 2:41 ♀ ☍	♒ 26 7:41		GC 26♐31.6 ⚶ 21♍10.3
☽0N 30 8:49		28 17:22 ♇ □	♒ 29 23:04	28 6:45 ♂ △	♓ 28 10:46		Eris 14♈28.0R ✱ 15♏39.3
				30 14:36 ♂ □	♈ 30 16:11		⚷ 5♉45.0 ⚵ 0♍44.3
							☽ Mean ☊ 18♎37.9

LONGITUDE September 1977

Day	Sid.Time	☉	0 hr ☽	Noon ☽	True ☊	☿	♀	♂	⚳	♃	♄	♅	♆	♇
1 Th	10 42 09	8♍55 52	17♈03 33	23♈20 42	15♎39.7	16♍05.8	4♌35.2	0♋18.0	26♎17.5	1♋54.4	22♌50.2	8♏37.7	13♐23.0	12♎44.2
2 F	10 46 05	9 53 57	29 33 25	5♉42 06	15 41.0	15R 11.1	5 46.6	0 55.1	26 41.0	2 03.3	22 57.7	8 40.0	13 23.3	12 46.2
3 Sa	10 50 02	10 52 03	11♉47 14	17 49 20	15 42.6	14 14.1	6 58.0	1 31.9	27 04.6	2 11.9	23 05.1	8 42.4	13 23.6	12 48.3
4 Su	10 53 58	11 50 11	23 48 58	29 46 42	15 44.1	13 15.9	8 09.6	2 08.7	27 28.3	2 20.5	23 12.6	8 44.8	13 23.9	12 50.3
5 M	10 57 55	12 48 22	5♊43 11	11♊39 01	15R 44.8	12 17.8	9 21.2	2 45.3	27 52.0	2 28.9	23 20.0	8 47.3	13 24.2	12 52.4
6 Tu	11 01 52	13 46 34	17 34 49	23 31 11	15 44.3	11 21.1	10 32.9	3 21.8	28 15.8	2 37.2	23 27.4	8 49.8	13 24.6	12 54.5
7 W	11 05 48	14 44 48	29 28 45	5♋28 03	15 42.4	10 27.0	11 44.7	3 58.2	28 39.6	2 45.4	23 34.7	8 52.3	13 25.0	12 56.7
8 Th	11 09 45	15 43 04	11♋29 40	17 34 03	15 39.3	9 36.8	12 56.6	4 34.4	29 03.5	2 53.4	23 42.1	8 54.9	13 25.4	12 58.8
9 F	11 13 41	16 41 22	23 41 41	29 52 57	15 35.2	8 51.7	14 08.5	5 10.4	29 27.4	3 01.4	23 49.4	8 57.5	13 25.9	13 01.0
10 Sa	11 17 38	17 39 43	6♌08 11	12♌27 37	15 30.7	8 12.9	15 20.6	5 46.3	29 51.4	3 09.1	23 56.6	9 00.1	13 26.4	13 03.1
11 Su	11 21 34	18 38 05	18 51 28	25 19 49	15 26.2	7 41.4	16 32.7	6 22.1	0♏15.5	3 16.7	24 03.9	9 02.8	13 26.9	13 05.3
12 M	11 25 31	19 36 29	1♍52 42	8♍30 02	15 22.4	7 17.8	17 44.9	6 57.7	0 39.6	3 24.2	24 11.1	9 05.6	13 27.5	13 07.5
13 Tu	11 29 27	20 34 55	15 11 42	21 57 29	15 19.7	7 02.9	18 57.1	7 33.1	1 03.8	3 31.6	24 18.3	9 08.3	13 28.1	13 09.7
14 W	11 33 24	21 33 22	28 47 07	5♎40 16	15D 18.2	6D 57.0	20 09.5	8 08.4	1 28.0	3 38.8	24 25.4	9 11.1	13 28.7	13 11.9
15 Th	11 37 21	22 31 52	12♎36 35	19 35 41	15 18.0	7 00.5	21 21.9	8 43.6	1 52.3	3 45.8	24 32.5	9 13.9	13 29.4	13 14.1
16 F	11 41 17	23 30 23	26 37 08	3♏40 33	15 18.7	7 13.5	22 34.3	9 18.5	2 16.6	3 52.7	24 39.6	9 16.8	13 30.1	13 16.4
17 Sa	11 45 14	24 28 56	10♏45 30	17 51 37	15 20.0	7 35.8	23 46.9	9 53.4	2 41.0	3 59.5	24 46.6	9 19.7	13 30.8	13 18.6
18 Su	11 49 10	25 27 31	24 58 31	2♐05 50	15 21.3	8 07.3	24 59.5	10 28.0	3 05.4	4 06.0	24 53.6	9 22.6	13 31.6	13 20.9
19 M	11 53 07	26 26 08	9♐13 15	16 20 26	15R 22.3	8 47.6	26 12.2	11 02.5	3 29.9	4 12.5	25 00.6	9 25.6	13 32.4	13 23.2
20 Tu	11 57 03	27 24 46	23 27 08	0♑33 01	15 22.5	9 36.3	27 24.9	11 36.8	3 54.4	4 18.8	25 07.5	9 28.6	13 33.2	13 25.4
21 W	12 01 00	28 23 25	7♑37 51	14 41 20	15 21.9	10 32.9	28 37.7	12 10.9	4 18.9	4 24.9	25 14.4	9 31.6	13 34.1	13 27.7
22 Th	12 04 56	29 22 07	21 43 14	28 43 16	15 20.6	11 36.9	29 50.6	12 44.9	4 43.5	4 30.9	25 21.2	9 34.7	13 34.9	13 30.0
23 F	12 08 53	0♎20 50	5♒41 10	12♒36 40	15 18.8	12 47.6	1♍03.6	13 18.7	5 08.2	4 36.7	25 28.0	9 37.8	13 35.9	13 32.3
24 Sa	12 12 50	1 19 34	19 29 32	26 19 28	15 16.8	14 04.3	2 16.6	13 52.3	5 32.8	4 42.3	25 34.7	9 40.9	13 36.8	13 34.6
25 Su	12 16 46	2 18 21	3♓06 16	9♓49 42	15 15.1	15 26.5	3 29.6	14 25.7	5 57.6	4 47.8	25 41.4	9 44.1	13 37.8	13 37.0
26 M	12 20 43	3 17 09	16 29 35	23 05 46	15 13.8	16 53.4	4 42.8	14 58.9	6 22.3	4 53.1	25 48.1	9 47.2	13 38.8	13 39.3
27 Tu	12 24 39	4 15 59	29 38 07	6♈06 35	15D 13.1	18 24.4	5 56.0	15 32.0	6 47.1	4 58.3	25 54.7	9 50.4	13 39.8	13 41.6
28 W	12 28 36	5 14 52	12♈31 08	18 51 49	15 13.0	19 59.0	7 09.2	16 04.9	7 11.9	5 03.3	26 01.2	9 53.7	13 40.9	13 43.9
29 Th	12 32 32	6 13 46	25 08 43	1♉21 59	15 13.3	21 36.5	8 22.6	16 37.5	7 36.8	5 08.1	26 07.7	9 56.9	13 42.0	13 46.3
30 F	12 36 29	7 12 42	7♉31 50	13 38 31	15 14.0	23 16.5	9 36.0	17 10.0	8 01.7	5 12.7	26 14.2	10 00.2	13 43.1	13 48.6

LONGITUDE October 1977

Day	Sid.Time	☉	0 hr ☽	Noon ☽	True ☊	☿	♀	♂	⚳	♃	♄	♅	♆	♇
1 Sa	12 40 25	8♎11 41	19♉42 20	25♉43 40	15♎14.8	24♍58.4	10♍49.4	17♋42.3	8♏26.6	5♋17.2	26♌20.6	10♏03.5	13♐44.3	13♎51.0
2 Su	12 44 22	9 10 42	1♊42 55	7♊40 32	15 15.5	26 41.9	12 02.9	18 14.4	8 51.6	5 21.5	26 26.9	10 06.8	13 45.5	13 53.3
3 M	12 48 19	10 09 45	13 37 00	19 32 50	15 16.0	28 26.5	13 16.5	18 46.3	9 16.6	5 25.6	26 33.2	10 10.2	13 46.7	13 55.7
4 Tu	12 52 15	11 08 51	25 28 35	1♋24 48	15R 16.3	0♎12.0	14 30.1	19 18.0	9 41.6	5 29.5	26 39.5	10 13.6	13 47.9	13 58.0
5 W	12 56 12	12 07 59	7♋22 06	13 21 01	15 16.4	1 58.1	15 43.8	19 49.5	10 06.7	5 33.3	26 45.6	10 17.0	13 49.2	14 00.4
6 Th	13 00 08	13 07 09	19 22 10	25 26 07	15 16.3	3 44.5	16 57.6	20 20.7	10 31.8	5 36.9	26 51.7	10 20.4	13 50.5	14 02.8
7 F	13 04 05	14 06 21	1♌33 25	7♌44 36	15 16.2	5 31.1	18 11.4	20 51.7	10 56.9	5 40.3	26 57.8	10 23.9	13 51.8	14 05.1
8 Sa	13 08 01	15 05 36	14 00 09	20 20 29	15D 16.2	7 17.6	19 25.2	21 22.5	11 22.1	5 43.5	27 03.8	10 27.3	13 53.2	14 07.5
9 Su	13 11 58	16 04 53	26 46 00	3♍16 57	15 16.2	9 03.9	20 39.1	21 53.1	11 47.2	5 46.5	27 09.7	10 30.8	13 54.5	14 09.8
10 M	13 15 54	17 04 12	9♍53 34	16 35 55	15 16.3	10 50.0	21 53.1	22 23.4	12 12.4	5 49.3	27 15.6	10 34.3	13 55.9	14 12.2
11 Tu	13 19 51	18 03 33	23 24 00	0♎17 40	15 16.5	12 35.7	23 07.1	22 53.5	12 37.7	5 52.0	27 21.4	10 37.8	13 57.4	14 14.5
12 W	13 23 47	19 02 57	7♎16 40	14 20 36	15R 16.6	14 20.9	24 21.2	23 23.3	13 03.0	5 54.4	27 27.2	10 41.4	13 58.8	14 16.9
13 Th	13 27 44	20 02 22	21 28 58	28 41 10	15 16.5	16 05.6	25 35.3	23 52.9	13 28.2	5 56.7	27 32.8	10 45.0	14 00.3	14 19.3
14 F	13 31 41	21 01 50	5♏56 30	13♏14 11	15 16.1	17 49.8	26 49.4	24 22.3	13 53.6	5 58.7	27 38.4	10 48.5	14 01.8	14 21.6
15 Sa	13 35 37	22 01 19	20 33 26	27 53 25	15 15.4	19 33.4	28 03.6	24 51.3	14 18.9	6 00.6	27 44.0	10 52.1	14 03.4	14 24.0
16 Su	13 39 34	23 00 51	5♐13 18	12♐32 20	15 14.6	21 16.3	29 17.9	25 20.1	14 44.3	6 02.3	27 49.5	10 55.7	14 04.9	14 26.3
17 M	13 43 30	24 00 24	19 49 48	27 05 04	15 13.7	22 58.7	0♎32.1	25 48.7	15 09.6	6 03.7	27 54.9	10 59.4	14 06.5	14 28.6
18 Tu	13 47 27	24 59 59	4♑17 36	11♑26 57	15 13.1	24 40.4	1 46.5	26 16.9	15 35.0	6 05.0	28 00.2	11 03.0	14 08.1	14 31.0
19 W	13 51 23	25 59 36	18 32 46	25 34 49	15D 12.8	26 21.5	3 00.8	26 44.9	16 00.5	6 06.1	28 05.4	11 06.7	14 09.8	14 33.3
20 Th	13 55 20	26 59 14	2♒32 56	9♒27 02	15 13.1	28 02.0	4 15.2	27 12.6	16 25.9	6 07.0	28 10.6	11 10.3	14 11.4	14 35.6
21 F	13 59 16	27 58 54	16 17 07	23 03 12	15 13.8	29 41.8	5 29.6	27 40.0	16 51.3	6 07.7	28 15.7	11 14.0	14 13.1	14 37.9
22 Sa	14 03 13	28 58 35	29 45 22	6♓23 44	15 15.0	1♏21.0	6 44.1	28 07.1	17 16.8	6 08.1	28 20.7	11 17.7	14 14.8	14 40.2
23 Su	14 07 10	29 58 19	12♓58 24	19 29 32	15 16.2	2 59.7	7 58.6	28 34.0	17 42.3	6R 08.4	28 25.7	11 21.4	14 16.5	14 42.5
24 M	14 11 06	0♏58 04	25 57 14	2♈21 39	15 17.1	4 37.7	9 13.1	29 00.5	18 07.8	6 08.5	28 30.5	11 25.1	14 18.3	14 44.8
25 Tu	14 15 03	1 57 51	8♈42 56	15 01 11	15R 17.5	6 15.2	10 27.7	29 26.7	18 33.3	6 08.4	28 35.3	11 28.8	14 20.1	14 47.1
26 W	14 18 59	2 57 40	21 16 34	27 29 11	15 17.1	7 52.1	11 42.3	29 52.6	18 58.8	6 08.1	28 40.0	11 32.5	14 21.8	14 49.4
27 Th	14 22 56	3 57 30	3♉39 11	9♉46 43	15 15.7	9 28.5	12 57.0	0♌18.2	19 24.3	6 07.6	28 44.6	11 36.2	14 23.7	14 51.7
28 F	14 26 52	4 57 23	15 51 55	21 55 00	15 13.3	11 04.3	14 11.7	0 43.4	19 49.9	6 06.9	28 49.2	11 39.9	14 25.5	14 53.9
29 Sa	14 30 49	5 57 18	27 56 08	3♊55 34	15 10.1	12 39.7	15 26.4	1 08.3	20 15.4	6 05.9	28 53.6	11 43.7	14 27.3	14 56.2
30 Su	14 34 45	6 57 15	9♊53 32	15 50 21	15 06.4	14 14.6	16 41.1	1 32.9	20 41.0	6 04.8	28 58.0	11 47.4	14 29.2	14 58.4
31 M	14 38 42	7 57 14	21 46 20	27 41 51	15 02.7	15 49.0	17 55.9	1 57.1	21 06.6	6 03.5	29 02.3	11 51.2	14 31.1	15 00.6

Astro Data	Dy Hr Mn
☽ 0S	13 19:06
☿ D	14 15:05
☉ 0S	23 3:30
♆ ⚹ ♇	26 2:58
☽ 0N	26 17:16
☿ 0S	6 17:54
☽ 0S	11 4:27
♀ 0S	19 22:39
☽ 0N	24 0:01
♃ R	24 10:13

Planet Ingress		Dy Hr Mn
♂	♋	1 0:20
⚳	♏	10 20:32
♀	♍	22 15:05
☉	♎	23 3:29
☿	♎	4 9:16
♀	♎	17 1:37
☿	♏	21 16:23
☉	♏	23 12:41
♂	♌	26 18:56

Last Aspect Dy Hr Mn		☽ Ingress	Dy Hr Mn
1 11:01	♄ △	♉	2 0:52
3 22:39	♄ □	♊	4 12:27
6 11:52	♄ ⚹	♋	7 1:03
8 8:02	☉ ⚹	♌	9 12:14
11 9:38	♄ ☌	♍	11 20:34
13 9:23	☉ ☌	♎	14 2:07
15 20:32	♄ ⚹	♏	16 5:45
17 23:59	☉ ⚹	♐	18 8:28
20 6:18	☉ □	♑	20 11:04
22 13:12	☉ △	♒	22 14:12
24 10:41	♄ ☍	♓	24 18:30
25 23:19	☿ ☍	♈	27 0:40
29 1:48	♄ △	♉	29 9:21

Last Aspect Dy Hr Mn		☽ Ingress	Dy Hr Mn
1 13:14	♄ □	♊	1 20:33
4 9:07	☿ □	♋	4 9:09
6 1:29	♂ ☌	♌	6 20:58
9 0:39	♄ ☌	♍	9 5:59
10 22:37	♂ ⚹	♎	11 11:29
13 10:06	♄ ⚹	♏	13 14:11
15 12:18	♀ ⚹	♐	15 15:27
17 13:23	♄ △	♑	17 16:51
19 14:04	♂ ☍	♒	19 19:36
21 21:31	☉ △	♓	22 0:26
24 5:29	♂ △	♈	24 7:34
26 16:48	♂ □	♉	26 16:53
29 1:51	♄ □	♊	29 4:08
31 14:44	♄ ⚹	♋	31 16:40

☽ Phases & Eclipses Dy Hr Mn	
5 14:33	☾ 12♊55
13 9:23	● 20♍29
20 6:18	☽ 27♐11
27 8:17	○ 4♈07
27 8:29	A 0.901
5 9:21	☾ 12♋01
12 20:31	● 19♎24
12 20:26:39	T 02'37"
19 12:46	☽ 26♑01
26 23:35	○ 3♉27

Astro Data

1 September 1977
Julian Day # 28368
SVP 5♓34'12"
GC 26♐31.6 ⚵ 4♎29.1
Eris 14♈16.7R ⚴ 20♏53.9
⚷ 5♉32.1R ⚶ 15♍34.3
☽ Mean ☊ 16♎59.4

1 October 1977
Julian Day # 28398
SVP 5♓34'10"
GC 26♐31.7 ⚵ 17♎43.5
Eris 13♈59.9R ⚴ 28♏35.5
⚷ 4♉34.8R ⚶ 0♎23.5
☽ Mean ☊ 15♎24.0

November 1977 — LONGITUDE

Day	Sid.Time	☉	0 hr ☽	Noon ☽	True ☊	☿	♀	♂	⚳	♃	♄	♅	♆	♇
1 Tu	14 42 39	8♏57 15	3♋37 19	9♋33 09	14♎59.3	17♏22.9	19♎10.8	2♌21.0	21♏32.2	6♋02.0	29♌06.5	11♏54.9	14♐33.0	15♎02.8
2 W	14 46 35	9 57 18	15 29 50	21 27 53	14R56.8	18 56.5	20 25.6	2 44.5	21 57.8	6R00.3	29 10.6	11 58.7	14 34.9	15 05.0
3 Th	14 50 32	10 57 23	27 27 50	3♌30 14	14D55.4	20 29.6	21 40.5	3 07.6	22 23.4	5 58.4	29 14.6	12 02.4	14 36.9	15 07.2
4 F	14 54 28	11 57 31	9♌35 40	15 44 43	14 55.2	22 02.3	22 55.4	3 30.3	22 49.0	5 56.2	29 18.6	12 06.2	14 38.8	15 09.4
5 Sa	14 58 25	12 57 40	21 57 57	28 15 56	14 56.1	23 34.5	24 10.3	3 52.7	23 14.6	5 53.9	29 22.4	12 09.9	14 40.8	15 11.5
6 Su	15 02 21	13 57 51	4♍39 12	11♍08 14	14 57.6	25 06.4	25 25.3	4 14.6	23 40.2	5 51.4	29 26.2	12 13.7	14 42.8	15 13.7
7 M	15 06 18	14 58 05	17 43 28	24 25 13	14 59.2	26 38.0	26 40.3	4 36.2	24 05.8	5 48.7	29 29.8	12 17.4	14 44.8	15 15.8
8 Tu	15 10 14	15 58 20	1♎13 43	8♎09 03	15R00.4	28 09.1	27 55.3	4 57.3	24 31.5	5 45.8	29 33.4	12 21.2	14 46.8	15 17.9
9 W	15 14 11	16 58 38	15 11 09	22 19 48	15 00.3	29 39.9	29 10.4	5 18.0	24 57.1	5 42.7	29 36.8	12 24.9	14 48.9	15 20.0
10 Th	15 18 08	17 58 57	29 34 35	6♏54 52	14 58.7	1♐10.3	0♏25.5	5 38.2	25 22.7	5 39.4	29 40.2	12 28.7	14 50.9	15 22.1
11 F	15 22 04	18 59 18	14♏19 53	21 48 40	14 55.4	2 40.3	1 40.6	5 58.0	25 48.4	5 35.9	29 43.5	12 32.4	14 53.0	15 24.1
12 Sa	15 26 01	19 59 41	29 20 07	6♐53 04	14 50.8	4 09.9	2 55.7	6 17.3	26 14.0	5 32.3	29 46.7	12 36.2	14 55.1	15 26.2
13 Su	15 29 57	21 00 06	14♐26 17	21 58 31	14 45.3	5 39.1	4 10.8	6 36.2	26 39.7	5 28.4	29 49.7	12 39.9	14 57.2	15 28.2
14 M	15 33 54	22 00 32	29 28 37	6♑55 30	14 39.8	7 07.9	5 26.0	6 54.6	27 05.3	5 24.3	29 52.7	12 43.6	14 59.3	15 30.2
15 Tu	15 37 50	23 00 59	14♑18 16	21 36 08	14 35.2	8 36.3	6 41.2	7 12.5	27 30.9	5 20.1	29 55.6	12 47.4	15 01.4	15 32.2
16 W	15 41 47	24 01 28	28 48 35	5♒55 12	14 32.0	10 04.2	7 56.3	7 29.9	27 56.6	5 15.7	29 58.4	12 51.1	15 03.6	15 34.2
17 Th	15 45 43	25 01 58	12♒55 47	19 50 17	14D30.5	11 31.6	9 11.5	7 46.8	28 22.2	5 11.1	0♍01.0	12 54.8	15 05.7	15 36.1
18 F	15 49 40	26 02 29	26 38 49	3♓21 34	14 30.6	12 58.5	10 26.8	8 03.2	28 47.8	5 06.4	0 03.6	12 58.5	15 07.9	15 38.0
19 Sa	15 53 37	27 03 01	9♓58 50	16 30 57	14 31.8	14 24.8	11 42.0	8 19.1	29 13.4	5 01.4	0 06.0	13 02.1	15 10.0	15 39.9
20 Su	15 57 33	28 03 35	22 58 20	29 21 23	14 33.3	15 50.4	12 57.2	8 34.4	29 39.0	4 56.3	0 08.4	13 05.8	15 12.2	15 41.8
21 M	16 01 30	29 04 09	5♈40 32	11♈56 10	14R34.2	17 15.3	14 12.5	8 49.2	0♐04.6	4 51.1	0 10.7	13 09.4	15 14.4	15 43.7
22 Tu	16 05 26	0♐04 45	18 08 41	24 18 26	14 33.7	18 39.3	15 27.8	9 03.5	0 30.2	4 45.6	0 12.8	13 13.1	15 16.6	15 45.5
23 W	16 09 23	1 05 23	0♉25 47	6♉31 00	14 31.1	20 02.5	16 43.0	9 17.1	0 55.8	4 40.0	0 14.8	13 16.7	15 18.8	15 47.3
24 Th	16 13 19	2 06 01	12 34 22	18 36 08	14 26.2	21 24.6	17 58.3	9 30.2	1 21.3	4 34.3	0 16.8	13 20.3	15 21.0	15 49.1
25 F	16 17 16	3 06 41	24 36 31	0♊35 41	14 19.1	22 45.5	19 13.6	9 42.8	1 46.9	4 28.4	0 18.6	13 23.9	15 23.2	15 50.9
26 Sa	16 21 12	4 07 23	6♊33 50	12 31 09	14 10.0	24 05.1	20 29.0	9 54.7	2 12.4	4 22.4	0 20.3	13 27.5	15 25.4	15 52.6
27 Su	16 25 09	5 08 05	18 27 47	24 23 56	13 59.7	25 23.1	21 44.3	10 06.0	2 37.9	4 16.2	0 21.9	13 31.1	15 27.7	15 54.4
28 M	16 29 06	6 08 49	0♋19 48	6♋15 36	13 49.2	26 39.4	22 59.7	10 16.7	3 03.4	4 09.9	0 23.4	13 34.6	15 29.9	15 56.0
29 Tu	16 33 02	7 09 35	12 11 35	18 08 01	13 39.3	27 53.7	24 15.0	10 26.7	3 29.0	4 03.4	0 24.8	13 38.2	15 32.2	15 57.7
30 W	16 36 59	8 10 22	24 05 15	0♌03 38	13 31.0	29 05.7	25 30.4	10 36.1	3 54.4	3 56.8	0 26.1	13 41.7	15 34.4	15 59.4

December 1977 — LONGITUDE

Day	Sid.Time	☉	0 hr ☽	Noon ☽	True ☊	☿	♀	♂	⚳	♃	♄	♅	♆	♇
1 Th	16 40 55	9♐11 10	6♌03 34	12♌05 30	13♎24.8	0♑15.0	26♏45.8	10♌44.9	4♐19.9	3♋50.1	0♍27.3	13♏45.2	15♐36.7	16♎01.0
2 F	16 44 52	10 12 00	18 09 56	24 17 22	13R21.0	1 21.3	28 01.2	10 52.9	4 45.4	3R43.2	0 28.4	13 48.7	15 38.9	16 02.6
3 Sa	16 48 48	11 12 51	0♍28 21	6♍43 28	13D19.5	2 24.0	29 16.6	11 00.3	5 10.8	3 36.3	0 29.3	13 52.1	15 41.2	16 04.1
4 Su	16 52 45	12 13 43	13 03 18	19 28 25	13 19.6	3 22.8	0♐32.0	11 07.0	5 36.2	3 29.2	0 30.2	13 55.5	15 43.4	16 05.7
5 M	16 56 41	13 14 37	25 59 21	2♎36 38	13R20.4	4 16.9	1 47.4	11 12.9	6 01.6	3 22.0	0 30.9	13 58.9	15 45.7	16 07.2
6 Tu	17 00 38	14 15 32	9♎20 41	16 11 50	13 20.7	5 05.9	3 02.9	11 18.1	6 27.0	3 14.7	0 31.5	14 02.3	15 47.9	16 08.7
7 W	17 04 35	15 16 28	23 10 17	0♏16 05	13 19.4	5 48.9	4 18.3	11 22.6	6 52.4	3 07.3	0 32.0	14 05.7	15 50.2	16 10.1
8 Th	17 08 31	16 17 26	7♏29 04	14 48 53	13 15.8	6 25.1	5 33.8	11 26.4	7 17.7	2 59.8	0 32.4	14 09.0	15 52.5	16 11.5
9 F	17 12 28	17 18 25	22 14 55	29 46 20	13 09.5	6 53.9	6 49.3	11 29.4	7 43.0	2 52.3	0 32.7	14 12.3	15 54.7	16 12.9
10 Sa	17 16 24	18 19 25	7♐22 03	15♐00 51	13 00.9	7 14.2	8 04.7	11 31.6	8 08.3	2 44.6	0 32.9	14 15.6	15 57.0	16 14.3
11 Su	17 20 21	19 20 25	22 41 17	0♑21 55	12 50.7	7R25.2	9 20.2	11 33.0	8 33.6	2 36.9	0R32.9	14 18.9	15 59.3	16 15.6
12 M	17 24 17	20 21 27	8♑01 13	15 37 45	12 40.3	7 26.1	10 35.7	11R33.6	8 58.9	2 29.1	0 32.9	14 22.1	16 01.5	16 16.9
13 Tu	17 28 14	21 22 29	23 10 13	0♒37 29	12 30.9	7 16.2	11 51.2	11 33.5	9 24.1	2 21.2	0 32.7	14 25.3	16 03.8	16 18.2
14 W	17 32 10	22 23 32	7♒58 40	15 13 04	12 23.5	6 55.0	13 06.7	11 32.5	9 49.3	2 13.3	0 32.4	14 28.5	16 06.1	16 19.5
15 Th	17 36 07	23 24 35	22 20 17	29 20 07	12 18.7	6 22.2	14 22.2	11 30.7	10 14.4	2 05.3	0 32.0	14 31.6	16 08.3	16 20.7
16 F	17 40 04	24 25 39	6♓12 35	12♓57 50	12D16.4	5 37.8	15 37.7	11 28.1	10 39.6	1 57.3	0 31.5	14 34.8	16 10.6	16 21.9
17 Sa	17 44 00	25 26 42	19 36 14	26 08 11	12 15.9	4 42.7	16 53.1	11 24.7	11 04.7	1 49.3	0 30.9	14 37.8	16 12.8	16 23.0
18 Su	17 47 57	26 27 47	2♈34 14	8♈54 54	12R16.1	3 37.7	18 08.6	11 20.5	11 29.7	1 41.2	0 30.2	14 40.9	16 15.0	16 24.1
19 M	17 51 53	27 28 51	15 10 48	21 22 32	12 15.8	2 24.8	19 24.1	11 15.5	11 54.7	1 33.1	0 29.3	14 43.9	16 17.3	16 25.2
20 Tu	17 55 50	28 29 56	27 30 40	3♉35 45	12 13.9	1 05.9	20 39.6	11 09.6	12 19.7	1 24.9	0 28.4	14 46.9	16 19.5	16 26.2
21 W	17 59 46	29 31 01	9♉38 19	15 38 52	12 09.5	29♐43.8	21 55.1	11 02.9	12 44.7	1 16.8	0 27.3	14 49.8	16 21.7	16 27.3
22 Th	18 03 43	0♑32 07	21 37 48	27 35 33	12 02.0	28 21.2	23 10.6	10 55.3	13 09.6	1 08.6	0 26.1	14 52.7	16 23.9	16 28.3
23 F	18 07 39	1 33 12	3♊32 27	9♊28 47	11 51.5	27 00.8	24 26.1	10 47.0	13 34.5	1 00.5	0 24.9	14 55.6	16 26.1	16 29.2
24 Sa	18 11 36	2 34 18	15 24 50	21 20 47	11 38.5	25 45.1	25 41.6	10 37.8	13 59.4	0 52.4	0 23.5	14 58.5	16 28.3	16 30.1
25 Su	18 15 33	3 35 25	27 16 52	3♋13 13	11 23.9	24 36.5	26 57.1	10 27.8	14 24.2	0 44.2	0 22.0	15 01.3	16 30.5	16 31.0
26 M	18 19 29	4 36 32	9♋10 00	15 07 21	11 08.8	23 36.4	28 12.6	10 17.0	14 49.0	0 36.1	0 20.4	15 04.0	16 32.7	16 31.9
27 Tu	18 23 26	5 37 39	21 05 25	27 04 23	10 54.4	22 46.1	29 28.1	10 05.3	15 13.7	0 28.0	0 18.7	15 06.8	16 34.9	16 32.7
28 W	18 27 22	6 38 46	3♌04 23	9♌05 40	10 41.9	22 06.2	0♑43.6	9 52.9	15 38.4	0 19.9	0 16.9	15 09.5	16 37.0	16 33.5
29 Th	18 31 19	7 39 54	15 08 26	21 13 00	10 32.2	21 36.9	1 59.1	9 39.6	16 03.0	0 11.9	0 15.0	15 12.1	16 39.2	16 34.2
30 F	18 35 15	8 41 02	27 19 40	3♍28 49	10 25.5	21 18.1	3 14.6	9 25.6	16 27.6	0 03.9	0 13.0	15 14.7	16 41.3	16 34.9
31 Sa	18 39 12	9 42 11	9♍40 51	15 56 12	10 21.7	21D09.3	4 30.1	9 10.8	16 52.2	29♊56.0	0 10.9	15 17.3	16 43.5	16 35.6

Astro Data	Dy Hr Mn
☽0S	7 14:56
☽0N	20 6:08
☽0S	5 1:07
♄R	11 12:11
☿R	12 2:09
♂R	12 19:12
☽0N	17 13:25
♆⚹♇	25 20:43
♃⚹♄	28 23:53
♃⚼♅	29 11:30
☿D	31 22:03

Planet Ingress	Dy Hr Mn
☿ ♐	9 17:20
♀ ♏	10 3:52
♄ ♍	17 2:43
⚳ ♐	21 7:41
☉ ♐	22 10:07
☿ ♑	1 6:43
♀ ♐	4 1:49
☿ ♐R	21 7:18
☉ ♑	21 23:23
♀ ♑	27 22:09
♃ ♊R	30 23:50

Last Aspect Dy Hr Mn		☽ Ingress Dy Hr Mn
2 9:40	♀ □	♌ 3 5:03
5 14:06	♄ ☌	♍ 5 15:17
7 16:25	☿ ⚹	♎ 7 21:51
10 0:24	♀ ☌	♏ 10 0:42
12 0:40	♄ □	♐ 12 1:03
14 0:36	♄ △	♑ 14 0:50
15 14:31	☉ ⚹	♒ 16 2:00
17 21:52	☉ □	♓ 18 5:58
20 9:20	☉ △	♈ 20 13:13
21 23:35	☿ △	♉ 22 23:09
24 10:36	♀ ☍	♊ 25 10:48
27 14:14	☿ ☍	♋ 27 23:20
30 1:47	♀ △	♌ 30 11:53

Last Aspect Dy Hr Mn		☽ Ingress Dy Hr Mn
2 20:04	♀ □	♍ 2 23:05
4 4:59	♆ □	♎ 5 7:18
6 11:54	♇ ☌	♏ 7 11:33
8 10:55	♅ ☌	♐ 9 12:22
10 17:33	☉ ☌	♑ 11 11:26
12 13:02	♇ □	♒ 13 10:59
15 1:02	☉ ⚹	♓ 15 13:09
17 10:37	☉ □	♈ 17 19:11
20 1:02	☉ △	♉ 20 4:54
21 10:21	♅ ☍	♊ 22 16:51
24 21:50	♀ ☍	♋ 25 5:30
26 14:50	♇ □	♌ 27 17:52
29 12:46	☿ △	♍ 30 5:13

☽ Phases & Eclipses Dy Hr Mn	
4 3:58	☾ 11♌37
11 7:09	● 18♏47
17 21:52	☽ 25♒27
25 17:31	○ 3♊21
3 21:16	☾ 11♍36
10 17:33	● 18♐34
17 10:37	☽ 25♓23
25 12:49	○ 3♋37

Astro Data

1 November 1977
Julian Day # 28429
SVP 5♓34'07"
GC 26♐31.8 ⚴ 1♏30.3
Eris 13♈41.4R ⚵ 8♐14.6
⚷ 3♉09.5R ⚶ 15♎56.5
☽ Mean ☊ 13♎45.5

1 December 1977
Julian Day # 28459
SVP 5♓34'02"
GC 26♐31.8 ⚴ 14♏38.4
Eris 13♈27.9R ⚵ 18♐33.1
⚷ 1♉52.4R ⚶ 0♏55.8
☽ Mean ☊ 12♎10.2

LONGITUDE — January 1978

Day	Sid.Time	☉	0 hr ☽	Noon ☽	True ☊	☿	♀	♂	⚳	♃	♄	♅	♆	♇
1 Su	18 43 08	10♑43 19	22♍15 22	28♍38 51	10♎20.3	21♐10.1	5♑45.6	8♌55.3	17♐16.7	29♊48.1	0♍08.6	15♏19.9	16♐45.6	16♎36.2
2 M	18 47 05	11 44 29	5♎07 09	11♎40 47	10R 20.1	21 19.6	7 01.1	8R 39.0	17 41.2	29R 40.3	0R 06.3	15 22.3	16 47.7	16 36.9
3 Tu	18 51 02	12 45 38	18 20 13	25 05 52	10 19.8	21 37.2	8 16.6	8 21.9	18 05.6	29 32.5	0 03.9	15 24.8	16 49.8	16 37.4
4 W	18 54 58	13 46 48	1♏58 05	8♏57 06	10 18.2	22 02.2	9 32.1	8 04.2	18 30.0	29 24.8	0 01.4	15 27.2	16 51.8	16 38.0
5 Th	18 58 55	14 47 58	16 02 58	23 15 36	10 14.3	22 33.9	10 47.6	7 45.8	18 54.3	29 17.2	29♌58.8	15 29.6	16 53.9	16 38.5
6 F	19 02 51	15 49 08	0♐34 42	7♐59 43	10 07.5	23 11.6	12 03.1	7 26.8	19 18.6	29 09.6	29 56.1	15 31.9	16 56.0	16 38.9
7 Sa	19 06 48	16 50 19	15 29 54	23 04 15	9 58.0	23 54.6	13 18.6	7 07.2	19 42.9	29 02.2	29 53.3	15 34.2	16 58.0	16 39.4
8 Su	19 10 44	17 51 29	0♑41 34	8♑20 31	9 46.8	24 42.4	14 34.1	6 46.9	20 07.0	28 54.8	29 50.4	15 36.4	17 00.0	16 39.8
9 M	19 14 41	18 52 40	15 59 37	23 37 26	9 35.0	25 34.5	15 49.6	6 26.1	20 31.2	28 47.6	29 47.4	15 38.6	17 02.0	16 40.1
10 Tu	19 18 38	19 53 50	1♒12 29	8♒43 28	9 24.1	26 30.5	17 05.1	6 04.8	20 55.2	28 40.4	29 44.3	15 40.7	17 04.0	16 40.5
11 W	19 22 34	20 54 59	16 09 14	23 28 50	9 15.3	27 29.8	18 20.6	5 43.1	21 19.2	28 33.4	29 41.1	15 42.8	17 06.0	16 40.7
12 Th	19 26 31	21 56 08	0♓41 33	7♓46 57	9 09.2	28 32.2	19 36.0	5 20.9	21 43.2	28 26.5	29 37.9	15 44.9	17 07.9	16 41.0
13 F	19 30 27	22 57 17	14 44 46	21 34 59	9 05.9	29 37.4	20 51.5	4 58.3	22 07.1	28 19.7	29 34.5	15 46.9	17 09.9	16 41.2
14 Sa	19 34 24	23 58 24	28 17 48	4♈53 30	9D 04.8	0♑45.0	22 07.0	4 35.4	22 30.9	28 13.0	29 31.1	15 48.8	17 11.8	16 41.4
15 Su	19 38 20	24 59 31	11♈22 32	17 45 26	9R 04.9	1 54.9	23 22.4	4 12.1	22 54.7	28 06.5	29 27.6	15 50.7	17 13.7	16 41.5
16 M	19 42 17	26 00 38	24 02 48	0♉15 16	9 04.9	3 06.7	24 37.9	3 48.7	23 18.4	28 00.1	29 24.0	15 52.6	17 15.5	16 41.6
17 Tu	19 46 13	27 01 43	6♉23 29	12 28 05	9 03.7	4 20.4	25 53.3	3 25.0	23 42.0	27 53.8	29 20.4	15 54.4	17 17.4	16 41.7
18 W	19 50 10	28 02 48	18 29 44	24 29 02	9 00.4	5 35.7	27 08.8	3 01.1	24 05.6	27 47.7	29 16.7	15 56.2	17 19.2	16R 41.7
19 Th	19 54 06	29 03 52	0♊26 33	6♊22 50	8 54.4	6 52.5	28 24.2	2 37.2	24 29.1	27 41.7	29 12.9	15 57.9	17 21.0	16 41.7
20 F	19 58 03	0♒04 55	12 18 23	18 13 38	8 45.6	8 10.8	29 39.6	2 13.2	24 52.5	27 35.9	29 09.0	15 59.5	17 22.8	16 41.7
21 Sa	20 02 00	1 05 57	24 08 59	0♋04 45	8 34.5	9 30.3	0♒55.0	1 49.1	25 15.8	27 30.2	29 05.0	16 01.1	17 24.6	16 41.6
22 Su	20 05 56	2 06 59	6♋01 16	11 58 45	8 21.9	10 51.0	2 10.4	1 25.1	25 39.1	27 24.7	29 01.0	16 02.7	17 26.4	16 41.5
23 M	20 09 53	3 08 00	17 57 25	23 57 27	8 08.7	12 12.8	3 25.8	1 01.2	26 02.4	27 19.3	28 57.0	16 04.2	17 28.1	16 41.4
24 Tu	20 13 49	4 09 00	29 58 59	6♌02 08	7 56.2	13 35.7	4 41.2	0 37.4	26 25.5	27 14.2	28 52.8	16 05.6	17 29.8	16 41.2
25 W	20 17 46	5 09 59	12♌07 01	18 13 45	7 45.3	14 59.5	5 56.6	0 13.7	26 48.6	27 09.1	28 48.6	16 07.0	17 31.5	16 41.0
26 Th	20 21 42	6 10 57	24 22 25	0♍33 10	7 36.8	16 24.3	7 12.0	29♋50.2	27 11.6	27 04.3	28 44.4	16 08.4	17 33.1	16 40.8
27 F	20 25 39	7 11 54	6♍46 09	13 01 32	7 31.1	17 50.0	8 27.3	29 27.0	27 34.5	26 59.6	28 40.1	16 09.7	17 34.8	16 40.5
28 Sa	20 29 35	8 12 51	19 19 31	25 40 21	7D 28.2	19 16.6	9 42.7	29 04.1	27 57.3	26 55.1	28 35.7	16 10.9	17 36.4	16 40.2
29 Su	20 33 32	9 13 47	2♎04 17	8♎31 39	7 27.5	20 44.0	10 58.0	28 41.6	28 20.1	26 50.8	28 31.3	16 12.1	17 37.9	16 39.8
30 M	20 37 29	10 14 43	15 02 44	21 37 53	7 28.1	22 12.2	12 13.4	28 19.4	28 42.8	26 46.6	28 26.9	16 13.2	17 39.5	16 39.4
31 Tu	20 41 25	11 15 37	28 17 25	5♏01 39	7R 28.9	23 41.2	13 28.7	27 57.6	29 05.4	26 42.7	28 22.4	16 14.3	17 41.0	16 39.0

LONGITUDE — February 1978

Day	Sid.Time	☉	0 hr ☽	Noon ☽	True ☊	☿	♀	♂	⚳	♃	♄	♅	♆	♇
1 W	20 45 22	12♒16 31	11♏50 50	18♏45 12	7♎28.9	25♑11.0	14♒44.0	27♋36.2	29♐27.9	26♊38.9	28♌17.8	16♏15.3	17♐42.5	16♎38.6
2 Th	20 49 18	13 17 24	25 44 51	2♐49 47	7R 27.1	26 41.5	15 59.3	27R 15.4	29 50.3	26R 35.3	28R 13.2	16 16.3	17 44.0	16R 38.1
3 F	20 53 15	14 18 17	9♐59 53	17 14 50	7 23.1	28 12.9	17 14.6	26 55.1	0♑12.7	26 31.9	28 08.6	16 17.2	17 45.5	16 37.6
4 Sa	20 57 11	15 19 09	24 34 13	1♑57 21	7 17.0	29 45.0	18 29.9	26 35.3	0 34.9	26 28.7	28 04.0	16 18.1	17 46.9	16 37.0
5 Su	21 01 08	16 19 59	9♑23 28	16 51 35	7 09.3	1♒17.8	19 45.2	26 16.1	0 57.1	26 25.7	27 59.3	16 18.9	17 48.3	16 36.4
6 M	21 05 05	17 20 49	24 20 39	1♒49 31	7 01.1	2 51.4	21 00.5	25 57.6	1 19.2	26 22.9	27 54.6	16 19.7	17 49.7	16 35.8
7 Tu	21 09 01	18 21 38	9♒17 00	16 41 57	6 53.4	4 25.8	22 15.8	25 39.6	1 41.2	26 20.3	27 49.8	16 20.4	17 51.0	16 35.2
8 W	21 12 58	19 22 25	24 03 17	1♓20 04	6 47.1	6 01.0	23 31.1	25 22.4	2 03.0	26 17.8	27 45.0	16 21.0	17 52.4	16 34.5
9 Th	21 16 54	20 23 11	8♓31 28	15 36 52	6 43.0	7 37.0	24 46.3	25 05.9	2 24.8	26 15.6	27 40.2	16 21.6	17 53.6	16 33.8
10 F	21 20 51	21 23 55	22 35 49	29 28 04	6D 41.0	9 13.7	26 01.5	24 50.0	2 46.5	26 13.6	27 35.4	16 22.1	17 54.9	16 33.0
11 Sa	21 24 47	22 24 38	6♈13 33	12♈52 21	6 40.9	10 51.3	27 16.7	24 34.9	3 08.1	26 11.8	27 30.6	16 22.6	17 56.1	16 32.2
12 Su	21 28 44	23 25 20	19 24 39	25 50 50	6 42.0	12 29.6	28 31.9	24 20.6	3 29.6	26 10.1	27 25.8	16 23.0	17 57.3	16 31.4
13 M	21 32 40	24 25 59	2♉11 20	8♉26 39	6 43.6	14 08.8	29 47.1	24 07.0	3 50.9	26 08.7	27 20.9	16 23.4	17 58.5	16 30.6
14 Tu	21 36 37	25 26 37	14 37 20	20 44 01	6R 44.6	15 48.9	1♓02.3	23 54.2	4 12.2	26 07.5	27 16.1	16 23.7	17 59.6	16 29.7
15 W	21 40 33	26 27 14	26 47 19	2♊47 51	6 44.5	17 29.8	2 17.4	23 42.2	4 33.4	26 06.5	27 11.2	16 24.0	18 00.7	16 28.8
16 Th	21 44 30	27 27 48	8♊46 16	14 43 09	6 42.7	19 11.5	3 32.6	23 31.0	4 54.4	26 05.7	27 06.3	16 24.2	18 01.8	16 27.9
17 F	21 48 27	28 28 21	20 39 06	26 34 41	6 39.2	20 54.2	4 47.7	23 20.5	5 15.4	26 05.0	27 01.5	16 24.3	18 02.9	16 27.0
18 Sa	21 52 23	29 28 52	2♋30 25	8♋26 47	6 34.1	22 37.7	6 02.8	23 10.9	5 36.2	26 04.6	26 56.6	16 24.4	18 03.9	16 26.0
19 Su	21 56 20	0♓29 22	14 24 14	20 23 08	6 27.9	24 22.2	7 17.9	23 02.0	5 56.9	26D 04.4	26 51.8	16R 24.4	18 04.9	16 25.0
20 M	22 00 16	1 29 49	26 23 50	2♌26 39	6 21.2	26 07.6	8 32.9	22 54.0	6 17.5	26 04.4	26 46.9	16 24.4	18 05.8	16 23.9
21 Tu	22 04 13	2 30 15	8♌31 48	14 39 29	6 14.8	27 54.0	9 48.0	22 46.7	6 38.0	26 04.6	26 42.1	16 24.3	18 06.8	16 22.9
22 W	22 08 09	3 30 39	20 49 53	27 03 05	6 09.3	29 41.2	11 03.0	22 40.3	6 58.3	26 05.0	26 37.3	16 24.2	18 07.6	16 21.8
23 Th	22 12 06	4 31 02	3♍19 10	9♍38 12	6 05.2	1♓29.5	12 18.0	22 34.6	7 18.6	26 05.6	26 32.5	16 24.0	18 08.5	16 20.7
24 F	22 16 02	5 31 23	16 00 14	22 25 15	6 02.8	3 18.6	13 33.0	22 29.7	7 38.7	26 06.3	26 27.7	16 23.8	18 09.3	16 19.5
25 Sa	22 19 59	6 31 42	28 53 16	5♎24 20	6D 01.9	5 08.7	14 47.9	22 25.6	7 58.7	26 07.3	26 23.0	16 23.5	18 10.1	16 18.3
26 Su	22 23 56	7 31 59	11♎58 25	18 35 33	6 02.5	6 59.7	16 02.9	22 22.3	8 18.5	26 08.5	26 18.2	16 23.1	18 10.9	16 17.1
27 M	22 27 52	8 32 15	25 15 47	1♏59 07	6 03.9	8 51.6	17 17.8	22 19.7	8 38.3	26 09.9	26 13.5	16 22.7	18 11.6	16 15.9
28 Tu	22 31 49	9 32 30	8♏45 35	15 35 14	6 05.5	10 44.4	18 32.7	22 17.9	8 57.9	26 11.4	26 08.9	16 22.3	18 12.3	16 14.7

Astro Data

	Dy Hr Mn
☽ 0S	1 9:39
☽ 0N	13 22:55
♇ R	19 0:47
☽ 0S	28 16:31
☽ 0N	10 9:52
♅ R	19 15:25
♅⊻♇	20 0:26
♃ D	20 1:24
☽ 0S	24 23:05
♃✶♄	28 2:10

Planet Ingress

	Dy Hr Mn
♄ ♌R	5 0:44
☿ ♑	13 20:07
☉ ♒	20 10:04
♀ ♒	20 18:29
♂ ♋R	26 1:59
⚳ ♑	2 22:23
☿ ♒	4 15:54
♀ ♓	13 16:07
☉ ♓	19 0:21
☿ ♓	22 16:11

Last Aspect / ☽ Ingress

Last Aspect Dy Hr Mn		☽ Ingress Dy Hr Mn
1 14:08 ♃ □	♎	1 14:31
3 19:43 ♃ △	♏	3 20:35
5 22:59 ♄ □	♐	5 23:03
7 22:42 ♄ △	♑	7 22:55
9 4:00 ☉ ☌	♒	9 22:05
11 22:16 ♄ ☍	♓	11 22:50
13 23:57 ♃ □	♈	14 3:05
16 10:21 ♄ △	♉	16 11:30
18 21:36 ♄ □	♊	18 23:06
21 10:00 ♄ ✶	♋	21 11:50
22 21:28 ♇ □	♌	24 0:02
26 8:30 ♄ ☌	♍	26 10:56
28 18:12 ♂ ✶	♎	28 20:08
31 0:13 ♄ ✶	♏	31 3:04

Last Aspect / ☽ Ingress

Last Aspect Dy Hr Mn		☽ Ingress Dy Hr Mn
2 4:15 ♄ □	♐	2 7:13
4 5:43 ♄ △	♑	4 8:50
6 2:47 ♂ ☍	♒	6 9:04
8 6:07 ♄ ☍	♓	8 9:47
10 6:20 ♃ □	♈	10 12:56
12 17:37 ♀ ✶	♉	12 19:50
15 0:52 ♄ □	♊	15 6:24
17 16:12 ☉ △	♋	17 18:56
19 17:14 ♂ ☌	♌	20 7:10
22 11:11 ♄ ☌	♍	22 17:39
24 18:51 ♃ □	♎	25 2:03
27 1:47 ♄ ✶	♏	27 8:28

☽ Phases & Eclipses

Dy Hr Mn	
2 12:07	☾ 11♎45
9 4:00	● 18♑32
16 3:03	☽ 25♈38
24 7:56	○ 3♌59
31 23:51	☾ 11♏46
7 14:54	● 18♒29
14 22:11	☽ 25♉52
23 1:26	○ 4♍04

Astro Data

1 January 1978
Julian Day # 28490
SVP 5♓33'57"
GC 26♐31.9 ⚴ 27♏33.9
Eris 13♈22.7 ⚵ 29♐38.7
⚷ 1♉09.2R ⚶ 15♏55.6
☽ Mean ☊ 10♎31.7

1 February 1978
Julian Day # 28521
SVP 5♓33'53"
GC 26♐32.0 ⚴ 9♐09.0
Eris 13♈28.2 ⚵ 10♑39.7
⚷ 1♉19.7 ⚶ 29♏45.2
☽ Mean ☊ 8♎53.2

March 1978 — LONGITUDE

Day	Sid.Time	☉	0 hr ☽	Noon ☽	True ☊	☿	♀	♂	⚳	♃	♄	♅	♆	♇
1 W	22 35 45	10♓32 43	22♏28 04	29♏24 05	6♎06.7	12♓38.0	19♓47.6	22♋16.9	9♑17.3	26♊13.2	26♌04.2	16♏21.8	18♐13.0	16♎13.4
2 Th	22 39 42	11 32 55	6♐23 13	13♐25 24	6R 07.1	14 32.3	21 02.5	22D 16.6	9 36.7	26 15.2	25R 59.6	16R 21.2	18 13.6	16R 12.2
3 F	22 43 38	12 33 06	20 30 28	27 38 11	6 06.4	16 27.3	22 17.3	22 17.0	9 55.9	26 17.3	25 55.1	16 20.6	18 14.2	16 10.8
4 Sa	22 47 35	13 33 14	4♑48 16	12♑00 19	6 04.6	18 22.8	23 32.2	22 18.2	10 15.0	26 19.7	25 50.5	16 20.0	18 14.8	16 09.5
5 Su	22 51 31	14 33 22	19 13 51	26 28 19	6 02.0	20 18.8	24 47.0	22 20.0	10 33.9	26 22.2	25 46.1	16 19.2	18 15.3	16 08.2
6 M	22 55 28	15 33 27	3♒43 06	10♒57 30	5 59.1	22 15.1	26 01.8	22 22.6	10 52.6	26 24.9	25 41.6	16 18.5	18 15.8	16 06.8
7 Tu	22 59 25	16 33 31	18 10 49	25 22 20	5 56.3	24 11.5	27 16.6	22 25.9	11 11.3	26 27.8	25 37.2	16 17.7	18 16.3	16 05.4
8 W	23 03 21	17 33 33	2♓31 18	9♓37 06	5 54.2	26 07.9	28 31.3	22 29.9	11 29.7	26 30.9	25 32.9	16 16.8	18 16.7	16 04.0
9 Th	23 07 18	18 33 34	16 39 04	23 36 43	5D 52.9	28 03.8	29 46.1	22 34.6	11 48.1	26 34.2	25 28.6	16 15.9	18 17.1	16 02.6
10 F	23 11 14	19 33 32	0♈29 36	7♈17 24	5 52.5	29 59.2	1♈00.8	22 39.9	12 06.2	26 37.7	25 24.4	16 14.9	18 17.5	16 01.1
11 Sa	23 15 11	20 33 28	13 59 55	20 37 02	5 53.0	1♈53.6	2 15.5	22 45.9	12 24.2	26 41.3	25 20.2	16 13.9	18 17.8	15 59.7
12 Su	23 19 07	21 33 23	27 08 47	3♉35 18	5 54.0	3 46.7	3 30.1	22 52.5	12 42.1	26 45.2	25 16.1	16 12.8	18 18.1	15 58.2
13 M	23 23 04	22 33 15	9♉56 46	16 13 31	5 55.3	5 38.1	4 44.8	22 59.8	12 59.7	26 49.2	25 12.1	16 11.7	18 18.4	15 56.7
14 Tu	23 27 00	23 33 05	22 25 55	28 34 24	5 56.4	7 27.4	5 59.4	23 07.7	13 17.3	26 53.4	25 08.1	16 10.5	18 18.6	15 55.2
15 W	23 30 57	24 32 53	4♊39 28	10♊41 38	5 57.3	9 14.1	7 13.9	23 16.3	13 34.6	26 57.8	25 04.2	16 09.3	18 18.8	15 53.7
16 Th	23 34 53	25 32 38	16 41 27	22 39 31	5R 57.7	10 57.7	8 28.5	23 25.4	13 51.8	27 02.3	25 00.3	16 08.0	18 18.9	15 52.1
17 F	23 38 50	26 32 22	28 36 24	4♋32 43	5 57.6	12 37.9	9 43.0	23 35.1	14 08.8	27 07.0	24 56.5	16 06.7	18 19.1	15 50.6
18 Sa	23 42 47	27 32 03	10♋29 02	16 25 56	5 57.0	14 14.1	10 57.5	23 45.4	14 25.6	27 11.9	24 52.8	16 05.4	18 19.2	15 49.0
19 Su	23 46 43	28 31 42	22 23 58	28 23 39	5 56.2	15 45.7	12 12.0	23 56.2	14 42.3	27 17.0	24 49.2	16 04.0	18 19.2	15 47.4
20 M	23 50 40	29 31 18	4♌25 30	10♌29 57	5 55.4	17 12.5	13 26.4	24 07.6	14 58.8	27 22.2	24 45.6	16 02.5	18R 19.2	15 45.8
21 Tu	23 54 36	0♈30 53	16 37 24	22 48 14	5 54.6	18 33.8	14 40.9	24 19.5	15 15.0	27 27.6	24 42.2	16 01.1	18 19.2	15 44.2
22 W	23 58 33	1 30 25	29 02 45	5♍21 10	5 54.0	19 49.4	15 55.2	24 32.0	15 31.1	27 33.1	24 38.8	15 59.5	18 19.2	15 42.6
23 Th	0 02 29	2 29 55	11♍43 40	18 10 21	5 53.6	20 58.9	17 09.6	24 44.9	15 47.1	27 38.8	24 35.5	15 58.0	18 19.1	15 41.0
24 F	0 06 26	3 29 22	24 41 17	1♎16 25	5D 53.5	22 01.8	18 23.9	24 58.4	16 02.8	27 44.7	24 32.2	15 56.4	18 19.0	15 39.4
25 Sa	0 10 22	4 28 48	7♎55 39	14 38 52	5 53.5	22 58.0	19 38.2	25 12.3	16 18.3	27 50.7	24 29.1	15 54.7	18 18.9	15 37.7
26 Su	0 14 19	5 28 12	21 25 50	28 16 17	5R 53.5	23 47.1	20 52.5	25 26.7	16 33.7	27 56.9	24 26.0	15 53.0	18 18.7	15 36.1
27 M	0 18 16	6 27 34	5♏09 57	12♏06 30	5 53.5	24 29.1	22 06.7	25 41.6	16 48.8	28 03.3	24 23.0	15 51.3	18 18.5	15 34.4
28 Tu	0 22 12	7 26 54	19 05 34	26 06 48	5 53.4	25 03.6	23 20.9	25 57.0	17 03.8	28 09.8	24 20.1	15 49.5	18 18.3	15 32.8
29 W	0 26 09	8 26 13	3♐09 50	10♐14 19	5 53.2	25 30.8	24 35.1	26 12.8	17 18.5	28 16.4	24 17.3	15 47.7	18 18.0	15 31.1
30 Th	0 30 05	9 25 29	17 19 52	24 26 08	5 53.0	25 50.4	25 49.2	26 29.0	17 33.0	28 23.2	24 14.6	15 45.9	18 17.7	15 29.5
31 F	0 34 02	10 24 44	1♑32 48	8♑39 33	5D 52.8	26 02.7	27 03.4	26 45.7	17 47.4	28 30.1	24 12.0	15 44.0	18 17.4	15 27.8

April 1978 — LONGITUDE

Day	Sid.Time	☉	0 hr ☽	Noon ☽	True ☊	☿	♀	♂	⚳	♃	♄	♅	♆	♇
1 Sa	0 37 58	11♈23 58	15♑46 03	22♑52 01	5♎52.9	26♈07.5	28♈17.5	27♋02.8	18♑01.5	28♊37.2	24♌09.5	15♏42.1	18♐17.0	15♎26.1
2 Su	0 41 55	12 23 09	29 57 10	7♒01 12	5 53.3	26R 05.3	29 31.5	27 20.2	18 15.4	28 44.4	24R 07.0	15R 40.1	18R 16.6	15R 24.4
3 M	0 45 51	13 22 19	14♒03 50	21 04 48	5 53.9	25 56.1	0♉45.6	27 38.1	18 29.0	28 51.8	24 04.7	15 38.1	18 16.2	15 22.8
4 Tu	0 49 48	14 21 27	28 03 48	5♓00 34	5 54.7	25 40.4	1 59.6	27 56.4	18 42.5	28 59.3	24 02.5	15 36.1	18 15.7	15 21.1
5 W	0 53 45	15 20 33	11♓54 49	18 46 17	5 55.3	25 18.6	3 13.6	28 15.1	18 55.7	29 07.0	24 00.3	15 34.1	18 15.2	15 19.4
6 Th	0 57 41	16 19 37	25 34 42	2♈19 50	5R 55.7	24 51.3	4 27.5	28 34.2	19 08.7	29 14.7	23 58.3	15 32.0	18 14.7	15 17.7
7 F	1 01 38	17 18 39	9♈01 29	15 39 26	5 55.5	24 19.0	5 41.4	28 53.6	19 21.4	29 22.7	23 56.3	15 29.9	18 14.1	15 16.0
8 Sa	1 05 34	18 17 39	22 13 34	28 43 48	5 54.8	23 42.4	6 55.3	29 13.4	19 33.9	29 30.7	23 54.5	15 27.8	18 13.5	15 14.3
9 Su	1 09 31	19 16 37	5♉10 04	11♉32 23	5 53.3	23 02.4	8 09.2	29 33.6	19 46.2	29 38.9	23 52.7	15 25.6	18 12.9	15 12.7
10 M	1 13 27	20 15 33	17 50 51	24 05 34	5 51.4	22 19.8	9 23.0	29 54.1	19 58.2	29 47.2	23 51.1	15 23.4	18 12.3	15 11.0
11 Tu	1 17 24	21 14 27	0♊16 44	6♊24 38	5 49.1	21 35.3	10 36.8	0♌15.0	20 10.0	29 55.7	23 49.6	15 21.2	18 11.6	15 09.3
12 W	1 21 20	22 13 18	12 29 33	18 31 52	5 46.8	20 50.0	11 50.6	0 36.1	20 21.5	0♋04.2	23 48.1	15 18.9	18 10.9	15 07.6
13 Th	1 25 17	23 12 08	24 31 59	0♋30 23	5 44.9	20 04.6	13 04.3	0 57.6	20 32.7	0 12.9	23 46.8	15 16.7	18 10.2	15 06.0
14 F	1 29 13	24 10 55	6♋27 32	12 23 59	5 43.6	19 20.0	14 18.0	1 19.5	20 43.7	0 21.7	23 45.6	15 14.4	18 09.4	15 04.3
15 Sa	1 33 10	25 09 40	18 20 18	24 17 02	5D 43.1	18 37.0	15 31.6	1 41.6	20 54.5	0 30.7	23 44.5	15 12.1	18 08.6	15 02.7
16 Su	1 37 07	26 08 23	0♌14 48	6♌14 12	5 43.5	17 56.4	16 45.3	2 04.1	21 05.0	0 39.7	23 43.5	15 09.7	18 07.8	15 01.0
17 M	1 41 03	27 07 04	12 15 47	18 20 10	5 44.6	17 18.7	17 58.8	2 26.8	21 15.2	0 48.9	23 42.5	15 07.4	18 07.0	14 59.4
18 Tu	1 45 00	28 05 42	24 27 53	0♍39 29	5 46.1	16 44.5	19 12.4	2 49.8	21 25.1	0 58.1	23 41.7	15 05.0	18 06.1	14 57.7
19 W	1 48 56	29 04 18	6♍55 25	13 16 07	5 47.7	16 14.3	20 25.9	3 13.1	21 34.8	1 07.5	23 41.0	15 02.6	18 05.2	14 56.1
20 Th	1 52 53	0♉02 52	19 41 57	26 13 10	5R 48.8	15 48.4	21 39.3	3 36.7	21 44.1	1 17.0	23 40.5	15 00.2	18 04.3	14 54.5
21 F	1 56 49	1 01 24	2♎49 57	9♎32 23	5 49.0	15 27.1	22 52.8	4 00.5	21 53.2	1 26.6	23 40.0	14 57.8	18 03.3	14 52.9
22 Sa	2 00 46	1 59 54	16 20 23	23 13 48	5 48.0	15 10.7	24 06.2	4 24.6	22 02.1	1 36.3	23 39.6	14 55.3	18 02.3	14 51.3
23 Su	2 04 42	2 58 22	0♏12 19	7♏15 32	5 45.8	14 59.3	25 19.5	4 49.0	22 10.6	1 46.1	23 39.3	14 52.9	18 01.3	14 49.7
24 M	2 08 39	3 56 48	14 22 54	21 33 46	5 42.4	14D 52.8	26 32.8	5 13.6	22 18.8	1 56.1	23 39.2	14 50.4	18 00.3	14 48.1
25 Tu	2 12 36	4 55 12	28 47 26	6♐03 07	5 38.3	14 51.4	27 46.1	5 38.4	22 26.8	2 06.1	23D 39.1	14 47.9	17 59.2	14 46.6
26 W	2 16 32	5 53 35	13♐20 00	20 37 18	5 34.1	14 55.0	28 59.3	6 03.5	22 34.4	2 16.2	23 39.2	14 45.4	17 58.2	14 45.0
27 Th	2 20 29	6 51 56	27 54 15	5♑10 08	5 30.4	15 03.4	0♊12.5	6 28.8	22 41.8	2 26.4	23 39.3	14 42.9	17 57.1	14 43.5
28 F	2 24 25	7 50 16	12♑24 19	19 36 16	5 27.8	15 16.7	1 25.7	6 54.4	22 48.8	2 36.7	23 39.6	14 40.4	17 55.9	14 42.0
29 Sa	2 28 22	8 48 34	26 45 32	3♒51 47	5D 26.6	15 34.6	2 38.8	7 20.2	22 55.5	2 47.1	23 40.0	14 37.9	17 54.8	14 40.5
30 Su	2 32 18	9 46 51	10♒54 47	17 54 21	5 26.7	15 57.1	3 51.9	7 46.2	23 01.9	2 57.6	23 40.4	14 35.4	17 53.6	14 39.0

Astro Data

	Dy Hr Mn
♂ D	2 9:56
☽ 0N	9 20:22
☿ 0N	10 22:48
♀ 0N	11 23:44
♆ R	20 18:47
☉ 0N	20 23:34
☽ 0S	24 6:47
☿ R	1 16:18
☽ 0N	6 5:00
♃□♅	13 20:07
☽ 0S	20 16:03
☿ D	25 6:47
♄ D	25 12:16
♅⚺♇	26 22:16

Planet Ingress

	Dy Hr Mn
♀ ♈	9 16:29
☿ ♈	10 12:10
☉ ♈	20 23:34
♀ ♉	2 21:14
♂ ♌	10 18:50
♃ ♋	12 0:12
☉ ♉	20 10:50
♀ ♊	27 7:53

Last Aspect / ☽ Ingress (March)

Last Aspect Dy Hr Mn		☽ Ingress Dy Hr Mn
1 6:17 ♄ □	♐	1 13:02
3 9:44 ♃ ☍	♑	3 15:58
5 8:56 ♀ ⚹	♒	5 17:51
7 13:50 ♃ △	♓	7 19:45
9 21:01 ☿ ☌	♈	9 23:08
11 23:13 ♃ ⚹	♉	12 5:18
14 5:18 ♄ □	♊	14 14:48
16 20:53 ♃ ☌	♋	17 2:49
19 12:17 ☉ △	♌	19 15:12
21 21:02 ♃ ⚹	♍	22 1:49
24 5:32 ♃ □	♎	24 9:41
26 11:26 ♃ △	♏	26 15:01
28 11:43 ♂ △	♐	28 18:37
30 18:43 ♃ ☍	♑	30 21:23

Last Aspect / ☽ Ingress (April)

Last Aspect Dy Hr Mn		☽ Ingress Dy Hr Mn
1 22:04 ♀ □	♒	2 0:05
4 1:30 ♃ △	♓	4 3:20
6 6:27 ♃ □	♈	6 7:51
8 13:28 ♃ ⚹	♉	8 14:21
10 11:32 ♄ □	♊	10 23:27
12 22:31 ♄ ⚹	♋	13 10:59
15 13:56 ☉ □	♌	15 23:30
18 6:38 ☉ △	♍	18 10:44
20 2:45 ♀ △	♎	20 18:53
22 12:45 ♄ ⚹	♏	22 23:39
24 21:03 ♀ ☍	♐	25 2:00
26 17:00 ♄ △	♑	27 3:27
28 4:39 ☿ □	♒	29 5:28

☽ Phases & Eclipses

Dy Hr Mn	
2 8:34	☾ 11♐24
9 2:36	● 18♓10
16 18:21	☽ 25♊48
24 16:20	○ 3♎40
24 16:22	T 1.451
31 15:11	☾ 10♑33
7 15:15	● 17♈27
7 15:02:58	P 0.788
15 13:56	☽ 25♋14
23 4:11	○ 2♏39
29 21:02	☾ 9♒11

Astro Data

1 March 1978
Julian Day # 28549
SVP 5♓33'50"
GC 26♐32.1 ⚴ 17♐33.7
Eris 13♈41.2 ⚵ 20♑03.8
⚷ 2♉14.0 ⚶ 10♐20.6
☽ Mean ☊ 7♎24.2

1 April 1978
Julian Day # 28580
SVP 5♓33'47"
GC 26♐32.1 ⚴ 23♐00.0
Eris 14♈00.8 ⚵ 29♑11.3
⚷ 3♉50.5 ⚶ 18♐20.9
☽ Mean ☊ 5♎45.7

LONGITUDE — May 1978

Day	Sid.Time	☉	0 hr ☽	Noon ☽	True ☊	☿	♀	♂	⚳	♃	♄	♅	♆	♇
1 M	2 36 15	10♉45 06	24♒50 26	1♓43 00	5♎27.8	16♈23.9	5♊05.0	8♌12.4	23♑08.0	3♋08.2	23♌41.0	14♏32.9	17♐52.4	14♎37.5
2 Tu	2 40 11	11 43 19	8♓32 05	15 17 44	5 29.3	16 54.9	6 18.0	8 38.9	23 13.8	3 18.9	23 41.7	14R 30.3	17R 51.2	14R 36.0
3 W	2 44 08	12 41 32	22 00 02	28 39 05	5R 30.4	17 30.0	7 31.0	9 05.5	23 19.3	3 29.7	23 42.5	14 27.8	17 50.0	14 34.6
4 Th	2 48 05	13 39 42	5♈14 56	11♈47 41	5 30.4	18 09.0	8 44.0	9 32.4	23 24.4	3 40.5	23 43.4	14 25.3	17 48.7	14 33.2
5 F	2 52 01	14 37 51	18 17 24	24 44 08	5 28.8	18 51.7	9 56.9	9 59.4	23 29.2	3 51.5	23 44.4	14 22.7	17 47.5	14 31.8
6 Sa	2 55 58	15 35 59	1♉07 55	7♉28 49	5 25.2	19 38.0	11 09.7	10 26.7	23 33.6	4 02.5	23 45.5	14 20.2	17 46.2	14 30.4
7 Su	2 59 54	16 34 05	13 46 51	20 02 05	5 19.7	20 27.7	12 22.6	10 54.2	23 37.7	4 13.6	23 46.8	14 17.6	17 44.8	14 29.0
8 M	3 03 51	17 32 09	26 14 34	2♊24 23	5 12.6	21 20.8	13 35.4	11 21.8	23 41.5	4 24.8	23 48.1	14 15.1	17 43.5	14 27.7
9 Tu	3 07 47	18 30 12	8♊31 39	14 36 30	5 04.7	22 17.1	14 48.1	11 49.7	23 44.9	4 36.1	23 49.5	14 12.6	17 42.2	14 26.3
10 W	3 11 44	19 28 13	20 39 07	26 39 45	4 56.6	23 16.4	16 00.9	12 17.7	23 48.0	4 47.4	23 51.0	14 10.1	17 40.8	14 25.0
11 Th	3 15 40	20 26 12	2♋38 39	8♋36 08	4 49.3	24 18.7	17 13.5	12 46.0	23 50.7	4 58.8	23 52.7	14 07.5	17 39.4	14 23.7
12 F	3 19 37	21 24 09	14 32 36	20 28 26	4 43.2	25 23.9	18 26.2	13 14.4	23 53.1	5 10.3	23 54.4	14 05.0	17 38.0	14 22.5
13 Sa	3 23 34	22 22 05	26 24 08	2♌20 10	4 39.1	26 31.9	19 38.7	13 42.9	23 55.1	5 21.9	23 56.3	14 02.5	17 36.6	14 21.2
14 Su	3 27 30	23 19 59	8♌17 06	14 15 30	4D 36.9	27 42.6	20 51.3	14 11.7	23 56.8	5 33.5	23 58.2	14 00.0	17 35.2	14 20.0
15 M	3 31 27	24 17 51	20 15 59	26 19 09	4 36.4	28 55.9	22 03.8	14 40.6	23 58.1	5 45.2	24 00.3	13 57.5	17 33.7	14 18.8
16 Tu	3 35 23	25 15 41	2♍25 38	8♍36 03	4 37.1	0♉11.8	23 16.2	15 09.7	23 59.1	5 57.0	24 02.4	13 55.1	17 32.3	14 17.6
17 W	3 39 20	26 13 30	14 51 02	21 11 08	4 38.2	1 30.2	24 28.6	15 38.9	23 59.7	6 08.9	24 04.7	13 52.6	17 30.8	14 16.5
18 Th	3 43 16	27 11 17	27 36 53	4♎08 44	4R 38.8	2 51.0	25 41.0	16 08.3	23R 59.9	6 20.8	24 07.0	13 50.1	17 29.3	14 15.4
19 F	3 47 13	28 09 02	10♎47 04	17 32 07	4 38.1	4 14.3	26 53.3	16 37.8	23 59.8	6 32.7	24 09.4	13 47.7	17 27.8	14 14.3
20 Sa	3 51 09	29 06 46	24 24 00	1♏22 41	4 35.3	5 40.0	28 05.5	17 07.5	23 59.3	6 44.8	24 12.0	13 45.3	17 26.3	14 13.2
21 Su	3 55 06	0♊04 28	8♏27 55	15 39 18	4 30.3	7 08.0	29 17.7	17 37.4	23 58.5	6 56.8	24 14.6	13 42.9	17 24.8	14 12.1
22 M	3 59 03	1 02 09	22 56 14	0♐17 56	4 23.3	8 38.5	0♋29.9	18 07.3	23 57.3	7 09.0	24 17.4	13 40.5	17 23.2	14 11.1
23 Tu	4 02 59	1 59 49	7♐43 27	15 11 42	4 14.9	10 11.2	1 42.0	18 37.5	23 55.7	7 21.2	24 20.2	13 38.1	17 21.7	14 10.1
24 W	4 06 56	2 57 27	22 41 31	0♑11 44	4 06.2	11 46.3	2 54.0	19 07.7	23 53.8	7 33.5	24 23.1	13 35.8	17 20.2	14 09.1
25 Th	4 10 52	3 55 05	7♑41 08	15 08 39	3 58.3	13 23.7	4 06.1	19 38.1	23 51.5	7 45.8	24 26.1	13 33.4	17 18.6	14 08.2
26 F	4 14 49	4 52 41	22 33 15	29 54 07	3 52.1	15 03.4	5 18.0	20 08.7	23 48.8	7 58.1	24 29.3	13 31.1	17 17.0	14 07.3
27 Sa	4 18 45	5 50 17	7♒10 34	14♒22 06	3 48.1	16 45.4	6 29.9	20 39.4	23 45.7	8 10.6	24 32.5	13 28.9	17 15.5	14 06.4
28 Su	4 22 42	6 47 51	21 28 23	28 29 16	3D 46.2	18 29.7	7 41.8	21 10.2	23 42.3	8 23.0	24 35.8	13 26.6	17 13.9	14 05.5
29 M	4 26 38	7 45 25	5♓24 45	12♓14 54	3 46.0	20 16.3	8 53.6	21 41.1	23 38.6	8 35.6	24 39.1	13 24.3	17 12.3	14 04.7
30 Tu	4 30 35	8 42 58	18 59 55	25 40 04	3R 46.5	22 05.1	10 05.3	22 12.2	23 34.4	8 48.1	24 42.6	13 22.1	17 10.7	14 03.9
31 W	4 34 32	9 40 29	2♈15 39	8♈47 01	3 46.6	23 56.3	11 17.1	22 43.4	23 29.9	9 00.8	24 46.2	13 19.9	17 09.1	14 03.1

LONGITUDE — June 1978

Day	Sid.Time	☉	0 hr ☽	Noon ☽	True ☊	☿	♀	♂	⚳	♃	♄	♅	♆	♇
1 Th	4 38 28	10♊38 01	15♈14 28	21♈38 22	3♎45.2	25♉49.7	12♋28.7	23♌14.7	23♑25.1	9♋13.4	24♌49.8	13♏17.8	17♐07.5	14♎02.4
2 F	4 42 25	11 35 31	27 59 00	4♉16 39	3R 41.5	27 45.3	13 40.3	23 46.1	23R 19.9	9 26.1	24 53.6	13R 15.6	17R 05.9	14R 01.7
3 Sa	4 46 21	12 33 01	10♉31 36	16 44 02	3 35.0	29 43.0	14 51.9	24 17.7	23 14.3	9 38.9	24 57.4	13 13.5	17 04.2	14 01.0
4 Su	4 50 18	13 30 29	22 54 11	29 02 12	3 25.9	1♊42.8	16 03.4	24 49.4	23 08.3	9 51.7	25 01.3	13 11.4	17 02.6	14 00.3
5 M	4 54 14	14 27 57	5♊08 13	11♊12 24	3 14.6	3 44.6	17 14.8	25 21.3	23 02.1	10 04.5	25 05.3	13 09.4	17 01.0	13 59.7
6 Tu	4 58 11	15 25 24	17 14 52	23 15 44	3 01.9	5 48.4	18 26.2	25 53.2	22 55.4	10 17.4	25 09.4	13 07.4	16 59.4	13 59.1
7 W	5 02 07	16 22 51	29 15 09	5♋13 17	2 48.9	7 53.8	19 37.6	26 25.3	22 48.5	10 30.3	25 13.6	13 05.4	16 57.8	13 58.5
8 Th	5 06 04	17 20 16	11♋10 19	17 06 29	2 36.7	10 00.9	20 48.8	26 57.4	22 41.2	10 43.3	25 17.9	13 03.4	16 56.1	13 58.0
9 F	5 10 01	18 17 40	23 02 01	28 57 14	2 26.3	12 09.4	22 00.1	27 29.7	22 33.5	10 56.3	25 22.2	13 01.5	16 54.5	13 57.5
10 Sa	5 13 57	19 15 03	4♌52 29	10♌48 10	2 18.3	14 19.1	23 11.2	28 02.1	22 25.6	11 09.3	25 26.6	12 59.6	16 52.9	13 57.0
11 Su	5 17 54	20 12 25	16 44 43	22 42 37	2 12.9	16 29.7	24 22.3	28 34.6	22 17.3	11 22.4	25 31.1	12 57.7	16 51.3	13 56.6
12 M	5 21 50	21 09 47	28 42 25	4♍44 41	2 10.1	18 41.1	25 33.3	29 07.3	22 08.7	11 35.5	25 35.7	12 55.9	16 49.6	13 56.2
13 Tu	5 25 47	22 07 07	10♍50 01	16 59 03	2D 09.1	20 52.9	26 44.3	29 40.0	21 59.8	11 48.6	25 40.4	12 54.1	16 48.0	13 55.8
14 W	5 29 43	23 04 26	23 12 23	29 30 41	2R 09.1	23 04.9	27 55.2	0♍12.8	21 50.6	12 01.7	25 45.1	12 52.4	16 46.4	13 55.5
15 Th	5 33 40	24 01 44	5♎54 34	12♎24 34	2 08.9	25 16.9	29 06.0	0 45.8	21 41.2	12 14.9	25 49.9	12 50.7	16 44.8	13 55.2
16 F	5 37 36	24 59 02	19 01 12	25 44 53	2 07.4	27 28.4	0♌16.8	1 18.8	21 31.4	12 28.1	25 54.8	12 49.0	16 43.2	13 54.9
17 Sa	5 41 33	25 56 19	2♏35 55	9♏34 25	2 03.7	29 39.3	1 27.4	1 51.9	21 21.4	12 41.3	25 59.7	12 47.4	16 41.6	13 54.7
18 Su	5 45 30	26 53 34	16 40 20	23 53 25	1 57.4	1♋49.3	2 38.0	2 25.2	21 11.1	12 54.6	26 04.8	12 45.8	16 40.0	13 54.4
19 M	5 49 26	27 50 50	1♐13 11	8♐38 55	1 48.8	3 58.3	3 48.6	2 58.5	21 00.6	13 07.9	26 09.9	12 44.3	16 38.4	13 54.3
20 Tu	5 53 23	28 48 04	16 09 41	23 44 21	1 38.6	6 05.9	4 59.0	3 31.9	20 49.8	13 21.2	26 15.0	12 42.8	16 36.8	13 54.1
21 W	5 57 19	29 45 19	1♑21 36	9♑00 02	1 27.8	8 12.1	6 09.4	4 05.4	20 38.8	13 34.5	26 20.3	12 41.3	16 35.3	13 54.0
22 Th	6 01 16	0♋42 33	16 38 15	24 14 49	1 17.8	10 16.6	7 19.7	4 39.0	20 27.5	13 47.8	26 25.6	12 39.9	16 33.7	13 53.9
23 F	6 05 12	1 39 46	1♒48 27	9♒17 59	1 09.6	12 19.4	8 29.9	5 12.7	20 16.0	14 01.2	26 31.0	12 38.5	16 32.2	13D 53.9
24 Sa	6 09 09	2 36 59	16 42 29	24 01 11	1 04.0	14 20.4	9 40.1	5 46.5	20 04.4	14 14.5	26 36.4	12 37.2	16 30.6	13 53.9
25 Su	6 13 05	3 34 13	1♓13 36	8♓19 24	1 01.0	16 19.4	10 50.1	6 20.4	19 52.5	14 27.9	26 41.9	12 35.9	16 29.1	13 53.9
26 M	6 17 02	4 31 26	15 18 30	22 10 57	0 59.9	18 16.5	12 00.1	6 54.4	19 40.5	14 41.3	26 47.5	12 34.6	16 27.5	13 54.0
27 Tu	6 20 59	5 28 39	28 56 58	5♈36 50	0 59.8	20 11.5	13 10.0	7 28.5	19 28.2	14 54.8	26 53.1	12 33.4	16 26.0	13 54.1
28 W	6 24 55	6 25 52	12♈10 59	18 39 50	0 59.4	22 04.4	14 19.8	8 02.6	19 15.8	15 08.2	26 58.8	12 32.2	16 24.5	13 54.2
29 Th	6 28 52	7 23 05	25 03 51	1♉23 33	0 57.8	23 55.3	15 29.6	8 36.9	19 03.3	15 21.6	27 04.6	12 31.1	16 23.0	13 54.3
30 F	6 32 48	8 20 19	7♉39 22	13 51 47	0 53.8	25 44.0	16 39.2	9 11.2	18 50.6	15 35.1	27 10.4	12 30.1	16 21.5	13 54.5

Astro Data	Planet Ingress	Last Aspect	☽ Ingress	Last Aspect	☽ Ingress	☽ Phases & Eclipses	Astro Data
Dy Hr Mn	Dy Hr Mn	Dy Hr Mn	Dy Hr Mn	Dy Hr Mn	Dy Hr Mn	Dy Hr Mn	
☽0N 3 11:48	☿ ♉ 16 8:20	30 21:59 ♄ ☍	♓ 1 9:00	1 18:03 ♄ △	♉ 2 3:50	7 4:47 ● 16♉17	1 May 1978
☽0S 18 2:10	☉ ♊ 21 10:08	2 16:34 ♆ □	♈ 3 14:27	4 4:06 ♄ □	♊ 4 13:53	15 7:39 ☽ 24♌07	Julian Day # 28610
⚳R 18 15:56	♀ ♋ 22 2:03	5 10:08 ♄ △	♉ 5 21:52	6 17:30 ♂ ✱	♋ 7 1:30	22 13:17 ○ 1♐05	SVP 5♓33'44"
☽0N 30 18:06		7 19:14 ♄ □	♊ 8 7:18	8 20:20 ♀ ☌	♌ 9 14:07	29 3:30 ☾ 7♓25	GC 26♐32.2 ⚴ 22♐17.0R
	☿ ♊ 3 15:26	10 6:22 ♄ ✱	♋ 10 18:41	12 0:18 ♂ ☌	♍ 12 2:35		Eris 14♈20.5 ⚵ 5♒45.8
♃∠♄ 5 14:14	♂ ♍ 14 2:38	12 23:01 ☿ □	♌ 13 7:17	14 8:41 ♀ ✱	♎ 14 12:55	5 19:01 ● 14♊45	⚷ 5♉41.1 ⚶ 20♐05.5R
☽0S 14 11:53	♀ ♌ 16 6:19	15 17:44 ☿ △	♍ 15 19:15	16 15:37 ☿ △	♏ 16 19:28	13 22:44 ☽ 22♍33	☽ Mean ☊ 4♎10.4
♃△♅ 17 21:49	☿ ♋ 17 15:49	17 22:11 ☉ △	♎ 18 4:24	18 15:37 ♄ □	♐ 18 22:01	20 20:30 ○ 29♐08	
♃□♇ 22 22:59	☉ ♋ 21 18:10	20 5:50 ♀ △	♏ 20 9:39	20 20:30 ☉ ☍	♑ 20 21:52	27 11:44 ☾ 5♈28	1 June 1978
♇ D 24 7:43		22 2:11 ♄ □	♐ 22 11:31	21 19:42 ♇ □	♒ 22 21:07		Julian Day # 28641
☽0N 27 1:26		24 2:41 ♄ △	♑ 24 11:41	24 16:19 ♄ ☍	♓ 24 21:57		SVP 5♓33'40"
		25 10:23 ♇ □	♒ 26 12:10	26 4:02 ☿ △	♈ 27 1:53		GC 26♐32.3 ⚴ 14♐58.3R
		28 5:18 ♄ ☍	♓ 28 14:36	29 3:44 ♄ △	♉ 29 9:21		Eris 14♈36.5 ⚵ 8♒43.3
		30 4:31 ☿ ✱	♈ 30 19:52				⚷ 7♉31.8 ⚶ 14♐51.1R
							☽ Mean ☊ 2♎31.9

July 1978 — LONGITUDE

Day	Sid.Time	☉	0 hr ☽	Noon ☽	True ☊	☿	♀	♂	⚳	♃	♄	♅	♆	♇
1 Sa	6 36 45	9♋17 32	20♉01 14	26♉08 05	0♎47.1	27♋30.6	17♌48.8	9♍45.7	18♑37.9	15♋48.6	27♌16.3	12♏29.0	16♐20.1	13♎54.8
2 Su	6 40 41	10 14 46	2♊12 43	8♊15 27	0R 37.6	29 15.1	18 58.3	10 20.2	18R 25.0	16 02.1	27 22.3	12R 28.1	16R 18.6	13 55.0
3 M	6 44 38	11 12 00	14 16 32	20 16 15	0 25.9	0♌57.5	20 07.7	10 54.8	18 12.0	16 15.6	27 28.3	12 27.1	16 17.2	13 55.3
4 Tu	6 48 34	12 09 14	26 14 49	2♋12 24	0 12.8	2 37.7	21 17.0	11 29.5	17 58.9	16 29.1	27 34.3	12 26.2	16 15.7	13 55.6
5 W	6 52 31	13 06 27	8♋09 13	14 05 25	29♍59.3	4 15.8	22 26.2	12 04.3	17 45.8	16 42.6	27 40.4	12 25.4	16 14.3	13 56.0
6 Th	6 56 28	14 03 41	20 01 12	25 56 43	29 46.5	5 51.7	23 35.3	12 39.2	17 32.6	16 56.1	27 46.6	12 24.6	16 12.9	13 56.4
7 F	7 00 24	15 00 55	1♌52 11	7♌47 50	29 35.5	7 25.5	24 44.3	13 14.1	17 19.4	17 09.6	27 52.8	12 23.9	16 11.6	13 56.8
8 Sa	7 04 21	15 58 09	13 43 54	19 40 41	29 27.0	8 57.1	25 53.3	13 49.2	17 06.2	17 23.1	27 59.1	12 23.2	16 10.2	13 57.3
9 Su	7 08 17	16 55 22	25 38 31	1♍37 46	29 21.3	10 26.5	27 02.1	14 24.3	16 52.9	17 36.6	28 05.5	12 22.6	16 08.9	13 57.8
10 M	7 12 14	17 52 36	7♍38 51	13 42 13	29 18.1	11 53.8	28 10.8	14 59.5	16 39.7	17 50.1	28 11.8	12 22.0	16 07.5	13 58.3
11 Tu	7 16 10	18 49 49	19 48 22	25 57 50	29D 17.1	13 18.8	29 19.4	15 34.8	16 26.5	18 03.6	28 18.3	12 21.5	16 06.2	13 58.8
12 W	7 20 07	19 47 03	2♎11 10	8♎28 56	29R 17.2	14 41.5	0♍27.9	16 10.1	16 13.3	18 17.1	28 24.7	12 21.0	16 04.9	13 59.4
13 Th	7 24 03	20 44 16	14 51 42	21 20 02	29 17.5	16 02.0	1 36.2	16 45.6	16 00.2	18 30.6	28 31.3	12 20.5	16 03.7	14 00.1
14 F	7 28 00	21 41 30	27 54 28	4♏35 25	29 16.8	17 20.1	2 44.5	17 21.1	15 47.1	18 44.1	28 37.8	12 20.2	16 02.4	14 00.7
15 Sa	7 31 57	22 38 44	11♏23 17	18 18 19	29 14.3	18 35.8	3 52.6	17 56.7	15 34.2	18 57.6	28 44.5	12 19.8	16 01.2	14 01.4
16 Su	7 35 53	23 35 57	25 20 36	2♐30 04	29 09.6	19 49.1	5 00.6	18 32.4	15 21.3	19 11.1	28 51.1	12 19.6	16 00.0	14 02.1
17 M	7 39 50	24 33 11	9♐46 26	17 09 10	29 02.7	20 59.9	6 08.5	19 08.2	15 08.5	19 24.5	28 57.8	12 19.3	15 58.8	14 02.9
18 Tu	7 43 46	25 30 25	24 37 34	2♑10 38	28 54.2	22 08.1	7 16.2	19 44.0	14 55.9	19 38.0	29 04.6	12 19.2	15 57.6	14 03.7
19 W	7 47 43	26 27 39	9♑47 14	17 26 03	28 45.1	23 13.6	8 23.8	20 19.9	14 43.3	19 51.5	29 11.4	12 19.0	15 56.5	14 04.5
20 Th	7 51 39	27 24 54	25 05 41	2♒44 42	28 36.6	24 16.4	9 31.3	20 55.9	14 31.0	20 04.9	29 18.2	12D 19.0	15 55.4	14 05.4
21 F	7 55 36	28 22 09	10♒21 41	17 55 20	28 29.7	25 16.3	10 38.6	21 31.9	14 18.7	20 18.3	29 25.1	12 18.9	15 54.3	14 06.3
22 Sa	7 59 33	29 19 25	25 24 31	2♓48 15	28 25.1	26 13.3	11 45.8	22 08.0	14 06.7	20 31.7	29 32.0	12 19.0	15 53.2	14 07.2
23 Su	8 03 29	0♌16 42	10♓05 48	17 16 40	28D 22.7	27 07.2	12 52.9	22 44.2	13 54.8	20 45.1	29 38.9	12 19.0	15 52.1	14 08.1
24 M	8 07 26	1 13 59	24 20 30	1♈17 14	28 22.2	27 57.9	13 59.8	23 20.5	13 43.1	20 58.5	29 45.9	12 19.2	15 51.1	14 09.1
25 Tu	8 11 22	2 11 17	8♈06 55	14 49 46	28 22.9	28 45.3	15 06.5	23 56.9	13 31.6	21 11.9	29 52.9	12 19.4	15 50.1	14 10.1
26 W	8 15 19	3 08 36	21 26 08	27 56 20	28R 23.7	29 29.2	16 13.1	24 33.3	13 20.4	21 25.2	29 60.0	12 19.6	15 49.1	14 11.1
27 Th	8 19 15	4 05 57	4♉20 58	10♉40 31	28 23.5	0♍09.4	17 19.6	25 09.8	13 09.3	21 38.6	0♍07.1	12 19.9	15 48.2	14 12.2
28 F	8 23 12	5 03 18	16 55 30	23 06 29	28 21.8	0 45.9	18 25.9	25 46.3	12 58.5	21 51.9	0 14.2	12 20.2	15 47.2	14 13.3
29 Sa	8 27 08	6 00 40	29 13 59	5♊18 31	28 18.0	1 18.4	19 32.0	26 23.0	12 47.9	22 05.2	0 21.3	12 20.6	15 46.3	14 14.4
30 Su	8 31 05	6 58 03	11♊20 36	17 20 40	28 12.0	1 46.8	20 38.0	26 59.7	12 37.6	22 18.4	0 28.5	12 21.1	15 45.5	14 15.6
31 M	8 35 01	7 55 27	23 19 08	29 16 24	28 04.3	2 10.8	21 43.8	27 36.5	12 27.5	22 31.7	0 35.7	12 21.6	15 44.6	14 16.8

August 1978 — LONGITUDE

Day	Sid.Time	☉	0 hr ☽	Noon ☽	True ☊	☿	♀	♂	⚳	♃	♄	♅	♆	♇
1 Tu	8 38 58	8♌52 53	5♋12 48	11♋08 40	27♍55.4	2♍30.3	22♍49.4	28♍13.4	12♑17.7	22♋44.9	0♍43.0	12♏22.1	15♐43.8	14♎18.0
2 W	8 42 55	9 50 19	17 04 15	22 59 50	27R 46.2	2 45.2	23 54.9	28 50.3	12R 08.2	22 58.1	0 50.3	12 22.7	15R 43.0	14 19.3
3 Th	8 46 51	10 47 46	28 55 39	4♌51 54	27 37.5	2 55.1	25 00.2	29 27.4	11 59.0	23 11.2	0 57.5	12 23.4	15 42.2	14 20.6
4 F	8 50 48	11 45 14	10♌48 47	16 46 31	27 30.0	3R 00.1	26 05.3	0♎04.5	11 50.1	23 24.4	1 04.9	12 24.1	15 41.5	14 21.9
5 Sa	8 54 44	12 42 43	22 45 19	28 45 22	27 24.5	2 59.9	27 10.2	0 41.6	11 41.5	23 37.5	1 12.2	12 24.9	15 40.8	14 23.2
6 Su	8 58 41	13 40 13	4♍46 56	10♍50 15	27 21.0	2 54.4	28 14.9	1 18.9	11 33.1	23 50.6	1 19.6	12 25.7	15 40.1	14 24.6
7 M	9 02 37	14 37 43	16 55 37	23 03 18	27D 19.5	2 43.7	29 19.4	1 56.2	11 25.1	24 03.6	1 27.0	12 26.5	15 39.4	14 26.0
8 Tu	9 06 34	15 35 15	29 13 41	5♎27 06	27 19.7	2 27.5	0♎23.7	2 33.6	11 17.5	24 16.6	1 34.4	12 27.4	15 38.8	14 27.4
9 W	9 10 30	16 32 47	11♎43 57	18 04 38	27 20.9	2 06.1	1 27.8	3 11.0	11 10.1	24 29.6	1 41.8	12 28.4	15 38.2	14 28.8
10 Th	9 14 27	17 30 21	24 29 34	0♏59 09	27 22.4	1 39.5	2 31.6	3 48.5	11 03.1	24 42.5	1 49.2	12 29.4	15 37.6	14 30.3
11 F	9 18 24	18 27 55	7♏33 48	14 13 52	27R 23.3	1 08.0	3 35.3	4 26.1	10 56.5	24 55.4	1 56.7	12 30.5	15 37.1	14 31.8
12 Sa	9 22 20	19 25 30	20 59 39	27 51 24	27 23.0	0 31.8	4 38.7	5 03.8	10 50.1	25 08.2	2 04.2	12 31.6	15 36.6	14 33.3
13 Su	9 26 17	20 23 06	4♐49 13	11♐53 08	27 21.3	29♌51.4	5 41.8	5 41.5	10 44.2	25 21.0	2 11.7	12 32.8	15 36.1	14 34.9
14 M	9 30 13	21 20 43	19 03 00	26 18 29	27 18.1	29 07.3	6 44.7	6 19.3	10 38.5	25 33.8	2 19.2	12 34.0	15 35.7	14 36.5
15 Tu	9 34 10	22 18 21	3♑39 07	11♑04 13	27 13.8	28 20.1	7 47.3	6 57.2	10 33.2	25 46.5	2 26.7	12 35.3	15 35.3	14 38.1
16 W	9 38 06	23 15 59	18 32 58	26 04 20	27 08.9	27 30.7	8 49.7	7 35.1	10 28.3	25 59.2	2 34.3	12 36.6	15 34.9	14 39.7
17 Th	9 42 03	24 13 39	3♒37 15	11♒10 31	27 04.4	26 39.8	9 51.8	8 13.1	10 23.7	26 11.9	2 41.8	12 38.0	15 34.5	14 41.4
18 F	9 45 59	25 11 21	18 42 54	26 13 14	27 00.7	25 48.4	10 53.6	8 51.2	10 19.5	26 24.5	2 49.4	12 39.4	15 34.2	14 43.1
19 Sa	9 49 56	26 09 03	3♓40 23	11♓03 21	26 58.4	24 57.6	11 55.1	9 29.3	10 15.7	26 37.0	2 56.9	12 40.8	15 33.9	14 44.8
20 Su	9 53 53	27 06 47	18 21 16	25 33 29	26D 57.6	24 08.2	12 56.3	10 07.5	10 12.1	26 49.5	3 04.5	12 42.4	15 33.7	14 46.5
21 M	9 57 49	28 04 32	2♈39 27	9♈38 51	26 58.0	23 21.5	13 57.2	10 45.7	10 09.0	27 01.9	3 12.1	12 43.9	15 33.4	14 48.2
22 Tu	10 01 46	29 02 19	16 31 33	23 17 32	26 59.3	22 38.3	14 57.8	11 24.1	10 06.2	27 14.3	3 19.7	12 45.5	15 33.3	14 50.0
23 W	10 05 42	0♍00 08	29 56 58	6♉30 04	27 00.9	21 59.6	15 58.0	12 02.5	10 03.8	27 26.7	3 27.3	12 47.2	15 33.1	14 51.8
24 Th	10 09 39	0 57 58	12♉57 13	19 18 51	27 02.1	21 26.3	16 58.0	12 40.9	10 01.7	27 39.0	3 34.9	12 48.9	15 33.0	14 53.6
25 F	10 13 35	1 55 50	25 35 26	1♊47 31	27R 02.7	20 59.2	17 57.6	13 19.5	10 00.0	27 51.2	3 42.5	12 50.6	15 32.9	14 55.5
26 Sa	10 17 32	2 53 44	7♊55 38	14 00 22	27 02.1	20 38.8	18 56.8	13 58.1	9 58.6	28 03.4	3 50.1	12 52.4	15 32.8	14 57.3
27 Su	10 21 28	3 51 40	20 02 14	26 01 49	27 00.5	20 25.9	19 55.7	14 36.8	9 57.6	28 15.5	3 57.7	12 54.3	15D 32.8	14 59.2
28 M	10 25 25	4 49 38	1♋59 39	7♋56 14	26 58.0	20D 20.6	20 54.2	15 15.5	9 57.0	28 27.5	4 05.3	12 56.2	15 32.8	15 01.1
29 Tu	10 29 22	5 47 37	13 52 02	19 47 32	26 54.9	20 23.5	21 52.3	15 54.3	9D 56.7	28 39.5	4 12.9	12 58.1	15 32.8	15 03.1
30 W	10 33 18	6 45 38	25 43 07	1♌39 12	26 51.6	20 34.5	22 50.0	16 33.2	9 56.8	28 51.5	4 20.5	13 00.1	15 32.9	15 05.0
31 Th	10 37 15	7 43 41	7♌36 06	13 34 10	26 48.4	20 53.9	23 47.3	17 12.2	9 57.2	29 03.3	4 28.1	13 02.1	15 32.9	15 07.0

Astro Data

	Dy Hr Mn
♃⚻♆	3 14:36
☽0S	11 20:09
♄∠♇	18 8:22
♅D	21 10:04
☽0N	24 10:30
☿R	4 23:08
♂0S	6 4:49
♀0S	7 20:35
☽0S	8 2:51
☽0N	20 20:52
♆D	28 0:54
☿D	28 15:42
⚳D	29 18:54

Planet Ingress

	Dy Hr Mn
☿ ♌	2 22:28
☊ ♍R	5 10:41
♀ ♍	12 2:14
☉ ♌	23 5:00
♄ ♍	26 12:02
☿ ♍	27 6:10
♂ ♎	4 9:07
♀ ♎	8 3:08
☿ ♌R	13 7:05
☉ ♍	23 11:57

Last Aspect / ☽ Ingress

Last Aspect Dy Hr Mn		☽ Ingress Dy Hr Mn
1 15:10	☿ ⚹	♊ 1 19:37
4 2:35	♄ ⚹	♋ 4 7:33
5 17:24	♃ ☌	♌ 6 20:13
9 4:51	♄ ☌	♍ 9 8:44
10 20:55	☉ ⚹	♎ 11 19:48
14 1:13	♄ ⚹	♏ 14 3:47
16 5:51	♄ □	♐ 16 7:50
18 7:03	♄ △	♑ 18 8:33
20 3:05	☉ ☍	♒ 20 7:41
22 6:38	♄ ☍	♓ 22 7:26
23 21:40	♂ ☍	♈ 24 9:46
26 15:03	☿ △	♉ 26 15:50
28 17:29	♂ △	♊ 29 1:31
31 8:28	♂ □	♋ 31 13:28

Last Aspect / ☽ Ingress

Last Aspect Dy Hr Mn		☽ Ingress Dy Hr Mn
3 0:28	♂ ⚹	♌ 3 2:10
4 9:49	♆ △	♍ 5 14:29
8 1:20	♀ ☌	♎ 8 1:30
10 0:12	♃ □	♏ 10 10:11
12 7:11	♃ △	♐ 12 15:43
14 16:23	☿ △	♑ 14 18:03
16 11:52	♃ ☍	♒ 16 18:15
18 11:22	☿ ☍	♓ 18 18:04
20 14:10	♃ △	♈ 20 19:29
22 23:10	☉ △	♉ 23 0:06
25 4:14	♃ ⚹	♊ 25 8:31
27 0:57	☿ ⚹	♋ 27 19:59
30 6:15	♃ ☌	♌ 30 8:40

☽ Phases & Eclipses

Dy Hr Mn	
5 9:50	● 13♋01
13 10:49	☽ 20♎41
20 3:05	○ 27♑04
26 22:31	☾ 3♉34
4 1:01	● 11♌19
11 20:06	☽ 18♏47
18 10:14	○ 25♒07
25 12:18	☾ 1♊57

Astro Data

1 July 1978
Julian Day # 28671
SVP 5♓33'36"
GC 26♐32.3 ⚴ 7♐08.5R
Eris 14♈44.3 ⚵ 6♒23.2R
⚷ 8♉55.8 ⚶ 8♐39.1R
☽ Mean ☊ 0♎56.6

1 August 1978
Julian Day # 28702
SVP 5♓33'31"
GC 26♐32.4 ⚴ 4♐51.4
Eris 14♈42.5R ⚵ 29♑35.1R
⚷ 9♉42.1 ⚶ 8♐28.1
☽ Mean ☊ 29♍18.1

LONGITUDE — September 1978

Day	Sid.Time	☉	0 hr ☽	Noon ☽	True ☊	☿	♀	♂	⚳	♃	♄	♅	♆	♇
1 F	10 41 11	8♍41 45	19♌33 39	25♌34 50	26♍45.8	21♌21.6	24♎44.1	17♎51.2	9♑58.0	29♋15.1	4♍35.7	13♏04.2	15♐33.1	15♎09.0
2 Sa	10 45 08	9 39 51	1♍37 55	7♍43 08	26R44.0	21 57.5	25 40.6	18 30.3	9 59.1	29 26.9	4 43.3	13 06.3	15 33.2	15 11.0
3 Su	10 49 04	10 37 59	13 50 39	20 00 39	26D43.2	22 41.4	26 36.5	19 09.4	10 00.6	29 38.6	4 50.9	13 08.5	15 33.4	15 13.0
4 M	10 53 01	11 36 09	26 13 17	2♎28 44	26 43.1	23 33.0	27 32.0	19 48.7	10 02.4	29 50.1	4 58.5	13 10.7	15 33.7	15 15.0
5 Tu	10 56 57	12 34 20	8♎47 09	15 08 41	26 43.7	24 31.9	28 27.0	20 28.0	10 04.6	0♌01.7	5 06.1	13 12.9	15 33.9	15 17.1
6 W	11 00 54	13 32 32	21 33 30	28 01 45	26 44.8	25 37.9	29 21.5	21 07.3	10 07.2	0 13.1	5 13.6	13 15.2	15 34.2	15 19.1
7 Th	11 04 51	14 30 46	4♏33 37	11♏09 14	26 45.9	26 50.4	0♏15.4	21 46.8	10 10.0	0 24.5	5 21.2	13 17.5	15 34.5	15 21.2
8 F	11 08 47	15 29 02	17 48 46	24 32 20	26 46.8	28 09.0	1 08.8	22 26.3	10 13.3	0 35.8	5 28.7	13 19.9	15 34.9	15 23.3
9 Sa	11 12 44	16 27 20	1♐20 03	8♐11 58	26R47.3	29 33.1	2 01.6	23 05.8	10 16.8	0 47.0	5 36.2	13 22.3	15 35.3	15 25.5
10 Su	11 16 40	17 25 38	15 08 07	22 08 27	26 47.4	1♍02.2	2 53.8	23 45.4	10 20.7	0 58.2	5 43.8	13 24.8	15 35.7	15 27.6
11 M	11 20 37	18 23 59	29 12 49	6♑21 02	26 47.0	2 35.7	3 45.4	24 25.1	10 24.9	1 09.2	5 51.3	13 27.3	15 36.2	15 29.8
12 Tu	11 24 33	19 22 20	13♑32 46	20 47 38	26 46.4	4 13.0	4 36.3	25 04.9	10 29.5	1 20.2	5 58.7	13 29.8	15 36.7	15 31.9
13 W	11 28 30	20 20 44	28 05 06	5♒24 33	26 45.7	5 53.7	5 26.5	25 44.7	10 34.3	1 31.1	6 06.2	13 32.4	15 37.2	15 34.1
14 Th	11 32 26	21 19 09	12♒45 18	20 06 35	26 45.0	7 37.3	6 16.1	26 24.6	10 39.5	1 41.9	6 13.7	13 35.0	15 37.7	15 36.3
15 F	11 36 23	22 17 35	27 27 33	4♓47 23	26 44.6	9 23.1	7 04.9	27 04.6	10 45.0	1 52.6	6 21.1	13 37.6	15 38.3	15 38.5
16 Sa	11 40 19	23 16 04	12♓05 14	19 20 19	26D44.4	11 10.8	7 52.9	27 44.6	10 50.8	2 03.2	6 28.5	13 40.3	15 38.9	15 40.7
17 Su	11 44 16	24 14 34	26 31 51	3♈39 10	26 44.4	12 59.9	8 40.2	28 24.6	10 56.9	2 13.8	6 35.9	13 43.0	15 39.6	15 43.0
18 M	11 48 13	25 13 06	10♈41 44	17 39 05	26 44.4	14 50.2	9 26.6	29 04.8	11 03.4	2 24.2	6 43.2	13 45.8	15 40.3	15 45.2
19 Tu	11 52 09	26 11 40	24 30 53	1♉16 57	26R44.5	16 41.1	10 12.2	29 45.0	11 10.1	2 34.6	6 50.6	13 48.5	15 41.0	15 47.5
20 W	11 56 06	27 10 16	7♉57 11	14 31 39	26 44.5	18 32.5	10 57.0	0♏25.3	11 17.1	2 44.8	6 57.9	13 51.4	15 41.7	15 49.7
21 Th	12 00 02	28 08 55	21 00 28	27 23 54	26 44.4	20 24.1	11 40.8	1 05.6	11 24.4	2 55.0	7 05.2	13 54.2	15 42.5	15 52.0
22 F	12 03 59	29 07 35	3♊42 18	9♊56 01	26 44.3	22 15.7	12 23.6	1 46.0	11 32.0	3 05.1	7 12.4	13 57.1	15 43.3	15 54.3
23 Sa	12 07 55	0♎06 18	16 05 34	22 11 25	26D44.1	24 07.1	13 05.5	2 26.5	11 39.9	3 15.1	7 19.7	14 00.0	15 44.2	15 56.6
24 Su	12 11 52	1 05 03	28 14 08	4♋14 17	26 44.1	25 58.1	13 46.4	3 07.0	11 48.1	3 24.9	7 26.9	14 03.0	15 45.0	15 58.9
25 M	12 15 48	2 03 51	10♋12 25	16 09 09	26 44.3	27 48.7	14 26.1	3 47.7	11 56.6	3 34.7	7 34.0	14 06.0	15 45.9	16 01.2
26 Tu	12 19 45	3 02 40	22 05 02	28 00 40	26 44.7	29 38.7	15 04.8	4 28.3	12 05.3	3 44.3	7 41.2	14 09.0	15 46.9	16 03.5
27 W	12 23 42	4 01 32	3♌56 35	9♌53 19	26 45.4	1♎28.0	15 42.4	5 09.1	12 14.3	3 53.9	7 48.3	14 12.1	15 47.8	16 05.8
28 Th	12 27 38	5 00 26	15 51 21	21 51 11	26 46.3	3 16.7	16 18.7	5 49.9	12 23.6	4 03.3	7 55.4	14 15.2	15 48.8	16 08.2
29 F	12 31 35	5 59 22	27 53 12	3♍57 48	26 47.1	5 04.6	16 53.8	6 30.8	12 33.1	4 12.7	8 02.4	14 18.3	15 49.8	16 10.5
30 Sa	12 35 31	6 58 21	10♍05 19	16 16 02	26R47.7	6 51.7	17 27.7	7 11.7	12 43.0	4 21.9	8 09.4	14 21.4	15 50.9	16 12.8

LONGITUDE — October 1978

Day	Sid.Time	☉	0 hr ☽	Noon ☽	True ☊	☿	♀	♂	⚳	♃	♄	♅	♆	♇
1 Su	12 39 28	7♎57 21	22♍30 10	28♍47 55	26♍47.9	8♎38.0	18♏00.1	7♏52.7	12♑53.0	4♌31.0	8♍16.4	14♏24.6	15♐52.0	16♎15.2
2 M	12 43 24	8 56 24	5♎09 23	11♎34 39	26R47.5	10 23.4	18 31.2	8 33.8	13 03.4	4 40.0	8 23.3	14 27.8	15 53.1	16 17.5
3 Tu	12 47 21	9 55 28	18 03 43	24 36 34	26 46.4	12 08.0	19 00.8	9 15.0	13 14.0	4 48.9	8 30.2	14 31.0	15 54.2	16 19.9
4 W	12 51 17	10 54 35	1♏13 06	7♏53 13	26 44.8	13 51.8	19 28.9	9 56.2	13 24.8	4 57.6	8 37.1	14 34.3	15 55.4	16 22.3
5 Th	12 55 14	11 53 43	14 36 45	21 23 32	26 42.7	15 34.8	19 55.5	10 37.5	13 35.9	5 06.2	8 43.9	14 37.5	15 56.6	16 24.6
6 F	12 59 11	12 52 53	28 13 21	5♐06 01	26 40.6	17 16.9	20 20.3	11 18.8	13 47.3	5 14.7	8 50.7	14 40.8	15 57.8	16 27.0
7 Sa	13 03 07	13 52 05	12♐01 17	18 58 56	26 38.8	18 58.3	20 43.5	12 00.2	13 58.8	5 23.1	8 57.4	14 44.2	15 59.1	16 29.4
8 Su	13 07 04	14 51 19	25 58 44	3♑00 27	26D37.6	20 38.8	21 05.0	12 41.7	14 10.7	5 31.4	9 04.1	14 47.5	16 00.4	16 31.7
9 M	13 11 00	15 50 35	10♑03 50	17 08 40	26 37.3	22 18.5	21 24.6	13 23.2	14 22.7	5 39.5	9 10.7	14 50.9	16 01.7	16 34.1
10 Tu	13 14 57	16 49 52	24 14 41	1♒21 38	26 37.8	23 57.5	21 42.3	14 04.8	14 35.0	5 47.5	9 17.3	14 54.3	16 03.1	16 36.5
11 W	13 18 53	17 49 11	8♒29 13	15 37 09	26 39.0	25 35.7	21 58.0	14 46.5	14 47.5	5 55.3	9 23.8	14 57.7	16 04.4	16 38.9
12 Th	13 22 50	18 48 32	22 45 06	29 52 42	26 40.4	27 13.2	22 11.7	15 28.2	15 00.2	6 03.0	9 30.3	15 01.2	16 05.8	16 41.2
13 F	13 26 46	19 47 55	6♓59 33	14♓05 16	26R41.5	28 49.9	22 23.3	16 10.0	15 13.2	6 10.6	9 36.7	15 04.6	16 07.2	16 43.6
14 Sa	13 30 43	20 47 19	21 09 23	28 11 29	26 41.9	0♏26.0	22 32.8	16 51.9	15 26.3	6 18.1	9 43.1	15 08.1	16 08.7	16 46.0
15 Su	13 34 39	21 46 45	5♈11 04	12♈07 44	26 41.2	2 01.4	22 40.1	17 33.8	15 39.7	6 25.4	9 49.4	15 11.6	16 10.2	16 48.3
16 M	13 38 36	22 46 13	19 01 03	25 50 38	26 39.1	3 36.1	22 45.1	18 15.7	15 53.3	6 32.6	9 55.7	15 15.1	16 11.7	16 50.7
17 Tu	13 42 33	23 45 44	2♉36 08	9♉17 18	26 35.7	5 10.1	22R47.8	18 57.8	16 07.1	6 39.6	10 01.9	15 18.7	16 13.2	16 53.1
18 W	13 46 29	24 45 16	15 53 55	22 25 52	26 31.3	6 43.5	22 48.2	19 39.9	16 21.0	6 46.5	10 08.1	15 22.2	16 14.7	16 55.4
19 Th	13 50 26	25 44 51	28 53 08	5♊15 46	26 26.5	8 16.3	22 46.2	20 22.0	16 35.2	6 53.2	10 14.2	15 25.8	16 16.3	16 57.8
20 F	13 54 22	26 44 27	11♊33 53	17 47 44	26 21.7	9 48.5	22 41.8	21 04.3	16 49.6	6 59.8	10 20.2	15 29.4	16 17.9	17 00.1
21 Sa	13 58 19	27 44 06	23 57 37	0♋03 53	26 17.7	11 20.1	22 35.1	21 46.6	17 04.2	7 06.2	10 26.2	15 33.0	16 19.5	17 02.5
22 Su	14 02 15	28 43 48	6♋06 59	12 07 24	26 14.8	12 51.1	22 25.9	22 28.9	17 18.9	7 12.5	10 32.1	15 36.6	16 21.2	17 04.8
23 M	14 06 12	29 43 31	18 05 40	24 02 22	26D13.3	14 21.5	22 14.3	23 11.4	17 33.9	7 18.6	10 38.0	15 40.2	16 22.9	17 07.2
24 Tu	14 10 08	0♏43 17	29 58 05	5♌53 28	26 13.3	15 51.3	22 00.3	23 53.8	17 49.0	7 24.6	10 43.8	15 43.9	16 24.6	17 09.5
25 W	14 14 05	1 43 05	11♌49 07	17 45 42	26 14.4	17 20.5	21 43.9	24 36.4	18 04.3	7 30.4	10 49.6	15 47.5	16 26.3	17 11.8
26 Th	14 18 02	2 42 55	23 43 48	29 44 04	26 16.1	18 49.1	21 25.3	25 19.0	18 19.8	7 36.1	10 55.2	15 51.2	16 28.0	17 14.1
27 F	14 21 58	3 42 47	5♍47 04	11♍53 21	26 17.7	20 17.1	21 04.3	26 01.7	18 35.5	7 41.6	11 00.8	15 54.9	16 29.8	17 16.4
28 Sa	14 25 55	4 42 42	18 03 26	24 17 44	26R18.5	21 44.5	20 41.3	26 44.4	18 51.3	7 46.9	11 06.4	15 58.5	16 31.6	17 18.7
29 Su	14 29 51	5 42 38	0♎36 38	7♎00 26	26 18.0	23 11.2	20 16.1	27 27.3	19 07.4	7 52.1	11 11.8	16 02.2	16 33.4	17 21.0
30 M	14 33 48	6 42 37	13 29 19	20 03 24	26 15.6	24 37.3	19 49.0	28 10.1	19 23.6	7 57.1	11 17.2	16 05.9	16 35.2	17 23.3
31 Tu	14 37 44	7 42 37	26 42 39	3♏26 58	26 11.2	26 02.7	19 20.1	28 53.1	19 39.9	8 01.9	11 22.5	16 09.7	16 37.0	17 25.5

Astro Data Dy Hr Mn	Planet Ingress Dy Hr Mn	Last Aspect Dy Hr Mn	☽ Ingress Dy Hr Mn	Last Aspect Dy Hr Mn	☽ Ingress Dy Hr Mn	☽ Phases & Eclipses Dy Hr Mn
☽0S 4 8:57	♃ ♌ 5 8:31	1 10:11 ♀ ✶	♍ 1 20:46	30 14:25 ♀ ✶	♎ 1 14:17	2 16:09 ● 9♍50
♃□♆ 8 10:01	♀ ♏ 7 5:07	4 6:52 ♃ ✶	♎ 4 7:15	2 20:46 ♇ ☌	♏ 3 21:48	10 3:20 ☽ 17♐05
♆✶♇ 15 9:09	☿ ♍ 9 19:23	6 14:38 ♀ ☌	♏ 6 15:38	5 9:19 ♀ ☌	♐ 6 3:07	16 19:01 ○ 23♓33
☽0N 17 7:19	♂ ♏ 19 20:57	8 19:06 ☿ □	♐ 8 21:39	7 11:59 ☿ ✶	♑ 8 6:52	16 19:04 ☍ T 1.327
☉0S 23 9:25	☉ ♎ 23 9:25	10 14:53 ♂ ✶	♑ 11 1:20	9 21:53 ☿ □	♒ 10 9:42	24 5:07 ☾ 0♋48
☿0S 28 13:45	☿ ♎ 26 16:40	12 19:24 ♂ □	♒ 13 3:09	12 6:57 ☿ △	♓ 12 12:12	
		14 22:46 ♂ △	♓ 15 4:09	14 2:16 ♀ △	♈ 14 15:06	2 6:41 ● 8♎43
☽0S 1 15:55	☿ ♏ 14 5:30	16 19:01 ☉ ☍	♈ 17 5:50	16 6:10 ☉ ☍	♉ 16 19:22	2 6:27:54 ✓ P 0.691
☽0N 14 16:37	☉ ♏ 23 18:37	19 9:08 ☿ ☍	♉ 19 9:43	18 12:41 ♀ ☍	♊ 19 2:05	9 9:38 ☽ 15♑45
♀R 18 3:58		21 13:32 ☉ △	♊ 21 16:56	21 7:00 ☉ △	♋ 21 11:52	16 6:10 ○ 22♈32
☽0S 29 0:41		23 16:30 ☿ □	♋ 24 3:31	23 10:10 ♂ △	♌ 24 0:04	24 0:34 ☾ 0♌15
		26 15:55 ☿ ✶	♌ 26 16:02	26 2:37 ♂ □	♍ 26 12:32	31 20:06 ● 8♏03
		28 0:31 ♇ ✶	♍ 29 4:11	28 16:57 ♂ ✶	♎ 28 22:51	
				30 7:08 ♇ ☌	♏ 31 5:53	

Astro Data

1 September 1978
Julian Day # 28733
SVP 5♓33'27"
GC 26♐32.5 ⚴ 8♐44.4
Eris 14♈31.3R ⚵ 24♑02.1R
⚷ 9♉36.7R ⚶ 14♐59.9
☽ Mean ☊ 27♍39.6

1 October 1978
Julian Day # 28763
SVP 5♓33'25"
GC 26♐32.5 ⚴ 16♐17.3
Eris 14♈14.5R ⚵ 24♑15.7
⚷ 8♉44.2R ⚶ 25♐26.0
☽ Mean ☊ 26♍04.2

November 1978 — LONGITUDE

Day	Sid.Time	☉	0 hr ☽	Noon ☽	True ☊	☿	♀	♂	⚳	♃	♄	♅	♆	♇
1 W	14 41 41	8♏42 40	10♏16 05	17♏09 41	26♍05.1	27♏27.4	18♏49.6	29♏36.1	19♑56.4	8♌06.6	11♍27.8	16♏13.4	16♐38.9	17♎27.8
2 Th	14 45 37	9 42 44	24 07 18	1♐08 26	25R 57.9	28 51.4	18R 17.5	0♐19.1	20 13.1	8 11.1	11 33.0	16 17.1	16 40.8	17 30.0
3 F	14 49 34	10 42 50	8♐12 30	15 18 51	25 50.5	0♐14.5	17 44.2	1 02.3	20 30.0	8 15.4	11 38.1	16 20.8	16 42.7	17 32.3
4 Sa	14 53 31	11 42 58	22 26 51	29 35 53	25 43.8	1 36.7	17 09.8	1 45.5	20 47.0	8 19.5	11 43.1	16 24.6	16 44.6	17 34.5
5 Su	14 57 27	12 43 08	6♑45 20	13♑54 41	25 38.7	2 58.0	16 34.4	2 28.7	21 04.1	8 23.5	11 48.1	16 28.3	16 46.5	17 36.7
6 M	15 01 24	13 43 19	21 03 26	28 11 10	25 35.5	4 18.3	15 58.5	3 12.0	21 21.4	8 27.2	11 52.9	16 32.1	16 48.5	17 38.9
7 Tu	15 05 20	14 43 31	5♒17 36	12♒22 26	25D 34.4	5 37.4	15 22.1	3 55.4	21 38.9	8 30.8	11 57.7	16 35.8	16 50.5	17 41.1
8 W	15 09 17	15 43 45	19 25 31	26 26 42	25 34.8	6 55.3	14 45.5	4 38.8	21 56.5	8 34.3	12 02.4	16 39.5	16 52.5	17 43.2
9 Th	15 13 13	16 44 00	3♓25 54	10♓23 04	25 35.8	8 11.8	14 09.1	5 22.3	22 14.2	8 37.5	12 07.0	16 43.3	16 54.5	17 45.4
10 F	15 17 10	17 44 17	17 18 08	24 11 04	25R 36.5	9 26.7	13 33.0	6 05.8	22 32.1	8 40.5	12 11.6	16 47.0	16 56.5	17 47.5
11 Sa	15 21 06	18 44 35	1♈01 48	7♈50 16	25 35.8	10 40.0	12 57.5	6 49.4	22 50.1	8 43.4	12 16.1	16 50.8	16 58.5	17 49.6
12 Su	15 25 03	19 44 55	14 36 21	21 19 56	25 32.9	11 51.3	12 22.8	7 33.1	23 08.3	8 46.1	12 20.4	16 54.5	17 00.6	17 51.7
13 M	15 29 00	20 45 16	28 00 53	4♉39 01	25 27.4	13 00.4	11 49.2	8 16.8	23 26.5	8 48.6	12 24.7	16 58.3	17 02.6	17 53.8
14 Tu	15 32 56	21 45 39	11♉14 11	17 46 12	25 19.5	14 07.2	11 16.9	9 00.6	23 44.9	8 50.9	12 28.9	17 02.0	17 04.7	17 55.9
15 W	15 36 53	22 46 03	24 14 55	0♊40 13	25 09.5	15 11.2	10 46.0	9 44.4	24 03.5	8 53.0	12 33.0	17 05.7	17 06.8	17 57.9
16 Th	15 40 49	23 46 29	7♊02 01	13 20 15	24 58.4	16 12.1	10 16.9	10 28.3	24 22.1	8 54.9	12 37.1	17 09.5	17 08.9	18 00.0
17 F	15 44 46	24 46 57	19 34 58	25 46 13	24 47.2	17 09.6	9 49.6	11 12.2	24 40.9	8 56.7	12 41.0	17 13.2	17 11.0	18 02.0
18 Sa	15 48 42	25 47 27	1♋54 10	7♋59 01	24 37.0	18 03.1	9 24.3	11 56.2	24 59.8	8 58.2	12 44.9	17 16.9	17 13.2	18 04.0
19 Su	15 52 39	26 47 58	14 01 04	20 00 40	24 28.7	18 52.1	9 01.2	12 40.3	25 18.9	8 59.6	12 48.6	17 20.6	17 15.3	18 05.9
20 M	15 56 35	27 48 31	25 58 13	1♌54 13	24 22.7	19 36.2	8 40.3	13 24.4	25 38.0	9 00.7	12 52.3	17 24.3	17 17.5	18 07.9
21 Tu	16 00 32	28 49 06	7♌49 11	13 43 42	24 19.1	20 14.5	8 21.7	14 08.6	25 57.3	9 01.7	12 55.9	17 28.0	17 19.6	18 09.8
22 W	16 04 29	29 49 42	19 38 23	25 33 53	24D 17.8	20 46.6	8 05.5	14 52.9	26 16.7	9 02.5	12 59.3	17 31.7	17 21.8	18 11.7
23 Th	16 08 25	0♐50 20	1♍30 52	7♍30 00	24 17.8	21 11.5	7 51.7	15 37.2	26 36.1	9 03.0	13 02.7	17 35.4	17 24.0	18 13.6
24 F	16 12 22	1 51 00	13 32 01	19 37 33	24R 18.3	21 28.6	7 40.4	16 21.5	26 55.7	9 03.4	13 06.0	17 39.1	17 26.2	18 15.5
25 Sa	16 16 18	2 51 41	25 47 16	2♎01 48	24 18.1	21R 37.0	7 31.6	17 05.9	27 15.4	9R 03.6	13 09.2	17 42.7	17 28.4	18 17.3
26 Su	16 20 15	3 52 24	8♎21 41	14 47 24	24 16.2	21 36.1	7 25.3	17 50.4	27 35.3	9 03.5	13 12.3	17 46.4	17 30.6	18 19.1
27 M	16 24 11	4 53 09	21 19 20	27 57 46	24 11.9	21 25.0	7 21.5	18 34.9	27 55.2	9 03.3	13 15.3	17 50.0	17 32.8	18 20.9
28 Tu	16 28 08	5 53 55	4♏42 47	11♏34 23	24 04.8	21 03.3	7D 20.2	19 19.5	28 15.2	9 02.9	13 18.2	17 53.6	17 35.0	18 22.7
29 W	16 32 04	6 54 42	18 32 20	25 36 15	23 55.2	20 30.7	7 21.3	20 04.2	28 35.3	9 02.3	13 21.0	17 57.2	17 37.2	18 24.5
30 Th	16 36 01	7 55 31	2♐45 35	9♐59 37	23 43.9	19 47.0	7 24.7	20 48.9	28 55.6	9 01.4	13 23.7	18 00.8	17 39.5	18 26.2

December 1978 — LONGITUDE

Day	Sid.Time	☉	0 hr ☽	Noon ☽	True ☊	☿	♀	♂	⚳	♃	♄	♅	♆	♇
1 F	16 39 58	8♐56 21	17♐17 27	24♐38 07	23♍32.1	18♐52.9	7♏30.6	21♐33.6	29♑15.9	9♌00.4	13♍26.3	18♏04.4	17♐41.7	18♎27.9
2 Sa	16 43 54	9 57 13	2♑00 36	9♑23 50	23R 21.2	17R 49.1	7 38.7	22 18.5	29 36.3	8R 59.2	13 28.8	18 07.9	17 44.0	18 29.6
3 Su	16 47 51	10 58 05	16 46 47	24 08 30	23 12.3	16 37.2	7 49.1	23 03.3	29 56.9	8 57.8	13 31.1	18 11.5	17 46.2	18 31.2
4 M	16 51 47	11 58 58	1♒28 09	8♒45 01	23 06.1	15 19.0	8 01.7	23 48.2	0♒17.5	8 56.1	13 33.4	18 15.0	17 48.5	18 32.8
5 Tu	16 55 44	12 59 52	15 58 32	23 08 18	23 02.7	13 57.2	8 16.4	24 33.2	0 38.2	8 54.3	13 35.6	18 18.5	17 50.7	18 34.4
6 W	16 59 40	14 00 46	0♓14 03	7♓15 41	23D 01.5	12 34.2	8 33.2	25 18.2	0 59.0	8 52.3	13 37.6	18 22.0	17 53.0	18 36.0
7 Th	17 03 37	15 01 41	14 13 08	21 06 30	23R 01.5	11 13.1	8 52.0	26 03.3	1 19.8	8 50.1	13 39.6	18 25.5	17 55.3	18 37.5
8 F	17 07 33	16 02 37	27 55 56	4♈41 35	23 01.2	9 56.5	9 12.8	26 48.4	1 40.8	8 47.7	13 41.5	18 28.9	17 57.5	18 39.0
9 Sa	17 11 30	17 03 34	11♈23 39	18 02 22	22 59.3	8 46.7	9 35.4	27 33.6	2 01.8	8 45.1	13 43.2	18 32.3	17 59.8	18 40.5
10 Su	17 15 27	18 04 31	24 37 55	1♉10 27	22 54.9	7 45.7	9 59.9	28 18.8	2 22.9	8 42.3	13 44.8	18 35.7	18 02.1	18 42.0
11 M	17 19 23	19 05 29	7♉40 09	14 07 06	22 47.4	6 54.7	10 26.1	29 04.0	2 44.1	8 39.3	13 46.4	18 39.1	18 04.3	18 43.4
12 Tu	17 23 20	20 06 28	20 31 23	26 53 03	22 36.9	6 14.7	10 54.1	29 49.3	3 05.4	8 36.2	13 47.8	18 42.4	18 06.6	18 44.8
13 W	17 27 16	21 07 27	3♊12 09	9♊28 40	22 23.9	5 46.0	11 23.7	0♑34.7	3 26.8	8 32.8	13 49.1	18 45.7	18 08.8	18 46.2
14 Th	17 31 13	22 08 27	15 42 37	21 54 00	22 09.5	5 28.3	11 54.9	1 20.1	3 48.2	8 29.3	13 50.3	18 49.0	18 11.1	18 47.5
15 F	17 35 09	23 09 28	28 02 52	4♋09 15	21 54.8	5D 21.5	12 27.6	2 05.6	4 09.7	8 25.5	13 51.4	18 52.3	18 13.4	18 48.8
16 Sa	17 39 06	24 10 30	10♋13 14	16 14 57	21 41.2	5 24.8	13 01.8	2 51.1	4 31.3	8 21.6	13 52.4	18 55.6	18 15.6	18 50.1
17 Su	17 43 02	25 11 32	22 14 34	28 12 20	21 29.6	5 37.5	13 37.5	3 36.6	4 52.9	8 17.6	13 53.3	18 58.8	18 17.9	18 51.3
18 M	17 46 59	26 12 36	4♌08 30	10♌03 27	21 20.7	5 58.8	14 14.5	4 22.2	5 14.6	8 13.3	13 54.0	19 02.0	18 20.1	18 52.5
19 Tu	17 50 56	27 13 40	15 57 33	21 51 17	21 14.9	6 27.9	14 52.8	5 07.9	5 36.4	8 08.9	13 54.7	19 05.1	18 22.4	18 53.7
20 W	17 54 52	28 14 44	27 45 09	3♍39 42	21 11.8	7 04.0	15 32.4	5 53.5	5 58.2	8 04.2	13 55.2	19 08.2	18 24.6	18 54.9
21 Th	17 58 49	29 15 50	9♍35 34	15 33 23	21D 10.7	7 46.4	16 13.2	6 39.3	6 20.1	7 59.5	13 55.7	19 11.3	18 26.9	18 56.0
22 F	18 02 45	0♑16 56	21 33 49	27 37 33	21R 10.7	8 34.2	16 55.2	7 25.1	6 42.1	7 54.5	13 56.0	19 14.4	18 29.1	18 57.1
23 Sa	18 06 42	1 18 03	3♎45 17	9♎57 43	21 10.5	9 27.0	17 38.3	8 10.9	7 04.1	7 49.4	13 56.2	19 17.4	18 31.3	18 58.1
24 Su	18 10 38	2 19 11	16 15 31	22 39 17	21 08.9	10 24.1	18 22.5	8 56.8	7 26.2	7 44.1	13R 56.3	19 20.4	18 33.5	18 59.1
25 M	18 14 35	3 20 19	29 09 35	5♏46 51	21 05.2	11 24.9	19 07.7	9 42.7	7 48.4	7 38.7	13 56.3	19 23.4	18 35.7	19 00.1
26 Tu	18 18 31	4 21 28	12♏31 27	19 23 31	20 58.7	12 29.2	19 53.9	10 28.7	8 10.6	7 33.1	13 56.2	19 26.3	18 37.9	19 01.1
27 W	18 22 28	5 22 38	26 23 04	3♐29 53	20 49.7	13 36.4	20 41.1	11 14.7	8 32.9	7 27.3	13 55.9	19 29.2	18 40.1	19 02.0
28 Th	18 26 25	6 23 48	10♐43 33	18 03 25	20 38.9	14 46.2	21 29.2	12 00.7	8 55.2	7 21.4	13 55.6	19 32.1	18 42.3	19 02.9
29 F	18 30 21	7 24 58	25 28 37	2♑58 05	20 27.3	15 58.3	22 18.1	12 46.8	9 17.6	7 15.4	13 55.1	19 34.9	18 44.5	19 03.7
30 Sa	18 34 18	8 26 09	10♑30 37	18 04 55	20 16.5	17 12.5	23 07.9	13 33.0	9 40.1	7 09.2	13 54.6	19 37.7	18 46.7	19 04.5
31 Su	18 38 14	9 27 20	25 39 39	3♒13 29	20 07.5	18 28.5	23 58.5	14 19.2	10 02.6	7 02.9	13 53.9	19 40.5	18 48.8	19 05.3

Astro Data

	Dy Hr Mn
☽0N	11 0:12
♅⊻♆	16 3:53
☽0S	25 10:55
♃ R	25 20:30
☿ R	25 21:43
♀ D	28 13:10
☽0N	8 6:48
♅⊻♇	13 17:12
☿ D	15 15:57
☽0S	22 21:03
♄ R	24 21:12

Planet Ingress

	Dy Hr Mn
♂ ♐	2 1:20
☿ ♐	3 7:48
☉ ♐	22 16:05
⚳ ♒	3 15:40
♂ ♑	12 17:39
☉ ♑	22 5:21

Last Aspect / ☽ Ingress

Last Aspect Dy Hr Mn		☽ Ingress Dy Hr Mn
2 7:40 ☿ ☌	♐	2 10:03
3 15:45 ♇ ⚹	♑	4 12:40
5 18:14 ♇ □	♒	6 15:04
7 21:03 ♇ △	♓	8 18:06
9 23:53 ☉ △	♈	10 22:11
12 5:47 ♇ ☍	♉	13 3:35
14 20:00 ☉ ☍	♊	15 10:45
16 20:58 ♇ △	♋	17 20:16
20 2:57 ☉ △	♌	20 8:09
22 1:53 ☿ △	♍	22 20:57
24 15:41 ☿ □	♎	25 8:07
27 0:22 ☿ ⚹	♏	27 15:39
28 22:57 ♅ ☌	♐	29 19:23

Last Aspect / ☽ Ingress

Last Aspect Dy Hr Mn		☽ Ingress Dy Hr Mn
1 6:43 ♂ ☌	♑	1 20:44
3 2:49 ♇ □	♒	3 21:35
5 14:31 ♂ ⚹	♓	5 23:36
7 21:12 ♂ □	♈	8 3:40
10 6:25 ♂ △	♉	10 9:50
11 20:31 ♅ ☍	♊	12 17:54
14 12:31 ☉ ☍	♋	15 3:50
16 17:23 ♅ △	♌	17 15:37
19 23:58 ☉ △	♍	20 4:34
21 19:18 ♅ ⚹	♎	22 16:40
24 5:08 ♇ ☌	♏	25 1:32
26 12:56 ♀ ☌	♐	27 6:07
28 13:37 ♇ ⚹	♑	29 7:15
30 20:28 ♀ ⚹	♒	31 6:53

☽ Phases & Eclipses

Dy Hr Mn	
7 16:18	☽ 14♒54
14 20:00	○ 22♉06
22 21:24	☾ 0♍13
30 8:19	● 7♐46
7 0:34	☽ 14♓33
14 12:31	○ 22♊10
22 17:42	☾ 0♎31
29 19:36	● 7♑44

Astro Data

1 November 1978
Julian Day # 28794
SVP 5♓33'23"
GC 26♐32.6 ⚴ 26♐18.3
Eris 13♈56.1R ⚵ 0♒09.1
⚷ 7♉19.4R ⚶ 8♑40.7
☽ Mean ☊ 24♍25.7

1 December 1978
Julian Day # 28824
SVP 5♓33'18"
GC 26♐32.7 ⚴ 7♑07.7
Eris 13♈42.4R ⚵ 9♒42.9
⚷ 5♉58.4R ⚶ 22♑51.3
☽ Mean ☊ 22♍50.4

LONGITUDE — January 1979

Day	Sid.Time	☉	0 hr ☽	Noon ☽	True ☊	☿	♀	♂	⚳	♃	♄	♅	♆	♇
1 M	18 42 11	10♑28 30	10♒45 13	18♒13 46	20♍01.2	19♐46.0	24♏49.8	15♑05.4	10♒25.1	6♌56.5	13♍53.1	19♏43.2	18♐51.0	19♎06.1
2 Tu	18 46 07	11 29 41	25 38 11	2♓57 45	19R57.8	21 05.0	25 41.9	15 51.6	10 47.7	6R49.9	13R52.2	19 45.9	18 53.1	19 06.8
3 W	18 50 04	12 30 51	10♓11 58	17 20 28	19D56.7	22 25.3	26 34.7	16 37.9	11 10.3	6 43.2	13 51.2	19 48.5	18 55.2	19 07.4
4 Th	18 54 00	13 32 01	24 23 08	1♈19 56	19R56.9	23 46.8	27 28.2	17 24.3	11 33.0	6 36.4	13 50.1	19 51.1	18 57.3	19 08.1
5 F	18 57 57	14 33 11	8♈11 00	14 56 33	19 57.3	25 09.3	28 22.3	18 10.6	11 55.8	6 29.5	13 48.8	19 53.7	18 59.4	19 08.7
6 Sa	19 01 54	15 34 20	21 36 53	28 12 21	19 56.5	26 32.8	29 17.1	18 57.0	12 18.5	6 22.4	13 47.5	19 56.2	19 01.5	19 09.3
7 Su	19 05 50	16 35 29	4♉43 17	11♉10 05	19 53.6	27 57.1	0♐12.4	19 43.5	12 41.3	6 15.3	13 46.1	19 58.7	19 03.6	19 09.8
8 M	19 09 47	17 36 37	17 33 06	23 52 40	19 48.1	29 22.3	1 08.4	20 29.9	13 04.2	6 08.1	13 44.5	20 01.1	19 05.6	19 10.3
9 Tu	19 13 43	18 37 45	0♊09 07	6♊22 44	19 40.0	0♑48.3	2 05.0	21 16.4	13 27.1	6 00.7	13 42.9	20 03.5	19 07.7	19 10.7
10 W	19 17 40	19 38 53	12 33 45	18 42 26	19 29.7	2 14.9	3 02.1	22 02.9	13 50.0	5 53.3	13 41.1	20 05.8	19 09.7	19 11.2
11 Th	19 21 36	20 40 00	24 48 56	0♋53 27	19 18.1	3 42.2	3 59.7	22 49.5	14 13.0	5 45.8	13 39.3	20 08.2	19 11.7	19 11.6
12 F	19 25 33	21 41 07	6♋56 08	12 57 07	19 06.3	5 10.2	4 57.8	23 36.1	14 36.0	5 38.3	13 37.3	20 10.4	19 13.7	19 11.9
13 Sa	19 29 30	22 42 14	18 56 34	24 54 37	18 55.3	6 38.8	5 56.5	24 22.7	14 59.0	5 30.6	13 35.3	20 12.6	19 15.7	19 12.2
14 Su	19 33 26	23 43 20	0♌51 26	6♌47 11	18 46.0	8 07.9	6 55.6	25 09.4	15 22.1	5 22.9	13 33.1	20 14.8	19 17.6	19 12.5
15 M	19 37 23	24 44 26	12 42 07	18 36 28	18 39.0	9 37.7	7 55.2	25 56.1	15 45.2	5 15.2	13 30.8	20 16.9	19 19.6	19 12.8
16 Tu	19 41 19	25 45 31	24 30 30	0♍24 34	18 34.5	11 08.0	8 55.2	26 42.8	16 08.3	5 07.3	13 28.5	20 19.0	19 21.5	19 13.0
17 W	19 45 16	26 46 36	6♍19 02	12 14 19	18D32.5	12 38.9	9 55.6	27 29.6	16 31.5	4 59.5	13 26.0	20 21.0	19 23.4	19 13.2
18 Th	19 49 12	27 47 41	18 10 52	24 09 12	18 32.4	14 10.3	10 56.5	28 16.3	16 54.7	4 51.6	13 23.5	20 23.0	19 25.3	19 13.3
19 F	19 53 09	28 48 45	0♎09 52	6♎13 26	18 33.5	15 42.4	11 57.8	29 03.2	17 17.9	4 43.6	13 20.8	20 25.0	19 27.2	19 13.4
20 Sa	19 57 05	29 49 50	12 20 30	18 31 41	18R34.8	17 14.9	12 59.4	29 50.0	17 41.2	4 35.6	13 18.1	20 26.8	19 29.0	19 13.5
21 Su	20 01 02	0♒50 53	24 47 37	1♏08 53	18 35.4	18 48.1	14 01.4	0♒36.9	18 04.5	4 27.6	13 15.3	20 28.7	19 30.8	19R13.5
22 M	20 04 58	1 51 57	7♏36 05	14 09 43	18 34.5	20 21.8	15 03.8	1 23.8	18 27.8	4 19.6	13 12.4	20 30.5	19 32.6	19 13.5
23 Tu	20 08 55	2 52 59	20 50 14	27 37 58	18 31.8	21 56.1	16 06.5	2 10.7	18 51.1	4 11.6	13 09.3	20 32.2	19 34.4	19 13.4
24 W	20 12 52	3 54 02	4♐33 07	11♐35 42	18 27.1	23 31.0	17 09.6	2 57.6	19 14.5	4 03.5	13 06.2	20 33.9	19 36.2	19 13.4
25 Th	20 16 48	4 55 04	18 45 33	26 02 19	18 21.0	25 06.5	18 12.9	3 44.6	19 37.9	3 55.5	13 03.1	20 35.6	19 37.9	19 13.3
26 F	20 20 45	5 56 06	3♑25 23	10♑53 58	18 14.2	26 42.6	19 16.6	4 31.6	20 01.3	3 47.5	12 59.8	20 37.1	19 39.6	19 13.1
27 Sa	20 24 41	6 57 06	18 27 01	26 03 23	18 07.6	28 19.3	20 20.5	5 18.7	20 24.7	3 39.4	12 56.5	20 38.7	19 41.3	19 12.9
28 Su	20 28 38	7 58 06	3♒41 44	11♒20 42	18 02.2	29 56.7	21 24.8	6 05.7	20 48.2	3 31.4	12 53.0	20 40.2	19 43.0	19 12.7
29 M	20 32 34	8 59 05	18 58 55	26 35 03	17 58.5	1♒34.7	22 29.3	6 52.8	21 11.6	3 23.4	12 49.5	20 41.6	19 44.6	19 12.5
30 Tu	20 36 31	10 00 03	4♓07 53	11♓36 22	17D56.9	3 13.4	23 34.0	7 39.9	21 35.1	3 15.5	12 45.9	20 43.0	19 46.2	19 12.2
31 W	20 40 28	11 01 00	18 59 37	26 16 59	17 56.9	4 52.7	24 39.1	8 27.0	21 58.6	3 07.6	12 42.3	20 44.3	19 47.8	19 11.9

LONGITUDE — February 1979

Day	Sid.Time	☉	0 hr ☽	Noon ☽	True ☊	☿	♀	♂	⚳	♃	♄	♅	♆	♇
1 Th	20 44 24	12♒01 55	3♈27 59	10♈32 21	17♍58.2	6♒32.8	25♐44.3	9♒14.1	22♒22.1	2♌59.7	12♍38.5	20♏45.6	19♐49.4	19♎11.5
2 F	20 48 21	13 02 49	17 29 58	24 20 55	17 59.7	8 13.6	26 49.8	10 01.3	22 45.7	2R51.8	12R34.7	20 46.8	19 50.9	19R11.1
3 Sa	20 52 17	14 03 42	1♉05 22	7♉43 36	18R00.8	9 55.1	27 55.5	10 48.4	23 09.2	2 44.1	12 30.9	20 48.0	19 52.5	19 10.7
4 Su	20 56 14	15 04 33	14 15 59	20 42 57	18 00.8	11 37.3	29 01.4	11 35.6	23 32.8	2 36.4	12 26.9	20 49.1	19 54.0	19 10.2
5 M	21 00 10	16 05 23	27 04 55	3♊22 23	17 59.4	13 20.2	0♑07.6	12 22.8	23 56.3	2 28.7	12 22.9	20 50.2	19 55.4	19 09.7
6 Tu	21 04 07	17 06 11	9♊35 48	15 45 39	17 56.5	15 04.0	1 13.9	13 10.0	24 19.9	2 21.1	12 18.9	20 51.2	19 56.9	19 09.2
7 W	21 08 03	18 06 58	21 52 22	27 56 23	17 52.2	16 48.4	2 20.5	13 57.2	24 43.5	2 13.7	12 14.7	20 52.2	19 58.3	19 08.6
8 Th	21 12 00	19 07 44	3♋58 07	9♋57 54	17 47.2	18 33.7	3 27.2	14 44.4	25 07.1	2 06.2	12 10.6	20 53.1	19 59.7	19 08.0
9 F	21 15 57	20 08 28	15 56 07	21 53 03	17 42.0	20 19.7	4 34.1	15 31.6	25 30.7	1 58.9	12 06.3	20 53.9	20 01.0	19 07.4
10 Sa	21 19 53	21 09 11	27 49 02	3♌44 18	17 37.2	22 06.4	5 41.3	16 18.9	25 54.3	1 51.7	12 02.0	20 54.7	20 02.3	19 06.8
11 Su	21 23 50	22 09 52	9♌39 07	15 33 44	17 33.1	23 53.9	6 48.5	17 06.2	26 17.9	1 44.5	11 57.7	20 55.4	20 03.6	19 06.1
12 M	21 27 46	23 10 32	21 28 23	27 23 18	17 30.3	25 42.1	7 56.0	17 53.4	26 41.5	1 37.5	11 53.3	20 56.1	20 04.9	19 05.3
13 Tu	21 31 43	24 11 11	3♍18 44	9♍14 55	17D28.8	27 31.0	9 03.7	18 40.7	27 05.1	1 30.6	11 48.9	20 56.8	20 06.2	19 04.6
14 W	21 35 39	25 11 48	15 12 09	21 10 40	17 28.6	29 20.5	10 11.5	19 28.0	27 28.7	1 23.8	11 44.4	20 57.3	20 07.4	19 03.8
15 Th	21 39 36	26 12 24	27 10 49	3♎12 55	17 29.4	1♓10.6	11 19.4	20 15.3	27 52.3	1 17.1	11 39.9	20 57.9	20 08.5	19 03.0
16 F	21 43 32	27 12 58	9♎17 20	15 24 27	17 30.8	3 01.1	12 27.5	21 02.6	28 15.9	1 10.5	11 35.4	20 58.3	20 09.7	19 02.2
17 Sa	21 47 29	28 13 31	21 34 39	27 48 23	17 32.4	4 52.1	13 35.8	21 49.9	28 39.5	1 04.0	11 30.8	20 58.7	20 10.8	19 01.3
18 Su	21 51 25	29 14 03	4♏06 05	10♏28 11	17 33.8	6 43.4	14 44.2	22 37.2	29 03.2	0 57.7	11 26.1	20 59.1	20 11.9	19 00.4
19 M	21 55 22	0♓14 34	16 55 07	23 27 18	17R34.6	8 34.9	15 52.8	23 24.6	29 26.8	0 51.5	11 21.5	20 59.4	20 13.0	18 59.4
20 Tu	21 59 19	1 15 04	0♐05 06	6♐48 50	17 34.7	10 26.3	17 01.4	24 11.9	29 50.4	0 45.4	11 16.8	20 59.6	20 14.0	18 58.5
21 W	22 03 15	2 15 32	13 38 45	20 34 58	17 34.0	12 17.5	18 10.3	24 59.3	0♓14.0	0 39.5	11 12.1	20 59.8	20 15.0	18 57.5
22 Th	22 07 12	3 15 59	27 37 30	4♑46 14	17 32.6	14 08.3	19 19.2	25 46.6	0 37.6	0 33.7	11 07.4	21 00.0	20 16.0	18 56.5
23 F	22 11 08	4 16 25	12♑00 53	19 20 58	17 31.0	15 58.3	20 28.3	26 34.0	1 01.2	0 28.1	11 02.6	21R00.1	20 16.9	18 55.4
24 Sa	22 15 05	5 16 49	26 45 52	4♒14 47	17 29.4	17 47.4	21 37.4	27 21.3	1 24.8	0 22.6	10 57.9	21 00.1	20 17.8	18 54.4
25 Su	22 19 01	6 17 12	11♒46 45	19 20 42	17 28.1	19 35.0	22 46.7	28 08.7	1 48.4	0 17.3	10 53.1	21 00.1	20 18.7	18 53.3
26 M	22 22 58	7 17 33	26 55 28	4♓29 52	17D27.3	21 20.8	23 56.1	28 56.0	2 12.0	0 12.1	10 48.3	21 00.0	20 19.5	18 52.1
27 Tu	22 26 54	8 17 52	12♓02 41	19 32 46	17 27.1	23 04.3	25 05.6	29 43.4	2 35.6	0 07.1	10 43.5	20 59.8	20 20.4	18 51.0
28 W	22 30 51	9 18 09	26 59 06	4♈20 44	17 27.4	24 45.2	26 15.2	0♓30.7	2 59.1	0 02.3	10 38.7	20 59.6	20 21.1	18 49.8

Astro Data

	Dy Hr Mn
☽0N	4 14:09
♆✱♇	11 9:43
☽0S	19 5:34
♃⊼♆	21 4:14
♇ R	21 20:47
☽0N	31 23:29
☽0S	15 12:13
♅ R	24 11:58
☽0N	28 10:23

Planet Ingress

		Dy Hr Mn
♀	♐	7 6:38
☿	♑	8 22:33
☉	♒	20 16:00
♂	♒	20 17:07
☿	♒	28 12:49
♀	♑	5 9:16
☿	♓	14 20:38
☉	♓	19 6:13
⚳	♓	20 21:47
♂	♓	27 20:25
♃	♋R	28 23:35

Last Aspect / ☽ Ingress

Last Aspect Dy Hr Mn			☽ Ingress	Dy Hr Mn
1 23:21	♀	□	♓	2 7:08
4 4:51	♀	△	♈	4 9:41
6 8:36	☿	△	♉	6 15:17
8 5:09	♂	△	♊	8 23:42
10 12:56	♇	△	♋	11 10:14
13 10:51	♂	☍	♌	13 22:16
15 15:25	♅	□	♍	16 11:10
18 20:48	♂	△	♎	18 23:40
20 13:51	♆	✱	♏	21 9:51
23 0:38	☿	✱	♐	23 16:08
25 1:26	♆	☌	♑	25 18:27
27 15:59	☿	☌	♒	27 18:12
29 5:02	♀	✱	♓	29 17:25
31 9:05	♀	□	♈	31 18:11

Last Aspect / ☽ Ingress

Last Aspect Dy Hr Mn			☽ Ingress	Dy Hr Mn
2 16:47	♀	△	♉	2 22:03
4 12:12	♅	☍	♊	5 5:33
6 20:14	♆	☍	♋	7 16:06
9 10:00	♅	△	♌	10 4:25
12 7:58	☿	☍	♍	12 17:18
14 11:33	♅	✱	♎	15 5:37
17 12:52	☉	△	♏	17 16:12
19 11:55	♂	□	♐	19 23:51
21 19:58	♂	✱	♑	22 4:00
23 14:41	♅	✱	♒	24 5:12
26 2:42	♂	☌	♓	26 4:52
27 21:42	♀	✱	♈	28 4:54

☽ Phases & Eclipses

Dy Hr Mn		
5 11:15	☽	14♈31
13 7:09	○	22♋30
21 11:23	☾	0♏49
28 6:20	●	7♒44
4 0:36	☽	14♉36
12 2:39	○	22♌47
20 1:17	☾	0♐48
26 16:45	●	7♓29
26 16:54:16	●	T 02'49"

Astro Data

1 January 1979
Julian Day # 28855
SVP 5♓33'13"
GC 26♐32.8 ⚴ 18♑46.0
Eris 13♈37.1 ⚵ 22♒13.8
⚷ 5♉08.2R ⚶ 8♒14.4
☽ Mean ☊ 21♍11.9

1 February 1979
Julian Day # 28886
SVP 5♓33'08"
GC 26♐32.8 ⚴ 0♒17.8
Eris 13♈42.4 ⚵ 6♓32.0
⚷ 5♉11.5 ⚶ 23♒54.3
☽ Mean ☊ 19♍33.4

March 1979 LONGITUDE

Day	Sid.Time	☉	0 hr ☽	Noon ☽	True ☊	☿	♀	♂	⚳	♃	♄	♅	♆	♇
1 Th	22 34 48	10♓18 25	11♈36 55	18♈47 04	17♍28.0	26♓22.7	27♑24.9	1♓18.1	3♓22.7	29♋57.6	10♍33.9	20♏59.4	20♐21.9	18♎48.6
2 F	22 38 44	11 18 38	25 50 44	2♉47 41	17 28.6	27 56.5	28 34.7	2 05.4	3 46.2	29R 53.1	10R 29.1	20R 59.1	20 22.6	18R 47.4
3 Sa	22 42 41	12 18 50	9♉37 51	16 21 17	17 29.2	29 25.9	29 44.5	2 52.8	4 09.7	29 48.8	10 24.3	20 58.7	20 23.3	18 46.1
4 Su	22 46 37	13 19 00	22 58 09	29 28 47	17 29.5	0♈50.3	0♒54.5	3 40.1	4 33.2	29 44.6	10 19.5	20 58.3	20 23.9	18 44.9
5 M	22 50 34	14 19 07	5♊53 32	12♊12 53	17R 29.6	2 09.1	2 04.5	4 27.4	4 56.7	29 40.7	10 14.7	20 57.9	20 24.5	18 43.6
6 Tu	22 54 30	15 19 12	18 27 18	24 37 19	17 29.6	3 21.9	3 14.6	5 14.8	5 20.2	29 36.9	10 09.9	20 57.3	20 25.1	18 42.3
7 W	22 58 27	16 19 16	0♋43 30	6♋46 23	17 29.5	4 28.0	4 24.8	6 02.1	5 43.6	29 33.3	10 05.1	20 56.8	20 25.6	18 40.9
8 Th	23 02 23	17 19 17	12 46 32	18 44 28	17D 29.5	5 26.9	5 35.1	6 49.4	6 07.1	29 29.8	10 00.4	20 56.2	20 26.2	18 39.6
9 F	23 06 20	18 19 16	24 40 44	0♌35 48	17 29.5	6 18.3	6 45.5	7 36.7	6 30.5	29 26.6	9 55.6	20 55.5	20 26.6	18 38.2
10 Sa	23 10 17	19 19 12	6♌30 09	12 24 14	17 29.7	7 01.6	7 55.9	8 23.9	6 53.9	29 23.5	9 50.9	20 54.8	20 27.1	18 36.8
11 Su	23 14 13	20 19 07	18 18 26	24 13 08	17 29.9	7 36.6	9 06.4	9 11.2	7 17.3	29 20.7	9 46.2	20 54.0	20 27.5	18 35.4
12 M	23 18 10	21 19 00	0♍08 42	6♍05 25	17R 30.2	8 03.1	10 16.9	9 58.5	7 40.6	29 18.0	9 41.5	20 53.2	20 27.9	18 34.0
13 Tu	23 22 06	22 18 50	12 03 36	18 03 30	17 30.2	8 20.9	11 27.6	10 45.7	8 03.9	29 15.5	9 36.9	20 52.3	20 28.2	18 32.5
14 W	23 26 03	23 18 39	24 05 21	0♎09 23	17 30.1	8R 30.0	12 38.3	11 32.9	8 27.2	29 13.2	9 32.3	20 51.4	20 28.5	18 31.0
15 Th	23 29 59	24 18 26	6♎15 47	12 24 46	17 29.6	8 30.5	13 49.1	12 20.2	8 50.5	29 11.0	9 27.7	20 50.4	20 28.8	18 29.6
16 F	23 33 56	25 18 11	18 36 30	24 51 10	17 28.7	8 22.5	14 59.9	13 07.4	9 13.8	29 09.1	9 23.2	20 49.4	20 29.0	18 28.0
17 Sa	23 37 52	26 17 54	1♏08 56	7♏30 00	17 27.6	8 06.4	16 10.8	13 54.5	9 37.0	29 07.4	9 18.7	20 48.3	20 29.3	18 26.5
18 Su	23 41 49	27 17 35	13 54 31	20 22 40	17 26.3	7 42.8	17 21.8	14 41.7	10 00.2	29 05.8	9 14.2	20 47.2	20 29.4	18 25.0
19 M	23 45 45	28 17 14	26 54 38	3♐30 34	17 25.2	7 12.2	18 32.8	15 28.9	10 23.4	29 04.5	9 09.8	20 46.0	20 29.6	18 23.5
20 Tu	23 49 42	29 16 52	10♐10 37	16 54 57	17D 24.4	6 35.4	19 43.9	16 16.0	10 46.6	29 03.3	9 05.4	20 44.8	20 29.7	18 21.9
21 W	23 53 39	0♈16 28	23 43 38	0♑36 45	17 24.1	5 53.2	20 55.0	17 03.2	11 09.7	29 02.3	9 01.1	20 43.6	20 29.8	18 20.3
22 Th	23 57 35	1 16 03	7♑34 20	14 36 18	17 24.4	5 06.7	22 06.2	17 50.3	11 32.8	29 01.5	8 56.8	20 42.3	20R 29.8	18 18.8
23 F	0 01 32	2 15 35	21 42 32	28 52 49	17 25.3	4 16.9	23 17.5	18 37.4	11 55.8	29 01.0	8 52.6	20 40.9	20 29.8	18 17.2
24 Sa	0 05 28	3 15 06	6♒06 50	13♒24 09	17 26.4	3 24.9	24 28.8	19 24.5	12 18.9	29 00.6	8 48.5	20 39.5	20 29.8	18 15.6
25 Su	0 09 25	4 14 35	20 44 15	28 06 27	17 27.5	2 31.9	25 40.1	20 11.6	12 41.9	29D 00.4	8 44.4	20 38.1	20 29.7	18 13.9
26 M	0 13 21	5 14 03	5♓30 03	12♓54 13	17R 28.1	1 38.9	26 51.5	20 58.6	13 04.8	29 00.4	8 40.3	20 36.6	20 29.6	18 12.3
27 Tu	0 17 18	6 13 28	20 18 04	27 40 42	17 28.0	0 47.0	28 02.9	21 45.6	13 27.8	29 00.5	8 36.3	20 35.1	20 29.5	18 10.7
28 W	0 21 14	7 12 51	5♈01 12	12♈18 41	17 26.7	29♓57.3	29 14.4	22 32.6	13 50.7	29 00.9	8 32.4	20 33.5	20 29.4	18 09.0
29 Th	0 25 11	8 12 12	19 32 20	26 41 25	17 24.5	29 10.5	0♓25.9	23 19.6	14 13.5	29 01.5	8 28.5	20 31.9	20 29.2	18 07.4
30 F	0 29 08	9 11 31	3♉45 20	10♉43 35	17 21.6	28 27.3	1 37.5	24 06.5	14 36.3	29 02.3	8 24.7	20 30.2	20 28.9	18 05.7
31 Sa	0 33 04	10 10 48	17 35 49	24 21 52	17 18.2	27 48.5	2 49.1	24 53.5	14 59.1	29 03.2	8 21.0	20 28.5	20 28.7	18 04.1

April 1979 LONGITUDE

Day	Sid.Time	☉	0 hr ☽	Noon ☽	True ☊	☿	♀	♂	⚳	♃	♄	♅	♆	♇
1 Su	0 37 01	11♈10 03	1♊01 38	7♊35 14	17♍15.0	27♓14.5	4♓00.7	25♓40.4	15♓21.8	29♋04.4	8♍17.3	20♏26.8	20♐28.4	18♎02.4
2 M	0 40 57	12 09 15	14 02 49	20 24 44	17R 12.4	26R 45.6	5 12.4	26 27.2	15 44.5	29 05.7	8R 13.8	20R 25.1	20R 28.1	18R 00.7
3 Tu	0 44 54	13 08 26	26 41 20	2♋53 06	17D 10.8	26 22.2	6 24.1	27 14.1	16 07.2	29 07.2	8 10.3	20 23.2	20 27.7	17 59.0
4 W	0 48 50	14 07 33	9♋00 34	15 04 18	17 10.3	26 04.2	7 35.8	28 00.9	16 29.8	29 08.9	8 06.8	20 21.4	20 27.3	17 57.4
5 Th	0 52 47	15 06 39	21 04 52	27 02 55	17 11.0	25 51.9	8 47.5	28 47.7	16 52.3	29 10.8	8 03.5	20 19.5	20 26.9	17 55.7
6 F	0 56 43	16 05 42	2♌59 04	8♌53 56	17 12.4	25D 45.2	9 59.3	29 34.4	17 14.9	29 12.9	8 00.2	20 17.6	20 26.5	17 54.0
7 Sa	1 00 40	17 04 43	14 48 07	20 42 13	17 14.2	25 44.0	11 11.1	0♈21.1	17 37.3	29 15.2	7 57.0	20 15.7	20 26.0	17 52.3
8 Su	1 04 37	18 03 41	26 36 48	2♍32 23	17 15.8	25 48.1	12 23.0	1 07.8	17 59.7	29 17.6	7 53.9	20 13.7	20 25.5	17 50.6
9 M	1 08 33	19 02 38	8♍29 28	14 28 30	17R 16.7	25 57.5	13 34.8	1 54.5	18 22.1	29 20.2	7 50.9	20 11.7	20 25.0	17 48.9
10 Tu	1 12 30	20 01 32	20 29 54	26 34 00	17 16.3	26 12.0	14 46.7	2 41.1	18 44.4	29 23.1	7 48.0	20 09.6	20 24.4	17 47.3
11 W	1 16 26	21 00 24	2♎41 08	8♎51 31	17 14.3	26 31.4	15 58.7	3 27.7	19 06.7	29 26.0	7 45.1	20 07.6	20 23.8	17 45.6
12 Th	1 20 23	21 59 14	15 05 21	21 22 46	17 10.7	26 55.4	17 10.6	4 14.3	19 28.9	29 29.2	7 42.4	20 05.5	20 23.1	17 43.9
13 F	1 24 19	22 58 02	27 43 50	4♏08 35	17 05.7	27 23.9	18 22.6	5 00.8	19 51.0	29 32.5	7 39.7	20 03.3	20 22.5	17 42.2
14 Sa	1 28 16	23 56 48	10♏36 59	17 08 59	16 59.7	27 56.6	19 34.6	5 47.3	20 13.2	29 36.0	7 37.1	20 01.2	20 21.8	17 40.5
15 Su	1 32 12	24 55 32	23 44 29	0♐23 20	16 53.3	28 33.4	20 46.7	6 33.7	20 35.2	29 39.7	7 34.6	19 59.0	20 21.1	17 38.9
16 M	1 36 09	25 54 15	7♐05 25	13 50 33	16 47.5	29 14.1	21 58.7	7 20.2	20 57.2	29 43.6	7 32.2	19 56.8	20 20.3	17 37.2
17 Tu	1 40 05	26 52 55	20 38 36	27 29 25	16 42.8	29 58.5	23 10.8	8 06.6	21 19.2	29 47.6	7 29.9	19 54.6	20 19.6	17 35.5
18 W	1 44 02	27 51 35	4♑22 50	11♑18 42	16 39.8	0♈46.3	24 23.0	8 52.9	21 41.0	29 51.8	7 27.7	19 52.3	20 18.8	17 33.9
19 Th	1 47 59	28 50 12	18 16 55	25 17 20	16D 38.6	1 37.5	25 35.1	9 39.3	22 02.9	29 56.1	7 25.6	19 50.0	20 17.9	17 32.2
20 F	1 51 55	29 48 48	2♒19 49	9♒24 13	16 38.8	2 31.9	26 47.3	10 25.6	22 24.7	0♌00.7	7 23.6	19 47.7	20 17.1	17 30.6
21 Sa	1 55 52	0♉47 22	16 30 23	23 38 06	16 40.0	3 29.3	27 59.5	11 11.8	22 46.4	0 05.4	7 21.7	19 45.4	20 16.2	17 29.0
22 Su	1 59 48	1 45 54	0♓47 08	7♓57 11	16R 41.1	4 29.6	29 11.7	11 58.0	23 08.0	0 10.2	7 19.8	19 43.0	20 15.3	17 27.3
23 M	2 03 45	2 44 25	15 07 53	22 18 50	16 41.2	5 32.8	0♈24.0	12 44.2	23 29.6	0 15.2	7 18.1	19 40.7	20 14.3	17 25.7
24 Tu	2 07 41	3 42 54	29 29 32	6♈39 27	16 39.6	6 38.5	1 36.2	13 30.4	23 51.1	0 20.4	7 16.5	19 38.3	20 13.4	17 24.1
25 W	2 11 38	4 41 22	13♈48 00	20 54 35	16 35.7	7 46.9	2 48.5	14 16.5	24 12.6	0 25.7	7 15.0	19 35.9	20 12.4	17 22.5
26 Th	2 15 34	5 39 47	27 58 34	4♉59 21	16 29.7	8 57.7	4 00.8	15 02.5	24 33.9	0 31.2	7 13.6	19 33.5	20 11.4	17 20.9
27 F	2 19 31	6 38 11	11♉56 22	18 49 07	16 22.0	10 10.9	5 13.1	15 48.5	24 55.3	0 36.8	7 12.2	19 31.0	20 10.3	17 19.3
28 Sa	2 23 28	7 36 33	25 37 10	2♊20 11	16 13.2	11 26.5	6 25.5	16 34.5	25 16.5	0 42.6	7 11.0	19 28.6	20 09.3	17 17.8
29 Su	2 27 24	8 34 53	8♊57 59	15 30 25	16 04.5	12 44.3	7 37.8	17 20.5	25 37.7	0 48.6	7 09.9	19 26.1	20 08.2	17 16.2
30 M	2 31 21	9 33 11	21 57 31	28 19 25	15 56.8	14 04.3	8 50.2	18 06.4	25 58.8	0 54.7	7 08.9	19 23.7	20 07.0	17 14.7

Astro Data	Dy Hr Mn
☿0N	2 20:25
☽0S	14 18:16
☿R	15 1:14
☉0N	21 5:21
♆R	23 7:34
♃D	26 0:55
☽0N	27 21:14
♅⊻♆	31 9:35
☿0S	2 0:56
☿D	7 5:21
♂0N	9 21:12
☽0S	11 1:17
☿0N	24 1:50
☽0N	24 6:36
♀0N	26 5:03

Planet Ingress		Dy Hr Mn
♀	♒	3 17:18
☿	♈	3 21:32
☉	♈	21 5:22
☿	♓R	28 10:39
♀	♓	29 3:18
♂	♈	7 1:08
☿	♈	17 12:48
♃	♌	20 8:30
☉	♉	20 16:35
♀	♈	23 4:02

Last Aspect Dy Hr Mn			☽ Ingress	Dy Hr Mn
2 6:59	♃	□	♉	2 7:09
4 12:29	♃	⚹	♊	4 12:58
6 3:48	♆	☍	♋	6 22:34
9 9:40	♃	☌	♌	9 10:47
11 5:16	♅	□	♍	11 23:42
14 10:09	♃	⚹	♎	14 11:42
16 20:11	♃	□	♏	16 21:49
19 3:58	♃	△	♐	19 5:38
20 18:19	♆	☌	♑	21 10:56
23 12:13	♃	☍	♒	23 13:52
25 7:41	♀	☌	♓	25 15:04
27 14:10	♃	△	♈	27 15:47
29 15:57	♃	□	♉	29 17:36
31 20:26	♃	⚹	♊	31 22:08

Last Aspect Dy Hr Mn			☽ Ingress	Dy Hr Mn
3 0:19	♂	□	♋	3 6:24
5 16:19	♃	☌	♌	5 17:58
7 11:27	♆	△	♍	8 6:52
10 17:34	♃	⚹	♎	10 18:45
13 3:22	♃	□	♏	13 4:16
15 10:41	♃	△	♐	15 11:18
17 10:51	☉	△	♑	17 16:23
19 19:58	♃	☍	♒	19 20:02
21 6:21	♆	⚹	♓	21 22:41
23 8:32	♆	□	♈	24 0:51
25 10:49	♆	△	♉	26 3:27
27 13:13	♅	☍	♊	28 7:49
29 20:35	♆	☍	♋	30 15:11

☽ Phases & Eclipses Dy Hr Mn		
5 16:23	☽	14♊30
13 21:14	○	22♍42
13 21:08	☋	P 0.854
21 11:22	☾	0♑15
28 3:00	●	6♈51
4 9:57	☽	14♋03
12 13:15	○	22♎02
19 18:30	☾	29♑06
26 13:15	●	5♉43

Astro Data

1 March 1979
Julian Day # 28914
SVP 5♓33'05"
GC 26♐32.9 ⚵ 10♒10.1
Eris 13♈55.2 ⚶ 20♓31.0
⚷ 6♉01.2 ⚴ 7♓59.0
☽ Mean ☊ 18♍04.4

1 April 1979
Julian Day # 28945
SVP 5♓33'03"
GC 26♐33.0 ⚵ 19♒56.3
Eris 14♈14.8 ⚶ 6♈49.6
⚷ 7♉35.5 ⚴ 23♓12.3
☽ Mean ☊ 16♍25.9

LONGITUDE — May 1979

Day	Sid.Time	☉	0 hr ☽	Noon ☽	True ☊	☿	♀	♂	⚳	♃	♄	♅	♆	♇
1 Tu	2 35 17	10♉31 28	4♋36 20	10♋48 36	15♍50.7	15♈26.4	10♈02.5	18♈52.2	26♓19.8	1♌00.9	7♍08.0	19♏21.2	20♐05.9	17♎13.2
2 W	2 39 14	11 29 42	16 56 37	23 00 52	15R46.7	16 50.7	11 14.9	19 38.0	26 40.7	1 07.3	7R07.2	19R18.7	20R04.8	17R11.7
3 Th	2 43 10	12 27 54	29 01 54	5♌00 19	15D44.7	18 17.0	12 27.3	20 23.8	27 01.6	1 13.8	7 06.5	19 16.2	20 03.6	17 10.2
4 F	2 47 07	13 26 04	10♌56 44	16 51 48	15 44.5	19 45.4	13 39.7	21 09.5	27 22.4	1 20.5	7 05.9	19 13.7	20 02.4	17 08.7
5 Sa	2 51 03	14 24 12	22 46 12	28 40 35	15 45.2	21 15.7	14 52.1	21 55.1	27 43.1	1 27.3	7 05.4	19 11.2	20 01.2	17 07.2
6 Su	2 55 00	15 22 18	4♍35 37	10♍31 57	15R46.0	22 48.1	16 04.6	22 40.7	28 03.7	1 34.3	7 05.1	19 08.7	19 59.9	17 05.8
7 M	2 58 57	16 20 22	16 30 13	22 31 01	15 45.8	24 22.5	17 17.0	23 26.3	28 24.2	1 41.4	7 04.8	19 06.1	19 58.6	17 04.4
8 Tu	3 02 53	17 18 25	28 34 52	4♎42 16	15 44.0	25 58.8	18 29.5	24 11.8	28 44.7	1 48.6	7 04.6	19 03.6	19 57.4	17 03.0
9 W	3 06 50	18 16 25	10♎53 39	17 09 21	15 39.9	27 37.1	19 41.9	24 57.3	29 05.1	1 55.9	7D04.6	19 01.1	19 56.1	17 01.6
10 Th	3 10 46	19 14 24	23 29 39	29 54 43	15 33.3	29 17.4	20 54.4	25 42.7	29 25.3	2 03.4	7 04.6	18 58.6	19 54.7	17 00.2
11 F	3 14 43	20 12 21	6♏24 36	12♏59 19	15 24.6	0♉59.7	22 06.9	26 28.1	29 45.5	2 11.0	7 04.7	18 56.0	19 53.4	16 58.9
12 Sa	3 18 39	21 10 16	19 38 42	26 22 32	15 14.3	2 43.9	23 19.4	27 13.4	0♈05.6	2 18.8	7 05.0	18 53.5	19 52.0	16 57.6
13 Su	3 22 36	22 08 11	3♐10 30	10♐02 14	15 03.5	4 30.1	24 32.0	27 58.7	0 25.7	2 26.6	7 05.3	18 51.0	19 50.7	16 56.2
14 M	3 26 32	23 06 03	16 57 16	23 55 06	14 53.3	6 18.3	25 44.5	28 43.9	0 45.6	2 34.6	7 05.8	18 48.5	19 49.3	16 55.0
15 Tu	3 30 29	24 03 55	0♑55 16	7♑57 15	14 44.8	8 08.5	26 57.1	29 29.1	1 05.4	2 42.7	7 06.4	18 46.0	19 47.9	16 53.7
16 W	3 34 26	25 01 45	15 00 34	22 04 47	14 38.7	10 00.7	28 09.7	0♉14.3	1 25.2	2 51.0	7 07.0	18 43.5	19 46.5	16 52.5
17 Th	3 38 22	25 59 33	29 09 31	6♒14 27	14 35.1	11 54.8	29 22.2	0 59.3	1 44.8	2 59.3	7 07.8	18 41.0	19 45.0	16 51.2
18 F	3 42 19	26 57 21	13♒19 19	20 23 52	14D33.7	13 50.9	0♉34.9	1 44.4	2 04.3	3 07.8	7 08.7	18 38.5	19 43.6	16 50.0
19 Sa	3 46 15	27 55 08	27 27 59	4♓31 29	14R33.6	15 48.9	1 47.5	2 29.4	2 23.8	3 16.4	7 09.7	18 36.0	19 42.1	16 48.9
20 Su	3 50 12	28 52 53	11♓34 17	18 36 17	14 33.7	17 48.8	3 00.1	3 14.3	2 43.1	3 25.1	7 10.7	18 33.5	19 40.6	16 47.7
21 M	3 54 08	29 50 37	25 37 21	2♈37 21	14 32.7	19 50.5	4 12.8	3 59.2	3 02.4	3 33.9	7 11.9	18 31.0	19 39.1	16 46.6
22 Tu	3 58 05	0♊48 21	9♈36 07	16 33 26	14 29.5	21 54.0	5 25.4	4 44.1	3 21.5	3 42.8	7 13.2	18 28.6	19 37.6	16 45.5
23 W	4 02 01	1 46 03	23 29 05	0♉22 45	14 23.6	23 59.1	6 38.1	5 28.8	3 40.5	3 51.8	7 14.6	18 26.1	19 36.1	16 44.4
24 Th	4 05 58	2 43 44	7♉14 08	14 02 53	14 14.9	26 05.8	7 50.8	6 13.6	3 59.4	4 01.0	7 16.1	18 23.7	19 34.6	16 43.4
25 F	4 09 55	3 41 24	20 48 41	27 31 10	14 03.9	28 13.8	9 03.5	6 58.3	4 18.2	4 10.2	7 17.7	18 21.3	19 33.0	16 42.4
26 Sa	4 13 51	4 39 03	4♊10 02	10♊45 01	13 51.5	0♊23.1	10 16.2	7 42.9	4 36.9	4 19.6	7 19.4	18 18.9	19 31.5	16 41.4
27 Su	4 17 48	5 36 40	17 15 55	23 42 35	13 39.0	2 33.4	11 28.9	8 27.5	4 55.5	4 29.0	7 21.2	18 16.5	19 29.9	16 40.4
28 M	4 21 44	6 34 17	0♋04 58	6♋23 04	13 27.5	4 44.5	12 41.7	9 12.0	5 13.9	4 38.6	7 23.1	18 14.1	19 28.4	16 39.5
29 Tu	4 25 41	7 31 52	12 37 02	18 47 02	13 17.9	6 56.2	13 54.4	9 56.5	5 32.3	4 48.2	7 25.1	18 11.8	19 26.8	16 38.5
30 W	4 29 37	8 29 26	24 53 22	0♌56 23	13 10.9	9 08.1	15 07.2	10 40.9	5 50.5	4 58.0	7 27.2	18 09.5	19 25.2	16 37.7
31 Th	4 33 34	9 26 58	6♌56 32	12 54 17	13 06.5	11 20.2	16 20.0	11 25.2	6 08.5	5 07.9	7 29.4	18 07.2	19 23.6	16 36.8

LONGITUDE — June 1979

Day	Sid.Time	☉	0 hr ☽	Noon ☽	True ☊	☿	♀	♂	⚳	♃	♄	♅	♆	♇
1 F	4 37 30	10♊24 29	18♌50 14	24♌44 56	13♍04.4	13♊31.9	17♉32.7	12♉09.5	6♈26.5	5♌17.8	7♍31.7	18♏04.9	19♐22.0	16♎36.0
2 Sa	4 41 27	11 21 59	0♍39 03	6♍33 14	13R03.8	15 43.2	18 45.5	12 53.7	6 44.3	5 27.8	7 34.1	18R02.6	19R20.4	16R35.2
3 Su	4 45 24	12 19 27	12 28 11	18 24 34	13 03.8	17 53.7	19 58.3	13 37.9	7 02.0	5 38.0	7 36.6	18 00.4	19 18.8	16 34.4
4 M	4 49 20	13 16 54	24 23 05	0♎24 24	13 03.2	20 03.1	21 11.1	14 22.0	7 19.6	5 48.2	7 39.2	17 58.2	19 17.2	16 33.7
5 Tu	4 53 17	14 14 20	6♎29 10	12 37 59	13 01.0	22 11.3	22 23.9	15 06.1	7 37.0	5 58.5	7 41.8	17 56.0	19 15.6	16 32.9
6 W	4 57 13	15 11 45	18 51 25	25 09 57	12 56.6	24 18.0	23 36.8	15 50.1	7 54.3	6 08.9	7 44.6	17 53.9	19 14.0	16 32.3
7 Th	5 01 10	16 09 09	1♏33 58	8♏03 46	12 49.7	26 23.0	24 49.6	16 34.0	8 11.4	6 19.3	7 47.5	17 51.7	19 12.4	16 31.6
8 F	5 05 06	17 06 32	14 39 30	21 21 14	12 40.3	28 26.2	26 02.4	17 17.9	8 28.5	6 29.9	7 50.5	17 49.6	19 10.8	16 31.0
9 Sa	5 09 03	18 03 53	28 08 52	5♐02 07	12 29.3	0♋27.5	27 15.3	18 01.8	8 45.3	6 40.5	7 53.5	17 47.6	19 09.1	16 30.4
10 Su	5 12 59	19 01 14	12♐00 37	19 03 51	12 17.7	2 26.6	28 28.2	18 45.5	9 02.1	6 51.3	7 56.7	17 45.5	19 07.5	16 29.9
11 M	5 16 56	19 58 34	26 11 09	3♑21 47	12 06.6	4 23.5	29 41.1	19 29.2	9 18.6	7 02.1	7 59.9	17 43.5	19 05.9	16 29.3
12 Tu	5 20 53	20 55 54	10♑34 57	17 49 52	11 57.3	6 18.2	0♊54.0	20 12.9	9 35.1	7 12.9	8 03.2	17 41.5	19 04.3	16 28.8
13 W	5 24 49	21 53 13	25 05 40	2♒21 37	11 50.5	8 10.6	2 06.9	20 56.5	9 51.4	7 23.9	8 06.6	17 39.6	19 02.7	16 28.4
14 Th	5 28 46	22 50 31	9♒36 59	16 51 10	11 46.4	10 00.6	3 19.9	21 40.0	10 07.5	7 34.9	8 10.1	17 37.7	19 01.0	16 27.9
15 F	5 32 42	23 47 49	24 03 39	1♓14 02	11D44.6	11 48.3	4 32.9	22 23.5	10 23.5	7 46.0	8 13.7	17 35.8	18 59.4	16 27.5
16 Sa	5 36 39	24 45 07	8♓21 59	15 27 20	11R44.4	13 33.5	5 45.8	23 07.0	10 39.3	7 57.2	8 17.4	17 33.9	18 57.8	16 27.2
17 Su	5 40 35	25 42 24	22 29 55	29 29 40	11 44.5	15 16.3	6 58.7	23 50.3	10 54.9	8 08.4	8 21.2	17 32.1	18 56.2	16 26.8
18 M	5 44 32	26 39 41	6♈26 35	13♈20 40	11 43.6	16 56.6	8 11.9	24 33.6	11 10.4	8 19.7	8 25.0	17 30.3	18 54.6	16 26.5
19 Tu	5 48 28	27 36 58	20 11 56	27 00 25	11 40.7	18 34.5	9 24.9	25 16.9	11 25.7	8 31.1	8 28.9	17 28.6	18 53.0	16 26.3
20 W	5 52 25	28 34 15	3♉46 06	10♉28 59	11 35.2	20 09.9	10 37.9	26 00.1	11 40.9	8 42.6	8 33.0	17 26.9	18 51.4	16 26.0
21 Th	5 56 22	29 31 31	17 09 02	23 46 13	11 27.1	21 42.8	11 51.0	26 43.2	11 55.9	8 54.1	8 37.1	17 25.2	18 49.8	16 25.8
22 F	6 00 18	0♋28 47	0♊20 26	6♊51 37	11 16.8	23 13.2	13 04.1	27 26.3	12 10.7	9 05.7	8 41.2	17 23.6	18 48.2	16 25.7
23 Sa	6 04 15	1 26 03	13 19 40	19 44 31	11 05.2	24 41.1	14 17.2	28 09.3	12 25.3	9 17.3	8 45.5	17 22.0	18 46.6	16 25.5
24 Su	6 08 11	2 23 19	26 06 05	2♋24 21	10 53.4	26 06.5	15 30.3	28 52.3	12 39.7	9 29.0	8 49.9	17 20.5	18 45.1	16 25.4
25 M	6 12 08	3 20 34	8♋39 18	14 50 59	10 42.5	27 29.2	16 43.5	29 35.2	12 54.0	9 40.8	8 54.3	17 19.0	18 43.5	16 25.4
26 Tu	6 16 04	4 17 49	20 59 29	27 04 58	10 33.4	28 49.3	17 56.6	0♊18.0	13 08.0	9 52.6	8 58.8	17 17.5	18 42.0	16D25.3
27 W	6 20 01	5 15 03	3♌07 37	9♌07 43	10 26.7	0♌06.8	19 09.8	1 00.7	13 21.9	10 04.5	9 03.4	17 16.1	18 40.4	16 25.3
28 Th	6 23 58	6 12 17	15 05 36	21 01 38	10 22.5	1 21.6	20 23.0	1 43.4	13 35.5	10 16.4	9 08.0	17 14.7	18 38.9	16 25.3
29 F	6 27 54	7 09 31	26 56 17	2♍50 03	10D20.5	2 33.5	21 36.2	2 26.1	13 49.0	10 28.4	9 12.7	17 13.4	18 37.4	16 25.4
30 Sa	6 31 51	8 06 44	8♍43 27	14 37 05	10 20.3	3 42.7	22 49.4	3 08.6	14 02.3	10 40.4	9 17.6	17 12.1	18 35.8	16 25.5

Astro Data	Dy Hr Mn
☽ 0S	8 9:53
♄ D	9 14:53
☽ 0N	21 14:09
♃⚼♆	27 13:59
☽ 0S	4 19:33
☽ 0N	17 20:42
♃⚺♄	19 4:59
♇ D	27 1:26

Planet Ingress		Dy Hr Mn
☿	♉	10 22:03
⚳	♈	12 5:16
♂	♉	16 4:25
♀	♉	18 0:29
☉	♊	21 15:54
☿	♊	26 7:44
☿	♋	9 6:32
♀	♊	11 18:13
☉	♋	21 23:56
♂	♊	26 1:55
☿	♌	27 9:51

Last Aspect Dy Hr Mn		☽ Ingress	Dy Hr Mn
2 4:51	♂ □	♌	3 1:56
4 21:19	♂ △	♍	5 14:41
7 6:57	♆ □	♎	8 2:48
10 10:40	☿ ☍	♏	10 12:10
12 2:01	☉ ☍	♐	12 18:25
14 20:43	♂ △	♑	14 22:25
16 23:16	♀ □	♒	17 1:26
18 23:57	☉ □	♓	19 4:18
21 6:53	☉ ⚹	♈	21 7:30
22 17:18	♆ △	♉	23 11:20
25 13:31	☿ ☌	♊	25 16:28
27 4:10	♆ ☍	♋	27 23:51
29 10:51	♅ △	♌	30 10:08

Last Aspect Dy Hr Mn		☽ Ingress	Dy Hr Mn
1 1:06	♆ △	♍	1 22:41
3 15:30	♀ △	♎	4 11:12
6 10:02	☿ △	♏	6 21:05
8 21:06	♀ ☍	♐	9 3:15
10 12:06	♆ ☌	♑	11 6:23
12 16:09	♂ △	♒	13 8:06
14 22:41	☉ △	♓	15 9:56
17 5:01	☉ □	♈	17 12:52
19 13:10	☉ ⚹	♉	19 17:18
21 17:41	♂ ☌	♊	21 23:23
23 10:12	♆ ☍	♋	24 7:24
26 15:52	☿ ☌	♌	26 17:47
28 10:33	♀ ⚹	♍	29 6:14

☽ Phases & Eclipses Dy Hr Mn	
4 4:25	☽ 13♌08
12 2:01	○ 20♏46
18 23:57	☾ 27♒26
26 0:00	● 4♊10
2 22:37	☽ 11♍47
10 11:55	○ 19♐01
17 5:01	☾ 25♓26
24 11:58	● 2♋23

Astro Data

1 May 1979
Julian Day # 28975
SVP 5♓33'00"
GC 26♐33.0 ⚳ 27♒30.5
Eris 14♈34.5 ⚵ 23♈11.6
⚷ 9♉27.2 ⚶ 7♈17.5
☽ Mean ☊ 14♍50.6

1 June 1979
Julian Day # 29006
SVP 5♓32'56"
GC 26♐33.1 ⚳ 2♓15.7
Eris 14♈50.6 ⚵ 10♉28.4
⚷ 11♉22.1 ⚶ 20♈50.1
☽ Mean ☊ 13♍12.1

July 1979 — LONGITUDE

Day	Sid.Time	☉	0 hr ☽	Noon ☽	True ☊	☿	♀	♂	⚳	♃	♄	♅	♆	♇
1 Su	6 35 47	9♋03 57	20♍31 33	26♍27 31	10♍21.0	4♌48.9	24♊02.6	3♊51.1	14♈15.3	10♌52.5	9♍22.4	17♏10.8	18♐34.3	16♎25.6
2 M	6 39 44	10 01 09	2♎25 38	8♎26 34	10R 21.5	5 52.2	25 15.9	4 33.6	14 28.2	11 04.6	9 27.4	17R 09.6	18R 32.9	16 25.8
3 Tu	6 43 40	10 58 21	14 31 00	20 39 35	10 21.0	6 52.3	26 29.2	5 16.0	14 40.8	11 16.8	9 32.4	17 08.5	18 31.4	16 26.0
4 W	6 47 37	11 55 33	26 52 55	3♏11 36	10 18.8	7 49.4	27 42.4	5 58.3	14 53.3	11 29.1	9 37.5	17 07.4	18 29.9	16 26.2
5 Th	6 51 33	12 52 44	9♏36 09	16 06 57	10 14.5	8 43.1	28 55.7	6 40.5	15 05.5	11 41.3	9 42.7	17 06.3	18 28.5	16 26.5
6 F	6 55 30	13 49 55	22 44 21	29 28 31	10 08.2	9 33.4	0♋09.1	7 22.7	15 17.5	11 53.7	9 47.9	17 05.3	18 27.0	16 26.8
7 Sa	6 59 26	14 47 06	6♐19 30	13♐17 09	10 00.5	10 20.3	1 22.4	8 04.8	15 29.2	12 06.0	9 53.2	17 04.3	18 25.6	16 27.1
8 Su	7 03 23	15 44 18	20 21 11	27 31 06	9 52.1	11 03.5	2 35.7	8 46.8	15 40.8	12 18.5	9 58.6	17 03.4	18 24.2	16 27.5
9 M	7 07 20	16 41 29	4♑46 16	12♑05 53	9 44.0	11 42.9	3 49.1	9 28.8	15 52.1	12 30.9	10 04.0	17 02.5	18 22.8	16 27.9
10 Tu	7 11 16	17 38 40	19 29 00	26 54 38	9 37.2	12 18.5	5 02.5	10 10.8	16 03.2	12 43.4	10 09.5	17 01.7	18 21.5	16 28.4
11 W	7 15 13	18 35 51	4♒21 43	11♒49 11	9 32.4	12 50.0	6 15.9	10 52.6	16 14.1	12 55.9	10 15.0	17 00.9	18 20.1	16 28.8
12 Th	7 19 09	19 33 03	19 16 00	26 41 16	9D 29.8	13 17.3	7 29.4	11 34.4	16 24.7	13 08.5	10 20.7	17 00.2	18 18.8	16 29.3
13 F	7 23 06	20 30 15	4♓04 07	11♓23 51	9 29.2	13 40.4	8 42.8	12 16.1	16 35.0	13 21.1	10 26.3	16 59.5	18 17.5	16 29.9
14 Sa	7 27 02	21 27 28	18 39 55	25 51 53	9 29.9	13 58.9	9 56.3	12 57.8	16 45.2	13 33.7	10 32.1	16 58.9	18 16.2	16 30.4
15 Su	7 30 59	22 24 41	2♈59 27	10♈02 26	9R 31.0	14 13.0	11 09.8	13 39.4	16 55.0	13 46.4	10 37.9	16 58.3	18 14.9	16 31.0
16 M	7 34 56	23 21 55	17 00 48	23 54 31	9 31.5	14 22.3	12 23.3	14 21.0	17 04.6	13 59.1	10 43.7	16 57.7	18 13.6	16 31.7
17 Tu	7 38 52	24 19 09	0♉43 41	7♉28 27	9 30.7	14R 26.9	13 36.9	15 02.4	17 14.0	14 11.9	10 49.7	16 57.3	18 12.4	16 32.3
18 W	7 42 49	25 16 24	14 08 56	20 45 20	9 28.1	14 26.6	14 50.5	15 43.8	17 23.1	14 24.6	10 55.6	16 56.8	18 11.2	16 33.0
19 Th	7 46 45	26 13 40	27 17 50	3♊46 36	9 23.6	14 21.5	16 04.0	16 25.2	17 31.9	14 37.4	11 01.7	16 56.4	18 10.0	16 33.8
20 F	7 50 42	27 10 57	10♊11 51	16 33 43	9 17.5	14 11.5	17 17.7	17 06.5	17 40.5	14 50.3	11 07.8	16 56.1	18 08.8	16 34.5
21 Sa	7 54 38	28 08 14	22 52 23	29 07 58	9 10.5	13 56.7	18 31.3	17 47.7	17 48.8	15 03.1	11 13.9	16 55.8	18 07.6	16 35.3
22 Su	7 58 35	29 05 32	5♋20 39	11♋30 33	9 03.3	13 37.2	19 45.0	18 28.8	17 56.8	15 16.0	11 20.1	16 55.6	18 06.5	16 36.2
23 M	8 02 31	0♌02 51	17 37 48	23 42 34	8 56.7	13 13.1	20 58.7	19 09.9	18 04.5	15 28.9	11 26.3	16 55.4	18 05.4	16 37.0
24 Tu	8 06 28	1 00 10	29 45 02	5♌45 21	8 51.2	12 44.8	22 12.4	19 50.9	18 11.9	15 41.9	11 32.6	16 55.3	18 04.3	16 37.9
25 W	8 10 25	1 57 30	11♌43 45	17 40 28	8 47.4	12 12.6	23 26.1	20 31.9	18 19.0	15 54.8	11 39.0	16D 55.2	18 03.3	16 38.8
26 Th	8 14 21	2 54 50	23 35 46	29 29 58	8D 45.4	11 36.8	24 39.9	21 12.7	18 25.9	16 07.8	11 45.4	16 55.2	18 02.2	16 39.8
27 F	8 18 18	3 52 11	5♍23 24	11♍16 28	8 44.9	10 57.9	25 53.6	21 53.5	18 32.4	16 20.8	11 51.8	16 55.2	18 01.2	16 40.8
28 Sa	8 22 14	4 49 32	17 09 35	23 03 12	8 45.8	10 16.7	27 07.4	22 34.3	18 38.7	16 33.8	11 58.3	16 55.3	18 00.2	16 41.8
29 Su	8 26 11	5 46 54	28 57 49	4♎53 58	8 47.3	9 33.5	28 21.2	23 14.9	18 44.6	16 46.8	12 04.9	16 55.4	17 59.2	16 42.9
30 M	8 30 07	6 44 16	10♎52 13	16 53 08	8 49.0	8 49.3	29 35.0	23 55.5	18 50.2	16 59.9	12 11.4	16 55.6	17 58.3	16 44.0
31 Tu	8 34 04	7 41 39	22 57 19	29 05 22	8R 50.2	8 04.8	0♌48.9	24 36.0	18 55.5	17 12.9	12 18.1	16 55.9	17 57.4	16 45.1

August 1979 — LONGITUDE

Day	Sid.Time	☉	0 hr ☽	Noon ☽	True ☊	☿	♀	♂	⚳	♃	♄	♅	♆	♇
1 W	8 38 00	8♌39 03	5♏17 53	11♏35 26	8♍50.5	7♌20.7	2♌02.7	25♊16.5	19♈00.5	17♌26.0	12♍24.7	16♏56.1	17♐56.5	16♎46.2
2 Th	8 41 57	9 36 27	17 58 34	24 27 45	8R 49.6	6R 37.9	3 16.6	25 56.8	19 05.2	17 39.1	12 31.4	16 56.5	17R 55.6	16 47.4
3 F	8 45 53	10 33 52	1♐03 26	7♐45 53	8 47.4	5 57.2	4 30.5	26 37.1	19 09.6	17 52.2	12 38.2	16 56.9	17 54.8	16 48.6
4 Sa	8 49 50	11 31 17	14 35 21	21 31 51	8 44.4	5 19.4	5 44.4	27 17.3	19 13.6	18 05.3	12 45.0	16 57.3	17 54.0	16 49.8
5 Su	8 53 47	12 28 44	28 35 17	5♑45 23	8 40.8	4 45.3	6 58.4	27 57.5	19 17.3	18 18.4	12 51.8	16 57.8	17 53.2	16 51.1
6 M	8 57 43	13 26 11	13♑01 42	20 23 33	8 37.3	4 15.4	8 12.3	28 37.6	19 20.7	18 31.6	12 58.7	16 58.4	17 52.5	16 52.4
7 Tu	9 01 40	14 23 38	27 50 09	5♒20 30	8 34.4	3 50.5	9 26.3	29 17.6	19 23.8	18 44.7	13 05.6	16 59.0	17 51.7	16 53.7
8 W	9 05 36	15 21 07	12♒53 33	20 28 07	8 32.5	3 31.1	10 40.3	29 57.5	19 26.5	18 57.9	13 12.5	16 59.6	17 51.0	16 55.1
9 Th	9 09 33	16 18 37	28 03 00	5♓37 02	8D 31.7	3 17.7	11 54.3	0♋37.4	19 28.9	19 11.0	13 19.5	17 00.3	17 50.4	16 56.4
10 F	9 13 29	17 16 08	13♓09 06	20 38 10	8 32.0	3D 10.6	13 08.3	1 17.2	19 30.9	19 24.2	13 26.5	17 01.1	17 49.7	16 57.8
11 Sa	9 17 26	18 13 40	28 03 21	5♈23 54	8 33.0	3 10.2	14 22.4	1 57.0	19 32.6	19 37.3	13 33.5	17 01.9	17 49.1	16 59.3
12 Su	9 21 22	19 11 14	12♈39 15	19 48 58	8 34.3	3 16.6	15 36.5	2 36.6	19 33.9	19 50.5	13 40.6	17 02.8	17 48.5	17 00.7
13 M	9 25 19	20 08 49	26 52 48	3♉50 35	8 35.4	3 30.1	16 50.6	3 16.2	19 34.9	20 03.6	13 47.7	17 03.7	17 48.0	17 02.2
14 Tu	9 29 16	21 06 26	10♉42 21	17 28 12	8R 36.0	3 50.8	18 04.7	3 55.7	19 35.5	20 16.8	13 54.8	17 04.6	17 47.5	17 03.7
15 W	9 33 12	22 04 04	24 08 19	0♊42 58	8 35.8	4 18.6	19 18.8	4 35.2	19R 35.8	20 29.9	14 02.0	17 05.6	17 47.0	17 05.3
16 Th	9 37 09	23 01 44	7♊12 27	13 37 08	8 34.9	4 53.5	20 33.0	5 14.5	19 35.7	20 43.1	14 09.2	17 06.7	17 46.5	17 06.8
17 F	9 41 05	23 59 25	19 57 21	26 13 30	8 33.4	5 35.5	21 47.2	5 53.8	19 35.2	20 56.2	14 16.4	17 07.8	17 46.1	17 08.4
18 Sa	9 45 02	24 57 08	2♋25 57	8♋35 04	8 31.6	6 24.5	23 01.4	6 33.1	19 34.4	21 09.4	14 23.6	17 09.0	17 45.7	17 10.1
19 Su	9 48 58	25 54 52	14 41 13	20 44 44	8 29.7	7 20.3	24 15.6	7 12.2	19 33.2	21 22.5	14 30.9	17 10.2	17 45.3	17 11.7
20 M	9 52 55	26 52 38	26 45 58	2♌45 12	8 28.0	8 22.6	25 29.9	7 51.3	19 31.7	21 35.7	14 38.2	17 11.5	17 45.0	17 13.4
21 Tu	9 56 51	27 50 25	8♌42 45	14 38 55	8 26.7	9 31.3	26 44.1	8 30.3	19 29.8	21 48.8	14 45.5	17 12.8	17 44.7	17 15.1
22 W	10 00 48	28 48 14	20 33 57	26 28 10	8 25.9	10 46.0	27 58.4	9 09.2	19 27.5	22 01.9	14 52.8	17 14.1	17 44.4	17 16.8
23 Th	10 04 45	29 46 04	2♍21 49	8♍15 12	8D 25.7	12 06.5	29 12.7	9 48.0	19 24.8	22 15.0	15 00.1	17 15.6	17 44.2	17 18.5
24 F	10 08 41	0♍43 56	14 08 36	20 02 18	8 25.9	13 32.2	0♍27.0	10 26.8	19 21.8	22 28.1	15 07.5	17 17.0	17 44.0	17 20.3
25 Sa	10 12 38	1 41 49	25 56 37	1♎51 55	8 26.3	15 03.0	1 41.4	11 05.5	19 18.4	22 41.2	15 14.9	17 18.5	17 43.8	17 22.1
26 Su	10 16 34	2 39 43	7♎48 31	13 46 49	8 27.0	16 38.3	2 55.7	11 44.1	19 14.6	22 54.3	15 22.3	17 20.1	17 43.6	17 23.9
27 M	10 20 31	3 37 38	19 47 13	25 50 07	8 27.5	18 17.6	4 10.1	12 22.6	19 10.5	23 07.3	15 29.7	17 21.7	17 43.5	17 25.7
28 Tu	10 24 27	4 35 35	1♏55 58	8♏05 14	8 28.0	20 00.6	5 24.4	13 01.0	19 06.0	23 20.3	15 37.1	17 23.3	17 43.4	17 27.6
29 W	10 28 24	5 33 34	14 18 22	20 35 51	8 28.2	21 46.8	6 38.8	13 39.3	19 01.1	23 33.3	15 44.6	17 25.0	17D 43.4	17 29.5
30 Th	10 32 20	6 31 33	26 58 07	3♐25 38	8R 28.3	23 35.6	7 53.2	14 17.6	18 55.9	23 46.3	15 52.0	17 26.8	17 43.4	17 31.4
31 F	10 36 17	7 29 34	9♐58 47	16 37 56	8D 28.3	25 26.6	9 07.6	14 55.8	18 50.3	23 59.3	15 59.5	17 28.6	17 43.4	17 33.3

Astro Data	Dy Hr Mn
☽0S	2 4:59
☽0N	15 3:42
☿R	17 22:43
♅D	26 10:59
♃✶♇	29 4:04
☽0S	29 13:05
♃□♅	30 4:03
♃△♆	3 16:27
☿D	11 1:31
☽0N	11 12:14
⚳R	15 17:59
♅⚻♇	16 5:19
☽0S	25 19:33
♆D	30 11:14

Planet Ingress	Dy Hr Mn
♀ ♋	6 9:02
☉ ♌	23 10:49
♀ ♌	30 20:07
♂ ♋	8 13:28
☉ ♍	23 17:47
♀ ♍	24 3:16

Last Aspect Dy Hr Mn		☽ Ingress	Dy Hr Mn
1 6:34	♀ □	♎	1 19:08
4 0:27	♀ △	♏	4 5:57
5 13:48	♅ ☌	♐	6 12:56
7 20:44	♆ ☌	♑	8 16:07
9 20:02	♅ ✶	♒	10 16:59
11 22:29	♆ ✶	♓	12 17:23
14 4:07	☉ △	♈	14 18:57
16 10:59	☉ □	♉	16 22:43
18 20:56	☉ ✶	♊	19 5:00
20 15:00	♆ ☍	♋	21 13:40
23 5:59	♀ ☌	♌	24 0:30
25 18:08	♂ ✶	♍	26 13:01
28 21:14	♀ ✶	♎	29 2:06
31 2:43	♂ △	♏	31 13:46

Last Aspect Dy Hr Mn		☽ Ingress	Dy Hr Mn
1 23:11	♃ □	♐	2 22:05
4 22:17	♂ ☍	♑	5 2:23
6 6:26	♅ ✶	♒	7 3:28
8 9:35	♃ ☍	♓	9 3:05
10 7:30	♆ □	♈	11 3:10
12 12:03	♃ △	♉	13 5:21
14 19:02	☉ □	♊	15 10:41
17 7:21	☉ ✶	♋	17 19:17
19 4:56	♇ □	♌	20 6:28
22 17:10	☉ ☌	♍	22 19:11
24 7:19	♆ □	♎	25 8:13
27 6:32	♃ ✶	♏	27 20:12
29 17:41	♃ □	♐	30 5:39

☽ Phases & Eclipses Dy Hr Mn	
2 15:24	☽ 10♎09
9 19:59	○ 17♑01
16 10:59	☾ 23♈19
24 1:41	● 0♌36
1 5:57	☽ 8♏25
8 3:21	○ 15♒00
14 19:02	☾ 21♉23
22 17:10	● 29♌01
22 17:21:48	● A 06'03"
30 18:09	☽ 6♐46

Astro Data

1 July 1979
Julian Day # 29036
SVP 5♓32'51"
GC 26♐33.2 ⚴ 2♓29.2R
Eris 14♈58.5 ⚵ 27♉17.8
⚷ 12♉52.8 ⚶ 2♉28.2
☽ Mean ☊ 11♍36.8

1 August 1979
Julian Day # 29067
SVP 5♓32'47"
GC 26♐33.2 ⚴ 27♒25.3R
Eris 14♈56.8R ⚵ 14♊23.8
⚷ 13♉47.3 ⚶ 12♉06.4
☽ Mean ☊ 9♍58.3

LONGITUDE — September 1979

Day	Sid.Time	☉	0 hr ☽	Noon ☽	True ☊	☿	♀	♂	⚳	♃	♄	♅	♆	♇
1 Sa	10 40 14	8♍27 37	23♐23 22	0♑15 16	8♍28.3	27♌19.5	10♍22.1	15♋33.9	18♈44.4	24♌12.3	16♍07.0	17♏30.4	17♐43.4	17♎35.2
2 Su	10 44 10	9 25 40	7♑13 43	14 18 40	8 28.4	29 13.8	11 36.5	16 11.9	18R 38.1	24 25.2	16 14.5	17 32.3	17 43.5	17 37.2
3 M	10 48 07	10 23 45	21 29 56	28 47 09	8 28.5	1♍09.1	12 51.0	16 49.8	18 31.4	24 38.1	16 22.0	17 34.3	17 43.6	17 39.2
4 Tu	10 52 03	11 21 52	6♒09 46	13♒37 07	8 28.7	3 05.1	14 05.4	17 27.7	18 24.4	24 50.9	16 29.5	17 36.2	17 43.8	17 41.2
5 W	10 56 00	12 20 00	21 08 19	28 42 24	8R 28.9	5 01.4	15 19.9	18 05.4	18 17.1	25 03.8	16 37.0	17 38.3	17 44.0	17 43.2
6 Th	10 59 56	13 18 10	6♓18 13	13♓54 36	8 28.9	6 57.9	16 34.4	18 43.1	18 09.5	25 16.6	16 44.5	17 40.3	17 44.2	17 45.2
7 F	11 03 53	14 16 21	21 30 21	29 04 16	8 28.7	8 54.2	17 48.8	19 20.7	18 01.5	25 29.4	16 52.0	17 42.4	17 44.4	17 47.3
8 Sa	11 07 49	15 14 34	6♈35 12	14♈02 07	8 28.1	10 50.3	19 03.3	19 58.2	17 53.1	25 42.2	16 59.6	17 44.6	17 44.7	17 49.3
9 Su	11 11 46	16 12 49	21 24 09	28 40 32	8 27.3	12 45.8	20 17.9	20 35.6	17 44.5	25 54.9	17 07.1	17 46.8	17 45.0	17 51.4
10 M	11 15 43	17 11 06	5♉50 42	12♉54 17	8 26.4	14 40.8	21 32.4	21 13.0	17 35.5	26 07.6	17 14.6	17 49.0	17 45.4	17 53.5
11 Tu	11 19 39	18 09 25	19 51 03	26 40 58	8 25.5	16 35.0	22 46.9	21 50.2	17 26.2	26 20.2	17 22.1	17 51.3	17 45.7	17 55.6
12 W	11 23 36	19 07 47	3♊24 07	10♊00 42	8D 24.9	18 28.4	24 01.5	22 27.4	17 16.6	26 32.9	17 29.7	17 53.6	17 46.1	17 57.8
13 Th	11 27 32	20 06 10	16 31 02	22 55 32	8 24.8	20 20.9	25 16.1	23 04.4	17 06.8	26 45.5	17 37.2	17 56.0	17 46.6	17 59.9
14 F	11 31 29	21 04 36	29 14 39	5♋28 52	8 25.2	22 12.5	26 30.6	23 41.4	16 56.6	26 58.0	17 44.7	17 58.4	17 47.1	18 02.1
15 Sa	11 35 25	22 03 04	11♋38 43	17 44 45	8 26.1	24 03.1	27 45.2	24 18.3	16 46.1	27 10.5	17 52.2	18 00.8	17 47.6	18 04.3
16 Su	11 39 22	23 01 34	23 47 29	29 47 28	8 27.4	25 52.7	28 59.8	24 55.1	16 35.4	27 23.0	17 59.8	18 03.3	17 48.1	18 06.5
17 M	11 43 18	24 00 06	5♌45 11	11♌41 10	8 28.7	27 41.3	0♎14.4	25 31.8	16 24.4	27 35.4	18 07.3	18 05.9	17 48.7	18 08.7
18 Tu	11 47 15	24 58 40	17 35 50	23 29 39	8 29.9	29 28.9	1 29.1	26 08.4	16 13.1	27 47.8	18 14.8	18 08.4	17 49.3	18 10.9
19 W	11 51 12	25 57 16	29 23 01	5♍16 18	8R 30.5	1♎15.4	2 43.7	26 45.0	16 01.6	28 00.2	18 22.3	18 11.0	17 49.9	18 13.1
20 Th	11 55 08	26 55 54	11♍09 52	17 04 00	8 30.3	3 00.9	3 58.4	27 21.4	15 49.9	28 12.5	18 29.7	18 13.7	17 50.6	18 15.4
21 F	11 59 05	27 54 33	22 59 02	28 55 13	8 29.1	4 45.4	5 13.0	27 57.7	15 38.0	28 24.7	18 37.2	18 16.3	17 51.3	18 17.6
22 Sa	12 03 01	28 53 15	4♎52 49	10♎52 04	8 26.9	6 28.9	6 27.7	28 33.9	15 25.8	28 36.9	18 44.7	18 19.0	17 52.0	18 19.9
23 Su	12 06 58	29 51 59	16 53 11	22 56 25	8 23.8	8 11.4	7 42.3	29 10.0	15 13.5	28 49.1	18 52.1	18 21.8	17 52.8	18 22.2
24 M	12 10 54	0♎50 45	29 01 58	5♏10 05	8 20.2	9 52.9	8 57.0	29 46.0	15 00.9	29 01.1	18 59.6	18 24.6	17 53.6	18 24.5
25 Tu	12 14 51	1 49 33	11♏21 00	17 34 57	8 16.5	11 33.4	10 11.7	0♌21.9	14 48.2	29 13.2	19 07.0	18 27.4	17 54.4	18 26.8
26 W	12 18 47	2 48 22	23 52 11	0♐12 58	8 13.2	13 13.0	11 26.4	0 57.7	14 35.4	29 25.2	19 14.4	18 30.3	17 55.2	18 29.1
27 Th	12 22 44	3 47 13	6♐37 35	13 06 18	8 10.6	14 51.7	12 41.0	1 33.4	14 22.4	29 37.1	19 21.8	18 33.2	17 56.1	18 31.4
28 F	12 26 40	4 46 06	19 39 23	26 17 06	8D 09.2	16 29.4	13 55.7	2 09.0	14 09.3	29 49.0	19 29.1	18 36.1	17 57.1	18 33.7
29 Sa	12 30 37	5 45 01	2♑59 42	9♑47 23	8 09.0	18 06.3	15 10.4	2 44.4	13 56.0	0♍00.8	19 36.5	18 39.0	17 58.0	18 36.0
30 Su	12 34 34	6 43 57	16 40 19	23 38 34	8 09.8	19 42.2	16 25.1	3 19.8	13 42.7	0 12.5	19 43.8	18 42.0	17 59.0	18 38.4

LONGITUDE — October 1979

Day	Sid.Time	☉	0 hr ☽	Noon ☽	True ☊	☿	♀	♂	⚳	♃	♄	♅	♆	♇
1 M	12 38 30	7♎42 55	0♒42 08	7♒50 56	8♍11.2	21♎17.3	17♎39.8	3♌55.1	13♈29.3	0♍24.2	19♍51.1	18♏45.0	18♐00.0	18♎40.7
2 Tu	12 42 27	8 41 55	15 04 45	22 23 12	8 12.6	22 51.6	18 54.5	4 30.2	13R 15.8	0 35.9	19 58.4	18 48.1	18 01.1	18 43.1
3 W	12 46 23	9 40 57	29 45 47	7♓11 51	8R 13.3	24 25.0	20 09.2	5 05.2	13 02.2	0 47.4	20 05.6	18 51.2	18 02.1	18 45.4
4 Th	12 50 20	10 40 00	14♓40 37	22 11 09	8 12.6	25 57.5	21 23.9	5 40.1	12 48.6	0 58.9	20 12.9	18 54.3	18 03.2	18 47.8
5 F	12 54 16	11 39 05	29 42 25	7♈13 19	8 10.4	27 29.3	22 38.6	6 14.9	12 35.0	1 10.3	20 20.1	18 57.4	18 04.4	18 50.2
6 Sa	12 58 13	12 38 12	14♈42 44	22 09 33	8 06.5	29 00.2	23 53.3	6 49.6	12 21.4	1 21.7	20 27.2	19 00.6	18 05.5	18 52.5
7 Su	13 02 09	13 37 22	29 32 42	6♉51 15	8 01.4	0♏30.3	25 08.0	7 24.2	12 07.8	1 33.0	20 34.4	19 03.8	18 06.7	18 54.9
8 M	13 06 06	14 36 33	14♉04 23	21 11 25	7 55.8	1 59.6	26 22.7	7 58.7	11 54.2	1 44.2	20 41.5	19 07.0	18 07.9	18 57.3
9 Tu	13 10 03	15 35 47	28 11 53	5♊05 30	7 50.3	3 28.1	27 37.4	8 33.0	11 40.6	1 55.3	20 48.6	19 10.2	18 09.2	18 59.7
10 W	13 13 59	16 35 03	11♊52 08	18 31 50	7 45.8	4 55.7	28 52.1	9 07.2	11 27.0	2 06.4	20 55.6	19 13.5	18 10.4	19 02.0
11 Th	13 17 56	17 34 22	25 04 46	1♋31 17	7 42.8	6 22.6	0♏06.9	9 41.3	11 13.6	2 17.4	21 02.7	19 16.8	18 11.7	19 04.4
12 F	13 21 52	18 33 43	7♋51 48	14 06 48	7D 41.4	7 48.6	1 21.6	10 15.3	11 00.2	2 28.3	21 09.7	19 20.1	18 13.1	19 06.8
13 Sa	13 25 49	19 33 06	20 16 51	26 22 36	7 41.5	9 13.7	2 36.3	10 49.1	10 46.9	2 39.1	21 16.6	19 23.5	18 14.4	19 09.2
14 Su	13 29 45	20 32 31	2♌24 39	8♌23 39	7 42.7	10 38.0	3 51.0	11 22.9	10 33.7	2 49.9	21 23.5	19 26.8	18 15.8	19 11.6
15 M	13 33 42	21 31 59	14 20 16	20 15 08	7 44.3	12 01.3	5 05.8	11 56.4	10 20.6	3 00.5	21 30.4	19 30.2	18 17.2	19 14.0
16 Tu	13 37 38	22 31 29	26 08 51	2♍02 01	7R 45.4	13 23.7	6 20.5	12 29.9	10 07.6	3 11.1	21 37.3	19 33.6	18 18.7	19 16.4
17 W	13 41 35	23 31 01	7♍55 11	13 48 52	7 45.4	14 45.1	7 35.3	13 03.2	9 54.8	3 21.6	21 44.1	19 37.1	18 20.1	19 18.7
18 Th	13 45 32	24 30 35	19 43 32	25 39 36	7 43.5	16 05.4	8 50.0	13 36.4	9 42.2	3 32.0	21 50.8	19 40.5	18 21.6	19 21.1
19 F	13 49 28	25 30 12	1♎37 27	7♎37 23	7 39.4	17 24.7	10 04.7	14 09.4	9 29.7	3 42.3	21 57.5	19 44.0	18 23.1	19 23.5
20 Sa	13 53 25	26 29 50	13 39 42	19 44 35	7 33.1	18 42.7	11 19.5	14 42.3	9 17.4	3 52.5	22 04.2	19 47.5	18 24.7	19 25.9
21 Su	13 57 21	27 29 31	25 52 13	2♏02 44	7 24.9	19 59.5	12 34.2	15 15.0	9 05.4	4 02.6	22 10.9	19 51.0	18 26.2	19 28.2
22 M	14 01 18	28 29 13	8♏16 13	14 32 43	7 15.5	21 14.9	13 49.0	15 47.6	8 53.5	4 12.7	22 17.4	19 54.5	18 27.8	19 30.6
23 Tu	14 05 14	29 28 58	20 52 16	27 14 52	7 05.7	22 28.9	15 03.7	16 20.1	8 41.9	4 22.6	22 24.0	19 58.1	18 29.5	19 33.0
24 W	14 09 11	0♏28 44	3♐40 32	10♐09 15	6 56.6	23 41.3	16 18.5	16 52.3	8 30.5	4 32.4	22 30.5	20 01.7	18 31.1	19 35.3
25 Th	14 13 07	1 28 32	16 41 02	23 15 54	6 49.0	24 51.9	17 33.2	17 24.5	8 19.4	4 42.2	22 36.9	20 05.2	18 32.8	19 37.7
26 F	14 17 04	2 28 22	29 53 53	6♑35 02	6 43.7	26 00.5	18 48.0	17 56.4	8 08.5	4 51.8	22 43.3	20 08.8	18 34.4	19 40.0
27 Sa	14 21 00	3 28 14	13♑19 25	20 07 07	6 40.7	27 07.1	20 02.7	18 28.2	7 57.9	5 01.3	22 49.6	20 12.5	18 36.2	19 42.4
28 Su	14 24 57	4 28 07	26 58 12	3♒52 46	6D 39.8	28 11.4	21 17.5	18 59.9	7 47.6	5 10.7	22 55.9	20 16.1	18 37.9	19 44.7
29 M	14 28 54	5 28 02	10♒50 51	17 52 27	6 40.3	29 13.0	22 32.2	19 31.4	7 37.6	5 20.0	23 02.2	20 19.7	18 39.6	19 47.0
30 Tu	14 32 50	6 27 59	24 57 34	2♓06 02	6R 41.0	0♐11.8	23 46.9	20 02.7	7 27.9	5 29.2	23 08.3	20 23.4	18 41.4	19 49.3
31 W	14 36 47	7 27 57	9♓17 41	16 32 11	6 40.6	1 07.3	25 01.7	20 33.8	7 18.5	5 38.3	23 14.5	20 27.0	18 43.2	19 51.6

Astro Data

	Dy Hr Mn
♆✱♇	5 22:25
☽0N	7 22:24
♅⊻♆	8 13:23
♄□♆	14 19:58
♄✱♅	17 5:12
♄⊻♇	17 18:24
♀0S	19 16:41
☿0S	20 4:39
☽0S	22 1:20
☉0S	23 15:17
♅⊻♇	24 6:11
☽0N	5 9:20
☽0S	19 7:54
♃∠♇	24 21:21

Planet Ingress

		Dy Hr Mn
☿	♍	2 21:39
♀	♎	17 7:21
☿	♎	18 18:59
☉	♎	23 15:16
♂	♌	24 21:21
♃	♍	29 10:23
☿	♏	7 3:55
♀	♏	11 9:48
☉	♏	24 0:28
☿	♐	30 7:06

Last Aspect / ☽ Ingress (September)

Last Aspect Dy Hr Mn			☽ Ingress	Dy Hr Mn
1 6:05	☿	△	♑	1 11:34
2 17:33	♇	□	♒	3 13:59
5 6:09	♃	☍	♓	5 14:03
6 19:55	♂	△	♈	7 13:29
9 7:22	♃	△	♉	9 14:12
11 11:23	♃	□	♊	11 17:54
13 19:23	♃	✱	♋	14 1:27
16 10:13	♀	✱	♌	16 12:25
18 20:55	♃	☌	♍	19 1:15
21 9:58	♂	✱	♎	21 14:11
24 0:54	♂	□	♏	24 1:54
26 10:29	♃	□	♐	26 11:36
28 18:26	♃	△	♑	28 18:40
30 5:13	♄	△	♒	30 22:49

Last Aspect / ☽ Ingress (October)

Last Aspect Dy Hr Mn			☽ Ingress	Dy Hr Mn
2 12:52	☿	△	♓	3 0:23
4 8:50	♄	☍	♈	5 0:28
7 0:23	☿	☍	♉	7 0:45
8 11:09	♄	△	♊	9 3:07
11 9:05	♀	△	♋	11 9:09
13 1:51	♄	✱	♌	13 19:12
15 14:51	☉	✱	♍	16 7:51
18 4:13	♄	☌	♎	18 20:44
21 2:23	☉	☌	♏	21 8:02
23 2:48	♄	✱	♐	23 17:09
25 10:49	♄	□	♑	26 0:11
28 1:18	☿	✱	♒	28 5:16
29 20:40	♀	□	♓	30 8:29

☽ Phases & Eclipses

Dy Hr Mn		
6 10:59	○	13♓16
6 10:54	☍	T 1.094
13 6:15	☾	19♊52
21 9:47	●	27♍49
29 4:20	☽	5♑26
5 19:35	○	11♈58
12 21:24	☾	18♋57
21 2:23	●	27♎06
28 13:06	☽	4♒31

Astro Data

1 September 1979
Julian Day # 29098
SVP 5♓32'43"
GC 26♐33.3 ⚵ 19♒42.5R
Eris 14♈45.8R ⚴ 0♋34.8
⚷ 13♉50.2R ⚶ 17♉47.1
☽ Mean ☊ 8♍19.8

1 October 1979
Julian Day # 29128
SVP 5♓32'41"
GC 26♐33.4 ⚵ 15♒00.0R
Eris 14♈29.1R ⚴ 14♋22.8
⚷ 13♉03.3R ⚶ 17♉29.8R
☽ Mean ☊ 6♍44.4

November 1979

LONGITUDE

Day	Sid.Time	☉	0 hr ☽	Noon ☽	True ☊	☿	♀	♂	⚳	♃	♄	♅	♆	♇
1 Th	14 40 43	8♏27 56	23♓49 06	1♈07 53	6♍38.4	1♐59.4	26♏16.4	21♌04.8	7♈09.4	5♍47.3	23♍20.5	20♏30.7	18♐45.0	19♎53.9
2 F	14 44 40	9 27 58	8♈27 52	15 48 17	6R 33.5	2 47.4	27 31.1	21 35.6	7R 00.6	5 56.1	23 26.5	20 34.4	18 46.9	19 56.2
3 Sa	14 48 36	10 28 01	23 08 16	0♉26 55	6 25.9	3 31.1	28 45.8	22 06.2	6 52.2	6 04.9	23 32.5	20 38.0	18 48.7	19 58.5
4 Su	14 52 33	11 28 05	7♉43 17	14 56 28	6 16.2	4 09.8	0♐00.5	22 36.6	6 44.1	6 13.5	23 38.3	20 41.7	18 50.6	20 00.7
5 M	14 56 29	12 28 12	22 05 37	29 09 59	6 05.3	4 43.0	1 15.2	23 06.9	6 36.4	6 22.0	23 44.2	20 45.4	18 52.5	20 03.0
6 Tu	15 00 26	13 28 21	6♊08 56	13♊02 00	5 54.5	5 10.2	2 29.9	23 37.0	6 29.0	6 30.4	23 49.9	20 49.1	18 54.4	20 05.2
7 W	15 04 23	14 28 32	19 48 50	26 29 18	5 44.8	5 30.6	3 44.6	24 06.8	6 21.9	6 38.6	23 55.6	20 52.9	18 56.3	20 07.5
8 Th	15 08 19	15 28 44	3♋03 23	9♋31 14	5 37.2	5 43.6	4 59.3	24 36.5	6 15.2	6 46.8	24 01.3	20 56.6	18 58.3	20 09.7
9 F	15 12 16	16 28 59	15 53 06	22 09 24	5 32.1	5R 48.6	6 14.0	25 06.0	6 08.9	6 54.8	24 06.8	21 00.3	19 00.3	20 11.9
10 Sa	15 16 12	17 29 16	28 20 36	4♌27 16	5 29.4	5 44.8	7 28.7	25 35.3	6 02.9	7 02.7	24 12.3	21 04.0	19 02.2	20 14.1
11 Su	15 20 09	18 29 34	10♌30 01	16 29 30	5D 28.6	5 31.7	8 43.4	26 04.4	5 57.3	7 10.4	24 17.8	21 07.8	19 04.2	20 16.2
12 M	15 24 05	19 29 55	22 26 26	28 21 29	5R 28.7	5 08.8	9 58.1	26 33.3	5 52.1	7 18.0	24 23.1	21 11.5	19 06.3	20 18.4
13 Tu	15 28 02	20 30 17	4♍15 23	10♍08 48	5 28.7	4 35.7	11 12.8	27 02.0	5 47.2	7 25.5	24 28.4	21 15.2	19 08.3	20 20.5
14 W	15 31 58	21 30 41	16 02 26	21 56 54	5 27.5	3 52.5	12 27.5	27 30.4	5 42.8	7 32.8	24 33.6	21 19.0	19 10.3	20 22.7
15 Th	15 35 55	22 31 08	27 52 49	3♎50 44	5 24.2	2 59.5	13 42.2	27 58.6	5 38.7	7 40.0	24 38.8	21 22.7	19 12.4	20 24.8
16 F	15 39 52	23 31 36	9♎51 10	15 54 33	5 18.1	1 57.4	14 56.9	28 26.6	5 35.0	7 47.1	24 43.8	21 26.4	19 14.5	20 26.9
17 Sa	15 43 48	24 32 05	22 01 15	28 11 33	5 09.2	0 47.4	16 11.6	28 54.4	5 31.7	7 54.0	24 48.8	21 30.2	19 16.6	20 28.9
18 Su	15 47 45	25 32 37	4♏25 42	10♏43 48	4 57.7	29♏31.3	17 26.2	29 21.9	5 28.7	8 00.8	24 53.7	21 33.9	19 18.7	20 31.0
19 M	15 51 41	26 33 10	17 05 54	23 32 00	4 44.6	28 11.4	18 40.9	29 49.2	5 26.2	8 07.4	24 58.6	21 37.6	19 20.8	20 33.0
20 Tu	15 55 38	27 33 45	0♐01 58	6♐35 38	4 30.9	26 50.0	19 55.6	0♍16.2	5 24.0	8 13.9	25 03.3	21 41.4	19 22.9	20 35.0
21 W	15 59 34	28 34 21	13 12 48	19 53 12	4 17.9	25 29.9	21 10.3	0 43.0	5 22.3	8 20.2	25 08.0	21 45.1	19 25.0	20 37.0
22 Th	16 03 31	29 34 59	26 36 33	3♑22 33	4 06.9	24 13.7	22 24.9	1 09.5	5 20.9	8 26.4	25 12.6	21 48.8	19 27.2	20 39.0
23 F	16 07 27	0♐35 38	10♑10 57	17 01 29	3 58.7	23 04.0	23 39.6	1 35.7	5 19.9	8 32.4	25 17.1	21 52.5	19 29.4	20 41.0
24 Sa	16 11 24	1 36 18	23 53 56	0♒48 07	3 53.6	22 02.7	24 54.3	2 01.7	5 19.3	8 38.3	25 21.6	21 56.2	19 31.5	20 42.9
25 Su	16 15 21	2 36 59	7♒43 53	14 41 08	3 51.2	21 11.4	26 08.9	2 27.4	5D 19.1	8 44.0	25 25.9	21 59.9	19 33.7	20 44.8
26 M	16 19 17	3 37 41	21 39 49	28 39 52	3 50.6	20 31.1	27 23.5	2 52.8	5 19.3	8 49.5	25 30.2	22 03.6	19 35.9	20 46.7
27 Tu	16 23 14	4 38 24	5♓41 16	12♓43 56	3 50.5	20 02.4	28 38.2	3 17.9	5 19.8	8 54.9	25 34.4	22 07.3	19 38.1	20 48.6
28 W	16 27 10	5 39 09	19 47 50	26 52 49	3 49.6	19 45.3	29 52.8	3 42.8	5 20.8	9 00.1	25 38.4	22 11.0	19 40.3	20 50.5
29 Th	16 31 07	6 39 54	3♈58 43	11♈05 17	3 46.5	19D 39.5	1♑07.4	4 07.3	5 22.1	9 05.2	25 42.4	22 14.6	19 42.5	20 52.3
30 F	16 35 03	7 40 40	18 12 12	25 19 03	3 40.7	19 44.5	2 22.0	4 31.6	5 23.7	9 10.1	25 46.4	22 18.2	19 44.7	20 54.1

December 1979

LONGITUDE

Day	Sid.Time	☉	0 hr ☽	Noon ☽	True ☊	☿	♀	♂	⚳	♃	♄	♅	♆	♇
1 Sa	16 39 00	8♐41 27	2♉25 21	9♉30 34	3♍31.8	19♏59.5	3♑36.5	4♍55.5	5♈25.8	9♍14.8	25♍50.2	22♏21.9	19♐47.0	20♎55.8
2 Su	16 42 56	9 42 15	16 34 05	23 35 18	3R 20.5	20 23.6	4 51.1	5 19.2	5 28.2	9 19.4	25 53.9	22 25.5	19 49.2	20 57.6
3 M	16 46 53	10 43 04	0♊33 35	7♊28 21	3 07.8	20 56.0	6 05.6	5 42.5	5 31.0	9 23.8	25 57.5	22 29.1	19 51.4	20 59.3
4 Tu	16 50 50	11 43 55	14 19 04	21 05 15	2 55.0	21 35.9	7 20.2	6 05.5	5 34.2	9 28.0	26 01.1	22 32.7	19 53.7	21 01.0
5 W	16 54 46	12 44 47	27 46 35	4♋22 46	2 43.2	22 22.3	8 34.7	6 28.2	5 37.7	9 32.0	26 04.5	22 36.3	19 55.9	21 02.7
6 Th	16 58 43	13 45 39	10♋53 43	17 19 23	2 33.6	23 14.6	9 49.2	6 50.5	5 41.5	9 35.9	26 07.9	22 39.8	19 58.2	21 04.4
7 F	17 02 39	14 46 33	23 39 54	29 55 29	2 26.8	24 11.9	11 03.7	7 12.5	5 45.8	9 39.6	26 11.2	22 43.4	20 00.4	21 06.0
8 Sa	17 06 36	15 47 29	6♌06 27	12♌13 13	2 22.7	25 13.8	12 18.2	7 34.2	5 50.3	9 43.1	26 14.3	22 46.9	20 02.7	21 07.6
9 Su	17 10 32	16 48 25	18 16 16	24 16 10	2D 21.0	26 19.5	13 32.7	7 55.4	5 55.2	9 46.5	26 17.4	22 50.4	20 05.0	21 09.1
10 M	17 14 29	17 49 22	0♍13 32	6♍09 00	2 20.8	27 28.5	14 47.2	8 16.3	6 00.5	9 49.6	26 20.4	22 53.9	20 07.2	21 10.7
11 Tu	17 18 25	18 50 21	12 03 15	17 56 59	2R 21.0	28 40.5	16 01.6	8 36.8	6 06.1	9 52.6	26 23.3	22 57.4	20 09.5	21 12.2
12 W	17 22 22	19 51 21	23 50 54	29 45 43	2 20.6	29 55.0	17 16.1	8 57.0	6 12.0	9 55.4	26 26.0	23 00.8	20 11.8	21 13.7
13 Th	17 26 19	20 52 21	5♎42 06	11♎40 42	2 18.4	1♐11.8	18 30.5	9 16.7	6 18.3	9 58.0	26 28.7	23 04.2	20 14.0	21 15.1
14 F	17 30 15	21 53 23	17 42 11	23 47 05	2 13.9	2 30.4	19 44.9	9 36.0	6 24.9	10 00.4	26 31.3	23 07.6	20 16.3	21 16.6
15 Sa	17 34 12	22 54 26	29 55 56	6♏09 11	2 06.7	3 50.7	20 59.3	9 54.9	6 31.8	10 02.7	26 33.7	23 11.0	20 18.6	21 18.0
16 Su	17 38 08	23 55 30	12♏27 11	18 50 11	1 57.1	5 12.5	22 13.7	10 13.4	6 39.0	10 04.7	26 36.1	23 14.4	20 20.8	21 19.3
17 M	17 42 05	24 56 35	25 18 21	1♐51 43	1 45.9	6 35.4	23 28.1	10 31.5	6 46.6	10 06.6	26 38.4	23 17.7	20 23.1	21 20.7
18 Tu	17 46 01	25 57 40	8♐30 13	15 13 39	1 33.9	7 59.5	24 42.4	10 49.1	6 54.5	10 08.3	26 40.5	23 21.0	20 25.3	21 22.0
19 W	17 49 58	26 58 46	22 01 44	28 54 03	1 22.6	9 24.6	25 56.8	11 06.2	7 02.7	10 09.7	26 42.6	23 24.3	20 27.6	21 23.3
20 Th	17 53 55	27 59 53	5♑50 08	12♑49 27	1 12.9	10 50.5	27 11.1	11 22.9	7 11.2	10 11.0	26 44.5	23 27.6	20 29.9	21 24.5
21 F	17 57 51	29 01 00	19 51 24	26 55 26	1 05.8	12 17.1	28 25.4	11 39.1	7 20.0	10 12.1	26 46.4	23 30.8	20 32.1	21 25.7
22 Sa	18 01 48	0♑02 08	4♒00 58	11♒07 27	1 01.5	13 44.4	29 39.7	11 54.9	7 29.1	10 13.0	26 48.1	23 34.0	20 34.4	21 26.9
23 Su	18 05 44	1 03 16	18 14 25	25 21 25	0D 59.8	15 12.3	0♒53.9	12 10.1	7 38.5	10 13.7	26 49.7	23 37.2	20 36.6	21 28.0
24 M	18 09 41	2 04 24	2♓28 07	9♓34 14	0 59.9	16 40.7	2 08.1	12 24.8	7 48.2	10 14.2	26 51.3	23 40.3	20 38.8	21 29.2
25 Tu	18 13 37	3 05 32	16 39 30	23 43 47	1R 00.7	18 09.6	3 22.3	12 39.0	7 58.1	10 14.6	26 52.7	23 43.4	20 41.1	21 30.2
26 W	18 17 34	4 06 40	0♈46 56	7♈48 51	1 00.9	19 38.9	4 36.5	12 52.7	8 08.4	10R 14.7	26 54.0	23 46.5	20 43.3	21 31.3
27 Th	18 21 30	5 07 48	14 49 25	21 48 34	0 59.5	21 08.7	5 50.6	13 05.9	8 18.9	10 14.6	26 55.2	23 49.5	20 45.5	21 32.3
28 F	18 25 27	6 08 56	28 46 10	5♉42 05	0 55.9	22 38.9	7 04.7	13 18.5	8 29.8	10 14.3	26 56.3	23 52.6	20 47.7	21 33.3
29 Sa	18 29 24	7 10 04	12♉36 10	19 28 12	0 49.9	24 09.4	8 18.8	13 30.6	8 40.8	10 13.9	26 57.2	23 55.5	20 49.9	21 34.2
30 Su	18 33 20	8 11 12	26 17 59	3♊05 16	0 41.9	25 40.3	9 32.8	13 42.1	8 52.2	10 13.2	26 58.1	23 58.5	20 52.1	21 35.1
31 M	18 37 17	9 12 20	9♊49 46	16 31 16	0 32.7	27 11.6	10 46.9	13 53.0	9 03.8	10 12.4	26 58.9	24 01.4	20 54.3	21 36.0

Astro Data

	Dy Hr Mn
☽0N	1 19:31
☿R	9 13:55
☽0S	15 16:12
⚳D	25 13:20
☽0N	29 3:51
☿D	29 12:41
☽0S	13 1:51
☽0N	26 10:32
♃R	26 14:59

Planet Ingress

		Dy Hr Mn
♀	♐	4 11:50
☿	♏R	18 3:08
♂	♍	19 21:36
☉	♐	22 21:54
♀	♑	28 14:20
☿	♐	12 13:34
☉	♑	22 11:10
♀	♒	22 18:35

Last Aspect / ☽ Ingress

Last Aspect Dy Hr Mn			☽ Ingress	Dy Hr Mn
1 3:17	♀	△	♈	1 10:09
2 21:49	♂	△	♉	3 11:16
5 2:43	♄	△	♊	5 13:25
7 7:33	♂	⚹	♋	7 18:24
9 15:49	♄	⚹	♌	10 3:14
12 8:11	♂	☌	♍	12 15:20
14 17:20	♄	☌	♎	15 4:16
17 13:26	♂	⚹	♏	17 15:29
19 19:48	☿	☌	♐	19 23:56
21 21:26	♄	□	♑	22 6:01
24 2:30	♄	△	♒	24 10:37
26 9:37	♀	⚹	♓	26 14:17
28 9:53	♄	☍	♈	28 17:17
30 4:32	♇	☍	♉	30 19:54

Last Aspect / ☽ Ingress

Last Aspect Dy Hr Mn			☽ Ingress	Dy Hr Mn
2 15:59	♄	△	♊	2 23:02
4 20:52	♄	□	♋	5 4:01
7 4:47	♄	⚹	♌	7 12:09
9 16:34	☿	□	♍	9 23:33
12 12:21	☿	⚹	♎	12 12:29
14 7:56	☉	⚹	♏	15 0:08
17 2:26	♄	⚹	♐	17 8:36
19 8:23	☉	☌	♑	19 13:55
21 14:47	♀	☌	♒	21 17:13
23 9:04	♅	□	♓	23 19:50
25 17:22	♄	☍	♈	25 22:40
27 11:32	♇	☍	♉	28 2:08
30 1:10	♄	△	♊	30 6:32

☽ Phases & Eclipses

Dy Hr Mn		
4 5:47	○	11♉13
11 16:24	☾	18♌41
19 18:04	●	26♏48
26 21:09	☽	4♓01
3 18:08	○	10♊59
11 13:59	☾	18♍55
19 8:23	●	26♐50
26 5:11	☽	3♈49

Astro Data

1 November 1979
Julian Day # 29159
SVP 5♓32'38"
GC 26♐33.5 ⚴ 15♒26.5
Eris 14♈10.6R ✱ 24♋58.3
⚷ 11♉39.7R ⚶ 11♉01.0R
☽ Mean ☊ 5♍05.9

1 December 1979
Julian Day # 29189
SVP 5♓32'34"
GC 26♐33.5 ⚴ 20♒08.0
Eris 13♈56.9R ✱ 29♋04.3
⚷ 10♉14.8R ⚶ 4♉23.0R
☽ Mean ☊ 3♍30.6

LONGITUDE — January 1980

Day	Sid.Time	☉	0 hr ☽	Noon☽	True☊	☿	♀	♂	⚳	♃	♄	♅	♆	♇
1 Tu	18 41 13	10♑13 28	23♊09 28	29♊44 10	0♍23.2	28♐43.2	12♒00.8	14♍03.4	9♈15.6	10♍11.3	26♍59.5	24♏04.3	20♐56.5	21♎36.9
2 W	18 45 10	11 14 36	6♋15 11	12♋42 20	0R 14.6	0♑15.2	13 14.8	14 13.2	9 27.8	10R 10.1	27 00.1	24 07.1	20 58.6	21 37.7
3 Th	18 49 06	12 15 44	19 05 34	25 24 50	0 07.6	1 47.5	14 28.7	14 22.3	9 40.1	10 08.7	27 00.5	24 10.0	21 00.8	21 38.5
4 F	18 53 03	13 16 52	1♌40 13	7♌51 48	0 02.8	3 20.2	15 42.5	14 30.9	9 52.7	10 07.1	27 00.8	24 12.7	21 02.9	21 39.2
5 Sa	18 56 59	14 18 01	13 59 48	20 04 28	0D 00.2	4 53.2	16 56.3	14 38.8	10 05.6	10 05.2	27 01.0	24 15.5	21 05.0	21 39.9
6 Su	19 00 56	15 19 09	26 06 09	2♍05 15	29♌59.6	6 26.7	18 10.1	14 46.0	10 18.6	10 03.2	27R 01.2	24 18.2	21 07.1	21 40.6
7 M	19 04 53	16 20 18	8♍02 12	13 57 32	0♍00.5	8 00.4	19 23.9	14 52.7	10 32.0	10 01.0	27 01.1	24 20.8	21 09.2	21 41.2
8 Tu	19 08 49	17 21 26	19 51 48	25 45 34	0 02.1	9 34.6	20 37.6	14 58.6	10 45.5	9 58.7	27 01.0	24 23.4	21 11.3	21 41.8
9 W	19 12 46	18 22 35	1♎39 28	7♎34 10	0 03.6	11 09.2	21 51.2	15 03.9	10 59.3	9 56.1	27 00.8	24 26.0	21 13.4	21 42.4
10 Th	19 16 42	19 23 43	13 30 17	19 28 31	0R 04.2	12 44.2	23 04.8	15 08.4	11 13.3	9 53.3	27 00.5	24 28.6	21 15.5	21 42.9
11 F	19 20 39	20 24 52	25 29 29	1♏33 52	0 03.4	14 19.6	24 18.4	15 12.3	11 27.5	9 50.4	27 00.0	24 31.1	21 17.5	21 43.4
12 Sa	19 24 35	21 26 01	7♏42 15	13 55 12	0 00.9	15 55.5	25 32.0	15 15.5	11 41.9	9 47.2	26 59.5	24 33.5	21 19.5	21 43.9
13 Su	19 28 32	22 27 09	20 13 14	26 36 47	29♌56.8	17 31.8	26 45.4	15 17.9	11 56.6	9 43.9	26 58.8	24 35.9	21 21.6	21 44.3
14 M	19 32 28	23 28 18	3♐06 11	9♐41 40	29 51.4	19 08.6	27 58.9	15 19.6	12 11.4	9 40.4	26 58.0	24 38.3	21 23.6	21 44.7
15 Tu	19 36 25	24 29 26	16 23 21	23 11 13	29 45.4	20 45.9	29 12.3	15R 20.6	12 26.5	9 36.7	26 57.2	24 40.6	21 25.5	21 45.0
16 W	19 40 22	25 30 34	0♑05 06	7♑04 40	29 39.5	22 23.7	0♓25.6	15 20.8	12 41.8	9 32.9	26 56.2	24 42.9	21 27.5	21 45.3
17 Th	19 44 18	26 31 42	14 09 30	21 18 59	29 34.5	24 02.0	1 38.9	15 20.2	12 57.2	9 28.8	26 55.1	24 45.2	21 29.5	21 45.6
18 F	19 48 15	27 32 49	28 32 26	5♒49 05	29 31.0	25 40.9	2 52.2	15 18.9	13 12.9	9 24.6	26 53.9	24 47.4	21 31.4	21 45.9
19 Sa	19 52 11	28 33 56	13♒08 04	20 28 31	29D 29.2	27 20.2	4 05.4	15 16.8	13 28.8	9 20.2	26 52.6	24 49.5	21 33.3	21 46.1
20 Su	19 56 08	29 35 02	27 49 34	5♓10 24	29 29.1	29 00.2	5 18.5	15 13.9	13 44.8	9 15.7	26 51.2	24 51.6	21 35.2	21 46.2
21 M	20 00 04	0♒36 07	12♓30 14	19 48 23	29 30.1	0♒40.6	6 31.6	15 10.2	14 01.1	9 10.9	26 49.6	24 53.7	21 37.1	21 46.4
22 Tu	20 04 01	1 37 11	27 04 16	4♈17 24	29 31.6	2 21.7	7 44.6	15 05.7	14 17.5	9 06.0	26 48.0	24 55.7	21 38.9	21 46.5
23 W	20 07 57	2 38 14	11♈27 22	18 33 54	29 32.9	4 03.3	8 57.5	15 00.4	14 34.1	9 01.0	26 46.3	24 57.7	21 40.8	21 46.5
24 Th	20 11 54	3 39 16	25 36 46	2♉35 53	29R 33.6	5 45.5	10 10.4	14 54.4	14 50.9	8 55.8	26 44.4	24 59.6	21 42.6	21R 46.5
25 F	20 15 51	4 40 17	9♉31 09	16 22 33	29 33.1	7 28.2	11 23.2	14 47.5	15 07.8	8 50.4	26 42.5	25 01.5	21 44.4	21 46.5
26 Sa	20 19 47	5 41 17	23 10 09	29 53 58	29 31.4	9 11.5	12 35.9	14 39.9	15 25.0	8 44.9	26 40.5	25 03.3	21 46.1	21 46.5
27 Su	20 23 44	6 42 16	6♊34 05	13♊10 34	29 28.6	10 55.4	13 48.5	14 31.4	15 42.3	8 39.3	26 38.4	25 05.1	21 47.9	21 46.4
28 M	20 27 40	7 43 13	19 43 32	26 13 03	29 25.3	12 39.7	15 01.1	14 22.2	15 59.7	8 33.5	26 36.1	25 06.8	21 49.6	21 46.3
29 Tu	20 31 37	8 44 10	2♋39 11	9♋02 03	29 21.8	14 24.6	16 13.6	14 12.2	16 17.3	8 27.6	26 33.8	25 08.5	21 51.3	21 46.1
30 W	20 35 33	9 45 06	15 21 44	21 38 19	29 18.7	16 09.8	17 26.0	14 01.4	16 35.1	8 21.5	26 31.4	25 10.1	21 53.0	21 45.9
31 Th	20 39 30	10 46 00	27 51 54	4♌02 36	29 16.3	17 55.5	18 38.4	13 49.8	16 53.0	8 15.3	26 28.9	25 11.7	21 54.6	21 45.7

LONGITUDE — February 1980

Day	Sid.Time	☉	0 hr ☽	Noon☽	True☊	☿	♀	♂	⚳	♃	♄	♅	♆	♇
1 F	20 43 26	11♒46 54	10♌10 34	16♌15 55	29♌14.8	19♒41.4	19♓50.6	13♍37.4	17♈11.1	8♍09.0	26♍26.3	25♏13.2	21♐56.3	21♎45.5
2 Sa	20 47 23	12 47 46	22 18 52	28 19 36	29D 14.3	21 27.6	21 02.8	13R 24.3	17 29.3	8R 02.5	26R 23.6	25 14.6	21 57.9	21R 45.2
3 Su	20 51 20	13 48 37	4♍18 23	10♍15 29	29 14.6	23 13.9	22 14.8	13 10.5	17 47.7	7 56.0	26 20.8	25 16.1	21 59.4	21 44.8
4 M	20 55 16	14 49 28	16 11 12	22 05 55	29 15.6	25 00.1	23 26.8	12 55.9	18 06.2	7 49.3	26 17.9	25 17.4	22 01.0	21 44.5
5 Tu	20 59 13	15 50 17	28 00 01	3♎53 54	29 16.9	26 46.2	24 38.7	12 40.5	18 24.9	7 42.5	26 15.0	25 18.7	22 02.5	21 44.1
6 W	21 03 09	16 51 05	9♎48 04	15 42 59	29 18.2	28 31.9	25 50.5	12 24.5	18 43.7	7 35.6	26 11.9	25 20.0	22 04.0	21 43.6
7 Th	21 07 06	17 51 53	21 39 11	27 37 14	29 19.3	0♓17.0	27 02.2	12 07.7	19 02.6	7 28.6	26 08.8	25 21.2	22 05.5	21 43.2
8 F	21 11 02	18 52 39	3♏37 41	9♏41 07	29R 19.9	2 01.2	28 13.8	11 50.3	19 21.7	7 21.5	26 05.6	25 22.4	22 06.9	21 42.7
9 Sa	21 14 59	19 53 25	15 48 08	21 59 17	29 20.1	3 44.2	29 25.3	11 32.2	19 40.9	7 14.3	26 02.3	25 23.5	22 08.4	21 42.1
10 Su	21 18 55	20 54 09	28 15 10	4♐36 16	29 19.8	5 25.6	0♈36.7	11 13.5	20 00.2	7 07.1	25 58.9	25 24.5	22 09.8	21 41.6
11 M	21 22 52	21 54 53	11♐03 05	17 36 01	29 19.2	7 05.1	1 48.0	10 54.2	20 19.7	6 59.7	25 55.5	25 25.5	22 11.1	21 41.0
12 Tu	21 26 49	22 55 35	24 15 24	1♑01 27	29 18.4	8 42.2	2 59.2	10 34.3	20 39.3	6 52.3	25 51.9	25 26.5	22 12.5	21 40.4
13 W	21 30 45	23 56 17	7♑54 15	14 53 46	29 17.7	10 16.3	4 10.3	10 13.9	20 59.0	6 44.8	25 48.3	25 27.4	22 13.8	21 39.7
14 Th	21 34 42	24 56 57	21 59 47	29 11 56	29 17.2	11 47.0	5 21.3	9 53.0	21 18.9	6 37.2	25 44.7	25 28.2	22 15.1	21 39.0
15 F	21 38 38	25 57 36	6♒29 40	13♒52 16	29 16.9	13 13.5	6 32.2	9 31.6	21 38.8	6 29.6	25 40.9	25 29.0	22 16.3	21 38.3
16 Sa	21 42 35	26 58 13	21 18 55	28 48 37	29D 16.8	14 35.3	7 43.0	9 09.7	21 58.9	6 21.9	25 37.1	25 29.7	22 17.6	21 37.5
17 Su	21 46 31	27 58 49	6♓20 18	13♓52 50	29 16.8	15 51.6	8 53.6	8 47.5	22 19.1	6 14.2	25 33.2	25 30.4	22 18.8	21 36.7
18 M	21 50 28	28 59 23	21 25 07	28 56 00	29R 16.9	17 01.9	10 04.2	8 24.9	22 39.4	6 06.4	25 29.3	25 31.0	22 19.9	21 35.9
19 Tu	21 54 24	29 59 56	6♈24 30	13♈49 39	29 16.8	18 05.2	11 14.6	8 02.0	22 59.8	5 58.6	25 25.3	25 31.6	22 21.1	21 35.0
20 W	21 58 21	1♓00 27	21 10 40	28 26 55	29 16.7	19 01.1	12 24.8	7 38.8	23 20.4	5 50.8	25 21.2	25 32.1	22 22.2	21 34.2
21 Th	22 02 18	2 00 55	5♉37 53	12♉43 14	29 16.5	19 48.9	13 35.0	7 15.4	23 41.0	5 43.0	25 17.1	25 32.5	22 23.2	21 33.2
22 F	22 06 14	3 01 23	19 42 47	26 36 27	29D 16.4	20 28.0	14 45.0	6 51.8	24 01.7	5 35.1	25 12.9	25 32.9	22 24.3	21 32.3
23 Sa	22 10 11	4 01 48	3♊24 19	10♊06 30	29 16.4	20 57.9	15 54.8	6 28.1	24 22.6	5 27.2	25 08.7	25 33.3	22 25.3	21 31.3
24 Su	22 14 07	5 02 11	16 43 16	23 14 52	29 16.6	21 18.2	17 04.5	6 04.3	24 43.5	5 19.3	25 04.4	25 33.6	22 26.3	21 30.3
25 M	22 18 04	6 02 32	29 41 40	6♋03 59	29 17.2	21R 28.7	18 14.1	5 40.5	25 04.6	5 11.4	25 00.1	25 33.8	22 27.2	21 29.3
26 Tu	22 22 00	7 02 52	12♋22 13	18 36 43	29 17.9	21 29.4	19 23.5	5 16.6	25 25.7	5 03.5	24 55.7	25 34.0	22 28.2	21 28.3
27 W	22 25 57	8 03 09	24 47 52	0♌56 00	29 18.8	21 20.2	20 32.7	4 52.9	25 46.9	4 55.7	24 51.3	25 34.1	22 29.0	21 27.2
28 Th	22 29 53	9 03 25	7♌01 29	13 04 38	29 19.6	21 01.6	21 41.8	4 29.2	26 08.2	4 47.8	24 46.9	25R 34.2	22 29.9	21 26.1
29 F	22 33 50	10 03 38	19 05 44	25 05 06	29R 20.0	20 33.9	22 50.7	4 05.6	26 29.6	4 40.0	24 42.4	25 34.2	22 30.7	21 25.0

Astro Data	Dy Hr Mn	Planet Ingress	Dy Hr Mn	Last Aspect Dy Hr Mn	☽ Ingress	Dy Hr Mn	Last Aspect Dy Hr Mn	☽ Ingress	Dy Hr Mn	☽ Phases & Eclipses Dy Hr Mn		Astro Data
♄ R	6 22:42	☿ ♑	2 8:02	1 9:54 ☿ ☍	♋	1 12:29	2 5:50 ♅ □	♍	2 15:21	2 9:02	○ 11♋07	1 January 1980
☽ 0S	9 11:25	☊ ♌R	5 14:53	3 15:03 ♄ ✶	♌	3 20:47	4 20:30 ♄ ☌	♎	5 4:04	10 11:50	☾ 19♎23	Julian Day # 29220
♂ R	16 6:18	☊ ♍	7 2:39	5 20:21 ♅ □	♍	6 7:48	7 0:52 ♆ ✶	♏	7 16:46	17 21:19	● 26♑55	SVP 5♓32'28"
☽ 0N	22 17:20	☊ ♌R	12 18:20	8 14:34 ♄ ☌	♎	8 20:38	9 19:45 ♄ ✶	♐	10 3:19	24 13:58	☽ 3♉44	GC 26♐33.6 ⚴ 27♒50.6
♇ R	24 15:49	♀ ♓	16 3:37	10 20:01 ♀ △	♏	11 8:55	12 2:55 ♄ □	♑	12 10:12			Eris 13♈51.4R ⚵ 25♋01.9R
♆✶♇	26 16:49	☉ ♒	20 21:49	13 12:41 ♄ ✶	♐	13 18:17	14 6:17 ♄ △	♒	14 13:20	1 2:21	○ 11♌22	⚷ 9♉17.4R ⚶ 3♉29.1
⚳0N	30 3:17	☿ ♒	21 2:18	15 23:29 ♀ ✶	♑	15 23:51	16 8:51 ☉ ☌	♓	16 13:54	9 7:35	☾ 19♏42	☽ Mean ☊ 1♍52.1
				17 21:19 ☉ ☌	♒	18 2:25	18 6:32 ♅ △	♈	18 13:42	16 8:51	● 26♒50	
☽ 0S	5 19:33	☿ ♓	7 8:07	19 19:07 ♅ □	♓	20 3:33	20 1:57 ♆ △	♉	20 14:35	16 8:53:11	● T 04'08"	1 February 1980
♀0N	11 0:49	♀ ♈	9 23:39	21 23:34 ♄ ☍	♈	22 4:52	22 10:09 ♅ ☍	♊	22 17:58	23 0:14	☽ 3♊32	Julian Day # 29251
♃∠♇	14 5:52	☉ ♓	19 12:02	23 17:27 ♇ ☍	♉	24 7:31	24 15:22 ♄ □	♋	25 0:34			SVP 5♓32'23"
♄✶♅	18 2:55			26 6:15 ♄ △	♊	26 12:11	27 1:30 ♅ △	♌	27 10:10			GC 26♐33.7 ⚴ 7♓16.2
☽ 0N	19 1:58			28 12:43 ♄ □	♋	28 19:02	29 12:58 ♅ □	♍	29 21:53			Eris 13♈56.5 ⚵ 17♋53.5R
☿ R	26 1:30			30 21:23 ♄ ✶	♌	31 4:08						⚷ 9♉13.1 ⚶ 8♉45.8
♅ R	29 6:39											☽ Mean ☊ 0♍13.6

March 1980 — LONGITUDE

Day	Sid.Time	☉	0 hr ☽	Noon ☽	True☊	☿	♀	♂	⚳	♃	♄	♅	♆	♇
1 Sa	22 37 46	11♓03 50	1♍03 00	6♍59 41	29♌19.9	19♓58.0	23♈59.5	3♍42.2	26♈51.1	4♍32.2	24♍37.9	25♏34.1	22♐31.5	21♎23.8
2 Su	22 41 43	12 04 00	12 55 25	18 50 27	29R 19.2	19R 14.8	25 08.0	3R 19.1	27 12.7	4R 24.4	24R 33.3	25R 34.1	22 32.3	21R 22.6
3 M	22 45 40	13 04 08	24 45 02	0♎39 26	29 17.7	18 25.2	26 16.4	2 56.2	27 34.4	4 16.7	24 28.7	25 33.9	22 33.0	21 21.4
4 Tu	22 49 36	14 04 14	6♎33 55	12 28 47	29 15.6	17 30.7	27 24.7	2 33.6	27 56.1	4 09.0	24 24.1	25 33.7	22 33.7	21 20.2
5 W	22 53 33	15 04 19	18 24 18	24 20 49	29 13.1	16 32.7	28 32.7	2 11.3	28 18.0	4 01.3	24 19.5	25 33.4	22 34.3	21 18.9
6 Th	22 57 29	16 04 22	0♏18 41	6♏18 16	29 10.5	15 32.4	29 40.5	1 49.4	28 39.9	3 53.7	24 14.8	25 33.1	22 35.0	21 17.7
7 F	23 01 26	17 04 23	12 19 59	18 24 14	29 08.2	14 31.4	0♉48.2	1 28.0	29 01.9	3 46.2	24 10.1	25 32.8	22 35.6	21 16.4
8 Sa	23 05 22	18 04 23	24 31 29	0♐42 12	29 06.4	13 31.1	1 55.6	1 07.0	29 23.9	3 38.7	24 05.4	25 32.4	22 36.1	21 15.0
9 Su	23 09 19	19 04 21	6♐56 52	13 15 57	29D 05.4	12 32.8	3 02.9	0 46.4	29 46.1	3 31.3	24 00.7	25 31.9	22 36.7	21 13.7
10 M	23 13 15	20 04 18	19 39 56	26 09 17	29 05.4	11 37.6	4 10.0	0 26.4	0♉08.3	3 24.0	23 56.0	25 31.4	22 37.2	21 12.3
11 Tu	23 17 12	21 04 13	2♑44 24	9♑25 40	29 06.3	10 46.4	5 16.8	0 07.0	0 30.6	3 16.8	23 51.2	25 30.8	22 37.6	21 11.0
12 W	23 21 09	22 04 06	16 13 23	23 07 43	29 07.7	10 00.2	6 23.4	29♌48.1	0 53.0	3 09.6	23 46.5	25 30.2	22 38.0	21 09.6
13 Th	23 25 05	23 03 57	0♒08 45	7♒16 26	29 09.1	9 19.4	7 29.8	29 29.8	1 15.4	3 02.5	23 41.7	25 29.5	22 38.4	21 08.1
14 F	23 29 02	24 03 47	14 30 32	21 50 38	29R 10.1	8 44.6	8 36.0	29 12.2	1 37.9	2 55.6	23 37.0	25 28.8	22 38.8	21 06.7
15 Sa	23 32 58	25 03 35	29 16 07	6♓46 14	29 10.1	8 15.9	9 42.0	28 55.2	2 00.5	2 48.7	23 32.2	25 28.0	22 39.1	21 05.2
16 Su	23 36 55	26 03 21	14♓20 01	21 56 21	29 08.7	7 53.6	10 47.7	28 38.9	2 23.1	2 41.9	23 27.5	25 27.2	22 39.4	21 03.8
17 M	23 40 51	27 03 05	29 34 00	7♈11 41	29 06.0	7 37.7	11 53.2	28 23.3	2 45.9	2 35.3	23 22.7	25 26.3	22 39.7	21 02.3
18 Tu	23 44 48	28 02 47	14♈48 04	22 21 55	29 02.2	7 28.0	12 58.4	28 08.4	3 08.6	2 28.7	23 18.0	25 25.4	22 39.9	21 00.8
19 W	23 48 44	29 02 27	29 52 02	7♉17 22	28 57.9	7D 24.5	14 03.4	27 54.3	3 31.5	2 22.3	23 13.3	25 24.4	22 40.1	20 59.2
20 Th	23 52 41	0♈02 05	14♉37 04	21 50 28	28 53.7	7 26.9	15 08.1	27 40.9	3 54.4	2 16.0	23 08.6	25 23.4	22 40.3	20 57.7
21 F	23 56 38	1 01 40	28 57 05	5♊56 39	28 50.2	7 35.1	16 12.6	27 28.3	4 17.3	2 09.8	23 03.9	25 22.3	22 40.4	20 56.2
22 Sa	0 00 34	2 01 14	12♊49 06	19 34 29	28 48.1	7 48.8	17 16.7	27 16.4	4 40.3	2 03.8	22 59.2	25 21.2	22 40.5	20 54.6
23 Su	0 04 31	3 00 45	26 13 03	2♋45 08	28D 47.4	8 07.6	18 20.6	27 05.3	5 03.4	1 57.9	22 54.6	25 20.0	22 40.5	20 53.0
24 M	0 08 27	4 00 13	9♋11 10	15 31 38	28 47.9	8 31.4	19 24.1	26 55.1	5 26.5	1 52.1	22 49.9	25 18.8	22R 40.6	20 51.4
25 Tu	0 12 24	4 59 39	21 47 04	27 58 03	28 49.4	8 59.9	20 27.3	26 45.5	5 49.7	1 46.5	22 45.4	25 17.5	22 40.5	20 49.8
26 W	0 16 20	5 59 03	4♌05 07	10♌08 52	28 51.1	9 32.8	21 30.2	26 36.8	6 12.9	1 41.0	22 40.8	25 16.2	22 40.5	20 48.2
27 Th	0 20 17	6 58 25	16 09 48	22 08 29	28R 52.3	10 09.9	22 32.8	26 28.9	6 36.2	1 35.7	22 36.3	25 14.9	22 40.4	20 46.6
28 F	0 24 13	7 57 44	28 05 23	4♍00 58	28 52.4	10 50.8	23 35.1	26 21.8	6 59.5	1 30.5	22 31.8	25 13.5	22 40.3	20 45.0
29 Sa	0 28 10	8 57 01	9♍55 38	15 49 48	28 50.8	11 35.5	24 36.9	26 15.4	7 22.9	1 25.5	22 27.3	25 12.0	22 40.2	20 43.3
30 Su	0 32 06	9 56 16	21 43 47	27 37 54	28 47.2	12 23.7	25 38.5	26 09.8	7 46.3	1 20.6	22 22.9	25 10.6	22 40.0	20 41.7
31 M	0 36 03	10 55 29	3♎32 27	9♎27 40	28 41.7	13 15.2	26 39.6	26 05.0	8 09.8	1 15.9	22 18.5	25 09.0	22 39.8	20 40.0

April 1980 — LONGITUDE

Day	Sid.Time	☉	0 hr ☽	Noon ☽	True☊	☿	♀	♂	⚳	♃	♄	♅	♆	♇
1 Tu	0 40 00	11♈54 40	15♎23 48	21♎21 01	28♌34.5	14♓09.8	27♉40.4	26♌01.0	8♉33.3	1♍11.3	22♍14.1	25♏07.5	22♐39.5	20♎38.4
2 W	0 43 56	12 53 49	27 19 34	3♏19 37	28R 26.2	15 07.4	28 40.7	25R 57.7	8 56.9	1R 06.9	22R 09.9	25R 05.9	22R 39.3	20R 36.7
3 Th	0 47 53	13 52 56	9♏21 22	15 25 02	28 17.5	16 07.8	29 40.7	25 55.2	9 20.5	1 02.7	22 05.6	25 04.2	22 39.0	20 35.0
4 F	0 51 49	14 52 01	21 30 49	27 38 57	28 09.4	17 10.8	0♊40.2	25 53.5	9 44.1	0 58.6	22 01.4	25 02.5	22 38.6	20 33.4
5 Sa	0 55 46	15 51 04	3♐49 43	10♐03 22	28 02.7	18 16.4	1 39.3	25D 52.5	10 07.8	0 54.7	21 57.3	25 00.8	22 38.3	20 31.7
6 Su	0 59 42	16 50 05	16 20 14	22 40 38	27 57.8	19 24.5	2 38.0	25 52.2	10 31.5	0 51.0	21 53.2	24 59.0	22 37.9	20 30.0
7 M	1 03 39	17 49 05	29 04 55	5♑33 27	27 55.0	20 34.8	3 36.2	25 52.7	10 55.3	0 47.4	21 49.2	24 57.2	22 37.4	20 28.3
8 Tu	1 07 35	18 48 03	12♑06 37	18 44 44	27D 54.2	21 47.4	4 34.0	25 53.9	11 19.1	0 44.1	21 45.2	24 55.4	22 37.0	20 26.6
9 W	1 11 32	19 46 59	25 28 10	2♒17 12	27 54.7	23 02.2	5 31.2	25 55.8	11 43.0	0 40.9	21 41.3	24 53.5	22 36.5	20 25.0
10 Th	1 15 29	20 45 54	9♒12 03	16 12 51	27R 55.7	24 19.0	6 28.0	25 58.4	12 06.9	0 37.8	21 37.4	24 51.6	22 36.0	20 23.3
11 F	1 19 25	21 44 46	23 19 37	0♓32 13	27 56.1	25 37.8	7 24.2	26 01.8	12 30.8	0 35.0	21 33.6	24 49.7	22 35.4	20 21.6
12 Sa	1 23 22	22 43 37	7♓50 23	15 13 38	27 54.9	26 58.6	8 19.9	26 05.8	12 54.8	0 32.3	21 29.9	24 47.7	22 34.8	20 19.9
13 Su	1 27 18	23 42 26	22 41 18	0♈12 33	27 51.4	28 21.3	9 15.1	26 10.4	13 18.7	0 29.9	21 26.3	24 45.7	22 34.2	20 18.2
14 M	1 31 15	24 41 13	7♈46 22	15 21 35	27 45.5	29 45.8	10 09.7	26 15.8	13 42.8	0 27.5	21 22.7	24 43.7	22 33.6	20 16.5
15 Tu	1 35 11	25 39 59	22 56 56	0♉31 07	27 37.6	1♈12.2	11 03.7	26 21.8	14 06.8	0 25.4	21 19.2	24 41.6	22 32.9	20 14.8
16 W	1 39 08	26 38 42	8♉02 50	15 30 51	27 28.6	2 40.4	11 57.1	26 28.5	14 30.9	0 23.5	21 15.7	24 39.5	22 32.2	20 13.1
17 Th	1 43 04	27 37 23	22 54 03	0♊11 32	27 19.5	4 10.3	12 49.8	26 35.8	14 55.1	0 21.8	21 12.4	24 37.4	22 31.4	20 11.5
18 F	1 47 01	28 36 03	7♊22 31	14 26 31	27 11.4	5 41.9	13 41.9	26 43.7	15 19.2	0 20.2	21 09.1	24 35.2	22 30.7	20 09.8
19 Sa	1 50 58	29 34 40	21 23 12	28 12 28	27 05.3	7 15.3	14 33.3	26 52.3	15 43.4	0 18.8	21 05.9	24 33.1	22 29.9	20 08.1
20 Su	1 54 54	0♉33 15	4♋54 24	11♋29 14	27 01.4	8 50.4	15 24.0	27 01.4	16 07.6	0 17.7	21 02.8	24 30.9	22 29.1	20 06.5
21 M	1 58 51	1 31 47	17 57 21	24 19 08	26D 59.6	10 27.2	16 14.0	27 11.2	16 31.8	0 16.7	20 59.7	24 28.6	22 28.2	20 04.8
22 Tu	2 02 47	2 30 18	0♌35 24	6♌46 32	26 59.5	12 05.7	17 03.2	27 21.5	16 56.1	0 15.8	20 56.8	24 26.4	22 27.4	20 03.2
23 W	2 06 44	3 28 46	12 53 15	18 56 12	27R 00.0	13 45.9	17 51.6	27 32.4	17 20.4	0 15.2	20 53.9	24 24.1	22 26.5	20 01.5
24 Th	2 10 40	4 27 12	24 56 05	0♍53 31	27 00.1	15 27.8	18 39.1	27 43.9	17 44.7	0 14.8	20 51.1	24 21.8	22 25.5	19 59.9
25 F	2 14 37	5 25 36	6♍49 09	12 43 35	26 58.9	17 11.4	19 25.8	27 55.9	18 09.0	0D 14.5	20 48.4	24 19.5	22 24.6	19 58.3
26 Sa	2 18 33	6 23 58	18 37 31	24 31 00	26 55.4	18 56.7	20 11.6	28 08.4	18 33.4	0 14.5	20 45.8	24 17.1	22 23.6	19 56.7
27 Su	2 22 30	7 22 18	0♎24 59	6♎19 42	26 49.4	20 43.8	20 56.4	28 21.5	18 57.7	0 14.6	20 43.3	24 14.8	22 22.6	19 55.1
28 M	2 26 27	8 20 36	12 15 33	18 12 50	26 40.7	22 32.6	21 40.3	28 35.0	19 22.1	0 14.9	20 40.8	24 12.4	22 21.6	19 53.5
29 Tu	2 30 23	9 18 52	24 11 49	0♏12 43	26 29.7	24 23.1	22 23.2	28 49.1	19 46.5	0 15.4	20 38.5	24 10.0	22 20.5	19 51.9
30 W	2 34 20	10 17 06	6♏15 43	12 20 57	26 17.1	26 15.4	23 05.1	29 03.7	20 11.0	0 16.0	20 36.3	24 07.6	22 19.4	19 50.4

Astro Data	Dy Hr Mn
☽0S	4 2:04
☽0N	17 12:33
☿ D	19 13:59
☉0N	20 11:10
♆ R	24 17:42
♄□♆	26 13:32
☽0S	31 8:01
♂ D	6 8:27
☽0N	13 23:40
☿0N	18 17:26
♃ D	26 8:47
☽0S	27 14:41

Planet Ingress	Dy Hr Mn
♀ ♉	6 18:54
⚳ ♉	10 3:03
♂ ♌R	11 20:46
☉ ♈	20 11:10
♀ ♊	3 19:46
☿ ♈	14 15:58
☉ ♉	19 22:23

Last Aspect Dy Hr Mn		☽ Ingress Dy Hr Mn
3 1:39	♅ ⚹	♎ 3 10:40
5 21:20	♀ ☍	♏ 5 23:22
8 1:59	♅ ☌	♐ 8 10:38
10 7:56	♄ □	♑ 10 19:02
12 16:05	♅ ⚹	♒ 12 23:45
14 23:40	♂ ☍	♓ 15 1:10
16 18:56	☉ ☌	♈ 17 0:41
18 21:05	♂ △	♉ 19 0:13
20 21:42	♂ □	♊ 21 1:47
23 1:44	♂ ⚹	♋ 23 6:55
25 6:48	♅ △	♌ 25 15:58
27 20:40	♂ ☌	♍ 28 3:52
30 7:34	♀ △	♎ 30 16:49

Last Aspect Dy Hr Mn		☽ Ingress Dy Hr Mn
1 21:20	♂ ⚹	♏ 2 5:21
4 8:35	♂ □	♐ 4 16:35
6 18:00	♂ △	♑ 7 1:43
8 23:00	♅ ⚹	♒ 9 8:00
11 4:29	♂ ☍	♓ 11 11:07
13 8:45	☿ ☌	♈ 13 11:40
15 5:22	♂ △	♉ 15 11:11
17 6:01	♂ □	♊ 17 11:41
19 14:38	☉ ⚹	♋ 19 15:11
21 12:18	♅ △	♌ 21 22:52
24 5:31	♂ ☌	♍ 24 10:12
26 11:32	♅ ⚹	♎ 26 23:09
29 9:10	♂ ⚹	♏ 29 11:35

☽ Phases & Eclipses Dy Hr Mn	
1 21:00	○ 11♍26
1 20:45	• A 0.654
9 23:49	☾ 19♐34
16 18:56	● 26♓21
23 12:31	☽ 3♋02
31 15:14	○ 11♎03
8 12:06	☾ 18♑48
15 3:46	● 25♈20
22 2:59	☽ 2♌08
30 7:35	○ 10♏06

Astro Data

1 March 1980
Julian Day # 29280
SVP 5♓32'20"
GC 26♐33.7 ⚴ 16♓54.8
Eris 14♈09.8 ⚵ 16♋24.8
⚷ 10♉00.0 ⚶ 17♉17.7
☽ Mean ☊ 28♌41.5

1 April 1980
Julian Day # 29311
SVP 5♓32'18"
GC 26♐33.8 ⚴ 27♓33.5
Eris 14♈29.5 ⚵ 21♋24.6
⚷ 11♉32.9 ⚶ 28♉35.9
☽ Mean ☊ 27♌03.0

LONGITUDE — May 1980

Day	Sid.Time	☉	0 hr ☽	Noon ☽	True ☊	☿	♀	♂	⚳	♃	♄	♅	♆	♇
1 Th	2 38 16	11♉15 19	18♏28 32	24♏38 33	26♌04.1	28♈09.5	23♊45.9	29♌18.7	20♉35.4	0♍16.9	20♍34.1	24♏05.2	22♐18.3	19♎48.8
2 F	2 42 13	12 13 30	0♐51 03	7♐06 08	25R51.7	0♉05.2	24 25.5	29 34.2	20 59.9	0 17.9	20R32.0	24R02.8	22R17.2	19R47.3
3 Sa	2 46 09	13 11 39	13 23 51	19 44 16	25 41.0	2 02.7	25 04.0	29 50.2	21 24.4	0 19.1	20 30.1	24 00.3	22 16.1	19 45.8
4 Su	2 50 06	14 09 47	26 07 31	2♑33 41	25 32.8	4 01.9	25 41.3	0♍06.6	21 48.9	0 20.5	20 28.2	23 57.9	22 14.9	19 44.3
5 M	2 54 02	15 07 53	9♑02 57	15 35 28	25 27.3	6 02.7	26 17.4	0 23.4	22 13.4	0 22.1	20 26.4	23 55.4	22 13.7	19 42.8
6 Tu	2 57 59	16 05 58	22 11 26	28 51 04	25 24.6	8 05.2	26 52.2	0 40.7	22 37.9	0 23.9	20 24.8	23 52.9	22 12.5	19 41.3
7 W	3 01 56	17 04 02	5♒34 36	12♒22 15	25 23.7	10 09.2	27 25.6	0 58.4	23 02.5	0 25.8	20 23.2	23 50.4	22 11.3	19 39.8
8 Th	3 05 52	18 02 04	19 14 12	26 10 37	25 23.7	12 14.6	27 57.6	1 16.6	23 27.0	0 27.9	20 21.7	23 47.9	22 10.0	19 38.4
9 F	3 09 49	19 00 04	3♓11 36	10♓17 08	25 23.2	14 21.4	28 28.2	1 35.1	23 51.6	0 30.2	20 20.3	23 45.4	22 08.7	19 37.0
10 Sa	3 13 45	19 58 04	17 27 07	24 41 20	25 21.1	16 29.5	28 57.3	1 54.0	24 16.2	0 32.7	20 19.0	23 42.9	22 07.5	19 35.6
11 Su	3 17 42	20 56 02	1♈59 22	9♈20 42	25 16.5	18 38.5	29 24.9	2 13.4	24 40.8	0 35.3	20 17.8	23 40.4	22 06.1	19 34.2
12 M	3 21 38	21 53 59	16 44 37	24 10 16	25 09.2	20 48.4	29 50.8	2 33.1	25 05.4	0 38.1	20 16.8	23 37.9	22 04.8	19 32.8
13 Tu	3 25 35	22 51 54	1♉36 40	9♉02 47	24 59.4	22 59.0	0♋15.1	2 53.2	25 30.1	0 41.1	20 15.8	23 35.4	22 03.5	19 31.5
14 W	3 29 31	23 49 48	16 27 30	23 49 41	24 48.2	25 10.0	0 37.7	3 13.6	25 54.7	0 44.2	20 14.9	23 32.9	22 02.1	19 30.1
15 Th	3 33 28	24 47 41	1♊08 19	8♊22 25	24 36.7	27 21.1	0 58.5	3 34.5	26 19.3	0 47.6	20 14.1	23 30.3	22 00.7	19 28.8
16 F	3 37 25	25 45 32	15 31 11	22 33 58	24 26.3	29 32.2	1 17.4	3 55.7	26 44.0	0 51.1	20 13.5	23 27.8	21 59.3	19 27.6
17 Sa	3 41 21	26 43 21	29 30 17	6♋19 53	24 17.9	1♊42.8	1 34.4	4 17.2	27 08.7	0 54.7	20 12.9	23 25.3	21 57.9	19 26.3
18 Su	3 45 18	27 41 09	13♋02 38	19 38 39	24 12.1	3 52.8	1 49.5	4 39.1	27 33.3	0 58.6	20 12.4	23 22.8	21 56.5	19 25.1
19 M	3 49 14	28 38 55	26 08 07	2♌31 25	24 08.8	6 01.8	2 02.5	5 01.4	27 58.0	1 02.5	20 12.1	23 20.3	21 55.0	19 23.8
20 Tu	3 53 11	29 36 40	8♌49 00	15 01 24	24D07.5	8 09.5	2 13.4	5 23.9	28 22.7	1 06.7	20 11.8	23 17.8	21 53.6	19 22.7
21 W	3 57 07	0♊34 23	21 09 14	27 13 08	24R07.4	10 15.8	2 22.2	5 46.8	28 47.3	1 11.0	20D11.7	23 15.3	21 52.1	19 21.5
22 Th	4 01 04	1 32 04	3♍13 47	9♍11 53	24 07.2	12 20.4	2 28.8	6 10.0	29 12.0	1 15.5	20 11.6	23 12.8	21 50.6	19 20.3
23 F	4 05 00	2 29 44	15 08 05	21 03 03	24 06.1	14 23.1	2 33.0	6 33.5	29 36.7	1 20.1	20 11.7	23 10.3	21 49.1	19 19.2
24 Sa	4 08 57	3 27 22	26 57 28	2♎51 54	24 02.9	16 23.6	2R35.0	6 57.3	0♊01.4	1 24.9	20 11.8	23 07.9	21 47.6	19 18.1
25 Su	4 12 54	4 24 59	8♎46 57	14 43 09	23 57.3	18 21.9	2 34.6	7 21.3	0 26.1	1 29.9	20 12.1	23 05.4	21 46.1	19 17.0
26 M	4 16 50	5 22 34	20 40 57	26 40 47	23 49.1	20 17.7	2 31.9	7 45.7	0 50.8	1 35.0	20 12.4	23 03.0	21 44.6	19 16.0
27 Tu	4 20 47	6 20 08	2♏43 01	8♏47 55	23 38.5	22 11.1	2 26.7	8 10.4	1 15.4	1 40.2	20 12.9	23 00.6	21 43.0	19 15.0
28 W	4 24 43	7 17 41	14 55 45	21 06 40	23 26.5	24 01.8	2 19.1	8 35.3	1 40.1	1 45.6	20 13.5	22 58.1	21 41.5	19 14.0
29 Th	4 28 40	8 15 13	27 20 46	3♐38 07	23 13.8	25 49.9	2 09.0	9 00.5	2 04.8	1 51.2	20 14.1	22 55.7	21 39.9	19 13.0
30 F	4 32 36	9 12 43	9♐58 43	16 22 32	23 01.8	27 35.2	1 56.6	9 26.0	2 29.5	1 56.9	20 14.9	22 53.4	21 38.3	19 12.1
31 Sa	4 36 33	10 10 13	22 49 29	29 19 30	22 51.4	29 17.7	1 41.7	9 51.7	2 54.2	2 02.7	20 15.8	22 51.0	21 36.8	19 11.2

LONGITUDE — June 1980

Day	Sid.Time	☉	0 hr ☽	Noon ☽	True ☊	☿	♀	♂	⚳	♃	♄	♅	♆	♇
1 Su	4 40 29	11♊07 41	5♑52 28	12♑28 17	22♌43.5	0♋57.4	1♋24.4	10♍17.7	3♊18.9	2♍08.7	20♍16.8	22♏48.6	21♐35.2	19♎10.3
2 M	4 44 26	12 05 09	19 06 53	25 48 11	22R38.3	2 34.3	1R04.9	10 43.9	3 43.5	2 14.8	20 17.8	22R46.3	21R33.6	19R09.5
3 Tu	4 48 23	13 02 36	2♒32 08	9♒18 44	22D35.7	4 08.2	0 43.1	11 10.4	4 08.2	2 21.1	20 19.0	22 44.0	21 32.0	19 08.6
4 W	4 52 19	14 00 02	16 07 58	22 59 51	22 35.0	5 39.3	0 19.1	11 37.1	4 32.9	2 27.5	20 20.3	22 41.7	21 30.4	19 07.8
5 Th	4 56 16	14 57 27	29 54 25	6♓51 41	22R35.4	7 07.4	29♊53.0	12 04.0	4 57.5	2 34.0	20 21.7	22 39.4	21 28.8	19 07.1
6 F	5 00 12	15 54 52	13♓51 39	20 54 17	22 35.4	8 32.5	29 25.0	12 31.2	5 22.2	2 40.7	20 23.2	22 37.2	21 27.2	19 06.3
7 Sa	5 04 09	16 52 16	27 59 30	5♈07 07	22 34.1	9 54.6	28 55.2	12 58.6	5 46.9	2 47.5	20 24.7	22 35.0	21 25.6	19 05.6
8 Su	5 08 05	17 49 40	12♈16 54	19 28 31	22 30.7	11 13.7	28 23.7	13 26.3	6 11.5	2 54.5	20 26.4	22 32.8	21 24.0	19 04.9
9 M	5 12 02	18 47 03	26 41 31	3♉55 22	22 24.9	12 29.7	27 50.8	13 54.1	6 36.1	3 01.6	20 28.2	22 30.6	21 22.3	19 04.3
10 Tu	5 15 58	19 44 26	11♉09 26	18 23 00	22 17.0	13 42.6	27 16.5	14 22.2	7 00.8	3 08.8	20 30.1	22 28.4	21 20.7	19 03.7
11 W	5 19 55	20 41 48	25 35 19	2♊45 37	22 07.7	14 52.2	26 41.2	14 50.5	7 25.4	3 16.1	20 32.1	22 26.3	21 19.1	19 03.1
12 Th	5 23 52	21 39 09	9♊53 08	16 57 08	21 58.1	15 58.7	26 04.9	15 19.1	7 50.0	3 23.6	20 34.1	22 24.2	21 17.5	19 02.5
13 F	5 27 48	22 36 30	23 56 57	0♋52 04	21 49.3	17 01.8	25 28.0	15 47.8	8 14.6	3 31.2	20 36.3	22 22.1	21 15.9	19 02.0
14 Sa	5 31 45	23 33 50	7♋42 00	14 26 29	21 42.3	18 01.5	24 50.7	16 16.7	8 39.2	3 38.9	20 38.6	22 20.1	21 14.2	19 01.5
15 Su	5 35 41	24 31 10	21 05 18	27 38 26	21 37.4	18 57.7	24 13.2	16 45.9	9 03.8	3 46.7	20 40.9	22 18.1	21 12.6	19 01.1
16 M	5 39 38	25 28 28	4♌05 59	10♌28 07	21D34.9	19 50.4	23 35.7	17 15.3	9 28.4	3 54.7	20 43.4	22 16.1	21 11.0	19 00.6
17 Tu	5 43 34	26 25 46	16 45 09	22 57 30	21 34.3	20 39.4	22 58.4	17 44.8	9 52.9	4 02.8	20 46.0	22 14.2	21 09.4	19 00.3
18 W	5 47 31	27 23 03	29 05 39	5♍10 06	21 34.9	21 24.6	22 21.7	18 14.5	10 17.5	4 11.0	20 48.6	22 12.3	21 07.8	18 59.9
19 Th	5 51 27	28 20 19	11♍11 27	17 10 19	21 35.9	22 06.0	21 45.7	18 44.5	10 42.0	4 19.3	20 51.4	22 10.4	21 06.2	18 59.6
20 F	5 55 24	29 17 35	23 07 20	29 03 10	21R36.5	22 43.3	21 10.7	19 14.6	11 06.5	4 27.7	20 54.2	22 08.6	21 04.6	18 59.3
21 Sa	5 59 21	0♋14 50	4♎58 27	10♎53 50	21 35.8	23 16.6	20 36.8	19 44.9	11 31.0	4 36.3	20 57.1	22 06.8	21 03.0	18 59.0
22 Su	6 03 17	1 12 04	16 49 57	22 47 22	21 33.3	23 45.7	20 04.3	20 15.4	11 55.5	4 44.9	21 00.1	22 05.0	21 01.4	18 58.8
23 M	6 07 14	2 09 17	28 46 41	4♏48 24	21 28.8	24 10.5	19 33.4	20 46.0	12 19.9	4 53.6	21 03.2	22 03.3	20 59.8	18 58.6
24 Tu	6 11 10	3 06 30	10♏52 58	17 00 50	21 22.6	24 30.9	19 04.2	21 16.8	12 44.3	5 02.5	21 06.4	22 01.6	20 58.2	18 58.4
25 W	6 15 07	4 03 42	23 12 19	29 27 43	21 15.2	24 46.8	18 36.8	21 47.8	13 08.7	5 11.5	21 09.7	21 59.9	20 56.6	18 58.3
26 Th	6 19 03	5 00 55	5♐47 11	12♐10 53	21 07.2	24 58.2	18 11.5	22 19.0	13 33.1	5 20.5	21 13.1	21 58.3	20 55.1	18 58.2
27 F	6 23 00	5 58 06	18 38 49	25 10 59	20 59.5	25R05.0	17 48.2	22 50.3	13 57.5	5 29.7	21 16.6	21 56.7	20 53.5	18 58.1
28 Sa	6 26 56	6 55 18	1♑47 15	8♑27 28	20 52.9	25 07.1	17 27.1	23 21.8	14 21.9	5 39.0	21 20.1	21 55.2	20 52.0	18D58.1
29 Su	6 30 53	7 52 29	15 11 23	21 58 45	20 48.1	25 04.7	17 08.4	23 53.5	14 46.2	5 48.4	21 23.8	21 53.7	20 50.4	18 58.1
30 M	6 34 50	8 49 40	28 49 15	5♒42 34	20 45.2	24 57.6	16 51.9	24 25.3	15 10.5	5 57.8	21 27.5	21 52.2	20 48.9	18 58.1

Astro Data

	Dy Hr Mn
☽0N	11 9:38
♄ D	22 11:50
♀ R	24 20:10
☽0S	24 22:41
☽0N	7 17:36
♃∠♇	17 4:51
☽0S	21 7:37
♄□♆	22 18:21
☿ R	28 11:12
♇ D	28 20:09

Planet Ingress

	Dy Hr Mn
☿ ♉	2 10:56
♂ ♍	4 2:27
♀ ♋	12 20:53
☿ ♊	16 17:06
☉ ♊	20 21:42
⚳ ♊	24 10:39
☿ ♋	31 22:05
♀ ♊R	5 5:44
☉ ♋	21 5:47

Last Aspect / ☽ Ingress

Last Aspect Dy Hr Mn		☽ Ingress Dy Hr Mn
1 21:13 ♂ □	♐	1 22:22
3 22:32 ♀ ☍	♑	4 7:14
6 3:05 ♅ ⚹	♒	6 14:03
8 15:11 ♀ △	♓	8 18:33
10 19:15 ♀ □	♈	10 20:44
12 8:38 ♆ △	♉	12 21:24
14 14:34 ☿ ☌	♊	14 22:07
16 11:01 ♆ ☍	♋	17 0:52
19 4:06 ☉ ⚹	♌	19 7:14
21 4:10 ♅ □	♍	21 17:32
23 16:18 ♅ ⚹	♎	24 6:11
26 2:09 ♆ ⚹	♏	26 18:37
28 15:34 ♅ ☌	♐	29 5:05
31 11:56 ☿ ☍	♑	31 13:14

Last Aspect / ☽ Ingress

Last Aspect Dy Hr Mn		☽ Ingress Dy Hr Mn
2 6:35 ♅ ⚹	♒	2 19:29
4 11:28 ♅ □	♓	5 0:10
7 1:55 ♀ □	♈	7 3:23
9 2:17 ♀ ⚹	♉	9 5:29
10 18:47 ♅ ☍	♊	11 7:22
13 3:01 ♀ ☌	♋	13 10:29
15 2:14 ♅ △	♌	15 16:22
17 19:21 ☉ ⚹	♍	18 1:47
20 12:32 ☉ □	♎	20 13:55
22 14:02 ☿ □	♏	23 2:26
25 2:51 ☿ △	♐	25 13:02
27 7:32 ♂ □	♑	27 20:46
29 17:25 ☿ ☍	♒	30 2:04

☽ Phases & Eclipses

Dy Hr Mn	
7 20:51	☾ 17♒25
14 12:00	● 23♉50
21 19:16	☽ 0♍52
29 21:28	○ 8♐38
6 2:53	☾ 15♓33
12 20:38	● 22♊00
20 12:32	☽ 29♍19
28 9:02	○ 6♑48

Astro Data

1 May 1980
Julian Day # 29341
SVP 5♓32'15"
GC 26♐33.9 ⚴ 7♈45.9
Eris 14♈49.1 ⚵ 0♌12.1
⚷ 13♉26.1 ⚶ 10♊43.2
☽ Mean ☊ 25♌27.6

1 June 1980
Julian Day # 29372
SVP 5♓32'11"
GC 26♐33.9 ⚴ 17♈45.7
Eris 15♈05.0 ⚵ 11♌21.3
⚷ 15♉25.0 ⚶ 23♊53.0
☽ Mean ☊ 23♌49.1

July 1980 LONGITUDE

Day	Sid.Time	☉	0 hr ☽	Noon ☽	True ☊	☿	♀	♂	⚳	♃	♄	♅	♆	♇
1 Tu	6 38 46	9♋46 51	12♒38 24	19♒36 24	20♌44.3	24♋46.2	16♊37.8	24♍57.2	15♊34.8	6♍07.4	21♍31.3	21♏50.8	20♐47.4	18♎58.2
2 W	6 42 43	10 44 03	26 36 17	3♓37 46	20D44.8	24R30.3	16R26.2	25 29.4	15 59.1	6 17.0	21 35.2	21R49.4	20R45.9	18 58.3
3 Th	6 46 39	11 41 14	10♓40 34	17 44 27	20 46.1	24 10.4	16 16.9	26 01.6	16 23.3	6 26.8	21 39.1	21 48.1	20 44.4	18 58.4
4 F	6 50 36	12 38 25	24 49 10	1♈54 31	20R47.3	23 46.6	16 10.0	26 34.0	16 47.5	6 36.6	21 43.2	21 46.8	20 42.9	18 58.6
5 Sa	6 54 32	13 35 37	9♈00 16	16 06 12	20 47.6	23 19.2	16 05.6	27 06.6	17 11.7	6 46.6	21 47.3	21 45.6	20 41.4	18 58.8
6 Su	6 58 29	14 32 50	23 12 05	0♉17 39	20 46.6	22 48.6	16D03.5	27 39.3	17 35.9	6 56.6	21 51.5	21 44.4	20 40.0	18 59.1
7 M	7 02 25	15 30 02	7♉22 36	14 26 37	20 44.1	22 15.4	16 03.8	28 12.2	18 00.0	7 06.7	21 55.8	21 43.2	20 38.6	18 59.3
8 Tu	7 06 22	16 27 15	21 29 23	28 30 30	20 40.2	21 39.9	16 06.3	28 45.2	18 24.1	7 16.9	22 00.2	21 42.1	20 37.1	18 59.6
9 W	7 10 19	17 24 29	5♊29 36	12♊26 16	20 35.4	21 02.7	16 11.2	29 18.4	18 48.2	7 27.2	22 04.6	21 41.0	20 35.7	19 00.0
10 Th	7 14 15	18 21 43	19 20 09	26 10 50	20 30.4	20 24.5	16 18.2	29 51.7	19 12.2	7 37.6	22 09.1	21 40.0	20 34.3	19 00.4
11 F	7 18 12	19 18 57	2♋58 00	9♋41 20	20 25.9	19 45.9	16 27.4	0♎25.1	19 36.3	7 48.0	22 13.8	21 39.1	20 32.9	19 00.8
12 Sa	7 22 08	20 16 11	16 20 36	22 55 38	20 22.3	19 07.6	16 38.6	0 58.7	20 00.3	7 58.5	22 18.4	21 38.1	20 31.6	19 01.2
13 Su	7 26 05	21 13 26	29 26 17	5♌52 33	20 20.0	18 30.1	16 51.9	1 32.5	20 24.2	8 09.2	22 23.2	21 37.3	20 30.2	19 01.7
14 M	7 30 01	22 10 41	12♌14 28	18 32 09	20D19.2	17 54.3	17 07.2	2 06.3	20 48.1	8 19.9	22 28.0	21 36.4	20 28.9	19 02.2
15 Tu	7 33 58	23 07 56	24 45 48	0♍55 41	20 19.6	17 20.6	17 24.4	2 40.3	21 12.0	8 30.6	22 32.9	21 35.7	20 27.6	19 02.8
16 W	7 37 54	24 05 11	7♍02 07	13 05 31	20 20.9	16 49.8	17 43.4	3 14.5	21 35.8	8 41.5	22 37.9	21 34.9	20 26.3	19 03.3
17 Th	7 41 51	25 02 27	19 06 17	25 04 56	20 22.5	16 22.4	18 04.2	3 48.7	21 59.6	8 52.4	22 42.9	21 34.2	20 25.1	19 03.9
18 F	7 45 48	25 59 42	1♎01 59	6♎58 00	20 24.1	15 58.9	18 26.7	4 23.1	22 23.4	9 03.4	22 48.0	21 33.6	20 23.8	19 04.6
19 Sa	7 49 44	26 56 58	12 53 32	18 49 11	20R25.1	15 39.8	18 50.9	4 57.6	22 47.1	9 14.4	22 53.2	21 33.0	20 22.6	19 05.3
20 Su	7 53 41	27 54 14	24 45 35	0♏43 18	20 25.4	15 25.4	19 16.8	5 32.3	23 10.8	9 25.5	22 58.4	21 32.5	20 21.4	19 06.0
21 M	7 57 37	28 51 30	6♏42 56	12 45 04	20 24.6	15 16.2	19 44.2	6 07.1	23 34.5	9 36.7	23 03.7	21 32.0	20 20.2	19 06.7
22 Tu	8 01 34	29 48 47	18 50 15	24 58 59	20 23.0	15D12.3	20 13.1	6 42.0	23 58.1	9 48.0	23 09.1	21 31.6	20 19.0	19 07.5
23 W	8 05 30	0♌46 04	1♐11 46	7♐29 00	20 20.7	15 14.1	20 43.4	7 17.0	24 21.6	9 59.3	23 14.5	21 31.2	20 17.9	19 08.3
24 Th	8 09 27	1 43 21	13 51 00	20 18 05	20 18.1	15 21.6	21 15.2	7 52.1	24 45.1	10 10.7	23 20.0	21 30.9	20 16.7	19 09.1
25 F	8 13 23	2 40 39	26 50 23	3♑28 01	20 15.6	15 35.1	21 48.3	8 27.4	25 08.6	10 22.1	23 25.6	21 30.6	20 15.6	19 10.0
26 Sa	8 17 20	3 37 58	10♑10 56	16 59 03	20 13.5	15 54.5	22 22.7	9 02.7	25 32.0	10 33.6	23 31.2	21 30.4	20 14.6	19 10.9
27 Su	8 21 17	4 35 17	23 52 08	0♒49 50	20 12.0	16 20.0	22 58.4	9 38.2	25 55.4	10 45.2	23 36.9	21 30.2	20 13.5	19 11.9
28 M	8 25 13	5 32 36	7♒51 46	14 57 25	20D11.4	16 51.5	23 35.3	10 13.8	26 18.7	10 56.8	23 42.6	21 30.1	20 12.5	19 12.8
29 Tu	8 29 10	6 29 57	22 06 13	29 17 34	20 11.4	17 29.1	24 13.4	10 49.5	26 42.0	11 08.5	23 48.4	21D30.0	20 11.5	19 13.8
30 W	8 33 06	7 27 18	6♓30 49	13♓45 18	20 12.1	18 12.6	24 52.6	11 25.4	27 05.2	11 20.2	23 54.3	21 30.0	20 10.5	19 14.9
31 Th	8 37 03	8 24 41	21 00 24	28 15 29	20 13.0	19 02.1	25 32.9	12 01.3	27 28.4	11 32.0	24 00.2	21 30.0	20 09.6	19 15.9

August 1980 LONGITUDE

Day	Sid.Time	☉	0 hr ☽	Noon ☽	True ☊	☿	♀	♂	⚳	♃	♄	♅	♆	♇
1 F	8 40 59	9♌22 04	5♈29 58	12♈43 18	20♌13.8	19♋57.5	26♊14.2	12♎37.3	27♊51.6	11♍43.9	24♍06.1	21♏30.1	20♐08.6	19♎17.0
2 Sa	8 44 56	10 19 29	19 55 02	27 04 45	20 14.5	20 58.7	26 56.6	13 13.5	28 14.6	11 55.8	24 12.2	21 30.2	20R07.7	19 18.1
3 Su	8 48 52	11 16 55	4♉12 05	11♉16 45	20R14.7	22 05.4	27 39.9	13 49.8	28 37.7	12 07.7	24 18.2	21 30.4	20 06.9	19 19.3
4 M	8 52 49	12 14 22	18 18 30	25 17 09	20 14.5	23 17.7	28 24.1	14 26.2	29 00.6	12 19.7	24 24.4	21 30.6	20 06.0	19 20.5
5 Tu	8 56 46	13 11 50	2♊12 33	9♊04 36	20 14.0	24 35.3	29 09.3	15 02.7	29 23.6	12 31.8	24 30.5	21 30.9	20 05.2	19 21.7
6 W	9 00 42	14 09 20	15 53 14	22 38 22	20 13.3	25 58.1	29 55.3	15 39.3	29 46.4	12 43.9	24 36.8	21 31.2	20 04.4	19 22.9
7 Th	9 04 39	15 06 51	29 19 59	5♋58 03	20 12.7	27 25.7	0♋42.2	16 16.0	0♋09.2	12 56.0	24 43.1	21 31.6	20 03.6	19 24.2
8 F	9 08 35	16 04 23	12♋32 36	19 03 36	20 12.1	28 58.0	1 29.8	16 52.9	0 32.0	13 08.2	24 49.4	21 32.1	20 02.9	19 25.5
9 Sa	9 12 32	17 01 57	25 31 07	1♌55 11	20 11.8	0♌34.7	2 18.2	17 29.8	0 54.6	13 20.4	24 55.8	21 32.6	20 02.2	19 26.8
10 Su	9 16 28	17 59 31	8♌15 51	14 33 13	20D11.7	2 15.4	3 07.4	18 06.8	1 17.2	13 32.7	25 02.2	21 33.1	20 01.5	19 28.2
11 M	9 20 25	18 57 07	20 47 23	26 58 29	20 11.7	3 59.9	3 57.3	18 44.0	1 39.8	13 45.0	25 08.7	21 33.7	20 00.8	19 29.6
12 Tu	9 24 21	19 54 44	3♍06 42	9♍12 12	20R11.7	5 47.7	4 47.8	19 21.3	2 02.3	13 57.4	25 15.2	21 34.4	20 00.2	19 31.0
13 W	9 28 18	20 52 22	15 15 15	21 16 05	20 11.7	7 38.5	5 39.0	19 58.6	2 24.7	14 09.8	25 21.7	21 35.1	19 59.6	19 32.4
14 Th	9 32 15	21 50 01	27 15 03	3♎12 27	20 11.6	9 31.8	6 30.9	20 36.1	2 47.0	14 22.2	25 28.3	21 35.8	19 59.1	19 33.9
15 F	9 36 11	22 47 41	9♎08 42	15 04 12	20 11.3	11 27.3	7 23.4	21 13.7	3 09.3	14 34.7	25 35.0	21 36.6	19 58.5	19 35.4
16 Sa	9 40 08	23 45 22	20 59 23	26 54 46	20 10.9	13 24.7	8 16.4	21 51.4	3 31.5	14 47.2	25 41.6	21 37.5	19 58.0	19 36.9
17 Su	9 44 04	24 43 04	2♏50 49	8♏48 06	20 10.6	15 23.4	9 10.1	22 29.1	3 53.6	14 59.7	25 48.4	21 38.4	19 57.5	19 38.5
18 M	9 48 01	25 40 48	14 47 08	20 48 30	20D10.4	17 23.1	10 04.3	23 07.0	4 15.6	15 12.3	25 55.1	21 39.4	19 57.1	19 40.1
19 Tu	9 51 57	26 38 32	26 52 45	3♐00 28	20 10.4	19 23.6	10 59.1	23 45.0	4 37.6	15 24.9	26 01.9	21 40.4	19 56.7	19 41.7
20 W	9 55 54	27 36 18	9♐12 11	15 28 25	20 10.7	21 24.4	11 54.4	24 23.1	4 59.5	15 37.5	26 08.8	21 41.4	19 56.3	19 43.3
21 Th	9 59 50	28 34 04	21 49 40	28 16 21	20 11.4	23 25.3	12 50.2	25 01.3	5 21.3	15 50.2	26 15.6	21 42.6	19 56.0	19 45.0
22 F	10 03 47	29 31 52	4♑48 51	11♑27 26	20 12.2	25 26.0	13 46.4	25 39.5	5 43.0	16 02.9	26 22.5	21 43.7	19 55.6	19 46.7
23 Sa	10 07 44	0♍29 41	18 12 18	25 03 30	20 13.0	27 26.4	14 43.2	26 17.9	6 04.6	16 15.6	26 29.5	21 44.9	19 55.4	19 48.4
24 Su	10 11 40	1 27 32	2♒00 57	9♒04 29	20R13.6	29 26.2	15 40.5	26 56.3	6 26.2	16 28.3	26 36.4	21 46.2	19 55.1	19 50.1
25 M	10 15 37	2 25 23	16 13 41	23 28 05	20 13.8	1♍25.3	16 38.2	27 34.9	6 47.6	16 41.1	26 43.4	21 47.5	19 54.9	19 51.8
26 Tu	10 19 33	3 23 17	0♓47 01	8♓09 40	20 13.3	3 23.6	17 36.3	28 13.5	7 09.0	16 53.8	26 50.4	21 48.9	19 54.7	19 53.6
27 W	10 23 30	4 21 11	15 35 10	23 02 31	20 12.2	5 20.9	18 34.9	28 52.3	7 30.3	17 06.6	26 57.5	21 50.3	19 54.5	19 55.4
28 Th	10 27 26	5 19 08	0♈30 42	7♈58 40	20 10.5	7 17.2	19 33.9	29 31.1	7 51.5	17 19.5	27 04.6	21 51.7	19 54.4	19 57.2
29 F	10 31 23	6 17 06	15 25 26	22 50 03	20 08.6	9 12.4	20 33.3	0♏10.0	8 12.6	17 32.3	27 11.7	21 53.2	19 54.3	19 59.1
30 Sa	10 35 19	7 15 06	0♉11 40	7♉29 34	20 06.7	11 06.4	21 33.1	0 49.0	8 33.6	17 45.2	27 18.8	21 54.8	19 54.2	20 00.9
31 Su	10 39 16	8 13 07	14 43 10	21 52 01	20 05.4	12 59.3	22 33.3	1 28.1	8 54.5	17 58.0	27 26.0	21 56.4	19D54.2	20 02.8

Astro Data

	Dy Hr Mn
☽0N	4 23:58
♄⚹♅	5 4:16
♀D	6 21:15
♂0S	12 5:07
☽0S	18 16:28
☿D	22 16:37
♅D	30 11:39
☽0N	1 6:15
☽0S	15 0:16
♆⚹♇	27 1:00
☽0N	28 14:02
♆D	31 23:39

Planet Ingress

	Dy Hr Mn
♂ ♎	10 17:59
☉ ♌	22 16:42
♀ ♋	6 14:25
⚳ ♋	7 2:18
☿ ♌	9 3:31
☉ ♍	22 23:41
☿ ♍	24 18:47
♂ ♏	29 5:50

Last Aspect / ☽ Ingress

Last Aspect Dy Hr Mn		☽ Ingress	Dy Hr Mn
1 15:50	♅ □	♓	2 5:48
4 2:36	♂ ☍	♈	4 8:46
5 23:47	☿ □	♉	6 11:30
8 12:26	♂ △	♊	8 14:33
10 4:53	♄ □	♋	10 18:44
12 10:52	♄ ⚹	♌	13 1:03
14 17:54	♅ □	♍	15 10:11
17 11:55	☉ ⚹	♎	17 21:55
20 5:51	☉ □	♏	20 10:33
22 8:25	♄ ⚹	♐	22 21:42
24 17:37	♄ □	♑	25 5:45
26 23:28	♄ △	♒	27 10:34
29 3:09	♀ △	♓	29 13:11
31 7:18	♀ □	♈	31 14:53

Last Aspect / ☽ Ingress

Last Aspect Dy Hr Mn		☽ Ingress	Dy Hr Mn
2 11:46	♀ ⚹	♉	2 16:55
4 10:28	♄ △	♊	4 20:10
6 15:33	♄ □	♋	7 1:12
8 22:47	♄ ⚹	♌	9 8:23
11 1:29	♅ □	♍	11 17:54
13 20:17	♄ ☌	♎	14 5:32
16 5:02	☉ ⚹	♏	16 18:15
18 22:28	☉ □	♐	19 6:08
21 12:35	☉ △	♑	21 15:11
23 14:30	♄ △	♒	23 20:32
25 19:04	♂ △	♓	25 22:43
27 18:21	♄ ☍	♈	27 23:11
29 8:02	♀ □	♉	29 23:41

☽ Phases & Eclipses

Dy Hr Mn	
5 7:27	☾ 13♈25
12 6:46	● 20♋04
20 5:51	☽ 27♎40
27 18:54	○ 4♒52
27 19:08	☍ A 0.253
3 12:00	☾ 11♉17
10 19:09	● 18♌17
10 19:11:30	☌ A 03'23"
18 22:28	☽ 26♏06
26 3:42	○ 3♓03
26 3:30	☍ A 0.709

Astro Data

1 July 1980
Julian Day # 29402
SVP 5♓32'06"
GC 26♐34.0 ⚴ 26♈19.0
Eris 15♈12.8 ⚵ 23♌05.6
⚷ 17♉01.7 ⚶ 6♋53.7
☽ Mean ☊ 22♌13.8

1 August 1980
Julian Day # 29433
SVP 5♓32'01"
GC 26♐34.1 ⚴ 2♉58.8
Eris 15♈10.9R ⚵ 5♍36.5
⚷ 18♉03.7 ⚶ 20♋21.4
☽ Mean ☊ 20♌35.3

LONGITUDE — September 1980

Day	Sid.Time	☉	0 hr ☽	Noon ☽	True ☊	☿	♀	♂	⚳	♃	♄	♅	♆	♇
1 M	10 43 13	9♍11 11	28♉55 49	5♊54 23	20♌04.7	14♍50.9	23♋33.8	2♏07.3	9♋15.4	18♍10.9	27♍33.2	21♏58.0	19♐54.2	20♎04.7
2 Tu	10 47 09	10 09 17	12♊47 40	19 35 43	20D 04.9	16 41.4	24 34.7	2 46.6	9 36.1	18 23.8	27 40.4	21 59.7	19 54.2	20 06.7
3 W	10 51 06	11 07 25	26 18 40	2♋56 42	20 05.9	18 30.7	25 36.0	3 26.0	9 56.7	18 36.8	27 47.6	22 01.5	19 54.3	20 08.6
4 Th	10 55 02	12 05 35	9♋30 06	15 59 07	20 07.3	20 18.7	26 37.6	4 05.5	10 17.2	18 49.7	27 54.9	22 03.3	19 54.4	20 10.6
5 F	10 58 59	13 03 47	22 24 02	28 45 11	20 08.9	22 05.5	27 39.6	4 45.1	10 37.6	19 02.7	28 02.2	22 05.1	19 54.5	20 12.6
6 Sa	11 02 55	14 02 00	5♌02 52	11♌17 21	20R 09.9	23 51.2	28 41.9	5 24.8	10 57.9	19 15.6	28 09.4	22 07.0	19 54.7	20 14.6
7 Su	11 06 52	15 00 16	17 28 56	23 37 52	20 10.2	25 35.6	29 44.4	6 04.5	11 18.1	19 28.6	28 16.8	22 08.9	19 54.9	20 16.6
8 M	11 10 48	15 58 33	29 44 24	5♍48 47	20 09.2	27 18.9	0♌47.3	6 44.4	11 38.1	19 41.6	28 24.1	22 10.9	19 55.1	20 18.7
9 Tu	11 14 45	16 56 52	11♍51 13	17 51 56	20 06.9	29 01.0	1 50.5	7 24.3	11 58.1	19 54.5	28 31.4	22 12.9	19 55.4	20 20.7
10 W	11 18 41	17 55 13	23 51 08	29 49 03	20 03.2	0♎41.9	2 54.0	8 04.4	12 17.9	20 07.5	28 38.8	22 15.0	19 55.7	20 22.8
11 Th	11 22 38	18 53 36	5♎45 53	11♎41 53	19 58.5	2 21.8	3 57.7	8 44.5	12 37.6	20 20.5	28 46.2	22 17.1	19 56.0	20 24.9
12 F	11 26 35	19 52 00	17 37 17	23 32 24	19 53.2	4 00.5	5 01.7	9 24.7	12 57.1	20 33.5	28 53.5	22 19.2	19 56.4	20 27.0
13 Sa	11 30 31	20 50 27	29 27 30	5♏22 57	19 47.8	5 38.1	6 06.0	10 05.0	13 16.6	20 46.5	29 00.9	22 21.4	19 56.7	20 29.2
14 Su	11 34 28	21 48 55	11♏19 06	17 16 21	19 43.0	7 14.7	7 10.5	10 45.4	13 35.9	20 59.5	29 08.3	22 23.7	19 57.2	20 31.3
15 M	11 38 24	22 47 24	23 15 08	29 15 55	19 39.3	8 50.1	8 15.3	11 25.9	13 55.0	21 12.5	29 15.8	22 26.0	19 57.6	20 33.5
16 Tu	11 42 21	23 45 55	5♐19 12	11♐25 31	19 37.0	10 24.6	9 20.3	12 06.5	14 14.1	21 25.5	29 23.2	22 28.3	19 58.1	20 35.7
17 W	11 46 17	24 44 28	17 35 22	23 49 20	19D 36.2	11 57.9	10 25.6	12 47.1	14 33.0	21 38.5	29 30.6	22 30.6	19 58.7	20 37.9
18 Th	11 50 14	25 43 03	0♑07 57	6♑31 45	19 36.7	13 30.3	11 31.1	13 27.8	14 51.7	21 51.5	29 38.0	22 33.0	19 59.2	20 40.1
19 F	11 54 10	26 41 39	13 01 15	19 36 53	19 38.0	15 01.5	12 36.9	14 08.7	15 10.4	22 04.4	29 45.5	22 35.5	19 59.8	20 42.3
20 Sa	11 58 07	27 40 17	26 19 02	3♒08 00	19 39.5	16 31.8	13 42.8	14 49.6	15 28.8	22 17.4	29 52.9	22 38.0	20 00.4	20 44.5
21 Su	12 02 04	28 38 57	10♒03 58	17 06 56	19R 40.3	18 01.0	14 49.0	15 30.5	15 47.2	22 30.4	0♎00.4	22 40.5	20 01.1	20 46.8
22 M	12 06 00	29 37 38	24 16 47	1♓33 11	19 39.8	19 29.2	15 55.4	16 11.6	16 05.3	22 43.3	0 07.8	22 43.1	20 01.8	20 49.0
23 Tu	12 09 57	0♎36 21	8♓55 35	16 23 15	19 37.5	20 56.3	17 02.1	16 52.7	16 23.3	22 56.3	0 15.3	22 45.7	20 02.5	20 51.3
24 W	12 13 53	1 35 06	23 55 16	1♈30 31	19 33.3	22 22.4	18 08.9	17 34.0	16 41.2	23 09.2	0 22.7	22 48.3	20 03.2	20 53.6
25 Th	12 17 50	2 33 53	9♈07 46	16 45 40	19 27.5	23 47.4	19 16.0	18 15.3	16 58.9	23 22.1	0 30.1	22 51.0	20 04.0	20 55.9
26 F	12 21 46	3 32 41	24 22 52	1♉58 02	19 20.9	25 11.2	20 23.2	18 56.6	17 16.4	23 35.0	0 37.6	22 53.7	20 04.8	20 58.2
27 Sa	12 25 43	4 31 33	9♉29 56	16 57 29	19 14.4	26 34.0	21 30.7	19 38.1	17 33.8	23 47.9	0 45.0	22 56.4	20 05.7	21 00.5
28 Su	12 29 39	5 30 26	24 19 44	1♊35 58	19 09.0	27 55.6	22 38.3	20 19.7	17 51.0	24 00.8	0 52.5	22 59.2	20 06.5	21 02.8
29 M	12 33 36	6 29 22	8♊45 43	15 48 39	19 05.1	29 16.1	23 46.2	21 01.3	18 08.1	24 13.6	0 59.9	23 02.0	20 07.5	21 05.1
30 Tu	12 37 33	7 28 20	22 44 41	29 33 52	19D 03.2	0♏35.2	24 54.2	21 43.0	18 24.9	24 26.5	1 07.3	23 04.9	20 08.4	21 07.5

LONGITUDE — October 1980

Day	Sid.Time	☉	0 hr ☽	Noon ☽	True ☊	☿	♀	♂	⚳	♃	♄	♅	♆	♇
1 W	12 41 29	8♎27 20	6♋16 25	12♋52 39	19♌03.0	1♏53.1	26♌02.4	22♏24.8	18♋41.6	24♍39.3	1♎14.7	23♏07.7	20♐09.4	21♎09.8
2 Th	12 45 26	9 26 23	19 22 59	25 47 53	19 03.9	3 09.7	27 10.8	23 06.7	18 58.1	24 52.1	1 22.1	23 10.7	20 10.4	21 12.1
3 F	12 49 22	10 25 28	2♌07 51	8♌23 25	19R 05.0	4 24.8	28 19.4	23 48.6	19 14.4	25 04.9	1 29.5	23 13.6	20 11.4	21 14.5
4 Sa	12 53 19	11 24 35	14 35 05	20 43 22	19 05.4	5 38.4	29 28.1	24 30.7	19 30.5	25 17.6	1 36.9	23 16.6	20 12.4	21 16.9
5 Su	12 57 15	12 23 45	26 48 46	2♍51 42	19 04.3	6 50.4	0♍37.0	25 12.8	19 46.5	25 30.3	1 44.3	23 19.6	20 13.5	21 19.2
6 M	13 01 12	13 22 56	8♍52 38	14 51 55	19 01.0	8 00.6	1 46.1	25 55.0	20 02.2	25 43.0	1 51.7	23 22.6	20 14.7	21 21.6
7 Tu	13 05 08	14 22 10	20 49 53	26 46 52	18 55.1	9 09.1	2 55.3	26 37.3	20 17.7	25 55.7	1 59.0	23 25.7	20 15.8	21 24.0
8 W	13 09 05	15 21 26	2♎43 06	8♎38 52	18 46.8	10 15.5	4 04.7	27 19.7	20 33.0	26 08.3	2 06.3	23 28.8	20 17.0	21 26.4
9 Th	13 13 01	16 20 44	14 34 20	20 29 44	18 36.5	11 19.7	5 14.2	28 02.1	20 48.1	26 20.9	2 13.6	23 32.0	20 18.2	21 28.8
10 F	13 16 58	17 20 04	26 25 15	2♏21 03	18 24.9	12 21.7	6 23.9	28 44.6	21 03.0	26 33.5	2 20.9	23 35.1	20 19.4	21 31.1
11 Sa	13 20 55	18 19 26	8♏17 20	14 14 19	18 13.1	13 21.0	7 33.7	29 27.2	21 17.7	26 46.0	2 28.2	23 38.3	20 20.7	21 33.5
12 Su	13 24 51	19 18 50	20 12 12	26 11 14	18 02.2	14 17.6	8 43.7	0♐09.9	21 32.1	26 58.5	2 35.5	23 41.5	20 22.0	21 35.9
13 M	13 28 48	20 18 16	2♐11 43	8♐13 56	17 53.0	15 11.1	9 53.8	0 52.6	21 46.3	27 11.0	2 42.7	23 44.8	20 23.3	21 38.3
14 Tu	13 32 44	21 17 44	14 18 17	20 25 07	17 46.1	16 01.3	11 04.0	1 35.5	22 00.3	27 23.4	2 49.9	23 48.0	20 24.6	21 40.7
15 W	13 36 41	22 17 13	26 34 53	2♑48 03	17 41.8	16 47.8	12 14.4	2 18.4	22 14.1	27 35.8	2 57.1	23 51.3	20 26.0	21 43.1
16 Th	13 40 37	23 16 45	9♑05 06	15 26 33	17D 40.0	17 30.2	13 24.9	3 01.3	22 27.6	27 48.2	3 04.3	23 54.6	20 27.4	21 45.5
17 F	13 44 34	24 16 18	21 52 54	28 24 41	17 39.7	18 08.2	14 35.5	3 44.4	22 40.8	28 00.5	3 11.4	23 58.0	20 28.9	21 47.9
18 Sa	13 48 30	25 15 53	5♒02 23	11♒46 24	17R 40.2	18 41.2	15 46.2	4 27.5	22 53.9	28 12.7	3 18.5	24 01.4	20 30.3	21 50.3
19 Su	13 52 27	26 15 29	18 37 06	25 34 43	17 40.0	19 08.9	16 57.1	5 10.7	23 06.6	28 25.0	3 25.6	24 04.7	20 31.8	21 52.7
20 M	13 56 24	27 15 07	2♓39 21	9♓50 57	17 38.2	19 30.6	18 08.1	5 54.0	23 19.1	28 37.1	3 32.6	24 08.1	20 33.3	21 55.1
21 Tu	14 00 20	28 14 47	17 09 14	24 33 43	17 34.0	19 45.9	19 19.2	6 37.3	23 31.4	28 49.3	3 39.6	24 11.6	20 34.8	21 57.5
22 W	14 04 17	29 14 29	2♈03 42	9♈38 12	17 27.1	19R 54.1	20 30.4	7 20.7	23 43.4	29 01.3	3 46.6	24 15.0	20 36.4	21 59.9
23 Th	14 08 13	0♏14 12	17 16 05	24 56 02	17 17.8	19 54.7	21 41.7	8 04.2	23 55.1	29 13.3	3 53.6	24 18.5	20 38.0	22 02.2
24 F	14 12 10	1 13 58	2♉36 35	10♉16 17	17 07.2	19 47.2	22 53.1	8 47.7	24 06.6	29 25.3	4 00.5	24 22.0	20 39.6	22 04.6
25 Sa	14 16 06	2 13 46	17 53 37	25 27 15	16 56.4	19 31.1	24 04.7	9 31.3	24 17.7	29 37.2	4 07.4	24 25.5	20 41.2	22 07.0
26 Su	14 20 03	3 13 35	2♊55 57	10♊18 42	16 46.9	19 06.0	25 16.4	10 15.0	24 28.6	29 49.1	4 14.2	24 29.0	20 42.9	22 09.4
27 M	14 23 59	4 13 27	17 34 44	24 43 28	16 39.5	18 31.7	26 28.1	10 58.7	24 39.3	0♎00.9	4 21.1	24 32.5	20 44.5	22 11.7
28 Tu	14 27 56	5 13 21	1♋44 38	8♋38 08	16 34.6	17 48.2	27 40.0	11 42.6	24 49.6	0 12.6	4 27.8	24 36.1	20 46.2	22 14.1
29 W	14 31 53	6 13 18	15 24 06	22 02 48	16 32.3	16 55.9	28 52.0	12 26.5	24 59.6	0 24.3	4 34.6	24 39.7	20 48.0	22 16.4
30 Th	14 35 49	7 13 16	28 34 38	5♌00 07	16 31.6	15 55.4	0♎04.1	13 10.4	25 09.3	0 36.0	4 41.3	24 43.3	20 49.7	22 18.8
31 F	14 39 46	8 13 17	11♌19 50	17 34 24	16 31.6	14 47.7	1 16.3	13 54.5	25 18.7	0 47.5	4 47.9	24 46.9	20 51.5	22 21.1

Astro Data (Dy Hr Mn)

♃□♆ 9 13:34
☿0S 10 21:36
☽0S 11 6:51
♃⚺♇ 11 21:43
♃⚹♅ 22 11:22
☉0S 22 21:09
☽0N 24 23:58

☽0S 8 12:51
☽0N 22 11:16
☿R 23 1:58

Planet Ingress (Dy Hr Mn)

♀ ♌ 7 17:57
☿ ♎ 10 2:00
♄ ♎ 21 10:48
☉ ♎ 22 21:09
☿ ♏ 30 1:16

♀ ♍ 4 23:07
♂ ♐ 12 6:27
☉ ♏ 23 6:18
♃ ♎ 27 10:10
♀ ♎ 30 10:38

Last Aspect Dy Hr Mn		☽ Ingress Dy Hr Mn
31 21:32	♄ △	♊ 1 1:50
3 2:35	♄ □	♋ 3 6:39
5 10:38	♄ ⚹	♌ 5 14:22
7 9:06	♅ □	♍ 8 0:31
10 9:37	♄ ☌	♎ 10 12:22
12 5:43	♇ ☌	♏ 13 1:06
15 12:00	♄ ⚹	♐ 15 13:28
17 22:56	♄ □	♑ 17 23:45
20 6:15	♄ △	♒ 20 6:31
21 21:21	♅ □	♓ 22 9:27
23 22:35	♃ ☍	♈ 24 9:37
26 0:11	☿ ☍	♉ 26 8:53
27 23:18	♃ △	♊ 28 9:21
30 3:02	♀ ⚹	♋ 30 12:46

Last Aspect Dy Hr Mn		☽ Ingress Dy Hr Mn
2 10:13	♃ ⚹	♌ 2 19:57
4 19:55	♂ □	♍ 5 6:19
7 11:39	♂ ⚹	♎ 7 18:30
9 14:00	♇ ☌	♏ 10 7:15
12 13:36	♃ ⚹	♐ 12 19:37
15 1:48	♃ □	♑ 15 6:37
17 11:15	♃ △	♒ 17 14:54
19 13:15	☉ △	♓ 19 19:31
21 18:55	♃ ☍	♈ 21 20:43
23 7:27	♇ ☍	♉ 23 19:55
25 18:45	♃ △	♊ 25 19:17
27 15:14	♀ □	♋ 27 21:00
30 1:49	♀ ⚹	♌ 30 2:38

☽ Phases & Eclipses (Dy Hr Mn)

1 18:08 ☾ 9♊26
9 10:00 ● 16♍52
17 13:54 ☽ 24♐49
24 12:08 ○ 1♈35

1 3:18 ☾ 8♋06
9 2:50 ● 15♎58
17 3:47 ☽ 23♑56
23 20:52 ○ 0♉36
30 16:33 ☾ 7♌25

Astro Data

1 September 1980
Julian Day # 29464
SVP 5♓31'58"
GC 26♐34.2 ⚴ 5♉37.0R
Eris 14♈59.8R ⚵ 18♍08.9
⚷ 18♉13.8R ⚶ 3♌34.0
☽ Mean ☊ 18♌56.8

1 October 1980
Julian Day # 29494
SVP 5♓31'55"
GC 26♐34.2 ⚴ 2♉05.6R
Eris 14♈43.0R ⚵ 0♎01.5
⚷ 17♉31.8R ⚶ 15♌44.4
☽ Mean ☊ 17♌21.5

November 1980 LONGITUDE

Day	Sid.Time	☉	0 hr ☽	Noon ☽	True ☊	☿	♀	♂	⚳	♃	♄	♅	♆	♇
1 Sa	14 43 42	9♏13 19	23♌44 27	29♌50 38	16♌31.1	13♏34.5	2♎28.6	14♐38.5	25♋27.8	0♎59.0	4♎54.5	24♏50.5	20♐53.3	22♎23.4
2 Su	14 47 39	10 13 24	5♍53 35	11♍53 54	16R 28.9	12R 17.7	3 41.0	15 22.7	25 36.6	1 10.5	5 01.1	24 54.1	20 55.1	22 25.7
3 M	14 51 35	11 13 31	17 52 09	23 48 53	16 24.2	10 59.3	4 53.4	16 07.0	25 45.0	1 21.9	5 07.6	24 57.7	20 56.9	22 28.0
4 Tu	14 55 32	12 13 40	29 44 35	5♎39 40	16 16.5	9 42.0	6 06.0	16 51.3	25 53.2	1 33.2	5 14.1	25 01.4	20 58.7	22 30.3
5 W	14 59 28	13 13 51	11♎34 32	17 29 31	16 05.8	8 28.1	7 18.6	17 35.6	26 01.0	1 44.4	5 20.5	25 05.1	21 00.6	22 32.6
6 Th	15 03 25	14 14 03	23 24 53	29 20 55	15 52.6	7 20.1	8 31.3	18 20.1	26 08.4	1 55.6	5 26.9	25 08.7	21 02.5	22 34.9
7 F	15 07 22	15 14 18	5♏17 48	11♏15 42	15 38.0	6 19.9	9 44.1	19 04.6	26 15.5	2 06.6	5 33.2	25 12.4	21 04.4	22 37.1
8 Sa	15 11 18	16 14 34	17 14 46	23 15 09	15 23.0	5 29.3	10 57.0	19 49.1	26 22.3	2 17.6	5 39.5	25 16.1	21 06.3	22 39.4
9 Su	15 15 15	17 14 53	29 16 57	5♐20 18	15 08.9	4 49.4	12 10.0	20 33.8	26 28.7	2 28.6	5 45.7	25 19.8	21 08.3	22 41.6
10 M	15 19 11	18 15 12	11♐25 20	17 32 13	14 56.7	4 21.0	13 23.0	21 18.5	26 34.7	2 39.4	5 51.9	25 23.5	21 10.2	22 43.8
11 Tu	15 23 08	19 15 34	23 41 07	29 52 15	14 47.4	4D 04.2	14 36.1	22 03.2	26 40.4	2 50.2	5 58.0	25 27.2	21 12.2	22 46.1
12 W	15 27 04	20 15 57	6♑05 53	12♑22 17	14 41.2	3 59.1	15 49.3	22 48.1	26 45.7	3 00.9	6 04.0	25 30.9	21 14.2	22 48.2
13 Th	15 31 01	21 16 21	18 41 48	25 04 47	14 37.9	4 05.0	17 02.5	23 32.9	26 50.7	3 11.5	6 10.0	25 34.6	21 16.2	22 50.4
14 F	15 34 57	22 16 47	1♒31 38	8♒02 44	14D 36.7	4 21.5	18 15.8	24 17.9	26 55.2	3 22.0	6 16.0	25 38.4	21 18.3	22 52.6
15 Sa	15 38 54	23 17 14	14 38 32	21 19 23	14R 36.7	4 47.6	19 29.2	25 02.9	26 59.4	3 32.5	6 21.9	25 42.1	21 20.3	22 54.7
16 Su	15 42 51	24 17 43	28 05 41	4♓57 43	14 36.4	5 22.6	20 42.6	25 48.0	27 03.3	3 42.8	6 27.7	25 45.8	21 22.4	22 56.9
17 M	15 46 47	25 18 12	11♓55 42	18 59 44	14 34.6	6 05.5	21 56.1	26 33.1	27 06.7	3 53.1	6 33.4	25 49.5	21 24.4	22 59.0
18 Tu	15 50 44	26 18 43	26 09 44	3♈25 30	14 30.5	6 55.4	23 09.6	27 18.2	27 09.7	4 03.2	6 39.1	25 53.2	21 26.5	23 01.1
19 W	15 54 40	27 19 15	10♈46 36	18 12 25	14 23.6	7 51.5	24 23.2	28 03.5	27 12.4	4 13.3	6 44.7	25 57.0	21 28.6	23 03.2
20 Th	15 58 37	28 19 48	25 42 06	3♉14 39	14 14.3	8 53.1	25 36.9	28 48.7	27 14.6	4 23.3	6 50.3	26 00.7	21 30.7	23 05.2
21 F	16 02 33	29 20 23	10♉48 51	18 23 27	14 03.4	9 59.3	26 50.6	29 34.1	27 16.5	4 33.1	6 55.8	26 04.4	21 32.8	23 07.3
22 Sa	16 06 30	0♐20 59	25 57 05	3♊28 25	13 52.2	11 09.6	28 04.4	0♑19.5	27 17.9	4 42.9	7 01.2	26 08.1	21 35.0	23 09.3
23 Su	16 10 26	1 21 37	10♊56 12	18 19 17	13 42.1	12 23.4	29 18.2	1 04.9	27 19.0	4 52.6	7 06.6	26 11.9	21 37.1	23 11.3
24 M	16 14 23	2 22 16	25 36 44	2♋47 46	13 34.0	13 40.2	0♏32.1	1 50.4	27 19.6	5 02.2	7 11.9	26 15.6	21 39.3	23 13.3
25 Tu	16 18 20	3 22 57	9♋51 53	16 48 45	13 28.6	14 59.6	1 46.0	2 36.0	27R 19.8	5 11.7	7 17.1	26 19.3	21 41.5	23 15.2
26 W	16 22 16	4 23 39	23 38 15	0♌20 29	13 25.9	16 21.1	3 00.0	3 21.6	27 19.6	5 21.0	7 22.3	26 23.0	21 43.6	23 17.2
27 Th	16 26 13	5 24 23	6♌55 41	13 24 13	13D 25.1	17 44.4	4 14.0	4 07.2	27 19.0	5 30.3	7 27.4	26 26.7	21 45.8	23 19.1
28 F	16 30 09	6 25 08	19 46 35	26 03 20	13R 25.5	19 09.3	5 28.1	4 53.0	27 18.0	5 39.4	7 32.4	26 30.4	21 48.0	23 21.0
29 Sa	16 34 06	7 25 55	2♍15 05	8♍22 29	13 25.8	20 35.5	6 42.3	5 38.7	27 16.5	5 48.5	7 37.3	26 34.1	21 50.2	23 22.9
30 Su	16 38 02	8 26 43	14 26 12	20 26 55	13 25.0	22 02.9	7 56.4	6 24.5	27 14.7	5 57.4	7 42.1	26 37.7	21 52.4	23 24.7

December 1980 LONGITUDE

Day	Sid.Time	☉	0 hr ☽	Noon ☽	True ☊	☿	♀	♂	⚳	♃	♄	♅	♆	♇
1 M	16 41 59	9♐27 32	26♍25 16	2♎21 54	13♌22.2	23♏31.1	9♏10.7	7♑10.4	27♋12.4	6♎06.2	7♎46.9	26♏41.4	21♐54.6	23♎26.6
2 Tu	16 45 55	10 28 23	8♎17 25	14 12 22	13R 16.8	25 00.1	10 24.9	7 56.3	27R 09.6	6 14.9	7 51.6	26 45.0	21 56.9	23 28.4
3 W	16 49 52	11 29 16	20 07 17	26 02 37	13 08.9	26 29.8	11 39.2	8 42.3	27 06.5	6 23.5	7 56.2	26 48.7	21 59.1	23 30.1
4 Th	16 53 49	12 30 10	1♏58 47	7♏56 10	12 58.8	28 00.0	12 53.6	9 28.3	27 02.9	6 32.0	8 00.8	26 52.3	22 01.3	23 31.9
5 F	16 57 45	13 31 05	13 55 05	19 55 45	12 47.3	29 30.6	14 08.0	10 14.4	26 58.9	6 40.3	8 05.2	26 55.9	22 03.6	23 33.6
6 Sa	17 01 42	14 32 01	25 58 24	2♐03 12	12 35.3	1♐01.7	15 22.4	11 00.5	26 54.4	6 48.5	8 09.6	26 59.5	22 05.8	23 35.3
7 Su	17 05 38	15 32 58	8♐10 15	14 19 40	12 24.1	2 33.1	16 36.8	11 46.7	26 49.6	6 56.6	8 13.9	27 03.1	22 08.1	23 37.0
8 M	17 09 35	16 33 56	20 31 30	26 45 47	12 14.5	4 04.7	17 51.3	12 32.9	26 44.3	7 04.6	8 18.1	27 06.7	22 10.4	23 38.7
9 Tu	17 13 31	17 34 55	3♑02 34	9♑21 55	12 07.2	5 36.6	19 05.8	13 19.2	26 38.6	7 12.4	8 22.2	27 10.3	22 12.6	23 40.3
10 W	17 17 28	18 35 55	15 43 52	22 08 29	12 02.7	7 08.7	20 20.4	14 05.5	26 32.5	7 20.1	8 26.2	27 13.8	22 14.9	23 41.9
11 Th	17 21 24	19 36 56	28 35 52	5♒06 09	12D 00.6	8 40.9	21 35.0	14 51.9	26 26.0	7 27.6	8 30.2	27 17.4	22 17.1	23 43.5
12 F	17 25 21	20 37 57	11♒39 28	18 16 00	12 00.5	10 13.3	22 49.6	15 38.2	26 19.1	7 35.1	8 34.0	27 20.9	22 19.4	23 45.0
13 Sa	17 29 18	21 38 59	24 55 55	1♓39 24	12 01.5	11 45.9	24 04.2	16 24.7	26 11.7	7 42.4	8 37.8	27 24.4	22 21.7	23 46.5
14 Su	17 33 14	22 40 01	8♓26 40	15 17 51	12R 02.6	13 18.6	25 18.8	17 11.1	26 04.0	7 49.5	8 41.4	27 27.8	22 23.9	23 48.0
15 M	17 37 11	23 41 03	22 13 05	29 12 26	12 02.6	14 51.4	26 33.5	17 57.7	25 55.9	7 56.5	8 45.0	27 31.3	22 26.2	23 49.5
16 Tu	17 41 07	24 42 06	6♈15 53	13♈23 18	12 01.0	16 24.4	27 48.2	18 44.2	25 47.4	8 03.4	8 48.5	27 34.7	22 28.5	23 50.9
17 W	17 45 04	25 43 09	20 34 27	27 48 58	11 57.3	17 57.5	29 02.9	19 30.8	25 38.6	8 10.1	8 51.9	27 38.1	22 30.7	23 52.3
18 Th	17 49 00	26 44 13	5♉06 20	12♉25 56	11 51.8	19 30.8	0♐17.6	20 17.4	25 29.4	8 16.7	8 55.2	27 41.5	22 33.0	23 53.6
19 F	17 52 57	27 45 17	19 47 00	27 08 41	11 44.9	21 04.2	1 32.3	21 04.0	25 19.8	8 23.1	8 58.4	27 44.9	22 35.3	23 55.0
20 Sa	17 56 53	28 46 21	4♊30 01	11♊50 04	11 37.8	22 37.8	2 47.1	21 50.7	25 09.9	8 29.4	9 01.5	27 48.2	22 37.5	23 56.3
21 Su	18 00 50	29 47 26	19 07 50	26 22 26	11 31.2	24 11.5	4 01.9	22 37.5	24 59.6	8 35.5	9 04.5	27 51.5	22 39.8	23 57.6
22 M	18 04 47	0♑48 32	3♋33 00	10♋38 49	11 26.1	25 45.5	5 16.7	23 24.2	24 49.0	8 41.5	9 07.4	27 54.8	22 42.0	23 58.8
23 Tu	18 08 43	1 49 38	17 39 18	24 34 00	11 22.8	27 19.6	6 31.6	24 11.0	24 38.1	8 47.3	9 10.3	27 58.1	22 44.3	24 00.0
24 W	18 12 40	2 50 44	1♌22 38	8♌05 05	11D 21.5	28 53.9	7 46.4	24 57.8	24 26.9	8 53.0	9 13.0	28 01.3	22 46.5	24 01.2
25 Th	18 16 36	3 51 51	14 41 21	21 11 35	11 21.9	0♑28.5	9 01.3	25 44.7	24 15.4	8 58.5	9 15.6	28 04.5	22 48.8	24 02.3
26 F	18 20 33	4 52 58	27 36 04	3♍55 10	11 23.3	2 03.3	10 16.2	26 31.6	24 03.6	9 03.9	9 18.1	28 07.7	22 51.0	24 03.5
27 Sa	18 24 29	5 54 06	10♍09 18	16 19 01	11 25.0	3 38.4	11 31.1	27 18.5	23 51.5	9 09.1	9 20.5	28 10.9	22 53.2	24 04.5
28 Su	18 28 26	6 55 14	22 24 52	28 27 27	11R 26.4	5 13.7	12 46.0	28 05.4	23 39.2	9 14.1	9 22.8	28 14.0	22 55.4	24 05.6
29 M	18 32 23	7 56 23	4♎27 24	10♎25 19	11 26.8	6 49.3	14 00.9	28 52.4	23 26.6	9 19.0	9 25.1	28 17.1	22 57.7	24 06.6
30 Tu	18 36 19	8 57 32	16 21 52	22 17 38	11 25.7	8 25.3	15 15.9	29 39.4	23 13.8	9 23.7	9 27.2	28 20.1	22 59.9	24 07.6
31 W	18 40 16	9 58 42	28 13 15	4♏09 17	11 23.2	10 01.5	16 30.9	0♒26.5	23 00.7	9 28.2	9 29.2	28 23.2	23 02.1	24 08.5

Astro Data

	Dy Hr Mn
♄0S	1 12:52
♀0S	2 11:46
☽0S	4 19:22
♃0S	10 4:08
☿ D	12 10:56
☽0N	18 22:03
⚳ R	25 13:02
☽0S	2 3:06
☽0N	16 6:33
☽0S	29 11:54
♃☌♄	31 21:23

Planet Ingress

	Dy Hr Mn
♂ ♑	22 1:42
☉ ♐	22 3:41
♀ ♏	24 1:35
☿ ♐	5 19:45
♀ ♐	18 6:21
☉ ♑	21 16:56
☿ ♑	25 4:46
♂ ♒	30 22:30

Last Aspect / ☽ Ingress

Last Aspect Dy Hr Mn		☽ Ingress Dy Hr Mn
1 2:06 ♅ □	♍	1 12:19
3 14:20 ♅ ⚹	♎	4 0:31
5 22:16 ♇ ☌	♏	6 13:19
8 16:02 ♅ ☌	♐	9 1:25
10 22:10 ♇ ⚹	♑	11 12:15
13 12:56 ♅ ⚹	♒	13 21:10
15 19:49 ♅ □	♓	16 3:21
18 1:20 ♂ □	♈	18 6:22
20 4:35 ♂ △	♉	20 6:51
22 0:15 ♅ ☍	♊	22 6:27
23 20:01 ♇ △	♋	24 7:18
26 4:51 ♅ △	♌	26 11:23
28 12:52 ♅ □	♍	28 19:37

Last Aspect / ☽ Ingress

Last Aspect Dy Hr Mn		☽ Ingress Dy Hr Mn
1 0:29 ♅ ⚹	♎	1 7:13
3 6:50 ♇ ☌	♏	3 20:00
6 1:58 ♅ ☌	♐	6 7:57
8 6:00 ♇ ⚹	♑	8 18:12
10 21:31 ♅ ⚹	♒	11 2:36
13 4:24 ♅ □	♓	13 9:03
15 9:06 ♅ △	♈	15 13:21
17 8:16 ☉ △	♉	17 15:36
19 12:59 ♅ ☍	♊	19 16:39
21 7:59 ♇ △	♋	21 18:03
23 18:00 ♅ △	♌	23 21:34
26 0:57 ♅ □	♍	26 4:32
28 11:33 ♅ ⚹	♎	28 15:05
30 15:43 ♇ ☌	♏	31 3:36

☽ Phases & Eclipses

Dy Hr Mn	
7 20:43	● 15♏36
15 15:47	☽ 23♒27
22 6:39	○ 0♊07
29 9:59	☾ 7♍21
7 14:35	● 15♐40
15 1:47	☽ 23♓15
21 18:08	○ 0♋03
29 6:32	☾ 7♎42

Astro Data

1 November 1980
Julian Day # 29525
SVP 5♓31'52"
GC 26♐34.3 ⚴ 23♈02.6R
Eris 14♈24.6R ⚵ 11♎41.8
⚷ 16♉09.4R ⚶ 27♌02.9
☽ Mean ☊ 15♌43.0

1 December 1980
Julian Day # 29555
SVP 5♓31'48"
GC 26♐34.4 ⚴ 16♈40.3R
Eris 14♈11.0R ⚵ 21♎56.8
⚷ 14♉41.3R ⚶ 5♍40.1
☽ Mean ☊ 14♌07.7

LONGITUDE — January 1981

Day	Sid.Time	☉	0 hr ☽	Noon ☽	True ☊	☿	♀	♂	⚳	♃	♄	♅	♆	♇
1 Th	18 44 12	10♑59 51	10♏06 16	16♏04 43	11♌19.3	11♑38.1	17♐45.9	1♒13.5	22♋47.5	9♎32.6	9♎31.1	28♏26.2	23♐04.2	24♎09.4
2 F	18 48 09	12 01 02	22 05 05	28 07 47	11R 14.4	13 15.0	19 00.9	2 00.6	22R 34.1	9 36.8	9 32.9	28 29.1	23 06.4	24 10.3
3 Sa	18 52 05	13 02 12	4♐13 10	10♐21 32	11 09.3	14 52.3	20 15.9	2 47.7	22 20.5	9 40.8	9 34.6	28 32.1	23 08.6	24 11.2
4 Su	18 56 02	14 03 23	16 33 07	22 48 06	11 04.3	16 30.0	21 30.9	3 34.9	22 06.8	9 44.6	9 36.2	28 35.0	23 10.7	24 12.0
5 M	18 59 58	15 04 34	29 06 37	5♑28 42	11 00.1	18 08.0	22 45.9	4 22.1	21 52.9	9 48.3	9 37.6	28 37.8	23 12.9	24 12.7
6 Tu	19 03 55	16 05 44	11♑54 24	18 23 38	10 57.2	19 46.3	24 01.0	5 09.3	21 38.9	9 51.8	9 39.0	28 40.7	23 15.0	24 13.5
7 W	19 07 52	17 06 55	24 56 22	1♒32 28	10D 55.6	21 25.1	25 16.0	5 56.5	21 24.9	9 55.1	9 40.3	28 43.5	23 17.1	24 14.2
8 Th	19 11 48	18 08 05	8♒11 49	14 54 16	10 55.3	23 04.2	26 31.1	6 43.7	21 10.7	9 58.3	9 41.4	28 46.2	23 19.3	24 14.9
9 F	19 15 45	19 09 15	21 39 39	28 27 48	10 56.1	24 43.7	27 46.1	7 31.0	20 56.5	10 01.2	9 42.5	28 48.9	23 21.4	24 15.5
10 Sa	19 19 41	20 10 24	5♓18 35	12♓11 49	10 57.5	26 23.5	29 01.2	8 18.3	20 42.3	10 04.0	9 43.4	28 51.6	23 23.4	24 16.1
11 Su	19 23 38	21 11 33	19 07 21	26 05 02	10 59.0	28 03.6	0♑16.2	9 05.6	20 28.0	10 06.6	9 44.3	28 54.3	23 25.5	24 16.6
12 M	19 27 34	22 12 41	3♈04 44	10♈06 16	11R 00.1	29 44.1	1 31.3	9 52.9	20 13.7	10 09.0	9 45.0	28 56.9	23 27.6	24 17.2
13 Tu	19 31 31	23 13 49	17 09 28	24 14 07	11 00.4	1♒24.8	2 46.4	10 40.2	19 59.5	10 11.2	9 45.6	28 59.4	23 29.6	24 17.7
14 W	19 35 27	24 14 56	1♉20 00	8♉26 50	10 59.9	3 05.8	4 01.4	11 27.5	19 45.3	10 13.3	9 46.1	29 01.9	23 31.6	24 18.1
15 Th	19 39 24	25 16 02	15 34 20	22 42 07	10 58.6	4 46.9	5 16.5	12 14.9	19 31.1	10 15.1	9 46.5	29 04.4	23 33.6	24 18.5
16 F	19 43 21	26 17 07	29 49 48	6♊56 56	10 56.9	6 28.0	6 31.6	13 02.3	19 17.1	10 16.8	9 46.8	29 06.9	23 35.6	24 18.9
17 Sa	19 47 17	27 18 12	14♊03 04	21 07 41	10 55.0	8 09.2	7 46.7	13 49.6	19 03.1	10 18.3	9 47.0	29 09.2	23 37.6	24 19.3
18 Su	19 51 14	28 19 16	28 10 18	5♋10 25	10 53.3	9 50.3	9 01.7	14 37.0	18 49.2	10 19.6	9R 47.0	29 11.6	23 39.5	24 19.6
19 M	19 55 10	29 20 19	12♋07 33	19 01 15	10 52.0	11 31.1	10 16.8	15 24.4	18 35.5	10 20.7	9 47.0	29 13.9	23 41.5	24 19.8
20 Tu	19 59 07	0♒21 22	25 51 09	2♌36 55	10D 51.3	13 11.5	11 31.9	16 11.8	18 21.9	10 21.6	9 46.9	29 16.2	23 43.4	24 20.1
21 W	20 03 03	1 22 24	9♌18 17	15 55 05	10 51.3	14 51.3	12 47.0	16 59.2	18 08.4	10 22.3	9 46.6	29 18.4	23 45.3	24 20.3
22 Th	20 07 00	2 23 25	22 27 14	28 54 42	10 51.7	16 30.3	14 02.1	17 46.7	17 55.2	10 22.8	9 46.3	29 20.6	23 47.2	24 20.4
23 F	20 10 56	3 24 26	5♍17 35	11♍36 03	10 52.4	18 08.2	15 17.2	18 34.1	17 42.1	10 23.2	9 45.8	29 22.7	23 49.0	24 20.6
24 Sa	20 14 53	4 25 26	17 50 19	24 00 42	10 53.1	19 44.7	16 32.3	19 21.5	17 29.3	10R 23.3	9 45.2	29 24.8	23 50.9	24 20.7
25 Su	20 18 50	5 26 25	0♎07 34	6♎11 21	10 53.8	21 19.5	17 47.4	20 09.0	17 16.6	10 23.3	9 44.6	29 26.8	23 52.7	24 20.7
26 M	20 22 46	6 27 24	12 12 31	18 11 36	10 54.3	22 52.1	19 02.5	20 56.4	17 04.2	10 23.1	9 43.8	29 28.8	23 54.5	24R 20.7
27 Tu	20 26 43	7 28 22	24 09 07	0♏05 39	10R 54.5	24 22.0	20 17.6	21 43.9	16 52.1	10 22.7	9 42.9	29 30.8	23 56.3	24 20.7
28 W	20 30 39	8 29 20	6♏01 47	11 58 07	10 54.5	25 48.7	21 32.7	22 31.3	16 40.2	10 22.0	9 41.9	29 32.7	23 58.0	24 20.7
29 Th	20 34 36	9 30 16	17 55 15	23 53 45	10 54.5	27 11.7	22 47.8	23 18.8	16 28.6	10 21.2	9 40.8	29 34.5	23 59.8	24 20.6
30 F	20 38 32	10 31 13	29 54 13	5♐57 11	10D 54.4	28 30.3	24 02.9	24 06.3	16 17.3	10 20.2	9 39.6	29 36.3	24 01.5	24 20.5
31 Sa	20 42 29	11 32 08	12♐03 11	18 12 40	10 54.4	29 43.7	25 18.0	24 53.8	16 06.3	10 19.1	9 38.3	29 38.1	24 03.2	24 20.3

LONGITUDE — February 1981

Day	Sid.Time	☉	0 hr ☽	Noon ☽	True ☊	☿	♀	♂	⚳	♃	♄	♅	♆	♇
1 Su	20 46 25	12♒33 03	24♐26 06	0♑43 49	10♌54.6	0♓51.3	26♑33.1	25♒41.2	15♋55.6	10♎17.7	9♎36.8	29♏39.8	24♐04.8	24♎20.1
2 M	20 50 22	13 33 57	7♑06 07	13 33 15	10 54.8	1 52.2	27 48.2	26 28.7	15R 45.3	10R 16.1	9R 35.3	29 41.5	24 06.5	24R 19.9
3 Tu	20 54 19	14 34 50	20 05 19	26 42 23	10 55.0	2 45.6	29 03.3	27 16.2	15 35.3	10 14.4	9 33.7	29 43.1	24 08.1	24 19.6
4 W	20 58 15	15 35 42	3♒24 25	10♒11 14	10R 55.2	3 30.8	0♒18.4	28 03.7	15 25.6	10 12.4	9 32.0	29 44.6	24 09.7	24 19.3
5 Th	21 02 12	16 36 32	17 02 37	23 58 14	10 55.0	4 07.0	1 33.5	28 51.2	15 16.4	10 10.3	9 30.2	29 46.1	24 11.2	24 19.0
6 F	21 06 08	17 37 22	0♓57 40	8♓00 27	10 54.6	4 33.5	2 48.6	29 38.6	15 07.5	10 08.0	9 28.2	29 47.6	24 12.8	24 18.6
7 Sa	21 10 05	18 38 10	15 06 02	22 13 52	10 53.8	4 49.8	4 03.7	0♓26.1	14 58.9	10 05.4	9 26.2	29 49.0	24 14.3	24 18.2
8 Su	21 14 01	19 38 57	29 23 21	6♈33 54	10 52.7	4R 55.4	5 18.7	1 13.6	14 50.8	10 02.7	9 24.1	29 50.3	24 15.8	24 17.8
9 M	21 17 58	20 39 42	13♈44 55	20 55 53	10 51.6	4 50.2	6 33.8	2 01.0	14 43.1	9 59.9	9 21.9	29 51.6	24 17.2	24 17.3
10 Tu	21 21 54	21 40 25	28 06 16	5♉15 39	10 50.8	4 34.2	7 48.9	2 48.4	14 35.7	9 56.8	9 19.6	29 52.9	24 18.7	24 16.8
11 W	21 25 51	22 41 07	12♉23 38	19 29 51	10D 50.4	4 07.7	9 03.9	3 35.9	14 28.8	9 53.6	9 17.1	29 54.1	24 20.1	24 16.2
12 Th	21 29 48	23 41 47	26 34 04	3♊36 02	10 50.5	3 31.3	10 19.0	4 23.3	14 22.3	9 50.2	9 14.7	29 55.2	24 21.5	24 15.7
13 F	21 33 44	24 42 26	10♊35 34	17 32 33	10 51.3	2 45.9	11 34.0	5 10.7	14 16.2	9 46.6	9 12.1	29 56.3	24 22.8	24 15.1
14 Sa	21 37 41	25 43 03	24 26 49	1♋18 19	10 52.4	1 52.8	12 49.0	5 58.1	14 10.6	9 42.8	9 09.4	29 57.3	24 24.1	24 14.4
15 Su	21 41 37	26 43 38	8♋06 58	14 52 41	10 53.7	0 53.3	14 04.0	6 45.5	14 05.3	9 38.9	9 06.6	29 58.3	24 25.4	24 13.8
16 M	21 45 34	27 44 12	21 35 23	28 15 03	10R 54.7	29♒49.2	15 19.1	7 32.9	14 00.5	9 34.8	9 03.8	29 59.2	24 26.7	24 13.1
17 Tu	21 49 30	28 44 44	4♌51 36	11♌24 58	10 55.1	28 42.1	16 34.1	8 20.2	13 56.1	9 30.5	9 00.8	0♐00.1	24 27.9	24 12.3
18 W	21 53 27	29 45 14	17 55 07	24 22 01	10 54.6	27 33.9	17 49.1	9 07.6	13 52.2	9 26.1	8 57.8	0 00.9	24 29.2	24 11.6
19 Th	21 57 23	0♓45 42	0♍45 40	7♍06 02	10 53.0	26 26.4	19 04.0	9 54.9	13 48.7	9 21.5	8 54.7	0 01.7	24 30.3	24 10.8
20 F	22 01 20	1 46 09	13 23 12	19 37 12	10 50.3	25 21.2	20 19.0	10 42.2	13 45.6	9 16.7	8 51.5	0 02.4	24 31.5	24 09.9
21 Sa	22 05 17	2 46 35	25 48 09	1♎56 13	10 46.9	24 19.7	21 34.0	11 29.5	13 42.9	9 11.8	8 48.3	0 03.1	24 32.6	24 09.1
22 Su	22 09 13	3 46 59	8♎01 36	14 04 31	10 43.0	23 23.0	22 49.0	12 16.8	13 40.7	9 06.8	8 44.9	0 03.7	24 33.7	24 08.2
23 M	22 13 10	4 47 21	20 05 18	26 04 17	10 39.1	22 32.2	24 03.9	13 04.0	13 38.9	9 01.5	8 41.5	0 04.2	24 34.7	24 07.3
24 Tu	22 17 06	5 47 42	2♏01 50	7♏58 25	10 35.7	21 47.9	25 18.9	13 51.3	13 37.5	8 56.2	8 38.0	0 04.7	24 35.8	24 06.3
25 W	22 21 03	6 48 02	13 54 30	19 50 35	10 33.2	21 10.5	26 33.8	14 38.5	13 36.6	8 50.7	8 34.5	0 05.1	24 36.8	24 05.4
26 Th	22 24 59	7 48 20	25 47 14	1♐45 00	10D 31.9	20 40.3	27 48.8	15 25.7	13D 36.1	8 45.0	8 30.8	0 05.5	24 37.7	24 04.4
27 F	22 28 56	8 48 37	7♐44 30	13 46 19	10 31.8	20 17.4	29 03.7	16 12.9	13 36.0	8 39.2	8 27.1	0 05.9	24 38.7	24 03.3
28 Sa	22 32 52	9 48 53	19 51 04	25 59 21	10 32.8	20 01.7	0♓18.7	17 00.1	13 36.4	8 33.3	8 23.4	0 06.1	24 39.6	24 02.3

Astro Data	Planet Ingress	Last Aspect	☽ Ingress	Last Aspect	☽ Ingress	☽ Phases & Eclipses
Dy Hr Mn	Dy Hr Mn	Dy Hr Mn	Dy Hr Mn	Dy Hr Mn	Dy Hr Mn	Dy Hr Mn
☽ 0N 12 12:46	♀ ♑ 11 6:48	2 12:42 ♅ ☌	♐ 2 15:42	1 1:45 ♂ ✱	♑ 1 10:37	6 7:24 ● 15♑54
♄ R 18 16:58	☿ ♒ 12 15:48	4 14:40 ♇ ✱	♑ 5 1:41	3 17:25 ♅ ✱	♒ 3 17:55	13 10:10 ☽ 23♈09
♃ R 24 19:23	☉ ♒ 20 3:36	7 6:52 ♅ ✱	♒ 7 9:12	5 21:59 ♅ □	♓ 5 22:21	20 7:39 ○ 0♌10
☽ 0S 25 20:50	☿ ♓ 31 17:35	9 12:37 ♅ □	♓ 9 14:42	8 0:44 ♅ △	♈ 8 1:01	20 7:50 • A 1.014
♇ R 26 12:51		11 16:52 ♅ △	♈ 11 18:43	9 17:37 ♆ △	♉ 10 3:11	28 4:19 ☾ 8♏10
	♀ ♒ 4 6:07	13 12:06 ♇ ☍	♉ 13 21:45	12 5:42 ♅ ☍	♊ 12 5:51	
☿ R 8 12:31	♂ ♓ 6 22:48	15 22:45 ♅ ☍	♊ 16 0:17	14 1:26 ☉ △	♋ 14 9:43	4 22:14 ● 16♒02
☽ 0N 8 18:44	☿ ♒R 16 8:02	17 17:26 ♇ △	♋ 18 3:08	16 15:09 ♅ △	♌ 16 15:10	4 22:08:31 • A 00'33"
♆✱♇ 9 12:39	♅ ♐ 17 9:02	20 6:02 ♅ △	♌ 20 7:21	18 17:30 ☿ ☍	♍ 18 22:34	11 17:49 ☽ 22♉56
☽ 0S 22 4:56	☉ ♓ 18 17:52	22 12:49 ♅ □	♍ 22 14:02	20 21:32 ♆ □	♎ 21 8:12	18 22:58 ○ 0♍13
⚳ D 27 3:44	♀ ♓ 28 6:01	24 22:38 ♅ ✱	♎ 24 23:45	23 9:00 ♆ ✱	♏ 23 19:54	27 1:14 ☾ 8♐22
		27 0:23 ♇ ☌	♏ 27 11:49	26 3:09 ♀ □	♐ 26 8:29	
		29 23:23 ♅ ☌	♐ 30 0:12	28 9:24 ♆ ☌	♑ 28 19:46	

Astro Data

1 January 1981
Julian Day # 29586
SVP 5♓31'43"
GC 26♐34.4 ⚴ 18♈09.3
Eris 14♈05.6 ⚵ 0♏42.5
⚷ 13♉37.8R ⚶ 10♍13.7
☽ Mean ☊ 12♌29.2

1 February 1981
Julian Day # 29617
SVP 5♓31'38"
GC 26♐34.5 ⚴ 26♈38.3
Eris 14♈10.9 ⚵ 6♏26.1
⚷ 13♉27.1 ⚶ 8♍02.5R
☽ Mean ☊ 10♌50.7

March 1981 LONGITUDE

Day	Sid.Time	☉	0 hr ☽	Noon ☽	True ☊	☿	♀	♂	⚳	♃	♄	♅	♆	♇
1 Su	22 36 49	10♓49 06	2♑11 45	8♑28 48	10♌34.4	19♒53.0	1♓33.6	17♓47.2	13♋37.2	8♎27.3	8♎19.5	0♐06.4	24♐40.4	24♎01.2
2 M	22 40 45	11 49 19	14 51 00	21 18 48	10 36.1	19D 51.0	2 48.5	18 34.4	13 38.4	8R 21.1	8R 15.6	0 06.5	24 41.3	24R 00.1
3 Tu	22 44 42	12 49 30	27 52 34	4♒32 32	10R 37.2	19 55.5	4 03.4	19 21.5	13 40.0	8 14.8	8 11.7	0 06.6	24 42.1	23 58.9
4 W	22 48 39	13 49 39	11♒18 50	18 11 30	10 37.1	20 06.1	5 18.3	20 08.6	13 42.1	8 08.4	8 07.7	0R 06.7	24 42.9	23 57.8
5 Th	22 52 35	14 49 46	25 10 21	2♓15 05	10 35.4	20 22.5	6 33.2	20 55.6	13 44.6	8 01.9	8 03.6	0 06.7	24 43.6	23 56.6
6 F	22 56 32	15 49 52	9♓25 14	16 40 09	10 32.0	20 44.4	7 48.1	21 42.7	13 47.5	7 55.2	7 59.5	0 06.7	24 44.3	23 55.4
7 Sa	23 00 28	16 49 55	23 59 05	1♈21 08	10 27.1	21 11.3	9 02.9	22 29.7	13 50.8	7 48.5	7 55.3	0 06.6	24 45.0	23 54.1
8 Su	23 04 25	17 49 57	8♈45 17	16 10 32	10 21.4	21 42.9	10 17.8	23 16.7	13 54.5	7 41.6	7 51.1	0 06.4	24 45.6	23 52.9
9 M	23 08 21	18 49 57	23 35 49	1♉00 07	10 15.6	22 19.0	11 32.6	24 03.6	13 58.6	7 34.7	7 46.8	0 06.2	24 46.2	23 51.6
10 Tu	23 12 18	19 49 54	8♉22 32	15 42 12	10 10.6	22 59.1	12 47.4	24 50.6	14 03.1	7 27.6	7 42.5	0 05.9	24 46.8	23 50.3
11 W	23 16 14	20 49 50	22 58 27	0♊10 44	10 07.1	23 43.2	14 02.2	25 37.5	14 08.0	7 20.5	7 38.1	0 05.6	24 47.4	23 49.0
12 Th	23 20 11	21 49 43	7♊18 38	14 21 55	10D 05.3	24 30.8	15 17.0	26 24.3	14 13.3	7 13.3	7 33.7	0 05.2	24 47.9	23 47.6
13 F	23 24 08	22 49 34	21 20 25	28 14 10	10 05.2	25 21.8	16 31.8	27 11.2	14 19.0	7 06.1	7 29.3	0 04.8	24 48.3	23 46.3
14 Sa	23 28 04	23 49 23	5♋03 13	11♋47 45	10 06.2	26 16.0	17 46.6	27 58.0	14 25.1	6 58.7	7 24.8	0 04.3	24 48.8	23 44.9
15 Su	23 32 01	24 49 09	18 27 57	25 04 05	10 07.6	27 13.1	19 01.3	28 44.7	14 31.5	6 51.4	7 20.3	0 03.8	24 49.2	23 43.5
16 M	23 35 57	25 48 53	1♌36 23	8♌05 07	10R 08.4	28 13.0	20 16.0	29 31.5	14 38.4	6 43.9	7 15.8	0 03.2	24 49.6	23 42.0
17 Tu	23 39 54	26 48 35	14 30 33	20 52 55	10 07.8	29 15.5	21 30.8	0♈18.2	14 45.5	6 36.4	7 11.2	0 02.6	24 49.9	23 40.6
18 W	23 43 50	27 48 15	27 12 24	3♍29 14	10 05.2	0♓20.4	22 45.4	1 04.8	14 53.1	6 28.8	7 06.6	0 01.9	24 50.2	23 39.1
19 Th	23 47 47	28 47 53	9♍43 33	15 55 30	10 00.2	1 27.7	24 00.1	1 51.5	15 01.0	6 21.2	7 02.0	0 01.2	24 50.5	23 37.7
20 F	23 51 43	29 47 28	22 05 14	28 12 50	9 53.0	2 37.3	25 14.8	2 38.1	15 09.2	6 13.6	6 57.4	0 00.4	24 50.7	23 36.2
21 Sa	23 55 40	0♈47 02	4♎18 27	10♎22 12	9 43.9	3 48.9	26 29.5	3 24.6	15 17.8	6 05.9	6 52.8	29♏59.6	24 50.9	23 34.7
22 Su	23 59 37	1 46 33	16 24 11	22 24 35	9 33.8	5 02.6	27 44.1	4 11.1	15 26.8	5 58.2	6 48.1	29 58.7	24 51.1	23 33.1
23 M	0 03 33	2 46 03	28 23 33	4♏21 19	9 23.5	6 18.2	28 58.7	4 57.6	15 36.1	5 50.5	6 43.5	29 57.7	24 51.2	23 31.6
24 Tu	0 07 30	3 45 31	10♏18 08	16 14 15	9 14.0	7 35.6	0♈13.3	5 44.1	15 45.7	5 42.8	6 38.8	29 56.8	24 51.4	23 30.0
25 W	0 11 26	4 44 57	22 10 03	28 05 53	9 06.1	8 54.9	1 27.9	6 30.5	15 55.6	5 35.0	6 34.1	29 55.7	24 51.4	23 28.5
26 Th	0 15 23	5 44 21	4♐02 12	9♐59 27	9 00.3	10 15.9	2 42.5	7 16.9	16 05.9	5 27.3	6 29.4	29 54.7	24R 51.5	23 26.9
27 F	0 19 19	6 43 43	15 58 09	21 58 53	8 56.9	11 38.6	3 57.1	8 03.2	16 16.4	5 19.5	6 24.7	29 53.5	24 51.5	23 25.3
28 Sa	0 23 16	7 43 04	28 02 11	4♑08 43	8D 55.6	13 02.9	5 11.7	8 49.6	16 27.3	5 11.8	6 20.0	29 52.4	24 51.5	23 23.7
29 Su	0 27 12	8 42 23	10♑19 03	16 33 51	8 55.8	14 28.9	6 26.2	9 35.8	16 38.5	5 04.0	6 15.3	29 51.1	24 51.4	23 22.1
30 M	0 31 09	9 41 40	22 53 43	29 19 14	8R 56.5	15 56.4	7 40.7	10 22.1	16 50.0	4 56.3	6 10.7	29 49.9	24 51.3	23 20.5
31 Tu	0 35 06	10 40 55	5♒50 56	12♒29 16	8 56.7	17 25.4	8 55.3	11 08.3	17 01.8	4 48.6	6 06.0	29 48.6	24 51.2	23 18.8

April 1981 LONGITUDE

Day	Sid.Time	☉	0 hr ☽	Noon ☽	True ☊	☿	♀	♂	⚳	♃	♄	♅	♆	♇
1 W	0 39 02	11♈40 09	19♒14 36	26♒07 09	8♌55.4	18♓56.0	10♈09.8	11♈54.4	17♋13.9	4♎40.9	6♎01.3	29♏47.2	24♐51.0	23♎17.2
2 Th	0 42 59	12 39 20	3♓06 59	10♓13 58	8R 51.9	20 28.1	11 24.3	12 40.5	17 26.3	4R 33.3	5R 56.7	29R 45.8	24R 50.8	23R 15.5
3 F	0 46 55	13 38 30	17 27 48	24 47 55	8 45.8	22 01.7	12 38.7	13 26.6	17 39.0	4 25.7	5 52.0	29 44.4	24 50.6	23 13.9
4 Sa	0 50 52	14 37 38	2♈13 34	9♈43 46	8 37.4	23 36.8	13 53.2	14 12.7	17 52.0	4 18.1	5 47.4	29 42.9	24 50.3	23 12.2
5 Su	0 54 48	15 36 43	17 17 22	24 53 05	8 27.6	25 13.4	15 07.7	14 58.7	18 05.2	4 10.6	5 42.8	29 41.4	24 50.1	23 10.6
6 M	0 58 45	16 35 47	2♉29 32	10♉05 21	8 17.5	26 51.4	16 22.1	15 44.6	18 18.7	4 03.2	5 38.2	29 39.8	24 49.7	23 08.9
7 Tu	1 02 41	17 34 49	17 39 13	25 09 53	8 08.3	28 30.9	17 36.5	16 30.5	18 32.5	3 55.8	5 33.7	29 38.2	24 49.4	23 07.2
8 W	1 06 38	18 33 48	2♊36 19	9♊57 38	8 01.1	0♈12.0	18 50.9	17 16.4	18 46.6	3 48.4	5 29.2	29 36.6	24 49.0	23 05.5
9 Th	1 10 34	19 32 45	17 13 12	24 22 35	7 56.5	1 54.5	20 05.3	18 02.2	19 00.9	3 41.2	5 24.7	29 34.9	24 48.6	23 03.8
10 F	1 14 31	20 31 40	1♋25 32	8♋22 00	7D 54.2	3 38.5	21 19.6	18 48.0	19 15.5	3 34.0	5 20.2	29 33.2	24 48.1	23 02.1
11 Sa	1 18 28	21 30 33	15 12 06	21 56 05	7 53.7	5 24.0	22 34.0	19 33.7	19 30.3	3 26.9	5 15.8	29 31.4	24 47.7	23 00.5
12 Su	1 22 24	22 29 23	28 34 15	5♌07 01	7R 53.9	7 11.0	23 48.3	20 19.4	19 45.4	3 19.9	5 11.4	29 29.6	24 47.1	22 58.8
13 M	1 26 21	23 28 11	11♌34 49	17 58 08	7 53.6	8 59.5	25 02.6	21 05.0	20 00.7	3 13.0	5 07.1	29 27.8	24 46.6	22 57.1
14 Tu	1 30 17	24 26 57	24 17 24	0♍33 06	7 51.6	10 49.6	26 16.9	21 50.6	20 16.2	3 06.1	5 02.8	29 25.9	24 46.0	22 55.4
15 W	1 34 14	25 25 40	6♍45 39	12 55 26	7 47.2	12 41.2	27 31.1	22 36.1	20 32.0	2 59.4	4 58.6	29 24.0	24 45.4	22 53.7
16 Th	1 38 10	26 24 21	19 02 50	25 08 10	7 39.9	14 34.4	28 45.4	23 21.6	20 48.0	2 52.8	4 54.4	29 22.1	24 44.8	22 52.0
17 F	1 42 07	27 23 00	1♎11 42	7♎13 41	7 29.8	16 29.1	29 59.6	24 07.1	21 04.2	2 46.3	4 50.2	29 20.1	24 44.1	22 50.3
18 Sa	1 46 03	28 21 37	13 14 20	19 13 51	7 17.4	18 25.4	1♉13.8	24 52.5	21 20.7	2 39.8	4 46.1	29 18.1	24 43.5	22 48.6
19 Su	1 50 00	29 20 12	25 12 23	1♏10 06	7 03.5	20 23.2	2 28.0	25 37.8	21 37.4	2 33.5	4 42.0	29 16.1	24 42.7	22 46.9
20 M	1 53 57	0♉18 46	7♏07 09	13 03 41	6 49.4	22 22.5	3 42.1	26 23.1	21 54.2	2 27.4	4 38.0	29 14.0	24 42.0	22 45.3
21 Tu	1 57 53	1 17 17	18 59 54	24 55 58	6 36.1	24 23.3	4 56.3	27 08.3	22 11.3	2 21.3	4 34.1	29 11.9	24 41.2	22 43.6
22 W	2 01 50	2 15 47	0♐52 07	6♐48 37	6 24.7	26 25.5	6 10.4	27 53.5	22 28.6	2 15.4	4 30.2	29 09.8	24 40.4	22 41.9
23 Th	2 05 46	3 14 15	12 45 46	18 43 55	6 15.9	28 29.0	7 24.6	28 38.7	22 46.1	2 09.6	4 26.4	29 07.7	24 39.6	22 40.3
24 F	2 09 43	4 12 41	24 43 26	0♑44 46	6 09.9	0♉33.8	8 38.7	29 23.8	23 03.8	2 03.9	4 22.6	29 05.5	24 38.7	22 38.6
25 Sa	2 13 39	5 11 05	6♑48 24	12 54 50	6 06.7	2 39.8	9 52.8	0♉08.9	23 21.7	1 58.4	4 18.9	29 03.3	24 37.8	22 37.0
26 Su	2 17 36	6 09 28	19 04 39	25 18 24	6 05.4	4 46.8	11 06.8	0 53.9	23 39.8	1 53.0	4 15.3	29 01.1	24 36.9	22 35.3
27 M	2 21 32	7 07 50	1♒36 41	8♒00 06	6 05.3	6 54.7	12 20.9	1 38.8	23 58.0	1 47.7	4 11.8	28 58.8	24 36.0	22 33.7
28 Tu	2 25 29	8 06 10	14 29 13	21 04 34	6 05.0	9 03.3	13 34.9	2 23.8	24 16.5	1 42.6	4 08.3	28 56.6	24 35.0	22 32.1
29 W	2 29 26	9 04 28	27 46 36	4♓35 43	6 03.5	11 12.4	14 49.0	3 08.6	24 35.1	1 37.6	4 04.8	28 54.3	24 34.0	22 30.5
30 Th	2 33 22	10 02 45	11♓32 08	18 35 55	5 59.7	13 21.7	16 03.0	3 53.4	24 53.9	1 32.8	4 01.5	28 52.0	24 33.0	22 28.9

Astro Data

	Dy Hr Mn
☿ D	2 7:05
♃☌♄	4 19:07
♅ R	5 1:46
☽ 0N	8 2:42
♂ 0N	19 9:29
☉ 0N	20 17:02
☽ 0S	21 11:54
♀ 0N	26 21:59
♆ R	27 6:08
♄ 0N	30 23:41
☽ 0N	4 12:57
♃ 0N	9 17:29
☿ 0N	11 9:40
☽ 0S	17 18:14

Planet Ingress

		Dy Hr Mn
♂	♈	17 2:40
☿	♓	18 4:33
☉	♈	20 17:03
♅	♏R	20 23:15
♀	♈	24 7:43
☿	♈	8 9:11
♀	♉	17 12:08
☉	♉	20 4:19
☿	♉	24 5:31
♂	♉	25 7:17

Last Aspect / ☽ Ingress

Dy Hr Mn				☽ Ingress Dy Hr Mn
2 16:56	♇	□	♒	3 3:51
4 23:14	♆	⚹	♓	5 8:12
7 1:14	♆	□	♈	7 9:48
9 1:54	♆	△	♉	9 10:22
11 3:58	♂	⚹	♊	11 11:42
13 10:03	♂	□	♋	13 15:06
15 19:10	♂	△	♌	15 21:02
17 19:29	♆	△	♍	18 5:20
20 15:22	☉	☍	♎	20 15:31
22 16:54	♆	⚹	♏	23 3:14
25 15:42	♅	☌	♐	25 15:51
27 17:43	♆	☌	♑	28 3:52
30 12:57	♅	⚹	♒	30 13:15

Last Aspect / ☽ Ingress

Dy Hr Mn				☽ Ingress Dy Hr Mn
1 18:18	♅	□	♓	1 18:41
3 19:59	♅	△	♈	3 20:25
5 11:55	♆	△	♉	5 20:04
7 19:11	♅	☍	♊	7 19:47
9 12:44	♆	☍	♋	9 21:34
12 1:42	♅	△	♌	12 2:36
14 9:51	♅	□	♍	14 10:56
16 20:21	♅	⚹	♎	16 21:38
19 7:59	☉	☍	♏	19 9:39
21 20:36	♅	☌	♐	21 22:15
24 9:08	♂	△	♑	24 10:31
26 19:04	♅	⚹	♒	26 20:57
29 2:02	♅	□	♓	29 3:56

☽ Phases & Eclipses

Dy Hr Mn		
6 10:31	●	15♓46
13 1:51	☽	22♊24
20 15:22	○	29♍56
28 19:34	☾	8♑02
4 20:19	●	14♈58
11 11:11	☽	21♋29
19 7:59	○	29♎10
27 10:14	☾	7♒04

Astro Data

1 March 1981
Julian Day # 29645
SVP 5♓31'35"
GC 26♐34.6 ⚳ 8♉14.4
Eris 14♈23.8 ⚵ 7♏41.7R
⚷ 14♉07.7 ⚶ 1♍14.8R
☽ Mean ☊ 9♌21.7

1 April 1981
Julian Day # 29676
SVP 5♓31'32"
GC 26♐34.6 ⚳ 23♉50.9
Eris 14♈43.4 ⚵ 3♏55.0R
⚷ 15♉37.7 ⚶ 25♌42.7R
☽ Mean ☊ 7♌43.2

LONGITUDE — May 1981

Day	Sid.Time	☉	0 hr ☽	Noon ☽	True ☊	☿	♀	♂	⚳	♃	♄	♅	♆	♇
1 F	2 37 19	11♉01 00	25♓46 59	3♈04 59	5♌53.3	15♉31.0	17♉17.0	4♉38.2	25♋12.9	1♎28.1	3♎58.2	28♏49.6	24♐32.0	22♎27.3
2 Sa	2 41 15	11 59 14	10♈29 22	17 59 19	5R 44.5	17 40.0	18 31.0	5 22.9	25 32.1	1R 23.6	3R 55.0	28R 47.3	24R 30.9	22R 25.7
3 Su	2 45 12	12 57 26	25 33 48	3♉11 36	5 34.0	19 48.4	19 45.0	6 07.6	25 51.5	1 19.3	3 51.9	28 44.9	24 29.8	22 24.2
4 M	2 49 08	13 55 36	10♉51 19	18 31 31	5 23.0	21 55.9	20 58.9	6 52.2	26 11.0	1 15.1	3 48.9	28 42.5	24 28.7	22 22.6
5 Tu	2 53 05	14 53 45	26 10 41	3♊47 24	5 13.0	24 02.3	22 12.9	7 36.8	26 30.6	1 11.1	3 45.9	28 40.1	24 27.6	22 21.1
6 W	2 57 01	15 51 52	11♊20 21	18 48 25	5 04.9	26 07.2	23 26.8	8 21.3	26 50.5	1 07.2	3 43.0	28 37.7	24 26.4	22 19.6
7 Th	3 00 58	16 49 57	26 10 41	3♋26 27	4 59.4	28 10.4	24 40.7	9 05.8	27 10.5	1 03.5	3 40.2	28 35.3	24 25.2	22 18.1
8 F	3 04 55	17 48 01	10♋35 15	17 36 53	4 56.5	0♊11.5	25 54.6	9 50.2	27 30.7	1 00.0	3 37.5	28 32.8	24 24.0	22 16.6
9 Sa	3 08 51	18 46 02	24 31 18	1♌18 40	4D 55.5	2 10.4	27 08.5	10 34.5	27 51.0	0 56.7	3 34.9	28 30.4	24 22.8	22 15.1
10 Su	3 12 48	19 44 02	7♌59 14	14 33 25	4R 55.6	4 06.8	28 22.3	11 18.8	28 11.4	0 53.5	3 32.4	28 27.9	24 21.6	22 13.6
11 M	3 16 44	20 41 59	21 01 41	27 24 33	4 55.5	6 00.5	29 36.2	12 03.0	28 32.0	0 50.5	3 29.9	28 25.5	24 20.3	22 12.2
12 Tu	3 20 41	21 39 55	3♍42 34	9♍56 18	4 54.1	7 51.4	0♊50.0	12 47.2	28 52.8	0 47.7	3 27.6	28 23.0	24 19.0	22 10.8
13 W	3 24 37	22 37 49	16 06 18	22 13 06	4 50.6	9 39.3	2 03.8	13 31.4	29 13.7	0 45.0	3 25.3	28 20.5	24 17.7	22 09.4
14 Th	3 28 34	23 35 41	28 17 12	4♎19 05	4 44.4	11 24.1	3 17.6	14 15.4	29 34.7	0 42.6	3 23.2	28 18.0	24 16.4	22 08.0
15 F	3 32 30	24 33 32	10♎19 11	16 17 52	4 35.7	13 05.8	4 31.3	14 59.5	29 55.9	0 40.3	3 21.1	28 15.5	24 15.1	22 06.6
16 Sa	3 36 27	25 31 21	22 15 31	28 12 24	4 24.9	14 44.2	5 45.1	15 43.4	0♌17.2	0 38.1	3 19.1	28 13.0	24 13.7	22 05.3
17 Su	3 40 24	26 29 08	4♏08 49	10♏04 59	4 12.7	16 19.2	6 58.8	16 27.4	0 38.6	0 36.2	3 17.2	28 10.5	24 12.4	22 04.0
18 M	3 44 20	27 26 54	16 01 09	21 57 28	4 00.2	17 50.8	8 12.5	17 11.2	1 00.2	0 34.4	3 15.4	28 08.0	24 11.0	22 02.6
19 Tu	3 48 17	28 24 38	27 54 08	3♐51 20	3 48.5	19 19.0	9 26.2	17 55.0	1 21.9	0 32.9	3 13.7	28 05.5	24 09.6	22 01.4
20 W	3 52 13	29 22 21	9♐49 15	15 48 03	3 38.4	20 43.7	10 39.9	18 38.8	1 43.7	0 31.5	3 12.1	28 03.0	24 08.1	22 00.1
21 Th	3 56 10	0♊20 03	21 47 58	27 49 13	3 30.7	22 04.8	11 53.5	19 22.5	2 05.6	0 30.2	3 10.6	28 00.5	24 06.7	21 58.9
22 F	4 00 06	1 17 44	3♑52 04	9♑56 50	3 25.6	23 22.3	13 07.2	20 06.1	2 27.7	0 29.2	3 09.2	27 58.0	24 05.3	21 57.7
23 Sa	4 04 03	2 15 24	16 03 50	22 13 26	3D 23.0	24 36.2	14 20.8	20 49.7	2 49.8	0 28.3	3 07.8	27 55.5	24 03.8	21 56.5
24 Su	4 07 59	3 13 02	28 26 04	4♒42 08	3 22.4	25 46.4	15 34.4	21 33.3	3 12.1	0 27.7	3 06.6	27 53.0	24 02.3	21 55.3
25 M	4 11 56	4 10 40	11♒02 07	17 26 28	3 23.0	26 52.8	16 48.1	22 16.8	3 34.5	0 27.2	3 05.5	27 50.5	24 00.8	21 54.2
26 Tu	4 15 53	5 08 16	23 55 40	0♓30 10	3R 23.6	27 55.4	18 01.6	23 00.2	3 57.0	0 26.8	3 04.5	27 48.0	23 59.3	21 53.0
27 W	4 19 49	6 05 52	7♓10 24	13 56 42	3 23.4	28 54.2	19 15.2	23 43.6	4 19.7	0D 26.7	3 03.5	27 45.6	23 57.8	21 51.9
28 Th	4 23 46	7 03 26	20 49 20	27 48 28	3 21.6	29 48.9	20 28.8	24 26.9	4 42.4	0 26.7	3 02.7	27 43.1	23 56.3	21 50.9
29 F	4 27 42	8 01 00	4♈54 06	12♈06 04	3 17.7	0♋39.7	21 42.4	25 10.2	5 05.2	0 27.0	3 02.0	27 40.6	23 54.8	21 49.8
30 Sa	4 31 39	8 58 33	19 24 02	26 47 26	3 11.8	1 26.4	22 55.9	25 53.5	5 28.2	0 27.4	3 01.4	27 38.2	23 53.2	21 48.8
31 Su	4 35 35	9 56 05	4♉15 31	11♉47 19	3 04.4	2 08.9	24 09.4	26 36.6	5 51.2	0 28.0	3 00.9	27 35.7	23 51.7	21 47.8

LONGITUDE — June 1981

Day	Sid.Time	☉	0 hr ☽	Noon ☽	True ☊	☿	♀	♂	⚳	♃	♄	♅	♆	♇
1 M	4 39 32	10♊53 37	19♉21 43	26♉57 29	2♌56.6	2♋47.2	25♊22.9	27♉19.8	6♌14.4	0♎28.7	3♎00.4	27♏33.3	23♐50.1	21♎46.9
2 Tu	4 43 28	11 51 07	4♊33 18	12♊07 49	2R 49.3	3 21.1	26 36.4	28 02.8	6 37.7	0 29.7	3R 00.1	27R 30.9	23R 48.5	21R 45.9
3 W	4 47 25	12 48 37	19 39 46	27 07 58	2 43.5	3 50.7	27 49.9	28 45.9	7 01.0	0 30.8	2 59.9	27 28.5	23 46.9	21 45.0
4 Th	4 51 22	13 46 05	4♋31 23	11♋49 11	2 39.7	4 15.7	29 03.4	29 28.8	7 24.5	0 32.1	2D 59.8	27 26.2	23 45.4	21 44.1
5 F	4 55 18	14 43 32	19 00 42	26 05 30	2D 37.9	4 36.3	0♋16.9	0♊11.7	7 48.0	0 33.6	2 59.8	27 23.8	23 43.8	21 43.3
6 Sa	4 59 15	15 40 58	3♌03 20	9♌54 10	2 38.0	4 52.2	1 30.3	0 54.6	8 11.7	0 35.3	2 59.9	27 21.5	23 42.2	21 42.5
7 Su	5 03 11	16 38 23	16 38 06	23 15 21	2 39.0	5 03.6	2 43.7	1 37.4	8 35.4	0 37.1	3 00.1	27 19.1	23 40.6	21 41.7
8 M	5 07 08	17 35 47	29 46 18	6♍11 22	2R 40.2	5R 10.4	3 57.2	2 20.1	8 59.3	0 39.1	3 00.4	27 16.8	23 39.0	21 40.9
9 Tu	5 11 04	18 33 10	12♍31 04	18 45 57	2 40.8	5 12.6	5 10.5	3 02.8	9 23.2	0 41.3	3 00.8	27 14.5	23 37.4	21 40.2
10 W	5 15 01	19 30 32	24 56 34	1♎03 30	2 40.0	5 10.3	6 23.9	3 45.4	9 47.2	0 43.6	3 01.3	27 12.3	23 35.7	21 39.5
11 Th	5 18 57	20 27 52	7♎07 19	13 08 35	2 37.5	5 03.5	7 37.3	4 28.0	10 11.2	0 46.2	3 01.9	27 10.0	23 34.1	21 38.8
12 F	5 22 54	21 25 12	19 07 50	25 05 34	2 33.2	4 52.5	8 50.6	5 10.5	10 35.4	0 48.9	3 02.6	27 07.8	23 32.5	21 38.2
13 Sa	5 26 51	22 22 30	1♏02 15	6♏58 20	2 27.5	4 37.4	10 03.9	5 52.9	10 59.7	0 51.7	3 03.4	27 05.6	23 30.9	21 37.5
14 Su	5 30 47	23 19 48	12 54 13	18 50 15	2 20.8	4 18.5	11 17.2	6 35.3	11 24.0	0 54.8	3 04.3	27 03.5	23 29.3	21 37.0
15 M	5 34 44	24 17 05	24 46 47	0♐44 04	2 13.8	3 56.0	12 30.5	7 17.7	11 48.4	0 58.0	3 05.3	27 01.3	23 27.6	21 36.4
16 Tu	5 38 40	25 14 22	6♐42 24	12 41 59	2 07.2	3 30.4	13 43.8	8 00.0	12 12.9	1 01.4	3 06.4	26 59.2	23 26.0	21 35.9
17 W	5 42 37	26 11 38	18 43 02	24 45 45	2 01.7	3 01.9	14 57.0	8 42.2	12 37.4	1 04.9	3 07.6	26 57.1	23 24.4	21 35.4
18 Th	5 46 33	27 08 53	0♑50 19	6♑56 54	1 57.7	2 31.2	16 10.2	9 24.4	13 02.0	1 08.6	3 08.9	26 55.1	23 22.8	21 35.0
19 F	5 50 30	28 06 08	13 05 40	19 16 48	1 55.3	1 58.6	17 23.4	10 06.5	13 26.7	1 12.5	3 10.3	26 53.1	23 21.2	21 34.5
20 Sa	5 54 26	29 03 22	25 30 31	1♒46 59	1D 54.6	1 24.8	18 36.6	10 48.6	13 51.5	1 16.5	3 11.8	26 51.1	23 19.6	21 34.1
21 Su	5 58 23	0♋00 37	8♒06 27	14 29 07	1 55.1	0 50.2	19 49.8	11 30.6	14 16.4	1 20.7	3 13.4	26 49.1	23 18.0	21 33.8
22 M	6 02 20	0 57 50	20 55 16	27 25 07	1 56.5	0 15.6	21 03.0	12 12.6	14 41.3	1 25.0	3 15.1	26 47.2	23 16.4	21 33.5
23 Tu	6 06 16	1 55 04	3♓58 57	10♓37 00	1 58.1	29♊41.4	22 16.1	12 54.5	15 06.2	1 29.5	3 16.8	26 45.3	23 14.8	21 33.2
24 W	6 10 13	2 52 18	17 19 30	24 06 39	1R 59.2	29 08.3	23 29.2	13 36.4	15 31.3	1 34.1	3 18.7	26 43.4	23 13.2	21 32.9
25 Th	6 14 09	3 49 31	0♈58 35	7♈55 21	1 59.4	28 36.8	24 42.4	14 18.2	15 56.4	1 38.9	3 20.7	26 41.6	23 11.6	21 32.7
26 F	6 18 06	4 46 45	14 56 59	22 03 19	1 58.4	28 07.5	25 55.4	15 00.0	16 21.6	1 43.9	3 22.8	26 39.8	23 10.0	21 32.5
27 Sa	6 22 02	5 43 58	29 14 09	6♉29 05	1 56.3	27 40.9	27 08.5	15 41.7	16 46.8	1 49.0	3 25.0	26 38.0	23 08.4	21 32.3
28 Su	6 25 59	6 41 12	13♉47 38	21 09 08	1 53.4	27 17.5	28 21.6	16 23.4	17 12.1	1 54.3	3 27.2	26 36.3	23 06.8	21 32.2
29 M	6 29 55	7 38 26	28 32 51	5♊57 54	1 50.2	26 57.6	29 34.7	17 05.0	17 37.5	1 59.7	3 29.6	26 34.6	23 05.3	21 32.1
30 Tu	6 33 52	8 35 39	13♊23 22	20 48 13	1 47.1	26 41.6	0♌47.7	17 46.5	18 02.9	2 05.2	3 32.1	26 32.9	23 03.7	21 32.1

Astro Data

	Dy Hr Mn
☽ 0N	2 0:05
☽ 0S	15 0:45
♃ D	27 18:26
☽ 0N	29 10:08
♄ D	5 2:13
☿ R	9 11:36
☽ 0S	11 8:04
☽ 0N	25 17:56

Planet Ingress

	Dy Hr Mn
☿ ♊	8 9:42
♀ ♊	11 19:45
⚳ ♌	15 16:39
☉ ♊	21 3:39
☿ ♋	28 17:04
♂ ♊	5 5:26
♀ ♋	5 6:29
☉ ♋	21 11:45
☿ ♊R	22 22:51
♀ ♌	29 20:20

Last Aspect / ☽ Ingress (May)

Last Aspect Dy Hr Mn		☽ Ingress	Dy Hr Mn
1 5:03	♅ △	♈	1 6:57
2 22:20	♆ △	♉	3 6:59
5 3:56	♅ ☍	♊	5 6:01
6 21:09	♆ ☍	♋	7 6:18
9 7:02	♅ △	♌	9 9:40
11 16:37	♀ □	♍	11 16:55
14 0:04	♅ ⚹	♎	14 3:24
16 3:59	♆ ⚹	♏	16 15:37
19 0:25	♆ ☌	♐	19 4:14
21 4:38	♅ ☌	♑	21 16:20
23 22:59	♅ ⚹	♒	24 3:01
26 7:06	♅ □	♓	26 11:05
28 15:38	☿ □	♈	28 15:44
30 7:18	♆ △	♉	30 17:10

Last Aspect / ☽ Ingress (June)

Last Aspect Dy Hr Mn		☽ Ingress	Dy Hr Mn
1 12:56	♅ ☍	♊	1 16:48
3 13:14	♀ ☌	♋	3 16:38
5 14:14	♅ △	♌	5 18:43
7 19:26	♅ □	♍	8 0:25
10 4:27	♅ ⚹	♎	10 9:55
12 8:53	♆ ⚹	♏	12 21:54
15 4:33	♅ ☌	♐	15 10:31
17 15:04	☉ ☍	♑	17 22:21
20 2:36	♅ ⚹	♒	20 8:36
22 10:50	♅ □	♓	22 16:44
24 20:28	☿ □	♈	24 22:18
26 21:50	☿ ⚹	♉	27 1:16
29 0:45	♀ ⚹	♊	29 2:21

☽ Phases & Eclipses

Dy Hr Mn	
4 4:19	● 13♉37
10 22:22	☽ 20♌09
19 0:04	○ 27♏56
26 21:00	☾ 5♓30
2 11:32	● 11♊50
9 11:33	☽ 18♍32
17 15:04	○ 26♐19
25 4:25	☾ 3♈31

Astro Data

1 May 1981
Julian Day # 29706
SVP 5♓31'29"
GC 26♐34.7 ⚴ 10♊40.2
Eris 15♈03.0 ⚵ 27♎15.7R
⚷ 17♉31.8 ⚶ 27♌08.6
☽ Mean ☊ 6♌07.9

1 June 1981
Julian Day # 29737
SVP 5♓31'25"
GC 26♐34.8 ⚴ 28♊57.9
Eris 15♈19.0 ⚵ 22♎31.4R
⚷ 19♉35.3 ⚶ 4♍33.6
☽ Mean ☊ 4♌29.4

July 1981 — LONGITUDE

Day	Sid.Time	☉	0 hr ☽	Noon ☽	True ☊	☿	♀	♂	⚳	♃	♄	♅	♆	♇
1 W	6 37 49	9♋32 53	28♊11 30	5♋32 15	1♌44.8	26♊29.9	2♌00.7	18♊28.0	18♌28.4	2♎10.9	3♎34.6	26♏31.3	23♐02.2	21♎32.0
2 Th	6 41 45	10 30 07	12♋49 34	20 02 39	1D 43.4	26R 22.6	3 13.7	19 09.5	18 54.0	2 16.8	3 37.3	26R 29.8	23R 00.7	21D 32.0
3 F	6 45 42	11 27 21	27 10 51	4♌13 36	1 43.1	26D 20.0	4 26.7	19 50.9	19 19.6	2 22.8	3 40.0	26 28.2	22 59.1	21 32.1
4 Sa	6 49 38	12 24 34	11♌10 32	18 01 25	1 43.6	26 22.3	5 39.7	20 32.2	19 45.3	2 28.9	3 42.8	26 26.7	22 57.6	21 32.2
5 Su	6 53 35	13 21 47	24 46 09	1♍24 46	1 44.8	26 29.5	6 52.6	21 13.5	20 11.0	2 35.2	3 45.8	26 25.3	22 56.1	21 32.3
6 M	6 57 31	14 19 00	7♍57 25	14 24 22	1 46.1	26 41.7	8 05.5	21 54.7	20 36.8	2 41.6	3 48.8	26 23.9	22 54.6	21 32.4
7 Tu	7 01 28	15 16 13	20 45 59	27 02 39	1 47.3	26 59.1	9 18.4	22 35.9	21 02.6	2 48.2	3 51.9	26 22.5	22 53.2	21 32.6
8 W	7 05 24	16 13 25	3♎14 52	9♎23 08	1R 48.0	27 21.5	10 31.3	23 17.0	21 28.5	2 54.8	3 55.1	26 21.2	22 51.7	21 32.8
9 Th	7 09 21	17 10 38	15 28 01	21 30 03	1 48.1	27 49.1	11 44.1	23 58.1	21 54.4	3 01.7	3 58.3	26 19.9	22 50.3	21 33.1
10 F	7 13 18	18 07 50	27 29 49	3♏27 53	1 47.5	28 21.8	12 57.0	24 39.1	22 20.4	3 08.6	4 01.7	26 18.6	22 48.8	21 33.3
11 Sa	7 17 14	19 05 02	9♏24 48	15 21 06	1 46.4	28 59.6	14 09.8	25 20.0	22 46.4	3 15.7	4 05.2	26 17.5	22 47.4	21 33.6
12 Su	7 21 11	20 02 15	21 17 18	27 13 54	1 44.9	29 42.4	15 22.5	26 00.9	23 12.5	3 22.9	4 08.7	26 16.3	22 46.0	21 34.0
13 M	7 25 07	20 59 27	3♐11 21	9♐10 04	1 43.4	0♋30.2	16 35.3	26 41.8	23 38.6	3 30.2	4 12.3	26 15.2	22 44.6	21 34.4
14 Tu	7 29 04	21 56 40	15 10 27	21 12 50	1 42.0	1 23.0	17 48.0	27 22.6	24 04.8	3 37.7	4 16.0	26 14.1	22 43.3	21 34.8
15 W	7 33 00	22 53 52	27 17 32	3♑24 49	1 40.9	2 20.7	19 00.7	28 03.3	24 31.0	3 45.3	4 19.8	26 13.1	22 41.9	21 35.3
16 Th	7 36 57	23 51 05	9♑34 54	15 47 59	1 40.2	3 23.2	20 13.4	28 44.0	24 57.2	3 53.0	4 23.7	26 12.2	22 40.6	21 35.7
17 F	7 40 54	24 48 19	22 04 13	28 23 42	1D 39.9	4 30.5	21 26.0	29 24.7	25 23.5	4 00.8	4 27.6	26 11.3	22 39.3	21 36.3
18 Sa	7 44 50	25 45 32	4♒46 33	11♒12 47	1 40.0	5 42.5	22 38.6	0♋05.2	25 49.9	4 08.7	4 31.7	26 10.4	22 38.0	21 36.8
19 Su	7 48 47	26 42 47	17 42 29	24 15 37	1 40.3	6 59.1	23 51.2	0 45.8	26 16.3	4 16.8	4 35.8	26 09.6	22 36.7	21 37.4
20 M	7 52 43	27 40 02	0♓52 11	7♓32 10	1 40.7	8 20.2	25 03.8	1 26.3	26 42.7	4 25.0	4 40.0	26 08.8	22 35.4	21 38.0
21 Tu	7 56 40	28 37 17	14 15 31	21 02 12	1 41.0	9 45.7	26 16.3	2 06.7	27 09.1	4 33.3	4 44.2	26 08.1	22 34.2	21 38.7
22 W	8 00 36	29 34 33	27 52 07	4♈45 11	1 41.2	11 15.5	27 28.8	2 47.1	27 35.6	4 41.7	4 48.6	26 07.4	22 33.0	21 39.3
23 Th	8 04 33	0♌31 50	11♈41 17	18 40 18	1 41.3	12 49.5	28 41.3	3 27.4	28 02.2	4 50.2	4 53.0	26 06.7	22 31.8	21 40.1
24 F	8 08 29	1 29 08	25 42 02	2♉46 18	1 41.4	14 27.5	29 53.8	4 07.7	28 28.7	4 58.8	4 57.5	26 06.2	22 30.6	21 40.8
25 Sa	8 12 26	2 26 27	9♉52 51	17 01 23	1 41.4	16 09.3	1♍06.2	4 47.9	28 55.4	5 07.6	5 02.1	26 05.6	22 29.4	21 41.6
26 Su	8 16 22	3 23 47	24 11 34	1♊22 59	1 41.5	17 54.7	2 18.6	5 28.1	29 22.0	5 16.4	5 06.7	26 05.1	22 28.3	21 42.4
27 M	8 20 19	4 21 08	8♊35 12	15 47 44	1 41.7	19 43.4	3 31.0	6 08.2	29 48.7	5 25.4	5 11.4	26 04.7	22 27.2	21 43.2
28 Tu	8 24 16	5 18 30	23 00 02	0♋11 32	1 42.0	21 35.2	4 43.3	6 48.3	0♍15.4	5 34.4	5 16.2	26 04.3	22 26.1	21 44.1
29 W	8 28 12	6 15 53	7♋21 40	14 29 51	1 42.3	23 29.8	5 55.7	7 28.3	0 42.2	5 43.6	5 21.1	26 04.0	22 25.0	21 45.0
30 Th	8 32 09	7 13 17	21 35 30	28 38 05	1R 42.5	25 26.8	7 08.0	8 08.3	1 09.0	5 52.8	5 26.0	26 03.7	22 24.0	21 46.0
31 F	8 36 05	8 10 42	5♌37 05	12♌32 05	1 42.4	27 26.0	8 20.2	8 48.2	1 35.8	6 02.2	5 31.0	26 03.5	22 23.0	21 47.0

August 1981 — LONGITUDE

Day	Sid.Time	☉	0 hr ☽	Noon ☽	True ☊	☿	♀	♂	⚳	♃	♄	♅	♆	♇
1 Sa	8 40 02	9♌08 07	19♌22 41	26♌08 37	1♌41.9	29♋27.0	9♍32.5	9♋28.1	2♍02.7	6♎11.7	5♎36.1	26♏03.3	22♐22.0	21♎48.0
2 Su	8 43 58	10 05 33	2♍49 40	9♍25 45	1R 41.1	1♌29.3	10 44.7	10 07.9	2 29.6	6 21.2	5 41.2	26R 03.2	22R 21.0	21 49.0
3 M	8 47 55	11 03 00	15 56 49	22 22 58	1 40.0	3 32.8	11 56.9	10 47.7	2 56.5	6 30.9	5 46.4	26D 03.1	22 20.1	21 50.1
4 Tu	8 51 52	12 00 28	28 44 22	5♎01 15	1 38.7	5 37.0	13 09.0	11 27.4	3 23.5	6 40.6	5 51.7	26 03.1	22 19.2	21 51.2
5 W	8 55 48	12 57 56	11♎13 56	17 22 47	1 37.4	7 41.6	14 21.1	12 07.0	3 50.4	6 50.5	5 57.0	26 03.1	22 18.3	21 52.3
6 Th	8 59 45	13 55 26	23 28 16	29 30 50	1 36.5	9 46.3	15 33.2	12 46.6	4 17.4	7 00.4	6 02.4	26 03.2	22 17.4	21 53.5
7 F	9 03 41	14 52 55	5♏31 02	11♏29 24	1D 36.0	11 50.9	16 45.2	13 26.2	4 44.5	7 10.4	6 07.9	26 03.3	22 16.6	21 54.7
8 Sa	9 07 38	15 50 26	17 26 30	23 22 55	1 36.2	13 55.2	17 57.2	14 05.7	5 11.5	7 20.6	6 13.4	26 03.5	22 15.8	21 55.9
9 Su	9 11 34	16 47 58	29 19 14	5♐16 03	1 36.9	15 58.8	19 09.1	14 45.1	5 38.6	7 30.8	6 19.0	26 03.8	22 15.0	21 57.1
10 M	9 15 31	17 45 30	11♐13 55	17 13 24	1 38.1	18 01.7	20 21.1	15 24.5	6 05.7	7 41.0	6 24.6	26 04.1	22 14.3	21 58.4
11 Tu	9 19 27	18 43 04	23 15 02	29 19 17	1 39.5	20 03.7	21 32.9	16 03.8	6 32.8	7 51.4	6 30.3	26 04.4	22 13.5	21 59.7
12 W	9 23 24	19 40 38	5♑26 38	11♑37 28	1 40.8	22 04.6	22 44.8	16 43.1	7 00.0	8 01.9	6 36.1	26 04.8	22 12.8	22 01.1
13 Th	9 27 20	20 38 14	17 52 10	24 10 59	1R 41.6	24 04.4	23 56.5	17 22.3	7 27.2	8 12.4	6 41.9	26 05.2	22 12.2	22 02.5
14 F	9 31 17	21 35 50	0♒34 10	7♒01 51	1 41.7	26 03.0	25 08.3	18 01.5	7 54.4	8 23.0	6 47.8	26 05.7	22 11.5	22 03.9
15 Sa	9 35 14	22 33 28	13 34 06	20 10 54	1 40.8	28 00.3	26 20.0	18 40.6	8 21.6	8 33.7	6 53.7	26 06.3	22 10.9	22 05.3
16 Su	9 39 10	23 31 07	26 52 08	3♓37 40	1 38.8	29 56.2	27 31.6	19 19.7	8 48.8	8 44.4	6 59.7	26 06.9	22 10.3	22 06.7
17 M	9 43 07	24 28 47	10♓27 12	17 20 27	1 36.1	1♍50.8	28 43.2	19 58.7	9 16.1	8 55.3	7 05.7	26 07.5	22 09.8	22 08.2
18 Tu	9 47 03	25 26 28	24 17 01	1♈16 29	1 32.8	3 44.0	29 54.8	20 37.7	9 43.3	9 06.2	7 11.8	26 08.2	22 09.3	22 09.7
19 W	9 51 00	26 24 11	8♈18 25	15 22 20	1 29.4	5 35.8	1♎06.3	21 16.6	10 10.6	9 17.2	7 17.9	26 09.0	22 08.8	22 11.3
20 Th	9 54 56	27 21 56	22 27 45	29 34 15	1 26.6	7 26.3	2 17.8	21 55.5	10 37.9	9 28.2	7 24.1	26 09.8	22 08.3	22 12.8
21 F	9 58 53	28 19 42	6♉41 22	13♉48 43	1 24.7	9 15.3	3 29.3	22 34.3	11 05.3	9 39.3	7 30.4	26 10.6	22 07.9	22 14.4
22 Sa	10 02 49	29 17 30	20 55 56	28 02 41	1D 24.0	11 02.9	4 40.6	23 13.1	11 32.6	9 50.5	7 36.6	26 11.6	22 07.5	22 16.0
23 Su	10 06 46	0♍15 20	5♊08 41	12♊13 41	1 24.4	12 49.2	5 52.0	23 51.8	12 00.0	10 01.8	7 43.0	26 12.5	22 07.1	22 17.7
24 M	10 10 43	1 13 12	19 17 26	26 19 45	1 25.7	14 34.1	7 03.3	24 30.5	12 27.4	10 13.1	7 49.3	26 13.5	22 06.8	22 19.3
25 Tu	10 14 39	2 11 06	3♋20 26	10♋19 16	1 27.1	16 17.6	8 14.6	25 09.1	12 54.8	10 24.5	7 55.8	26 14.6	22 06.5	22 21.0
26 W	10 18 36	3 09 01	17 16 06	24 10 41	1R 28.2	17 59.9	9 25.8	25 47.7	13 22.2	10 36.0	8 02.2	26 15.7	22 06.2	22 22.7
27 Th	10 22 32	4 06 58	1♌02 52	7♌52 24	1 28.2	19 40.8	10 37.0	26 26.2	13 49.6	10 47.5	8 08.7	26 16.9	22 06.0	22 24.5
28 F	10 26 29	5 04 56	14 39 05	21 22 42	1 26.8	21 20.3	11 48.1	27 04.6	14 17.1	10 59.1	8 15.3	26 18.1	22 05.8	22 26.2
29 Sa	10 30 25	6 02 57	28 03 03	4♍39 57	1 23.6	22 58.6	12 59.2	27 43.1	14 44.5	11 10.8	8 21.9	26 19.3	22 05.6	22 28.0
30 Su	10 34 22	7 00 58	11♍13 14	17 42 47	1 18.8	24 35.6	14 10.2	28 21.4	15 12.0	11 22.5	8 28.5	26 20.6	22 05.5	22 29.8
31 M	10 38 18	7 59 02	24 08 31	0♎30 25	1 12.7	26 11.3	15 21.2	28 59.7	15 39.5	11 34.2	8 35.2	26 22.0	22 05.3	22 31.7

Astro Data	Planet Ingress	Last Aspect	☽ Ingress	Last Aspect	☽ Ingress	☽ Phases & Eclipses	Astro Data
Dy Hr Mn	Dy Hr Mn	Dy Hr Mn	Dy Hr Mn	Dy Hr Mn	Dy Hr Mn	Dy Hr Mn	
♇ D 1 16:12	☿ ♋ 12 21:08	30 21:25 ☿ ☌	♋ 1 2:57	1 11:51 ♅ □	♍ 1 18:54	1 19:03 ● 9♋50	1 July 1981
☿ D 3 12:58	♂ ♋ 18 8:54	2 22:49 ♅ △	♌ 3 4:47	3 18:55 ♅ ✶	♎ 4 2:24	9 2:39 ☽ 16♎48	Julian Day # 29767
♃0S 8 15:38	☉ ♌ 22 22:40	5 3:00 ☿ ✶	♍ 5 9:26	5 21:41 ♆ ✶	♏ 6 12:58	17 4:39 ○ 24♑31	SVP 5♓31'19"
☽0S 8 16:10	♀ ♍ 24 14:04	7 11:53 ☿ □	♎ 7 17:42	8 17:25 ♅ ☌	♐ 9 1:22	17 4:47 ◐ P 0.548	GC 26♐34.9 ⚳ 16♋52.4
☽0N 22 23:46	⚳ ♍ 27 22:09	10 1:14 ☿ △	♏ 10 5:02	10 21:59 ♆ ☌	♑ 11 13:20	24 9:40 ☾ 1♉24	Eris 15♈26.9 ⚵ 22♎40.8
♃☌♄ 24 4:15		12 10:04 ♅ ☌	♐ 12 17:35	13 15:36 ♅ ✶	♒ 13 22:56	31 3:52 ● 7♌51	⚷ 21♉19.3 ⚶ 15♍20.7
♄0S 29 6:48	☿ ♌ 1 18:30	15 0:53 ♂ ☍	♑ 15 5:19	16 4:23 ☿ ☍	♓ 16 5:34	31 3:45:44 ◐ T 02'03"	☽ Mean ☊ 2♌54.1
	☿ ♍ 16 12:47	17 7:50 ♅ ✶	♒ 17 15:02	18 9:27 ♀ ☍	♈ 18 9:49		1 August 1981
♅ D 4 10:49	♀ ♎ 18 13:44	19 15:27 ♅ □	♓ 19 22:26	20 8:01 ☉ △	♉ 20 12:43	7 19:26 ☽ 15♏11	Julian Day # 29798
☽0S 5 0:34	☉ ♍ 23 5:38	22 2:19 ☉ △	♈ 22 3:43	22 14:16 ☉ □	♊ 22 15:18	15 16:37 ○ 22♒45	SVP 5♓31'14"
♆✶♇ 18 6:43		24 6:40 ♀ △	♉ 24 7:18	24 5:09 ♇ △	♋ 24 18:17	22 14:16 ☾ 29♉23	GC 26♐34.9 ⚳ 5♌01.5
☽0N 19 5:18		26 3:10 ♅ ☍	♊ 26 9:42	26 15:38 ♅ △	♌ 26 22:10	29 14:43 ● 6♍10	Eris 15♈25.2R ⚵ 27♎07.2
♀0S 19 23:26		27 23:04 ♆ ☍	♋ 28 11:41	28 20:51 ♅ □	♍ 29 3:32		⚷ 22♉31.0 ⚶ 28♍44.8
♃∠♅ 30 7:47		30 7:36 ♅ △	♌ 30 14:20	31 8:59 ♂ ✶	♎ 31 11:02		☽ Mean ☊ 1♌15.6

LONGITUDE — September 1981

Day	Sid.Time	☉	0 hr ☽	Noon ☽	True ☊	☿	♀	♂	⚳	♃	♄	♅	♆	♇
1 Tu	10 42 15	8♍57 06	6♎48 31	13♎02 54	1♌06.2	27♍45.8	16♎32.1	29♋37.9	16♍06.9	11♎46.0	8♎41.9	26♏23.4	22♐05.3	22♎33.5
2 W	10 46 12	9 55 13	19 13 45	25 21 17	0R 59.7	29 19.0	17 43.0	0♌16.1	16 34.4	11 57.9	8 48.6	26 24.9	22D 05.2	22 35.4
3 Th	10 50 08	10 53 21	1♏25 47	7♏27 38	0 54.1	0♎50.9	18 53.8	0 54.3	17 01.9	12 09.8	8 55.4	26 26.4	22 05.2	22 37.3
4 F	10 54 05	11 51 30	13 27 13	19 25 00	0 49.9	2 21.6	20 04.5	1 32.3	17 29.5	12 21.8	9 02.2	26 27.9	22 05.2	22 39.2
5 Sa	10 58 01	12 49 41	25 21 30	1♐17 16	0 47.3	3 51.0	21 15.2	2 10.3	17 57.0	12 33.8	9 09.1	26 29.5	22 05.3	22 41.2
6 Su	11 01 58	13 47 53	7♐12 54	13 08 59	0D 46.5	5 19.1	22 25.9	2 48.3	18 24.5	12 45.9	9 16.0	26 31.2	22 05.3	22 43.1
7 M	11 05 54	14 46 07	19 06 09	25 05 02	0 47.0	6 46.0	23 36.4	3 26.2	18 52.0	12 58.1	9 22.9	26 32.9	22 05.5	22 45.1
8 Tu	11 09 51	15 44 22	1♑06 16	7♑10 30	0 48.4	8 11.6	24 46.9	4 04.1	19 19.6	13 10.2	9 29.8	26 34.6	22 05.6	22 47.1
9 W	11 13 47	16 42 39	13 18 18	19 30 15	0R 49.7	9 35.8	25 57.4	4 41.8	19 47.1	13 22.4	9 36.8	26 36.4	22 05.8	22 49.1
10 Th	11 17 44	17 40 58	25 46 52	2♒08 37	0 50.2	10 58.7	27 07.8	5 19.6	20 14.7	13 34.7	9 43.8	26 38.3	22 06.0	22 51.2
11 F	11 21 41	18 39 18	8♒35 51	15 08 51	0 49.2	12 20.3	28 18.1	5 57.3	20 42.2	13 47.0	9 50.8	26 40.1	22 06.3	22 53.2
12 Sa	11 25 37	19 37 40	21 47 47	28 32 43	0 46.1	13 40.4	29 28.3	6 34.9	21 09.7	13 59.3	9 57.9	26 42.1	22 06.5	22 55.3
13 Su	11 29 34	20 36 03	5♓23 30	12♓19 56	0 41.0	14 59.1	0♏38.5	7 12.4	21 37.3	14 11.7	10 04.9	26 44.0	22 06.9	22 57.4
14 M	11 33 30	21 34 28	19 21 36	26 27 58	0 34.0	16 16.3	1 48.5	7 50.0	22 04.8	14 24.1	10 12.0	26 46.0	22 07.2	22 59.5
15 Tu	11 37 27	22 32 55	3♈38 24	10♈52 06	0 25.9	17 31.9	2 58.6	8 27.4	22 32.4	14 36.6	10 19.2	26 48.1	22 07.6	23 01.6
16 W	11 41 23	23 31 24	18 08 16	25 25 59	0 17.6	18 45.9	4 08.5	9 04.8	22 59.9	14 49.1	10 26.3	26 50.2	22 08.0	23 03.8
17 Th	11 45 20	24 29 55	2♉44 23	10♉02 37	0 10.3	19 58.2	5 18.4	9 42.2	23 27.5	15 01.6	10 33.5	26 52.4	22 08.4	23 05.9
18 F	11 49 16	25 28 29	17 19 53	24 35 29	0 04.7	21 08.8	6 28.2	10 19.5	23 55.0	15 14.2	10 40.7	26 54.5	22 08.9	23 08.1
19 Sa	11 53 13	26 27 04	1♊48 50	8♊59 27	0 01.2	22 17.4	7 37.9	10 56.7	24 22.6	15 26.8	10 47.9	26 56.8	22 09.4	23 10.3
20 Su	11 57 09	27 25 42	16 06 59	23 11 12	29♋59.9	23 24.1	8 47.5	11 33.9	24 50.1	15 39.4	10 55.1	26 59.1	22 10.0	23 12.5
21 M	12 01 06	28 24 22	0♋11 57	7♋09 13	0♌00.0	24 28.6	9 57.1	12 11.0	25 17.7	15 52.1	11 02.4	27 01.4	22 10.5	23 14.7
22 Tu	12 05 03	29 23 05	14 02 59	20 53 21	0 00.8	25 30.9	11 06.6	12 48.1	25 45.2	16 04.8	11 09.6	27 03.7	22 11.1	23 17.0
23 W	12 08 59	0♎21 49	27 40 23	4♌24 13	0 00.9	26 30.7	12 16.0	13 25.1	26 12.8	16 17.5	11 16.9	27 06.1	22 11.8	23 19.2
24 Th	12 12 56	1 20 36	11♌04 58	17 42 43	29♋59.5	27 28.0	13 25.3	14 02.0	26 40.3	16 30.3	11 24.2	27 08.6	22 12.5	23 21.5
25 F	12 16 52	2 19 25	24 17 35	0♍49 35	29 55.6	28 22.4	14 34.6	14 38.9	27 07.9	16 43.0	11 31.5	27 11.1	22 13.2	23 23.7
26 Sa	12 20 49	3 18 16	7♍18 47	13 45 11	29 49.1	29 13.8	15 43.7	15 15.7	27 35.4	16 55.8	11 38.8	27 13.6	22 13.9	23 26.0
27 Su	12 24 45	4 17 09	20 08 48	26 29 36	29 39.9	0♏01.9	16 52.8	15 52.5	28 02.9	17 08.7	11 46.1	27 16.1	22 14.7	23 28.3
28 M	12 28 42	5 16 04	2♎47 36	9♎02 46	29 28.6	0 46.4	18 01.8	16 29.2	28 30.4	17 21.5	11 53.5	27 18.7	22 15.5	23 30.6
29 Tu	12 32 38	6 15 01	15 15 07	21 24 43	29 16.3	1 27.1	19 10.7	17 05.8	28 57.9	17 34.4	12 00.8	27 21.4	22 16.3	23 32.9
30 W	12 36 35	7 14 01	27 31 38	3♏35 59	29 03.9	2 03.5	20 19.5	17 42.4	29 25.4	17 47.3	12 08.2	27 24.0	22 17.2	23 35.2

LONGITUDE — October 1981

Day	Sid.Time	☉	0 hr ☽	Noon ☽	True ☊	☿	♀	♂	⚳	♃	♄	♅	♆	♇
1 Th	12 40 32	8♎13 02	9♏37 57	15♏37 45	28♋52.6	2♏35.4	21♏28.1	18♌18.9	29♍52.9	18♎00.2	12♎15.5	27♏26.7	22♐18.0	23♎37.6
2 F	12 44 28	9 12 05	21 35 42	27 32 06	28R 43.3	3 02.4	22 36.7	18 55.4	0♎20.3	18 13.1	12 22.9	27 29.5	22 19.0	23 39.9
3 Sa	12 48 25	10 11 09	3♐27 23	9♐22 00	28 36.6	3 23.9	23 45.2	19 31.7	0 47.8	18 26.0	12 30.3	27 32.3	22 19.9	23 42.2
4 Su	12 52 21	11 10 16	15 16 26	21 11 16	28 32.4	3 39.6	24 53.6	20 08.0	1 15.2	18 39.0	12 37.6	27 35.1	22 20.9	23 44.6
5 M	12 56 18	12 09 25	27 07 04	3♑04 30	28D 30.6	3R 49.1	26 01.9	20 44.3	1 42.7	18 52.0	12 45.0	27 37.9	22 21.9	23 47.0
6 Tu	13 00 14	13 08 35	9♑04 11	15 06 49	28 30.2	3 51.8	27 10.0	21 20.4	2 10.1	19 04.9	12 52.4	27 40.8	22 23.0	23 49.3
7 W	13 04 11	14 07 47	21 13 05	27 23 39	28R 30.4	3 47.3	28 18.0	21 56.6	2 37.5	19 17.9	12 59.7	27 43.7	22 24.1	23 51.7
8 Th	13 08 07	15 07 01	3♒39 09	10♒00 13	28 30.0	3 35.2	29 25.9	22 32.6	3 04.9	19 30.9	13 07.1	27 46.7	22 25.2	23 54.1
9 F	13 12 04	16 06 16	16 27 23	23 01 08	28 27.9	3 15.2	0♐33.7	23 08.6	3 32.2	19 43.9	13 14.5	27 49.6	22 26.3	23 56.5
10 Sa	13 16 01	17 05 34	29 41 46	6♓29 33	28 23.3	2 47.1	1 41.3	23 44.5	3 59.6	19 57.0	13 21.8	27 52.6	22 27.5	23 58.9
11 Su	13 19 57	18 04 53	13♓24 29	20 26 28	28 16.1	2 10.7	2 48.8	24 20.3	4 26.9	20 10.0	13 29.2	27 55.7	22 28.7	24 01.2
12 M	13 23 54	19 04 14	27 35 10	4♈50 00	28 06.5	1 26.3	3 56.1	24 56.0	4 54.2	20 23.0	13 36.5	27 58.7	22 29.9	24 03.6
13 Tu	13 27 50	20 03 37	12♈10 15	19 34 59	27 55.4	0 34.1	5 03.3	25 31.7	5 21.5	20 36.0	13 43.9	28 01.8	22 31.1	24 06.0
14 W	13 31 47	21 03 02	27 03 06	4♉33 25	27 43.9	29♎34.9	6 10.4	26 07.3	5 48.7	20 49.0	13 51.2	28 05.0	22 32.4	24 08.4
15 Th	13 35 43	22 02 29	12♉04 41	19 35 40	27 33.4	28 29.6	7 17.3	26 42.9	6 16.0	21 02.1	13 58.6	28 08.1	22 33.7	24 10.8
16 F	13 39 40	23 01 58	27 05 09	4♊32 05	27 25.0	27 19.7	8 24.0	27 18.4	6 43.2	21 15.1	14 05.9	28 11.3	22 35.1	24 13.2
17 Sa	13 43 36	24 01 30	11♊55 33	19 14 47	27 19.4	26 06.8	9 30.6	27 53.8	7 10.4	21 28.1	14 13.2	28 14.5	22 36.4	24 15.7
18 Su	13 47 33	25 01 04	26 29 14	3♋38 31	27 16.4	24 52.8	10 37.0	28 29.1	7 37.6	21 41.1	14 20.5	28 17.8	22 37.8	24 18.1
19 M	13 51 30	26 00 40	10♋42 27	17 40 58	27 15.4	23 39.9	11 43.3	29 04.4	8 04.7	21 54.2	14 27.8	28 21.0	22 39.2	24 20.5
20 Tu	13 55 26	27 00 19	24 34 08	1♌22 09	27 15.4	22 30.2	12 49.4	29 39.6	8 31.8	22 07.2	14 35.0	28 24.3	22 40.7	24 22.9
21 W	13 59 23	28 00 00	8♌05 16	14 43 45	27 14.9	21 25.9	13 55.3	0♍14.7	8 58.9	22 20.2	14 42.3	28 27.6	22 42.1	24 25.3
22 Th	14 03 19	28 59 43	21 17 58	27 48 14	27 12.7	20 28.9	15 01.0	0 49.7	9 26.0	22 33.2	14 49.5	28 31.0	22 43.6	24 27.7
23 F	14 07 16	29 59 28	4♍14 51	10♍38 10	27 07.9	19 40.8	16 06.6	1 24.7	9 53.1	22 46.2	14 56.7	28 34.3	22 45.2	24 30.1
24 Sa	14 11 12	0♏59 15	16 58 25	23 15 51	27 00.1	19 02.7	17 11.9	1 59.6	10 20.1	22 59.2	15 03.9	28 37.7	22 46.7	24 32.5
25 Su	14 15 09	1 59 05	29 30 42	5♎43 06	26 49.3	18 35.6	18 17.1	2 34.4	10 47.1	23 12.2	15 11.1	28 41.1	22 48.3	24 34.9
26 M	14 19 05	2 58 57	11♎53 14	18 01 12	26 36.3	18D 19.8	19 22.0	3 09.1	11 14.0	23 25.1	15 18.3	28 44.5	22 49.9	24 37.3
27 Tu	14 23 02	3 58 50	24 07 07	0♏11 05	26 21.9	18 15.5	20 26.8	3 43.7	11 40.9	23 38.1	15 25.4	28 48.0	22 51.5	24 39.6
28 W	14 26 58	4 58 46	6♏13 12	12 13 34	26 07.5	18 22.3	21 31.3	4 18.3	12 07.8	23 51.0	15 32.5	28 51.4	22 53.1	24 42.0
29 Th	14 30 55	5 58 44	18 12 20	24 09 40	25 54.1	18 39.9	22 35.5	4 52.7	12 34.7	24 03.9	15 39.6	28 54.9	22 54.8	24 44.4
30 F	14 34 52	6 58 43	0♐05 44	6♐00 48	25 42.9	19 07.5	23 39.6	5 27.1	13 01.5	24 16.8	15 46.7	28 58.4	22 56.5	24 46.8
31 Sa	14 38 48	7 58 44	11 55 08	17 49 04	25 34.4	19 44.3	24 43.4	6 01.3	13 28.3	24 29.7	15 53.7	29 01.9	22 58.2	24 49.1

Astro Data Dy Hr Mn	Planet Ingress Dy Hr Mn	Last Aspect Dy Hr Mn	☽ Ingress Dy Hr Mn	Last Aspect Dy Hr Mn	☽ Ingress Dy Hr Mn	☽ Phases & Eclipses Dy Hr Mn
☽0S 1 8:39	♂ ♌ 2 1:52	2 6:33 ♇ ☌	♏ 2 21:10	2 11:55 ♅ ☌	♐ 2 16:59	6 13:26 ☽ 13♐51
☿0S 2 22:03	☿ ♎ 2 22:40	5 2:16 ♅ ☌	♐ 5 9:24	4 17:12 ♇ ✶	♑ 5 5:49	14 3:09 ○ 21♓16
♆D 3 11:07	♀ ♏ 12 22:51	7 8:43 ♀ ✶	♑ 7 21:48	7 13:55 ♀ ✶	♒ 7 17:01	20 19:47 ☾ 27♊45
☽0N 15 12:33	☊ ♋R 20 7:19	10 1:36 ♅ ✶	♒ 10 7:59	9 20:42 ♅ □	♓ 10 0:32	28 4:07 ● 4♎57
☉0S 23 3:05	☊ ♌ 21 10:24	12 13:47 ♀ △	♓ 12 14:34	12 0:37 ♅ △	♈ 12 4:01	
☽0S 28 16:01	☉ ♎ 23 3:05	14 12:30 ♅ △	♈ 14 17:55	14 4:33 ♅ ☍	♉ 14 4:43	6 7:45 ☽ 12♑58
	☊ ♋R 24 6:27	16 8:06 ♇ ☍	♉ 16 19:30	16 1:44 ♅ ☍	♊ 16 4:41	13 12:49 ○ 20♈06
♄∠♅ 3 22:29	☿ ♏ 27 11:02	18 15:51 ♅ ☍	♊ 18 20:59	18 2:58 ♂ ✶	♋ 18 5:52	20 3:40 ☾ 26♋40
☿R 6 9:15		20 19:47 ☉ □	♋ 20 23:39	20 6:44 ♅ △	♌ 20 9:34	27 20:13 ● 4♏19
☽0N 12 22:20	⚳ ♎ 1 18:13	22 22:57 ♅ △	♌ 23 4:08	22 14:24 ☉ ✶	♍ 22 16:05	
♃✶♆ 23 9:49	♀ ♐ 9 0:04	25 7:09 ♅ ✶	♍ 25 10:29	24 22:21 ♅ ✶	♎ 25 0:56	
☽0S 25 22:40	☿ ♎R 14 2:09	27 13:29 ♅ ✶	♎ 27 18:40	27 1:02 ♇ ☌	♏ 27 11:38	
☿D 27 9:09	♂ ♍ 21 1:56	29 16:12 ♇ ☌	♏ 30 4:53	29 21:39 ♅ ☌	♐ 29 23:48	
	☉ ♏ 23 12:13					

Astro Data

1 September 1981
Julian Day # 29829
SVP 5♓31'11"
GC 26♐35.0 ⚴ 22♌23.7
Eris 15♈14.2R ⚵ 4♏28.0
⚷ 22♉51.1R ⚶ 13♎36.3
☽ Mean ☊ 29♋37.1

1 October 1981
Julian Day # 29859
SVP 5♓31'09"
GC 26♐35.1 ⚴ 8♍09.6
Eris 14♈57.5R ⚵ 13♏17.0
⚷ 22♉16.6R ⚶ 28♎53.6
☽ Mean ☊ 28♋01.7

November 1981 — LONGITUDE

Day	Sid.Time	☉	0 hr ☽	Noon ☽	True ☊	☿	♀	♂	⚳	♃	♄	♅	♆	♇
1 Su	14 42 45	8♏58 47	23♐43 00	29♐37 22	25♋28.9	20♎29.5	25♐46.9	6♍35.5	13♎55.0	24♎42.5	16♎00.7	29♏05.5	23♐00.0	24♎51.5
2 M	14 46 41	9 58 52	5♑32 38	11♑29 22	25R 26.1	21 22.2	26 50.2	7 09.6	14 21.7	24 55.4	16 07.7	29 09.0	23 01.7	24 53.8
3 Tu	14 50 38	10 58 58	17 28 07	23 29 31	25D 25.3	22 21.5	27 53.2	7 43.6	14 48.4	25 08.2	16 14.6	29 12.6	23 03.5	24 56.2
4 W	14 54 34	11 59 06	29 34 11	5♒42 49	25R 25.5	23 26.7	28 55.9	8 17.5	15 15.0	25 21.0	16 21.5	29 16.2	23 05.3	24 58.5
5 Th	14 58 31	12 59 15	11♒56 04	18 14 35	25 25.4	24 37.0	29 58.3	8 51.3	15 41.6	25 33.7	16 28.4	29 19.8	23 07.1	25 00.8
6 F	15 02 28	13 59 26	24 39 00	1♓09 53	25 24.2	25 51.6	1♑00.4	9 25.0	16 08.1	25 46.4	16 35.2	29 23.4	23 09.0	25 03.1
7 Sa	15 06 24	14 59 39	7♓47 45	14 32 59	25 20.8	27 10.0	2 02.1	9 58.6	16 34.6	25 59.1	16 42.0	29 27.0	23 10.8	25 05.4
8 Su	15 10 21	15 59 52	21 25 49	28 26 20	25 14.9	28 31.5	3 03.6	10 32.1	17 01.1	26 11.8	16 48.8	29 30.6	23 12.7	25 07.7
9 M	15 14 17	17 00 08	5♈34 25	12♈49 43	25 06.6	29 55.6	4 04.6	11 05.5	17 27.5	26 24.4	16 55.5	29 34.3	23 14.6	25 10.0
10 Tu	15 18 14	18 00 24	20 11 40	27 39 27	24 56.8	1♏22.0	5 05.3	11 38.9	17 53.8	26 37.0	17 02.2	29 37.9	23 16.5	25 12.3
11 W	15 22 10	19 00 43	5♉12 02	12♉48 11	24 46.4	2 50.2	6 05.7	12 12.1	18 20.1	26 49.6	17 08.9	29 41.6	23 18.5	25 14.5
12 Th	15 26 07	20 01 03	20 26 34	28 05 45	24 36.9	4 19.9	7 05.6	12 45.2	18 46.4	27 02.1	17 15.5	29 45.2	23 20.4	25 16.8
13 F	15 30 03	21 01 25	5♊44 19	13♊20 51	24 29.3	5 50.9	8 05.1	13 18.2	19 12.6	27 14.6	17 22.1	29 48.9	23 22.4	25 19.0
14 Sa	15 34 00	22 01 49	20 54 08	28 23 04	24 24.1	7 22.9	9 04.2	13 51.1	19 38.7	27 27.1	17 28.6	29 52.6	23 24.4	25 21.2
15 Su	15 37 57	23 02 14	5♋46 47	13♋04 36	24D 21.6	8 55.7	10 02.9	14 23.9	20 04.8	27 39.5	17 35.1	29 56.3	23 26.4	25 23.4
16 M	15 41 53	24 02 42	20 16 04	27 20 57	24 21.1	10 29.1	11 01.1	14 56.6	20 30.9	27 51.8	17 41.5	29 60.0	23 28.4	25 25.6
17 Tu	15 45 50	25 03 11	4♌19 11	11♌10 52	24 21.8	12 03.0	11 58.9	15 29.1	20 56.9	28 04.2	17 47.9	0♐03.7	23 30.4	25 27.8
18 W	15 49 46	26 03 42	17 56 12	24 35 31	24R 22.3	13 37.2	12 56.2	16 01.6	21 22.8	28 16.5	17 54.2	0 07.4	23 32.5	25 29.9
19 Th	15 53 43	27 04 15	1♍09 13	7♍37 42	24 21.8	15 11.7	13 53.0	16 33.9	21 48.7	28 28.7	18 00.5	0 11.1	23 34.6	25 32.1
20 F	15 57 39	28 04 50	14 01 27	20 20 54	24 19.2	16 46.4	14 49.2	17 06.1	22 14.5	28 40.9	18 06.8	0 14.8	23 36.6	25 34.2
21 Sa	16 01 36	29 05 26	26 36 31	2♎48 45	24 14.2	18 21.3	15 45.0	17 38.2	22 40.3	28 53.0	18 13.0	0 18.5	23 38.7	25 36.3
22 Su	16 05 32	0♐06 04	8♎57 58	15 04 35	24 06.8	19 56.2	16 40.2	18 10.2	23 06.0	29 05.1	18 19.1	0 22.3	23 40.8	25 38.4
23 M	16 09 29	1 06 44	21 08 54	27 11 15	23 57.5	21 31.1	17 34.7	18 42.1	23 31.6	29 17.2	18 25.2	0 25.9	23 43.0	25 40.4
24 Tu	16 13 25	2 07 25	3♏11 54	9♏11 06	23 47.1	23 06.0	18 28.7	19 13.8	23 57.2	29 29.1	18 31.2	0 29.7	23 45.1	25 42.5
25 W	16 17 22	3 08 07	15 09 03	21 05 58	23 36.6	24 40.8	19 22.1	19 45.4	24 22.7	29 41.1	18 37.2	0 33.4	23 47.2	25 44.5
26 Th	16 21 19	4 08 52	27 02 02	2♐57 27	23 26.8	26 15.6	20 14.8	20 16.8	24 48.1	29 52.9	18 43.1	0 37.1	23 49.4	25 46.5
27 F	16 25 15	5 09 37	8♐52 23	14 47 04	23 18.7	27 50.4	21 06.8	20 48.2	25 13.5	0♏04.8	18 49.0	0 40.8	23 51.6	25 48.5
28 Sa	16 29 12	6 10 24	20 41 41	26 36 29	23 12.8	29 25.1	21 58.2	21 19.3	25 38.8	0 16.5	18 54.8	0 44.5	23 53.7	25 50.5
29 Su	16 33 08	7 11 12	2♑31 45	8♑27 47	23 09.2	0♐59.7	22 48.7	21 50.4	26 04.0	0 28.2	19 00.5	0 48.2	23 55.9	25 52.4
30 M	16 37 05	8 12 01	14 24 55	20 23 33	23D 07.9	2 34.2	23 38.5	22 21.3	26 29.2	0 39.8	19 06.2	0 51.9	23 58.1	25 54.3

December 1981 — LONGITUDE

Day	Sid.Time	☉	0 hr ☽	Noon ☽	True ☊	☿	♀	♂	⚳	♃	♄	♅	♆	♇
1 Tu	16 41 01	9♐12 51	26♑24 06	2♒27 01	23♋08.3	4♐08.6	24♑27.5	22♍52.0	26♎54.2	0♏51.4	19♎11.8	0♐55.6	24♐00.3	25♎56.2
2 W	16 44 58	10 13 42	8♒32 49	14 42 00	23 09.7	5 43.0	25 15.7	23 22.6	27 19.2	1 02.9	19 17.3	0 59.3	24 02.5	25 58.1
3 Th	16 48 55	11 14 34	20 55 07	27 12 44	23 11.2	7 17.3	26 03.0	23 53.0	27 44.1	1 14.3	19 22.8	1 03.0	24 04.8	26 00.0
4 F	16 52 51	12 15 26	3♓35 24	10♓03 39	23R 12.0	8 51.6	26 49.3	24 23.3	28 09.0	1 25.7	19 28.2	1 06.6	24 07.0	26 01.8
5 Sa	16 56 48	13 16 19	16 37 58	23 18 47	23 11.5	10 25.8	27 34.7	24 53.4	28 33.7	1 37.0	19 33.6	1 10.3	24 09.2	26 03.6
6 Su	17 00 44	14 17 13	0♈06 27	7♈01 10	23 09.3	12 00.0	28 19.1	25 23.4	28 58.4	1 48.2	19 38.8	1 13.9	24 11.4	26 05.4
7 M	17 04 41	15 18 08	14 03 02	21 11 57	23 05.5	13 34.2	29 02.4	25 53.2	29 23.0	1 59.3	19 44.0	1 17.6	24 13.7	26 07.1
8 Tu	17 08 37	16 19 04	28 27 37	5♉49 33	23 00.4	15 08.4	29 44.7	26 22.9	29 47.5	2 10.4	19 49.2	1 21.2	24 15.9	26 08.9
9 W	17 12 34	17 20 00	13♉17 01	20 49 06	22 54.8	16 42.7	0♒25.8	26 52.3	0♏11.9	2 21.3	19 54.2	1 24.8	24 18.2	26 10.6
10 Th	17 16 30	18 20 57	28 24 42	6♊02 36	22 49.6	18 16.9	1 05.7	27 21.7	0 36.2	2 32.3	19 59.2	1 28.4	24 20.4	26 12.3
11 F	17 20 27	19 21 55	13♊41 26	21 19 52	22 45.5	19 51.2	1 44.4	27 50.8	1 00.4	2 43.1	20 04.1	1 32.0	24 22.7	26 13.9
12 Sa	17 24 24	20 22 54	28 56 31	6♋30 09	22 42.9	21 25.6	2 21.8	28 19.8	1 24.6	2 53.8	20 09.0	1 35.6	24 25.0	26 15.5
13 Su	17 28 20	21 23 54	13♋59 39	21 24 01	22D 42.0	23 00.1	2 57.9	28 48.6	1 48.6	3 04.5	20 13.7	1 39.2	24 27.2	26 17.1
14 M	17 32 17	22 24 54	28 42 31	5♌54 35	22 42.5	24 34.6	3 32.6	29 17.2	2 12.6	3 15.1	20 18.4	1 42.7	24 29.5	26 18.7
15 Tu	17 36 13	23 25 56	12♌59 50	19 58 07	22 43.9	26 09.3	4 05.9	29 45.6	2 36.4	3 25.5	20 23.0	1 46.2	24 31.8	26 20.3
16 W	17 40 10	24 26 58	26 49 24	3♍33 50	22 45.5	27 44.1	4 37.7	0♎13.8	3 00.2	3 35.9	20 27.6	1 49.7	24 34.0	26 21.8
17 Th	17 44 06	25 28 01	10♍11 41	16 43 19	22R 46.7	29 19.0	5 07.9	0 41.8	3 23.8	3 46.3	20 32.0	1 53.2	24 36.3	26 23.3
18 F	17 48 03	26 29 06	23 09 08	29 29 38	22 47.0	0♑54.1	5 36.6	1 09.7	3 47.4	3 56.5	20 36.4	1 56.7	24 38.6	26 24.7
19 Sa	17 51 59	27 30 11	5♎45 20	11♎56 45	22 46.1	2 29.4	6 03.5	1 37.3	4 10.8	4 06.6	20 40.7	2 00.2	24 40.8	26 26.1
20 Su	17 55 56	28 31 17	18 04 26	24 08 53	22 44.0	4 04.8	6 28.8	2 04.7	4 34.2	4 16.6	20 44.9	2 03.6	24 43.1	26 27.5
21 M	17 59 53	29 32 23	0♏10 37	6♏10 08	22 40.8	5 40.3	6 52.2	2 31.9	4 57.4	4 26.5	20 49.0	2 07.0	24 45.4	26 28.9
22 Tu	18 03 49	0♑33 31	12 07 52	18 04 16	22 37.1	7 16.1	7 13.8	2 58.9	5 20.5	4 36.4	20 53.0	2 10.4	24 47.6	26 30.2
23 W	18 07 46	1 34 39	23 59 42	29 54 33	22 33.2	8 52.0	7 33.5	3 25.7	5 43.5	4 46.1	20 56.9	2 13.8	24 49.9	26 31.5
24 Th	18 11 42	2 35 47	5♐49 09	11♐43 47	22 29.7	10 28.1	7 51.2	3 52.2	6 06.4	4 55.7	21 00.8	2 17.1	24 52.1	26 32.8
25 F	18 15 39	3 36 56	17 38 45	23 34 18	22 26.9	12 04.3	8 06.8	4 18.5	6 29.2	5 05.2	21 04.6	2 20.5	24 54.4	26 34.1
26 Sa	18 19 35	4 38 06	29 30 41	5♑28 07	22 25.0	13 40.6	8 20.3	4 44.6	6 51.8	5 14.7	21 08.3	2 23.8	24 56.6	26 35.3
27 Su	18 23 32	5 39 16	11♑26 49	17 27 02	22D 24.1	15 17.1	8 31.6	5 10.4	7 14.3	5 24.0	21 11.8	2 27.0	24 58.9	26 36.5
28 M	18 27 28	6 40 26	23 28 58	29 32 53	22 24.2	16 53.6	8 40.7	5 36.0	7 36.7	5 33.1	21 15.3	2 30.3	25 01.1	26 37.6
29 Tu	18 31 25	7 41 36	5♒39 00	11♒47 36	22 25.0	18 30.2	8 47.5	6 01.3	7 59.0	5 42.2	21 18.7	2 33.5	25 03.4	26 38.7
30 W	18 35 22	8 42 46	17 58 58	24 13 23	22 26.2	20 06.8	8 51.9	6 26.4	8 21.1	5 51.2	21 22.0	2 36.7	25 05.6	26 39.8
31 Th	18 39 18	9 43 56	0♓31 11	6♓52 41	22 27.4	21 43.3	8R 54.0	6 51.1	8 43.1	6 00.0	21 25.3	2 39.8	25 07.8	26 40.8

Astro Data	Planet Ingress	Last Aspect	☽ Ingress	Last Aspect	☽ Ingress	☽ Phases & Eclipses
Dy Hr Mn	Dy Hr Mn	Dy Hr Mn	Dy Hr Mn	Dy Hr Mn	Dy Hr Mn	Dy Hr Mn
♃☌♇ 2 8:27	♀ ♑ 5 12:39	1 3:26 ♀ ☌	♑ 1 12:46	30 23:02 ♇ □	♒ 1 7:09	5 1:09 ☽ 12♒32
☽0N 9 9:40	☿ ♏ 9 13:14	3 23:21 ♅ ✶	♒ 4 0:51	3 9:42 ♇ △	♓ 3 17:16	11 22:26 ○ 19♉27
⚳0S 11 12:53	♅ ♐ 16 12:05	6 8:44 ♅ □	♓ 6 9:52	5 20:00 ♀ ✶	♈ 5 23:49	18 14:54 ☾ 26♌11
☽0S 22 5:07	☉ ♐ 22 9:36	8 13:49 ♅ △	♈ 8 14:39	8 1:36 ♀ □	♉ 8 2:31	26 14:38 ● 4♐16
	♃ ♏ 27 2:19	10 10:19 ♃ ☍	♉ 10 15:44	9 21:53 ♂ △	♊ 10 2:30	
♃✶♅ 2 0:55	☿ ♐ 28 20:52	12 14:37 ♅ ☍	♊ 12 14:59	11 22:36 ♂ □	♋ 12 1:40	4 16:22 ☽ 12♓27
☽0N 6 20:15		14 10:29 ♃ △	♋ 14 14:37	14 0:35 ♂ ✶	♌ 14 2:08	11 8:41 ○ 19♊14
☽0S 19 12:06	♀ ♒ 8 20:52	16 12:54 ♃ □	♌ 16 16:32	16 0:15 ☿ △	♍ 16 5:38	18 5:47 ☾ 26♍13
♂0S 27 17:06	⚳ ♏ 9 0:19	18 18:49 ♃ ✶	♍ 18 21:53	18 5:47 ☉ □	♎ 18 12:58	26 10:10 ● 4♑33
♀R 31 19:45	♂ ♎ 16 0:14	21 4:09 ☉ ✶	♎ 21 6:33	20 21:30 ☉ ✶	♏ 20 23:39	
	☿ ♑ 17 22:21	23 16:15 ♃ ☌	♏ 23 17:36	21 13:27 ♀ □	♐ 23 12:11	
	☉ ♑ 21 22:51	25 20:21 ♅ ☌	♐ 26 6:00	25 18:04 ♇ ✶	♑ 26 0:59	
		28 10:26 ♇ ✶	♑ 28 18:53	28 6:13 ♇ □	♒ 28 12:53	
				30 16:40 ♇ △	♓ 30 23:01	

Astro Data

1 November 1981
Julian Day # 29890
SVP 5♓31'05"
GC 26♐35.1 ⚴ 23♍03.2
Eris 14♈39.1R ⚵ 23♏24.5
⚷ 20♉56.9R ⚶ 15♏17.1
☽ Mean ☊ 26♋23.2

1 December 1981
Julian Day # 29920
SVP 5♓31'01"
GC 26♐35.2 ⚴ 5♎37.5
Eris 14♈25.4R ⚵ 3♐38.5
⚷ 19♉25.7R ⚶ 1♐26.1
☽ Mean ☊ 24♋47.9

LONGITUDE — January 1982

Day	Sid.Time	☉	0 hr ☽	Noon ☽	True ☊	☿	♀	♂	⚳	♃	♄	♅	♆	♇
1 F	18 43 15	10♑45 06	13♓18 13	19♓48 06	22♋28.5	23♑19.6	8♒53.5	7♎15.7	9♏05.0	6♏08.8	21♎28.4	2♐43.0	25♐10.0	26♎41.8
2 Sa	18 47 11	11 46 15	26 22 41	3♈02 13	22R 29.1	24 55.7	8R 50.6	7 39.9	9 26.7	6 17.4	21 31.4	2 46.1	25 12.2	26 42.8
3 Su	18 51 08	12 47 24	9♈46 58	16 37 08	22 29.2	26 31.4	8 45.1	8 03.9	9 48.3	6 25.9	21 34.3	2 49.2	25 14.4	26 43.8
4 M	18 55 04	13 48 33	23 32 48	0♉34 01	22 28.8	28 06.6	8 37.2	8 27.5	10 09.8	6 34.2	21 37.1	2 52.2	25 16.6	26 44.7
5 Tu	18 59 01	14 49 42	7♉40 39	14 52 30	22 28.2	29 41.1	8 26.6	8 50.9	10 31.1	6 42.5	21 39.9	2 55.2	25 18.7	26 45.5
6 W	19 02 57	15 50 50	22 09 10	29 30 08	22 27.4	1♒14.8	8 13.6	9 14.0	10 52.2	6 50.6	21 42.5	2 58.2	25 20.9	26 46.4
7 Th	19 06 54	16 51 58	6♊54 45	14♊22 12	22 26.7	2 47.4	7 58.1	9 36.8	11 13.2	6 58.6	21 45.0	3 01.1	25 23.1	26 47.2
8 F	19 10 51	17 53 06	21 51 33	29 21 49	22 26.2	4 18.7	7 40.1	9 59.3	11 34.1	7 06.4	21 47.5	3 04.0	25 25.2	26 48.0
9 Sa	19 14 47	18 54 14	6♋51 54	14♋20 44	22D 26.0	5 48.3	7 19.7	10 21.5	11 54.8	7 14.2	21 49.8	3 06.9	25 27.3	26 48.7
10 Su	19 18 44	19 55 21	21 47 16	29 10 28	22 25.9	7 15.9	6 57.0	10 43.3	12 15.4	7 21.8	21 52.1	3 09.8	25 29.4	26 49.4
11 M	19 22 40	20 56 28	6♌29 27	13♌43 25	22 26.0	8 41.0	6 32.2	11 04.8	12 35.7	7 29.2	21 54.2	3 12.6	25 31.5	26 50.1
12 Tu	19 26 37	21 57 34	20 51 47	27 54 01	22R 26.1	10 03.2	6 05.2	11 26.0	12 56.0	7 36.6	21 56.2	3 15.3	25 33.6	26 50.7
13 W	19 30 33	22 58 41	4♍49 51	11♍39 05	22 26.1	11 22.0	5 36.4	11 46.9	13 16.0	7 43.7	21 58.2	3 18.1	25 35.7	26 51.3
14 Th	19 34 30	23 59 47	18 21 45	24 57 56	22 26.0	12 36.7	5 05.7	12 07.3	13 35.9	7 50.8	22 00.0	3 20.8	25 37.8	26 51.9
15 F	19 38 27	25 00 53	1♎27 54	7♎51 59	22 25.8	13 46.6	4 33.6	12 27.5	13 55.7	7 57.7	22 01.7	3 23.4	25 39.8	26 52.4
16 Sa	19 42 23	26 01 59	14 10 37	20 24 16	22D 25.7	14 51.1	4 00.0	12 47.2	14 15.2	8 04.5	22 03.3	3 26.1	25 41.8	26 52.9
17 Su	19 46 20	27 03 04	26 33 28	2♏38 47	22 25.7	15 49.2	3 25.3	13 06.6	14 34.6	8 11.1	22 04.8	3 28.6	25 43.8	26 53.3
18 M	19 50 16	28 04 10	8♏40 49	14 40 08	22 25.9	16 40.2	2 49.6	13 25.6	14 53.8	8 17.5	22 06.2	3 31.2	25 45.8	26 53.7
19 Tu	19 54 13	29 05 15	20 37 19	26 32 59	22 26.5	17 23.1	2 13.3	13 44.2	15 12.8	8 23.9	22 07.5	3 33.7	25 47.8	26 54.1
20 W	19 58 09	0♒06 19	2♐27 39	8♐21 52	22 27.3	17 57.2	1 36.6	14 02.4	15 31.7	8 30.0	22 08.7	3 36.1	25 49.8	26 54.4
21 Th	20 02 06	1 07 24	14 16 08	20 10 57	22 28.2	18 21.5	0 59.6	14 20.1	15 50.3	8 36.1	22 09.8	3 38.6	25 51.7	26 54.8
22 F	20 06 02	2 08 28	26 06 43	2♑03 52	22 29.1	18R 35.4	0 22.8	14 37.5	16 08.8	8 41.9	22 10.8	3 40.9	25 53.7	26 55.0
23 Sa	20 09 59	3 09 31	8♑02 44	14 03 39	22R 29.7	18 38.3	29♑46.3	14 54.4	16 27.0	8 47.6	22 11.7	3 43.3	25 55.6	26 55.3
24 Su	20 13 56	4 10 34	20 06 54	26 12 43	22 29.8	18 29.7	29 10.3	15 10.9	16 45.1	8 53.2	22 12.5	3 45.6	25 57.5	26 55.5
25 M	20 17 52	5 11 35	2♒21 17	8♒32 47	22 29.3	18 09.6	28 35.2	15 26.9	17 02.9	8 58.6	22 13.1	3 47.8	25 59.3	26 55.6
26 Tu	20 21 49	6 12 36	14 47 21	21 05 04	22 28.0	17 38.1	28 01.1	15 42.4	17 20.6	9 03.8	22 13.7	3 50.0	26 01.2	26 55.7
27 W	20 25 45	7 13 36	27 26 01	3♓50 17	22 26.2	16 56.0	27 28.3	15 57.5	17 38.0	9 08.9	22 14.1	3 52.2	26 03.0	26 55.8
28 Th	20 29 42	8 14 35	10♓17 52	16 48 49	22 23.8	16 04.2	26 57.0	16 12.1	17 55.2	9 13.8	22 14.5	3 54.3	26 04.8	26R 55.9
29 F	20 33 38	9 15 33	23 23 09	0♈00 52	22 21.4	15 04.1	26 27.3	16 26.1	18 12.2	9 18.5	22 14.7	3 56.3	26 06.6	26 55.9
30 Sa	20 37 35	10 16 30	6♈42 00	13 26 32	22 19.3	13 57.3	25 59.4	16 39.7	18 29.0	9 23.1	22R 14.8	3 58.4	26 08.4	26 55.9
31 Su	20 41 31	11 17 25	20 14 27	27 05 46	22 17.8	12 46.0	25 33.5	16 52.8	18 45.6	9 27.5	22 14.8	4 00.3	26 10.1	26 55.8

LONGITUDE — February 1982

Day	Sid.Time	☉	0 hr ☽	Noon ☽	True ☊	☿	♀	♂	⚳	♃	♄	♅	♆	♇
1 M	20 45 28	12♒18 19	4♉00 25	10♉58 22	22♋17.2	11♒32.3	25♑09.7	17♎05.4	19♏01.9	9♏31.7	22♎14.8	4♐02.3	26♐11.8	26♎55.7
2 Tu	20 49 24	13 19 12	17 59 31	25 03 43	22D 17.6	10R 18.2	24R 48.0	17 17.4	19 18.0	9 35.8	22R 14.6	4 04.1	26 13.5	26R 55.6
3 W	20 53 21	14 20 03	2♊10 48	9♊20 31	22 18.7	9 05.8	24 28.7	17 28.9	19 33.9	9 39.7	22 14.3	4 06.0	26 15.2	26 55.4
4 Th	20 57 18	15 20 53	16 32 32	23 46 29	22 20.2	7 57.1	24 11.8	17 39.8	19 49.5	9 43.4	22 13.9	4 07.8	26 16.9	26 55.2
5 F	21 01 14	16 21 42	1♋01 52	8♋18 10	22R 21.5	6 53.5	23 57.2	17 50.2	20 04.9	9 46.9	22 13.3	4 09.5	26 18.5	26 55.0
6 Sa	21 05 11	17 22 29	15 34 45	22 50 57	22 22.0	5 56.3	23 45.2	18 00.0	20 20.0	9 50.3	22 12.7	4 11.2	26 20.1	26 54.7
7 Su	21 09 07	18 23 15	0♌06 04	7♌19 21	22 21.3	5 06.4	23 35.6	18 09.2	20 34.9	9 53.5	22 12.0	4 12.8	26 21.7	26 54.4
8 M	21 13 04	19 24 00	14 30 05	21 37 33	22 19.1	4 24.4	23 28.5	18 17.8	20 49.6	9 56.5	22 11.2	4 14.4	26 23.2	26 54.1
9 Tu	21 17 00	20 24 43	28 41 07	5♍40 12	22 15.7	3 50.5	23 23.9	18 25.8	21 04.0	9 59.3	22 10.3	4 15.9	26 24.7	26 53.7
10 W	21 20 57	21 25 25	12♍34 20	19 23 09	22 11.1	3 24.8	23D 21.8	18 33.3	21 18.1	10 02.0	22 09.2	4 17.4	26 26.2	26 53.3
11 Th	21 24 54	22 26 05	26 06 23	2♎43 55	22 06.1	3 07.3	23 22.1	18 40.0	21 32.0	10 04.5	22 08.1	4 18.8	26 27.7	26 52.8
12 F	21 28 50	23 26 45	9♎15 44	15 41 59	22 01.3	2D 57.5	23 24.9	18 46.2	21 45.6	10 06.8	22 06.8	4 20.2	26 29.2	26 52.4
13 Sa	21 32 47	24 27 23	22 02 51	28 18 40	21 57.3	2 55.3	23 30.0	18 51.6	21 58.9	10 08.9	22 05.5	4 21.6	26 30.6	26 51.9
14 Su	21 36 43	25 28 01	4♏29 51	10♏36 51	21 54.6	3 00.2	23 37.5	18 56.5	22 11.9	10 10.8	22 04.1	4 22.8	26 32.0	26 51.3
15 M	21 40 40	26 28 37	16 40 13	22 40 31	21D 53.3	3 11.7	23 47.2	19 00.6	22 24.7	10 12.5	22 02.5	4 24.1	26 33.3	26 50.7
16 Tu	21 44 36	27 29 12	28 38 22	4♐34 24	21 53.5	3 29.5	23 59.1	19 04.1	22 37.2	10 14.1	22 00.9	4 25.2	26 34.7	26 50.1
17 W	21 48 33	28 29 46	10♐29 17	16 23 37	21 54.8	3 53.0	24 13.2	19 06.8	22 49.4	10 15.5	21 59.1	4 26.4	26 36.0	26 49.5
18 Th	21 52 29	29 30 18	22 18 05	28 13 17	21 56.6	4 21.8	24 29.3	19 08.9	23 01.3	10 16.6	21 57.3	4 27.4	26 37.3	26 48.8
19 F	21 56 26	0♓30 49	4♑09 49	10♑08 16	21R 58.2	4 55.6	24 47.5	19 10.2	23 12.9	10 17.6	21 55.3	4 28.4	26 38.5	26 48.1
20 Sa	22 00 22	1 31 19	16 09 08	22 12 54	21 58.8	5 33.9	25 07.6	19R 10.8	23 24.2	10 18.4	21 53.3	4 29.4	26 39.7	26 47.4
21 Su	22 04 19	2 31 48	28 20 00	4♒30 46	21 57.9	6 16.4	25 29.6	19 10.6	23 35.2	10 19.1	21 51.2	4 30.3	26 40.9	26 46.6
22 M	22 08 16	3 32 15	10♒45 30	17 04 25	21 55.1	7 02.8	25 53.3	19 09.7	23 45.9	10 19.5	21 49.0	4 31.2	26 42.1	26 45.8
23 Tu	22 12 12	4 32 40	23 27 38	29 55 12	21 50.2	7 52.7	26 18.8	19 08.1	23 56.3	10R 19.7	21 46.6	4 32.0	26 43.2	26 45.0
24 W	22 16 09	5 33 04	6♓27 05	13♓03 11	21 43.6	8 46.0	26 46.0	19 05.7	24 06.3	10 19.8	21 44.2	4 32.7	26 44.3	26 44.1
25 Th	22 20 05	6 33 26	19 43 17	26 27 09	21 35.8	9 42.2	27 14.8	19 02.5	24 16.0	10 19.6	21 41.7	4 33.4	26 45.4	26 43.2
26 F	22 24 02	7 33 46	3♈14 29	10♈04 56	21 27.8	10 41.4	27 45.0	18 58.5	24 25.4	10 19.3	21 39.1	4 34.1	26 46.4	26 42.3
27 Sa	22 27 58	8 34 04	16 58 08	23 53 44	21 20.5	11 43.2	28 17.0	18 53.8	24 34.5	10 18.8	21 36.4	4 34.6	26 47.4	26 41.3
28 Su	22 31 55	9 34 20	0♉51 21	7♉50 38	21 14.6	12 47.4	28 50.3	18 48.3	24 43.2	10 18.1	21 33.7	4 35.2	26 48.4	26 40.3

Astro Data

	Dy Hr Mn
☽ 0N	3 4:08
☽ 0S	15 20:07
☿ R	23 6:01
♇ R	29 8:18
☽ 0N	30 9:33
♄ R	31 3:46
♀ D	10 20:38
☽ 0S	12 5:00
☿ D	13 7:17
♂ R	20 19:13
♃ R	24 5:41
♆ ✶ ♇	24 9:04
☽ 0N	26 14:58

Planet Ingress

	Dy Hr Mn
☿ ♒	5 16:49
☉ ♒	20 9:31
♀ ♑R	23 2:56
☉ ♓	18 23:47

Last Aspect / ☽ Ingress

Last Aspect Dy Hr Mn		☽ Ingress Dy Hr Mn
1 21:50	♆ □	♈ 2 6:33
4 7:17	♆ □	♉ 4 11:02
5 11:55	☉ △	♊ 6 12:49
8 7:54	♇ △	♋ 8 13:01
10 8:10	♇ □	♌ 10 13:21
12 10:11	♇ ✶	♍ 12 15:37
14 13:13	♆ □	♎ 14 21:17
17 0:39	♇ ☌	♏ 17 6:46
19 17:38	☉ ✶	♐ 19 19:00
22 1:37	♇ ✶	♑ 22 7:51
24 17:32	♀ ☌	♒ 24 19:25
26 23:03	♇ △	♓ 27 4:49
29 5:48	♀ ✶	♈ 29 11:58
31 11:43	♇ ☍	♉ 31 17:03

Last Aspect / ☽ Ingress

Last Aspect Dy Hr Mn		☽ Ingress Dy Hr Mn
2 11:34	♀ △	♊ 2 20:20
4 17:12	♇ △	♋ 4 22:18
6 18:43	♇ □	♌ 6 23:50
8 20:57	♇ ✶	♍ 9 2:15
11 0:37	♆ □	♎ 11 7:02
13 9:13	♇ ☌	♏ 13 15:16
15 20:21	☉ □	♐ 16 2:45
18 14:50	☉ ✶	♑ 18 15:36
20 20:58	♇ □	♒ 21 3:15
23 6:08	♇ △	♓ 23 12:09
25 13:28	♀ ✶	♈ 25 18:17
27 19:53	♀ □	♉ 27 22:32

☽ Phases & Eclipses

Dy Hr Mn		
3 4:45	☽	12♈29
9 19:53	○	19♋14
9 19:56	☍	T 1.331
16 23:58	☾	26♎32
25 4:56	●	4♒54
25 4:41:59	☌	P 0.566
1 14:28	☽	12♉25
8 7:57	○	19♌14
15 20:21	☾	26♏50
23 21:13	●	4♓56

Astro Data

1 January 1982
Julian Day # 29951
SVP 5♓30'55"
GC 26♐35.3 ⚴ 15♎45.5
Eris 14♈19.9R ⚵ 14♐08.5
⚷ 18♉14.3R ⚶ 18♐06.3
☽ Mean ☊ 23♋09.4

1 February 1982
Julian Day # 29982
SVP 5♓30'51"
GC 26♐35.3 ⚴ 21♎12.8
Eris 14♈25.0 ⚵ 23♐58.0
⚷ 17♉54.8 ⚶ 4♑23.5
☽ Mean ☊ 21♋31.0

March 1982

LONGITUDE

Day	Sid.Time	☉	0 hr ☽	Noon ☽	True ☊	☿	♀	♂	⚳	♃	♄	♅	♆	♇
1 M	22 35 51	10♓34 35	14♉51 16	21♉52 58	21♋10.9	13♒53.9	29♑24.9	18♎42.0	24♏51.6	10♏17.2	21♎30.8	4♐35.7	26♐49.4	26♎39.3
2 Tu	22 39 48	11 34 47	28 55 30	5♊58 40	21D 09.3	15 02.6	0♒00.9	18R 35.0	24 59.6	10R 16.1	21R 27.9	4 36.1	26 50.3	26R 38.3
3 W	22 43 45	12 34 57	13♊02 16	20 06 08	21 09.3	16 13.4	0 38.1	18 27.2	25 07.3	10 14.8	21 24.9	4 36.4	26 51.2	26 37.2
4 Th	22 47 41	13 35 06	27 10 09	4♋14 09	21 10.3	17 26.0	1 16.6	18 18.6	25 14.6	10 13.3	21 21.8	4 36.8	26 52.0	26 36.1
5 F	22 51 38	14 35 12	11♋17 59	18 21 27	21R 11.0	18 40.5	1 56.2	18 09.2	25 21.6	10 11.7	21 18.6	4 37.0	26 52.8	26 35.0
6 Sa	22 55 34	15 35 16	25 24 19	2♌26 21	21 10.5	19 56.8	2 37.0	17 59.1	25 28.2	10 09.8	21 15.4	4 37.2	26 53.6	26 33.9
7 Su	22 59 31	16 35 17	9♌27 13	16 26 34	21 07.9	21 14.7	3 18.8	17 48.2	25 34.5	10 07.8	21 12.0	4 37.4	26 54.4	26 32.7
8 M	23 03 27	17 35 17	23 24 01	0♍19 10	21 02.7	22 34.2	4 01.7	17 36.6	25 40.4	10 05.6	21 08.6	4 37.5	26 55.1	26 31.5
9 Tu	23 07 24	18 35 15	7♍11 35	14 00 50	20 55.0	23 55.2	4 45.6	17 24.2	25 45.9	10 03.2	21 05.2	4R 37.5	26 55.8	26 30.3
10 W	23 11 20	19 35 10	20 46 33	27 28 21	20 45.3	25 17.7	5 30.5	17 11.0	25 51.1	10 00.7	21 01.6	4 37.5	26 56.5	26 29.1
11 Th	23 15 17	20 35 04	4♎05 58	10♎39 09	20 34.6	26 41.7	6 16.3	16 57.2	25 55.9	9 57.9	20 58.0	4 37.5	26 57.1	26 27.8
12 F	23 19 14	21 34 56	17 07 47	23 31 49	20 23.8	28 07.0	7 03.0	16 42.6	26 00.3	9 55.0	20 54.3	4 37.3	26 57.7	26 26.5
13 Sa	23 23 10	22 34 47	29 51 17	6♏06 21	20 14.2	29 33.8	7 50.6	16 27.4	26 04.3	9 51.9	20 50.6	4 37.2	26 58.2	26 25.2
14 Su	23 27 07	23 34 35	12♏17 14	18 24 15	20 06.4	1♓01.9	8 39.0	16 11.4	26 07.9	9 48.6	20 46.8	4 37.0	26 58.8	26 23.9
15 M	23 31 03	24 34 22	24 27 48	0♐28 23	20 01.0	2 31.3	9 28.2	15 54.8	26 11.2	9 45.2	20 42.9	4 36.7	26 59.2	26 22.5
16 Tu	23 35 00	25 34 07	6♐26 29	12 22 43	19 58.0	4 02.0	10 18.1	15 37.5	26 14.0	9 41.6	20 39.0	4 36.4	26 59.7	26 21.2
17 W	23 38 56	26 33 51	18 17 41	24 12 03	19D 57.0	5 34.1	11 08.8	15 19.6	26 16.5	9 37.8	20 35.0	4 36.0	27 00.1	26 19.8
18 Th	23 42 53	27 33 33	0♑06 30	6♑01 41	19 57.2	7 07.4	12 00.2	15 01.1	26 18.5	9 33.8	20 31.0	4 35.5	27 00.5	26 18.4
19 F	23 46 49	28 33 13	11 58 20	17 57 06	19R 57.6	8 42.0	12 52.3	14 42.0	26 20.2	9 29.7	20 26.9	4 35.1	27 00.9	26 16.9
20 Sa	23 50 46	29 32 51	23 58 38	0♒03 35	19 57.2	10 17.9	13 45.0	14 22.4	26 21.4	9 25.4	20 22.8	4 34.5	27 01.2	26 15.5
21 Su	23 54 43	0♈32 27	6♒12 31	12 25 56	19 54.9	11 55.0	14 38.4	14 02.2	26 22.3	9 21.0	20 18.6	4 33.9	27 01.5	26 14.0
22 M	23 58 39	1 32 02	18 44 17	25 07 56	19 50.2	13 33.4	15 32.3	13 41.6	26R 22.7	9 16.4	20 14.4	4 33.3	27 01.8	26 12.6
23 Tu	0 02 36	2 31 35	1♓37 06	8♓11 56	19 42.8	15 13.2	16 26.8	13 20.5	26 22.7	9 11.6	20 10.1	4 32.6	27 02.0	26 11.1
24 W	0 06 32	3 31 06	14 52 26	21 38 28	19 32.9	16 54.2	17 21.9	12 59.0	26 22.3	9 06.7	20 05.8	4 31.9	27 02.2	26 09.5
25 Th	0 10 29	4 30 34	28 29 44	5♈25 52	19 21.5	18 36.5	18 17.5	12 37.2	26 21.5	9 01.6	20 01.4	4 31.1	27 02.3	26 08.0
26 F	0 14 25	5 30 01	12♈26 21	19 30 32	19 09.5	20 20.1	19 13.5	12 15.0	26 20.3	8 56.4	19 57.0	4 30.2	27 02.5	26 06.5
27 Sa	0 18 22	6 29 26	26 37 44	3♉47 13	18 58.4	22 05.1	20 10.1	11 52.5	26 18.7	8 51.0	19 52.6	4 29.3	27 02.5	26 04.9
28 Su	0 22 18	7 28 49	10♉58 15	18 10 04	18 49.2	23 51.4	21 07.2	11 29.8	26 16.6	8 45.5	19 48.2	4 28.4	27 02.6	26 03.3
29 M	0 26 15	8 28 09	25 22 01	2♊33 29	18 42.7	25 39.0	22 04.7	11 06.8	26 14.2	8 39.9	19 43.7	4 27.4	27R 02.6	26 01.7
30 Tu	0 30 11	9 27 27	9♊43 56	16 52 57	18 39.0	27 28.0	23 02.6	10 43.8	26 11.3	8 34.1	19 39.2	4 26.4	27 02.6	26 00.2
31 W	0 34 08	10 26 43	24 00 12	1♋05 28	18D 37.5	29 18.3	24 01.0	10 20.6	26 08.0	8 28.2	19 34.6	4 25.3	27 02.6	25 58.5

April 1982

LONGITUDE

Day	Sid.Time	☉	0 hr ☽	Noon ☽	True ☊	☿	♀	♂	⚳	♃	♄	♅	♆	♇
1 Th	0 38 05	11♈25 56	8♋08 35	15♋09 27	18♋37.4	1♈10.0	24♒59.7	9♎57.4	26♏04.4	8♏22.2	19♎30.1	4♐24.2	27♐02.5	25♎56.9
2 F	0 42 01	12 25 08	22 08 03	29 04 23	18R 37.2	3 03.1	25 58.9	9R 34.1	26R 00.3	8R 16.0	19R 25.5	4R 23.0	27R 02.4	25R 55.3
3 Sa	0 45 58	13 24 16	5♌58 27	12♌50 16	18 35.6	4 57.6	26 58.4	9 10.9	25 55.8	8 09.8	19 20.9	4 21.8	27 02.2	25 53.7
4 Su	0 49 54	14 23 23	19 39 48	26 27 02	18 31.8	6 53.4	27 58.3	8 47.7	25 51.0	8 03.4	19 16.3	4 20.5	27 02.1	25 52.0
5 M	0 53 51	15 22 27	3♍11 55	9♍54 21	18 25.0	8 50.6	28 58.5	8 24.7	25 45.7	7 56.9	19 11.7	4 19.2	27 01.9	25 50.4
6 Tu	0 57 47	16 21 29	16 34 12	23 11 19	18 15.3	10 49.1	29 59.1	8 01.8	25 40.0	7 50.3	19 07.1	4 17.8	27 01.6	25 48.7
7 W	1 01 44	17 20 28	29 45 33	6♎16 45	18 03.3	12 48.9	1♓00.1	7 39.1	25 34.0	7 43.6	19 02.5	4 16.4	27 01.3	25 47.1
8 Th	1 05 40	18 19 26	12♎44 44	19 09 23	17 50.0	14 49.9	2 01.3	7 16.7	25 27.6	7 36.8	18 57.8	4 15.0	27 01.0	25 45.4
9 F	1 09 37	19 18 21	25 30 36	1♏48 20	17 36.6	16 52.2	3 02.9	6 54.5	25 20.8	7 30.0	18 53.2	4 13.5	27 00.7	25 43.7
10 Sa	1 13 34	20 17 15	8♏02 35	14 13 24	17 24.3	18 55.5	4 04.8	6 32.7	25 13.6	7 23.0	18 48.6	4 12.0	27 00.3	25 42.0
11 Su	1 17 30	21 16 07	20 20 56	26 25 24	17 14.0	20 59.7	5 06.9	6 11.2	25 06.1	7 16.0	18 44.0	4 10.4	26 59.9	25 40.3
12 M	1 21 27	22 14 57	2♐27 02	8♐26 13	17 06.3	23 04.9	6 09.4	5 50.1	24 58.2	7 08.9	18 39.3	4 08.8	26 59.5	25 38.6
13 Tu	1 25 23	23 13 45	14 23 19	20 18 50	17 01.4	25 10.7	7 12.1	5 29.4	24 49.9	7 01.7	18 34.7	4 07.2	26 59.0	25 37.0
14 W	1 29 20	24 12 32	26 13 16	2♑07 12	16 59.0	27 17.0	8 15.1	5 09.3	24 41.3	6 54.4	18 30.1	4 05.5	26 58.5	25 35.3
15 Th	1 33 16	25 11 17	8♑01 15	13 56 03	16D 58.3	29 23.6	9 18.4	4 49.6	24 32.4	6 47.1	18 25.5	4 03.8	26 58.0	25 33.6
16 F	1 37 13	26 10 00	19 52 17	25 50 37	16R 58.4	1♉30.3	10 21.9	4 30.4	24 23.1	6 39.7	18 20.9	4 02.0	26 57.5	25 31.9
17 Sa	1 41 09	27 08 41	1♒51 47	7♒56 26	16 58.0	3 36.7	11 25.6	4 11.8	24 13.5	6 32.3	18 16.4	4 00.2	26 56.9	25 30.2
18 Su	1 45 06	28 07 21	14 05 16	20 18 53	16 56.2	5 42.6	12 29.6	3 53.8	24 03.6	6 24.8	18 11.9	3 58.4	26 56.3	25 28.5
19 M	1 49 03	29 05 59	26 37 51	3♓02 42	16 52.2	7 47.7	13 33.8	3 36.5	23 53.4	6 17.3	18 07.3	3 56.5	26 55.6	25 26.8
20 Tu	1 52 59	0♉04 35	9♓33 48	16 11 28	16 45.6	9 51.7	14 38.2	3 19.7	23 42.9	6 09.7	18 02.8	3 54.6	26 54.9	25 25.1
21 W	1 56 56	1 03 09	22 55 49	29 46 52	16 36.7	11 54.2	15 42.8	3 03.7	23 32.1	6 02.1	17 58.4	3 52.7	26 54.2	25 23.4
22 Th	2 00 52	2 01 42	6♈44 25	13♈48 06	16 26.1	13 54.9	16 47.6	2 48.3	23 21.0	5 54.5	17 53.9	3 50.7	26 53.5	25 21.7
23 F	2 04 49	3 00 13	20 57 24	28 11 37	16 14.9	15 53.4	17 52.6	2 33.6	23 09.7	5 46.8	17 49.5	3 48.7	26 52.7	25 20.1
24 Sa	2 08 45	3 58 42	5♉29 53	12♉51 15	16 04.4	17 49.6	18 57.8	2 19.7	22 58.1	5 39.2	17 45.2	3 46.7	26 51.9	25 18.4
25 Su	2 12 42	4 57 09	20 14 42	27 39 12	15 55.6	19 43.1	20 03.2	2 06.5	22 46.3	5 31.5	17 40.8	3 44.7	26 51.1	25 16.7
26 M	2 16 38	5 55 35	5♊03 41	12♊27 13	15 49.4	21 33.6	21 08.8	1 54.1	22 34.3	5 23.8	17 36.6	3 42.6	26 50.3	25 15.1
27 Tu	2 20 35	6 53 58	19 48 55	27 08 03	15 45.9	23 20.9	22 14.5	1 42.5	22 22.1	5 16.2	17 32.3	3 40.5	26 49.4	25 13.4
28 W	2 24 32	7 52 19	4♋24 02	11♋36 23	15D 44.7	25 04.8	23 20.4	1 31.6	22 09.7	5 08.5	17 28.1	3 38.3	26 48.5	25 11.8
29 Th	2 28 28	8 50 38	18 44 48	25 49 05	15 44.8	26 45.1	24 26.4	1 21.6	21 57.1	5 00.8	17 23.9	3 36.1	26 47.6	25 10.1
30 F	2 32 25	9 48 55	2♌49 10	9♌45 02	15R 45.1	28 21.7	25 32.6	1 12.3	21 44.3	4 53.2	17 19.8	3 34.0	26 46.6	25 08.5

Astro Data

	Dy Hr Mn
♅ R	9 19:41
☽ 0S	11 13:52
☉ 0N	20 22:56
⚳ R	23 1:04
☽ 0N	25 22:32
♆ R	29 16:38
☿ 0N	3 3:12
♄ ∠ ♅	3 5:59
☽ 0S	7 21:48
♂ 0N	11 20:12
☽ 0N	22 8:23

Planet Ingress

	Dy Hr Mn
♀ ♒	2 11:25
☿ ♓	13 19:11
☉ ♈	20 22:56
☿ ♈	31 20:59
♀ ♓	6 12:20
☿ ♉	15 18:54
☉ ♉	20 10:07

Last Aspect / ☽ Ingress

Last Aspect Dy Hr Mn		☽ Ingress Dy Hr Mn
2 1:24	♀ △	♊ 2 1:50
3 23:28	♆ ☍	♋ 4 4:48
6 1:59	♇ □	♌ 6 7:50
8 6:05	♆ △	♍ 8 11:27
10 11:03	♆ □	♎ 10 16:34
12 21:49	☿ △	♏ 13 0:17
14 23:09	☉ △	♐ 15 11:03
17 17:42	♆ ☌	♑ 17 23:47
20 10:54	☉ ⚹	♒ 20 11:53
22 15:32	♆ ⚹	♓ 22 21:01
24 21:28	♆ □	♈ 25 2:37
27 0:42	♆ △	♉ 27 5:39
28 22:50	☿ ⚹	♊ 29 7:44
31 8:31	☿ □	♋ 31 10:09

Last Aspect / ☽ Ingress

Last Aspect Dy Hr Mn		☽ Ingress Dy Hr Mn
2 6:33	♇ □	♌ 2 13:36
4 14:55	♀ ☍	♍ 4 18:18
6 19:00	♆ □	♎ 7 0:26
9 2:51	♆ ⚹	♏ 9 8:33
9 22:51	♃ ☌	♐ 11 19:07
14 1:33	♆ ☌	♑ 14 7:41
16 12:42	☉ □	♒ 16 20:18
19 4:02	☉ ⚹	♓ 19 6:20
21 6:59	♆ □	♈ 21 12:23
23 9:50	♆ △	♉ 23 14:59
24 22:43	♀ ⚹	♊ 25 15:48
27 11:29	♆ ☍	♋ 27 16:43
29 13:48	☿ ⚹	♌ 29 19:09

☽ Phases & Eclipses

Dy Hr Mn	
2 22:15	☽ 12♊00
9 20:45	○ 18♍57
17 17:15	☾ 26♐47
25 10:17	● 4♈26
1 5:08	☽ 11♋09
8 10:18	○ 18♎15
16 12:42	☾ 26♑12
23 20:29	● 3♉21
30 12:07	☽ 9♌49

Astro Data

1 March 1982
Julian Day # 30010
SVP 5♓30'47"
GC 26♐35.4 ⚵ 20♎02.5R
Eris 14♈37.7 ⚶ 1♑36.8
⚷ 18♉29.0 ⚴ 18♑23.8
☽ Mean ☊ 20♋02.0

1 April 1982
Julian Day # 30041
SVP 5♓30'44"
GC 26♐35.5 ⚵ 11♎58.3R
Eris 14♈57.2 ⚶ 7♑43.4
⚷ 19♉55.7 ⚴ 2♒33.3
☽ Mean ☊ 18♋23.5

LONGITUDE — May 1982

Day	Sid.Time	☉	0 hr ☽	Noon ☽	True ☊	☿	♀	♂	⚳	♃	♄	♅	♆	♇
1 Sa	2 36 21	10♉47 10	16♌36 47	23♌24 31	15♋44.4	29♉54.4	26♓38.9	1♎03.8	21♏31.4	4♏45.6	17♎15.8	3♐31.7	26♐45.7	25♎06.9
2 Su	2 40 18	11 45 23	0♍08 25	6♍48 37	15R41.8	1♊23.1	27 45.4	0R56.2	21R18.4	4R38.0	17R11.8	3R29.5	26R44.7	25R05.3
3 M	2 44 14	12 43 34	13 25 18	19 58 36	15 36.7	2 47.7	28 52.0	0 49.3	21 05.3	4 30.5	17 07.8	3 27.2	26 43.6	25 03.7
4 Tu	2 48 11	13 41 43	26 28 41	2♎55 40	15 29.2	4 08.0	29 58.8	0 43.2	20 52.0	4 23.0	17 03.9	3 25.0	26 42.6	25 02.1
5 W	2 52 07	14 39 50	9♎19 37	15 40 39	15 19.7	5 24.1	1♈05.7	0 38.0	20 38.7	4 15.5	17 00.1	3 22.6	26 41.5	25 00.5
6 Th	2 56 04	15 37 55	21 58 49	28 14 10	15 09.1	6 35.9	2 12.7	0 33.5	20 25.3	4 08.1	16 56.3	3 20.3	26 40.4	24 59.0
7 F	3 00 01	16 35 58	4♏26 47	10♏36 44	14 58.3	7 43.2	3 19.9	0 29.8	20 11.9	4 00.8	16 52.6	3 18.0	26 39.3	24 57.4
8 Sa	3 03 57	17 34 00	16 44 05	22 48 58	14 48.4	8 46.1	4 27.1	0 26.9	19 58.4	3 53.5	16 48.9	3 15.6	26 38.1	24 55.9
9 Su	3 07 54	18 32 00	28 51 29	4♐51 51	14 40.1	9 44.3	5 34.6	0 24.7	19 44.9	3 46.2	16 45.3	3 13.3	26 37.0	24 54.4
10 M	3 11 50	19 29 59	10♐50 16	16 47 00	14 34.1	10 38.0	6 42.1	0 23.4	19 31.4	3 39.1	16 41.8	3 10.9	26 35.8	24 52.8
11 Tu	3 15 47	20 27 56	22 42 21	28 36 40	14 30.5	11 27.0	7 49.8	0D22.8	19 17.9	3 32.0	16 38.4	3 08.5	26 34.6	24 51.4
12 W	3 19 43	21 25 52	4♑30 23	10♑23 56	14D29.0	12 11.2	8 57.5	0 23.0	19 04.4	3 25.0	16 35.0	3 06.0	26 33.3	24 49.9
13 Th	3 23 40	22 23 46	16 17 48	22 12 34	14 29.2	12 50.7	10 05.4	0 23.9	18 51.0	3 18.0	16 31.7	3 03.6	26 32.1	24 48.4
14 F	3 27 36	23 21 40	28 08 45	4♒07 00	14 30.2	13 25.3	11 13.4	0 25.6	18 37.6	3 11.2	16 28.4	3 01.2	26 30.8	24 47.0
15 Sa	3 31 33	24 19 32	10♒07 56	16 12 11	14R31.3	13 55.0	12 21.5	0 28.0	18 24.3	3 04.4	16 25.3	2 58.7	26 29.5	24 45.6
16 Su	3 35 30	25 17 22	22 20 24	28 33 13	14 31.6	14 19.8	13 29.7	0 31.1	18 11.1	2 57.7	16 22.2	2 56.3	26 28.2	24 44.2
17 M	3 39 26	26 15 12	4♓51 14	11♓15 01	14 30.3	14 39.6	14 38.0	0 34.9	17 58.0	2 51.2	16 19.1	2 53.8	26 26.9	24 42.8
18 Tu	3 43 23	27 13 00	17 45 05	24 21 48	14 27.3	14 54.6	15 46.4	0 39.5	17 45.0	2 44.7	16 16.2	2 51.3	26 25.6	24 41.4
19 W	3 47 19	28 10 47	1♈05 30	7♈56 19	14 22.5	15 04.6	16 54.9	0 44.7	17 32.2	2 38.4	16 13.3	2 48.8	26 24.2	24 40.1
20 Th	3 51 16	29 08 33	14 54 16	21 59 09	14 16.3	15R09.8	18 03.5	0 50.7	17 19.4	2 32.1	16 10.6	2 46.3	26 22.8	24 38.7
21 F	3 55 12	0♊06 18	29 10 37	6♉28 05	14 09.5	15 10.2	19 12.2	0 57.3	17 06.9	2 26.0	16 07.9	2 43.9	26 21.4	24 37.4
22 Sa	3 59 09	1 04 02	13♉50 48	21 17 51	14 03.0	15 06.0	20 21.0	1 04.6	16 54.5	2 20.0	16 05.3	2 41.4	26 20.0	24 36.2
23 Su	4 03 05	2 01 44	28 48 10	6♊20 35	13 57.6	14 57.3	21 29.8	1 12.6	16 42.4	2 14.1	16 02.7	2 38.9	26 18.6	24 34.9
24 M	4 07 02	2 59 25	13♊53 55	21 26 57	13 54.0	14 44.3	22 38.8	1 21.3	16 30.4	2 08.4	16 00.3	2 36.4	26 17.1	24 33.7
25 Tu	4 10 59	3 57 05	28 58 33	6♋27 40	13D52.3	14 27.4	23 47.8	1 30.5	16 18.6	2 02.7	15 58.0	2 33.9	26 15.7	24 32.4
26 W	4 14 55	4 54 44	13♋53 22	21 14 54	13 52.3	14 06.7	24 56.9	1 40.5	16 07.1	1 57.3	15 55.7	2 31.4	26 14.2	24 31.3
27 Th	4 18 52	5 52 21	28 31 38	5♌43 10	13 53.4	13 42.8	26 06.0	1 51.0	15 55.8	1 51.9	15 53.5	2 28.9	26 12.7	24 30.1
28 F	4 22 48	6 49 57	12♌49 12	19 49 36	13 54.7	13 15.9	27 15.2	2 02.2	15 44.8	1 46.7	15 51.5	2 26.4	26 11.2	24 29.0
29 Sa	4 26 45	7 47 31	26 44 20	3♍33 31	13R55.6	12 46.6	28 24.5	2 13.9	15 34.1	1 41.6	15 49.5	2 23.9	26 09.7	24 27.8
30 Su	4 30 41	8 45 03	10♍17 17	16 55 54	13 55.4	12 15.4	29 33.9	2 26.3	15 23.6	1 36.7	15 47.6	2 21.4	26 08.2	24 26.7
31 M	4 34 38	9 42 34	23 29 36	29 58 44	13 53.7	11 42.8	0♉43.3	2 39.2	15 13.4	1 32.0	15 45.8	2 19.0	26 06.7	24 25.7

LONGITUDE — June 1982

Day	Sid.Time	☉	0 hr ☽	Noon ☽	True ☊	☿	♀	♂	⚳	♃	♄	♅	♆	♇
1 Tu	4 38 34	10♊40 04	6♎23 34	12♎44 27	13♋50.5	11♊09.3	1♉52.8	2♎52.6	15♏03.5	1♏27.3	15♎44.1	2♐16.5	26♐05.1	24♎24.6
2 W	4 42 31	11 37 33	19 01 42	25 15 36	13R46.1	10R35.7	3 02.4	3 06.7	14R54.0	1R22.9	15R42.5	2R14.0	26R03.6	24R23.6
3 Th	4 46 28	12 35 00	1♏26 27	7♏34 31	13 41.0	10 02.4	4 12.0	3 21.2	14 44.7	1 18.6	15 40.9	2 11.6	26 02.0	24 22.6
4 F	4 50 24	13 32 27	13 40 04	19 43 22	13 35.8	9 30.0	5 21.7	3 36.3	14 35.7	1 14.4	15 39.5	2 09.2	26 00.5	24 21.7
5 Sa	4 54 21	14 29 52	25 44 37	1♐44 05	13 31.0	8 59.0	6 31.5	3 51.9	14 27.1	1 10.5	15 38.2	2 06.7	25 58.9	24 20.7
6 Su	4 58 17	15 27 16	7♐41 58	13 38 32	13 27.1	8 30.1	7 41.3	4 08.1	14 18.8	1 06.6	15 37.0	2 04.3	25 57.3	24 19.8
7 M	5 02 14	16 24 40	19 34 00	25 28 37	13 24.5	8 03.6	8 51.2	4 24.7	14 10.8	1 03.0	15 35.8	2 01.9	25 55.7	24 19.0
8 Tu	5 06 10	17 22 02	1♑22 41	7♑16 28	13D23.3	7 40.1	10 01.2	4 41.8	14 03.2	0 59.5	15 34.8	1 59.6	25 54.1	24 18.1
9 W	5 10 07	18 19 24	13 10 17	19 04 30	13 23.2	7 19.8	11 11.2	4 59.4	13 56.0	0 56.2	15 33.9	1 57.2	25 52.5	24 17.3
10 Th	5 14 03	19 16 45	24 59 29	0♒55 38	13 24.2	7 03.2	12 21.3	5 17.4	13 49.1	0 53.0	15 33.0	1 54.9	25 50.9	24 16.5
11 F	5 18 00	20 14 06	6♒53 23	12 53 13	13 25.7	6 50.4	13 31.4	5 35.9	13 42.5	0 50.0	15 32.3	1 52.5	25 49.3	24 15.7
12 Sa	5 21 57	21 11 26	18 55 35	25 01 01	13 27.3	6 41.8	14 41.6	5 54.9	13 36.3	0 47.2	15 31.6	1 50.2	25 47.7	24 15.0
13 Su	5 25 53	22 08 46	1♓10 03	7♓23 11	13 28.5	6D37.5	15 51.9	6 14.3	13 30.5	0 44.5	15 31.1	1 47.9	25 46.1	24 14.3
14 M	5 29 50	23 06 05	13 40 58	20 03 54	13R29.2	6 37.7	17 02.2	6 34.1	13 25.0	0 42.1	15 30.6	1 45.6	25 44.5	24 13.6
15 Tu	5 33 46	24 03 23	26 32 27	3♈07 03	13 29.0	6 42.3	18 12.6	6 54.4	13 19.9	0 39.8	15 30.3	1 43.4	25 42.9	24 13.0
16 W	5 37 43	25 00 42	9♈48 03	16 35 42	13 27.9	6 51.5	19 23.0	7 15.1	13 15.2	0 37.7	15 30.0	1 41.2	25 41.2	24 12.4
17 Th	5 41 39	25 58 00	23 30 09	0♉31 24	13 26.2	7 05.4	20 33.5	7 36.2	13 10.9	0 35.7	15D29.9	1 38.9	25 39.6	24 11.8
18 F	5 45 36	26 55 17	7♉39 19	14 53 33	13 24.2	7 23.8	21 44.1	7 57.7	13 06.9	0 33.9	15 29.8	1 36.8	25 38.0	24 11.3
19 Sa	5 49 32	27 52 35	22 13 36	29 38 48	13 22.3	7 46.8	22 54.7	8 19.6	13 03.3	0 32.4	15 29.9	1 34.6	25 36.4	24 10.7
20 Su	5 53 29	28 49 52	7♊08 18	14♊41 06	13 20.7	8 14.4	24 05.3	8 41.9	13 00.1	0 30.9	15 30.1	1 32.5	25 34.8	24 10.3
21 M	5 57 26	29 47 09	22 16 04	29 52 03	13D19.7	8 46.4	25 16.1	9 04.6	12 57.3	0 29.7	15 30.3	1 30.4	25 33.2	24 09.8
22 Tu	6 01 22	0♋44 26	7♋27 48	15♋02 09	13 19.5	9 22.9	26 26.8	9 27.7	12 54.9	0 28.7	15 30.7	1 28.3	25 31.5	24 09.4
23 W	6 05 19	1 41 42	22 33 56	0♌02 09	13 19.8	10 03.7	27 37.6	9 51.1	12 52.9	0 27.8	15 31.1	1 26.3	25 29.9	24 09.0
24 Th	6 09 15	2 38 57	7♌25 53	14 44 24	13 20.6	10 48.9	28 48.5	10 14.9	12 51.2	0 27.1	15 31.7	1 24.2	25 28.3	24 08.7
25 F	6 13 12	3 36 12	21 57 08	29 03 40	13 21.4	11 38.2	29 59.4	10 39.1	12 49.9	0 26.6	15 32.4	1 22.2	25 26.7	24 08.3
26 Sa	6 17 08	4 33 26	6♍03 47	12♍57 23	13 22.1	12 31.8	1♊10.3	11 03.6	12 49.0	0 26.3	15 33.1	1 20.3	25 25.1	24 08.1
27 Su	6 21 05	5 30 40	19 44 31	26 25 21	13R22.5	13 29.4	2 21.3	11 28.5	12D48.5	0D26.2	15 34.0	1 18.4	25 23.5	24 07.8
28 M	6 25 01	6 27 53	3♎00 08	9♎29 13	13 22.6	14 31.1	3 32.3	11 53.7	12 48.4	0 26.2	15 34.9	1 16.5	25 21.9	24 07.6
29 Tu	6 28 58	7 25 05	15 52 58	22 11 49	13 22.4	15 36.8	4 43.4	12 19.2	12 48.6	0 26.5	15 36.0	1 14.6	25 20.4	24 07.4
30 W	6 32 55	8 22 17	28 26 13	4♏36 39	13 22.0	16 46.5	5 54.5	12 45.0	12 49.3	0 26.9	15 37.1	1 12.8	25 18.8	24 07.2

Astro Data

	Dy Hr Mn
☽0S	5 4:37
♀0N	7 13:34
♂ D	11 18:36
♃⚺♅	16 20:35
☽0N	19 18:59
☿ R	21 2:05
♂0S	26 22:43
☽0S	1 10:49
☿ D	13 23:22
☽0N	16 4:23
♄ D	18 11:05
♃ D	27 18:16
⚳ D	28 8:30
☽0S	28 17:19

Planet Ingress

	Dy Hr Mn
☿ ♊	1 13:29
♀ ♈	4 12:27
☉ ♊	21 9:23
♀ ♉	30 21:02
☉ ♋	21 17:23
♀ ♊	25 12:13

Last Aspect / ☽ Ingress

Last Aspect Dy Hr Mn		☽ Ingress Dy Hr Mn
1 17:57	♆ △	♍ 1 23:45
4 5:59	♀ ☍	♎ 4 6:32
6 9:00	♆ ⚹	♏ 6 15:24
8 0:45	☉ ☍	♐ 9 2:17
11 7:52	♆ ☌	♑ 11 14:50
13 17:15	♇ □	♒ 14 3:44
16 8:00	♆ ⚹	♓ 16 14:46
18 17:30	☉ ⚹	♈ 18 22:04
20 19:20	♆ △	♉ 21 1:22
21 5:25	♃ ☍	♊ 23 1:54
24 19:42	♆ ☍	♋ 25 1:38
26 18:36	♀ □	♌ 27 2:27
29 2:05	♀ △	♍ 29 5:43
31 4:50	♆ □	♎ 31 12:02

Last Aspect / ☽ Ingress

Last Aspect Dy Hr Mn		☽ Ingress Dy Hr Mn
2 13:33	♆ ⚹	♏ 2 21:12
3 4:42	♀ ☍	♐ 5 8:31
7 12:55	♆ ☌	♑ 7 21:12
9 22:34	♇ □	♒ 10 10:08
12 13:31	♆ ⚹	♓ 12 21:44
14 22:30	♆ □	♈ 15 6:20
17 3:43	♆ △	♉ 17 11:07
19 0:10	♀ ☌	♊ 19 12:34
21 11:52	☉ ☌	♋ 21 12:13
23 7:47	♀ ⚹	♌ 23 11:57
25 5:53	♆ △	♍ 25 13:36
27 10:09	♆ □	♎ 27 18:30
29 18:01	♆ ⚹	♏ 30 3:02

☽ Phases & Eclipses

Dy Hr Mn	
8 0:45	○ 17♏07
16 5:11	☾ 25♒01
23 4:40	● 1♊44
29 20:07	☽ 8♍07
6 15:59	○ 15♐37
14 18:06	☾ 23♓21
21 11:52	● 29♊47
21 12:03:42	● P 0.617
28 5:56	☽ 6♎13

Astro Data

1 May 1982
Julian Day # 30071
SVP 5♓30'41"
GC 26♐35.5 ⚴ 4♎08.1R
Eris 15♈16.9 ⚵ 9♑56.1R
⚷ 21♉50.5 ⚶ 14♒04.3
☽ Mean ☊ 16♋48.1

1 June 1982
Julian Day # 30102
SVP 5♓30'37"
GC 26♐35.6 ⚴ 2♎45.2
Eris 15♈33.0 ⚵ 7♑09.0R
⚷ 23♉58.6 ⚶ 22♒14.7
☽ Mean ☊ 15♋09.7

July 1982 — LONGITUDE

Day	Sid.Time	☉	0 hr ☽	Noon☽	True☊	☿	♀	♂	⚳	♃	♄	♅	♆	♇
1 Th	6 36 51	9♋19 29	10♏43 34	16♏47 26	13♋21.5	18♊00.0	7♊05.7	13♎11.2	12♏50.2	0♏27.4	15♎38.4	1♐11.0	25♐17.2	24♎07.1
2 F	6 40 48	10 16 40	22 48 42	28 47 47	13R 21.0	19 17.4	8 16.9	13 37.7	12 51.6	0 28.2	15 39.7	1R 09.2	25R 15.7	24R 07.0
3 Sa	6 44 44	11 13 52	4♐45 07	10♐41 03	13 20.7	20 38.6	9 28.2	14 04.4	12 53.3	0 29.2	15 41.2	1 07.5	25 14.1	24 07.0
4 Su	6 48 41	12 11 03	16 36 00	22 30 16	13 20.6	22 03.6	10 39.5	14 31.5	12 55.4	0 30.3	15 42.7	1 05.8	25 12.6	24D 07.0
5 M	6 52 37	13 08 14	28 24 13	4♑18 08	13 20.5	23 32.2	11 50.8	14 58.9	12 57.9	0 31.6	15 44.4	1 04.2	25 11.1	24 07.0
6 Tu	6 56 34	14 05 25	10♑12 20	16 07 05	13 20.5	25 04.5	13 02.2	15 26.5	13 00.7	0 33.0	15 46.1	1 02.6	25 09.6	24 07.0
7 W	7 00 31	15 02 36	22 02 41	27 59 25	13 20.5	26 40.3	14 13.7	15 54.4	13 03.8	0 34.7	15 48.0	1 01.0	25 08.1	24 07.1
8 Th	7 04 27	15 59 47	3♒57 32	9♒57 21	13 20.3	28 19.7	15 25.2	16 22.6	13 07.3	0 36.5	15 49.9	0 59.5	25 06.6	24 07.2
9 F	7 08 24	16 56 58	15 59 08	22 03 12	13 20.0	0♋02.5	16 36.7	16 51.1	13 11.2	0 38.5	15 51.9	0 58.0	25 05.1	24 07.4
10 Sa	7 12 20	17 54 10	28 09 52	4♓19 26	13 19.5	1 48.5	17 48.3	17 19.8	13 15.4	0 40.7	15 54.0	0 56.6	25 03.6	24 07.5
11 Su	7 16 17	18 51 22	10♓32 15	16 48 40	13 18.9	3 37.7	19 00.0	17 48.8	13 19.9	0 43.0	15 56.2	0 55.2	25 02.2	24 07.8
12 M	7 20 13	19 48 34	23 09 01	29 33 39	13 18.3	5 29.8	20 11.7	18 18.0	13 24.8	0 45.5	15 58.5	0 53.8	25 00.7	24 08.0
13 Tu	7 24 10	20 45 47	6♈02 54	12♈37 05	13D 17.9	7 24.7	21 23.4	18 47.6	13 30.0	0 48.2	16 00.9	0 52.5	24 59.3	24 08.3
14 W	7 28 06	21 43 00	19 16 29	26 01 22	13 17.9	9 22.3	22 35.2	19 17.3	13 35.5	0 51.1	16 03.4	0 51.2	24 57.9	24 08.6
15 Th	7 32 03	22 40 14	2♉51 52	9♉48 06	13 18.2	11 22.1	23 47.0	19 47.3	13 41.3	0 54.1	16 06.0	0 50.0	24 56.5	24 09.0
16 F	7 36 00	23 37 29	16 50 04	23 57 39	13 18.9	13 24.0	24 58.9	20 17.6	13 47.5	0 57.3	16 08.7	0 48.8	24 55.1	24 09.4
17 Sa	7 39 56	24 34 45	1♊10 37	8♊28 34	13 19.7	15 27.7	26 10.9	20 48.1	13 54.0	1 00.7	16 11.5	0 47.6	24 53.8	24 09.8
18 Su	7 43 53	25 32 01	15 51 00	23 17 12	13 20.5	17 32.8	27 22.8	21 18.8	14 00.8	1 04.2	16 14.3	0 46.6	24 52.4	24 10.2
19 M	7 47 49	26 29 18	0♋46 22	8♋17 36	13R 21.0	19 39.1	28 34.9	21 49.8	14 08.0	1 07.9	16 17.3	0 45.5	24 51.1	24 10.7
20 Tu	7 51 46	27 26 35	15 49 50	23 21 59	13 20.9	21 46.2	29 46.9	22 21.0	14 15.4	1 11.8	16 20.3	0 44.5	24 49.8	24 11.2
21 W	7 55 42	28 23 53	0♌52 57	8♌21 39	13 20.1	23 53.8	0♋59.1	22 52.4	14 23.1	1 15.8	16 23.4	0 43.5	24 48.5	24 11.8
22 Th	7 59 39	29 21 11	15 47 01	23 08 08	13 18.5	26 01.7	2 11.2	23 24.1	14 31.2	1 20.0	16 26.6	0 42.6	24 47.2	24 12.4
23 F	8 03 35	0♌18 29	0♍24 11	7♍34 30	13 16.4	28 09.5	3 23.4	23 56.0	14 39.5	1 24.3	16 29.9	0 41.8	24 46.0	24 13.0
24 Sa	8 07 32	1 15 48	14 38 35	21 36 07	13 14.2	0♌16.9	4 35.6	24 28.1	14 48.2	1 28.8	16 33.3	0 40.9	24 44.8	24 13.7
25 Su	8 11 29	2 13 08	28 26 54	5♎10 57	13 12.1	2 23.9	5 47.9	25 00.4	14 57.1	1 33.5	16 36.8	0 40.2	24 43.5	24 14.4
26 M	8 15 25	3 10 27	11♎48 23	18 19 27	13 10.6	4 30.0	7 00.2	25 32.9	15 06.3	1 38.3	16 40.3	0 39.4	24 42.4	24 15.1
27 Tu	8 19 22	4 07 47	24 44 30	1♏03 57	13D 09.9	6 35.2	8 12.6	26 05.7	15 15.8	1 43.3	16 44.0	0 38.8	24 41.2	24 15.8
28 W	8 23 18	5 05 08	7♏18 18	13 28 06	13 10.2	8 39.4	9 25.0	26 38.6	15 25.6	1 48.4	16 47.7	0 38.1	24 40.0	24 16.6
29 Th	8 27 15	6 02 29	19 33 54	25 36 17	13 11.2	10 42.3	10 37.5	27 11.8	15 35.6	1 53.7	16 51.5	0 37.6	24 38.9	24 17.5
30 F	8 31 11	6 59 51	1♐35 50	7♐33 08	13 12.7	12 43.9	11 49.9	27 45.1	15 45.9	1 59.1	16 55.4	0 37.0	24 37.8	24 18.3
31 Sa	8 35 08	7 57 13	13 28 45	19 23 12	13 14.4	14 44.1	13 02.5	28 18.6	15 56.5	2 04.7	16 59.4	0 36.6	24 36.8	24 19.2

August 1982 — LONGITUDE

Day	Sid.Time	☉	0 hr ☽	Noon☽	True☊	☿	♀	♂	⚳	♃	♄	♅	♆	♇
1 Su	8 39 04	8♌54 36	25♐17 02	1♑10 43	13♋15.7	16♌42.8	14♋15.0	28♎52.4	16♏07.3	2♏10.4	17♎03.4	0♐36.1	24♐35.7	24♎20.1
2 M	8 43 01	9 51 59	7♑04 43	12 59 25	13R 16.3	18 40.0	15 27.7	29 26.3	16 18.4	2 16.3	17 07.5	0R 35.8	24R 34.7	24 21.1
3 Tu	8 46 58	10 49 24	18 55 13	24 52 28	13 15.7	20 35.7	16 40.3	0♏00.3	16 29.7	2 22.3	17 11.7	0 35.4	24 33.7	24 22.1
4 W	8 50 54	11 46 49	0♒51 28	6♒52 29	13 13.8	22 29.8	17 53.0	0 34.6	16 41.3	2 28.5	17 16.0	0 35.2	24 32.7	24 23.1
5 Th	8 54 51	12 44 15	12 55 44	19 01 27	13 10.5	24 22.4	19 05.8	1 09.1	16 53.1	2 34.8	17 20.4	0 34.9	24 31.8	24 24.1
6 F	8 58 47	13 41 42	25 09 48	1♓20 56	13 06.0	26 13.4	20 18.6	1 43.7	17 05.2	2 41.2	17 24.8	0 34.8	24 30.8	24 25.2
7 Sa	9 02 44	14 39 10	7♓35 00	13 52 07	13 00.9	28 02.8	21 31.4	2 18.5	17 17.5	2 47.8	17 29.3	0 34.6	24 29.9	24 26.3
8 Su	9 06 40	15 36 40	20 12 23	26 35 55	12 55.7	29 50.6	22 44.3	2 53.5	17 30.0	2 54.5	17 33.8	0D 34.6	24 29.0	24 27.4
9 M	9 10 37	16 34 10	3♈02 50	9♈33 13	12 50.9	1♍36.9	23 57.2	3 28.6	17 42.8	3 01.4	17 38.5	0 34.6	24 28.2	24 28.6
10 Tu	9 14 33	17 31 42	16 07 11	22 44 51	12 47.3	3 21.6	25 10.2	4 03.9	17 55.8	3 08.4	17 43.2	0 34.6	24 27.4	24 29.8
11 W	9 18 30	18 29 15	29 26 20	6♉11 42	12D 45.1	5 04.8	26 23.2	4 39.4	18 09.0	3 15.5	17 48.0	0 34.7	24 26.6	24 31.0
12 Th	9 22 27	19 26 50	13♉01 04	19 54 30	12 44.4	6 46.5	27 36.3	5 15.0	18 22.4	3 22.7	17 52.9	0 34.8	24 25.8	24 32.3
13 F	9 26 23	20 24 26	26 52 00	3♊53 34	12 45.0	8 26.6	28 49.4	5 50.9	18 36.0	3 30.1	17 57.8	0 35.0	24 25.1	24 33.6
14 Sa	9 30 20	21 22 04	10♊59 07	18 08 29	12 46.3	10 05.2	0♌02.6	6 26.8	18 49.9	3 37.6	18 02.8	0 35.2	24 24.4	24 34.9
15 Su	9 34 16	22 19 43	25 21 25	2♋37 33	12R 47.5	11 42.4	1 15.8	7 03.0	19 03.9	3 45.3	18 07.9	0 35.5	24 23.7	24 36.3
16 M	9 38 13	23 17 24	9♋56 26	17 17 28	12 47.7	13 18.1	2 29.0	7 39.3	19 18.2	3 53.0	18 13.0	0 35.9	24 23.0	24 37.6
17 Tu	9 42 09	24 15 07	24 39 59	2♌03 10	12 46.4	14 52.2	3 42.3	8 15.8	19 32.7	4 00.9	18 18.2	0 36.3	24 22.4	24 39.1
18 W	9 46 06	25 12 50	9♌26 11	16 48 06	12 43.1	16 24.9	4 55.7	8 52.4	19 47.4	4 08.9	18 23.5	0 36.7	24 21.8	24 40.5
19 Th	9 50 02	26 10 35	24 07 59	1♍24 55	12 37.8	17 56.1	6 09.0	9 29.2	20 02.3	4 17.1	18 28.8	0 37.2	24 21.3	24 41.9
20 F	9 53 59	27 08 22	8♍38 03	15 46 36	12 31.2	19 25.8	7 22.5	10 06.1	20 17.3	4 25.3	18 34.2	0 37.7	24 20.7	24 43.4
21 Sa	9 57 56	28 06 09	22 49 54	29 47 27	12 23.9	20 54.0	8 35.9	10 43.2	20 32.6	4 33.7	18 39.6	0 38.3	24 20.2	24 45.0
22 Su	10 01 52	29 03 58	6♎38 53	13♎23 58	12 16.9	22 20.7	9 49.4	11 20.4	20 48.0	4 42.2	18 45.1	0 39.0	24 19.7	24 46.5
23 M	10 05 49	0♍01 48	20 02 39	26 35 01	12 11.0	23 45.9	11 02.9	11 57.8	21 03.7	4 50.8	18 50.7	0 39.7	24 19.3	24 48.1
24 Tu	10 09 45	0 59 39	3♏01 18	9♏21 47	12 06.7	25 09.4	12 16.5	12 35.4	21 19.5	4 59.5	18 56.3	0 40.5	24 18.9	24 49.7
25 W	10 13 42	1 57 32	15 36 57	21 47 16	12D 04.4	26 31.4	13 30.1	13 13.1	21 35.5	5 08.3	19 02.0	0 41.3	24 18.5	24 51.3
26 Th	10 17 38	2 55 25	27 53 18	3♐55 41	12 03.8	27 51.8	14 43.7	13 50.9	21 51.6	5 17.3	19 07.8	0 42.1	24 18.2	24 52.9
27 F	10 21 35	3 53 20	9♐55 03	15 52 03	12 04.4	29 10.5	15 57.4	14 28.8	22 08.0	5 26.3	19 13.6	0 43.0	24 17.8	24 54.6
28 Sa	10 25 31	4 51 17	21 47 21	27 41 36	12 05.6	0♎27.5	17 11.1	15 06.9	22 24.5	5 35.5	19 19.4	0 44.0	24 17.6	24 56.3
29 Su	10 29 28	5 49 15	3♑35 26	9♑29 29	12R 06.3	1 42.7	18 24.9	15 45.2	22 41.2	5 44.7	19 25.4	0 45.0	24 17.3	24 58.0
30 M	10 33 25	6 47 14	15 24 18	21 20 28	12 05.9	2 56.1	19 38.7	16 23.5	22 58.0	5 54.1	19 31.3	0 46.1	24 17.1	24 59.8
31 Tu	10 37 21	7 45 14	27 18 27	3♒18 43	12 03.5	4 07.6	20 52.5	17 02.1	23 15.0	6 03.6	19 37.3	0 47.2	24 16.9	25 01.6

Astro Data

	Dy Hr Mn
♇ D	4 13:11
♄∠♅	11 5:01
☽ 0N	13 11:28
♃⊻♅	14 12:44
☽ 0S	26 0:51
♆✶♇	9 7:02
♅ D	9 10:21
☽ 0N	9 16:41
☽ 0S	22 9:28
☿0S	26 14:41

Planet Ingress

	Dy Hr Mn
☿ ♋	9 11:26
♀ ♋	20 16:21
☉ ♌	23 4:15
☿ ♌	24 8:48
♂ ♏	3 11:45
☿ ♍	8 14:06
♀ ♌	14 11:09
☉ ♍	23 11:15
☿ ♎	28 3:22

Last Aspect — ☽ Ingress

Dy Hr Mn			Dy Hr Mn
30 19:59	☉ △	♐	2 14:25
4 17:29	♆ ☌	♑	5 3:15
7 4:11	♇ □	♒	7 16:03
9 17:57	♆ ✶	♓	10 3:35
12 3:31	♆ □	♈	12 12:49
14 10:08	♆ △	♉	14 19:00
16 11:24	☉ ✶	♊	16 22:03
18 19:09	♀ ☌	♋	18 22:46
20 18:57	☉ ☌	♌	20 22:35
22 14:43	♆ △	♍	22 23:20
24 17:29	♆ □	♎	25 2:45
27 2:08	♂ ☌	♏	27 9:58
28 3:14	♀ △	♐	29 20:48

Last Aspect — ☽ Ingress

Dy Hr Mn			Dy Hr Mn
1 7:04	♂ ✶	♑	1 9:36
3 10:59	♇ □	♒	3 22:17
6 0:19	☿ ☍	♓	6 9:23
8 8:03	♆ □	♈	8 18:21
10 16:48	♀ □	♉	11 1:00
13 2:32	♀ ✶	♊	13 5:22
14 22:44	♇ △	♋	15 7:40
16 23:57	♇ □	♌	17 8:40
19 2:45	☉ ☌	♍	19 9:40
21 2:35	♆ □	♎	21 12:22
23 8:42	♇ ☌	♏	23 18:21
25 22:28	☿ ✶	♐	26 4:11
28 6:23	♇ ✶	♑	28 16:42
30 19:23	♇ □	♒	31 5:23

☽ Phases & Eclipses

Dy Hr Mn	
6 7:32	○ 13♑55
6 7:31	• T 1.718
14 3:47	☾ 21♈23
20 18:57	● 27♋43
20 18:43:50	• P 0.464
27 18:22	☽ 4♏23
4 22:34	○ 12♒12
12 11:08	☾ 19♉25
19 2:45	● 25♌48
26 9:49	☽ 2♐50

Astro Data

1 July 1982
Julian Day # 30132
SVP 5♓30'32"
GC 26♐35.7 ⚴ 7♎31.7
Eris 15♈41.0 ⚵ 0♑43.0R
⚷ 25♉50.4 ⚶ 24♒27.5R
☽ Mean ☊ 13♋34.3

1 August 1982
Julian Day # 30163
SVP 5♓30'26"
GC 26♐35.8 ⚴ 16♎23.5
Eris 15♈39.5R ⚵ 25♐12.1R
⚷ 27♉12.5 ⚶ 19♒42.0R
☽ Mean ☊ 11♋55.9

LONGITUDE — September 1982

Day	Sid.Time	☉	0 hr ☽	Noon☽	True☊	☿	♀	♂	⚳	♃	♄	♅	♆	♇
1 W	10 41 18	8♍43 16	9♒21 39	15♒27 35	11♋58.9	5♎17.1	22♌06.3	17♏40.7	23♏32.2	6♏13.1	19♎43.4	0♐48.3	24♐16.7	25♎03.4
2 Th	10 45 14	9 41 19	21 36 46	27 49 26	11R 51.9	6 24.5	23 20.2	18 19.4	23 49.5	6 22.8	19 49.5	0 49.6	24R 16.6	25 05.2
3 F	10 49 11	10 39 24	4♓05 41	10♓25 35	11 42.9	7 29.8	24 34.2	18 58.3	24 06.9	6 32.5	19 55.7	0 50.8	24 16.5	25 07.0
4 Sa	10 53 07	11 37 31	16 49 10	23 16 22	11 32.7	8 32.7	25 48.1	19 37.3	24 24.5	6 42.4	20 01.9	0 52.1	24 16.4	25 08.9
5 Su	10 57 04	12 35 39	29 47 06	6♈21 13	11 22.1	9 33.2	27 02.2	20 16.5	24 42.3	6 52.4	20 08.2	0 53.5	24D 16.4	25 10.8
6 M	11 01 00	13 33 50	12♈58 33	19 38 58	11 12.4	10 31.2	28 16.2	20 55.7	25 00.2	7 02.4	20 14.5	0 54.9	24 16.4	25 12.7
7 Tu	11 04 57	14 32 02	26 22 14	3♉08 13	11 04.4	11 26.4	29 30.3	21 35.1	25 18.2	7 12.5	20 20.8	0 56.3	24 16.4	25 14.6
8 W	11 08 53	15 30 16	9♉56 44	16 47 39	10 58.8	12 18.7	0♍44.4	22 14.6	25 36.4	7 22.8	20 27.2	0 57.8	24 16.5	25 16.6
9 Th	11 12 50	16 28 32	23 40 51	0♊36 16	10 55.6	13 07.9	1 58.6	22 54.3	25 54.7	7 33.1	20 33.6	0 59.4	24 16.6	25 18.5
10 F	11 16 47	17 26 51	7♊33 48	14 33 24	10D 54.6	13 53.8	3 12.7	23 34.0	26 13.2	7 43.5	20 40.1	1 01.0	24 16.7	25 20.5
11 Sa	11 20 43	18 25 11	21 35 00	28 38 32	10R 54.8	14 36.1	4 27.0	24 13.9	26 31.8	7 54.0	20 46.6	1 02.7	24 16.9	25 22.5
12 Su	11 24 40	19 23 34	5♋43 54	12♋50 56	10 55.0	15 14.6	5 41.3	24 53.9	26 50.5	8 04.6	20 53.2	1 04.4	24 17.1	25 24.6
13 M	11 28 36	20 21 59	19 59 26	27 09 07	10 54.1	15 49.0	6 55.6	25 34.0	27 09.3	8 15.2	20 59.8	1 06.1	24 17.3	25 26.6
14 Tu	11 32 33	21 20 26	4♌19 39	11♌30 33	10 51.0	16 19.0	8 09.9	26 14.3	27 28.3	8 26.0	21 06.4	1 07.9	24 17.6	25 28.7
15 W	11 36 29	22 18 55	18 41 20	25 51 23	10 45.1	16 44.3	9 24.3	26 54.7	27 47.4	8 36.8	21 13.1	1 09.7	24 17.9	25 30.8
16 Th	11 40 26	23 17 26	3♍00 04	10♍06 41	10 36.6	17 04.5	10 38.7	27 35.1	28 06.7	8 47.7	21 19.8	1 11.6	24 18.2	25 32.9
17 F	11 44 22	24 15 59	17 10 34	24 11 04	10 25.9	17 19.3	11 53.1	28 15.7	28 26.0	8 58.7	21 26.6	1 13.5	24 18.6	25 35.0
18 Sa	11 48 19	25 14 33	1♎07 32	7♎59 28	10 14.1	17R 28.4	13 07.5	28 56.4	28 45.5	9 09.8	21 33.4	1 15.5	24 19.0	25 37.1
19 Su	11 52 16	26 13 10	14 46 25	21 28 04	10 02.4	17 31.3	14 22.0	29 37.3	29 05.1	9 21.0	21 40.2	1 17.5	24 19.4	25 39.3
20 M	11 56 12	27 11 48	28 04 13	4♏34 49	9 52.0	17 27.7	15 36.5	0♐18.2	29 24.8	9 32.2	21 47.0	1 19.6	24 19.9	25 41.4
21 Tu	12 00 09	28 10 29	10♏59 55	17 19 42	9 43.7	17 17.4	16 51.1	0 59.3	29 44.6	9 43.5	21 53.9	1 21.7	24 20.4	25 43.6
22 W	12 04 05	29 09 11	23 34 28	29 44 36	9 38.1	17 00.1	18 05.6	1 40.4	0♐04.6	9 54.8	22 00.8	1 23.8	24 20.9	25 45.8
23 Th	12 08 02	0♎07 54	5♐50 35	11♐52 56	9 34.9	16 35.5	19 20.2	2 21.7	0 24.6	10 06.3	22 07.7	1 26.0	24 21.5	25 48.0
24 F	12 11 58	1 06 40	17 52 17	23 49 16	9D 33.7	16 03.7	20 34.9	3 03.1	0 44.8	10 17.8	22 14.7	1 28.3	24 22.1	25 50.3
25 Sa	12 15 55	2 05 27	29 44 32	5♑38 48	9R 33.6	15 24.7	21 49.5	3 44.5	1 05.0	10 29.3	22 21.7	1 30.5	24 22.7	25 52.5
26 Su	12 19 51	3 04 16	11♑32 44	17 27 04	9 33.5	14 38.9	23 04.2	4 26.1	1 25.4	10 41.0	22 28.7	1 32.9	24 23.4	25 54.8
27 M	12 23 48	4 03 07	23 22 26	29 19 31	9 32.2	13 46.5	24 18.8	5 07.8	1 45.8	10 52.7	22 35.7	1 35.2	24 24.0	25 57.0
28 Tu	12 27 45	5 01 59	5♒18 56	11♒21 14	9 29.0	12 48.5	25 33.6	5 49.6	2 06.4	11 04.4	22 42.8	1 37.6	24 24.8	25 59.3
29 W	12 31 41	6 00 53	17 26 58	23 36 34	9 23.2	11 45.8	26 48.3	6 31.5	2 27.0	11 16.3	22 49.9	1 40.0	24 25.5	26 01.6
30 Th	12 35 38	6 59 49	29 50 25	6♓08 47	9 14.7	10 39.7	28 03.0	7 13.5	2 47.8	11 28.1	22 57.0	1 42.5	24 26.3	26 03.9

LONGITUDE — October 1982

Day	Sid.Time	☉	0 hr ☽	Noon☽	True☊	☿	♀	♂	⚳	♃	♄	♅	♆	♇
1 F	12 39 34	7♎58 47	12♓31 52	18♓59 46	9♋03.7	9♎31.6	29♍17.8	7♐55.5	3♐08.6	11♏40.1	23♎04.1	1♐45.0	24♐27.1	26♎06.2
2 Sa	12 43 31	8 57 47	25 32 27	2♈09 49	8R 51.3	8R 23.2	0♎32.6	8 37.7	3 29.6	11 52.1	23 11.2	1 47.6	24 28.0	26 08.5
3 Su	12 47 27	9 56 49	8♈51 38	15 37 37	8 38.5	7 16.3	1 47.4	9 20.0	3 50.6	12 04.1	23 18.4	1 50.2	24 28.8	26 10.8
4 M	12 51 24	10 55 53	22 27 22	29 20 26	8 26.5	6 12.8	3 02.3	10 02.3	4 11.7	12 16.2	23 25.6	1 52.8	24 29.8	26 13.2
5 Tu	12 55 20	11 54 59	6♉16 23	13♉14 41	8 16.5	5 14.4	4 17.1	10 44.8	4 32.9	12 28.4	23 32.8	1 55.5	24 30.7	26 15.5
6 W	12 59 17	12 54 07	20 14 52	27 16 28	8 09.2	4 22.8	5 32.0	11 27.3	4 54.2	12 40.6	23 40.0	1 58.2	24 31.7	26 17.9
7 Th	13 03 13	13 53 17	4♊19 05	11♊22 21	8 04.9	3 39.3	6 46.9	12 10.0	5 15.6	12 52.9	23 47.2	2 00.9	24 32.7	26 20.3
8 F	13 07 10	14 52 30	18 25 58	25 29 41	8D 03.0	3 05.2	8 01.8	12 52.7	5 37.0	13 05.2	23 54.4	2 03.7	24 33.7	26 22.6
9 Sa	13 11 07	15 51 46	2♋33 18	9♋36 42	8R 02.7	2 41.3	9 16.8	13 35.5	5 58.6	13 17.6	24 01.7	2 06.5	24 34.8	26 25.0
10 Su	13 15 03	16 51 03	16 39 46	23 42 24	8 02.7	2D 28.0	10 31.8	14 18.5	6 20.2	13 30.0	24 08.9	2 09.3	24 35.9	26 27.4
11 M	13 19 00	17 50 23	0♌44 31	7♌46 01	8 01.5	2 25.6	11 46.8	15 01.5	6 41.9	13 42.5	24 16.2	2 12.2	24 37.0	26 29.8
12 Tu	13 22 56	18 49 46	14 46 45	21 46 34	7 58.2	2 33.9	13 01.8	15 44.6	7 03.7	13 55.0	24 23.5	2 15.1	24 38.1	26 32.2
13 W	13 26 53	19 49 10	28 45 15	5♍42 32	7 52.1	2 52.8	14 16.8	16 27.8	7 25.5	14 07.5	24 30.8	2 18.1	24 39.3	26 34.6
14 Th	13 30 49	20 48 37	12♍38 06	19 31 37	7 43.2	3 21.7	15 31.8	17 11.0	7 47.4	14 20.1	24 38.1	2 21.1	24 40.5	26 37.0
15 F	13 34 46	21 48 06	26 22 43	3♎10 59	7 32.0	3 59.9	16 46.9	17 54.4	8 09.5	14 32.7	24 45.3	2 24.1	24 41.8	26 39.4
16 Sa	13 38 42	22 47 37	9♎56 05	16 37 37	7 19.6	4 46.9	18 02.0	18 37.9	8 31.5	14 45.4	24 52.6	2 27.1	24 43.0	26 41.8
17 Su	13 42 39	23 47 10	23 15 18	29 48 51	7 07.2	5 41.7	19 17.1	19 21.4	8 53.7	14 58.1	24 59.9	2 30.2	24 44.3	26 44.2
18 M	13 46 36	24 46 45	6♏18 07	12♏42 58	6 56.1	6 43.6	20 32.2	20 05.0	9 15.9	15 10.9	25 07.2	2 33.3	24 45.7	26 46.6
19 Tu	13 50 32	25 46 22	19 03 23	25 19 28	6 47.0	7 51.7	21 47.3	20 48.8	9 38.2	15 23.7	25 14.5	2 36.4	24 47.0	26 49.0
20 W	13 54 29	26 46 01	1♐31 23	7♐39 22	6 40.6	9 05.3	23 02.5	21 32.6	10 00.6	15 36.5	25 21.8	2 39.5	24 48.4	26 51.4
21 Th	13 58 25	27 45 42	13 43 46	19 45 00	6 36.9	10 23.7	24 17.6	22 16.4	10 23.0	15 49.3	25 29.1	2 42.7	24 49.8	26 53.8
22 F	14 02 22	28 45 25	25 43 32	1♑39 55	6D 35.5	11 46.1	25 32.8	23 00.4	10 45.5	16 02.2	25 36.4	2 45.9	24 51.2	26 56.3
23 Sa	14 06 18	29 45 09	7♑34 44	13 28 37	6 35.5	13 12.0	26 47.9	23 44.4	11 08.0	16 15.2	25 43.7	2 49.2	24 52.7	26 58.7
24 Su	14 10 15	0♏44 55	19 22 13	25 16 12	6R 36.1	14 40.8	28 03.1	24 28.6	11 30.6	16 28.1	25 51.0	2 52.4	24 54.2	27 01.1
25 M	14 14 11	1 44 43	1♒11 18	7♒08 10	6 36.0	16 12.0	29 18.3	25 12.7	11 53.3	16 41.1	25 58.3	2 55.7	24 55.7	27 03.5
26 Tu	14 18 08	2 44 33	13 07 29	19 09 57	6 34.5	17 45.1	0♏33.5	25 57.0	12 16.0	16 54.1	26 05.6	2 59.0	24 57.2	27 05.9
27 W	14 22 05	3 44 24	25 16 09	1♓26 41	6 30.8	19 19.8	1 48.7	26 41.3	12 38.8	17 07.1	26 12.8	3 02.3	24 58.8	27 08.3
28 Th	14 26 01	4 44 17	7♓42 03	14 02 42	6 24.8	20 55.7	3 03.9	27 25.7	13 01.7	17 20.1	26 20.1	3 05.7	25 00.4	27 10.7
29 F	14 29 58	5 44 11	20 28 58	27 01 04	6 16.6	22 32.7	4 19.1	28 10.2	13 24.6	17 33.2	26 27.3	3 09.1	25 02.0	27 13.1
30 Sa	14 33 54	6 44 07	3♈39 08	10♈23 07	6 06.9	24 10.3	5 34.3	28 54.8	13 47.5	17 46.3	26 34.6	3 12.5	25 03.6	27 15.5
31 Su	14 37 51	7 44 05	17 12 52	24 08 03	5 56.8	25 48.5	6 49.6	29 39.4	14 10.5	17 59.4	26 41.8	3 15.9	25 05.3	27 17.9

Astro Data	Dy Hr Mn
☽0N	5 21:52
♆D	5 23:36
☽0S	18 18:32
♃∠♆	19 8:35
☿R	19 11:03
⊙0S	23 8:47
☽0N	3 4:56
♀0S	4 17:08
☿D	11 5:20
♄✶♆	14 21:50
☽0S	16 3:05
☽0N	30 14:26

Planet Ingress		Dy Hr Mn
♀	♍	7 21:38
♂	♐	20 1:20
⚳	♐	22 6:32
⊙	♎	23 8:46
♀	♎	2 1:32
⊙	♏	23 17:58
♀	♏	26 1:19
♂	♑	31 23:05

Last Aspect Dy Hr Mn		☽ Ingress	Dy Hr Mn
2 6:43	♇ △	♓	2 16:11
4 13:51	♆ □	♈	5 0:24
7 4:55	♀ △	♉	7 6:27
8 21:59	♂ ☍	♊	9 10:57
11 6:26	♇ △	♋	11 14:18
13 9:13	♂ △	♌	13 16:46
15 13:51	♂ □	♍	15 18:57
17 19:24	♂ ✶	♎	17 22:03
19 19:37	♇ ☌	♏	20 3:32
22 10:45	⊙ ✶	♐	22 12:30
24 16:06	♇ ✶	♑	25 0:31
27 5:11	♇ □	♒	27 13:21
29 16:41	♇ △	♓	30 0:18

Last Aspect Dy Hr Mn		☽ Ingress	Dy Hr Mn
1 22:01	♆ □	♈	2 8:06
4 6:33	♇ ☍	♉	4 13:09
5 10:39	♃ ☍	♊	6 16:39
8 13:30	♇ △	♋	8 19:39
10 16:42	♇ □	♌	10 22:44
12 20:12	♇ ✶	♍	13 2:09
14 21:01	♆ □	♎	15 6:23
17 6:20	♇ ☌	♏	17 12:21
18 16:44	♃ ☌	♐	19 21:02
22 5:35	⊙ ✶	♑	22 8:38
24 18:19	♀ □	♒	24 21:36
27 3:37	♇ △	♓	27 9:12
29 14:13	♂ △	♈	29 17:25
31 22:00	♂ △	♉	31 22:04

☽ Phases & Eclipses Dy Hr Mn		
3 12:28	○	10♓41
10 17:19	☾	17♊40
17 12:09	●	24♍16
25 4:07	☽	1♑46
3 1:09	○	9♈30
9 23:26	☾	16♋20
17 0:04	●	23♎18
25 0:08	☽	1♒15

Astro Data

1 September 1982
Julian Day # 30194
SVP 5♓30'23"
GC 26♐35.8 ⚴ 27♎34.2
Eris 15♈28.6R ⚵ 24♐47.4
⚷ 27♉43.7 ⚶ 12♒43.1R
☽ Mean ☊ 10♋17.4

1 October 1982
Julian Day # 30224
SVP 5♓30'20"
GC 26♐35.9 ⚴ 9♏39.4
Eris 15♈12.0R ⚵ 29♐15.0
⚷ 27♉18.0R ⚶ 11♒11.5
☽ Mean ☊ 8♋42.0

November 1982 — LONGITUDE

Day	Sid.Time	☉	0 hr ☽	Noon ☽	True ☊	☿	♀	♂	⚳	♃	♄	♅	♆	♇
1 M	14 41 47	8♏44 05	1♉08 14	8♉12 52	5♋47.3	27♎27.0	8♏04.8	0♑24.1	14♐33.6	18♏12.5	26♎49.0	3♐19.3	25♐07.0	27♎20.2
2 Tu	14 45 44	9 44 07	15 21 16	22 32 42	5R39.4	29 05.7	9 20.0	1 08.8	14 56.7	18 25.7	26 56.2	3 22.8	25 08.7	27 22.6
3 W	14 49 40	10 44 11	29 46 24	7♊01 34	5 33.8	0♏44.6	10 35.3	1 53.6	15 19.8	18 38.8	27 03.4	3 26.2	25 10.4	27 25.0
4 Th	14 53 37	11 44 17	14♊17 25	21 33 14	5D30.7	2 23.5	11 50.6	2 38.5	15 43.0	18 52.0	27 10.5	3 29.7	25 12.2	27 27.4
5 F	14 57 34	12 44 24	28 48 23	6♋02 16	5 29.9	4 02.2	13 05.8	3 23.5	16 06.3	19 05.2	27 17.7	3 33.2	25 13.9	27 29.7
6 Sa	15 01 30	13 44 34	13♋14 25	20 24 28	5 30.5	5 40.9	14 21.1	4 08.5	16 29.5	19 18.4	27 24.8	3 36.8	25 15.7	27 32.1
7 Su	15 05 27	14 44 46	27 32 07	4♌37 09	5R31.6	7 19.4	15 36.4	4 53.5	16 52.9	19 31.6	27 31.9	3 40.3	25 17.5	27 34.4
8 M	15 09 23	15 45 00	11♌39 27	18 38 55	5 31.9	8 57.6	16 51.7	5 38.7	17 16.3	19 44.8	27 39.0	3 43.9	25 19.4	27 36.7
9 Tu	15 13 20	16 45 16	25 35 31	2♍29 12	5 30.7	10 35.6	18 07.0	6 23.9	17 39.7	19 58.1	27 46.0	3 47.4	25 21.2	27 39.0
10 W	15 17 16	17 45 35	9♍19 58	16 07 49	5 27.4	12 13.4	19 22.4	7 09.2	18 03.2	20 11.3	27 53.0	3 51.0	25 23.1	27 41.3
11 Th	15 21 13	18 45 55	22 52 43	29 34 39	5 21.9	13 50.9	20 37.7	7 54.5	18 26.7	20 24.6	28 00.0	3 54.6	25 25.0	27 43.6
12 F	15 25 09	19 46 16	6♎13 34	12♎49 24	5 14.8	15 28.0	21 53.0	8 39.9	18 50.2	20 37.8	28 07.0	3 58.2	25 26.9	27 45.9
13 Sa	15 29 06	20 46 40	19 22 07	25 51 39	5 06.6	17 04.9	23 08.3	9 25.3	19 13.8	20 51.1	28 14.0	4 01.9	25 28.8	27 48.2
14 Su	15 33 03	21 47 06	2♏17 55	8♏40 53	4 58.5	18 41.5	24 23.7	10 10.9	19 37.4	21 04.3	28 20.9	4 05.5	25 30.8	27 50.5
15 M	15 36 59	22 47 33	15 00 31	21 16 49	4 51.1	20 17.9	25 39.0	10 56.4	20 01.1	21 17.6	28 27.8	4 09.1	25 32.8	27 52.7
16 Tu	15 40 56	23 48 02	27 29 51	3♐39 40	4 45.2	21 53.9	26 54.4	11 42.1	20 24.8	21 30.9	28 34.6	4 12.8	25 34.7	27 54.9
17 W	15 44 52	24 48 33	9♐46 25	15 50 17	4 41.3	23 29.7	28 09.8	12 27.8	20 48.6	21 44.1	28 41.5	4 16.5	25 36.7	27 57.2
18 Th	15 48 49	25 49 05	21 51 29	27 50 19	4D39.4	25 05.2	29 25.1	13 13.5	21 12.3	21 57.4	28 48.3	4 20.1	25 38.8	27 59.4
19 F	15 52 45	26 49 38	3♑47 08	9♑42 19	4 39.3	26 40.4	0♐40.5	13 59.3	21 36.1	22 10.6	28 55.0	4 23.8	25 40.8	28 01.6
20 Sa	15 56 42	27 50 13	15 36 19	21 29 37	4 40.4	28 15.5	1 55.8	14 45.2	22 00.0	22 23.9	29 01.7	4 27.5	25 42.8	28 03.7
21 Su	16 00 38	28 50 49	27 22 46	3♒16 19	4 42.2	29 50.3	3 11.2	15 31.1	22 23.8	22 37.1	29 08.4	4 31.2	25 44.9	28 05.9
22 M	16 04 35	29 51 26	9♒10 52	15 07 03	4 43.9	1♐24.9	4 26.6	16 17.0	22 47.7	22 50.3	29 15.1	4 34.9	25 47.0	28 08.0
23 Tu	16 08 32	0♐52 05	21 05 30	27 06 52	4R44.9	2 59.3	5 41.9	17 03.0	23 11.7	23 03.6	29 21.7	4 38.6	25 49.1	28 10.2
24 W	16 12 28	1 52 44	3♓11 47	9♓20 53	4 44.6	4 33.6	6 57.3	17 49.0	23 35.6	23 16.8	29 28.2	4 42.3	25 51.2	28 12.3
25 Th	16 16 25	2 53 25	15 34 46	21 53 59	4 43.0	6 07.7	8 12.7	18 35.1	23 59.6	23 30.0	29 34.8	4 46.0	25 53.3	28 14.3
26 F	16 20 21	3 54 06	28 19 01	4♈50 17	4 39.9	7 41.6	9 28.0	19 21.2	24 23.6	23 43.1	29 41.2	4 49.7	25 55.4	28 16.4
27 Sa	16 24 18	4 54 49	11♈28 04	18 12 34	4 35.8	9 15.5	10 43.4	20 07.4	24 47.6	23 56.3	29 47.7	4 53.3	25 57.6	28 18.5
28 Su	16 28 14	5 55 33	25 03 49	2♉01 43	4 31.3	10 49.2	11 58.7	20 53.6	25 11.6	24 09.4	29 54.1	4 57.1	25 59.7	28 20.5
29 M	16 32 11	6 56 18	9♉05 58	16 16 10	4 27.0	12 22.8	13 14.1	21 39.9	25 35.7	24 22.6	0♏00.4	5 00.8	26 01.9	28 22.5
30 Tu	16 36 07	7 57 04	23 31 41	0♊51 46	4 23.4	13 56.3	14 29.5	22 26.2	25 59.8	24 35.7	0 06.7	5 04.5	26 04.0	28 24.5

December 1982 — LONGITUDE

Day	Sid.Time	☉	0 hr ☽	Noon ☽	True ☊	☿	♀	♂	⚳	♃	♄	♅	♆	♇
1 W	16 40 04	8♐57 52	8♊15 32	15♊42 01	4♋21.1	15♐29.8	15♐44.8	23♑12.5	26♐23.9	24♏48.7	0♏12.9	5♐08.2	26♐06.2	28♎26.5
2 Th	16 44 01	9 58 40	23 10 10	0♋38 57	4D20.1	17 03.2	17 00.2	23 58.9	26 48.0	25 01.8	0 19.1	5 11.9	26 08.4	28 28.4
3 F	16 47 57	10 59 30	8♋07 19	15 34 19	4 20.4	18 36.6	18 15.5	24 45.3	27 12.2	25 14.9	0 25.3	5 15.6	26 10.6	28 30.3
4 Sa	16 51 54	12 00 21	22 59 03	0♌20 43	4 21.5	20 09.9	19 30.9	25 31.7	27 36.3	25 27.9	0 31.4	5 19.2	26 12.8	28 32.2
5 Su	16 55 50	13 01 14	7♌38 43	14 52 30	4 22.9	21 43.1	20 46.3	26 18.2	28 00.5	25 40.9	0 37.4	5 22.9	26 15.0	28 34.1
6 M	16 59 47	14 02 08	22 01 42	29 06 03	4 24.2	23 16.4	22 01.6	27 04.7	28 24.7	25 53.8	0 43.4	5 26.6	26 17.3	28 36.0
7 Tu	17 03 43	15 03 03	6♍05 26	12♍59 47	4R24.8	24 49.5	23 17.0	27 51.3	28 48.9	26 06.8	0 49.3	5 30.3	26 19.5	28 37.8
8 W	17 07 40	16 03 59	19 49 10	26 33 41	4 24.4	26 22.7	24 32.4	28 37.8	29 13.1	26 19.7	0 55.2	5 33.9	26 21.7	28 39.6
9 Th	17 11 36	17 04 56	3♎13 29	9♎48 48	4 23.2	27 55.7	25 47.7	29 24.5	29 37.4	26 32.5	1 01.0	5 37.6	26 24.0	28 41.4
10 F	17 15 33	18 05 55	16 19 49	22 46 48	4 21.3	29 28.8	27 03.1	0♒11.1	0♑01.6	26 45.4	1 06.8	5 41.2	26 26.2	28 43.2
11 Sa	17 19 30	19 06 55	29 09 59	5♏29 35	4 19.1	1♑01.7	28 18.5	0 57.8	0 25.9	26 58.2	1 12.5	5 44.9	26 28.5	28 44.9
12 Su	17 23 26	20 07 56	11♏45 52	17 59 03	4 16.7	2 34.4	29 33.8	1 44.5	0 50.2	27 11.0	1 18.1	5 48.5	26 30.7	28 46.6
13 M	17 27 23	21 08 58	24 09 20	0♐16 57	4 14.7	4 07.1	0♑49.2	2 31.3	1 14.5	27 23.7	1 23.7	5 52.1	26 33.0	28 48.3
14 Tu	17 31 19	22 10 01	6♐22 06	12 24 59	4 13.2	5 39.5	2 04.6	3 18.1	1 38.8	27 36.4	1 29.2	5 55.7	26 35.2	28 49.9
15 W	17 35 16	23 11 04	18 25 49	24 24 48	4D12.4	7 11.6	3 20.0	4 04.9	2 03.1	27 49.0	1 34.7	5 59.3	26 37.5	28 51.6
16 Th	17 39 12	24 12 09	0♑22 10	6♑18 10	4 12.2	8 43.4	4 35.3	4 51.7	2 27.4	28 01.6	1 40.0	6 02.9	26 39.8	28 53.2
17 F	17 43 09	25 13 14	12 13 03	18 07 06	4 12.6	10 14.8	5 50.7	5 38.6	2 51.7	28 14.2	1 45.3	6 06.4	26 42.1	28 54.7
18 Sa	17 47 06	26 14 19	24 00 38	29 53 59	4 13.2	11 45.7	7 06.0	6 25.5	3 16.0	28 26.7	1 50.6	6 10.0	26 44.3	28 56.3
19 Su	17 51 02	27 15 25	5♒47 31	11♒41 39	4 14.1	13 15.9	8 21.4	7 12.4	3 40.3	28 39.2	1 55.8	6 13.5	26 46.6	28 57.8
20 M	17 54 59	28 16 32	17 36 49	23 33 28	4 14.8	14 45.4	9 36.8	7 59.3	4 04.7	28 51.6	2 00.9	6 17.0	26 48.9	28 59.3
21 Tu	17 58 55	29 17 38	29 32 07	5♓33 15	4 15.4	16 13.9	10 52.1	8 46.2	4 29.0	29 04.0	2 05.9	6 20.5	26 51.1	29 00.7
22 W	18 02 52	0♑18 45	11♓37 25	17 45 11	4 15.8	17 41.3	12 07.4	9 33.2	4 53.3	29 16.3	2 10.8	6 24.0	26 53.4	29 02.2
23 Th	18 06 48	1 19 52	23 57 05	0♈13 40	4R15.9	19 07.2	13 22.8	10 20.2	5 17.7	29 28.6	2 15.7	6 27.4	26 55.7	29 03.6
24 F	18 10 45	2 20 59	6♈35 27	13 02 57	4 15.8	20 31.6	14 38.1	11 07.2	5 42.0	29 40.8	2 20.5	6 30.9	26 57.9	29 04.9
25 Sa	18 14 41	3 22 06	19 36 34	26 16 41	4D15.7	21 53.9	15 53.4	11 54.2	6 06.3	29 53.0	2 25.3	6 34.3	27 00.2	29 06.3
26 Su	18 18 38	4 23 14	3♉03 34	9♉57 23	4 15.7	23 13.9	17 08.7	12 41.2	6 30.6	0♐05.1	2 29.9	6 37.7	27 02.4	29 07.6
27 M	18 22 35	5 24 21	16 58 08	24 05 40	4 15.8	24 31.2	18 24.0	13 28.3	6 54.9	0 17.1	2 34.5	6 41.1	27 04.7	29 08.8
28 Tu	18 26 31	6 25 29	1♊19 43	8♊39 45	4 15.9	25 45.2	19 39.3	14 15.3	7 19.2	0 29.1	2 39.0	6 44.4	27 06.9	29 10.1
29 W	18 30 28	7 26 36	16 05 06	23 34 57	4R16.1	26 55.4	20 54.6	15 02.4	7 43.5	0 41.0	2 43.4	6 47.7	27 09.2	29 11.3
30 Th	18 34 24	8 27 44	1♋08 16	8♋43 57	4 16.1	28 01.2	22 09.8	15 49.5	8 07.8	0 52.9	2 47.8	6 51.0	27 11.4	29 12.5
31 F	18 38 21	9 28 52	16 20 47	23 57 31	4 15.9	29 01.9	23 25.1	16 36.5	8 32.1	1 04.7	2 52.0	6 54.3	27 13.7	29 13.6

Astro Data	Planet Ingress	Last Aspect	☽ Ingress	Last Aspect	☽ Ingress	☽ Phases & Eclipses	Astro Data
Dy Hr Mn	Dy Hr Mn	Dy Hr Mn	Dy Hr Mn	Dy Hr Mn	Dy Hr Mn	Dy Hr Mn	1 November 1982
♄☌♇ 8 0:44	☿ ♏ 3 1:10	2 5:02 ♃ ☍	♊ 3 0:23	2 8:30 ♇ △	♋ 2 10:58	1 12:57 ○ 8♉46	Julian Day # 30255
☽0S 12 10:17	♀ ♐ 18 23:07	4 21:47 ♇ △	♋ 5 1:59	4 9:02 ♇ □	♌ 4 11:26	8 6:38 ☾ 15♌32	SVP 5♓30'17"
☽0N 27 1:05	☿ ♐ 21 14:28	7 0:02 ♇ □	♌ 7 4:10	6 11:09 ♇ ⚹	♍ 6 13:32	15 15:10 ● 22♏56	GC 26♐36.0 ⚵ 22♏51.0
	☉ ♐ 22 15:23	9 3:42 ♄ ⚹	♍ 9 7:40	8 15:57 ♂ △	♎ 8 18:11	23 20:06 ☽ 1♓13	Eris 14♈53.6R ⚴ 7♑27.3
♃⚺♆ 8 16:39	♄ ♏ 29 10:29	11 4:31 ♆ □	♎ 11 12:46	10 23:11 ♇ ☌	♏ 11 1:34		⚷ 26♉02.4R ⚶ 16♒15.4
☽0S 9 16:19		13 16:27 ♄ ☌	♏ 13 19:42	13 6:14 ♃ ☌	♐ 13 11:27	1 0:21 ○ 8♊28	☽ Mean ☊ 7♋03.5
♃⚺♇ 21 4:50	♂ ♒ 10 6:17	15 21:22 ♀ ☌	♐ 16 4:52	15 20:58 ♇ ⚹	♑ 15 23:15	7 15:53 ☾ 15♍13	
☽0N 24 10:30	⚳ ♑ 10 10:23	18 13:58 ♄ ⚹	♑ 18 16:21	18 10:02 ♇ □	♒ 18 12:12	15 9:18 ● 23♐04	1 December 1982
	☿ ♑ 10 20:04	21 3:56 ☿ ⚹	♒ 21 5:20	20 22:56 ♇ △	♓ 21 0:56	15 9:31:18 ● P 0.735	Julian Day # 30285
	♀ ♑ 12 20:20	23 16:29 ♄ △	♓ 23 17:43	23 10:33 ♃ △	♈ 23 11:34	23 14:17 ☽ 1♈26	SVP 5♓30'12"
	☉ ♑ 22 4:38	25 19:30 ♆ □	♈ 26 3:07	25 17:02 ♇ ☍	♉ 25 18:37	30 11:33 ○ 8♋27	GC 26♐36.0 ⚵ 5♐50.7
	♃ ♐ 26 1:57	28 8:19 ♄ ☍	♉ 28 8:31	27 12:47 ☿ △	♊ 27 21:49	30 11:29 ● T 1.182	Eris 14♈39.8R ⚴ 17♑41.9
		30 1:36 ♃ ☍	♊ 30 10:36	29 20:55 ♇ △	♋ 29 22:12		⚷ 24♉28.5R ⚶ 25♒29.0
				31 20:33 ☿ ☍	♌ 31 21:33		☽ Mean ☊ 5♋28.2

LONGITUDE — January 1983

Day	Sid.Time	☉	0 hr ☽	Noon ☽	True ☊	☿	♀	♂	⚳	♃	♄	♅	♆	♇
1 Sa	18 42 17	10♑30 00	1♌32 55	9♌05 48	4♋15.4	29♑56.7	24♑40.4	17♒23.6	8♑56.4	1♐16.4	2♏56.2	6♐57.6	27♐15.9	29♎14.7
2 Su	18 46 14	11 31 08	16 35 06	23 59 53	4R 14.7	0♒44.8	25 55.6	18 10.7	9 20.7	1 28.0	3 00.3	7 00.8	27 18.1	29 15.8
3 M	18 50 10	12 32 17	1♍19 20	8♍32 54	4 13.7	1 25.4	27 10.8	18 57.8	9 44.9	1 39.6	3 04.3	7 04.0	27 20.3	29 16.8
4 Tu	18 54 07	13 33 26	15 40 07	22 40 45	4 12.9	1 57.4	28 26.1	19 44.9	10 09.2	1 51.1	3 08.2	7 07.2	27 22.5	29 17.8
5 W	18 58 04	14 34 34	29 34 44	6♎22 07	4D 12.3	2 20.0	29 41.3	20 32.0	10 33.4	2 02.6	3 12.0	7 10.3	27 24.7	29 18.8
6 Th	19 02 00	15 35 44	13♎03 05	19 37 55	4 12.2	2R 32.4	0♒56.5	21 19.2	10 57.6	2 14.0	3 15.8	7 13.4	27 26.9	29 19.8
7 F	19 05 57	16 36 53	26 06 58	2♏30 40	4 12.7	2 33.8	2 11.7	22 06.3	11 21.9	2 25.3	3 19.4	7 16.5	27 29.1	29 20.7
8 Sa	19 09 53	17 38 03	8♏49 28	15 03 49	4 13.7	2 23.6	3 26.9	22 53.4	11 46.1	2 36.5	3 23.0	7 19.6	27 31.3	29 21.5
9 Su	19 13 50	18 39 12	21 14 14	27 21 11	4 15.0	2 01.6	4 42.1	23 40.6	12 10.2	2 47.6	3 26.5	7 22.6	27 33.4	29 22.4
10 M	19 17 46	19 40 22	3♐25 06	9♐26 28	4 16.4	1 27.9	5 57.3	24 27.7	12 34.4	2 58.7	3 29.9	7 25.6	27 35.6	29 23.2
11 Tu	19 21 43	20 41 31	15 25 42	21 23 10	4 17.5	0 42.9	7 12.5	25 14.9	12 58.6	3 09.7	3 33.2	7 28.5	27 37.7	29 24.0
12 W	19 25 39	21 42 41	27 19 16	3♑14 19	4R 18.0	29♑47.5	8 27.6	26 02.0	13 22.7	3 20.6	3 36.4	7 31.5	27 39.8	29 24.7
13 Th	19 29 36	22 43 50	9♑08 38	15 02 32	4 17.6	28 43.2	9 42.8	26 49.1	13 46.8	3 31.4	3 39.5	7 34.4	27 41.9	29 25.4
14 F	19 33 33	23 44 59	20 56 15	26 50 04	4 16.2	27 31.8	10 57.9	27 36.3	14 10.9	3 42.1	3 42.5	7 37.2	27 44.0	29 26.0
15 Sa	19 37 29	24 46 07	2♒44 14	8♒39 00	4 13.6	26 15.6	12 13.0	28 23.4	14 35.0	3 52.7	3 45.4	7 40.0	27 46.1	29 26.7
16 Su	19 41 26	25 47 15	14 34 35	20 31 16	4 10.2	24 57.1	13 28.2	29 10.6	14 59.0	4 03.3	3 48.3	7 42.8	27 48.2	29 27.3
17 M	19 45 22	26 48 22	26 29 17	2♓28 56	4 06.3	23 38.6	14 43.2	29 57.7	15 23.1	4 13.7	3 51.0	7 45.6	27 50.2	29 27.8
18 Tu	19 49 19	27 49 28	8♓30 30	14 34 18	4 02.2	22 22.6	15 58.3	0♓44.8	15 47.1	4 24.0	3 53.6	7 48.3	27 52.3	29 28.3
19 W	19 53 15	28 50 34	20 40 42	26 50 02	3 58.6	21 11.1	17 13.4	1 31.9	16 11.0	4 34.3	3 56.1	7 51.0	27 54.3	29 28.8
20 Th	19 57 12	29 51 39	3♈02 42	9♈19 06	3 55.8	20 05.9	18 28.4	2 19.1	16 35.0	4 44.4	3 58.6	7 53.6	27 56.3	29 29.3
21 F	20 01 08	0♒52 43	15 39 40	22 04 48	3D 54.2	19 08.2	19 43.4	3 06.1	16 58.9	4 54.5	4 00.9	7 56.2	27 58.3	29 29.7
22 Sa	20 05 05	1 53 46	28 34 55	5♉10 26	3 53.9	18 19.1	20 58.4	3 53.2	17 22.8	5 04.4	4 03.1	7 58.7	28 00.2	29 30.0
23 Su	20 09 02	2 54 48	11♉51 40	18 38 57	3 54.8	17 39.0	22 13.4	4 40.3	17 46.7	5 14.3	4 05.2	8 01.3	28 02.2	29 30.4
24 M	20 12 58	3 55 49	25 32 31	2♊32 27	3 56.2	17 08.0	23 28.4	5 27.4	18 10.5	5 24.0	4 07.3	8 03.7	28 04.1	29 30.7
25 Tu	20 16 55	4 56 49	9♊38 48	16 51 23	3 57.8	16 46.2	24 43.3	6 14.4	18 34.3	5 33.7	4 09.2	8 06.2	28 06.0	29 30.9
26 W	20 20 51	5 57 48	24 09 55	1♋33 54	3R 58.6	16 33.3	25 58.2	7 01.4	18 58.0	5 43.2	4 11.0	8 08.6	28 07.9	29 31.2
27 Th	20 24 48	6 58 46	9♋02 39	16 35 18	3 58.0	16D 28.7	27 13.1	7 48.5	19 21.8	5 52.6	4 12.8	8 10.9	28 09.8	29 31.4
28 F	20 28 44	7 59 43	24 10 51	1♌48 05	3 55.8	16 32.1	28 28.0	8 35.5	19 45.5	6 01.9	4 14.4	8 13.2	28 11.7	29 31.5
29 Sa	20 32 41	9 00 39	9♌25 46	17 02 34	3 51.9	16 43.0	29 42.8	9 22.4	20 09.1	6 11.1	4 15.9	8 15.5	28 13.5	29 31.6
30 Su	20 36 38	10 01 34	24 37 10	2♍08 21	3 46.7	17 00.6	0♓57.6	10 09.4	20 32.8	6 20.2	4 17.3	8 17.7	28 15.3	29 31.7
31 M	20 40 34	11 02 28	9♍34 57	16 56 00	3 40.8	17 24.6	2 12.4	10 56.3	20 56.3	6 29.2	4 18.6	8 19.9	28 17.1	29R 31.8

LONGITUDE — February 1983

Day	Sid.Time	☉	0 hr ☽	Noon ☽	True ☊	☿	♀	♂	⚳	♃	♄	♅	♆	♇
1 Tu	20 44 31	12♒03 21	24♍10 45	1♎18 36	3♋35.2	17♑54.3	3♓27.1	11♓43.3	21♑19.9	6♐38.0	4♏19.9	8♐22.0	28♐18.9	29♎31.8
2 W	20 48 27	13 04 13	8♎19 11	15 12 21	3R 30.6	18 29.3	4 41.9	12 30.2	21 43.4	6 46.8	4 21.0	8 24.1	28 20.7	29R 31.7
3 Th	20 52 24	14 05 05	21 58 08	28 36 42	3 27.5	19 09.1	5 56.6	13 17.1	22 06.9	6 55.4	4 22.0	8 26.2	28 22.4	29 31.7
4 F	20 56 20	15 05 56	5♏08 23	11♏33 37	3D 26.2	19 53.3	7 11.3	14 03.9	22 30.3	7 03.9	4 22.9	8 28.2	28 24.1	29 31.6
5 Sa	21 00 17	16 06 46	17 52 56	24 06 53	3 26.5	20 41.5	8 25.9	14 50.8	22 53.7	7 12.2	4 23.6	8 30.1	28 25.8	29 31.5
6 Su	21 04 13	17 07 35	0♐16 05	6♐21 12	3 27.7	21 33.3	9 40.6	15 37.6	23 17.0	7 20.5	4 24.3	8 32.0	28 27.4	29 31.3
7 M	21 08 10	18 08 23	12 22 50	18 21 37	3 29.3	22 28.4	10 55.2	16 24.4	23 40.3	7 28.6	4 24.9	8 33.9	28 29.1	29 31.1
8 Tu	21 12 06	19 09 10	24 18 10	0♑13 03	3R 30.3	23 26.6	12 09.8	17 11.2	24 03.6	7 36.6	4 25.4	8 35.7	28 30.7	29 30.8
9 W	21 16 03	20 09 56	6♑06 49	11 59 59	3 29.9	24 27.6	13 24.3	17 58.0	24 26.8	7 44.4	4 25.8	8 37.5	28 32.3	29 30.6
10 Th	21 20 00	21 10 41	17 52 59	23 46 14	3 27.5	25 31.2	14 38.8	18 44.7	24 50.0	7 52.1	4 26.0	8 39.2	28 33.8	29 30.3
11 F	21 23 56	22 11 25	29 40 08	5♒34 59	3 22.8	26 37.1	15 53.3	19 31.5	25 13.1	7 59.7	4R 26.2	8 40.8	28 35.4	29 29.9
12 Sa	21 27 53	23 12 07	11♒31 04	17 28 38	3 15.7	27 45.2	17 07.8	20 18.2	25 36.2	8 07.1	4 26.2	8 42.5	28 36.9	29 29.5
13 Su	21 31 49	24 12 48	23 27 53	29 29 00	3 06.7	28 55.3	18 22.2	21 04.8	25 59.2	8 14.4	4 26.2	8 44.0	28 38.4	29 29.1
14 M	21 35 46	25 13 28	5♓32 08	11♓37 25	2 56.5	0♒07.3	19 36.6	21 51.5	26 22.2	8 21.6	4 26.0	8 45.5	28 39.8	29 28.7
15 Tu	21 39 42	26 14 06	17 44 58	23 54 55	2 45.9	1 21.0	20 51.0	22 38.1	26 45.1	8 28.6	4 25.7	8 47.0	28 41.3	29 28.2
16 W	21 43 39	27 14 43	0♈07 23	6♈22 31	2 36.1	2 36.5	22 05.3	23 24.7	27 07.9	8 35.5	4 25.4	8 48.4	28 42.7	29 27.7
17 Th	21 47 35	28 15 17	12 40 28	19 01 25	2 27.9	3 53.5	23 19.6	24 11.2	27 30.7	8 42.2	4 24.9	8 49.8	28 44.0	29 27.1
18 F	21 51 32	29 15 50	25 25 34	1♉53 09	2 22.0	5 11.9	24 33.9	24 57.8	27 53.4	8 48.7	4 24.3	8 51.1	28 45.4	29 26.5
19 Sa	21 55 29	0♓16 22	8♉24 25	14 59 38	2 18.5	6 31.8	25 48.1	25 44.3	28 16.1	8 55.2	4 23.6	8 52.3	28 46.7	29 25.9
20 Su	21 59 25	1 16 51	21 39 03	28 22 58	2D 17.3	7 53.1	27 02.2	26 30.7	28 38.7	9 01.4	4 22.8	8 53.5	28 48.0	29 25.3
21 M	22 03 22	2 17 19	5♊11 37	12♊05 12	2 17.6	9 15.6	28 16.4	27 17.2	29 01.3	9 07.6	4 21.9	8 54.7	28 49.3	29 24.6
22 Tu	22 07 18	3 17 45	19 03 52	26 07 41	2R 18.3	10 39.4	29 30.5	28 03.5	29 23.8	9 13.5	4 20.9	8 55.8	28 50.5	29 23.9
23 W	22 11 15	4 18 09	3♋16 36	10♋30 26	2 18.1	12 04.3	0♈44.5	28 49.9	29 46.2	9 19.3	4 19.9	8 56.8	28 51.7	29 23.1
24 Th	22 15 11	5 18 31	17 48 51	25 11 22	2 16.1	13 30.5	1 58.5	29 36.2	0♒08.6	9 25.0	4 18.7	8 57.8	28 52.9	29 22.4
25 F	22 19 08	6 18 51	2♌37 19	10♌05 51	2 11.6	14 57.8	3 12.4	0♈22.5	0 30.9	9 30.5	4 17.4	8 58.8	28 54.0	29 21.5
26 Sa	22 23 04	7 19 09	17 36 00	25 06 40	2 04.3	16 26.2	4 26.3	1 08.8	0 53.1	9 35.8	4 16.0	8 59.7	28 55.2	29 20.7
27 Su	22 27 01	8 19 25	2♍36 39	10♍04 46	1 54.9	17 55.8	5 40.2	1 55.0	1 15.2	9 41.0	4 14.5	9 00.5	28 56.2	29 19.8
28 M	22 30 58	9 19 40	17 29 50	24 50 45	1 44.2	19 26.4	6 54.0	2 41.1	1 37.3	9 46.0	4 12.9	9 01.3	28 57.3	29 18.9

Astro Data	Planet Ingress	Last Aspect	☽ Ingress	Last Aspect	☽ Ingress	☽ Phases & Eclipses	Astro Data
Dy Hr Mn	Dy Hr Mn	Dy Hr Mn	Dy Hr Mn	Dy Hr Mn	Dy Hr Mn	Dy Hr Mn	1 January 1983
☽0S 5 22:30	☿ ♒ 1 13:32	2 20:37 ♇ ⚹	♍ 2 21:49	1 6:56 ♆ □	♎ 1 9:47	6 4:00 ☾ 15♎15	Julian Day # 30316
☿R 7 2:57	♀ ♒ 5 17:58	4 23:00 ♀ △	♎ 5 0:44	3 13:40 ♇ ☌	♏ 3 14:32	14 5:08 ● 23♑27	SVP 5♓30'06"
♃⚺♄ 14 13:20	☿ ♑R 12 6:55	7 6:02 ♇ ☌	♏ 7 7:16	5 4:55 ☿ ⚹	♐ 5 23:28	22 5:33 ☽ 1♉37	GC 26♐36.1 ⚴ 19♐02.8
☽0N 20 17:15	♂ ♓ 17 13:10	9 4:17 ♂ □	♐ 9 17:14	8 10:34 ♇ ⚹	♑ 8 11:33	28 22:26 ○ 8♌26	Eris 14♈34.1R ⚵ 29♑49.2
☿D 27 13:26	☉ ♒ 20 15:17	12 4:14 ♇ ⚹	♑ 12 5:26	10 23:40 ♇ □	♒ 11 0:40		⚷ 23♉09.1R ⚶ 7♓34.6
	♀ ♓ 29 17:31	14 17:17 ♇ □	♒ 14 18:26	13 12:00 ♇ △	♓ 13 13:02	4 19:17 ☾ 15♏24	☽ Mean ☊ 3♋49.7
♇R 1 5:53		17 6:37 ♂ ☌	♓ 17 7:02	15 21:15 ♆ □	♈ 15 23:46	13 0:32 ● 23♒44	
☽0S 2 6:18	☿ ♒ 14 9:36	19 16:15 ☉ ⚹	♈ 19 18:08	18 7:29 ♇ ☍	♉ 18 8:30	20 17:32 ☽ 1♊31	1 February 1983
♄R 12 11:17	☉ ♓ 19 5:31	22 1:41 ♇ ☍	♉ 22 2:36	20 9:22 ♀ ⚹	♊ 20 14:52	27 8:58 ○ 8♍12	Julian Day # 30347
☽0N 16 22:10	♀ ♈ 22 21:35	23 18:52 ♀ □	♊ 24 7:40	22 18:14 ♀ □	♋ 22 18:31		SVP 5♓30'01"
♃☌♅ 18 22:41	⚳ ♒ 24 2:49	26 8:42 ♇ △	♋ 26 9:28	24 19:32 ♂ △	♌ 24 19:47		GC 26♐36.2 ⚴ 1♑28.7
♀0N 24 18:24	♂ ♈ 25 0:19	28 8:25 ♇ □	♌ 28 9:10	26 18:46 ♇ ⚹	♍ 26 19:49		Eris 14♈39.1 ⚵ 12♒55.5
♂0N 26 19:50		30 7:49 ♇ ⚹	♍ 30 8:35	28 18:47 ♆ □	♎ 28 20:30		⚷ 22♉39.9 ⚶ 21♓04.1
							☽ Mean ☊ 2♋11.3

March 1983 LONGITUDE

Day	Sid.Time	☉	0 hr ☽	Noon ☽	True ☊	☿	♀	♂	⚳	♃	♄	♅	♆	♇
1 Tu	22 34 54	10♓19 53	2♎06 32	9♎16 24	1♋33.6	20♒58.1	8♈07.7	3♈27.3	1♒59.4	9♐50.9	4♏11.2	9♐02.0	28♐58.3	29♎18.0
2 W	22 38 51	11 20 04	16 19 44	23 16 06	1R 24.2	22 31.0	9 21.4	4 13.4	2 21.3	9 55.6	4R 09.4	9 02.7	28 59.3	29R 17.1
3 Th	22 42 47	12 20 14	0♏05 17	6♏47 17	1 17.0	24 04.8	10 35.1	4 59.4	2 43.2	10 00.1	4 07.5	9 03.3	29 00.3	29 16.1
4 F	22 46 44	13 20 22	13 22 15	19 50 27	1 12.2	25 39.8	11 48.7	5 45.5	3 05.0	10 04.5	4 05.6	9 03.9	29 01.2	29 15.1
5 Sa	22 50 40	14 20 28	26 12 19	2♐28 22	1 09.8	27 15.9	13 02.2	6 31.5	3 26.7	10 08.6	4 03.5	9 04.4	29 02.1	29 14.0
6 Su	22 54 37	15 20 34	8♐39 13	14 45 29	1D 09.2	28 53.0	14 15.7	7 17.4	3 48.4	10 12.7	4 01.3	9 04.9	29 03.0	29 13.0
7 M	22 58 33	16 20 37	20 47 51	26 47 02	1R 09.4	0♓31.3	15 29.2	8 03.3	4 10.0	10 16.5	3 59.1	9 05.3	29 03.8	29 11.9
8 Tu	23 02 30	17 20 39	2♑43 44	8♑38 37	1 09.2	2 10.6	16 42.6	8 49.2	4 31.5	10 20.2	3 56.7	9 05.6	29 04.6	29 10.7
9 W	23 06 27	18 20 39	14 32 22	20 25 36	1 07.6	3 51.1	17 56.0	9 35.1	4 52.9	10 23.7	3 54.3	9 05.9	29 05.4	29 09.6
10 Th	23 10 23	19 20 38	26 18 56	2♒12 54	1 03.8	5 32.6	19 09.3	10 20.9	5 14.2	10 27.0	3 51.8	9 06.2	29 06.1	29 08.4
11 F	23 14 20	20 20 35	8♒08 02	14 04 45	0 57.1	7 15.4	20 22.5	11 06.6	5 35.5	10 30.1	3 49.2	9 06.4	29 06.8	29 07.2
12 Sa	23 18 16	21 20 30	20 03 27	26 04 27	0 47.6	8 59.2	21 35.7	11 52.4	5 56.6	10 33.1	3 46.5	9 06.5	29 07.5	29 06.0
13 Su	23 22 13	22 20 23	2♓08 01	8♓14 22	0 35.6	10 44.2	22 48.9	12 38.0	6 17.7	10 35.8	3 43.7	9 06.6	29 08.1	29 04.8
14 M	23 26 09	23 20 14	14 23 37	20 35 53	0 22.0	12 30.4	24 02.0	13 23.7	6 38.7	10 38.4	3 40.8	9R 06.6	29 08.7	29 03.5
15 Tu	23 30 06	24 20 04	26 51 10	3♈09 31	0 08.0	14 17.8	25 15.0	14 09.3	6 59.6	10 40.9	3 37.9	9 06.6	29 09.3	29 02.2
16 W	23 34 02	25 19 51	9♈30 51	15 55 08	29♊54.7	16 06.4	26 28.0	14 54.8	7 20.4	10 43.1	3 34.8	9 06.5	29 09.9	29 00.9
17 Th	23 37 59	26 19 36	22 22 19	28 52 19	29 43.4	17 56.2	27 40.9	15 40.3	7 41.1	10 45.1	3 31.7	9 06.4	29 10.4	28 59.6
18 F	23 41 56	27 19 19	5♉25 07	12♉00 39	29 34.8	19 47.1	28 53.7	16 25.8	8 01.7	10 47.0	3 28.6	9 06.2	29 10.8	28 58.2
19 Sa	23 45 52	28 19 00	18 38 56	25 20 00	29 29.3	21 39.3	0♉06.5	17 11.2	8 22.2	10 48.7	3 25.3	9 06.0	29 11.3	28 56.8
20 Su	23 49 49	29 18 39	2♊03 54	8♊50 43	29 26.6	23 32.7	1 19.2	17 56.6	8 42.7	10 50.2	3 22.0	9 05.7	29 11.7	28 55.4
21 M	23 53 45	0♈18 16	15 40 32	22 33 28	29 25.8	25 27.3	2 31.9	18 41.9	9 03.0	10 51.5	3 18.6	9 05.3	29 12.0	28 54.0
22 Tu	23 57 42	1 17 50	29 29 36	6♋29 01	29 25.7	27 23.1	3 44.5	19 27.2	9 23.2	10 52.6	3 15.1	9 04.9	29 12.4	28 52.6
23 W	0 01 38	2 17 22	13♋31 42	20 37 36	29 25.0	29 20.0	4 57.0	20 12.5	9 43.3	10 53.5	3 11.6	9 04.5	29 12.7	28 51.1
24 Th	0 05 35	3 16 51	27 46 35	4♌58 24	29 22.5	1♈18.0	6 09.4	20 57.7	10 03.3	10 54.3	3 08.0	9 04.0	29 13.0	28 49.7
25 F	0 09 31	4 16 19	12♌12 41	19 28 56	29 17.4	3 17.1	7 21.8	21 42.8	10 23.2	10 54.8	3 04.3	9 03.5	29 13.2	28 48.2
26 Sa	0 13 28	5 15 43	26 46 32	4♍04 45	29 09.5	5 17.2	8 34.1	22 27.9	10 43.0	10 55.2	3 00.6	9 02.9	29 13.4	28 46.7
27 Su	0 17 25	6 15 06	11♍22 46	18 39 42	28 59.2	7 18.1	9 46.3	23 12.9	11 02.7	10R 55.4	2 56.8	9 02.2	29 13.6	28 45.2
28 M	0 21 21	7 14 27	25 54 37	3♎06 39	28 47.4	9 19.9	10 58.4	23 57.9	11 22.2	10 55.4	2 52.9	9 01.5	29 13.7	28 43.6
29 Tu	0 25 18	8 13 45	10♎14 57	17 18 44	28 35.6	11 22.2	12 10.5	24 42.9	11 41.7	10 55.2	2 49.0	9 00.8	29 13.8	28 42.1
30 W	0 29 14	9 13 01	24 17 22	1♏10 22	28 24.9	13 25.1	13 22.4	25 27.8	12 01.0	10 54.8	2 45.1	9 00.0	29 13.9	28 40.5
31 Th	0 33 11	10 12 16	7♏57 23	14 38 13	28 16.2	15 28.2	14 34.3	26 12.6	12 20.3	10 54.3	2 41.1	8 59.1	29R 13.9	28 39.0

April 1983 LONGITUDE

Day	Sid.Time	☉	0 hr ☽	Noon ☽	True ☊	☿	♀	♂	⚳	♃	♄	♅	♆	♇
1 F	0 37 07	11♈11 29	21♏12 50	27♏41 22	28♊10.3	17♈31.4	15♉46.2	26♈57.4	12♒39.4	10♐53.5	2♏37.0	8♐58.2	29♐13.9	28♎37.4
2 Sa	0 41 04	12 10 39	4♐04 03	10♐21 15	28R 06.9	19 34.4	16 57.9	27 42.2	12 58.4	10R 52.6	2R 32.9	8R 57.3	29R 13.9	28R 35.8
3 Su	0 45 00	13 09 49	16 33 26	22 41 06	28D 05.7	21 36.9	18 09.6	28 26.9	13 17.2	10 51.5	2 28.8	8 56.3	29 13.9	28 34.2
4 M	0 48 57	14 08 56	28 44 53	4♑45 24	28R 05.7	23 38.6	19 21.2	29 11.6	13 36.0	10 50.2	2 24.6	8 55.2	29 13.8	28 32.6
5 Tu	0 52 53	15 08 02	10♑43 19	16 39 20	28 05.8	25 39.2	20 32.7	29 56.2	13 54.6	10 48.7	2 20.3	8 54.2	29 13.6	28 30.9
6 W	0 56 50	16 07 05	22 34 09	28 28 25	28 05.1	27 38.3	21 44.1	0♉40.8	14 13.1	10 47.0	2 16.1	8 53.0	29 13.5	28 29.3
7 Th	1 00 47	17 06 07	4♒22 50	10♒18 00	28 02.5	29 35.6	22 55.4	1 25.3	14 31.5	10 45.1	2 11.7	8 51.9	29 13.3	28 27.6
8 F	1 04 43	18 05 08	16 14 34	22 13 04	27 57.6	1♉30.6	24 06.7	2 09.8	14 49.7	10 43.1	2 07.4	8 50.6	29 13.1	28 26.0
9 Sa	1 08 40	19 04 06	28 14 01	4♓17 51	27 50.1	3 23.0	25 17.9	2 54.2	15 07.8	10 40.9	2 03.0	8 49.4	29 12.8	28 24.3
10 Su	1 12 36	20 03 02	10♓24 58	16 35 40	27 40.4	5 12.5	26 29.0	3 38.6	15 25.7	10 38.4	1 58.6	8 48.0	29 12.5	28 22.7
11 M	1 16 33	21 01 57	22 50 11	29 08 41	27 29.1	6 58.7	27 40.0	4 22.9	15 43.5	10 35.8	1 54.2	8 46.7	29 12.2	28 21.0
12 Tu	1 20 29	22 00 50	5♈31 12	11♈57 45	27 17.4	8 41.3	28 50.9	5 07.2	16 01.2	10 33.1	1 49.7	8 45.3	29 11.8	28 19.3
13 W	1 24 26	22 59 40	18 28 16	25 02 34	27 06.2	10 20.0	0♊01.7	5 51.4	16 18.7	10 30.1	1 45.2	8 43.8	29 11.5	28 17.6
14 Th	1 28 22	23 58 29	1♉40 29	8♉21 46	26 56.7	11 54.5	1 12.4	6 35.6	16 36.1	10 27.0	1 40.7	8 42.3	29 11.0	28 15.9
15 F	1 32 19	24 57 16	15 06 09	21 53 22	26 49.6	13 24.6	2 23.0	7 19.7	16 53.3	10 23.7	1 36.2	8 40.8	29 10.6	28 14.2
16 Sa	1 36 16	25 56 01	28 43 06	5♊35 08	26 45.2	14 50.1	3 33.6	8 03.8	17 10.4	10 20.2	1 31.6	8 39.3	29 10.1	28 12.5
17 Su	1 40 12	26 54 43	12♊29 12	19 25 06	26D 43.4	16 10.8	4 44.0	8 47.9	17 27.3	10 16.6	1 27.1	8 37.6	29 09.6	28 10.9
18 M	1 44 09	27 53 24	26 22 39	3♋21 43	26 43.3	17 26.4	5 54.3	9 31.9	17 44.1	10 12.7	1 22.5	8 36.0	29 09.1	28 09.2
19 Tu	1 48 05	28 52 02	10♋22 09	17 23 51	26R 44.0	18 37.0	7 04.5	10 15.8	18 00.7	10 08.8	1 17.9	8 34.3	29 08.5	28 07.5
20 W	1 52 02	29 50 38	24 26 43	1♌30 37	26 44.4	19 42.3	8 14.6	10 59.7	18 17.2	10 04.6	1 13.4	8 32.6	29 07.9	28 05.8
21 Th	1 55 58	0♉49 12	8♌35 25	15 40 56	26 43.4	20 42.2	9 24.6	11 43.5	18 33.4	10 00.3	1 08.8	8 30.8	29 07.3	28 04.1
22 F	1 59 55	1 47 43	22 46 57	29 53 10	26 40.3	21 36.6	10 34.5	12 27.3	18 49.6	9 55.8	1 04.2	8 29.0	29 06.6	28 02.4
23 Sa	2 03 51	2 46 13	6♍59 15	14♍04 48	26 35.1	22 25.5	11 44.3	13 11.0	19 05.5	9 51.2	0 59.6	8 27.2	29 05.9	28 00.7
24 Su	2 07 48	3 44 40	21 09 20	28 12 23	26 27.9	23 08.8	12 53.9	13 54.7	19 21.3	9 46.4	0 55.0	8 25.3	29 05.2	27 59.0
25 M	2 11 45	4 43 05	5♎13 25	12♎11 53	26 19.6	23 46.5	14 03.4	14 38.3	19 36.9	9 41.5	0 50.5	8 23.5	29 04.4	27 57.3
26 Tu	2 15 41	5 41 28	19 07 17	25 59 07	26 11.1	24 18.4	15 12.8	15 21.9	19 52.3	9 36.5	0 45.9	8 21.5	29 03.7	27 55.6
27 W	2 19 38	6 39 49	2♏46 59	9♏30 29	26 03.4	24 44.6	16 22.1	16 05.4	20 07.6	9 31.2	0 41.4	8 19.6	29 02.9	27 54.0
28 Th	2 23 34	7 38 08	16 09 23	22 43 28	25 57.3	25 05.1	17 31.3	16 48.8	20 22.7	9 25.9	0 36.8	8 17.6	29 02.0	27 52.3
29 F	2 27 31	8 36 26	29 12 42	5♐37 04	25 53.2	25 20.0	18 40.3	17 32.2	20 37.6	9 20.4	0 32.3	8 15.5	29 01.2	27 50.6
30 Sa	2 31 27	9 34 42	11♐56 43	18 11 51	25D 51.2	25 29.2	19 49.2	18 15.6	20 52.3	9 14.8	0 27.8	8 13.5	29 00.3	27 49.0

Astro Data	Dy Hr Mn
☽0S	1 15:53
♆✶♇	11 17:16
♅R	14 13:03
☽0N	16 3:33
☉0N	21 4:39
☿0N	25 10:26
♃R	27 23:56
☽0S	29 1:54
♆R	1 4:28
☽0N	12 10:56
☽0S	25 10:44

Planet Ingress		Dy Hr Mn
☿	♓	7 4:24
☊	♊R	16 2:05
♀	♉	19 9:51
☉	♈	21 4:39
☿	♈	23 20:09
♂	♉	5 14:03
☿	♉	7 17:04
♀	♊	13 11:26
☉	♉	20 15:50

Last Aspect Dy Hr Mn			☽ Ingress	Dy Hr Mn
2 22:34	♇	☌	♏	2 23:51
5 0:34	☿	□	♐	5 7:15
7 16:51	♇	✶	♑	7 18:29
10 5:46	♇	□	♒	10 7:30
12 18:03	♆	✶	♓	12 19:47
15 4:23	♆	□	♈	15 6:00
17 12:33	♆	△	♉	17 14:04
19 17:45	☉	✶	♊	19 20:20
21 23:30	♆	☍	♋	22 0:52
24 1:47	♇	□	♌	24 3:43
26 4:01	♆	△	♍	26 5:18
28 5:31	♆	□	♎	28 6:48
30 8:36	♆	✶	♏	30 9:57

Last Aspect Dy Hr Mn			☽ Ingress	Dy Hr Mn
31 11:52	♀	☍	♐	1 16:20
4 0:58	♆	☌	♑	4 2:30
6 12:02	♇	□	♒	6 15:06
9 1:57	♆	✶	♓	9 3:30
11 12:07	♆	□	♈	11 13:37
13 19:31	♆	△	♉	13 20:59
14 19:08	☿	☌	♊	16 2:15
18 4:46	♆	☍	♋	18 6:14
20 8:58	☉	□	♌	20 9:26
22 10:41	♆	△	♍	22 12:12
24 13:30	♆	□	♎	24 15:04
26 17:25	♆	✶	♏	26 19:04
28 16:27	☿	☍	♐	29 1:28

☽ Phases & Eclipses Dy Hr Mn		
6 13:16	☾	15♐24
14 17:43	●	23♓35
22 2:25	☽	0♋54
28 19:27	○	7♎33
5 8:38	☾	15♑00
13 7:58	●	22♈50
20 8:58	☽	29♋43
27 6:31	○	6♏26

Astro Data

1 March 1983
Julian Day # 30375
SVP 5♓29'58"
GC 26♐36.2 ⚴ 11♑27.3
Eris 14♈51.7 ⚵ 25♒14.8
⚷ 23♉07.0 ⚶ 3♈49.6
☽ Mean ☊ 0♋42.3

1 April 1983
Julian Day # 30406
SVP 5♓29'55"
GC 26♐36.3 ⚴ 20♑10.3
Eris 15♈11.1 ⚵ 9♓06.6
⚷ 24♉29.5 ⚶ 18♈08.3
☽ Mean ☊ 29♊03.8

LONGITUDE — May 1983

Day	Sid.Time	☉	0 hr ☽	Noon ☽	True ☊	☿	♀	♂	⚳	♃	♄	♅	♆	♇
1 Su	2 35 24	10♉32 57	24♐22 46	0♑29 52	25♊51.0	25♉32.9	20♊57.9	18♉58.9	21♒06.8	9♐09.0	0♏23.4	8♐11.4	28♐59.4	27♎47.4
2 M	2 39 20	11 31 10	6♑33 34	12 34 23	25 52.0	25R 31.3	22 06.6	19 42.2	21 21.1	9R 03.1	0R 18.9	8R 09.3	28R 58.5	27R 45.7
3 Tu	2 43 17	12 29 21	18 32 52	24 29 36	25 53.5	25 24.5	23 15.0	20 25.4	21 35.3	8 57.1	0 14.5	8 07.2	28 57.5	27 44.1
4 W	2 47 14	13 27 31	0♒25 11	6♒20 16	25R 54.7	25 12.8	24 23.4	21 08.6	21 49.2	8 51.0	0 10.1	8 05.0	28 56.5	27 42.5
5 Th	2 51 10	14 25 39	12 15 29	18 11 28	25 54.9	24 56.5	25 31.6	21 51.7	22 03.0	8 44.7	0 05.7	8 02.8	28 55.5	27 40.9
6 F	2 55 07	15 23 46	24 08 52	0♓08 16	25 53.6	24 35.9	26 39.7	22 34.8	22 16.5	8 38.4	0 01.3	8 00.6	28 54.5	27 39.3
7 Sa	2 59 03	16 21 52	6♓10 17	12 15 28	25 50.6	24 11.5	27 47.6	23 17.8	22 29.8	8 31.9	29♎57.0	7 58.4	28 53.4	27 37.7
8 Su	3 03 00	17 19 56	18 24 17	24 37 11	25 46.2	23 43.7	28 55.4	24 00.8	22 43.0	8 25.3	29 52.8	7 56.1	28 52.3	27 36.1
9 M	3 06 56	18 17 59	0♈54 33	7♈16 39	25 40.6	23 13.1	0♋03.0	24 43.7	22 55.9	8 18.6	29 48.5	7 53.8	28 51.2	27 34.5
10 Tu	3 10 53	19 16 00	13 43 43	20 15 50	25 34.5	22 40.2	1 10.4	25 26.5	23 08.5	8 11.9	29 44.3	7 51.5	28 50.1	27 33.0
11 W	3 14 49	20 14 00	26 53 00	3♉35 09	25 28.6	22 05.7	2 17.8	26 09.4	23 21.0	8 05.0	29 40.2	7 49.2	28 48.9	27 31.4
12 Th	3 18 46	21 11 58	10♉22 04	17 13 29	25 23.7	21 30.0	3 24.9	26 52.1	23 33.3	7 58.0	29 36.1	7 46.9	28 47.7	27 29.9
13 F	3 22 43	22 09 55	24 09 00	1♊08 13	25 20.2	20 54.0	4 31.9	27 34.9	23 45.3	7 51.0	29 32.0	7 44.5	28 46.5	27 28.4
14 Sa	3 26 39	23 07 51	8♊10 36	15 15 39	25D 18.3	20 18.2	5 38.7	28 17.6	23 57.1	7 43.9	29 28.0	7 42.2	28 45.3	27 26.9
15 Su	3 30 36	24 05 45	22 22 50	29 31 34	25 18.0	19 43.2	6 45.3	29 00.2	24 08.6	7 36.7	29 24.1	7 39.8	28 44.1	27 25.5
16 M	3 34 32	25 03 37	6♋41 20	13♋51 39	25 18.9	19 09.6	7 51.8	29 42.8	24 19.9	7 29.5	29 20.2	7 37.4	28 42.8	27 24.0
17 Tu	3 38 29	26 01 27	21 02 02	28 12 04	25 20.3	18 38.0	8 58.1	0♊25.3	24 31.0	7 22.1	29 16.3	7 35.0	28 41.5	27 22.6
18 W	3 42 25	26 59 16	5♌21 23	12♌29 38	25 21.6	18 08.9	10 04.1	1 07.8	24 41.9	7 14.8	29 12.5	7 32.6	28 40.2	27 21.1
19 Th	3 46 22	27 57 03	19 36 32	26 41 50	25R 22.2	17 42.7	11 10.0	1 50.2	24 52.4	7 07.4	29 08.8	7 30.1	28 38.9	27 19.7
20 F	3 50 18	28 54 48	3♍45 18	10♍46 43	25 21.7	17 19.9	12 15.7	2 32.6	25 02.8	6 59.9	29 05.1	7 27.7	28 37.6	27 18.4
21 Sa	3 54 15	29 52 32	17 45 53	24 42 37	25 20.1	17 00.7	13 21.1	3 14.9	25 12.9	6 52.4	29 01.5	7 25.2	28 36.2	27 17.0
22 Su	3 58 12	0♊50 14	1♎36 45	8♎28 07	25 17.4	16 45.4	14 26.4	3 57.1	25 22.7	6 44.9	28 58.0	7 22.8	28 34.8	27 15.7
23 M	4 02 08	1 47 54	15 16 31	22 01 49	25 14.2	16 34.3	15 31.4	4 39.4	25 32.3	6 37.3	28 54.5	7 20.3	28 33.5	27 14.3
24 Tu	4 06 05	2 45 33	28 43 51	5♏22 30	25 10.8	16 27.5	16 36.2	5 21.5	25 41.6	6 29.7	28 51.1	7 17.8	28 32.1	27 13.0
25 W	4 10 01	3 43 10	11♏57 37	18 29 08	25 07.8	16D 25.1	17 40.8	6 03.6	25 50.6	6 22.1	28 47.7	7 15.4	28 30.6	27 11.7
26 Th	4 13 58	4 40 47	24 57 00	1♐21 11	25 05.5	16 27.2	18 45.1	6 45.7	25 59.4	6 14.5	28 44.5	7 12.9	28 29.2	27 10.5
27 F	4 17 54	5 38 22	7♐41 42	13 58 37	25D 04.2	16 33.8	19 49.2	7 27.7	26 07.9	6 06.8	28 41.3	7 10.4	28 27.8	27 09.3
28 Sa	4 21 51	6 35 56	20 12 03	26 22 10	25 03.8	16 45.0	20 53.0	8 09.7	26 16.1	5 59.2	28 38.1	7 07.9	28 26.3	27 08.0
29 Su	4 25 47	7 33 28	2♑29 11	8♑33 22	25 04.3	17 00.6	21 56.6	8 51.6	26 24.1	5 51.6	28 35.1	7 05.4	28 24.8	27 06.9
30 M	4 29 44	8 31 00	14 35 01	20 34 30	25 05.4	17 20.6	22 59.9	9 33.5	26 31.8	5 43.9	28 32.1	7 02.9	28 23.3	27 05.7
31 Tu	4 33 41	9 28 31	26 32 13	2♒28 36	25 06.7	17 44.9	24 02.9	10 15.3	26 39.2	5 36.3	28 29.2	7 00.5	28 21.8	27 04.6

LONGITUDE — June 1983

Day	Sid.Time	☉	0 hr ☽	Noon ☽	True ☊	☿	♀	♂	⚳	♃	♄	♅	♆	♇
1 W	4 37 37	10♊26 01	8♒24 09	14♒19 22	25♊08.0	18♉13.6	25♋05.7	10♊57.1	26♒46.3	5♐28.7	28♎26.4	6♐58.0	28♐20.3	27♎03.4
2 Th	4 41 34	11 23 31	20 14 47	26 10 58	25 09.0	18 46.4	26 08.2	11 38.9	26 53.1	5R 21.2	28R 23.7	6R 55.5	28R 18.8	27R 02.3
3 F	4 45 30	12 20 59	2♓08 29	8♓07 55	25R 09.5	19 23.3	27 10.4	12 20.6	26 59.6	5 13.6	28 21.0	6 53.0	28 17.3	27 01.3
4 Sa	4 49 27	13 18 27	14 09 51	20 14 52	25 09.5	20 04.1	28 12.3	13 02.2	27 05.8	5 06.1	28 18.4	6 50.6	28 15.7	27 00.2
5 Su	4 53 23	14 15 54	26 23 31	2♈36 20	25 08.9	20 48.9	29 13.8	13 43.8	27 11.7	4 58.6	28 15.9	6 48.1	28 14.2	26 59.2
6 M	4 57 20	15 13 20	8♈53 48	15 16 20	25 08.0	21 37.5	0♌15.1	14 25.4	27 17.3	4 51.1	28 13.5	6 45.6	28 12.6	26 58.2
7 Tu	5 01 16	16 10 46	21 44 19	28 18 02	25 06.9	22 29.7	1 16.1	15 06.9	27 22.6	4 43.8	28 11.2	6 43.2	28 11.0	26 57.3
8 W	5 05 13	17 08 11	4♉57 39	11♉43 15	25 05.8	23 25.6	2 16.7	15 48.3	27 27.5	4 36.4	28 09.0	6 40.7	28 09.5	26 56.3
9 Th	5 09 10	18 05 35	18 34 48	25 32 08	25 05.0	24 25.0	3 17.0	16 29.8	27 32.2	4 29.1	28 06.8	6 38.3	28 07.9	26 55.4
10 F	5 13 06	19 02 59	2♊34 55	9♊42 44	25 04.5	25 27.8	4 16.9	17 11.1	27 36.5	4 21.9	28 04.8	6 35.9	28 06.3	26 54.6
11 Sa	5 17 03	20 00 22	16 55 03	24 11 36	25D 04.4	26 34.1	5 16.5	17 52.5	27 40.5	4 14.8	28 02.8	6 33.5	28 04.7	26 53.7
12 Su	5 20 59	20 57 44	1♋30 21	8♋51 45	25 04.5	27 43.7	6 15.7	18 33.8	27 44.2	4 07.7	28 00.9	6 31.1	28 03.1	26 52.9
13 M	5 24 56	21 55 06	16 14 32	23 37 48	25 04.7	28 56.5	7 14.5	19 15.0	27 47.5	4 00.7	27 59.1	6 28.8	28 01.5	26 52.1
14 Tu	5 28 52	22 52 26	1♌00 42	8♌22 24	25 05.0	0♊12.6	8 12.9	19 56.2	27 50.6	3 53.8	27 57.5	6 26.4	27 59.9	26 51.4
15 W	5 32 49	23 49 46	15 42 10	22 59 20	25 05.1	1 31.9	9 10.9	20 37.3	27 53.2	3 47.0	27 55.9	6 24.1	27 58.3	26 50.6
16 Th	5 36 46	24 47 05	0♍13 19	7♍23 41	25R 05.2	2 54.3	10 08.5	21 18.4	27 55.6	3 40.2	27 54.4	6 21.7	27 56.7	26 49.9
17 F	5 40 42	25 44 23	14 30 02	21 32 09	25D 05.2	4 19.8	11 05.6	21 59.5	27 57.6	3 33.6	27 52.9	6 19.4	27 55.0	26 49.3
18 Sa	5 44 39	26 41 39	28 29 51	5♎23 05	25 05.2	5 48.4	12 02.2	22 40.5	27 59.2	3 27.1	27 51.6	6 17.1	27 53.4	26 48.6
19 Su	5 48 35	27 38 55	12♎11 48	18 56 06	25 05.3	7 20.1	12 58.4	23 21.5	28 00.5	3 20.6	27 50.4	6 14.9	27 51.8	26 48.0
20 M	5 52 32	28 36 11	25 36 04	2♏11 50	25 05.6	8 54.8	13 54.1	24 02.4	28 01.5	3 14.3	27 49.3	6 12.6	27 50.2	26 47.4
21 Tu	5 56 28	29 33 25	8♏43 34	15 11 27	25 06.0	10 32.6	14 49.2	24 43.2	28 02.1	3 08.1	27 48.3	6 10.4	27 48.6	26 46.9
22 W	6 00 25	0♋30 39	21 35 40	27 56 25	25 06.5	12 13.3	15 43.8	25 24.1	28R 02.4	3 02.0	27 47.3	6 08.2	27 46.9	26 46.4
23 Th	6 04 21	1 27 53	4♐13 53	10♐28 17	25 06.9	13 57.0	16 37.9	26 04.8	28 02.3	2 56.1	27 46.5	6 06.1	27 45.3	26 45.9
24 F	6 08 18	2 25 06	16 39 49	22 48 39	25R 07.1	15 43.5	17 31.4	26 45.6	28 01.9	2 50.2	27 45.8	6 03.9	27 43.7	26 45.5
25 Sa	6 12 15	3 22 18	28 55 01	4♑59 07	25 07.0	17 32.9	18 24.3	27 26.3	28 01.1	2 44.5	27 45.1	6 01.8	27 42.1	26 45.1
26 Su	6 16 11	4 19 31	11♑01 09	17 01 22	25 06.4	19 24.9	19 16.6	28 06.9	28 00.0	2 38.9	27 44.6	5 59.7	27 40.5	26 44.7
27 M	6 20 08	5 16 43	23 00 00	28 57 19	25 05.4	21 19.7	20 08.2	28 47.5	27 58.5	2 33.5	27 44.1	5 57.6	27 38.9	26 44.3
28 Tu	6 24 04	6 13 55	4♒53 36	10♒49 11	25 04.0	23 16.9	20 59.2	29 28.1	27 56.6	2 28.2	27 43.8	5 55.6	27 37.3	26 44.0
29 W	6 28 01	7 11 06	16 44 23	22 39 34	25 02.3	25 16.5	21 49.5	0♋08.6	27 54.4	2 23.0	27 43.6	5 53.6	27 35.7	26 43.7
30 Th	6 31 57	8 08 18	28 35 09	4♓31 33	25 00.6	27 18.3	22 39.2	0 49.1	27 51.9	2 18.0	27 43.4	5 51.6	27 34.1	26 43.5

Astro Data	Dy Hr Mn
☿ R	1 16:37
☽ 0N	9 20:02
♃☌♅	14 20:36
☽ 0S	22 17:40
☿ D	25 12:49
☽ 0N	6 5:26
♄✱♆	7 17:33
☽ 0S	18 23:18
♄✱♆	21 22:59
⚳ R	22 18:48

Planet Ingress	Dy Hr Mn
♄ ♎R	6 19:29
♀ ♋	9 10:56
♂ ♊	16 21:43
☉ ♊	21 15:06
♀ ♌	6 6:04
☿ ♊	14 8:06
☉ ♋	21 23:09
♂ ♋	29 6:54

Last Aspect Dy Hr Mn	☽ Ingress Dy Hr Mn
1 9:02 ♆ ☌	♑ 1 11:01
3 18:33 ♇ □	♒ 3 23:09
6 9:33 ♆ ✱	♓ 6 11:43
8 21:02 ♀ □	♈ 8 22:16
11 5:02 ♄ ☍	♉ 11 5:36
13 5:35 ♂ ☌	♊ 13 10:03
15 11:47 ♄ △	♋ 15 12:48
17 13:47 ♄ □	♌ 17 15:01
19 16:08 ♄ ✱	♍ 19 17:37
21 18:45 ♆ □	♎ 21 21:11
24 0:16 ♄ ☌	♏ 24 2:17
25 10:23 ♀ △	♐ 26 9:27
28 16:25 ♄ ✱	♑ 28 19:07
31 3:58 ♄ □	♒ 31 7:00

Last Aspect Dy Hr Mn	☽ Ingress Dy Hr Mn
2 16:27 ♄ △	♓ 2 19:42
5 4:55 ♀ △	♈ 5 6:59
7 11:48 ♄ ☍	♉ 7 15:05
9 9:56 ☿ ☌	♊ 9 19:37
11 18:23 ♆ ☍	♋ 11 21:32
13 21:26 ☿ ✱	♌ 13 22:21
15 20:14 ♆ △	♍ 15 23:38
17 22:58 ♆ □	♎ 18 2:36
20 4:56 ☉ △	♏ 20 7:59
21 11:15 ♀ □	♐ 22 15:55
24 21:43 ♄ ✱	♑ 25 2:08
27 9:32 ♄ □	♒ 27 14:07
29 22:15 ♄ △	♓ 30 2:52

☽ Phases & Eclipses Dy Hr Mn	
5 3:43	☾ 14♒06
12 19:25	● 21♉30
19 14:17	☽ 28♌03
26 18:48	○ 4♐57
3 21:07	☾ 12♓43
11 4:37	● 19♊43
11 4:42:41	● T 05'11"
17 19:46	☽ 26♍03
25 8:32	○ 3♑14
25 8:22	● P 0.335

Astro Data

1 May 1983
Julian Day # 30436
SVP 5♓29'51"
GC 26♐36.4 ⚴ 24♑52.5
Eris 15♈30.8 ⚵ 22♓27.7
⚷ 26♉24.6 ⚶ 1♉51.3
☽ Mean ☊ 27♊28.4

1 June 1983
Julian Day # 30467
SVP 5♓29'47"
GC 26♐36.5 ⚴ 24♑00.7R
Eris 15♈47.0 ⚵ 5♈49.7
⚷ 28♉37.4 ⚶ 15♉36.7
☽ Mean ☊ 25♊50.0

July 1983 LONGITUDE

Day	Sid.Time	☉	0 hr ☽	Noon ☽	True ☊	☿	♀	♂	⚳	♃	♄	♅	♆	♇
1 F	6 35 54	9♋05 30	10♓29 13	16♓28 39	24♊59.1	29♊22.0	23♌28.1	1♋29.5	27♒49.0	2♐13.1	27♎43.4	5♐49.7	27♐32.5	26♎43.2
2 Sa	6 39 50	10 02 42	22 30 20	28 34 47	24R 58.1	1♋27.5	24 16.3	2 09.9	27R 45.7	2R 08.3	27D 43.4	5R 47.7	27R 31.0	26R 43.1
3 Su	6 43 47	10 59 54	4♈42 33	10♈54 10	24D 57.7	3 34.5	25 03.6	2 50.3	27 42.0	2 03.7	27 43.5	5 45.9	27 29.4	26 42.9
4 M	6 47 44	11 57 06	17 10 08	23 30 59	24 58.0	5 42.7	25 50.2	3 30.6	27 38.1	1 59.3	27 43.8	5 44.0	27 27.8	26 42.8
5 Tu	6 51 40	12 54 19	29 57 11	6♉29 10	24 59.0	7 51.8	26 36.0	4 10.9	27 33.7	1 55.0	27 44.1	5 42.2	27 26.3	26 42.7
6 W	6 55 37	13 51 31	13♉07 17	19 51 50	25 00.3	10 01.5	27 20.9	4 51.2	27 29.0	1 50.9	27 44.6	5 40.4	27 24.7	26D 42.6
7 Th	6 59 33	14 48 45	26 42 58	3♊40 44	25 01.5	12 11.6	28 04.9	5 31.4	27 23.9	1 47.0	27 45.1	5 38.7	27 23.2	26 42.6
8 F	7 03 30	15 45 58	10♊45 03	17 55 38	25R 02.3	14 21.8	28 48.0	6 11.5	27 18.5	1 43.2	27 45.8	5 37.0	27 21.7	26 42.6
9 Sa	7 07 26	16 43 12	25 12 04	2♋33 45	25 02.3	16 31.7	29 30.1	6 51.7	27 12.8	1 39.6	27 46.5	5 35.3	27 20.2	26 42.7
10 Su	7 11 23	17 40 26	9♋59 53	17 29 35	25 01.2	18 41.2	0♍11.2	7 31.7	27 06.7	1 36.1	27 47.4	5 33.6	27 18.7	26 42.8
11 M	7 15 19	18 37 40	25 01 46	2♌35 18	24 59.1	20 49.9	0 51.3	8 11.8	27 00.2	1 32.8	27 48.3	5 32.1	27 17.2	26 42.9
12 Tu	7 19 16	19 34 54	10♌08 59	17 41 38	24 56.1	22 57.8	1 30.2	8 51.8	26 53.5	1 29.7	27 49.3	5 30.5	27 15.7	26 43.1
13 W	7 23 13	20 32 09	25 12 07	2♍39 23	24 52.8	25 04.5	2 08.1	9 31.8	26 46.4	1 26.8	27 50.5	5 29.0	27 14.3	26 43.3
14 Th	7 27 09	21 29 23	10♍02 30	17 20 43	24 49.6	27 10.0	2 44.8	10 11.7	26 38.9	1 24.0	27 51.7	5 27.5	27 12.8	26 43.5
15 F	7 31 06	22 26 37	24 33 26	1♎40 14	24 47.2	29 14.1	3 20.2	10 51.6	26 31.1	1 21.4	27 53.0	5 26.1	27 11.4	26 43.7
16 Sa	7 35 02	23 23 51	8♎40 53	15 35 17	24D 45.9	1♌16.8	3 54.4	11 31.4	26 23.1	1 19.0	27 54.5	5 24.7	27 10.0	26 44.0
17 Su	7 38 59	24 21 06	22 23 30	29 05 42	24 45.7	3 17.8	4 27.3	12 11.2	26 14.7	1 16.8	27 56.0	5 23.3	27 08.6	26 44.3
18 M	7 42 55	25 18 20	5♏42 07	12♏13 08	24 46.6	5 17.2	4 58.8	12 51.0	26 06.0	1 14.7	27 57.6	5 22.0	27 07.2	26 44.7
19 Tu	7 46 52	26 15 35	18 39 05	25 00 26	24 48.2	7 15.0	5 28.8	13 30.7	25 57.0	1 12.9	27 59.3	5 20.7	27 05.8	26 45.1
20 W	7 50 48	27 12 50	1♐17 34	7♐30 57	24 49.7	9 11.0	5 57.4	14 10.4	25 47.7	1 11.2	28 01.1	5 19.5	27 04.5	26 45.5
21 Th	7 54 45	28 10 05	13 41 00	19 48 08	24R 50.7	11 05.2	6 24.4	14 50.0	25 38.1	1 09.7	28 03.0	5 18.3	27 03.1	26 46.0
22 F	7 58 42	29 07 21	25 52 43	1♑55 09	24 50.6	12 57.8	6 49.8	15 29.6	25 28.3	1 08.4	28 05.1	5 17.2	27 01.8	26 46.5
23 Sa	8 02 38	0♌04 37	7♑55 44	13 54 47	24 48.9	14 48.5	7 13.6	16 09.2	25 18.2	1 07.2	28 07.1	5 16.1	27 00.5	26 47.0
24 Su	8 06 35	1 01 53	19 52 36	25 49 27	24 45.5	16 37.5	7 35.7	16 48.7	25 07.8	1 06.2	28 09.3	5 15.1	26 59.2	26 47.6
25 M	8 10 31	1 59 10	1♒45 35	7♒41 13	24 40.5	18 24.7	7 56.0	17 28.2	24 57.2	1 05.5	28 11.6	5 14.1	26 58.0	26 48.2
26 Tu	8 14 28	2 56 28	13 36 40	19 31 58	24 34.2	20 10.2	8 14.4	18 07.7	24 46.3	1 04.9	28 14.0	5 13.1	26 56.7	26 48.8
27 W	8 18 24	3 53 46	25 27 31	1♓23 33	24 27.1	21 53.9	8 31.0	18 47.1	24 35.2	1 04.4	28 16.5	5 12.2	26 55.5	26 49.5
28 Th	8 22 21	4 51 05	7♓20 17	13 18 02	24 19.9	23 35.8	8 45.7	19 26.5	24 23.9	1D 04.2	28 19.0	5 11.3	26 54.3	26 50.2
29 F	8 26 17	5 48 25	19 17 05	25 17 47	24 13.4	25 16.1	8 58.3	20 05.9	24 12.4	1 04.2	28 21.7	5 10.5	26 53.1	26 50.9
30 Sa	8 30 14	6 45 46	1♈20 30	7♈25 37	24 08.2	26 54.6	9 08.9	20 45.2	24 00.6	1 04.3	28 24.4	5 09.7	26 52.0	26 51.6
31 Su	8 34 11	7 43 08	13 33 36	19 44 52	24 04.6	28 31.3	9 17.3	21 24.5	23 48.7	1 04.6	28 27.2	5 09.0	26 50.9	26 52.4

August 1983 LONGITUDE

Day	Sid.Time	☉	0 hr ☽	Noon ☽	True ☊	☿	♀	♂	⚳	♃	♄	♅	♆	♇
1 M	8 38 07	8♌40 31	25♈59 54	2♉19 11	24♊03.0	0♍06.4	9♍23.7	22♋03.7	23♒36.6	1♐05.1	28♎30.1	5♐08.4	26♐49.7	26♎53.3
2 Tu	8 42 04	9 37 56	8♉43 12	15 12 28	24D 02.9	1 39.7	9 27.8	22 42.9	23R 24.3	1 05.8	28 33.1	5R 07.7	26R 48.7	26 54.1
3 W	8 46 00	10 35 21	21 47 23	28 28 24	24 03.8	3 11.3	9R 29.7	23 22.1	23 11.9	1 06.6	28 36.2	5 07.2	26 47.6	26 55.0
4 Th	8 49 57	11 32 48	5♊15 49	12♊09 54	24R 05.0	4 41.2	9 29.2	24 01.3	22 59.3	1 07.7	28 39.4	5 06.6	26 46.6	26 55.9
5 F	8 53 53	12 30 16	19 10 47	26 18 25	24 05.4	6 09.3	9 26.5	24 40.4	22 46.2	1 08.9	28 42.6	5 06.2	26 45.5	26 56.9
6 Sa	8 57 50	13 27 45	3♋32 38	10♋53 01	24 04.3	7 35.6	9 21.5	25 19.5	22 33.7	1 10.3	28 46.0	5 05.7	26 44.6	26 57.9
7 Su	9 01 46	14 25 16	18 19 00	25 49 46	24 01.1	9 00.2	9 14.0	25 58.5	22 20.8	1 11.9	28 49.4	5 05.4	26 43.6	26 58.9
8 M	9 05 43	15 22 47	3♌24 19	11♌01 29	23 55.8	10 22.9	9 04.2	26 37.5	22 07.8	1 13.7	28 53.0	5 05.1	26 42.6	27 00.0
9 Tu	9 09 40	16 20 20	18 39 59	26 18 25	23 48.7	11 43.8	8 52.1	27 16.5	21 54.7	1 15.6	28 56.6	5 04.8	26 41.7	27 01.0
10 W	9 13 36	17 17 53	3♍55 24	11♍29 37	23 40.8	13 02.8	8 37.5	27 55.5	21 41.5	1 17.7	29 00.2	5 04.6	26 40.8	27 02.2
11 Th	9 17 33	18 15 28	18 59 49	26 24 56	23 33.0	14 19.8	8 20.7	28 34.4	21 28.2	1 20.0	29 04.0	5 04.4	26 40.0	27 03.3
12 F	9 21 29	19 13 03	3♎44 05	10♎56 38	23 26.4	15 34.9	8 01.5	29 13.2	21 15.0	1 22.5	29 07.8	5 04.3	26 39.1	27 04.5
13 Sa	9 25 26	20 10 39	18 02 08	25 00 22	23 21.7	16 47.9	7 40.1	29 52.1	21 01.7	1 25.2	29 11.8	5D 04.2	26 38.3	27 05.7
14 Su	9 29 22	21 08 16	1♏51 18	8♏35 06	23 19.0	17 58.7	7 16.6	0♌30.9	20 48.4	1 28.0	29 15.8	5 04.2	26 37.6	27 06.9
15 M	9 33 19	22 05 55	15 12 02	21 42 32	23D 18.3	19 07.4	6 50.9	1 09.6	20 35.1	1 31.0	29 19.9	5 04.2	26 36.8	27 08.2
16 Tu	9 37 15	23 03 34	28 07 03	4♐26 09	23 18.7	20 13.7	6 23.3	1 48.4	20 21.9	1 34.2	29 24.0	5 04.3	26 36.1	27 09.5
17 W	9 41 12	24 01 14	10♐40 25	16 50 26	23R 19.4	21 17.7	5 53.9	2 27.1	20 08.7	1 37.6	29 28.3	5 04.5	26 35.4	27 10.8
18 Th	9 45 09	24 58 55	22 56 47	29 00 03	23 19.4	22 19.1	5 22.7	3 05.7	19 55.5	1 41.1	29 32.6	5 04.7	26 34.7	27 12.2
19 F	9 49 05	25 56 38	5♑00 47	10♑59 31	23 17.8	23 18.0	4 50.1	3 44.4	19 42.4	1 44.8	29 37.0	5 04.9	26 34.1	27 13.6
20 Sa	9 53 02	26 54 21	16 56 43	22 52 49	23 13.9	24 14.0	4 16.1	4 23.0	19 29.4	1 48.7	29 41.4	5 05.2	26 33.5	27 15.0
21 Su	9 56 58	27 52 06	28 48 14	4♒43 19	23 07.3	25 07.2	3 41.1	5 01.5	19 16.5	1 52.7	29 46.0	5 05.5	26 32.9	27 16.4
22 M	10 00 55	28 49 52	10♒38 22	16 33 41	22 58.3	25 57.3	3 05.0	5 40.0	19 03.7	1 56.9	29 50.6	5 05.9	26 32.4	27 17.9
23 Tu	10 04 51	29 47 39	22 29 28	28 25 57	22 47.2	26 44.1	2 28.4	6 18.5	18 51.0	2 01.3	29 55.3	5 06.4	26 31.8	27 19.4
24 W	10 08 48	0♍45 28	4♓23 20	10♓21 45	22 34.9	27 27.5	1 51.2	6 57.0	18 38.4	2 05.8	0♏00.0	5 06.9	26 31.4	27 20.9
25 Th	10 12 44	1 43 18	16 21 25	22 22 27	22 22.4	28 07.3	1 13.9	7 35.4	18 26.0	2 10.5	0 04.8	5 07.4	26 30.9	27 22.4
26 F	10 16 41	2 41 10	28 25 03	4♈29 25	22 10.8	28 43.1	0 36.6	8 13.8	18 13.7	2 15.3	0 09.7	5 08.0	26 30.5	27 24.0
27 Sa	10 20 38	3 39 04	10♈35 44	16 44 14	22 00.9	29 14.9	29♌59.6	8 52.2	18 01.6	2 20.4	0 14.7	5 08.7	26 30.1	27 25.6
28 Su	10 24 34	4 36 59	22 55 13	29 08 59	21 53.6	29 42.3	29 23.1	9 30.6	17 49.6	2 25.5	0 19.7	5 09.4	26 29.7	27 27.3
29 M	10 28 31	5 34 56	5♉25 51	11♉46 12	21 49.0	0♎05.1	28 47.4	10 08.9	17 37.9	2 30.8	0 24.8	5 10.2	26 29.4	27 28.9
30 Tu	10 32 27	6 32 55	18 10 24	24 38 54	21D 46.8	0 23.1	28 12.7	10 47.1	17 26.4	2 36.3	0 29.9	5 11.0	26 29.1	27 30.6
31 W	10 36 24	7 30 56	1♊12 06	7♊50 24	21 46.3	0 35.8	27 39.1	11 25.4	17 15.0	2 41.9	0 35.2	5 11.8	26 28.8	27 32.3

Astro Data (Dy Hr Mn)

♄ D 1 12:31
☽0N 3 13:37
♇ D 7 11:25
☽0S 16 5:09
♃ D 29 7:04
♆✶♇ 30 16:25
☽0N 30 19:53

♀ R 3 19:44
☽0S 12 12:36
♅ D 14 7:10
☿0S 21 3:01
☽0N 27 0:55

Planet Ingress (Dy Hr Mn)

☿ ♋ 1 19:18
♀ ♍ 10 5:25
☿ ♌ 15 20:57
☉ ♌ 23 10:04

☿ ♍ 1 10:22
♂ ♌ 13 16:54
☉ ♍ 23 17:07
♄ ♏ 24 11:54
♀ ♌R 27 11:43
☿ ♎ 29 6:07

Last Aspect / ☽ Ingress

Last Aspect Dy Hr Mn			☽ Ingress Dy Hr Mn
2 9:55	♆ □	♈	2 14:47
4 19:53	♄ ☍	♉	5 0:05
7 1:50	♀ □	♊	7 5:41
9 6:47	♀ ✶	♋	9 7:50
11 4:24	♄ □	♌	11 7:54
13 4:14	♄ ✶	♍	13 7:43
15 7:10	☿ ✶	♎	15 9:10
17 9:54	♄ ☌	♏	17 13:38
19 14:35	☉ △	♐	19 21:31
22 4:21	♄ ✶	♑	22 8:11
24 16:44	♄ □	♒	24 20:26
27 5:40	♄ △	♓	27 9:11
29 15:09	♆ □	♈	29 21:21

Last Aspect / ☽ Ingress

Last Aspect Dy Hr Mn			☽ Ingress Dy Hr Mn
1 7:13	☿ △	♉	1 7:37
3 2:23	♂ ✶	♊	3 14:43
5 16:01	♄ △	♋	5 18:09
7 16:46	♄ □	♌	7 18:37
9 16:10	♄ ✶	♍	9 17:49
11 15:41	♂ ✶	♎	11 17:51
13 19:21	♄ ☌	♏	13 20:44
15 12:47	☉ □	♐	16 3:33
18 13:05	♄ ✶	♑	18 13:59
21 1:53	♄ □	♒	21 2:25
23 15:01	♄ △	♓	23 15:10
26 0:01	☿ ☍	♈	26 3:08
28 12:26	♀ △	♉	28 13:38
30 18:16	♀ □	♊	30 21:49

☽ Phases & Eclipses (Dy Hr Mn)

3 12:12 ☾ 11♈00
10 12:18 ● 17♋41
17 2:50 ☽ 23♎59
24 23:27 ○ 1♒29

2 0:52 ☾ 9♉11
8 19:18 ● 15♌40
15 12:47 ☽ 22♏08
23 14:59 ○ 29♒55
31 11:22 ☾ 7♊29

Astro Data

1 July 1983
Julian Day # 30497
SVP 5♓29'41"
GC 26♐36.5 ⚳ 17♑24.5R
Eris 15♈55.1 ⚵ 17♈49.1
⚷ 0♊37.4 ⚶ 28♉14.1
☽ Mean ☊ 24♊14.7

1 August 1983
Julian Day # 30528
SVP 5♓29'37"
GC 26♐36.6 ⚳ 9♑30.5R
Eris 15♈53.8R ⚵ 28♈13.2
⚷ 2♊10.8 ⚶ 10♊08.6
☽ Mean ☊ 22♊36.2

LONGITUDE — September 1983

Day	Sid.Time	☉	0 hr ☽	Noon ☽	True ☊	☿	♀	♂	⚳	♃	♄	♅	♆	♇
1 Th	10 40 20	8♍28 58	14♊34 11	21♊23 46	21♊46.4	0♎43.1	27♌07.0	12♌03.6	17♒03.9	2♐47.7	0♏40.5	5♐12.7	26♐28.5	27♎34.0
2 F	10 44 17	9 27 03	28 19 24	5♋21 14	21R45.9	0R44.7	26R36.5	12 41.8	16R53.0	2 53.7	0 45.8	5 13.7	26R28.3	27 35.8
3 Sa	10 48 13	10 25 10	12♋29 16	19 43 21	21 43.7	0 40.4	26 07.7	13 20.0	16 42.4	2 59.8	0 51.2	5 14.7	26 28.2	27 37.6
4 Su	10 52 10	11 23 19	27 03 07	4♌28 03	21 38.9	0 30.0	25 40.7	13 58.1	16 32.0	3 06.0	0 56.7	5 15.8	26 28.0	27 39.4
5 M	10 56 07	12 21 29	11♌57 23	19 30 08	21 31.5	0 13.2	25 15.8	14 36.2	16 21.9	3 12.4	1 02.2	5 16.9	26 27.9	27 41.2
6 Tu	11 00 03	13 19 41	27 05 13	4♍41 20	21 21.7	29♍50.1	24 53.0	15 14.3	16 12.1	3 18.9	1 07.8	5 18.1	26 27.8	27 43.1
7 W	11 04 00	14 17 55	12♍17 08	19 51 15	21 10.7	29 20.6	24 32.4	15 52.3	16 02.5	3 25.6	1 13.5	5 19.3	26D27.8	27 44.9
8 Th	11 07 56	15 16 11	27 22 22	4♎49 14	20 59.7	28 44.8	24 14.0	16 30.3	15 53.3	3 32.4	1 19.2	5 20.5	26 27.8	27 46.8
9 F	11 11 53	16 14 28	12♎10 49	19 26 14	20 50.0	28 03.1	23 58.0	17 08.3	15 44.3	3 39.4	1 24.9	5 21.8	26 27.8	27 48.7
10 Sa	11 15 49	17 12 47	26 34 50	3♏36 13	20 42.5	27 15.8	23 44.3	17 46.3	15 35.6	3 46.5	1 30.7	5 23.2	26 27.8	27 50.7
11 Su	11 19 46	18 11 08	10♏30 10	17 16 41	20 37.6	26 23.5	23 33.0	18 24.2	15 27.3	3 53.7	1 36.6	5 24.6	26 27.9	27 52.6
12 M	11 23 42	19 09 30	23 55 58	0♐28 19	20 35.1	25 27.1	23 24.1	19 02.0	15 19.3	4 01.1	1 42.5	5 26.1	26 28.0	27 54.6
13 Tu	11 27 39	20 07 54	6♐54 12	13 14 09	20 34.4	24 27.6	23 17.7	19 39.9	15 11.5	4 08.6	1 48.5	5 27.6	26 28.2	27 56.6
14 W	11 31 36	21 06 20	19 28 45	25 38 39	20 34.3	23 26.1	23 13.6	20 17.7	15 04.2	4 16.3	1 54.5	5 29.1	26 28.4	27 58.6
15 Th	11 35 32	22 04 47	1♑44 31	7♑47 00	20 33.8	22 24.0	23D11.9	20 55.5	14 57.1	4 24.1	2 00.6	5 30.7	26 28.6	28 00.7
16 F	11 39 29	23 03 16	13 46 46	19 44 27	20 31.7	21 22.6	23 12.5	21 33.2	14 50.5	4 32.0	2 06.7	5 32.4	26 28.9	28 02.7
17 Sa	11 43 25	24 01 46	25 40 39	1♒35 54	20 27.2	20 23.5	23 15.5	22 10.9	14 44.1	4 40.0	2 12.9	5 34.1	26 29.1	28 04.8
18 Su	11 47 22	25 00 18	7♒30 46	13 25 40	20 20.0	19 28.1	23 20.7	22 48.6	14 38.1	4 48.2	2 19.1	5 35.8	26 29.5	28 06.9
19 M	11 51 18	25 58 52	19 21 03	25 17 17	20 10.0	18 38.0	23 28.2	23 26.2	14 32.4	4 56.5	2 25.4	5 37.6	26 29.8	28 09.0
20 Tu	11 55 15	26 57 27	1♓14 40	7♓13 27	19 57.8	17 54.2	23 37.9	24 03.9	14 27.1	5 04.9	2 31.7	5 39.5	26 30.2	28 11.1
21 W	11 59 11	27 56 04	13 13 53	19 16 07	19 44.2	17 18.1	23 49.7	24 41.4	14 22.2	5 13.4	2 38.0	5 41.3	26 30.6	28 13.3
22 Th	12 03 08	28 54 44	25 20 17	1♈26 31	19 30.4	16 50.5	24 03.7	25 19.0	14 17.6	5 22.1	2 44.4	5 43.3	26 31.0	28 15.4
23 F	12 07 04	29 53 25	7♈34 52	13 45 26	19 17.5	16 32.2	24 19.6	25 56.5	14 13.4	5 30.9	2 50.8	5 45.2	26 31.5	28 17.6
24 Sa	12 11 01	0♎52 08	19 58 17	26 13 30	19 06.6	16D23.5	24 37.6	26 34.0	14 09.5	5 39.8	2 57.3	5 47.3	26 32.0	28 19.8
25 Su	12 14 58	1 50 53	2♉31 09	8♉51 23	18 58.3	16 24.9	24 57.4	27 11.5	14 06.0	5 48.8	3 03.8	5 49.3	26 32.6	28 22.0
26 M	12 18 54	2 49 41	15 14 20	21 40 09	18 52.9	16 36.2	25 19.1	27 48.9	14 02.8	5 57.9	3 10.4	5 51.4	26 33.2	28 24.2
27 Tu	12 22 51	3 48 31	28 09 04	4♊41 18	18 50.3	16 57.4	25 42.6	28 26.3	14 00.0	6 07.1	3 17.0	5 53.6	26 33.8	28 26.5
28 W	12 26 47	4 47 23	11♊17 06	17 56 44	18D49.6	17 28.3	26 07.9	29 03.7	13 57.6	6 16.5	3 23.6	5 55.8	26 34.4	28 28.7
29 Th	12 30 44	5 46 17	24 40 28	1♋28 33	18R49.8	18 08.2	26 34.8	29 41.0	13 55.5	6 25.9	3 30.3	5 58.0	26 35.1	28 31.0
30 F	12 34 40	6 45 14	8♋21 12	15 18 33	18 49.6	18 56.7	27 03.4	0♍18.3	13 53.8	6 35.5	3 37.0	6 00.3	26 35.8	28 33.2

LONGITUDE — October 1983

Day	Sid.Time	☉	0 hr ☽	Noon ☽	True ☊	☿	♀	♂	⚳	♃	♄	♅	♆	♇
1 Sa	12 38 37	7♎44 13	22♋20 41	29♋27 33	18♊47.9	19♍53.3	27♌33.5	0♍55.6	13♒52.5	6♐45.2	3♏43.7	6♐02.6	26♐36.5	28♎35.5
2 Su	12 42 33	8 43 15	6♌38 59	13♌54 40	18R43.8	20 57.1	28 05.1	1 32.9	13R51.5	6 55.0	3 50.5	6 04.9	26 37.3	28 37.8
3 M	12 46 30	9 42 18	21 14 07	28 36 40	18 37.2	22 07.5	28 38.2	2 10.1	13 50.9	7 04.9	3 57.3	6 07.3	26 38.1	28 40.1
4 Tu	12 50 27	10 41 24	6♍01 33	13♍27 48	18 28.4	23 23.7	29 12.6	2 47.3	13D50.7	7 14.9	4 04.1	6 09.8	26 38.9	28 42.5
5 W	12 54 23	11 40 32	20 54 22	28 20 10	18 18.3	24 45.1	29 48.4	3 24.5	13 50.8	7 25.0	4 11.0	6 12.2	26 39.8	28 44.8
6 Th	12 58 20	12 39 42	5♎44 03	13♎04 56	18 08.0	26 11.0	0♍25.5	4 01.6	13 51.3	7 35.2	4 17.8	6 14.8	26 40.7	28 47.1
7 F	13 02 16	13 38 54	20 21 48	27 33 48	17 58.8	27 40.6	1 03.8	4 38.7	13 52.1	7 45.4	4 24.7	6 17.3	26 41.6	28 49.5
8 Sa	13 06 13	14 38 09	4♏40 10	11♏40 22	17 51.7	29 13.6	1 43.3	5 15.7	13 53.3	7 55.8	4 31.7	6 19.9	26 42.6	28 51.8
9 Su	13 10 09	15 37 25	18 34 04	25 21 02	17 47.0	0♎49.2	2 24.0	5 52.7	13 54.9	8 06.3	4 38.7	6 22.5	26 43.6	28 54.2
10 M	13 14 06	16 36 43	2♐01 19	8♐35 01	17D44.8	2 27.0	3 05.8	6 29.7	13 56.8	8 16.9	4 45.6	6 25.2	26 44.6	28 56.6
11 Tu	13 18 02	17 36 03	15 02 27	21 24 00	17 44.4	4 06.5	3 48.6	7 06.7	13 59.0	8 27.6	4 52.7	6 27.9	26 45.7	28 58.9
12 W	13 21 59	18 35 25	27 40 09	3♑51 29	17 45.1	5 47.4	4 32.5	7 43.6	14 01.7	8 38.4	4 59.7	6 30.7	26 46.7	29 01.3
13 Th	13 25 56	19 34 48	9♑58 34	16 02 05	17R45.8	7 29.4	5 17.3	8 20.4	14 04.6	8 49.2	5 06.7	6 33.4	26 47.9	29 03.7
14 F	13 29 52	20 34 13	22 02 40	28 00 59	17 45.5	9 12.1	6 03.2	8 57.3	14 07.9	9 00.2	5 13.8	6 36.2	26 49.0	29 06.1
15 Sa	13 33 49	21 33 40	3♒57 41	9♒53 25	17 43.5	10 55.3	6 49.9	9 34.1	14 11.6	9 11.2	5 20.9	6 39.1	26 50.2	29 08.5
16 Su	13 37 45	22 33 09	15 48 45	21 44 18	17 39.3	12 38.8	7 37.5	10 10.8	14 15.6	9 22.3	5 28.0	6 42.0	26 51.4	29 10.9
17 M	13 41 42	23 32 40	27 40 34	3♓38 03	17 32.9	14 22.4	8 26.0	10 47.6	14 19.9	9 33.5	5 35.1	6 44.9	26 52.6	29 13.3
18 Tu	13 45 38	24 32 12	9♓37 11	15 38 21	17 24.6	16 06.1	9 15.3	11 24.3	14 24.5	9 44.8	5 42.3	6 47.8	26 53.9	29 15.7
19 W	13 49 35	25 31 46	21 41 51	27 47 58	17 15.0	17 49.5	10 05.5	12 00.9	14 29.5	9 56.1	5 49.4	6 50.8	26 55.1	29 18.1
20 Th	13 53 31	26 31 22	3♈56 53	10♈08 46	17 05.2	19 32.8	10 56.4	12 37.5	14 34.8	10 07.5	5 56.6	6 53.8	26 56.4	29 20.6
21 F	13 57 28	27 31 00	16 23 43	22 41 45	16 56.0	21 15.7	11 48.0	13 14.1	14 40.4	10 19.1	6 03.8	6 56.8	26 57.8	29 23.0
22 Sa	14 01 25	28 30 40	29 02 54	5♉27 08	16 48.3	22 58.3	12 40.4	13 50.7	14 46.3	10 30.6	6 11.0	6 59.9	26 59.2	29 25.4
23 Su	14 05 21	29 30 22	11♉54 24	18 24 38	16 42.7	24 40.4	13 33.5	14 27.2	14 52.6	10 42.3	6 18.2	7 03.0	27 00.5	29 27.8
24 M	14 09 18	0♏30 07	24 57 46	1♊33 45	16 39.5	26 22.2	14 27.2	15 03.7	14 59.1	10 54.0	6 25.4	7 06.1	27 02.0	29 30.2
25 Tu	14 13 14	1 29 53	8♊12 32	14 54 03	16D38.3	28 03.4	15 21.6	15 40.1	15 06.0	11 05.8	6 32.6	7 09.2	27 03.4	29 32.6
26 W	14 17 11	2 29 42	21 38 18	28 25 17	16 38.8	29 44.1	16 16.7	16 16.5	15 13.1	11 17.7	6 39.8	7 12.4	27 04.9	29 35.1
27 Th	14 21 07	3 29 32	5♋15 00	12♋07 27	16 40.1	1♏24.4	17 12.4	16 52.9	15 20.6	11 29.7	6 47.0	7 15.6	27 06.4	29 37.5
28 F	14 25 04	4 29 26	19 02 40	26 00 36	16R41.3	3 04.1	18 08.6	17 29.2	15 28.4	11 41.7	6 54.3	7 18.8	27 07.9	29 39.9
29 Sa	14 29 00	5 29 21	3♌01 15	10♌04 29	16 41.5	4 43.4	19 05.4	18 05.5	15 36.4	11 53.8	7 01.5	7 22.1	27 09.5	29 42.3
30 Su	14 32 57	6 29 18	17 10 12	24 18 08	16 40.1	6 22.1	20 02.8	18 41.8	15 44.7	12 05.9	7 08.7	7 25.4	27 11.1	29 44.7
31 M	14 36 54	7 29 18	1♍28 01	8♍39 26	16 36.9	8 00.4	21 00.7	19 18.0	15 53.4	12 18.1	7 16.0	7 28.7	27 12.7	29 47.1

Astro Data

	Dy Hr Mn
☿R	2 6:41
♆D	8 11:00
☽0S	8 21:59
☿0N	15 13:23
♀D	15 17:22
☽0N	23 6:19
☉0S	23 14:41
☿D	24 20:51
♃☌♅	25 13:54
⚳D	4 16:16
☽0S	6 8:19
☿0S	11 17:35
☽0N	20 13:22

Planet Ingress

	Dy Hr Mn
☿ ♍R	6 2:30
☉ ♎	23 14:42
♂ ♍	30 0:12
♀ ♍	5 19:35
☿ ♎	8 23:44
☉ ♏	23 23:54
☿ ♏	26 15:47

Last Aspect / ☽ Ingress

Last Aspect Dy Hr Mn		☽ Ingress Dy Hr Mn
1 22:43 ♇ △	♋	2 2:53
4 0:58 ♇ □	♌	4 4:47
6 0:58 ♇ ✶	♍	6 4:36
8 2:36 ☿ ☌	♎	8 4:13
10 2:07 ♇ ☌	♏	10 5:49
12 3:24 ☿ ✶	♐	12 11:08
14 16:35 ♇ ✶	♑	14 20:34
17 4:51 ♇ □	♒	17 8:46
19 17:47 ♇ △	♓	19 21:30
22 6:36 ☉ ☍	♈	22 9:10
24 16:02 ♇ ☍	♉	24 19:12
26 23:57 ♂ □	♊	27 3:24
29 8:42 ♂ ✶	♋	29 9:24

Last Aspect / ☽ Ingress

Last Aspect Dy Hr Mn		☽ Ingress Dy Hr Mn
1 10:32 ♇ □	♌	1 12:54
3 12:06 ♇ ✶	♍	3 14:15
5 9:18 ♆ □	♎	5 14:42
7 14:08 ♇ ☌	♏	7 16:06
8 0:30 ♂ ✶	♐	9 20:21
12 2:35 ♇ ✶	♑	12 4:30
14 14:12 ♇ □	♒	14 16:00
17 3:05 ♇ △	♓	17 4:41
19 10:16 ♆ □	♈	19 16:18
22 0:40 ♇ ☍	♉	22 1:47
23 4:21 ♂ △	♊	24 9:10
26 14:38 ☿ △	♋	26 14:47
28 18:17 ♇ □	♌	28 18:50
30 21:09 ♇ ✶	♍	30 21:33

☽ Phases & Eclipses

Dy Hr Mn	
7 2:35	● 13♍55
14 2:24	☽ 20♐43
22 6:36	○ 28♓42
29 20:05	☾ 6♋06
6 11:16	● 12♎38
13 19:42	☽ 19♑54
21 21:53	○ 27♈56
29 3:37	☾ 5♌08

Astro Data

1 September 1983
Julian Day # 30559
SVP 5♓29'33"
GC 26♐36.7 ⚵ 6♑32.9
Eris 15♈43.1R ✳ 4♉40.6
⚷ 2♊54.5 ⚶ 20♊09.7
☽ Mean ☊ 20♊57.7

1 October 1983
Julian Day # 30589
SVP 5♓29'29"
GC 26♐36.7 ⚵ 9♑10.0
Eris 15♈26.6R ✳ 4♉33.7R
⚷ 2♊39.2R ⚶ 26♊49.4
☽ Mean ☊ 19♊22.3

November 1983 LONGITUDE

Day	Sid.Time	☉	0 hr ☽	Noon ☽	True ☊	☿	♀	♂	⚳	♃	♄	♅	♆	♇
1 Tu	14 40 50	8♏29 20	15♍51 54	23♍04 52	16♊32.2	9♏38.2	21♍59.1	19♍54.2	16♒02.3	12♐30.4	7♏23.2	7♐32.0	27♐14.3	29♎49.5
2 W	14 44 47	9 29 24	0♎17 42	7♎29 42	16R26.5	11 15.5	22 58.1	20 30.3	16 11.5	12 42.7	7 30.5	7 35.3	27 15.9	29 51.9
3 Th	14 48 43	10 29 29	14 40 09	21 48 20	16 20.6	12 52.3	23 57.5	21 06.4	16 20.9	12 55.1	7 37.7	7 38.7	27 17.6	29 54.3
4 F	14 52 40	11 29 37	28 53 34	5♏55 11	16 15.3	14 28.7	24 57.3	21 42.5	16 30.6	13 07.5	7 44.9	7 42.1	27 19.3	29 56.7
5 Sa	14 56 36	12 29 47	12♏52 38	19 45 25	16 11.3	16 04.7	25 57.6	22 18.5	16 40.7	13 20.0	7 52.2	7 45.5	27 21.0	29 59.1
6 Su	15 00 33	13 29 59	26 33 11	3♐15 41	16D08.9	17 40.3	26 58.3	22 54.4	16 50.9	13 32.6	7 59.4	7 49.0	27 22.8	0♏01.5
7 M	15 04 29	14 30 12	9♐52 47	16 24 28	16 08.2	19 15.4	27 59.5	23 30.4	17 01.5	13 45.2	8 06.6	7 52.4	27 24.5	0 03.8
8 Tu	15 08 26	15 30 27	22 50 50	29 12 06	16 08.8	20 50.2	29 01.0	24 06.2	17 12.3	13 57.9	8 13.8	7 55.9	27 26.3	0 06.2
9 W	15 12 23	16 30 44	5♑28 33	11♑40 35	16 10.4	22 24.6	0♎02.9	24 42.1	17 23.3	14 10.6	8 21.0	7 59.4	27 28.1	0 08.6
10 Th	15 16 19	17 31 02	17 48 37	23 53 11	16 12.2	23 58.7	1 05.2	25 17.8	17 34.6	14 23.4	8 28.2	8 02.9	27 30.0	0 10.9
11 F	15 20 16	18 31 22	29 54 48	5♒54 05	16 13.7	25 32.5	2 07.9	25 53.6	17 46.1	14 36.2	8 35.4	8 06.4	27 31.8	0 13.2
12 Sa	15 24 12	19 31 43	11♒51 37	17 48 01	16R14.4	27 05.9	3 10.9	26 29.3	17 57.9	14 49.1	8 42.5	8 09.9	27 33.7	0 15.6
13 Su	15 28 09	20 32 05	23 43 54	29 39 53	16 14.0	28 39.0	4 14.3	27 04.9	18 10.0	15 02.0	8 49.7	8 13.5	27 35.6	0 17.9
14 M	15 32 05	21 32 29	5♓36 35	11♓34 34	16 12.4	0♐11.8	5 18.0	27 40.5	18 22.2	15 14.9	8 56.8	8 17.0	27 37.5	0 20.2
15 Tu	15 36 02	22 32 54	17 34 22	23 36 31	16 09.8	1 44.4	6 22.0	28 16.0	18 34.7	15 27.9	9 03.9	8 20.6	27 39.4	0 22.4
16 W	15 39 58	23 33 20	29 41 30	5♈49 42	16 06.4	3 16.7	7 26.3	28 51.5	18 47.4	15 40.9	9 11.0	8 24.2	27 41.3	0 24.7
17 Th	15 43 55	24 33 48	12♈01 29	18 17 10	16 02.8	4 48.7	8 31.0	29 26.9	19 00.4	15 54.0	9 18.1	8 27.8	27 43.3	0 27.0
18 F	15 47 52	25 34 18	24 36 57	1♉00 59	15 59.4	6 20.4	9 35.9	0♎02.3	19 13.5	16 07.1	9 25.2	8 31.4	27 45.3	0 29.2
19 Sa	15 51 48	26 34 48	7♉29 22	14 02 04	15 56.7	7 51.9	10 41.2	0 37.6	19 26.9	16 20.2	9 32.2	8 35.0	27 47.3	0 31.5
20 Su	15 55 45	27 35 21	20 39 03	27 20 08	15 54.8	9 23.1	11 46.7	1 12.9	19 40.5	16 33.4	9 39.2	8 38.7	27 49.3	0 33.7
21 M	15 59 41	28 35 54	4♊05 09	10♊53 49	15D54.0	10 54.1	12 52.5	1 48.2	19 54.3	16 46.6	9 46.2	8 42.3	27 51.3	0 35.9
22 Tu	16 03 38	29 36 30	17 45 50	24 40 52	15 54.1	12 24.8	13 58.6	2 23.4	20 08.3	16 59.9	9 53.2	8 46.0	27 53.3	0 38.1
23 W	16 07 34	0♐37 07	1♋38 34	8♋38 34	15 54.9	13 55.3	15 04.9	2 58.5	20 22.5	17 13.1	10 00.1	8 49.6	27 55.4	0 40.3
24 Th	16 11 31	1 37 46	15 40 28	22 43 55	15 56.0	15 25.4	16 11.5	3 33.6	20 37.0	17 26.4	10 07.1	8 53.3	27 57.5	0 42.4
25 F	16 15 27	2 38 26	29 48 33	6♌54 02	15 57.2	16 55.2	17 18.4	4 08.6	20 51.6	17 39.8	10 14.0	8 57.0	27 59.6	0 44.6
26 Sa	16 19 24	3 39 08	14♌00 02	21 06 16	15R58.0	18 24.7	18 25.4	4 43.6	21 06.4	17 53.1	10 20.8	9 00.7	28 01.7	0 46.7
27 Su	16 23 21	4 39 51	28 12 26	5♍18 14	15 58.2	19 53.9	19 32.8	5 18.5	21 21.4	18 06.5	10 27.7	9 04.3	28 03.8	0 48.8
28 M	16 27 17	5 40 36	12♍23 26	19 27 44	15 57.9	21 22.6	20 40.3	5 53.4	21 36.6	18 20.0	10 34.5	9 08.0	28 05.9	0 50.9
29 Tu	16 31 14	6 41 23	26 30 53	3♎32 37	15 57.2	22 50.8	21 48.0	6 28.2	21 51.9	18 33.4	10 41.2	9 11.7	28 08.0	0 53.0
30 W	16 35 10	7 42 11	10♎32 39	17 30 44	15 56.2	24 18.5	22 56.0	7 02.9	22 07.5	18 46.9	10 48.0	9 15.4	28 10.2	0 55.0

December 1983 LONGITUDE

Day	Sid.Time	☉	0 hr ☽	Noon ☽	True ☊	☿	♀	♂	⚳	♃	♄	♅	♆	♇
1 Th	16 39 07	8♐43 01	24♎26 33	1♏19 51	15♊55.2	25♐45.6	24♎04.2	7♎37.6	22♒23.3	19♐00.3	10♏54.7	9♐19.1	28♐12.3	0♏57.1
2 F	16 43 03	9 43 52	8♏10 21	14 57 48	15R54.4	27 12.0	25 12.5	8 12.2	22 39.2	19 13.8	11 01.3	9 22.8	28 14.5	0 59.1
3 Sa	16 47 00	10 44 44	21 41 57	28 22 35	15 53.9	28 37.6	26 21.1	8 46.8	22 55.3	19 27.4	11 08.0	9 26.5	28 16.7	1 01.1
4 Su	16 50 56	11 45 38	4♐59 33	11♐32 41	15D53.7	0♑02.2	27 29.8	9 21.3	23 11.5	19 40.9	11 14.6	9 30.2	28 18.9	1 03.0
5 M	16 54 53	12 46 32	18 01 54	24 27 10	15 53.7	1 25.7	28 38.7	9 55.7	23 28.0	19 54.5	11 21.1	9 33.8	28 21.1	1 05.0
6 Tu	16 58 50	13 47 28	0♑48 31	7♑06 01	15 53.9	2 48.0	29 47.8	10 30.1	23 44.6	20 08.0	11 27.6	9 37.5	28 23.3	1 06.9
7 W	17 02 46	14 48 25	13 19 48	19 30 06	15 54.0	4 08.8	0♏57.0	11 04.3	24 01.4	20 21.6	11 34.1	9 41.2	28 25.5	1 08.8
8 Th	17 06 43	15 49 22	25 37 08	1♒41 16	15R54.1	5 27.9	2 06.4	11 38.6	24 18.3	20 35.2	11 40.5	9 44.9	28 27.7	1 10.7
9 F	17 10 39	16 50 21	7♒42 49	13 42 15	15 54.0	6 45.0	3 16.0	12 12.7	24 35.4	20 48.8	11 46.9	9 48.6	28 29.9	1 12.6
10 Sa	17 14 36	17 51 20	19 39 59	25 36 32	15 53.9	7 59.7	4 25.7	12 46.8	24 52.7	21 02.4	11 53.3	9 52.2	28 32.2	1 14.4
11 Su	17 18 32	18 52 19	1♓32 27	7♓28 15	15 53.7	9 11.8	5 35.5	13 20.8	25 10.1	21 16.1	11 59.6	9 55.9	28 34.4	1 16.2
12 M	17 22 29	19 53 19	13 24 33	19 21 54	15D53.6	10 20.7	6 45.5	13 54.7	25 27.6	21 29.7	12 05.8	9 59.6	28 36.7	1 18.0
13 Tu	17 26 25	20 54 20	25 20 56	1♈22 14	15 53.7	11 26.1	7 55.6	14 28.5	25 45.3	21 43.3	12 12.0	10 03.2	28 38.9	1 19.7
14 W	17 30 22	21 55 21	7♈26 22	13 33 53	15 54.1	12 27.2	9 05.9	15 02.3	26 03.2	21 56.9	12 18.1	10 06.8	28 41.2	1 21.5
15 Th	17 34 19	22 56 23	19 45 21	26 01 13	15 54.7	13 23.6	10 16.3	15 36.0	26 21.2	22 10.6	12 24.2	10 10.5	28 43.4	1 23.2
16 F	17 38 15	23 57 25	2♉21 55	8♉47 50	15 55.6	14 14.4	11 26.8	16 09.6	26 39.3	22 24.2	12 30.3	10 14.1	28 45.7	1 24.9
17 Sa	17 42 12	24 58 27	15 19 13	21 56 15	15 56.4	14 59.0	12 37.4	16 43.1	26 57.5	22 37.8	12 36.3	10 17.7	28 48.0	1 26.5
18 Su	17 46 08	25 59 31	28 39 02	5♊27 31	15R57.0	15 36.5	13 48.2	17 16.6	27 15.9	22 51.5	12 42.2	10 21.3	28 50.2	1 28.1
19 M	17 50 05	27 00 34	12♊21 33	19 20 49	15 57.1	16 06.1	14 59.1	17 50.0	27 34.5	23 05.1	12 48.1	10 24.9	28 52.5	1 29.7
20 Tu	17 54 01	28 01 39	26 24 56	3♋33 21	15 56.6	16 26.8	16 10.1	18 23.3	27 53.1	23 18.7	12 53.9	10 28.4	28 54.8	1 31.3
21 W	17 57 58	29 02 44	10♋45 27	18 00 30	15 55.5	16R37.7	17 21.2	18 56.5	28 11.9	23 32.3	12 59.7	10 32.0	28 57.0	1 32.9
22 Th	18 01 55	0♑03 49	25 17 43	2♌36 17	15 53.8	16 38.1	18 32.4	19 29.6	28 30.8	23 45.9	13 05.4	10 35.5	28 59.3	1 34.4
23 F	18 05 51	1 04 55	9♌55 22	17 14 11	15 51.9	16 27.2	19 43.8	20 02.6	28 49.8	23 59.5	13 11.0	10 39.1	29 01.6	1 35.9
24 Sa	18 09 48	2 06 02	24 31 57	1♍47 59	15 50.0	16 04.7	20 55.2	20 35.6	29 09.0	24 13.1	13 16.6	10 42.6	29 03.9	1 37.3
25 Su	18 13 44	3 07 09	9♍01 43	16 12 37	15 48.5	15 30.4	22 06.7	21 08.5	29 28.3	24 26.7	13 22.1	10 46.1	29 06.1	1 38.7
26 M	18 17 41	4 08 17	23 20 18	0♎24 29	15D47.8	14 44.6	23 18.4	21 41.2	29 47.6	24 40.3	13 27.6	10 49.5	29 08.4	1 40.1
27 Tu	18 21 37	5 09 26	7♎24 57	14 21 37	15 48.0	13 48.0	24 30.1	22 13.9	0♓07.2	24 53.8	13 33.0	10 53.0	29 10.6	1 41.5
28 W	18 25 34	6 10 35	21 14 25	28 03 23	15 49.0	12 42.1	25 41.9	22 46.5	0 26.8	25 07.3	13 38.3	10 56.4	29 12.9	1 42.8
29 Th	18 29 30	7 11 45	4♏48 34	11♏30 05	15 50.5	11 28.6	26 53.8	23 19.0	0 46.5	25 20.9	13 43.6	10 59.9	29 15.2	1 44.1
30 F	18 33 27	8 12 55	18 08 03	24 42 34	15 52.0	10 09.8	28 05.8	23 51.4	1 06.3	25 34.4	13 48.8	11 03.3	29 17.4	1 45.4
31 Sa	18 37 24	9 14 06	1♐13 46	7♐41 46	15R53.1	8 48.3	29 17.9	24 23.6	1 26.3	25 47.9	13 53.9	11 06.6	29 19.7	1 46.6

Astro Data

	Dy Hr Mn
☽0S	2 17:46
♄⊻♅	3 18:24
♀0S	12 1:36
♃∠♇	14 23:49
☽0N	16 22:07
♂0S	24 10:19
☽0S	30 0:59
☽0N	14 7:14
☿R	22 0:51
☽0S	27 6:18

Planet Ingress

		Dy Hr Mn
♇	♏	5 21:07
♀	♎	9 10:52
☿	♐	14 8:56
♂	♎	18 10:26
☉	♐	22 21:18
☿	♑	4 11:22
♀	♏	6 16:15
☉	♑	22 10:30
⚳	♓	27 3:13

Last Aspect / ☽ Ingress (November)

Last Aspect Dy Hr Mn			☽ Ingress	Dy Hr Mn
1 18:56	♆	□	♎	1 23:31
4 1:46	♇	☌	♏	4 1:53
5 23:50	♀	⚹	♐	6 6:09
8 11:37	♀	□	♑	8 13:31
10 14:57	♂	△	♒	11 0:10
13 9:38	☿	□	♓	13 12:41
15 21:40	♂	☍	♈	16 0:36
18 5:53	♆	△	♉	18 10:06
20 12:29	☉	☍	♊	20 16:45
22 17:33	♆	☍	♋	22 21:10
23 23:56	♀	□	♌	25 0:19
26 23:44	♆	△	♍	27 3:02
29 2:44	♆	□	♎	29 5:57

Last Aspect / ☽ Ingress (December)

Last Aspect Dy Hr Mn			☽ Ingress	Dy Hr Mn
1 6:32	♆	⚹	♏	1 9:41
2 4:58	♄	☌	♐	3 14:56
5 20:41	♀	⚹	♑	5 22:28
6 20:28	♄	⚹	♒	8 8:39
10 17:56	♆	⚹	♓	10 20:53
13 6:34	♆	□	♈	13 9:17
15 17:09	♆	△	♉	15 19:33
16 22:39	☿	△	♊	18 2:23
20 4:11	♆	☍	♋	20 6:02
21 13:36	♂	□	♌	22 7:44
24 7:28	♆	△	♍	24 9:01
26 9:50	♆	□	♎	26 11:18
28 14:03	♆	⚹	♏	28 15:27
30 18:51	♀	☌	♐	30 21:44

☽ Phases & Eclipses

Dy Hr Mn		
4 22:21	●	11♏56
12 15:49	☽	19♒41
20 12:29	○	27♉37
27 10:50	☾	4♍37
4 12:26	●	11♐47
4 12:30:22	✔	A 04'01"
12 13:09	☽	19♓56
20 2:00	○	27♊36
20 1:49	✔	A 0.889
26 18:52	☾	4♎26

Astro Data

1 November 1983
Julian Day # 30620
SVP 5♓29'26"
GC 26♐36.8 ⚴ 15♑45.9
Eris 15♈08.1R ⚵ 28♈17.6R
⚷ 1♊29.2R ⚶ 28♊33.6R
☽ Mean ☊ 17♊43.8

1 December 1983
Julian Day # 30650
SVP 5♓29'21"
GC 26♐36.9 ⚴ 24♑22.4
Eris 14♈54.2R ⚵ 24♈27.0R
⚷ 29♉53.7R ⚶ 23♊53.4R
☽ Mean ☊ 16♊08.5

LONGITUDE — January 1984

Day	Sid.Time	☉	0 hr ☽	Noon ☽	True ☊	☿	♀	♂	⚳	♃	♄	♅	♆	♇
1 Su	18 41 20	10♑15 17	14♐06 42	20♐28 38	15♊53.3	7♑26.9	0♐30.1	24♎55.8	1♓46.3	26♐01.3	13♏59.0	11♐10.0	29♐21.9	1♏47.8
2 M	18 45 17	11 16 28	26 47 42	3♑03 58	15R52.1	6R08.0	1 42.3	25 27.9	2 06.5	26 14.8	14 03.9	11 13.3	29 24.1	1 49.0
3 Tu	18 49 13	12 17 39	9♑17 32	15 28 29	15 49.5	4 54.2	2 54.6	25 59.8	2 26.8	26 28.2	14 08.9	11 16.6	29 26.4	1 50.2
4 W	18 53 10	13 18 50	21 36 57	27 43 03	15 45.6	3 47.4	4 07.0	26 31.7	2 47.1	26 41.6	14 13.7	11 19.9	29 28.6	1 51.3
5 Th	18 57 06	14 20 01	3♒46 56	9♒48 46	15 40.6	2 49.1	5 19.4	27 03.4	3 07.6	26 54.9	14 18.5	11 23.2	29 30.8	1 52.3
6 F	19 01 03	15 21 12	15 48 45	21 47 10	15 35.0	2 00.1	6 31.9	27 35.0	3 28.1	27 08.3	14 23.2	11 26.4	29 33.0	1 53.4
7 Sa	19 04 59	16 22 23	27 44 18	3♓40 27	15 29.5	1 21.2	7 44.5	28 06.5	3 48.8	27 21.6	14 27.8	11 29.6	29 35.2	1 54.4
8 Su	19 08 56	17 23 33	9♓36 01	15 31 25	15 24.6	0 52.4	8 57.1	28 37.8	4 09.5	27 34.8	14 32.3	11 32.8	29 37.4	1 55.4
9 M	19 12 53	18 24 43	21 27 07	27 23 36	15 20.9	0 33.5	10 09.7	29 09.1	4 30.4	27 48.1	14 36.8	11 35.9	29 39.6	1 56.3
10 Tu	19 16 49	19 25 52	3♈21 24	9♈21 05	15D18.8	0D24.2	11 22.5	29 40.2	4 51.3	28 01.3	14 41.1	11 39.1	29 41.8	1 57.2
11 W	19 20 46	20 27 01	15 23 15	21 28 30	15 18.2	0 24.0	12 35.2	0♏11.2	5 12.3	28 14.5	14 45.4	11 42.1	29 43.9	1 58.1
12 Th	19 24 42	21 28 09	27 37 26	3♉50 40	15 18.9	0 32.1	13 48.1	0 42.0	5 33.4	28 27.6	14 49.6	11 45.2	29 46.1	1 58.9
13 F	19 28 39	22 29 17	10♉08 46	16 32 18	15 20.5	0 48.1	15 00.9	1 12.7	5 54.5	28 40.7	14 53.8	11 48.2	29 48.2	1 59.7
14 Sa	19 32 35	23 30 24	23 01 47	29 37 36	15 22.0	1 11.1	16 13.9	1 43.3	6 15.8	28 53.7	14 57.8	11 51.2	29 50.3	2 00.5
15 Su	19 36 32	24 31 30	6♊20 07	13♊09 32	15R22.9	1 40.5	17 26.9	2 13.8	6 37.1	29 06.7	15 01.8	11 54.2	29 52.5	2 01.2
16 M	19 40 28	25 32 36	20 05 54	27 09 09	15 22.3	2 15.8	18 39.9	2 44.1	6 58.5	29 19.7	15 05.7	11 57.1	29 54.6	2 01.9
17 Tu	19 44 25	26 33 41	4♋18 58	11♋34 53	15 19.8	2 56.4	19 52.9	3 14.3	7 20.0	29 32.6	15 09.5	12 00.0	29 56.6	2 02.5
18 W	19 48 22	27 34 46	18 56 14	26 22 10	15 15.3	3 41.7	21 06.1	3 44.3	7 41.5	29 45.5	15 13.2	12 02.9	29 58.7	2 03.2
19 Th	19 52 18	28 35 50	3♌51 39	11♌23 32	15 09.2	4 31.2	22 19.2	4 14.2	8 03.2	29 58.4	15 16.8	12 05.7	0♑00.8	2 03.7
20 F	19 56 15	29 36 54	18 56 35	26 29 32	15 02.2	5 24.7	23 32.4	4 43.9	8 24.8	0♑11.2	15 20.3	12 08.5	0 02.8	2 04.3
21 Sa	20 00 11	0♒37 56	4♍01 10	11♍30 18	14 55.2	6 21.5	24 45.7	5 13.5	8 46.6	0 23.9	15 23.8	12 11.3	0 04.8	2 04.8
22 Su	20 04 08	1 38 59	18 55 56	26 17 12	14 49.2	7 21.5	25 59.0	5 43.0	9 08.4	0 36.6	15 27.1	12 14.0	0 06.9	2 05.3
23 M	20 08 04	2 40 01	3♎33 23	10♎44 01	14 45.0	8 24.3	27 12.3	6 12.2	9 30.3	0 49.2	15 30.4	12 16.7	0 08.9	2 05.7
24 Tu	20 12 01	3 41 02	17 48 48	24 47 35	14D42.8	9 29.7	28 25.6	6 41.3	9 52.3	1 01.8	15 33.6	12 19.4	0 10.8	2 06.1
25 W	20 15 57	4 42 03	1♏40 24	8♏27 23	14 42.5	10 37.4	29 39.1	7 10.3	10 14.3	1 14.3	15 36.7	12 22.0	0 12.8	2 06.5
26 Th	20 19 54	5 43 04	15 08 49	21 44 59	14 43.3	11 47.3	0♑52.5	7 39.1	10 36.4	1 26.8	15 39.6	12 24.5	0 14.7	2 06.8
27 F	20 23 51	6 44 04	28 16 16	4♐43 05	14R44.4	12 59.0	2 06.0	8 07.7	10 58.6	1 39.2	15 42.5	12 27.1	0 16.7	2 07.1
28 Sa	20 27 47	7 45 04	11♐05 50	17 24 55	14 44.8	14 12.6	3 19.5	8 36.1	11 20.8	1 51.5	15 45.3	12 29.6	0 18.6	2 07.4
29 Su	20 31 44	8 46 02	23 40 44	29 53 37	14 43.5	15 27.7	4 33.0	9 04.3	11 43.1	2 03.8	15 48.0	12 32.0	0 20.5	2 07.6
30 M	20 35 40	9 47 00	6♑03 55	12♑11 56	14 39.8	16 44.4	5 46.6	9 32.3	12 05.4	2 16.1	15 50.6	12 34.5	0 22.3	2 07.8
31 Tu	20 39 37	10 47 58	18 17 54	24 22 04	14 33.4	18 02.5	7 00.2	10 00.2	12 27.8	2 28.2	15 53.2	12 36.8	0 24.2	2 08.0

LONGITUDE — February 1984

Day	Sid.Time	☉	0 hr ☽	Noon ☽	True ☊	☿	♀	♂	⚳	♃	♄	♅	♆	♇
1 W	20 43 33	11♒48 54	0♒24 37	6♒25 44	14♊24.4	19♑22.0	8♑13.8	10♏27.8	12♓50.3	2♑40.3	15♏55.6	12♐39.2	0♑26.0	2♏08.1
2 Th	20 47 30	12 49 49	12 25 34	18 24 16	14R13.4	20 42.6	9 27.4	10 55.3	13 12.8	2 52.4	15 57.9	12 41.4	0 27.8	2 08.1
3 F	20 51 26	13 50 43	24 22 00	0♓18 54	14 01.2	22 04.5	10 41.1	11 22.5	13 35.3	3 04.3	16 00.1	12 43.7	0 29.6	2R08.2
4 Sa	20 55 23	14 51 36	6♓15 10	12 10 58	13 48.9	23 27.4	11 54.8	11 49.5	13 57.9	3 16.2	16 02.2	12 45.9	0 31.4	2 08.2
5 Su	20 59 20	15 52 27	18 06 34	24 02 12	13 37.5	24 51.4	13 08.5	12 16.4	14 20.6	3 28.0	16 04.2	12 48.0	0 33.1	2 08.2
6 M	21 03 16	16 53 18	29 58 11	5♈54 52	13 28.0	26 16.5	14 22.2	12 42.9	14 43.3	3 39.8	16 06.1	12 50.1	0 34.8	2 08.1
7 Tu	21 07 13	17 54 06	11♈52 40	17 52 00	13 21.0	27 42.5	15 35.9	13 09.3	15 06.0	3 51.4	16 07.9	12 52.2	0 36.5	2 08.0
8 W	21 11 09	18 54 54	23 53 22	29 57 18	13 16.7	29 09.4	16 49.7	13 35.4	15 28.8	4 03.0	16 09.6	12 54.2	0 38.2	2 07.8
9 Th	21 15 06	19 55 39	6♉04 22	12♉15 08	13D14.8	0♒37.3	18 03.5	14 01.3	15 51.6	4 14.5	16 11.3	12 56.2	0 39.8	2 07.7
10 F	21 19 02	20 56 24	18 30 14	24 50 17	13 14.5	2 06.1	19 17.2	14 27.0	16 14.5	4 25.9	16 12.8	12 58.1	0 41.4	2 07.5
11 Sa	21 22 59	21 57 07	1♊15 51	7♊47 32	13R14.9	3 35.8	20 31.0	14 52.4	16 37.4	4 37.3	16 14.2	13 00.0	0 43.0	2 07.2
12 Su	21 26 55	22 57 48	14 25 50	21 11 10	13 14.8	5 06.4	21 44.9	15 17.6	17 00.4	4 48.5	16 15.5	13 01.8	0 44.6	2 06.9
13 M	21 30 52	23 58 27	28 03 50	5♋04 01	13 13.0	6 37.9	22 58.7	15 42.6	17 23.4	4 59.7	16 16.7	13 03.6	0 46.2	2 06.6
14 Tu	21 34 49	24 59 05	12♋11 42	19 26 38	13 08.7	8 10.2	24 12.5	16 07.2	17 46.4	5 10.8	16 17.8	13 05.4	0 47.7	2 06.3
15 W	21 38 45	25 59 41	26 48 23	4♌16 14	13 01.7	9 43.5	25 26.4	16 31.6	18 09.5	5 21.8	16 18.8	13 07.0	0 49.2	2 05.9
16 Th	21 42 42	27 00 16	11♌49 15	19 26 17	12 52.3	11 17.6	26 40.3	16 55.8	18 32.6	5 32.7	16 19.7	13 08.7	0 50.7	2 05.5
17 F	21 46 38	28 00 49	27 06 00	4♍46 56	12 41.4	12 52.5	27 54.1	17 19.7	18 55.7	5 43.5	16 20.4	13 10.3	0 52.1	2 05.0
18 Sa	21 50 35	29 01 20	12♍27 34	20 06 25	12 30.4	14 28.4	29 08.0	17 43.3	19 18.9	5 54.2	16 21.1	13 11.8	0 53.5	2 04.5
19 Su	21 54 31	0♓01 50	27 42 05	5♎13 18	12 20.5	16 05.2	0♒21.9	18 06.6	19 42.1	6 04.9	16 21.7	13 13.3	0 54.9	2 04.0
20 M	21 58 28	1 02 19	12♎39 03	19 58 30	12 12.9	17 42.9	1 35.9	18 29.6	20 05.3	6 15.4	16 22.2	13 14.7	0 56.3	2 03.4
21 Tu	22 02 24	2 02 46	27 11 06	4♏16 30	12 07.9	19 21.5	2 49.8	18 52.3	20 28.6	6 25.9	16 22.6	13 16.1	0 57.6	2 02.9
22 W	22 06 21	3 03 12	11♏14 35	18 05 27	12 05.5	21 01.0	4 03.8	19 14.7	20 51.9	6 36.2	16 22.8	13 17.5	0 58.9	2 02.2
23 Th	22 10 18	4 03 37	24 49 19	1♐26 33	12 04.8	22 41.5	5 17.7	19 36.8	21 15.2	6 46.4	16 23.0	13 18.8	1 00.2	2 01.6
24 F	22 14 14	5 04 01	7♐57 37	14 23 01	12 04.8	24 22.9	6 31.7	19 58.6	21 38.5	6 56.6	16R23.1	13 20.0	1 01.4	2 00.9
25 Sa	22 18 11	6 04 23	20 43 20	26 59 06	12 04.2	26 05.4	7 45.7	20 20.0	22 01.9	7 06.6	16 23.0	13 21.2	1 02.7	2 00.2
26 Su	22 22 07	7 04 43	3♑10 55	9♑19 19	12 01.9	27 48.8	8 59.7	20 41.1	22 25.3	7 16.5	16 22.9	13 22.3	1 03.8	1 59.4
27 M	22 26 04	8 05 02	15 24 49	21 27 54	11 56.8	29 33.2	10 13.7	21 01.9	22 48.8	7 26.4	16 22.6	13 23.4	1 05.0	1 58.7
28 Tu	22 30 00	9 05 20	27 29 00	3♒28 32	11 48.8	1♓18.6	11 27.7	21 22.3	23 12.2	7 36.1	16 22.3	13 24.4	1 06.1	1 57.8
29 W	22 33 57	10 05 36	9♒26 50	15 24 12	11 37.7	3 05.1	12 41.7	21 42.3	23 35.7	7 45.7	16 21.8	13 25.4	1 07.2	1 57.0

Astro Data

	Dy Hr Mn
☽ 0N	10 15:06
♄∠♆	10 19:00
☿ D	11 0:37
♃☌♆	19 17:23
♃∠♄	21 11:44
☽ 0S	23 12:01
♃⚹♇	29 19:31
♇ R	4 2:05
☽ 0N	6 21:10
☽ 0S	19 20:12
♄ R	24 14:36

Planet Ingress

		Dy Hr Mn
♀	♐	1 2:00
♂	♏	11 3:20
♆	♑	19 2:55
♃	♑	19 15:04
☉	♒	20 21:05
♀	♑	25 18:51
☿	♒	9 1:50
♀	♒	19 4:53
☉	♓	19 11:16
☿	♓	27 18:07

Last Aspect / ☽ Ingress (January)

Last Aspect Dy Hr Mn			☽ Ingress	Dy Hr Mn
2 4:57	♆	☌	♑	2 6:07
4 9:33	♂	□	♒	4 16:30
7 3:43	♆	⚹	♓	7 4:34
9 16:35	♆	□	♈	9 17:15
12 4:08	♆	△	♉	12 4:36
13 23:56	☉	△	♊	14 12:40
16 16:39	♆	☍	♋	16 16:47
18 14:05	☉	☍	♌	18 17:50
20 6:54	♀	△	♍	20 17:35
22 11:27	♀	□	♎	22 18:07
24 18:56	♀	⚹	♏	24 21:04
26 0:53	♄	☌	♐	27 3:12
28 2:37	♅	☌	♑	29 12:12
30 22:00	☿	☌	♒	31 23:11

Last Aspect / ☽ Ingress (February)

Last Aspect Dy Hr Mn			☽ Ingress	Dy Hr Mn
2 7:05	♄	□	♓	3 11:22
5 13:53	☿	⚹	♈	6 0:04
8 10:13	☿	□	♉	8 12:05
10 4:00	☉	□	♊	10 21:39
12 15:22	☉	△	♋	13 3:20
14 20:30	♀	☍	♌	15 5:09
17 0:41	☉	☍	♍	17 4:32
19 3:33	♀	△	♎	19 3:39
20 7:49	☿	△	♏	21 4:44
22 17:56	☿	□	♐	23 9:22
25 10:00	☿	⚹	♑	25 17:49
27 11:07	♂	⚹	♒	28 5:02

☽ Phases & Eclipses

Dy Hr Mn		
3 5:16	●	12♑00
11 9:48	☽	20♈21
18 14:05	○	27♋40
25 4:48	☾	4♏24
1 23:46	●	12♒19
10 4:00	☽	20♉36
17 0:41	○	27♌32
23 17:12	☾	4♐17

Astro Data

1 January 1984
Julian Day # 30681
SVP 5♓29'16"
GC 26♐36.9 ⚴ 4♒29.1
Eris 14♈48.4R ⚵ 28♈42.9
⚷ 28♉26.1R ⚶ 16♊10.0R
☽ Mean ☊ 14♊30.1

1 February 1984
Julian Day # 30712
SVP 5♓29'10"
GC 26♐37.0 ⚴ 15♒04.9
Eris 14♈53.3 ⚵ 9♉31.7
⚷ 27♉46.3R ⚶ 13♊00.1
☽ Mean ☊ 12♊51.6

March 1984

LONGITUDE

Day	Sid.Time	☉	0 hr ☽	Noon ☽	True ☊	☿	♀	♂	⚳	♃	♄	♅	♆	♇
1 Th	22 37 53	11♓05 50	21♒20 54	27♒17 10	11♊24.3	4♓52.6	13♒55.8	22♏02.0	23♓59.2	7♑55.2	16♏21.2	13♐26.3	1♑08.3	1♏56.1
2 F	22 41 50	12 06 03	3♓13 11	9♓09 07	11R 09.5	6 41.1	15 09.8	22 21.2	24 22.7	8 04.5	16R 20.6	13 27.2	1 09.3	1R 55.2
3 Sa	22 45 47	13 06 13	15 05 09	21 01 25	10 54.4	8 30.7	16 23.8	22 40.1	24 46.2	8 13.8	16 19.8	13 28.0	1 10.3	1 54.3
4 Su	22 49 43	14 06 22	26 58 05	2♈55 19	10 40.3	10 21.3	17 37.9	22 58.6	25 09.8	8 22.9	16 18.9	13 28.8	1 11.3	1 53.3
5 M	22 53 40	15 06 29	8♈53 18	14 52 15	10 28.2	12 13.0	18 51.9	23 16.6	25 33.4	8 31.9	16 18.0	13 29.5	1 12.3	1 52.3
6 Tu	22 57 36	16 06 34	20 52 25	26 54 07	10 19.0	14 05.6	20 05.9	23 34.3	25 56.9	8 40.8	16 16.9	13 30.1	1 13.2	1 51.3
7 W	23 01 33	17 06 37	2♉57 39	9♉03 26	10 12.9	15 59.3	21 20.0	23 51.5	26 20.5	8 49.6	16 15.7	13 30.7	1 14.1	1 50.3
8 Th	23 05 29	18 06 37	15 11 51	21 23 23	10 09.6	17 53.9	22 34.0	24 08.3	26 44.2	8 58.2	16 14.5	13 31.3	1 14.9	1 49.2
9 F	23 09 26	19 06 36	27 38 32	3♊57 48	10D 08.4	19 49.4	23 48.0	24 24.6	27 07.8	9 06.8	16 13.1	13 31.8	1 15.7	1 48.1
10 Sa	23 13 22	20 06 33	10♊21 45	16 50 54	10R 08.4	21 45.8	25 02.1	24 40.5	27 31.4	9 15.1	16 11.6	13 32.2	1 16.5	1 47.0
11 Su	23 17 19	21 06 27	23 25 46	0♋06 50	10 08.2	23 43.0	26 16.1	24 56.0	27 55.1	9 23.4	16 10.1	13 32.6	1 17.3	1 45.8
12 M	23 21 16	22 06 19	6♋54 28	13 49 00	10 06.6	25 40.8	27 30.2	25 10.9	28 18.7	9 31.5	16 08.4	13 33.0	1 18.0	1 44.7
13 Tu	23 25 12	23 06 09	20 50 34	27 59 10	10 02.8	27 39.2	28 44.2	25 25.4	28 42.4	9 39.5	16 06.7	13 33.2	1 18.7	1 43.5
14 W	23 29 09	24 05 57	5♌14 36	12♌36 27	9 56.4	29 38.0	29 58.2	25 39.4	29 06.1	9 47.4	16 04.8	13 33.5	1 19.3	1 42.2
15 Th	23 33 05	25 05 42	20 04 04	27 36 33	9 47.6	1♈37.0	1♓12.2	25 52.9	29 29.8	9 55.1	16 02.9	13 33.6	1 19.9	1 41.0
16 F	23 37 02	26 05 25	5♍12 49	12♍51 33	9 37.2	3 36.0	2 26.3	26 05.9	29 53.5	10 02.7	16 00.9	13 33.8	1 20.5	1 39.7
17 Sa	23 40 58	27 05 06	20 31 23	28 10 49	9 26.5	5 34.8	3 40.3	26 18.4	0♈17.2	10 10.2	15 58.7	13R 33.8	1 21.1	1 38.4
18 Su	23 44 55	28 04 45	5♎48 24	13♎22 44	9 16.8	7 33.1	4 54.3	26 30.3	0 40.8	10 17.5	15 56.5	13 33.8	1 21.6	1 37.1
19 M	23 48 51	29 04 22	20 52 35	28 16 53	9 09.1	9 30.5	6 08.4	26 41.7	1 04.6	10 24.6	15 54.2	13 33.8	1 22.1	1 35.8
20 Tu	23 52 48	0♈03 57	5♏34 49	12♏45 46	9 04.0	11 26.9	7 22.4	26 52.6	1 28.3	10 31.6	15 51.8	13 33.7	1 22.5	1 34.4
21 W	23 56 45	1 03 31	19 49 24	26 45 32	9D 01.5	13 21.7	8 36.4	27 02.9	1 52.0	10 38.5	15 49.4	13 33.6	1 23.0	1 33.0
22 Th	0 00 41	2 03 03	3♐34 15	10♐15 45	9 00.9	15 14.5	9 50.5	27 12.6	2 15.7	10 45.3	15 46.8	13 33.4	1 23.4	1 31.6
23 F	0 04 38	3 02 33	16 50 24	23 18 38	9R 01.3	17 05.1	11 04.5	27 21.7	2 39.4	10 51.8	15 44.2	13 33.1	1 23.7	1 30.2
24 Sa	0 08 34	4 02 01	29 41 00	5♑58 05	9 01.6	18 52.8	12 18.5	27 30.2	3 03.1	10 58.3	15 41.4	13 32.8	1 24.0	1 28.8
25 Su	0 12 31	5 01 28	12♑10 28	18 18 48	9 00.6	20 37.4	13 32.6	27 38.1	3 26.8	11 04.6	15 38.6	13 32.5	1 24.3	1 27.3
26 M	0 16 27	6 00 53	24 23 40	0♒25 41	8 57.6	22 18.3	14 46.6	27 45.3	3 50.5	11 10.7	15 35.7	13 32.1	1 24.6	1 25.9
27 Tu	0 20 24	7 00 16	6♒25 24	12 23 21	8 52.1	23 55.2	16 00.6	27 51.9	4 14.3	11 16.7	15 32.8	13 31.6	1 24.8	1 24.4
28 W	0 24 20	7 59 37	18 20 02	24 15 54	8 44.2	25 27.6	17 14.7	27 57.9	4 38.0	11 22.5	15 29.7	13 31.1	1 25.0	1 22.9
29 Th	0 28 17	8 58 56	0♓11 19	6♓06 41	8 34.2	26 55.1	18 28.7	28 03.2	5 01.7	11 28.1	15 26.6	13 30.6	1 25.2	1 21.4
30 F	0 32 14	9 58 13	12 02 17	17 58 24	8 22.9	28 17.5	19 42.7	28 07.8	5 25.4	11 33.6	15 23.4	13 29.9	1 25.3	1 19.8
31 Sa	0 36 10	10 57 29	23 55 16	29 53 06	8 11.4	29 34.4	20 56.7	28 11.8	5 49.1	11 39.0	15 20.1	13 29.3	1 25.4	1 18.3

April 1984

LONGITUDE

Day	Sid.Time	☉	0 hr ☽	Noon ☽	True ☊	☿	♀	♂	⚳	♃	♄	♅	♆	♇
1 Su	0 40 07	11♈56 42	5♈52 03	11♈52 18	8♊00.6	0♉45.5	22♓10.7	28♏15.0	6♈12.8	11♑44.1	15♏16.8	13♐28.6	1♑25.4	1♏16.7
2 M	0 44 03	12 55 53	17 54 00	23 57 18	7R 51.5	1 50.6	23 24.7	28 17.5	6 36.5	11 49.1	15R 13.4	13R 27.8	1R 25.4	1R 15.1
3 Tu	0 48 00	13 55 02	0♉02 21	6♉09 20	7 44.7	2 49.4	24 38.7	28 19.3	7 00.1	11 54.0	15 09.9	13 27.0	1 25.4	1 13.5
4 W	0 51 56	14 54 09	12 18 25	18 29 51	7 40.3	3 41.8	25 52.7	28 20.5	7 23.8	11 58.6	15 06.3	13 26.1	1 25.4	1 11.9
5 Th	0 55 53	15 53 14	24 43 50	1♊00 41	7D 38.4	4 27.7	27 06.7	28R 20.8	7 47.4	12 03.1	15 02.7	13 25.2	1 25.3	1 10.3
6 F	0 59 49	16 52 17	7♊20 40	13 44 08	7 38.3	5 06.9	28 20.7	28 20.5	8 11.1	12 07.5	14 59.1	13 24.3	1 25.2	1 08.7
7 Sa	1 03 46	17 51 18	20 11 26	26 42 54	7 39.3	5 39.3	29 34.7	28 19.4	8 34.7	12 11.6	14 55.3	13 23.3	1 25.0	1 07.1
8 Su	1 07 42	18 50 16	3♋18 54	9♋59 46	7R 40.4	6 04.9	0♈48.6	28 17.5	8 58.3	12 15.6	14 51.5	13 22.2	1 24.9	1 05.4
9 M	1 11 39	19 49 12	16 45 48	23 37 14	7 40.6	6 23.8	2 02.6	28 15.0	9 21.9	12 19.4	14 47.7	13 21.1	1 24.7	1 03.8
10 Tu	1 15 36	20 48 05	0♌34 14	7♌36 50	7 39.3	6 35.9	3 16.5	28 11.6	9 45.5	12 23.0	14 43.8	13 20.0	1 24.4	1 02.1
11 W	1 19 32	21 46 57	14 44 56	21 58 19	7 36.1	6R 41.4	4 30.5	28 07.5	10 09.1	12 26.5	14 39.9	13 18.8	1 24.1	1 00.5
12 Th	1 23 29	22 45 45	29 16 34	6♍39 06	7 31.1	6 40.5	5 44.4	28 02.7	10 32.6	12 29.8	14 35.9	13 17.6	1 23.8	0 58.8
13 F	1 27 25	23 44 32	14♍05 10	21 33 51	7 24.9	6 33.3	6 58.3	27 57.1	10 56.2	12 32.9	14 31.8	13 16.3	1 23.5	0 57.1
14 Sa	1 31 22	24 43 16	29 04 07	6♎34 49	7 18.4	6 20.2	8 12.2	27 50.7	11 19.7	12 35.8	14 27.7	13 15.0	1 23.1	0 55.4
15 Su	1 35 18	25 41 59	14♎04 47	21 32 51	7 12.3	6 01.6	9 26.1	27 43.6	11 43.2	12 38.6	14 23.6	13 13.6	1 22.7	0 53.8
16 M	1 39 15	26 40 39	28 57 53	6♏18 52	7 07.6	5 37.9	10 40.0	27 35.7	12 06.7	12 41.1	14 19.4	13 12.2	1 22.3	0 52.1
17 Tu	1 43 11	27 39 18	13♏34 55	20 45 20	7 04.7	5 09.5	11 53.9	27 27.1	12 30.1	12 43.5	14 15.2	13 10.8	1 21.8	0 50.4
18 W	1 47 08	28 37 54	27 49 34	4♐47 17	7D 03.6	4 37.3	13 07.8	27 17.7	12 53.6	12 45.7	14 10.9	13 09.3	1 21.3	0 48.7
19 Th	1 51 05	29 36 29	11♐38 17	18 22 35	7 04.1	4 01.7	14 21.7	27 07.5	13 17.0	12 47.8	14 06.7	13 07.8	1 20.8	0 47.0
20 F	1 55 01	0♉35 03	25 00 17	1♑31 41	7 05.4	3 23.5	15 35.6	26 56.6	13 40.4	12 49.6	14 02.3	13 06.2	1 20.3	0 45.3
21 Sa	1 58 58	1 33 34	7♑57 07	14 17 03	7 07.0	2 43.4	16 49.5	26 45.0	14 03.8	12 51.3	13 58.0	13 04.6	1 19.7	0 43.6
22 Su	2 02 54	2 32 04	20 31 59	26 42 29	7R 08.1	2 02.2	18 03.4	26 32.6	14 27.1	12 52.7	13 53.6	13 02.9	1 19.1	0 41.9
23 M	2 06 51	3 30 33	2♒49 07	8♒52 28	7 08.1	1 20.7	19 17.2	26 19.5	14 50.4	12 54.0	13 49.2	13 01.3	1 18.4	0 40.2
24 Tu	2 10 47	4 29 00	14 53 10	20 51 47	7 06.7	0 39.6	20 31.1	26 05.7	15 13.7	12 55.1	13 44.8	12 59.5	1 17.7	0 38.5
25 W	2 14 44	5 27 25	26 48 53	2♓45 02	7 03.9	29♈59.7	21 45.0	25 51.2	15 37.0	12 56.0	13 40.3	12 57.8	1 17.0	0 36.8
26 Th	2 18 40	6 25 48	8♓40 44	14 36 29	6 59.9	29 21.6	22 58.8	25 36.1	16 00.3	12 56.7	13 35.9	12 56.0	1 16.3	0 35.2
27 F	2 22 37	7 24 10	20 32 43	26 29 52	6 55.1	28 45.9	24 12.7	25 20.3	16 23.5	12 57.2	13 31.4	12 54.1	1 15.6	0 33.5
28 Sa	2 26 34	8 22 30	2♈28 15	8♈28 14	6 50.0	28 13.3	25 26.5	25 03.8	16 46.7	12 57.6	13 26.9	12 52.3	1 14.8	0 31.8
29 Su	2 30 30	9 20 48	14 30 06	20 34 04	6 45.2	27 44.0	26 40.4	24 46.8	17 09.9	12R 57.7	13 22.3	12 50.4	1 13.9	0 30.1
30 M	2 34 27	10 19 05	26 40 21	2♉49 08	6 41.3	27 18.7	27 54.2	24 29.2	17 33.0	12 57.7	13 17.8	12 48.5	1 13.1	0 28.4

Astro Data Dy Hr Mn	Planet Ingress Dy Hr Mn	Last Aspect Dy Hr Mn	☽ Ingress Dy Hr Mn	Last Aspect Dy Hr Mn	☽ Ingress Dy Hr Mn	☽ Phases & Eclipses Dy Hr Mn
☽0N 5 2:26	♀ ♓ 14 12:35	1 1:05 ♂ □	♓ 1 17:29	1 15:12 ♅ △	♉ 2 23:55	2 18:31 ● 12♓22
♄∠♆ 8 7:11	☿ ♈ 14 16:27	3 15:25 ♂ △	♈ 4 6:07	5 6:55 ♂ ☍	♊ 5 10:04	10 18:27 ☽ 20♊23
☿0N 15 14:28	⚳ ♈ 16 18:37	5 20:54 ♀ ⚹	♉ 6 18:09	7 17:46 ♀ □	♋ 7 17:59	17 10:10 ○ 27♍01
♅ R 18 6:13	☉ ♈ 20 10:24	8 17:25 ♂ ☍	♊ 9 4:30	9 19:59 ♂ △	♌ 9 23:01	24 7:58 ☾ 3♑52
☽0S 18 6:42	☿ ♉ 31 20:25	11 4:25 ♀ △	♋ 11 11:48	11 22:04 ♂ □	♍ 12 1:11	
☉0N 20 10:24		13 11:21 ☿ △	♌ 13 15:21	13 22:09 ♂ ⚹	♎ 14 1:29	1 12:10 ● 11♈57
♆⚹♇ 27 5:55	♀ ♈ 7 20:13	15 9:13 ♂ □	♍ 15 15:47	15 19:11 ☉ ☍	♏ 16 1:41	9 4:51 ☽ 19♋32
☽0N 1 8:15	☉ ♉ 19 21:38	17 10:10 ☉ ☍	♎ 17 14:51	17 23:14 ♂ ☌	♐ 18 3:44	15 19:11 ○ 26♎00
♆ R 2 14:04	☿ ♈R 25 11:49	18 12:18 ♅ ⚹	♏ 19 14:49	19 4:06 ♀ △	♑ 20 9:10	23 0:26 ☾ 3♒02
♂ R 5 12:22		21 12:31 ♂ ☌	♐ 21 17:41	22 11:41 ♂ ⚹	♒ 22 18:27	
♀0N 10 16:14		22 22:34 ☿ △	♑ 24 0:36	24 22:20 ♂ □	♓ 25 6:26	
☿ R 11 20:25		26 6:37 ♂ ⚹	♒ 26 11:09	27 9:43 ♂ △	♈ 27 19:03	
☽0S 14 17:33		28 19:33 ♂ □	♓ 28 23:37	30 1:36 ☿ ☌	♉ 30 6:30	
♃⚺♅ 26 4:47		31 8:35 ♂ △	♈ 31 12:14			
☽0N 28 15:16	♃ R29 18:37					

Astro Data

1 March 1984
Julian Day # 30741
SVP 5♓29'06"
GC 26♐37.1 ⚴ 24♒54.2
Eris 15♈06.3 ⚵ 22♉54.0
⚷ 28♉06.8 ⚶ 16♊05.9
☽ Mean ☊ 11♊19.4

1 April 1984
Julian Day # 30772
SVP 5♓29'03"
GC 26♐37.2 ⚴ 4♓47.0
Eris 15♈25.8 ⚵ 8♊49.0
⚷ 29♉25.8 ⚶ 24♊01.4
☽ Mean ☊ 9♊40.9

LONGITUDE — May 1984

Day	Sid.Time	☉	0 hr ☽	Noon ☽	True ☊	☿	♀	♂	⚳	♃	♄	♅	♆	♇
1 Tu	2 38 23	11♉17 20	9♉00 33	15♉14 44	6♊38.5	26♈57.5	29♈08.0	24♏11.0	17♈56.1	12♑57.5	13♏13.3	12♐46.5	1♑12.2	0♏26.8
2 W	2 42 20	12 15 34	21 31 46	27 51 46	6D 37.0	26R 40.7	0♉21.9	23R 52.4	18 19.2	12R 57.0	13R 08.8	12R 44.5	1R 11.3	0R 25.1
3 Th	2 46 16	13 13 45	4♊14 48	10♊40 57	6 36.8	26 28.5	1 35.7	23 33.3	18 42.2	12 56.4	13 04.2	12 42.5	1 10.4	0 23.5
4 F	2 50 13	14 11 55	17 10 18	23 42 55	6 37.5	26 20.9	2 49.5	23 13.7	19 05.2	12 55.6	12 59.7	12 40.4	1 09.5	0 21.8
5 Sa	2 54 09	15 10 03	0♋18 53	6♋58 18	6 38.9	26D 18.1	4 03.3	22 53.7	19 28.1	12 54.6	12 55.2	12 38.3	1 08.5	0 20.2
6 Su	2 58 06	16 08 09	13 41 13	20 27 43	6 40.3	26 20.1	5 17.1	22 33.4	19 51.1	12 53.5	12 50.6	12 36.2	1 07.5	0 18.6
7 M	3 02 03	17 06 13	27 17 50	4♌11 36	6R 41.4	26 26.8	6 30.9	22 12.7	20 14.0	12 52.1	12 46.1	12 34.1	1 06.5	0 17.0
8 Tu	3 05 59	18 04 15	11♌08 59	18 09 54	6 41.8	26 38.1	7 44.7	21 51.8	20 36.8	12 50.6	12 41.6	12 31.9	1 05.4	0 15.4
9 W	3 09 56	19 02 15	25 14 14	2♍21 45	6 41.4	26 54.0	8 58.4	21 30.7	20 59.6	12 48.8	12 37.1	12 29.8	1 04.3	0 13.8
10 Th	3 13 52	20 00 14	9♍32 09	16 45 04	6 40.2	27 14.4	10 12.2	21 09.3	21 22.4	12 46.9	12 32.6	12 27.6	1 03.2	0 12.2
11 F	3 17 49	20 58 10	24 00 00	1♎16 24	6 38.5	27 39.1	11 25.9	20 47.8	21 45.1	12 44.8	12 28.2	12 25.3	1 02.1	0 10.7
12 Sa	3 21 45	21 56 04	8♎33 38	15 50 58	6 36.6	28 08.1	12 39.7	20 26.2	22 07.8	12 42.5	12 23.7	12 23.1	1 01.0	0 09.1
13 Su	3 25 42	22 53 57	23 07 41	0♏23 01	6 34.9	28 41.1	13 53.4	20 04.5	22 30.4	12 40.1	12 19.3	12 20.8	0 59.8	0 07.6
14 M	3 29 38	23 51 48	7♏36 12	14 46 32	6 33.7	29 18.2	15 07.2	19 42.9	22 53.0	12 37.4	12 14.9	12 18.5	0 58.6	0 06.1
15 Tu	3 33 35	24 49 38	21 53 19	28 56 00	6D 33.0	29 59.0	16 20.9	19 21.2	23 15.5	12 34.6	12 10.5	12 16.2	0 57.4	0 04.6
16 W	3 37 32	25 47 27	5♐54 03	12♐47 05	6 33.0	0♉43.6	17 34.6	18 59.6	23 38.1	12 31.6	12 06.2	12 13.9	0 56.2	0 03.1
17 Th	3 41 28	26 45 14	19 34 51	26 17 10	6 33.5	1 31.7	18 48.4	18 38.1	24 00.5	12 28.4	12 01.9	12 11.5	0 54.9	0 01.6
18 F	3 45 25	27 42 59	2♑53 59	9♑25 22	6 34.2	2 23.3	20 02.1	18 16.8	24 22.9	12 25.1	11 57.6	12 09.2	0 53.7	0 00.2
19 Sa	3 49 21	28 40 44	15 51 28	22 12 33	6 35.0	3 18.3	21 15.8	17 55.7	24 45.3	12 21.6	11 53.3	12 06.8	0 52.4	29♎58.7
20 Su	3 53 18	29 38 27	28 28 56	4♒41 01	6 35.7	4 16.4	22 29.5	17 34.8	25 07.6	12 17.9	11 49.1	12 04.4	0 51.1	29 57.3
21 M	3 57 14	0♊36 10	10♒49 15	16 54 08	6 36.2	5 17.8	23 43.2	17 14.2	25 29.9	12 14.0	11 45.0	12 02.0	0 49.7	29 55.9
22 Tu	4 01 11	1 33 51	22 56 11	28 55 58	6R 36.4	6 22.2	24 57.0	16 53.9	25 52.1	12 10.0	11 40.8	11 59.6	0 48.4	29 54.5
23 W	4 05 07	2 31 31	4♓54 04	10♓51 01	6 36.3	7 29.5	26 10.7	16 34.0	26 14.2	12 05.8	11 36.7	11 57.2	0 47.0	29 53.2
24 Th	4 09 04	3 29 10	16 47 25	22 43 51	6 36.1	8 39.8	27 24.4	16 14.5	26 36.4	12 01.5	11 32.7	11 54.7	0 45.7	29 51.8
25 F	4 13 01	4 26 48	28 40 50	4♈38 54	6 35.9	9 52.8	28 38.1	15 55.5	26 58.4	11 56.9	11 28.7	11 52.3	0 44.3	29 50.5
26 Sa	4 16 57	5 24 25	10♈38 34	16 40 18	6 35.7	11 08.7	29 51.8	15 36.9	27 20.4	11 52.3	11 24.7	11 49.8	0 42.9	29 49.2
27 Su	4 20 54	6 22 01	22 44 31	28 51 36	6D 35.6	12 27.3	1♊05.5	15 18.8	27 42.3	11 47.4	11 20.8	11 47.4	0 41.4	29 47.9
28 M	4 24 50	7 19 36	5♉01 54	11♉15 41	6 35.6	13 48.5	2 19.3	15 01.4	28 04.2	11 42.4	11 17.0	11 44.9	0 40.0	29 46.6
29 Tu	4 28 47	8 17 10	17 33 12	23 54 35	6R 35.7	15 12.4	3 33.0	14 44.5	28 26.1	11 37.3	11 13.2	11 42.4	0 38.5	29 45.4
30 W	4 32 43	9 14 43	0♊19 58	6♊49 24	6 35.8	16 39.0	4 46.7	14 28.2	28 47.8	11 32.0	11 09.4	11 40.0	0 37.1	29 44.2
31 Th	4 36 40	10 12 16	13 22 52	20 00 19	6 35.7	18 08.1	6 00.4	14 12.5	29 09.5	11 26.6	11 05.8	11 37.5	0 35.6	29 43.0

LONGITUDE — June 1984

Day	Sid.Time	☉	0 hr ☽	Noon ☽	True ☊	☿	♀	♂	⚳	♃	♄	♅	♆	♇
1 F	4 40 36	11♊09 47	26♊41 36	3♋26 35	6♊35.4	19♉39.8	7♊14.1	13♏57.6	29♈31.2	11♑21.1	11♏02.2	11♐35.0	0♑34.1	29♎41.8
2 Sa	4 44 33	12 07 17	10♋15 03	17 06 44	6R 34.9	21 14.0	8 27.8	13R 43.4	29 52.7	11R 15.4	10R 58.6	11R 32.5	0R 32.6	29R 40.7
3 Su	4 48 30	13 04 45	24 01 24	0♌58 44	6 34.2	22 50.8	9 41.5	13 29.9	0♉14.2	11 09.5	10 55.1	11 30.1	0 31.1	29 39.6
4 M	4 52 26	14 02 13	7♌58 26	15 00 11	6 33.4	24 30.1	10 55.2	13 17.1	0 35.7	11 03.6	10 51.7	11 27.6	0 29.5	29 38.5
5 Tu	4 56 23	14 59 39	22 03 39	29 08 32	6 32.9	26 11.9	12 08.9	13 05.1	0 57.0	10 57.5	10 48.3	11 25.1	0 28.0	29 37.4
6 W	5 00 19	15 57 04	6♍14 30	13♍21 13	6D 32.6	27 56.3	13 22.6	12 53.9	1 18.3	10 51.3	10 45.0	11 22.6	0 26.5	29 36.4
7 Th	5 04 16	16 54 28	20 28 24	27 35 43	6 32.7	29 43.1	14 36.3	12 43.4	1 39.6	10 45.0	10 41.8	11 20.2	0 24.9	29 35.4
8 F	5 08 12	17 51 51	4♎42 51	11♎49 29	6 33.3	1♊32.4	15 50.0	12 33.8	2 00.7	10 38.5	10 38.7	11 17.7	0 23.3	29 34.4
9 Sa	5 12 09	18 49 12	18 55 17	25 59 55	6 34.2	3 24.1	17 03.7	12 25.0	2 21.8	10 32.0	10 35.6	11 15.3	0 21.8	29 33.4
10 Su	5 16 05	19 46 33	3♏03 03	10♏04 20	6 35.2	5 18.3	18 17.4	12 17.0	2 42.8	10 25.4	10 32.6	11 12.8	0 20.2	29 32.5
11 M	5 20 02	20 43 53	17 03 25	24 00 00	6R 35.9	7 14.7	19 31.1	12 09.8	3 03.7	10 18.6	10 29.7	11 10.4	0 18.6	29 31.6
12 Tu	5 23 59	21 41 11	0♐53 43	7♐44 17	6 36.2	9 13.4	20 44.8	12 03.5	3 24.5	10 11.8	10 26.8	11 08.0	0 17.0	29 30.7
13 W	5 27 55	22 38 30	14 31 23	21 14 48	6 35.8	11 14.2	21 58.5	11 57.9	3 45.3	10 04.9	10 24.1	11 05.5	0 15.4	29 29.9
14 Th	5 31 52	23 35 47	27 54 19	4♑29 47	6 34.5	13 17.1	23 12.2	11 53.2	4 06.0	9 57.9	10 21.4	11 03.1	0 13.8	29 29.1
15 F	5 35 48	24 33 04	11♑01 05	17 28 12	6 32.4	15 21.8	24 25.8	11 49.3	4 26.6	9 50.8	10 18.8	11 00.8	0 12.2	29 28.3
16 Sa	5 39 45	25 30 20	23 51 08	0♒10 00	6 29.8	17 28.2	25 39.6	11 46.3	4 47.2	9 43.6	10 16.2	10 58.4	0 10.6	29 27.6
17 Su	5 43 41	26 27 36	6♒24 58	12 36 15	6 26.8	19 36.1	26 53.3	11 44.0	5 07.6	9 36.4	10 13.8	10 56.0	0 09.0	29 26.8
18 M	5 47 38	27 24 52	18 44 08	24 48 58	6 24.0	21 45.2	28 07.0	11 42.6	5 28.0	9 29.1	10 11.4	10 53.7	0 07.4	29 26.1
19 Tu	5 51 35	28 22 07	0♓51 10	6♓51 10	6 21.8	23 55.4	29 20.7	11D 42.0	5 48.2	9 21.8	10 09.2	10 51.3	0 05.7	29 25.5
20 W	5 55 31	29 19 22	12 49 28	18 46 35	6D 20.3	26 06.3	0♋34.4	11 42.2	6 08.4	9 14.3	10 07.0	10 49.0	0 04.1	29 24.8
21 Th	5 59 28	0♋16 36	24 43 06	0♈39 33	6 19.8	28 17.7	1 48.1	11 43.2	6 28.5	9 06.9	10 04.9	10 46.7	0 02.5	29 24.2
22 F	6 03 24	1 13 51	6♈36 33	12 34 41	6 20.3	0♋29.3	3 01.8	11 45.0	6 48.5	8 59.3	10 02.8	10 44.5	0 00.9	29 23.6
23 Sa	6 07 21	2 11 05	18 34 33	24 36 44	6 21.6	2 40.8	4 15.5	11 47.5	7 08.4	8 51.8	10 00.9	10 42.2	29♐59.3	29 23.1
24 Su	6 11 17	3 08 20	0♉41 48	6♉50 17	6 23.2	4 51.9	5 29.3	11 50.9	7 28.2	8 44.2	9 59.1	10 40.0	29 57.6	29 22.6
25 M	6 15 14	4 05 34	13 02 40	19 19 23	6 24.7	7 02.5	6 43.0	11 55.1	7 48.0	8 36.6	9 57.3	10 37.8	29 56.0	29 22.1
26 Tu	6 19 10	5 02 48	25 40 50	2♊07 20	6R 25.6	9 12.1	7 56.8	12 00.0	8 07.6	8 28.9	9 55.7	10 35.6	29 54.4	29 21.7
27 W	6 23 07	6 00 02	8♊39 03	15 16 09	6 25.4	11 20.8	9 10.5	12 05.8	8 27.1	8 21.2	9 54.1	10 33.4	29 52.8	29 21.2
28 Th	6 27 04	6 57 17	21 58 37	28 46 22	6 23.8	13 28.1	10 24.3	12 12.2	8 46.5	8 13.6	9 52.6	10 31.3	29 51.2	29 20.9
29 F	6 31 00	7 54 31	5♋39 09	12♋36 40	6 20.7	15 34.1	11 38.0	12 19.5	9 05.8	8 05.9	9 51.3	10 29.2	29 49.6	29 20.5
30 Sa	6 34 57	8 51 44	19 38 27	26 43 58	6 16.5	17 38.5	12 51.8	12 27.4	9 25.0	7 58.2	9 50.0	10 27.1	29 48.0	29 20.2

Astro Data	Planet Ingress	Last Aspect	☽ Ingress	Last Aspect	☽ Ingress	☽ Phases & Eclipses	Astro Data
Dy Hr Mn	Dy Hr Mn	Dy Hr Mn	Dy Hr Mn	Dy Hr Mn	Dy Hr Mn	Dy Hr Mn	1 May 1984
⚳0N 1 22:17	♀ ♉ 2 4:53	2 4:38 ♂ ☍	♊ 2 16:02	1 5:22 ♇ △	♋ 1 5:54	1 3:45 ● 10♉57	Julian Day # 30802
☿ D 5 14:06	☿ ♉ 15 12:33	4 16:46 ☿ ⚹	♋ 4 23:26	3 9:44 ♇ □	♌ 3 10:19	8 11:50 ☽ 18♌04	SVP 5♓29'00"
♃⚹♄ 5 15:38	♇ ♎R 18 14:35	6 22:23 ☿ □	♌ 7 4:43	5 12:49 ♇ ⚹	♍ 5 13:27	15 4:29 ○ 24♏32	GC 26♐37.2 ⚵ 13♓09.5
☽0S 12 2:40	☉ ♊ 20 20:58	9 2:37 ☿ △	♍ 9 8:02	6 16:42 ☉ □	♎ 7 16:03	15 4:40 • A 0.807	Eris 15♈45.4 ⚴ 24♊46.8
♄⚺♅ 12 19:12	♀ ♊ 26 14:40	10 19:07 ♂ ⚹	♎ 11 9:54	9 18:03 ♇ ☌	♏ 9 18:48	22 17:45 ☾ 1♓48	⚷ 1♊21.7 ⚶ 4♋24.8
☽0N 25 23:09		13 9:04 ☿ ☍	♏ 13 11:22	10 15:45 ♂ ☌	♐ 11 22:26	30 16:48 ● 9♊26	☽ Mean ☊ 8♊05.6
♃⚺♅ 27 12:33	⚳ ♉ 2 20:06	15 4:29 ☉ ☍	♐ 15 13:50	14 2:52 ♇ ⚹	♑ 14 3:48	30 16:44:47 • A 00'11"	
	☿ ♊ 7 15:45	16 11:02 ♅ ☌	♑ 17 18:43	16 10:39 ♇ □	♒ 16 11:41		1 June 1984
☽0S 8 9:16	♀ ♋ 20 0:48	20 2:51 ♇ □	♒ 20 2:55	18 21:10 ♇ △	♓ 18 22:18	6 16:42 ☽ 16♍08	Julian Day # 30833
♃⚹♄ 8 11:04	☉ ♋ 21 5:02	22 13:57 ♇ △	♓ 22 14:09	21 6:09 ☿ □	♈ 21 10:40	13 14:42 ○ 22♐45	SVP 5♓28'55"
♂ D 19 18:17	☿ ♋ 22 6:39	24 22:31 ♀ ⚹	♈ 25 2:39	23 22:35 ♆ △	♉ 23 22:38	13 14:26 • A 0.064	GC 26♐37.3 ⚵ 19♓45.8
☽0N 22 7:04	♆ ♐R 23 1:10	27 13:50 ♇ ☍	♉ 27 14:13	24 21:45 ♂ ☍	♊ 26 8:04	21 11:10 ☾ 0♈15	Eris 16♈01.5 ⚴ 11♋14.0
		28 19:02 ♂ ☍	♊ 29 23:23	28 13:53 ♆ ☍	♋ 28 14:09	29 3:18 ● 7♋34	⚷ 3♊39.4 ⚶ 16♋47.1
				30 16:23 ♇ □	♌ 30 17:30		☽ Mean ☊ 6♊27.1

July 1984 LONGITUDE

Day	Sid.Time	☉	0 hr ☽	Noon ☽	True ☊	☿	♀	♂	⚳	♃	♄	♅	♆	♇
1 Su	6 38 53	9♋48 58	3♌52 36	11♌03 39	6♊11.7	19♋41.3	14♋05.5	12♏36.1	9♉44.1	7♑50.5	9♏48.8	10♐25.0	29♐46.4	29♎19.9
2 M	6 42 50	10 46 11	18 16 25	25 30 12	6R 06.8	21 42.3	15 19.3	12 45.5	10 03.1	7R 42.8	9R 47.7	10R 23.0	29R 44.8	29R 19.7
3 Tu	6 46 46	11 43 24	2♍44 16	9♍57 58	6 02.7	23 41.5	16 33.1	12 55.7	10 22.0	7 35.1	9 46.7	10 21.0	29 43.3	29 19.5
4 W	6 50 43	12 40 37	17 10 42	24 21 58	5 59.9	25 38.8	17 46.8	13 06.5	10 40.7	7 27.5	9 45.8	10 19.0	29 41.7	29 19.3
5 Th	6 54 39	13 37 49	1♎31 18	8♎38 22	5D 58.7	27 34.1	19 00.6	13 18.0	10 59.3	7 19.9	9 45.0	10 17.1	29 40.1	29 19.1
6 F	6 58 36	14 35 01	15 42 53	22 44 40	5 58.8	29 27.6	20 14.4	13 30.2	11 17.8	7 12.3	9 44.3	10 15.2	29 38.6	29 19.0
7 Sa	7 02 33	15 32 12	29 43 35	6♏39 34	5 59.9	1♌19.0	21 28.1	13 43.1	11 36.2	7 04.7	9 43.7	10 13.3	29 37.0	29 18.9
8 Su	7 06 29	16 29 24	13♏32 34	20 22 35	6 01.2	3 08.5	22 41.9	13 56.6	11 54.5	6 57.2	9 43.2	10 11.5	29 35.5	29D 18.9
9 M	7 10 26	17 26 36	27 09 38	3♐53 41	6R 02.0	4 56.0	23 55.7	14 10.7	12 12.6	6 49.7	9 42.7	10 09.7	29 34.0	29 18.9
10 Tu	7 14 22	18 23 47	10♐34 47	17 12 55	6 01.5	6 41.5	25 09.5	14 25.5	12 30.7	6 42.3	9 42.4	10 07.9	29 32.4	29 18.9
11 W	7 18 19	19 20 59	23 48 03	0♑20 12	5 59.1	8 25.1	26 23.2	14 40.8	12 48.6	6 35.0	9 42.2	10 06.2	29 30.9	29 19.0
12 Th	7 22 15	20 18 10	6♑49 19	13 15 22	5 54.7	10 06.6	27 37.0	14 56.8	13 06.3	6 27.7	9D 42.1	10 04.5	29 29.4	29 19.0
13 F	7 26 12	21 15 22	19 38 21	25 58 15	5 48.3	11 46.2	28 50.8	15 13.4	13 23.9	6 20.5	9 42.1	10 02.8	29 28.0	29 19.2
14 Sa	7 30 08	22 12 34	2♒15 05	8♒28 52	5 40.5	13 23.8	0♌04.6	15 30.5	13 41.4	6 13.3	9 42.1	10 01.2	29 26.5	29 19.3
15 Su	7 34 05	23 09 47	14 39 43	20 47 44	5 32.0	14 59.4	1 18.4	15 48.2	13 58.8	6 06.2	9 42.3	9 59.6	29 25.1	29 19.5
16 M	7 38 02	24 07 00	26 53 05	2♓55 59	5 23.7	16 33.0	2 32.2	16 06.4	14 16.0	5 59.2	9 42.6	9 58.0	29 23.6	29 19.7
17 Tu	7 41 58	25 04 14	8♓56 43	14 55 35	5 16.2	18 04.6	3 46.0	16 25.2	14 33.1	5 52.3	9 42.9	9 56.5	29 22.2	29 20.0
18 W	7 45 55	26 01 28	20 52 59	26 49 20	5 10.3	19 34.2	4 59.8	16 44.5	14 50.0	5 45.5	9 43.4	9 55.1	29 20.8	29 20.3
19 Th	7 49 51	26 58 42	2♈45 06	8♈40 49	5 06.4	21 01.7	6 13.6	17 04.3	15 06.8	5 38.8	9 43.9	9 53.6	29 19.4	29 20.6
20 F	7 53 48	27 55 58	14 37 02	20 34 21	5D 04.5	22 27.3	7 27.4	17 24.7	15 23.4	5 32.1	9 44.6	9 52.2	29 18.0	29 21.0
21 Sa	7 57 44	28 53 14	26 33 21	2♉34 42	5 04.2	23 50.7	8 41.2	17 45.5	15 39.9	5 25.6	9 45.3	9 50.9	29 16.6	29 21.4
22 Su	8 01 41	29 50 31	8♉39 01	14 46 56	5 05.0	25 12.0	9 55.0	18 06.9	15 56.2	5 19.2	9 46.2	9 49.6	29 15.3	29 21.8
23 M	8 05 37	0♌47 49	20 59 05	27 16 03	5R 05.9	26 31.2	11 08.8	18 28.7	16 12.4	5 12.9	9 47.2	9 48.3	29 14.0	29 22.3
24 Tu	8 09 34	1 45 08	3♊38 22	10♊06 31	5 06.0	27 48.2	12 22.7	18 51.0	16 28.4	5 06.7	9 48.2	9 47.1	29 12.7	29 22.8
25 W	8 13 31	2 42 28	16 40 52	23 21 43	5 04.5	29 03.0	13 36.5	19 13.8	16 44.2	5 00.6	9 49.3	9 45.9	29 11.4	29 23.3
26 Th	8 17 27	3 39 49	0♋09 10	7♋03 15	5 00.8	0♍15.4	14 50.3	19 37.1	16 59.9	4 54.7	9 50.6	9 44.8	29 10.1	29 23.9
27 F	8 21 24	4 37 10	14 03 46	21 10 23	4 54.8	1 25.5	16 04.2	20 00.8	17 15.4	4 48.9	9 51.9	9 43.7	29 08.9	29 24.5
28 Sa	8 25 20	5 34 33	28 22 32	5♌39 33	4 46.8	2 33.1	17 18.0	20 25.0	17 30.7	4 43.2	9 53.4	9 42.7	29 07.6	29 25.1
29 Su	8 29 17	6 31 56	13♌00 31	20 24 30	4 37.6	3 38.2	18 31.9	20 49.6	17 45.9	4 37.7	9 54.9	9 41.7	29 06.4	29 25.8
30 M	8 33 13	7 29 19	27 50 23	5♍17 05	4 28.4	4 40.7	19 45.7	21 14.6	18 00.8	4 32.3	9 56.5	9 40.7	29 05.2	29 26.5
31 Tu	8 37 10	8 26 44	12♍43 29	20 08 34	4 20.2	5 40.4	20 59.6	21 40.1	18 15.6	4 27.0	9 58.2	9 39.8	29 04.1	29 27.2

August 1984 LONGITUDE

Day	Sid.Time	☉	0 hr ☽	Noon ☽	True ☊	☿	♀	♂	⚳	♃	♄	♅	♆	♇
1 W	8 41 07	9♌24 09	27♍31 21	4♎51 04	4♊14.0	6♍37.2	22♌13.4	22♏06.0	18♉30.2	4♑21.9	10♏00.1	9♐39.0	29♐02.9	29♎28.0
2 Th	8 45 03	10 21 34	12♎07 02	19 18 45	4R 10.1	7 31.1	23 27.2	22 32.2	18 44.6	4R 16.9	10 02.0	9R 38.2	29R 01.8	29 28.8
3 F	8 49 00	11 19 00	26 25 54	3♏28 16	4D 08.4	8 21.8	24 41.1	22 58.9	18 58.8	4 12.1	10 04.0	9 37.4	29 00.7	29 29.6
4 Sa	8 52 56	12 16 27	10♏25 50	17 18 37	4 08.3	9 09.3	25 54.9	23 26.0	19 12.8	4 07.5	10 06.1	9 36.7	28 59.6	29 30.5
5 Su	8 56 53	13 13 55	24 06 45	0♐50 28	4R 08.6	9 53.3	27 08.8	23 53.4	19 26.6	4 03.0	10 08.3	9 36.0	28 58.6	29 31.4
6 M	9 00 49	14 11 23	7♐29 59	14 05 34	4 08.3	10 33.7	28 22.6	24 21.3	19 40.2	3 58.7	10 10.6	9 35.4	28 57.5	29 32.3
7 Tu	9 04 46	15 08 52	20 37 29	27 05 59	4 06.2	11 10.3	29 36.4	24 49.5	19 53.6	3 54.5	10 12.9	9 34.9	28 56.5	29 33.2
8 W	9 08 42	16 06 22	3♑31 19	9♑53 41	4 01.7	11 42.9	0♍50.2	25 18.0	20 06.8	3 50.5	10 15.4	9 34.4	28 55.6	29 34.2
9 Th	9 12 39	17 03 53	16 13 17	22 30 15	3 54.4	12 11.3	2 04.1	25 46.9	20 19.8	3 46.7	10 18.0	9 33.9	28 54.6	29 35.3
10 F	9 16 36	18 01 25	28 44 45	4♒56 54	3 44.4	12 35.4	3 17.9	26 16.1	20 32.6	3 43.0	10 20.6	9 33.5	28 53.7	29 36.3
11 Sa	9 20 32	18 58 57	11♒06 42	17 14 20	3 32.4	12 54.8	4 31.7	26 45.7	20 45.2	3 39.5	10 23.3	9 33.1	28 52.8	29 37.4
12 Su	9 24 29	19 56 31	23 19 53	29 23 26	3 19.4	13 09.4	5 45.5	27 15.6	20 57.5	3 36.2	10 26.2	9 32.8	28 51.9	29 38.5
13 M	9 28 25	20 54 06	5♓25 07	11♓25 04	3 06.3	13 19.0	6 59.3	27 45.8	21 09.6	3 33.1	10 29.1	9 32.5	28 51.1	29 39.7
14 Tu	9 32 22	21 51 43	17 23 28	23 20 34	2 54.4	13R 23.3	8 13.1	28 16.3	21 21.5	3 30.1	10 32.1	9 32.3	28 50.2	29 40.9
15 W	9 36 18	22 49 21	29 16 36	5♈11 54	2 44.4	13 22.3	9 26.9	28 47.1	21 33.1	3 27.3	10 35.2	9 32.2	28 49.4	29 42.1
16 Th	9 40 15	23 47 00	11♈06 51	17 01 50	2 37.1	13 15.8	10 40.7	29 18.2	21 44.6	3 24.7	10 38.3	9 32.0	28 48.7	29 43.3
17 F	9 44 11	24 44 41	22 57 20	28 53 53	2 32.4	13 03.6	11 54.5	29 49.7	21 55.7	3 22.3	10 41.6	9D 32.0	28 47.9	29 44.6
18 Sa	9 48 08	25 42 23	4♉52 00	10♉52 19	2 30.1	12 45.8	13 08.3	0♐21.4	22 06.6	3 20.0	10 44.9	9 32.0	28 47.2	29 45.9
19 Su	9 52 04	26 40 07	16 55 26	23 02 00	2 29.5	12 22.3	14 22.1	0 53.4	22 17.3	3 17.9	10 48.4	9 32.0	28 46.5	29 47.2
20 M	9 56 01	27 37 52	29 12 41	5♊28 08	2 29.4	11 53.3	15 35.9	1 25.7	22 27.8	3 16.1	10 51.9	9 32.1	28 45.9	29 48.6
21 Tu	9 59 58	28 35 40	11♊48 58	18 15 48	2 28.9	11 18.9	16 49.7	1 58.3	22 37.9	3 14.4	10 55.5	9 32.2	28 45.3	29 50.0
22 W	10 03 54	29 33 29	24 49 08	1♋29 25	2 26.8	10 39.5	18 03.5	2 31.2	22 47.8	3 12.9	10 59.1	9 32.4	28 44.7	29 51.4
23 Th	10 07 51	0♍31 20	8♋16 57	15 11 55	2 22.3	9 55.6	19 17.3	3 04.3	22 57.5	3 11.5	11 02.9	9 32.7	28 44.1	29 52.8
24 F	10 11 47	1 29 12	22 14 17	29 23 51	2 15.2	9 07.7	20 31.1	3 37.7	23 06.8	3 10.4	11 06.7	9 33.0	28 43.6	29 54.3
25 Sa	10 15 44	2 27 06	6♌40 10	14♌02 34	2 05.7	8 16.6	21 44.9	4 11.4	23 15.9	3 09.5	11 10.7	9 33.3	28 43.1	29 55.8
26 Su	10 19 40	3 25 02	21 30 11	29 01 55	1 54.9	7 23.1	22 58.6	4 45.3	23 24.7	3 08.7	11 14.7	9 33.7	28 42.6	29 57.3
27 M	10 23 37	4 22 59	6♍36 32	14♍12 42	1 43.8	6 28.2	24 12.4	5 19.5	23 33.3	3 08.1	11 18.7	9 34.2	28 42.2	29 58.9
28 Tu	10 27 33	5 20 58	21 49 03	29 24 11	1 33.7	5 32.9	25 26.2	5 53.9	23 41.5	3 07.8	11 22.9	9 34.7	28 41.7	0♏00.5
29 W	10 31 30	6 18 58	6♎56 52	14♎25 57	1 25.9	4 38.4	26 39.9	6 28.6	23 49.4	3D 07.6	11 27.1	9 35.2	28 41.4	0 02.1
30 Th	10 35 27	7 16 59	21 50 30	29 09 46	1 20.7	3 46.0	27 53.7	7 03.6	23 57.1	3 07.6	11 31.4	9 35.9	28 41.0	0 03.7
31 F	10 39 23	8 15 02	6♏23 13	13♏30 31	1 18.1	2 56.7	29 07.4	7 38.8	24 04.4	3 07.8	11 35.8	9 36.5	28 40.7	0 05.4

Astro Data	Dy Hr Mn
☽0S	5 14:17
♇D	9 8:22
♄D	13 6:16
♆⚹♇	18 18:49
☽0N	19 14:13
♄⚺♅	24 0:26
☽0S	1 19:49
☿R	14 19:34
☽0N	15 20:25
♅D	18 5:40
☽0S	29 3:37
♃D	29 23:02

Planet Ingress		Dy Hr Mn
☿	♌	6 18:56
♀	♌	14 10:30
☉	♌	22 15:58
☿	♍	26 6:49
♀	♍	7 19:40
♂	♐	17 19:50
☉	♍	22 23:00
♇	♏	28 4:44

Last Aspect Dy Hr Mn			☽ Ingress	Dy Hr Mn
2 19:02	♆	△	♍	2 19:28
4 20:55	♆	□	♎	4 21:27
6 23:50	♆	⚹	♏	7 0:28
8 16:30	♀	△	♐	9 5:03
11 10:29	♆	☌	♑	11 11:23
13 18:23	♇	□	♒	13 19:41
16 4:59	♆	⚹	♓	16 6:10
18 17:06	♆	□	♈	18 18:26
21 5:35	♇	☍	♉	21 6:52
23 10:25	☿	□	♊	23 17:10
25 23:03	☿	⚹	♋	25 23:44
28 1:43	♇	□	♌	28 2:41
30 2:34	♇	⚹	♍	30 3:29

Last Aspect Dy Hr Mn			☽ Ingress	Dy Hr Mn
1 2:30	♆	□	♎	1 4:03
3 5:12	♇	☌	♏	3 6:04
5 4:44	♀	□	♐	5 10:30
7 17:10	♀	△	♑	7 17:24
10 1:39	♇	□	♒	10 2:25
12 12:30	♇	△	♓	12 13:13
14 23:06	♆	□	♈	15 1:28
17 13:42	♇	☍	♉	17 14:13
19 19:41	☉	□	♊	20 1:31
22 9:04	♇	△	♋	22 9:20
24 12:51	♇	□	♌	24 13:00
26 13:28	♇	⚹	♍	26 13:32
28 10:53	♆	□	♎	28 12:57
30 11:13	♆	⚹	♏	30 13:23

☽ Phases & Eclipses Dy Hr Mn		
5 21:04	☽	13♎59
13 2:20	○	20♑52
21 4:01	☾	28♈34
28 11:51	●	5♌34
4 2:33	☽	11♏54
11 15:43	○	19♒08
19 19:41	☾	26♉59
26 19:25	●	3♍43

Astro Data

1 July 1984
Julian Day # 30863
SVP 5♓28'49"
GC 26♐37.4 ⚴ 23♓00.4
Eris 16♈09.5 ⚵ 26♋47.4
⚷ 5♊47.5 ⚶ 29♋42.8
☽ Mean ☊ 4♊51.8

1 August 1984
Julian Day # 30894
SVP 5♓28'44"
GC 26♐37.4 ⚴ 21♓37.1R
Eris 16♈08.0R ⚵ 12♌17.0
⚷ 7♊31.9 ⚶ 13♌40.7
☽ Mean ☊ 3♊13.3

LONGITUDE September 1984

Day	Sid.Time	☉	0 hr ☽	Noon☽	True☊	☿	♀	♂	⚳	♃	♄	♅	♆	♇
1 Sa	10 43 20	9♍13 06	20♏31 33	27♏26 19	1♊17.3	2♍11.6	0♎21.2	8♐14.2	24♉11.5	3♑08.2	11♏40.3	9♐37.2	28♐40.4	0♏07.1
2 Su	10 47 16	10 11 12	4♐14 59	10♐57 49	1R 17.3	1R 32.0	1 34.9	8 49.8	24 18.2	3 08.8	11 44.8	9 38.0	28R 40.2	0 08.8
3 M	10 51 13	11 09 19	17 35 10	24 07 26	1 16.9	0 58.6	2 48.6	9 25.7	24 24.7	3 09.5	11 49.4	9 38.8	28 39.9	0 10.5
4 Tu	10 55 09	12 07 27	0♑35 00	6♑58 20	1 14.7	0 32.4	4 02.3	10 01.7	24 30.8	3 10.5	11 54.1	9 39.7	28 39.7	0 12.3
5 W	10 59 06	13 05 37	13 17 50	19 33 55	1 10.2	0 13.9	5 16.0	10 38.0	24 36.6	3 11.7	11 58.8	9 40.6	28 39.6	0 14.1
6 Th	11 03 02	14 03 49	25 46 57	1♒57 17	1 02.8	0D 03.7	6 29.7	11 14.5	24 42.0	3 13.0	12 03.6	9 41.6	28 39.5	0 15.9
7 F	11 06 59	15 02 02	8♒05 13	14 11 02	0 52.8	0 02.3	7 43.3	11 51.2	24 47.2	3 14.5	12 08.5	9 42.6	28 39.4	0 17.7
8 Sa	11 10 56	16 00 16	20 14 58	26 17 13	0 40.8	0 09.7	8 57.0	12 28.1	24 52.0	3 16.2	12 13.5	9 43.6	28 39.3	0 19.6
9 Su	11 14 52	16 58 32	2♓17 58	8♓17 24	0 27.6	0 26.1	10 10.6	13 05.2	24 56.5	3 18.1	12 18.5	9 44.8	28D 39.3	0 21.5
10 M	11 18 49	17 56 50	14 15 41	20 12 58	0 14.4	0 51.4	11 24.3	13 42.5	25 00.7	3 20.2	12 23.5	9 45.9	28 39.3	0 23.4
11 Tu	11 22 45	18 55 10	26 09 24	2♈05 11	0 02.3	1 25.5	12 37.9	14 20.0	25 04.5	3 22.5	12 28.7	9 47.1	28 39.3	0 25.3
12 W	11 26 42	19 53 32	8♈00 30	13 55 37	29♉52.2	2 08.1	13 51.5	14 57.7	25 07.9	3 24.9	12 33.9	9 48.4	28 39.4	0 27.2
13 Th	11 30 38	20 51 55	19 50 46	25 46 17	29 44.6	2 58.8	15 05.1	15 35.5	25 11.1	3 27.6	12 39.2	9 49.7	28 39.5	0 29.2
14 F	11 34 35	21 50 21	1♉42 30	7♉39 49	29 39.8	3 57.2	16 18.7	16 13.6	25 13.8	3 30.4	12 44.5	9 51.1	28 39.6	0 31.2
15 Sa	11 38 31	22 48 49	13 38 40	19 39 33	29D 37.5	5 02.7	17 32.2	16 51.8	25 16.2	3 33.4	12 49.9	9 52.5	28 39.8	0 33.2
16 Su	11 42 28	23 47 19	25 42 59	1♊49 31	29 37.1	6 14.9	18 45.8	17 30.2	25 18.3	3 36.5	12 55.3	9 54.0	28 40.0	0 35.2
17 M	11 46 25	24 45 51	7♊59 44	14 14 14	29R 37.5	7 33.1	19 59.4	18 08.8	25 20.0	3 39.9	13 00.9	9 55.5	28 40.2	0 37.2
18 Tu	11 50 21	25 44 25	20 33 37	26 58 30	29 37.9	8 56.8	21 12.9	18 47.5	25 21.3	3 43.4	13 06.4	9 57.0	28 40.5	0 39.3
19 W	11 54 18	26 43 02	3♋29 24	10♋06 50	29 37.0	10 25.3	22 26.5	19 26.4	25 22.3	3 47.1	13 12.1	9 58.6	28 40.8	0 41.4
20 Th	11 58 14	27 41 40	16 51 13	23 42 50	29 34.2	11 57.9	23 40.0	20 05.5	25 22.8	3 51.0	13 17.7	10 00.3	28 41.1	0 43.5
21 F	12 02 11	28 40 21	0♌41 51	7♌48 13	29 29.2	13 34.2	24 53.5	20 44.7	25R 23.0	3 55.1	13 23.5	10 02.0	28 41.5	0 45.6
22 Sa	12 06 07	29 39 05	15 01 44	22 21 56	29 22.0	15 13.6	26 07.0	21 24.2	25 22.9	3 59.3	13 29.3	10 03.7	28 41.9	0 47.7
23 Su	12 10 04	0♎37 50	29 48 09	7♍19 28	29 13.5	16 55.4	27 20.5	22 03.7	25 22.3	4 03.7	13 35.1	10 05.5	28 42.3	0 49.9
24 M	12 14 00	1 36 37	14♍54 46	22 32 47	29 04.5	18 39.4	28 34.0	22 43.5	25 21.4	4 08.3	13 41.0	10 07.4	28 42.8	0 52.1
25 Tu	12 17 57	2 35 27	0♎12 09	7♎51 25	28 56.4	20 24.9	29 47.5	23 23.3	25 20.1	4 13.1	13 47.0	10 09.2	28 43.3	0 54.2
26 W	12 21 54	3 34 18	15 29 10	23 04 05	28 50.1	22 11.7	1♏01.0	24 03.4	25 18.3	4 18.0	13 53.0	10 11.2	28 43.8	0 56.4
27 Th	12 25 50	4 33 11	0♏34 58	8♏00 49	28 46.1	23 59.4	2 14.4	24 43.6	25 16.3	4 23.1	13 59.1	10 13.1	28 44.4	0 58.7
28 F	12 29 47	5 32 06	15 20 51	22 34 27	28D 44.3	25 47.7	3 27.9	25 23.9	25 13.8	4 28.4	14 05.2	10 15.2	28 45.0	1 00.9
29 Sa	12 33 43	6 31 03	29 41 18	6♐41 12	28 44.4	27 36.3	4 41.3	26 04.4	25 10.9	4 33.8	14 11.3	10 17.2	28 45.6	1 03.1
30 Su	12 37 40	7 30 02	13♐34 10	20 20 22	28 45.4	29 25.0	5 54.7	26 45.1	25 07.7	4 39.4	14 17.5	10 19.3	28 46.3	1 05.4

LONGITUDE October 1984

Day	Sid.Time	☉	0 hr ☽	Noon☽	True☊	☿	♀	♂	⚳	♃	♄	♅	♆	♇
1 M	12 41 36	8♎29 03	27♐00 06	3♑33 43	28♉46.3	1♎13.7	7♏08.1	27♐25.9	25♉04.0	4♑45.1	14♏23.8	10♐21.5	28♐47.0	1♏07.6
2 Tu	12 45 33	9 28 05	10♑01 39	16 24 25	28R 46.1	3 02.1	8 21.5	28 06.8	25R 00.0	4 51.0	14 30.0	10 23.7	28 47.7	1 09.9
3 W	12 49 29	10 27 09	22 42 29	28 56 24	28 44.2	4 50.2	9 34.8	28 47.8	24 55.6	4 57.1	14 36.4	10 25.9	28 48.4	1 12.2
4 Th	12 53 26	11 26 15	5♒06 40	11♒13 45	28 40.3	6 37.9	10 48.2	29 29.0	24 50.8	5 03.3	14 42.7	10 28.2	28 49.2	1 14.5
5 F	12 57 23	12 25 22	17 18 08	23 20 15	28 34.3	8 25.0	12 01.5	0♑10.3	24 45.7	5 09.7	14 49.2	10 30.5	28 50.1	1 16.8
6 Sa	13 01 19	13 24 31	29 20 29	5♓19 14	28 26.8	10 11.6	13 14.8	0 51.7	24 40.1	5 16.3	14 55.6	10 32.9	28 50.9	1 19.2
7 Su	13 05 16	14 23 43	11♓16 48	17 13 30	28 18.4	11 57.5	14 28.1	1 33.2	24 34.2	5 23.0	15 02.1	10 35.3	28 51.8	1 21.5
8 M	13 09 12	15 22 56	23 09 36	29 05 20	28 09.9	13 42.7	15 41.3	2 14.9	24 27.9	5 29.8	15 08.6	10 37.7	28 52.7	1 23.8
9 Tu	13 13 09	16 22 11	5♈00 57	10♈56 39	28 02.2	15 27.3	16 54.6	2 56.7	24 21.3	5 36.8	15 15.2	10 40.2	28 53.6	1 26.2
10 W	13 17 05	17 21 28	16 52 39	22 49 09	27 55.8	17 11.2	18 07.8	3 38.6	24 14.3	5 43.9	15 21.8	10 42.7	28 54.6	1 28.5
11 Th	13 21 02	18 20 47	28 46 22	4♉44 33	27 51.3	18 54.3	19 21.0	4 20.6	24 06.9	5 51.2	15 28.4	10 45.3	28 55.6	1 30.9
12 F	13 24 58	19 20 08	10♉43 54	16 44 44	27D 48.8	20 36.8	20 34.2	5 02.7	23 59.1	5 58.6	15 35.1	10 47.8	28 56.7	1 33.3
13 Sa	13 28 55	20 19 32	22 47 18	28 51 58	27 48.2	22 18.5	21 47.3	5 44.9	23 51.1	6 06.2	15 41.8	10 50.5	28 57.7	1 35.7
14 Su	13 32 51	21 18 58	4♊59 05	11♊09 01	27 48.9	23 59.5	23 00.5	6 27.2	23 42.6	6 13.9	15 48.5	10 53.1	28 58.8	1 38.1
15 M	13 36 48	22 18 26	17 22 11	23 39 01	27 50.4	25 39.8	24 13.6	7 09.6	23 33.8	6 21.8	15 55.3	10 55.8	29 00.0	1 40.5
16 Tu	13 40 45	23 17 56	29 59 59	6♋25 30	27 52.0	27 19.4	25 26.7	7 52.2	23 24.7	6 29.8	16 02.1	10 58.6	29 01.1	1 42.9
17 W	13 44 41	24 17 29	12♋56 01	19 31 56	27R 53.0	28 58.4	26 39.8	8 34.8	23 15.3	6 37.9	16 08.9	11 01.4	29 02.3	1 45.3
18 Th	13 48 38	25 17 04	26 13 37	3♌01 23	27 52.9	0♏36.7	27 52.9	9 17.6	23 05.5	6 46.1	16 15.8	11 04.2	29 03.5	1 47.7
19 F	13 52 34	26 16 41	9♌55 23	16 55 44	27 51.3	2 14.4	29 06.0	10 00.4	22 55.4	6 54.5	16 22.7	11 07.0	29 04.8	1 50.1
20 Sa	13 56 31	27 16 21	24 02 22	1♍15 03	27 48.4	3 51.4	0♐19.0	10 43.4	22 45.0	7 03.1	16 29.6	11 09.9	29 06.0	1 52.5
21 Su	14 00 27	28 16 02	8♍33 23	15 56 48	27 44.6	5 27.9	1 32.0	11 26.4	22 34.3	7 11.7	16 36.5	11 12.8	29 07.3	1 54.9
22 M	14 04 24	29 15 46	23 24 30	0♎55 33	27 40.4	7 03.7	2 45.0	12 09.5	22 23.3	7 20.5	16 43.5	11 15.7	29 08.7	1 57.3
23 Tu	14 08 20	0♏15 32	8♎28 53	16 03 19	27 36.5	8 39.0	3 58.0	12 52.8	22 12.0	7 29.4	16 50.4	11 18.7	29 10.0	1 59.8
24 W	14 12 17	1 15 21	23 37 38	1♏10 34	27 33.6	10 13.7	5 11.0	13 36.1	22 00.5	7 38.5	16 57.4	11 21.7	29 11.4	2 02.2
25 Th	14 16 14	2 15 11	8♏40 57	16 07 41	27D 31.9	11 47.9	6 23.9	14 19.5	21 48.7	7 47.6	17 04.4	11 24.7	29 12.8	2 04.6
26 F	14 20 10	3 15 03	23 29 48	0♐46 30	27 31.6	13 21.5	7 36.9	15 03.0	21 36.7	7 56.9	17 11.5	11 27.8	29 14.3	2 07.0
27 Sa	14 24 07	4 14 57	7♐57 12	15 01 25	27 32.3	14 54.7	8 49.8	15 46.6	21 24.4	8 06.3	17 18.5	11 30.9	29 15.7	2 09.5
28 Su	14 28 03	5 14 53	21 58 56	28 49 39	27 33.7	16 27.3	10 02.6	16 30.3	21 12.0	8 15.9	17 25.6	11 34.0	29 17.2	2 11.9
29 M	14 32 00	6 14 50	5♑33 37	12♑11 04	27 35.2	17 59.5	11 15.5	17 14.1	20 59.3	8 25.5	17 32.7	11 37.1	29 18.7	2 14.3
30 Tu	14 35 56	7 14 49	18 42 17	25 07 39	27 36.4	19 31.1	12 28.3	17 57.9	20 46.4	8 35.3	17 39.8	11 40.3	29 20.3	2 16.7
31 W	14 39 53	8 14 50	1♒27 38	7♒42 45	27R 36.9	21 02.3	13 41.1	18 41.9	20 33.4	8 45.2	17 46.9	11 43.5	29 21.9	2 19.2

Astro Data

	Dy Hr Mn
♀0S	3 5:39
☿ D	7 4:00
♆ D	9 22:13
☽0N	12 2:08
⚳ R	21 13:05
☉0S	22 20:33
♄∠♆	24 19:42
☽0S	25 13:51
☿0S	2 23:14
☽0N	9 8:07
☽0S	23 0:58

Planet Ingress

		Dy Hr Mn
♀	♎	1 5:07
☊	♉R	11 17:01
☉	♎	22 20:33
♀	♏	25 16:05
☿	♎	30 19:44
♂	♑	5 6:02
☿	♏	18 3:01
♀	♐	20 5:45
☉	♏	23 5:46

Last Aspect / ☽ Ingress

Dy Hr Mn	Aspect	☽ Ingress	Dy Hr Mn
31 8:45	♄ ☌	♐	1 16:30
3 20:25	♆ ☌	♑	3 22:55
4 22:35	☉ △	♒	6 8:11
8 16:43	♆ ⚹	♓	8 19:24
11 5:03	♆ □	♈	11 7:47
13 17:50	♆ △	♉	13 20:33
15 18:49	☉ △	♊	16 8:26
18 15:09	♆ ☍	♋	18 17:36
20 19:23	☉ ⚹	♌	20 22:49
22 22:14	♆ △	♍	23 0:19
24 21:40	♆ □	♎	24 23:41
26 21:02	♆ ⚹	♏	26 23:04
28 18:12	☿ ⚹	♐	29 0:32

Last Aspect / ☽ Ingress

Dy Hr Mn	Aspect	☽ Ingress	Dy Hr Mn
1 3:14	♆ ☌	♑	1 5:28
2 8:22	♄ ⚹	♒	3 14:03
5 23:00	♆ ⚹	♓	6 1:19
8 11:34	♆ □	♈	8 13:51
11 0:18	♆ △	♉	11 2:28
12 20:27	♀ ☍	♊	13 14:14
15 22:08	♆ ☍	♋	16 0:00
18 2:03	♀ △	♌	18 6:41
20 8:26	♆ △	♍	20 9:56
22 9:09	♆ □	♎	22 10:32
24 8:50	♆ ⚹	♏	24 10:08
25 13:33	♄ ☌	♐	26 10:43
28 12:49	♆ ☌	♑	28 14:05
30 0:07	☿ ⚹	♒	30 21:13

☽ Phases & Eclipses

Dy Hr Mn		
2 10:30	☽	10♐08
10 7:01	○	17♓45
18 9:31	☾	25♊38
25 3:11	●	2♎14
1 21:52	☽	8♑53
9 23:58	○	16♈52
17 21:14	☾	24♋40
24 12:08	●	1♏16
31 13:07	☽	8♒18

Astro Data

1 September 1984
Julian Day # 30925
SVP 5♓28'40"
GC 26♐37.5 ⚴ 15♓13.2R
Eris 15♈57.1R ⚵ 27♌01.2
⚷ 8♊27.7 ⚶ 28♌00.1
☽ Mean ☊ 1♊34.8

1 October 1984
Julian Day # 30955
SVP 5♓28'37"
GC 26♐37.6 ⚴ 7♓57.1R
Eris 15♈40.6R ⚵ 10♍21.4
⚷ 8♊22.8R ⚶ 11♍58.4
☽ Mean ☊ 29♉59.5

November 1984 LONGITUDE

Day	Sid.Time	☉	0 hr ☽	Noon ☽	True ☊	☿	♀	♂	⚳	♃	♄	♅	♆	♇
1 Th	14 43 49	9♏14 52	13♒53 31	20♒00 30	27♉36.4	22♏33.0	14♐53.8	19♑25.9	20♉20.2	8♑55.2	17♏54.1	11♐46.7	29♐23.4	2♏21.6
2 F	14 47 46	10 14 56	26 04 15	2♓05 19	27R35.2	24 03.3	16 06.6	20 09.9	20R06.8	9 05.3	18 01.2	11 50.0	29 25.1	2 24.0
3 Sa	14 51 43	11 15 02	8♓04 14	14 01 32	27 33.2	25 33.1	17 19.3	20 54.1	19 53.4	9 15.5	18 08.3	11 53.3	29 26.7	2 26.4
4 Su	14 55 39	12 15 09	19 57 41	25 53 09	27 30.9	27 02.3	18 31.9	21 38.3	19 39.8	9 25.8	18 15.5	11 56.6	29 28.4	2 28.8
5 M	14 59 36	13 15 17	1♈48 22	7♈43 44	27 28.5	28 31.1	19 44.5	22 22.5	19 26.1	9 36.2	18 22.6	11 59.9	29 30.1	2 31.2
6 Tu	15 03 32	14 15 27	13 39 36	19 36 17	27 26.4	29 59.5	20 57.1	23 06.9	19 12.3	9 46.7	18 29.8	12 03.2	29 31.8	2 33.6
7 W	15 07 29	15 15 39	25 34 07	1♉33 20	27 24.7	1♐27.2	22 09.7	23 51.3	18 58.5	9 57.3	18 37.0	12 06.6	29 33.5	2 36.0
8 Th	15 11 25	16 15 53	7♉34 12	13 36 55	27 23.7	2 54.5	23 22.2	24 35.7	18 44.6	10 08.1	18 44.2	12 10.0	29 35.2	2 38.3
9 F	15 15 22	17 16 09	19 41 41	25 48 43	27D23.4	4 21.2	24 34.6	25 20.2	18 30.6	10 18.9	18 51.3	12 13.4	29 37.0	2 40.7
10 Sa	15 19 18	18 16 26	1♊58 11	8♊10 14	27 23.6	5 47.3	25 47.1	26 04.8	18 16.7	10 29.8	18 58.5	12 16.8	29 38.8	2 43.1
11 Su	15 23 15	19 16 45	14 25 04	20 42 50	27 24.1	7 12.8	26 59.5	26 49.4	18 02.7	10 40.8	19 05.7	12 20.3	29 40.6	2 45.4
12 M	15 27 12	20 17 06	27 03 43	3♋27 54	27 24.8	8 37.5	28 11.8	27 34.1	17 48.7	10 51.9	19 12.9	12 23.7	29 42.5	2 47.8
13 Tu	15 31 08	21 17 29	9♋55 35	16 26 55	27 25.6	10 01.6	29 24.1	28 18.9	17 34.8	11 03.1	19 20.1	12 27.2	29 44.3	2 50.1
14 W	15 35 05	22 17 54	23 02 06	29 41 17	27 26.1	11 24.8	0♑36.4	29 03.7	17 20.9	11 14.4	19 27.3	12 30.7	29 46.2	2 52.4
15 Th	15 39 01	23 18 21	6♌24 39	13♌12 18	27R26.4	12 47.0	1 48.7	29 48.5	17 07.1	11 25.8	19 34.4	12 34.2	29 48.1	2 54.8
16 F	15 42 58	24 18 49	20 04 19	27 00 43	27 26.4	14 08.3	3 00.8	0♒33.4	16 53.3	11 37.3	19 41.6	12 37.7	29 50.0	2 57.1
17 Sa	15 46 54	25 19 19	4♍01 29	11♍06 29	27 26.4	15 28.4	4 13.0	1 18.4	16 39.6	11 48.9	19 48.8	12 41.3	29 52.0	2 59.3
18 Su	15 50 51	26 19 52	18 15 30	25 28 14	27 26.2	16 47.3	5 25.1	2 03.4	16 26.1	12 00.5	19 56.0	12 44.8	29 53.9	3 01.6
19 M	15 54 47	27 20 26	2♎44 14	10♎02 59	27D26.2	18 04.7	6 37.2	2 48.4	16 12.6	12 12.2	20 03.1	12 48.4	29 55.9	3 03.9
20 Tu	15 58 44	28 21 01	17 23 50	24 46 03	27 26.2	19 20.5	7 49.2	3 33.5	15 59.3	12 24.0	20 10.3	12 52.0	29 57.9	3 06.1
21 W	16 02 41	29 21 39	2♏08 51	9♏31 20	27 26.3	20 34.5	9 01.1	4 18.7	15 46.1	12 35.9	20 17.4	12 55.6	29 59.9	3 08.4
22 Th	16 06 37	0♐22 18	16 52 38	24 11 53	27R26.4	21 46.3	10 13.0	5 03.9	15 33.1	12 47.9	20 24.5	12 59.2	0♑01.9	3 10.6
23 F	16 10 34	1 22 59	1♐28 12	8♐40 50	27 26.4	22 55.8	11 24.9	5 49.1	15 20.3	13 00.0	20 31.6	13 02.8	0 03.9	3 12.8
24 Sa	16 14 30	2 23 41	15 49 03	22 52 17	27 26.1	24 02.6	12 36.7	6 34.4	15 07.7	13 12.1	20 38.7	13 06.4	0 06.0	3 15.0
25 Su	16 18 27	3 24 24	29 50 03	6♑42 03	27 25.5	25 06.3	13 48.5	7 19.7	14 55.3	13 24.3	20 45.8	13 10.1	0 08.1	3 17.2
26 M	16 22 23	4 25 08	13♑28 04	20 08 00	27 24.6	26 06.4	15 00.2	8 05.1	14 43.2	13 36.6	20 52.9	13 13.7	0 10.2	3 19.4
27 Tu	16 26 20	5 25 54	26 42 01	3♒10 12	27 23.7	27 02.5	16 11.8	8 50.5	14 31.2	13 48.9	20 59.9	13 17.4	0 12.3	3 21.5
28 W	16 30 17	6 26 41	9♒32 51	15 50 20	27 22.8	27 54.0	17 23.3	9 35.9	14 19.6	14 01.3	21 07.0	13 21.0	0 14.4	3 23.6
29 Th	16 34 13	7 27 28	22 03 06	28 11 37	27D22.1	28 40.3	18 34.8	10 21.4	14 08.2	14 13.8	21 14.0	13 24.7	0 16.5	3 25.7
30 F	16 38 10	8 28 17	4♓16 27	10♓18 10	27 22.0	29 20.7	19 46.2	11 06.9	13 57.0	14 26.4	21 21.0	13 28.4	0 18.6	3 27.8

December 1984 LONGITUDE

Day	Sid.Time	☉	0 hr ☽	Noon ☽	True ☊	☿	♀	♂	⚳	♃	♄	♅	♆	♇
1 Sa	16 42 06	9♐29 06	16♓17 20	22♓14 34	27♉22.4	29♐54.5	20♑57.6	11♒52.4	13♉46.2	14♑39.0	21♏27.9	13♐32.0	0♑20.8	3♏29.9
2 Su	16 46 03	10 29 56	28 10 29	4♈05 39	27 23.3	0♑20.8	22 08.8	12 37.9	13R35.7	14 51.7	21 34.9	13 35.7	0 22.9	3 32.0
3 M	16 49 59	11 30 47	10♈00 40	15 56 05	27 24.5	0 38.8	23 20.0	13 23.5	13 25.4	15 04.4	21 41.8	13 39.4	0 25.1	3 34.0
4 Tu	16 53 56	12 31 39	21 52 25	27 50 10	27 26.0	0R47.8	24 31.1	14 09.1	13 15.5	15 17.2	21 48.7	13 43.0	0 27.2	3 36.0
5 W	16 57 52	13 32 32	3♉49 47	9♉51 42	27 27.2	0 46.8	25 42.1	14 54.7	13 05.9	15 30.1	21 55.5	13 46.7	0 29.4	3 38.0
6 Th	17 01 49	14 33 26	15 56 16	22 03 47	27R28.0	0 35.2	26 53.0	15 40.4	12 56.7	15 43.0	22 02.4	13 50.4	0 31.6	3 40.0
7 F	17 05 46	15 34 21	28 14 32	4♊28 43	27 27.9	0 12.5	28 03.8	16 26.0	12 47.8	15 56.0	22 09.2	13 54.1	0 33.8	3 41.9
8 Sa	17 09 42	16 35 17	10♊46 29	17 07 55	27 26.8	29♐38.4	29 14.6	17 11.7	12 39.2	16 09.0	22 16.0	13 57.7	0 36.0	3 43.8
9 Su	17 13 39	17 36 13	23 33 04	0♋01 56	27 24.8	28 53.0	0♒25.2	17 57.4	12 31.0	16 22.1	22 22.7	14 01.4	0 38.3	3 45.7
10 M	17 17 35	18 37 11	6♋34 27	13 10 31	27 21.8	27 57.0	1 35.7	18 43.1	12 23.2	16 35.2	22 29.4	14 05.1	0 40.5	3 47.6
11 Tu	17 21 32	19 38 10	19 50 00	26 32 46	27 18.4	26 51.4	2 46.1	19 28.8	12 15.7	16 48.4	22 36.1	14 08.8	0 42.7	3 49.5
12 W	17 25 28	20 39 10	3♌18 37	10♌07 23	27 15.0	25 37.8	3 56.5	20 14.6	12 08.6	17 01.6	22 42.8	14 12.4	0 45.0	3 51.3
13 Th	17 29 25	21 40 10	16 58 51	23 52 51	27 12.0	24 18.5	5 06.7	21 00.3	12 01.9	17 14.9	22 49.4	14 16.1	0 47.2	3 53.1
14 F	17 33 21	22 41 12	0♍49 10	7♍47 38	27 10.0	22 56.0	6 16.8	21 46.1	11 55.5	17 28.2	22 56.0	14 19.7	0 49.5	3 54.9
15 Sa	17 37 18	23 42 15	14 48 04	21 50 17	27D09.2	21 33.1	7 26.7	22 31.9	11 49.6	17 41.6	23 02.5	14 23.4	0 51.7	3 56.7
16 Su	17 41 15	24 43 18	28 54 06	5♎59 18	27 09.6	20 12.6	8 36.6	23 17.7	11 44.0	17 55.0	23 09.0	14 27.0	0 54.0	3 58.4
17 M	17 45 11	25 44 23	13♎05 42	20 13 01	27 10.8	18 57.2	9 46.4	24 03.5	11 38.8	18 08.4	23 15.5	14 30.7	0 56.2	4 00.1
18 Tu	17 49 08	26 45 29	27 21 00	4♏29 20	27 12.4	17 48.9	10 56.0	24 49.3	11 34.0	18 21.9	23 21.9	14 34.3	0 58.5	4 01.8
19 W	17 53 04	27 46 35	11♏37 39	18 45 33	27R13.6	16 49.6	12 05.5	25 35.1	11 29.7	18 35.5	23 28.2	14 37.9	1 00.8	4 03.4
20 Th	17 57 01	28 47 42	25 52 34	2♐58 14	27 13.7	16 00.3	13 14.8	26 21.0	11 25.7	18 49.0	23 34.6	14 41.5	1 03.0	4 05.1
21 F	18 00 57	29 48 50	10♐02 03	17 03 28	27 12.3	15 21.7	14 24.1	27 06.8	11 22.1	19 02.7	23 40.9	14 45.1	1 05.3	4 06.7
22 Sa	18 04 54	0♑49 59	24 01 59	0♑57 06	27 09.0	14 54.0	15 33.2	27 52.7	11 19.0	19 16.3	23 47.1	14 48.7	1 07.6	4 08.2
23 Su	18 08 50	1 51 08	7♑48 23	14 35 25	27 04.1	14 37.1	16 42.1	28 38.5	11 16.2	19 30.0	23 53.3	14 52.2	1 09.9	4 09.8
24 M	18 12 47	2 52 17	21 17 54	27 55 35	26 58.0	14D30.5	17 50.9	29 24.4	11 13.9	19 43.7	23 59.4	14 55.8	1 12.1	4 11.3
25 Tu	18 16 44	3 53 27	4♒28 20	10♒56 06	26 51.3	14 33.5	18 59.5	0♓10.3	11 12.0	19 57.5	24 05.5	14 59.3	1 14.4	4 12.8
26 W	18 20 40	4 54 37	17 18 58	23 37 04	26 45.0	14 45.5	20 08.0	0 56.1	11 10.4	20 11.2	24 11.6	15 02.9	1 16.7	4 14.2
27 Th	18 24 37	5 55 46	29 50 40	6♓00 05	26 39.6	15 05.7	21 16.3	1 42.0	11 09.3	20 25.0	24 17.6	15 06.4	1 18.9	4 15.6
28 F	18 28 33	6 56 56	12♓05 45	18 08 08	26 35.8	15 33.4	22 24.4	2 27.9	11 08.6	20 38.9	24 23.5	15 09.9	1 21.2	4 17.0
29 Sa	18 32 30	7 58 06	24 07 46	0♈05 13	26D33.7	16 07.7	23 32.3	3 13.7	11D08.3	20 52.7	24 29.4	15 13.3	1 23.5	4 18.4
30 Su	18 36 26	8 59 15	6♈01 07	11 56 06	26 33.3	16 48.1	24 40.0	3 59.6	11 08.4	21 06.6	24 35.2	15 16.8	1 25.7	4 19.7
31 M	18 40 23	10 00 24	17 50 49	23 45 55	26 34.3	17 33.8	25 47.6	4 45.4	11 08.9	21 20.5	24 41.0	15 20.2	1 28.0	4 21.0

Astro Data Dy Hr Mn	Planet Ingress Dy Hr Mn	Last Aspect Dy Hr Mn	☽ Ingress Dy Hr Mn	Last Aspect Dy Hr Mn	☽ Ingress Dy Hr Mn	☽ Phases & Eclipses Dy Hr Mn
☽0N 5 14:51	☿ ♐ 6 12:09	2 6:39 ♆ ⚹	♓ 2 7:50	1 10:25 ♄ △	♈ 2 3:42	8 17:43 ○ 16♉30
☽0S 19 10:33	♀ ♑ 13 23:54	4 19:17 ♆ □	♈ 4 20:20	4 4:36 ♀ □	♉ 4 16:20	8 17:55 • A 0.899
♃⚹♅ 23 20:03	♂ ♒ 15 18:09	7 8:00 ♆ △	♉ 7 8:53	6 22:21 ♀ △	♊ 7 3:24	16 6:59 ☾ 24♌06
	♆ ♑ 21 13:21	9 11:01 ♂ △	♊ 9 20:10	9 10:01 ☿ ☍	♋ 9 11:56	22 22:57 ● 0♐50
☽0N 2 22:15	☉ ♐ 22 3:11	12 4:57 ♆ ☍	♋ 12 5:31	11 4:54 ♄ △	♌ 11 18:08	22 22:53:22 • T 01'60"
☿R 4 21:47		14 10:48 ♂ ☍	♌ 14 12:34	13 12:40 ☿ △	♍ 13 22:35	30 8:01 ☽ 8♓18
☽0S 16 17:10	☿ ♑ 1 16:29	16 16:51 ♆ △	♍ 16 17:08	15 15:25 ☉ □	♎ 16 1:52	
☿D 24 16:12	☿ ♐R 7 21:46	18 19:20 ♆ □	♎ 18 19:29	17 22:00 ☉ ⚹	♏ 18 4:27	8 10:53 ○ 16♊32
⚳D 29 18:08	♀ ♒ 9 3:26	20 20:28 ♆ ⚹	♏ 20 20:31	20 0:10 ♂ □	♐ 20 6:58	15 15:25 ☾ 23♍51
☽0N 30 5:49	☉ ♑ 21 16:23	22 5:44 ♄ ☌	♐ 22 21:34	22 6:21 ♂ ⚹	♑ 22 10:21	22 11:47 ● 0♑49
	♂ ♓ 25 6:38	24 14:11 ☿ ☌	♑ 25 0:17	24 4:48 ♄ ⚹	♒ 24 15:47	30 5:27 ☽ 8♈43
		26 13:22 ♄ ⚹	♒ 27 6:06	26 13:07 ♄ □	♓ 27 0:18	
		29 13:00 ☿ ⚹	♓ 29 15:33	29 0:38 ♄ △	♈ 29 11:49	

Astro Data

1 November 1984
Julian Day # 30986
SVP 5♓28'33"
GC 26♐37.6 ⚵ 4♓35.7R
Eris 15♈22.2R ⚴ 22♍49.3
⚷ 7♊18.9R ⚶ 26♍13.4
☽ Mean ☊ 28♉21.0

1 December 1984
Julian Day # 31016
SVP 5♓28'28"
GC 26♐37.7 ⚵ 6♓40.6
Eris 15♈08.4R ⚴ 3♎00.3
⚷ 5♊42.4R ⚶ 9♎23.2
☽ Mean ☊ 26♉45.7

LONGITUDE — January 1985

Day	Sid.Time	☉	0 hr ☽	Noon ☽	True ☊	☿	♀	♂	⚳	♃	♄	♅	♆	♇
1 Tu	18 44 19	11♑01 34	29♈42 04	5♉39 54	26♉35.9	18♐24.2	26♒54.9	5♓31.3	11♉09.8	21♑34.4	24♏46.7	15♐23.6	1♑30.2	4♏22.3
2 W	18 48 16	12 02 43	11♉40 02	17 43 04	26R 37.2	19 18.9	28 02.0	6 17.1	11 11.1	21 48.3	24 52.3	15 27.0	1 32.5	4 23.5
3 Th	18 52 13	13 03 52	23 49 32	29 59 56	26 37.5	20 17.3	29 08.9	7 03.0	11 12.8	22 02.3	24 57.9	15 30.4	1 34.7	4 24.7
4 F	18 56 09	14 05 01	6♊14 40	12♊34 04	26 36.1	21 19.1	0♓15.6	7 48.8	11 14.9	22 16.3	25 03.4	15 33.8	1 36.9	4 25.9
5 Sa	19 00 06	15 06 09	18 58 25	25 27 51	26 32.5	22 23.9	1 22.0	8 34.6	11 17.3	22 30.2	25 08.9	15 37.1	1 39.2	4 27.0
6 Su	19 04 02	16 07 18	2♋02 26	8♋42 05	26 26.6	23 31.2	2 28.2	9 20.4	11 20.2	22 44.2	25 14.3	15 40.4	1 41.4	4 28.1
7 M	19 07 59	17 08 26	15 26 37	22 15 47	26 18.8	24 41.0	3 34.1	10 06.1	11 23.4	22 58.3	25 19.6	15 43.7	1 43.6	4 29.2
8 Tu	19 11 55	18 09 34	29 09 09	6♌06 17	26 09.8	25 52.9	4 39.8	10 51.9	11 27.0	23 12.3	25 24.9	15 46.9	1 45.8	4 30.2
9 W	19 15 52	19 10 42	13♌06 38	20 09 36	26 00.7	27 06.7	5 45.2	11 37.7	11 31.0	23 26.3	25 30.1	15 50.2	1 48.0	4 31.2
10 Th	19 19 49	20 11 50	27 14 35	4♍20 59	25 52.5	28 22.2	6 50.4	12 23.4	11 35.3	23 40.4	25 35.3	15 53.4	1 50.2	4 32.2
11 F	19 23 45	21 12 57	11♍28 12	18 35 44	25 46.1	29 39.2	7 55.2	13 09.1	11 40.1	23 54.4	25 40.3	15 56.6	1 52.4	4 33.1
12 Sa	19 27 42	22 14 05	25 43 05	2♎49 51	25 42.0	0♑57.6	8 59.8	13 54.8	11 45.1	24 08.5	25 45.3	15 59.7	1 54.5	4 34.0
13 Su	19 31 38	23 15 12	9♎55 44	17 00 29	25D40.3	2 17.4	10 04.0	14 40.5	11 50.6	24 22.5	25 50.3	16 02.8	1 56.7	4 34.9
14 M	19 35 35	24 16 20	24 03 54	1♏05 52	25 40.2	3 38.3	11 08.0	15 26.2	11 56.3	24 36.6	25 55.1	16 05.9	1 58.8	4 35.7
15 Tu	19 39 31	25 17 27	8♏06 17	15 05 07	25R41.0	5 00.3	12 11.6	16 11.8	12 02.5	24 50.6	25 59.9	16 09.0	2 01.0	4 36.5
16 W	19 43 28	26 18 35	22 02 18	28 57 47	25 41.2	6 23.3	13 14.9	16 57.4	12 09.0	25 04.7	26 04.6	16 12.1	2 03.1	4 37.3
17 Th	19 47 24	27 19 42	5♐51 29	12♐43 19	25 39.9	7 47.2	14 17.9	17 43.1	12 15.8	25 18.8	26 09.3	16 15.1	2 05.2	4 38.0
18 F	19 51 21	28 20 49	19 33 09	26 20 49	25 36.1	9 12.1	15 20.6	18 28.7	12 23.0	25 32.9	26 13.8	16 18.0	2 07.3	4 38.7
19 Sa	19 55 18	29 21 55	3♑06 07	9♑48 51	25 29.4	10 37.7	16 22.8	19 14.3	12 30.5	25 46.9	26 18.3	16 21.0	2 09.4	4 39.4
20 Su	19 59 14	0♒23 01	16 28 47	23 05 39	25 19.9	12 04.2	17 24.7	19 59.8	12 38.4	26 01.0	26 22.7	16 23.9	2 11.4	4 40.0
21 M	20 03 11	1 24 06	29 39 14	6♒09 20	25 08.4	13 31.4	18 26.2	20 45.4	12 46.5	26 15.1	26 27.1	16 26.8	2 13.5	4 40.6
22 Tu	20 07 07	2 25 10	12♒35 47	18 58 28	24 55.8	14 59.4	19 27.3	21 30.9	12 55.0	26 29.1	26 31.3	16 29.6	2 15.5	4 41.1
23 W	20 11 04	3 26 14	25 17 20	1♓32 25	24 43.2	16 28.1	20 28.0	22 16.4	13 03.9	26 43.1	26 35.5	16 32.4	2 17.5	4 41.6
24 Th	20 15 00	4 27 17	7♓43 48	13 51 39	24 31.9	17 57.5	21 28.3	23 01.9	13 13.0	26 57.2	26 39.6	16 35.2	2 19.5	4 42.1
25 F	20 18 57	5 28 18	19 56 13	25 57 50	24 22.8	19 27.5	22 28.1	23 47.4	13 22.5	27 11.2	26 43.6	16 37.9	2 21.5	4 42.5
26 Sa	20 22 53	6 29 19	1♈56 54	7♈53 52	24 16.3	20 58.3	23 27.4	24 32.8	13 32.2	27 25.2	26 47.5	16 40.6	2 23.5	4 42.9
27 Su	20 26 50	7 30 18	13 49 16	19 43 39	24 12.6	22 29.7	24 26.3	25 18.2	13 42.3	27 39.2	26 51.3	16 43.3	2 25.4	4 43.3
28 M	20 30 47	8 31 17	25 37 40	1♉31 58	24D11.0	24 01.8	25 24.6	26 03.6	13 52.6	27 53.1	26 55.1	16 45.9	2 27.4	4 43.6
29 Tu	20 34 43	9 32 14	7♉27 12	13 24 06	24R10.8	25 34.6	26 22.5	26 48.9	14 03.3	28 07.1	26 58.7	16 48.5	2 29.3	4 43.9
30 W	20 38 40	10 33 10	19 23 20	25 25 37	24 11.0	27 08.0	27 19.7	27 34.2	14 14.2	28 21.0	27 02.3	16 51.1	2 31.2	4 44.1
31 Th	20 42 36	11 34 05	1♊31 37	7♊41 59	24 10.3	28 42.1	28 16.5	28 19.5	14 25.4	28 34.9	27 05.8	16 53.6	2 33.1	4 44.4

LONGITUDE — February 1985

Day	Sid.Time	☉	0 hr ☽	Noon ☽	True ☊	☿	♀	♂	⚳	♃	♄	♅	♆	♇
1 F	20 46 33	12♒34 58	13♊57 19	20♊18 08	24♉07.7	0♒17.0	29♓12.6	29♓04.8	14♉36.9	28♑48.8	27♏09.2	16♐56.0	2♑34.9	4♏44.5
2 Sa	20 50 29	13 35 50	26 44 52	3♋17 51	24R02.6	1 52.5	0♈08.1	29 50.0	14 48.7	29 02.7	27 12.5	16 58.5	2 36.8	4 44.7
3 Su	20 54 26	14 36 41	9♋57 18	16 43 15	23 54.7	3 28.7	1 03.0	0♈35.2	15 00.8	29 16.6	27 15.7	17 00.9	2 38.6	4 44.8
4 M	20 58 22	15 37 31	23 35 36	0♌34 04	23 44.3	5 05.7	1 57.2	1 20.3	15 13.1	29 30.4	27 18.9	17 03.2	2 40.4	4 44.9
5 Tu	21 02 19	16 38 19	7♌38 13	14 47 26	23 32.3	6 43.4	2 50.8	2 05.4	15 25.6	29 44.2	27 21.9	17 05.5	2 42.1	4R44.9
6 W	21 06 16	17 39 06	22 00 56	29 17 52	23 20.0	8 21.8	3 43.7	2 50.5	15 38.5	29 57.9	27 24.8	17 07.8	2 43.9	4 44.9
7 Th	21 10 12	18 39 52	6♍37 16	13♍58 08	23 08.7	10 01.0	4 35.8	3 35.6	15 51.5	0♒11.7	27 27.7	17 10.0	2 45.6	4 44.9
8 F	21 14 09	19 40 37	21 19 28	28 40 19	22 59.5	11 41.0	5 27.2	4 20.6	16 04.9	0 25.4	27 30.4	17 12.1	2 47.3	4 44.8
9 Sa	21 18 05	20 41 21	5♎59 50	13♎17 16	22 53.2	13 21.8	6 17.7	5 05.6	16 18.4	0 39.1	27 33.1	17 14.3	2 49.0	4 44.7
10 Su	21 22 02	21 42 03	20 32 01	27 43 36	22 49.8	15 03.4	7 07.5	5 50.5	16 32.3	0 52.7	27 35.7	17 16.4	2 50.7	4 44.6
11 M	21 25 58	22 42 45	4♏51 42	11♏56 06	22 48.5	16 45.8	7 56.5	6 35.4	16 46.3	1 06.3	27 38.1	17 18.4	2 52.3	4 44.4
12 Tu	21 29 55	23 43 25	18 56 43	25 53 34	22 48.4	18 29.1	8 44.6	7 20.3	17 00.6	1 19.9	27 40.5	17 20.4	2 53.9	4 44.2
13 W	21 33 51	24 44 05	2♐46 44	9♐36 18	22 48.0	20 13.3	9 31.7	8 05.2	17 15.1	1 33.4	27 42.8	17 22.3	2 55.5	4 43.9
14 Th	21 37 48	25 44 43	16 22 27	23 05 20	22 46.0	21 58.2	10 18.0	8 50.0	17 29.9	1 47.0	27 45.0	17 24.2	2 57.0	4 43.6
15 F	21 41 45	26 45 21	29 45 07	6♑21 54	22 41.5	23 44.1	11 03.2	9 34.8	17 44.8	2 00.4	27 47.1	17 26.1	2 58.6	4 43.3
16 Sa	21 45 41	27 45 57	12♑55 50	19 26 58	22 33.9	25 30.8	11 47.5	10 19.5	18 00.0	2 13.8	27 49.1	17 27.9	3 00.1	4 43.0
17 Su	21 49 38	28 46 31	25 55 21	2♒21 01	22 23.3	27 18.4	12 30.7	11 04.2	18 15.4	2 27.2	27 51.0	17 29.7	3 01.6	4 42.6
18 M	21 53 34	29 47 05	8♒43 57	15 04 09	22 10.4	29 06.9	13 12.9	11 48.9	18 31.0	2 40.6	27 52.7	17 31.4	3 03.0	4 42.1
19 Tu	21 57 31	0♓47 36	21 21 34	27 36 13	21 56.3	0♓56.2	13 53.8	12 33.5	18 46.9	2 53.9	27 54.4	17 33.1	3 04.5	4 41.7
20 W	22 01 27	1 48 06	3♓48 04	9♓57 10	21 42.1	2 46.3	14 33.7	13 18.1	19 02.9	3 07.1	27 56.0	17 34.7	3 05.9	4 41.2
21 Th	22 05 24	2 48 35	16 03 34	22 07 23	21 29.2	4 37.2	15 12.2	14 02.7	19 19.1	3 20.3	27 57.5	17 36.2	3 07.2	4 40.7
22 F	22 09 20	3 49 01	28 08 47	4♈07 57	21 18.5	6 28.9	15 49.5	14 47.2	19 35.6	3 33.4	27 58.9	17 37.7	3 08.6	4 40.1
23 Sa	22 13 17	4 49 26	10♈05 11	16 00 48	21 10.5	8 21.2	16 25.5	15 31.7	19 52.2	3 46.5	28 00.2	17 39.2	3 09.9	4 39.5
24 Su	22 17 14	5 49 49	21 55 11	27 48 48	21 05.5	10 14.2	17 00.1	16 16.2	20 09.0	3 59.6	28 01.3	17 40.6	3 11.2	4 38.9
25 M	22 21 10	6 50 11	3♉42 08	9♉35 45	21D03.1	12 07.8	17 33.2	17 00.6	20 26.1	4 12.5	28 02.4	17 42.0	3 12.4	4 38.2
26 Tu	22 25 07	7 50 30	15 30 14	21 26 14	21 02.6	14 01.7	18 04.9	17 44.9	20 43.3	4 25.5	28 03.4	17 43.3	3 13.7	4 37.5
27 W	22 29 03	8 50 47	27 24 23	3♊25 24	21R02.8	15 55.9	18 35.0	18 29.3	21 00.6	4 38.3	28 04.3	17 44.6	3 14.9	4 36.8
28 Th	22 33 00	9 51 03	9♊29 58	15 38 46	21 02.8	17 50.3	19 03.4	19 13.5	21 18.2	4 51.2	28 05.0	17 45.8	3 16.0	4 36.0

Astro Data	Dy Hr Mn
☽0S	12 21:52
♃✶♄	22 17:26
☽0N	26 13:02
♀0N	30 19:34
♂0N	4 1:55
♇R	5 23:58
☽0S	9 3:37
♃∠♅	17 17:03
♃⊻♆	20 9:30
☽0N	22 19:46
♃□♇	27 9:16

Planet Ingress	Dy Hr Mn
♀ ♓	4 6:23
☿ ♑	11 18:25
☉ ♒	20 2:58
☿ ♒	1 7:43
♀ ♈	2 8:29
♂ ♈	2 17:19
♃ ♒	6 15:35
☉ ♓	18 17:07
☿ ♓	18 23:41

Last Aspect Dy Hr Mn		☽ Ingress Dy Hr Mn
31 16:32	♀ ✶	♉ 1 0:36
3 10:12	♀ □	♊ 3 12:00
5 5:50	☿ ☍	♋ 5 20:18
7 17:23	♄ △	♌ 8 1:28
10 0:55	☿ △	♍ 10 4:40
11 24:00	♄ ✶	♎ 12 7:13
14 0:44	♃ □	♏ 14 10:07
16 7:02	☉ ✶	♐ 16 13:48
17 21:17	♂ □	♑ 18 18:29
20 18:02	♄ ✶	♒ 21 0:38
23 2:26	♄ □	♓ 23 9:02
25 14:30	♃ ✶	♈ 25 20:05
28 4:27	♃ □	♉ 28 8:53
30 17:53	♃ △	♊ 30 21:01

Last Aspect Dy Hr Mn		☽ Ingress Dy Hr Mn
2 5:48	♀ □	♋ 2 5:59
4 10:09	♃ ☍	♌ 4 11:02
6 8:54	♄ □	♍ 6 13:09
8 10:05	♄ ✶	♎ 8 14:10
10 1:11	☉ △	♏ 10 15:49
12 15:06	♄ ☌	♐ 12 19:09
14 17:10	☉ ✶	♑ 15 0:27
17 3:34	♄ ✶	♒ 17 7:36
19 12:35	♄ □	♓ 19 16:38
21 23:39	♄ △	♈ 22 3:43
23 15:20	♅ △	♉ 24 16:27
27 1:19	♄ ☍	♊ 27 5:11

☽ Phases & Eclipses Dy Hr Mn	
7 2:16	○ 16♋44
13 23:27	☾ 23♎44
21 2:28	● 1♒00
29 3:29	☽ 9♉11
5 15:19	○ 16♌47
12 7:57	☾ 23♏33
19 18:43	● 1♓05
27 23:41	☽ 9♊20

Astro Data

1 January 1985
Julian Day # 31047
SVP 5♓28'23"
GC 26♐37.8 ⚴ 13♓02.2
Eris 15♈02.8R ⚵ 10♎29.4
⚷ 4♊07.6R ⚶ 21♎33.6
☽ Mean ☊ 25♉07.2

1 February 1985
Julian Day # 31078
SVP 5♓28'17"
GC 26♐37.9 ⚴ 22♓10.4
Eris 15♈07.8 ⚵ 13♎14.1R
⚷ 3♊17.9R ⚶ 0♏54.4
☽ Mean ☊ 23♉28.8

March 1985 LONGITUDE

Day	Sid.Time	☉	0 hr ☽	Noon ☽	True ☊	☿	♀	♂	⚳	♃	♄	♅	♆	♇
1 F	22 36 56	10♓51 16	21♊52 29	28♊11 44	21♉01.3	19♓44.6	19♈30.2	19♈57.8	21♉35.9	5♒03.9	28♏05.7	17♐46.9	3♑17.2	4♏35.3
2 Sa	22 40 53	11 51 27	4♋37 07	11♋09 06	20R57.8	21 38.5	19 55.2	20 42.0	21 53.8	5 16.6	28 06.3	17 48.0	3 18.3	4R34.4
3 Su	22 44 49	12 51 36	17 48 05	24 34 19	20 51.8	23 31.9	20 18.5	21 26.1	22 11.9	5 29.2	28 06.7	17 49.1	3 19.4	4 33.6
4 M	22 48 46	13 51 43	1♌27 53	8♌28 42	20 43.4	25 24.4	20 39.8	22 10.2	22 30.1	5 41.8	28 07.1	17 50.1	3 20.4	4 32.7
5 Tu	22 52 43	14 51 49	15 36 29	22 50 43	20 33.6	27 15.7	20 59.2	22 54.3	22 48.5	5 54.3	28 07.4	17 51.1	3 21.5	4 31.8
6 W	22 56 39	15 51 52	0♍10 42	7♍35 32	20 23.2	29 05.4	21 16.7	23 38.3	23 07.1	6 06.7	28 07.5	17 52.0	3 22.4	4 30.9
7 Th	23 00 36	16 51 53	15 04 09	22 35 24	20 13.6	0♈53.0	21 32.0	24 22.3	23 25.8	6 19.1	28R07.6	17 52.8	3 23.4	4 29.9
8 F	23 04 32	17 51 52	0♎08 00	7♎40 43	20 05.7	2 38.2	21 45.2	25 06.2	23 44.7	6 31.4	28 07.5	17 53.6	3 24.3	4 28.9
9 Sa	23 08 29	18 51 49	15 12 21	22 41 47	20 00.4	4 20.3	21 56.3	25 50.1	24 03.7	6 43.6	28 07.4	17 54.3	3 25.2	4 27.9
10 Su	23 12 25	19 51 45	0♏08 01	7♏30 16	19D57.7	5 59.0	22 05.1	26 33.9	24 22.9	6 55.7	28 07.1	17 55.0	3 26.1	4 26.9
11 M	23 16 22	20 51 39	14 47 54	22 00 28	19 57.1	7 33.7	22 11.6	27 17.7	24 42.2	7 07.8	28 06.8	17 55.7	3 26.9	4 25.8
12 Tu	23 20 18	21 51 31	29 07 39	6♐09 22	19 57.7	9 03.9	22 15.9	28 01.5	25 01.6	7 19.8	28 06.3	17 56.2	3 27.7	4 24.7
13 W	23 24 15	22 51 22	13♐05 35	19 56 26	19R58.4	10 29.1	22R17.7	28 45.2	25 21.2	7 31.8	28 05.8	17 56.8	3 28.5	4 23.6
14 Th	23 28 12	23 51 12	26 42 05	3♑22 49	19 58.0	11 48.7	22 17.1	29 28.9	25 41.0	7 43.6	28 05.1	17 57.3	3 29.2	4 22.4
15 F	23 32 08	24 50 59	9♑58 54	16 30 39	19 55.6	13 02.3	22 14.1	0♉12.5	26 00.8	7 55.4	28 04.4	17 57.7	3 29.9	4 21.2
16 Sa	23 36 05	25 50 45	22 58 22	29 22 22	19 51.0	14 09.5	22 08.6	0 56.1	26 20.8	8 07.1	28 03.5	17 58.1	3 30.6	4 20.0
17 Su	23 40 01	26 50 29	5♒42 55	12♒00 18	19 44.1	15 09.9	22 00.6	1 39.7	26 41.0	8 18.7	28 02.5	17 58.4	3 31.2	4 18.8
18 M	23 43 58	27 50 11	18 14 45	24 26 29	19 35.3	16 03.0	21 50.2	2 23.2	27 01.3	8 30.2	28 01.5	17 58.6	3 31.8	4 17.6
19 Tu	23 47 54	28 49 51	0♓35 41	6♓42 33	19 25.5	16 48.7	21 37.3	3 06.6	27 21.7	8 41.6	28 00.3	17 58.8	3 32.4	4 16.3
20 W	23 51 51	29 49 30	12 47 13	18 49 52	19 15.7	17 26.7	21 21.9	3 50.0	27 42.2	8 53.0	27 59.1	17 59.0	3 33.0	4 15.0
21 Th	23 55 47	0♈49 06	24 50 38	0♈49 42	19 06.7	17 56.8	21 04.1	4 33.4	28 02.8	9 04.2	27 57.7	17 59.1	3 33.5	4 13.7
22 F	23 59 44	1 48 40	6♈47 13	12 43 24	18 59.3	18 18.9	20 43.9	5 16.8	28 23.6	9 15.4	27 56.3	17R59.2	3 33.9	4 12.3
23 Sa	0 03 41	2 48 13	18 38 28	24 32 40	18 54.0	18 33.0	20 21.4	6 00.0	28 44.5	9 26.4	27 54.7	17 59.1	3 34.4	4 11.0
24 Su	0 07 37	3 47 43	0♉26 18	6♉19 43	18 51.0	18R39.2	19 56.7	6 43.3	29 05.5	9 37.4	27 53.1	17 59.1	3 34.8	4 09.6
25 M	0 11 34	4 47 11	12 13 15	18 07 20	18D50.0	18 37.6	19 29.9	7 26.5	29 26.6	9 48.3	27 51.4	17 59.0	3 35.1	4 08.2
26 Tu	0 15 30	5 46 36	24 02 47	29 59 03	18 50.6	18 28.5	19 01.2	8 09.6	29 47.9	9 59.1	27 49.5	17 58.8	3 35.5	4 06.7
27 W	0 19 27	6 46 00	5♊57 42	11♊58 57	18 52.0	18 12.2	18 30.6	8 52.7	0♊09.2	10 09.8	27 47.6	17 58.6	3 35.8	4 05.3
28 Th	0 23 23	7 45 21	18 03 24	24 11 40	18 53.5	17 49.2	17 58.3	9 35.8	0 30.7	10 20.3	27 45.6	17 58.3	3 36.0	4 03.9
29 F	0 27 20	8 44 40	0♋24 19	6♋42 00	18R54.3	17 20.2	17 24.6	10 18.8	0 52.2	10 30.8	27 43.5	17 58.0	3 36.3	4 02.4
30 Sa	0 31 16	9 43 57	13 05 16	19 34 39	18 53.8	16 45.7	16 49.5	11 01.8	1 13.9	10 41.2	27 41.3	17 57.7	3 36.5	4 00.9
31 Su	0 35 13	10 43 11	26 10 37	2♌53 32	18 51.7	16 06.5	16 13.4	11 44.7	1 35.7	10 51.5	27 39.1	17 57.2	3 36.7	3 59.4

April 1985 LONGITUDE

Day	Sid.Time	☉	0 hr ☽	Noon ☽	True ☊	☿	♀	♂	⚳	♃	♄	♅	♆	♇
1 M	0 39 10	11♈42 23	9♌43 39	16♌41 05	18♉48.1	15♈23.5	15♈36.5	12♉27.6	1♊57.5	11♒01.6	27♏36.7	17♐56.8	3♑36.8	3♏57.9
2 Tu	0 43 06	12 41 33	23 45 46	0♍57 26	18R43.3	14R37.7	14R59.0	13 10.4	2 19.5	11 11.7	27R34.3	17R56.3	3 36.9	3R56.3
3 W	0 47 03	13 40 40	8♍15 39	15 39 44	18 38.0	13 50.0	14 21.1	13 53.2	2 41.6	11 21.6	27 31.7	17 55.7	3 37.0	3 54.8
4 Th	0 50 59	14 39 45	23 08 50	0♎41 54	18 33.0	13 01.4	13 43.2	14 35.9	3 03.7	11 31.4	27 29.1	17 55.1	3R37.0	3 53.2
5 F	0 54 56	15 38 48	8♎17 47	15 55 12	18 29.0	12 12.8	13 05.4	15 18.6	3 25.9	11 41.2	27 26.4	17 54.4	3 37.0	3 51.6
6 Sa	0 58 52	16 37 49	23 32 51	1♏09 26	18 26.5	11 25.1	12 28.1	16 01.2	3 48.3	11 50.8	27 23.7	17 53.7	3 37.0	3 50.0
7 Su	1 02 49	17 36 48	8♏43 43	16 14 37	18D25.5	10 39.4	11 51.5	16 43.8	4 10.7	12 00.3	27 20.8	17 52.9	3 36.9	3 48.4
8 M	1 06 45	18 35 45	23 41 09	1♐02 33	18 25.9	9 56.2	11 15.8	17 26.4	4 33.2	12 09.6	27 17.9	17 52.1	3 36.8	3 46.8
9 Tu	1 10 42	19 34 41	8♐18 12	15 27 41	18 27.2	9 16.3	10 41.2	18 08.9	4 55.8	12 18.9	27 14.9	17 51.2	3 36.7	3 45.2
10 W	1 14 38	20 33 35	22 30 47	29 27 23	18 28.7	8 40.3	10 08.0	18 51.3	5 18.5	12 28.0	27 11.8	17 50.3	3 36.5	3 43.6
11 Th	1 18 35	21 32 27	6♑17 33	13♑01 28	18R29.8	8 08.6	9 36.4	19 33.8	5 41.3	12 37.0	27 08.6	17 49.3	3 36.3	3 41.9
12 F	1 22 32	22 31 17	19 39 23	26 11 37	18 30.1	7 41.7	9 06.6	20 16.1	6 04.1	12 45.9	27 05.4	17 48.3	3 36.1	3 40.3
13 Sa	1 26 28	23 30 06	2♒38 33	9♒00 37	18 29.1	7 19.7	8 38.6	20 58.5	6 27.0	12 54.7	27 02.1	17 47.3	3 35.9	3 38.6
14 Su	1 30 25	24 28 52	15 18 14	21 31 50	18 27.1	7 02.8	8 12.6	21 40.7	6 50.0	13 03.3	26 58.7	17 46.2	3 35.6	3 37.0
15 M	1 34 21	25 27 38	27 41 50	3♓48 40	18 24.1	6 51.2	7 48.8	22 23.0	7 13.1	13 11.8	26 55.3	17 45.0	3 35.3	3 35.3
16 Tu	1 38 18	26 26 21	9♓52 44	15 54 24	18 20.6	6D44.8	7 27.2	23 05.2	7 36.3	13 20.2	26 51.8	17 43.8	3 34.9	3 33.6
17 W	1 42 14	27 25 02	21 54 02	27 51 58	18 17.0	6 43.6	7 07.9	23 47.4	7 59.5	13 28.4	26 48.2	17 42.6	3 34.5	3 32.0
18 Th	1 46 11	28 23 42	3♈48 31	9♈43 58	18 13.7	6 47.6	6 51.0	24 29.5	8 22.9	13 36.5	26 44.6	17 41.3	3 34.1	3 30.3
19 F	1 50 07	29 22 19	15 38 36	21 32 42	18 11.2	6 56.6	6 36.5	25 11.5	8 46.3	13 44.5	26 40.9	17 40.0	3 33.6	3 28.6
20 Sa	1 54 04	0♉20 55	27 26 32	3♉20 21	18 09.6	7 10.5	6 24.4	25 53.6	9 09.7	13 52.3	26 37.2	17 38.6	3 33.2	3 26.9
21 Su	1 58 01	1 19 29	9♉14 25	15 09 00	18D08.9	7 29.2	6 14.8	26 35.6	9 33.3	14 00.0	26 33.4	17 37.2	3 32.7	3 25.2
22 M	2 01 57	2 18 01	21 04 25	27 00 57	18 09.1	7 52.4	6 07.6	27 17.5	9 56.9	14 07.6	26 29.5	17 35.7	3 32.1	3 23.5
23 Tu	2 05 54	3 16 31	2♊58 56	8♊58 42	18 09.9	8 20.0	6 02.8	27 59.4	10 20.5	14 15.0	26 25.6	17 34.2	3 31.5	3 21.8
24 W	2 09 50	4 14 59	15 00 37	21 05 05	18 11.1	8 51.8	6D00.4	28 41.3	10 44.3	14 22.2	26 21.7	17 32.7	3 30.9	3 20.1
25 Th	2 13 47	5 13 25	27 12 30	3♋23 19	18 12.3	9 27.7	6 00.4	29 23.1	11 08.1	14 29.3	26 17.7	17 31.1	3 30.3	3 18.4
26 F	2 17 43	6 11 49	9♋37 57	15 56 51	18 13.3	10 07.4	6 02.7	0♊04.8	11 31.9	14 36.3	26 13.6	17 29.5	3 29.7	3 16.7
27 Sa	2 21 40	7 10 11	22 20 27	28 49 11	18R13.9	10 50.8	6 07.3	0 46.6	11 55.9	14 43.1	26 09.5	17 27.9	3 29.0	3 15.0
28 Su	2 25 36	8 08 31	5♌23 27	12♌03 34	18 14.0	11 37.8	6 14.1	1 28.2	12 19.8	14 49.8	26 05.4	17 26.2	3 28.2	3 13.3
29 M	2 29 33	9 06 49	18 49 48	25 42 22	18 13.7	12 28.1	6 23.2	2 09.9	12 43.9	14 56.3	26 01.2	17 24.5	3 27.5	3 11.6
30 Tu	2 33 30	10 05 04	2♍41 18	9♍46 35	18 13.0	13 21.8	6 34.3	2 51.5	13 08.0	15 02.7	25 57.0	17 22.7	3 26.7	3 10.0

Astro Data Dy Hr Mn	Planet Ingress Dy Hr Mn	Last Aspect Dy Hr Mn	☽ Ingress Dy Hr Mn	Last Aspect Dy Hr Mn	☽ Ingress Dy Hr Mn	☽ Phases & Eclipses Dy Hr Mn
☿0N 7 0:10	☿ ♈ 7 0:07	28 19:21 ♂ ⚹	♋ 1 15:23	2 6:23 ♄ □	♍ 2 10:25	7 2:13 ○ 16♍27
♄ R 7 12:38	♂ ♉ 15 5:06	3 18:11 ♄ △	♌ 3 21:28	4 6:55 ♄ ⚹	♎ 4 10:54	13 17:34 ☾ 23♐05
☽0S 8 12:21	☉ ♈ 20 16:14	5 20:39 ♄ □	♍ 5 23:43	5 15:07 ♅ ⚹	♏ 6 10:10	21 11:59 ● 0♈49
♀ R 13 18:18	⚳ ♊ 27 1:38	7 20:48 ♄ ⚹	♎ 7 23:47	8 5:54 ♄ ☌	♐ 8 10:17	29 16:11 ☽ 8♋55
☉0N 20 16:14		9 17:19 ♂ ☍	♏ 9 23:47	9 19:30 ☉ △	♑ 10 12:57	
☽0N 22 2:06	☉ ♉ 20 3:26	11 22:17 ♄ ☌	♐ 12 1:29	12 13:39 ♄ ⚹	♒ 12 19:04	5 11:32 ○ 15♎38
♅ R 22 22:02	♂ ♊ 26 9:13	14 4:34 ♂ △	♑ 14 5:55	14 22:33 ♄ □	♓ 15 4:30	12 4:41 ☾ 22♑13
☿ R 24 19:01		16 9:32 ♄ ⚹	♒ 16 13:11	17 9:52 ♄ △	♈ 17 16:18	20 5:22 ● 0♉05
		18 18:58 ♄ □	♓ 18 22:50	19 4:08 ♅ △	♉ 20 5:12	28 4:25 ☽ 7♌50
☽0S 4 23:19		21 6:15 ♄ △	♈ 21 10:20	22 12:35 ♂ ☌	♊ 22 18:01	
♆ R 5 1:27		23 3:45 ♀ ☌	♉ 23 23:06	24 5:02 ♅ ☍	♋ 25 5:26	
♆⚹♇ 15 12:59		26 7:40 ♄ ☍	♊ 26 12:02	27 7:07 ♄ △	♌ 27 14:10	
☿ D 17 5:22		28 0:21 ♀ ⚹	♋ 28 23:13	29 12:32 ♄ □	♍ 29 19:24	
☽0N 18 8:15		31 2:41 ♄ △	♌ 31 6:51			
♀ D 25 0:09						

Astro Data

1 March 1985
Julian Day # 31106
SVP 5♓28'13"
GC 26♐37.9 ⚴ 1♈56.4
Eris 15♈20.4 ⚵ 10♎29.0R
⚷ 3♊29.2 ⚶ 5♏03.4
☽ Mean ☊ 21♉59.8

1 April 1985
Julian Day # 31137
SVP 5♓28'10"
GC 26♐38.0 ⚴ 13♈50.1
Eris 15♈39.8 ⚵ 3♎26.9R
⚷ 4♊42.0 ⚶ 2♏44.6R
☽ Mean ☊ 20♉21.3

LONGITUDE May 1985

Day	Sid.Time	☉	0 hr ☽	Noon ☽	True ☊	☿	♀	♂	⚳	♃	♄	♅	♆	♇
1 W	2 37 26	11♉03 17	16♍57 58	24♍15 08	18♉12.2	14♈18.5	6♈47.6	3♊33.0	13♊32.1	15♒08.9	25♏52.8	17♐20.9	3♑25.9	3♏08.3
2 Th	2 41 23	12 01 29	1♎37 30	9♎04 24	18R 11.4	15 18.2	7 02.8	4 14.5	13 56.3	15 14.9	25R 48.5	17R 19.1	3R 25.1	3R 06.6
3 F	2 45 19	12 59 38	16 34 58	24 08 12	18 10.9	16 20.8	7 20.0	4 56.0	14 20.6	15 20.8	25 44.2	17 17.2	3 24.2	3 04.9
4 Sa	2 49 16	13 57 46	1♏43 01	9♏18 15	18D 10.7	17 26.2	7 39.2	5 37.4	14 44.9	15 26.5	25 39.9	17 15.3	3 23.3	3 03.3
5 Su	2 53 12	14 55 52	16 52 42	24 25 13	18 10.6	18 34.3	8 00.1	6 18.7	15 09.3	15 32.1	25 35.5	17 13.4	3 22.4	3 01.6
6 M	2 57 09	15 53 56	1♐54 41	9♐20 07	18 10.8	19 45.0	8 22.9	7 00.1	15 33.7	15 37.5	25 31.1	17 11.4	3 21.5	3 00.0
7 Tu	3 01 05	16 51 59	16 40 38	23 55 32	18 10.9	20 58.2	8 47.3	7 41.4	15 58.2	15 42.8	25 26.7	17 09.4	3 20.5	2 58.3
8 W	3 05 02	17 50 01	1♑04 17	8♑06 31	18R 11.0	22 13.9	9 13.5	8 22.6	16 22.7	15 47.8	25 22.3	17 07.4	3 19.6	2 56.7
9 Th	3 08 59	18 48 01	15 02 01	21 50 44	18 11.0	23 32.0	9 41.2	9 03.8	16 47.3	15 52.8	25 17.9	17 05.4	3 18.5	2 55.1
10 F	3 12 55	19 46 00	28 32 46	5♒08 20	18 10.9	24 52.4	10 10.4	9 45.0	17 11.9	15 57.5	25 13.4	17 03.3	3 17.5	2 53.5
11 Sa	3 16 52	20 43 57	11♒37 45	18 01 22	18D 10.8	26 15.2	10 41.2	10 26.1	17 36.6	16 02.1	25 09.0	17 01.2	3 16.5	2 51.9
12 Su	3 20 48	21 41 53	24 19 41	0♓33 10	18 10.9	27 40.2	11 13.3	11 07.2	18 01.3	16 06.5	25 04.5	16 59.1	3 15.4	2 50.3
13 M	3 24 45	22 39 48	6♓42 21	12 47 46	18 11.1	29 07.5	11 46.8	11 48.2	18 26.1	16 10.7	25 00.0	16 56.9	3 14.3	2 48.7
14 Tu	3 28 41	23 37 41	18 49 58	24 49 29	18 11.6	0♉36.9	12 21.7	12 29.3	18 50.9	16 14.8	24 55.5	16 54.7	3 13.1	2 47.2
15 W	3 32 38	24 35 34	0♈46 51	6♈42 32	18 12.2	2 08.6	12 57.8	13 10.2	19 15.7	16 18.7	24 51.0	16 52.5	3 12.0	2 45.6
16 Th	3 36 34	25 33 25	12 37 04	18 30 52	18 12.9	3 42.4	13 35.1	13 51.2	19 40.6	16 22.4	24 46.5	16 50.3	3 10.8	2 44.1
17 F	3 40 31	26 31 14	24 24 23	0♉17 59	18 13.6	5 18.4	14 13.5	14 32.1	20 05.6	16 25.9	24 42.0	16 48.0	3 09.6	2 42.6
18 Sa	3 44 28	27 29 03	6♉12 05	12 06 58	18R 14.0	6 56.5	14 53.1	15 12.9	20 30.5	16 29.2	24 37.5	16 45.8	3 08.4	2 41.1
19 Su	3 48 24	28 26 50	18 03 00	24 00 26	18 14.0	8 36.8	15 33.7	15 53.7	20 55.6	16 32.4	24 33.0	16 43.5	3 07.1	2 39.6
20 M	3 52 21	29 24 36	29 59 33	6♊00 37	18 13.5	10 19.3	16 15.4	16 34.5	21 20.6	16 35.4	24 28.6	16 41.2	3 05.9	2 38.1
21 Tu	3 56 17	0♊22 20	12♊03 50	18 09 26	18 12.4	12 03.9	16 58.0	17 15.3	21 45.7	16 38.2	24 24.1	16 38.9	3 04.6	2 36.6
22 W	4 00 14	1 20 03	24 17 38	0♋28 39	18 10.8	13 50.7	17 41.6	17 56.0	22 10.9	16 40.8	24 19.6	16 36.5	3 03.3	2 35.2
23 Th	4 04 10	2 17 45	6♋42 41	12 59 56	18 08.8	15 39.6	18 26.1	18 36.6	22 36.1	16 43.2	24 15.2	16 34.2	3 02.0	2 33.8
24 F	4 08 07	3 15 25	19 20 38	25 44 58	18 06.8	17 30.6	19 11.4	19 17.3	23 01.3	16 45.5	24 10.8	16 31.8	3 00.6	2 32.4
25 Sa	4 12 03	4 13 04	2♌13 10	8♌45 25	18 05.1	19 23.7	19 57.6	19 57.9	23 26.5	16 47.6	24 06.4	16 29.4	2 59.3	2 31.0
26 Su	4 16 00	5 10 41	15 21 55	22 02 50	18 03.9	21 19.0	20 44.6	20 38.4	23 51.8	16 49.4	24 02.0	16 27.0	2 57.9	2 29.7
27 M	4 19 57	6 08 17	28 48 21	5♍38 33	18D 03.5	23 16.3	21 32.4	21 18.9	24 17.1	16 51.1	23 57.7	16 24.6	2 56.5	2 28.3
28 Tu	4 23 53	7 05 51	12♍33 31	19 33 15	18 03.8	25 15.6	22 20.9	21 59.4	24 42.5	16 52.6	23 53.4	16 22.2	2 55.1	2 27.0
29 W	4 27 50	8 03 24	26 37 40	3♎46 37	18 04.8	27 16.8	23 10.1	22 39.8	25 07.9	16 53.9	23 49.1	16 19.7	2 53.7	2 25.7
30 Th	4 31 46	9 00 55	10♎59 49	18 16 53	18 06.1	29 20.0	24 00.0	23 20.2	25 33.3	16 55.0	23 44.8	16 17.3	2 52.3	2 24.4
31 F	4 35 43	9 58 25	25 37 20	3♏00 33	18 07.2	1♊24.8	24 50.6	24 00.6	25 58.7	16 56.0	23 40.6	16 14.9	2 50.8	2 23.2

LONGITUDE June 1985

Day	Sid.Time	☉	0 hr ☽	Noon ☽	True ☊	☿	♀	♂	⚳	♃	♄	♅	♆	♇
1 Sa	4 39 39	10♊55 54	10♏25 47	17♏52 14	18♉07.7	3♊31.3	25♈41.9	24♊40.9	26♊24.2	16♒56.7	23♏36.4	16♐12.4	2♑49.4	2♏21.9
2 Su	4 43 36	11 53 21	25 18 58	2♐45 04	18R 07.2	5 39.2	26 33.7	25 21.2	26 49.7	16 57.3	23R 32.2	16R 10.0	2R 47.9	2R 20.7
3 M	4 47 32	12 50 48	10♐09 32	17 31 24	18 05.4	7 48.5	27 26.2	26 01.4	27 15.2	16 57.6	23 28.1	16 07.5	2 46.4	2 19.5
4 Tu	4 51 29	13 48 14	24 49 47	2♑03 51	18 02.6	9 58.8	28 19.3	26 41.7	27 40.7	16R 57.8	23 24.0	16 05.0	2 44.9	2 18.4
5 W	4 55 26	14 45 39	9♑12 52	16 16 16	17 58.9	12 09.9	29 12.9	27 21.8	28 06.3	16 57.8	23 20.0	16 02.6	2 43.4	2 17.2
6 Th	4 59 22	15 43 03	23 13 38	0♒04 39	17 55.0	14 21.7	0♉07.1	28 02.0	28 31.9	16 57.6	23 16.0	16 00.1	2 41.9	2 16.1
7 F	5 03 19	16 40 27	6♒49 11	13 27 17	17 51.4	16 33.7	1 01.8	28 42.1	28 57.6	16 57.2	23 12.1	15 57.6	2 40.4	2 15.0
8 Sa	5 07 15	17 37 50	19 59 04	26 24 47	17 48.5	18 45.8	1 57.0	29 22.2	29 23.2	16 56.6	23 08.2	15 55.2	2 38.8	2 14.0
9 Su	5 11 12	18 35 12	2♓44 50	8♓59 38	17D 46.8	20 57.7	2 52.6	0♋02.2	29 48.9	16 55.8	23 04.4	15 52.7	2 37.3	2 12.9
10 M	5 15 08	19 32 33	15 09 43	21 15 38	17 46.3	23 09.1	3 48.8	0 42.2	0♋14.6	16 54.9	23 00.6	15 50.2	2 35.7	2 11.9
11 Tu	5 19 05	20 29 54	27 17 57	3♈17 20	17 47.0	25 19.7	4 45.4	1 22.2	0 40.3	16 53.7	22 56.8	15 47.8	2 34.1	2 10.9
12 W	5 23 02	21 27 15	9♈14 22	15 09 41	17 48.5	27 29.4	5 42.4	2 02.2	1 06.1	16 52.3	22 53.1	15 45.3	2 32.6	2 10.0
13 Th	5 26 58	22 24 35	21 03 53	26 57 35	17 50.2	29 37.8	6 39.9	2 42.1	1 31.9	16 50.8	22 49.5	15 42.9	2 31.0	2 09.0
14 F	5 30 55	23 21 55	2♉51 20	8♉45 40	17R 51.6	1♋44.8	7 37.8	3 22.0	1 57.7	16 49.1	22 46.0	15 40.4	2 29.4	2 08.1
15 Sa	5 34 51	24 19 15	14 41 06	20 38 04	17 51.9	3 50.2	8 36.0	4 01.8	2 23.5	16 47.1	22 42.5	15 38.0	2 27.8	2 07.3
16 Su	5 38 48	25 16 33	26 37 01	2♊38 17	17 50.8	5 53.9	9 34.7	4 41.7	2 49.3	16 45.0	22 39.0	15 35.6	2 26.2	2 06.4
17 M	5 42 44	26 13 52	8♊42 11	14 49 00	17 47.9	7 55.7	10 33.7	5 21.4	3 15.2	16 42.7	22 35.7	15 33.1	2 24.6	2 05.6
18 Tu	5 46 41	27 11 10	20 58 56	27 12 09	17 43.3	9 55.5	11 33.0	6 01.2	3 41.1	16 40.2	22 32.4	15 30.7	2 23.0	2 04.8
19 W	5 50 37	28 08 28	3♋28 46	9♋48 50	17 37.2	11 53.3	12 32.7	6 41.0	4 07.0	16 37.6	22 29.1	15 28.3	2 21.4	2 04.1
20 Th	5 54 34	29 05 45	16 12 23	22 39 25	17 30.3	13 49.0	13 32.7	7 20.7	4 32.9	16 34.7	22 26.0	15 26.0	2 19.8	2 03.4
21 F	5 58 31	0♋03 01	29 09 53	5♌43 44	17 23.2	15 42.5	14 33.1	8 00.3	4 58.9	16 31.7	22 22.9	15 23.6	2 18.1	2 02.7
22 Sa	6 02 27	1 00 17	12♌20 53	19 01 17	17 16.9	17 33.9	15 33.7	8 40.0	5 24.8	16 28.5	22 19.9	15 21.2	2 16.5	2 02.0
23 Su	6 06 24	1 57 32	25 44 49	2♍31 26	17 11.9	19 23.0	16 34.7	9 19.6	5 50.8	16 25.1	22 16.9	15 18.9	2 14.9	2 01.4
24 M	6 10 20	2 54 46	9♍21 03	16 13 37	17 08.8	21 09.9	17 35.9	9 59.2	6 16.8	16 21.5	22 14.1	15 16.6	2 13.3	2 00.8
25 Tu	6 14 17	3 52 00	23 09 03	0♎07 17	17D 07.5	22 54.5	18 37.4	10 38.7	6 42.7	16 17.8	22 11.3	15 14.3	2 11.7	2 00.2
26 W	6 18 13	4 49 13	7♎08 14	14 11 48	17 07.8	24 36.9	19 39.2	11 18.2	7 08.8	16 13.9	22 08.6	15 12.0	2 10.0	1 59.6
27 Th	6 22 10	5 46 26	21 17 52	28 26 14	17 08.8	26 17.0	20 41.2	11 57.7	7 34.8	16 09.8	22 05.9	15 09.7	2 08.4	1 59.1
28 F	6 26 06	6 43 38	5♏36 40	12♏48 51	17R 09.6	27 54.8	21 43.5	12 37.2	8 00.8	16 05.5	22 03.4	15 07.5	2 06.8	1 58.7
29 Sa	6 30 03	7 40 50	20 02 23	27 16 50	17 09.3	29 30.3	22 46.1	13 16.6	8 26.8	16 01.1	22 00.9	15 05.3	2 05.2	1 58.2
30 Su	6 34 00	8 38 02	4♐31 38	11♐46 11	17 07.0	1♌03.6	23 48.9	13 56.0	8 52.9	15 56.5	21 58.5	15 03.1	2 03.6	1 57.8

Astro Data

	Dy Hr Mn
☽ 0S	2 10:10
☽ 0N	15 14:30
♃⚹♅	21 15:10
☽ 0S	29 18:50
♃ R	4 22:24
☽ 0N	11 21:05
☽ 0S	26 0:48

Planet Ingress

	Dy Hr Mn
☿ ♉	14 2:10
☉ ♊	21 2:43
☿ ♊	30 19:44
♀ ♉	6 8:53
♂ ♋	9 10:40
⚳ ♋	9 22:23
☿ ♋	13 16:11
☉ ♋	21 10:44
☿ ♌	29 19:34

Last Aspect / ☽ Ingress

Last Aspect Dy Hr Mn		☽ Ingress	Dy Hr Mn
1 14:39	♄ ⚹	♎	1 21:22
3 1:09	♅ ⚹	♏	3 21:17
5 13:52	♄ ☌	♐	5 20:56
7 6:38	☿ △	♑	7 22:11
9 18:08	♄ ⚹	♒	10 2:38
12 5:42	☿ ⚹	♓	12 10:56
14 12:12	♄ △	♈	14 22:25
16 8:36	♅ △	♉	17 11:23
19 21:41	☉ ☌	♊	20 0:01
21 10:07	♂ ☌	♋	22 11:05
24 9:05	♄ △	♌	24 19:54
26 15:31	♄ □	♍	27 2:06
28 23:17	☿ △	♎	29 5:41
30 21:55	♀ ☍	♏	31 7:07

Last Aspect / ☽ Ingress

Last Aspect Dy Hr Mn		☽ Ingress	Dy Hr Mn
1 21:12	♄ ☌	♐	2 7:33
4 5:22	♀ △	♑	4 8:34
6 0:08	♄ ⚹	♒	6 11:52
8 17:53	♂ △	♓	8 18:46
10 16:34	☿ □	♈	11 5:24
13 1:55	☉ ⚹	♉	13 18:11
15 16:09	♄ ☍	♊	16 6:45
18 11:58	☉ ☌	♋	18 17:22
20 11:35	♄ △	♌	21 1:32
22 17:54	♄ □	♍	23 7:32
24 22:23	♄ ⚹	♎	25 11:48
27 7:55	☿ □	♏	27 14:37
29 16:08	☿ △	♐	29 16:30

☽ Phases & Eclipses

Dy Hr Mn	
4 19:53	○ 14♏17
4 19:56	T 1.237
11 17:34	☾ 20♒57
19 21:41	● 28♉50
19 21:28:42	P 0.841
27 12:56	☽ 6♍11
3 3:50	○ 12♐31
10 8:19	☾ 19♓24
18 11:58	● 27♊11
25 18:53	☽ 4♎08

Astro Data

1 May 1985
Julian Day # 31167
SVP 5♓28'06"
GC 26♐38.1 ⚴ 26♈04.0
Eris 15♈59.4 ⚵ 28♍11.4R
⚷ 6♊37.1 ⚶ 25♎41.1R
☽ Mean ☊ 18♉46.0

1 June 1985
Julian Day # 31198
SVP 5♓28'02"
GC 26♐38.1 ⚴ 9♉12.8
Eris 16♈15.6 ⚵ 27♍58.1
⚷ 8♊59.5 ⚶ 21♎48.2R
☽ Mean ☊ 17♉07.5

July 1985 — LONGITUDE

Day	Sid.Time	☉	0 hr ☽	Noon ☽	True ☊	☿	♀	♂	⚳	♃	♄	♅	♆	♇
1 M	6 37 56	9♋35 13	18♐59 47	26♐11 44	17♉02.6	2♌34.5	24♉51.9	14♋35.4	9♋19.0	15♒51.8	21♏56.2	15♐00.9	2♑02.0	1♏57.4
2 Tu	6 41 53	10 32 24	3♑21 19	10♑27 49	16R 55.9	4 03.1	25 55.2	15 14.7	9 45.0	15R 46.9	21R 54.0	14R 58.7	2R 00.4	1R 57.1
3 W	6 45 49	11 29 35	17 30 33	24 28 56	16 47.7	5 29.4	26 58.8	15 54.0	10 11.1	15 41.9	21 51.9	14 56.6	1 58.8	1 56.8
4 Th	6 49 46	12 26 46	1♒22 26	8♒10 40	16 38.7	6 53.3	28 02.5	16 33.3	10 37.2	15 36.7	21 49.8	14 54.5	1 57.2	1 56.5
5 F	6 53 42	13 23 57	14 53 21	21 30 19	16 30.0	8 14.7	29 06.5	17 12.6	11 03.3	15 31.3	21 47.9	14 52.4	1 55.6	1 56.3
6 Sa	6 57 39	14 21 08	28 01 34	4♓27 11	16 22.4	9 33.8	0♊10.7	17 51.8	11 29.4	15 25.8	21 46.0	14 50.4	1 54.1	1 56.0
7 Su	7 01 36	15 18 19	10♓47 24	17 02 32	16 16.7	10 50.3	1 15.0	18 31.0	11 55.5	15 20.2	21 44.2	14 48.4	1 52.5	1 55.9
8 M	7 05 32	16 15 31	23 13 01	29 19 18	16 13.1	12 04.3	2 19.6	19 10.2	12 21.7	15 14.4	21 42.5	14 46.4	1 50.9	1 55.7
9 Tu	7 09 29	17 12 43	5♈21 58	11♈21 36	16D 11.5	13 15.7	3 24.4	19 49.4	12 47.8	15 08.5	21 40.9	14 44.4	1 49.4	1 55.6
10 W	7 13 25	18 09 56	17 18 51	23 14 23	16 11.4	14 24.4	4 29.4	20 28.5	13 13.9	15 02.5	21 39.4	14 42.5	1 47.8	1 55.5
11 Th	7 17 22	19 07 09	29 08 50	5♉02 55	16R 12.0	15 30.4	5 34.6	21 07.6	13 40.1	14 56.3	21 38.0	14 40.6	1 46.3	1D 55.5
12 F	7 21 18	20 04 22	10♉57 16	16 52 32	16 12.4	16 33.5	6 40.0	21 46.7	14 06.2	14 50.0	21 36.6	14 38.7	1 44.8	1 55.5
13 Sa	7 25 15	21 01 36	22 49 20	28 48 17	16 11.6	17 33.8	7 45.5	22 25.8	14 32.4	14 43.6	21 35.4	14 36.9	1 43.3	1 55.5
14 Su	7 29 11	21 58 51	4♊49 52	10♊54 36	16 08.8	18 31.0	8 51.2	23 04.8	14 58.6	14 37.0	21 34.3	14 35.1	1 41.8	1 55.5
15 M	7 33 08	22 56 06	17 02 54	23 15 07	16 03.6	19 25.1	9 57.1	23 43.9	15 24.7	14 30.4	21 33.2	14 33.3	1 40.3	1 55.6
16 Tu	7 37 05	23 53 22	29 31 30	5♋52 14	15 56.0	20 15.9	11 03.2	24 22.9	15 50.9	14 23.6	21 32.3	14 31.6	1 38.8	1 55.8
17 W	7 41 01	24 50 38	12♋17 26	18 47 06	15 46.2	21 03.3	12 09.4	25 01.8	16 17.1	14 16.8	21 31.4	14 29.9	1 37.3	1 55.9
18 Th	7 44 58	25 47 54	25 21 08	1♌59 22	15 35.1	21 47.2	13 15.8	25 40.8	16 43.3	14 09.8	21 30.7	14 28.3	1 35.9	1 56.1
19 F	7 48 54	26 45 11	8♌41 35	15 27 27	15 23.7	22 27.4	14 22.3	26 19.7	17 09.4	14 02.8	21 30.0	14 26.7	1 34.5	1 56.3
20 Sa	7 52 51	27 42 28	22 16 38	29 08 45	15 13.3	23 03.9	15 29.0	26 58.6	17 35.6	13 55.7	21 29.4	14 25.1	1 33.0	1 56.6
21 Su	7 56 47	28 39 46	6♍03 24	13♍00 12	15 04.9	23 36.3	16 35.8	27 37.5	18 01.8	13 48.4	21 29.0	14 23.5	1 31.6	1 56.9
22 M	8 00 44	29 37 04	19 58 47	26 58 48	14 58.9	24 04.6	17 42.7	28 16.4	18 28.0	13 41.1	21 28.6	14 22.0	1 30.3	1 57.2
23 Tu	8 04 40	0♌34 22	3♎59 59	11♎02 04	14 55.6	24 28.6	18 49.8	28 55.2	18 54.1	13 33.8	21 28.3	14 20.6	1 28.9	1 57.6
24 W	8 08 37	1 31 40	18 04 51	25 08 09	14D 54.4	24 48.1	19 57.0	29 34.0	19 20.3	13 26.3	21 28.1	14 19.1	1 27.5	1 58.0
25 Th	8 12 34	2 28 59	2♏11 51	9♏15 49	14R 54.3	25 02.9	21 04.4	0♌12.8	19 46.4	13 18.9	21D 28.1	14 17.8	1 26.2	1 58.4
26 F	8 16 30	3 26 18	16 19 55	23 24 03	14 54.2	25 13.1	22 11.9	0 51.6	20 12.6	13 11.3	21 28.1	14 16.4	1 24.9	1 58.9
27 Sa	8 20 27	4 23 38	0♐28 01	7♐31 39	14 52.8	25R 18.2	23 19.6	1 30.3	20 38.7	13 03.7	21 28.2	14 15.1	1 23.6	1 59.4
28 Su	8 24 23	5 20 58	14 34 42	21 36 52	14 49.1	25 18.4	24 27.3	2 09.1	21 04.9	12 56.1	21 28.4	14 13.9	1 22.3	1 59.9
29 M	8 28 20	6 18 19	28 37 49	5♑37 08	14 42.6	25 13.5	25 35.2	2 47.8	21 31.0	12 48.4	21 28.7	14 12.7	1 21.0	2 00.5
30 Tu	8 32 16	7 15 40	12♑34 24	19 29 10	14 33.5	25 03.5	26 43.2	3 26.5	21 57.1	12 40.7	21 29.1	14 11.5	1 19.8	2 01.1
31 W	8 36 13	8 13 02	26 20 59	3♒09 24	14 22.2	24 48.3	27 51.4	4 05.1	22 23.2	12 32.9	21 29.6	14 10.4	1 18.6	2 01.7

August 1985 — LONGITUDE

Day	Sid.Time	☉	0 hr ☽	Noon ☽	True ☊	☿	♀	♂	⚳	♃	♄	♅	♆	♇
1 Th	8 40 09	9♌10 25	9♒54 01	16♒34 29	14♉10.0	24♌28.1	28♊59.7	4♌43.8	22♋49.4	12♒25.2	21♏30.2	14♐09.3	1♑17.4	2♏02.4
2 F	8 44 06	10 07 48	23 10 32	29 41 59	13R 57.9	24R 03.0	0♋08.1	5 22.4	23 15.5	12R 17.4	21 30.9	14R 08.3	1R 16.2	2 03.1
3 Sa	8 48 03	11 05 13	6♓08 43	12♓30 45	13 47.1	23 33.2	1 16.6	6 01.0	23 41.6	12 09.6	21 31.7	14 07.3	1 15.1	2 03.9
4 Su	8 51 59	12 02 38	18 48 11	25 01 12	13 38.4	22 59.1	2 25.3	6 39.6	24 07.6	12 01.8	21 32.6	14 06.4	1 13.9	2 04.6
5 M	8 55 56	13 00 05	1♈10 07	7♈15 17	13 32.3	22 21.0	3 34.0	7 18.2	24 33.7	11 54.0	21 33.6	14 05.5	1 12.8	2 05.4
6 Tu	8 59 52	13 57 33	13 17 09	19 16 14	13 28.8	21 39.4	4 42.9	7 56.7	24 59.8	11 46.2	21 34.7	14 04.6	1 11.7	2 06.3
7 W	9 03 49	14 55 02	25 13 07	1♉08 24	13 27.3	20 55.1	5 51.9	8 35.3	25 25.8	11 38.4	21 35.9	14 03.8	1 10.7	2 07.1
8 Th	9 07 45	15 52 33	7♉02 43	12 56 46	13 27.0	20 08.5	7 01.0	9 13.8	25 51.9	11 30.6	21 37.1	14 03.1	1 09.6	2 08.0
9 F	9 11 42	16 50 05	18 51 14	24 46 47	13 26.9	19 20.7	8 10.3	9 52.3	26 17.9	11 22.9	21 38.5	14 02.4	1 08.6	2 09.0
10 Sa	9 15 38	17 47 38	0♊44 07	6♊43 54	13 25.9	18 32.3	9 19.6	10 30.8	26 43.9	11 15.1	21 40.0	14 01.7	1 07.6	2 09.9
11 Su	9 19 35	18 45 13	12 46 46	18 53 19	13 23.1	17 44.3	10 29.1	11 09.3	27 09.9	11 07.5	21 41.5	14 01.1	1 06.6	2 10.9
12 M	9 23 32	19 42 49	25 04 05	1♋19 34	13 17.8	16 57.7	11 38.6	11 47.7	27 35.9	10 59.8	21 43.2	14 00.6	1 05.7	2 11.9
13 Tu	9 27 28	20 40 26	7♋40 07	14 06 02	13 10.0	16 13.3	12 48.3	12 26.2	28 01.9	10 52.2	21 45.0	14 00.1	1 04.8	2 13.0
14 W	9 31 25	21 38 05	20 37 30	27 14 34	12 59.9	15 32.0	13 58.1	13 04.6	28 27.9	10 44.6	21 46.8	13 59.6	1 03.9	2 14.1
15 Th	9 35 21	22 35 46	3♌57 10	10♌45 07	12 48.4	14 54.8	15 07.9	13 43.0	28 53.8	10 37.1	21 48.8	13 59.2	1 03.0	2 15.2
16 F	9 39 18	23 33 27	17 38 02	24 35 32	12 36.5	14 22.4	16 17.9	14 21.4	29 19.7	10 29.7	21 50.8	13 58.8	1 02.2	2 16.4
17 Sa	9 43 14	24 31 10	1♍37 01	8♍41 52	12 25.5	13 55.5	17 28.0	14 59.8	29 45.7	10 22.3	21 52.9	13 58.5	1 01.4	2 17.6
18 Su	9 47 11	25 28 54	15 49 25	22 58 57	12 16.5	13 34.7	18 38.1	15 38.2	0♌11.5	10 15.0	21 55.1	13 58.3	1 00.6	2 18.8
19 M	9 51 07	26 26 39	0♎09 47	7♎21 15	12 10.2	13 20.6	19 48.4	16 16.5	0 37.4	10 07.7	21 57.5	13 58.1	0 59.8	2 20.0
20 Tu	9 55 04	27 24 25	14 32 44	21 43 43	12 06.6	13D 13.6	20 58.7	16 54.8	1 03.2	10 00.6	21 59.9	13 57.9	0 59.1	2 21.3
21 W	9 59 01	28 22 12	28 53 45	6♏02 27	12D 05.3	13 14.0	22 09.2	17 33.2	1 29.0	9 53.5	22 02.4	13 57.8	0 58.4	2 22.6
22 Th	10 02 57	29 20 01	13♏09 34	20 14 53	12R 05.3	13 22.0	23 19.7	18 11.5	1 54.8	9 46.6	22 04.9	13D 57.7	0 57.8	2 23.9
23 F	10 06 54	0♍17 51	27 18 15	4♐19 35	12 05.4	13 37.8	24 30.3	18 49.8	2 20.6	9 39.7	22 07.6	13 57.7	0 57.1	2 25.3
24 Sa	10 10 50	1 15 42	11♐18 49	18 15 53	12 04.3	14 01.4	25 41.0	19 28.0	2 46.3	9 32.9	22 10.4	13 57.8	0 56.5	2 26.7
25 Su	10 14 47	2 13 34	25 10 45	2♑03 22	12 01.2	14 32.8	26 51.8	20 06.3	3 12.0	9 26.3	22 13.3	13 57.9	0 55.9	2 28.1
26 M	10 18 43	3 11 27	8♑53 38	15 41 27	11 55.4	15 11.9	28 02.7	20 44.5	3 37.7	9 19.8	22 16.2	13 58.1	0 55.4	2 29.6
27 Tu	10 22 40	4 09 22	22 26 42	29 09 14	11 47.2	15 58.6	29 13.7	21 22.7	4 03.4	9 13.3	22 19.2	13 58.3	0 54.9	2 31.1
28 W	10 26 36	5 07 18	5♒48 52	12♒25 27	11 37.0	16 52.6	0♌24.8	22 01.0	4 29.0	9 07.0	22 22.3	13 58.5	0 54.4	2 32.6
29 Th	10 30 33	6 05 15	18 58 48	25 28 45	11 25.8	17 53.6	1 35.9	22 39.1	4 54.6	9 00.9	22 25.5	13 58.8	0 53.9	2 34.1
30 F	10 34 30	7 03 14	1♓55 12	8♓18 02	11 14.8	19 01.3	2 47.1	23 17.3	5 20.2	8 54.8	22 28.8	13 59.2	0 53.5	2 35.7
31 Sa	10 38 26	8 01 15	14 37 13	20 52 45	11 04.8	20 15.4	3 58.5	23 55.5	5 45.7	8 48.9	22 32.2	13 59.6	0 53.1	2 37.3

Astro Data

	Dy Hr Mn
♆✶♇	5 0:45
☽0N	9 4:05
♇D	12 8:41
♃✶♅	14 21:33
☽0S	23 5:24
♄D	25 19:34
☿R	28 0:51
☽0N	5 11:25
☽0S	19 11:01
☿D	20 22:49
♅D	23 0:18

Planet Ingress

	Dy Hr Mn
♀ ♊	6 8:01
☉ ♌	22 21:36
♂ ♌	25 4:04
♀ ♋	2 9:10
⚳ ♌	18 1:18
☉ ♍	23 4:36
♀ ♌	28 3:39

Last Aspect / ☽ Ingress

Last Aspect Dy Hr Mn		☽ Ingress Dy Hr Mn
30 18:53	♃ ✶	♑ 1 18:22
3 16:42	♀ △	♒ 3 21:36
6 3:16	♀ □	♓ 6 3:40
7 21:05	♄ △	♈ 8 13:20
10 6:04	♂ □	♉ 11 1:44
12 22:28	♂ ✶	♊ 13 14:23
15 4:02	☿ ✶	♋ 16 0:54
18 0:00	♂ ☌	♌ 18 8:25
20 0:54	☿ ☌	♍ 20 13:29
22 16:51	☉ ✶	♎ 22 17:10
24 19:54	♂ □	♏ 24 20:16
26 15:07	☿ □	♐ 26 23:12
28 18:17	☿ △	♑ 29 2:21
30 15:29	♄ ✶	♒ 31 6:25

Last Aspect / ☽ Ingress

Last Aspect Dy Hr Mn		☽ Ingress Dy Hr Mn
2 1:56	☿ ☍	♓ 2 12:33
4 5:16	♄ △	♈ 4 21:43
6 16:32	☿ △	♉ 7 9:41
9 5:38	♄ ☍	♊ 9 22:31
11 11:43	☉ ✶	♋ 12 9:28
14 2:05	♄ △	♌ 14 16:57
16 10:05	☉ ☌	♍ 16 21:15
18 10:13	♄ ✶	♎ 18 23:44
20 22:11	☉ ✶	♏ 21 1:51
22 17:42	♀ △	♐ 23 4:36
24 14:11	♂ △	♑ 25 8:24
27 12:09	♀ ☍	♒ 27 13:31
29 6:30	♂ ☍	♓ 29 20:25

☽ Phases & Eclipses

Dy Hr Mn	
2 12:08	○ 10♑33
10 0:49	☾ 17♈43
17 23:56	● 25♋19
24 23:39	☽ 1♏59
31 21:41	○ 8♒36
8 18:29	☾ 16♉08
16 10:05	● 23♌29
23 4:36	☽ 0♐00
30 9:27	○ 6♓57

Astro Data

1 July 1985
Julian Day # 31228
SVP 5♓27'56"
GC 26♐38.2 ⚴ 22♉14.9
Eris 16♈23.7 ⚵ 2♎12.7
⚷ 11♊16.8 ⚶ 25♎08.0
☽ Mean ☊ 15♉32.2

1 August 1985
Julian Day # 31259
SVP 5♓27'50"
GC 26♐38.3 ⚴ 5♊47.5
Eris 16♈22.4R ⚵ 9♎34.7
⚷ 13♊14.7 ⚶ 4♏08.0
☽ Mean ☊ 13♉53.7

LONGITUDE — September 1985

Day	Sid.Time	☉	0 hr ☽	Noon ☽	True ☊	☿	♀	♂	⚳	♃	♄	♅	♆	♇
1 Su	10 42 23	8♍59 17	27♓04 43	3♈13 14	10♉56.8	21♌35.3	5♌09.9	24♌33.7	6♌11.2	8♒43.1	22♏35.7	14♐00.0	0♑52.7	2♏38.9
2 M	10 46 19	9 57 21	9♈18 31	15 20 51	10R51.2	23 00.7	6 21.4	25 11.8	6 36.7	8R37.4	22 39.2	14 00.5	0R52.4	2 40.5
3 Tu	10 50 16	10 55 26	21 20 32	27 17 59	10 48.1	24 31.1	7 32.9	25 49.9	7 02.1	8 31.9	22 42.8	14 01.1	0 52.1	2 42.2
4 W	10 54 12	11 53 34	3♉13 39	9♉08 03	10D47.1	26 05.9	8 44.6	26 28.1	7 27.5	8 26.6	22 46.5	14 01.7	0 51.8	2 43.9
5 Th	10 58 09	12 51 44	15 01 43	20 55 15	10 47.5	27 44.6	9 56.4	27 06.2	7 52.9	8 21.4	22 50.3	14 02.4	0 51.6	2 45.6
6 F	11 02 05	13 49 55	26 49 17	2♊44 28	10 48.4	29 26.8	11 08.2	27 44.3	8 18.2	8 16.3	22 54.1	14 03.1	0 51.4	2 47.3
7 Sa	11 06 02	14 48 09	8♊41 26	14 40 54	10R48.9	1♍11.9	12 20.1	28 22.4	8 43.5	8 11.4	22 58.1	14 03.9	0 51.2	2 49.1
8 Su	11 09 59	15 46 24	20 43 31	26 49 55	10 48.2	2 59.4	13 32.1	29 00.5	9 08.8	8 06.7	23 02.1	14 04.7	0 51.1	2 50.9
9 M	11 13 55	16 44 42	3♋00 45	9♋16 34	10 45.6	4 48.9	14 44.2	29 38.5	9 34.0	8 02.1	23 06.2	14 05.6	0 51.0	2 52.7
10 Tu	11 17 52	17 43 02	15 37 53	22 05 09	10 41.0	6 39.9	15 56.4	0♍16.6	9 59.2	7 57.7	23 10.4	14 06.5	0 50.9	2 54.5
11 W	11 21 48	18 41 24	28 38 40	5♌18 38	10 34.5	8 32.1	17 08.6	0 54.7	10 24.3	7 53.5	23 14.6	14 07.5	0D50.8	2 56.4
12 Th	11 25 45	19 39 48	12♌05 09	18 58 06	10 26.7	10 25.1	18 20.9	1 32.7	10 49.4	7 49.5	23 18.9	14 08.5	0 50.8	2 58.3
13 F	11 29 41	20 38 13	25 57 15	3♍02 12	10 18.5	12 18.6	19 33.3	2 10.8	11 14.5	7 45.6	23 23.3	14 09.6	0 50.8	3 00.2
14 Sa	11 33 38	21 36 41	10♍12 23	17 27 05	10 10.8	14 12.3	20 45.7	2 48.8	11 39.5	7 41.9	23 27.8	14 10.7	0 50.9	3 02.1
15 Su	11 37 34	22 35 11	24 45 29	2♎06 39	10 04.6	16 06.0	21 58.2	3 26.8	12 04.4	7 38.3	23 32.4	14 11.8	0 51.0	3 04.1
16 M	11 41 31	23 33 42	9♎29 40	16 53 32	10 00.4	17 59.6	23 10.8	4 04.8	12 29.3	7 35.0	23 37.0	14 13.1	0 51.1	3 06.0
17 Tu	11 45 27	24 32 15	24 17 19	1♏40 08	9D58.5	19 52.7	24 23.5	4 42.8	12 54.2	7 31.8	23 41.7	14 14.3	0 51.2	3 08.0
18 W	11 49 24	25 30 50	9♏01 12	16 19 50	9 58.3	21 45.4	25 36.2	5 20.8	13 19.0	7 28.8	23 46.4	14 15.7	0 51.4	3 10.0
19 Th	11 53 21	26 29 27	23 35 28	0♐47 41	9 59.3	23 37.4	26 49.0	5 58.7	13 43.7	7 26.0	23 51.3	14 17.0	0 51.7	3 12.1
20 F	11 57 17	27 28 05	7♐56 08	15 00 37	10R00.6	25 28.7	28 01.9	6 36.7	14 08.4	7 23.4	23 56.2	14 18.5	0 51.9	3 14.1
21 Sa	12 01 14	28 26 45	22 01 00	28 57 16	10 01.1	27 19.3	29 14.8	7 14.7	14 33.1	7 21.0	24 01.1	14 19.9	0 52.2	3 16.2
22 Su	12 05 10	29 25 27	5♑49 25	12♑37 31	10 00.3	29 09.0	0♍27.7	7 52.6	14 57.7	7 18.8	24 06.2	14 21.4	0 52.5	3 18.3
23 M	12 09 07	0♎24 10	19 21 39	26 01 57	9 57.7	0♎57.9	1 40.8	8 30.5	15 22.2	7 16.8	24 11.3	14 23.0	0 52.9	3 20.4
24 Tu	12 13 03	1 22 55	2♒38 31	9♒11 29	9 53.4	2 45.8	2 53.9	9 08.4	15 46.6	7 15.0	24 16.4	14 24.6	0 53.3	3 22.5
25 W	12 17 00	2 21 42	15 40 57	22 07 03	9 47.7	4 32.9	4 07.1	9 46.3	16 11.0	7 13.3	24 21.7	14 26.3	0 53.7	3 24.6
26 Th	12 20 56	3 20 30	28 29 52	4♓49 31	9 41.4	6 19.0	5 20.3	10 24.2	16 35.4	7 11.9	24 26.9	14 28.0	0 54.1	3 26.8
27 F	12 24 53	4 19 20	11♓06 05	17 19 40	9 35.0	8 04.2	6 33.6	11 02.1	16 59.6	7 10.6	24 32.3	14 29.7	0 54.6	3 29.0
28 Sa	12 28 50	5 18 12	23 30 23	29 38 21	9 29.4	9 48.5	7 46.9	11 40.0	17 23.8	7 09.6	24 37.7	14 31.5	0 55.1	3 31.2
29 Su	12 32 46	6 17 06	5♈43 43	11♈46 38	9 25.0	11 31.9	9 00.3	12 17.8	17 48.0	7 08.7	24 43.1	14 33.4	0 55.7	3 33.4
30 M	12 36 43	7 16 03	17 47 18	23 45 56	9 22.2	13 14.4	10 13.8	12 55.7	18 12.0	7 08.1	24 48.7	14 35.3	0 56.2	3 35.6

LONGITUDE — October 1985

Day	Sid.Time	☉	0 hr ☽	Noon ☽	True ☊	☿	♀	♂	⚳	♃	♄	♅	♆	♇
1 Tu	12 40 39	8♎15 01	29♈42 49	5♉38 14	9♉21.0	14♎56.0	11♍27.3	13♍33.5	18♌36.0	7♒07.6	24♏54.3	14♐37.2	0♑56.8	3♏37.8
2 W	12 44 36	9 14 01	11♉32 31	17 26 04	9D21.2	16 36.7	12 40.9	14 11.4	19 00.0	7D07.3	24 59.9	14 39.2	0 57.5	3 40.0
3 Th	12 48 32	10 13 04	23 19 17	29 12 38	9 22.5	18 16.6	13 54.5	14 49.2	19 23.8	7 07.3	25 05.6	14 41.2	0 58.2	3 42.3
4 F	12 52 29	11 12 09	5♊06 37	11♊01 46	9 24.3	19 55.6	15 08.2	15 27.1	19 47.6	7 07.4	25 11.3	14 43.2	0 58.9	3 44.6
5 Sa	12 56 25	12 11 16	16 58 37	22 57 47	9 26.0	21 33.9	16 22.0	16 04.9	20 11.4	7 07.7	25 17.1	14 45.4	0 59.6	3 46.9
6 Su	13 00 22	13 10 26	28 59 50	5♋05 22	9R27.1	23 11.3	17 35.8	16 42.7	20 35.0	7 08.3	25 23.0	14 47.5	1 00.4	3 49.2
7 M	13 04 19	14 09 38	11♋15 01	17 29 22	9 27.4	24 47.9	18 49.7	17 20.5	20 58.6	7 09.0	25 28.9	14 49.7	1 01.2	3 51.5
8 Tu	13 08 15	15 08 52	23 48 57	0♌14 18	9 26.5	26 23.8	20 03.6	17 58.3	21 22.0	7 09.9	25 34.9	14 51.9	1 02.0	3 53.8
9 W	13 12 12	16 08 08	6♌45 51	13 23 59	9 24.6	27 58.9	21 17.6	18 36.1	21 45.4	7 11.0	25 40.9	14 54.2	1 02.9	3 56.1
10 Th	13 16 08	17 07 27	20 08 56	27 00 49	9 21.9	29 33.3	22 31.6	19 13.9	22 08.8	7 12.3	25 46.9	14 56.5	1 03.8	3 58.5
11 F	13 20 05	18 06 48	3♍59 38	11♍05 11	9 18.9	1♏06.9	23 45.7	19 51.7	22 32.0	7 13.8	25 53.0	14 58.9	1 04.7	4 00.8
12 Sa	13 24 01	19 06 11	18 17 06	25 34 50	9 16.0	2 39.8	24 59.8	20 29.4	22 55.1	7 15.5	25 59.2	15 01.3	1 05.7	4 03.2
13 Su	13 27 58	20 05 36	2♎57 40	10♎24 45	9 13.7	4 12.1	26 14.0	21 07.2	23 18.2	7 17.4	26 05.4	15 03.7	1 06.7	4 05.5
14 M	13 31 54	21 05 04	17 55 04	25 27 31	9D12.4	5 43.6	27 28.2	21 45.0	23 41.1	7 19.5	26 11.6	15 06.2	1 07.7	4 07.9
15 Tu	13 35 51	22 04 33	3♏00 57	10♏34 13	9 12.0	7 14.5	28 42.4	22 22.7	24 04.0	7 21.8	26 17.9	15 08.7	1 08.8	4 10.3
16 W	13 39 48	23 04 05	18 06 11	25 35 48	9 12.4	8 44.6	29 56.7	23 00.4	24 26.7	7 24.3	26 24.3	15 11.3	1 09.9	4 12.7
17 Th	13 43 44	24 03 38	3♐02 09	10♐24 24	9 13.4	10 14.1	1♎11.1	23 38.2	24 49.4	7 27.0	26 30.6	15 13.9	1 11.0	4 15.1
18 F	13 47 41	25 03 13	17 41 56	24 54 12	9 14.6	11 42.9	2 25.4	24 15.9	25 11.9	7 29.9	26 37.1	15 16.5	1 12.1	4 17.5
19 Sa	13 51 37	26 02 50	2♑00 54	9♑01 49	9 15.5	13 11.0	3 39.8	24 53.6	25 34.4	7 33.0	26 43.5	15 19.2	1 13.3	4 19.9
20 Su	13 55 34	27 02 29	15 56 53	22 46 08	9R16.0	14 38.4	4 54.3	25 31.3	25 56.7	7 36.2	26 50.0	15 21.9	1 14.5	4 22.3
21 M	13 59 30	28 02 09	29 29 43	6♒07 50	9 15.9	16 05.1	6 08.8	26 09.0	26 18.9	7 39.7	26 56.5	15 24.6	1 15.7	4 24.7
22 Tu	14 03 27	29 01 51	12♒40 46	19 08 49	9 15.3	17 31.0	7 23.3	26 46.7	26 41.0	7 43.3	27 03.1	15 27.4	1 17.0	4 27.1
23 W	14 07 23	0♏01 35	25 32 19	1♓51 39	9 14.3	18 56.2	8 37.9	27 24.3	27 03.0	7 47.1	27 09.7	15 30.2	1 18.3	4 29.5
24 Th	14 11 20	1 01 20	8♓07 08	14 19 09	9 13.2	20 20.5	9 52.4	28 02.0	27 24.9	7 51.1	27 16.3	15 33.1	1 19.6	4 32.0
25 F	14 15 17	2 01 07	20 28 01	26 34 05	9 12.1	21 44.1	11 07.1	28 39.6	27 46.7	7 55.3	27 23.0	15 35.9	1 21.0	4 34.4
26 Sa	14 19 13	3 00 56	2♈37 40	8♈39 03	9 11.2	23 06.8	12 21.7	29 17.3	28 08.3	7 59.6	27 29.7	15 38.8	1 22.3	4 36.8
27 Su	14 23 10	4 00 47	14 38 33	20 36 25	9 10.6	24 28.5	13 36.4	29 54.9	28 29.9	8 04.2	27 36.4	15 41.8	1 23.7	4 39.2
28 M	14 27 06	5 00 39	26 32 57	2♉28 22	9D10.3	25 49.3	14 51.1	0♎32.5	28 51.3	8 08.9	27 43.2	15 44.7	1 25.2	4 41.7
29 Tu	14 31 03	6 00 34	8♉22 58	14 17 01	9 10.3	27 09.0	16 05.9	1 10.1	29 12.6	8 13.8	27 50.0	15 47.7	1 26.6	4 44.1
30 W	14 34 59	7 00 30	20 10 46	26 04 30	9 10.4	28 27.6	17 20.7	1 47.7	29 33.7	8 18.9	27 56.8	15 50.8	1 28.1	4 46.5
31 Th	14 38 56	8 00 29	1♊58 32	7♊53 11	9 10.6	29 44.9	18 35.5	2 25.3	29 54.7	8 24.1	28 03.6	15 53.8	1 29.6	4 48.9

Astro Data Dy Hr Mn	Planet Ingress Dy Hr Mn	Last Aspect Dy Hr Mn	☽ Ingress Dy Hr Mn	Last Aspect Dy Hr Mn	☽ Ingress Dy Hr Mn	☽ Phases & Eclipses Dy Hr Mn	Astro Data
☽0N 1 18:43	☿ ♍ 6 19:39	31 15:13 ♄ △	♈ 1 5:42	29 17:33 ♅ △	♉ 1 0:35	7 12:16 ☾ 14♊49	1 September 1985
♆D 12 9:17	♂ ♍ 10 1:31	3 8:52 ♂ △	♉ 3 17:28	3 3:33 ♄ ☍	♊ 3 13:36	14 19:20 ● 21♍55	Julian Day # 31290
☽0S 15 19:15	♀ ♍ 22 2:53	6 4:12 ☿ □	♊ 6 6:27	5 8:46 ☿ △	♋ 6 1:59	21 11:03 ☽ 28♐24	SVP 5♓27'46"
⊙0S 23 2:07	☿ ♎ 22 23:13	8 16:28 ♂ ✶	♋ 8 18:10	8 3:50 ☿ □	♌ 8 11:33	29 0:08 ○ 5♈48	GC 26♐38.3 ⚴ 18♊53.9
☿0S 24 15:42	⊙ ♎ 23 2:07	10 14:01 ♄ △	♌ 11 2:27	10 16:57 ☿ ✶	♍ 10 17:09		Eris 16♈11.6R ⚵ 18♎44.7
☽0N 29 1:37		12 19:32 ♄ □	♍ 13 6:52	12 12:40 ♄ ✶	♎ 12 19:12	7 5:04 ☾ 13♋53	⚷ 14♊26.2 ⚶ 16♏32.0
	☿ ♏ 10 18:50	14 21:56 ♄ ✶	♎ 15 8:34	14 4:33 ⊙ ☌	♏ 14 19:13	14 4:33 ● 20♎47	☽ Mean ☊ 12♉15.2
♃D 3 8:17	♀ ♎ 16 13:04	16 23:07 ♀ ✶	♏ 17 9:17	16 13:19 ♄ ☌	♐ 16 19:05	20 20:13 ☽ 27♑23	
☽0S 13 5:50	⊙ ♏ 23 11:22	19 4:45 ♀ □	♐ 19 10:40	18 12:16 ⊙ ✶	♑ 18 20:35	28 17:38 ○ 5♉15	1 October 1985
♀0S 19 9:52	♂ ♎ 27 15:16	21 12:33 ♀ △	♑ 21 13:49	20 20:13 ⊙ □	♒ 21 0:54	28 17:42 T 1.074	Julian Day # 31320
☽0N 26 7:55	☿ ♐ 31 16:44	23 8:39 ♀ ✶	♒ 23 19:11	23 8:12 ⊙ △	♓ 23 8:27		SVP 5♓27'43"
	⚳ ♍ 31 18:03	25 16:14 ♄ □	♓ 26 2:50	25 16:22 ♂ ☍	♈ 25 18:47		GC 26♐38.4 ⚴ 0♋04.7
		28 2:07 ♄ △	♈ 28 12:43	27 2:05 ♅ △	♉ 28 6:59		Eris 15♈55.2R ⚵ 28♎34.3
				30 17:27 ☿ ☍	♊ 30 19:59		⚷ 14♊36.0R ⚶ 0♐26.3
							☽ Mean ☊ 10♉39.9

November 1985 LONGITUDE

Day	Sid.Time	☉	0 hr ☽	Noon ☽	True ☊	☿	♀	♂	⚳	♃	♄	♅	♆	♇
1 F	14 42 52	9♏00 30	13♊48 47	19♊45 42	9♉10.7	1♐00.9	19♎50.4	3♎02.9	0♍15.6	8♒29.6	28♏10.5	15♐56.9	1♑31.1	4♏51.4
2 Sa	14 46 49	10 00 32	25 44 19	1♋45 02	9R 10.6	2 15.4	21 05.2	3 40.5	0 36.4	8 35.2	28 17.4	16 00.0	1 32.7	4 53.8
3 Su	14 50 46	11 00 37	7♋48 19	13 54 36	9 10.5	3 28.3	22 20.1	4 18.1	0 57.0	8 40.9	28 24.3	16 03.2	1 34.3	4 56.2
4 M	14 54 42	12 00 44	20 04 22	26 18 06	9 10.3	4 39.3	23 35.1	4 55.7	1 17.4	8 46.9	28 31.2	16 06.4	1 35.9	4 58.6
5 Tu	14 58 39	13 00 53	2♌36 16	8♌59 20	9D 10.2	5 48.3	24 50.1	5 33.2	1 37.8	8 53.0	28 38.2	16 09.6	1 37.5	5 01.1
6 W	15 02 35	14 01 04	15 27 47	22 02 00	9 10.2	6 55.1	26 05.1	6 10.8	1 57.9	8 59.2	28 45.1	16 12.8	1 39.2	5 03.5
7 Th	15 06 32	15 01 17	28 42 22	5♍29 09	9 10.5	7 59.4	27 20.1	6 48.3	2 17.9	9 05.7	28 52.1	16 16.0	1 40.8	5 05.9
8 F	15 10 28	16 01 32	12♍22 31	19 22 35	9 11.0	9 00.8	28 35.1	7 25.9	2 37.8	9 12.2	28 59.2	16 19.3	1 42.5	5 08.3
9 Sa	15 14 25	17 01 49	26 29 14	3♎42 15	9 11.7	9 59.1	29 50.2	8 03.4	2 57.5	9 19.0	29 06.2	16 22.6	1 44.3	5 10.7
10 Su	15 18 21	18 02 07	11♎01 15	18 25 38	9 12.4	10 53.8	1♏05.3	8 40.9	3 17.0	9 25.9	29 13.2	16 25.9	1 46.0	5 13.0
11 M	15 22 18	19 02 28	25 54 38	3♏27 22	9R 12.8	11 44.6	2 20.4	9 18.4	3 36.4	9 33.0	29 20.3	16 29.2	1 47.8	5 15.4
12 Tu	15 26 15	20 02 51	11♏02 45	18 39 37	9 12.7	12 30.9	3 35.6	9 55.9	3 55.6	9 40.2	29 27.4	16 32.6	1 49.6	5 17.8
13 W	15 30 11	21 03 16	26 16 43	3♐52 49	9 12.0	13 12.1	4 50.7	10 33.4	4 14.6	9 47.6	29 34.5	16 36.0	1 51.4	5 20.2
14 Th	15 34 08	22 03 42	11♐26 40	18 57 07	9 10.7	13 47.8	6 05.9	11 10.9	4 33.5	9 55.1	29 41.6	16 39.4	1 53.2	5 22.5
15 F	15 38 04	23 04 09	26 23 09	3♑43 54	9 09.0	14 17.1	7 21.1	11 48.4	4 52.1	10 02.8	29 48.7	16 42.8	1 55.1	5 24.9
16 Sa	15 42 01	24 04 38	10♑58 39	18 06 55	9 07.2	14 39.4	8 36.3	12 25.8	5 10.6	10 10.7	29 55.8	16 46.3	1 56.9	5 27.2
17 Su	15 45 57	25 05 09	25 08 21	2♒02 49	9 05.5	14 54.0	9 51.6	13 03.3	5 28.9	10 18.7	0♐02.9	16 49.7	1 58.8	5 29.5
18 M	15 49 54	26 05 40	8♒50 21	15 31 04	9D 04.4	15R 00.1	11 06.8	13 40.7	5 47.0	10 26.8	0 10.1	16 53.2	2 00.8	5 31.9
19 Tu	15 53 50	27 06 13	22 05 17	28 33 22	9 04.1	14 57.0	12 22.1	14 18.1	6 04.9	10 35.1	0 17.2	16 56.7	2 02.7	5 34.2
20 W	15 57 47	28 06 47	4♓55 44	11♓12 55	9 04.7	14 44.0	13 37.3	14 55.5	6 22.6	10 43.5	0 24.3	17 00.2	2 04.6	5 36.5
21 Th	16 01 44	29 07 22	17 25 25	23 33 48	9 05.9	14 20.7	14 52.6	15 32.9	6 40.1	10 52.1	0 31.5	17 03.7	2 06.6	5 38.7
22 F	16 05 40	0♐07 58	29 38 36	5♈40 21	9 07.5	13 46.7	16 07.9	16 10.3	6 57.4	11 00.8	0 38.6	17 07.3	2 08.6	5 41.0
23 Sa	16 09 37	1 08 35	11♈39 36	17 36 50	9 09.2	13 02.1	17 23.2	16 47.6	7 14.5	11 09.6	0 45.8	17 10.8	2 10.6	5 43.2
24 Su	16 13 33	2 09 14	23 32 32	29 27 08	9R 10.4	12 07.2	18 38.5	17 25.0	7 31.3	11 18.5	0 52.9	17 14.4	2 12.6	5 45.5
25 M	16 17 30	3 09 54	5♉21 03	11♉14 40	9 10.8	11 03.1	19 53.8	18 02.3	7 48.0	11 27.6	1 00.0	17 17.9	2 14.6	5 47.7
26 Tu	16 21 26	4 10 35	17 08 18	23 02 17	9 09.9	9 51.0	21 09.2	18 39.6	8 04.4	11 36.9	1 07.2	17 21.5	2 16.7	5 49.9
27 W	16 25 23	5 11 18	28 56 54	4♊52 25	9 07.7	8 33.0	22 24.5	19 16.9	8 20.6	11 46.2	1 14.3	17 25.1	2 18.7	5 52.1
28 Th	16 29 19	6 12 02	10♊49 04	16 47 04	9 04.1	7 11.4	23 39.9	19 54.2	8 36.6	11 55.7	1 21.4	17 28.7	2 20.8	5 54.3
29 F	16 33 16	7 12 47	22 46 38	28 47 59	8 59.5	5 48.9	24 55.3	20 31.5	8 52.4	12 05.3	1 28.6	17 32.3	2 22.9	5 56.5
30 Sa	16 37 13	8 13 34	4♋51 20	10♋56 53	8 54.2	4 28.3	26 10.6	21 08.8	9 07.9	12 15.1	1 35.7	17 36.0	2 25.0	5 58.6

December 1985 LONGITUDE

Day	Sid.Time	☉	0 hr ☽	Noon ☽	True ☊	☿	♀	♂	⚳	♃	♄	♅	♆	♇
1 Su	16 41 09	9♐14 22	17♋04 51	23♋15 30	8♉48.9	3♐12.3	27♏26.0	21♎46.1	9♍23.2	12♒24.9	1♐42.8	17♐39.6	2♑27.1	6♏00.7
2 M	16 45 06	10 15 11	29 29 05	5♌45 51	8R 44.2	2R 03.2	28 41.4	22 23.3	9 38.2	12 34.9	1 49.9	17 43.2	2 29.2	6 02.8
3 Tu	16 49 02	11 16 02	12♌06 07	18 30 10	8 40.6	1 03.0	29 56.9	23 00.6	9 53.0	12 45.0	1 57.0	17 46.9	2 31.4	6 04.9
4 W	16 52 59	12 16 53	24 58 20	1♍30 55	8D 38.4	0 13.1	1♐12.3	23 37.8	10 07.5	12 55.2	2 04.1	17 50.5	2 33.5	6 07.0
5 Th	16 56 55	13 17 47	8♍08 15	14 50 35	8 37.9	29♏34.3	2 27.7	24 15.0	10 21.7	13 05.5	2 11.1	17 54.2	2 35.7	6 09.1
6 F	17 00 52	14 18 41	21 38 12	28 31 18	8 38.6	29 07.0	3 43.2	24 52.2	10 35.7	13 15.9	2 18.2	17 57.8	2 37.9	6 11.1
7 Sa	17 04 48	15 19 37	5♎30 00	12♎34 20	8 40.0	28D 51.0	4 58.6	25 29.4	10 49.4	13 26.5	2 25.2	18 01.5	2 40.0	6 13.1
8 Su	17 08 45	16 20 34	19 44 12	26 59 24	8R 41.4	28 46.0	6 14.1	26 06.6	11 02.9	13 37.2	2 32.2	18 05.2	2 42.2	6 15.1
9 M	17 12 42	17 21 33	4♏19 32	11♏44 02	8 41.8	28 51.3	7 29.6	26 43.7	11 16.0	13 47.9	2 39.2	18 08.8	2 44.4	6 17.1
10 Tu	17 16 38	18 22 33	19 12 14	26 43 13	8 40.5	29 06.2	8 45.1	27 20.8	11 28.9	13 58.8	2 46.2	18 12.4	2 46.6	6 19.0
11 W	17 20 35	19 23 33	4♐15 58	11♐49 22	8 37.3	29 29.8	10 00.5	27 58.0	11 41.5	14 09.8	2 53.2	18 16.1	2 48.9	6 20.9
12 Th	17 24 31	20 24 35	19 22 12	26 53 15	8 32.0	0♐01.3	11 16.0	28 35.1	11 53.8	14 20.9	3 00.1	18 19.8	2 51.1	6 22.8
13 F	17 28 28	21 25 37	4♑21 19	11♑45 17	8 25.3	0 39.9	12 31.5	29 12.2	12 05.7	14 32.1	3 07.1	18 23.5	2 53.3	6 24.7
14 Sa	17 32 24	22 26 41	19 04 11	26 17 11	8 18.0	1 24.8	13 47.0	29 49.2	12 17.4	14 43.4	3 14.0	18 27.2	2 55.6	6 26.6
15 Su	17 36 21	23 27 44	3♒23 40	10♒23 10	8 11.1	2 15.2	15 02.5	0♏26.3	12 28.8	14 54.8	3 20.8	18 30.8	2 57.8	6 28.4
16 M	17 40 18	24 28 48	17 15 28	24 00 31	8 05.5	3 10.5	16 18.0	1 03.3	12 39.8	15 06.3	3 27.7	18 34.5	3 00.1	6 30.2
17 Tu	17 44 14	25 29 53	0♓38 26	7♓09 29	8 01.6	4 10.1	17 33.5	1 40.3	12 50.5	15 17.8	3 34.5	18 38.1	3 02.3	6 32.0
18 W	17 48 11	26 30 57	13 34 05	19 52 42	7D 59.7	5 13.4	18 49.0	2 17.2	13 00.9	15 29.5	3 41.3	18 41.8	3 04.6	6 33.8
19 Th	17 52 07	27 32 02	26 05 54	2♈14 19	7 59.6	6 20.1	20 04.5	2 54.2	13 10.9	15 41.3	3 48.0	18 45.4	3 06.8	6 35.5
20 F	17 56 04	28 33 08	8♈18 35	14 19 23	8 00.6	7 29.6	21 20.0	3 31.1	13 20.7	15 53.1	3 54.8	18 49.0	3 09.1	6 37.2
21 Sa	18 00 00	29 34 13	20 17 22	26 13 12	8 01.8	8 41.6	22 35.5	4 08.0	13 30.0	16 05.1	4 01.5	18 52.6	3 11.4	6 38.9
22 Su	18 03 57	0♑35 19	2♉07 31	8♉00 56	8R 02.5	9 55.9	23 51.0	4 44.9	13 39.1	16 17.1	4 08.1	18 56.3	3 13.6	6 40.5
23 M	18 07 53	1 36 25	13 54 01	19 47 18	8 01.6	11 12.1	25 06.5	5 21.8	13 47.8	16 29.2	4 14.8	18 59.9	3 15.9	6 42.1
24 Tu	18 11 50	2 37 31	25 41 14	1♊36 18	7 58.5	12 30.0	26 22.0	5 58.6	13 56.1	16 41.4	4 21.4	19 03.5	3 18.2	6 43.7
25 W	18 15 47	3 38 38	7♊32 50	13 31 12	7 52.9	13 49.5	27 37.5	6 35.4	14 04.1	16 53.7	4 27.9	19 07.0	3 20.4	6 45.3
26 Th	18 19 43	4 39 45	19 31 39	25 34 25	7 44.8	15 10.3	28 53.0	7 12.2	14 11.7	17 06.0	4 34.4	19 10.6	3 22.7	6 46.8
27 F	18 23 40	5 40 52	1♋39 40	7♋47 32	7 34.6	16 32.2	0♑08.5	7 49.0	14 18.9	17 18.4	4 40.9	19 14.2	3 25.0	6 48.3
28 Sa	18 27 36	6 42 00	13 58 06	20 11 26	7 23.2	17 55.3	1 24.0	8 25.8	14 25.8	17 30.9	4 47.4	19 17.7	3 27.3	6 49.8
29 Su	18 31 33	7 43 07	26 27 35	2♌46 32	7 11.6	19 19.3	2 39.5	9 02.5	14 32.3	17 43.5	4 53.8	19 21.2	3 29.5	6 51.3
30 M	18 35 29	8 44 16	9♌08 20	15 32 58	7 00.9	20 44.1	3 55.0	9 39.2	14 38.4	17 56.2	5 00.1	19 24.8	3 31.8	6 52.7
31 Tu	18 39 26	9 45 24	22 00 30	28 30 57	6 52.0	22 09.7	5 10.5	10 15.9	14 44.1	18 08.9	5 06.5	19 28.3	3 34.1	6 54.1

Astro Data

	Dy Hr Mn
♂0S	1 1:13
☽0S	9 16:47
☿R	18 16:10
☽0N	22 13:48
☽0S	7 1:35
☿D	8 11:23
♄×♆	10 14:06
☽0N	19 19:58

Planet Ingress

		Dy Hr Mn
♀	♏	9 15:08
♂	♐	17 2:10
☉	♐	22 8:51
♀	♐	3 13:00
☿	♏R	4 19:23
☿	♐	12 11:05
♂	♏	14 18:59
☉	♑	21 22:08
♀	♑	27 9:17

Last Aspect / ☽ Ingress

Last Aspect Dy Hr Mn			☽ Ingress	Dy Hr Mn
1 12:10	♀	△	♋	2 8:31
4 16:17	♄	△	♌	4 19:04
7 0:11	♄	□	♍	7 2:18
9 4:18	♄	⚹	♎	9 5:52
10 8:46	♅	⚹	♏	11 6:31
13 5:09	♄	☌	♐	13 5:52
14 8:18	♅	☌	♑	15 5:53
16 22:58	☉	⚹	♒	17 8:25
19 9:04	☉	□	♓	19 14:42
21 23:58	☉	△	♈	22 0:42
23 11:07	♅	△	♉	24 13:07
26 7:43	♀	☍	♊	27 2:08
28 18:36	♂	△	♋	29 14:23

Last Aspect / ☽ Ingress

Last Aspect Dy Hr Mn			☽ Ingress	Dy Hr Mn
1 20:58	♀	△	♌	2 0:59
3 20:48	♂	⚹	♍	4 9:14
6 13:00	♀	⚹	♎	6 14:33
8 10:29	♂	☌	♏	8 16:56
10 15:53	☿	☌	♐	10 17:13
12 14:50	♂	⚹	♑	12 16:59
14 18:13	♂	□	♒	14 18:15
16 12:55	☉	⚹	♓	16 22:50
19 1:58	☉	□	♈	19 7:37
21 19:27	☉	△	♉	21 19:41
23 5:09	♃	□	♊	24 8:45
26 19:17	♀	☍	♋	26 20:44
27 12:03	♂	△	♌	29 6:44
30 22:50	☿	△	♍	31 14:43

☽ Phases & Eclipses

Dy Hr Mn		
5 20:07	☾	13♌21
12 14:20	●	20♏09
12 14:10:31	✔	T 01'59"
19 9:04	☽	26♒59
27 12:42	○	5♊13
5 9:01	☾	13♍10
12 0:54	●	19♐56
19 1:58	☽	27♓06
27 7:30	○	5♋29

Astro Data

1 November 1985
Julian Day # 31351
SVP 5♓27'39"
GC 26♐38.5 ⚴ 7♋34.5
Eris 15♈36.8R ⚵ 9♏09.7
⚷ 13♊42.2R ⚶ 15♐58.4
☽ Mean ☊ 9♉01.4

1 December 1985
Julian Day # 31381
SVP 5♓27'34"
GC 26♐38.6 ⚴ 6♋45.7R
Eris 15♈22.9R ⚵ 19♏21.8
⚷ 12♊06.9R ⚶ 1♑38.6
☽ Mean ☊ 7♉26.1

LONGITUDE — January 1986

Day	Sid.Time	☉	0 hr ☽	Noon ☽	True ☊	☿	♀	♂	⚳	♃	♄	♅	♆	♇
1 W	18 43 22	10♑46 32	5♍04 23	11♍40 55	6♉45.7	23♐36.1	6♑26.0	10♏52.6	14♍49.4	18♒21.7	5♐12.7	19♐31.8	3♑36.3	6♏55.4
2 Th	18 47 19	11 47 41	18 20 39	25 03 44	6R 42.1	25 03.1	7 41.5	11 29.2	14 54.3	18 34.5	5 19.0	19 35.2	3 38.6	6 56.7
3 F	18 51 16	12 48 50	1♎50 17	8♎40 29	6D 40.7	26 30.7	8 57.0	12 05.8	14 58.8	18 47.5	5 25.1	19 38.7	3 40.8	6 58.0
4 Sa	18 55 12	13 50 00	15 34 27	22 32 18	6 40.9	27 58.9	10 12.5	12 42.4	15 03.0	19 00.4	5 31.3	19 42.1	3 43.1	6 59.3
5 Su	18 59 09	14 51 10	29 34 04	6♏39 44	6R 41.2	29 27.7	11 28.0	13 19.0	15 06.6	19 13.5	5 37.4	19 45.5	3 45.3	7 00.5
6 M	19 03 05	15 52 20	13♏49 12	21 02 15	6 40.4	0♑57.0	12 43.5	13 55.5	15 09.9	19 26.6	5 43.4	19 48.9	3 47.5	7 01.7
7 Tu	19 07 02	16 53 30	28 18 29	5♐37 27	6 37.5	2 26.8	13 59.0	14 32.0	15 12.8	19 39.8	5 49.4	19 52.3	3 49.8	7 02.9
8 W	19 10 58	17 54 41	12♐58 30	20 20 52	6 31.7	3 57.1	15 14.5	15 08.5	15 15.2	19 53.1	5 55.3	19 55.7	3 52.0	7 04.0
9 Th	19 14 55	18 55 51	27 43 40	5♑05 56	6 23.1	5 27.8	16 30.0	15 44.9	15 17.2	20 06.4	6 01.2	19 59.0	3 54.2	7 05.1
10 F	19 18 52	19 57 01	12♑26 39	19 44 48	6 12.2	6 59.1	17 45.5	16 21.4	15 18.8	20 19.7	6 07.0	20 02.3	3 56.4	7 06.2
11 Sa	19 22 48	20 58 11	26 59 24	4♒09 34	6 00.1	8 30.8	19 01.0	16 57.7	15 19.9	20 33.1	6 12.8	20 05.6	3 58.6	7 07.2
12 Su	19 26 45	21 59 21	11♒14 32	18 13 40	5 48.3	10 02.9	20 16.5	17 34.1	15 20.6	20 46.6	6 18.5	20 08.9	4 00.8	7 08.2
13 M	19 30 41	23 00 30	25 06 31	1♓52 49	5 37.9	11 35.6	21 32.0	18 10.4	15R 20.9	21 00.1	6 24.2	20 12.1	4 03.0	7 09.2
14 Tu	19 34 38	24 01 38	8♓32 27	15 05 30	5 29.8	13 08.7	22 47.5	18 46.6	15 20.7	21 13.7	6 29.8	20 15.3	4 05.2	7 10.1
15 W	19 38 34	25 02 46	21 32 11	27 52 49	5 24.4	14 42.3	24 02.9	19 22.9	15 20.1	21 27.3	6 35.3	20 18.5	4 07.3	7 11.0
16 Th	19 42 31	26 03 53	4♈07 52	10♈17 53	5 21.7	16 16.4	25 18.4	19 59.0	15 19.0	21 40.9	6 40.8	20 21.6	4 09.5	7 11.9
17 F	19 46 27	27 04 59	16 23 28	22 25 17	5D 20.8	17 51.0	26 33.8	20 35.2	15 17.5	21 54.6	6 46.2	20 24.8	4 11.6	7 12.7
18 Sa	19 50 24	28 06 05	28 24 00	4♉20 21	5R 20.7	19 26.1	27 49.3	21 11.3	15 15.6	22 08.4	6 51.5	20 27.9	4 13.7	7 13.5
19 Su	19 54 21	29 07 09	10♉15 02	16 08 46	5 20.4	21 01.7	29 04.7	21 47.4	15 13.2	22 22.2	6 56.8	20 30.9	4 15.9	7 14.2
20 M	19 58 17	0♒08 13	22 02 12	27 56 01	5 18.7	22 37.9	0♒20.1	22 23.4	15 10.4	22 36.0	7 02.0	20 34.0	4 18.0	7 15.0
21 Tu	20 02 14	1 09 16	3♊50 49	9♊47 12	5 14.6	24 14.6	1 35.6	22 59.4	15 07.2	22 49.9	7 07.2	20 37.0	4 20.0	7 15.6
22 W	20 06 10	2 10 18	15 45 39	21 46 39	5 07.7	25 51.9	2 51.0	23 35.4	15 03.5	23 03.8	7 12.3	20 40.0	4 22.1	7 16.3
23 Th	20 10 07	3 11 19	27 50 35	3♋57 46	4 58.0	27 29.8	4 06.4	24 11.3	14 59.3	23 17.7	7 17.3	20 42.9	4 24.2	7 16.9
24 F	20 14 03	4 12 20	10♋08 28	16 22 49	4 45.8	29 08.2	5 21.8	24 47.2	14 54.8	23 31.7	7 22.2	20 45.8	4 26.2	7 17.5
25 Sa	20 18 00	5 13 19	22 40 56	29 02 49	4 32.1	0♒47.3	6 37.1	25 23.0	14 49.8	23 45.7	7 27.1	20 48.7	4 28.2	7 18.0
26 Su	20 21 56	6 14 18	5♌28 25	11♌57 37	4 18.0	2 27.1	7 52.5	25 58.8	14 44.4	23 59.8	7 31.9	20 51.6	4 30.2	7 18.5
27 M	20 25 53	7 15 16	18 30 15	25 06 07	4 04.9	4 07.4	9 07.9	26 34.6	14 38.5	24 13.9	7 36.6	20 54.4	4 32.2	7 19.0
28 Tu	20 29 50	8 16 13	1♍44 59	8♍26 38	3 53.9	5 48.4	10 23.2	27 10.3	14 32.3	24 28.0	7 41.3	20 57.2	4 34.2	7 19.4
29 W	20 33 46	9 17 09	15 10 49	21 57 21	3 45.8	7 30.1	11 38.6	27 46.0	14 25.6	24 42.1	7 45.9	20 59.9	4 36.2	7 19.8
30 Th	20 37 43	10 18 04	28 46 02	5♎36 45	3 40.8	9 12.5	12 53.9	28 21.6	14 18.5	24 56.2	7 50.4	21 02.6	4 38.1	7 20.2
31 F	20 41 39	11 18 58	12♎29 22	19 23 50	3 38.5	10 55.5	14 09.2	28 57.2	14 11.0	25 10.4	7 54.8	21 05.3	4 40.0	7 20.5

LONGITUDE — February 1986

Day	Sid.Time	☉	0 hr ☽	Noon ☽	True ☊	☿	♀	♂	⚳	♃	♄	♅	♆	♇
1 Sa	20 45 36	12♒19 52	26♎20 06	3♏18 10	3♉38.0	12♒39.3	15♒24.5	29♏32.7	14♍03.1	25♒24.6	7♐59.1	21♐07.9	4♑41.9	7♏20.8
2 Su	20 49 32	13 20 46	10♏17 59	17 19 34	3R 38.0	14 23.7	16 39.9	0♐08.2	13R 54.8	25 38.9	8 03.4	21 10.5	4 43.8	7 21.0
3 M	20 53 29	14 21 38	24 22 52	1♐27 45	3 37.1	16 08.8	17 55.2	0 43.6	13 46.1	25 53.1	8 07.6	21 13.1	4 45.7	7 21.2
4 Tu	20 57 25	15 22 30	8♐34 06	15 41 40	3 34.2	17 54.5	19 10.5	1 19.0	13 37.1	26 07.4	8 11.7	21 15.6	4 47.5	7 21.4
5 W	21 01 22	16 23 21	22 50 08	29 59 05	3 28.5	19 40.9	20 25.8	1 54.4	13 27.6	26 21.7	8 15.8	21 18.1	4 49.4	7 21.6
6 Th	21 05 19	17 24 11	7♑08 02	14♑16 25	3 20.0	21 27.9	21 41.0	2 29.6	13 17.8	26 36.0	8 19.7	21 20.6	4 51.2	7 21.7
7 F	21 09 15	18 25 00	21 23 35	28 28 52	3 09.1	23 15.5	22 56.3	3 04.9	13 07.7	26 50.4	8 23.6	21 23.0	4 53.0	7 21.7
8 Sa	21 13 12	19 25 47	5♒31 36	12♒31 06	2 57.0	25 03.6	24 11.6	3 40.0	12 57.2	27 04.7	8 27.4	21 25.3	4 54.7	7R 21.8
9 Su	21 17 08	20 26 34	19 26 45	26 18 02	2 44.9	26 52.2	25 26.8	4 15.1	12 46.4	27 19.1	8 31.1	21 27.6	4 56.5	7 21.8
10 M	21 21 05	21 27 19	3♓04 28	9♓45 46	2 34.1	28 41.1	26 42.0	4 50.2	12 35.3	27 33.5	8 34.7	21 29.9	4 58.2	7 21.7
11 Tu	21 25 01	22 28 02	16 21 41	22 52 09	2 25.4	0♓30.2	27 57.3	5 25.2	12 23.9	27 47.8	8 38.2	21 32.1	4 59.9	7 21.6
12 W	21 28 58	23 28 44	29 17 14	5♈37 05	2 19.6	2 19.5	29 12.5	6 00.1	12 12.2	28 02.2	8 41.7	21 34.3	5 01.5	7 21.5
13 Th	21 32 54	24 29 25	11♈51 58	18 02 16	2 16.3	4 08.8	0♓27.6	6 34.9	12 00.2	28 16.6	8 45.0	21 36.5	5 03.2	7 21.4
14 F	21 36 51	25 30 04	24 08 26	0♉11 00	2D 15.3	5 57.8	1 42.8	7 09.7	11 48.0	28 31.0	8 48.3	21 38.6	5 04.8	7 21.2
15 Sa	21 40 48	26 30 41	6♉10 34	12 07 45	2 15.6	7 46.4	2 57.9	7 44.4	11 35.5	28 45.5	8 51.4	21 40.6	5 06.4	7 21.0
16 Su	21 44 44	27 31 16	18 03 12	23 57 37	2R 16.1	9 34.3	4 13.1	8 19.0	11 22.8	28 59.9	8 54.5	21 42.6	5 07.9	7 20.7
17 M	21 48 41	28 31 50	29 51 41	5♊46 06	2 15.9	11 21.2	5 28.2	8 53.6	11 09.9	29 14.3	8 57.5	21 44.6	5 09.5	7 20.4
18 Tu	21 52 37	29 32 22	11♊41 31	17 38 38	2 13.9	13 06.8	6 43.3	9 28.1	10 56.8	29 28.7	9 00.4	21 46.5	5 11.0	7 20.1
19 W	21 56 34	0♓32 52	23 38 02	29 40 19	2 09.8	14 50.6	7 58.4	10 02.6	10 43.6	29 43.1	9 03.2	21 48.4	5 12.5	7 19.7
20 Th	22 00 30	1 33 21	5♋46 01	11♋55 35	2 03.2	16 32.2	9 13.4	10 36.9	10 30.2	29 57.5	9 05.9	21 50.2	5 14.0	7 19.3
21 F	22 04 27	2 33 48	18 09 26	24 27 50	1 54.5	18 11.2	10 28.5	11 11.2	10 16.7	0♓12.0	9 08.5	21 52.0	5 15.4	7 18.9
22 Sa	22 08 23	3 34 12	0♌51 01	7♌19 06	1 44.4	19 47.0	11 43.5	11 45.4	10 03.0	0 26.4	9 11.1	21 53.7	5 16.8	7 18.4
23 Su	22 12 20	4 34 35	13 52 05	20 29 52	1 33.9	21 19.0	12 58.5	12 19.6	9 49.2	0 40.8	9 13.5	21 55.4	5 18.2	7 17.9
24 M	22 16 17	5 34 57	27 12 16	3♍59 00	1 24.1	22 46.7	14 13.4	12 53.7	9 35.4	0 55.2	9 15.8	21 57.1	5 19.6	7 17.4
25 Tu	22 20 13	6 35 16	10♍49 41	17 43 55	1 15.9	24 09.4	15 28.4	13 27.7	9 21.5	1 09.6	9 18.1	21 58.7	5 20.9	7 16.8
26 W	22 24 10	7 35 34	24 41 12	1♎41 04	1 10.0	25 26.5	16 43.3	14 01.6	9 07.5	1 23.9	9 20.2	22 00.2	5 22.2	7 16.2
27 Th	22 28 06	8 35 50	8♎42 59	15 46 30	1 06.6	26 37.4	17 58.3	14 35.4	8 53.5	1 38.3	9 22.2	22 01.7	5 23.5	7 15.6
28 F	22 32 03	9 36 05	22 51 10	29 56 32	1D 05.5	27 41.4	19 13.1	15 09.2	8 39.5	1 52.7	9 24.2	22 03.1	5 24.7	7 15.0

Astro Data Dy Hr Mn	Planet Ingress Dy Hr Mn	Last Aspect Dy Hr Mn	☽ Ingress Dy Hr Mn	Last Aspect Dy Hr Mn	☽ Ingress Dy Hr Mn	☽ Phases & Eclipses Dy Hr Mn
♃∠♆ 2 21:06	☿ ♑ 5 20:42	2 11:59 ☿ □	♎ 2 20:45	31 22:10 ♃ △	♏ 1 6:19	3 19:47 ☾ 13♎09
☽0S 3 7:19	♀ ♒ 20 5:36	4 22:24 ☿ ✶	♏ 5 0:44	3 2:23 ♃ □	♐ 3 9:32	10 12:22 ● 19♑58
♃✶♅ 8 18:17	☉ ♒ 20 8:46	6 9:19 ♃ □	♐ 7 2:47	5 5:49 ♃ ✶	♑ 5 12:02	17 22:13 ☽ 27♈31
⚳R 13 14:20	☿ ♒ 25 0:33	8 11:19 ♅ ☌	♑ 9 3:42	6 0:23 ♇ ✶	♒ 7 14:35	26 0:31 ○ 5♌45
☽0N 16 3:11		10 12:22 ☉ ☌	♒ 11 5:01	9 13:50 ♃ ☌	♓ 9 18:32	
♄⊻♇ 23 9:58	♂ ♐ 2 6:27	12 16:30 ♃ ☌	♓ 13 8:39	11 9:31 ♅ □	♈ 12 1:21	2 4:41 ☾ 13♏02
☽0S 30 11:48	☿ ♓ 11 5:21	15 6:09 ☉ ✶	♈ 15 16:03	14 8:37 ♃ ✶	♉ 14 11:38	9 0:55 ● 19♒59
	♀ ♓ 13 3:11	17 22:13 ☉ □	♉ 18 3:14	16 22:27 ♃ □	♊ 17 0:17	16 19:55 ☽ 27♉51
♇R 8 20:17	☉ ♓ 18 22:58	20 0:56 ♃ □	♊ 20 16:12	19 12:06 ♃ △	♋ 19 12:39	24 15:02 ○ 5♍43
☽0N 12 11:26	♃ ♓ 20 16:05	22 14:36 ♃ △	♋ 23 4:15	20 22:15 ☿ △	♌ 21 22:25	
☽0S 26 17:58		25 4:46 ♂ △	♌ 25 13:47	23 14:34 ♅ △	♍ 24 4:58	
☿0N 27 17:46		27 14:48 ♂ □	♍ 27 20:51	26 0:14 ☿ ☍	♎ 26 9:07	
		29 22:42 ♂ ✶	♎ 30 2:10	27 22:37 ♅ ✶	♏ 28 12:06	

Astro Data

1 January 1986
Julian Day # 31412
SVP 5♓27'28"
GC 26♐38.6 ⚴ 27♊30.2R
Eris 15♈17.2R ⚵ 29♏18.4
⚷ 10♊24.2R ⚶ 18♑06.5
☽ Mean ☊ 5♉47.6

1 February 1986
Julian Day # 31443
SVP 5♓27'23"
GC 26♐38.7 ⚴ 22♊42.8
Eris 15♈22.0 ⚵ 7♐55.1
⚷ 9♊21.5R ⚶ 4♒30.6
☽ Mean ☊ 4♉09.1

March 1986 — LONGITUDE

Day	Sid.Time	☉	0 hr ☽	Noon ☽	True ☊	☿	♀	♂	⚳	♃	♄	♅	♆	♇
1 Sa	22 35 59	10♓36 18	7♏02 17	14♏08 05	1♉06.1	28♓38.1	20♓28.0	15♐42.8	8♍25.6	2♓07.0	9♐26.0	22♐04.5	5♑25.9	7♏14.3
2 Su	22 39 56	11 36 30	21 13 41	28 18 51	1 07.1	29 26.8	21 42.9	16 16.4	8R11.6	2 21.4	9 27.8	22 05.8	5 27.1	7R13.5
3 M	22 43 52	12 36 41	5♐23 26	12♐27 15	1R07.7	0♈07.1	22 57.7	16 49.9	7 57.7	2 35.7	9 29.5	22 07.1	5 28.3	7 12.8
4 Tu	22 47 49	13 36 50	19 30 09	26 32 00	1 06.9	0 38.7	24 12.6	17 23.3	7 43.8	2 50.0	9 31.0	22 08.4	5 29.4	7 12.0
5 W	22 51 46	14 36 57	3♑32 37	10♑31 50	1 04.2	1 01.3	25 27.4	17 56.6	7 30.0	3 04.3	9 32.5	22 09.6	5 30.5	7 11.2
6 Th	22 55 42	15 37 03	17 29 26	24 25 11	0 59.4	1R14.7	26 42.2	18 29.8	7 16.4	3 18.5	9 33.8	22 10.7	5 31.6	7 10.3
7 F	22 59 39	16 37 07	1♒18 50	8♒10 05	0 52.9	1 18.8	27 56.9	19 02.9	7 02.8	3 32.8	9 35.1	22 11.8	5 32.6	7 09.4
8 Sa	23 03 35	17 37 10	14 58 39	21 44 15	0 45.4	1 13.9	29 11.7	19 36.0	6 49.4	3 47.0	9 36.2	22 12.8	5 33.6	7 08.5
9 Su	23 07 32	18 37 10	28 26 35	5♓05 25	0 37.9	1 00.2	0♈26.4	20 08.8	6 36.1	4 01.2	9 37.3	22 13.8	5 34.6	7 07.6
10 M	23 11 28	19 37 09	11♓40 30	18 11 41	0 31.1	0 38.0	1 41.1	20 41.6	6 23.1	4 15.4	9 38.2	22 14.7	5 35.5	7 06.6
11 Tu	23 15 25	20 37 06	24 38 50	1♈01 54	0 25.9	0 08.0	2 55.7	21 14.3	6 10.2	4 29.6	9 39.1	22 15.6	5 36.4	7 05.6
12 W	23 19 21	21 37 01	7♈20 54	13 35 56	0 22.5	29♓31.0	4 10.4	21 46.9	5 57.5	4 43.7	9 39.8	22 16.4	5 37.3	7 04.6
13 Th	23 23 18	22 36 54	19 47 10	25 54 49	0D21.0	28 47.9	5 25.0	22 19.3	5 45.0	4 57.8	9 40.5	22 17.2	5 38.1	7 03.6
14 F	23 27 14	23 36 44	1♉59 12	8♉00 42	0 21.2	27 59.7	6 39.6	22 51.6	5 32.8	5 11.9	9 41.0	22 17.9	5 39.0	7 02.5
15 Sa	23 31 11	24 36 33	13 59 43	19 56 45	0 22.5	27 07.6	7 54.2	23 23.8	5 20.8	5 25.9	9 41.5	22 18.6	5 39.7	7 01.4
16 Su	23 35 08	25 36 20	25 52 18	1♊46 57	0 24.3	26 12.8	9 08.7	23 55.9	5 09.1	5 39.9	9 41.8	22 19.2	5 40.5	7 00.2
17 M	23 39 04	26 36 04	7♊41 16	13 35 54	0 25.9	25 16.6	10 23.2	24 27.9	4 57.7	5 53.9	9 42.1	22 19.8	5 41.2	6 59.1
18 Tu	23 43 01	27 35 46	19 31 27	25 28 34	0R26.7	24 20.1	11 37.7	24 59.7	4 46.6	6 07.8	9R42.2	22 20.3	5 41.9	6 57.9
19 W	23 46 57	28 35 26	1♋27 54	7♋30 03	0 26.3	23 24.7	12 52.2	25 31.4	4 35.8	6 21.7	9 42.2	22 20.7	5 42.5	6 56.7
20 Th	23 50 54	29 35 03	13 35 37	19 45 10	0 24.5	22 31.3	14 06.6	26 02.9	4 25.4	6 35.6	9 42.2	22 21.1	5 43.2	6 55.5
21 F	23 54 50	0♈34 39	25 59 14	2♌18 16	0 21.4	21 41.0	15 21.0	26 34.4	4 15.2	6 49.4	9 42.0	22 21.5	5 43.7	6 54.2
22 Sa	23 58 47	1 34 12	8♌42 39	15 12 39	0 17.4	20 54.6	16 35.4	27 05.7	4 05.6	7 03.2	9 41.7	22 21.8	5 44.3	6 52.9
23 Su	0 02 43	2 33 42	21 48 29	28 30 13	0 13.0	20 12.7	17 49.7	27 36.8	3 56.0	7 16.9	9 41.4	22 22.0	5 44.8	6 51.6
24 M	0 06 40	3 33 11	5♍17 47	12♍11 02	0 08.7	19 35.9	19 04.0	28 07.8	3 46.9	7 30.6	9 40.9	22 22.2	5 45.3	6 50.3
25 Tu	0 10 37	4 32 37	19 09 39	26 13 12	0 05.3	19 04.6	20 18.3	28 38.7	3 38.2	7 44.3	9 40.4	22 22.3	5 45.8	6 49.0
26 W	0 14 33	5 32 01	3♎21 09	10♎32 51	0 02.9	18 39.1	21 32.5	29 09.4	3 29.8	7 57.9	9 39.7	22 22.4	5 46.2	6 47.6
27 Th	0 18 30	6 31 23	17 47 35	25 04 36	0D01.9	18 19.4	22 46.7	29 40.0	3 21.9	8 11.5	9 38.9	22R22.4	5 46.6	6 46.2
28 F	0 22 26	7 30 43	2♏23 07	9♏42 19	0 02.1	18 05.7	24 00.9	0♑10.4	3 14.3	8 25.0	9 38.1	22 22.4	5 46.9	6 44.8
29 Sa	0 26 23	8 30 02	17 01 28	24 19 51	0 03.1	17D57.8	25 15.0	0 40.7	3 07.1	8 38.5	9 37.1	22 22.3	5 47.2	6 43.4
30 Su	0 30 19	9 29 19	1♐36 49	8♐51 49	0 04.4	17 55.8	26 29.2	1 10.8	3 00.4	8 51.9	9 36.1	22 22.2	5 47.5	6 42.0
31 M	0 34 16	10 28 34	16 04 22	23 14 03	0 05.6	17 59.3	27 43.3	1 40.7	2 54.0	9 05.3	9 34.9	22 22.1	5 47.8	6 40.5

April 1986 — LONGITUDE

Day	Sid.Time	☉	0 hr ☽	Noon ☽	True ☊	☿	♀	♂	⚳	♃	♄	♅	♆	♇
1 Tu	0 38 12	11♈27 47	0♑20 34	7♑23 41	0♉06.3	18♓08.3	28♈57.3	2♑10.5	2♍48.0	9♓18.6	9♐33.7	22♐21.8	5♑48.0	6♏39.0
2 W	0 42 09	12 26 58	14 23 15	21 19 08	0R06.1	18 22.6	0♉11.4	2 40.0	2R42.5	9 31.8	9R32.3	22R21.5	5 48.2	6R37.5
3 Th	0 46 06	13 26 08	28 11 17	4♒59 40	0 05.2	18 41.8	1 25.4	3 09.4	2 37.4	9 45.1	9 30.9	22 21.2	5 48.3	6 36.0
4 F	0 50 02	14 25 16	11♒44 20	18 25 16	0 03.5	19 05.9	2 39.3	3 38.6	2 32.6	9 58.2	9 29.4	22 20.8	5 48.5	6 34.5
5 Sa	0 53 59	15 24 22	25 02 33	1♓36 14	0 01.5	19 34.5	3 53.3	4 07.6	2 28.4	10 11.3	9 27.7	22 20.4	5 48.6	6 33.0
6 Su	0 57 55	16 23 26	8♓06 22	14 33 03	29♈59.5	20 07.4	5 07.2	4 36.4	2 24.5	10 24.3	9 26.0	22 19.9	5 48.6	6 31.4
7 M	1 01 52	17 22 29	20 56 20	27 16 20	29 57.7	20 44.4	6 21.1	5 05.0	2 21.1	10 37.3	9 24.2	22 19.4	5R48.6	6 29.9
8 Tu	1 05 48	18 21 29	3♈33 07	9♈46 50	29 56.4	21 25.2	7 34.9	5 33.4	2 18.1	10 50.2	9 22.3	22 18.8	5 48.6	6 28.3
9 W	1 09 45	19 20 27	15 57 35	22 05 32	29D55.8	22 09.8	8 48.8	6 01.6	2 15.5	11 03.1	9 20.3	22 18.2	5 48.6	6 26.7
10 Th	1 13 41	20 19 24	28 10 51	4♉13 44	29 55.7	22 57.8	10 02.6	6 29.6	2 13.4	11 15.9	9 18.2	22 17.5	5 48.5	6 25.1
11 F	1 17 38	21 18 18	10♉14 26	16 13 12	29 56.1	23 49.2	11 16.3	6 57.3	2 11.7	11 28.6	9 16.1	22 16.7	5 48.4	6 23.5
12 Sa	1 21 35	22 17 10	22 10 21	28 06 12	29 56.7	24 43.7	12 30.0	7 24.8	2 10.4	11 41.2	9 13.8	22 15.9	5 48.2	6 21.8
13 Su	1 25 31	23 16 00	4♊01 08	9♊55 34	29 57.5	25 41.2	13 43.7	7 52.1	2 09.6	11 53.8	9 11.5	22 15.1	5 48.0	6 20.2
14 M	1 29 28	24 14 48	15 49 56	21 44 41	29 58.2	26 41.5	14 57.4	8 19.1	2D09.2	12 06.3	9 09.0	22 14.2	5 47.8	6 18.6
15 Tu	1 33 24	25 13 34	27 40 22	3♋37 28	29 58.7	27 44.6	16 11.0	8 45.9	2 09.2	12 18.7	9 06.5	22 13.3	5 47.6	6 16.9
16 W	1 37 21	26 12 18	9♋36 33	15 38 10	29R59.0	28 50.2	17 24.6	9 12.4	2 09.7	12 31.1	9 03.9	22 12.3	5 47.3	6 15.3
17 Th	1 41 17	27 10 59	21 42 54	27 51 19	29 59.1	29 58.4	18 38.1	9 38.7	2 10.5	12 43.4	9 01.2	22 11.3	5 47.0	6 13.6
18 F	1 45 14	28 09 38	4♌03 57	10♌21 21	29 59.0	1♈09.0	19 51.6	10 04.7	2 11.8	12 55.6	8 58.5	22 10.2	5 46.7	6 11.9
19 Sa	1 49 10	29 08 15	16 44 00	23 12 21	29D58.9	2 21.9	21 05.1	10 30.4	2 13.5	13 07.7	8 55.7	22 09.1	5 46.3	6 10.3
20 Su	1 53 07	0♉06 50	29 46 45	6♍27 30	29 58.9	3 37.0	22 18.5	10 55.9	2 15.7	13 19.8	8 52.8	22 08.0	5 45.9	6 08.6
21 M	1 57 04	1 05 22	13♍14 45	20 08 35	29 59.0	4 54.4	23 31.9	11 21.1	2 18.2	13 31.7	8 49.8	22 06.8	5 45.5	6 06.9
22 Tu	2 01 00	2 03 52	27 08 53	4♎15 26	29 59.1	6 13.8	24 45.2	11 46.0	2 21.1	13 43.6	8 46.7	22 05.5	5 45.0	6 05.2
23 W	2 04 57	3 02 20	11♎27 50	18 45 32	29R59.3	7 35.3	25 58.5	12 10.6	2 24.5	13 55.4	8 43.6	22 04.2	5 44.5	6 03.5
24 Th	2 08 53	4 00 47	26 07 49	3♏33 50	29 59.3	8 58.8	27 11.8	12 35.0	2 28.2	14 07.1	8 40.4	22 02.9	5 44.0	6 01.8
25 F	2 12 50	4 59 11	11♏02 38	18 33 12	29 59.1	10 24.3	28 25.0	12 59.0	2 32.3	14 18.8	8 37.1	22 01.5	5 43.4	6 00.1
26 Sa	2 16 46	5 57 34	26 04 25	3♐35 13	29 58.7	11 51.7	29 38.2	13 22.7	2 36.8	14 30.3	8 33.8	22 00.1	5 42.8	5 58.4
27 Su	2 20 43	6 55 55	11♐04 31	18 31 22	29 58.0	13 21.0	0♊51.3	13 46.1	2 41.7	14 41.8	8 30.4	21 58.6	5 42.2	5 56.7
28 M	2 24 39	7 54 15	25 54 52	3♑14 16	29 57.2	14 52.3	2 04.4	14 09.2	2 47.0	14 53.1	8 26.9	21 57.1	5 41.6	5 55.0
29 Tu	2 28 36	8 52 33	10♑28 56	17 38 26	29 56.4	16 25.4	3 17.5	14 31.9	2 52.7	15 04.4	8 23.4	21 55.6	5 40.9	5 53.3
30 W	2 32 33	9 50 49	24 42 27	1♒40 48	29D55.9	18 00.4	4 30.5	14 54.3	2 58.7	15 15.6	8 19.8	21 54.0	5 40.2	5 51.7

Astro Data

	Dy Hr Mn
♅∠♇	6 7:23
☿R	7 10:56
♀0N	11 10:33
☽0N	11 19:45
♃✶♆	16 13:02
♄R	19 9:27
☿0S	19 20:42
☉0N	20 22:02
♃△♇	21 19:38
☽0S	26 2:57
♅R	27 14:17
☿D	30 8:42
♃□♄	2 12:49
♆R	7 12:52
☽0N	8 3:01

Planet Ingress

	Dy Hr Mn
☿ ♈	3 7:22
♀ ♈	9 3:32
☿ ♓R	11 17:36
☉ ♈	20 22:03
♂ ♑	28 3:47
♀ ♉	2 8:19
☊ ♈R	6 5:31
☿ ♈	17 12:33
☉ ♉	20 9:12
♀ ♊	26 19:10
⚳ D	14 22:35
☽0S	22 13:29
☿0N	22 13:40

Last Aspect / ☽ Ingress

Last Aspect Dy Hr Mn		☽ Ingress Dy Hr Mn
2 14:01 ☿ △	♐	2 14:51
4 7:39 ♀ □	♑	4 17:56
6 16:22 ♀ ✶	♒	6 21:42
8 12:51 ♅ ✶	♓	9 2:48
10 19:32 ♅ □	♈	11 10:03
13 4:53 ♅ △	♉	13 20:04
16 1:31 ☿ ✶	♊	16 8:23
18 16:39 ☉ □	♋	18 21:04
20 17:00 ☿ △	♌	21 7:38
23 10:21 ♂ △	♍	23 14:39
25 16:15 ♂ □	♎	25 18:22
27 19:49 ♂ ✶	♏	27 20:05
29 1:37 ☿ △	♐	29 21:20
31 20:17 ♀ △	♑	31 23:25

Last Aspect / ☽ Ingress

Last Aspect Dy Hr Mn		☽ Ingress Dy Hr Mn
2 6:47 ☿ ✶	♒	3 3:11
4 19:06 ♅ ✶	♓	5 9:03
7 2:37 ♅ □	♈	7 17:12
9 12:25 ♅ △	♉	10 3:36
12 4:35 ☿ ✶	♊	12 15:51
14 22:59 ☿ □	♋	15 4:42
17 10:35 ☉ □	♌	17 16:10
19 23:42 ☉ △	♍	20 0:24
21 18:23 ♀ △	♎	22 4:50
23 17:24 ♅ ✶	♏	24 6:15
26 5:08 ☿ ☍	♐	26 6:16
27 17:35 ♅ ☌	♑	28 6:41
29 9:42 ☿ □	♒	30 9:06

☽ Phases & Eclipses

Dy Hr Mn	
3 12:17	☾ 12♐37
10 14:52	● 19♓44
18 16:39	☽ 27♊47
26 3:02	○ 5♎10
1 19:30	☾ 11♑46
9 6:08	● 19♈06
9 6:20:27	● P 0.824
17 10:35	☽ 27♋08
24 12:46	○ 4♏03
24 12:43	• T 1.202

Astro Data

1 March 1986
Julian Day # 31471
SVP 5♓27'19"
GC 26♐38.8 ⚴ 27♊15.5
Eris 15♈34.5 ⚵ 13♐41.6
⚷ 9♊21.7 ⚶ 19♒00.0
☽ Mean ☊ 2♉40.2

1 April 1986
Julian Day # 31502
SVP 5♓27'15"
GC 26♐38.8 ⚴ 8♋11.9
Eris 15♈53.8 ⚵ 16♐35.1
⚷ 10♊26.6 ⚶ 4♓22.2
☽ Mean ☊ 1♉01.7

LONGITUDE May 1986

Day	Sid.Time	☉	0 hr ☽	Noon☽	True☊	☿	♀	♂	⚳	♃	♄	♅	♆	♇
1 Th	2 36 29	10♉49 04	8♒33 25	15♒20 23	29♈55.9	19♈37.3	5♊43.5	15♑16.3	3♍05.1	15♓26.7	8♐16.2	21♐52.4	5♑39.5	5♏50.0
2 F	2 40 26	11 47 17	22 01 51	28 38 03	29 56.3	21 16.0	6 56.5	15 38.0	3 11.8	15 37.7	8R 12.4	21R 50.8	5R 38.7	5R 48.3
3 Sa	2 44 22	12 45 29	5♓09 15	11♓35 45	29 57.2	22 56.6	8 09.4	15 59.2	3 19.0	15 48.6	8 08.7	21 49.1	5 37.9	5 46.6
4 Su	2 48 19	13 43 40	17 57 56	24 16 07	29 58.3	24 39.0	9 22.3	16 20.1	3 26.4	15 59.4	8 04.9	21 47.3	5 37.1	5 44.9
5 M	2 52 15	14 41 49	0♈30 41	6♈41 57	29 59.5	26 23.3	10 35.1	16 40.6	3 34.3	16 10.1	8 01.0	21 45.6	5 36.3	5 43.2
6 Tu	2 56 12	15 39 56	12 50 17	18 55 59	0♉00.4	28 09.4	11 47.9	17 00.7	3 42.4	16 20.7	7 57.1	21 43.8	5 35.4	5 41.6
7 W	3 00 08	16 38 02	24 59 22	1♉00 43	0R 00.7	29 57.5	13 00.7	17 20.3	3 50.9	16 31.1	7 53.1	21 41.9	5 34.5	5 39.9
8 Th	3 04 05	17 36 06	7♉00 20	12 58 27	0 00.2	1♉47.4	14 13.4	17 39.5	3 59.8	16 41.5	7 49.1	21 40.1	5 33.6	5 38.3
9 F	3 08 02	18 34 09	18 55 20	24 51 14	29♈58.8	3 39.1	15 26.1	17 58.3	4 09.0	16 51.8	7 45.0	21 38.2	5 32.6	5 36.6
10 Sa	3 11 58	19 32 10	0♊46 25	6♊41 07	29 56.4	5 32.8	16 38.7	18 16.6	4 18.5	17 01.9	7 40.9	21 36.2	5 31.6	5 35.0
11 Su	3 15 55	20 30 09	12 35 38	18 30 13	29 53.3	7 28.2	17 51.3	18 34.5	4 28.3	17 12.0	7 36.8	21 34.3	5 30.6	5 33.3
12 M	3 19 51	21 28 07	24 25 11	0♋20 52	29 49.8	9 25.6	19 03.9	18 51.9	4 38.5	17 21.9	7 32.6	21 32.3	5 29.6	5 31.7
13 Tu	3 23 48	22 26 03	6♋17 36	12 15 45	29 46.3	11 24.7	20 16.4	19 08.8	4 49.0	17 31.7	7 28.4	21 30.3	5 28.6	5 30.1
14 W	3 27 44	23 23 58	18 15 43	24 17 57	29 43.3	13 25.6	21 28.8	19 25.3	4 59.7	17 41.4	7 24.2	21 28.2	5 27.5	5 28.5
15 Th	3 31 41	24 21 50	0♌22 53	6♌30 59	29 41.0	15 28.2	22 41.3	19 41.2	5 10.8	17 51.0	7 19.9	21 26.1	5 26.4	5 26.9
16 F	3 35 37	25 19 41	12 42 45	18 58 40	29D 39.8	17 32.5	23 53.6	19 56.6	5 22.2	18 00.5	7 15.6	21 24.0	5 25.3	5 25.4
17 Sa	3 39 34	26 17 30	25 19 14	1♍44 56	29 39.8	19 38.2	25 05.9	20 11.6	5 33.9	18 09.8	7 11.3	21 21.9	5 24.1	5 23.8
18 Su	3 43 31	27 15 18	8♍16 13	14 53 29	29 40.7	21 45.4	26 18.2	20 25.9	5 45.8	18 19.0	7 06.9	21 19.7	5 23.0	5 22.3
19 M	3 47 27	28 13 03	21 37 06	28 27 19	29 42.1	23 53.8	27 30.4	20 39.8	5 58.1	18 28.1	7 02.6	21 17.6	5 21.8	5 20.7
20 Tu	3 51 24	29 10 47	5♎24 16	12♎27 58	29 43.5	26 03.4	28 42.6	20 53.1	6 10.6	18 37.1	6 58.2	21 15.4	5 20.6	5 19.2
21 W	3 55 20	0♊08 30	19 38 18	26 54 57	29R 44.3	28 13.8	29 54.7	21 05.9	6 23.4	18 45.9	6 53.8	21 13.1	5 19.3	5 17.7
22 Th	3 59 17	1 06 11	4♏17 24	11♏44 59	29 43.9	0♊25.0	1♋06.8	21 18.1	6 36.5	18 54.7	6 49.3	21 10.9	5 18.1	5 16.2
23 F	4 03 13	2 03 50	19 16 49	26 51 51	29 41.9	2 36.5	2 18.8	21 29.7	6 49.8	19 03.2	6 44.9	21 08.6	5 16.8	5 14.7
24 Sa	4 07 10	3 01 29	4♐28 56	12♐06 46	29 38.6	4 48.3	3 30.7	21 40.7	7 03.4	19 11.7	6 40.5	21 06.3	5 15.5	5 13.3
25 Su	4 11 06	3 59 06	19 44 03	27 19 29	29 34.1	6 59.9	4 42.6	21 51.1	7 17.2	19 20.0	6 36.0	21 04.0	5 14.2	5 11.9
26 M	4 15 03	4 56 42	4♑51 49	12♑19 57	29 29.1	9 11.2	5 54.5	22 00.9	7 31.3	19 28.2	6 31.6	21 01.7	5 12.9	5 10.5
27 Tu	4 19 00	5 54 17	19 42 55	26 59 57	29 24.4	11 21.8	7 06.3	22 10.1	7 45.6	19 36.3	6 27.1	20 59.4	5 11.6	5 09.1
28 W	4 22 56	6 51 51	4♒10 30	11♒14 11	29 20.7	13 31.5	8 18.0	22 18.6	8 00.2	19 44.2	6 22.7	20 57.1	5 10.2	5 07.7
29 Th	4 26 53	7 49 25	18 10 50	25 00 28	29 18.3	15 40.0	9 29.7	22 26.5	8 15.0	19 52.0	6 18.2	20 54.7	5 08.8	5 06.3
30 F	4 30 49	8 46 57	1♓43 13	8♓19 23	29D 17.5	17 47.2	10 41.4	22 33.7	8 30.0	19 59.6	6 13.7	20 52.3	5 07.4	5 05.0
31 Sa	4 34 46	9 44 28	14 49 21	21 13 34	29 18.1	19 52.7	11 53.0	22 40.2	8 45.3	20 07.1	6 09.3	20 49.9	5 06.0	5 03.7

LONGITUDE June 1986

Day	Sid.Time	☉	0 hr ☽	Noon☽	True☊	☿	♀	♂	⚳	♃	♄	♅	♆	♇
1 Su	4 38 42	10♊41 59	27♓32 32	3♈46 48	29♈19.4	21♊56.4	13♋04.5	22♑46.0	9♍00.8	20♓14.4	6♐04.8	20♐47.5	5♑04.6	5♏02.4
2 M	4 42 39	11 39 29	9♈56 55	16 03 24	29 20.8	23 58.1	14 16.0	22 51.2	9 16.5	20 21.6	6R 00.4	20R 45.1	5R 03.2	5R 01.1
3 Tu	4 46 35	12 36 58	22 06 49	28 07 39	29R 21.6	25 57.7	15 27.4	22 55.6	9 32.5	20 28.6	5 56.0	20 42.7	5 01.7	4 59.8
4 W	4 50 32	13 34 26	4♉06 23	10♉03 29	29 20.9	27 55.0	16 38.8	22 59.3	9 48.6	20 35.5	5 51.5	20 40.2	5 00.2	4 58.6
5 Th	4 54 29	14 31 54	15 59 22	21 54 23	29 18.4	29 50.1	17 50.1	23 02.2	10 05.0	20 42.3	5 47.1	20 37.8	4 58.7	4 57.4
6 F	4 58 25	15 29 21	27 48 53	3♊43 10	29 13.7	1♋42.7	19 01.3	23 04.4	10 21.6	20 48.9	5 42.8	20 35.3	4 57.3	4 56.2
7 Sa	5 02 22	16 26 47	9♊37 32	15 32 13	29 07.1	3 32.8	20 12.5	23 05.9	10 38.4	20 55.3	5 38.4	20 32.9	4 55.7	4 55.0
8 Su	5 06 18	17 24 12	21 27 27	27 23 28	28 58.8	5 20.5	21 23.7	23R 06.6	10 55.4	21 01.6	5 34.1	20 30.4	4 54.2	4 53.9
9 M	5 10 15	18 21 36	3♋20 27	9♋18 37	28 49.6	7 05.6	22 34.8	23 06.6	11 12.6	21 07.7	5 29.8	20 28.0	4 52.7	4 52.8
10 Tu	5 14 11	19 18 59	15 18 11	21 19 23	28 40.3	8 48.1	23 45.8	23 05.9	11 30.0	21 13.7	5 25.5	20 25.5	4 51.2	4 51.7
11 W	5 18 08	20 16 22	27 22 26	3♌27 37	28 31.8	10 28.0	24 56.7	23 04.3	11 47.5	21 19.5	5 21.3	20 23.1	4 49.6	4 50.6
12 Th	5 22 05	21 13 43	9♌35 12	15 45 32	28 24.9	12 05.3	26 07.6	23 02.0	12 05.3	21 25.1	5 17.0	20 20.6	4 48.1	4 49.6
13 F	5 26 01	22 11 04	21 58 57	28 15 48	28 20.0	13 39.9	27 18.4	22 59.0	12 23.3	21 30.5	5 12.9	20 18.1	4 46.5	4 48.6
14 Sa	5 29 58	23 08 23	4♍36 30	11♍01 28	28D 17.4	15 11.9	28 29.1	22 55.2	12 41.4	21 35.8	5 08.7	20 15.7	4 44.9	4 47.6
15 Su	5 33 54	24 05 42	17 31 05	24 05 48	28 16.6	16 41.1	29 39.8	22 50.7	12 59.7	21 41.0	5 04.6	20 13.2	4 43.3	4 46.7
16 M	5 37 51	25 03 00	0♎45 58	7♎31 56	28 17.1	18 07.7	0♌50.4	22 45.5	13 18.2	21 45.9	5 00.5	20 10.8	4 41.8	4 45.7
17 Tu	5 41 47	26 00 16	14 24 00	21 22 20	28R 17.8	19 31.5	2 00.9	22 39.5	13 36.8	21 50.7	4 56.5	20 08.3	4 40.2	4 44.8
18 W	5 45 44	26 57 32	28 27 00	5♏37 58	28 17.8	20 52.6	3 11.4	22 32.8	13 55.6	21 55.3	4 52.5	20 05.9	4 38.6	4 44.0
19 Th	5 49 40	27 54 48	12♏54 57	20 17 32	28 16.0	22 10.8	4 21.7	22 25.3	14 14.6	21 59.8	4 48.6	20 03.4	4 37.0	4 43.1
20 F	5 53 37	28 52 02	27 45 06	5♐16 49	28 11.9	23 26.1	5 32.0	22 17.2	14 33.7	22 04.0	4 44.7	20 01.0	4 35.4	4 42.3
21 Sa	5 57 34	29 49 16	12♐51 39	20 28 26	28 05.5	24 38.6	6 42.2	22 08.4	14 53.0	22 08.1	4 40.9	19 58.6	4 33.8	4 41.5
22 Su	6 01 30	0♋46 30	28 05 53	5♑42 37	27 57.2	25 48.1	7 52.3	21 58.9	15 12.5	22 12.1	4 37.1	19 56.2	4 32.1	4 40.8
23 M	6 05 27	1 43 43	13♑17 17	20 48 35	27 48.0	26 54.5	9 02.4	21 48.7	15 32.1	22 15.8	4 33.4	19 53.8	4 30.5	4 40.1
24 Tu	6 09 23	2 40 56	28 15 20	5♒36 32	27 39.0	27 57.9	10 12.3	21 37.9	15 51.8	22 19.4	4 29.7	19 51.4	4 28.9	4 39.4
25 W	6 13 20	3 38 09	12♒51 22	19 59 15	27 31.2	28 58.0	11 22.2	21 26.4	16 11.7	22 22.8	4 26.1	19 49.1	4 27.3	4 38.7
26 Th	6 17 16	4 35 21	26 59 49	3♓52 53	27 25.4	29 54.8	12 32.0	21 14.3	16 31.7	22 26.0	4 22.6	19 46.7	4 25.7	4 38.1
27 F	6 21 13	5 32 34	10♓38 31	17 16 55	27 22.0	0♌48.3	13 41.7	21 01.6	16 51.9	22 29.0	4 19.1	19 44.4	4 24.1	4 37.5
28 Sa	6 25 09	6 29 46	23 48 26	0♈13 31	27D 20.5	1 38.3	14 51.3	20 48.3	17 12.2	22 31.8	4 15.6	19 42.0	4 22.4	4 36.9
29 Su	6 29 06	7 26 59	6♈32 43	12 46 37	27 20.4	2 24.7	16 00.8	20 34.5	17 32.6	22 34.4	4 12.3	19 39.7	4 20.8	4 36.4
30 M	6 33 03	8 24 11	18 55 52	25 01 07	27R 20.7	3 07.4	17 10.2	20 20.1	17 53.2	22 36.9	4 09.0	19 37.4	4 19.2	4 35.9

Astro Data	Planet Ingress	Last Aspect	☽ Ingress	Last Aspect	☽ Ingress	☽ Phases & Eclipses	Astro Data
Dy Hr Mn	Dy Hr Mn	Dy Hr Mn	Dy Hr Mn	Dy Hr Mn	Dy Hr Mn	Dy Hr Mn	
☽0N 5 8:58	☊ ♉ 5 22:57	1 23:42 ♅ ⚹	♓ 2 14:30	31 14:45 ♂ ⚹	♈ 1 4:43	1 3:22 ☾ 10♒28	1 May 1986
♆⚹♇ 16 17:11	☿ ♉ 7 12:33	4 7:17 ♅ □	♈ 4 23:01	3 6:49 ☿ ⚹	♉ 3 15:45	8 22:10 ● 18♉01	Julian Day # 31532
☽0S 19 23:24	☊ ♈R 8 17:11	7 9:31 ☿ ☌	♉ 7 9:59	5 14:18 ♂ △	♊ 6 4:26	17 1:00 ☽ 25♌51	SVP 5♓27'11"
♃⚼♇ 31 2:38	☉ ♊ 21 8:28	8 22:10 ☉ ☌	♊ 9 22:26	7 23:01 ♃ □	♋ 8 17:16	23 20:45 ○ 2♐25	GC 26♐38.9 ⚴ 21♋24.1
	♀ ♋ 21 13:46	11 18:12 ♅ ☍	♋ 12 11:18	10 17:22 ♀ ☌	♌ 11 5:11	30 12:55 ☾ 8♓49	Eris 16♈13.4 ⚵ 14♐40.4R
☽0N 1 14:17	☿ ♊ 22 7:26	14 10:04 ☉ ⚹	♌ 14 23:15	12 23:26 ☉ ⚹	♍ 13 15:18		⚷ 12♊19.9 ⚶ 18♓12.4
♃□♅ 5 0:12		17 1:00 ☉ □	♍ 17 8:45	15 12:00 ☉ □	♎ 15 22:38	7 14:00 ● 16♊32	☽ Mean ☊ 29♈26.4
♂ R 8 23:25	☿ ♋ 5 14:06	19 11:33 ☉ △	♎ 19 14:41	17 20:26 ☉ △	♏ 18 2:36	15 12:00 ☽ 24♍06	
♆⚹♇ 9 8:02	♀ ♌ 15 18:52	21 2:39 ♅ ⚹	♏ 21 17:02	19 15:24 ♂ ⚹	♐ 20 3:36	22 3:42 ○ 0♑27	1 June 1986
☽0S 16 7:03	☉ ♋ 21 16:30	23 3:24 ♂ ⚹	♐ 23 16:57	21 14:38 ♃ □	♑ 22 3:00	29 0:53 ☾ 7♈00	Julian Day # 31563
♄⚺♇ 21 7:05	☿ ♌ 26 14:15	25 2:08 ♅ ☌	♑ 25 16:15	23 22:35 ☿ ☍	♒ 24 2:50		SVP 5♓27'07"
♄⚺♆ 24 21:49		27 3:56 ♂ ☌	♒ 27 17:00	25 11:43 ♅ ⚹	♓ 26 5:12		GC 26♐39.0 ⚴ 6♌01.6
☽0N 28 20:12		29 4:48 ♅ ⚹	♓ 29 20:54	27 21:35 ♃ ☌	♈ 28 11:35		Eris 16♈29.7 ⚵ 8♐31.6R
				30 2:56 ♂ □	♉ 30 21:54		⚷ 14♊46.4 ⚶ 0♈52.6
							☽ Mean ☊ 27♈47.9

July 1986 — LONGITUDE

Day	Sid.Time	☉	0 hr ☽	Noon ☽	True ☊	☿	♀	♂	⚳	♃	♄	♅	♆	♇
1 Tu	6 36 59	9♋21 24	1♉03 00	7♉02 10	27♈20.4	3♌46.3	18♌19.5	20♑05.3	18♍13.9	22♓39.2	4♐05.7	19♐35.1	4♑17.6	4♏35.4
2 W	6 40 56	10 18 37	12 59 13	18 54 45	27R18.4	4 21.2	19 28.8	19R50.0	18 34.8	22 41.2	4R02.6	19R32.9	4R16.0	4R34.9
3 Th	6 44 52	11 15 50	24 49 17	0♊43 20	27 14.0	4 52.1	20 38.0	19 34.3	18 55.8	22 43.1	3 59.5	19 30.7	4 14.4	4 34.5
4 F	6 48 49	12 13 04	6♊37 20	12 31 41	27 06.9	5 18.8	21 47.0	19 18.2	19 16.9	22 44.8	3 56.4	19 28.4	4 12.8	4 34.1
5 Sa	6 52 45	13 10 17	18 26 46	24 22 52	26 57.2	5 41.1	22 56.0	19 01.8	19 38.1	22 46.3	3 53.5	19 26.3	4 11.2	4 33.8
6 Su	6 56 42	14 07 31	0♋20 14	6♋19 07	26 45.4	5 59.0	24 04.8	18 45.0	19 59.4	22 47.7	3 50.6	19 24.1	4 09.6	4 33.5
7 M	7 00 38	15 04 44	12 19 41	18 22 04	26 32.3	6 12.4	25 13.6	18 28.0	20 20.9	22 48.8	3 47.8	19 21.9	4 08.0	4 33.2
8 Tu	7 04 35	16 01 58	24 26 26	0♌32 52	26 19.0	6 21.1	26 22.3	18 10.9	20 42.5	22 49.7	3 45.1	19 19.8	4 06.4	4 33.0
9 W	7 08 32	16 59 12	6♌41 30	12 52 26	26 06.8	6R25.1	27 30.8	17 53.5	21 04.2	22 50.4	3 42.4	19 17.7	4 04.8	4 32.8
10 Th	7 12 28	17 56 25	19 05 48	25 21 44	25 56.4	6 24.4	28 39.2	17 36.1	21 26.0	22 51.0	3 39.8	19 15.7	4 03.3	4 32.6
11 F	7 16 25	18 53 39	1♍40 23	8♍01 58	25 48.7	6 19.0	29 47.5	17 18.6	21 47.9	22 51.3	3 37.4	19 13.6	4 01.7	4 32.4
12 Sa	7 20 21	19 50 53	14 26 41	20 54 48	25 43.8	6 08.8	0♍55.7	17 01.0	22 09.9	22R51.4	3 35.0	19 11.6	4 00.2	4 32.3
13 Su	7 24 18	20 48 06	27 26 35	4♎02 19	25 41.5	5 54.0	2 03.8	16 43.5	22 32.1	22 51.4	3 32.6	19 09.6	3 58.6	4 32.2
14 M	7 28 14	21 45 20	10♎42 18	17 26 49	25 40.8	5 34.8	3 11.8	16 26.1	22 54.3	22 51.1	3 30.4	19 07.7	3 57.1	4D32.2
15 Tu	7 32 11	22 42 33	24 16 08	1♏10 27	25 40.8	5 11.3	4 19.6	16 08.9	23 16.6	22 50.7	3 28.2	19 05.8	3 55.6	4 32.2
16 W	7 36 07	23 39 47	8♏09 56	15 14 37	25 40.1	4 43.7	5 27.3	15 51.8	23 39.1	22 50.0	3 26.2	19 03.9	3 54.1	4 32.2
17 Th	7 40 04	24 37 01	22 24 24	29 39 06	25 37.6	4 12.5	6 34.8	15 34.9	24 01.6	22 49.2	3 24.2	19 02.0	3 52.6	4 32.3
18 F	7 44 01	25 34 15	6♐58 18	14♐21 27	25 32.6	3 38.1	7 42.3	15 18.3	24 24.3	22 48.2	3 22.3	19 00.2	3 51.1	4 32.4
19 Sa	7 47 57	26 31 29	21 47 49	29 16 29	25 25.0	3 00.9	8 49.5	15 02.0	24 47.0	22 46.9	3 20.5	18 58.4	3 49.6	4 32.5
20 Su	7 51 54	27 28 44	6♑46 26	14♑16 29	25 15.2	2 21.6	9 56.7	14 46.0	25 09.8	22 45.5	3 18.8	18 56.7	3 48.2	4 32.7
21 M	7 55 50	28 25 59	21 45 28	29 12 10	25 04.3	1 40.7	11 03.7	14 30.4	25 32.7	22 43.9	3 17.2	18 55.0	3 46.7	4 32.9
22 Tu	7 59 47	29 23 14	6♒35 26	13♒54 14	24 53.4	0 58.9	12 10.5	14 15.3	25 55.7	22 42.1	3 15.6	18 53.3	3 45.3	4 33.1
23 W	8 03 43	0♌20 30	21 07 40	28 15 00	24 43.8	0 17.1	13 17.2	14 00.6	26 18.8	22 40.1	3 14.2	18 51.7	3 43.9	4 33.4
24 Th	8 07 40	1 17 47	5♓15 45	12♓09 34	24 36.4	29♋35.8	14 23.7	13 46.3	26 41.9	22 38.0	3 12.8	18 50.0	3 42.5	4 33.7
25 F	8 11 37	2 15 05	18 56 20	25 36 05	24 31.5	28 55.8	15 30.0	13 32.6	27 05.2	22 35.6	3 11.6	18 48.5	3 41.1	4 34.0
26 Sa	8 15 33	3 12 23	2♈09 04	8♈35 35	24 29.0	28 18.0	16 36.2	13 19.5	27 28.5	22 33.0	3 10.4	18 46.9	3 39.8	4 34.4
27 Su	8 19 30	4 09 42	14 56 07	21 11 11	24D28.3	27 42.9	17 42.3	13 06.9	27 51.9	22 30.3	3 09.3	18 45.4	3 38.4	4 34.8
28 M	8 23 26	5 07 03	27 21 24	3♉27 24	24R28.3	27 11.3	18 48.1	12 55.0	28 15.4	22 27.3	3 08.3	18 44.0	3 37.1	4 35.2
29 Tu	8 27 23	6 04 24	9♉29 52	15 29 27	24 28.0	26 43.8	19 53.8	12 43.7	28 39.0	22 24.2	3 07.5	18 42.6	3 35.8	4 35.7
30 W	8 31 19	7 01 46	21 26 49	27 22 39	24 26.4	26 20.9	20 59.4	12 33.1	29 02.6	22 20.9	3 06.7	18 41.2	3 34.5	4 36.2
31 Th	8 35 16	7 59 10	3♊17 33	9♊12 07	24 22.6	26 03.2	22 04.7	12 23.1	29 26.4	22 17.4	3 06.0	18 39.9	3 33.2	4 36.7

August 1986 — LONGITUDE

Day	Sid.Time	☉	0 hr ☽	Noon ☽	True ☊	☿	♀	♂	⚳	♃	♄	♅	♆	♇
1 F	8 39 12	8♌56 35	15♊06 54	21♊02 26	24♈16.3	25♋50.9	23♍09.9	12♑13.9	29♍50.2	22♓13.7	3♐05.4	18♐38.6	3♑32.0	4♏37.3
2 Sa	8 43 09	9 54 00	26 59 08	2♋57 26	24R07.4	25D44.6	24 14.8	12R05.4	0♎14.1	22R09.8	3R04.9	18R37.4	3R30.7	4 37.9
3 Su	8 47 06	10 51 27	8♋57 39	15 00 06	23 56.4	25 44.4	25 19.6	11 57.7	0 38.0	22 05.8	3 04.5	18 36.2	3 29.5	4 38.5
4 M	8 51 02	11 48 55	21 05 00	27 12 31	23 44.1	25 50.6	26 24.2	11 50.8	1 02.0	22 01.6	3 04.1	18 35.0	3 28.3	4 39.2
5 Tu	8 54 59	12 46 24	3♌22 48	9♌35 54	23 31.6	26 03.2	27 28.6	11 44.7	1 26.1	21 57.2	3 03.9	18 33.9	3 27.2	4 39.9
6 W	8 58 55	13 43 53	15 51 52	22 10 43	23 20.1	26 22.5	28 32.8	11 39.4	1 50.3	21 52.6	3D03.8	18 32.8	3 26.0	4 40.6
7 Th	9 02 52	14 41 24	28 32 27	4♍57 02	23 10.3	26 48.5	29 36.7	11 34.9	2 14.5	21 47.9	3 03.8	18 31.8	3 24.9	4 41.4
8 F	9 06 48	15 38 56	11♍24 27	17 54 41	23 03.2	27 21.1	0♎40.4	11 31.2	2 38.8	21 43.0	3 03.9	18 30.8	3 23.8	4 42.2
9 Sa	9 10 45	16 36 28	24 27 45	1♎03 40	22 58.7	28 00.3	1 43.9	11 28.4	3 03.2	21 38.0	3 04.1	18 29.9	3 22.7	4 43.0
10 Su	9 14 41	17 34 01	7♎42 30	14 24 17	22D56.8	28 46.1	2 47.2	11 26.4	3 27.6	21 32.7	3 04.3	18 29.0	3 21.7	4 43.9
11 M	9 18 38	18 31 36	21 09 09	27 57 09	22 56.6	29 38.4	3 50.2	11D25.3	3 52.1	21 27.4	3 04.7	18 28.2	3 20.6	4 44.8
12 Tu	9 22 35	19 29 11	4♏48 26	11♏43 04	22R57.1	0♌37.0	4 53.0	11 25.0	4 16.6	21 21.8	3 05.2	18 27.4	3 19.6	4 45.8
13 W	9 26 31	20 26 47	18 41 06	25 42 33	22 57.1	1 41.8	5 55.5	11 25.6	4 41.2	21 16.2	3 05.7	18 26.7	3 18.7	4 46.7
14 Th	9 30 28	21 24 24	2♐47 21	9♐55 21	22 55.7	2 52.5	6 57.7	11 27.0	5 05.9	21 10.4	3 06.4	18 26.0	3 17.7	4 47.7
15 F	9 34 24	22 22 02	17 06 19	24 19 53	22 52.2	4 09.0	7 59.7	11 29.3	5 30.6	21 04.4	3 07.2	18 25.3	3 16.8	4 48.8
16 Sa	9 38 21	23 19 41	1♑35 34	8♑52 46	22 46.4	5 30.9	9 01.3	11 32.4	5 55.4	20 58.3	3 08.0	18 24.7	3 15.9	4 49.8
17 Su	9 42 17	24 17 21	16 10 48	23 28 51	22 38.7	6 57.9	10 02.7	11 36.3	6 20.2	20 52.1	3 09.0	18 24.2	3 15.0	4 50.9
18 M	9 46 14	25 15 02	0♒46 05	8♒01 36	22 29.9	8 29.8	11 03.7	11 41.0	6 45.1	20 45.8	3 10.0	18 23.7	3 14.2	4 52.1
19 Tu	9 50 10	26 12 44	15 14 32	22 24 05	22 21.1	10 06.2	12 04.5	11 46.6	7 10.0	20 39.3	3 11.2	18 23.2	3 13.3	4 53.2
20 W	9 54 07	27 10 28	29 29 28	6♓30 03	22 13.3	11 46.6	13 04.9	11 52.9	7 35.0	20 32.7	3 12.4	18 22.8	3 12.5	4 54.4
21 Th	9 58 04	28 08 12	13♓25 19	20 14 55	22 07.3	13 30.7	14 04.9	12 00.1	8 00.0	20 26.0	3 13.8	18 22.5	3 11.8	4 55.6
22 F	10 02 00	29 05 59	26 58 36	3♈36 17	22 03.6	15 17.9	15 04.7	12 08.0	8 25.0	20 19.1	3 15.2	18 22.2	3 11.0	4 56.9
23 Sa	10 05 57	0♍03 47	10♈08 03	16 34 04	22D01.9	17 08.0	16 04.0	12 16.6	8 50.2	20 12.2	3 16.7	18 21.9	3 10.3	4 58.1
24 Su	10 09 53	1 01 37	22 54 38	29 10 09	22 02.0	19 00.4	17 03.0	12 26.1	9 15.3	20 05.2	3 18.3	18 21.7	3 09.6	4 59.5
25 M	10 13 50	1 59 28	5♉21 04	11♉27 56	22 03.0	20 54.8	18 01.7	12 36.3	9 40.5	19 58.0	3 20.1	18 21.6	3 09.0	5 00.8
26 Tu	10 17 46	2 57 21	17 31 20	23 31 51	22R04.2	22 50.6	18 59.9	12 47.2	10 05.8	19 50.8	3 21.9	18 21.5	3 08.3	5 02.2
27 W	10 21 43	3 55 16	29 30 09	5♊26 52	22 04.6	24 47.6	19 57.8	12 58.9	10 31.1	19 43.5	3 23.8	18D21.5	3 07.8	5 03.6
28 Th	10 25 39	4 53 13	11♊22 38	17 18 06	22 03.6	26 45.4	20 55.2	13 11.3	10 56.4	19 36.1	3 25.8	18 21.5	3 07.2	5 05.0
29 F	10 29 36	5 51 12	23 13 52	29 10 32	22 00.8	28 43.7	21 52.3	13 24.4	11 21.8	19 28.6	3 27.9	18 21.5	3 06.7	5 06.4
30 Sa	10 33 33	6 49 12	5♋08 38	11♋08 41	21 56.2	0♍42.1	22 48.8	13 38.2	11 47.3	19 21.0	3 30.1	18 21.6	3 06.2	5 07.9
31 Su	10 37 29	7 47 15	17 11 09	23 16 25	21 49.9	2 40.5	23 45.0	13 52.7	12 12.8	19 13.4	3 32.3	18 21.8	3 05.7	5 09.4

Astro Data

	Dy Hr Mn
♅∠♇	1 8:54
☿R	9 20:28
♃R	12 17:01
☽0S	13 12:24
♇D	15 6:31
☽0N	26 3:33
☿D	3 0:47
♄D	7 4:50
♀0S	7 11:44
☽0S	9 17:02
♂D	12 7:45
♄⚺♆	20 13:14
☽0N	22 12:13
♃⚼♇	25 4:13
♅D	27 21:16

Planet Ingress

		Dy Hr Mn
♀	♍	11 16:23
☉	♌	23 3:24
☿	♋R	23 21:51
⚳	♎	1 21:53
♀	♎	7 20:46
☿	♌	11 21:09
☉	♍	23 10:26
☿	♍	30 3:28

Last Aspect / ☽ Ingress

Last Aspect Dy Hr Mn			☽ Ingress	Dy Hr Mn
2 19:41	♃	⚹	♊	3 10:32
5 8:46	♀	⚹	♋	5 23:19
7 20:48	♃	△	♌	8 10:56
10 18:54	♀	☌	♍	10 20:50
12 15:35	♃	☍	♎	13 4:40
14 20:10	☉	☐	♏	15 9:58
17 3:05	☉	△	♐	17 12:34
19 1:36	♃	☐	♑	19 13:10
21 10:40	☉	☍	♒	21 13:17
22 20:15	♅	⚹	♓	23 14:59
25 17:47	♅	△	♈	25 20:02
28 0:10	☿	☐	♉	28 5:11
30 9:58	☿	⚹	♊	30 17:19

Last Aspect / ☽ Ingress

Last Aspect Dy Hr Mn			☽ Ingress	Dy Hr Mn
1 16:43	♀	☐	♋	2 6:04
4 10:17	♀	⚹	♌	4 17:26
6 5:07	♅	△	♍	7 2:44
9 6:09	☿	⚹	♎	9 10:05
11 15:11	☿	☐	♏	11 15:36
13 4:29	♃	△	♐	13 19:17
15 8:31	☉	△	♑	15 21:22
17 7:44	♃	⚹	♒	17 22:44
19 18:54	☉	☍	♓	20 0:52
21 12:20	♃	☌	♈	22 5:27
23 15:23	♅	△	♉	24 13:36
26 10:21	☿	☐	♊	27 1:00
29 10:55	☿	⚹	♋	29 13:40

☽ Phases & Eclipses

Dy Hr Mn		
7 4:55	●	14♋48
14 20:10	☽	22♎05
21 10:40	○	28♑23
28 15:34	☾	5♉16
5 18:36	●	13♌02
13 2:21	☽	20♏04
19 18:54	○	26♒29
27 8:39	☾	3♊47

Astro Data

1 July 1986
Julian Day # 31593
SVP 5♓27'01"
GC 26♐39.0 ⚴ 20♌25.8
Eris 16♈38.0 ⚵ 2♐41.8R
⚷ 17♊13.3 ⚶ 10♈41.4
☽ Mean ☊ 26♈12.6

1 August 1986
Julian Day # 31624
SVP 5♓26'56"
GC 26♐39.1 ⚴ 5♍16.6
Eris 16♈36.8R ⚵ 0♐59.3
⚷ 19♊25.8 ⚶ 16♈44.7
☽ Mean ☊ 24♈34.1

LONGITUDE — September 1986

Day	Sid.Time	☉	0 hr ☽	Noon ☽	True ☊	☿	♀	♂	⚳	♃	♄	♅	♆	♇
1 M	10 41 26	8♍45 19	29♋24 51	5♌36 43	21♈42.6	4♍38.6	24♎40.6	14♑07.8	12♎38.3	19♓05.7	3♐34.7	18♐22.0	3♑05.2	5♏11.0
2 Tu	10 45 22	9 43 25	11♌52 14	18 11 32	21R35.0	6 36.2	25 35.8	14 23.7	13 03.8	18R58.0	3 37.2	18 22.3	3R04.8	5 12.5
3 W	10 49 19	10 41 32	24 34 42	1♍01 44	21 27.9	8 33.2	26 30.5	14 40.2	13 29.4	18 50.2	3 39.7	18 22.6	3 04.4	5 14.1
4 Th	10 53 15	11 39 42	7♍32 35	14 07 09	21 22.1	10 29.4	27 24.7	14 57.4	13 55.1	18 42.4	3 42.4	18 22.9	3 04.1	5 15.7
5 F	10 57 12	12 37 53	20 45 16	27 26 46	21 18.0	12 24.8	28 18.3	15 15.2	14 20.7	18 34.5	3 45.1	18 23.4	3 03.8	5 17.4
6 Sa	11 01 08	13 36 05	4♎11 25	10♎59 01	21D15.8	14 19.3	29 11.3	15 33.6	14 46.4	18 26.6	3 47.9	18 23.8	3 03.5	5 19.1
7 Su	11 05 05	14 34 20	17 49 20	24 42 08	21 15.4	16 12.8	0♏03.8	15 52.6	15 12.2	18 18.6	3 50.8	18 24.3	3 03.2	5 20.8
8 M	11 09 01	15 32 35	1♏37 12	8♏34 21	21 16.3	18 05.2	0 55.7	16 12.3	15 37.9	18 10.7	3 53.8	18 24.9	3 03.0	5 22.5
9 Tu	11 12 58	16 30 53	15 33 23	22 34 06	21 17.8	19 56.6	1 46.9	16 32.5	16 03.7	18 02.7	3 56.9	18 25.5	3 02.8	5 24.2
10 W	11 16 55	17 29 12	29 36 21	6♐39 56	21R19.0	21 46.8	2 37.5	16 53.3	16 29.6	17 54.8	4 00.1	18 26.2	3 02.7	5 26.0
11 Th	11 20 51	18 27 32	13♐44 40	20 50 21	21 19.4	23 36.0	3 27.4	17 14.7	16 55.4	17 46.8	4 03.3	18 26.9	3 02.5	5 27.8
12 F	11 24 48	19 25 54	27 56 45	5♑03 34	21 18.4	25 24.0	4 16.5	17 36.7	17 21.3	17 38.8	4 06.7	18 27.7	3 02.4	5 29.6
13 Sa	11 28 44	20 24 18	12♑10 30	19 17 13	21 16.1	27 10.9	5 05.0	17 59.1	17 47.3	17 30.9	4 10.1	18 28.6	3 02.4	5 31.5
14 Su	11 32 41	21 22 43	26 23 17	3♒28 17	21 12.6	28 56.7	5 52.6	18 22.1	18 13.2	17 22.9	4 13.6	18 29.4	3D02.4	5 33.3
15 M	11 36 37	22 21 10	10♒31 46	17 33 14	21 08.4	0♎41.5	6 39.5	18 45.6	18 39.2	17 15.0	4 17.2	18 30.4	3 02.4	5 35.2
16 Tu	11 40 34	23 19 38	24 32 14	1♓28 18	21 04.1	2 25.1	7 25.5	19 09.6	19 05.2	17 07.2	4 20.9	18 31.3	3 02.4	5 37.1
17 W	11 44 31	24 18 08	8♓20 59	15 09 55	21 00.4	4 07.6	8 10.6	19 34.1	19 31.2	16 59.3	4 24.6	18 32.4	3 02.5	5 39.1
18 Th	11 48 27	25 16 40	21 54 46	28 35 17	20 57.7	5 49.2	8 54.9	19 59.0	19 57.3	16 51.5	4 28.5	18 33.5	3 02.6	5 41.0
19 F	11 52 24	26 15 14	5♈11 16	11♈42 39	20D56.2	7 29.6	9 38.2	20 24.4	20 23.3	16 43.7	4 32.4	18 34.6	3 02.7	5 43.0
20 Sa	11 56 20	27 13 50	18 09 24	24 31 37	20 55.9	9 09.1	10 20.5	20 50.3	20 49.4	16 36.0	4 36.3	18 35.8	3 02.9	5 45.0
21 Su	12 00 17	28 12 28	0♉49 26	7♉03 06	20 56.7	10 47.5	11 01.8	21 16.6	21 15.5	16 28.4	4 40.4	18 37.0	3 03.1	5 47.0
22 M	12 04 13	29 11 08	13 12 55	19 19 15	20 58.1	12 25.0	11 42.1	21 43.3	21 41.7	16 20.8	4 44.6	18 38.3	3 03.3	5 49.0
23 Tu	12 08 10	0♎09 50	25 22 32	1♊23 15	20 59.7	14 01.5	12 21.3	22 10.4	22 07.8	16 13.2	4 48.8	18 39.6	3 03.6	5 51.1
24 W	12 12 06	1 08 34	7♊21 53	13 19 01	21 01.2	15 37.0	12 59.4	22 38.0	22 34.0	16 05.8	4 53.1	18 41.0	3 03.9	5 53.1
25 Th	12 16 03	2 07 21	19 15 12	25 11 01	21R02.1	17 11.6	13 36.2	23 05.9	23 00.2	15 58.4	4 57.4	18 42.4	3 04.2	5 55.2
26 F	12 19 59	3 06 10	1♋07 06	7♋04 01	21 02.2	18 45.3	14 11.9	23 34.3	23 26.4	15 51.1	5 01.9	18 43.9	3 04.6	5 57.3
27 Sa	12 23 56	4 05 02	13 02 23	19 02 46	21 01.5	20 18.0	14 46.3	24 03.0	23 52.7	15 43.9	5 06.4	18 45.4	3 05.0	5 59.5
28 Su	12 27 53	5 03 55	25 05 44	1♌11 47	21 00.1	21 49.9	15 19.4	24 32.1	24 19.0	15 36.8	5 11.0	18 47.0	3 05.4	6 01.6
29 M	12 31 49	6 02 51	7♌21 26	13 35 05	20 58.2	23 20.8	15 51.1	25 01.6	24 45.2	15 29.8	5 15.7	18 48.6	3 05.9	6 03.8
30 Tu	12 35 46	7 01 49	19 53 08	26 15 51	20 56.2	24 50.9	16 21.4	25 31.4	25 11.5	15 22.9	5 20.4	18 50.2	3 06.4	6 05.9

LONGITUDE — October 1986

Day	Sid.Time	☉	0 hr ☽	Noon ☽	True ☊	☿	♀	♂	⚳	♃	♄	♅	♆	♇
1 W	12 39 42	8♎00 49	2♍43 28	9♍16 08	20♈54.3	26♎20.0	16♏50.2	26♑01.6	25♎37.8	15♓16.1	5♐25.2	18♐51.9	3♑06.9	6♏08.1
2 Th	12 43 39	8 59 51	15 53 52	22 36 37	20R52.8	27 48.2	17 17.5	26 32.1	26 04.2	15R09.5	5 30.1	18 53.7	3 07.5	6 10.3
3 F	12 47 35	9 58 55	29 24 15	6♎16 30	20 51.9	29 15.6	17 43.1	27 03.0	26 30.5	15 02.9	5 35.0	18 55.5	3 08.1	6 12.6
4 Sa	12 51 32	10 58 02	13♎13 02	20 13 27	20D51.6	0♏41.9	18 07.2	27 34.2	26 56.9	14 56.5	5 40.0	18 57.4	3 08.7	6 14.8
5 Su	12 55 28	11 57 10	27 17 15	4♏23 55	20 51.8	2 07.4	18 29.5	28 05.8	27 23.2	14 50.2	5 45.1	18 59.2	3 09.4	6 17.0
6 M	12 59 25	12 56 21	11♏32 52	18 43 32	20 52.3	3 31.9	18 50.0	28 37.6	27 49.6	14 44.1	5 50.2	19 01.2	3 10.1	6 19.3
7 Tu	13 03 22	13 55 33	25 55 18	3♐07 36	20 53.0	4 55.4	19 08.7	29 09.8	28 16.0	14 38.1	5 55.4	19 03.2	3 10.8	6 21.6
8 W	13 07 18	14 54 47	10♐19 53	17 31 39	20 53.5	6 17.8	19 25.4	29 42.3	28 42.4	14 32.2	6 00.7	19 05.2	3 11.6	6 23.9
9 Th	13 11 15	15 54 03	24 42 25	1♑51 47	20 53.9	7 39.2	19 40.2	0♒15.0	29 08.8	14 26.5	6 06.0	19 07.3	3 12.3	6 26.2
10 F	13 15 11	16 53 21	8♑59 24	16 04 55	20R54.0	8 59.6	19 52.9	0 48.1	29 35.2	14 20.9	6 11.4	19 09.4	3 13.2	6 28.5
11 Sa	13 19 08	17 52 40	23 08 07	0♒08 45	20 54.0	10 18.7	20 03.5	1 21.4	0♏01.7	14 15.5	6 16.9	19 11.6	3 14.0	6 30.8
12 Su	13 23 04	18 52 01	7♒06 39	14 01 41	20 53.8	11 36.6	20 12.0	1 55.0	0 28.1	14 10.3	6 22.4	19 13.8	3 14.9	6 33.1
13 M	13 27 01	19 51 24	20 53 42	27 42 37	20 53.7	12 53.2	20 18.2	2 28.8	0 54.5	14 05.2	6 27.9	19 16.0	3 15.8	6 35.5
14 Tu	13 30 57	20 50 48	4♓28 20	11♓10 48	20D53.6	14 08.4	20 22.2	3 02.9	1 20.9	14 00.3	6 33.5	19 18.3	3 16.8	6 37.8
15 W	13 34 54	21 50 15	17 49 56	24 25 42	20 53.6	15 22.2	20R23.8	3 37.3	1 47.4	13 55.5	6 39.2	19 20.6	3 17.8	6 40.2
16 Th	13 38 51	22 49 43	0♈58 05	7♈27 02	20 53.7	16 34.3	20 23.0	4 11.9	2 13.8	13 51.0	6 44.9	19 23.0	3 18.8	6 42.6
17 F	13 42 47	23 49 13	13 52 34	20 14 43	20R53.8	17 44.7	20 19.9	4 46.7	2 40.3	13 46.6	6 50.7	19 25.4	3 19.8	6 44.9
18 Sa	13 46 44	24 48 45	26 33 32	2♉49 04	20 53.7	18 53.3	20 14.4	5 21.7	3 06.7	13 42.3	6 56.6	19 27.8	3 20.9	6 47.3
19 Su	13 50 40	25 48 19	9♉01 28	15 10 51	20 53.4	19 59.8	20 06.4	5 57.0	3 33.2	13 38.3	7 02.4	19 30.3	3 22.0	6 49.7
20 M	13 54 37	26 47 56	21 17 26	27 21 25	20 52.8	21 04.0	19 56.0	6 32.4	3 59.6	13 34.4	7 08.4	19 32.8	3 23.1	6 52.1
21 Tu	13 58 33	27 47 34	3♊23 05	9♊22 45	20 51.9	22 05.9	19 43.2	7 08.1	4 26.1	13 30.7	7 14.4	19 35.4	3 24.3	6 54.5
22 W	14 02 30	28 47 15	15 20 46	21 17 32	20 50.8	23 05.0	19 28.0	7 44.0	4 52.5	13 27.3	7 20.4	19 38.0	3 25.5	6 56.9
23 Th	14 06 26	29 46 58	27 13 29	3♋09 04	20 49.7	24 01.2	19 10.5	8 20.1	5 19.0	13 24.0	7 26.5	19 40.6	3 26.7	6 59.3
24 F	14 10 23	0♏46 43	9♋04 48	15 01 13	20 48.9	24 54.0	18 50.7	8 56.3	5 45.4	13 20.8	7 32.6	19 43.3	3 27.9	7 01.7
25 Sa	14 14 20	1 46 30	20 58 52	26 58 18	20D48.4	25 43.3	18 28.7	9 32.8	6 11.9	13 17.9	7 38.8	19 46.0	3 29.2	7 04.2
26 Su	14 18 16	2 46 20	3♌00 07	9♌04 54	20 48.4	26 28.4	18 04.5	10 09.4	6 38.3	13 15.2	7 45.0	19 48.7	3 30.5	7 06.6
27 M	14 22 13	3 46 12	15 13 13	21 25 37	20 49.0	27 09.2	17 38.4	10 46.2	7 04.7	13 12.7	7 51.3	19 51.5	3 31.9	7 09.0
28 Tu	14 26 09	4 46 06	27 42 39	4♍04 46	20 50.1	27 44.9	17 10.3	11 23.3	7 31.2	13 10.3	7 57.6	19 54.3	3 33.2	7 11.4
29 W	14 30 06	5 46 02	10♍32 25	17 05 56	20 51.3	28 15.2	16 40.6	12 00.4	7 57.6	13 08.2	8 04.0	19 57.1	3 34.6	7 13.9
30 Th	14 34 02	6 46 00	23 45 35	0♎31 30	20 52.5	28 39.4	16 09.2	12 37.8	8 24.0	13 06.3	8 10.3	20 00.0	3 36.0	7 16.3
31 F	14 37 59	7 46 00	7♎23 44	14 22 07	20R53.2	28 57.0	15 36.5	13 15.3	8 50.5	13 04.5	8 16.8	20 02.9	3 37.5	7 18.7

Astro Data

	Dy Hr Mn
☽ 0S	5 23:00
♃□♅	6 19:52
⚳0S	7 21:21
♆ D	14 19:38
☿0S	16 6:46
☽ 0N	18 21:07
☉0S	23 7:59
☽ 0S	3 7:22
♀ R	15 16:33
♄⊻♇	15 19:04
☽ 0N	16 4:55
☽ 0S	30 17:25

Planet Ingress

		Dy Hr Mn
♀	♏	7 10:15
☿	♎	15 2:28
☉	♎	23 7:59
☿	♏	4 0:19
♂	♒	9 1:01
⚳	♏	11 10:30
☉	♏	23 17:14

Last Aspect / ☽ Ingress

Last Aspect Dy Hr Mn			☽ Ingress	Dy Hr Mn
31 13:01	♀	□	♌	1 1:08
3 2:58	♀	⚹	♍	3 10:06
4 20:14	♃	☍	♎	5 16:33
7 1:01	♅	⚹	♏	7 21:12
9 6:50	☿	⚹	♐	10 0:40
11 17:21	☿	□	♑	12 3:28
14 3:15	☿	△	♒	14 6:07
15 13:38	♅	⚹	♓	16 9:27
18 5:34	☉	☍	♈	18 14:33
20 4:47	♂	□	♉	20 22:25
22 16:56	♂	△	♊	23 9:13
24 22:52	♅	☍	♋	25 21:44
27 22:21	♂	☍	♌	28 9:39
30 9:00	☿	⚹	♍	30 18:57

Last Aspect / ☽ Ingress

Last Aspect Dy Hr Mn			☽ Ingress	Dy Hr Mn
2 19:13	♂	△	♎	3 1:03
5 0:57	♂	□	♏	5 4:35
7 5:09	♂	⚹	♐	7 6:48
8 14:37	♅	☌	♑	9 8:52
10 18:33	♀	⚹	♒	11 11:45
12 22:52	♀	□	♓	13 16:03
15 4:39	♀	△	♈	15 22:13
17 19:22	☉	☍	♉	18 6:35
19 22:22	☿	☍	♊	20 17:15
23 4:33	☉	△	♋	23 5:37
25 9:19	☿	△	♌	25 18:02
27 23:30	☿	□	♍	28 4:20
30 8:37	☿	⚹	♎	30 11:05

☽ Phases & Eclipses

Dy Hr Mn		
4 7:10	●	11♍28
11 7:41	☽	18♐17
18 5:34	○	25♓01
26 3:17	☾	2♋45
3 18:55	●	10♎16
3 19:05:19	●	AT00'00"
10 13:28	☽	16♑57
17 19:22	○	24♈07
17 19:18	●	T 1.246
25 22:26	☾	2♌12

Astro Data

1 September 1986
Julian Day # 31655
SVP 5♓26'51"
GC 26♐39.2 ⚴ 19♍57.7
Eris 16♈26.2R ⚵ 4♐12.1
⚷ 20♊55.3 ⚶ 16♈30.1R
☽ Mean ☊ 22♈55.6

1 October 1986
Julian Day # 31685
SVP 5♓26'48"
GC 26♐39.3 ⚴ 3♎56.1
Eris 16♈09.9R ⚵ 10♐47.6
⚷ 21♊22.5R ⚶ 10♈12.2R
☽ Mean ☊ 21♈20.3

November 1986 LONGITUDE

Day	Sid.Time	☉	0 hr ☽	Noon ☽	True ☊	☿	♀	♂	⚳	♃	♄	♅	♆	♇
1 Sa	14 41 55	8♏46 03	21♎26 25	28♎36 13	20♈53.2	29♏07.2	15♏02.6	13♒53.0	9♏16.9	13♓03.0	8♐23.2	20♐05.9	3♑38.9	7♏21.2
2 Su	14 45 52	9 46 07	5♏50 55	13♏09 49	20R 52.2	29R 09.5	14R 27.8	14 30.8	9 43.3	13R 01.7	8 29.8	20 08.8	3 40.4	7 23.6
3 M	14 49 49	10 46 13	20 32 04	27 56 45	20 50.2	29 03.3	13 52.1	15 08.8	10 09.7	13 00.6	8 36.3	20 11.8	3 41.9	7 26.0
4 Tu	14 53 45	11 46 21	5♐22 50	12♐49 20	20 47.5	28 48.1	13 16.0	15 47.0	10 36.1	12 59.7	8 42.9	20 14.9	3 43.5	7 28.5
5 W	14 57 42	12 46 31	20 15 12	27 39 30	20 44.5	28 23.3	12 39.6	16 25.3	11 02.4	12 59.0	8 49.5	20 17.9	3 45.1	7 30.9
6 Th	15 01 38	13 46 42	5♑01 21	12♑19 58	20 41.8	27 48.7	12 03.1	17 03.7	11 28.8	12 58.5	8 56.2	20 21.0	3 46.7	7 33.3
7 F	15 05 35	14 46 55	19 34 44	26 45 10	20 39.7	27 04.4	11 26.8	17 42.3	11 55.2	12D 58.2	9 02.8	20 24.1	3 48.3	7 35.7
8 Sa	15 09 31	15 47 09	3♒50 55	10♒51 46	20D 38.7	26 10.7	10 51.0	18 21.0	12 21.5	12 58.1	9 09.5	20 27.3	3 49.9	7 38.1
9 Su	15 13 28	16 47 25	17 47 36	24 38 28	20 38.8	25 08.4	10 15.9	18 59.8	12 47.8	12 58.2	9 16.3	20 30.5	3 51.6	7 40.6
10 M	15 17 24	17 47 42	1♓24 27	8♓05 44	20 39.9	23 58.6	9 41.7	19 38.8	13 14.1	12 58.6	9 23.1	20 33.6	3 53.3	7 43.0
11 Tu	15 21 21	18 48 00	14 42 31	21 15 04	20 41.5	22 43.1	9 08.7	20 17.9	13 40.4	12 59.1	9 29.8	20 36.9	3 55.0	7 45.4
12 W	15 25 18	19 48 20	27 43 40	4♈08 34	20 43.1	21 24.0	8 37.1	20 57.1	14 06.6	12 59.8	9 36.7	20 40.1	3 56.8	7 47.8
13 Th	15 29 14	20 48 41	10♈30 03	16 48 23	20R 44.1	20 03.6	8 07.0	21 36.4	14 32.9	13 00.8	9 43.5	20 43.4	3 58.5	7 50.1
14 F	15 33 11	21 49 04	23 03 48	29 16 32	20 43.8	18 44.7	7 38.6	22 15.8	14 59.1	13 01.9	9 50.4	20 46.7	4 00.3	7 52.5
15 Sa	15 37 07	22 49 28	5♉26 48	11♉34 46	20 41.9	17 29.8	7 12.2	22 55.3	15 25.3	13 03.3	9 57.3	20 50.0	4 02.1	7 54.9
16 Su	15 41 04	23 49 54	17 40 38	23 44 34	20 38.3	16 21.3	6 47.8	23 34.9	15 51.5	13 04.8	10 04.2	20 53.3	4 03.9	7 57.3
17 M	15 45 00	24 50 22	29 46 44	5♊47 18	20 33.1	15 21.3	6 25.6	24 14.6	16 17.7	13 06.6	10 11.1	20 56.7	4 05.8	7 59.6
18 Tu	15 48 57	25 50 51	11♊46 26	17 44 21	20 26.7	14 31.3	6 05.6	24 54.4	16 43.8	13 08.6	10 18.1	21 00.1	4 07.6	8 02.0
19 W	15 52 53	26 51 22	23 41 16	29 37 25	20 19.7	13 52.4	5 48.0	25 34.3	17 09.9	13 10.7	10 25.0	21 03.4	4 09.5	8 04.3
20 Th	15 56 50	27 51 55	5♋33 05	11♋28 35	20 12.7	13 25.0	5 32.8	26 14.3	17 36.0	13 13.1	10 32.0	21 06.9	4 11.4	8 06.6
21 F	16 00 47	28 52 29	17 24 15	23 20 29	20 06.6	13D 09.4	5 20.1	26 54.3	18 02.1	13 15.7	10 39.0	21 10.3	4 13.3	8 08.9
22 Sa	16 04 43	29 53 05	29 17 43	5♌16 24	20 01.8	13 05.2	5 09.8	27 34.5	18 28.2	13 18.4	10 46.1	21 13.8	4 15.3	8 11.2
23 Su	16 08 40	0♐53 42	11♌17 03	17 20 12	19 58.8	13 11.9	5 02.1	28 14.7	18 54.2	13 21.4	10 53.1	21 17.2	4 17.2	8 13.5
24 M	16 12 36	1 54 22	23 26 25	29 36 16	19D 57.7	13 28.7	4 56.9	28 55.0	19 20.2	13 24.5	11 00.1	21 20.7	4 19.2	8 15.8
25 Tu	16 16 33	2 55 02	5♍50 22	12♍09 16	19 58.0	13 54.9	4D 54.1	29 35.4	19 46.2	13 27.9	11 07.2	21 24.2	4 21.2	8 18.1
26 W	16 20 29	3 55 45	18 33 33	25 03 45	19 59.3	14 29.4	4 53.8	0♓15.9	20 12.1	13 31.4	11 14.3	21 27.7	4 23.2	8 20.3
27 Th	16 24 26	4 56 29	1♎40 20	8♎23 40	20R 00.7	15 11.5	4 56.0	0 56.4	20 38.0	13 35.1	11 21.4	21 31.2	4 25.2	8 22.6
28 F	16 28 22	5 57 15	15 14 04	22 11 38	20 01.1	16 00.3	5 00.5	1 37.0	21 03.9	13 39.1	11 28.4	21 34.8	4 27.3	8 24.8
29 Sa	16 32 19	6 58 02	29 16 23	6♏28 04	19 59.9	16 55.0	5 07.4	2 17.7	21 29.8	13 43.2	11 35.5	21 38.3	4 29.3	8 27.0
30 Su	16 36 16	7 58 50	13♏46 19	21 10 27	19 56.5	17 54.7	5 16.6	2 58.5	21 55.6	13 47.5	11 42.6	21 41.9	4 31.4	8 29.2

December 1986 LONGITUDE

Day	Sid.Time	☉	0 hr ☽	Noon ☽	True ☊	☿	♀	♂	⚳	♃	♄	♅	♆	♇
1 M	16 40 12	8♐59 40	28♏39 40	6♐12 53	19♈50.9	18♏59.0	5♏28.0	3♓39.3	22♏21.4	13♓52.0	11♐49.8	21♐45.5	4♑33.5	8♏31.4
2 Tu	16 44 09	10 00 32	13♐48 55	21 26 26	19R 43.5	20 07.1	5 41.6	4 20.2	22 47.1	13 56.7	11 56.9	21 49.1	4 35.6	8 33.5
3 W	16 48 05	11 01 24	29 04 03	6♑40 22	19 35.3	21 18.6	5 57.2	5 01.1	23 12.9	14 01.6	12 04.0	21 52.7	4 37.7	8 35.7
4 Th	16 52 02	12 02 18	14♑14 05	21 44 00	19 27.3	22 33.0	6 15.0	5 42.2	23 38.5	14 06.6	12 11.1	21 56.3	4 39.8	8 37.8
5 F	16 55 58	13 03 12	29 09 07	6♒28 35	19 20.7	23 49.8	6 34.7	6 23.2	24 04.2	14 11.8	12 18.2	21 59.9	4 42.0	8 39.9
6 Sa	16 59 55	14 04 07	13♒41 49	20 48 26	19 16.0	25 08.8	6 56.3	7 04.4	24 29.8	14 17.3	12 25.4	22 03.5	4 44.1	8 42.0
7 Su	17 03 52	15 05 02	27 48 16	4♓41 18	19D 13.5	26 29.6	7 19.8	7 45.6	24 55.4	14 22.9	12 32.5	22 07.2	4 46.3	8 44.1
8 M	17 07 48	16 05 58	11♓27 41	18 07 44	19 13.0	27 52.0	7 45.1	8 26.8	25 20.9	14 28.6	12 39.6	22 10.8	4 48.4	8 46.1
9 Tu	17 11 45	17 06 55	24 41 49	1♈10 23	19 13.6	29 15.7	8 12.1	9 08.1	25 46.3	14 34.6	12 46.7	22 14.4	4 50.6	8 48.2
10 W	17 15 41	18 07 53	7♈33 55	13 52 56	19R 14.4	0♐40.6	8 40.8	9 49.4	26 11.8	14 40.7	12 53.8	22 18.1	4 52.8	8 50.2
11 Th	17 19 38	19 08 51	20 07 56	26 19 26	19 14.3	2 06.5	9 11.1	10 30.7	26 37.2	14 47.0	13 00.9	22 21.7	4 55.0	8 52.2
12 F	17 23 34	20 09 50	2♉27 54	8♉33 46	19 12.3	3 33.2	9 42.9	11 12.1	27 02.5	14 53.4	13 08.0	22 25.4	4 57.2	8 54.1
13 Sa	17 27 31	21 10 49	14 37 27	20 39 18	19 07.6	5 00.7	10 16.3	11 53.6	27 27.8	15 00.1	13 15.0	22 29.0	4 59.4	8 56.1
14 Su	17 31 27	22 11 50	26 39 39	2♊38 48	19 00.2	6 28.8	10 51.1	12 35.0	27 53.1	15 06.9	13 22.1	22 32.7	5 01.7	8 58.0
15 M	17 35 24	23 12 51	8♊36 57	14 34 21	18 50.0	7 57.5	11 27.3	13 16.5	28 18.3	15 13.8	13 29.2	22 36.3	5 03.9	8 59.9
16 Tu	17 39 21	24 13 52	20 31 12	26 27 38	18 37.9	9 26.7	12 04.9	13 58.1	28 43.4	15 20.9	13 36.2	22 40.0	5 06.1	9 01.8
17 W	17 43 17	25 14 55	2♋23 50	8♋19 58	18 24.5	10 56.4	12 43.8	14 39.6	29 08.5	15 28.2	13 43.2	22 43.6	5 08.4	9 03.6
18 Th	17 47 14	26 15 58	14 16 11	20 12 41	18 11.1	12 26.4	13 23.9	15 21.2	29 33.6	15 35.7	13 50.2	22 47.3	5 10.6	9 05.4
19 F	17 51 10	27 17 01	26 09 40	2♌07 21	17 58.8	13 56.8	14 05.2	16 02.8	29 58.6	15 43.2	13 57.2	22 50.9	5 12.9	9 07.3
20 Sa	17 55 07	28 18 06	8♌06 01	14 05 59	17 48.6	15 27.5	14 47.6	16 44.5	0♐23.5	15 51.0	14 04.2	22 54.5	5 15.1	9 09.0
21 Su	17 59 03	29 19 11	20 07 37	26 11 17	17 41.0	16 58.5	15 31.2	17 26.1	0 48.4	15 58.9	14 11.2	22 58.2	5 17.4	9 10.8
22 M	18 03 00	0♑20 17	2♍17 26	8♍26 34	17 36.3	18 29.8	16 15.8	18 07.8	1 13.3	16 06.9	14 18.1	23 01.8	5 19.6	9 12.5
23 Tu	18 06 56	1 21 23	14 39 11	20 55 51	17D 34.2	20 01.4	17 01.4	18 49.5	1 38.0	16 15.1	14 25.1	23 05.4	5 21.9	9 14.2
24 W	18 10 53	2 22 30	27 17 06	3♎43 31	17 33.7	21 33.3	17 48.0	19 31.3	2 02.8	16 23.5	14 32.0	23 09.1	5 24.2	9 15.9
25 Th	18 14 50	3 23 38	10♎15 39	16 53 59	17R 33.9	23 05.4	18 35.6	20 13.0	2 27.4	16 32.0	14 38.8	23 12.7	5 26.4	9 17.5
26 F	18 18 46	4 24 47	23 38 59	0♏30 59	17 33.4	24 37.8	19 24.0	20 54.8	2 52.1	16 40.6	14 45.7	23 16.3	5 28.7	9 19.1
27 Sa	18 22 43	5 25 56	7♏30 13	14 36 44	17 31.0	26 10.5	20 13.4	21 36.6	3 16.6	16 49.4	14 52.5	23 19.9	5 31.0	9 20.7
28 Su	18 26 39	6 27 06	21 50 25	29 10 53	17 25.9	27 43.4	21 03.5	22 18.4	3 41.1	16 58.3	14 59.3	23 23.5	5 33.3	9 22.3
29 M	18 30 36	7 28 16	6♐37 35	14♐09 39	17 18.0	29 16.6	21 54.5	23 00.3	4 05.5	17 07.3	15 06.1	23 27.0	5 35.5	9 23.8
30 Tu	18 34 32	8 29 27	21 46 02	29 25 28	17 07.8	0♑50.1	22 46.2	23 42.1	4 29.9	17 16.5	15 12.9	23 30.6	5 37.8	9 25.3
31 W	18 38 29	9 30 38	7♑06 30	14♑47 38	16 56.1	2 23.8	23 38.7	24 24.0	4 54.2	17 25.9	15 19.6	23 34.2	5 40.1	9 26.8

Astro Data	Planet Ingress	Last Aspect	☽ Ingress	Last Aspect	☽ Ingress	☽ Phases & Eclipses	Astro Data
Dy Hr Mn	Dy Hr Mn	Dy Hr Mn	Dy Hr Mn	Dy Hr Mn	Dy Hr Mn	Dy Hr Mn	1 November 1986
☿R 2 6:47	☉ ♐ 22 14:44	31 21:41 ♅ ⚹	♏ 1 14:19	30 6:20 ☿ ☌	♐ 1 2:08	2 6:02 ● 9♏31	Julian Day # 31716
♃D 8 9:27	♂ ♓ 26 2:35	3 13:46 ☿ ☌	♐ 3 15:19	2 12:36 ♅ ☌	♑ 3 1:28	8 21:11 ☽ 16♒10	SVP 5♓26'44"
☽0N 12 10:55		5 0:02 ♅ ☌	♑ 5 15:48	4 13:26 ☿ ⚹	♒ 5 1:23	16 12:12 ○ 23♉50	GC 26♐39.3 ⚴ 17♎59.3
☿D 22 9:02	☿ ♐ 10 0:34	7 12:31 ☿ ⚹	♒ 7 17:28	6 20:12 ☿ □	♓ 7 3:48	24 16:50 ☾ 2♍07	Eris 15♈51.5R ⚵ 19♐57.9
♀D 26 2:46	⚳ ♐ 19 13:22	9 12:49 ☿ □	♓ 9 21:30	9 8:00 ☿ △	♈ 9 9:49		⚷ 20♊42.1R ⚶ 3♈38.4R
☽0S 27 3:07	☉ ♑ 22 4:02	11 14:28 ☿ △	♈ 12 4:14	11 4:16 ♅ △	♉ 11 19:10	1 16:43 ● 9♐12	☽ Mean ☊ 19♈41.8
	☿ ♑ 29 23:09	13 21:42 ♂ ⚹	♉ 14 13:24	13 0:39 ♃ ⚹	♊ 14 6:41	8 8:02 ☽ 15♓56	
☽0N 9 15:53		16 12:12 ☉ ☍	♊ 17 0:26	16 7:04 ☉ ☍	♋ 16 19:09	16 7:04 ○ 24♊01	1 December 1986
☽0S 24 10:33		19 3:19 ♂ △	♋ 19 12:46	18 2:35 ♃ △	♌ 19 7:44	24 9:17 ☾ 2♎16	Julian Day # 31746
		22 0:11 ☉ △	♌ 22 1:25	21 18:44 ☉ △	♍ 21 19:30	31 3:10 ● 9♑08	SVP 5♓26'39"
		24 10:36 ♂ ☍	♍ 24 12:46	23 16:07 ♅ □	♎ 24 5:05		GC 26♐39.4 ⚴ 0♏57.4
		26 5:21 ♅ □	♎ 26 20:59	26 0:25 ☿ ⚹	♏ 26 11:06		Eris 15♈37.5R ⚵ 0♑17.2
		28 10:57 ♅ ⚹	♏ 29 1:13	28 0:12 ♂ △	♐ 28 13:20		⚷ 19♊10.8R ⚶ 3♈14.5
				30 2:42 ♅ ☌	♑ 30 12:54		☽ Mean ☊ 18♈06.5

LONGITUDE — January 1987

Day	Sid.Time	☉	0 hr ☽	Noon ☽	True ☊	☿	♀	♂	⚳	♃	♄	♅	♆	♇
1 Th	18 42 26	10♑31 49	22♑27 21	0♒04 10	16♈44.5	3♑57.9	24♏31.8	25♓05.9	5♐18.4	17♓35.3	15♐26.3	23♐37.7	5♑42.4	9♏28.3
2 F	18 46 22	11 33 00	7♒36 44	15 03 55	16R34.3	5 32.3	25 25.6	25 47.8	5 42.5	17 44.9	15 32.9	23 41.2	5 44.6	9 29.7
3 Sa	18 50 19	12 34 10	22 24 47	29 38 39	16 26.6	7 07.0	26 20.1	26 29.7	6 06.6	17 54.6	15 39.6	23 44.8	5 46.9	9 31.1
4 Su	18 54 15	13 35 21	6♓45 05	13♓43 55	16 21.6	8 42.1	27 15.2	27 11.6	6 30.6	18 04.5	15 46.2	23 48.3	5 49.1	9 32.4
5 M	18 58 12	14 36 31	20 35 08	27 18 56	16 19.2	10 17.5	28 10.9	27 53.6	6 54.6	18 14.5	15 52.7	23 51.7	5 51.4	9 33.7
6 Tu	19 02 08	15 37 40	3♈55 42	10♈25 51	16 18.6	11 53.3	29 07.1	28 35.5	7 18.4	18 24.5	15 59.2	23 55.2	5 53.6	9 35.0
7 W	19 06 05	16 38 50	16 49 58	23 08 36	16 18.5	13 29.4	0♐04.0	29 17.5	7 42.2	18 34.8	16 05.7	23 58.6	5 55.9	9 36.3
8 Th	19 10 01	17 39 59	29 22 24	5♉32 01	16 17.8	15 06.0	1 01.3	29 59.4	8 05.9	18 45.1	16 12.1	24 02.1	5 58.1	9 37.5
9 F	19 13 58	18 41 07	11♉38 02	17 41 04	16 15.2	16 43.0	1 59.2	0♈41.4	8 29.5	18 55.5	16 18.5	24 05.5	6 00.4	9 38.7
10 Sa	19 17 55	19 42 15	23 41 42	29 40 27	16 09.9	18 20.4	2 57.6	1 23.3	8 53.0	19 06.1	16 24.9	24 08.9	6 02.6	9 39.8
11 Su	19 21 51	20 43 23	5♊37 49	11♊34 13	16 01.6	19 58.2	3 56.5	2 05.3	9 16.5	19 16.8	16 31.2	24 12.3	6 04.8	9 41.0
12 M	19 25 48	21 44 30	17 30 02	23 25 38	15 50.3	21 36.5	4 55.8	2 47.2	9 39.9	19 27.6	16 37.5	24 15.6	6 07.0	9 42.1
13 Tu	19 29 44	22 45 37	29 21 16	5♋17 12	15 36.8	23 15.3	5 55.6	3 29.1	10 03.1	19 38.4	16 43.7	24 18.9	6 09.2	9 43.1
14 W	19 33 41	23 46 43	11♋13 39	17 10 47	15 22.1	24 54.6	6 55.8	4 11.1	10 26.3	19 49.5	16 49.9	24 22.2	6 11.4	9 44.1
15 Th	19 37 37	24 47 49	23 08 45	29 07 42	15 07.1	26 34.3	7 56.4	4 53.0	10 49.4	20 00.6	16 56.0	24 25.5	6 13.6	9 45.1
16 F	19 41 34	25 48 55	5♌07 45	11♌09 02	14 53.4	28 14.5	8 57.5	5 34.9	11 12.5	20 11.8	17 02.1	24 28.8	6 15.8	9 46.1
17 Sa	19 45 30	26 50 00	17 11 41	23 15 54	14 41.7	29 55.2	9 58.9	6 16.9	11 35.4	20 23.1	17 08.1	24 32.0	6 17.9	9 47.0
18 Su	19 49 27	27 51 04	29 21 51	5♍29 45	14 32.9	1♒36.4	11 00.8	6 58.8	11 58.2	20 34.5	17 14.1	24 35.2	6 20.1	9 47.9
19 M	19 53 24	28 52 08	11♍39 53	17 52 33	14 27.3	3 18.1	12 03.0	7 40.7	12 21.0	20 46.0	17 20.0	24 38.4	6 22.2	9 48.8
20 Tu	19 57 20	29 53 12	24 08 05	0♎26 52	14 24.4	5 00.2	13 05.5	8 22.6	12 43.6	20 57.6	17 25.9	24 41.6	6 24.4	9 49.6
21 W	20 01 17	0♒54 15	6♎49 20	13 15 53	14D23.6	6 42.8	14 08.4	9 04.5	13 06.2	21 09.3	17 31.7	24 44.7	6 26.5	9 50.4
22 Th	20 05 13	1 55 18	19 46 58	26 23 03	14R23.8	8 25.7	15 11.6	9 46.4	13 28.7	21 21.1	17 37.5	24 47.8	6 28.6	9 51.1
23 F	20 09 10	2 56 21	3♏04 32	9♏51 46	14 23.7	10 09.1	16 15.1	10 28.2	13 51.0	21 33.0	17 43.2	24 50.9	6 30.7	9 51.8
24 Sa	20 13 06	3 57 23	16 45 04	23 44 35	14 22.2	11 52.7	17 19.0	11 10.1	14 13.3	21 44.9	17 48.9	24 53.9	6 32.8	9 52.5
25 Su	20 17 03	4 58 25	0♐50 23	8♐02 21	14 18.3	13 36.6	18 23.1	11 52.0	14 35.4	21 57.0	17 54.5	24 57.0	6 34.8	9 53.2
26 M	20 20 59	5 59 26	15 20 10	22 43 19	14 11.8	15 20.7	19 27.5	12 33.8	14 57.5	22 09.1	18 00.0	24 59.9	6 36.9	9 53.8
27 Tu	20 24 56	7 00 27	0♑11 05	7♑42 33	14 03.0	17 04.8	20 32.2	13 15.7	15 19.4	22 21.4	18 05.5	25 02.9	6 38.9	9 54.3
28 W	20 28 53	8 01 27	15 16 34	22 51 55	13 52.7	18 48.9	21 37.1	13 57.5	15 41.2	22 33.7	18 11.0	25 05.8	6 40.9	9 54.9
29 Th	20 32 49	9 02 27	0♒27 14	8♒01 10	13 42.4	20 32.7	22 42.3	14 39.3	16 03.0	22 46.1	18 16.3	25 08.7	6 42.9	9 55.4
30 F	20 36 46	10 03 25	15 32 23	22 59 39	13 33.1	22 16.1	23 47.8	15 21.2	16 24.6	22 58.6	18 21.6	25 11.6	6 44.9	9 55.8
31 Sa	20 40 42	11 04 22	0♓21 53	7♓38 13	13 25.9	23 58.9	24 53.4	16 03.0	16 46.0	23 11.2	18 26.8	25 14.4	6 46.9	9 56.3

LONGITUDE — February 1987

Day	Sid.Time	☉	0 hr ☽	Noon ☽	True ☊	☿	♀	♂	⚳	♃	♄	♅	♆	♇
1 Su	20 44 39	12♒05 18	14♓47 58	21♓50 41	13♈21.4	25♒40.9	25♐59.3	16♈44.8	17♐07.4	23♓23.8	18♐32.0	25♐17.2	6♑48.8	9♏56.6
2 M	20 48 35	13 06 12	28 46 08	5♈34 16	13D19.3	27 21.6	27 05.4	17 26.5	17 28.6	23 36.5	18 37.1	25 20.0	6 50.8	9 57.0
3 Tu	20 52 32	14 07 06	12♈15 15	18 49 21	13 19.1	29 00.9	28 11.7	18 08.3	17 49.8	23 49.3	18 42.1	25 22.7	6 52.7	9 57.3
4 W	20 56 28	15 07 58	25 16 58	1♉38 38	13 19.9	0♓38.2	29 18.2	18 50.1	18 10.8	24 02.1	18 47.1	25 25.3	6 54.6	9 57.6
5 Th	21 00 25	16 08 48	7♉54 53	14 06 21	13R20.6	2 13.1	0♑24.9	19 31.8	18 31.6	24 15.1	18 52.0	25 28.0	6 56.4	9 57.8
6 F	21 04 22	17 09 37	20 13 40	26 17 29	13 20.1	3 45.2	1 31.8	20 13.5	18 52.4	24 28.0	18 56.8	25 30.6	6 58.3	9 58.0
7 Sa	21 08 18	18 10 25	2♊18 25	8♊17 07	13 17.6	5 13.9	2 38.8	20 55.2	19 13.0	24 41.1	19 01.5	25 33.2	7 00.1	9 58.2
8 Su	21 12 15	19 11 11	14 14 11	20 10 09	13 12.9	6 38.5	3 46.1	21 36.9	19 33.4	24 54.2	19 06.2	25 35.7	7 01.9	9 58.3
9 M	21 16 11	20 11 56	26 05 34	2♋00 54	13 06.0	7 58.4	4 53.5	22 18.5	19 53.8	25 07.4	19 10.8	25 38.2	7 03.7	9 58.4
10 Tu	21 20 08	21 12 39	7♋56 34	13 52 59	12 57.1	9 12.9	6 01.1	23 00.2	20 14.0	25 20.6	19 15.3	25 40.7	7 05.5	9 58.5
11 W	21 24 04	22 13 21	19 50 27	25 49 17	12 47.2	10 21.3	7 08.9	23 41.8	20 34.1	25 33.9	19 19.8	25 43.1	7 07.2	9R58.5
12 Th	21 28 01	23 14 02	1♌49 41	7♌51 54	12 37.1	11 22.8	8 16.8	24 23.4	20 54.0	25 47.3	19 24.2	25 45.4	7 09.0	9 58.5
13 F	21 31 57	24 14 40	13 56 03	20 02 17	12 27.7	12 16.6	9 24.9	25 05.0	21 13.8	26 00.7	19 28.5	25 47.8	7 10.7	9 58.5
14 Sa	21 35 54	25 15 18	26 10 43	2♍21 25	12 19.9	13 02.2	10 33.1	25 46.5	21 33.4	26 14.2	19 32.7	25 50.1	7 12.3	9 58.4
15 Su	21 39 51	26 15 54	8♍34 31	14 50 03	12 14.3	13 38.8	11 41.4	26 28.0	21 52.9	26 27.7	19 36.8	25 52.3	7 14.0	9 58.3
16 M	21 43 47	27 16 28	21 08 08	27 28 53	12 10.9	14 05.9	12 50.0	27 09.5	22 12.3	26 41.3	19 40.9	25 54.5	7 15.6	9 58.1
17 Tu	21 47 44	28 17 02	3♎52 25	10♎18 52	12D09.8	14 23.0	13 58.6	27 51.0	22 31.5	26 54.9	19 44.9	25 56.7	7 17.2	9 57.9
18 W	21 51 40	29 17 34	16 48 25	23 21 16	12 10.2	14R30.0	15 07.4	28 32.4	22 50.5	27 08.6	19 48.8	25 58.8	7 18.8	9 57.7
19 Th	21 55 37	0♓18 04	29 57 35	6♏37 36	12 11.6	14 26.6	16 16.3	29 13.9	23 09.4	27 22.3	19 52.6	26 00.8	7 20.4	9 57.4
20 F	21 59 33	1 18 34	13♏21 31	20 09 30	12R12.9	14 13.0	17 25.4	29 55.3	23 28.1	27 36.1	19 56.3	26 02.9	7 21.9	9 57.1
21 Sa	22 03 30	2 19 02	27 01 43	3♐58 16	12 13.4	13 49.5	18 34.5	0♉36.7	23 46.7	27 49.9	20 00.0	26 04.9	7 23.4	9 56.8
22 Su	22 07 26	3 19 29	10♐59 08	18 04 17	12 12.4	13 16.8	19 43.8	1 18.0	24 05.1	28 03.7	20 03.5	26 06.8	7 24.9	9 56.4
23 M	22 11 23	4 19 55	25 13 31	2♑26 31	12 09.7	12 35.6	20 53.2	1 59.4	24 23.4	28 17.7	20 07.0	26 08.7	7 26.3	9 56.0
24 Tu	22 15 20	5 20 19	9♑42 51	17 01 57	12 05.5	11 47.0	22 02.7	2 40.7	24 41.4	28 31.6	20 10.4	26 10.6	7 27.8	9 55.6
25 W	22 19 16	6 20 42	24 23 06	1♒45 29	12 00.2	10 52.3	23 12.3	3 22.0	24 59.3	28 45.6	20 13.7	26 12.4	7 29.2	9 55.1
26 Th	22 23 13	7 21 03	9♒08 12	16 30 18	11 54.7	9 53.0	24 22.0	4 03.3	25 17.1	28 59.6	20 16.9	26 14.1	7 30.5	9 54.6
27 F	22 27 09	8 21 23	23 50 47	1♓08 44	11 49.7	8 50.6	25 31.8	4 44.6	25 34.6	29 13.7	20 20.1	26 15.8	7 31.9	9 54.1
28 Sa	22 31 06	9 21 41	8♓23 15	15 33 30	11 46.0	7 46.7	26 41.7	5 25.8	25 52.0	29 27.8	20 23.1	26 17.5	7 33.2	9 53.5

Astro Data

	Dy Hr Mn
☽0N	5 21:49
♂0N	9 11:07
☽0S	20 15:44
♅∠♇	23 21:30
☽0N	2 6:08
♃⚼♇	8 19:34
♇R	11 16:56
♃□♅	12 7:56
☽0S	16 20:39
☿R	18 16:08

Planet Ingress

	Dy Hr Mn
♀ ♐	7 10:20
♂ ♈	8 12:20
☿ ♒	17 13:08
☉ ♒	20 14:40
☿ ♓	4 2:31
♀ ♑	5 3:03
☉ ♓	19 4:50
♂ ♉	20 14:44

Last Aspect / ☽ Ingress

Last Aspect Dy Hr Mn		☽ Ingress Dy Hr Mn
1 3:47	♂ ✶	♒ 1 11:53
3 6:07	♀ □	♓ 3 12:36
5 13:41	♀ △	♈ 5 16:51
7 13:36	♅ △	♉ 8 1:13
9 14:30	♃ ✶	♊ 10 12:39
12 13:42	♅ ☍	♋ 13 1:18
15 6:03	♅ ☍	♌ 15 13:45
17 14:31	♅ △	♍ 18 1:15
20 10:51	☉ △	♎ 20 11:09
22 9:07	♅ ✶	♏ 22 18:30
24 8:33	♃ △	♐ 24 22:35
26 15:41	♅ ☌	♑ 26 23:42
28 11:31	♃ ✶	♒ 28 23:17
30 15:35	♅ ✶	♓ 30 23:24

Last Aspect / ☽ Ingress

Last Aspect Dy Hr Mn		☽ Ingress Dy Hr Mn
1 19:47	♀ □	♈ 2 2:09
4 7:08	♀ △	♉ 4 8:53
6 8:19	♃ ✶	♊ 6 19:23
8 23:02	♅ ☍	♋ 9 7:55
11 11:29	♃ △	♌ 11 20:21
13 23:17	♅ △	♍ 14 7:26
16 10:29	♃ ☍	♎ 16 16:44
18 23:41	☉ △	♏ 19 0:04
21 1:13	♃ △	♐ 21 5:09
23 5:00	♃ □	♑ 23 7:57
25 7:03	♃ ✶	♒ 25 9:08
27 3:57	♅ ✶	♓ 27 10:07

☽ Phases & Eclipses

Dy Hr Mn	
6 22:34	☽ 16♈05
15 2:30	○ 24♋24
22 22:45	☾ 2♏23
29 13:45	● 9♒07
5 16:21	☽ 16♉20
13 20:58	○ 24♌37
21 8:56	☾ 2♐11
28 0:51	● 8♓54

Astro Data

1 January 1987
Julian Day # 31777
SVP 5♓26'33"
GC 26♐39.5 ⚴ 13♏12.6
Eris 15♈31.6R ⚵ 11♑49.0
⚷ 17♊21.0R ⚶ 8♈55.0
☽ Mean ☊ 16♈28.0

1 February 1987
Julian Day # 31808
SVP 5♓26'27"
GC 26♐39.5 ⚴ 23♏24.7
Eris 15♈36.3 ⚵ 23♑42.6
⚷ 16♊04.2R ⚶ 18♈29.9
☽ Mean ☊ 14♈49.5

March 1987 — LONGITUDE

Day	Sid.Time	☉	0 hr ☽	Noon ☽	True ☊	☿	♀	♂	⚳	♃	♄	♅	♆	♇
1 Su	22 35 02	10♓21 57	22♓38 51	29♓38 44	11♈43.8	6♓42.9	27♑51.7	6♉07.0	26♐09.1	29♓41.9	20♐26.0	26♐19.1	7♑34.5	9♏52.9
2 M	22 38 59	11 22 11	6♈32 47	13♈20 45	11D43.2	5R40.6	29 01.8	6 48.2	26 26.1	29 56.1	20 28.9	26 20.6	7 35.7	9R52.3
3 Tu	22 42 55	12 22 23	20 02 34	26 38 16	11 44.0	4 41.1	0♒11.9	7 29.4	26 42.9	0♈10.2	20 31.6	26 22.1	7 36.9	9 51.6
4 W	22 46 52	13 22 34	3♉08 01	9♉32 08	11 45.5	3 45.7	1 22.2	8 10.5	26 59.5	0 24.5	20 34.3	26 23.6	7 38.1	9 50.9
5 Th	22 50 49	14 22 42	15 50 59	22 05 01	11 47.3	2 55.1	2 32.5	8 51.6	27 15.9	0 38.7	20 36.9	26 25.0	7 39.3	9 50.2
6 F	22 54 45	15 22 48	28 14 44	4♊20 42	11R48.6	2 10.3	3 42.9	9 32.7	27 32.1	0 53.0	20 39.4	26 26.4	7 40.4	9 49.4
7 Sa	22 58 42	16 22 52	10♊23 30	16 23 44	11 49.1	1 31.6	4 53.3	10 13.8	27 48.2	1 07.3	20 41.8	26 27.7	7 41.6	9 48.6
8 Su	23 02 38	17 22 54	22 22 00	28 18 55	11 48.6	0 59.4	6 03.8	10 54.8	28 04.0	1 21.6	20 44.1	26 28.9	7 42.6	9 47.8
9 M	23 06 35	18 22 54	4♋15 03	10♋11 00	11 46.9	0 34.0	7 14.4	11 35.8	28 19.6	1 35.9	20 46.2	26 30.2	7 43.7	9 47.0
10 Tu	23 10 31	19 22 52	16 07 18	22 04 28	11 44.2	0 15.2	8 25.1	12 16.8	28 34.9	1 50.3	20 48.4	26 31.3	7 44.7	9 46.1
11 W	23 14 28	20 22 47	28 02 58	4♌03 16	11 40.9	0 03.1	9 35.8	12 57.7	28 50.1	2 04.7	20 50.4	26 32.4	7 45.7	9 45.2
12 Th	23 18 24	21 22 41	10♌05 44	16 10 43	11 37.5	29♒57.5	10 46.6	13 38.6	29 05.1	2 19.1	20 52.3	26 33.5	7 46.6	9 44.2
13 F	23 22 21	22 22 32	22 18 30	28 29 20	11 34.3	29D58.1	11 57.5	14 19.5	29 19.8	2 33.5	20 54.1	26 34.5	7 47.6	9 43.3
14 Sa	23 26 18	23 22 21	4♍43 24	11♍00 50	11 31.7	0♓04.8	13 08.4	15 00.4	29 34.3	2 47.9	20 55.8	26 35.4	7 48.5	9 42.3
15 Su	23 30 14	24 22 08	17 21 45	23 46 09	11 30.0	0 17.2	14 19.4	15 41.2	29 48.6	3 02.4	20 57.4	26 36.3	7 49.3	9 41.2
16 M	23 34 11	25 21 53	0♎14 05	6♎45 29	11D29.3	0 35.1	15 30.4	16 22.0	0♑02.7	3 16.8	20 58.9	26 37.2	7 50.1	9 40.2
17 Tu	23 38 07	26 21 37	13 20 18	19 58 28	11 29.4	0 58.1	16 41.5	17 02.8	0 16.5	3 31.3	21 00.3	26 38.0	7 50.9	9 39.1
18 W	23 42 04	27 21 18	26 39 51	3♏24 22	11 30.1	1 25.9	17 52.7	17 43.5	0 30.1	3 45.8	21 01.7	26 38.7	7 51.7	9 38.0
19 Th	23 46 00	28 20 58	10♏11 52	17 02 14	11 31.2	1 58.3	19 03.9	18 24.2	0 43.5	4 00.3	21 02.9	26 39.4	7 52.4	9 36.8
20 F	23 49 57	29 20 36	23 55 19	0♐50 58	11 32.2	2 35.0	20 15.1	19 04.9	0 56.6	4 14.8	21 04.0	26 40.1	7 53.1	9 35.7
21 Sa	23 53 53	0♈20 12	7♐49 03	14 49 22	11 33.0	3 15.6	21 26.5	19 45.6	1 09.5	4 29.3	21 05.0	26 40.7	7 53.8	9 34.5
22 Su	23 57 50	1 19 46	21 51 45	28 56 00	11R33.4	4 00.1	22 37.8	20 26.2	1 22.1	4 43.8	21 06.0	26 41.2	7 54.4	9 33.3
23 M	0 01 47	2 19 19	6♑01 52	13♑09 04	11 33.2	4 48.0	23 49.3	21 06.8	1 34.5	4 58.4	21 06.8	26 41.7	7 55.0	9 32.1
24 Tu	0 05 43	3 18 50	20 17 17	27 26 11	11 32.7	5 39.3	25 00.7	21 47.4	1 46.6	5 12.9	21 07.5	26 42.1	7 55.6	9 30.8
25 W	0 09 40	4 18 20	4♒35 22	11♒44 22	11 31.9	6 33.8	26 12.3	22 27.9	1 58.5	5 27.4	21 08.2	26 42.5	7 56.1	9 29.5
26 Th	0 13 36	5 17 47	18 52 45	26 00 01	11 31.1	7 31.2	27 23.8	23 08.5	2 10.0	5 42.0	21 08.7	26 42.8	7 56.6	9 28.2
27 F	0 17 33	6 17 13	3♓05 38	10♓09 07	11 30.5	8 31.3	28 35.4	23 49.0	2 21.4	5 56.5	21 09.1	26 43.1	7 57.1	9 26.9
28 Sa	0 21 29	7 16 36	17 09 57	24 07 39	11 30.1	9 34.2	29 47.1	24 29.4	2 32.4	6 11.0	21 09.4	26 43.3	7 57.5	9 25.6
29 Su	0 25 26	8 15 58	1♈01 48	7♈52 02	11D29.9	10 39.5	0♓58.7	25 09.9	2 43.2	6 25.5	21 09.6	26 43.5	7 57.9	9 24.2
30 M	0 29 22	9 15 18	14 38 01	21 19 31	11 30.0	11 47.2	2 10.5	25 50.3	2 53.7	6 40.1	21R09.8	26 43.6	7 58.3	9 22.8
31 Tu	0 33 19	10 14 35	27 56 24	4♉28 33	11 30.1	12 57.2	3 22.2	26 30.7	3 03.9	6 54.6	21 09.8	26R43.7	7 58.6	9 21.4

April 1987 — LONGITUDE

Day	Sid.Time	☉	0 hr ☽	Noon ☽	True ☊	☿	♀	♂	⚳	♃	♄	♅	♆	♇
1 W	0 37 15	11♈13 50	10♉56 01	17♉18 53	11♈30.1	14♓09.3	4♓34.0	27♉11.1	3♑13.8	7♈09.1	21♐09.7	26♐43.7	7♑59.0	9♏20.0
2 Th	0 41 12	12 13 04	23 37 19	29 51 34	11R30.1	15 23.6	5 45.8	27 51.4	3 23.4	7 23.6	21R09.5	26R43.6	7 59.2	9R18.5
3 F	0 45 09	13 12 15	6♊01 57	12♊08 52	11 30.0	16 39.8	6 57.6	28 31.7	3 32.7	7 38.1	21 09.2	26 43.5	7 59.5	9 17.1
4 Sa	0 49 05	14 11 24	18 12 44	24 14 01	11 29.7	17 58.0	8 09.5	29 12.0	3 41.8	7 52.6	21 08.9	26 43.4	7 59.7	9 15.6
5 Su	0 53 02	15 10 30	0♋13 15	6♋10 58	11D29.6	19 18.1	9 21.4	29 52.3	3 50.5	8 07.0	21 08.4	26 43.2	7 59.8	9 14.1
6 M	0 56 58	16 09 34	12 07 44	18 04 07	11 29.5	20 40.0	10 33.3	0♊32.5	3 58.9	8 21.5	21 07.8	26 42.9	8 00.0	9 12.6
7 Tu	1 00 55	17 08 36	24 00 44	29 58 08	11 29.7	22 03.6	11 45.3	1 12.7	4 07.0	8 36.0	21 07.1	26 42.6	8 00.1	9 11.1
8 W	1 04 51	18 07 36	5♌56 55	11♌57 38	11 30.1	23 29.0	12 57.3	1 52.8	4 14.8	8 50.4	21 06.4	26 42.3	8 00.1	9 09.5
9 Th	1 08 48	19 06 33	18 00 48	24 06 57	11 30.8	24 56.2	14 09.3	2 33.0	4 22.3	9 04.8	21 05.5	26 41.9	8R00.2	9 08.0
10 F	1 12 44	20 05 28	0♍16 32	6♍29 57	11 31.6	26 24.9	15 21.3	3 13.1	4 29.5	9 19.2	21 04.5	26 41.4	8 00.2	9 06.4
11 Sa	1 16 41	21 04 20	12 47 33	19 09 39	11 32.4	27 55.4	16 33.3	3 53.2	4 36.4	9 33.6	21 03.5	26 40.9	8 00.1	9 04.8
12 Su	1 20 38	22 03 11	25 36 26	2♎08 03	11R33.0	29 27.5	17 45.4	4 33.2	4 42.9	9 47.9	21 02.3	26 40.4	8 00.1	9 03.3
13 M	1 24 34	23 01 59	8♎44 31	15 25 50	11 33.1	1♈01.2	18 57.5	5 13.2	4 49.1	10 02.2	21 01.1	26 39.8	8 00.0	9 01.7
14 Tu	1 28 31	24 00 46	22 11 50	29 02 18	11 32.6	2 36.5	20 09.6	5 53.2	4 55.0	10 16.5	20 59.7	26 39.1	7 59.8	9 00.0
15 W	1 32 27	24 59 30	5♏56 55	12♏55 19	11 31.5	4 13.4	21 21.8	6 33.1	5 00.5	10 30.8	20 58.3	26 38.4	7 59.7	8 58.4
16 Th	1 36 24	25 58 13	19 57 01	27 01 32	11 29.8	5 52.0	22 34.0	7 13.1	5 05.7	10 45.1	20 56.7	26 37.7	7 59.5	8 56.8
17 F	1 40 20	26 56 54	4♐08 18	11♐16 47	11 27.9	7 32.1	23 46.2	7 53.0	5 10.6	10 59.3	20 55.1	26 36.9	7 59.3	8 55.1
18 Sa	1 44 17	27 55 33	18 26 24	25 36 36	11 26.0	9 13.9	24 58.4	8 32.9	5 15.1	11 13.6	20 53.4	26 36.0	7 59.0	8 53.5
19 Su	1 48 13	28 54 11	2♑46 52	9♑56 43	11 24.5	10 57.3	26 10.7	9 12.7	5 19.2	11 27.7	20 51.6	26 35.1	7 58.7	8 51.8
20 M	1 52 10	29 52 47	17 05 44	24 13 31	11D23.7	12 42.3	27 23.0	9 52.5	5 23.1	11 41.9	20 49.7	26 34.2	7 58.4	8 50.2
21 Tu	1 56 07	0♉51 21	1♒19 45	8♒24 09	11 23.8	14 29.0	28 35.3	10 32.3	5 26.5	11 56.0	20 47.7	26 33.2	7 58.0	8 48.5
22 W	2 00 03	1 49 53	15 26 29	22 26 35	11 24.6	16 17.3	29 47.6	11 12.1	5 29.6	12 10.1	20 45.7	26 32.2	7 57.6	8 46.8
23 Th	2 04 00	2 48 24	29 24 17	6♓19 26	11 25.9	18 07.3	0♈59.9	11 51.8	5 32.4	12 24.2	20 43.5	26 31.1	7 57.2	8 45.2
24 F	2 07 56	3 46 54	13♓11 56	20 01 41	11 27.3	19 58.9	2 12.3	12 31.6	5 34.7	12 38.2	20 41.2	26 30.0	7 56.8	8 43.5
25 Sa	2 11 53	4 45 21	26 48 34	3♈32 29	11R28.3	21 52.1	3 24.7	13 11.3	5 36.7	12 52.2	20 38.9	26 28.8	7 56.3	8 41.8
26 Su	2 15 49	5 43 47	10♈13 22	16 51 05	11 28.4	23 47.1	4 37.1	13 50.9	5 38.4	13 06.2	20 36.5	26 27.6	7 55.8	8 40.1
27 M	2 19 46	6 42 11	23 25 35	29 56 47	11 27.3	25 43.6	5 49.5	14 30.6	5 39.6	13 20.1	20 34.0	26 26.3	7 55.2	8 38.4
28 Tu	2 23 42	7 40 33	6♉24 37	12♉49 03	11 24.8	27 41.8	7 01.9	15 10.2	5 40.5	13 34.0	20 31.4	26 25.0	7 54.7	8 36.7
29 W	2 27 39	8 38 54	19 10 06	25 27 46	11 21.1	29 41.6	8 14.3	15 49.8	5R41.1	13 47.8	20 28.7	26 23.7	7 54.1	8 35.0
30 Th	2 31 36	9 37 13	1♊42 09	7♊53 21	11 16.6	1♉43.0	9 26.8	16 29.4	5 41.2	14 01.6	20 26.0	26 22.3	7 53.4	8 33.3

Astro Data	Dy Hr Mn
☽0N	1 16:08
☿D	12 21:23
♃0N	13 6:31
☽0S	16 3:16
☉0N	21 3:52
☽0N	29 1:43
♄R	31 4:43
♅R	1 4:35
♃□♆	4 23:53
♃⚻♇	9 16:49
♆R	10 0:12
☽0S	12 11:47
☿0N	16 10:02
☽0N	25 9:14
♀0N	25 16:56

Planet Ingress	Dy Hr Mn
♃ ♈	2 18:41
♀ ♒	3 7:55
☿ ♒R	11 21:55
☿ ♓	13 21:09
⚳ ♑	16 7:23
☉ ♈	21 3:52
♀ ♓	28 16:20
♂ ♊	5 16:37
☿ ♈	12 20:23
☉ ♉	20 14:58
♀ ♈	22 16:07
☿ ♉	29 15:39
⚳ R30	9:22

Last Aspect Dy Hr Mn		☽ Ingress	Dy Hr Mn
1 12:06	♃ ☌	♈	1 12:37
3 11:30	♅ △	♉	3 18:11
4 19:55	☉ ⚹	♊	6 3:26
8 8:18	♅ ☍	♋	8 15:24
10 6:05	☉ △	♌	11 3:54
13 14:52	☿ ☍	♍	13 14:55
15 17:17	♅ □	♎	15 23:34
17 23:57	♅ ⚹	♏	18 5:57
20 9:12	☉ △	♐	20 10:32
22 8:11	♅ ☌	♑	22 13:48
24 2:03	♂ △	♒	24 16:18
26 14:35	♀ ☌	♓	26 18:46
28 16:30	♅ □	♈	28 22:12
30 21:47	♅ △	♉	31 3:46

Last Aspect Dy Hr Mn		☽ Ingress	Dy Hr Mn
2 7:55	♂ ☌	♊	2 12:16
4 16:59	♅ ☍	♋	4 23:33
6 17:56	☿ △	♌	7 12:04
9 17:03	♅ △	♍	9 23:28
12 6:26	☿ ☍	♎	12 8:06
14 7:50	♅ ⚹	♏	14 13:41
16 3:45	♀ △	♐	16 17:02
18 16:10	☉ △	♑	18 19:21
20 17:49	♀ ⚹	♒	20 21:45
22 19:02	♅ ⚹	♓	23 1:02
24 23:26	♅ □	♈	25 5:41
27 5:33	♅ △	♉	27 12:06
28 4:08	♇ ☍	♊	29 20:43

☽ Phases & Eclipses Dy Hr Mn	
7 11:58	☽ 16♊23
15 13:13	○ 24♍25
22 16:22	☾ 1♑31
29 12:46	● 8♈18
29 12:48:52	● AT00'08"
6 7:48	☽ 15♋59
14 2:31	○ 23♎38
14 2:19	● A 0.777
20 22:15	☾ 0♒18
28 1:34	● 7♉15

Astro Data

1 March 1987
Julian Day # 31836
SVP 5♓26'23"
GC 26♐39.6 ⚴ 29♏35.6
Eris 15♈48.6 ⚵ 4♒22.0
⚷ 15♊51.2 ⚶ 29♈02.5
☽ Mean ☊ 13♈20.6

1 April 1987
Julian Day # 31867
SVP 5♓26'20"
GC 26♐39.7 ⚴ 0♐56.2R
Eris 16♈07.9 ⚵ 15♒35.3
⚷ 16♊45.9 ⚶ 11♉49.5
☽ Mean ☊ 11♈42.1

LONGITUDE — May 1987

Day	Sid.Time	☉	0 hr ☽	Noon ☽	True ☊	☿	♀	♂	⚳	♃	♄	♅	♆	♇
1 F	2 35 32	10♉35 30	14♊01 32	20♊06 56	11♈11.6	3♉45.9	10♈39.3	17♊08.9	5♑41.0	14♈15.4	20♐23.2	26♐20.9	7♑52.8	8♏31.6
2 Sa	2 39 29	11 33 45	26 09 49	2♋10 30	11R 06.8	5 50.2	11 51.7	17 48.5	5R 40.4	14 29.1	20R 20.3	26R 19.4	7R 52.1	8R 29.9
3 Su	2 43 25	12 31 57	8♋09 21	14 06 49	11 02.7	7 55.9	13 04.2	18 28.0	5 39.4	14 42.7	20 17.3	26 17.9	7 51.4	8 28.2
4 M	2 47 22	13 30 08	20 03 20	25 59 25	10 59.8	10 02.7	14 16.7	19 07.4	5 38.0	14 56.3	20 14.3	26 16.4	7 50.6	8 26.5
5 Tu	2 51 18	14 28 17	1♌55 36	7♌52 28	10D 58.3	12 10.7	15 29.2	19 46.9	5 36.3	15 09.9	20 11.2	26 14.8	7 49.8	8 24.9
6 W	2 55 15	15 26 24	13 50 35	19 50 35	10 58.1	14 19.6	16 41.7	20 26.3	5 34.2	15 23.4	20 08.0	26 13.2	7 49.0	8 23.2
7 Th	2 59 11	16 24 29	25 53 02	1♍58 35	10 59.1	16 29.3	17 54.3	21 05.7	5 31.7	15 36.9	20 04.7	26 11.5	7 48.2	8 21.5
8 F	3 03 08	17 22 32	8♍07 49	14 21 17	11 00.7	18 39.4	19 06.8	21 45.1	5 28.8	15 50.3	20 01.4	26 09.8	7 47.4	8 19.8
9 Sa	3 07 05	18 20 34	20 39 31	27 02 59	11 02.1	20 49.8	20 19.4	22 24.4	5 25.6	16 03.7	19 58.0	26 08.1	7 46.5	8 18.2
10 Su	3 11 01	19 18 33	3♎32 05	10♎07 08	11R 02.8	23 00.3	21 31.9	23 03.7	5 22.0	16 17.0	19 54.6	26 06.3	7 45.6	8 16.5
11 M	3 14 58	20 16 30	16 48 20	23 35 46	11 02.2	25 10.4	22 44.5	23 43.0	5 18.0	16 30.2	19 51.1	26 04.5	7 44.6	8 14.8
12 Tu	3 18 54	21 14 26	0♏29 21	7♏28 53	10 59.7	27 20.1	23 57.1	24 22.3	5 13.6	16 43.4	19 47.5	26 02.6	7 43.7	8 13.2
13 W	3 22 51	22 12 20	14 34 00	21 44 11	10 55.5	29 28.9	25 09.7	25 01.5	5 08.9	16 56.6	19 43.9	26 00.8	7 42.7	8 11.6
14 Th	3 26 47	23 10 13	28 58 44	6♐16 53	10 49.8	1♊36.6	26 22.3	25 40.7	5 03.8	17 09.6	19 40.2	25 58.9	7 41.7	8 09.9
15 F	3 30 44	24 08 05	13♐37 44	21 00 18	10 43.3	3 42.8	27 34.9	26 19.9	4 58.4	17 22.6	19 36.4	25 56.9	7 40.6	8 08.3
16 Sa	3 34 40	25 05 55	28 23 37	5♑46 41	10 37.0	5 47.5	28 47.6	26 59.1	4 52.6	17 35.6	19 32.7	25 55.0	7 39.6	8 06.7
17 Su	3 38 37	26 03 44	13♑08 34	20 28 27	10 31.5	7 50.2	0♉00.2	27 38.2	4 46.4	17 48.5	19 28.8	25 53.0	7 38.5	8 05.1
18 M	3 42 34	27 01 31	27 45 36	4♒59 25	10 27.7	9 50.9	1 12.9	28 17.4	4 39.9	18 01.3	19 24.9	25 51.0	7 37.4	8 03.6
19 Tu	3 46 30	27 59 18	12♒09 26	19 15 21	10D 25.7	11 49.2	2 25.6	28 56.5	4 33.0	18 14.1	19 21.0	25 48.9	7 36.2	8 02.0
20 W	3 50 27	28 57 03	26 16 57	3♓14 10	10 25.4	13 45.1	3 38.3	29 35.6	4 25.8	18 26.8	19 17.0	25 46.8	7 35.1	8 00.4
21 Th	3 54 23	29 54 47	10♓07 01	16 55 35	10 26.3	15 38.4	4 51.0	0♋14.6	4 18.3	18 39.4	19 13.0	25 44.7	7 33.9	7 58.9
22 F	3 58 20	0♊52 30	23 40 01	0♈20 30	10R 27.3	17 29.0	6 03.7	0 53.7	4 10.4	18 52.0	19 08.9	25 42.6	7 32.7	7 57.3
23 Sa	4 02 16	1 50 12	6♈57 15	13 30 27	10 27.6	19 16.8	7 16.5	1 32.7	4 02.1	19 04.5	19 04.8	25 40.5	7 31.5	7 55.8
24 Su	4 06 13	2 47 53	20 00 19	26 27 03	10 26.4	21 01.7	8 29.2	2 11.7	3 53.6	19 16.9	19 00.6	25 38.3	7 30.2	7 54.3
25 M	4 10 09	3 45 33	2♉50 48	9♉11 43	10 22.9	22 43.6	9 42.0	2 50.7	3 44.7	19 29.2	18 56.4	25 36.1	7 29.0	7 52.8
26 Tu	4 14 06	4 43 12	15 29 56	21 45 34	10 16.9	24 22.5	10 54.7	3 29.6	3 35.6	19 41.5	18 52.2	25 33.8	7 27.7	7 51.4
27 W	4 18 03	5 40 50	27 58 42	4♊09 25	10 08.8	25 58.4	12 07.5	4 08.6	3 26.1	19 53.7	18 48.0	25 31.6	7 26.4	7 49.9
28 Th	4 21 59	6 38 26	10♊17 49	16 24 00	9 58.9	27 31.1	13 20.3	4 47.5	3 16.3	20 05.8	18 43.7	25 29.3	7 25.1	7 48.5
29 F	4 25 56	7 36 02	22 28 04	28 30 11	9 48.1	29 00.8	14 33.1	5 26.4	3 06.3	20 17.9	18 39.4	25 27.1	7 23.8	7 47.1
30 Sa	4 29 52	8 33 36	4♋30 30	10♋29 14	9 37.5	0♋27.2	15 46.0	6 05.3	2 56.0	20 29.8	18 35.1	25 24.8	7 22.4	7 45.7
31 Su	4 33 49	9 31 09	16 26 38	22 22 59	9 27.9	1 50.5	16 58.8	6 44.2	2 45.4	20 41.7	18 30.7	25 22.4	7 21.0	7 44.3

LONGITUDE — June 1987

Day	Sid.Time	☉	0 hr ☽	Noon ☽	True ☊	☿	♀	♂	⚳	♃	♄	♅	♆	♇
1 M	4 37 45	10♊28 40	28♋18 39	4♌14 00	9♈20.2	3♋10.5	18♉11.6	7♋23.0	2♑34.5	20♈53.5	18♐26.4	25♐20.1	7♑19.7	7♏42.9
2 Tu	4 41 42	11 26 11	10♌09 29	16 05 35	9R 14.7	4 27.2	19 24.5	8 01.9	2R 23.5	21 05.2	18R 22.0	25R 17.8	7R 18.2	7R 41.6
3 W	4 45 39	12 23 40	22 02 50	28 01 48	9 11.6	5 40.6	20 37.3	8 40.7	2 12.2	21 16.8	18 17.6	25 15.4	7 16.8	7 40.3
4 Th	4 49 35	13 21 08	4♍03 05	10♍07 17	9D 10.5	6 50.6	21 50.2	9 19.5	2 00.6	21 28.3	18 13.2	25 13.0	7 15.4	7 39.0
5 F	4 53 32	14 18 34	16 15 04	22 27 02	9 10.6	7 57.1	23 03.0	9 58.2	1 48.9	21 39.7	18 08.7	25 10.6	7 13.9	7 37.7
6 Sa	4 57 28	15 15 59	28 43 51	5♎06 06	9R 11.1	9 00.2	24 15.9	10 37.0	1 37.0	21 51.0	18 04.3	25 08.2	7 12.5	7 36.5
7 Su	5 01 25	16 13 23	11♎34 19	18 09 01	9 10.9	9 59.6	25 28.8	11 15.7	1 24.9	22 02.3	17 59.9	25 05.8	7 11.0	7 35.2
8 M	5 05 21	17 10 46	24 50 33	1♏39 11	9 08.9	10 55.4	26 41.7	11 54.4	1 12.6	22 13.4	17 55.4	25 03.4	7 09.5	7 34.0
9 Tu	5 09 18	18 08 08	8♏35 03	15 38 03	9 04.7	11 47.4	27 54.6	12 33.1	1 00.2	22 24.5	17 51.0	25 01.0	7 08.0	7 32.8
10 W	5 13 14	19 05 29	22 47 57	0♐04 16	8 58.0	12 35.7	29 07.6	13 11.8	0 47.6	22 35.4	17 46.5	24 58.5	7 06.5	7 31.7
11 Th	5 17 11	20 02 50	7♐26 18	14 53 12	8 49.2	13 19.9	0♊20.5	13 50.5	0 34.9	22 46.3	17 42.1	24 56.1	7 05.0	7 30.5
12 F	5 21 08	21 00 09	22 23 51	29 57 05	8 39.2	14 00.2	1 33.5	14 29.1	0 22.0	22 57.1	17 37.7	24 53.7	7 03.5	7 29.4
13 Sa	5 25 04	21 57 28	7♑31 34	15♑06 00	8 29.2	14 36.4	2 46.4	15 07.7	0 09.1	23 07.7	17 33.2	24 51.2	7 01.9	7 28.4
14 Su	5 29 01	22 54 46	22 39 05	0♒09 37	8 20.3	15 08.4	3 59.4	15 46.3	29♐56.1	23 18.3	17 28.8	24 48.8	7 00.4	7 27.3
15 M	5 32 57	23 52 04	7♒36 32	14 58 57	8 13.6	15 36.1	5 12.4	16 24.9	29 43.0	23 28.7	17 24.4	24 46.3	6 58.8	7 26.3
16 Tu	5 36 54	24 49 21	22 16 11	29 27 44	8 09.3	15 59.4	6 25.5	17 03.5	29 29.8	23 39.0	17 20.0	24 43.9	6 57.2	7 25.3
17 W	5 40 50	25 46 38	6♓33 20	13♓32 51	8D 07.3	16 18.2	7 38.5	17 42.1	29 16.6	23 49.3	17 15.7	24 41.4	6 55.7	7 24.3
18 Th	5 44 47	26 43 54	20 26 21	27 13 58	8R 06.9	16 32.6	8 51.6	18 20.6	29 03.3	23 59.4	17 11.3	24 39.0	6 54.1	7 23.3
19 F	5 48 43	27 41 11	3♈55 59	10♈32 45	8 07.0	16 42.4	10 04.6	18 59.1	28 50.0	24 09.4	17 07.0	24 36.5	6 52.5	7 22.4
20 Sa	5 52 40	28 38 27	17 04 37	23 32 01	8 06.3	16R 47.7	11 17.7	19 37.7	28 36.7	24 19.3	17 02.6	24 34.0	6 50.9	7 21.5
21 Su	5 56 37	29 35 43	29 55 21	6♉15 01	8 03.8	16 48.4	12 30.8	20 16.2	28 23.4	24 29.1	16 58.3	24 31.6	6 49.3	7 20.6
22 M	6 00 33	0♋32 58	12♉31 23	18 44 49	7 58.7	16 44.6	13 44.0	20 54.7	28 10.2	24 38.8	16 54.1	24 29.2	6 47.7	7 19.8
23 Tu	6 04 30	1 30 14	24 55 37	1♊04 04	7 50.8	16 36.4	14 57.1	21 33.2	27 57.0	24 48.4	16 49.8	24 26.7	6 46.1	7 19.0
24 W	6 08 26	2 27 29	7♊10 26	13 14 55	7 40.1	16 23.8	16 10.3	22 11.6	27 43.8	24 57.8	16 45.6	24 24.3	6 44.5	7 18.2
25 Th	6 12 23	3 24 44	19 17 42	25 18 57	7 27.4	16 07.2	17 23.4	22 50.1	27 30.7	25 07.1	16 41.5	24 21.9	6 42.9	7 17.5
26 F	6 16 19	4 21 59	1♋18 49	7♋17 29	7 13.6	15 46.6	18 36.6	23 28.5	27 17.6	25 16.3	16 37.3	24 19.5	6 41.2	7 16.7
27 Sa	6 20 16	5 19 14	13 15 03	19 11 44	6 59.9	15 22.5	19 49.9	24 07.0	27 04.7	25 25.4	16 33.2	24 17.1	6 39.6	7 16.0
28 Su	6 24 13	6 16 28	25 07 41	1♌03 08	6 47.3	14 55.1	21 03.1	24 45.4	26 51.9	25 34.3	16 29.2	24 14.7	6 38.0	7 15.4
29 M	6 28 09	7 13 42	6♌58 18	12 53 31	6 36.7	14 24.8	22 16.3	25 23.8	26 39.2	25 43.1	16 25.2	24 12.3	6 36.4	7 14.8
30 Tu	6 32 06	8 10 55	18 49 04	24 45 21	6 28.9	13 52.2	23 29.6	26 02.2	26 26.6	25 51.8	16 21.2	24 10.0	6 34.8	7 14.2

Astro Data

	Dy Hr Mn
☽ 0S	9 21:00
☽ 0N	22 14:37
♃△♄	23 12:26
☽ 0S	6 5:21
☽ 0N	18 19:24
☿ R	21 3:43
♃△♅	21 16:52

Planet Ingress

	Dy Hr Mn
☿ ♊	13 17:50
♀ ♉	17 11:56
♂ ♋	21 3:01
☉ ♊	21 14:10
☿ ♋	30 4:21
♀ ♊	11 5:15
⚳ ♐R	14 4:48
☉ ♋	21 22:11

Last Aspect / ☽ Ingress

Last Aspect Dy Hr Mn		☽ Ingress	Dy Hr Mn
2 0:21	♅ ☍	♋	2 7:39
3 13:14	♃ □	♌	4 20:06
7 0:38	♅ △	♍	7 8:07
9 10:18	♅ □	♎	9 17:29
11 16:19	♅ ⚹	♏	11 23:09
13 12:50	☉ ☍	♐	14 1:41
15 23:38	♀ △	♑	16 2:37
17 21:51	☉ △	♒	18 3:42
20 5:23	♂ △	♓	20 6:24
22 3:41	♅ □	♈	22 11:23
24 10:29	♅ △	♉	24 18:39
25 13:03	♀ ☌	♊	27 3:55
29 13:09	☿ ☌	♋	29 14:59

Last Aspect Dy Hr Mn		☽ Ingress	Dy Hr Mn
31 8:32	♃ □	♌	1 3:25
3 6:28	♅ △	♍	3 15:56
5 17:13	♅ □	♎	6 2:24
8 0:25	♅ ⚹	♏	8 9:06
10 10:18	♀ ☍	♐	10 11:53
12 4:00	♅ ☌	♑	12 12:05
14 0:55	♃ □	♒	14 11:45
16 4:07	♅ ⚹	♓	16 12:54
18 11:03	☉ □	♈	18 16:56
20 22:22	☉ ⚹	♉	21 0:09
22 16:25	♂ ⚹	♊	23 9:54
25 11:36	♃ ⚹	♋	25 21:22
28 0:45	♃ □	♌	28 9:52
30 14:16	♃ △	♍	30 22:34

☽ Phases & Eclipses

Dy Hr Mn	
6 2:26	☽ 15♌03
13 12:50	○ 22♏14
20 4:02	☾ 28♒38
27 15:13	● 5♊49
4 18:53	☽ 13♍38
11 20:49	○ 20♐24
18 11:03	☾ 26♓42
26 5:37	● 4♋07

Astro Data

1 May 1987
Julian Day # 31897
SVP 5♓26'16"
GC 26♐39.7 ⚵ 25♏17.0R
Eris 16♈27.5 ⚶ 25♒15.3
⚷ 18♊35.9 ⚴ 24♉43.5
☽ Mean ☊ 10♈06.7

1 June 1987
Julian Day # 31928
SVP 5♓26'11"
GC 26♐39.8 ⚵ 16♏23.4R
Eris 16♈43.9 ⚶ 2♓59.7
⚷ 21♊06.0 ⚴ 8♊12.9
☽ Mean ☊ 8♈28.3

July 1987 — LONGITUDE

Day	Sid.Time	☉	0 hr ☽	Noon ☽	True ☊	☿	♀	♂	⚳	♃	♄	♅	♆	♇
1 W	6 36 02	9♋08 08	0♍42 47	6♍41 50	6♈23.9	13♋17.7	24♊42.8	26♋40.6	26♐14.2	26♈00.3	16♐17.3	24♐07.6	6♑33.1	7♏13.6
2 Th	6 39 59	10 05 21	12 43 00	18 46 51	6R 21.4	12R 41.8	25 56.1	27 19.0	26R 01.9	26 08.7	16R 13.4	24R 05.3	6R 31.5	7R 13.1
3 F	6 43 55	11 02 33	24 53 57	1♎04 55	6 20.6	12 05.3	27 09.4	27 57.4	25 49.9	26 17.0	16 09.5	24 02.9	6 29.9	7 12.5
4 Sa	6 47 52	11 59 45	7♎20 22	13 40 55	6 20.6	11 28.7	28 22.8	28 35.7	25 38.0	26 25.1	16 05.8	24 00.6	6 28.3	7 12.1
5 Su	6 51 48	12 56 56	20 07 10	26 39 39	6 20.1	10 52.6	29 36.1	29 14.0	25 26.3	26 33.1	16 02.0	23 58.4	6 26.7	7 11.6
6 M	6 55 45	13 54 08	3♏18 53	10♏05 14	6 18.2	10 17.7	0♋49.4	29 52.4	25 14.8	26 41.0	15 58.4	23 56.1	6 25.1	7 11.2
7 Tu	6 59 42	14 51 19	16 58 59	24 00 14	6 14.0	9 44.5	2 02.8	0♌30.7	25 03.6	26 48.7	15 54.8	23 53.9	6 23.5	7 10.9
8 W	7 03 38	15 48 30	1♐08 54	8♐24 41	6 07.3	9 13.8	3 16.2	1 09.0	24 52.6	26 56.3	15 51.2	23 51.6	6 21.9	7 10.5
9 Th	7 07 35	16 45 41	15 47 05	23 15 18	5 58.5	8 45.9	4 29.6	1 47.3	24 41.8	27 03.7	15 47.7	23 49.4	6 20.3	7 10.2
10 F	7 11 31	17 42 52	0♑48 22	8♑25 05	5 48.3	8 21.4	5 43.0	2 25.6	24 31.3	27 11.0	15 44.3	23 47.3	6 18.7	7 09.9
11 Sa	7 15 28	18 40 03	16 04 08	23 44 02	5 38.0	8 00.8	6 56.5	3 03.9	24 21.0	27 18.2	15 40.9	23 45.1	6 17.1	7 09.7
12 Su	7 19 24	19 37 15	1♒23 22	9♒00 41	5 28.8	7 44.5	8 09.9	3 42.1	24 11.0	27 25.1	15 37.6	23 43.0	6 15.6	7 09.5
13 M	7 23 21	20 34 26	16 34 42	24 04 15	5 21.7	7 32.8	9 23.4	4 20.4	24 01.3	27 32.0	15 34.4	23 40.9	6 14.0	7 09.3
14 Tu	7 27 17	21 31 38	1♓28 24	8♓46 25	5 17.0	7D 26.0	10 36.9	4 58.6	23 51.9	27 38.7	15 31.2	23 38.8	6 12.4	7 09.2
15 W	7 31 14	22 28 51	15 57 49	23 02 19	5D 14.8	7 24.3	11 50.4	5 36.9	23 42.7	27 45.2	15 28.1	23 36.7	6 10.9	7 09.1
16 Th	7 35 11	23 26 04	29 59 50	6♈50 28	5 14.4	7 27.8	13 04.0	6 15.1	23 33.9	27 51.6	15 25.1	23 34.7	6 09.4	7 09.0
17 F	7 39 07	24 23 18	13♈34 27	20 12 07	5R 14.6	7 36.9	14 17.5	6 53.3	23 25.3	27 57.8	15 22.1	23 32.7	6 07.8	7D 08.9
18 Sa	7 43 04	25 20 32	26 43 53	3♉10 13	5 14.5	7 51.4	15 31.1	7 31.6	23 17.1	28 03.8	15 19.2	23 30.7	6 06.3	7 08.9
19 Su	7 47 00	26 17 47	9♉31 37	15 48 38	5 12.8	8 11.6	16 44.7	8 09.8	23 09.2	28 09.7	15 16.4	23 28.8	6 04.8	7 09.0
20 M	7 50 57	27 15 03	22 01 44	28 11 26	5 08.9	8 37.4	17 58.4	8 48.0	23 01.6	28 15.5	15 13.7	23 26.9	6 03.3	7 09.0
21 Tu	7 54 53	28 12 20	4♊18 12	10♊22 27	5 02.4	9 08.7	19 12.0	9 26.2	22 54.3	28 21.0	15 11.0	23 25.0	6 01.9	7 09.1
22 W	7 58 50	29 09 37	16 24 36	22 25 00	4 53.5	9 45.8	20 25.7	10 04.4	22 47.4	28 26.4	15 08.5	23 23.2	6 00.4	7 09.2
23 Th	8 02 46	0♌06 55	28 23 59	4♋21 50	4 42.8	10 28.4	21 39.4	10 42.7	22 40.8	28 31.7	15 06.0	23 21.4	5 59.0	7 09.4
24 F	8 06 43	1 04 14	10♋18 47	16 15 06	4 31.0	11 16.5	22 53.2	11 20.9	22 34.6	28 36.7	15 03.6	23 19.6	5 57.5	7 09.6
25 Sa	8 10 40	2 01 34	22 10 58	28 06 36	4 19.2	12 10.1	24 06.9	11 59.1	22 28.7	28 41.6	15 01.2	23 17.9	5 56.1	7 09.8
26 Su	8 14 36	2 58 54	4♌02 10	9♌57 52	4 08.4	13 09.1	25 20.7	12 37.2	22 23.1	28 46.3	14 59.0	23 16.2	5 54.7	7 10.1
27 M	8 18 33	3 56 14	15 53 55	21 50 31	3 59.5	14 13.4	26 34.5	13 15.4	22 18.0	28 50.8	14 56.8	23 14.5	5 53.3	7 10.4
28 Tu	8 22 29	4 53 36	27 47 55	3♍46 24	3 53.0	15 22.9	27 48.3	13 53.6	22 13.1	28 55.2	14 54.7	23 12.8	5 51.9	7 10.7
29 W	8 26 26	5 50 57	9♍46 15	15 47 48	3 49.0	16 37.5	29 02.1	14 31.8	22 08.7	28 59.4	14 52.7	23 11.2	5 50.6	7 11.1
30 Th	8 30 22	6 48 20	21 51 27	27 57 37	3D 47.2	17 57.0	0♌15.9	15 10.0	22 04.6	29 03.4	14 50.8	23 09.7	5 49.2	7 11.5
31 F	8 34 19	7 45 43	4♎06 44	10♎19 17	3 47.2	19 21.4	1 29.8	15 48.1	22 00.8	29 07.2	14 49.0	23 08.2	5 47.9	7 11.9

August 1987 — LONGITUDE

Day	Sid.Time	☉	0 hr ☽	Noon ☽	True ☊	☿	♀	♂	⚳	♃	♄	♅	♆	♇
1 Sa	8 38 15	8♌43 06	16♎35 46	22♎56 42	3♈48.1	20♋50.4	2♌43.7	16♌26.3	21♐57.4	29♈10.8	14♐47.3	23♐06.7	5♑46.6	7♏12.4
2 Su	8 42 12	9 40 31	29 22 36	5♏53 58	3R 48.8	22 23.9	3 57.6	17 04.5	21R 54.4	29 14.3	14R 45.6	23R 05.3	5R 45.3	7 12.9
3 M	8 46 09	10 37 56	12♏31 15	19 14 50	3 48.5	24 01.5	5 11.5	17 42.6	21 51.8	29 17.5	14 44.1	23 03.9	5 44.1	7 13.5
4 Tu	8 50 05	11 35 21	26 05 03	3♐02 04	3 46.5	25 43.1	6 25.4	18 20.8	21 49.5	29 20.6	14 42.6	23 02.5	5 42.8	7 14.0
5 W	8 54 02	12 32 47	10♐05 56	17 16 33	3 42.6	27 28.4	7 39.4	18 58.9	21 47.6	29 23.5	14 41.3	23 01.2	5 41.6	7 14.7
6 Th	8 57 58	13 30 14	24 33 34	1♑56 27	3 36.8	29 17.0	8 53.3	19 37.1	21 46.0	29 26.2	14 40.0	22 59.9	5 40.4	7 15.3
7 F	9 01 55	14 27 42	9♑24 30	16 56 44	3 30.0	1♌08.6	10 07.3	20 15.2	21 44.8	29 28.7	14 38.8	22 58.7	5 39.2	7 16.0
8 Sa	9 05 51	15 25 11	24 32 03	2♒09 12	3 22.8	3 02.8	11 21.3	20 53.4	21 44.0	29 31.0	14 37.7	22 57.5	5 38.1	7 16.7
9 Su	9 09 48	16 22 40	9♒46 50	17 23 37	3 16.4	4 59.3	12 35.4	21 31.5	21D 43.5	29 33.2	14 36.7	22 56.4	5 36.9	7 17.4
10 M	9 13 44	17 20 11	24 58 12	2♓29 23	3 11.5	6 57.7	13 49.4	22 09.7	21 43.4	29 35.1	14 35.8	22 55.3	5 35.8	7 18.2
11 Tu	9 17 41	18 17 42	9♓56 03	17 17 19	3 08.6	8 57.7	15 03.5	22 47.8	21 43.7	29 36.9	14 35.0	22 54.2	5 34.7	7 19.0
12 W	9 21 38	19 15 15	24 32 29	1♈41 02	3D 07.6	10 58.8	16 17.5	23 26.0	21 44.3	29 38.4	14 34.3	22 53.2	5 33.7	7 19.8
13 Th	9 25 34	20 12 50	8♈42 41	15 37 19	3 08.1	13 00.7	17 31.6	24 04.1	21 45.2	29 39.8	14 33.7	22 52.2	5 32.6	7 20.7
14 F	9 29 31	21 10 25	22 25 00	29 05 54	3 09.3	15 03.1	18 45.8	24 42.2	21 46.5	29 41.0	14 33.2	22 51.3	5 31.6	7 21.6
15 Sa	9 33 27	22 08 03	5♉40 22	12♉08 47	3R 10.6	17 05.7	19 59.9	25 20.4	21 48.1	29 41.9	14 32.7	22 50.4	5 30.6	7 22.6
16 Su	9 37 24	23 05 42	18 31 37	24 49 24	3 11.0	19 08.2	21 14.1	25 58.5	21 50.1	29 42.7	14 32.4	22 49.6	5 29.6	7 23.5
17 M	9 41 20	24 03 22	1♊02 39	7♊11 55	3 10.0	21 10.5	22 28.3	26 36.7	21 52.4	29 43.3	14 32.2	22 48.8	5 28.7	7 24.5
18 Tu	9 45 17	25 01 04	13 17 47	19 20 45	3 07.4	23 12.2	23 42.5	27 14.8	21 55.1	29 43.7	14D 32.1	22 48.1	5 27.8	7 25.6
19 W	9 49 13	25 58 48	25 21 21	1♋20 04	3 03.2	25 13.2	24 56.7	27 53.0	21 58.1	29R 43.8	14 32.0	22 47.4	5 26.9	7 26.6
20 Th	9 53 10	26 56 33	7♋17 22	13 13 40	2 57.7	27 13.4	26 11.0	28 31.2	22 01.5	29 43.8	14 32.1	22 46.8	5 26.0	7 27.7
21 F	9 57 07	27 54 20	19 09 22	25 04 49	2 51.5	29 12.6	27 25.2	29 09.3	22 05.2	29 43.6	14 32.2	22 46.2	5 25.2	7 28.9
22 Sa	10 01 03	28 52 08	1♌00 21	6♌56 14	2 45.2	1♍10.8	28 39.5	29 47.5	22 09.2	29 43.2	14 32.5	22 45.7	5 24.4	7 30.0
23 Su	10 05 00	29 49 58	12 52 46	18 50 09	2 39.5	3 07.9	29 53.8	0♍25.7	22 13.5	29 42.5	14 32.9	22 45.2	5 23.6	7 31.2
24 M	10 08 56	0♍47 49	24 48 39	0♍48 27	2 34.9	5 03.7	1♍08.1	1 03.9	22 18.2	29 41.7	14 33.3	22 44.8	5 22.8	7 32.4
25 Tu	10 12 53	1 45 42	6♍49 46	12 52 49	2 31.7	6 58.3	2 22.4	1 42.0	22 23.2	29 40.7	14 33.8	22 44.4	5 22.1	7 33.7
26 W	10 16 49	2 43 36	18 57 47	25 04 54	2D 30.1	8 51.7	3 36.8	2 20.2	22 28.5	29 39.4	14 34.5	22 44.0	5 21.4	7 35.0
27 Th	10 20 46	3 41 31	1♎14 24	7♎26 31	2 30.0	10 43.8	4 51.1	2 58.4	22 34.2	29 38.0	14 35.2	22 43.7	5 20.8	7 36.3
28 F	10 24 42	4 39 28	13 41 32	19 59 44	2 30.9	12 34.5	6 05.5	3 36.6	22 40.1	29 36.4	14 36.1	22 43.5	5 20.1	7 37.6
29 Sa	10 28 39	5 37 26	26 21 24	2♏46 52	2 32.4	14 24.0	7 19.9	4 14.8	22 46.4	29 34.5	14 37.0	22 43.3	5 19.5	7 39.0
30 Su	10 32 36	6 35 26	9♏16 25	15 50 22	2 34.0	16 12.2	8 34.3	4 53.0	22 52.9	29 32.5	14 38.1	22 43.2	5 18.9	7 40.4
31 M	10 36 32	7 33 27	22 29 01	29 12 36	2R 35.0	17 59.1	9 48.7	5 31.2	22 59.8	29 30.3	14 39.2	22 43.1	5 18.4	7 41.8

Astro Data

	Dy Hr Mn
☽0S	3 11:59
☿D	15 7:51
☽0N	16 1:33
♇D	18 6:11
☽0S	30 17:15
⚳D	10 7:56
♃⚼♄	10 18:20
☽0N	12 10:04
♄D	19 8:53
♃R	19 21:07
☽0S	26 22:26
♃⚼♄	28 14:44

Planet Ingress

		Dy Hr Mn
♀	♋	5 19:50
♂	♌	6 16:46
☉	♌	23 9:06
♀	♌	30 6:49
☿	♌	6 21:20
☿	♍	21 21:36
♂	♍	22 19:51
♀	♍	23 14:00
☉	♍	23 16:10

Last Aspect / ☽ Ingress (July)

Last Aspect Dy Hr Mn			☽ Ingress Dy Hr Mn
3 5:37	♂ ⚹	♎	3 9:55
5 17:52	♀ △	♏	5 18:03
6 19:10	☉ △	♐	7 22:05
9 18:07	♃ △	♑	9 22:43
11 17:38	♃ □	♒	11 21:49
13 17:38	♃ ⚹	♓	13 21:36
15 12:59	♅ □	♈	16 0:00
18 2:24	♃ ☌	♉	18 6:04
20 10:00	☉ ⚹	♊	20 15:33
23 0:10	♃ ⚹	♋	23 3:13
25 13:11	♃ □	♌	25 15:50
28 2:12	♃ △	♍	28 4:26
30 2:35	♅ □	♎	30 15:59

Last Aspect / ☽ Ingress (August)

Last Aspect Dy Hr Mn			☽ Ingress Dy Hr Mn
1 23:41	♃ ☍	♏	2 1:09
3 21:34	♃ △	♐	4 6:47
6 7:56	♃ △	♑	6 8:52
8 7:50	♃ □	♒	8 8:37
10 7:21	♃ ⚹	♓	10 8:01
11 21:16	♅ □	♈	12 9:09
14 13:04	♃ ☌	♉	14 13:38
16 14:20	♂ □	♊	16 21:59
19 8:46	♃ ⚹	♋	19 9:19
21 21:24	♃ □	♌	21 21:58
24 9:47	♃ △	♍	24 10:23
26 7:24	♅ □	♎	26 21:35
29 6:03	♃ ☍	♏	29 6:49
30 12:46	☿ ⚹	♐	31 13:24

☽ Phases & Eclipses

Dy Hr Mn		
4 8:34	☽	11♎52
11 3:33	○	18♑20
17 20:17	☾	24♈43
25 20:38	●	2♌22
2 19:24	☽	9♏58
9 10:17	○	16♒19
16 8:25	☾	22♉57
24 11:59	●	0♍48

Astro Data

1 July 1987
Julian Day # 31958
SVP 5♓26'05"
GC 26♐39.9 ⚴ 12♏27.4R
Eris 16♈52.3 ⚵ 6♓45.6
⚷ 23♊42.5 ⚶ 21♊09.0
☽ Mean ☊ 6♈53.0

1 August 1987
Julian Day # 31989
SVP 5♓26'00"
GC 26♐40.0 ⚴ 15♏09.6
Eris 16♈51.3R ⚵ 4♓52.9R
⚷ 26♊10.8 ⚶ 4♋07.2
☽ Mean ☊ 5♈14.5

LONGITUDE — September 1987

Day	Sid.Time	☉	0 hr ☽	Noon ☽	True ☊	☿	♀	♂	⚳	♃	♄	♅	♆	♇
1 Tu	10 40 29	8♍31 29	6♐01 20	12♐55 20	2♈35.1	19♍44.7	11♍03.1	6♍09.4	23♐07.0	29♈27.9	14♐40.4	22♐43.1	5♑17.9	7♏43.3
2 W	10 44 25	9 29 33	19 54 40	26 59 15	2R34.3	21 29.1	12 17.6	6 47.6	23 14.4	29R25.3	14 41.7	22D43.1	5R17.4	7 44.8
3 Th	10 48 22	10 27 38	4♑08 55	11♑23 19	2 32.4	23 12.2	13 32.0	7 25.8	23 22.2	29 22.5	14 43.2	22 43.2	5 16.9	7 46.3
4 F	10 52 18	11 25 45	18 42 00	26 04 21	2 29.9	24 54.1	14 46.5	8 04.0	23 30.2	29 19.5	14 44.7	22 43.3	5 16.5	7 47.8
5 Sa	10 56 15	12 23 53	3♒29 35	10♒56 50	2 27.3	26 34.7	16 00.9	8 42.2	23 38.5	29 16.3	14 46.3	22 43.5	5 16.1	7 49.4
6 Su	11 00 11	13 22 02	18 25 08	25 53 27	2 24.9	28 14.2	17 15.4	9 20.4	23 47.1	29 12.9	14 48.0	22 43.7	5 15.7	7 51.0
7 M	11 04 08	14 20 13	3♓20 43	10♓45 54	2 23.1	29 52.4	18 29.9	9 58.7	23 56.0	29 09.4	14 49.8	22 44.0	5 15.4	7 52.6
8 Tu	11 08 05	15 18 26	18 08 00	25 26 09	2D22.3	1♎29.5	19 44.4	10 36.9	24 05.2	29 05.6	14 51.7	22 44.3	5 15.1	7 54.3
9 W	11 12 01	16 16 40	2♈39 34	9♈47 37	2 22.3	3 05.4	20 58.9	11 15.1	24 14.6	29 01.7	14 53.7	22 44.6	5 14.8	7 55.9
10 Th	11 15 58	17 14 57	16 49 50	23 45 52	2 23.0	4 40.2	22 13.4	11 53.4	24 24.2	28 57.6	14 55.8	22 45.1	5 14.6	7 57.6
11 F	11 19 54	18 13 15	0♉35 34	7♉18 54	2 24.1	6 13.9	23 27.9	12 31.6	24 34.2	28 53.3	14 57.9	22 45.6	5 14.4	7 59.3
12 Sa	11 23 51	19 11 36	13 55 59	20 27 00	2 25.2	7 46.4	24 42.5	13 09.9	24 44.3	28 48.8	15 00.2	22 46.1	5 14.2	8 01.1
13 Su	11 27 47	20 09 59	26 52 18	3♊12 15	2 26.2	9 17.7	25 57.0	13 48.2	24 54.8	28 44.2	15 02.6	22 46.7	5 14.0	8 02.9
14 M	11 31 44	21 08 24	9♊27 19	15 38 01	2R26.7	10 48.0	27 11.6	14 26.4	25 05.5	28 39.4	15 05.0	22 47.3	5 13.9	8 04.7
15 Tu	11 35 40	22 06 51	21 44 52	27 48 26	2 26.7	12 17.1	28 26.2	15 04.7	25 16.4	28 34.4	15 07.6	22 48.0	5 13.9	8 06.5
16 W	11 39 37	23 05 20	3♋49 17	9♋48 00	2 26.2	13 45.1	29 40.7	15 43.0	25 27.6	28 29.3	15 10.2	22 48.7	5D13.8	8 08.3
17 Th	11 43 34	24 03 51	15 45 07	21 41 11	2 25.4	15 12.0	0♎55.3	16 21.3	25 39.0	28 23.9	15 12.9	22 49.5	5 13.8	8 10.2
18 F	11 47 30	25 02 24	27 36 45	3♌32 17	2 24.4	16 37.7	2 09.9	16 59.7	25 50.7	28 18.5	15 15.7	22 50.3	5 13.8	8 12.1
19 Sa	11 51 27	26 01 00	9♌28 15	15 25 06	2 23.5	18 02.2	3 24.6	17 38.0	26 02.6	28 12.8	15 18.6	22 51.2	5 13.9	8 14.0
20 Su	11 55 23	26 59 38	21 23 14	27 22 59	2 22.7	19 25.5	4 39.2	18 16.3	26 14.7	28 07.0	15 21.6	22 52.2	5 14.0	8 15.9
21 M	11 59 20	27 58 17	3♍24 42	9♍28 40	2 22.1	20 47.6	5 53.8	18 54.7	26 27.1	28 01.1	15 24.7	22 53.2	5 14.1	8 17.9
22 Tu	12 03 16	28 56 59	15 35 06	21 44 15	2D21.9	22 08.5	7 08.5	19 33.0	26 39.6	27 55.0	15 27.8	22 54.2	5 14.2	8 19.9
23 W	12 07 13	29 55 42	27 56 16	4♎11 19	2 21.8	23 28.0	8 23.1	20 11.4	26 52.4	27 48.8	15 31.1	22 55.3	5 14.4	8 21.9
24 Th	12 11 09	0♎54 28	10♎29 30	16 50 55	2 21.8	24 46.2	9 37.8	20 49.8	27 05.5	27 42.4	15 34.4	22 56.4	5 14.6	8 23.9
25 F	12 15 06	1 53 15	23 15 38	29 43 43	2R21.9	26 03.0	10 52.4	21 28.2	27 18.7	27 35.9	15 37.8	22 57.6	5 14.9	8 25.9
26 Sa	12 19 03	2 52 05	6♏15 12	12♏50 07	2 21.9	27 18.3	12 07.1	22 06.6	27 32.1	27 29.3	15 41.3	22 58.8	5 15.2	8 28.0
27 Su	12 22 59	3 50 56	19 28 29	26 10 17	2 21.8	28 32.1	13 21.8	22 45.0	27 45.8	27 22.5	15 44.9	23 00.1	5 15.5	8 30.0
28 M	12 26 56	4 49 49	2♐55 33	9♐44 13	2 21.6	29 44.2	14 36.4	23 23.4	27 59.7	27 15.7	15 48.6	23 01.5	5 15.8	8 32.1
29 Tu	12 30 52	5 48 44	16 36 17	23 31 39	2D21.4	0♏54.5	15 51.1	24 01.8	28 13.7	27 08.7	15 52.3	23 02.9	5 16.2	8 34.3
30 W	12 34 49	6 47 41	0♑30 15	7♑31 56	2 21.3	2 03.1	17 05.8	24 40.2	28 28.0	27 01.6	15 56.2	23 04.3	5 16.7	8 36.4

LONGITUDE — October 1987

Day	Sid.Time	☉	0 hr ☽	Noon ☽	True ☊	☿	♀	♂	⚳	♃	♄	♅	♆	♇
1 Th	12 38 45	7♎46 39	14♑36 31	21♑43 46	2♈21.5	3♏09.6	18♎20.5	25♍18.7	28♐42.4	26♈54.4	16♐00.1	23♐05.8	5♑17.1	8♏38.5
2 F	12 42 42	8 45 39	28 53 24	6♒05 04	2 21.9	4 14.0	19 35.1	25 57.1	28 57.1	26R47.1	16 04.1	23 07.3	5 17.6	8 40.7
3 Sa	12 46 38	9 44 41	13♒18 19	20 32 40	2 22.5	5 16.1	20 49.8	26 35.6	29 11.9	26 39.7	16 08.1	23 08.9	5 18.1	8 42.9
4 Su	12 50 35	10 43 44	27 47 36	5♓02 30	2 23.1	6 15.7	22 04.5	27 14.1	29 26.9	26 32.2	16 12.3	23 10.5	5 18.7	8 45.1
5 M	12 54 32	11 42 49	12♓16 43	19 29 38	2R23.7	7 12.7	23 19.2	27 52.5	29 42.1	26 24.7	16 16.5	23 12.2	5 19.2	8 47.3
6 Tu	12 58 28	12 41 56	26 40 32	3♈48 49	2 23.9	8 06.7	24 33.8	28 31.0	29 57.5	26 17.0	16 20.8	23 13.9	5 19.9	8 49.5
7 W	13 02 25	13 41 05	10♈53 50	17 55 03	2 23.5	8 57.5	25 48.5	29 09.5	0♑13.1	26 09.3	16 25.1	23 15.7	5 20.5	8 51.7
8 Th	13 06 21	14 40 17	24 51 57	1♉44 09	2 22.6	9 44.8	27 03.2	29 48.0	0 28.8	26 01.5	16 29.6	23 17.5	5 21.2	8 54.0
9 F	13 10 18	15 39 30	8♉31 19	15 13 15	2 21.0	10 28.4	28 17.9	0♎26.6	0 44.7	25 53.7	16 34.1	23 19.3	5 21.9	8 56.2
10 Sa	13 14 14	16 38 46	21 49 52	28 21 09	2 19.1	11 07.7	29 32.6	1 05.1	1 00.7	25 45.8	16 38.7	23 21.2	5 22.6	8 58.5
11 Su	13 18 11	17 38 04	4♊47 13	11♊08 15	2 17.0	11 42.6	0♏47.3	1 43.7	1 17.0	25 37.8	16 43.3	23 23.2	5 23.4	9 00.8
12 M	13 22 07	18 37 24	17 24 33	23 36 28	2 15.1	12 12.5	2 02.0	2 22.2	1 33.4	25 29.9	16 48.1	23 25.2	5 24.2	9 03.1
13 Tu	13 26 04	19 36 46	29 44 26	5♋48 55	2 13.7	12 36.9	3 16.7	3 00.8	1 49.9	25 21.8	16 52.9	23 27.2	5 25.1	9 05.4
14 W	13 30 01	20 36 11	11♋50 28	17 49 38	2D13.1	12 55.4	4 31.4	3 39.4	2 06.6	25 13.8	16 57.7	23 29.3	5 25.9	9 07.8
15 Th	13 33 57	21 35 38	23 47 00	29 43 10	2 13.3	13 07.5	5 46.1	4 18.0	2 23.5	25 05.7	17 02.7	23 31.4	5 26.9	9 10.1
16 F	13 37 54	22 35 08	5♌38 44	11♌34 19	2 14.2	13R12.6	7 00.8	4 56.7	2 40.5	24 57.6	17 07.7	23 33.6	5 27.8	9 12.4
17 Sa	13 41 50	23 34 39	17 30 31	23 27 54	2 15.8	13 10.3	8 15.5	5 35.3	2 57.7	24 49.5	17 12.7	23 35.8	5 28.8	9 14.8
18 Su	13 45 47	24 34 13	29 27 01	5♍28 23	2 17.5	13 00.1	9 30.2	6 14.0	3 15.0	24 41.4	17 17.9	23 38.0	5 29.7	9 17.1
19 M	13 49 43	25 33 49	11♍32 30	17 39 47	2 18.9	12 41.5	10 44.9	6 52.6	3 32.5	24 33.2	17 23.1	23 40.3	5 30.8	9 19.5
20 Tu	13 53 40	26 33 27	23 50 36	0♎05 18	2R19.6	12 14.2	11 59.6	7 31.3	3 50.1	24 25.1	17 28.3	23 42.6	5 31.8	9 21.9
21 W	13 57 36	27 33 07	6♎24 06	12 47 11	2 19.2	11 38.2	13 14.4	8 10.0	4 07.8	24 17.0	17 33.7	23 45.0	5 32.9	9 24.3
22 Th	14 01 33	28 32 50	19 14 40	25 46 32	2 17.5	10 53.5	14 29.1	8 48.7	4 25.7	24 08.9	17 39.0	23 47.4	5 34.0	9 26.7
23 F	14 05 29	29 32 34	2♏22 45	9♏03 10	2 14.4	10 00.4	15 43.8	9 27.4	4 43.8	24 00.9	17 44.5	23 49.9	5 35.2	9 29.1
24 Sa	14 09 26	0♏32 21	15 47 36	22 35 45	2 10.4	8 59.7	16 58.5	10 06.2	5 02.0	23 52.8	17 50.0	23 52.4	5 36.4	9 31.5
25 Su	14 13 23	1 32 09	29 27 18	6♐21 54	2 05.8	7 52.5	18 13.2	10 44.9	5 20.3	23 44.8	17 55.6	23 54.9	5 37.6	9 33.9
26 M	14 17 19	2 31 59	13♐19 08	20 18 38	2 01.3	6 40.2	19 28.0	11 23.7	5 38.7	23 36.9	18 01.2	23 57.5	5 38.8	9 36.3
27 Tu	14 21 16	3 31 51	27 19 57	4♑22 44	1 57.5	5 24.7	20 42.7	12 02.5	5 57.3	23 29.0	18 06.9	24 00.1	5 40.1	9 38.7
28 W	14 25 12	4 31 45	11♑26 35	18 31 10	1 55.0	4 08.1	21 57.4	12 41.3	6 16.0	23 21.2	18 12.6	24 02.7	5 41.4	9 41.1
29 Th	14 29 09	5 31 40	25 36 12	2♒41 22	1D53.9	2 52.7	23 12.1	13 20.1	6 34.8	23 13.4	18 18.4	24 05.4	5 42.7	9 43.6
30 F	14 33 05	6 31 37	9♒46 28	16 51 15	1 54.3	1 40.8	24 26.8	13 58.9	6 53.7	23 05.7	18 24.2	24 08.1	5 44.1	9 46.0
31 Sa	14 37 02	7 31 35	23 55 32	0♓59 06	1 55.6	0 34.9	25 41.5	14 37.7	7 12.8	22 58.1	18 30.1	24 10.8	5 45.4	9 48.4

Astro Data Dy Hr Mn	Planet Ingress Dy Hr Mn	Last Aspect Dy Hr Mn	☽ Ingress Dy Hr Mn	Last Aspect Dy Hr Mn	☽ Ingress Dy Hr Mn	☽ Phases & Eclipses Dy Hr Mn
♅∠♇ 1 8:32	☿ ♎ 7 13:52	2 16:05 ♃ △	♑ 2 17:04	1 20:37 ♃ □	♒ 2 1:51	1 3:48 ☽ 8♐12
♅D 1 14:23	♀ ♎ 16 18:12	4 17:15 ♃ □	♒ 4 18:22	3 22:02 ♃ ✱	♓ 4 3:39	7 18:13 ○ 14♓35
☿0S 8 2:06	☉ ♎ 23 13:45	6 17:20 ♃ ✱	♓ 6 18:37	6 2:40 ♂ ☍	♈ 6 5:35	14 23:44 ☾ 21♊37
☽0N 8 20:16	☿ ♏ 28 17:21	8 7:33 ♅ □	♈ 8 19:34	8 3:00 ♀ ☍	♉ 8 8:57	23 3:08 ● 29♍34
♆D 17 8:23		10 21:04 ♃ ☌	♉ 10 22:57	9 3:00 ☿ ☍	♊ 10 15:03	23 3:11:26 ● A 03'49"
♀0S 19 3:20	⚳ ♑ 6 15:52	12 20:47 ♀ △	♊ 13 5:54	12 15:39 ♃ ✱	♋ 13 0:31	30 10:39 ☽ 6♑44
☽0S 23 4:46	♂ ♎ 8 19:27	15 13:31 ♃ ✱	♋ 15 16:22	15 2:45 ♃ □	♌ 15 12:34	
☉0S 23 13:45	♀ ♏ 10 20:49	18 1:29 ♃ □	♌ 18 4:50	17 14:42 ♃ △	♍ 18 1:06	7 4:12 ○ 13♈22
	☉ ♏ 23 23:01	20 13:27 ♃ △	♍ 20 17:13	19 23:42 ♅ □	♎ 20 11:50	7 4:02 ◐ A 0.987
☽0N 6 6:17		23 3:08 ☉ ☌	♎ 23 3:58	22 17:28 ☉ ☌	♏ 22 19:41	14 18:06 ☾ 20♋51
♂0S 12 8:49		25 8:06 ♃ ☍	♏ 25 12:30	24 1:05 ♀ ☌	♐ 25 0:57	22 17:28 ● 28♎46
☿R 16 16:46		27 5:34 ♂ ✱	♐ 27 18:49	26 18:15 ♅ ☌	♑ 27 4:33	29 17:10 ☽ 5♒45
☽0S 20 12:36		29 18:11 ♃ △	♑ 29 23:08	28 20:07 ♃ □	♒ 29 7:27	
♃△♅ 24 13:04				31 2:08 ♀ □	♓ 31 10:19	

Astro Data

1 September 1987
Julian Day # 32020
SVP 5♓25'56"
GC 26♐40.0 ⚴ 22♏35.4
Eris 16♈40.8R ⚵ 27♒56.2R
⚷ 28♊00.2 ⚶ 16♋18.6
☽ Mean ☊ 3♈36.0

1 October 1987
Julian Day # 32050
SVP 5♓25'52"
GC 26♐40.1 ⚴ 2♐22.7
Eris 16♈24.6R ⚵ 22♒43.7R
⚷ 28♊48.2 ⚶ 26♋45.9
☽ Mean ☊ 2♈00.7

November 1987 LONGITUDE

Day	Sid.Time	☉	0 hr ☽	Noon ☽	True ☊	☿	♀	♂	⚳	♃	♄	♅	♆	♇
1 Su	14 40 58	8♏31 35	8♓01 45	15♓03 18	1♈57.0	29♎36.7	26♏56.2	15♎16.5	7♑31.9	22♈50.6	18♐36.1	24♐13.6	5♑46.8	9♏50.9
2 M	14 44 55	9 31 37	22 03 31	29 02 09	1R57.9	28R47.9	28 10.9	15 55.4	7 51.2	22R43.1	18 42.1	24 16.4	5 48.3	9 53.3
3 Tu	14 48 52	10 31 40	5♈58 56	12♈53 35	1 57.4	28 09.8	29 25.6	16 34.2	8 10.6	22 35.8	18 48.1	24 19.3	5 49.7	9 55.7
4 W	14 52 48	11 31 45	19 45 49	26 35 17	1 55.1	27 43.0	0♐40.2	17 13.1	8 30.1	22 28.5	18 54.2	24 22.1	5 51.2	9 58.1
5 Th	14 56 45	12 31 51	3♉21 42	10♉04 46	1 50.7	27D27.8	1 54.9	17 52.0	8 49.7	22 21.3	19 00.3	24 25.0	5 52.7	10 00.6
6 F	15 00 41	13 32 00	16 44 13	23 19 48	1 44.4	27 24.2	3 09.6	18 30.9	9 09.4	22 14.3	19 06.5	24 28.0	5 54.3	10 03.0
7 Sa	15 04 38	14 32 10	29 51 23	6♊18 48	1 36.9	27 31.7	4 24.3	19 09.9	9 29.2	22 07.4	19 12.7	24 31.0	5 55.8	10 05.4
8 Su	15 08 34	15 32 23	12♊42 02	19 01 06	1 28.8	27 49.8	5 38.9	19 48.8	9 49.2	22 00.5	19 19.0	24 34.0	5 57.4	10 07.9
9 M	15 12 31	16 32 37	25 16 08	1♋27 17	1 21.0	28 17.6	6 53.6	20 27.8	10 09.2	21 53.8	19 25.3	24 37.0	5 59.0	10 10.3
10 Tu	15 16 28	17 32 53	7♋34 49	13 39 06	1 14.4	28 54.4	8 08.2	21 06.7	10 29.3	21 47.3	19 31.6	24 40.1	6 00.7	10 12.7
11 W	15 20 24	18 33 11	19 40 30	25 39 30	1 09.5	29 39.3	9 22.9	21 45.7	10 49.5	21 40.8	19 38.0	24 43.1	6 02.3	10 15.1
12 Th	15 24 21	19 33 31	1♌36 37	7♌32 25	1 06.6	0♏31.3	10 37.6	22 24.7	11 09.9	21 34.5	19 44.5	24 46.3	6 04.0	10 17.5
13 F	15 28 17	20 33 53	13 27 30	19 22 29	1D05.6	1 29.6	11 52.2	23 03.8	11 30.3	21 28.4	19 50.9	24 49.4	6 05.7	10 19.9
14 Sa	15 32 14	21 34 17	25 18 01	1♍14 47	1 06.0	2 33.3	13 06.9	23 42.8	11 50.8	21 22.4	19 57.4	24 52.6	6 07.4	10 22.3
15 Su	15 36 10	22 34 43	7♍13 26	13 14 38	1 07.2	3 41.9	14 21.5	24 21.9	12 11.4	21 16.5	20 04.0	24 55.8	6 09.2	10 24.7
16 M	15 40 07	23 35 10	19 19 00	25 27 09	1R08.2	4 54.6	15 36.1	25 01.0	12 32.1	21 10.8	20 10.6	24 59.0	6 10.9	10 27.1
17 Tu	15 44 03	24 35 40	1♎39 38	7♎56 56	1 08.1	6 10.7	16 50.8	25 40.1	12 52.9	21 05.3	20 17.2	25 02.2	6 12.7	10 29.5
18 W	15 48 00	25 36 11	14 19 29	20 47 37	1 06.1	7 29.9	18 05.4	26 19.2	13 13.7	20 59.9	20 23.8	25 05.5	6 14.6	10 31.9
19 Th	15 51 56	26 36 44	27 21 31	4♏01 18	1 01.8	8 51.6	19 20.1	26 58.3	13 34.7	20 54.6	20 30.5	25 08.8	6 16.4	10 34.2
20 F	15 55 53	27 37 19	10♏46 54	17 38 10	0 54.9	10 15.4	20 34.7	27 37.4	13 55.7	20 49.6	20 37.2	25 12.1	6 18.2	10 36.6
21 Sa	15 59 50	28 37 55	24 34 45	1♐36 11	0 46.2	11 41.1	21 49.3	28 16.6	14 16.9	20 44.7	20 43.9	25 15.4	6 20.1	10 38.9
22 Su	16 03 46	29 38 33	8♐41 52	15 51 07	0 36.2	13 08.2	23 03.9	28 55.8	14 38.1	20 40.0	20 50.7	25 18.8	6 22.0	10 41.3
23 M	16 07 43	0♐39 12	23 03 09	0♑17 08	0 26.4	14 36.5	24 18.6	29 35.0	14 59.4	20 35.5	20 57.5	25 22.2	6 23.9	10 43.6
24 Tu	16 11 39	1 39 52	7♑32 13	14 47 37	0 17.6	16 05.9	25 33.2	0♏14.2	15 20.7	20 31.2	21 04.3	25 25.6	6 25.9	10 45.9
25 W	16 15 36	2 40 34	22 02 33	29 16 22	0 11.0	17 36.1	26 47.8	0 53.4	15 42.2	20 27.0	21 11.2	25 29.0	6 27.8	10 48.2
26 Th	16 19 32	3 41 17	6♒28 29	13♒38 26	0 06.9	19 07.0	28 02.4	1 32.6	16 03.7	20 23.1	21 18.0	25 32.4	6 29.8	10 50.5
27 F	16 23 29	4 42 00	20 45 52	27 50 33	0D05.2	20 38.5	29 17.0	2 11.9	16 25.3	20 19.3	21 24.9	25 35.8	6 31.8	10 52.8
28 Sa	16 27 26	5 42 45	4♓52 20	11♓51 10	0 05.1	22 10.4	0♑31.5	2 51.1	16 46.9	20 15.7	21 31.8	25 39.3	6 33.8	10 55.1
29 Su	16 31 22	6 43 30	18 47 04	25 40 02	0R05.6	23 42.7	1 46.1	3 30.4	17 08.7	20 12.4	21 38.8	25 42.8	6 35.8	10 57.3
30 M	16 35 19	7 44 17	2♈30 11	9♈17 34	0 05.3	25 15.2	3 00.6	4 09.7	17 30.5	20 09.2	21 45.7	25 46.3	6 37.8	10 59.5

December 1987 LONGITUDE

Day	Sid.Time	☉	0 hr ☽	Noon ☽	True ☊	☿	♀	♂	⚳	♃	♄	♅	♆	♇
1 Tu	16 39 15	8♐45 04	16♈02 15	22♈44 19	0♈03.2	26♏48.0	4♑15.2	4♏49.0	17♑52.3	20♈06.2	21♐52.7	25♐49.8	6♑39.9	11♏01.8
2 W	16 43 12	9 45 53	29 23 47	6♉00 39	29♓58.3	28 20.9	5 29.7	5 28.3	18 14.2	20R03.4	21 59.7	25 53.3	6 42.0	11 04.0
3 Th	16 47 08	10 46 42	12♉34 52	19 06 25	29R50.5	29 54.0	6 44.2	6 07.6	18 36.2	20 00.8	22 06.7	25 56.8	6 44.0	11 06.2
4 F	16 51 05	11 47 33	25 35 11	2♊01 07	29 39.9	1♐27.2	7 58.7	6 47.0	18 58.3	19 58.4	22 13.7	26 00.4	6 46.1	11 08.3
5 Sa	16 55 01	12 48 24	8♊24 07	14 44 06	29 27.3	3 00.5	9 13.2	7 26.3	19 20.4	19 56.3	22 20.7	26 04.0	6 48.2	11 10.5
6 Su	16 58 58	13 49 17	21 01 01	27 14 52	29 13.6	4 33.8	10 27.6	8 05.7	19 42.5	19 54.3	22 27.7	26 07.5	6 50.4	11 12.6
7 M	17 02 55	14 50 11	3♋25 38	9♋33 26	29 00.2	6 07.2	11 42.1	8 45.1	20 04.8	19 52.5	22 34.8	26 11.1	6 52.5	11 14.8
8 Tu	17 06 51	15 51 06	15 38 22	21 40 40	28 48.2	7 40.7	12 56.5	9 24.5	20 27.0	19 51.0	22 41.8	26 14.7	6 54.6	11 16.9
9 W	17 10 48	16 52 02	27 40 33	3♌38 23	28 38.4	9 14.2	14 10.9	10 04.0	20 49.4	19 49.6	22 48.9	26 18.3	6 56.8	11 18.9
10 Th	17 14 44	17 52 59	9♌34 31	15 29 26	28 31.4	10 47.8	15 25.4	10 43.4	21 11.8	19 48.5	22 56.0	26 21.9	6 59.0	11 21.0
11 F	17 18 41	18 53 57	21 23 37	27 17 37	28 27.2	12 21.4	16 39.7	11 22.9	21 34.2	19 47.5	23 03.1	26 25.5	7 01.1	11 23.1
12 Sa	17 22 37	19 54 56	3♍12 04	9♍07 35	28D25.4	13 55.1	17 54.1	12 02.4	21 56.7	19 46.8	23 10.2	26 29.1	7 03.3	11 25.1
13 Su	17 26 34	20 55 56	15 04 51	21 04 33	28R25.0	15 28.8	19 08.5	12 41.9	22 19.3	19 46.3	23 17.3	26 32.7	7 05.5	11 27.1
14 M	17 30 30	21 56 58	27 07 24	3♎14 05	28 25.0	17 02.6	20 22.8	13 21.4	22 41.9	19 45.9	23 24.4	26 36.4	7 07.7	11 29.1
15 Tu	17 34 27	22 58 00	9♎25 17	15 41 39	28 24.1	18 36.6	21 37.2	14 01.0	23 04.5	19D45.8	23 31.5	26 40.0	7 09.9	11 31.0
16 W	17 38 24	23 59 03	22 03 46	28 32 10	28 21.3	20 10.6	22 51.5	14 40.5	23 27.2	19 45.9	23 38.6	26 43.6	7 12.1	11 33.0
17 Th	17 42 20	25 00 08	5♏07 14	11♏49 17	28 15.9	21 44.7	24 05.8	15 20.1	23 49.9	19 46.2	23 45.7	26 47.3	7 14.4	11 34.9
18 F	17 46 17	26 01 13	18 38 27	25 34 40	28 07.7	23 19.0	25 20.1	15 59.7	24 12.7	19 46.8	23 52.8	26 50.9	7 16.6	11 36.8
19 Sa	17 50 13	27 02 19	2♐37 43	9♐47 11	27 57.0	24 53.4	26 34.4	16 39.3	24 35.6	19 47.5	23 59.9	26 54.5	7 18.8	11 38.7
20 Su	17 54 10	28 03 26	17 02 24	24 22 34	27 44.9	26 27.9	27 48.6	17 18.9	24 58.5	19 48.4	24 07.0	26 58.2	7 21.1	11 40.5
21 M	17 58 06	29 04 34	1♑46 41	9♑13 39	27 32.6	28 02.7	29 02.9	17 58.5	25 21.4	19 49.6	24 14.1	27 01.8	7 23.3	11 42.3
22 Tu	18 02 03	0♑05 42	16 42 16	24 11 20	27 21.5	29 37.6	0♒17.1	18 38.2	25 44.4	19 51.0	24 21.1	27 05.5	7 25.6	11 44.1
23 W	18 06 00	1 06 50	1♒39 40	9♒06 13	27 12.9	1♑12.7	1 31.3	19 17.9	26 07.4	19 52.5	24 28.2	27 09.1	7 27.9	11 45.9
24 Th	18 09 56	2 07 58	16 30 00	23 50 14	27 07.1	2 48.0	2 45.4	19 57.5	26 30.4	19 54.3	24 35.3	27 12.7	7 30.1	11 47.7
25 F	18 13 53	3 09 07	1♓06 18	8♓17 46	27 04.2	4 23.6	3 59.5	20 37.2	26 53.5	19 56.3	24 42.3	27 16.4	7 32.4	11 49.4
26 Sa	18 17 49	4 10 15	15 24 20	22 25 55	27 03.3	5 59.4	5 13.6	21 16.9	27 16.6	19 58.5	24 49.4	27 20.0	7 34.7	11 51.1
27 Su	18 21 46	5 11 23	29 22 30	6♈14 12	27 03.3	7 35.4	6 27.7	21 56.6	27 39.7	20 00.9	24 56.4	27 23.6	7 36.9	11 52.7
28 M	18 25 42	6 12 32	13♈01 14	19 43 49	27 02.7	9 11.7	7 41.7	22 36.4	28 02.9	20 03.4	25 03.4	27 27.2	7 39.2	11 54.4
29 Tu	18 29 39	7 13 40	26 22 14	2♉56 47	27 00.4	10 48.3	8 55.7	23 16.1	28 26.1	20 06.2	25 10.4	27 30.8	7 41.5	11 56.0
30 W	18 33 35	8 14 49	9♉27 45	15 55 22	26 55.5	12 25.2	10 09.7	23 55.8	28 49.3	20 09.2	25 17.4	27 34.4	7 43.7	11 57.6
31 Th	18 37 32	9 15 57	22 19 54	28 41 33	26 47.5	14 02.3	11 23.6	24 35.6	29 12.6	20 12.4	25 24.4	27 38.0	7 46.0	11 59.1

Astro Data	Planet Ingress	Last Aspect	☽ Ingress	Last Aspect	☽ Ingress	☽ Phases & Eclipses	Astro Data
Dy Hr Mn	Dy Hr Mn	Dy Hr Mn	Dy Hr Mn	Dy Hr Mn	Dy Hr Mn	Dy Hr Mn	1 November 1987
☽0N 2 14:15	☿ ♎R 1 1:57	2 10:23 ♀ △	♈ 2 13:40	1 17:35 ♅ △	♉ 2 1:06	5 16:46 ○ 12♉44	Julian Day # 32081
☿D 6 7:38	♀ ♐ 3 23:04	4 13:57 ☿ ☍	♉ 4 18:02	2 21:15 ♇ ☍	♊ 4 8:13	13 14:38 ☾ 20♌41	SVP 5♓25'48"
♇0S 12 23:20	☿ ♏ 11 21:57	5 16:46 ☉ ☍	♊ 7 0:16	6 9:49 ♅ ☍	♋ 6 17:20	21 6:33 ● 28♏24	GC 26♐40.2 ⚵ 13♐57.6
☽0S 16 21:11	☉ ♐ 22 20:29	9 5:35 ☿ △	♋ 9 9:10	8 8:22 ♃ □	♌ 9 4:40	28 0:37 ☽ 5♓14	Eris 16♈06.2R ⚴ 24♒09.5
♃△♄ 21 13:39	♂ ♏ 24 3:19	11 20:39 ☿ □	♌ 11 20:45	11 10:14 ♅ △	♍ 11 17:30		⚷ 28♊25.6R ⚶ 5♌04.6
☽0N 29 19:38	♀ ♑ 28 1:51	13 23:05 ♅ △	♍ 14 9:29	13 22:55 ♅ □	♎ 14 5:40	5 8:01 ○ 12♊38	☽ Mean ☊ 0♈22.2
		16 11:05 ♅ □	♎ 16 20:48	16 8:39 ♅ ⚹	♏ 16 14:41	13 11:41 ☾ 20♍55	
♅∠♇ 9 22:20	☊ ♓R 2 5:13	18 22:38 ♂ ☌	♏ 19 4:47	18 11:32 ♀ ⚹	♐ 18 19:33	20 18:25 ● 28♐20	1 December 1987
☽0S 14 5:08	☿ ♐ 3 13:33	21 6:33 ☉ ☌	♐ 21 9:16	20 18:25 ☉ ☌	♑ 20 21:08	27 10:01 ☽ 5♈06	Julian Day # 32111
♃D 15 12:22	♀ ♒ 22 6:29	23 10:47 ♂ ⚹	♑ 23 11:32	22 5:02 ♃ □	♒ 22 21:20		SVP 5♓25'43"
☽0N 27 0:13	☉ ♑ 22 9:46	24 21:26 ♃ □	♒ 25 13:13	24 17:35 ♅ ⚹	♓ 24 22:10		GC 26♐40.2 ⚵ 25♐51.0
	☿ ♑ 22 17:40	27 14:41 ♀ ⚹	♓ 27 15:40	26 20:30 ♅ □	♈ 27 1:05		Eris 15♈52.1R ⚴ 1♓40.7
		29 12:05 ♅ □	♈ 29 19:36	29 2:02 ♅ △	♉ 29 6:37		⚷ 27♊02.0R ⚶ 8♌54.6
				31 3:50 ♂ ☍	♊ 31 14:29		☽ Mean ☊ 28♓46.9

LONGITUDE — January 1988

Day	Sid.Time	☉	0 hr ☽	Noon ☽	True ☊	☿	♀	♂	⚳	♃	♄	♅	♆	♇
1 F	18 41 29	10♑17 05	5♊00 29	11♊16 51	26♓36.7	15♑39.7	12♒37.5	25♏15.4	29♑35.9	20♈15.8	25♐31.4	27♐41.6	7♑48.3	12♏00.7
2 Sa	18 45 25	11 18 14	17 30 45	23 42 17	26R 23.8	17 17.4	13 51.4	25 55.2	29 59.2	20 19.4	25 38.3	27 45.1	7 50.6	12 02.2
3 Su	18 49 22	12 19 22	29 51 33	5♋58 35	26 09.9	18 55.4	15 05.2	26 35.0	0♒22.6	20 23.1	25 45.2	27 48.7	7 52.8	12 03.6
4 M	18 53 18	13 20 30	12♋03 30	18 06 21	25 56.0	20 33.6	16 19.0	27 14.9	0 45.9	20 27.1	25 52.1	27 52.2	7 55.1	12 05.1
5 Tu	18 57 15	14 21 38	24 07 16	0♌06 22	25 43.5	22 12.1	17 32.7	27 54.7	1 09.3	20 31.3	25 59.0	27 55.8	7 57.4	12 06.5
6 W	19 01 11	15 22 47	6♌03 52	11 59 58	25 33.2	23 50.8	18 46.4	28 34.6	1 32.8	20 35.6	26 05.8	27 59.3	7 59.6	12 07.9
7 Th	19 05 08	16 23 55	17 54 55	23 49 05	25 25.7	25 29.7	20 00.0	29 14.4	1 56.2	20 40.1	26 12.7	28 02.8	8 01.9	12 09.2
8 F	19 09 04	17 25 03	29 42 47	5♍36 29	25 21.1	27 08.7	21 13.7	29 54.3	2 19.7	20 44.9	26 19.5	28 06.3	8 04.1	12 10.5
9 Sa	19 13 01	18 26 11	11♍30 39	17 25 48	25D 19.0	28 47.9	22 27.2	0♐34.3	2 43.1	20 49.8	26 26.2	28 09.8	8 06.4	12 11.8
10 Su	19 16 58	19 27 19	23 22 30	29 21 22	25 18.8	0♒27.0	23 40.7	1 14.2	3 06.6	20 54.8	26 33.0	28 13.2	8 08.6	12 13.0
11 M	19 20 54	20 28 28	5♎23 02	11♎28 10	25R 19.4	2 06.0	24 54.2	1 54.1	3 30.2	21 00.1	26 39.7	28 16.7	8 10.9	12 14.3
12 Tu	19 24 51	21 29 36	17 37 27	23 51 32	25 19.6	3 44.9	26 07.6	2 34.1	3 53.7	21 05.5	26 46.4	28 20.1	8 13.1	12 15.4
13 W	19 28 47	22 30 44	0♏11 04	6♏36 41	25 18.5	5 23.5	27 21.0	3 14.1	4 17.3	21 11.2	26 53.0	28 23.5	8 15.3	12 16.6
14 Th	19 32 44	23 31 52	13 08 54	19 48 11	25 15.4	7 01.6	28 34.3	3 54.1	4 40.8	21 17.0	26 59.7	28 26.9	8 17.5	12 17.7
15 F	19 36 40	24 33 00	26 34 51	3♐29 06	25 09.8	8 39.1	29 47.6	4 34.1	5 04.4	21 22.9	27 06.3	28 30.3	8 19.7	12 18.8
16 Sa	19 40 37	25 34 08	10♐30 55	17 40 07	25 02.1	10 15.8	1♓00.8	5 14.1	5 28.0	21 29.1	27 12.8	28 33.6	8 21.9	12 19.9
17 Su	19 44 33	26 35 16	24 56 16	2♑18 42	24 53.0	11 51.3	2 14.0	5 54.1	5 51.7	21 35.4	27 19.3	28 36.9	8 24.1	12 20.9
18 M	19 48 30	27 36 23	9♑46 35	17 18 49	24 43.4	13 25.5	3 27.1	6 34.2	6 15.3	21 41.9	27 25.8	28 40.2	8 26.3	12 21.9
19 Tu	19 52 27	28 37 30	24 54 10	2♒31 19	24 34.8	14 57.9	4 40.2	7 14.2	6 38.9	21 48.5	27 32.3	28 43.5	8 28.5	12 22.8
20 W	19 56 23	29 38 36	10♒08 53	17 45 29	24 28.0	16 28.2	5 53.2	7 54.3	7 02.6	21 55.4	27 38.7	28 46.8	8 30.6	12 23.8
21 Th	20 00 20	0♒39 42	25 19 51	2♓50 49	24 23.6	17 55.8	7 06.1	8 34.4	7 26.3	22 02.3	27 45.0	28 50.0	8 32.8	12 24.6
22 F	20 04 16	1 40 46	10♓17 25	17 38 52	24D 21.7	19 20.4	8 19.0	9 14.5	7 49.9	22 09.5	27 51.3	28 53.2	8 34.9	12 25.5
23 Sa	20 08 13	2 41 50	24 54 34	2♈04 10	24 21.7	20 41.2	9 31.8	9 54.6	8 13.6	22 16.8	27 57.6	28 56.4	8 37.0	12 26.3
24 Su	20 12 09	3 42 52	9♈07 26	16 04 22	24 22.7	21 57.7	10 44.6	10 34.7	8 37.3	22 24.2	28 03.8	28 59.6	8 39.2	12 27.1
25 M	20 16 06	4 43 53	22 55 04	29 39 45	24R 23.6	23 09.2	11 57.2	11 14.8	9 00.9	22 31.9	28 10.0	29 02.7	8 41.3	12 27.8
26 Tu	20 20 02	5 44 54	6♉18 43	12♉52 20	24 23.5	24 14.8	13 09.8	11 54.9	9 24.6	22 39.6	28 16.2	29 05.8	8 43.3	12 28.5
27 W	20 23 59	6 45 53	19 20 59	25 45 06	24 21.5	25 13.8	14 22.3	12 35.1	9 48.3	22 47.6	28 22.3	29 08.9	8 45.4	12 29.2
28 Th	20 27 56	7 46 51	2♊05 04	8♊21 20	24 17.4	26 05.3	15 34.7	13 15.2	10 12.0	22 55.6	28 28.3	29 11.9	8 47.5	12 29.8
29 F	20 31 52	8 47 49	14 34 15	20 44 12	24 11.2	26 48.5	16 47.1	13 55.4	10 35.7	23 03.8	28 34.3	29 15.0	8 49.5	12 30.4
30 Sa	20 35 49	9 48 44	26 51 31	2♋56 31	24 03.5	27 22.6	17 59.4	14 35.6	10 59.4	23 12.2	28 40.2	29 18.0	8 51.5	12 31.0
31 Su	20 39 45	10 49 39	8♋59 27	15 00 35	23 54.9	27 46.9	19 11.5	15 15.8	11 23.0	23 20.7	28 46.1	29 20.9	8 53.5	12 31.5

LONGITUDE — February 1988

Day	Sid.Time	☉	0 hr ☽	Noon ☽	True ☊	☿	♀	♂	⚳	♃	♄	♅	♆	♇
1 M	20 43 42	11♒50 33	21♋00 10	26♋58 22	23♓46.4	28♒00.7	20♓23.6	15♐56.0	11♒46.7	23♈29.4	28♐52.0	29♐23.8	8♑55.5	12♏32.0
2 Tu	20 47 38	12 51 26	2♌55 26	8♌51 31	23R 38.7	28R 03.6	21 35.6	16 36.2	12 10.4	23 38.1	28 57.7	29 26.7	8 57.5	12 32.5
3 W	20 51 35	13 52 17	14 46 51	20 41 39	23 32.5	27 55.4	22 47.5	17 16.4	12 34.1	23 47.0	29 03.5	29 29.6	8 59.5	12 32.9
4 Th	20 55 32	14 53 07	26 36 06	2♍30 29	23 28.2	27 36.0	23 59.3	17 56.7	12 57.7	23 56.1	29 09.1	29 32.4	9 01.4	12 33.3
5 F	20 59 28	15 53 57	8♍25 02	14 20 06	23D 25.9	27 05.8	25 11.0	18 36.9	13 21.4	24 05.3	29 14.8	29 35.2	9 03.3	12 33.6
6 Sa	21 03 25	16 54 45	20 15 58	26 13 03	23 25.5	26 25.4	26 22.6	19 17.2	13 45.0	24 14.6	29 20.3	29 38.0	9 05.2	12 33.9
7 Su	21 07 21	17 55 32	2♎11 44	8♎12 28	23 26.4	25 35.9	27 34.1	19 57.5	14 08.7	24 24.0	29 25.8	29 40.7	9 07.1	12 34.2
8 M	21 11 18	18 56 18	14 15 44	20 22 02	23 28.1	24 38.5	28 45.5	20 37.8	14 32.3	24 33.6	29 31.2	29 43.4	9 08.9	12 34.4
9 Tu	21 15 14	19 57 03	26 31 55	2♏45 54	23 29.8	23 35.0	29 56.9	21 18.1	14 55.9	24 43.3	29 36.6	29 46.0	9 10.8	12 34.6
10 W	21 19 11	20 57 47	9♏04 32	15 28 22	23R 30.9	22 27.1	1♈08.1	21 58.4	15 19.6	24 53.1	29 41.9	29 48.7	9 12.6	12 34.8
11 Th	21 23 07	21 58 30	21 57 54	28 33 36	23 30.9	21 16.8	2 19.1	22 38.7	15 43.2	25 03.1	29 47.2	29 51.2	9 14.4	12 34.9
12 F	21 27 04	22 59 13	5♐15 51	12♐04 57	23 29.4	20 06.0	3 30.1	23 19.1	16 06.8	25 13.1	29 52.4	29 53.8	9 16.2	12 35.0
13 Sa	21 31 01	23 59 54	19 01 03	26 04 10	23 26.7	18 56.5	4 41.0	23 59.4	16 30.4	25 23.3	29 57.5	29 56.3	9 17.9	12 35.1
14 Su	21 34 57	25 00 34	3♑14 10	10♑30 42	23 22.9	17 50.2	5 51.8	24 39.8	16 53.9	25 33.6	0♑02.6	29 58.8	9 19.7	12R 35.1
15 M	21 38 54	26 01 13	17 53 13	25 20 57	23 18.8	16 48.4	7 02.4	25 20.2	17 17.5	25 44.0	0 07.5	0♑01.2	9 21.4	12 35.1
16 Tu	21 42 50	27 01 50	2♒53 00	10♒28 15	23 15.0	15 52.2	8 12.9	26 00.6	17 41.0	25 54.5	0 12.5	0 03.6	9 23.1	12 35.0
17 W	21 46 47	28 02 27	18 05 29	25 43 23	23 12.1	15 02.6	9 23.3	26 40.9	18 04.5	26 05.2	0 17.3	0 05.9	9 24.8	12 34.9
18 Th	21 50 43	29 03 01	3♓20 40	10♓56 02	23D 10.4	14 20.2	10 33.6	27 21.3	18 28.1	26 15.9	0 22.1	0 08.2	9 26.4	12 34.8
19 F	21 54 40	0♓03 34	18 28 18	25 56 23	23 10.0	13 45.3	11 43.8	28 01.7	18 51.5	26 26.8	0 26.8	0 10.5	9 28.0	12 34.7
20 Sa	21 58 36	1 04 05	3♈19 24	10♈36 38	23 10.7	13 18.0	12 53.8	28 42.1	19 15.0	26 37.7	0 31.4	0 12.7	9 29.6	12 34.5
21 Su	22 02 33	2 04 35	17 47 33	24 51 49	23 12.1	12 58.3	14 03.6	29 22.5	19 38.4	26 48.8	0 36.0	0 14.9	9 31.2	12 34.2
22 M	22 06 29	3 05 02	1♉49 15	8♉39 53	23 13.5	12 46.1	15 13.3	0♑03.0	20 01.9	26 59.9	0 40.5	0 17.0	9 32.7	12 34.0
23 Tu	22 10 26	4 05 28	15 23 49	22 01 19	23 14.6	12D 41.0	16 22.9	0 43.4	20 25.3	27 11.2	0 44.9	0 19.1	9 34.2	12 33.7
24 W	22 14 23	5 05 52	28 32 44	4♊58 27	23R 15.0	12 42.8	17 32.3	1 23.8	20 48.6	27 22.5	0 49.2	0 21.1	9 35.7	12 33.3
25 Th	22 18 19	6 06 14	11♊18 57	17 34 42	23 14.6	12 51.1	18 41.6	2 04.2	21 12.0	27 34.0	0 53.4	0 23.1	9 37.2	12 32.9
26 F	22 22 16	7 06 34	23 46 12	29 54 00	23 13.4	13 05.5	19 50.7	2 44.7	21 35.3	27 45.5	0 57.6	0 25.1	9 38.6	12 32.5
27 Sa	22 26 12	8 06 52	5♋58 34	12♋00 23	23 11.5	13 25.7	20 59.7	3 25.1	21 58.6	27 57.1	1 01.7	0 27.0	9 40.0	12 32.1
28 Su	22 30 09	9 07 08	17 59 57	23 57 42	23 09.4	13 51.2	22 08.4	4 05.5	22 21.8	28 08.9	1 05.7	0 28.8	9 41.4	12 31.6
29 M	22 34 05	10 07 22	29 54 02	5♌49 21	23 07.2	14 21.6	23 17.0	4 46.0	22 45.1	28 20.7	1 09.7	0 30.7	9 42.7	12 31.1

Astro Data

	Dy Hr Mn
☽0S	10 11:41
♄∠♇	17 18:49
☽0N	23 6:54
☿R	2 6:16
☽0S	6 17:19
♀0N	10 13:21
♄☌♅	13 0:58
♇R	14 14:50
☽0N	19 16:39
☿D	23 17:30
♇0N	26 23:24

Planet Ingress

	Dy Hr Mn
⚳ ♒	2 12:48
♂ ♐	8 15:24
☿ ♒	10 5:28
♀ ♓	15 16:04
☉ ♒	20 20:24
♀ ♈	9 13:04
♄ ♑	13 23:51
♅ ♑	15 0:11
☉ ♓	19 10:35
♂ ♑	22 10:15

Last Aspect / ☽ Ingress

Last Aspect Dy Hr Mn		☽ Ingress Dy Hr Mn
2 19:55	♅☍	♋ 3 0:17
5 7:20	♂△	♌ 5 11:47
7 23:42	♂□	♍ 8 0:35
10 9:43	♅□	♎ 10 13:17
12 20:33	♅⚹	♏ 12 23:39
15 4:59	♀□	♐ 15 5:58
17 5:59	♅☌	♑ 17 8:15
19 5:26	☉☌	♒ 19 8:02
21 5:33	♅⚹	♓ 21 7:27
23 6:43	♅□	♈ 23 8:31
25 10:53	♅△	♉ 25 12:36
27 10:56	☿□	♊ 27 20:02
30 4:47	♅☍	♋ 30 6:11

Last Aspect / ☽ Ingress

Last Aspect Dy Hr Mn		☽ Ingress Dy Hr Mn
1 4:54	♃□	♌ 1 18:06
4 5:57	♅△	♍ 4 6:54
6 18:53	♅□	♎ 6 19:36
9 6:14	♅⚹	♏ 9 6:42
10 23:50	☿□	♐ 11 14:36
13 18:34	♄☌	♑ 13 18:36
15 12:37	♃□	♒ 15 19:25
17 15:54	☉☌	♓ 17 18:44
19 15:33	♂□	♈ 19 18:35
21 20:09	♂△	♉ 21 20:50
22 19:13	☿□	♊ 24 2:42
26 7:44	♃⚹	♋ 26 12:12
28 20:36	♃□	♌ 29 0:12

☽ Phases & Eclipses

Dy Hr Mn	
4 1:40	○ 12♋54
12 7:04	☾ 21♎17
19 5:26	● 28♑21
25 21:54	☽ 5♉09
2 20:52	○ 13♌14
10 23:01	☾ 21♏26
17 15:54	● 28♒12
24 12:15	☽ 5♊07

Astro Data

1 January 1988
Julian Day # 32142
SVP 5♓25'37"
GC 26♐40.3 ⚴ 8♑16.1
Eris 15♈46.1R ⚵ 13♓44.1
⚷ 25♊07.2R ⚶ 6♌23.1R
☽ Mean ☊ 27♓08.4

1 February 1988
Julian Day # 32173
SVP 5♓25'31"
GC 26♐40.4 ⚴ 20♑18.1
Eris 15♈50.6 ⚵ 28♓34.7
⚷ 23♊35.3R ⚶ 28♋44.5R
☽ Mean ☊ 25♓29.9

March 1988 — LONGITUDE

Day	Sid.Time	☉	0 hr ☽	Noon ☽	True ☊	☿	♀	♂	⚳	♃	♄	♅	♆	♇
1 Tu	22 38 02	11♓07 34	11♌44 01	17♌38 22	23♓05.3	14♒56.7	24♈25.4	5♑26.5	23♒08.3	28♈32.6	1♑13.5	0♑32.4	9♑44.1	12♏30.6
2 W	22 41 59	12 07 45	23 32 43	29 27 20	23R 03.9	15 36.0	25 33.6	6 06.9	23 31.4	28 44.5	1 17.3	0 34.2	9 45.4	12R 30.0
3 Th	22 45 55	13 07 53	5♍22 31	11♍18 31	23D 03.1	16 19.4	26 41.7	6 47.4	23 54.6	28 56.6	1 21.0	0 35.8	9 46.6	12 29.4
4 F	22 49 52	14 07 59	17 15 35	23 13 58	23 02.9	17 06.4	27 49.5	7 27.9	24 17.7	29 08.7	1 24.6	0 37.5	9 47.9	12 28.8
5 Sa	22 53 48	15 08 04	29 13 54	5♎15 39	23 03.1	17 56.9	28 57.2	8 08.4	24 40.7	29 20.9	1 28.1	0 39.0	9 49.1	12 28.1
6 Su	22 57 45	16 08 07	11♎19 27	17 25 36	23 03.6	18 50.6	0♉04.6	8 48.9	25 03.8	29 33.2	1 31.5	0 40.6	9 50.3	12 27.4
7 M	23 01 41	17 08 08	23 34 21	29 46 00	23 04.2	19 47.3	1 11.9	9 29.4	25 26.8	29 45.6	1 34.9	0 42.0	9 51.4	12 26.7
8 Tu	23 05 38	18 08 08	6♏00 52	12♏19 16	23 04.8	20 46.8	2 18.9	10 09.9	25 49.7	29 58.1	1 38.1	0 43.5	9 52.5	12 25.9
9 W	23 09 34	19 08 06	18 41 31	25 07 56	23 05.3	21 48.9	3 25.8	10 50.4	26 12.7	0♉10.6	1 41.3	0 44.9	9 53.6	12 25.1
10 Th	23 13 31	20 08 02	1♐38 52	8♐14 35	23 05.5	22 53.5	4 32.4	11 30.9	26 35.6	0 23.2	1 44.4	0 46.2	9 54.7	12 24.3
11 F	23 17 27	21 07 57	14 55 22	21 41 26	23R 05.6	24 00.5	5 38.8	12 11.4	26 58.4	0 35.8	1 47.4	0 47.5	9 55.7	12 23.4
12 Sa	23 21 24	22 07 50	28 32 57	5♑29 59	23D 05.6	25 09.6	6 44.9	12 51.9	27 21.2	0 48.6	1 50.3	0 48.7	9 56.7	12 22.5
13 Su	23 25 21	23 07 42	12♑32 32	19 40 26	23 05.5	26 20.8	7 50.9	13 32.5	27 44.0	1 01.4	1 53.1	0 49.9	9 57.7	12 21.6
14 M	23 29 17	24 07 32	26 53 28	4♒11 12	23 05.6	27 34.0	8 56.5	14 13.0	28 06.7	1 14.2	1 55.9	0 51.0	9 58.6	12 20.7
15 Tu	23 33 14	25 07 20	11♒33 06	18 58 28	23 05.7	28 49.1	10 02.0	14 53.5	28 29.4	1 27.1	1 58.5	0 52.1	9 59.5	12 19.7
16 W	23 37 10	26 07 06	26 26 31	3♓56 18	23 05.9	0♓06.0	11 07.2	15 34.0	28 52.1	1 40.1	2 01.0	0 53.1	10 00.4	12 18.7
17 Th	23 41 07	27 06 50	11♓26 48	18 56 59	23R 06.1	1 24.6	12 12.1	16 14.6	29 14.7	1 53.2	2 03.5	0 54.1	10 01.3	12 17.7
18 F	23 45 03	28 06 33	26 25 44	3♈52 02	23 06.0	2 44.9	13 16.8	16 55.1	29 37.2	2 06.3	2 05.8	0 55.0	10 02.1	12 16.6
19 Sa	23 49 00	29 06 13	11♈14 54	18 33 25	23 05.7	4 06.8	14 21.2	17 35.6	29 59.7	2 19.5	2 08.1	0 55.9	10 02.8	12 15.5
20 Su	23 52 56	0♈05 51	25 46 51	2♉54 35	23 05.0	5 30.3	15 25.3	18 16.1	0♓22.2	2 32.7	2 10.2	0 56.7	10 03.6	12 14.4
21 M	23 56 53	1 05 27	9♉56 09	16 51 15	23 04.0	6 55.3	16 29.1	18 56.6	0 44.6	2 46.0	2 12.3	0 57.5	10 04.3	12 13.3
22 Tu	0 00 50	2 05 01	23 39 45	0♊21 39	23 03.0	8 21.8	17 32.7	19 37.1	1 06.9	2 59.3	2 14.3	0 58.2	10 05.0	12 12.1
23 W	0 04 46	3 04 33	6♊57 06	13 26 21	23 02.1	9 49.8	18 35.9	20 17.6	1 29.2	3 12.7	2 16.2	0 58.9	10 05.6	12 10.9
24 Th	0 08 43	4 04 02	19 49 44	26 07 43	23D 01.5	11 19.2	19 38.8	20 58.0	1 51.5	3 26.1	2 17.9	0 59.5	10 06.2	12 09.7
25 F	0 12 39	5 03 29	2♋20 46	8♋29 25	23 01.4	12 50.1	20 41.3	21 38.5	2 13.6	3 39.6	2 19.6	1 00.1	10 06.8	12 08.5
26 Sa	0 16 36	6 02 54	14 34 14	20 35 48	23 01.9	14 22.3	21 43.5	22 19.0	2 35.8	3 53.1	2 21.2	1 00.6	10 07.4	12 07.2
27 Su	0 20 32	7 02 17	26 34 43	2♌31 34	23 02.8	15 56.0	22 45.4	22 59.4	2 57.8	4 06.7	2 22.7	1 01.1	10 07.9	12 06.0
28 M	0 24 29	8 01 37	8♌26 54	14 21 18	23 04.2	17 31.1	23 46.9	23 39.9	3 19.8	4 20.3	2 24.1	1 01.5	10 08.4	12 04.6
29 Tu	0 28 25	9 00 55	20 15 16	26 09 19	23 05.6	19 07.5	24 48.0	24 20.3	3 41.8	4 33.9	2 25.4	1 01.8	10 08.8	12 03.3
30 W	0 32 22	10 00 10	2♍03 54	7♍59 28	23 06.8	20 45.3	25 48.7	25 00.8	4 03.7	4 47.6	2 26.6	1 02.1	10 09.2	12 02.0
31 Th	0 36 19	10 59 24	13 56 24	19 55 03	23R 07.4	22 24.6	26 49.0	25 41.2	4 25.5	5 01.4	2 27.7	1 02.4	10 09.6	12 00.6

April 1988 — LONGITUDE

Day	Sid.Time	☉	0 hr ☽	Noon ☽	True ☊	☿	♀	♂	⚳	♃	♄	♅	♆	♇
1 F	0 40 15	11♈58 35	25♍55 45	1♎58 46	23♓07.1	24♓05.2	27♉48.9	26♑21.6	4♓47.3	5♉15.1	2♑28.7	1♑02.6	10♑10.0	11♏59.2
2 Sa	0 44 12	12 57 44	8♎04 20	14 12 39	23R 05.9	25 47.3	28 48.4	27 02.0	5 09.0	5 28.9	2 29.6	1 02.7	10 10.3	11R 57.8
3 Su	0 48 08	13 56 51	20 23 54	26 38 12	23 03.7	27 30.7	29 47.5	27 42.4	5 30.6	5 42.8	2 30.4	1 02.8	10 10.6	11 56.4
4 M	0 52 05	14 55 56	2♏55 41	9♏16 26	23 00.7	29 15.6	0♊46.0	28 22.8	5 52.2	5 56.6	2 31.1	1R 02.8	10 10.8	11 55.0
5 Tu	0 56 01	15 54 59	15 40 30	22 07 57	22 57.1	1♈01.9	1 44.2	29 03.2	6 13.7	6 10.6	2 31.7	1 02.8	10 11.0	11 53.5
6 W	0 59 58	16 54 01	28 38 49	5♐13 08	22 53.6	2 49.7	2 41.8	29 43.6	6 35.1	6 24.5	2 32.2	1 02.8	10 11.2	11 52.0
7 Th	1 03 54	17 53 01	11♐50 57	18 32 16	22 50.5	4 38.9	3 39.0	0♒24.0	6 56.5	6 38.5	2 32.6	1 02.7	10 11.4	11 50.5
8 F	1 07 51	18 51 59	25 17 07	2♑05 30	22 48.3	6 29.6	4 35.6	1 04.3	7 17.8	6 52.5	2 32.9	1 02.5	10 11.5	11 49.0
9 Sa	1 11 48	19 50 55	8♑57 24	15 52 49	22D 47.4	8 21.8	5 31.7	1 44.7	7 39.0	7 06.5	2 33.1	1 02.3	10 11.6	11 47.5
10 Su	1 15 44	20 49 49	22 51 42	29 53 56	22 47.6	10 15.5	6 27.3	2 25.0	8 00.2	7 20.6	2R 33.2	1 02.0	10 11.6	11 46.0
11 M	1 19 41	21 48 42	6♒59 24	14♒07 54	22 48.7	12 10.6	7 22.3	3 05.3	8 21.3	7 34.7	2 33.2	1 01.7	10R 11.7	11 44.4
12 Tu	1 23 37	22 47 33	21 19 10	28 32 52	22 50.1	14 07.2	8 16.8	3 45.6	8 42.3	7 48.8	2 33.1	1 01.3	10 11.6	11 42.9
13 W	1 27 34	23 46 22	5♓48 34	13♓05 45	22R 51.3	16 05.3	9 10.6	4 25.9	9 03.2	8 02.9	2 32.9	1 00.9	10 11.6	11 41.3
14 Th	1 31 30	24 45 10	20 23 49	27 42 08	22 51.5	18 04.7	10 03.8	5 06.2	9 24.0	8 17.0	2 32.6	1 00.4	10 11.5	11 39.7
15 F	1 35 27	25 43 55	4♈59 56	12♈16 29	22 50.2	20 05.6	10 56.4	5 46.4	9 44.8	8 31.2	2 32.2	0 59.9	10 11.4	11 38.1
16 Sa	1 39 23	26 42 39	19 30 58	26 42 39	22 47.3	22 07.8	11 48.4	6 26.6	10 05.5	8 45.4	2 31.8	0 59.3	10 11.2	11 36.5
17 Su	1 43 20	27 41 21	3♉50 47	10♉54 42	22 42.8	24 11.2	12 39.6	7 06.7	10 26.1	8 59.6	2 31.2	0 58.7	10 11.1	11 34.8
18 M	1 47 17	28 40 01	17 53 49	24 47 40	22 37.2	26 15.8	13 30.1	7 46.9	10 46.6	9 13.9	2 30.5	0 58.1	10 10.9	11 33.2
19 Tu	1 51 13	29 38 38	1♊35 56	8♊18 22	22 31.2	28 21.5	14 19.9	8 27.0	11 07.0	9 28.1	2 29.7	0 57.3	10 10.6	11 31.6
20 W	1 55 10	0♉37 14	14 54 54	21 25 35	22 25.6	0♉28.0	15 08.9	9 07.1	11 27.3	9 42.4	2 28.8	0 56.6	10 10.3	11 29.9
21 Th	1 59 06	1 35 48	27 50 35	4♋10 10	22 21.0	2 35.4	15 57.1	9 47.1	11 47.6	9 56.6	2 27.9	0 55.8	10 10.0	11 28.3
22 F	2 03 03	2 34 19	10♋24 42	16 34 39	22 17.9	4 43.2	16 44.5	10 27.2	12 07.7	10 10.9	2 26.8	0 54.9	10 09.7	11 26.6
23 Sa	2 06 59	3 32 49	22 40 30	28 42 51	22D 16.4	6 51.4	17 31.0	11 07.1	12 27.8	10 25.2	2 25.6	0 54.0	10 09.3	11 24.9
24 Su	2 10 56	4 31 16	4♌42 17	10♌39 26	22 16.5	8 59.7	18 16.6	11 47.1	12 47.8	10 39.5	2 24.4	0 53.0	10 08.9	11 23.3
25 M	2 14 52	5 29 40	16 34 56	22 29 28	22 17.6	11 07.9	19 01.2	12 27.0	13 07.6	10 53.8	2 23.0	0 52.0	10 08.5	11 21.6
26 Tu	2 18 49	6 28 03	28 23 38	4♍18 05	22 19.2	13 15.6	19 44.9	13 06.9	13 27.4	11 08.1	2 21.6	0 51.0	10 08.0	11 19.9
27 W	2 22 46	7 26 24	10♍13 26	16 10 15	22R 20.3	15 22.5	20 27.5	13 46.8	13 47.0	11 22.4	2 20.0	0 49.9	10 07.5	11 18.2
28 Th	2 26 42	8 24 43	22 09 03	28 10 22	22 20.3	17 28.3	21 09.2	14 26.6	14 06.6	11 36.8	2 18.4	0 48.7	10 07.0	11 16.5
29 F	2 30 39	9 22 59	4♎14 36	10♎22 09	22 18.6	19 32.8	21 49.7	15 06.3	14 26.1	11 51.1	2 16.7	0 47.6	10 06.4	11 14.8
30 Sa	2 34 35	10 21 14	16 33 20	22 48 24	22 14.7	21 35.6	22 29.1	15 46.1	14 45.4	12 05.4	2 14.9	0 46.3	10 05.8	11 13.1

Astro Data Dy Hr Mn	Planet Ingress Dy Hr Mn	Last Aspect Dy Hr Mn	☽ Ingress Dy Hr Mn	Last Aspect Dy Hr Mn	☽ Ingress Dy Hr Mn	☽ Phases & Eclipses Dy Hr Mn	Astro Data
☽0S 4 23:06	♀ ♉ 6 10:21	2 10:32 ♃ △	♍ 2 13:06	1 3:01 ♀ △	♎ 1 8:05	3 16:01 ○ 13♍18	1 March 1988
♃△♅ 12 12:19	♃ ♉ 8 15:44	3 16:01 ☉ ☍	♎ 5 1:32	3 14:10 ♂ □	♏ 3 18:26	3 16:13 ☍ A 1.091	Julian Day # 32202
☽0N 18 3:48	☿ ♓ 16 10:09	7 11:59 ♃ ☍	♏ 7 12:27	6 1:26 ♂ ⚹	♐ 6 2:29	11 10:56 ☾ 21♐05	SVP 5♓25'27"
♃△♄ 18 10:57	⚳ ♓ 19 12:18	9 5:17 ☿ □	♐ 9 20:59	7 10:44 ☉ △	♑ 8 8:19	18 2:02 ● 27♓42	GC 26♐40.4 ⚵ 0♒42.7
☉0N 20 9:38	☉ ♈ 20 9:39	11 16:26 ☿ ⚹	♑ 12 2:31	9 19:21 ☉ □	♒ 10 12:10	18 1:58:00 ☌ T 03'47"	Eris 16♈03.4 ⚴ 14♈05.3
		13 18:11 ☉ ⚹	♒ 14 5:08	12 1:45 ☉ ⚹	♓ 12 14:24	25 4:42 ☽ 4♋45	⚷ 23♊06.9 ⚶ 23♋45.2R
☽0S 1 5:42	♀ ♊ 3 17:07	16 5:17 ☿ ☌	♓ 16 5:42	13 9:41 ♇ △	♈ 14 15:47		☽ Mean ☊ 23♓57.8
♅ R 4 19:25	☿ ♈ 4 22:04	18 2:02 ☉ ☌	♈ 18 5:45	16 12:00 ☉ ☌	♉ 16 17:31	2 9:21 ○ 12♎51	
☿0N 7 14:28	♂ ♒ 6 21:44	19 10:20 ♂ □	♉ 20 7:05	17 13:09 ♇ ☍	♊ 18 21:10	9 19:21 ☾ 20♑09	1 April 1988
♄ R 11 2:08	☉ ♉ 19 20:45	21 15:51 ♂ △	♊ 22 11:21	19 23:40 ♀ ☌	♋ 21 4:04	16 12:00 ● 26♈43	Julian Day # 32233
♆ R 11 13:17	☿ ♉ 20 6:42	23 4:27 ☿ □	♋ 24 19:27	22 2:01 ♇ △	♌ 23 14:34	23 22:32 ☽ 3♌58	SVP 5♓25'24"
☽0N 14 13:44		26 15:39 ♂ ☍	♌ 27 6:54	25 4:29 ♀ ⚹	♍ 26 3:16		GC 26♐40.5 ⚵ 10♒16.4
♃△♆ 22 9:59		29 8:59 ♀ □	♍ 29 19:49	27 21:09 ♀ □	♎ 28 15:37		Eris 16♈22.7 ⚴ 1♉45.5
♃☍♇ 27 5:39							⚷ 23♊50.8 ⚶ 25♋09.1
☽0S 28 13:01							☽ Mean ☊ 22♓19.3

LONGITUDE — May 1988

Day	Sid.Time	☉	0 hr ☽	Noon ☽	True ☊	☿	♀	♂	⚳	♃	♄	♅	♆	♇
1 Su	2 38 32	11♉19 27	29♎07 30	5♏30 45	22♓08.8	23♉36.4	23♊07.3	16♒25.8	15♓04.7	12♉19.7	2♑13.0	0♑45.1	10♑05.2	11♏11.4
2 M	2 42 28	12 17 38	11♏58 10	18 29 41	22R 01.2	25 35.0	23 44.2	17 05.4	15 23.8	12 34.1	2R 11.0	0R 43.8	10R 04.6	11R 09.7
3 Tu	2 46 25	13 15 48	25 05 12	1♐44 31	21 52.6	27 31.0	24 20.0	17 45.1	15 42.9	12 48.4	2 08.9	0 42.4	10 03.9	11 08.1
4 W	2 50 21	14 13 56	8♐27 24	15 13 35	21 43.9	29 24.4	24 54.3	18 24.6	16 01.8	13 02.7	2 06.8	0 41.0	10 03.2	11 06.4
5 Th	2 54 18	15 12 02	22 02 46	28 54 39	21 36.0	1♊14.8	25 27.4	19 04.2	16 20.6	13 17.0	2 04.5	0 39.6	10 02.5	11 04.7
6 F	2 58 15	16 10 07	5♑48 55	12♑45 16	21 29.9	3 02.2	25 59.0	19 43.7	16 39.3	13 31.3	2 02.2	0 38.1	10 01.7	11 03.0
7 Sa	3 02 11	17 08 11	19 43 26	26 43 11	21 25.9	4 46.3	26 29.2	20 23.1	16 57.9	13 45.6	1 59.8	0 36.6	10 00.9	11 01.3
8 Su	3 06 08	18 06 13	3♒44 17	10♒46 33	21D 24.1	6 27.0	26 57.8	21 02.5	17 16.4	13 59.9	1 57.3	0 35.0	10 00.1	10 59.6
9 M	3 10 04	19 04 14	17 49 50	24 53 58	21 24.0	8 04.3	27 24.9	21 41.8	17 34.8	14 14.2	1 54.7	0 33.5	9 59.3	10 58.0
10 Tu	3 14 01	20 02 13	1♓58 48	9♓04 12	21R 24.6	9 38.0	27 50.3	22 21.1	17 53.0	14 28.5	1 52.1	0 31.8	9 58.4	10 56.3
11 W	3 17 57	21 00 11	16 09 57	23 15 52	21 25.0	11 08.0	28 14.1	23 00.3	18 11.1	14 42.8	1 49.4	0 30.2	9 57.5	10 54.6
12 Th	3 21 54	21 58 08	0♈21 42	7♈27 07	21 24.0	12 34.3	28 36.1	23 39.5	18 29.1	14 57.1	1 46.5	0 28.4	9 56.6	10 53.0
13 F	3 25 50	22 56 03	14 31 46	21 35 16	21 20.7	13 56.8	28 56.3	24 18.6	18 46.9	15 11.3	1 43.7	0 26.7	9 55.6	10 51.3
14 Sa	3 29 47	23 53 58	28 37 07	5♉36 52	21 14.8	15 15.5	29 14.6	24 57.6	19 04.6	15 25.5	1 40.7	0 24.9	9 54.6	10 49.7
15 Su	3 33 44	24 51 51	12♉34 01	19 28 04	21 06.4	16 30.3	29 31.1	25 36.5	19 22.2	15 39.8	1 37.7	0 23.1	9 53.6	10 48.0
16 M	3 37 40	25 49 42	26 18 32	3♊05 00	20 56.3	17 41.2	29 45.5	26 15.4	19 39.7	15 54.0	1 34.6	0 21.3	9 52.6	10 46.4
17 Tu	3 41 37	26 47 32	9♊47 08	16 24 37	20 45.2	18 48.0	29 57.9	26 54.2	19 57.0	16 08.2	1 31.4	0 19.4	9 51.6	10 44.8
18 W	3 45 33	27 45 21	22 57 18	29 25 05	20 34.5	19 50.7	0♋08.2	27 32.9	20 14.2	16 22.3	1 28.1	0 17.5	9 50.5	10 43.2
19 Th	3 49 30	28 43 08	5♋47 59	12♋06 07	20 25.1	20 49.4	0 16.4	28 11.5	20 31.2	16 36.5	1 24.8	0 15.6	9 49.4	10 41.6
20 F	3 53 26	29 40 53	18 19 43	24 29 06	20 17.8	21 43.8	0 22.3	28 50.1	20 48.1	16 50.6	1 21.5	0 13.6	9 48.3	10 40.0
21 Sa	3 57 23	0♊38 37	0♌34 39	6♌36 51	20 12.8	22 33.9	0 25.9	29 28.5	21 04.8	17 04.7	1 18.0	0 11.6	9 47.1	10 38.5
22 Su	4 01 19	1 36 19	12 36 14	18 33 22	20 10.2	23 19.7	0R 27.2	0♓06.9	21 21.4	17 18.8	1 14.5	0 09.6	9 46.0	10 36.9
23 M	4 05 16	2 34 00	24 28 53	0♍23 26	20D 09.4	24 01.0	0 26.2	0 45.2	21 37.8	17 32.9	1 11.0	0 07.5	9 44.8	10 35.4
24 Tu	4 09 13	3 31 39	6♍17 42	12 12 21	20R 09.6	24 37.9	0 22.7	1 23.3	21 54.1	17 46.9	1 07.3	0 05.4	9 43.6	10 33.8
25 W	4 13 09	4 29 16	18 08 05	24 05 33	20 09.6	25 10.3	0 16.9	2 01.4	22 10.2	18 00.9	1 03.7	0 03.3	9 42.3	10 32.3
26 Th	4 17 06	5 26 52	0♎05 25	6♎08 18	20 08.6	25 38.0	0 08.6	2 39.4	22 26.2	18 14.9	0 59.9	0 01.2	9 41.1	10 30.8
27 F	4 21 02	6 24 27	12 14 45	18 25 18	20 05.6	26 01.1	29♊57.8	3 17.3	22 42.0	18 28.8	0 56.2	29♐59.0	9 39.8	10 29.3
28 Sa	4 24 59	7 22 00	24 40 24	1♏00 23	20 00.2	26 19.5	29 44.7	3 55.1	22 57.6	18 42.7	0 52.3	29 56.9	9 38.5	10 27.9
29 Su	4 28 55	8 19 32	7♏25 32	13 56 00	19 52.2	26 33.2	29 29.1	4 32.8	23 13.1	18 56.6	0 48.4	29 54.7	9 37.2	10 26.4
30 M	4 32 52	9 17 03	20 31 49	27 12 55	19 42.0	26 42.2	29 11.1	5 10.4	23 28.4	19 10.4	0 44.5	29 52.4	9 35.9	10 25.0
31 Tu	4 36 48	10 14 33	3♐59 06	10♐50 03	19 30.5	26R 46.6	28 50.9	5 47.9	23 43.6	19 24.3	0 40.6	29 50.2	9 34.5	10 23.6

LONGITUDE — June 1988

Day	Sid.Time	☉	0 hr ☽	Noon ☽	True ☊	☿	♀	♂	⚳	♃	♄	♅	♆	♇
1 W	4 40 45	11♊12 02	17♐45 19	24♐44 25	19♓18.7	26♊46.3	28♊28.3	6♓25.3	23♓58.5	19♉38.0	0♑36.5	29♐47.9	9♑33.2	10♏22.2
2 Th	4 44 42	12 09 29	1♑46 44	8♑51 40	19R 08.1	26R 41.6	28R 03.7	7 02.6	24 13.3	19 51.8	0R 32.5	29R 45.7	9R 31.8	10R 20.8
3 F	4 48 38	13 06 56	15 58 33	23 06 46	18 59.4	26 32.5	27 36.9	7 39.7	24 28.0	20 05.5	0 28.4	29 43.4	9 30.4	10 19.5
4 Sa	4 52 35	14 04 23	0♒15 41	7♒24 47	18 53.4	26 19.3	27 08.3	8 16.8	24 42.4	20 19.2	0 24.3	29 41.1	9 29.0	10 18.1
5 Su	4 56 31	15 01 48	14 33 34	21 41 40	18 50.1	26 02.2	26 37.9	8 53.7	24 56.6	20 32.8	0 20.1	29 38.7	9 27.6	10 16.8
6 M	5 00 28	15 59 13	28 48 43	5♓54 31	18 48.9	25 41.4	26 05.9	9 30.4	25 10.7	20 46.4	0 15.9	29 36.4	9 26.1	10 15.5
7 Tu	5 04 24	16 56 37	12♓58 53	20 01 41	18 48.8	25 17.4	25 32.4	10 07.1	25 24.6	20 59.9	0 11.7	29 34.0	9 24.7	10 14.3
8 W	5 08 21	17 54 00	27 02 49	4♈02 15	18 48.4	24 50.5	24 57.7	10 43.6	25 38.3	21 13.4	0 07.4	29 31.6	9 23.2	10 13.0
9 Th	5 12 17	18 51 23	10♈59 55	17 55 44	18 46.7	24 21.3	24 22.0	11 19.9	25 51.7	21 26.9	0 03.1	29 29.3	9 21.7	10 11.8
10 F	5 16 14	19 48 46	24 49 39	1♉41 31	18 42.5	23 50.0	23 45.5	11 56.1	26 05.0	21 40.3	29♐58.8	29 26.9	9 20.2	10 10.6
11 Sa	5 20 11	20 46 08	8♉31 12	15 18 32	18 35.5	23 17.4	23 08.4	12 32.1	26 18.1	21 53.7	29 54.5	29 24.5	9 18.7	10 09.4
12 Su	5 24 07	21 43 29	22 03 18	28 45 18	18 25.8	22 43.9	22 30.9	13 08.0	26 31.0	22 07.0	29 50.1	29 22.0	9 17.2	10 08.2
13 M	5 28 04	22 40 50	5♊24 16	12♊00 00	18 14.0	22 10.1	21 53.4	13 43.7	26 43.6	22 20.3	29 45.7	29 19.6	9 15.7	10 07.1
14 Tu	5 32 00	23 38 10	18 32 17	25 00 56	18 01.3	21 36.7	21 15.9	14 19.2	26 56.1	22 33.5	29 41.4	29 17.2	9 14.2	10 06.0
15 W	5 35 57	24 35 30	1♋25 50	7♋46 54	17 48.8	21 04.1	20 38.9	14 54.6	27 08.3	22 46.7	29 37.0	29 14.8	9 12.6	10 04.9
16 Th	5 39 53	25 32 49	14 04 07	20 17 33	17 37.6	20 32.9	20 02.4	15 29.8	27 20.3	22 59.8	29 32.5	29 12.3	9 11.0	10 03.9
17 F	5 43 50	26 30 08	26 27 19	2♌33 39	17 28.5	20 03.7	19 26.7	16 04.7	27 32.1	23 12.9	29 28.1	29 09.9	9 09.5	10 02.8
18 Sa	5 47 47	27 27 25	8♌36 50	14 37 13	17 22.1	19 36.9	18 52.1	16 39.5	27 43.6	23 25.9	29 23.7	29 07.4	9 07.9	10 01.8
19 Su	5 51 43	28 24 42	20 35 12	26 31 18	17 18.3	19 13.0	18 18.7	17 14.1	27 55.0	23 38.8	29 19.3	29 05.0	9 06.3	10 00.8
20 M	5 55 40	29 21 58	2♍26 02	8♍19 59	17D 16.7	18 52.4	17 46.8	17 48.5	28 06.0	23 51.7	29 14.8	29 02.5	9 04.7	9 59.9
21 Tu	5 59 36	0♋19 13	14 13 47	20 08 04	17R 16.5	18 35.5	17 16.4	18 22.7	28 16.9	24 04.5	29 10.4	29 00.1	9 03.1	9 59.0
22 W	6 03 33	1 16 28	26 03 30	2♎00 48	17 16.6	18 22.6	16 47.8	18 56.6	28 27.5	24 17.3	29 05.9	28 57.6	9 01.5	9 58.1
23 Th	6 07 29	2 13 42	8♎00 38	14 03 40	17 16.0	18 13.8	16 21.1	19 30.4	28 37.9	24 30.0	29 01.5	28 55.2	8 59.9	9 57.2
24 F	6 11 26	3 10 55	20 10 34	26 21 57	17 13.9	18D 09.5	15 56.4	20 03.9	28 48.0	24 42.6	28 57.1	28 52.7	8 58.3	9 56.4
25 Sa	6 15 22	4 08 08	2♏38 21	9♏00 17	17 09.5	18 09.8	15 33.9	20 37.3	28 57.9	24 55.2	28 52.7	28 50.3	8 56.7	9 55.6
26 Su	6 19 19	5 05 21	15 28 09	22 02 13	17 02.8	18 14.7	15 13.5	21 10.3	29 07.5	25 07.7	28 48.3	28 47.9	8 55.1	9 54.8
27 M	6 23 16	6 02 33	28 42 38	5♐29 27	16 53.9	18 24.5	14 55.4	21 43.2	29 16.9	25 20.2	28 43.9	28 45.5	8 53.5	9 54.0
28 Tu	6 27 12	6 59 44	12♐22 31	19 21 32	16 43.7	18 39.0	14 39.7	22 15.8	29 26.0	25 32.5	28 39.5	28 43.0	8 51.9	9 53.3
29 W	6 31 09	7 56 56	26 26 01	3♑35 24	16 33.3	18 58.5	14 26.3	22 48.2	29 34.8	25 44.8	28 35.2	28 40.6	8 50.3	9 52.6
30 Th	6 35 05	8 54 07	10♑48 55	18 05 45	16 23.7	19 22.7	14 15.4	23 20.3	29 43.4	25 57.1	28 30.9	28 38.2	8 48.6	9 52.0

Astro Data	Dy Hr Mn
☽ 0N	11 20:55
♃□♅	14 11:05
♃□♄	18 19:59
♀ R	22 13:26
☽ 0S	25 20:30
☿ R	31 22:44
☽ 0N	8 1:50
♃□♆	21 9:41
☽ 0S	22 3:37
☿ D	24 22:41
♄☌♅	26 17:06

Planet Ingress		Dy Hr Mn
☿	♊	4 19:40
♀	♋	17 16:26
☉	♊	20 19:57
♂	♓	22 7:42
♅	♐R	27 1:17
♀	♊R	27 7:36
♄	♐R	10 5:22
☉	♋	21 3:57

Last Aspect Dy Hr Mn		☽ Ingress Dy Hr Mn
30 11:21	♀ △	♏ 1 1:39
3 3:07	☿ ☍	♐ 3 8:52
5 5:43	♀ ☍	♑ 5 13:54
6 18:19	☉ △	♒ 7 17:37
9 16:24	♀ △	♓ 9 20:39
11 20:38	♀ □	♈ 11 23:23
14 0:50	♀ ✶	♉ 14 2:22
15 23:18	♂ □	♊ 16 6:31
18 8:20	♂ △	♋ 18 13:05
19 20:50	♃ ✶	♌ 20 22:51
22 22:17	☿ ✶	♍ 23 11:12
25 14:15	☿ □	♎ 25 23:49
28 10:01	♅ ✶	♏ 28 10:06
29 21:17	♃ ☍	♐ 30 16:57

Last Aspect Dy Hr Mn		☽ Ingress Dy Hr Mn
1 20:37	♅ ☌	♑ 1 20:58
3 6:50	♃ △	♒ 3 23:34
6 1:22	♅ ✶	♓ 6 2:00
8 4:16	♅ □	♈ 8 5:04
10 9:01	♄ △	♉ 10 9:02
11 23:55	♃ ☌	♊ 12 14:14
14 20:41	♄ ☍	♋ 14 21:19
16 17:21	♃ ✶	♌ 17 6:57
19 17:39	♄ △	♍ 19 19:03
22 6:10	♄ □	♎ 22 7:57
24 16:56	♄ ✶	♏ 24 18:58
26 17:40	♃ ☍	♐ 27 2:18
29 3:48	♅ ☌	♑ 29 6:00

☽ Phases & Eclipses Dy Hr Mn	
1 23:41	○ 11♏48
9 1:23	☾ 18♒39
15 22:11	● 25♉16
23 16:49	☽ 2♍46
31 10:53	○ 10♐12
7 6:22	☾ 16♓43
14 9:14	● 23♊32
22 10:23	☽ 1♎13
29 19:46	○ 8♑15

Astro Data

1 May 1988
Julian Day # 32263
SVP 5♓25'20"
GC 26♐40.6 ⚴ 17♒04.4
Eris 16♈42.2 ⚵ 19♉27.1
⚷ 25♊36.8 ⚶ 1♌58.6
☽ Mean ☊ 20♓44.0

1 June 1988
Julian Day # 32294
SVP 5♓25'15"
GC 26♐40.6 ⚴ 20♒10.7
Eris 16♈58.5 ⚵ 7♊55.0
⚷ 28♊10.1 ⚶ 12♌32.6
☽ Mean ☊ 19♓05.5

July 1988 — LONGITUDE

Day	Sid.Time	☉	0 hr ☽	Noon ☽	True ☊	☿	♀	♂	⚳	♃	♄	♅	♆	♇
1 F	6 39 02	9♋51 18	25♑24 59	2♒45 40	16♓16.0	19♊51.8	14♊06.8	23♓52.1	29♓51.7	26♉09.2	28♐26.6	28♐35.9	8♑47.0	9♏51.4
2 Sa	6 42 58	10 48 29	10♒06 54	17 27 48	16R 10.7	20 25.7	14R 00.7	24 23.7	29 59.8	26 21.3	28R 22.3	28R 33.5	8R 45.4	9R 50.8
3 Su	6 46 55	11 45 40	24 47 33	2♓05 28	16D 08.0	21 04.4	13 56.9	24 55.0	0♈07.5	26 33.3	28 18.0	28 31.1	8 43.8	9 50.2
4 M	6 50 51	12 42 51	9♓20 58	16 33 36	16 07.3	21 47.8	13D 55.5	25 26.1	0 15.0	26 45.2	28 13.8	28 28.8	8 42.2	9 49.7
5 Tu	6 54 48	13 40 03	23 43 01	0♈48 58	16R 07.7	22 35.8	13 56.5	25 56.8	0 22.2	26 57.1	28 09.6	28 26.4	8 40.5	9 49.2
6 W	6 58 45	14 37 14	7♈51 20	14 50 02	16 08.1	23 28.4	13 59.8	26 27.2	0 29.1	27 08.9	28 05.4	28 24.1	8 38.9	9 48.7
7 Th	7 02 41	15 34 27	21 45 06	28 36 33	16 07.3	24 25.6	14 05.3	26 57.3	0 35.7	27 20.6	28 01.3	28 21.8	8 37.3	9 48.2
8 F	7 06 38	16 31 39	5♉24 29	12♉08 56	16 04.6	25 27.3	14 13.0	27 27.1	0 42.0	27 32.2	27 57.2	28 19.5	8 35.7	9 47.8
9 Sa	7 10 34	17 28 53	18 50 02	25 27 49	15 59.6	26 33.5	14 22.8	27 56.5	0 48.0	27 43.7	27 53.1	28 17.2	8 34.1	9 47.5
10 Su	7 14 31	18 26 06	2♊02 23	8♊33 45	15 52.3	27 44.0	14 34.7	28 25.6	0 53.7	27 55.1	27 49.1	28 15.0	8 32.5	9 47.1
11 M	7 18 27	19 23 20	15 01 58	21 27 03	15 43.4	28 58.8	14 48.7	28 54.4	0 59.1	28 06.5	27 45.2	28 12.7	8 30.9	9 46.8
12 Tu	7 22 24	20 20 34	27 49 01	4♋07 54	15 33.6	0♋17.8	15 04.6	29 22.7	1 04.2	28 17.8	27 41.2	28 10.5	8 29.4	9 46.5
13 W	7 26 20	21 17 49	10♋23 44	16 36 32	15 23.8	1 41.1	15 22.4	29 50.8	1 09.0	28 28.9	27 37.4	28 08.3	8 27.8	9 46.3
14 Th	7 30 17	22 15 04	22 46 24	28 53 26	15 15.2	3 08.4	15 42.0	0♈18.4	1 13.4	28 40.0	27 33.5	28 06.2	8 26.2	9 46.1
15 F	7 34 14	23 12 19	4♌57 45	10♌59 33	15 08.3	4 39.7	16 03.4	0 45.6	1 17.6	28 51.0	27 29.7	28 04.0	8 24.7	9 45.9
16 Sa	7 38 10	24 09 34	16 59 03	22 56 32	15 03.5	6 14.9	16 26.6	1 12.4	1 21.4	29 01.9	27 26.0	28 01.9	8 23.1	9 45.8
17 Su	7 42 07	25 06 50	28 52 20	4♍46 48	15D 01.0	7 53.9	16 51.3	1 38.8	1 24.8	29 12.7	27 22.3	27 59.8	8 21.6	9 45.7
18 M	7 46 03	26 04 06	10♍40 23	16 33 33	15 00.4	9 36.5	17 17.7	2 04.8	1 28.0	29 23.4	27 18.7	27 57.7	8 20.0	9 45.6
19 Tu	7 50 00	27 01 22	22 26 48	28 20 41	15 01.2	11 22.5	17 45.6	2 30.4	1 30.8	29 34.0	27 15.2	27 55.7	8 18.5	9D 45.6
20 W	7 53 56	27 58 38	4♎15 48	10♎12 46	15 02.5	13 11.8	18 15.0	2 55.5	1 33.2	29 44.5	27 11.7	27 53.7	8 17.0	9 45.6
21 Th	7 57 53	28 55 55	16 12 13	22 14 46	15R 03.5	15 04.2	18 45.8	3 20.2	1 35.3	29 54.8	27 08.2	27 51.7	8 15.5	9 45.6
22 F	8 01 49	29 53 12	28 21 06	4♏31 49	15 03.6	16 59.3	19 18.0	3 44.4	1 37.1	0♊05.1	27 04.9	27 49.7	8 14.0	9 45.7
23 Sa	8 05 46	0♌50 29	10♏47 32	17 08 49	15 02.2	18 56.8	19 51.6	4 08.2	1 38.6	0 15.3	27 01.5	27 47.8	8 12.5	9 45.7
24 Su	8 09 43	1 47 46	23 36 10	0♐09 58	14 59.1	20 56.6	20 26.4	4 31.5	1 39.7	0 25.4	26 58.3	27 45.9	8 11.1	9 45.9
25 M	8 13 39	2 45 04	6♐50 33	13 38 05	14 54.4	22 58.3	21 02.4	4 54.3	1 40.4	0 35.3	26 55.1	27 44.0	8 09.6	9 46.0
26 Tu	8 17 36	3 42 23	20 32 36	27 33 57	14 48.7	25 01.5	21 39.7	5 16.6	1R 40.8	0 45.2	26 52.0	27 42.2	8 08.2	9 46.3
27 W	8 21 32	4 39 42	4♑41 48	11♑55 41	14 42.5	27 05.9	22 18.1	5 38.3	1 40.9	0 54.9	26 49.0	27 40.4	8 06.8	9 46.5
28 Th	8 25 29	5 37 02	19 14 54	26 38 38	14 36.9	29 11.2	22 57.6	5 59.6	1 40.6	1 04.5	26 46.0	27 38.7	8 05.4	9 46.8
29 F	8 29 25	6 34 22	4♒05 53	11♒35 37	14 32.4	1♌17.1	23 38.2	6 20.3	1 39.9	1 14.0	26 43.2	27 36.9	8 04.0	9 47.1
30 Sa	8 33 22	7 31 43	19 06 41	26 37 58	14 29.6	3 23.2	24 19.8	6 40.5	1 38.9	1 23.4	26 40.3	27 35.2	8 02.7	9 47.4
31 Su	8 37 19	8 29 05	4♓08 23	11♓36 54	14D 28.5	5 29.3	25 02.4	7 00.1	1 37.6	1 32.7	26 37.6	27 33.6	8 01.3	9 47.8

August 1988 — LONGITUDE

Day	Sid.Time	☉	0 hr ☽	Noon ☽	True ☊	☿	♀	♂	⚳	♃	♄	♅	♆	♇
1 M	8 41 15	9♌26 28	19♓02 36	26♓24 44	14♓28.9	7♌35.1	25♊45.9	7♈19.2	1♈35.8	1♊41.8	26♐34.9	27♐32.0	8♑00.0	9♏48.2
2 Tu	8 45 12	10 23 51	3♈42 40	10♈55 54	14 30.1	9 40.4	26 30.4	7 37.6	1R 33.7	1 50.9	26R 32.4	27R 30.4	7R 58.7	9 48.6
3 W	8 49 08	11 21 17	18 04 07	25 07 05	14 31.5	11 45.0	27 15.8	7 55.5	1 31.3	1 59.8	26 29.9	27 28.8	7 57.4	9 49.1
4 Th	8 53 05	12 18 43	2♉04 45	8♉57 07	14R 32.3	13 48.7	28 02.1	8 12.7	1 28.5	2 08.5	26 27.4	27 27.3	7 56.1	9 49.6
5 F	8 57 01	13 16 11	15 44 16	22 26 24	14 32.0	15 51.4	28 49.1	8 29.3	1 25.3	2 17.2	26 25.1	27 25.9	7 54.9	9 50.1
6 Sa	9 00 58	14 13 40	29 03 42	5♊36 24	14 30.4	17 53.0	29 37.0	8 45.2	1 21.7	2 25.7	26 22.8	27 24.4	7 53.6	9 50.7
7 Su	9 04 54	15 11 10	12♊04 48	18 29 07	14 27.4	19 53.3	0♋25.6	9 00.5	1 17.8	2 34.1	26 20.7	27 23.1	7 52.4	9 51.3
8 M	9 08 51	16 08 42	24 49 39	1♋06 40	14 23.5	21 52.4	1 15.0	9 15.1	1 13.6	2 42.4	26 18.6	27 21.7	7 51.2	9 52.0
9 Tu	9 12 48	17 06 15	7♋20 25	13 31 09	14 19.0	23 50.0	2 05.1	9 28.9	1 09.0	2 50.5	26 16.6	27 20.4	7 50.1	9 52.6
10 W	9 16 44	18 03 49	19 39 05	25 44 28	14 14.5	25 46.2	2 55.8	9 42.1	1 04.0	2 58.5	26 14.7	27 19.1	7 48.9	9 53.3
11 Th	9 20 41	19 01 25	1♌47 32	7♌48 28	14 10.6	27 41.0	3 47.3	9 54.6	0 58.6	3 06.3	26 12.8	27 17.9	7 47.8	9 54.1
12 F	9 24 37	19 59 01	13 47 31	19 44 55	14 07.7	29 34.3	4 39.3	10 06.3	0 52.9	3 14.0	26 11.1	27 16.8	7 46.7	9 54.9
13 Sa	9 28 34	20 56 39	25 40 54	1♍35 43	14 05.9	1♍26.2	5 32.0	10 17.2	0 46.9	3 21.5	26 09.4	27 15.6	7 45.6	9 55.7
14 Su	9 32 30	21 54 18	7♍29 40	13 23 02	14D 05.3	3 16.6	6 25.2	10 27.4	0 40.5	3 29.0	26 07.9	27 14.5	7 44.5	9 56.5
15 M	9 36 27	22 51 58	19 16 09	25 09 23	14 05.7	5 05.5	7 19.0	10 36.9	0 33.7	3 36.2	26 06.4	27 13.5	7 43.5	9 57.4
16 Tu	9 40 23	23 49 39	1♎03 06	6♎57 44	14 06.8	6 52.9	8 13.4	10 45.5	0 26.6	3 43.3	26 05.0	27 12.5	7 42.5	9 58.3
17 W	9 44 20	24 47 21	12 53 44	18 51 35	14 08.3	8 38.9	9 08.3	10 53.4	0 19.2	3 50.3	26 03.8	27 11.5	7 41.5	9 59.2
18 Th	9 48 17	25 45 04	24 51 46	0♏54 49	14 09.8	10 23.5	10 03.7	11 00.5	0 11.5	3 57.1	26 02.6	27 10.6	7 40.6	10 00.2
19 F	9 52 13	26 42 49	7♏01 16	13 11 42	14 10.9	12 06.6	10 59.7	11 06.8	0 03.4	4 03.8	26 01.5	27 09.8	7 39.6	10 01.2
20 Sa	9 56 10	27 40 34	19 26 37	25 46 33	14R 11.4	13 48.3	11 56.1	11 12.3	29♓55.0	4 10.3	26 00.5	27 09.0	7 38.7	10 02.3
21 Su	10 00 06	28 38 21	2♐12 02	8♐43 30	14 11.1	15 28.6	12 52.9	11 16.9	29 46.3	4 16.6	25 59.6	27 08.2	7 37.8	10 03.3
22 M	10 04 03	29 36 09	15 21 19	22 05 48	14 10.2	17 07.5	13 50.3	11 20.8	29 37.3	4 22.8	25 58.8	27 07.5	7 37.0	10 04.4
23 Tu	10 07 59	0♍33 58	28 57 09	5♑55 25	14 08.9	18 45.0	14 48.1	11 23.8	29 28.0	4 28.8	25 58.0	27 06.8	7 36.2	10 05.6
24 W	10 11 56	1 31 48	13♑00 30	20 12 09	14 07.3	20 21.2	15 46.3	11 26.0	29 18.4	4 34.7	25 57.4	27 06.2	7 35.4	10 06.7
25 Th	10 15 52	2 29 40	27 29 55	4♒53 12	14 05.9	21 56.0	16 44.9	11 27.3	29 08.5	4 40.4	25 56.9	27 05.6	7 34.6	10 07.9
26 F	10 19 49	3 27 33	12♒21 13	19 53 00	14 04.8	23 29.4	17 44.0	11R 27.8	28 58.3	4 45.9	25 56.5	27 05.1	7 33.9	10 09.1
27 Sa	10 23 46	4 25 27	27 27 30	5♓03 32	14D 04.3	25 01.5	18 43.4	11 27.5	28 47.9	4 51.3	25 56.2	27 04.7	7 33.2	10 10.4
28 Su	10 27 42	5 23 23	12♓39 55	20 15 25	14 04.2	26 32.2	19 43.3	11 26.3	28 37.2	4 56.5	25 55.9	27 04.2	7 32.5	10 11.7
29 M	10 31 39	6 21 20	27 48 53	5♈19 14	14 04.6	28 01.5	20 43.5	11 24.3	28 26.2	5 01.5	25D 55.8	27 03.9	7 31.8	10 13.0
30 Tu	10 35 35	7 19 19	12♈45 30	20 06 53	14 05.1	29 29.5	21 44.1	11 21.4	28 15.0	5 06.4	25 55.7	27 03.5	7 31.2	10 14.3
31 W	10 39 32	8 17 21	27 22 44	4♉32 33	14 05.7	0♎56.1	22 45.0	11 17.7	28 03.6	5 11.1	25 55.8	27 03.3	7 30.6	10 15.7

Astro Data	Dy Hr Mn
♀ D	4 14:09
☽ 0N	5 6:38
♃⊼♄	10 2:38
♃⊼♅	11 23:04
☽ 0S	19 10:09
♇ D	20 4:21
⚳ R	27 3:40
☽ 0N	1 13:30
☽ 0S	15 16:14
♂ R	26 14:40
☽ 0N	28 23:03
☿ 0S	30 7:50
♄ D	30 10:06

Planet Ingress	Dy Hr Mn
⚳ ♈	2 12:44
☿ ♋	12 6:42
♂ ♈	13 20:00
♃ ♊	21 24:00
☉ ♌	22 14:51
☿ ♌	28 21:19
♀ ♋	6 23:24
☿ ♍	12 17:29
⚳ ♓R	19 21:48
☉ ♍	22 21:54
☿ ♎	30 20:25

Last Aspect Dy Hr Mn		☽ Ingress	Dy Hr Mn
1 1:03	♃ △	♒	1 7:30
3 6:08	♅ ⚹	♓	3 8:33
5 7:59	♅ □	♈	5 10:37
7 11:34	♅ △	♉	7 14:27
9 16:41	♂ ⚹	♊	9 20:16
12 3:50	☿ ☌	♋	12 4:08
14 11:33	♃ ⚹	♌	14 14:11
17 0:31	♃ □	♍	17 2:17
19 14:31	♃ △	♎	19 15:22
22 2:14	☉ □	♏	22 3:13
23 15:59	☿ △	♐	24 11:42
26 12:14	♅ ☌	♑	26 16:07
28 16:46	☿ ☍	♒	28 17:25
30 13:31	♅ ⚹	♓	30 17:23

Last Aspect Dy Hr Mn		☽ Ingress	Dy Hr Mn
1 13:50	♅ □	♈	1 17:53
3 16:03	♅ △	♉	3 20:24
4 22:07	☿ □	♊	6 1:43
8 4:50	♅ ☍	♋	8 9:52
9 4:55	♇ △	♌	10 20:26
13 3:13	♅ △	♍	13 8:46
15 16:12	♅ □	♎	15 21:52
18 4:37	♅ ⚹	♏	18 10:12
20 15:51	☉ □	♐	20 19:55
22 20:49	♅ ☌	♑	23 1:49
24 12:17	☿ △	♒	25 4:05
26 23:24	♅ ⚹	♓	27 4:01
28 23:04	☿ ☍	♈	29 3:29
30 23:28	♅ △	♉	31 4:22

☽ Phases & Eclipses Dy Hr Mn	
6 11:36	☾ 14♈36
13 21:53	● 21♋41
22 2:14	☽ 29♎30
29 3:25	○ 6♒14
4 18:22	☾ 12♉34
12 12:31	● 20♌00
20 15:51	☽ 27♏50
27 10:56	○ 4♓23
27 11:05	• P 0.291

Astro Data

1 July 1988
Julian Day # 32324
SVP 5♓25'09"
GC 26♐40.7 ⚵ 17♒58.0R
Eris 17♈06.7 ⚴ 25♊35.1
⚷ 0♋56.4 ⚶ 24♌50.1
☽ Mean ☊ 17♓30.2

1 August 1988
Julian Day # 32355
SVP 5♓25'04"
GC 26♐40.8 ⚵ 10♒51.5R
Eris 17♈05.5R ⚴ 13♋15.1
⚷ 3♋40.6 ⚶ 8♍53.6
☽ Mean ☊ 15♓51.7

LONGITUDE — September 1988

Day	Sid.Time	☉	0 hr ☽	Noon ☽	True ☊	☿	♀	♂	⚳	♃	♄	♅	♆	♇
1 Th	10 43 28	9♍15 24	11♉36 04	18♉33 05	14♓06.1	2♎21.3	23♋46.3	11♈13.2	27♓51.9	5♊15.6	25♐56.0	27♐03.0	7♑30.0	10♏17.1
2 F	10 47 25	10 13 29	25 23 37	2♊07 46	14R 06.3	3 45.1	24 48.0	11R 07.8	27R 40.1	5 20.0	25 56.2	27R 02.9	7R 29.5	10 18.5
3 Sa	10 51 21	11 11 36	8♊45 45	15 17 53	14 06.4	5 07.4	25 50.0	11 01.5	27 28.0	5 24.1	25 56.6	27 02.7	7 29.0	10 20.0
4 Su	10 55 18	12 09 45	21 44 30	28 06 00	14 06.3	6 28.3	26 52.3	10 54.5	27 15.8	5 28.1	25 57.0	27D 02.7	7 28.5	10 21.5
5 M	10 59 15	13 07 56	4♋22 51	10♋35 30	14D 06.2	7 47.6	27 54.9	10 46.6	27 03.3	5 31.9	25 57.6	27 02.6	7 28.1	10 23.0
6 Tu	11 03 11	14 06 08	16 44 23	22 49 58	14 06.1	9 05.4	28 57.8	10 37.9	26 50.7	5 35.5	25 58.2	27 02.7	7 27.7	10 24.5
7 W	11 07 08	15 04 23	28 52 41	4♌52 59	14 06.2	10 21.6	0♌01.0	10 28.4	26 38.0	5 39.0	25 58.9	27 02.8	7 27.3	10 26.1
8 Th	11 11 04	16 02 40	10♌51 14	16 47 51	14 06.3	11 36.2	1 04.5	10 18.2	26 25.1	5 42.2	25 59.8	27 02.9	7 26.9	10 27.7
9 F	11 15 01	17 00 59	22 43 10	28 37 34	14 06.5	12 48.9	2 08.3	10 07.3	26 12.1	5 45.3	26 00.7	27 03.1	7 26.6	10 29.3
10 Sa	11 18 57	17 59 19	4♍31 20	10♍24 47	14R 06.7	13 59.9	3 12.3	9 55.6	25 58.9	5 48.1	26 01.8	27 03.3	7 26.3	10 31.0
11 Su	11 22 54	18 57 41	16 18 14	22 11 56	14 06.6	15 08.9	4 16.6	9 43.3	25 45.7	5 50.8	26 02.9	27 03.6	7 26.1	10 32.7
12 M	11 26 50	19 56 06	28 06 11	4♎01 15	14 06.3	16 16.0	5 21.2	9 30.3	25 32.4	5 53.3	26 04.1	27 03.9	7 25.8	10 34.4
13 Tu	11 30 47	20 54 31	9♎57 26	15 54 59	14 05.6	17 20.9	6 26.0	9 16.7	25 19.0	5 55.6	26 05.4	27 04.3	7 25.6	10 36.1
14 W	11 34 43	21 52 59	21 54 14	27 55 29	14 04.7	18 23.5	7 31.0	9 02.5	25 05.6	5 57.7	26 06.9	27 04.7	7 25.5	10 37.8
15 Th	11 38 40	22 51 29	3♏59 03	10♏05 17	14 03.5	19 23.7	8 36.3	8 47.8	24 52.1	5 59.6	26 08.4	27 05.2	7 25.4	10 39.6
16 F	11 42 37	23 50 00	16 14 32	22 27 11	14 02.3	20 21.3	9 41.9	8 32.6	24 38.6	6 01.3	26 10.0	27 05.8	7 25.3	10 41.4
17 Sa	11 46 33	24 48 33	28 43 37	5♐04 12	14 01.3	21 16.2	10 47.6	8 16.9	24 25.1	6 02.8	26 11.7	27 06.4	7 25.2	10 43.2
18 Su	11 50 30	25 47 07	11♐29 20	17 59 23	14D 00.7	22 08.2	11 53.6	8 00.8	24 11.6	6 04.1	26 13.5	27 07.0	7D 25.2	10 45.1
19 M	11 54 26	26 45 43	24 34 42	1♑15 36	14 00.6	22 56.9	12 59.8	7 44.4	23 58.2	6 05.2	26 15.4	27 07.7	7 25.2	10 47.0
20 Tu	11 58 23	27 44 21	8♑02 19	14 55 03	14 01.1	23 42.2	14 06.2	7 27.6	23 44.7	6 06.1	26 17.4	27 08.5	7 25.2	10 48.8
21 W	12 02 19	28 43 01	21 53 52	28 58 46	14 02.1	24 23.8	15 12.8	7 10.6	23 31.4	6 06.8	26 19.5	27 09.3	7 25.3	10 50.8
22 Th	12 06 16	29 41 42	6♒09 35	13♒26 00	14 03.2	25 01.4	16 19.6	6 53.3	23 18.0	6 07.4	26 21.7	27 10.1	7 25.4	10 52.7
23 F	12 10 12	0♎40 25	20 47 34	28 13 40	14 04.2	25 34.6	17 26.7	6 35.8	23 04.8	6 07.7	26 24.0	27 11.0	7 25.5	10 54.7
24 Sa	12 14 09	1 39 10	5♓43 30	13♓16 10	14R 04.6	26 03.2	18 33.9	6 18.2	22 51.7	6R 07.8	26 26.3	27 12.0	7 25.7	10 56.6
25 Su	12 18 06	2 37 56	20 50 35	28 25 38	14 04.2	26 26.7	19 41.3	6 00.5	22 38.6	6 07.7	26 28.8	27 13.0	7 25.9	10 58.6
26 M	12 22 02	3 36 44	6♈00 07	13♈32 51	14 02.8	26 44.8	20 48.9	5 42.8	22 25.7	6 07.4	26 31.3	27 14.0	7 26.2	11 00.6
27 Tu	12 25 59	4 35 35	21 02 42	28 28 34	14 00.5	26 57.0	21 56.7	5 25.1	22 12.9	6 06.9	26 34.0	27 15.1	7 26.4	11 02.7
28 W	12 29 55	5 34 27	5♉49 32	13♉04 48	13 57.6	27R 03.0	23 04.7	5 07.4	22 00.3	6 06.3	26 36.7	27 16.3	7 26.7	11 04.7
29 Th	12 33 52	6 33 22	20 13 47	27 16 03	13 54.6	27 02.3	24 12.9	4 49.8	21 47.8	6 05.4	26 39.5	27 17.5	7 27.1	11 06.8
30 F	12 37 48	7 32 20	4♊11 21	10♊59 36	13 52.0	26 54.5	25 21.3	4 32.3	21 35.5	6 04.3	26 42.4	27 18.7	7 27.4	11 08.9

LONGITUDE — October 1988

Day	Sid.Time	☉	0 hr ☽	Noon ☽	True ☊	☿	♀	♂	⚳	♃	♄	♅	♆	♇
1 Sa	12 41 45	8♎31 19	17♊40 54	24♊15 28	13♓50.1	26♎39.4	26♌29.8	4♈15.1	21♓23.4	6♊03.0	26♐45.4	27♐20.0	7♑27.8	11♏11.0
2 Su	12 45 41	9 30 21	0♋43 37	7♋05 48	13D 49.3	26R 16.7	27 38.5	3R 58.0	21R 11.5	6R 01.5	26 48.5	27 21.4	7 28.3	11 13.2
3 M	12 49 38	10 29 25	13 22 30	19 34 16	13 49.6	25 46.2	28 47.4	3 41.3	20 59.8	5 59.8	26 51.7	27 22.8	7 28.7	11 15.3
4 Tu	12 53 35	11 28 32	25 41 40	1♌45 19	13 50.9	25 07.9	29 56.4	3 24.8	20 48.3	5 57.9	26 54.9	27 24.2	7 29.2	11 17.5
5 W	12 57 31	12 27 41	7♌45 49	13 43 44	13 52.6	24 22.0	1♍05.6	3 08.7	20 37.0	5 55.8	26 58.3	27 25.7	7 29.8	11 19.6
6 Th	13 01 28	13 26 51	19 39 40	25 34 10	13 54.3	23 29.1	2 15.0	2 53.1	20 26.0	5 53.5	27 01.7	27 27.3	7 30.3	11 21.8
7 F	13 05 24	14 26 05	1♍27 44	7♍20 53	13R 55.5	22 29.8	3 24.5	2 37.9	20 15.2	5 51.0	27 05.2	27 28.8	7 30.9	11 24.1
8 Sa	13 09 21	15 25 20	13 14 04	19 07 41	13 55.6	21 25.1	4 34.1	2 23.1	20 04.7	5 48.4	27 08.8	27 30.5	7 31.6	11 26.3
9 Su	13 13 17	16 24 37	25 02 07	0♎57 42	13 54.1	20 16.4	5 43.9	2 08.9	19 54.5	5 45.5	27 12.5	27 32.2	7 32.2	11 28.5
10 M	13 17 14	17 23 57	6♎54 44	12 53 28	13 51.0	19 05.3	6 53.9	1 55.3	19 44.5	5 42.4	27 16.3	27 33.9	7 32.9	11 30.8
11 Tu	13 21 10	18 23 19	18 54 10	24 57 00	13 46.3	17 53.6	8 03.9	1 42.3	19 34.8	5 39.1	27 20.1	27 35.7	7 33.7	11 33.0
12 W	13 25 07	19 22 42	1♏02 08	7♏09 46	13 40.3	16 43.4	9 14.2	1 29.9	19 25.5	5 35.6	27 24.0	27 37.5	7 34.4	11 35.3
13 Th	13 29 04	20 22 08	13 20 01	19 33 01	13 33.7	15 36.7	10 24.5	1 18.1	19 16.5	5 32.0	27 28.0	27 39.3	7 35.2	11 37.6
14 F	13 33 00	21 21 36	25 48 55	2♐07 50	13 27.0	14 35.4	11 35.0	1 07.1	19 07.7	5 28.1	27 32.1	27 41.3	7 36.0	11 39.9
15 Sa	13 36 57	22 21 06	8♐29 56	14 55 21	13 21.2	13 41.3	12 45.6	0 56.8	18 59.3	5 24.1	27 36.3	27 43.2	7 36.9	11 42.2
16 Su	13 40 53	23 20 37	21 24 15	27 56 50	13 16.7	12 55.9	13 56.3	0 47.1	18 51.3	5 19.9	27 40.5	27 45.2	7 37.8	11 44.5
17 M	13 44 50	24 20 10	4♑33 16	11♑13 44	13 14.1	12 20.3	15 07.1	0 38.3	18 43.6	5 15.5	27 44.8	27 47.3	7 38.7	11 46.9
18 Tu	13 48 46	25 19 45	17 58 25	24 47 29	13D 13.2	11 55.5	16 18.1	0 30.2	18 36.2	5 10.9	27 49.2	27 49.4	7 39.7	11 49.2
19 W	13 52 43	26 19 22	1♒41 02	8♒39 12	13 13.8	11D 41.8	17 29.2	0 22.9	18 29.1	5 06.2	27 53.7	27 51.5	7 40.7	11 51.6
20 Th	13 56 39	27 19 00	15 41 57	22 49 15	13 15.0	11 39.3	18 40.4	0 16.3	18 22.5	5 01.2	27 58.2	27 53.7	7 41.7	11 53.9
21 F	14 00 36	28 18 40	0♓00 55	7♓16 41	13R 16.1	11 47.8	19 51.7	0 10.6	18 16.1	4 56.1	28 02.8	27 55.9	7 42.7	11 56.3
22 Sa	14 04 33	29 18 22	14 36 05	21 58 36	13 15.9	12 06.9	21 03.1	0 05.6	18 10.2	4 50.9	28 07.5	27 58.1	7 43.8	11 58.7
23 Su	14 08 29	0♏18 05	29 23 32	6♈50 02	13 13.8	12 36.1	22 14.6	0 01.5	18 04.6	4 45.4	28 12.3	28 00.4	7 44.9	12 01.1
24 M	14 12 26	1 17 50	14♈17 11	21 43 58	13 09.5	13 14.5	23 26.2	29♓58.1	17 59.3	4 39.9	28 17.1	28 02.8	7 46.0	12 03.5
25 Tu	14 16 22	2 17 37	29 09 20	6♉32 12	13 03.0	14 01.3	24 37.9	29 55.6	17 54.5	4 34.1	28 22.0	28 05.1	7 47.2	12 05.9
26 W	14 20 19	3 17 27	13♉51 35	21 06 31	12 55.1	14 55.8	25 49.8	29 53.8	17 50.0	4 28.2	28 26.9	28 07.6	7 48.4	12 08.3
27 Th	14 24 15	4 17 18	28 16 13	5♊20 01	12 46.6	15 57.0	27 01.7	29D 52.9	17 45.9	4 22.2	28 31.9	28 10.0	7 49.6	12 10.7
28 F	14 28 12	5 17 11	12♊17 26	19 08 10	12 38.6	17 04.1	28 13.8	29 52.7	17 42.1	4 16.0	28 37.0	28 12.5	7 50.9	12 13.1
29 Sa	14 32 08	6 17 07	25 52 04	2♋29 09	12 32.0	18 16.4	29 25.9	29 53.3	17 38.7	4 09.7	28 42.2	28 15.0	7 52.2	12 15.5
30 Su	14 36 05	7 17 05	8♋59 38	15 23 49	12 27.3	19 33.2	0♎38.2	29 54.7	17 35.7	4 03.2	28 47.4	28 17.6	7 53.5	12 17.9
31 M	14 40 02	8 17 05	21 42 07	27 55 03	12D 24.7	20 53.8	1 50.5	29 56.9	17 33.1	3 56.6	28 52.7	28 20.2	7 54.8	12 20.4

Astro Data
Dy Hr Mn
♇0S 5 6:53
♅D 5 9:41
☽0S 11 22:13
♆D 18 18:19
☉0S 22 19:28
♃R 24 13:58
☽0N 25 10:06
☿R 28 21:37

☽0S 9 4:26
♄☌♅ 18 13:26
☿D 20 5:20
☽0N 22 20:22
♂D 28 5:07

Planet Ingress
Dy Hr Mn
♀ ♌ 7 11:37
☉ ♎ 22 19:29

♀ ♍ 4 13:15
☉ ♏ 23 4:44
♂ ♓R 23 22:01
♀ ♎ 29 23:20

Last Aspect / ☽ Ingress
Last Aspect Dy Hr Mn			☽ Ingress Dy Hr Mn
1 21:53	♀ ✶	♊	2 8:11
4 10:00	♅ ☍	♋	4 15:37
7 1:20	♀ ☌	♌	7 2:14
9 8:48	♅ △	♍	9 14:48
11 21:53	♅ □	♎	12 3:51
14 10:19	♅ ✶	♏	14 16:07
16 14:52	☉ ✶	♐	17 2:25
19 4:36	♅ ☌	♑	19 9:45
21 11:31	☉ △	♒	21 13:43
23 10:19	♅ ✶	♓	23 14:51
25 10:05	♅ □	♈	25 14:29
27 10:01	♅ △	♉	27 14:29
29 6:19	♀ □	♊	29 16:43

Last Aspect / ☽ Ingress
Last Aspect Dy Hr Mn			☽ Ingress Dy Hr Mn
1 17:42	♅ ☍	♋	1 22:39
3 23:34	☿ □	♌	4 8:31
6 15:51	♅ △	♍	6 21:01
9 5:03	♅ □	♎	9 10:03
11 17:14	♅ ✶	♏	11 21:58
12 20:39	♇ ☌	♐	14 7:58
16 11:39	♅ ☌	♑	16 15:44
18 13:01	☉ □	♒	18 21:05
20 20:39	♄ ✶	♓	20 23:58
22 22:00	♄ □	♈	23 0:59
24 22:39	♄ △	♉	25 1:22
27 2:44	♂ ✶	♊	27 2:55
29 7:16	♂ □	♋	29 7:28
31 15:58	♂ △	♌	31 16:03

☽ Phases & Eclipses
Dy Hr Mn
3 3:50 ☾ 10♊52
11 4:49 ● 18♍40
11 4:43:33 ● A 06'57"
19 3:18 ☽ 26♐24
25 19:07 ○ 2♈55

2 16:59 ☾ 9♋43
10 21:49 ● 17♎48
18 13:01 ☽ 25♑22
25 4:36 ○ 1♉59

Astro Data
1 September 1988
Julian Day # 32386
SVP 5♓25'00"
GC 26♐40.9 ⚴ 3♒49.3R
Eris 16♈55.0R ⚵ 29♋54.4
⚷ 5♋50.9 ⚶ 23♍52.7
☽ Mean ☊ 14♓13.2

1 October 1988
Julian Day # 32416
SVP 5♓24'56"
GC 26♐40.9 ⚴ 1♒38.4
Eris 16♈38.6R ⚵ 14♌34.8
⚷ 7♋01.2 ⚶ 8♎58.6
☽ Mean ☊ 12♓37.9

November 1988 LONGITUDE

Day	Sid.Time	☉	0 hr ☽	Noon ☽	True ☊	☿	♀	♂	⚳	♃	♄	♅	♆	♇
1 Tu	14 43 58	9♏17 07	4♌03 13	10♌07 13	12♓24.1	22♎17.5	3♎02.9	29♓59.9	17♓30.8	3♊49.9	28♐58.0	28♐22.9	7♑56.2	12♏22.8
2 W	14 47 55	10 17 11	16 07 44	22 05 26	12 24.6	23 44.0	4 15.5	0♈03.6	17R 29.0	3R 43.0	29 03.4	28 25.5	7 57.6	12 25.2
3 Th	14 51 51	11 17 17	28 01 01	3♍55 09	12R 25.6	25 12.7	5 28.1	0 08.1	17 27.5	3 36.0	29 08.9	28 28.3	7 59.0	12 27.6
4 F	14 55 48	12 17 25	9♍48 30	15 41 41	12 25.8	26 43.2	6 40.8	0 13.3	17 26.3	3 28.9	29 14.4	28 31.0	8 00.4	12 30.1
5 Sa	14 59 44	13 17 36	21 35 19	27 29 56	12 24.4	28 15.3	7 53.5	0 19.3	17 25.6	3 21.7	29 20.0	28 33.8	8 01.9	12 32.5
6 Su	15 03 41	14 17 48	3♎26 02	9♎24 06	12 20.8	29 48.5	9 06.4	0 26.0	17D 25.2	3 14.4	29 25.6	28 36.6	8 03.4	12 34.9
7 M	15 07 37	15 18 02	15 24 31	21 27 36	12 14.5	1♏22.7	10 19.3	0 33.4	17 25.2	3 07.0	29 31.3	28 39.4	8 04.9	12 37.4
8 Tu	15 11 34	16 18 18	27 33 38	3♏42 49	12 05.5	2 57.6	11 32.3	0 41.6	17 25.6	2 59.5	29 37.1	28 42.3	8 06.5	12 39.8
9 W	15 15 31	17 18 36	9♏55 17	16 11 07	11 54.5	4 33.0	12 45.4	0 50.5	17 26.4	2 51.9	29 42.9	28 45.2	8 08.1	12 42.2
10 Th	15 19 27	18 18 56	22 30 21	28 52 56	11 42.3	6 08.9	13 58.6	1 00.1	17 27.5	2 44.2	29 48.8	28 48.2	8 09.7	12 44.6
11 F	15 23 24	19 19 18	5♐18 48	11♐47 51	11 30.1	7 45.1	15 11.8	1 10.3	17 29.0	2 36.5	29 54.7	28 51.2	8 11.3	12 47.1
12 Sa	15 27 20	20 19 41	18 19 59	24 55 04	11 18.9	9 21.4	16 25.1	1 21.3	17 30.9	2 28.7	0♑00.6	28 54.2	8 12.9	12 49.5
13 Su	15 31 17	21 20 05	1♑32 58	8♑13 35	11 09.9	10 57.9	17 38.5	1 32.9	17 33.1	2 20.8	0 06.7	28 57.2	8 14.6	12 51.9
14 M	15 35 13	22 20 31	14 56 50	21 42 39	11 03.6	12 34.3	18 51.9	1 45.2	17 35.7	2 12.8	0 12.7	29 00.3	8 16.3	12 54.3
15 Tu	15 39 10	23 20 59	28 31 01	5♒21 54	11 00.1	14 10.7	20 05.4	1 58.1	17 38.7	2 04.8	0 18.8	29 03.4	8 18.0	12 56.7
16 W	15 43 06	24 21 27	12♒15 21	19 11 22	10D 58.8	15 47.1	21 18.9	2 11.6	17 42.0	1 56.8	0 25.0	29 06.5	8 19.8	12 59.1
17 Th	15 47 03	25 21 57	26 09 58	3♓11 11	10R 58.8	17 23.3	22 32.5	2 25.8	17 45.7	1 48.7	0 31.2	29 09.6	8 21.6	13 01.5
18 F	15 51 00	26 22 28	10♓14 58	17 21 13	10 58.8	18 59.4	23 46.1	2 40.5	17 49.7	1 40.6	0 37.4	29 12.8	8 23.3	13 03.9
19 Sa	15 54 56	27 23 01	24 29 47	1♈40 25	10 57.5	20 35.4	24 59.8	2 55.9	17 54.0	1 32.5	0 43.7	29 16.0	8 25.1	13 06.3
20 Su	15 58 53	28 23 34	8♈52 47	16 06 24	10 53.7	22 11.1	26 13.6	3 11.7	17 58.7	1 24.3	0 50.0	29 19.2	8 27.0	13 08.6
21 M	16 02 49	29 24 09	23 20 43	0♉35 05	10 47.0	23 46.8	27 27.4	3 28.2	18 03.8	1 16.1	0 56.4	29 22.4	8 28.8	13 11.0
22 Tu	16 06 46	0♐24 45	7♉48 47	15 01 00	10 37.4	25 22.2	28 41.3	3 45.2	18 09.2	1 08.0	1 02.8	29 25.7	8 30.7	13 13.4
23 W	16 10 42	1 25 22	22 10 56	29 17 47	10 25.8	26 57.5	29 55.2	4 02.7	18 14.9	0 59.8	1 09.3	29 29.0	8 32.6	13 15.7
24 Th	16 14 39	2 26 01	6♊20 49	13♊19 22	10 13.2	28 32.6	1♏09.2	4 20.7	18 20.9	0 51.6	1 15.8	29 32.3	8 34.5	13 18.0
25 F	16 18 35	3 26 42	20 12 50	27 00 49	10 00.9	0♐07.6	2 23.2	4 39.2	18 27.3	0 43.4	1 22.3	29 35.6	8 36.4	13 20.4
26 Sa	16 22 32	4 27 24	3♋43 00	10♋19 15	9 50.2	1 42.5	3 37.2	4 58.2	18 34.0	0 35.3	1 28.8	29 39.0	8 38.4	13 22.7
27 Su	16 26 29	5 28 07	16 49 33	23 14 03	9 41.9	3 17.2	4 51.4	5 17.7	18 41.0	0 27.2	1 35.4	29 42.4	8 40.3	13 25.0
28 M	16 30 25	6 28 52	29 32 59	5♌46 44	9 36.3	4 51.7	6 05.5	5 37.7	18 48.3	0 19.1	1 42.1	29 45.8	8 42.3	13 27.3
29 Tu	16 34 22	7 29 38	11♌55 46	18 00 37	9 33.4	6 26.2	7 19.7	5 58.1	18 55.9	0 11.0	1 48.7	29 49.2	8 44.3	13 29.5
30 W	16 38 18	8 30 26	24 01 54	0♍00 15	9 32.3	8 00.6	8 34.0	6 18.9	19 03.8	0 03.0	1 55.4	29 52.6	8 46.3	13 31.8

December 1988 LONGITUDE

Day	Sid.Time	☉	0 hr ☽	Noon ☽	True ☊	☿	♀	♂	⚳	♃	♄	♅	♆	♇
1 Th	16 42 15	9♐31 15	5♍56 22	11♍50 55	9♓32.2	9♐34.9	9♏48.3	6♈40.2	19♓12.0	29♉55.0	2♑02.1	29♐56.0	8♑48.3	13♏34.0
2 F	16 46 11	10 32 06	17 44 40	23 38 16	9R 31.9	11 09.1	11 02.6	7 01.9	19 20.5	29R 47.1	2 08.9	29 59.5	8 50.4	13 36.3
3 Sa	16 50 08	11 32 57	29 32 27	5♎27 52	9 30.2	12 43.3	12 17.0	7 24.0	19 29.4	29 39.2	2 15.7	0♑03.0	8 52.4	13 38.5
4 Su	16 54 04	12 33 51	11♎25 09	17 24 53	9 26.2	14 17.5	13 31.4	7 46.5	19 38.5	29 31.4	2 22.5	0 06.4	8 54.5	13 40.7
5 M	16 58 01	13 34 45	23 27 37	29 33 48	9 19.4	15 51.7	14 45.9	8 09.5	19 47.9	29 23.7	2 29.3	0 09.9	8 56.6	13 42.9
6 Tu	17 01 58	14 35 41	5♏43 51	11♏58 03	9 09.8	17 25.8	16 00.4	8 32.8	19 57.6	29 16.0	2 36.1	0 13.5	8 58.7	13 45.0
7 W	17 05 54	15 36 38	18 16 39	24 39 45	8 57.8	19 00.0	17 14.9	8 56.5	20 07.5	29 08.5	2 43.0	0 17.0	9 00.8	13 47.2
8 Th	17 09 51	16 37 36	1♐07 24	7♐39 30	8 44.5	20 34.2	18 29.4	9 20.6	20 17.8	29 01.0	2 49.9	0 20.5	9 02.9	13 49.3
9 F	17 13 47	17 38 36	14 15 56	20 56 25	8 30.9	22 08.4	19 44.0	9 45.0	20 28.3	28 53.6	2 56.8	0 24.1	9 05.1	13 51.5
10 Sa	17 17 44	18 39 36	27 40 40	4♑28 17	8 18.5	23 42.7	20 58.6	10 09.8	20 39.1	28 46.3	3 03.8	0 27.7	9 07.2	13 53.6
11 Su	17 21 40	19 40 37	11♑18 54	18 12 04	8 08.3	25 17.0	22 13.3	10 34.9	20 50.1	28 39.2	3 10.8	0 31.2	9 09.4	13 55.6
12 M	17 25 37	20 41 38	25 07 24	2♒04 30	8 01.1	26 51.4	23 27.9	11 00.4	21 01.5	28 32.1	3 17.7	0 34.8	9 11.6	13 57.7
13 Tu	17 29 34	21 42 40	9♒03 00	16 02 36	7 56.9	28 25.9	24 42.6	11 26.2	21 13.0	28 25.2	3 24.7	0 38.4	9 13.8	13 59.8
14 W	17 33 30	22 43 43	23 03 03	0♓04 10	7D 55.3	0♑00.4	25 57.3	11 52.3	21 24.9	28 18.4	3 31.7	0 42.0	9 16.0	14 01.8
15 Th	17 37 27	23 44 46	7♓05 46	14 07 45	7R 55.2	1 35.1	27 12.0	12 18.7	21 36.9	28 11.7	3 38.8	0 45.6	9 18.2	14 03.8
16 F	17 41 23	24 45 49	21 10 03	28 12 33	7 55.3	3 09.8	28 26.8	12 45.5	21 49.3	28 05.1	3 45.8	0 49.2	9 20.4	14 05.8
17 Sa	17 45 20	25 46 53	5♈15 12	12♈17 52	7 54.2	4 44.5	29 41.5	13 12.5	22 01.8	27 58.7	3 52.8	0 52.8	9 22.6	14 07.7
18 Su	17 49 16	26 47 57	19 20 26	26 22 43	7 51.0	6 19.3	0♐56.3	13 39.8	22 14.6	27 52.5	3 59.9	0 56.4	9 24.8	14 09.6
19 M	17 53 13	27 49 01	3♉24 27	10♉25 20	7 45.0	7 54.2	2 11.1	14 07.3	22 27.7	27 46.3	4 07.0	1 00.0	9 27.0	14 11.6
20 Tu	17 57 09	28 50 06	17 25 02	24 23 08	7 36.4	9 29.1	3 25.9	14 35.2	22 40.9	27 40.4	4 14.0	1 03.7	9 29.3	14 13.4
21 W	18 01 06	29 51 11	1♊19 12	8♊12 45	7 25.6	11 03.9	4 40.8	15 03.3	22 54.4	27 34.6	4 21.1	1 07.3	9 31.5	14 15.3
22 Th	18 05 03	0♑52 16	15 03 20	21 50 30	7 13.9	12 38.7	5 55.6	15 31.6	23 08.1	27 28.9	4 28.2	1 10.9	9 33.8	14 17.2
23 F	18 08 59	1 53 22	28 33 52	5♋13 06	7 02.4	14 13.4	7 10.5	16 00.2	23 22.0	27 23.4	4 35.3	1 14.5	9 36.0	14 19.0
24 Sa	18 12 56	2 54 28	11♋47 54	18 18 07	6 52.2	15 47.9	8 25.4	16 29.1	23 36.2	27 18.1	4 42.4	1 18.2	9 38.3	14 20.8
25 Su	18 16 52	3 55 35	24 43 40	1♌04 33	6 44.2	17 22.2	9 40.3	16 58.1	23 50.5	27 12.9	4 49.5	1 21.8	9 40.6	14 22.5
26 M	18 20 49	4 56 42	7♌20 54	13 32 55	6 38.9	18 56.2	10 55.3	17 27.4	24 05.1	27 07.9	4 56.6	1 25.4	9 42.8	14 24.3
27 Tu	18 24 45	5 57 50	19 40 54	25 45 14	6D 36.1	20 29.7	12 10.2	17 56.9	24 19.9	27 03.1	5 03.7	1 29.0	9 45.1	14 26.0
28 W	18 28 42	6 58 58	1♍46 23	7♍44 50	6 35.4	22 02.7	13 25.2	18 26.6	24 34.8	26 58.4	5 10.8	1 32.6	9 47.4	14 27.7
29 Th	18 32 38	8 00 06	13 41 11	19 36 02	6 36.1	23 35.0	14 40.2	18 56.5	24 50.0	26 54.0	5 17.9	1 36.2	9 49.6	14 29.3
30 F	18 36 35	9 01 15	25 30 02	1♎23 51	6R 37.0	25 06.3	15 55.1	19 26.6	25 05.4	26 49.7	5 25.0	1 39.8	9 51.9	14 31.0
31 Sa	18 40 32	10 02 24	7♎18 10	13 13 40	6 37.2	26 36.5	17 10.2	19 57.0	25 20.9	26 45.6	5 32.1	1 43.4	9 54.2	14 32.6

Astro Data

	Dy Hr Mn
♀0S	2 0:18
☽0S	5 11:02
⚳D	6 23:30
♂0N	17 11:08
☽0N	19 3:53
♃⊼♄	22 20:25
♃⊼♅	1 9:48
☽0S	2 17:59
☽0N	16 8:46
☽0S	30 1:08

Planet Ingress

	Dy Hr Mn
♂ ♈	1 12:57
☿ ♏	6 14:57
♄ ♑	12 9:26
☉ ♐	22 2:12
♀ ♏	23 13:34
☿ ♐	25 10:04
♃ ♉R	30 20:53
♅ ♑	2 15:35
☿ ♑	14 11:53
♀ ♐	17 17:56
☉ ♑	21 15:28

Last Aspect / ☽ Ingress

Last Aspect Dy Hr Mn		☽ Ingress Dy Hr Mn
3 2:13	♄ △	♍ 3 4:02
5 15:45	♄ □	♎ 5 17:04
8 3:58	♄ ⚹	♏ 8 4:46
9 14:20	☉ ☌	♐ 10 14:06
12 19:15	♅ ☌	♑ 12 21:12
14 13:12	☉ ⚹	♒ 15 2:36
17 5:06	♅ ⚹	♓ 17 6:34
19 7:58	♅ □	♈ 19 9:12
21 9:59	♅ △	♉ 21 11:02
23 7:33	♅ ☍	♊ 23 13:12
25 16:37	♅ ☍	♋ 25 17:19
26 17:38	♇ △	♌ 28 0:52
30 11:44	♅ △	♍ 30 11:59

Last Aspect / ☽ Ingress

Last Aspect Dy Hr Mn		☽ Ingress Dy Hr Mn
3 0:21	♃ △	♎ 3 0:56
4 4:49	☿ ⚹	♏ 5 12:51
7 20:15	♃ ☍	♐ 7 21:55
9 14:26	☿ ☌	♑ 10 4:07
12 5:57	♃ △	♒ 12 8:25
14 11:53	☿ ⚹	♓ 14 11:53
16 12:27	♀ △	♈ 16 15:03
18 12:46	☉ △	♉ 18 18:11
20 17:38	♃ ☌	♊ 20 21:43
22 0:26	♂ ⚹	♋ 23 2:35
25 4:44	♃ ⚹	♌ 25 9:57
27 14:34	♃ □	♍ 27 20:27
30 2:45	♃ △	♎ 30 9:09

☽ Phases & Eclipses

Dy Hr Mn		
1 10:11	☾	9♌13
9 14:20	●	17♏24
16 21:35	☽	24♒46
23 15:53	○	1♊35
1 6:49	☾	9♍18
9 5:36	●	17♐22
16 5:40	☽	24♓30
23 5:29	○	1♋37
31 4:57	☾	9♎44

Astro Data

1 November 1988
Julian Day # 32447
SVP 5♓24'52"
GC 26♐41.0 ⚴ 4♒31.0
Eris 16♈20.3R ⚵ 27♌29.6
⚷ 6♋59.2R ⚶ 24♎56.7
☽ Mean ☊ 10♓59.4

1 December 1988
Julian Day # 32477
SVP 5♓24'47"
GC 26♐41.1 ⚴ 10♒46.4
Eris 16♈06.4R ⚵ 6♍36.8
⚷ 5♋46.7R ⚶ 10♏29.0
☽ Mean ☊ 9♓24.1

LONGITUDE — January 1989

Day	Sid.Time	☉	0 hr ☽	Noon ☽	True ☊	☿	♀	♂	⚳	♃	♄	♅	♆	♇
1 Su	18 44 28	11♑03 33	19♎11 02	25♎10 57	6♓35.9	28♑05.3	18♐25.2	20♈27.5	25♓36.7	26♉41.7	5♑39.1	1♑47.0	9♑56.4	14♏34.2
2 M	18 48 25	12 04 43	1♏14 02	7♏20 52	6R32.5	29 32.5	19 40.2	20 58.2	25 52.6	26R38.0	5 46.2	1 50.6	9 58.7	14 35.7
3 Tu	18 52 21	13 05 54	13 32 01	19 47 56	6 26.9	0♒57.6	20 55.3	21 29.1	26 08.7	26 34.4	5 53.3	1 54.2	10 01.0	14 37.2
4 W	18 56 18	14 07 04	26 08 59	2♐35 30	6 19.3	2 20.4	22 10.3	22 00.1	26 25.0	26 31.1	6 00.3	1 57.8	10 03.3	14 38.7
5 Th	19 00 14	15 08 15	9♐07 38	15 45 27	6 10.4	3 40.2	23 25.4	22 31.4	26 41.5	26 28.0	6 07.4	2 01.3	10 05.5	14 40.2
6 F	19 04 11	16 09 25	22 28 52	29 17 43	6 01.2	4 56.6	24 40.5	23 02.8	26 58.1	26 25.1	6 14.4	2 04.9	10 07.8	14 41.6
7 Sa	19 08 08	17 10 36	6♑11 38	13♑10 13	5 52.6	6 09.0	25 55.5	23 34.4	27 15.0	26 22.3	6 21.5	2 08.4	10 10.1	14 43.0
8 Su	19 12 04	18 11 47	20 12 55	27 19 05	5 45.7	7 16.7	27 10.6	24 06.2	27 32.0	26 19.8	6 28.5	2 11.9	10 12.3	14 44.4
9 M	19 16 01	19 12 57	4♒28 04	11♒39 09	5 41.0	8 19.1	28 25.7	24 38.1	27 49.1	26 17.5	6 35.5	2 15.5	10 14.6	14 45.7
10 Tu	19 19 57	20 14 07	18 51 37	26 04 47	5D38.7	9 15.1	29 40.8	25 10.2	28 06.5	26 15.3	6 42.5	2 19.0	10 16.8	14 47.0
11 W	19 23 54	21 15 16	3♓18 02	10♓30 48	5 38.4	10 04.2	0♑55.9	25 42.4	28 23.9	26 13.4	6 49.4	2 22.4	10 19.1	14 48.3
12 Th	19 27 50	22 16 25	17 42 33	24 52 55	5 39.4	10 45.2	2 11.0	26 14.8	28 41.6	26 11.7	6 56.4	2 25.9	10 21.3	14 49.6
13 F	19 31 47	23 17 33	2♈01 31	9♈08 07	5 40.7	11 17.4	3 26.1	26 47.4	28 59.4	26 10.2	7 03.3	2 29.4	10 23.5	14 50.8
14 Sa	19 35 43	24 18 40	16 12 31	23 14 33	5R41.4	11 39.9	4 41.2	27 20.0	29 17.3	26 08.9	7 10.2	2 32.8	10 25.8	14 51.9
15 Su	19 39 40	25 19 46	0♉14 07	7♉11 08	5 40.8	11R51.9	5 56.3	27 52.8	29 35.4	26 07.8	7 17.1	2 36.2	10 28.0	14 53.1
16 M	19 43 37	26 20 52	14 05 32	20 57 15	5 38.3	11 52.7	7 11.4	28 25.8	29 53.7	26 06.9	7 23.9	2 39.6	10 30.2	14 54.2
17 Tu	19 47 33	27 21 57	27 46 14	4♊32 24	5 34.0	11 41.9	8 26.6	28 58.8	0♈12.1	26 06.2	7 30.8	2 43.0	10 32.4	14 55.3
18 W	19 51 30	28 23 02	11♊15 40	17 55 57	5 28.3	11 19.4	9 41.7	29 32.0	0 30.6	26 05.8	7 37.6	2 46.4	10 34.6	14 56.3
19 Th	19 55 26	29 24 05	24 33 08	1♋07 09	5 21.9	10 45.4	10 56.8	0♉05.3	0 49.2	26D05.5	7 44.4	2 49.7	10 36.8	14 57.4
20 F	19 59 23	0♒25 08	7♋37 53	14 05 16	5 15.6	10 00.5	12 11.9	0 38.7	1 08.0	26 05.5	7 51.1	2 53.1	10 39.0	14 58.3
21 Sa	20 03 19	1 26 10	20 29 15	26 49 48	5 10.0	9 05.7	13 27.0	1 12.2	1 27.0	26 05.6	7 57.8	2 56.4	10 41.1	14 59.3
22 Su	20 07 16	2 27 12	3♌06 55	9♌20 40	5 05.8	8 02.5	14 42.1	1 45.8	1 46.0	26 06.0	8 04.5	2 59.6	10 43.3	15 00.2
23 M	20 11 12	3 28 12	15 31 08	21 38 28	5 03.2	6 52.8	15 57.2	2 19.6	2 05.2	26 06.5	8 11.2	3 02.9	10 45.4	15 01.1
24 Tu	20 15 09	4 29 12	27 42 53	3♍44 37	5D02.3	5 38.7	17 12.3	2 53.4	2 24.5	26 07.3	8 17.8	3 06.1	10 47.5	15 01.9
25 W	20 19 06	5 30 11	9♍43 59	15 41 21	5 02.8	4 22.5	18 27.5	3 27.3	2 44.0	26 08.3	8 24.4	3 09.3	10 49.6	15 02.7
26 Th	20 23 02	6 31 10	21 37 07	27 31 44	5 04.3	3 06.4	19 42.6	4 01.3	3 03.5	26 09.4	8 31.0	3 12.5	10 51.7	15 03.5
27 F	20 26 59	7 32 08	3♎25 43	9♎19 35	5 06.2	1 52.8	20 57.7	4 35.4	3 23.2	26 10.8	8 37.5	3 15.7	10 53.8	15 04.2
28 Sa	20 30 55	8 33 05	15 13 55	21 09 17	5 07.9	0 43.3	22 12.8	5 09.7	3 43.0	26 12.4	8 44.0	3 18.8	10 55.9	15 04.9
29 Su	20 34 52	9 34 01	27 06 19	3♏05 39	5R09.0	29♑39.8	23 27.9	5 43.9	4 02.9	26 14.2	8 50.5	3 21.9	10 58.0	15 05.6
30 M	20 38 48	10 34 57	9♏07 53	15 13 39	5 09.1	28 43.3	24 43.1	6 18.3	4 22.9	26 16.2	8 56.9	3 25.0	11 00.0	15 06.2
31 Tu	20 42 45	11 35 53	21 23 33	27 38 10	5 08.1	27 54.8	25 58.2	6 52.8	4 43.0	26 18.3	9 03.3	3 28.0	11 02.0	15 06.8

LONGITUDE — February 1989

Day	Sid.Time	☉	0 hr ☽	Noon ☽	True ☊	☿	♀	♂	⚳	♃	♄	♅	♆	♇
1 W	20 46 41	12♒36 47	3♐57 59	10♐23 28	5♓06.0	27♑14.7	27♑13.3	7♉27.4	5♈03.3	26♉20.7	9♑09.6	3♑31.1	11♑04.1	15♏07.4
2 Th	20 50 38	13 37 41	16 55 01	23 32 52	5R03.2	26R43.2	28 28.4	8 02.0	5 23.6	26 23.3	9 15.9	3 34.1	11 06.1	15 07.9
3 F	20 54 35	14 38 34	0♑17 11	7♑08 00	5 00.1	26 20.3	29 43.6	8 36.7	5 44.1	26 26.1	9 22.1	3 37.0	11 08.0	15 08.4
4 Sa	20 58 31	15 39 26	14 05 12	21 08 29	4 57.2	26 05.8	0♒58.7	9 11.5	6 04.7	26 29.0	9 28.4	3 40.0	11 10.0	15 08.8
5 Su	21 02 28	16 40 16	28 17 26	5♒31 28	4 54.9	25D59.3	2 13.8	9 46.4	6 25.3	26 32.2	9 34.5	3 42.9	11 12.0	15 09.2
6 M	21 06 24	17 41 06	12♒49 52	20 11 48	4D53.4	26 00.5	3 28.9	10 21.4	6 46.1	26 35.6	9 40.6	3 45.7	11 13.9	15 09.6
7 Tu	21 10 21	18 41 55	27 36 21	5♓02 32	4 53.0	26 08.9	4 44.0	10 56.4	7 07.0	26 39.1	9 46.7	3 48.6	11 15.8	15 09.9
8 W	21 14 17	19 42 41	12♓29 22	19 55 52	4 53.4	26 23.9	5 59.1	11 31.5	7 27.9	26 42.9	9 52.7	3 51.4	11 17.7	15 10.2
9 Th	21 18 14	20 43 27	27 21 08	4♈44 17	4 54.3	26 45.0	7 14.2	12 06.7	7 49.0	26 46.8	9 58.7	3 54.1	11 19.6	15 10.5
10 F	21 22 10	21 44 11	12♈04 35	19 21 25	4 55.4	27 11.9	8 29.3	12 41.9	8 10.1	26 50.9	10 04.6	3 56.9	11 21.4	15 10.7
11 Sa	21 26 07	22 44 53	26 34 16	3♉42 45	4 56.3	27 44.0	9 44.4	13 17.2	8 31.3	26 55.2	10 10.4	3 59.6	11 23.2	15 10.9
12 Su	21 30 04	23 45 34	10♉46 36	17 45 41	4R56.9	28 20.9	10 59.4	13 52.6	8 52.7	26 59.7	10 16.3	4 02.2	11 25.0	15 11.1
13 M	21 34 00	24 46 13	24 39 54	1♊29 19	4 56.8	29 02.3	12 14.5	14 28.0	9 14.1	27 04.4	10 22.0	4 04.8	11 26.8	15 11.2
14 Tu	21 37 57	25 46 51	8♊13 59	14 54 04	4 56.3	29 47.7	13 29.6	15 03.5	9 35.6	27 09.2	10 27.7	4 07.4	11 28.6	15 11.3
15 W	21 41 53	26 47 26	21 29 44	28 01 11	4 55.5	0♒36.8	14 44.6	15 39.1	9 57.1	27 14.2	10 33.3	4 10.0	11 30.3	15R11.4
16 Th	21 45 50	27 48 01	4♋28 39	10♋52 21	4 54.5	1 29.3	15 59.6	16 14.7	10 18.8	27 19.4	10 38.9	4 12.5	11 32.1	15 11.4
17 F	21 49 46	28 48 33	17 12 30	23 29 21	4 53.6	2 25.1	17 14.7	16 50.3	10 40.5	27 24.8	10 44.4	4 15.0	11 33.8	15 11.3
18 Sa	21 53 43	29 49 03	29 43 06	5♌53 58	4 52.9	3 23.7	18 29.7	17 26.0	11 02.3	27 30.4	10 49.9	4 17.4	11 35.4	15 11.3
19 Su	21 57 39	0♓49 32	12♌02 11	18 07 56	4 52.5	4 25.0	19 44.7	18 01.7	11 24.2	27 36.1	10 55.3	4 19.8	11 37.1	15 11.2
20 M	22 01 36	1 49 59	24 11 25	0♍12 53	4D52.3	5 28.8	20 59.7	18 37.5	11 46.2	27 41.9	11 00.7	4 22.1	11 38.7	15 11.1
21 Tu	22 05 33	2 50 25	6♍12 31	12 10 34	4 52.3	6 34.9	22 14.7	19 13.3	12 08.2	27 48.0	11 05.9	4 24.4	11 40.3	15 10.9
22 W	22 09 29	3 50 49	18 07 15	24 02 52	4 52.4	7 43.3	23 29.6	19 49.2	12 30.3	27 54.2	11 11.1	4 26.7	11 41.9	15 10.7
23 Th	22 13 26	4 51 11	29 57 42	5♎52 02	4R52.5	8 53.6	24 44.6	20 25.1	12 52.5	28 00.6	11 16.3	4 28.9	11 43.4	15 10.5
24 F	22 17 22	5 51 32	11♎46 14	17 40 39	4 52.4	10 05.9	25 59.6	21 01.1	13 14.7	28 07.1	11 21.4	4 31.1	11 45.0	15 10.2
25 Sa	22 21 19	6 51 52	23 35 42	29 31 48	4 52.2	11 19.9	27 14.5	21 37.1	13 37.0	28 13.8	11 26.4	4 33.3	11 46.5	15 09.9
26 Su	22 25 15	7 52 09	5♏29 25	11♏29 02	4 51.9	12 35.7	28 29.5	22 13.1	13 59.4	28 20.6	11 31.3	4 35.4	11 47.9	15 09.5
27 M	22 29 12	8 52 26	17 31 09	23 36 18	4 51.6	13 53.1	29 44.4	22 49.1	14 21.8	28 27.6	11 36.2	4 37.4	11 49.4	15 09.2
28 Tu	22 33 08	9 52 41	29 45 01	5♐57 51	4D51.4	15 12.1	0♓59.4	23 25.3	14 44.3	28 34.8	11 41.0	4 39.4	11 50.8	15 08.8

Astro Data

	Dy Hr Mn
☽0N	12 13:39
☿R	16 1:43
♃D	20 6:12
☽0S	26 8:20
☿D	5 20:08
☽0N	8 21:16
♇R	16 9:46
☽0S	22 15:15

Planet Ingress

	Dy Hr Mn
☿ ♒	2 19:41
♀ ♑	10 18:08
⚳ ♈	16 20:17
♂ ♉	19 8:11
☉ ♒	20 2:07
☿ ♑R	29 4:06
♀ ♒	3 17:15
☿ ♒	14 18:11
☉ ♓	18 16:21
♀ ♓	27 16:59

Last Aspect / ☽ Ingress

Last Aspect Dy Hr Mn		☽ Ingress Dy Hr Mn
1 18:34 ☿ □	♏	1 21:34
4 0:44 ♃ ☍	♐	4 7:12
6 3:03 ♀ ☌	♑	6 13:14
8 10:20 ♃ △	♒	8 16:31
10 12:18 ♃ □	♓	10 18:31
12 14:12 ♃ ⚹	♈	12 20:36
14 19:18 ♂ ☌	♉	14 23:36
16 22:15 ☉ △	♊	17 3:57
18 0:29 ☿ △	♋	19 9:57
21 10:36 ♃ ⚹	♌	21 18:02
23 20:50 ♃ □	♍	24 4:32
26 9:12 ♃ △	♎	26 17:01
29 5:40 ☿ □	♏	29 5:49
31 12:30 ☿ ⚹	♐	31 16:30

Last Aspect / ☽ Ingress

Last Aspect Dy Hr Mn		☽ Ingress Dy Hr Mn
1 16:27 ☉ ⚹	♑	2 23:30
4 21:01 ♃ △	♒	5 2:51
6 22:24 ♃ □	♓	7 3:52
8 23:01 ♃ ⚹	♈	9 4:18
11 1:32 ☿ □	♉	11 5:45
13 7:26 ☿ △	♊	13 9:22
15 9:32 ☉ △	♋	15 15:40
17 19:36 ♃ ⚹	♌	18 0:33
20 6:56 ♃ □	♍	20 11:34
22 19:53 ♃ △	♎	23 0:05
25 6:50 ♀ △	♏	25 12:57
27 21:35 ♃ ☍	♐	28 0:29

☽ Phases & Eclipses

Dy Hr Mn	
7 19:22	● 17♑29
14 13:58	☽ 24♈24
21 21:34	○ 1♌50
30 2:02	☾ 10♏10
6 7:37	● 17♒30
12 23:15	☽ 24♉14
20 15:32	○ 1♍59
20 15:35	• T 1.275
28 20:08	☾ 10♐13

Astro Data

1 January 1989
Julian Day # 32508
SVP 5♓24'41"
GC 26♐41.1 ⚵ 19♒23.6
Eris 16♈00.5R ✱ 10♍34.1
⚷ 3♋49.7R ⚶ 26♏15.6
☽ Mean ☊ 7♓45.6

1 February 1989
Julian Day # 32539
SVP 5♓24'36"
GC 26♐41.2 ⚵ 29♒12.0
Eris 16♈05.1 ✱ 7♍14.5R
⚷ 2♋03.8R ⚶ 11♐13.9
☽ Mean ☊ 6♓07.2

March 1989 LONGITUDE

Day	Sid.Time	☉	0 hr ☽	Noon ☽	True ☊	☿	♀	♂	⚳	♃	♄	♅	♆	♇
1 W	22 37 05	10♓52 55	12♐15 18	18♐37 54	4♓51.5	16♒32.5	2♓14.3	24♉01.4	15♈06.9	28♉42.1	11♑45.8	4♑41.4	11♑52.2	15♏08.3
2 Th	22 41 02	11 53 07	25 06 06	1♑40 21	4 51.8	17 54.4	3 29.2	24 37.6	15 29.5	28 49.6	11 50.5	4 43.3	11 53.6	15R 07.8
3 F	22 44 58	12 53 17	8♑20 59	15 08 15	4 52.4	19 17.7	4 44.2	25 13.8	15 52.2	28 57.2	11 55.1	4 45.2	11 54.9	15 07.3
4 Sa	22 48 55	13 53 27	22 02 18	29 03 08	4 53.2	20 42.3	5 59.1	25 50.1	16 14.9	29 04.9	11 59.6	4 47.0	11 56.2	15 06.8
5 Su	22 52 51	14 53 34	6♒10 37	13♒24 26	4 54.0	22 08.2	7 14.0	26 26.4	16 37.7	29 12.8	12 04.1	4 48.8	11 57.5	15 06.2
6 M	22 56 48	15 53 40	20 44 05	28 08 55	4R54.5	23 35.3	8 28.8	27 02.7	17 00.6	29 20.9	12 08.4	4 50.6	11 58.7	15 05.6
7 Tu	23 00 44	16 53 43	5♓38 04	13♓10 34	4 54.5	25 03.7	9 43.7	27 39.0	17 23.5	29 29.0	12 12.7	4 52.3	12 00.0	15 05.0
8 W	23 04 41	17 53 45	20 45 18	28 21 04	4 53.8	26 33.4	10 58.6	28 15.4	17 46.4	29 37.4	12 16.9	4 53.9	12 01.2	15 04.3
9 Th	23 08 37	18 53 45	5♈56 38	13♈30 48	4 52.4	28 04.3	12 13.4	28 51.8	18 09.5	29 45.8	12 21.1	4 55.5	12 02.3	15 03.6
10 F	23 12 34	19 53 43	21 02 24	28 30 22	4 50.6	29 36.3	13 28.3	29 28.3	18 32.5	29 54.4	12 25.2	4 57.0	12 03.5	15 02.8
11 Sa	23 16 31	20 53 39	5♉53 47	13♉11 53	4 48.6	1♓09.6	14 43.1	0♊04.8	18 55.6	0♊03.1	12 29.1	4 58.5	12 04.6	15 02.1
12 Su	23 20 27	21 53 33	20 24 07	27 30 05	4 46.8	2 44.0	15 57.9	0 41.3	19 18.8	0 12.0	12 33.0	5 00.0	12 05.6	15 01.3
13 M	23 24 24	22 53 25	4♊29 32	11♊22 26	4D45.6	4 19.6	17 12.7	1 17.8	19 42.0	0 21.0	12 36.9	5 01.4	12 06.7	15 00.4
14 Tu	23 28 20	23 53 14	18 08 51	24 48 59	4 45.3	5 56.5	18 27.5	1 54.4	20 05.2	0 30.1	12 40.6	5 02.7	12 07.7	14 59.6
15 W	23 32 17	24 53 01	1♋23 07	7♋51 38	4 45.8	7 34.5	19 42.2	2 31.0	20 28.5	0 39.3	12 44.3	5 04.1	12 08.7	14 58.7
16 Th	23 36 13	25 52 46	14 14 56	20 33 30	4 47.0	9 13.7	20 57.0	3 07.6	20 51.9	0 48.7	12 47.8	5 05.3	12 09.6	14 57.8
17 F	23 40 10	26 52 29	26 47 46	2♌58 13	4 48.6	10 54.1	22 11.7	3 44.2	21 15.3	0 58.1	12 51.3	5 06.5	12 10.6	14 56.8
18 Sa	23 44 06	27 52 09	9♌05 20	15 09 33	4 50.2	12 35.8	23 26.4	4 20.8	21 38.7	1 07.7	12 54.7	5 07.7	12 11.4	14 55.9
19 Su	23 48 03	28 51 47	21 11 19	27 11 02	4R51.3	14 18.6	24 41.1	4 57.5	22 02.1	1 17.4	12 58.0	5 08.8	12 12.3	14 54.8
20 M	23 52 00	29 51 23	3♍09 04	9♍05 46	4 51.4	16 02.8	25 55.8	5 34.2	22 25.6	1 27.2	13 01.3	5 09.8	12 13.1	14 53.8
21 Tu	23 55 56	0♈50 57	15 01 29	20 56 30	4 50.3	17 48.1	27 10.4	6 10.8	22 49.1	1 37.1	13 04.4	5 10.8	12 13.9	14 52.8
22 W	23 59 53	1 50 29	26 51 05	2♎45 31	4 47.9	19 34.8	28 25.1	6 47.5	23 12.7	1 47.2	13 07.5	5 11.8	12 14.7	14 51.7
23 Th	0 03 49	2 49 58	8♎40 03	14 34 54	4 44.0	21 22.7	29 39.7	7 24.3	23 36.3	1 57.3	13 10.4	5 12.7	12 15.4	14 50.6
24 F	0 07 46	3 49 26	20 30 20	26 26 35	4 39.2	23 11.9	0♈54.3	8 01.0	23 59.9	2 07.6	13 13.3	5 13.5	12 16.1	14 49.4
25 Sa	0 11 42	4 48 52	2♏23 53	8♏22 31	4 33.8	25 02.4	2 08.9	8 37.7	24 23.6	2 17.9	13 16.1	5 14.3	12 16.7	14 48.3
26 Su	0 15 39	5 48 16	14 22 46	20 24 56	4 28.4	26 54.2	3 23.5	9 14.5	24 47.3	2 28.4	13 18.8	5 15.0	12 17.4	14 47.1
27 M	0 19 35	6 47 38	26 29 21	2♐36 22	4 23.6	28 47.4	4 38.1	9 51.3	25 11.0	2 38.9	13 21.4	5 15.7	12 18.0	14 45.9
28 Tu	0 23 32	7 46 59	8♐46 21	14 59 42	4 19.9	0♈41.8	5 52.6	10 28.1	25 34.8	2 49.6	13 23.9	5 16.4	12 18.5	14 44.6
29 W	0 27 28	8 46 17	21 16 51	27 38 14	4D17.7	2 37.6	7 07.2	11 04.9	25 58.5	3 00.4	13 26.3	5 17.0	12 19.1	14 43.4
30 Th	0 31 25	9 45 34	4♑04 15	10♑35 22	4 17.1	4 34.6	8 21.7	11 41.7	26 22.4	3 11.2	13 28.7	5 17.5	12 19.6	14 42.1
31 F	0 35 22	10 44 49	17 11 57	23 54 23	4 17.8	6 32.8	9 36.2	12 18.6	26 46.2	3 22.2	13 30.9	5 18.0	12 20.0	14 40.8

April 1989 LONGITUDE

Day	Sid.Time	☉	0 hr ☽	Noon ☽	True ☊	☿	♀	♂	⚳	♃	♄	♅	♆	♇
1 Sa	0 39 18	11♈44 03	0♒42 57	7♒37 52	4♓19.1	8♈32.3	10♈50.7	12♊55.4	27♈10.1	3♊33.2	13♑33.1	5♑18.4	12♑20.5	14♏39.5
2 Su	0 43 15	12 43 14	14 39 16	21 47 05	4R 20.5	10 32.9	12 05.2	13 32.3	27 34.0	3 44.4	13 35.1	5 18.8	12 20.9	14R 38.1
3 M	0 47 11	13 42 24	29 01 09	6♓21 07	4 21.0	12 34.6	13 19.7	14 09.2	27 57.9	3 55.6	13 37.1	5 19.2	12 21.2	14 36.8
4 Tu	0 51 08	14 41 32	13♓46 26	21 16 22	4 19.9	14 37.3	14 34.2	14 46.1	28 21.9	4 06.9	13 38.9	5 19.4	12 21.6	14 35.4
5 W	0 55 04	15 40 38	28 49 57	6♈26 08	4 16.9	16 40.8	15 48.6	15 23.0	28 45.9	4 18.3	13 40.7	5 19.7	12 21.9	14 34.0
6 Th	0 59 01	16 39 42	14♈03 40	21 41 14	4 12.0	18 45.0	17 03.1	15 59.9	29 09.9	4 29.8	13 42.3	5 19.8	12 22.1	14 32.5
7 F	1 02 57	17 38 44	29 17 31	6♉51 11	4 05.7	20 49.9	18 17.5	16 36.9	29 33.9	4 41.3	13 43.9	5 20.0	12 22.4	14 31.1
8 Sa	1 06 54	18 37 44	14♉21 01	21 45 56	3 58.8	22 55.0	19 31.9	17 13.8	29 57.9	4 53.0	13 45.4	5R 20.0	12 22.6	14 29.6
9 Su	1 10 51	19 36 42	29 05 02	6♊17 35	3 52.4	25 00.3	20 46.3	17 50.8	0♉22.0	5 04.7	13 46.7	5 20.0	12 22.7	14 28.2
10 M	1 14 47	20 35 37	13♊23 07	20 21 21	3 47.1	27 05.5	22 00.6	18 27.8	0 46.1	5 16.5	13 48.0	5 20.0	12 22.9	14 26.7
11 Tu	1 18 44	21 34 30	27 12 12	3♋55 45	3 43.6	29 10.3	23 15.0	19 04.7	1 10.2	5 28.4	13 49.2	5 19.9	12 23.0	14 25.2
12 W	1 22 40	22 33 21	10♋32 17	17 02 09	3D42.0	1♉14.4	24 29.3	19 41.7	1 34.3	5 40.4	13 50.3	5 19.8	12 23.0	14 23.6
13 Th	1 26 37	23 32 10	23 25 49	29 43 51	3 42.1	3 17.4	25 43.6	20 18.7	1 58.4	5 52.4	13 51.3	5 19.6	12R 23.1	14 22.1
14 F	1 30 33	24 30 57	5♌56 48	12♌05 19	3 43.1	5 19.0	26 57.9	20 55.7	2 22.5	6 04.5	13 52.1	5 19.4	12 23.1	14 20.6
15 Sa	1 34 30	25 29 41	18 10 00	24 11 29	3R44.2	7 19.0	28 12.1	21 32.8	2 46.7	6 16.7	13 52.9	5 19.1	12 23.0	14 19.0
16 Su	1 38 26	26 28 22	0♍10 22	6♍07 12	3 44.6	9 16.9	29 26.4	22 09.8	3 10.9	6 28.9	13 53.6	5 18.7	12 23.0	14 17.4
17 M	1 42 23	27 27 02	12 02 34	17 56 57	3 43.4	11 12.4	0♉40.6	22 46.8	3 35.0	6 41.2	13 54.2	5 18.3	12 22.9	14 15.8
18 Tu	1 46 20	28 25 40	23 50 48	29 44 34	3 40.0	13 05.2	1 54.8	23 23.8	3 59.2	6 53.6	13 54.7	5 17.9	12 22.7	14 14.2
19 W	1 50 16	29 24 15	5♎38 36	11♎33 15	3 34.1	14 54.9	3 09.0	24 00.8	4 23.4	7 06.0	13 55.1	5 17.4	12 22.6	14 12.6
20 Th	1 54 13	0♉22 49	17 28 48	23 25 30	3 26.0	16 41.4	4 23.2	24 37.9	4 47.6	7 18.5	13 55.4	5 16.9	12 22.4	14 11.0
21 F	1 58 09	1 21 20	29 23 34	5♏23 11	3 16.0	18 24.3	5 37.3	25 14.9	5 11.8	7 31.0	13 55.5	5 16.3	12 22.1	14 09.4
22 Sa	2 02 06	2 19 50	11♏24 32	17 27 46	3 04.9	20 03.5	6 51.4	25 51.9	5 36.1	7 43.7	13R 55.6	5 15.6	12 21.9	14 07.7
23 Su	2 06 02	3 18 18	23 33 00	29 40 25	2 53.8	21 38.7	8 05.6	26 29.0	6 00.3	7 56.3	13 55.6	5 15.0	12 21.6	14 06.1
24 M	2 09 59	4 16 44	5♐50 08	12♐02 20	2 43.6	23 09.8	9 19.7	27 06.0	6 24.5	8 09.0	13 55.5	5 14.2	12 21.3	14 04.4
25 Tu	2 13 55	5 15 09	18 17 11	24 34 54	2 35.2	24 36.6	10 33.7	27 43.1	6 48.8	8 21.8	13 55.3	5 13.4	12 20.9	14 02.8
26 W	2 17 52	6 13 32	0♑55 42	7♑19 52	2 29.2	25 59.0	11 47.8	28 20.2	7 13.1	8 34.7	13 55.1	5 12.6	12 20.5	14 01.1
27 Th	2 21 49	7 11 53	13 47 40	20 19 23	2 25.7	27 16.8	13 01.9	28 57.2	7 37.3	8 47.5	13 54.7	5 11.7	12 20.1	13 59.4
28 F	2 25 45	8 10 13	26 55 22	3♒35 53	2D 24.4	28 30.1	14 15.9	29 34.3	8 01.6	9 00.5	13 54.2	5 10.8	12 19.7	13 57.8
29 Sa	2 29 42	9 08 32	10♒21 15	17 11 43	2 24.5	29 38.5	15 29.9	0♋11.4	8 25.9	9 13.5	13 53.6	5 09.9	12 19.2	13 56.1
30 Su	2 33 38	10 06 48	24 07 30	1♓08 41	2R 24.8	0♊42.2	16 43.9	0 48.5	8 50.2	9 26.5	13 52.9	5 08.8	12 18.7	13 54.4

Astro Data Dy Hr Mn	Planet Ingress Dy Hr Mn	Last Aspect Dy Hr Mn	☽ Ingress Dy Hr Mn	Last Aspect Dy Hr Mn	☽ Ingress Dy Hr Mn	☽ Phases & Eclipses Dy Hr Mn
♄☌♆ 3 10:44	☿ ♓ 10 18:07	1 7:37 ☿ ⚹	♑ 2 8:58	1 23:59 ♇ □	♓ 3 1:37	7 18:19 ● 17♓10
⚳0N 3 12:14	♃ ♊ 11 3:26	4 12:03 ♃ △	♒ 4 13:36	4 1:20 ♇ △	♈ 5 1:51	7 18:07:44 ● P 0.827
☽0N 8 7:46	♂ ♊ 11 8:51	6 13:57 ♃ □	♓ 6 14:59	6 6:39 ☿ ☌	♉ 7 1:07	14 10:11 ☽ 23♊49
☉0N 20 15:28	☉ ♈ 20 15:28	8 14:02 ♃ ⚹	♈ 8 14:36	8 0:15 ♇ ☍	♊ 9 1:31	22 9:58 ○ 1♎45
☽0S 21 21:38	♀ ♈ 23 18:32	10 13:59 ☿ ⚹	♉ 10 14:25	11 1:57 ☿ ⚹	♋ 11 4:58	30 10:21 ☾ 9♑42
♀0N 26 8:38	☿ ♈ 28 3:16	12 1:47 ☉ ⚹	♊ 12 16:16	13 3:31 ♀ □	♌ 13 12:31	
☿0N 30 2:43		14 10:11 ☉ □	♋ 14 21:27	15 20:58 ♀ △	♍ 15 23:39	6 3:33 ● 16♈19
	⚳ ♉ 8 14:05	16 23:07 ☉ △	♌ 17 6:13	17 22:22 ♂ □	♎ 18 12:31	12 23:13 ☽ 23♋01
☽0N 4 18:57	☿ ♉ 11 21:36	18 11:33 ♇ □	♍ 19 17:39	20 14:34 ♂ △	♏ 21 1:13	21 3:13 ○ 1♏00
♅R 9 8:54	♀ ♉ 16 22:52	22 2:09 ♀ ☍	♎ 22 6:24	22 17:54 ☿ ☍	♐ 23 12:38	28 20:46 ☾ 8♒32
♃⚻♅ 10 18:59	☉ ♉ 20 2:39	23 9:08 ♄ □	♏ 24 19:10	25 18:15 ♂ ☍	♑ 25 22:15	
♆R 13 23:36	♂ ♋ 29 4:37	27 3:09 ☿ △	♐ 27 6:54	28 1:57 ☿ △	♒ 28 5:33	
☽0S 18 3:33	☿ ♊ 29 19:53	28 2:50 ♂ ☍	♑ 29 16:25	29 8:45 ♀ □	♓ 30 10:03	
♄R 22 23:37		30 19:28 ♇ ⚹	♒ 31 22:45			

Astro Data

1 March 1989
Julian Day # 32567
SVP 5♓24'32"
GC 26♐41.3 ⚴ 8♓28.7
Eris 16♈17.5 ⚵ 0♍19.4R
⚷ 1♋19.0R ⚶ 23♐24.8
☽ Mean ☊ 4♓38.2

1 April 1989
Julian Day # 32598
SVP 5♓24'28"
GC 26♐41.3 ⚴ 18♓42.4
Eris 16♈36.7 ⚵ 25♌30.3R
⚷ 1♋46.0 ⚶ 4♑16.0
☽ Mean ☊ 2♓59.7

LONGITUDE — May 1989

Day	Sid.Time	☉	0 hr ☽	Noon☽	True☊	☿	♀	♂	⚳	♃	♄	♅	♆	♇
1 M	2 37 35	11♉05 04	8♓15 19	15♓27 16	2♓24.2	1♊41.0	17♉57.9	1♋25.6	9♉14.4	9♊39.6	13♑52.1	5♑07.8	12♑18.1	13♏52.7
2 Tu	2 41 31	12 03 17	22 44 15	0♈05 51	2R 21.7	2 34.9	19 11.9	2 02.7	9 38.7	9 52.7	13R 51.2	5R 06.7	12R 17.5	13R 51.0
3 W	2 45 28	13 01 29	7♈31 25	15 00 10	2 16.6	3 23.7	20 25.9	2 39.8	10 03.0	10 05.9	13 50.3	5 05.5	12 16.9	13 49.3
4 Th	2 49 24	13 59 40	22 31 08	0♉03 12	2 08.9	4 07.5	21 39.8	3 16.9	10 27.3	10 19.1	13 49.2	5 04.3	12 16.3	13 47.6
5 F	2 53 21	14 57 49	7♉35 10	15 05 47	1 59.1	4 46.1	22 53.8	3 54.0	10 51.6	10 32.3	13 48.0	5 03.1	12 15.6	13 45.9
6 Sa	2 57 18	15 55 57	22 33 50	29 58 08	1 48.4	5 19.6	24 07.7	4 31.1	11 15.9	10 45.6	13 46.8	5 01.8	12 15.0	13 44.3
7 Su	3 01 14	16 54 03	7♊17 38	14♊31 27	1 37.9	5 47.8	25 21.6	5 08.3	11 40.2	10 59.0	13 45.4	5 00.5	12 14.2	13 42.6
8 M	3 05 11	17 52 07	21 38 53	28 39 27	1 28.9	6 10.9	26 35.5	5 45.4	12 04.4	11 12.3	13 44.0	4 59.1	12 13.5	13 40.9
9 Tu	3 09 07	18 50 09	5♋32 51	12♋19 01	1 22.1	6 28.7	27 49.3	6 22.6	12 28.7	11 25.8	13 42.4	4 57.7	12 12.7	13 39.2
10 W	3 13 04	19 48 10	18 58 01	25 30 08	1 17.8	6 41.4	29 03.2	6 59.7	12 53.0	11 39.2	13 40.8	4 56.3	12 11.9	13 37.5
11 Th	3 17 00	20 46 08	1♌55 43	8♌15 17	1 15.7	6R 48.9	0♊17.0	7 36.9	13 17.3	11 52.7	13 39.1	4 54.8	12 11.1	13 35.9
12 F	3 20 57	21 44 05	14 29 23	20 38 38	1 15.2	6 51.3	1 30.8	8 14.0	13 41.5	12 06.2	13 37.3	4 53.3	12 10.2	13 34.2
13 Sa	3 24 53	22 41 59	26 43 43	2♍45 18	1 15.3	6 48.9	2 44.6	8 51.2	14 05.8	12 19.7	13 35.4	4 51.7	12 09.3	13 32.5
14 Su	3 28 50	23 39 52	8♍44 04	14 40 41	1 14.7	6 41.7	3 58.4	9 28.3	14 30.0	12 33.3	13 33.4	4 50.1	12 08.4	13 30.9
15 M	3 32 47	24 37 44	20 35 48	26 30 02	1 12.6	6 29.9	5 12.1	10 05.5	14 54.2	12 46.9	13 31.3	4 48.4	12 07.5	13 29.2
16 Tu	3 36 43	25 35 33	2♎23 58	8♎18 09	1 08.1	6 13.9	6 25.9	10 42.6	15 18.4	13 00.5	13 29.2	4 46.8	12 06.5	13 27.6
17 W	3 40 40	26 33 21	14 13 04	20 09 08	1 00.9	5 54.0	7 39.6	11 19.8	15 42.7	13 14.1	13 26.9	4 45.1	12 05.5	13 25.9
18 Th	3 44 36	27 31 07	26 06 46	2♏06 16	0 51.0	5 30.5	8 53.3	11 57.0	16 06.9	13 27.8	13 24.6	4 43.3	12 04.5	13 24.3
19 F	3 48 33	28 28 52	8♏07 56	14 11 57	0 39.0	5 03.9	10 07.0	12 34.1	16 31.0	13 41.5	13 22.2	4 41.5	12 03.5	13 22.7
20 Sa	3 52 29	29 26 36	20 18 29	26 27 40	0 25.7	4 34.6	11 20.6	13 11.3	16 55.2	13 55.2	13 19.7	4 39.7	12 02.4	13 21.1
21 Su	3 56 26	0♊24 18	2♐39 35	8♐54 15	0 12.3	4 03.2	12 34.3	13 48.5	17 19.4	14 08.9	13 17.1	4 37.9	12 01.3	13 19.5
22 M	4 00 22	1 21 59	15 11 42	21 31 56	29♒60.0	3 30.3	13 47.9	14 25.6	17 43.6	14 22.7	13 14.5	4 36.0	12 00.2	13 17.9
23 Tu	4 04 19	2 19 39	27 54 57	4♑20 46	29 49.6	2 56.4	15 01.5	15 02.8	18 07.7	14 36.4	13 11.8	4 34.1	11 59.1	13 16.3
24 W	4 08 16	3 17 17	10♑49 24	17 20 52	29 42.0	2 22.1	16 15.1	15 40.0	18 31.8	14 50.2	13 09.0	4 32.1	11 57.9	13 14.7
25 Th	4 12 12	4 14 55	23 55 16	0♒32 39	29 37.2	1 48.0	17 28.7	16 17.2	18 55.9	15 04.0	13 06.1	4 30.2	11 56.8	13 13.2
26 F	4 16 09	5 12 31	7♒13 10	13 56 56	29 35.0	1 14.7	18 42.3	16 54.4	19 20.1	15 17.9	13 03.1	4 28.2	11 55.6	13 11.6
27 Sa	4 20 05	6 10 07	20 44 05	27 34 47	29 34.4	0 42.8	19 55.8	17 31.6	19 44.1	15 31.7	13 00.1	4 26.1	11 54.4	13 10.1
28 Su	4 24 02	7 07 42	4♓29 09	11♓27 17	29 34.4	0 12.8	21 09.4	18 08.8	20 08.2	15 45.5	12 57.0	4 24.1	11 53.1	13 08.6
29 M	4 27 58	8 05 15	18 29 12	25 34 53	29 33.7	29♉45.2	22 22.9	18 46.0	20 32.3	15 59.4	12 53.9	4 22.0	11 51.9	13 07.1
30 Tu	4 31 55	9 02 48	2♈44 11	9♈56 50	29 31.0	29 20.5	23 36.4	19 23.2	20 56.3	16 13.3	12 50.6	4 19.9	11 50.6	13 05.6
31 W	4 35 51	10 00 21	17 12 29	24 30 36	29 25.9	28 58.9	24 49.9	20 00.4	21 20.3	16 27.2	12 47.3	4 17.8	11 49.3	13 04.2

LONGITUDE — June 1989

Day	Sid.Time	☉	0 hr ☽	Noon☽	True☊	☿	♀	♂	⚳	♃	♄	♅	♆	♇
1 Th	4 39 48	10♊57 52	1♉50 31	9♉11 30	29♒18.1	28♉41.0	26♊03.4	20♋37.6	21♉44.3	16♊41.1	12♑44.0	4♑15.6	11♑48.0	13♏02.7
2 F	4 43 45	11 55 23	16 32 38	23 52 59	29R 08.3	28R 26.8	27 16.9	21 14.8	22 08.3	16 55.0	12R 40.5	4R 13.4	11R 46.6	13R 01.3
3 Sa	4 47 41	12 52 52	1♊11 35	8♊27 28	28 57.3	28 16.8	28 30.4	21 52.1	22 32.3	17 08.9	12 37.0	4 11.2	11 45.3	12 59.9
4 Su	4 51 38	13 50 21	15 39 42	22 47 30	28 46.5	28D 10.9	29 43.8	22 29.3	22 56.2	17 22.8	12 33.5	4 09.0	11 43.9	12 58.5
5 M	4 55 34	14 47 49	29 50 08	6♋47 05	28 37.0	28 09.4	0♋57.3	23 06.6	23 20.1	17 36.7	12 29.9	4 06.8	11 42.5	12 57.1
6 Tu	4 59 31	15 45 16	13♋37 56	20 22 29	28 29.7	28 12.4	2 10.7	23 43.8	23 44.0	17 50.6	12 26.2	4 04.5	11 41.1	12 55.8
7 W	5 03 27	16 42 42	27 00 40	3♌32 35	28 24.9	28 19.8	3 24.1	24 21.1	24 07.9	18 04.5	12 22.5	4 02.2	11 39.7	12 54.4
8 Th	5 07 24	17 40 07	9♌58 28	16 18 38	28D 22.5	28 31.7	4 37.5	24 58.4	24 31.7	18 18.4	12 18.7	3 59.9	11 38.3	12 53.1
9 F	5 11 21	18 37 30	22 33 34	28 43 46	28 21.9	28 48.2	5 50.8	25 35.6	24 55.5	18 32.4	12 14.9	3 57.6	11 36.8	12 51.8
10 Sa	5 15 17	19 34 52	4♍49 50	10♍52 22	28R 22.2	29 09.1	7 04.2	26 12.9	25 19.3	18 46.3	12 11.0	3 55.3	11 35.4	12 50.6
11 Su	5 19 14	20 32 14	16 52 02	22 49 31	28 22.4	29 34.4	8 17.5	26 50.2	25 43.0	19 00.2	12 07.1	3 52.9	11 33.9	12 49.3
12 M	5 23 10	21 29 34	28 45 29	4♎40 34	28 21.5	0♊04.0	9 30.8	27 27.5	26 06.7	19 14.1	12 03.1	3 50.6	11 32.4	12 48.1
13 Tu	5 27 07	22 26 54	10♎35 27	16 30 43	28 18.7	0 38.0	10 44.1	28 04.7	26 30.4	19 28.0	11 59.1	3 48.2	11 30.9	12 46.9
14 W	5 31 03	23 24 12	22 26 58	28 24 45	28 13.6	1 16.1	11 57.3	28 42.0	26 54.1	19 41.9	11 55.0	3 45.8	11 29.4	12 45.7
15 Th	5 35 00	24 21 30	4♏24 31	10♏26 44	28 06.2	1 58.4	13 10.6	29 19.3	27 17.7	19 55.7	11 51.0	3 43.4	11 27.8	12 44.6
16 F	5 38 56	25 18 47	16 31 45	22 39 53	27 56.9	2 44.8	14 23.8	29 56.6	27 41.3	20 09.6	11 46.8	3 41.0	11 26.3	12 43.4
17 Sa	5 42 53	26 16 03	28 51 22	5♐06 22	27 46.4	3 35.2	15 37.0	0♌33.9	28 04.9	20 23.5	11 42.7	3 38.6	11 24.8	12 42.3
18 Su	5 46 50	27 13 19	11♐25 00	17 47 18	27 35.8	4 29.4	16 50.2	1 11.2	28 28.4	20 37.3	11 38.5	3 36.2	11 23.2	12 41.3
19 M	5 50 46	28 10 34	24 13 13	0♑42 42	27 25.9	5 27.6	18 03.4	1 48.5	28 51.9	20 51.2	11 34.3	3 33.8	11 21.7	12 40.2
20 Tu	5 54 43	29 07 49	7♑15 38	13 51 50	27 17.8	6 29.5	19 16.6	2 25.9	29 15.3	21 05.0	11 30.0	3 31.4	11 20.1	12 39.2
21 W	5 58 39	0♋05 03	20 31 10	27 13 26	27 11.9	7 35.1	20 29.7	3 03.2	29 38.8	21 18.8	11 25.7	3 28.9	11 18.5	12 38.2
22 Th	6 02 36	1 02 17	3♒58 28	10♒46 05	27 08.6	8 44.4	21 42.8	3 40.5	0♊02.2	21 32.6	11 21.4	3 26.5	11 16.9	12 37.2
23 F	6 06 32	1 59 30	17 36 07	24 28 28	27D 07.4	9 57.3	22 55.9	4 17.9	0 25.5	21 46.4	11 17.1	3 24.1	11 15.3	12 36.3
24 Sa	6 10 29	2 56 44	1♓23 00	8♓19 38	27 07.7	11 13.8	24 09.0	4 55.2	0 48.8	22 00.1	11 12.7	3 21.6	11 13.7	12 35.3
25 Su	6 14 25	3 53 57	15 18 16	22 18 50	27R 08.6	12 33.8	25 22.0	5 32.6	1 12.1	22 13.9	11 08.4	3 19.2	11 12.1	12 34.4
26 M	6 18 22	4 51 11	29 21 13	6♈25 19	27 09.0	13 57.4	26 35.1	6 09.9	1 35.3	22 27.6	11 04.0	3 16.7	11 10.5	12 33.6
27 Tu	6 22 19	5 48 24	13♈30 58	20 37 58	27 08.1	15 24.3	27 48.1	6 47.3	1 58.5	22 41.3	10 59.6	3 14.3	11 08.9	12 32.7
28 W	6 26 15	6 45 38	27 46 02	4♉54 52	27 05.2	16 54.7	29 01.1	7 24.7	2 21.7	22 55.0	10 55.2	3 11.9	11 07.3	12 31.9
29 Th	6 30 12	7 42 51	12♉04 01	19 13 04	27 00.3	18 28.5	0♌14.1	8 02.1	2 44.8	23 08.6	10 50.7	3 09.4	11 05.7	12 31.2
30 F	6 34 08	8 40 05	26 21 27	3♊28 36	26 53.8	20 05.6	1 27.1	8 39.5	3 07.9	23 22.3	10 46.3	3 07.0	11 04.1	12 30.4

Astro Data

	Dy Hr Mn
☽ 0N	2 4:23
♄✶♇	2 5:26
☿ R	12 11:52
♃⚻♆	12 18:45
☽ 0S	15 9:27
♃⚻♇	18 6:30
♃⚻♄	18 7:13
♄✶♇	18 21:50
☽ 0N	29 11:00
☿ D	5 8:06
☽ 0S	11 15:56
♄☌♆	24 3:11
☽ 0N	25 15:48

Planet Ingress

	Dy Hr Mn
♀ ♊	11 6:28
☉ ♊	21 1:54
☊ ♒R	22 11:56
☿ ♉R	28 22:53
♀ ♋	4 17:17
☿ ♊	12 8:56
♂ ♌	16 14:10
☉ ♋	21 9:53
⚳ ♊	22 9:47
♀ ♌	29 7:21

Last Aspect / ☽ Ingress

Last Aspect Dy Hr Mn		☽ Ingress Dy Hr Mn
1 16:32	♀ ✶	♈ 2 11:51
3 10:08	♄ □	♉ 4 11:55
6 1:40	♀ ☌	♊ 6 12:03
7 6:01	♃ ☌	♋ 8 14:19
10 19:18	♀ ✶	♌ 10 20:23
12 14:20	☉ □	♍ 13 6:30
15 7:51	☉ △	♎ 15 19:07
16 22:29	♄ □	♏ 18 7:48
20 18:16	☉ ☍	♐ 20 18:52
21 22:12	♃ ☍	♑ 23 3:54
24 8:46	♂ ☍	♒ 25 11:01
26 21:15	♀ △	♓ 27 16:13
29 18:48	☿ ✶	♈ 29 19:25
31 12:35	♀ ✶	♉ 31 20:59

Last Aspect / ☽ Ingress

Last Aspect Dy Hr Mn		☽ Ingress Dy Hr Mn
2 19:23	☿ ☌	♊ 2 22:02
4 2:44	♃ ☌	♋ 5 0:17
7 2:18	☿ ✶	♌ 7 5:28
9 12:09	☿ □	♍ 9 14:29
12 2:14	☿ △	♎ 12 2:31
14 12:37	♂ □	♏ 14 15:11
15 18:00	♀ △	♐ 17 2:12
19 6:57	☉ ☍	♑ 19 10:41
20 22:45	♀ ☍	♒ 21 16:57
23 7:13	♃ △	♓ 23 21:36
25 17:42	♀ △	♈ 26 1:06
28 1:11	♀ □	♉ 28 3:45
29 0:46	♇ ☍	♊ 30 6:08

☽ Phases & Eclipses

Dy Hr Mn	
5 11:46	● 14♉57
12 14:20	☽ 21♌50
20 18:16	○ 29♏42
28 4:01	☾ 6♓49
3 19:53	● 13♊12
11 6:59	☽ 20♍20
19 6:57	○ 27♐59
26 9:09	☾ 4♈44

Astro Data

1 May 1989
Julian Day # 32628
SVP 5♓24'24"
GC 26♐41.4 ⚵ 28♓05.3
Eris 16♈56.3 ⚶ 26♌46.7
⚷ 3♋23.3 ⚴ 10♑19.3
☽ Mean ☊ 1♓24.4

1 June 1989
Julian Day # 32659
SVP 5♓24'20"
GC 26♐41.5 ⚵ 6♈39.7
Eris 17♈12.6 ⚶ 2♍45.7
⚷ 5♋56.8 ⚴ 9♑39.6R
☽ Mean ☊ 29♒45.9

July 1989 — LONGITUDE

Day	Sid.Time	☉	0 hr ☽	Noon☽	True☊	☿	♀	♂	⚳	♃	♄	♅	♆	♇
1 Sa	6 38 05	9♋37 19	10♊33 55	17♊36 48	26♒46.4	21♊46.0	2♌40.1	9♌16.9	3♊30.9	23♊35.9	10♑41.9	3♑04.6	11♑02.5	12♏29.7
2 Su	6 42 01	10 34 33	24 36 39	1♋32 56	26R 39.0	23 29.5	3 53.0	9 54.3	3 53.9	23 49.5	10R 37.5	3R 02.2	11R 00.8	12R 29.0
3 M	6 45 58	11 31 47	8♋25 08	15 12 53	26 32.5	25 16.2	5 06.0	10 31.7	4 16.8	24 03.0	10 33.0	2 59.7	10 59.2	12 28.4
4 Tu	6 49 55	12 29 01	21 55 50	28 33 47	26 27.6	27 05.8	6 18.9	11 09.2	4 39.7	24 16.6	10 28.6	2 57.3	10 57.6	12 27.7
5 W	6 53 51	13 26 14	5♌06 39	11♌34 25	26 24.7	28 58.3	7 31.8	11 46.7	5 02.5	24 30.1	10 24.2	2 55.0	10 56.0	12 27.1
6 Th	6 57 48	14 23 28	17 57 12	24 15 13	26D 23.6	0♋53.6	8 44.6	12 24.1	5 25.3	24 43.5	10 19.7	2 52.6	10 54.4	12 26.6
7 F	7 01 44	15 20 41	0♍28 45	6♍38 11	26 24.0	2 51.3	9 57.5	13 01.6	5 48.0	24 57.0	10 15.3	2 50.2	10 52.7	12 26.1
8 Sa	7 05 41	16 17 54	12 43 58	18 46 35	26 25.3	4 51.4	11 10.3	13 39.1	6 10.6	25 10.4	10 10.9	2 47.8	10 51.1	12 25.6
9 Su	7 09 37	17 15 07	24 46 35	0♎44 33	26 26.9	6 53.6	12 23.1	14 16.6	6 33.2	25 23.7	10 06.5	2 45.5	10 49.5	12 25.1
10 M	7 13 34	18 12 20	6♎41 04	12 36 48	26R 27.9	8 57.6	13 35.8	14 54.1	6 55.8	25 37.0	10 02.2	2 43.2	10 47.9	12 24.6
11 Tu	7 17 30	19 09 33	18 32 20	24 28 19	26 27.9	11 03.2	14 48.6	15 31.6	7 18.3	25 50.3	9 57.8	2 40.9	10 46.3	12 24.2
12 W	7 21 27	20 06 46	0♏25 21	6♏24 01	26 26.5	13 10.1	16 01.3	16 09.1	7 40.7	26 03.6	9 53.5	2 38.6	10 44.7	12 23.9
13 Th	7 25 23	21 03 59	12 24 55	18 28 34	26 23.6	15 17.9	17 14.0	16 46.6	8 03.1	26 16.8	9 49.2	2 36.3	10 43.1	12 23.5
14 F	7 29 20	22 01 12	24 35 26	0♐45 58	26 19.4	17 26.4	18 26.6	17 24.1	8 25.4	26 29.9	9 44.9	2 34.0	10 41.5	12 23.2
15 Sa	7 33 17	22 58 25	7♐00 31	13 19 24	26 14.4	19 35.2	19 39.2	18 01.7	8 47.7	26 43.0	9 40.6	2 31.8	10 39.9	12 23.0
16 Su	7 37 13	23 55 38	19 42 48	26 10 52	26 09.1	21 44.1	20 51.8	18 39.2	9 09.9	26 56.1	9 36.4	2 29.6	10 38.4	12 22.7
17 M	7 41 10	24 52 52	2♑43 39	9♑21 06	26 04.2	23 52.8	22 04.4	19 16.8	9 32.0	27 09.1	9 32.2	2 27.4	10 36.8	12 22.5
18 Tu	7 45 06	25 50 06	16 03 06	22 49 26	26 00.2	26 01.1	23 17.0	19 54.4	9 54.1	27 22.1	9 28.0	2 25.2	10 35.3	12 22.4
19 W	7 49 03	26 47 20	29 39 51	6♒33 59	25 57.6	28 08.7	24 29.5	20 32.0	10 16.1	27 35.1	9 23.9	2 23.0	10 33.7	12 22.2
20 Th	7 52 59	27 44 35	13♒31 26	20 31 49	25D 56.4	0♌15.4	25 42.0	21 09.6	10 38.0	27 48.0	9 19.8	2 20.9	10 32.2	12 22.1
21 F	7 56 56	28 41 50	27 34 39	4♓39 29	25 56.5	2 21.1	26 54.4	21 47.2	10 59.9	28 00.8	9 15.7	2 18.8	10 30.7	12 22.0
22 Sa	8 00 53	29 39 06	11♓45 53	18 53 24	25 57.6	4 25.5	28 06.8	22 24.8	11 21.7	28 13.6	9 11.7	2 16.7	10 29.1	12D 22.0
23 Su	8 04 49	0♌36 23	26 01 38	3♈10 10	25 59.0	6 28.7	29 19.2	23 02.4	11 43.4	28 26.3	9 07.7	2 14.6	10 27.6	12 22.0
24 M	8 08 46	1 33 40	10♈18 40	17 26 46	26 00.2	8 30.5	0♍31.6	23 40.1	12 05.0	28 39.0	9 03.8	2 12.6	10 26.1	12 22.0
25 Tu	8 12 42	2 30 59	24 34 12	1♉40 39	26R 00.7	10 30.7	1 43.9	24 17.8	12 26.6	28 51.6	8 59.9	2 10.6	10 24.7	12 22.1
26 W	8 16 39	3 28 19	8♉45 52	15 49 34	26 00.2	12 29.4	2 56.2	24 55.4	12 48.1	29 04.2	8 56.1	2 08.6	10 23.2	12 22.2
27 Th	8 20 35	4 25 39	22 51 30	29 51 27	25 58.8	14 26.6	4 08.5	25 33.1	13 09.5	29 16.7	8 52.3	2 06.7	10 21.7	12 22.3
28 F	8 24 32	5 23 01	6♊49 08	13♊44 20	25 56.6	16 22.1	5 20.8	26 10.9	13 30.9	29 29.2	8 48.5	2 04.8	10 20.3	12 22.5
29 Sa	8 28 28	6 20 24	20 36 49	27 26 20	25 53.9	18 16.0	6 33.0	26 48.6	13 52.2	29 41.6	8 44.9	2 02.9	10 18.9	12 22.7
30 Su	8 32 25	7 17 47	4♋12 41	10♋55 40	25 51.3	20 08.2	7 45.2	27 26.3	14 13.4	29 53.9	8 41.2	2 01.1	10 17.5	12 22.9
31 M	8 36 22	8 15 12	17 35 06	24 10 51	25 49.0	21 58.8	8 57.4	28 04.1	14 34.5	0♋06.2	8 37.7	1 59.2	10 16.1	12 23.2

August 1989 — LONGITUDE

Day	Sid.Time	☉	0 hr ☽	Noon☽	True☊	☿	♀	♂	⚳	♃	♄	♅	♆	♇
1 Tu	8 40 18	9♌12 37	0♌42 49	7♌10 55	25♒47.4	23♌47.8	10♍09.5	28♌41.9	14♊55.5	0♋18.4	8♑34.2	1♑57.5	10♑14.7	12♏23.5
2 W	8 44 15	10 10 04	13 35 10	19 55 34	25D 46.7	25 35.1	11 21.6	29 19.7	15 16.4	0 30.6	8R 30.7	1R 55.7	10R 13.4	12 23.8
3 Th	8 48 11	11 07 31	26 12 14	2♍25 17	25 46.7	27 20.7	12 33.7	29 57.5	15 37.2	0 42.6	8 27.3	1 54.0	10 12.0	12 24.2
4 F	8 52 08	12 04 59	8♍34 57	14 41 27	25 47.3	29 04.7	13 45.7	0♍35.3	15 58.0	0 54.6	8 24.0	1 52.3	10 10.7	12 24.6
5 Sa	8 56 04	13 02 27	20 45 07	26 46 17	25 48.4	0♍47.1	14 57.7	1 13.2	16 18.6	1 06.6	8 20.8	1 50.7	10 09.4	12 25.1
6 Su	9 00 01	13 59 57	2♎45 22	8♎42 48	25 49.5	2 27.9	16 09.7	1 51.0	16 39.2	1 18.4	8 17.6	1 49.0	10 08.1	12 25.5
7 M	9 03 57	14 57 27	14 39 03	20 34 38	25 50.6	4 07.1	17 21.6	2 28.9	16 59.6	1 30.2	8 14.5	1 47.5	10 06.8	12 26.0
8 Tu	9 07 54	15 54 58	26 30 06	2♏25 59	25 51.3	5 44.7	18 33.5	3 06.8	17 20.0	1 41.9	8 11.4	1 45.9	10 05.6	12 26.6
9 W	9 11 51	16 52 30	8♏22 53	14 21 22	25R 51.6	7 20.7	19 45.3	3 44.7	17 40.2	1 53.6	8 08.4	1 44.5	10 04.4	12 27.2
10 Th	9 15 47	17 50 03	20 22 01	26 25 24	25 51.5	8 55.1	20 57.1	4 22.6	18 00.4	2 05.1	8 05.6	1 43.0	10 03.2	12 27.8
11 F	9 19 44	18 47 36	2♐32 05	8♐42 36	25 51.1	10 27.9	22 08.9	5 00.5	18 20.4	2 16.6	8 02.7	1 41.6	10 02.0	12 28.4
12 Sa	9 23 40	19 45 11	14 57 26	21 17 02	25 50.4	11 59.1	23 20.6	5 38.5	18 40.4	2 28.0	8 00.0	1 40.2	10 00.8	12 29.1
13 Su	9 27 37	20 42 47	27 41 46	4♑11 57	25 49.8	13 28.7	24 32.2	6 16.5	19 00.2	2 39.3	7 57.3	1 38.9	9 59.7	12 29.8
14 M	9 31 33	21 40 23	10♑47 48	17 29 25	25 49.3	14 56.7	25 43.9	6 54.4	19 19.9	2 50.6	7 54.7	1 37.6	9 58.6	12 30.6
15 Tu	9 35 30	22 38 01	24 16 50	1♒09 56	25 48.9	16 23.1	26 55.4	7 32.4	19 39.5	3 01.7	7 52.2	1 36.4	9 57.5	12 31.3
16 W	9 39 26	23 35 40	8♒08 27	15 12 04	25D 48.7	17 47.8	28 07.0	8 10.5	19 59.0	3 12.8	7 49.8	1 35.2	9 56.4	12 32.2
17 Th	9 43 23	24 33 19	22 20 18	29 32 32	25 48.7	19 10.8	29 18.4	8 48.5	20 18.4	3 23.8	7 47.5	1 34.0	9 55.4	12 33.0
18 F	9 47 20	25 31 01	6♓48 08	14♓06 19	25R 48.7	20 32.1	0♎29.9	9 26.5	20 37.7	3 34.6	7 45.2	1 32.9	9 54.4	12 33.9
19 Sa	9 51 16	26 28 43	21 26 18	28 47 16	25 48.7	21 51.7	1 41.2	10 04.6	20 56.8	3 45.4	7 43.0	1 31.8	9 53.4	12 34.8
20 Su	9 55 13	27 26 27	6♈08 22	13♈28 49	25 48.6	23 09.5	2 52.6	10 42.7	21 15.9	3 56.1	7 40.9	1 30.8	9 52.4	12 35.7
21 M	9 59 09	28 24 13	20 47 52	28 04 53	25 48.4	24 25.5	4 03.9	11 20.8	21 34.8	4 06.8	7 38.9	1 29.8	9 51.4	12 36.7
22 Tu	10 03 06	29 22 01	5♉19 14	12♉30 28	25 48.1	25 39.6	5 15.1	11 58.9	21 53.5	4 17.3	7 37.0	1 28.9	9 50.5	12 37.7
23 W	10 07 02	0♍19 50	19 38 10	26 42 03	25D 48.0	26 51.7	6 26.3	12 37.1	22 12.2	4 27.7	7 35.2	1 28.0	9 49.6	12 38.7
24 Th	10 10 59	1 17 41	3♊41 54	10♊37 36	25 48.1	28 01.8	7 37.5	13 15.3	22 30.7	4 38.0	7 33.4	1 27.1	9 48.8	12 39.8
25 F	10 14 55	2 15 34	17 29 07	24 26 26	25 48.4	29 09.8	8 48.6	13 53.5	22 49.1	4 48.2	7 31.8	1 26.4	9 47.9	12 40.9
26 Sa	10 18 52	3 13 29	0♋59 38	7♋38 47	25 49.0	0♎15.6	9 59.6	14 31.7	23 07.3	4 58.4	7 30.2	1 25.6	9 47.1	12 42.0
27 Su	10 22 49	4 11 25	14 14 01	20 45 28	25 49.8	1 19.0	11 10.6	15 09.9	23 25.4	5 08.4	7 28.7	1 24.9	9 46.3	12 43.2
28 M	10 26 45	5 09 23	27 13 17	3♌37 37	25 50.5	2 20.1	12 21.6	15 48.2	23 43.4	5 18.3	7 27.4	1 24.3	9 45.6	12 44.4
29 Tu	10 30 42	6 07 23	9♌58 37	16 16 27	25R 51.1	3 18.5	13 32.5	16 26.5	24 01.2	5 28.1	7 26.1	1 23.6	9 44.8	12 45.6
30 W	10 34 38	7 05 24	22 31 16	28 43 14	25 51.2	4 14.2	14 43.3	17 04.8	24 18.9	5 37.8	7 24.9	1 23.1	9 44.1	12 46.9
31 Th	10 38 35	8 03 27	4♍52 31	10♍59 17	25 50.8	5 07.0	15 54.1	17 43.2	24 36.4	5 47.4	7 23.8	1 22.6	9 43.5	12 48.2

Astro Data Dy Hr Mn	Planet Ingress Dy Hr Mn	Last Aspect Dy Hr Mn	☽ Ingress Dy Hr Mn	Last Aspect Dy Hr Mn	☽ Ingress Dy Hr Mn	☽ Phases & Eclipses Dy Hr Mn
☽0S 8 23:11	☿ ♋ 6 0:55	1 22:26 ♃ ☌	♋ 2 9:19	3 6:59 ♂ ☌	♍ 3 7:19	3 4:59 ● 11♋15
♃□♇ 18 12:24	☿ ♌ 20 9:04	3 7:09 ♇ △	♌ 4 14:37	4 9:58 ♀ ☌	♎ 5 18:28	11 0:19 ☽ 18♎42
☽0N 22 21:01	☉ ♌ 22 20:45	6 12:55 ♃ ⚹	♍ 6 23:04	6 23:37 ☉ ⚹	♏ 8 7:05	18 17:42 ○ 26♑04
♇ D 23 3:55	♀ ♍ 24 1:31	9 1:02 ♃ □	♎ 9 10:30	9 23:58 ♀ ⚹	♐ 10 19:02	25 13:31 ☾ 2♉35
	♃ ♋ 30 23:50	11 14:49 ♃ △	♏ 11 23:09	12 16:16 ♀ □	♑ 13 4:16	
☽0S 5 6:51		13 17:32 ☉ △	♐ 14 10:31	15 3:55 ♀ △	♒ 15 9:59	1 16:06 ● 9♌22
♃☍♅ 8 19:18	♂ ♍ 3 13:35	16 13:25 ♃ ☍	♑ 16 19:01	17 3:07 ☉ ☍	♓ 17 12:46	9 17:29 ☽ 17♏06
☽0N 19 4:29	☿ ♍ 5 0:54	18 18:39 ☿ ☍	♒ 19 0:35	18 23:35 ☿ ☍	♈ 19 13:59	17 3:07 ○ 24♒12
♀0S 19 11:05	♀ ♎ 18 1:58	21 0:34 ♃ △	♓ 21 4:07	21 12:34 ☉ △	♉ 21 15:10	17 3:08 ☍ T 1.598
☿0S 23 12:50	☉ ♍ 23 3:46	23 3:56 ♃ □	♈ 23 6:41	23 12:18 ☿ △	♊ 23 17:39	23 18:40 ☾ 0♊36
	☿ ♎ 26 6:14	25 7:10 ♃ ⚹	♉ 25 9:10	25 21:30 ☿ □	♋ 25 22:13	31 5:45 ● 7♍48
		27 4:16 ♂ □	♊ 27 12:15	27 1:11 ♂ ⚹	♌ 28 5:12	31 5:30:50 ☌ P 0.634
		29 16:03 ♃ ☌	♋ 29 16:32	29 6:14 ♀ ⚹	♍ 30 14:29	
		30 14:37 ♇ △	♌ 31 22:41			

Astro Data

1 July 1989
Julian Day # 32689
SVP 5♓24'14"
GC 26♐41.6 ⚴ 13♈02.5
Eris 17♈21.0 ⚵ 11♍11.9
⚷ 8♋52.0 ⚶ 3♑14.8R
☽ Mean ☊ 28♒10.6

1 August 1989
Julian Day # 32720
SVP 5♓24'08"
GC 26♐41.6 ⚴ 16♈16.4
Eris 17♈19.9R ⚵ 21♍24.4
⚷ 11♋53.6 ⚶ 28♐20.6R
☽ Mean ☊ 26♒32.1

LONGITUDE — September 1989

Day	Sid.Time	☉	0 hr ☽	Noon ☽	True ☊	☿	♀	♂	⚳	♃	♄	♅	♆	♇
1 F	10 42 31	9♍01 32	17♍03 43	23♍06 02	25♒49.6	5♎56.8	17♎04.9	18♍21.5	24♊53.7	5♋56.8	7♑22.8	1♑22.1	9♑42.8	12♏49.5
2 Sa	10 46 28	9 59 38	29 06 26	5♎05 11	25R47.9	6 43.3	18 15.6	18 59.9	25 10.9	6 06.2	7R21.9	1R21.7	9R42.2	12 50.8
3 Su	10 50 24	10 57 46	11♎02 33	16 58 49	25 45.7	7 26.3	19 26.2	19 38.3	25 27.9	6 15.4	7 21.1	1 21.3	9 41.6	12 52.2
4 M	10 54 21	11 55 55	22 54 20	28 49 28	25 43.2	8 05.6	20 36.7	20 16.7	25 44.8	6 24.5	7 20.3	1 21.0	9 41.1	12 53.6
5 Tu	10 58 18	12 54 06	4♏44 37	10♏40 12	25 40.9	8 40.9	21 47.2	20 55.1	26 01.5	6 33.5	7 19.7	1 20.8	9 40.6	12 55.0
6 W	11 02 14	13 52 18	16 36 42	22 34 35	25 38.9	9 12.0	22 57.7	21 33.6	26 18.0	6 42.4	7 19.2	1 20.6	9 40.1	12 56.5
7 Th	11 06 11	14 50 32	28 34 24	4♐36 40	25D37.7	9 38.5	24 08.1	22 12.1	26 34.3	6 51.1	7 18.8	1 20.4	9 39.6	12 58.0
8 F	11 10 07	15 48 48	10♐41 57	16 50 48	25 37.4	10 00.3	25 18.4	22 50.6	26 50.5	6 59.7	7 18.5	1 20.3	9 39.2	12 59.5
9 Sa	11 14 04	16 47 05	23 03 46	29 21 24	25 37.9	10 16.8	26 28.6	23 29.1	27 06.5	7 08.2	7 18.2	1D20.3	9 38.8	13 01.1
10 Su	11 18 00	17 45 23	5♑44 13	12♑12 41	25 39.0	10 27.9	27 38.8	24 07.7	27 22.3	7 16.6	7D18.1	1 20.3	9 38.4	13 02.6
11 M	11 21 57	18 43 43	18 47 13	25 28 07	25 40.5	10R33.2	28 48.9	24 46.3	27 38.0	7 24.8	7 18.1	1 20.3	9 38.1	13 04.2
12 Tu	11 25 53	19 42 05	2♒15 39	9♒09 54	25 41.9	10 32.4	29 58.9	25 24.9	27 53.4	7 32.9	7 18.1	1 20.4	9 37.8	13 05.9
13 W	11 29 50	20 40 28	16 10 50	23 18 15	25R42.5	10 25.2	1♏08.9	26 03.5	28 08.6	7 40.9	7 18.3	1 20.6	9 37.5	13 07.5
14 Th	11 33 47	21 38 53	0♓31 48	7♓50 55	25 42.1	10 11.4	2 18.7	26 42.2	28 23.7	7 48.8	7 18.6	1 20.7	9 37.3	13 09.2
15 F	11 37 43	22 37 20	15 14 53	22 42 50	25 40.4	9 50.8	3 28.5	27 20.8	28 38.5	7 56.4	7 18.9	1 21.0	9 37.1	13 10.9
16 Sa	11 41 40	23 35 48	0♈13 44	7♈46 27	25 37.5	9 23.3	4 38.2	27 59.5	28 53.2	8 04.0	7 19.4	1 21.3	9 36.9	13 12.6
17 Su	11 45 36	24 34 18	15 19 47	22 52 33	25 33.6	8 49.0	5 47.8	28 38.2	29 07.6	8 11.4	7 19.9	1 21.6	9 36.8	13 14.4
18 M	11 49 33	25 32 51	0♉23 35	7♉51 47	25 29.5	8 08.1	6 57.4	29 17.0	29 21.9	8 18.7	7 20.6	1 22.1	9 36.6	13 16.1
19 Tu	11 53 29	26 31 26	15 16 11	22 36 00	25 25.7	7 20.8	8 06.8	29 55.8	29 35.9	8 25.8	7 21.4	1 22.5	9 36.6	13 17.9
20 W	11 57 26	27 30 03	29 50 35	6♊59 28	25 22.9	6 27.8	9 16.2	0♎34.6	29 49.7	8 32.8	7 22.2	1 23.0	9D36.5	13 19.8
21 Th	12 01 22	28 28 42	14♊02 22	20 59 11	25D21.3	5 29.9	10 25.5	1 13.4	0♋03.3	8 39.7	7 23.2	1 23.6	9 36.5	13 21.6
22 F	12 05 19	29 27 24	27 49 55	4♋34 42	25 21.2	4 28.0	11 34.7	1 52.3	0 16.6	8 46.4	7 24.2	1 24.2	9 36.5	13 23.5
23 Sa	12 09 16	0♎26 07	11♋13 48	17 47 31	25 22.2	3 23.5	12 43.9	2 31.1	0 29.8	8 52.9	7 25.4	1 24.8	9 36.6	13 25.4
24 Su	12 13 12	1 24 53	24 16 13	0♌40 17	25 23.8	2 17.7	13 52.9	3 10.1	0 42.7	8 59.3	7 26.6	1 25.6	9 36.7	13 27.3
25 M	12 17 09	2 23 42	7♌00 10	13 16 15	25R25.2	1 12.3	15 01.9	3 49.0	0 55.3	9 05.5	7 27.9	1 26.3	9 36.8	13 29.2
26 Tu	12 21 05	3 22 32	19 28 56	25 38 37	25 25.8	0 08.9	16 10.7	4 28.0	1 07.7	9 11.6	7 29.4	1 27.1	9 37.0	13 31.2
27 W	12 25 02	4 21 24	1♍45 40	7♍50 24	25 25.0	29♍09.1	17 19.5	5 07.0	1 19.9	9 17.5	7 30.9	1 28.0	9 37.1	13 33.2
28 Th	12 28 58	5 20 19	13 53 09	19 54 09	25 22.3	28 14.7	18 28.1	5 46.0	1 31.8	9 23.2	7 32.5	1 28.9	9 37.4	13 35.2
29 F	12 32 55	6 19 15	25 53 42	1♎52 00	25 17.5	27 27.1	19 36.7	6 25.1	1 43.4	9 28.8	7 34.3	1 29.9	9 37.6	13 37.2
30 Sa	12 36 51	7 18 14	7♎49 18	13 45 46	25 10.9	26 47.4	20 45.2	7 04.1	1 54.8	9 34.2	7 36.1	1 30.9	9 37.9	13 39.2

LONGITUDE — October 1989

Day	Sid.Time	☉	0 hr ☽	Noon ☽	True ☊	☿	♀	♂	⚳	♃	♄	♅	♆	♇
1 Su	12 40 48	8♎17 15	19♎41 39	25♎37 07	25♒03.0	26♍16.9	21♏53.5	7♎43.3	2♋05.9	9♋39.5	7♑38.0	1♑31.9	9♑38.2	13♏41.3
2 M	12 44 44	9 16 17	1♏32 24	7♏27 45	24R54.3	25R56.2	23 01.8	8 22.4	2 16.7	9 44.5	7 40.0	1 33.1	9 38.6	13 43.3
3 Tu	12 48 41	10 15 22	13 23 23	19 19 38	24 45.8	25D45.7	24 09.9	9 01.6	2 27.3	9 49.4	7 42.1	1 34.2	9 39.0	13 45.4
4 W	12 52 38	11 14 29	25 16 47	1♐15 11	24 38.3	25 45.8	25 17.9	9 40.8	2 37.6	9 54.2	7 44.3	1 35.4	9 39.4	13 47.6
5 Th	12 56 34	12 13 37	7♐15 14	13 17 21	24 32.5	25 56.4	26 25.8	10 20.0	2 47.6	9 58.7	7 46.6	1 36.7	9 39.8	13 49.7
6 F	13 00 31	13 12 47	19 22 00	25 29 40	24 28.6	26 17.2	27 33.6	10 59.3	2 57.3	10 03.1	7 49.0	1 38.0	9 40.3	13 51.8
7 Sa	13 04 27	14 11 59	1♑40 52	7♑56 08	24D26.8	26 47.8	28 41.3	11 38.5	3 06.7	10 07.3	7 51.5	1 39.4	9 40.9	13 54.0
8 Su	13 08 24	15 11 13	14 16 02	20 41 05	24 26.8	27 27.7	29 48.8	12 17.8	3 15.9	10 11.4	7 54.1	1 40.8	9 41.4	13 56.2
9 M	13 12 20	16 10 29	27 11 49	3♒48 42	24 27.7	28 16.2	0♐56.2	12 57.2	3 24.7	10 15.2	7 56.8	1 42.3	9 42.0	13 58.4
10 Tu	13 16 17	17 09 46	10♒32 10	17 22 31	24R28.6	29 12.5	2 03.4	13 36.5	3 33.2	10 18.9	7 59.5	1 43.8	9 42.6	14 00.6
11 W	13 20 13	18 09 05	24 19 59	1♓24 37	24 28.6	0♎16.0	3 10.5	14 15.9	3 41.4	10 22.4	8 02.4	1 45.3	9 43.3	14 02.8
12 Th	13 24 10	19 08 25	8♓36 17	15 54 42	24 26.8	1 25.8	4 17.4	14 55.4	3 49.3	10 25.7	8 05.3	1 46.9	9 43.9	14 05.0
13 F	13 28 07	20 07 48	23 19 18	0♈49 21	24 22.6	2 41.2	5 24.2	15 34.8	3 56.9	10 28.8	8 08.3	1 48.6	9 44.7	14 07.3
14 Sa	13 32 03	21 07 12	8♈23 50	16 01 37	24 16.1	4 01.4	6 30.8	16 14.3	4 04.2	10 31.7	8 11.4	1 50.3	9 45.4	14 09.6
15 Su	13 36 00	22 06 39	23 41 21	1♉21 38	24 07.8	5 25.8	7 37.2	16 53.8	4 11.1	10 34.5	8 14.6	1 52.0	9 46.2	14 11.8
16 M	13 39 56	23 06 07	9♉00 58	16 37 58	23 58.8	6 53.7	8 43.5	17 33.3	4 17.7	10 37.0	8 17.9	1 53.8	9 47.0	14 14.1
17 Tu	13 43 53	24 05 38	24 11 18	1♊39 47	23 50.1	8 24.6	9 49.6	18 12.9	4 24.0	10 39.4	8 21.3	1 55.6	9 47.8	14 16.4
18 W	13 47 49	25 05 11	9♊02 28	16 18 37	23 42.9	9 58.0	10 55.5	18 52.5	4 29.9	10 41.6	8 24.7	1 57.5	9 48.7	14 18.7
19 Th	13 51 46	26 04 47	23 27 44	0♋29 31	23 37.9	11 33.3	12 01.2	19 32.2	4 35.5	10 43.6	8 28.3	1 59.4	9 49.6	14 21.1
20 F	13 55 42	27 04 25	7♋23 55	14 11 02	23 35.1	13 10.3	13 06.8	20 11.8	4 40.7	10 45.4	8 31.9	2 01.4	9 50.6	14 23.4
21 Sa	13 59 39	28 04 05	20 51 09	27 24 40	23D34.3	14 48.5	14 12.1	20 51.5	4 45.6	10 47.0	8 35.6	2 03.4	9 51.5	14 25.8
22 Su	14 03 36	29 03 47	3♌52 02	10♌13 49	23 34.6	16 27.7	15 17.3	21 31.3	4 50.1	10 48.4	8 39.4	2 05.5	9 52.5	14 28.1
23 M	14 07 32	0♏03 31	16 30 34	22 42 53	23R35.1	18 07.6	16 22.2	22 11.1	4 54.2	10 49.6	8 43.3	2 07.6	9 53.6	14 30.5
24 Tu	14 11 29	1 03 18	28 51 22	4♍56 35	23 34.4	19 47.9	17 27.0	22 50.9	4 58.0	10 50.6	8 47.2	2 09.7	9 54.6	14 32.8
25 W	14 15 25	2 03 07	10♍59 05	16 59 22	23 31.8	21 28.6	18 31.5	23 30.7	5 01.4	10 51.4	8 51.3	2 11.9	9 55.7	14 35.2
26 Th	14 19 22	3 02 58	22 57 54	28 55 07	23 26.5	23 09.4	19 35.8	24 10.6	5 04.4	10 52.0	8 55.4	2 14.1	9 56.9	14 37.6
27 F	14 23 18	4 02 51	4♎51 23	10♎47 04	23 18.2	24 50.3	20 39.9	24 50.5	5 07.1	10 52.4	8 59.6	2 16.4	9 58.0	14 40.0
28 Sa	14 27 15	5 02 46	16 42 25	22 37 42	23 07.3	26 31.1	21 43.7	25 30.4	5 09.3	10R52.6	9 03.8	2 18.7	9 59.2	14 42.4
29 Su	14 31 11	6 02 43	28 33 09	4♏28 56	22 54.3	28 11.7	22 47.3	26 10.4	5 11.2	10 52.6	9 08.2	2 21.0	10 00.4	14 44.8
30 M	14 35 08	7 02 42	10♏25 14	16 22 13	22 40.2	29 52.1	23 50.6	26 50.4	5 12.7	10 52.4	9 12.6	2 23.4	10 01.6	14 47.2
31 Tu	14 39 05	8 02 43	22 20 02	28 18 50	22 26.2	1♏32.3	24 53.7	27 30.4	5 13.7	10 52.0	9 17.1	2 25.8	10 02.9	14 49.6

Astro Data	Dy Hr Mn	Planet Ingress	Dy Hr Mn	Last Aspect Dy Hr Mn		☽ Ingress	Dy Hr Mn	Last Aspect Dy Hr Mn		☽ Ingress	Dy Hr Mn	☽ Phases & Eclipses Dy Hr Mn	
☽ 0S	1 14:12	♀ ♏	12 12:22	1 2:03	♂ ☌	♎	2 1:47	30 3:39	♆ □	♏	1 20:53	8 9:49	☽ 15♐44
♅ D	10 1:14	♂ ♎	19 14:38	3 17:31	♀ ☌	♏	4 14:23	4 0:56	☿ ⚹	♐	4 9:29	15 11:50	○ 22♓37
♃☍♄	10 16:19	⚳ ♋	21 6:11	6 9:51	♂ ⚹	♐	7 2:51	6 13:36	☿ □	♑	6 20:45	22 2:10	☾ 29♊03
♄ D	11 7:10	☉ ♎	23 1:20	9 5:58	♀ ⚹	♑	9 13:13	9 1:16	☿ △	♒	9 5:07	29 21:47	● 6♎43
☿ R	11 20:58	☿ ♍R	26 15:28	11 18:30	♀ □	♒	11 20:02	10 11:36	☉ △	♓	11 9:37		
☽ 0N	15 14:24			12 18:46	♇ □	♓	13 23:08	12 9:00	♇ △	♈	13 10:41	8 0:52	☽ 14♑44
♆ D	21 6:53	♀ ♐	8 16:00	15 19:44	♂ ☍	♈	15 23:38	14 20:32	☉ ☍	♉	15 9:52	14 20:32	○ 21♈28
♂ 0S	22 13:31	☿ ♎	11 6:11	16 14:55	♆ □	♉	17 23:22	16 8:12	♇ ☍	♊	17 9:19	21 13:19	☾ 28♋07
☉ 0S	23 1:20	☉ ♏	23 10:35	19 18:57	☉ △	♊	20 0:16	19 3:52	☉ △	♋	19 11:09	29 15:27	● 6♏11
☽ 0S	28 20:39	☿ ♏	30 13:53	22 2:10	☉ □	♋	22 3:50	21 13:19	☉ □	♌	21 16:47		
☿ 0N	29 18:25			23 3:58	♇ △	♌	24 10:44	23 10:55	♂ ⚹	♍	24 2:15		
♃☍♆	1 5:52			25 15:44	♀ □	♍	26 20:32	25 15:23	♀ □	♎	26 14:11		
☿ D	3 23:50			29 3:39	☿ ☌	♎	29 8:15	28 21:11	☿ ☌	♏	29 2:56		
☽ 0N	13 1:19	☽ 0S26	2:12					30 8:48	♇ ☌	♐	31 15:23		
☿ 0S	14 20:26	♃ R29	0:03										

Astro Data

1 September 1989
Julian Day # 32751
SVP 5♓24'04"
GC 26♐41.7 ⚴ 14♈14.8R
Eris 17♈09.5R ⚵ 2♎23.3
⚷ 14♉28.6 ⚶ 0♑29.9
☽ Mean ☊ 24♒53.6

1 October 1989
Julian Day # 32781
SVP 5♓24'01"
GC 26♐41.8 ⚴ 7♈04.6R
Eris 16♈53.2R ⚵ 13♎17.2
⚷ 16♉07.4 ⚶ 8♑12.9
☽ Mean ☊ 23♒18.3

November 1989 LONGITUDE

Day	Sid.Time	☉	0 hr ☽	Noon ☽	True ☊	☿	♀	♂	⚴	♃	♄	♅	♆	♇
1 W	14 43 01	9♏02 46	4♐18 49	10♐20 09	22♒13.5	3♏12.1	25♐56.5	28♎10.5	5♋14.4	10♋51.4	9♑21.7	2♑28.3	10♑04.2	14♏52.0
2 Th	14 46 58	10 02 50	16 23 05	22 27 53	22R 03.0	4 51.6	26 59.0	28 50.6	5R 14.7	10R 50.6	9 26.3	2 30.8	10 05.5	14 54.5
3 F	14 50 54	11 02 56	28 34 49	4♑44 15	21 55.3	6 30.7	28 01.1	29 30.7	5 14.6	10 49.6	9 31.1	2 33.3	10 06.9	14 56.9
4 Sa	14 54 51	12 03 04	10♑56 34	17 12 10	21 50.5	8 09.5	29 03.0	0♏10.9	5 14.0	10 48.4	9 35.8	2 35.9	10 08.3	14 59.3
5 Su	14 58 47	13 03 14	23 31 30	29 55 04	21 48.4	9 47.9	0♑04.6	0 51.1	5 13.1	10 47.0	9 40.7	2 38.5	10 09.7	15 01.7
6 M	15 02 44	14 03 25	6♒23 19	12♒56 46	21 47.9	11 25.8	1 05.8	1 31.3	5 11.8	10 45.4	9 45.6	2 41.2	10 11.1	15 04.2
7 Tu	15 06 40	15 03 37	19 35 51	26 20 59	21 47.8	13 03.4	2 06.6	2 11.6	5 10.0	10 43.5	9 50.6	2 43.9	10 12.6	15 06.6
8 W	15 10 37	16 03 51	3♓12 31	10♓10 42	21 47.0	14 40.7	3 07.1	2 51.9	5 07.9	10 41.5	9 55.7	2 46.6	10 14.1	15 09.0
9 Th	15 14 34	17 04 06	17 15 37	24 27 12	21 44.2	16 17.5	4 07.2	3 32.2	5 05.3	10 39.3	10 00.8	2 49.3	10 15.6	15 11.4
10 F	15 18 30	18 04 23	1♈45 13	9♈09 10	21 38.8	17 54.0	5 06.9	4 12.6	5 02.3	10 36.9	10 06.0	2 52.1	10 17.1	15 13.9
11 Sa	15 22 27	19 04 41	16 38 22	24 11 52	21 30.5	19 30.1	6 06.2	4 52.9	4 58.9	10 34.3	10 11.3	2 54.9	10 18.7	15 16.3
12 Su	15 26 23	20 05 01	1♉48 34	9♉27 08	21 20.0	21 05.9	7 05.0	5 33.4	4 55.1	10 31.5	10 16.6	2 57.8	10 20.3	15 18.7
13 M	15 30 20	21 05 22	17 06 10	24 44 12	21 08.4	22 41.4	8 03.5	6 13.8	4 50.9	10 28.6	10 22.0	3 00.7	10 21.9	15 21.1
14 Tu	15 34 16	22 05 45	2♊19 47	9♊51 34	20 57.0	24 16.6	9 01.4	6 54.3	4 46.3	10 25.4	10 27.4	3 03.6	10 23.5	15 23.6
15 W	15 38 13	23 06 10	17 18 22	24 39 11	20 47.2	25 51.5	9 58.9	7 34.8	4 41.3	10 22.0	10 32.9	3 06.6	10 25.2	15 26.0
16 Th	15 42 09	24 06 37	1♋53 14	9♋00 00	20 39.8	27 26.1	10 55.9	8 15.4	4 35.9	10 18.5	10 38.5	3 09.5	10 26.9	15 28.4
17 F	15 46 06	25 07 06	15 59 11	22 50 43	20 35.1	29 00.5	11 52.3	8 56.0	4 30.1	10 14.7	10 44.1	3 12.5	10 28.6	15 30.8
18 Sa	15 50 03	26 07 36	29 34 44	6♌11 29	20 33.0	0♐34.6	12 48.3	9 36.7	4 23.9	10 10.8	10 49.8	3 15.6	10 30.3	15 33.2
19 Su	15 53 59	27 08 08	12♌41 25	19 05 02	20 32.5	2 08.5	13 43.7	10 17.3	4 17.3	10 06.7	10 55.5	3 18.6	10 32.1	15 35.6
20 M	15 57 56	28 08 42	25 22 55	1♍35 43	20 32.5	3 42.2	14 38.5	10 58.0	4 10.3	10 02.4	11 01.3	3 21.7	10 33.9	15 38.0
21 Tu	16 01 52	29 09 17	7♍44 06	13 48 43	20 31.7	5 15.7	15 32.7	11 38.8	4 02.9	9 57.9	11 07.1	3 24.8	10 35.7	15 40.4
22 W	16 05 49	0♐09 55	19 50 14	25 49 17	20 29.2	6 49.1	16 26.3	12 19.6	3 55.1	9 53.3	11 13.0	3 28.0	10 37.5	15 42.7
23 Th	16 09 45	1 10 34	1♎46 28	7♎42 20	20 24.0	8 22.2	17 19.3	13 00.4	3 46.9	9 48.4	11 19.0	3 31.2	10 39.3	15 45.1
24 F	16 13 42	2 11 14	13 37 26	19 32 12	20 16.0	9 55.2	18 11.6	13 41.2	3 38.4	9 43.4	11 25.0	3 34.4	10 41.2	15 47.5
25 Sa	16 17 38	3 11 56	25 27 05	1♏22 26	20 05.1	11 28.1	19 03.2	14 22.1	3 29.4	9 38.3	11 31.0	3 37.6	10 43.1	15 49.8
26 Su	16 21 35	4 12 40	7♏18 34	13 15 45	19 52.1	13 00.8	19 54.1	15 03.1	3 20.2	9 32.9	11 37.1	3 40.8	10 45.0	15 52.1
27 M	16 25 32	5 13 25	19 14 12	25 14 05	19 37.9	14 33.4	20 44.2	15 44.0	3 10.6	9 27.4	11 43.2	3 44.1	10 46.9	15 54.5
28 Tu	16 29 28	6 14 12	1♐15 33	7♐18 44	19 23.8	16 05.8	21 33.6	16 25.0	3 00.6	9 21.8	11 49.4	3 47.4	10 48.8	15 56.8
29 W	16 33 25	7 15 00	13 23 43	19 30 36	19 10.8	17 38.2	22 22.1	17 06.1	2 50.3	9 16.0	11 55.7	3 50.7	10 50.8	15 59.1
30 Th	16 37 21	8 15 49	25 39 28	1♑50 26	19 00.1	19 10.4	23 09.8	17 47.1	2 39.7	9 10.0	12 02.0	3 54.0	10 52.8	16 01.4

December 1989 LONGITUDE

Day	Sid.Time	☉	0 hr ☽	Noon ☽	True ☊	☿	♀	♂	⚴	♃	♄	♅	♆	♇
1 F	16 41 18	9♐16 39	8♑03 37	14♑19 10	18♒52.3	20♐42.4	23♑56.6	18♏28.2	2♋28.7	9♋03.9	12♑08.3	3♑57.4	10♑54.8	16♏03.7
2 Sa	16 45 14	10 17 30	20 37 15	26 58 07	18R 47.4	22 14.3	24 42.5	19 09.4	2R 17.5	8R 57.7	12 14.7	4 00.7	10 56.8	16 06.0
3 Su	16 49 11	11 18 22	3♒21 58	9♒49 07	18D 45.2	23 46.0	25 27.4	19 50.5	2 06.0	8 51.3	12 21.1	4 04.1	10 58.8	16 08.2
4 M	16 53 08	12 19 15	16 19 52	22 54 32	18 45.0	25 17.5	26 11.3	20 31.7	1 54.2	8 44.8	12 27.5	4 07.5	11 00.8	16 10.5
5 Tu	16 57 04	13 20 08	29 33 27	6♓16 55	18R 45.4	26 48.8	26 54.1	21 13.0	1 42.1	8 38.1	12 34.0	4 11.0	11 02.9	16 12.7
6 W	17 01 01	14 21 03	13♓05 15	19 58 39	18 45.5	28 19.9	27 35.9	21 54.2	1 29.8	8 31.3	12 40.5	4 14.4	11 05.0	16 14.9
7 Th	17 04 57	15 21 57	26 57 18	4♈01 13	18 43.9	29 50.6	28 16.4	22 35.5	1 17.3	8 24.4	12 47.1	4 17.8	11 07.0	16 17.1
8 F	17 08 54	16 22 53	11♈10 20	18 24 24	18 40.1	1♑21.0	28 55.8	23 16.9	1 04.5	8 17.4	12 53.7	4 21.3	11 09.1	16 19.3
9 Sa	17 12 50	17 23 50	25 43 00	3♉05 34	18 33.8	2 50.9	29 33.9	23 58.3	0 51.5	8 10.3	13 00.3	4 24.8	11 11.2	16 21.4
10 Su	17 16 47	18 24 47	10♉31 20	17 59 22	18 25.4	4 20.3	0♒10.8	24 39.7	0 38.3	8 03.1	13 06.9	4 28.3	11 13.4	16 23.6
11 M	17 20 43	19 25 45	25 28 36	2♊57 54	18 15.9	5 49.1	0 46.2	25 21.1	0 25.0	7 55.8	13 13.6	4 31.8	11 15.5	16 25.7
12 Tu	17 24 40	20 26 43	10♊26 03	17 51 53	18 06.5	7 17.2	1 20.3	26 02.6	0 11.5	7 48.3	13 20.4	4 35.3	11 17.7	16 27.8
13 W	17 28 37	21 27 43	25 14 16	2♋32 11	17 58.3	8 44.4	1 52.8	26 44.1	29♊57.9	7 40.8	13 27.1	4 38.9	11 19.8	16 29.9
14 Th	17 32 33	22 28 43	9♋44 48	16 51 24	17 52.1	10 10.6	2 23.9	27 25.7	29 44.1	7 33.3	13 33.9	4 42.4	11 22.0	16 32.0
15 F	17 36 30	23 29 44	23 51 31	0♌44 51	17 48.3	11 35.6	2 53.4	28 07.3	29 30.2	7 25.6	13 40.7	4 46.0	11 24.2	16 34.1
16 Sa	17 40 26	24 30 46	7♌31 16	14 10 51	17D 46.9	12 59.2	3 21.2	28 48.9	29 16.2	7 17.8	13 47.5	4 49.5	11 26.4	16 36.1
17 Su	17 44 23	25 31 49	20 43 48	27 10 27	17 47.2	14 21.0	3 47.3	29 30.6	29 02.1	7 10.0	13 54.4	4 53.1	11 28.6	16 38.1
18 M	17 48 19	26 32 53	3♍31 14	9♍46 42	17 48.3	15 40.8	4 11.7	0♐12.3	28 48.0	7 02.2	14 01.3	4 56.7	11 30.8	16 40.1
19 Tu	17 52 16	27 33 57	15 57 23	22 03 57	17R 49.3	16 58.3	4 34.2	0 54.0	28 33.8	6 54.2	14 08.2	5 00.3	11 33.0	16 42.1
20 W	17 56 12	28 35 03	28 07 01	4♎07 15	17 49.3	18 13.0	4 54.9	1 35.8	28 19.5	6 46.3	14 15.1	5 03.8	11 35.2	16 44.0
21 Th	18 00 09	29 36 09	10♎05 18	16 01 48	17 47.6	19 24.5	5 13.6	2 17.6	28 05.3	6 38.2	14 22.0	5 07.4	11 37.4	16 46.0
22 F	18 04 06	0♑37 16	21 57 21	27 52 33	17 43.7	20 32.2	5 30.3	2 59.5	27 51.1	6 30.2	14 29.0	5 11.0	11 39.7	16 47.9
23 Sa	18 08 02	1 38 23	3♏47 56	9♏44 01	17 37.8	21 35.6	5 44.9	3 41.4	27 36.9	6 22.1	14 36.0	5 14.6	11 41.9	16 49.7
24 Su	18 11 59	2 39 32	15 41 14	21 39 59	17 30.3	22 33.9	5 57.3	4 23.3	27 22.7	6 14.0	14 43.0	5 18.2	11 44.1	16 51.6
25 M	18 15 55	3 40 41	27 40 39	3♐43 29	17 21.8	23 26.5	6 07.6	5 05.2	27 08.6	6 05.8	14 50.0	5 21.9	11 46.4	16 53.4
26 Tu	18 19 52	4 41 50	9♐48 46	15 56 39	17 13.1	24 12.4	6 15.6	5 47.3	26 54.6	5 57.7	14 57.0	5 25.5	11 48.7	16 55.3
27 W	18 23 48	5 43 00	22 07 18	28 20 48	17 05.2	24 50.9	6 21.3	6 29.3	26 40.7	5 49.5	15 04.1	5 29.1	11 50.9	16 57.0
28 Th	18 27 45	6 44 10	4♑37 12	10♑56 32	16 58.8	25 21.0	6R 24.6	7 11.4	26 26.9	5 41.4	15 11.1	5 32.7	11 53.2	16 58.8
29 F	18 31 41	7 45 20	17 18 49	23 44 00	16 54.3	25 41.8	6 25.5	7 53.5	26 13.3	5 33.3	15 18.2	5 36.3	11 55.5	17 00.5
30 Sa	18 35 38	8 46 31	0♒12 07	6♒43 07	16D 51.9	25R 52.4	6 23.9	8 35.6	25 59.7	5 25.1	15 25.3	5 39.9	11 57.7	17 02.3
31 Su	18 39 35	9 47 41	13 16 59	19 53 46	16 51.5	25 52.1	6 19.9	9 17.8	25 46.4	5 17.0	15 32.4	5 43.5	12 00.0	17 03.9

Astro Data	Dy Hr Mn	Planet Ingress	Dy Hr Mn
⚴ R	2 16:36	♂ ♏	4 5:29
☽ 0N	9 10:57	♀ ♑	5 10:13
♄☌♆	13 11:39	☿ ♐	18 3:10
♃☍♄	14 6:27	☉ ♐	22 8:05
♃☍♆	14 20:54		
☽ 0S	22 7:36	☿ ♑	7 14:30
		♀ ♒	10 4:54
☽ 0N	6 17:46	⚴ ♊R	13 8:15
☽ 0S	19 14:05	♂ ♐	18 4:57
♃☍♅	29 5:46	☉ ♑	21 21:22
♀ R	29 8:50		
☿ R	30 23:31		

Last Aspect Dy Hr Mn		☽ Ingress Dy Hr Mn
3 1:14	♂ ✶	♑ 3 2:46
4 7:45	♇ ✶	♒ 5 12:09
6 15:52	♇ □	♓ 7 18:25
8 22:45	☉ △	♈ 9 21:08
10 14:21	♃ □	♉ 11 21:09
13 8:24	☿ ☍	♊ 13 20:19
13 8:24	☿ ☍	♋ 15 20:51
18 0:26	☿ △	♌ 18 0:45
20 4:44	☉ □	♍ 20 8:54
21 15:43	♀ △	♎ 22 20:25
24 9:03	♀ □	♏ 25 9:13
27 2:20	♀ ✶	♐ 27 21:30
29 7:48	☿ ☌	♑ 30 8:26

Last Aspect Dy Hr Mn		☽ Ingress Dy Hr Mn
2 7:28	♀ ☌	♒ 2 17:42
4 16:53	☿ ✶	♓ 5 0:48
7 4:04	☿ □	♈ 7 5:11
9 6:01	♀ □	♉ 9 6:59
10 23:13	♂ ☍	♊ 11 7:15
12 16:30	☉ ☍	♋ 13 7:49
15 7:10	♂ △	♌ 15 10:41
17 16:39	♂ □	♍ 17 17:19
19 23:55	☉ □	♎ 20 3:45
21 19:35	☿ □	♏ 22 16:18
24 13:57	☿ ✶	♐ 25 4:37
25 16:48	♀ ✶	♑ 27 15:10
29 15:43	☿ ☌	♒ 29 23:38

☽ Phases & Eclipses Dy Hr Mn	
6 14:11	☽ 14♒09
13 5:51	○ 20♉50
20 4:44	☾ 27♌50
28 9:41	● 6♐08
6 1:26	☽ 13♓54
12 16:30	○ 20♊38
19 23:55	☾ 28♍04
28 3:20	● 6♑22

Astro Data

1 November 1989
Julian Day # 32812
SVP 5♓23'57"
GC 26♐41.8 ⚳ 29♓18.6R
Eris 16♈34.8R ⚵ 24♎25.4
⚷ 16♋34.6R ⚶ 19♑43.5
☽ Mean ☊ 21♒39.8

1 December 1989
Julian Day # 32842
SVP 5♓23'52"
GC 26♐41.9 ⚳ 27♓15.3
Eris 16♈20.9R ⚵ 4♏38.3
⚷ 15♋42.1R ⚶ 2♒49.0
☽ Mean ☊ 20♒04.5

LONGITUDE — January 1990

Day	Sid.Time	☉	0 hr ☽	Noon ☽	True ☊	☿	♀	♂	⚳	♃	♄	♅	♆	♇
1 M	18 43 31	10♑48 51	26♒33 26	3♓16 04	16♒52.4	25♑40.4	6♒13.3	10♐00.0	25♊33.2	5♋08.9	15♑39.4	5♑47.1	12♑02.3	17♏05.6
2 Tu	18 47 28	11 50 01	10♓01 40	16 50 18	16 54.0	25R 16.7	6R 04.2	10 42.2	25R 20.3	5R 00.9	15 46.5	5 50.7	12 04.6	17 07.2
3 W	18 51 24	12 51 11	23 42 00	0♈36 49	16R 55.4	24 41.3	5 52.6	11 24.5	25 07.6	4 52.9	15 53.7	5 54.3	12 06.8	17 08.8
4 Th	18 55 21	13 52 20	7♈34 44	14 35 41	16 55.9	23 54.5	5 38.5	12 06.8	24 55.1	4 44.9	16 00.8	5 57.9	12 09.1	17 10.4
5 F	18 59 17	14 53 30	21 39 36	28 46 17	16 55.1	22 57.2	5 21.9	12 49.2	24 42.8	4 37.0	16 07.9	6 01.5	12 11.4	17 11.9
6 Sa	19 03 14	15 54 38	5♉55 28	13♉06 50	16 52.8	21 50.9	5 02.9	13 31.5	24 30.8	4 29.1	16 15.0	6 05.1	12 13.6	17 13.4
7 Su	19 07 10	16 55 47	20 19 54	27 34 09	16 49.3	20 37.7	4 41.6	14 14.0	24 19.1	4 21.3	16 22.1	6 08.6	12 15.9	17 14.9
8 M	19 11 07	17 56 55	4♊48 57	12♊03 37	16 45.0	19 19.6	4 18.0	14 56.4	24 07.7	4 13.6	16 29.2	6 12.2	12 18.2	17 16.4
9 Tu	19 15 04	18 58 03	19 17 26	26 29 37	16 40.6	17 59.4	3 52.2	15 38.9	23 56.5	4 06.0	16 36.3	6 15.7	12 20.5	17 17.8
10 W	19 19 00	19 59 10	3♋39 26	10♋46 10	16 36.8	16 39.6	3 24.4	16 21.4	23 45.7	3 58.4	16 43.4	6 19.3	12 22.7	17 19.2
11 Th	19 22 57	21 00 17	17 49 10	24 47 51	16 34.1	15 22.6	2 54.7	17 04.0	23 35.2	3 50.9	16 50.5	6 22.8	12 25.0	17 20.6
12 F	19 26 53	22 01 24	1♌41 45	8♌30 30	16D 32.6	14 10.7	2 23.3	17 46.6	23 25.0	3 43.5	16 57.6	6 26.3	12 27.2	17 21.9
13 Sa	19 30 50	23 02 30	15 13 53	21 51 47	16 32.5	13 05.6	1 50.5	18 29.2	23 15.2	3 36.2	17 04.7	6 29.8	12 29.5	17 23.2
14 Su	19 34 46	24 03 36	28 24 11	4♍51 12	16 33.4	12 08.6	1 16.3	19 11.8	23 05.7	3 29.1	17 11.8	6 33.3	12 31.7	17 24.5
15 M	19 38 43	25 04 42	11♍13 04	17 30 04	16 34.9	11 20.7	0 41.1	19 54.5	22 56.5	3 22.0	17 18.9	6 36.8	12 33.9	17 25.7
16 Tu	19 42 40	26 05 47	23 42 36	29 51 06	16 36.6	10 42.2	0 05.1	20 37.3	22 47.8	3 15.0	17 25.9	6 40.3	12 36.2	17 26.9
17 W	19 46 36	27 06 52	5♎56 05	11♎58 06	16 38.0	10 13.4	29♑28.5	21 20.1	22 39.4	3 08.1	17 33.0	6 43.7	12 38.4	17 28.1
18 Th	19 50 33	28 07 58	17 57 43	23 55 31	16R 38.7	9 54.1	28 51.6	22 02.9	22 31.4	3 01.4	17 40.0	6 47.1	12 40.6	17 29.2
19 F	19 54 29	29 09 02	29 52 07	5♏48 08	16 38.6	9D 43.8	28 14.7	22 45.7	22 23.7	2 54.8	17 47.1	6 50.5	12 42.8	17 30.3
20 Sa	19 58 26	0♒10 07	11♏44 10	17 40 47	16 37.7	9 42.2	27 37.9	23 28.6	22 16.5	2 48.3	17 54.1	6 53.9	12 45.0	17 31.4
21 Su	20 02 22	1 11 11	23 38 35	29 38 05	16 36.1	9 48.7	27 01.7	24 11.5	22 09.6	2 41.9	18 01.1	6 57.3	12 47.2	17 32.4
22 M	20 06 19	2 12 15	5♐39 47	11♐44 10	16 34.1	10 02.7	26 26.1	24 54.5	22 03.2	2 35.7	18 08.1	7 00.7	12 49.4	17 33.4
23 Tu	20 10 15	3 13 18	17 51 37	24 02 29	16 31.9	10 23.5	25 51.5	25 37.5	21 57.2	2 29.6	18 15.0	7 04.0	12 51.5	17 34.4
24 W	20 14 12	4 14 20	0♑17 05	6♑35 38	16 30.0	10 50.6	25 18.0	26 20.5	21 51.6	2 23.7	18 22.0	7 07.4	12 53.7	17 35.3
25 Th	20 18 09	5 15 22	12 58 18	19 25 09	16 28.5	11 23.5	24 45.9	27 03.5	21 46.4	2 18.0	18 28.9	7 10.7	12 55.9	17 36.2
26 F	20 22 05	6 16 24	25 56 14	2♒31 28	16 27.6	12 01.5	24 15.4	27 46.6	21 41.6	2 12.3	18 35.8	7 13.9	12 58.0	17 37.1
27 Sa	20 26 02	7 17 24	9♒10 47	15 53 58	16D 27.3	12 44.2	23 46.6	28 29.8	21 37.3	2 06.9	18 42.7	7 17.2	13 00.1	17 38.0
28 Su	20 29 58	8 18 23	22 40 48	29 31 02	16 27.5	13 31.3	23 19.8	29 12.9	21 33.4	2 01.6	18 49.6	7 20.4	13 02.2	17 38.7
29 M	20 33 55	9 19 22	6♓24 21	13♓20 26	16 28.0	14 22.1	22 54.9	29 56.1	21 29.9	1 56.5	18 56.4	7 23.6	13 04.3	17 39.5
30 Tu	20 37 51	10 20 19	20 18 56	27 19 30	16 28.7	15 16.5	22 32.2	0♑39.3	21 26.8	1 51.5	19 03.2	7 26.8	13 06.4	17 40.2
31 W	20 41 48	11 21 15	4♈21 47	11♈25 27	16 29.2	16 14.1	22 11.8	1 22.5	21 24.2	1 46.7	19 10.0	7 30.0	13 08.5	17 40.9

LONGITUDE — February 1990

Day	Sid.Time	☉	0 hr ☽	Noon ☽	True ☊	☿	♀	♂	⚳	♃	♄	♅	♆	♇
1 Th	20 45 44	12♒22 09	18♈30 10	25♈35 37	16♒29.6	17♑14.6	21♑53.7	2♑05.8	21♊22.0	1♋42.1	19♑16.7	7♑33.1	13♑10.5	17♏41.6
2 F	20 49 41	13 23 03	2♉41 29	9♉47 30	16R 29.7	18 17.7	21R 38.0	2 49.1	21R 20.3	1R 37.7	19 23.4	7 36.2	13 12.5	17 42.2
3 Sa	20 53 38	14 23 55	16 53 21	23 58 47	16 29.7	19 23.3	21 24.7	3 32.5	21 18.9	1 33.4	19 30.1	7 39.3	13 14.6	17 42.8
4 Su	20 57 34	15 24 45	1♊03 29	8♊07 13	16 29.6	20 31.1	21 13.8	4 15.8	21 18.0	1 29.4	19 36.8	7 42.3	13 16.6	17 43.3
5 M	21 01 31	16 25 35	15 09 41	22 10 35	16D 29.6	21 40.9	21 05.5	4 59.2	21D 17.5	1 25.5	19 43.4	7 45.4	13 18.6	17 43.9
6 Tu	21 05 27	17 26 22	29 09 39	6♋06 35	16 29.6	22 52.7	20 59.6	5 42.7	21 17.5	1 21.8	19 50.0	7 48.4	13 20.5	17 44.3
7 W	21 09 24	18 27 09	13♋01 05	19 52 52	16 29.8	24 06.2	20D 56.2	6 26.1	21 17.9	1 18.3	19 56.6	7 51.3	13 22.5	17 44.8
8 Th	21 13 20	19 27 54	26 41 40	3♌27 13	16R 29.9	25 21.4	20 55.3	7 09.6	21 18.6	1 15.0	20 03.1	7 54.3	13 24.4	17 45.2
9 F	21 17 17	20 28 37	10♌09 18	16 47 43	16 30.0	26 38.1	20 56.8	7 53.2	21 19.8	1 11.9	20 09.6	7 57.2	13 26.3	17 45.5
10 Sa	21 21 13	21 29 19	23 22 19	29 53 00	16 29.9	27 56.2	21 00.6	8 36.7	21 21.5	1 08.9	20 16.0	8 00.0	13 28.2	17 45.9
11 Su	21 25 10	22 30 00	6♍19 42	12♍42 26	16 29.4	29 15.7	21 06.9	9 20.3	21 23.5	1 06.2	20 22.4	8 02.9	13 30.1	17 46.2
12 M	21 29 07	23 30 40	19 01 16	25 16 20	16 28.7	0♒36.6	21 15.4	10 03.9	21 25.9	1 03.6	20 28.8	8 05.7	13 32.0	17 46.4
13 Tu	21 33 03	24 31 18	1♎27 49	7♎35 58	16 27.6	1 58.7	21 26.1	10 47.6	21 28.8	1 01.3	20 35.1	8 08.4	13 33.8	17 46.7
14 W	21 37 00	25 31 55	13 41 06	19 43 35	16 26.3	3 21.9	21 39.1	11 31.3	21 32.0	0 59.1	20 41.4	8 11.2	13 35.6	17 46.8
15 Th	21 40 56	26 32 31	25 43 49	1♏42 16	16 25.2	4 46.4	21 54.1	12 15.0	21 35.6	0 57.2	20 47.6	8 13.9	13 37.4	17 47.0
16 F	21 44 53	27 33 06	7♏39 25	13 35 48	16 24.2	6 11.9	22 11.2	12 58.8	21 39.6	0 55.4	20 53.8	8 16.5	13 39.2	17 47.1
17 Sa	21 48 49	28 33 39	19 31 59	25 28 33	16D 23.8	7 38.5	22 30.3	13 42.6	21 44.1	0 53.8	21 00.0	8 19.2	13 40.9	17 47.2
18 Su	21 52 46	29 34 11	1♐26 03	7♐25 08	16 23.9	9 06.2	22 51.3	14 26.4	21 48.9	0 52.5	21 06.1	8 21.8	13 42.7	17R 47.2
19 M	21 56 42	0♓34 43	13 26 21	19 30 18	16 24.6	10 34.9	23 14.2	15 10.2	21 54.1	0 51.3	21 12.1	8 24.3	13 44.4	17 47.2
20 Tu	22 00 39	1 35 12	25 37 32	1♑48 36	16 25.8	12 04.6	23 38.9	15 54.1	21 59.6	0 50.3	21 18.1	8 26.8	13 46.1	17 47.2
21 W	22 04 36	2 35 41	8♑03 58	14 24 05	16 27.2	13 35.4	24 05.2	16 38.0	22 05.6	0 49.6	21 24.1	8 29.3	13 47.7	17 47.2
22 Th	22 08 32	3 36 08	20 49 17	27 19 53	16 28.5	15 07.1	24 33.3	17 22.0	22 11.9	0 49.0	21 30.0	8 31.8	13 49.4	17 47.1
23 F	22 12 29	4 36 33	3♒56 02	10♒37 50	16R 29.3	16 39.9	25 02.9	18 05.9	22 18.6	0 48.7	21 35.8	8 34.2	13 51.0	17 46.9
24 Sa	22 16 25	5 36 57	17 25 15	24 18 07	16 29.2	18 13.6	25 34.1	18 49.9	22 25.6	0D 48.5	21 41.6	8 36.5	13 52.6	17 46.8
25 Su	22 20 22	6 37 20	1♓16 10	8♓18 58	16 28.1	19 48.3	26 06.7	19 34.0	22 33.0	0 48.5	21 47.4	8 38.8	13 54.1	17 46.6
26 M	22 24 18	7 37 40	15 26 00	22 36 39	16 26.0	21 24.1	26 40.7	20 18.0	22 40.8	0 48.8	21 53.1	8 41.1	13 55.7	17 46.3
27 Tu	22 28 15	8 37 59	29 50 12	7♈05 52	16 23.0	23 00.8	27 16.1	21 02.1	22 48.9	0 49.2	21 58.7	8 43.4	13 57.2	17 46.0
28 W	22 32 11	9 38 16	14♈22 52	21 40 23	16 19.7	24 38.5	27 52.7	21 46.2	22 57.4	0 49.9	22 04.2	8 45.6	13 58.7	17 45.7

Astro Data	Planet Ingress	Last Aspect	☽ Ingress	Last Aspect	☽ Ingress	☽ Phases & Eclipses	Astro Data
Dy Hr Mn	Dy Hr Mn	Dy Hr Mn	Dy Hr Mn	Dy Hr Mn	Dy Hr Mn	Dy Hr Mn	1 January 1990
☽ 0N 2 22:37	♀ ♑R 16 15:23	31 6:52 ♇ □	♓ 1 6:10	1 5:52 ♀ □	♉ 1 19:27	4 10:40 ☽ 13♈49	Julian Day # 32873
☽ 0S 15 22:14	☉ ♒ 20 8:02	3 2:11 ☿ ⚹	♈ 3 10:56	3 7:43 ♀ △	♊ 3 22:12	11 4:57 ○ 20♋42	SVP 5♓23'46"
♄⚹♇ 16 15:56	♂ ♑ 29 14:10	5 2:50 ☿ □	♉ 5 14:04	5 1:24 ☉ △	♋ 6 1:27	18 21:17 ☾ 28♎32	GC 26♐42.0 ⚵ 1♈33.6
☿ D 20 4:31		7 1:24 ☿ △	♊ 7 16:02	7 20:10 ☿ ☍	♌ 8 5:51	26 19:20 ● 6♒35	Eris 16♈14.8R ⚶ 13♏59.5
♃□♇ 22 19:42	☿ ♒ 12 1:11	8 17:01 ♂ ☍	♋ 9 17:52	9 19:16 ☉ ☍	♍ 10 12:13	26 19:30:24 ● A 02'03"	⚷ 13♋48.8R ⚴ 17♒26.6
☽ 0N 30 4:11	☉ ♓ 18 22:14	11 4:57 ☉ ☍	♌ 11 21:02	12 4:11 ♀ △	♎ 12 21:09		☽ Mean ☊ 18♒26.0
		13 5:31 ♂ △	♍ 14 2:57	15 0:40 ☉ △	♏ 15 8:34	2 18:32 ☽ 13♉40	
⚳ D 6 2:55		16 3:59 ☉ △	♎ 16 12:17	17 18:48 ☉ □	♐ 17 21:07	9 19:16 ○ 20♌47	1 February 1990
♀ D 8 9:16		18 21:28 ♀ □	♏ 19 0:16	18 15:50 ☿ ⚹	♑ 20 8:30	9 19:11 ● T 1.075	Julian Day # 32904
☽ 0S 12 7:10		21 7:02 ♀ ⚹	♐ 21 12:44	22 6:42 ♀ ☌	♒ 22 16:52	17 18:48 ☾ 28♏51	SVP 5♓23'41"
♇ R 19 6:31		23 15:14 ♂ ☌	♑ 23 23:27	24 0:38 ♇ □	♓ 24 21:49	25 8:54 ● 6♓30	GC 26♐42.0 ⚵ 10♈35.0
♃ D 24 19:14		25 21:29 ♀ ☌	♒ 26 7:25	26 19:03 ♀ ⚹	♈ 27 0:16		Eris 16♈19.3 ⚶ 21♏11.4
☽ 0N 26 12:18		28 11:27 ♂ ⚹	♓ 28 12:51				⚷ 11♋48.6R ⚴ 2♓34.8
		30 4:01 ♀ ⚹	♈ 30 16:34				☽ Mean ☊ 16♒47.6

March 1990 — LONGITUDE

Day	Sid.Time	☉	0 hr ☽	Noon ☽	True ☊	☿	♀	♂	⚳	♃	♄	♅	♆	♇
1 Th	22 36 08	10♓38 31	28♈57 39	6♉13 56	16♒16.6	26♒17.3	28♑30.6	22♑30.3	23♊06.2	0♋50.7	22♑09.8	8♑47.7	14♑00.1	17♏45.4
2 F	22 40 05	11 38 43	13♉28 35	20 41 02	16R 14.2	27 57.0	29 09.7	23 14.4	23 15.3	0 51.7	22 15.2	8 49.8	14 01.6	17R 45.0
3 Sa	22 44 01	12 38 54	27 50 48	4♊57 33	16D 12.9	29 37.8	29 50.0	23 58.6	23 24.8	0 53.0	22 20.6	8 51.9	14 03.0	17 44.6
4 Su	22 47 58	13 39 03	12♊01 01	19 01 00	16 12.8	1♓19.7	0♒31.4	24 42.8	23 34.6	0 54.4	22 25.9	8 53.9	14 04.3	17 44.1
5 M	22 51 54	14 39 10	25 57 25	2♋50 14	16 13.7	3 02.6	1 13.8	25 27.0	23 44.7	0 56.0	22 31.2	8 55.9	14 05.7	17 43.6
6 Tu	22 55 51	15 39 14	9♋39 29	16 25 14	16 15.3	4 46.7	1 57.2	26 11.2	23 55.2	0 57.9	22 36.4	8 57.8	14 07.0	17 43.1
7 W	22 59 47	16 39 17	23 07 32	29 46 30	16 16.8	6 31.8	2 41.6	26 55.5	24 05.9	0 59.9	22 41.5	8 59.7	14 08.3	17 42.6
8 Th	23 03 44	17 39 17	6♌22 14	12♌54 49	16R 17.7	8 18.0	3 27.0	27 39.8	24 17.0	1 02.1	22 46.6	9 01.6	14 09.6	17 42.0
9 F	23 07 40	18 39 15	19 24 20	25 50 53	16 17.3	10 05.3	4 13.3	28 24.1	24 28.3	1 04.5	22 51.6	9 03.4	14 10.8	17 41.4
10 Sa	23 11 37	19 39 11	2♍14 30	8♍35 17	16 15.3	11 53.7	5 00.4	29 08.4	24 39.9	1 07.1	22 56.5	9 05.1	14 12.0	17 40.7
11 Su	23 15 34	20 39 05	14 53 15	21 08 29	16 11.6	13 43.3	5 48.4	29 52.8	24 51.9	1 09.8	23 01.4	9 06.8	14 13.2	17 40.1
12 M	23 19 30	21 38 58	27 21 02	3♎31 01	16 06.2	15 34.1	6 37.2	0♒37.2	25 04.1	1 12.8	23 06.2	9 08.5	14 14.3	17 39.4
13 Tu	23 23 27	22 38 48	9♎38 30	15 43 39	15 59.7	17 25.9	7 26.8	1 21.6	25 16.6	1 15.9	23 10.9	9 10.1	14 15.4	17 38.6
14 W	23 27 23	23 38 36	21 46 38	27 47 38	15 52.6	19 18.9	8 17.2	2 06.0	25 29.4	1 19.3	23 15.6	9 11.7	14 16.5	17 37.8
15 Th	23 31 20	24 38 23	3♏46 56	9♏44 49	15 45.7	21 13.1	9 08.2	2 50.5	25 42.4	1 22.8	23 20.1	9 13.2	14 17.6	17 37.0
16 F	23 35 16	25 38 08	15 41 38	21 37 45	15 39.7	23 08.3	10 00.0	3 35.0	25 55.7	1 26.4	23 24.6	9 14.6	14 18.6	17 36.2
17 Sa	23 39 13	26 37 51	27 33 38	3♐29 45	15 35.1	25 04.6	10 52.4	4 19.5	26 09.3	1 30.3	23 29.1	9 16.1	14 19.6	17 35.4
18 Su	23 43 09	27 37 33	9♐26 36	15 24 46	15 32.4	27 01.9	11 45.5	5 04.0	26 23.1	1 34.3	23 33.4	9 17.4	14 20.6	17 34.5
19 M	23 47 06	28 37 13	21 24 48	27 27 20	15D 31.4	29 00.2	12 39.1	5 48.5	26 37.2	1 38.6	23 37.7	9 18.8	14 21.5	17 33.5
20 Tu	23 51 03	29 36 51	3♑32 58	9♑42 19	15 31.9	0♈59.3	13 33.4	6 33.1	26 51.6	1 43.0	23 41.9	9 20.0	14 22.4	17 32.6
21 W	23 54 59	0♈36 27	15 56 00	22 14 36	15 33.2	2 59.2	14 28.3	7 17.7	27 06.2	1 47.5	23 46.1	9 21.3	14 23.3	17 31.6
22 Th	23 58 56	1 36 02	28 38 40	5♒08 42	15R 34.5	4 59.8	15 23.6	8 02.3	27 21.0	1 52.3	23 50.1	9 22.4	14 24.1	17 30.6
23 F	0 02 52	2 35 34	11♒45 05	18 28 07	15 34.9	7 00.9	16 19.5	8 46.9	27 36.1	1 57.2	23 54.1	9 23.6	14 24.9	17 29.6
24 Sa	0 06 49	3 35 05	25 17 59	2♓14 42	15 33.6	9 02.3	17 16.0	9 31.6	27 51.5	2 02.2	23 58.0	9 24.6	14 25.7	17 28.5
25 Su	0 10 45	4 34 34	9♓18 08	16 27 56	15 30.1	11 03.8	18 12.8	10 16.2	28 07.0	2 07.5	24 01.8	9 25.7	14 26.5	17 27.4
26 M	0 14 42	5 34 01	23 43 34	1♈04 20	15 24.6	13 05.2	19 10.2	11 00.9	28 22.8	2 12.9	24 05.5	9 26.6	14 27.2	17 26.3
27 Tu	0 18 38	6 33 26	8♈29 19	15 57 30	15 17.2	15 06.3	20 08.0	11 45.6	28 38.8	2 18.5	24 09.2	9 27.6	14 27.8	17 25.2
28 W	0 22 35	7 32 49	23 27 43	0♉58 45	15 09.1	17 06.6	21 06.2	12 30.3	28 55.0	2 24.2	24 12.7	9 28.4	14 28.5	17 24.0
29 Th	0 26 31	8 32 10	8♉29 24	15 58 30	15 01.1	19 05.9	22 04.9	13 15.0	29 11.5	2 30.1	24 16.2	9 29.2	14 29.1	17 22.8
30 F	0 30 28	9 31 29	23 24 57	0♊47 51	14 54.3	21 03.8	23 03.9	13 59.7	29 28.2	2 36.1	24 19.6	9 30.0	14 29.7	17 21.6
31 Sa	0 34 25	10 30 45	8♊06 25	15 20 03	14 49.5	22 59.9	24 03.3	14 44.5	29 45.1	2 42.4	24 22.9	9 30.7	14 30.2	17 20.4

April 1990 — LONGITUDE

Day	Sid.Time	☉	0 hr ☽	Noon ☽	True ☊	☿	♀	♂	⚳	♃	♄	♅	♆	♇
1 Su	0 38 21	11♈30 00	22♊28 22	29♊31 07	14♒46.9	24♈53.9	25♒03.1	15♒29.2	0♋02.1	2♋48.7	24♑26.1	9♑31.4	14♑30.7	17♏19.1
2 M	0 42 18	12 29 11	6♋28 15	13♋19 48	14D 46.3	26 45.4	26 03.2	16 14.0	0 19.4	2 55.2	24 29.3	9 32.0	14 31.2	17R 17.8
3 Tu	0 46 14	13 28 21	20 05 57	26 46 58	14 46.8	28 33.9	27 03.7	16 58.7	0 36.9	3 01.9	24 32.3	9 32.6	14 31.7	17 16.5
4 W	0 50 11	14 27 28	3♌23 08	9♌54 49	14R 47.5	0♉19.1	28 04.5	17 43.5	0 54.6	3 08.7	24 35.3	9 33.1	14 32.1	17 15.2
5 Th	0 54 07	15 26 33	16 22 23	22 46 11	14 47.3	2 00.6	29 05.7	18 28.3	1 12.5	3 15.7	24 38.1	9 33.5	14 32.5	17 13.9
6 F	0 58 04	16 25 35	29 06 35	5♍23 55	14 45.2	3 38.0	0♓07.1	19 13.1	1 30.5	3 22.8	24 40.9	9 33.9	14 32.8	17 12.5
7 Sa	1 02 00	17 24 35	11♍38 28	17 50 30	14 40.6	5 11.1	1 08.9	19 57.9	1 48.8	3 30.0	24 43.6	9 34.3	14 33.1	17 11.1
8 Su	1 05 57	18 23 33	24 00 16	0♎07 58	14 33.3	6 39.5	2 10.9	20 42.7	2 07.2	3 37.4	24 46.2	9 34.6	14 33.4	17 09.7
9 M	1 09 54	19 22 29	6♎13 48	12 17 53	14 23.5	8 03.0	3 13.3	21 27.5	2 25.8	3 44.9	24 48.7	9 34.9	14 33.7	17 08.3
10 Tu	1 13 50	20 21 23	18 20 23	24 21 26	14 11.8	9 21.4	4 15.9	22 12.3	2 44.5	3 52.5	24 51.1	9 35.1	14 33.9	17 06.9
11 W	1 17 47	21 20 15	0♏21 10	6♏19 45	13 59.1	10 34.4	5 18.8	22 57.2	3 03.5	4 00.3	24 53.4	9 35.2	14 34.0	17 05.4
12 Th	1 21 43	22 19 05	12 17 19	18 14 05	13 46.6	11 41.9	6 22.0	23 42.0	3 22.6	4 08.3	24 55.6	9 35.3	14 34.2	17 03.9
13 F	1 25 40	23 17 53	24 10 15	0♐06 06	13 35.2	12 43.7	7 25.4	24 26.9	3 41.9	4 16.3	24 57.8	9R 35.3	14 34.3	17 02.4
14 Sa	1 29 36	24 16 39	6♐01 56	11 58 05	13 25.8	13 39.7	8 29.0	25 11.7	4 01.3	4 24.5	24 59.8	9 35.3	14 34.4	17 00.9
15 Su	1 33 33	25 15 24	17 54 58	23 53 00	13 19.0	14 29.7	9 32.9	25 56.6	4 20.9	4 32.8	25 01.8	9 35.3	14 34.4	16 59.4
16 M	1 37 29	26 14 07	29 52 41	5♑54 33	13 14.9	15 13.7	10 37.1	26 41.5	4 40.7	4 41.2	25 03.6	9 35.2	14R 34.5	16 57.9
17 Tu	1 41 26	27 12 48	11♑59 09	18 07 06	13D 13.1	15 51.7	11 41.4	27 26.4	5 00.6	4 49.8	25 05.4	9 35.0	14 34.4	16 56.3
18 W	1 45 23	28 11 27	24 19 00	0♒35 28	13R 12.8	16 23.5	12 46.0	28 11.3	5 20.6	4 58.5	25 07.0	9 34.8	14 34.4	16 54.8
19 Th	1 49 19	29 10 05	6♒57 08	13 24 35	13 12.9	16 49.2	13 50.7	28 56.1	5 40.8	5 07.3	25 08.6	9 34.6	14 34.3	16 53.2
20 F	1 53 16	0♉08 41	19 58 21	26 38 55	13 12.4	17 08.8	14 55.7	29 41.0	6 01.2	5 16.2	25 10.1	9 34.2	14 34.2	16 51.6
21 Sa	1 57 12	1 07 15	3♓26 37	10♓21 42	13 10.0	17 22.3	16 00.9	0♓25.9	6 21.7	5 25.2	25 11.4	9 33.9	14 34.1	16 50.0
22 Su	2 01 09	2 05 48	17 24 14	24 34 05	13 05.2	17R 29.8	17 06.2	1 10.8	6 42.3	5 34.4	25 12.7	9 33.5	14 33.9	16 48.4
23 M	2 05 05	3 04 19	1♈50 53	9♈14 04	12 57.8	17 31.5	18 11.8	1 55.7	7 03.1	5 43.6	25 13.9	9 33.0	14 33.7	16 46.8
24 Tu	2 09 02	4 02 48	16 42 50	24 16 07	12 48.1	17 27.4	19 17.5	2 40.5	7 24.1	5 53.0	25 15.0	9 32.5	14 33.4	16 45.2
25 W	2 12 58	5 01 16	1♉52 43	9♉31 15	12 37.1	17 18.0	20 23.3	3 25.4	7 45.1	6 02.5	25 15.9	9 31.9	14 33.1	16 43.5
26 Th	2 16 55	5 59 42	17 10 17	24 48 21	12 26.3	17 03.4	21 29.4	4 10.3	8 06.3	6 12.1	25 16.8	9 31.3	14 32.8	16 41.9
27 F	2 20 52	6 58 06	2♊24 05	9♊56 11	12 16.8	16 44.1	22 35.5	4 55.1	8 27.7	6 21.8	25 17.6	9 30.7	14 32.5	16 40.2
28 Sa	2 24 48	7 56 28	17 23 34	24 45 22	12 09.5	16 20.3	23 41.9	5 39.9	8 49.1	6 31.6	25 18.3	9 30.0	14 32.1	16 38.6
29 Su	2 28 45	8 54 47	2♋00 55	9♋09 49	12 05.0	15 52.7	24 48.3	6 24.8	9 10.7	6 41.5	25 18.9	9 29.2	14 31.7	16 36.9
30 M	2 32 41	9 53 05	16 11 49	23 06 56	12 02.9	15 21.8	25 55.0	7 09.6	9 32.4	6 51.5	25 19.4	9 28.4	14 31.3	16 35.2

Astro Data

	Dy Hr Mn
☽0S	11 15:15
⊙0N	20 21:20
☿0N	21 7:49
☽0N	25 22:29
♃□♇	28 11:22
☽0S	7 21:34
♅R	13 22:21
♆R	16 12:55
☽0N	22 8:42
☿R	23 6:54

Planet Ingress

	Dy Hr Mn
☿ ♓	3 17:14
♀ ♒	3 17:52
♂ ♒	11 15:54
☿ ♈	20 0:04
⊙ ♈	20 21:19
⚳ ♋	1 9:01
☿ ♉	4 7:35
♀ ♓	6 9:13
⊙ ♉	20 8:27
♂ ♓	20 22:09

Last Aspect / ☽ Ingress

Last Aspect Dy Hr Mn		☽ Ingress Dy Hr Mn
28 22:41	♀ □	♉ 1 1:43
3 2:55	♀ △	♊ 3 3:37
4 2:05	⊙ □	♋ 5 7:02
7 6:33	♂ ☍	♌ 7 12:24
8 20:50	♇ □	♍ 9 19:47
11 15:39	♄ △	♎ 12 5:09
14 2:54	♄ □	♏ 14 16:25
16 20:51	⊙ △	♐ 17 4:56
19 15:39	♄ ☌	♑ 19 17:01
21 14:53	♄ ☌	♒ 22 2:31
23 10:16	♇ □	♓ 24 8:09
26 0:33	♄ ⚹	♈ 26 10:15
28 1:09	♄ □	♉ 28 10:26
30 1:26	♄ △	♊ 30 10:42

Last Aspect / ☽ Ingress

Last Aspect Dy Hr Mn		☽ Ingress Dy Hr Mn
1 3:48	♀ △	♋ 1 12:50
3 15:44	☿ □	♌ 3 17:50
6 1:02	♀ ☍	♍ 6 1:42
8 1:27	♄ △	♎ 8 11:44
10 12:59	♄ □	♏ 10 23:18
13 1:34	♄ ⚹	♐ 13 11:48
15 16:24	♂ ⚹	♑ 16 0:15
18 7:03	⊙ □	♒ 18 10:53
20 17:42	♂ ☌	♓ 20 17:57
22 13:04	♄ ⚹	♈ 22 20:58
24 13:33	♄ □	♉ 24 21:03
26 12:45	♄ △	♊ 26 20:12
28 10:08	♀ □	♋ 28 20:39

☽ Phases & Eclipses

Dy Hr Mn	
4 2:05	☽ 13♊14
11 10:59	○ 20♍37
19 14:30	☾ 28♐43
26 19:48	● 5♈53
2 10:24	☽ 12♋25
10 3:18	○ 20♎00
18 7:03	☾ 27♑59
25 4:27	● 4♉43

Astro Data

1 March 1990
Julian Day # 32932
SVP 5♓23'37"
GC 26♐42.1 ⚴ 21♈27.2
Eris 16♈31.5 ⚵ 24♏44.1
⚷ 10♋42.6R ⚶ 16♓19.8
☽ Mean ☊ 15♒18.6

1 April 1990
Julian Day # 32963
SVP 5♓23'33"
GC 26♐42.2 ⚴ 5♉36.1
Eris 16♈50.7 ⚵ 24♏02.5R
⚷ 10♋47.6 ⚶ 1♈19.6
☽ Mean ☊ 13♒40.1

LONGITUDE — May 1990

Day	Sid.Time	☉	0 hr ☽	Noon ☽	True ☊	☿	♀	♂	⚳	♃	♄	♅	♆	♇
1 Tu	2 36 38	10♉51 21	29♋55 18	6♌37 11	12♒02.3	14♉48.1	27♓01.7	7♓54.4	9♋54.3	7♋01.6	25♑19.8	9♑27.6	14♑30.8	16♏33.6
2 W	2 40 34	11 49 34	13♌12 59	19 43 09	12R 02.3	14R 12.3	28 08.6	8 39.2	10 16.2	7 11.8	25 20.0	9R 26.7	14R 30.3	16R 31.9
3 Th	2 44 31	12 47 46	26 08 09	2♍28 30	12 01.4	13 35.1	29 15.6	9 23.9	10 38.3	7 22.1	25 20.2	9 25.7	14 29.8	16 30.2
4 F	2 48 27	13 45 55	8♍44 44	14 57 20	11 58.8	12 57.1	0♈22.8	10 08.7	11 00.4	7 32.5	25R 20.3	9 24.8	14 29.2	16 28.5
5 Sa	2 52 24	14 44 03	21 06 48	27 13 34	11 53.5	12 19.0	1 30.0	10 53.4	11 22.7	7 43.0	25 20.3	9 23.7	14 28.6	16 26.8
6 Su	2 56 21	15 42 08	3♎18 02	9♎20 35	11 45.4	11 41.5	2 37.4	11 38.2	11 45.1	7 53.6	25 20.2	9 22.6	14 28.0	16 25.2
7 M	3 00 17	16 40 12	15 21 32	21 21 11	11 34.5	11 05.3	3 44.9	12 22.9	12 07.6	8 04.2	25 20.0	9 21.5	14 27.4	16 23.5
8 Tu	3 04 14	17 38 14	27 19 46	3♏17 31	11 21.7	10 30.9	4 52.6	13 07.6	12 30.2	8 15.0	25 19.7	9 20.4	14 26.7	16 21.8
9 W	3 08 10	18 36 14	9♏14 38	15 11 16	11 07.8	9 59.0	6 00.3	13 52.3	12 52.9	8 25.8	25 19.3	9 19.1	14 26.0	16 20.1
10 Th	3 12 07	19 34 13	21 07 37	27 03 51	10 54.0	9 29.9	7 08.2	14 37.0	13 15.7	8 36.7	25 18.8	9 17.9	14 25.2	16 18.4
11 F	3 16 03	20 32 11	3♐00 07	8♐56 37	10 41.4	9 04.1	8 16.2	15 21.6	13 38.7	8 47.7	25 18.3	9 16.6	14 24.5	16 16.7
12 Sa	3 20 00	21 30 07	14 53 33	20 51 11	10 30.9	8 42.1	9 24.2	16 06.2	14 01.7	8 58.8	25 17.6	9 15.3	14 23.7	16 15.1
13 Su	3 23 56	22 28 01	26 49 47	2♑49 40	10 23.1	8 24.0	10 32.4	16 50.9	14 24.8	9 10.0	25 16.8	9 13.9	14 22.9	16 13.4
14 M	3 27 53	23 25 54	8♑51 10	14 54 43	10 18.1	8 10.2	11 40.7	17 35.5	14 48.0	9 21.2	25 15.9	9 12.5	14 22.0	16 11.7
15 Tu	3 31 50	24 23 46	21 00 44	27 09 43	10 15.7	8 00.7	12 49.1	18 20.0	15 11.3	9 32.5	25 15.0	9 11.0	14 21.2	16 10.0
16 W	3 35 46	25 21 37	3♒22 10	9♒38 38	10D 15.1	7D 55.8	13 57.6	19 04.6	15 34.7	9 43.9	25 13.9	9 09.5	14 20.3	16 08.4
17 Th	3 39 43	26 19 26	15 59 39	22 25 47	10R 15.2	7 55.4	15 06.2	19 49.1	15 58.2	9 55.4	25 12.7	9 08.0	14 19.4	16 06.7
18 F	3 43 39	27 17 14	28 57 33	5♓35 27	10 15.0	7 59.6	16 14.8	20 33.6	16 21.7	10 06.9	25 11.5	9 06.4	14 18.4	16 05.1
19 Sa	3 47 36	28 15 01	12♓19 53	19 11 12	10 13.4	8 08.4	17 23.6	21 18.1	16 45.4	10 18.5	25 10.1	9 04.8	14 17.4	16 03.4
20 Su	3 51 32	29 12 47	26 09 34	3♈15 03	10 09.6	8 21.7	18 32.5	22 02.5	17 09.1	10 30.2	25 08.7	9 03.2	14 16.4	16 01.8
21 M	3 55 29	0♊10 32	10♈27 29	17 46 31	10 03.4	8 39.5	19 41.4	22 46.9	17 33.0	10 41.9	25 07.2	9 01.5	14 15.4	16 00.2
22 Tu	3 59 25	1 08 16	25 11 32	2♉41 45	9 55.1	9 01.6	20 50.4	23 31.3	17 56.9	10 53.7	25 05.6	8 59.8	14 14.3	15 58.6
23 W	4 03 22	2 05 58	10♉16 07	17 53 25	9 45.6	9 28.1	21 59.5	24 15.6	18 20.9	11 05.6	25 03.8	8 58.0	14 13.3	15 56.9
24 Th	4 07 19	3 03 40	25 32 19	3♊11 21	9 35.9	9 58.7	23 08.7	24 59.9	18 45.0	11 17.5	25 02.0	8 56.2	14 12.2	15 55.4
25 F	4 11 15	4 01 20	10♊49 07	18 24 13	9 27.4	10 33.4	24 17.9	25 44.2	19 09.2	11 29.5	25 00.2	8 54.4	14 11.1	15 53.8
26 Sa	4 15 12	4 58 59	25 55 25	3♋21 36	9 20.8	11 12.0	25 27.2	26 28.4	19 33.4	11 41.6	24 58.2	8 52.5	14 09.9	15 52.2
27 Su	4 19 08	5 56 37	10♋41 56	17 55 43	9 16.8	11 54.5	26 36.6	27 12.6	19 57.8	11 53.7	24 56.1	8 50.7	14 08.7	15 50.6
28 M	4 23 05	6 54 13	25 02 33	2♌02 14	9D 15.0	12 40.7	27 46.1	27 56.7	20 22.2	12 05.9	24 54.0	8 48.7	14 07.6	15 49.1
29 Tu	4 27 01	7 51 48	8♌54 42	15 40 08	9 14.9	13 30.5	28 55.6	28 40.8	20 46.6	12 18.1	24 51.7	8 46.8	14 06.4	15 47.6
30 W	4 30 58	8 49 21	22 18 48	28 51 06	9R 15.6	14 23.9	0♉05.2	29 24.8	21 11.2	12 30.4	24 49.4	8 44.8	14 05.1	15 46.0
31 Th	4 34 54	9 46 53	5♍17 30	11♍38 31	9 15.9	15 20.7	1 14.8	0♈08.8	21 35.8	12 42.8	24 47.0	8 42.8	14 03.9	15 44.5

LONGITUDE — June 1990

Day	Sid.Time	☉	0 hr ☽	Noon ☽	True ☊	☿	♀	♂	⚳	♃	♄	♅	♆	♇
1 F	4 38 51	10♊44 24	17♍54 42	24♍06 38	9♒14.9	16♉20.8	2♉24.5	0♈52.8	22♋00.5	12♋55.2	24♑44.5	8♑40.8	14♑02.6	15♏43.0
2 Sa	4 42 48	11 41 53	0♎14 53	6♎19 59	9R 11.9	17 24.2	3 34.3	1 36.7	22 25.2	13 07.6	24R 42.0	8R 38.7	14R 01.3	15R 41.6
3 Su	4 46 44	12 39 21	12 22 29	18 22 51	9 06.7	18 30.7	4 44.1	2 20.5	22 50.1	13 20.1	24 39.3	8 36.6	14 00.0	15 40.1
4 M	4 50 41	13 36 48	24 21 35	0♏19 05	8 59.3	19 40.4	5 54.0	3 04.3	23 14.9	13 32.6	24 36.6	8 34.5	13 58.7	15 38.7
5 Tu	4 54 37	14 34 14	6♏15 45	12 11 55	8 50.3	20 53.2	7 03.9	3 48.0	23 39.9	13 45.2	24 33.8	8 32.4	13 57.3	15 37.2
6 W	4 58 34	15 31 39	18 07 52	24 03 55	8 40.4	22 09.0	8 13.9	4 31.7	24 04.9	13 57.9	24 30.9	8 30.2	13 56.0	15 35.8
7 Th	5 02 30	16 29 02	0♐00 17	5♐57 12	8 30.5	23 27.7	9 24.0	5 15.4	24 30.0	14 10.5	24 28.0	8 28.0	13 54.6	15 34.5
8 F	5 06 27	17 26 25	11 54 51	17 53 26	8 21.5	24 49.4	10 34.1	5 59.0	24 55.1	14 23.3	24 25.0	8 25.8	13 53.2	15 33.1
9 Sa	5 10 24	18 23 47	23 53 09	29 54 09	8 14.1	26 14.0	11 44.3	6 42.5	25 20.3	14 36.0	24 21.9	8 23.6	13 51.8	15 31.7
10 Su	5 14 20	19 21 09	5♑56 40	12♑00 54	8 08.8	27 41.5	12 54.6	7 26.0	25 45.5	14 48.8	24 18.7	8 21.4	13 50.4	15 30.4
11 M	5 18 17	20 18 29	18 07 05	24 15 28	8 05.7	29 11.9	14 04.9	8 09.4	26 10.9	15 01.7	24 15.5	8 19.1	13 48.9	15 29.1
12 Tu	5 22 13	21 15 49	0♒26 21	6♒40 03	8D 04.7	0♊45.1	15 15.2	8 52.8	26 36.2	15 14.5	24 12.2	8 16.8	13 47.5	15 27.8
13 W	5 26 10	22 13 09	12 56 54	19 17 15	8 05.2	2 21.1	16 25.6	9 36.1	27 01.6	15 27.4	24 08.8	8 14.6	13 46.0	15 26.6
14 Th	5 30 06	23 10 28	25 41 31	2♓10 03	8 06.4	3 59.9	17 36.1	10 19.3	27 27.1	15 40.4	24 05.4	8 12.2	13 44.5	15 25.3
15 F	5 34 03	24 07 46	8♓43 15	15 21 29	8R 07.5	5 41.4	18 46.7	11 02.5	27 52.7	15 53.4	24 01.9	8 09.9	13 43.0	15 24.1
16 Sa	5 37 59	25 05 05	22 05 03	28 54 15	8 07.8	7 25.8	19 57.2	11 45.6	28 18.2	16 06.4	23 58.4	8 07.6	13 41.5	15 22.9
17 Su	5 41 56	26 02 22	5♈49 13	12♈50 02	8 06.5	9 12.8	21 07.9	12 28.6	28 43.9	16 19.4	23 54.8	8 05.2	13 40.0	15 21.7
18 M	5 45 53	26 59 40	19 56 39	27 08 51	8 03.6	11 02.5	22 18.6	13 11.6	29 09.6	16 32.5	23 51.1	8 02.8	13 38.5	15 20.6
19 Tu	5 49 49	27 56 58	4♉26 15	11♉48 18	7 59.2	12 54.8	23 29.3	13 54.5	29 35.3	16 45.6	23 47.4	8 00.5	13 36.9	15 19.4
20 W	5 53 46	28 54 15	19 14 14	26 43 12	7 53.8	14 49.7	24 40.1	14 37.3	0♌01.1	16 58.8	23 43.6	7 58.1	13 35.4	15 18.3
21 Th	5 57 42	29 51 32	4♊14 09	11♊45 56	7 48.3	16 46.9	25 51.0	15 20.0	0 27.0	17 11.9	23 39.8	7 55.7	13 33.8	15 17.3
22 F	6 01 39	0♋48 49	19 17 24	26 47 21	7 43.4	18 46.5	27 01.9	16 02.6	0 52.9	17 25.1	23 35.9	7 53.3	13 32.3	15 16.2
23 Sa	6 05 35	1 46 05	4♋14 38	11♋38 13	7 39.7	20 48.2	28 12.8	16 45.2	1 18.8	17 38.4	23 32.0	7 50.9	13 30.7	15 15.2
24 Su	6 09 32	2 43 21	18 57 09	26 10 42	7D 37.6	22 51.9	29 23.8	17 27.7	1 44.8	17 51.6	23 28.0	7 48.5	13 29.1	15 14.2
25 M	6 13 28	3 40 37	3♌18 16	10♌19 28	7 37.2	24 57.4	0♊34.8	18 10.1	2 10.9	18 04.9	23 24.0	7 46.0	13 27.5	15 13.2
26 Tu	6 17 25	4 37 51	17 14 02	24 01 56	7 38.0	27 04.5	1 45.9	18 52.3	2 37.0	18 18.1	23 20.0	7 43.6	13 25.9	15 12.3
27 W	6 21 22	5 35 06	0♍43 15	7♍18 12	7 39.5	29 12.9	2 57.0	19 34.5	3 03.1	18 31.5	23 15.9	7 41.2	13 24.3	15 11.4
28 Th	6 25 18	6 32 20	13 47 06	20 10 21	7 41.0	1♋22.3	4 08.2	20 16.6	3 29.2	18 44.8	23 11.7	7 38.7	13 22.7	15 10.5
29 F	6 29 15	7 29 33	26 28 25	2♎41 51	7R 41.9	3 32.5	5 19.4	20 58.6	3 55.4	18 58.1	23 07.6	7 36.3	13 21.1	15 09.6
30 Sa	6 33 11	8 26 46	8♎51 09	14 56 56	7 41.8	5 43.1	6 30.6	21 40.6	4 21.7	19 11.5	23 03.4	7 33.9	13 19.5	15 08.8

Astro Data

	Dy Hr Mn
♄ R	4 22:43
☽ 0S	5 2:36
♀ 0N	7 5:08
♃☍♅	13 19:31
☿ D	17 2:01
☽ 0N	19 17:09
☽ 0S	1 7:52
♃☍♆	6 8:45
♂ 0N	6 9:20
♃△♇	13 10:30
☽ 0N	15 23:23
☽ 0S	28 14:43

Planet Ingress

		Dy Hr Mn
♀	♈	4 3:52
☉	♊	21 7:37
♀	♉	30 10:13
♂	♈	31 7:11
☿	♊	12 0:29
⚳	♌	20 10:57
☉	♋	21 15:33
♀	♊	25 0:14
☿	♋	27 20:46

Last Aspect / ☽ Ingress

Last Aspect Dy Hr Mn			☽ Ingress	Dy Hr Mn
30 17:21	♀	△	♌	1 0:08
2 6:07	♇	□	♍	3 7:18
5 8:17	♄	△	♎	5 17:28
7 19:59	♄	□	♏	8 5:22
10 8:28	♄	✱	♐	10 17:56
12 1:48	♂	□	♑	13 6:21
15 8:17	♄	☌	♒	15 17:30
17 19:45	☉	□	♓	18 1:54
20 4:42	☉	✱	♈	20 6:31
21 23:52	♄	□	♉	22 7:42
23 23:14	♄	△	♊	24 7:00
26 0:18	♂	□	♋	26 6:34
28 4:34	♂	△	♌	28 8:29
29 12:13	♇	□	♍	30 14:08

Last Aspect / ☽ Ingress

Last Aspect Dy Hr Mn			☽ Ingress	Dy Hr Mn
1 13:13	♄	△	♎	1 23:31
4 0:33	♄	□	♏	4 11:22
6 12:54	♄	✱	♐	6 23:59
8 11:01	☉	☍	♑	9 12:12
11 22:58	☿	△	♒	11 23:09
13 17:57	☉	△	♓	14 8:00
16 4:48	☉	□	♈	16 13:55
18 11:44	☉	✱	♉	18 16:43
20 8:26	♀	☌	♊	20 17:15
21 21:13	☿	☌	♋	22 17:09
24 17:53	♀	✱	♌	24 18:25
26 18:28	☿	✱	♍	26 22:42
28 17:42	♄	△	♎	29 6:47

☽ Phases & Eclipses

Dy Hr Mn		
1 20:18	☽	11♌11
9 19:31	○	18♏54
17 19:45	☾	26♒38
24 11:47	●	3♊03
31 8:11	☽	9♍38
8 11:01	○	17♐24
16 4:48	☾	24♓48
22 18:55	●	1♋05
29 22:07	☽	7♎54

Astro Data

1 May 1990
Julian Day # 32993
SVP 5♓23'29"
GC 26♐42.3 ⚴ 20♉53.1
Eris 17♈10.2 ⚵ 18♏46.8R
⚷ 12♋11.4 ⚶ 15♈20.8
☽ Mean ☊ 12♒04.8

1 June 1990
Julian Day # 33024
SVP 5♓23'25"
GC 26♐42.3 ⚴ 7♊56.8
Eris 17♈26.6 ⚵ 12♏14.8R
⚷ 14♋41.6 ⚶ 29♈00.9
☽ Mean ☊ 10♒26.3

July 1990

LONGITUDE

Day	Sid.Time	☉	0 hr ☽	Noon ☽	True ☊	☿	♀	♂	⚳	♃	♄	♅	♆	♇
1 Su	6 37 08	9♋23 58	20♎59 44	27♎00 07	7♒40.4	7♋54.0	7♊41.9	22♈22.4	4♌48.0	19♋24.8	22♑59.1	7♑31.4	13♑17.9	15♏08.0
2 M	6 41 04	10 21 10	2♏58 39	8♏55 51	7R37.9	10 04.8	8 53.2	23 04.1	5 14.3	19 38.2	22R 54.9	7R 29.0	13R 16.3	15R 07.2
3 Tu	6 45 01	11 18 22	14 52 12	20 48 12	7 34.4	12 15.2	10 04.6	23 45.7	5 40.7	19 51.6	22 50.6	7 26.6	13 14.6	15 06.5
4 W	6 48 57	12 15 34	26 44 16	2♐40 49	7 30.4	14 25.1	11 16.0	24 27.2	6 07.1	20 05.0	22 46.3	7 24.1	13 13.0	15 05.8
5 Th	6 52 54	13 12 45	8♐38 12	14 36 44	7 26.3	16 34.1	12 27.5	25 08.6	6 33.5	20 18.4	22 41.9	7 21.7	13 11.4	15 05.1
6 F	6 56 51	14 09 56	20 36 45	26 38 29	7 22.6	18 42.0	13 39.0	25 49.9	7 00.0	20 31.9	22 37.6	7 19.3	13 09.8	15 04.4
7 Sa	7 00 47	15 07 08	2♑42 10	8♑48 00	7 19.7	20 48.8	14 50.6	26 31.1	7 26.5	20 45.3	22 33.2	7 16.9	13 08.2	15 03.8
8 Su	7 04 44	16 04 19	14 56 11	21 06 53	7 17.8	22 54.3	16 02.2	27 12.2	7 53.0	20 58.8	22 28.8	7 14.5	13 06.5	15 03.2
9 M	7 08 40	17 01 31	27 20 13	3♒36 22	7D17.0	24 58.2	17 13.8	27 53.2	8 19.6	21 12.2	22 24.4	7 12.1	13 04.9	15 02.7
10 Tu	7 12 37	17 58 42	9♒55 27	16 17 35	7 17.2	27 00.6	18 25.5	28 34.0	8 46.2	21 25.7	22 20.0	7 09.7	13 03.3	15 02.1
11 W	7 16 33	18 55 54	22 42 56	29 11 37	7 18.1	29 01.3	19 37.2	29 14.8	9 12.8	21 39.1	22 15.6	7 07.4	13 01.7	15 01.6
12 Th	7 20 30	19 53 06	5♓43 46	12♓19 32	7 19.4	1♌00.2	20 49.0	29 55.4	9 39.5	21 52.6	22 11.1	7 05.0	13 00.1	15 01.2
13 F	7 24 26	20 50 19	18 59 01	25 42 21	7 20.6	2 57.4	22 00.9	0♉35.9	10 06.2	22 06.0	22 06.7	7 02.7	12 58.5	15 00.7
14 Sa	7 28 23	21 47 32	2♈29 38	9♈20 54	7R21.5	4 52.8	23 12.7	1 16.3	10 32.9	22 19.5	22 02.3	7 00.3	12 56.9	15 00.3
15 Su	7 32 20	22 44 46	16 16 11	23 15 25	7 21.8	6 46.4	24 24.7	1 56.5	10 59.7	22 32.9	21 57.8	6 58.0	12 55.3	15 00.0
16 M	7 36 16	23 42 01	0♉18 32	7♉25 18	7 21.4	8 38.1	25 36.7	2 36.6	11 26.5	22 46.4	21 53.4	6 55.7	12 53.7	14 59.6
17 Tu	7 40 13	24 39 16	14 35 29	21 48 40	7 20.5	10 28.0	26 48.7	3 16.6	11 53.3	22 59.9	21 48.9	6 53.4	12 52.1	14 59.3
18 W	7 44 09	25 36 32	29 04 24	6♊22 07	7 19.3	12 16.0	28 00.7	3 56.5	12 20.2	23 13.3	21 44.5	6 51.1	12 50.5	14 59.1
19 Th	7 48 06	26 33 49	13♊41 09	21 00 47	7 18.0	14 02.2	29 12.9	4 36.2	12 47.1	23 26.8	21 40.1	6 48.9	12 49.0	14 58.8
20 F	7 52 02	27 31 06	28 20 14	5♋38 43	7 16.9	15 46.6	0♋25.0	5 15.8	13 14.0	23 40.3	21 35.7	6 46.7	12 47.4	14 58.6
21 Sa	7 55 59	28 28 24	12♋55 23	20 09 29	7 16.2	17 29.1	1 37.2	5 55.2	13 40.9	23 53.7	21 31.3	6 44.5	12 45.8	14 58.5
22 Su	7 59 56	29 25 43	27 20 17	4♌27 06	7D15.9	19 09.8	2 49.5	6 34.4	14 07.9	24 07.1	21 26.9	6 42.3	12 44.3	14 58.3
23 M	8 03 52	0♌23 02	11♌29 23	18 26 41	7 16.0	20 48.6	4 01.8	7 13.5	14 34.9	24 20.6	21 22.5	6 40.1	12 42.8	14 58.2
24 Tu	8 07 49	1 20 21	25 18 39	2♍05 04	7 16.4	22 25.6	5 14.1	7 52.5	15 01.9	24 34.0	21 18.2	6 38.0	12 41.3	14 58.2
25 W	8 11 45	2 17 41	8♍45 50	15 20 59	7 16.9	24 00.8	6 26.4	8 31.2	15 28.9	24 47.4	21 13.8	6 35.8	12 39.7	14D 58.1
26 Th	8 15 42	3 15 01	21 50 36	28 14 56	7 17.3	25 34.1	7 38.8	9 09.8	15 56.0	25 00.8	21 09.5	6 33.7	12 38.2	14 58.1
27 F	8 19 38	4 12 22	4♎34 17	10♎49 01	7 17.7	27 05.6	8 51.3	9 48.3	16 23.1	25 14.1	21 05.2	6 31.7	12 36.8	14 58.1
28 Sa	8 23 35	5 09 43	16 59 35	23 06 28	7 17.8	28 35.3	10 03.8	10 26.6	16 50.1	25 27.5	21 01.0	6 29.6	12 35.3	14 58.2
29 Su	8 27 31	6 07 04	29 10 11	5♏11 16	7R17.9	0♍03.0	11 16.3	11 04.7	17 17.3	25 40.8	20 56.8	6 27.6	12 33.8	14 58.3
30 M	8 31 28	7 04 27	11♏10 18	17 07 50	7D17.9	1 28.9	12 28.9	11 42.6	17 44.4	25 54.2	20 52.6	6 25.6	12 32.4	14 58.5
31 Tu	8 35 25	8 01 49	23 04 28	29 00 44	7 17.9	2 52.8	13 41.5	12 20.3	18 11.6	26 07.5	20 48.4	6 23.7	12 30.9	14 58.6

August 1990

LONGITUDE

Day	Sid.Time	☉	0 hr ☽	Noon ☽	True ☊	☿	♀	♂	⚳	♃	♄	♅	♆	♇
1 W	8 39 21	8♌59 13	4♐57 12	10♐54 23	7♒18.0	4♍14.8	14♋54.1	12♉57.9	18♌38.7	26♋20.7	20♑44.3	6♑21.7	12♑29.5	14♏58.8
2 Th	8 43 18	9 56 37	16 52 48	22 52 53	7 18.3	5 34.9	16 06.8	13 35.3	19 05.9	26 34.0	20R 40.3	6R 19.8	12R 28.1	14 59.1
3 F	8 47 14	10 54 02	28 55 06	4♑59 49	7 18.6	6 52.9	17 19.6	14 12.5	19 33.1	26 47.3	20 36.2	6 18.0	12 26.8	14 59.3
4 Sa	8 51 11	11 51 27	11♑07 24	17 18 09	7 19.0	8 08.8	18 32.3	14 49.5	20 00.3	27 00.5	20 32.2	6 16.1	12 25.4	14 59.7
5 Su	8 55 07	12 48 53	23 32 17	29 50 02	7R19.2	9 22.5	19 45.1	15 26.3	20 27.6	27 13.7	20 28.3	6 14.3	12 24.0	15 00.0
6 M	8 59 04	13 46 21	6♒11 31	12♒36 51	7 19.3	10 34.1	20 58.0	16 03.0	20 54.8	27 26.8	20 24.4	6 12.6	12 22.7	15 00.4
7 Tu	9 03 00	14 43 49	19 06 02	25 39 04	7 19.0	11 43.4	22 10.9	16 39.4	21 22.1	27 40.0	20 20.5	6 10.8	12 21.4	15 00.8
8 W	9 06 57	15 41 18	2♓15 54	8♓56 25	7 18.3	12 50.4	23 23.9	17 15.6	21 49.4	27 53.1	20 16.7	6 09.1	12 20.1	15 01.2
9 Th	9 10 54	16 38 48	15 40 27	22 27 51	7 17.2	13 54.9	24 36.8	17 51.6	22 16.7	28 06.1	20 13.0	6 07.5	12 18.8	15 01.7
10 F	9 14 50	17 36 20	29 18 24	6♈11 52	7 16.0	14 56.8	25 49.9	18 27.4	22 44.0	28 19.2	20 09.3	6 05.8	12 17.6	15 02.2
11 Sa	9 18 47	18 33 53	13♈08 01	20 06 35	7 14.8	15 56.1	27 03.0	19 03.0	23 11.3	28 32.2	20 05.7	6 04.3	12 16.3	15 02.7
12 Su	9 22 43	19 31 27	27 07 18	4♉09 54	7 14.0	16 52.6	28 16.1	19 38.4	23 38.6	28 45.2	20 02.1	6 02.7	12 15.1	15 03.3
13 M	9 26 40	20 29 03	11♉14 07	18 19 39	7D13.6	17 46.2	29 29.3	20 13.5	24 06.0	28 58.2	19 58.6	6 01.2	12 13.9	15 03.9
14 Tu	9 30 36	21 26 40	25 26 14	2♊33 34	7 13.8	18 36.7	0♌42.5	20 48.4	24 33.3	29 11.1	19 55.1	5 59.7	12 12.7	15 04.6
15 W	9 34 33	22 24 19	9♊41 19	16 49 11	7 14.5	19 24.0	1 55.7	21 23.1	25 00.7	29 24.0	19 51.7	5 58.3	12 11.6	15 05.3
16 Th	9 38 29	23 22 00	23 56 50	1♋03 54	7 15.7	20 07.9	3 09.0	21 57.5	25 28.1	29 36.8	19 48.4	5 56.9	12 10.5	15 06.0
17 F	9 42 26	24 19 42	8♋10 00	15 14 45	7 16.8	20 48.2	4 22.4	22 31.7	25 55.5	29 49.6	19 45.1	5 55.5	12 09.4	15 06.7
18 Sa	9 46 23	25 17 26	22 17 45	29 18 35	7R17.6	21 24.6	5 35.8	23 05.6	26 22.9	0♌02.4	19 41.9	5 54.2	12 08.3	15 07.5
19 Su	9 50 19	26 15 11	6♌16 52	13♌12 11	7 17.6	21 57.1	6 49.2	23 39.3	26 50.3	0 15.1	19 38.8	5 52.9	12 07.2	15 08.3
20 M	9 54 16	27 12 57	20 04 11	26 52 30	7 16.7	22 25.3	8 02.7	24 12.6	27 17.7	0 27.8	19 35.7	5 51.7	12 06.2	15 09.2
21 Tu	9 58 12	28 10 44	3♍36 53	10♍17 04	7 14.8	22 49.0	9 16.2	24 45.7	27 45.1	0 40.4	19 32.7	5 50.5	12 05.2	15 10.0
22 W	10 02 09	29 08 33	16 52 54	23 24 16	7 11.9	23 08.0	10 29.7	25 18.6	28 12.5	0 53.0	19 29.8	5 49.4	12 04.2	15 11.0
23 Th	10 06 05	0♍06 24	29 51 10	6♎13 37	7 08.4	23 22.0	11 43.3	25 51.1	28 39.9	1 05.6	19 27.0	5 48.3	12 03.2	15 11.9
24 F	10 10 02	1 04 15	12♎31 47	18 45 52	7 04.8	23 30.7	12 56.9	26 23.3	29 07.4	1 18.1	19 24.2	5 47.2	12 02.3	15 12.9
25 Sa	10 13 58	2 02 08	24 56 08	1♏02 55	7 01.5	23R34.0	14 10.6	26 55.3	29 34.8	1 30.5	19 21.5	5 46.2	12 01.4	15 13.9
26 Su	10 17 55	3 00 02	7♏06 39	13 07 45	6 58.9	23 31.7	15 24.3	27 26.9	0♍02.2	1 42.9	19 18.9	5 45.2	12 00.5	15 14.9
27 M	10 21 51	3 57 57	19 06 46	25 04 12	6D57.4	23 23.5	16 38.0	27 58.3	0 29.7	1 55.2	19 16.4	5 44.3	11 59.7	15 16.0
28 Tu	10 25 48	4 55 54	1♐00 38	6♐56 40	6 57.0	23 09.2	17 51.7	28 29.3	0 57.1	2 07.5	19 14.0	5 43.5	11 58.8	15 17.1
29 W	10 29 45	5 53 52	12 52 53	18 49 54	6 57.7	22 48.9	19 05.5	29 00.0	1 24.6	2 19.8	19 11.6	5 42.6	11 58.1	15 18.2
30 Th	10 33 41	6 51 52	24 48 20	0♑48 46	6 59.2	22 22.6	20 19.4	29 30.4	1 52.0	2 31.9	19 09.4	5 41.9	11 57.3	15 19.4
31 F	10 37 38	7 49 52	6♑51 46	12 57 54	7 00.9	21 50.3	21 33.2	0♊00.4	2 19.4	2 44.1	19 07.2	5 41.1	11 56.5	15 20.6

Astro Data	Planet Ingress	Last Aspect	☽ Ingress	Last Aspect	☽ Ingress	☽ Phases & Eclipses	Astro Data
Dy Hr Mn	Dy Hr Mn	Dy Hr Mn	Dy Hr Mn	Dy Hr Mn	Dy Hr Mn	Dy Hr Mn	
☽0N 13 4:29	☿ ♌ 11 23:48	1 4:01 ♄ □	♏ 1 18:01	1 7:48 ☉ △	♑ 3 2:09	8 1:23 ○ 15♑39	1 July 1990
♃☍♄ 13 12:53	♂ ♉ 12 14:44	3 16:06 ♄ ⚹	♐ 4 6:35	5 6:57 ♃ ☍	♒ 5 12:19	15 11:04 ☾ 22♈43	Julian Day # 33054
☽0S 25 23:17	♀ ♋ 20 3:41	6 10:18 ♂ △	♑ 6 18:39	6 18:41 ♂ □	♓ 7 19:54	22 2:54 ● 29♋04	SVP 5♓23'19"
♇ D 26 1:25	☉ ♌ 23 2:22	9 0:25 ♂ □	♒ 9 5:07	9 22:03 ♃ △	♈ 10 1:13	22 3:02:08 ● T 02'33"	GC 26♐42.4 ⚴ 25♊20.4
	☿ ♍ 29 11:10	11 12:06 ♂ ⚹	♓ 11 13:29	12 2:38 ♃ □	♉ 12 4:55	29 14:01 ☽ 6♏12	Eris 17♈35.1 ⚵ 9♏22.9R
☽0N 9 10:15		13 5:38 ♄ ⚹	♈ 13 19:36	14 6:14 ♃ ⚹	♊ 14 7:41		⚷ 17♋43.6 ⚶ 11♉03.0
☿0S 20 10:18	♀ ♌ 13 22:05	15 14:09 ♀ ⚹	♉ 15 23:29	15 22:05 ☉ ⚹	♋ 16 10:12	6 14:19 ○ 13♒52	☽ Mean ☊ 8♒51.0
☽0S 22 8:31	♃ ♌ 18 7:30	17 17:02 ☉ ⚹	♊ 18 1:32	18 0:55 ♂ ⚹	♌ 18 13:11	6 14:12 ● P 0.676	
☿ R 25 14:08	☉ ♍ 23 9:21	20 2:39 ♀ ☌	♋ 20 2:44	20 12:39 ☉ ☌	♍ 20 17:33	13 15:54 ☾ 20♉38	1 August 1990
	⚳ ♍ 26 10:02	22 2:54 ☉ ☌	♌ 22 4:29	22 15:41 ♂ △	♎ 23 0:17	20 12:39 ● 27♌15	Julian Day # 33085
	♂ ♊ 31 11:40	23 16:40 ☿ ☌	♍ 24 8:17	24 13:14 ♄ □	♏ 25 9:56	28 7:34 ☽ 4♐45	SVP 5♓23'14"
		26 5:49 ♃ ⚹	♎ 26 15:18	27 18:07 ♂ ☍	♐ 27 21:57		GC 26♐42.5 ⚴ 13♋45.6
		29 0:21 ☿ ⚹	♏ 29 1:39	29 19:45 ☿ □	♑ 30 10:23		Eris 17♈34.3R ⚵ 11♏16.7
		31 6:03 ♃ △	♐ 31 14:00				⚷ 21♋02.3 ⚶ 21♉34.2
							☽ Mean ☊ 7♒12.5

LONGITUDE — September 1990

Day	Sid.Time	☉	0 hr ☽	Noon☽	True☊	☿	♀	♂	⚳	♃	♄	♅	♆	♇
1 Sa	10 41 34	8♍47 55	19♑07 40	25♑21 31	7♒02.3	21♍12.2	22♌47.1	0♊30.1	2♍46.9	2♌56.1	19♑05.1	5♑40.4	11♑55.8	15♏21.8
2 Su	10 45 31	9 45 58	1♒39 50	8♒02 56	7R 02.8	20R 28.8	24 01.1	0 59.5	3 14.3	3 08.1	19R 03.1	5R 39.8	11R 55.1	15 23.1
3 M	10 49 27	10 44 03	14 31 04	21 04 23	7 02.0	19 40.5	25 15.1	1 28.5	3 41.7	3 20.0	19 01.1	5 39.2	11 54.5	15 24.4
4 Tu	10 53 24	11 42 10	27 42 54	4♓26 33	6 59.6	18 48.0	26 29.1	1 57.2	4 09.2	3 31.9	18 59.3	5 38.7	11 53.9	15 25.7
5 W	10 57 20	12 40 18	11♓15 09	18 08 26	6 55.5	17 52.2	27 43.1	2 25.5	4 36.6	3 43.7	18 57.6	5 38.2	11 53.3	15 27.0
6 Th	11 01 17	13 38 28	25 05 59	2♈07 20	6 50.3	16 54.2	28 57.2	2 53.5	5 04.0	3 55.4	18 55.9	5 37.8	11 52.7	15 28.4
7 F	11 05 14	14 36 39	9♈11 55	16 19 06	6 44.5	15 54.9	0♍11.3	3 21.0	5 31.4	4 07.1	18 54.3	5 37.4	11 52.2	15 29.8
8 Sa	11 09 10	15 34 53	23 28 16	0♉38 44	6 38.9	14 55.8	1 25.4	3 48.2	5 58.8	4 18.7	18 52.9	5 37.0	11 51.7	15 31.2
9 Su	11 13 07	16 33 09	7♉49 52	15 01 05	6 34.3	13 58.2	2 39.6	4 15.0	6 26.2	4 30.3	18 51.5	5 36.7	11 51.2	15 32.7
10 M	11 17 03	17 31 26	22 11 48	29 21 33	6 31.1	13 03.4	3 53.8	4 41.3	6 53.6	4 41.7	18 50.2	5 36.5	11 50.7	15 34.2
11 Tu	11 21 00	18 29 46	6♊29 57	13♊36 38	6D 29.7	12 12.7	5 08.1	5 07.3	7 21.0	4 53.1	18 49.0	5 36.3	11 50.3	15 35.7
12 W	11 24 56	19 28 08	20 41 22	27 43 57	6 29.9	11 27.4	6 22.4	5 32.8	7 48.4	5 04.4	18 47.9	5 36.2	11 49.9	15 37.2
13 Th	11 28 53	20 26 33	4♋44 15	11♋42 11	6 31.0	10 48.6	7 36.7	5 57.9	8 15.8	5 15.7	18 46.9	5 36.1	11 49.6	15 38.8
14 F	11 32 49	21 24 59	18 37 40	25 30 40	6R 32.2	10 17.3	8 51.1	6 22.5	8 43.1	5 26.8	18 46.0	5D 36.0	11 49.3	15 40.4
15 Sa	11 36 46	22 23 28	2♌21 09	9♌09 02	6 32.6	9 54.3	10 05.5	6 46.6	9 10.5	5 37.9	18 45.2	5 36.0	11 49.0	15 42.0
16 Su	11 40 43	23 21 58	15 54 18	22 36 50	6 31.3	9 40.2	11 19.9	7 10.3	9 37.9	5 48.9	18 44.5	5 36.1	11 48.7	15 43.7
17 M	11 44 39	24 20 30	29 16 35	5♍53 25	6 28.0	9D 35.4	12 34.3	7 33.5	10 05.2	5 59.8	18 43.9	5 36.2	11 48.5	15 45.4
18 Tu	11 48 36	25 19 05	12♍27 15	18 57 57	6 22.3	9 40.2	13 48.8	7 56.2	10 32.5	6 10.7	18 43.4	5 36.4	11 48.3	15 47.1
19 W	11 52 32	26 17 41	25 25 26	1♎49 37	6 14.6	9 54.5	15 03.3	8 18.4	10 59.8	6 21.4	18 42.9	5 36.6	11 48.2	15 48.8
20 Th	11 56 29	27 16 19	8♎10 27	14 27 55	6 05.4	10 18.3	16 17.9	8 40.1	11 27.1	6 32.1	18 42.6	5 36.9	11 48.0	15 50.5
21 F	12 00 25	28 15 00	20 42 02	26 52 54	5 55.7	10 51.4	17 32.4	9 01.2	11 54.4	6 42.6	18 42.4	5 37.2	11 47.9	15 52.3
22 Sa	12 04 22	29 13 41	3♏00 39	9♏05 30	5 46.4	11 33.3	18 47.0	9 21.9	12 21.7	6 53.1	18D 42.3	5 37.6	11 47.9	15 54.1
23 Su	12 08 18	0♎12 25	15 07 43	21 07 36	5 38.3	12 23.5	20 01.6	9 41.9	12 48.9	7 03.5	18 42.3	5 38.0	11D 47.9	15 55.9
24 M	12 12 15	1 11 11	27 05 33	3♐02 01	5 32.2	13 21.6	21 16.3	10 01.4	13 16.1	7 13.8	18 42.3	5 38.4	11 47.9	15 57.8
25 Tu	12 16 12	2 09 58	8♐57 30	14 52 31	5 28.3	14 26.9	22 30.9	10 20.4	13 43.3	7 24.0	18 42.5	5 39.0	11 47.9	15 59.7
26 W	12 20 08	3 08 47	20 47 39	26 43 32	5D 26.5	15 38.8	23 45.6	10 38.7	14 10.5	7 34.1	18 42.8	5 39.6	11 48.0	16 01.6
27 Th	12 24 05	4 07 38	2♑40 48	8♑40 07	5 26.4	16 56.5	25 00.3	10 56.5	14 37.7	7 44.0	18 43.2	5 40.2	11 48.1	16 03.5
28 F	12 28 01	5 06 31	14 42 07	20 47 29	5 27.1	18 19.5	26 15.0	11 13.7	15 04.8	7 53.9	18 43.6	5 40.9	11 48.2	16 05.4
29 Sa	12 31 58	6 05 25	26 56 51	3♒10 50	5R 27.7	19 47.0	27 29.8	11 30.2	15 31.9	8 03.7	18 44.2	5 41.6	11 48.4	16 07.4
30 Su	12 35 54	7 04 21	9♒30 00	15 54 50	5 27.2	21 18.4	28 44.6	11 46.2	15 59.0	8 13.4	18 44.9	5 42.4	11 48.6	16 09.4

LONGITUDE — October 1990

Day	Sid.Time	☉	0 hr ☽	Noon☽	True☊	☿	♀	♂	⚳	♃	♄	♅	♆	♇
1 M	12 39 51	8♎03 19	22♒25 45	29♒03 02	5♒24.8	22♍53.2	29♍59.3	12♊01.5	16♍26.1	8♌23.0	18♑45.7	5♑43.2	11♑48.8	16♏11.4
2 Tu	12 43 47	9 02 18	5♓46 53	12♓37 19	5R 19.9	24 30.7	1♎14.1	12 16.1	16 53.1	8 32.4	18 46.5	5 44.1	11 49.1	16 13.4
3 W	12 47 44	10 01 20	19 34 10	26 37 09	5 12.6	26 10.5	2 29.0	12 30.1	17 20.2	8 41.8	18 47.5	5 45.0	11 49.4	16 15.4
4 Th	12 51 41	11 00 23	3♈45 46	10♈59 21	5 03.3	27 52.2	3 43.8	12 43.4	17 47.1	8 51.0	18 48.6	5 46.0	11 49.8	16 17.5
5 F	12 55 37	11 59 28	18 17 06	25 38 04	4 53.0	29 35.2	4 58.7	12 56.1	18 14.1	9 00.2	18 49.7	5 47.0	11 50.1	16 19.5
6 Sa	12 59 34	12 58 36	3♉01 14	10♉25 31	4 42.8	1♎19.3	6 13.6	13 08.0	18 41.0	9 09.2	18 51.0	5 48.1	11 50.5	16 21.6
7 Su	13 03 30	13 57 46	17 49 53	25 13 20	4 34.0	3 04.2	7 28.5	13 19.2	19 08.0	9 18.1	18 52.4	5 49.2	11 51.0	16 23.7
8 M	13 07 27	14 56 58	2♊34 55	9♊53 52	4 27.5	4 49.7	8 43.4	13 29.7	19 34.8	9 26.9	18 53.8	5 50.4	11 51.4	16 25.9
9 Tu	13 11 23	15 56 12	17 09 32	24 21 25	4 23.5	6 35.3	9 58.4	13 39.5	20 01.7	9 35.6	18 55.4	5 51.6	11 52.0	16 28.0
10 W	13 15 20	16 55 29	1♋29 10	8♋32 37	4D 21.8	8 21.1	11 13.3	13 48.5	20 28.5	9 44.1	18 57.1	5 52.9	11 52.5	16 30.2
11 Th	13 19 16	17 54 48	15 31 39	22 26 20	4R 21.6	10 06.9	12 28.3	13 56.7	20 55.3	9 52.5	18 58.8	5 54.3	11 53.1	16 32.4
12 F	13 23 13	18 54 10	29 16 45	6♌03 06	4 21.8	11 52.4	13 43.3	14 04.1	21 22.1	10 00.8	19 00.7	5 55.6	11 53.7	16 34.6
13 Sa	13 27 10	19 53 33	12♌45 33	19 24 21	4 21.0	13 37.7	14 58.4	14 10.7	21 48.8	10 09.0	19 02.6	5 57.1	11 54.3	16 36.8
14 Su	13 31 06	20 52 59	25 59 42	2♍31 49	4 18.1	15 22.5	16 13.4	14 16.6	22 15.5	10 17.0	19 04.7	5 58.5	11 55.0	16 39.0
15 M	13 35 03	21 52 28	9♍00 54	15 27 06	4 12.5	17 07.0	17 28.5	14 21.5	22 42.1	10 24.9	19 06.8	6 00.0	11 55.7	16 41.2
16 Tu	13 38 59	22 51 58	21 50 32	28 11 18	4 03.8	18 50.9	18 43.6	14 25.7	23 08.8	10 32.7	19 09.0	6 01.6	11 56.4	16 43.5
17 W	13 42 56	23 51 30	4♎29 29	10♎45 08	3 52.4	20 34.3	19 58.6	14 29.0	23 35.3	10 40.3	19 11.3	6 03.2	11 57.2	16 45.7
18 Th	13 46 52	24 51 05	16 58 17	23 08 58	3 39.1	22 17.2	21 13.8	14 31.4	24 01.9	10 47.8	19 13.8	6 04.9	11 58.0	16 48.0
19 F	13 50 49	25 50 42	29 17 15	5♏23 10	3 24.8	23 59.4	22 28.9	14 33.0	24 28.4	10 55.2	19 16.3	6 06.6	11 58.8	16 50.3
20 Sa	13 54 45	26 50 20	11♏26 50	17 28 21	3 10.9	25 41.1	23 44.0	14R 33.7	24 54.8	11 02.4	19 18.9	6 08.4	11 59.7	16 52.6
21 Su	13 58 42	27 50 01	23 27 55	29 25 42	2 58.5	27 22.2	24 59.2	14 33.6	25 21.2	11 09.5	19 21.6	6 10.2	12 00.6	16 54.9
22 M	14 02 38	28 49 43	5♐22 00	11♐17 08	2 48.4	29 02.6	26 14.3	14 32.5	25 47.6	11 16.4	19 24.4	6 12.0	12 01.5	16 57.2
23 Tu	14 06 35	29 49 28	17 11 28	23 05 26	2 41.2	0♏42.5	27 29.5	14 30.6	26 13.9	11 23.2	19 27.3	6 13.9	12 02.4	16 59.6
24 W	14 10 32	0♏49 14	28 59 32	4♑54 16	2 36.8	2 21.8	28 44.7	14 27.8	26 40.2	11 29.8	19 30.3	6 15.8	12 03.4	17 01.9
25 Th	14 14 28	1 49 02	10♑50 15	16 48 05	2 34.9	4 00.5	29 59.8	14 24.1	27 06.4	11 36.3	19 33.3	6 17.8	12 04.5	17 04.3
26 F	14 18 25	2 48 51	22 48 25	28 51 56	2 34.4	5 38.7	1♏15.0	14 19.5	27 32.5	11 42.6	19 36.5	6 19.8	12 05.5	17 06.6
27 Sa	14 22 21	3 48 42	4♒59 20	11♒11 17	2 34.3	7 16.3	2 30.2	14 14.0	27 58.7	11 48.8	19 39.7	6 21.9	12 06.6	17 09.0
28 Su	14 26 18	4 48 35	17 28 26	23 51 27	2 33.5	8 53.4	3 45.4	14 07.6	28 24.7	11 54.8	19 43.0	6 24.0	12 07.7	17 11.4
29 M	14 30 14	5 48 29	0♓20 52	6♓57 11	2 30.8	10 29.9	5 00.6	14 00.3	28 50.7	12 00.7	19 46.5	6 26.2	12 08.8	17 13.8
30 Tu	14 34 11	6 48 25	13 40 45	20 31 48	2 25.5	12 06.0	6 15.9	13 52.2	29 16.7	12 06.4	19 50.0	6 28.4	12 10.0	17 16.2
31 W	14 38 07	7 48 23	27 30 22	4♈36 18	2 17.6	13 41.5	7 31.1	13 43.2	29 42.5	12 11.9	19 53.5	6 30.6	12 11.2	17 18.5

Astro Data	Dy Hr Mn	Planet Ingress	Dy Hr Mn
☿0N	3 8:08	♀ ♍	7 8:21
☽0N	5 17:54	☉ ♎	23 6:56
♅ D	14 18:29		
♃⚻♅	15 7:55	♀ ♎	1 12:13
☿ D	17 12:06	☿ ♎	5 17:44
☽0S	18 16:51	☿ ♏	23 1:46
♄ D	23 5:10	☉ ♏	23 16:14
☉0S	23 6:55	♀ ♏	25 12:03
♆ D	23 18:37		
☽0N	3 3:21		
♀0S	4 3:38		
☿0S	8 4:34		
☽0S	15 23:15		
♂ R	20 19:30		
☽0N	30 13:12	♃⚻⚻	31 8:04

Last Aspect Dy Hr Mn		☽ Ingress Dy Hr Mn	
1 4:25	☿ △	♒	1 20:51
3 20:20	☿ ☍	♓	4 4:06
5 13:25	♄ ⚹	♈	6 8:23
7 16:20	♄ □	♉	8 10:55
9 18:24	♄ △	♊	10 13:05
11 20:53	☉ □	♋	12 15:53
14 4:19	☉ ⚹	♌	14 19:52
15 23:40	♇ □	♍	17 1:19
19 0:46	☉ ☌	♎	19 8:34
20 20:09	♄ □	♏	21 18:06
23 9:32	♀ ⚹	♐	24 5:52
26 5:18	♀ □	♑	26 18:36
28 23:50	♀ △	♒	29 5:54

Last Aspect Dy Hr Mn		☽ Ingress Dy Hr Mn	
30 12:27	♇ □	♓	1 13:42
3 11:09	☿ ☍	♈	3 17:42
5 0:53	♄ □	♉	5 19:06
7 1:40	♄ △	♊	7 19:47
8 20:57	☉ △	♋	9 21:29
11 5:58	♄ ☍	♌	12 1:16
13 12:57	☉ ⚹	♍	14 7:21
15 18:53	♄ △	♎	16 15:26
18 15:37	☉ ☌	♏	19 1:24
20 15:42	♄ ⚹	♐	21 13:09
23 22:01	♀ ⚹	♑	24 2:03
25 17:32	♄ ☌	♒	26 14:14
27 23:25	♇ □	♓	28 23:22
30 10:47	♄ ⚹	♈	31 4:14

☽ Phases & Eclipses Dy Hr Mn	
5 1:46	○ 12♓15
11 20:53	☾ 18♊51
19 0:46	● 25♍50
27 2:06	☽ 3♑43
4 12:02	○ 11♈00
11 3:31	☾ 17♋34
18 15:37	● 25♎00
26 20:26	☽ 3♒10

Astro Data

1 September 1990
Julian Day # 33116
SVP 5♓23'10"
GC 26♐42.5 ⚴ 2♌01.2
Eris 17♈24.0R ⚵ 17♏00.7
⚷ 24♋03.4 ⚶ 28♉54.6
☽ Mean ☊ 5♒34.0

1 October 1990
Julian Day # 33146
SVP 5♓23'06"
GC 26♐42.6 ⚴ 18♌49.2
Eris 17♈07.7R ⚵ 24♏57.4
⚷ 26♋14.4 ⚶ 1♊06.9R
☽ Mean ☊ 3♒58.7

November 1990 — LONGITUDE

Day	Sid.Time	☉	0 hr ☽	Noon ☽	True ☊	☿	♀	♂	⚳	♃	♄	♅	♆	♇
1 Th	14 42 04	8♏48 22	11♈49 15	19♈08 36	2♒07.4	15♏16.6	8♏46.3	13♊33.3	0♎08.4	12♌17.3	19♑57.2	6♑32.9	12♑12.4	17♏20.9
2 F	14 46 01	9 48 24	26 33 33	4♉03 04	1R 56.0	16 51.3	10 01.5	13R 22.6	0 34.2	12 22.5	20 01.0	6 35.2	12 13.7	17 23.3
3 Sa	14 49 57	10 48 27	11♉35 58	19 10 58	1 44.6	18 25.5	11 16.8	13 11.1	0 59.9	12 27.6	20 04.8	6 37.6	12 15.0	17 25.8
4 Su	14 53 54	11 48 32	26 46 40	4♊21 45	1 34.5	19 59.3	12 32.0	12 58.7	1 25.5	12 32.4	20 08.7	6 39.9	12 16.3	17 28.2
5 M	14 57 50	12 48 39	11♊54 54	19 24 59	1 26.8	21 32.6	13 47.3	12 45.5	1 51.1	12 37.2	20 12.7	6 42.4	12 17.6	17 30.6
6 Tu	15 01 47	13 48 48	26 51 01	4♋12 11	1 21.9	23 05.6	15 02.6	12 31.5	2 16.7	12 41.7	20 16.8	6 44.9	12 19.0	17 33.0
7 W	15 05 43	14 48 59	11♋27 54	18 37 47	1D 19.7	24 38.3	16 17.9	12 16.7	2 42.1	12 46.1	20 21.0	6 47.4	12 20.4	17 35.4
8 Th	15 09 40	15 49 12	25 41 39	2♌39 27	1 19.2	26 10.5	17 33.1	12 01.1	3 07.6	12 50.3	20 25.2	6 49.9	12 21.8	17 37.9
9 F	15 13 37	16 49 27	9♌31 19	16 17 27	1R 19.4	27 42.4	18 48.4	11 44.9	3 32.9	12 54.3	20 29.5	6 52.5	12 23.3	17 40.3
10 Sa	15 17 33	17 49 44	22 58 09	29 33 47	1 18.9	29 14.0	20 03.7	11 27.9	3 58.2	12 58.2	20 33.9	6 55.1	12 24.8	17 42.7
11 Su	15 21 30	18 50 04	6♍04 43	12♍31 21	1 16.5	0♐45.2	21 19.0	11 10.2	4 23.4	13 01.8	20 38.4	6 57.8	12 26.3	17 45.1
12 M	15 25 26	19 50 25	18 54 06	25 13 19	1 11.6	2 16.0	22 34.4	10 51.9	4 48.5	13 05.3	20 42.9	7 00.5	12 27.8	17 47.6
13 Tu	15 29 23	20 50 48	1♎29 21	7♎42 32	1 03.8	3 46.5	23 49.7	10 32.9	5 13.5	13 08.6	20 47.5	7 03.2	12 29.4	17 50.0
14 W	15 33 19	21 51 12	13 53 08	20 01 24	0 53.3	5 16.7	25 05.0	10 13.4	5 38.5	13 11.7	20 52.2	7 06.0	12 30.9	17 52.4
15 Th	15 37 16	22 51 39	26 07 33	2♏11 45	0 41.0	6 46.5	26 20.3	9 53.3	6 03.4	13 14.7	20 57.0	7 08.8	12 32.5	17 54.8
16 F	15 41 12	23 52 07	8♏14 12	14 15 01	0 27.8	8 16.0	27 35.7	9 32.8	6 28.2	13 17.4	21 01.8	7 11.6	12 34.2	17 57.2
17 Sa	15 45 09	24 52 37	20 14 22	26 12 22	0 14.8	9 45.0	28 51.0	9 11.8	6 53.0	13 20.0	21 06.7	7 14.4	12 35.8	17 59.7
18 Su	15 49 06	25 53 09	2♐09 11	8♐05 00	0 03.2	11 13.7	0♐06.4	8 50.4	7 17.6	13 22.4	21 11.7	7 17.3	12 37.5	18 02.1
19 M	15 53 02	26 53 42	14 00 00	19 54 24	29♑53.7	12 41.9	1 21.7	8 28.7	7 42.2	13 24.5	21 16.8	7 20.3	12 39.2	18 04.5
20 Tu	15 56 59	27 54 17	25 48 29	1♑42 34	29 47.0	14 09.6	2 37.1	8 06.7	8 06.7	13 26.5	21 21.9	7 23.2	12 40.9	18 06.9
21 W	16 00 55	28 54 53	7♑36 59	13 32 09	29 43.1	15 36.9	3 52.4	7 44.4	8 31.0	13 28.3	21 27.1	7 26.2	12 42.7	18 09.3
22 Th	16 04 52	29 55 30	19 28 30	25 26 33	29D 41.5	17 03.5	5 07.8	7 22.0	8 55.3	13 29.9	21 32.3	7 29.2	12 44.5	18 11.7
23 F	16 08 48	0♐56 08	1♒26 49	7♒29 53	29 41.7	18 29.5	6 23.1	6 59.4	9 19.5	13 31.4	21 37.6	7 32.3	12 46.3	18 14.1
24 Sa	16 12 45	1 56 48	13 36 21	19 46 50	29 42.6	19 54.8	7 38.5	6 36.7	9 43.6	13 32.6	21 43.0	7 35.3	12 48.1	18 16.4
25 Su	16 16 41	2 57 28	26 01 58	2♓22 23	29R 43.1	21 19.3	8 53.8	6 13.9	10 07.7	13 33.6	21 48.4	7 38.4	12 49.9	18 18.8
26 M	16 20 38	3 58 10	8♓48 41	15 21 24	29 42.4	22 42.9	10 09.2	5 51.2	10 31.6	13 34.4	21 53.9	7 41.5	12 51.8	18 21.2
27 Tu	16 24 35	4 58 53	22 01 00	28 47 53	29 39.7	24 05.4	11 24.5	5 28.6	10 55.4	13 35.0	21 59.5	7 44.7	12 53.6	18 23.5
28 W	16 28 31	5 59 36	5♈42 16	12♈44 13	29 34.9	25 26.8	12 39.9	5 06.0	11 19.1	13 35.5	22 05.1	7 47.9	12 55.5	18 25.9
29 Th	16 32 28	7 00 21	19 53 38	27 10 09	29 28.1	26 46.7	13 55.2	4 43.7	11 42.7	13R 35.7	22 10.7	7 51.1	12 57.4	18 28.2
30 F	16 36 24	8 01 07	4♉33 14	12♉02 03	29 20.1	28 05.2	15 10.6	4 21.6	12 06.2	13 35.8	22 16.5	7 54.3	12 59.4	18 30.5

December 1990 — LONGITUDE

Day	Sid.Time	☉	0 hr ☽	Noon ☽	True ☊	☿	♀	♂	⚳	♃	♄	♅	♆	♇
1 Sa	16 40 21	9♐01 54	19♉35 37	27♉12 43	29♑12.0	29♐21.8	16♐25.9	3♊59.7	12♎29.6	13♌35.6	22♑22.3	7♑57.5	13♑01.3	18♏32.8
2 Su	16 44 17	10 02 42	4♊52 01	12♊32 06	29R 04.7	0♑36.3	17 41.3	3R 38.1	12 52.8	13R 35.3	22 28.1	8 00.8	13 03.3	18 35.1
3 M	16 48 14	11 03 31	20 11 31	27 48 55	28 59.2	1 48.5	18 56.6	3 16.9	13 16.0	13 34.7	22 34.0	8 04.1	13 05.3	18 37.4
4 Tu	16 52 10	12 04 22	5♋23 01	12♋52 42	28 56.0	2 58.0	20 12.0	2 56.1	13 39.1	13 34.0	22 39.9	8 07.4	13 07.3	18 39.7
5 W	16 56 07	13 05 14	20 17 03	27 35 22	28D 54.9	4 04.2	21 27.3	2 35.7	14 02.0	13 33.0	22 45.9	8 10.7	13 09.3	18 42.0
6 Th	17 00 04	14 06 07	4♌47 10	11♌52 09	28 55.4	5 06.9	22 42.7	2 15.8	14 24.8	13 31.9	22 52.0	8 14.1	13 11.3	18 44.2
7 F	17 04 00	15 07 01	18 50 14	25 41 29	28 56.8	6 05.4	23 58.0	1 56.4	14 47.6	13 30.5	22 58.1	8 17.4	13 13.4	18 46.4
8 Sa	17 07 57	16 07 56	2♍26 05	9♍04 22	28R 57.9	6 59.1	25 13.3	1 37.5	15 10.1	13 29.0	23 04.2	8 20.8	13 15.4	18 48.7
9 Su	17 11 53	17 08 53	15 36 41	22 03 30	28 58.0	7 47.4	26 28.7	1 19.2	15 32.6	13 27.3	23 10.4	8 24.2	13 17.5	18 50.9
10 M	17 15 50	18 09 51	28 25 18	4♎42 33	28 56.5	8 29.6	27 44.0	1 01.5	15 54.9	13 25.3	23 16.6	8 27.6	13 19.6	18 53.1
11 Tu	17 19 46	19 10 50	10♎55 46	17 05 26	28 53.1	9 04.7	28 59.4	0 44.4	16 17.1	13 23.2	23 22.9	8 31.1	13 21.7	18 55.2
12 W	17 23 43	20 11 50	23 11 59	29 15 54	28 47.9	9 32.1	0♑14.7	0 28.1	16 39.2	13 20.9	23 29.2	8 34.5	13 23.8	18 57.4
13 Th	17 27 39	21 12 52	5♏17 33	11♏17 20	28 41.3	9 50.7	1 30.1	0 12.4	17 01.1	13 18.4	23 35.6	8 38.0	13 26.0	18 59.5
14 F	17 31 36	22 13 54	17 15 35	23 12 37	28 34.1	9R 59.8	2 45.4	29♉57.4	17 22.9	13 15.6	23 42.0	8 41.5	13 28.1	19 01.7
15 Sa	17 35 33	23 14 57	29 08 43	5♐04 09	28 27.0	9 58.5	4 00.8	29 43.2	17 44.6	13 12.7	23 48.5	8 45.0	13 30.3	19 03.8
16 Su	17 39 29	24 16 01	10♐59 08	16 53 54	28 20.7	9 46.1	5 16.1	29 29.7	18 06.1	13 09.6	23 55.0	8 48.5	13 32.4	19 05.9
17 M	17 43 26	25 17 06	22 48 41	28 43 41	28 15.7	9 22.3	6 31.5	29 17.1	18 27.4	13 06.4	24 01.5	8 52.0	13 34.6	19 07.9
18 Tu	17 47 22	26 18 11	4♑39 07	10♑35 14	28 12.4	8 46.8	7 46.8	29 05.2	18 48.6	13 02.9	24 08.1	8 55.5	13 36.8	19 10.0
19 W	17 51 19	27 19 17	16 32 17	22 30 32	28D 10.9	7 59.8	9 02.2	28 54.1	19 09.7	12 59.2	24 14.7	8 59.0	13 39.0	19 12.0
20 Th	17 55 15	28 20 24	28 30 17	4♒31 51	28 10.9	7 02.3	10 17.5	28 43.8	19 30.6	12 55.4	24 21.3	9 02.6	13 41.2	19 14.0
21 F	17 59 12	29 21 30	10♒35 36	16 41 55	28 12.1	5 55.3	11 32.8	28 34.4	19 51.3	12 51.4	24 28.0	9 06.2	13 43.4	19 16.0
22 Sa	18 03 08	0♑22 37	22 51 12	29 03 56	28 13.8	4 40.8	12 48.2	28 25.8	20 11.9	12 47.2	24 34.7	9 09.7	13 45.6	19 18.0
23 Su	18 07 05	1 23 44	5♓20 31	11♓41 28	28 15.5	3 21.1	14 03.5	28 18.0	20 32.3	12 42.8	24 41.4	9 13.3	13 47.8	19 19.9
24 M	18 11 02	2 24 52	18 07 12	24 38 12	28R 16.7	1 58.8	15 18.8	28 11.1	20 52.5	12 38.3	24 48.2	9 16.9	13 50.1	19 21.8
25 Tu	18 14 58	3 25 59	1♈14 51	7♈57 30	28 16.8	0 36.7	16 34.1	28 05.0	21 12.6	12 33.5	24 55.0	9 20.4	13 52.3	19 23.7
26 W	18 18 55	4 27 07	14 46 27	21 41 52	28 15.8	29♐17.4	17 49.4	27 59.7	21 32.5	12 28.6	25 01.8	9 24.0	13 54.6	19 25.6
27 Th	18 22 51	5 28 14	28 43 47	5♉52 07	28 13.7	28 03.5	19 04.6	27 55.2	21 52.2	12 23.6	25 08.7	9 27.6	13 56.8	19 27.5
28 F	18 26 48	6 29 22	13♉06 35	20 26 44	28 11.0	26 56.8	20 19.9	27 51.6	22 11.8	12 18.4	25 15.5	9 31.2	13 59.1	19 29.3
29 Sa	18 30 44	7 30 29	27 51 56	5♊21 22	28 08.0	25 59.1	21 35.2	27 48.8	22 31.1	12 13.0	25 22.4	9 34.8	14 01.3	19 31.1
30 Su	18 34 41	8 31 37	12♊54 04	20 28 54	28 05.4	25 11.1	22 50.4	27 46.8	22 50.3	12 07.5	25 29.3	9 38.4	14 03.6	19 32.9
31 M	18 38 38	9 32 45	28 04 40	5♋40 07	28 03.5	24 33.6	24 05.7	27 45.6	23 09.3	12 01.8	25 36.3	9 42.0	14 05.9	19 34.6

Astro Data

	Dy Hr Mn
☽ 0S	12 4:05
☽ 0N	26 21:45
♃ R	30 5:03
☽ 0S	9 9:15
♃⚻♆	11 20:13
☿ R	14 21:10
☽ 0N	24 4:10

Planet Ingress

	Dy Hr Mn
⚳ ♎	1 4:12
☿ ♐	11 0:06
♀ ♐	18 9:58
☊ ♑R	18 19:23
☉ ♐	22 13:47
☿ ♑	2 0:13
♀ ♑	12 7:18
♂ ♉R	14 7:46
☉ ♑	22 3:07
☿ ♐R	25 22:57

Last Aspect / ☽ Ingress (November)

Last Aspect Dy Hr Mn		☽ Ingress Dy Hr Mn
1 13:19	♄ □	♉ 2 5:31
3 13:25	♄ △	♊ 4 5:06
5 1:30	♂ ☌	♋ 6 5:07
7 23:27	☿ △	♌ 8 7:24
10 11:19	☿ □	♍ 10 12:48
12 6:24	♀ ⚹	♎ 12 21:08
14 13:40	♄ □	♏ 15 7:39
17 17:58	♀ ☌	♐ 17 19:39
18 22:46	♃ △	♑ 20 8:31
22 4:06	♄ ☌	♒ 22 21:07
24 12:17	☿ ⚹	♓ 25 7:32
27 2:45	☿ □	♈ 27 14:06
29 11:18	☿ △	♉ 29 16:37

Last Aspect / ☽ Ingress (December)

Last Aspect Dy Hr Mn		☽ Ingress Dy Hr Mn
1 4:20	♄ △	♊ 1 16:23
2 20:48	♀ ☍	♋ 3 15:27
5 4:00	♄ ☍	♌ 5 16:00
7 8:39	♀ △	♍ 7 19:39
9 21:14	♀ □	♎ 10 3:00
12 0:28	♄ □	♏ 12 13:28
15 1:22	♂ ☍	♐ 15 1:44
17 4:22	☉ ☌	♑ 17 14:35
20 0:37	♂ △	♒ 20 2:59
22 10:47	♂ □	♓ 22 13:48
24 18:25	♂ ⚹	♈ 24 21:45
26 23:54	☿ △	♉ 27 2:09
28 23:57	♂ ☌	♊ 29 3:26
30 19:07	☿ ☍	♋ 31 3:02

☽ Phases & Eclipses

Dy Hr Mn	
2 21:48	○ 10♉13
9 13:02	☾ 16♌52
17 9:05	● 24♏45
25 13:11	☽ 3♓00
2 7:50	○ 9♊52
9 2:04	☾ 16♍44
17 4:22	● 24♐58
25 3:16	☽ 3♈04
31 18:35	○ 9♋50

Astro Data

1 November 1990
Julian Day # 33177
SVP 5♓23'03"
GC 26♐42.7 ⚳ 4♍23.7
Eris 16♈49.3R ⚵ 4♐42.0
⚷ 27♋17.8 ⚶ 26♉47.8R
☽ Mean ☊ 2♒20.2

1 December 1990
Julian Day # 33207
SVP 5♓22'58"
GC 26♐42.7 ⚳ 16♍35.2
Eris 16♈35.3R ⚵ 14♐58.3
⚷ 26♋54.6R ⚶ 19♉17.5R
☽ Mean ☊ 0♒44.9

LONGITUDE — January 1991

Day	Sid.Time	☉	0 hr ☽	Noon ☽	True ☊	☿	♀	♂	⚳	♃	♄	♅	♆	♇
1 Tu	18 42 34	10♑33 53	13♋14 02	20♋45 11	28♑02.5	24♐06.5	25♑20.9	27♉45.2	23♎28.1	11♌56.0	25♑43.3	9♑45.6	14♑08.1	19♏36.3
2 W	18 46 31	11 35 01	28 12 31	5♌35 04	28D02.5	23R49.7	26 36.1	27D45.6	23 46.7	11R50.1	25 50.2	9 49.2	14 10.4	19 38.0
3 Th	18 50 27	12 36 09	12♌52 04	20 02 55	28 03.3	23D42.7	27 51.4	27 46.7	24 05.1	11 43.9	25 57.2	9 52.8	14 12.7	19 39.7
4 F	18 54 24	13 37 17	27 07 11	4♍04 37	28 04.5	23 45.0	29 06.6	27 48.6	24 23.3	11 37.7	26 04.3	9 56.4	14 15.0	19 41.4
5 Sa	18 58 20	14 38 25	10♍55 10	17 38 54	28 05.7	23 55.8	0♒21.8	27 51.2	24 41.3	11 31.3	26 11.3	10 00.0	14 17.2	19 43.0
6 Su	19 02 17	15 39 34	24 16 01	0♎46 50	28 06.6	24 14.6	1 37.0	27 54.5	24 59.1	11 24.8	26 18.3	10 03.5	14 19.5	19 44.6
7 M	19 06 13	16 40 43	7♎11 44	13 31 12	28R07.0	24 40.4	2 52.1	27 58.6	25 16.7	11 18.2	26 25.4	10 07.1	14 21.8	19 46.1
8 Tu	19 10 10	17 41 52	19 45 44	25 55 53	28 06.9	25 12.8	4 07.3	28 03.4	25 34.0	11 11.4	26 32.5	10 10.7	14 24.1	19 47.7
9 W	19 14 07	18 43 01	2♏02 11	8♏05 12	28 06.3	25 50.9	5 22.5	28 08.9	25 51.2	11 04.6	26 39.6	10 14.3	14 26.3	19 49.2
10 Th	19 18 03	19 44 10	14 05 29	20 03 36	28 05.4	26 34.3	6 37.6	28 15.2	26 08.1	10 57.6	26 46.7	10 17.8	14 28.6	19 50.6
11 F	19 22 00	20 45 19	26 00 02	1♐55 17	28 04.3	27 22.4	7 52.8	28 22.0	26 24.8	10 50.5	26 53.8	10 21.4	14 30.9	19 52.1
12 Sa	19 25 56	21 46 28	7♐49 49	13 44 04	28 03.3	28 14.7	9 07.9	28 29.6	26 41.2	10 43.3	27 00.9	10 24.9	14 33.1	19 53.5
13 Su	19 29 53	22 47 37	19 38 25	25 33 16	28 02.4	29 10.7	10 23.0	28 37.8	26 57.4	10 36.1	27 08.0	10 28.5	14 35.4	19 54.9
14 M	19 33 49	23 48 46	1♑28 54	7♑25 40	28 01.9	0♑10.0	11 38.2	28 46.7	27 13.4	10 28.7	27 15.1	10 32.0	14 37.6	19 56.3
15 Tu	19 37 46	24 49 54	13 23 49	19 23 36	28D01.7	1 12.4	12 53.3	28 56.2	27 29.1	10 21.2	27 22.3	10 35.5	14 39.9	19 57.6
16 W	19 41 42	25 51 02	25 25 15	1♒28 58	28 01.6	2 17.5	14 08.3	29 06.3	27 44.6	10 13.7	27 29.4	10 39.1	14 42.1	19 58.9
17 Th	19 45 39	26 52 10	7♒34 57	13 43 24	28 01.7	3 25.0	15 23.4	29 17.1	27 59.8	10 06.1	27 36.6	10 42.6	14 44.4	20 00.1
18 F	19 49 36	27 53 16	19 54 28	26 08 22	28R01.8	4 34.8	16 38.5	29 28.4	28 14.8	9 58.4	27 43.7	10 46.0	14 46.6	20 01.4
19 Sa	19 53 32	28 54 22	2♓25 16	8♓45 22	28 01.7	5 46.5	17 53.5	29 40.4	28 29.5	9 50.7	27 50.8	10 49.5	14 48.8	20 02.6
20 Su	19 57 29	29 55 27	15 08 49	21 35 51	28 01.5	7 00.0	19 08.5	29 52.9	28 43.9	9 42.9	27 58.0	10 53.0	14 51.1	20 03.7
21 M	20 01 25	0♒56 32	28 06 38	4♈41 23	28 01.3	8 15.2	20 23.5	0♊05.9	28 58.0	9 35.1	28 05.1	10 56.4	14 53.3	20 04.8
22 Tu	20 05 22	1 57 35	11♈20 15	18 03 25	28 01.0	9 31.9	21 38.5	0 19.5	29 11.9	9 27.2	28 12.2	10 59.8	14 55.5	20 05.9
23 W	20 09 18	2 58 38	24 50 59	1♉43 05	28D00.9	10 50.0	22 53.4	0 33.7	29 25.5	9 19.2	28 19.4	11 03.2	14 57.7	20 07.0
24 Th	20 13 15	3 59 39	8♉39 43	15 40 52	28 01.0	12 09.3	24 08.3	0 48.3	29 38.8	9 11.3	28 26.5	11 06.6	14 59.8	20 08.0
25 F	20 17 11	5 00 40	22 46 25	29 56 08	28 01.4	13 29.9	25 23.3	1 03.5	29 51.9	9 03.3	28 33.6	11 10.0	15 02.0	20 09.0
26 Sa	20 21 08	6 01 39	7♊09 45	14♊26 47	28 02.1	14 51.7	26 38.1	1 19.2	0♏04.6	8 55.3	28 40.7	11 13.4	15 04.2	20 10.0
27 Su	20 25 05	7 02 37	21 46 44	29 08 57	28 02.8	16 14.4	27 53.0	1 35.3	0 17.0	8 47.3	28 47.8	11 16.7	15 06.3	20 10.9
28 M	20 29 01	8 03 35	6♋32 39	13♋57 03	28R03.5	17 38.2	29 07.8	1 52.0	0 29.2	8 39.3	28 54.9	11 20.0	15 08.5	20 11.8
29 Tu	20 32 58	9 04 31	21 21 13	28 44 16	28 03.7	19 03.0	0♓22.6	2 09.0	0 41.0	8 31.3	29 02.0	11 23.3	15 10.6	20 12.7
30 W	20 36 54	10 05 26	6♌05 15	13♌23 19	28 03.4	20 28.7	1 37.4	2 26.6	0 52.6	8 23.3	29 09.0	11 26.6	15 12.7	20 13.5
31 Th	20 40 51	11 06 20	20 37 36	27 47 23	28 02.3	21 55.3	2 52.2	2 44.5	1 03.8	8 15.3	29 16.1	11 29.8	15 14.8	20 14.3

LONGITUDE — February 1991

Day	Sid.Time	☉	0 hr ☽	Noon ☽	True ☊	☿	♀	♂	⚳	♃	♄	♅	♆	♇
1 F	20 44 47	12♒07 13	4♍52 02	11♍51 05	28♑00.7	23♑22.7	4♓06.9	3♊02.9	1♏14.7	8♌07.3	29♑23.1	11♑33.1	15♑16.9	20♏15.0
2 Sa	20 48 44	13 08 05	18 44 09	25 31 03	27R58.6	24 51.0	5 21.6	3 21.7	1 25.3	7R59.3	29 30.1	11 36.3	15 19.0	20 15.8
3 Su	20 52 40	14 08 57	2♎11 42	8♎46 09	27 56.4	26 20.1	6 36.2	3 40.8	1 35.5	7 51.4	29 37.1	11 39.4	15 21.0	20 16.4
4 M	20 56 37	15 09 47	15 14 36	21 37 20	27 54.4	27 50.0	7 50.9	4 00.4	1 45.4	7 43.5	29 44.1	11 42.6	15 23.1	20 17.1
5 Tu	21 00 34	16 10 37	27 54 44	4♏07 14	27 53.1	29 20.7	9 05.5	4 20.4	1 55.0	7 35.6	29 51.1	11 45.7	15 25.1	20 17.7
6 W	21 04 30	17 11 25	10♏15 22	16 19 41	27D52.5	0♒52.2	10 20.1	4 40.7	2 04.3	7 27.8	29 58.0	11 48.8	15 27.1	20 18.3
7 Th	21 08 27	18 12 13	22 20 47	28 19 16	27 52.9	2 24.5	11 34.7	5 01.4	2 13.1	7 20.0	0♒04.9	11 51.9	15 29.1	20 18.8
8 F	21 12 23	19 13 00	4♐15 45	10♐10 52	27 54.1	3 57.6	12 49.2	5 22.5	2 21.7	7 12.3	0 11.8	11 55.0	15 31.1	20 19.3
9 Sa	21 16 20	20 13 46	16 05 13	21 59 22	27 55.8	5 31.5	14 03.7	5 43.9	2 29.9	7 04.6	0 18.7	11 58.0	15 33.0	20 19.8
10 Su	21 20 16	21 14 31	27 53 55	3♑49 23	27 57.6	7 06.2	15 18.2	6 05.7	2 37.7	6 57.0	0 25.6	12 01.0	15 35.0	20 20.2
11 M	21 24 13	22 15 15	9♑46 16	15 45 02	27 59.0	8 41.7	16 32.6	6 27.8	2 45.2	6 49.5	0 32.4	12 04.0	15 36.9	20 20.6
12 Tu	21 28 09	23 15 57	21 46 05	27 49 47	27R59.5	10 18.1	17 47.0	6 50.2	2 52.2	6 42.0	0 39.2	12 06.9	15 38.8	20 21.0
13 W	21 32 06	24 16 39	3♒56 26	10♒06 19	27 58.9	11 55.2	19 01.4	7 13.0	2 59.0	6 34.7	0 46.0	12 09.8	15 40.7	20 21.3
14 Th	21 36 03	25 17 19	16 19 36	22 36 27	27 56.9	13 33.2	20 15.8	7 36.1	3 05.3	6 27.4	0 52.7	12 12.7	15 42.6	20 21.6
15 F	21 39 59	26 17 57	28 56 56	5♓21 05	27 53.4	15 12.0	21 30.1	7 59.4	3 11.2	6 20.2	0 59.4	12 15.5	15 44.4	20 21.9
16 Sa	21 43 56	27 18 34	11♓48 54	18 20 19	27 48.9	16 51.8	22 44.4	8 23.1	3 16.8	6 13.2	1 06.1	12 18.3	15 46.2	20 22.1
17 Su	21 47 52	28 19 09	24 55 14	1♈33 33	27 43.8	18 32.3	23 58.6	8 47.1	3 22.0	6 06.2	1 12.7	12 21.1	15 48.0	20 22.3
18 M	21 51 49	29 19 43	8♈15 05	14 59 43	27 38.7	20 13.8	25 12.8	9 11.3	3 26.7	5 59.3	1 19.3	12 23.8	15 49.8	20 22.4
19 Tu	21 55 45	0♓20 15	21 47 15	28 37 34	27 34.4	21 56.2	26 26.9	9 35.8	3 31.1	5 52.6	1 25.9	12 26.5	15 51.6	20 22.5
20 W	21 59 42	1 20 45	5♉30 28	12♉25 49	27 31.3	23 39.5	27 41.1	10 00.6	3 35.1	5 45.9	1 32.4	12 29.2	15 53.3	20 22.6
21 Th	22 03 38	2 21 13	19 23 28	26 23 17	27D29.9	25 23.7	28 55.1	10 25.7	3 38.6	5 39.4	1 38.9	12 31.8	15 55.1	20R22.6
22 F	22 07 35	3 21 40	3♊25 07	10♊28 50	27 29.9	27 08.9	0♈09.2	10 51.0	3 41.8	5 33.1	1 45.4	12 34.4	15 56.7	20 22.6
23 Sa	22 11 32	4 22 04	17 34 14	24 41 09	27 31.0	28 55.0	1 23.1	11 16.6	3 44.6	5 26.8	1 51.8	12 37.0	15 58.4	20 22.6
24 Su	22 15 28	5 22 27	1♋49 19	8♋58 30	27 32.5	0♓42.1	2 37.1	11 42.4	3 46.9	5 20.7	1 58.1	12 39.5	16 00.1	20 22.5
25 M	22 19 25	6 22 47	16 08 19	23 18 25	27R33.5	2 30.2	3 51.0	12 08.4	3 48.9	5 14.8	2 04.5	12 42.0	16 01.7	20 22.4
26 Tu	22 23 21	7 23 06	0♌28 19	7♌37 33	27 33.1	4 19.2	5 04.8	12 34.7	3 50.4	5 09.0	2 10.8	12 44.5	16 03.3	20 22.3
27 W	22 27 18	8 23 23	14 45 33	21 51 44	27 30.9	6 09.2	6 18.6	13 01.2	3 51.5	5 03.3	2 17.0	12 46.9	16 04.9	20 22.1
28 Th	22 31 14	9 23 38	28 55 32	5♍56 21	27 26.6	8 00.1	7 32.3	13 27.9	3 52.2	4 57.7	2 23.2	12 49.2	16 06.4	20 21.9

Astro Data

	Dy Hr Mn
♂ D	1 12:49
☿ D	3 17:52
☽ 0S	5 16:47
⚳0S	8 12:39
♃⚻♅	14 4:40
☽ 0N	20 9:33
☽ 0S	2 2:46
☽ 0N	16 15:44
♇ R	22 1:29
♀0N	24 5:30

Planet Ingress

		Dy Hr Mn
♀	♒	5 5:03
☿	♑	14 8:02
☉	♒	20 13:47
♂	♊	21 1:15
⚳	♏	26 3:17
♀	♓	29 4:44
☿	♒	5 22:20
♄	♒	6 18:51
☉	♓	19 3:58
♀	♈	22 9:02
☿	♓	24 2:35

Last Aspect / ☽ Ingress (January)

Last Aspect Dy Hr Mn		☽ Ingress Dy Hr Mn
1 23:16 ♂ ✶	♌	2 2:54
4 1:09 ♂ □	♍	4 4:57
6 6:40 ♂ △	♎	6 10:33
8 13:12 ♄ □	♏	8 19:59
11 4:43 ♂ ☍	♐	11 8:06
13 20:00 ☿ ☌	♑	13 21:00
16 7:14 ♂ △	♒	16 9:04
18 18:29 ♂ □	♓	18 19:23
20 23:51 ♄ ✶	♈	21 3:28
23 6:02 ♄ □	♉	23 9:01
25 9:41 ♄ △	♊	25 12:06
27 9:45 ♀ △	♋	27 13:23
29 12:29 ♄ ☍	♌	29 14:03
30 23:21 ♇ □	♍	31 15:44

Last Aspect / ☽ Ingress (February)

Last Aspect Dy Hr Mn		☽ Ingress Dy Hr Mn
2 19:12 ♄ △	♎	2 20:02
5 3:39 ♄ □	♏	5 4:01
6 19:55 ♇ ☌	♐	7 15:23
9 8:05 ☉ ✶	♑	10 4:16
11 21:10 ♇ ✶	♒	12 16:16
14 17:32 ☉ ☌	♓	15 1:59
16 20:52 ♀ ☌	♈	17 9:11
18 22:35 ☿ ✶	♉	19 14:24
21 16:45 ♀ ✶	♊	21 18:10
23 20:08 ☿ △	♋	23 20:56
25 7:05 ♇ △	♌	25 23:13
27 9:28 ♇ □	♍	28 1:50

☽ Phases & Eclipses

Dy Hr Mn	
7 18:36	☾ 16♎58
15 23:50	● 25♑20
15 23:52:53	◐ A 07'36"
23 14:21	☽ 3♉05
30 6:10	○ 9♌51
30 5:59	◐ A 0.881
6 13:52	☾ 17♏16
14 17:32	● 25♒31
21 22:58	☽ 2♊49
28 18:25	○ 9♍40

Astro Data

1 January 1991
Julian Day # 33238
SVP 5♓22'52"
GC 26♐42.8 ⚴ 24♍17.3
Eris 16♈29.1R ⚵ 25♐54.6
⚷ 25♋14.4R ⚶ 15♉33.6R
☽ Mean ☊ 29♑06.4

1 February 1991
Julian Day # 33269
SVP 5♓22'47"
GC 26♐42.9 ⚴ 24♍11.2R
Eris 16♈33.4 ⚵ 6♑38.4
⚷ 23♋04.2R ⚶ 18♉31.1
☽ Mean ☊ 27♑27.9

March 1991

LONGITUDE

Day	Sid.Time	☉	0 hr ☽	Noon ☽	True ☊	☿	♀	♂	⚳	♃	♄	♅	♆	♇
1 F	22 35 11	10♓23 51	12♍53 39	19♍46 54	27♑20.4	9♓52.0	8♈46.0	13♊54.8	3♏52.5	4♌52.4	2♒29.4	12♑51.6	16♑07.9	20♏21.6
2 Sa	22 39 07	11 24 02	26 35 41	3♎19 38	27R12.9	11 44.8	9 59.6	14 21.9	3R52.3	4R47.2	2 35.5	12 53.8	16 09.4	20R21.4
3 Su	22 43 04	12 24 12	9♎58 32	16 32 13	27 04.9	13 38.4	11 13.2	14 49.2	3 51.7	4 42.1	2 41.5	12 56.1	16 10.9	20 21.0
4 M	22 47 01	13 24 20	23 00 40	29 23 57	26 57.3	15 32.8	12 26.7	15 16.7	3 50.7	4 37.2	2 47.5	12 58.3	16 12.3	20 20.7
5 Tu	22 50 57	14 24 26	5♏42 16	11♏55 52	26 50.9	17 28.0	13 40.2	15 44.4	3 49.3	4 32.5	2 53.5	13 00.5	16 13.8	20 20.3
6 W	22 54 54	15 24 31	18 05 10	24 10 34	26 46.4	19 23.9	14 53.6	16 12.3	3 47.5	4 27.9	2 59.4	13 02.6	16 15.1	20 19.9
7 Th	22 58 50	16 24 34	0♐12 36	6♐11 50	26D43.8	21 20.3	16 07.0	16 40.3	3 45.2	4 23.5	3 05.2	13 04.7	16 16.5	20 19.4
8 F	23 02 47	17 24 36	12 08 53	18 04 21	26 43.1	23 17.1	17 20.3	17 08.6	3 42.5	4 19.3	3 11.0	13 06.7	16 17.8	20 19.0
9 Sa	23 06 43	18 24 36	23 58 56	29 53 17	26 43.7	25 14.1	18 33.6	17 37.0	3 39.3	4 15.2	3 16.8	13 08.7	16 19.2	20 18.4
10 Su	23 10 40	19 24 35	5♑48 04	11♑43 57	26 44.9	27 11.2	19 46.8	18 05.6	3 35.8	4 11.3	3 22.5	13 10.6	16 20.4	20 17.9
11 M	23 14 36	20 24 32	17 41 34	23 41 31	26R45.8	29 08.2	21 00.0	18 34.4	3 31.8	4 07.6	3 28.1	13 12.6	16 21.7	20 17.3
12 Tu	23 18 33	21 24 27	29 44 25	5♒50 44	26 45.3	1♈04.7	22 13.1	19 03.3	3 27.4	4 04.1	3 33.7	13 14.4	16 22.9	20 16.7
13 W	23 22 30	22 24 20	12♒00 58	18 15 30	26 42.9	3 00.4	23 26.1	19 32.4	3 22.6	4 00.8	3 39.2	13 16.2	16 24.1	20 16.0
14 Th	23 26 26	23 24 12	24 34 38	0♓58 35	26 38.1	4 55.1	24 39.1	20 01.6	3 17.3	3 57.6	3 44.7	13 18.0	16 25.3	20 15.4
15 F	23 30 23	24 24 01	7♓27 28	14 01 18	26 30.9	6 48.4	25 52.1	20 31.0	3 11.7	3 54.6	3 50.1	13 19.7	16 26.4	20 14.7
16 Sa	23 34 19	25 23 49	20 40 00	27 23 21	26 21.7	8 39.9	27 04.9	21 00.6	3 05.6	3 51.8	3 55.4	13 21.4	16 27.5	20 13.9
17 Su	23 38 16	26 23 35	4♈11 03	11♈02 45	26 11.4	10 29.0	28 17.7	21 30.3	2 59.2	3 49.3	4 00.7	13 23.0	16 28.6	20 13.1
18 M	23 42 12	27 23 18	17 57 57	24 56 10	26 01.1	12 15.5	29 30.5	22 00.2	2 52.3	3 46.8	4 05.9	13 24.6	16 29.6	20 12.3
19 Tu	23 46 09	28 23 00	1♉56 52	8♉59 29	25 52.0	13 58.8	0♉43.2	22 30.2	2 45.1	3 44.6	4 11.0	13 26.1	16 30.6	20 11.5
20 W	23 50 05	29 22 39	16 03 31	23 08 26	25 44.9	15 38.4	1 55.8	23 00.3	2 37.5	3 42.6	4 16.1	13 27.6	16 31.6	20 10.6
21 Th	23 54 02	0♈22 16	0♊13 50	7♊19 18	25 40.3	17 13.9	3 08.3	23 30.6	2 29.5	3 40.8	4 21.1	13 29.1	16 32.5	20 09.7
22 F	23 57 59	1 21 51	14 24 32	21 29 16	25D38.1	18 44.9	4 20.8	24 01.0	2 21.1	3 39.1	4 26.0	13 30.4	16 33.4	20 08.8
23 Sa	0 01 55	2 21 24	28 33 18	5♋36 31	25 37.8	20 10.8	5 33.2	24 31.5	2 12.4	3 37.7	4 30.9	13 31.8	16 34.3	20 07.9
24 Su	0 05 52	3 20 54	12♋38 46	19 39 59	25R38.2	21 31.3	6 45.5	25 02.2	2 03.3	3 36.4	4 35.7	13 33.1	16 35.2	20 06.9
25 M	0 09 48	4 20 22	26 40 05	3♌38 59	25 38.1	22 46.1	7 57.8	25 32.9	1 53.9	3 35.4	4 40.4	13 34.3	16 36.0	20 05.9
26 Tu	0 13 45	5 19 48	10♌36 32	17 32 38	25 36.2	23 54.7	9 09.9	26 03.8	1 44.2	3 34.5	4 45.1	13 35.5	16 36.8	20 04.8
27 W	0 17 41	6 19 11	24 27 05	1♍19 39	25 31.9	24 56.9	10 22.0	26 34.8	1 34.1	3 33.8	4 49.7	13 36.7	16 37.6	20 03.8
28 Th	0 21 38	7 18 32	8♍10 06	14 58 09	25 24.7	25 52.3	11 34.0	27 06.0	1 23.7	3 33.3	4 54.2	13 37.7	16 38.3	20 02.7
29 F	0 25 34	8 17 50	21 43 29	28 25 49	25 14.8	26 40.9	12 46.0	27 37.2	1 13.1	3 33.0	4 58.6	13 38.8	16 39.0	20 01.6
30 Sa	0 29 31	9 17 07	5♎04 49	11♎40 16	25 02.9	27 22.4	13 57.8	28 08.5	1 02.1	3D32.9	5 03.0	13 39.8	16 39.6	20 00.4
31 Su	0 33 27	10 16 22	18 11 54	24 39 33	24 50.2	27 56.7	15 09.6	28 39.9	0 50.9	3 33.0	5 07.3	13 40.7	16 40.3	19 59.3

April 1991

LONGITUDE

Day	Sid.Time	☉	0 hr ☽	Noon ☽	True ☊	☿	♀	♂	⚳	♃	♄	♅	♆	♇
1 M	0 37 24	11♈15 34	1♏03 07	7♏22 36	24♑37.9	28♈23.7	16♉21.3	29♊11.4	0♏39.4	3♌33.3	5♒11.5	13♑41.6	16♑40.8	19♏58.1
2 Tu	0 41 21	12 14 45	13 38 01	19 49 31	24R26.9	28 43.4	17 32.9	29 43.1	0R27.7	3 33.8	5 15.6	13 42.5	16 41.4	19R56.9
3 W	0 45 17	13 13 54	25 57 19	2♐01 45	24 18.3	28 55.8	18 44.4	0♋14.8	0 15.7	3 34.4	5 19.7	13 43.2	16 41.9	19 55.6
4 Th	0 49 14	14 13 01	8♐03 09	14 02 00	24 12.2	29R01.1	19 55.8	0 46.6	0 03.5	3 35.3	5 23.7	13 44.0	16 42.4	19 54.4
5 F	0 53 10	15 12 07	19 58 47	25 54 05	24 08.8	28 59.5	21 07.2	1 18.5	29♎51.0	3 36.3	5 27.6	13 44.7	16 42.9	19 53.1
6 Sa	0 57 07	16 11 10	1♑48 29	7♑42 39	24D07.4	28 51.1	22 18.4	1 50.6	29 38.4	3 37.5	5 31.4	13 45.3	16 43.3	19 51.8
7 Su	1 01 03	17 10 12	13 37 15	19 32 57	24R07.2	28 36.3	23 29.6	2 22.7	29 25.6	3 38.9	5 35.1	13 45.9	16 43.7	19 50.5
8 M	1 05 00	18 09 12	25 30 29	1♒30 30	24 07.1	28 15.6	24 40.7	2 54.9	29 12.7	3 40.5	5 38.8	13 46.4	16 44.1	19 49.1
9 Tu	1 08 56	19 08 11	7♒33 42	13 40 44	24 06.0	27 49.4	25 51.7	3 27.1	28 59.6	3 42.3	5 42.4	13 46.9	16 44.4	19 47.8
10 W	1 12 53	20 07 07	19 52 12	26 08 37	24 03.0	27 18.3	27 02.6	3 59.5	28 46.3	3 44.3	5 45.8	13 47.4	16 44.7	19 46.4
11 Th	1 16 50	21 06 02	2♓30 29	8♓58 08	23 57.3	26 43.1	28 13.4	4 32.0	28 33.0	3 46.4	5 49.3	13 47.7	16 45.0	19 45.0
12 F	1 20 46	22 04 54	15 31 50	22 11 42	23 49.0	26 04.4	29 24.2	5 04.5	28 19.5	3 48.7	5 52.6	13 48.1	16 45.2	19 43.6
13 Sa	1 24 43	23 03 45	28 57 43	5♈49 43	23 38.4	25 23.0	0♊34.8	5 37.1	28 06.0	3 51.2	5 55.8	13 48.3	16 45.4	19 42.1
14 Su	1 28 39	24 02 34	12♈47 21	19 50 09	23 26.4	24 39.8	1 45.3	6 09.8	27 52.4	3 53.9	5 58.9	13 48.6	16 45.6	19 40.7
15 M	1 32 36	25 01 22	26 57 28	4♉08 35	23 14.4	23 55.7	2 55.8	6 42.6	27 38.7	3 56.8	6 02.0	13 48.7	16 45.7	19 39.2
16 Tu	1 36 32	26 00 07	11♉22 40	18 38 50	23 03.5	23 11.3	4 06.1	7 15.5	27 25.0	3 59.9	6 05.0	13 48.9	16 45.8	19 37.7
17 W	1 40 29	26 58 50	25 56 12	3♊13 54	22 54.8	22 27.7	5 16.3	7 48.4	27 11.3	4 03.1	6 07.8	13R48.9	16 45.9	19 36.2
18 Th	1 44 25	27 57 31	10♊31 07	17 47 09	22 49.0	21 45.4	6 26.4	8 21.5	26 57.7	4 06.5	6 10.6	13 49.0	16R45.9	19 34.7
19 F	1 48 22	28 56 10	25 01 23	2♋13 20	22 45.9	21 05.4	7 36.5	8 54.6	26 44.0	4 10.1	6 13.3	13 48.9	16 45.9	19 33.2
20 Sa	1 52 19	29 54 47	9♋22 37	16 29 00	22D44.9	20 28.1	8 46.4	9 27.7	26 30.4	4 13.8	6 15.9	13 48.8	16 45.9	19 31.6
21 Su	1 56 15	0♉53 21	23 32 18	0♌32 27	22R44.9	19 54.2	9 56.1	10 01.0	26 16.9	4 17.7	6 18.5	13 48.7	16 45.8	19 30.1
22 M	2 00 12	1 51 53	7♌29 27	14 23 19	22 44.5	19 24.0	11 05.8	10 34.3	26 03.4	4 21.8	6 20.9	13 48.5	16 45.7	19 28.5
23 Tu	2 04 08	2 50 23	21 14 09	28 02 01	22 42.5	18 58.1	12 15.3	11 07.6	25 50.0	4 26.1	6 23.2	13 48.3	16 45.6	19 26.9
24 W	2 08 05	3 48 51	4♍46 58	11♍29 04	22 38.1	18 36.7	13 24.8	11 41.1	25 36.7	4 30.5	6 25.4	13 48.0	16 45.4	19 25.3
25 Th	2 12 01	4 47 16	18 08 21	24 44 50	22 30.9	18 19.9	14 34.0	12 14.6	25 23.6	4 35.1	6 27.6	13 47.7	16 45.2	19 23.7
26 F	2 15 58	5 45 39	1♎18 30	7♎49 18	22 21.1	18 08.0	15 43.2	12 48.1	25 10.6	4 39.8	6 29.6	13 47.3	16 45.0	19 22.1
27 Sa	2 19 54	6 44 01	14 17 12	20 42 07	22 09.3	18D01.1	16 52.2	13 21.7	24 57.8	4 44.7	6 31.6	13 46.9	16 44.7	19 20.5
28 Su	2 23 51	7 42 21	27 04 01	3♏22 51	21 56.6	17 59.0	18 01.1	13 55.4	24 45.1	4 49.8	6 33.5	13 46.4	16 44.4	19 18.8
29 M	2 27 48	8 40 39	9♏38 34	15 51 13	21 44.2	18 01.9	19 09.9	14 29.1	24 32.6	4 55.0	6 35.2	13 45.8	16 44.1	19 17.2
30 Tu	2 31 44	9 38 55	22 00 50	28 07 31	21 33.1	18 09.7	20 18.5	15 02.9	24 20.3	5 00.4	6 36.9	13 45.3	16 43.7	19 15.5

Astro Data Dy Hr Mn	Planet Ingress Dy Hr Mn	Last Aspect Dy Hr Mn	☽ Ingress Dy Hr Mn	Last Aspect Dy Hr Mn	☽ Ingress Dy Hr Mn	☽ Phases & Eclipses Dy Hr Mn	Astro Data
☽0S 1 13:09	☿ ♈ 11 22:40	1 13:01 ♇ ⚹	♎ 2 6:03	2 12:14 ♇ ☌	♐ 3 7:59	8 10:32 ☾ 17♐21	1 March 1991
⚳R 1 15:18	♀ ♉ 18 21:45	3 11:21 ♆ □	♏ 4 13:08	5 18:13 ☿ △	♑ 5 20:19	16 8:10 ● 25♓14	Julian Day # 33297
⚳0N 8 17:38	☉ ♈ 21 3:02	6 4:25 ♇ ☌	♐ 6 23:35	8 5:43 ☿ □	♒ 8 9:00	23 6:03 ☽ 2♋07	SVP 5♓22'43"
☿0N 12 12:51		9 0:41 ☿ □	♑ 9 12:14	10 14:07 ☿ ⚹	♓ 10 19:18	30 7:17 ○ 9♎05	GC 26♐43.0 ⚴ 16♍51.5R
☽0N 15 23:37	♂ ♋ 3 0:49	11 6:01 ♀ □	♒ 12 0:31	12 7:35 ♇ △	♈ 13 1:49		Eris 16♈45.5 ⚵ 15♑38.4
♃☍♄ 16 1:26	⚳ ♎R 4 18:44	13 22:53 ♀ ⚹	♓ 14 10:11	14 19:45 ☿ ☌	♉ 15 5:06	7 6:45 ☾ 16♑57	⚷ 21♋35.2R ⚶ 25♉24.8
☉0N 21 3:02	♀ ♊ 13 0:10	16 8:10 ☉ ☌	♈ 16 16:38	16 13:37 ♇ ☍	♊ 17 6:41	14 19:38 ● 24♈21	☽ Mean ☊ 25♑59.0
☽0S 28 21:40	☉ ♉ 20 14:08	18 20:34 ♀ ☌	♉ 18 20:40	19 6:07 ☉ ⚹	♋ 19 8:17	21 12:39 ☽ 0♌55	
♃D 30 13:15		20 23:21 ☉ ⚹	♊ 20 23:37	20 18:30 ☿ □	♌ 21 11:04	28 20:59 ○ 8♏04	1 April 1991
☿R 4 18:10		22 16:27 ♂ ☌	♋ 23 2:27	22 20:53 ♇ □	♍ 23 15:29		Julian Day # 33328
☽0N 12 8:34		24 15:30 ☿ □	♌ 25 5:43	25 2:18 ♇ ⚹	♎ 25 21:36		SVP 5♓22'40"
♅R 18 10:33		27 3:23 ♂ ⚹	♍ 27 9:41	27 7:00 ☿ ☍	♏ 28 5:34		GC 26♐43.0 ⚴ 8♍09.4R
♆R 19 0:11		29 10:29 ♂ □	♎ 29 14:49	29 18:40 ♇ ☌	♐ 30 15:42		Eris 17♈04.5 ⚵ 24♑05.1
☽0S 25 3:37		31 19:50 ♂ △	♏ 31 22:01				⚷ 21♋11.9 ⚶ 5♊49.3
☿D 28 9:49							☽ Mean ☊ 24♑20.4

LONGITUDE — May 1991

Day	Sid.Time	☉	0 hr ☽	Noon ☽	True ☊	☿	♀	♂	⚳	♃	♄	♅	♆	♇
1 W	2 35 41	10♉37 09	4♐11 25	10♐12 46	21♑24.2	18♈22.2	21♊27.0	15♋36.7	24♎08.3	5♌05.9	6♒38.5	13♑44.6	16♑43.3	19♏13.9
2 Th	2 39 37	11 35 22	16 11 50	22 08 56	21R17.8	18 39.4	22 35.3	16 10.6	23R56.4	5 11.6	6 40.0	13R44.0	16R42.9	19R12.2
3 F	2 43 34	12 33 33	28 04 28	3♑58 53	21 14.1	19 01.1	23 43.5	16 44.6	23 44.8	5 17.4	6 41.4	13 43.3	16 42.5	19 10.6
4 Sa	2 47 30	13 31 43	9♑52 41	15 46 24	21D12.7	19 27.2	24 51.5	17 18.6	23 33.4	5 23.4	6 42.6	13 42.5	16 42.0	19 08.9
5 Su	2 51 27	14 29 51	21 40 38	27 36 00	21 12.7	19 57.5	25 59.4	17 52.7	23 22.3	5 29.5	6 43.8	13 41.7	16 41.5	19 07.2
6 M	2 55 23	15 27 58	3♒33 09	9♒32 45	21R13.2	20 31.8	27 07.2	18 26.8	23 11.5	5 35.8	6 44.9	13 40.8	16 40.9	19 05.6
7 Tu	2 59 20	16 26 03	15 35 29	21 42 01	21 13.2	21 10.1	28 14.8	19 00.9	23 00.9	5 42.2	6 45.9	13 39.9	16 40.4	19 03.9
8 W	3 03 17	17 24 07	27 53 01	4♓09 06	21 11.8	21 52.2	29 22.2	19 35.2	22 50.7	5 48.8	6 46.8	13 38.9	16 39.8	19 02.2
9 Th	3 07 13	18 22 10	10♓30 49	16 58 41	21 08.3	22 37.9	0♋29.5	20 09.4	22 40.7	5 55.5	6 47.6	13 37.9	16 39.1	19 00.5
10 F	3 11 10	19 20 11	23 33 05	0♈14 18	21 02.6	23 27.1	1 36.6	20 43.8	22 31.1	6 02.3	6 48.3	13 36.9	16 38.5	18 58.8
11 Sa	3 15 06	20 18 11	7♈02 29	13 57 36	20 54.9	24 19.6	2 43.5	21 18.1	22 21.8	6 09.3	6 48.9	13 35.8	16 37.8	18 57.1
12 Su	3 19 03	21 16 09	20 59 27	28 07 38	20 45.9	25 15.4	3 50.3	21 52.6	22 12.8	6 16.4	6 49.5	13 34.7	16 37.1	18 55.5
13 M	3 22 59	22 14 06	5♉21 34	12♉40 31	20 36.6	26 14.3	4 56.9	22 27.1	22 04.2	6 23.7	6 49.9	13 33.5	16 36.3	18 53.8
14 Tu	3 26 56	23 12 02	20 03 34	27 29 42	20 28.2	27 16.2	6 03.3	23 01.6	21 55.9	6 31.0	6 50.2	13 32.3	16 35.5	18 52.1
15 W	3 30 52	24 09 56	4♊57 49	12♊26 46	20 21.6	28 21.1	7 09.6	23 36.2	21 48.0	6 38.6	6 50.4	13 31.0	16 34.7	18 50.4
16 Th	3 34 49	25 07 49	19 55 27	27 22 51	20 17.3	29 28.8	8 15.6	24 10.8	21 40.4	6 46.2	6R50.5	13 29.7	16 33.9	18 48.8
17 F	3 38 46	26 05 40	4♋47 59	12♋10 04	20D15.4	0♉39.2	9 21.4	24 45.5	21 33.2	6 54.0	6 50.5	13 28.3	16 33.1	18 47.1
18 Sa	3 42 42	27 03 29	19 28 27	26 42 35	20 15.3	1 52.3	10 27.1	25 20.2	21 26.4	7 01.9	6 50.4	13 27.0	16 32.2	18 45.4
19 Su	3 46 39	28 01 17	3♌52 10	10♌56 56	20 16.1	3 08.0	11 32.5	25 55.0	21 20.0	7 09.9	6 50.3	13 25.5	16 31.3	18 43.8
20 M	3 50 35	28 59 03	17 56 49	24 51 48	20R16.9	4 26.3	12 37.7	26 29.8	21 13.9	7 18.0	6 50.0	13 24.1	16 30.3	18 42.1
21 Tu	3 54 32	29 56 47	1♍42 00	8♍27 33	20 16.6	5 47.1	13 42.7	27 04.7	21 08.2	7 26.3	6 49.6	13 22.5	16 29.4	18 40.5
22 W	3 58 28	0♊54 29	15 08 38	21 45 28	20 14.6	7 10.4	14 47.5	27 39.5	21 03.0	7 34.7	6 49.1	13 21.0	16 28.4	18 38.8
23 Th	4 02 25	1 52 10	28 18 18	4♎47 20	20 10.5	8 36.2	15 52.0	28 14.5	20 58.1	7 43.2	6 48.6	13 19.4	16 27.4	18 37.2
24 F	4 06 21	2 49 50	11♎12 47	17 34 53	20 04.5	10 04.3	16 56.3	28 49.5	20 53.6	7 51.8	6 47.9	13 17.8	16 26.3	18 35.6
25 Sa	4 10 18	3 47 28	23 53 48	0♏09 43	19 57.0	11 34.9	18 00.4	29 24.5	20 49.5	8 00.5	6 47.1	13 16.1	16 25.3	18 34.0
26 Su	4 14 15	4 45 04	6♏22 49	12 33 13	19 48.9	13 07.9	19 04.1	29 59.5	20 45.8	8 09.3	6 46.3	13 14.4	16 24.2	18 32.4
27 M	4 18 11	5 42 39	18 41 05	24 46 34	19 40.9	14 43.2	20 07.7	0♌34.6	20 42.5	8 18.2	6 45.3	13 12.7	16 23.1	18 30.8
28 Tu	4 22 08	6 40 14	0♐49 49	6♐51 01	19 33.8	16 20.9	21 10.9	1 09.8	20 39.5	8 27.3	6 44.3	13 10.9	16 21.9	18 29.2
29 W	4 26 04	7 37 47	12 50 19	18 47 57	19 28.2	18 01.0	22 13.9	1 44.9	20 37.0	8 36.4	6 43.1	13 09.2	16 20.8	18 27.7
30 Th	4 30 01	8 35 19	24 44 10	0♑39 12	19 24.5	19 43.4	23 16.6	2 20.1	20 34.9	8 45.7	6 41.9	13 07.3	16 19.6	18 26.1
31 F	4 33 57	9 32 49	6♑33 24	12 27 05	19D22.7	21 28.2	24 19.0	2 55.4	20 33.2	8 55.1	6 40.6	13 05.5	16 18.4	18 24.6

LONGITUDE — June 1991

Day	Sid.Time	☉	0 hr ☽	Noon ☽	True ☊	☿	♀	♂	⚳	♃	♄	♅	♆	♇
1 Sa	4 37 54	10♊30 19	18♑20 38	24♑14 30	19♑22.5	23♉15.3	25♋21.2	3♌30.7	20♎31.8	9♌04.5	6♒39.2	13♑03.6	16♑17.2	18♏23.0
2 Su	4 41 50	11 27 48	0♒09 07	6♒05 00	19 23.6	25 04.8	26 23.0	4 06.0	20R30.9	9 14.1	6R37.6	13R01.7	16R15.9	18R21.5
3 M	4 45 47	12 25 17	12 02 40	18 02 42	19 25.2	26 56.5	27 24.5	4 41.4	20D30.3	9 23.7	6 36.0	12 59.7	16 14.7	18 20.0
4 Tu	4 49 44	13 22 44	24 05 40	0♓12 09	19 26.7	28 50.5	28 25.6	5 16.8	20 30.1	9 33.5	6 34.4	12 57.7	16 13.4	18 18.5
5 W	4 53 40	14 20 11	6♓22 47	12 38 07	19R27.4	0♊46.8	29 26.5	5 52.2	20 30.4	9 43.3	6 32.6	12 55.7	16 12.1	18 17.1
6 Th	4 57 37	15 17 37	18 58 45	25 25 11	19 26.9	2 45.2	0♌27.0	6 27.7	20 31.0	9 53.3	6 30.7	12 53.7	16 10.8	18 15.6
7 F	5 01 33	16 15 02	1♈57 53	8♈37 15	19 25.1	4 45.7	1 27.2	7 03.2	20 31.9	10 03.3	6 28.7	12 51.6	16 09.5	18 14.2
8 Sa	5 05 30	17 12 27	15 23 31	22 16 52	19 21.9	6 48.2	2 27.0	7 38.7	20 33.3	10 13.5	6 26.7	12 49.5	16 08.1	18 12.7
9 Su	5 09 26	18 09 52	29 17 15	6♉24 30	19 17.9	8 52.6	3 26.4	8 14.3	20 35.1	10 23.7	6 24.5	12 47.4	16 06.7	18 11.3
10 M	5 13 23	19 07 15	13♉38 14	20 57 53	19 13.6	10 58.7	4 25.5	8 50.0	20 37.2	10 34.0	6 22.3	12 45.3	16 05.3	18 10.0
11 Tu	5 17 19	20 04 39	28 22 44	5♊51 50	19 09.6	13 06.3	5 24.2	9 25.6	20 39.7	10 44.4	6 20.0	12 43.1	16 03.9	18 08.6
12 W	5 21 16	21 02 01	13♊24 09	20 58 31	19 06.5	15 15.2	6 22.5	10 01.4	20 42.6	10 54.9	6 17.6	12 40.9	16 02.5	18 07.3
13 Th	5 25 13	21 59 23	28 33 43	6♋08 33	19D04.7	17 25.3	7 20.3	10 37.1	20 45.8	11 05.4	6 15.2	12 38.7	16 01.1	18 05.9
14 F	5 29 09	22 56 44	13♋41 49	21 12 28	19 04.3	19 36.3	8 17.7	11 12.9	20 49.5	11 16.1	6 12.6	12 36.5	15 59.7	18 04.6
15 Sa	5 33 06	23 54 04	28 39 30	6♌02 06	19 05.0	21 47.8	9 14.7	11 48.7	20 53.4	11 26.8	6 10.0	12 34.3	15 58.2	18 03.4
16 Su	5 37 02	24 51 24	13♌19 38	20 31 36	19 06.2	23 59.7	10 11.2	12 24.6	20 57.8	11 37.6	6 07.3	12 32.0	15 56.7	18 02.1
17 M	5 40 59	25 48 42	27 37 40	4♍37 41	19 07.6	26 11.6	11 07.3	13 00.5	21 02.5	11 48.5	6 04.5	12 29.7	15 55.2	18 00.9
18 Tu	5 44 55	26 46 00	11♍31 35	18 19 29	19R08.5	28 23.3	12 02.8	13 36.4	21 07.5	11 59.4	6 01.6	12 27.4	15 53.7	17 59.6
19 W	5 48 52	27 43 16	25 01 31	1♎37 57	19 08.7	0♋34.5	12 57.8	14 12.4	21 12.9	12 10.5	5 58.7	12 25.1	15 52.2	17 58.4
20 Th	5 52 49	28 40 32	8♎09 06	14 35 18	19 07.9	2 45.0	13 52.3	14 48.4	21 18.7	12 21.6	5 55.7	12 22.8	15 50.7	17 57.3
21 F	5 56 45	29 37 47	20 56 55	27 14 20	19 06.2	4 54.5	14 46.2	15 24.4	21 24.7	12 32.7	5 52.6	12 20.4	15 49.2	17 56.1
22 Sa	6 00 42	0♋35 02	3♏27 58	9♏38 09	19 03.9	7 02.8	15 39.5	16 00.4	21 31.2	12 44.0	5 49.4	12 18.1	15 47.6	17 55.0
23 Su	6 04 38	1 32 16	15 45 17	21 49 43	19 01.3	9 09.8	16 32.2	16 36.5	21 37.9	12 55.3	5 46.2	12 15.7	15 46.1	17 53.9
24 M	6 08 35	2 29 29	27 51 48	3♐51 50	18 58.7	11 15.2	17 24.3	17 12.7	21 45.0	13 06.7	5 42.9	12 13.3	15 44.5	17 52.8
25 Tu	6 12 31	3 26 42	9♐50 08	15 47 01	18 56.5	13 19.0	18 15.8	17 48.8	21 52.4	13 18.1	5 39.5	12 11.0	15 42.9	17 51.8
26 W	6 16 28	4 23 55	21 42 45	27 37 36	18 54.9	15 21.0	19 06.6	18 25.0	22 00.1	13 29.6	5 36.1	12 08.6	15 41.4	17 50.8
27 Th	6 20 24	5 21 07	3♑31 52	9♑25 49	18D54.0	17 21.1	19 56.7	19 01.2	22 08.1	13 41.2	5 32.6	12 06.2	15 39.8	17 49.8
28 F	6 24 21	6 18 19	15 19 43	21 13 53	18 53.8	19 19.3	20 46.1	19 37.5	22 16.4	13 52.8	5 29.1	12 03.8	15 38.2	17 48.8
29 Sa	6 28 18	7 15 31	27 08 35	3♒04 10	18 54.2	21 15.6	21 34.8	20 13.8	22 25.0	14 04.5	5 25.5	12 01.4	15 36.6	17 47.9
30 Su	6 32 14	8 12 42	9♒00 58	14 59 20	18 55.0	23 09.8	22 22.7	20 50.1	22 33.9	14 16.2	5 21.8	11 58.9	15 35.0	17 47.0

Astro Data	Dy Hr Mn
☽0N	9 17:20
♃☍♄	17 1:24
♄R	17 4:04
☽0S	22 8:17
⚳D	4 10:33
☽0N	6 0:58
⚳0S	16 5:18
☽0S	18 13:53
♃⚻♅	20 14:10

Planet Ingress		Dy Hr Mn
♀	♋	9 1:28
☿	♉	16 22:45
☉	♊	21 13:20
♂	♌	26 12:19
☿	♊	5 2:24
♀	♌	6 1:16
☿	♋	19 5:40
☉	♋	21 21:19

Last Aspect Dy Hr Mn		☽ Ingress	Dy Hr Mn
2 12:59	♀ ☍	♑	3 3:54
4 19:48	☿ □	♒	5 16:51
8 1:57	♀ △	♓	8 4:04
9 18:06	♂ △	♈	10 11:35
12 6:51	☿ ☌	♉	12 15:07
14 4:36	☉ ☌	♊	14 16:02
16 15:40	☿ ✶	♋	16 16:14
18 12:37	☉ ✶	♌	18 17:30
20 19:46	☉ □	♍	20 21:00
22 23:19	♂ ✶	♎	23 3:08
25 10:29	♂ □	♏	25 11:41
27 1:58	♀ △	♐	27 22:21
28 15:15	♃ △	♑	30 10:40

Last Aspect Dy Hr Mn		☽ Ingress	Dy Hr Mn
1 14:28	♀ ☍	♒	1 23:42
4 8:51	☿ □	♓	4 11:36
5 22:40	♇ △	♈	6 20:25
8 2:31	☉ ✶	♉	9 1:13
10 7:26	♇ ☍	♊	11 2:36
12 12:06	☉ ☌	♋	13 2:16
14 7:00	♇ △	♌	15 2:10
16 19:49	☉ ✶	♍	17 4:03
19 4:19	☉ □	♎	19 9:01
21 16:58	☉ △	♏	21 17:18
23 4:14	♇ ☌	♐	24 4:16
25 17:24	♀ △	♑	26 16:49
28 7:21	☿ ☍	♒	29 5:47

☽ Phases & Eclipses Dy Hr Mn	
7 0:46	☾ 15♒59
14 4:36	● 22♉54
20 19:46	☽ 29♌18
28 11:37	○ 6♐39
5 15:30	☾ 14♓29
12 12:06	● 21♊02
19 4:19	☽ 27♍25
27 2:58	○ 5♑00
27 3:15	• A 0.312

Astro Data

1 May 1991
Julian Day # 33358
SVP 5♓22'37"
GC 26♐43.1 ⚴ 6♍33.9
Eris 17♈24.1 ⚵ 29♑39.8
⚷ 22♋15.7 ⚶ 17♊28.9
☽ Mean ☊ 22♑45.1

1 June 1991
Julian Day # 33389
SVP 5♓22'31"
GC 26♐43.2 ⚴ 11♍32.3
Eris 17♈40.6 ⚵ 1♒10.4R
⚷ 24♋36.8 ⚶ 0♋26.1
☽ Mean ☊ 21♑06.6

July 1991 — LONGITUDE

Day	Sid.Time	☉	0 hr ☽	Noon ☽	True ☊	☿	♀	♂	⚳	♃	♄	♅	♆	♇
1 M	6 36 11	9♋09 54	20♒59 39	27♒02 19	18♑56.0	25♋01.9	23♌09.8	21♌26.4	22♎43.1	14♌28.0	5♒18.1	11♑56.5	15♑33.4	17♏46.1
2 Tu	6 40 07	10 07 06	3♓07 45	9♓16 24	18 56.9	26 52.0	23 56.1	22 02.8	22 52.6	14 39.9	5R14.4	11R54.1	15R31.8	17R45.2
3 W	6 44 04	11 04 18	15 28 42	21 45 07	18 57.5	28 40.0	24 41.6	22 39.2	23 02.4	14 51.8	5 10.5	11 51.7	15 30.1	17 44.4
4 Th	6 48 00	12 01 30	28 06 06	4♈32 05	18R57.9	0♌25.9	25 26.1	23 15.7	23 12.5	15 03.8	5 06.7	11 49.2	15 28.5	17 43.6
5 F	6 51 57	12 58 42	11♈03 29	17 40 38	18 58.0	2 09.7	26 09.8	23 52.2	23 22.8	15 15.8	5 02.7	11 46.8	15 26.9	17 42.8
6 Sa	6 55 53	13 55 54	24 23 51	1♉13 22	18 57.7	3 51.5	26 52.5	24 28.7	23 33.4	15 27.9	4 58.8	11 44.4	15 25.3	17 42.1
7 Su	6 59 50	14 53 07	8♉09 17	15 11 35	18 57.4	5 31.1	27 34.2	25 05.3	23 44.3	15 40.0	4 54.8	11 42.0	15 23.7	17 41.4
8 M	7 03 47	15 50 21	22 20 09	29 34 39	18 57.0	7 08.7	28 15.0	25 41.9	23 55.5	15 52.2	4 50.7	11 39.5	15 22.0	17 40.7
9 Tu	7 07 43	16 47 35	6♊54 39	14♊19 30	18 56.8	8 44.1	28 54.6	26 18.5	24 06.9	16 04.4	4 46.6	11 37.1	15 20.4	17 40.1
10 W	7 11 40	17 44 49	21 48 26	29 20 29	18 56.7	10 17.5	29 33.2	26 55.2	24 18.6	16 16.7	4 42.5	11 34.7	15 18.8	17 39.4
11 Th	7 15 36	18 42 03	6♋54 37	14♋29 42	18 56.6	11 48.7	0♍10.6	27 31.9	24 30.5	16 29.0	4 38.3	11 32.3	15 17.2	17 38.9
12 F	7 19 33	19 39 18	22 04 34	29 38 02	18 56.6	13 17.8	0 46.9	28 08.6	24 42.7	16 41.4	4 34.1	11 29.9	15 15.6	17 38.3
13 Sa	7 23 29	20 36 33	7♌08 58	14♌36 20	18 56.6	14 44.7	1 21.9	28 45.4	24 55.1	16 53.8	4 29.8	11 27.5	15 13.9	17 37.8
14 Su	7 27 26	21 33 47	21 59 13	29 16 50	18 56.4	16 09.4	1 55.6	29 22.2	25 07.8	17 06.2	4 25.6	11 25.1	15 12.3	17 37.3
15 M	7 31 22	22 31 02	6♍28 35	13♍34 00	18 56.0	17 32.0	2 28.0	29 59.1	25 20.7	17 18.7	4 21.3	11 22.8	15 10.7	17 36.8
16 Tu	7 35 19	23 28 17	20 32 50	27 24 58	18 55.6	18 52.2	2 59.1	0♍36.0	25 33.9	17 31.2	4 16.9	11 20.4	15 09.1	17 36.4
17 W	7 39 16	24 25 32	4♎10 25	10♎49 22	18 55.3	20 10.2	3 28.6	1 12.9	25 47.3	17 43.8	4 12.6	11 18.0	15 07.5	17 36.0
18 Th	7 43 12	25 22 47	17 22 04	23 48 51	18D55.1	21 25.9	3 56.7	1 49.8	26 00.9	17 56.4	4 08.2	11 15.7	15 05.9	17 35.6
19 F	7 47 09	26 20 02	0♏10 10	6♏26 29	18 55.2	22 39.1	4 23.2	2 26.8	26 14.7	18 09.0	4 03.8	11 13.4	15 04.3	17 35.3
20 Sa	7 51 05	27 17 18	12 38 16	18 46 04	18 55.7	23 49.8	4 48.1	3 03.8	26 28.8	18 21.6	3 59.4	11 11.1	15 02.8	17 35.0
21 Su	7 55 02	28 14 34	24 50 24	0♐51 48	18 56.5	24 58.1	5 11.3	3 40.8	26 43.1	18 34.3	3 55.0	11 08.8	15 01.2	17 34.7
22 M	7 58 58	29 11 50	6♐50 46	12 47 47	18 57.5	26 03.6	5 32.8	4 17.9	26 57.5	18 47.1	3 50.6	11 06.5	14 59.6	17 34.5
23 Tu	8 02 55	0♌09 06	18 43 21	24 37 54	18 58.4	27 06.5	5 52.5	4 55.0	27 12.2	18 59.8	3 46.1	11 04.3	14 58.1	17 34.3
24 W	8 06 52	1 06 23	0♑31 50	6♑25 35	18 59.2	28 06.6	6 10.3	5 32.1	27 27.1	19 12.6	3 41.7	11 02.0	14 56.5	17 34.1
25 Th	8 10 48	2 03 40	12 19 30	18 13 55	18R59.5	29 03.7	6 26.2	6 09.3	27 42.2	19 25.4	3 37.2	10 59.8	14 55.0	17 34.0
26 F	8 14 45	3 00 58	24 09 09	0♒05 30	18 59.3	29 57.8	6 40.2	6 46.5	27 57.5	19 38.2	3 32.8	10 57.6	14 53.5	17 33.9
27 Sa	8 18 41	3 58 17	6♒03 13	12 02 35	18 58.2	0♍48.7	6 52.1	7 23.8	28 13.0	19 51.1	3 28.3	10 55.4	14 51.9	17 33.8
28 Su	8 22 38	4 55 36	18 03 51	24 07 13	18 56.5	1 36.4	7 01.9	8 01.0	28 28.7	20 04.0	3 23.8	10 53.3	14 50.4	17D33.8
29 M	8 26 34	5 52 56	0♓12 57	6♓21 15	18 54.2	2 20.5	7 09.6	8 38.3	28 44.5	20 16.9	3 19.4	10 51.2	14 48.9	17 33.8
30 Tu	8 30 31	6 50 17	12 32 22	18 46 31	18 51.6	3 01.0	7 15.1	9 15.7	29 00.6	20 29.8	3 14.9	10 49.1	14 47.5	17 33.8
31 W	8 34 27	7 47 39	25 03 57	1♈24 55	18 49.0	3 37.8	7R18.4	9 53.1	29 16.8	20 42.8	3 10.5	10 47.0	14 46.0	17 33.9

August 1991 — LONGITUDE

Day	Sid.Time	☉	0 hr ☽	Noon ☽	True ☊	☿	♀	♂	⚳	♃	♄	♅	♆	♇
1 Th	8 38 24	8♌45 02	7♈49 39	14♈18 23	18♑46.9	4♍10.6	7♍19.4	10♍30.5	29♎33.2	20♌55.7	3♒06.1	10♑44.9	14♑44.5	17♏34.0
2 F	8 42 20	9 42 26	20 51 23	27 28 52	18D45.5	4 39.2	7R18.1	11 07.9	29 49.8	21 08.7	3R01.6	10R42.9	14R43.1	17 34.1
3 Sa	8 46 17	10 39 51	4♉11 03	10♉58 06	18 45.0	5 03.6	7 14.5	11 45.4	0♏06.5	21 21.7	2 57.2	10 40.9	14 41.7	17 34.3
4 Su	8 50 14	11 37 18	17 50 08	24 47 14	18 45.5	5 23.4	7 08.5	12 22.9	0 23.5	21 34.8	2 52.8	10 38.9	14 40.3	17 34.5
5 M	8 54 10	12 34 46	1♊49 24	8♊56 30	18 46.6	5 38.5	7 00.2	13 00.5	0 40.6	21 47.8	2 48.5	10 37.0	14 38.9	17 34.8
6 Tu	8 58 07	13 32 15	16 08 21	23 24 37	18 48.0	5 48.7	6 49.5	13 38.1	0 57.8	22 00.9	2 44.1	10 35.0	14 37.5	17 35.0
7 W	9 02 03	14 29 45	0♋44 50	8♋08 25	18R49.1	5R53.9	6 36.4	14 15.7	1 15.3	22 13.9	2 39.8	10 33.2	14 36.1	17 35.4
8 Th	9 06 00	15 27 17	15 34 39	23 02 41	18 49.3	5 53.9	6 21.0	14 53.4	1 32.8	22 27.0	2 35.5	10 31.3	14 34.8	17 35.7
9 F	9 09 56	16 24 49	0♌31 35	8♌00 21	18 48.3	5 48.5	6 03.3	15 31.1	1 50.6	22 40.1	2 31.2	10 29.5	14 33.5	17 36.1
10 Sa	9 13 53	17 22 23	15 27 56	22 53 18	18 45.9	5 37.8	5 43.3	16 08.9	2 08.5	22 53.2	2 27.0	10 27.7	14 32.2	17 36.5
11 Su	9 17 50	18 19 58	0♍15 26	7♍33 25	18 42.3	5 21.7	5 21.2	16 46.7	2 26.5	23 06.3	2 22.7	10 26.0	14 30.9	17 36.9
12 M	9 21 46	19 17 34	14 46 28	21 53 53	18 38.0	5 00.2	4 56.9	17 24.5	2 44.7	23 19.5	2 18.6	10 24.2	14 29.6	17 37.4
13 Tu	9 25 43	20 15 10	28 55 11	5♎50 00	18 33.4	4 33.4	4 30.6	18 02.3	3 03.1	23 32.6	2 14.4	10 22.5	14 28.4	17 37.9
14 W	9 29 39	21 12 48	12♎38 09	19 19 37	18 29.3	4 01.5	4 02.3	18 40.2	3 21.6	23 45.7	2 10.3	10 20.9	14 27.1	17 38.5
15 Th	9 33 36	22 10 27	25 54 31	2♏23 06	18 26.3	3 24.9	3 32.3	19 18.2	3 40.2	23 58.8	2 06.2	10 19.3	14 25.9	17 39.0
16 F	9 37 32	23 08 07	8♏45 43	15 02 49	18D24.6	2 43.9	3 00.7	19 56.1	3 59.0	24 12.0	2 02.2	10 17.7	14 24.8	17 39.7
17 Sa	9 41 29	24 05 47	21 14 55	27 22 34	18 24.4	1 59.1	2 27.6	20 34.1	4 17.9	24 25.1	1 58.3	10 16.2	14 23.6	17 40.3
18 Su	9 45 25	25 03 29	3♐26 23	9♐26 59	18 25.3	1 11.1	1 53.3	21 12.2	4 36.9	24 38.2	1 54.3	10 14.7	14 22.5	17 41.0
19 M	9 49 22	26 01 12	15 24 58	21 21 00	18 26.8	0 20.8	1 17.9	21 50.3	4 56.1	24 51.4	1 50.5	10 13.2	14 21.3	17 41.7
20 Tu	9 53 19	26 58 56	27 15 39	3♑09 33	18 28.4	29♌28.9	0 41.6	22 28.4	5 15.4	25 04.5	1 46.6	10 11.8	14 20.3	17 42.5
21 W	9 57 15	27 56 41	9♑03 14	14 57 13	18R29.4	28 36.5	0 04.8	23 06.5	5 34.8	25 17.6	1 42.9	10 10.4	14 19.2	17 43.2
22 Th	10 01 12	28 54 28	20 52 02	26 48 06	18 29.0	27 44.6	29♌27.6	23 44.7	5 54.4	25 30.7	1 39.1	10 09.1	14 18.1	17 44.1
23 F	10 05 08	29 52 16	2♒45 49	8♒45 34	18 27.0	26 54.3	28 50.2	24 22.9	6 14.1	25 43.9	1 35.5	10 07.8	14 17.1	17 44.9
24 Sa	10 09 05	0♍50 04	14 47 39	20 52 18	18 23.0	26 06.6	28 12.9	25 01.2	6 33.9	25 57.0	1 31.9	10 06.6	14 16.1	17 45.8
25 Su	10 13 01	1 47 55	26 59 45	3♓10 10	18 17.2	25 22.5	27 36.0	25 39.5	6 53.8	26 10.1	1 28.3	10 05.3	14 15.2	17 46.7
26 M	10 16 58	2 45 47	9♓23 40	15 40 19	18 10.0	24 43.1	26 59.8	26 17.8	7 13.8	26 23.1	1 24.8	10 04.2	14 14.2	17 47.6
27 Tu	10 20 54	3 43 40	22 00 10	28 23 16	18 02.1	24 09.2	26 24.3	26 56.2	7 33.9	26 36.2	1 21.4	10 03.0	14 13.3	17 48.6
28 W	10 24 51	4 41 35	4♈49 36	11♈19 08	17 54.2	23 41.6	25 49.9	27 34.6	7 54.2	26 49.3	1 18.1	10 02.0	14 12.4	17 49.6
29 Th	10 28 47	5 39 32	17 51 54	24 27 50	17 47.3	23 21.1	25 16.7	28 13.0	8 14.5	27 02.3	1 14.8	10 00.9	14 11.5	17 50.6
30 F	10 32 44	6 37 30	1♉06 57	7♉49 15	17 42.0	23 08.1	24 45.0	28 51.5	8 35.0	27 15.4	1 11.6	9 59.9	14 10.7	17 51.7
31 Sa	10 36 41	7 35 31	14 34 44	21 23 25	17 38.7	23D03.2	24 15.0	29 30.1	8 55.6	27 28.4	1 08.4	9 59.0	14 09.9	17 52.8

Astro Data

	Dy Hr Mn
☽ 0N	3 7:19
♃⚻♆	6 7:28
☽ 0S	15 21:50
♃□♇	16 21:37
♇ D	28 23:47
☽ 0N	30 13:06
♀ R	1 10:35
☿ R	7 23:58
☽ 0S	12 7:48
♃⚼♅	21 0:06
☽ 0N	26 19:17
☿ D	31 14:35

Planet Ingress

	Dy Hr Mn
☿ ♌	4 6:05
♀ ♍	11 5:06
♂ ♍	15 12:36
☉ ♌	23 8:11
☿ ♍	26 13:00
⚳ ♏	3 2:39
☿ ♌R	19 21:40
♀ ♌R	21 15:06
☉ ♍	23 15:13

Last Aspect / ☽ Ingress (July)

Last Aspect Dy Hr Mn		☽ Ingress Dy Hr Mn
1 3:47 ♀ ☍	♓	1 17:51
4 3:09 ☿ △	♈	4 3:33
6 3:58 ♀ △	♉	6 9:52
8 9:42 ♀ □	♊	8 12:42
10 12:21 ♀ ⚹	♋	10 13:03
11 19:06 ☉ ☌	♌	12 12:35
14 12:09 ♂ ☌	♍	14 13:12
16 4:34 ☉ ⚹	♎	16 16:34
18 15:11 ☉ □	♏	18 23:41
21 6:19 ☉ △	♐	21 10:16
23 17:31 ☿ △	♑	23 22:55
25 10:39 ♇ ⚹	♒	26 11:49
28 3:50 ♃ ☍	♓	28 23:35
30 9:41 ♇ △	♈	31 9:20

Last Aspect / ☽ Ingress (August)

Last Aspect Dy Hr Mn		☽ Ingress Dy Hr Mn
2 0:20 ♃ △	♉	2 16:32
4 6:24 ♃ □	♊	4 20:54
6 9:40 ♃ ⚹	♋	6 22:47
8 3:15 ♇ △	♌	8 23:09
10 12:00 ♃ ☌	♍	10 23:35
12 4:47 ♇ ⚹	♎	13 1:52
14 20:12 ♃ ⚹	♏	15 7:34
17 6:05 ♃ □	♐	17 17:11
20 5:02 ☿ △	♑	20 5:34
22 5:29 ♂ △	♒	22 18:27
25 1:42 ♀ ☍	♓	25 5:51
27 9:08 ♂ ☍	♈	27 15:01
29 16:44 ♃ △	♉	29 22:00

☽ Phases & Eclipses

Dy Hr Mn	
5 2:50	☾ 12♈37
11 19:06	● 18♋59
11 19:06:03	● T 06'53"
18 15:11	☽ 25♎30
26 18:24	○ 3♒16
26 18:08	◐ A 0.254
3 11:25	☾ 10♉38
10 2:28	● 17♌00
17 5:01	☽ 23♏49
25 9:07	○ 1♓41

Astro Data

1 July 1991
Julian Day # 33419
SVP 5♓22'26"
GC 26♐43.2 ⚴ 20♍12.0
Eris 17♈49.2 ⚵ 27♑24.3R
⚷ 27♋41.9 ⚶ 13♋26.5
☽ Mean ☊ 19♑31.3

1 August 1991
Julian Day # 33450
SVP 5♓22'21"
GC 26♐43.3 ⚴ 1♎22.9
Eris 17♈48.5R ⚵ 20♑19.2R
⚷ 1♌15.4 ⚶ 27♋05.0
☽ Mean ☊ 17♑52.9

LONGITUDE — September 1991

Day	Sid.Time	☉	0 hr ☽	Noon ☽	True ☊	☿	♀	♂	⚳	♃	♄	♅	♆	♇
1 Su	10 40 37	8♍33 33	28♉15 19	5♊10 26	17♑37.5	23♌06.4	23♌46.7	0♎08.6	9♏16.2	27♌41.4	1♒05.3	9♑58.1	14♑09.1	17♏54.0
2 M	10 44 34	9 31 38	12♊08 47	19 10 20	17D37.7	23 18.2	23R20.4	0 47.2	9 37.0	27 54.4	1R02.3	9R57.2	14R08.3	17 55.1
3 Tu	10 48 30	10 29 44	26 15 00	3♋22 39	17R38.6	23 38.4	22 56.2	1 25.9	9 57.9	28 07.4	0 59.4	9 56.4	14 07.6	17 56.3
4 W	10 52 27	11 27 52	10♋33 06	17 46 03	17 39.2	24 07.1	22 34.1	2 04.6	10 18.9	28 20.4	0 56.5	9 55.7	14 06.9	17 57.6
5 Th	10 56 23	12 26 03	25 01 07	2♌17 48	17 38.3	24 44.1	22 14.2	2 43.3	10 40.0	28 33.3	0 53.8	9 55.0	14 06.2	17 58.8
6 F	11 00 20	13 24 15	9♌35 32	16 53 37	17 35.3	25 29.2	21 56.7	3 22.1	11 01.2	28 46.2	0 51.1	9 54.3	14 05.6	18 00.1
7 Sa	11 04 16	14 22 29	24 11 18	1♍27 46	17 29.8	26 22.0	21 41.5	4 00.9	11 22.4	28 59.1	0 48.4	9 53.7	14 05.0	18 01.4
8 Su	11 08 13	15 20 45	8♍42 10	15 53 42	17 22.0	27 22.2	21 28.6	4 39.8	11 43.8	29 12.0	0 45.9	9 53.1	14 04.4	18 02.8
9 M	11 12 10	16 19 02	23 01 33	0♎05 00	17 12.7	28 29.5	21 18.2	5 18.7	12 05.3	29 24.8	0 43.4	9 52.6	14 03.9	18 04.1
10 Tu	11 16 06	17 17 21	7♎03 27	13 56 24	17 02.9	29 43.1	21 10.2	5 57.7	12 26.8	29 37.6	0 41.1	9 52.1	14 03.3	18 05.5
11 W	11 20 03	18 15 42	20 43 30	27 24 34	16 53.6	1♍02.8	21 04.6	6 36.6	12 48.5	29 50.4	0 38.8	9 51.7	14 02.8	18 07.0
12 Th	11 23 59	19 14 05	3♏59 31	10♏28 28	16 45.8	2 27.8	21D01.3	7 15.7	13 10.2	0♍03.2	0 36.6	9 51.3	14 02.4	18 08.4
13 F	11 27 56	20 12 29	16 51 35	23 09 14	16 40.2	3 57.6	21 00.4	7 54.7	13 32.0	0 15.9	0 34.4	9 51.0	14 01.9	18 09.9
14 Sa	11 31 52	21 10 55	29 21 50	5♐29 52	16 36.8	5 31.8	21 01.9	8 33.9	13 53.9	0 28.6	0 32.4	9 50.7	14 01.6	18 11.4
15 Su	11 35 49	22 09 23	11♐33 56	17 34 38	16D35.5	7 09.6	21 05.7	9 13.0	14 15.9	0 41.3	0 30.5	9 50.5	14 01.2	18 13.0
16 M	11 39 45	23 07 52	23 32 39	29 28 37	16 35.5	8 50.6	21 11.7	9 52.2	14 38.0	0 53.9	0 28.6	9 50.3	14 00.9	18 14.6
17 Tu	11 43 42	24 06 23	5♑23 15	11♑17 13	16R36.0	10 34.2	21 19.9	10 31.4	15 00.1	1 06.5	0 26.9	9 50.2	14 00.6	18 16.2
18 W	11 47 39	25 04 55	17 11 11	23 05 49	16 35.9	12 19.9	21 30.3	11 10.7	15 22.3	1 19.0	0 25.2	9D50.2	14 00.3	18 17.8
19 Th	11 51 35	26 03 29	29 01 42	4♒59 27	16 34.3	14 07.4	21 42.8	11 50.0	15 44.6	1 31.5	0 23.7	9 50.1	14 00.1	18 19.4
20 F	11 55 32	27 02 05	10♒59 34	17 02 31	16 30.4	15 56.2	21 57.4	12 29.4	16 06.9	1 44.0	0 22.2	9 50.2	13 59.8	18 21.1
21 Sa	11 59 28	28 00 42	23 08 44	29 18 32	16 23.9	17 45.9	22 14.0	13 08.8	16 29.4	1 56.4	0 20.8	9 50.2	13 59.7	18 22.8
22 Su	12 03 25	28 59 21	5♓32 11	11♓49 52	16 14.8	19 36.3	22 32.5	13 48.2	16 51.9	2 08.8	0 19.5	9 50.4	13 59.5	18 24.5
23 M	12 07 21	29 58 02	18 11 41	24 37 39	16 03.6	21 27.0	22 52.9	14 27.7	17 14.4	2 21.1	0 18.3	9 50.6	13 59.4	18 26.3
24 Tu	12 11 18	0♎56 45	1♈07 41	7♈41 40	15 51.4	23 17.9	23 15.1	15 07.2	17 37.1	2 33.4	0 17.2	9 50.8	13 59.3	18 28.1
25 W	12 15 14	1 55 30	14 19 23	21 00 35	15 39.2	25 08.7	23 39.1	15 46.7	17 59.8	2 45.6	0 16.2	9 51.1	13D59.3	18 29.9
26 Th	12 19 11	2 54 18	27 44 58	4♉32 15	15 28.3	26 59.2	24 04.8	16 26.4	18 22.6	2 57.8	0 15.3	9 51.4	13 59.3	18 31.7
27 F	12 23 08	3 53 07	11♉22 06	18 14 12	15 19.5	28 49.4	24 32.2	17 06.0	18 45.4	3 10.0	0 14.5	9 51.8	13 59.3	18 33.5
28 Sa	12 27 04	4 51 59	25 08 18	2♊04 07	15 13.6	0♎39.1	25 01.2	17 45.7	19 08.3	3 22.1	0 13.8	9 52.3	13 59.4	18 35.4
29 Su	12 31 01	5 50 52	9♊01 28	16 00 09	15 10.3	2 28.2	25 31.8	18 25.4	19 31.3	3 34.1	0 13.2	9 52.7	13 59.5	18 37.3
30 M	12 34 57	6 49 49	23 00 04	0♋01 06	15D09.2	4 16.7	26 03.8	19 05.2	19 54.3	3 46.1	0 12.7	9 53.3	13 59.6	18 39.2

LONGITUDE — October 1991

Day	Sid.Time	☉	0 hr ☽	Noon ☽	True ☊	☿	♀	♂	⚳	♃	♄	♅	♆	♇
1 Tu	12 38 54	7♎48 47	7♋03 09	14♋06 10	15♑09.1	6♎04.5	26♌37.3	19♎45.1	20♏17.4	3♍58.0	0♒12.3	9♑53.9	13♑59.7	18♏41.1
2 W	12 42 50	8 47 48	21 10 03	28 14 40	15R08.8	7 51.5	27 12.1	20 24.9	20 40.5	4 09.9	0R11.9	9 54.5	13 59.9	18 43.1
3 Th	12 46 47	9 46 51	5♌19 53	12♌25 28	15 06.9	9 37.8	27 48.3	21 04.9	21 03.7	4 21.7	0 11.7	9 55.2	14 00.2	18 45.1
4 F	12 50 43	10 45 57	19 31 10	26 36 36	15 02.5	11 23.3	28 25.8	21 44.8	21 27.0	4 33.5	0D11.6	9 56.0	14 00.4	18 47.1
5 Sa	12 54 40	11 45 04	3♍41 23	10♍45 02	14 55.1	13 07.9	29 04.4	22 24.9	21 50.3	4 45.2	0 11.6	9 56.8	14 00.7	18 49.1
6 Su	12 58 37	12 44 14	17 47 01	24 46 47	14 45.0	14 51.8	29 44.3	23 04.9	22 13.7	4 56.8	0 11.7	9 57.6	14 01.0	18 51.1
7 M	13 02 33	13 43 26	1♎43 47	8♎37 27	14 33.0	16 34.9	0♍25.3	23 45.0	22 37.1	5 08.4	0 11.9	9 58.5	14 01.4	18 53.2
8 Tu	13 06 30	14 42 40	15 27 17	22 12 51	14 20.1	18 17.2	1 07.4	24 25.2	23 00.6	5 19.9	0 12.2	9 59.5	14 01.8	18 55.3
9 W	13 10 26	15 41 56	28 53 46	5♏29 48	14 07.6	19 58.7	1 50.6	25 05.4	23 24.2	5 31.3	0 12.5	10 00.5	14 02.2	18 57.4
10 Th	13 14 23	16 41 14	12♏00 46	18 26 40	13 56.9	21 39.4	2 34.7	25 45.6	23 47.7	5 42.7	0 13.0	10 01.5	14 02.7	18 59.5
11 F	13 18 19	17 40 34	24 47 32	1♐03 34	13 48.5	23 19.4	3 19.9	26 25.9	24 11.4	5 54.0	0 13.6	10 02.6	14 03.1	19 01.6
12 Sa	13 22 16	18 39 56	7♐15 03	13 22 22	13 43.0	24 58.6	4 06.0	27 06.3	24 35.1	6 05.2	0 14.3	10 03.8	14 03.7	19 03.7
13 Su	13 26 12	19 39 20	19 25 58	25 26 22	13 40.0	26 37.1	4 53.0	27 46.6	24 58.8	6 16.4	0 15.1	10 05.0	14 04.2	19 05.9
14 M	13 30 09	20 38 45	1♑24 10	7♑19 59	13D38.9	28 14.8	5 40.8	28 27.1	25 22.6	6 27.4	0 16.0	10 06.2	14 04.8	19 08.1
15 Tu	13 34 05	21 38 13	13 14 30	19 08 22	13R38.9	29 51.9	6 29.5	29 07.5	25 46.4	6 38.4	0 17.0	10 07.5	14 05.4	19 10.3
16 W	13 38 02	22 37 42	25 02 19	0♒57 02	13 38.7	1♏28.3	7 19.1	29 48.0	26 10.3	6 49.3	0 18.1	10 08.9	14 06.1	19 12.5
17 Th	13 41 59	23 37 12	6♒53 13	12 51 31	13 37.3	3 04.0	8 09.4	0♏28.6	26 34.2	7 00.2	0 19.3	10 10.3	14 06.8	19 14.7
18 F	13 45 55	24 36 45	18 52 35	24 57 02	13 33.8	4 39.0	9 00.5	1 09.2	26 58.1	7 10.9	0 20.6	10 11.7	14 07.5	19 16.9
19 Sa	13 49 52	25 36 19	1♓05 23	7♓18 07	13 27.7	6 13.5	9 52.3	1 49.8	27 22.1	7 21.6	0 22.0	10 13.2	14 08.3	19 19.2
20 Su	13 53 48	26 35 55	13 35 37	19 58 12	13 19.0	7 47.3	10 44.8	2 30.5	27 46.1	7 32.2	0 23.5	10 14.7	14 09.0	19 21.4
21 M	13 57 45	27 35 33	26 26 02	2♈59 12	13 08.2	9 20.5	11 38.0	3 11.3	28 10.2	7 42.7	0 25.1	10 16.3	14 09.9	19 23.7
22 Tu	14 01 41	28 35 13	9♈37 40	16 21 16	12 56.2	10 53.1	12 31.9	3 52.0	28 34.3	7 53.1	0 26.7	10 17.9	14 10.7	19 26.0
23 W	14 05 38	29 34 54	23 09 43	0♉02 37	12 44.1	12 25.1	13 26.4	4 32.9	28 58.4	8 03.4	0 28.5	10 19.6	14 11.6	19 28.3
24 Th	14 09 34	0♏34 38	6♉59 30	13 59 49	12 33.2	13 56.6	14 21.6	5 13.7	29 22.6	8 13.6	0 30.4	10 21.3	14 12.5	19 30.6
25 F	14 13 31	1 34 24	21 02 57	28 08 17	12 24.6	15 27.5	15 17.3	5 54.7	29 46.8	8 23.8	0 32.4	10 23.1	14 13.4	19 32.9
26 Sa	14 17 28	2 34 12	5♊15 11	12♊23 05	12 18.6	16 57.8	16 13.7	6 35.6	0♐11.0	8 33.8	0 34.5	10 24.9	14 14.4	19 35.3
27 Su	14 21 24	3 34 02	19 31 25	26 39 44	12 15.5	18 27.6	17 10.6	7 16.7	0 35.3	8 43.7	0 36.6	10 26.8	14 15.4	19 37.6
28 M	14 25 21	4 33 54	3♋47 36	10♋54 42	12D14.6	19 56.8	18 08.1	7 57.7	0 59.6	8 53.6	0 38.9	10 28.7	14 16.5	19 40.0
29 Tu	14 29 17	5 33 49	18 00 47	25 05 39	12R14.9	21 25.4	19 06.0	8 38.8	1 23.9	9 03.3	0 41.3	10 30.7	14 17.5	19 42.3
30 W	14 33 14	6 33 45	2♌09 09	9♌11 12	12 15.1	22 53.5	20 04.6	9 20.0	1 48.3	9 13.0	0 43.7	10 32.6	14 18.6	19 44.7
31 Th	14 37 10	7 33 44	16 11 42	23 10 35	12 14.1	24 21.0	21 03.6	10 01.2	2 12.7	9 22.5	0 46.3	10 34.7	14 19.8	19 47.0

Astro Data

	Dy Hr Mn
♂0S	3 17:37
♃☍♆	7 22:27
☽0S	8 18:08
♀ D	13 8:55
♃⊼♄	14 18:16
♅ D	19 8:37
☽0N	23 2:32
☉0S	23 12:49
♆ D	26 7:13
☿0S	30 2:19
♄ D	5 3:57
☽0S	6 2:53
☽0N	20 10:46

Planet Ingress

		Dy Hr Mn
♂	♎	1 6:38
☿	♍	10 17:14
♃	♍	12 6:00
☉	♎	23 12:48
☿	♎	28 3:26
♀	♍	6 21:15
☿	♏	15 14:01
♂	♏	16 19:05
☉	♏	23 22:05
⚳	♐	26 1:06

Last Aspect / ☽ Ingress

Dy Hr Mn	Last Aspect	☽ Ingress	Dy Hr Mn
1 2:52	♂ △	♊	1 3:02
3 3:02	♃ ⚹	♋	3 6:19
4 12:19	♇ △	♌	5 8:13
7 7:51	♃ ☌	♍	7 9:35
8 15:37	♇ ⚹	♎	9 11:51
11 16:29	♃ ⚹	♏	11 16:42
13 7:53	♀ □	♐	14 1:14
15 22:01	☉ □	♑	16 13:04
18 16:23	☉ △	♒	19 1:58
20 21:53	♀ ☍	♓	21 13:20
23 5:06	☿ ☍	♈	23 21:56
25 16:52	♀ △	♉	26 3:59
27 23:21	♀ □	♊	28 8:25
30 4:58	♀ ⚹	♋	30 11:58

Last Aspect / ☽ Ingress

Dy Hr Mn	Last Aspect	☽ Ingress	Dy Hr Mn
1 22:04	♂ □	♌	2 14:58
4 15:14	♀ ☌	♍	4 17:45
6 1:48	♇ ⚹	♎	6 21:00
8 16:09	♂ ☌	♏	9 2:00
10 13:02	♇ ☌	♐	11 9:58
13 16:59	♂ ⚹	♑	13 21:10
16 9:32	♂ □	♒	16 10:04
18 11:17	☉ △	♓	18 21:53
20 10:51	♇ △	♈	21 6:33
23 11:08	☉ ☍	♉	23 11:55
24 21:25	♇ ☍	♊	25 15:09
26 18:55	♀ □	♋	27 17:37
29 5:03	☿ △	♌	29 20:20
31 14:15	☿ □	♍	31 23:47

☽ Phases & Eclipses

Dy Hr Mn		
1 18:16	☾	8♊49
8 11:01	●	15♍18
15 22:01	☽	22♐34
23 22:40	○	0♈24
1 0:30	☾	7♋21
7 21:39	●	14♎07
15 17:33	☽	21♑52
23 11:08	○	29♈33
30 7:11	☾	6♌22

Astro Data

1 September 1991
Julian Day # 33481
SVP 5♓22'17"
GC 26♐43.4 ⚴ 13♎52.7
Eris 17♈38.3R ⚵ 15♑58.4R
⚷ 4♌42.7 ⚶ 10♌40.9
☽ Mean ☊ 16♑14.4

1 October 1991
Julian Day # 33511
SVP 5♓22'14"
GC 26♐43.4 ⚴ 26♎41.9
Eris 17♈22.2R ⚵ 17♑27.9
⚷ 7♌28.7 ⚶ 23♌29.8
☽ Mean ☊ 14♑39.0

November 1991 — LONGITUDE

Day	Sid.Time	☉	0 hr ☽	Noon ☽	True ☊	☿	♀	♂	⚳	♃	♄	♅	♆	♇
1 F	14 41 07	8♏33 45	0♍07 46	7♍03 09	12♑10.8	25♏47.9	22♍03.0	10♏42.5	2♐37.1	9♍32.0	0♒48.9	10♑36.8	14♑20.9	19♏49.4
2 Sa	14 45 03	9 33 48	13 56 36	20 47 59	12R 05.0	27 14.1	23 03.0	11 23.8	3 01.5	9 41.3	0 51.7	10 38.9	14 22.1	19 51.8
3 Su	14 49 00	10 33 54	27 37 06	4♎23 44	11 56.7	28 39.7	24 03.3	12 05.2	3 26.0	9 50.5	0 54.5	10 41.1	14 23.3	19 54.2
4 M	14 52 57	11 34 01	11♎07 39	17 48 38	11 46.6	0♐04.6	25 04.1	12 46.6	3 50.5	9 59.6	0 57.4	10 43.3	14 24.6	19 56.6
5 Tu	14 56 53	12 34 10	24 26 25	1♏00 46	11 35.7	1 28.8	26 05.4	13 28.0	4 15.1	10 08.6	1 00.4	10 45.5	14 25.8	19 59.0
6 W	15 00 50	13 34 21	7♏31 32	13 58 31	11 25.1	2 52.2	27 07.0	14 09.5	4 39.6	10 17.5	1 03.6	10 47.8	14 27.1	20 01.4
7 Th	15 04 46	14 34 34	20 21 39	26 40 52	11 16.0	4 14.7	28 09.0	14 51.1	5 04.2	10 26.3	1 06.8	10 50.1	14 28.5	20 03.8
8 F	15 08 43	15 34 49	2♐56 13	9♐07 48	11 08.9	5 36.3	29 11.4	15 32.7	5 28.8	10 34.9	1 10.0	10 52.5	14 29.8	20 06.2
9 Sa	15 12 39	16 35 06	15 15 48	21 20 27	11 04.3	6 56.9	0♎14.1	16 14.3	5 53.4	10 43.4	1 13.4	10 54.9	14 31.2	20 08.6
10 Su	15 16 36	17 35 24	27 22 04	3♑21 03	11D 02.1	8 16.3	1 17.2	16 56.0	6 18.1	10 51.8	1 16.9	10 57.4	14 32.6	20 11.1
11 M	15 20 32	18 35 43	9♑17 50	15 12 56	11 01.8	9 34.5	2 20.7	17 37.8	6 42.7	11 00.1	1 20.4	10 59.8	14 34.1	20 13.5
12 Tu	15 24 29	19 36 04	21 06 53	27 00 18	11 02.7	10 51.3	3 24.4	18 19.6	7 07.4	11 08.3	1 24.1	11 02.4	14 35.6	20 15.9
13 W	15 28 26	20 36 27	2♒53 47	8♒48 00	11 04.0	12 06.6	4 28.5	19 01.4	7 32.1	11 16.3	1 27.8	11 04.9	14 37.1	20 18.3
14 Th	15 32 22	21 36 50	14 43 37	20 41 18	11R 04.7	13 20.2	5 32.9	19 43.3	7 56.8	11 24.2	1 31.6	11 07.5	14 38.6	20 20.8
15 F	15 36 19	22 37 15	26 41 44	2♓45 34	11 04.0	14 31.8	6 37.6	20 25.2	8 21.5	11 31.9	1 35.5	11 10.2	14 40.1	20 23.2
16 Sa	15 40 15	23 37 42	8♓53 26	15 05 56	11 01.5	15 41.2	7 42.6	21 07.2	8 46.2	11 39.6	1 39.5	11 12.8	14 41.7	20 25.6
17 Su	15 44 12	24 38 10	21 23 35	27 46 50	10 57.0	16 48.1	8 47.9	21 49.2	9 11.0	11 47.1	1 43.5	11 15.5	14 43.3	20 28.0
18 M	15 48 08	25 38 39	4♈16 04	10♈51 32	10 50.9	17 52.3	9 53.4	22 31.3	9 35.7	11 54.4	1 47.7	11 18.3	14 44.9	20 30.4
19 Tu	15 52 05	26 39 09	17 33 21	24 21 30	10 43.6	18 53.2	10 59.2	23 13.4	10 00.5	12 01.6	1 51.9	11 21.0	14 46.6	20 32.8
20 W	15 56 01	27 39 41	1♉15 50	8♉16 02	10 36.1	19 50.6	12 05.3	23 55.6	10 25.3	12 08.7	1 56.2	11 23.8	14 48.2	20 35.2
21 Th	15 59 58	28 40 14	15 21 37	22 31 59	10 29.3	20 44.0	13 11.7	24 37.8	10 50.1	12 15.6	2 00.5	11 26.7	14 49.9	20 37.6
22 F	16 03 55	29 40 49	29 46 26	7♊04 06	10 24.0	21 32.7	14 18.3	25 20.0	11 14.9	12 22.4	2 05.0	11 29.5	14 51.6	20 40.0
23 Sa	16 07 51	0♐41 26	14♊24 08	21 45 36	10 20.7	22 16.2	15 25.1	26 02.3	11 39.7	12 29.1	2 09.5	11 32.4	14 53.4	20 42.4
24 Su	16 11 48	1 42 04	29 07 37	6♋29 19	10D 19.3	22 53.9	16 32.2	26 44.7	12 04.5	12 35.6	2 14.1	11 35.4	14 55.1	20 44.8
25 M	16 15 44	2 42 43	13♋49 53	21 08 39	10 19.7	23 25.1	17 39.5	27 27.1	12 29.3	12 42.0	2 18.8	11 38.3	14 56.9	20 47.2
26 Tu	16 19 41	3 43 24	28 25 00	5♌38 26	10 21.0	23 48.9	18 47.1	28 09.5	12 54.2	12 48.2	2 23.5	11 41.3	14 58.7	20 49.6
27 W	16 23 37	4 44 07	12♌48 35	19 55 10	10 22.4	24 04.5	19 54.9	28 52.1	13 19.0	12 54.2	2 28.4	11 44.3	15 00.6	20 52.0
28 Th	16 27 34	5 44 51	26 58 01	3♍57 01	10R 23.2	24R 11.3	21 02.8	29 34.6	13 43.8	13 00.1	2 33.2	11 47.4	15 02.4	20 54.3
29 F	16 31 30	6 45 36	10♍52 07	17 43 21	10 22.7	24 08.4	22 11.0	0♐17.2	14 08.7	13 05.9	2 38.2	11 50.5	15 04.3	20 56.7
30 Sa	16 35 27	7 46 24	24 30 46	1♎14 25	10 20.6	23 55.1	23 19.4	0 59.9	14 33.5	13 11.4	2 43.2	11 53.6	15 06.1	20 59.0

December 1991 — LONGITUDE

Day	Sid.Time	☉	0 hr ☽	Noon ☽	True ☊	☿	♀	♂	⚳	♃	♄	♅	♆	♇
1 Su	16 39 24	8♐47 13	7♎54 23	14♎30 47	10♑17.0	23♐31.0	24♎28.0	1♐42.6	14♐58.4	13♍16.9	2♒48.3	11♑56.7	15♑08.0	21♏01.4
2 M	16 43 20	9 48 03	21 03 41	27 33 11	10R 12.3	22R 55.8	25 36.7	2 25.3	15 23.2	13 22.1	2 53.5	11 59.8	15 10.0	21 03.7
3 Tu	16 47 17	10 48 54	3♏59 21	10♏22 16	10 07.1	22 09.6	26 45.7	3 08.1	15 48.1	13 27.2	2 58.7	12 03.0	15 11.9	21 06.0
4 W	16 51 13	11 49 47	16 42 01	22 58 40	10 02.0	21 12.9	27 54.8	3 51.0	16 12.9	13 32.2	3 04.0	12 06.2	15 13.9	21 08.3
5 Th	16 55 10	12 50 41	29 12 18	5♐23 02	9 57.7	20 06.9	29 04.0	4 33.9	16 37.8	13 36.9	3 09.4	12 09.4	15 15.9	21 10.6
6 F	16 59 06	13 51 37	11♐30 59	17 36 16	9 54.5	18 53.1	0♏13.5	5 16.8	17 02.6	13 41.5	3 14.8	12 12.7	15 17.9	21 12.9
7 Sa	17 03 03	14 52 33	23 39 04	29 39 35	9D 52.7	17 33.7	1 23.1	5 59.8	17 27.5	13 45.9	3 20.3	12 15.9	15 19.9	21 15.2
8 Su	17 07 00	15 53 30	5♑38 03	11♑34 45	9 52.2	16 11.3	2 32.8	6 42.8	17 52.3	13 50.2	3 25.9	12 19.2	15 21.9	21 17.4
9 M	17 10 56	16 54 28	17 29 59	23 24 07	9 52.9	14 48.5	3 42.7	7 25.9	18 17.2	13 54.3	3 31.5	12 22.5	15 23.9	21 19.7
10 Tu	17 14 53	17 55 27	29 17 33	5♒10 43	9 54.4	13 28.2	4 52.7	8 09.1	18 42.0	13 58.2	3 37.2	12 25.9	15 26.0	21 21.9
11 W	17 18 49	18 56 26	11♒04 05	16 58 11	9 56.1	12 13.1	6 02.9	8 52.2	19 06.8	14 01.9	3 42.9	12 29.2	15 28.1	21 24.1
12 Th	17 22 46	19 57 27	22 53 33	28 50 44	9 57.8	11 05.3	7 13.2	9 35.5	19 31.6	14 05.5	3 48.7	12 32.6	15 30.2	21 26.3
13 F	17 26 42	20 58 27	4♓50 21	10♓53 00	9R 58.9	10 06.6	8 23.6	10 18.7	19 56.4	14 08.8	3 54.5	12 36.0	15 32.3	21 28.5
14 Sa	17 30 39	21 59 28	16 59 16	23 09 46	9 59.2	9 18.2	9 34.1	11 02.0	20 21.2	14 12.0	4 00.4	12 39.4	15 34.4	21 30.7
15 Su	17 34 35	23 00 30	29 25 05	5♈45 45	9 58.7	8 40.8	10 44.8	11 45.4	20 46.0	14 15.0	4 06.4	12 42.8	15 36.5	21 32.8
16 M	17 38 32	24 01 32	12♈12 17	18 45 04	9 57.4	8 14.5	11 55.6	12 28.8	21 10.7	14 17.8	4 12.4	12 46.2	15 38.6	21 34.9
17 Tu	17 42 29	25 02 35	25 24 28	2♉10 42	9 55.7	7D 59.3	13 06.5	13 12.2	21 35.5	14 20.5	4 18.5	12 49.7	15 40.8	21 37.0
18 W	17 46 25	26 03 37	9♉03 51	16 03 51	9 53.7	7 54.5	14 17.5	13 55.7	22 00.2	14 22.9	4 24.6	12 53.1	15 43.0	21 39.1
19 Th	17 50 22	27 04 41	23 10 30	0♊23 22	9 52.0	7 59.7	15 28.7	14 39.3	22 24.9	14 25.2	4 30.7	12 56.6	15 45.1	21 41.2
20 F	17 54 18	28 05 45	7♊41 55	15 05 23	9 50.6	8 14.0	16 39.9	15 22.8	22 49.7	14 27.3	4 36.9	13 00.1	15 47.3	21 43.3
21 Sa	17 58 15	29 06 49	22 32 54	0♋03 26	9D 49.9	8 36.6	17 51.3	16 06.5	23 14.3	14 29.2	4 43.2	13 03.6	15 49.5	21 45.3
22 Su	18 02 11	0♑07 54	7♋35 55	15 09 11	9 49.9	9 06.8	19 02.7	16 50.1	23 39.0	14 30.9	4 49.5	13 07.1	15 51.7	21 47.3
23 M	18 06 08	1 09 00	22 42 06	0♌13 32	9 50.3	9 43.7	20 14.3	17 33.9	24 03.7	14 32.5	4 55.8	13 10.6	15 53.9	21 49.4
24 Tu	18 10 04	2 10 06	7♌42 29	15 08 01	9 50.9	10 26.7	21 25.9	18 17.6	24 28.3	14 33.8	5 02.2	13 14.1	15 56.1	21 51.3
25 W	18 14 01	3 11 12	22 29 21	29 45 51	9 51.6	11 15.0	22 37.7	19 01.4	24 52.9	14 34.9	5 08.6	13 17.7	15 58.4	21 53.3
26 Th	18 17 58	4 12 19	6♍57 03	14♍02 36	9 52.1	12 08.0	23 49.5	19 45.3	25 17.5	14 35.9	5 15.1	13 21.2	16 00.6	21 55.2
27 F	18 21 54	5 13 27	21 02 20	27 56 12	9R 52.4	13 05.3	25 01.4	20 29.2	25 42.1	14 36.6	5 21.6	13 24.8	16 02.8	21 57.1
28 Sa	18 25 51	6 14 36	4♎44 15	11♎26 39	9 52.4	14 06.2	26 13.4	21 13.2	26 06.6	14 37.2	5 28.1	13 28.3	16 05.1	21 59.0
29 Su	18 29 47	7 15 44	18 03 38	24 35 28	9 52.3	15 10.5	27 25.6	21 57.2	26 31.2	14 37.6	5 34.7	13 31.9	16 07.3	22 00.9
30 M	18 33 44	8 16 54	1♏02 29	7♏25 03	9 52.1	16 17.6	28 37.7	22 41.2	26 55.7	14R 37.7	5 41.3	13 35.5	16 09.6	22 02.7
31 Tu	18 37 40	9 18 04	13 43 29	19 58 11	9D 52.0	17 27.2	29 50.0	23 25.3	27 20.2	14 37.7	5 48.0	13 39.0	16 11.8	22 04.5

Astro Data

	Dy Hr Mn
☽0S	2 9:05
♃△♅	11 10:51
♀0S	11 22:41
☽0N	16 19:15
☿R	28 17:01
☽0S	29 13:46
☽0N	14 3:04
☿D	18 11:12
☽0S	26 19:38
♃R	30 21:33

Planet Ingress

	Dy Hr Mn
☿ ♐	4 10:41
♀ ♎	9 6:37
☉ ♐	22 19:36
♂ ♐	29 2:19
♀ ♏	6 7:21
☉ ♑	22 8:54
♀ ♐	31 15:19

Last Aspect / ☽ Ingress

Last Aspect Dy Hr Mn		☽ Ingress Dy Hr Mn
3 0:39	☿ ⚹	♎ 3 4:13
4 5:52	♆ □	♏ 5 10:09
7 15:04	♀ ⚹	♐ 7 18:21
8 14:52	♃ □	♑ 10 5:16
11 22:13	♇ ⚹	♒ 12 18:06
14 14:02	☉ □	♓ 15 6:33
17 5:37	☉ △	♈ 17 16:08
19 1:36	☿ △	♉ 19 21:49
21 22:56	☉ ☍	♊ 22 0:22
23 12:52	☿ ☍	♋ 24 1:25
25 22:56	♂ △	♌ 26 2:37
28 4:04	♂ □	♍ 28 5:12
29 23:12	☿ □	♎ 30 9:47

Last Aspect / ☽ Ingress

Last Aspect Dy Hr Mn		☽ Ingress Dy Hr Mn
2 8:03	♀ ☌	♏ 2 16:33
4 8:28	♇ ☌	♐ 5 1:32
6 14:18	☿ ☌	♑ 7 12:41
9 7:46	♇ ⚹	♒ 10 1:27
11 21:01	♇ □	♓ 12 14:19
14 9:32	☉ □	♈ 15 1:06
16 22:18	☉ △	♉ 17 8:10
18 21:28	♇ ☍	♊ 19 11:21
21 10:23	☉ ☍	♋ 21 11:55
22 22:34	♇ △	♌ 23 11:38
24 23:11	♀ □	♍ 25 12:23
27 6:26	♀ ⚹	♎ 27 15:37
29 6:51	♂ ⚹	♏ 29 22:03

☽ Phases & Eclipses

Dy Hr Mn	
6 11:11	● 13♏32
14 14:02	☽ 21♒42
21 22:56	○ 29♉08
28 15:21	☾ 5♍53
6 3:56	● 13♐31
14 9:32	☽ 21♓53
21 10:23	○ 29♊03
21 10:33	• P 0.087
28 1:55	☾ 5♎49

Astro Data

1 November 1991
Julian Day # 33542
SVP 5♓22'10"
GC 26♐43.5 ⚴ 10♏18.7
Eris 17♈03.8R ⚵ 24♑06.7
⚷ 9♌14.8 ⚶ 5♍53.6
☽ Mean ☊ 13♑00.5

1 December 1991
Julian Day # 33572
SVP 5♓22'06"
GC 26♐43.6 ⚴ 23♏29.5
Eris 16♈49.6R ⚵ 3♒56.9
⚷ 9♌31.5R ⚶ 16♍15.0
☽ Mean ☊ 11♑25.2

LONGITUDE — January 1992

Day	Sid.Time	☉	0 hr ☽	Noon ☽	True ☊	☿	♀	♂	⚳	♃	♄	♅	♆	♇
1 W	18 41 37	10♑19 14	26♏09 30	2♐17 45	9♑52.0	18♐39.2	1♐02.3	24♐09.5	27♐44.6	14♍37.5	5♒54.7	13♑42.6	16♑14.1	22♏06.3
2 Th	18 45 33	11 20 25	8♐23 18	14 26 27	9 52.1	19 53.1	2 14.7	24 53.6	28 09.1	14R37.1	6 01.4	13 46.2	16 16.4	22 08.1
3 F	18 49 30	12 21 35	20 27 29	26 26 42	9 52.2	21 08.9	3 27.2	25 37.9	28 33.5	14 36.5	6 08.2	13 49.8	16 18.6	22 09.9
4 Sa	18 53 27	13 22 46	2♑24 22	8♑20 45	9R52.3	22 26.2	4 39.8	26 22.1	28 57.8	14 35.7	6 15.0	13 53.4	16 20.9	22 11.6
5 Su	18 57 23	14 23 57	14 16 04	20 10 37	9 52.3	23 45.0	5 52.4	27 06.5	29 22.2	14 34.7	6 21.8	13 57.0	16 23.2	22 13.3
6 M	19 01 20	15 25 08	26 04 37	1♒58 22	9 51.9	25 05.0	7 05.0	27 50.8	29 46.5	14 33.5	6 28.6	14 00.5	16 25.5	22 14.9
7 Tu	19 05 16	16 26 18	7♒52 07	13 46 10	9 51.2	26 26.3	8 17.7	28 35.2	0♑10.8	14 32.1	6 35.5	14 04.1	16 27.8	22 16.6
8 W	19 09 13	17 27 28	19 40 49	25 36 26	9 50.1	27 48.6	9 30.5	29 19.6	0 35.0	14 30.5	6 42.4	14 07.7	16 30.0	22 18.2
9 Th	19 13 09	18 28 38	1♓33 21	7♓31 59	9 48.9	29 11.8	10 43.3	0♑04.1	0 59.2	14 28.8	6 49.3	14 11.3	16 32.3	22 19.8
10 F	19 17 06	19 29 48	13 32 43	19 36 01	9 47.6	0♑36.0	11 56.2	0 48.6	1 23.4	14 26.8	6 56.3	14 14.9	16 34.6	22 21.3
11 Sa	19 21 02	20 30 57	25 42 20	1♈52 09	9 46.6	2 01.0	13 09.1	1 33.2	1 47.5	14 24.6	7 03.2	14 18.4	16 36.8	22 22.8
12 Su	19 24 59	21 32 05	8♈05 58	14 24 15	9D45.9	3 26.8	14 22.1	2 17.8	2 11.6	14 22.3	7 10.2	14 22.0	16 39.1	22 24.3
13 M	19 28 56	22 33 13	20 47 31	27 16 14	9 45.9	4 53.3	15 35.1	3 02.4	2 35.7	14 19.7	7 17.3	14 25.6	16 41.4	22 25.8
14 Tu	19 32 52	23 34 20	3♉50 48	10♉31 36	9 46.4	6 20.5	16 48.2	3 47.1	2 59.7	14 17.0	7 24.3	14 29.1	16 43.6	22 27.2
15 W	19 36 49	24 35 26	17 18 55	24 12 58	9 47.5	7 48.4	18 01.3	4 31.8	3 23.6	14 14.1	7 31.3	14 32.7	16 45.9	22 28.6
16 Th	19 40 45	25 36 32	1♊13 48	8♊21 22	9 48.7	9 16.9	19 14.4	5 16.6	3 47.6	14 11.0	7 38.4	14 36.2	16 48.2	22 30.0
17 F	19 44 42	26 37 38	15 35 25	22 55 33	9 49.8	10 46.1	20 27.6	6 01.4	4 11.5	14 07.8	7 45.5	14 39.7	16 50.4	22 31.3
18 Sa	19 48 38	27 38 42	0♋21 10	7♋51 29	9R50.3	12 15.8	21 40.9	6 46.2	4 35.3	14 04.3	7 52.6	14 43.3	16 52.7	22 32.7
19 Su	19 52 35	28 39 46	15 25 32	23 02 14	9 50.0	13 46.2	22 54.1	7 31.1	4 59.1	14 00.7	7 59.7	14 46.8	16 54.9	22 33.9
20 M	19 56 32	29 40 49	0♌40 20	8♌18 34	9 48.6	15 17.1	24 07.4	8 16.0	5 22.9	13 56.9	8 06.8	14 50.3	16 57.1	22 35.2
21 Tu	20 00 28	0♒41 52	15 55 37	23 30 14	9 46.2	16 48.7	25 20.8	9 00.9	5 46.6	13 52.9	8 13.9	14 53.8	16 59.4	22 36.4
22 W	20 04 25	1 42 53	1♍01 13	8♍27 31	9 43.2	18 20.8	26 34.2	9 45.9	6 10.2	13 48.7	8 21.1	14 57.2	17 01.6	22 37.6
23 Th	20 08 21	2 43 55	15 48 16	23 02 45	9 40.0	19 53.5	27 47.6	10 31.0	6 33.8	13 44.4	8 28.2	15 00.7	17 03.8	22 38.7
24 F	20 12 18	3 44 56	0♎10 30	7♎11 13	9 37.3	21 26.8	29 01.1	11 16.0	6 57.4	13 39.9	8 35.4	15 04.1	17 06.0	22 39.9
25 Sa	20 16 14	4 45 56	14 04 47	20 51 15	9 35.4	23 00.7	0♑14.6	12 01.1	7 20.9	13 35.2	8 42.6	15 07.6	17 08.2	22 41.0
26 Su	20 20 11	5 46 56	27 30 49	4♏03 49	9D34.6	24 35.3	1 28.1	12 46.3	7 44.4	13 30.4	8 49.7	15 11.0	17 10.4	22 42.0
27 M	20 24 07	6 47 56	10♏30 40	16 51 49	9 35.0	26 10.4	2 41.7	13 31.5	8 07.8	13 25.4	8 56.9	15 14.4	17 12.6	22 43.0
28 Tu	20 28 04	7 48 55	23 07 49	29 19 13	9 36.3	27 46.2	3 55.3	14 16.7	8 31.1	13 20.3	9 04.1	15 17.8	17 14.7	22 44.0
29 W	20 32 01	8 49 53	5♐26 35	11♐30 28	9 38.1	29 22.7	5 08.9	15 02.0	8 54.4	13 15.0	9 11.3	15 21.1	17 16.9	22 45.0
30 Th	20 35 57	9 50 51	17 31 27	23 30 01	9 39.9	0♒59.8	6 22.6	15 47.3	9 17.7	13 09.5	9 18.4	15 24.5	17 19.0	22 45.9
31 F	20 39 54	10 51 47	29 26 42	5♑21 58	9R40.9	2 37.5	7 36.3	16 32.6	9 40.8	13 03.9	9 25.6	15 27.8	17 21.2	22 46.8

LONGITUDE — February 1992

Day	Sid.Time	☉	0 hr ☽	Noon ☽	True ☊	☿	♀	♂	⚳	♃	♄	♅	♆	♇
1 Sa	20 43 50	11♒52 43	11♑16 14	17♑09 54	9♑40.7	4♒16.0	8♑50.0	17♑18.0	10♑04.0	12♍58.2	9♒32.8	15♑31.1	17♑23.3	22♏47.6
2 Su	20 47 47	12 53 39	23 03 19	28 56 50	9R38.8	5 55.2	10 03.7	18 03.4	10 27.0	12R52.3	9 40.0	15 34.4	17 25.4	22 48.4
3 M	20 51 43	13 54 33	4♒50 44	10♒45 16	9 35.2	7 35.0	11 17.5	18 48.8	10 50.0	12 46.3	9 47.2	15 37.7	17 27.5	22 49.2
4 Tu	20 55 40	14 55 25	16 40 40	22 37 11	9 29.9	9 15.6	12 31.3	19 34.3	11 13.0	12 40.1	9 54.3	15 41.0	17 29.6	22 50.0
5 W	20 59 36	15 56 17	28 35 01	4♓34 21	9 23.3	10 57.0	13 45.0	20 19.8	11 35.8	12 33.8	10 01.5	15 44.2	17 31.6	22 50.7
6 Th	21 03 33	16 57 07	10♓35 23	16 38 20	9 16.0	12 39.1	14 58.9	21 05.4	11 58.6	12 27.4	10 08.7	15 47.4	17 33.7	22 51.4
7 F	21 07 30	17 57 56	22 43 25	28 50 51	9 08.7	14 21.9	16 12.7	21 50.9	12 21.4	12 20.9	10 15.8	15 50.6	17 35.7	22 52.0
8 Sa	21 11 26	18 58 44	5♈00 54	11♈13 50	9 02.3	16 05.6	17 26.5	22 36.5	12 44.0	12 14.2	10 22.9	15 53.7	17 37.7	22 52.6
9 Su	21 15 23	19 59 30	17 29 57	23 49 34	8 57.4	17 50.0	18 40.4	23 22.2	13 06.6	12 07.5	10 30.1	15 56.8	17 39.7	22 53.2
10 M	21 19 19	21 00 15	0♉13 02	6♉40 41	8 54.4	19 35.2	19 54.2	24 07.8	13 29.1	12 00.6	10 37.2	15 59.9	17 41.7	22 53.7
11 Tu	21 23 16	22 00 58	13 12 53	19 49 59	8D53.3	21 21.2	21 08.1	24 53.5	13 51.6	11 53.7	10 44.3	16 03.0	17 43.7	22 54.2
12 W	21 27 12	23 01 40	26 32 19	3♊20 09	8 53.7	23 08.0	22 22.0	25 39.2	14 14.0	11 46.6	10 51.4	16 06.1	17 45.6	22 54.7
13 Th	21 31 09	24 02 20	10♊13 45	17 13 14	8 54.9	24 55.6	23 35.9	26 25.0	14 36.2	11 39.5	10 58.4	16 09.1	17 47.6	22 55.1
14 F	21 35 05	25 02 58	24 18 39	1♋29 54	8R56.0	26 43.9	24 49.8	27 10.7	14 58.5	11 32.2	11 05.5	16 12.1	17 49.5	22 55.5
15 Sa	21 39 02	26 03 35	8♋46 45	16 08 47	8 56.0	28 32.9	26 03.8	27 56.5	15 20.6	11 24.9	11 12.5	16 15.1	17 51.4	22 55.8
16 Su	21 42 59	27 04 09	23 35 23	1♌05 47	8 54.1	0♓22.6	27 17.7	28 42.4	15 42.7	11 17.6	11 19.5	16 18.0	17 53.3	22 56.1
17 M	21 46 55	28 04 43	8♌39 02	16 13 59	8 49.9	2 13.0	28 31.6	29 28.2	16 04.7	11 10.1	11 26.5	16 20.9	17 55.1	22 56.4
18 Tu	21 50 52	29 05 14	23 49 27	1♍24 07	8 43.5	4 03.9	29 45.6	0♒14.1	16 26.5	11 02.6	11 33.5	16 23.8	17 57.0	22 56.7
19 W	21 54 48	0♓05 44	8♍56 43	16 25 59	8 35.6	5 55.3	0♒59.6	1 00.0	16 48.4	10 55.0	11 40.4	16 26.6	17 58.8	22 56.9
20 Th	21 58 45	1 06 13	23 50 47	1♎10 07	8 27.1	7 47.1	2 13.6	1 45.9	17 10.1	10 47.4	11 47.4	16 29.4	18 00.6	22 57.1
21 F	22 02 41	2 06 40	8♎23 10	15 29 22	8 19.0	9 39.2	3 27.6	2 31.9	17 31.7	10 39.7	11 54.3	16 32.2	18 02.3	22 57.2
22 Sa	22 06 38	3 07 05	22 28 18	29 19 47	8 12.4	11 31.4	4 41.6	3 17.9	17 53.3	10 32.0	12 01.1	16 34.9	18 04.1	22 57.3
23 Su	22 10 34	4 07 30	6♏03 52	12♏40 41	8 07.9	13 23.6	5 55.6	4 03.9	18 14.8	10 24.2	12 08.0	16 37.6	18 05.8	22 57.4
24 M	22 14 31	5 07 53	19 10 36	25 34 02	8D05.5	15 15.4	7 09.6	4 50.0	18 36.2	10 16.4	12 14.8	16 40.3	18 07.5	22R57.4
25 Tu	22 18 28	6 08 15	1♐51 32	8♐03 42	8 05.0	17 06.8	8 23.7	5 36.0	18 57.4	10 08.6	12 21.6	16 42.9	18 09.2	22 57.4
26 W	22 22 24	7 08 35	14 11 11	20 14 39	8 05.6	18 57.3	9 37.7	6 22.1	19 18.6	10 00.7	12 28.4	16 45.6	18 10.9	22 57.3
27 Th	22 26 21	8 08 54	26 14 47	2♑12 14	8R06.4	20 46.7	10 51.8	7 08.3	19 39.7	9 52.9	12 35.1	16 48.1	18 12.5	22 57.3
28 F	22 30 17	9 09 11	8♑07 39	14 01 41	8 06.4	22 34.5	12 05.9	7 54.4	20 00.8	9 45.0	12 41.8	16 50.7	18 14.1	22 57.2
29 Sa	22 34 14	10 09 27	19 54 55	25 47 53	8 04.6	24 20.4	13 20.0	8 40.6	20 21.7	9 37.1	12 48.5	16 53.1	18 15.7	22 57.0

Astro Data	Planet Ingress	Last Aspect	☽ Ingress	Last Aspect	☽ Ingress	☽ Phases & Eclipses	Astro Data
Dy Hr Mn	Dy Hr Mn	Dy Hr Mn	Dy Hr Mn	Dy Hr Mn	Dy Hr Mn	Dy Hr Mn	1 January 1992
☽0N 10 9:52	⚳ ♑ 7 1:21	31 16:05 ♇ ☌	♐ 1 7:30	1 23:29 ♇ ⚹	♒ 2 14:09	4 23:10 ● 13♑51	Julian Day # 33603
♃△♅ 12 13:07	♂ ♑ 9 9:47	3 10:15 ♂ ☌	♑ 3 19:09	4 12:26 ♇ □	♓ 5 2:51	4 23:04:39 ● A 10'58"	SVP 5♓22'00"
☽0S 23 4:36	☿ ♑ 10 1:46	5 16:10 ♇ ⚹	♒ 6 7:59	7 0:16 ♇ △	♈ 7 14:15	13 2:32 ☽ 22♈09	GC 26♐43.7 ♀ 6♐40.7
	☉ ♒ 20 19:32	8 20:01 ♂ ⚹	♓ 8 20:52	9 11:05 ♂ □	♉ 9 23:36	19 21:28 ○ 29♋04	Eris 16♈43.2R ✱ 16♒26.1
☽0N 6 16:08	♀ ♑ 25 7:14	10 17:26 ♇ △	♈ 11 8:22	11 21:37 ♂ △	♊ 12 6:08	26 15:27 ☾ 5♏56	⚷ 8♌17.7R ⚵ 23♍44.5
♃⚻♄ 16 8:43	☿ ♒ 29 21:15	13 2:32 ☉ □	♉ 13 17:00	14 2:55 ☿ △	♋ 14 9:31		☽ Mean ☊ 9♑46.7
☽0S 19 15:49		15 12:42 ☉ △	♊ 15 21:55	16 7:59 ♂ ☍	♌ 16 10:15	3 19:00 ● 14♒12	
♇ R 24 21:33	☿ ♓ 16 7:04	17 7:37 ♀ ☍	♋ 17 23:26	18 8:04 ☉ ☍	♍ 18 9:47	11 16:15 ☽ 22♉12	1 February 1992
	♂ ♒ 18 4:38	19 21:28 ☉ ☍	♌ 19 22:57	19 22:32 ♇ ⚹	♎ 20 10:04	18 8:04 ○ 28♌55	Julian Day # 33634
	♀ ♒ 18 16:40	21 15:12 ♀ △	♍ 21 22:22	21 16:22 ♆ □	♏ 22 13:11	25 7:56 ☾ 5♐58	SVP 5♓21'54"
	☉ ♓ 19 9:43	23 20:43 ♀ □	♎ 23 23:42	24 7:04 ♇ ☌	♐ 24 20:26		GC 26♐43.7 ♀ 18♐49.6
		25 16:23 ☿ □	♏ 26 4:32	26 8:59 ☿ □	♑ 27 7:33		Eris 16♈47.4 ✱ 0♓30.2
		28 8:32 ☿ ⚹	♐ 28 13:20	29 8:30 ☿ ⚹	♒ 29 20:34		⚷ 6♌06.9R ⚵ 25♍35.1R
		29 15:26 ♃ □	♑ 31 1:07				☽ Mean ☊ 8♑08.3

March 1992 — LONGITUDE

Day	Sid.Time	☉	0 hr ☽	Noon ☽	True ☊	☿	♀	♂	⚳	♃	♄	♅	♆	♇
1 Su	22 38 10	11♓09 41	1♒41 06	7♒35 01	8♑00.3	26♓03.9	14♒34.0	9♒26.8	20♑42.5	9♍29.2	12♒55.1	16♑55.6	18♑17.2	22♏56.8
2 M	22 42 07	12 09 54	13 30 01	19 26 29	7R 53.3	27 44.5	15 48.1	10 13.0	21 03.2	9R 21.4	13 01.7	16 58.0	18 18.8	22R 56.6
3 Tu	22 46 03	13 10 05	25 24 40	1♓24 51	7 43.8	29 21.6	17 02.2	10 59.2	21 23.8	9 13.5	13 08.3	17 00.4	18 20.3	22 56.4
4 W	22 50 00	14 10 14	7♓27 12	13 31 54	7 32.1	0♈54.8	18 16.3	11 45.4	21 44.3	9 05.7	13 14.8	17 02.7	18 21.8	22 56.1
5 Th	22 53 56	15 10 21	19 39 02	25 48 42	7 19.3	2 23.5	19 30.4	12 31.7	22 04.6	8 57.9	13 21.3	17 05.0	18 23.2	22 55.8
6 F	22 57 53	16 10 26	2♈00 57	8♈15 51	7 06.5	3 47.1	20 44.5	13 18.0	22 24.9	8 50.1	13 27.7	17 07.3	18 24.7	22 55.4
7 Sa	23 01 50	17 10 29	14 33 26	20 53 45	6 54.9	5 05.0	21 58.6	14 04.3	22 45.1	8 42.4	13 34.1	17 09.5	18 26.1	22 55.0
8 Su	23 05 46	18 10 31	27 16 52	3♉42 51	6 45.4	6 16.7	23 12.7	14 50.6	23 05.1	8 34.7	13 40.5	17 11.7	18 27.4	22 54.6
9 M	23 09 43	19 10 30	10♉11 50	16 43 56	6 38.6	7 21.7	24 26.8	15 36.9	23 25.0	8 27.0	13 46.8	17 13.8	18 28.8	22 54.1
10 Tu	23 13 39	20 10 27	23 19 18	29 58 08	6 34.6	8 19.5	25 40.9	16 23.3	23 44.9	8 19.4	13 53.1	17 15.9	18 30.1	22 53.6
11 W	23 17 36	21 10 22	6♊40 37	13♊26 59	6D 33.1	9 09.7	26 55.0	17 09.6	24 04.6	8 11.9	13 59.3	17 17.9	18 31.4	22 53.1
12 Th	23 21 32	22 10 15	20 17 23	27 12 01	6R 32.9	9 52.0	28 09.0	17 56.0	24 24.1	8 04.4	14 05.5	17 19.9	18 32.6	22 52.6
13 F	23 25 29	23 10 05	4♋10 59	11♋14 20	6 33.0	10 26.1	29 23.1	18 42.4	24 43.6	7 57.0	14 11.6	17 21.9	18 33.9	22 52.0
14 Sa	23 29 25	24 09 54	18 22 02	25 33 54	6 31.9	10 51.8	0♓37.2	19 28.7	25 02.9	7 49.7	14 17.7	17 23.8	18 35.1	22 51.3
15 Su	23 33 22	25 09 39	2♌49 40	10♌08 52	6 28.6	11 08.9	1 51.3	20 15.1	25 22.1	7 42.5	14 23.8	17 25.7	18 36.3	22 50.7
16 M	23 37 19	26 09 23	17 30 54	24 55 01	6 22.5	11R 17.6	3 05.4	21 01.6	25 41.2	7 35.3	14 29.7	17 27.5	18 37.4	22 50.0
17 Tu	23 41 15	27 09 05	2♍20 20	9♍45 51	6 13.7	11 17.8	4 19.4	21 48.0	26 00.1	7 28.2	14 35.7	17 29.3	18 38.5	22 49.3
18 W	23 45 12	28 08 44	17 10 31	24 33 14	6 02.8	11 09.7	5 33.5	22 34.4	26 18.9	7 21.2	14 41.5	17 31.0	18 39.6	22 48.5
19 Th	23 49 08	29 08 21	1♎52 55	9♎08 34	5 50.9	10 53.9	6 47.6	23 20.8	26 37.6	7 14.4	14 47.4	17 32.7	18 40.7	22 47.8
20 F	23 53 05	0♈07 56	16 19 19	23 24 24	5 39.4	10 30.6	8 01.6	24 07.3	26 56.1	7 07.6	14 53.1	17 34.4	18 41.7	22 47.0
21 Sa	23 57 01	1 07 30	0♏23 16	7♏15 33	5 29.4	10 00.6	9 15.7	24 53.8	27 14.5	7 00.9	14 58.9	17 36.0	18 42.7	22 46.1
22 Su	0 00 58	2 07 02	14 01 01	20 39 40	5 21.9	9 24.6	10 29.8	25 40.2	27 32.8	6 54.4	15 04.5	17 37.5	18 43.6	22 45.3
23 M	0 04 54	3 06 32	27 11 39	3♐37 14	5 17.0	8 43.3	11 43.9	26 26.7	27 50.9	6 47.9	15 10.1	17 39.0	18 44.6	22 44.4
24 Tu	0 08 51	4 06 00	9♐56 50	16 10 57	5 14.6	7 57.9	12 57.9	27 13.2	28 08.9	6 41.6	15 15.7	17 40.5	18 45.5	22 43.4
25 W	0 12 48	5 05 26	22 20 10	28 25 07	5 13.8	7 09.2	14 12.0	27 59.7	28 26.7	6 35.4	15 21.2	17 41.9	18 46.3	22 42.5
26 Th	0 16 44	6 04 51	4♑26 27	10♑24 54	5 13.8	6 18.4	15 26.1	28 46.2	28 44.4	6 29.3	15 26.6	17 43.2	18 47.2	22 41.5
27 F	0 20 41	7 04 14	16 21 09	22 15 53	5 13.3	5 26.5	16 40.1	29 32.7	29 01.9	6 23.4	15 31.9	17 44.5	18 48.0	22 40.5
28 Sa	0 24 37	8 03 35	28 09 47	4♒03 31	5 11.2	4 34.6	17 54.2	0♓19.2	29 19.3	6 17.6	15 37.2	17 45.8	18 48.8	22 39.5
29 Su	0 28 34	9 02 54	9♒57 41	15 52 52	5 06.8	3 43.8	19 08.3	1 05.8	29 36.5	6 11.9	15 42.5	17 47.0	18 49.5	22 38.4
30 M	0 32 30	10 02 11	21 49 35	27 48 19	4 59.5	2 55.0	20 22.3	1 52.3	29 53.6	6 06.4	15 47.7	17 48.2	18 50.2	22 37.3
31 Tu	0 36 27	11 01 27	3♓49 28	9♓53 23	4 49.6	2 09.0	21 36.4	2 38.8	0♒10.5	6 01.0	15 52.8	17 49.3	18 50.9	22 36.2

April 1992 — LONGITUDE

Day	Sid.Time	☉	0 hr ☽	Noon ☽	True ☊	☿	♀	♂	⚳	♃	♄	♅	♆	♇
1 W	0 40 23	12♈00 40	16♓00 19	22♓10 30	4♑37.5	1♈26.6	22♓50.4	3♓25.3	0♒27.2	5♍55.7	15♒57.8	17♑50.3	18♑51.5	22♏35.1
2 Th	0 44 20	12 59 52	28 24 04	4♈41 04	4R 24.1	0R 48.4	24 04.5	4 11.9	0 43.8	5R 50.7	16 02.8	17 51.4	18 52.1	22R 33.9
3 F	0 48 17	13 59 01	11♈01 32	17 25 23	4 10.7	0 14.8	25 18.5	4 58.4	1 00.2	5 45.7	16 07.7	17 52.3	18 52.7	22 32.7
4 Sa	0 52 13	14 58 09	23 52 34	0♉22 57	3 58.3	29♓46.2	26 32.6	5 44.9	1 16.4	5 41.0	16 12.5	17 53.2	18 53.2	22 31.5
5 Su	0 56 10	15 57 14	6♉56 22	13 32 42	3 48.2	29 22.9	27 46.6	6 31.4	1 32.4	5 36.3	16 17.3	17 54.1	18 53.8	22 30.3
6 M	1 00 06	16 56 18	20 11 47	26 53 30	3 40.9	29 05.0	29 00.6	7 17.9	1 48.3	5 31.9	16 22.0	17 54.9	18 54.2	22 29.0
7 Tu	1 04 03	17 55 19	3♊37 44	10♊24 24	3 36.5	28 52.6	0♈14.6	8 04.4	2 04.0	5 27.6	16 26.6	17 55.7	18 54.7	22 27.7
8 W	1 07 59	18 54 18	17 13 28	24 04 53	3D 34.7	28D 45.8	1 28.6	8 50.9	2 19.5	5 23.5	16 31.1	17 56.4	18 55.1	22 26.4
9 Th	1 11 56	19 53 14	0♋58 40	7♋54 50	3R 34.4	28 44.3	2 42.6	9 37.4	2 34.8	5 19.6	16 35.6	17 57.0	18 55.5	22 25.1
10 F	1 15 52	20 52 09	14 53 23	21 54 18	3 34.6	28 48.2	3 56.6	10 23.9	2 49.9	5 15.8	16 40.0	17 57.6	18 55.8	22 23.8
11 Sa	1 19 49	21 51 01	28 57 33	6♌03 02	3 33.9	28 57.3	5 10.6	11 10.3	3 04.9	5 12.2	16 44.3	17 58.2	18 56.1	22 22.4
12 Su	1 23 46	22 49 50	13♌10 35	20 19 57	3 31.3	29 11.4	6 24.5	11 56.8	3 19.6	5 08.8	16 48.6	17 58.7	18 56.4	22 21.0
13 M	1 27 42	23 48 37	27 30 47	4♍42 40	3 26.1	29 30.3	7 38.5	12 43.2	3 34.1	5 05.5	16 52.7	17 59.2	18 56.7	22 19.6
14 Tu	1 31 39	24 47 22	11♍55 02	19 07 17	3 18.4	29 53.9	8 52.4	13 29.7	3 48.5	5 02.4	16 56.8	17 59.6	18 56.9	22 18.2
15 W	1 35 35	25 46 05	26 18 43	3♎28 36	3 08.8	0♈21.9	10 06.4	14 16.1	4 02.6	4 59.5	17 00.8	17 59.9	18 57.1	22 16.8
16 Th	1 39 32	26 44 46	10♎36 12	17 40 46	2 58.2	0 54.2	11 20.3	15 02.5	4 16.6	4 56.8	17 04.8	18 00.2	18 57.2	22 15.3
17 F	1 43 28	27 43 24	24 41 38	1♏38 11	2 47.9	1 30.5	12 34.2	15 48.9	4 30.3	4 54.3	17 08.6	18 00.5	18 57.3	22 13.8
18 Sa	1 47 25	28 42 01	8♏29 54	15 16 24	2 38.8	2 10.8	13 48.1	16 35.3	4 43.8	4 51.9	17 12.4	18 00.7	18 57.4	22 12.4
19 Su	1 51 21	29 40 36	21 57 26	28 32 51	2 31.9	2 54.7	15 02.1	17 21.7	4 57.1	4 49.7	17 16.1	18 00.8	18 57.4	22 10.9
20 M	1 55 18	0♉39 10	5♐02 40	11♐26 59	2 27.4	3 42.1	16 16.0	18 08.1	5 10.2	4 47.8	17 19.7	18 00.9	18R 57.5	22 09.3
21 Tu	1 59 14	1 37 41	17 46 04	24 00 15	2D 25.3	4 32.9	17 29.9	18 54.4	5 23.1	4 45.9	17 23.2	18R 01.0	18 57.4	22 07.8
22 W	2 03 11	2 36 11	0♑09 58	6♑15 42	2 25.0	5 27.0	18 43.8	19 40.8	5 35.7	4 44.3	17 26.6	18 01.0	18 57.4	22 06.3
23 Th	2 07 08	3 34 39	12 18 01	18 17 32	2 25.8	6 24.1	19 57.7	20 27.1	5 48.2	4 42.9	17 30.0	18 00.9	18 57.3	22 04.7
24 F	2 11 04	4 33 06	24 14 52	0♒10 41	2R 26.5	7 24.1	21 11.6	21 13.4	6 00.4	4 41.6	17 33.3	18 00.8	18 57.2	22 03.2
25 Sa	2 15 01	5 31 31	6♒05 40	12 00 27	2 26.4	8 26.9	22 25.4	21 59.7	6 12.3	4 40.5	17 36.4	18 00.6	18 57.0	22 01.6
26 Su	2 18 57	6 29 54	17 55 42	23 52 05	2 24.6	9 32.5	23 39.3	22 46.0	6 24.0	4 39.6	17 39.5	18 00.4	18 56.9	22 00.0
27 M	2 22 54	7 28 16	29 50 10	5♓50 32	2 20.7	10 40.7	24 53.2	23 32.3	6 35.5	4 38.9	17 42.5	18 00.2	18 56.7	21 58.4
28 Tu	2 26 50	8 26 36	11♓53 42	18 00 09	2 14.7	11 51.3	26 07.1	24 18.5	6 46.8	4 38.4	17 45.5	17 59.9	18 56.4	21 56.8
29 W	2 30 47	9 24 54	24 10 15	0♈24 22	2 07.0	13 04.4	27 20.9	25 04.8	6 57.7	4 38.1	17 48.3	17 59.5	18 56.1	21 55.1
30 Th	2 34 43	10 23 11	6♈42 43	13 05 28	1 58.1	14 19.9	28 34.8	25 51.0	7 08.5	4D 37.9	17 51.0	17 59.1	18 55.8	21 53.5

Astro Data

	Dy Hr Mn
☿0N	3 6:02
☽0N	4 22:31
☿R	17 0:31
☽0S	18 2:44
☉0N	20 8:49
☽0N	1 5:26
☿0S	6 18:18
☿D	9 6:26
♀0N	10 3:05
☽0S	14 11:12
♆R	20 12:14
♅R	21 23:19
☿0N	22 21:43
☽0N	28 12:53
♃D	30 19:38

Planet Ingress

		Dy Hr Mn
☿	♈	3 21:45
♀	♓	13 23:57
☉	♈	20 8:48
♂	♓	28 2:04
⚳	♒	30 21:04
☿	♓R	3 23:52
♀	♈	7 7:16
☿	♈	14 17:35
☉	♉	19 19:57

Last Aspect / ☽ Ingress

Last Aspect Dy Hr Mn			☽ Ingress	Dy Hr Mn
2 19:03	♇	□	♓	3 9:11
5 6:24	♇	△	♈	5 20:07
7 14:15	♀	⚹	♉	8 5:05
10 3:29	♀	□	♊	10 12:03
12 13:48	♀	△	♋	12 16:50
14 9:30	☉	△	♌	14 19:20
16 8:38	♇	□	♍	16 20:13
18 18:18	☉	☍	♎	18 20:55
20 13:18	♂	△	♏	20 23:20
22 21:46	♂	□	♐	23 5:13
25 11:06	♂	⚹	♑	25 15:08
27 12:50	♇	⚹	♒	28 3:44
30 1:37	♇	□	♓	30 16:23

Last Aspect / ☽ Ingress

Last Aspect Dy Hr Mn			☽ Ingress	Dy Hr Mn
1 13:26	♀	☌	♈	2 3:04
3 14:43	♆	□	♉	4 11:18
6 16:10	♀	⚹	♊	6 17:33
8 20:07	☿	□	♋	8 22:18
10 23:51	☿	△	♌	11 1:46
12 16:29	☉	△	♍	13 4:09
14 17:18	♇	⚹	♎	15 6:10
17 4:43	☉	☍	♏	17 9:10
19 0:26	♇	☌	♐	19 14:40
21 1:32	♂	□	♑	21 23:40
23 19:36	♇	⚹	♒	24 11:38
26 11:31	♀	⚹	♓	27 0:20
29 1:05	♂	☌	♈	29 11:13

☽ Phases & Eclipses

Dy Hr Mn		
4 13:22	●	14♓14
12 2:36	☽	21♊47
18 18:18	○	28♍24
26 2:30	☾	5♑41
3 5:01	●	13♈42
10 10:06	☽	20♋47
17 4:43	○	27♎26
24 21:40	☾	4♒57

Astro Data

1 March 1992
Julian Day # 33663
SVP 5♓21'51"
GC 26♐43.8 ⚳ 28♐28.0
Eris 16♈59.9 ✱ 14♓38.8
⚷ 4♌12.7R ⚶ 20♍49.8R
☽ Mean ☊ 6♑36.1

1 April 1992
Julian Day # 33694
SVP 5♓21'48"
GC 26♐43.9 ⚳ 5♑36.7
Eris 17♈19.0 ✱ 0♈29.7
⚷ 3♌18.0R ⚶ 13♍22.5R
☽ Mean ☊ 4♑57.6

LONGITUDE — May 1992

Day	Sid.Time	☉	0 hr ☽	Noon ☽	True ☊	☿	♀	♂	⚳	♃	♄	♅	♆	♇
1 F	2 38 40	11♉21 27	19♈32 41	26♈04 23	1♑49.0	15♈37.7	29♈48.7	26♓37.1	7♒19.0	4♍38.0	17♒53.7	17♑58.7	18♑55.5	21♏51.9
2 Sa	2 42 37	12 19 40	2♉40 27	9♉20 42	1R 40.7	16 57.7	1♉02.5	27 23.3	7 29.2	4 38.2	17 56.2	17R 58.2	18R 55.1	21R 50.2
3 Su	2 46 33	13 17 52	16 04 54	22 52 44	1 33.9	18 19.9	2 16.3	28 09.4	7 39.1	4 38.6	17 58.7	17 57.6	18 54.7	21 48.6
4 M	2 50 30	14 16 02	29 43 53	6♊37 57	1 29.3	19 44.2	3 30.2	28 55.5	7 48.8	4 39.2	18 01.1	17 57.0	18 54.3	21 46.9
5 Tu	2 54 26	15 14 11	13♊34 34	20 33 21	1D 26.8	21 10.6	4 44.0	29 41.6	7 58.3	4 39.9	18 03.3	17 56.4	18 53.8	21 45.3
6 W	2 58 23	16 12 18	27 33 56	4♋35 58	1 26.4	22 39.2	5 57.8	0♈27.6	8 07.4	4 40.9	18 05.5	17 55.7	18 53.3	21 43.6
7 Th	3 02 19	17 10 22	11♋39 10	18 43 13	1 27.2	24 09.8	7 11.6	1 13.6	8 16.3	4 42.0	18 07.6	17 54.9	18 52.8	21 41.9
8 F	3 06 16	18 08 25	25 47 54	2♌52 58	1 28.5	25 42.4	8 25.4	1 59.6	8 24.9	4 43.4	18 09.6	17 54.1	18 52.2	21 40.3
9 Sa	3 10 12	19 06 26	9♌58 13	17 03 27	1R 29.2	27 17.0	9 39.2	2 45.6	8 33.2	4 44.9	18 11.5	17 53.3	18 51.6	21 38.6
10 Su	3 14 09	20 04 25	24 08 29	1♍13 05	1 28.7	28 53.7	10 53.0	3 31.5	8 41.2	4 46.6	18 13.3	17 52.4	18 51.0	21 36.9
11 M	3 18 06	21 02 22	8♍17 01	15 20 03	1 26.5	0♉32.4	12 06.8	4 17.3	8 48.9	4 48.4	18 15.0	17 51.5	18 50.4	21 35.2
12 Tu	3 22 02	22 00 17	22 21 52	29 22 11	1 22.5	2 13.1	13 20.6	5 03.2	8 56.4	4 50.5	18 16.7	17 50.5	18 49.7	21 33.6
13 W	3 25 59	22 58 10	6♎20 38	13♎16 53	1 17.3	3 55.8	14 34.3	5 49.0	9 03.5	4 52.7	18 18.2	17 49.5	18 49.0	21 31.9
14 Th	3 29 55	23 56 02	20 10 35	27 01 21	1 11.4	5 40.6	15 48.1	6 34.8	9 10.4	4 55.1	18 19.6	17 48.4	18 48.2	21 30.2
15 F	3 33 52	24 53 52	3♏48 51	10♏32 47	1 05.6	7 27.3	17 01.8	7 20.5	9 17.0	4 57.6	18 20.9	17 47.3	18 47.5	21 28.5
16 Sa	3 37 48	25 51 40	17 12 53	23 48 55	1 00.5	9 16.1	18 15.6	8 06.2	9 23.2	5 00.3	18 22.2	17 46.2	18 46.7	21 26.9
17 Su	3 41 45	26 49 27	0♐20 46	6♐48 20	0 56.8	11 06.9	19 29.3	8 51.9	9 29.2	5 03.3	18 23.3	17 45.0	18 45.9	21 25.2
18 M	3 45 41	27 47 13	13 11 37	19 30 41	0D 54.7	12 59.7	20 43.1	9 37.5	9 34.8	5 06.3	18 24.3	17 43.7	18 45.0	21 23.5
19 Tu	3 49 38	28 44 58	25 45 41	1♑56 51	0 54.1	14 54.6	21 56.8	10 23.1	9 40.1	5 09.6	18 25.3	17 42.5	18 44.2	21 21.9
20 W	3 53 35	29 42 41	8♑04 28	14 08 52	0 54.8	16 51.3	23 10.5	11 08.7	9 45.1	5 13.0	18 26.1	17 41.1	18 43.3	21 20.2
21 Th	3 57 31	0♊40 23	20 10 28	26 09 45	0 56.3	18 50.1	24 24.2	11 54.2	9 49.8	5 16.6	18 26.9	17 39.8	18 42.4	21 18.6
22 F	4 01 28	1 38 04	2♒07 11	8♒03 20	0 58.0	20 50.7	25 38.0	12 39.7	9 54.2	5 20.3	18 27.5	17 38.4	18 41.4	21 16.9
23 Sa	4 05 24	2 35 44	13 58 46	19 54 03	0 59.4	22 53.1	26 51.7	13 25.2	9 58.2	5 24.2	18 28.1	17 36.9	18 40.4	21 15.3
24 Su	4 09 21	3 33 23	25 49 50	1♓46 41	1R 00.1	24 57.3	28 05.4	14 10.6	10 01.9	5 28.3	18 28.5	17 35.5	18 39.4	21 13.7
25 M	4 13 17	4 31 00	7♓45 14	13 46 05	0 59.8	27 03.1	29 19.2	14 55.9	10 05.2	5 32.5	18 28.9	17 33.9	18 38.4	21 12.0
26 Tu	4 17 14	5 28 37	19 49 48	25 56 57	0 58.3	29 10.4	0♊32.9	15 41.3	10 08.3	5 36.9	18 29.1	17 32.4	18 37.4	21 10.4
27 W	4 21 10	6 26 13	2♈08 02	8♈23 30	0 55.8	1♊19.1	1 46.6	16 26.6	10 11.0	5 41.4	18 29.3	17 30.8	18 36.3	21 08.8
28 Th	4 25 07	7 23 48	14 43 45	21 09 05	0 52.6	3 28.9	3 00.3	17 11.8	10 13.3	5 46.1	18R 29.3	17 29.2	18 35.2	21 07.2
29 F	4 29 04	8 21 22	27 39 45	4♉15 52	0 49.2	5 39.6	4 14.1	17 57.0	10 15.3	5 51.0	18 29.3	17 27.5	18 34.1	21 05.6
30 Sa	4 33 00	9 18 56	10♉57 28	17 44 27	0 46.1	7 51.1	5 27.8	18 42.1	10 16.9	5 56.0	18 29.1	17 25.8	18 32.9	21 04.1
31 Su	4 36 57	10 16 28	24 36 38	1♊33 42	0 43.6	10 03.0	6 41.5	19 27.2	10 18.2	6 01.2	18 28.9	17 24.0	18 31.8	21 02.5

LONGITUDE — June 1992

Day	Sid.Time	☉	0 hr ☽	Noon ☽	True ☊	☿	♀	♂	⚳	♃	♄	♅	♆	♇
1 M	4 40 53	11♊13 59	8♊35 16	15♊40 48	0♑42.1	12♊15.0	7♊55.2	20♈12.3	10♒19.2	6♍06.5	18♒28.6	17♑22.3	18♑30.6	21♏00.9
2 Tu	4 44 50	12 11 30	22 49 45	0♋01 29	0D 41.6	14 27.1	9 09.0	20 57.3	10 19.8	6 12.0	18R 28.1	17R 20.5	18R 29.4	20R 59.4
3 W	4 48 46	13 08 59	7♋15 19	14 30 34	0 41.9	16 38.7	10 22.7	21 42.2	10R 20.0	6 17.6	18 27.6	17 18.6	18 28.1	20 57.9
4 Th	4 52 43	14 06 27	21 46 33	29 02 38	0 42.9	18 49.7	11 36.4	22 27.1	10 19.9	6 23.4	18 27.0	17 16.8	18 26.9	20 56.4
5 F	4 56 40	15 03 54	6♌18 09	13♌32 35	0 44.0	20 59.9	12 50.1	23 11.9	10 19.4	6 29.3	18 26.3	17 14.9	18 25.6	20 54.9
6 Sa	5 00 36	16 01 19	20 45 24	27 56 11	0 45.0	23 08.9	14 03.8	23 56.7	10 18.6	6 35.4	18 25.4	17 12.9	18 24.3	20 53.4
7 Su	5 04 33	16 58 44	5♍04 32	12♍10 10	0R 45.5	25 16.5	15 17.5	24 41.4	10 17.4	6 41.6	18 24.5	17 11.0	18 23.0	20 51.9
8 M	5 08 29	17 56 07	19 12 50	26 12 21	0 45.4	27 22.6	16 31.2	25 26.0	10 15.8	6 47.9	18 23.5	17 09.0	18 21.7	20 50.5
9 Tu	5 12 26	18 53 29	3♎08 32	10♎01 19	0 44.8	29 26.9	17 44.9	26 10.6	10 13.9	6 54.4	18 22.4	17 07.0	18 20.3	20 49.1
10 W	5 16 22	19 50 50	16 50 37	23 36 23	0 43.7	1♋29.4	18 58.6	26 55.2	10 11.6	7 01.0	18 21.2	17 04.9	18 19.0	20 47.6
11 Th	5 20 19	20 48 10	0♏18 36	6♏57 14	0 42.5	3 29.9	20 12.3	27 39.7	10 09.0	7 07.7	18 19.9	17 02.9	18 17.6	20 46.2
12 F	5 24 15	21 45 29	13 32 19	20 03 52	0 41.3	5 28.3	21 26.0	28 24.1	10 06.0	7 14.6	18 18.5	17 00.8	18 16.2	20 44.9
13 Sa	5 28 12	22 42 48	26 31 55	2♐56 30	0 40.3	7 24.4	22 39.7	29 08.4	10 02.7	7 21.6	18 17.0	16 58.7	18 14.8	20 43.5
14 Su	5 32 09	23 40 05	9♐17 43	15 35 37	0 39.7	9 18.4	23 53.4	29 52.8	9 59.0	7 28.8	18 15.4	16 56.5	18 13.4	20 42.2
15 M	5 36 05	24 37 22	21 50 20	28 02 00	0D 39.5	11 10.1	25 07.1	0♉37.0	9 54.9	7 36.0	18 13.8	16 54.4	18 11.9	20 40.9
16 Tu	5 40 02	25 34 39	4♑10 45	10♑16 48	0 39.6	12 59.4	26 20.8	1 21.2	9 50.5	7 43.4	18 12.0	16 52.2	18 10.5	20 39.6
17 W	5 43 58	26 31 55	16 20 22	22 21 42	0 39.8	14 46.4	27 34.5	2 05.3	9 45.8	7 51.0	18 10.2	16 50.0	18 09.0	20 38.3
18 Th	5 47 55	27 29 10	28 21 05	4♒18 52	0 40.2	16 31.0	28 48.2	2 49.4	9 40.7	7 58.6	18 08.3	16 47.7	18 07.5	20 37.0
19 F	5 51 51	28 26 25	10♒15 24	16 11 05	0 40.5	18 13.2	0♋01.9	3 33.4	9 35.2	8 06.4	18 06.2	16 45.5	18 06.1	20 35.8
20 Sa	5 55 48	29 23 40	22 06 21	28 01 39	0 40.7	19 53.0	1 15.6	4 17.3	9 29.4	8 14.2	18 04.1	16 43.2	18 04.5	20 34.6
21 Su	5 59 44	0♋20 54	3♓57 28	9♓54 21	0R 40.8	21 30.4	2 29.4	5 01.2	9 23.2	8 22.2	18 01.9	16 41.0	18 03.0	20 33.4
22 M	6 03 41	1 18 08	15 52 49	21 53 24	0D 40.8	23 05.3	3 43.1	5 45.0	9 16.7	8 30.4	17 59.7	16 38.7	18 01.5	20 32.2
23 Tu	6 07 38	2 15 22	27 56 40	4♈03 12	0 40.8	24 37.9	4 56.8	6 28.8	9 09.9	8 38.6	17 57.3	16 36.4	18 00.0	20 31.1
24 W	6 11 34	3 12 37	10♈13 31	16 28 09	0 40.8	26 07.9	6 10.5	7 12.5	9 02.7	8 46.9	17 54.8	16 34.0	17 58.4	20 30.0
25 Th	6 15 31	4 09 51	22 47 37	29 12 21	0 41.1	27 35.5	7 24.3	7 56.1	8 55.2	8 55.4	17 52.3	16 31.7	17 56.9	20 28.9
26 F	6 19 27	5 07 05	5♉42 45	12♉19 07	0 41.4	29 00.6	8 38.0	8 39.6	8 47.4	9 04.0	17 49.7	16 29.3	17 55.3	20 27.8
27 Sa	6 23 24	6 04 19	19 01 42	25 50 35	0 41.9	0♌23.2	9 51.7	9 23.1	8 39.3	9 12.7	17 47.0	16 27.0	17 53.7	20 26.8
28 Su	6 27 20	7 01 33	2♊45 46	9♊47 05	0 42.4	1 43.2	11 05.5	10 06.5	8 30.8	9 21.5	17 44.2	16 24.6	17 52.1	20 25.8
29 M	6 31 17	7 58 47	16 54 16	24 06 50	0R 42.7	3 00.6	12 19.2	10 49.8	8 22.1	9 30.4	17 41.4	16 22.2	17 50.5	20 24.8
30 Tu	6 35 13	8 56 01	1♋24 12	8♋45 38	0 42.7	4 15.3	13 33.0	11 33.1	8 13.0	9 39.4	17 38.5	16 19.8	17 49.0	20 23.8

Astro Data Dy Hr Mn	Planet Ingress Dy Hr Mn	Last Aspect Dy Hr Mn	☽ Ingress Dy Hr Mn	Last Aspect Dy Hr Mn	☽ Ingress Dy Hr Mn	☽ Phases & Eclipses Dy Hr Mn	Astro Data
♄⊻♅ 3 3:19	♀ ♉ 1 15:41	30 22:52 ♆ □	♉ 1 19:09	1 20:01 ♂ ⚹	♋ 2 11:58	2 17:44 ● 12♉34	1 May 1992
♂0N 9 22:29	♂ ♈ 5 21:36	3 21:48 ♂ ⚹	♊ 4 0:28	4 0:31 ♂ □	♌ 4 13:35	9 15:44 ☽ 19♌15	Julian Day # 33724
☽0S 11 17:01	☿ ♉ 11 4:10	5 13:11 ☿ ⚹	♋ 6 4:09	6 4:57 ♂ △	♍ 6 15:28	16 16:03 ○ 26♏01	SVP 5♓21'45"
☽0N 25 20:36	☉ ♊ 20 19:12	7 22:21 ☿ □	♌ 8 7:07	8 14:22 ☿ □	♎ 8 18:33	24 15:53 ☾ 3♓43	GC 26♐43.9 ⚵ 7♑32.4R
♄ R 28 13:36	♀ ♊ 26 1:18	10 7:33 ☿ △	♍ 10 9:56	10 18:16 ♂ ☍	♏ 10 23:27		Eris 17♈38.5 ⚴ 16♈19.5
	☿ ♊ 26 21:16	11 22:39 ♇ ⚹	♎ 12 13:05	12 13:16 ♇ ☌	♐ 13 6:29	1 3:57 ● 10♊55	⚷ 3♌55.8 ⚶ 11♍26.7
⚳R 3 15:51		13 21:37 ♆ □	♏ 14 17:15	15 5:43 ♀ ☍	♑ 15 15:50	7 20:47 ☽ 17♍20	☽ Mean ☊ 3♑22.3
♄⊻♆ 4 8:16	☿ ♋ 9 18:27	16 16:03 ☉ ☍	♐ 16 23:22	17 8:34 ♇ ⚹	♒ 18 3:19	15 4:50 ○ 24♐20	
☽0S 7 21:57	♂ ♉ 14 15:56	18 9:53 ♄ ⚹	♑ 19 8:13	20 15:01 ☉ △	♓ 20 16:00	15 4:57 • P 0.682	1 June 1992
♄⊻♆ 19 19:35	♀ ♋ 19 11:22	21 8:04 ♀ △	♒ 21 19:43	22 14:44 ☿ △	♈ 23 4:03	23 8:11 ☾ 2♈06	Julian Day # 33755
☽0N 22 4:12	☉ ♋ 21 3:14	24 3:42 ♀ □	♓ 24 8:25	25 8:37 ☿ □	♉ 25 13:28	30 12:18 ● 8♋57	SVP 5♓21'40"
	☿ ♌ 27 5:11	26 19:35 ☿ ⚹	♈ 26 19:52	27 2:31 ♇ ☍	♊ 27 19:14	30 12:10:24 • T 05'20"	GC 26♐44.0 ⚵ 2♑47.4R
		28 7:14 ♆ □	♉ 29 4:16	29 1:21 ♄ △	♋ 29 21:42		Eris 17♈54.9 ⚴ 2♉59.2
		30 17:49 ♇ ☍	♊ 31 9:19				⚷ 6♌01.6 ⚶ 16♍28.0
							☽ Mean ☊ 1♑43.8

July 1992 LONGITUDE

Day	Sid.Time	☉	0 hr ☽	Noon ☽	True ☊	☿	♀	♂	⚳	♃	♄	♅	♆	♇
1 W	6 39 10	9♋53 15	16♋10 18	23♋37 14	0♑42.2	5♌27.4	14♋46.8	12♉16.2	8♒03.7	9♍48.5	17♒35.5	16♑17.4	17♑47.4	20♏22.9
2 Th	6 43 07	10 50 28	1♌05 26	8♌33 53	0R 41.3	6 36.6	16 00.5	12 59.3	7R 54.0	9 57.7	17R 32.4	16R 15.0	17R 45.8	20R 22.0
3 F	6 47 03	11 47 42	16 01 33	23 27 29	0 40.1	7 43.0	17 14.3	13 42.3	7 44.1	10 07.0	17 29.3	16 12.6	17 44.1	20 21.1
4 Sa	6 51 00	12 44 55	0♍50 47	8♍10 39	0 38.9	8 46.4	18 28.1	14 25.3	7 33.9	10 16.4	17 26.1	16 10.2	17 42.5	20 20.2
5 Su	6 54 56	13 42 07	15 26 28	22 37 42	0 37.7	9 46.8	19 41.8	15 08.1	7 23.5	10 26.0	17 22.8	16 07.8	17 40.9	20 19.4
6 M	6 58 53	14 39 20	29 43 58	6♎45 02	0D 37.1	10 44.1	20 55.6	15 50.9	7 12.8	10 35.6	17 19.4	16 05.4	17 39.3	20 18.6
7 Tu	7 02 49	15 36 32	13♎40 47	20 31 12	0 37.0	11 38.2	22 09.4	16 33.6	7 01.9	10 45.3	17 16.0	16 02.9	17 37.7	20 17.9
8 W	7 06 46	16 33 44	27 16 22	3♏56 27	0 37.6	12 28.9	23 23.1	17 16.2	6 50.7	10 55.1	17 12.5	16 00.5	17 36.0	20 17.1
9 Th	7 10 42	17 30 56	10♏31 41	17 02 18	0 38.7	13 16.1	24 36.9	17 58.7	6 39.4	11 04.9	17 09.0	15 58.1	17 34.4	20 16.4
10 F	7 14 39	18 28 08	23 28 37	29 50 56	0 40.0	13 59.8	25 50.7	18 41.1	6 27.8	11 14.9	17 05.4	15 55.7	17 32.8	20 15.7
11 Sa	7 18 36	19 25 20	6♐09 32	12♐24 46	0 41.3	14 39.7	27 04.4	19 23.4	6 16.0	11 25.0	17 01.7	15 53.3	17 31.2	20 15.1
12 Su	7 22 32	20 22 32	18 36 55	24 46 16	0R 42.0	15 15.7	28 18.2	20 05.7	6 04.1	11 35.1	16 58.0	15 50.9	17 29.6	20 14.5
13 M	7 26 29	21 19 44	0♑53 05	6♑57 39	0 42.0	15 47.8	29 32.0	20 47.9	5 52.0	11 45.4	16 54.2	15 48.5	17 27.9	20 13.9
14 Tu	7 30 25	22 16 57	13 00 13	19 01 00	0 41.0	16 15.6	0♌45.8	21 30.0	5 39.7	11 55.7	16 50.4	15 46.1	17 26.3	20 13.4
15 W	7 34 22	23 14 09	25 00 16	0♒58 14	0 38.8	16 39.2	1 59.5	22 12.0	5 27.3	12 06.1	16 46.5	15 43.7	17 24.7	20 12.8
16 Th	7 38 18	24 11 22	6♒55 09	12 51 16	0 35.7	16 58.4	3 13.3	22 53.9	5 14.7	12 16.5	16 42.6	15 41.3	17 23.1	20 12.4
17 F	7 42 15	25 08 36	18 46 49	24 42 07	0 31.8	17 12.9	4 27.1	23 35.7	5 02.0	12 27.1	16 38.7	15 38.9	17 21.5	20 11.9
18 Sa	7 46 11	26 05 50	0♓37 25	6♓33 04	0 27.6	17 22.8	5 40.9	24 17.5	4 49.2	12 37.7	16 34.6	15 36.5	17 19.9	20 11.5
19 Su	7 50 08	27 03 04	12 29 25	18 26 50	0 23.6	17R 27.8	6 54.7	24 59.1	4 36.3	12 48.4	16 30.6	15 34.2	17 18.3	20 11.1
20 M	7 54 05	28 00 20	24 25 43	0♈26 31	0 20.1	17 28.0	8 08.5	25 40.7	4 23.3	12 59.2	16 26.5	15 31.8	17 16.7	20 10.7
21 Tu	7 58 01	28 57 36	6♈29 41	12 35 43	0 17.7	17 23.3	9 22.3	26 22.2	4 10.2	13 10.1	16 22.3	15 29.5	17 15.1	20 10.4
22 W	8 01 58	29 54 52	18 45 06	24 58 22	0D 16.6	17 13.6	10 36.1	27 03.5	3 57.1	13 21.0	16 18.1	15 27.1	17 13.5	20 10.1
23 Th	8 05 54	0♌52 10	1♉16 01	7♉38 35	0 16.6	16 59.0	11 49.9	27 44.8	3 43.9	13 32.0	16 13.9	15 24.8	17 12.0	20 09.8
24 F	8 09 51	1 49 29	14 06 31	20 40 18	0 17.7	16 39.7	13 03.7	28 26.0	3 30.7	13 43.1	16 09.7	15 22.5	17 10.4	20 09.6
25 Sa	8 13 47	2 46 48	27 20 17	4♊06 49	0 19.2	16 15.7	14 17.5	29 07.1	3 17.5	13 54.2	16 05.4	15 20.2	17 08.9	20 09.4
26 Su	8 17 44	3 44 09	11♊00 03	18 00 07	0R 20.5	15 47.3	15 31.3	29 48.1	3 04.3	14 05.5	16 01.1	15 18.0	17 07.3	20 09.2
27 M	8 21 40	4 41 30	25 06 54	2♋20 10	0 20.9	15 14.9	16 45.1	0♊29.0	2 51.1	14 16.7	15 56.7	15 15.7	17 05.8	20 09.1
28 Tu	8 25 37	5 38 53	9♋39 30	17 04 16	0 19.9	14 38.8	17 58.9	1 09.8	2 37.9	14 28.1	15 52.4	15 13.5	17 04.3	20 09.0
29 W	8 29 34	6 36 16	24 33 39	2♌06 40	0 17.3	13 59.5	19 12.8	1 50.4	2 24.7	14 39.5	15 48.0	15 11.3	17 02.8	20 08.9
30 Th	8 33 30	7 33 40	9♌42 10	17 18 54	0 13.1	13 17.7	20 26.6	2 31.0	2 11.6	14 51.0	15 43.6	15 09.1	17 01.3	20D 08.9
31 F	8 37 27	8 31 05	24 55 35	2♍30 53	0 07.9	12 33.8	21 40.4	3 11.5	1 58.6	15 02.5	15 39.1	15 07.0	16 59.8	20 08.9

August 1992 LONGITUDE

Day	Sid.Time	☉	0 hr ☽	Noon ☽	True ☊	☿	♀	♂	⚳	♃	♄	♅	♆	♇
1 Sa	8 41 23	9♌28 30	10♍03 35	17♍32 31	0♑02.3	11♌48.8	22♌54.3	3♊51.8	1♒45.6	15♍14.1	15♒34.7	15♑04.8	16♑58.3	20♏08.9
2 Su	8 45 20	10 25 56	24 56 42	2♎15 19	29♐57.1	11R 03.3	24 08.1	4 32.0	1R 32.8	15 25.7	15R 30.2	15R 02.7	16R 56.8	20 09.0
3 M	8 49 16	11 23 23	9♎27 47	16 33 40	29R 53.2	10 18.2	25 21.9	5 12.1	1 20.0	15 37.4	15 25.7	15 00.6	16 55.4	20 09.1
4 Tu	8 53 13	12 20 50	23 32 45	0♏25 01	29D 50.9	9 34.3	26 35.7	5 52.1	1 07.4	15 49.2	15 21.3	14 58.5	16 54.0	20 09.3
5 W	8 57 09	13 18 18	7♏10 34	13 49 40	29 50.2	8 52.4	27 49.5	6 32.0	0 54.9	16 01.0	15 16.8	14 56.5	16 52.5	20 09.4
6 Th	9 01 06	14 15 47	20 22 39	26 49 57	29 50.9	8 13.5	29 03.3	7 11.8	0 42.6	16 12.9	15 12.3	14 54.5	16 51.1	20 09.6
7 F	9 05 03	15 13 17	3♐12 01	9♐29 24	29 52.1	7 38.2	0♍17.1	7 51.5	0 30.4	16 24.8	15 07.8	14 52.5	16 49.8	20 09.9
8 Sa	9 08 59	16 10 47	15 42 34	21 52 04	29R 53.3	7 07.3	1 30.9	8 31.0	0 18.4	16 36.8	15 03.3	14 50.6	16 48.4	20 10.2
9 Su	9 12 56	17 08 19	27 58 23	4♑02 01	29 53.5	6 41.5	2 44.7	9 10.4	0 06.6	16 48.8	14 58.8	14 48.6	16 47.0	20 10.5
10 M	9 16 52	18 05 51	10♑03 23	16 02 56	29 52.0	6 21.2	3 58.5	9 49.7	29♑55.0	17 00.9	14 54.3	14 46.7	16 45.7	20 10.8
11 Tu	9 20 49	19 03 24	22 01 01	27 58 00	29 48.5	6 07.1	5 12.3	10 28.9	29 43.6	17 13.0	14 49.9	14 44.9	16 44.4	20 11.2
12 W	9 24 45	20 00 58	3♒54 11	9♒49 52	29 42.7	5D 59.4	6 26.1	11 08.0	29 32.4	17 25.1	14 45.4	14 43.0	16 43.1	20 11.6
13 Th	9 28 42	20 58 33	15 45 17	21 40 40	29 34.8	5 58.6	7 39.9	11 46.9	29 21.5	17 37.3	14 40.9	14 41.2	16 41.8	20 12.1
14 F	9 32 38	21 56 10	27 36 14	3♓32 11	29 25.5	6 04.8	8 53.7	12 25.7	29 10.7	17 49.6	14 36.5	14 39.5	16 40.6	20 12.5
15 Sa	9 36 35	22 53 48	9♓28 44	15 26 05	29 15.4	6 18.3	10 07.4	13 04.4	29 00.3	18 01.8	14 32.1	14 37.7	16 39.3	20 13.1
16 Su	9 40 32	23 51 27	21 24 27	27 24 03	29 05.5	6 39.0	11 21.2	13 43.0	28 50.0	18 14.2	14 27.7	14 36.0	16 38.1	20 13.6
17 M	9 44 28	24 49 07	3♈25 10	9♈28 05	28 56.6	7 07.1	12 35.0	14 21.4	28 40.1	18 26.5	14 23.3	14 34.4	16 36.9	20 14.2
18 Tu	9 48 25	25 46 49	15 33 05	21 40 34	28 49.6	7 42.5	13 48.7	14 59.8	28 30.4	18 38.9	14 18.9	14 32.7	16 35.7	20 14.8
19 W	9 52 21	26 44 33	27 50 52	4♉04 26	28 44.9	8 25.2	15 02.5	15 37.9	28 21.0	18 51.4	14 14.6	14 31.1	16 34.6	20 15.4
20 Th	9 56 18	27 42 18	10♉21 41	16 43 06	28D 42.4	9 14.9	16 16.2	16 16.0	28 11.8	19 03.8	14 10.3	14 29.6	16 33.5	20 16.1
21 F	10 00 14	28 40 06	23 09 07	29 40 13	28 41.8	10 11.5	17 30.0	16 53.9	28 03.0	19 16.3	14 06.0	14 28.0	16 32.4	20 16.8
22 Sa	10 04 11	29 37 54	6♊16 51	12♊59 25	28 42.2	11 14.7	18 43.7	17 31.7	27 54.5	19 28.9	14 01.7	14 26.6	16 31.3	20 17.6
23 Su	10 08 07	0♍35 45	19 48 15	26 43 38	28R 42.7	12 24.4	19 57.5	18 09.3	27 46.3	19 41.5	13 57.5	14 25.1	16 30.2	20 18.4
24 M	10 12 04	1 33 37	3♋45 39	10♋54 20	28 42.2	13 40.1	21 11.2	18 46.8	27 38.4	19 54.1	13 53.3	14 23.7	16 29.2	20 19.2
25 Tu	10 16 01	2 31 31	18 09 29	25 30 42	28 39.7	15 01.5	22 25.0	19 24.1	27 30.8	20 06.7	13 49.2	14 22.4	16 28.2	20 20.0
26 W	10 19 57	3 29 27	2♌57 24	10♌28 45	28 34.7	16 28.3	23 38.7	20 01.3	27 23.5	20 19.4	13 45.1	14 21.1	16 27.2	20 20.9
27 Th	10 23 54	4 27 24	18 03 46	25 41 13	28 27.3	17 59.9	24 52.4	20 38.4	27 16.6	20 32.1	13 41.0	14 19.8	16 26.2	20 21.8
28 F	10 27 50	5 25 23	3♍19 48	10♍58 06	28 18.1	19 35.9	26 06.1	21 15.2	27 10.0	20 44.8	13 37.0	14 18.5	16 25.3	20 22.8
29 Sa	10 31 47	6 23 24	18 34 42	26 08 14	28 08.1	21 15.9	27 19.9	21 52.0	27 03.8	20 57.5	13 33.0	14 17.3	16 24.4	20 23.7
30 Su	10 35 43	7 21 25	3♎37 28	11♎01 19	27 58.7	22 59.4	28 33.6	22 28.5	26 57.9	21 10.3	13 29.1	14 16.2	16 23.5	20 24.8
31 M	10 39 40	8 19 29	18 18 55	25 29 38	27 50.8	24 45.9	29 47.3	23 04.9	26 52.3	21 23.1	13 25.3	14 15.1	16 22.6	20 25.8

Astro Data	Planet Ingress	Last Aspect	☽ Ingress	Last Aspect	☽ Ingress	☽ Phases & Eclipses	Astro Data
Dy Hr Mn	Dy Hr Mn	Dy Hr Mn	Dy Hr Mn	Dy Hr Mn	Dy Hr Mn	Dy Hr Mn	
☽0S 5 4:17	♀ ♌ 13 21:07	1 6:48 ♇ △	♌ 1 22:15	1 16:13 ♇ ⚹	♎ 2 8:17	7 2:43 ☽ 15♎14	1 July 1992
☽0N 19 11:20	☉ ♌ 22 14:09	3 6:59 ♇ □	♍ 3 22:37	4 4:39 ♀ ⚹	♏ 4 11:16	14 19:06 ○ 22♑34	Julian Day # 33785
☿R 20 0:53	♂ ♊ 26 18:59	5 8:09 ♇ ⚹	♎ 6 0:27	6 16:37 ♀ □	♐ 6 17:57	22 22:12 ☾ 0♉19	SVP 5♓21'34"
♇D 30 21:34		7 15:11 ♀ □	♏ 8 4:53	8 1:35 ♃ □	♑ 9 4:00	29 19:35 ● 6♌54	GC 26♐44.1 ⚴ 24♐24.8R
♃△♅ 31 19:49	☊ ♐R 1 22:09	10 3:38 ♀ △	♐ 10 12:17	10 20:18 ♇ ⚹	♒ 11 16:06		Eris 18♈03.3 ⚵ 19♉09.7
	♀ ♍ 7 6:26	11 20:53 ♄ ⚹	♑ 12 22:16	13 10:27 ☉ ☍	♓ 14 4:51	5 10:59 ☽ 13♏16	⚷ 9♌04.7 ⚶ 25♍59.0
☽0S 1 13:06	⚳ ♑R 10 1:39	14 19:06 ☉ ☍	♒ 15 10:03	15 21:37 ♇ △	♈ 16 17:11	13 10:27 ○ 20♒55	☽ Mean ☊ 0♑08.5
♃⚻♄ 2 18:39	☉ ♍ 22 21:10	17 9:37 ♂ □	♓ 17 22:44	18 20:40 ☉ △	♉ 19 4:10	21 10:01 ☾ 28♉35	
♃△♆ 9 8:51	♀ ♎ 31 16:09	20 6:44 ☉ △	♈ 20 11:07	21 10:01 ☉ □	♊ 21 12:36	28 2:42 ● 5♍03	1 August 1992
☿D 13 2:52		21 21:15 ☿ △	♉ 22 21:36	22 23:37 ♃ □	♋ 23 17:36		Julian Day # 33816
♄⚺♅ 13 9:29		25 2:42 ♂ ☌	♊ 25 4:44	25 6:30 ♀ ⚹	♌ 25 19:15		SVP 5♓21'29"
☽0N 15 17:54		26 8:38 ♄ △	♋ 27 8:08	27 3:44 ♂ ⚹	♍ 27 18:46		GC 26♐44.1 ⚴ 19♐07.9R
♃⚹♇ 26 15:08		28 16:57 ♇ △	♌ 29 8:39	29 14:05 ♀ ☌	♎ 29 18:10		Eris 18♈02.4R ⚵ 5♊31.3
☽0S 28 23:46		30 17:22 ♀ ☌	♍ 31 8:01	31 10:36 ☿ ⚹	♏ 31 19:38		⚷ 12♌49.1 ⚶ 8♎42.7
							☽ Mean ☊ 28♐30.0

LONGITUDE — September 1992

Day	Sid.Time	☉	0 hr ☽	Noon ☽	True ☊	☿	♀	♂	⚳	♃	♄	♅	♆	♇
1 Tu	10 43 36	9♍17 33	2♏33 03	9♏28 59	27♐45.2	26♌34.9	1♎01.0	23♊41.2	26♑47.1	21♍35.9	13♒21.4	14♑14.0	16♑21.8	20♏26.9
2 W	10 47 33	10 15 40	16 17 27	22 58 39	27R42.0	28 25.9	2 14.6	24 17.2	26R42.3	21 48.7	13R17.7	14R13.0	16R21.0	20 28.0
3 Th	10 51 30	11 13 47	29 32 53	6♐00 38	27D40.9	0♍18.7	3 28.3	24 53.2	26 37.8	22 01.6	13 14.0	14 12.0	16 20.3	20 29.1
4 F	10 55 26	12 11 56	12♐22 25	18 38 49	27R40.9	2 12.7	4 42.0	25 28.9	26 33.7	22 14.5	13 10.3	14 11.1	16 19.5	20 30.3
5 Sa	10 59 23	13 10 07	24 50 27	0♑57 58	27 40.9	4 07.6	5 55.6	26 04.5	26 30.0	22 27.3	13 06.8	14 10.2	16 18.8	20 31.5
6 Su	11 03 19	14 08 19	7♑02 00	13 03 10	27 40.0	6 03.0	7 09.2	26 39.8	26 26.6	22 40.2	13 03.2	14 09.4	16 18.1	20 32.7
7 M	11 07 16	15 06 32	19 02 04	24 59 14	27 37.1	7 58.7	8 22.9	27 15.1	26 23.5	22 53.1	12 59.8	14 08.6	16 17.5	20 34.0
8 Tu	11 11 12	16 04 47	0♒55 11	6♒50 25	27 31.6	9 54.5	9 36.5	27 50.1	26 20.9	23 06.1	12 56.4	14 07.9	16 16.8	20 35.2
9 W	11 15 09	17 03 04	12 45 19	18 40 18	27 23.3	11 50.1	10 50.1	28 25.0	26 18.5	23 19.0	12 53.1	14 07.2	16 16.2	20 36.6
10 Th	11 19 05	18 01 22	24 35 40	0♓31 42	27 12.3	13 45.3	12 03.6	28 59.6	26 16.6	23 31.9	12 49.8	14 06.6	16 15.7	20 37.9
11 F	11 23 02	18 59 42	6♓28 39	12 26 43	26 59.4	15 40.0	13 17.2	29 34.1	26 15.0	23 44.9	12 46.6	14 06.0	16 15.1	20 39.3
12 Sa	11 26 59	19 58 04	18 26 03	24 26 50	26 45.5	17 34.0	14 30.8	0♋08.4	26 13.8	23 57.9	12 43.5	14 05.4	16 14.6	20 40.7
13 Su	11 30 55	20 56 27	0♈29 11	6♈33 13	26 31.8	19 27.3	15 44.3	0 42.6	26 12.9	24 10.8	12 40.5	14 04.9	16 14.2	20 42.1
14 M	11 34 52	21 54 53	12 39 04	18 46 52	26 19.3	21 19.8	16 57.8	1 16.5	26D12.4	24 23.8	12 37.5	14 04.5	16 13.7	20 43.6
15 Tu	11 38 48	22 53 20	24 56 47	1♉09 00	26 09.1	23 11.4	18 11.3	1 50.2	26 12.2	24 36.8	12 34.6	14 04.1	16 13.3	20 45.1
16 W	11 42 45	23 51 50	7♉23 42	13 41 09	26 01.7	25 02.1	19 24.9	2 23.7	26 12.4	24 49.8	12 31.8	14 03.7	16 12.9	20 46.6
17 Th	11 46 41	24 50 22	20 01 37	26 25 25	25 57.3	26 51.8	20 38.3	2 57.1	26 12.9	25 02.7	12 29.1	14 03.4	16 12.6	20 48.1
18 F	11 50 38	25 48 56	2♊52 52	9♊24 22	25 55.2	28 40.5	21 51.8	3 30.2	26 13.8	25 15.7	12 26.4	14 03.2	16 12.3	20 49.7
19 Sa	11 54 34	26 47 32	16 00 15	22 40 52	25 54.8	0♎28.3	23 05.3	4 03.1	26 15.1	25 28.7	12 23.9	14 03.0	16 12.0	20 51.3
20 Su	11 58 31	27 46 11	29 26 35	6♋17 41	25 54.7	2 15.0	24 18.8	4 35.8	26 16.7	25 41.7	12 21.4	14 02.8	16 11.7	20 52.9
21 M	12 02 28	28 44 51	13♋14 21	20 16 44	25 53.7	4 00.8	25 32.2	5 08.3	26 18.7	25 54.7	12 19.0	14 02.7	16 11.5	20 54.6
22 Tu	12 06 24	29 43 34	27 24 47	4♌38 21	25 50.7	5 45.5	26 45.7	5 40.5	26 20.9	26 07.7	12 16.7	14D02.7	16 11.3	20 56.2
23 W	12 10 21	0♎42 19	11♌57 05	19 20 27	25 45.1	7 29.3	27 59.1	6 12.5	26 23.6	26 20.6	12 14.4	14 02.7	16 11.2	20 57.9
24 Th	12 14 17	1 41 07	26 47 42	4♍17 55	25 36.7	9 12.1	29 12.5	6 44.3	26 26.6	26 33.6	12 12.3	14 02.7	16 11.0	20 59.7
25 F	12 18 14	2 39 56	11♍50 02	19 22 49	25 26.3	10 53.9	0♏25.9	7 15.8	26 29.9	26 46.6	12 10.2	14 02.8	16 10.9	21 01.4
26 Sa	12 22 10	3 38 47	26 55 01	4♎25 20	25 15.0	12 34.8	1 39.3	7 47.1	26 33.5	26 59.5	12 08.3	14 03.0	16 10.9	21 03.2
27 Su	12 26 07	4 37 41	11♎52 31	19 15 25	25 04.0	14 14.7	2 52.7	8 18.2	26 37.5	27 12.5	12 06.4	14 03.2	16D10.8	21 05.0
28 M	12 30 03	5 36 36	26 33 04	3♏44 39	24 54.7	15 53.8	4 06.1	8 49.0	26 41.9	27 25.4	12 04.6	14 03.4	16 10.9	21 06.8
29 Tu	12 34 00	6 35 34	10♏49 34	17 47 27	24 47.7	17 31.9	5 19.4	9 19.5	26 46.5	27 38.3	12 02.9	14 03.7	16 10.9	21 08.7
30 W	12 37 56	7 34 33	24 38 06	1♐21 34	24 43.4	19 09.2	6 32.8	9 49.8	26 51.5	27 51.2	12 01.3	14 04.1	16 11.0	21 10.5

LONGITUDE — October 1992

Day	Sid.Time	☉	0 hr ☽	Noon ☽	True ☊	☿	♀	♂	⚳	♃	♄	♅	♆	♇
1 Th	12 41 53	8♎33 34	7♐58 01	14♐27 47	24♐41.5	20♎45.6	7♏46.1	10♋19.8	26♑56.8	28♍04.1	11♒59.9	14♑04.5	16♑11.1	21♏12.4
2 F	12 45 50	9 32 37	20 51 19	27 09 08	24D41.2	22 21.2	8 59.4	10 49.5	27 02.4	28 17.0	11R58.5	14 05.0	16 11.2	21 14.3
3 Sa	12 49 46	10 31 41	3♑21 51	9♑30 05	24R41.4	23 55.9	10 12.7	11 18.9	27 08.3	28 29.9	11 57.2	14 05.5	16 11.4	21 16.3
4 Su	12 53 43	11 30 47	15 34 31	21 35 49	24 41.0	25 29.8	11 25.9	11 48.1	27 14.6	28 42.7	11 56.0	14 06.0	16 11.6	21 18.2
5 M	12 57 39	12 29 55	27 34 38	3♒31 37	24 38.9	27 03.0	12 39.2	12 17.0	27 21.1	28 55.5	11 54.8	14 06.7	16 11.9	21 20.2
6 Tu	13 01 36	13 29 05	9♒27 24	15 22 33	24 34.5	28 35.3	13 52.4	12 45.6	27 28.0	29 08.3	11 53.8	14 07.3	16 12.1	21 22.2
7 W	13 05 32	14 28 17	21 17 36	27 13 03	24 27.4	0♏06.8	15 05.6	13 13.9	27 35.2	29 21.1	11 52.9	14 08.1	16 12.4	21 24.2
8 Th	13 09 29	15 27 30	3♓09 21	9♓06 53	24 17.9	1 37.5	16 18.8	13 41.9	27 42.6	29 33.8	11 52.1	14 08.8	16 12.8	21 26.2
9 F	13 13 25	16 26 45	15 05 58	21 06 54	24 06.5	3 07.5	17 32.0	14 09.6	27 50.4	29 46.5	11 51.4	14 09.6	16 13.2	21 28.3
10 Sa	13 17 22	17 26 02	27 09 53	3♈15 07	23 54.0	4 36.6	18 45.1	14 36.9	27 58.4	29 59.2	11 50.8	14 10.5	16 13.6	21 30.4
11 Su	13 21 19	18 25 21	9♈22 43	15 32 47	23 41.7	6 05.0	19 58.2	15 04.0	28 06.7	0♎11.9	11 50.3	14 11.4	16 14.0	21 32.5
12 M	13 25 15	19 24 43	21 45 22	28 00 31	23 30.6	7 32.6	21 11.3	15 30.8	28 15.3	0 24.5	11 49.8	14 12.4	16 14.5	21 34.6
13 Tu	13 29 12	20 24 06	4♉18 14	10♉38 35	23 21.5	8 59.4	22 24.4	15 57.2	28 24.2	0 37.1	11 49.5	14 13.4	16 15.0	21 36.7
14 W	13 33 08	21 23 31	17 01 33	23 27 12	23 15.1	10 25.4	23 37.5	16 23.2	28 33.3	0 49.7	11 49.3	14 14.5	16 15.5	21 38.8
15 Th	13 37 05	22 22 59	29 55 35	6♊26 47	23 11.3	11 50.6	24 50.5	16 49.0	28 42.7	1 02.3	11D49.2	14 15.6	16 16.1	21 41.0
16 F	13 41 01	23 22 29	13♊00 55	19 38 07	23D10.0	13 14.9	26 03.5	17 14.4	28 52.4	1 14.8	11 49.2	14 16.8	16 16.7	21 43.2
17 Sa	13 44 58	24 22 01	26 18 32	3♋02 20	23 10.3	14 38.3	27 16.5	17 39.4	29 02.4	1 27.2	11 49.3	14 18.0	16 17.4	21 45.3
18 Su	13 48 54	25 21 36	9♋49 42	16 40 46	23R11.0	16 00.7	28 29.5	18 04.0	29 12.6	1 39.7	11 49.5	14 19.3	16 18.0	21 47.6
19 M	13 52 51	26 21 13	23 35 40	0♌34 28	23 11.2	17 22.3	29 42.4	18 28.3	29 23.0	1 52.1	11 49.8	14 20.6	16 18.7	21 49.8
20 Tu	13 56 48	27 20 52	7♌37 09	14 43 40	23 09.8	18 42.7	0♐55.4	18 52.2	29 33.8	2 04.4	11 50.2	14 21.9	16 19.5	21 52.0
21 W	14 00 44	28 20 33	21 53 46	29 07 10	23 06.3	20 02.1	2 08.3	19 15.7	29 44.7	2 16.8	11 50.7	14 23.3	16 20.2	21 54.3
22 Th	14 04 41	29 20 17	6♍23 23	13♍41 50	23 00.6	21 20.4	3 21.2	19 38.8	29 55.9	2 29.0	11 51.3	14 24.8	16 21.0	21 56.5
23 F	14 08 37	0♏20 03	21 01 48	28 22 28	22 53.0	22 37.4	4 34.1	20 01.5	0♒07.4	2 41.3	11 52.0	14 26.3	16 21.9	21 58.8
24 Sa	14 12 34	1 19 51	5♎42 55	13♎02 13	22 44.6	23 53.0	5 46.9	20 23.7	0 19.1	2 53.4	11 52.8	14 27.9	16 22.7	22 01.1
25 Su	14 16 30	2 19 41	20 19 25	27 33 34	22 36.4	25 07.2	6 59.8	20 45.5	0 31.0	3 05.6	11 53.7	14 29.5	16 23.6	22 03.4
26 M	14 20 27	3 19 33	4♏43 51	11♏49 30	22 29.3	26 19.8	8 12.6	21 06.9	0 43.2	3 17.7	11 54.7	14 31.1	16 24.6	22 05.7
27 Tu	14 24 23	4 19 27	18 49 54	25 44 36	22 24.2	27 30.6	9 25.4	21 27.8	0 55.6	3 29.7	11 55.8	14 32.8	16 25.5	22 08.0
28 W	14 28 20	5 19 23	2♐33 17	9♐15 48	22D21.3	28 39.5	10 38.1	21 48.3	1 08.3	3 41.7	11 57.0	14 34.6	16 26.5	22 10.3
29 Th	14 32 17	6 19 20	15 52 10	22 22 29	22 20.4	29 46.3	11 50.9	22 08.3	1 21.1	3 53.6	11 58.3	14 36.4	16 27.6	22 12.6
30 F	14 36 13	7 19 20	28 47 01	5♑06 09	22 21.1	0♐50.7	13 03.6	22 27.8	1 34.2	4 05.5	11 59.8	14 38.2	16 28.6	22 15.0
31 Sa	14 40 10	8 19 21	11♑20 18	17 30 00	22 22.5	1 52.5	14 16.2	22 46.8	1 47.5	4 17.3	12 01.3	14 40.1	16 29.7	22 17.3

Astro Data

	Dy Hr Mn
♀0S	2 16:25
☽0N	12 0:07
⚳ D	15 10:53
☿0S	20 17:23
☉0S	22 18:43
♅ D	22 23:45
☽0S	25 10:29
♃♀♄	27 2:07
♆ D	27 18:36
☽0N	9 6:28
♄ D	16 2:06
♃0S	22 17:55
☽0S	22 19:19

Planet Ingress

	Dy Hr Mn
☿ ♍	3 8:03
♂ ♋	12 6:05
☿ ♎	19 5:41
☉ ♎	22 18:43
♀ ♏	25 3:31
☿ ♏	7 10:13
♃ ♎	10 13:26
♀ ♐	19 17:47
⚳ ♒	22 20:34
☉ ♏	23 3:57
☿ ♐	29 17:02

Last Aspect / ☽ Ingress (September)

Last Aspect Dy Hr Mn		☽ Ingress Dy Hr Mn
2 23:37	☿ □	♐ 3 0:50
5 1:55	♂ ☍	♑ 5 10:06
7 7:41	♃ △	♒ 7 22:08
10 8:44	♂ △	♓ 10 10:56
12 11:01	♃ ☍	♈ 12 23:02
14 8:03	♀ ☍	♉ 15 9:47
17 12:57	☿ △	♊ 17 18:40
19 19:53	☉ □	♋ 20 0:59
22 3:16	☉ ⚹	♌ 22 4:19
24 3:09	♀ ⚹	♍ 24 5:08
25 23:57	♃ ☌	♎ 26 4:55
27 6:59	♆ □	♏ 28 5:44
30 5:37	♃ ⚹	♐ 30 9:33

Last Aspect / ☽ Ingress (October)

Last Aspect Dy Hr Mn		☽ Ingress Dy Hr Mn
2 14:13	♃ □	♑ 2 17:29
5 2:33	♃ △	♒ 5 4:53
7 0:11	♇ □	♓ 7 17:38
10 5:28	♃ ☍	♈ 10 5:36
11 18:03	☉ ☍	♉ 12 15:48
14 12:21	♀ ☍	♊ 15 0:08
16 19:17	☉ △	♋ 17 6:36
19 10:22	♀ △	♌ 19 11:01
21 10:37	☉ ⚹	♍ 21 13:27
23 1:42	☿ ⚹	♎ 23 14:39
25 0:26	♂ □	♏ 25 16:04
27 15:23	☿ ☌	♐ 27 19:29
28 16:52	♄ ⚹	♑ 30 2:18

☽ Phases & Eclipses

Dy Hr Mn	
3 22:39	☽ 11♐40
12 2:17	○ 19♓34
19 19:53	☾ 27♊07
26 10:40	● 3♎36
3 14:12	☽ 10♑37
11 18:03	○ 18♈40
19 4:12	☾ 26♋02
25 20:34	● 2♏41

Astro Data

1 September 1992
Julian Day # 33847
SVP 5♓21'26"
GC 26♐44.2 ⚵ 20♐15.4
Eris 17♈52.1R ⚹ 20♊47.7
⚷ 16♌39.6 ⚶ 23♎14.6
☽ Mean ☊ 26♐51.5

1 October 1992
Julian Day # 33877
SVP 5♓21'23"
GC 26♐44.3 ⚵ 25♐57.7
Eris 17♈35.9R ⚹ 3♋17.0
⚷ 19♌59.5 ⚶ 8♏23.6
☽ Mean ☊ 25♐16.2

November 1992 — LONGITUDE

Day	Sid.Time	☉	0 hr ☽	Noon ☽	True ☊	☿	♀	♂	⚳	♃	♄	♅	♆	♇
1 Su	14 44 06	9♏19 23	23♑35 50	29♑38 23	22♐23.8	2♐51.4	15♐28.9	23♋05.3	2♒01.0	4♎29.1	12♒02.9	14♑42.0	16♑30.8	22♏19.7
2 M	14 48 03	10 19 28	5♒38 16	11♒36 10	22R 24.3	3 47.0	16 41.5	23 23.3	2 14.7	4 40.8	12 04.6	14 44.0	16 32.0	22 22.1
3 Tu	14 51 59	11 19 33	17 32 42	23 28 29	22 23.3	4 39.0	17 54.1	23 40.8	2 28.7	4 52.4	12 06.4	14 46.0	16 33.1	22 24.4
4 W	14 55 56	12 19 40	29 24 09	5♓20 17	22 20.6	5 26.9	19 06.6	23 57.8	2 42.8	5 04.0	12 08.3	14 48.0	16 34.3	22 26.8
5 Th	14 59 52	13 19 49	11♓17 26	17 16 07	22 16.1	6 10.3	20 19.1	24 14.3	2 57.1	5 15.5	12 10.4	14 50.1	16 35.6	22 29.2
6 F	15 03 49	14 20 00	23 16 48	29 19 53	22 10.3	6 48.7	21 31.5	24 30.1	3 11.7	5 26.9	12 12.5	14 52.3	16 36.8	22 31.6
7 Sa	15 07 46	15 20 12	5♈25 44	11♈34 38	22 03.7	7 21.4	22 44.0	24 45.5	3 26.4	5 38.3	12 14.7	14 54.4	16 38.1	22 34.0
8 Su	15 11 42	16 20 25	17 46 51	24 02 31	21 57.0	7 47.8	23 56.3	25 00.3	3 41.3	5 49.6	12 17.0	14 56.7	16 39.4	22 36.4
9 M	15 15 39	17 20 40	0♉21 46	6♉44 38	21 50.9	8 07.3	25 08.7	25 14.5	3 56.4	6 00.9	12 19.4	14 58.9	16 40.8	22 38.8
10 Tu	15 19 35	18 20 58	13 11 08	19 41 11	21 46.1	8R 19.2	26 21.0	25 28.1	4 11.6	6 12.0	12 21.9	15 01.2	16 42.2	22 41.2
11 W	15 23 32	19 21 16	26 14 43	2♊51 34	21 43.0	8 22.8	27 33.2	25 41.1	4 27.1	6 23.1	12 24.5	15 03.6	16 43.6	22 43.6
12 Th	15 27 28	20 21 37	9♊31 37	16 14 41	21D 41.6	8 17.4	28 45.4	25 53.4	4 42.7	6 34.1	12 27.2	15 06.0	16 45.0	22 46.0
13 F	15 31 25	21 21 59	23 00 36	29 49 11	21 41.7	8 02.4	29 57.6	26 05.2	4 58.6	6 45.1	12 29.9	15 08.4	16 46.5	22 48.4
14 Sa	15 35 21	22 22 23	6♋40 16	13♋33 42	21 42.9	7 37.3	1♑09.7	26 16.3	5 14.5	6 56.0	12 32.8	15 10.8	16 48.0	22 50.9
15 Su	15 39 18	23 22 49	20 29 19	27 27 00	21 44.5	7 02.0	2 21.8	26 26.8	5 30.7	7 06.7	12 35.8	15 13.3	16 49.5	22 53.3
16 M	15 43 15	24 23 17	4♌26 35	11♌27 57	21R 45.8	6 16.4	3 33.8	26 36.6	5 47.0	7 17.5	12 38.9	15 15.9	16 51.0	22 55.7
17 Tu	15 47 11	25 23 47	18 30 54	25 35 17	21 46.3	5 21.0	4 45.8	26 45.7	6 03.5	7 28.1	12 42.0	15 18.4	16 52.6	22 58.1
18 W	15 51 08	26 24 19	2♍40 53	9♍47 27	21 45.7	4 16.7	5 57.7	26 54.1	6 20.2	7 38.6	12 45.2	15 21.1	16 54.1	23 00.5
19 Th	15 55 04	27 24 52	16 54 40	24 02 13	21 43.9	3 04.8	7 09.6	27 01.8	6 37.0	7 49.1	12 48.6	15 23.7	16 55.8	23 02.9
20 F	15 59 01	28 25 27	1♎09 42	8♎16 41	21 41.2	1 47.3	8 21.4	27 08.8	6 53.9	7 59.4	12 52.0	15 26.4	16 57.4	23 05.3
21 Sa	16 02 57	29 26 04	15 22 41	22 27 13	21 37.9	0 26.3	9 33.2	27 15.0	7 11.1	8 09.7	12 55.5	15 29.1	16 59.1	23 07.7
22 Su	16 06 54	0♐26 43	29 29 44	6♏29 46	21 34.7	29♏04.7	10 44.9	27 20.5	7 28.4	8 19.9	12 59.1	15 31.8	17 00.7	23 10.1
23 M	16 10 50	1 27 23	13♏26 47	20 20 21	21 32.0	27 45.0	11 56.6	27 25.3	7 45.8	8 30.0	13 02.8	15 34.6	17 02.4	23 12.5
24 Tu	16 14 47	2 28 04	27 10 04	3♐55 35	21 30.1	26 30.0	13 08.2	27 29.3	8 03.4	8 40.0	13 06.6	15 37.4	17 04.2	23 14.9
25 W	16 18 44	3 28 47	10♐36 39	17 13 04	21D 29.3	25 21.9	14 19.8	27 32.4	8 21.1	8 49.9	13 10.4	15 40.3	17 05.9	23 17.3
26 Th	16 22 40	4 29 32	23 44 46	0♑11 44	21 29.5	24 22.8	15 31.3	27 34.8	8 39.0	8 59.7	13 14.4	15 43.2	17 07.7	23 19.7
27 F	16 26 37	5 30 17	6♑34 05	12 51 57	21 30.3	23 34.0	16 42.7	27 36.5	8 57.0	9 09.4	13 18.4	15 46.1	17 09.5	23 22.1
28 Sa	16 30 33	6 31 04	19 05 37	25 15 24	21 31.7	22 56.4	17 54.0	27R 37.3	9 15.1	9 19.0	13 22.5	15 49.0	17 11.3	23 24.5
29 Su	16 34 30	7 31 52	1♒21 40	7♒24 53	21 33.1	22 30.4	19 05.3	27 37.2	9 33.4	9 28.5	13 26.7	15 52.0	17 13.2	23 26.8
30 M	16 38 26	8 32 40	13 25 31	19 24 08	21 34.2	22D 15.9	20 16.5	27 36.4	9 51.8	9 37.9	13 31.0	15 55.0	17 15.0	23 29.2

December 1992 — LONGITUDE

Day	Sid.Time	☉	0 hr ☽	Noon ☽	True ☊	☿	♀	♂	⚳	♃	♄	♅	♆	♇
1 Tu	16 42 23	9♐33 30	25♒21 15	1♓17 29	21♐34.9	22♏12.5	21♑27.6	27♋34.7	10♒10.4	9♎47.1	13♒35.3	15♑58.0	17♑16.9	23♏31.5
2 W	16 46 19	10 34 20	7♓13 24	13 09 37	21R 35.1	22 19.6	22 38.7	27R 32.2	10 29.1	9 56.3	13 39.7	16 01.0	17 18.8	23 33.9
3 Th	16 50 16	11 35 11	19 06 44	25 05 20	21 34.7	22 36.4	23 49.6	27 28.9	10 47.9	10 05.3	13 44.2	16 04.1	17 20.7	23 36.2
4 F	16 54 13	12 36 03	1♈06 01	7♈09 18	21 33.9	23 02.2	25 00.5	27 24.7	11 06.8	10 14.3	13 48.8	16 07.2	17 22.7	23 38.5
5 Sa	16 58 09	13 36 56	13 15 42	19 25 41	21 32.9	23 35.9	26 11.2	27 19.7	11 25.8	10 23.1	13 53.5	16 10.3	17 24.6	23 40.8
6 Su	17 02 06	14 37 50	25 39 41	1♉58 02	21 31.9	24 16.8	27 21.9	27 13.9	11 45.0	10 31.8	13 58.2	16 13.5	17 26.6	23 43.1
7 M	17 06 02	15 38 44	8♉21 01	14 48 51	21 31.0	25 04.0	28 32.5	27 07.2	12 04.3	10 40.4	14 03.0	16 16.7	17 28.6	23 45.4
8 Tu	17 09 59	16 39 40	21 21 38	27 59 23	21 30.4	25 56.9	29 42.9	26 59.6	12 23.7	10 48.9	14 07.9	16 19.9	17 30.6	23 47.7
9 W	17 13 55	17 40 36	4♊42 03	11♊29 28	21D 30.1	26 54.6	0♒53.3	26 51.2	12 43.2	10 57.2	14 12.9	16 23.1	17 32.6	23 49.9
10 Th	17 17 52	18 41 33	18 21 22	25 17 26	21 30.1	27 56.7	2 03.5	26 42.0	13 02.8	11 05.5	14 17.9	16 26.4	17 34.6	23 52.2
11 F	17 21 48	19 42 31	2♋17 14	9♋20 17	21 30.2	29 02.4	3 13.7	26 31.9	13 22.5	11 13.6	14 23.0	16 29.6	17 36.7	23 54.4
12 Sa	17 25 45	20 43 30	16 26 05	23 34 03	21R 30.3	0♐11.5	4 23.7	26 21.0	13 42.4	11 21.5	14 28.1	16 32.9	17 38.8	23 56.6
13 Su	17 29 42	21 44 30	0♌43 36	7♌54 11	21 30.3	1 23.3	5 33.6	26 09.3	14 02.3	11 29.4	14 33.4	16 36.2	17 40.8	23 58.8
14 M	17 33 38	22 45 31	15 05 14	22 16 13	21 30.3	2 37.7	6 43.4	25 56.7	14 22.3	11 37.1	14 38.7	16 39.6	17 42.9	24 01.0
15 Tu	17 37 35	23 46 33	29 26 39	6♍36 06	21 30.1	3 54.2	7 53.1	25 43.4	14 42.5	11 44.7	14 44.0	16 42.9	17 45.0	24 03.2
16 W	17 41 31	24 47 36	13♍44 10	20 50 31	21D 30.0	5 12.5	9 02.6	25 29.2	15 02.7	11 52.2	14 49.4	16 46.3	17 47.2	24 05.4
17 Th	17 45 28	25 48 40	27 54 53	4♎57 01	21 30.1	6 32.5	10 12.0	25 14.3	15 23.1	11 59.5	14 54.9	16 49.6	17 49.3	24 07.5
18 F	17 49 24	26 49 45	11♎56 45	18 53 54	21 30.4	7 53.9	11 21.3	24 58.5	15 43.5	12 06.6	15 00.5	16 53.0	17 51.4	24 09.6
19 Sa	17 53 21	27 50 50	25 48 20	2♏39 58	21 30.9	9 16.5	12 30.4	24 42.1	16 04.0	12 13.7	15 06.1	16 56.5	17 53.6	24 11.7
20 Su	17 57 17	28 51 57	9♏28 41	16 14 24	21 31.6	10 40.3	13 39.4	24 24.9	16 24.7	12 20.6	15 11.8	16 59.9	17 55.8	24 13.8
21 M	18 01 14	29 53 04	22 57 03	29 36 33	21 32.3	12 05.0	14 48.3	24 07.0	16 45.4	12 27.3	15 17.5	17 03.3	17 58.0	24 15.9
22 Tu	18 05 11	0♑54 12	6♐12 51	12♐45 53	21R 32.8	13 30.5	15 57.0	23 48.4	17 06.2	12 33.9	15 23.3	17 06.8	18 00.1	24 17.9
23 W	18 09 07	1 55 21	19 15 37	25 42 00	21 32.9	14 56.8	17 05.5	23 29.2	17 27.1	12 40.4	15 29.2	17 10.3	18 02.4	24 20.0
24 Th	18 13 04	2 56 30	2♑05 03	8♑24 46	21 32.4	16 23.8	18 13.9	23 09.4	17 48.1	12 46.7	15 35.1	17 13.7	18 04.6	24 22.0
25 F	18 17 00	3 57 39	14 41 13	20 54 29	21 31.2	17 51.4	19 22.1	22 49.0	18 09.1	12 52.9	15 41.0	17 17.2	18 06.8	24 24.0
26 Sa	18 20 57	4 58 48	27 04 41	3♒11 59	21 29.4	19 19.5	20 30.1	22 28.0	18 30.3	12 58.9	15 47.1	17 20.7	18 09.0	24 25.9
27 Su	18 24 53	5 59 58	9♒16 37	15 18 49	21 27.2	20 48.2	21 38.0	22 06.6	18 51.5	13 04.7	15 53.1	17 24.3	18 11.2	24 27.9
28 M	18 28 50	7 01 08	21 18 55	27 17 16	21 24.7	22 17.4	22 45.6	21 44.7	19 12.8	13 10.4	15 59.2	17 27.8	18 13.5	24 29.8
29 Tu	18 32 47	8 02 17	3♓14 16	9♓10 20	21 22.5	23 46.9	23 53.1	21 22.4	19 34.2	13 16.0	16 05.4	17 31.3	18 15.7	24 31.7
30 W	18 36 43	9 03 27	15 05 59	21 01 43	21 20.7	25 17.0	25 00.4	20 59.7	19 55.7	13 21.3	16 11.6	17 34.8	18 18.0	24 33.6
31 Th	18 40 40	10 04 36	26 58 05	2♈55 40	21D 19.6	26 47.4	26 07.4	20 36.7	20 17.2	13 26.5	16 17.9	17 38.4	18 20.2	24 35.4

Astro Data	Dy Hr Mn
☽0N	5 13:27
☿R	11 9:49
☽0S	19 1:33
♃∠♇	21 5:57
♂R	28 23:31
☿D	1 7:30
☽0N	2 21:12
☽0S	16 6:42
☽0N	30 5:24

Planet Ingress	Dy Hr Mn
♀ ♑	13 12:48
☿ ♏R	21 19:44
☉ ♐	22 1:26
♀ ♒	8 17:49
☿ ♐	12 8:05
☉ ♑	21 14:43

Last Aspect Dy Hr Mn		☽ Ingress	Dy Hr Mn
31 22:39	♂ ☍	♒	1 12:43
3 9:50	♇ □	♓	4 1:13
6 2:13	♂ △	♈	6 13:19
8 13:52	♂ □	♉	8 23:19
10 22:46	♂ ⚹	♊	11 6:49
13 12:16	♀ ☍	♋	13 12:19
15 10:15	♂ ☌	♌	15 16:23
17 11:39	☉ □	♍	17 19:28
19 18:07	☉ ⚹	♎	19 22:03
21 20:13	♂ □	♏	22 0:52
24 0:31	♂ △	♐	24 5:01
25 4:36	♄ ⚹	♑	26 11:38
28 16:38	♂ ☍	♒	28 21:19

Last Aspect Dy Hr Mn		☽ Ingress	Dy Hr Mn
30 20:15	♇ □	♓	1 9:23
3 16:46	♂ △	♈	3 21:49
6 3:04	♂ □	♉	6 8:16
8 15:24	♀ △	♊	8 15:37
9 23:41	☉ ☍	♋	10 20:05
12 16:36	♂ ☌	♌	12 22:47
14 14:56	♇ □	♍	15 0:56
16 19:44	♂ ⚹	♎	17 3:33
19 2:53	☉ ⚹	♏	19 7:20
21 2:20	♇ ☌	♐	21 12:42
22 18:26	♀ ⚹	♑	23 20:04
25 18:48	♇ ⚹	♒	26 5:43
28 6:22	♇ □	♓	28 17:28
30 21:51	☿ □	♈	31 6:07

☽ Phases & Eclipses Dy Hr Mn	
2 9:11	☽ 10♒12
10 9:20	○ 18♉14
17 11:39	☾ 25♌23
24 9:11	● 2♐21
2 6:17	☽ 10♓20
9 23:41	○ 18♊10
9 23:44	☊ T 1.271
16 19:13	☾ 25♍06
24 0:43	● 2♑28
24 0:30:43	☋ P 0.842

Astro Data

1 November 1992
Julian Day # 33908
SVP 5♓21'19"
GC 26♐44.4 ⚳ 4♑42.0
Eris 17♈17.6R ⚵ 11♋31.4
⚷ 22♌30.2 ⚶ 24♏45.0
☽ Mean ☊ 23♐37.7

1 December 1992
Julian Day # 33938
SVP 5♓21'15"
GC 26♐44.4 ⚳ 14♑40.3
Eris 17♈03.5R ⚵ 12♋02.1R
⚷ 23♌33.7 ⚶ 10♐56.2
☽ Mean ☊ 22♐02.4

LONGITUDE — January 1993

Day	Sid.Time	☉	0 hr ☽	Noon ☽	True ☊	☿	♀	♂	⚳	♃	♄	♅	♆	♇
1 F	18 44 36	11♑05 45	8♈55 02	14♈56 47	21♐19.5	28♐18.2	27♒14.2	20♋13.4	20♒38.8	13♎31.6	16♒24.2	17♑41.9	18♑22.5	24♏37.3
2 Sa	18 48 33	12 06 54	21 01 31	27 09 51	21 20.2	29 49.4	28 20.8	19R49.9	21 00.5	13 36.5	16 30.6	17 45.5	18 24.7	24 39.1
3 Su	18 52 29	13 08 03	3♉22 20	9♉39 30	21 21.6	1♑20.9	29 27.2	19 26.2	21 22.3	13 41.2	16 37.0	17 49.1	18 27.0	24 40.9
4 M	18 56 26	14 09 12	16 01 52	22 29 50	21 23.3	2 52.9	0♓33.3	19 02.4	21 44.1	13 45.8	16 43.4	17 52.6	18 29.3	24 42.6
5 Tu	19 00 22	15 10 20	29 03 46	5♊43 54	21 24.7	4 25.2	1 39.2	18 38.5	22 05.9	13 50.1	16 49.9	17 56.2	18 31.5	24 44.3
6 W	19 04 19	16 11 28	12♊30 23	19 23 12	21R25.4	5 58.0	2 44.8	18 14.5	22 27.9	13 54.4	16 56.4	17 59.8	18 33.8	24 46.1
7 Th	19 08 16	17 12 36	26 22 14	3♋27 09	21 25.0	7 31.1	3 50.1	17 50.6	22 49.9	13 58.4	17 03.0	18 03.3	18 36.1	24 47.7
8 F	19 12 12	18 13 44	10♋37 30	17 52 41	21 23.1	9 04.6	4 55.2	17 26.6	23 12.0	14 02.3	17 09.6	18 06.9	18 38.4	24 49.4
9 Sa	19 16 09	19 14 51	25 11 55	2♌34 20	21 20.0	10 38.5	6 00.0	17 02.8	23 34.1	14 06.0	17 16.3	18 10.5	18 40.6	24 51.0
10 Su	19 20 05	20 15 58	9♌58 57	17 24 44	21 15.9	12 12.8	7 04.4	16 39.2	23 56.3	14 09.5	17 23.0	18 14.0	18 42.9	24 52.6
11 M	19 24 02	21 17 05	24 50 40	2♍15 43	21 11.4	13 47.6	8 08.6	16 15.7	24 18.5	14 12.9	17 29.7	18 17.6	18 45.2	24 54.2
12 Tu	19 27 58	22 18 12	9♍38 56	16 59 29	21 07.3	15 22.8	9 12.4	15 52.5	24 40.8	14 16.1	17 36.4	18 21.2	18 47.5	24 55.7
13 W	19 31 55	23 19 19	24 16 38	1♎29 48	21 04.1	16 58.5	10 16.0	15 29.5	25 03.2	14 19.1	17 43.2	18 24.7	18 49.7	24 57.2
14 Th	19 35 51	24 20 26	8♎38 34	15 42 38	21D02.4	18 34.7	11 19.2	15 06.9	25 25.6	14 21.9	17 50.0	18 28.3	18 52.0	24 58.7
15 F	19 39 48	25 21 32	22 41 50	29 36 10	21 02.1	20 11.4	12 22.0	14 44.6	25 48.0	14 24.5	17 56.9	18 31.8	18 54.3	25 00.2
16 Sa	19 43 45	26 22 39	6♏25 40	13♏10 28	21 03.1	21 48.5	13 24.5	14 22.7	26 10.6	14 26.9	18 03.7	18 35.4	18 56.5	25 01.6
17 Su	19 47 41	27 23 45	19 50 48	26 26 53	21 04.7	23 26.2	14 26.6	14 01.3	26 33.1	14 29.2	18 10.6	18 38.9	18 58.8	25 03.0
18 M	19 51 38	28 24 51	2♐59 00	9♐27 23	21R06.2	25 04.4	15 28.4	13 40.3	26 55.7	14 31.3	18 17.6	18 42.5	19 01.1	25 04.4
19 Tu	19 55 34	29 25 57	15 52 21	22 14 07	21 06.7	26 43.2	16 29.8	13 19.9	27 18.4	14 33.2	18 24.5	18 46.0	19 03.3	25 05.7
20 W	19 59 31	0♒27 02	28 32 55	4♑48 59	21 05.7	28 22.5	17 30.7	13 00.0	27 41.1	14 34.9	18 31.5	18 49.5	19 05.6	25 07.0
21 Th	20 03 27	1 28 06	11♑02 30	17 13 38	21 02.6	0♒02.4	18 31.3	12 40.8	28 03.9	14 36.4	18 38.5	18 53.0	19 07.8	25 08.3
22 F	20 07 24	2 29 10	23 22 31	29 29 19	20 57.4	1 42.9	19 31.4	12 22.1	28 26.7	14 37.8	18 45.6	18 56.5	19 10.0	25 09.5
23 Sa	20 11 20	3 30 14	5♒34 08	11♒37 08	20 50.3	3 24.0	20 31.0	12 04.1	28 49.6	14 38.9	18 52.6	19 00.0	19 12.3	25 10.7
24 Su	20 15 17	4 31 16	17 38 25	23 38 11	20 41.8	5 05.7	21 30.2	11 46.8	29 12.4	14 39.8	18 59.7	19 03.5	19 14.5	25 11.9
25 M	20 19 14	5 32 18	29 36 35	5♓33 49	20 32.6	6 48.0	22 28.9	11 30.1	29 35.4	14 40.6	19 06.8	19 07.0	19 16.7	25 13.0
26 Tu	20 23 10	6 33 18	11♓30 10	17 25 52	20 23.8	8 30.8	23 27.1	11 14.2	29 58.3	14 41.2	19 13.9	19 10.4	19 18.9	25 14.1
27 W	20 27 07	7 34 18	23 21 16	29 16 44	20 16.0	10 14.3	24 24.8	10 59.1	0♓21.3	14 41.5	19 21.0	19 13.9	19 21.1	25 15.2
28 Th	20 31 03	8 35 16	5♈12 41	11♈09 34	20 10.0	11 58.3	25 21.9	10 44.6	0 44.4	14R41.7	19 28.2	19 17.3	19 23.3	25 16.3
29 F	20 35 00	9 36 13	17 07 52	23 08 09	20 06.2	13 43.0	26 18.5	10 31.0	1 07.5	14 41.7	19 35.3	19 20.7	19 25.4	25 17.3
30 Sa	20 38 56	10 37 10	29 10 59	5♉16 56	20D04.5	15 28.1	27 14.5	10 18.1	1 30.6	14 41.5	19 42.5	19 24.1	19 27.6	25 18.2
31 Su	20 42 53	11 38 04	11♉26 39	17 40 45	20 04.5	17 13.7	28 09.8	10 06.0	1 53.7	14 41.1	19 49.7	19 27.5	19 29.7	25 19.2

LONGITUDE — February 1993

Day	Sid.Time	☉	0 hr ☽	Noon ☽	True ☊	☿	♀	♂	⚳	♃	♄	♅	♆	♇
1 M	20 46 49	12♒38 58	23♉59 49	0♊24 28	20♐05.5	18♒59.8	29♓04.5	9♋54.8	2♓16.9	14♎40.6	19♒56.9	19♑30.9	19♑31.9	25♏20.1
2 Tu	20 50 46	13 39 50	6♊55 14	13 32 34	20R06.5	20 46.3	29 58.6	9R44.3	2 40.1	14R39.8	20 04.1	19 34.2	19 34.0	25 21.0
3 W	20 54 43	14 40 41	20 16 54	27 08 26	20 06.4	22 33.0	0♈52.0	9 34.6	3 03.3	14 38.8	20 11.3	19 37.5	19 36.1	25 21.8
4 Th	20 58 39	15 41 31	4♋07 19	11♋13 29	20 04.5	24 20.0	1 44.7	9 25.8	3 26.6	14 37.7	20 18.5	19 40.8	19 38.2	25 22.6
5 F	21 02 36	16 42 19	18 26 38	25 46 18	20 00.1	26 07.0	2 36.6	9 17.7	3 49.9	14 36.4	20 25.7	19 44.1	19 40.3	25 23.4
6 Sa	21 06 32	17 43 06	3♌11 46	10♌42 06	19 53.3	27 54.0	3 27.8	9 10.4	4 13.2	14 34.8	20 32.9	19 47.4	19 42.4	25 24.1
7 Su	21 10 29	18 43 51	18 16 12	25 52 46	19 44.7	29 40.8	4 18.1	9 04.0	4 36.5	14 33.1	20 40.2	19 50.6	19 44.4	25 24.8
8 M	21 14 25	19 44 36	3♍30 27	11♍07 50	19 35.2	1♓27.1	5 07.6	8 58.3	4 59.9	14 31.2	20 47.4	19 53.8	19 46.5	25 25.5
9 Tu	21 18 22	20 45 19	18 43 32	26 16 15	19 26.1	3 12.8	5 56.3	8 53.4	5 23.3	14 29.1	20 54.6	19 57.0	19 48.5	25 26.1
10 W	21 22 18	21 46 01	3♎44 51	11♎08 24	19 18.4	4 57.5	6 44.1	8 49.4	5 46.7	14 26.9	21 01.8	20 00.2	19 50.5	25 26.7
11 Th	21 26 15	22 46 42	18 26 09	25 37 35	19 13.0	6 40.9	7 31.0	8 46.1	6 10.1	14 24.4	21 09.1	20 03.4	19 52.5	25 27.3
12 F	21 30 12	23 47 22	2♏42 24	9♏40 30	19 10.0	8 22.6	8 16.9	8 43.5	6 33.5	14 21.8	21 16.3	20 06.5	19 54.5	25 27.8
13 Sa	21 34 08	24 48 00	16 31 57	23 16 58	19D09.1	10 02.2	9 01.8	8 41.8	6 57.0	14 18.9	21 23.5	20 09.6	19 56.4	25 28.3
14 Su	21 38 05	25 48 38	29 55 52	6♐29 03	19R09.4	11 39.2	9 45.7	8D40.8	7 20.5	14 15.9	21 30.8	20 12.7	19 58.4	25 28.7
15 M	21 42 01	26 49 15	12♐56 59	19 20 08	19 09.7	13 13.1	10 28.6	8 40.5	7 44.0	14 12.8	21 38.0	20 15.7	20 00.3	25 29.2
16 Tu	21 45 58	27 49 50	25 39 02	1♑54 09	19 09.0	14 43.4	11 10.3	8 41.0	8 07.5	14 09.4	21 45.2	20 18.7	20 02.2	25 29.5
17 W	21 49 54	28 50 24	8♑05 58	14 14 54	19 06.1	16 09.3	11 50.9	8 42.3	8 31.1	14 05.8	21 52.4	20 21.7	20 04.1	25 29.9
18 Th	21 53 51	29 50 57	20 21 22	26 25 44	19 00.4	17 30.3	12 30.3	8 44.3	8 54.6	14 02.1	21 59.6	20 24.7	20 05.9	25 30.2
19 F	21 57 47	0♓51 29	2♒28 18	8♒29 22	18 51.7	18 45.7	13 08.4	8 46.9	9 18.2	13 58.2	22 06.8	20 27.6	20 07.8	25 30.5
20 Sa	22 01 44	1 51 59	14 29 10	20 27 55	18 40.3	19 54.8	13 45.2	8 50.3	9 41.8	13 54.2	22 14.0	20 30.5	20 09.6	25 30.7
21 Su	22 05 41	2 52 27	26 25 46	2♓22 56	18 26.9	20 56.9	14 20.7	8 54.4	10 05.4	13 50.0	22 21.1	20 33.4	20 11.4	25 30.9
22 M	22 09 37	3 52 53	8♓19 31	14 15 42	18 12.4	21 51.4	14 54.9	8 59.2	10 29.0	13 45.6	22 28.3	20 36.3	20 13.2	25 31.1
23 Tu	22 13 34	4 53 18	20 11 39	26 07 31	17 58.2	22 37.7	15 27.5	9 04.7	10 52.6	13 41.0	22 35.4	20 39.1	20 15.0	25 31.2
24 W	22 17 30	5 53 42	2♈03 31	7♈59 52	17 45.3	23 15.3	15 58.6	9 10.8	11 16.2	13 36.3	22 42.5	20 41.9	20 16.7	25 31.3
25 Th	22 21 27	6 54 03	13 56 50	19 54 45	17 34.7	23 43.8	16 28.2	9 17.6	11 39.9	13 31.4	22 49.6	20 44.6	20 18.4	25 31.3
26 F	22 25 23	7 54 22	25 53 57	1♉54 50	17 27.0	24 02.7	16 56.1	9 25.0	12 03.5	13 26.4	22 56.7	20 47.3	20 20.1	25R31.4
27 Sa	22 29 20	8 54 40	7♉57 51	14 03 31	17 22.3	24R12.0	17 22.4	9 33.1	12 27.2	13 21.2	23 03.8	20 50.0	20 21.8	25 31.4
28 Su	22 33 16	9 54 56	20 12 19	26 24 51	17 20.1	24 11.5	17 46.8	9 41.8	12 50.8	13 15.9	23 10.8	20 52.6	20 23.4	25 31.3

Astro Data

	Dy Hr Mn
☽0S	12 13:29
♄⊻♅	25 13:18
☽0N	26 13:19
♄⊻♆	27 12:16
♃R	28 23:09
♀0N	30 15:24
♅☌♆	2 8:06
☽0S	8 23:11
♂D	15 7:43
☽0N	22 20:17
♇R	26 14:29
☿0N	26 14:52
☿R	27 22:56

Planet Ingress

	Dy Hr Mn
☿ ♑	2 14:47
♀ ♓	3 23:54
☉ ♒	20 1:23
☿ ♒	21 11:25
⚳ ♓	26 13:44
♀ ♈	2 12:37
☿ ♓	7 16:19
☉ ♓	18 15:35

Last Aspect / ☽ Ingress

Last Aspect Dy Hr Mn		☽ Ingress Dy Hr Mn
2 14:31	♀ ⚹	♉ 2 17:30
4 16:04	♇ ☍	♊ 5 1:42
6 7:43	♄ △	♋ 7 6:10
8 23:24	♇ △	♌ 9 7:49
11 0:04	♇ □	♍ 11 8:20
13 1:06	♇ ⚹	♎ 13 9:30
15 4:01	☉ □	♏ 15 12:42
17 13:53	☉ ⚹	♐ 17 18:30
19 4:42	♄ ⚹	♑ 20 2:46
22 3:29	♇ ⚹	♒ 22 13:00
24 15:08	♇ □	♓ 25 0:47
27 3:50	♇ △	♈ 27 13:28
29 4:51	♄ ⚹	♉ 30 1:37

Last Aspect / ☽ Ingress

Last Aspect Dy Hr Mn		☽ Ingress Dy Hr Mn
1 9:20	♀ ⚹	♊ 1 11:15
3 2:48	☿ △	♋ 3 16:56
5 11:23	♇ △	♌ 5 18:51
7 11:16	♇ □	♍ 7 18:29
9 10:40	♇ ⚹	♎ 9 17:58
11 6:52	☉ △	♏ 11 19:23
13 15:56	♇ ☌	♐ 14 0:08
16 3:29	☉ ⚹	♑ 16 8:20
18 10:10	♇ ⚹	♒ 18 19:05
20 22:09	♇ □	♓ 21 7:12
23 10:47	♇ △	♈ 23 19:50
25 17:54	♄ ⚹	♉ 26 8:11
28 10:17	♇ ☍	♊ 28 18:52

☽ Phases & Eclipses

Dy Hr Mn	
1 3:38	☽ 10♈44
8 12:37	○ 18♋15
15 4:01	☾ 25♎01
22 18:27	● 2♒46
30 23:20	☽ 11♉06
6 23:55	○ 18♌13
13 14:57	☾ 24♏55
21 13:05	● 2♓55

Astro Data

1 January 1993
Julian Day # 33969
SVP 5♓21'10"
GC 26♐44.5 ⚴ 25♑41.9
Eris 16♈57.3R ⚵ 5♋31.2R
⚷ 22♌59.2R ⚶ 27♐43.0
☽ Mean ☊ 20♐23.9

1 February 1993
Julian Day # 34000
SVP 5♓21'04"
GC 26♐44.6 ⚴ 6♒50.0
Eris 17♈01.6 ⚵ 1♋05.6R
⚷ 21♌02.3R ⚶ 14♑12.8
☽ Mean ☊ 18♐45.4

March 1993 LONGITUDE

Day	Sid.Time	☉	0 hr ☽	Noon ☽	True ☊	☿	♀	♂	⚳	♃	♄	♅	♆	♇
1 M	22 37 13	10♓55 09	2♊41 41	9♊03 25	17♐19.6	24♓01.5	18♈09.5	9♋51.0	13♓14.5	13♎10.4	23♒17.8	20♑55.2	20♑25.0	25♏31.2
2 Tu	22 41 10	11 55 21	15 30 37	22 03 52	17R 19.6	23R 42.3	18 30.2	10 00.9	13 38.1	13R 04.8	23 24.8	20 57.8	20 26.6	25R 31.1
3 W	22 45 06	12 55 31	28 43 39	5♋30 24	17 18.8	23 14.3	18 49.0	10 11.3	14 01.8	12 59.0	23 31.8	21 00.3	20 28.2	25 30.9
4 Th	22 49 03	13 55 38	12♋24 25	19 25 53	17 16.1	22 38.3	19 05.8	10 22.3	14 25.4	12 53.2	23 38.8	21 02.8	20 29.7	25 30.8
5 F	22 52 59	14 55 43	26 34 45	3♌50 49	17 10.8	21 55.2	19 20.5	10 33.9	14 49.1	12 47.2	23 45.7	21 05.3	20 31.3	25 30.5
6 Sa	22 56 56	15 55 47	11♌13 38	18 42 28	17 02.8	21 06.2	19 33.0	10 46.0	15 12.7	12 41.0	23 52.6	21 07.7	20 32.8	25 30.3
7 Su	23 00 52	16 55 48	26 16 24	3♍54 15	16 52.6	20 12.4	19 43.3	10 58.6	15 36.4	12 34.8	23 59.5	21 10.1	20 34.2	25 30.0
8 M	23 04 49	17 55 47	11♍34 40	19 16 10	16 41.2	19 15.2	19 51.3	11 11.7	16 00.0	12 28.4	24 06.3	21 12.4	20 35.7	25 29.7
9 Tu	23 08 45	18 55 44	26 57 15	4♎36 23	16 30.0	18 16.0	19 57.1	11 25.3	16 23.6	12 21.9	24 13.1	21 14.7	20 37.1	25 29.3
10 W	23 12 42	19 55 39	12♎12 09	19 43 17	16 20.3	17 16.1	20R 00.4	11 39.4	16 47.3	12 15.3	24 19.9	21 17.0	20 38.5	25 28.9
11 Th	23 16 38	20 55 33	27 08 46	4♏27 45	16 13.0	16 17.0	20 01.4	11 54.0	17 10.9	12 08.6	24 26.7	21 19.2	20 39.8	25 28.5
12 F	23 20 35	21 55 25	11♏39 40	18 44 12	16 08.5	15 19.8	19 59.9	12 09.1	17 34.5	12 01.8	24 33.4	21 21.4	20 41.2	25 28.0
13 Sa	23 24 32	22 55 16	25 41 14	2♐30 51	16 06.4	14 25.6	19 55.9	12 24.6	17 58.2	11 54.9	24 40.1	21 23.6	20 42.5	25 27.5
14 Su	23 28 28	23 55 04	9♐13 18	15 48 58	16 06.0	13 35.5	19 49.5	12 40.5	18 21.8	11 48.0	24 46.7	21 25.7	20 43.7	25 27.0
15 M	23 32 25	24 54 52	22 18 19	28 41 53	16 06.0	12 50.2	19 40.6	12 56.9	18 45.4	11 40.9	24 53.3	21 27.7	20 45.0	25 26.4
16 Tu	23 36 21	25 54 37	5♑00 16	11♑14 03	16 05.2	12 10.2	19 29.2	13 13.7	19 09.0	11 33.7	24 59.9	21 29.7	20 46.2	25 25.8
17 W	23 40 18	26 54 21	17 23 50	23 30 12	16 02.5	11 36.0	19 15.3	13 31.0	19 32.6	11 26.5	25 06.4	21 31.7	20 47.4	25 25.2
18 Th	23 44 14	27 54 03	29 33 43	5♒34 53	15 57.2	11 07.9	18 59.0	13 48.6	19 56.2	11 19.2	25 12.9	21 33.6	20 48.6	25 24.6
19 F	23 48 11	28 53 43	11♒34 11	17 32 05	15 49.0	10 46.0	18 40.3	14 06.7	20 19.7	11 11.8	25 19.4	21 35.5	20 49.7	25 23.9
20 Sa	23 52 07	29 53 21	23 28 56	29 25 07	15 38.2	10 30.4	18 19.3	14 25.2	20 43.3	11 04.4	25 25.8	21 37.4	20 50.8	25 23.2
21 Su	23 56 04	0♈52 57	5♓20 53	11♓16 33	15 25.3	10 20.9	17 56.0	14 44.0	21 06.8	10 56.9	25 32.2	21 39.1	20 51.8	25 22.4
22 M	0 00 01	1 52 32	17 12 18	23 08 21	15 11.4	10D 17.5	17 30.5	15 03.2	21 30.4	10 49.4	25 38.5	21 40.9	20 52.9	25 21.6
23 Tu	0 03 57	2 52 04	29 04 52	5♈02 00	14 57.6	10 20.0	17 03.0	15 22.8	21 53.9	10 41.8	25 44.8	21 42.6	20 53.9	25 20.8
24 W	0 07 54	3 51 34	10♈59 56	16 58 48	14 45.2	10 28.1	16 33.6	15 42.8	22 17.4	10 34.2	25 51.0	21 44.2	20 54.9	25 20.0
25 Th	0 11 50	4 51 03	22 58 48	29 00 06	14 34.9	10 41.7	16 02.4	16 03.1	22 40.8	10 26.5	25 57.2	21 45.9	20 55.8	25 19.1
26 F	0 15 47	5 50 29	5♉02 56	11♉07 33	14 27.3	11 00.4	15 29.6	16 23.7	23 04.3	10 18.8	26 03.3	21 47.4	20 56.7	25 18.2
27 Sa	0 19 43	6 49 53	17 14 15	23 23 20	14 22.7	11 24.1	14 55.4	16 44.7	23 27.7	10 11.1	26 09.4	21 48.9	20 57.6	25 17.3
28 Su	0 23 40	7 49 15	29 35 11	5♊50 12	14D 20.7	11 52.4	14 20.0	17 06.1	23 51.2	10 03.4	26 15.5	21 50.4	20 58.5	25 16.3
29 M	0 27 36	8 48 34	12♊08 49	18 31 30	14 20.4	12 25.0	13 43.7	17 27.7	24 14.6	9 55.6	26 21.4	21 51.8	20 59.3	25 15.3
30 Tu	0 31 33	9 47 52	24 58 42	1♋30 53	14R 20.9	13 01.9	13 06.6	17 49.7	24 37.9	9 47.9	26 27.4	21 53.2	21 00.1	25 14.3
31 W	0 35 30	10 47 06	8♋08 31	14 51 59	14 21.0	13 42.6	12 29.0	18 11.9	25 01.3	9 40.2	26 33.3	21 54.5	21 00.8	25 13.3

April 1993 LONGITUDE

Day	Sid.Time	☉	0 hr ☽	Noon ☽	True ☊	☿	♀	♂	⚳	♃	♄	♅	♆	♇
1 Th	0 39 26	11♈46 19	21♋41 37	28♋37 39	14♐19.8	14♓27.1	11♈51.1	18♋34.5	25♓24.6	9♎32.4	26♒39.1	21♑55.8	21♑01.5	25♏12.2
2 F	0 43 23	12 45 29	5♌40 11	12♌49 11	14R 16.4	15 15.1	11R 13.3	18 57.4	25 47.9	9R 24.7	26 44.8	21 57.0	21 02.2	25R 11.2
3 Sa	0 47 19	13 44 37	20 04 24	27 25 24	14 10.7	16 06.3	10 35.7	19 20.5	26 11.2	9 17.0	26 50.6	21 58.2	21 02.9	25 10.0
4 Su	0 51 16	14 43 43	4♍51 34	12♍22 00	14 03.0	17 00.7	9 58.6	19 43.9	26 34.4	9 09.3	26 56.2	21 59.3	21 03.5	25 08.9
5 M	0 55 12	15 42 46	19 55 42	27 31 26	13 54.3	17 58.1	9 22.3	20 07.6	26 57.6	9 01.7	27 01.8	22 00.4	21 04.1	25 07.7
6 Tu	0 59 09	16 41 47	5♎07 55	12♎43 46	13 45.5	18 58.3	8 47.0	20 31.5	27 20.8	8 54.0	27 07.3	22 01.4	21 04.7	25 06.5
7 W	1 03 05	17 40 46	20 17 39	27 48 17	13 37.8	20 01.2	8 12.9	20 55.7	27 44.0	8 46.4	27 12.8	22 02.4	21 05.2	25 05.3
8 Th	1 07 02	18 39 43	5♏14 31	12♏35 23	13 32.1	21 06.7	7 40.2	21 20.1	28 07.1	8 38.9	27 18.2	22 03.4	21 05.7	25 04.1
9 F	1 10 59	19 38 38	19 50 06	26 58 07	13 28.7	22 14.6	7 09.2	21 44.8	28 30.2	8 31.4	27 23.6	22 04.2	21 06.2	25 02.8
10 Sa	1 14 55	20 37 32	3♐59 05	10♐52 50	13D 27.5	23 24.9	6 40.0	22 09.8	28 53.3	8 24.0	27 28.9	22 05.1	21 06.6	25 01.6
11 Su	1 18 52	21 36 24	17 39 27	24 19 05	13 27.9	24 37.4	6 12.7	22 34.9	29 16.3	8 16.6	27 34.1	22 05.9	21 07.0	25 00.3
12 M	1 22 48	22 35 14	0♑52 04	7♑18 50	13 29.0	25 52.2	5 47.5	23 00.3	29 39.4	8 09.2	27 39.3	22 06.6	21 07.3	24 59.0
13 Tu	1 26 45	23 34 02	13 39 52	19 55 45	13R 29.9	27 09.0	5 24.5	23 25.9	0♈02.3	8 02.0	27 44.4	22 07.3	21 07.7	24 57.6
14 W	1 30 41	24 32 49	26 07 03	2♒14 23	13 29.6	28 27.9	5 03.7	23 51.8	0 25.3	7 54.8	27 49.4	22 07.9	21 08.0	24 56.3
15 Th	1 34 38	25 31 34	8♒18 22	14 19 35	13 27.6	29 48.7	4 45.3	24 17.8	0 48.2	7 47.7	27 54.4	22 08.5	21 08.2	24 54.9
16 F	1 38 34	26 30 17	20 18 37	26 16 00	13 23.5	1♈11.5	4 29.3	24 44.1	1 11.0	7 40.6	27 59.3	22 09.0	21 08.5	24 53.5
17 Sa	1 42 31	27 28 58	2♓12 16	8♓07 53	13 17.6	2 36.2	4 15.7	25 10.6	1 33.9	7 33.7	28 04.1	22 09.5	21 08.7	24 52.1
18 Su	1 46 28	28 27 38	14 03 18	19 58 53	13 10.1	4 02.7	4 04.6	25 37.3	1 56.7	7 26.8	28 08.8	22 09.9	21 08.8	24 50.6
19 M	1 50 24	29 26 16	25 55 01	1♈51 59	13 01.9	5 31.1	3 55.9	26 04.2	2 19.4	7 20.1	28 13.5	22 10.3	21 09.0	24 49.2
20 Tu	1 54 21	0♉24 52	7♈50 04	13 49 30	12 53.6	7 01.2	3 49.7	26 31.3	2 42.1	7 13.4	28 18.1	22 10.6	21 09.1	24 47.7
21 W	1 58 17	1 23 26	19 50 30	25 53 14	12 46.1	8 33.2	3 45.9	26 58.5	3 04.8	7 06.9	28 22.7	22 10.9	21 09.1	24 46.2
22 Th	2 02 14	2 21 58	1♉57 51	8♉04 32	12 40.1	10 06.9	3D 44.5	27 26.0	3 27.4	7 00.4	28 27.1	22 11.1	21R 09.1	24 44.7
23 F	2 06 10	3 20 29	14 13 23	20 24 35	12 35.9	11 42.3	3 45.4	27 53.7	3 50.0	6 54.1	28 31.5	22 11.3	21 09.1	24 43.2
24 Sa	2 10 07	4 18 57	26 38 15	2♊54 35	12D 33.7	13 19.5	3 48.7	28 21.5	4 12.6	6 47.9	28 35.8	22 11.4	21 09.1	24 41.7
25 Su	2 14 03	5 17 24	9♊13 43	15 35 53	12 33.3	14 58.4	3 54.2	28 49.6	4 35.0	6 41.8	28 40.1	22R 11.5	21 09.0	24 40.1
26 M	2 18 00	6 15 48	22 01 17	28 30 09	12 34.2	16 39.1	4 02.0	29 17.8	4 57.5	6 35.8	28 44.2	22 11.5	21 08.9	24 38.6
27 Tu	2 21 56	7 14 11	5♋02 44	11♋39 14	12 35.7	18 21.5	4 11.9	29 46.1	5 19.9	6 30.0	28 48.3	22 11.5	21 08.8	24 37.0
28 W	2 25 53	8 12 31	18 19 56	25 05 01	12 37.1	20 05.7	4 24.0	0♌14.7	5 42.2	6 24.3	28 52.3	22 11.4	21 08.7	24 35.4
29 Th	2 29 50	9 10 49	1♌54 40	8♌49 01	12R 37.7	21 51.6	4 38.1	0 43.4	6 04.5	6 18.7	28 56.2	22 11.3	21 08.5	24 33.9
30 F	2 33 46	10 09 06	15 48 05	22 51 50	12 37.0	23 39.3	4 54.1	1 12.3	6 26.8	6 13.3	29 00.0	22 11.1	21 08.2	24 32.3

Astro Data

	Dy Hr Mn
☿0S	5 23:28
☽0S	8 10:35
♀R	11 9:28
♄□♇	20 3:09
☉0N	20 14:41
☽0N	22 2:20
☿D	22 13:44
♃⚻♄	23 6:50
♃∠♇	26 14:09
☽0S	4 21:18
☽0N	18 8:11
☿0N	19 22:06
♀D	22 14:14
♆R	22 22:32
♅R	26 10:03

Planet Ingress

	Dy Hr Mn
☉ ♈	20 14:41
⚳ ♈	13 9:34
☿ ♈	15 15:18
☉ ♉	20 1:49
♂ ♌	27 23:40

Last Aspect / ☽ Ingress

Last Aspect Dy Hr Mn		☽ Ingress	Dy Hr Mn
2 14:53	☿ □	♋	3 2:16
4 22:13	♇ △	♌	5 5:40
6 22:47	♇ □	♍	7 5:52
8 21:43	♇ ⚹	♎	9 4:46
10 19:29	♄ △	♏	11 4:40
12 23:37	♇ ☌	♐	13 7:33
15 4:46	♄ ⚹	♑	15 14:28
17 19:20	☉ ⚹	♒	18 0:52
20 3:52	♄ ☌	♓	20 13:11
22 16:29	♇ △	♈	23 1:51
25 5:53	♄ ⚹	♉	25 13:59
27 17:25	♄ □	♊	28 0:48
30 2:39	♄ △	♋	30 9:14

Last Aspect / ☽ Ingress

Last Aspect Dy Hr Mn		☽ Ingress	Dy Hr Mn
1 6:06	♇ △	♌	1 14:21
3 11:03	♄ ☍	♍	3 16:10
5 8:13	♇ ⚹	♎	5 15:54
7 11:03	♄ △	♏	7 15:32
9 12:44	♄ □	♐	9 17:10
11 17:58	♄ ⚹	♑	11 22:24
14 3:41	☿ ⚹	♒	14 7:36
16 15:30	♄ ☌	♓	16 19:32
18 23:51	♂ △	♈	19 8:14
21 16:57	♄ ⚹	♉	21 20:08
24 3:43	♄ □	♊	24 6:27
26 12:26	♄ △	♋	26 14:45
28 11:08	♇ △	♌	28 20:39

☽ Phases & Eclipses

Dy Hr Mn	
1 15:47	☽ 11♊05
8 9:46	○ 17♍50
15 4:17	☾ 24♐36
23 7:14	● 2♈40
31 4:10	☽ 10♋28
6 18:43	○ 16♎58
13 19:39	☾ 23♑53
21 23:49	● 1♉52
29 12:40	☽ 9♌12

Astro Data

1 March 1993
Julian Day # 34028
SVP 5♓21'01"
GC 26♐44.6 ⚴ 16♒31.3
Eris 17♈13.7 ⚵ 3♋37.4
⚷ 18♌56.6R ⚶ 28♑32.8
☽ Mean ☊ 17♐16.4

1 April 1993
Julian Day # 34059
SVP 5♓20'58"
GC 26♐44.7 ⚴ 26♒18.8
Eris 17♈32.7 ⚵ 11♋47.9
⚷ 17♌23.9R ⚶ 13♒20.7
☽ Mean ☊ 15♐37.9

LONGITUDE — May 1993

Day	Sid.Time	☉	0 hr ☽	Noon ☽	True ☊	☿	♀	♂	⚳	♃	♄	♅	♆	♇
1 Sa	2 37 43	11♉07 20	0♍00 06	7♍12 37	12♐35.0	25♈28.7	5♈12.1	1♌41.3	6♈48.9	6♎08.0	29♒03.8	22♑10.8	21♑08.0	24♏30.7
2 Su	2 41 39	12 05 32	14 28 58	21 48 34	12R31.8	27 19.9	5 32.0	2 10.4	7 11.1	6R02.9	29 07.4	22R10.6	21R07.7	24R29.0
3 M	2 45 36	13 03 42	29 10 46	6♎34 44	12 27.8	29 12.9	5 53.7	2 39.8	7 33.1	5 57.9	29 11.0	22 10.2	21 07.3	24 27.4
4 Tu	2 49 32	14 01 50	13♎59 34	21 24 18	12 23.7	1♉07.7	6 17.1	3 09.2	7 55.2	5 53.0	29 14.5	22 09.8	21 07.0	24 25.8
5 W	2 53 29	14 59 56	28 47 58	6♏09 32	12 20.2	3 04.2	6 42.2	3 38.8	8 17.1	5 48.3	29 17.9	22 09.4	21 06.6	24 24.1
6 Th	2 57 25	15 58 00	13♏28 06	20 42 48	12 17.6	5 02.4	7 08.9	4 08.6	8 39.0	5 43.8	29 21.3	22 08.9	21 06.2	24 22.5
7 F	3 01 22	16 56 03	27 52 54	4♐57 46	12D16.4	7 02.4	7 37.2	4 38.4	9 00.9	5 39.4	29 24.5	22 08.4	21 05.7	24 20.9
8 Sa	3 05 19	17 54 05	11♐56 57	18 50 09	12 16.3	9 04.0	8 07.1	5 08.5	9 22.7	5 35.2	29 27.7	22 07.9	21 05.2	24 19.2
9 Su	3 09 15	18 52 05	25 37 11	2♑18 02	12 17.3	11 07.3	8 38.4	5 38.6	9 44.4	5 31.1	29 30.8	22 07.2	21 04.7	24 17.5
10 M	3 13 12	19 50 04	8♑52 49	15 21 45	12 18.7	13 12.1	9 11.1	6 08.9	10 06.1	5 27.2	29 33.7	22 06.6	21 04.2	24 15.9
11 Tu	3 17 08	20 48 01	21 45 08	28 03 22	12 20.2	15 18.2	9 45.1	6 39.3	10 27.7	5 23.5	29 36.6	22 05.9	21 03.6	24 14.2
12 W	3 21 05	21 45 57	4♒16 56	10♒26 19	12 21.4	17 25.7	10 20.4	7 09.8	10 49.3	5 19.9	29 39.4	22 05.1	21 03.0	24 12.5
13 Th	3 25 01	22 43 52	16 32 04	22 34 47	12R21.8	19 34.4	10 57.0	7 40.5	11 10.7	5 16.5	29 42.2	22 04.3	21 02.4	24 10.9
14 F	3 28 58	23 41 45	28 35 00	4♓33 19	12 21.4	21 44.0	11 34.8	8 11.3	11 32.1	5 13.3	29 44.8	22 03.4	21 01.7	24 09.2
15 Sa	3 32 54	24 39 37	10♓30 19	16 26 34	12 20.1	23 54.4	12 13.7	8 42.2	11 53.5	5 10.2	29 47.3	22 02.5	21 01.0	24 07.5
16 Su	3 36 51	25 37 28	22 22 34	28 18 52	12 18.3	26 05.4	12 53.8	9 13.2	12 14.8	5 07.3	29 49.8	22 01.6	21 00.3	24 05.9
17 M	3 40 48	26 35 17	4♈15 56	10♈14 14	12 16.0	28 16.7	13 34.8	9 44.4	12 36.0	5 04.6	29 52.1	22 00.6	20 59.6	24 04.2
18 Tu	3 44 44	27 33 06	16 14 08	22 16 03	12 13.7	0♊28.0	14 16.9	10 15.6	12 57.1	5 02.1	29 54.4	21 59.5	20 58.8	24 02.5
19 W	3 48 41	28 30 53	28 20 16	4♉27 06	12 11.7	2 39.1	15 00.0	10 47.0	13 18.2	4 59.7	29 56.5	21 58.5	20 58.0	24 00.9
20 Th	3 52 37	29 28 39	10♉36 45	16 49 27	12 10.1	4 49.6	15 44.0	11 18.5	13 39.2	4 57.5	29 58.6	21 57.3	20 57.2	23 59.2
21 F	3 56 34	0♊26 24	23 05 19	29 24 29	12D09.2	6 59.4	16 28.9	11 50.1	14 00.1	4 55.5	0♓00.6	21 56.2	20 56.3	23 57.5
22 Sa	4 00 30	1 24 07	5♊47 03	12♊13 01	12 08.9	9 08.1	17 14.7	12 21.9	14 20.9	4 53.7	0 02.4	21 55.0	20 55.4	23 55.9
23 Su	4 04 27	2 21 49	18 42 26	25 15 18	12 09.2	11 15.5	18 01.2	12 53.7	14 41.7	4 52.1	0 04.2	21 53.7	20 54.5	23 54.2
24 M	4 08 23	3 19 30	1♋51 34	8♋31 12	12 09.8	13 21.3	18 48.6	13 25.6	15 02.3	4 50.6	0 05.9	21 52.4	20 53.6	23 52.6
25 Tu	4 12 20	4 17 09	15 14 10	22 00 22	12 10.5	15 25.4	19 36.7	13 57.7	15 22.9	4 49.3	0 07.5	21 51.1	20 52.6	23 50.9
26 W	4 16 17	5 14 47	28 49 45	5♌42 12	12 11.2	17 27.4	20 25.6	14 29.8	15 43.4	4 48.2	0 09.0	21 49.7	20 51.6	23 49.3
27 Th	4 20 13	6 12 23	12♌37 36	19 35 49	12 11.7	19 27.3	21 15.2	15 02.1	16 03.9	4 47.3	0 10.4	21 48.3	20 50.6	23 47.7
28 F	4 24 10	7 09 58	26 36 42	3♍40 03	12R11.9	21 24.9	22 05.4	15 34.4	16 24.2	4 46.6	0 11.7	21 46.8	20 49.6	23 46.1
29 Sa	4 28 06	8 07 32	10♍45 38	17 53 11	12 11.8	23 20.1	22 56.3	16 06.9	16 44.4	4 46.0	0 12.9	21 45.3	20 48.5	23 44.5
30 Su	4 32 03	9 05 04	25 02 22	2♎12 50	12 11.6	25 12.8	23 47.8	16 39.4	17 04.6	4 45.7	0 14.0	21 43.8	20 47.4	23 42.9
31 M	4 35 59	10 02 34	9♎24 09	16 35 51	12 11.4	27 02.9	24 40.0	17 12.1	17 24.6	4D45.5	0 15.0	21 42.2	20 46.3	23 41.3

LONGITUDE — June 1993

Day	Sid.Time	☉	0 hr ☽	Noon ☽	True ☊	☿	♀	♂	⚳	♃	♄	♅	♆	♇
1 Tu	4 39 56	11♊00 03	23♎47 26	0♏58 22	12♐11.2	28♊50.3	25♈32.7	17♌44.8	17♈44.6	4♎45.5	0♓15.9	21♑40.6	20♑45.2	23♏39.7
2 W	4 43 52	11 57 31	8♏08 05	15 16 01	12D11.2	0♋35.1	26 26.0	18 17.6	18 04.5	4 45.6	0 16.7	21R39.0	20R44.0	23R38.1
3 Th	4 47 49	12 54 58	22 21 36	29 24 19	12R11.2	2 17.1	27 19.8	18 50.5	18 24.2	4 46.0	0 17.4	21 37.3	20 42.9	23 36.6
4 F	4 51 46	13 52 24	6♐23 39	13♐19 11	12 11.2	3 56.3	28 14.2	19 23.5	18 43.9	4 46.5	0 18.0	21 35.6	20 41.7	23 35.0
5 Sa	4 55 42	14 49 49	20 10 30	26 57 19	12 11.1	5 32.7	29 09.1	19 56.6	19 03.5	4 47.2	0 18.6	21 33.8	20 40.5	23 33.5
6 Su	4 59 39	15 47 14	3♑39 25	10♑16 39	12 10.9	7 06.3	0♉04.5	20 29.7	19 23.0	4 48.1	0 19.0	21 32.1	20 39.2	23 32.0
7 M	5 03 35	16 44 37	16 49 00	23 16 29	12 10.5	8 37.0	1 00.4	21 03.0	19 42.4	4 49.2	0 19.3	21 30.3	20 38.0	23 30.5
8 Tu	5 07 32	17 42 00	29 39 14	5♒57 28	12 09.8	10 04.9	1 56.7	21 36.3	20 01.7	4 50.4	0 19.5	21 28.4	20 36.7	23 29.0
9 W	5 11 28	18 39 22	12♒11 29	18 21 36	12 09.1	11 29.8	2 53.5	22 09.7	20 20.9	4 51.9	0R19.6	21 26.5	20 35.4	23 27.5
10 Th	5 15 25	19 36 43	24 28 14	0♓31 51	12 08.5	12 51.8	3 50.8	22 43.2	20 39.9	4 53.4	0 19.7	21 24.6	20 34.1	23 26.1
11 F	5 19 22	20 34 04	6♓32 56	12 32 02	12D08.0	14 10.9	4 48.4	23 16.8	20 58.9	4 55.2	0 19.6	21 22.7	20 32.7	23 24.6
12 Sa	5 23 18	21 31 24	18 29 40	24 26 26	12 07.9	15 26.9	5 46.4	23 50.5	21 17.8	4 57.2	0 19.4	21 20.7	20 31.4	23 23.2
13 Su	5 27 15	22 28 44	0♈22 54	6♈19 38	12 08.3	16 39.8	6 44.9	24 24.3	21 36.5	4 59.3	0 19.1	21 18.7	20 30.0	23 21.8
14 M	5 31 11	23 26 04	12 17 14	18 16 15	12 09.0	17 49.6	7 43.7	24 58.1	21 55.1	5 01.6	0 18.8	21 16.7	20 28.6	23 20.4
15 Tu	5 35 08	24 23 23	24 17 12	0♉20 38	12 10.1	18 56.3	8 42.9	25 32.0	22 13.6	5 04.0	0 18.3	21 14.7	20 27.2	23 19.0
16 W	5 39 04	25 20 42	6♉27 00	12 36 43	12 11.2	19 59.7	9 42.4	26 06.0	22 32.0	5 06.7	0 17.7	21 12.6	20 25.8	23 17.7
17 Th	5 43 01	26 18 00	18 50 12	25 07 45	12 12.2	20 59.7	10 42.2	26 40.1	22 50.3	5 09.5	0 17.1	21 10.5	20 24.4	23 16.3
18 F	5 46 57	27 15 18	1♊29 37	7♊56 00	12R12.7	21 56.3	11 42.4	27 14.2	23 08.4	5 12.4	0 16.3	21 08.4	20 22.9	23 15.0
19 Sa	5 50 54	28 12 36	14 26 59	21 02 36	12 12.6	22 49.5	12 42.9	27 48.5	23 26.5	5 15.6	0 15.4	21 06.2	20 21.5	23 13.7
20 Su	5 54 51	29 09 53	27 42 49	4♋27 27	12 11.7	23 39.0	13 43.7	28 22.8	23 44.4	5 18.9	0 14.5	21 04.1	20 20.0	23 12.5
21 M	5 58 47	0♋07 10	11♋16 18	18 09 05	12 09.9	24 24.8	14 44.8	28 57.2	24 02.1	5 22.4	0 13.4	21 01.9	20 18.5	23 11.2
22 Tu	6 02 44	1 04 26	25 05 24	2♌04 53	12 07.6	25 06.8	15 46.2	29 31.6	24 19.7	5 26.0	0 12.3	20 59.7	20 17.0	23 10.0
23 W	6 06 40	2 01 42	9♌07 03	16 11 26	12 05.0	25 44.9	16 47.9	0♍06.2	24 37.2	5 29.8	0 11.0	20 57.4	20 15.5	23 08.8
24 Th	6 10 37	2 58 57	23 17 32	0♍24 52	12 02.6	26 19.0	17 49.8	0 40.8	24 54.6	5 33.8	0 09.7	20 55.2	20 14.0	23 07.6
25 F	6 14 33	3 56 11	7♍32 57	14 41 20	12 00.7	26 48.8	18 52.0	1 15.5	25 11.8	5 37.9	0 08.3	20 52.9	20 12.5	23 06.4
26 Sa	6 18 30	4 53 25	21 49 37	28 57 24	11D59.8	27 14.5	19 54.4	1 50.2	25 28.9	5 42.2	0 06.7	20 50.6	20 10.9	23 05.3
27 Su	6 22 26	5 50 38	6♎04 23	13♎10 15	11 59.8	27 35.7	20 57.1	2 25.1	25 45.8	5 46.6	0 05.1	20 48.3	20 09.4	23 04.2
28 M	6 26 23	6 47 51	20 14 44	27 17 37	12 00.8	27 52.5	22 00.0	3 00.0	26 02.6	5 51.2	0 03.4	20 46.0	20 07.8	23 03.1
29 Tu	6 30 20	7 45 03	4♏18 41	11♏17 44	12 02.1	28 04.8	23 03.2	3 34.9	26 19.2	5 56.0	0 01.6	20 43.7	20 06.2	23 02.0
30 W	6 34 16	8 42 15	18 14 36	25 09 06	12 03.5	28 12.4	24 06.5	4 10.0	26 35.7	6 00.9	29♒59.7	20 41.4	20 04.6	23 01.0

Astro Data

	Dy Hr Mn
☽0S	2 5:39
☽0N	15 14:46
☽0S	29 11:46
♃D	1 1:09
♄R	10 5:27
☽0N	11 22:31
⚳0N	15 0:40
☽0S	25 17:19

Planet Ingress

	Dy Hr Mn
☿ ♉	3 21:54
☿ ♊	18 6:53
☉ ♊	21 1:02
♄ ♓	21 4:58
☿ ♋	2 3:54
♀ ♉	6 10:03
☉ ♋	21 9:00
♂ ♍	23 7:42
♄ ♒R	30 8:29

Last Aspect / ☽ Ingress (May)

Last Aspect Dy Hr Mn		☽ Ingress Dy Hr Mn
2 16:21	♇ ⚹	♎ 3 1:20
5 0:46	♄ △	♏ 5 1:57
7 2:32	♄ □	♐ 7 3:34
9 6:57	♄ ⚹	♑ 9 7:51
11 4:44	♇ ⚹	♒ 11 15:44
14 2:18	♄ ☌	♓ 14 2:50
16 6:30	☿ ⚹	♈ 16 15:24
19 3:08	♄ ⚹	♉ 19 3:16
21 1:41	♇ ☍	♊ 21 13:07
22 21:53	♀ ⚹	♋ 23 20:38
25 15:15	♇ △	♌ 26 2:03
27 19:11	♇ □	♍ 28 5:46
29 22:32	☿ □	♎ 30 8:18

Last Aspect / ☽ Ingress (June)

Last Aspect Dy Hr Mn		☽ Ingress Dy Hr Mn
1 7:56	☿ △	♏ 1 10:22
3 2:08	♇ ☌	♐ 3 13:01
5 16:12	♀ △	♑ 5 17:26
7 12:26	♇ ⚹	♒ 8 0:39
9 21:59	♇ □	♓ 10 10:57
12 9:53	♇ △	♈ 12 23:14
15 2:01	♂ △	♉ 15 11:19
17 15:03	♂ □	♊ 17 21:12
20 1:52	☉ ☌	♋ 20 4:05
21 23:25	☿ ☌	♌ 22 8:26
23 23:44	♇ □	♍ 24 11:18
26 9:02	☿ ⚹	♎ 26 13:45
28 13:01	☿ □	♏ 28 16:37
30 20:26	♄ □	♐ 30 20:28

☽ Phases & Eclipses

Dy Hr Mn	
6 3:34	○ 15♏38
13 12:20	☾ 22♒45
21 14:06	● 0♊31
21 14:19:11	● P 0.735
28 18:21	☽ 7♍25
4 13:02	○ 13♐55
4 13:00	● T 1.562
12 5:36	☾ 21♓16
20 1:52	● 28♊46
26 22:43	☽ 5♎19

Astro Data

1 May 1993
Julian Day # 34089
SVP 5♓20'55"
GC 26♐44.8 ⚴ 4♓11.9
Eris 17♈52.2 ⚵ 22♋34.5
⚷ 17♌22.6 ⚶ 25♒58.2
☽ Mean ☊ 14♐02.6

1 June 1993
Julian Day # 34120
SVP 5♓20'51"
GC 26♐44.8 ⚴ 9♓43.0
Eris 18♈08.7 ⚵ 5♌04.8
⚷ 18♌58.8 ⚶ 6♓12.0
☽ Mean ☊ 12♐24.1

July 1993 — LONGITUDE

Day	Sid.Time	☉	0 hr ☽	Noon ☽	True ☊	☿	♀	♂	⚳	♃	♄	♅	♆	♇
1 Th	6 38 13	9♋39 26	2♐01 03	8♐50 18	12♐04.2	28♋15.4	25♉10.1	4♍45.1	26♈52.0	6♎06.0	29♒57.7	20♑39.0	20♑03.1	23♏00.0
2 F	6 42 09	10 36 38	15 36 39	22 19 56	12R 03.9	28R 13.7	26 14.0	5 20.2	27 08.2	6 11.2	29R 55.7	20R 36.7	20R 01.5	22R 59.0
3 Sa	6 46 06	11 33 49	29 00 00	5♑36 42	12 02.2	28 07.5	27 18.0	5 55.5	27 24.2	6 16.5	29 53.5	20 34.3	19 59.9	22 58.1
4 Su	6 50 02	12 31 00	12♑09 55	18 39 32	11 59.0	27 56.7	28 22.3	6 30.8	27 40.1	6 22.0	29 51.3	20 31.9	19 58.3	22 57.1
5 M	6 53 59	13 28 11	25 05 29	1♒27 47	11 54.6	27 41.4	29 26.7	7 06.1	27 55.8	6 27.7	29 49.0	20 29.5	19 56.7	22 56.2
6 Tu	6 57 55	14 25 22	7♒46 26	14 01 31	11 49.3	27 22.0	0♊31.4	7 41.6	28 11.3	6 33.5	29 46.6	20 27.2	19 55.1	22 55.4
7 W	7 01 52	15 22 33	20 13 11	26 21 39	11 43.8	26 58.5	1 36.3	8 17.0	28 26.6	6 39.4	29 44.1	20 24.8	19 53.4	22 54.5
8 Th	7 05 49	16 19 45	2♓27 08	8♓29 58	11 38.6	26 31.3	2 41.3	8 52.6	28 41.8	6 45.5	29 41.5	20 22.4	19 51.8	22 53.7
9 F	7 09 45	17 16 57	14 30 32	20 29 15	11 34.3	26 00.8	3 46.5	9 28.2	28 56.9	6 51.7	29 38.8	20 19.9	19 50.2	22 52.9
10 Sa	7 13 42	18 14 09	26 26 34	2♈23 00	11 31.4	25 27.5	4 52.0	10 03.9	29 11.7	6 58.1	29 36.1	20 17.5	19 48.6	22 52.1
11 Su	7 17 38	19 11 21	8♈19 06	14 15 26	11D 30.0	24 51.7	5 57.6	10 39.7	29 26.3	7 04.6	29 33.3	20 15.1	19 47.0	22 51.4
12 M	7 21 35	20 08 34	20 12 36	26 11 13	11 30.1	24 14.1	7 03.3	11 15.5	29 40.8	7 11.2	29 30.4	20 12.7	19 45.3	22 50.7
13 Tu	7 25 31	21 05 48	2♉11 54	8♉15 16	11 31.2	23 35.3	8 09.3	11 51.4	29 55.1	7 17.9	29 27.4	20 10.3	19 43.7	22 50.0
14 W	7 29 28	22 03 02	14 21 55	20 32 24	11 32.7	22 55.9	9 15.4	12 27.3	0♉09.2	7 24.8	29 24.4	20 07.9	19 42.1	22 49.4
15 Th	7 33 24	23 00 17	26 47 18	3♊07 04	11R 33.9	22 16.6	10 21.7	13 03.4	0 23.1	7 31.9	29 21.2	20 05.5	19 40.5	22 48.8
16 F	7 37 21	23 57 33	9♊32 07	16 02 48	11 34.1	21 38.2	11 28.1	13 39.4	0 36.8	7 39.0	29 18.1	20 03.0	19 38.9	22 48.2
17 Sa	7 41 18	24 54 49	22 39 21	29 21 52	11 32.7	21 01.1	12 34.7	14 15.6	0 50.3	7 46.3	29 14.8	20 00.6	19 37.2	22 47.6
18 Su	7 45 14	25 52 05	6♋10 21	13♋04 38	11 29.4	20 26.3	13 41.4	14 51.8	1 03.6	7 53.7	29 11.5	19 58.2	19 35.6	22 47.1
19 M	7 49 11	26 49 22	20 04 25	27 09 16	11 24.2	19 54.2	14 48.3	15 28.1	1 16.7	8 01.3	29 08.1	19 55.8	19 34.0	22 46.6
20 Tu	7 53 07	27 46 40	4♌18 35	11♌31 41	11 17.6	19 25.5	15 55.3	16 04.5	1 29.6	8 08.9	29 04.6	19 53.4	19 32.4	22 46.2
21 W	7 57 04	28 43 58	18 47 44	26 05 54	11 10.4	19 00.7	17 02.5	16 40.9	1 42.3	8 16.7	29 01.1	19 51.1	19 30.8	22 45.8
22 Th	8 01 00	29 41 16	3♍25 14	10♍44 53	11 03.4	18 40.2	18 09.7	17 17.3	1 54.7	8 24.6	28 57.5	19 48.7	19 29.2	22 45.4
23 F	8 04 57	0♌38 34	18 03 58	25 21 43	10 57.7	18 24.6	19 17.2	17 53.9	2 07.0	8 32.7	28 53.8	19 46.3	19 27.6	22 45.0
24 Sa	8 08 53	1 35 53	2♎37 25	9♎50 31	10 53.8	18 14.2	20 24.7	18 30.5	2 19.0	8 40.8	28 50.1	19 44.0	19 26.0	22 44.7
25 Su	8 12 50	2 33 12	17 00 34	24 07 13	10D 51.9	18D 09.3	21 32.4	19 07.1	2 30.7	8 49.1	28 46.3	19 41.6	19 24.5	22 44.4
26 M	8 16 47	3 30 32	1♏10 15	8♏09 34	10 51.6	18 10.0	22 40.2	19 43.8	2 42.3	8 57.4	28 42.5	19 39.3	19 22.9	22 44.1
27 Tu	8 20 43	4 27 52	15 05 07	21 56 57	10 52.4	18 16.7	23 48.1	20 20.6	2 53.6	9 05.9	28 38.6	19 37.0	19 21.3	22 43.9
28 W	8 24 40	5 25 12	28 45 08	5♐29 49	10R 53.2	18 29.4	24 56.2	20 57.4	3 04.7	9 14.5	28 34.7	19 34.7	19 19.8	22 43.7
29 Th	8 28 36	6 22 33	12♐11 05	18 49 07	10 53.1	18 48.3	26 04.3	21 34.3	3 15.5	9 23.2	28 30.7	19 32.4	19 18.3	22 43.6
30 F	8 32 33	7 19 55	25 24 00	1♑55 52	10 51.1	19 13.4	27 12.6	22 11.3	3 26.1	9 32.1	28 26.7	19 30.2	19 16.7	22 43.4
31 Sa	8 36 29	8 17 17	8♑24 48	14 50 52	10 46.7	19 44.6	28 21.0	22 48.3	3 36.4	9 41.0	28 22.6	19 27.9	19 15.2	22 43.3

August 1993 — LONGITUDE

Day	Sid.Time	☉	0 hr ☽	Noon ☽	True ☊	☿	♀	♂	⚳	♃	♄	♅	♆	♇
1 Su	8 40 26	9♌14 40	21♑14 08	27♑34 38	10♐39.8	20♋22.1	29♊29.6	23♍25.4	3♉46.5	9♎50.0	28♒18.5	19♑25.7	19♑13.7	22♏43.3
2 M	8 44 22	10 12 04	3♒52 24	10♒07 27	10R 30.8	21 05.7	0♋38.2	24 02.5	3 56.3	9 59.1	28R 14.4	19R 23.5	19R 12.2	22D 43.3
3 Tu	8 48 19	11 09 28	16 19 51	22 29 39	10 20.2	21 55.4	1 47.0	24 39.7	4 05.9	10 08.4	28 10.2	19 21.3	19 10.7	22 43.3
4 W	8 52 16	12 06 54	28 36 56	4♓41 49	10 09.0	22 51.1	2 55.9	25 16.9	4 15.2	10 17.7	28 05.9	19 19.1	19 09.3	22 43.3
5 Th	8 56 12	13 04 20	10♓44 27	16 45 03	9 58.2	23 52.6	4 04.9	25 54.2	4 24.3	10 27.1	28 01.7	19 17.0	19 07.8	22 43.4
6 F	9 00 09	14 01 48	22 43 51	28 41 10	9 48.8	25 00.0	5 14.0	26 31.6	4 33.0	10 36.6	27 57.4	19 14.8	19 06.4	22 43.5
7 Sa	9 04 05	14 59 17	4♈37 21	10♈32 49	9 41.4	26 12.9	6 23.2	27 09.0	4 41.5	10 46.3	27 53.0	19 12.7	19 05.0	22 43.6
8 Su	9 08 02	15 56 47	16 28 00	22 23 26	9 36.4	27 31.2	7 32.6	27 46.5	4 49.8	10 56.0	27 48.7	19 10.6	19 03.5	22 43.8
9 M	9 11 58	16 54 19	28 19 38	4♉17 13	9 33.7	28 54.7	8 42.0	28 24.0	4 57.7	11 05.8	27 44.3	19 08.6	19 02.2	22 44.0
10 Tu	9 15 55	17 51 51	10♉16 47	16 18 58	9D 32.8	0♌23.1	9 51.6	29 01.6	5 05.3	11 15.7	27 39.9	19 06.6	19 00.8	22 44.2
11 W	9 19 51	18 49 26	22 24 27	28 33 51	9R 33.1	1 56.2	11 01.2	29 39.3	5 12.7	11 25.7	27 35.4	19 04.6	18 59.4	22 44.5
12 Th	9 23 48	19 47 01	4♊47 51	11♊07 02	9 33.3	3 33.7	12 11.0	0♎17.0	5 19.8	11 35.8	27 31.0	19 02.6	18 58.1	22 44.8
13 F	9 27 45	20 44 39	17 31 58	24 03 11	9 32.5	5 15.1	13 20.9	0 54.8	5 26.5	11 45.9	27 26.5	19 00.7	18 56.7	22 45.2
14 Sa	9 31 41	21 42 17	0♋41 03	7♋25 51	9 29.7	7 00.2	14 30.8	1 32.7	5 33.0	11 56.2	27 22.0	18 58.7	18 55.4	22 45.6
15 Su	9 35 38	22 39 57	14 17 44	21 16 41	9 24.5	8 48.5	15 40.9	2 10.6	5 39.1	12 06.5	27 17.5	18 56.9	18 54.2	22 46.0
16 M	9 39 34	23 37 39	28 22 27	5♌34 38	9 16.7	10 39.7	16 51.1	2 48.5	5 45.0	12 17.0	27 13.0	18 55.0	18 52.9	22 46.4
17 Tu	9 43 31	24 35 22	12♌52 35	20 15 30	9 07.0	12 33.3	18 01.3	3 26.6	5 50.5	12 27.5	27 08.5	18 53.2	18 51.6	22 46.9
18 W	9 47 27	25 33 06	27 42 22	5♍12 04	8 56.3	14 29.0	19 11.7	4 04.7	5 55.7	12 38.1	27 04.0	18 51.4	18 50.4	22 47.4
19 Th	9 51 24	26 30 51	12♍43 21	20 14 58	8 45.8	16 26.2	20 22.1	4 42.8	6 00.5	12 48.7	26 59.4	18 49.6	18 49.2	22 48.0
20 F	9 55 20	27 28 38	27 45 43	5♎14 25	8 36.9	18 24.8	21 32.6	5 21.0	6 05.0	12 59.5	26 54.9	18 47.9	18 48.0	22 48.6
21 Sa	9 59 17	28 26 26	12♎40 04	20 01 47	8 30.3	20 24.2	22 43.2	5 59.3	6 09.3	13 10.3	26 50.4	18 46.2	18 46.9	22 49.2
22 Su	10 03 14	29 24 15	27 18 55	4♏30 58	8 26.3	22 24.2	23 53.9	6 37.6	6 13.1	13 21.2	26 45.8	18 44.6	18 45.7	22 49.8
23 M	10 07 10	0♍22 05	11♏37 37	18 38 44	8D 24.6	24 24.5	25 04.7	7 16.0	6 16.7	13 32.2	26 41.3	18 43.0	18 44.6	22 50.5
24 Tu	10 11 07	1 19 56	25 34 20	2♐24 31	8R 24.3	26 24.8	26 15.6	7 54.5	6 19.8	13 43.2	26 36.8	18 41.4	18 43.5	22 51.2
25 W	10 15 03	2 17 49	9♐09 31	15 49 36	8 24.2	28 24.8	27 26.6	8 33.0	6 22.7	13 54.4	26 32.3	18 39.9	18 42.4	22 52.0
26 Th	10 19 00	3 15 43	22 25 07	28 56 24	8 23.1	0♍24.4	28 37.6	9 11.5	6 25.2	14 05.5	26 27.8	18 38.4	18 41.4	22 52.8
27 F	10 22 56	4 13 38	5♑23 46	11♑47 36	8 20.0	2 23.3	29 48.7	9 50.1	6 27.4	14 16.8	26 23.4	18 36.9	18 40.4	22 53.6
28 Sa	10 26 53	5 11 34	18 08 11	24 25 49	8 14.1	4 21.5	0♌59.9	10 28.8	6 29.2	14 28.1	26 18.9	18 35.5	18 39.4	22 54.4
29 Su	10 30 49	6 09 32	0♒40 44	6♒53 11	8 05.3	6 18.9	2 11.2	11 07.5	6 30.6	14 39.5	26 14.5	18 34.1	18 38.4	22 55.3
30 M	10 34 46	7 07 31	13 03 20	19 11 21	7 53.9	8 15.2	3 22.6	11 46.3	6 31.7	14 50.9	26 10.1	18 32.8	18 37.5	22 56.2
31 Tu	10 38 43	8 05 31	25 17 22	1♓21 32	7 40.7	10 10.6	4 34.1	12 25.2	6 32.4	15 02.5	26 05.7	18 31.5	18 36.5	22 57.2

Astro Data

	Dy Hr Mn
☿ R	1 15:29
☽ 0N	9 7:00
♃∠♇	17 16:03
☽ 0S	23 0:10
☿ D	25 20:51
♇ D	2 19:29
☽ 0N	5 15:14
♂ 0S	14 1:14
♃□♄	16 5:41
☽ 0S	19 9:11
♅☌♆	20 7:56

Planet Ingress

		Dy Hr Mn
♀	♊	6 0:21
⚳	♉	13 20:17
☉	♌	22 19:51
♀	♋	1 22:38
☿	♌	10 5:51
♂	♎	12 1:10
☉	♍	23 2:50
☿	♍	26 7:06
♀	♌	27 15:48

Last Aspect / ☽ Ingress

Last Aspect Dy Hr Mn		☽ Ingress	Dy Hr Mn
3 1:38	♄ ⚹	♑	3 1:48
5 7:50	♀ △	♒	5 9:14
7 18:37	♄ ☌	♓	7 19:09
9 22:39	☿ △	♈	10 7:11
12 18:37	♄ ⚹	♉	12 19:37
15 4:55	♄ □	♊	15 6:07
17 11:47	♄ △	♋	17 13:08
19 11:24	☉ ☌	♌	19 16:47
21 16:46	♄ ☍	♍	21 18:24
23 7:42	♇ ⚹	♎	23 19:39
25 19:52	♄ △	♏	25 22:00
27 23:45	♄ □	♐	28 2:13
30 5:37	♄ ⚹	♑	30 8:27

Last Aspect / ☽ Ingress

Last Aspect Dy Hr Mn		☽ Ingress	Dy Hr Mn
1 3:44	♂ △	♒	1 16:36
3 23:04	♄ ☌	♓	4 2:44
6 7:24	♂ ☍	♈	6 14:39
8 23:43	☿ □	♉	9 3:22
11 14:13	♂ △	♊	11 14:47
13 18:07	♄ △	♋	13 22:46
15 14:32	♇ △	♌	16 2:43
17 23:02	♄ ☍	♍	18 3:41
19 16:04	♇ ⚹	♎	20 3:35
22 2:51	☉ ⚹	♏	22 4:27
24 1:52	♄ □	♐	24 7:45
26 7:27	♄ ⚹	♑	26 13:58
28 9:05	♇ ⚹	♒	28 22:42
31 1:39	♄ ☌	♓	31 9:18

☽ Phases & Eclipses

Dy Hr Mn	
3 23:45	○ 12♑02
11 22:49	☾ 19♈37
19 11:24	● 26♋48
26 3:25	☽ 3♏10
2 12:10	○ 10♒12
10 15:19	☾ 18♉00
17 19:28	● 24♌53
24 9:57	☽ 1♐15

Astro Data

1 July 1993
Julian Day # 34150
SVP 5♓20'45"
GC 26♐44.9 ⚴ 11♓11.2R
Eris 18♈17.3 ⚵ 17♌43.1
⚷ 21♌48.2 ⚶ 11♓41.9
☽ Mean ☊ 10♐48.8

1 August 1993
Julian Day # 34181
SVP 5♓20'40"
GC 26♐45.0 ⚴ 7♓31.2R
Eris 18♈16.5R ⚵ 0♍53.4
⚷ 25♌34.3 ⚶ 10♓41.3R
☽ Mean ☊ 9♐10.3

LONGITUDE — September 1993

Day	Sid.Time	☉	0 hr ☽	Noon☽	True☊	☿	♀	♂	⯲	♃	♄	♅	♆	♇
1 W	10 42 39	9♍03 34	7♓23 57	13♓24 44	7♐26.7	12♍04.8	5♌45.6	13♎04.1	6♉32.8	15♎14.0	26♒01.3	18♑30.2	18♑35.6	22♏58.1
2 Th	10 46 36	10 01 38	19 24 02	25 22 01	7R13.1	13 57.9	6 57.3	13 43.0	6R32.8	15 25.7	25R57.0	18R29.0	18R34.8	22 59.1
3 F	10 50 32	10 59 43	1♈18 50	7♈14 42	7 01.0	15 49.9	8 09.0	14 22.0	6 32.5	15 37.3	25 52.7	18 27.8	18 33.9	23 00.2
4 Sa	10 54 29	11 57 50	13 09 54	19 04 43	6 51.2	17 40.6	9 20.8	15 01.1	6 31.7	15 49.1	25 48.4	18 26.7	18 33.1	23 01.3
5 Su	10 58 25	12 56 00	24 59 30	0♉54 39	6 44.1	19 30.2	10 32.6	15 40.2	6 30.6	16 00.9	25 44.2	18 25.6	18 32.3	23 02.4
6 M	11 02 22	13 54 11	6♉50 36	12 47 50	6 39.9	21 18.6	11 44.6	16 19.4	6 29.1	16 12.8	25 40.0	18 24.6	18 31.6	23 03.5
7 Tu	11 06 18	14 52 24	18 46 55	24 48 25	6D38.0	23 05.8	12 56.6	16 58.7	6 27.3	16 24.7	25 35.8	18 23.6	18 30.9	23 04.7
8 W	11 10 15	15 50 40	0♊52 56	7♊01 06	6R37.6	24 51.8	14 08.7	17 38.0	6 25.1	16 36.6	25 31.7	18 22.6	18 30.2	23 05.9
9 Th	11 14 12	16 48 57	13 13 33	19 30 58	6 37.6	26 36.7	15 20.9	18 17.4	6 22.5	16 48.7	25 27.7	18 21.7	18 29.5	23 07.1
10 F	11 18 08	17 47 16	25 53 56	2♋23 04	6 37.0	28 20.4	16 33.2	18 56.8	6 19.5	17 00.7	25 23.6	18 20.9	18 28.8	23 08.3
11 Sa	11 22 05	18 45 38	8♋58 51	15 41 45	6 34.6	0♎03.0	17 45.5	19 36.3	6 16.2	17 12.9	25 19.7	18 20.1	18 28.2	23 09.6
12 Su	11 26 01	19 44 02	22 32 02	29 29 52	6 29.8	1 44.4	18 58.0	20 15.9	6 12.4	17 25.0	25 15.7	18 19.3	18 27.7	23 10.9
13 M	11 29 58	20 42 27	6♌35 12	13♌47 49	6 22.4	3 24.7	20 10.4	20 55.5	6 08.3	17 37.2	25 11.9	18 18.6	18 27.1	23 12.3
14 Tu	11 33 54	21 40 55	21 07 13	28 32 41	6 13.1	5 04.0	21 23.0	21 35.2	6 03.8	17 49.5	25 08.1	18 17.9	18 26.6	23 13.7
15 W	11 37 51	22 39 25	6♍03 18	13♍37 56	6 02.5	6 42.2	22 35.6	22 14.9	5 59.0	18 01.8	25 04.3	18 17.3	18 26.1	23 15.1
16 Th	11 41 47	23 37 56	21 15 16	28 53 54	5 52.2	8 19.3	23 48.3	22 54.7	5 53.7	18 14.1	25 00.6	18 16.7	18 25.6	23 16.5
17 F	11 45 44	24 36 30	6♎32 25	14♎09 24	5 43.2	9 55.4	25 01.1	23 34.6	5 48.1	18 26.5	24 57.0	18 16.2	18 25.2	23 18.0
18 Sa	11 49 40	25 35 05	21 43 33	29 13 43	5 36.5	11 30.4	26 13.9	24 14.5	5 42.1	18 39.0	24 53.4	18 15.7	18 24.8	23 19.4
19 Su	11 53 37	26 33 42	6♏38 55	13♏58 24	5 32.4	13 04.4	27 26.8	24 54.5	5 35.8	18 51.4	24 49.9	18 15.3	18 24.4	23 21.0
20 M	11 57 34	27 32 21	21 11 40	28 18 22	5D30.8	14 37.5	28 39.8	25 34.5	5 29.1	19 03.9	24 46.4	18 14.9	18 24.1	23 22.5
21 Tu	12 01 30	28 31 01	5♐18 23	12♐11 46	5 30.7	16 09.5	29 52.8	26 14.6	5 22.0	19 16.5	24 43.0	18 14.6	18 23.8	23 24.1
22 W	12 05 27	29 29 43	18 58 43	25 39 30	5R31.1	17 40.5	1♍05.9	26 54.8	5 14.6	19 29.1	24 39.7	18 14.3	18 23.5	23 25.7
23 Th	12 09 23	0♎28 27	2♑14 30	8♑44 09	5 30.9	19 10.4	2 19.0	27 35.0	5 06.9	19 41.7	24 36.5	18 14.1	18 23.3	23 27.3
24 F	12 13 20	1 27 13	15 08 54	21 29 15	5 28.9	20 39.4	3 32.2	28 15.3	4 58.8	19 54.3	24 33.3	18 13.9	18 23.1	23 28.9
25 Sa	12 17 16	2 26 00	27 45 38	3♒58 32	5 24.7	22 07.4	4 45.4	28 55.6	4 50.3	20 07.0	24 30.3	18 13.8	18 22.9	23 30.6
26 Su	12 21 13	3 24 49	10♒08 21	16 15 29	5 17.8	23 34.4	5 58.8	29 36.0	4 41.6	20 19.7	24 27.2	18 13.7	18 22.8	23 32.3
27 M	12 25 09	4 23 39	22 20 19	28 23 10	5 08.7	25 00.3	7 12.1	0♏16.4	4 32.5	20 32.4	24 24.3	18D13.7	18 22.7	23 34.0
28 Tu	12 29 06	5 22 32	4♓24 19	10♓24 02	4 58.0	26 25.2	8 25.6	0 56.9	4 23.1	20 45.2	24 21.5	18 13.7	18 22.6	23 35.8
29 W	12 33 03	6 21 26	16 22 32	22 20 03	4 46.5	27 49.0	9 39.0	1 37.5	4 13.4	20 57.9	24 18.7	18 13.8	18D22.6	23 37.6
30 Th	12 36 59	7 20 22	28 16 45	4♈12 51	4 35.4	29 11.7	10 52.6	2 18.1	4 03.4	21 10.7	24 16.0	18 13.9	18 22.6	23 39.4

LONGITUDE — October 1993

Day	Sid.Time	☉	0 hr ☽	Noon☽	True☊	☿	♀	♂	⯲	♃	♄	♅	♆	♇
1 F	12 40 56	8♎19 21	10♈08 31	16♈03 57	4♐25.5	0♏33.3	12♍06.2	2♏58.8	3♉53.1	21♎23.6	24♒13.4	18♑14.1	18♑22.6	23♏41.2
2 Sa	12 44 52	9 18 21	21 59 20	27 54 55	4R17.6	1 53.7	13 19.8	3 39.5	3R42.5	21 36.4	24R10.8	18 14.3	18 22.6	23 43.0
3 Su	12 48 49	10 17 24	3♉50 56	9♉47 41	4 12.1	3 13.0	14 33.5	4 20.3	3 31.6	21 49.3	24 08.4	18 14.6	18 22.7	23 44.9
4 M	12 52 45	11 16 28	15 45 29	21 44 42	4 09.1	4 30.9	15 47.3	5 01.2	3 20.5	22 02.2	24 06.1	18 14.9	18 22.9	23 46.8
5 Tu	12 56 42	12 15 35	27 45 42	3♊48 57	4D08.2	5 47.5	17 01.1	5 42.1	3 09.1	22 15.1	24 03.8	18 15.3	18 23.0	23 48.7
6 W	13 00 38	13 14 44	9♊54 56	16 04 07	4 08.7	7 02.7	18 15.0	6 23.1	2 57.4	22 28.0	24 01.6	18 15.7	18 23.2	23 50.6
7 Th	13 04 35	14 13 56	22 17 04	28 34 18	4 09.9	8 16.4	19 28.9	7 04.1	2 45.6	22 41.0	23 59.5	18 16.2	18 23.4	23 52.6
8 F	13 08 32	15 13 10	4♋56 24	11♋23 51	4R10.8	9 28.5	20 42.9	7 45.2	2 33.5	22 53.9	23 57.5	18 16.8	18 23.7	23 54.5
9 Sa	13 12 28	16 12 26	17 57 11	24 36 51	4 10.5	10 38.9	21 57.0	8 26.3	2 21.1	23 06.9	23 55.6	18 17.3	18 24.0	23 56.5
10 Su	13 16 25	17 11 45	1♌23 12	8♌16 29	4 08.5	11 47.4	23 11.0	9 07.6	2 08.6	23 19.9	23 53.8	18 18.0	18 24.3	23 58.5
11 M	13 20 21	18 11 05	15 16 49	22 24 09	4 04.6	12 54.0	24 25.2	9 48.8	1 55.9	23 32.9	23 52.1	18 18.7	18 24.7	24 00.6
12 Tu	13 24 18	19 10 28	29 38 14	6♍58 39	3 59.0	13 58.4	25 39.4	10 30.2	1 43.0	23 45.9	23 50.5	18 19.4	18 25.1	24 02.6
13 W	13 28 14	20 09 54	14♍24 41	21 55 30	3 52.4	15 00.4	26 53.6	11 11.6	1 30.0	23 59.0	23 48.9	18 20.2	18 25.5	24 04.7
14 Th	13 32 11	21 09 21	29 30 01	7♎07 01	3 45.7	15 59.9	28 07.9	11 53.1	1 16.8	24 12.0	23 47.5	18 21.0	18 26.0	24 06.8
15 F	13 36 07	22 08 51	14♎45 11	22 23 08	3 40.0	16 56.6	29 22.2	12 34.6	1 03.5	24 25.0	23 46.2	18 21.9	18 26.5	24 08.9
16 Sa	13 40 04	23 08 22	29 59 31	7♏33 04	3 35.8	17 50.2	0♎36.5	13 16.2	0 50.1	24 38.1	23 44.9	18 22.9	18 27.0	24 11.0
17 Su	13 44 01	24 07 56	15♏02 37	22 27 10	3D33.5	18 40.3	1 50.9	13 57.8	0 36.5	24 51.1	23 43.8	18 23.9	18 27.5	24 13.1
18 M	13 47 57	25 07 32	29 45 57	6♐58 21	3 33.1	19 26.8	3 05.3	14 39.5	0 22.9	25 04.2	23 42.8	18 24.9	18 28.1	24 15.3
19 Tu	13 51 54	26 07 09	14♐04 01	21 02 44	3 34.0	20 09.1	4 19.8	15 21.3	0 09.2	25 17.2	23 41.8	18 26.0	18 28.8	24 17.5
20 W	13 55 50	27 06 48	27 54 29	4♑39 25	3 35.5	20 46.9	5 34.3	16 03.1	29♈55.5	25 30.3	23 41.0	18 27.1	18 29.4	24 19.7
21 Th	13 59 47	28 06 29	11♑17 47	17 49 56	3R36.8	21 19.6	6 48.9	16 45.0	29 41.7	25 43.3	23 40.3	18 28.3	18 30.1	24 21.9
22 F	14 03 43	29 06 11	24 16 19	0♒37 24	3 37.3	21 46.9	8 03.4	17 26.9	29 27.9	25 56.4	23 39.6	18 29.6	18 30.8	24 24.1
23 Sa	14 07 40	0♏05 56	6♒53 42	13 05 46	3 36.4	22 08.0	9 18.0	18 08.9	29 14.1	26 09.4	23 39.1	18 30.9	18 31.6	24 26.3
24 Su	14 11 36	1 05 42	19 14 06	25 19 15	3 33.9	22 22.6	10 32.7	18 51.0	29 00.3	26 22.4	23 38.7	18 32.2	18 32.4	24 28.5
25 M	14 15 33	2 05 29	1♓21 43	7♓21 59	3 30.1	22R29.9	11 47.3	19 33.1	28 46.5	26 35.5	23 38.4	18 33.6	18 33.2	24 30.8
26 Tu	14 19 30	3 05 18	13 20 30	19 17 42	3 25.2	22 29.4	13 02.0	20 15.2	28 32.8	26 48.5	23 38.1	18 35.0	18 34.1	24 33.1
27 W	14 23 26	4 05 09	25 13 57	1♈09 37	3 19.8	22 20.6	14 16.8	20 57.5	28 19.1	27 01.5	23D38.0	18 36.5	18 35.0	24 35.3
28 Th	14 27 23	5 05 02	7♈05 01	13 00 28	3 14.5	22 03.0	15 31.5	21 39.7	28 05.5	27 14.5	23 38.0	18 38.0	18 35.9	24 37.6
29 F	14 31 19	6 04 57	18 56 13	24 52 31	3 09.9	21 36.1	16 46.3	22 22.1	27 52.0	27 27.5	23 38.1	18 39.6	18 36.8	24 39.9
30 Sa	14 35 16	7 04 53	0♉49 37	6♉47 42	3 06.4	21 00.0	18 01.1	23 04.5	27 38.6	27 40.5	23 38.3	18 41.2	18 37.8	24 42.2
31 Su	14 39 12	8 04 52	12 47 01	18 47 46	3 04.2	20 14.5	19 16.0	23 46.9	27 25.3	27 53.4	23 38.6	18 42.9	18 38.8	24 44.6

Astro Data Dy Hr Mn	Planet Ingress Dy Hr Mn	Last Aspect Dy Hr Mn	☽ Ingress Dy Hr Mn	Last Aspect Dy Hr Mn	☽ Ingress Dy Hr Mn	☽ Phases & Eclipses Dy Hr Mn
☽0N 1 22:23	☿ ♎ 11 11:18	2 7:12 ♇ △	♈ 2 21:21	2 4:28 ♄ ✱	♉ 2 16:13	1 2:33 ○ 8♓41
⯲R 2 0:23	♀ ♍ 21 14:22	5 1:34 ♄ ✱	♉ 5 10:09	4 16:42 ♄ □	♊ 5 4:27	9 6:26 ☾ 16♊35
☿0S 12 9:35	☉ ♎ 23 0:22	7 13:34 ♄ □	♊ 7 22:16	7 3:18 ♄ △	♋ 7 14:42	16 3:10 ● 23♍16
☽0S 15 19:47	♂ ♏ 27 2:15	10 3:24 ☿ □	♋ 10 7:37	9 10:48 ♇ △	♌ 9 21:34	22 19:32 ☽ 29♐48
♃□♅ 16 16:47		12 1:07 ♇ △	♌ 12 12:51	11 14:41 ♇ □	♍ 12 0:36	30 18:54 ○ 7♈37
♃□♆ 17 9:30	☿ ♏ 1 2:09	14 6:32 ♄ ☍	♍ 14 14:20	13 20:35 ♀ ☌	♎ 14 0:47	
☉0S 23 0:23	♀ ♎ 16 0:13	16 3:10 ☉ ☌	♎ 16 13:44	15 15:15 ♃ ☌	♏ 16 0:01	8 19:35 ☾ 15♋32
♅ D 27 12:29	⯲ ♈R 20 4:06	18 6:46 ♀ ✱	♏ 18 13:14	17 14:54 ♇ ☌	♐ 18 0:23	15 11:36 ● 22♎08
☽0N 29 4:22	☉ ♏ 23 9:37	20 12:40 ♀ □	♐ 20 14:53	19 21:33 ☉ ✱	♑ 20 3:42	22 8:52 ☽ 28♑58
♆ D 30 6:09		22 19:32 ☉ □	♑ 22 19:54	22 8:52 ☉ □	♒ 22 10:49	30 12:38 ○ 7♉06
♄□♇ 9 6:23	♀0S 18 20:52	25 1:41 ♂ □	♒ 25 4:19	24 14:07 ♃ △	♓ 24 21:17	
⯲0S 11 15:24	♅☌☌ 24 20:07	27 4:23 ☿ △	♓ 27 15:13	26 22:39 ♇ △	♈ 27 9:39	
♃△♄ 12 19:28	☿ R 25 22:40	29 14:37 ♇ △	♈ 30 3:29	29 17:18 ♃ ☍	♉ 29 22:20	
☽0S 13 6:22	☽0N 26 9:57					
♃⚺♇ 14 0:35	♄ D 28 3:39					

Astro Data

1 September 1993
Julian Day # 34212
SVP 5♓20'37"
GC 26♐45.0 ⚳ 0♓01.6R
Eris 18♈06.3R ⚴ 13♍53.6
⚷ 29♌42.1 ⚵ 3♓46.8R
☽ Mean ☊ 7♐31.8

1 October 1993
Julian Day # 34242
SVP 5♓20'34"
GC 26♐45.1 ⚳ 24♒06.2R
Eris 17♈50.2R ⚴ 26♍04.1
⚷ 3♍33.3 ⚵ 28♒29.2R
☽ Mean ☊ 5♐56.5

November 1993 LONGITUDE

Day	Sid.Time	☉	0 hr ☽	Noon☽	True☊	☿	♀	♂	⚳	♃	♄	♅	♆	♇
1 M	14 43 09	9♏04 52	24♉50 11	0♊54 28	3♐03.3	19♏20.1	20♎30.9	24♏29.4	27♈12.2	28♎06.4	23♒39.0	18♑44.6	18♑39.8	24♏46.9
2 Tu	14 47 05	10 04 55	7♊00 54	13 09 43	3D 03.7	18R 17.6	21 45.8	25 12.0	26R 59.2	28 19.3	23 39.5	18 46.4	18 40.9	24 49.2
3 W	14 51 02	11 04 59	19 21 12	25 35 40	3 04.8	17 08.1	23 00.7	25 54.6	26 46.3	28 32.2	23 40.1	18 48.2	18 42.0	24 51.6
4 Th	14 54 58	12 05 06	1♋53 25	8♋14 47	3 06.4	15 53.4	24 15.7	26 37.3	26 33.6	28 45.1	23 40.8	18 50.0	18 43.2	24 53.9
5 F	14 58 55	13 05 14	14 40 06	21 09 43	3 07.9	14 35.4	25 30.7	27 20.1	26 21.1	28 58.0	23 41.6	18 51.9	18 44.3	24 56.3
6 Sa	15 02 52	14 05 25	27 43 58	4♌23 08	3R 08.9	13 16.5	26 45.7	28 02.9	26 08.8	29 10.8	23 42.5	18 53.9	18 45.5	24 58.7
7 Su	15 06 48	15 05 37	11♌07 29	17 57 13	3 09.2	11 59.2	28 00.8	28 45.8	25 56.7	29 23.7	23 43.5	18 55.9	18 46.7	25 01.0
8 M	15 10 45	16 05 52	24 52 28	1♍53 14	3 08.6	10 46.0	29 15.9	29 28.7	25 44.9	29 36.5	23 44.7	18 57.9	18 48.0	25 03.4
9 Tu	15 14 41	17 06 09	8♍59 27	16 10 52	3 07.2	9 39.2	0♏31.0	0♐11.7	25 33.3	29 49.2	23 45.9	19 00.0	18 49.3	25 05.8
10 W	15 18 38	18 06 27	23 27 08	0♎47 43	3 05.4	8 40.8	1 46.1	0 54.7	25 21.9	0♏02.0	23 47.2	19 02.1	18 50.6	25 08.2
11 Th	15 22 34	19 06 48	8♎11 56	15 39 00	3 03.6	7 52.4	3 01.2	1 37.8	25 10.8	0 14.7	23 48.6	19 04.2	18 51.9	25 10.6
12 F	15 26 31	20 07 11	23 07 56	0♏37 46	3 02.0	7 14.9	4 16.4	2 21.0	24 59.9	0 27.4	23 50.2	19 06.4	18 53.3	25 13.0
13 Sa	15 30 27	21 07 35	8♏07 23	15 35 42	3 00.9	6 49.1	5 31.6	3 04.2	24 49.4	0 40.1	23 51.8	19 08.7	18 54.7	25 15.4
14 Su	15 34 24	22 08 01	23 01 40	0♐24 16	3D 00.5	6D 34.9	6 46.8	3 47.5	24 39.1	0 52.7	23 53.5	19 10.9	18 56.1	25 17.8
15 M	15 38 21	23 08 29	7♐42 38	14 56 00	3 00.6	6 32.3	8 02.0	4 30.8	24 29.2	1 05.3	23 55.4	19 13.3	18 57.5	25 20.2
16 Tu	15 42 17	24 08 58	22 03 44	29 05 24	3 01.2	6 40.6	9 17.2	5 14.2	24 19.5	1 17.9	23 57.3	19 15.6	18 59.0	25 22.6
17 W	15 46 14	25 09 29	6♑00 41	12♑49 29	3 02.0	6 59.1	10 32.5	5 57.7	24 10.2	1 30.4	23 59.3	19 18.0	19 00.5	25 25.0
18 Th	15 50 10	26 10 01	19 31 46	26 07 42	3 02.8	7 27.1	11 47.8	6 41.2	24 01.3	1 42.9	24 01.5	19 20.5	19 02.0	25 27.4
19 F	15 54 07	27 10 34	2♒37 32	9♒01 36	3 03.3	8 03.6	13 03.0	7 24.8	23 52.6	1 55.3	24 03.7	19 22.9	19 03.6	25 29.8
20 Sa	15 58 03	28 11 08	15 20 20	21 34 13	3R 03.6	8 47.8	14 18.3	8 08.4	23 44.3	2 07.7	24 06.1	19 25.5	19 05.2	25 32.2
21 Su	16 02 00	29 11 44	27 43 46	3♓49 32	3 03.6	9 38.7	15 33.6	8 52.0	23 36.4	2 20.0	24 08.5	19 28.0	19 06.8	25 34.6
22 M	16 05 56	0♐12 20	9♓52 07	15 52 04	3 03.5	10 35.6	16 48.9	9 35.8	23 28.8	2 32.3	24 11.0	19 30.6	19 08.4	25 37.0
23 Tu	16 09 53	1 12 58	21 49 58	27 46 23	3 03.3	11 37.7	18 04.3	10 19.5	23 21.6	2 44.6	24 13.6	19 33.2	19 10.1	25 39.4
24 W	16 13 50	2 13 37	3♈41 51	9♈36 53	3D 03.1	12 44.3	19 19.6	11 03.4	23 14.8	2 56.8	24 16.4	19 35.9	19 11.7	25 41.8
25 Th	16 17 46	3 14 18	15 31 58	21 27 34	3 03.1	13 54.7	20 34.9	11 47.2	23 08.3	3 09.0	24 19.2	19 38.5	19 13.4	25 44.2
26 F	16 21 43	4 14 59	27 24 07	3♉21 59	3 03.2	15 08.5	21 50.3	12 31.2	23 02.2	3 21.1	24 22.1	19 41.3	19 15.1	25 46.6
27 Sa	16 25 39	5 15 42	9♉21 30	15 23 01	3 03.3	16 25.2	23 05.7	13 15.2	22 56.5	3 33.1	24 25.1	19 44.0	19 16.9	25 49.0
28 Su	16 29 36	6 16 25	21 26 46	27 32 59	3R 03.5	17 44.4	24 21.0	13 59.2	22 51.2	3 45.1	24 28.2	19 46.8	19 18.7	25 51.4
29 M	16 33 32	7 17 10	3♊41 53	9♊53 38	3 03.4	19 05.6	25 36.4	14 43.3	22 46.2	3 57.1	24 31.4	19 49.6	19 20.4	25 53.7
30 Tu	16 37 29	8 17 57	16 08 21	22 26 09	3 03.2	20 28.6	26 51.8	15 27.5	22 41.7	4 09.0	24 34.7	19 52.5	19 22.3	25 56.1

December 1993 LONGITUDE

Day	Sid.Time	☉	0 hr ☽	Noon☽	True☊	☿	♀	♂	⚳	♃	♄	♅	♆	♇
1 W	16 41 26	9♐18 44	28♊47 08	5♋11 21	3♐02.6	21♏53.1	28♏07.2	16♐11.7	22♈37.5	4♏20.8	24♒38.0	19♑55.4	19♑24.1	25♏58.5
2 Th	16 45 22	10 19 33	11♋38 53	18 09 44	3R 01.7	23 18.8	29 22.6	16 55.9	22R 33.7	4 32.6	24 41.5	19 58.3	19 25.9	26 00.8
3 F	16 49 19	11 20 24	24 43 58	1♌21 36	3 00.7	24 45.7	0♐38.1	17 40.2	22 30.4	4 44.3	24 45.1	20 01.2	19 27.8	26 03.2
4 Sa	16 53 15	12 21 15	8♌02 39	14 47 09	2 59.6	26 13.5	1 53.5	18 24.6	22 27.4	4 56.0	24 48.7	20 04.2	19 29.7	26 05.5
5 Su	16 57 12	13 22 08	21 35 04	28 26 24	2 58.8	27 42.0	3 08.9	19 09.0	22 24.8	5 07.6	24 52.4	20 07.2	19 31.6	26 07.8
6 M	17 01 08	14 23 02	5♍21 08	12♍19 10	2D 58.5	29 11.2	4 24.4	19 53.5	22 22.6	5 19.1	24 56.2	20 10.2	19 33.5	26 10.2
7 Tu	17 05 05	15 23 57	19 20 25	26 24 43	2 58.7	0♐41.0	5 39.8	20 38.0	22 20.8	5 30.6	25 00.1	20 13.3	19 35.5	26 12.5
8 W	17 09 01	16 24 54	3♎31 53	10♎41 38	2 59.4	2 11.2	6 55.3	21 22.6	22 19.3	5 41.9	25 04.1	20 16.4	19 37.5	26 14.8
9 Th	17 12 58	17 25 52	17 53 38	25 07 28	3 00.5	3 41.8	8 10.8	22 07.2	22 18.3	5 53.3	25 08.2	20 19.5	19 39.4	26 17.1
10 F	17 16 55	18 26 51	2♏22 39	9♏38 37	3 01.7	5 12.8	9 26.3	22 51.9	22 17.7	6 04.5	25 12.4	20 22.6	19 41.4	26 19.3
11 Sa	17 20 51	19 27 52	16 54 45	24 10 24	3R 02.5	6 44.0	10 41.8	23 36.7	22D 17.5	6 15.7	25 16.6	20 25.8	19 43.5	26 21.6
12 Su	17 24 48	20 28 53	1♐24 50	8♐37 21	3 02.6	8 15.6	11 57.3	24 21.4	22 17.6	6 26.8	25 20.9	20 29.0	19 45.5	26 23.8
13 M	17 28 44	21 29 55	15 47 15	22 53 50	3 01.7	9 47.3	13 12.8	25 06.3	22 18.2	6 37.8	25 25.3	20 32.2	19 47.5	26 26.1
14 Tu	17 32 41	22 30 58	29 56 30	6♑54 43	2 59.8	11 19.3	14 28.3	25 51.2	22 19.2	6 48.7	25 29.8	20 35.4	19 49.6	26 28.3
15 W	17 36 37	23 32 02	13♑48 02	20 36 05	2 57.0	12 51.5	15 43.8	26 36.1	22 20.5	6 59.6	25 34.4	20 38.7	19 51.7	26 30.5
16 Th	17 40 34	24 33 06	27 18 40	3♒55 40	2 53.6	14 23.8	16 59.3	27 21.1	22 22.2	7 10.4	25 39.0	20 41.9	19 53.8	26 32.7
17 F	17 44 30	25 34 11	10♒27 05	16 53 03	2 50.2	15 56.3	18 14.8	28 06.1	22 24.3	7 21.1	25 43.7	20 45.2	19 55.9	26 34.9
18 Sa	17 48 27	26 35 16	23 13 46	29 29 34	2 47.1	17 29.0	19 30.3	28 51.2	22 26.8	7 31.7	25 48.5	20 48.5	19 58.0	26 37.1
19 Su	17 52 24	27 36 21	5♓40 50	11♓48 02	2 44.9	19 01.8	20 45.8	29 36.4	22 29.7	7 42.2	25 53.4	20 51.9	20 00.1	26 39.2
20 M	17 56 20	28 37 26	17 51 42	23 52 22	2D 43.8	20 34.8	22 01.3	0♑21.5	22 32.9	7 52.6	25 58.3	20 55.2	20 02.3	26 41.3
21 Tu	18 00 17	29 38 32	29 50 39	5♈47 10	2 43.9	22 08.0	23 16.8	1 06.7	22 36.5	8 02.9	26 03.3	20 58.6	20 04.4	26 43.4
22 W	18 04 13	0♑39 38	11♈42 32	17 37 24	2 45.0	23 41.4	24 32.3	1 52.0	22 40.5	8 13.2	26 08.4	21 02.0	20 06.6	26 45.5
23 Th	18 08 10	1 40 45	23 32 22	29 28 03	2 46.7	25 14.9	25 47.9	2 37.3	22 44.8	8 23.3	26 13.6	21 05.4	20 08.8	26 47.6
24 F	18 12 06	2 41 51	5♉25 03	11♉23 55	2 48.6	26 48.7	27 03.4	3 22.7	22 49.5	8 33.4	26 18.8	21 08.8	20 11.0	26 49.7
25 Sa	18 16 03	3 42 58	17 25 09	23 29 14	2R 50.0	28 22.7	28 18.9	4 08.1	22 54.6	8 43.3	26 24.1	21 12.2	20 13.2	26 51.7
26 Su	18 19 59	4 44 05	29 36 35	5♊47 34	2 50.3	29 56.9	29 34.4	4 53.5	23 00.0	8 53.2	26 29.4	21 15.6	20 15.4	26 53.7
27 M	18 23 56	5 45 12	12♊02 28	18 21 31	2 49.2	1♑31.4	0♑49.9	5 39.0	23 05.8	9 02.9	26 34.9	21 19.1	20 17.6	26 55.7
28 Tu	18 27 53	6 46 19	24 44 49	1♋12 28	2 46.3	3 06.1	2 05.4	6 24.5	23 11.9	9 12.6	26 40.3	21 22.6	20 19.8	26 57.7
29 W	18 31 49	7 47 26	7♋44 27	14 20 38	2 41.8	4 41.1	3 20.9	7 10.1	23 18.3	9 22.1	26 45.9	21 26.0	20 22.0	26 59.7
30 Th	18 35 46	8 48 34	21 00 53	27 44 56	2 36.0	6 16.4	4 36.4	7 55.7	23 25.1	9 31.6	26 51.5	21 29.5	20 24.3	27 01.6
31 F	18 39 42	9 49 42	4♌32 32	11♌23 18	2 29.7	7 52.0	5 51.9	8 41.4	23 32.2	9 40.9	26 57.2	21 33.0	20 26.5	27 03.5

Astro Data

	Dy Hr Mn
☽0S	9 15:15
☿D	15 5:37
☽0N	22 16:28
☽0S	6 21:55
⚳0N	9 1:45
⚳D	11 13:46
☽0N	20 0:44

Planet Ingress

	Dy Hr Mn
♀ ♏	9 2:07
♂ ♐	9 5:29
♃ ♏	10 8:15
☉ ♐	22 7:07
♀ ♐	2 23:54
☿ ♐	7 1:04
♂ ♑	20 0:34
☉ ♑	21 20:26
☿ ♑	26 12:47
♀ ♑	26 20:09

Last Aspect / ☽ Ingress

Last Aspect Dy Hr Mn		☽ Ingress Dy Hr Mn
31 23:51 ♇ ☍	♊	1 10:13
3 17:43 ♃ △	♋	3 20:25
6 2:28 ♃ □	♌	6 4:06
8 8:03 ♃ ⚹	♍	8 8:47
10 2:44 ♇ ⚹	♎	10 10:42
12 1:06 ♄ △	♏	12 11:00
14 3:39 ♇ ☌	♐	14 11:20
16 3:12 ♄ ⚹	♑	16 13:34
18 12:05 ☉ ⚹	♒	18 19:08
21 2:03 ☉ □	♓	21 4:27
23 7:42 ♇ △	♈	23 16:30
25 17:48 ♄ ⚹	♉	26 5:14
28 8:40 ♇ ☍	♊	28 16:48

Last Aspect / ☽ Ingress

Last Aspect Dy Hr Mn		☽ Ingress Dy Hr Mn
30 16:05 ♄ △	♋	1 2:17
3 2:22 ♇ △	♌	3 9:33
5 10:33 ☿ □	♍	5 14:43
7 11:39 ♇ ⚹	♎	7 18:03
9 12:01 ♄ △	♏	9 20:04
11 15:38 ♇ ☌	♐	11 21:39
13 16:19 ♄ ⚹	♑	14 0:06
15 22:35 ♇ ⚹	♒	16 4:51
18 10:41 ♂ ⚹	♓	18 12:59
20 22:26 ☉ □	♈	21 0:19
23 5:24 ♄ ⚹	♉	23 13:05
25 18:39 ♇ ☍	♊	26 0:46
28 3:32 ♄ △	♋	28 9:46
30 10:43 ♇ △	♌	30 15:59

☽ Phases & Eclipses

Dy Hr Mn	
7 6:36	☾ 14♌52
13 21:34	● 21♏32
13 21:44:48	P 0.928
21 2:03	☽ 28♒47
29 6:31	○ 7♊03
29 6:26	T 1.087
6 15:49	☾ 14♍33
13 9:27	● 21♐23
20 22:26	☽ 29♓04
28 23:05	○ 7♋15

Astro Data

1 November 1993
Julian Day # 34273
SVP 5♓20'31"
GC 26♐45.2 ⚵ 23♒04.1
Eris 17♈31.8R ⚶ 7♎54.4
⚷ 6♍50.9 ⚴ 29♒42.8
☽ Mean ☊ 4♐18.0

1 December 1993
Julian Day # 34303
SVP 5♓20'26"
GC 26♐45.3 ⚵ 26♒47.0
Eris 17♈17.7R ⚶ 18♎09.9
⚷ 8♍50.3 ⚴ 6♓29.9
☽ Mean ☊ 2♐42.6

LONGITUDE — January 1994

Day	Sid.Time	☉	0 hr ☽	Noon ☽	True ☊	☿	♀	♂	⚳	♃	♄	♅	♆	♇
1 Sa	18 43 39	10♑50 50	18♌16 54	25♌12 56	2♐23.5	9♑27.9	7♑07.3	9♑27.1	23♈39.6	9♏50.1	27♒02.9	21♑36.5	20♑28.7	27♏05.4
2 Su	18 47 35	11 51 58	2♍11 03	9♍10 51	2R 18.3	11 04.1	8 22.8	10 12.8	23 47.3	9 59.3	27 08.7	21 40.0	20 31.0	27 07.3
3 M	18 51 32	12 53 07	16 12 01	23 14 14	2 14.7	12 40.7	9 38.3	10 58.6	23 55.4	10 08.3	27 14.6	21 43.6	20 33.3	27 09.1
4 Tu	18 55 28	13 54 15	0♎17 12	7♎20 43	2D 13.0	14 17.7	10 53.8	11 44.4	24 03.8	10 17.1	27 20.5	21 47.1	20 35.5	27 10.9
5 W	18 59 25	14 55 24	14 24 33	21 28 31	2 12.9	15 55.0	12 09.3	12 30.3	24 12.5	10 25.9	27 26.4	21 50.6	20 37.8	27 12.7
6 Th	19 03 22	15 56 34	28 32 27	5♏36 12	2 14.0	17 32.7	13 24.8	13 16.2	24 21.5	10 34.6	27 32.5	21 54.2	20 40.0	27 14.5
7 F	19 07 18	16 57 44	12♏39 36	19 42 28	2R 15.3	19 10.8	14 40.3	14 02.2	24 30.8	10 43.1	27 38.5	21 57.7	20 42.3	27 16.2
8 Sa	19 11 15	17 58 53	26 44 35	3♐45 42	2 15.8	20 49.3	15 55.8	14 48.2	24 40.4	10 51.5	27 44.7	22 01.3	20 44.6	27 18.0
9 Su	19 15 11	19 00 03	10♐45 34	17 43 50	2 14.7	22 28.3	17 11.3	15 34.2	24 50.3	10 59.8	27 50.9	22 04.8	20 46.9	27 19.7
10 M	19 19 08	20 01 13	24 40 10	1♑34 12	2 11.3	24 07.6	18 26.8	16 20.3	25 00.5	11 08.0	27 57.1	22 08.4	20 49.2	27 21.3
11 Tu	19 23 04	21 02 23	8♑25 33	15 13 49	2 05.5	25 47.3	19 42.3	17 06.4	25 10.9	11 16.0	28 03.4	22 11.9	20 51.4	27 23.0
12 W	19 27 01	22 03 32	21 58 39	28 39 42	1 57.5	27 27.4	20 57.8	17 52.6	25 21.7	11 23.9	28 09.7	22 15.5	20 53.7	27 24.6
13 Th	19 30 57	23 04 41	5♒16 42	11♒49 27	1 48.1	29 07.9	22 13.3	18 38.8	25 32.8	11 31.7	28 16.1	22 19.0	20 56.0	27 26.2
14 F	19 34 54	24 05 49	18 17 46	24 41 38	1 38.2	0♒48.7	23 28.7	19 25.0	25 44.1	11 39.3	28 22.5	22 22.6	20 58.3	27 27.7
15 Sa	19 38 51	25 06 57	1♓01 04	7♓16 11	1 28.8	2 29.9	24 44.2	20 11.2	25 55.7	11 46.8	28 29.0	22 26.2	21 00.5	27 29.2
16 Su	19 42 47	26 08 04	13 27 12	19 34 26	1 20.8	4 11.3	25 59.7	20 57.5	26 07.5	11 54.1	28 35.5	22 29.7	21 02.8	27 30.7
17 M	19 46 44	27 09 10	25 38 14	1♈39 03	1 15.0	5 53.0	27 15.1	21 43.8	26 19.6	12 01.4	28 42.1	22 33.3	21 05.1	27 32.2
18 Tu	19 50 40	28 10 16	7♈37 24	13 33 51	1 11.4	7 34.8	28 30.6	22 30.2	26 32.0	12 08.4	28 48.6	22 36.8	21 07.3	27 33.7
19 W	19 54 37	29 11 20	19 28 59	25 23 27	1D 10.0	9 16.8	29 46.0	23 16.6	26 44.7	12 15.4	28 55.3	22 40.4	21 09.6	27 35.1
20 Th	19 58 33	0♒12 24	1♉17 55	7♉13 04	1 10.2	10 58.7	1♒01.4	24 03.0	26 57.6	12 22.2	29 02.0	22 43.9	21 11.9	27 36.4
21 F	20 02 30	1 13 27	13 09 34	19 08 07	1R 11.0	12 40.5	2 16.8	24 49.4	27 10.7	12 28.8	29 08.7	22 47.4	21 14.1	27 37.8
22 Sa	20 06 26	2 14 30	25 09 23	1♊13 58	1 11.5	14 22.0	3 32.2	25 35.9	27 24.1	12 35.3	29 15.4	22 51.0	21 16.4	27 39.1
23 Su	20 10 23	3 15 31	7♊22 29	13 35 29	1 10.7	16 03.1	4 47.6	26 22.4	27 37.7	12 41.7	29 22.2	22 54.5	21 18.6	27 40.4
24 M	20 14 20	4 16 31	19 53 24	26 16 39	1 07.7	17 43.6	6 03.0	27 09.0	27 51.5	12 47.9	29 29.0	22 58.0	21 20.8	27 41.7
25 Tu	20 18 16	5 17 30	2♋45 29	9♋20 05	1 02.1	19 23.1	7 18.4	27 55.5	28 05.6	12 54.0	29 35.9	23 01.5	21 23.1	27 42.9
26 W	20 22 13	6 18 29	16 00 28	22 46 33	0 54.0	21 01.5	8 33.8	28 42.1	28 19.9	12 59.9	29 42.8	23 05.0	21 25.3	27 44.1
27 Th	20 26 09	7 19 26	29 38 05	6♌34 42	0 43.8	22 38.4	9 49.1	29 28.7	28 34.4	13 05.6	29 49.7	23 08.5	21 27.5	27 45.3
28 F	20 30 06	8 20 23	13♌35 52	20 40 58	0 32.5	24 13.4	11 04.5	0♒15.4	28 49.1	13 11.2	29 56.6	23 11.9	21 29.7	27 46.4
29 Sa	20 34 02	9 21 18	27 49 18	5♍00 05	0 21.4	25 46.1	12 19.8	1 02.0	29 04.1	13 16.6	0♓03.6	23 15.4	21 31.9	27 47.5
30 Su	20 37 59	10 22 13	12♍12 31	19 25 51	0 11.7	27 16.0	13 35.1	1 48.7	29 19.2	13 21.9	0 10.6	23 18.8	21 34.1	27 48.5
31 M	20 41 55	11 23 07	26 39 17	3♎52 11	0 04.3	28 42.6	14 50.4	2 35.5	29 34.6	13 27.0	0 17.6	23 22.3	21 36.3	27 49.6

LONGITUDE — February 1994

Day	Sid.Time	☉	0 hr ☽	Noon ☽	True ☊	☿	♀	♂	⚳	♃	♄	♅	♆	♇
1 Tu	20 45 52	12♒24 00	11♎03 56	18♎14 03	29♏59.6	0♓05.2	16♒05.7	3♒22.2	29♈50.2	13♏32.0	0♓24.6	23♑25.7	21♑38.4	27♏50.6
2 W	20 49 49	13 24 52	25 22 11	2♏28 02	29D 57.4	1 23.1	17 21.0	4 09.0	0♉05.9	13 36.8	0 31.7	23 29.1	21 40.6	27 51.5
3 Th	20 53 45	14 25 44	9♏31 25	16 32 16	29R 57.1	2 35.7	18 36.3	4 55.8	0 21.9	13 41.4	0 38.8	23 32.5	21 42.7	27 52.5
4 F	20 57 42	15 26 35	23 30 33	0♐26 15	29 57.2	3 42.2	19 51.6	5 42.6	0 38.1	13 45.9	0 45.9	23 35.9	21 44.9	27 53.4
5 Sa	21 01 38	16 27 25	7♐19 27	14 10 10	29 56.6	4 41.8	21 06.9	6 29.5	0 54.4	13 50.1	0 53.0	23 39.2	21 47.0	27 54.2
6 Su	21 05 35	17 28 14	20 58 27	27 44 20	29 53.9	5 33.8	22 22.2	7 16.4	1 11.0	13 54.3	1 00.2	23 42.6	21 49.1	27 55.1
7 M	21 09 31	18 29 02	4♑27 48	11♑08 49	29 48.4	6 17.3	23 37.4	8 03.3	1 27.7	13 58.2	1 07.4	23 45.9	21 51.2	27 55.9
8 Tu	21 13 28	19 29 50	17 47 20	24 23 14	29 39.8	6 51.7	24 52.7	8 50.2	1 44.6	14 02.0	1 14.6	23 49.2	21 53.3	27 56.6
9 W	21 17 25	20 30 36	0♒56 23	7♒26 40	29 28.4	7 16.4	26 07.9	9 37.2	2 01.7	14 05.6	1 21.8	23 52.5	21 55.3	27 57.3
10 Th	21 21 21	21 31 20	13 53 57	20 18 05	29 15.0	7R 30.8	27 23.1	10 24.1	2 19.0	14 09.0	1 29.0	23 55.7	21 57.4	27 58.0
11 F	21 25 18	22 32 04	26 38 35	2♓56 35	29 00.7	7 34.5	28 38.3	11 11.1	2 36.5	14 12.2	1 36.2	23 59.0	21 59.4	27 58.7
12 Sa	21 29 14	23 32 46	9♓10 51	15 21 48	28 46.9	7 27.6	29 53.5	11 58.1	2 54.1	14 15.3	1 43.5	24 02.2	22 01.4	27 59.3
13 Su	21 33 11	24 33 26	21 29 34	27 34 18	28 34.8	7 10.1	1♓08.7	12 45.1	3 11.9	14 18.2	1 50.7	24 05.4	22 03.4	27 59.9
14 M	21 37 07	25 34 05	3♈36 14	9♈35 39	28 25.1	6 42.3	2 23.8	13 32.1	3 29.8	14 20.9	1 58.0	24 08.5	22 05.4	28 00.4
15 Tu	21 41 04	26 34 42	15 32 57	21 28 33	28 18.4	6 04.9	3 39.0	14 19.2	3 47.9	14 23.4	2 05.3	24 11.7	22 07.4	28 00.9
16 W	21 45 00	27 35 18	27 22 58	3♉16 42	28 14.4	5 18.9	4 54.1	15 06.2	4 06.2	14 25.7	2 12.5	24 14.8	22 09.3	28 01.4
17 Th	21 48 57	28 35 52	9♉10 24	15 04 40	28 12.8	4 25.5	6 09.2	15 53.3	4 24.6	14 27.9	2 19.8	24 17.9	22 11.2	28 01.9
18 F	21 52 53	29 36 24	21 00 12	26 57 39	28 12.5	3 26.2	7 24.3	16 40.4	4 43.2	14 29.9	2 27.1	24 21.0	22 13.2	28 02.3
19 Sa	21 56 50	0♓36 54	2♊57 46	9♊01 13	28 12.3	2 22.5	8 39.4	17 27.4	5 01.9	14 31.7	2 34.4	24 24.0	22 15.0	28 02.6
20 Su	22 00 47	1 37 23	15 08 43	21 20 55	28 11.3	1 16.2	9 54.4	18 14.5	5 20.8	14 33.3	2 41.7	24 27.1	22 16.9	28 03.0
21 M	22 04 43	2 37 50	27 38 26	4♋01 50	28 08.2	0 09.1	11 09.4	19 01.7	5 39.8	14 34.7	2 49.0	24 30.0	22 18.8	28 03.3
22 Tu	22 08 40	3 38 14	10♋31 34	17 07 59	28 02.6	29♒02.8	12 24.4	19 48.8	5 59.0	14 35.9	2 56.3	24 33.0	22 20.6	28 03.5
23 W	22 12 36	4 38 37	23 51 18	0♌41 34	27 54.3	27 58.8	13 39.4	20 35.9	6 18.3	14 37.0	3 03.6	24 35.9	22 22.4	28 03.8
24 Th	22 16 33	5 38 59	7♌38 41	14 42 19	27 43.8	26 58.6	14 54.4	21 23.0	6 37.7	14 37.8	3 10.9	24 38.8	22 24.2	28 04.0
25 F	22 20 29	6 39 18	21 52 00	29 07 02	27 32.0	26 03.3	16 09.3	22 10.2	6 57.2	14 38.5	3 18.2	24 41.7	22 26.0	28 04.1
26 Sa	22 24 26	7 39 35	6♍26 34	13♍49 36	27 20.2	25 13.7	17 24.2	22 57.3	7 16.9	14 39.0	3 25.5	24 44.6	22 27.7	28 04.2
27 Su	22 28 22	8 39 51	21 15 04	28 41 50	27 09.7	24 30.5	18 39.1	23 44.5	7 36.7	14 39.3	3 32.7	24 47.4	22 29.4	28 04.3
28 M	22 32 19	9 40 05	6♎08 47	13♎34 50	27 01.6	23 54.2	19 54.0	24 31.6	7 56.7	14R 39.4	3 40.0	24 50.1	22 31.1	28R 04.4

Astro Data

	Dy Hr Mn
♄□♇	2 3:11
☽0S	3 3:49
☽0N	16 10:12
☽0S	30 11:06
☿R	11 8:29
☽0N	12 19:16
☽0S	26 20:38
♃R	28 13:50

Planet Ingress

	Dy Hr Mn
☿ ♒	14 0:25
♀ ♒	19 16:28
☉ ♒	20 7:07
♂ ♒	28 4:05
♄ ♓	28 23:43
☊ ♏R	1 9:14
☿ ♓	1 10:28
⚳ ♉	2 2:59
♀ ♓	12 14:04
☉ ♓	18 21:22
☿ ♒R	21 15:15

Last Aspect / ☽ Ingress (January)

Last Aspect Dy Hr Mn		☽ Ingress Dy Hr Mn
1 15:14 ♇ □	♍	1 20:15
3 18:41 ♇ ✶	♎	3 23:31
5 22:12 ♄ △	♏	6 2:29
8 1:38 ♄ □	♐	8 5:34
10 5:39 ♄ ✶	♑	10 9:16
12 9:44 ♇ ✶	♒	12 14:25
14 19:02 ♄ ☌	♓	14 22:04
17 3:46 ♇ △	♈	17 8:42
19 20:27 ☉ □	♉	19 21:22
22 8:04 ♄ □	♊	22 9:35
24 18:01 ♄ △	♋	24 18:55
26 23:00 ♂ ☍	♌	27 0:38
28 23:56 ♇ □	♍	29 3:39
31 1:56 ♇ ✶	♎	31 5:34

Last Aspect / ☽ Ingress (February)

Last Aspect Dy Hr Mn		☽ Ingress Dy Hr Mn
1 20:46 ♅ □	♏	2 7:49
4 7:34 ♇ ☌	♐	4 11:14
6 1:30 ♀ ✶	♑	6 16:02
8 18:31 ♇ ✶	♒	8 22:16
11 2:52 ♀ ☌	♓	11 6:22
13 12:51 ♇ △	♈	13 16:49
15 23:20 ☉ ✶	♉	16 5:20
18 17:47 ☉ □	♊	18 18:05
20 5:36 ♂ △	♋	21 4:27
23 7:24 ♇ △	♌	23 10:48
25 10:16 ♇ □	♍	25 13:27
27 11:00 ♇ ✶	♎	27 14:06

☽ Phases & Eclipses

Dy Hr Mn		
5 0:01	☾	14♎25
11 23:10	●	21♑31
19 20:27	☽	29♈33
27 13:23	○	7♌23
3 8:06	☾	14♏16
10 14:30	●	21♒38
18 17:47	☽	29♉51
26 1:15	○	7♍13

Astro Data

1 January 1994
Julian Day # 34334
SVP 5♓20'21"
GC 26♐45.3 ⚴ 3♓58.0
Eris 17♈11.3R ⚵ 26♎44.0
⚷ 9♍13.0R ⚶ 17♓02.3
☽ Mean ☊ 1♐04.2

1 February 1994
Julian Day # 34365
SVP 5♓20'16"
GC 26♐45.4 ⚴ 13♓14.7
Eris 17♈15.5 ⚵ 1♏58.5
⚷ 7♍52.6R ⚶ 29♓33.5
☽ Mean ☊ 29♏25.7

March 1994 LONGITUDE

Day	Sid.Time	☉	0 hr ☽	Noon ☽	True ☊	☿	♀	♂	⚳	♃	♄	♅	♆	♇
1 Tu	22 36 16	10♓40 18	20♎59 01	28♎20 30	26♏56.3	23♒24.9	21♓08.9	25♒18.8	8♉16.8	14♏39.3	3♓47.3	24♑52.9	22♑32.8	28♏04.4
2 W	22 40 12	11 40 29	5♏38 35	12♏52 44	26D 53.7	23R 02.7	22 23.7	26 06.0	8 36.9	14R 39.0	3 54.5	24 55.6	22 34.5	28R 04.4
3 Th	22 44 09	12 40 39	20 02 36	27 07 56	26 53.1	22 47.6	23 38.5	26 53.1	8 57.3	14 38.6	4 01.8	24 58.3	22 36.1	28 04.3
4 F	22 48 05	13 40 47	4♐08 40	11♐04 48	26R 53.3	22D 39.3	24 53.3	27 40.3	9 17.7	14 37.9	4 09.0	25 00.9	22 37.7	28 04.2
5 Sa	22 52 02	14 40 54	17 56 27	24 43 47	26 53.0	22 37.8	26 08.1	28 27.5	9 38.2	14 37.1	4 16.3	25 03.5	22 39.3	28 04.1
6 Su	22 55 58	15 40 59	1♑26 59	8♑06 18	26 50.9	22 42.5	27 22.9	29 14.7	9 58.9	14 36.1	4 23.5	25 06.1	22 40.9	28 03.9
7 M	22 59 55	16 41 03	14 41 56	21 14 07	26 46.4	22 53.3	28 37.6	0♓01.9	10 19.7	14 34.9	4 30.7	25 08.7	22 42.4	28 03.8
8 Tu	23 03 51	17 41 05	27 43 03	4♒08 55	26 39.0	23 09.9	29 52.3	0 49.1	10 40.6	14 33.5	4 37.9	25 11.2	22 43.9	28 03.5
9 W	23 07 48	18 41 05	10♒31 50	16 51 56	26 29.1	23 31.7	1♈07.0	1 36.3	11 01.5	14 31.9	4 45.0	25 13.6	22 45.4	28 03.3
10 Th	23 11 45	19 41 03	23 09 19	29 24 04	26 17.3	23 58.6	2 21.7	2 23.5	11 22.6	14 30.1	4 52.2	25 16.1	22 46.8	28 03.0
11 F	23 15 41	20 41 00	5♓36 15	11♓45 56	26 04.7	24 30.2	3 36.4	3 10.7	11 43.9	14 28.1	4 59.3	25 18.5	22 48.3	28 02.6
12 Sa	23 19 38	21 40 55	17 53 10	23 58 03	25 52.4	25 06.2	4 51.0	3 57.9	12 05.2	14 26.0	5 06.4	25 20.8	22 49.7	28 02.3
13 Su	23 23 34	22 40 47	0♈00 41	6♈01 14	25 41.6	25 46.4	6 05.6	4 45.1	12 26.6	14 23.7	5 13.5	25 23.1	22 51.0	28 01.9
14 M	23 27 31	23 40 38	11 59 51	17 56 45	25 32.9	26 30.3	7 20.2	5 32.3	12 48.1	14 21.2	5 20.6	25 25.4	22 52.4	28 01.4
15 Tu	23 31 27	24 40 27	23 52 13	29 46 34	25 26.9	27 17.9	8 34.7	6 19.4	13 09.7	14 18.5	5 27.6	25 27.6	22 53.7	28 00.9
16 W	23 35 24	25 40 14	5♉40 09	11♉33 24	25 23.5	28 08.8	9 49.2	7 06.6	13 31.4	14 15.6	5 34.7	25 29.8	22 55.0	28 00.4
17 Th	23 39 20	26 39 58	17 26 47	23 20 49	25D 22.3	29 02.8	11 03.7	7 53.8	13 53.2	14 12.5	5 41.6	25 32.0	22 56.2	27 59.9
18 F	23 43 17	27 39 40	29 16 04	5♊13 06	25 22.7	29 59.9	12 18.2	8 40.9	14 15.1	14 09.3	5 48.6	25 34.1	22 57.5	27 59.3
19 Sa	23 47 13	28 39 20	11♊12 35	17 15 08	25 23.6	0♓59.7	13 32.6	9 28.0	14 37.0	14 05.9	5 55.6	25 36.1	22 58.7	27 58.8
20 Su	23 51 10	29 38 58	23 21 26	29 32 09	25R 24.2	2 02.1	14 47.0	10 15.2	14 59.1	14 02.4	6 02.5	25 38.2	22 59.8	27 58.1
21 M	23 55 07	0♈38 34	5♋47 54	12♋09 20	25 23.4	3 07.0	16 01.4	11 02.3	15 21.2	13 58.6	6 09.4	25 40.1	23 01.0	27 57.5
22 Tu	23 59 03	1 38 07	18 36 59	25 11 20	25 20.7	4 14.3	17 15.7	11 49.4	15 43.5	13 54.7	6 16.2	25 42.1	23 02.1	27 56.8
23 W	0 03 00	2 37 38	1♌52 46	8♌41 32	25 16.0	5 23.8	18 30.0	12 36.5	16 05.8	13 50.6	6 23.0	25 44.0	23 03.2	27 56.1
24 Th	0 06 56	3 37 07	15 37 42	22 41 12	25 09.4	6 35.4	19 44.3	13 23.6	16 28.1	13 46.4	6 29.8	25 45.8	23 04.2	27 55.3
25 F	0 10 53	4 36 33	29 51 43	7♍08 45	25 01.7	7 49.1	20 58.6	14 10.6	16 50.6	13 42.0	6 36.6	25 47.6	23 05.3	27 54.5
26 Sa	0 14 49	5 35 57	14♍31 36	21 59 21	24 53.8	9 04.7	22 12.8	14 57.7	17 13.1	13 37.5	6 43.3	25 49.4	23 06.2	27 53.7
27 Su	0 18 46	6 35 19	29 30 56	7♎05 08	24 46.7	10 22.2	23 26.9	15 44.7	17 35.8	13 32.8	6 49.9	25 51.1	23 07.2	27 52.9
28 M	0 22 42	7 34 39	14♎40 41	22 16 18	24 41.3	11 41.6	24 41.1	16 31.7	17 58.4	13 27.9	6 56.6	25 52.8	23 08.1	27 52.0
29 Tu	0 26 39	8 33 57	29 50 42	7♏22 44	24 38.0	13 02.7	25 55.2	17 18.7	18 21.2	13 22.9	7 03.2	25 54.4	23 09.0	27 51.1
30 W	0 30 36	9 33 14	14♏51 22	22 15 44	24D 36.8	14 25.5	27 09.3	18 05.7	18 44.0	13 17.7	7 09.8	25 56.0	23 09.9	27 50.2
31 Th	0 34 32	10 32 28	29 35 08	6♐49 03	24 37.2	15 50.0	28 23.3	18 52.7	19 06.9	13 12.4	7 16.3	25 57.5	23 10.7	27 49.2

April 1994 LONGITUDE

Day	Sid.Time	☉	0 hr ☽	Noon ☽	True ☊	☿	♀	♂	⚳	♃	♄	♅	♆	♇
1 F	0 38 29	11♈31 41	13♐57 10	20♐59 19	24♏38.5	17♓16.1	29♈37.4	19♓39.7	19♉29.9	13♏07.0	7♓22.8	25♑59.0	23♑11.5	27♏48.2
2 Sa	0 42 25	12 30 52	27 55 28	4♑45 43	24R 39.6	18 43.9	0♉51.4	20 26.6	19 53.0	13R 01.4	7 29.2	26 00.4	23 12.3	27R 47.2
3 Su	0 46 22	13 30 01	11♑30 15	18 09 20	24 39.8	20 13.2	2 05.3	21 13.5	20 16.1	12 55.7	7 35.6	26 01.8	23 13.0	27 46.2
4 M	0 50 18	14 29 09	24 43 16	1♒12 25	24 38.4	21 44.1	3 19.3	22 00.4	20 39.2	12 49.9	7 42.0	26 03.1	23 13.8	27 45.1
5 Tu	0 54 15	15 28 14	7♒37 07	13 57 45	24 35.2	23 16.5	4 33.2	22 47.3	21 02.5	12 43.9	7 48.3	26 04.4	23 14.4	27 44.0
6 W	0 58 11	16 27 18	20 14 40	26 28 13	24 30.3	24 50.4	5 47.1	23 34.2	21 25.8	12 37.8	7 54.6	26 05.7	23 15.1	27 42.9
7 Th	1 02 08	17 26 20	2♓38 42	8♓46 26	24 24.2	26 25.9	7 00.9	24 21.0	21 49.2	12 31.6	8 00.8	26 06.9	23 15.7	27 41.8
8 F	1 06 05	18 25 20	14 51 41	20 54 44	24 17.5	28 02.9	8 14.7	25 07.9	22 12.6	12 25.2	8 06.9	26 08.0	23 16.3	27 40.6
9 Sa	1 10 01	19 24 19	26 55 49	2♈55 10	24 11.0	29 41.4	9 28.5	25 54.7	22 36.1	12 18.8	8 13.0	26 09.1	23 16.8	27 39.4
10 Su	1 13 58	20 23 15	8♈53 00	14 49 31	24 05.2	1♈21.4	10 42.2	26 41.4	22 59.6	12 12.2	8 19.1	26 10.2	23 17.3	27 38.2
11 M	1 17 54	21 22 09	20 44 59	26 39 35	24 00.8	3 02.9	11 55.9	27 28.2	23 23.2	12 05.6	8 25.1	26 11.2	23 17.8	27 37.0
12 Tu	1 21 51	22 21 02	2♉33 35	8♉27 16	23 58.0	4 46.0	13 09.6	28 14.9	23 46.9	11 58.8	8 31.1	26 12.1	23 18.2	27 35.7
13 W	1 25 47	23 19 52	14 20 53	20 14 46	23D 56.8	6 30.5	14 23.3	29 01.6	24 10.6	11 52.0	8 37.0	26 13.0	23 18.6	27 34.4
14 Th	1 29 44	24 18 40	26 09 15	2♊04 44	23 57.0	8 16.7	15 36.9	29 48.3	24 34.4	11 45.0	8 42.8	26 13.9	23 19.0	27 33.1
15 F	1 33 40	25 17 26	8♊01 38	14 00 22	23 58.3	10 04.4	16 50.4	0♈34.9	24 58.2	11 38.0	8 48.6	26 14.7	23 19.4	27 31.8
16 Sa	1 37 37	26 16 10	20 01 25	26 05 18	24 00.0	11 53.6	18 04.0	1 21.5	25 22.1	11 30.9	8 54.4	26 15.4	23 19.7	27 30.5
17 Su	1 41 34	27 14 52	2♋12 32	8♋23 39	24 01.6	13 44.4	19 17.5	2 08.1	25 46.0	11 23.8	9 00.1	26 16.1	23 20.0	27 29.1
18 M	1 45 30	28 13 32	14 39 12	20 59 43	24R 02.7	15 36.8	20 30.9	2 54.7	26 09.9	11 16.5	9 05.7	26 16.8	23 20.2	27 27.7
19 Tu	1 49 27	29 12 09	27 25 42	3♌57 37	24 02.8	17 30.7	21 44.3	3 41.2	26 34.0	11 09.2	9 11.2	26 17.4	23 20.4	27 26.3
20 W	1 53 23	0♉10 44	10♌35 54	17 20 51	24 01.8	19 26.2	22 57.7	4 27.6	26 58.0	11 01.9	9 16.7	26 17.9	23 20.6	27 24.9
21 Th	1 57 20	1 09 17	24 12 41	1♍11 29	23 59.8	21 23.3	24 11.0	5 14.1	27 22.1	10 54.5	9 22.2	26 18.4	23 20.7	27 23.5
22 F	2 01 16	2 07 48	8♍17 12	15 29 34	23 57.2	23 21.9	25 24.3	6 00.5	27 46.3	10 47.0	9 27.6	26 18.9	23 20.9	27 22.0
23 Sa	2 05 13	3 06 16	22 48 09	0♎12 20	23 54.4	25 22.1	26 37.6	6 46.9	28 10.4	10 39.5	9 32.9	26 19.3	23 20.9	27 20.6
24 Su	2 09 09	4 04 43	7♎41 19	15 14 07	23 51.8	27 23.7	27 50.8	7 33.2	28 34.7	10 32.0	9 38.1	26 19.6	23R 21.0	27 19.1
25 M	2 13 06	5 03 07	22 49 37	0♏26 38	23 50.0	29 26.7	29 03.9	8 19.5	28 58.9	10 24.4	9 43.3	26 19.9	23 21.0	27 17.6
26 Tu	2 17 02	6 01 30	8♏03 53	15 40 08	23D 49.0	1♉31.1	0♊17.1	9 05.8	29 23.3	10 16.8	9 48.4	26 20.1	23 21.0	27 16.1
27 W	2 20 59	6 59 51	23 14 10	0♐44 52	23 49.0	3 36.7	1 30.2	9 52.0	29 47.6	10 09.2	9 53.5	26 20.3	23 20.9	27 14.6
28 Th	2 24 56	7 58 10	8♐11 15	15 32 30	23 49.7	5 43.4	2 43.2	10 38.2	0♊12.0	10 01.5	9 58.4	26 20.5	23 20.8	27 13.0
29 F	2 28 52	8 56 28	22 47 59	29 57 13	23 50.7	7 51.1	3 56.2	11 24.4	0 36.4	9 53.9	10 03.4	26 20.6	23 20.7	27 11.5
30 Sa	2 32 49	9 54 44	6♑59 55	13♑55 57	23 51.9	9 59.6	5 09.2	12 10.6	1 00.9	9 46.2	10 08.2	26R 20.6	23 20.6	27 09.9

Astro Data

	Dy Hr Mn
♇ R	1 10:01
☿ D	5 5:48
♀0N	10 21:16
☽0N	12 2:37
☉0N	20 20:29
☽0S	26 7:24
☽0N	8 8:18
♄∠♆	10 4:12
☿0N	12 20:26
♂0N	17 20:26
☽0S	22 17:38
♆ R	25 10:37
♃△♄	28 17:56
♅ R	30 22:18

Planet Ingress

		Dy Hr Mn
♂	♓	7 11:01
♀	♈	8 14:28
☿	♓	18 12:04
☉	♈	20 20:28
♀	♉	1 19:20
☿	♈	9 16:30
♂	♈	14 18:02
☉	♉	20 7:36
☿	♉	25 18:27
♀	♊	26 6:24
⚳	♊	28 0:12

Last Aspect / ☽ Ingress (March)

Last Aspect Dy Hr Mn			☽ Ingress	Dy Hr Mn
1 6:46	♂	△	♏	1 14:43
3 13:36	♇	☌	♐	3 16:54
5 19:03	♂	⚹	♑	5 21:24
8 3:09	♀	⚹	♒	8 4:15
10 9:24	♇	□	♓	10 13:09
12 20:04	♇	△	♈	12 23:59
15 6:35	☿	⚹	♉	15 12:27
18 0:33	☿	□	♊	18 1:29
20 12:14	☉	□	♋	20 12:54
22 16:58	♇	△	♌	22 20:39
24 20:46	♇	□	♍	25 0:14
26 21:25	♇	⚹	♎	27 0:46
28 17:43	♅	□	♏	29 0:15
30 21:07	♇	☌	♐	31 0:41

Last Aspect / ☽ Ingress (April)

Last Aspect Dy Hr Mn			☽ Ingress	Dy Hr Mn
1 9:35	♂	□	♑	2 3:37
4 5:36	♇	⚹	♒	4 9:45
6 14:24	♇	□	♓	6 18:51
9 4:29	☿	☌	♈	9 6:09
11 11:02	♅	□	♉	11 18:48
14 7:05	♂	⚹	♊	14 7:48
16 12:23	☉	⚹	♋	16 19:41
19 2:34	☉	□	♌	19 4:45
21 5:30	♇	□	♍	21 9:58
23 7:23	♇	⚹	♎	23 11:40
25 10:11	☿	☍	♏	25 11:18
27 6:24	♇	☌	♐	27 10:48
28 3:32	♂	△	♑	29 12:05

☽ Phases & Eclipses

Dy Hr Mn		
4 16:53	☾	13♐53
12 7:05	●	21♓29
20 12:14	☽	29♊40
27 11:10	○	6♎33
3 2:55	☾	13♑08
11 0:17	●	20♈53
19 2:34	☽	28♋49
25 19:45	○	5♏22

Astro Data

1 March 1994
Julian Day # 34393
SVP 5♓20'13"
GC 26♐45.5 ⚴ 22♓40.7
Eris 17♈27.4 ⚵ 2♏30.8R
⚷ 5♍46.9R ⚶ 11♈44.9
☽ Mean ☊ 27♏56.7

1 April 1994
Julian Day # 34424
SVP 5♓20'10"
GC 26♐45.5 ⚴ 3♈44.2
Eris 17♈46.4 ⚵ 27♎55.6R
⚷ 3♍40.0R ⚶ 25♈39.4
☽ Mean ☊ 26♏18.2

LONGITUDE — May 1994

Day	Sid.Time	☉	0 hr ☽	Noon ☽	True ☊	☿	♀	♂	⚳	♃	♄	♅	♆	♇
1 Su	2 36 45	10♉52 59	20♑45 19	27♑28 10	23♏52.7	12♉08.7	6♊22.1	12♈56.7	1♊25.4	9♏38.6	10♓13.0	26♑20.6	23♑20.4	27♏08.4
2 M	2 40 42	11 51 12	4♒04 45	10♒35 24	23R 53.0	14 18.3	7 35.0	13 42.7	1 49.9	9R 30.9	10 17.7	26R 20.6	23R 20.2	27R 06.8
3 Tu	2 44 38	12 49 24	17 00 29	23 20 28	23 52.8	16 27.9	8 47.8	14 28.8	2 14.5	9 23.3	10 22.3	26 20.5	23 20.0	27 05.2
4 W	2 48 35	13 47 34	29 35 47	5♓46 57	23 52.1	18 37.4	10 00.6	15 14.7	2 39.1	9 15.7	10 26.9	26 20.3	23 19.7	27 03.6
5 Th	2 52 31	14 45 42	11♓54 25	17 58 41	23 51.1	20 46.6	11 13.4	16 00.7	3 03.8	9 08.1	10 31.3	26 20.1	23 19.4	27 02.0
6 F	2 56 28	15 43 50	24 00 12	29 59 26	23 50.0	22 55.0	12 26.1	16 46.6	3 28.4	9 00.5	10 35.7	26 19.8	23 19.0	27 00.4
7 Sa	3 00 25	16 41 55	5♈56 48	11♈52 42	23 48.9	25 02.4	13 38.8	17 32.5	3 53.1	8 52.9	10 40.1	26 19.5	23 18.7	26 58.7
8 Su	3 04 21	17 40 00	17 47 32	23 41 39	23 48.1	27 08.5	14 51.5	18 18.3	4 17.9	8 45.4	10 44.3	26 19.2	23 18.2	26 57.1
9 M	3 08 18	18 38 02	29 35 22	5♉29 01	23 47.5	29 13.1	16 04.1	19 04.1	4 42.6	8 37.9	10 48.5	26 18.8	23 17.8	26 55.5
10 Tu	3 12 14	19 36 04	11♉22 53	17 17 17	23D 47.2	1♊15.8	17 16.6	19 49.8	5 07.4	8 30.5	10 52.6	26 18.3	23 17.3	26 53.8
11 W	3 16 11	20 34 03	23 12 28	29 08 44	23 47.2	3 16.4	18 29.2	20 35.5	5 32.3	8 23.1	10 56.6	26 17.8	23 16.9	26 52.2
12 Th	3 20 07	21 32 01	5♊06 19	11♊05 31	23 47.4	5 14.7	19 41.6	21 21.2	5 57.1	8 15.8	11 00.5	26 17.3	23 16.3	26 50.5
13 F	3 24 04	22 29 58	17 06 37	23 09 54	23 47.5	7 10.5	20 54.1	22 06.8	6 22.0	8 08.5	11 04.4	26 16.7	23 15.8	26 48.8
14 Sa	3 28 00	23 27 53	29 15 39	5♋24 12	23R 47.6	9 03.6	22 06.4	22 52.3	6 46.9	8 01.3	11 08.1	26 16.0	23 15.2	26 47.2
15 Su	3 31 57	24 25 46	11♋35 53	17 51 00	23 47.6	10 53.9	23 18.8	23 37.8	7 11.9	7 54.2	11 11.8	26 15.4	23 14.6	26 45.5
16 M	3 35 54	25 23 38	24 09 56	0♌33 00	23 47.5	12 41.2	24 31.1	24 23.3	7 36.8	7 47.2	11 15.4	26 14.6	23 13.9	26 43.9
17 Tu	3 39 50	26 21 27	7♌00 33	13 32 54	23 47.4	14 25.5	25 43.3	25 08.7	8 01.8	7 40.2	11 18.9	26 13.8	23 13.3	26 42.2
18 W	3 43 47	27 19 15	20 10 21	26 53 09	23D 47.3	16 06.6	26 55.5	25 54.0	8 26.8	7 33.3	11 22.4	26 13.0	23 12.5	26 40.5
19 Th	3 47 43	28 17 02	3♍41 30	10♍35 32	23 47.4	17 44.5	28 07.6	26 39.4	8 51.8	7 26.5	11 25.7	26 12.1	23 11.8	26 38.9
20 F	3 51 40	29 14 46	17 35 17	24 40 41	23 47.7	19 19.1	29 19.7	27 24.6	9 16.8	7 19.9	11 28.9	26 11.2	23 11.1	26 37.2
21 Sa	3 55 36	0♊12 29	1♎51 32	9♎07 30	23 48.2	20 50.4	0♋31.7	28 09.8	9 41.9	7 13.3	11 32.1	26 10.2	23 10.3	26 35.5
22 Su	3 59 33	1 10 10	16 28 06	23 52 44	23 48.8	22 18.3	1 43.7	28 55.0	10 07.0	7 06.8	11 35.2	26 09.2	23 09.4	26 33.9
23 M	4 03 29	2 07 50	1♏20 38	8♏50 56	23R 49.3	23 42.8	2 55.6	29 40.1	10 32.1	7 00.4	11 38.2	26 08.2	23 08.6	26 32.2
24 Tu	4 07 26	3 05 29	16 22 37	23 54 38	23 49.5	25 03.8	4 07.4	0♉25.1	10 57.2	6 54.1	11 41.1	26 07.1	23 07.7	26 30.6
25 W	4 11 23	4 03 06	1♐25 54	8♐55 20	23 49.2	26 21.3	5 19.2	1 10.1	11 22.3	6 48.0	11 43.9	26 05.9	23 06.8	26 28.9
26 Th	4 15 19	5 00 42	16 21 51	23 44 32	23 48.4	27 35.3	6 31.0	1 55.1	11 47.5	6 42.0	11 46.6	26 04.7	23 05.9	26 27.3
27 F	4 19 16	5 58 17	1♑02 29	8♑15 00	23 47.2	28 45.6	7 42.7	2 40.0	12 12.6	6 36.0	11 49.3	26 03.5	23 05.0	26 25.6
28 Sa	4 23 12	6 55 51	15 21 31	22 21 39	23 45.6	29 52.3	8 54.3	3 24.9	12 37.8	6 30.3	11 51.8	26 02.3	23 04.0	26 24.0
29 Su	4 27 09	7 53 24	29 15 08	6♒01 55	23 44.0	0♋55.2	10 05.9	4 09.7	13 03.0	6 24.6	11 54.3	26 00.9	23 03.0	26 22.4
30 M	4 31 05	8 50 56	12♒42 02	19 15 42	23 42.7	1 54.4	11 17.4	4 54.4	13 28.2	6 19.1	11 56.6	25 59.6	23 02.0	26 20.8
31 Tu	4 35 02	9 48 28	25 43 11	2♓04 54	23D 41.8	2 49.6	12 28.9	5 39.1	13 53.4	6 13.7	11 58.9	25 58.2	23 00.9	26 19.1

LONGITUDE — June 1994

Day	Sid.Time	☉	0 hr ☽	Noon ☽	True ☊	☿	♀	♂	⚳	♃	♄	♅	♆	♇
1 W	4 38 59	10♊45 58	8♓21 17	14♓32 52	23♏41.7	3♋41.0	13♋40.3	6♉23.8	14♊18.7	6♏08.4	12♓01.1	25♑56.8	22♑59.9	26♏17.5
2 Th	4 42 55	11 43 28	20 40 12	26 43 50	23 42.3	4 28.3	14 51.6	7 08.4	14 43.9	6R 03.3	12 03.1	25R 55.3	22R 58.8	26R 15.9
3 F	4 46 52	12 40 57	2♈44 22	8♈42 23	23 43.5	5 11.6	16 02.9	7 52.9	15 09.2	5 58.3	12 05.1	25 53.8	22 57.6	26 14.4
4 Sa	4 50 48	13 38 25	14 38 27	20 33 07	23 45.0	5 50.7	17 14.1	8 37.4	15 34.5	5 53.5	12 07.0	25 52.3	22 56.5	26 12.8
5 Su	4 54 45	14 35 52	26 26 57	2♉20 25	23 46.6	6 25.5	18 25.3	9 21.8	15 59.8	5 48.8	12 08.8	25 50.7	22 55.3	26 11.2
6 M	4 58 41	15 33 19	8♉14 01	14 08 12	23R 47.7	6 56.0	19 36.4	10 06.2	16 25.1	5 44.3	12 10.5	25 49.0	22 54.2	26 09.7
7 Tu	5 02 38	16 30 45	20 03 22	25 59 52	23 48.0	7 22.0	20 47.5	10 50.5	16 50.4	5 39.9	12 12.1	25 47.4	22 53.0	26 08.1
8 W	5 06 34	17 28 10	1♊58 04	7♊58 14	23 47.2	7 43.6	21 58.5	11 34.8	17 15.7	5 35.7	12 13.6	25 45.7	22 51.7	26 06.6
9 Th	5 10 31	18 25 35	14 00 40	20 05 33	23 45.2	8 00.7	23 09.4	12 19.0	17 41.1	5 31.7	12 15.0	25 44.0	22 50.5	26 05.1
10 F	5 14 28	19 22 58	26 13 07	2♋23 31	23 42.2	8 13.2	24 20.3	13 03.2	18 06.4	5 27.8	12 16.3	25 42.2	22 49.2	26 03.6
11 Sa	5 18 24	20 20 21	8♋36 55	14 53 26	23 38.2	8 21.2	25 31.1	13 47.2	18 31.7	5 24.1	12 17.5	25 40.4	22 47.9	26 02.1
12 Su	5 22 21	21 17 43	21 13 10	27 36 13	23 33.9	8R 24.5	26 41.8	14 31.3	18 57.1	5 20.5	12 18.6	25 38.6	22 46.6	26 00.7
13 M	5 26 17	22 15 04	4♌02 42	10♌32 42	23 29.6	8 23.4	27 52.5	15 15.2	19 22.5	5 17.1	12 19.6	25 36.8	22 45.3	25 59.2
14 Tu	5 30 14	23 12 24	17 06 17	23 43 32	23 26.1	8 17.8	29 03.0	15 59.1	19 47.8	5 13.9	12 20.5	25 34.9	22 44.0	25 57.8
15 W	5 34 10	24 09 43	0♍24 33	7♍09 23	23 23.6	8 07.8	0♌13.6	16 43.0	20 13.2	5 10.9	12 21.3	25 32.9	22 42.6	25 56.3
16 Th	5 38 07	25 07 02	13 58 06	20 50 44	23D 22.5	7 53.8	1 24.0	17 26.7	20 38.5	5 08.0	12 22.0	25 31.0	22 41.2	25 54.9
17 F	5 42 03	26 04 19	27 47 18	4♎47 45	23 22.7	7 35.7	2 34.3	18 10.4	21 03.9	5 05.3	12 22.6	25 29.0	22 39.8	25 53.6
18 Sa	5 46 00	27 01 35	11♎52 00	18 59 53	23 23.8	7 14.1	3 44.6	18 54.1	21 29.3	5 02.8	12 23.1	25 27.0	22 38.4	25 52.2
19 Su	5 49 57	27 58 51	26 11 12	3♏25 37	23 25.2	6 49.1	4 54.8	19 37.7	21 54.6	5 00.4	12 23.5	25 25.0	22 37.0	25 50.9
20 M	5 53 53	28 56 06	10♏42 42	18 01 58	23R 26.1	6 21.1	6 04.9	20 21.2	22 20.0	4 58.3	12 23.8	25 22.9	22 35.5	25 49.5
21 Tu	5 57 50	29 53 20	25 22 46	2♐44 24	23 25.9	5 50.7	7 14.9	21 04.7	22 45.4	4 56.3	12 24.1	25 20.9	22 34.1	25 48.2
22 W	6 01 46	0♋50 34	10♐06 06	17 27 00	23 24.1	5 18.2	8 24.8	21 48.1	23 10.8	4 54.4	12R 24.2	25 18.8	22 32.6	25 46.9
23 Th	6 05 43	1 47 48	24 46 16	2♑03 00	23 20.5	4 44.3	9 34.7	22 31.4	23 36.1	4 52.8	12 24.2	25 16.6	22 31.1	25 45.7
24 F	6 09 39	2 45 01	9♑16 23	16 25 38	23 15.4	4 09.5	10 44.4	23 14.7	24 01.5	4 51.3	12 24.1	25 14.5	22 29.7	25 44.4
25 Sa	6 13 36	3 42 13	23 30 06	0♒29 13	23 09.2	3 34.3	11 54.1	23 57.9	24 26.9	4 50.1	12 23.9	25 12.3	22 28.2	25 43.2
26 Su	6 17 32	4 39 26	7♒22 32	14 09 49	23 02.9	2 59.5	13 03.7	24 41.0	24 52.2	4 49.0	12 23.6	25 10.1	22 26.6	25 42.0
27 M	6 21 29	5 36 38	20 50 53	27 25 46	22 57.0	2 25.6	14 13.2	25 24.1	25 17.6	4 48.0	12 23.3	25 07.9	22 25.1	25 40.8
28 Tu	6 25 26	6 33 50	3♓54 35	10♓17 35	22 52.4	1 53.1	15 22.5	26 07.2	25 43.0	4 47.3	12 22.8	25 05.7	22 23.6	25 39.7
29 W	6 29 22	7 31 02	16 35 09	22 47 42	22 49.5	1 22.7	16 31.8	26 50.1	26 08.3	4 46.7	12 22.2	25 03.5	22 22.0	25 38.6
30 Th	6 33 19	8 28 15	28 55 46	4♈59 54	22D 48.2	0 54.8	17 41.0	27 33.0	26 33.7	4 46.3	12 21.5	25 01.2	22 20.5	25 37.5

Astro Data

	Dy Hr Mn
☽0N	5 13:44
♄∠♅	16 7:36
☽0S	20 2:06
☽0N	1 20:29
☿R	12 17:49
☽0S	16 8:52
♄R	23 3:57
☽0N	29 5:05

Planet Ingress

	Dy Hr Mn
☿ ♊	9 21:08
♀ ♋	21 1:26
☉ ♊	21 6:48
♂ ♉	23 22:37
☿ ♋	28 14:52
♀ ♌	15 7:23
☉ ♋	21 14:48

Last Aspect / ☽ Ingress

Last Aspect Dy Hr Mn		☽ Ingress	Dy Hr Mn
1 11:24	♇ ⚹	♒	1 16:34
3 19:09	♇ □	♓	4 0:47
6 6:01	♇ △	♈	6 12:01
8 17:20	♅ □	♉	9 0:50
11 7:25	♇ ☍	♊	11 13:43
13 9:47	♂ ⚹	♋	14 1:27
16 4:51	♇ △	♌	16 10:58
18 12:50	☉ □	♍	18 17:31
20 20:30	♀ □	♎	20 20:54
22 20:32	♂ ☍	♏	22 21:51
24 16:08	♇ ☌	♐	24 21:43
26 18:52	☿ ☍	♑	26 22:17
28 19:00	♇ ⚹	♒	29 1:19
31 1:09	♇ □	♓	31 8:03

Last Aspect / ☽ Ingress

Last Aspect Dy Hr Mn		☽ Ingress	Dy Hr Mn
2 11:05	♇ △	♈	2 18:31
4 22:48	♅ □	♉	5 7:14
7 12:17	♇ ☍	♊	7 20:03
9 8:26	☉ ☌	♋	10 7:22
12 10:08	♀ ☌	♌	12 16:29
14 16:01	♇ □	♍	14 23:16
16 20:46	♇ ⚹	♎	17 3:48
19 2:21	☉ △	♏	19 6:20
21 0:43	♇ ☌	♐	21 7:32
22 3:45	♄ □	♑	23 8:37
25 3:48	♇ ⚹	♒	25 11:10
27 8:48	♇ □	♓	27 16:44
29 20:23	♂ ⚹	♈	30 2:06

☽ Phases & Eclipses

Dy Hr Mn	
2 14:32	☾ 11♒57
10 17:07	● 19♉48
10 17:11:25	A 06'14"
18 12:50	☽ 27♌21
25 3:39	○ 3♐43
25 3:30	P 0.243
1 4:02	☾ 10♓27
9 8:26	● 18♊17
16 19:56	☽ 25♍26
23 11:33	○ 1♑47
30 19:31	☾ 8♈46

Astro Data

1 May 1994
Julian Day # 34454
SVP 5♓20'07"
GC 26♐45.6 ⚴ 14♈39.9
Eris 18♈05.9 ⚵ 21♎12.5R
⚷ 2♍51.0R ⚶ 9♉09.5
☽ Mean ☊ 24♏42.9

1 June 1994
Julian Day # 34485
SVP 5♓20'02"
GC 26♐45.7 ⚴ 25♈50.0
Eris 18♈22.4 ⚵ 17♎13.7R
⚷ 3♍42.9 ⚶ 22♉51.6
☽ Mean ☊ 23♏04.4

July 1994 — LONGITUDE

Day	Sid.Time	☉	0 hr ☽	Noon ☽	True ☊	☿	♀	♂	⚳	♃	♄	♅	♆	♇
1 F	6 37 15	9♋25 27	11♈00 42	16♈58 50	22♏48.4	0♋30.0	18♌50.1	28♉15.9	26♊59.0	4♏46.1	12♓20.7	24♑58.9	22♑18.9	25♏36.4
2 Sa	6 41 12	10 22 40	22 54 56	28 49 39	22 49.5	0R 08.7	19 59.1	28 58.6	27 24.4	4D 46.1	12R 19.9	24R 56.6	22R 17.3	25R 35.3
3 Su	6 45 08	11 19 53	4♉43 37	10♉37 29	22 50.8	29♊51.3	21 08.0	29 41.3	27 49.7	4 46.2	12 18.9	24 54.3	22 15.7	25 34.3
4 M	6 49 05	12 17 06	16 31 50	22 27 16	22R51.4	29 38.1	22 16.8	0♊24.0	28 15.0	4 46.6	12 17.8	24 52.0	22 14.2	25 33.3
5 Tu	6 53 01	13 14 19	28 24 17	4♊23 25	22 50.7	29 29.4	23 25.6	1 06.5	28 40.4	4 47.1	12 16.7	24 49.6	22 12.6	25 32.3
6 W	6 56 58	14 11 32	10♊25 04	16 29 38	22 48.0	29D 25.3	24 34.1	1 49.0	29 05.7	4 47.8	12 15.4	24 47.3	22 11.0	25 31.3
7 Th	7 00 55	15 08 46	22 37 26	28 48 43	22 43.1	29 26.2	25 42.6	2 31.5	29 31.0	4 48.7	12 14.0	24 44.9	22 09.4	25 30.4
8 F	7 04 51	16 06 00	5♋03 41	11♋22 28	22 36.0	29 32.2	26 51.0	3 13.8	29 56.3	4 49.7	12 12.6	24 42.6	22 07.8	25 29.5
9 Sa	7 08 48	17 03 14	17 45 05	24 11 33	22 27.4	29 43.2	27 59.3	3 56.1	0♋21.6	4 51.0	12 11.1	24 40.2	22 06.1	25 28.7
10 Su	7 12 44	18 00 28	0♌41 47	7♌15 41	22 18.0	29 59.5	29 07.4	4 38.4	0 46.9	4 52.4	12 09.4	24 37.8	22 04.5	25 27.8
11 M	7 16 41	18 57 42	13 53 05	20 33 47	22 08.7	0♋20.9	0♍15.4	5 20.5	1 12.2	4 54.0	12 07.7	24 35.4	22 02.9	25 27.0
12 Tu	7 20 37	19 54 56	27 17 35	4♍04 16	22 00.5	0 47.6	1 23.3	6 02.6	1 37.4	4 55.7	12 05.9	24 33.0	22 01.3	25 26.2
13 W	7 24 34	20 52 10	10♍53 37	17 45 26	21 54.3	1 19.6	2 31.1	6 44.6	2 02.6	4 57.7	12 03.9	24 30.6	21 59.7	25 25.5
14 Th	7 28 30	21 49 24	24 39 34	1♎35 49	21 50.4	1 56.8	3 38.8	7 26.5	2 27.9	4 59.8	12 01.9	24 28.2	21 58.0	25 24.7
15 F	7 32 27	22 46 38	8♎34 04	15 34 11	21D 48.7	2 39.1	4 46.3	8 08.4	2 53.1	5 02.1	11 59.8	24 25.8	21 56.4	25 24.0
16 Sa	7 36 24	23 43 52	22 36 04	29 39 35	21 48.6	3 26.6	5 53.6	8 50.2	3 18.3	5 04.6	11 57.6	24 23.4	21 54.8	25 23.4
17 Su	7 40 20	24 41 06	6♏44 38	13♏51 04	21R 49.1	4 19.1	7 00.9	9 31.9	3 43.4	5 07.2	11 55.4	24 21.0	21 53.2	25 22.7
18 M	7 44 17	25 38 21	20 58 41	28 07 14	21 49.1	5 16.7	8 07.9	10 13.5	4 08.6	5 10.0	11 53.0	24 18.6	21 51.5	25 22.1
19 Tu	7 48 13	26 35 35	5♐16 26	12♐25 54	21 47.6	6 19.3	9 14.9	10 55.1	4 33.7	5 13.0	11 50.6	24 16.2	21 49.9	25 21.6
20 W	7 52 10	27 32 50	19 35 11	26 43 48	21 43.6	7 26.7	10 21.6	11 36.6	4 58.9	5 16.2	11 48.0	24 13.8	21 48.3	25 21.0
21 Th	7 56 06	28 30 05	3♑51 11	10♑56 43	21 37.1	8 38.9	11 28.2	12 18.0	5 24.0	5 19.5	11 45.4	24 11.4	21 46.7	25 20.5
22 F	8 00 03	29 27 21	17 59 49	24 59 52	21 28.2	9 55.9	12 34.7	12 59.4	5 49.0	5 23.0	11 42.8	24 09.0	21 45.1	25 20.0
23 Sa	8 03 59	0♌24 37	1♒56 16	8♒48 32	21 17.8	11 17.5	13 41.0	13 40.7	6 14.1	5 26.6	11 40.0	24 06.6	21 43.5	25 19.6
24 Su	8 07 56	1 21 54	15 36 11	22 18 54	21 06.7	12 43.6	14 47.1	14 21.9	6 39.1	5 30.4	11 37.1	24 04.2	21 41.9	25 19.2
25 M	8 11 53	2 19 11	28 56 26	5♓28 39	20 56.2	14 14.0	15 53.1	15 03.0	7 04.2	5 34.4	11 34.2	24 01.8	21 40.3	25 18.8
26 Tu	8 15 49	3 16 29	11♓55 33	18 17 15	20 47.3	15 48.6	16 58.8	15 44.0	7 29.2	5 38.5	11 31.2	23 59.4	21 38.7	25 18.4
27 W	8 19 46	4 13 48	24 33 58	0♈46 01	20 40.6	17 27.3	18 04.4	16 25.0	7 54.1	5 42.8	11 28.1	23 57.1	21 37.1	25 18.1
28 Th	8 23 42	5 11 08	6♈53 48	12 57 49	20 36.4	19 09.7	19 09.8	17 05.9	8 19.1	5 47.3	11 25.0	23 54.7	21 35.6	25 17.8
29 F	8 27 39	6 08 29	18 58 36	24 56 46	20 34.3	20 55.8	20 15.1	17 46.8	8 44.0	5 51.9	11 21.7	23 52.4	21 34.0	25 17.5
30 Sa	8 31 35	7 05 51	0♉52 55	6♉47 45	20D 33.8	22 45.1	21 20.1	18 27.5	9 08.9	5 56.7	11 18.4	23 50.0	21 32.5	25 17.3
31 Su	8 35 32	8 03 14	12 41 56	18 36 09	20R 33.9	24 37.4	22 25.0	19 08.2	9 33.8	6 01.6	11 15.1	23 47.7	21 30.9	25 17.1

August 1994 — LONGITUDE

Day	Sid.Time	☉	0 hr ☽	Noon ☽	True ☊	☿	♀	♂	⚳	♃	♄	♅	♆	♇
1 M	8 39 28	9♌00 38	24♉31 05	0♊27 24	20♏33.6	26♋32.5	23♍29.6	19♊48.8	9♋58.6	6♏06.7	11♓11.6	23♑45.4	21♑29.4	25♏17.0
2 Tu	8 43 25	9 58 04	6♊25 45	12 26 44	20R 31.9	28 29.9	24 34.1	20 29.4	10 23.5	6 11.9	11R 08.1	23R 43.1	21R 27.9	25R 16.8
3 W	8 47 22	10 55 30	18 30 54	24 38 46	20 28.0	0♌29.2	25 38.3	21 09.8	10 48.3	6 17.3	11 04.5	23 40.9	21 26.3	25 16.7
4 Th	8 51 18	11 52 58	0♋50 46	7♋07 15	20 21.4	2 30.3	26 42.4	21 50.2	11 13.0	6 22.8	11 00.9	23 38.6	21 24.8	25 16.7
5 F	8 55 15	12 50 26	13 28 28	19 54 36	20 12.3	4 32.6	27 46.2	22 30.5	11 37.8	6 28.5	10 57.2	23 36.4	21 23.4	25D 16.7
6 Sa	8 59 11	13 47 56	26 25 42	3♌01 43	20 01.2	6 35.9	28 49.8	23 10.7	12 02.5	6 34.3	10 53.5	23 34.1	21 21.9	25 16.7
7 Su	9 03 08	14 45 27	9♌42 29	16 27 46	19 49.0	8 39.8	29 53.1	23 50.8	12 27.2	6 40.3	10 49.6	23 31.9	21 20.4	25 16.7
8 M	9 07 04	15 42 58	23 17 12	0♍10 22	19 37.0	10 43.9	0♎56.3	24 30.9	12 51.8	6 46.4	10 45.8	23 29.8	21 19.0	25 16.8
9 Tu	9 11 01	16 40 31	7♍06 46	14 05 54	19 26.3	12 48.1	1 59.1	25 10.8	13 16.4	6 52.7	10 41.8	23 27.6	21 17.5	25 16.9
10 W	9 14 57	17 38 05	21 07 13	28 10 03	19 17.8	14 52.1	3 01.8	25 50.7	13 41.0	6 59.1	10 37.9	23 25.5	21 16.1	25 17.0
11 Th	9 18 54	18 35 39	5♎14 24	12♎19 19	19 12.2	16 55.6	4 04.1	26 30.5	14 05.5	7 05.7	10 33.8	23 23.4	21 14.7	25 17.2
12 F	9 22 51	19 33 15	19 24 36	26 29 55	19 09.3	18 58.5	5 06.2	27 10.2	14 30.0	7 12.4	10 29.8	23 21.3	21 13.3	25 17.4
13 Sa	9 26 47	20 30 51	3♏35 00	10♏39 40	19 08.3	21 00.5	6 08.0	27 49.8	14 54.4	7 19.2	10 25.6	23 19.2	21 12.0	25 17.7
14 Su	9 30 44	21 28 28	17 43 44	24 47 07	19 08.3	23 01.6	7 09.5	28 29.3	15 18.8	7 26.1	10 21.5	23 17.2	21 10.6	25 18.0
15 M	9 34 40	22 26 07	1♐49 40	8♐51 20	19 07.8	25 01.6	8 10.7	29 08.8	15 43.2	7 33.2	10 17.3	23 15.2	21 09.3	25 18.3
16 Tu	9 38 37	23 23 46	15 51 59	22 51 29	19 05.6	27 00.5	9 11.6	29 48.1	16 07.5	7 40.5	10 13.0	23 13.2	21 08.0	25 18.6
17 W	9 42 33	24 21 26	29 49 40	6♑46 21	19 01.0	28 58.1	10 12.2	0♋27.4	16 31.8	7 47.8	10 08.7	23 11.2	21 06.7	25 19.0
18 Th	9 46 30	25 19 08	13♑41 16	20 34 08	18 53.6	0♍54.5	11 12.5	1 06.6	16 56.0	7 55.3	10 04.4	23 09.3	21 05.4	25 19.4
19 F	9 50 26	26 16 50	27 24 40	4♒12 30	18 43.6	2 49.5	12 12.4	1 45.7	17 20.2	8 02.9	10 00.1	23 07.4	21 04.1	25 19.9
20 Sa	9 54 23	27 14 34	10♒57 19	17 38 48	18 31.8	4 43.1	13 11.9	2 24.7	17 44.4	8 10.7	9 55.7	23 05.6	21 02.9	25 20.4
21 Su	9 58 20	28 12 19	24 16 38	0♓50 35	18 19.4	6 35.4	14 11.1	3 03.6	18 08.5	8 18.5	9 51.3	23 03.7	21 01.7	25 20.9
22 M	10 02 16	29 10 05	7♓20 27	13 46 07	18 07.5	8 26.4	15 09.9	3 42.4	18 32.5	8 26.5	9 46.9	23 01.9	21 00.5	25 21.4
23 Tu	10 06 13	0♍07 53	20 07 31	26 24 42	17 57.2	10 15.9	16 08.3	4 21.2	18 56.5	8 34.6	9 42.4	23 00.2	20 59.3	25 22.0
24 W	10 10 09	1 05 42	2♈37 47	8♈46 59	17 49.2	12 04.1	17 06.4	4 59.8	19 20.5	8 42.9	9 37.9	22 58.4	20 58.2	25 22.6
25 Th	10 14 06	2 03 33	14 52 36	20 54 58	17 43.9	13 50.9	18 04.0	5 38.4	19 44.4	8 51.2	9 33.4	22 56.7	20 57.0	25 23.3
26 F	10 18 02	3 01 26	26 54 33	2♉51 49	17 41.0	15 36.4	19 01.2	6 16.9	20 08.2	8 59.7	9 28.9	22 55.0	20 55.9	25 24.0
27 Sa	10 21 59	3 59 20	8♉47 20	14 41 42	17D 40.1	17 20.6	19 57.9	6 55.3	20 32.0	9 08.2	9 24.4	22 53.4	20 54.8	25 24.7
28 Su	10 25 55	4 57 17	20 35 33	26 29 32	17R 40.2	19 03.4	20 54.3	7 33.6	20 55.8	9 16.9	9 19.8	22 51.8	20 53.8	25 25.4
29 M	10 29 52	5 55 15	2♊24 20	8♊20 38	17 40.4	20 44.9	21 50.1	8 11.8	21 19.5	9 25.7	9 15.2	22 50.3	20 52.7	25 26.2
30 Tu	10 33 49	6 53 15	14 19 08	20 20 29	17 39.5	22 25.2	22 45.5	8 49.9	21 43.1	9 34.7	9 10.7	22 48.8	20 51.7	25 27.0
31 W	10 37 45	7 51 17	26 25 20	2♋34 18	17 36.8	24 04.2	23 40.4	9 27.9	22 06.7	9 43.7	9 06.1	22 47.3	20 50.7	25 27.9

Astro Data Dy Hr Mn	Planet Ingress Dy Hr Mn	Last Aspect Dy Hr Mn	☽ Ingress Dy Hr Mn	Last Aspect Dy Hr Mn	☽ Ingress Dy Hr Mn	☽ Phases & Eclipses Dy Hr Mn
♃ D 2 3:33	☿ ♊R 2 23:18	2 4:08 ♅ □	♉ 2 14:23	1 2:34 ☿ ⚹	♊ 1 11:05	8 21:37 ● 16♋29
☿ D 6 19:43	♂ ♊ 3 22:30	4 18:15 ♇ ☍	♊ 5 3:12	3 14:07 ♀ □	♋ 3 22:22	16 1:12 ☽ 23♎18
☽0S 13 15:03	⚳ ♋ 8 15:30	7 13:13 ☿ ☌	♋ 7 14:17	6 3:43 ☿ ⚹	♌ 6 6:31	22 20:16 ○ 29♑47
☽0N 26 14:44	☿ ♋ 10 12:41	9 14:23 ♇ △	♌ 9 22:43	8 3:29 ♇ □	♍ 8 11:42	30 12:40 ☾ 7♉07
	♀ ♍ 11 6:33	11 20:43 ♇ □	♍ 12 4:48	10 7:51 ♂ □	♎ 10 15:07	
♇ D 5 17:08	☉ ♌ 23 1:41	14 1:19 ♇ ⚹	♎ 14 9:15	12 13:12 ♂ △	♏ 12 17:56	7 8:45 ● 14♌38
♀0S 7 2:56		16 3:04 ♅ □	♏ 16 12:35	14 12:53 ♇ ☌	♐ 14 20:53	14 5:57 ☽ 21♏14
☽0S 9 22:01	☿ ♌ 3 6:09	18 7:32 ☉ △	♐ 18 15:09	16 20:19 ☿ △	♑ 17 0:18	21 6:47 ○ 28♒00
☽0N 22 23:57	♀ ♎ 7 14:36	19 11:01 ♄ □	♑ 20 17:30	18 20:20 ♇ ⚹	♒ 19 4:34	29 6:41 ☾ 5♊42
♃△♄ 28 17:10	♂ ♋ 16 19:15	22 20:16 ☉ ☍	♒ 22 20:38	21 6:47 ☉ ☍	♓ 21 10:27	
	☿ ♍ 18 0:44	24 17:25 ♇ □	♓ 25 1:56	23 10:00 ♇ △	♈ 23 18:55	
	☉ ♍ 23 8:44	27 1:25 ♇ △	♈ 27 10:30	25 16:03 ♅ □	♉ 26 6:13	
		29 9:51 ♅ □	♉ 29 22:13	28 9:50 ♇ ☍	♊ 28 19:07	
				30 17:10 ♀ △	♋ 31 7:00	

Astro Data

1 July 1994
Julian Day # 34515
SVP 5♓19'58"
GC 26♐45.7 ⚴ 6♉07.3
Eris 18♈31.1 ⚵ 18♎13.7
⚷ 6♍03.8 ⚶ 5♊36.7
☽ Mean ☊ 21♏29.1

1 August 1994
Julian Day # 34546
SVP 5♓19'53"
GC 26♐45.8 ⚴ 15♉32.4
Eris 18♈30.5R ⚵ 23♎18.0
⚷ 9♍37.7 ⚶ 17♊54.3
☽ Mean ☊ 19♏50.6

LONGITUDE — September 1994

Day	Sid.Time	☉	0 hr ☽	Noon ☽	True ☊	☿	♀	♂	⚳	♃	♄	♅	♆	♇
1 Th	10 41 42	8♍49 21	8♋47 57	15♋06 44	17♏31.8	25♍41.9	24♎34.7	10♋05.8	22♋30.2	9♏52.8	9♓01.5	22♑45.8	20♑49.8	25♏28.8
2 F	10 45 38	9 47 26	21 31 03	28 01 13	17R 24.4	27 18.4	25 28.6	10 43.6	22 53.7	10 02.1	8R 57.0	22R 44.4	20R 48.9	25 29.7
3 Sa	10 49 35	10 45 34	4♌37 23	11♌19 36	17 15.1	28 53.6	26 21.8	11 21.3	23 17.1	10 11.4	8 52.4	22 43.1	20 47.9	25 30.6
4 Su	10 53 31	11 43 43	18 07 46	25 01 37	17 04.6	0♎27.6	27 14.6	11 58.9	23 40.4	10 20.9	8 47.8	22 41.8	20 47.1	25 31.6
5 M	10 57 28	12 41 54	2♍00 47	9♍04 44	16 54.2	2 00.4	28 06.7	12 36.4	24 03.6	10 30.4	8 43.2	22 40.5	20 46.2	25 32.6
6 Tu	11 01 24	13 40 07	16 12 48	23 24 17	16 44.9	3 31.9	28 58.2	13 13.9	24 26.8	10 40.1	8 38.7	22 39.2	20 45.4	25 33.6
7 W	11 05 21	14 38 21	0♎38 22	7♎54 13	16 37.7	5 02.2	29 49.1	13 51.2	24 49.9	10 49.9	8 34.1	22 38.0	20 44.6	25 34.7
8 Th	11 09 17	15 36 37	15 11 03	22 28 03	16 33.0	6 31.3	0♏39.3	14 28.3	25 13.0	10 59.7	8 29.6	22 36.9	20 43.8	25 35.8
9 F	11 13 14	16 34 55	29 44 31	6♏59 49	16D 30.8	7 59.2	1 28.8	15 05.4	25 36.0	11 09.7	8 25.1	22 35.8	20 43.1	25 36.9
10 Sa	11 17 11	17 33 14	14♏13 25	21 24 53	16 30.6	9 25.8	2 17.6	15 42.4	25 58.9	11 19.7	8 20.6	22 34.7	20 42.4	25 38.1
11 Su	11 21 07	18 31 35	28 33 53	5♐40 11	16R 31.2	10 51.2	3 05.6	16 19.3	26 21.7	11 29.9	8 16.1	22 33.7	20 41.7	25 39.3
12 M	11 25 04	19 29 57	12♐43 36	19 44 03	16 31.7	12 15.2	3 52.9	16 56.0	26 44.4	11 40.1	8 11.7	22 32.7	20 41.0	25 40.5
13 Tu	11 29 00	20 28 21	26 41 29	3♑35 53	16 30.9	13 38.0	4 39.3	17 32.7	27 07.1	11 50.4	8 07.3	22 31.8	20 40.4	25 41.8
14 W	11 32 57	21 26 47	10♑27 16	17 15 37	16 28.1	14 59.4	5 24.9	18 09.2	27 29.6	12 00.9	8 02.9	22 30.9	20 39.8	25 43.1
15 Th	11 36 53	22 25 14	24 00 57	0♒43 16	16 23.0	16 19.5	6 09.6	18 45.6	27 52.1	12 11.4	7 58.5	22 30.1	20 39.2	25 44.4
16 F	11 40 50	23 23 42	7♒22 33	13 58 46	16 15.8	17 38.1	6 53.4	19 21.9	28 14.6	12 21.9	7 54.2	22 29.3	20 38.7	25 45.7
17 Sa	11 44 46	24 22 13	20 31 52	27 01 48	16 07.2	18 55.2	7 36.3	19 58.1	28 36.9	12 32.6	7 49.9	22 28.6	20 38.2	25 47.1
18 Su	11 48 43	25 20 45	3♓28 32	9♓52 00	15 58.0	20 10.8	8 18.1	20 34.2	28 59.1	12 43.4	7 45.6	22 27.9	20 37.7	25 48.5
19 M	11 52 40	26 19 18	16 12 12	22 29 07	15 49.2	21 24.9	8 58.9	21 10.1	29 21.3	12 54.2	7 41.4	22 27.2	20 37.3	25 49.9
20 Tu	11 56 36	27 17 54	28 42 48	4♈53 17	15 41.6	22 37.2	9 38.6	21 46.0	29 43.3	13 05.1	7 37.2	22 26.6	20 36.9	25 51.4
21 W	12 00 33	28 16 32	11♈00 44	17 05 17	15 35.8	23 47.8	10 17.2	22 21.7	0♌05.3	13 16.1	7 33.1	22 26.1	20 36.5	25 52.9
22 Th	12 04 29	29 15 12	23 07 09	29 06 36	15 32.2	24 56.5	10 54.7	22 57.3	0 27.1	13 27.2	7 29.0	22 25.6	20 36.1	25 54.4
23 F	12 08 26	0♎13 54	5♉03 58	10♉59 38	15D 30.6	26 03.2	11 30.9	23 32.8	0 48.9	13 38.3	7 25.0	22 25.1	20 35.8	25 55.9
24 Sa	12 12 22	1 12 38	16 54 01	22 47 36	15 30.8	27 07.8	12 05.9	24 08.2	1 10.6	13 49.5	7 21.0	22 24.7	20 35.5	25 57.5
25 Su	12 16 19	2 11 24	28 40 53	4♊34 26	15 32.0	28 10.1	12 39.6	24 43.4	1 32.2	14 00.8	7 17.0	22 24.4	20 35.3	25 59.1
26 M	12 20 15	3 10 13	10♊28 50	16 24 43	15 33.5	29 10.1	13 12.0	25 18.5	1 53.6	14 12.2	7 13.2	22 24.1	20 35.1	26 00.7
27 Tu	12 24 12	4 09 03	22 22 42	28 23 26	15R 34.7	0♏07.4	13 43.0	25 53.5	2 15.0	14 23.6	7 09.3	22 23.8	20 34.9	26 02.4
28 W	12 28 09	5 07 57	4♋27 34	10♋35 45	15 34.7	1 01.9	14 12.5	26 28.4	2 36.3	14 35.2	7 05.6	22 23.6	20 34.7	26 04.0
29 Th	12 32 05	6 06 52	16 48 34	23 06 36	15 33.2	1 53.3	14 40.5	27 03.1	2 57.4	14 46.7	7 01.9	22 23.5	20 34.6	26 05.7
30 F	12 36 02	7 05 50	29 30 22	6♌00 17	15 30.0	2 41.4	15 06.9	27 37.7	3 18.5	14 58.4	6 58.2	22 23.4	20 34.5	26 07.5

LONGITUDE — October 1994

Day	Sid.Time	☉	0 hr ☽	Noon ☽	True ☊	☿	♀	♂	⚳	♃	♄	♅	♆	♇
1 Sa	12 39 58	8♎04 49	12♌36 42	19♌19 49	15♏25.4	3♏26.0	15♏31.7	28♋12.1	3♌39.4	15♏10.1	6♓54.6	22♑23.3	20♑34.5	26♏09.2
2 Su	12 43 55	9 03 51	26 09 45	3♍06 22	15R 20.0	4 06.6	15 54.9	28 46.4	4 00.2	15 21.9	6R 51.1	22D 23.3	20D 34.4	26 11.0
3 M	12 47 51	10 02 56	10♍09 28	17 18 38	15 14.3	4 43.0	16 16.2	29 20.6	4 20.9	15 33.7	6 47.7	22 23.3	20 34.4	26 12.8
4 Tu	12 51 48	11 02 02	24 33 15	1♎52 37	15 09.2	5 14.7	16 35.8	29 54.6	4 41.4	15 45.6	6 44.3	22 23.4	20 34.5	26 14.6
5 W	12 55 44	12 01 11	9♎15 50	16 41 57	15 05.4	5 41.4	16 53.6	0♌28.5	5 01.9	15 57.6	6 41.0	22 23.6	20 34.6	26 16.4
6 Th	12 59 41	13 00 21	24 09 54	1♏38 39	15D 03.2	6 02.6	17 09.3	1 02.2	5 22.2	16 09.6	6 37.7	22 23.8	20 34.7	26 18.3
7 F	13 03 37	13 59 34	9♏07 07	16 34 21	15 02.6	6 17.9	17 23.1	1 35.8	5 42.3	16 21.7	6 34.6	22 24.0	20 34.8	26 20.2
8 Sa	13 07 34	14 58 48	23 59 25	1♐21 33	15 03.3	6R 26.8	17 34.9	2 09.2	6 02.4	16 33.8	6 31.5	22 24.3	20 35.0	26 22.1
9 Su	13 11 31	15 58 05	8♐40 05	15 54 29	15 04.7	6 28.8	17 44.5	2 42.5	6 22.3	16 46.0	6 28.5	22 24.7	20 35.2	26 24.0
10 M	13 15 27	16 57 23	23 04 23	0♑09 30	15 06.1	6 23.4	17 51.9	3 15.6	6 42.0	16 58.2	6 25.6	22 25.1	20 35.4	26 26.0
11 Tu	13 19 24	17 56 42	7♑09 42	14 04 56	15R 06.9	6 10.3	17 57.1	3 48.5	7 01.6	17 10.5	6 22.7	22 25.6	20 35.7	26 27.9
12 W	13 23 20	18 56 04	20 55 15	27 40 44	15 06.7	5 49.2	18R 00.0	4 21.3	7 21.1	17 22.9	6 20.0	22 26.1	20 36.0	26 29.9
13 Th	13 27 17	19 55 27	4♒21 33	10♒57 54	15 05.3	5 19.7	18 00.6	4 53.9	7 40.4	17 35.3	6 17.3	22 26.6	20 36.4	26 31.9
14 F	13 31 13	20 54 52	17 29 58	23 58 00	15 02.7	4 41.8	17 58.7	5 26.4	7 59.6	17 47.7	6 14.7	22 27.3	20 36.8	26 34.0
15 Sa	13 35 10	21 54 19	0♓22 14	6♓42 52	14 59.4	3 55.7	17 54.5	5 58.6	8 18.6	18 00.2	6 12.2	22 27.9	20 37.2	26 36.0
16 Su	13 39 06	22 53 47	13 00 08	19 14 16	14 55.7	3 01.9	17 47.9	6 30.8	8 37.5	18 12.7	6 09.8	22 28.6	20 37.6	26 38.1
17 M	13 43 03	23 53 18	25 25 27	1♈33 54	14 52.2	2 01.0	17 38.8	7 02.7	8 56.2	18 25.3	6 07.5	22 29.4	20 38.1	26 40.1
18 Tu	13 47 00	24 52 50	7♈39 48	13 43 22	14 49.3	0 54.1	17 27.3	7 34.5	9 14.7	18 37.9	6 05.3	22 30.2	20 38.6	26 42.2
19 W	13 50 56	25 52 24	19 44 47	25 44 18	14 47.3	29♎42.8	17 13.4	8 06.0	9 33.1	18 50.6	6 03.1	22 31.1	20 39.2	26 44.4
20 Th	13 54 53	26 52 01	1♉42 06	7♉38 26	14D 46.2	28 28.8	16 57.0	8 37.4	9 51.3	19 03.3	6 01.1	22 32.0	20 39.7	26 46.5
21 F	13 58 49	27 51 39	13 33 35	19 27 49	14 46.1	27 14.1	16 38.4	9 08.7	10 09.4	19 16.0	5 59.1	22 33.0	20 40.3	26 48.6
22 Sa	14 02 46	28 51 20	25 21 27	1♊14 50	14 46.8	26 01.0	16 17.5	9 39.7	10 27.2	19 28.8	5 57.2	22 34.0	20 41.0	26 50.8
23 Su	14 06 42	29 51 02	7♊08 21	13 02 24	14 48.0	24 51.5	15 54.4	10 10.6	10 44.9	19 41.6	5 55.5	22 35.0	20 41.7	26 53.0
24 M	14 10 39	0♏50 47	18 57 25	24 53 53	14 49.4	23 48.0	15 29.3	10 41.2	11 02.4	19 54.4	5 53.8	22 36.1	20 42.4	26 55.2
25 Tu	14 14 35	1 50 34	0♋52 17	6♋53 08	14 50.6	22 52.2	15 02.2	11 11.7	11 19.7	20 07.3	5 52.2	22 37.3	20 43.1	26 57.4
26 W	14 18 32	2 50 24	12 57 00	19 04 25	14 51.5	22 05.8	14 33.2	11 41.9	11 36.9	20 20.2	5 50.8	22 38.5	20 43.9	26 59.6
27 Th	14 22 29	3 50 15	25 15 57	1♌32 08	14R 51.9	21 29.7	14 02.6	12 12.0	11 53.8	20 33.2	5 49.4	22 39.8	20 44.7	27 01.9
28 F	14 26 25	4 50 09	7♌53 31	14 20 34	14 51.8	21 04.8	13 30.6	12 41.8	12 10.6	20 46.1	5 48.1	22 41.1	20 45.5	27 04.1
29 Sa	14 30 22	5 50 05	20 53 44	27 33 22	14 51.2	20D 51.5	12 57.2	13 11.4	12 27.1	20 59.1	5 46.9	22 42.5	20 46.4	27 06.4
30 Su	14 34 18	6 50 03	4♍19 45	11♍13 01	14 50.3	20 49.5	12 22.7	13 40.8	12 43.4	21 12.2	5 45.8	22 43.9	20 47.3	27 08.6
31 M	14 38 15	7 50 03	18 13 12	25 20 08	14 49.4	20 58.7	11 47.4	14 10.0	12 59.6	21 25.2	5 44.9	22 45.3	20 48.2	27 10.9

Astro Data

	Dy Hr Mn
☿0S	4 8:23
☽0S	6 6:36
☽0N	19 7:35
☉0S	23 6:19
♄∠♅	23 10:54
♅ D	2 1:47
♆ D	2 17:47
☽0S	3 16:36
☿ R	9 6:43
♀ R	13 5:41
☽0N	16 13:30
♃⚹♆	28 10:50
♄∠♆	29 18:10
☿ D	30 4:04
☽0S	31 2:53

Planet Ingress

	Dy Hr Mn
☿ ♎	4 4:55
♀ ♏	7 17:12
⚳ ♌	21 6:13
☉ ♎	23 6:19
☿ ♏	27 8:51
♂ ♌	4 15:48
☿ ♎R	19 6:19
☉ ♏	23 15:36

Last Aspect / ☽ Ingress

Last Aspect Dy Hr Mn		☽ Ingress Dy Hr Mn
2 10:30 ☿ ⚹	♌	2 15:37
4 16:05 ♀ ⚹	♍	4 20:33
6 15:35 ♇ ⚹	♎	6 22:57
8 12:15 ♅ □	♏	9 0:26
10 19:05 ♇ ☌	♐	11 2:25
12 11:34 ☉ □	♑	13 5:44
15 3:04 ♇ ⚹	♒	15 10:42
17 9:41 ♇ □	♓	17 17:31
19 20:01 ☉ ☍	♈	20 2:30
22 2:46 ☿ ☍	♉	22 13:47
24 18:28 ♇ ☍	♊	25 2:41
25 17:29 ♄ □	♋	27 15:12
29 19:46 ♂ ☌	♌	30 0:55

Last Aspect / ☽ Ingress

Last Aspect Dy Hr Mn		☽ Ingress Dy Hr Mn
2 0:01 ♇ □	♍	2 6:39
4 8:40 ♂ ⚹	♎	4 8:56
5 21:09 ♅ □	♏	6 9:22
8 3:51 ♇ ☌	♐	8 9:47
9 12:07 ☉ ⚹	♑	10 11:44
12 9:53 ♇ ⚹	♒	12 16:09
14 16:52 ♇ □	♓	14 23:18
17 2:24 ♇ △	♈	17 8:56
19 19:15 ☿ ☍	♉	19 20:34
22 3:00 ♇ ☍	♊	22 9:28
24 9:58 ☿ △	♋	24 22:15
27 3:22 ♇ △	♌	27 9:05
29 11:12 ♇ □	♍	29 16:21
31 15:05 ♇ ⚹	♎	31 19:46

☽ Phases & Eclipses

Dy Hr Mn	
5 18:33	● 12♍58
12 11:34	☽ 19♐29
19 20:01	○ 26♓39
28 0:23	☾ 4♋39
5 3:55	● 11♎41
11 19:17	☽ 18♑15
19 12:18	○ 25♈53
27 16:44	☾ 4♌02

Astro Data

1 September 1994
Julian Day # 34577
SVP 5♓19'49"
GC 26♐45.9 ⚴ 22♉24.6
Eris 18♈20.5R ⚵ 1♏02.2
⚷ 13♍51.0 ⚶ 28♊42.5
☽ Mean ☊ 18♏12.1

1 October 1994
Julian Day # 34607
SVP 5♓19'47"
GC 26♐46.0 ⚴ 24♉17.1R
Eris 18♈04.4R ⚵ 10♏03.6
⚷ 18♍03.8 ⚶ 6♋44.5
☽ Mean ☊ 16♏36.7

November 1994 LONGITUDE

Day	Sid.Time	☉	0 hr ☽	Noon ☽	True ☊	☿	♀	♂	⚳	♃	♄	♅	♆	♇
1 Tu	14 42 11	8♏50 05	2♎33 31	9♎52 51	14♏48.7	21♎18.4	11♏11.5	14♌39.0	13♌15.5	21♏38.3	5♓44.0	22♑46.8	20♑49.2	27♏13.2
2 W	14 46 08	9 50 09	17 17 28	24 46 30	14R 48.2	21 48.0	10R 35.2	15 07.7	13 31.2	21 51.4	5R 43.2	22 48.4	20 50.2	27 15.5
3 Th	14 50 04	10 50 16	2♏18 59	9♏53 49	14D 48.0	22 26.5	9 58.7	15 36.2	13 46.6	22 04.5	5 42.6	22 50.0	20 51.2	27 17.8
4 F	14 54 01	11 50 24	17 29 47	25 05 41	14 48.0	23 13.2	9 22.4	16 04.4	14 01.9	22 17.7	5 42.0	22 51.6	20 52.3	27 20.2
5 Sa	14 57 58	12 50 34	2♐40 18	10♐12 30	14 48.2	24 07.1	8 46.3	16 32.4	14 16.9	22 30.8	5 41.5	22 53.3	20 53.4	27 22.5
6 Su	15 01 54	13 50 46	17 41 14	25 05 36	14 48.3	25 07.4	8 10.8	17 00.1	14 31.7	22 44.0	5 41.2	22 55.0	20 54.5	27 24.8
7 M	15 05 51	14 50 59	2♑24 49	9♑38 19	14R 48.4	26 13.3	7 36.2	17 27.6	14 46.2	22 57.2	5 40.9	22 56.8	20 55.7	27 27.2
8 Tu	15 09 47	15 51 14	16 45 40	23 46 39	14 48.3	27 24.1	7 02.6	17 54.8	15 00.5	23 10.5	5D 40.8	22 58.7	20 56.8	27 29.5
9 W	15 13 44	16 51 30	0♒41 09	7♒29 14	14D 48.2	28 39.0	6 30.2	18 21.7	15 14.5	23 23.7	5 40.8	23 00.5	20 58.1	27 31.9
10 Th	15 17 40	17 51 47	14 11 02	20 46 49	14 48.2	29 57.4	5 59.3	18 48.4	15 28.3	23 36.9	5 40.8	23 02.5	20 59.3	27 34.3
11 F	15 21 37	18 52 06	27 16 56	3♓41 45	14 48.3	1♏18.9	5 29.9	19 14.8	15 41.8	23 50.2	5 41.0	23 04.4	21 00.6	27 36.6
12 Sa	15 25 33	19 52 27	10♓01 41	16 17 12	14 48.7	2 42.9	5 02.5	19 40.9	15 55.1	24 03.4	5 41.3	23 06.4	21 01.9	27 39.0
13 Su	15 29 30	20 52 49	22 28 45	28 36 47	14 49.3	4 09.0	4 36.9	20 06.7	16 08.1	24 16.7	5 41.7	23 08.5	21 03.2	27 41.4
14 M	15 33 27	21 53 12	4♈41 44	10♈44 03	14 50.1	5 36.8	4 13.4	20 32.3	16 20.8	24 30.0	5 42.1	23 10.6	21 04.5	27 43.8
15 Tu	15 37 23	22 53 37	16 44 06	22 42 19	14 50.8	7 06.1	3 52.2	20 57.5	16 33.3	24 43.3	5 42.7	23 12.7	21 05.9	27 46.2
16 W	15 41 20	23 54 03	28 39 01	4♉34 34	14R 51.4	8 36.6	3 33.2	21 22.5	16 45.4	24 56.6	5 43.4	23 14.9	21 07.3	27 48.6
17 Th	15 45 16	24 54 31	10♉29 16	16 23 26	14 51.5	10 08.1	3 16.6	21 47.1	16 57.3	25 09.9	5 44.2	23 17.1	21 08.8	27 51.0
18 F	15 49 13	25 55 00	22 17 19	28 11 13	14 51.2	11 40.3	3 02.4	22 11.4	17 08.9	25 23.1	5 45.1	23 19.3	21 10.2	27 53.4
19 Sa	15 53 09	26 55 31	4♊05 23	10♊00 04	14 50.2	13 13.1	2 50.7	22 35.4	17 20.3	25 36.4	5 46.2	23 21.6	21 11.7	27 55.8
20 Su	15 57 06	27 56 03	15 55 33	21 52 05	14 48.6	14 46.4	2 41.5	22 59.1	17 31.3	25 49.7	5 47.3	23 24.0	21 13.2	27 58.2
21 M	16 01 02	28 56 38	27 49 57	3♋49 26	14 46.5	16 20.1	2 34.8	23 22.5	17 42.0	26 03.0	5 48.5	23 26.3	21 14.8	28 00.5
22 Tu	16 04 59	29 57 13	9♋50 52	15 54 33	14 44.1	17 54.1	2 30.6	23 45.5	17 52.4	26 16.3	5 49.8	23 28.8	21 16.4	28 02.9
23 W	16 08 56	0♐57 51	22 00 52	28 10 09	14 41.8	19 28.2	2D 28.8	24 08.1	18 02.5	26 29.6	5 51.2	23 31.2	21 17.9	28 05.3
24 Th	16 12 52	1 58 30	4♌22 49	10♌39 15	14 40.0	21 02.5	2 29.6	24 30.4	18 12.3	26 42.9	5 52.8	23 33.7	21 19.6	28 07.7
25 F	16 16 49	2 59 10	16 59 53	23 25 06	14D 38.8	22 36.9	2 32.7	24 52.4	18 21.7	26 56.2	5 54.4	23 36.2	21 21.2	28 10.1
26 Sa	16 20 45	3 59 53	29 55 19	6♍30 54	14 38.5	24 11.3	2 38.2	25 13.9	18 30.8	27 09.4	5 56.1	23 38.8	21 22.9	28 12.5
27 Su	16 24 42	5 00 36	13♍12 11	19 59 28	14 39.1	25 45.7	2 46.1	25 35.1	18 39.6	27 22.7	5 58.0	23 41.4	21 24.6	28 14.9
28 M	16 28 38	6 01 22	26 52 57	3♎52 42	14 40.4	27 20.2	2 56.2	25 55.9	18 48.1	27 35.9	5 59.9	23 44.0	21 26.3	28 17.3
29 Tu	16 32 35	7 02 09	10♎58 44	18 10 53	14 41.8	28 54.6	3 08.5	26 16.2	18 56.1	27 49.2	6 02.0	23 46.7	21 28.0	28 19.7
30 W	16 36 31	8 02 57	25 28 50	2♏52 04	14R 43.0	0♐28.9	3 23.1	26 36.2	19 03.9	28 02.4	6 04.1	23 49.4	21 29.8	28 22.0

December 1994 LONGITUDE

Day	Sid.Time	☉	0 hr ☽	Noon ☽	True ☊	☿	♀	♂	⚳	♃	♄	♅	♆	♇
1 Th	16 40 28	9♐03 47	10♏19 55	17♏51 34	14♏43.3	2♐03.3	3♏39.7	26♌55.7	19♌11.3	28♏15.6	6♓06.4	23♑52.1	21♑31.5	28♏24.4
2 F	16 44 25	10 04 39	25 26 00	3♐02 05	14R 42.4	3 37.6	3 58.3	27 14.9	19 18.3	28 28.8	6 08.7	23 54.9	21 33.3	28 26.8
3 Sa	16 48 21	11 05 31	10♐38 36	18 14 17	14 40.1	5 11.8	4 18.9	27 33.5	19 24.9	28 42.0	6 11.1	23 57.7	21 35.2	28 29.1
4 Su	16 52 18	12 06 25	25 47 52	3♑18 10	14 36.6	6 46.1	4 41.4	27 51.7	19 31.2	28 55.2	6 13.7	24 00.5	21 37.0	28 31.5
5 M	16 56 14	13 07 20	10♑44 04	18 04 38	14 32.4	8 20.2	5 05.7	28 09.5	19 37.1	29 08.3	6 16.3	24 03.4	21 38.9	28 33.8
6 Tu	17 00 11	14 08 15	25 19 07	2♒26 55	14 28.0	9 54.4	5 31.7	28 26.8	19 42.7	29 21.4	6 19.1	24 06.3	21 40.8	28 36.2
7 W	17 04 07	15 09 11	9♒27 40	16 21 12	14 24.3	11 28.5	5 59.5	28 43.6	19 47.8	29 34.5	6 21.9	24 09.2	21 42.7	28 38.5
8 Th	17 08 04	16 10 08	23 07 30	29 46 44	14 21.6	13 02.7	6 28.9	29 00.0	19 52.5	29 47.6	6 24.9	24 12.2	21 44.6	28 40.8
9 F	17 12 00	17 11 06	6♓19 11	12♓45 16	14D 20.4	14 36.8	6 59.9	29 15.8	19 56.9	0♐00.6	6 27.9	24 15.2	21 46.5	28 43.1
10 Sa	17 15 57	18 12 04	19 05 28	25 20 18	14 20.5	16 11.0	7 32.5	29 31.1	20 00.9	0 13.6	6 31.0	24 18.2	21 48.5	28 45.4
11 Su	17 19 54	19 13 03	1♈30 23	7♈36 20	14 21.8	17 45.2	8 06.5	29 46.0	20 04.4	0 26.6	6 34.2	24 21.2	21 50.5	28 47.7
12 M	17 23 50	20 14 02	13 38 44	19 38 14	14 23.6	19 19.5	8 41.9	0♍00.3	20 07.6	0 39.5	6 37.5	24 24.3	21 52.5	28 50.0
13 Tu	17 27 47	21 15 02	25 35 24	1♉30 49	14 25.2	20 53.8	9 18.7	0 14.0	20 10.3	0 52.4	6 40.9	24 27.4	21 54.5	28 52.3
14 W	17 31 43	22 16 02	7♉25 01	13 18 30	14R 26.0	22 28.2	9 56.8	0 27.3	20 12.7	1 05.3	6 44.4	24 30.5	21 56.5	28 54.5
15 Th	17 35 40	23 17 04	19 11 45	25 05 11	14 25.3	24 02.7	10 36.1	0 40.0	20 14.6	1 18.2	6 48.0	24 33.6	21 58.5	28 56.7
16 F	17 39 36	24 18 05	0♊59 10	6♊54 03	14 22.7	25 37.4	11 16.7	0 52.1	20 16.1	1 31.0	6 51.7	24 36.8	22 00.6	28 59.0
17 Sa	17 43 33	25 19 08	12 50 08	18 47 40	14 18.1	27 12.1	11 58.5	1 03.6	20 17.2	1 43.8	6 55.5	24 40.0	22 02.7	29 01.2
18 Su	17 47 29	26 20 11	24 46 53	0♋47 58	14 11.6	28 47.0	12 41.4	1 14.6	20 17.9	1 56.5	6 59.3	24 43.2	22 04.8	29 03.4
19 M	17 51 26	27 21 15	6♋51 05	12 56 24	14 03.6	0♑22.1	13 25.4	1 24.9	20R 18.1	2 09.2	7 03.3	24 46.4	22 06.9	29 05.6
20 Tu	17 55 23	28 22 19	19 04 01	25 14 06	13 54.9	1 57.3	14 10.4	1 34.7	20 17.9	2 21.8	7 07.3	24 49.7	22 09.0	29 07.7
21 W	17 59 19	29 23 24	1♌26 45	7♌42 08	13 46.4	3 32.7	14 56.4	1 43.8	20 17.3	2 34.5	7 11.4	24 52.9	22 11.1	29 09.9
22 Th	18 03 16	0♑24 30	14 00 22	20 21 38	13 39.0	5 08.3	15 43.4	1 52.3	20 16.3	2 47.0	7 15.6	24 56.2	22 13.2	29 12.0
23 F	18 07 12	1 25 36	26 46 08	3♍14 02	13 33.3	6 44.1	16 31.3	2 00.1	20 14.8	2 59.5	7 19.9	24 59.5	22 15.4	29 14.1
24 Sa	18 11 09	2 26 43	9♍45 36	16 21 03	13 29.7	8 20.1	17 20.2	2 07.3	20 12.9	3 12.0	7 24.2	25 02.9	22 17.6	29 16.2
25 Su	18 15 05	3 27 50	23 00 37	29 44 33	13D 28.3	9 56.3	18 09.8	2 13.8	20 10.5	3 24.4	7 28.7	25 06.2	22 19.7	29 18.3
26 M	18 19 02	4 28 58	6♎33 05	13♎26 22	13 28.5	11 32.7	19 00.3	2 19.6	20 07.7	3 36.8	7 33.2	25 09.6	22 21.9	29 20.4
27 Tu	18 22 58	5 30 07	20 24 34	27 27 43	13 29.6	13 09.3	19 51.6	2 24.7	20 04.5	3 49.1	7 37.8	25 12.9	22 24.1	29 22.4
28 W	18 26 55	6 31 17	4♏35 47	11♏48 35	13R 30.3	14 46.0	20 43.7	2 29.1	20 00.8	4 01.4	7 42.4	25 16.3	22 26.3	29 24.4
29 Th	18 30 52	7 32 27	19 05 49	26 27 02	13 29.6	16 23.0	21 36.5	2 32.8	19 56.7	4 13.6	7 47.2	25 19.8	22 28.5	29 26.4
30 F	18 34 48	8 33 37	3♐51 36	11♐18 45	13 26.6	18 00.0	22 30.0	2 35.7	19 52.2	4 25.8	7 52.0	25 23.2	22 30.7	29 28.4
31 Sa	18 38 45	9 34 48	18 47 34	26 16 59	13 21.1	19 37.2	23 24.1	2 37.9	19 47.2	4 37.9	7 57.0	25 26.6	22 33.0	29 30.4

Astro Data Dy Hr Mn	Planet Ingress Dy Hr Mn	Last Aspect Dy Hr Mn	☽ Ingress Dy Hr Mn	Last Aspect Dy Hr Mn	☽ Ingress Dy Hr Mn	☽ Phases & Eclipses Dy Hr Mn	Astro Data
♃✶♅ 7 11:09	☿ ♏ 10 12:46	2 8:51 ♅ □	♏ 2 20:19	2 4:44 ♇ ☌	♐ 2 7:13	3 13:35 ● 10♏54	1 November 1994
♄D 9 8:36	☉ ♐ 22 13:06	4 15:33 ♇ ☌	♐ 4 19:46	4 3:07 ♂ △	♑ 4 6:42	3 13:39:05 ● T 04'24"	Julian Day # 34638
☽0N 12 19:01	☿ ♐ 30 4:38	6 12:03 ☿ ⚹	♑ 6 20:02	6 6:42 ♃ ⚹	♒ 6 7:51	10 6:14 ☽ 17♒37	SVP 5♓19'44"
♀D 23 16:57		8 18:53 ☿ □	♒ 8 22:48	8 12:02 ♃ □	♓ 8 12:24	18 6:57 ○ 25♉42	GC 26♐46.0 ⚴ 18♉31.9R
☽0S 27 12:01	♃ ♐ 9 10:54	11 0:35 ♇ □	♓ 11 5:04	10 18:39 ♇ △	♈ 10 21:03	18 6:44 ☍ A 0.881	Eris 17♈46.1R ⚵ 20♏16.3
	♂ ♍ 12 11:32	13 10:11 ♇ △	♈ 13 14:44	12 21:39 ♅ □	♉ 13 8:56	26 7:04 ☾ 3♍47	⚷ 22♍01.0 ⚶ 10♋46.7
♃☌♇ 2 7:30	☿ ♑ 19 6:26	15 13:01 ♅ □	♉ 16 2:44	15 19:53 ♇ ☍	♊ 15 22:00		☽ Mean ☊ 14♏58.2
☽0N 10 2:01	☉ ♑ 22 2:23	18 11:24 ♇ ☍	♊ 18 15:41	18 7:23 ☿ ☍	♋ 18 10:25	2 23:54 ● 10♐35	
⚳R 19 13:44		20 14:20 ♂ ⚹	♋ 21 4:21	20 19:33 ♇ △	♌ 20 21:13	9 21:06 ☽ 17♓34	1 December 1994
♄∠♆ 21 8:36		23 11:51 ♇ △	♌ 23 15:33	23 4:34 ♇ □	♍ 23 6:01	18 2:17 ○ 25♊55	Julian Day # 34668
☽0S 24 19:25		25 20:48 ♇ □	♍ 26 0:09	25 11:13 ♇ ⚹	♎ 25 12:27	25 19:06 ☾ 3♎46	SVP 5♓19'40"
		28 2:24 ♇ ⚹	♎ 28 5:22	27 8:11 ♅ □	♏ 27 16:17		GC 26♐46.1 ⚴ 9♉02.0R
		30 1:36 ♂ ⚹	♏ 30 7:21	29 16:52 ♇ ☌	♐ 29 17:46		Eris 17♈31.8R ⚵ 0♐29.0
				30 6:26 ♄ □	♑ 31 17:57		⚷ 24♍54.2 ⚶ 8♋34.4R
							☽ Mean ☊ 13♏22.9

LONGITUDE — January 1995

Day	Sid.Time	☉	0 hr ☽	Noon ☽	True ☊	☿	♀	♂	⚳	♃	♄	♅	♆	♇
1 Su	18 42 41	10♑35 59	3♑45 54	11♑13 08	13♏13.2	21♑14.4	24♏18.9	2♍39.4	19♌41.8	4♐49.9	8♓01.9	25♑30.1	22♑35.2	29♏32.3
2 M	18 46 38	11 37 10	18 37 34	25 58 05	13R03.7	22 51.6	25 14.3	2R40.1	19R36.0	5 01.9	8 07.0	25 33.5	22 37.4	29 34.3
3 Tu	18 50 34	12 38 21	3♒13 45	10♒23 44	12 53.7	24 28.8	26 10.3	2 40.0	19 29.7	5 13.8	8 12.1	25 37.0	22 39.7	29 36.2
4 W	18 54 31	13 39 32	17 27 22	24 24 15	12 44.3	26 05.8	27 06.9	2 39.1	19 23.1	5 25.7	8 17.3	25 40.5	22 41.9	29 38.0
5 Th	18 58 28	14 40 43	1♓14 05	7♓56 49	12 36.6	27 42.5	28 04.0	2 37.5	19 16.0	5 37.4	8 22.6	25 44.0	22 44.2	29 39.9
6 F	19 02 24	15 41 53	14 32 33	21 01 33	12 31.2	29 18.9	29 01.6	2 35.1	19 08.5	5 49.2	8 28.0	25 47.5	22 46.5	29 41.7
7 Sa	19 06 21	16 43 03	27 24 12	3♈40 59	12 28.2	0♒54.7	29 59.7	2 31.8	19 00.6	6 00.8	8 33.4	25 51.0	22 48.7	29 43.5
8 Su	19 10 17	17 44 12	9♈52 28	15 59 18	12D27.3	2 29.9	0♐58.4	2 27.8	18 52.3	6 12.4	8 38.8	25 54.5	22 51.0	29 45.3
9 M	19 14 14	18 45 21	22 02 09	28 01 41	12 27.5	4 04.2	1 57.5	2 23.0	18 43.7	6 23.9	8 44.4	25 58.0	22 53.3	29 47.1
10 Tu	19 18 10	19 46 29	3♉58 38	9♉53 40	12R28.0	5 37.3	2 57.0	2 17.4	18 34.6	6 35.3	8 50.0	26 01.6	22 55.5	29 48.8
11 W	19 22 07	20 47 37	15 47 28	21 40 41	12 27.6	7 09.1	3 57.0	2 10.9	18 25.3	6 46.6	8 55.7	26 05.1	22 57.8	29 50.5
12 Th	19 26 03	21 48 45	27 33 55	3♊27 46	12 25.4	8 39.0	4 57.4	2 03.7	18 15.5	6 57.9	9 01.4	26 08.6	23 00.1	29 52.2
13 F	19 30 00	22 49 52	9♊22 44	15 19 18	12 20.5	10 06.9	5 58.3	1 55.7	18 05.4	7 09.1	9 07.2	26 12.2	23 02.4	29 53.8
14 Sa	19 33 57	23 50 58	21 17 52	27 18 47	12 12.8	11 32.1	6 59.5	1 46.8	17 55.0	7 20.2	9 13.0	26 15.7	23 04.6	29 55.5
15 Su	19 37 53	24 52 04	3♋22 20	9♋28 45	12 02.4	12 54.3	8 01.1	1 37.2	17 44.2	7 31.2	9 19.0	26 19.3	23 06.9	29 57.1
16 M	19 41 50	25 53 10	15 38 11	21 50 45	11 50.0	14 12.9	9 03.1	1 26.7	17 33.1	7 42.2	9 24.9	26 22.8	23 09.2	29 58.6
17 Tu	19 45 46	26 54 15	28 06 28	4♌25 20	11 36.4	15 27.2	10 05.5	1 15.5	17 21.8	7 53.0	9 30.9	26 26.3	23 11.5	0♐00.2
18 W	19 49 43	27 55 19	10♌47 20	17 12 22	11 23.0	16 36.5	11 08.2	1 03.5	17 10.1	8 03.8	9 37.0	26 29.9	23 13.7	0 01.7
19 Th	19 53 39	28 56 23	23 40 22	0♍11 13	11 10.9	17 40.1	12 11.2	0 50.7	16 58.1	8 14.5	9 43.2	26 33.4	23 16.0	0 03.2
20 F	19 57 36	29 57 26	6♍44 52	13 21 12	11 01.2	18 37.1	13 14.6	0 37.1	16 45.9	8 25.1	9 49.3	26 37.0	23 18.3	0 04.6
21 Sa	20 01 32	0♒58 29	20 00 12	26 41 51	10 54.4	19 26.7	14 18.3	0 22.8	16 33.5	8 35.6	9 55.6	26 40.5	23 20.5	0 06.1
22 Su	20 05 29	1 59 32	3♎26 08	10♎13 06	10 50.5	20 08.0	15 22.3	0 07.7	16 20.8	8 46.0	10 01.9	26 44.1	23 22.8	0 07.5
23 M	20 09 26	3 00 34	17 02 50	23 55 24	10D49.1	20 40.2	16 26.5	29♌51.9	16 07.9	8 56.3	10 08.2	26 47.6	23 25.1	0 08.8
24 Tu	20 13 22	4 01 35	0♏50 52	7♏49 19	10R48.9	21 02.5	17 31.1	29 35.3	15 54.7	9 06.5	10 14.6	26 51.1	23 27.3	0 10.2
25 W	20 17 19	5 02 37	14 50 46	21 55 12	10 48.7	21R14.2	18 35.9	29 18.1	15 41.4	9 16.7	10 21.0	26 54.6	23 29.6	0 11.5
26 Th	20 21 15	6 03 38	29 02 30	6♐12 31	10 47.0	21 14.8	19 41.0	29 00.2	15 27.9	9 26.7	10 27.5	26 58.2	23 31.8	0 12.7
27 F	20 25 12	7 04 38	13♐24 54	20 39 16	10 42.9	21 03.9	20 46.4	28 41.7	15 14.3	9 36.6	10 34.0	27 01.7	23 34.0	0 14.0
28 Sa	20 29 08	8 05 38	27 55 04	5♑11 38	10 35.8	20 41.7	21 52.0	28 22.5	15 00.5	9 46.4	10 40.6	27 05.2	23 36.3	0 15.2
29 Su	20 33 05	9 06 37	12♑28 14	19 44 01	10 25.8	20 08.4	22 57.8	28 02.7	14 46.6	9 56.1	10 47.2	27 08.7	23 38.5	0 16.4
30 M	20 37 01	10 07 35	26 58 07	4♒09 40	10 13.8	19 24.6	24 03.8	27 42.4	14 32.6	10 05.7	10 53.9	27 12.2	23 40.7	0 17.5
31 Tu	20 40 58	11 08 32	11♒17 48	18 21 44	10 01.0	18 31.6	25 10.1	27 21.5	14 18.6	10 15.2	11 00.6	27 15.6	23 42.9	0 18.7

LONGITUDE — February 1995

Day	Sid.Time	☉	0 hr ☽	Noon ☽	True ☊	☿	♀	♂	⚳	♃	♄	♅	♆	♇
1 W	20 44 55	12♒09 28	25♒20 48	2♓14 26	9♏48.6	17♒30.7	26♐16.5	27♌00.2	14♌04.4	10♐24.6	11♓07.3	27♑19.1	23♑45.1	0♐19.7
2 Th	20 48 51	13 10 22	9♓02 15	15 43 59	9R38.0	16R23.7	27 23.2	26R38.4	13R50.3	10 33.9	11 14.1	27 22.5	23 47.3	0 20.8
3 F	20 52 48	14 11 16	22 19 34	28 49 03	9 30.0	15 12.6	28 30.0	26 16.2	13 36.1	10 43.0	11 20.9	27 26.0	23 49.4	0 21.8
4 Sa	20 56 44	15 12 08	5♈12 37	11♈30 36	9 24.9	13 59.4	29 37.1	25 53.6	13 21.9	10 52.1	11 27.8	27 29.4	23 51.6	0 22.8
5 Su	21 00 41	16 12 59	17 43 26	23 51 37	9 22.3	12 46.4	0♑44.3	25 30.7	13 07.7	11 01.0	11 34.6	27 32.8	23 53.7	0 23.7
6 M	21 04 37	17 13 48	29 55 44	5♉56 25	9D21.6	11 35.3	1 51.7	25 07.5	12 53.6	11 09.8	11 41.6	27 36.2	23 55.9	0 24.7
7 Tu	21 08 34	18 14 36	11♉54 21	17 50 13	9R21.6	10 28.1	2 59.2	24 44.0	12 39.6	11 18.4	11 48.5	27 39.6	23 58.0	0 25.5
8 W	21 12 30	19 15 23	23 44 43	29 38 35	9 21.2	9 26.1	4 06.9	24 20.4	12 25.6	11 27.0	11 55.5	27 43.0	24 00.1	0 26.4
9 Th	21 16 27	20 16 08	5♊32 29	11♊27 06	9 19.3	8 30.5	5 14.8	23 56.6	12 11.7	11 35.4	12 02.5	27 46.3	24 02.2	0 27.2
10 F	21 20 24	21 16 51	17 23 04	23 20 59	9 15.2	7 42.2	6 22.9	23 32.7	11 57.9	11 43.7	12 09.5	27 49.6	24 04.3	0 28.0
11 Sa	21 24 20	22 17 33	29 21 23	5♋24 45	9 08.3	7 01.6	7 31.0	23 08.8	11 44.3	11 51.9	12 16.6	27 53.0	24 06.4	0 28.7
12 Su	21 28 17	23 18 14	11♋31 32	17 42 03	8 58.8	6 29.0	8 39.4	22 44.8	11 30.8	11 59.9	12 23.7	27 56.3	24 08.4	0 29.5
13 M	21 32 13	24 18 53	23 56 34	0♌15 16	8 47.2	6 04.5	9 47.8	22 20.9	11 17.4	12 07.8	12 30.8	27 59.5	24 10.4	0 30.1
14 Tu	21 36 10	25 19 30	6♌38 14	13 05 27	8 34.4	5 48.0	10 56.4	21 57.0	11 04.3	12 15.6	12 37.9	28 02.8	24 12.5	0 30.8
15 W	21 40 06	26 20 06	19 36 51	26 12 15	8 21.6	5D39.1	12 05.2	21 33.3	10 51.4	12 23.3	12 45.1	28 06.0	24 14.5	0 31.4
16 Th	21 44 03	27 20 40	2♍51 26	9♍34 07	8 10.1	5 37.6	13 14.1	21 09.7	10 38.6	12 30.8	12 52.3	28 09.2	24 16.5	0 32.0
17 F	21 47 59	28 21 13	16 19 59	23 08 40	8 00.8	5 43.0	14 23.1	20 46.4	10 26.1	12 38.1	12 59.5	28 12.4	24 18.4	0 32.5
18 Sa	21 51 56	29 21 44	29 59 51	6♎53 12	7 54.4	5 54.9	15 32.2	20 23.2	10 13.9	12 45.4	13 06.7	28 15.6	24 20.4	0 33.0
19 Su	21 55 52	0♓22 14	13♎48 23	20 45 09	7 50.8	6 13.0	16 41.4	20 00.4	10 01.9	12 52.5	13 13.9	28 18.7	24 22.3	0 33.5
20 M	21 59 49	1 22 43	27 43 17	4♏42 34	7D49.6	6 36.7	17 50.8	19 37.9	9 50.1	12 59.4	13 21.2	28 21.8	24 24.3	0 33.9
21 Tu	22 03 46	2 23 10	11♏42 52	18 44 05	7 49.8	7 05.7	19 00.3	19 15.8	9 38.7	13 06.2	13 28.4	28 24.9	24 26.2	0 34.3
22 W	22 07 42	3 23 37	25 46 05	2♐48 49	7R50.2	7 39.6	20 09.9	18 54.0	9 27.6	13 12.9	13 35.7	28 28.0	24 28.0	0 34.6
23 Th	22 11 39	4 24 02	9♐52 09	16 56 00	7 49.6	8 17.9	21 19.6	18 32.8	9 16.7	13 19.4	13 43.0	28 31.1	24 29.9	0 35.0
24 F	22 15 35	5 24 25	24 00 11	1♑04 29	7 46.9	9 00.4	22 29.4	18 11.9	9 06.2	13 25.8	13 50.3	28 34.1	24 31.7	0 35.3
25 Sa	22 19 32	6 24 48	8♑08 40	15 12 23	7 41.7	9 46.8	23 39.3	17 51.7	8 56.1	13 32.0	13 57.7	28 37.1	24 33.6	0 35.5
26 Su	22 23 28	7 25 09	22 15 16	29 16 52	7 34.0	10 36.7	24 49.3	17 31.9	8 46.2	13 38.0	14 05.0	28 40.0	24 35.4	0 35.7
27 M	22 27 25	8 25 28	6♒16 43	13♒14 18	7 24.6	11 29.9	25 59.4	17 12.7	8 36.8	13 43.9	14 12.3	28 43.0	24 37.2	0 35.9
28 Tu	22 31 21	9 25 45	20 09 08	27 00 42	7 14.3	12 26.1	27 09.6	16 54.2	8 27.7	13 49.7	14 19.7	28 45.9	24 38.9	0 36.1

Astro Data

	Dy Hr Mn
♂ R	2 21:27
☽ 0N	6 11:25
♃∠♆	19 16:20
☽ 0S	21 1:55
☿ R	26 1:13
☽ 0N	2 22:07
☿ D	16 5:06
☽ 0S	17 9:07
♄∠♅	20 15:55
♃∠♅	27 4:13

Planet Ingress

	Dy Hr Mn
☿ ♒	6 22:17
♀ ♐	7 12:07
♇ ♐	17 9:16
☉ ♒	20 13:00
♂ ♌R	22 23:48
♀ ♑	4 20:12
☉ ♓	19 3:11

Last Aspect / ☽ Ingress (January)

Last Aspect Dy Hr Mn		☽ Ingress Dy Hr Mn
2 17:57	♇ ⚹	♒ 2 18:39
4 21:11	♇ □	♓ 4 21:49
7 4:24	♇ △	♈ 7 4:56
9 7:50	♅ □	♉ 9 15:58
12 4:40	♇ ☍	♊ 12 4:57
13 0:01	☿ △	♋ 14 17:20
17 3:36	♇ △	♌ 17 3:36
18 10:47	☿ ☍	♍ 19 11:39
21 11:58	♅ △	♎ 21 17:53
23 22:06	♂ ⚹	♏ 23 22:32
26 0:11	♂ □	♐ 26 1:37
28 1:00	♂ △	♑ 28 3:26
30 0:21	♅ ☌	♒ 30 5:03

Last Aspect / ☽ Ingress (February)

Last Aspect Dy Hr Mn		☽ Ingress Dy Hr Mn
1 3:06	♂ ☍	♓ 1 8:05
3 11:21	♀ □	♈ 3 14:12
5 19:19	♅ □	♉ 6 0:08
8 8:04	♅ △	♊ 8 12:44
10 12:23	♂ ⚹	♋ 11 1:17
13 7:42	♅ ☍	♌ 13 11:31
15 12:15	☉ ☍	♍ 15 18:52
17 20:54	♅ △	♎ 18 0:00
20 1:04	♅ □	♏ 20 3:55
22 4:34	♅ ⚹	♐ 22 7:13
23 14:40	♂ △	♑ 24 10:11
26 10:57	♅ ☌	♒ 26 13:14
27 18:44	♂ ☍	♓ 28 17:16

☽ Phases & Eclipses

Dy Hr Mn	
1 10:56	● 10♑33
8 15:46	☽ 17♈54
16 20:26	○ 26♋15
24 4:58	☾ 3♏44
30 22:48	● 10♒35
7 12:54	☽ 18♉17
15 12:15	○ 26♌21
22 13:04	☾ 3♐26

Astro Data

1 January 1995
Julian Day # 34699
SVP 5♓19'34"
GC 26♐46.2 ⚴ 6♉00.5
Eris 17♈25.3R ⚵ 10♐51.1
⚷ 26♍21.9 ⚶ 1♋05.4R
☽ Mean ☊ 11♏44.4

1 February 1995
Julian Day # 34730
SVP 5♓19'29"
GC 26♐46.2 ⚴ 12♉32.2
Eris 17♈29.3 ⚵ 20♐24.6
⚷ 25♍58.5R ⚶ 25♊30.6R
☽ Mean ☊ 10♏05.9

March 1995 LONGITUDE

Day	Sid.Time	☉	0 hr ☽	Noon ☽	True ☊	☿	♀	♂	⚳	♃	♄	♅	♆	♇
1 W	22 35 18	10♓26 01	3♓48 34	10♓32 19	7♏04.4	13♒25.2	28♑19.8	16♌36.3	8♌19.0	13♐55.3	14♓27.1	28♑48.8	24♑40.6	0♐36.2
2 Th	22 39 15	11 26 15	17 11 40	23 46 22	6R 55.8	14 26.9	29 30.2	16R 19.0	8R 10.6	14 00.7	14 34.4	28 51.6	24 42.4	0 36.3
3 F	22 43 11	12 26 27	0♈16 17	6♈41 24	6 49.3	15 31.1	0♒40.6	16 02.4	8 02.7	14 05.9	14 41.8	28 54.4	24 44.0	0R 36.3
4 Sa	22 47 08	13 26 38	13 01 45	19 17 32	6 45.3	16 37.6	1 51.0	15 46.5	7 55.1	14 11.0	14 49.1	28 57.2	24 45.7	0 36.3
5 Su	22 51 04	14 26 46	25 29 01	1♉36 30	6D 43.6	17 46.3	3 01.6	15 31.4	7 48.0	14 16.0	14 56.5	28 59.9	24 47.4	0 36.3
6 M	22 55 01	15 26 52	7♉40 27	13 41 20	6 43.7	18 57.0	4 12.2	15 17.0	7 41.3	14 20.7	15 03.9	29 02.7	24 49.0	0 36.2
7 Tu	22 58 57	16 26 57	19 39 41	25 36 06	6 44.8	20 09.7	5 22.9	15 03.3	7 35.0	14 25.3	15 11.3	29 05.3	24 50.6	0 36.1
8 W	23 02 54	17 26 59	1♊31 11	7♊25 37	6R 46.0	21 24.2	6 33.7	14 50.4	7 29.1	14 29.8	15 18.6	29 08.0	24 52.1	0 36.0
9 Th	23 06 50	18 26 59	13 20 01	19 15 05	6 46.6	22 40.5	7 44.5	14 38.3	7 23.7	14 34.0	15 26.0	29 10.6	24 53.7	0 35.8
10 F	23 10 47	19 26 57	25 11 27	1♋09 48	6 45.6	23 58.5	8 55.4	14 26.9	7 18.7	14 38.1	15 33.4	29 13.2	24 55.2	0 35.6
11 Sa	23 14 44	20 26 52	7♋10 44	13 14 51	6 42.8	25 18.1	10 06.3	14 16.3	7 14.1	14 42.1	15 40.7	29 15.7	24 56.7	0 35.4
12 Su	23 18 40	21 26 46	19 22 41	25 34 43	6 38.2	26 39.2	11 17.3	14 06.6	7 09.9	14 45.8	15 48.1	29 18.2	24 58.1	0 35.1
13 M	23 22 37	22 26 37	1♌51 23	8♌13 00	6 31.9	28 01.9	12 28.4	13 57.6	7 06.2	14 49.4	15 55.4	29 20.7	24 59.6	0 34.8
14 Tu	23 26 33	23 26 26	14 39 49	21 11 57	6 24.6	29 26.0	13 39.5	13 49.3	7 02.9	14 52.8	16 02.7	29 23.1	25 01.0	0 34.4
15 W	23 30 30	24 26 13	27 49 27	4♍32 12	6 17.2	0♓51.6	14 50.6	13 41.9	7 00.1	14 56.0	16 10.1	29 25.5	25 02.4	0 34.1
16 Th	23 34 26	25 25 58	11♍20 01	18 12 36	6 10.4	2 18.5	16 01.9	13 35.3	6 57.7	14 59.1	16 17.4	29 27.9	25 03.7	0 33.7
17 F	23 38 23	26 25 41	25 09 32	2♎10 20	6 05.1	3 46.8	17 13.1	13 29.4	6 55.7	15 01.9	16 24.7	29 30.2	25 05.1	0 33.2
18 Sa	23 42 19	27 25 22	9♎14 27	16 21 16	6 01.6	5 16.5	18 24.5	13 24.4	6 54.1	15 04.6	16 32.0	29 32.5	25 06.4	0 32.7
19 Su	23 46 16	28 25 01	23 30 11	0♏40 36	6D 00.1	6 47.5	19 35.9	13 20.1	6 53.0	15 07.1	16 39.2	29 34.7	25 07.6	0 32.2
20 M	23 50 13	29 24 38	7♏51 53	15 03 30	6 00.3	8 19.9	20 47.3	13 16.5	6 52.3	15 09.5	16 46.5	29 36.9	25 08.9	0 31.7
21 Tu	23 54 09	0♈24 14	22 14 57	29 25 45	6 01.5	9 53.5	21 58.8	13 13.7	6D 52.1	15 11.6	16 53.8	29 39.1	25 10.1	0 31.1
22 W	23 58 06	1 23 48	6♐35 32	13♐43 57	6 02.9	11 28.5	23 10.3	13 11.7	6 52.3	15 13.6	17 01.0	29 41.2	25 11.3	0 30.5
23 Th	0 02 02	2 23 20	20 50 44	27 55 39	6R 03.9	13 04.8	24 21.9	13 10.5	6 52.9	15 15.4	17 08.2	29 43.3	25 12.4	0 29.9
24 F	0 05 59	3 22 50	4♑58 30	11♑59 08	6 03.6	14 42.4	25 33.5	13D 09.9	6 53.9	15 17.0	17 15.4	29 45.3	25 13.6	0 29.2
25 Sa	0 09 55	4 22 19	18 57 24	25 53 10	6 02.0	16 21.3	26 45.2	13 10.1	6 55.4	15 18.4	17 22.6	29 47.3	25 14.7	0 28.5
26 Su	0 13 52	5 21 46	2♒46 18	9♒36 41	5 58.9	18 01.5	27 56.9	13 11.1	6 57.2	15 19.6	17 29.7	29 49.2	25 15.7	0 27.8
27 M	0 17 48	6 21 11	16 24 11	23 08 41	5 54.7	19 43.1	29 08.7	13 12.7	6 59.5	15 20.7	17 36.8	29 51.1	25 16.8	0 27.1
28 Tu	0 21 45	7 20 34	29 50 02	6♓28 08	5 50.1	21 25.9	0♓20.4	13 15.1	7 02.2	15 21.5	17 44.0	29 53.0	25 17.8	0 26.3
29 W	0 25 41	8 19 55	13♓02 52	19 34 08	5 45.5	23 10.2	1 32.3	13 18.1	7 05.3	15 22.2	17 51.0	29 54.8	25 18.8	0 25.5
30 Th	0 29 38	9 19 14	26 01 51	2♈26 00	5 41.7	24 55.7	2 44.1	13 21.9	7 08.9	15 22.6	17 58.1	29 56.6	25 19.7	0 24.6
31 F	0 33 35	10 18 32	8♈46 35	15 03 36	5 38.9	26 42.7	3 56.0	13 26.3	7 12.8	15 22.9	18 05.1	29 58.3	25 20.6	0 23.7

April 1995 LONGITUDE

Day	Sid.Time	☉	0 hr ☽	Noon ☽	True ☊	☿	♀	♂	⚳	♃	♄	♅	♆	♇
1 Sa	0 37 31	11♈17 47	21♈17 10	27♈27 25	5♏37.5	28♓31.0	5♓07.9	13♌31.4	7♌17.2	15♐23.0	18♓12.1	29♑60.0	25♑21.5	0♐22.8
2 Su	0 41 28	12 17 00	3♉34 31	9♉38 43	5D 37.3	0♈20.7	6 19.9	13 37.2	7 21.9	15R 22.9	18 19.1	0♒01.6	25 22.3	0R 21.9
3 M	0 45 24	13 16 11	15 40 17	21 39 35	5 38.1	2 11.8	7 31.8	13 43.6	7 27.0	15 22.6	18 26.0	0 03.2	25 23.2	0 20.9
4 Tu	0 49 21	14 15 20	27 36 59	3♊32 56	5 39.6	4 04.3	8 43.8	13 50.7	7 32.6	15 22.2	18 32.9	0 04.8	25 23.9	0 19.9
5 W	0 53 17	15 14 26	9♊27 53	15 22 21	5 41.2	5 58.2	9 55.9	13 58.4	7 38.5	15 21.5	18 39.8	0 06.3	25 24.7	0 18.9
6 Th	0 57 14	16 13 31	21 16 52	27 12 01	5 42.7	7 53.5	11 07.9	14 06.7	7 44.8	15 20.7	18 46.7	0 07.7	25 25.4	0 17.9
7 F	1 01 10	17 12 33	3♋08 22	9♋06 31	5R 43.7	9 50.2	12 20.0	14 15.6	7 51.4	15 19.6	18 53.5	0 09.1	25 26.1	0 16.8
8 Sa	1 05 07	18 11 33	15 07 05	21 10 39	5 43.9	11 48.3	13 32.1	14 25.1	7 58.5	15 18.4	19 00.2	0 10.5	25 26.8	0 15.7
9 Su	1 09 04	19 10 30	27 17 50	3♌29 09	5 43.2	13 47.7	14 44.2	14 35.1	8 05.9	15 17.0	19 07.0	0 11.8	25 27.4	0 14.6
10 M	1 13 00	20 09 25	9♌45 09	16 06 19	5 42.0	15 48.3	15 56.3	14 45.8	8 13.6	15 15.4	19 13.7	0 13.0	25 28.0	0 13.5
11 Tu	1 16 57	21 08 18	22 33 01	29 05 37	5 40.2	17 50.2	17 08.5	14 57.0	8 21.7	15 13.7	19 20.3	0 14.2	25 28.5	0 12.3
12 W	1 20 53	22 07 09	5♍44 18	12♍29 12	5 38.3	19 53.3	18 20.7	15 08.7	8 30.2	15 11.7	19 27.0	0 15.4	25 29.1	0 11.1
13 Th	1 24 50	23 05 57	19 20 18	26 17 27	5 36.6	21 57.4	19 32.9	15 21.0	8 39.0	15 09.6	19 33.5	0 16.5	25 29.6	0 09.9
14 F	1 28 46	24 04 43	3♎20 22	10♎28 37	5 35.4	24 02.5	20 45.1	15 33.8	8 48.2	15 07.2	19 40.1	0 17.6	25 30.0	0 08.7
15 Sa	1 32 43	25 03 27	17 41 40	24 58 47	5D 34.7	26 08.3	21 57.4	15 47.0	8 57.6	15 04.7	19 46.6	0 18.6	25 30.4	0 07.4
16 Su	1 36 39	26 02 10	2♏19 14	9♏42 08	5 34.6	28 14.8	23 09.7	16 00.8	9 07.4	15 02.1	19 53.0	0 19.6	25 30.8	0 06.2
17 M	1 40 36	27 00 50	17 06 34	24 31 38	5 34.9	0♉21.7	24 22.0	16 15.1	9 17.6	14 59.2	19 59.4	0 20.5	25 31.2	0 04.9
18 Tu	1 44 33	27 59 29	1♐56 23	9♐20 00	5 35.5	2 28.8	25 34.3	16 29.8	9 28.0	14 56.2	20 05.8	0 21.3	25 31.5	0 03.5
19 W	1 48 29	28 58 06	16 41 38	24 00 36	5 36.1	4 35.8	26 46.6	16 45.0	9 38.8	14 53.0	20 12.1	0 22.2	25 31.8	0 02.2
20 Th	1 52 26	29 56 41	1♑16 18	8♑28 14	5 36.6	6 42.5	27 59.0	17 00.7	9 49.9	14 49.6	20 18.4	0 22.9	25 32.1	0 00.9
21 F	1 56 22	0♉55 15	15 36 00	22 39 21	5R 36.9	8 48.6	29 11.4	17 16.8	10 01.2	14 46.1	20 24.6	0 23.7	25 32.3	29♏59.5
22 Sa	2 00 19	1 53 47	29 38 07	6♒32 12	5 36.9	10 53.7	0♈23.8	17 33.3	10 12.9	14 42.4	20 30.7	0 24.3	25 32.5	29 58.1
23 Su	2 04 15	2 52 17	13♒21 37	20 06 25	5 36.8	12 57.6	1 36.2	17 50.3	10 24.9	14 38.5	20 36.9	0 25.0	25 32.7	29 56.7
24 M	2 08 12	3 50 46	26 46 43	3♓22 41	5 36.6	14 59.9	2 48.7	18 07.7	10 37.1	14 34.4	20 42.9	0 25.5	25 32.8	29 55.2
25 Tu	2 12 08	4 49 13	9♓54 28	16 22 18	5D 36.5	17 00.2	4 01.1	18 25.5	10 49.7	14 30.2	20 48.9	0 26.0	25 32.9	29 53.8
26 W	2 16 05	5 47 38	22 46 22	29 06 52	5 36.5	18 58.4	5 13.6	18 43.7	11 02.5	14 25.8	20 54.9	0 26.5	25 33.0	29 52.3
27 Th	2 20 02	6 46 02	5♈24 03	11♈38 06	5 36.5	20 54.0	6 26.1	19 02.4	11 15.6	14 21.3	21 00.8	0 26.9	25R 33.0	29 50.9
28 F	2 23 58	7 44 24	17 49 14	23 57 40	5R 36.6	22 47.0	7 38.6	19 21.4	11 29.0	14 16.6	21 06.7	0 27.3	25 33.0	29 49.4
29 Sa	2 27 55	8 42 45	0♉03 35	6♉07 14	5 36.7	24 36.9	8 51.1	19 40.7	11 42.7	14 11.7	21 12.4	0 27.6	25 33.0	29 47.8
30 Su	2 31 51	9 41 03	12 08 48	18 08 31	5 36.6	26 23.6	10 03.7	20 00.5	11 56.6	14 06.7	21 18.2	0 27.9	25 32.9	29 46.3

Astro Data	Dy Hr Mn
☽0N	2 8:00
♇R	4 2:34
☽0S	16 17:51
⊙0N	21 2:14
⚳D	21 13:59
♂D	24 17:18
☽0N	29 15:40
♃R	1 12:03
☿0N	4 16:32
♅✶♇	10 16:39
♃∠♅	11 7:23
☽0S	13 3:41
♀0N	25 4:46
☽0N	25 21:29
♆R	27 22:14

Planet Ingress		Dy Hr Mn
♀	♒	2 22:10
☿	♓	14 21:35
⊙	♈	21 2:14
♀	♓	28 5:10
♅	♒	1 12:11
☿	♈	2 7:29
☿	♉	17 7:54
⊙	♉	20 13:21
♇	♏R	21 2:56
♀	♈	22 4:07

Last Aspect Dy Hr Mn			☽ Ingress	Dy Hr Mn
2 21:25	♅	✶	♈	2 23:30
5 6:51	♅	□	♉	5 8:50
7 19:06	♅	△	♊	7 20:55
9 19:46	☿	△	♋	10 9:40
12 19:10	♅	☍	♌	12 20:28
14 0:21	♃	△	♍	15 3:54
17 7:26	♅	△	♎	17 8:18
19 10:10	♅	□	♏	19 10:52
21 12:22	♅	✶	♐	21 12:57
23 5:24	♀	✶	♑	23 15:31
25 18:48	♅	☌	♒	25 19:10
27 23:49	♀	☌	♓	28 0:18
30 7:19	♅	✶	♈	30 7:26

Last Aspect Dy Hr Mn			☽ Ingress	Dy Hr Mn
1 7:54	♆	□	♉	1 16:59
3 19:31	♆	△	♊	4 4:49
5 18:45	♄	□	♋	6 17:40
8 20:23	♆	☍	♌	9 5:16
10 20:11	⊙	△	♍	11 13:39
13 10:38	♆	△	♎	13 18:20
15 14:13	☿	☍	♏	15 20:13
17 13:36	♆	✶	♐	17 20:51
19 20:46	⊙	△	♑	19 21:53
22 0:36	♇	✶	♒	22 0:38
24 5:43	♇	□	♓	24 5:50
26 13:26	♇	△	♈	26 13:41
28 15:07	♆	□	♉	28 23:53

☽ Phases & Eclipses Dy Hr Mn	
1 11:48	● 10♓26
9 10:14	☽ 18♊23
17 1:26	○ 25♍59
23 20:10	☾ 2♑44
31 2:09	● 9♈54
8 5:35	☽ 17♋56
15 12:08	○ 25♎04
15 12:18	P 0.111
22 3:18	☾ 1♒33
29 17:36	● 8♉56
29 17:32:20	A 06'37"

Astro Data

1 March 1995
Julian Day # 34758
SVP 5♓19'26"
GC 26♐46.3 ⚴ 23♉50.8
Eris 17♈41.1 ⚵ 27♐39.5
⚷ 24♍16.5R ⚶ 26♊14.1
☽ Mean ☊ 8♏37.0

1 April 1995
Julian Day # 34789
SVP 5♓19'24"
GC 26♐46.4 ⚴ 9♊37.9
Eris 18♈00.0 ⚵ 3♑05.0
⚷ 21♍52.5R ⚶ 2♋30.5
☽ Mean ☊ 6♏58.4

LONGITUDE — May 1995

Day	Sid.Time	☉	0 hr ☽	Noon ☽	True ☊	☿	♀	♂	⚳	♃	♄	♅	♆	♇
1 M	2 35 48	10♉39 20	24♉06 39	0♊03 26	5♏36.2	28♉06.9	11♈16.2	20♌20.6	12♌10.8	14♐01.6	21♓23.9	0♒28.1	25♑32.8	29♏44.8
2 Tu	2 39 44	11 37 35	5♊59 09	11 54 07	5R 35.6	29 46.6	12 28.8	20 41.1	12 25.2	13R 56.3	21 29.5	0 28.3	25R 32.7	29R 43.2
3 W	2 43 41	12 35 48	17 48 40	23 43 08	5 34.7	1♊22.6	13 41.3	21 02.0	12 39.9	13 50.9	21 35.0	0 28.4	25 32.5	29 41.7
4 Th	2 47 37	13 33 59	29 37 56	5♋33 28	5 33.7	2 54.8	14 53.9	21 23.2	12 54.9	13 45.3	21 40.5	0R 28.4	25 32.3	29 40.1
5 F	2 51 34	14 32 09	11♋30 10	17 28 32	5 32.6	4 23.1	16 06.5	21 44.7	13 10.1	13 39.6	21 45.9	0 28.5	25 32.1	29 38.5
6 Sa	2 55 31	15 30 16	23 29 03	29 32 14	5 31.8	5 47.4	17 19.1	22 06.5	13 25.5	13 33.8	21 51.3	0 28.4	25 31.8	29 37.0
7 Su	2 59 27	16 28 21	5♌38 36	11♌48 42	5D 31.4	7 07.5	18 31.7	22 28.7	13 41.1	13 27.8	21 56.6	0 28.3	25 31.5	29 35.4
8 M	3 03 24	17 26 25	18 03 03	24 22 11	5 31.4	8 23.5	19 44.3	22 51.2	13 57.0	13 21.7	22 01.8	0 28.2	25 31.2	29 33.8
9 Tu	3 07 20	18 24 26	0♍46 35	7♍16 41	5 32.0	9 35.2	20 56.9	23 14.0	14 13.1	13 15.5	22 07.0	0 28.0	25 30.9	29 32.1
10 W	3 11 17	19 22 26	13 52 54	20 35 32	5 33.0	10 42.6	22 09.6	23 37.1	14 29.5	13 09.2	22 12.1	0 27.8	25 30.5	29 30.5
11 Th	3 15 13	20 20 24	27 24 47	4♎20 45	5 34.1	11 45.7	23 22.2	24 00.5	14 46.0	13 02.8	22 17.1	0 27.5	25 30.0	29 28.9
12 F	3 19 10	21 18 19	11♎23 23	18 32 29	5 35.1	12 44.3	24 34.8	24 24.1	15 02.8	12 56.3	22 22.1	0 27.2	25 29.6	29 27.2
13 Sa	3 23 06	22 16 14	25 47 42	3♏08 28	5R 35.6	13 38.4	25 47.5	24 48.1	15 19.8	12 49.7	22 27.0	0 26.8	25 29.1	29 25.6
14 Su	3 27 03	23 14 06	10♏34 04	18 03 38	5 35.3	14 27.9	27 00.2	25 12.3	15 36.9	12 43.0	22 31.8	0 26.4	25 28.6	29 24.0
15 M	3 30 59	24 11 58	25 36 09	3♐10 29	5 34.1	15 12.8	28 12.9	25 36.8	15 54.3	12 36.1	22 36.5	0 25.9	25 28.1	29 22.3
16 Tu	3 34 56	25 09 47	10♐45 27	18 19 51	5 32.1	15 53.0	29 25.6	26 01.5	16 11.9	12 29.3	22 41.2	0 25.4	25 27.5	29 20.7
17 W	3 38 53	26 07 36	25 52 28	3♑22 14	5 29.5	16 28.4	0♉38.3	26 26.5	16 29.6	12 22.3	22 45.8	0 24.8	25 26.9	29 19.0
18 Th	3 42 49	27 05 23	10♑48 07	18 09 18	5 26.9	16 59.1	1 51.0	26 51.8	16 47.6	12 15.2	22 50.3	0 24.2	25 26.3	29 17.4
19 F	3 46 46	28 03 09	25 25 04	2♒34 57	5 24.6	17 25.0	3 03.8	27 17.3	17 05.7	12 08.1	22 54.8	0 23.5	25 25.6	29 15.7
20 Sa	3 50 42	29 00 54	9♒38 35	16 35 50	5D 23.1	17 46.0	4 16.5	27 43.1	17 24.1	12 00.9	22 59.2	0 22.8	25 24.9	29 14.0
21 Su	3 54 39	29 58 38	23 26 40	0♓11 14	5 22.6	18 02.1	5 29.3	28 09.0	17 42.6	11 53.6	23 03.5	0 22.1	25 24.2	29 12.4
22 M	3 58 35	0♊56 20	6♓49 43	13 22 28	5 23.1	18 13.4	6 42.1	28 35.3	18 01.3	11 46.3	23 07.7	0 21.3	25 23.5	29 10.7
23 Tu	4 02 32	1 54 02	19 49 50	26 12 15	5 24.4	18R 19.9	7 54.8	29 01.7	18 20.1	11 38.9	23 11.8	0 20.4	25 22.7	29 09.1
24 W	4 06 28	2 51 43	2♈30 08	8♈43 58	5 26.0	18 21.7	9 07.6	29 28.4	18 39.2	11 31.4	23 15.9	0 19.5	25 21.9	29 07.4
25 Th	4 10 25	3 49 22	14 54 12	21 01 15	5 27.5	18 18.8	10 20.5	29 55.3	18 58.4	11 23.9	23 19.9	0 18.6	25 21.1	29 05.8
26 F	4 14 22	4 47 01	27 05 33	3♉07 31	5R 28.2	18 11.5	11 33.3	0♍22.5	19 17.8	11 16.4	23 23.8	0 17.6	25 20.2	29 04.1
27 Sa	4 18 18	5 44 38	9♉07 29	15 05 50	5 27.8	17 59.8	12 46.1	0 49.8	19 37.3	11 08.9	23 27.6	0 16.5	25 19.3	29 02.5
28 Su	4 22 15	6 42 15	21 02 53	26 58 55	5 25.9	17 44.1	13 59.0	1 17.4	19 57.0	11 01.3	23 31.3	0 15.5	25 18.4	29 00.8
29 M	4 26 11	7 39 50	2♊54 13	8♊49 02	5 22.5	17 24.7	15 11.8	1 45.1	20 16.9	10 53.7	23 35.0	0 14.3	25 17.5	28 59.2
30 Tu	4 30 08	8 37 24	14 43 38	20 38 15	5 17.6	17 01.8	16 24.7	2 13.1	20 36.9	10 46.0	23 38.5	0 13.2	25 16.5	28 57.5
31 W	4 34 04	9 34 57	26 33 08	2♋28 31	5 11.7	16 36.0	17 37.6	2 41.3	20 57.1	10 38.4	23 42.0	0 12.0	25 15.5	28 55.9

LONGITUDE — June 1995

Day	Sid.Time	☉	0 hr ☽	Noon ☽	True ☊	☿	♀	♂	⚳	♃	♄	♅	♆	♇
1 Th	4 38 01	10♊32 29	8♋24 40	14♋21 51	5♏05.4	16♊07.5	18♉50.5	3♍09.7	21♌17.4	10♐30.7	23♓45.4	0♒10.7	25♑14.5	28♏54.3
2 F	4 41 58	11 30 00	20 20 21	26 20 30	4R 59.3	15R 37.0	20 03.4	3 38.3	21 37.9	10R 23.1	23 48.7	0R 09.5	25R 13.5	28R 52.7
3 Sa	4 45 54	12 27 29	2♌22 38	8♌27 08	4 54.0	15 04.9	21 16.3	4 07.1	21 58.5	10 15.5	23 51.9	0 08.1	25 12.4	28 51.1
4 Su	4 49 51	13 24 58	14 34 22	20 44 47	4 50.1	14 31.8	22 29.2	4 36.0	22 19.2	10 07.8	23 55.0	0 06.8	25 11.3	28 49.5
5 M	4 53 47	14 22 25	26 58 49	3♍16 55	4D 47.8	13 58.3	23 42.1	5 05.2	22 40.1	10 00.2	23 58.1	0 05.3	25 10.2	28 47.9
6 Tu	4 57 44	15 19 50	9♍39 33	16 07 11	4 47.2	13 24.9	24 55.1	5 34.5	23 01.2	9 52.6	24 01.0	0 03.9	25 09.1	28 46.3
7 W	5 01 40	16 17 15	22 40 16	29 19 11	4 47.8	12 52.2	26 08.0	6 04.0	23 22.3	9 45.0	24 03.9	0 02.4	25 08.0	28 44.7
8 Th	5 05 37	17 14 38	6♎04 18	12♎55 53	4 49.1	12 20.7	27 21.0	6 33.7	23 43.6	9 37.5	24 06.6	0 00.9	25 06.8	28 43.2
9 F	5 09 33	18 12 01	19 54 07	26 59 01	4R 50.2	11 51.1	28 33.9	7 03.5	24 05.0	9 30.0	24 09.3	29♑59.3	25 05.6	28 41.6
10 Sa	5 13 30	19 09 22	4♏10 29	11♏28 13	4 50.2	11 23.8	29 46.9	7 33.5	24 26.6	9 22.5	24 11.9	29 57.7	25 04.4	28 40.1
11 Su	5 17 27	20 06 42	18 51 45	26 20 24	4 48.5	10 59.2	0♊59.9	8 03.7	24 48.2	9 15.1	24 14.4	29 56.1	25 03.1	28 38.6
12 M	5 21 23	21 04 02	3♐53 16	11♐29 18	4 44.9	10 37.8	2 12.9	8 34.1	25 10.0	9 07.8	24 16.8	29 54.4	25 01.9	28 37.1
13 Tu	5 25 20	22 01 20	19 07 17	26 45 54	4 39.4	10 19.9	3 25.9	9 04.6	25 31.9	9 00.5	24 19.1	29 52.7	25 00.6	28 35.6
14 W	5 29 16	22 58 38	4♑23 48	11♑59 37	4 32.6	10 05.9	4 38.9	9 35.2	25 54.0	8 53.2	24 21.3	29 51.0	24 59.3	28 34.1
15 Th	5 33 13	23 55 56	19 32 03	26 59 58	4 25.4	9 55.9	5 52.0	10 06.0	26 16.1	8 46.0	24 23.4	29 49.2	24 58.0	28 32.7
16 F	5 37 09	24 53 13	4♒22 22	11♒39 28	4 18.8	9D 50.2	7 05.0	10 37.0	26 38.3	8 38.9	24 25.4	29 47.4	24 56.7	28 31.2
17 Sa	5 41 06	25 50 30	18 47 43	25 49 45	4 13.5	9 48.9	8 18.1	11 08.1	27 00.7	8 31.9	24 27.3	29 45.6	24 55.3	28 29.8
18 Su	5 45 02	26 47 46	2♓44 25	9♓31 46	4 10.1	9 52.1	9 31.2	11 39.3	27 23.2	8 24.9	24 29.2	29 43.7	24 54.0	28 28.4
19 M	5 48 59	27 45 02	16 12 01	22 45 29	4D 08.7	9 59.9	10 44.3	12 10.7	27 45.7	8 18.1	24 30.9	29 41.8	24 52.6	28 27.0
20 Tu	5 52 56	28 42 17	29 12 36	5♈33 53	4 08.7	10 12.4	11 57.4	12 42.3	28 08.4	8 11.3	24 32.5	29 39.9	24 51.2	28 25.6
21 W	5 56 52	29 39 33	11♈49 55	18 01 16	4 09.6	10 29.5	13 10.6	13 14.0	28 31.2	8 04.6	24 34.1	29 38.0	24 49.7	28 24.3
22 Th	6 00 49	0♋36 48	24 08 33	0♉12 23	4R 10.4	10 51.3	14 23.8	13 45.8	28 54.1	7 58.0	24 35.5	29 36.0	24 48.3	28 22.9
23 F	6 04 45	1 34 03	6♉13 19	12 11 57	4 10.1	11 17.7	15 36.9	14 17.8	29 17.1	7 51.5	24 36.8	29 34.0	24 46.9	28 21.6
24 Sa	6 08 42	2 31 18	18 08 46	24 04 18	4 08.0	11 48.7	16 50.1	14 49.9	29 40.2	7 45.1	24 38.1	29 31.9	24 45.4	28 20.3
25 Su	6 12 38	3 28 33	29 58 58	5♊53 12	4 03.6	12 24.2	18 03.4	15 22.1	0♍03.3	7 38.8	24 39.2	29 29.9	24 43.9	28 19.0
26 M	6 16 35	4 25 48	11♊47 20	17 41 42	3 56.6	13 04.1	19 16.6	15 54.5	0 26.6	7 32.7	24 40.3	29 27.8	24 42.5	28 17.8
27 Tu	6 20 31	5 23 02	23 36 35	29 32 14	3 47.4	13 48.5	20 29.8	16 27.1	0 50.0	7 26.6	24 41.2	29 25.7	24 41.0	28 16.5
28 W	6 24 28	6 20 17	5♋28 52	11♋26 41	3 36.5	14 37.2	21 43.1	16 59.7	1 13.5	7 20.7	24 42.0	29 23.6	24 39.4	28 15.3
29 Th	6 28 25	7 17 31	17 25 51	23 26 33	3 24.8	15 30.2	22 56.4	17 32.5	1 37.0	7 14.9	24 42.8	29 21.4	24 37.9	28 14.1
30 F	6 32 21	8 14 44	29 28 56	5♌33 11	3 13.3	16 27.4	24 09.7	18 05.5	2 00.7	7 09.3	24 43.4	29 19.2	24 36.4	28 13.0

Astro Data (Dy Hr Mn)

♅ R	5 7:48
☽ 0S	10 13:33
☽ 0N	23 3:14
☿ R	24 9:01
♃∠♆	3 23:04
☽ 0S	6 22:25
☿ D	17 6:58
☽ 0N	19 10:38
♄⚹♆	27 9:32

Planet Ingress (Dy Hr Mn)

☿ ♊	2 15:18
♀ ♉	16 23:22
☉ ♊	21 12:34
♂ ♍	25 16:09
♅ ♑R	9 1:42
♀ ♊	10 16:18
☉ ♋	21 20:34
⚳ ♍	25 8:33

Last Aspect / ☽ Ingress (May)

Last Aspect Dy Hr Mn		☽ Ingress Dy Hr Mn
1 11:22 ♇ ☍	♊	1 11:53
3 7:38 ♄ □	♋	4 0:45
6 12:09 ♇ △	♌	6 12:55
8 21:43 ♇ □	♍	8 22:33
11 3:37 ♇ ⚹	♎	11 4:30
12 23:30 ♆ □	♏	13 6:53
15 5:59 ♇ ☌	♐	15 6:58
17 0:35 ♂ △	♑	17 6:36
19 6:26 ♇ ⚹	♒	19 7:39
21 11:36 ☉ □	♓	21 11:40
23 17:35 ♇ △	♈	23 19:13
25 20:32 ♆ □	♉	26 5:46
28 16:06 ♇ ☍	♊	28 18:07
30 18:08 ♄ □	♋	31 6:59

Last Aspect / ☽ Ingress (June)

Last Aspect Dy Hr Mn		☽ Ingress Dy Hr Mn
2 17:02 ♇ △	♌	2 19:17
5 3:30 ♇ □	♍	5 5:46
7 10:58 ♇ ⚹	♎	7 13:13
9 17:02 ♅ □	♏	9 17:03
11 17:43 ♅ ⚹	♐	11 17:50
13 8:09 ♄ □	♑	13 17:05
15 16:34 ♅ ☌	♒	15 16:52
17 16:36 ♇ □	♓	17 19:13
20 0:53 ♅ ⚹	♈	20 1:29
22 10:48 ♅ □	♉	22 11:35
24 23:03 ♅ △	♊	25 0:02
27 2:10 ♄ □	♋	27 12:56
29 23:43 ♅ ☍	♌	30 1:02

☽ Phases & Eclipses (Dy Hr Mn)

7 21:44	☽ 16♌52
14 20:48	○ 23♏35
21 11:36	☾ 29♒58
29 9:27	● 7♊34
6 10:26	☽ 15♍16
13 4:03	○ 21♐42
19 22:01	☾ 28♓09
28 0:50	● 5♋54

Astro Data

1 May 1995
Julian Day # 34819
SVP 5♓19'21"
GC 26♐46.4 ⚴ 26♊27.3
Eris 18♈19.5 ⚵ 4♑21.7R
⚷ 20♍15.5R ⚶ 12♋02.3
☽ Mean ☊ 5♏23.1

1 June 1995
Julian Day # 34850
SVP 5♓19'17"
GC 26♐46.5 ⚴ 14♋17.0
Eris 18♈36.1 ⚵ 0♑37.0R
⚷ 20♍10.3 ⚶ 23♋59.2
☽ Mean ☊ 3♏44.6

July 1995 LONGITUDE

Day	Sid.Time	☉	0 hr ☽	Noon ☽	True ☊	☿	♀	♂	⚳	♃	♄	♅	♆	♇
1 Sa	6 36 18	9♋11 58	11♌39 30	17♌48 04	3♏03.0	17♊28.8	25♊23.0	18♍38.5	2♍24.4	7♐03.8	24♓44.0	29♑17.0	24♑34.8	28♏11.8
2 Su	6 40 14	10 09 11	23 59 07	0♍12 54	2R 54.8	18 34.3	26 36.3	19 11.7	2 48.2	6R 58.4	24 44.4	29R 14.8	24R 33.3	28R 10.7
3 M	6 44 11	11 06 24	6♍29 43	12 49 53	2 49.1	19 43.8	27 49.6	19 45.0	3 12.1	6 53.1	24 44.7	29 12.6	24 31.7	28 09.6
4 Tu	6 48 07	12 03 36	19 13 44	25 41 38	2 45.9	20 57.4	29 03.0	20 18.4	3 36.1	6 48.0	24 45.0	29 10.3	24 30.2	28 08.5
5 W	6 52 04	13 00 48	2♎13 57	8♎51 03	2D 44.8	22 14.9	0♋16.4	20 52.0	4 00.2	6 43.1	24R 45.1	29 08.1	24 28.6	28 07.5
6 Th	6 56 00	13 58 00	15 33 18	22 21 01	2R 44.9	23 36.3	1 29.8	21 25.6	4 24.3	6 38.2	24 45.1	29 05.8	24 27.0	28 06.4
7 F	6 59 57	14 55 12	29 14 27	6♏13 47	2 45.0	25 01.5	2 43.2	21 59.4	4 48.5	6 33.6	24 45.1	29 03.5	24 25.4	28 05.4
8 Sa	7 03 54	15 52 23	13♏19 04	20 30 13	2 44.0	26 30.5	3 56.6	22 33.3	5 12.8	6 29.1	24 44.9	29 01.2	24 23.8	28 04.5
9 Su	7 07 50	16 49 34	27 47 01	5♐09 00	2 41.0	28 03.3	5 10.0	23 07.3	5 37.2	6 24.7	24 44.6	28 58.8	24 22.2	28 03.5
10 M	7 11 47	17 46 46	12♐35 34	20 05 55	2 35.3	29 39.6	6 23.5	23 41.5	6 01.6	6 20.6	24 44.3	28 56.5	24 20.6	28 02.6
11 Tu	7 15 43	18 43 57	27 39 00	5♑13 43	2 27.2	1♋19.6	7 36.9	24 15.7	6 26.1	6 16.5	24 43.8	28 54.2	24 19.0	28 01.7
12 W	7 19 40	19 41 08	12♑48 46	20 22 50	2 17.3	3 02.9	8 50.4	24 50.0	6 50.7	6 12.7	24 43.2	28 51.8	24 17.4	28 00.9
13 Th	7 23 36	20 38 20	27 54 37	5♒22 52	2 06.7	4 49.6	10 03.9	25 24.5	7 15.4	6 09.0	24 42.6	28 49.4	24 15.8	28 00.0
14 F	7 27 33	21 35 32	12♒46 25	20 04 21	1 56.6	6 39.4	11 17.5	25 59.0	7 40.1	6 05.5	24 41.8	28 47.1	24 14.1	27 59.2
15 Sa	7 31 29	22 32 44	27 15 53	4♓20 28	1 48.2	8 32.1	12 31.0	26 33.7	8 04.8	6 02.1	24 40.9	28 44.7	24 12.5	27 58.4
16 Su	7 35 26	23 29 57	11♓17 46	18 07 41	1 42.1	10 27.6	13 44.6	27 08.5	8 29.7	5 58.9	24 40.0	28 42.3	24 10.9	27 57.7
17 M	7 39 23	24 27 10	24 50 16	1♈25 44	1 38.5	12 25.7	14 58.2	27 43.3	8 54.6	5 55.9	24 38.9	28 39.9	24 09.3	27 57.0
18 Tu	7 43 19	25 24 24	7♈54 30	14 16 59	1D 36.9	14 25.9	16 11.8	28 18.3	9 19.5	5 53.0	24 37.8	28 37.5	24 07.7	27 56.3
19 W	7 47 16	26 21 39	20 33 48	26 45 31	1R 36.6	16 28.2	17 25.4	28 53.4	9 44.6	5 50.3	24 36.5	28 35.1	24 06.0	27 55.6
20 Th	7 51 12	27 18 54	2♉52 49	8♉56 20	1 36.6	18 32.0	18 39.1	29 28.6	10 09.7	5 47.8	24 35.2	28 32.7	24 04.4	27 55.0
21 F	7 55 09	28 16 11	14 56 47	20 54 46	1 35.6	20 37.3	19 52.8	0♎03.9	10 34.8	5 45.5	24 33.7	28 30.3	24 02.8	27 54.4
22 Sa	7 59 05	29 13 28	26 50 58	2♊45 57	1 32.7	22 43.5	21 06.5	0 39.3	11 00.0	5 43.4	24 32.2	28 27.9	24 01.2	27 53.8
23 Su	8 03 02	0♌10 45	8♊40 18	14 34 31	1 27.3	24 50.5	22 20.2	1 14.8	11 25.3	5 41.4	24 30.5	28 25.5	23 59.6	27 53.3
24 M	8 06 58	1 08 04	20 29 05	26 24 24	1 19.2	26 57.8	23 33.9	1 50.4	11 50.6	5 39.6	24 28.8	28 23.1	23 58.0	27 52.8
25 Tu	8 10 55	2 05 23	2♋20 52	8♋18 46	1 08.5	29 05.3	24 47.7	2 26.2	12 16.0	5 38.0	24 27.0	28 20.7	23 56.3	27 52.3
26 W	8 14 52	3 02 43	14 18 22	20 19 53	0 55.8	1♌12.5	26 01.5	3 02.0	12 41.4	5 36.6	24 25.1	28 18.3	23 54.7	27 51.8
27 Th	8 18 48	4 00 04	26 23 30	2♌29 20	0 42.3	3 19.4	27 15.3	3 37.9	13 06.9	5 35.4	24 23.1	28 15.9	23 53.1	27 51.4
28 F	8 22 45	4 57 26	8♌37 29	14 48 01	0 28.9	5 25.6	28 29.1	4 13.9	13 32.5	5 34.3	24 21.0	28 13.5	23 51.6	27 51.0
29 Sa	8 26 41	5 54 48	21 01 01	27 16 33	0 16.9	7 31.0	29 43.0	4 50.0	13 58.1	5 33.5	24 18.8	28 11.1	23 50.0	27 50.7
30 Su	8 30 38	6 52 11	3♍34 39	9♍55 24	0 07.1	9 35.4	0♌56.9	5 26.2	14 23.7	5 32.8	24 16.5	28 08.7	23 48.4	27 50.4
31 M	8 34 34	7 49 34	16 18 55	22 45 17	0 00.1	11 38.7	2 10.7	6 02.6	14 49.4	5 32.3	24 14.1	28 06.4	23 46.8	27 50.1

August 1995 LONGITUDE

Day	Sid.Time	☉	0 hr ☽	Noon ☽	True ☊	☿	♀	♂	⚳	♃	♄	♅	♆	♇
1 Tu	8 38 31	8♌46 58	29♍14 41	5♎47 16	29♎56.0	13♌40.7	3♌24.6	6♎39.0	15♍15.2	5♐32.0	24♓11.7	28♑04.0	23♑45.3	27♏49.8
2 W	8 42 27	9 44 23	12♎23 15	19 02 51	29D 54.3	15 41.3	4 38.6	7 15.5	15 40.9	5D 31.8	24R 09.1	28R 01.7	23R 43.7	27R 49.6
3 Th	8 46 24	10 41 48	25 46 17	2♏33 46	29R 54.0	17 40.6	5 52.5	7 52.1	16 06.8	5 31.9	24 06.5	27 59.3	23 42.2	27 49.4
4 F	8 50 21	11 39 14	9♏25 29	16 21 37	29 54.0	19 38.4	7 06.4	8 28.8	16 32.6	5 32.1	24 03.8	27 57.0	23 40.7	27 49.3
5 Sa	8 54 17	12 36 40	23 22 14	0♐27 19	29 53.1	21 34.7	8 20.4	9 05.5	16 58.6	5 32.6	24 01.0	27 54.7	23 39.1	27 49.1
6 Su	8 58 14	13 34 07	7♐36 47	14 50 22	29 50.2	23 29.5	9 34.4	9 42.4	17 24.5	5 33.2	23 58.1	27 52.4	23 37.6	27 49.1
7 M	9 02 10	14 31 35	22 07 41	29 28 11	29 44.8	25 22.7	10 48.4	10 19.4	17 50.5	5 34.0	23 55.2	27 50.2	23 36.1	27 49.0
8 Tu	9 06 07	15 29 04	6♑51 09	14♑15 45	29 36.9	27 14.4	12 02.4	10 56.4	18 16.6	5 34.9	23 52.1	27 47.9	23 34.7	27D 49.0
9 W	9 10 03	16 26 34	21 41 02	29 05 58	29 27.2	29 04.5	13 16.5	11 33.6	18 42.7	5 36.1	23 49.0	27 45.7	23 33.2	27 49.0
10 Th	9 14 00	17 24 05	6♒29 27	13♒50 25	29 16.7	0♍53.1	14 30.5	12 10.8	19 08.8	5 37.4	23 45.9	27 43.4	23 31.7	27 49.0
11 F	9 17 56	18 21 36	21 07 51	28 20 51	29 06.7	2 40.2	15 44.6	12 48.1	19 34.9	5 39.0	23 42.6	27 41.2	23 30.3	27 49.1
12 Sa	9 21 53	19 19 09	5♓28 37	12♓30 33	28 58.1	4 25.7	16 58.7	13 25.5	20 01.1	5 40.6	23 39.3	27 39.0	23 28.9	27 49.2
13 Su	9 25 50	20 16 43	19 26 11	26 15 16	28 51.9	6 09.7	18 12.8	14 03.0	20 27.3	5 42.5	23 35.9	27 36.9	23 27.5	27 49.4
14 M	9 29 46	21 14 18	2♈57 42	9♈33 34	28 48.1	7 52.2	19 26.9	14 40.5	20 53.6	5 44.6	23 32.4	27 34.7	23 26.1	27 49.6
15 Tu	9 33 43	22 11 55	16 03 05	22 26 34	28D 46.5	9 33.2	20 41.1	15 18.2	21 19.9	5 46.8	23 28.9	27 32.6	23 24.7	27 49.8
16 W	9 37 39	23 09 34	28 44 29	4♉57 21	28 46.5	11 12.7	21 55.2	15 56.0	21 46.2	5 49.2	23 25.3	27 30.5	23 23.3	27 50.0
17 Th	9 41 36	24 07 14	11♉05 44	17 10 16	28R 47.0	12 50.7	23 09.4	16 33.8	22 12.6	5 51.8	23 21.6	27 28.4	23 22.0	27 50.3
18 F	9 45 32	25 04 55	23 11 36	29 10 23	28 47.1	14 27.3	24 23.6	17 11.7	22 39.0	5 54.6	23 17.9	27 26.4	23 20.6	27 50.6
19 Sa	9 49 29	26 02 38	5♊07 19	11♊03 01	28 45.8	16 02.4	25 37.8	17 49.7	23 05.4	5 57.5	23 14.1	27 24.4	23 19.3	27 51.0
20 Su	9 53 25	27 00 23	16 58 07	22 53 14	28 42.5	17 36.1	26 52.1	18 27.8	23 31.9	6 00.6	23 10.2	27 22.4	23 18.1	27 51.3
21 M	9 57 22	27 58 09	28 48 56	4♋45 43	28 36.9	19 08.4	28 06.4	19 06.0	23 58.4	6 03.9	23 06.3	27 20.4	23 16.8	27 51.8
22 Tu	10 01 19	28 55 57	10♋44 04	16 44 24	28 29.1	20 39.1	29 20.6	19 44.3	24 24.9	6 07.4	23 02.4	27 18.5	23 15.5	27 52.2
23 W	10 05 15	29 53 47	22 47 05	28 52 25	28 19.6	22 08.5	0♍34.9	20 22.7	24 51.5	6 11.0	22 58.3	27 16.6	23 14.3	27 52.7
24 Th	10 09 12	0♍51 38	5♌00 39	11♌11 56	28 09.2	23 36.3	1 49.3	21 01.1	25 18.1	6 14.8	22 54.3	27 14.7	23 13.1	27 53.2
25 F	10 13 08	1 49 31	17 26 24	23 44 08	27 58.8	25 02.7	3 03.6	21 39.7	25 44.7	6 18.8	22 50.2	27 12.8	23 11.9	27 53.8
26 Sa	10 17 05	2 47 25	0♍05 08	6♍29 22	27 49.5	26 27.5	4 17.9	22 18.3	26 11.4	6 22.9	22 46.0	27 11.0	23 10.7	27 54.4
27 Su	10 21 01	3 45 20	12 56 47	19 27 19	27 42.1	27 50.9	5 32.3	22 57.0	26 38.0	6 27.2	22 41.8	27 09.2	23 09.6	27 55.0
28 M	10 24 58	4 43 17	26 00 52	2♎37 21	27 37.1	29 12.7	6 46.7	23 35.8	27 04.7	6 31.7	22 37.5	27 07.5	23 08.5	27 55.6
29 Tu	10 28 54	5 41 16	9♎16 39	15 58 44	27D 34.4	0♎32.9	8 01.1	24 14.7	27 31.4	6 36.4	22 33.2	27 05.8	23 07.4	27 56.3
30 W	10 32 51	6 39 16	22 43 31	29 30 57	27 33.8	1 51.4	9 15.4	24 53.7	27 58.2	6 41.2	22 28.9	27 04.1	23 06.3	27 57.0
31 Th	10 36 47	7 37 17	6♏21 02	13♏13 44	27 34.5	3 08.3	10 29.9	25 32.7	28 24.9	6 46.1	22 24.5	27 02.5	23 05.3	27 57.8

Astro Data	Dy Hr Mn
☽0S	4 5:53
♄R	6 7:46
☽0N	16 20:03
♂0S	22 23:25
☽0S	31 12:25
♃D	2 16:44
♅⚹♇	8 0:26
♇D	8 13:33
☽0N	13 6:32
♄⚹♆	17 8:10
☽0S	27 19:05
☿0S	27 21:30

Planet Ingress	Dy Hr Mn
♀ ♋	5 6:39
☿ ♋	10 16:58
♂ ♎	21 9:21
☉ ♌	23 7:30
☿ ♌	25 22:19
♀ ♌	29 17:32
☊ ♎R	31 12:33
☿ ♍	10 0:13
♀ ♍	23 0:43
☉ ♍	23 14:35
☿ ♎	29 2:07

Last Aspect Dy Hr Mn		☽ Ingress Dy Hr Mn
2 8:06	♇ □	♍ 2 11:35
4 18:49	♀ □	♎ 4 19:55
6 23:43	♅ □	♏ 7 1:19
9 1:59	♅ ⚹	♐ 9 3:37
10 19:22	♄ □	♑ 11 3:43
13 1:29	♅ ☌	♒ 13 3:21
15 1:12	♇ □	♓ 15 4:37
17 6:58	♅ ⚹	♈ 17 9:23
19 15:33	♅ □	♉ 19 18:20
22 4:11	☉ ⚹	♊ 22 6:23
24 8:07	♄ □	♋ 24 19:16
27 3:43	♅ ☍	♌ 27 7:07
29 13:05	♇ □	♍ 29 17:12

Last Aspect Dy Hr Mn		☽ Ingress Dy Hr Mn
31 21:52	♅ △	♎ 1 1:23
3 3:57	♅ □	♏ 3 7:29
5 7:43	♅ ⚹	♐ 5 11:14
7 4:21	☿ △	♑ 7 12:52
9 9:55	♇ ⚹	♒ 9 13:28
11 11:07	♇ □	♓ 11 14:46
13 14:47	♇ △	♈ 13 18:41
15 21:41	♅ □	♉ 16 2:25
18 9:19	♇ ☍	♊ 18 13:40
20 21:05	☉ ⚹	♋ 21 2:24
23 10:03	♇ △	♌ 23 14:13
25 19:53	♇ □	♍ 25 23:50
28 5:07	☿ ☌	♎ 28 7:15
30 7:42	♅ □	♏ 30 12:51

☽ Phases & Eclipses Dy Hr Mn	
5 20:02	☽ 13♎20
12 10:49	○ 19♑38
19 11:10	☾ 26♈20
27 15:13	● 4♌08
4 3:16	☽ 11♏18
10 18:16	○ 17♒39
18 3:04	☾ 24♉43
26 4:31	● 2♍29

Astro Data

1 July 1995
Julian Day # 34880
SVP 5♓19'12"
GC 26♐46.6 ⚴ 1♌18.8
Eris 18♈45.0 ⚵ 24♐00.7R
⚷ 21♍45.6 ⚶ 6♌47.3
☽ Mean ☊ 2♏09.3

1 August 1995
Julian Day # 34911
SVP 5♓19'07"
GC 26♐46.7 ⚴ 18♌19.8
Eris 18♈44.6R ⚵ 19♐16.6R
⚷ 24♍49.5 ⚶ 20♌49.9
☽ Mean ☊ 0♏30.8

LONGITUDE — September 1995

Day	Sid.Time	☉	0 hr ☽	Noon ☽	True ☊	☿	♀	♂	⚳	♃	♄	♅	♆	♇
1 F	10 40 44	8♍35 20	20♏09 04	27♏06 58	27♎35.6	4♎23.4	11♍44.3	26♎11.8	28♍51.7	6♐51.3	22♓20.1	27♑00.8	23♑04.2	27♏58.6
2 Sa	10 44 41	9 33 24	4♐07 26	11♐10 22	27R36.0	5 36.8	12 58.7	26 51.0	29 18.5	6 56.5	22R15.7	26R59.3	23R03.2	27 59.4
3 Su	10 48 37	10 31 29	18 15 38	25 23 03	27 35.0	6 48.2	14 13.2	27 30.3	29 45.4	7 02.0	22 11.2	26 57.7	23 02.3	28 00.2
4 M	10 52 34	11 29 36	2♑32 20	9♑43 09	27 32.2	7 57.7	15 27.6	28 09.7	0♎12.2	7 07.6	22 06.8	26 56.2	23 01.3	28 01.1
5 Tu	10 56 30	12 27 44	16 55 01	24 07 27	27 27.4	9 05.2	16 42.1	28 49.1	0 39.1	7 13.3	22 02.2	26 54.8	23 00.4	28 02.0
6 W	11 00 27	13 25 54	1♒19 51	8♒31 32	27 21.3	10 10.4	17 56.5	29 28.7	1 05.9	7 19.2	21 57.7	26 53.4	22 59.5	28 03.0
7 Th	11 04 23	14 24 05	15 41 49	22 50 00	27 14.5	11 13.4	19 11.0	0♏08.3	1 32.8	7 25.3	21 53.2	26 52.0	22 58.7	28 04.0
8 F	11 08 20	15 22 18	29 55 24	6♓57 21	27 08.0	12 14.0	20 25.5	0 47.9	1 59.7	7 31.5	21 48.6	26 50.7	22 57.8	28 05.0
9 Sa	11 12 16	16 20 32	13♓55 17	20 48 42	27 02.5	13 12.0	21 40.0	1 27.7	2 26.7	7 37.8	21 44.0	26 49.4	22 57.0	28 06.0
10 Su	11 16 13	17 18 48	27 37 11	4♈20 30	26 58.6	14 07.3	22 54.5	2 07.5	2 53.6	7 44.3	21 39.4	26 48.1	22 56.2	28 07.1
11 M	11 20 10	18 17 07	10♈58 27	17 31 01	26D56.5	14 59.7	24 09.0	2 47.4	3 20.6	7 51.0	21 34.8	26 46.9	22 55.5	28 08.2
12 Tu	11 24 06	19 15 27	23 58 16	0♉20 22	26 56.1	15 48.9	25 23.5	3 27.4	3 47.5	7 57.8	21 30.2	26 45.7	22 54.7	28 09.3
13 W	11 28 03	20 13 49	6♉37 37	12 50 22	26 57.0	16 34.9	26 38.1	4 07.5	4 14.5	8 04.7	21 25.6	26 44.6	22 54.0	28 10.5
14 Th	11 31 59	21 12 13	18 59 02	25 04 08	26 58.6	17 17.2	27 52.6	4 47.6	4 41.5	8 11.8	21 20.9	26 43.5	22 53.4	28 11.7
15 F	11 35 56	22 10 40	1♊06 11	7♊05 45	27 00.2	17 55.8	29 07.2	5 27.9	5 08.5	8 19.0	21 16.3	26 42.5	22 52.7	28 12.9
16 Sa	11 39 52	23 09 08	13 03 28	18 59 56	27R01.2	18 30.1	0♎21.7	6 08.2	5 35.5	8 26.3	21 11.7	26 41.5	22 52.1	28 14.1
17 Su	11 43 49	24 07 39	24 55 46	0♋51 35	27 01.1	19 00.1	1 36.3	6 48.6	6 02.6	8 33.8	21 07.1	26 40.5	22 51.5	28 15.4
18 M	11 47 45	25 06 12	6♋48 01	12 45 38	26 59.5	19 25.3	2 50.9	7 29.0	6 29.6	8 41.4	21 02.5	26 39.6	22 51.0	28 16.7
19 Tu	11 51 42	26 04 47	18 45 00	24 46 39	26 56.7	19 45.3	4 05.5	8 09.6	6 56.7	8 49.2	20 57.9	26 38.8	22 50.5	28 18.1
20 W	11 55 39	27 03 24	0♌51 05	6♌58 42	26 52.7	19 59.9	5 20.1	8 50.2	7 23.7	8 57.1	20 53.3	26 38.0	22 50.0	28 19.5
21 Th	11 59 35	28 02 03	13 09 53	19 24 58	26 48.0	20R08.6	6 34.7	9 30.9	7 50.8	9 05.1	20 48.7	26 37.2	22 49.5	28 20.9
22 F	12 03 32	29 00 45	25 44 10	2♍07 39	26 43.3	20 11.1	7 49.3	10 11.7	8 17.9	9 13.2	20 44.1	26 36.5	22 49.1	28 22.3
23 Sa	12 07 28	29 59 28	8♍35 30	15 07 45	26 39.1	20 07.0	9 03.9	10 52.6	8 45.0	9 21.5	20 39.6	26 35.8	22 48.7	28 23.7
24 Su	12 11 25	0♎58 14	21 44 19	28 25 03	26 35.8	19 56.0	10 18.6	11 33.5	9 12.1	9 29.9	20 35.0	26 35.2	22 48.3	28 25.2
25 M	12 15 21	1 57 01	5♎09 46	11♎58 13	26 33.8	19 37.8	11 33.2	12 14.5	9 39.2	9 38.4	20 30.5	26 34.6	22 48.0	28 26.7
26 Tu	12 19 18	2 55 51	18 50 04	25 45 00	26D33.2	19 12.3	12 47.9	12 55.6	10 06.3	9 47.1	20 26.1	26 34.1	22 47.7	28 28.3
27 W	12 23 14	3 54 42	2♏42 39	9♏42 39	26 33.6	18 39.5	14 02.5	13 36.8	10 33.4	9 55.8	20 21.6	26 33.6	22 47.4	28 29.8
28 Th	12 27 11	4 53 35	16 44 37	23 48 12	26 34.8	17 59.3	15 17.2	14 18.0	11 00.5	10 04.7	20 17.2	26 33.2	22 47.2	28 31.4
29 F	12 31 08	5 52 30	0♐53 02	7♐58 47	26 36.2	17 12.1	16 31.8	14 59.4	11 27.6	10 13.7	20 12.8	26 32.8	22 47.0	28 33.1
30 Sa	12 35 04	6 51 27	15 05 07	22 11 45	26 37.3	16 18.5	17 46.5	15 40.8	11 54.7	10 22.9	20 08.5	26 32.5	22 46.8	28 34.7

LONGITUDE — October 1995

Day	Sid.Time	☉	0 hr ☽	Noon ☽	True ☊	☿	♀	♂	⚳	♃	♄	♅	♆	♇
1 Su	12 39 01	7♎50 26	29♐18 23	6♑24 44	26♎37.8	15♎19.1	19♎01.1	16♏22.2	12♎21.8	10♐32.1	20♓04.2	26♑32.2	22♑46.7	28♏36.4
2 M	12 42 57	8 49 26	13♑30 32	20 35 30	26R37.5	14R15.1	20 15.8	17 03.8	12 49.0	10 41.5	19R59.9	26R32.0	22R46.6	28 38.1
3 Tu	12 46 54	9 48 28	27 39 22	4♒41 51	26 36.3	13 07.7	21 30.5	17 45.4	13 16.1	10 50.9	19 55.7	26 31.8	22 46.5	28 39.8
4 W	12 50 50	10 47 32	11♒42 39	18 41 29	26 34.6	11 58.6	22 45.1	18 27.1	13 43.2	11 00.5	19 51.6	26 31.7	22D46.5	28 41.5
5 Th	12 54 47	11 46 37	25 38 03	2♓32 03	26 32.6	10 49.4	23 59.8	19 08.8	14 10.3	11 10.2	19 47.4	26 31.6	22 46.5	28 43.3
6 F	12 58 43	12 45 45	9♓23 13	16 11 15	26 30.7	9 42.2	25 14.4	19 50.7	14 37.4	11 20.0	19 43.4	26D31.6	22 46.5	28 45.1
7 Sa	13 02 40	13 44 54	22 55 56	29 37 01	26 29.1	8 38.6	26 29.1	20 32.6	15 04.5	11 29.9	19 39.4	26 31.6	22 46.5	28 46.9
8 Su	13 06 36	14 44 05	6♈14 21	12♈47 46	26 28.2	7 40.6	27 43.7	21 14.5	15 31.6	11 39.8	19 35.4	26 31.7	22 46.6	28 48.7
9 M	13 10 33	15 43 18	19 17 13	25 42 39	26D27.8	6 49.7	28 58.4	21 56.6	15 58.6	11 49.9	19 31.5	26 31.8	22 46.8	28 50.6
10 Tu	13 14 30	16 42 33	2♉04 06	8♉21 39	26 28.1	6 07.5	0♏13.1	22 38.7	16 25.7	12 00.1	19 27.6	26 32.0	22 46.9	28 52.5
11 W	13 18 26	17 41 51	14 35 28	20 45 46	26 28.7	5 34.9	1 27.7	23 20.9	16 52.8	12 10.4	19 23.8	26 32.2	22 47.1	28 54.4
12 Th	13 22 23	18 41 11	26 52 48	2♊56 54	26 29.5	5 12.7	2 42.4	24 03.2	17 19.9	12 20.8	19 20.1	26 32.5	22 47.3	28 56.3
13 F	13 26 19	19 40 33	8♊58 27	14 57 52	26 30.3	5D01.3	3 57.1	24 45.5	17 46.9	12 31.3	19 16.4	26 32.8	22 47.6	28 58.2
14 Sa	13 30 16	20 39 57	20 55 35	26 52 09	26 30.9	5 01.0	5 11.7	25 27.9	18 14.0	12 41.9	19 12.8	26 33.2	22 47.9	29 00.2
15 Su	13 34 12	21 39 23	2♋48 03	8♋43 52	26 31.3	5 11.4	6 26.4	26 10.4	18 41.0	12 52.6	19 09.3	26 33.6	22 48.2	29 02.2
16 M	13 38 09	22 38 52	14 40 09	20 37 30	26R31.5	5 32.3	7 41.1	26 52.9	19 08.1	13 03.3	19 05.8	26 34.1	22 48.6	29 04.2
17 Tu	13 42 05	23 38 23	26 36 31	2♌37 45	26 31.5	6 03.2	8 55.7	27 35.5	19 35.1	13 14.2	19 02.4	26 34.6	22 49.0	29 06.2
18 W	13 46 02	24 37 57	8♌41 47	14 49 11	26 31.3	6 43.3	10 10.4	28 18.2	20 02.1	13 25.2	18 59.1	26 35.2	22 49.4	29 08.3
19 Th	13 49 59	25 37 32	21 00 28	27 16 05	26D31.2	7 31.8	11 25.1	29 01.0	20 29.1	13 36.2	18 55.9	26 35.8	22 49.9	29 10.3
20 F	13 53 55	26 37 10	3♍36 29	10♍02 00	26 31.1	8 28.0	12 39.8	29 43.8	20 56.1	13 47.3	18 52.7	26 36.5	22 50.4	29 12.4
21 Sa	13 57 52	27 36 50	16 32 55	23 09 24	26 31.2	9 31.0	13 54.5	0♐26.8	21 23.1	13 58.5	18 49.6	26 37.3	22 50.9	29 14.5
22 Su	14 01 48	28 36 32	29 51 32	6♎39 17	26 31.3	10 40.0	15 09.2	1 09.7	21 50.1	14 09.8	18 46.6	26 38.1	22 51.5	29 16.6
23 M	14 05 45	29 36 17	13♎32 30	20 30 54	26R31.5	11 54.3	16 23.8	1 52.8	22 17.0	14 21.2	18 43.7	26 38.9	22 52.1	29 18.7
24 Tu	14 09 41	0♏36 03	27 34 07	4♏41 37	26 31.4	13 13.2	17 38.5	2 35.9	22 44.0	14 32.6	18 40.8	26 39.8	22 52.7	29 20.9
25 W	14 13 38	1 35 52	11♏52 49	19 07 02	26 31.2	14 35.9	18 53.2	3 19.1	23 10.9	14 44.2	18 38.1	26 40.7	22 53.4	29 23.0
26 Th	14 17 34	2 35 42	26 23 31	3♐41 29	26 30.6	16 01.9	20 07.9	4 02.4	23 37.8	14 55.8	18 35.4	26 41.7	22 54.1	29 25.2
27 F	14 21 31	3 35 34	11♐00 08	18 18 43	26 29.9	17 30.6	21 22.6	4 45.7	24 04.7	15 07.5	18 32.8	26 42.8	22 54.8	29 27.4
28 Sa	14 25 28	4 35 28	25 36 28	2♑52 44	26 29.0	19 01.5	22 37.3	5 29.1	24 31.5	15 19.3	18 30.3	26 43.9	22 55.6	29 29.6
29 Su	14 29 24	5 35 24	10♑06 55	17 18 29	26 28.3	20 34.3	23 52.0	6 12.6	24 58.4	15 31.1	18 27.9	26 45.0	22 56.3	29 31.8
30 M	14 33 21	6 35 21	24 27 02	1♒32 14	26D27.9	22 08.6	25 06.6	6 56.1	25 25.2	15 43.0	18 25.6	26 46.2	22 57.2	29 34.1
31 Tu	14 37 17	7 35 20	8♒33 52	15 31 46	26 28.0	23 44.1	26 21.3	7 39.7	25 52.0	15 55.0	18 23.4	26 47.4	22 58.0	29 36.3

Astro Data Dy Hr Mn	Planet Ingress Dy Hr Mn	Last Aspect Dy Hr Mn	☽ Ingress Dy Hr Mn	Last Aspect Dy Hr Mn	☽ Ingress Dy Hr Mn	☽ Phases & Eclipses Dy Hr Mn
☽0N 9 16:29	⚳ ♎ 4 1:06	1 13:29 ♇ ☌	♐ 1 16:57	30 8:33 ♄ □	♑ 1 1:10	2 9:03 ☽ 9♐26
♃∠♆ 12 2:19	♂ ♏ 7 7:00	3 15:44 ♂ ✶	♑ 3 19:45	3 1:42 ♇ ✶	♒ 3 3:59	9 3:37 ○ 16♓00
♀0S 18 13:58	♀ ♎ 16 5:01	5 20:11 ♂ □	♒ 5 21:47	5 5:21 ♇ □	♓ 5 7:35	16 21:09 ☾ 23♊31
☿R 22 9:15	☉ ♎ 23 12:13	7 20:51 ♇ □	♓ 8 0:08	7 10:29 ♇ △	♈ 7 12:41	24 16:55 ● 1♎10
☉0S 23 12:12		10 0:52 ♇ △	♈ 10 4:14	9 18:49 ♀ ☍	♉ 9 20:05	
☽0S 24 2:55	♀ ♏ 10 7:48	12 5:15 ♅ □	♉ 12 11:21	12 4:02 ♇ ☍	♊ 12 6:09	1 14:36 ☽ 7♑57
	♂ ♐ 20 21:02	14 18:13 ♇ ☍	♊ 14 21:48	13 22:20 ☉ △	♋ 14 18:20	8 15:52 ○ 14♈54
♆D 5 3:56	☉ ♏ 23 21:32	16 21:09 ☉ □	♋ 17 10:16	17 4:58 ♇ △	♌ 17 6:46	8 16:04 • A 0.825
♅D 6 12:58		19 18:59 ♇ △	♌ 19 22:19	19 15:38 ♇ □	♍ 19 17:11	16 16:26 ☾ 22♋50
☽0N 7 0:41		22 4:57 ♇ □	♍ 22 8:01	21 22:56 ♇ ✶	♎ 22 0:15	24 4:36 ● 0♏18
♃∠♅ 7 16:12		24 12:00 ♇ ✶	♎ 24 14:50	23 22:27 ♅ □	♏ 24 4:06	24 4:32:29 • T 02'10"
⚳0S 10 4:05		26 13:25 ♅ □	♏ 26 19:20	26 4:58 ♇ ☌	♐ 26 5:56	30 21:17 ☽ 6♒59
☿D 14 0:45		28 20:01 ♇ ☌	♐ 28 22:30	27 12:23 ♄ □	♑ 28 7:15	
☽0S 21 12:13				30 8:39 ♇ ✶	♒ 30 9:23	

Astro Data

1 September 1995
Julian Day # 34942
SVP 5♓19'04"
GC 26♐46.7 ⚴ 4♍36.1
Eris 18♈34.6R ⚵ 19♐45.9
⚷ 28♍51.2 ⚶ 5♍24.6
☽ Mean ☊ 28♎52.3

1 October 1995
Julian Day # 34972
SVP 5♓19'01"
GC 26♐46.8 ⚴ 19♍33.0
Eris 18♈18.7R ⚵ 24♐46.0
⚷ 3♎10.5 ⚶ 19♍48.1
☽ Mean ☊ 27♎17.0

November 1995 LONGITUDE

Day	Sid.Time	☉	0 hr ☽	Noon ☽	True☊	☿	♀	♂	⚳	♃	♄	♅	♆	♇
1 W	14 41 14	8♏35 20	22♒25 52	29♒16 07	26♎28.5	25♎20.4	27♏36.0	8♐23.3	26♎18.7	16♐07.0	18♓21.3	26♑48.7	22♑58.9	29♏38.6
2 Th	14 45 10	9 35 22	6♓02 34	12♓45 15	26 29.6	26 57.5	28 50.6	9 07.1	26 45.5	16 19.1	18R19.2	26 50.0	22 59.8	29 40.8
3 F	14 49 07	10 35 25	19 24 17	25 59 44	26 30.7	28 35.0	0♐05.3	9 50.8	27 12.2	16 31.3	18 17.3	26 51.4	23 00.8	29 43.1
4 Sa	14 53 03	11 35 31	2♈31 44	9♈00 22	26 31.8	0♏12.9	1 19.9	10 34.7	27 38.9	16 43.5	18 15.5	26 52.9	23 01.8	29 45.4
5 Su	14 57 00	12 35 37	15 25 46	21 48 02	26R32.5	1 51.0	2 34.6	11 18.6	28 05.5	16 55.8	18 13.7	26 54.3	23 02.8	29 47.7
6 M	15 00 57	13 35 46	28 07 16	4♉23 35	26 32.3	3 29.2	3 49.2	12 02.6	28 32.2	17 08.2	18 12.1	26 55.9	23 03.8	29 50.0
7 Tu	15 04 53	14 35 56	10♉37 05	16 47 54	26 31.3	5 07.4	5 03.8	12 46.6	28 58.8	17 20.6	18 10.5	26 57.4	23 04.9	29 52.3
8 W	15 08 50	15 36 09	22 56 10	29 02 02	26 29.2	6 45.5	6 18.5	13 30.7	29 25.4	17 33.1	18 09.1	26 59.1	23 06.0	29 54.6
9 Th	15 12 46	16 36 23	5♊05 40	11♊07 15	26 26.3	8 23.5	7 33.1	14 14.9	29 51.9	17 45.6	18 07.8	27 00.7	23 07.2	29 57.0
10 F	15 16 43	17 36 39	17 07 03	23 05 19	26 22.8	10 01.4	8 47.7	14 59.1	0♏18.4	17 58.2	18 06.5	27 02.4	23 08.3	29 59.3
11 Sa	15 20 39	18 36 56	29 02 20	4♋58 27	26 19.0	11 39.1	10 02.3	15 43.4	0 44.9	18 10.8	18 05.4	27 04.2	23 09.5	0♐01.6
12 Su	15 24 36	19 37 16	10♋54 03	16 49 32	26 15.6	13 16.5	11 16.9	16 27.7	1 11.4	18 23.5	18 04.3	27 06.0	23 10.8	0 04.0
13 M	15 28 32	20 37 38	22 45 22	28 42 03	26 12.8	14 53.7	12 31.5	17 12.1	1 37.8	18 36.3	18 03.4	27 07.9	23 12.0	0 06.4
14 Tu	15 32 29	21 38 01	4♌40 05	10♌40 01	26D11.0	16 30.7	13 46.1	17 56.6	2 04.2	18 49.1	18 02.6	27 09.7	23 13.3	0 08.7
15 W	15 36 26	22 38 27	16 42 26	22 47 54	26 10.4	18 07.4	15 00.8	18 41.1	2 30.6	19 01.9	18 01.9	27 11.7	23 14.6	0 11.1
16 Th	15 40 22	23 38 54	28 57 00	5♍10 21	26 10.9	19 43.8	16 15.4	19 25.7	2 56.9	19 14.8	18 01.2	27 13.7	23 16.0	0 13.5
17 F	15 44 19	24 39 23	11♍28 28	17 51 55	26 12.3	21 20.0	17 29.9	20 10.4	3 23.2	19 27.7	18 00.7	27 15.7	23 17.3	0 15.8
18 Sa	15 48 15	25 39 54	24 21 10	0♎56 37	26 14.0	22 56.0	18 44.5	20 55.1	3 49.4	19 40.7	18 00.3	27 17.7	23 18.7	0 18.2
19 Su	15 52 12	26 40 27	7♎38 36	14 27 19	26R15.4	24 31.7	19 59.1	21 39.9	4 15.6	19 53.8	18 00.0	27 19.9	23 20.1	0 20.6
20 M	15 56 08	27 41 01	21 22 49	28 25 03	26 15.8	26 07.1	21 13.7	22 24.7	4 41.8	20 06.8	17 59.8	27 22.0	23 21.6	0 23.0
21 Tu	16 00 05	28 41 37	5♏33 45	12♏48 28	26 14.8	27 42.4	22 28.3	23 09.6	5 08.0	20 19.9	17D59.7	27 24.2	23 23.1	0 25.4
22 W	16 04 01	29 42 15	20 08 34	27 33 15	26 12.1	29 17.4	23 42.9	23 54.6	5 34.0	20 33.1	17 59.7	27 26.4	23 24.6	0 27.8
23 Th	16 07 58	0♐42 55	5♐01 33	12♐32 23	26 07.9	0♐52.3	24 57.5	24 39.6	6 00.1	20 46.3	17 59.9	27 28.7	23 26.1	0 30.2
24 F	16 11 55	1 43 35	20 04 34	27 36 53	26 02.6	2 26.9	26 12.0	25 24.7	6 26.1	20 59.5	18 00.1	27 31.0	23 27.7	0 32.5
25 Sa	16 15 51	2 44 17	5♑08 08	12♑37 09	25 57.0	4 01.4	27 26.6	26 09.8	6 52.0	21 12.8	18 00.4	27 33.4	23 29.3	0 34.9
26 Su	16 19 48	3 45 00	20 02 57	27 24 36	25 52.0	5 35.7	28 41.2	26 55.0	7 17.9	21 26.1	18 00.9	27 35.8	23 30.9	0 37.3
27 M	16 23 44	4 45 45	4♒41 26	11♒52 54	25 48.2	7 10.0	29 55.7	27 40.3	7 43.8	21 39.4	18 01.4	27 38.2	23 32.5	0 39.7
28 Tu	16 27 41	5 46 30	18 58 39	25 58 31	25D46.1	8 44.0	1♑10.2	28 25.6	8 09.6	21 52.8	18 02.1	27 40.7	23 34.2	0 42.1
29 W	16 31 37	6 47 16	2♓52 27	9♓40 34	25 45.7	10 18.0	2 24.7	29 10.9	8 35.3	22 06.1	18 02.9	27 43.2	23 35.8	0 44.5
30 Th	16 35 34	7 48 03	16 23 04	23 00 15	25 46.6	11 51.9	3 39.2	29 56.3	9 01.0	22 19.6	18 03.8	27 45.7	23 37.5	0 46.9

December 1995 LONGITUDE

Day	Sid.Time	☉	0 hr ☽	Noon ☽	True☊	☿	♀	♂	⚳	♃	♄	♅	♆	♇
1 F	16 39 30	8♐48 51	29♓32 27	6♈00 04	25♎48.0	13♐25.7	4♑53.7	0♑41.7	9♏26.7	22♐33.0	18♓04.7	27♑48.3	23♑39.3	0♐49.2
2 Sa	16 43 27	9 49 40	12♈23 28	18 43 04	25R49.3	14 59.4	6 08.2	1 27.2	9 52.3	22 46.5	18 05.8	27 50.9	23 41.0	0 51.6
3 Su	16 47 24	10 50 30	24 59 16	1♉12 24	25 49.3	16 33.1	7 22.7	2 12.8	10 17.8	22 59.9	18 07.0	27 53.6	23 42.8	0 54.0
4 M	16 51 20	11 51 20	7♉22 51	13 30 53	25 47.6	18 06.8	8 37.1	2 58.4	10 43.3	23 13.4	18 08.3	27 56.2	23 44.6	0 56.3
5 Tu	16 55 17	12 52 12	19 36 48	25 40 51	25 43.5	19 40.4	9 51.6	3 44.0	11 08.7	23 27.0	18 09.7	27 59.0	23 46.4	0 58.7
6 W	16 59 13	13 53 05	1♊43 15	7♊44 12	25 37.1	21 14.0	11 06.0	4 29.7	11 34.1	23 40.5	18 11.3	28 01.7	23 48.2	1 01.0
7 Th	17 03 10	14 53 59	13 43 53	19 42 27	25 28.6	22 47.6	12 20.4	5 15.5	11 59.4	23 54.1	18 12.9	28 04.5	23 50.1	1 03.3
8 F	17 07 06	15 54 54	25 40 06	1♋36 58	25 18.6	24 21.1	13 34.8	6 01.3	12 24.6	24 07.7	18 14.6	28 07.3	23 52.0	1 05.7
9 Sa	17 11 03	16 55 50	7♋33 16	13 29 11	25 08.1	25 54.7	14 49.1	6 47.1	12 49.8	24 21.3	18 16.4	28 10.2	23 53.9	1 08.0
10 Su	17 14 59	17 56 47	19 24 57	25 20 50	24 57.8	27 28.2	16 03.5	7 33.0	13 14.9	24 34.9	18 18.3	28 13.0	23 55.8	1 10.3
11 M	17 18 56	18 57 45	1♌17 07	7♌14 09	24 48.9	29 01.8	17 17.8	8 18.9	13 40.0	24 48.5	18 20.4	28 15.9	23 57.7	1 12.6
12 Tu	17 22 53	19 58 44	13 12 19	19 12 01	24 41.9	0♑35.3	18 32.2	9 04.9	14 04.9	25 02.2	18 22.5	28 18.9	23 59.7	1 14.9
13 W	17 26 49	20 59 44	25 13 44	1♍17 57	24 37.3	2 08.7	19 46.5	9 50.9	14 29.9	25 15.8	18 24.7	28 21.8	24 01.6	1 17.2
14 Th	17 30 46	22 00 45	7♍25 14	13 36 08	24D35.0	3 42.1	21 00.7	10 37.0	14 54.7	25 29.5	18 27.1	28 24.8	24 03.6	1 19.5
15 F	17 34 42	23 01 47	19 51 14	26 11 08	24 34.6	5 15.3	22 15.0	11 23.2	15 19.5	25 43.1	18 29.5	28 27.8	24 05.6	1 21.7
16 Sa	17 38 39	24 02 51	2♎36 24	9♎07 36	24 35.3	6 48.5	23 29.3	12 09.3	15 44.2	25 56.8	18 32.1	28 30.9	24 07.6	1 24.0
17 Su	17 42 35	25 03 55	15 45 13	22 29 42	24R35.9	8 21.4	24 43.5	12 55.5	16 08.9	26 10.5	18 34.7	28 34.0	24 09.7	1 26.2
18 M	17 46 32	26 05 00	29 21 22	6♏20 23	24 35.3	9 54.1	25 57.7	13 41.8	16 33.4	26 24.2	18 37.4	28 37.1	24 11.7	1 28.5
19 Tu	17 50 28	27 06 06	13♏26 46	20 40 21	24 32.6	11 26.5	27 11.9	14 28.1	16 57.9	26 37.9	18 40.3	28 40.2	24 13.8	1 30.7
20 W	17 54 25	28 07 13	28 00 44	5♐27 16	24 27.3	12 58.5	28 26.1	15 14.5	17 22.3	26 51.6	18 43.2	28 43.3	24 15.9	1 32.9
21 Th	17 58 22	29 08 20	12♐59 04	20 35 04	24 19.4	14 29.9	29 40.3	16 00.8	17 46.7	27 05.3	18 46.2	28 46.5	24 18.0	1 35.1
22 F	18 02 18	0♑09 29	28 13 58	5♑54 21	24 09.6	16 00.7	0♒54.4	16 47.3	18 10.9	27 19.0	18 49.4	28 49.7	24 20.1	1 37.2
23 Sa	18 06 15	1 10 37	13♑34 44	21 13 37	23 59.1	17 30.7	2 08.5	17 33.8	18 35.1	27 32.7	18 52.6	28 52.9	24 22.2	1 39.4
24 Su	18 10 11	2 11 46	28 49 35	6♒21 22	23 49.2	18 59.8	3 22.6	18 20.3	18 59.2	27 46.3	18 55.9	28 56.1	24 24.4	1 41.5
25 M	18 14 08	3 12 55	13♒47 52	21 08 14	23 41.0	20 27.6	4 36.7	19 06.8	19 23.2	28 00.0	18 59.3	28 59.4	24 26.5	1 43.6
26 Tu	18 18 04	4 14 04	28 21 49	5♓28 14	23 35.2	21 54.1	5 50.7	19 53.4	19 47.1	28 13.7	19 02.8	29 02.7	24 28.7	1 45.7
27 W	18 22 01	5 15 13	12♓27 19	19 19 07	23 32.1	23 18.8	7 04.7	20 40.0	20 10.9	28 27.4	19 06.4	29 06.0	24 30.8	1 47.8
28 Th	18 25 57	6 16 22	26 03 50	2♈41 47	23D31.0	24 41.4	8 18.7	21 26.7	20 34.7	28 41.0	19 10.1	29 09.3	24 33.0	1 49.9
29 F	18 29 54	7 17 32	9♈13 26	15 39 18	23R31.1	26 01.7	9 32.6	22 13.4	20 58.3	28 54.6	19 13.9	29 12.6	24 35.2	1 51.9
30 Sa	18 33 51	8 18 41	21 59 55	28 15 53	23 31.2	27 19.0	10 46.5	23 00.1	21 21.8	29 08.3	19 17.8	29 16.0	24 37.4	1 54.0
31 Su	18 37 47	9 19 49	4♉27 46	10♉36 09	23 29.9	28 32.9	12 00.3	23 46.8	21 45.3	29 21.9	19 21.7	29 19.3	24 39.6	1 56.0

Astro Data

	Dy Hr Mn
☽ 0N	3 7:05
♃□♄	11 2:30
☽ 0S	17 22:19
♄ D	21 19:48
☽ 0N	30 13:07
♃⚺♆	7 3:48
☽ 0S	15 7:50
☽ 0N	27 20:48
♃⚺♅	31 6:02

Planet Ingress

	Dy Hr Mn
♀ ♐	3 10:18
☿ ♏	4 8:50
⚳ ♏	9 19:18
♇ ♐	10 19:11
☉ ♐	22 19:01
☿ ♐	22 22:46
♀ ♑	27 13:23
♂ ♑	30 13:57
☿ ♑	12 2:57
♀ ♒	21 18:23
☉ ♑	22 8:17

Last Aspect / ☽ Ingress

Last Aspect Dy Hr Mn		☽ Ingress Dy Hr Mn
1 12:40 ♇ □	♓	1 13:17
3 18:51 ♇ △	♈	3 19:21
5 21:42 ♅ □	♉	6 3:35
8 13:44 ♇ ☍	♊	8 13:54
10 2:00 ♄ □	♋	11 1:56
13 8:50 ♅ ☍	♌	13 14:37
15 11:40 ☉ □	♍	16 2:02
18 5:22 ♅ △	♎	18 10:18
20 10:13 ♅ □	♏	20 14:40
22 15:43 ☉ ☌	♐	22 15:56
24 9:33 ♀ ☌	♑	24 15:48
26 12:18 ♅ ☌	♒	26 16:15
28 16:29 ♂ ⚹	♓	28 18:59

Last Aspect / ☽ Ingress

Last Aspect Dy Hr Mn		☽ Ingress Dy Hr Mn
30 20:45 ♅ ⚹	♈	1 0:51
3 5:34 ♅ □	♉	3 9:40
5 16:35 ♅ △	♊	5 20:35
7 20:36 ♃ ☍	♋	8 8:44
10 17:50 ♅ ☍	♌	10 21:24
12 23:50 ♃ △	♍	13 9:26
15 16:18 ♅ △	♎	15 19:09
17 22:40 ♅ □	♏	18 1:07
20 1:07 ♅ ⚹	♐	20 3:13
22 2:22 ☉ ☌	♑	22 2:46
24 0:08 ♅ ☌	♒	24 1:52
25 23:35 ♃ ⚹	♓	26 2:45
28 5:32 ♅ ⚹	♈	28 7:06
30 13:56 ♅ □	♉	30 15:21

☽ Phases & Eclipses

Dy Hr Mn	
7 7:20	○ 14♉24
15 11:40	☾ 22♌38
22 15:43	● 29♏52
29 6:28	☽ 6♓33
7 1:27	○ 14♊27
15 5:31	☾ 22♍45
22 2:22	● 29♐45
28 19:06	☽ 6♈34

Astro Data

1 November 1995
Julian Day # 35003
SVP 5♓18'58"
GC 26♐46.9 ⚴ 4♎01.5
Eris 18♈00.3R ⚵ 3♑12.0
⚷ 7♎32.9 ⚶ 4♎42.5
☽ Mean ☊ 25♎38.4

1 December 1995
Julian Day # 35033
SVP 5♓18'54"
GC 26♐46.9 ⚴ 16♎47.2
Eris 17♈45.9R ⚵ 13♑26.1
⚷ 11♎08.7 ⚶ 18♎49.0
☽ Mean ☊ 24♎03.1

LONGITUDE — January 1996

Day	Sid.Time	☉	0 hr ☽	Noon ☽	True ☊	☿	♀	♂	⚳	♃	♄	♅	♆	♇
1 M	18 41 44	10♑20 58	16♉41 33	22♉44 29	23♎26.4	29♑42.9	13♒14.2	24♑33.6	22♏08.6	29♐35.5	19♓25.8	29♑22.7	24♑41.8	1♐58.0
2 Tu	18 45 40	11 22 07	28 45 26	4♊44 47	23R 20.0	0♒48.3	14 27.9	25 20.4	22 31.9	29 49.1	19 29.9	29 26.1	24 44.0	1 59.9
3 W	18 49 37	12 23 16	10♊42 55	16 40 10	23 10.6	1 48.3	15 41.7	26 07.3	22 55.1	0♑02.6	19 34.1	29 29.5	24 46.3	2 01.9
4 Th	18 53 33	13 24 24	22 36 49	28 33 06	22 58.3	2 42.2	16 55.4	26 54.1	23 18.1	0 16.2	19 38.4	29 32.9	24 48.5	2 03.8
5 F	18 57 30	14 25 33	4♋29 13	10♋25 22	22 44.1	3 29.1	18 09.0	27 41.0	23 41.1	0 29.7	19 42.8	29 36.4	24 50.8	2 05.7
6 Sa	19 01 26	15 26 41	16 21 42	22 18 22	22 29.0	4 08.2	19 22.6	28 28.0	24 03.9	0 43.2	19 47.3	29 39.8	24 53.0	2 07.6
7 Su	19 05 23	16 27 50	28 15 30	4♌13 16	22 14.3	4 38.5	20 36.2	29 14.9	24 26.6	0 56.6	19 51.8	29 43.3	24 55.3	2 09.5
8 M	19 09 20	17 28 58	10♌11 50	16 11 23	22 01.0	4 59.1	21 49.7	0♒01.9	24 49.3	1 10.1	19 56.4	29 46.7	24 57.5	2 11.3
9 Tu	19 13 16	18 30 06	22 12 09	28 14 24	21 50.2	5R 09.2	23 03.1	0 48.9	25 11.8	1 23.5	20 01.1	29 50.2	24 59.8	2 13.1
10 W	19 17 13	19 31 14	4♍18 25	10♍24 33	21 42.4	5 08.2	24 16.5	1 36.0	25 34.2	1 36.9	20 05.9	29 53.7	25 02.1	2 14.9
11 Th	19 21 09	20 32 22	16 33 12	22 44 47	21 37.7	4 55.5	25 29.9	2 23.0	25 56.5	1 50.3	20 10.8	29 57.2	25 04.3	2 16.7
12 F	19 25 06	21 33 30	28 59 47	5♎18 42	21 35.5	4 30.9	26 43.2	3 10.1	26 18.7	2 03.6	20 15.7	0♒00.7	25 06.6	2 18.4
13 Sa	19 29 02	22 34 38	11♎42 02	18 10 20	21 35.0	3 54.8	27 56.5	3 57.2	26 40.7	2 16.9	20 20.7	0 04.2	25 08.9	2 20.1
14 Su	19 32 59	23 35 46	24 44 06	1♏23 50	21 34.9	3 07.5	29 09.7	4 44.4	27 02.7	2 30.2	20 25.8	0 07.7	25 11.2	2 21.8
15 M	19 36 55	24 36 54	8♏09 56	15 02 44	21 33.9	2 10.3	0♓22.8	5 31.5	27 24.5	2 43.4	20 31.0	0 11.2	25 13.4	2 23.5
16 Tu	19 40 52	25 38 02	22 02 28	29 09 11	21 30.9	1 04.7	1 35.9	6 18.7	27 46.2	2 56.7	20 36.2	0 14.8	25 15.7	2 25.1
17 W	19 44 49	26 39 09	6♐22 45	13♐42 50	21 25.2	29♑52.6	2 49.0	7 05.9	28 07.8	3 09.8	20 41.5	0 18.3	25 18.0	2 26.7
18 Th	19 48 45	27 40 16	21 08 51	28 39 59	21 16.7	28 36.2	4 02.0	7 53.2	28 29.2	3 23.0	20 46.9	0 21.8	25 20.3	2 28.3
19 F	19 52 42	28 41 23	6♑15 14	13♑53 19	21 06.0	27 18.1	5 14.9	8 40.4	28 50.5	3 36.0	20 52.3	0 25.4	25 22.5	2 29.9
20 Sa	19 56 38	29 42 30	21 32 54	29 12 28	20 54.2	26 00.5	6 27.8	9 27.7	29 11.7	3 49.1	20 57.9	0 28.9	25 24.8	2 31.4
21 Su	20 00 35	0♒43 36	6♒50 33	14♒25 42	20 42.9	24 45.8	7 40.6	10 15.0	29 32.7	4 02.1	21 03.4	0 32.4	25 27.1	2 32.9
22 M	20 04 31	1 44 41	21 56 37	29 22 09	20 33.2	23 36.0	8 53.3	11 02.3	29 53.6	4 15.1	21 09.1	0 36.0	25 29.4	2 34.4
23 Tu	20 08 28	2 45 45	6♓41 25	13♓53 43	20 26.2	22 32.7	10 06.0	11 49.7	0♐14.3	4 28.0	21 14.8	0 39.5	25 31.6	2 35.8
24 W	20 12 24	3 46 48	20 58 38	27 55 58	20 21.9	21 37.0	11 18.6	12 37.0	0 34.9	4 40.8	21 20.6	0 43.0	25 33.9	2 37.2
25 Th	20 16 21	4 47 50	4♈45 43	11♈28 05	20D 20.2	20 49.7	12 31.1	13 24.3	0 55.4	4 53.6	21 26.4	0 46.6	25 36.2	2 38.6
26 F	20 20 18	5 48 51	18 03 24	24 32 07	20R 20.0	20 11.4	13 43.6	14 11.7	1 15.7	5 06.4	21 32.3	0 50.1	25 38.4	2 40.0
27 Sa	20 24 14	6 49 51	0♉54 47	7♉11 59	20 20.1	19 42.2	14 55.9	14 59.1	1 35.8	5 19.1	21 38.3	0 53.6	25 40.7	2 41.3
28 Su	20 28 11	7 50 49	13 24 22	19 32 34	20 19.5	19 21.9	16 08.2	15 46.5	1 55.8	5 31.8	21 44.3	0 57.1	25 42.9	2 42.6
29 M	20 32 07	8 51 47	25 37 14	1♊38 59	20 17.0	19D 10.2	17 20.4	16 33.9	2 15.7	5 44.4	21 50.3	1 00.6	25 45.1	2 43.9
30 Tu	20 36 04	9 52 44	7♊38 26	13 36 07	20 12.0	19 06.8	18 32.5	17 21.3	2 35.4	5 56.9	21 56.5	1 04.1	25 47.4	2 45.1
31 W	20 40 00	10 53 39	19 32 34	25 28 16	20 04.1	19 11.2	19 44.5	18 08.7	2 54.9	6 09.4	22 02.6	1 07.6	25 49.6	2 46.3

LONGITUDE — February 1996

Day	Sid.Time	☉	0 hr ☽	Noon ☽	True ☊	☿	♀	♂	⚳	♃	♄	♅	♆	♇
1 Th	20 43 57	11♒54 33	1♋23 38	7♋19 03	19♎53.8	19♑22.8	20♓56.4	18♒56.1	3♐14.2	6♑21.8	22♓08.9	1♒11.1	25♑51.8	2♐47.4
2 F	20 47 53	12 55 26	13 14 50	19 11 15	19R 41.5	19 41.0	22 08.2	19 43.5	3 33.4	6 34.2	22 15.2	1 14.6	25 54.0	2 48.6
3 Sa	20 51 50	13 56 17	25 08 34	1♌06 58	19 28.4	20 05.5	23 20.0	20 30.9	3 52.5	6 46.5	22 21.5	1 18.1	25 56.2	2 49.7
4 Su	20 55 47	14 57 08	7♌06 38	13 07 41	19 15.5	20 35.5	24 31.6	21 18.4	4 11.3	6 58.7	22 27.9	1 21.6	25 58.4	2 50.8
5 M	20 59 43	15 57 57	19 10 15	25 14 28	19 04.0	21 10.8	25 43.1	22 05.8	4 30.0	7 10.9	22 34.3	1 25.0	26 00.5	2 51.8
6 Tu	21 03 40	16 58 45	1♍20 26	7♍28 17	18 54.6	21 50.7	26 54.5	22 53.2	4 48.5	7 23.0	22 40.8	1 28.5	26 02.7	2 52.8
7 W	21 07 36	17 59 32	13 38 10	19 50 16	18 47.9	22 35.0	28 05.8	23 40.7	5 06.8	7 35.0	22 47.4	1 31.9	26 04.9	2 53.8
8 Th	21 11 33	19 00 18	26 04 46	2♎21 54	18 44.1	23 23.2	29 17.0	24 28.1	5 25.0	7 47.0	22 53.9	1 35.3	26 07.0	2 54.7
9 F	21 15 29	20 01 03	8♎41 56	15 05 10	18D 42.6	24 15.0	0♈28.1	25 15.6	5 43.0	7 58.9	23 00.5	1 38.7	26 09.1	2 55.6
10 Sa	21 19 26	21 01 47	21 31 56	28 02 34	18 42.9	25 10.1	1 39.1	26 03.0	6 00.7	8 10.7	23 07.2	1 42.1	26 11.2	2 56.5
11 Su	21 23 22	22 02 30	4♏37 24	11♏16 49	18R 43.7	26 08.3	2 49.9	26 50.5	6 18.3	8 22.5	23 13.9	1 45.5	26 13.4	2 57.3
12 M	21 27 19	23 03 12	18 01 07	24 50 34	18 44.1	27 09.2	4 00.7	27 38.0	6 35.7	8 34.2	23 20.7	1 48.8	26 15.4	2 58.1
13 Tu	21 31 16	24 03 53	1♐45 23	8♐45 41	18 43.1	28 12.6	5 11.3	28 25.4	6 52.9	8 45.8	23 27.5	1 52.2	26 17.5	2 58.9
14 W	21 35 12	25 04 32	15 51 27	23 02 31	18 39.9	29 18.5	6 21.8	29 12.9	7 09.9	8 57.3	23 34.3	1 55.5	26 19.6	2 59.6
15 Th	21 39 09	26 05 11	0♑18 35	7♑39 09	18 34.6	0♒26.5	7 32.2	0♓00.3	7 26.7	9 08.7	23 41.2	1 58.8	26 21.6	3 00.3
16 F	21 43 05	27 05 48	15 03 33	22 30 54	18 27.4	1 36.6	8 42.5	0 47.8	7 43.3	9 20.1	23 48.1	2 02.1	26 23.7	3 01.0
17 Sa	21 47 02	28 06 25	0♒00 15	7♒30 28	18 19.3	2 48.5	9 52.6	1 35.3	7 59.6	9 31.4	23 55.0	2 05.4	26 25.7	3 01.6
18 Su	21 50 58	29 06 59	15 00 21	22 28 44	18 11.4	4 02.3	11 02.6	2 22.7	8 15.8	9 42.5	24 02.0	2 08.6	26 27.7	3 02.2
19 M	21 54 55	0♓07 32	29 54 26	7♓16 21	18 04.5	5 17.7	12 12.5	3 10.1	8 31.7	9 53.6	24 09.0	2 11.9	26 29.7	3 02.8
20 Tu	21 58 51	1 08 04	14♓33 32	21 45 13	17 59.6	6 34.7	13 22.2	3 57.6	8 47.4	10 04.6	24 16.0	2 15.1	26 31.6	3 03.3
21 W	22 02 48	2 08 33	28 50 46	5♈49 45	17D 56.9	7 53.2	14 31.8	4 45.0	9 02.9	10 15.6	24 23.1	2 18.3	26 33.6	3 03.8
22 Th	22 06 45	3 09 01	12♈41 58	19 27 21	17 56.2	9 13.1	15 41.2	5 32.4	9 18.2	10 26.4	24 30.2	2 21.4	26 35.5	3 04.2
23 F	22 10 41	4 09 28	26 06 00	2♉38 09	17 57.0	10 34.4	16 50.5	6 19.8	9 33.2	10 37.1	24 37.3	2 24.6	26 37.4	3 04.7
24 Sa	22 14 38	5 09 52	9♉04 11	15 24 32	17 58.4	11 57.1	17 59.6	7 07.2	9 48.0	10 47.7	24 44.5	2 27.7	26 39.3	3 05.0
25 Su	22 18 34	6 10 14	21 39 44	27 50 21	17R 59.7	13 20.9	19 08.5	7 54.6	10 02.5	10 58.3	24 51.6	2 30.8	26 41.2	3 05.4
26 M	22 22 31	7 10 35	3♊56 59	10♊00 15	18 00.0	14 46.1	20 17.3	8 42.0	10 16.8	11 08.7	24 58.8	2 33.8	26 43.0	3 05.7
27 Tu	22 26 27	8 10 53	16 00 48	21 59 15	17 58.8	16 12.4	21 25.9	9 29.3	10 30.9	11 19.1	25 06.1	2 36.9	26 44.9	3 06.0
28 W	22 30 24	9 11 10	27 56 10	3♋52 10	17 55.8	17 39.9	22 34.3	10 16.7	10 44.7	11 29.3	25 13.3	2 39.9	26 46.7	3 06.2
29 Th	22 34 20	10 11 24	9♋47 46	15 43 30	17 51.2	19 08.5	23 42.6	11 04.0	10 58.2	11 39.4	25 20.6	2 42.9	26 48.5	3 06.4

Astro Data	Dy Hr Mn	Planet Ingress	Dy Hr Mn
☿ R	9 21:53	☿ ♒	1 18:06
☽ 0S	11 15:50	♃ ♑	3 7:22
♃⚺♇	13 18:38	♂ ♒	8 11:02
☽ 0N	24 6:55	♅ ♒	12 7:13
☿ D	30 10:17	♀ ♓	15 4:30
		☿ ♑R	17 9:37
☽ 0S	7 22:33	☉ ♒	20 18:52
♀0N	10 1:54	⚳ ♐	22 19:24
☽ 0N	20 18:13		
		♀ ♈	9 2:30
		☿ ♒	15 2:44
		♂ ♓	15 11:50
		☉ ♓	19 9:01

Last Aspect Dy Hr Mn		☽ Ingress Dy Hr Mn	
2 1:18	♅ △	♊	2 2:29
3 17:53	♄ □	♋	4 14:56
7 2:54	♅ ☍	♌	7 3:30
9 0:32	♀ ☍	♍	9 15:29
12 1:53	♅ △	♎	12 1:55
14 7:35	♀ △	♏	14 9:30
16 5:38	☉ ⚹	♐	16 13:25
17 23:20	♄ □	♑	18 14:07
20 12:51	☉ ☌	♒	20 13:15
21 5:01	♂ ☌	♓	22 13:02
24 7:53	♆ ⚹	♈	24 15:37
26 14:04	♆ □	♉	26 22:16
29 0:13	♆ △	♊	29 8:42
31 5:00	♄ □	♋	31 21:11

Last Aspect Dy Hr Mn		☽ Ingress Dy Hr Mn	
3 1:34	♆ ☍	♌	3 9:46
5 5:22	♂ ☍	♍	5 21:22
8 5:31	♀ ☍	♎	8 7:30
10 8:35	♆ □	♏	10 15:35
12 17:09	♂ □	♐	12 20:58
14 22:47	♂ ⚹	♑	14 23:29
16 18:14	♆ ☌	♒	16 24:00
18 23:30	☉ ☌	♓	19 0:09
20 20:05	♆ ⚹	♈	21 1:58
23 0:56	♆ □	♉	23 7:08
25 9:45	♆ △	♊	25 16:14
27 18:20	♄ □	♋	28 4:10

☽ Phases & Eclipses Dy Hr Mn	
5 20:51	○ 14♋48
13 20:45	☾ 22♎57
20 12:51	● 29♑45
27 11:14	☽ 6♉48
4 15:58	○ 15♌07
12 8:37	☾ 22♏55
18 23:30	● 29♒36
26 5:52	☽ 6♊55

Astro Data

1 January 1996
Julian Day # 35064
SVP 5♓18'49"
GC 26♐47.0 ⚴ 28♎01.2
Eris 17♈39.3R ⚵ 25♑22.5
⚷ 13♎37.1 ⚶ 2♏29.4
☽ Mean ☊ 22♎24.6

1 February 1996
Julian Day # 35095
SVP 5♓18'44"
GC 26♐47.1 ⚴ 5♏59.6
Eris 17♈43.1 ⚵ 8♒08.5
⚷ 14♎20.2R ⚶ 14♏16.1
☽ Mean ☊ 20♎46.2

March 1996

LONGITUDE

Day	Sid.Time	☉	0 hr ☽	Noon ☽	True ☊	☿	♀	♂	⚳	♃	♄	♅	♆	♇
1 F	22 38 17	11♓11 37	21♋39 49	27♋37 09	17♎45.3	20♒38.3	24♈50.6	11♓51.3	11♐11.5	11♑49.4	25♓27.9	2♒45.9	26♑50.2	3♐06.6
2 Sa	22 42 14	12 11 47	3♌35 52	9♌36 18	17R 38.7	22 09.2	25 58.5	12 38.6	11 24.6	11 59.4	25 35.2	2 48.8	26 52.0	3 06.7
3 Su	22 46 10	13 11 56	15 38 44	21 43 25	17 32.1	23 41.3	27 06.1	13 25.9	11 37.4	12 09.2	25 42.5	2 51.7	26 53.7	3 06.8
4 M	22 50 07	14 12 02	27 50 31	4♍00 12	17 26.2	25 14.4	28 13.6	14 13.1	11 49.9	12 18.9	25 49.8	2 54.6	26 55.4	3 06.9
5 Tu	22 54 03	15 12 07	10♍12 35	16 27 45	17 21.5	26 48.7	29 20.8	15 00.4	12 02.1	12 28.5	25 57.2	2 57.4	26 57.1	3R06.9
6 W	22 58 00	16 12 09	22 45 47	29 06 44	17 18.5	28 24.0	0♉27.9	15 47.6	12 14.1	12 37.9	26 04.5	3 00.2	26 58.7	3 06.9
7 Th	23 01 56	17 12 10	5♎30 37	11♎57 29	17D 17.1	0♓00.5	1 34.7	16 34.8	12 25.8	12 47.3	26 11.9	3 03.0	27 00.3	3 06.9
8 F	23 05 53	18 12 10	18 27 22	25 00 19	17 17.2	1 38.0	2 41.3	17 21.9	12 37.2	12 56.5	26 19.3	3 05.7	27 01.9	3 06.8
9 Sa	23 09 49	19 12 07	1♏36 23	8♏15 37	17 18.4	3 16.8	3 47.6	18 09.1	12 48.3	13 05.7	26 26.7	3 08.5	27 03.5	3 06.7
10 Su	23 13 46	20 12 03	14 58 06	21 43 51	17 19.9	4 56.6	4 53.8	18 56.2	12 59.1	13 14.7	26 34.1	3 11.1	27 05.1	3 06.6
11 M	23 17 42	21 11 57	28 32 58	5♐25 27	17 21.4	6 37.6	5 59.7	19 43.4	13 09.7	13 23.6	26 41.5	3 13.8	27 06.6	3 06.4
12 Tu	23 21 39	22 11 50	12♐21 19	19 20 33	17R 22.1	8 19.7	7 05.3	20 30.5	13 19.9	13 32.3	26 49.0	3 16.4	27 08.1	3 06.2
13 W	23 25 36	23 11 41	26 23 02	3♑28 37	17 21.8	10 03.0	8 10.7	21 17.6	13 29.9	13 41.0	26 56.4	3 19.0	27 09.6	3 05.9
14 Th	23 29 32	24 11 30	10♑37 04	17 48 04	17 20.4	11 47.5	9 15.9	22 04.6	13 39.5	13 49.5	27 03.8	3 21.5	27 11.1	3 05.7
15 F	23 33 29	25 11 18	25 01 11	2♒15 56	17 18.0	13 33.2	10 20.8	22 51.7	13 48.8	13 57.9	27 11.3	3 24.1	27 12.5	3 05.3
16 Sa	23 37 25	26 11 04	9♒31 42	16 47 50	17 15.2	15 20.1	11 25.4	23 38.7	13 57.9	14 06.1	27 18.7	3 26.5	27 13.9	3 05.0
17 Su	23 41 22	27 10 48	24 03 36	1♓18 16	17 12.3	17 08.2	12 29.7	24 25.6	14 06.5	14 14.3	27 26.2	3 29.0	27 15.2	3 04.6
18 M	23 45 18	28 10 30	8♓31 03	15 41 14	17 09.9	18 57.5	13 33.8	25 12.6	14 14.9	14 22.2	27 33.6	3 31.4	27 16.6	3 04.2
19 Tu	23 49 15	29 10 10	22 48 07	29 51 04	17 08.2	20 48.1	14 37.6	25 59.5	14 22.9	14 30.1	27 41.1	3 33.7	27 17.9	3 03.8
20 W	23 53 11	0♈09 49	6♈49 34	13♈43 09	17D 07.6	22 39.9	15 41.0	26 46.4	14 30.6	14 37.8	27 48.5	3 36.1	27 19.2	3 03.3
21 Th	23 57 08	1 09 25	20 31 32	27 14 30	17 07.8	24 32.9	16 44.2	27 33.3	14 38.0	14 45.4	27 56.0	3 38.3	27 20.4	3 02.8
22 F	0 01 05	2 08 59	3♉51 59	10♉23 59	17 08.6	26 27.1	17 47.0	28 20.2	14 45.0	14 52.8	28 03.4	3 40.6	27 21.7	3 02.2
23 Sa	0 05 01	3 08 31	16 50 40	23 12 16	17 09.8	28 22.6	18 49.5	29 07.0	14 51.7	15 00.1	28 10.8	3 42.8	27 22.9	3 01.6
24 Su	0 08 58	4 08 00	29 29 06	5♊41 32	17 11.1	0♈19.3	19 51.7	29 53.8	14 58.1	15 07.3	28 18.3	3 45.0	27 24.0	3 01.0
25 M	0 12 54	5 07 27	11♊50 02	17 55 07	17 12.1	2 17.1	20 53.5	0♈40.5	15 04.0	15 14.3	28 25.7	3 47.1	27 25.2	3 00.4
26 Tu	0 16 51	6 06 53	23 57 17	29 57 07	17R 12.6	4 16.0	21 54.9	1 27.2	15 09.7	15 21.1	28 33.1	3 49.2	27 26.3	2 59.7
27 W	0 20 47	7 06 15	5♋55 12	11♋52 07	17 12.6	6 16.0	22 56.0	2 13.9	15 15.0	15 27.8	28 40.5	3 51.2	27 27.4	2 59.0
28 Th	0 24 44	8 05 36	17 48 27	23 44 47	17 12.2	8 16.9	23 56.7	3 00.5	15 19.9	15 34.4	28 47.9	3 53.2	27 28.4	2 58.3
29 F	0 28 40	9 04 54	29 41 41	5♌39 41	17 11.4	10 18.7	24 57.0	3 47.2	15 24.5	15 40.8	28 55.3	3 55.2	27 29.5	2 57.5
30 Sa	0 32 37	10 04 10	11♌39 19	17 41 04	17 10.5	12 21.3	25 56.8	4 33.7	15 28.7	15 47.1	29 02.6	3 57.1	27 30.4	2 56.7
31 Su	0 36 34	11 03 23	23 45 20	29 52 33	17 09.6	14 24.4	26 56.2	5 20.3	15 32.5	15 53.2	29 10.0	3 58.9	27 31.4	2 55.9

April 1996

LONGITUDE

Day	Sid.Time	☉	0 hr ☽	Noon ☽	True ☊	☿	♀	♂	⚳	♃	♄	♅	♆	♇
1 M	0 40 30	12♈02 34	6♍03 03	12♍17 08	17♎08.9	16♈27.9	27♉55.2	6♈06.8	15♐36.0	15♑59.1	29♓17.3	4♒00.8	27♑32.3	2♐55.1
2 Tu	0 44 27	13 01 43	18 35 00	24 56 50	17R 08.4	18 31.7	28 53.7	6 53.2	15 39.1	16 04.9	29 24.6	4 02.5	27 33.2	2R54.2
3 W	0 48 23	14 00 50	1♎22 44	7♎52 45	17D 08.2	20 35.4	29 51.7	7 39.6	15 41.8	16 10.5	29 31.9	4 04.3	27 34.1	2 53.3
4 Th	0 52 20	14 59 55	14 26 51	21 04 58	17 08.1	22 38.8	0♊49.3	8 26.0	15 44.2	16 16.0	29 39.2	4 06.0	27 34.9	2 52.3
5 F	0 56 16	15 58 58	27 46 57	4♏32 37	17 08.2	24 41.6	1 46.3	9 12.4	15 46.1	16 21.3	29 46.5	4 07.6	27 35.7	2 51.4
6 Sa	1 00 13	16 57 59	11♏21 45	18 14 05	17R 08.3	26 43.4	2 42.9	9 58.7	15 47.7	16 26.5	29 53.7	4 09.2	27 36.5	2 50.4
7 Su	1 04 09	17 56 58	25 09 19	2♐07 08	17 08.2	28 44.1	3 38.9	10 45.0	15 48.9	16 31.4	0♈01.0	4 10.8	27 37.2	2 49.4
8 M	1 08 06	18 55 55	9♐07 12	16 09 12	17 08.1	0♉43.1	4 34.3	11 31.2	15 49.8	16 36.3	0 08.2	4 12.3	27 37.9	2 48.3
9 Tu	1 12 03	19 54 51	23 12 48	0♑17 39	17 07.9	2 40.1	5 29.2	12 17.4	15R 50.2	16 40.9	0 15.3	4 13.8	27 38.6	2 47.3
10 W	1 15 59	20 53 45	7♑23 27	14 29 52	17D 07.8	4 34.8	6 23.5	13 03.6	15 50.3	16 45.4	0 22.5	4 15.2	27 39.3	2 46.2
11 Th	1 19 56	21 52 37	21 36 35	28 43 18	17 07.8	6 26.8	7 17.1	13 49.7	15 49.9	16 49.7	0 29.6	4 16.5	27 39.9	2 45.1
12 F	1 23 52	22 51 27	5♒49 43	12♒55 31	17 08.0	8 15.7	8 10.2	14 35.8	15 49.2	16 53.9	0 36.7	4 17.9	27 40.4	2 43.9
13 Sa	1 27 49	23 50 16	20 00 24	27 04 03	17 08.5	10 01.3	9 02.6	15 21.9	15 48.0	16 57.8	0 43.8	4 19.1	27 41.0	2 42.8
14 Su	1 31 45	24 49 03	4♓06 10	11♓06 26	17 09.2	11 43.3	9 54.3	16 07.9	15 46.5	17 01.6	0 50.8	4 20.4	27 41.5	2 41.6
15 M	1 35 42	25 47 48	18 04 32	25 00 08	17 09.9	13 21.3	10 45.3	16 53.8	15 44.6	17 05.2	0 57.9	4 21.5	27 42.0	2 40.4
16 Tu	1 39 38	26 46 32	1♈52 58	8♈42 42	17R 10.3	14 55.2	11 35.6	17 39.7	15 42.3	17 08.7	1 04.8	4 22.7	27 42.4	2 39.1
17 W	1 43 35	27 45 13	15 29 06	22 11 55	17 10.4	16 24.6	12 25.2	18 25.6	15 39.5	17 11.9	1 11.8	4 23.8	27 42.8	2 37.9
18 Th	1 47 31	28 43 53	28 50 57	5♉26 04	17 09.9	17 49.5	13 14.0	19 11.5	15 36.4	17 15.0	1 18.7	4 24.8	27 43.2	2 36.6
19 F	1 51 28	29 42 30	11♉57 08	18 24 07	17 08.7	19 09.7	14 02.0	19 57.3	15 32.9	17 17.9	1 25.6	4 25.8	27 43.5	2 35.3
20 Sa	1 55 25	0♉41 06	24 47 02	1♊05 58	17 07.0	20 24.9	14 49.1	20 43.0	15 29.1	17 20.6	1 32.4	4 26.7	27 43.9	2 34.0
21 Su	1 59 21	1 39 40	7♊21 04	13 32 32	17 04.9	21 35.2	15 35.4	21 28.7	15 24.8	17 23.2	1 39.3	4 27.6	27 44.1	2 32.6
22 M	2 03 18	2 38 11	19 40 39	25 45 43	17 02.8	22 40.3	16 20.7	22 14.4	15 20.1	17 25.5	1 46.0	4 28.4	27 44.4	2 31.3
23 Tu	2 07 14	3 36 40	1♋48 08	7♋48 20	17 00.8	23 40.2	17 05.1	23 00.0	15 15.1	17 27.7	1 52.8	4 29.2	27 44.6	2 29.9
24 W	2 11 11	4 35 08	13 46 47	19 43 59	16 59.3	24 34.7	17 48.6	23 45.5	15 09.7	17 29.7	1 59.5	4 30.0	27 44.8	2 28.5
25 Th	2 15 07	5 33 33	25 40 30	1♌36 52	16D 58.6	25 23.9	18 31.0	24 31.0	15 03.9	17 31.5	2 06.1	4 30.6	27 44.9	2 27.1
26 F	2 19 04	6 31 56	7♌33 41	13 31 32	16 58.8	26 07.5	19 12.3	25 16.5	14 57.7	17 33.1	2 12.7	4 31.3	27 45.0	2 25.7
27 Sa	2 23 00	7 30 17	19 31 01	25 32 42	16 59.6	26 45.7	19 52.5	26 01.9	14 51.2	17 34.5	2 19.3	4 31.9	27 45.1	2 24.2
28 Su	2 26 57	8 28 36	1♍37 11	7♍45 00	17 01.1	27 18.3	20 31.6	26 47.3	14 44.3	17 35.8	2 25.8	4 32.4	27R 45.2	2 22.8
29 M	2 30 54	9 26 52	13 56 39	20 12 36	17 02.6	27 45.3	21 09.5	27 32.6	14 37.1	17 36.8	2 32.3	4 32.9	27 45.2	2 21.3
30 Tu	2 34 50	10 25 07	26 33 16	2♎58 59	17 03.9	28 06.8	21 46.2	28 17.8	14 29.5	17 37.7	2 38.7	4 33.3	27 45.2	2 19.8

Astro Data Dy Hr Mn	Planet Ingress Dy Hr Mn	Last Aspect Dy Hr Mn	☽ Ingress Dy Hr Mn	Last Aspect Dy Hr Mn	☽ Ingress Dy Hr Mn	☽ Phases & Eclipses Dy Hr Mn
♇R 5 20:18	♀ ♉ 6 2:01	1 10:25 ♆ ☍	♌ 1 16:47	2 20:25 ♄ ☍	♎ 2 21:26	5 9:23 ○ 15♍06
☽0S 6 5:14	☿ ♓ 7 11:53	3 23:37 ♀ △	♍ 4 4:13	4 23:39 ♆ □	♏ 5 3:57	12 17:15 ☾ 22♐25
♅✶♇ 8 21:05	☉ ♈ 20 8:03	6 7:58 ♆ △	♎ 6 13:40	7 8:21 ♄ △	♐ 7 8:21	19 10:45 ● 29♓07
♄✶♆ 15 16:44	☿ ♈ 24 8:03	8 15:42 ♆ □	♏ 8 21:05	8 17:05 ☉ △	♑ 9 11:30	27 1:31 ☽ 6♋40
☽0N 19 4:37	♂ ♈ 24 15:12	10 21:27 ♆ ✶	♐ 11 2:32	11 10:13 ♆ ☌	♒ 11 14:09	
☉0N 20 8:03		13 0:51 ♄ □	♑ 13 6:08	13 6:06 ☉ ✶	♓ 13 17:00	4 0:07 ○ 14♎31
☿0N 26 0:59	♀ ♊ 3 15:26	15 3:37 ♆ ☌	♒ 15 8:15	15 16:42 ♆ ✶	♈ 15 20:42	4 0:10 • T 1.379
♂0N 27 2:54	♄ ♈ 7 8:49	16 2:25 ♀ □	♓ 17 9:50	17 22:49 ☉ ☌	♉ 18 2:05	10 23:36 ☾ 21♑22
☽0S 2 13:01	☿ ♉ 8 3:16	19 10:45 ☉ ☌	♈ 19 12:15	20 5:35 ♆ △	♊ 20 9:54	17 22:49 ● 28♈12
⚳R 10 2:56	☉ ♉ 19 19:10	21 12:11 ♆ □	♉ 21 16:59	22 4:35 ♂ ✶	♋ 22 20:25	17 22:37:10 • P 0.880
☽0N 15 12:50		24 0:03 ♂ ✶	♊ 24 0:59	25 4:11 ♆ ☍	♌ 25 8:44	25 20:40 ☽ 5♌55
♃∠♇ 24 3:35		26 9:10 ♄ □	♋ 26 12:06	27 14:32 ☿ □	♍ 27 20:49	
♄△♇ 28 2:49		28 22:18 ♄ △	♌ 29 0:37	30 2:41 ☿ △	♎ 30 6:27	
♆R 29 9:52		31 5:45 ♀ □	♍ 31 12:15			
☽0S 29 22:06						

Astro Data

1 March 1996
Julian Day # 35124
SVP 5♓18'41"
GC 26♐47.1 ⚴ 8♏35.5R
Eris 17♈55.4 ⚵ 20♒27.1
⚷ 13♎20.6R ⚶ 22♏06.7
☽ Mean ☊ 19♎14.0

1 April 1996
Julian Day # 35155
SVP 5♓18'39"
GC 26♐47.2 ⚴ 4♏10.1R
Eris 18♈14.3 ⚵ 3♓38.9
⚷ 11♎06.5R ⚶ 24♏44.7R
☽ Mean ☊ 17♎35.5

LONGITUDE May 1996

Day	Sid.Time	☉	0 hr ☽	Noon ☽	True ☊	☿	♀	♂	⚳	♃	♄	♅	♆	♇
1 W	2 38 47	11♉23 20	9♎29 59	16♎06 26	17♎04.5	28♉22.7	22♊21.5	29♈03.1	14♐21.5	17♑38.4	2♈45.1	4♒33.7	27♑45.1	2♐18.3
2 Th	2 42 43	12 21 31	22 48 24	29 35 48	17R04.0	28 33.1	22 55.6	29 48.2	14R13.3	17 38.9	2 51.5	4 34.1	27R45.0	2R16.8
3 F	2 46 40	13 19 40	6♏28 27	13♏26 04	17 02.2	28R38.1	23 28.2	0♉33.3	14 04.7	17 39.2	2 57.8	4 34.3	27 44.9	2 15.3
4 Sa	2 50 36	14 17 48	20 28 13	27 34 23	16 59.3	28 37.8	23 59.4	1 18.4	13 55.8	17R39.3	3 04.0	4 34.6	27 44.8	2 13.7
5 Su	2 54 33	15 15 54	4♐43 57	11♐56 12	16 55.5	28 32.4	24 29.1	2 03.4	13 46.5	17 39.2	3 10.2	4 34.8	27 44.6	2 12.2
6 M	2 58 29	16 13 58	19 10 26	26 25 51	16 51.3	28 22.1	24 57.3	2 48.4	13 37.0	17 39.0	3 16.3	4 34.9	27 44.4	2 10.6
7 Tu	3 02 26	17 12 01	3♑41 44	10♑57 19	16 47.5	28 07.3	25 23.9	3 33.3	13 27.2	17 38.6	3 22.4	4 35.0	27 44.1	2 09.0
8 W	3 06 23	18 10 03	18 11 58	25 25 05	16 44.6	27 48.1	25 48.8	4 18.2	13 17.1	17 37.9	3 28.5	4R35.0	27 43.9	2 07.5
9 Th	3 10 19	19 08 03	2♒36 08	9♒44 44	16D42.9	27 25.1	26 12.0	5 03.0	13 06.6	17 37.1	3 34.4	4 35.0	27 43.6	2 05.9
10 F	3 14 16	20 06 02	16 50 33	23 53 21	16 42.6	26 58.7	26 33.4	5 47.8	12 56.0	17 36.1	3 40.4	4 35.0	27 43.2	2 04.3
11 Sa	3 18 12	21 03 59	0♓52 59	7♓49 21	16 43.5	26 29.3	26 53.0	6 32.5	12 45.0	17 34.9	3 46.2	4 34.9	27 42.8	2 02.6
12 Su	3 22 09	22 01 56	14 42 26	21 32 13	16 44.9	25 57.5	27 10.8	7 17.2	12 33.8	17 33.5	3 52.1	4 34.7	27 42.4	2 01.0
13 M	3 26 05	22 59 51	28 18 44	5♈02 03	16R46.2	25 23.9	27 26.5	8 01.8	12 22.4	17 31.9	3 57.8	4 34.5	27 42.0	1 59.4
14 Tu	3 30 02	23 57 44	11♈42 12	18 19 15	16 46.7	24 49.0	27 40.3	8 46.4	12 10.7	17 30.2	4 03.5	4 34.2	27 41.5	1 57.8
15 W	3 33 58	24 55 37	24 53 13	1♉24 10	16 45.7	24 13.6	27 52.0	9 30.9	11 58.8	17 28.2	4 09.1	4 33.9	27 41.0	1 56.1
16 Th	3 37 55	25 53 28	7♉52 05	14 17 01	16 42.9	23 38.2	28 01.7	10 15.3	11 46.8	17 26.1	4 14.7	4 33.6	27 40.5	1 54.5
17 F	3 41 52	26 51 18	20 38 59	26 57 59	16 38.1	23 03.5	28 09.1	10 59.8	11 34.5	17 23.8	4 20.2	4 33.2	27 40.0	1 52.9
18 Sa	3 45 48	27 49 06	3♊14 04	9♊27 17	16 31.7	22 30.0	28 14.3	11 44.1	11 22.1	17 21.3	4 25.7	4 32.7	27 39.4	1 51.2
19 Su	3 49 45	28 46 53	15 37 44	21 45 29	16 24.2	21 58.2	28R17.2	12 28.4	11 09.5	17 18.6	4 31.0	4 32.2	27 38.8	1 49.6
20 M	3 53 41	29 44 38	27 50 44	3♋53 39	16 16.4	21 28.8	28 17.8	13 12.7	10 56.7	17 15.7	4 36.3	4 31.7	27 38.1	1 47.9
21 Tu	3 57 38	0♊42 22	9♋54 29	15 53 31	16 08.9	21 02.2	28 16.0	13 56.9	10 43.8	17 12.7	4 41.6	4 31.1	27 37.5	1 46.3
22 W	4 01 34	1 40 05	21 51 05	27 47 36	16 02.6	20 38.7	28 11.9	14 41.0	10 30.8	17 09.5	4 46.8	4 30.4	27 36.8	1 44.6
23 Th	4 05 31	2 37 46	3♌43 28	9♌39 11	15 58.0	20 18.7	28 05.3	15 25.1	10 17.7	17 06.1	4 51.9	4 29.7	27 36.0	1 42.9
24 F	4 09 27	3 35 25	15 35 17	21 32 18	15 55.2	20 02.6	27 56.3	16 09.1	10 04.6	17 02.5	4 56.9	4 29.0	27 35.3	1 41.3
25 Sa	4 13 24	4 33 03	27 30 49	3♍31 28	15D54.3	19 50.5	27 44.8	16 53.1	9 51.3	16 58.8	5 01.9	4 28.2	27 34.5	1 39.6
26 Su	4 17 21	5 30 39	9♍34 52	15 41 38	15 54.8	19 42.6	27 31.0	17 37.0	9 38.0	16 54.9	5 06.8	4 27.4	27 33.7	1 38.0
27 M	4 21 17	6 28 14	21 52 24	28 07 45	15 55.9	19D39.1	27 14.7	18 20.9	9 24.7	16 50.8	5 11.6	4 26.5	27 32.8	1 36.3
28 Tu	4 25 14	7 25 47	4♎28 16	10♎54 26	15R56.8	19 40.1	26 56.0	19 04.7	9 11.3	16 46.6	5 16.4	4 25.6	27 31.9	1 34.7
29 W	4 29 10	8 23 19	17 26 43	24 05 26	15 56.6	19 45.5	26 35.1	19 48.4	8 57.9	16 42.2	5 21.0	4 24.6	27 31.1	1 33.1
30 Th	4 33 07	9 20 50	0♏50 48	7♏42 55	15 54.6	19 55.4	26 11.9	20 32.1	8 44.5	16 37.7	5 25.6	4 23.6	27 30.1	1 31.4
31 F	4 37 03	10 18 20	14 41 41	21 46 52	15 50.4	20 09.8	25 46.5	21 15.8	8 31.2	16 32.9	5 30.2	4 22.6	27 29.2	1 29.8

LONGITUDE June 1996

Day	Sid.Time	☉	0 hr ☽	Noon ☽	True ☊	☿	♀	♂	⚳	♃	♄	♅	♆	♇
1 Sa	4 41 00	11♊15 48	28♏58 00	6♐14 29	15♎44.1	20♉28.6	25♊19.2	21♉59.3	8♐17.9	16♑28.1	5♈34.6	4♒21.5	27♑28.2	1♐28.2
2 Su	4 44 56	12 13 16	13♐35 30	21 00 08	15R36.2	20 51.8	24R49.9	22 42.9	8R04.6	16R23.1	5 39.0	4R20.3	27R27.2	1R26.6
3 M	4 48 53	13 10 42	28 27 17	5♑55 51	15 27.7	21 19.3	24 18.9	23 26.4	7 51.4	16 17.9	5 43.3	4 19.2	27 26.2	1 24.9
4 Tu	4 52 50	14 08 08	13♑24 38	20 52 33	15 19.5	21 51.0	23 46.4	24 09.8	7 38.3	16 12.6	5 47.5	4 17.9	27 25.2	1 23.3
5 W	4 56 46	15 05 33	28 18 30	5♒41 35	15 12.7	22 26.9	23 12.4	24 53.1	7 25.3	16 07.2	5 51.7	4 16.7	27 24.1	1 21.7
6 Th	5 00 43	16 02 57	13♒00 59	20 16 05	15 08.0	23 06.8	22 37.3	25 36.4	7 12.3	16 01.6	5 55.7	4 15.4	27 23.0	1 20.2
7 F	5 04 39	17 00 21	27 26 26	4♓31 44	15D05.5	23 50.7	22 01.2	26 19.7	6 59.5	15 55.9	5 59.7	4 14.0	27 21.9	1 18.6
8 Sa	5 08 36	17 57 44	11♓31 52	18 26 48	15 04.8	24 38.5	21 24.4	27 02.9	6 46.8	15 50.0	6 03.6	4 12.7	27 20.7	1 17.0
9 Su	5 12 32	18 55 06	25 16 38	2♈01 35	15R05.2	25 30.0	20 47.1	27 46.0	6 34.3	15 44.0	6 07.4	4 11.2	27 19.6	1 15.4
10 M	5 16 29	19 52 28	8♈41 53	15 17 49	15 05.6	26 25.2	20 09.5	28 29.1	6 21.9	15 37.9	6 11.1	4 09.8	27 18.4	1 13.9
11 Tu	5 20 25	20 49 50	21 49 42	28 17 49	15 04.8	27 24.0	19 31.9	29 12.2	6 09.7	15 31.7	6 14.8	4 08.3	27 17.2	1 12.4
12 W	5 24 22	21 47 11	4♉42 30	11♉04 00	15 02.0	28 26.4	18 54.5	29 55.2	5 57.7	15 25.4	6 18.4	4 06.7	27 16.0	1 10.8
13 Th	5 28 19	22 44 31	17 22 34	23 38 27	14 56.6	29 32.3	18 17.6	0♊38.1	5 45.9	15 18.9	6 21.8	4 05.2	27 14.7	1 09.3
14 F	5 32 15	23 41 51	29 51 49	6♊02 50	14 48.5	0♊41.5	17 41.4	1 21.0	5 34.2	15 12.3	6 25.2	4 03.5	27 13.4	1 07.8
15 Sa	5 36 12	24 39 11	12♊11 40	18 18 26	14 38.0	1 54.2	17 06.0	2 03.8	5 22.9	15 05.7	6 28.5	4 01.9	27 12.2	1 06.3
16 Su	5 40 08	25 36 30	24 23 15	0♋26 15	14 25.8	3 10.1	16 31.8	2 46.5	5 11.7	14 58.9	6 31.7	4 00.2	27 10.9	1 04.9
17 M	5 44 05	26 33 48	6♋27 32	12 27 16	14 12.9	4 29.3	15 58.9	3 29.2	5 00.8	14 52.0	6 34.8	3 58.5	27 09.5	1 03.4
18 Tu	5 48 01	27 31 06	18 25 37	24 22 45	14 00.5	5 51.8	15 27.5	4 11.9	4 50.2	14 45.1	6 37.9	3 56.7	27 08.2	1 02.0
19 W	5 51 58	28 28 23	0♌18 56	6♌14 26	13 49.6	7 17.5	14 57.8	4 54.5	4 39.8	14 38.0	6 40.8	3 55.0	27 06.8	1 00.6
20 Th	5 55 54	29 25 39	12 09 34	18 04 43	13 40.8	8 46.3	14 29.8	5 37.0	4 29.7	14 30.9	6 43.6	3 53.1	27 05.5	0 59.2
21 F	5 59 51	0♋22 55	24 00 18	29 56 45	13 34.7	10 18.3	14 03.8	6 19.4	4 19.9	14 23.7	6 46.4	3 51.3	27 04.1	0 57.8
22 Sa	6 03 48	1 20 10	5♍54 37	11♍54 27	13 31.2	11 53.4	13 39.9	7 01.9	4 10.4	14 16.4	6 49.0	3 49.4	27 02.7	0 56.4
23 Su	6 07 44	2 17 24	17 56 49	24 02 20	13D29.8	13 31.5	13 18.1	7 44.2	4 01.1	14 09.1	6 51.6	3 47.5	27 01.2	0 55.1
24 M	6 11 41	3 14 38	0♎11 39	6♎25 24	13R29.6	15 12.8	12 58.5	8 26.5	3 52.2	14 01.7	6 54.1	3 45.6	26 59.8	0 53.7
25 Tu	6 15 37	4 11 51	12 44 13	19 08 43	13 29.6	16 57.0	12 41.2	9 08.7	3 43.7	13 54.3	6 56.5	3 43.6	26 58.3	0 52.4
26 W	6 19 34	5 09 04	25 39 26	2♏16 52	13 28.6	18 44.1	12 26.3	9 50.9	3 35.4	13 46.8	6 58.7	3 41.6	26 56.9	0 51.1
27 Th	6 23 30	6 06 16	9♏01 25	15 53 19	13 25.7	20 34.1	12 13.7	10 33.0	3 27.5	13 39.3	7 00.9	3 39.6	26 55.4	0 49.8
28 F	6 27 27	7 03 28	22 52 40	29 59 49	13 20.3	22 26.8	12 03.5	11 15.0	3 19.9	13 31.7	7 03.0	3 37.6	26 53.9	0 48.6
29 Sa	6 31 23	8 00 39	7♐13 10	14♐33 29	13 12.5	24 22.2	11 55.7	11 57.0	3 12.6	13 24.1	7 05.0	3 35.5	26 52.4	0 47.4
30 Su	6 35 20	8 57 50	21 59 34	29 30 27	13 02.6	26 20.0	11 50.3	12 39.0	3 05.7	13 16.4	7 06.9	3 33.4	26 50.9	0 46.2

Astro Data

	Dy Hr Mn
☿R	3 22:41
♃R	4 15:37
♅R	8 19:36
☽0N	12 19:18
♄✶♅	19 16:50
♀R	20 6:08
♄0N	25 3:37
☽0S	27 7:48
☿D	27 19:03
♃∠♇	1 11:27
☽0N	9 1:37
☽0S	23 17:01

Planet Ingress

	Dy Hr Mn
♂ ♉	2 18:16
☉ ♊	20 18:23
♂ ♊	12 14:42
☿ ♊	13 21:45
☉ ♋	21 2:24

Last Aspect / ☽ Ingress

Last Aspect Dy Hr Mn		☽ Ingress Dy Hr Mn
2 12:23	♂ ☍	♏ 2 12:42
4 13:46	☿ ☍	♐ 4 16:05
6 9:29	♀ ☍	♑ 6 17:54
8 15:53	☿ △	♒ 8 19:39
10 17:07	☿ □	♓ 10 22:29
12 22:55	♀ ✶	♈ 13 3:00
15 5:23	♀ ✶	♉ 15 9:25
17 13:20	♆ △	♊ 17 17:48
20 0:54	♀ ☌	♋ 20 4:16
22 11:38	♆ ☍	♌ 22 16:28
25 0:40	♀ ✶	♍ 25 4:58
27 10:53	♆ △	♎ 27 15:33
29 18:06	♆ □	♏ 29 22:30

Last Aspect / ☽ Ingress

Last Aspect Dy Hr Mn		☽ Ingress Dy Hr Mn
31 21:32	♆ ✶	♐ 1 1:43
2 17:58	♀ ☍	♑ 3 2:29
4 22:33	♆ ☌	♒ 5 2:44
6 21:24	♂ □	♓ 7 4:19
9 3:59	♂ ✶	♈ 9 8:23
11 10:07	♆ □	♉ 11 15:11
13 18:56	♆ △	♊ 14 0:16
16 1:36	☉ ☌	♋ 16 11:08
18 17:34	♆ ☍	♌ 18 23:22
20 5:00	♀ ✶	♍ 21 12:07
23 17:49	♆ △	♎ 23 23:37
26 2:22	♆ □	♏ 26 7:53
28 6:49	♆ ✶	♐ 28 12:01
30 6:11	☿ ☍	♑ 30 12:47

☽ Phases & Eclipses

Dy Hr Mn	
3 11:48	○ 13♏19
10 5:04	☾ 19♒49
17 11:46	● 26♉51
25 14:13	☽ 4♍38
1 20:47	○ 11♐37
8 11:06	☾ 17♓56
16 1:36	● 25♊12
24 5:23	☽ 2♎59

Astro Data

1 May 1996
Julian Day # 35185
SVP 5♓18'36"
GC 26♐47.3 ⚵ 25♎19.4R
Eris 18♈33.8 ✱ 16♓06.1
⚷ 8♎57.5R ⚶ 20♏17.1R
☽ Mean ☊ 16♎00.1

1 June 1996
Julian Day # 35216
SVP 5♓18'32"
GC 26♐47.4 ⚵ 19♎47.7R
Eris 18♈50.3 ✱ 28♓09.3
⚷ 7♎55.3R ⚶ 13♏25.1R
☽ Mean ☊ 14♎21.6

July 1996 LONGITUDE

Day	Sid.Time	☉	0 hr ☽	Noon ☽	True ☊	☿	♀	♂	⚳	♃	♄	♅	♆	♇
1 M	6 39 17	9♋55 01	7♑04 58	14♑41 49	12♎51.9	28♊20.2	11♊47.3	13♊20.9	2♐59.1	13♑08.8	7♈08.7	3♒31.3	26♑49.4	0♐45.0
2 Tu	6 43 13	10 52 12	22 19 36	29 56 54	12R 41.5	0♋22.5	11D 46.6	14 02.7	2R 52.9	13R 01.1	7 10.4	3R 29.2	26R 47.8	0R 43.8
3 W	6 47 10	11 49 23	7♒32 21	15♒04 43	12 32.6	2 26.7	11 48.3	14 44.5	2 47.0	12 53.4	7 12.0	3 27.0	26 46.3	0 42.7
4 Th	6 51 06	12 46 34	22 32 54	29 55 59	12 26.1	4 32.5	11 52.2	15 26.2	2 41.5	12 45.7	7 13.5	3 24.8	26 44.7	0 41.6
5 F	6 55 03	13 43 45	7♓13 18	14♓24 23	12 22.2	6 39.8	11 58.4	16 07.8	2 36.3	12 38.0	7 14.9	3 22.6	26 43.2	0 40.5
6 Sa	6 58 59	14 40 56	21 28 58	28 27 00	12 20.5	8 48.1	12 06.7	16 49.4	2 31.6	12 30.3	7 16.2	3 20.4	26 41.6	0 39.4
7 Su	7 02 56	15 38 08	5♈18 33	12♈03 51	12 20.2	10 57.2	12 17.2	17 31.0	2 27.1	12 22.6	7 17.4	3 18.2	26 40.0	0 38.4
8 M	7 06 52	16 35 20	18 43 12	25 17 01	12 20.1	13 06.9	12 29.8	18 12.5	2 23.0	12 15.0	7 18.5	3 15.9	26 38.4	0 37.3
9 Tu	7 10 49	17 32 33	1♉45 43	8♉09 47	12 19.0	15 16.7	12 44.4	18 53.9	2 19.3	12 07.3	7 19.6	3 13.6	26 36.8	0 36.3
10 W	7 14 46	18 29 46	14 29 39	20 45 46	12 15.9	17 26.5	13 00.9	19 35.3	2 16.0	11 59.7	7 20.5	3 11.4	26 35.2	0 35.4
11 Th	7 18 42	19 26 59	26 58 36	3♊08 31	12 10.1	19 36.0	13 19.3	20 16.6	2 13.0	11 52.1	7 21.3	3 09.1	26 33.6	0 34.4
12 F	7 22 39	20 24 13	9♊15 54	15 21 04	12 01.4	21 44.9	13 39.6	20 57.9	2 10.4	11 44.5	7 22.0	3 06.7	26 32.0	0 33.5
13 Sa	7 26 35	21 21 28	21 24 20	27 25 55	11 50.3	23 53.0	14 01.6	21 39.1	2 08.2	11 37.0	7 22.6	3 04.4	26 30.4	0 32.6
14 Su	7 30 32	22 18 42	3♋26 05	9♋25 01	11 37.5	26 00.1	14 25.3	22 20.2	2 06.4	11 29.5	7 23.1	3 02.1	26 28.8	0 31.8
15 M	7 34 28	23 15 58	15 22 54	21 19 54	11 23.9	28 06.0	14 50.6	23 01.3	2 04.9	11 22.1	7 23.5	2 59.7	26 27.2	0 30.9
16 Tu	7 38 25	24 13 13	27 16 12	3♌11 58	11 10.8	0♌10.7	15 17.5	23 42.4	2 03.8	11 14.7	7 23.8	2 57.4	26 25.5	0 30.1
17 W	7 42 22	25 10 29	9♌07 23	15 02 40	10 59.1	2 13.9	15 46.0	24 23.4	2 03.0	11 07.4	7 23.9	2 55.0	26 23.9	0 29.4
18 Th	7 46 18	26 07 45	20 58 03	26 53 48	10 49.6	4 15.7	16 15.9	25 04.3	2D 02.7	11 00.2	7R 24.0	2 52.6	26 22.3	0 28.6
19 F	7 50 15	27 05 01	2♍50 14	8♍47 42	10 42.9	6 15.8	16 47.2	25 45.1	2 02.7	10 53.1	7 24.0	2 50.2	26 20.7	0 27.9
20 Sa	7 54 11	28 02 18	14 46 36	20 47 22	10 38.9	8 14.3	17 19.9	26 25.9	2 03.0	10 46.0	7 23.9	2 47.8	26 19.0	0 27.2
21 Su	7 58 08	28 59 35	26 50 29	2♎56 28	10D 37.3	10 11.2	17 53.8	27 06.7	2 03.7	10 39.0	7 23.7	2 45.5	26 17.4	0 26.6
22 M	8 02 04	29 56 52	9♎05 52	15 19 15	10 37.1	12 06.3	18 29.1	27 47.3	2 04.8	10 32.1	7 23.4	2 43.1	26 15.8	0 25.9
23 Tu	8 06 01	0♌54 10	21 37 13	28 00 21	10R 37.4	13 59.7	19 05.5	28 27.9	2 06.3	10 25.3	7 22.9	2 40.7	26 14.2	0 25.3
24 W	8 09 57	1 51 28	4♏29 12	11♏04 17	10 37.1	15 51.4	19 43.2	29 08.5	2 08.1	10 18.5	7 22.4	2 38.3	26 12.6	0 24.8
25 Th	8 13 54	2 48 46	17 46 04	24 34 54	10 35.2	17 41.4	20 21.9	29 49.0	2 10.2	10 11.9	7 21.8	2 35.9	26 10.9	0 24.2
26 F	8 17 50	3 46 05	1♐30 59	8♐34 26	10 31.2	19 29.6	21 01.8	0♋29.4	2 12.7	10 05.4	7 21.1	2 33.5	26 09.3	0 23.7
27 Sa	8 21 47	4 43 24	15 45 05	23 02 38	10 24.9	21 16.0	21 42.7	1 09.8	2 15.6	9 59.1	7 20.2	2 31.1	26 07.7	0 23.3
28 Su	8 25 44	5 40 44	0♑26 31	7♑55 55	10 16.7	23 00.8	22 24.6	1 50.1	2 18.8	9 52.8	7 19.3	2 28.7	26 06.1	0 22.8
29 M	8 29 40	6 38 04	15 29 52	23 07 08	10 07.6	24 43.8	23 07.5	2 30.4	2 22.3	9 46.6	7 18.3	2 26.3	26 04.5	0 22.4
30 Tu	8 33 37	7 35 25	0♒46 23	8♒26 12	9 58.7	26 25.2	23 51.3	3 10.6	2 26.2	9 40.6	7 17.2	2 23.9	26 03.0	0 22.1
31 W	8 37 33	8 32 47	16 05 09	23 41 49	9 51.1	28 04.8	24 36.0	3 50.7	2 30.4	9 34.7	7 16.0	2 21.5	26 01.4	0 21.7

August 1996 LONGITUDE

Day	Sid.Time	☉	0 hr ☽	Noon ☽	True ☊	☿	♀	♂	⚳	♃	♄	♅	♆	♇
1 Th	8 41 30	9♌30 09	1♓14 56	8♓43 24	9♎45.5	29♌42.7	25♊21.6	4♋30.8	2♐34.9	9♑28.9	7♈14.6	2♒19.1	25♑59.8	0♐21.4
2 F	8 45 26	10 27 33	16 06 17	23 22 54	9R 42.3	1♍18.9	26 08.1	5 10.9	2 39.8	9R 23.3	7R 13.2	2R 16.7	25R 58.2	0R 21.1
3 Sa	8 49 23	11 24 58	0♈32 46	7♈35 37	9D 41.2	2 53.5	26 55.4	5 50.8	2 45.0	9 17.7	7 11.7	2 14.4	25 56.7	0 20.9
4 Su	8 53 19	12 22 24	14 31 24	21 20 12	9 41.6	4 26.3	27 43.5	6 30.7	2 50.5	9 12.4	7 10.1	2 12.0	25 55.1	0 20.6
5 M	8 57 16	13 19 51	28 02 16	4♉37 55	9R 42.4	5 57.5	28 32.3	7 10.6	2 56.3	9 07.1	7 08.4	2 09.7	25 53.6	0 20.5
6 Tu	9 01 13	14 17 20	11♉07 37	17 31 49	9 42.6	7 26.9	29 21.9	7 50.4	3 02.4	9 02.1	7 06.6	2 07.3	25 52.1	0 20.3
7 W	9 05 09	15 14 49	23 51 03	0♊05 51	9 41.4	8 54.7	0♋12.1	8 30.2	3 08.8	8 57.1	7 04.7	2 05.0	25 50.6	0 20.2
8 Th	9 09 06	16 12 21	6♊16 44	12 24 14	9 38.2	10 20.7	1 03.1	9 09.8	3 15.6	8 52.4	7 02.7	2 02.7	25 49.1	0 20.1
9 F	9 13 02	17 09 53	18 28 51	24 31 03	9 32.8	11 44.9	1 54.7	9 49.5	3 22.6	8 47.7	7 00.6	2 00.4	25 47.6	0 20.1
10 Sa	9 16 59	18 07 27	0♋31 17	6♋29 55	9 25.4	13 07.4	2 46.9	10 29.1	3 30.0	8 43.3	6 58.5	1 58.1	25 46.1	0D 20.0
11 Su	9 20 55	19 05 02	12 27 20	18 23 52	9 16.6	14 28.0	3 39.7	11 08.6	3 37.6	8 39.0	6 56.2	1 55.9	25 44.6	0 20.0
12 M	9 24 52	20 02 39	24 19 48	0♌15 24	9 07.1	15 46.8	4 33.2	11 48.0	3 45.6	8 34.8	6 53.9	1 53.6	25 43.2	0 20.1
13 Tu	9 28 48	21 00 16	6♌10 56	12 06 35	8 58.0	17 03.7	5 27.2	12 27.4	3 53.8	8 30.9	6 51.4	1 51.4	25 41.8	0 20.2
14 W	9 32 45	21 57 55	18 02 36	23 59 09	8 49.9	18 18.6	6 21.7	13 06.7	4 02.3	8 27.1	6 48.9	1 49.2	25 40.3	0 20.3
15 Th	9 36 42	22 55 35	29 56 29	5♍54 46	8 43.5	19 31.5	7 16.8	13 46.0	4 11.1	8 23.4	6 46.3	1 47.0	25 38.9	0 20.4
16 F	9 40 38	23 53 17	11♍54 16	17 55 12	8 39.2	20 42.3	8 12.4	14 25.2	4 20.2	8 20.0	6 43.5	1 44.8	25 37.5	0 20.6
17 Sa	9 44 35	24 50 59	23 57 52	0♎02 33	8D 37.1	21 50.9	9 08.4	15 04.4	4 29.5	8 16.7	6 40.8	1 42.7	25 36.2	0 20.8
18 Su	9 48 31	25 48 43	6♎09 36	12 19 21	8 36.8	22 57.3	10 05.0	15 43.4	4 39.1	8 13.6	6 37.9	1 40.5	25 34.8	0 21.1
19 M	9 52 28	26 46 27	18 32 12	24 48 34	8 37.7	24 01.3	11 02.0	16 22.5	4 49.0	8 10.7	6 34.9	1 38.4	25 33.5	0 21.4
20 Tu	9 56 24	27 44 13	1♏08 52	7♏33 33	8 39.1	25 02.8	11 59.4	17 01.4	4 59.2	8 08.0	6 31.9	1 36.3	25 32.2	0 21.7
21 W	10 00 21	28 42 00	14 03 03	20 37 47	8R 40.3	26 01.7	12 57.3	17 40.3	5 09.6	8 05.4	6 28.8	1 34.3	25 30.9	0 22.0
22 Th	10 04 17	29 39 49	27 18 07	4♐04 21	8 40.5	26 57.8	13 55.6	18 19.1	5 20.3	8 03.0	6 25.6	1 32.2	25 29.6	0 22.4
23 F	10 08 14	0♍37 38	10♐56 44	17 55 22	8 39.2	27 51.1	14 54.4	18 57.9	5 31.2	8 00.9	6 22.3	1 30.2	25 28.3	0 22.9
24 Sa	10 12 11	1 35 29	25 00 16	2♑11 15	8 36.4	28 41.3	15 53.5	19 36.6	5 42.3	7 58.9	6 19.0	1 28.3	25 27.1	0 23.3
25 Su	10 16 07	2 33 21	9♑27 57	16 49 53	8 32.2	29 28.3	16 53.0	20 15.3	5 53.7	7 57.1	6 15.6	1 26.3	25 25.9	0 23.8
26 M	10 20 04	3 31 14	24 16 18	1♒46 19	8 27.3	0♎11.8	17 52.9	20 53.8	6 05.4	7 55.4	6 12.1	1 24.4	25 24.7	0 24.3
27 Tu	10 24 00	4 29 08	9♒18 55	16 52 56	8 22.5	0 51.7	18 53.2	21 32.3	6 17.3	7 54.0	6 08.5	1 22.5	25 23.5	0 24.9
28 W	10 27 57	5 27 04	24 27 09	2♓00 19	8 18.3	1 27.7	19 53.8	22 10.8	6 29.4	7 52.7	6 04.9	1 20.7	25 22.3	0 25.5
29 Th	10 31 53	6 25 01	9♓31 14	16 58 47	8 15.4	1 59.6	20 54.8	22 49.2	6 41.7	7 51.7	6 01.2	1 18.8	25 21.2	0 26.1
30 F	10 35 50	7 23 00	24 21 57	1♈39 54	8D 14.0	2 27.1	21 56.2	23 27.5	6 54.3	7 50.8	5 57.5	1 17.0	25 20.1	0 26.7
31 Sa	10 39 46	8 21 01	8♈51 58	15 57 41	8 14.1	2 49.9	22 57.9	24 05.8	7 07.1	7 50.1	5 53.6	1 15.3	25 19.0	0 27.4

Astro Data

	Dy Hr Mn
♀ D	2 6:51
☽ 0N	6 9:19
♄ R	18 20:29
⚳ D	18 23:57
☽ 0S	21 0:54
☽ 0N	2 18:54
♇ D	10 12:35
☽ 0S	17 7:29
☿ 0S	20 22:25
☽ 0N	30 5:40
♄ 0S	30 16:56

Planet Ingress

	Dy Hr Mn
☿ ♋	2 7:37
☿ ♌	16 9:56
☉ ♌	22 13:19
♂ ♋	25 18:32
☿ ♍	1 16:17
♀ ♋	7 6:15
☉ ♍	22 20:23
☿ ♎	26 5:17

Last Aspect / ☽ Ingress (July)

Last Aspect Dy Hr Mn		☽ Ingress Dy Hr Mn
2 7:03 ♆ ☌	♒	2 12:05
3 11:26 ♂ △	♓	4 12:07
6 8:58 ♆ ⚹	♈	6 14:42
8 14:30 ♆ □	♉	8 20:43
10 23:13 ♆ △	♊	11 5:52
12 23:48 ♂ ☌	♋	13 17:08
16 4:35 ☿ ☌	♌	16 5:31
18 8:05 ♂ ⚹	♍	18 18:16
21 3:35 ☉ ⚹	♎	21 6:14
23 12:54 ♂ △	♏	23 15:43
25 14:47 ♆ ⚹	♐	25 21:24
27 9:43 ♀ ☍	♑	27 23:17
29 16:38 ♆ ☌	♒	29 22:47
31 19:48 ☿ ☍	♓	31 22:00

Last Aspect / ☽ Ingress (August)

Last Aspect Dy Hr Mn		☽ Ingress Dy Hr Mn
2 16:51 ♀ □	♈	2 23:05
5 0:11 ♀ ⚹	♉	5 3:33
7 3:50 ♆ △	♊	7 11:49
8 20:08 ☉ ⚹	♋	9 22:57
12 2:50 ♆ ☍	♌	12 11:29
14 7:34 ☉ ☌	♍	15 0:07
17 3:15 ♆ △	♎	17 11:55
19 16:02 ☉ ⚹	♏	19 21:50
22 3:36 ☉ □	♐	22 4:48
24 5:49 ☿ □	♑	24 8:22
26 1:51 ♆ ☌	♒	26 9:10
26 19:01 ♄ ⚹	♓	28 8:49
30 1:36 ♆ ⚹	♈	30 9:15

☽ Phases & Eclipses

Dy Hr Mn	
1 3:58	○ 9♑36
7 18:55	☾ 15♈55
15 16:15	● 23♋26
23 17:49	☽ 1♏08
30 10:35	○ 7♒32
6 5:25	☾ 14♉02
14 7:34	● 21♌47
22 3:36	☽ 29♏20
28 17:52	○ 5♓41

Astro Data

1 July 1996
Julian Day # 35246
SVP 5♓18'27"
GC 26♐47.4 ⚴ 21♎17.3
Eris 18♈59.0 ⚵ 8♈16.0
⚷ 8♎34.7 ⚶ 12♏18.2
☽ Mean ☊ 12♎46.3

1 August 1996
Julian Day # 35277
SVP 5♓18'22"
GC 26♐47.5 ⚴ 28♎05.1
Eris 18♈58.4R ⚵ 15♈40.4
⚷ 10♎53.0 ⚶ 18♏06.3
☽ Mean ☊ 11♎07.9

LONGITUDE — September 1996

Day	Sid.Time	☉	0 hr ☽	Noon ☽	True ☊	☿	♀	♂	⚳	♃	♄	♅	♆	♇
1 Su	10 43 43	9♍19 03	22♈56 43	29♈48 59	8♎15.1	3♎07.8	23♋59.9	24♋44.0	7♐20.1	7♑49.6	5♈49.8	1♒13.5	25♑18.0	0♐28.1
2 M	10 47 40	10 17 08	6♉34 30	13♉13 25	8 16.7	3 20.5	25 02.2	25 22.1	7 33.3	7R 49.3	5R 45.8	1R 11.8	25R 16.9	0 28.9
3 Tu	10 51 36	11 15 14	19 46 02	26 12 43	8 18.1	3R 27.7	26 04.8	26 00.2	7 46.7	7D 49.2	5 41.8	1 10.2	25 15.9	0 29.7
4 W	10 55 33	12 13 22	2♊33 55	8♊50 08	8R 18.9	3 29.1	27 07.8	26 38.2	8 00.4	7 49.3	5 37.8	1 08.6	25 14.9	0 30.5
5 Th	10 59 29	13 11 33	15 01 53	21 09 44	8 18.7	3 24.5	28 11.0	27 16.2	8 14.2	7 49.5	5 33.7	1 07.0	25 14.0	0 31.3
6 F	11 03 26	14 09 45	27 14 14	3♋15 56	8 17.3	3 13.7	29 14.5	27 54.1	8 28.2	7 50.0	5 29.6	1 05.4	25 13.0	0 32.2
7 Sa	11 07 22	15 08 00	9♋15 23	15 13 06	8 15.0	2 56.4	0♌18.3	28 31.9	8 42.5	7 50.6	5 25.4	1 03.9	25 12.1	0 33.1
8 Su	11 11 19	16 06 16	21 09 36	27 05 19	8 11.8	2 32.7	1 22.4	29 09.7	8 56.9	7 51.5	5 21.1	1 02.4	25 11.2	0 34.1
9 M	11 15 15	17 04 34	3♌00 42	8♌56 10	8 08.4	2 02.4	2 26.7	29 47.4	9 11.6	7 52.5	5 16.8	1 01.0	25 10.4	0 35.1
10 Tu	11 19 12	18 02 55	14 52 05	20 48 46	8 05.0	1 25.8	3 31.3	0♌25.0	9 26.4	7 53.7	5 12.5	0 59.6	25 09.5	0 36.1
11 W	11 23 09	19 01 17	26 46 32	2♍45 40	8 02.0	0 43.1	4 36.2	1 02.6	9 41.4	7 55.1	5 08.1	0 58.2	25 08.7	0 37.1
12 Th	11 27 05	19 59 41	8♍46 23	14 48 56	7 59.8	29♍54.8	5 41.3	1 40.1	9 56.7	7 56.7	5 03.7	0 56.9	25 08.0	0 38.2
13 F	11 31 02	20 58 07	20 53 31	27 00 19	7D 58.6	29 01.4	6 46.6	2 17.5	10 12.0	7 58.5	4 59.3	0 55.6	25 07.2	0 39.3
14 Sa	11 34 58	21 56 34	3♎09 32	9♎21 19	7 58.3	28 03.9	7 52.1	2 54.9	10 27.6	8 00.5	4 54.8	0 54.4	25 06.5	0 40.4
15 Su	11 38 55	22 55 04	15 35 51	21 53 18	7 58.7	27 03.3	8 57.9	3 32.1	10 43.4	8 02.6	4 50.3	0 53.2	25 05.8	0 41.6
16 M	11 42 51	23 53 35	28 13 52	4♏37 43	7 59.6	26 00.7	10 03.9	4 09.3	10 59.3	8 05.0	4 45.7	0 52.1	25 05.2	0 42.8
17 Tu	11 46 48	24 52 08	11♏05 03	17 36 03	8 00.8	24 57.6	11 10.1	4 46.5	11 15.4	8 07.5	4 41.2	0 51.0	25 04.5	0 44.0
18 W	11 50 44	25 50 43	24 10 54	0♐49 46	8 01.9	23 55.5	12 16.5	5 23.5	11 31.7	8 10.2	4 36.6	0 49.9	25 03.9	0 45.2
19 Th	11 54 41	26 49 20	7♐32 49	14 20 10	8R 02.6	22 55.9	13 23.2	6 00.5	11 48.1	8 13.1	4 32.0	0 48.9	25 03.4	0 46.5
20 F	11 58 37	27 47 58	21 11 56	28 08 06	8 02.8	22 00.2	14 30.0	6 37.5	12 04.7	8 16.2	4 27.3	0 47.9	25 02.8	0 47.8
21 Sa	12 02 34	28 46 38	5♑08 40	12♑13 30	8 02.6	21 10.1	15 37.0	7 14.3	12 21.4	8 19.5	4 22.7	0 47.0	25 02.3	0 49.2
22 Su	12 06 31	29 45 19	19 22 22	26 34 57	8 02.0	20 26.7	16 44.2	7 51.1	12 38.4	8 23.0	4 18.1	0 46.1	25 01.9	0 50.6
23 M	12 10 27	0♎44 02	3♒50 50	11♒09 28	8 01.2	19 51.2	17 51.6	8 27.8	12 55.4	8 26.6	4 13.4	0 45.3	25 01.4	0 52.0
24 Tu	12 14 24	1 42 47	18 30 12	25 52 19	8 00.4	19 24.5	18 59.2	9 04.4	13 12.6	8 30.4	4 08.7	0 44.5	25 01.0	0 53.4
25 W	12 18 20	2 41 33	3♓14 58	10♓37 19	7 59.8	19 07.4	20 07.0	9 40.9	13 30.0	8 34.4	4 04.0	0 43.8	25 00.6	0 54.8
26 Th	12 22 17	3 40 22	17 58 29	25 17 36	7D 59.5	19D 00.1	21 15.0	10 17.4	13 47.5	8 38.5	3 59.4	0 43.1	25 00.3	0 56.3
27 F	12 26 13	4 39 12	2♈33 48	9♈46 21	7 59.4	19 03.0	22 23.1	10 53.8	14 05.2	8 42.9	3 54.7	0 42.4	25 00.0	0 57.8
28 Sa	12 30 10	5 38 04	16 54 32	23 57 48	7 59.5	19 16.1	23 31.5	11 30.1	14 22.9	8 47.4	3 50.0	0 41.8	24 59.7	0 59.4
29 Su	12 34 06	6 36 59	0♉55 41	7♉47 53	7 59.7	19 39.1	24 40.0	12 06.4	14 40.9	8 52.0	3 45.3	0 41.3	24 59.4	1 00.9
30 M	12 38 03	7 35 56	14 34 12	21 14 33	7R 59.7	20 11.6	25 48.6	12 42.5	14 58.9	8 56.9	3 40.7	0 40.8	24 59.2	1 02.5

LONGITUDE — October 1996

Day	Sid.Time	☉	0 hr ☽	Noon ☽	True ☊	☿	♀	♂	⚳	♃	♄	♅	♆	♇
1 Tu	12 42 00	8♎34 55	27♉49 02	4♊17 47	7♎59.7	20♍53.3	26♌57.5	13♌18.6	15♐17.1	9♑01.9	3♈36.0	0♒40.3	24♑59.0	1♐04.1
2 W	12 45 56	9 33 56	10♊41 05	16 59 17	7R 59.6	21 43.4	28 06.5	13 54.6	15 35.5	9 07.1	3R 31.4	0R 39.9	24R 58.9	1 05.8
3 Th	12 49 53	10 33 00	23 12 48	29 22 06	7D 59.5	22 41.3	29 15.6	14 30.6	15 53.9	9 12.4	3 26.7	0 39.6	24 58.8	1 07.4
4 F	12 53 49	11 32 05	5♋27 43	11♋30 12	7 59.4	23 46.4	0♍25.0	15 06.4	16 12.5	9 17.9	3 22.1	0 39.3	24 58.7	1 09.1
5 Sa	12 57 46	12 31 14	17 30 07	23 28 03	7 59.5	24 57.9	1 34.5	15 42.2	16 31.3	9 23.6	3 17.5	0 39.0	24 58.6	1 10.9
6 Su	13 01 42	13 30 24	29 24 35	5♌20 18	7 59.9	26 15.0	2 44.1	16 17.9	16 50.1	9 29.5	3 12.9	0 38.8	24D 58.6	1 12.6
7 M	13 05 39	14 29 37	11♌15 46	17 11 31	8 00.5	27 37.0	3 53.9	16 53.5	17 09.1	9 35.5	3 08.4	0 38.7	24 58.6	1 14.4
8 Tu	13 09 35	15 28 52	23 08 04	29 05 55	8 01.2	29 03.3	5 03.8	17 29.1	17 28.2	9 41.6	3 03.8	0 38.6	24 58.7	1 16.1
9 W	13 13 32	16 28 09	5♍05 31	11♍07 16	8 02.1	0♎33.3	6 13.8	18 04.5	17 47.4	9 47.9	2 59.3	0D 38.5	24 58.7	1 18.0
10 Th	13 17 29	17 27 28	17 11 33	23 18 40	8 02.8	2 06.3	7 24.0	18 39.9	18 06.7	9 54.4	2 54.9	0 38.5	24 58.8	1 19.8
11 F	13 21 25	18 26 50	29 28 55	5♎42 29	8R 03.1	3 41.8	8 34.4	19 15.1	18 26.2	10 01.0	2 50.4	0 38.6	24 59.0	1 21.6
12 Sa	13 25 22	19 26 13	11♎59 34	18 20 17	8 02.9	5 19.3	9 44.8	19 50.3	18 45.7	10 07.8	2 46.0	0 38.7	24 59.2	1 23.5
13 Su	13 29 18	20 25 39	24 44 40	1♏12 46	8 02.1	6 58.5	10 55.4	20 25.4	19 05.4	10 14.8	2 41.7	0 38.8	24 59.4	1 25.4
14 M	13 33 15	21 25 07	7♏44 33	14 19 56	8 00.7	8 39.0	12 06.1	21 00.4	19 25.2	10 21.8	2 37.4	0 39.0	24 59.6	1 27.3
15 Tu	13 37 11	22 24 36	20 58 51	27 41 08	7 58.8	10 20.4	13 16.9	21 35.3	19 45.1	10 29.1	2 33.1	0 39.3	24 59.9	1 29.3
16 W	13 41 08	23 24 08	4♐26 40	11♐15 16	7 56.7	12 02.5	14 27.9	22 10.1	20 05.1	10 36.5	2 28.9	0 39.6	25 00.2	1 31.2
17 Th	13 45 04	24 23 41	18 06 45	25 00 57	7 54.8	13 45.1	15 38.9	22 44.8	20 25.2	10 44.0	2 24.7	0 39.9	25 00.6	1 33.2
18 F	13 49 01	25 23 16	1♑57 38	8♑56 37	7 53.4	15 27.9	16 50.1	23 19.4	20 45.4	10 51.7	2 20.6	0 40.4	25 01.0	1 35.2
19 Sa	13 52 57	26 22 53	15 57 43	23 00 42	7D 52.7	17 10.8	18 01.4	23 53.9	21 05.7	10 59.5	2 16.5	0 40.8	25 01.4	1 37.2
20 Su	13 56 54	27 22 32	0♒05 20	7♒11 25	7 52.9	18 53.7	19 12.8	24 28.3	21 26.1	11 07.4	2 12.5	0 41.3	25 01.8	1 39.3
21 M	14 00 51	28 22 12	14 18 39	21 26 46	7 53.9	20 36.4	20 24.3	25 02.6	21 46.6	11 15.5	2 08.6	0 41.9	25 02.3	1 41.3
22 Tu	14 04 47	29 21 54	28 35 27	5♓44 22	7 55.3	22 18.9	21 35.9	25 36.8	22 07.2	11 23.8	2 04.7	0 42.5	25 02.8	1 43.4
23 W	14 08 44	0♏21 37	12♓53 06	20 01 14	7 56.6	24 01.1	22 47.6	26 10.9	22 27.9	11 32.1	2 00.8	0 43.2	25 03.4	1 45.5
24 Th	14 12 40	1 21 23	27 08 20	4♈13 55	7R 57.3	25 42.9	23 59.4	26 44.9	22 48.6	11 40.6	1 57.1	0 43.9	25 03.9	1 47.6
25 F	14 16 37	2 21 10	11♈17 29	18 18 34	7 57.0	27 24.4	25 11.3	27 18.8	23 09.5	11 49.3	1 53.3	0 44.7	25 04.6	1 49.7
26 Sa	14 20 33	3 20 59	25 16 39	2♉11 18	7 55.4	29 05.4	26 23.3	27 52.6	23 30.4	11 58.0	1 49.7	0 45.5	25 05.2	1 51.9
27 Su	14 24 30	4 20 50	9♉02 06	15 48 42	7 52.5	0♏46.0	27 35.4	28 26.2	23 51.4	12 06.9	1 46.1	0 46.3	25 05.9	1 54.0
28 M	14 28 26	5 20 43	22 30 49	29 08 13	7 48.5	2 26.1	28 47.6	28 59.8	24 12.6	12 15.9	1 42.6	0 47.2	25 06.6	1 56.2
29 Tu	14 32 23	6 20 38	5♊40 50	12♊08 35	7 43.8	4 05.7	29 59.9	29 33.3	24 33.8	12 25.0	1 39.2	0 48.2	25 07.3	1 58.4
30 W	14 36 20	7 20 36	18 31 34	24 49 56	7 39.0	5 44.9	1♎12.3	0♍06.6	24 55.0	12 34.3	1 35.9	0 49.2	25 08.1	2 00.6
31 Th	14 40 16	8 20 35	1♋03 55	7♋13 49	7 34.7	7 23.6	2 24.8	0 39.9	25 16.4	12 43.7	1 32.6	0 50.3	25 08.9	2 02.8

Astro Data	Dy Hr Mn
♃ D	3 14:37
☿ R	4 5:47
☽ 0S	13 13:40
☿ 0N	18 20:31
♅ ✶ ♇	20 12:44
☉ 0S	22 18:00
☽ 0N	26 16:12
☿ D	26 17:10
♆ D	6 15:55
♅ D	10 0:55
☽ 0S	10 20:48
☿ 0S	12 0:39
☽ 0N	24 1:15
♄ △ ♇	26 3:03

Planet Ingress	Dy Hr Mn
♀ ♌	7 5:07
♂ ♌	9 20:02
☿ ♍R	12 9:32
☉ ♎	22 18:00
♀ ♍	4 3:22
☿ ♎	9 3:13
☉ ♏	23 3:19
☿ ♏	27 1:01
♀ ♎	29 12:02
♂ ♍	30 7:13

Last Aspect Dy Hr Mn		☽ Ingress	Dy Hr Mn
1 4:06	♆ □	♉	1 12:19
3 11:44	♀ ✶	♊	3 19:08
4 19:06	☉ □	♋	6 5:29
8 16:26	♂ ☌	♌	8 17:54
9 4:38	♄ △	♍	11 6:28
13 15:40	☿ ☌	♎	13 17:51
15 18:05	♆ □	♏	16 3:20
18 2:18	☉ ✶	♐	18 10:31
20 11:23	☉ □	♑	20 15:12
22 17:38	☉ △	♒	22 17:39
23 23:52	♀ ☍	♓	24 18:43
26 11:32	♆ ✶	♈	26 19:46
28 13:46	♆ □	♉	28 22:23

Last Aspect Dy Hr Mn		☽ Ingress	Dy Hr Mn
30 21:07	♀ □	♊	1 4:01
3 11:46	♀ ✶	♋	3 13:14
5 15:22	☿ ✶	♌	6 1:12
7 11:22	♂ ☌	♍	8 13:49
10 15:15	♆ △	♎	11 1:00
13 0:27	♆ □	♏	13 9:46
15 7:12	♆ ✶	♐	15 16:07
17 10:50	☉ ✶	♑	17 20:37
19 18:09	☉ □	♒	19 23:51
22 0:30	☉ △	♓	22 2:22
23 20:29	♆ ✶	♈	24 4:50
26 5:52	☿ ☍	♉	26 8:11
28 11:44	♂ □	♊	28 13:34
28 17:08	♇ ☍	♋	30 21:56

☽ Phases & Eclipses Dy Hr Mn	
4 19:06	☾ 12♊31
12 23:07	● 20♍27
20 11:23	☽ 27♐46
27 2:51	○ 4♈17
27 2:54	◑ T 1.240
4 12:04	☾ 11♋32
12 14:14	● 19♎32
12 14:02:02	◐ P 0.758
19 18:09	☽ 26♑38
26 14:11	○ 3♉26

Astro Data

1 September 1996
Julian Day # 35308
SVP 5♓18'19"
GC 26♐47.6 ⚴ 8♏02.8
Eris 18♈48.4R ⚵ 17♈36.4R
⚷ 14♎26.1 ⚶ 28♏36.2
☽ Mean ☊ 9♎29.3

1 October 1996
Julian Day # 35338
SVP 5♓18'17"
GC 26♐47.6 ⚴ 19♏23.9
Eris 18♈32.3R ⚵ 12♈51.9R
⚷ 18♎34.8 ⚶ 11♐22.9
☽ Mean ☊ 7♎54.0

November 1996 LONGITUDE

Day	Sid.Time	☉	0 hr ☽	Noon ☽	True ☊	☿	♀	♂	⚳	♃	♄	♅	♆	♇
1 F	14 44 13	9♏20 36	13♋20 04	19♋23 05	7♎31.4	9♏01.8	3♎37.4	1♍13.0	25♐37.8	12♑53.2	1♈29.4	0♒51.4	25♑09.8	2♐05.0
2 Sa	14 48 09	10 20 40	25 23 23	1♌21 31	7D 29.5	10 39.6	4 50.0	1 46.0	25 59.3	13 02.8	1R 26.3	0 52.6	25 10.7	2 07.2
3 Su	14 52 06	11 20 46	7♌18 04	13 13 39	7 29.1	12 16.9	6 02.8	2 18.9	26 20.9	13 12.6	1 23.3	0 53.8	25 11.6	2 09.5
4 M	14 56 02	12 20 53	19 08 54	25 04 26	7 29.9	13 53.8	7 15.6	2 51.7	26 42.6	13 22.4	1 20.3	0 55.1	25 12.5	2 11.7
5 Tu	14 59 59	13 21 03	1♍00 54	6♍58 55	7 31.4	15 30.3	8 28.5	3 24.4	27 04.3	13 32.4	1 17.4	0 56.4	25 13.5	2 14.0
6 W	15 03 55	14 21 15	12 59 06	19 02 01	7 33.2	17 06.3	9 41.5	3 56.9	27 26.1	13 42.5	1 14.7	0 57.7	25 14.5	2 16.3
7 Th	15 07 52	15 21 29	25 08 12	1♎18 08	7R 34.4	18 42.0	10 54.6	4 29.3	27 48.0	13 52.6	1 12.0	0 59.1	25 15.5	2 18.6
8 F	15 11 49	16 21 45	7♎32 16	13 50 56	7 34.4	20 17.3	12 07.7	5 01.6	28 10.0	14 02.9	1 09.4	1 00.6	25 16.6	2 20.9
9 Sa	15 15 45	17 22 02	20 14 25	26 42 54	7 32.6	21 52.2	13 20.9	5 33.7	28 32.0	14 13.4	1 06.9	1 02.1	25 17.7	2 23.2
10 Su	15 19 42	18 22 22	3♏16 27	9♏55 04	7 28.9	23 26.8	14 34.2	6 05.7	28 54.1	14 23.9	1 04.4	1 03.6	25 18.8	2 25.5
11 M	15 23 38	19 22 43	16 38 35	23 26 47	7 23.3	25 01.1	15 47.5	6 37.5	29 16.2	14 34.5	1 02.1	1 05.2	25 19.9	2 27.8
12 Tu	15 27 35	20 23 06	0♐19 19	7♐15 45	7 16.4	26 35.1	17 01.0	7 09.3	29 38.5	14 45.2	0 59.9	1 06.9	25 21.1	2 30.1
13 W	15 31 31	21 23 31	14 15 35	21 18 14	7 08.9	28 08.8	18 14.4	7 40.8	0♑00.7	14 56.0	0 57.8	1 08.6	25 22.3	2 32.5
14 Th	15 35 28	22 23 58	28 23 09	5♑29 42	7 01.8	29 42.1	19 28.0	8 12.3	0 23.1	15 07.0	0 55.7	1 10.3	25 23.6	2 34.8
15 F	15 39 24	23 24 25	12♑37 18	19 45 23	6 56.0	1♐15.3	20 41.6	8 43.5	0 45.5	15 18.0	0 53.8	1 12.1	25 24.9	2 37.2
16 Sa	15 43 21	24 24 54	26 53 28	4♒01 07	6 52.0	2 48.1	21 55.2	9 14.7	1 08.0	15 29.1	0 51.9	1 13.9	25 26.2	2 39.5
17 Su	15 47 18	25 25 24	11♒07 57	18 13 40	6D 50.2	4 20.7	23 08.9	9 45.6	1 30.5	15 40.3	0 50.2	1 15.8	25 27.5	2 41.9
18 M	15 51 14	26 25 56	25 18 03	2♓20 55	6 50.1	5 53.1	24 22.6	10 16.5	1 53.0	15 51.6	0 48.6	1 17.7	25 28.9	2 44.3
19 Tu	15 55 11	27 26 28	9♓22 09	16 21 39	6 51.0	7 25.2	25 36.4	10 47.1	2 15.7	16 03.0	0 47.0	1 19.7	25 30.2	2 46.6
20 W	15 59 07	28 27 02	23 19 21	0♈15 11	6R 52.0	8 57.1	26 50.3	11 17.6	2 38.3	16 14.5	0 45.6	1 21.7	25 31.7	2 49.0
21 Th	16 03 04	29 27 37	7♈09 04	14 00 56	6 51.9	10 28.8	28 04.2	11 47.9	3 01.1	16 26.1	0 44.3	1 23.7	25 33.1	2 51.4
22 F	16 07 00	0♐28 14	20 50 38	27 38 04	6 49.9	12 00.2	29 18.2	12 18.1	3 23.8	16 37.7	0 43.0	1 25.8	25 34.6	2 53.7
23 Sa	16 10 57	1 28 51	4♉23 03	11♉05 24	6 45.4	13 31.4	0♏32.2	12 48.1	3 46.7	16 49.5	0 41.9	1 28.0	25 36.1	2 56.1
24 Su	16 14 53	2 29 30	17 44 55	24 21 24	6 38.3	15 02.4	1 46.2	13 18.0	4 09.5	17 01.3	0 40.9	1 30.1	25 37.6	2 58.5
25 M	16 18 50	3 30 10	0♊54 40	7♊24 31	6 28.9	16 33.2	3 00.3	13 47.6	4 32.5	17 13.2	0 40.0	1 32.3	25 39.1	3 00.9
26 Tu	16 22 47	4 30 52	13 50 49	20 13 29	6 18.1	18 03.6	4 14.5	14 17.1	4 55.4	17 25.2	0 39.2	1 34.6	25 40.7	3 03.3
27 W	16 26 43	5 31 35	26 32 26	2♋47 44	6 06.9	19 33.8	5 28.7	14 46.4	5 18.4	17 37.2	0 38.5	1 36.9	25 42.3	3 05.6
28 Th	16 30 40	6 32 20	8♋59 26	15 07 43	5 56.3	21 03.7	6 42.9	15 15.6	5 41.5	17 49.4	0 37.9	1 39.2	25 43.9	3 08.0
29 F	16 34 36	7 33 05	21 12 47	27 14 58	5 47.2	22 33.2	7 57.2	15 44.5	6 04.6	18 01.6	0 37.4	1 41.6	25 45.6	3 10.4
30 Sa	16 38 33	8 33 53	3♌14 37	9♌12 10	5 40.4	24 02.3	9 11.5	16 13.3	6 27.7	18 13.9	0 37.0	1 44.0	25 47.2	3 12.8

December 1996 LONGITUDE

Day	Sid.Time	☉	0 hr ☽	Noon ☽	True ☊	☿	♀	♂	⚳	♃	♄	♅	♆	♇
1 Su	16 42 29	9♐34 41	15♌08 08	21♌03 03	5♎36.1	25♐31.0	10♏25.9	16♍41.8	6♑50.9	18♑26.2	0♈36.8	1♒46.4	25♑48.9	3♐15.1
2 M	16 46 26	10 35 32	26 57 30	2♍52 08	5D 34.1	26 59.1	11 40.3	17 10.2	7 14.1	18 38.6	0R 36.6	1 48.9	25 50.7	3 17.5
3 Tu	16 50 22	11 36 23	8♍47 36	14 44 34	5 33.8	28 26.7	12 54.7	17 38.4	7 37.4	18 51.1	0D 36.5	1 51.4	25 52.4	3 19.8
4 W	16 54 19	12 37 16	20 43 44	26 45 48	5R 34.2	29 53.5	14 09.2	18 06.3	8 00.6	19 03.7	0 36.6	1 54.0	25 54.2	3 22.2
5 Th	16 58 16	13 38 10	2♎51 25	9♎01 15	5 34.4	1♑19.5	15 23.7	18 34.1	8 24.0	19 16.3	0 36.7	1 56.6	25 55.9	3 24.5
6 F	17 02 12	14 39 06	15 15 53	21 35 53	5 33.2	2 44.6	16 38.2	19 01.6	8 47.3	19 29.0	0 37.0	1 59.2	25 57.7	3 26.9
7 Sa	17 06 09	15 40 02	28 01 41	4♏33 40	5 29.7	4 08.6	17 52.8	19 28.9	9 10.7	19 41.8	0 37.4	2 01.9	25 59.6	3 29.2
8 Su	17 10 05	16 41 00	11♏12 03	17 56 57	5 23.5	5 31.3	19 07.4	19 56.0	9 34.2	19 54.6	0 37.9	2 04.6	26 01.4	3 31.6
9 M	17 14 02	17 42 00	24 48 17	1♐45 51	5 14.7	6 52.5	20 22.1	20 22.8	9 57.6	20 07.5	0 38.5	2 07.3	26 03.3	3 33.9
10 Tu	17 17 58	18 43 00	8♐49 13	15 57 49	5 03.8	8 11.9	21 36.8	20 49.4	10 21.1	20 20.5	0 39.2	2 10.1	26 05.2	3 36.2
11 W	17 21 55	19 44 01	23 10 56	0♑27 42	4 51.9	9 29.3	22 51.4	21 15.8	10 44.7	20 33.5	0 40.0	2 12.9	26 07.1	3 38.5
12 Th	17 25 51	20 45 03	7♑47 09	15 08 17	4 40.4	10 44.3	24 06.2	21 41.9	11 08.2	20 46.5	0 40.9	2 15.7	26 09.0	3 40.8
13 F	17 29 48	21 46 05	22 30 05	29 51 35	4 30.6	11 56.5	25 20.9	22 07.8	11 31.8	20 59.6	0 42.0	2 18.6	26 11.0	3 43.1
14 Sa	17 33 45	22 47 08	7♒11 50	14♒30 05	4 23.3	13 05.4	26 35.7	22 33.4	11 55.4	21 12.8	0 43.1	2 21.5	26 12.9	3 45.4
15 Su	17 37 41	23 48 12	21 45 39	28 58 02	4 18.9	14 10.6	27 50.5	22 58.7	12 19.1	21 26.0	0 44.4	2 24.4	26 14.9	3 47.7
16 M	17 41 38	24 49 16	6♓06 50	13♓11 50	4D 17.0	15 11.4	29 05.3	23 23.8	12 42.7	21 39.3	0 45.7	2 27.3	26 16.9	3 49.9
17 Tu	17 45 34	25 50 20	20 12 55	27 10 05	4R 16.6	16 07.3	0♐20.1	23 48.6	13 06.4	21 52.6	0 47.2	2 30.3	26 18.9	3 52.2
18 W	17 49 31	26 51 24	4♈03 23	10♈52 58	4 16.6	16 57.4	1 34.9	24 13.1	13 30.1	22 06.0	0 48.8	2 33.3	26 21.0	3 54.4
19 Th	17 53 27	27 52 29	17 39 00	24 21 39	4 15.4	17 41.0	2 49.8	24 37.3	13 53.8	22 19.4	0 50.4	2 36.3	26 23.0	3 56.6
20 F	17 57 24	28 53 34	1♉01 07	7♉37 32	4 12.1	18 17.3	4 04.6	25 01.3	14 17.6	22 32.8	0 52.2	2 39.4	26 25.1	3 58.9
21 Sa	18 01 20	29 54 40	14 11 04	20 41 50	4 05.7	18 45.3	5 19.5	25 25.0	14 41.3	22 46.3	0 54.1	2 42.5	26 27.1	4 01.1
22 Su	18 05 17	0♑55 45	27 09 53	3♊35 17	3 56.3	19 04.1	6 34.4	25 48.3	15 05.1	22 59.8	0 56.1	2 45.6	26 29.2	4 03.2
23 M	18 09 14	1 56 51	9♊58 03	16 18 12	3 44.1	19R 13.0	7 49.3	26 11.4	15 28.9	23 13.4	0 58.2	2 48.7	26 31.3	4 05.4
24 Tu	18 13 10	2 57 58	22 35 41	28 50 31	3 30.1	19 11.0	9 04.3	26 34.2	15 52.7	23 27.0	1 00.4	2 51.9	26 33.5	4 07.6
25 W	18 17 07	3 59 05	5♋02 41	11♋12 12	3 15.3	18 57.6	10 19.2	26 56.6	16 16.5	23 40.7	1 02.7	2 55.0	26 35.6	4 09.7
26 Th	18 21 03	5 00 12	17 19 08	23 23 33	3 01.2	18 32.4	11 34.2	27 18.7	16 40.4	23 54.4	1 05.1	2 58.2	26 37.7	4 11.8
27 F	18 25 00	6 01 19	29 25 35	5♌25 25	2 48.8	17 55.4	12 49.2	27 40.5	17 04.2	24 08.1	1 07.6	3 01.4	26 39.9	4 13.9
28 Sa	18 28 56	7 02 27	11♌23 19	17 19 33	2 39.0	17 07.1	14 04.2	28 02.0	17 28.1	24 21.8	1 10.2	3 04.7	26 42.0	4 16.0
29 Su	18 32 53	8 03 35	23 14 30	29 08 34	2 32.2	16 08.3	15 19.2	28 23.1	17 52.0	24 35.6	1 12.9	3 07.9	26 44.2	4 18.1
30 M	18 36 49	9 04 44	5♍02 15	10♍56 04	2 28.2	15 00.5	16 34.2	28 43.8	18 15.9	24 49.4	1 15.7	3 11.2	26 46.4	4 20.1
31 Tu	18 40 46	10 05 53	16 50 35	22 46 26	2D 26.5	13 45.7	17 49.3	29 04.2	18 39.8	25 03.2	1 18.6	3 14.5	26 48.6	4 22.2

Astro Data Dy Hr Mn	Planet Ingress Dy Hr Mn	Last Aspect Dy Hr Mn	☽ Ingress Dy Hr Mn	Last Aspect Dy Hr Mn	☽ Ingress Dy Hr Mn	☽ Phases & Eclipses Dy Hr Mn
♀0S 1 12:52	⚳ ♑ 13 11:12	1 23:34 ♆ ☍	♌ 2 9:16	1 22:22 ☿ △	♍ 2 6:11	3 7:50 ☾ 11♌10
☽0S 7 5:35	☿ ♐ 14 16:36	3 9:47 ☿ □	♍ 4 21:57	4 10:17 ♆ △	♎ 4 18:23	11 4:16 ● 19♏03
♄✱♅ 10 16:50	☉ ♐ 22 0:49	7 0:13 ♆ △	♎ 7 9:29	6 20:11 ♆ □	♏ 7 3:39	18 1:09 ☽ 25♒59
☽0N 20 8:28	♀ ♏ 23 1:34	9 9:23 ♆ □	♏ 9 18:02	9 2:09 ♆ ✱	♐ 9 8:58	25 4:10 ○ 3♊10
♃∠♇ 30 9:19		11 15:18 ♆ ✱	♐ 11 23:26	10 20:21 ♂ □	♑ 11 11:14	
	☿ ♑ 4 13:48	13 6:18 ♀ ✱	♑ 14 2:44	13 5:59 ♆ ☌	♒ 13 12:14	3 5:06 ☾ 11♍19
♄ D 3 12:39	♀ ♐ 17 5:34	15 21:32 ♆ ☌	♒ 16 5:14	15 9:56 ♀ □	♓ 15 13:44	10 16:56 ● 18♐56
☽0S 4 15:34	☉ ♑ 21 14:06	18 1:09 ☉ □	♓ 18 8:00	17 10:31 ♆ ✱	♈ 17 16:55	17 9:31 ☽ 25♓44
☽0N 17 15:01		20 8:38 ☉ △	♈ 20 11:34	19 18:51 ☉ △	♉ 19 22:09	24 20:41 ○ 3♋20
☿ R 23 19:47		22 15:15 ♀ ☍	♉ 22 16:12	21 22:42 ♆ △	♊ 22 5:17	
		24 14:19 ♆ △	♊ 24 22:20	24 7:29 ♂ □	♋ 24 14:14	
		26 7:22 ☿ ☍	♋ 27 6:37	26 20:02 ♂ ✱	♌ 27 1:09	
		29 9:01 ♆ ☍	♌ 29 17:30	28 4:38 ♀ △	♍ 29 13:45	

Astro Data

1 November 1996
Julian Day # 35369
SVP 5♓18'14"
GC 26♐47.7 ⚴ 2♐05.1
Eris 18♈14.0R ⚵ 6♈27.5R
⚷ 23♎03.7 ⚶ 26♐09.5
☽ Mean ☊ 6♎15.5

1 December 1996
Julian Day # 35399
SVP 5♓18'09"
GC 26♐47.8 ⚴ 14♐44.3
Eris 17♈59.7R ⚵ 6♈48.6
⚷ 27♎03.6 ⚶ 11♑19.2
☽ Mean ☊ 4♎40.2

LONGITUDE — January 1997

Day	Sid.Time	☉	0 hr ☽	Noon ☽	True ☊	☿	♀	♂	⚳	♃	♄	♅	♆	♇
1 W	18 44 43	11♑07 02	28♍44 17	4♎44 47	2♎26.3	12♑26.3	19♐04.3	29♍24.2	19♑03.7	25♑17.1	1♈21.6	3♒17.8	26♑50.8	4♐24.2
2 Th	18 48 39	12 08 12	10♎48 39	16 56 35	2R 26.3	11R 04.9	20 19.4	29 43.8	19 27.6	25 31.0	1 24.8	3 21.2	26 53.0	4 26.2
3 F	18 52 36	13 09 22	23 09 16	29 27 21	2 25.3	9 44.1	21 34.5	0♎03.0	19 51.5	25 44.9	1 27.9	3 24.5	26 55.2	4 28.1
4 Sa	18 56 32	14 10 32	5♏51 27	12♏22 06	2 22.4	8 26.6	22 49.5	0 21.9	20 15.4	25 58.9	1 31.2	3 27.9	26 57.5	4 30.1
5 Su	19 00 29	15 11 42	18 59 44	25 44 39	2 16.9	7 14.5	24 04.6	0 40.3	20 39.4	26 12.8	1 34.6	3 31.3	26 59.7	4 32.0
6 M	19 04 25	16 12 53	2♐37 01	9♐36 46	2 08.7	6 09.7	25 19.8	0 58.3	21 03.3	26 26.8	1 38.1	3 34.6	27 01.9	4 34.0
7 Tu	19 08 22	17 14 04	16 43 41	23 57 18	1 58.3	5 13.6	26 34.9	1 15.9	21 27.2	26 40.8	1 41.7	3 38.1	27 04.2	4 35.8
8 W	19 12 19	18 15 15	1♑16 58	8♑41 46	1 46.8	4 26.9	27 50.0	1 33.0	21 51.2	26 54.8	1 45.4	3 41.5	27 06.5	4 37.7
9 Th	19 16 15	19 16 25	16 10 40	23 42 27	1 35.5	3 50.1	29 05.1	1 49.7	22 15.1	27 08.9	1 49.2	3 44.9	27 08.7	4 39.6
10 F	19 20 12	20 17 36	1♒15 50	8♒49 31	1 25.7	3 23.3	0♑20.3	2 06.0	22 39.1	27 22.9	1 53.0	3 48.4	27 11.0	4 41.4
11 Sa	19 24 08	21 18 45	16 22 13	23 52 45	1 18.4	3 06.3	1 35.4	2 21.7	23 03.0	27 37.0	1 57.0	3 51.8	27 13.3	4 43.2
12 Su	19 28 05	22 19 55	1♓20 04	8♓43 19	1 13.9	2D 58.7	2 50.5	2 37.0	23 27.0	27 51.1	2 01.0	3 55.3	27 15.5	4 45.0
13 M	19 32 01	23 21 03	16 01 48	23 15 02	1D 12.0	2 59.8	4 05.7	2 51.8	23 50.9	28 05.2	2 05.1	3 58.8	27 17.8	4 46.7
14 Tu	19 35 58	24 22 11	0♈22 43	7♈24 42	1 11.9	3 09.2	5 20.8	3 06.2	24 14.8	28 19.3	2 09.3	4 02.2	27 20.1	4 48.4
15 W	19 39 54	25 23 19	14 21 01	21 11 47	1R 12.3	3 26.1	6 35.9	3 20.0	24 38.8	28 33.4	2 13.6	4 05.7	27 22.3	4 50.1
16 Th	19 43 51	26 24 25	27 57 13	4♉37 37	1 12.1	3 49.9	7 51.1	3 33.3	25 02.7	28 47.5	2 18.0	4 09.2	27 24.6	4 51.8
17 F	19 47 48	27 25 31	11♉13 17	17 44 35	1 10.0	4 19.9	9 06.2	3 46.0	25 26.6	29 01.6	2 22.5	4 12.7	27 26.9	4 53.4
18 Sa	19 51 44	28 26 36	24 11 52	0♊35 27	1 05.5	4 55.7	10 21.4	3 58.3	25 50.5	29 15.7	2 27.0	4 16.2	27 29.2	4 55.1
19 Su	19 55 41	29 27 40	6♊55 40	13 12 49	0 58.3	5 36.6	11 36.5	4 10.0	26 14.4	29 29.9	2 31.7	4 19.7	27 31.5	4 56.7
20 M	19 59 37	0♒28 43	19 27 09	25 38 53	0 48.8	6 22.1	12 51.6	4 21.2	26 38.3	29 44.0	2 36.4	4 23.3	27 33.7	4 58.2
21 Tu	20 03 34	1 29 46	1♋48 15	7♋55 23	0 37.6	7 11.8	14 06.8	4 31.7	27 02.2	29 58.1	2 41.2	4 26.8	27 36.0	4 59.8
22 W	20 07 30	2 30 48	14 00 29	20 03 40	0 25.8	8 05.3	15 21.9	4 41.8	27 26.0	0♒12.2	2 46.0	4 30.3	27 38.3	5 01.3
23 Th	20 11 27	3 31 49	26 05 05	2♌04 51	0 14.4	9 02.1	16 37.1	4 51.2	27 49.9	0 26.3	2 51.0	4 33.8	27 40.6	5 02.8
24 F	20 15 23	4 32 49	8♌03 08	14 00 06	0 04.5	10 02.1	17 52.2	5 00.0	28 13.7	0 40.5	2 56.0	4 37.3	27 42.8	5 04.2
25 Sa	20 19 20	5 33 48	19 55 56	25 50 51	29♍56.7	11 04.8	19 07.3	5 08.3	28 37.5	0 54.6	3 01.1	4 40.9	27 45.1	5 05.6
26 Su	20 23 17	6 34 47	1♍45 07	7♍39 02	29 51.4	12 10.1	20 22.5	5 15.9	29 01.3	1 08.7	3 06.3	4 44.4	27 47.3	5 07.0
27 M	20 27 13	7 35 45	13 32 56	19 27 14	29D 48.4	13 17.7	21 37.6	5 22.9	29 25.1	1 22.8	3 11.5	4 47.9	27 49.6	5 08.4
28 Tu	20 31 10	8 36 42	25 22 20	1♎18 44	29 47.9	14 27.3	22 52.8	5 29.2	29 48.9	1 36.9	3 16.8	4 51.4	27 51.8	5 09.7
29 W	20 35 06	9 37 38	7♎16 57	13 17 32	29 48.7	15 39.0	24 07.9	5 34.9	0♒12.6	1 50.9	3 22.2	4 54.9	27 54.1	5 11.1
30 Th	20 39 03	10 38 34	19 21 05	25 28 13	29 50.0	16 52.4	25 23.0	5 39.9	0 36.4	2 05.0	3 27.7	4 58.4	27 56.3	5 12.3
31 F	20 42 59	11 39 29	1♏39 32	7♏55 41	29R 50.9	18 07.4	26 38.2	5 44.2	1 00.1	2 19.0	3 33.2	5 01.9	27 58.6	5 13.6

LONGITUDE — February 1997

Day	Sid.Time	☉	0 hr ☽	Noon ☽	True ☊	☿	♀	♂	⚳	♃	♄	♅	♆	♇
1 Sa	20 46 56	12♒40 23	14♏17 16	20♏44 51	29♍50.6	19♑24.0	27♑53.3	5♎47.8	1♒23.8	2♒33.1	3♈38.8	5♒05.4	28♑00.8	5♐14.8
2 Su	20 50 52	13 41 17	27 18 57	4♐00 00	29R 48.6	20 42.0	29 08.5	5 50.8	1 47.4	2 47.1	3 44.5	5 08.9	28 03.0	5 16.0
3 M	20 54 49	14 42 10	10♐48 18	17 44 02	29 44.6	22 01.4	0♒23.6	5 53.0	2 11.1	3 01.1	3 50.2	5 12.4	28 05.2	5 17.1
4 Tu	20 58 46	15 43 02	24 47 11	1♑57 36	29 38.9	23 22.0	1 38.8	5 54.5	2 34.7	3 15.1	3 56.0	5 15.9	28 07.4	5 18.2
5 W	21 02 42	16 43 53	9♑14 50	16 38 17	29 32.2	24 43.8	2 53.9	5R 55.3	2 58.3	3 29.1	4 01.8	5 19.4	28 09.6	5 19.3
6 Th	21 06 39	17 44 43	24 07 07	1♒40 17	29 25.4	26 06.8	4 09.0	5 55.3	3 21.9	3 43.0	4 07.8	5 22.9	28 11.8	5 20.4
7 F	21 10 35	18 45 32	9♒16 36	16 54 45	29 19.5	27 30.8	5 24.2	5 54.5	3 45.5	3 57.0	4 13.7	5 26.3	28 14.0	5 21.4
8 Sa	21 14 32	19 46 19	24 33 21	2♓11 04	29 15.1	28 55.9	6 39.3	5 53.1	4 09.0	4 10.9	4 19.8	5 29.8	28 16.1	5 22.4
9 Su	21 18 28	20 47 05	9♓46 35	17 18 43	29D 12.7	0♒22.0	7 54.4	5 50.8	4 32.5	4 24.7	4 25.9	5 33.2	28 18.3	5 23.4
10 M	21 22 25	21 47 50	24 46 28	2♈08 58	29 12.2	1 49.1	9 09.5	5 47.8	4 56.0	4 38.6	4 32.0	5 36.6	28 20.4	5 24.3
11 Tu	21 26 21	22 48 33	9♈25 36	16 35 54	29 13.1	3 17.1	10 24.6	5 44.0	5 19.4	4 52.4	4 38.2	5 40.0	28 22.5	5 25.2
12 W	21 30 18	23 49 14	23 39 39	0♉36 45	29 14.6	4 46.1	11 39.7	5 39.4	5 42.8	5 06.2	4 44.5	5 43.4	28 24.6	5 26.0
13 Th	21 34 14	24 49 54	7♉27 17	14 11 25	29R 16.0	6 16.0	12 54.8	5 34.0	6 06.2	5 19.9	4 50.8	5 46.8	28 26.7	5 26.8
14 F	21 38 11	25 50 32	20 49 27	27 21 45	29 16.4	7 46.8	14 09.8	5 27.9	6 29.5	5 33.7	4 57.2	5 50.2	28 28.8	5 27.6
15 Sa	21 42 08	26 51 09	3♊48 43	10♊10 47	29 15.5	9 18.5	15 24.9	5 21.0	6 52.8	5 47.4	5 03.6	5 53.5	28 30.9	5 28.4
16 Su	21 46 04	27 51 44	16 28 26	22 42 05	29 13.1	10 51.1	16 40.0	5 13.3	7 16.0	6 01.0	5 10.1	5 56.9	28 32.9	5 29.1
17 M	21 50 01	28 52 17	28 52 13	4♋59 15	29 09.3	12 24.6	17 55.0	5 04.8	7 39.3	6 14.6	5 16.6	6 00.2	28 35.0	5 29.8
18 Tu	21 53 57	29 52 48	11♋03 35	17 05 37	29 04.5	13 59.1	19 10.0	4 55.6	8 02.4	6 28.2	5 23.2	6 03.5	28 37.0	5 30.4
19 W	21 57 54	0♓53 17	23 05 42	29 04 10	28 59.3	15 34.4	20 25.1	4 45.6	8 25.6	6 41.8	5 29.8	6 06.8	28 39.0	5 31.0
20 Th	22 01 50	1 53 45	5♌01 18	10♌57 25	28 54.2	17 10.7	21 40.1	4 34.8	8 48.7	6 55.2	5 36.5	6 10.0	28 41.0	5 31.6
21 F	22 05 47	2 54 11	16 52 46	22 47 35	28 49.9	18 47.9	22 55.1	4 23.2	9 11.7	7 08.7	5 43.2	6 13.3	28 43.0	5 32.2
22 Sa	22 09 43	3 54 35	28 42 08	4♍36 38	28 46.6	20 26.0	24 10.1	4 10.9	9 34.7	7 22.1	5 49.9	6 16.5	28 44.9	5 32.7
23 Su	22 13 40	4 54 58	10♍31 20	16 26 29	28 44.7	22 05.1	25 25.1	3 57.8	9 57.7	7 35.5	5 56.7	6 19.7	28 46.9	5 33.2
24 M	22 17 37	5 55 19	22 22 21	28 19 12	28D 44.0	23 45.1	26 40.1	3 44.0	10 20.6	7 48.8	6 03.5	6 22.9	28 48.8	5 33.6
25 Tu	22 21 33	6 55 38	4♎17 20	10♎17 04	28 44.5	25 26.1	27 55.0	3 29.5	10 43.5	8 02.1	6 10.4	6 26.1	28 50.7	5 34.0
26 W	22 25 30	7 55 56	16 18 46	22 22 48	28 45.7	27 08.2	29 10.0	3 14.3	11 06.4	8 15.3	6 17.3	6 29.2	28 52.5	5 34.4
27 Th	22 29 26	8 56 12	28 29 33	4♏39 29	28 47.3	28 51.2	0♓24.9	2 58.3	11 29.2	8 28.5	6 24.2	6 32.3	28 54.4	5 34.7
28 F	22 33 23	9 56 27	10♏53 00	17 10 34	28 48.8	0♓35.2	1 39.9	2 41.7	11 51.9	8 41.6	6 31.2	6 35.4	28 56.2	5 35.0

Astro Data Dy Hr Mn	Planet Ingress Dy Hr Mn	Last Aspect Dy Hr Mn	☽ Ingress Dy Hr Mn	Last Aspect Dy Hr Mn	☽ Ingress Dy Hr Mn	☽ Phases & Eclipses Dy Hr Mn	Astro Data
☽0S 1 1:17	♂ ♎ 3 8:10	1 1:02 ♂ ☌	♎ 1 2:32	2 2:24 ♀ ✶	♐ 2 4:51	2 1:45 ☾ 11♎42	1 January 1997
♃☌♆ 9 11:39	♀ ♑ 10 5:32	3 7:11 ♆ □	♏ 3 13:02	3 6:22 ☉ ✶	♑ 4 8:44	9 4:26 ● 18♑57	Julian Day # 35430
☿D 12 20:42	☉ ♒ 20 0:43	5 14:12 ♆ ✶	♐ 5 19:27	6 6:29 ♆ ☌	♒ 6 9:21	15 20:02 ☽ 25♈44	SVP 5♓18'04"
☽0N 13 22:50	♃ ♒ 21 15:13	7 16:43 ♀ ☌	♑ 7 21:55	7 15:06 ☉ ☌	♓ 8 8:34	23 15:11 ○ 3♌40	GC 26♐47.8 ⚴ 27♐42.7
☽0S 28 9:28	☊ ♍R 25 0:51	9 17:33 ♃ ☌	♒ 9 22:00	10 5:46 ♆ ✶	♈ 10 8:29	31 19:40 ☾ 11♏59	Eris 17♈53.3R ⚵ 14♈51.0
	⚳ ♒ 28 23:15	10 5:25 ♇ ✶	♓ 11 21:51	12 8:10 ♆ □	♉ 12 10:56		⚷ 0♏15.2 ⚶ 27♑24.5
♅✶♇ 5 11:21		13 20:16 ♃ ✶	♈ 13 23:22	14 14:04 ♆ △	♊ 14 16:53	7 15:06 ● 18♒53	☽ Mean ☊ 3♎01.7
♂R 6 0:37	♀ ♒ 3 4:28	16 1:19 ♃ □	♉ 16 3:40	16 22:56 ☉ △	♋ 17 2:13	14 8:58 ☽ 25♉43	
♃✶♄ 9 15:33	☿ ♒ 9 5:53	18 9:27 ♃ △	♊ 18 10:53	19 11:09 ♆ ☍	♌ 19 13:52	22 10:27 ○ 3♍51	1 February 1997
☽0N 10 8:50	☉ ♓ 18 14:51	18 20:12 ♇ ☍	♋ 20 20:29	21 12:17 ♀ ☍	♍ 22 2:38		Julian Day # 35461
♃✶♇ 14 0:47	♀ ♓ 27 4:01	23 3:09 ♆ ☍	♌ 23 7:50	24 13:00 ♆ △	♎ 24 15:23		SVP 5♓18'00"
♃☌♅ 16 2:22	☿ ♓ 28 3:54	23 17:58 ♇ △	♍ 25 20:26	27 2:49 ♀ △	♏ 27 2:57		GC 26♐47.9 ⚴ 10♑03.7
♄0N 16 5:26		28 5:01 ♆ △	♎ 28 9:21				Eris 17♈57.3 ⚵ 27♈54.6
♄△♇ 19 16:56		30 16:49 ♆ □	♏ 30 20:48				⚷ 1♏55.8 ⚶ 13♒33.2
☽0S 24 16:04							☽ Mean ☊ 1♎23.2

March 1997 — LONGITUDE

Day	Sid.Time	☉	0 hr ☽	Noon ☽	True ☊	☿	♀	♂	⚳	♃	♄	♅	♆	♇
1 Sa	22 37 19	10♓56 41	23♏32 38	29♏59 39	28♍49.9	2♓20.3	2♓54.8	2♎24.4	12♒14.6	8♒54.7	6♈38.2	6♒38.5	28♑58.1	5♐35.3
2 Su	22 41 16	11 56 53	6♐32 02	13♐10 10	28R50.2	4 06.4	4 09.8	2R06.5	12 37.3	9 07.7	6 45.3	6 41.5	28 59.9	5 35.5
3 M	22 45 12	12 57 03	19 54 21	26 44 49	28 49.8	5 53.6	5 24.7	1 48.0	12 59.9	9 20.7	6 52.4	6 44.5	29 01.6	5 35.7
4 Tu	22 49 09	13 57 12	3♑41 41	10♑44 58	28 48.6	7 41.8	6 39.6	1 28.8	13 22.4	9 33.6	6 59.5	6 47.5	29 03.4	5 35.9
5 W	22 53 06	14 57 19	17 54 31	25 10 00	28 47.0	9 31.1	7 54.5	1 09.2	13 44.9	9 46.5	7 06.6	6 50.5	29 05.1	5 36.0
6 Th	22 57 02	15 57 25	2♒30 57	9♒56 41	28 45.3	11 21.5	9 09.4	0 48.9	14 07.3	9 59.3	7 13.8	6 53.4	29 06.8	5 36.1
7 F	23 00 59	16 57 29	17 26 23	24 59 04	28 43.9	13 13.0	10 24.3	0 28.2	14 29.7	10 12.0	7 21.0	6 56.3	29 08.5	5 36.1
8 Sa	23 04 55	17 57 31	2♓33 37	10♓08 52	28 42.9	15 05.5	11 39.2	0 07.0	14 52.0	10 24.7	7 28.2	6 59.2	29 10.2	5R36.2
9 Su	23 08 52	18 57 32	17 43 37	25 16 39	28D42.5	16 59.0	12 54.0	29♍45.4	15 14.3	10 37.3	7 35.5	7 02.0	29 11.8	5 36.1
10 M	23 12 48	19 57 30	2♈46 49	10♈13 06	28 42.6	18 53.6	14 08.9	29 23.4	15 36.5	10 49.8	7 42.8	7 04.9	29 13.5	5 36.1
11 Tu	23 16 45	20 57 26	17 34 36	24 50 33	28 43.1	20 49.1	15 23.7	29 01.0	15 58.6	11 02.3	7 50.1	7 07.6	29 15.0	5 36.0
12 W	23 20 41	21 57 21	2♉00 23	9♉03 42	28 43.8	22 45.5	16 38.5	28 38.4	16 20.7	11 14.7	7 57.4	7 10.4	29 16.6	5 35.9
13 Th	23 24 38	22 57 13	16 00 17	22 50 05	28 44.4	24 42.8	17 53.3	28 15.5	16 42.7	11 27.0	8 04.8	7 13.1	29 18.2	5 35.7
14 F	23 28 35	23 57 03	29 33 09	6♊09 42	28 44.8	26 40.8	19 08.1	27 52.3	17 04.7	11 39.3	8 12.1	7 15.8	29 19.7	5 35.5
15 Sa	23 32 31	24 56 51	12♊40 03	19 04 34	28R45.0	28 39.5	20 22.9	27 29.1	17 26.5	11 51.5	8 19.5	7 18.4	29 21.2	5 35.3
16 Su	23 36 28	25 56 36	25 23 43	1♋37 59	28 45.0	0♈38.7	21 37.6	27 05.6	17 48.3	12 03.6	8 26.9	7 21.1	29 22.6	5 35.1
17 M	23 40 24	26 56 19	7♋47 55	13 54 03	28 44.9	2 38.2	22 52.4	26 42.1	18 10.1	12 15.6	8 34.3	7 23.7	29 24.1	5 34.8
18 Tu	23 44 21	27 56 00	19 56 55	25 57 04	28D44.8	4 37.9	24 07.1	26 18.6	18 31.7	12 27.6	8 41.8	7 26.2	29 25.5	5 34.5
19 W	23 48 17	28 55 39	1♌55 02	7♌51 18	28 44.8	6 37.6	25 21.8	25 55.1	18 53.3	12 39.4	8 49.2	7 28.7	29 26.9	5 34.1
20 Th	23 52 14	29 55 15	13 46 23	19 40 43	28 44.9	8 36.9	26 36.5	25 31.6	19 14.9	12 51.2	8 56.7	7 31.2	29 28.2	5 33.7
21 F	23 56 10	0♈54 50	25 34 45	1♍28 51	28 45.1	10 35.6	27 51.1	25 08.2	19 36.3	13 03.0	9 04.1	7 33.6	29 29.5	5 33.3
22 Sa	0 00 07	1 54 22	7♍23 24	13 18 44	28 45.3	12 33.4	29 05.8	24 45.0	19 57.7	13 14.6	9 11.6	7 36.0	29 30.8	5 32.8
23 Su	0 04 03	2 53 51	19 15 11	25 13 00	28R45.4	14 29.8	0♈20.4	24 21.9	20 19.0	13 26.1	9 19.1	7 38.4	29 32.1	5 32.3
24 M	0 08 00	3 53 19	1♎12 28	7♎13 48	28 45.4	16 24.7	1 35.0	23 59.1	20 40.2	13 37.6	9 26.6	7 40.7	29 33.3	5 31.8
25 Tu	0 11 57	4 52 45	13 17 15	19 23 02	28 45.0	18 17.4	2 49.6	23 36.5	21 01.3	13 49.0	9 34.1	7 43.0	29 34.6	5 31.3
26 W	0 15 53	5 52 09	25 31 20	1♏42 21	28 44.3	20 07.7	4 04.2	23 14.2	21 22.4	14 00.2	9 41.6	7 45.3	29 35.7	5 30.7
27 Th	0 19 50	6 51 31	7♏56 17	14 13 20	28 43.3	21 55.0	5 18.8	22 52.3	21 43.4	14 11.4	9 49.1	7 47.5	29 36.9	5 30.1
28 F	0 23 46	7 50 51	20 33 41	26 57 33	28 42.2	23 39.1	6 33.4	22 30.8	22 04.3	14 22.5	9 56.6	7 49.6	29 38.0	5 29.4
29 Sa	0 27 43	8 50 09	3♐25 07	9♐56 35	28 41.0	25 19.3	7 47.9	22 09.6	22 25.1	14 33.6	10 04.2	7 51.8	29 39.1	5 28.8
30 Su	0 31 39	9 49 26	16 32 09	23 11 58	28 40.1	26 55.5	9 02.5	21 48.9	22 45.8	14 44.5	10 11.7	7 53.9	29 40.2	5 28.1
31 M	0 35 36	10 48 41	29 56 11	6♑44 57	28D39.6	28 27.1	10 17.0	21 28.8	23 06.5	14 55.3	10 19.2	7 55.9	29 41.2	5 27.3

April 1997 — LONGITUDE

Day	Sid.Time	☉	0 hr ☽	Noon ☽	True ☊	☿	♀	♂	⚳	♃	♄	♅	♆	♇
1 Tu	0 39 32	11♈47 54	13♑38 20	20♑36 20	28♍39.7	29♈53.9	11♈31.5	21♍09.1	23♒27.0	15♒06.0	10♈26.7	7♒57.9	29♑42.2	5♐26.6
2 W	0 43 29	12 47 05	27 38 54	4♒45 55	28 40.4	1♉15.5	12 46.0	20R49.9	23 47.5	15 16.6	10 34.3	7 59.9	29 43.2	5R25.8
3 Th	0 47 26	13 46 15	11♒57 07	19 12 12	28 41.5	2 31.6	14 00.4	20 31.4	24 07.8	15 27.1	10 41.8	8 01.8	29 44.1	5 24.9
4 F	0 51 22	14 45 23	26 30 40	3♓51 59	28 42.6	3 42.0	15 14.9	20 13.5	24 28.1	15 37.6	10 49.3	8 03.7	29 45.1	5 24.1
5 Sa	0 55 19	15 44 28	11♓15 27	18 40 18	28R43.4	4 46.5	16 29.4	19 56.1	24 48.3	15 47.9	10 56.8	8 05.5	29 45.9	5 23.2
6 Su	0 59 15	16 43 32	26 05 41	3♈30 40	28 43.5	5 44.9	17 43.8	19 39.5	25 08.4	15 58.1	11 04.3	8 07.3	29 46.8	5 22.3
7 M	1 03 12	17 42 34	10♈54 19	18 15 43	28 42.8	6 36.9	18 58.2	19 23.5	25 28.4	16 08.2	11 11.8	8 09.1	29 47.6	5 21.4
8 Tu	1 07 08	18 41 34	25 33 56	2♉48 10	28 41.0	7 22.6	20 12.6	19 08.3	25 48.3	16 18.1	11 19.3	8 10.8	29 48.4	5 20.4
9 W	1 11 05	19 40 32	9♉57 40	17 01 50	28 38.3	8 01.7	21 27.0	18 53.7	26 08.0	16 28.0	11 26.8	8 12.4	29 49.1	5 19.4
10 Th	1 15 01	20 39 28	24 00 12	0♊52 26	28 35.2	8 34.2	22 41.3	18 39.9	26 27.7	16 37.8	11 34.3	8 14.1	29 49.9	5 18.4
11 F	1 18 58	21 38 22	7♊38 22	14 17 57	28 32.0	9 00.2	23 55.7	18 26.9	26 47.3	16 47.4	11 41.7	8 15.6	29 50.6	5 17.3
12 Sa	1 22 55	22 37 13	20 51 18	27 18 37	28 29.3	9 19.5	25 10.0	18 14.6	27 06.7	16 56.9	11 49.2	8 17.1	29 51.2	5 16.3
13 Su	1 26 51	23 36 02	3♋40 13	9♋56 32	28 27.4	9 32.2	26 24.3	18 03.1	27 26.1	17 06.3	11 56.6	8 18.6	29 51.8	5 15.2
14 M	1 30 48	24 34 49	16 08 01	22 15 14	28D26.6	9R38.6	27 38.6	17 52.3	27 45.3	17 15.6	12 04.1	8 20.1	29 52.4	5 14.1
15 Tu	1 34 44	25 33 34	28 18 44	4♌19 07	28 26.9	9 38.6	28 52.8	17 42.4	28 04.4	17 24.8	12 11.5	8 21.4	29 53.0	5 12.9
16 W	1 38 41	26 32 16	10♌17 01	16 13 02	28 28.1	9 32.5	0♉07.1	17 33.2	28 23.4	17 33.8	12 18.8	8 22.8	29 53.5	5 11.7
17 Th	1 42 37	27 30 56	22 07 48	28 01 54	28 29.9	9 20.6	1 21.3	17 24.9	28 42.3	17 42.7	12 26.2	8 24.1	29 54.0	5 10.6
18 F	1 46 34	28 29 34	3♍55 55	9♍50 25	28 31.6	9 03.3	2 35.5	17 17.3	29 01.1	17 51.5	12 33.6	8 25.3	29 54.5	5 09.3
19 Sa	1 50 30	29 28 10	15 45 53	21 42 49	28R32.8	8 40.9	3 49.7	17 10.5	29 19.8	18 00.2	12 40.9	8 26.5	29 54.9	5 08.1
20 Su	1 54 27	0♉26 43	27 41 40	3♎42 48	28 32.8	8 14.0	5 03.8	17 04.5	29 38.3	18 08.7	12 48.2	8 27.6	29 55.3	5 06.9
21 M	1 58 23	1 25 15	9♎46 34	15 53 16	28 31.5	7 43.2	6 18.0	16 59.3	29 56.7	18 17.1	12 55.5	8 28.7	29 55.6	5 05.6
22 Tu	2 02 20	2 23 45	22 03 07	28 16 19	28 28.5	7 08.9	7 32.1	16 54.9	0♓15.0	18 25.4	13 02.7	8 29.8	29 56.0	5 04.3
23 W	2 06 17	3 22 12	4♏33 00	10♏53 13	28 24.0	6 32.0	8 46.2	16 51.3	0 33.1	18 33.5	13 10.0	8 30.8	29 56.3	5 03.0
24 Th	2 10 13	4 20 38	17 17 02	23 44 25	28 18.3	5 53.1	10 00.3	16 48.4	0 51.1	18 41.5	13 17.2	8 31.7	29 56.5	5 01.6
25 F	2 14 10	5 19 02	0♐15 19	6♐49 41	28 12.1	5 13.0	11 14.4	16 46.3	1 09.0	18 49.4	13 24.4	8 32.6	29 56.8	5 00.3
26 Sa	2 18 06	6 17 25	13 27 25	20 08 22	28 06.2	4 32.4	12 28.4	16 44.9	1 26.8	18 57.1	13 31.5	8 33.5	29 57.0	4 58.9
27 Su	2 22 03	7 15 46	26 52 27	3♑39 32	28 01.1	3 52.1	13 42.5	16D44.3	1 44.4	19 04.7	13 38.7	8 34.3	29 57.1	4 57.5
28 M	2 25 59	8 14 05	10♑29 30	17 22 13	27 57.6	3 12.7	14 56.5	16 44.5	2 01.9	19 12.1	13 45.8	8 35.0	29 57.3	4 56.1
29 Tu	2 29 56	9 12 23	24 17 36	1♒15 31	27D55.8	2 35.1	16 10.5	16 45.4	2 19.3	19 19.4	13 52.8	8 35.8	29 57.4	4 54.7
30 W	2 33 52	10 10 39	8♒15 53	15 18 33	27 55.6	1 59.6	17 24.5	16 47.0	2 36.5	19 26.6	13 59.9	8 36.4	29 57.4	4 53.2

Astro Data

	Dy Hr Mn
♄⚹♅	1 13:23
♇ R	8 12:54
☽ 0N	9 20:06
☿ 0N	17 5:09
☉ 0N	20 13:55
☽ 0S	23 22:16
♀ 0N	25 19:22
☽ 0N	6 6:52
☿ R	14 24:00
☽ 0S	20 5:23
♂ D	27 19:09

Planet Ingress

	Dy Hr Mn
♂ ♍R	8 19:49
☿ ♈	16 4:13
☉ ♈	20 13:55
♀ ♈	23 5:26
☿ ♉	1 13:45
♀ ♉	16 9:43
☉ ♉	20 1:03
⚳ ♓	21 16:20

Last Aspect / ☽ Ingress

Last Aspect Dy Hr Mn		☽ Ingress Dy Hr Mn
1 10:06 ♆ ⚹	♐	1 12:01
2 9:37 ☉ □	♑	3 17:38
5 18:26 ♆ ☌	♒	5 19:54
6 12:04 ♃ ☌	♓	7 19:57
9 18:59 ♂ ☍	♈	9 19:33
11 19:23 ♆ □	♉	11 20:37
13 23:34 ♆ △	♊	14 0:48
16 3:31 ♂ □	♋	16 8:51
18 19:00 ♆ ☍	♌	18 20:08
19 21:54 ♃ ☍	♍	21 8:59
23 20:40 ♆ △	♎	23 21:35
26 7:55 ♆ □	♏	26 8:42
28 16:59 ♆ ⚹	♐	28 17:40
30 19:31 ☿ △	♑	31 0:07

Last Aspect / ☽ Ingress

Last Aspect Dy Hr Mn		☽ Ingress Dy Hr Mn
2 3:30 ♆ ☌	♒	2 3:59
3 5:44 ♃ ☌	♓	4 5:42
6 5:57 ♆ ⚹	♈	6 6:19
8 7:01 ♆ □	♉	8 7:20
10 10:10 ♆ △	♊	10 10:28
12 7:34 ♀ ⚹	♋	12 17:03
15 3:07 ♆ ☍	♌	15 3:22
17 10:51 ☉ △	♍	17 16:00
20 4:27 ♆ △	♎	20 4:36
22 15:11 ♆ □	♏	22 15:19
24 23:26 ♆ ⚹	♐	24 23:32
26 9:51 ♃ ⚹	♑	27 5:32
29 9:46 ♆ ☌	♒	29 9:50

☽ Phases & Eclipses

Dy Hr Mn	
2 9:37	☾ 11♐51
9 1:15	● 18♓31
9 1:23:48	● T 02'50"
16 0:06	☽ 25♊27
24 4:45	○ 3♎35
24 4:39	● P 0.919
31 19:38	☾ 11♑08
7 11:02	● 17♈40
14 17:00	☽ 24♋47
22 20:33	○ 2♏45
30 2:37	☾ 9♒48

Astro Data

1 March 1997
Julian Day # 35489
SVP 5♓17'57"
GC 26♐48.0 ⚵ 20♑09.4
Eris 18♈09.1 ⚴ 12♉05.2
⚷ 1♏51.7R ⚶ 27♒54.4
☽ Mean ☊ 29♍54.2

1 April 1997
Julian Day # 35520
SVP 5♓17'54"
GC 26♐48.1 ⚵ 29♑22.0
Eris 18♈28.0 ⚴ 29♉03.7
⚷ 0♏13.8R ⚶ 13♓15.5
☽ Mean ☊ 28♍15.7

LONGITUDE — May 1997

Day	Sid.Time	☉	0 hr ☽	Noon ☽	True ☊	☿	♀	♂	⚳	♃	♄	♅	♆	♇
1 Th	2 37 49	11♉08 54	22♒23 24	29♒30 14	27♍56.5	1♉27.0	18♉38.5	16♍49.3	2♓53.6	19♒33.6	14♈06.9	8♒37.0	29♑57.5	4♐51.8
2 F	2 41 46	12 07 07	6♓38 52	13♓49 01	27R57.7	0R57.7	19 52.4	16 52.4	3 10.5	19 40.5	14 13.9	8 37.6	29R57.5	4R50.3
3 Sa	2 45 42	13 05 19	21 00 21	28 12 29	27 58.3	0 32.1	21 06.4	16 56.1	3 27.2	19 47.2	14 20.8	8 38.1	29 57.4	4 48.8
4 Su	2 49 39	14 03 29	5♈24 57	12♈37 13	27 57.4	0 10.5	22 20.3	17 00.6	3 43.9	19 53.7	14 27.7	8 38.5	29 57.4	4 47.3
5 M	2 53 35	15 01 38	19 48 42	26 58 47	27 54.5	29♈53.2	23 34.2	17 05.7	4 00.3	20 00.1	14 34.6	8 39.0	29 57.3	4 45.8
6 Tu	2 57 32	15 59 45	4♉06 48	11♉12 05	27 49.4	29 40.4	24 48.1	17 11.6	4 16.6	20 06.4	14 41.4	8 39.3	29 57.1	4 44.3
7 W	3 01 28	16 57 51	18 14 02	25 12 01	27 42.3	29 32.2	26 02.0	17 18.1	4 32.8	20 12.4	14 48.2	8 39.6	29 57.0	4 42.7
8 Th	3 05 25	17 55 55	2♊05 34	8♊54 14	27 34.0	29D28.6	27 15.9	17 25.2	4 48.7	20 18.4	14 54.9	8 39.9	29 56.8	4 41.2
9 F	3 09 21	18 53 57	15 37 41	22 15 44	27 25.5	29 29.8	28 29.7	17 33.0	5 04.5	20 24.1	15 01.6	8 40.1	29 56.5	4 39.6
10 Sa	3 13 18	19 51 58	28 48 18	5♋15 25	27 17.5	29 35.6	29 43.6	17 41.5	5 20.2	20 29.7	15 08.3	8 40.2	29 56.3	4 38.1
11 Su	3 17 15	20 49 57	11♋37 13	17 53 58	27 11.0	29 46.1	0♊57.4	17 50.6	5 35.7	20 35.2	15 14.9	8 40.4	29 56.0	4 36.5
12 M	3 21 11	21 47 54	24 06 02	0♌13 49	27 06.5	0♉01.1	2 11.2	18 00.3	5 51.0	20 40.5	15 21.5	8R40.4	29 55.7	4 34.9
13 Tu	3 25 08	22 45 49	6♌17 51	12 18 41	27D04.0	0 20.6	3 25.0	18 10.6	6 06.1	20 45.6	15 28.0	8 40.4	29 55.3	4 33.3
14 W	3 29 04	23 43 42	18 16 55	24 13 11	27 03.4	0 44.5	4 38.7	18 21.5	6 21.0	20 50.5	15 34.5	8 40.4	29 54.9	4 31.7
15 Th	3 33 01	24 41 33	0♍08 10	6♍02 30	27 03.9	1 12.6	5 52.5	18 33.0	6 35.8	20 55.3	15 41.0	8 40.3	29 54.5	4 30.1
16 F	3 36 57	25 39 23	11 56 51	17 51 55	27R04.8	1 44.8	7 06.2	18 45.0	6 50.4	20 59.9	15 47.4	8 40.1	29 54.1	4 28.5
17 Sa	3 40 54	26 37 11	23 48 17	29 46 36	27 05.1	2 21.1	8 19.9	18 57.6	7 04.7	21 04.3	15 53.7	8 40.0	29 53.6	4 26.8
18 Su	3 44 50	27 34 58	5♎47 26	11♎51 18	27 03.9	3 01.1	9 33.5	19 10.7	7 18.9	21 08.6	16 00.0	8 39.7	29 53.1	4 25.2
19 M	3 48 47	28 32 43	17 58 40	24 09 56	27 00.6	3 45.0	10 47.2	19 24.4	7 33.0	21 12.7	16 06.2	8 39.4	29 52.5	4 23.6
20 Tu	3 52 44	29 30 26	0♏25 27	6♏45 25	26 54.9	4 32.4	12 00.8	19 38.6	7 46.8	21 16.6	16 12.4	8 39.1	29 52.0	4 21.9
21 W	3 56 40	0♊28 08	13 10 02	19 39 20	26 46.9	5 23.3	13 14.5	19 53.3	8 00.4	21 20.3	16 18.5	8 38.7	29 51.4	4 20.3
22 Th	4 00 37	1 25 48	26 13 16	2♐51 44	26 37.1	6 17.7	14 28.1	20 08.5	8 13.8	21 23.9	16 24.6	8 38.3	29 50.7	4 18.6
23 F	4 04 33	2 23 28	9♐34 29	16 21 14	26 26.5	7 15.3	15 41.7	20 24.2	8 27.1	21 27.2	16 30.6	8 37.8	29 50.1	4 17.0
24 Sa	4 08 30	3 21 06	23 11 36	0♑05 10	26 16.0	8 16.1	16 55.2	20 40.4	8 40.1	21 30.5	16 36.6	8 37.3	29 49.4	4 15.4
25 Su	4 12 26	4 18 43	7♑01 30	14 00 08	26 06.9	9 20.1	18 08.8	20 57.1	8 52.9	21 33.5	16 42.5	8 36.7	29 48.7	4 13.7
26 M	4 16 23	5 16 19	21 00 37	28 02 31	26 00.0	10 27.1	19 22.3	21 14.2	9 05.5	21 36.3	16 48.4	8 36.1	29 47.9	4 12.1
27 Tu	4 20 19	6 13 54	5♒05 28	12♒09 06	25 55.6	11 37.0	20 35.9	21 31.8	9 17.9	21 39.0	16 54.2	8 35.4	29 47.2	4 10.4
28 W	4 24 16	7 11 28	19 13 08	26 17 21	25D53.5	12 49.8	21 49.4	21 49.8	9 30.0	21 41.5	16 59.9	8 34.7	29 46.4	4 08.8
29 Th	4 28 13	8 09 01	3♓21 32	10♓25 33	25 53.1	14 05.5	23 02.9	22 08.2	9 42.0	21 43.7	17 05.6	8 34.0	29 45.5	4 07.1
30 F	4 32 09	9 06 33	17 29 16	24 32 33	25R53.3	15 23.9	24 16.4	22 27.1	9 53.7	21 45.8	17 11.2	8 33.2	29 44.7	4 05.5
31 Sa	4 36 06	10 04 05	1♈35 17	8♈37 20	25 52.9	16 45.1	25 29.8	22 46.4	10 05.2	21 47.8	17 16.7	8 32.3	29 43.8	4 03.9

LONGITUDE — June 1997

Day	Sid.Time	☉	0 hr ☽	Noon ☽	True ☊	☿	♀	♂	⚳	♃	♄	♅	♆	♇
1 Su	4 40 02	11♊01 36	15♈38 32	22♈38 39	25♍50.6	18♉09.0	26♊43.3	23♍06.1	10♓16.4	21♒49.5	17♈22.2	8♒31.4	29♑42.9	4♐02.2
2 M	4 43 59	11 59 06	29 37 27	6♉34 39	25R45.7	19 35.6	27 56.7	23 26.2	10 27.5	21 51.0	17 27.7	8R30.5	29R42.0	4R00.6
3 Tu	4 47 55	12 56 35	13♉29 53	20 22 49	25 38.1	21 04.9	29 10.1	23 46.8	10 38.2	21 52.4	17 33.0	8 29.5	29 41.0	3 59.0
4 W	4 51 52	13 54 04	27 13 03	4♊00 13	25 27.9	22 36.8	0♋23.6	24 07.7	10 48.8	21 53.5	17 38.3	8 28.4	29 40.0	3 57.3
5 Th	4 55 48	14 51 31	10♊43 56	17 23 54	25 16.0	24 11.3	1 37.0	24 29.0	10 59.1	21 54.5	17 43.5	8 27.4	29 39.0	3 55.7
6 F	4 59 45	15 48 58	23 59 48	0♋31 26	25 03.6	25 48.4	2 50.3	24 50.7	11 09.1	21 55.3	17 48.7	8 26.3	29 38.0	3 54.1
7 Sa	5 03 42	16 46 24	6♋58 40	13 21 27	24 51.8	27 28.1	4 03.7	25 12.7	11 18.9	21 55.8	17 53.8	8 25.1	29 36.9	3 52.5
8 Su	5 07 38	17 43 48	19 39 50	25 53 57	24 41.7	29 10.4	5 17.1	25 35.2	11 28.4	21 56.2	17 58.8	8 23.9	29 35.8	3 50.9
9 M	5 11 35	18 41 12	2♌04 00	8♌10 19	24 34.0	0♊55.3	6 30.4	25 58.0	11 37.7	21R56.4	18 03.7	8 22.7	29 34.7	3 49.4
10 Tu	5 15 31	19 38 35	14 13 16	20 13 20	24 28.8	2 42.7	7 43.7	26 21.1	11 46.7	21 56.4	18 08.6	8 21.4	29 33.6	3 47.8
11 W	5 19 28	20 35 56	26 11 01	2♍06 53	24 26.1	4 32.6	8 57.0	26 44.6	11 55.4	21 56.2	18 13.3	8 20.1	29 32.5	3 46.2
12 Th	5 23 24	21 33 17	8♍01 33	13 55 41	24 25.2	6 25.0	10 10.3	27 08.4	12 03.9	21 55.9	18 18.1	8 18.7	29 31.3	3 44.7
13 F	5 27 21	22 30 37	19 49 56	25 45 00	24 25.1	8 19.8	11 23.5	27 32.5	12 12.0	21 55.3	18 22.7	8 17.3	29 30.1	3 43.1
14 Sa	5 31 17	23 27 55	1♎41 34	7♎40 19	24 24.8	10 16.9	12 36.7	27 57.0	12 20.0	21 54.5	18 27.3	8 15.8	29 28.9	3 41.6
15 Su	5 35 14	24 25 13	13 41 55	19 47 00	24 23.2	12 16.2	13 50.0	28 21.7	12 27.6	21 53.6	18 31.7	8 14.4	29 27.6	3 40.1
16 M	5 39 11	25 22 30	25 56 08	2♏09 53	24 19.5	14 17.7	15 03.1	28 46.8	12 34.9	21 52.4	18 36.2	8 12.8	29 26.4	3 38.6
17 Tu	5 43 07	26 19 46	8♏28 40	14 52 53	24 13.4	16 21.2	16 16.3	29 12.2	12 42.0	21 51.1	18 40.5	8 11.3	29 25.1	3 37.1
18 W	5 47 04	27 17 02	21 22 46	27 58 28	24 04.7	18 26.5	17 29.5	29 37.8	12 48.8	21 49.6	18 44.7	8 09.7	29 23.8	3 35.6
19 Th	5 51 00	28 14 17	4♐40 01	11♐27 15	23 54.1	20 33.4	18 42.6	0♎03.8	12 55.2	21 47.8	18 48.9	8 08.1	29 22.5	3 34.2
20 F	5 54 57	29 11 31	18 19 55	25 17 37	23 42.5	22 41.7	19 55.7	0 30.0	13 01.4	21 45.9	18 53.0	8 06.4	29 21.2	3 32.7
21 Sa	5 58 53	0♋08 45	2♑19 49	9♑25 53	23 31.0	24 51.2	21 08.8	0 56.6	13 07.3	21 43.9	18 57.0	8 04.7	29 19.8	3 31.3
22 Su	6 02 50	1 05 58	16 35 07	23 46 44	23 21.0	27 01.5	22 21.9	1 23.4	13 12.9	21 41.6	19 00.9	8 03.0	29 18.5	3 29.9
23 M	6 06 46	2 03 11	0♒59 59	8♒14 05	23 13.2	29 12.5	23 34.9	1 50.4	13 18.2	21 39.1	19 04.8	8 01.2	29 17.1	3 28.5
24 Tu	6 10 43	3 00 24	15 28 20	22 42 04	23 08.1	1♋23.9	24 47.9	2 17.7	13 23.1	21 36.5	19 08.5	7 59.4	29 15.7	3 27.1
25 W	6 14 40	3 57 37	29 54 44	7♓05 52	23 05.6	3 35.3	26 00.9	2 45.3	13 27.8	21 33.7	19 12.2	7 57.6	29 14.3	3 25.8
26 Th	6 18 36	4 54 50	14♓15 06	21 22 10	23D04.9	5 46.5	27 13.9	3 13.2	13 32.1	21 30.7	19 15.8	7 55.7	29 12.8	3 24.4
27 F	6 22 33	5 52 03	28 26 52	5♈29 06	23R05.0	7 57.2	28 26.9	3 41.3	13 36.1	21 27.5	19 19.3	7 53.9	29 11.4	3 23.1
28 Sa	6 26 29	6 49 16	12♈28 47	19 25 54	23 04.5	10 07.2	29 39.9	4 09.6	13 39.8	21 24.1	19 22.7	7 51.9	29 09.9	3 21.8
29 Su	6 30 26	7 46 29	26 20 26	3♉12 22	23 02.4	12 16.3	0♌52.8	4 38.2	13 43.1	21 20.6	19 26.0	7 50.0	29 08.4	3 20.5
30 M	6 34 22	8 43 42	10♉01 43	16 48 26	22 57.9	14 24.2	2 05.7	5 07.0	13 46.2	21 16.8	19 29.2	7 48.0	29 07.0	3 19.2

Astro Data	Dy Hr Mn	Planet Ingress	Dy Hr Mn
♆ R	1 23:21	☿ ♈R	5 1:48
☽ 0N	3 15:52	♀ ♊	10 17:20
☿ D	8 18:06	☿ ♉	12 10:25
♅ R	13 4:05	☉ ♊	21 0:18
☽ 0S	17 13:58		
☽ 0N	30 23:05	♀ ♋	4 4:18
		☿ ♊	8 23:25
♃ R	10 0:24	♂ ♎	19 8:30
☽ 0S	13 23:28	☉ ♋	21 8:20
♄□♇	16 22:00	☿ ♋	23 20:41
♂ 0S	21 6:05	♀ ♌	28 18:38
☽ 0N	27 5:39		

Last Aspect Dy Hr Mn		☽ Ingress	Dy Hr Mn
30 19:04	♃ ☌	♓	1 12:50
3 14:55	♆ ⚹	♈	3 14:59
5 17:00	♆ □	♉	5 17:04
7 20:15	♆ △	♊	7 20:21
10 1:22	☿ ⚹	♋	10 2:13
12 11:24	♆ ☍	♌	12 11:33
14 10:55	☉ □	♍	14 23:43
17 12:14	♆ △	♎	17 12:27
19 22:57	♆ □	♏	19 23:11
22 6:34	♆ ⚹	♐	22 6:51
23 21:00	♃ ⚹	♑	24 11:51
26 14:59	♆ ☌	♒	26 15:20
28 4:10	♃ ☌	♓	28 18:18
30 20:51	♆ ⚹	♈	30 21:18

Last Aspect Dy Hr Mn		☽ Ingress	Dy Hr Mn
2 0:09	♆ □	♉	2 0:39
4 4:20	♆ △	♊	4 4:55
6 1:15	♂ □	♋	6 11:02
8 19:24	☿ ⚹	♌	8 19:58
10 15:27	♃ ☍	♍	11 7:43
13 19:34	♆ △	♎	13 20:35
16 6:47	♆ □	♏	16 7:51
18 15:05	♂ ⚹	♐	18 15:39
20 19:09	☉ ☍	♑	20 20:02
22 21:11	♆ ☌	♒	22 22:20
24 10:11	♃ ☌	♓	25 0:09
27 1:17	♆ ⚹	♈	27 2:38
29 4:54	♆ □	♉	29 6:23

☽ Phases & Eclipses Dy Hr Mn	
6 20:47	● 16♉21
14 10:55	☽ 23♌41
22 9:13	○ 1♐19
29 7:51	☾ 7♓59
5 7:04	● 14♊40
13 4:51	☽ 22♍14
20 19:09	○ 29♐29
27 12:42	☾ 5♈54

Astro Data

1 May 1997
Julian Day # 35550
SVP 5♓17'51"
GC 26♐48.1 ⚵ 5♒09.6
Eris 18♈47.5 ⚴ 15♊56.1
⚷ 27♎56.9R ⚶ 27♓15.5
☽ Mean ☊ 26♍40.4

1 June 1997
Julian Day # 35581
SVP 5♓17'47"
GC 26♐48.2 ⚵ 6♒14.0R
Eris 19♈04.0 ⚴ 3♋15.9
⚷ 26♎06.9R ⚶ 10♈24.0
☽ Mean ☊ 25♍01.9

July 1997 — LONGITUDE

Day	Sid.Time	☉	0 hr ☽	Noon ☽	True☊	☿	♀	♂	⚳	♃	♄	♅	♆	♇
1 Tu	6 38 19	9♋40 55	23♉32 28	0♊13 44	22♍50.6	16♋30.9	3♌18.6	5♎36.1	13♓48.8	21♒12.9	19♈32.4	7♒46.0	29♑05.5	3♐18.0
2 W	6 42 15	10 38 09	6♊52 10	13 27 38	22R 41.0	18 36.0	4 31.5	6 05.4	13 51.2	21R 08.9	19 35.4	7R 44.0	29R 03.9	3R 16.8
3 Th	6 46 12	11 35 22	20 00 01	26 29 13	22 29.7	20 39.6	5 44.4	6 34.9	13 53.2	21 04.6	19 38.4	7 41.9	29 02.4	3 15.6
4 F	6 50 09	12 32 36	2♋55 06	9♋17 35	22 17.8	22 41.5	6 57.2	7 04.7	13 54.9	21 00.2	19 41.2	7 39.9	29 00.9	3 14.4
5 Sa	6 54 05	13 29 49	15 36 39	21 52 16	22 06.5	24 41.7	8 10.0	7 34.7	13 56.2	20 55.6	19 44.0	7 37.8	28 59.4	3 13.2
6 Su	6 58 02	14 27 02	28 04 28	4♌13 22	21 56.7	26 40.0	9 22.8	8 04.9	13 57.2	20 50.9	19 46.7	7 35.6	28 57.8	3 12.1
7 M	7 01 58	15 24 16	10♌19 08	16 21 59	21 49.1	28 36.5	10 35.6	8 35.3	13 57.8	20 46.0	19 49.3	7 33.5	28 56.2	3 11.0
8 Tu	7 05 55	16 21 29	22 22 12	28 20 09	21 44.1	0♌31.0	11 48.3	9 06.0	13R 58.0	20 41.0	19 51.7	7 31.3	28 54.7	3 09.9
9 W	7 09 51	17 18 42	4♍16 13	10♍10 52	21D 41.5	2 23.6	13 01.1	9 36.8	13 58.0	20 35.8	19 54.1	7 29.1	28 53.1	3 08.8
10 Th	7 13 48	18 15 56	16 04 39	21 58 05	21 40.8	4 14.3	14 13.8	10 07.9	13 57.5	20 30.4	19 56.4	7 26.9	28 51.5	3 07.8
11 F	7 17 45	19 13 09	27 51 48	3♎46 24	21 41.2	6 03.1	15 26.4	10 39.2	13 56.7	20 24.9	19 58.6	7 24.7	28 49.9	3 06.8
12 Sa	7 21 41	20 10 22	9♎42 34	15 40 57	21R 41.8	7 49.9	16 39.1	11 10.7	13 55.6	20 19.2	20 00.7	7 22.4	28 48.3	3 05.8
13 Su	7 25 38	21 07 35	21 42 14	27 47 05	21 41.7	9 34.7	17 51.7	11 42.3	13 54.1	20 13.5	20 02.7	7 20.2	28 46.7	3 04.8
14 M	7 29 34	22 04 48	3♏56 09	10♏10 01	21 40.0	11 17.6	19 04.3	12 14.2	13 52.2	20 07.5	20 04.6	7 17.9	28 45.1	3 03.9
15 Tu	7 33 31	23 02 01	16 29 17	22 54 24	21 36.3	12 58.6	20 16.8	12 46.2	13 50.0	20 01.5	20 06.4	7 15.6	28 43.5	3 03.0
16 W	7 37 27	23 59 14	29 25 47	6♐03 42	21 30.5	14 37.6	21 29.4	13 18.5	13 47.5	19 55.3	20 08.1	7 13.3	28 41.9	3 02.1
17 Th	7 41 24	24 56 28	12♐48 18	19 39 36	21 22.9	16 14.7	22 41.9	13 50.9	13 44.5	19 49.0	20 09.7	7 11.0	28 40.3	3 01.3
18 F	7 45 20	25 53 42	26 37 26	3♑41 27	21 14.4	17 49.8	23 54.3	14 23.5	13 41.3	19 42.6	20 11.2	7 08.7	28 38.6	3 00.5
19 Sa	7 49 17	26 50 56	10♑51 09	18 05 52	21 06.0	19 22.9	25 06.8	14 56.3	13 37.6	19 36.1	20 12.6	7 06.3	28 37.0	2 59.7
20 Su	7 53 14	27 48 10	25 24 47	2♒47 00	20 58.5	20 54.1	26 19.2	15 29.2	13 33.7	19 29.4	20 14.0	7 04.0	28 35.4	2 58.9
21 M	7 57 10	28 45 25	10♒11 31	17 37 18	20 52.9	22 23.3	27 31.5	16 02.3	13 29.3	19 22.7	20 15.2	7 01.6	28 33.8	2 58.2
22 Tu	8 01 07	29 42 41	25 03 19	2♓28 38	20 49.4	23 50.6	28 43.9	16 35.6	13 24.6	19 15.8	20 16.3	6 59.3	28 32.1	2 57.5
23 W	8 05 03	0♌39 57	9♓52 20	17 13 38	20D 48.1	25 15.8	29 56.2	17 09.1	13 19.6	19 08.9	20 17.3	6 56.9	28 30.5	2 56.8
24 Th	8 09 00	1 37 14	24 31 55	1♈46 38	20 48.4	26 39.0	1♍08.4	17 42.7	13 14.2	19 01.8	20 18.2	6 54.5	28 28.9	2 56.1
25 F	8 12 56	2 34 32	8♈57 24	16 03 58	20 49.5	28 00.1	2 20.7	18 16.5	13 08.4	18 54.7	20 19.0	6 52.1	28 27.3	2 55.5
26 Sa	8 16 53	3 31 51	23 06 10	0♉03 56	20R 50.2	29 19.1	3 32.9	18 50.5	13 02.4	18 47.5	20 19.6	6 49.7	28 25.7	2 54.9
27 Su	8 20 49	4 29 11	6♉57 19	13 46 21	20 49.9	0♍35.9	4 45.1	19 24.6	12 55.9	18 40.2	20 20.2	6 47.3	28 24.0	2 54.3
28 M	8 24 46	5 26 32	20 31 10	27 11 54	20 47.8	1 50.5	5 57.2	19 58.9	12 49.1	18 32.8	20 20.7	6 44.9	28 22.4	2 53.8
29 Tu	8 28 43	6 23 55	3♊48 43	10♊21 46	20 43.8	3 02.9	7 09.4	20 33.3	12 42.0	18 25.4	20 21.1	6 42.5	28 20.8	2 53.3
30 W	8 32 39	7 21 18	16 51 12	23 17 10	20 38.1	4 12.9	8 21.4	21 07.9	12 34.6	18 17.9	20 21.4	6 40.1	28 19.2	2 52.8
31 Th	8 36 36	8 18 42	29 39 48	5♋59 15	20 31.2	5 20.5	9 33.5	21 42.7	12 26.8	18 10.3	20 21.6	6 37.7	28 17.6	2 52.4

August 1997 — LONGITUDE

Day	Sid.Time	☉	0 hr ☽	Noon ☽	True☊	☿	♀	♂	⚳	♃	♄	♅	♆	♇
1 F	8 40 32	9♌16 07	12♋15 37	18♋29 02	20♍23.8	6♍25.6	10♍45.5	22♎17.6	12♓18.7	18♒02.7	20♈21.6	6♒35.4	28♑16.0	2♐52.0
2 Sa	8 44 29	10 13 33	24 39 37	0♌47 29	20R 16.8	7 28.1	11 57.5	22 52.7	12R 10.3	17R 55.0	20R 21.6	6R 33.0	28R 14.4	2R 51.6
3 Su	8 48 25	11 11 00	6♌52 47	12 55 41	20 10.8	8 27.9	13 09.5	23 27.9	12 01.6	17 47.3	20 21.5	6 30.6	28 12.9	2 51.3
4 M	8 52 22	12 08 28	18 56 22	24 55 02	20 06.3	9 24.8	14 21.4	24 03.3	11 52.6	17 39.6	20 21.2	6 28.2	28 11.3	2 51.0
5 Tu	8 56 18	13 05 57	0♍51 56	6♍47 21	20 03.6	10 18.8	15 33.3	24 38.9	11 43.3	17 31.8	20 20.9	6 25.8	28 09.7	2 50.7
6 W	9 00 15	14 03 26	12 41 36	18 35 03	20D 02.6	11 09.7	16 45.1	25 14.5	11 33.7	17 24.0	20 20.4	6 23.4	28 08.2	2 50.5
7 Th	9 04 12	15 00 57	24 28 06	0♎21 10	20 03.1	11 57.4	17 56.9	25 50.4	11 23.8	17 16.2	20 19.9	6 21.1	28 06.6	2 50.3
8 F	9 08 08	15 58 28	6♎14 46	12 09 23	20 04.5	12 41.6	19 08.7	26 26.3	11 13.6	17 08.4	20 19.2	6 18.7	28 05.1	2 50.1
9 Sa	9 12 05	16 56 00	18 05 35	24 03 55	20 06.2	13 22.2	20 20.4	27 02.4	11 03.2	17 00.5	20 18.5	6 16.3	28 03.6	2 49.9
10 Su	9 16 01	17 53 33	0♏04 59	6♏09 24	20 07.6	13 59.1	21 32.1	27 38.7	10 52.5	16 52.7	20 17.6	6 14.0	28 02.1	2 49.8
11 M	9 19 58	18 51 07	12 17 47	18 30 42	20R 08.2	14 32.0	22 43.7	28 15.1	10 41.6	16 44.9	20 16.7	6 11.7	28 00.6	2 49.7
12 Tu	9 23 54	19 48 42	24 48 44	1♐12 26	20 07.6	15 00.6	23 55.3	28 51.6	10 30.4	16 37.1	20 15.6	6 09.4	27 59.1	2D 49.7
13 W	9 27 51	20 46 18	7♐42 16	14 18 38	20 05.7	15 24.9	25 06.9	29 28.3	10 19.1	16 29.3	20 14.5	6 07.1	27 57.6	2 49.7
14 Th	9 31 47	21 43 55	21 01 50	27 52 01	20 02.8	15 44.6	26 18.4	0♏05.1	10 07.5	16 21.5	20 13.2	6 04.8	27 56.2	2 49.7
15 F	9 35 44	22 41 32	4♑49 14	11♑53 20	19 59.2	15 59.4	27 29.8	0 42.0	9 55.7	16 13.7	20 11.8	6 02.5	27 54.7	2 49.8
16 Sa	9 39 40	23 39 11	19 04 01	26 20 45	19 55.4	16 09.1	28 41.2	1 19.0	9 43.7	16 06.0	20 10.4	6 00.3	27 53.3	2 49.8
17 Su	9 43 37	24 36 51	3♒42 54	11♒09 36	19 52.1	16R 13.6	29 52.5	1 56.2	9 31.5	15 58.4	20 08.8	5 58.0	27 51.9	2 50.0
18 M	9 47 34	25 34 32	18 39 52	26 12 37	19 49.7	16 12.6	1♎03.8	2 33.5	9 19.2	15 50.7	20 07.2	5 55.8	27 50.5	2 50.1
19 Tu	9 51 30	26 32 15	3♓46 41	11♓20 53	19D 48.5	16 06.1	2 15.1	3 10.9	9 06.7	15 43.2	20 05.4	5 53.6	27 49.1	2 50.3
20 W	9 55 27	27 29 58	18 54 05	26 25 10	19 48.4	15 53.8	3 26.3	3 48.5	8 54.1	15 35.6	20 03.6	5 51.4	27 47.7	2 50.5
21 Th	9 59 23	28 27 44	3♈53 10	11♈17 14	19 49.2	15 35.7	4 37.4	4 26.2	8 41.3	15 28.2	20 01.6	5 49.3	27 46.4	2 50.8
22 F	10 03 20	29 25 31	18 36 40	25 50 55	19 50.5	15 11.9	5 48.5	5 04.0	8 28.5	15 20.8	19 59.6	5 47.1	27 45.1	2 51.1
23 Sa	10 07 16	0♍23 19	2♉59 36	10♉02 28	19 51.7	14 42.4	6 59.5	5 41.9	8 15.5	15 13.5	19 57.5	5 45.0	27 43.8	2 51.4
24 Su	10 11 13	1 21 10	16 59 25	23 50 29	19R 52.5	14 07.5	8 10.5	6 19.9	8 02.4	15 06.2	19 55.2	5 42.9	27 42.5	2 51.7
25 M	10 15 09	2 19 02	0♊35 45	7♊15 27	19 52.6	13 27.4	9 21.4	6 58.1	7 49.2	14 59.0	19 52.9	5 40.9	27 41.2	2 52.1
26 Tu	10 19 06	3 16 56	13 49 49	20 19 09	19 51.9	12 42.7	10 32.3	7 36.4	7 36.0	14 52.0	19 50.5	5 38.8	27 39.9	2 52.5
27 W	10 23 03	4 14 52	26 43 48	3♋04 06	19 50.5	11 53.9	11 43.1	8 14.8	7 22.7	14 45.0	19 48.0	5 36.8	27 38.7	2 53.0
28 Th	10 26 59	5 12 50	9♋20 25	15 33 07	19 48.6	11 01.8	12 53.9	8 53.3	7 09.4	14 38.1	19 45.4	5 34.8	27 37.5	2 53.5
29 F	10 30 56	6 10 49	21 42 32	27 49 01	19 46.6	10 07.3	14 04.6	9 32.0	6 56.0	14 31.3	19 42.8	5 32.9	27 36.3	2 54.0
30 Sa	10 34 52	7 08 50	3♌52 53	9♌54 26	19 44.7	9 11.3	15 15.3	10 10.7	6 42.7	14 24.6	19 40.0	5 30.9	27 35.2	2 54.6
31 Su	10 38 49	8 06 53	15 54 00	21 51 50	19 43.1	8 15.0	16 25.9	10 49.6	6 29.3	14 18.0	19 37.1	5 29.0	27 34.0	2 55.2

Astro Data

	Dy Hr Mn
⚳R	8 18:26
☽0S	11 8:42
♃✶♄	14 20:57
☽0N	24 13:02
♄R	1 16:56
☽0S	7 16:38
♇D	13 8:31
☿R	17 19:49
♀0S	18 23:01
☽0N	20 22:07

Planet Ingress

	Dy Hr Mn
☿ ♌	8 5:28
☉ ♌	22 19:15
♀ ♍	23 13:16
☿ ♍	27 0:42
♂ ♏	14 8:42
♀ ♎	17 14:31
☉ ♍	23 2:19

Last Aspect / ☽ Ingress

Last Aspect Dy Hr Mn		☽ Ingress Dy Hr Mn
1 9:57 ♆ △	♊	1 11:35
3 2:02 ♃ △	♋	3 18:33
6 1:45 ♆ ☍	♌	6 3:45
7 20:44 ♃ ☍	♍	8 15:22
11 2:00 ♆ △	♎	11 4:21
13 13:57 ♆ □	♏	13 16:20
15 22:41 ♆ ✶	♐	16 1:02
17 17:45 ♀ △	♑	18 5:45
20 5:12 ♆ ☌	♒	20 7:29
22 5:24 ♀ ☍	♓	22 7:59
24 6:32 ♆ ✶	♈	24 9:03
26 10:34 ☿ △	♉	26 11:53
28 14:07 ♆ △	♊	28 17:04
30 7:47 ♂ △	♋	31 0:38

Last Aspect / ☽ Ingress

Last Aspect Dy Hr Mn		☽ Ingress Dy Hr Mn
2 7:01 ♆ ☍	♌	2 10:27
4 10:11 ♂ ✶	♍	4 22:15
7 7:26 ♆ △	♎	7 11:17
9 19:58 ♆ □	♏	9 23:50
12 5:59 ♆ ✶	♐	12 9:45
14 9:01 ♀ □	♑	14 15:42
16 16:10 ♀ △	♒	16 17:58
18 10:55 ☉ ☍	♓	18 18:01
20 14:12 ♆ ✶	♈	20 17:45
22 18:25 ☉ △	♉	22 18:57
24 18:50 ♆ △	♊	24 22:56
26 11:07 ♄ ✶	♋	27 6:10
29 11:35 ♆ ☍	♌	29 16:19

☽ Phases & Eclipses

Dy Hr Mn		
4 18:40	●	12♋48
12 21:44	☽	20♎34
20 3:20	○	27♑28
26 18:28	☾	3♉47
3 8:14	●	11♌02
11 12:42	☽	18♏53
18 10:55	○	25♒32
25 2:24	☾	1♊56

Astro Data

1 July 1997
Julian Day # 35611
SVP 5♓17'43"
GC 26♐48.3 ⚴ 1♒28.2R
Eris 19♈12.9 ⚵ 19♋36.0
⚷ 25♎44.0 ⚶ 21♈09.9
☽ Mean ☊ 23♍26.6

1 August 1997
Julian Day # 35642
SVP 5♓17'38"
GC 26♐48.3 ⚴ 23♑20.0R
Eris 19♈12.4R ⚵ 5♌48.2
⚷ 27♎02.0 ⚶ 29♈03.9
☽ Mean ☊ 21♍48.1

LONGITUDE — September 1997

Day	Sid.Time	☉	0 hr ☽	Noon ☽	True ☊	☿	♀	♂	⚳	♃	♄	♅	♆	♇
1 M	10 42 45	9♍04 58	27♌48 14	3♍43 29	19♍42.1	7♍19.6	17♎36.5	11♏28.6	6♓16.0	14♒11.6	19♈34.2	5♒27.1	27♑32.9	2♐55.8
2 Tu	10 46 42	10 03 04	9♍37 49	15 31 32	19D41.7	6R 26.3	18 47.0	12 07.8	6R 02.7	14R 05.3	19R 31.2	5R 25.3	27R 31.8	2 56.4
3 W	10 50 38	11 01 12	21 24 54	27 18 13	19 41.7	5 36.2	19 57.4	12 47.0	5 49.4	13 59.1	19 28.1	5 23.5	27 30.7	2 57.1
4 Th	10 54 35	11 59 21	3♎11 48	9♎05 57	19 42.2	4 50.7	21 07.8	13 26.3	5 36.3	13 53.0	19 24.9	5 21.7	27 29.7	2 57.8
5 F	10 58 32	12 57 32	15 01 02	20 57 24	19 42.8	4 10.7	22 18.1	14 05.8	5 23.1	13 47.0	19 21.6	5 20.0	27 28.6	2 58.6
6 Sa	11 02 28	13 55 45	26 55 27	2♏55 37	19 43.5	3 37.2	23 28.3	14 45.4	5 10.1	13 41.2	19 18.3	5 18.2	27 27.6	2 59.4
7 Su	11 06 25	14 53 59	8♏58 18	15 03 59	19 44.1	3 11.1	24 38.5	15 25.1	4 57.2	13 35.6	19 14.9	5 16.6	27 26.7	3 00.2
8 M	11 10 21	15 52 15	21 13 08	27 26 13	19 44.4	2 53.0	25 48.6	16 04.8	4 44.5	13 30.1	19 11.4	5 14.9	27 25.7	3 01.0
9 Tu	11 14 18	16 50 32	3♐43 44	10♐06 09	19R44.6	2D43.5	26 58.6	16 44.7	4 31.8	13 24.7	19 07.8	5 13.3	27 24.8	3 01.9
10 W	11 18 14	17 48 51	16 33 54	23 07 25	19 44.6	2 42.9	28 08.6	17 24.8	4 19.3	13 19.5	19 04.2	5 11.8	27 23.9	3 02.8
11 Th	11 22 11	18 47 11	29 47 02	6♑33 03	19D44.6	2 51.3	29 18.5	18 04.9	4 07.0	13 14.4	19 00.5	5 10.2	27 23.0	3 03.8
12 F	11 26 07	19 45 33	13♑25 38	20 24 52	19 44.5	3 08.9	0♏28.3	18 45.1	3 54.8	13 09.5	18 56.8	5 08.7	27 22.2	3 04.8
13 Sa	11 30 04	20 43 56	27 30 40	4♒42 49	19 44.6	3 35.6	1 38.0	19 25.4	3 42.8	13 04.8	18 52.9	5 07.3	27 21.4	3 05.8
14 Su	11 34 01	21 42 21	12♒00 56	19 24 26	19 44.7	4 11.0	2 47.6	20 05.8	3 31.1	13 00.2	18 49.1	5 05.9	27 20.6	3 06.8
15 M	11 37 57	22 40 48	26 52 37	4♓24 33	19 44.9	4 55.0	3 57.2	20 46.3	3 19.5	12 55.8	18 45.1	5 04.5	27 19.8	3 07.9
16 Tu	11 41 54	23 39 16	11♓59 15	19 35 33	19R45.0	5 47.1	5 06.6	21 26.9	3 08.1	12 51.6	18 41.1	5 03.2	27 19.1	3 09.0
17 W	11 45 50	24 37 46	27 12 15	4♈48 08	19 44.9	6 46.9	6 16.0	22 07.6	2 57.0	12 47.6	18 37.0	5 01.9	27 18.4	3 10.1
18 Th	11 49 47	25 36 19	12♈21 59	19 52 43	19 44.5	7 53.7	7 25.3	22 48.4	2 46.1	12 43.7	18 32.9	5 00.6	27 17.7	3 11.3
19 F	11 53 43	26 34 53	27 19 16	4♉40 48	19 43.8	9 07.0	8 34.5	23 29.4	2 35.5	12 40.0	18 28.7	4 59.4	27 17.1	3 12.5
20 Sa	11 57 40	27 33 29	11♉56 34	19 06 04	19 43.0	10 26.2	9 43.6	24 10.4	2 25.1	12 36.5	18 24.5	4 58.2	27 16.5	3 13.7
21 Su	12 01 36	28 32 08	26 08 55	3♊04 58	19 42.1	11 50.7	10 52.6	24 51.5	2 15.0	12 33.1	18 20.2	4 57.1	27 15.9	3 15.0
22 M	12 05 33	29 30 49	9♊54 09	16 36 36	19 41.4	13 19.8	12 01.5	25 32.7	2 05.1	12 30.0	18 15.9	4 56.0	27 15.3	3 16.2
23 Tu	12 09 29	0♎29 32	23 12 33	29 42 20	19D41.2	14 53.0	13 10.4	26 14.0	1 55.6	12 27.0	18 11.6	4 55.0	27 14.8	3 17.5
24 W	12 13 26	1 28 18	6♋06 21	12♋25 04	19 41.4	16 29.5	14 19.1	26 55.4	1 46.3	12 24.2	18 07.2	4 54.0	27 14.3	3 18.9
25 Th	12 17 23	2 27 05	18 38 59	24 48 37	19 42.2	18 09.0	15 27.8	27 36.9	1 37.3	12 21.6	18 02.7	4 53.1	27 13.9	3 20.3
26 F	12 21 19	3 25 55	0♌54 29	6♌57 09	19 43.3	19 50.8	16 36.3	28 18.4	1 28.7	12 19.2	17 58.2	4 52.2	27 13.4	3 21.7
27 Sa	12 25 16	4 24 47	12 57 06	18 54 50	19 44.6	21 34.5	17 44.7	29 00.1	1 20.3	12 17.0	17 53.7	4 51.3	27 13.0	3 23.1
28 Su	12 29 12	5 23 42	24 50 51	0♍45 35	19 45.9	23 19.7	18 53.1	29 41.9	1 12.3	12 14.9	17 49.2	4 50.5	27 12.7	3 24.5
29 M	12 33 09	6 22 38	6♍39 27	12 32 51	19R46.7	25 06.0	20 01.3	0♐23.8	1 04.6	12 13.1	17 44.6	4 49.8	27 12.3	3 26.0
30 Tu	12 37 05	7 21 36	18 26 09	24 19 40	19 46.7	26 53.1	21 09.4	1 05.8	0 57.2	12 11.5	17 40.0	4 49.0	27 12.0	3 27.5

LONGITUDE — October 1997

Day	Sid.Time	☉	0 hr ☽	Noon ☽	True ☊	☿	♀	♂	⚳	♃	♄	♅	♆	♇
1 W	12 41 02	8♎20 37	0♎13 43	6♎08 35	19♍45.9	28♍40.7	22♏17.4	1♐47.8	0♓50.2	12♒10.0	17♈35.3	4♒48.4	27♑11.8	3♐29.1
2 Th	12 44 58	9 19 40	12 04 33	18 01 50	19R44.1	0♎28.6	23 25.3	2 30.0	0R 43.5	12R 08.8	17R 30.7	4R 47.8	27R 11.5	3 30.6
3 F	12 48 55	10 18 44	24 00 42	0♏01 23	19 41.3	2 16.6	24 33.1	3 12.2	0 37.2	12 07.7	17 26.0	4 47.2	27 11.3	3 32.2
4 Sa	12 52 52	11 17 51	6♏04 06	12 09 05	19 37.9	4 04.5	25 40.7	3 54.6	0 31.2	12 06.9	17 21.3	4 46.7	27 11.2	3 33.8
5 Su	12 56 48	12 16 59	18 16 36	24 26 53	19 34.3	5 52.1	26 48.3	4 37.0	0 25.6	12 06.3	17 16.6	4 46.2	27 11.0	3 35.5
6 M	13 00 45	13 16 10	0♐40 12	6♐56 50	19 30.8	7 39.4	27 55.6	5 19.5	0 20.3	12 05.8	17 11.9	4 45.8	27 10.9	3 37.1
7 Tu	13 04 41	14 15 22	13 17 03	19 41 09	19 27.9	9 26.3	29 02.9	6 02.1	0 15.4	12D 05.6	17 07.2	4 45.4	27 10.9	3 38.8
8 W	13 08 38	15 14 36	26 09 27	2♑42 14	19 26.1	11 12.6	0♐10.0	6 44.8	0 10.9	12 05.5	17 02.4	4 45.1	27D 10.8	3 40.5
9 Th	13 12 34	16 13 52	9♑19 47	16 02 22	19D25.5	12 58.3	1 17.0	7 27.6	0 06.7	12 05.7	16 57.7	4 44.8	27 10.8	3 42.3
10 F	13 16 31	17 13 09	22 50 12	29 43 27	19 26.0	14 43.5	2 23.8	8 10.5	0 02.9	12 06.1	16 53.0	4 44.6	27 10.8	3 44.0
11 Sa	13 20 27	18 12 29	6♒42 11	13♒46 27	19 27.3	16 28.0	3 30.4	8 53.4	29♒59.5	12 06.6	16 48.2	4 44.4	27 10.9	3 45.8
12 Su	13 24 24	19 11 49	20 56 06	28 10 54	19 28.8	18 11.8	4 36.9	9 36.5	29 56.5	12 07.4	16 43.5	4 44.3	27 11.0	3 47.6
13 M	13 28 21	20 11 12	5♓30 28	12♓54 16	19R29.8	19 54.9	5 43.2	10 19.6	29 53.8	12 08.3	16 38.8	4D 44.2	27 11.1	3 49.4
14 Tu	13 32 17	21 10 37	20 21 36	27 51 37	19 29.7	21 37.4	6 49.3	11 02.7	29 51.5	12 09.5	16 34.0	4 44.2	27 11.3	3 51.3
15 W	13 36 14	22 10 03	5♈23 23	12♈55 48	19 28.1	23 19.1	7 55.3	11 46.0	29 49.5	12 10.9	16 29.3	4 44.2	27 11.5	3 53.2
16 Th	13 40 10	23 09 31	20 27 44	27 58 02	19 24.8	25 00.2	9 01.0	12 29.3	29 47.9	12 12.4	16 24.6	4 44.3	27 11.7	3 55.1
17 F	13 44 07	24 09 02	5♉25 33	12♉49 13	19 20.1	26 40.6	10 06.6	13 12.8	29 46.7	12 14.1	16 20.0	4 44.4	27 12.0	3 57.0
18 Sa	13 48 03	25 08 35	20 08 05	27 21 20	19 14.6	28 20.3	11 12.0	13 56.2	29 45.9	12 16.1	16 15.3	4 44.6	27 12.3	3 58.9
19 Su	13 52 00	26 08 09	4♊28 20	11♊28 37	19 09.1	29 59.4	12 17.2	14 39.8	29D 45.4	12 18.2	16 10.7	4 44.8	27 12.6	4 00.9
20 M	13 55 56	27 07 46	18 21 55	25 08 09	19 04.2	1♏37.9	13 22.2	15 23.5	29 45.3	12 20.6	16 06.0	4 45.1	27 13.0	4 02.8
21 Tu	13 59 53	28 07 26	1♋47 23	8♋19 50	19 00.7	3 15.7	14 26.9	16 07.2	29 45.6	12 23.1	16 01.5	4 45.5	27 13.4	4 04.8
22 W	14 03 49	29 07 08	14 45 50	21 05 51	18D58.8	4 53.0	15 31.5	16 51.0	29 46.2	12 25.8	15 56.9	4 45.9	27 13.8	4 06.8
23 Th	14 07 46	0♏06 51	27 20 24	3♌30 03	18 58.5	6 29.6	16 35.8	17 34.9	29 47.2	12 28.7	15 52.4	4 46.3	27 14.3	4 08.9
24 F	14 11 43	1 06 37	9♌35 25	15 37 10	18 59.4	8 05.7	17 39.9	18 18.9	29 48.5	12 31.8	15 47.9	4 46.8	27 14.8	4 10.9
25 Sa	14 15 39	2 06 26	21 35 56	27 32 21	19 01.0	9 41.2	18 43.8	19 02.9	29 50.2	12 35.1	15 43.4	4 47.3	27 15.3	4 13.0
26 Su	14 19 36	3 06 16	3♍27 04	9♍20 41	19R02.4	11 16.2	19 47.4	19 47.0	29 52.3	12 38.6	15 39.0	4 47.9	27 15.9	4 15.1
27 M	14 23 32	4 06 09	15 13 46	21 06 52	19 02.8	12 50.7	20 50.7	20 31.2	29 54.7	12 42.2	15 34.6	4 48.5	27 16.5	4 17.2
28 Tu	14 27 29	5 06 04	27 00 28	2♎55 03	19 01.6	14 24.6	21 53.8	21 15.5	29 57.4	12 46.1	15 30.3	4 49.2	27 17.1	4 19.3
29 W	14 31 25	6 06 00	8♎50 59	14 48 39	18 58.3	15 58.1	22 56.7	21 59.8	0♓00.5	12 50.1	15 26.0	4 50.0	27 17.8	4 21.4
30 Th	14 35 22	7 05 59	20 48 20	26 50 18	18 52.7	17 31.1	23 59.2	22 44.2	0 04.0	12 54.3	15 21.8	4 50.8	27 18.5	4 23.6
31 F	14 39 18	8 06 00	2♏54 46	9♏01 52	18 45.0	19 03.6	25 01.5	23 28.7	0 07.8	12 58.7	15 17.6	4 51.6	27 19.2	4 25.7

Astro Data

	Dy Hr Mn
☽0S	3 23:08
☿D	10 1:41
☽0N	17 8:47
♄⚼♇	22 10:42
☉0S	22 23:55
☽0S	1 5:05
☿0S	4 11:03
♃D	8 4:37
♆D	9 1:28
♅D	14 10:48
☽0N	14 19:50
⚳D	20 7:10
☽0S	28 11:52

Planet Ingress

		Dy Hr Mn
♀	♏	12 2:17
☉	♎	22 23:56
♂	♐	28 22:22
☿	♎	2 5:38
♀	♐	8 8:25
⚳	♒R	11 8:28
☿	♏	19 12:08
☉	♏	23 9:15
⚳	♓	29 8:07

Last Aspect / ☽ Ingress

Last Aspect Dy Hr Mn		☽ Ingress	Dy Hr Mn
31 7:30	♄ △	♍	1 4:27
3 12:25	♆ △	♎	3 17:30
6 1:05	♆ □	♏	6 6:10
8 11:59	♆ ⚹	♐	8 16:54
10 21:55	♀ ⚹	♑	11 0:23
12 23:45	♆ ☌	♒	13 4:10
14 13:10	♂ □	♓	15 4:59
17 0:10	♆ ⚹	♈	17 4:25
18 23:57	♆ □	♉	19 4:21
21 3:31	☉ △	♊	21 6:38
22 14:59	♄ ⚹	♋	23 12:33
25 17:50	♂ △	♌	25 22:12
28 9:42	♂ □	♍	28 10:27
30 18:08	☿ ☌	♎	30 23:32

Last Aspect / ☽ Ingress

Last Aspect Dy Hr Mn		☽ Ingress	Dy Hr Mn
3 6:21	♆ □	♏	3 11:57
5 17:17	♆ ⚹	♐	5 22:43
7 7:14	♄ △	♑	8 7:04
10 7:35	♆ ☌	♒	10 12:29
11 20:00	☉ △	♓	12 14:59
14 10:56	♆ ⚹	♈	14 15:25
16 10:46	♆ □	♉	16 15:16
18 11:45	♆ △	♊	18 16:26
20 15:52	☉ △	♋	20 20:45
23 4:48	☉ □	♌	23 5:10
24 17:45	♂ △	♍	25 16:59
28 0:33	♆ △	♎	28 6:05
30 12:56	♆ □	♏	30 18:15

☽ Phases & Eclipses

Dy Hr Mn		
1 23:52	●	9♍34
2 0:03:46		P 0.899
10 1:31	☽	17♐23
16 18:50	○	23♓56
16 18:47		T 1.191
23 13:35	☾	0♋33
1 16:52	●	8♎33
9 12:22	☽	16♑15
16 3:46	○	22♈49
23 4:48	☾	29♋49
31 10:01	●	8♏01

Astro Data

1 September 1997
Julian Day # 35673
SVP 5♓17'34"
GC 26♐48.4 ⚴ 18♑13.7R
Eris 19♈02.5R ⚵ 21♌07.6
⚷ 29♎49.1 ⚶ 1♉43.2R
☽ Mean ☊ 20♍09.6

1 October 1997
Julian Day # 35703
SVP 5♓17'32"
GC 26♐48.5 ⚴ 18♑46.4
Eris 18♈46.6R ⚵ 4♍53.3
⚷ 3♏29.8 ⚶ 27♈45.7R
☽ Mean ☊ 18♍34.2

November 1997 LONGITUDE

Day	Sid.Time	☉	0 hr ☽	Noon ☽	True ☊	☿	♀	♂	⚳	♃	♄	♅	♆	♇
1 Sa	14 43 15	9♏06 03	15♏11 45	21♏24 30	18♍35.8	20♏35.7	26♐03.4	24♐13.3	0♓11.9	13♒03.3	15♈13.4	4♒52.5	27♑20.0	4♐27.9
2 Su	14 47 12	10 06 07	27 40 09	3♐58 46	18R 26.0	22 07.3	27 05.1	24 57.9	0 16.4	13 08.1	15R 09.4	4 53.4	27 20.8	4 30.1
3 M	14 51 08	11 06 13	10♐20 21	16 44 58	18 16.5	23 38.5	28 06.4	25 42.6	0 21.2	13 13.1	15 05.3	4 54.4	27 21.6	4 32.3
4 Tu	14 55 05	12 06 21	23 12 36	29 43 17	18 08.2	25 09.2	29 07.4	26 27.3	0 26.4	13 18.2	15 01.4	4 55.5	27 22.5	4 34.5
5 W	14 59 01	13 06 31	6♑17 06	12♑54 06	18 02.0	26 39.5	0♑08.0	27 12.2	0 31.9	13 23.5	14 57.5	4 56.6	27 23.4	4 36.7
6 Th	15 02 58	14 06 42	19 34 23	26 18 01	17 58.1	28 09.4	1 08.2	27 57.1	0 37.7	13 29.0	14 53.7	4 57.7	27 24.3	4 39.0
7 F	15 06 54	15 06 55	3♒05 08	9♒55 51	17D 56.6	29 38.8	2 08.1	28 42.0	0 43.8	13 34.6	14 49.9	4 58.9	27 25.2	4 41.2
8 Sa	15 10 51	16 07 09	16 50 14	23 48 23	17 56.7	1♐07.8	3 07.6	29 27.0	0 50.3	13 40.5	14 46.2	5 00.2	27 26.2	4 43.5
9 Su	15 14 47	17 07 25	0♓50 18	7♓55 57	17R 57.4	2 36.3	4 06.6	0♑12.1	0 57.1	13 46.5	14 42.6	5 01.5	27 27.3	4 45.8
10 M	15 18 44	18 07 41	15 05 13	22 17 52	17 57.6	4 04.3	5 05.2	0 57.3	1 04.1	13 52.6	14 39.0	5 02.8	27 28.3	4 48.0
11 Tu	15 22 41	19 08 00	29 33 34	6♈51 51	17 56.1	5 31.8	6 03.4	1 42.5	1 11.5	13 58.9	14 35.6	5 04.2	27 29.4	4 50.3
12 W	15 26 37	20 08 19	14♈12 07	21 33 39	17 52.3	6 58.7	7 01.0	2 27.7	1 19.2	14 05.4	14 32.2	5 05.6	27 30.5	4 52.6
13 Th	15 30 34	21 08 41	28 55 38	6♉17 08	17 45.6	8 25.1	7 58.2	3 13.0	1 27.2	14 12.1	14 28.8	5 07.1	27 31.6	4 54.9
14 F	15 34 30	22 09 04	13♉37 13	20 54 54	17 36.6	9 50.9	8 54.9	3 58.4	1 35.5	14 18.9	14 25.6	5 08.6	27 32.8	4 57.2
15 Sa	15 38 27	23 09 28	28 09 15	5♊19 23	17 26.1	11 16.0	9 51.1	4 43.8	1 44.0	14 25.9	14 22.4	5 10.2	27 34.0	4 59.6
16 Su	15 42 23	24 09 55	12♊24 32	19 24 05	17 15.1	12 40.3	10 46.7	5 29.3	1 52.9	14 33.0	14 19.4	5 11.8	27 35.2	5 01.9
17 M	15 46 20	25 10 23	26 17 33	3♋04 38	17 04.9	14 03.9	11 41.8	6 14.9	2 02.0	14 40.3	14 16.4	5 13.5	27 36.5	5 04.2
18 Tu	15 50 16	26 10 53	9♋45 11	16 19 13	16 56.5	15 26.5	12 36.2	7 00.4	2 11.4	14 47.7	14 13.5	5 15.2	27 37.8	5 06.6
19 W	15 54 13	27 11 24	22 46 56	29 08 36	16 50.5	16 48.1	13 30.1	7 46.1	2 21.1	14 55.3	14 10.7	5 17.0	27 39.1	5 08.9
20 Th	15 58 10	28 11 58	5♌24 40	11♌35 36	16 47.1	18 08.6	14 23.3	8 31.8	2 31.1	15 03.1	14 07.9	5 18.8	27 40.5	5 11.3
21 F	16 02 06	29 12 33	17 42 00	23 44 30	16D 45.7	19 27.8	15 15.9	9 17.6	2 41.3	15 11.0	14 05.3	5 20.6	27 41.8	5 13.6
22 Sa	16 06 03	0♐13 09	29 43 46	5♍40 30	16R 45.7	20 45.6	16 07.8	10 03.4	2 51.8	15 19.0	14 02.7	5 22.5	27 43.2	5 16.0
23 Su	16 09 59	1 13 48	11♍35 24	17 29 11	16 45.9	22 01.7	16 59.0	10 49.3	3 02.5	15 27.2	14 00.3	5 24.5	27 44.7	5 18.3
24 M	16 13 56	2 14 28	23 22 31	29 16 04	16 45.2	23 16.0	17 49.4	11 35.2	3 13.5	15 35.5	13 57.9	5 26.5	27 46.1	5 20.7
25 Tu	16 17 52	3 15 09	5♎10 29	11♎06 21	16 42.6	24 28.1	18 39.1	12 21.2	3 24.8	15 44.0	13 55.7	5 28.5	27 47.6	5 23.1
26 W	16 21 49	4 15 53	17 04 12	23 04 32	16 37.5	25 37.7	19 28.0	13 07.2	3 36.3	15 52.6	13 53.5	5 30.5	27 49.1	5 25.4
27 Th	16 25 45	5 16 37	29 07 45	5♏14 13	16 29.4	26 44.6	20 16.1	13 53.3	3 48.1	16 01.3	13 51.4	5 32.7	27 50.6	5 27.8
28 F	16 29 42	6 17 24	11♏24 13	17 37 55	16 18.6	27 48.3	21 03.3	14 39.4	4 00.1	16 10.2	13 49.5	5 34.8	27 52.2	5 30.2
29 Sa	16 33 39	7 18 11	23 55 28	0♐16 53	16 05.8	28 48.3	21 49.6	15 25.6	4 12.4	16 19.3	13 47.6	5 37.0	27 53.8	5 32.5
30 Su	16 37 35	8 19 00	6♐42 08	13 11 07	15 52.0	29 44.2	22 34.9	16 11.8	4 24.9	16 28.4	13 45.8	5 39.2	27 55.4	5 34.9

December 1997 LONGITUDE

Day	Sid.Time	☉	0 hr ☽	Noon ☽	True ☊	☿	♀	♂	⚳	♃	♄	♅	♆	♇
1 M	16 41 32	9♐19 50	19♐43 41	26♐19 38	15♍38.5	0♑35.3	23♑19.3	16♑58.1	4♓37.6	16♒37.7	13♈44.2	5♒41.5	27♑57.0	5♐37.2
2 Tu	16 45 28	10 20 41	2♑58 42	9♑40 39	15R 26.5	1 21.0	24 02.7	17 44.4	4 50.5	16 47.1	13R 42.6	5 43.8	27 58.7	5 39.6
3 W	16 49 25	11 21 34	16 25 14	23 12 12	15 17.1	2 00.6	24 45.0	18 30.7	5 03.7	16 56.7	13 41.2	5 46.2	28 00.4	5 42.0
4 Th	16 53 21	12 22 27	0♒01 20	6♒52 28	15 10.8	2 33.4	25 26.2	19 17.1	5 17.1	17 06.4	13 39.8	5 48.6	28 02.1	5 44.3
5 F	16 57 18	13 23 21	13 45 28	20 40 13	15 07.4	2 58.4	26 06.2	20 03.6	5 30.8	17 16.2	13 38.6	5 51.0	28 03.8	5 46.7
6 Sa	17 01 14	14 24 15	27 36 39	4♓34 44	15 06.3	3 14.9	26 45.0	20 50.1	5 44.6	17 26.1	13 37.4	5 53.5	28 05.6	5 49.0
7 Su	17 05 11	15 25 11	11♓34 27	18 35 45	15 06.2	3R 22.0	27 22.5	21 36.6	5 58.7	17 36.1	13 36.4	5 56.0	28 07.4	5 51.4
8 M	17 09 08	16 26 07	25 38 37	2♈42 58	15 05.7	3 18.9	27 58.7	22 23.1	6 12.9	17 46.3	13 35.5	5 58.5	28 09.2	5 53.7
9 Tu	17 13 04	17 27 03	9♈48 40	16 55 30	15 03.6	3 04.9	28 33.5	23 09.7	6 27.4	17 56.6	13 34.7	6 01.1	28 11.0	5 56.0
10 W	17 17 01	18 28 01	24 03 14	1♉11 28	14 58.8	2 39.6	29 06.9	23 56.4	6 42.1	18 07.0	13 34.0	6 03.7	28 12.8	5 58.4
11 Th	17 20 57	19 28 59	8♉19 46	15 27 36	14 51.1	2 02.9	29 38.8	24 43.0	6 56.9	18 17.5	13 33.4	6 06.3	28 14.7	6 00.7
12 F	17 24 54	20 29 57	22 34 22	29 39 27	14 40.6	1 14.9	0♒09.1	25 29.7	7 12.0	18 28.1	13 32.9	6 09.0	28 16.6	6 03.0
13 Sa	17 28 50	21 30 57	6♊42 09	13♊41 50	14 28.3	0 16.4	0 37.8	26 16.4	7 27.2	18 38.8	13 32.5	6 11.7	28 18.5	6 05.3
14 Su	17 32 47	22 31 57	20 37 52	27 29 42	14 15.3	29♐08.7	1 04.9	27 03.2	7 42.7	18 49.6	13 32.3	6 14.5	28 20.4	6 07.6
15 M	17 36 43	23 32 58	4♋16 52	10♋58 59	14 03.1	27 53.5	1 30.2	27 50.0	7 58.3	19 00.6	13D 32.1	6 17.3	28 22.3	6 09.9
16 Tu	17 40 40	24 34 00	17 35 49	24 07 15	13 52.7	26 33.1	1 53.7	28 36.8	8 14.1	19 11.6	13 32.1	6 20.1	28 24.3	6 12.2
17 W	17 44 37	25 35 02	0♌33 18	6♌54 03	13 44.8	25 10.3	2 15.3	29 23.6	8 30.1	19 22.8	13 32.1	6 22.9	28 26.3	6 14.4
18 Th	17 48 33	26 36 05	13 09 47	19 20 50	13 39.9	23 47.8	2 35.0	0♒10.5	8 46.3	19 34.0	13 32.3	6 25.8	28 28.3	6 16.7
19 F	17 52 30	27 37 09	25 27 37	1♍30 40	13 37.4	22 28.4	2 52.8	0 57.4	9 02.6	19 45.3	13 32.6	6 28.7	28 30.3	6 18.9
20 Sa	17 56 26	28 38 14	7♍30 33	13 27 53	13D 36.8	21 14.6	3 08.4	1 44.4	9 19.1	19 56.8	13 33.0	6 31.6	28 32.3	6 21.2
21 Su	18 00 23	29 39 20	19 23 20	25 17 35	13R 37.0	20 08.4	3 22.0	2 31.3	9 35.8	20 08.3	13 33.5	6 34.6	28 34.3	6 23.4
22 M	18 04 19	0♑40 26	1♎11 21	7♎05 18	13 36.9	19 11.4	3 33.4	3 18.3	9 52.6	20 20.0	13 34.1	6 37.5	28 36.4	6 25.6
23 Tu	18 08 16	1 41 34	13 00 10	18 56 37	13 35.4	18 24.5	3 42.5	4 05.3	10 09.6	20 31.7	13 34.8	6 40.6	28 38.4	6 27.8
24 W	18 12 12	2 42 41	24 55 18	0♏56 50	13 31.7	17 48.4	3 49.4	4 52.4	10 26.8	20 43.5	13 35.6	6 43.6	28 40.5	6 30.0
25 Th	18 16 09	3 43 50	7♏01 46	13 10 36	13 25.4	17 23.1	3 53.9	5 39.5	10 44.1	20 55.4	13 36.6	6 46.7	28 42.6	6 32.1
26 F	18 20 06	4 44 59	19 23 45	25 41 34	13 16.5	17D 08.3	3R 56.1	6 26.6	11 01.6	21 07.4	13 37.6	6 49.7	28 44.7	6 34.3
27 Sa	18 24 02	5 46 09	2♐04 17	8♐32 03	13 05.6	17 03.6	3 55.8	7 13.7	11 19.2	21 19.5	13 38.8	6 52.9	28 46.9	6 36.4
28 Su	18 27 59	6 47 19	15 04 51	21 42 38	12 53.6	17 08.3	3 53.1	8 00.8	11 37.0	21 31.6	13 40.0	6 56.0	28 49.0	6 38.5
29 M	18 31 55	7 48 29	28 25 12	5♑12 14	12 41.9	17 21.7	3 47.9	8 48.0	11 54.9	21 43.9	13 41.4	6 59.2	28 51.2	6 40.6
30 Tu	18 35 52	8 49 40	12♑03 21	18 58 06	12 31.4	17 43.1	3 40.2	9 35.2	12 13.0	21 56.2	13 42.9	7 02.3	28 53.3	6 42.7
31 W	18 39 48	9 50 50	25 55 58	2♒56 25	12 23.2	18 11.8	3 30.0	10 22.4	12 31.2	22 08.6	13 44.5	7 05.5	28 55.5	6 44.8

Astro Data	Planet Ingress	Last Aspect	☽ Ingress	Last Aspect	☽ Ingress	☽ Phases & Eclipses	Astro Data
Dy Hr Mn	Dy Hr Mn	Dy Hr Mn	Dy Hr Mn	Dy Hr Mn	Dy Hr Mn	Dy Hr Mn	
☽0N 11 5:47	♀ ♑ 5 8:50	1 23:22 ♆ ⚹	♐ 2 4:27	30 18:07 ♃ ⚹	♑ 1 18:38	7 21:43 ☽ 15♒31	1 November 1997
♃⚹♄ 15 3:53	☿ ♐ 7 17:42	4 10:48 ♀ ☌	♑ 4 12:31	3 20:29 ♆ ☌	♒ 3 23:58	14 14:12 ○ 22♉15	Julian Day # 35734
☽0S 24 20:17	♂ ♑ 9 5:33	6 15:42 ☿ ⚹	♒ 6 18:33	5 6:02 ♃ ☌	♓ 6 4:07	21 23:58 ☾ 29♌43	SVP 5♓17'30"
	☉ ♐ 22 6:48	8 22:11 ♂ ⚹	♓ 8 22:35	8 4:15 ♆ ⚹	♈ 8 7:24	30 2:14 ● 7♐54	GC 26♐48.5 ⚴ 23♑50.9
☿ R 7 16:57	☿ ♑ 30 19:11	10 20:34 ♆ ⚹	♈ 11 0:44	10 8:22 ♀ □	♉ 10 10:00		Eris 18♈28.2R ⚵ 17♍36.1
☽0N 8 13:42		12 21:42 ♆ □	♉ 13 1:45	12 9:39 ♆ △	♊ 12 12:35	7 6:09 ☽ 15♓10	⚷ 7♏47.9 ⚶ 20♈06.4R
♄ D 16 10:29	♀ ♒ 12 4:39	14 23:00 ♆ △	♊ 15 3:05	14 14:40 ☿ ☍	♋ 14 16:25	14 2:37 ○ 22♊08	☽ Mean ☊ 16♍55.7
☽0S 22 5:57	☿ ♐R 13 18:06	16 3:35 ♃ △	♋ 17 6:32	16 20:54 ♂ ☍	♌ 16 22:58	21 21:43 ☾ 0♎04	
♀ R 26 21:21	♂ ♒ 18 6:37	19 9:10 ♆ ☍	♌ 19 13:38	19 3:34 ☉ △	♍ 19 9:00	29 16:56 ● 8♑01	1 December 1997
☿ D 27 11:41	☉ ♑ 21 20:07	21 23:58 ☉ □	♍ 22 0:33	21 18:42 ♆ △	♎ 21 21:35		Julian Day # 35764
		24 8:57 ♆ △	♎ 24 13:29	24 7:28 ♆ □	♏ 24 10:07		SVP 5♓17'25"
		26 21:26 ♆ □	♏ 27 1:43	26 17:47 ♆ ⚹	♐ 26 20:07		GC 26♐48.6 ⚴ 1♒29.5
		29 7:30 ♆ ⚹	♐ 29 11:28	28 11:40 ♃ ⚹	♑ 29 2:48		Eris 18♈13.9R ⚵ 27♍45.9
				31 5:07 ♆ ☌	♒ 31 6:58		⚷ 11♏55.2 ⚶ 16♈31.8R
							☽ Mean ☊ 15♍20.4

LONGITUDE — January 1998

Day	Sid.Time	☉	0 hr ☽	Noon ☽	True ☊	☿	♀	♂	⚳	♃	♄	♅	♆	♇
1 Th	18 43 45	10♑52 01	9♒58 54	17♒02 53	12♍17.9	18♐46.9	3♒17.2	11♒09.6	12♓49.6	22♒21.1	13♈46.2	7♒08.8	28♑57.7	6♐46.9
2 F	18 47 42	11 53 11	24 07 52	1♓13 26	12D 15.2	19 27.8	3R 02.1	11 56.8	13 08.1	22 33.7	13 48.0	7 12.0	28 59.9	6 48.9
3 Sa	18 51 38	12 54 21	8♓19 11	15 24 48	12 14.8	20 13.9	2 44.4	12 44.1	13 26.7	22 46.3	13 49.9	7 15.3	29 02.1	6 50.9
4 Su	18 55 35	13 55 31	22 30 01	29 34 39	12 15.4	21 04.6	2 24.4	13 31.3	13 45.4	22 59.1	13 52.0	7 18.6	29 04.3	6 52.9
5 M	18 59 31	14 56 41	6♈38 31	13♈41 31	12R 16.0	21 59.4	2 02.1	14 18.6	14 04.3	23 11.8	13 54.1	7 21.9	29 06.5	6 54.9
6 Tu	19 03 28	15 57 50	20 43 32	27 44 28	12 15.3	22 57.9	1 37.5	15 05.9	14 23.4	23 24.7	13 56.3	7 25.2	29 08.7	6 56.8
7 W	19 07 24	16 58 59	4♉44 11	11♉42 34	12 12.6	23 59.7	1 10.9	15 53.2	14 42.5	23 37.6	13 58.7	7 28.5	29 11.0	6 58.8
8 Th	19 11 21	18 00 07	18 39 27	25 34 38	12 07.5	25 04.4	0 42.3	16 40.5	15 01.8	23 50.6	14 01.1	7 31.9	29 13.2	7 00.7
9 F	19 15 17	19 01 15	2♊27 53	9♊18 56	12 00.2	26 11.6	0 11.9	17 27.8	15 21.1	24 03.6	14 03.7	7 35.2	29 15.4	7 02.6
10 Sa	19 19 14	20 02 23	16 07 32	22 53 21	11 51.3	27 21.2	29♑39.9	18 15.1	15 40.6	24 16.7	14 06.3	7 38.6	29 17.7	7 04.5
11 Su	19 23 11	21 03 30	29 36 06	6♋15 32	11 41.9	28 32.9	29 06.5	19 02.4	16 00.2	24 29.9	14 09.1	7 42.0	29 20.0	7 06.3
12 M	19 27 07	22 04 37	12♋51 21	19 23 23	11 32.9	29 46.5	28 31.8	19 49.7	16 20.0	24 43.2	14 11.9	7 45.4	29 22.2	7 08.1
13 Tu	19 31 04	23 05 43	25 51 27	2♌15 29	11 25.3	1♑01.8	27 56.2	20 37.0	16 39.8	24 56.4	14 14.9	7 48.8	29 24.5	7 10.0
14 W	19 35 00	24 06 49	8♌35 26	14 51 22	11 19.7	2 18.6	27 19.9	21 24.4	16 59.7	25 09.8	14 17.9	7 52.3	29 26.8	7 11.7
15 Th	19 38 57	25 07 55	21 03 25	27 11 48	11 16.3	3 36.9	26 43.1	22 11.7	17 19.8	25 23.2	14 21.1	7 55.7	29 29.0	7 13.5
16 F	19 42 53	26 09 00	3♍16 46	9♍18 42	11D 15.1	4 56.4	26 06.2	22 59.0	17 40.0	25 36.6	14 24.3	7 59.2	29 31.3	7 15.2
17 Sa	19 46 50	27 10 06	15 17 59	21 15 06	11 15.6	6 17.1	25 29.2	23 46.4	18 00.2	25 50.1	14 27.6	8 02.6	29 33.6	7 16.9
18 Su	19 50 46	28 11 10	27 10 34	3♎04 57	11 17.1	7 38.9	24 52.6	24 33.7	18 20.6	26 03.7	14 31.1	8 06.1	29 35.9	7 18.6
19 M	19 54 43	29 12 15	8♎58 52	14 52 55	11 18.7	9 01.8	24 16.6	25 21.0	18 41.0	26 17.3	14 34.6	8 09.5	29 38.1	7 20.3
20 Tu	19 58 40	0♒13 19	20 47 45	26 44 03	11R 19.7	10 25.6	23 41.4	26 08.4	19 01.6	26 31.0	14 38.2	8 13.0	29 40.4	7 21.9
21 W	20 02 36	1 14 23	2♏42 28	8♏43 39	11 19.4	11 50.3	23 07.3	26 55.7	19 22.2	26 44.7	14 42.0	8 16.5	29 42.7	7 23.5
22 Th	20 06 33	2 15 26	14 48 13	20 56 47	11 17.5	13 15.9	22 34.4	27 43.0	19 43.0	26 58.4	14 45.8	8 20.0	29 45.0	7 25.1
23 F	20 10 29	3 16 29	27 09 54	3♐28 04	11 13.8	14 42.3	22 03.1	28 30.4	20 03.8	27 12.2	14 49.7	8 23.5	29 47.2	7 26.6
24 Sa	20 14 26	4 17 31	9♐51 41	16 21 04	11 08.8	16 09.5	21 33.4	29 17.7	20 24.8	27 26.1	14 53.7	8 27.0	29 49.5	7 28.1
25 Su	20 18 22	5 18 33	22 56 26	29 37 54	11 02.9	17 37.5	21 05.5	0♓05.0	20 45.8	27 39.9	14 57.8	8 30.5	29 51.8	7 29.6
26 M	20 22 19	6 19 35	6♑25 24	13♑18 45	10 56.8	19 06.2	20 39.7	0 52.4	21 06.9	27 53.9	15 01.9	8 34.0	29 54.1	7 31.1
27 Tu	20 26 15	7 20 35	20 17 39	27 21 38	10 51.4	20 35.7	20 15.9	1 39.7	21 28.1	28 07.8	15 06.2	8 37.6	29 56.3	7 32.5
28 W	20 30 12	8 21 35	4♒30 08	11♒42 28	10 47.3	22 05.9	19 54.4	2 27.0	21 49.4	28 21.8	15 10.5	8 41.1	29 58.6	7 34.0
29 Th	20 34 09	9 22 34	18 57 51	26 15 30	10D 44.9	23 36.7	19 35.1	3 14.3	22 10.8	28 35.8	15 15.0	8 44.6	0♒00.9	7 35.3
30 F	20 38 05	10 23 32	3♓34 34	10♓54 14	10 44.1	25 08.3	19 18.2	4 01.6	22 32.2	28 49.9	15 19.5	8 48.1	0 03.1	7 36.7
31 Sa	20 42 02	11 24 28	18 13 42	25 32 16	10 44.7	26 40.6	19 03.7	4 48.9	22 53.7	29 04.0	15 24.1	8 51.6	0 05.4	7 38.0

LONGITUDE — February 1998

Day	Sid.Time	☉	0 hr ☽	Noon ☽	True ☊	☿	♀	♂	⚳	♃	♄	♅	♆	♇
1 Su	20 45 58	12♒25 24	2♈49 14	10♈04 06	10♍46.1	28♑13.6	18♑51.7	5♓36.2	23♓15.3	29♒18.1	15♈28.8	8♒55.1	0♒07.6	7♐39.3
2 M	20 49 55	13 26 17	17 16 21	24 25 39	10 47.6	29 47.3	18R 42.1	6 23.5	23 37.0	29 32.3	15 33.5	8 58.6	0 09.8	7 40.5
3 Tu	20 53 51	14 27 10	1♉31 43	8♉34 20	10R 48.6	1♒21.7	18 35.0	7 10.7	23 58.8	29 46.5	15 38.4	9 02.1	0 12.1	7 41.8
4 W	20 57 48	15 28 01	15 33 23	22 28 47	10 48.5	2 56.8	18 30.4	7 57.9	24 20.6	0♓00.7	15 43.3	9 05.6	0 14.3	7 43.0
5 Th	21 01 44	16 28 51	29 20 31	6♊08 36	10 47.3	4 32.7	18D 28.2	8 45.1	24 42.5	0 14.9	15 48.3	9 09.1	0 16.5	7 44.1
6 F	21 05 41	17 29 39	12♊53 03	19 33 55	10 44.9	6 09.3	18 28.5	9 32.3	25 04.4	0 29.2	15 53.4	9 12.6	0 18.7	7 45.3
7 Sa	21 09 38	18 30 26	26 11 14	2♋45 06	10 41.7	7 46.7	18 31.1	10 19.5	25 26.4	0 43.4	15 58.6	9 16.1	0 20.9	7 46.4
8 Su	21 13 34	19 31 12	9♋15 33	15 42 39	10 38.3	9 24.8	18 36.2	11 06.7	25 48.5	0 57.7	16 03.8	9 19.5	0 23.1	7 47.4
9 M	21 17 31	20 31 56	22 06 27	28 27 02	10 35.0	11 03.7	18 43.5	11 53.8	26 10.7	1 12.1	16 09.1	9 23.0	0 25.3	7 48.5
10 Tu	21 21 27	21 32 39	4♌44 29	10♌58 52	10 32.3	12 43.4	18 53.1	12 41.0	26 32.9	1 26.4	16 14.5	9 26.5	0 27.4	7 49.5
11 W	21 25 24	22 33 20	17 10 18	23 18 54	10 30.5	14 23.9	19 04.9	13 28.1	26 55.2	1 40.7	16 19.9	9 29.9	0 29.6	7 50.5
12 Th	21 29 20	23 34 00	29 24 50	5♍28 17	10D 29.6	16 05.3	19 18.8	14 15.1	27 17.5	1 55.1	16 25.4	9 33.4	0 31.7	7 51.4
13 F	21 33 17	24 34 38	11♍29 26	17 28 34	10 29.7	17 47.5	19 34.8	15 02.2	27 39.9	2 09.5	16 31.0	9 36.8	0 33.8	7 52.3
14 Sa	21 37 13	25 35 15	23 25 56	29 21 54	10 30.5	19 30.5	19 52.9	15 49.2	28 02.3	2 23.9	16 36.7	9 40.2	0 35.9	7 53.2
15 Su	21 41 10	26 35 51	5♎16 48	11♎11 03	10 31.7	21 14.5	20 12.9	16 36.2	28 24.8	2 38.3	16 42.4	9 43.6	0 38.0	7 54.0
16 M	21 45 06	27 36 26	17 05 04	22 59 22	10 33.0	22 59.3	20 34.8	17 23.2	28 47.4	2 52.7	16 48.2	9 47.0	0 40.1	7 54.8
17 Tu	21 49 03	28 36 59	28 54 25	4♏50 46	10 34.2	24 44.9	20 58.5	18 10.2	29 10.0	3 07.1	16 54.0	9 50.4	0 42.2	7 55.6
18 W	21 53 00	29 37 31	10♏48 58	16 49 36	10 35.0	26 31.5	21 24.0	18 57.2	29 32.7	3 21.6	16 59.9	9 53.7	0 44.3	7 56.3
19 Th	21 56 56	0♓38 02	22 53 14	29 00 29	10R 35.4	28 19.0	21 51.2	19 44.1	29 55.4	3 36.0	17 05.9	9 57.1	0 46.3	7 57.0
20 F	22 00 53	1 38 32	5♐11 54	11♐28 03	10 35.2	0♓07.4	22 20.1	20 31.0	0♈18.2	3 50.5	17 11.9	10 00.4	0 48.3	7 57.7
21 Sa	22 04 49	2 39 00	17 49 27	24 16 33	10 34.7	1 56.7	22 50.5	21 17.9	0 41.0	4 04.9	17 18.0	10 03.7	0 50.4	7 58.3
22 Su	22 08 46	3 39 27	0♑49 46	7♑29 24	10 33.9	3 46.8	23 22.4	22 04.7	1 03.9	4 19.4	17 24.2	10 07.0	0 52.4	7 58.9
23 M	22 12 42	4 39 53	14 15 39	21 08 35	10 33.1	5 37.8	23 55.8	22 51.5	1 26.8	4 33.8	17 30.4	10 10.3	0 54.3	7 59.5
24 Tu	22 16 39	5 40 17	28 08 09	5♒14 07	10 32.5	7 29.6	24 30.5	23 38.3	1 49.7	4 48.3	17 36.7	10 13.6	0 56.3	8 00.0
25 W	22 20 35	6 40 40	12♒26 05	19 43 30	10 32.1	9 22.1	25 06.6	24 25.1	2 12.7	5 02.8	17 43.0	10 16.8	0 58.3	8 00.5
26 Th	22 24 32	7 41 01	27 05 40	4♓31 44	10D 31.9	11 15.3	25 44.0	25 11.9	2 35.8	5 17.2	17 49.4	10 20.0	1 00.2	8 01.0
27 F	22 28 29	8 41 20	12♓00 42	19 31 33	10 31.9	13 09.2	26 22.5	25 58.6	2 58.9	5 31.7	17 55.8	10 23.2	1 02.1	8 01.4
28 Sa	22 32 25	9 41 37	27 03 10	4♈34 27	10R 32.0	15 03.6	27 02.3	26 45.3	3 22.0	5 46.1	18 02.3	10 26.4	1 04.0	8 01.8

Astro Data Dy Hr Mn	Planet Ingress Dy Hr Mn	Last Aspect Dy Hr Mn	☽ Ingress Dy Hr Mn	Last Aspect Dy Hr Mn	☽ Ingress Dy Hr Mn	☽ Phases & Eclipses Dy Hr Mn	Astro Data
☽ 0N 4 20:19	♀ ♑R 9 21:03	1 21:07 ♃ ☌	♓ 2 9:56	2 20:46 ♃ ⚹	♉ 2 21:25	5 14:18 ☽ 15♈03	1 January 1998
☽ 0S 18 15:28	☿ ♑ 12 16:20	4 11:08 ♆ ⚹	♈ 4 12:43	4 5:08 ♀ △	♊ 5 1:09	12 17:24 ○ 22♋18	Julian Day # 35795
	☉ ♒ 20 6:46	6 14:25 ♆ □	♉ 6 15:52	6 7:58 ☉ △	♋ 7 6:57	20 19:40 ☾ 0♏33	SVP 5♓17'20"
☽ 0N 1 3:34	♂ ♓ 25 9:26	8 18:21 ♆ △	♊ 8 19:42	8 17:27 ♀ ☍	♌ 9 14:57	28 6:01 ● 8♒06	GC 26♐48.7 ⚴ 10♒58.5
♃⚺♆ 5 15:10	♆ ♒ 29 2:52	10 20:45 ☿ ☍	♋ 11 0:43	11 10:23 ☉ ☍	♍ 12 1:09		Eris 18♈07.3R ⚵ 4♎49.8
♀ D 5 21:27		13 6:38 ♆ ☍	♌ 13 7:45	13 16:20 ♀ △	♎ 14 13:17	3 22:53 ☽ 14♉55	⚷ 15♏33.9 ⚶ 19♈30.4
♃∠♄ 9 4:06	☿ ♒ 2 15:15	15 8:23 ♃ ☍	♍ 15 17:31	16 22:14 ☉ △	♏ 17 2:13	11 10:23 ○ 22♌29	☽ Mean ☊ 13♍41.9
☽ 0S 14 23:37	♃ ♓ 4 10:52	18 4:54 ♆ △	♎ 18 5:44	19 10:25 ♆ □	♐ 19 13:56	19 15:27 ☾ 0♐47	
☽ 0N 28 12:51	☉ ♓ 18 20:55	20 17:56 ♆ □	♏ 20 18:34	21 6:08 ♂ □	♑ 21 22:30	26 17:26 ● 7♓55	1 February 1998
	⚳ ♈ 19 16:51	23 4:59 ♆ ⚹	♐ 23 5:25	23 17:00 ♀ ☌	♒ 24 3:10	26 17:28:24 ● T 04'09"	Julian Day # 35826
	☿ ♓ 20 10:22	25 8:26 ♃ ⚹	♑ 25 12:39	25 8:41 ♄ ⚹	♓ 26 4:42		SVP 5♓17'15"
		27 16:21 ♆ ☌	♒ 27 16:27	27 23:25 ♀ ⚹	♈ 28 4:42		GC 26♐48.8 ⚴ 21♒13.0
		29 15:54 ♃ ☌	♓ 29 18:08				Eris 18♈11.2 ⚵ 6♎36.7R
		31 14:06 ☿ ⚹	♈ 31 19:21				⚷ 18♏00.2 ⚶ 27♈24.8
							☽ Mean ☊ 12♍03.4

March 1998

LONGITUDE

Day	Sid.Time	☉	0 hr ☽	Noon ☽	True ☊	☿	♀	♂	⚳	♃	♄	♅	♆	♇
1 Su	22 36 22	10♓41 53	12♈04 19	19♈31 46	10♍32.0	16♓58.4	27♑43.2	27♓31.9	3♈45.2	6♓00.5	18♈08.8	10♒29.6	1♒05.8	8♐02.2
2 M	22 40 18	11 42 07	26 55 55	4♉16 00	10R 32.0	18 53.4	28 25.1	28 18.5	4 08.4	6 15.0	18 15.4	10 32.7	1 07.7	8 02.5
3 Tu	22 44 15	12 42 18	11♉31 24	18 41 37	10 31.8	20 48.5	29 08.1	29 05.1	4 31.6	6 29.4	18 22.1	10 35.8	1 09.5	8 02.8
4 W	22 48 11	13 42 28	25 46 22	2♊45 26	10D 31.6	22 43.4	29 52.1	29 51.7	4 54.9	6 43.8	18 28.7	10 38.9	1 11.3	8 03.0
5 Th	22 52 08	14 42 35	9♊38 47	16 26 28	10 31.6	24 38.0	0♒37.1	0♈38.2	5 18.2	6 58.2	18 35.5	10 42.0	1 13.1	8 03.2
6 F	22 56 04	15 42 40	23 08 38	29 45 29	10 31.7	26 31.9	1 23.0	1 24.7	5 41.5	7 12.6	18 42.2	10 45.0	1 14.9	8 03.4
7 Sa	23 00 01	16 42 44	6♋17 19	12♋44 26	10 32.2	28 24.8	2 09.7	2 11.1	6 04.9	7 27.0	18 49.0	10 48.0	1 16.6	8 03.6
8 Su	23 03 58	17 42 45	19 07 11	25 25 54	10 32.8	0♈16.3	2 57.3	2 57.5	6 28.3	7 41.3	18 55.9	10 51.0	1 18.3	8 03.7
9 M	23 07 54	18 42 44	1♌40 57	7♌52 41	10 33.7	2 06.1	3 45.8	3 43.9	6 51.7	7 55.7	19 02.8	10 54.0	1 20.0	8 03.8
10 Tu	23 11 51	19 42 40	14 01 25	20 07 29	10 34.5	3 53.7	4 35.0	4 30.2	7 15.2	8 10.0	19 09.7	10 56.9	1 21.7	8R 03.8
11 W	23 15 47	20 42 35	26 11 12	2♍12 51	10R 35.0	5 38.6	5 25.0	5 16.5	7 38.7	8 24.3	19 16.7	10 59.8	1 23.4	8 03.8
12 Th	23 19 44	21 42 28	8♍12 42	14 11 02	10 35.1	7 20.5	6 15.7	6 02.7	8 02.2	8 38.6	19 23.7	11 02.7	1 25.0	8 03.8
13 F	23 23 40	22 42 18	20 08 06	26 04 09	10 34.6	8 58.7	7 07.1	6 48.9	8 25.7	8 52.8	19 30.7	11 05.5	1 26.6	8 03.7
14 Sa	23 27 37	23 42 07	1♎59 26	7♎54 11	10 33.4	10 32.7	7 59.2	7 35.1	8 49.3	9 07.0	19 37.8	11 08.3	1 28.2	8 03.6
15 Su	23 31 33	24 41 54	13 48 42	19 43 15	10 31.6	12 02.2	8 52.0	8 21.2	9 12.9	9 21.2	19 44.9	11 11.1	1 29.7	8 03.5
16 M	23 35 30	25 41 39	25 38 06	1♏33 36	10 29.3	13 26.4	9 45.4	9 07.3	9 36.5	9 35.4	19 52.1	11 13.8	1 31.3	8 03.3
17 Tu	23 39 27	26 41 22	7♏30 03	13 27 51	10 26.8	14 45.1	10 39.4	9 53.4	10 00.1	9 49.6	19 59.3	11 16.6	1 32.8	8 03.1
18 W	23 43 23	27 41 04	19 27 22	25 29 00	10 24.3	15 57.7	11 34.0	10 39.4	10 23.8	10 03.7	20 06.5	11 19.3	1 34.2	8 02.9
19 Th	23 47 20	28 40 43	1♐33 14	7♐40 30	10 22.4	17 03.9	12 29.1	11 25.4	10 47.4	10 17.8	20 13.7	11 21.9	1 35.7	8 02.6
20 F	23 51 16	29 40 21	13 51 16	20 06 03	10D 21.2	18 03.3	13 24.8	12 11.3	11 11.1	10 31.9	20 21.0	11 24.5	1 37.1	8 02.3
21 Sa	23 55 13	0♈39 58	26 25 20	2♑49 35	10 20.9	18 55.6	14 21.0	12 57.2	11 34.8	10 45.9	20 28.3	11 27.1	1 38.5	8 02.0
22 Su	23 59 09	1 39 32	9♑19 17	15 54 49	10 21.5	19 40.4	15 17.7	13 43.0	11 58.6	10 59.9	20 35.6	11 29.7	1 39.9	8 01.6
23 M	0 03 06	2 39 05	22 36 34	29 24 49	10 22.7	20 17.7	16 14.9	14 28.9	12 22.3	11 13.9	20 42.9	11 32.2	1 41.2	8 01.2
24 Tu	0 07 02	3 38 36	6♒19 44	13♒21 23	10 24.2	20 47.3	17 12.5	15 14.6	12 46.1	11 27.9	20 50.3	11 34.7	1 42.5	8 00.8
25 W	0 10 59	4 38 05	20 29 41	27 44 21	10R 25.4	21 09.1	18 10.6	16 00.4	13 09.9	11 41.8	20 57.7	11 37.1	1 43.8	8 00.4
26 Th	0 14 55	5 37 32	5♓04 58	12♓30 54	10 25.8	21 23.0	19 09.1	16 46.0	13 33.7	11 55.6	21 05.1	11 39.5	1 45.1	7 59.9
27 F	0 18 52	6 36 58	20 01 20	27 35 18	10 25.0	21R 29.3	20 08.1	17 31.7	13 57.5	12 09.5	21 12.5	11 41.9	1 46.3	7 59.3
28 Sa	0 22 49	7 36 21	5♈11 40	12♈49 12	10 22.8	21 27.9	21 07.4	18 17.3	14 21.3	12 23.2	21 20.0	11 44.2	1 47.5	7 58.8
29 Su	0 26 45	8 35 43	20 26 35	28 02 33	10 19.4	21 19.3	22 07.0	19 02.8	14 45.1	12 37.0	21 27.5	11 46.5	1 48.7	7 58.2
30 M	0 30 42	9 35 02	5♉35 49	13♉05 14	10 15.3	21 03.7	23 07.1	19 48.4	15 09.0	12 50.7	21 34.9	11 48.8	1 49.8	7 57.6
31 Tu	0 34 38	10 34 19	20 29 49	27 48 43	10 11.0	20 41.6	24 07.5	20 33.8	15 32.8	13 04.3	21 42.4	11 51.0	1 50.9	7 56.9

April 1998

LONGITUDE

Day	Sid.Time	☉	0 hr ☽	Noon ☽	True ☊	☿	♀	♂	⚳	♃	♄	♅	♆	♇
1 W	0 38 35	11♈33 34	5♊01 17	12♊07 07	10♍07.4	20♈13.5	25♒08.2	21♈19.2	15♈56.7	13♓17.9	21♈50.0	11♒53.2	1♒52.0	7♐56.2
2 Th	0 42 31	12 32 46	19 05 56	25 57 42	10R 04.8	19R 40.1	26 09.3	22 04.6	16 20.6	13 31.5	21 57.5	11 55.3	1 53.0	7R 55.5
3 F	0 46 28	13 31 56	2♋42 31	9♋20 37	10D 03.7	19 02.1	27 10.6	22 49.9	16 44.5	13 45.0	22 05.0	11 57.4	1 54.1	7 54.8
4 Sa	0 50 24	14 31 04	15 52 20	22 18 07	10 03.8	18 20.5	28 12.3	23 35.2	17 08.3	13 58.5	22 12.6	11 59.5	1 55.0	7 54.0
5 Su	0 54 21	15 30 10	28 38 28	4♌53 52	10 05.1	17 35.9	29 14.3	24 20.4	17 32.2	14 11.9	22 20.2	12 01.5	1 56.0	7 53.2
6 M	0 58 18	16 29 13	11♌04 55	17 12 09	10 06.7	16 49.5	0♓16.5	25 05.6	17 56.1	14 25.2	22 27.7	12 03.5	1 56.9	7 52.4
7 Tu	1 02 14	17 28 13	23 16 06	29 17 20	10R 08.2	16 02.0	1 19.1	25 50.7	18 20.0	14 38.5	22 35.3	12 05.4	1 57.8	7 51.5
8 W	1 06 11	18 27 12	5♍16 18	11♍13 31	10 08.7	15 14.5	2 21.9	26 35.8	18 43.9	14 51.7	22 42.9	12 07.3	1 58.7	7 50.6
9 Th	1 10 07	19 26 08	17 09 25	23 04 23	10 07.8	14 27.9	3 24.9	27 20.8	19 07.8	15 04.9	22 50.5	12 09.1	1 59.5	7 49.7
10 F	1 14 04	20 25 03	28 58 47	4♎52 58	10 04.9	13 42.9	4 28.3	28 05.8	19 31.7	15 18.1	22 58.1	12 10.9	2 00.3	7 48.8
11 Sa	1 18 00	21 23 55	10♎47 14	16 41 51	10 00.1	13 00.5	5 31.8	28 50.7	19 55.6	15 31.1	23 05.7	12 12.7	2 01.1	7 47.8
12 Su	1 21 57	22 22 45	22 37 03	28 33 05	9 53.5	12 21.1	6 35.6	29 35.6	20 19.5	15 44.1	23 13.3	12 14.4	2 01.8	7 46.8
13 M	1 25 53	23 21 33	4♏30 08	10♏28 25	9 45.7	11 45.4	7 39.7	0♉20.4	20 43.3	15 57.1	23 20.9	12 16.1	2 02.5	7 45.8
14 Tu	1 29 50	24 20 19	16 28 09	22 29 31	9 37.2	11 14.0	8 44.0	1 05.2	21 07.2	16 10.0	23 28.5	12 17.7	2 03.2	7 44.7
15 W	1 33 47	25 19 04	28 32 45	4♐38 05	9 29.0	10 47.0	9 48.5	1 49.9	21 31.1	16 22.8	23 36.1	12 19.3	2 03.8	7 43.7
16 Th	1 37 43	26 17 47	10♐45 47	16 56 06	9 21.8	10 24.9	10 53.2	2 34.6	21 55.0	16 35.5	23 43.7	12 20.8	2 04.5	7 42.6
17 F	1 41 40	27 16 28	23 09 22	29 25 54	9 16.4	10 07.9	11 58.1	3 19.2	22 18.9	16 48.2	23 51.3	12 22.3	2 05.0	7 41.5
18 Sa	1 45 36	28 15 07	5♑46 03	12♑10 12	9 13.0	9 55.9	13 03.2	4 03.8	22 42.8	17 00.8	23 58.8	12 23.7	2 05.6	7 40.3
19 Su	1 49 33	29 13 44	18 38 44	25 12 01	9D 11.6	9D 49.2	14 08.5	4 48.3	23 06.7	17 13.4	24 06.4	12 25.1	2 06.1	7 39.1
20 M	1 53 29	0♉12 20	1♒50 26	8♒34 19	9 11.8	9 47.6	15 14.0	5 32.8	23 30.5	17 25.9	24 14.0	12 26.5	2 06.6	7 38.0
21 Tu	1 57 26	1 10 55	15 23 58	22 19 34	9 12.7	9 51.0	16 19.6	6 17.3	23 54.4	17 38.3	24 21.6	12 27.8	2 07.0	7 36.7
22 W	2 01 22	2 09 27	29 21 17	6♓29 04	9R 13.5	9 59.5	17 25.5	7 01.6	24 18.2	17 50.6	24 29.2	12 29.1	2 07.4	7 35.5
23 Th	2 05 19	3 07 58	13♓42 48	21 02 08	9 12.9	10 12.9	18 31.5	7 46.0	24 42.1	18 02.8	24 36.7	12 30.3	2 07.8	7 34.3
24 F	2 09 16	4 06 27	28 26 34	5♈55 23	9 10.4	10 31.0	19 37.7	8 30.3	25 05.9	18 15.0	24 44.3	12 31.4	2 08.1	7 33.0
25 Sa	2 13 12	5 04 55	13♈27 42	21 02 27	9 05.4	10 53.6	20 44.0	9 14.5	25 29.8	18 27.1	24 51.8	12 32.5	2 08.5	7 31.7
26 Su	2 17 09	6 03 21	28 38 27	6♉14 23	8 58.3	11 20.6	21 50.5	9 58.7	25 53.6	18 39.1	24 59.3	12 33.6	2 08.7	7 30.4
27 M	2 21 05	7 01 45	13♉48 55	21 20 46	8 49.7	11 51.9	22 57.1	10 42.8	26 17.4	18 51.1	25 06.8	12 34.6	2 09.0	7 29.0
28 Tu	2 25 02	8 00 07	28 48 43	6♊11 40	8 40.7	12 27.2	24 03.8	11 26.9	26 41.2	19 02.9	25 14.3	12 35.6	2 09.2	7 27.7
29 W	2 28 58	8 58 27	13♊28 42	20 39 08	8 32.3	13 06.4	25 10.7	12 11.0	27 04.9	19 14.7	25 21.8	12 36.5	2 09.4	7 26.3
30 Th	2 32 55	9 56 45	27 42 29	4♋38 27	8 25.6	13 49.3	26 17.8	12 55.0	27 28.7	19 26.4	25 29.2	12 37.4	2 09.5	7 24.9

Astro Data	Dy Hr Mn
♂0N	6 16:12
☿0N	8 13:09
♃□♇	10 1:36
♇ R	11 4:55
☽0S	14 6:15
☉0N	20 19:54
♃⚺♅	25 2:17
☿ R	27 19:43
☽0N	27 23:47
⚳0N	2 22:57
♄⚼♇	9 9:49
☽0S	10 12:22
♃∠♆	18 21:27
☿ D	20 7:31
☽0N	24 10:50

Planet Ingress		Dy Hr Mn
♀	♒	4 16:14
♂	♈	4 16:18
☿	♈	8 8:28
☉	♈	20 19:55
♀	♓	6 5:38
♂	♉	13 1:05
☉	♉	20 6:57

Last Aspect Dy Hr Mn			☽ Ingress	Dy Hr Mn
2 1:57	♀	□	♉	2 5:00
4 6:44	♀	△	♊	4 7:15
6 5:09	☿	□	♋	6 12:27
7 23:32	♄	□	♌	8 20:46
10 10:05	♄	△	♍	11 7:35
13 4:34	☉	☍	♎	13 19:58
15 12:03	♄	☍	♏	16 8:51
18 16:45	☉	△	♐	18 20:56
20 12:29	♄	△	♑	21 6:43
22 20:29	♄	□	♒	23 13:02
25 0:50	☿	⚹	♓	25 15:43
26 11:02	♃	☌	♈	27 15:49
29 1:59	♀	⚹	♉	29 15:06
31 5:29	♀	□	♊	31 15:37

Last Aspect Dy Hr Mn			☽ Ingress	Dy Hr Mn
2 12:22	♀	△	♋	2 19:09
4 14:34	♂	□	♌	5 2:36
7 4:40	♂	△	♍	7 13:25
8 19:30	♃	☍	♎	10 2:04
12 14:15	♂	☍	♏	12 14:55
13 23:10	♃	△	♐	15 2:52
17 7:32	☉	△	♑	17 13:05
19 19:53	☉	□	♒	19 20:41
21 15:31	♄	⚹	♓	22 1:06
23 7:34	♀	☌	♈	24 2:30
25 18:05	♄	☌	♉	26 2:09
27 14:47	♀	⚹	♊	28 1:55
29 20:20	♀	□	♋	30 3:57

☽ Phases & Eclipses Dy Hr Mn	
5 8:41	☽ 14♊34
13 4:34	○ 22♍24
13 4:20	☍ A 0.709
21 7:38	☾ 0♑29
28 3:14	● 7♈15
3 20:18	☽ 13♋52
11 22:23	○ 21♎49
19 19:53	☾ 29♑33
26 11:41	● 6♉03

Astro Data

1 March 1998
Julian Day # 35854
SVP 5♓17'12"
GC 26♐48.8 ⚴ 0♓35.1
Eris 18♈22.8 ⚵ 2♎46.6R
⚷ 18♏46.8 ⚶ 7♉02.5
☽ Mean ☊ 10♍34.4

1 April 1998
Julian Day # 35885
SVP 5♓17'10"
GC 26♐48.9 ⚴ 10♓35.0
Eris 18♈41.6 ⚵ 25♍27.0R
⚷ 17♏57.9R ⚶ 19♉13.0
☽ Mean ☊ 8♍55.9

LONGITUDE — May 1998

Day	Sid.Time	☉	0 hr ☽	Noon ☽	True ☊	☿	♀	♂	⚳	♃	♄	♅	♆	♇
1 F	2 36 51	10♉55 02	11♋27 00	18♋08 14	8♍21.1	14♈35.8	27♓24.9	13♉38.9	27♈52.5	19♓38.0	25♈36.7	12♒38.2	2♒09.6	7♐23.5
2 Sa	2 40 48	11 53 16	24 42 25	1♌09 57	8D18.8	15 25.7	28 32.2	14 22.8	28 16.2	19 49.5	25 44.1	12 39.0	2 09.7	7R22.1
3 Su	2 44 45	12 51 28	7♌31 19	13 47 07	8 18.2	16 18.9	29 39.6	15 06.6	28 39.9	20 00.9	25 51.5	12 39.7	2R09.8	7 20.6
4 M	2 48 41	13 49 38	19 57 56	26 04 26	8 18.6	17 15.3	0♈47.1	15 50.4	29 03.6	20 12.2	25 58.9	12 40.4	2 09.8	7 19.2
5 Tu	2 52 38	14 47 46	2♍07 17	8♍07 07	8R19.0	18 14.6	1 54.7	16 34.1	29 27.3	20 23.4	26 06.2	12 41.0	2 09.8	7 17.7
6 W	2 56 34	15 45 52	14 04 35	20 00 19	8 18.3	19 16.9	3 02.4	17 17.7	29 50.9	20 34.5	26 13.6	12 41.5	2 09.7	7 16.2
7 Th	3 00 31	16 43 56	25 54 51	1♎48 46	8 15.7	20 22.0	4 10.3	18 01.3	0♉14.5	20 45.6	26 20.9	12 42.1	2 09.6	7 14.7
8 F	3 04 27	17 41 58	7♎42 32	13 36 36	8 10.6	21 29.9	5 18.2	18 44.9	0 38.2	20 56.5	26 28.1	12 42.5	2 09.5	7 13.2
9 Sa	3 08 24	18 39 59	19 31 24	25 27 14	8 02.8	22 40.3	6 26.3	19 28.4	1 01.7	21 07.3	26 35.4	12 43.0	2 09.4	7 11.7
10 Su	3 12 20	19 37 58	1♏24 26	7♏23 14	7 52.6	23 53.4	7 34.5	20 11.8	1 25.3	21 18.1	26 42.6	12 43.3	2 09.2	7 10.2
11 M	3 16 17	20 35 55	13 23 51	19 26 27	7 40.6	25 08.9	8 42.7	20 55.2	1 48.8	21 28.7	26 49.8	12 43.7	2 09.0	7 08.6
12 Tu	3 20 13	21 33 51	25 31 11	1♐38 09	7 27.7	26 26.9	9 51.1	21 38.6	2 12.4	21 39.2	26 57.0	12 43.9	2 08.7	7 07.1
13 W	3 24 10	22 31 45	7♐47 26	13 59 09	7 15.1	27 47.3	10 59.6	22 21.8	2 35.9	21 49.6	27 04.1	12 44.2	2 08.5	7 05.5
14 Th	3 28 07	23 29 38	20 13 22	26 30 11	7 03.8	29 10.1	12 08.1	23 05.1	2 59.3	22 00.0	27 11.2	12 44.4	2 08.2	7 03.9
15 F	3 32 03	24 27 29	2♑49 41	9♑12 02	6 54.7	0♉35.1	13 16.8	23 48.3	3 22.8	22 10.2	27 18.3	12 44.5	2 07.8	7 02.3
16 Sa	3 36 00	25 25 20	15 37 22	22 05 52	6 48.4	2 02.5	14 25.5	24 31.4	3 46.2	22 20.3	27 25.3	12 44.6	2 07.4	7 00.7
17 Su	3 39 56	26 23 09	28 37 45	5♒13 14	6 44.8	3 32.1	15 34.4	25 14.5	4 09.6	22 30.3	27 32.4	12R44.6	2 07.0	6 59.1
18 M	3 43 53	27 20 56	11♒52 34	18 36 00	6D43.4	5 03.9	16 43.3	25 57.6	4 33.0	22 40.1	27 39.3	12 44.6	2 06.6	6 57.5
19 Tu	3 47 49	28 18 43	25 23 46	2♓16 05	6R43.3	6 38.0	17 52.3	26 40.6	4 56.3	22 49.9	27 46.3	12 44.5	2 06.2	6 55.9
20 W	3 51 46	29 16 29	9♓13 06	16 14 54	6 43.1	8 14.3	19 01.4	27 23.5	5 19.6	22 59.5	27 53.1	12 44.4	2 05.7	6 54.3
21 Th	3 55 42	0♊14 13	23 21 29	0♈32 43	6 41.7	9 52.8	20 10.5	28 06.4	5 42.9	23 09.1	28 00.0	12 44.2	2 05.1	6 52.7
22 F	3 59 39	1 11 56	7♈48 19	15 07 52	6 38.1	11 33.5	21 19.8	28 49.2	6 06.1	23 18.5	28 06.8	12 44.0	2 04.6	6 51.0
23 Sa	4 03 36	2 09 39	22 30 46	29 56 16	6 31.8	13 16.4	22 29.1	29 32.0	6 29.4	23 27.7	28 13.6	12 43.7	2 04.0	6 49.4
24 Su	4 07 32	3 07 20	7♉23 26	14♉51 17	6 22.9	15 01.5	23 38.5	0♊14.8	6 52.5	23 36.9	28 20.3	12 43.4	2 03.4	6 47.8
25 M	4 11 29	4 05 00	22 18 40	29 44 26	6 12.2	16 48.8	24 48.0	0 57.5	7 15.7	23 45.9	28 27.0	12 43.1	2 02.7	6 46.1
26 Tu	4 15 25	5 02 39	7♊07 29	14♊26 44	6 00.7	18 38.3	25 57.5	1 40.1	7 38.8	23 54.8	28 33.7	12 42.7	2 02.1	6 44.5
27 W	4 19 22	6 00 17	21 41 14	28 50 10	5 50.0	20 30.0	27 07.1	2 22.7	8 01.9	24 03.6	28 40.3	12 42.2	2 01.4	6 42.9
28 Th	4 23 18	6 57 53	5♋52 55	12♋49 03	5 40.9	22 23.8	28 16.8	3 05.2	8 24.9	24 12.2	28 46.8	12 41.7	2 00.6	6 41.2
29 F	4 27 15	7 55 28	19 38 19	26 20 40	5 34.3	24 19.8	29 26.5	3 47.7	8 47.9	24 20.8	28 53.3	12 41.1	1 59.9	6 39.6
30 Sa	4 31 12	8 53 02	2♌56 12	9♌25 11	5 30.3	26 17.8	0♉36.3	4 30.1	9 10.9	24 29.1	28 59.8	12 40.5	1 59.1	6 37.9
31 Su	4 35 08	9 50 34	15 48 00	22 05 08	5 28.5	28 17.9	1 46.1	5 12.5	9 33.8	24 37.4	29 06.2	12 39.9	1 58.3	6 36.3

LONGITUDE — June 1998

Day	Sid.Time	☉	0 hr ☽	Noon ☽	True ☊	☿	♀	♂	⚳	♃	♄	♅	♆	♇
1 M	4 39 05	10♊48 05	28♌17 08	4♍24 38	5♍28.1	0♊19.8	2♉56.0	5♊54.8	9♉56.7	24♓45.5	29♈12.5	12♒39.2	1♒57.4	6♐34.7
2 Tu	4 43 01	11 45 35	10♍28 16	16 28 44	5R28.0	2 23.7	4 05.9	6 37.1	10 19.5	24 53.4	29 18.8	12R38.5	1R56.6	6R33.0
3 W	4 46 58	12 43 03	22 26 42	28 22 51	5 27.3	4 29.2	5 15.9	7 19.3	10 42.3	25 01.3	29 25.1	12 37.7	1 55.7	6 31.4
4 Th	4 50 54	13 40 30	4♎17 50	10♎12 17	5 24.8	6 36.3	6 26.0	8 01.5	11 05.0	25 08.9	29 31.3	12 36.8	1 54.8	6 29.8
5 F	4 54 51	14 37 56	16 06 48	22 01 55	5 19.9	8 44.8	7 36.1	8 43.6	11 27.7	25 16.5	29 37.4	12 36.0	1 53.8	6 28.2
6 Sa	4 58 47	15 35 21	27 58 10	3♏56 00	5 12.5	10 54.5	8 46.3	9 25.7	11 50.3	25 23.9	29 43.5	12 35.0	1 52.8	6 26.5
7 Su	5 02 44	16 32 45	9♏55 47	15 57 54	5 02.6	13 05.2	9 56.5	10 07.7	12 12.9	25 31.1	29 49.6	12 34.1	1 51.8	6 24.9
8 M	5 06 40	17 30 07	22 02 35	28 10 04	4 50.8	15 16.6	11 06.8	10 49.7	12 35.5	25 38.2	29 55.5	12 33.1	1 50.8	6 23.3
9 Tu	5 10 37	18 27 29	4♐20 30	10♐34 00	4 38.2	17 28.5	12 17.2	11 31.6	12 58.0	25 45.2	0♉01.4	12 32.0	1 49.8	6 21.7
10 W	5 14 34	19 24 50	16 50 36	23 10 18	4 25.8	19 40.6	13 27.6	12 13.4	13 20.5	25 52.0	0 07.3	12 30.9	1 48.7	6 20.1
11 Th	5 18 30	20 22 11	29 33 05	5♑58 54	4 14.7	21 52.6	14 38.0	12 55.2	13 42.9	25 58.6	0 13.1	12 29.8	1 47.6	6 18.6
12 F	5 22 27	21 19 30	12♑27 41	18 59 21	4 05.8	24 04.3	15 48.5	13 37.0	14 05.2	26 05.1	0 18.8	12 28.6	1 46.5	6 17.0
13 Sa	5 26 23	22 16 49	25 33 52	2♒11 10	3 59.6	26 15.3	16 59.1	14 18.7	14 27.5	26 11.5	0 24.5	12 27.4	1 45.4	6 15.4
14 Su	5 30 20	23 14 08	8♒51 13	15 34 01	3 56.1	28 25.5	18 09.7	15 00.4	14 49.8	26 17.7	0 30.1	12 26.1	1 44.2	6 13.9
15 M	5 34 16	24 11 26	22 19 36	29 08 00	3D54.8	0♋34.6	19 20.4	15 42.0	15 12.0	26 23.7	0 35.7	12 24.8	1 43.0	6 12.3
16 Tu	5 38 13	25 08 43	5♓59 15	12♓53 26	3R54.9	2 42.4	20 31.1	16 23.6	15 34.1	26 29.5	0 41.2	12 23.5	1 41.8	6 10.8
17 W	5 42 10	26 06 01	19 50 34	26 50 41	3 55.2	4 48.7	21 41.9	17 05.1	15 56.2	26 35.2	0 46.6	12 22.1	1 40.6	6 09.3
18 Th	5 46 06	27 03 18	3♈53 44	10♈59 37	3 54.4	6 53.4	22 52.7	17 46.6	16 18.2	26 40.8	0 51.9	12 20.7	1 39.3	6 07.8
19 F	5 50 03	28 00 34	18 08 11	25 19 08	3 51.8	8 56.3	24 03.6	18 28.0	16 40.2	26 46.1	0 57.2	12 19.2	1 38.1	6 06.3
20 Sa	5 53 59	28 57 51	2♉32 06	9♉46 35	3 46.8	10 57.3	25 14.5	19 09.4	17 02.1	26 51.4	1 02.4	12 17.7	1 36.8	6 04.8
21 Su	5 57 56	29 55 07	17 02 01	24 17 42	3 39.5	12 56.3	26 25.5	19 50.7	17 24.0	26 56.4	1 07.6	12 16.2	1 35.5	6 03.3
22 M	6 01 52	0♋52 24	1♊32 53	8♊46 45	3 30.5	14 53.3	27 36.5	20 32.0	17 45.8	27 01.2	1 12.6	12 14.6	1 34.2	6 01.9
23 Tu	6 05 49	1 49 40	15 58 28	23 07 16	3 20.9	16 48.2	28 47.5	21 13.3	18 07.5	27 05.9	1 17.6	12 13.0	1 32.8	6 00.4
24 W	6 09 45	2 46 55	0♋12 22	7♋13 08	3 11.7	18 41.0	29 58.6	21 54.5	18 29.1	27 10.5	1 22.6	12 11.4	1 31.5	5 59.0
25 Th	6 13 42	3 44 11	14 08 58	20 59 27	3 04.0	20 31.6	1♊09.8	22 35.6	18 50.7	27 14.8	1 27.4	12 09.7	1 30.1	5 57.6
26 F	6 17 39	4 41 26	27 44 17	4♌23 19	2 58.3	22 20.0	2 21.0	23 16.7	19 12.2	27 19.0	1 32.2	12 08.0	1 28.7	5 56.2
27 Sa	6 21 35	5 38 40	10♌56 33	17 24 03	2 55.0	24 06.2	3 32.2	23 57.8	19 33.7	27 22.9	1 36.9	12 06.2	1 27.3	5 54.9
28 Su	6 25 32	6 35 54	23 46 06	0♍03 00	2D53.8	25 50.3	4 43.5	24 38.8	19 55.1	27 26.7	1 41.5	12 04.4	1 25.9	5 53.5
29 M	6 29 28	7 33 07	6♍15 11	12 23 09	2 54.1	27 32.1	5 54.8	25 19.8	20 16.4	27 30.4	1 46.1	12 02.6	1 24.4	5 52.2
30 Tu	6 33 25	8 30 20	18 27 26	24 28 40	2 55.1	29 11.6	7 06.2	26 00.7	20 37.6	27 33.8	1 50.5	12 00.8	1 23.0	5 50.8

Astro Data	Planet Ingress	Last Aspect	☽ Ingress	Last Aspect	☽ Ingress	☽ Phases & Eclipses	Astro Data
Dy Hr Mn	Dy Hr Mn	Dy Hr Mn	Dy Hr Mn	Dy Hr Mn	Dy Hr Mn	Dy Hr Mn	
♆R 4 10:39	♀ ♈ 3 19:16	2 6:37 ♀ △	♌ 2 9:49	1 2:24 ☿ □	♍ 1 3:21	3 10:04 ☽ 12♌47	1 May 1998
♀0N 6 20:40	⚳ ♉ 6 21:14	4 11:49 ♄ △	♍ 4 19:47	3 5:08 ♃ ☍	♎ 3 15:17	11 14:29 ○ 20♏42	Julian Day # 35915
☽0S 7 19:11	☿ ♉ 15 2:10	6 13:10 ♃ ☍	♎ 7 8:19	6 3:28 ♄ ☍	♏ 6 4:06	19 4:35 ☾ 28♒01	SVP 5♓17'07"
♅R 17 15:01	☉ ♊ 21 6:05	9 14:19 ♄ ☍	♏ 9 21:10	8 7:00 ♃ △	♐ 8 15:34	25 19:32 ● 4♊23	GC 26♐49.0 ⚴ 19♓21.6
☽0N 21 20:27	♂ ♊ 24 3:42	11 16:05 ♃ △	♐ 12 8:48	10 17:08 ♃ □	♑ 11 0:50		Eris 19♈01.2 ⚵ 21♍12.0R
	♀ ♉ 29 23:32	14 17:42 ☿ △	♑ 14 18:39	13 1:03 ♃ ⚹	♒ 13 8:03	2 1:45 ☽ 11♍21	⚷ 15♏58.6R ⚶ 1♊47.8
☽0S 4 3:19		16 21:53 ♄ □	♒ 17 2:30	15 2:38 ☉ △	♓ 15 13:31	10 4:18 ○ 19♐06	☽ Mean ☊ 7♍20.6
☽0N 18 4:04	☿ ♊ 1 8:07	19 4:35 ☉ □	♓ 19 8:03	17 11:33 ♃ ☌	♈ 17 17:23	17 10:38 ☾ 26♓03	
♃∠♅ 24 15:34	♄ ♉ 9 6:07	21 7:44 ♂ ⚹	♈ 21 11:06	19 16:48 ☉ ⚹	♉ 19 19:47	24 3:50 ● 2♋27	1 June 1998
♄□♆ 25 22:24	☿ ♋ 15 5:33	23 9:13 ♄ ☌	♉ 23 12:06	21 16:24 ♃ ⚹	♊ 21 21:26		Julian Day # 35946
	☉ ♋ 21 14:03	25 2:15 ♃ ⚹	♊ 25 12:25	23 18:46 ♃ □	♋ 23 23:39		SVP 5♓17'02"
	♀ ♊ 24 12:27	27 11:43 ♄ ⚹	♋ 27 13:58	25 23:11 ♃ △	♌ 26 4:04		GC 26♐49.0 ⚴ 26♓46.9
	☿ ♌ 30 23:52	29 18:09 ♀ □	♌ 29 18:38	28 1:05 ♂ ⚹	♍ 28 11:54		Eris 19♈17.8 ⚵ 22♍17.8
				30 22:57 ☿ ⚹	♎ 30 23:05		⚷ 13♏45.2R ⚶ 15♊09.2
							☽ Mean ☊ 5♍42.1

July 1998 LONGITUDE

Day	Sid.Time	☉	0 hr ☽	Noon ☽	True ☊	☿	♀	♂	⚳	♃	♄	♅	♆	♇
1 W	6 37 21	9♋27 33	0♎27 27	6♎24 26	2♍55.8	0♌49.0	8♊17.6	26♊41.5	20♉58.7	27♓37.0	1♉54.9	11♒58.9	1♒21.5	5♐49.5
2 Th	6 41 18	10 24 45	12 20 16	18 15 36	2R55.5	2 24.1	9 29.0	27 22.3	21 19.8	27 40.1	1 59.2	11R57.0	1R20.0	5R48.3
3 F	6 45 14	11 21 57	24 11 04	0♏07 18	2 53.5	3 56.9	10 40.5	28 03.1	21 40.8	27 43.0	2 03.4	11 55.1	1 18.5	5 47.0
4 Sa	6 49 11	12 19 09	6♏04 51	12 04 17	2 49.5	5 27.5	11 52.0	28 43.8	22 01.7	27 45.7	2 07.6	11 53.1	1 17.0	5 45.8
5 Su	6 53 08	13 16 20	18 06 06	24 10 45	2 43.7	6 55.8	13 03.6	29 24.5	22 22.5	27 48.2	2 11.6	11 51.1	1 15.5	5 44.6
6 M	6 57 04	14 13 31	0♐18 37	6♐30 00	2 36.3	8 21.8	14 15.2	0♋05.1	22 43.3	27 50.6	2 15.6	11 49.1	1 14.0	5 43.4
7 Tu	7 01 01	15 10 42	12 45 11	19 04 20	2 28.2	9 45.5	15 26.8	0 45.6	23 04.0	27 52.7	2 19.5	11 47.1	1 12.4	5 42.2
8 W	7 04 57	16 07 53	25 27 33	1♑54 52	2 20.2	11 06.8	16 38.5	1 26.2	23 24.5	27 54.6	2 23.3	11 45.0	1 10.9	5 41.1
9 Th	7 08 54	17 05 05	8♑26 14	15 01 32	2 13.0	12 25.7	17 50.3	2 06.7	23 45.0	27 56.4	2 27.0	11 42.9	1 09.3	5 39.9
10 F	7 12 50	18 02 16	21 40 38	28 23 17	2 07.4	13 42.1	19 02.1	2 47.1	24 05.4	27 58.0	2 30.7	11 40.8	1 07.8	5 38.8
11 Sa	7 16 47	18 59 27	5♒09 16	11♒58 19	2 03.7	14 56.1	20 13.9	3 27.5	24 25.8	27 59.4	2 34.2	11 38.7	1 06.2	5 37.8
12 Su	7 20 43	19 56 39	18 50 08	25 44 26	2D02.1	16 07.5	21 25.7	4 07.8	24 46.0	28 00.5	2 37.7	11 36.5	1 04.6	5 36.7
13 M	7 24 40	20 53 51	2♓40 57	9♓39 26	2 02.1	17 16.2	22 37.7	4 48.1	25 06.1	28 01.5	2 41.0	11 34.4	1 03.0	5 35.7
14 Tu	7 28 37	21 51 04	16 39 38	23 41 19	2 03.2	18 22.3	23 49.6	5 28.4	25 26.2	28 02.3	2 44.3	11 32.2	1 01.4	5 34.7
15 W	7 32 33	22 48 17	0♈44 16	7♈48 18	2 04.5	19 25.5	25 01.6	6 08.6	25 46.1	28 02.9	2 47.5	11 29.9	0 59.8	5 33.7
16 Th	7 36 30	23 45 31	14 53 12	21 58 46	2R05.2	20 25.9	26 13.7	6 48.8	26 06.0	28 03.3	2 50.6	11 27.7	0 58.2	5 32.7
17 F	7 40 26	24 42 45	29 04 48	6♉11 01	2 04.7	21 23.3	27 25.8	7 28.9	26 25.7	28R03.6	2 53.6	11 25.5	0 56.6	5 31.8
18 Sa	7 44 23	25 40 00	13♉17 10	20 22 56	2 02.6	22 17.5	28 37.9	8 09.0	26 45.4	28 03.6	2 56.5	11 23.2	0 55.0	5 30.9
19 Su	7 48 19	26 37 16	27 27 58	4♊31 53	1 59.1	23 08.6	29 50.1	8 49.1	27 04.9	28 03.4	2 59.3	11 20.9	0 53.4	5 30.0
20 M	7 52 16	27 34 33	11♊34 17	18 34 44	1 54.4	23 56.3	1♋02.4	9 29.1	27 24.3	28 03.0	3 02.0	11 18.6	0 51.8	5 29.2
21 Tu	7 56 12	28 31 50	25 32 47	2♋28 02	1 49.3	24 40.5	2 14.6	10 09.1	27 43.7	28 02.4	3 04.7	11 16.3	0 50.1	5 28.4
22 W	8 00 09	29 29 09	9♋20 02	16 08 27	1 44.4	25 21.1	3 27.0	10 49.0	28 02.9	28 01.7	3 07.2	11 14.0	0 48.5	5 27.6
23 Th	8 04 06	0♌26 27	22 52 56	29 33 14	1 40.3	25 57.9	4 39.3	11 28.9	28 22.0	28 00.7	3 09.6	11 11.7	0 46.9	5 26.8
24 F	8 08 02	1 23 46	6♌09 10	12♌40 35	1 37.5	26 30.7	5 51.7	12 08.7	28 41.0	27 59.5	3 12.0	11 09.3	0 45.3	5 26.1
25 Sa	8 11 59	2 21 06	19 07 29	25 29 55	1D36.2	26 59.4	7 04.2	12 48.5	28 59.9	27 58.1	3 14.2	11 07.0	0 43.6	5 25.4
26 Su	8 15 55	3 18 26	1♍48 00	8♍01 57	1 36.2	27 23.8	8 16.6	13 28.3	29 18.6	27 56.6	3 16.3	11 04.6	0 42.0	5 24.7
27 M	8 19 52	4 15 47	14 12 03	20 18 39	1 37.2	27 43.8	9 29.2	14 08.0	29 37.2	27 54.8	3 18.4	11 02.2	0 40.4	5 24.1
28 Tu	8 23 48	5 13 08	26 22 09	2♎23 00	1 38.8	27 59.0	10 41.7	14 47.6	29 55.7	27 52.9	3 20.3	10 59.8	0 38.8	5 23.5
29 W	8 27 45	6 10 30	8♎21 43	14 18 50	1 40.5	28 09.6	11 54.3	15 27.2	0♊14.1	27 50.7	3 22.2	10 57.5	0 37.1	5 22.9
30 Th	8 31 41	7 07 52	20 14 55	26 10 34	1R41.7	28R15.1	13 07.0	16 06.8	0 32.4	27 48.4	3 23.9	10 55.1	0 35.5	5 22.3
31 F	8 35 38	8 05 15	2♏06 21	8♏02 53	1 42.2	28 15.6	14 19.6	16 46.3	0 50.5	27 45.9	3 25.5	10 52.7	0 33.9	5 21.8

August 1998 LONGITUDE

Day	Sid.Time	☉	0 hr ☽	Noon ☽	True ☊	☿	♀	♂	⚳	♃	♄	♅	♆	♇
1 Sa	8 39 35	9♌02 39	14♏00 47	20♏00 38	1♍41.7	28♌11.0	15♋32.4	17♋25.8	1♊08.5	27♓43.2	3♉27.1	10♒50.3	0♒32.3	5♐21.3
2 Su	8 43 31	10 00 03	26 02 59	2♐08 24	1R40.2	28R01.2	16 45.1	18 05.3	1 26.3	27R40.3	3 28.5	10R47.9	0R30.7	5R20.9
3 M	8 47 28	10 57 27	8♐17 22	14 30 20	1 38.0	27 46.2	17 57.9	18 44.7	1 44.0	27 37.2	3 29.8	10 45.5	0 29.1	5 20.4
4 Tu	8 51 24	11 54 53	20 47 42	27 09 47	1 35.3	27 26.0	19 10.7	19 24.0	2 01.6	27 33.9	3 31.0	10 43.1	0 27.5	5 20.0
5 W	8 55 21	12 52 19	3♑36 51	10♑09 02	1 32.5	27 00.9	20 23.6	20 03.3	2 19.0	27 30.4	3 32.2	10 40.7	0 25.9	5 19.7
6 Th	8 59 17	13 49 46	16 46 25	23 28 57	1 30.1	26 30.9	21 36.5	20 42.6	2 36.3	27 26.8	3 33.2	10 38.3	0 24.4	5 19.3
7 F	9 03 14	14 47 14	0♒16 30	7♒08 51	1 28.3	25 56.4	22 49.5	21 21.8	2 53.5	27 23.0	3 34.1	10 35.9	0 22.8	5 19.0
8 Sa	9 07 10	15 44 43	14 05 40	21 06 32	1D27.3	25 17.9	24 02.5	22 01.0	3 10.5	27 19.0	3 34.9	10 33.6	0 21.3	5 18.8
9 Su	9 11 07	16 42 13	28 10 59	5♓18 28	1 27.1	24 35.7	25 15.6	22 40.2	3 27.3	27 14.8	3 35.6	10 31.2	0 19.7	5 18.5
10 M	9 15 04	17 39 44	12♓28 24	19 40 11	1 27.6	23 50.6	26 28.6	23 19.3	3 44.0	27 10.5	3 36.2	10 28.8	0 18.2	5 18.3
11 Tu	9 19 00	18 37 16	26 53 11	4♈06 49	1 28.5	23 03.2	27 41.8	23 58.4	4 00.5	27 06.0	3 36.7	10 26.4	0 16.6	5 18.2
12 W	9 22 57	19 34 50	11♈20 30	18 33 42	1 29.4	22 14.4	28 54.9	24 37.4	4 16.9	27 01.3	3 37.1	10 24.1	0 15.1	5 18.0
13 Th	9 26 53	20 32 25	25 45 54	2♉56 40	1 30.2	21 24.9	0♌08.2	25 16.4	4 33.1	26 56.4	3 37.4	10 21.7	0 13.6	5 17.9
14 F	9 30 50	21 30 02	10♉05 36	17 12 23	1R30.6	20 35.9	1 21.4	25 55.3	4 49.2	26 51.4	3 37.6	10 19.4	0 12.1	5 17.8
15 Sa	9 34 46	22 27 40	24 16 44	1♊18 23	1 30.5	19 48.1	2 34.7	26 34.3	5 05.1	26 46.2	3R37.7	10 17.1	0 10.6	5D17.8
16 Su	9 38 43	23 25 20	8♊17 10	15 12 54	1 30.1	19 02.6	3 48.1	27 13.2	5 20.8	26 40.9	3 37.7	10 14.7	0 09.2	5 17.8
17 M	9 42 39	24 23 01	22 05 29	28 54 47	1 29.4	18 20.3	5 01.5	27 52.0	5 36.3	26 35.4	3 37.5	10 12.4	0 07.7	5 17.8
18 Tu	9 46 36	25 20 44	5♋40 45	12♋23 17	1 28.6	17 42.1	6 14.9	28 30.8	5 51.6	26 29.8	3 37.3	10 10.1	0 06.3	5 17.9
19 W	9 50 33	26 18 29	19 02 22	25 37 58	1 27.9	17 08.9	7 28.4	29 09.6	6 06.8	26 24.0	3 37.0	10 07.9	0 04.9	5 17.9
20 Th	9 54 29	27 16 15	2♌10 02	8♌38 36	1 27.5	16 41.3	8 41.9	29 48.3	6 21.8	26 18.0	3 36.5	10 05.6	0 03.5	5 18.1
21 F	9 58 26	28 14 02	15 03 40	21 25 18	1D27.2	16 20.0	9 55.5	0♌27.0	6 36.6	26 12.0	3 36.0	10 03.4	0 02.1	5 18.2
22 Sa	10 02 22	29 11 51	27 43 33	3♍58 30	1 27.2	16 05.6	11 09.0	1 05.6	6 51.2	26 05.8	3 35.3	10 01.1	0 00.7	5 18.4
23 Su	10 06 19	0♍09 41	10♍10 19	16 19 08	1 27.2	15D58.4	12 22.7	1 44.2	7 05.6	25 59.4	3 34.6	9 58.9	29♑59.3	5 18.6
24 M	10 10 15	1 07 33	22 25 09	28 28 37	1R27.3	15 58.9	13 36.3	2 22.8	7 19.8	25 52.9	3 33.7	9 56.7	29 58.0	5 18.9
25 Tu	10 14 12	2 05 25	4♎29 49	10♎29 02	1 27.3	16 07.2	14 50.0	3 01.3	7 33.8	25 46.3	3 32.7	9 54.6	29 56.7	5 19.2
26 W	10 18 08	3 03 20	16 26 39	22 23 04	1 27.1	16 23.5	16 03.8	3 39.8	7 47.6	25 39.6	3 31.7	9 52.4	29 55.4	5 19.5
27 Th	10 22 05	4 01 15	28 18 41	4♏13 59	1 26.9	16 47.7	17 17.5	4 18.2	8 01.1	25 32.8	3 30.5	9 50.3	29 54.1	5 19.9
28 F	10 26 01	4 59 12	10♏09 27	16 05 37	1 26.6	17 19.9	18 31.3	4 56.6	8 14.5	25 25.9	3 29.2	9 48.2	29 52.8	5 20.3
29 Sa	10 29 58	5 57 10	22 03 01	28 02 12	1D26.4	18 00.0	19 45.2	5 35.0	8 27.6	25 18.8	3 27.8	9 46.1	29 51.6	5 20.7
30 Su	10 33 55	6 55 10	4♐03 45	10♐08 13	1 26.3	18 47.6	20 59.1	6 13.3	8 40.6	25 11.7	3 26.4	9 44.1	29 50.4	5 21.1
31 M	10 37 51	7 53 11	16 16 10	22 28 10	1 26.5	19 42.7	22 13.0	6 51.5	8 53.3	25 04.4	3 24.8	9 42.0	29 49.2	5 21.6

Astro Data	Planet Ingress	Last Aspect	☽ Ingress	Last Aspect	☽ Ingress	☽ Phases & Eclipses	Astro Data
Dy Hr Mn	Dy Hr Mn	Dy Hr Mn	Dy Hr Mn	Dy Hr Mn	Dy Hr Mn	Dy Hr Mn	
☽0S 1 12:23	♂ ♋ 6 9:00	3 7:34 ♂ △	♏ 3 11:45	2 4:01 ☿ □	♐ 2 7:48	1 18:43 ☽ 9♎44	1 July 1998
☽0N 15 10:24	♀ ♋ 19 15:17	5 19:08 ♃ △	♐ 5 23:24	4 12:45 ♃ □	♑ 4 17:18	9 16:01 ○ 17♑15	Julian Day # 35976
♃R 18 1:49	☉ ♌ 23 0:55	8 4:33 ♃ □	♑ 8 8:27	6 18:59 ♃ ⚹	♒ 6 23:31	16 15:13 ☾ 23♈53	SVP 5♓16'58"
☽0S 28 21:21	⚳ ♊ 28 17:33	10 11:15 ♃ ⚹	♒ 10 14:52	8 18:47 ☿ ☍	♓ 9 3:04	23 13:44 ● 0♌31	GC 26♐49.1 ⚴ 1♈20.3
☿R 31 2:27		12 3:48 ♀ △	♓ 12 19:22	11 0:25 ♃ ☌	♈ 11 5:10	31 12:05 ☽ 8♏05	Eris 19♈26.8 ⚵ 27♍30.5
	♀ ♌ 13 9:19	14 19:25 ♃ ☌	♈ 14 22:45	13 6:52 ♀ □	♉ 13 7:04		⚷ 12♏30.7R ⚶ 28♊08.0
☽0N 11 17:01	♂ ♌ 20 19:16	16 19:51 ♀ ⚹	♉ 17 1:33	15 4:18 ♃ ⚹	♊ 15 9:46	8 2:10 ○ 15♒21	☽ Mean ☊ 4♍06.8
♄R 15 19:09	♆ ♑R 23 0:13	19 1:00 ♃ ⚹	♊ 19 4:18	17 7:56 ♃ □	♋ 17 13:55	8 2:25 • A 0.120	
♇D 16 6:08	☉ ♍ 23 7:59	21 4:19 ♃ □	♋ 21 7:43	19 18:48 ♂ ☌	♌ 19 20:00	14 19:48 ☾ 21♉49	1 August 1998
☿D 23 22:37		23 9:13 ♃ △	♌ 23 12:48	22 2:03 ☉ ☌	♍ 22 4:21	22 2:03 ● 28♌48	Julian Day # 36007
☽0S 25 5:19		25 14:56 ☿ ☌	♍ 25 20:34	24 14:57 ♆ △	♎ 24 15:02	22 2:06:07 • A 03'14"	SVP 5♓16'53"
		28 3:02 ♃ ☍	♎ 28 7:14	27 3:14 ♆ □	♏ 27 3:25	30 5:06 ☽ 6♐39	GC 26♐49.2 ⚴ 1♈49.0R
		30 16:13 ☿ ⚹	♏ 30 19:44	29 15:38 ♆ ⚹	♐ 29 15:55		Eris 19♈26.5R ⚵ 5♎32.7
							⚷ 12♏46.9 ⚶ 11♋20.4
							☽ Mean ☊ 2♍28.3

LONGITUDE — September 1998

Day	Sid.Time	☉	0 hr ☽	Noon ☽	True ☊	☿	♀	♂	⚳	♃	♄	♅	♆	♇
1 Tu	10 41 48	8♍51 13	28♐44 43	5♑06 17	1♍27.1	20♌44.9	23♌26.9	7♌29.8	9♊05.7	24♓57.1	3♉23.1	9♒40.0	29♑48.0	5♐22.2
2 W	10 45 44	9 49 17	11♑33 18	18 06 07	1 27.8	21 53.7	24 40.9	8 08.0	9 18.0	24R 49.7	3R 21.3	9R 38.1	29R 46.8	5 22.7
3 Th	10 49 41	10 47 22	24 45 00	1♒30 06	1 28.6	23 08.8	25 54.9	8 46.1	9 30.0	24 42.2	3 19.5	9 36.1	29 45.7	5 23.3
4 F	10 53 37	11 45 28	8♒21 27	15 18 58	1 29.3	24 29.8	27 08.9	9 24.2	9 41.8	24 34.7	3 17.5	9 34.2	29 44.6	5 23.9
5 Sa	10 57 34	12 43 36	22 22 25	29 31 25	1R 29.6	25 56.1	28 23.0	10 02.3	9 53.3	24 27.1	3 15.4	9 32.3	29 43.5	5 24.6
6 Su	11 01 30	13 41 46	6♓45 27	14♓03 50	1 29.4	27 27.3	29 37.1	10 40.3	10 04.6	24 19.4	3 13.3	9 30.5	29 42.4	5 25.3
7 M	11 05 27	14 39 57	21 25 46	28 50 24	1 28.5	29 02.7	0♍51.3	11 18.3	10 15.6	24 11.6	3 11.0	9 28.6	29 41.4	5 26.0
8 Tu	11 09 24	15 38 10	6♈16 43	13♈43 45	1 27.1	0♍41.9	2 05.4	11 56.3	10 26.4	24 03.8	3 08.7	9 26.9	29 40.4	5 26.8
9 W	11 13 20	16 36 26	21 10 28	28 35 56	1 25.3	2 24.4	3 19.6	12 34.2	10 36.9	23 56.0	3 06.2	9 25.1	29 39.4	5 27.6
10 Th	11 17 17	17 34 43	5♉59 14	13♉19 33	1 23.4	4 09.6	4 33.9	13 12.1	10 47.2	23 48.1	3 03.7	9 23.4	29 38.4	5 28.4
11 F	11 21 13	18 33 02	20 36 13	27 48 41	1 21.9	5 57.1	5 48.2	13 49.9	10 57.1	23 40.2	3 01.1	9 21.7	29 37.5	5 29.2
12 Sa	11 25 10	19 31 24	4♊56 33	11♊59 30	1D 21.0	7 46.4	7 02.5	14 27.7	11 06.9	23 32.3	2 58.3	9 20.0	29 36.6	5 30.1
13 Su	11 29 06	20 29 47	18 57 25	25 50 13	1 21.0	9 37.2	8 16.8	15 05.5	11 16.3	23 24.3	2 55.5	9 18.4	29 35.7	5 31.0
14 M	11 33 03	21 28 13	2♋37 59	9♋20 51	1 21.7	11 28.9	9 31.2	15 43.2	11 25.5	23 16.3	2 52.6	9 16.8	29 34.8	5 32.0
15 Tu	11 36 59	22 26 41	15 58 59	22 32 37	1 23.0	13 21.4	10 45.6	16 20.9	11 34.3	23 08.3	2 49.7	9 15.3	29 34.0	5 33.0
16 W	11 40 56	23 25 11	29 02 01	5♌27 28	1 24.5	15 14.2	12 00.1	16 58.5	11 42.9	23 00.3	2 46.6	9 13.8	29 33.2	5 34.0
17 Th	11 44 53	24 23 43	11♌49 14	18 07 36	1 25.8	17 07.2	13 14.5	17 36.1	11 51.2	22 52.3	2 43.5	9 12.3	29 32.4	5 35.0
18 F	11 48 49	25 22 17	24 22 49	0♍35 10	1R 26.4	19 00.2	14 29.1	18 13.7	11 59.2	22 44.3	2 40.2	9 10.9	29 31.7	5 36.1
19 Sa	11 52 46	26 20 53	6♍44 52	12 52 09	1 25.9	20 52.8	15 43.6	18 51.2	12 06.9	22 36.4	2 36.9	9 09.5	29 31.0	5 37.2
20 Su	11 56 42	27 19 31	18 57 14	25 00 19	1 24.0	22 45.1	16 58.1	19 28.7	12 14.2	22 28.4	2 33.5	9 08.1	29 30.3	5 38.3
21 M	12 00 39	28 18 11	1♎01 36	7♎01 18	1 20.9	24 36.9	18 12.7	20 06.2	12 21.3	22 20.5	2 30.1	9 06.8	29 29.6	5 39.5
22 Tu	12 04 35	29 16 53	12 59 36	18 56 46	1 16.5	26 28.0	19 27.3	20 43.5	12 28.0	22 12.6	2 26.5	9 05.5	29 29.0	5 40.7
23 W	12 08 32	0♎15 37	24 52 59	0♏48 33	1 11.4	28 18.5	20 42.0	21 20.9	12 34.4	22 04.7	2 22.9	9 04.3	29 28.4	5 41.9
24 Th	12 12 28	1 14 23	6♏43 44	12 38 52	1 06.1	0♎08.2	21 56.6	21 58.2	12 40.5	21 56.9	2 19.2	9 03.1	29 27.8	5 43.1
25 F	12 16 25	2 13 10	18 34 16	24 30 21	1 01.2	1 57.0	23 11.3	22 35.5	12 46.3	21 49.2	2 15.5	9 02.0	29 27.3	5 44.4
26 Sa	12 20 21	3 11 59	0♐27 31	6♐26 13	0 57.1	3 45.0	24 26.0	23 12.7	12 51.7	21 41.5	2 11.7	9 00.9	29 26.8	5 45.7
27 Su	12 24 18	4 10 51	12 26 56	18 30 11	0 54.3	5 32.2	25 40.7	23 49.9	12 56.8	21 33.8	2 07.8	8 59.8	29 26.3	5 47.1
28 M	12 28 15	5 09 43	24 36 31	0♑46 27	0D 53.1	7 18.4	26 55.5	24 27.0	13 01.5	21 26.3	2 03.8	8 58.8	29 25.9	5 48.4
29 Tu	12 32 11	6 08 38	7♑00 33	13 19 23	0 53.2	9 03.8	28 10.2	25 04.1	13 05.9	21 18.8	1 59.8	8 57.9	29 25.5	5 49.8
30 W	12 36 08	7 07 34	19 43 30	26 13 22	0 54.4	10 48.3	29 25.0	25 41.2	13 10.0	21 11.4	1 55.8	8 56.9	29 25.1	5 51.3

LONGITUDE — October 1998

Day	Sid.Time	☉	0 hr ☽	Noon ☽	True ☊	☿	♀	♂	⚳	♃	♄	♅	♆	♇
1 Th	12 40 04	8♎06 32	2♒49 28	9♒32 09	0♍55.9	12♎31.8	0♎39.8	26♌18.2	13♊13.6	21♓04.1	1♉51.6	8♒56.1	29♑24.7	5♐52.7
2 F	12 44 01	9 05 32	16 21 42	23 18 17	0R 57.1	14 14.5	1 54.7	26 55.1	13 17.0	20R 56.8	1R 47.4	8R 55.2	29R 24.4	5 54.2
3 Sa	12 47 57	10 04 34	0♓21 52	7♓32 18	0 57.1	15 56.4	3 09.5	27 32.1	13 20.0	20 49.7	1 43.2	8 54.5	29 24.1	5 55.7
4 Su	12 51 54	11 03 37	14 49 13	22 12 02	0 55.5	17 37.3	4 24.3	28 08.9	13 22.6	20 42.7	1 38.9	8 53.7	29 23.9	5 57.2
5 M	12 55 50	12 02 42	29 40 00	7♈12 09	0 51.9	19 17.5	5 39.2	28 45.8	13 24.8	20 35.8	1 34.6	8 53.1	29 23.7	5 58.8
6 Tu	12 59 47	13 01 50	14♈47 21	22 24 21	0 46.7	20 56.8	6 54.1	29 22.5	13 26.7	20 28.9	1 30.2	8 52.4	29 23.5	6 00.4
7 W	13 03 44	14 00 59	0♉01 48	7♉38 21	0 40.3	22 35.3	8 09.0	29 59.3	13 28.2	20 22.2	1 25.8	8 51.8	29 23.3	6 02.0
8 Th	13 07 40	15 00 11	15 12 44	22 43 41	0 33.7	24 13.0	9 24.0	0♍36.0	13 29.4	20 15.7	1 21.3	8 51.3	29 23.2	6 03.6
9 F	13 11 37	15 59 24	0♊10 11	7♊31 21	0 27.8	25 50.0	10 38.9	1 12.6	13 30.1	20 09.2	1 16.8	8 50.8	29 23.1	6 05.3
10 Sa	13 15 33	16 58 41	14 46 29	21 55 10	0 23.4	27 26.2	11 53.9	1 49.3	13R 30.5	20 02.9	1 12.3	8 50.3	29 23.1	6 07.0
11 Su	13 19 30	17 57 59	28 57 06	5♋52 13	0D 20.8	29 01.7	13 08.9	2 25.8	13 30.5	19 56.7	1 07.7	8 50.0	29D 23.1	6 08.7
12 M	13 23 26	18 57 20	12♋40 37	19 22 32	0 20.0	0♏36.5	14 23.9	3 02.4	13 30.1	19 50.7	1 03.1	8 49.6	29 23.1	6 10.4
13 Tu	13 27 23	19 56 43	25 58 17	2♌28 17	0 20.6	2 10.5	15 38.9	3 38.8	13 29.3	19 44.8	0 58.4	8 49.3	29 23.1	6 12.2
14 W	13 31 19	20 56 09	8♌53 00	15 12 56	0 21.8	3 43.9	16 54.0	4 15.3	13 28.2	19 39.0	0 53.8	8 49.1	29 23.2	6 13.9
15 Th	13 35 16	21 55 37	21 28 35	27 40 27	0R 22.6	5 16.6	18 09.0	4 51.7	13 26.6	19 33.4	0 49.1	8 48.9	29 23.3	6 15.7
16 F	13 39 13	22 55 07	3♍49 03	9♍54 49	0 22.2	6 48.6	19 24.1	5 28.0	13 24.6	19 27.9	0 44.4	8 48.7	29 23.4	6 17.6
17 Sa	13 43 09	23 54 39	15 58 12	21 59 35	0 19.6	8 20.0	20 39.2	6 04.3	13 22.2	19 22.6	0 39.6	8 48.6	29 23.6	6 19.4
18 Su	13 47 06	24 54 13	27 59 20	3♎57 46	0 14.6	9 50.7	21 54.3	6 40.5	13 19.5	19 17.5	0 34.9	8D 48.6	29 23.8	6 21.3
19 M	13 51 02	25 53 49	9♎55 09	15 51 46	0 07.1	11 20.8	23 09.4	7 16.7	13 16.3	19 12.5	0 30.1	8 48.6	29 24.1	6 23.2
20 Tu	13 54 59	26 53 28	21 47 49	27 43 31	29♌57.3	12 50.2	24 24.6	7 52.9	13 12.7	19 07.8	0 25.3	8 48.6	29 24.4	6 25.1
21 W	13 58 55	27 53 08	3♏39 03	9♏34 35	29 46.1	14 19.0	25 39.7	8 29.0	13 08.8	19 03.1	0 20.5	8 48.8	29 24.7	6 27.0
22 Th	14 02 52	28 52 51	15 30 20	21 26 28	29 34.2	15 47.0	26 54.9	9 05.0	13 04.4	18 58.7	0 15.7	8 48.9	29 25.0	6 29.0
23 F	14 06 48	29 52 35	27 23 12	3♐20 46	29 22.8	17 14.5	28 10.0	9 41.0	12 59.6	18 54.4	0 10.9	8 49.1	29 25.4	6 30.9
24 Sa	14 10 45	0♏52 22	9♐19 27	15 19 31	29 12.9	18 41.2	29 25.2	10 16.9	12 54.5	18 50.3	0 06.1	8 49.4	29 25.8	6 32.9
25 Su	14 14 42	1 52 10	21 21 20	27 25 15	29 05.1	20 07.2	0♏40.4	10 52.8	12 48.9	18 46.4	0 01.3	8 49.7	29 26.3	6 34.9
26 M	14 18 38	2 51 59	3♑31 41	9♑41 06	29 00.0	21 32.5	1 55.6	11 28.6	12 43.0	18 42.7	29♈56.5	8 50.1	29 26.8	6 37.0
27 Tu	14 22 35	3 51 51	15 54 00	22 10 52	28D 57.3	22 57.1	3 10.8	12 04.4	12 36.7	18 39.2	29 51.8	8 50.5	29 27.3	6 39.0
28 W	14 26 31	4 51 44	28 32 14	4♒58 39	28 56.7	24 20.8	4 26.0	12 40.1	12 30.0	18 35.9	29 47.0	8 51.0	29 27.8	6 41.1
29 Th	14 30 28	5 51 39	11♒30 38	18 08 39	28R 57.0	25 43.7	5 41.2	13 15.7	12 22.9	18 32.7	29 42.2	8 51.5	29 28.4	6 43.1
30 F	14 34 24	6 51 35	24 53 10	1♓44 29	28 57.2	27 05.7	6 56.4	13 51.3	12 15.5	18 29.8	29 37.5	8 52.1	29 29.1	6 45.2
31 Sa	14 38 21	7 51 33	8♓42 52	15 48 23	28 56.2	28 26.7	8 11.7	14 26.9	12 07.7	18 27.1	29 32.8	8 52.7	29 29.7	6 47.3

Astro Data

	Dy Hr Mn
♃∠♅	4 13:56
☽0N	8 1:22
☽0S	21 12:05
☉0S	23 5:38
☿0S	26 4:33
♀0S	3 14:29
☽0N	5 11:47
⚳R	10 23:36
♆D	11 14:03
☽0S	18 18:17
♅D	18 21:24

Planet Ingress

	Dy Hr Mn
♀ ♍	6 19:24
☿ ♍	8 1:58
☉ ♎	23 5:37
☿ ♎	24 10:13
♀ ♎	30 23:13
♂ ♍	7 12:28
☿ ♏	12 2:44
☊ ♌R	20 5:51
☉ ♏	23 14:59
♀ ♏	24 23:06
♄ ♈R	25 18:41

Last Aspect / ☽ Ingress

Last Aspect Dy Hr Mn		☽ Ingress Dy Hr Mn
31 16:57	♃ □	♑ 1 2:23
3 8:56	♆ ☌	♒ 3 9:21
5 9:55	♀ ☍	♓ 5 12:48
7 13:22	♆ ⚹	♈ 7 13:52
9 13:43	♆ □	♉ 9 14:16
11 15:02	♆ △	♊ 11 15:40
13 7:47	♃ □	♋ 13 19:20
16 0:59	♆ ☍	♌ 16 1:48
17 10:57	♂ ☌	♍ 18 10:52
20 20:57	♆ △	♎ 20 21:57
23 9:18	♆ □	♏ 23 10:22
25 21:58	♆ ⚹	♐ 25 23:05
28 3:41	♀ □	♑ 28 10:30
30 18:26	♀ △	♒ 30 18:53

Last Aspect / ☽ Ingress

Last Aspect Dy Hr Mn		☽ Ingress Dy Hr Mn
2 18:27	♂ ☍	♓ 2 23:23
4 23:34	♆ ⚹	♈ 5 0:32
6 23:26	♂ △	♉ 6 23:57
8 22:44	♆ △	♊ 8 23:43
10 22:37	☿ △	♋ 11 1:48
13 6:17	♆ ☍	♌ 13 7:25
14 23:54	☉ ⚹	♍ 15 16:32
18 2:49	♆ △	♎ 18 4:02
20 15:24	♆ □	♏ 20 16:36
23 4:06	♆ ⚹	♐ 23 5:16
24 18:58	♃ □	♑ 25 17:05
28 2:24	♄ □	♒ 28 2:44
30 8:20	♄ ⚹	♓ 30 8:58

☽ Phases & Eclipses

Dy Hr Mn	
6 11:21	○ 13♓40
6 11:10	• A 0.812
13 1:58	☾ 20♊05
20 17:01	● 27♍32
28 21:11	☽ 5♑32
5 20:12	○ 12♈23
12 11:11	☾ 18♋55
20 10:09	● 26♎49
28 11:46	☽ 4♒51

Astro Data

1 September 1998
Julian Day # 36038
SVP 5♓16'50"
GC 26♐49.2 ⚴ 26♓53.1R
Eris 19♈16.8R ⚵ 15♎08.3
⚷ 14♏39.2 ⚶ 24♋00.9
☽ Mean ☊ 0♍49.8

1 October 1998
Julian Day # 36068
SVP 5♓16'47"
GC 26♐49.3 ⚴ 19♓08.9R
Eris 19♈00.9R ⚵ 25♎13.0
⚷ 17♏40.2 ⚶ 5♌17.9
☽ Mean ☊ 29♌14.4

November 1998 LONGITUDE

Day	Sid.Time	☉	0 hr ☽	Noon ☽	True ☊	☿	♀	♂	⚳	♃	♄	♅	♆	♇
1 Su	14 42 17	8♏51 33	23♓00 56	0♈20 13	28♌52.8	29♏46.6	9♏26.9	15♍02.4	11♊59.5	18♓24.5	29♈28.1	8♒53.3	29♑30.4	6♐49.5
2 M	14 46 14	9 51 34	7♈45 43	15 16 39	28R 46.8	1♐05.5	10 42.1	15 37.8	11R 51.0	18R 22.2	29R 23.4	8 54.1	29 31.1	6 51.6
3 Tu	14 50 10	10 51 37	22 52 02	0♉30 40	28 38.3	2 23.1	11 57.4	16 13.1	11 42.1	18 20.0	29 18.7	8 54.8	29 31.9	6 53.8
4 W	14 54 07	11 51 42	8♉11 11	15 52 08	28 28.0	3 39.3	13 12.6	16 48.5	11 32.9	18 18.1	29 14.1	8 55.7	29 32.6	6 55.9
5 Th	14 58 04	12 51 48	23 31 59	1♊09 18	28 17.0	4 54.1	14 27.9	17 23.7	11 23.4	18 16.3	29 09.5	8 56.5	29 33.4	6 58.1
6 F	15 02 00	13 51 57	8♊42 41	16 10 58	28 06.9	6 07.2	15 43.1	17 58.9	11 13.5	18 14.8	29 04.9	8 57.5	29 34.3	7 00.3
7 Sa	15 05 57	14 52 08	23 33 09	0♋48 30	27 58.6	7 18.5	16 58.4	18 34.0	11 03.3	18 13.4	29 00.4	8 58.4	29 35.2	7 02.5
8 Su	15 09 53	15 52 20	7♋56 31	14 56 55	27 52.9	8 27.7	18 13.7	19 09.1	10 52.8	18 12.3	28 55.9	8 59.5	29 36.1	7 04.7
9 M	15 13 50	16 52 35	21 49 41	28 34 56	27 49.7	9 34.7	19 28.9	19 44.1	10 42.0	18 11.4	28 51.5	9 00.5	29 37.0	7 07.0
10 Tu	15 17 46	17 52 51	5♌12 59	11♌44 17	27D 48.5	10 39.1	20 44.2	20 19.1	10 30.9	18 10.6	28 47.1	9 01.7	29 38.0	7 09.2
11 W	15 21 43	18 53 10	18 09 19	24 28 40	27R 48.5	11 40.7	21 59.5	20 54.0	10 19.5	18 10.1	28 42.7	9 02.8	29 39.0	7 11.5
12 Th	15 25 40	19 53 31	0♍43 00	6♍52 54	27 48.3	12 39.0	23 14.8	21 28.8	10 07.8	18 09.8	28 38.4	9 04.1	29 40.0	7 13.7
13 F	15 29 36	20 53 53	12 59 02	19 02 01	27 46.8	13 33.6	24 30.1	22 03.6	9 55.9	18D 09.7	28 34.1	9 05.3	29 41.1	7 16.0
14 Sa	15 33 33	21 54 17	25 02 27	1♎00 51	27 42.9	14 24.2	25 45.4	22 38.3	9 43.7	18 09.8	28 29.9	9 06.6	29 42.2	7 18.3
15 Su	15 37 29	22 54 44	6♎57 47	12 53 40	27 36.2	15 10.1	27 00.8	23 12.9	9 31.3	18 10.1	28 25.8	9 08.0	29 43.3	7 20.5
16 M	15 41 26	23 55 12	18 48 56	24 43 58	27 26.4	15 50.9	28 16.1	23 47.5	9 18.7	18 10.6	28 21.7	9 09.4	29 44.5	7 22.8
17 Tu	15 45 22	24 55 41	0♏39 03	6♏34 29	27 13.9	16 25.9	29 31.4	24 21.9	9 05.8	18 11.3	28 17.7	9 10.9	29 45.7	7 25.1
18 W	15 49 19	25 56 13	12 30 29	18 27 14	26 59.5	16 54.4	0♐46.8	24 56.4	8 52.8	18 12.2	28 13.7	9 12.4	29 46.9	7 27.5
19 Th	15 53 15	26 56 46	24 24 55	0♐23 40	26 44.3	17 15.6	2 02.1	25 30.7	8 39.5	18 13.3	28 09.8	9 13.9	29 48.2	7 29.8
20 F	15 57 12	27 57 20	6♐23 36	12 24 53	26 29.6	17R 28.9	3 17.4	26 05.0	8 26.2	18 14.7	28 05.9	9 15.6	29 49.4	7 32.1
21 Sa	16 01 08	28 57 56	18 27 36	24 31 57	26 16.6	17 33.4	4 32.8	26 39.1	8 12.6	18 16.2	28 02.2	9 17.2	29 50.7	7 34.4
22 Su	16 05 05	29 58 34	0♑38 04	6♑46 11	26 06.1	17 28.4	5 48.1	27 13.2	7 59.0	18 18.0	27 58.5	9 18.9	29 52.1	7 36.8
23 M	16 09 02	0♐59 12	12 56 31	19 09 21	25 58.7	17 13.4	7 03.5	27 47.3	7 45.2	18 19.9	27 54.9	9 20.6	29 53.4	7 39.1
24 Tu	16 12 58	1 59 52	25 25 00	1♒43 50	25 54.4	16 47.8	8 18.8	28 21.2	7 31.3	18 22.1	27 51.3	9 22.4	29 54.8	7 41.5
25 W	16 16 55	3 00 33	8♒06 13	14 32 36	25D 52.6	16 11.4	9 34.2	28 55.1	7 17.4	18 24.5	27 47.9	9 24.3	29 56.3	7 43.8
26 Th	16 20 51	4 01 15	21 03 23	27 39 01	25R 52.3	15 24.3	10 49.5	29 28.9	7 03.3	18 27.0	27 44.5	9 26.1	29 57.7	7 46.1
27 F	16 24 48	5 01 58	4♓19 54	11♓06 25	25 52.2	14 27.1	12 04.8	0♎02.6	6 49.3	18 29.8	27 41.2	9 28.1	29 59.2	7 48.5
28 Sa	16 28 44	6 02 42	17 58 52	24 57 27	25 51.1	13 20.7	13 20.2	0 36.2	6 35.2	18 32.7	27 37.9	9 30.0	0♒00.7	7 50.8
29 Su	16 32 41	7 03 27	2♈02 16	9♈13 14	25 47.9	12 06.9	14 35.5	1 09.7	6 21.1	18 35.9	27 34.8	9 32.0	0 02.2	7 53.2
30 M	16 36 37	8 04 13	16 30 06	23 52 24	25 42.0	10 47.5	15 50.8	1 43.1	6 06.9	18 39.2	27 31.7	9 34.1	0 03.7	7 55.5

December 1998 LONGITUDE

Day	Sid.Time	☉	0 hr ☽	Noon ☽	True ☊	☿	♀	♂	⚳	♃	♄	♅	♆	♇
1 Tu	16 40 34	9♐05 00	1♉19 29	8♉50 26	25♌33.5	9♐25.2	17♐06.2	2♎16.5	5♊52.9	18♓42.8	27♈28.8	9♒36.2	0♒05.3	7♐57.9
2 W	16 44 31	10 05 48	16 24 12	23 59 34	25R 23.0	8R 02.8	18 21.5	2 49.8	5R 38.8	18 46.5	27R 25.9	9 38.3	0 06.9	8 00.2
3 Th	16 48 27	11 06 37	1♊35 11	9♊09 42	25 11.7	6 42.9	19 36.8	3 23.0	5 24.8	18 50.4	27 23.1	9 40.5	0 08.6	8 02.6
4 F	16 52 24	12 07 27	16 41 43	24 10 00	25 01.0	5 28.3	20 52.2	3 56.0	5 10.9	18 54.6	27 20.4	9 42.7	0 10.2	8 05.0
5 Sa	16 56 20	13 08 19	1♋33 25	8♋51 01	24 52.1	4 21.1	22 07.5	4 29.1	4 57.0	18 58.9	27 17.8	9 45.0	0 11.9	8 07.3
6 Su	17 00 17	14 09 11	16 02 04	23 06 03	24 45.7	3 23.2	23 22.8	5 02.0	4 43.3	19 03.4	27 15.3	9 47.3	0 13.6	8 09.6
7 M	17 04 13	15 10 05	0♌02 42	6♌51 55	24 42.1	2 35.9	24 38.1	5 34.8	4 29.7	19 08.1	27 12.9	9 49.6	0 15.3	8 12.0
8 Tu	17 08 10	16 11 00	13 33 50	20 08 42	24D 40.7	1 59.7	25 53.5	6 07.5	4 16.2	19 12.9	27 10.6	9 52.0	0 17.0	8 14.3
9 W	17 12 07	17 11 56	26 36 55	2♍59 00	24 40.8	1 34.9	27 08.8	6 40.1	4 02.8	19 18.0	27 08.4	9 54.4	0 18.8	8 16.7
10 Th	17 16 03	18 12 54	9♍15 29	15 27 02	24R 41.3	1D 21.3	28 24.1	7 12.6	3 49.6	19 23.2	27 06.2	9 56.8	0 20.6	8 19.0
11 F	17 20 00	19 13 52	21 34 17	27 37 55	24 40.9	1 18.5	29 39.4	7 45.1	3 36.6	19 28.6	27 04.2	9 59.3	0 22.4	8 21.3
12 Sa	17 23 56	20 14 52	3♎38 34	9♎36 55	24 38.8	1 25.7	0♑54.8	8 17.4	3 23.8	19 34.2	27 02.3	10 01.8	0 24.2	8 23.6
13 Su	17 27 53	21 15 53	15 33 33	21 29 05	24 34.3	1 42.3	2 10.1	8 49.6	3 11.2	19 40.0	27 00.5	10 04.4	0 26.1	8 25.9
14 M	17 31 49	22 16 54	27 24 04	3♏18 59	24 27.2	2 07.3	3 25.4	9 21.7	2 58.8	19 45.9	26 58.8	10 07.0	0 28.0	8 28.2
15 Tu	17 35 46	23 17 57	9♏14 18	15 10 24	24 17.7	2 40.0	4 40.8	9 53.6	2 46.7	19 52.0	26 57.2	10 09.6	0 29.9	8 30.5
16 W	17 39 42	24 19 01	21 07 39	27 06 20	24 06.4	3 19.5	5 56.1	10 25.5	2 34.8	19 58.3	26 55.7	10 12.3	0 31.8	8 32.8
17 Th	17 43 39	25 20 05	3♐06 42	9♐08 57	23 54.4	4 05.0	7 11.4	10 57.3	2 23.2	20 04.8	26 54.3	10 15.0	0 33.7	8 35.1
18 F	17 47 36	26 21 10	15 13 13	21 19 38	23 42.7	4 55.9	8 26.7	11 28.9	2 11.8	20 11.4	26 53.0	10 17.7	0 35.6	8 37.4
19 Sa	17 51 32	27 22 16	27 28 18	3♑39 16	23 32.4	5 51.5	9 42.1	12 00.4	2 00.8	20 18.2	26 51.8	10 20.4	0 37.6	8 39.6
20 Su	17 55 29	28 23 23	9♑52 37	16 08 23	23 24.2	6 51.3	10 57.4	12 31.8	1 50.0	20 25.1	26 50.7	10 23.2	0 39.6	8 41.9
21 M	17 59 25	29 24 30	22 26 38	28 47 28	23 18.6	7 54.7	12 12.7	13 03.0	1 39.6	20 32.3	26 49.8	10 26.1	0 41.6	8 44.1
22 Tu	18 03 22	0♑25 37	5♒10 57	11♒33 47	23D 15.7	9 01.4	13 28.0	13 34.2	1 29.5	20 39.6	26 48.9	10 28.9	0 43.6	8 46.4
23 W	18 07 18	1 26 45	18 06 29	24 38 50	23 14.9	10 10.8	14 43.3	14 05.2	1 19.7	20 47.0	26 48.2	10 31.8	0 45.7	8 48.6
24 Th	18 11 15	2 27 52	1♓14 30	7♓53 42	23 15.7	11 22.7	15 58.6	14 36.0	1 10.3	20 54.6	26 47.6	10 34.7	0 47.7	8 50.8
25 F	18 15 11	3 29 00	14 36 38	21 23 32	23R 16.8	12 36.8	17 13.9	15 06.7	1 01.2	21 02.4	26 47.0	10 37.7	0 49.8	8 53.0
26 Sa	18 19 08	4 30 08	28 14 34	5♈09 52	23 17.4	13 52.7	18 29.1	15 37.3	0 52.5	21 10.3	26 46.6	10 40.6	0 51.9	8 55.1
27 Su	18 23 05	5 31 16	12♈09 30	19 13 27	23 16.4	15 10.4	19 44.4	16 07.8	0 44.1	21 18.3	26 46.3	10 43.6	0 54.0	8 57.3
28 M	18 27 01	6 32 23	26 21 34	3♉33 37	23 13.5	16 29.6	20 59.7	16 38.0	0 36.1	21 26.5	26 46.1	10 46.6	0 56.1	8 59.5
29 Tu	18 30 58	7 33 31	10♉49 12	18 07 47	23 08.6	17 50.0	22 14.9	17 08.2	0 28.5	21 34.9	26D 46.1	10 49.7	0 58.2	9 01.6
30 W	18 34 54	8 34 39	25 28 40	2♊51 05	23 02.2	19 11.7	23 30.1	17 38.2	0 21.3	21 43.4	26 46.1	10 52.8	1 00.3	9 03.7
31 Th	18 38 51	9 35 47	10♊14 07	17 36 47	22 55.0	20 34.5	24 45.4	18 08.1	0 14.5	21 52.0	26 46.3	10 55.9	1 02.5	9 05.8

Astro Data	Dy Hr Mn
♄□♆	1 1:36
☽0N	1 23:12
♃ D	13 13:02
☽0S	15 0:59
☿R	21 11:46
☽0N	29 9:39
♂0S	4 13:44
☿D	11 6:29
☽0S	12 8:56
☽0N	26 17:41
♄ D	29 15:45

Planet Ingress	Dy Hr Mn
☿ ♐	1 16:02
♀ ♐	17 21:06
☉ ♐	22 12:34
♂ ♎	27 10:10
♆ ♒	28 1:19
♀ ♑	11 18:33
☉ ♑	22 1:56

Last Aspect Dy Hr Mn		☽ Ingress Dy Hr Mn
1 11:00 ♆ △	♈	1 11:27
3 10:28 ♆ □	♉	3 11:12
5 9:29 ♆ △	♊	5 10:11
7 9:01 ♄ ⚹	♋	7 10:39
9 13:52 ♆ ☍	♌	9 14:33
11 20:05 ♄ △	♍	11 22:37
14 9:21 ♆ △	♎	14 9:58
16 22:10 ♆ □	♏	16 22:41
19 10:49 ♆ ⚹	♐	19 11:13
21 18:52 ♄ △	♑	21 22:45
24 8:33 ♆ ☌	♒	24 8:43
26 12:10 ♄ ⚹	♓	26 16:14
28 0:56 ♃ ☌	♈	28 20:34
30 17:53 ♄ ☌	♉	30 21:52

Last Aspect Dy Hr Mn		☽ Ingress Dy Hr Mn
2 3:43 ♃ ⚹	♊	2 21:30
4 17:07 ♄ ⚹	♋	4 21:28
6 19:08 ♄ □	♌	6 23:55
9 1:01 ♄ △	♍	9 6:21
11 16:30 ♀ □	♎	11 16:43
13 23:10 ♄ ☍	♏	14 5:16
15 21:33 ♃ △	♐	16 17:47
18 22:50 ♄ △	♑	19 4:55
21 8:18 ♄ □	♒	21 14:17
23 15:56 ♄ ⚹	♓	23 21:45
25 11:22 ♃ ☌	♈	26 3:03
28 0:41 ♄ ☌	♉	28 6:05
29 19:22 ♀ △	♊	30 7:22

☽ Phases & Eclipses Dy Hr Mn	
4 5:18	○ 11♉35
11 0:28	☾ 18♌24
19 4:27	● 26♏38
27 0:23	☽ 4♓33
3 15:19	○ 11♊15
10 17:54	☾ 18♍28
18 22:42	● 26♐48
26 10:46	☽ 4♈27

Astro Data

1 November 1998
Julian Day # 36099
SVP 5♓16'45"
GC 26♐49.4 ⚴ 13♓55.3R
Eris 18♈42.5R ⚵ 5♏56.3
⚷ 21♏33.3 ⚶ 15♌04.0
☽ Mean ☊ 27♌35.9

1 December 1998
Julian Day # 36129
SVP 5♓16'41"
GC 26♐49.4 ⚴ 14♓29.7
Eris 18♈28.1R ⚵ 16♏09.3
⚷ 25♏32.9 ⚶ 21♌12.7
☽ Mean ☊ 26♌00.6

LONGITUDE — January 1999

Day	Sid.Time	☉	0 hr ☽	Noon ☽	True ☊	☿	♀	♂	⚳	♃	♄	♅	♆	♇
1 F	18 42 47	10♑36 55	24♊58 05	2♋17 01	22♌48.1	21♐58.2	26♑00.6	18♎37.8	0♊08.1	22♓00.8	26♈46.5	10♒59.0	1♒04.6	9♐07.9
2 Sa	18 46 44	11 38 02	9♋32 40	16 44 09	22R 42.4	23 22.8	27 15.8	19 07.3	0R 02.0	22 09.8	26 46.9	11 02.1	1 06.8	9 10.0
3 Su	18 50 40	12 39 10	23 50 44	0♌51 51	22 38.5	24 48.1	28 31.0	19 36.7	29♉56.4	22 18.8	26 47.4	11 05.3	1 09.0	9 12.0
4 M	18 54 37	13 40 18	7♌47 03	14 36 04	22D 36.5	26 14.3	29 46.2	20 06.0	29 51.2	22 28.0	26 48.0	11 08.5	1 11.2	9 14.1
5 Tu	18 58 34	14 41 26	21 18 47	27 55 14	22 36.3	27 41.1	1♒01.3	20 35.0	29 46.4	22 37.3	26 48.7	11 11.7	1 13.3	9 16.1
6 W	19 02 30	15 42 35	4♍25 36	10♍50 08	22 37.4	29 08.5	2 16.5	21 03.9	29 41.9	22 46.8	26 49.5	11 14.9	1 15.6	9 18.1
7 Th	19 06 27	16 43 43	17 09 15	23 23 24	22 39.2	0♑36.5	3 31.6	21 32.7	29 37.9	22 56.4	26 50.4	11 18.2	1 17.8	9 20.1
8 F	19 10 23	17 44 51	29 33 07	5♎38 57	22 40.7	2 05.2	4 46.8	22 01.2	29 34.3	23 06.1	26 51.5	11 21.4	1 20.0	9 22.0
9 Sa	19 14 20	18 46 00	11♎41 32	17 41 29	22R 41.4	3 34.3	6 01.9	22 29.6	29 31.1	23 16.0	26 52.6	11 24.7	1 22.2	9 24.0
10 Su	19 18 16	19 47 08	23 39 24	29 35 57	22 40.9	5 04.0	7 17.0	22 57.8	29 28.4	23 25.9	26 53.9	11 28.0	1 24.5	9 25.9
11 M	19 22 13	20 48 17	5♏31 44	11♏27 20	22 38.8	6 34.3	8 32.2	23 25.8	29 26.0	23 36.0	26 55.2	11 31.4	1 26.7	9 27.8
12 Tu	19 26 09	21 49 26	17 23 20	23 20 15	22 35.3	8 05.0	9 47.3	23 53.6	29 24.1	23 46.2	26 56.7	11 34.7	1 29.0	9 29.6
13 W	19 30 06	22 50 34	29 18 35	5♐18 46	22 30.7	9 36.2	11 02.4	24 21.2	29 22.5	23 56.6	26 58.3	11 38.0	1 31.2	9 31.5
14 Th	19 34 03	23 51 43	11♐21 13	17 26 16	22 25.6	11 08.0	12 17.4	24 48.7	29 21.4	24 07.0	27 00.0	11 41.4	1 33.5	9 33.3
15 F	19 37 59	24 52 51	23 34 12	29 45 15	22 20.4	12 40.2	13 32.5	25 15.9	29 20.7	24 17.6	27 01.8	11 44.8	1 35.7	9 35.1
16 Sa	19 41 56	25 53 59	5♑59 35	12♑17 19	22 15.9	14 13.0	14 47.6	25 42.9	29D 20.4	24 28.3	27 03.7	11 48.2	1 38.0	9 36.9
17 Su	19 45 52	26 55 06	18 38 31	25 03 12	22 12.5	15 46.3	16 02.6	26 09.6	29 20.6	24 39.1	27 05.7	11 51.6	1 40.3	9 38.7
18 M	19 49 49	27 56 13	1♒31 20	8♒02 52	22 10.4	17 20.0	17 17.6	26 36.2	29 21.1	24 50.0	27 07.8	11 55.0	1 42.6	9 40.4
19 Tu	19 53 45	28 57 19	14 37 43	21 15 46	22D 09.7	18 54.3	18 32.6	27 02.5	29 22.1	25 01.0	27 10.1	11 58.4	1 44.8	9 42.2
20 W	19 57 42	29 58 25	27 56 54	4♓40 58	22 10.1	20 29.2	19 47.6	27 28.6	29 23.4	25 12.1	27 12.4	12 01.9	1 47.1	9 43.8
21 Th	20 01 38	0♒59 30	11♓27 53	18 17 28	22 11.3	22 04.6	21 02.6	27 54.4	29 25.2	25 23.3	27 14.9	12 05.3	1 49.4	9 45.5
22 F	20 05 35	2 00 34	25 09 38	2♈04 15	22 12.8	23 40.5	22 17.5	28 20.1	29 27.4	25 34.6	27 17.4	12 08.8	1 51.7	9 47.1
23 Sa	20 09 32	3 01 36	9♈01 12	16 00 20	22 14.1	25 17.0	23 32.4	28 45.4	29 29.9	25 46.0	27 20.1	12 12.2	1 53.9	9 48.7
24 Su	20 13 28	4 02 38	23 01 30	0♉04 34	22R 14.8	26 54.1	24 47.3	29 10.5	29 32.9	25 57.6	27 22.8	12 15.7	1 56.2	9 50.3
25 M	20 17 25	5 03 39	7♉09 19	14 15 31	22 14.6	28 31.8	26 02.2	29 35.4	29 36.2	26 09.2	27 25.7	12 19.2	1 58.5	9 51.9
26 Tu	20 21 21	6 04 39	21 22 53	28 31 06	22 13.6	0♒10.1	27 17.1	0♏00.0	29 40.0	26 20.9	27 28.6	12 22.7	2 00.8	9 53.4
27 W	20 25 18	7 05 37	5♊39 48	12♊48 33	22 12.0	1 49.1	28 31.9	0 24.4	29 44.1	26 32.7	27 31.7	12 26.2	2 03.0	9 54.9
28 Th	20 29 14	8 06 35	19 56 52	27 04 16	22 10.1	3 28.7	29 46.7	0 48.4	29 48.6	26 44.6	27 34.8	12 29.7	2 05.3	9 56.4
29 F	20 33 11	9 07 31	4♋10 13	11♋14 10	22 08.3	5 08.9	1♓01.4	1 12.2	29 53.5	26 56.6	27 38.1	12 33.2	2 07.6	9 57.8
30 Sa	20 37 07	10 08 27	18 15 37	25 14 02	22 06.8	6 49.9	2 16.2	1 35.8	29 58.8	27 08.6	27 41.5	12 36.7	2 09.9	9 59.3
31 Su	20 41 04	11 09 21	2♌08 58	9♌00 00	22D 05.9	8 31.5	3 30.9	1 59.0	0♊04.4	27 20.8	27 44.9	12 40.2	2 12.1	10 00.6

LONGITUDE — February 1999

Day	Sid.Time	☉	0 hr ☽	Noon ☽	True ☊	☿	♀	♂	⚳	♃	♄	♅	♆	♇
1 M	20 45 01	12♒10 14	15♌46 48	22♌29 06	22♌05.7	10♒13.8	4♓45.6	2♏21.9	0♊10.3	27♓33.0	27♈48.4	12♒43.7	2♒14.4	10♐02.0
2 Tu	20 48 57	13 11 06	29 06 43	5♍39 34	22 05.9	11 56.8	6 00.2	2 44.6	0 16.7	27 45.3	27 52.1	12 47.1	2 16.6	10 03.3
3 W	20 52 54	14 11 58	12♍07 38	18 31 01	22 06.5	13 40.5	7 14.9	3 06.9	0 23.4	27 57.7	27 55.8	12 50.6	2 18.9	10 04.6
4 Th	20 56 50	15 12 48	24 49 53	1♎04 29	22 07.3	15 25.0	8 29.5	3 29.0	0 30.4	28 10.2	27 59.6	12 54.1	2 21.1	10 05.9
5 F	21 00 47	16 13 37	7♎15 07	13 22 12	22 08.0	17 10.1	9 44.0	3 50.7	0 37.8	28 22.8	28 03.6	12 57.6	2 23.3	10 07.1
6 Sa	21 04 43	17 14 26	19 26 09	25 27 27	22 08.6	18 56.0	10 58.6	4 12.0	0 45.5	28 35.4	28 07.6	13 01.1	2 25.6	10 08.4
7 Su	21 08 40	18 15 13	1♏26 37	7♏24 13	22 08.9	20 42.5	12 13.1	4 33.1	0 53.5	28 48.1	28 11.7	13 04.6	2 27.8	10 09.5
8 M	21 12 36	19 16 00	13 20 49	19 17 00	22R 09.0	22 29.7	13 27.6	4 53.8	1 01.9	29 00.9	28 15.8	13 08.1	2 30.0	10 10.7
9 Tu	21 16 33	20 16 45	25 13 22	1♐10 31	22 08.9	24 17.5	14 42.0	5 14.1	1 10.6	29 13.7	28 20.1	13 11.6	2 32.2	10 11.8
10 W	21 20 30	21 17 30	7♐09 02	13 09 28	22D 08.8	26 05.9	15 56.5	5 34.1	1 19.7	29 26.7	28 24.5	13 15.1	2 34.4	10 12.9
11 Th	21 24 26	22 18 13	19 12 23	25 18 16	22 08.8	27 54.8	17 10.9	5 53.7	1 29.1	29 39.6	28 28.9	13 18.5	2 36.5	10 13.9
12 F	21 28 23	23 18 56	1♑27 36	7♑40 47	22 08.9	29 44.2	18 25.2	6 12.9	1 38.7	29 52.7	28 33.5	13 22.0	2 38.7	10 14.9
13 Sa	21 32 19	24 19 37	13 58 11	20 20 04	22 09.1	1♓33.9	19 39.5	6 31.8	1 48.7	0♈05.8	28 38.1	13 25.5	2 40.9	10 15.9
14 Su	21 36 16	25 20 17	26 46 40	3♒18 07	22 09.3	3 23.9	20 53.8	6 50.2	1 59.0	0 19.0	28 42.8	13 28.9	2 43.0	10 16.9
15 M	21 40 12	26 20 56	9♒54 25	16 35 33	22R 09.5	5 14.0	22 08.1	7 08.2	2 09.6	0 32.2	28 47.6	13 32.4	2 45.2	10 17.8
16 Tu	21 44 09	27 21 33	23 21 22	0♓11 38	22 09.5	7 04.0	23 22.3	7 25.9	2 20.5	0 45.6	28 52.4	13 35.8	2 47.3	10 18.7
17 W	21 48 05	28 22 09	7♓06 03	14 04 11	22 09.2	8 53.7	24 36.5	7 43.0	2 31.7	0 58.9	28 57.4	13 39.2	2 49.4	10 19.6
18 Th	21 52 02	29 22 43	21 05 37	28 09 51	22 08.5	10 42.9	25 50.6	7 59.8	2 43.2	1 12.3	29 02.4	13 42.6	2 51.5	10 20.4
19 F	21 55 59	0♓23 15	5♈16 19	12♈24 29	22 07.5	12 31.3	27 04.7	8 16.1	2 55.0	1 25.8	29 07.5	13 46.0	2 53.6	10 21.2
20 Sa	21 59 55	1 23 46	19 33 47	26 43 40	22 06.5	14 18.6	28 18.8	8 31.9	3 07.0	1 39.3	29 12.7	13 49.4	2 55.6	10 21.9
21 Su	22 03 52	2 24 15	3♉53 39	11♉03 14	22 05.5	16 04.5	29 32.8	8 47.3	3 19.4	1 52.9	29 18.0	13 52.8	2 57.7	10 22.6
22 M	22 07 48	3 24 42	18 12 00	25 19 34	22D 04.9	17 48.5	0♈46.8	9 02.2	3 32.0	2 06.6	29 23.3	13 56.1	2 59.7	10 23.3
23 Tu	22 11 45	4 25 07	2♊25 38	9♊29 53	22 04.9	19 30.2	2 00.7	9 16.7	3 44.8	2 20.2	29 28.7	13 59.5	3 01.7	10 24.0
24 W	22 15 41	5 25 30	16 32 07	23 32 08	22 05.4	21 09.0	3 14.6	9 30.6	3 58.0	2 34.0	29 34.2	14 02.8	3 03.7	10 24.6
25 Th	22 19 38	6 25 51	0♋29 46	7♋24 53	22 06.4	22 44.5	4 28.4	9 44.1	4 11.4	2 47.7	29 39.7	14 06.1	3 05.7	10 25.2
26 F	22 23 34	7 26 11	14 17 21	21 07 06	22 07.6	24 16.0	5 42.2	9 57.0	4 25.0	3 01.6	29 45.3	14 09.4	3 07.7	10 25.7
27 Sa	22 27 31	8 26 28	27 53 59	4♌37 56	22 08.8	25 43.0	6 55.9	10 09.5	4 38.9	3 15.4	29 51.0	14 12.7	3 09.7	10 26.2
28 Su	22 31 28	9 26 43	11♌18 51	17 56 39	22R 09.4	27 04.9	8 09.6	10 21.4	4 53.0	3 29.3	29 56.8	14 15.9	3 11.6	10 26.7

Astro Data	Dy Hr Mn	Planet Ingress	Dy Hr Mn
☽ 0S	8 18:03	⚳ ♉R	2 20:31
⚳ D	16 16:16	♀ ♒	4 16:25
☽ 0N	22 23:46	☿ ♑	7 2:04
		☉ ♒	20 12:37
♃∠♅	2 16:53	☿ ♒	26 9:32
♃⚺♄	3 6:40	♂ ♏	26 11:59
☽ 0S	5 3:20	♀ ♓	28 16:17
☽ 0N	19 6:10	⚳ ♊	30 17:28
♀0N	23 16:56		
♃0N	24 11:41	☿ ♓	12 15:28
♃✶♆	27 0:24	♃ ♈	13 1:23
☿0N	28 21:15	☉ ♓	19 2:47
		♀ ♈	21 20:49

Last Aspect Dy Hr Mn		☽ Ingress Dy Hr Mn
1 2:57	♄ ✶	♋ 1 8:15
3 7:34	♀ ☍	♌ 3 10:31
5 11:31	☿ △	♍ 5 15:49
7 11:07	♃ ☍	♎ 8 0:53
10 6:32	♄ ☍	♏ 10 12:49
12 12:53	♃ △	♐ 13 1:23
15 6:43	♄ △	♑ 15 12:29
17 15:49	♄ □	♒ 17 21:11
19 22:44	♂ △	♓ 20 3:40
22 0:34	♃ ☌	♈ 22 8:25
24 10:25	♂ ☍	♉ 24 11:52
26 9:44	♀ □	♊ 26 14:29
28 12:52	♄ ✶	♋ 28 16:57
30 16:16	♄ □	♌ 30 20:16

Last Aspect Dy Hr Mn		☽ Ingress Dy Hr Mn
1 21:40	♄ △	♍ 2 1:37
4 6:18	♃ ☍	♎ 4 9:56
6 17:22	♄ ☍	♏ 6 21:06
9 8:00	♃ △	♐ 9 9:38
11 20:39	♃ □	♑ 11 21:10
14 3:31	♄ □	♒ 14 5:57
16 9:41	♄ ✶	♓ 16 11:40
18 7:42	♀ ☌	♈ 18 15:06
20 16:11	♄ ☌	♉ 20 17:29
21 21:36	☿ ✶	♊ 22 19:54
24 22:28	♄ ✶	♋ 24 23:09
27 3:24	♄ □	♌ 27 3:44

☽ Phases & Eclipses Dy Hr Mn	
2 2:50	○ 11♋15
9 14:22	☾ 18♎52
17 15:46	● 27♑05
24 19:15	☽ 4♉21
31 16:07	○ 11♌20
31 16:17	• A 1.003
8 11:58	☾ 19♏16
16 6:39	● 27♒08
16 6:33:34	• A 00'39"
23 2:43	☽ 4♊02

Astro Data

1 January 1999
Julian Day # 36160
SVP 5♓16'35"
GC 26♐49.5 ⚴ 20♓05.5
Eris 18♈21.4R ⚵ 25♏59.4
⚷ 29♏21.3 ⚶ 21♌51.2R
☽ Mean ☊ 24♌22.1

1 February 1999
Julian Day # 36191
SVP 5♓16'30"
GC 26♐49.6 ⚴ 29♓07.4
Eris 18♈25.1 ⚵ 4♐19.7
⚷ 2♐15.8 ⚶ 15♌47.5R
☽ Mean ☊ 22♌43.6

March 1999 — LONGITUDE

Day	Sid.Time	☉	0 hr ☽	Noon ☽	True ☊	☿	♀	♂	⚳	♃	♄	♅	♆	♇
1 M	22 35 24	10♓26 57	24♌31 15	1♍02 34	22♌09.2	28♓21.0	9♈23.2	10♏32.7	5♊07.4	3♈43.2	0♉02.6	14♒19.2	3♒13.5	10♐27.2
2 Tu	22 39 21	11 27 09	7♍30 34	13 55 13	22R 08.0	29 30.7	10 36.7	10 43.6	5 22.0	3 57.2	0 08.4	14 22.4	3 15.4	10 27.6
3 W	22 43 17	12 27 18	20 16 30	26 34 28	22 05.8	0♈33.6	11 50.2	10 53.8	5 36.9	4 11.2	0 14.4	14 25.6	3 17.3	10 28.0
4 Th	22 47 14	13 27 27	2♎49 10	9♎00 42	22 02.7	1 28.9	13 03.7	11 03.5	5 51.9	4 25.3	0 20.4	14 28.7	3 19.1	10 28.3
5 F	22 51 10	14 27 33	15 09 16	21 15 02	21 59.0	2 16.4	14 17.1	11 12.6	6 07.2	4 39.4	0 26.5	14 31.9	3 21.0	10 28.6
6 Sa	22 55 07	15 27 38	27 18 16	3♏19 17	21 55.1	2 55.4	15 30.4	11 21.1	6 22.7	4 53.5	0 32.6	14 35.0	3 22.8	10 28.9
7 Su	22 59 03	16 27 41	9♏18 27	15 16 09	21 51.5	3 25.8	16 43.7	11 29.0	6 38.5	5 07.6	0 38.8	14 38.1	3 24.6	10 29.1
8 M	23 03 00	17 27 42	21 12 50	27 09 00	21 48.8	3 47.3	17 56.9	11 36.3	6 54.4	5 21.8	0 45.0	14 41.2	3 26.4	10 29.3
9 Tu	23 06 56	18 27 42	3♐05 10	9♐01 53	21D 47.1	3R 59.8	19 10.1	11 42.9	7 10.6	5 36.0	0 51.3	14 44.3	3 28.1	10 29.5
10 W	23 10 53	19 27 41	14 59 45	20 59 20	21 46.7	4 03.2	20 23.3	11 48.9	7 26.9	5 50.3	0 57.7	14 47.3	3 29.8	10 29.6
11 Th	23 14 50	20 27 37	27 01 15	3♑06 07	21 47.4	3 57.7	21 36.3	11 54.2	7 43.5	6 04.5	1 04.1	14 50.3	3 31.6	10 29.7
12 F	23 18 46	21 27 33	9♑14 31	15 27 01	21 48.8	3 43.7	22 49.3	11 58.9	8 00.3	6 18.8	1 10.5	14 53.3	3 33.2	10 29.8
13 Sa	23 22 43	22 27 26	21 44 10	28 06 27	21 50.6	3 21.5	24 02.3	12 02.9	8 17.2	6 33.2	1 17.1	14 56.3	3 34.9	10R 29.8
14 Su	23 26 39	23 27 18	4♒34 17	11♒08 01	21R 51.9	2 51.7	25 15.2	12 06.2	8 34.4	6 47.5	1 23.6	14 59.2	3 36.5	10 29.8
15 M	23 30 36	24 27 08	17 47 53	24 33 59	21 52.3	2 15.2	26 28.0	12 08.7	8 51.7	7 01.9	1 30.2	15 02.1	3 38.2	10 29.8
16 Tu	23 34 32	25 26 56	1♓26 19	8♓24 43	21 51.2	1 32.7	27 40.8	12 10.6	9 09.3	7 16.2	1 36.9	15 05.0	3 39.7	10 29.7
17 W	23 38 29	26 26 42	15 28 51	22 38 14	21 48.5	0 45.4	28 53.5	12 11.8	9 27.0	7 30.6	1 43.6	15 07.8	3 41.3	10 29.6
18 Th	23 42 25	27 26 26	29 52 15	7♈10 08	21 44.1	29♓54.3	0♉06.1	12R 12.2	9 44.9	7 45.1	1 50.4	15 10.7	3 42.8	10 29.4
19 F	23 46 22	28 26 08	14♈30 59	21 53 52	21 38.7	29 00.6	1 18.7	12 11.9	10 03.0	7 59.5	1 57.2	15 13.4	3 44.4	10 29.3
20 Sa	23 50 19	29 25 48	29 17 45	6♉41 39	21 32.9	28 05.5	2 31.2	12 10.8	10 21.3	8 14.0	2 04.0	15 16.2	3 45.8	10 29.1
21 Su	23 54 15	0♈25 26	14♉04 36	21 25 42	21 27.6	27 10.3	3 43.6	12 09.0	10 39.7	8 28.4	2 10.9	15 18.9	3 47.3	10 28.8
22 M	23 58 12	1 25 01	28 44 10	5♊59 21	21 23.6	26 16.0	4 56.0	12 06.4	10 58.3	8 42.9	2 17.9	15 21.6	3 48.7	10 28.5
23 Tu	0 02 08	2 24 35	13♊10 44	20 17 56	21D 21.2	25 23.8	6 08.3	12 03.1	11 17.1	8 57.4	2 24.8	15 24.3	3 50.2	10 28.2
24 W	0 06 05	3 24 06	27 20 43	4♋18 57	21 20.5	24 34.4	7 20.5	11 59.1	11 36.0	9 11.9	2 31.9	15 26.9	3 51.5	10 27.9
25 Th	0 10 01	4 23 34	11♋12 39	18 01 52	21 21.2	23 48.9	8 32.6	11 54.2	11 55.1	9 26.4	2 38.9	15 29.5	3 52.9	10 27.5
26 F	0 13 58	5 23 01	24 46 45	1♌27 30	21 22.6	23 07.8	9 44.6	11 48.6	12 14.4	9 40.9	2 46.0	15 32.0	3 54.2	10 27.1
27 Sa	0 17 54	6 22 25	8♌04 19	14 37 27	21R 23.7	22 31.6	10 56.6	11 42.3	12 33.8	9 55.4	2 53.1	15 34.6	3 55.5	10 26.7
28 Su	0 21 51	7 21 47	21 07 07	27 33 33	21 23.7	22 00.8	12 08.5	11 35.1	12 53.4	10 09.9	3 00.3	15 37.0	3 56.8	10 26.2
29 M	0 25 48	8 21 06	3♍56 58	10♍17 31	21 21.9	21 35.5	13 20.3	11 27.2	13 13.1	10 24.4	3 07.5	15 39.5	3 58.0	10 25.7
30 Tu	0 29 44	9 20 23	16 35 23	22 50 43	21 17.8	21 16.1	14 32.0	11 18.6	13 32.9	10 39.0	3 14.7	15 41.9	3 59.2	10 25.2
31 W	0 33 41	10 19 38	29 03 37	5♎14 13	21 11.5	21 02.4	15 43.6	11 09.2	13 52.9	10 53.5	3 21.9	15 44.3	4 00.4	10 24.6

April 1999 — LONGITUDE

Day	Sid.Time	☉	0 hr ☽	Noon ☽	True ☊	☿	♀	♂	⚳	♃	♄	♅	♆	♇
1 Th	0 37 37	11♈18 51	11♎22 36	17♎28 54	21♌03.1	20♓54.5	16♉55.2	10♏59.0	14♊13.0	11♈08.0	3♉29.2	15♒46.6	4♒01.6	10♐24.0
2 F	0 41 34	12 18 02	23 33 12	29 35 39	20R 53.5	20D 52.3	18 06.7	10R 48.1	14 33.3	11 22.5	3 36.5	15 48.9	4 02.7	10R 23.4
3 Sa	0 45 30	13 17 11	5♏36 24	11♏35 38	20 43.3	20 55.7	19 18.0	10 36.4	14 53.7	11 37.0	3 43.9	15 51.2	4 03.8	10 22.7
4 Su	0 49 27	14 16 19	17 33 35	23 30 29	20 33.6	21 04.5	20 29.3	10 24.0	15 14.2	11 51.5	3 51.2	15 53.4	4 04.8	10 22.0
5 M	0 53 23	15 15 24	29 26 40	5♐22 28	20 25.3	21 18.4	21 40.5	10 10.9	15 34.9	12 06.1	3 58.6	15 55.6	4 05.9	10 21.3
6 Tu	0 57 20	16 14 28	11♐18 18	17 14 36	20 18.9	21 37.4	22 51.6	9 57.0	15 55.6	12 20.6	4 06.1	15 57.7	4 06.9	10 20.5
7 W	1 01 17	17 13 29	23 11 51	29 10 35	20 14.8	22 01.1	24 02.6	9 42.5	16 16.6	12 35.1	4 13.5	15 59.8	4 07.9	10 19.8
8 Th	1 05 13	18 12 29	5♑11 23	11♑14 49	20D 12.9	22 29.3	25 13.5	9 27.2	16 37.6	12 49.6	4 21.0	16 01.9	4 08.8	10 19.0
9 F	1 09 10	19 11 28	17 21 32	23 32 08	20 12.8	23 01.8	26 24.3	9 11.3	16 58.8	13 04.0	4 28.4	16 03.9	4 09.7	10 18.1
10 Sa	1 13 06	20 10 24	29 47 16	6♒07 31	20 13.4	23 38.5	27 35.1	8 54.8	17 20.1	13 18.5	4 35.9	16 05.9	4 10.6	10 17.3
11 Su	1 17 03	21 09 19	12♒33 29	19 05 40	20R 14.0	24 19.0	28 45.7	8 37.6	17 41.5	13 33.0	4 43.5	16 07.8	4 11.4	10 16.4
12 M	1 20 59	22 08 12	25 44 31	2♓30 21	20 13.3	25 03.3	29 56.2	8 19.8	18 03.0	13 47.4	4 51.0	16 09.7	4 12.3	10 15.5
13 Tu	1 24 56	23 07 03	9♓23 23	16 23 37	20 10.6	25 51.0	1♊06.7	8 01.4	18 24.6	14 01.8	4 58.6	16 11.6	4 13.0	10 14.5
14 W	1 28 52	24 05 52	23 30 55	0♈44 55	20 05.5	26 42.1	2 17.0	7 42.5	18 46.4	14 16.3	5 06.1	16 13.4	4 13.8	10 13.5
15 Th	1 32 49	25 04 40	8♈05 03	15 30 31	19 57.9	27 36.3	3 27.2	7 23.0	19 08.2	14 30.7	5 13.7	16 15.2	4 14.5	10 12.5
16 F	1 36 45	26 03 25	23 00 20	0♉33 19	19 48.6	28 33.6	4 37.4	7 03.1	19 30.2	14 45.0	5 21.3	16 16.9	4 15.2	10 11.5
17 Sa	1 40 42	27 02 09	8♉08 13	15 43 40	19 38.5	29 33.7	5 47.4	6 42.7	19 52.3	14 59.4	5 28.9	16 18.6	4 15.9	10 10.5
18 Su	1 44 39	28 00 51	23 18 20	0♊50 55	19 29.0	0♈36.6	6 57.3	6 22.0	20 14.5	15 13.7	5 36.6	16 20.2	4 16.5	10 09.4
19 M	1 48 35	28 59 30	8♊20 15	15 45 21	19 21.2	1 42.2	8 07.1	6 00.8	20 36.8	15 28.1	5 44.2	16 21.8	4 17.1	10 08.3
20 Tu	1 52 32	29 58 08	23 05 22	0♋19 44	19 15.7	2 50.2	9 16.8	5 39.4	20 59.2	15 42.4	5 51.8	16 23.3	4 17.6	10 07.2
21 W	1 56 28	0♉56 43	7♋28 02	14 30 04	19 12.7	4 00.7	10 26.3	5 17.6	21 21.7	15 56.6	5 59.5	16 24.8	4 18.2	10 06.0
22 Th	2 00 25	1 55 16	21 25 49	28 15 23	19D 11.7	5 13.6	11 35.7	4 55.7	21 44.2	16 10.9	6 07.2	16 26.3	4 18.7	10 04.9
23 F	2 04 21	2 53 47	4♌59 01	11♌37 03	19R 11.8	6 28.7	12 45.0	4 33.5	22 06.9	16 25.1	6 14.8	16 27.7	4 19.1	10 03.7
24 Sa	2 08 18	3 52 15	18 09 52	24 37 53	19 11.8	7 46.0	13 54.2	4 11.2	22 29.7	16 39.3	6 22.5	16 29.1	4 19.5	10 02.5
25 Su	2 12 14	4 50 41	1♍01 34	7♍21 21	19 10.6	9 05.4	15 03.3	3 48.8	22 52.6	16 53.4	6 30.1	16 30.4	4 19.9	10 01.2
26 M	2 16 11	5 49 06	13 37 39	19 50 52	19 07.1	10 27.0	16 12.2	3 26.3	23 15.5	17 07.5	6 37.8	16 31.6	4 20.3	10 00.0
27 Tu	2 20 08	6 47 28	26 01 23	2♎09 31	19 00.9	11 50.6	17 20.9	3 03.8	23 38.6	17 21.6	6 45.5	16 32.9	4 20.6	9 58.7
28 W	2 24 04	7 45 48	8♎15 34	14 19 48	18 51.8	13 16.2	18 29.6	2 41.3	24 01.7	17 35.7	6 53.1	16 34.0	4 20.9	9 57.4
29 Th	2 28 01	8 44 06	20 22 26	26 23 39	18 40.2	14 43.8	19 38.0	2 18.9	24 24.9	17 49.7	7 00.8	16 35.2	4 21.2	9 56.1
30 F	2 31 57	9 42 22	2♏23 38	8♏22 33	18 26.9	16 13.3	20 46.4	1 56.6	24 48.2	18 03.7	7 08.5	16 36.2	4 21.4	9 54.7

Astro Data Dy Hr Mn	Planet Ingress Dy Hr Mn	Last Aspect Dy Hr Mn	☽ Ingress Dy Hr Mn	Last Aspect Dy Hr Mn	☽ Ingress Dy Hr Mn	☽ Phases & Eclipses Dy Hr Mn
☽0S 4 11:44	♄ ♉ 1 1:26	28 5:18 ♅ ☍	♍ 1 10:04	1 8:38 ♅ △	♏ 2 12:48	2 6:58 ○ 11♍15
☿R 10 9:10	☿ ♈ 2 22:50	2 6:58 ⊙ ☍	♎ 3 18:34	4 7:01 ☿ △	♐ 5 1:07	10 8:40 ☾ 19♐19
♇R 13 21:34	☿ ♓R 18 9:23	4 22:43 ♅ △	♏ 6 5:22	6 21:07 ☿ □	♑ 7 13:39	17 18:48 ● 26♓44
♂R 18 13:41	♀ ♉ 18 9:59	7 14:38 ⊙ △	♐ 8 17:46	9 18:06 ♀ △	♒ 10 0:24	24 10:18 ☽ 3♋20
☽0N 18 14:41	⊙ ♈ 21 1:46	10 10:40 ♀ △	♑ 11 5:54	12 7:02 ♀ □	♓ 12 7:35	31 22:49 ○ 10♎46
⊙0N 21 1:47		13 3:33 ♀ □	♒ 13 15:32	14 4:53 ☿ ☌	♈ 14 10:46	
☿0S 24 19:32	♀ ♊ 12 13:17	15 15:40 ♀ ⚹	♓ 15 21:30	16 4:22 ⊙ ☌	♉ 16 11:07	9 2:51 ☾ 18♑49
♃△♇ 29 14:00	☿ ♈ 17 22:09	17 18:48 ⊙ ☌	♈ 18 0:13	17 12:55 ♅ □	♊ 18 10:39	16 4:22 ● 25♈45
☽0S 31 18:53	⊙ ♉ 20 12:46	19 1:07 ♅ ⚹	♉ 20 1:09	20 11:21 ⊙ ⚹	♋ 20 11:27	22 19:02 ☽ 2♌12
☿D 2 9:19		21 20:52 ♅ ⚹	♊ 22 2:05	21 14:32 ♃ □	♌ 22 15:06	30 14:55 ○ 9♏49
♄□♆ 6 15:05		23 20:11 ☿ □	♋ 24 4:33	23 20:57 ♃ △	♍ 24 22:04	
☽0N 15 1:13		25 21:46 ☿ △	♌ 26 9:22	26 4:14 ♀ □	♎ 27 7:46	
☿0N 23 9:02		27 13:45 ♅ ☍	♍ 28 16:34	28 21:07 ♀ △	♏ 29 19:12	
♃⚹♅ 23 16:55		30 9:02 ♅ ☍	♎ 31 1:49			
☽0S 28 1:18						

Astro Data

1 March 1999
Julian Day # 36219
SVP 5♓16'27"
GC 26♐49.7 ⚴ 9♈13.1
Eris 18♈36.6 ⚵ 9♐40.1
⚷ 3♐41.1 ⚶ 9♌07.1R
☽ Mean ☊ 21♌14.7

1 April 1999
Julian Day # 36250
SVP 5♓16'25"
GC 26♐49.7 ⚴ 21♈52.0
Eris 18♈55.4 ⚵ 11♐49.4R
⚷ 3♐39.7R ⚶ 7♌21.6
☽ Mean ☊ 19♌36.1

LONGITUDE — May 1999

Day	Sid.Time	☉	0 hr ☽	Noon ☽	True ☊	☿	♀	♂	⚳	♃	♄	♅	♆	♇
1 Sa	2 35 54	10♉40 37	14♏20 32	20♏17 45	18♌12.9	17♈44.8	21♊54.6	1♏34.5	25♊11.6	18♈17.7	7♉16.1	16♒37.3	4♒21.6	9♐53.4
2 Su	2 39 50	11 38 50	26 14 21	2♐10 32	17R59.3	19 18.2	23 02.6	1R12.5	25 35.0	18 31.6	7 23.8	16 38.2	4 21.8	9R52.0
3 M	2 43 47	12 37 01	8♐06 30	14 02 29	17 47.3	20 53.5	24 10.5	0 50.8	25 58.5	18 45.5	7 31.5	16 39.2	4 21.9	9 50.6
4 Tu	2 47 43	13 35 11	19 58 46	25 55 41	17 37.7	22 30.7	25 18.2	0 29.4	26 22.2	18 59.3	7 39.1	16 40.1	4 22.0	9 49.2
5 W	2 51 40	14 33 19	1♑53 35	7♑52 52	17 30.9	24 09.8	26 25.8	0 08.3	26 45.8	19 13.1	7 46.7	16 40.9	4 22.1	9 47.8
6 Th	2 55 37	15 31 26	13 54 02	19 57 32	17 26.9	25 50.8	27 33.2	29♎47.5	27 09.6	19 26.9	7 54.4	16 41.7	4R 22.1	9 46.4
7 F	2 59 33	16 29 31	26 03 57	2♒13 50	17 25.1	27 33.7	28 40.4	29 27.2	27 33.5	19 40.6	8 02.0	16 42.4	4 22.1	9 44.9
8 Sa	3 03 30	17 27 35	8♒27 46	14 46 22	17 24.7	29 18.6	29 47.5	29 07.3	27 57.4	19 54.3	8 09.6	16 43.1	4 22.1	9 43.4
9 Su	3 07 26	18 25 38	21 10 14	27 39 55	17 24.6	1♉05.3	0♋54.4	28 47.9	28 21.4	20 07.9	8 17.2	16 43.8	4 22.0	9 42.0
10 M	3 11 23	19 23 39	4♓15 59	10♓58 50	17 23.6	2 53.9	2 01.1	28 28.9	28 45.4	20 21.5	8 24.8	16 44.4	4 21.9	9 40.5
11 Tu	3 15 19	20 21 39	17 48 51	24 46 14	17 20.7	4 44.4	3 07.7	28 10.6	29 09.6	20 35.0	8 32.4	16 44.9	4 21.8	9 39.0
12 W	3 19 16	21 19 37	1♈51 01	9♈03 04	17 15.2	6 36.9	4 14.1	27 52.8	29 33.8	20 48.5	8 39.9	16 45.4	4 21.6	9 37.4
13 Th	3 23 12	22 17 34	16 21 59	23 47 10	17 07.2	8 31.2	5 20.2	27 35.6	29 58.0	21 01.9	8 47.5	16 45.8	4 21.4	9 35.9
14 F	3 27 09	23 15 30	1♉17 46	8♉52 42	16 57.2	10 27.4	6 26.2	27 19.0	0♋22.4	21 15.3	8 55.0	16 46.2	4 21.2	9 34.4
15 Sa	3 31 06	24 13 24	16 30 43	24 10 24	16 46.3	12 25.5	7 32.0	27 03.1	0 46.8	21 28.6	9 02.5	16 46.6	4 20.9	9 32.8
16 Su	3 35 02	25 11 17	1♊50 18	9♊28 57	16 35.8	14 25.4	8 37.6	26 47.9	1 11.2	21 41.9	9 10.0	16 46.9	4 20.6	9 31.2
17 M	3 38 59	26 09 09	17 04 57	24 37 00	16 27.0	16 27.1	9 43.0	26 33.4	1 35.8	21 55.1	9 17.5	16 47.1	4 20.3	9 29.7
18 Tu	3 42 55	27 06 59	2♋04 03	9♋25 13	16 20.6	18 30.5	10 48.2	26 19.6	2 00.4	22 08.2	9 24.9	16 47.3	4 20.0	9 28.1
19 W	3 46 52	28 04 47	16 39 52	23 47 35	16 16.8	20 35.5	11 53.2	26 06.6	2 25.0	22 21.3	9 32.4	16 47.5	4 19.6	9 26.5
20 Th	3 50 48	29 02 33	0♌48 12	7♌41 42	16D15.3	22 42.0	12 57.9	25 54.4	2 49.7	22 34.4	9 39.8	16 47.6	4 19.2	9 24.9
21 F	3 54 45	0♊00 18	14 28 17	21 08 13	16R15.2	24 49.8	14 02.4	25 42.9	3 14.5	22 47.3	9 47.2	16R47.6	4 18.7	9 23.3
22 Sa	3 58 41	0 58 01	27 41 55	4♍09 50	16 15.3	26 58.9	15 06.7	25 32.2	3 39.3	23 00.3	9 54.5	16 47.6	4 18.2	9 21.7
23 Su	4 02 38	1 55 43	10♍32 31	16 50 30	16 14.4	29 09.0	16 10.7	25 22.3	4 04.2	23 13.1	10 01.8	16 47.5	4 17.7	9 20.1
24 M	4 06 35	2 53 23	23 04 18	29 14 29	16 11.6	1♊19.9	17 14.4	25 13.3	4 29.1	23 25.9	10 09.1	16 47.4	4 17.2	9 18.5
25 Tu	4 10 31	3 51 01	5♎21 33	11♎25 59	16 06.3	3 31.4	18 17.9	25 05.0	4 54.1	23 38.6	10 16.4	16 47.3	4 16.6	9 16.9
26 W	4 14 28	4 48 38	17 28 13	23 28 41	15 58.4	5 43.2	19 21.1	24 57.5	5 19.1	23 51.2	10 23.6	16 47.1	4 16.0	9 15.2
27 Th	4 18 24	5 46 14	29 27 44	5♏25 41	15 48.1	7 55.0	20 24.0	24 50.9	5 44.2	24 03.8	10 30.8	16 46.8	4 15.4	9 13.6
28 F	4 22 21	6 43 48	11♏22 50	17 19 27	15 36.2	10 06.7	21 26.7	24 45.1	6 09.3	24 16.3	10 38.0	16 46.5	4 14.7	9 12.0
29 Sa	4 26 17	7 41 21	23 15 44	29 11 54	15 23.7	12 17.8	22 29.0	24 40.1	6 34.5	24 28.7	10 45.2	16 46.2	4 14.0	9 10.3
30 Su	4 30 14	8 38 53	5♐08 09	11♐04 38	15 11.6	14 28.2	23 31.1	24 35.9	6 59.7	24 41.1	10 52.3	16 45.8	4 13.3	9 08.7
31 M	4 34 10	9 36 24	17 01 33	22 59 05	15 00.9	16 37.5	24 32.8	24 32.5	7 25.0	24 53.4	10 59.3	16 45.4	4 12.6	9 07.1

LONGITUDE — June 1999

Day	Sid.Time	☉	0 hr ☽	Noon ☽	True ☊	☿	♀	♂	⚳	♃	♄	♅	♆	♇
1 Tu	4 38 07	10♊33 54	28♐57 27	4♑56 51	14♌52.3	18♊45.6	25♋34.2	24♎29.9	7♋50.4	25♈05.6	11♉06.4	16♒44.9	4♒11.8	9♐05.4
2 W	4 42 04	11 31 23	10♑57 34	16 59 51	14R46.3	20 52.2	26 35.3	24R28.1	8 15.7	25 17.7	11 13.4	16R44.4	4R11.0	9R03.8
3 Th	4 46 00	12 28 51	23 04 04	29 10 33	14 42.9	22 57.0	27 36.1	24D27.1	8 41.1	25 29.8	11 20.4	16 43.8	4 10.2	9 02.2
4 F	4 49 57	13 26 18	5♒19 42	11♒31 56	14D41.7	25 00.1	28 36.5	24 26.9	9 06.6	25 41.7	11 27.3	16 43.2	4 09.3	9 00.6
5 Sa	4 53 53	14 23 45	17 47 45	24 07 36	14 41.9	27 01.1	29 36.5	24 27.5	9 32.1	25 53.6	11 34.2	16 42.5	4 08.5	8 58.9
6 Su	4 57 50	15 21 10	0♓31 59	7♓01 23	14R42.6	28 59.9	0♌36.2	24 28.8	9 57.7	26 05.4	11 41.0	16 41.8	4 07.6	8 57.3
7 M	5 01 46	16 18 35	13 36 15	20 17 02	14 42.8	0♋56.5	1 35.5	24 31.0	10 23.3	26 17.1	11 47.8	16 41.0	4 06.6	8 55.7
8 Tu	5 05 43	17 16 00	27 04 04	3♈57 37	14 41.5	2 50.8	2 34.5	24 33.9	10 48.9	26 28.8	11 54.6	16 40.2	4 05.7	8 54.1
9 W	5 09 39	18 13 24	10♈57 48	18 04 37	14 38.3	4 42.7	3 33.0	24 37.5	11 14.6	26 40.3	12 01.3	16 39.3	4 04.7	8 52.5
10 Th	5 13 36	19 10 47	25 17 51	2♉37 07	14 32.9	6 32.2	4 31.1	24 41.9	11 40.3	26 51.8	12 08.0	16 38.4	4 03.7	8 50.9
11 F	5 17 33	20 08 10	10♉01 49	17 31 08	14 25.9	8 19.2	5 28.8	24 47.1	12 06.1	27 03.2	12 14.6	16 37.5	4 02.6	8 49.3
12 Sa	5 21 29	21 05 32	25 04 03	2♊39 26	14 18.1	10 03.7	6 26.1	24 52.9	12 31.9	27 14.4	12 21.2	16 36.5	4 01.6	8 47.7
13 Su	5 25 26	22 02 54	10♊15 59	17 52 21	14 10.4	11 45.7	7 22.9	24 59.6	12 57.7	27 25.6	12 27.7	16 35.5	4 00.5	8 46.1
14 M	5 29 22	23 00 15	25 27 12	2♋59 15	14 03.9	13 25.1	8 19.3	25 06.9	13 23.6	27 36.7	12 34.2	16 34.4	3 59.4	8 44.5
15 Tu	5 33 19	23 57 36	10♋27 20	17 50 27	13 59.3	15 01.9	9 15.1	25 14.9	13 49.5	27 47.7	12 40.7	16 33.3	3 58.3	8 43.0
16 W	5 37 15	24 54 56	25 07 47	2♌18 43	13D56.9	16 36.1	10 10.5	25 23.7	14 15.4	27 58.6	12 47.1	16 32.1	3 57.1	8 41.4
17 Th	5 41 12	25 52 14	9♌22 52	16 20 02	13 56.3	18 07.8	11 05.3	25 33.1	14 41.4	28 09.4	12 53.4	16 30.9	3 56.0	8 39.9
18 F	5 45 08	26 49 32	23 10 10	29 53 25	13 57.1	19 36.8	11 59.6	25 43.2	15 07.4	28 20.1	12 59.7	16 29.7	3 54.8	8 38.3
19 Sa	5 49 05	27 46 49	6♍30 03	13♍00 27	13 58.3	21 03.1	12 53.4	25 54.0	15 33.5	28 30.7	13 05.9	16 28.4	3 53.5	8 36.8
20 Su	5 53 02	28 44 06	19 25 04	25 44 23	13R59.1	22 26.8	13 46.5	26 05.4	15 59.6	28 41.1	13 12.1	16 27.1	3 52.3	8 35.3
21 M	5 56 58	29 41 21	1♎58 59	8♎09 24	13 58.8	23 47.8	14 39.1	26 17.4	16 25.7	28 51.5	13 18.2	16 25.7	3 51.0	8 33.8
22 Tu	6 00 55	0♋38 36	14 16 13	20 19 59	13 56.7	25 06.0	15 31.0	26 30.1	16 51.8	29 01.8	13 24.2	16 24.3	3 49.8	8 32.3
23 W	6 04 51	1 35 50	26 21 15	2♏20 32	13 52.9	26 21.4	16 22.3	26 43.4	17 18.0	29 11.9	13 30.2	16 22.8	3 48.5	8 30.8
24 Th	6 08 48	2 33 03	8♏18 20	14 15 05	13 47.5	27 33.9	17 12.9	26 57.3	17 44.2	29 22.0	13 36.1	16 21.4	3 47.2	8 29.4
25 F	6 12 44	3 30 16	20 11 13	26 07 07	13 40.9	28 43.5	18 02.8	27 11.8	18 10.4	29 31.9	13 42.0	16 19.8	3 45.8	8 27.9
26 Sa	6 16 41	4 27 29	2♐03 07	7♐59 32	13 33.7	29 50.1	18 52.0	27 26.9	18 36.6	29 41.7	13 47.8	16 18.3	3 44.5	8 26.5
27 Su	6 20 37	5 24 41	13 56 39	19 54 42	13 26.8	0♌53.7	19 40.4	27 42.5	19 02.9	29 51.4	13 53.6	16 16.7	3 43.1	8 25.1
28 M	6 24 34	6 21 53	25 53 55	1♑54 30	13 20.7	1 54.1	20 28.1	27 58.7	19 29.2	0♉01.0	13 59.3	16 15.1	3 41.7	8 23.7
29 Tu	6 28 31	7 19 05	7♑56 39	14 00 33	13 16.0	2 51.3	21 14.9	28 15.4	19 55.5	0 10.5	14 04.9	16 13.4	3 40.3	8 22.3
30 W	6 32 27	8 16 16	20 06 23	26 14 21	13 13.0	3 45.2	22 00.9	28 32.7	20 21.9	0 19.8	14 10.5	16 11.7	3 38.9	8 21.0

Astro Data

	Dy Hr Mn
♆R	7 0:51
☽0N	12 12:12
♄⊼♇	18 20:24
♅R	21 22:25
☽0S	25 7:56
♃⚼♇	28 4:39
♂D	4 6:10
☽0N	8 21:52
☽0S	21 15:28

Planet Ingress

	Dy Hr Mn
♂ ♎R	5 21:32
♀ ♋	8 16:29
☿ ♉	8 21:22
⚳ ♋	13 13:57
☉ ♊	21 11:52
☿ ♊	23 21:22
♀ ♌	5 21:25
☿ ♋	7 0:18
☉ ♋	21 19:49
☿ ♌	26 15:39
♃ ♉	28 9:29

Last Aspect / ☽ Ingress (May)

Last Aspect Dy Hr Mn		☽ Ingress	Dy Hr Mn
1 4:35	♅ □	♐	2 7:36
4 10:37	♀ ☍	♑	4 20:12
7 6:45	♂ □	♒	7 7:40
9 14:01	♂ △	♓	9 16:16
11 3:51	☉ ⚹	♈	11 20:53
13 17:59	♂ ☍	♉	13 21:56
15 12:05	☉ ☌	♊	15 21:07
17 15:04	♂ △	♋	17 20:39
19 19:51	☉ ⚹	♌	19 22:37
21 20:14	♂ ⚹	♍	22 4:15
23 10:37	♀ ⚹	♎	24 13:29
26 14:56	♂ ☌	♏	27 1:05
28 21:08	♀ △	♐	29 13:37

Last Aspect / ☽ Ingress (June)

Last Aspect Dy Hr Mn		☽ Ingress	Dy Hr Mn
31 15:54	♃ △	♑	1 2:05
3 8:38	♀ ☍	♒	3 13:37
5 18:26	☿ △	♓	5 23:00
7 4:20	☉ □	♈	8 5:08
10 2:27	♃ ☌	♉	10 7:44
11 10:34	♅ □	♊	12 7:48
14 3:19	♃ ⚹	♋	14 7:14
16 4:39	♃ □	♌	16 8:07
18 9:10	♃ △	♍	18 12:12
20 18:13	☉ □	♎	20 20:10
23 5:36	♃ ☍	♏	23 7:18
25 17:50	☿ △	♐	25 19:51
28 8:11	♃ △	♑	28 8:12
30 16:36	♂ □	♒	30 19:19

☽ Phases & Eclipses

Dy Hr Mn	
8 17:29	☾ 17♒41
15 12:05	● 24♉14
22 5:34	☽ 0♍43
30 6:40	○ 8♐26
7 4:20	☾ 16♓00
13 19:03	● 22♊20
20 18:13	☽ 28♍59
28 21:37	○ 6♑45

Astro Data

1 May 1999
Julian Day # 36280
SVP 5♓16'22"
GC 26♐49.8 ⚴ 5♉12.0
Eris 19♈14.9 ⚵ 9♐06.1R
⚷ 2♐12.4R ⚶ 12♌07.7
☽ Mean ☊ 18♌00.8

1 June 1999
Julian Day # 36311
SVP 5♓16'17"
GC 26♐49.9 ⚴ 19♉53.5
Eris 19♈31.7 ⚵ 2♐37.2R
⚷ 29♏59.6R ⚶ 21♌33.7
☽ Mean ☊ 16♌22.3

July 1999 LONGITUDE

Day	Sid.Time	☉	0 hr ☽	Noon ☽	True ☊	☿	♀	♂	⚳	♃	♄	♅	♆	♇
1 Th	6 36 24	9♋13 27	2♒24 39	8♒37 28	13♌11.7	4♌35.6	22♌46.1	28♎50.5	20♋48.3	0♉29.0	14♉16.0	16♒10.0	3♒37.5	8♐19.6
2 F	6 40 20	10 10 39	14 53 04	21 11 40	13D 11.9	5 22.5	23 30.3	29 08.8	21 14.7	0 38.1	14 21.4	16R 08.2	3R 36.0	8R 18.3
3 Sa	6 44 17	11 07 50	27 33 33	3♓58 58	13 13.0	6 05.7	24 13.6	29 27.6	21 41.1	0 47.1	14 26.7	16 06.4	3 34.6	8 17.0
4 Su	6 48 13	12 05 01	10♓28 13	17 01 35	13 14.6	6 45.1	24 56.0	29 46.9	22 07.6	0 56.0	14 32.0	16 04.6	3 33.1	8 15.7
5 M	6 52 10	13 02 13	23 39 20	0♈21 43	13 15.9	7 20.6	25 37.3	0♏06.7	22 34.0	1 04.7	14 37.3	16 02.7	3 31.6	8 14.4
6 Tu	6 56 07	13 59 25	7♈08 56	14 01 09	13R 16.4	7 52.0	26 17.6	0 26.9	23 00.5	1 13.3	14 42.4	16 00.9	3 30.1	8 13.2
7 W	7 00 03	14 56 37	20 58 26	28 00 45	13 15.8	8 19.3	26 56.9	0 47.6	23 27.1	1 21.7	14 47.5	15 58.9	3 28.6	8 11.9
8 Th	7 04 00	15 53 50	5♉08 00	12♉19 54	13 14.0	8 42.3	27 35.0	1 08.8	23 53.6	1 30.1	14 52.5	15 57.0	3 27.1	8 10.7
9 F	7 07 56	16 51 03	19 36 03	26 55 55	13 11.3	9 00.8	28 12.0	1 30.5	24 20.2	1 38.3	14 57.4	15 55.0	3 25.5	8 09.6
10 Sa	7 11 53	17 48 17	4♊18 49	11♊43 56	13 07.9	9 14.8	28 47.8	1 52.6	24 46.7	1 46.3	15 02.3	15 53.0	3 24.0	8 08.4
11 Su	7 15 49	18 45 31	19 10 22	26 37 08	13 04.6	9 24.2	29 22.3	2 15.1	25 13.4	1 54.2	15 07.1	15 51.0	3 22.4	8 07.3
12 M	7 19 46	19 42 45	4♋03 12	11♋27 33	13 01.9	9R 28.9	29 55.5	2 38.1	25 40.0	2 02.0	15 11.8	15 48.9	3 20.9	8 06.1
13 Tu	7 23 42	20 40 00	18 49 12	26 07 14	13 00.1	9 28.8	0♍27.4	3 01.5	26 06.6	2 09.6	15 16.4	15 46.9	3 19.3	8 05.1
14 W	7 27 39	21 37 14	3♌20 52	10♌29 25	12D 59.4	9 23.9	0 57.9	3 25.3	26 33.3	2 17.1	15 20.9	15 44.8	3 17.7	8 04.0
15 Th	7 31 36	22 34 29	17 32 22	24 29 22	12 59.7	9 14.3	1 27.0	3 49.5	27 00.0	2 24.4	15 25.4	15 42.7	3 16.1	8 02.9
16 F	7 35 32	23 31 44	1♍20 11	8♍04 45	13 00.7	8 59.9	1 54.5	4 14.2	27 26.7	2 31.6	15 29.8	15 40.5	3 14.6	8 01.9
17 Sa	7 39 29	24 28 59	14 43 07	21 15 30	13 02.1	8 41.0	2 20.4	4 39.2	27 53.4	2 38.6	15 34.1	15 38.3	3 13.0	8 00.9
18 Su	7 43 25	25 26 15	27 42 08	4♎03 26	13 03.4	8 17.7	2 44.8	5 04.6	28 20.1	2 45.5	15 38.3	15 36.2	3 11.3	8 00.0
19 M	7 47 22	26 23 30	10♎19 48	16 31 43	13R 04.2	7 50.3	3 07.4	5 30.4	28 46.8	2 52.2	15 42.4	15 33.9	3 09.7	7 59.0
20 Tu	7 51 18	27 20 46	22 39 44	28 44 24	13 04.5	7 19.1	3 28.3	5 56.5	29 13.6	2 58.8	15 46.5	15 31.7	3 08.1	7 58.1
21 W	7 55 15	28 18 01	4♏46 15	10♏45 52	13 04.0	6 44.5	3 47.3	6 23.0	29 40.3	3 05.2	15 50.5	15 29.5	3 06.5	7 57.2
22 Th	7 59 11	29 15 17	16 43 49	22 40 38	13 03.0	6 07.0	4 04.5	6 49.9	0♌07.1	3 11.5	15 54.3	15 27.2	3 04.9	7 56.3
23 F	8 03 08	0♌12 34	28 36 51	4♐32 59	13 01.5	5 27.2	4 19.8	7 17.1	0 33.9	3 17.6	15 58.1	15 24.9	3 03.3	7 55.5
24 Sa	8 07 05	1 09 51	10♐29 29	16 26 48	12 59.8	4 45.6	4 33.0	7 44.7	1 00.6	3 23.5	16 01.8	15 22.7	3 01.6	7 54.7
25 Su	8 11 01	2 07 08	22 25 21	28 25 31	12 58.2	4 03.1	4 44.2	8 12.6	1 27.4	3 29.3	16 05.4	15 20.4	3 00.0	7 53.9
26 M	8 14 58	3 04 26	4♑27 36	10♑31 55	12 56.9	3 20.2	4 53.3	8 40.8	1 54.2	3 34.9	16 09.0	15 18.1	2 58.4	7 53.2
27 Tu	8 18 54	4 01 44	16 38 44	22 48 14	12 55.9	2 37.9	5 00.2	9 09.3	2 21.1	3 40.3	16 12.4	15 15.7	2 56.8	7 52.5
28 W	8 22 51	4 59 03	29 00 38	5♒16 05	12D 55.5	1 56.8	5 05.0	9 38.1	2 47.9	3 45.6	16 15.8	15 13.4	2 55.1	7 51.8
29 Th	8 26 47	5 56 23	11♒34 41	17 56 33	12 55.4	1 17.7	5R 07.4	10 07.3	3 14.7	3 50.7	16 19.0	15 11.0	2 53.5	7 51.1
30 F	8 30 44	6 53 43	24 21 44	0♓50 19	12 55.7	0 41.4	5 07.6	10 36.7	3 41.6	3 55.6	16 22.2	15 08.7	2 51.9	7 50.5
31 Sa	8 34 40	7 51 04	7♓22 17	13 57 42	12 56.1	0 08.5	5 05.4	11 06.5	4 08.4	4 00.4	16 25.2	15 06.3	2 50.3	7 49.9

August 1999 LONGITUDE

Day	Sid.Time	☉	0 hr ☽	Noon ☽	True ☊	☿	♀	♂	⚳	♃	♄	♅	♆	♇
1 Su	8 38 37	8♌48 26	20♓36 32	27♓18 48	12♌56.6	29♋39.7	5♍00.9	11♏36.5	4♌35.3	4♉05.0	16♉28.2	15♒04.0	2♒48.6	7♐49.3
2 M	8 42 34	9 45 50	4♈04 27	10♈53 29	12 56.9	29R 15.7	4R 54.0	12 06.8	5 02.1	4 09.4	16 31.1	15R 01.6	2R 47.0	7R 48.7
3 Tu	8 46 30	10 43 14	17 45 48	24 41 19	12 57.1	28 56.8	4 44.7	12 37.4	5 29.0	4 13.6	16 33.9	14 59.2	2 45.4	7 48.2
4 W	8 50 27	11 40 40	1♉39 57	8♉41 32	12R 57.2	28 43.6	4 33.1	13 08.3	5 55.8	4 17.7	16 36.6	14 56.8	2 43.8	7 47.7
5 Th	8 54 23	12 38 07	15 45 52	22 52 44	12D 57.2	28D 36.4	4 19.1	13 39.5	6 22.7	4 21.6	16 39.2	14 54.4	2 42.2	7 47.3
6 F	8 58 20	13 35 35	0♊01 48	7♊12 43	12 57.2	28 35.4	4 02.8	14 10.9	6 49.6	4 25.3	16 41.7	14 52.0	2 40.6	7 46.8
7 Sa	9 02 16	14 33 05	14 25 06	21 38 27	12 57.3	28 41.1	3 44.2	14 42.6	7 16.5	4 28.8	16 44.1	14 49.6	2 39.0	7 46.5
8 Su	9 06 13	15 30 36	28 52 14	6♋05 54	12 57.5	28 53.3	3 23.4	15 14.6	7 43.4	4 32.1	16 46.4	14 47.2	2 37.4	7 46.1
9 M	9 10 09	16 28 08	13♋18 51	20 30 26	12 57.8	29 12.4	3 00.4	15 46.8	8 10.3	4 35.3	16 48.6	14 44.8	2 35.9	7 45.8
10 Tu	9 14 06	17 25 41	27 40 03	4♌47 05	12R 58.0	29 38.3	2 35.3	16 19.3	8 37.2	4 38.2	16 50.7	14 42.4	2 34.3	7 45.5
11 W	9 18 03	18 23 16	11♌50 57	18 51 07	12 58.0	0♌11.1	2 08.3	16 52.1	9 04.1	4 41.0	16 52.7	14 40.1	2 32.8	7 45.2
12 Th	9 21 59	19 20 51	25 47 09	2♍38 38	12 57.7	0 50.6	1 39.4	17 25.0	9 31.0	4 43.5	16 54.6	14 37.7	2 31.2	7 45.0
13 F	9 25 56	20 18 28	9♍25 17	16 06 55	12 57.1	1 36.9	1 08.8	17 58.3	9 57.9	4 45.9	16 56.4	14 35.3	2 29.7	7 44.8
14 Sa	9 29 52	21 16 05	22 43 25	29 14 48	12 56.1	2 29.7	0 36.6	18 31.8	10 24.8	4 48.1	16 58.0	14 32.9	2 28.1	7 44.6
15 Su	9 33 49	22 13 44	5♎41 07	12♎02 36	12 55.0	3 29.0	0 03.1	19 05.5	10 51.7	4 50.1	16 59.6	14 30.5	2 26.6	7 44.5
16 M	9 37 45	23 11 24	18 19 28	24 32 05	12 53.8	4 34.6	29♌28.4	19 39.4	11 18.5	4 51.9	17 01.1	14 28.2	2 25.1	7 44.4
17 Tu	9 41 42	24 09 05	0♏40 50	6♏46 10	12 52.8	5 46.2	28 52.7	20 13.6	11 45.4	4 53.5	17 02.5	14 25.8	2 23.6	7 44.3
18 W	9 45 38	25 06 46	12 48 36	18 48 38	12D 52.3	7 03.5	28 16.3	20 48.0	12 12.3	4 54.9	17 03.8	14 23.5	2 22.2	7D 44.3
19 Th	9 49 35	26 04 29	24 46 52	0♐43 50	12 52.2	8 26.3	27 39.3	21 22.6	12 39.2	4 56.1	17 04.9	14 21.1	2 20.7	7 44.3
20 F	9 53 31	27 02 13	6♐40 09	12 36 24	12 52.8	9 54.3	27 02.1	21 57.5	13 06.0	4 57.1	17 06.0	14 18.8	2 19.3	7 44.3
21 Sa	9 57 28	27 59 59	18 33 08	24 30 57	12 53.8	11 27.0	26 24.7	22 32.5	13 32.9	4 57.9	17 07.0	14 16.5	2 17.8	7 44.4
22 Su	10 01 25	28 57 45	0♑30 22	6♑31 56	12 55.2	13 04.1	25 47.6	23 07.8	13 59.7	4 58.5	17 07.8	14 14.2	2 16.4	7 44.5
23 M	10 05 21	29 55 33	12 36 06	18 43 19	12 56.5	14 45.2	25 10.9	23 43.2	14 26.6	4 58.9	17 08.6	14 11.9	2 15.0	7 44.6
24 Tu	10 09 18	0♍53 21	24 53 58	1♒08 24	12R 57.5	16 29.8	24 34.9	24 18.9	14 53.4	4R 59.2	17 09.2	14 09.7	2 13.6	7 44.8
25 W	10 13 14	1 51 11	7♒26 53	13 49 36	12 57.9	18 17.4	23 59.7	24 54.7	15 20.2	4 59.2	17 09.7	14 07.4	2 12.3	7 45.0
26 Th	10 17 11	2 49 03	20 16 43	26 48 16	12 57.3	20 07.7	23 25.7	25 30.8	15 47.0	4 59.0	17 10.2	14 05.2	2 10.9	7 45.2
27 F	10 21 07	3 46 56	3♓24 14	10♓04 31	12 55.8	22 00.2	22 53.0	26 07.0	16 13.8	4 58.6	17 10.5	14 03.0	2 09.6	7 45.4
28 Sa	10 25 04	4 44 50	16 48 57	23 37 17	12 53.3	23 54.5	22 21.8	26 43.5	16 40.6	4 58.1	17 10.7	14 00.8	2 08.3	7 45.7
29 Su	10 29 00	5 42 46	0♈29 13	7♈24 25	12 50.2	25 50.1	21 52.3	27 20.1	17 07.4	4 57.3	17R 10.8	13 58.6	2 07.0	7 46.1
30 M	10 32 57	6 40 44	14 22 28	21 22 59	12 46.9	27 46.8	21 24.6	27 56.9	17 34.1	4 56.3	17 10.8	13 56.5	2 05.7	7 46.4
31 Tu	10 36 54	7 38 44	28 25 30	5♉29 38	12 43.9	29 44.1	20 58.9	28 33.8	18 00.9	4 55.1	17 10.7	13 54.3	2 04.4	7 46.8

Astro Data	Dy Hr Mn
☽0N	6 5:18
☿R	12 23:34
♄□♅	18 3:54
☽0S	18 23:56
♃□♆	21 15:52
♀R	30 1:41
☽0N	2 11:03
☿D	6 3:26
☽0S	15 8:46
♇D	19 1:46
♃R	25 2:37
☽0N	29 16:54
♄R	30 1:23

Planet Ingress		Dy Hr Mn
♂	♏	5 3:59
♀	♍	12 15:18
⚳	♌	22 5:40
☉	♌	23 6:44
☿	♋R	31 18:44
☿	♌	11 4:25
♀	♌R	15 14:12
☉	♍	23 13:51
☿	♍	31 15:15

Last Aspect Dy Hr Mn		☽ Ingress	Dy Hr Mn
3 3:21	♂ △	♓	3 4:34
4 7:25	♄ ⚹	♈	5 11:21
7 10:06	♀ △	♉	7 15:22
9 14:09	♀ □	♊	9 17:00
11 16:37	♀ ⚹	♋	11 17:27
13 2:24	☉ ☌	♌	13 18:26
14 20:55	♅ ☍	♍	15 21:39
17 18:28	☉ ⚹	♎	18 4:19
20 9:00	☉ □	♏	20 14:30
23 2:27	☉ △	♐	23 2:48
24 9:51	♅ ⚹	♑	25 15:08
26 23:05	♄ △	♒	28 1:54
29 8:56	♄ □	♓	30 10:27

Last Aspect Dy Hr Mn		☽ Ingress	Dy Hr Mn
1 16:03	☿ △	♈	1 16:47
3 19:12	☿ □	♉	3 21:09
5 21:35	☿ ⚹	♊	5 23:57
7 0:43	♅ △	♋	8 1:52
10 3:01	☿ ☌	♌	10 3:55
11 11:09	☉ ☌	♍	12 7:21
13 15:30	♂ ⚹	♎	14 13:24
16 21:12	♀ ⚹	♏	16 22:40
19 6:06	♀ □	♐	19 10:31
21 19:36	☉ △	♑	21 22:59
23 22:12	♂ ⚹	♒	24 9:49
26 9:31	♂ □	♓	26 17:50
28 17:41	♂ △	♈	28 23:09
31 0:39	☿ △	♉	31 2:41

☽ Phases & Eclipses Dy Hr Mn	
6 11:57	☾ 13♈59
13 2:24	● 20♋17
20 9:00	☽ 27♎14
28 11:25	○ 4♒58
28 11:34	☍ P 0.396
4 17:27	☾ 11♉54
11 11:09	● 18♌21
11 11:03:05	● T 02'23"
19 1:47	☽ 25♏40
26 23:48	○ 3♓17

Astro Data

1 July 1999
Julian Day # 36341
SVP 5♓16'12"
GC 26♐49.9 ⚴ 4♊51.5
Eris 19♈40.7 ⚵ 27♏18.0R
⚷ 28♏12.5R ⚶ 3♍20.5
☽ Mean ☊ 14♌47.0

1 August 1999
Julian Day # 36372
SVP 5♓16'08"
GC 26♐50.0 ⚴ 20♊55.1
Eris 19♈40.6R ⚵ 26♏23.9
⚷ 27♏36.0 ⚶ 17♍12.9
☽ Mean ☊ 13♌08.5

LONGITUDE — September 1999

Day	Sid.Time	☉	0 hr ☽	Noon ☽	True ☊	☿	♀	♂	⚳	♃	♄	♅	♆	♇
1 W	10 40 50	8♍36 45	12♉34 56	19♉41 02	12♌41.7	1♍41.7	20♌35.3	29♏11.0	18♌27.6	4♉53.8	17♉10.5	13♒52.2	2♒03.2	7♐47.2
2 Th	10 44 47	9 34 49	26 47 33	3♊54 08	12D 40.6	3 39.5	20R 13.9	29 48.3	18 54.4	4R 52.2	17R 10.2	13R 50.1	2R 02.0	7 47.7
3 F	10 48 43	10 32 55	11♊00 31	18 06 24	12 40.7	5 37.1	19 54.8	0♐25.8	19 21.1	4 50.4	17 09.8	13 48.1	2 00.8	7 48.2
4 Sa	10 52 40	11 31 02	25 11 31	2♋15 40	12 41.7	7 34.4	19 38.0	1 03.5	19 47.8	4 48.4	17 09.3	13 46.0	1 59.6	7 48.7
5 Su	10 56 36	12 29 12	9♋18 37	16 20 08	12 43.2	9 31.1	19 23.6	1 41.4	20 14.5	4 46.3	17 08.7	13 44.0	1 58.5	7 49.3
6 M	11 00 33	13 27 24	23 20 01	0♌18 02	12R 44.5	11 27.2	19 11.6	2 19.4	20 41.1	4 43.9	17 07.9	13 42.0	1 57.4	7 49.9
7 Tu	11 04 29	14 25 37	7♌13 57	14 07 30	12 45.0	13 22.5	19 02.0	2 57.6	21 07.8	4 41.3	17 07.1	13 40.1	1 56.3	7 50.5
8 W	11 08 26	15 23 52	20 58 29	27 46 35	12 44.1	15 17.0	18 54.8	3 36.0	21 34.4	4 38.6	17 06.1	13 38.1	1 55.2	7 51.2
9 Th	11 12 23	16 22 10	4♍31 36	11♍13 17	12 41.5	17 10.5	18 50.0	4 14.5	22 01.0	4 35.6	17 05.1	13 36.2	1 54.1	7 51.9
10 F	11 16 19	17 20 29	17 51 24	24 25 47	12 37.3	19 03.1	18D 47.6	4 53.2	22 27.6	4 32.5	17 03.9	13 34.4	1 53.1	7 52.6
11 Sa	11 20 16	18 18 49	0♎56 18	7♎22 51	12 31.8	20 54.6	18 47.5	5 32.0	22 54.2	4 29.1	17 02.6	13 32.5	1 52.1	7 53.3
12 Su	11 24 12	19 17 12	13 45 26	20 04 03	12 25.4	22 45.1	18 49.8	6 11.0	23 20.7	4 25.6	17 01.3	13 30.7	1 51.1	7 54.1
13 M	11 28 09	20 15 36	26 18 50	2♏29 58	12 18.9	24 34.4	18 54.4	6 50.2	23 47.2	4 21.9	16 59.8	13 28.9	1 50.2	7 55.0
14 Tu	11 32 05	21 14 02	8♏37 40	14 42 15	12 13.1	26 22.7	19 01.2	7 29.5	24 13.7	4 18.0	16 58.2	13 27.2	1 49.2	7 55.8
15 W	11 36 02	22 12 29	20 44 07	26 43 40	12 08.5	28 10.0	19 10.2	8 09.0	24 40.2	4 13.9	16 56.5	13 25.5	1 48.4	7 56.7
16 Th	11 39 58	23 10 58	2♐41 24	8♐37 50	12 05.5	29 56.1	19 21.3	8 48.6	25 06.6	4 09.6	16 54.8	13 23.8	1 47.5	7 57.6
17 F	11 43 55	24 09 29	14 33 32	20 29 06	12D 04.2	1♎41.2	19 34.5	9 28.4	25 33.0	4 05.2	16 52.9	13 22.2	1 46.6	7 58.6
18 Sa	11 47 52	25 08 02	26 25 09	2♑22 20	12 04.4	3 25.2	19 49.8	10 08.3	25 59.4	4 00.5	16 50.9	13 20.6	1 45.8	7 59.6
19 Su	11 51 48	26 06 36	8♑21 15	14 22 34	12 05.6	5 08.1	20 07.0	10 48.3	26 25.7	3 55.8	16 48.8	13 19.0	1 45.0	8 00.6
20 M	11 55 45	27 05 12	20 26 53	26 34 49	12 07.0	6 50.0	20 26.1	11 28.5	26 52.0	3 50.8	16 46.6	13 17.5	1 44.3	8 01.6
21 Tu	11 59 41	28 03 49	2♒46 53	9♒03 37	12R 07.9	8 30.9	20 47.1	12 08.8	27 18.3	3 45.7	16 44.4	13 16.0	1 43.5	8 02.7
22 W	12 03 38	29 02 29	15 25 27	21 52 43	12 07.5	10 10.8	21 09.9	12 49.2	27 44.6	3 40.4	16 42.0	13 14.6	1 42.8	8 03.8
23 Th	12 07 34	0♎01 10	28 25 42	5♓04 30	12 05.2	11 49.7	21 34.4	13 29.8	28 10.8	3 34.9	16 39.6	13 13.2	1 42.2	8 04.9
24 F	12 11 31	0 59 53	11♓49 09	18 39 32	12 00.7	13 27.6	22 00.6	14 10.5	28 37.0	3 29.3	16 37.0	13 11.8	1 41.5	8 06.1
25 Sa	12 15 27	1 58 37	25 35 23	2♈36 18	11 54.3	15 04.6	22 28.5	14 51.3	29 03.1	3 23.6	16 34.4	13 10.5	1 40.9	8 07.3
26 Su	12 19 24	2 57 24	9♈41 45	16 51 04	11 46.4	16 40.6	22 57.9	15 32.3	29 29.2	3 17.6	16 31.6	13 09.2	1 40.3	8 08.5
27 M	12 23 20	3 56 13	24 03 30	1♉18 15	11 38.1	18 15.7	23 28.9	16 13.3	29 55.3	3 11.6	16 28.8	13 08.0	1 39.8	8 09.7
28 Tu	12 27 17	4 55 04	8♉34 28	15 51 19	11 30.3	19 50.0	24 01.3	16 54.5	0♍21.3	3 05.4	16 25.9	13 06.8	1 39.3	8 11.0
29 W	12 31 14	5 53 57	23 07 59	0♊23 43	11 24.0	21 23.3	24 35.1	17 35.8	0 47.3	2 59.0	16 22.9	13 05.6	1 38.8	8 12.3
30 Th	12 35 10	6 52 52	7♊37 53	14 49 56	11 19.7	22 55.7	25 10.3	18 17.3	1 13.3	2 52.6	16 19.8	13 04.5	1 38.3	8 13.7

LONGITUDE — October 1999

Day	Sid.Time	☉	0 hr ☽	Noon ☽	True ☊	☿	♀	♂	⚳	♃	♄	♅	♆	♇
1 F	12 39 07	7♎51 50	21♊59 26	29♊06 04	11♌17.7	24♎27.3	25♌46.9	18♐58.8	1♍39.2	2♉46.0	16♉16.6	13♒03.4	1♒37.9	8♐15.0
2 Sa	12 43 03	8 50 51	6♋09 37	13♋09 58	11D 17.4	25 58.0	26 24.7	19 40.5	2 05.1	2R 39.2	16R 13.4	13R 02.4	1R 37.5	8 16.4
3 Su	12 47 00	9 49 53	20 07 04	27 00 57	11 18.1	27 27.8	27 03.7	20 22.3	2 30.9	2 32.4	16 10.0	13 01.4	1 37.1	8 17.9
4 M	12 50 56	10 48 58	3♌51 38	10♌39 15	11R 18.6	28 56.8	27 43.9	21 04.2	2 56.7	2 25.4	16 06.6	13 00.5	1 36.8	8 19.3
5 Tu	12 54 53	11 48 05	17 23 50	24 05 31	11 17.9	0♏24.8	28 25.2	21 46.2	3 22.4	2 18.3	16 03.1	12 59.6	1 36.5	8 20.8
6 W	12 58 49	12 47 15	0♍44 20	7♍20 20	11 15.0	1 52.0	29 07.6	22 28.3	3 48.1	2 11.1	15 59.5	12 58.7	1 36.2	8 22.3
7 Th	13 02 46	13 46 26	13 53 33	20 23 59	11 09.4	3 18.3	29 51.1	23 10.6	4 13.8	2 03.8	15 55.9	12 57.9	1 36.0	8 23.8
8 F	13 06 43	14 45 40	26 51 37	3♎16 24	11 01.0	4 43.7	0♍35.6	23 52.9	4 39.4	1 56.4	15 52.2	12 57.2	1 35.8	8 25.4
9 Sa	13 10 39	15 44 56	9♎38 18	15 57 18	10 50.4	6 08.2	1 21.0	24 35.4	5 04.9	1 48.9	15 48.4	12 56.5	1 35.6	8 27.0
10 Su	13 14 36	16 44 14	22 13 21	28 26 28	10 38.3	7 31.7	2 07.3	25 18.0	5 30.4	1 41.4	15 44.5	12 55.8	1 35.5	8 28.6
11 M	13 18 32	17 43 34	4♏36 41	10♏44 06	10 25.9	8 54.2	2 54.6	26 00.6	5 55.8	1 33.7	15 40.6	12 55.2	1 35.4	8 30.2
12 Tu	13 22 29	18 42 55	16 48 50	22 51 03	10 14.1	10 15.7	3 42.7	26 43.4	6 21.2	1 26.0	15 36.6	12 54.6	1 35.3	8 31.9
13 W	13 26 25	19 42 19	28 51 02	4♐49 03	10 04.1	11 36.1	4 31.7	27 26.3	6 46.5	1 18.2	15 32.5	12 54.1	1D 35.3	8 33.5
14 Th	13 30 22	20 41 45	10♐45 28	16 40 43	9 56.5	12 55.3	5 21.4	28 09.3	7 11.8	1 10.3	15 28.4	12 53.7	1 35.3	8 35.3
15 F	13 34 18	21 41 12	22 35 16	28 29 38	9 51.5	14 13.4	6 11.9	28 52.3	7 37.0	1 02.4	15 24.2	12 53.3	1 35.3	8 37.0
16 Sa	13 38 15	22 40 42	4♑24 24	10♑20 11	9 49.0	15 30.2	7 03.2	29 35.5	8 02.1	0 54.5	15 20.0	12 52.9	1 35.4	8 38.7
17 Su	13 42 12	23 40 13	16 17 38	22 17 23	9D 48.3	16 45.6	7 55.2	0♑18.8	8 27.2	0 46.5	15 15.7	12 52.6	1 35.5	8 40.5
18 M	13 46 08	24 39 46	28 20 09	4♒26 36	9R 48.4	17 59.5	8 47.9	1 02.1	8 52.2	0 38.4	15 11.4	12 52.3	1 35.6	8 42.3
19 Tu	13 50 05	25 39 20	10♒37 25	16 53 13	9 48.3	19 11.9	9 41.3	1 45.6	9 17.1	0 30.4	15 07.0	12 52.1	1 35.7	8 44.1
20 W	13 54 01	26 38 56	23 14 39	29 42 12	9 46.9	20 22.5	10 35.3	2 29.1	9 42.0	0 22.3	15 02.6	12 51.9	1 35.9	8 46.0
21 Th	13 57 58	27 38 34	6♓16 19	12♓57 20	9 43.2	21 31.2	11 29.9	3 12.7	10 06.8	0 14.2	14 58.1	12 51.8	1 36.2	8 47.8
22 F	14 01 54	28 38 14	19 45 26	26 40 38	9 36.8	22 37.9	12 25.2	3 56.4	10 31.5	0 06.0	14 53.6	12D 51.8	1 36.4	8 49.7
23 Sa	14 05 51	29 37 56	3♈42 44	10♈51 25	9 27.9	23 42.4	13 21.1	4 40.2	10 56.2	29♈57.9	14 49.0	12 51.8	1 36.7	8 51.6
24 Su	14 09 47	0♏37 39	18 06 04	25 25 55	9 17.0	24 44.4	14 17.5	5 24.1	11 20.8	29 49.8	14 44.4	12 51.8	1 37.1	8 53.6
25 M	14 13 44	1 37 25	2♉50 03	10♉17 22	9 05.4	25 43.6	15 14.5	6 08.0	11 45.3	29 41.6	14 39.8	12 51.9	1 37.4	8 55.5
26 Tu	14 17 41	2 37 12	17 46 41	25 16 47	8 54.3	26 39.8	16 12.0	6 52.0	12 09.7	29 33.5	14 35.1	12 52.0	1 37.8	8 57.5
27 W	14 21 37	3 37 02	2♊46 26	10♊14 32	8 44.9	27 32.7	17 10.1	7 36.1	12 34.1	29 25.4	14 30.4	12 52.2	1 38.3	8 59.4
28 Th	14 25 34	4 36 54	17 40 02	25 02 04	8 38.2	28 21.9	18 08.7	8 20.3	12 58.3	29 17.4	14 25.7	12 52.5	1 38.8	9 01.4
29 F	14 29 30	5 36 48	2♋19 57	9♋33 09	8 34.3	29 06.9	19 07.8	9 04.6	13 22.5	29 09.3	14 20.9	12 52.7	1 39.3	9 03.5
30 Sa	14 33 27	6 36 44	16 41 20	23 44 21	8 32.7	29 47.4	20 07.3	9 48.9	13 46.7	29 01.3	14 16.2	12 53.1	1 39.8	9 05.5
31 Su	14 37 23	7 36 42	0♌42 09	7♌34 49	8 32.4	0♐22.8	21 07.3	10 33.3	14 10.7	28 53.4	14 11.4	12 53.5	1 40.4	9 07.6

Astro Data

	Dy Hr Mn
♀ D	11 0:23
☽ 0S	11 17:14
☿ 0S	17 19:26
☉ 0S	23 11:32
☽ 0N	26 0:40
☽ 0S	9 0:49
♃□♆	11 6:47
♆ D	14 1:36
♅ D	23 6:12
☽ 0N	23 10:50

Planet Ingress

	Dy Hr Mn
♂ ♐	2 19:29
☿ ♎	16 12:53
☉ ♎	23 11:31
⚳ ♍	27 16:21
☿ ♏	5 5:12
♀ ♍	7 16:51
♂ ♑	17 1:35
♃ ♈R	23 5:48
☉ ♏	23 20:52
☿ ♐	30 20:08

Last Aspect / ☽ Ingress

Last Aspect Dy Hr Mn		☽ Ingress	Dy Hr Mn
2 4:46	♂ ☍	♊	2 5:25
3 15:00	♀ ⚹	♋	4 8:09
5 13:23	♄ ⚹	♌	6 11:29
7 20:30	♀ ☌	♍	8 15:57
10 0:33	☿ ☌	♎	10 22:16
12 9:38	♀ ⚹	♏	13 7:08
15 15:24	☿ ⚹	♐	15 18:35
17 20:06	☉ □	♑	18 7:13
20 13:04	☉ △	♒	20 18:38
22 10:38	♀ ☍	♓	23 2:51
24 8:27	♄ ⚹	♈	25 7:34
26 22:33	♀ △	♉	27 9:51
29 2:00	♀ □	♊	29 11:21

Last Aspect / ☽ Ingress

Last Aspect Dy Hr Mn		☽ Ingress	Dy Hr Mn
1 6:08	♀ ⚹	♋	1 13:31
3 12:53	☿ □	♌	3 17:13
5 20:14	♀ ☌	♍	5 22:40
7 17:27	♂ □	♎	8 5:52
10 5:33	♂ ⚹	♏	10 15:01
11 21:42	♄ ☍	♐	13 2:18
15 12:49	♂ ☌	♑	15 15:04
17 15:00	☉ □	♒	18 3:17
20 5:53	☉ △	♓	20 12:33
22 4:24	☿ △	♈	22 17:42
24 19:05	♃ ☌	♉	24 19:25
26 14:21	☿ ☍	♊	26 19:33
28 18:55	♃ ⚹	♋	28 20:09
30 21:00	♃ □	♌	30 22:47

☽ Phases & Eclipses

Dy Hr Mn	
2 22:17	☾ 10♊00
9 22:02	● 16♍47
17 20:06	☽ 24♐29
25 10:51	○ 1♈56
2 4:02	☾ 8♋31
9 11:34	● 15♎44
17 15:00	☽ 23♑48
24 21:02	○ 1♉00
31 12:04	☾ 7♌37

Astro Data

1 September 1999
Julian Day # 36403
SVP 5♓16'04"
GC 26♐50.1 ⚴ 7♋12.3
Eris 19♈31.0R ⚵ 0♐12.2
⚷ 28♏33.6 ⚶ 2♎13.7
☽ Mean ☊ 11♌30.0

1 October 1999
Julian Day # 36433
SVP 5♓16'02"
GC 26♐50.1 ⚴ 22♋25.7
Eris 19♈15.2R ⚵ 7♐06.0
⚷ 0♐49.9 ⚶ 17♎29.5
☽ Mean ☊ 9♌54.7

November 1999 LONGITUDE

Day	Sid.Time	☉	0 hr ☽	Noon☽	True☊	☿	♀	♂	⚳	♃	♄	♅	♆	♇
1 M	14 41 20	8♏36 43	14♌22 32	21♌05 34	8♌32.2	0♐52.5	22♍07.8	11♑17.8	14♍34.6	28♈45.5	14♉06.6	12♒53.9	1♒41.0	9♐09.6
2 Tu	14 45 16	9 36 46	27 44 12	4♍18 43	8R30.8	1 16.1	23 08.6	12 02.3	14 58.5	28R37.6	14R01.8	12 54.4	1 41.6	9 11.7
3 W	14 49 13	10 36 51	10♍49 27	17 16 41	8 27.0	1 32.8	24 09.9	12 46.9	15 22.2	28 29.8	13 56.9	12 55.0	1 42.3	9 13.8
4 Th	14 53 10	11 36 58	23 40 42	0♎01 45	8 20.2	1R41.9	25 11.6	13 31.6	15 45.9	28 22.1	13 52.1	12 55.6	1 43.0	9 15.9
5 F	14 57 06	12 37 06	6♎20 02	12 35 44	8 10.4	1 43.0	26 13.7	14 16.4	16 09.5	28 14.4	13 47.2	12 56.2	1 43.7	9 18.1
6 Sa	15 01 03	13 37 17	18 49 00	24 59 57	7 57.9	1 35.2	27 16.2	15 01.2	16 32.9	28 06.8	13 42.4	12 56.9	1 44.5	9 20.2
7 Su	15 04 59	14 37 30	1♏08 40	7♏15 16	7 43.8	1 18.2	28 19.0	15 46.1	16 56.3	27 59.3	13 37.5	12 57.7	1 45.3	9 22.4
8 M	15 08 56	15 37 45	13 19 48	19 22 24	7 29.2	0 51.5	29 22.2	16 31.1	17 19.6	27 51.9	13 32.7	12 58.5	1 46.1	9 24.5
9 Tu	15 12 52	16 38 01	25 23 09	1♐22 11	7 15.3	0 14.8	0♎25.7	17 16.1	17 42.7	27 44.6	13 27.8	12 59.3	1 47.0	9 26.7
10 W	15 16 49	17 38 19	7♐19 40	13 15 48	7 03.2	29♏28.3	1 29.5	18 01.2	18 05.8	27 37.4	13 23.0	13 00.2	1 47.9	9 28.9
11 Th	15 20 45	18 38 39	19 10 51	25 05 07	6 53.6	28 32.4	2 33.7	18 46.3	18 28.7	27 30.4	13 18.2	13 01.2	1 48.8	9 31.1
12 F	15 24 42	19 39 00	0♑58 55	6♑52 42	6 47.1	27 28.0	3 38.1	19 31.5	18 51.6	27 23.4	13 13.4	13 02.2	1 49.8	9 33.4
13 Sa	15 28 39	20 39 23	12 46 53	18 41 59	6 43.4	26 16.5	4 42.9	20 16.8	19 14.3	27 16.5	13 08.6	13 03.3	1 50.7	9 35.6
14 Su	15 32 35	21 39 47	24 38 34	0♒37 13	6D42.0	24 59.6	5 47.9	21 02.1	19 36.9	27 09.8	13 03.8	13 04.4	1 51.8	9 37.8
15 M	15 36 32	22 40 13	6♒38 34	12 43 17	6R42.0	23 39.5	6 53.3	21 47.5	19 59.3	27 03.2	12 59.0	13 05.5	1 52.8	9 40.1
16 Tu	15 40 28	23 40 40	18 52 01	25 05 28	6 42.1	22 18.9	7 58.9	22 32.9	20 21.7	26 56.7	12 54.3	13 06.7	1 53.9	9 42.4
17 W	15 44 25	24 41 08	1♓24 16	7♓49 04	6 41.4	21 00.3	9 04.7	23 18.4	20 43.9	26 50.4	12 49.6	13 08.0	1 55.0	9 44.6
18 Th	15 48 21	25 41 38	14 20 25	20 58 48	6 38.7	19 46.4	10 10.8	24 03.9	21 06.0	26 44.2	12 44.9	13 09.3	1 56.2	9 46.9
19 F	15 52 18	26 42 08	27 44 36	4♈38 02	6 33.6	18 39.5	11 17.2	24 49.5	21 28.0	26 38.2	12 40.3	13 10.6	1 57.4	9 49.2
20 Sa	15 56 14	27 42 40	11♈39 09	18 47 47	6 26.1	17 41.6	12 23.9	25 35.1	21 49.8	26 32.3	12 35.7	13 12.0	1 58.6	9 51.5
21 Su	16 00 11	28 43 14	26 03 34	3♉25 53	6 16.6	16 53.9	13 30.7	26 20.8	22 11.5	26 26.6	12 31.1	13 13.5	1 59.8	9 53.8
22 M	16 04 07	29 43 48	10♉53 54	18 26 32	6 06.2	16 17.6	14 37.8	27 06.5	22 33.1	26 21.0	12 26.6	13 15.0	2 01.1	9 56.1
23 Tu	16 08 04	0♐44 25	26 02 33	3♊40 37	5 56.1	15 52.8	15 45.2	27 52.2	22 54.6	26 15.6	12 22.1	13 16.5	2 02.4	9 58.4
24 W	16 12 01	1 45 02	11♊19 18	18 57 11	5 47.6	15D39.7	16 52.7	28 38.0	23 15.9	26 10.3	12 17.7	13 18.1	2 03.7	10 00.7
25 Th	16 15 57	2 45 41	26 32 55	4♋05 17	5 41.4	15 37.9	18 00.5	29 23.8	23 37.0	26 05.3	12 13.3	13 19.7	2 05.0	10 03.0
26 F	16 19 54	3 46 22	11♋33 15	18 55 58	5 38.0	15 46.8	19 08.5	0♒09.7	23 58.0	26 00.4	12 09.0	13 21.4	2 06.4	10 05.4
27 Sa	16 23 50	4 47 04	26 12 49	3♌23 23	5D36.8	16 05.5	20 16.7	0 55.6	24 18.9	25 55.6	12 04.7	13 23.1	2 07.8	10 07.7
28 Su	16 27 47	5 47 48	10♌27 27	17 24 58	5 37.2	16 33.3	21 25.1	1 41.5	24 39.6	25 51.1	12 00.5	13 24.9	2 09.3	10 10.0
29 M	16 31 43	6 48 33	24 16 04	1♍00 59	5R37.9	17 09.2	22 33.7	2 27.5	25 00.1	25 46.7	11 56.3	13 26.7	2 10.7	10 12.4
30 Tu	16 35 40	7 49 20	7♍40 01	14 13 33	5 37.8	17 52.4	23 42.4	3 13.5	25 20.5	25 42.5	11 52.2	13 28.6	2 12.2	10 14.7

December 1999 LONGITUDE

Day	Sid.Time	☉	0 hr ☽	Noon☽	True☊	☿	♀	♂	⚳	♃	♄	♅	♆	♇
1 W	16 39 37	8♐50 09	20♍42 01	27♍05 52	5♌36.0	18♏42.0	24♎51.4	3♒59.5	25♍40.8	25♈38.5	11♉48.1	13♒30.5	2♒13.7	10♐17.0
2 Th	16 43 33	9 50 58	3♎25 32	9♎41 27	5R31.8	19 37.3	26 00.5	4 45.6	26 00.8	25R34.7	11R44.1	13 32.4	2 15.2	10 19.4
3 F	16 47 30	10 51 50	15 54 02	22 03 40	5 25.2	20 37.5	27 09.8	5 31.7	26 20.7	25 31.1	11 40.2	13 34.4	2 16.8	10 21.7
4 Sa	16 51 26	11 52 42	28 10 42	4♏15 28	5 16.5	21 42.0	28 19.3	6 17.9	26 40.4	25 27.7	11 36.4	13 36.4	2 18.4	10 24.0
5 Su	16 55 23	12 53 36	10♏18 14	16 19 17	5 06.3	22 50.2	29 28.9	7 04.0	27 00.0	25 24.4	11 32.6	13 38.5	2 20.0	10 26.4
6 M	16 59 19	13 54 31	22 18 48	28 17 02	4 55.6	24 01.7	0♏38.7	7 50.3	27 19.3	25 21.4	11 28.9	13 40.6	2 21.7	10 28.7
7 Tu	17 03 16	14 55 27	4♐14 09	10♐10 20	4 45.4	25 15.9	1 48.6	8 36.5	27 38.5	25 18.6	11 25.2	13 42.8	2 23.3	10 31.1
8 W	17 07 12	15 56 24	16 05 47	22 00 40	4 36.7	26 32.6	2 58.7	9 22.8	27 57.5	25 15.9	11 21.7	13 45.0	2 25.0	10 33.4
9 Th	17 11 09	16 57 23	27 55 12	3♑49 37	4 29.9	27 51.3	4 08.9	10 09.1	28 16.3	25 13.5	11 18.2	13 47.2	2 26.7	10 35.7
10 F	17 15 06	17 58 22	9♑44 09	15 39 05	4 25.5	29 11.8	5 19.3	10 55.4	28 34.9	25 11.3	11 14.8	13 49.5	2 28.5	10 38.1
11 Sa	17 19 02	18 59 21	21 34 46	27 31 32	4D23.4	0♐33.8	6 29.7	11 41.7	28 53.3	25 09.3	11 11.5	13 51.8	2 30.2	10 40.4
12 Su	17 22 59	20 00 22	3♒29 47	9♒29 57	4 23.3	1 57.2	7 40.3	12 28.1	29 11.5	25 07.5	11 08.3	13 54.2	2 32.0	10 42.7
13 M	17 26 55	21 01 23	15 32 33	21 38 03	4 24.4	3 21.7	8 51.0	13 14.5	29 29.5	25 05.9	11 05.1	13 56.6	2 33.8	10 45.0
14 Tu	17 30 52	22 02 25	27 47 01	4♓00 01	4 26.0	4 47.2	10 01.9	14 00.9	29 47.3	25 04.5	11 02.1	13 59.0	2 35.6	10 47.3
15 W	17 34 48	23 03 27	10♓17 36	16 40 19	4R27.1	6 13.6	11 12.8	14 47.3	0♎04.9	25 03.3	10 59.1	14 01.5	2 37.5	10 49.6
16 Th	17 38 45	24 04 29	23 08 45	29 43 21	4 27.2	7 40.7	12 23.9	15 33.7	0 22.2	25 02.4	10 56.2	14 04.0	2 39.3	10 51.9
17 F	17 42 41	25 05 32	6♈24 35	13♈12 45	4 25.6	9 08.4	13 35.0	16 20.2	0 39.4	25 01.6	10 53.5	14 06.5	2 41.2	10 54.2
18 Sa	17 46 38	26 06 35	20 08 04	27 10 37	4 22.3	10 36.8	14 46.3	17 06.6	0 56.3	25 01.1	10 50.8	14 09.1	2 43.1	10 56.5
19 Su	17 50 35	27 07 39	4♉20 15	11♉36 40	4 17.6	12 05.6	15 57.7	17 53.1	1 12.9	25 00.7	10 48.2	14 11.7	2 45.1	10 58.7
20 M	17 54 31	28 08 43	18 59 19	26 27 29	4 12.0	13 34.9	17 09.2	18 39.6	1 29.4	25D00.6	10 45.7	14 14.4	2 47.0	11 01.0
21 Tu	17 58 28	29 09 47	4♊00 47	11♊36 20	4 06.6	15 04.7	18 20.7	19 26.1	1 45.6	25 00.7	10 43.3	14 17.0	2 49.0	11 03.3
22 W	18 02 24	0♑10 52	19 14 39	26 53 46	4 01.9	16 34.8	19 32.4	20 12.6	2 01.6	25 01.0	10 41.0	14 19.8	2 50.9	11 05.5
23 Th	18 06 21	1 11 57	4♋32 20	12♋08 59	3 58.7	18 05.2	20 44.2	20 59.1	2 17.3	25 01.5	10 38.8	14 22.5	2 52.9	11 07.7
24 F	18 10 17	2 13 03	19 42 31	27 11 46	3D57.2	19 36.0	21 56.0	21 45.6	2 32.8	25 02.2	10 36.7	14 25.3	2 55.0	11 10.0
25 Sa	18 14 14	3 14 10	4♌35 50	11♌53 57	3 57.2	21 07.2	23 08.0	22 32.1	2 48.0	25 03.1	10 34.7	14 28.1	2 57.0	11 12.2
26 Su	18 18 10	4 15 16	19 05 36	26 10 26	3 58.4	22 38.6	24 20.0	23 18.6	3 03.0	25 04.2	10 32.9	14 30.9	2 59.0	11 14.4
27 M	18 22 07	5 16 24	3♍08 18	9♍59 12	4 00.0	24 10.3	25 32.1	24 05.1	3 17.7	25 05.5	10 31.1	14 33.8	3 01.1	11 16.6
28 Tu	18 26 04	6 17 32	16 43 18	23 20 52	4 01.4	25 42.3	26 44.4	24 51.7	3 32.2	25 07.0	10 29.4	14 36.7	3 03.2	11 18.7
29 W	18 30 00	7 18 40	29 52 15	6♎17 54	4R02.1	27 14.6	27 56.6	25 38.2	3 46.3	25 08.8	10 27.8	14 39.6	3 05.2	11 20.9
30 Th	18 33 57	8 19 49	12♎38 18	18 53 57	4 01.6	28 47.2	29 09.0	26 24.7	4 00.2	25 10.7	10 26.4	14 42.6	3 07.3	11 23.0
31 F	18 37 53	9 20 58	25 05 22	1♏13 04	3 59.8	0♑20.1	0♐21.4	27 11.3	4 13.8	25 12.8	10 25.0	14 45.5	3 09.5	11 25.2

Astro Data	Planet Ingress	Last Aspect	☽ Ingress	Last Aspect	☽ Ingress	☽ Phases & Eclipses
Dy Hr Mn	Dy Hr Mn	Dy Hr Mn	Dy Hr Mn	Dy Hr Mn	Dy Hr Mn	Dy Hr Mn
☿R 5 2:58	♀ ♎ 9 2:19	2 1:43 ♃ △	♍ 2 4:07	30 19:11 ☿ ⚹	♎ 1 17:29	8 3:53 ● 15♏17
☽0S 5 7:33	☿ ♏R 9 20:13	4 2:03 ♀ ☌	♎ 4 11:57	3 23:03 ♀ ☌	♏ 4 3:35	16 9:03 ☽ 23♒33
♀0S 11 19:37	☉ ♐ 22 18:25	6 18:01 ♃ ☍	♏ 6 21:46	6 2:29 ☿ ☌	♐ 6 15:27	23 7:04 ○ 0♊32
♄□♅ 14 9:36	♂ ♒ 26 6:56	8 5:57 ♂ ⚹	♐ 9 9:15	8 18:35 ♃ △	♑ 9 4:14	29 23:19 ☾ 7♍17
☽0N 19 22:09		11 16:53 ♃ △	♑ 11 22:00	11 7:14 ♃ □	♒ 11 16:59	
☿D 25 3:53	♀ ♏ 5 22:41	14 5:08 ♃ □	♒ 14 10:46	13 18:46 ♃ ⚹	♓ 14 4:18	7 22:32 ● 15♐22
	☿ ♐ 11 2:09	16 15:31 ♃ ⚹	♓ 16 21:21	16 0:50 ☉ □	♈ 16 12:30	16 0:50 ☽ 23♓36
☽0S 2 14:05	⚳ ♎ 15 5:19	18 21:04 ☉ △	♈ 19 3:57	18 10:03 ☉ △	♉ 18 16:45	22 17:31 ○ 0♋25
♃Q♇ 5 3:29	☉ ♑ 22 7:44	21 0:42 ♃ ☌	♉ 21 6:26	19 22:47 ♂ □	♊ 20 17:39	29 14:04 ☾ 7♎24
☽0N 17 8:16	♀ ♐ 31 4:54	23 2:24 ♂ △	♊ 23 6:13	22 9:03 ♃ ⚹	♋ 22 16:52	
♄⚻♇ 17 8:29	☿ ♑ 31 6:48	24 23:20 ♃ ⚹	♋ 25 5:29	24 8:31 ♃ □	♌ 24 16:32	
♃D 20 14:48		26 23:36 ♃ □	♌ 27 6:19	26 10:07 ♃ △	♍ 26 18:34	
☽0S 29 21:21		29 2:43 ♃ △	♍ 29 10:11	28 18:51 ♀ ⚹	♎ 29 0:14	
				31 3:34 ♂ △	♏ 31 9:36	

Astro Data

1 November 1999
Julian Day # 36464
SVP 5♓15'58"
GC 26♐50.2 ⚴ 6♌03.5
Eris 18♈56.9R ⚵ 16♐22.7
⚷ 4♐09.8 ⚶ 3♏44.3
☽ Mean ☊ 8♌16.2

1 December 1999
Julian Day # 36494
SVP 5♓15'54"
GC 26♐50.3 ⚴ 14♌28.9
Eris 18♈42.4R ⚵ 26♐39.0
⚷ 7♐51.4 ⚶ 19♏39.2
☽ Mean ☊ 6♌40.8

LONGITUDE — January 2000

Day	Sid.Time	☉	0 hr ☽	Noon ☽	True ☊	☿	♀	♂	⚳	♃	♄	♅	♆	♇
1 Sa	18 41 50	10♑22 08	7♏17 36	13♏19 26	3♌57.0	1♑53.4	1♐33.9	27♒57.8	4♎27.2	25♈15.2	10♉23.7	14♒48.6	3♒11.6	11♐27.3
2 Su	18 45 46	11 23 18	19 19 02	25 16 51	3R53.4	3 26.9	2 46.5	28 44.3	4 40.2	25 17.7	10R22.6	14 51.6	3 13.7	11 29.4
3 M	18 49 43	12 24 29	1♐13 19	7♐08 47	3 49.5	5 00.8	3 59.2	29 30.9	4 52.9	25 20.5	10 21.6	14 54.6	3 15.9	11 31.5
4 Tu	18 53 39	13 25 39	13 03 37	18 58 09	3 45.8	6 35.0	5 11.9	0♓17.4	5 05.4	25 23.4	10 20.6	14 57.7	3 18.0	11 33.5
5 W	18 57 36	14 26 50	24 52 40	0♑47 26	3 42.7	8 09.5	6 24.6	1 04.0	5 17.5	25 26.6	10 19.8	15 00.8	3 20.2	11 35.6
6 Th	19 01 33	15 28 01	6♑42 43	12 38 45	3 40.5	9 44.4	7 37.5	1 50.5	5 29.3	25 29.9	10 19.1	15 04.0	3 22.4	11 37.6
7 F	19 05 29	16 29 11	18 35 46	24 34 00	3D39.2	11 19.7	8 50.3	2 37.0	5 40.8	25 33.5	10 18.6	15 07.1	3 24.6	11 39.7
8 Sa	19 09 26	17 30 22	0♒33 40	6♒35 01	3 39.0	12 55.4	10 03.3	3 23.6	5 52.0	25 37.2	10 18.1	15 10.3	3 26.8	11 41.7
9 Su	19 13 22	18 31 32	12 38 18	18 43 46	3 39.6	14 31.5	11 16.2	4 10.1	6 02.8	25 41.1	10 17.7	15 13.5	3 29.0	11 43.6
10 M	19 17 19	19 32 42	24 51 43	1♓02 26	3 40.7	16 08.0	12 29.3	4 56.6	6 13.3	25 45.3	10 17.5	15 16.7	3 31.2	11 45.6
11 Tu	19 21 15	20 33 51	7♓16 15	13 33 29	3 42.0	17 44.9	13 42.3	5 43.1	6 23.5	25 49.6	10D17.3	15 20.0	3 33.5	11 47.5
12 W	19 25 12	21 35 00	19 54 29	26 19 36	3 43.1	19 22.3	14 55.4	6 29.6	6 33.3	25 54.1	10 17.3	15 23.2	3 35.7	11 49.4
13 Th	19 29 08	22 36 08	2♈49 11	9♈23 34	3 43.9	21 00.1	16 08.6	7 16.1	6 42.8	25 58.8	10 17.4	15 26.5	3 37.9	11 51.3
14 F	19 33 05	23 37 15	16 03 03	22 47 53	3R44.2	22 38.4	17 21.8	8 02.5	6 51.9	26 03.6	10 17.6	15 29.8	3 40.2	11 53.2
15 Sa	19 37 02	24 38 22	29 38 17	6♉34 20	3 44.0	24 17.2	18 35.0	8 49.0	7 00.7	26 08.7	10 17.9	15 33.1	3 42.4	11 55.1
16 Su	19 40 58	25 39 28	13♉36 03	20 43 21	3 43.4	25 56.5	19 48.3	9 35.4	7 09.1	26 13.9	10 18.4	15 36.4	3 44.7	11 56.9
17 M	19 44 55	26 40 34	27 55 57	5♊13 29	3 42.6	27 36.3	21 01.6	10 21.8	7 17.2	26 19.4	10 18.9	15 39.7	3 47.0	11 58.7
18 Tu	19 48 51	27 41 38	12♊35 25	20 01 01	3 41.9	29 16.7	22 15.0	11 08.2	7 24.9	26 24.9	10 19.5	15 43.1	3 49.2	12 00.5
19 W	19 52 48	28 42 42	27 29 28	4♋59 49	3 41.3	0♒57.5	23 28.4	11 54.6	7 32.2	26 30.7	10 20.3	15 46.5	3 51.5	12 02.3
20 Th	19 56 44	29 43 46	12♋31 02	20 02 00	3D41.0	2 38.8	24 41.8	12 41.0	7 39.1	26 36.7	10 21.2	15 49.8	3 53.8	12 04.0
21 F	20 00 41	0♒44 48	27 31 38	4♌58 51	3 40.9	4 20.7	25 55.3	13 27.3	7 45.7	26 42.8	10 22.2	15 53.2	3 56.1	12 05.7
22 Sa	20 04 38	1 45 50	12♌22 37	19 42 03	3 41.0	6 03.0	27 08.8	14 13.6	7 51.9	26 49.1	10 23.3	15 56.6	3 58.3	12 07.4
23 Su	20 08 34	2 46 51	26 56 22	4♍04 56	3R41.1	7 45.9	28 22.3	14 59.9	7 57.7	26 55.5	10 24.5	16 00.1	4 00.6	12 09.1
24 M	20 12 31	3 47 52	11♍07 18	18 03 09	3 41.1	9 29.2	29 35.9	15 46.2	8 03.0	27 02.1	10 25.8	16 03.5	4 02.9	12 10.7
25 Tu	20 16 27	4 48 52	24 52 22	1♎34 56	3 41.0	11 12.9	0♑49.5	16 32.4	8 08.0	27 08.9	10 27.3	16 06.9	4 05.2	12 12.4
26 W	20 20 24	5 49 52	8♎11 00	14 40 49	3 40.9	12 57.0	2 03.1	17 18.7	8 12.6	27 15.8	10 28.8	16 10.4	4 07.4	12 13.9
27 Th	20 24 20	6 50 50	21 04 45	27 23 13	3D40.7	14 41.4	3 16.8	18 04.9	8 16.8	27 22.9	10 30.4	16 13.8	4 09.7	12 15.5
28 F	20 28 17	7 51 49	3♏36 43	9♏45 46	3 40.7	16 26.1	4 30.4	18 51.1	8 20.6	27 30.2	10 32.2	16 17.3	4 12.0	12 17.0
29 Sa	20 32 13	8 52 47	15 50 58	21 52 53	3 40.8	18 10.9	5 44.2	19 37.2	8 23.9	27 37.6	10 34.1	16 20.7	4 14.3	12 18.6
30 Su	20 36 10	9 53 44	27 52 05	3♐49 11	3 41.3	19 55.8	6 57.9	20 23.4	8 26.8	27 45.2	10 36.0	16 24.2	4 16.5	12 20.0
31 M	20 40 06	10 54 40	9♐44 44	15 39 18	3 42.0	21 40.5	8 11.7	21 09.5	8 29.3	27 52.9	10 38.1	16 27.7	4 18.8	12 21.5

LONGITUDE — February 2000

Day	Sid.Time	☉	0 hr ☽	Noon ☽	True ☊	☿	♀	♂	⚳	♃	♄	♅	♆	♇
1 Tu	20 44 03	11♒55 36	21♐33 24	27♐27 31	3♌42.9	23♒25.1	9♑25.5	21♓55.6	8♎31.4	28♈00.8	10♉40.3	16♒31.2	4♒21.1	12♐22.9
2 W	20 48 00	12 56 31	3♑22 08	9♑17 41	3 43.8	25 09.1	10 39.3	22 41.7	8 33.0	28 08.8	10 42.6	16 34.7	4 23.3	12 24.3
3 Th	20 51 56	13 57 25	15 14 31	21 13 02	3 44.5	26 52.5	11 53.2	23 27.7	8 34.2	28 17.0	10 45.0	16 38.1	4 25.6	12 25.7
4 F	20 55 53	14 58 18	27 13 31	3♒16 15	3R44.8	28 35.0	13 07.0	24 13.7	8 35.0	28 25.3	10 47.5	16 41.6	4 27.9	12 27.0
5 Sa	20 59 49	15 59 09	9♒21 28	15 29 22	3 44.5	0♓16.2	14 20.9	24 59.7	8R35.3	28 33.8	10 50.2	16 45.1	4 30.1	12 28.3
6 Su	21 03 46	17 00 00	21 40 07	27 53 51	3 43.5	1 55.7	15 34.8	25 45.7	8 35.2	28 42.4	10 52.9	16 48.6	4 32.3	12 29.6
7 M	21 07 42	18 00 49	4♓10 41	10♓30 42	3 41.8	3 33.2	16 48.7	26 31.6	8 34.7	28 51.1	10 55.7	16 52.1	4 34.6	12 30.9
8 Tu	21 11 39	19 01 37	16 53 59	23 20 36	3 39.7	5 08.2	18 02.6	27 17.5	8 33.7	29 00.0	10 58.6	16 55.6	4 36.8	12 32.1
9 W	21 15 35	20 02 24	29 50 35	6♈23 59	3 37.2	6 40.2	19 16.6	28 03.4	8 32.3	29 09.0	11 01.6	16 59.1	4 39.0	12 33.3
10 Th	21 19 32	21 03 09	13♈00 50	19 41 10	3 35.0	8 08.5	20 30.5	28 49.3	8 30.4	29 18.2	11 04.8	17 02.6	4 41.2	12 34.4
11 F	21 23 29	22 03 52	26 25 02	3♉12 26	3 33.2	9 32.6	21 44.5	29 35.1	8 28.1	29 27.5	11 08.0	17 06.0	4 43.4	12 35.6
12 Sa	21 27 25	23 04 34	10♉03 22	16 57 50	3D32.3	10 51.8	22 58.4	0♈20.8	8 25.4	29 36.9	11 11.3	17 09.5	4 45.6	12 36.7
13 Su	21 31 22	24 05 15	23 55 46	0♊57 07	3 32.4	12 05.4	24 12.4	1 06.6	8 22.2	29 46.4	11 14.7	17 13.0	4 47.8	12 37.7
14 M	21 35 18	25 05 53	8♊01 44	15 09 25	3 33.2	13 12.7	25 26.4	1 52.3	8 18.6	29 56.1	11 18.3	17 16.5	4 50.0	12 38.7
15 Tu	21 39 15	26 06 30	22 19 55	29 32 55	3 34.6	14 12.9	26 40.4	2 38.0	8 14.5	0♉05.9	11 21.9	17 19.9	4 52.2	12 39.8
16 W	21 43 11	27 07 05	6♋47 59	14♋04 36	3 36.0	15 05.3	27 54.4	3 23.6	8 10.0	0 15.8	11 25.6	17 23.4	4 54.3	12 40.7
17 Th	21 47 08	28 07 39	21 22 13	28 40 11	3R36.9	15 49.3	29 08.4	4 09.2	8 05.1	0 25.8	11 29.4	17 26.8	4 56.4	12 41.7
18 F	21 51 04	29 08 11	5♌57 46	13♌14 14	3 36.7	16 24.3	0♒22.5	4 54.7	7 59.8	0 35.9	11 33.3	17 30.3	4 58.6	12 42.6
19 Sa	21 55 01	0♓08 41	20 28 48	27 40 44	3 35.1	16 49.7	1 36.5	5 40.3	7 54.1	0 46.2	11 37.3	17 33.7	5 00.7	12 43.4
20 Su	21 58 58	1 09 10	4♍49 17	11♍53 47	3 32.1	17 05.3	2 50.5	6 25.7	7 47.9	0 56.6	11 41.3	17 37.1	5 02.8	12 44.3
21 M	22 02 54	2 09 37	18 53 40	25 48 27	3 28.0	17R10.7	4 04.6	7 11.2	7 41.3	1 07.0	11 45.5	17 40.5	5 04.9	12 45.1
22 Tu	22 06 51	3 10 02	2♎37 45	9♎21 20	3 23.2	17 06.0	5 18.7	7 56.6	7 34.4	1 17.6	11 49.8	17 43.9	5 06.9	12 45.8
23 W	22 10 47	4 10 26	15 59 06	22 31 04	3 18.3	16 51.2	6 32.7	8 41.9	7 27.0	1 28.3	11 54.1	17 47.3	5 09.0	12 46.6
24 Th	22 14 44	5 10 49	28 57 20	5♏18 10	3 14.1	16 26.8	7 46.8	9 27.3	7 19.2	1 39.1	11 58.5	17 50.7	5 11.0	12 47.3
25 F	22 18 40	6 11 10	11♏33 54	17 44 57	3 10.9	15 53.5	9 00.9	10 12.5	7 11.0	1 50.0	12 03.0	17 54.1	5 13.1	12 47.9
26 Sa	22 22 37	7 11 30	23 51 49	29 55 02	3D09.2	15 12.0	10 15.0	10 57.8	7 02.5	2 01.0	12 07.6	17 57.4	5 15.1	12 48.6
27 Su	22 26 33	8 11 48	5♐55 11	11♐52 54	3 09.0	14 23.4	11 29.1	11 43.0	6 53.6	2 12.1	12 12.3	18 00.8	5 17.1	12 49.2
28 M	22 30 30	9 12 05	17 48 49	23 43 34	3 10.0	13 29.1	12 43.3	12 28.2	6 44.3	2 23.3	12 17.1	18 04.1	5 19.1	12 49.7
29 Tu	22 34 27	10 12 21	29 37 49	5♑32 10	3 11.6	12 30.4	13 57.4	13 13.3	6 34.7	2 34.6	12 21.9	18 07.4	5 21.0	12 50.3

Astro Data (Dy Hr Mn)	Planet Ingress (Dy Hr Mn)	Last Aspect (Dy Hr Mn)	☽ Ingress (Dy Hr Mn)	Last Aspect (Dy Hr Mn)	☽ Ingress (Dy Hr Mn)	☽ Phases & Eclipses (Dy Hr Mn)	Astro Data
♄ D 12 4:59	♂ ♓ 4 3:01	2 19:28 ♂ □	♐ 2 21:32	1 13:08 ♃ △	♑ 1 17:10	6 18:14 ● 15♑44	1 January 2000
☽ 0N 13 15:37	☿ ♒ 18 22:20	5 1:06 ♃ △	♑ 5 10:24	4 2:16 ♃ □	♒ 4 5:31	14 13:34 ☽ 23♈41	Julian Day # 36525
♃□♇ 26 3:36	☉ ♒ 20 18:23	7 14:00 ♃ □	♒ 7 22:53	6 13:34 ♃ ✶	♓ 6 16:02	21 4:40 ○ 0♌26	SVP 5♓15'49"
☽ 0S 26 5:57	♀ ♑ 24 19:52	10 1:41 ♃ ✶	♓ 10 9:59	8 19:46 ♂ ☌	♈ 9 0:17	21 4:43 • T 1.325	GC 26♐50.4 ⚴ 14♌02.6R
		12 2:23 ☉ ✶	♈ 12 18:48	11 5:19 ♃ ☌	♉ 11 6:21	28 7:57 ☾ 7♏42	Eris 18♈35.5R ⚵ 7♑59.8
⚳ R 5 18:11	☿ ♓ 5 8:09	14 17:47 ♃ ☌	♉ 15 0:38	12 23:22 ♀ △	♊ 13 10:23		⚷ 11♐37.0 ⚶ 5♐58.3
☽ 0N 9 20:59	♂ ♈ 12 1:04	16 21:50 ☿ △	♊ 17 3:25	15 5:51 ☉ △	♋ 15 12:45	5 13:03 ● 16♒02	☽ Mean ☊ 5♌02.4
♂ 0N 13 14:03	♃ ♉ 14 21:40	18 22:21 ♃ ✶	♋ 19 4:01	17 12:51 ♀ ☍	♌ 17 14:11	5 12:49:22 • P 0.580	
☿ R 21 12:47	♀ ♒ 18 4:43	20 22:36 ♃ □	♌ 21 3:58	18 19:05 ♅ ☍	♍ 19 15:53	12 23:21 ☽ 23♉33	1 February 2000
☽ 0S 22 15:25	☉ ♓ 19 8:33	23 1:30 ♀ △	♍ 23 5:07	20 20:59 ☿ ☍	♎ 21 19:21	19 16:27 ○ 0♍20	Julian Day # 36556
		24 7:48 ♂ ☍	♎ 25 9:09	23 3:16 ♅ △	♏ 24 1:58	27 3:54 ☾ 7♐51	SVP 5♓15'44"
		27 11:59 ♃ ☍	♏ 27 17:01	25 12:18 ♅ □	♐ 26 12:10		GC 26♐50.4 ⚴ 4♌40.9R
		29 7:11 ♂ △	♐ 30 4:17	28 0:28 ♅ ✶	♑ 29 0:45		Eris 18♈39.0 ⚵ 19♑34.1
							⚷ 14♐45.3 ⚶ 21♐43.8
							☽ Mean ☊ 3♌23.9

March 2000 — LONGITUDE

Day	Sid.Time	☉	0 hr ☽	Noon ☽	True ☊	☿	♀	♂	⚳	♃	♄	♅	♆	♇
1 W	22 38 23	11♓12 35	11♑27 16	17♑23 41	3♌13.4	11♓28.8	15♒11.5	13♈58.4	6♎24.7	2♉46.0	12♉26.9	18♒10.7	5♒23.0	12♐50.8
2 Th	22 42 20	12 12 48	23 21 58	29 22 38	3R 14.4	10R 25.9	16 25.7	14 43.4	6R 14.4	2 57.5	12 31.9	18 13.9	5 24.9	12 51.2
3 F	22 46 16	13 12 58	5♒26 10	11♒32 57	3 14.1	9 23.2	17 39.8	15 28.5	6 03.7	3 09.1	12 37.0	18 17.2	5 26.8	12 51.7
4 Sa	22 50 13	14 13 07	17 43 19	23 57 33	3 12.0	8 22.1	18 54.0	16 13.4	5 52.8	3 20.8	12 42.1	18 20.4	5 28.7	12 52.1
5 Su	22 54 09	15 13 15	0♓15 51	6♓38 21	3 07.8	7 23.9	20 08.1	16 58.4	5 41.5	3 32.5	12 47.4	18 23.6	5 30.5	12 52.4
6 M	22 58 06	16 13 20	13 05 04	19 35 59	3 01.8	6 29.7	21 22.2	17 43.2	5 30.0	3 44.4	12 52.7	18 26.8	5 32.4	12 52.8
7 Tu	23 02 02	17 13 24	26 11 00	2♈49 55	2 54.4	5 40.3	22 36.4	18 28.1	5 18.2	3 56.3	12 58.1	18 30.0	5 34.2	12 53.0
8 W	23 05 59	18 13 26	9♈32 32	16 18 33	2 46.4	4 56.4	23 50.5	19 12.9	5 06.1	4 08.3	13 03.6	18 33.2	5 36.0	12 53.3
9 Th	23 09 56	19 13 25	23 07 40	29 59 33	2 38.8	4 18.7	25 04.7	19 57.7	4 53.9	4 20.4	13 09.1	18 36.3	5 37.8	12 53.5
10 F	23 13 52	20 13 23	6♉53 51	13♉50 17	2 32.4	3 47.3	26 18.8	20 42.4	4 41.3	4 32.6	13 14.7	18 39.4	5 39.6	12 53.7
11 Sa	23 17 49	21 13 18	20 48 30	27 48 14	2 27.9	3 22.4	27 33.0	21 27.0	4 28.6	4 44.9	13 20.4	18 42.5	5 41.3	12 53.9
12 Su	23 21 45	22 13 12	4♊49 14	11♊51 17	2D 25.5	3 04.2	28 47.1	22 11.7	4 15.7	4 57.2	13 26.1	18 45.5	5 43.0	12 54.0
13 M	23 25 42	23 13 03	18 54 12	25 57 48	2 25.1	2 52.5	0♓01.2	22 56.3	4 02.7	5 09.6	13 31.9	18 48.6	5 44.7	12 54.1
14 Tu	23 29 38	24 12 52	3♋01 57	10♋06 30	2 25.8	2D 47.1	1 15.4	23 40.8	3 49.4	5 22.1	13 37.8	18 51.6	5 46.4	12R 54.1
15 W	23 33 35	25 12 38	17 11 16	24 16 05	2R 26.8	2 48.0	2 29.5	24 25.3	3 36.1	5 34.6	13 43.8	18 54.6	5 48.0	12 54.1
16 Th	23 37 31	26 12 22	1♌20 44	8♌24 57	2 26.9	2 54.7	3 43.6	25 09.7	3 22.6	5 47.3	13 49.8	18 57.5	5 49.7	12 54.1
17 F	23 41 28	27 12 04	15 28 26	22 30 50	2 25.1	3 07.2	4 57.7	25 54.1	3 09.0	5 59.9	13 55.8	19 00.4	5 51.3	12 54.1
18 Sa	23 45 25	28 11 44	29 31 45	6♍30 46	2 20.9	3 25.0	6 11.8	26 38.4	2 55.3	6 12.7	14 01.9	19 03.3	5 52.8	12 54.0
19 Su	23 49 21	29 11 22	13♍27 25	20 21 14	2 14.2	3 47.8	7 25.9	27 22.7	2 41.6	6 25.5	14 08.1	19 06.2	5 54.4	12 53.8
20 M	23 53 18	0♈10 57	27 11 47	3♎58 39	2 05.3	4 15.5	8 40.1	28 07.0	2 27.8	6 38.4	14 14.4	19 09.1	5 55.9	12 53.7
21 Tu	23 57 14	1 10 31	10♎41 27	17 19 53	1 55.0	4 47.7	9 54.2	28 51.2	2 14.0	6 51.3	14 20.7	19 11.9	5 57.4	12 53.5
22 W	0 01 11	2 10 02	23 53 44	0♏22 53	1 44.4	5 24.2	11 08.3	29 35.3	2 00.2	7 04.3	14 27.0	19 14.7	5 58.9	12 53.3
23 Th	0 05 07	3 09 32	6♏47 17	13 07 00	1 34.5	6 04.7	12 22.4	0♉19.4	1 46.4	7 17.4	14 33.4	19 17.4	6 00.3	12 53.0
24 F	0 09 04	4 09 00	19 22 11	25 33 07	1 26.2	6 48.9	13 36.5	1 03.5	1 32.6	7 30.5	14 39.9	19 20.1	6 01.8	12 52.7
25 Sa	0 13 00	5 08 26	1♐40 08	7♐43 38	1 20.1	7 36.7	14 50.6	1 47.5	1 18.8	7 43.6	14 46.4	19 22.8	6 03.1	12 52.4
26 Su	0 16 57	6 07 51	13 44 08	19 42 09	1 16.4	8 27.8	16 04.7	2 31.5	1 05.1	7 56.9	14 53.0	19 25.5	6 04.5	12 52.1
27 M	0 20 53	7 07 13	25 38 19	1♑33 15	1D 14.9	9 22.1	17 18.8	3 15.4	0 51.5	8 10.1	14 59.6	19 28.1	6 05.9	12 51.7
28 Tu	0 24 50	8 06 34	7♑27 35	13 22 02	1 14.8	10 19.3	18 32.9	3 59.3	0 37.9	8 23.5	15 06.3	19 30.7	6 07.2	12 51.3
29 W	0 28 47	9 05 53	19 17 17	25 13 59	1R 15.3	11 19.3	19 47.0	4 43.1	0 24.5	8 36.8	15 13.0	19 33.3	6 08.5	12 50.8
30 Th	0 32 43	10 05 11	1♒12 50	7♒14 28	1 15.3	12 22.0	21 01.1	5 26.9	0 11.2	8 50.3	15 19.8	19 35.8	6 09.7	12 50.3
31 F	0 36 40	11 04 26	13 19 30	19 28 28	1 13.7	13 27.3	22 15.2	6 10.6	29♍58.0	9 03.7	15 26.6	19 38.3	6 10.9	12 49.8

April 2000 — LONGITUDE

Day	Sid.Time	☉	0 hr ☽	Noon ☽	True ☊	☿	♀	♂	⚳	♃	♄	♅	♆	♇
1 Sa	0 40 36	12♈03 40	25♒41 54	2♓00 11	1♌09.9	14♓34.9	23♓29.2	6♉54.3	29♍45.1	9♉17.3	15♉33.5	19♒40.7	6♒12.1	12♐49.3
2 Su	0 44 33	13 02 51	8♓23 40	14 52 34	1R 03.4	15 44.8	24 43.3	7 38.0	29R 32.2	9 30.8	15 40.4	19 43.1	6 13.3	12R 48.7
3 M	0 48 29	14 02 01	21 27 00	28 06 55	0 54.4	16 57.0	25 57.4	8 21.6	29 19.6	9 44.4	15 47.3	19 45.5	6 14.4	12 48.1
4 Tu	0 52 26	15 01 09	4♈52 11	11♈42 32	0 43.5	18 11.2	27 11.5	9 05.1	29 07.2	9 58.1	15 54.3	19 47.9	6 15.5	12 47.5
5 W	0 56 22	16 00 15	18 37 34	25 36 46	0 31.6	19 27.5	28 25.5	9 48.6	28 55.0	10 11.8	16 01.3	19 50.2	6 16.6	12 46.8
6 Th	1 00 19	16 59 19	2♉39 33	9♉45 14	0 20.1	20 45.8	29 39.6	10 32.1	28 43.1	10 25.5	16 08.4	19 52.4	6 17.7	12 46.1
7 F	1 04 16	17 58 20	16 53 08	24 02 33	0 10.2	22 06.0	0♈53.6	11 15.5	28 31.4	10 39.3	16 15.5	19 54.7	6 18.7	12 45.4
8 Sa	1 08 12	18 57 20	1♊12 48	8♊23 14	0 02.7	23 28.0	2 07.6	11 58.9	28 20.0	10 53.1	16 22.6	19 56.9	6 19.7	12 44.6
9 Su	1 12 09	19 56 17	15 33 20	22 42 35	29♋58.0	24 51.8	3 21.7	12 42.2	28 08.9	11 06.9	16 29.8	19 59.0	6 20.6	12 43.8
10 M	1 16 05	20 55 12	29 50 37	6♋57 08	29 55.9	26 17.4	4 35.7	13 25.5	27 58.1	11 20.8	16 37.0	20 01.1	6 21.6	12 43.0
11 Tu	1 20 02	21 54 05	14♋01 55	21 04 50	29 55.4	27 44.7	5 49.7	14 08.7	27 47.6	11 34.7	16 44.3	20 03.2	6 22.5	12 42.2
12 W	1 23 58	22 52 55	28 05 48	5♌04 46	29 55.4	29 13.8	7 03.7	14 51.8	27 37.4	11 48.6	16 51.6	20 05.2	6 23.3	12 41.3
13 Th	1 27 55	23 51 43	12♌01 43	18 56 38	29 54.5	0♈44.5	8 17.7	15 35.0	27 27.5	12 02.6	16 58.9	20 07.2	6 24.1	12 40.4
14 F	1 31 51	24 50 29	25 49 29	2♍40 14	29 51.6	2 16.9	9 31.7	16 18.0	27 18.0	12 16.5	17 06.2	20 09.2	6 24.9	12 39.5
15 Sa	1 35 48	25 49 12	9♍28 48	16 15 05	29 46.0	3 50.9	10 45.6	17 01.0	27 08.8	12 30.6	17 13.6	20 11.1	6 25.7	12 38.5
16 Su	1 39 45	26 47 54	22 58 57	29 40 13	29 37.4	5 26.6	11 59.6	17 44.0	27 00.0	12 44.6	17 21.0	20 12.9	6 26.4	12 37.6
17 M	1 43 41	27 46 33	6♎18 44	12♎54 17	29 26.3	7 03.9	13 13.5	18 26.9	26 51.6	12 58.6	17 28.4	20 14.7	6 27.1	12 36.6
18 Tu	1 47 38	28 45 10	19 26 40	25 55 44	29 13.5	8 42.9	14 27.5	19 09.8	26 43.5	13 12.7	17 35.8	20 16.5	6 27.8	12 35.5
19 W	1 51 34	29 43 45	2♏21 19	8♏43 19	29 00.2	10 23.5	15 41.4	19 52.6	26 35.8	13 26.8	17 43.3	20 18.2	6 28.5	12 34.5
20 Th	1 55 31	0♉42 18	15 01 41	21 16 25	28 47.5	12 05.8	16 55.4	20 35.4	26 28.4	13 40.9	17 50.8	20 19.9	6 29.1	12 33.4
21 F	1 59 27	1 40 50	27 27 36	3♐35 24	28 36.6	13 49.7	18 09.3	21 18.1	26 21.5	13 55.1	17 58.3	20 21.6	6 29.6	12 32.3
22 Sa	2 03 24	2 39 20	9♐40 01	15 41 45	28 28.2	15 35.3	19 23.2	22 00.8	26 14.9	14 09.2	18 05.8	20 23.2	6 30.2	12 31.2
23 Su	2 07 20	3 37 48	21 40 57	27 38 04	28 22.5	17 22.5	20 37.1	22 43.4	26 08.8	14 23.4	18 13.4	20 24.7	6 30.7	12 30.0
24 M	2 11 17	4 36 15	3♑33 35	9♑28 02	28 19.4	19 11.5	21 51.0	23 26.0	26 03.0	14 37.6	18 21.0	20 26.3	6 31.2	12 28.9
25 Tu	2 15 14	5 34 40	15 22 00	21 16 07	28D 18.3	21 02.1	23 04.9	24 08.5	25 57.6	14 51.8	18 28.6	20 27.7	6 31.6	12 27.7
26 W	2 19 10	6 33 03	27 11 02	3♒07 27	28R 18.2	22 54.4	24 18.8	24 51.0	25 52.7	15 06.0	18 36.2	20 29.1	6 32.0	12 26.5
27 Th	2 23 07	7 31 25	9♒06 02	15 07 29	28 18.1	24 48.4	25 32.7	25 33.4	25 48.1	15 20.3	18 43.8	20 30.5	6 32.4	12 25.2
28 F	2 27 03	8 29 45	21 12 29	27 21 41	28 16.8	26 44.1	26 46.6	26 15.8	25 44.0	15 34.5	18 51.4	20 31.8	6 32.8	12 24.0
29 Sa	2 31 00	9 28 03	3♓35 42	9♓55 04	28 13.5	28 41.4	28 00.5	26 58.2	25 40.3	15 48.8	18 59.1	20 33.1	6 33.1	12 22.7
30 Su	2 34 56	10 26 20	16 20 17	22 51 43	28 07.8	0♉40.4	29 14.4	27 40.5	25 37.0	16 03.0	19 06.8	20 34.4	6 33.3	12 21.4

Astro Data	Dy Hr Mn
♄⊼♇	6 12:14
☽0N	8 2:47
☿ D	14 20:40
♇ R	15 11:51
♃□♆	16 17:14
☉0N	20 7:35
☽0S	21 0:36
☽0N	4 10:46
♀0N	9 14:16
♃⊼♇	16 0:47
☿0N	16 18:11
☽0S	17 8:37

Planet Ingress		Dy Hr Mn
♀	♓	13 11:36
☉	♈	20 7:35
♂	♉	23 1:25
⚳	♍R	31 8:25
♀	♈	6 18:37
☊	♋R	9 0:11
☿	♈	13 0:17
☉	♉	19 18:40
☿	♉	30 3:53

Last Aspect Dy Hr Mn		☽ Ingress	Dy Hr Mn
1 4:38	♂ □	♒	2 13:14
4 1:12	♀ ☌	♓	4 23:30
6 5:17	☉ ☌	♈	7 6:54
9 2:34	♀ ⚹	♉	9 12:01
11 11:31	♀ □	♊	11 15:46
13 6:59	☉ □	♋	13 18:51
15 13:43	☉ △	♌	15 21:43
17 18:07	♂ △	♍	18 0:48
20 4:44	☉ ☍	♎	20 4:57
22 10:26	♂ ☍	♏	22 11:17
23 23:53	♅ □	♐	24 20:43
26 11:26	♅ ⚹	♑	27 8:51
28 23:43	♀ ⚹	♒	29 21:34

Last Aspect Dy Hr Mn		☽ Ingress	Dy Hr Mn
31 12:19	♅ ☌	♓	1 8:12
3 7:44	♀ ☌	♈	3 15:22
5 2:04	♅ ⚹	♉	5 19:29
7 8:24	☿ ⚹	♊	7 21:58
9 16:01	☿ □	♋	10 0:16
12 0:45	☿ △	♌	12 3:16
13 21:14	☉ △	♍	14 7:19
15 13:45	♄ △	♎	16 12:36
18 17:42	☉ ☍	♏	18 19:35
20 10:36	♂ ☍	♐	21 4:58
22 21:25	♅ ⚹	♑	23 16:47
25 18:12	♂ △	♒	26 5:42
28 10:44	♀ ⚹	♓	28 17:06

☽ Phases & Eclipses Dy Hr Mn	
6 5:17	● 15♓57
13 6:59	☽ 23♊01
20 4:44	○ 29♍53
28 0:21	☾ 7♑38
4 18:12	● 15♈16
11 13:30	☽ 21♋58
18 17:42	○ 28♎59
26 19:30	☾ 6♒51

Astro Data

1 March 2000
Julian Day # 36585
SVP 5♓15'41"
GC 26♐50.5 ⚳ 28♋42.3R
Eris 18♈51.0 ⚵ 0♒09.0
⚷ 16♐39.2 ⚶ 5♑26.4
☽ Mean ☊ 1♌51.7

1 April 2000
Julian Day # 36616
SVP 5♓15'38"
GC 26♐50.6 ⚳ 1♌06.6
Eris 19♈09.8 ⚵ 10♒38.6
⚷ 17♐13.2R ⚶ 18♑09.6
☽ Mean ☊ 0♌13.2

LONGITUDE — May 2000

Day	Sid.Time	☉	0 hr ☽	Noon ☽	True ☊	☿	♀	♂	⚳	♃	♄	♅	♆	♇
1 M	2 38 53	11♉24 36	29♓29 36	6♈14 04	27♋59.6	2♉41.0	0♉28.3	28♉22.8	25♍34.1	16♉17.3	19♉14.4	20♒35.5	6♒33.6	12♐20.1
2 Tu	2 42 49	12 22 49	13♈05 04	20 02 23	27R49.4	4 43.2	1 42.1	29 05.0	25R31.6	16 31.6	19 22.1	20 36.7	6 33.8	12R18.7
3 W	2 46 46	13 21 02	27 05 39	4♉14 18	27 38.3	6 46.9	2 56.0	29 47.2	25 29.6	16 45.9	19 29.8	20 37.8	6 34.0	12 17.4
4 Th	2 50 42	14 19 12	11♉27 38	18 44 49	27 27.4	8 52.0	4 09.9	0♊29.3	25 27.9	17 00.1	19 37.5	20 38.8	6 34.1	12 16.0
5 F	2 54 39	15 17 21	26 04 55	3♊26 56	27 17.8	10 58.4	5 23.7	1 11.4	25 26.7	17 14.4	19 45.2	20 39.8	6 34.2	12 14.6
6 Sa	2 58 36	16 15 29	10♊49 52	18 12 44	27 10.7	13 06.0	6 37.6	1 53.4	25 25.9	17 28.7	19 53.0	20 40.8	6 34.3	12 13.2
7 Su	3 02 32	17 13 34	25 34 38	2♋54 46	27 06.2	15 14.6	7 51.4	2 35.4	25D25.5	17 43.0	20 00.7	20 41.7	6 34.4	12 11.8
8 M	3 06 29	18 11 38	10♋12 26	17 27 06	27D04.2	17 24.1	9 05.2	3 17.4	25 25.6	17 57.3	20 08.4	20 42.5	6R34.4	12 10.4
9 Tu	3 10 25	19 09 39	24 38 19	1♌45 50	27 04.0	19 34.3	10 19.0	3 59.3	25 26.0	18 11.6	20 16.1	20 43.3	6 34.4	12 08.9
10 W	3 14 22	20 07 39	8♌49 27	15 49 07	27R04.4	21 44.8	11 32.9	4 41.1	25 26.9	18 25.9	20 23.9	20 44.1	6 34.3	12 07.5
11 Th	3 18 18	21 05 37	22 44 50	29 36 40	27 04.2	23 55.6	12 46.7	5 22.9	25 28.1	18 40.1	20 31.6	20 44.8	6 34.2	12 06.0
12 F	3 22 15	22 03 32	6♍24 43	13♍09 08	27 02.3	26 06.2	14 00.4	6 04.7	25 29.8	18 54.4	20 39.3	20 45.4	6 34.1	12 04.5
13 Sa	3 26 12	23 01 26	19 50 01	26 27 32	26 58.1	28 16.4	15 14.2	6 46.4	25 31.9	19 08.7	20 47.0	20 46.0	6 34.0	12 03.0
14 Su	3 30 08	23 59 19	3♎01 47	9♎32 53	26 51.4	0♊26.0	16 28.0	7 28.0	25 34.3	19 22.9	20 54.8	20 46.6	6 33.8	12 01.5
15 M	3 34 05	24 57 09	16 00 54	22 25 54	26 42.5	2 34.6	17 41.8	8 09.7	25 37.2	19 37.1	21 02.5	20 47.1	6 33.6	11 59.9
16 Tu	3 38 01	25 54 58	28 47 57	5♏07 05	26 32.1	4 42.0	18 55.5	8 51.2	25 40.4	19 51.4	21 10.2	20 47.5	6 33.3	11 58.4
17 W	3 41 58	26 52 46	11♏23 19	17 36 44	26 21.3	6 47.9	20 09.3	9 32.7	25 44.1	20 05.6	21 17.9	20 48.0	6 33.1	11 56.9
18 Th	3 45 54	27 50 32	23 47 21	29 55 17	26 11.0	8 52.0	21 23.0	10 14.2	25 48.1	20 19.8	21 25.6	20 48.3	6 32.8	11 55.3
19 F	3 49 51	28 48 16	6♐00 36	12♐03 29	26 02.1	10 54.2	22 36.8	10 55.7	25 52.4	20 34.0	21 33.3	20 48.6	6 32.4	11 53.7
20 Sa	3 53 47	29 46 00	18 04 06	24 02 41	25 55.3	12 54.3	23 50.5	11 37.1	25 57.2	20 48.2	21 41.0	20 48.9	6 32.1	11 52.2
21 Su	3 57 44	0♊43 42	29 59 30	5♑54 53	25 50.9	14 52.0	25 04.3	12 18.4	26 02.3	21 02.3	21 48.7	20 49.1	6 31.7	11 50.6
22 M	4 01 41	1 41 23	11♑49 13	17 42 55	25D48.7	16 47.2	26 18.0	12 59.7	26 07.8	21 16.5	21 56.3	20 49.3	6 31.2	11 49.0
23 Tu	4 05 37	2 39 03	23 36 27	29 30 21	25 48.4	18 39.8	27 31.8	13 41.0	26 13.7	21 30.6	22 04.0	20 49.4	6 30.8	11 47.4
24 W	4 09 34	3 36 42	5♒25 09	11♒21 28	25 49.3	20 29.7	28 45.5	14 22.2	26 19.8	21 44.7	22 11.6	20R49.5	6 30.3	11 45.8
25 Th	4 13 30	4 34 19	17 19 53	23 21 04	25 50.4	22 16.8	29 59.2	15 03.4	26 26.4	21 58.8	22 19.2	20 49.5	6 29.7	11 44.2
26 F	4 17 27	5 31 56	29 25 40	5♓34 18	25R51.0	24 01.1	1♊13.0	15 44.5	26 33.3	22 12.8	22 26.8	20 49.4	6 29.2	11 42.6
27 Sa	4 21 23	6 29 32	11♓47 37	18 06 13	25 50.2	25 42.5	2 26.7	16 25.6	26 40.5	22 26.9	22 34.4	20 49.4	6 28.6	11 41.0
28 Su	4 25 20	7 27 07	24 30 38	1♈01 22	25 47.7	27 20.9	3 40.4	17 06.7	26 48.1	22 40.9	22 42.0	20 49.2	6 28.0	11 39.3
29 M	4 29 16	8 24 41	7♈38 47	14 23 09	25 43.3	28 56.3	4 54.2	17 47.7	26 56.0	22 54.9	22 49.6	20 49.0	6 27.4	11 37.7
30 Tu	4 33 13	9 22 14	21 14 36	28 13 05	25 37.4	0♋28.7	6 07.9	18 28.7	27 04.2	23 08.9	22 57.1	20 48.8	6 26.7	11 36.1
31 W	4 37 09	10 19 46	5♉18 23	12♉30 07	25 30.6	1 58.1	7 21.6	19 09.6	27 12.8	23 22.8	23 04.6	20 48.5	6 26.0	11 34.5

LONGITUDE — June 2000

Day	Sid.Time	☉	0 hr ☽	Noon ☽	True ☊	☿	♀	♂	⚳	♃	♄	♅	♆	♇
1 Th	4 41 06	11♊17 18	19♉47 39	27♉10 14	25♋23.8	3♋24.3	8♊35.4	19♊50.5	27♍21.7	23♉36.7	23♉12.1	20♒48.2	6♒25.3	11♐32.8
2 F	4 45 03	12 14 49	4♊36 54	12♊06 38	25R17.9	4 47.4	9 49.1	20 31.4	27 30.9	23 50.6	23 19.6	20R47.8	6R24.5	11R31.2
3 Sa	4 48 59	13 12 18	19 38 15	27 10 35	25 13.5	6 07.4	11 02.8	21 12.2	27 40.4	24 04.5	23 27.0	20 47.4	6 23.7	11 29.6
4 Su	4 52 56	14 09 47	4♋42 28	12♋12 49	25D11.1	7 24.1	12 16.6	21 53.0	27 50.3	24 18.3	23 34.5	20 47.0	6 22.9	11 28.0
5 M	4 56 52	15 07 14	19 40 36	27 04 58	25 10.5	8 37.6	13 30.3	22 33.7	28 00.4	24 32.1	23 41.9	20 46.4	6 22.1	11 26.3
6 Tu	5 00 49	16 04 41	4♌25 12	11♌40 44	25 11.2	9 47.8	14 44.0	23 14.4	28 10.9	24 45.8	23 49.2	20 45.9	6 21.2	11 24.7
7 W	5 04 45	17 02 06	18 51 10	25 56 15	25 12.6	10 54.6	15 57.7	23 55.1	28 21.6	24 59.6	23 56.6	20 45.3	6 20.3	11 23.1
8 Th	5 08 42	17 59 30	2♍55 51	9♍49 59	25R13.7	11 57.9	17 11.5	24 35.7	28 32.6	25 13.2	24 03.9	20 44.6	6 19.4	11 21.5
9 F	5 12 39	18 56 52	16 38 44	23 22 16	25 13.8	12 57.8	18 25.2	25 16.3	28 43.9	25 26.9	24 11.2	20 43.9	6 18.4	11 19.9
10 Sa	5 16 35	19 54 14	0♎00 49	6♎34 37	25 12.6	13 54.0	19 38.9	25 56.8	28 55.5	25 40.5	24 18.4	20 43.2	6 17.5	11 18.3
11 Su	5 20 32	20 51 35	13 03 58	19 29 09	25 09.8	14 46.6	20 52.6	26 37.3	29 07.4	25 54.0	24 25.6	20 42.4	6 16.5	11 16.7
12 M	5 24 28	21 48 54	25 50 28	2♏08 13	25 05.7	15 35.4	22 06.3	27 17.8	29 19.5	26 07.5	24 32.8	20 41.5	6 15.4	11 15.1
13 Tu	5 28 25	22 46 13	8♏22 39	14 34 04	25 00.6	16 20.4	23 20.0	27 58.2	29 31.9	26 21.0	24 40.0	20 40.6	6 14.4	11 13.5
14 W	5 32 21	23 43 31	20 42 42	26 48 47	24 55.2	17 01.4	24 33.7	28 38.5	29 44.5	26 34.4	24 47.1	20 39.7	6 13.3	11 11.9
15 Th	5 36 18	24 40 48	2♐52 34	8♐54 15	24 50.1	17 38.4	25 47.4	29 18.9	29 57.4	26 47.8	24 54.2	20 38.7	6 12.2	11 10.3
16 F	5 40 14	25 38 05	14 54 04	20 52 15	24 45.8	18 11.2	27 01.1	29 59.2	0♎10.6	27 01.1	25 01.2	20 37.7	6 11.1	11 08.8
17 Sa	5 44 11	26 35 21	26 49 00	2♑44 36	24 42.7	18 39.7	28 14.8	0♋39.4	0 24.0	27 14.4	25 08.2	20 36.7	6 10.0	11 07.2
18 Su	5 48 08	27 32 36	8♑39 16	14 33 19	24D40.9	19 04.0	29 28.5	1 19.7	0 37.7	27 27.7	25 15.2	20 35.6	6 08.8	11 05.7
19 M	5 52 04	28 29 51	20 27 02	26 20 44	24 40.5	19 23.8	0♋42.2	1 59.8	0 51.5	27 40.9	25 22.1	20 34.4	6 07.6	11 04.2
20 Tu	5 56 01	29 27 06	2♒14 48	8♒09 38	24 41.2	19 39.1	1 56.0	2 40.0	1 05.7	27 54.0	25 29.0	20 33.3	6 06.4	11 02.6
21 W	5 59 57	0♋24 20	14 05 38	20 03 15	24 42.5	19 49.8	3 09.7	3 20.1	1 20.0	28 07.1	25 35.8	20 32.0	6 05.2	11 01.1
22 Th	6 03 54	1 21 34	26 02 59	2♓05 19	24 44.2	19R56.0	4 23.4	4 00.2	1 34.6	28 20.1	25 42.6	20 30.8	6 04.0	10 59.6
23 F	6 07 50	2 18 48	8♓10 48	14 19 57	24 45.6	19 57.7	5 37.1	4 40.2	1 49.4	28 33.1	25 49.4	20 29.5	6 02.7	10 58.1
24 Sa	6 11 47	3 16 02	20 33 19	26 51 26	24R46.5	19 54.7	6 50.8	5 20.3	2 04.4	28 46.0	25 56.1	20 28.1	6 01.4	10 56.6
25 Su	6 15 43	4 13 16	3♈14 48	9♈43 54	24 46.5	19 47.3	8 04.6	6 00.2	2 19.7	28 58.9	26 02.8	20 26.7	6 00.1	10 55.2
26 M	6 19 40	5 10 29	16 19 09	23 00 53	24 45.7	19 35.6	9 18.3	6 40.2	2 35.1	29 11.7	26 09.4	20 25.3	5 58.8	10 53.7
27 Tu	6 23 37	6 07 43	29 49 22	6♉44 41	24 44.1	19 19.6	10 32.0	7 20.1	2 50.8	29 24.4	26 15.9	20 23.8	5 57.4	10 52.3
28 W	6 27 33	7 04 57	13♉46 50	20 55 37	24 42.0	18 59.6	11 45.8	8 00.0	3 06.7	29 37.1	26 22.5	20 22.3	5 56.1	10 50.9
29 Th	6 31 30	8 02 11	28 10 42	5♊31 31	24 39.9	18 35.9	12 59.5	8 39.8	3 22.7	29 49.7	26 28.9	20 20.8	5 54.7	10 49.5
30 F	6 35 26	8 59 24	12♊57 22	20 27 21	24 38.0	18 08.9	14 13.3	9 19.6	3 39.0	0♊02.3	26 35.4	20 19.2	5 53.3	10 48.1

Astro Data

	Dy Hr Mn
☽0N	1 20:44
⚳D	7 21:51
♆R	8 12:30
♄□♅	13 8:34
☽0S	14 15:22
♃□♅	20 13:16
♅R	25 8:20
♃☌♄	28 16:04
☽0N	29 7:06
☽0S	10 21:37
☿R	23 8:32
☽0N	25 16:05

Planet Ingress

	Dy Hr Mn
♀ ♉	1 2:49
♂ ♊	3 19:18
☿ ♊	14 7:10
☉ ♊	20 17:49
♀ ♊	25 12:15
☿ ♋	30 4:27
⚳ ♎	15 16:42
♂ ♋	16 12:30
♀ ♋	18 22:15
☉ ♋	21 1:48
♃ ♊	30 7:35

Last Aspect / ☽ Ingress

Last Aspect Dy Hr Mn		☽ Ingress Dy Hr Mn
30 21:13 ♂ ✶	♈	1 0:55
2 12:59 ♅ ✶	♉	3 4:54
4 15:07 ♅ □	♊	5 6:23
6 16:01 ♅ △	♋	7 7:14
8 16:31 ♄ ✶	♌	9 9:01
11 0:11 ☿ □	♍	11 12:41
13 15:57 ♅ △	♎	13 18:27
15 8:55 ♅ △	♏	16 2:16
18 7:34 ☉ ☍	♐	18 12:09
20 5:30 ♅ ✶	♑	21 0:01
23 7:31 ♀ △	♒	23 13:00
25 9:56 ♄ □	♓	26 1:07
28 4:17 ☿ □	♈	28 10:08
29 23:15 ♅ ✶	♉	30 15:02

Last Aspect / ☽ Ingress

Last Aspect Dy Hr Mn		☽ Ingress Dy Hr Mn
1 6:08 ♃ ☌	♊	1 16:34
3 2:03 ♂ ☌	♋	3 16:30
5 7:48 ♃ ✶	♌	5 16:45
7 10:22 ♃ □	♍	7 18:57
9 15:48 ♃ △	♎	9 23:59
12 2:15 ♂ △	♏	12 7:55
14 11:31 ♃ ☍	♐	14 18:18
17 1:50 ♀ ☍	♑	17 6:26
19 14:46 ♃ △	♒	19 19:26
22 4:35 ♃ □	♓	22 7:52
24 15:40 ♃ ✶	♈	24 17:55
26 7:23 ♅ ✶	♉	27 0:19
29 2:34 ♃ ☌	♊	29 2:59

☽ Phases & Eclipses

Dy Hr Mn		
4 4:12	●	14♉00
10 20:01	☽	20♌27
18 7:34	○	27♏40
26 11:55	☾	5♓32
2 12:14	●	12♊15
9 3:29	☽	18♍37
16 22:27	○	26♐03
25 1:00	☾	3♈47

Astro Data

1 May 2000
Julian Day # 36646
SVP 5♓15'35"
GC 26♐50.6 ⚴ 9♌08.1
Eris 19♈29.3 ⚵ 19♒15.0
⚷ 16♐18.3R ⚶ 27♑15.5
☽ Mean ☊ 28♋37.9

1 June 2000
Julian Day # 36677
SVP 5♓15'31"
GC 26♐50.7 ⚴ 20♌20.1
Eris 19♈45.9 ⚵ 25♒20.3
⚷ 14♐20.2R ⚶ 1♒12.4
☽ Mean ☊ 26♋59.4

July 2000

LONGITUDE

Day	Sid.Time	☉	0 hr ☽	Noon ☽	True ☊	☿	♀	♂	⚳	♃	♄	♅	♆	♇
1 Sa	6 39 23	9♋56 38	28♊00 28	5♋35 35	24♋36.8	17♋38.8	15♋27.0	9♋59.4	3♎55.5	0♊14.8	26♉41.7	20♒17.6	5♒51.9	10♐46.7
2 Su	6 43 19	10 53 52	13♋11 30	20 46 59	24D 36.2	17R 06.2	16 40.8	10 39.2	4 12.2	0 27.2	26 48.0	20R 16.0	5R 50.5	10R 45.4
3 M	6 47 16	11 51 06	28 20 53	5♌52 05	24 36.4	16 31.5	17 54.6	11 18.9	4 29.0	0 39.6	26 54.3	20 14.3	5 49.0	10 44.0
4 Tu	6 51 12	12 48 19	13♌19 34	20 42 29	24 37.0	15 55.4	19 08.3	11 58.6	4 46.1	0 51.9	27 00.5	20 12.6	5 47.6	10 42.7
5 W	6 55 09	13 45 33	28 00 07	5♍11 56	24 37.9	15 18.4	20 22.1	12 38.2	5 03.3	1 04.1	27 06.6	20 10.8	5 46.1	10 41.4
6 Th	6 59 06	14 42 46	12♍17 35	19 16 50	24 38.8	14 41.1	21 35.8	13 17.9	5 20.7	1 16.2	27 12.7	20 09.0	5 44.6	10 40.2
7 F	7 03 02	15 39 58	26 09 39	2♎56 05	24 39.3	14 04.2	22 49.6	13 57.4	5 38.3	1 28.3	27 18.7	20 07.2	5 43.1	10 38.9
8 Sa	7 06 59	16 37 11	9♎36 18	16 10 36	24R 39.5	13 28.3	24 03.4	14 37.0	5 56.1	1 40.3	27 24.7	20 05.4	5 41.6	10 37.7
9 Su	7 10 55	17 34 23	22 39 17	29 02 45	24 39.4	12 54.0	25 17.1	15 16.5	6 14.0	1 52.2	27 30.6	20 03.5	5 40.1	10 36.4
10 M	7 14 52	18 31 35	5♏21 26	11♏35 45	24 38.9	12 22.1	26 30.9	15 56.0	6 32.1	2 04.0	27 36.4	20 01.6	5 38.6	10 35.2
11 Tu	7 18 48	19 28 47	17 46 11	23 53 10	24 38.3	11 52.9	27 44.7	16 35.4	6 50.4	2 15.8	27 42.2	19 59.7	5 37.0	10 34.1
12 W	7 22 45	20 26 00	29 57 09	5♐58 33	24 37.8	11 27.1	28 58.4	17 14.8	7 08.8	2 27.4	27 47.9	19 57.7	5 35.5	10 32.9
13 Th	7 26 41	21 23 12	11♐57 48	17 55 17	24 37.3	11 05.1	0♌12.2	17 54.2	7 27.4	2 39.0	27 53.6	19 55.7	5 33.9	10 31.8
14 F	7 30 38	22 20 24	23 51 23	29 46 26	24 37.0	10 47.4	1 26.0	18 33.6	7 46.1	2 50.5	27 59.2	19 53.7	5 32.4	10 30.7
15 Sa	7 34 35	23 17 37	5♑40 47	11♑34 45	24 36.9	10 34.3	2 39.7	19 12.9	8 05.0	3 01.9	28 04.7	19 51.7	5 30.8	10 29.6
16 Su	7 38 31	24 14 50	17 28 37	23 22 43	24 36.8	10 26.2	3 53.5	19 52.2	8 24.0	3 13.3	28 10.1	19 49.6	5 29.2	10 28.6
17 M	7 42 28	25 12 04	29 17 18	5♒12 39	24 36.8	10D 23.2	5 07.2	20 31.5	8 43.2	3 24.5	28 15.5	19 47.5	5 27.6	10 27.5
18 Tu	7 46 24	26 09 17	11♒09 05	17 06 51	24 36.8	10 25.6	6 21.0	21 10.7	9 02.5	3 35.7	28 20.8	19 45.4	5 26.0	10 26.5
19 W	7 50 21	27 06 32	23 06 15	29 07 37	24 36.6	10 33.6	7 34.8	21 49.9	9 21.9	3 46.7	28 26.0	19 43.3	5 24.4	10 25.5
20 Th	7 54 17	28 03 46	5♓11 14	11♓17 26	24 36.2	10 47.2	8 48.6	22 29.1	9 41.5	3 57.7	28 31.2	19 41.1	5 22.8	10 24.6
21 F	7 58 14	29 01 02	17 26 35	23 39 01	24 35.7	11 06.5	10 02.3	23 08.3	10 01.2	4 08.6	28 36.3	19 38.9	5 21.2	10 23.6
22 Sa	8 02 10	29 58 18	29 55 07	6♈15 13	24 35.2	11 31.6	11 16.1	23 47.4	10 21.1	4 19.4	28 41.3	19 36.7	5 19.6	10 22.7
23 Su	8 06 07	0♌55 35	12♈39 43	19 08 58	24D 34.8	12 02.5	12 29.9	24 26.5	10 41.1	4 30.0	28 46.3	19 34.5	5 18.0	10 21.8
24 M	8 10 04	1 52 53	25 43 16	2♉22 57	24 34.7	12 39.1	13 43.7	25 05.6	11 01.2	4 40.6	28 51.1	19 32.3	5 16.3	10 21.0
25 Tu	8 14 00	2 50 12	9♉08 14	15 59 19	24 34.9	13 21.5	14 57.4	25 44.6	11 21.5	4 51.1	28 55.9	19 30.0	5 14.7	10 20.2
26 W	8 17 57	3 47 32	22 56 17	29 59 08	24 35.4	14 09.5	16 11.2	26 23.6	11 41.9	5 01.5	29 00.6	19 27.8	5 13.1	10 19.4
27 Th	8 21 53	4 44 53	7♊07 42	14♊21 45	24 36.2	15 03.2	17 25.0	27 02.6	12 02.4	5 11.8	29 05.3	19 25.5	5 11.5	10 18.6
28 F	8 25 50	5 42 15	21 40 51	29 04 27	24 37.0	16 02.4	18 38.8	27 41.6	12 23.0	5 21.9	29 09.8	19 23.2	5 09.8	10 17.8
29 Sa	8 29 46	6 39 38	6♋31 49	14♋02 06	24R 37.6	17 07.1	19 52.6	28 20.6	12 43.7	5 32.0	29 14.3	19 20.9	5 08.2	10 17.1
30 Su	8 33 43	7 37 02	21 34 20	29 07 28	24 37.7	18 17.0	21 06.4	28 59.5	13 04.6	5 42.0	29 18.7	19 18.6	5 06.6	10 16.5
31 M	8 37 40	8 34 26	6♌40 21	14♌11 52	24 37.2	19 32.2	22 20.2	29 38.4	13 25.6	5 51.8	29 23.0	19 16.3	5 04.9	10 15.8

August 2000

LONGITUDE

Day	Sid.Time	☉	0 hr ☽	Noon ☽	True ☊	☿	♀	♂	⚳	♃	♄	♅	♆	♇
1 Tu	8 41 36	9♌31 52	21♌40 55	29♌06 27	24♋35.9	20♋52.4	23♌34.0	0♌17.3	13♎46.7	6♊01.5	29♉27.3	19♒13.9	5♒03.3	10♐15.2
2 W	8 45 33	10 29 18	6♍27 32	13♍43 23	24R 34.1	22 17.5	24 47.8	0 56.1	14 07.9	6 11.1	29 31.4	19R 11.6	5R 01.7	10R 14.6
3 Th	8 49 29	11 26 45	20 53 21	27 56 58	24 32.0	23 47.3	26 01.6	1 34.9	14 29.2	6 20.6	29 35.4	19 09.2	5 00.1	10 14.0
4 F	8 53 26	12 24 12	4♎53 56	11♎44 07	24 30.0	25 21.5	27 15.4	2 13.7	14 50.6	6 30.0	29 39.4	19 06.8	4 58.5	10 13.5
5 Sa	8 57 22	13 21 40	18 27 31	25 04 19	24 28.4	26 59.9	28 29.2	2 52.5	15 12.1	6 39.3	29 43.3	19 04.4	4 56.8	10 13.0
6 Su	9 01 19	14 19 09	1♏34 45	7♏59 14	24D 27.5	28 42.2	29 43.0	3 31.2	15 33.8	6 48.4	29 47.1	19 02.1	4 55.2	10 12.5
7 M	9 05 15	15 16 39	14 18 10	20 32 04	24 27.4	0♌28.1	0♍56.7	4 09.9	15 55.5	6 57.4	29 50.8	18 59.7	4 53.6	10 12.0
8 Tu	9 09 12	16 14 10	26 41 28	2♐46 58	24 28.2	2 17.3	2 10.5	4 48.6	16 17.3	7 06.3	29 54.4	18 57.3	4 52.0	10 11.6
9 W	9 13 08	17 11 41	8♐49 06	14 48 29	24 29.6	4 09.3	3 24.3	5 27.3	16 39.2	7 15.1	29 57.9	18 54.9	4 50.5	10 11.2
10 Th	9 17 05	18 09 13	20 45 39	26 41 11	24 31.3	6 03.9	4 38.0	6 05.9	17 01.3	7 23.7	0♊01.4	18 52.5	4 48.9	10 10.9
11 F	9 21 02	19 06 46	2♑35 35	8♑29 23	24 32.8	8 00.7	5 51.8	6 44.5	17 23.4	7 32.2	0 04.7	18 50.1	4 47.3	10 10.6
12 Sa	9 24 58	20 04 21	14 23 01	20 16 56	24R 33.6	9 59.1	7 05.6	7 23.1	17 45.6	7 40.6	0 07.9	18 47.7	4 45.8	10 10.3
13 Su	9 28 55	21 01 56	26 11 33	2♒07 13	24 33.5	11 59.0	8 19.3	8 01.7	18 07.9	7 48.8	0 11.1	18 45.3	4 44.2	10 10.0
14 M	9 32 51	21 59 32	8♒04 15	14 02 57	24 32.0	13 59.9	9 33.0	8 40.2	18 30.2	7 56.9	0 14.2	18 42.9	4 42.7	10 09.8
15 Tu	9 36 48	22 57 10	20 03 36	26 06 24	24 29.2	16 01.4	10 46.8	9 18.7	18 52.7	8 04.9	0 17.1	18 40.6	4 41.1	10 09.6
16 W	9 40 44	23 54 48	2♓11 34	8♓19 17	24 25.2	18 03.4	12 00.5	9 57.2	19 15.2	8 12.7	0 20.0	18 38.2	4 39.6	10 09.5
17 Th	9 44 41	24 52 28	14 29 42	20 42 59	24 20.4	20 05.4	13 14.2	10 35.7	19 37.9	8 20.4	0 22.7	18 35.8	4 38.1	10 09.3
18 F	9 48 37	25 50 10	26 59 15	3♈18 39	24 15.2	22 07.3	14 27.9	11 14.1	20 00.6	8 27.9	0 25.4	18 33.4	4 36.6	10 09.2
19 Sa	9 52 34	26 47 53	9♈41 18	16 07 20	24 10.3	24 08.7	15 41.6	11 52.6	20 23.4	8 35.4	0 28.0	18 31.1	4 35.1	10 09.2
20 Su	9 56 31	27 45 37	22 36 54	29 10 07	24 06.3	26 09.6	16 55.3	12 31.0	20 46.2	8 42.6	0 30.5	18 28.7	4 33.7	10D 09.1
21 M	10 00 27	28 43 23	5♉47 09	12♉28 07	24 03.6	28 09.7	18 09.0	13 09.4	21 09.2	8 49.7	0 32.8	18 26.3	4 32.2	10 09.1
22 Tu	10 04 24	29 41 11	19 13 09	26 02 22	24D 02.5	0♍09.0	19 22.7	13 47.7	21 32.2	8 56.7	0 35.1	18 24.0	4 30.8	10 09.2
23 W	10 08 20	0♍39 01	2♊55 50	9♊53 37	24 02.8	2 07.3	20 36.4	14 26.1	21 55.3	9 03.5	0 37.3	18 21.7	4 29.3	10 09.2
24 Th	10 12 17	1 36 53	16 55 41	24 01 58	24 03.9	4 04.5	21 50.1	15 04.4	22 18.5	9 10.2	0 39.4	18 19.4	4 27.9	10 09.3
25 F	10 16 13	2 34 46	1♋12 16	8♋26 19	24 05.2	6 00.6	23 03.8	15 42.8	22 41.7	9 16.7	0 41.3	18 17.1	4 26.5	10 09.5
26 Sa	10 20 10	3 32 41	15 43 45	23 04 03	24R 05.9	7 55.5	24 17.5	16 21.1	23 05.0	9 23.0	0 43.2	18 14.8	4 25.2	10 09.6
27 Su	10 24 06	4 30 38	0♌26 35	7♌50 38	24 05.2	9 49.2	25 31.2	16 59.3	23 28.4	9 29.2	0 45.0	18 12.5	4 23.8	10 09.8
28 M	10 28 03	5 28 36	15 15 20	22 39 47	24 02.7	11 41.6	26 44.8	17 37.6	23 51.9	9 35.3	0 46.6	18 10.3	4 22.4	10 10.1
29 Tu	10 32 00	6 26 36	0♍03 01	7♍24 04	23 58.2	13 32.8	27 58.5	18 15.8	24 15.4	9 41.1	0 48.2	18 08.0	4 21.1	10 10.4
30 W	10 35 56	7 24 38	14 42 00	21 55 54	23 52.0	15 22.7	29 12.2	18 54.0	24 39.0	9 46.8	0 49.6	18 05.8	4 19.8	10 10.7
31 Th	10 39 53	8 22 41	29 05 01	6♎08 42	23 45.0	17 11.4	0♎25.8	19 32.2	25 02.7	9 52.3	0 51.0	18 03.6	4 18.5	10 11.0

Astro Data (Dy Hr Mn)	Planet Ingress (Dy Hr Mn)
☽0S 8 4:25	♀ ♌ 13 8:02
☿D 17 13:20	☉ ♌ 22 12:43
☽0N 22 22:50	
♃△♆ 27 11:22	♂ ♌ 1 1:21
	♀ ♍ 6 17:32
☽0S 4 12:27	☿ ♌ 7 5:42
⚳0S 6 20:11	♄ ♊ 10 2:26
☽0N 19 4:01	☿ ♍ 22 10:11
♇D 20 22:43	☉ ♍ 22 19:49
☽0S 31 21:37	♀ ♎ 31 3:35

Last Aspect (Dy Hr Mn)	☽ Ingress (Dy Hr Mn)
30 11:47 ♅ △	♋ 1 3:09
2 21:36 ♄ ⚹	♌ 3 2:38
4 22:26 ♄ □	♍ 5 3:19
7 1:57 ♄ △	♎ 7 6:47
9 4:10 ♀ □	♏ 9 13:48
11 20:29 ♀ △	♐ 12 0:06
13 16:03 ♅ ⚹	♑ 14 12:28
16 21:48 ♄ △	♒ 17 1:27
19 10:37 ♄ □	♓ 19 13:44
21 23:08 ☉ △	♈ 22 0:09
23 22:11 ♂ □	♉ 24 7:44
26 10:20 ♄ ☌	♊ 26 12:01
27 20:18 ♅ △	♋ 28 13:30
30 12:18 ♄ ⚹	♌ 30 13:23

Last Aspect (Dy Hr Mn)	☽ Ingress (Dy Hr Mn)
1 12:34 ♄ □	♍ 1 13:27
3 14:50 ♄ △	♎ 3 15:31
5 18:56 ♀ ⚹	♏ 5 21:04
8 6:17 ♄ ☍	♐ 8 6:30
9 20:15 ♅ ⚹	♑ 10 18:44
11 6:02 ♀ △	♒ 13 7:43
15 5:13 ☉ ☍	♓ 15 19:41
16 19:58 ♀ ☍	♈ 18 5:44
20 9:14 ☉ △	♉ 20 13:31
22 18:51 ☉ □	♊ 22 18:55
24 7:57 ♀ □	♋ 24 22:00
26 14:11 ♀ ⚹	♌ 26 23:17
28 4:44 ♅ ☍	♍ 28 23:55
31 1:21 ♀ ☌	♎ 31 1:33

☽ Phases & Eclipses (Dy Hr Mn)	
1 19:20	● 10♋14
1 19:32:32	☽ P 0.477
8 12:53	☽ 16♎39
16 13:55	○ 24♑19
16 13:56	☽ T 1.768
24 11:02	☾ 1♉51
31 2:25	● 8♌12
31 2:13:02	☽ P 0.603
7 1:02	☽ 14♏50
15 5:13	○ 22♒41
22 18:51	☾ 29♉58
29 10:19	● 6♍23

Astro Data

1 July 2000
Julian Day # 36707
SVP 5♓15'25"
GC 26♐50.8 ⚵ 2♍33.3
Eris 19♈54.9 ⚶ 26♒48.9R
⚷ 12♐20.6R ⚴ 28♑02.2R
☽ Mean ☊ 25♋24.1

1 August 2000
Julian Day # 36738
SVP 5♓15'20"
GC 26♐50.8 ⚵ 15♍54.8
Eris 19♈54.6R ⚶ 22♒29.1R
⚷ 11♐08.5R ⚴ 20♑54.8R
☽ Mean ☊ 23♋45.6

LONGITUDE — September 2000

Day	Sid.Time	☉	0 hr ☽	Noon ☽	True ☊	☿	♀	♂	⚳	♃	♄	♅	♆	♇
1 F	10 43 49	9♍20 46	13♎06 25	19♎57 50	23♋37.9	18♍58.7	1♎39.4	20♌10.4	25♎26.4	9♊57.7	0♊52.2	18♒01.4	4♒17.3	10♐11.3
2 Sa	10 47 46	10 18 52	26 42 45	3♏21 10	23R31.7	20 44.9	2 53.1	20 48.6	25 50.2	10 02.9	0 53.3	17R59.2	4R16.0	10 11.7
3 Su	10 51 42	11 16 59	9♏53 10	16 19 01	23 26.9	22 29.7	4 06.7	21 26.7	26 14.1	10 07.9	0 54.4	17 57.1	4 14.8	10 12.2
4 M	10 55 39	12 15 08	22 39 04	28 53 46	23 24.0	24 13.4	5 20.3	22 04.8	26 38.0	10 12.8	0 55.3	17 55.0	4 13.6	10 12.7
5 Tu	10 59 35	13 13 19	5♐03 39	11♐09 18	23D23.0	25 55.8	6 33.9	22 42.9	27 01.9	10 17.5	0 56.1	17 52.9	4 12.4	10 13.2
6 W	11 03 32	14 11 31	17 11 19	23 10 23	23 23.3	27 37.1	7 47.5	23 21.0	27 26.0	10 22.0	0 56.8	17 50.8	4 11.2	10 13.7
7 Th	11 07 29	15 09 44	29 07 08	5♑02 14	23 24.5	29 17.1	9 01.0	23 59.0	27 50.1	10 26.3	0 57.4	17 48.8	4 10.1	10 14.3
8 F	11 11 25	16 07 59	10♑56 20	16 50 04	23R25.5	0♎56.0	10 14.6	24 37.0	28 14.2	10 30.5	0 57.9	17 46.7	4 09.0	10 14.9
9 Sa	11 15 22	17 06 16	22 44 02	28 38 48	23 25.5	2 33.7	11 28.1	25 15.0	28 38.4	10 34.4	0 58.2	17 44.7	4 07.9	10 15.5
10 Su	11 19 18	18 04 34	4♒34 54	10♒32 48	23 23.9	4 10.3	12 41.6	25 53.0	29 02.6	10 38.2	0 58.5	17 42.8	4 06.8	10 16.2
11 M	11 23 15	19 02 54	16 32 56	22 35 41	23 20.0	5 45.8	13 55.1	26 31.0	29 26.9	10 41.8	0R58.7	17 40.8	4 05.8	10 16.8
12 Tu	11 27 11	20 01 15	28 41 21	4♓50 11	23 13.7	7 20.1	15 08.6	27 08.9	29 51.2	10 45.2	0 58.7	17 38.9	4 04.8	10 17.6
13 W	11 31 08	20 59 38	11♓02 21	17 18 00	23 05.3	8 53.4	16 22.1	27 46.9	0♏15.6	10 48.5	0 58.7	17 37.0	4 03.8	10 18.3
14 Th	11 35 04	21 58 03	23 37 10	29 59 53	22 55.3	10 25.5	17 35.6	28 24.8	0 40.0	10 51.5	0 58.5	17 35.2	4 02.8	10 19.1
15 F	11 39 01	22 56 30	6♈26 05	12♈55 42	22 44.8	11 56.6	18 49.0	29 02.7	1 04.5	10 54.4	0 58.2	17 33.4	4 01.9	10 19.9
16 Sa	11 42 57	23 54 59	19 28 36	26 04 40	22 34.6	13 26.5	20 02.5	29 40.6	1 29.1	10 57.1	0 57.8	17 31.6	4 01.0	10 20.8
17 Su	11 46 54	24 53 30	2♉43 44	9♉25 40	22 25.9	14 55.4	21 15.9	0♍18.4	1 53.6	10 59.6	0 57.4	17 29.8	4 00.1	10 21.7
18 M	11 50 51	25 52 03	16 10 20	22 57 37	22 19.3	16 23.1	22 29.3	0 56.3	2 18.2	11 01.8	0 56.8	17 28.1	3 59.2	10 22.6
19 Tu	11 54 47	26 50 39	29 47 25	6♊39 40	22 15.3	17 49.7	23 42.7	1 34.1	2 42.9	11 03.9	0 56.1	17 26.4	3 58.4	10 23.6
20 W	11 58 44	27 49 16	13♊34 18	20 31 17	22D13.6	19 15.3	24 56.1	2 11.9	3 07.6	11 05.9	0 55.3	17 24.8	3 57.6	10 24.5
21 Th	12 02 40	28 47 56	27 30 35	4♋32 10	22 13.5	20 39.6	26 09.5	2 49.7	3 32.4	11 07.6	0 54.3	17 23.2	3 56.8	10 25.6
22 F	12 06 37	29 46 38	11♋35 57	18 41 50	22R13.9	22 02.8	27 22.8	3 27.5	3 57.1	11 09.1	0 53.3	17 21.6	3 56.1	10 26.6
23 Sa	12 10 33	0♎45 23	25 49 39	2♌59 12	22 13.5	23 24.8	28 36.2	4 05.3	4 22.0	11 10.4	0 52.2	17 20.1	3 55.4	10 27.7
24 Su	12 14 30	1 44 10	10♌10 09	17 22 06	22 11.3	24 45.6	29 49.5	4 43.0	4 46.8	11 11.5	0 50.9	17 18.6	3 54.7	10 28.8
25 M	12 18 26	2 42 58	24 34 35	1♍47 00	22 06.5	26 05.1	1♏02.9	5 20.8	5 11.8	11 12.4	0 49.6	17 17.1	3 54.0	10 29.9
26 Tu	12 22 23	3 41 49	8♍58 43	16 09 02	21 58.9	27 23.3	2 16.2	5 58.5	5 36.7	11 13.2	0 48.2	17 15.7	3 53.4	10 31.1
27 W	12 26 20	4 40 42	23 17 13	0♎22 33	21 48.8	28 40.1	3 29.5	6 36.2	6 01.7	11 13.7	0 46.6	17 14.3	3 52.8	10 32.3
28 Th	12 30 16	5 39 37	7♎24 20	14 21 55	21 37.3	29 55.5	4 42.8	7 13.9	6 26.7	11 14.0	0 44.9	17 12.9	3 52.2	10 33.5
29 F	12 34 13	6 38 34	21 14 45	28 02 25	21 25.4	1♏09.3	5 56.0	7 51.5	6 51.8	11R14.1	0 43.2	17 11.6	3 51.7	10 34.7
30 Sa	12 38 09	7 37 33	4♏44 36	11♏21 06	21 14.5	2 21.5	7 09.3	8 29.2	7 16.8	11 14.0	0 41.3	17 10.4	3 51.2	10 36.0

LONGITUDE — October 2000

Day	Sid.Time	☉	0 hr ☽	Noon ☽	True ☊	☿	♀	♂	⚳	♃	♄	♅	♆	♇
1 Su	12 42 06	8♎36 34	17♏51 53	24♏17 03	21♋05.5	3♏32.0	8♏22.5	9♍06.8	7♏42.0	11♊13.7	0♊39.3	17♒09.1	3♒50.7	10♐37.3
2 M	12 46 02	9 35 37	0♐36 47	6♐51 25	20R59.0	4 40.6	9 35.8	9 44.4	8 07.1	11R13.2	0R37.3	17R08.0	3R50.2	10 38.7
3 Tu	12 49 59	10 34 41	13 01 23	19 07 09	20 55.1	5 47.3	10 49.0	10 22.0	8 32.3	11 12.5	0 35.1	17 06.8	3 49.8	10 40.1
4 W	12 53 55	11 33 48	25 09 18	1♑08 27	20D53.3	6 51.8	12 02.2	10 59.6	8 57.5	11 11.6	0 32.8	17 05.8	3 49.4	10 41.4
5 Th	12 57 52	12 32 56	7♑05 15	13 00 22	20R53.0	7 54.0	13 15.3	11 37.1	9 22.8	11 10.5	0 30.5	17 04.7	3 49.1	10 42.9
6 F	13 01 49	13 32 06	18 54 32	24 48 25	20 53.0	8 53.8	14 28.5	12 14.7	9 48.0	11 09.2	0 28.0	17 03.7	3 48.8	10 44.3
7 Sa	13 05 45	14 31 17	0♒42 43	6♒38 06	20 52.2	9 50.8	15 41.6	12 52.2	10 13.3	11 07.7	0 25.5	17 02.8	3 48.5	10 45.8
8 Su	13 09 42	15 30 31	12 35 14	18 34 41	20 49.7	10 45.0	16 54.7	13 29.7	10 38.6	11 06.0	0 22.8	17 01.9	3 48.3	10 47.3
9 M	13 13 38	16 29 46	24 37 02	0♓42 47	20 44.7	11 35.8	18 07.8	14 07.2	11 04.0	11 04.1	0 20.1	17 01.0	3 48.0	10 48.8
10 Tu	13 17 35	17 29 03	6♓52 21	13 06 04	20 36.9	12 23.2	19 20.8	14 44.6	11 29.3	11 02.0	0 17.3	17 00.2	3 47.8	10 50.4
11 W	13 21 31	18 28 22	19 24 14	25 46 59	20 26.6	13 06.7	20 33.9	15 22.1	11 54.7	10 59.7	0 14.3	16 59.4	3 47.7	10 52.0
12 Th	13 25 28	19 27 43	2♈14 25	8♈46 29	20 14.3	13 46.0	21 46.9	15 59.5	12 20.1	10 57.2	0 11.3	16 58.7	3 47.6	10 53.6
13 F	13 29 24	20 27 06	15 23 03	22 03 54	20 01.3	14 20.7	22 59.8	16 36.9	12 45.6	10 54.5	0 08.2	16 58.0	3 47.5	10 55.2
14 Sa	13 33 21	21 26 30	28 48 45	5♉37 12	19 48.7	14 50.3	24 12.8	17 14.3	13 11.0	10 51.6	0 05.0	16 57.4	3 47.4	10 56.9
15 Su	13 37 18	22 25 57	12♉28 52	19 23 16	19 37.7	15 14.3	25 25.7	17 51.6	13 36.5	10 48.5	0 01.8	16 56.8	3D47.4	10 58.5
16 M	13 41 14	23 25 27	26 19 59	3♊18 34	19 29.3	15 32.3	26 38.7	18 29.0	14 02.0	10 45.2	29♉58.4	16 56.3	3 47.4	11 00.2
17 Tu	13 45 11	24 24 58	10♊18 36	17 19 42	19 23.9	15 43.7	27 51.6	19 06.3	14 27.5	10 41.8	29 55.0	16 55.8	3 47.5	11 02.0
18 W	13 49 07	25 24 32	24 21 36	1♋23 59	19 21.1	15R47.9	29 04.4	19 43.7	14 53.0	10 38.1	29 51.5	16 55.4	3 47.6	11 03.7
19 Th	13 53 04	26 24 08	8♋26 42	15 29 33	19 20.4	15 44.6	0♐17.3	20 21.0	15 18.6	10 34.3	29 47.9	16 55.0	3 47.7	11 05.5
20 F	13 57 00	27 23 47	22 32 26	29 35 16	19 20.4	15 33.1	1 30.1	20 58.3	15 44.1	10 30.2	29 44.2	16 54.6	3 47.8	11 07.3
21 Sa	14 00 57	28 23 28	6♌37 57	13♌40 24	19 19.8	15 13.0	2 42.9	21 35.6	16 09.7	10 26.0	29 40.5	16 54.4	3 48.0	11 09.1
22 Su	14 04 53	29 23 11	20 42 29	27 44 04	19 17.3	14 44.2	3 55.7	22 12.8	16 35.3	10 21.6	29 36.7	16 54.1	3 48.2	11 10.9
23 M	14 08 50	0♏22 56	4♍44 56	11♍44 50	19 12.2	14 06.4	5 08.5	22 50.1	17 00.9	10 17.0	29 32.8	16 53.9	3 48.5	11 12.8
24 Tu	14 12 47	1 22 43	18 43 28	25 40 29	19 04.3	13 19.8	6 21.2	23 27.3	17 26.6	10 12.3	29 28.8	16 53.8	3 48.7	11 14.7
25 W	14 16 43	2 22 33	2♎35 29	9♎28 03	18 53.7	12 24.8	7 33.9	24 04.5	17 52.2	10 07.4	29 24.8	16 53.7	3 49.1	11 16.6
26 Th	14 20 40	3 22 25	16 17 46	23 04 13	18 41.6	11 22.3	8 46.6	24 41.7	18 17.8	10 02.3	29 20.7	16D53.7	3 49.4	11 18.5
27 F	14 24 36	4 22 18	29 47 01	6♏25 48	18 29.0	10 13.4	9 59.3	25 18.8	18 43.5	9 57.0	29 16.6	16 53.7	3 49.8	11 20.4
28 Sa	14 28 33	5 22 14	13♏00 20	19 30 25	18 17.2	8 59.7	11 11.9	25 56.0	19 09.2	9 51.5	29 12.3	16 53.8	3 50.2	11 22.4
29 Su	14 32 29	6 22 11	25 55 56	2♐16 53	18 07.3	7 43.1	12 24.6	26 33.1	19 34.9	9 45.9	29 08.1	16 53.9	3 50.7	11 24.4
30 M	14 36 26	7 22 11	8♐33 22	14 45 33	18 00.0	6 26.0	13 37.1	27 10.2	20 00.6	9 40.2	29 03.8	16 54.1	3 51.2	11 26.4
31 Tu	14 40 22	8 22 12	20 53 44	26 58 15	17 55.4	5 10.6	14 49.7	27 47.3	20 26.3	9 34.3	28 59.4	16 54.3	3 51.7	11 28.4

Astro Data

	Dy Hr Mn
♀0S	2 3:34
♃☍♇	4 11:14
☿0S	8 13:44
♄ R	12 11:34
☽0N	15 9:30
☉0S	22 17:28
☽0S	28 7:05
♃ R	29 12:52
☽0N	12 17:00
♃☍♇	13 8:04
♆ D	15 14:12
☿ R	18 13:41
☽0S	25 15:44
♅ D	26 15:24

Planet Ingress

		Dy Hr Mn
☿	♎	7 22:22
⚳	♏	12 20:38
♂	♍	17 0:19
☉	♎	22 17:28
♀	♏	24 15:26
☿	♏	28 13:28
♄	♉R	16 0:44
♀	♐	19 6:18
☉	♏	23 2:47

Last Aspect / ☽ Ingress

Last Aspect Dy Hr Mn			☽ Ingress	Dy Hr Mn
1 12:23	♂	⚹	♏	2 5:55
4 1:34	☿	⚹	♐	4 14:08
6 22:26	☿	□	♑	7 1:47
8 10:27	☉	△	♒	9 14:44
11 20:09	♂	☍	♓	12 2:34
13 19:37	☉	☍	♈	14 12:00
16 18:50	♂	△	♉	16 19:05
18 17:31	☉	△	♊	19 0:22
21 1:28	☉	□	♋	21 4:16
23 3:58	♀	□	♌	23 7:00
25 1:33	☿	⚹	♍	25 9:02
26 3:44	♃	□	♎	27 11:22
28 16:57	♅	△	♏	29 15:29

Last Aspect Dy Hr Mn			☽ Ingress	Dy Hr Mn
30 22:42	♅	□	♐	1 22:50
3 8:03	♅	⚹	♑	4 9:42
5 12:34	♀	⚹	♒	6 22:33
8 8:55	♅	☌	♓	9 10:36
11 1:09	♀	△	♈	11 19:51
13 8:53	☉	☍	♉	14 2:06
16 6:17	♄	☌	♊	16 6:19
18 1:01	☉	△	♋	18 9:37
20 12:15	♄	⚹	♌	20 12:42
22 15:12	♄	□	♍	22 15:52
24 18:34	♄	△	♎	24 19:30
26 1:03	♅	△	♏	27 0:23
29 6:04	♄	☍	♐	29 7:40
31 13:43	♂	□	♑	31 18:01

☽ Phases & Eclipses

Dy Hr Mn		
5 16:27	☽	13♐24
13 19:37	○	21♓18
21 1:28	☾	28♊22
27 19:53	●	5♎00
5 10:59	☽	12♑30
13 8:53	○	20♈19
20 7:59	☾	27♋14
27 7:58	●	4♏12

Astro Data

1 September 2000
Julian Day # 36769
SVP 5♓15'17"
GC 26♐50.9 ⚴ 29♍39.7
Eris 19♈44.8R ⚵ 15♒12.8R
⚷ 11♐21.2 ⚶ 18♑08.4
☽ Mean ☊ 22♋07.1

1 October 2000
Julian Day # 36799
SVP 5♓15'14"
GC 26♐51.0 ⚴ 13♎07.5
Eris 19♈29.0R ⚵ 12♒00.0
⚷ 12♐56.1 ⚶ 22♑10.3
☽ Mean ☊ 20♋31.8

November 2000 — LONGITUDE

Day	Sid.Time	☉	0 hr ☽	Noon ☽	True ☊	☿	♀	♂	⚳	♃	♄	♅	♆	♇
1 W	14 44 19	9♏22 15	2♑59 32	8♑58 05	17♋53.2	3♏59.4	16♐02.2	28♍24.4	20♏52.0	9♊28.2	28♉55.0	16♒54.6	3♒52.2	11♐30.4
2 Th	14 48 16	10 22 19	14 54 29	20 49 18	17D 52.9	2R 54.5	17 14.7	29 01.4	21 17.7	9R 22.0	28R 50.5	16 54.9	3 52.8	11 32.5
3 F	14 52 12	11 22 25	26 43 11	2♒36 49	17R 53.4	1 58.0	18 27.1	29 38.4	21 43.4	9 15.7	28 46.0	16 55.3	3 53.5	11 34.5
4 Sa	14 56 09	12 22 33	8♒30 53	14 26 04	17 53.6	1 11.3	19 39.5	0♎15.4	22 09.1	9 09.2	28 41.4	16 55.7	3 54.1	11 36.6
5 Su	15 00 05	13 22 42	20 23 04	26 22 33	17 52.6	0 35.5	20 51.9	0 52.4	22 34.9	9 02.6	28 36.8	16 56.2	3 54.8	11 38.7
6 M	15 04 02	14 22 53	2♓25 10	8♓31 34	17 49.6	0 11.2	22 04.2	1 29.3	23 00.6	8 55.8	28 32.2	16 56.7	3 55.5	11 40.8
7 Tu	15 07 58	15 23 05	14 42 16	20 57 47	17 44.3	29♎58.5	23 16.5	2 06.2	23 26.3	8 49.0	28 27.5	16 57.3	3 56.3	11 42.9
8 W	15 11 55	16 23 18	27 18 31	3♈44 49	17 36.6	29D 57.3	24 28.8	2 43.1	23 52.0	8 42.0	28 22.8	16 58.0	3 57.1	11 45.1
9 Th	15 15 51	17 23 34	10♈16 51	16 54 43	17 27.2	0♏07.1	25 41.0	3 20.0	24 17.7	8 34.9	28 18.0	16 58.6	3 57.9	11 47.2
10 F	15 19 48	18 23 50	23 38 21	0♉27 36	17 16.9	0 27.3	26 53.1	3 56.9	24 43.5	8 27.7	28 13.3	16 59.4	3 58.7	11 49.4
11 Sa	15 23 44	19 24 09	7♉22 06	14 21 26	17 06.9	0 57.0	28 05.2	4 33.7	25 09.2	8 20.4	28 08.5	17 00.2	3 59.6	11 51.6
12 Su	15 27 41	20 24 29	21 25 02	28 32 14	16 58.1	1 35.4	29 17.3	5 10.5	25 34.9	8 13.0	28 03.7	17 01.0	4 00.5	11 53.7
13 M	15 31 38	21 24 51	5♊42 20	12♊54 36	16 51.6	2 21.5	0♑29.3	5 47.3	26 00.6	8 05.5	27 58.8	17 01.9	4 01.5	11 55.9
14 Tu	15 35 34	22 25 15	20 08 14	27 22 33	16 47.5	3 14.5	1 41.2	6 24.1	26 26.3	7 57.9	27 54.0	17 02.8	4 02.4	11 58.2
15 W	15 39 31	23 25 40	4♋36 52	11♋50 33	16D 45.9	4 13.6	2 53.1	7 00.9	26 52.0	7 50.2	27 49.1	17 03.8	4 03.5	12 00.4
16 Th	15 43 27	24 26 08	19 03 05	26 14 03	16 46.1	5 17.9	4 05.0	7 37.6	27 17.8	7 42.5	27 44.2	17 04.8	4 04.5	12 02.6
17 F	15 47 24	25 26 37	3♌23 06	10♌29 57	16 47.1	6 26.9	5 16.8	8 14.3	27 43.5	7 34.7	27 39.4	17 05.9	4 05.6	12 04.9
18 Sa	15 51 20	26 27 08	17 34 25	24 36 23	16R 47.8	7 39.7	6 28.6	8 51.0	28 09.2	7 26.8	27 34.5	17 07.1	4 06.7	12 07.1
19 Su	15 55 17	27 27 41	1♍35 45	8♍32 28	16 47.2	8 55.9	7 40.3	9 27.7	28 34.8	7 18.8	27 29.6	17 08.3	4 07.8	12 09.4
20 M	15 59 14	28 28 16	15 26 30	22 17 49	16 44.7	10 15.0	8 51.9	10 04.3	29 00.5	7 10.8	27 24.7	17 09.5	4 09.0	12 11.6
21 Tu	16 03 10	29 28 52	29 06 23	5♎52 08	16 40.0	11 36.4	10 03.5	10 40.9	29 26.2	7 02.8	27 19.8	17 10.8	4 10.2	12 13.9
22 W	16 07 07	0♐29 30	12♎35 02	19 15 00	16 33.3	13 00.0	11 15.0	11 17.5	29 51.9	6 54.7	27 14.9	17 12.1	4 11.4	12 16.2
23 Th	16 11 03	1 30 10	25 51 56	2♏25 45	16 25.4	14 25.2	12 26.5	11 54.1	0♐17.5	6 46.6	27 10.0	17 13.5	4 12.6	12 18.5
24 F	16 15 00	2 30 52	8♏56 22	15 23 41	16 17.1	15 51.9	13 37.9	12 30.6	0 43.2	6 38.4	27 05.1	17 14.9	4 13.9	12 20.8
25 Sa	16 18 56	3 31 34	21 47 37	28 08 10	16 09.3	17 19.9	14 49.2	13 07.1	1 08.8	6 30.3	27 00.3	17 16.4	4 15.2	12 23.1
26 Su	16 22 53	4 32 19	4♐25 17	10♐39 01	16 02.8	18 48.8	16 00.5	13 43.6	1 34.4	6 22.1	26 55.4	17 17.9	4 16.6	12 25.4
27 M	16 26 49	5 33 04	16 49 27	22 56 43	15 58.2	20 18.5	17 11.7	14 20.1	2 00.0	6 13.9	26 50.6	17 19.5	4 17.9	12 27.7
28 Tu	16 30 46	6 33 51	29 01 00	5♑02 32	15D 55.6	21 48.9	18 22.9	14 56.5	2 25.6	6 05.7	26 45.8	17 21.1	4 19.3	12 30.0
29 W	16 34 43	7 34 39	11♑01 38	16 58 38	15 54.9	23 19.9	19 33.9	15 32.9	2 51.2	5 57.5	26 41.1	17 22.7	4 20.8	12 32.3
30 Th	16 38 39	8 35 28	22 53 58	28 48 05	15 55.7	24 51.3	20 44.9	16 09.2	3 16.7	5 49.3	26 36.3	17 24.5	4 22.2	12 34.7

December 2000 — LONGITUDE

Day	Sid.Time	☉	0 hr ☽	Noon ☽	True ☊	☿	♀	♂	⚳	♃	♄	♅	♆	♇
1 F	16 42 36	9♐36 18	4♒41 29	10♒34 43	15♋57.3	26♏23.1	21♑55.8	16♎45.6	3♐42.3	5♊41.2	26♉31.6	17♒26.2	4♒23.7	12♐37.0
2 Sa	16 46 32	10 37 09	16 28 21	22 23 01	15 59.2	27 55.2	23 06.6	17 21.8	4 07.8	5R 33.0	26R 26.9	17 28.0	4 25.2	12 39.3
3 Su	16 50 29	11 38 00	28 19 19	4♓17 55	16R 00.4	29 27.5	24 17.3	17 58.1	4 33.3	5 24.9	26 22.3	17 29.9	4 26.7	12 41.6
4 M	16 54 25	12 38 53	10♓19 28	16 24 35	16 00.6	1♐00.0	25 27.9	18 34.3	4 58.7	5 16.9	26 17.7	17 31.7	4 28.3	12 43.9
5 Tu	16 58 22	13 39 46	22 33 55	28 48 02	15 59.4	2 32.7	26 38.4	19 10.5	5 24.2	5 08.8	26 13.1	17 33.7	4 29.9	12 46.3
6 W	17 02 18	14 40 40	5♈07 29	11♈32 46	15 56.8	4 05.6	27 48.8	19 46.7	5 49.6	5 00.9	26 08.6	17 35.6	4 31.5	12 48.6
7 Th	17 06 15	15 41 35	18 04 14	24 42 11	15 52.9	5 38.5	28 59.1	20 22.8	6 15.0	4 53.0	26 04.1	17 37.7	4 33.1	12 50.9
8 F	17 10 12	16 42 30	1♉26 47	8♉18 03	15 48.4	7 11.5	0♒09.3	20 58.9	6 40.4	4 45.1	25 59.7	17 39.7	4 34.7	12 53.2
9 Sa	17 14 08	17 43 27	15 15 51	22 19 54	15 43.9	8 44.6	1 19.4	21 35.0	7 05.7	4 37.3	25 55.3	17 41.8	4 36.4	12 55.6
10 Su	17 18 05	18 44 24	29 29 45	6♊44 45	15 39.9	10 17.9	2 29.4	22 11.0	7 31.1	4 29.6	25 51.0	17 44.0	4 38.1	12 57.9
11 M	17 22 01	19 45 22	14♊04 11	21 27 10	15 37.1	11 51.1	3 39.2	22 47.0	7 56.4	4 22.0	25 46.8	17 46.1	4 39.9	13 00.2
12 Tu	17 25 58	20 46 21	28 52 43	6♋19 52	15D 35.6	13 24.5	4 49.0	23 23.0	8 21.6	4 14.4	25 42.6	17 48.4	4 41.6	13 02.5
13 W	17 29 54	21 47 21	13♋47 33	21 14 46	15 35.4	14 58.0	5 58.6	23 58.9	8 46.9	4 07.0	25 38.4	17 50.6	4 43.4	13 04.8
14 Th	17 33 51	22 48 22	28 40 37	6♌04 13	15 36.3	16 31.5	7 08.0	24 34.8	9 12.1	3 59.6	25 34.4	17 52.9	4 45.2	13 07.1
15 F	17 37 47	23 49 23	13♌24 50	20 41 51	15 37.7	18 05.1	8 17.3	25 10.6	9 37.3	3 52.3	25 30.4	17 55.3	4 47.0	13 09.4
16 Sa	17 41 44	24 50 26	27 54 47	5♍03 16	15 39.1	19 38.9	9 26.5	25 46.5	10 02.5	3 45.2	25 26.4	17 57.7	4 48.8	13 11.7
17 Su	17 45 41	25 51 29	12♍07 04	19 06 03	15R 39.9	21 12.8	10 35.6	26 22.2	10 27.6	3 38.1	25 22.5	18 00.1	4 50.7	13 14.0
18 M	17 49 37	26 52 34	26 00 10	2♎49 28	15 40.0	22 46.8	11 44.5	26 58.0	10 52.7	3 31.2	25 18.7	18 02.5	4 52.6	13 16.3
19 Tu	17 53 34	27 53 39	9♎34 04	16 14 06	15 39.1	24 21.0	12 53.2	27 33.7	11 17.7	3 24.4	25 15.0	18 05.0	4 54.4	13 18.5
20 W	17 57 30	28 54 45	22 49 45	29 21 14	15 37.4	25 55.3	14 01.9	28 09.4	11 42.8	3 17.7	25 11.4	18 07.5	4 56.4	13 20.8
21 Th	18 01 27	29 55 52	5♏48 45	12♏12 32	15 35.2	27 29.8	15 10.3	28 45.0	12 07.7	3 11.1	25 07.8	18 10.1	4 58.3	13 23.0
22 F	18 05 23	0♑57 00	18 32 48	24 49 45	15 32.8	29 04.5	16 18.6	29 20.6	12 32.7	3 04.7	25 04.3	18 12.7	5 00.2	13 25.3
23 Sa	18 09 20	1 58 08	1♐03 37	7♐14 35	15 30.7	0♑39.4	17 26.7	29 56.1	12 57.6	2 58.4	25 00.9	18 15.3	5 02.2	13 27.5
24 Su	18 13 16	2 59 17	13 22 50	19 28 35	15 29.0	2 14.5	18 34.7	0♏31.6	13 22.5	2 52.3	24 57.6	18 18.0	5 04.2	13 29.8
25 M	18 17 13	4 00 26	25 32 01	1♑33 20	15 27.9	3 49.9	19 42.4	1 07.1	13 47.3	2 46.3	24 54.3	18 20.7	5 06.2	13 32.0
26 Tu	18 21 10	5 01 36	7♑32 44	13 30 27	15D 27.5	5 25.5	20 50.0	1 42.5	14 12.1	2 40.5	24 51.2	18 23.4	5 08.2	13 34.2
27 W	18 25 06	6 02 45	19 26 44	25 21 50	15 27.7	7 01.3	21 57.4	2 17.8	14 36.9	2 34.9	24 48.1	18 26.2	5 10.3	13 36.4
28 Th	18 29 03	7 03 55	1♒16 02	7♒09 41	15 28.3	8 37.5	23 04.6	2 53.1	15 01.6	2 29.3	24 45.1	18 29.0	5 12.3	13 38.6
29 F	18 32 59	8 05 05	13 03 05	18 56 39	15 29.1	10 13.9	24 11.5	3 28.4	15 26.2	2 24.0	24 42.2	18 31.8	5 14.4	13 40.7
30 Sa	18 36 56	9 06 15	24 50 47	0♓45 56	15 29.9	11 50.6	25 18.3	4 03.6	15 50.9	2 18.8	24 39.5	18 34.7	5 16.5	13 42.9
31 Su	18 40 52	10 07 25	6♓42 34	12 41 12	15 30.6	13 27.7	26 24.8	4 38.7	16 15.4	2 13.8	24 36.8	18 37.6	5 18.6	13 45.0

Astro Data

	Dy Hr Mn
☿ D	8 2:26
♂ 0S	8 23:23
☽ 0N	9 2:42
☽ 0S	21 22:49
☽ 0N	6 13:06
♃△♆	9 14:16
☽ 0S	19 4:50

Planet Ingress

	Dy Hr Mn
♂ ♎	4 2:00
☿ ♎R	7 7:28
♀ ♑	13 2:14
☉ ♐	22 0:19
⚳ ♐	22 19:37
☿ ♐	3 20:26
♀ ♒	8 8:48
☉ ♑	21 13:37
☿ ♑	23 2:03
♂ ♏	23 14:37

Last Aspect / ☽ Ingress

Dy Hr Mn	Last Aspect	☽ Ingress	Dy Hr Mn
3 5:37	♂ △	♒	3 6:41
5 16:26	♄ □	♓	5 19:13
8 2:04	♄ ⚹	♈	8 5:02
10 5:07	♀ △	♉	10 11:12
12 11:12	♄ ☌	♊	12 14:27
13 18:51	♅ △	♋	14 16:21
16 14:30	♄ ⚹	♌	16 18:19
18 17:03	♄ □	♍	18 21:15
20 23:45	☉ ⚹	♎	21 1:35
22 8:18	♅ △	♏	23 7:33
25 9:52	♄ ☍	♐	25 15:33
27 0:57	♅ ⚹	♑	28 1:57
30 7:34	♄ △	♒	30 14:26

Last Aspect / ☽ Ingress

Dy Hr Mn	Last Aspect	☽ Ingress	Dy Hr Mn
3 0:51	☿ □	♓	3 3:23
5 7:26	♀ ⚹	♈	5 14:17
7 20:22	♀ □	♉	7 21:27
9 18:00	♄ ☌	♊	10 0:50
11 14:15	♂ △	♋	12 1:48
13 19:04	♄ ⚹	♌	14 2:09
15 19:57	♄ □	♍	16 3:30
18 0:41	☉ □	♎	18 7:01
20 11:07	☉ ⚹	♏	20 13:12
22 12:28	♄ ☍	♐	22 21:57
24 10:03	♀ ⚹	♑	25 8:54
27 10:52	♄ △	♒	27 21:25
29 23:47	♀ ☌	♓	30 10:27

☽ Phases & Eclipses

Dy Hr Mn	
4 7:27	☽ 12♒11
11 21:15	○ 19♉47
18 15:24	☾ 26♌36
25 23:11	● 4♐00
4 3:55	☽ 12♓18
11 9:03	○ 19♊38
18 0:41	☾ 26♍24
25 17:22	● 4♑14
25 17:34:55	● P 0.723

Astro Data

1 November 2000
Julian Day # 36830
SVP 5♓15'11"
GC 26♐51.1 ⚵ 26♎59.3
Eris 19♈10.6R ⚴ 15♒25.6
⚷ 15♐41.7 ⚶ 1♒17.5
☽ Mean ☊ 18♋53.2

1 December 2000
Julian Day # 36860
SVP 5♓15'06"
GC 26♐51.1 ⚵ 10♏04.5
Eris 18♈56.3R ⚴ 23♒57.5
⚷ 19♐00.8 ⚶ 12♒56.3
☽ Mean ☊ 17♋17.9

LONGITUDE — January 2001

Day	Sid.Time	☉	0 hr ☽	Noon ☽	True ☊	☿	♀	♂	⚳	♃	♄	♅	♆	♇
1 M	18 44 49	11♑08 35	18♓42 21	24♓46 33	15♋31.0	15♑05.0	27♒31.1	5♏13.8	16♐39.9	2♊09.0	24♉34.2	18♒40.5	5♒20.7	13♐47.1
2 Tu	18 48 45	12 09 45	0♈54 23	7♈06 24	15R 31.2	16 42.6	28 37.2	5 48.8	17 04.4	2R 04.4	24R 31.7	18 43.4	5 22.8	13 49.3
3 W	18 52 42	13 10 54	13 23 08	19 45 07	15 31.2	18 20.6	29 43.0	6 23.8	17 28.8	1 59.9	24 29.3	18 46.4	5 24.9	13 51.4
4 Th	18 56 39	14 12 03	26 12 50	2♉46 44	15 31.1	19 58.9	0♓48.5	6 58.8	17 53.2	1 55.6	24 27.0	18 49.4	5 27.1	13 53.4
5 F	19 00 35	15 13 12	9♉27 09	16 14 21	15D 31.0	21 37.4	1 53.8	7 33.6	18 17.5	1 51.6	24 24.8	18 52.4	5 29.3	13 55.5
6 Sa	19 04 32	16 14 20	23 08 29	0♊09 32	15 31.0	23 16.3	2 58.8	8 08.5	18 41.8	1 47.7	24 22.7	18 55.4	5 31.4	13 57.5
7 Su	19 08 28	17 15 28	7♊17 22	14 31 38	15 31.2	24 55.4	4 03.5	8 43.2	19 06.0	1 43.9	24 20.7	18 58.5	5 33.6	13 59.6
8 M	19 12 25	18 16 36	21 51 49	29 17 15	15 31.4	26 34.8	5 07.8	9 17.9	19 30.1	1 40.4	24 18.9	19 01.6	5 35.8	14 01.6
9 Tu	19 16 21	19 17 44	6♋47 04	14♋20 15	15R 31.5	28 14.3	6 11.9	9 52.6	19 54.2	1 37.1	24 17.1	19 04.7	5 38.0	14 03.6
10 W	19 20 18	20 18 51	21 55 40	29 32 08	15 31.4	29 54.1	7 15.7	10 27.2	20 18.2	1 34.0	24 15.4	19 07.9	5 40.2	14 05.6
11 Th	19 24 15	21 19 58	7♌08 25	14♌43 15	15 31.0	1♒33.9	8 19.1	11 01.7	20 42.2	1 31.1	24 13.9	19 11.0	5 42.4	14 07.5
12 F	19 28 11	22 21 04	22 15 32	29 44 09	15 30.3	3 13.7	9 22.2	11 36.2	21 06.1	1 28.3	24 12.4	19 14.2	5 44.7	14 09.5
13 Sa	19 32 08	23 22 11	7♍08 14	14♍27 01	15 29.4	4 53.5	10 24.9	12 10.6	21 30.0	1 25.8	24 11.1	19 17.4	5 46.9	14 11.4
14 Su	19 36 04	24 23 17	21 39 54	28 46 31	15 28.5	6 33.0	11 27.3	12 45.0	21 53.8	1 23.4	24 09.8	19 20.6	5 49.1	14 13.3
15 M	19 40 01	25 24 23	5♎46 37	12♎40 08	15 27.8	8 12.3	12 29.3	13 19.3	22 17.5	1 21.3	24 08.7	19 23.9	5 51.4	14 15.2
16 Tu	19 43 57	26 25 29	19 27 09	26 07 51	15D 27.5	9 51.1	13 30.9	13 53.5	22 41.2	1 19.4	24 07.7	19 27.1	5 53.6	14 17.0
17 W	19 47 54	27 26 35	2♏42 31	9♏11 30	15 27.8	11 29.2	14 32.2	14 27.6	23 04.8	1 17.7	24 06.8	19 30.4	5 55.9	14 18.9
18 Th	19 51 50	28 27 41	15 35 13	21 54 07	15 28.6	13 06.4	15 33.0	15 01.7	23 28.3	1 16.1	24 06.0	19 33.7	5 58.1	14 20.7
19 F	19 55 47	29 28 46	28 08 40	4♐19 19	15 29.8	14 42.4	16 33.4	15 35.7	23 51.8	1 14.8	24 05.3	19 37.0	6 00.4	14 22.5
20 Sa	19 59 44	0♒29 51	10♐26 33	16 30 48	15 31.2	16 16.9	17 33.3	16 09.7	24 15.2	1 13.7	24 04.7	19 40.3	6 02.7	14 24.2
21 Su	20 03 40	1 30 55	22 32 31	28 32 05	15 32.5	17 49.6	18 32.8	16 43.5	24 38.5	1 12.8	24 04.3	19 43.7	6 04.9	14 26.0
22 M	20 07 37	2 31 59	4♑29 54	10♑26 18	15R 33.2	19 20.1	19 31.8	17 17.3	25 01.7	1 12.1	24 03.9	19 47.0	6 07.2	14 27.7
23 Tu	20 11 33	3 33 03	16 21 38	22 16 11	15 33.2	20 47.8	20 30.4	17 51.0	25 24.9	1 11.6	24 03.7	19 50.4	6 09.5	14 29.4
24 W	20 15 30	4 34 05	28 10 15	4♒04 05	15 32.1	22 12.2	21 28.4	18 24.7	25 48.0	1D 11.3	24D 03.6	19 53.8	6 11.8	14 31.1
25 Th	20 19 26	5 35 07	9♒57 57	15 52 06	15 29.9	23 32.7	22 25.9	18 58.2	26 11.0	1 11.3	24 03.6	19 57.2	6 14.1	14 32.7
26 F	20 23 23	6 36 08	21 46 46	27 42 13	15 26.8	24 48.6	23 22.9	19 31.7	26 34.0	1 11.4	24 03.7	20 00.6	6 16.3	14 34.3
27 Sa	20 27 19	7 37 08	3♓38 41	9♓36 27	15 23.0	25 59.3	24 19.3	20 05.1	26 56.8	1 11.7	24 03.9	20 04.0	6 18.6	14 35.9
28 Su	20 31 16	8 38 07	15 35 49	21 37 05	15 19.0	27 04.0	25 15.0	20 38.3	27 19.6	1 12.3	24 04.3	20 07.4	6 20.9	14 37.5
29 M	20 35 13	9 39 05	27 40 35	3♈46 40	15 15.1	28 01.7	26 10.2	21 11.5	27 42.3	1 13.0	24 04.7	20 10.9	6 23.2	14 39.0
30 Tu	20 39 09	10 40 01	9♈55 44	16 08 10	15 12.0	28 51.8	27 04.8	21 44.6	28 04.9	1 14.0	24 05.3	20 14.3	6 25.4	14 40.6
31 W	20 43 06	11 40 56	22 24 24	28 44 51	15 10.0	29 33.4	27 58.7	22 17.6	28 27.4	1 15.1	24 06.0	20 17.7	6 27.7	14 42.0

LONGITUDE — February 2001

Day	Sid.Time	☉	0 hr ☽	Noon ☽	True ☊	☿	♀	♂	⚳	♃	♄	♅	♆	♇
1 Th	20 47 02	12♒41 50	5♉09 57	11♉40 09	15♋09.3	0♓05.7	28♓51.9	22♏50.6	28♐49.9	1♊16.5	24♉06.7	20♒21.2	6♒30.0	14♐43.5
2 F	20 50 59	13 42 43	18 15 49	24 57 21	15D 09.7	0 28.0	29 44.3	23 23.4	29 12.2	1 18.1	24 07.7	20 24.7	6 32.3	14 44.9
3 Sa	20 54 55	14 43 34	1♊45 01	8♊39 04	15 11.1	0R 39.8	0♈36.1	23 56.1	29 34.4	1 19.8	24 08.7	20 28.1	6 34.5	14 46.3
4 Su	20 58 52	15 44 24	15 39 36	22 46 36	15 12.7	0 40.7	1 27.0	24 28.8	29 56.6	1 21.8	24 09.8	20 31.6	6 36.8	14 47.7
5 M	21 02 48	16 45 13	29 59 55	7♋19 13	15R 13.8	0 30.5	2 17.2	25 01.3	0♑18.7	1 24.0	24 11.1	20 35.1	6 39.0	14 49.1
6 Tu	21 06 45	17 46 00	14♋43 58	22 13 28	15 13.8	0 09.4	3 06.5	25 33.7	0 40.6	1 26.4	24 12.4	20 38.6	6 41.3	14 50.4
7 W	21 10 42	18 46 46	29 46 49	7♌22 57	15 12.3	29♒37.6	3 54.9	26 06.1	1 02.5	1 28.9	24 13.9	20 42.0	6 43.5	14 51.7
8 Th	21 14 38	19 47 30	15♌00 41	22 38 44	15 09.0	28 56.0	4 42.4	26 38.3	1 24.3	1 31.7	24 15.4	20 45.5	6 45.8	14 52.9
9 F	21 18 35	20 48 13	0♍15 45	7♍50 25	15 04.2	28 05.7	5 29.0	27 10.4	1 46.0	1 34.6	24 17.1	20 49.0	6 48.0	14 54.2
10 Sa	21 22 31	21 48 55	15 21 30	22 47 53	14 58.6	27 07.9	6 14.6	27 42.4	2 07.5	1 37.8	24 18.9	20 52.5	6 50.2	14 55.4
11 Su	21 26 28	22 49 36	0♎08 38	7♎22 57	14 52.8	26 04.3	6 59.2	28 14.3	2 29.0	1 41.1	24 20.8	20 55.9	6 52.4	14 56.5
12 M	21 30 24	23 50 15	14 30 20	21 30 25	14 47.8	24 56.8	7 42.7	28 46.1	2 50.4	1 44.6	24 22.8	20 59.4	6 54.6	14 57.7
13 Tu	21 34 21	24 50 54	28 23 04	5♏08 21	14 44.2	23 47.2	8 25.2	29 17.8	3 11.6	1 48.3	24 24.9	21 02.9	6 56.8	14 58.8
14 W	21 38 17	25 51 31	11♏46 28	18 17 46	14D 42.3	22 37.3	9 06.5	29 49.4	3 32.8	1 52.2	24 27.2	21 06.4	6 59.0	14 59.8
15 Th	21 42 14	26 52 07	24 42 40	1♐01 43	14 42.1	21 29.1	9 46.7	0♐20.8	3 53.9	1 56.3	24 29.5	21 09.8	7 01.2	15 00.9
16 F	21 46 11	27 52 42	7♐15 29	13 24 35	14 43.1	20 24.1	10 25.7	0 52.1	4 14.8	2 00.5	24 31.9	21 13.3	7 03.4	15 01.9
17 Sa	21 50 07	28 53 16	19 29 39	25 31 18	14 44.7	19 23.7	11 03.3	1 23.3	4 35.6	2 05.0	24 34.5	21 16.8	7 05.5	15 02.9
18 Su	21 54 04	29 53 49	1♑30 09	7♑26 48	14R 45.9	18 29.0	11 39.7	1 54.4	4 56.3	2 09.6	24 37.1	21 20.2	7 07.7	15 03.8
19 M	21 58 00	0♓54 20	13 21 48	19 15 42	14 46.1	17 40.7	12 14.7	2 25.3	5 16.9	2 14.4	24 39.9	21 23.7	7 09.8	15 04.8
20 Tu	22 01 57	1 54 50	25 08 59	1♒02 04	14 44.4	16 59.6	12 48.3	2 56.1	5 37.4	2 19.4	24 42.7	21 27.1	7 11.9	15 05.6
21 W	22 05 53	2 55 18	6♒55 23	12 49 17	14 40.6	16 25.8	13 20.4	3 26.7	5 57.7	2 24.6	24 45.7	21 30.6	7 14.0	15 06.5
22 Th	22 09 50	3 55 45	18 44 04	24 40 01	14 34.3	15 59.5	13 51.0	3 57.2	6 18.0	2 29.9	24 48.7	21 34.0	7 16.1	15 07.3
23 F	22 13 46	4 56 10	0♓37 21	6♓36 17	14 26.0	15 40.7	14 20.0	4 27.6	6 38.0	2 35.4	24 51.9	21 37.4	7 18.2	15 08.1
24 Sa	22 17 43	5 56 33	12 37 00	18 39 38	14 16.1	15 29.2	14 47.4	4 57.8	6 58.0	2 41.1	24 55.1	21 40.8	7 20.3	15 08.8
25 Su	22 21 39	6 56 55	24 44 21	0♈51 16	14 05.6	15D 24.7	15 13.0	5 27.8	7 17.8	2 46.9	24 58.5	21 44.2	7 22.3	15 09.6
26 M	22 25 36	7 57 15	7♈00 31	13 12 16	13 55.5	15 27.0	15 36.9	5 57.7	7 37.6	2 52.9	25 01.9	21 47.6	7 24.4	15 10.2
27 Tu	22 29 33	8 57 33	19 26 40	25 43 54	13 46.7	15 35.6	15 58.9	6 27.4	7 57.1	2 59.1	25 05.5	21 51.0	7 26.4	15 10.9
28 W	22 33 29	9 57 49	2♉04 10	8♉27 42	13 40.0	15 50.3	16 19.0	6 57.0	8 16.5	3 05.4	25 09.1	21 54.3	7 28.4	15 11.5

Astro Data

	Dy Hr Mn
☽ 0N	2 22:01
☽ 0S	15 11:24
♄ D	25 0:24
♃ D	25 8:38
☽ 0N	30 4:23
♀ 0N	30 12:18
☿ R	4 1:56
☽ 0S	11 19:53
☿ D	25 15:42
☽ 0N	26 9:24

Planet Ingress

		Dy Hr Mn
♀	♓	3 18:14
☿	♒	10 13:26
☉	♒	20 0:16
☿	♓	1 7:13
♀	♈	2 19:14
⚳	♑	4 15:41
☿	♒R	6 19:57
♂	♐	14 20:06
☉	♓	18 14:27

Last Aspect / ☽ Ingress (January)

Last Aspect Dy Hr Mn			☽ Ingress	Dy Hr Mn
1 11:36	♄	⚹	♈	1 22:14
3 10:09	♅	⚹	♉	4 6:57
6 2:09	♄	☌	♊	6 11:44
7 19:19	♅	△	♋	8 13:09
10 12:39	☿	☍	♌	10 12:44
12 3:08	♄	□	♍	12 12:26
14 4:13	♄	△	♎	14 14:05
16 12:35	☉	□	♏	16 19:02
19 1:44	☉	⚹	♐	19 3:36
20 18:18	♅	⚹	♑	21 14:57
23 15:39	♄	△	♒	24 3:43
26 5:28	☿	☌	♓	26 16:39
28 19:48	♀	☌	♈	29 4:35
31 13:36	☿	⚹	♉	31 14:21

Last Aspect / ☽ Ingress (February)

Last Aspect Dy Hr Mn			☽ Ingress	Dy Hr Mn
2 10:31	♄	☌	♊	2 20:56
4 8:13	♅	△	♋	5 0:00
6 17:30	♂	△	♌	7 0:21
8 21:25	☿	☍	♍	8 23:35
10 20:18	♂	⚹	♎	10 23:46
12 17:31	☿	△	♏	13 2:51
15 3:24	☉	□	♐	15 10:02
17 19:22	☉	⚹	♑	17 20:59
19 23:03	♄	△	♒	20 9:53
22 12:18	♄	□	♓	22 22:45
25 0:25	♄	⚹	♈	25 10:20
27 4:34	♅	⚹	♉	27 20:06

☽ Phases & Eclipses

Dy Hr Mn		
2 22:32	☽	12♈37
9 20:24	○	19♋39
9 20:21	☊	T 1.189
16 12:35	☾	26♎27
24 13:07	●	4♒37
1 14:02	☽	12♉47
8 7:12	○	19♌35
15 3:24	☾	26♏30
23 8:21	●	4♓47

Astro Data

1 January 2001
Julian Day # 36891
SVP 5♓15'01"
GC 26♐51.2 ⚴ 22♏48.4
Eris 18♈49.5R ⚵ 6♓21.1
⚷ 22♐35.3 ⚶ 26♒35.2
☽ Mean ☊ 15♋39.5

1 February 2001
Julian Day # 36922
SVP 5♓14'56"
GC 26♐51.3 ⚴ 3♐59.4
Eris 18♈53.2 ⚵ 21♓07.6
⚷ 25♐45.8 ⚶ 11♓04.0
☽ Mean ☊ 14♋01.0

March 2001 — LONGITUDE

Day	Sid.Time	☉	0 hr ☽	Noon ☽	True ☊	☿	♀	♂	⚳	♃	♄	♅	♆	♇
1 Th	22 37 26	10♓58 03	14♉54 46	21♉25 37	13♋35.7	16♒10.6	16♈37.1	7♐26.3	8♑35.8	3♊11.9	25♉12.9	21♒57.7	7♒30.4	15♐12.1
2 F	22 41 22	11 58 15	28 00 34	4♊39 53	13D33.8	16 36.2	16 53.2	7 55.6	8 55.0	3 18.6	25 16.7	22 01.0	7 32.3	15 12.6
3 Sa	22 45 19	12 58 25	11♊23 52	18 12 47	13 33.7	17 06.7	17 07.2	8 24.6	9 14.0	3 25.4	25 20.6	22 04.3	7 34.3	15 13.1
4 Su	22 49 15	13 58 33	25 06 49	2♋06 08	13R34.3	17 41.8	17 19.0	8 53.5	9 32.8	3 32.4	25 24.6	22 07.6	7 36.2	15 13.6
5 M	22 53 12	14 58 39	9♋10 47	16 20 42	13 34.6	18 21.1	17 28.6	9 22.2	9 51.6	3 39.5	25 28.7	22 10.9	7 38.1	15 14.1
6 Tu	22 57 08	15 58 42	23 35 40	0♌55 20	13 33.4	19 04.4	17 35.9	9 50.7	10 10.1	3 46.8	25 32.9	22 14.1	7 40.0	15 14.5
7 W	23 01 05	16 58 44	8♌19 10	15 46 27	13 29.9	19 51.3	17 40.8	10 19.0	10 28.5	3 54.2	25 37.2	22 17.4	7 41.9	15 14.9
8 Th	23 05 02	17 58 43	23 16 17	0♍47 40	13 23.7	20 41.7	17R43.4	10 47.1	10 46.8	4 01.7	25 41.6	22 20.6	7 43.8	15 15.2
9 F	23 08 58	18 58 41	8♍19 26	15 50 23	13 15.1	21 35.3	17 43.5	11 15.0	11 04.9	4 09.4	25 46.1	22 23.8	7 45.6	15 15.5
10 Sa	23 12 55	19 58 36	23 19 16	0♎44 55	13 04.9	22 31.9	17 41.2	11 42.8	11 22.8	4 17.3	25 50.6	22 27.0	7 47.4	15 15.8
11 Su	23 16 51	20 58 30	8♎06 13	15 22 12	12 54.3	23 31.3	17 36.3	12 10.3	11 40.6	4 25.3	25 55.2	22 30.2	7 49.2	15 16.0
12 M	23 20 48	21 58 21	22 32 05	29 35 16	12 44.5	24 33.4	17 29.0	12 37.6	11 58.3	4 33.4	26 00.0	22 33.3	7 51.0	15 16.2
13 Tu	23 24 44	22 58 11	6♏31 23	13♏20 15	12 36.6	25 37.9	17 19.1	13 04.8	12 15.7	4 41.7	26 04.7	22 36.4	7 52.7	15 16.4
14 W	23 28 41	23 58 00	20 01 52	26 36 24	12 31.0	26 44.8	17 06.8	13 31.7	12 33.0	4 50.1	26 09.6	22 39.6	7 54.4	15 16.5
15 Th	23 32 37	24 57 47	3♐04 11	9♐25 40	12 27.9	27 53.8	16 52.0	13 58.3	12 50.1	4 58.6	26 14.6	22 42.6	7 56.1	15 16.6
16 F	23 36 34	25 57 32	15 41 23	21 51 56	12D26.9	29 05.0	16 34.7	14 24.8	13 07.1	5 07.2	26 19.6	22 45.7	7 57.8	15 16.7
17 Sa	23 40 31	26 57 15	27 57 58	4♑00 10	12R26.9	0♓18.2	16 15.1	14 51.0	13 23.9	5 16.0	26 24.7	22 48.7	7 59.5	15R16.8
18 Su	23 44 27	27 56 57	9♑59 14	15 55 52	12 27.0	1 33.3	15 53.2	15 17.0	13 40.4	5 24.9	26 29.9	22 51.7	8 01.1	15 16.8
19 M	23 48 24	28 56 37	21 50 44	27 44 30	12 26.0	2 50.3	15 29.0	15 42.7	13 56.9	5 34.0	26 35.2	22 54.7	8 02.7	15 16.7
20 Tu	23 52 20	29 56 15	3♒37 47	9♒31 09	12 23.0	4 09.0	15 02.7	16 08.1	14 13.1	5 43.2	26 40.5	22 57.7	8 04.3	15 16.7
21 W	23 56 17	0♈55 51	15 25 08	21 20 15	12 17.3	5 29.4	14 34.4	16 33.3	14 29.1	5 52.4	26 46.0	23 00.6	8 05.9	15 16.6
22 Th	0 00 13	1 55 25	27 16 54	3♓15 27	12 08.8	6 51.4	14 04.3	16 58.3	14 45.0	6 01.9	26 51.4	23 03.5	8 07.4	15 16.4
23 F	0 04 10	2 54 58	9♓16 13	15 19 27	11 57.6	8 15.1	13 32.5	17 22.9	15 00.6	6 11.4	26 57.0	23 06.4	8 08.9	15 16.3
24 Sa	0 08 06	3 54 28	21 25 20	27 34 01	11 44.5	9 40.3	12 59.2	17 47.3	15 16.1	6 21.0	27 02.6	23 09.2	8 10.4	15 16.1
25 Su	0 12 03	4 53 57	3♈45 34	10♈00 03	11 30.5	11 07.0	12 24.6	18 11.3	15 31.3	6 30.8	27 08.3	23 12.0	8 11.9	15 15.8
26 M	0 16 00	5 53 23	16 17 27	22 37 45	11 16.9	12 35.2	11 48.8	18 35.1	15 46.4	6 40.7	27 14.1	23 14.8	8 13.3	15 15.6
27 Tu	0 19 56	6 52 47	29 00 56	5♉26 57	11 04.9	14 04.9	11 12.2	18 58.6	16 01.2	6 50.6	27 19.9	23 17.6	8 14.7	15 15.3
28 W	0 23 53	7 52 10	11♉55 47	18 27 25	10 55.3	15 36.1	10 35.0	19 21.7	16 15.8	7 00.7	27 25.8	23 20.3	8 16.1	15 14.9
29 Th	0 27 49	8 51 30	25 01 50	1♊39 07	10 48.8	17 08.7	9 57.3	19 44.6	16 30.3	7 10.9	27 31.8	23 23.0	8 17.5	15 14.6
30 F	0 31 46	9 50 47	8♊19 17	15 02 28	10 45.1	18 42.7	9 19.5	20 07.1	16 44.5	7 21.2	27 37.8	23 25.7	8 18.8	15 14.2
31 Sa	0 35 42	10 50 03	21 48 44	28 38 15	10 43.8	20 18.2	8 41.9	20 29.3	16 58.5	7 31.6	27 43.9	23 28.3	8 20.1	15 13.7

April 2001 — LONGITUDE

Day	Sid.Time	☉	0 hr ☽	Noon ☽	True ☊	☿	♀	♂	⚳	♃	♄	♅	♆	♇
1 Su	0 39 39	11♈49 16	5♋31 07	12♋27 26	10♋43.6	21♓55.0	8♈04.5	20♐51.2	17♑12.2	7♊42.1	27♉50.1	23♒30.9	8♒21.3	15♐13.3
2 M	0 43 35	12 48 27	19 27 16	26 30 39	10R43.3	23 33.3	7R27.8	21 12.7	17 25.8	7 52.8	27 56.3	23 33.4	8 22.6	15R12.8
3 Tu	0 47 32	13 47 35	3♌37 30	10♌47 38	10 41.6	25 13.1	6 51.9	21 33.9	17 39.1	8 03.5	28 02.6	23 36.0	8 23.8	15 12.3
4 W	0 51 29	14 46 42	18 00 48	25 16 33	10 37.5	26 54.2	6 17.0	21 54.7	17 52.2	8 14.3	28 08.9	23 38.5	8 25.0	15 11.7
5 Th	0 55 25	15 45 45	2♍34 23	9♍53 36	10 30.7	28 36.8	5 43.5	22 15.1	18 05.0	8 25.1	28 15.3	23 40.9	8 26.1	15 11.1
6 F	0 59 22	16 44 47	17 13 26	24 33 00	10 21.2	0♈20.8	5 11.4	22 35.2	18 17.6	8 36.1	28 21.7	23 43.3	8 27.2	15 10.5
7 Sa	1 03 18	17 43 46	1♎51 23	9♎07 36	10 10.0	2 06.3	4 41.0	22 54.9	18 30.0	8 47.2	28 28.2	23 45.7	8 28.3	15 09.9
8 Su	1 07 15	18 42 43	16 20 45	23 29 57	9 58.2	3 53.2	4 12.5	23 14.2	18 42.1	8 58.3	28 34.8	23 48.1	8 29.4	15 09.2
9 M	1 11 11	19 41 39	0♏34 27	7♏33 37	9 47.1	5 41.7	3 45.9	23 33.2	18 54.0	9 09.6	28 41.4	23 50.4	8 30.4	15 08.5
10 Tu	1 15 08	20 40 32	14 26 57	21 14 07	9 37.8	7 31.6	3 21.5	23 51.7	19 05.6	9 20.9	28 48.0	23 52.6	8 31.4	15 07.8
11 W	1 19 04	21 39 24	27 54 59	4♐29 32	9 31.0	9 23.0	2 59.3	24 09.8	19 17.0	9 32.3	28 54.7	23 54.9	8 32.4	15 07.0
12 Th	1 23 01	22 38 14	10♐57 55	17 20 25	9 26.8	11 16.0	2 39.3	24 27.4	19 28.2	9 43.8	29 01.5	23 57.1	8 33.3	15 06.2
13 F	1 26 57	23 37 02	23 37 23	29 49 20	9D25.0	13 10.4	2 21.8	24 44.7	19 39.0	9 55.4	29 08.2	23 59.2	8 34.2	15 05.4
14 Sa	1 30 54	24 35 48	5♑56 48	12♑00 24	9 24.7	15 06.3	2 06.7	25 01.4	19 49.6	10 07.1	29 15.1	24 01.4	8 35.1	15 04.5
15 Su	1 34 51	25 34 33	18 00 47	23 58 37	9R24.9	17 03.7	1 54.0	25 17.7	20 00.0	10 18.8	29 22.0	24 03.4	8 36.0	15 03.7
16 M	1 38 47	26 33 16	29 54 36	5♒49 25	9 24.5	19 02.6	1 43.8	25 33.6	20 10.0	10 30.6	29 28.9	24 05.5	8 36.8	15 02.8
17 Tu	1 42 44	27 31 57	11♒43 43	17 38 12	9 22.6	21 02.9	1 36.1	25 48.9	20 19.8	10 42.5	29 35.9	24 07.5	8 37.6	15 01.8
18 W	1 46 40	28 30 36	23 33 27	29 30 05	9 18.5	23 04.6	1 30.8	26 03.8	20 29.3	10 54.4	29 42.9	24 09.4	8 38.3	15 00.9
19 Th	1 50 37	29 29 14	5♓28 38	11♓29 35	9 11.8	25 07.6	1D28.0	26 18.1	20 38.6	11 06.5	29 49.9	24 11.3	8 39.1	14 59.9
20 F	1 54 33	0♉27 50	17 33 22	23 40 30	9 02.7	27 11.9	1 27.5	26 31.9	20 47.5	11 18.6	29 57.0	24 13.2	8 39.7	14 58.9
21 Sa	1 58 30	1 26 24	29 50 46	6♈04 54	8 51.8	29 17.3	1 29.4	26 45.2	20 56.2	11 30.7	0♊04.2	24 15.0	8 40.4	14 57.9
22 Su	2 02 26	2 24 57	12♈22 51	18 44 41	8 40.0	1♉23.7	1 33.6	26 57.9	21 04.5	11 43.0	0 11.3	24 16.8	8 41.0	14 56.8
23 M	2 06 23	3 23 28	25 10 24	1♉39 54	8 28.5	3 30.9	1 40.1	27 10.1	21 12.6	11 55.3	0 18.5	24 18.6	8 41.6	14 55.7
24 Tu	2 10 20	4 21 56	8♉13 04	14 49 42	8 18.3	5 38.9	1 48.8	27 21.7	21 20.3	12 07.6	0 25.8	24 20.3	8 42.2	14 54.6
25 W	2 14 16	5 20 23	21 29 36	28 12 32	8 10.3	7 47.3	1 59.6	27 32.7	21 27.8	12 20.1	0 33.1	24 21.9	8 42.7	14 53.5
26 Th	2 18 13	6 18 49	4♊58 15	11♊46 31	8 04.9	9 56.0	2 12.5	27 43.2	21 34.9	12 32.6	0 40.4	24 23.5	8 43.2	14 52.3
27 F	2 22 09	7 17 12	18 37 07	25 29 51	8D02.2	12 04.6	2 27.5	27 53.0	21 41.7	12 45.1	0 47.7	24 25.1	8 43.6	14 51.2
28 Sa	2 26 06	8 15 33	2♋24 34	9♋21 07	8 01.5	14 13.0	2 44.4	28 02.3	21 48.3	12 57.7	0 55.1	24 26.6	8 44.1	14 50.0
29 Su	2 30 02	9 13 52	16 19 23	23 19 16	8 02.0	16 20.8	3 03.2	28 10.9	21 54.5	13 10.4	1 02.5	24 28.1	8 44.5	14 48.8
30 M	2 33 59	10 12 09	0♌20 41	7♌23 32	8R02.6	18 27.7	3 23.8	28 18.9	22 00.3	13 23.1	1 09.9	24 29.5	8 44.8	14 47.5

Astro Data

	Dy Hr Mn
♀ R	9 1:06
☽ 0S	11 6:01
♇ R	18 2:38
☉ 0N	20 13:31
☽ 0N	25 15:08
♃△♆	5 14:24
☽ 0S	7 16:12
☿ 0N	9 2:43
♀ D	20 4:34
☽ 0N	21 22:45

Planet Ingress

	Dy Hr Mn
☿ ♓	17 6:05
☉ ♈	20 13:31
☿ ♈	6 7:14
☉ ♉	20 0:36
♄ ♊	20 21:59
☿ ♉	21 20:08

Last Aspect / ☽ Ingress

Last Aspect Dy Hr Mn		☽ Ingress Dy Hr Mn
1 18:57	♄ ☌	♊ 2 3:36
3 18:45	♅ △	♋ 4 8:24
6 3:10	♄ ⚹	♌ 6 10:30
8 3:50	♄ □	♍ 8 10:44
10 4:01	♄ △	♎ 10 10:47
12 2:44	☿ △	♏ 12 12:42
14 12:17	☿ □	♐ 14 18:17
17 3:48	☿ ⚹	♑ 17 4:02
19 14:40	☉ ⚹	♒ 19 16:36
21 23:03	♄ □	♓ 22 5:28
24 10:58	♄ ⚹	♈ 24 16:44
26 13:10	♅ ⚹	♉ 27 1:51
29 4:29	♄ ☌	♊ 29 9:01
31 2:54	♅ △	♋ 31 14:23

Last Aspect Dy Hr Mn		☽ Ingress Dy Hr Mn
2 14:26	♄ ⚹	♌ 2 17:54
4 16:46	♄ □	♍ 4 19:46
6 18:18	♄ △	♎ 6 20:57
8 12:31	♅ △	♏ 8 23:01
11 1:43	♄ ☍	♐ 11 3:47
13 1:56	♂ ☌	♑ 13 12:21
15 23:00	♄ △	♒ 16 0:11
18 12:26	♄ □	♓ 18 13:00
20 17:40	♂ □	♈ 21 0:18
23 3:34	♂ △	♉ 23 8:56
25 5:08	♅ □	♊ 25 15:11
27 16:12	♂ ☍	♋ 27 19:49
28 21:53	☿ ⚹	♌ 29 23:25

☽ Phases & Eclipses

Dy Hr Mn	
3 2:03	☽ 12♊33
9 17:23	○ 19♍12
16 20:45	☾ 26♐19
25 1:21	● 4♈28
1 10:49	☽ 11♋46
8 3:22	○ 18♎22
15 15:31	☾ 25♑43
23 15:26	● 3♉32
30 17:08	☽ 10♌25

Astro Data

1 March 2001
Julian Day # 36950
SVP 5♓14'53"
GC 26♐51.3 ⚵ 11♐44.6
Eris 19♈04.8 ⚴ 5♈51.3
⚷ 27♐50.7 ⚶ 24♓24.6
☽ Mean ☊ 12♋32.0

1 April 2001
Julian Day # 36981
SVP 5♓14'50"
GC 26♐51.4 ⚵ 15♐55.1
Eris 19♈23.5 ⚴ 23♈11.6
⚷ 28♐53.6 ⚶ 9♈07.4
☽ Mean ☊ 10♋53.5

LONGITUDE — May 2001

Day	Sid.Time	☉	0 hr ☽	Noon ☽	True ☊	☿	♀	♂	⚳	♃	♄	♅	♆	♇
1 Tu	2 37 55	11♉10 23	14♌27 43	21♌33 04	8♋02.2	20♉33.4	3♈46.2	28♐26.3	22♑05.9	13♊35.9	1♊17.4	24♒30.9	8♒45.2	14♐46.3
2 W	2 41 52	12 08 36	28 39 23	5♍46 26	7R59.9	22 37.6	4 10.4	28 33.0	22 11.1	13 48.7	1 24.8	24 32.2	8 45.4	14R45.0
3 Th	2 45 49	13 06 47	12♍53 52	20 01 20	7 55.4	24 40.0	4 36.1	28 39.0	22 16.0	14 01.5	1 32.3	24 33.5	8 45.7	14 43.7
4 F	2 49 45	14 04 55	27 08 21	4♎14 27	7 48.9	26 40.4	5 03.5	28 44.5	22 20.6	14 14.5	1 39.9	24 34.8	8 45.9	14 42.4
5 Sa	2 53 42	15 03 02	11♎19 03	18 21 35	7 40.9	28 38.5	5 32.4	28 49.2	22 24.8	14 27.4	1 47.4	24 36.0	8 46.1	14 41.0
6 Su	2 57 38	16 01 07	25 21 31	2♏18 15	7 32.3	0♊34.0	6 02.9	28 53.2	22 28.7	14 40.4	1 55.0	24 37.1	8 46.3	14 39.7
7 M	3 01 35	16 59 10	9♏11 17	16 00 12	7 24.3	2 26.7	6 34.7	28 56.6	22 32.2	14 53.5	2 02.6	24 38.2	8 46.4	14 38.3
8 Tu	3 05 31	17 57 12	22 44 35	29 24 13	7 17.6	4 16.5	7 07.9	28 59.3	22 35.5	15 06.6	2 10.2	24 39.3	8 46.5	14 36.9
9 W	3 09 28	18 55 12	5♐58 53	12♐28 32	7 12.8	6 03.3	7 42.5	29 01.2	22 38.3	15 19.7	2 17.8	24 40.3	8 46.6	14 35.5
10 Th	3 13 24	19 53 11	18 53 13	25 13 04	7D10.1	7 46.8	8 18.3	29 02.4	22 40.8	15 32.9	2 25.4	24 41.2	8R46.6	14 34.1
11 F	3 17 21	20 51 08	1♑28 19	7♑39 18	7 09.3	9 26.9	8 55.4	29R02.9	22 43.0	15 46.1	2 33.1	24 42.2	8 46.6	14 32.7
12 Sa	3 21 18	21 49 04	13 46 25	19 50 07	7 10.0	11 03.7	9 33.6	29 02.7	22 44.8	15 59.4	2 40.8	24 43.0	8 46.6	14 31.3
13 Su	3 25 14	22 46 58	25 50 56	1♒49 25	7 11.4	12 36.9	10 13.0	29 01.7	22 46.3	16 12.7	2 48.5	24 43.8	8 46.5	14 29.8
14 M	3 29 11	23 44 52	7♒46 11	13 41 50	7R12.7	14 06.5	10 53.5	29 00.0	22 47.4	16 26.0	2 56.2	24 44.6	8 46.4	14 28.3
15 Tu	3 33 07	24 42 44	19 37 01	25 32 21	7 13.2	15 32.5	11 35.0	28 57.4	22 48.1	16 39.4	3 03.9	24 45.3	8 46.3	14 26.8
16 W	3 37 04	25 40 34	1♓28 30	7♓26 05	7 12.4	16 54.9	12 17.5	28 54.2	22R48.5	16 52.8	3 11.6	24 46.0	8 46.1	14 25.3
17 Th	3 41 00	26 38 24	13 25 42	19 27 55	7 09.9	18 13.4	13 01.0	28 50.1	22 48.5	17 06.2	3 19.3	24 46.6	8 45.9	14 23.8
18 F	3 44 57	27 36 12	25 33 16	1♈42 13	7 05.7	19 28.2	13 45.4	28 45.3	22 48.1	17 19.7	3 27.1	24 47.2	8 45.7	14 22.3
19 Sa	3 48 53	28 33 59	7♈55 12	14 12 34	7 00.3	20 39.1	14 30.7	28 39.8	22 47.4	17 33.2	3 34.8	24 47.7	8 45.5	14 20.8
20 Su	3 52 50	29 31 45	20 34 34	27 01 23	6 54.2	21 46.1	15 16.8	28 33.4	22 46.3	17 46.7	3 42.6	24 48.2	8 45.2	14 19.2
21 M	3 56 47	0♊29 30	3♉33 07	10♉09 45	6 48.0	22 49.1	16 03.8	28 26.3	22 44.9	18 00.2	3 50.4	24 48.6	8 44.8	14 17.7
22 Tu	4 00 43	1 27 14	16 51 10	23 37 12	6 42.6	23 48.1	16 51.5	28 18.5	22 43.0	18 13.8	3 58.1	24 49.0	8 44.5	14 16.1
23 W	4 04 40	2 24 57	0♊27 33	7♊21 51	6 38.5	24 43.0	17 40.0	28 09.9	22 40.8	18 27.4	4 05.9	24 49.3	8 44.1	14 14.5
24 Th	4 08 36	3 22 38	14 19 42	21 20 38	6 36.0	25 33.7	18 29.2	28 00.5	22 38.2	18 41.0	4 13.7	24 49.6	8 43.7	14 13.0
25 F	4 12 33	4 20 18	28 24 10	5♋29 46	6D35.1	26 20.1	19 19.1	27 50.5	22 35.3	18 54.7	4 21.4	24 49.8	8 43.2	14 11.4
26 Sa	4 16 29	5 17 56	12♋36 58	19 45 16	6 35.6	27 02.3	20 09.7	27 39.7	22 32.0	19 08.4	4 29.2	24 50.0	8 42.8	14 09.8
27 Su	4 20 26	6 15 33	26 54 13	4♌03 24	6 36.9	27 40.0	21 00.9	27 28.2	22 28.3	19 22.1	4 37.0	24 50.1	8 42.3	14 08.2
28 M	4 24 22	7 13 09	11♌12 25	18 20 55	6 38.3	28 13.3	21 52.7	27 16.1	22 24.3	19 35.8	4 44.8	24 50.2	8 41.7	14 06.6
29 Tu	4 28 19	8 10 43	25 28 37	2♍35 12	6R39.2	28 42.1	22 45.2	27 03.3	22 19.9	19 49.5	4 52.5	24R50.3	8 41.2	14 05.0
30 W	4 32 16	9 08 16	9♍40 27	16 44 06	6 39.1	29 06.3	23 38.2	26 49.8	22 15.1	20 03.2	5 00.3	24 50.2	8 40.6	14 03.4
31 Th	4 36 12	10 05 47	23 45 56	0♎45 44	6 37.8	29 25.9	24 31.7	26 35.8	22 10.0	20 17.0	5 08.1	24 50.2	8 39.9	14 01.8

LONGITUDE — June 2001

Day	Sid.Time	☉	0 hr ☽	Noon ☽	True ☊	☿	♀	♂	⚳	♃	♄	♅	♆	♇
1 F	4 40 09	11♊03 17	7♎43 18	14♎38 25	6♋35.4	29♊40.8	25♈25.8	26♐21.1	22♑04.5	20♊30.8	5♊15.8	24♒50.1	8♒39.3	14♐00.1
2 Sa	4 44 05	12 00 46	21 30 52	28 20 27	6R32.2	29 51.0	26 20.4	26R05.9	21R58.7	20 44.5	5 23.5	24R49.9	8R38.6	13R58.5
3 Su	4 48 02	12 58 13	5♏06 58	11♏50 14	6 28.7	29R56.7	27 15.5	25 50.2	21 52.5	20 58.3	5 31.3	24 49.7	8 37.9	13 56.9
4 M	4 51 58	13 55 39	18 30 05	25 06 22	6 25.4	29 57.7	28 11.1	25 34.0	21 46.0	21 12.1	5 39.0	24 49.4	8 37.1	13 55.3
5 Tu	4 55 55	14 53 05	1♐38 59	8♐07 50	6 22.8	29 54.2	29 07.2	25 17.3	21 39.2	21 25.9	5 46.7	24 49.1	8 36.3	13 53.7
6 W	4 59 51	15 50 29	14 32 55	20 54 13	6 21.1	29 46.3	0♉03.7	25 00.1	21 32.0	21 39.8	5 54.4	24 48.8	8 35.6	13 52.1
7 Th	5 03 48	16 47 53	27 11 48	3♑25 48	6D20.4	29 34.2	1 00.7	24 42.5	21 24.5	21 53.6	6 02.1	24 48.4	8 34.7	13 50.4
8 F	5 07 45	17 45 16	9♑36 23	15 43 46	6 20.6	29 18.2	1 58.1	24 24.6	21 16.6	22 07.4	6 09.8	24 47.9	8 33.9	13 48.8
9 Sa	5 11 41	18 42 38	21 48 14	27 50 07	6 21.5	28 58.4	2 55.9	24 06.3	21 08.5	22 21.3	6 17.5	24 47.4	8 33.0	13 47.2
10 Su	5 15 38	19 39 59	3♒49 46	9♒47 38	6 22.9	28 35.2	3 54.1	23 47.7	21 00.0	22 35.1	6 25.1	24 46.9	8 32.1	13 45.6
11 M	5 19 34	20 37 20	15 44 09	21 39 49	6 24.3	28 09.0	4 52.7	23 28.8	20 51.2	22 48.9	6 32.7	24 46.3	8 31.2	13 44.0
12 Tu	5 23 31	21 34 40	27 35 09	3♓30 43	6 25.4	27 40.3	5 51.7	23 09.7	20 42.1	23 02.8	6 40.3	24 45.7	8 30.2	13 42.4
13 W	5 27 27	22 32 00	9♓27 04	15 24 47	6R26.1	27 09.4	6 51.0	22 50.4	20 32.7	23 16.6	6 47.9	24 45.0	8 29.2	13 40.8
14 Th	5 31 24	23 29 20	21 24 28	27 26 41	6 26.2	26 36.9	7 50.7	22 31.0	20 23.1	23 30.5	6 55.5	24 44.2	8 28.2	13 39.2
15 F	5 35 20	24 26 39	3♈32 00	9♈40 58	6 25.7	26 03.4	8 50.7	22 11.5	20 13.1	23 44.3	7 03.1	24 43.5	8 27.2	13 37.6
16 Sa	5 39 17	25 23 57	15 54 07	22 11 54	6 24.8	25 29.4	9 51.1	21 51.9	20 02.9	23 58.2	7 10.6	24 42.6	8 26.1	13 36.1
17 Su	5 43 14	26 21 16	28 34 45	5♉03 00	6 23.6	24 55.5	10 51.7	21 32.4	19 52.4	24 12.0	7 18.1	24 41.8	8 25.0	13 34.5
18 M	5 47 10	27 18 34	11♉36 54	18 16 38	6 22.4	24 22.3	11 52.7	21 12.9	19 41.7	24 25.8	7 25.6	24 40.9	8 23.9	13 32.9
19 Tu	5 51 07	28 15 51	25 02 14	1♊53 39	6 21.4	23 50.4	12 53.9	20 53.5	19 30.7	24 39.7	7 33.1	24 39.9	8 22.8	13 31.4
20 W	5 55 03	29 13 09	8♊50 41	15 53 00	6 20.7	23 20.3	13 55.5	20 34.2	19 19.5	24 53.5	7 40.5	24 38.9	8 21.7	13 29.8
21 Th	5 59 00	0♋10 26	23 00 12	0♋11 42	6D20.4	22 52.5	14 57.3	20 15.1	19 08.0	25 07.3	7 47.9	24 37.9	8 20.5	13 28.3
22 F	6 02 56	1 07 43	7♋26 51	14 44 54	6 20.4	22 27.4	15 59.4	19 56.3	18 56.4	25 21.1	7 55.3	24 36.8	8 19.3	13 26.8
23 Sa	6 06 53	2 04 59	22 05 04	29 26 30	6 20.7	22 05.6	17 01.7	19 37.8	18 44.6	25 34.9	8 02.7	24 35.7	8 18.1	13 25.3
24 Su	6 10 50	3 02 15	6♌48 23	14♌09 52	6 21.0	21 47.4	18 04.3	19 19.6	18 32.5	25 48.7	8 10.0	24 34.5	8 16.8	13 23.8
25 M	6 14 46	3 59 30	21 30 12	28 48 40	6 21.3	21 33.1	19 07.1	19 01.8	18 20.3	26 02.5	8 17.3	24 33.3	8 15.6	13 22.3
26 Tu	6 18 43	4 56 44	6♍04 39	13♍17 36	6 21.4	21 22.9	20 10.1	18 44.4	18 08.0	26 16.2	8 24.5	24 32.0	8 14.3	13 20.8
27 W	6 22 39	5 53 58	20 27 05	27 32 46	6 21.5	21D17.2	21 13.4	18 27.5	17 55.5	26 29.9	8 31.8	24 30.7	8 13.0	13 19.3
28 Th	6 26 36	6 51 11	4♎34 24	11♎31 50	6 21.5	21 16.1	22 16.9	18 11.1	17 42.8	26 43.7	8 38.9	24 29.4	8 11.7	13 17.9
29 F	6 30 32	7 48 24	18 25 00	25 13 51	6 21.5	21 19.7	23 20.6	17 55.3	17 30.1	26 57.4	8 46.1	24 28.0	8 10.4	13 16.4
30 Sa	6 34 29	8 45 36	1♏58 27	8♏38 53	6 21.7	21 28.1	24 24.5	17 40.0	17 17.2	27 11.0	8 53.2	24 26.6	8 09.0	13 15.0

Astro Data

	Dy Hr Mn
☽0S	5 0:54
♃☍♇	6 10:47
♆R	11 1:13
♂R	11 16:08
⚳R	17 0:29
☽0N	19 7:48
♅R	29 15:11
☽0S	1 7:38
☿R	4 5:21
♃⚼♆	14 8:20
☽0N	15 16:56
♃△♅	19 12:25
♄△♆	25 7:15
☿D	28 5:48
☽0S	28 13:16

Planet Ingress

	Dy Hr Mn
☿ ♊	6 4:53
☉ ♊	20 23:44
♀ ♉	6 10:25
☉ ♋	21 7:38

Last Aspect / ☽ Ingress

Last Aspect Dy Hr Mn		☽ Ingress Dy Hr Mn
1 23:44 ♂ △	♍	2 2:16
4 2:39 ♂ □	♎	4 4:50
6 6:03 ♂ ⚹	♏	6 8:00
8 3:25 ♅ □	♐	8 13:05
10 19:20 ♂ ☌	♑	10 21:10
12 16:17 ☉ △	♒	13 8:20
15 18:53 ♂ ⚹	♓	15 21:01
18 6:18 ♂ □	♈	18 8:41
20 14:48 ♂ △	♉	20 17:29
22 14:07 ♅ □	♊	22 23:12
24 23:12 ♂ ☍	♋	25 2:42
26 12:44 ♀ □	♌	27 5:12
29 5:13 ☿ ⚹	♍	29 7:38
31 9:40 ☿ □	♎	31 10:41

Last Aspect / ☽ Ingress

Last Aspect Dy Hr Mn		☽ Ingress Dy Hr Mn
2 14:42 ☿ △	♏	2 14:56
4 11:29 ♅ □	♐	4 20:58
7 4:41 ☿ ☍	♑	7 5:23
7 6:57 ♀ △	♒	9 16:20
12 0:39 ☿ △	♓	12 4:53
14 10:26 ☿ □	♈	14 17:03
16 18:32 ☉ ⚹	♉	17 2:39
18 23:22 ♅ □	♊	19 8:42
21 3:24 ♃ ☌	♋	21 11:41
22 14:11 ♀ ⚹	♌	23 12:55
25 7:22 ♃ ⚹	♍	25 13:57
27 10:12 ♃ □	♎	27 16:11
29 15:07 ♃ △	♏	29 20:28

☽ Phases & Eclipses

Dy Hr Mn		
7 13:53	○	17♏04
15 10:11	☾	24♒38
23 2:46	●	2♊03
29 22:09	☽	8♍35
6 1:39	○	15♐26
14 3:28	☾	23♓09
21 11:58	●	0♋10
21 12:03:43	●	T 04'56"
28 3:20	☽	6♎31

Astro Data

1 May 2001
Julian Day # 37011
SVP 5♓14'46"
GC 26♐51.5 ⚴ 13♐27.1R
Eris 19♈43.0 ⚵ 10♉38.1
⚷ 28♐29.9R ⚶ 23♈01.2
☽ Mean ☊ 9♋18.2

1 June 2001
Julian Day # 37042
SVP 5♓14'42"
GC 26♐51.5 ⚴ 5♐04.4R
Eris 19♈59.7 ⚵ 28♉59.2
⚷ 26♐54.0R ⚶ 6♉44.6
☽ Mean ☊ 7♋39.7

July 2001 LONGITUDE

Day	Sid.Time	☉	0 hr ☽	Noon ☽	True ☊	☿	♀	♂	⚳	♃	♄	♅	♆	♇
1 Su	6 38 25	9♋42 48	15♏15 14	21♏47 41	6♋22.0	21♊41.4	25♉28.6	17♐25.3	17♑04.3	27♊24.7	9♊00.3	24♒25.2	8♒07.6	13♐13.6
2 M	6 42 22	10 40 00	28 16 21	4♐41 24	6 22.4	21 59.6	26 33.0	17R 11.2	16R 51.2	27 38.3	9 07.3	24R 23.7	8R 06.2	13R 12.2
3 Tu	6 46 19	11 37 11	11♐03 01	17 21 21	6 22.8	22 22.8	27 37.5	16 57.8	16 38.1	27 51.9	9 14.3	24 22.2	8 04.8	13 10.8
4 W	6 50 15	12 34 23	23 36 36	29 48 56	6R 23.0	22 50.9	28 42.3	16 45.1	16 25.0	28 05.5	9 21.3	24 20.6	8 03.4	13 09.5
5 Th	6 54 12	13 31 34	5♑58 31	12♑05 34	6 23.0	23 24.0	29 47.2	16 33.0	16 11.8	28 19.1	9 28.2	24 19.0	8 02.0	13 08.1
6 F	6 58 08	14 28 45	18 10 16	24 12 49	6 22.7	24 01.8	0♊52.3	16 21.7	15 58.6	28 32.6	9 35.1	24 17.4	8 00.6	13 06.8
7 Sa	7 02 05	15 25 57	0♒13 28	6♒12 27	6 21.9	24 44.6	1 57.6	16 11.2	15 45.4	28 46.2	9 41.9	24 15.7	7 59.1	13 05.5
8 Su	7 06 01	16 23 08	12 10 02	18 06 31	6 20.7	25 32.1	3 03.1	16 01.3	15 32.2	28 59.7	9 48.7	24 14.0	7 57.6	13 04.2
9 M	7 09 58	17 20 20	24 02 14	29 57 32	6 19.2	26 24.3	4 08.7	15 52.3	15 19.0	29 13.1	9 55.4	24 12.3	7 56.1	13 03.0
10 Tu	7 13 54	18 17 32	5♓52 47	11♓48 25	6 17.6	27 21.2	5 14.5	15 44.0	15 05.8	29 26.5	10 02.1	24 10.5	7 54.6	13 01.7
11 W	7 17 51	19 14 44	17 44 51	23 42 35	6 16.1	28 22.8	6 20.5	15 36.6	14 52.6	29 39.9	10 08.8	24 08.7	7 53.1	13 00.5
12 Th	7 21 48	20 11 57	29 42 05	5♈43 53	6 15.0	29 28.9	7 26.7	15 29.9	14 39.6	29 53.3	10 15.4	24 06.9	7 51.6	12 59.3
13 F	7 25 44	21 09 10	11♈48 31	17 56 31	6D 14.5	0♋39.4	8 33.0	15 24.1	14 26.6	0♋06.6	10 21.9	24 05.0	7 50.1	12 58.1
14 Sa	7 29 41	22 06 24	24 08 24	0♉24 44	6 14.6	1 54.4	9 39.5	15 19.1	14 13.6	0 19.9	10 28.4	24 03.1	7 48.5	12 56.9
15 Su	7 33 37	23 03 39	6♉46 00	13 12 40	6 15.4	3 13.8	10 46.1	15 14.9	14 00.8	0 33.2	10 34.9	24 01.2	7 46.9	12 55.8
16 M	7 37 34	24 00 54	19 45 10	26 23 51	6 16.6	4 37.4	11 52.9	15 11.5	13 48.1	0 46.4	10 41.3	23 59.3	7 45.4	12 54.7
17 Tu	7 41 30	24 58 10	3♊08 57	10♊00 38	6 17.9	6 05.3	12 59.8	15 09.0	13 35.5	0 59.6	10 47.6	23 57.3	7 43.8	12 53.6
18 W	7 45 27	25 55 26	16 58 55	24 03 39	6R 18.9	7 37.2	14 06.9	15 07.4	13 23.1	1 12.8	10 53.9	23 55.3	7 42.2	12 52.5
19 Th	7 49 23	26 52 43	1♋14 35	8♋31 13	6 19.2	9 13.0	15 14.1	15D 06.6	13 10.8	1 25.9	11 00.2	23 53.3	7 40.6	12 51.5
20 F	7 53 20	27 50 01	15 52 57	23 18 58	6 18.5	10 52.7	16 21.5	15 06.6	12 58.6	1 39.0	11 06.3	23 51.2	7 39.0	12 50.4
21 Sa	7 57 17	28 47 19	0♌48 20	8♌20 00	6 16.8	12 35.9	17 28.9	15 07.5	12 46.7	1 52.0	11 12.4	23 49.1	7 37.4	12 49.4
22 Su	8 01 13	29 44 38	15 52 49	23 25 38	6 14.2	14 22.7	18 36.5	15 09.3	12 34.9	2 05.0	11 18.5	23 47.0	7 35.8	12 48.5
23 M	8 05 10	0♌41 57	0♍57 15	8♍26 36	6 11.0	16 12.6	19 44.3	15 11.8	12 23.4	2 17.9	11 24.5	23 44.9	7 34.2	12 47.5
24 Tu	8 09 06	1 39 16	15 52 39	23 14 32	6 07.9	18 05.6	20 52.1	15 15.3	12 12.0	2 30.8	11 30.4	23 42.7	7 32.6	12 46.6
25 W	8 13 03	2 36 35	0♎31 32	7♎43 05	6 05.2	20 01.2	22 00.1	15 19.5	12 00.9	2 43.6	11 36.3	23 40.6	7 31.0	12 45.7
26 Th	8 16 59	3 33 55	14 48 50	21 48 32	6D 03.6	21 59.2	23 08.2	15 24.6	11 50.0	2 56.4	11 42.1	23 38.4	7 29.4	12 44.8
27 F	8 20 56	4 31 16	28 42 09	5♏29 44	6 03.1	23 59.3	24 16.4	15 30.5	11 39.4	3 09.1	11 47.8	23 36.2	7 27.7	12 44.0
28 Sa	8 24 52	5 28 37	12♏11 28	18 47 36	6 03.7	26 01.2	25 24.7	15 37.2	11 29.0	3 21.8	11 53.5	23 34.0	7 26.1	12 43.2
29 Su	8 28 49	6 25 58	25 18 28	1♐44 28	6 05.1	28 04.5	26 33.1	15 44.7	11 18.9	3 34.4	11 59.1	23 31.7	7 24.5	12 42.4
30 M	8 32 46	7 23 20	8♐05 58	14 23 24	6 06.7	0♌08.9	27 41.7	15 53.0	11 09.0	3 47.0	12 04.6	23 29.5	7 22.8	12 41.6
31 Tu	8 36 42	8 20 42	20 37 10	26 47 40	6R 08.0	2 14.0	28 50.4	16 02.0	10 59.4	3 59.5	12 10.1	23 27.2	7 21.2	12 40.9

August 2001 LONGITUDE

Day	Sid.Time	☉	0 hr ☽	Noon ☽	True ☊	☿	♀	♂	⚳	♃	♄	♅	♆	♇
1 W	8 40 39	9♌18 06	2♑55 19	9♑00 27	6♋08.3	4♌19.5	29♊59.1	16♐11.8	10♑50.2	4♋11.9	12♊15.5	23♒24.9	7♒19.6	12♐40.2
2 Th	8 44 35	10 15 29	15 03 25	21 04 33	6R 07.2	6 25.2	1♋08.0	16 22.4	10R 41.2	4 24.3	12 20.9	23R 22.6	7R 18.0	12R 39.5
3 F	8 48 32	11 12 54	27 04 06	3♒02 22	6 04.5	8 30.7	2 17.0	16 33.6	10 32.5	4 36.7	12 26.1	23 20.3	7 16.3	12 38.9
4 Sa	8 52 28	12 10 20	8♒59 37	14 56 03	6 00.0	10 35.9	3 26.1	16 45.6	10 24.1	4 48.9	12 31.3	23 18.0	7 14.7	12 38.3
5 Su	8 56 25	13 07 46	20 51 55	26 47 26	5 54.2	12 40.4	4 35.4	16 58.3	10 16.0	5 01.2	12 36.4	23 15.6	7 13.1	12 37.7
6 M	9 00 21	14 05 14	2♓42 51	8♓38 23	5 47.4	14 44.2	5 44.7	17 11.7	10 08.3	5 13.3	12 41.4	23 13.3	7 11.5	12 37.1
7 Tu	9 04 18	15 02 42	14 34 19	20 30 54	5 40.3	16 47.1	6 54.1	17 25.8	10 00.8	5 25.4	12 46.4	23 10.9	7 09.9	12 36.6
8 W	9 08 15	16 00 12	26 28 26	2♈27 15	5 33.6	18 48.9	8 03.7	17 40.5	9 53.7	5 37.4	12 51.3	23 08.5	7 08.2	12 36.1
9 Th	9 12 11	16 57 43	8♈27 42	14 30 11	5 28.0	20 49.5	9 13.3	17 55.9	9 47.0	5 49.3	12 56.1	23 06.2	7 06.6	12 35.6
10 F	9 16 08	17 55 15	20 35 07	26 42 56	5 24.0	22 48.9	10 23.1	18 12.0	9 40.5	6 01.2	13 00.8	23 03.8	7 05.0	12 35.2
11 Sa	9 20 04	18 52 49	2♉54 07	9♉09 10	5D 21.8	24 46.9	11 32.9	18 28.7	9 34.4	6 13.0	13 05.5	23 01.4	7 03.5	12 34.8
12 Su	9 24 01	19 50 24	15 28 34	21 52 50	5 21.3	26 43.6	12 42.9	18 46.0	9 28.7	6 24.8	13 10.1	22 59.0	7 01.9	12 34.4
13 M	9 27 57	20 48 00	28 22 27	4♊57 53	5 22.1	28 38.9	13 52.9	19 03.9	9 23.3	6 36.4	13 14.5	22 56.6	7 00.3	12 34.0
14 Tu	9 31 54	21 45 38	11♊39 31	18 27 41	5 23.3	0♍32.8	15 03.1	19 22.5	9 18.2	6 48.0	13 18.9	22 54.2	6 58.7	12 33.7
15 W	9 35 50	22 43 18	25 22 37	2♋24 25	5R 24.1	2 25.2	16 13.3	19 41.6	9 13.5	6 59.5	13 23.3	22 51.8	6 57.2	12 33.5
16 Th	9 39 47	23 40 59	9♋33 03	16 48 15	5 23.6	4 16.2	17 23.7	20 01.3	9 09.1	7 10.9	13 27.5	22 49.5	6 55.6	12 33.2
17 F	9 43 44	24 38 42	24 09 36	1♌36 28	5 21.2	6 05.7	18 34.1	20 21.6	9 05.2	7 22.3	13 31.7	22 47.1	6 54.1	12 33.0
18 Sa	9 47 40	25 36 26	9♌08 00	16 43 09	5 16.6	7 53.8	19 44.6	20 42.5	9 01.5	7 33.6	13 35.7	22 44.7	6 52.6	12 32.8
19 Su	9 51 37	26 34 11	24 20 44	1♍59 24	5 10.2	9 40.5	20 55.2	21 03.9	8 58.3	7 44.7	13 39.7	22 42.3	6 51.0	12 32.7
20 M	9 55 33	27 31 58	9♍37 47	17 14 30	5 02.5	11 25.7	22 05.9	21 25.9	8 55.4	7 55.8	13 43.6	22 39.9	6 49.5	12 32.5
21 Tu	9 59 30	28 29 46	24 48 12	2♎17 42	4 54.6	13 09.6	23 16.7	21 48.4	8 52.8	8 06.8	13 47.4	22 37.5	6 48.0	12 32.5
22 W	10 03 26	29 27 35	9♎41 58	17 00 09	4 47.6	14 52.0	24 27.6	22 11.4	8 50.6	8 17.8	13 51.1	22 35.1	6 46.6	12 32.4
23 Th	10 07 23	0♍25 25	24 11 41	1♏16 08	4 42.3	16 33.1	25 38.5	22 35.0	8 48.8	8 28.6	13 54.7	22 32.8	6 45.1	12D 32.4
24 F	10 11 19	1 23 17	8♏13 21	15 03 20	4 39.0	18 12.7	26 49.6	22 59.0	8 47.4	8 39.3	13 58.2	22 30.4	6 43.6	12 32.4
25 Sa	10 15 16	2 21 09	21 46 16	28 22 28	4D 37.7	19 51.1	28 00.7	23 23.6	8 46.3	8 50.0	14 01.7	22 28.1	6 42.2	12 32.4
26 Su	10 19 13	3 19 03	4♐52 20	11♐16 22	4 37.9	21 28.1	29 11.9	23 48.6	8 45.5	9 00.5	14 05.0	22 25.7	6 40.8	12 32.5
27 M	10 23 09	4 16 59	17 35 08	23 49 10	4R 38.7	23 03.7	0♌23.2	24 14.1	8D 45.2	9 11.0	14 08.2	22 23.4	6 39.4	12 32.6
28 Tu	10 27 06	5 14 55	29 59 05	6♑05 27	4 39.0	24 38.0	1 34.5	24 40.0	8 45.2	9 21.3	14 11.4	22 21.1	6 38.0	12 32.8
29 W	10 31 02	6 12 53	12♑08 49	18 09 45	4 38.1	26 11.0	2 46.0	25 06.4	8 45.5	9 31.6	14 14.4	22 18.8	6 36.6	12 32.9
30 Th	10 34 59	7 10 52	24 08 42	0♒06 10	4 34.9	27 42.7	3 57.5	25 33.2	8 46.2	9 41.7	14 17.4	22 16.5	6 35.3	12 33.2
31 F	10 38 55	8 08 53	6♒02 33	11 58 13	4 29.3	29 13.0	5 09.1	26 00.5	8 47.3	9 51.8	14 20.3	22 14.2	6 33.9	12 33.4

Astro Data

	Dy Hr Mn
☽0N	13 0:48
♂ D	19 22:45
☽0S	25 19:26
♄☍♇	5 17:20
☽0N	9 6:54
♃⚻♆	15 7:41
♃⚼♅	19 7:39
☽0S	22 3:26
♇ D	23 16:08
⚳ D	28 0:41
☿0S	31 17:11

Planet Ingress

	Dy Hr Mn
♀ ♊	5 16:44
☿ ♋	12 22:47
♃ ♋	13 0:03
☉ ♌	22 18:26
☿ ♌	30 10:18
♀ ♋	1 12:18
☿ ♍	14 5:04
☉ ♍	23 1:27
♀ ♌	27 4:12

Last Aspect / ☽ Ingress

Last Aspect Dy Hr Mn	☽ Ingress Dy Hr Mn
1 19:25 ♀ ☍	♐ 2 3:13
4 8:36 ♃ ☍	♑ 4 12:21
5 15:04 ☉ ☍	♒ 6 23:33
9 10:28 ♃ △	♓ 9 12:05
12 0:09 ♃ □	♈ 12 0:36
13 23:52 ♅ ⚹	♉ 14 11:13
16 7:41 ♅ □	♊ 16 18:26
18 11:46 ♅ △	♋ 18 21:56
20 19:44 ☉ ☌	♌ 20 22:43
22 12:34 ♅ ☍	♍ 22 22:29
24 7:48 ♀ □	♎ 24 23:08
26 15:10 ♅ △	♏ 27 2:17
29 3:50 ☿ △	♐ 29 8:44
31 16:24 ♀ ☍	♑ 31 18:16

Last Aspect / ☽ Ingress

Last Aspect Dy Hr Mn	☽ Ingress Dy Hr Mn
1 2:21 ♃ ☍	♒ 3 5:53
5 4:52 ♅ ☌	♓ 5 18:30
7 5:39 ♂ □	♈ 8 7:05
10 4:53 ♅ ⚹	♉ 10 18:23
12 22:32 ♅ □	♊ 13 2:59
14 19:43 ♅ △	♋ 15 7:55
16 13:03 ♀ ☌	♌ 17 9:25
19 2:55 ☉ ☌	♍ 19 8:53
20 20:21 ♀ ⚹	♎ 21 8:19
23 1:34 ♀ □	♏ 23 9:50
25 11:16 ♀ △	♐ 25 14:59
27 12:50 ♂ ☌	♑ 28 0:02
30 6:28 ☿ △	♒ 30 11:48

☽ Phases & Eclipses

Dy Hr Mn	
5 15:04	○ 13♑39
5 14:55	• P 0.495
13 18:45	☾ 21♈25
20 19:44	● 28♋08
27 10:08	☽ 4♏27
4 5:56	○ 11♒56
12 7:53	☾ 19♉41
19 2:55	● 26♌12
25 19:55	☽ 2♐40

Astro Data

1 July 2001
Julian Day # 37072
SVP 5♓14'37"
GC 26♐51.6 ⚴ 28♏18.4R
Eris 20♈08.8 ⚵ 16♊42.9
⚷ 24♐54.1R ⚶ 19♉04.2
☽ Mean ☊ 6♋04.4

1 August 2001
Julian Day # 37103
SVP 5♓14'31"
GC 26♐51.7 ⚴ 27♏54.0
Eris 20♈08.7R ⚵ 4♋35.5
⚷ 23♐18.3R ⚶ 0♊16.1
☽ Mean ☊ 4♋25.9

LONGITUDE — September 2001

Day	Sid.Time	☉	0 hr ☽	Noon ☽	True ☊	☿	♀	♂	⚳	♃	♄	♅	♆	♇
1 Sa	10 42 52	9♍06 55	17♒53 32	23♒48 45	4♋21.0	0♎42.1	6♌20.7	26♐28.1	8♑48.7	10♋01.7	14♊23.0	22♒11.9	6♒32.6	12♐33.7
2 Su	10 46 48	10 04 59	29 44 09	5♓39 57	4R 10.5	2 09.7	7 32.5	26 56.2	8 50.4	10 11.6	14 25.7	22R 09.7	6R 31.3	12 34.0
3 M	10 50 45	11 03 04	11♓36 21	17 33 33	3 58.5	3 36.1	8 44.3	27 24.7	8 52.5	10 21.3	14 28.2	22 07.5	6 30.0	12 34.3
4 Tu	10 54 42	12 01 11	23 31 42	29 30 58	3 45.9	5 01.0	9 56.2	27 53.5	8 54.9	10 30.9	14 30.7	22 05.2	6 28.8	12 34.7
5 W	10 58 38	12 59 19	5♈31 33	11♈33 36	3 33.8	6 24.6	11 08.2	28 22.7	8 57.7	10 40.4	14 33.0	22 03.0	6 27.6	12 35.1
6 Th	11 02 35	13 57 30	17 37 21	23 43 02	3 23.3	7 46.7	12 20.3	28 52.3	9 00.8	10 49.8	14 35.3	22 00.9	6 26.3	12 35.5
7 F	11 06 31	14 55 42	29 50 53	6♉01 13	3 15.1	9 07.4	13 32.4	29 22.3	9 04.2	10 59.1	14 37.5	21 58.7	6 25.1	12 36.0
8 Sa	11 10 28	15 53 57	12♉14 22	18 30 42	3 09.6	10 26.7	14 44.7	29 52.6	9 08.0	11 08.3	14 39.5	21 56.6	6 24.0	12 36.5
9 Su	11 14 24	16 52 13	24 50 36	1♊14 30	3 06.6	11 44.4	15 57.0	0♑23.2	9 12.1	11 17.3	14 41.5	21 54.5	6 22.8	12 37.0
10 M	11 18 21	17 50 32	7♊42 49	14 16 01	3D 05.6	13 00.5	17 09.3	0 54.2	9 16.5	11 26.3	14 43.3	21 52.4	6 21.7	12 37.6
11 Tu	11 22 17	18 48 53	20 54 30	27 38 39	3R 05.7	14 14.9	18 21.8	1 25.6	9 21.2	11 35.1	14 45.0	21 50.3	6 20.6	12 38.2
12 W	11 26 14	19 47 16	4♋28 49	11♋25 14	3 05.6	15 27.7	19 34.3	1 57.2	9 26.3	11 43.8	14 46.7	21 48.3	6 19.5	12 38.9
13 Th	11 30 10	20 45 41	18 28 01	25 37 10	3 04.1	16 38.6	20 46.9	2 29.2	9 31.7	11 52.3	14 48.2	21 46.3	6 18.5	12 39.5
14 F	11 34 07	21 44 08	2♌52 30	10♌13 36	3 00.2	17 47.7	21 59.6	3 01.5	9 37.4	12 00.8	14 49.6	21 44.3	6 17.4	12 40.2
15 Sa	11 38 04	22 42 37	17 39 55	25 10 36	2 53.7	18 54.7	23 12.3	3 34.1	9 43.4	12 09.1	14 50.9	21 42.4	6 16.4	12 41.0
16 Su	11 42 00	23 41 08	2♍44 39	10♍20 54	2 44.6	19 59.7	24 25.1	4 07.1	9 49.7	12 17.3	14 52.1	21 40.5	6 15.4	12 41.7
17 M	11 45 57	24 39 41	17 58 00	25 34 36	2 33.9	21 02.4	25 37.9	4 40.3	9 56.3	12 25.3	14 53.2	21 38.6	6 14.5	12 42.5
18 Tu	11 49 53	25 38 16	3♎09 16	10♎40 41	2 22.7	22 02.7	26 50.9	5 13.8	10 03.2	12 33.2	14 54.2	21 36.7	6 13.6	12 43.3
19 W	11 53 50	26 36 53	18 07 38	25 29 04	2 12.3	23 00.4	28 03.8	5 47.6	10 10.5	12 41.0	14 55.1	21 34.9	6 12.6	12 44.2
20 Th	11 57 46	27 35 32	2♏44 10	9♏52 17	2 04.0	23 55.4	29 16.9	6 21.7	10 18.0	12 48.6	14 55.9	21 33.1	6 11.8	12 45.1
21 F	12 01 43	28 34 12	16 53 05	23 46 23	1 58.2	24 47.4	0♍30.0	6 56.1	10 25.8	12 56.1	14 56.5	21 31.3	6 10.9	12 46.0
22 Sa	12 05 39	29 32 54	0♐32 13	7♐10 49	1 55.0	25 36.2	1 43.2	7 30.7	10 33.9	13 03.5	14 57.1	21 29.6	6 10.1	12 47.0
23 Su	12 09 36	0♎31 38	13 42 32	20 07 49	1 53.8	26 21.6	2 56.4	8 05.6	10 42.3	13 10.7	14 57.5	21 27.9	6 09.3	12 48.0
24 M	12 13 33	1 30 24	26 27 15	2♑41 25	1 53.6	27 03.2	4 09.7	8 40.8	10 50.9	13 17.7	14 57.8	21 26.2	6 08.6	12 49.0
25 Tu	12 17 29	2 29 11	8♑50 59	14 56 35	1 53.3	27 40.8	5 23.0	9 16.2	10 59.9	13 24.6	14 58.1	21 24.6	6 07.8	12 50.0
26 W	12 21 26	3 28 00	20 58 55	26 58 36	1 51.9	28 14.0	6 36.4	9 51.8	11 09.1	13 31.4	14R 58.2	21 23.0	6 07.1	12 51.1
27 Th	12 25 22	4 26 50	2♒56 15	8♒52 28	1 48.2	28 42.4	7 49.8	10 27.7	11 18.6	13 38.0	14 58.2	21 21.4	6 06.5	12 52.2
28 F	12 29 19	5 25 43	14 47 47	20 42 42	1 41.8	29 05.8	9 03.3	11 03.8	11 28.3	13 44.5	14 58.1	21 19.9	6 05.8	12 53.4
29 Sa	12 33 15	6 24 37	26 37 40	2♓33 04	1 32.5	29 23.6	10 16.9	11 40.2	11 38.3	13 50.8	14 57.8	21 18.5	6 05.2	12 54.5
30 Su	12 37 12	7 23 33	8♓29 17	14 26 34	1 20.8	29 35.4	11 30.5	12 16.7	11 48.5	13 56.9	14 57.5	21 17.0	6 04.6	12 55.7

LONGITUDE — October 2001

Day	Sid.Time	☉	0 hr ☽	Noon ☽	True ☊	☿	♀	♂	⚳	♃	♄	♅	♆	♇
1 M	12 41 08	8♎22 31	20♓25 11	26♓25 20	1♋07.4	29♎40.8	12♍44.2	12♑53.5	11♑59.1	14♋02.9	14♊57.1	21♒15.6	6♒04.1	12♐56.9
2 Tu	12 45 05	9 21 31	2♈27 10	8♈30 51	0R 53.3	29R 39.5	13 57.9	13 30.4	12 09.8	14 08.7	14R 56.5	21R 14.3	6R 03.5	12 58.2
3 W	12 49 02	10 20 33	14 36 27	20 44 04	0 39.8	29 30.9	15 11.7	14 07.6	12 20.8	14 14.4	14 55.9	21 12.9	6 03.0	12 59.5
4 Th	12 52 58	11 19 37	26 53 48	3♉05 43	0 27.9	29 14.8	16 25.5	14 45.0	12 32.0	14 19.9	14 55.1	21 11.7	6 02.6	13 00.8
5 F	12 56 55	12 18 43	9♉19 56	15 36 33	0 18.5	28 51.0	17 39.4	15 22.5	12 43.5	14 25.3	14 54.2	21 10.4	6 02.2	13 02.1
6 Sa	13 00 51	13 17 51	21 55 43	28 17 37	0 12.1	28 19.1	18 53.3	16 00.3	12 55.2	14 30.4	14 53.2	21 09.2	6 01.8	13 03.5
7 Su	13 04 48	14 17 02	4♊42 26	11♊10 25	0 08.5	27 39.4	20 07.3	16 38.2	13 07.2	14 35.4	14 52.1	21 08.1	6 01.4	13 04.9
8 M	13 08 44	15 16 15	17 41 50	24 16 58	0D 07.2	26 52.1	21 21.3	17 16.3	13 19.4	14 40.3	14 51.0	21 07.0	6 01.1	13 06.3
9 Tu	13 12 41	16 15 30	0♋56 06	7♋39 33	0R 07.1	25 57.5	22 35.4	17 54.6	13 31.8	14 45.0	14 49.6	21 05.9	6 00.8	13 07.8
10 W	13 16 37	17 14 48	14 27 33	21 20 21	0 07.2	24 56.6	23 49.6	18 33.1	13 44.4	14 49.5	14 48.2	21 04.9	6 00.5	13 09.2
11 Th	13 20 34	18 14 08	28 18 06	5♌20 51	0 06.2	23 50.4	25 03.7	19 11.7	13 57.3	14 53.8	14 46.7	21 03.9	6 00.3	13 10.7
12 F	13 24 31	19 13 30	12♌28 35	19 41 05	0 03.0	22 40.4	26 18.0	19 50.5	14 10.3	14 57.9	14 45.1	21 03.0	6 00.1	13 12.3
13 Sa	13 28 27	20 12 55	26 58 01	4♍18 50	29♊57.2	21 28.3	27 32.2	20 29.5	14 23.6	15 01.9	14 43.4	21 02.1	5 59.9	13 13.8
14 Su	13 32 24	21 12 22	11♍42 52	19 09 16	29 49.0	20 16.0	28 46.6	21 08.7	14 37.1	15 05.7	14 41.5	21 01.3	5 59.8	13 15.4
15 M	13 36 20	22 11 50	26 37 00	4♎05 01	29 39.2	19 05.5	0♎00.9	21 48.0	14 50.8	15 09.3	14 39.6	21 00.5	5 59.6	13 17.0
16 Tu	13 40 17	23 11 22	11♎32 08	18 57 11	29 28.7	17 58.9	1 15.3	22 27.4	15 04.7	15 12.7	14 37.6	20 59.8	5 59.6	13 18.6
17 W	13 44 13	24 10 55	26 19 03	3♏36 44	29 18.9	16 58.3	2 29.8	23 07.1	15 18.8	15 15.9	14 35.4	20 59.1	5D 59.5	13 20.3
18 Th	13 48 10	25 10 30	10♏49 20	17 56 07	29 10.9	16 05.3	3 44.2	23 46.8	15 33.1	15 18.9	14 33.2	20 58.4	5 59.5	13 22.0
19 F	13 52 06	26 10 07	24 56 35	1♐50 21	29 05.3	15 21.5	4 58.7	24 26.7	15 47.6	15 21.8	14 30.8	20 57.8	5 59.6	13 23.7
20 Sa	13 56 03	27 09 46	8♐37 18	15 17 27	29 02.2	14 47.8	6 13.3	25 06.8	16 02.3	15 24.5	14 28.4	20 57.3	5 59.6	13 25.4
21 Su	14 00 00	28 09 27	21 50 57	28 18 09	29D 01.3	14 25.1	7 27.9	25 47.0	16 17.2	15 26.9	14 25.8	20 56.8	5 59.7	13 27.1
22 M	14 03 56	29 09 10	4♑39 26	10♑55 20	29 01.8	14D 13.6	8 42.5	26 27.4	16 32.3	15 29.2	14 23.2	20 56.4	5 59.9	13 28.9
23 Tu	14 07 53	0♏08 54	17 06 26	23 13 19	29R 02.6	14 13.4	9 57.1	27 07.8	16 47.5	15 31.3	14 20.5	20 56.0	6 00.0	13 30.7
24 W	14 11 49	1 08 40	29 16 39	5♒17 06	29 02.7	14 24.2	11 11.8	27 48.4	17 02.9	15 33.2	14 17.7	20 55.6	6 00.2	13 32.5
25 Th	14 15 46	2 08 27	11♒15 19	17 11 57	29 01.2	14 45.5	12 26.5	28 29.1	17 18.6	15 34.9	14 14.7	20 55.3	6 00.5	13 34.3
26 F	14 19 42	3 08 17	23 07 38	29 02 57	28 57.7	15 16.6	13 41.3	29 10.0	17 34.3	15 36.4	14 11.7	20 55.1	6 00.7	13 36.2
27 Sa	14 23 39	4 08 08	4♓58 28	10♓54 42	28 51.8	15 56.8	14 56.0	29 50.9	17 50.3	15 37.8	14 08.6	20 54.9	6 01.0	13 38.1
28 Su	14 27 35	5 08 00	16 52 07	22 51 08	28 43.9	16 45.2	16 10.8	0♒32.0	18 06.4	15 38.9	14 05.5	20 54.7	6 01.4	13 40.0
29 M	14 31 32	6 07 55	28 52 07	4♈55 22	28 34.5	17 40.9	17 25.6	1 13.1	18 22.7	15 39.8	14 02.2	20 54.6	6 01.8	13 41.9
30 Tu	14 35 28	7 07 51	11♈01 07	17 09 35	28 24.5	18 43.1	18 40.5	1 54.4	18 39.1	15 40.5	13 58.8	20D 54.6	6 02.2	13 43.8
31 W	14 39 25	8 07 49	23 20 53	29 35 07	28 14.8	19 50.9	19 55.4	2 35.8	18 55.8	15 41.0	13 55.4	20 54.6	6 02.6	13 45.8

Astro Data

	Dy Hr Mn
☽ 0N	5 12:04
☽ 0S	18 13:20
♃⊼♇	19 23:23
☉0S	22 23:05
♄ R	27 0:04
☿ R	1 19:24
☽ 0N	2 17:45
♃⊻♄	10 7:03
☽ 0S	15 23:55
♆ D	18 1:48
♀0S	18 8:11
☿ D	23 0:20
☽ 0N	30 1:03
♅ D	30 22:55

Planet Ingress

	Dy Hr Mn
☿ ♎	1 0:37
♂ ♑	8 17:51
♀ ♍	21 2:09
☉ ♎	22 23:04
☊ ♊R	13 1:46
♀ ♎	15 11:42
☉ ♏	23 8:26
♂ ♒	27 17:19

Last Aspect / ☽ Ingress

Last Aspect Dy Hr Mn		☽ Ingress Dy Hr Mn
1 17:36 ♂ ⚹	♓	2 0:32
4 8:37 ♂ □	♈	4 12:58
6 22:31 ♂ △	♉	7 0:18
8 18:30 ♅ □	♊	9 9:41
11 1:42 ♅ △	♋	11 16:09
13 3:16 ☉ ⚹	♌	13 19:16
15 8:35 ♀ ☌	♍	15 19:39
17 10:27 ☉ ☌	♎	17 19:00
19 16:38 ♀ ⚹	♏	19 19:27
21 21:09 ☉ ⚹	♐	21 23:02
24 0:32 ☿ ⚹	♑	24 6:48
26 14:38 ☿ □	♒	26 18:05
29 5:28 ☿ △	♓	29 6:50

Last Aspect / ☽ Ingress

Last Aspect Dy Hr Mn		☽ Ingress Dy Hr Mn
30 13:02 ♄ □	♈	1 19:08
4 4:45 ☿ ☍	♉	4 6:01
5 22:33 ♅ □	♊	6 15:12
8 16:24 ☿ △	♋	8 22:19
10 17:47 ☿ □	♌	11 2:54
12 16:34 ☿ ⚹	♍	13 4:58
15 4:52 ♀ ☌	♎	15 5:26
16 19:23 ☉ ☌	♏	17 6:03
18 22:30 ♂ ⚹	♐	19 8:47
21 11:42 ☉ ⚹	♑	21 15:11
23 20:11 ♂ ☌	♒	24 1:26
25 19:32 ♅ ☌	♓	26 13:56
27 21:31 ♃ △	♈	29 2:15
30 19:17 ♅ ⚹	♉	31 12:48

☽ Phases & Eclipses

Dy Hr Mn	
2 21:43	○ 10♓28
10 19:00	☾ 18♊08
17 10:27	● 24♍36
24 9:31	☽ 1♑24
2 13:49	○ 9♈26
10 4:20	☾ 16♋56
16 19:23	● 23♎30
24 2:58	☽ 0♒46

Astro Data

1 September 2001
Julian Day # 37134
SVP 5♓14'27"
GC 26♐51.8 ⚴ 3♐13.5
Eris 19♈59.1R ⚵ 21♋31.5
⚷ 22♐53.0 ⚶ 8♊55.2
☽ Mean ☊ 2♋47.4

1 October 2001
Julian Day # 37164
SVP 5♓14'25"
GC 26♐51.8 ⚴ 11♐42.0
Eris 19♈43.3R ⚵ 6♌23.3
⚷ 23♐48.7 ⚶ 13♊15.7
☽ Mean ☊ 1♋12.1

November 2001 — LONGITUDE

Day	Sid.Time	☉	0 hr ☽	Noon ☽	True ☊	☿	♀	♂	⚳	♃	♄	♅	♆	♇
1 Th	14 43 22	9♏07 49	5♉52 19	12♉12 30	28♊06.4	21♎03.8	21♎10.3	3♒17.2	19♑12.5	15♋41.4	13♊51.9	20♒54.6	6♒03.1	13♐47.7
2 F	14 47 18	10 07 50	18 35 40	25 01 45	27R 59.9	22 20.8	22 25.2	3 58.8	19 29.4	15R 41.5	13R 48.3	20 54.7	6 03.6	13 49.7
3 Sa	14 51 15	11 07 54	1♊30 45	8♊02 35	27 55.7	23 41.5	23 40.2	4 40.5	19 46.5	15 41.4	13 44.6	20 54.9	6 04.1	13 51.7
4 Su	14 55 11	12 08 00	14 37 14	21 14 42	27D 53.8	25 05.2	24 55.2	5 22.2	20 03.7	15 41.2	13 40.9	20 55.1	6 04.7	13 53.8
5 M	14 59 08	13 08 08	27 54 57	4♋38 00	27 53.8	26 31.5	26 10.2	6 04.0	20 21.1	15 40.7	13 37.0	20 55.4	6 05.3	13 55.8
6 Tu	15 03 04	14 08 18	11♋23 54	18 12 40	27 54.9	27 59.9	27 25.2	6 46.0	20 38.6	15 40.0	13 33.1	20 55.7	6 05.9	13 57.9
7 W	15 07 01	15 08 30	25 04 22	1♌59 01	27 56.2	29 30.1	28 40.3	7 28.0	20 56.3	15 39.1	13 29.2	20 56.0	6 06.6	13 59.9
8 Th	15 10 58	16 08 44	8♌56 37	15 57 09	27R 56.8	1♏01.7	29 55.4	8 10.1	21 14.1	15 38.1	13 25.2	20 56.4	6 07.3	14 02.0
9 F	15 14 54	17 09 00	23 00 33	0♍06 38	27 56.1	2 34.4	1♏10.5	8 52.3	21 32.0	15 36.8	13 21.1	20 56.9	6 08.0	14 04.1
10 Sa	15 18 51	18 09 18	7♍15 12	14 25 54	27 53.5	4 08.0	2 25.7	9 34.5	21 50.1	15 35.3	13 16.9	20 57.4	6 08.8	14 06.2
11 Su	15 22 47	19 09 38	21 38 21	28 52 00	27 49.3	5 42.3	3 40.8	10 16.8	22 08.3	15 33.6	13 12.7	20 58.0	6 09.6	14 08.4
12 M	15 26 44	20 09 59	6♎06 17	13♎20 30	27 43.8	7 17.2	4 56.0	10 59.3	22 26.6	15 31.8	13 08.4	20 58.6	6 10.4	14 10.5
13 Tu	15 30 40	21 10 23	20 33 55	27 45 48	27 37.8	8 52.5	6 11.2	11 41.8	22 45.1	15 29.7	13 04.0	20 59.3	6 11.3	14 12.7
14 W	15 34 37	22 10 49	4♏55 23	12♏01 55	27 32.2	10 28.0	7 26.4	12 24.3	23 03.7	15 27.4	12 59.6	21 00.0	6 12.2	14 14.8
15 Th	15 38 33	23 11 16	19 04 45	26 03 18	27 27.6	12 03.8	8 41.7	13 07.0	23 22.4	15 24.9	12 55.2	21 00.7	6 13.1	14 17.0
16 F	15 42 30	24 11 45	2♐57 03	9♐45 38	27 24.6	13 39.6	9 56.9	13 49.7	23 41.3	15 22.3	12 50.7	21 01.6	6 14.1	14 19.2
17 Sa	15 46 26	25 12 16	16 28 50	23 06 29	27D 23.3	15 15.5	11 12.2	14 32.5	24 00.2	15 19.4	12 46.1	21 02.4	6 15.1	14 21.4
18 Su	15 50 23	26 12 48	29 38 36	6♑05 19	27 23.5	16 51.3	12 27.5	15 15.3	24 19.3	15 16.3	12 41.6	21 03.4	6 16.1	14 23.6
19 M	15 54 20	27 13 21	12♑26 50	18 43 27	27 24.8	18 27.2	13 42.8	15 58.2	24 38.5	15 13.1	12 36.9	21 04.3	6 17.2	14 25.8
20 Tu	15 58 16	28 13 55	24 55 36	1♒03 43	27 26.6	20 02.9	14 58.1	16 41.2	24 57.9	15 09.7	12 32.3	21 05.4	6 18.3	14 28.1
21 W	16 02 13	29 14 31	7♒08 19	13 09 59	27 28.3	21 38.5	16 13.4	17 24.2	25 17.3	15 06.0	12 27.5	21 06.4	6 19.4	14 30.3
22 Th	16 06 09	0♐15 08	19 09 16	25 06 49	27R 29.3	23 14.0	17 28.7	18 07.3	25 36.9	15 02.2	12 22.8	21 07.6	6 20.6	14 32.6
23 F	16 10 06	1 15 46	1♓03 13	6♓59 07	27 29.3	24 49.4	18 44.1	18 50.4	25 56.5	14 58.2	12 18.0	21 08.7	6 21.7	14 34.8
24 Sa	16 14 02	2 16 25	12 55 06	18 51 47	27 28.0	26 24.7	19 59.4	19 33.6	26 16.3	14 54.0	12 13.2	21 09.9	6 23.0	14 37.1
25 Su	16 17 59	3 17 06	24 49 44	0♈49 30	27 25.6	27 59.8	21 14.8	20 16.8	26 36.1	14 49.7	12 08.4	21 11.2	6 24.2	14 39.4
26 M	16 21 56	4 17 47	6♈51 34	12 56 24	27 22.4	29 34.7	22 30.2	21 00.1	26 56.1	14 45.1	12 03.6	21 12.5	6 25.5	14 41.6
27 Tu	16 25 52	5 18 30	19 04 24	25 15 54	27 18.8	1♐09.6	23 45.5	21 43.4	27 16.2	14 40.4	11 58.7	21 13.9	6 26.8	14 43.9
28 W	16 29 49	6 19 13	1♉31 13	7♉50 31	27 15.2	2 44.3	25 00.9	22 26.7	27 36.3	14 35.5	11 53.8	21 15.3	6 28.1	14 46.2
29 Th	16 33 45	7 19 58	14 13 58	20 41 38	27 12.1	4 18.9	26 16.3	23 10.1	27 56.6	14 30.5	11 48.9	21 16.8	6 29.4	14 48.5
30 F	16 37 42	8 20 44	27 13 31	3♊49 31	27 09.9	5 53.4	27 31.7	23 53.5	28 16.9	14 25.3	11 44.0	21 18.3	6 30.8	14 50.8

December 2001 — LONGITUDE

Day	Sid.Time	☉	0 hr ☽	Noon ☽	True ☊	☿	♀	♂	⚳	♃	♄	♅	♆	♇
1 Sa	16 41 38	9♐21 32	10♊29 32	17♊13 22	27♊08.7	7♐27.8	28♏47.1	24♒37.0	28♑37.4	14♋19.9	11♊39.1	21♒19.8	6♒32.2	14♐53.1
2 Su	16 45 35	10 22 20	24 00 46	0♋51 27	27D 08.5	9 02.2	0♐02.5	25 20.5	28 57.9	14R 14.3	11R 34.2	21 21.4	6 33.7	14 55.4
3 M	16 49 31	11 23 10	7♋45 07	14 41 26	27 09.1	10 36.4	1 18.0	26 04.0	29 18.6	14 08.7	11 29.3	21 23.1	6 35.2	14 57.7
4 Tu	16 53 28	12 24 01	21 40 04	28 40 39	27 10.1	12 10.7	2 33.4	26 47.6	29 39.3	14 02.8	11 24.3	21 24.8	6 36.6	15 00.0
5 W	16 57 25	13 24 54	5♌42 54	12♌46 26	27 11.3	13 44.9	3 48.9	27 31.1	0♒00.1	13 56.8	11 19.4	21 26.5	6 38.2	15 02.3
6 Th	17 01 21	14 25 47	19 51 00	26 56 15	27 12.3	15 19.1	5 04.3	28 14.7	0 21.0	13 50.7	11 14.5	21 28.3	6 39.7	15 04.6
7 F	17 05 18	15 26 42	4♍01 56	11♍07 45	27R 12.8	16 53.3	6 19.8	28 58.4	0 41.9	13 44.4	11 09.6	21 30.1	6 41.3	15 06.9
8 Sa	17 09 14	16 27 38	18 13 26	25 18 44	27 12.7	18 27.5	7 35.3	29 42.0	1 03.0	13 38.0	11 04.7	21 32.0	6 42.9	15 09.3
9 Su	17 13 11	17 28 36	2♎23 22	9♎27 03	27 12.1	20 01.8	8 50.7	0♓25.7	1 24.1	13 31.4	10 59.8	21 33.9	6 44.5	15 11.6
10 M	17 17 07	18 29 34	16 29 31	23 30 26	27 11.1	21 36.1	10 06.2	1 09.4	1 45.4	13 24.7	10 54.9	21 35.8	6 46.1	15 13.9
11 Tu	17 21 04	19 30 34	0♏29 32	7♏26 30	27 10.1	23 10.4	11 21.7	1 53.2	2 06.6	13 17.9	10 50.1	21 37.8	6 47.8	15 16.2
12 W	17 25 00	20 31 35	14 21 01	21 12 46	27 09.2	24 44.9	12 37.2	2 36.9	2 28.0	13 11.0	10 45.2	21 39.9	6 49.5	15 18.5
13 Th	17 28 57	21 32 37	28 01 30	4♐46 54	27 08.6	26 19.4	13 52.7	3 20.7	2 49.5	13 04.0	10 40.4	21 42.0	6 51.2	15 20.8
14 F	17 32 54	22 33 40	11♐28 46	18 06 53	27D 08.3	27 54.0	15 08.2	4 04.5	3 11.0	12 56.8	10 35.6	21 44.1	6 53.0	15 23.1
15 Sa	17 36 50	23 34 43	24 41 06	1♑11 18	27 08.2	29 28.8	16 23.8	4 48.4	3 32.6	12 49.6	10 30.9	21 46.3	6 54.7	15 25.4
16 Su	17 40 47	24 35 48	7♑37 28	13 59 35	27 08.3	1♑03.6	17 39.3	5 32.2	3 54.3	12 42.2	10 26.2	21 48.5	6 56.5	15 27.7
17 M	17 44 43	25 36 53	20 17 46	26 32 08	27 08.5	2 38.5	18 54.8	6 16.1	4 16.0	12 34.8	10 21.5	21 50.7	6 58.3	15 30.0
18 Tu	17 48 40	26 37 58	2♒42 55	8♒50 21	27R 08.7	4 13.6	20 10.3	7 00.0	4 37.8	12 27.2	10 16.9	21 53.0	7 00.1	15 32.2
19 W	17 52 36	27 39 04	14 54 48	20 56 37	27 08.7	5 48.7	21 25.8	7 43.9	4 59.7	12 19.6	10 12.3	21 55.4	7 02.0	15 34.5
20 Th	17 56 33	28 40 10	26 56 13	2♓54 07	27 08.5	7 23.9	22 41.4	8 27.8	5 21.6	12 11.9	10 07.7	21 57.7	7 03.9	15 36.8
21 F	18 00 29	29 41 16	8♓50 47	14 46 47	27 08.4	8 59.3	23 56.9	9 11.7	5 43.6	12 04.2	10 03.2	22 00.1	7 05.8	15 39.0
22 Sa	18 04 26	0♑42 22	20 42 39	26 39 00	27D 08.2	10 34.6	25 12.4	9 55.6	6 05.6	11 56.3	9 58.8	22 02.6	7 07.7	15 41.3
23 Su	18 08 23	1 43 29	2♈36 24	8♈35 28	27 08.3	12 10.1	26 27.9	10 39.5	6 27.8	11 48.4	9 54.4	22 05.0	7 09.6	15 43.5
24 M	18 12 19	2 44 36	14 36 46	20 40 54	27 08.6	13 45.5	27 43.4	11 23.4	6 49.9	11 40.5	9 50.0	22 07.6	7 11.5	15 45.8
25 Tu	18 16 16	3 45 43	26 48 25	2♉59 49	27 09.1	15 20.9	28 58.9	12 07.4	7 12.1	11 32.5	9 45.7	22 10.1	7 13.5	15 48.0
26 W	18 20 12	4 46 50	9♉15 36	15 36 10	27 09.9	16 56.2	0♑14.4	12 51.3	7 34.4	11 24.5	9 41.5	22 12.7	7 15.5	15 50.2
27 Th	18 24 09	5 47 57	22 01 53	28 32 59	27 10.7	18 31.3	1 29.9	13 35.2	7 56.8	11 16.5	9 37.3	22 15.3	7 17.5	15 52.4
28 F	18 28 05	6 49 05	5♊09 40	11♊52 00	27 11.4	20 06.3	2 45.4	14 19.2	8 19.1	11 08.4	9 33.2	22 18.0	7 19.5	15 54.6
29 Sa	18 32 02	7 50 12	18 39 54	25 33 14	27R 11.7	21 40.9	4 00.9	15 03.1	8 41.6	11 00.3	9 29.2	22 20.6	7 21.5	15 56.8
30 Su	18 35 58	8 51 20	2♋31 42	9♋34 52	27 11.5	23 15.0	5 16.4	15 47.0	9 04.1	10 52.2	9 25.2	22 23.4	7 23.6	15 59.0
31 M	18 39 55	9 52 27	16 42 15	23 53 13	27 10.6	24 48.6	6 31.9	16 30.9	9 26.6	10 44.1	9 21.4	22 26.1	7 25.6	16 01.1

Astro Data (Dy Hr Mn)	Planet Ingress (Dy Hr Mn)	Last Aspect (Dy Hr Mn)	☽ Ingress (Dy Hr Mn)	Last Aspect (Dy Hr Mn)	☽ Ingress (Dy Hr Mn)	☽ Phases & Eclipses (Dy Hr Mn)	Astro Data
♄☍♇ 2 5:50	☿ ♏ 7 19:53	2 4:20 ♅ □	♊ 2 21:13	2 1:48 ♂ △	♋ 2 10:30	1 5:41 ○ 8♉52	1 November 2001
♃ R 2 15:35	♀ ♏ 8 13:28	4 19:45 ☿ △	♋ 5 3:44	3 11:04 ♃ ☌	♌ 4 14:15	8 12:21 ☾ 16♌10	Julian Day # 37195
☽ 0S 12 9:15	☉ ♐ 22 6:00	7 7:10 ☿ □	♌ 7 8:34	6 14:20 ♂ ☍	♍ 6 17:11	15 6:40 ● 22♏58	SVP 5♓14'22"
☽ 0N 26 9:46	☿ ♐ 26 18:23	8 20:30 ♅ ☍	♍ 9 11:49	7 22:57 ☿ □	♎ 8 19:57	22 23:21 ☽ 0♓44	GC 26♐51.9 ⚴ 22♐21.9
♃⚻♇ 27 0:02		10 18:40 ☉ ⚹	♎ 11 13:53	10 8:43 ♅ △	♏ 10 23:09	30 20:49 ○ 8♊43	Eris 19♈24.9R ⚵ 19♌12.2
	♀ ♐ 2 11:11	13 0:42 ♅ △	♏ 13 15:44	12 12:48 ♅ □	♐ 13 3:30		⚷ 25♐59.2 ⚶ 11♊32.2R
☽ 0S 9 16:09	⚳ ♒ 5 11:54	15 6:40 ☉ ☌	♐ 15 18:51	15 8:24 ☿ ☌	♑ 15 9:48	7 19:52 ☾ 15♍47	☽ Mean ☊ 29♊33.5
☽ 0N 23 18:37	♂ ♓ 8 21:52	17 8:14 ♅ ⚹	♑ 18 0:40	16 9:35 ♃ ☍	♒ 17 18:43	14 20:47 ● 22♐56	
	☿ ♑ 15 19:55	20 5:57 ☉ ⚹	♒ 20 9:55	20 2:41 ☉ ⚹	♓ 20 6:09	14 20:51:58 ● A 03'53"	1 December 2001
	☉ ♑ 21 19:21	22 7:38 ☿ □	♓ 22 21:52	22 8:44 ♀ □	♈ 22 18:45	22 20:56 ☽ 1♈05	Julian Day # 37225
	♀ ♑ 26 7:25	25 5:29 ☿ △	♈ 25 10:21	25 3:21 ♀ △	♉ 25 6:12	30 10:40 ○ 8♋48	SVP 5♓14'17"
		27 4:43 ♂ ⚹	♉ 27 21:06	27 0:23 ♅ □	♊ 27 14:39	30 10:29 ◐ A 0.893	GC 26♐52.0 ⚴ 3♑37.8
		29 23:21 ♀ ☍	♊ 30 5:04	29 6:25 ♅ △	♋ 29 19:40		Eris 19♈10.5R ⚵ 27♌37.0
				31 13:43 ☿ ☍	♌ 31 22:09		⚷ 28♐53.3 ⚶ 4♊31.2R
							☽ Mean ☊ 27♊58.2

LONGITUDE — January 2002

Day	Sid.Time	☉	0 hr ☽	Noon☽	True☊	☿	♀	♂	⚳	♃	♄	♅	♆	♇
1 Tu	18 43 52	10♑53 35	1♌07 03	8♌23 00	27♊09.1	26♑21.4	7♑47.4	17♓14.8	9♒49.2	10♋35.9	9♊17.5	22♒28.9	7♒27.7	16♐03.3
2 W	18 47 48	11 54 44	15 40 17	22 58 05	27R 07.2	27 53.3	9 02.9	17 58.7	10 11.8	10R 27.8	9R 13.8	22 31.7	7 29.8	16 05.4
3 Th	18 51 45	12 55 52	0♍15 40	7♍32 17	27 05.2	29 24.0	10 18.4	18 42.6	10 34.5	10 19.7	9 10.1	22 34.5	7 31.9	16 07.5
4 F	18 55 41	13 57 00	14 47 18	22 00 08	27 03.6	0♒53.2	11 33.9	19 26.5	10 57.2	10 11.6	9 06.5	22 37.4	7 34.0	16 09.7
5 Sa	18 59 38	14 58 09	29 10 18	6♎17 27	27D 02.6	2 20.8	12 49.4	20 10.4	11 20.0	10 03.5	9 03.0	22 40.3	7 36.2	16 11.7
6 Su	19 03 34	15 59 18	13♎21 17	20 21 37	27 02.4	3 46.1	14 04.9	20 54.3	11 42.8	9 55.5	8 59.6	22 43.2	7 38.3	16 13.8
7 M	19 07 31	17 00 27	27 18 20	4♏11 23	27 03.1	5 09.0	15 20.4	21 38.2	12 05.6	9 47.4	8 56.2	22 46.2	7 40.4	16 15.9
8 Tu	19 11 27	18 01 37	11♏00 47	17 46 35	27 04.5	6 28.8	16 35.9	22 22.0	12 28.5	9 39.4	8 53.0	22 49.2	7 42.6	16 17.9
9 W	19 15 24	19 02 46	24 28 50	1♐07 39	27 06.1	7 45.0	17 51.4	23 05.9	12 51.4	9 31.5	8 49.8	22 52.2	7 44.8	16 20.0
10 Th	19 19 21	20 03 56	7♐43 08	14 15 21	27R 07.4	8 57.0	19 06.9	23 49.7	13 14.4	9 23.6	8 46.7	22 55.2	7 47.0	16 22.0
11 F	19 23 17	21 05 05	20 44 25	27 10 26	27 07.9	10 04.2	20 22.4	24 33.6	13 37.4	9 15.8	8 43.7	22 58.3	7 49.2	16 24.0
12 Sa	19 27 14	22 06 15	3♑33 26	9♑53 32	27 07.2	11 05.7	21 37.9	25 17.4	14 00.4	9 08.0	8 40.8	23 01.4	7 51.4	16 25.9
13 Su	19 31 10	23 07 24	16 10 47	22 25 16	27 05.2	12 00.7	22 53.3	26 01.2	14 23.5	9 00.3	8 38.0	23 04.5	7 53.6	16 27.9
14 M	19 35 07	24 08 32	28 37 04	4♒46 17	27 01.7	12 48.4	24 08.8	26 45.1	14 46.6	8 52.7	8 35.3	23 07.6	7 55.8	16 29.8
15 Tu	19 39 03	25 09 41	10♒53 01	16 57 27	26 57.1	13 27.8	25 24.3	27 28.9	15 09.7	8 45.2	8 32.7	23 10.7	7 58.1	16 31.8
16 W	19 43 00	26 10 48	22 59 44	29 00 06	26 51.6	13 58.2	26 39.8	28 12.6	15 32.9	8 37.7	8 30.2	23 13.9	8 00.3	16 33.7
17 Th	19 46 57	27 11 55	4♓58 47	10♓56 07	26 46.1	14 18.6	27 55.2	28 56.4	15 56.1	8 30.4	8 27.8	23 17.1	8 02.5	16 35.5
18 F	19 50 53	28 13 01	16 52 25	22 48 05	26 40.9	14R 28.3	29 10.6	29 40.2	16 19.3	8 23.1	8 25.5	23 20.3	8 04.8	16 37.4
19 Sa	19 54 50	29 14 06	28 43 33	4♈39 16	26 36.8	14 26.8	0♒26.1	0♈23.9	16 42.6	8 16.0	8 23.3	23 23.6	8 07.0	16 39.2
20 Su	19 58 46	0♒15 11	10♈35 47	16 33 36	26 34.2	14 13.7	1 41.5	1 07.6	17 05.8	8 08.9	8 21.2	23 26.8	8 09.3	16 41.0
21 M	20 02 43	1 16 14	22 33 20	28 35 33	26D 33.1	13 48.9	2 56.9	1 51.3	17 29.1	8 02.0	8 19.2	23 30.1	8 11.6	16 42.8
22 Tu	20 06 39	2 17 17	4♉40 51	10♉49 53	26 33.4	13 12.8	4 12.3	2 35.0	17 52.4	7 55.2	8 17.3	23 33.4	8 13.8	16 44.6
23 W	20 10 36	3 18 19	17 03 14	23 21 28	26 34.8	12 26.0	5 27.7	3 18.6	18 15.8	7 48.5	8 15.5	23 36.7	8 16.1	16 46.3
24 Th	20 14 32	4 19 20	29 45 10	6♊14 48	26 36.4	11 29.8	6 43.1	4 02.3	18 39.1	7 41.9	8 13.8	23 40.0	8 18.4	16 48.1
25 F	20 18 29	5 20 19	12♊50 46	19 33 24	26R 37.6	10 25.7	7 58.5	4 45.9	19 02.5	7 35.5	8 12.2	23 43.3	8 20.7	16 49.8
26 Sa	20 22 26	6 21 18	26 22 54	3♋19 16	26 37.7	9 15.6	9 13.9	5 29.4	19 25.9	7 29.2	8 10.8	23 46.6	8 22.9	16 51.4
27 Su	20 26 22	7 22 16	10♋22 26	17 32 04	26 35.9	8 01.6	10 29.2	6 13.0	19 49.3	7 23.0	8 09.4	23 50.0	8 25.2	16 53.1
28 M	20 30 19	8 23 13	24 47 40	2♌08 34	26 32.1	6 45.9	11 44.6	6 56.5	20 12.8	7 17.0	8 08.2	23 53.4	8 27.5	16 54.7
29 Tu	20 34 15	9 24 08	9♌33 54	17 02 38	26 26.5	5 30.9	12 59.9	7 40.0	20 36.2	7 11.2	8 07.1	23 56.8	8 29.8	16 56.3
30 W	20 38 12	10 25 03	24 33 38	2♍05 41	26 19.7	4 18.5	14 15.2	8 23.5	20 59.7	7 05.5	8 06.0	24 00.2	8 32.1	16 57.9
31 Th	20 42 08	11 25 57	9♍37 33	17 08 01	26 12.6	3 10.6	15 30.5	9 06.9	21 23.2	6 59.9	8 05.1	24 03.6	8 34.3	16 59.4

LONGITUDE — February 2002

Day	Sid.Time	☉	0 hr ☽	Noon☽	True☊	☿	♀	♂	⚳	♃	♄	♅	♆	♇
1 F	20 46 05	12♒26 50	24♍36 00	2♎00 30	26♊06.2	2♒08.8	16♒45.8	9♈50.4	21♒46.7	6♋54.5	8♊04.3	24♒07.0	8♒36.6	17♐00.9
2 Sa	20 50 01	13 27 42	9♎20 40	16 35 53	26R 01.3	1R 14.0	18 01.1	10 33.8	22 10.2	6R 49.3	8R 03.6	24 10.4	8 38.9	17 02.4
3 Su	20 53 58	14 28 34	23 45 40	0♏49 44	25 58.3	0 27.1	19 16.4	11 17.1	22 33.7	6 44.2	8 03.1	24 13.8	8 41.1	17 03.9
4 M	20 57 55	15 29 24	7♏47 59	14 40 27	25D 57.4	29♑48.6	20 31.7	12 00.5	22 57.2	6 39.3	8 02.6	24 17.2	8 43.4	17 05.3
5 Tu	21 01 51	16 30 14	21 27 17	28 08 43	25 57.9	29 18.5	21 47.0	12 43.8	23 20.8	6 34.6	8 02.3	24 20.7	8 45.7	17 06.7
6 W	21 05 48	17 31 03	4♐45 04	11♐16 42	25 59.1	28 56.9	23 02.2	13 27.1	23 44.3	6 30.0	8 02.0	24 24.1	8 47.9	17 08.1
7 Th	21 09 44	18 31 51	17 43 59	24 07 19	25R 59.8	28 43.5	24 17.5	14 10.3	24 07.9	6 25.6	8D 01.9	24 27.6	8 50.2	17 09.5
8 F	21 13 41	19 32 38	0♑27 06	6♑43 39	25 59.2	28D 38.0	25 32.7	14 53.6	24 31.4	6 21.4	8 01.9	24 31.1	8 52.5	17 10.8
9 Sa	21 17 37	20 33 24	12 57 21	19 08 28	25 56.4	28 40.0	26 47.9	15 36.8	24 55.0	6 17.4	8 02.0	24 34.5	8 54.7	17 12.1
10 Su	21 21 34	21 34 09	25 17 17	1♒24 02	25 51.0	28 49.0	28 03.2	16 20.0	25 18.6	6 13.6	8 02.2	24 38.0	8 57.0	17 13.4
11 M	21 25 30	22 34 53	7♒28 56	13 32 09	25 42.9	29 04.5	29 18.3	17 03.1	25 42.2	6 09.9	8 02.6	24 41.5	8 59.2	17 14.6
12 Tu	21 29 27	23 35 35	19 33 51	25 34 12	25 32.7	29 26.1	0♓33.5	17 46.3	26 05.8	6 06.4	8 03.0	24 45.0	9 01.4	17 15.8
13 W	21 33 24	24 36 16	1♓33 18	7♓31 20	25 20.9	29 53.2	1 48.7	18 29.4	26 29.3	6 03.2	8 03.6	24 48.4	9 03.6	17 17.0
14 Th	21 37 20	25 36 55	13 28 27	19 24 50	25 08.6	0♒25.6	3 03.9	19 12.4	26 52.9	6 00.1	8 04.2	24 51.9	9 05.8	17 18.2
15 F	21 41 17	26 37 33	25 20 41	1♈16 15	24 56.9	1 02.6	4 19.0	19 55.5	27 16.5	5 57.2	8 05.0	24 55.4	9 08.0	17 19.3
16 Sa	21 45 13	27 38 09	7♈11 48	13 07 40	24 46.7	1 44.1	5 34.1	20 38.5	27 40.1	5 54.5	8 05.9	24 58.8	9 10.2	17 20.4
17 Su	21 49 10	28 38 43	19 04 13	25 01 52	24 38.9	2 29.5	6 49.2	21 21.5	28 03.7	5 52.0	8 06.9	25 02.3	9 12.4	17 21.4
18 M	21 53 06	29 39 16	1♉01 04	7♉02 20	24 33.7	3 18.7	8 04.3	22 04.4	28 27.3	5 49.7	8 08.1	25 05.8	9 14.6	17 22.4
19 Tu	21 57 03	0♓39 47	13 06 13	19 13 18	24D 31.1	4 11.2	9 19.3	22 47.3	28 50.8	5 47.6	8 09.3	25 09.2	9 16.7	17 23.4
20 W	22 00 59	1 40 16	25 24 10	1♊39 26	24 30.4	5 06.9	10 34.4	23 30.2	29 14.4	5 45.7	8 10.6	25 12.7	9 18.9	17 24.4
21 Th	22 04 56	2 40 43	7♊59 44	14 25 40	24R 30.8	6 05.4	11 49.4	24 13.1	29 38.0	5 43.9	8 12.1	25 16.1	9 21.0	17 25.3
22 F	22 08 53	3 41 09	20 57 46	27 36 34	24 30.9	7 06.7	13 04.4	24 55.9	0♓01.5	5 42.4	8 13.7	25 19.6	9 23.2	17 26.2
23 Sa	22 12 49	4 41 33	4♋22 28	11♋15 45	24 29.8	8 10.5	14 19.4	25 38.7	0 25.1	5 41.1	8 15.4	25 23.0	9 25.3	17 27.1
24 Su	22 16 46	5 41 54	18 16 33	25 24 49	24 26.5	9 16.5	15 34.3	26 21.4	0 48.6	5 40.0	8 17.2	25 26.5	9 27.4	17 27.9
25 M	22 20 42	6 42 14	2♌40 18	10♌02 29	24 20.5	10 24.8	16 49.3	27 04.1	1 12.1	5 39.1	8 19.1	25 29.9	9 29.5	17 28.7
26 Tu	22 24 39	7 42 32	17 30 39	25 03 50	24 11.9	11 35.1	18 04.2	27 46.8	1 35.6	5 38.4	8 21.1	25 33.3	9 31.5	17 29.4
27 W	22 28 35	8 42 48	2♍40 51	10♍20 20	24 01.5	12 47.3	19 19.1	28 29.4	1 59.1	5 37.9	8 23.2	25 36.7	9 33.6	17 30.2
28 Th	22 32 32	9 43 02	18 00 51	25 40 54	23 50.5	14 01.4	20 33.9	29 12.0	2 22.6	5 37.5	8 25.4	25 40.1	9 35.6	17 30.9

Astro Data

	Dy Hr Mn
☽0S	5 21:26
♃⚺♄	18 0:33
♃⚼♅	18 18:25
☿R	18 20:52
♂0N	20 1:11
☽0N	20 2:12
♃⚻♆	20 10:58
♄△♆	23 8:19
☽0S	2 3:35
♄D	8 1:32
☿D	8 17:28
☽0N	16 8:16

Planet Ingress

	Dy Hr Mn
☿ ♒	3 21:38
♂ ♈	18 22:53
♀ ♒	19 3:42
☉ ♒	20 6:02
☿ ♑R	4 4:19
♀ ♓	12 1:18
☿ ♒	13 17:20
☉ ♓	18 20:13
⚳ ♓	22 10:27

Last Aspect / ☽ Ingress

Last Aspect Dy Hr Mn		☽ Ingress Dy Hr Mn
2 11:17 ♅ ☍	♍	2 23:34
4 7:30 ♂ ☍	♎	5 1:23
6 16:05 ♅ △	♏	7 4:41
8 21:03 ♅ □	♐	9 9:57
11 6:49 ♂ □	♑	11 17:18
13 19:24 ♂ ⚹	♒	14 2:41
16 0:25 ♅ ☌	♓	16 14:00
19 2:27 ♀ ⚹	♈	19 2:35
21 1:50 ♅ ⚹	♉	21 14:47
23 12:29 ♅ □	♊	24 0:28
25 19:23 ♅ △	♋	26 6:17
26 19:03 ♃ ☌	♌	28 8:31
29 23:04 ♅ ☍	♍	30 8:40

Last Aspect / ☽ Ingress

Last Aspect Dy Hr Mn		☽ Ingress Dy Hr Mn
31 11:46 ♇ □	♎	1 8:44
3 0:45 ♅ △	♏	3 10:35
5 14:02 ☿ ⚹	♐	5 15:21
7 12:38 ♅ ⚹	♑	7 23:08
10 6:50 ☿ ☌	♒	10 9:15
12 10:21 ♅ ☌	♓	12 20:53
14 7:44 ♇ □	♈	15 9:26
17 19:55 ☉ ⚹	♉	17 21:58
19 23:34 ♅ □	♊	20 8:50
22 7:53 ♅ △	♋	22 16:16
24 13:39 ♂ □	♌	24 19:36
26 16:30 ♂ △	♍	26 19:47
28 3:17 ♀ ☍	♎	28 18:47

☽ Phases & Eclipses

Dy Hr Mn	
6 3:55	☾ 15♎39
13 13:29	● 23♑11
21 17:47	☽ 1♉31
28 22:50	○ 8♌51
4 13:33	☾ 15♏33
12 7:41	● 23♒25
20 12:02	☽ 1♊40
27 9:17	○ 8♍36

Astro Data

1 January 2002
Julian Day # 37256
SVP 5♓14'11"
GC 26♐52.0 ⚵ 15♑35.4
Eris 19♈03.6R ⚴ 29♌52.3R
⚷ 2♑13.1 ⚶ 28♉27.2R
☽ Mean ☊ 26♊19.8

1 February 2002
Julian Day # 37287
SVP 5♓14'06"
GC 26♐52.1 ⚵ 27♑19.9
Eris 19♈07.1 ⚴ 24♌34.4R
⚷ 5♑21.1 ⚶ 28♉52.2
☽ Mean ☊ 24♊41.3

March 2002

LONGITUDE

Day	Sid.Time	☉	0 hr ☽	Noon ☽	True ☊	☿	♀	♂	⚳	♃	♄	♅	♆	♇
1 F	22 36 28	10♓43 15	3♎18 59	10♎53 45	23♊40.2	15♒17.2	21♓48.8	29♈54.5	2♓46.1	5♋37.4	8♊27.7	25♒43.5	9♒37.6	17♐31.5
2 Sa	22 40 25	11 43 26	18 24 01	25 48 45	23R 31.7	16 34.6	23 03.6	0♉37.1	3 09.6	5D 37.5	8 30.2	25 46.9	9 39.7	17 32.2
3 Su	22 44 21	12 43 35	3♏07 12	10♏18 50	23 25.8	17 53.6	24 18.4	1 19.5	3 33.0	5 37.8	8 32.7	25 50.2	9 41.6	17 32.8
4 M	22 48 18	13 43 43	17 23 21	24 20 41	23 22.6	19 14.1	25 33.2	2 02.0	3 56.5	5 38.2	8 35.3	25 53.6	9 43.6	17 33.3
5 Tu	22 52 15	14 43 50	1♐10 55	7♐54 18	23D 21.4	20 36.1	26 47.9	2 44.4	4 19.9	5 38.9	8 38.1	25 56.9	9 45.6	17 33.9
6 W	22 56 11	15 43 55	14 31 12	21 02 05	23R 21.4	21 59.5	28 02.7	3 26.8	4 43.3	5 39.7	8 40.9	26 00.3	9 47.5	17 34.4
7 Th	23 00 08	16 43 58	27 27 27	3♑47 52	23 21.1	23 24.2	29 17.4	4 09.1	5 06.7	5 40.8	8 43.9	26 03.6	9 49.4	17 34.8
8 F	23 04 04	17 44 00	10♑03 52	16 15 59	23 19.5	24 50.3	0♈32.1	4 51.4	5 30.0	5 42.1	8 46.9	26 06.9	9 51.4	17 35.2
9 Sa	23 08 01	18 44 00	22 24 47	28 30 45	23 15.5	26 17.7	1 46.7	5 33.7	5 53.4	5 43.5	8 50.1	26 10.1	9 53.2	17 35.6
10 Su	23 11 57	19 43 59	4♒34 19	10♒35 56	23 08.5	27 46.3	3 01.4	6 16.0	6 16.7	5 45.1	8 53.3	26 13.4	9 55.1	17 36.0
11 M	23 15 54	20 43 55	16 35 57	22 34 42	22 58.5	29 16.2	4 16.0	6 58.2	6 40.0	5 47.0	8 56.7	26 16.6	9 56.9	17 36.3
12 Tu	23 19 50	21 43 50	28 32 28	4♓29 30	22 45.9	0♓47.4	5 30.6	7 40.4	7 03.3	5 49.0	9 00.1	26 19.9	9 58.8	17 36.6
13 W	23 23 47	22 43 43	10♓26 00	16 22 10	22 31.6	2 19.8	6 45.2	8 22.5	7 26.6	5 51.2	9 03.6	26 23.1	10 00.6	17 36.9
14 Th	23 27 44	23 43 34	22 18 10	28 14 09	22 16.5	3 53.4	7 59.7	9 04.6	7 49.8	5 53.6	9 07.3	26 26.3	10 02.4	17 37.1
15 F	23 31 40	24 43 23	4♈10 16	10♈06 42	22 02.1	5 28.2	9 14.3	9 46.7	8 13.0	5 56.2	9 11.0	26 29.4	10 04.1	17 37.3
16 Sa	23 35 37	25 43 10	16 03 37	22 01 13	21 49.4	7 04.3	10 28.8	10 28.7	8 36.2	5 59.0	9 14.8	26 32.6	10 05.9	17 37.4
17 Su	23 39 33	26 42 55	27 59 45	3♉59 29	21 39.2	8 41.6	11 43.2	11 10.7	8 59.3	6 02.0	9 18.7	26 35.7	10 07.6	17 37.6
18 M	23 43 30	27 42 38	10♉00 44	16 03 51	21 32.1	10 20.1	12 57.7	11 52.7	9 22.4	6 05.1	9 22.8	26 38.8	10 09.3	17 37.7
19 Tu	23 47 26	28 42 18	22 09 14	28 17 21	21 27.9	11 59.8	14 12.1	12 34.6	9 45.5	6 08.4	9 26.9	26 41.9	10 10.9	17 37.7
20 W	23 51 23	29 41 57	4♊28 40	10♊43 42	21D 26.1	13 40.8	15 26.5	13 16.5	10 08.6	6 12.0	9 31.1	26 44.9	10 12.6	17R 37.7
21 Th	23 55 19	0♈41 33	17 03 00	23 27 07	21R 25.8	15 23.0	16 40.8	13 58.3	10 31.6	6 15.7	9 35.3	26 48.0	10 14.2	17 37.7
22 F	23 59 16	1 41 07	29 56 35	6♋31 55	21 25.8	17 06.5	17 55.1	14 40.2	10 54.6	6 19.5	9 39.7	26 51.0	10 15.8	17 37.7
23 Sa	0 03 13	2 40 38	13♋13 36	20 02 01	21 24.9	18 51.2	19 09.4	15 21.9	11 17.6	6 23.6	9 44.2	26 54.0	10 17.4	17 37.6
24 Su	0 07 09	3 40 08	26 57 26	3♌59 59	21 21.9	20 37.2	20 23.7	16 03.7	11 40.5	6 27.8	9 48.7	26 56.9	10 18.9	17 37.5
25 M	0 11 06	4 39 35	11♌09 39	18 26 12	21 16.5	22 24.6	21 37.9	16 45.4	12 03.4	6 32.2	9 53.3	26 59.8	10 20.4	17 37.3
26 Tu	0 15 02	5 38 59	25 49 08	3♍17 46	21 08.5	24 13.2	22 52.1	17 27.0	12 26.2	6 36.8	9 58.0	27 02.7	10 21.9	17 37.2
27 W	0 18 59	6 38 22	10♍51 10	18 28 11	20 58.6	26 03.2	24 06.2	18 08.6	12 49.0	6 41.5	10 02.8	27 05.6	10 23.4	17 36.9
28 Th	0 22 55	7 37 42	26 07 31	3♎47 42	20 47.9	27 54.5	25 20.3	18 50.2	13 11.8	6 46.4	10 07.7	27 08.4	10 24.9	17 36.7
29 F	0 26 52	8 37 00	11♎27 17	19 04 47	20 37.8	29 47.1	26 34.4	19 31.7	13 34.5	6 51.5	10 12.7	27 11.3	10 26.3	17 36.4
30 Sa	0 30 48	9 36 16	26 38 51	4♏08 15	20 29.4	1♈41.0	27 48.5	20 13.2	13 57.2	6 56.7	10 17.7	27 14.0	10 27.7	17 36.1
31 Su	0 34 45	10 35 30	11♏31 59	18 49 14	20 23.4	3 36.3	29 02.5	20 54.7	14 19.9	7 02.1	10 22.8	27 16.8	10 29.0	17 35.8

April 2002

LONGITUDE

Day	Sid.Time	☉	0 hr ☽	Noon ☽	True ☊	☿	♀	♂	⚳	♃	♄	♅	♆	♇
1 M	0 38 42	11♈34 43	25♏59 28	3♐02 21	20♊20.0	5♈32.9	0♉16.5	21♉36.1	14♓42.5	7♋07.7	10♊28.0	27♒19.5	10♒30.4	17♐35.4
2 Tu	0 42 38	12 33 53	9♐57 47	16 45 50	20D 18.8	7 30.7	1 30.4	22 17.5	15 05.0	7 13.4	10 33.2	27 22.2	10 31.7	17R 35.0
3 W	0 46 35	13 33 03	23 26 45	0♑00 54	20 19.0	9 29.9	2 44.3	22 58.8	15 27.6	7 19.3	10 38.6	27 24.9	10 33.0	17 34.5
4 Th	0 50 31	14 32 10	6♑28 44	12 50 49	20R 19.4	11 30.2	3 58.2	23 40.2	15 50.1	7 25.3	10 44.0	27 27.5	10 34.2	17 34.1
5 F	0 54 28	15 31 15	19 07 43	25 20 01	20 18.9	13 31.7	5 12.1	24 21.4	16 12.5	7 31.5	10 49.5	27 30.1	10 35.4	17 33.6
6 Sa	0 58 24	16 30 19	1♒28 21	7♒33 18	20 16.7	15 34.2	6 25.9	25 02.7	16 34.9	7 37.8	10 55.0	27 32.7	10 36.6	17 33.0
7 Su	1 02 21	17 29 21	13 35 27	19 35 21	20 12.0	17 37.7	7 39.7	25 43.9	16 57.2	7 44.3	11 00.6	27 35.2	10 37.8	17 32.5
8 M	1 06 17	18 28 21	25 33 30	1♓30 22	20 04.8	19 42.0	8 53.5	26 25.1	17 19.5	7 51.0	11 06.3	27 37.7	10 38.9	17 31.9
9 Tu	1 10 14	19 27 19	7♓26 24	13 21 57	19 55.5	21 47.0	10 07.2	27 06.2	17 41.8	7 57.7	11 12.1	27 40.2	10 40.0	17 31.3
10 W	1 14 11	20 26 15	19 17 23	25 12 59	19 44.5	23 52.4	11 20.9	27 47.3	18 03.9	8 04.7	11 17.9	27 42.6	10 41.1	17 30.6
11 Th	1 18 07	21 25 10	1♈09 01	7♈05 42	19 33.0	25 58.2	12 34.6	28 28.4	18 26.1	8 11.7	11 23.8	27 45.0	10 42.2	17 29.9
12 F	1 22 04	22 24 02	13 03 14	19 01 48	19 21.8	28 04.0	13 48.2	29 09.4	18 48.2	8 19.0	11 29.8	27 47.3	10 43.2	17 29.2
13 Sa	1 26 00	23 22 53	25 01 34	1♉02 41	19 12.1	0♉09.5	15 01.8	29 50.4	19 10.2	8 26.3	11 35.8	27 49.7	10 44.2	17 28.5
14 Su	1 29 57	24 21 41	7♉05 19	13 09 38	19 04.4	2 14.6	16 15.4	0♊31.4	19 32.2	8 33.8	11 41.9	27 51.9	10 45.1	17 27.7
15 M	1 33 53	25 20 28	19 15 51	25 24 09	18 59.2	4 18.8	17 28.9	1 12.3	19 54.1	8 41.4	11 48.0	27 54.2	10 46.0	17 26.9
16 Tu	1 37 50	26 19 12	1♊34 47	7♊48 02	18D 56.4	6 21.8	18 42.4	1 53.2	20 15.9	8 49.2	11 54.2	27 56.4	10 46.9	17 26.1
17 W	1 41 46	27 17 55	14 04 11	20 23 34	18 55.8	8 23.4	19 55.8	2 34.1	20 37.7	8 57.1	12 00.5	27 58.5	10 47.8	17 25.2
18 Th	1 45 43	28 16 35	26 46 33	3♋13 30	18 56.5	10 23.1	21 09.2	3 14.9	20 59.4	9 05.1	12 06.8	28 00.7	10 48.6	17 24.3
19 F	1 49 40	29 15 13	9♋44 48	16 20 48	18 57.6	12 20.7	22 22.6	3 55.7	21 21.1	9 13.3	12 13.2	28 02.7	10 49.4	17 23.4
20 Sa	1 53 36	0♉13 49	23 01 52	29 48 18	18R 58.2	14 15.7	23 35.9	4 36.5	21 42.7	9 21.6	12 19.6	28 04.8	10 50.2	17 22.5
21 Su	1 57 33	1 12 22	6♌40 21	13♌38 08	18 57.5	16 08.0	24 49.2	5 17.2	22 04.3	9 30.0	12 26.1	28 06.8	10 50.9	17 21.5
22 M	2 01 29	2 10 54	20 41 43	27 50 57	18 54.9	17 57.2	26 02.4	5 57.9	22 25.7	9 38.5	12 32.7	28 08.8	10 51.6	17 20.6
23 Tu	2 05 26	3 09 23	5♍05 36	12♍25 11	18 50.5	19 43.1	27 15.6	6 38.5	22 47.1	9 47.1	12 39.3	28 10.7	10 52.3	17 19.6
24 W	2 09 22	4 07 49	19 49 06	27 16 32	18 44.6	21 25.4	28 28.8	7 19.1	23 08.5	9 55.9	12 45.9	28 12.5	10 52.9	17 18.5
25 Th	2 13 19	5 06 14	4♎46 32	12♎18 01	18 38.1	23 03.9	29 41.9	7 59.7	23 29.7	10 04.8	12 52.6	28 14.4	10 53.5	17 17.5
26 F	2 17 15	6 04 37	19 49 47	27 20 39	18 31.7	24 38.6	0♊55.0	8 40.2	23 50.9	10 13.8	12 59.4	28 16.2	10 54.1	17 16.4
27 Sa	2 21 12	7 02 58	4♏49 25	12♏14 57	18 26.5	26 09.1	2 08.0	9 20.7	24 12.0	10 22.9	13 06.1	28 17.9	10 54.7	17 15.3
28 Su	2 25 08	8 01 17	19 36 15	26 52 26	18 22.9	27 35.4	3 21.0	10 01.2	24 33.1	10 32.1	13 13.0	28 19.6	10 55.2	17 14.1
29 M	2 29 05	8 59 35	4♐02 49	11♐06 54	18D 21.2	28 57.4	4 33.9	10 41.6	24 54.1	10 41.4	13 19.9	28 21.3	10 55.6	17 13.0
30 Tu	2 33 02	9 57 51	18 04 21	24 55 01	18 21.1	0♊15.0	5 46.8	11 22.0	25 15.0	10 50.9	13 26.8	28 22.9	10 56.1	17 11.8

Astro Data	Dy Hr Mn
☽0S	1 12:23
♃ D	1 15:15
♀0N	10 8:17
☽0N	15 13:45
♇ R	20 14:55
☉0N	20 19:16
☽0S	28 23:14
☿0N	31 16:53
♄△♆	2 2:37
☽0N	11 19:47
☽0S	25 10:01

Planet Ingress		Dy Hr Mn
♂	♉	1 15:05
♀	♈	8 1:42
☿	♓	11 23:34
☉	♈	20 19:16
☿	♈	29 14:44
♀	♉	1 6:39
☿	♉	13 10:10
♂	♊	13 17:36
☉	♉	20 6:20
♀	♊	25 17:57
☿	♊	30 7:15

Last Aspect Dy Hr Mn			☽ Ingress	Dy Hr Mn
2 11:57	♅	△	♏	2 18:51
4 14:43	♅	□	♐	4 21:55
7 2:31	♀	□	♑	7 4:48
8 15:06	☉	⚹	♒	9 14:56
11 19:28	♅	☌	♓	12 2:56
14 2:03	☉	☌	♈	14 15:34
16 21:08	♅	⚹	♉	17 4:01
19 12:53	☉	⚹	♊	19 15:20
21 18:14	♅	△	♋	22 0:06
23 10:19	♀	□	♌	24 5:13
26 1:57	♅	☍	♍	26 6:44
28 1:31	☿	☍	♎	28 6:04
30 0:57	♀	☍	♏	30 5:21

Last Aspect Dy Hr Mn			☽ Ingress	Dy Hr Mn
1 2:14	♅	□	♐	1 6:48
3 7:13	♅	⚹	♑	3 11:58
5 9:59	♂	△	♒	5 21:07
8 4:09	♅	☌	♓	8 8:57
10 17:31	♂	⚹	♈	10 21:41
13 9:52	☿	☌	♉	13 9:55
15 16:53	♅	□	♊	15 20:56
18 2:17	♅	△	♋	18 6:01
19 23:55	♀	⚹	♌	20 12:21
22 12:30	♅	☍	♍	22 15:35
24 14:06	♀	△	♎	24 16:22
26 13:29	♅	△	♏	26 16:15
28 14:25	♅	□	♐	28 17:13
30 18:10	♅	⚹	♑	30 21:03

☽ Phases & Eclipses Dy Hr Mn		
6 1:25	☾	15♐17
14 2:03	●	23♓19
22 2:28	☽	1♋17
28 18:25	○	7♎54
4 15:29	☾	14♑41
12 19:21	●	22♈42
20 12:48	☽	0♌16
27 3:00	○	6♏41

Astro Data

1 March 2002
Julian Day # 37315
SVP 5♓14'02"
GC 26♐52.2 ⚴ 7♒18.1
Eris 19♈18.6 ⚵ 17♌49.1R
⚷ 7♑34.7 ⚶ 4♊15.3
☽ Mean ☊ 23♊12.3

1 April 2002
Julian Day # 37346
SVP 5♓13'59"
GC 26♐52.2 ⚴ 17♒03.1
Eris 19♈37.2 ⚵ 15♌19.4
⚷ 8♑57.9 ⚶ 13♊41.8
☽ Mean ☊ 21♊33.8

LONGITUDE — May 2002

Day	Sid.Time	☉	0 hr ☽	Noon ☽	True ☊	☿	♀	♂	⚳	♃	♄	♅	♆	♇
1 W	2 36 58	10♉56 06	1♑38 56	8♑16 15	18♊22.2	1♊28.0	6♊59.7	12♊02.4	25♓35.8	11♋00.4	13♊33.8	28♒24.5	10♒56.5	17♐10.6
2 Th	2 40 55	11 54 18	14 47 15	21 12 20	18 23.8	2 36.4	8 12.5	12 42.7	25 56.6	11 10.1	13 40.8	28 26.0	10 56.9	17R 09.4
3 F	2 44 51	12 52 30	27 31 56	3♒46 36	18R 25.1	3 40.1	9 25.3	13 23.0	26 17.2	11 19.8	13 47.8	28 27.5	10 57.2	17 08.2
4 Sa	2 48 48	13 50 40	9♒56 52	16 03 20	18 25.4	4 39.1	10 38.0	14 03.3	26 37.8	11 29.7	13 54.9	28 29.0	10 57.5	17 06.9
5 Su	2 52 44	14 48 48	22 06 35	28 07 12	18 24.5	5 33.2	11 50.7	14 43.5	26 58.3	11 39.7	14 02.0	28 30.4	10 57.8	17 05.6
6 M	2 56 41	15 46 55	4♓05 47	10♓02 52	18 22.0	6 22.4	13 03.3	15 23.7	27 18.8	11 49.7	14 09.2	28 31.7	10 58.1	17 04.3
7 Tu	3 00 38	16 45 01	15 59 00	21 54 41	18 18.3	7 06.7	14 15.9	16 03.9	27 39.1	11 59.9	14 16.4	28 33.0	10 58.3	17 03.0
8 W	3 04 34	17 43 05	27 50 24	3♈46 33	18 13.5	7 46.0	15 28.5	16 44.0	27 59.4	12 10.1	14 23.7	28 34.3	10 58.5	17 01.7
9 Th	3 08 31	18 41 08	9♈43 33	15 41 45	18 08.4	8 20.3	16 41.0	17 24.1	28 19.5	12 20.4	14 30.9	28 35.5	10 58.6	17 00.3
10 F	3 12 27	19 39 09	21 41 27	27 42 55	18 03.3	8 49.4	17 53.5	18 04.2	28 39.6	12 30.9	14 38.2	28 36.6	10 58.7	16 59.0
11 Sa	3 16 24	20 37 09	3♉46 24	9♉52 05	17 58.9	9 13.5	19 05.9	18 44.2	28 59.6	12 41.4	14 45.6	28 37.8	10 58.8	16 57.6
12 Su	3 20 20	21 35 07	16 00 10	22 10 47	17 55.7	9 32.5	20 18.3	19 24.3	29 19.5	12 52.0	14 53.0	28 38.8	10 58.9	16 56.2
13 M	3 24 17	22 33 04	28 24 05	4♊40 09	17 53.7	9 46.3	21 30.7	20 04.3	29 39.3	13 02.7	15 00.4	28 39.8	10R 58.9	16 54.8
14 Tu	3 28 13	23 30 59	10♊59 07	17 21 05	17D 53.0	9 55.1	22 42.9	20 44.2	29 59.0	13 13.5	15 07.8	28 40.8	10 58.9	16 53.3
15 W	3 32 10	24 28 53	23 46 10	0♋14 27	17 53.5	9R 59.0	23 55.2	21 24.2	0♈18.6	13 24.4	15 15.3	28 41.8	10 58.8	16 51.9
16 Th	3 36 06	25 26 45	6♋46 03	13 21 05	17 54.7	9 57.9	25 07.4	22 04.1	0 38.1	13 35.3	15 22.7	28 42.6	10 58.7	16 50.4
17 F	3 40 03	26 24 36	19 59 40	26 41 54	17 56.2	9 52.2	26 19.5	22 43.9	0 57.5	13 46.4	15 30.3	28 43.5	10 58.6	16 49.0
18 Sa	3 44 00	27 22 24	3♌27 53	10♌17 40	17 57.4	9 41.9	27 31.6	23 23.8	1 16.8	13 57.5	15 37.8	28 44.2	10 58.5	16 47.5
19 Su	3 47 56	28 20 11	17 11 19	24 08 49	17R 58.1	9 27.4	28 43.7	24 03.6	1 35.9	14 08.7	15 45.3	28 45.0	10 58.3	16 46.0
20 M	3 51 53	29 17 57	1♍10 04	8♍14 58	17 57.9	9 08.8	29 55.6	24 43.4	1 55.0	14 19.9	15 52.9	28 45.7	10 58.1	16 44.5
21 Tu	3 55 49	0♊15 40	15 23 16	22 34 39	17 56.9	8 46.6	1♋07.6	25 23.1	2 14.0	14 31.3	16 00.5	28 46.3	10 57.8	16 43.0
22 W	3 59 46	1 13 22	29 48 42	7♎04 56	17 55.3	8 21.2	2 19.4	26 02.8	2 32.8	14 42.7	16 08.1	28 46.9	10 57.6	16 41.4
23 Th	4 03 42	2 11 02	14♎22 43	21 41 23	17 53.4	7 53.0	3 31.3	26 42.5	2 51.6	14 54.2	16 15.8	28 47.4	10 57.2	16 39.9
24 F	4 07 39	3 08 41	29 00 11	6♏18 20	17 51.5	7 22.5	4 43.0	27 22.2	3 10.2	15 05.7	16 23.4	28 47.9	10 56.9	16 38.3
25 Sa	4 11 35	4 06 19	13♏35 02	20 49 30	17 50.0	6 50.3	5 54.7	28 01.8	3 28.7	15 17.3	16 31.1	28 48.3	10 56.5	16 36.8
26 Su	4 15 32	5 03 55	28 00 57	5♐08 44	17D 49.1	6 17.0	7 06.3	28 41.4	3 47.1	15 29.0	16 38.8	28 48.7	10 56.1	16 35.2
27 M	4 19 29	6 01 30	12♐12 15	19 10 58	17 48.9	5 43.0	8 17.9	29 20.9	4 05.4	15 40.8	16 46.5	28 49.1	10 55.7	16 33.7
28 Tu	4 23 25	6 59 04	26 04 31	2♑52 39	17 49.2	5 09.1	9 29.4	0♋00.5	4 23.6	15 52.6	16 54.2	28 49.4	10 55.2	16 32.1
29 W	4 27 22	7 56 37	9♑35 11	16 12 07	17 49.9	4 35.7	10 40.9	0 40.0	4 41.6	16 04.5	17 01.9	28 49.6	10 54.8	16 30.5
30 Th	4 31 18	8 54 09	22 43 32	29 09 35	17 50.8	4 03.6	11 52.3	1 19.5	4 59.5	16 16.4	17 09.7	28 49.8	10 54.2	16 28.9
31 F	4 35 15	9 51 40	5♒30 33	11♒46 48	17 51.6	3 33.1	13 03.6	1 58.9	5 17.3	16 28.4	17 17.4	28 50.0	10 53.7	16 27.3

LONGITUDE — June 2002

Day	Sid.Time	☉	0 hr ☽	Noon ☽	True ☊	☿	♀	♂	⚳	♃	♄	♅	♆	♇
1 Sa	4 39 11	10♊49 11	17♒58 43	24♒06 47	17♊52.1	3♊04.9	14♋14.9	2♋38.4	5♈35.0	16♋40.5	17♊25.2	28♒50.1	10♒53.1	16♐25.7
2 Su	4 43 08	11 46 40	0♓11 30	6♓13 24	17R 52.4	2R 39.3	15 26.1	3 17.8	5 52.5	16 52.6	17 33.0	28R 50.1	10R 52.5	16R 24.1
3 M	4 47 05	12 44 09	12 13 04	18 11 02	17 52.5	2 16.8	16 37.3	3 57.2	6 09.9	17 04.8	17 40.8	28 50.1	10 51.9	16 22.5
4 Tu	4 51 01	13 41 37	24 07 55	0♈04 15	17 52.2	1 57.8	17 48.4	4 36.5	6 27.2	17 17.0	17 48.5	28 50.1	10 51.2	16 20.9
5 W	4 54 58	14 39 04	6♈00 36	11 57 32	17 51.9	1 42.5	18 59.4	5 15.8	6 44.3	17 29.3	17 56.3	28 50.0	10 50.5	16 19.3
6 Th	4 58 54	15 36 30	17 55 32	23 55 06	17 51.6	1 31.2	20 10.4	5 55.2	7 01.3	17 41.6	18 04.1	28 49.8	10 49.7	16 17.7
7 F	5 02 51	16 33 56	29 56 42	6♉00 43	17 51.4	1 24.1	21 21.3	6 34.4	7 18.1	17 54.0	18 11.9	28 49.6	10 49.0	16 16.1
8 Sa	5 06 47	17 31 22	12♉07 33	18 17 30	17D 51.3	1D 21.3	22 32.1	7 13.7	7 34.8	18 06.4	18 19.7	28 49.4	10 48.2	16 14.5
9 Su	5 10 44	18 28 46	24 30 50	0♊47 47	17 51.3	1 22.9	23 42.9	7 53.0	7 51.4	18 18.9	18 27.5	28 49.1	10 47.4	16 12.9
10 M	5 14 40	19 26 10	7♊08 31	13 33 07	17R 51.4	1 29.1	24 53.6	8 32.2	8 07.8	18 31.4	18 35.3	28 48.8	10 46.6	16 11.3
11 Tu	5 18 37	20 23 33	20 01 38	26 34 05	17 51.4	1 39.7	26 04.3	9 11.4	8 24.0	18 44.0	18 43.1	28 48.4	10 45.7	16 09.7
12 W	5 22 34	21 20 56	3♋10 25	9♋50 30	17 51.2	1 54.9	27 14.8	9 50.6	8 40.1	18 56.6	18 50.9	28 47.9	10 44.8	16 08.1
13 Th	5 26 30	22 18 17	16 34 13	23 21 23	17 50.8	2 14.6	28 25.3	10 29.7	8 56.0	19 09.3	18 58.7	28 47.5	10 43.9	16 06.5
14 F	5 30 27	23 15 38	0♌11 47	7♌05 11	17 50.3	2 38.8	29 35.7	11 08.8	9 11.8	19 22.0	19 06.5	28 46.9	10 42.9	16 04.9
15 Sa	5 34 23	24 12 58	14 01 19	20 59 56	17 49.6	3 07.3	0♌46.1	11 47.9	9 27.4	19 34.7	19 14.3	28 46.4	10 42.0	16 03.3
16 Su	5 38 20	25 10 17	28 00 45	5♍03 27	17 49.0	3 40.3	1 56.4	12 27.0	9 42.8	19 47.5	19 22.1	28 45.7	10 41.0	16 01.7
17 M	5 42 16	26 07 35	12♍07 46	19 13 24	17D 48.7	4 17.5	3 06.5	13 06.1	9 58.1	20 00.3	19 29.8	28 45.1	10 39.9	16 00.1
18 Tu	5 46 13	27 04 52	26 20 02	3♎27 21	17 48.7	4 58.9	4 16.6	13 45.1	10 13.1	20 13.2	19 37.6	28 44.4	10 38.9	15 58.5
19 W	5 50 09	28 02 08	10♎35 04	17 42 49	17 49.1	5 44.5	5 26.6	14 24.1	10 28.1	20 26.1	19 45.4	28 43.6	10 37.8	15 57.0
20 Th	5 54 06	28 59 24	24 50 17	1♏57 06	17 49.8	6 34.1	6 36.6	15 03.1	10 42.8	20 39.0	19 53.1	28 42.8	10 36.7	15 55.4
21 F	5 58 03	29 56 39	9♏02 55	16 07 21	17 50.8	7 27.8	7 46.4	15 42.1	10 57.4	20 52.0	20 00.8	28 41.9	10 35.6	15 53.8
22 Sa	6 01 59	0♋53 53	23 10 02	0♐10 34	17 51.6	8 25.4	8 56.1	16 21.0	11 11.7	21 04.9	20 08.5	28 41.1	10 34.5	15 52.3
23 Su	6 05 56	1 51 07	7♐08 34	14 03 42	17R 52.1	9 26.9	10 05.8	16 59.9	11 25.9	21 18.0	20 16.2	28 40.1	10 33.3	15 50.8
24 M	6 09 52	2 48 20	20 55 36	27 43 57	17 51.9	10 32.2	11 15.3	17 38.8	11 39.9	21 31.0	20 23.9	28 39.1	10 32.1	15 49.2
25 Tu	6 13 49	3 45 33	4♑28 30	11♑09 01	17 51.0	11 41.2	12 24.8	18 17.7	11 53.8	21 44.1	20 31.6	28 38.1	10 30.9	15 47.7
26 W	6 17 45	4 42 45	17 45 20	24 17 21	17 49.3	12 54.0	13 34.1	18 56.6	12 07.4	21 57.2	20 39.3	28 37.0	10 29.7	15 46.2
27 Th	6 21 42	5 39 58	0♒45 01	7♒08 23	17 46.9	14 10.5	14 43.4	19 35.4	12 20.8	22 10.3	20 46.9	28 35.9	10 28.5	15 44.7
28 F	6 25 38	6 37 10	13 27 34	19 42 44	17 44.2	15 30.6	15 52.6	20 14.2	12 34.0	22 23.5	20 54.5	28 34.8	10 27.2	15 43.3
29 Sa	6 29 35	7 34 22	25 54 07	2♓02 02	17 41.5	16 54.3	17 01.6	20 53.0	12 47.1	22 36.6	21 02.1	28 33.6	10 25.9	15 41.8
30 Su	6 33 32	8 31 34	8♓06 51	14 09 00	17 39.1	18 21.5	18 10.6	21 31.8	12 59.9	22 49.8	21 09.7	28 32.4	10 24.6	15 40.3

Astro Data

	Dy Hr Mn
♃⚻♆	1 1:44
☽0N	9 2:51
♆R	13 12:10
☿R	15 18:51
♃⚼♅	17 5:10
☽0S	22 18:50
♄☍♇	26 2:44
♃⚻♇	31 10:05
♅R	3 0:11
☽0N	5 10:38
☿D	8 15:12
♃⚺♄	11 7:36
☽0S	19 1:09

Planet Ingress

		Dy Hr Mn
⚳	♈	14 13:15
♀	♋	20 13:27
☉	♊	21 5:29
♂	♋	28 11:43
♀	♌	14 20:16
☉	♋	21 13:24

Last Aspect / ☽ Ingress

Last Aspect Dy Hr Mn		☽ Ingress	Dy Hr Mn
1 17:17	☉ △	♒	3 4:43
5 12:46	♅ ☌	♓	5 15:46
7 2:11	♇ □	♈	8 4:22
10 13:47	♅ ✶	♉	10 16:32
13 0:29	♅ □	♊	13 3:04
15 9:08	♅ △	♋	15 11:33
17 11:27	☉ ✶	♌	17 17:52
19 20:34	♀ ✶	♍	19 22:01
21 16:53	♂ □	♎	22 0:19
23 23:39	♅ △	♏	24 1:38
26 1:20	♅ □	♐	26 3:20
28 6:40	♂ ☍	♑	28 6:54
29 11:46	♃ ☍	♒	30 13:35

Last Aspect / ☽ Ingress

Last Aspect Dy Hr Mn		☽ Ingress	Dy Hr Mn
1 21:19	♅ ☌	♓	1 23:37
3 10:58	♄ □	♈	4 11:51
6 21:47	♅ ✶	♉	7 0:07
9 8:14	♅ □	♊	9 10:29
11 16:05	♅ △	♋	11 18:15
13 21:44	♀ ☌	♌	13 23:39
16 1:17	♅ ☍	♍	16 3:23
18 0:29	☉ □	♎	18 6:11
20 6:38	☉ △	♏	20 8:42
22 9:27	♅ □	♐	22 11:42
24 13:38	♅ ✶	♑	24 16:01
26 7:37	♃ ☍	♒	26 22:36
29 5:12	♅ ☌	♓	29 8:00

☽ Phases & Eclipses

Dy Hr Mn	
4 7:16	☾ 13♒39
12 10:45	● 21♉32
19 19:42	☽ 28♌39
26 11:51	○ 5♐04
26 12:03	• A 0.689
3 0:05	☾ 12♓16
10 23:47	● 19♊54
10 23:44:17	• A 00'22"
18 0:29	☽ 26♍37
24 21:42	○ 3♑11
24 21:27	• A 0.209

Astro Data

1 May 2002
Julian Day # 37376
SVP 5♓13'56"
GC 26♐52.3 ⚴ 24♒25.5
Eris 19♈56.7 ⚵ 18♌51.5
⚷ 9♑00.2R ⚶ 24♊51.9
☽ Mean ☊ 19♊58.5

1 June 2002
Julian Day # 37407
SVP 5♓13'51"
GC 26♐52.4 ⚴ 28♒42.9
Eris 20♈13.5 ⚵ 26♌28.9
⚷ 7♑47.6R ⚶ 7♋36.4
☽ Mean ☊ 18♊20.0

July 2002 LONGITUDE

Day	Sid.Time	☉	0 hr ☽	Noon ☽	True ☊	☿	♀	♂	⚳	♃	♄	♅	♆	♇
1 M	6 37 28	9♋28 47	20♓08 56	26♓07 09	17♊37.5	19♊52.2	19♌19.4	22♋10.6	13♈12.5	23♋03.0	21♊17.3	28♒31.1	10♒23.3	15♐38.9
2 Tu	6 41 25	10 25 59	2♈04 12	8♈00 39	17D36.8	21 26.4	20 28.2	22 49.3	13 24.9	23 16.3	21 24.8	28R29.8	10R21.9	15R37.5
3 W	6 45 21	11 23 12	13 57 04	19 54 04	17 37.1	23 04.0	21 36.8	23 28.0	13 37.1	23 29.5	21 32.3	28 28.4	10 20.6	15 36.1
4 Th	6 49 18	12 20 24	25 52 14	1♉52 09	17 38.1	24 44.9	22 45.4	24 06.8	13 49.1	23 42.8	21 39.8	28 27.0	10 19.2	15 34.7
5 F	6 53 14	13 17 38	7♉54 23	13 59 31	17 39.7	26 29.0	23 53.8	24 45.5	14 00.8	23 56.1	21 47.3	28 25.6	10 17.8	15 33.3
6 Sa	6 57 11	14 14 51	20 08 03	26 20 28	17 41.3	28 16.3	25 02.1	25 24.2	14 12.3	24 09.4	21 54.7	28 24.1	10 16.4	15 31.9
7 Su	7 01 07	15 12 04	2♊37 12	8♊58 35	17R42.4	0♋06.6	26 10.3	26 02.8	14 23.6	24 22.7	22 02.1	28 22.6	10 15.0	15 30.6
8 M	7 05 04	16 09 18	15 24 55	21 56 23	17 42.6	1 59.7	27 18.4	26 41.5	14 34.7	24 36.1	22 09.5	28 21.1	10 13.5	15 29.2
9 Tu	7 09 01	17 06 33	28 33 06	5♋15 03	17 41.5	3 55.6	28 26.3	27 20.1	14 45.5	24 49.4	22 16.9	28 19.5	10 12.1	15 27.9
10 W	7 12 57	18 03 47	12♋02 07	18 54 05	17 39.1	5 53.9	29 34.2	27 58.8	14 56.0	25 02.8	22 24.2	28 17.9	10 10.6	15 26.6
11 Th	7 16 54	19 01 01	25 50 36	2♌51 15	17 35.3	7 54.5	0♍41.9	28 37.4	15 06.4	25 16.2	22 31.5	28 16.2	10 09.1	15 25.4
12 F	7 20 50	19 58 16	9♌55 29	17 02 44	17 30.7	9 57.2	1 49.5	29 16.0	15 16.4	25 29.5	22 38.7	28 14.5	10 07.6	15 24.1
13 Sa	7 24 47	20 55 31	24 12 20	1♍23 37	17 25.9	12 01.5	2 56.9	29 54.6	15 26.2	25 42.9	22 45.9	28 12.8	10 06.1	15 22.9
14 Su	7 28 43	21 52 45	8♍35 54	15 48 32	17 21.6	14 07.4	4 04.3	0♌33.1	15 35.8	25 56.3	22 53.1	28 11.0	10 04.6	15 21.7
15 M	7 32 40	22 50 00	23 00 55	0♎12 29	17 18.4	16 14.3	5 11.4	1 11.7	15 45.1	26 09.7	23 00.3	28 09.2	10 03.1	15 20.5
16 Tu	7 36 37	23 47 15	7♎22 45	14 31 18	17D16.6	18 22.1	6 18.4	1 50.2	15 54.1	26 23.1	23 07.4	28 07.4	10 01.5	15 19.3
17 W	7 40 33	24 44 29	21 37 50	28 42 04	17 16.3	20 30.5	7 25.3	2 28.7	16 02.9	26 36.5	23 14.4	28 05.6	10 00.0	15 18.1
18 Th	7 44 30	25 41 44	5♏43 49	12♏42 57	17 17.2	22 39.0	8 32.0	3 07.2	16 11.4	26 49.9	23 21.4	28 03.7	9 58.4	15 17.0
19 F	7 48 26	26 38 59	19 39 24	26 33 05	17 18.6	24 47.5	9 38.6	3 45.7	16 19.6	27 03.3	23 28.4	28 01.8	9 56.8	15 15.9
20 Sa	7 52 23	27 36 15	3♐23 59	10♐12 03	17R19.6	26 55.7	10 45.0	4 24.2	16 27.6	27 16.7	23 35.4	27 59.8	9 55.3	15 14.8
21 Su	7 56 19	28 33 30	16 57 16	23 39 36	17 19.7	29 03.4	11 51.2	5 02.7	16 35.2	27 30.1	23 42.3	27 57.9	9 53.7	15 13.8
22 M	8 00 16	29 30 46	0♑19 01	6♑55 28	17 18.0	1♌10.3	12 57.3	5 41.1	16 42.6	27 43.5	23 49.1	27 55.9	9 52.1	15 12.7
23 Tu	8 04 12	0♌28 03	13 28 53	19 59 13	17 14.4	3 16.2	14 03.2	6 19.5	16 49.7	27 56.9	23 56.0	27 53.9	9 50.5	15 11.7
24 W	8 08 09	1 25 20	26 26 25	2♒50 25	17 08.7	5 21.0	15 08.9	6 58.0	16 56.5	28 10.3	24 02.7	27 51.8	9 48.9	15 10.8
25 Th	8 12 06	2 22 37	9♒11 14	15 28 50	17 01.5	7 24.6	16 14.4	7 36.4	17 03.0	28 23.7	24 09.4	27 49.8	9 47.3	15 09.8
26 F	8 16 02	3 19 55	21 43 16	27 54 37	16 53.4	9 26.9	17 19.7	8 14.8	17 09.3	28 37.0	24 16.1	27 47.7	9 45.7	15 08.9
27 Sa	8 19 59	4 17 14	4♓03 01	10♓08 37	16 45.0	11 27.7	18 24.8	8 53.2	17 15.2	28 50.4	24 22.7	27 45.6	9 44.0	15 07.9
28 Su	8 23 55	5 14 34	16 11 41	22 12 30	16 37.3	13 27.1	19 29.8	9 31.5	17 20.8	29 03.7	24 29.3	27 43.4	9 42.4	15 07.1
29 M	8 27 52	6 11 55	28 11 23	4♈08 46	16 31.1	15 24.8	20 34.5	10 09.9	17 26.1	29 17.1	24 35.8	27 41.3	9 40.8	15 06.2
30 Tu	8 31 48	7 09 16	10♈05 04	16 00 47	16 26.6	17 21.1	21 39.1	10 48.3	17 31.1	29 30.4	24 42.3	27 39.1	9 39.2	15 05.4
31 W	8 35 45	8 06 39	21 56 28	27 52 41	16D24.2	19 15.7	22 43.4	11 26.6	17 35.7	29 43.7	24 48.7	27 36.9	9 37.5	15 04.6

August 2002 LONGITUDE

Day	Sid.Time	☉	0 hr ☽	Noon ☽	True ☊	☿	♀	♂	⚳	♃	♄	♅	♆	♇
1 Th	8 39 41	9♌04 03	3♉50 01	9♉49 07	16♊23.5	21♌08.7	23♍47.5	12♌05.0	17♈40.1	29♋57.0	24♊55.1	27♒34.7	9♒35.9	15♐03.8
2 F	8 43 38	10 01 28	15 50 36	21 55 07	16 24.1	23 00.0	24 51.4	12 43.3	17 44.1	0♌10.3	25 01.4	27R32.4	9R34.3	15R03.0
3 Sa	8 47 35	10 58 54	28 03 19	4♊15 47	16R25.1	24 49.8	25 55.1	13 21.6	17 47.8	0 23.6	25 07.6	27 30.2	9 32.6	15 02.3
4 Su	8 51 31	11 56 21	10♊33 06	16 55 48	16 25.6	26 37.9	26 58.5	14 00.0	17 51.1	0 36.9	25 13.8	27 27.9	9 31.0	15 01.6
5 M	8 55 28	12 53 50	23 24 19	29 59 01	16 24.7	28 24.4	28 01.7	14 38.3	17 54.2	0 50.1	25 20.0	27 25.6	9 29.4	15 01.0
6 Tu	8 59 24	13 51 20	6♋40 09	13♋27 49	16 21.8	0♍09.3	29 04.7	15 16.6	17 56.8	1 03.3	25 26.1	27 23.3	9 27.7	15 00.3
7 W	9 03 21	14 48 51	20 22 00	27 22 27	16 16.6	1 52.7	0♎07.4	15 54.9	17 59.2	1 16.5	25 32.1	27 21.0	9 26.1	14 59.7
8 Th	9 07 17	15 46 23	4♌28 49	11♌40 32	16 09.2	3 34.4	1 09.9	16 33.2	18 01.2	1 29.7	25 38.0	27 18.7	9 24.5	14 59.1
9 F	9 11 14	16 43 56	18 56 53	26 16 59	16 00.4	5 14.6	2 12.1	17 11.5	18 02.8	1 42.9	25 43.9	27 16.4	9 22.9	14 58.6
10 Sa	9 15 10	17 41 30	3♍39 52	11♍04 30	15 51.0	6 53.1	3 14.1	17 49.8	18 04.1	1 56.0	25 49.7	27 14.0	9 21.3	14 58.1
11 Su	9 19 07	18 39 04	18 29 47	25 54 41	15 42.4	8 30.2	4 15.7	18 28.0	18 05.0	2 09.1	25 55.5	27 11.7	9 19.7	14 57.6
12 M	9 23 04	19 36 40	3♎18 11	10♎39 25	15 35.4	10 05.7	5 17.1	19 06.3	18 05.6	2 22.2	26 01.2	27 09.3	9 18.1	14 57.1
13 Tu	9 27 00	20 34 17	17 57 38	25 12 13	15 30.8	11 39.6	6 18.1	19 44.5	18R05.8	2 35.2	26 06.8	27 06.9	9 16.5	14 56.7
14 W	9 30 57	21 31 55	2♏22 42	9♏28 49	15D28.4	13 11.9	7 18.9	20 22.8	18 05.7	2 48.2	26 12.4	27 04.5	9 14.9	14 56.3
15 Th	9 34 53	22 29 33	16 30 22	23 27 20	15 27.9	14 42.7	8 19.3	21 01.0	18 05.2	3 01.2	26 17.9	27 02.2	9 13.3	14 55.9
16 F	9 38 50	23 27 13	0♐19 47	7♐07 50	15R28.2	16 12.0	9 19.4	21 39.3	18 04.4	3 14.2	26 23.3	26 59.8	9 11.7	14 55.6
17 Sa	9 42 46	24 24 54	13 51 40	20 31 32	15 28.3	17 39.6	10 19.1	22 17.5	18 03.1	3 27.1	26 28.6	26 57.4	9 10.1	14 55.3
18 Su	9 46 43	25 22 36	27 07 39	3♑40 15	15 26.9	19 05.7	11 18.5	22 55.7	18 01.6	3 40.0	26 33.9	26 55.0	9 08.6	14 55.0
19 M	9 50 39	26 20 18	10♑09 34	16 35 49	15 23.3	20 30.1	12 17.5	23 33.9	17 59.6	3 52.8	26 39.1	26 52.6	9 07.1	14 54.8
20 Tu	9 54 36	27 18 02	22 59 09	29 19 45	15 17.0	21 52.9	13 16.1	24 12.1	17 57.3	4 05.6	26 44.2	26 50.2	9 05.5	14 54.6
21 W	9 58 33	28 15 47	5♒37 42	11♒53 09	15 07.9	23 14.1	14 14.4	24 50.3	17 54.7	4 18.4	26 49.3	26 47.8	9 04.0	14 54.4
22 Th	10 02 29	29 13 34	18 06 09	24 16 47	14 56.5	24 33.5	15 12.2	25 28.5	17 51.6	4 31.1	26 54.2	26 45.4	9 02.5	14 54.3
23 F	10 06 26	0♍11 22	0♓25 07	6♓31 15	14 43.7	25 51.1	16 09.6	26 06.7	17 48.2	4 43.8	26 59.1	26 43.0	9 01.0	14 54.2
24 Sa	10 10 22	1 09 11	12 35 16	18 37 18	14 30.6	27 07.0	17 06.5	26 44.9	17 44.5	4 56.5	27 04.0	26 40.7	8 59.5	14 54.1
25 Su	10 14 19	2 07 02	24 37 29	0♈36 01	14 18.2	28 21.0	18 03.0	27 23.1	17 40.4	5 09.1	27 08.7	26 38.3	8 58.0	14D54.1
26 M	10 18 15	3 04 54	6♈33 09	12 29 09	14 07.5	29 33.0	18 59.1	28 01.3	17 35.9	5 21.6	27 13.3	26 35.9	8 56.6	14 54.0
27 Tu	10 22 12	4 02 48	18 24 22	24 19 11	13 59.3	0♎43.1	19 54.7	28 39.5	17 31.0	5 34.2	27 17.9	26 33.5	8 55.1	14 54.1
28 W	10 26 08	5 00 44	0♉14 02	6♉09 25	13 53.8	1 51.0	20 49.8	29 17.6	17 25.8	5 46.6	27 22.4	26 31.2	8 53.7	14 54.1
29 Th	10 30 05	5 58 41	12 05 51	18 03 56	13 50.8	2 56.8	21 44.3	29 55.8	17 20.2	5 59.0	27 26.8	26 28.8	8 52.3	14 54.2
30 F	10 34 01	6 56 41	24 04 15	0♊07 28	13D49.8	4 00.2	22 38.4	0♍34.0	17 14.3	6 11.4	27 31.2	26 26.5	8 50.9	14 54.3
31 Sa	10 37 58	7 54 42	6♊14 14	12 25 12	13R49.7	5 01.2	23 31.9	1 12.2	17 08.0	6 23.7	27 35.4	26 24.1	8 49.5	14 54.5

Astro Data

	Dy Hr Mn
☽0N	2 18:25
☽0S	16 6:09
♃⊼♅	23 7:18
☽0N	30 1:33
♄□♆	30 2:39
♃□♇	1 23:30
♀0S	6 18:38
☽0S	12 12:01
⚳R	13 14:59
♄△♅	21 7:18
☿0S	24 16:50
☽0N	26 7:53
♇D	26 11:01

Planet Ingress

		Dy Hr Mn
☿	♋	7 10:35
♀	♍	10 21:09
♂	♌	13 15:23
☿	♌	21 22:41
☉	♌	23 0:15
♃	♌	1 17:20
☿	♍	6 9:51
♀	♎	7 9:09
☉	♍	23 7:17
☿	♎	26 21:10
♂	♍	29 14:38

Last Aspect / ☽ Ingress

Last Aspect Dy Hr Mn			☽ Ingress	Dy Hr Mn
1 5:43	♃	△	♈	1 19:49
4 5:11	♅	⚹	♉	4 8:16
6 15:57	♅	□	♊	6 19:01
8 23:37	♅	△	♋	9 2:36
11 4:25	♂	☌	♌	11 7:08
13 6:42	♅	☍	♍	13 9:41
15 5:08	♃	⚹	♎	15 11:39
17 10:58	♅	△	♏	17 14:13
19 14:35	♅	□	♐	19 18:02
21 19:44	♅	⚹	♑	21 23:26
24 3:05	♃	☍	♒	24 6:40
26 11:47	♅	☌	♓	26 16:04
29 2:01	♃	△	♈	29 3:39
31 15:48	♃	□	♉	31 16:17

Last Aspect / ☽ Ingress

Last Aspect Dy Hr Mn			☽ Ingress	Dy Hr Mn
2 22:58	♅	□	♊	3 3:47
5 8:42	♅	⚹	♋	5 12:02
5 8:42	♅	⚹	♌	7 16:27
9 13:36	♅	☍	♍	9 18:03
11 12:01	♄	□	♎	11 18:38
13 15:11	♅	△	♏	13 20:01
15 18:13	♅	□	♐	15 23:25
17 23:39	♅	⚹	♑	18 5:15
19 20:13	♅	△	♒	20 13:16
22 22:29	☉	☍	♓	22 23:11
25 6:58	♅	☌	♈	25 10:48
27 21:18	♂	△	♉	27 23:32
30 4:44	♅	□	♊	30 11:45

☽ Phases & Eclipses

Dy Hr Mn		
2 17:19	☾	10♈39
10 10:26	●	18♋00
17 4:47	☽	24♎27
24 9:07	○	1♒18
1 10:22	☾	9♉00
8 19:15	●	16♌04
15 10:12	☽	22♏25
22 22:29	○	29♒39
31 2:31	☾	7♊32

Astro Data

1 July 2002
Julian Day # 37437
SVP 5♓13'46"
GC 26♐52.4 ⚴ 28♒12.2R
Eris 20♈22.7 ⚵ 5♍58.4
⚷ 5♓55.9R ⚶ 20♋36.4
☽ Mean ☊ 16♊44.7

1 August 2002
Julian Day # 37468
SVP 5♓13'41"
GC 26♐52.5 ⚴ 22♒24.7R
Eris 20♈22.7R ⚵ 16♍54.8
⚷ 4♓08.1R ⚶ 4♌25.0
☽ Mean ☊ 15♊06.2

LONGITUDE — September 2002

Day	Sid.Time	☉	0 hr ☽	Noon☽	True☊	☿	♀	♂	⚳	♃	♄	♅	♆	♇
1 Su	10 41 55	8♍52 46	18♊41 02	25♊02 22	13♊49.4	5♎59.7	24♎24.8	1♍50.4	17♈01.4	6♌36.0	27♊39.5	26♒21.8	8♒48.1	14♐54.6
2 M	10 45 51	9 50 51	1♋29 46	8♋03 45	13R47.9	6 55.5	25 17.2	2 28.5	16R54.4	6 48.2	27 43.6	26R19.5	8R46.8	14 54.9
3 Tu	10 49 48	10 48 58	14 44 45	21 33 00	13 44.2	7 48.4	26 09.0	3 06.7	16 47.1	7 00.4	27 47.6	26 17.2	8 45.5	14 55.1
4 W	10 53 44	11 47 07	28 28 41	5♌31 43	13 37.9	8 38.2	27 00.1	3 44.9	16 39.4	7 12.5	27 51.5	26 14.9	8 44.2	14 55.4
5 Th	10 57 41	12 45 18	12♌41 51	19 58 36	13 29.1	9 24.8	27 50.6	4 23.1	16 31.4	7 24.5	27 55.3	26 12.6	8 42.9	14 55.7
6 F	11 01 37	13 43 31	27 21 16	4♍48 56	13 18.5	10 07.9	28 40.4	5 01.3	16 23.0	7 36.5	27 59.0	26 10.4	8 41.6	14 56.1
7 Sa	11 05 34	14 41 45	12♍20 29	19 54 41	13 07.2	10 47.2	29 29.5	5 39.4	16 14.4	7 48.5	28 02.6	26 08.1	8 40.3	14 56.4
8 Su	11 09 30	15 40 01	27 30 11	5♎05 38	12 56.5	11 22.6	0♏17.9	6 17.6	16 05.4	8 00.3	28 06.1	26 05.9	8 39.1	14 56.8
9 M	11 13 27	16 38 19	12♎39 42	20 11 10	12 47.7	11 53.7	1 05.5	6 55.8	15 56.1	8 12.1	28 09.5	26 03.7	8 37.9	14 57.3
10 Tu	11 17 24	17 36 38	27 38 57	5♏02 09	12 41.5	12 20.3	1 52.4	7 33.9	15 46.5	8 23.8	28 12.9	26 01.5	8 36.7	14 57.8
11 W	11 21 20	18 34 59	12♏20 05	19 32 16	12 38.0	12 41.9	2 38.4	8 12.1	15 36.6	8 35.5	28 16.1	25 59.4	8 35.6	14 58.3
12 Th	11 25 17	19 33 22	26 38 25	3♐38 25	12D36.7	12 58.4	3 23.5	8 50.3	15 26.4	8 47.1	28 19.2	25 57.2	8 34.4	14 58.8
13 F	11 29 13	20 31 46	10♐32 20	17 20 21	12R36.6	13 09.3	4 07.8	9 28.5	15 15.9	8 58.6	28 22.3	25 55.1	8 33.3	14 59.4
14 Sa	11 33 10	21 30 12	24 02 42	0♑39 46	12 36.4	13R14.3	4 51.1	10 06.6	15 05.2	9 10.1	28 25.2	25 53.0	8 32.2	15 00.0
15 Su	11 37 06	22 28 39	7♑11 55	13 39 33	12 35.0	13 13.2	5 33.5	10 44.8	14 54.2	9 21.5	28 28.1	25 51.0	8 31.1	15 00.7
16 M	11 41 03	23 27 08	20 03 06	26 22 56	12 31.2	13 05.5	6 14.8	11 23.0	14 43.0	9 32.8	28 30.8	25 48.9	8 30.1	15 01.3
17 Tu	11 44 59	24 25 39	2♒39 28	8♒53 01	12 24.8	12 51.1	6 55.1	12 01.1	14 31.6	9 44.0	28 33.4	25 46.9	8 29.1	15 02.0
18 W	11 48 56	25 24 11	15 03 55	21 12 26	12 15.5	12 29.8	7 34.3	12 39.3	14 19.9	9 55.1	28 36.0	25 44.9	8 28.1	15 02.8
19 Th	11 52 53	26 22 45	27 18 50	3♓23 18	12 03.9	12 01.5	8 12.3	13 17.5	14 07.9	10 06.2	28 38.4	25 43.0	8 27.1	15 03.6
20 F	11 56 49	27 21 20	9♓26 03	15 27 14	11 50.9	11 26.2	8 49.2	13 55.6	13 55.8	10 17.2	28 40.8	25 41.0	8 26.2	15 04.4
21 Sa	12 00 46	28 19 58	21 27 01	27 25 33	11 37.4	10 44.1	9 24.8	14 33.8	13 43.5	10 28.1	28 43.0	25 39.1	8 25.3	15 05.2
22 Su	12 04 42	29 18 37	3♈22 58	9♈19 27	11 24.7	9 55.6	9 59.2	15 12.0	13 31.0	10 38.9	28 45.1	25 37.3	8 24.4	15 06.0
23 M	12 08 39	0♎17 19	15 15 12	21 10 23	11 13.7	9 01.4	10 32.2	15 50.1	13 18.4	10 49.7	28 47.1	25 35.4	8 23.5	15 06.9
24 Tu	12 12 35	1 16 02	27 05 17	3♉00 10	11 05.1	8 02.1	11 03.8	16 28.3	13 05.6	11 00.3	28 49.1	25 33.6	8 22.7	15 07.9
25 W	12 16 32	2 14 48	8♉55 22	14 51 15	10 59.3	6 59.0	11 34.0	17 06.5	12 52.6	11 10.9	28 50.9	25 31.8	8 21.9	15 08.8
26 Th	12 20 28	3 13 36	20 48 13	26 46 45	10 56.2	5 53.3	12 02.7	17 44.7	12 39.5	11 21.4	28 52.6	25 30.1	8 21.1	15 09.8
27 F	12 24 25	4 12 26	2♊47 21	8♊50 34	10D55.2	4 46.5	12 29.9	18 22.9	12 26.3	11 31.7	28 54.2	25 28.4	8 20.4	15 10.8
28 Sa	12 28 22	5 11 18	14 56 57	21 07 07	10 55.5	3 40.3	12 55.5	19 01.1	12 13.0	11 42.0	28 55.7	25 26.7	8 19.6	15 11.9
29 Su	12 32 18	6 10 13	27 21 42	3♋41 18	10R56.0	2 36.4	13 19.5	19 39.3	11 59.6	11 52.2	28 57.1	25 25.1	8 18.9	15 13.0
30 M	12 36 15	7 09 10	10♋06 30	16 37 52	10 55.6	1 36.6	13 41.7	20 17.5	11 46.1	12 02.3	28 58.3	25 23.5	8 18.3	15 14.1

LONGITUDE — October 2002

Day	Sid.Time	☉	0 hr ☽	Noon☽	True☊	☿	♀	♂	⚳	♃	♄	♅	♆	♇
1 Tu	12 40 11	8♎08 09	23♋15 54	0♌00 59	10♊53.5	0♎42.4	14♏02.1	20♍55.7	11♈32.5	12♌12.3	28♊59.5	25♒21.9	8♒17.7	15♐15.2
2 W	12 44 08	9 07 11	6♌53 25	13 53 19	10R49.1	29♍55.3	14 20.7	21 33.9	11R19.0	12 22.2	29 00.6	25R20.4	8R17.1	15 16.4
3 Th	12 48 04	10 06 14	21 00 38	28 15 06	10 42.5	29R16.7	14 37.5	22 12.1	11 05.3	12 32.0	29 01.5	25 18.9	8 16.5	15 17.6
4 F	12 52 01	11 05 20	5♍36 12	13♍03 14	10 34.2	28 47.5	14 52.2	22 50.3	10 51.7	12 41.7	29 02.4	25 17.4	8 16.0	15 18.8
5 Sa	12 55 57	12 04 28	20 35 15	28 11 06	10 25.1	28 28.3	15 05.0	23 28.6	10 38.1	12 51.3	29 03.1	25 16.0	8 15.4	15 20.1
6 Su	12 59 54	13 03 39	5♎49 29	13♎28 59	10 16.4	28D19.7	15 15.7	24 06.8	10 24.4	13 00.8	29 03.7	25 14.6	8 15.0	15 21.3
7 M	13 03 51	14 02 51	21 08 11	28 45 41	10 09.2	28 21.7	15 24.2	24 45.0	10 10.8	13 10.2	29 04.2	25 13.3	8 14.5	15 22.7
8 Tu	13 07 47	15 02 05	6♏20 09	13♏50 26	10 04.3	28 34.3	15 30.6	25 23.3	9 57.3	13 19.4	29 04.6	25 12.0	8 14.1	15 24.0
9 W	13 11 44	16 01 21	21 15 34	28 34 48	10D01.7	28 57.1	15 34.7	26 01.5	9 43.8	13 28.6	29 04.9	25 10.8	8 13.7	15 25.4
10 Th	13 15 40	17 00 39	5♐47 35	12♐53 35	10 01.2	29 29.7	15R36.5	26 39.8	9 30.4	13 37.6	29 05.1	25 09.5	8 13.4	15 26.8
11 F	13 19 37	17 59 59	19 52 41	26 44 56	10 02.0	0♎11.3	15 36.0	27 18.0	9 17.1	13 46.5	29R05.1	25 08.4	8 13.1	15 28.2
12 Sa	13 23 33	18 59 21	3♑30 29	10♑09 39	10R03.0	1 01.5	15 33.0	27 56.3	9 03.9	13 55.3	29 05.1	25 07.3	8 12.8	15 29.6
13 Su	13 27 30	19 58 44	16 42 50	23 10 26	10 03.2	1 59.2	15 27.7	28 34.5	8 50.9	14 04.0	29 04.9	25 06.2	8 12.5	15 31.1
14 M	13 31 26	20 58 10	29 32 58	5♒50 56	10 02.0	3 03.9	15 20.0	29 12.8	8 37.9	14 12.6	29 04.6	25 05.2	8 12.3	15 32.6
15 Tu	13 35 23	21 57 36	12♒04 49	18 15 07	9 58.6	4 14.7	15 09.8	29 51.0	8 25.2	14 21.0	29 04.2	25 04.2	8 12.1	15 34.1
16 W	13 39 20	22 57 05	24 22 19	0♓26 52	9 53.2	5 30.8	14 57.2	0♎29.3	8 12.5	14 29.3	29 03.7	25 03.2	8 12.0	15 35.7
17 Th	13 43 16	23 56 35	6♓29 10	12 29 36	9 46.0	6 51.5	14 42.2	1 07.6	8 00.1	14 37.5	29 03.1	25 02.4	8 11.9	15 37.3
18 F	13 47 13	24 56 07	18 28 31	24 26 14	9 37.7	8 16.2	14 24.8	1 45.8	7 47.8	14 45.5	29 02.4	25 01.5	8 11.8	15 38.9
19 Sa	13 51 09	25 55 41	0♈23 02	6♈19 11	9 29.0	9 44.3	14 05.1	2 24.1	7 35.8	14 53.5	29 01.6	25 00.7	8 11.7	15 40.5
20 Su	13 55 06	26 55 17	12 14 55	18 10 26	9 20.7	11 15.1	13 43.1	3 02.4	7 24.0	15 01.2	29 00.7	25 00.0	8D11.7	15 42.2
21 M	13 59 02	27 54 55	24 05 57	0♉01 41	9 13.7	12 48.3	13 19.1	3 40.7	7 12.3	15 08.9	28 59.6	24 59.2	8 11.7	15 43.8
22 Tu	14 02 59	28 54 35	5♉57 51	11 54 39	9 08.5	14 23.3	12 52.9	4 19.0	7 01.0	15 16.4	28 58.5	24 58.6	8 11.8	15 45.5
23 W	14 06 55	29 54 17	17 52 19	23 51 08	9 05.2	15 59.8	12 24.9	4 57.3	6 49.8	15 23.8	28 57.2	24 58.0	8 11.9	15 47.2
24 Th	14 10 52	0♏54 01	29 51 23	5♊53 21	9D03.9	17 37.5	11 55.1	5 35.6	6 39.0	15 31.0	28 55.8	24 57.4	8 12.0	15 49.0
25 F	14 14 48	1 53 48	11♊57 24	18 03 55	9 04.3	19 16.1	11 23.7	6 13.9	6 28.4	15 38.1	28 54.3	24 56.9	8 12.1	15 50.8
26 Sa	14 18 45	2 53 36	24 13 17	0♋25 57	9 05.6	20 55.4	10 51.0	6 52.2	6 18.1	15 45.1	28 52.8	24 56.4	8 12.3	15 52.5
27 Su	14 22 42	3 53 27	6♋42 23	13 03 01	9 07.3	22 35.1	10 17.0	7 30.5	6 08.0	15 51.9	28 51.1	24 56.0	8 12.5	15 54.4
28 M	14 26 38	4 53 20	19 28 19	25 58 46	9R08.6	24 15.0	9 42.0	8 08.9	5 58.3	15 58.6	28 49.3	24 55.7	8 12.8	15 56.2
29 Tu	14 30 35	5 53 15	2♌34 46	9♌16 41	9 08.9	25 55.1	9 06.3	8 47.2	5 48.8	16 05.1	28 47.4	24 55.3	8 13.1	15 58.0
30 W	14 34 31	6 53 12	16 04 49	22 59 22	9 07.8	27 35.3	8 30.1	9 25.6	5 39.7	16 11.5	28 45.4	24 55.1	8 13.4	15 59.9
31 Th	14 38 28	7 53 11	0♍00 24	7♍07 51	9 05.3	29 15.4	7 53.6	10 03.9	5 30.9	16 17.7	28 43.3	24 54.9	8 13.7	16 01.8

Astro Data

	Dy Hr Mn
☽0S	8 20:18
♃☍♆	11 12:06
☿R	14 19:39
☽0N	22 13:49
☉0S	23 4:55
☿0N	4 5:59
☽0S	6 6:55
☿D	6 19:28
♀R	10 18:35
♄R	11 13:01
♃∠♄	13 14:24
☿0S	15 13:36
♂0S	19 14:00
☽0N	19 19:58
♆D	20 13:53

Planet Ingress

		Dy Hr Mn
♀	♏	8 3:05
☉	♎	23 4:55
☿	♍R	2 9:26
☿	♎	11 5:56
♂	♎	15 17:38
☉	♏	23 14:18
☿	♏	31 22:43
♃△△		28 0:01

Last Aspect / ☽ Ingress (September)

Last Aspect Dy Hr Mn		☽ Ingress	Dy Hr Mn
1 16:55	♄ ☌	♋	1 21:14
3 20:31	♀ □	♌	4 2:36
6 1:33	♀ ⚹	♍	6 4:16
8 0:54	♄ □	♎	8 3:57
10 0:52	♄ △	♏	10 3:48
11 22:52	♅ □	♐	12 5:44
14 7:54	♄ ☍	♑	14 10:47
16 5:58	☉ △	♒	16 18:54
19 2:35	♄ △	♓	19 5:18
21 14:36	♄ □	♈	21 17:11
24 3:29	♄ ⚹	♉	24 5:55
26 9:27	♅ □	♊	26 18:26
29 3:01	♄ ☌	♋	29 5:01

Last Aspect / ☽ Ingress (October)

Last Aspect Dy Hr Mn		☽ Ingress	Dy Hr Mn
30 18:59	♂ ⚹	♌	1 11:58
3 13:16	♄ ⚹	♍	3 14:52
5 13:22	♄ □	♎	5 14:51
7 12:29	♄ △	♏	7 13:57
9 12:38	☿ ⚹	♐	9 14:21
11 16:08	♄ ☍	♑	11 17:45
13 22:42	♂ △	♒	14 0:51
16 9:16	♄ △	♓	16 11:07
18 21:17	♄ □	♈	18 23:13
21 9:55	♄ ⚹	♉	21 11:57
23 14:14	♅ □	♊	24 0:17
26 9:01	♄ ☌	♋	26 11:10
28 8:22	☿ □	♌	28 19:20
30 21:51	♄ ⚹	♍	30 23:59

☽ Phases & Eclipses

Dy Hr Mn	
7 3:10	● 14♍20
13 18:08	☽ 20♐47
21 13:59	○ 28♓25
29 17:03	☾ 6♋23
6 11:18	● 13♎02
13 5:33	☽ 19♑43
21 7:20	○ 27♈43
29 5:28	☾ 5♌37

Astro Data

1 September 2002
Julian Day # 37499
SVP 5♓13'37"
GC 26♐52.6 ⚴ 14♒45.5R
Eris 20♈13.3R ⚵ 28♍23.4
⚷ 3♑14.8R ⚶ 18♌22.0
☽ Mean ☊ 13♊27.7

1 October 2002
Julian Day # 37529
SVP 5♓13'33"
GC 26♐52.7 ⚴ 10♒48.5R
Eris 19♈57.5R ⚵ 9♎36.3
⚷ 3♑37.6 ⚶ 1♍44.4
☽ Mean ☊ 11♊52.4

November 2002 — LONGITUDE

Day	Sid.Time	☉	0 hr ☽	Noon ☽	True ☊	☿	♀	♂	⚳	♃	♄	♅	♆	♇
1 F	14 42 24	8♏53 13	14♍21 27	21♍40 47	9♊01.6	0♏55.3	7♏17.1	10♎42.3	5♈22.4	16♌23.7	28♊41.0	24♒54.7	8♒14.1	16♐03.7
2 Sa	14 46 21	9 53 17	29 05 14	6♎33 59	8R 57.4	2 35.0	6R 40.8	11 20.7	5R 14.3	16 29.6	28R 38.7	24R 54.6	8 14.5	16 05.6
3 Su	14 50 17	10 53 22	14♎06 03	21 40 21	8 53.3	4 14.5	6 04.9	11 59.1	5 06.5	16 35.4	28 36.3	24D 54.5	8 15.0	16 07.6
4 M	14 54 14	11 53 30	29 15 39	6♏50 42	8 49.9	5 53.7	5 29.8	12 37.5	4 59.0	16 41.0	28 33.8	24 54.5	8 15.5	16 09.5
5 Tu	14 58 11	12 53 39	14♏24 15	21 55 05	8 47.7	7 32.6	4 55.6	13 15.9	4 51.9	16 46.4	28 31.2	24 54.5	8 16.0	16 11.5
6 W	15 02 07	13 53 51	29 22 07	6♐44 24	8D 46.9	9 11.2	4 22.6	13 54.3	4 45.2	16 51.6	28 28.5	24 54.6	8 16.6	16 13.5
7 Th	15 06 04	14 54 04	14♐01 08	21 11 44	8 47.3	10 49.4	3 50.8	14 32.7	4 38.8	16 56.7	28 25.7	24 54.8	8 17.2	16 15.6
8 F	15 10 00	15 54 19	28 15 47	5♑13 04	8 48.5	12 27.2	3 20.7	15 11.1	4 32.8	17 01.6	28 22.8	24 55.0	8 17.8	16 17.6
9 Sa	15 13 57	16 54 35	12♑03 29	18 47 09	8 50.0	14 04.7	2 52.2	15 49.5	4 27.2	17 06.4	28 19.8	24 55.2	8 18.5	16 19.6
10 Su	15 17 53	17 54 53	25 24 17	1♒55 11	8 51.4	15 41.9	2 25.6	16 27.9	4 22.0	17 11.0	28 16.7	24 55.5	8 19.1	16 21.7
11 M	15 21 50	18 55 12	8♒20 16	14 39 59	8R 52.1	17 18.7	2 01.0	17 06.3	4 17.1	17 15.4	28 13.5	24 55.9	8 19.9	16 23.8
12 Tu	15 25 47	19 55 32	20 54 52	27 05 27	8 52.0	18 55.1	1 38.6	17 44.8	4 12.6	17 19.6	28 10.3	24 56.3	8 20.6	16 25.9
13 W	15 29 43	20 55 54	3♓12 16	9♓15 54	8 51.0	20 31.3	1 18.3	18 23.2	4 08.5	17 23.7	28 06.9	24 56.7	8 21.4	16 28.0
14 Th	15 33 40	21 56 18	15 16 52	21 15 42	8 49.2	22 07.1	1 00.4	19 01.6	4 04.8	17 27.6	28 03.5	24 57.2	8 22.2	16 30.1
15 F	15 37 36	22 56 42	27 12 55	3♈08 59	8 46.9	23 42.6	0 44.8	19 40.1	4 01.4	17 31.3	28 00.0	24 57.8	8 23.1	16 32.2
16 Sa	15 41 33	23 57 08	9♈04 21	14 59 27	8 44.4	25 17.9	0 31.7	20 18.5	3 58.5	17 34.8	27 56.4	24 58.4	8 24.0	16 34.4
17 Su	15 45 29	24 57 36	20 54 39	26 50 18	8 42.1	26 52.8	0 21.1	20 57.0	3 55.9	17 38.1	27 52.7	24 59.0	8 24.9	16 36.6
18 M	15 49 26	25 58 05	2♉46 43	8♉44 12	8 40.2	28 27.5	0 12.9	21 35.4	3 53.7	17 41.3	27 49.0	24 59.7	8 25.8	16 38.7
19 Tu	15 53 22	26 58 35	14 43 01	20 43 23	8 39.0	0♐02.0	0 07.2	22 13.9	3 51.9	17 44.3	27 45.2	25 00.5	8 26.8	16 40.9
20 W	15 57 19	27 59 07	26 45 32	2♊49 40	8D 38.4	1 36.3	0D 04.0	22 52.4	3 50.5	17 47.1	27 41.3	25 01.3	8 27.8	16 43.1
21 Th	16 01 15	28 59 41	8♊55 59	15 04 39	8 38.4	3 10.3	0 03.3	23 30.8	3 49.4	17 49.7	27 37.3	25 02.1	8 28.9	16 45.3
22 F	16 05 12	0♐00 16	21 15 53	27 29 50	8 38.8	4 44.2	0 05.0	24 09.3	3 48.8	17 52.1	27 33.3	25 03.0	8 30.0	16 47.5
23 Sa	16 09 09	1 00 53	3♋46 43	10♋06 42	8 39.6	6 17.8	0 09.1	24 47.8	3D 48.5	17 54.4	27 29.2	25 04.0	8 31.1	16 49.7
24 Su	16 13 05	2 01 31	16 30 01	22 56 51	8 40.3	7 51.4	0 15.5	25 26.3	3 48.6	17 56.4	27 25.0	25 05.0	8 32.2	16 52.0
25 M	16 17 02	3 02 11	29 27 25	6♌01 55	8 40.9	9 24.7	0 24.3	26 04.8	3 49.1	17 58.3	27 20.8	25 06.0	8 33.4	16 54.2
26 Tu	16 20 58	4 02 52	12♌40 34	19 23 27	8 41.3	10 58.0	0 35.4	26 43.4	3 49.9	18 00.0	27 16.5	25 07.2	8 34.6	16 56.4
27 W	16 24 55	5 03 35	26 10 49	3♍02 43	8R 41.5	12 31.1	0 48.6	27 21.9	3 51.2	18 01.4	27 12.2	25 08.3	8 35.8	16 58.7
28 Th	16 28 51	6 04 20	9♍59 11	17 00 11	8 41.4	14 04.1	1 04.0	28 00.4	3 52.8	18 02.7	27 07.8	25 09.5	8 37.1	17 01.0
29 F	16 32 48	7 05 06	24 05 37	1♎15 15	8 41.3	15 37.0	1 21.4	28 39.0	3 54.7	18 03.8	27 03.3	25 10.8	8 38.3	17 03.2
30 Sa	16 36 45	8 05 54	8♎28 46	15 45 42	8D 41.2	17 09.8	1 40.9	29 17.5	3 57.1	18 04.7	26 58.8	25 12.1	8 39.7	17 05.5

December 2002 — LONGITUDE

Day	Sid.Time	☉	0 hr ☽	Noon ☽	True ☊	☿	♀	♂	⚳	♃	♄	♅	♆	♇
1 Su	16 40 41	9♐06 43	23♎05 31	0♏27 31	8♊41.2	18♐42.5	2♏02.3	29♎56.1	3♈59.8	18♌05.4	26♊54.2	25♒13.4	8♒41.0	17♐07.8
2 M	16 44 38	10 07 34	7♏50 59	15 15 02	8 41.3	20 15.1	2 25.6	0♏34.6	4 02.9	18 05.9	26R 49.6	25 14.8	8 42.4	17 10.0
3 Tu	16 48 34	11 08 26	22 38 46	0♐01 18	8R 41.4	21 47.6	2 50.7	1 13.2	4 06.3	18 06.2	26 45.0	25 16.2	8 43.8	17 12.3
4 W	16 52 31	12 09 19	7♐21 41	14 39 03	8 41.4	23 20.0	3 17.6	1 51.8	4 10.1	18R 06.3	26 40.3	25 17.7	8 45.2	17 14.6
5 Th	16 56 27	13 10 14	21 52 36	29 01 38	8 41.2	24 52.3	3 46.1	2 30.4	4 14.2	18 06.2	26 35.6	25 19.3	8 46.7	17 16.9
6 F	17 00 24	14 11 09	6♑05 32	13♑03 50	8 40.7	26 24.4	4 16.2	3 09.0	4 18.8	18 05.9	26 30.9	25 20.9	8 48.2	17 19.2
7 Sa	17 04 20	15 12 06	19 56 14	26 42 32	8 40.0	27 56.4	4 47.9	3 47.5	4 23.6	18 05.4	26 26.1	25 22.5	8 49.7	17 21.5
8 Su	17 08 17	16 13 03	3♒22 40	9♒56 44	8 39.1	29 28.1	5 21.1	4 26.1	4 28.8	18 04.7	26 21.2	25 24.2	8 51.2	17 23.8
9 M	17 12 14	17 14 00	16 24 55	22 47 31	8 38.1	0♑59.7	5 55.7	5 04.7	4 34.4	18 03.8	26 16.4	25 25.9	8 52.8	17 26.1
10 Tu	17 16 10	18 14 59	29 04 54	5♓17 32	8 37.4	2 30.9	6 31.8	5 43.3	4 40.2	18 02.7	26 11.5	25 27.7	8 54.3	17 28.4
11 W	17 20 07	19 15 58	11♓25 54	17 30 34	8D 37.1	4 01.8	7 09.1	6 21.9	4 46.5	18 01.4	26 06.7	25 29.5	8 56.0	17 30.7
12 Th	17 24 03	20 16 57	23 32 06	29 31 07	8 37.3	5 32.2	7 47.8	7 00.5	4 53.0	17 59.9	26 01.8	25 31.4	8 57.6	17 33.0
13 F	17 28 00	21 17 57	5♈28 11	11♈23 56	8 38.0	7 02.2	8 27.7	7 39.1	4 59.9	17 58.3	25 56.8	25 33.3	8 59.3	17 35.3
14 Sa	17 31 56	22 18 58	17 18 56	23 13 46	8 39.2	8 31.6	9 08.7	8 17.7	5 07.1	17 56.4	25 51.9	25 35.2	9 00.9	17 37.6
15 Su	17 35 53	23 19 59	29 09 00	5♉05 07	8 40.6	10 00.2	9 51.0	8 56.3	5 14.6	17 54.3	25 47.0	25 37.2	9 02.6	17 39.8
16 M	17 39 49	24 21 01	11♉02 37	17 01 57	8 42.0	11 27.9	10 34.3	9 34.9	5 22.4	17 52.1	25 42.0	25 39.2	9 04.4	17 42.1
17 Tu	17 43 46	25 22 03	23 03 31	29 07 41	8R 42.9	12 54.6	11 18.7	10 13.5	5 30.5	17 49.6	25 37.1	25 41.3	9 06.1	17 44.4
18 W	17 47 43	26 23 06	5♊14 43	11♊24 54	8 43.1	14 20.1	12 04.1	10 52.2	5 39.0	17 47.0	25 32.1	25 43.4	9 07.9	17 46.7
19 Th	17 51 39	27 24 10	17 38 26	23 55 27	8 42.4	15 44.0	12 50.6	11 30.8	5 47.7	17 44.1	25 27.2	25 45.6	9 09.7	17 49.0
20 F	17 55 36	28 25 14	0♋16 03	6♋40 16	8 40.7	17 06.2	13 37.9	12 09.4	5 56.7	17 41.1	25 22.2	25 47.8	9 11.5	17 51.2
21 Sa	17 59 32	29 26 18	13 08 07	19 39 32	8 38.1	18 26.4	14 26.2	12 48.1	6 06.0	17 37.9	25 17.3	25 50.0	9 13.4	17 53.5
22 Su	18 03 29	0♑27 23	26 14 28	2♌52 47	8 34.8	19 44.0	15 15.4	13 26.7	6 15.7	17 34.5	25 12.4	25 52.3	9 15.2	17 55.8
23 M	18 07 25	1 28 29	9♌34 21	16 19 02	8 31.2	20 58.8	16 05.4	14 05.4	6 25.5	17 30.9	25 07.5	25 54.6	9 17.1	17 58.0
24 Tu	18 11 22	2 29 36	23 06 40	29 57 06	8 28.0	22 10.2	16 56.2	14 44.0	6 35.7	17 27.2	25 02.6	25 56.9	9 19.0	18 00.2
25 W	18 15 18	3 30 43	6♍50 10	13♍45 41	8 25.6	23 17.7	17 47.8	15 22.7	6 46.2	17 23.2	24 57.7	25 59.3	9 20.9	18 02.5
26 Th	18 19 15	4 31 50	20 43 32	27 43 32	8D 24.3	24 20.6	18 40.1	16 01.3	6 56.9	17 19.1	24 52.9	26 01.8	9 22.9	18 04.7
27 F	18 23 12	5 32 58	4♎45 31	11♎49 19	8 24.3	25 18.3	19 33.2	16 40.0	7 07.9	17 14.8	24 48.0	26 04.2	9 24.8	18 06.9
28 Sa	18 27 08	6 34 07	18 54 44	26 01 35	8 25.3	26 09.9	20 27.0	17 18.7	7 19.1	17 10.3	24 43.2	26 06.7	9 26.8	18 09.1
29 Su	18 31 05	7 35 17	3♏09 34	10♏18 26	8 26.8	26 54.7	21 21.4	17 57.4	7 30.7	17 05.7	24 38.5	26 09.3	9 28.8	18 11.3
30 M	18 35 01	8 36 27	17 27 49	24 37 21	8R 28.2	27 31.8	22 16.5	18 36.0	7 42.4	17 00.9	24 33.7	26 11.8	9 30.8	18 13.5
31 Tu	18 38 58	9 37 37	1♐46 35	8♐55 01	8 28.8	28 00.1	23 12.2	19 14.7	7 54.5	16 55.9	24 29.0	26 14.4	9 32.8	18 15.7

Astro Data

	Dy Hr Mn
☽0S	2 18:02
♅ D	4 6:27
☽0N	16 2:44
♀ D	21 7:12
⚳ D	23 17:25
☽0S	30 3:17
♃ R	4 12:22
☽0N	13 10:04
♄△♅	16 21:35
♃△♇	18 13:19
☽0S	27 9:28
♄⚼♆	30 22:30

Planet Ingress

	Dy Hr Mn
☿ ♐	19 11:29
☉ ♐	22 11:54
♂ ♏	1 14:26
☿ ♑	8 20:21
☉ ♑	22 1:14

Last Aspect / ☽ Ingress

Dy Hr Mn	Aspect	☽ Ingress Dy Hr Mn
1 23:19	♄ □	♎ 2 1:28
3 22:56	♄ △	♏ 4 1:10
5 16:48	♅ □	♐ 6 1:01
8 0:14	♄ ☍	♑ 8 2:59
9 8:22	☉ ⚹	♒ 10 8:27
12 14:06	♄ △	♓ 12 17:42
15 1:38	♄ □	♈ 15 5:38
17 14:06	♄ ⚹	♉ 17 18:23
20 1:34	☉ ☍	♊ 20 6:25
22 12:07	♄ ☌	♋ 22 16:48
24 16:51	♂ □	♌ 25 1:00
27 1:51	♄ ⚹	♍ 27 6:42
29 5:01	♄ □	♎ 29 9:54

Last Aspect / ☽ Ingress

Dy Hr Mn	Aspect	☽ Ingress Dy Hr Mn
1 11:07	♂ ☌	♏ 1 11:15
3 4:15	♅ □	♐ 3 11:58
5 7:55	♄ ☍	♑ 5 13:39
5 20:20	♀ ⚹	♒ 7 17:54
9 18:35	♄ △	♓ 10 1:46
12 5:02	♄ □	♈ 12 12:58
14 17:18	♄ ⚹	♉ 15 1:43
17 5:11	♅ □	♊ 17 13:43
19 19:10	☉ ☍	♋ 19 23:30
21 9:31	☿ ☍	♌ 22 6:48
24 4:58	♅ ☍	♍ 24 12:05
26 7:10	♄ □	♎ 26 15:53
28 12:15	☿ □	♏ 28 18:41
30 17:04	☿ ⚹	♐ 30 21:01

☽ Phases & Eclipses

Dy Hr Mn	
4 20:34	● 12♏15
11 20:52	☽ 19♒17
20 1:34	○ 27♉33
20 1:47	• A 0.860
27 15:46	☾ 5♍13
4 7:34	● 11♐58
4 7:31:11	• T 02'04"
11 15:49	☽ 19♓26
19 19:10	○ 27♊42
27 0:31	☾ 5♎04

Astro Data

1 November 2002
Julian Day # 37560
SVP 5♓13'30"
GC 26♐52.7 ⚴ 12♒03.3
Eris 19♈39.2R ⚵ 20♎55.8
⚷ 5♑15.8 ⚶ 15♍02.6
☽ Mean ☊ 10♊13.9

1 December 2002
Julian Day # 37590
SVP 5♓13'25"
GC 26♐52.8 ⚴ 17♒16.3
Eris 19♈24.6R ⚵ 1♏11.9
⚷ 7♑45.1 ⚶ 26♍47.6
☽ Mean ☊ 8♊38.6

LONGITUDE January 2003

Day	Sid.Time	☉	0 hr ☽	Noon ☽	True ☊	☿	♀	♂	⚳	♃	♄	♅	♆	♇
1 W	18 42 54	10♑38 48	16♐02 09	23♐07 25	8♊28.0	28♑18.9	24♏08.5	19♏53.4	8♈06.8	16♌50.7	24♊24.4	26♒17.1	9♒34.9	18♐17.9
2 Th	18 46 51	11 39 59	0♑10 16	7♑10 09	8R25.4	28R27.4	25 05.3	20 32.1	8 19.3	16R45.4	24R19.8	26 19.7	9 36.9	18 20.0
3 F	18 50 48	12 41 10	14 06 33	20 58 58	8 21.1	28 24.6	26 02.7	21 10.8	8 32.1	16 40.0	24 15.2	26 22.5	9 39.0	18 22.2
4 Sa	18 54 44	13 42 21	27 47 01	4♒30 22	8 15.4	28 10.3	27 00.6	21 49.5	8 45.1	16 34.4	24 10.7	26 25.2	9 41.1	18 24.3
5 Su	18 58 41	14 43 32	11♒08 46	17 42 05	8 08.9	27 44.1	27 59.0	22 28.2	8 58.4	16 28.6	24 06.2	26 28.0	9 43.2	18 26.4
6 M	19 02 37	15 44 42	24 10 17	0♓33 28	8 02.4	27 06.1	28 57.9	23 06.9	9 11.9	16 22.7	24 01.7	26 30.8	9 45.3	18 28.5
7 Tu	19 06 34	16 45 52	6♓51 46	13 05 28	7 56.6	26 17.0	29 57.2	23 45.5	9 25.6	16 16.6	23 57.4	26 33.6	9 47.4	18 30.6
8 W	19 10 30	17 47 02	19 14 56	25 20 35	7 52.2	25 17.8	0♐57.0	24 24.2	9 39.5	16 10.4	23 53.1	26 36.5	9 49.6	18 32.7
9 Th	19 14 27	18 48 11	1♈22 55	7♈22 28	7 49.6	24 10.1	1 57.2	25 02.9	9 53.7	16 04.1	23 48.8	26 39.3	9 51.7	18 34.7
10 F	19 18 23	19 49 20	13 19 49	19 15 37	7D48.7	22 55.9	2 57.9	25 41.6	10 08.1	15 57.7	23 44.6	26 42.3	9 53.9	18 36.8
11 Sa	19 22 20	20 50 29	25 10 30	1♉05 07	7 49.3	21 37.6	3 58.9	26 20.2	10 22.7	15 51.1	23 40.5	26 45.2	9 56.0	18 38.8
12 Su	19 26 17	21 51 37	7♉00 07	12 56 11	7 50.8	20 17.8	5 00.3	26 58.9	10 37.5	15 44.4	23 36.4	26 48.2	9 58.2	18 40.8
13 M	19 30 13	22 52 44	18 53 55	24 53 57	7 52.3	18 58.9	6 02.1	27 37.6	10 52.5	15 37.6	23 32.4	26 51.2	10 00.4	18 42.8
14 Tu	19 34 10	23 53 51	0♊56 52	7♊03 10	7R53.1	17 43.3	7 04.3	28 16.3	11 07.7	15 30.7	23 28.5	26 54.2	10 02.6	18 44.7
15 W	19 38 06	24 54 57	13 13 21	19 27 48	7 52.3	16 33.1	8 06.8	28 54.9	11 23.1	15 23.6	23 24.7	26 57.2	10 04.8	18 46.7
16 Th	19 42 03	25 56 02	25 46 51	2♋10 45	7 49.4	15 30.0	9 09.7	29 33.6	11 38.7	15 16.5	23 20.9	27 00.3	10 07.1	18 48.6
17 F	19 45 59	26 57 07	8♋39 37	15 13 29	7 44.3	14 35.0	10 12.9	0♐12.3	11 54.5	15 09.3	23 17.2	27 03.4	10 09.3	18 50.5
18 Sa	19 49 56	27 58 12	21 52 18	28 35 53	7 37.1	13 49.1	11 16.4	0 51.0	12 10.5	15 02.0	23 13.6	27 06.5	10 11.5	18 52.4
19 Su	19 53 52	28 59 16	5♌23 57	12♌16 08	7 28.4	13 12.6	12 20.2	1 29.6	12 26.6	14 54.6	23 10.1	27 09.7	10 13.8	18 54.3
20 M	19 57 49	0♒00 19	19 11 57	26 10 54	7 19.2	12 45.6	13 24.4	2 08.3	12 43.0	14 47.1	23 06.6	27 12.8	10 16.0	18 56.2
21 Tu	20 01 46	1 01 22	3♍12 26	10♍15 59	7 10.5	12 27.8	14 28.8	2 47.0	12 59.5	14 39.6	23 03.2	27 16.0	10 18.3	18 58.0
22 W	20 05 42	2 02 24	17 20 58	24 26 52	7 03.3	12D19.0	15 33.5	3 25.7	13 16.2	14 32.0	23 00.0	27 19.2	10 20.5	18 59.8
23 Th	20 09 39	3 03 26	1♎33 10	8♎39 28	6 58.4	12 18.6	16 38.4	4 04.3	13 33.1	14 24.3	22 56.8	27 22.4	10 22.8	19 01.6
24 F	20 13 35	4 04 27	15 45 22	22 50 36	6D55.8	12 26.0	17 43.7	4 43.0	13 50.1	14 16.5	22 53.7	27 25.7	10 25.0	19 03.4
25 Sa	20 17 32	5 05 28	29 54 56	6♏58 11	6 55.2	12 40.8	18 49.2	5 21.7	14 07.4	14 08.7	22 50.6	27 28.9	10 27.3	19 05.1
26 Su	20 21 28	6 06 28	14♏00 15	21 01 01	6 55.8	13 02.3	19 54.9	6 00.4	14 24.7	14 00.9	22 47.7	27 32.2	10 29.6	19 06.8
27 M	20 25 25	7 07 28	28 00 26	4♐58 26	6R56.4	13 29.9	21 00.8	6 39.0	14 42.3	13 53.0	22 44.9	27 35.5	10 31.9	19 08.5
28 Tu	20 29 21	8 08 28	11♐54 55	18 49 48	6 55.8	14 03.1	22 07.0	7 17.7	15 00.0	13 45.1	22 42.2	27 38.8	10 34.1	19 10.2
29 W	20 33 18	9 09 27	25 42 56	2♑34 10	6 53.0	14 41.4	23 13.4	7 56.4	15 17.9	13 37.1	22 39.5	27 42.1	10 36.4	19 11.9
30 Th	20 37 15	10 10 25	9♑23 16	16 10 02	6 47.4	15 24.4	24 20.0	8 35.0	15 35.9	13 29.2	22 37.0	27 45.4	10 38.7	19 13.5
31 F	20 41 11	11 11 22	22 54 12	29 35 29	6 39.0	16 11.5	25 26.9	9 13.7	15 54.0	13 21.2	22 34.6	27 48.8	10 41.0	19 15.1

LONGITUDE February 2003

Day	Sid.Time	☉	0 hr ☽	Noon ☽	True ☊	☿	♀	♂	⚳	♃	♄	♅	♆	♇
1 Sa	20 45 08	12♒12 18	6♒13 38	12♒48 23	6♊28.2	17♑02.4	26♐33.9	9♐52.3	16♈12.4	13♌13.2	22♊32.2	27♒52.2	10♒43.3	19♐16.7
2 Su	20 49 04	13 13 13	19 19 31	25 46 51	6R15.9	17 56.9	27 41.0	10 30.9	16 30.8	13R05.2	22R30.0	27 55.5	10 45.5	19 18.2
3 M	20 53 01	14 14 07	2♓10 18	8♓29 47	6 03.3	18 54.4	28 48.4	11 09.6	16 49.5	12 57.2	22 27.9	27 58.9	10 47.8	19 19.8
4 Tu	20 56 57	15 15 00	14 45 20	20 57 04	5 51.6	19 54.9	29 55.9	11 48.2	17 08.2	12 49.2	22 25.8	28 02.3	10 50.1	19 21.3
5 W	21 00 54	16 15 51	27 05 10	3♈09 54	5 41.8	20 57.9	1♑03.6	12 26.8	17 27.1	12 41.2	22 23.9	28 05.7	10 52.4	19 22.7
6 Th	21 04 50	17 16 41	9♈11 36	15 10 43	5 34.5	22 03.4	2 11.5	13 05.4	17 46.1	12 33.2	22 22.1	28 09.1	10 54.6	19 24.2
7 F	21 08 47	18 17 29	21 07 42	27 03 05	5 29.9	23 11.2	3 19.5	13 44.0	18 05.3	12 25.3	22 20.4	28 12.5	10 56.9	19 25.6
8 Sa	21 12 44	19 18 16	2♉57 29	8♉51 30	5D27.7	24 20.9	4 27.6	14 22.5	18 24.6	12 17.4	22 18.8	28 16.0	10 59.2	19 27.0
9 Su	21 16 40	20 19 02	14 45 49	20 41 07	5 27.2	25 32.6	5 36.0	15 01.1	18 44.0	12 09.5	22 17.3	28 19.4	11 01.4	19 28.3
10 M	21 20 37	21 19 46	26 38 05	2♊37 26	5R27.4	26 46.1	6 44.4	15 39.6	19 03.5	12 01.7	22 15.9	28 22.9	11 03.7	19 29.7
11 Tu	21 24 33	22 20 29	8♊39 51	14 46 00	5 27.1	28 01.2	7 53.0	16 18.2	19 23.2	11 53.9	22 14.7	28 26.3	11 05.9	19 31.0
12 W	21 28 30	23 21 10	20 56 30	27 11 58	5 25.3	29 17.8	9 01.7	16 56.7	19 43.0	11 46.2	22 13.5	28 29.8	11 08.2	19 32.2
13 Th	21 32 26	24 21 49	3♋32 52	9♋59 38	5 21.1	0♒36.0	10 10.6	17 35.3	20 02.9	11 38.5	22 12.5	28 33.2	11 10.4	19 33.5
14 F	21 36 23	25 22 27	16 32 34	23 11 51	5 14.1	1 55.5	11 19.5	18 13.8	20 22.9	11 30.9	22 11.6	28 36.7	11 12.6	19 34.7
15 Sa	21 40 19	26 23 03	29 57 30	6♌49 23	5 04.5	3 16.3	12 28.7	18 52.3	20 43.1	11 23.4	22 10.7	28 40.1	11 14.9	19 35.9
16 Su	21 44 16	27 23 37	13♌47 14	20 50 35	4 53.0	4 38.5	13 37.9	19 30.8	21 03.3	11 16.0	22 10.0	28 43.6	11 17.1	19 37.0
17 M	21 48 13	28 24 10	27 58 48	5♍11 10	4 40.7	6 01.8	14 47.2	20 09.3	21 23.7	11 08.6	22 09.4	28 47.1	11 19.3	19 38.2
18 Tu	21 52 09	29 24 42	12♍26 47	19 44 45	4 28.8	7 26.3	15 56.7	20 47.8	21 44.1	11 01.3	22 08.9	28 50.5	11 21.5	19 39.2
19 W	21 56 06	0♓25 12	27 04 06	4♎23 53	4 18.8	8 51.9	17 06.2	21 26.2	22 04.7	10 54.1	22 08.6	28 54.0	11 23.7	19 40.3
20 Th	22 00 02	1 25 40	11♎43 12	19 01 15	4 11.4	10 18.7	18 15.9	22 04.7	22 25.4	10 47.0	22 08.3	28 57.4	11 25.8	19 41.3
21 F	22 03 59	2 26 08	26 17 20	3♏30 54	4 06.9	11 46.5	19 25.7	22 43.2	22 46.1	10 40.0	22D08.1	29 00.9	11 28.0	19 42.3
22 Sa	22 07 55	3 26 34	10♏41 29	17 48 49	4 05.0	13 15.4	20 35.6	23 21.6	23 07.0	10 33.2	22 08.1	29 04.4	11 30.2	19 43.3
23 Su	22 11 52	4 26 59	24 52 41	1♐53 02	4 04.6	14 45.4	21 45.6	24 00.0	23 28.0	10 26.4	22 08.2	29 07.8	11 32.3	19 44.2
24 M	22 15 48	5 27 22	8♐49 52	15 43 14	4 04.5	16 16.4	22 55.7	24 38.5	23 49.1	10 19.7	22 08.4	29 11.3	11 34.4	19 45.2
25 Tu	22 19 45	6 27 44	22 33 16	29 20 04	4 03.2	17 48.4	24 05.9	25 16.9	24 10.2	10 13.2	22 08.7	29 14.7	11 36.6	19 46.0
26 W	22 23 42	7 28 05	6♑03 47	12♑44 32	3 59.8	19 21.4	25 16.2	25 55.3	24 31.5	10 06.8	22 09.1	29 18.2	11 38.7	19 46.9
27 Th	22 27 38	8 28 24	19 22 24	25 57 29	3 53.3	20 55.5	26 26.5	26 33.6	24 52.8	10 00.5	22 09.6	29 21.6	11 40.8	19 47.7
28 F	22 31 35	9 28 42	2♒29 49	8♒59 25	3 43.9	22 30.6	27 36.9	27 12.0	25 14.3	9 54.3	22 10.3	29 25.0	11 42.8	19 48.5

Astro Data (Dy Hr Mn)

☿ R	2 18:21
☽ 0N	9 17:38
☿ D	23 1:08
☽ 0S	23 14:11
♆ R	30 17:14
♆ D	31 6:44
⚳ 0N	1 21:18
☽ 0N	6 1:02
♃☍♆	16 9:12
☽ 0S	19 20:23
♄ D	22 7:41

Planet Ingress (Dy Hr Mn)

♀	♐	7 13:07
♂	♐	17 4:22
☉	♒	20 11:53
♀	♑	4 13:27
☿	♒	13 1:00
☉	♓	19 2:00

Last Aspect / ☽ Ingress (Dy Hr Mn)

Last Aspect			☽ Ingress	
1 17:23	♅ ⚹		♑	1 23:42
4 0:56	☿ ☌		♒	4 3:56
6 8:44	♀ □		♓	6 10:57
8 11:55	☿ ⚹		♈	8 21:15
11 3:10	♅ ⚹		♉	11 9:48
13 17:44	♂ ☍		♊	13 22:08
16 2:16	♅ △		♋	16 7:56
18 10:48	☉ ☍		♌	18 14:29
20 13:46	♅ ☍		♍	20 18:32
22 9:34	♄ □		♎	22 21:23
24 19:48	♅ △		♏	25 0:09
26 23:14	♅ □		♐	27 3:26
29 3:26	♅ ⚹		♑	29 7:30
30 10:34	☿ ☌		♒	31 12:44

Last Aspect / ☽ Ingress (Dy Hr Mn)

Last Aspect			☽ Ingress	
2 16:02	♅ ☌		♓	2 19:55
4 14:53	♄ □		♈	5 5:44
7 14:22	♅ ⚹		♉	7 17:59
10 3:28	♅ □		♊	10 6:45
12 14:29	♅ △		♋	12 17:19
13 12:22	♀ ☍		♌	15 0:04
17 1:18	♅ ☍		♍	17 3:22
18 15:56	♄ □		♎	19 4:48
21 4:29	♅ △		♏	21 6:09
23 7:15	♅ □		♐	23 8:46
25 11:50	♅ ⚹		♑	25 13:11
27 12:58	♀ ☌		♒	27 19:24

☽ Phases & Eclipses (Dy Hr Mn)

2 20:23	●	12♑01
10 13:15	☽	19♈53
18 10:48	○	27♋55
25 8:33	☾	4♏57
1 10:48	●	12♒09
9 11:11	☽	20♉17
16 23:51	○	27♌54
23 16:46	☾	4♐39

Astro Data

1 January 2003
Julian Day # 37621
SVP 5♓13'19"
GC 26♐52.9 ⚴ 25♒17.0
Eris 19♈17.6R ⚵ 10♏26.9
⚷ 10♑48.4 ⚶ 6♎38.2
☽ Mean ☊ 7♊00.1

1 February 2003
Julian Day # 37652
SVP 5♓13'14"
GC 26♐52.9 ⚴ 4♓49.6
Eris 19♈21.0 ⚵ 17♏19.7
⚷ 13♑50.2 ⚶ 12♎10.0
☽ Mean ☊ 5♊21.6

March 2003 — LONGITUDE

Day	Sid.Time	☉	0 hr ☽	Noon ☽	True ☊	☿	♀	♂	⚳	♃	♄	♅	♆	♇
1 Sa	22 35 31	10♓28 58	15♒26 15	21♒50 18	3♊31.9	24♒06.7	28♑47.5	27♐50.3	25♈35.8	9♌48.3	22♊11.0	29♒28.5	11♒44.9	19♐49.2
2 Su	22 39 28	11 29 12	28 11 32	4♓29 54	3R 18.2	25 43.9	29 58.0	28 28.6	25 57.5	9R 42.4	22 11.9	29 31.9	11 46.9	19 49.9
3 M	22 43 24	12 29 25	10♓45 21	16 57 55	3 04.0	27 22.1	1♒08.7	29 06.9	26 19.2	9 36.7	22 12.9	29 35.3	11 49.0	19 50.6
4 Tu	22 47 21	13 29 35	23 07 36	29 14 28	2 50.7	29 01.3	2 19.4	29 45.2	26 40.9	9 31.1	22 14.0	29 38.7	11 51.0	19 51.2
5 W	22 51 17	14 29 44	5♈18 38	11♈20 16	2 39.3	0♓41.6	3 30.2	0♑23.5	27 02.8	9 25.6	22 15.2	29 42.0	11 53.0	19 51.8
6 Th	22 55 14	15 29 51	17 19 36	23 16 56	2 30.5	2 23.0	4 41.1	1 01.7	27 24.8	9 20.3	22 16.5	29 45.4	11 55.0	19 52.4
7 F	22 59 11	16 29 56	29 12 36	5♉07 01	2 24.6	4 05.5	5 52.0	1 39.9	27 46.8	9 15.2	22 17.9	29 48.8	11 56.9	19 53.0
8 Sa	23 03 07	17 29 58	11♉00 38	16 54 00	2 21.4	5 49.0	7 03.0	2 18.0	28 08.9	9 10.3	22 19.5	29 52.1	11 58.9	19 53.5
9 Su	23 07 04	18 29 59	22 47 39	28 42 13	2D 20.3	7 33.7	8 14.0	2 56.2	28 31.1	9 05.5	22 21.1	29 55.5	12 00.8	19 53.9
10 M	23 11 00	19 29 58	4♊38 21	10♊36 41	2R 20.4	9 19.5	9 25.1	3 34.3	28 53.3	9 00.8	22 22.9	29 58.8	12 02.7	19 54.4
11 Tu	23 14 57	20 29 54	16 37 57	22 42 49	2 20.6	11 06.4	10 36.3	4 12.4	29 15.7	8 56.4	22 24.7	0♓02.1	12 04.6	19 54.8
12 W	23 18 53	21 29 48	28 51 59	5♋06 06	2 19.7	12 54.5	11 47.5	4 50.5	29 38.1	8 52.1	22 26.7	0 05.4	12 06.5	19 55.2
13 Th	23 22 50	22 29 40	11♋25 49	17 51 39	2 16.9	14 43.7	12 58.7	5 28.5	0♉00.5	8 47.9	22 28.8	0 08.6	12 08.4	19 55.5
14 F	23 26 46	23 29 30	24 24 05	1♌03 30	2 11.7	16 34.1	14 10.0	6 06.6	0 23.1	8 44.0	22 31.0	0 11.9	12 10.2	19 55.8
15 Sa	23 30 43	24 29 18	7♌50 05	14 43 55	2 04.1	18 25.7	15 21.4	6 44.6	0 45.7	8 40.2	22 33.3	0 15.1	12 12.0	19 56.1
16 Su	23 34 40	25 29 03	21 44 52	28 52 37	1 54.7	20 18.4	16 32.8	7 22.5	1 08.3	8 36.6	22 35.7	0 18.4	12 13.8	19 56.3
17 M	23 38 36	26 28 46	6♍06 39	13♍26 13	1 44.3	22 12.2	17 44.3	8 00.5	1 31.0	8 33.2	22 38.2	0 21.6	12 15.6	19 56.5
18 Tu	23 42 33	27 28 27	20 50 25	28 18 12	1 34.3	24 07.2	18 55.8	8 38.4	1 53.8	8 30.0	22 40.8	0 24.7	12 17.3	19 56.7
19 W	23 46 29	28 28 07	5♎48 25	13♎19 51	1 25.7	26 03.3	20 07.3	9 16.3	2 16.6	8 26.9	22 43.5	0 27.9	12 19.0	19 56.8
20 Th	23 50 26	29 27 44	20 51 16	28 21 31	1 19.5	28 00.5	21 18.9	9 54.1	2 39.5	8 24.1	22 46.3	0 31.0	12 20.7	19 56.9
21 F	23 54 22	0♈27 19	5♏49 33	13♏14 26	1 15.9	29 58.7	22 30.5	10 32.0	3 02.5	8 21.4	22 49.2	0 34.2	12 22.4	19 57.0
22 Sa	23 58 19	1 26 53	20 35 24	27 51 52	1D 14.6	1♈57.8	23 42.2	11 09.8	3 25.5	8 18.9	22 52.2	0 37.3	12 24.1	19R 57.1
23 Su	0 02 15	2 26 25	5♐03 25	12♐09 47	1 14.8	3 57.8	24 54.0	11 47.6	3 48.6	8 16.6	22 55.3	0 40.3	12 25.7	19 57.1
24 M	0 06 12	3 25 55	19 10 52	26 06 40	1R 15.6	5 58.6	26 05.8	12 25.3	4 11.7	8 14.5	22 58.5	0 43.4	12 27.3	19 57.0
25 Tu	0 10 09	4 25 24	2♑57 19	9♑42 58	1 15.6	8 00.0	27 17.6	13 03.0	4 34.9	8 12.5	23 01.9	0 46.4	12 28.9	19 57.0
26 W	0 14 05	5 24 50	16 23 52	23 00 18	1 14.1	10 01.8	28 29.4	13 40.7	4 58.1	8 10.8	23 05.3	0 49.4	12 30.5	19 56.9
27 Th	0 18 02	6 24 15	29 32 32	6♒00 51	1 10.3	12 03.9	29 41.3	14 18.3	5 21.4	8 09.2	23 08.8	0 52.4	12 32.0	19 56.8
28 F	0 21 58	7 23 38	12♒25 32	18 46 50	1 04.1	14 06.0	0♓53.3	14 55.9	5 44.7	8 07.9	23 12.4	0 55.4	12 33.5	19 56.6
29 Sa	0 25 55	8 23 00	25 05 00	1♓20 14	0 56.0	16 07.9	2 05.2	15 33.5	6 08.1	8 06.7	23 16.1	0 58.3	12 35.0	19 56.4
30 Su	0 29 51	9 22 19	7♓32 43	13 42 39	0 46.5	18 09.3	3 17.2	16 11.0	6 31.5	8 05.7	23 19.8	1 01.2	12 36.5	19 56.2
31 M	0 33 48	10 21 36	19 50 10	25 55 26	0 36.6	20 09.9	4 29.2	16 48.4	6 55.0	8 04.9	23 23.7	1 04.1	12 37.9	19 55.9

April 2003 — LONGITUDE

Day	Sid.Time	☉	0 hr ☽	Noon ☽	True ☊	☿	♀	♂	⚳	♃	♄	♅	♆	♇
1 Tu	0 37 44	11♈20 52	1♈58 34	7♈59 44	0♊27.2	22♈09.3	5♓41.3	17♑25.8	7♉18.5	8♌04.3	23♊27.7	1♓06.9	12♒39.3	19♐55.6
2 W	0 41 41	12 20 05	13 59 06	19 56 50	0R 19.3	24 07.2	6 53.4	18 03.2	7 42.1	8R 03.9	23 31.7	1 09.7	12 40.7	19R 55.3
3 Th	0 45 37	13 19 17	25 53 09	1♉48 16	0 13.3	26 03.2	8 05.5	18 40.5	8 05.7	8D 03.7	23 35.9	1 12.5	12 42.0	19 54.9
4 F	0 49 34	14 18 26	7♉42 28	13 36 03	0 09.5	27 57.0	9 17.6	19 17.8	8 29.4	8 03.7	23 40.1	1 15.3	12 43.3	19 54.6
5 Sa	0 53 31	15 17 33	19 29 22	25 22 49	0D 07.9	29 48.0	10 29.8	19 55.0	8 53.1	8 03.8	23 44.5	1 18.0	12 44.6	19 54.1
6 Su	0 57 27	16 16 38	1♊16 49	7♊11 51	0 08.0	1♉36.1	11 42.0	20 32.1	9 16.8	8 04.2	23 48.9	1 20.7	12 45.9	19 53.7
7 M	1 01 24	17 15 40	13 08 26	19 07 07	0 09.2	3 20.7	12 54.2	21 09.2	9 40.6	8 04.7	23 53.4	1 23.4	12 47.1	19 53.2
8 Tu	1 05 20	18 14 41	25 08 28	1♋13 06	0 10.7	5 01.6	14 06.4	21 46.2	10 04.4	8 05.5	23 58.0	1 26.0	12 48.3	19 52.7
9 W	1 09 17	19 13 39	7♋21 38	13 34 40	0R 11.8	6 38.3	15 18.6	22 23.2	10 28.2	8 06.4	24 02.6	1 28.6	12 49.5	19 52.2
10 Th	1 13 13	20 12 35	19 52 48	26 16 36	0 11.8	8 10.7	16 30.9	23 00.2	10 52.1	8 07.5	24 07.4	1 31.2	12 50.7	19 51.6
11 F	1 17 10	21 11 29	2♌46 37	9♌23 17	0 10.2	9 38.5	17 43.2	23 37.0	11 16.0	8 08.8	24 12.2	1 33.7	12 51.8	19 51.0
12 Sa	1 21 06	22 10 20	16 06 56	22 57 48	0 07.0	11 01.4	18 55.5	24 13.8	11 40.0	8 10.3	24 17.1	1 36.2	12 52.9	19 50.3
13 Su	1 25 03	23 09 09	29 55 59	7♍01 21	0 02.5	12 19.2	20 07.8	24 50.6	12 03.9	8 12.0	24 22.1	1 38.7	12 54.0	19 49.7
14 M	1 29 00	24 07 55	14♍13 39	21 32 21	29♉57.3	13 31.7	21 20.1	25 27.2	12 28.0	8 13.8	24 27.2	1 41.1	12 55.0	19 49.0
15 Tu	1 32 56	25 06 40	28 56 47	6♎26 03	29 52.0	14 38.8	22 32.5	26 03.9	12 52.0	8 15.9	24 32.3	1 43.5	12 56.0	19 48.3
16 W	1 36 53	26 05 22	13♎59 07	21 34 46	29 47.5	15 40.3	23 44.8	26 40.4	13 16.1	8 18.1	24 37.6	1 45.8	12 56.9	19 47.5
17 Th	1 40 49	27 04 03	29 11 47	6♏48 49	29 44.4	16 36.1	24 57.2	27 16.9	13 40.2	8 20.5	24 42.9	1 48.2	12 57.9	19 46.7
18 F	1 44 46	28 02 41	14♏24 39	21 58 04	29D 42.9	17 26.2	26 09.6	27 53.3	14 04.3	8 23.1	24 48.2	1 50.4	12 58.8	19 45.9
19 Sa	1 48 42	29 01 18	29 28 00	6♐53 33	29 42.8	18 10.3	27 22.1	28 29.7	14 28.4	8 25.8	24 53.7	1 52.7	12 59.7	19 45.1
20 Su	1 52 39	29 59 53	14♐13 56	21 28 37	29 43.9	18 48.6	28 34.5	29 06.0	14 52.6	8 28.7	24 59.2	1 54.9	13 00.5	19 44.3
21 M	1 56 35	0♉58 27	28 37 13	5♑39 31	29 45.4	19 20.8	29 47.0	29 42.2	15 16.8	8 31.8	25 04.8	1 57.1	13 01.3	19 43.4
22 Tu	2 00 32	1 56 59	12♑35 26	19 25 03	29 46.7	19 47.1	0♈59.5	0♒18.4	15 41.1	8 35.1	25 10.4	1 59.2	13 02.1	19 42.5
23 W	2 04 29	2 55 29	26 08 32	2♒46 09	29R 47.2	20 07.5	2 12.0	0 54.4	16 05.3	8 38.6	25 16.1	2 01.3	13 02.9	19 41.5
24 Th	2 08 25	3 53 57	9♒18 14	15 45 08	29 46.6	20 21.9	3 24.6	1 30.4	16 29.6	8 42.2	25 21.9	2 03.4	13 03.6	19 40.6
25 F	2 12 22	4 52 24	22 07 15	28 25 02	29 44.9	20R 30.4	4 37.1	2 06.3	16 53.9	8 46.0	25 27.8	2 05.4	13 04.3	19 39.6
26 Sa	2 16 18	5 50 50	4♓38 51	10♓49 08	29 42.1	20 33.2	5 49.7	2 42.1	17 18.2	8 49.9	25 33.7	2 07.3	13 04.9	19 38.6
27 Su	2 20 15	6 49 13	16 56 17	23 00 41	29 38.7	20 30.4	7 02.2	3 17.8	17 42.6	8 54.1	25 39.7	2 09.3	13 05.6	19 37.5
28 M	2 24 11	7 47 35	29 02 41	5♈02 37	29 35.0	20 22.3	8 14.8	3 53.4	18 07.0	8 58.3	25 45.7	2 11.2	13 06.2	19 36.5
29 Tu	2 28 08	8 45 56	11♈00 50	16 57 36	29 31.5	20 09.2	9 27.4	4 28.9	18 31.4	9 02.8	25 51.8	2 13.0	13 06.7	19 35.4
30 W	2 32 04	9 44 14	22 53 12	28 47 57	29 28.6	19 51.2	10 40.0	5 04.3	18 55.8	9 07.4	25 58.0	2 14.8	13 07.2	19 34.3

Astro Data Dy Hr Mn	Planet Ingress Dy Hr Mn	Last Aspect Dy Hr Mn	☽ Ingress Dy Hr Mn	Last Aspect Dy Hr Mn	☽ Ingress Dy Hr Mn	☽ Phases & Eclipses Dy Hr Mn	Astro Data
☽0N 5 8:02	♀ ♒ 2 12:40	2 2:30 ♅ ☌	♓ 2 3:26	2 22:05 ☿ ☌	♉ 3 8:20	3 2:35 ● 12♓06	1 March 2003
☽0S 19 5:33	♂ ♑ 4 21:17	4 13:04 ♂ □	♈ 4 13:30	5 0:15 ♂ △	♊ 5 21:24	11 7:15 ☽ 20♊18	Julian Day # 37680
☉0N 21 0:59	☿ ♓ 5 2:04	7 1:10 ♅ ⚹	♉ 7 1:36	7 21:35 ♄ ☌	♋ 8 9:36	18 10:35 ○ 27♍25	SVP 5♓13'10"
☿0N 22 22:40	♅ ♓ 10 20:53	9 14:29 ♅ □	♊ 9 14:38	10 5:34 ♂ ☍	♌ 10 18:54	25 1:51 ☾ 4♑00	GC 26♐53.0 ⚴ 14♓06.6
♇R 23 5:13	⚳ ♉ 13 11:26	11 11:24 ♄ ☌	♋ 12 2:12	12 14:18 ♄ ⚹	♍ 13 0:07		Eris 19♈32.3 ⚵ 20♏20.5
♃∠♄ 27 14:14	☉ ♈ 21 1:00	13 21:13 ☉ △	♌ 14 10:06	14 18:38 ♂ △	♎ 15 1:42	1 19:19 ● 11♈39	⚷ 16♑07.4 ⚶ 11♎20.3R
	☿ ♈ 21 12:16	16 1:24 ♄ ⚹	♍ 16 13:52	16 20:22 ♂ □	♏ 17 1:16	9 23:40 ☽ 19♋42	☽ Mean ☊ 3♊52.7
☽0N 1 14:31	♀ ♓ 27 18:14	18 10:35 ☉ ☍	♎ 18 14:43	18 21:52 ♂ ⚹	♐ 19 0:51	16 19:36 ○ 26♎24	
♃D 4 3:04		20 3:02 ♄ △	♏ 20 14:38	21 1:02 ♀ □	♑ 21 2:20	23 12:18 ☾ 2♒56	1 April 2003
☽0S 15 16:35	☿ ♉ 5 14:37	22 4:30 ♀ □	♐ 22 15:33	22 12:40 ☿ △	♒ 23 6:58		Julian Day # 37711
♀0N 24 16:46	☊ ♉R 13 23:43	24 11:58 ♀ ⚹	♑ 24 18:48	25 6:19 ♄ △	♓ 25 15:02		SVP 5♓13'07"
☿R 26 11:59	☉ ♉ 20 12:03	25 18:16 ♂ ☌	♒ 27 0:51	27 17:18 ♄ □	♈ 28 1:54		GC 26♐53.1 ⚴ 24♓35.7
☽0N 28 20:40	♀ ♈ 21 16:18	28 20:27 ♄ △	♓ 29 9:26	30 6:12 ♄ ⚹	♉ 30 14:26		Eris 19♈50.9 ⚵ 18♏51.0R
	♂ ♒ 21 23:48	31 6:59 ♄ □	♈ 31 20:04				⚷ 17♑44.6 ⚶ 4♎27.5R
							☽ Mean ☊ 2♊14.1

LONGITUDE — May 2003

Day	Sid.Time	☉	0 hr ☽	Noon ☽	True ☊	☿	♀	♂	⚳	♃	♄	♅	♆	♇
1 Th	2 36 01	10♉42 31	4♉42 04	10♉35 51	29♉26.6	19♉29.0	11♈52.7	5♒39.6	19♉20.2	9♌12.2	26♊04.2	2♓16.6	13♒07.7	19♐33.1
2 F	2 39 58	11 40 46	16 29 33	22 23 26	29D 25.6	19R 02.8	13 05.3	6 14.8	19 44.6	9 17.1	26 10.5	2 18.3	13 08.2	19R 32.0
3 Sa	2 43 54	12 39 00	28 17 48	4♊12 56	29 25.5	18 33.3	14 18.0	6 49.8	20 09.1	9 22.2	26 16.9	2 19.9	13 08.6	19 30.8
4 Su	2 47 51	13 37 11	10♊09 10	16 06 50	29 26.2	18 00.9	15 30.6	7 24.8	20 33.6	9 27.5	26 23.3	2 21.6	13 09.0	19 29.6
5 M	2 51 47	14 35 21	22 06 16	28 07 54	29 27.3	17 26.3	16 43.3	7 59.6	20 58.1	9 32.9	26 29.7	2 23.2	13 09.4	19 28.4
6 Tu	2 55 44	15 33 29	4♋12 07	10♋19 20	29 28.6	16 50.2	17 56.0	8 34.4	21 22.6	9 38.5	26 36.2	2 24.7	13 09.7	19 27.1
7 W	2 59 40	16 31 35	16 30 01	22 44 37	29 29.7	16 13.1	19 08.6	9 09.0	21 47.1	9 44.2	26 42.8	2 26.2	13 10.0	19 25.9
8 Th	3 03 37	17 29 39	29 03 36	5♌27 24	29R 30.5	15 35.7	20 21.3	9 43.4	22 11.7	9 50.1	26 49.4	2 27.7	13 10.3	19 24.6
9 F	3 07 33	18 27 41	11♌56 27	18 31 10	29 30.8	14 58.8	21 34.0	10 17.8	22 36.2	9 56.1	26 56.1	2 29.1	13 10.5	19 23.3
10 Sa	3 11 30	19 25 42	25 11 51	1♍58 48	29 30.5	14 23.0	22 46.7	10 52.0	23 00.8	10 02.3	27 02.8	2 30.4	13 10.7	19 22.0
11 Su	3 15 27	20 23 40	8♍52 10	15 52 01	29 29.9	13 48.7	23 59.4	11 26.1	23 25.3	10 08.6	27 09.5	2 31.7	13 10.8	19 20.7
12 M	3 19 23	21 21 36	22 58 16	0♎10 41	29 29.0	13 16.7	25 12.2	12 00.0	23 49.9	10 15.0	27 16.3	2 33.0	13 11.0	19 19.3
13 Tu	3 23 20	22 19 31	7♎28 51	14 52 13	29 28.2	12 47.4	26 24.9	12 33.8	24 14.5	10 21.6	27 23.2	2 34.2	13 11.1	19 17.9
14 W	3 27 16	23 17 24	22 20 03	29 51 26	29 27.5	12 21.3	27 37.6	13 07.5	24 39.0	10 28.3	27 30.1	2 35.4	13 11.1	19 16.6
15 Th	3 31 13	24 15 15	7♏25 22	15♏00 44	29D 27.1	11 58.6	28 50.4	13 41.0	25 03.6	10 35.2	27 37.0	2 36.5	13R 11.2	19 15.2
16 F	3 35 09	25 13 05	22 36 19	0♐10 58	29 27.0	11 39.9	0♉03.1	14 14.4	25 28.2	10 42.2	27 44.0	2 37.6	13 11.2	19 13.7
17 Sa	3 39 06	26 10 53	7♐43 29	15 12 47	29 27.1	11 25.2	1 15.9	14 47.7	25 52.9	10 49.3	27 51.0	2 38.6	13 11.1	19 12.3
18 Su	3 43 02	27 08 40	22 37 53	29 57 58	29 27.3	11 14.9	2 28.7	15 20.7	26 17.5	10 56.6	27 58.1	2 39.6	13 11.1	19 10.9
19 M	3 46 59	28 06 26	7♑12 19	14♑20 28	29 27.5	11D 08.9	3 41.5	15 53.7	26 42.1	11 04.0	28 05.2	2 40.6	13 11.0	19 09.4
20 Tu	3 50 56	29 04 11	21 22 02	28 16 52	29R 27.6	11 07.5	4 54.3	16 26.4	27 06.7	11 11.5	28 12.3	2 41.5	13 10.9	19 08.0
21 W	3 54 52	0♊01 54	5♒04 56	11♒46 22	29 27.6	11 10.6	6 07.1	16 59.0	27 31.3	11 19.1	28 19.5	2 42.3	13 10.7	19 06.5
22 Th	3 58 49	0 59 37	18 21 22	24 50 17	29D 27.5	11 18.3	7 19.9	17 31.4	27 56.0	11 26.9	28 26.7	2 43.1	13 10.5	19 05.0
23 F	4 02 45	1 57 18	1♓13 29	7♓31 27	29 27.5	11 30.5	8 32.8	18 03.6	28 20.6	11 34.8	28 34.0	2 43.9	13 10.3	19 03.5
24 Sa	4 06 42	2 54 59	13 44 40	19 53 39	29 27.7	11 47.2	9 45.6	18 35.6	28 45.3	11 42.8	28 41.3	2 44.6	13 10.0	19 02.0
25 Su	4 10 38	3 52 38	25 58 57	2♈01 04	29 28.0	12 08.3	10 58.5	19 07.4	29 09.9	11 51.0	28 48.6	2 45.2	13 09.7	19 00.5
26 M	4 14 35	4 50 16	8♈00 33	13 57 54	29 28.5	12 33.7	12 11.4	19 39.0	29 34.5	11 59.2	28 55.9	2 45.8	13 09.4	18 58.9
27 Tu	4 18 31	5 47 53	19 53 37	25 48 09	29 29.1	13 03.3	13 24.3	20 10.4	29 59.2	12 07.6	29 03.3	2 46.4	13 09.0	18 57.4
28 W	4 22 28	6 45 30	1♉41 57	7♉35 26	29 29.8	13 37.0	14 37.2	20 41.6	0♊23.8	12 16.1	29 10.7	2 46.9	13 08.7	18 55.8
29 Th	4 26 25	7 43 05	13 28 58	19 22 56	29R 30.3	14 14.7	15 50.1	21 12.6	0 48.5	12 24.7	29 18.2	2 47.3	13 08.2	18 54.3
30 F	4 30 21	8 40 39	25 17 39	1♊13 26	29 30.4	14 56.3	17 03.0	21 43.3	1 13.1	12 33.4	29 25.6	2 47.7	13 07.8	18 52.7
31 Sa	4 34 18	9 38 13	7♊10 33	13 09 16	29 30.1	15 41.8	18 16.0	22 13.8	1 37.8	12 42.3	29 33.1	2 48.1	13 07.3	18 51.1

LONGITUDE — June 2003

Day	Sid.Time	☉	0 hr ☽	Noon ☽	True ☊	☿	♀	♂	⚳	♃	♄	♅	♆	♇
1 Su	4 38 14	10♊35 45	19♊09 51	25♊12 33	29♉29.2	16♉30.9	19♉28.9	22♒44.1	2♊02.4	12♌51.2	29♊40.6	2♓48.4	13♒06.8	18♐49.6
2 M	4 42 11	11 33 16	1♋17 34	7♋25 09	29R 27.9	17 23.6	20 41.8	23 14.1	2 27.0	13 00.2	29 48.2	2 48.7	13R 06.3	18R 48.0
3 Tu	4 46 07	12 30 46	13 35 31	19 48 53	29 26.1	18 19.7	21 54.8	23 43.8	2 51.6	13 09.4	29 55.7	2 48.9	13 05.7	18 46.4
4 W	4 50 04	13 28 15	26 05 31	2♌25 36	29 24.3	19 19.3	23 07.8	24 13.3	3 16.3	13 18.7	0♋03.3	2 49.0	13 05.1	18 44.8
5 Th	4 54 00	14 25 42	8♌49 24	15 17 09	29 22.5	20 22.2	24 20.8	24 42.5	3 40.9	13 28.0	0 10.9	2 49.2	13 04.5	18 43.2
6 F	4 57 57	15 23 09	21 49 03	28 25 21	29 21.2	21 28.4	25 33.7	25 11.5	4 05.5	13 37.5	0 18.6	2R 49.2	13 03.8	18 41.6
7 Sa	5 01 54	16 20 34	5♍06 14	11♍51 52	29D 20.5	22 37.8	26 46.7	25 40.1	4 30.1	13 47.1	0 26.2	2 49.2	13 03.1	18 40.0
8 Su	5 05 50	17 17 58	18 42 23	25 37 50	29 20.7	23 50.3	27 59.7	26 08.5	4 54.7	13 56.7	0 33.9	2 49.2	13 02.4	18 38.4
9 M	5 09 47	18 15 20	2♎38 15	9♎43 32	29 21.5	25 05.9	29 12.7	26 36.6	5 19.2	14 06.5	0 41.6	2 49.1	13 01.7	18 36.8
10 Tu	5 13 43	19 12 42	16 53 30	24 07 52	29 22.7	26 24.6	0♊25.8	27 04.4	5 43.8	14 16.3	0 49.2	2 49.0	13 00.9	18 35.2
11 W	5 17 40	20 10 03	1♏26 12	8♏48 00	29 23.9	27 46.2	1 38.8	27 31.9	6 08.3	14 26.3	0 57.0	2 48.8	13 00.1	18 33.6
12 Th	5 21 36	21 07 23	16 12 35	23 39 12	29R 24.6	29 10.9	2 51.8	27 59.1	6 32.9	14 36.3	1 04.7	2 48.6	12 59.3	18 32.0
13 F	5 25 33	22 04 41	1♐06 57	8♐34 54	29 24.5	0♊38.5	4 04.9	28 26.0	6 57.4	14 46.4	1 12.4	2 48.3	12 58.4	18 30.4
14 Sa	5 29 30	23 02 00	16 02 04	23 27 26	29 23.2	2 09.0	5 18.0	28 52.5	7 21.9	14 56.6	1 20.2	2 48.0	12 57.6	18 28.8
15 Su	5 33 26	23 59 17	0♑50 02	8♑08 56	29 20.9	3 42.4	6 31.1	29 18.8	7 46.4	15 06.9	1 27.9	2 47.6	12 56.7	18 27.2
16 M	5 37 23	24 56 34	15 23 19	22 32 28	29 17.6	5 18.8	7 44.2	29 44.6	8 10.9	15 17.3	1 35.7	2 47.2	12 55.7	18 25.7
17 Tu	5 41 19	25 53 51	29 35 50	6♒32 59	29 13.9	6 58.0	8 57.3	0♓10.1	8 35.4	15 27.7	1 43.5	2 46.7	12 54.8	18 24.1
18 W	5 45 16	26 51 07	13♒23 40	20 07 48	29 10.2	8 40.0	10 10.4	0 35.3	8 59.9	15 38.3	1 51.2	2 46.2	12 53.8	18 22.5
19 Th	5 49 12	27 48 23	26 45 25	3♓16 40	29 07.2	10 24.8	11 23.5	1 00.0	9 24.3	15 48.9	1 59.0	2 45.7	12 52.8	18 20.9
20 F	5 53 09	28 45 38	9♓41 52	16 01 24	29 05.2	12 12.4	12 36.7	1 24.4	9 48.7	15 59.6	2 06.8	2 45.1	12 51.8	18 19.3
21 Sa	5 57 05	29 42 53	22 15 43	28 25 21	29D 04.4	14 02.7	13 49.9	1 48.4	10 13.2	16 10.4	2 14.6	2 44.4	12 50.7	18 17.8
22 Su	6 01 02	0♋40 08	4♈30 52	10♈32 52	29 04.9	15 55.7	15 03.1	2 11.9	10 37.6	16 21.2	2 22.4	2 43.7	12 49.6	18 16.2
23 M	6 04 59	1 37 23	16 31 58	22 28 47	29 06.2	17 51.1	16 16.3	2 35.1	11 01.9	16 32.2	2 30.2	2 43.0	12 48.5	18 14.7
24 Tu	6 08 55	2 34 38	28 23 55	4♉18 00	29 07.9	19 49.0	17 29.5	2 57.8	11 26.3	16 43.2	2 38.0	2 42.2	12 47.4	18 13.1
25 W	6 12 52	3 31 52	10♉11 36	16 05 16	29 09.4	21 49.2	18 42.8	3 20.0	11 50.7	16 54.3	2 45.8	2 41.4	12 46.2	18 11.6
26 Th	6 16 48	4 29 07	21 59 31	27 54 51	29R 10.1	23 51.5	19 56.0	3 41.8	12 15.0	17 05.4	2 53.6	2 40.5	12 45.1	18 10.1
27 F	6 20 45	5 26 21	3♊51 41	9♊50 26	29 09.5	25 55.8	21 09.3	4 03.1	12 39.3	17 16.6	3 01.5	2 39.6	12 43.9	18 08.6
28 Sa	6 24 41	6 23 36	15 51 26	21 55 00	29 07.3	28 01.7	22 22.6	4 23.9	13 03.6	17 27.9	3 09.3	2 38.6	12 42.6	18 07.1
29 Su	6 28 38	7 20 50	28 01 23	4♋10 47	29 03.3	0♋09.2	23 35.9	4 44.3	13 27.0	17 39.3	3 17.1	2 37.6	12 41.4	18 05.6
30 M	6 32 34	8 18 04	10♋23 21	16 39 13	28 57.8	2 17.8	24 49.3	5 04.1	13 52.1	17 50.7	3 24.9	2 36.5	12 40.2	18 04.1

Astro Data

	Dy Hr Mn
☽0S	13 3:10
♆R	16 0:48
♄⚼♆	20 7:06
☿D	20 7:32
☽0N	26 2:51
♃☍♆	3 2:55
♅R	7 6:58
☽0S	9 11:24
☽0N	22 9:28
♄△♅	24 23:34

Planet Ingress

	Dy Hr Mn
♀ ♉	16 10:58
☉ ♊	21 11:12
⚳ ♊	27 12:48
♄ ♋	4 1:28
♀ ♊	10 3:32
☿ ♊	13 1:34
♂ ♓	17 2:25
☉ ♋	21 19:10
☿ ♋	29 10:17

Last Aspect / ☽ Ingress (May)

Last Aspect Dy Hr Mn		☽ Ingress Dy Hr Mn
2 5:27	☿ ☌	♊ 3 3:27
5 8:43	♄ ☌	♋ 5 15:42
7 4:21	♀ □	♌ 8 1:46
10 3:13	♄ ⚹	♍ 10 8:31
12 7:09	♄ □	♎ 12 11:42
14 8:13	♄ △	♏ 14 12:14
16 3:36	☉ ☍	♐ 16 11:43
18 8:41	♄ ☍	♑ 18 12:03
20 13:29	☉ △	♒ 20 15:01
22 18:49	♄ △	♓ 22 21:41
25 5:33	♄ □	♈ 25 7:59
27 18:41	♄ ⚹	♉ 27 20:32
29 15:53	♂ □	♊ 30 9:32

Last Aspect / ☽ Ingress (June)

Last Aspect Dy Hr Mn		☽ Ingress Dy Hr Mn
1 20:55	♄ ☌	♋ 1 21:27
3 16:27	♀ ⚹	♌ 4 7:25
6 6:18	♀ □	♍ 6 14:51
8 16:27	♀ △	♎ 8 19:30
10 17:00	♂ △	♏ 10 21:39
12 21:51	☿ ☍	♐ 12 22:12
14 21:05	♂ ⚹	♑ 14 22:38
15 3:12	♅ ⚹	♒ 17 0:41
19 1:08	☉ △	♓ 19 5:57
21 14:45	☉ □	♈ 21 15:06
23 3:28	♇ △	♉ 24 3:15
25 13:41	♃ □	♊ 26 16:13
29 2:31	☿ ☌	♋ 29 3:52

☽ Phases & Eclipses

Dy Hr Mn	
1 12:15	● 10♉43
9 11:53	☽ 18♌27
16 3:36	○ 24♏53
16 3:40	● T 1.128
23 0:31	☾ 1♓30
31 4:20	● 9♊20
31 4:08:16	● A 03'37"
7 20:28	☽ 16♍41
14 11:16	○ 23♐00
21 14:45	☾ 29♓49
29 18:39	● 7♋37

Astro Data

1 May 2003
Julian Day # 37741
SVP 5♓13'04"
GC 26♐53.1 ⚴ 4♈30.7
Eris 20♈10.4 ⚵ 13♏03.8R
⚷ 18♑07.4R ⚶ 28♍55.3R
☽ Mean ☊ 0♊38.8

1 June 2003
Julian Day # 37772
SVP 5♓12'59"
GC 26♐53.2 ⚴ 14♈01.5
Eris 20♈27.3 ⚵ 6♏49.3R
⚷ 17♑16.5R ⚶ 0♎16.8
☽ Mean ☊ 29♉00.3

July 2003 — LONGITUDE

Day	Sid.Time	☉	0 hr ☽	Noon ☽	True ☊	☿	♀	♂	⚳	♃	♄	♅	♆	♇
1 Tu	6 36 31	9♋15 18	22♋58 25	29♋21 02	28♉51.2	4♋27.4	26♊02.6	5♓23.4	14♊16.3	18♌02.2	3♋32.6	2♓35.4	12♒38.9	18♐02.6
2 W	6 40 28	10 12 32	5♌47 02	12♌16 26	28R 44.2	6 37.6	27 16.0	5 42.2	14 40.5	18 13.8	3 40.4	2R 34.3	12R 37.6	18R 01.2
3 Th	6 44 24	11 09 45	18 49 12	25 25 16	28 37.7	8 48.1	28 29.4	6 00.4	15 04.6	18 25.4	3 48.2	2 33.1	12 36.3	17 59.7
4 F	6 48 21	12 06 58	2♍04 37	8♍47 11	28 32.3	10 58.8	29 42.7	6 18.1	15 28.7	18 37.0	3 56.0	2 31.9	12 34.9	17 58.3
5 Sa	6 52 17	13 04 11	15 32 57	22 21 52	28 28.6	13 09.2	0♋56.1	6 35.2	15 52.8	18 48.8	4 03.7	2 30.6	12 33.6	17 56.9
6 Su	6 56 14	14 01 23	29 13 54	6♎09 01	28D 26.8	15 19.2	2 09.6	6 51.7	16 16.9	19 00.5	4 11.4	2 29.3	12 32.2	17 55.5
7 M	7 00 10	14 58 35	13♎07 11	20 08 18	28 26.6	17 28.5	3 23.0	7 07.7	16 40.9	19 12.4	4 19.2	2 28.0	12 30.8	17 54.1
8 Tu	7 04 07	15 55 47	27 12 19	4♏19 03	28 27.5	19 36.8	4 36.5	7 23.1	17 05.0	19 24.3	4 26.9	2 26.6	12 29.4	17 52.7
9 W	7 08 03	16 52 59	11♏28 21	18 39 55	28R 28.5	21 44.1	5 49.9	7 37.8	17 28.9	19 36.2	4 34.6	2 25.2	12 28.0	17 51.4
10 Th	7 12 00	17 50 10	25 53 26	3♐08 28	28 28.7	23 50.1	7 03.4	7 52.0	17 52.9	19 48.2	4 42.3	2 23.7	12 26.6	17 50.1
11 F	7 15 57	18 47 22	10♐24 30	17 40 56	28 27.3	25 54.6	8 16.9	8 05.5	18 16.8	20 00.3	4 49.9	2 22.2	12 25.1	17 48.7
12 Sa	7 19 53	19 44 34	24 57 07	2♑12 19	28 23.7	27 57.7	9 30.4	8 18.4	18 40.7	20 12.4	4 57.6	2 20.7	12 23.7	17 47.4
13 Su	7 23 50	20 41 46	9♑25 45	16 36 41	28 17.9	29 59.2	10 44.0	8 30.7	19 04.5	20 24.5	5 05.2	2 19.1	12 22.2	17 46.2
14 M	7 27 46	21 38 58	23 44 21	0♒48 04	28 10.2	1♌59.0	11 57.5	8 42.2	19 28.3	20 36.7	5 12.8	2 17.5	12 20.7	17 44.9
15 Tu	7 31 43	22 36 10	7♒47 13	14 41 16	28 01.6	3 57.1	13 11.1	8 53.2	19 52.1	20 48.9	5 20.4	2 15.9	12 19.2	17 43.7
16 W	7 35 39	23 33 23	21 29 52	28 12 42	27 52.8	5 53.4	14 24.7	9 03.4	20 15.8	21 01.2	5 28.0	2 14.2	12 17.7	17 42.4
17 Th	7 39 36	24 30 36	4♓49 41	11♓20 49	27 45.0	7 47.9	15 38.3	9 12.9	20 39.5	21 13.6	5 35.5	2 12.5	12 16.2	17 41.2
18 F	7 43 32	25 27 50	17 46 12	24 06 07	27 38.7	9 40.6	16 51.9	9 21.7	21 03.2	21 25.9	5 43.0	2 10.8	12 14.6	17 40.1
19 Sa	7 47 29	26 25 04	0♈20 55	6♈31 01	27 34.6	11 31.5	18 05.6	9 29.7	21 26.8	21 38.3	5 50.5	2 09.0	12 13.1	17 38.9
20 Su	7 51 26	27 22 19	12 36 57	18 39 16	27D 32.5	13 20.6	19 19.3	9 37.1	21 50.4	21 50.8	5 58.0	2 07.2	12 11.5	17 37.8
21 M	7 55 22	28 19 35	24 38 36	0♉35 36	27 32.1	15 07.9	20 33.0	9 43.6	22 13.9	22 03.2	6 05.4	2 05.4	12 10.0	17 36.6
22 Tu	7 59 19	29 16 52	6♉30 55	12 25 14	27 32.7	16 53.3	21 46.7	9 49.4	22 37.4	22 15.8	6 12.8	2 03.5	12 08.4	17 35.6
23 W	8 03 15	0♌14 10	18 19 13	24 13 32	27R 33.3	18 37.0	23 00.4	9 54.5	23 00.9	22 28.3	6 20.2	2 01.6	12 06.8	17 34.5
24 Th	8 07 12	1 11 28	0♊08 47	6♊05 37	27 32.9	20 18.8	24 14.2	9 58.7	23 24.3	22 40.9	6 27.6	1 59.7	12 05.2	17 33.4
25 F	8 11 08	2 08 47	12 04 34	18 06 10	27 30.9	21 58.8	25 28.0	10 02.2	23 47.6	22 53.6	6 34.9	1 57.7	12 03.6	17 32.4
26 Sa	8 15 05	3 06 07	24 10 52	0♋19 04	27 26.5	23 37.1	26 41.8	10 04.8	24 11.0	23 06.2	6 42.2	1 55.7	12 02.0	17 31.4
27 Su	8 19 02	4 03 28	6♋31 05	12 47 11	27 19.6	25 13.6	27 55.6	10 06.7	24 34.2	23 18.9	6 49.5	1 53.7	12 00.4	17 30.4
28 M	8 22 58	5 00 50	19 07 31	25 32 09	27 10.4	26 48.2	29 09.5	10R 07.8	24 57.5	23 31.6	6 56.7	1 51.7	11 58.8	17 29.5
29 Tu	8 26 55	5 58 12	2♌01 06	8♌34 16	26 59.6	28 21.1	0♌23.3	10 08.0	25 20.6	23 44.4	7 03.9	1 49.6	11 57.2	17 28.6
30 W	8 30 51	6 55 36	15 11 28	21 52 30	26 48.3	29 52.2	1 37.2	10 07.5	25 43.7	23 57.2	7 11.1	1 47.5	11 55.5	17 27.7
31 Th	8 34 48	7 53 00	28 37 04	5♍24 51	26 37.4	1♍21.4	2 51.1	10 06.1	26 06.8	24 10.0	7 18.2	1 45.4	11 53.9	17 26.8

August 2003 — LONGITUDE

Day	Sid.Time	☉	0 hr ☽	Noon ☽	True ☊	☿	♀	♂	⚳	♃	♄	♅	♆	♇
1 F	8 38 44	8♌50 24	12♍15 29	19♍08 38	26♉28.2	2♍48.8	4♌05.0	10♓04.0	26♊29.8	24♌22.8	7♋25.2	1♓43.3	11♒52.3	17♐26.0
2 Sa	8 42 41	9 47 49	26 03 57	3♎01 07	26R 21.3	4 14.4	5 19.0	10R 01.0	26 52.8	24 35.7	7 32.3	1R 41.1	11R 50.6	17R 25.1
3 Su	8 46 37	10 45 15	9♎59 51	16 59 54	26 17.1	5 38.1	6 32.9	9 57.3	27 15.6	24 48.5	7 39.3	1 39.0	11 49.0	17 24.3
4 M	8 50 34	11 42 41	24 01 04	1♏03 09	26D 15.2	6 59.8	7 46.9	9 52.8	27 38.5	25 01.4	7 46.2	1 36.8	11 47.4	17 23.6
5 Tu	8 54 30	12 40 08	8♏06 02	15 09 36	26R 14.9	8 19.6	9 00.9	9 47.6	28 01.2	25 14.4	7 53.1	1 34.6	11 45.7	17 22.8
6 W	8 58 27	13 37 36	22 13 43	29 18 16	26 15.0	9 37.5	10 14.9	9 41.6	28 24.0	25 27.3	8 00.0	1 32.3	11 44.1	17 22.1
7 Th	9 02 24	14 35 05	6♐23 06	13♐28 03	26 14.2	10 53.2	11 28.9	9 34.9	28 46.6	25 40.3	8 06.8	1 30.1	11 42.5	17 21.5
8 F	9 06 20	15 32 34	20 32 52	27 37 17	26 11.4	12 06.9	12 43.0	9 27.5	29 09.2	25 53.2	8 13.6	1 27.8	11 40.9	17 20.8
9 Sa	9 10 17	16 30 04	4♑40 58	11♑43 29	26 05.9	13 18.4	13 57.0	9 19.3	29 31.7	26 06.2	8 20.3	1 25.6	11 39.2	17 20.2
10 Su	9 14 13	17 27 35	18 44 25	25 43 17	25 57.7	14 27.7	15 11.1	9 10.5	29 54.2	26 19.2	8 27.0	1 23.3	11 37.6	17 19.6
11 M	9 18 10	18 25 07	2♒39 34	9♒32 48	25 47.1	15 34.6	16 25.2	9 01.0	0♋16.6	26 32.2	8 33.6	1 21.0	11 36.0	17 19.0
12 Tu	9 22 06	19 22 40	16 22 30	23 08 14	25 35.1	16 39.1	17 39.3	8 50.9	0 38.9	26 45.3	8 40.2	1 18.6	11 34.4	17 18.5
13 W	9 26 03	20 20 14	29 49 39	6♓26 27	25 22.9	17 41.1	18 53.4	8 40.1	1 01.1	26 58.3	8 46.7	1 16.3	11 32.8	17 18.0
14 Th	9 30 00	21 17 50	12♓58 28	19 25 36	25 11.6	18 40.4	20 07.5	8 28.8	1 23.3	27 11.3	8 53.2	1 14.0	11 31.2	17 17.5
15 F	9 33 56	22 15 26	25 47 53	2♈05 26	25 02.2	19 37.0	21 21.7	8 16.8	1 45.4	27 24.4	8 59.6	1 11.6	11 29.6	17 17.1
16 Sa	9 37 53	23 13 05	8♈18 28	14 27 19	24 55.3	20 30.7	22 35.8	8 04.4	2 07.5	27 37.5	9 06.0	1 09.3	11 28.0	17 16.7
17 Su	9 41 49	24 10 44	20 32 22	26 34 06	24 51.0	21 21.3	23 50.0	7 51.4	2 29.4	27 50.5	9 12.3	1 06.9	11 26.4	17 16.3
18 M	9 45 46	25 08 25	2♉33 02	8♉29 46	24 48.9	22 08.7	25 04.2	7 37.9	2 51.3	28 03.6	9 18.6	1 04.5	11 24.8	17 15.9
19 Tu	9 49 42	26 06 08	14 24 56	20 19 12	24 48.4	22 52.7	26 18.5	7 23.9	3 13.1	28 16.7	9 24.8	1 02.1	11 23.2	17 15.6
20 W	9 53 39	27 03 52	26 13 14	2♊07 43	24 48.3	23 33.1	27 32.7	7 09.6	3 34.9	28 29.8	9 30.9	0 59.8	11 21.7	17 15.3
21 Th	9 57 35	28 01 39	8♊03 22	14 00 50	24 47.7	24 09.7	28 47.0	6 54.9	3 56.5	28 42.9	9 37.0	0 57.4	11 20.1	17 15.0
22 F	10 01 32	28 59 26	20 00 48	26 03 53	24 45.5	24 42.2	0♍01.3	6 39.8	4 18.1	28 56.0	9 43.0	0 55.0	11 18.6	17 14.8
23 Sa	10 05 28	29 57 16	2♋10 39	8♋21 38	24 41.0	25 10.5	1 15.6	6 24.5	4 39.6	29 09.0	9 49.0	0 52.6	11 17.0	17 14.6
24 Su	10 09 25	0♍55 07	14 37 17	20 57 57	24 33.8	25 34.3	2 29.9	6 08.9	5 01.0	29 22.1	9 54.9	0 50.2	11 15.5	17 14.5
25 M	10 13 22	1 53 00	27 23 53	3♌55 15	24 24.3	25 53.4	3 44.2	5 53.2	5 22.3	29 35.2	10 00.7	0 47.8	11 14.0	17 14.3
26 Tu	10 17 18	2 50 54	10♌32 04	17 14 15	24 12.9	26 07.4	4 58.6	5 37.3	5 43.5	29 48.3	10 06.5	0 45.4	11 12.5	17 14.2
27 W	10 21 15	3 48 50	24 01 35	0♍53 42	24 00.8	26 16.2	6 12.9	5 21.3	6 04.6	0♍01.4	10 12.1	0 43.0	11 11.0	17 14.2
28 Th	10 25 11	4 46 47	7♍50 10	14 50 27	23 49.2	26R 19.4	7 27.3	5 05.2	6 25.6	0 14.5	10 17.8	0 40.6	11 09.6	17D 14.1
29 F	10 29 08	5 44 46	21 53 57	28 59 59	23 39.3	26 16.9	8 41.7	4 49.2	6 46.5	0 27.5	10 23.3	0 38.2	11 08.1	17 14.1
30 Sa	10 33 04	6 42 46	6♎07 55	13♎17 06	23 31.9	26 08.5	9 56.1	4 33.2	7 07.3	0 40.6	10 28.8	0 35.8	11 06.7	17 14.1
31 Su	10 37 01	7 40 48	20 26 54	27 36 48	23 27.3	25 53.9	11 10.5	4 17.3	7 28.1	0 53.6	10 34.2	0 33.5	11 05.3	17 14.2

Astro Data Dy Hr Mn	Planet Ingress Dy Hr Mn	Last Aspect Dy Hr Mn	☽ Ingress Dy Hr Mn	Last Aspect Dy Hr Mn	☽ Ingress Dy Hr Mn	☽ Phases & Eclipses Dy Hr Mn	Astro Data
♃△♇ 1 12:47	♀ ♋ 4 17:39	29 18:39 ☉ ☌	♌ 1 13:13	1 9:02 ♇ □	♎ 2 6:48	7 2:32 ☽ 14♎36	1 July 2003
☽0S 6 17:04	☿ ♌ 13 12:10	3 18:06 ♀ ⚹	♍ 3 20:16	4 1:34 ♃ ⚹	♏ 4 10:12	13 19:21 ○ 20♑59	Julian Day # 37802
♃∠♄ 9 2:42	☉ ♌ 23 6:04	5 4:15 ♇ □	♎ 6 1:20	6 5:22 ♃ □	♐ 6 13:11	21 7:01 ☾ 28♈08	SVP 5♓12'53"
☽0N 19 16:41	♀ ♌ 29 4:25	7 10:23 ♃ ⚹	♏ 8 4:43	8 9:01 ♃ △	♑ 8 16:02	29 6:53 ● 5♌46	GC 26♐53.3 ⚴ 21♈51.5
♂R 29 7:36	☿ ♍ 30 14:05	9 17:58 ☿ △	♐ 10 6:48	9 14:57 ☿ △	♒ 10 19:23		Eris 20♈36.6 ⚵ 4♏43.2
		11 15:53 ♃ △	♑ 12 8:21	12 18:35 ♃ ☍	♓ 13 0:19	5 7:28 ☽ 12♏29	⚷ 15♑37.0R ⚶ 7♎37.4
☽0S 2 21:42	⚳ ♋ 10 18:14	13 19:21 ☉ ☍	♒ 14 10:38	14 10:29 ☿ ☍	♈ 15 8:00	12 4:48 ○ 19♒05	☽ Mean ☊ 27♉25.0
☽0N 16 0:18	♀ ♍ 22 11:36	15 22:57 ♃ ☍	♓ 16 15:14	17 14:36 ♃ △	♉ 17 18:52	20 0:48 ☾ 26♉37	
☿0S 20 8:57	☉ ♍ 23 13:08	18 14:49 ☉ △	♈ 18 23:20	20 4:29 ♃ □	♊ 20 7:41	27 17:26 ● 4♍02	1 August 2003
☿R 28 13:41	♃ ♍ 27 9:26	21 7:01 ☉ □	♉ 21 10:48	22 18:15 ☉ ⚹	♋ 22 19:44		Julian Day # 37833
♇D 29 3:34		23 9:14 ♀ ⚹	♊ 23 23:42	24 20:51 ☿ ⚹	♌ 25 4:48		SVP 5♓12'48"
☽0S 30 3:38		25 21:38 ♃ ⚹	♋ 26 11:23	26 12:00 ♇ △	♍ 27 10:27		GC 26♐53.4 ⚴ 27♈23.3
♃☍♅ 30 4:37		28 19:25 ♀ ☌	♌ 28 20:17	29 7:26 ☿ ☌	♎ 29 13:41		Eris 20♈36.8R ⚵ 7♏18.8
		30 15:46 ♃ ☌	♍ 31 2:27	30 18:37 ♇ ⚹	♏ 31 16:00		⚷ 13♑45.6R ⚶ 19♎05.6
							☽ Mean ☊ 25♉46.6

LONGITUDE — September 2003

Day	Sid.Time	☉	0 hr ☽	Noon ☽	True ☊	☿	♀	♂	⚳	♃	♄	♅	♆	♇
1 M	10 40 57	8♍38 51	4♏46 17	11♏54 58	23♉25.2	25♍33.2	12♍24.9	4♓01.6	7♋48.7	1♍06.7	10♋39.6	0♓31.1	11♒03.8	17♐14.3
2 Tu	10 44 54	9 36 55	19 02 33	26 08 45	23D 24.9	25R 06.4	13 39.3	3R 46.1	8 09.2	1 19.7	10 44.8	0R 28.7	11R 02.5	17 14.4
3 W	10 48 51	10 35 01	3♐13 25	10♐16 25	23R 25.0	24 33.4	14 53.8	3 30.9	8 29.6	1 32.7	10 50.0	0 26.4	11 01.1	17 14.6
4 Th	10 52 47	11 33 09	17 17 39	24 17 03	23 24.5	23 54.6	16 08.2	3 16.0	8 49.9	1 45.7	10 55.2	0 24.1	10 59.7	17 14.8
5 F	10 56 44	12 31 17	1♑14 33	8♑10 04	23 22.1	23 10.3	17 22.7	3 01.4	9 10.1	1 58.7	11 00.2	0 21.7	10 58.4	17 15.0
6 Sa	11 00 40	13 29 27	15 03 33	21 54 50	23 17.2	22 21.0	18 37.2	2 47.2	9 30.1	2 11.6	11 05.2	0 19.4	10 57.1	17 15.3
7 Su	11 04 37	14 27 39	28 43 49	5♒30 18	23 09.8	21 27.5	19 51.6	2 33.4	9 50.1	2 24.6	11 10.1	0 17.1	10 55.8	17 15.6
8 M	11 08 33	15 25 52	12♒14 07	18 55 03	23 00.1	20 30.7	21 06.1	2 20.0	10 09.9	2 37.5	11 14.9	0 14.8	10 54.5	17 15.9
9 Tu	11 12 30	16 24 07	25 32 53	2♓07 25	22 49.0	19 31.5	22 20.6	2 07.2	10 29.6	2 50.4	11 19.6	0 12.6	10 53.2	17 16.2
10 W	11 16 26	17 22 23	8♓38 29	15 05 55	22 37.6	18 31.3	23 35.1	1 54.9	10 49.2	3 03.3	11 24.2	0 10.3	10 52.0	17 16.6
11 Th	11 20 23	18 20 41	21 29 36	27 49 30	22 27.1	17 31.2	24 49.6	1 43.1	11 08.7	3 16.1	11 28.8	0 08.0	10 50.8	17 17.1
12 F	11 24 20	19 19 01	4♈05 38	10♈18 03	22 18.3	16 32.8	26 04.1	1 31.9	11 28.0	3 29.0	11 33.3	0 05.8	10 49.6	17 17.5
13 Sa	11 28 16	20 17 23	16 26 55	22 32 27	22 11.8	15 37.3	27 18.6	1 21.3	11 47.2	3 41.8	11 37.7	0 03.6	10 48.4	17 18.0
14 Su	11 32 13	21 15 47	28 34 55	4♉34 41	22 07.9	14 46.2	28 33.1	1 11.3	12 06.3	3 54.6	11 42.0	0 01.4	10 47.3	17 18.5
15 M	11 36 09	22 14 13	10♉32 11	16 27 52	22D 06.2	14 00.8	29 47.7	1 01.9	12 25.3	4 07.3	11 46.2	29♒59.3	10 46.1	17 19.1
16 Tu	11 40 06	23 12 41	22 22 15	28 15 56	22 06.2	13 22.2	1♎02.2	0 53.3	12 44.1	4 20.0	11 50.3	29 57.1	10 45.0	17 19.6
17 W	11 44 02	24 11 12	4♊09 30	10♊03 36	22 07.0	12 51.3	2 16.8	0 45.3	13 02.7	4 32.7	11 54.4	29 55.0	10 43.9	17 20.3
18 Th	11 47 59	25 09 44	15 58 53	21 56 02	22R 07.7	12 29.0	3 31.4	0 38.1	13 21.3	4 45.4	11 58.4	29 52.9	10 42.9	17 20.9
19 F	11 51 55	26 08 19	27 55 43	3♋58 36	22 07.4	12D 15.9	4 45.9	0 31.6	13 39.7	4 58.0	12 02.2	29 50.8	10 41.9	17 21.6
20 Sa	11 55 52	27 06 56	10♋05 19	16 16 31	22 05.4	12 12.3	6 00.5	0 25.8	13 57.9	5 10.6	12 06.0	29 48.8	10 40.8	17 22.3
21 Su	11 59 49	28 05 35	22 32 43	28 54 26	22 01.4	12 18.5	7 15.1	0 20.8	14 16.0	5 23.2	12 09.7	29 46.7	10 39.9	17 23.0
22 M	12 03 45	29 04 16	5♌22 03	11♌55 54	21 55.3	12 34.3	8 29.7	0 16.5	14 33.9	5 35.7	12 13.3	29 44.7	10 38.9	17 23.8
23 Tu	12 07 42	0♎02 59	18 36 08	25 22 47	21 47.6	12 59.8	9 44.3	0 13.0	14 51.7	5 48.2	12 16.8	29 42.8	10 38.0	17 24.6
24 W	12 11 38	1 01 45	2♍15 45	9♍14 46	21 39.2	13 34.5	10 58.9	0 10.4	15 09.3	6 00.6	12 20.2	29 40.8	10 37.1	17 25.5
25 Th	12 15 35	2 00 32	16 19 23	23 29 03	21 31.0	14 18.0	12 13.6	0 08.5	15 26.7	6 13.0	12 23.5	29 38.9	10 36.2	17 26.3
26 F	12 19 31	2 59 22	0♎43 01	8♎00 30	21 24.0	15 09.9	13 28.2	0D 07.4	15 44.0	6 25.4	12 26.7	29 37.0	10 35.3	17 27.2
27 Sa	12 23 28	3 58 13	15 20 35	22 42 21	21 19.0	16 09.4	14 42.8	0 07.1	16 01.1	6 37.7	12 29.8	29 35.2	10 34.5	17 28.2
28 Su	12 27 24	4 57 06	0♏04 51	7♏27 12	21D 16.2	17 16.0	15 57.4	0 07.7	16 18.0	6 50.0	12 32.8	29 33.3	10 33.7	17 29.1
29 M	12 31 21	5 56 02	14 48 34	22 08 12	21 15.4	18 29.0	17 12.1	0 09.0	16 34.7	7 02.2	12 35.7	29 31.6	10 33.0	17 30.1
30 Tu	12 35 18	6 54 59	29 25 28	6♐39 51	21 16.1	19 47.7	18 26.7	0 11.2	16 51.3	7 14.4	12 38.5	29 29.8	10 32.2	17 31.1

LONGITUDE — October 2003

Day	Sid.Time	☉	0 hr ☽	Noon ☽	True ☊	☿	♀	♂	⚳	♃	♄	♅	♆	♇
1 W	12 39 14	7♎53 58	13♐50 57	20♐58 28	21♉17.3	21♍11.4	19♎41.4	0♓14.2	17♋07.6	7♍26.5	12♋41.3	29♒28.1	10♒31.5	17♐32.2
2 Th	12 43 11	8 52 58	28 02 13	5♑02 06	21R 18.2	22 39.5	20 56.0	0 18.0	17 23.8	7 38.6	12 43.9	29R 26.4	10R 30.9	17 33.3
3 F	12 47 07	9 52 01	11♑58 03	18 50 05	21 17.9	24 11.3	22 10.6	0 22.6	17 39.8	7 50.6	12 46.4	29 24.7	10 30.2	17 34.4
4 Sa	12 51 04	10 51 05	25 38 17	2♒22 42	21 15.9	25 46.2	23 25.3	0 27.9	17 55.6	8 02.6	12 48.8	29 23.1	10 29.6	17 35.5
5 Su	12 55 00	11 50 11	9♒03 25	15 40 34	21 12.1	27 23.7	24 39.9	0 34.1	18 11.2	8 14.5	12 51.1	29 21.6	10 29.0	17 36.7
6 M	12 58 57	12 49 18	22 14 12	28 44 26	21 06.7	29 03.3	25 54.5	0 40.9	18 26.6	8 26.3	12 53.3	29 20.0	10 28.5	17 37.9
7 Tu	13 02 53	13 48 27	5♓11 21	11♓35 00	21 00.4	0♎44.6	27 09.2	0 48.6	18 41.8	8 38.2	12 55.4	29 18.5	10 28.0	17 39.1
8 W	13 06 50	14 47 39	17 55 28	24 12 50	20 53.8	2 27.3	28 23.8	0 57.0	18 56.7	8 49.9	12 57.3	29 17.1	10 27.5	17 40.4
9 Th	13 10 47	15 46 52	0♈27 11	6♈38 36	20 47.8	4 10.9	29 38.4	1 06.1	19 11.5	9 01.6	12 59.2	29 15.6	10 27.0	17 41.7
10 F	13 14 43	16 46 07	12 47 11	18 53 05	20 42.8	5 55.2	0♏53.1	1 15.9	19 26.0	9 13.2	13 01.0	29 14.2	10 26.6	17 43.0
11 Sa	13 18 40	17 45 24	24 56 27	0♉57 29	20 39.4	7 39.9	2 07.7	1 26.5	19 40.4	9 24.7	13 02.6	29 12.9	10 26.2	17 44.3
12 Su	13 22 36	18 44 43	6♉56 24	12 53 29	20D 37.6	9 24.8	3 22.3	1 37.7	19 54.5	9 36.2	13 04.2	29 11.6	10 25.8	17 45.7
13 M	13 26 33	19 44 05	18 49 02	24 43 24	20 37.4	11 09.9	4 37.0	1 49.6	20 08.3	9 47.6	13 05.6	29 10.3	10 25.5	17 47.1
14 Tu	13 30 29	20 43 29	0♊36 59	6♊30 13	20 38.4	12 54.8	5 51.6	2 02.2	20 22.0	9 59.0	13 07.0	29 09.1	10 25.2	17 48.5
15 W	13 34 26	21 42 55	12 23 33	18 17 32	20 40.1	14 39.6	7 06.2	2 15.4	20 35.4	10 10.2	13 08.2	29 07.9	10 24.9	17 50.0
16 Th	13 38 22	22 42 23	24 12 41	0♋09 34	20 41.9	16 24.0	8 20.9	2 29.3	20 48.5	10 21.5	13 09.3	29 06.8	10 24.7	17 51.4
17 F	13 42 19	23 41 53	6♋08 48	12 10 58	20 43.3	18 08.1	9 35.5	2 43.8	21 01.4	10 32.6	13 10.3	29 05.7	10 24.5	17 52.9
18 Sa	13 46 16	24 41 26	18 16 41	24 26 33	20R 43.9	19 51.8	10 50.2	2 58.9	21 14.1	10 43.7	13 11.2	29 04.7	10 24.3	17 54.5
19 Su	13 50 12	25 41 01	0♌41 11	7♌01 07	20 43.3	21 34.9	12 04.8	3 14.6	21 26.5	10 54.6	13 12.0	29 03.7	10 24.2	17 56.0
20 M	13 54 09	26 40 39	13 26 51	19 58 50	20 41.7	23 17.6	13 19.5	3 31.0	21 38.6	11 05.6	13 12.7	29 02.7	10 24.1	17 57.6
21 Tu	13 58 05	27 40 18	26 37 24	3♍22 48	20 39.1	24 59.7	14 34.1	3 47.9	21 50.5	11 16.4	13 13.3	29 01.8	10 24.0	17 59.2
22 W	14 02 02	28 40 00	10♍15 08	17 14 20	20 36.0	26 41.3	15 48.8	4 05.4	22 02.1	11 27.1	13 13.7	29 00.9	10D 24.0	18 00.8
23 Th	14 05 58	29 39 44	24 20 12	1♎32 20	20 32.9	28 22.3	17 03.4	4 23.5	22 13.4	11 37.8	13 14.0	29 00.1	10 24.0	18 02.5
24 F	14 09 55	0♏39 30	8♎50 11	16 13 00	20 30.3	0♏02.8	18 18.1	4 42.1	22 24.5	11 48.4	13 14.3	28 59.4	10 24.0	18 04.1
25 Sa	14 13 51	1 39 18	23 39 54	1♏09 52	20 28.6	1 42.7	19 32.7	5 01.3	22 35.2	11 58.9	13R 14.4	28 58.6	10 24.1	18 05.8
26 Su	14 17 48	2 39 08	8♏41 50	16 14 38	20D 27.8	3 22.0	20 47.4	5 21.0	22 45.7	12 09.3	13 14.4	28 58.0	10 24.2	18 07.6
27 M	14 21 44	3 39 01	23 47 08	1♐18 14	20 28.0	5 00.8	22 02.0	5 41.2	22 55.8	12 19.6	13 14.3	28 57.3	10 24.3	18 09.3
28 Tu	14 25 41	4 38 55	8♐46 56	16 12 19	20 28.9	6 39.0	23 16.7	6 02.0	23 05.7	12 29.8	13 14.0	28 56.8	10 24.5	18 11.1
29 W	14 29 38	5 38 50	23 33 36	0♑50 11	20 30.0	8 16.8	24 31.3	6 23.2	23 15.3	12 39.9	13 13.7	28 56.2	10 24.7	18 12.9
30 Th	14 33 34	6 38 48	8♑01 35	15 07 29	20 31.1	9 54.0	25 45.9	6 45.0	23 24.5	12 50.0	13 13.3	28 55.8	10 24.9	18 14.7
31 F	14 37 31	7 38 47	22 07 42	29 02 11	20R 31.8	11 30.7	27 00.6	7 07.2	23 33.5	12 59.9	13 12.7	28 55.3	10 25.2	18 16.5

Astro Data

	Dy Hr Mn
♄⊼♆	5 5:09
☿0N	8 9:50
☽0N	12 7:54
♀0S	18 0:44
☿D	20 8:52
⊙0S	23 10:47
☽0S	26 12:15
♂D	27 7:52
☿0S	9 14:41
☽0N	9 14:57
♃⊼♆	16 18:48
♆D	23 1:54
☽0S	23 22:59
♄R	25 23:42

Planet Ingress

	Dy Hr Mn
♅ ♒R	15 3:47
♀ ♎	15 15:58
⊙ ♎	23 10:47
☿ ♎	7 1:28
♀ ♏	9 18:56
⊙ ♏	23 20:08
☿ ♏	24 11:20

Last Aspect / ☽ Ingress (September)

Last Aspect Dy Hr Mn		☽ Ingress Dy Hr Mn
2 10:18	☿ ⚹	♐ 2 18:32
4 11:23	☿ □	♑ 4 21:51
6 12:43	☿ △	♒ 7 2:15
8 9:01	♇ ⚹	♓ 9 8:07
11 5:41	♀ ☍	♈ 11 16:09
13 1:40	♇ △	♉ 14 2:50
16 15:25	♅ □	♊ 16 15:32
19 3:51	♅ △	♋ 19 4:07
21 10:21	⊙ ⚹	♌ 21 14:03
23 19:33	♅ ☍	♍ 23 20:05
25 1:52	♇ □	♎ 25 22:49
27 23:10	♅ △	♏ 27 23:52
30 0:09	♅ □	♐ 30 0:57

Last Aspect / ☽ Ingress (October)

Last Aspect Dy Hr Mn		☽ Ingress Dy Hr Mn
2 2:25	♅ ⚹	♑ 2 3:21
3 22:40	♅ △	♒ 4 7:45
6 13:06	♅ ☌	♓ 6 14:20
7 23:30	♇ □	♈ 8 23:08
11 8:31	♅ ⚹	♉ 11 10:05
13 21:03	♅ □	♊ 13 22:45
16 9:54	♅ △	♋ 16 11:41
18 12:31	⊙ □	♌ 18 22:41
21 4:18	♅ ☍	♍ 21 6:01
22 13:19	♇ □	♎ 23 9:27
25 8:31	♅ △	♏ 25 10:08
27 8:15	♅ □	♐ 27 9:55
29 8:51	♅ ⚹	♑ 29 10:37
31 8:07	♀ ⚹	♒ 31 13:41

☽ Phases & Eclipses

Dy Hr Mn		
3 12:34	☽	10♐36
10 16:36	○	17♓34
18 19:03	☾	25♊27
26 3:09	●	2♎38
2 19:09	☽	9♑11
10 7:28	○	16♈35
18 12:31	☾	24♋43
25 12:50	●	1♏41

Astro Data

1 September 2003
Julian Day # 37864
SVP 5♓12'44"
GC 26♐53.4 ⚴ 28♈24.4R
Eris 20♈27.4R ⚵ 13♏29.5
⚷ 12♑33.2R ⚶ 2♏55.0
☽ Mean ☊ 24♉08.1

1 October 2003
Julian Day # 37894
SVP 5♓12'41"
GC 26♐53.5 ⚴ 23♈20.3R
Eris 20♈11.8R ⚵ 21♏40.1
⚷ 12♑29.2 ⚶ 17♏39.7
☽ Mean ☊ 22♉32.7

November 2003 — LONGITUDE

Day	Sid.Time	☉	0 hr ☽	Noon ☽	True ☊	☿	♀	♂	⚳	♃	♄	♅	♆	♇
1 Sa	14 41 27	8♏38 47	5♒50 59	12♒34 15	20♉31.9	13♏06.9	28♏15.2	7♓29.9	23♋42.1	13♍09.7	13♋12.0	28♒55.0	10♒25.5	18♐18.3
2 Su	14 45 24	9 38 49	19 12 10	25 45 02	20R 31.4	14 42.6	29 29.8	7 53.0	23 50.4	13 19.5	13R 11.2	28R 54.6	10 25.8	18 20.2
3 M	14 49 20	10 38 53	2♓13 08	8♓36 47	20 30.5	16 17.9	0♐44.5	8 16.6	23 58.3	13 29.1	13 10.3	28 54.3	10 26.2	18 22.1
4 Tu	14 53 17	11 38 58	14 56 21	21 12 09	20 29.3	17 52.8	1 59.1	8 40.6	24 06.0	13 38.6	13 09.3	28 54.1	10 26.6	18 24.0
5 W	14 57 13	12 39 05	27 24 31	3♈33 47	20 28.1	19 27.2	3 13.7	9 05.0	24 13.2	13 48.1	13 08.2	28 53.9	10 27.1	18 25.9
6 Th	15 01 10	13 39 13	9♈40 16	15 44 15	20 27.1	21 01.3	4 28.3	9 29.8	24 20.2	13 57.4	13 07.0	28 53.8	10 27.5	18 27.9
7 F	15 05 07	14 39 23	21 46 03	27 45 55	20 26.4	22 34.9	5 42.9	9 55.0	24 26.8	14 06.6	13 05.7	28 53.7	10 28.0	18 29.8
8 Sa	15 09 03	15 39 35	3♉44 07	9♉40 55	20D 26.0	24 08.2	6 57.4	10 20.6	24 33.1	14 15.7	13 04.2	28D 53.7	10 28.6	18 31.8
9 Su	15 13 00	16 39 49	15 36 35	21 31 21	20 25.9	25 41.1	8 12.0	10 46.5	24 39.0	14 24.7	13 02.7	28 53.7	10 29.2	18 33.8
10 M	15 16 56	17 40 04	27 25 29	3♊19 16	20 26.0	27 13.7	9 26.6	11 12.8	24 44.5	14 33.5	13 01.0	28 53.8	10 29.8	18 35.8
11 Tu	15 20 53	18 40 21	9♊12 59	15 06 56	20 26.2	28 46.0	10 41.2	11 39.5	24 49.7	14 42.3	12 59.2	28 53.9	10 30.4	18 37.8
12 W	15 24 49	19 40 40	21 01 27	26 56 53	20R 26.3	0♐17.9	11 55.7	12 06.5	24 54.5	14 50.9	12 57.4	28 54.1	10 31.1	18 39.9
13 Th	15 28 46	20 41 01	2♋53 36	8♋52 00	20 26.4	1 49.5	13 10.3	12 33.8	24 59.0	14 59.5	12 55.4	28 54.3	10 31.8	18 41.9
14 F	15 32 43	21 41 24	14 52 31	20 55 36	20 26.3	3 20.8	14 24.9	13 01.5	25 03.0	15 07.9	12 53.3	28 54.6	10 32.5	18 44.0
15 Sa	15 36 39	22 41 49	27 01 43	3♌11 20	20 26.1	4 51.8	15 39.4	13 29.5	25 06.7	15 16.1	12 51.1	28 55.0	10 33.3	18 46.1
16 Su	15 40 36	23 42 15	9♌24 59	15 43 08	20D 26.0	6 22.5	16 54.0	13 57.7	25 10.0	15 24.3	12 48.9	28 55.3	10 34.1	18 48.2
17 M	15 44 32	24 42 44	22 06 16	28 34 51	20 25.9	7 52.8	18 08.5	14 26.3	25 12.9	15 32.3	12 46.5	28 55.8	10 35.0	18 50.3
18 Tu	15 48 29	25 43 14	5♍09 18	11♍49 58	20 26.1	9 22.8	19 23.1	14 55.2	25 15.4	15 40.2	12 44.0	28 56.3	10 35.8	18 52.4
19 W	15 52 25	26 43 46	18 37 09	25 31 00	20 26.6	10 52.5	20 37.6	15 24.3	25 17.5	15 48.0	12 41.4	28 56.8	10 36.7	18 54.6
20 Th	15 56 22	27 44 20	2♎31 36	9♎38 50	20 27.2	12 21.9	21 52.1	15 53.8	25 19.2	15 55.6	12 38.7	28 57.4	10 37.7	18 56.7
21 F	16 00 18	28 44 55	16 52 28	24 12 05	20 27.9	13 50.8	23 06.7	16 23.5	25 20.5	16 03.1	12 35.9	28 58.0	10 38.6	18 58.9
22 Sa	16 04 15	29 45 32	1♏37 04	9♏06 38	20R 28.4	15 19.4	24 21.2	16 53.5	25 21.3	16 10.5	12 33.1	28 58.7	10 39.6	19 01.1
23 Su	16 08 11	0♐46 11	16 39 51	24 15 37	20 28.6	16 47.5	25 35.7	17 23.8	25R 21.8	16 17.7	12 30.1	28 59.4	10 40.7	19 03.2
24 M	16 12 08	1 46 52	1♐52 44	9♐29 59	20 28.1	18 15.1	26 50.2	17 54.3	25 21.8	16 24.8	12 27.0	29 00.2	10 41.7	19 05.4
25 Tu	16 16 05	2 47 34	17 06 05	24 39 48	20 27.1	19 42.1	28 04.8	18 25.1	25 21.5	16 31.7	12 23.9	29 01.1	10 42.8	19 07.6
26 W	16 20 01	3 48 17	2♑10 00	9♑35 41	20 25.5	21 08.6	29 19.3	18 56.1	25 20.7	16 38.5	12 20.7	29 02.0	10 44.0	19 09.9
27 Th	16 23 58	4 49 01	16 55 59	24 10 13	20 23.7	22 34.3	0♑33.8	19 27.4	25 19.5	16 45.2	12 17.3	29 02.9	10 45.1	19 12.1
28 F	16 27 54	5 49 46	1♒17 56	8♒18 49	20 21.9	23 59.2	1 48.2	19 58.9	25 17.8	16 51.7	12 13.9	29 03.9	10 46.3	19 14.3
29 Sa	16 31 51	6 50 32	15 12 44	21 59 44	20 20.6	25 23.3	3 02.7	20 30.6	25 15.8	16 58.0	12 10.4	29 05.0	10 47.5	19 16.5
30 Su	16 35 47	7 51 20	28 39 59	5♓13 47	20D 20.0	26 46.2	4 17.2	21 02.5	25 13.3	17 04.2	12 06.8	29 06.0	10 48.8	19 18.8

December 2003 — LONGITUDE

Day	Sid.Time	☉	0 hr ☽	Noon ☽	True ☊	☿	♀	♂	⚳	♃	♄	♅	♆	♇
1 M	16 39 44	8♐52 08	11♓41 31	18♓03 37	20♉20.3	28♐08.0	5♑31.6	21♓34.6	25♋10.4	17♍10.3	12♋03.2	29♒07.2	10♒50.1	19♐21.0
2 Tu	16 43 41	9 52 56	24 20 36	0♈32 59	20 21.3	29 28.4	6 46.0	22 07.0	25R 07.0	17 16.2	11R 59.4	29 08.4	10 51.4	19 23.3
3 W	16 47 37	10 53 46	6♈41 19	12 46 07	20 22.8	0♑47.2	8 00.4	22 39.5	25 03.3	17 21.9	11 55.6	29 09.6	10 52.7	19 25.5
4 Th	16 51 34	11 54 37	18 47 56	24 47 16	20 24.6	2 04.1	9 14.8	23 12.3	24 59.1	17 27.5	11 51.8	29 10.9	10 54.1	19 27.8
5 F	16 55 30	12 55 29	0♉44 38	6♉40 27	20 26.0	3 19.0	10 29.2	23 45.2	24 54.5	17 32.9	11 47.8	29 12.2	10 55.4	19 30.1
6 Sa	16 59 27	13 56 21	12 35 11	18 29 13	20R 26.7	4 31.4	11 43.6	24 18.3	24 49.5	17 38.2	11 43.8	29 13.6	10 56.9	19 32.3
7 Su	17 03 23	14 57 15	24 22 54	0♊16 34	20 26.3	5 40.9	12 57.9	24 51.5	24 44.1	17 43.3	11 39.7	29 15.1	10 58.3	19 34.6
8 M	17 07 20	15 58 09	6♊10 33	12 05 05	20 24.5	6 47.2	14 12.2	25 25.0	24 38.3	17 48.2	11 35.5	29 16.5	10 59.8	19 36.9
9 Tu	17 11 16	16 59 05	18 00 28	23 56 53	20 21.4	7 49.7	15 26.6	25 58.6	24 32.1	17 53.0	11 31.3	29 18.1	11 01.3	19 39.1
10 W	17 15 13	18 00 01	29 54 36	5♋53 49	20 17.1	8 47.9	16 40.9	26 32.3	24 25.4	17 57.6	11 27.0	29 19.6	11 02.8	19 41.4
11 Th	17 19 10	19 00 59	11♋54 44	17 57 36	20 12.0	9 41.2	17 55.1	27 06.3	24 18.4	18 02.0	11 22.7	29 21.3	11 04.3	19 43.7
12 F	17 23 06	20 01 57	24 02 37	0♌10 02	20 06.6	10 28.8	19 09.4	27 40.3	24 10.9	18 06.3	11 18.3	29 22.9	11 05.9	19 46.0
13 Sa	17 27 03	21 02 57	6♌20 06	12 33 06	20 01.5	11 10.0	20 23.6	28 14.5	24 03.1	18 10.4	11 13.9	29 24.6	11 07.5	19 48.3
14 Su	17 30 59	22 03 57	18 49 19	25 09 04	19 57.4	11 43.9	21 37.9	28 48.9	23 54.9	18 14.3	11 09.4	29 26.4	11 09.1	19 50.5
15 M	17 34 56	23 04 58	1♍32 40	8♍00 28	19 54.7	12 09.8	22 52.1	29 23.4	23 46.3	18 18.1	11 04.8	29 28.2	11 10.8	19 52.8
16 Tu	17 38 52	24 06 01	14 32 48	21 09 59	19D 53.6	12 26.6	24 06.2	29 58.0	23 37.3	18 21.6	11 00.2	29 30.0	11 12.5	19 55.1
17 W	17 42 49	25 07 04	27 52 20	4♎40 06	19 53.9	12R 33.6	25 20.4	0♈32.7	23 28.0	18 25.0	10 55.6	29 31.9	11 14.2	19 57.4
18 Th	17 46 45	26 08 08	11♎33 30	18 32 40	19 55.2	12 30.0	26 34.5	1 07.6	23 18.2	18 28.2	10 50.9	29 33.9	11 15.9	19 59.6
19 F	17 50 42	27 09 14	25 37 37	2♏48 16	19 56.7	12 15.1	27 48.7	1 42.6	23 08.2	18 31.3	10 46.2	29 35.8	11 17.6	20 01.9
20 Sa	17 54 39	28 10 20	10♏04 20	17 25 27	19R 57.6	11 48.5	29 02.8	2 17.8	22 57.8	18 34.1	10 41.4	29 37.8	11 19.4	20 04.2
21 Su	17 58 35	29 11 27	24 51 01	2♐20 17	19 57.0	11 10.3	0♒16.9	2 53.0	22 47.1	18 36.8	10 36.6	29 39.9	11 21.2	20 06.4
22 M	18 02 32	0♑12 34	9♐52 20	17 26 07	19 54.5	10 20.8	1 30.9	3 28.4	22 36.0	18 39.3	10 31.8	29 42.0	11 23.0	20 08.7
23 Tu	18 06 28	1 13 43	25 00 27	2♑34 07	19 50.0	9 20.9	2 44.9	4 03.9	22 24.7	18 41.5	10 27.0	29 44.2	11 24.8	20 11.0
24 W	18 10 25	2 14 52	10♑05 50	17 34 25	19 43.7	8 12.1	3 59.0	4 39.6	22 13.0	18 43.7	10 22.1	29 46.3	11 26.7	20 13.2
25 Th	18 14 21	3 16 01	24 58 45	2♒17 50	19 36.6	6 56.3	5 12.9	5 15.3	22 01.1	18 45.6	10 17.2	29 48.6	11 28.6	20 15.4
26 F	18 18 18	4 17 10	9♒30 52	16 37 15	19 29.5	5 35.9	6 26.9	5 51.1	21 48.9	18 47.3	10 12.3	29 50.8	11 30.5	20 17.7
27 Sa	18 22 15	5 18 19	23 36 33	0♓28 34	19 23.3	4 13.6	7 40.8	6 27.1	21 36.4	18 48.8	10 07.4	29 53.1	11 32.4	20 19.9
28 Su	18 26 11	6 19 28	7♓13 16	13 50 49	19 18.7	2 52.2	8 54.7	7 03.1	21 23.8	18 50.2	10 02.4	29 55.5	11 34.3	20 22.1
29 M	18 30 08	7 20 37	20 21 30	26 45 44	19D 16.2	1 34.2	10 08.5	7 39.2	21 10.9	18 51.3	9 57.5	29 57.9	11 36.3	20 24.3
30 Tu	18 34 04	8 21 46	3♈04 01	9♈16 55	19 15.5	0 22.1	11 22.3	8 15.5	20 57.7	18 52.3	9 52.5	0♓00.3	11 38.2	20 26.5
31 W	18 38 01	9 22 55	15 25 05	21 29 10	19 16.2	29♐17.6	12 36.1	8 51.8	20 44.4	18 53.0	9 47.6	0 02.7	11 40.2	20 28.7

Astro Data	Dy Hr Mn
♃⚹♄	1 17:13
☽0N	5 21:12
♅D	8 12:44
☽0S	20 9:40
⚳R	24 2:33
☽0N	3 3:00
♄⚻♆	14 12:48
☿R	17 16:02
☽0S	17 17:56
♂0N	17 19:18
☽0N	30 9:20

Planet Ingress		Dy Hr Mn
♀	♐	2 21:42
☿	♐	12 7:19
☉	♐	22 17:43
♀	♑	27 1:07
☿	♑	2 21:34
♂	♈	16 13:24
♀	♒	21 6:32
☉	♑	22 7:04
♅	♓	30 9:14
☿	♐R	30 19:52

Last Aspect Dy Hr Mn			☽ Ingress	Dy Hr Mn
2 19:40	♀	□	♓	2 19:52
4 6:36	♇	□	♈	5 5:02
7 14:16	♅	⚹	♉	7 16:29
10 3:00	♅	□	♊	10 5:14
12 15:57	♅	△	♋	12 18:10
14 13:39	☉	△	♌	15 5:48
17 12:38	♅	☍	♍	17 14:36
19 14:15	☉	⚹	♎	19 19:42
21 19:44	♅	△	♏	21 21:24
23 19:28	♅	□	♐	23 21:03
25 18:58	♅	⚹	♑	25 20:31
27 3:52	♂	⚹	♒	27 21:48
30 0:46	♅	☌	♓	30 2:25

Last Aspect Dy Hr Mn			☽ Ingress	Dy Hr Mn
2 9:39	☿	□	♈	2 10:56
4 20:52	♅	⚹	♉	4 22:30
7 9:55	♅	□	♊	7 11:26
9 22:48	♅	△	♋	10 0:11
12 6:53	♂	△	♌	12 11:40
14 20:05	♅	☍	♍	14 21:07
16 17:49	♀	△	♎	17 3:46
19 6:39	♅	△	♏	19 7:20
21 7:43	♅	□	♐	21 8:16
23 7:29	♅	⚹	♑	23 7:55
24 13:52	♃	△	♒	25 8:13
27 10:58	♅	☌	♓	27 11:10
29 0:03	♇	□	♈	29 18:08

☽ Phases & Eclipses Dy Hr Mn	
1 4:25	☽ 8♒20
9 1:13	○ 16♉13
9 1:19	• T 1.018
17 4:15	☾ 24♌23
23 22:59	● 1♐14
23 22:49:16	• T 01'58"
30 17:16	☽ 8♓05
8 20:37	○ 16♊20
16 17:42	☾ 24♍21
23 9:43	● 1♑08
30 10:03	☽ 8♈17

Astro Data

1 November 2003
Julian Day # 37925
SVP 5♓12'37"
GC 26♐53.6 ⚴ 14♈19.1R
Eris 19♈53.4R ⚵ 1♐30.0
⚷ 13♑39.0 ⚶ 3♐45.6
☽ Mean ☊ 20♉54.2

1 December 2003
Julian Day # 37955
SVP 5♓12'32"
GC 26♐53.6 ⚴ 9♈25.3R
Eris 19♈38.8R ⚵ 11♐44.4
⚷ 15♑45.0 ⚶ 19♐48.0
☽ Mean ☊ 19♉18.9

LONGITUDE — January 2004

Day	Sid.Time	☉	0 hr ☽	Noon☽	True☊	☿	♀	♂	⚳	♃	♄	♅	♆	♇
1 Th	18 41 57	10♑24 04	27♈29 49	3♉27 42	19♉17.5	28♐22.1	13♒49.8	9♈28.2	20♋31.0	18♍53.6	9♋42.6	0♓05.2	11♒42.2	20♐30.9
2 F	18 45 54	11 25 13	9♉23 29	15 17 46	19R 18.5	27R 36.5	15 03.5	10 04.7	20R 17.3	18 54.0	9R 37.7	0 07.7	11 44.2	20 33.0
3 Sa	18 49 50	12 26 22	21 11 10	27 04 15	19 18.2	27 01.3	16 17.2	10 41.2	20 03.6	18R 54.2	9 32.7	0 10.3	11 46.3	20 35.2
4 Su	18 53 47	13 27 30	2♊57 30	8♊51 24	19 15.9	26 36.3	17 30.8	11 17.9	19 49.7	18 54.2	9 27.8	0 12.9	11 48.3	20 37.3
5 M	18 57 44	14 28 39	14 46 22	20 42 46	19 11.2	26 21.5	18 44.3	11 54.6	19 35.7	18 54.0	9 22.9	0 15.5	11 50.4	20 39.5
6 Tu	19 01 40	15 29 47	26 40 55	2♋41 05	19 03.9	26D 16.2	19 57.8	12 31.4	19 21.6	18 53.6	9 18.0	0 18.2	11 52.5	20 41.6
7 W	19 05 37	16 30 55	8♋43 28	14 48 14	18 54.3	26 19.9	21 11.3	13 08.2	19 07.5	18 53.0	9 13.1	0 20.9	11 54.6	20 43.7
8 Th	19 09 33	17 32 03	20 55 31	27 05 24	18 43.2	26 32.0	22 24.7	13 45.1	18 53.3	18 52.3	9 08.2	0 23.6	11 56.7	20 45.8
9 F	19 13 30	18 33 11	3♌17 57	9♌33 14	18 31.5	26 51.8	23 38.0	14 22.1	18 39.0	18 51.3	9 03.3	0 26.4	11 58.8	20 47.9
10 Sa	19 17 26	19 34 18	15 51 15	22 12 04	18 20.3	27 18.4	24 51.3	14 59.1	18 24.8	18 50.1	8 58.5	0 29.2	12 00.9	20 49.9
11 Su	19 21 23	20 35 26	28 35 42	5♍02 14	18 10.6	27 51.4	26 04.6	15 36.2	18 10.5	18 48.8	8 53.7	0 32.0	12 03.1	20 52.0
12 M	19 25 19	21 36 33	11♍31 42	18 04 14	18 03.3	28 30.0	27 17.8	16 13.4	17 56.3	18 47.2	8 48.9	0 34.8	12 05.2	20 54.0
13 Tu	19 29 16	22 37 40	24 39 57	1♎18 59	17 58.7	29 13.7	28 30.9	16 50.6	17 42.1	18 45.5	8 44.2	0 37.7	12 07.4	20 56.0
14 W	19 33 13	23 38 48	8♎01 30	14 47 42	17D 56.6	0♑02.0	29 44.0	17 27.9	17 28.0	18 43.6	8 39.4	0 40.6	12 09.6	20 58.0
15 Th	19 37 09	24 39 55	21 37 43	28 31 44	17 56.3	0 54.4	0♓57.0	18 05.2	17 13.9	18 41.5	8 34.8	0 43.5	12 11.8	21 00.0
16 F	19 41 06	25 41 02	5♏29 51	12♏32 06	17R 56.7	1 50.5	2 10.0	18 42.6	16 59.9	18 39.2	8 30.1	0 46.5	12 14.0	21 02.0
17 Sa	19 45 02	26 42 09	19 38 30	26 48 53	17 56.5	2 49.8	3 22.9	19 20.0	16 46.1	18 36.7	8 25.6	0 49.5	12 16.2	21 03.9
18 Su	19 48 59	27 43 16	4♐03 02	11♐20 32	17 54.5	3 52.2	4 35.7	19 57.5	16 32.3	18 34.0	8 21.0	0 52.5	12 18.4	21 05.9
19 M	19 52 55	28 44 22	18 40 52	26 03 21	17 49.8	4 57.2	5 48.5	20 35.0	16 18.8	18 31.1	8 16.5	0 55.5	12 20.6	21 07.8
20 Tu	19 56 52	29 45 28	3♑27 10	10♑51 24	17 42.3	6 04.6	7 01.3	21 12.6	16 05.3	18 28.0	8 12.1	0 58.6	12 22.8	21 09.7
21 W	20 00 48	0♒46 34	18 15 00	25 36 58	17 32.1	7 14.2	8 13.9	21 50.3	15 52.1	18 24.8	8 07.7	1 01.7	12 25.1	21 11.6
22 Th	20 04 45	1 47 39	2♒56 12	10♒11 44	17 20.5	8 25.7	9 26.5	22 27.9	15 39.1	18 21.4	8 03.4	1 04.8	12 27.3	21 13.4
23 F	20 08 42	2 48 43	17 22 38	24 28 10	17 08.5	9 39.1	10 39.0	23 05.7	15 26.3	18 17.8	7 59.1	1 07.9	12 29.6	21 15.2
24 Sa	20 12 38	3 49 46	1♓27 41	8♓20 46	16 57.5	10 54.2	11 51.5	23 43.4	15 13.7	18 14.0	7 54.9	1 11.1	12 31.8	21 17.1
25 Su	20 16 35	4 50 49	15 07 09	21 46 47	16 48.6	12 10.7	13 03.8	24 21.2	15 01.3	18 10.0	7 50.7	1 14.2	12 34.1	21 18.8
26 M	20 20 31	5 51 50	28 19 44	4♈46 15	16 42.4	13 28.7	14 16.1	24 59.1	14 49.3	18 05.9	7 46.7	1 17.4	12 36.4	21 20.6
27 Tu	20 24 28	6 52 50	11♈06 41	17 21 33	16 38.8	14 48.0	15 28.3	25 37.0	14 37.5	18 01.6	7 42.6	1 20.6	12 38.6	21 22.3
28 W	20 28 24	7 53 49	23 31 22	29 36 46	16D 37.4	16 08.5	16 40.4	26 14.9	14 26.0	17 57.1	7 38.7	1 23.9	12 40.9	21 24.1
29 Th	20 32 21	8 54 47	5♉38 26	11♉37 03	16R 37.2	17 30.2	17 52.5	26 52.9	14 14.8	17 52.5	7 34.8	1 27.1	12 43.2	21 25.8
30 F	20 36 17	9 55 44	17 33 19	23 27 57	16 37.1	18 52.9	19 04.4	27 30.8	14 03.9	17 47.7	7 31.0	1 30.4	12 45.5	21 27.4
31 Sa	20 40 14	10 56 40	29 21 39	5♊15 06	16 36.0	20 16.7	20 16.2	28 08.9	13 53.4	17 42.7	7 27.3	1 33.7	12 47.7	21 29.1

LONGITUDE — February 2004

Day	Sid.Time	☉	0 hr ☽	Noon☽	True☊	☿	♀	♂	⚳	♃	♄	♅	♆	♇
1 Su	20 44 11	11♒57 34	11♊08 55	17♊03 43	16♉32.8	21♑41.4	21♓28.0	28♈46.9	13♋43.2	17♍37.6	7♋23.7	1♓37.0	12♒50.0	21♐30.7
2 M	20 48 07	12 58 27	23 00 04	28 58 27	16R 26.9	23 07.1	22 39.6	29 25.0	13R 33.3	17R 32.4	7R 20.2	1 40.3	12 52.2	21 32.3
3 Tu	20 52 04	13 59 19	4♋59 19	11♋03 02	16 18.0	24 33.7	23 51.1	0♉03.1	13 23.8	17 27.0	7 16.7	1 43.6	12 54.6	21 33.9
4 W	20 56 00	15 00 10	17 09 55	23 20 11	16 06.6	26 01.2	25 02.6	0 41.2	13 14.7	17 21.4	7 13.3	1 46.9	12 56.9	21 35.5
5 Th	20 59 57	16 00 59	29 34 00	5♌51 26	15 53.3	27 29.6	26 13.9	1 19.3	13 05.9	17 15.7	7 10.0	1 50.3	12 59.1	21 37.0
6 F	21 03 53	17 01 47	12♌12 30	18 37 08	15 39.2	28 58.8	27 25.1	1 57.5	12 57.5	17 09.9	7 06.8	1 53.7	13 01.4	21 38.5
7 Sa	21 07 50	18 02 34	25 05 16	1♍36 42	15 25.6	0♒28.9	28 36.2	2 35.6	12 49.5	17 03.9	7 03.7	1 57.0	13 03.7	21 40.0
8 Su	21 11 46	19 03 20	8♍11 17	14 48 48	15 13.7	1 59.7	29 47.2	3 13.8	12 41.9	16 57.8	7 00.6	2 00.4	13 06.0	21 41.4
9 M	21 15 43	20 04 04	21 29 04	28 11 54	15 04.5	3 31.5	0♈58.0	3 52.0	12 34.7	16 51.5	6 57.7	2 03.8	13 08.2	21 42.8
10 Tu	21 19 40	21 04 48	4♎57 06	11♎44 33	14 58.3	5 04.0	2 08.8	4 30.3	12 27.9	16 45.2	6 54.8	2 07.2	13 10.5	21 44.2
11 W	21 23 36	22 05 30	18 34 09	25 25 49	14 55.1	6 37.3	3 19.4	5 08.5	12 21.6	16 38.7	6 52.1	2 10.6	13 12.8	21 45.6
12 Th	21 27 33	23 06 12	2♏19 32	9♏15 16	14D 54.1	8 11.5	4 29.9	5 46.8	12 15.6	16 32.1	6 49.4	2 14.0	13 15.0	21 46.9
13 F	21 31 29	24 06 52	16 13 03	23 12 51	14R 54.1	9 46.6	5 40.3	6 25.0	12 10.0	16 25.4	6 46.8	2 17.5	13 17.3	21 48.2
14 Sa	21 35 26	25 07 31	0♐14 41	7♐18 28	14 53.7	11 22.4	6 50.5	7 03.3	12 04.9	16 18.6	6 44.4	2 20.9	13 19.5	21 49.5
15 Su	21 39 22	26 08 10	14 24 07	21 31 26	14 51.6	12 59.1	8 00.7	7 41.7	12 00.2	16 11.6	6 42.0	2 24.3	13 21.7	21 50.7
16 M	21 43 19	27 08 47	28 40 11	5♑49 59	14 47.1	14 36.7	9 10.6	8 20.0	11 56.0	16 04.6	6 39.8	2 27.8	13 24.0	21 52.0
17 Tu	21 47 15	28 09 23	13♑00 23	20 10 52	14 39.6	16 15.2	10 20.5	8 58.3	11 52.1	15 57.5	6 37.6	2 31.2	13 26.2	21 53.2
18 W	21 51 12	29 09 58	27 20 47	4♒29 29	14 29.6	17 54.5	11 30.2	9 36.7	11 48.7	15 50.3	6 35.6	2 34.7	13 28.4	21 54.3
19 Th	21 55 09	0♓10 31	11♒36 14	18 40 19	14 17.9	19 34.7	12 39.8	10 15.1	11 45.8	15 43.0	6 33.6	2 38.2	13 30.6	21 55.5
20 F	21 59 05	1 11 02	25 41 03	2♓37 47	14 05.8	21 15.9	13 49.2	10 53.5	11 43.2	15 35.7	6 31.8	2 41.6	13 32.8	21 56.6
21 Sa	22 03 02	2 11 32	9♓29 59	16 17 11	13 54.5	22 57.9	14 58.5	11 31.9	11 41.2	15 28.2	6 30.0	2 45.1	13 35.0	21 57.6
22 Su	22 06 58	3 12 01	22 59 03	29 35 26	13 45.1	24 40.9	16 07.6	12 10.3	11 39.5	15 20.7	6 28.4	2 48.5	13 37.2	21 58.7
23 M	22 10 55	4 12 27	6♈06 13	12♈31 31	13 38.3	26 24.9	17 16.5	12 48.7	11 38.3	15 13.2	6 26.9	2 52.0	13 39.4	21 59.7
24 Tu	22 14 51	5 12 52	18 51 29	25 06 26	13 34.3	28 09.8	18 25.3	13 27.1	11 37.5	15 05.6	6 25.5	2 55.4	13 41.5	22 00.7
25 W	22 18 48	6 13 15	1♉16 45	7♉22 56	13D 32.6	29 55.7	19 33.9	14 05.6	11D 37.2	14 57.9	6 24.2	2 58.9	13 43.7	22 01.6
26 Th	22 22 44	7 13 36	13 25 30	19 25 03	13 32.6	1♓42.6	20 42.3	14 44.0	11 37.3	14 50.2	6 23.0	3 02.3	13 45.8	22 02.5
27 F	22 26 41	8 13 55	25 22 15	1♊17 45	13R 33.1	3 30.4	21 50.6	15 22.5	11 37.8	14 42.5	6 21.9	3 05.8	13 47.9	22 03.4
28 Sa	22 30 38	9 14 12	7♊12 14	13 06 24	13 33.2	5 19.3	22 58.7	16 00.9	11 38.8	14 34.7	6 20.9	3 09.2	13 50.1	22 04.2
29 Su	22 34 34	10 14 27	19 00 55	24 56 29	13 31.0	7 00.1	24 06.5	16 39.4	11 40.2	14 26.9	6 20.0	3 12.7	13 52.2	22 05.1

Astro Data	Dy Hr Mn
♃ R	3 23:57
☿ D	6 13:44
☽ 0S	13 23:17
☽ 0N	26 16:58
♀0N	9 14:45
☽ 0S	10 3:53
☽ 0N	23 1:39
⚳ D	25 18:38

Planet Ingress		Dy Hr Mn
☿	♑	14 11:02
♀	♓	14 17:16
☉	♒	20 17:42
♂	♉	3 10:04
☿	♒	7 4:20
♀	♈	8 16:20
☉	♓	19 7:50
☿	♓	25 12:58

Last Aspect Dy Hr Mn			☽ Ingress	Dy Hr Mn
1 2:27	☿	△	♉	1 5:02
2 19:21	♃	△	♊	3 17:58
5 23:14	☿	☍	♋	6 6:39
7 20:00	♃	⚹	♌	8 17:38
10 22:00	☿	△	♍	11 2:37
13 8:01	☿	□	♎	13 9:38
15 4:46	☉	□	♏	15 14:33
17 11:48	☉	⚹	♐	17 17:18
19 3:58	♇	☌	♑	19 18:24
21 5:34	♂	□	♒	21 19:11
23 9:33	♂	⚹	♓	23 21:29
25 11:09	♇	□	♈	26 3:06
28 4:59	♂	☌	♉	28 12:46
30 2:04	♀	⚹	♊	31 1:18

Last Aspect Dy Hr Mn			☽ Ingress	Dy Hr Mn
2 12:56	♂	⚹	♋	2 14:03
4 17:53	☿	☍	♌	5 0:50
6 17:38	♇	△	♍	7 9:03
9 0:23	♇	□	♎	9 15:12
11 5:42	☉	△	♏	11 19:58
13 13:40	☉	□	♐	13 23:35
15 20:20	☉	⚹	♑	16 2:14
17 5:00	♃	△	♒	18 4:27
19 17:34	♇	⚹	♓	20 7:27
21 22:10	♇	□	♈	22 12:45
24 18:55	☿	⚹	♉	24 21:30
26 2:55	♃	△	♊	27 9:22
29 10:08	♀	⚹	♋	29 22:12

☽ Phases & Eclipses Dy Hr Mn	
7 15:40	○ 16♋40
15 4:46	☾ 24♎21
21 21:05	● 1♒10
29 6:03	☽ 8♉40
6 8:47	○ 16♌54
13 13:40	☾ 24♏11
20 9:18	● 1♓04
28 3:24	☽ 8♊53

Astro Data

1 January 2004
Julian Day # 37986
SVP 5♓12'26"
GC 26♐53.7 ⚴ 11♈56.4
Eris 19♈31.6R ⚵ 22♐31.8
⚷ 18♑31.2 ⚶ 6♑31.0
☽ Mean ☊ 17♉40.5

1 February 2004
Julian Day # 38017
SVP 5♓12'21"
GC 26♐53.8 ⚴ 20♈34.7
Eris 19♈34.8 ⚵ 2♑59.1
⚷ 21♑24.7 ⚶ 23♑03.0
☽ Mean ☊ 16♉02.0

March 2004

LONGITUDE

Day	Sid.Time	☉	0 hr ☽	Noon☽	True☊	☿	♀	♂	⚳	♃	♄	♅	♆	♇
1 M	22 38 31	11♓14 40	0♋53 43	6♋53 14	13♉28.5	9♓00.0	25♈14.2	17♉17.9	11♋42.0	14♍19.1	6♋19.3	3♓16.1	13♒54.2	22♐05.9
2 Tu	22 42 27	12 14 51	12 55 36	19 01 20	13R 22.7	10 51.8	26 21.7	17 56.3	11 44.2	14R 11.2	6R 18.7	3 19.5	13 56.3	22 06.6
3 W	22 46 24	13 15 00	25 10 52	1♌24 34	13 14.7	12 44.5	27 28.9	18 34.8	11 46.8	14 03.4	6 18.1	3 23.0	13 58.4	22 07.3
4 Th	22 50 20	14 15 07	7♌42 44	14 05 32	13 04.9	14 38.2	28 36.0	19 13.3	11 49.9	13 55.5	6 17.7	3 26.4	14 00.4	22 08.0
5 F	22 54 17	15 15 12	20 33 05	27 05 22	12 54.4	16 32.7	29 42.8	19 51.7	11 53.3	13 47.7	6 17.4	3 29.8	14 02.4	22 08.7
6 Sa	22 58 13	16 15 15	3♍42 18	10♍23 41	12 44.2	18 28.0	0♉49.4	20 30.2	11 57.2	13 39.9	6 17.2	3 33.2	14 04.4	22 09.3
7 Su	23 02 10	17 15 16	17 09 14	23 58 36	12 35.3	20 24.1	1 55.7	21 08.6	12 01.5	13 32.0	6D 17.2	3 36.6	14 06.4	22 09.9
8 M	23 06 07	18 15 15	0♎51 24	7♎47 11	12 28.5	22 20.8	3 01.8	21 47.1	12 06.1	13 24.2	6 17.2	3 39.9	14 08.4	22 10.4
9 Tu	23 10 03	19 15 13	14 45 29	21 45 51	12 24.2	24 18.0	4 07.7	22 25.6	12 11.2	13 16.4	6 17.3	3 43.3	14 10.4	22 11.0
10 W	23 14 00	20 15 08	28 47 51	5♏51 05	12D 22.3	26 15.6	5 13.3	23 04.0	12 16.6	13 08.7	6 17.6	3 46.7	14 12.3	22 11.4
11 Th	23 17 56	21 15 02	12♏55 11	19 59 49	12 22.4	28 13.3	6 18.7	23 42.5	12 22.4	13 01.0	6 18.0	3 50.0	14 14.2	22 11.9
12 F	23 21 53	22 14 55	27 04 42	4♐09 38	12 23.3	0♈11.1	7 23.8	24 20.9	12 28.6	12 53.3	6 18.5	3 53.3	14 16.1	22 12.3
13 Sa	23 25 49	23 14 46	11♐14 24	18 18 49	12R 24.2	2 08.6	8 28.7	24 59.4	12 35.2	12 45.7	6 19.1	3 56.7	14 18.0	22 12.7
14 Su	23 29 46	24 14 35	25 22 44	2♑26 01	12 24.0	4 05.6	9 33.2	25 37.8	12 42.1	12 38.1	6 19.8	4 00.0	14 19.9	22 13.1
15 M	23 33 42	25 14 23	9♑28 27	16 29 53	12 22.0	6 01.7	10 37.5	26 16.3	12 49.4	12 30.5	6 20.6	4 03.2	14 21.7	22 13.4
16 Tu	23 37 39	26 14 08	23 30 06	0♒28 51	12 18.0	7 56.6	11 41.5	26 54.7	12 57.1	12 23.1	6 21.5	4 06.5	14 23.5	22 13.7
17 W	23 41 36	27 13 53	7♒25 52	14 20 50	12 12.1	9 50.0	12 45.3	27 33.2	13 05.1	12 15.7	6 22.6	4 09.8	14 25.3	22 14.0
18 Th	23 45 32	28 13 35	21 13 27	28 03 23	12 04.9	11 41.4	13 48.7	28 11.6	13 13.5	12 08.3	6 23.7	4 13.0	14 27.1	22 14.2
19 F	23 49 29	29 13 15	4♓50 17	11♓33 52	11 57.3	13 30.4	14 51.8	28 50.1	13 22.2	12 01.1	6 25.0	4 16.2	14 28.9	22 14.4
20 Sa	23 53 25	0♈12 54	18 13 51	24 49 59	11 50.2	15 16.5	15 54.6	29 28.5	13 31.3	11 53.9	6 26.3	4 19.4	14 30.6	22 14.5
21 Su	23 57 22	1 12 30	1♈22 05	7♈50 01	11 44.4	16 59.3	16 57.0	0♊07.0	13 40.7	11 46.8	6 27.8	4 22.6	14 32.3	22 14.6
22 M	0 01 18	2 12 04	14 13 46	20 33 20	11 40.4	18 38.4	17 59.1	0 45.4	13 50.4	11 39.8	6 29.4	4 25.8	14 34.0	22 14.7
23 Tu	0 05 15	3 11 37	26 48 49	3♉00 24	11D 38.3	20 13.2	19 00.9	1 23.8	14 00.5	11 32.9	6 31.1	4 28.9	14 35.7	22 14.8
24 W	0 09 11	4 11 07	9♉08 21	15 12 58	11 38.0	21 43.4	20 02.3	2 02.3	14 10.9	11 26.2	6 32.9	4 32.0	14 37.3	22R 14.8
25 Th	0 13 08	5 10 35	21 14 39	27 13 49	11 38.9	23 08.5	21 03.3	2 40.7	14 21.6	11 19.5	6 34.8	4 35.1	14 39.0	22 14.8
26 F	0 17 05	6 10 00	3♊10 59	9♊06 41	11 40.6	24 28.2	22 03.9	3 19.1	14 32.6	11 12.9	6 36.9	4 38.2	14 40.6	22 14.7
27 Sa	0 21 01	7 09 24	15 01 29	20 55 59	11 42.3	25 42.1	23 04.1	3 57.5	14 44.0	11 06.4	6 39.0	4 41.3	14 42.1	22 14.7
28 Su	0 24 58	8 08 45	26 50 49	2♋46 35	11R 43.4	26 49.9	24 03.9	4 35.9	14 55.6	11 00.1	6 41.2	4 44.3	14 43.7	22 14.6
29 M	0 28 54	9 08 04	8♋43 57	14 43 33	11 43.4	27 51.4	25 03.3	5 14.3	15 07.6	10 53.9	6 43.6	4 47.3	14 45.2	22 14.4
30 Tu	0 32 51	10 07 21	20 45 58	26 51 49	11 42.0	28 46.3	26 02.2	5 52.7	15 19.8	10 47.8	6 46.0	4 50.3	14 46.7	22 14.2
31 W	0 36 47	11 06 35	3♌01 38	9♌15 56	11 39.3	29 34.4	27 00.6	6 31.1	15 32.4	10 41.8	6 48.6	4 53.2	14 48.2	22 14.0

April 2004

LONGITUDE

Day	Sid.Time	☉	0 hr ☽	Noon☽	True☊	☿	♀	♂	⚳	♃	♄	♅	♆	♇
1 Th	0 40 44	12♈05 47	15♌35 08	21♌59 36	11♉35.4	0♉15.5	27♉58.6	7♊09.5	15♋45.2	10♍36.0	6♋51.2	4♓56.2	14♒49.6	22♐13.8
2 F	0 44 40	13 04 56	28 29 37	5♍05 19	11R 31.0	0 49.6	28 56.1	7 47.9	15 58.3	10R 30.3	6 54.0	4 59.1	14 51.0	22R 13.5
3 Sa	0 48 37	14 04 04	11♍46 47	18 33 57	11 26.6	1 16.6	29 53.0	8 26.2	16 11.6	10 24.8	6 56.8	5 01.9	14 52.4	22 13.2
4 Su	0 52 34	15 03 09	25 26 37	2♎24 28	11 22.8	1 36.5	0♊49.5	9 04.6	16 25.3	10 19.4	6 59.8	5 04.8	14 53.8	22 12.9
5 M	0 56 30	16 02 12	9♎27 05	16 33 56	11 20.0	1 49.3	1 45.4	9 42.9	16 39.2	10 14.1	7 02.8	5 07.6	14 55.1	22 12.5
6 Tu	1 00 27	17 01 13	23 44 24	0♏57 47	11D 18.5	1R 55.1	2 40.7	10 21.2	16 53.3	10 09.0	7 06.0	5 10.4	14 56.4	22 12.1
7 W	1 04 23	18 00 12	8♏13 22	15 30 24	11 18.2	1 54.1	3 35.4	10 59.5	17 07.8	10 04.1	7 09.2	5 13.1	14 57.7	22 11.7
8 Th	1 08 20	18 59 09	22 48 08	0♐05 52	11 18.9	1 46.6	4 29.6	11 37.8	17 22.4	9 59.3	7 12.5	5 15.9	14 58.9	22 11.2
9 F	1 12 16	19 58 05	7♐22 55	14 38 41	11 20.2	1 32.8	5 23.1	12 16.1	17 37.3	9 54.6	7 16.0	5 18.6	15 00.2	22 10.7
10 Sa	1 16 13	20 56 59	21 52 39	29 04 20	11 21.5	1 13.2	6 16.0	12 54.4	17 52.5	9 50.2	7 19.5	5 21.2	15 01.4	22 10.2
11 Su	1 20 09	21 55 51	6♑13 23	13♑19 29	11R 22.4	0 48.2	7 08.2	13 32.7	18 07.9	9 45.8	7 23.1	5 23.9	15 02.5	22 09.7
12 M	1 24 06	22 54 41	20 22 25	27 21 59	11 22.6	0 18.4	7 59.7	14 11.0	18 23.6	9 41.7	7 26.9	5 26.5	15 03.7	22 09.1
13 Tu	1 28 03	23 53 30	4♒18 06	11♒10 40	11 21.9	29♈44.5	8 50.6	14 49.2	18 39.4	9 37.7	7 30.7	5 29.1	15 04.8	22 08.5
14 W	1 31 59	24 52 17	17 59 39	24 45 02	11 20.4	29 07.2	9 40.7	15 27.5	18 55.5	9 33.9	7 34.6	5 31.6	15 05.9	22 07.8
15 Th	1 35 56	25 51 02	1♓26 49	8♓05 01	11 18.4	28 27.1	10 30.0	16 05.8	19 11.9	9 30.2	7 38.6	5 34.1	15 06.9	22 07.1
16 F	1 39 52	26 49 45	14 39 41	21 10 50	11 16.3	27 45.1	11 18.6	16 44.0	19 28.4	9 26.7	7 42.6	5 36.6	15 07.9	22 06.4
17 Sa	1 43 49	27 48 27	27 38 30	4♈02 46	11 14.4	27 02.1	12 06.3	17 22.2	19 45.2	9 23.4	7 46.8	5 39.0	15 08.9	22 05.7
18 Su	1 47 45	28 47 06	10♈23 42	16 41 22	11 12.9	26 18.8	12 53.2	18 00.5	20 02.2	9 20.3	7 51.1	5 41.4	15 09.9	22 05.0
19 M	1 51 42	29 45 44	22 55 52	29 07 20	11D 12.0	25 36.0	13 39.2	18 38.7	20 19.4	9 17.3	7 55.4	5 43.8	15 10.8	22 04.2
20 Tu	1 55 38	0♉44 20	5♉15 55	11♉21 46	11 11.7	24 54.5	14 24.3	19 16.9	20 36.8	9 14.6	7 59.9	5 46.1	15 11.7	22 03.4
21 W	1 59 35	1 42 54	17 25 07	23 26 12	11 11.9	24 14.9	15 08.5	19 55.1	20 54.4	9 12.0	8 04.4	5 48.4	15 12.5	22 02.5
22 Th	2 03 31	2 41 26	29 25 17	5♊22 41	11 12.6	23 38.1	15 51.6	20 33.3	21 12.2	9 09.6	8 09.0	5 50.6	15 13.4	22 01.7
23 F	2 07 28	3 39 56	11♊18 45	17 13 52	11 13.4	23 04.3	16 33.8	21 11.5	21 30.2	9 07.3	8 13.7	5 52.9	15 14.2	22 00.8
24 Sa	2 11 25	4 38 24	23 08 27	29 02 58	11 14.1	22 34.3	17 14.8	21 49.7	21 48.4	9 05.3	8 18.4	5 55.0	15 14.9	21 59.8
25 Su	2 15 21	5 36 50	4♋57 53	10♋53 43	11 14.8	22 08.3	17 54.8	22 27.9	22 06.8	9 03.4	8 23.3	5 57.2	15 15.7	21 58.9
26 M	2 19 18	6 35 14	16 51 02	22 50 21	11 15.2	21 46.6	18 33.6	23 06.0	22 25.3	9 01.7	8 28.2	5 59.3	15 16.4	21 57.9
27 Tu	2 23 14	7 33 36	28 52 14	4♌57 17	11R 15.3	21 29.5	19 11.2	23 44.2	22 44.1	9 00.2	8 33.2	6 01.3	15 17.0	21 56.9
28 W	2 27 11	8 31 55	11♌06 03	17 19 05	11 15.3	21 17.2	19 47.5	24 22.3	23 03.0	8 58.9	8 38.3	6 03.3	15 17.7	21 55.9
29 Th	2 31 07	9 30 13	23 36 53	29 59 58	11 15.1	21 09.6	20 22.5	25 00.5	23 22.1	8 57.8	8 43.4	6 05.3	15 18.3	21 54.9
30 F	2 35 04	10 28 28	6♍28 45	13♍03 34	11D 15.0	21D 07.0	20 56.2	25 38.6	23 41.4	8 56.9	8 48.7	6 07.3	15 18.9	21 53.8

Astro Data	Planet Ingress	Last Aspect	☽ Ingress	Last Aspect	☽ Ingress	☽ Phases & Eclipses	Astro Data
Dy Hr Mn	Dy Hr Mn	Dy Hr Mn	Dy Hr Mn	Dy Hr Mn	Dy Hr Mn	Dy Hr Mn	1 March 2004
♃⊼♆ 4 0:12	♀ ♉ 5 18:12	3 3:42 ♀ □	♌ 3 9:18	1 23:56 ♀ □	♍ 2 2:45	6 23:14 ○ 16♍43	Julian Day # 38046
♄D 7 16:51	☿ ♈ 12 9:44	5 17:13 ♀ △	♍ 5 17:18	3 18:24 ♇ □	♎ 4 7:52	13 21:01 ☾ 23♐37	SVP 5♓12'17"
☽0S 8 10:26	☉ ♈ 20 6:49	7 8:49 ♇ □	♎ 7 22:31	5 21:26 ♇ ⚹	♏ 6 10:24	20 22:41 ● 0♈39	GC 26♐53.8 ⚴ 2♉19.0
☿0N 13 3:13	♂ ♊ 21 7:39	9 12:43 ♇ ⚹	♏ 10 2:03	7 11:06 ♆ □	♐ 8 11:50	28 23:48 ☽ 8♋38	Eris 19♈46.6 ⚵ 11♑52.3
☉0N 20 6:49		12 4:11 ☿ △	♐ 12 4:57	10 0:30 ♇ ☌	♑ 10 13:33		⚷ 23♑46.7 ⚶ 8♒02.7
☽0N 21 10:10	☿ ♉ 1 2:27	13 21:01 ☉ □	♑ 14 7:51	12 3:46 ☉ □	♒ 12 16:33	5 11:03 ○ 16♎00	☽ Mean ☊ 14♉29.9
♇R 24 15:09	♀ ♊ 3 14:57	16 5:34 ♂ △	♒ 16 11:10	14 19:27 ☿ ⚹	♓ 14 21:24	12 3:46 ☾ 22♑35	
	☿ ♈R 13 1:23	18 12:15 ♂ □	♓ 18 15:26	16 13:43 ♇ □	♈ 17 4:24	19 13:21 ● 29♈49	1 April 2004
☽0S 4 19:36	☉ ♉ 19 17:50	20 20:57 ♂ ⚹	♈ 20 21:29	19 13:21 ☉ ☌	♉ 19 13:43	19 13:34:01 ● P 0.737	Julian Day # 38077
☿R 6 20:28		22 15:14 ♇ △	♉ 23 6:10	20 19:36 ♅ □	♊ 22 1:10	27 17:32 ☽ 7♌47	SVP 5♓12'13"
☽0N 17 17:22		24 22:29 ♀ ☌	♊ 25 17:35	23 23:22 ☿ ⚹	♋ 24 13:56		GC 26♐53.9 ⚴ 17♉27.2
☿D 30 13:05		27 22:44 ☿ ⚹	♋ 28 6:23	26 9:56 ☿ □	♌ 27 2:14		Eris 20♈05.2 ⚵ 19♑34.3
		30 16:00 ☿ □	♌ 30 18:07	29 2:08 ♂ ⚹	♍ 29 12:00		⚷ 25♑31.3 ⚶ 23♒11.2
							☽ Mean ☊ 12♉51.3

LONGITUDE — May 2004

Day	Sid.Time	☉	0 hr ☽	Noon ☽	True ☊	☿	♀	♂	⚳	♃	♄	♅	♆	♇
1 Sa	2 39 00	11♉26 41	19♍44 41	26♍32 15	11♉15.0	21♈09.2	21♊28.5	26♊16.7	24♋00.9	8♍56.1	8♋54.0	6♓09.1	15♒19.4	21♐52.7
2 Su	2 42 57	12 24 53	3♎26 18	10♎26 44	11 15.1	21 16.2	21 59.3	26 54.8	24 20.5	8R55.5	8 59.3	6 11.0	15 19.9	21R51.6
3 M	2 46 54	13 23 02	17 33 16	24 45 30	11 15.2	21 28.0	22 28.6	27 32.9	24 40.2	8 55.1	9 04.8	6 12.8	15 20.4	21 50.5
4 Tu	2 50 50	14 21 10	2♏02 51	9♏24 37	11R15.3	21 44.3	22 56.3	28 11.0	25 00.2	8D54.9	9 10.3	6 14.6	15 20.8	21 49.3
5 W	2 54 47	15 19 16	16 49 58	24 17 56	11 15.2	22 05.2	23 22.4	28 49.0	25 20.3	8 54.9	9 15.9	6 16.3	15 21.2	21 48.1
6 Th	2 58 43	16 17 20	1♐47 30	9♐17 37	11 14.9	22 30.5	23 46.8	29 27.1	25 40.5	8 55.1	9 21.5	6 18.0	15 21.6	21 46.9
7 F	3 02 40	17 15 23	16 47 13	24 15 18	11 14.3	23 00.0	24 09.5	0♋05.1	26 00.9	8 55.4	9 27.3	6 19.6	15 22.0	21 45.7
8 Sa	3 06 36	18 13 25	1♑40 54	9♑03 12	11 13.6	23 33.6	24 30.4	0 43.2	26 21.4	8 55.9	9 33.1	6 21.2	15 22.3	21 44.5
9 Su	3 10 33	19 11 25	16 21 27	23 35 06	11 12.9	24 11.2	24 49.4	1 21.2	26 42.1	8 56.6	9 38.9	6 22.8	15 22.6	21 43.2
10 M	3 14 30	20 09 24	0♒43 41	7♒46 57	11D12.4	24 52.6	25 06.5	1 59.2	27 03.0	8 57.5	9 44.8	6 24.3	15 22.8	21 42.0
11 Tu	3 18 26	21 07 21	14 44 42	21 36 55	11 12.2	25 37.6	25 21.7	2 37.2	27 23.9	8 58.6	9 50.8	6 25.8	15 23.0	21 40.7
12 W	3 22 23	22 05 17	28 23 39	5♓05 03	11 12.4	26 26.2	25 34.8	3 15.3	27 45.0	8 59.8	9 56.8	6 27.2	15 23.2	21 39.3
13 Th	3 26 19	23 03 12	11♓41 20	18 12 46	11 13.1	27 18.1	25 45.8	3 53.3	28 06.3	9 01.2	10 02.9	6 28.5	15 23.4	21 38.0
14 F	3 30 16	24 01 06	24 39 38	1♈02 17	11 14.2	28 13.4	25 54.7	4 31.2	28 27.7	9 02.8	10 09.1	6 29.9	15 23.5	21 36.7
15 Sa	3 34 12	24 58 58	7♈21 01	13 36 10	11 15.3	29 11.8	26 01.4	5 09.2	28 49.2	9 04.6	10 15.3	6 31.2	15 23.5	21 35.3
16 Su	3 38 09	25 56 49	19 48 05	25 57 04	11 16.3	0♉13.3	26 05.9	5 47.2	29 10.8	9 06.6	10 21.6	6 32.4	15 23.6	21 33.9
17 M	3 42 05	26 54 39	2♉03 24	8♉07 25	11R16.8	1 17.8	26R08.1	6 25.2	29 32.6	9 08.7	10 27.9	6 33.6	15R23.6	21 32.5
18 Tu	3 46 02	27 52 27	14 09 21	20 09 29	11 16.6	2 25.1	26 07.9	7 03.2	29 54.5	9 11.0	10 34.3	6 34.7	15 23.6	21 31.1
19 W	3 49 58	28 50 14	26 08 03	2♊05 20	11 15.6	3 35.3	26 05.4	7 41.1	0♌16.5	9 13.5	10 40.8	6 35.8	15 23.5	21 29.7
20 Th	3 53 55	29 48 00	8♊01 33	13 56 59	11 13.6	4 48.2	26 00.5	8 19.1	0 38.7	9 16.2	10 47.3	6 36.9	15 23.5	21 28.2
21 F	3 57 52	0♊45 44	19 51 52	25 46 29	11 10.9	6 03.7	25 53.2	8 57.0	1 01.0	9 19.0	10 53.8	6 37.9	15 23.4	21 26.8
22 Sa	4 01 48	1 43 27	1♋41 08	7♋36 06	11 07.6	7 21.9	25 43.4	9 35.0	1 23.4	9 22.0	11 00.4	6 38.8	15 23.2	21 25.3
23 Su	4 05 45	2 41 09	13 31 46	19 28 27	11 04.2	8 42.7	25 31.2	10 12.9	1 45.9	9 25.2	11 07.1	6 39.7	15 23.0	21 23.9
24 M	4 09 41	3 38 49	25 26 34	1♌26 31	11 01.1	10 06.0	25 16.7	10 50.9	2 08.5	9 28.5	11 13.8	6 40.6	15 22.8	21 22.4
25 Tu	4 13 38	4 36 27	7♌28 46	13 33 45	10 58.7	11 31.8	24 59.7	11 28.8	2 31.2	9 32.1	11 20.5	6 41.4	15 22.6	21 20.9
26 W	4 17 34	5 34 04	19 41 58	25 53 56	10D57.2	13 00.0	24 40.3	12 06.7	2 54.0	9 35.7	11 27.3	6 42.2	15 22.3	21 19.4
27 Th	4 21 31	6 31 40	2♍10 08	8♍31 04	10 56.9	14 30.8	24 18.7	12 44.6	3 17.0	9 39.6	11 34.2	6 42.9	15 22.0	21 17.8
28 F	4 25 28	7 29 14	14 57 14	21 29 04	10 57.5	16 04.0	23 54.9	13 22.5	3 40.0	9 43.6	11 41.1	6 43.5	15 21.7	21 16.3
29 Sa	4 29 24	8 26 47	28 06 58	4♎51 17	10 58.8	17 39.6	23 29.0	14 00.4	4 03.2	9 47.7	11 48.0	6 44.1	15 21.3	21 14.8
30 Su	4 33 21	9 24 18	11♎42 15	18 39 59	11 00.3	19 17.6	23 01.1	14 38.3	4 26.4	9 52.1	11 55.0	6 44.7	15 20.9	21 13.2
31 M	4 37 17	10 21 48	25 44 29	2♏55 34	11R01.4	20 58.1	22 31.3	15 16.1	4 49.8	9 56.5	12 02.0	6 45.2	15 20.5	21 11.7

LONGITUDE — June 2004

Day	Sid.Time	☉	0 hr ☽	Noon ☽	True ☊	☿	♀	♂	⚳	♃	♄	♅	♆	♇
1 Tu	4 41 14	11♊19 16	10♏12 54	17♏35 57	11♉01.4	22♉40.9	21♊59.8	15♋54.0	5♌13.2	10♍01.2	12♋09.0	6♓45.7	15♒20.0	21♐10.1
2 W	4 45 10	12 16 44	25 03 59	2♐36 05	11R00.1	24 26.2	21R26.7	16 31.9	5 36.7	10 06.0	12 16.1	6 46.1	15R19.5	21R08.6
3 Th	4 49 07	13 14 11	10♐11 13	17 48 10	10 57.3	26 13.9	20 52.4	17 09.7	6 00.4	10 10.9	12 23.2	6 46.5	15 19.0	21 07.0
4 F	4 53 03	14 11 36	25 25 40	3♑02 25	10 53.3	28 03.9	20 16.9	17 47.6	6 24.1	10 16.0	12 30.4	6 46.8	15 18.4	21 05.4
5 Sa	4 57 00	15 09 01	10♑37 06	18 08 34	10 48.5	29 56.3	19 40.5	18 25.4	6 47.9	10 21.3	12 37.6	6 47.1	15 17.9	21 03.8
6 Su	5 00 57	16 06 25	25 35 41	2♒57 35	10 43.8	1♊50.9	19 03.4	19 03.2	7 11.8	10 26.7	12 44.8	6 47.3	15 17.3	21 02.3
7 M	5 04 53	17 03 49	10♒13 31	17 22 57	10 39.8	3 47.8	18 25.9	19 41.1	7 35.8	10 32.2	12 52.1	6 47.5	15 16.6	21 00.7
8 Tu	5 08 50	18 01 12	24 25 35	1♓21 16	10 37.1	5 46.9	17 48.2	20 18.9	7 59.8	10 37.9	12 59.4	6 47.6	15 16.0	20 59.1
9 W	5 12 46	18 58 34	8♓10 02	14 52 04	10D35.9	7 48.1	17 10.6	20 56.7	8 24.0	10 43.7	13 06.7	6 47.7	15 15.3	20 57.5
10 Th	5 16 43	19 55 55	21 27 39	27 57 11	10 36.0	9 51.3	16 33.2	21 34.5	8 48.2	10 49.7	13 14.1	6R47.8	15 14.5	20 55.9
11 F	5 20 39	20 53 17	4♈21 06	10♈39 55	10 37.2	11 56.2	15 56.4	22 12.4	9 12.5	10 55.8	13 21.5	6 47.7	15 13.8	20 54.3
12 Sa	5 24 36	21 50 37	16 54 09	23 04 21	10 38.7	14 02.9	15 20.4	22 50.2	9 36.9	11 02.1	13 28.9	6 47.7	15 13.0	20 52.7
13 Su	5 28 32	22 47 57	29 11 01	5♉14 41	10R39.8	16 11.0	14 45.4	23 28.0	10 01.4	11 08.5	13 36.4	6 47.6	15 12.2	20 51.1
14 M	5 32 29	23 45 17	11♉15 50	17 14 56	10 39.7	18 20.4	14 11.5	24 05.8	10 26.0	11 15.0	13 43.8	6 47.4	15 11.3	20 49.6
15 Tu	5 36 26	24 42 37	23 12 23	29 08 37	10 37.8	20 30.7	13 39.1	24 43.6	10 50.6	11 21.7	13 51.3	6 47.2	15 10.5	20 48.0
16 W	5 40 22	25 39 56	5♊03 57	10♊58 44	10 34.0	22 41.9	13 08.2	25 21.4	11 15.3	11 28.5	13 58.9	6 46.9	15 09.6	20 46.4
17 Th	5 44 19	26 37 14	16 53 14	22 47 45	10 28.1	24 53.5	12 39.0	25 59.2	11 40.1	11 35.5	14 06.4	6 46.6	15 08.7	20 44.8
18 F	5 48 15	27 34 32	28 42 30	4♋37 42	10 20.4	27 05.3	12 11.7	26 37.1	12 05.0	11 42.5	14 14.0	6 46.3	15 07.7	20 43.2
19 Sa	5 52 12	28 31 49	10♋33 36	16 30 24	10 11.6	29 17.1	11 46.4	27 14.9	12 29.9	11 49.7	14 21.6	6 45.9	15 06.8	20 41.6
20 Su	5 56 08	29 29 06	22 28 18	28 27 33	10 02.4	1♋28.5	11 23.2	27 52.7	12 54.9	11 57.1	14 29.2	6 45.4	15 05.8	20 40.1
21 M	6 00 05	0♋26 22	4♌28 22	10♌31 01	9 53.7	3 39.4	11 02.2	28 30.5	13 20.0	12 04.5	14 36.8	6 44.9	15 04.7	20 38.5
22 Tu	6 04 01	1 23 38	16 35 47	22 42 59	9 46.4	5 49.3	10 43.4	29 08.3	13 45.1	12 12.1	14 44.5	6 44.4	15 03.7	20 37.0
23 W	6 07 58	2 20 53	28 52 58	5♍06 05	9 40.9	7 58.2	10 26.9	29 46.1	14 10.3	12 19.8	14 52.1	6 43.8	15 02.6	20 35.4
24 Th	6 11 55	3 18 07	11♍22 45	17 43 22	9 37.6	10 05.9	10 12.8	0♌23.9	14 35.6	12 27.6	14 59.8	6 43.2	15 01.5	20 33.9
25 F	6 15 51	4 15 21	24 08 22	0♎38 11	9D36.3	12 12.1	10 01.0	1 01.7	15 00.9	12 35.6	15 07.5	6 42.5	15 00.4	20 32.3
26 Sa	6 19 48	5 12 34	7♎13 15	13 53 57	9 36.6	14 16.8	9 51.7	1 39.5	15 26.3	12 43.7	15 15.2	6 41.8	14 59.3	20 30.8
27 Su	6 23 44	6 09 46	20 40 38	27 33 33	9R37.4	16 19.8	9 44.7	2 17.2	15 51.8	12 51.8	15 22.9	6 41.0	14 58.1	20 29.3
28 M	6 27 41	7 06 59	4♏32 54	11♏38 43	9 37.7	18 20.9	9 40.1	2 55.0	16 17.3	13 00.1	15 30.7	6 40.2	14 56.9	20 27.8
29 Tu	6 31 37	8 04 10	18 50 55	26 09 11	9 36.7	20 20.2	9D37.8	3 32.8	16 42.9	13 08.5	15 38.4	6 39.3	14 55.7	20 26.3
30 W	6 35 34	9 01 22	3♐33 04	11♐01 53	9 33.5	22 17.6	9 37.9	4 10.6	17 08.5	13 17.1	15 46.2	6 38.4	14 54.5	20 24.8

Astro Data Dy Hr Mn	Planet Ingress Dy Hr Mn	Last Aspect Dy Hr Mn	☽ Ingress Dy Hr Mn	Last Aspect Dy Hr Mn	☽ Ingress Dy Hr Mn	☽ Phases & Eclipses Dy Hr Mn
♃✶♄ 1 20:31	♂ ♋ 7 8:46	1 11:31 ♂ □	♎ 1 18:03	1 21:16 ☿ ☍	♐ 2 7:52	4 20:33 ○ 14♏42
☽0S 2 5:59	☿ ♉ 16 6:54	3 16:49 ♂ △	♏ 3 20:39	3 17:12 ♇ ☌	♑ 4 7:12	4 20:30 ● T 1.303
♃D 5 3:06	⚳ ♌ 18 18:00	4 21:37 ♆ □	♐ 5 21:08	5 12:28 ♂ ☍	♒ 6 7:10	11 11:04 ☾ 21♒05
☽0N 14 23:09	☉ ♊ 20 16:59	7 11:50 ♀ ☍	♑ 7 21:17	7 18:09 ♇ ✶	♓ 8 9:38	19 4:52 ● 28♉33
♆R 17 12:13		9 13:03 ☿ □	♒ 9 22:46	9 23:37 ♂ △	♈ 10 15:49	27 7:57 ☽ 6♍22
♀R 17 22:29	☿ ♊ 5 12:47	11 19:31 ☿ ✶	♓ 12 2:52	12 11:31 ♂ □	♉ 13 1:37	
☽0S 29 15:27	☿ ♋ 19 19:49	14 2:14 ♀ ✶	♈ 14 10:02	15 2:34 ♂ ✶	♊ 15 13:44	3 4:20 ○ 12♐56
	☉ ♋ 21 0:57	16 12:17 ♀ ✶	♉ 16 19:57	17 20:27 ☉ ☌	♋ 18 2:37	9 20:02 ☾ 19♓18
♅R 10 15:47	♂ ♌ 23 20:50	19 4:52 ☉ ☌	♊ 19 7:47	20 10:46 ♂ ☌	♌ 20 15:05	17 20:27 ● 26♊57
☽0N 11 4:28		21 12:13 ♀ ☌	♋ 21 20:35	22 7:54 ♇ △	♍ 23 2:10	25 19:08 ☽ 4♎32
♄⊼♆ 24 16:40		22 18:58 ♄ ☌	♌ 24 9:07	24 17:19 ♇ □	♎ 25 10:50	
☽0S 25 22:39		26 9:42 ♀ ✶	♍ 26 19:52	26 23:41 ♇ ✶	♏ 27 16:13	
♀D 29 23:16		28 16:17 ♀ □	♎ 29 3:22	29 0:57 ☿ △	♐ 29 18:15	
		30 19:09 ♀ △	♏ 31 7:08			

Astro Data

1 May 2004
Julian Day # 38107
SVP 5♓12'10"
GC 26♐54.0 ⚴ 3♊49.3
Eris 20♈24.7 ⚵ 24♑03.7
⚷ 26♑07.9 ⚶ 6♓29.1
☽ Mean ☊ 11♉16.0

1 June 2004
Julian Day # 38138
SVP 5♓12'05"
GC 26♐54.1 ⚴ 21♊50.2
Eris 20♈41.4 ⚵ 24♑04.3R
⚷ 25♑33.9R ⚶ 18♓02.1
☽ Mean ☊ 9♉37.5

July 2004

LONGITUDE

Day	Sid.Time	☉	0 hr ☽	Noon ☽	True ☊	☿	♀	♂	⚳	♃	♄	♅	♆	♇
1 Th	6 39 31	9♋58 33	18♐34 45	26♐10 35	9♉27.9	24♋13.0	9♊40.2	4♌48.4	17♌34.2	13♍25.7	15♋53.9	6♓37.5	14♒53.3	20♐23.3
2 F	6 43 27	10 55 44	3♑48 11	11♑26 11	9R 20.3	26 06.4	9 44.9	5 26.2	17 59.9	13 34.4	16 01.7	6R 36.5	14R 52.0	20R 21.8
3 Sa	6 47 24	11 52 55	19 03 15	26 37 58	9 11.4	27 57.8	9 51.7	6 03.9	18 25.7	13 43.3	16 09.5	6 35.4	14 50.7	20 20.4
4 Su	6 51 20	12 50 06	4♒09 05	11♒35 26	9 02.3	29 47.1	10 00.7	6 41.7	18 51.5	13 52.2	16 17.2	6 34.4	14 49.4	20 18.9
5 M	6 55 17	13 47 17	18 56 02	26 10 07	8 54.1	1♌34.4	10 11.9	7 19.5	19 17.4	14 01.2	16 25.0	6 33.2	14 48.1	20 17.5
6 Tu	6 59 13	14 44 28	3♓17 08	10♓16 46	8 47.8	3 19.6	10 25.1	7 57.3	19 43.4	14 10.4	16 32.8	6 32.1	14 46.7	20 16.1
7 W	7 03 10	15 41 39	17 08 54	23 53 37	8 43.6	5 02.8	10 40.2	8 35.1	20 09.4	14 19.6	16 40.6	6 30.9	14 45.4	20 14.7
8 Th	7 07 06	16 38 51	0♈31 10	7♈01 54	8D 41.7	6 43.9	10 57.4	9 12.9	20 35.4	14 29.0	16 48.4	6 29.6	14 44.0	20 13.3
9 F	7 11 03	17 36 03	13 26 18	19 44 56	8 41.3	8 23.0	11 16.4	9 50.6	21 01.5	14 38.4	16 56.2	6 28.3	14 42.6	20 11.9
10 Sa	7 15 00	18 33 16	25 58 24	2♉07 20	8R 41.6	10 00.0	11 37.2	10 28.4	21 27.7	14 48.0	17 04.0	6 27.0	14 41.2	20 10.6
11 Su	7 18 56	19 30 29	8♉12 21	14 14 08	8 41.6	11 35.0	11 59.7	11 06.2	21 53.9	14 57.6	17 11.7	6 25.6	14 39.8	20 09.2
12 M	7 22 53	20 27 43	20 13 16	26 10 22	8 40.2	13 07.9	12 24.0	11 44.1	22 20.1	15 07.4	17 19.5	6 24.2	14 38.3	20 07.9
13 Tu	7 26 49	21 24 57	2♊06 00	8♊00 39	8 36.7	14 38.7	12 49.8	12 21.9	22 46.4	15 17.2	17 27.3	6 22.8	14 36.9	20 06.6
14 W	7 30 46	22 22 11	13 54 50	19 48 58	8 30.5	16 07.4	13 17.3	12 59.7	23 12.7	15 27.1	17 35.1	6 21.3	14 35.4	20 05.3
15 Th	7 34 42	23 19 27	25 43 25	1♋38 31	8 21.6	17 34.0	13 46.2	13 37.5	23 39.1	15 37.1	17 42.9	6 19.8	14 33.9	20 04.1
16 F	7 38 39	24 16 42	7♋34 35	13 31 49	8 10.4	18 58.5	14 16.6	14 15.3	24 05.5	15 47.2	17 50.6	6 18.2	14 32.4	20 02.8
17 Sa	7 42 35	25 13 58	19 30 28	25 30 42	7 57.6	20 20.8	14 48.4	14 53.2	24 32.0	15 57.4	17 58.4	6 16.6	14 30.9	20 01.6
18 Su	7 46 32	26 11 15	1♌32 39	7♌36 27	7 44.3	21 40.9	15 21.6	15 31.0	24 58.5	16 07.7	18 06.1	6 15.0	14 29.4	20 00.4
19 M	7 50 29	27 08 31	13 42 14	19 50 08	7 31.6	22 58.7	15 56.0	16 08.8	25 25.1	16 18.0	18 13.9	6 13.4	14 27.9	19 59.2
20 Tu	7 54 25	28 05 48	26 00 16	2♍12 47	7 20.5	24 14.2	16 31.7	16 46.7	25 51.6	16 28.4	18 21.6	6 11.7	14 26.3	19 58.0
21 W	7 58 22	29 03 06	8♍27 51	14 45 40	7 11.9	25 27.4	17 08.6	17 24.5	26 18.3	16 38.9	18 29.3	6 09.9	14 24.8	19 56.9
22 Th	8 02 18	0♌00 24	21 06 27	27 30 27	7 06.0	26 38.1	17 46.6	18 02.4	26 44.9	16 49.5	18 37.0	6 08.2	14 23.2	19 55.8
23 F	8 06 15	0 57 42	3♎57 57	10♎29 16	7 02.9	27 46.3	18 25.7	18 40.3	27 11.6	17 00.2	18 44.7	6 06.4	14 21.6	19 54.7
24 Sa	8 10 11	1 55 00	17 04 43	23 44 37	7 01.8	28 52.0	19 05.9	19 18.1	27 38.4	17 10.9	18 52.4	6 04.5	14 20.0	19 53.6
25 Su	8 14 08	2 52 19	0♏29 16	7♏18 57	7 01.7	29 55.0	19 47.2	19 56.0	28 05.1	17 21.8	19 00.0	6 02.7	14 18.5	19 52.5
26 M	8 18 04	3 49 38	14 13 52	21 14 11	7 01.4	0♍55.1	20 29.4	20 33.9	28 31.9	17 32.7	19 07.7	6 00.8	14 16.9	19 51.5
27 Tu	8 22 01	4 46 58	28 19 55	5♐30 58	6 59.6	1 52.4	21 12.6	21 11.7	28 58.8	17 43.6	19 15.3	5 58.9	14 15.3	19 50.5
28 W	8 25 58	5 44 18	12♐47 05	20 07 49	6 55.5	2 46.7	21 56.7	21 49.6	29 25.6	17 54.7	19 22.9	5 56.9	14 13.7	19 49.5
29 Th	8 29 54	6 41 39	27 32 35	5♑00 33	6 48.8	3 37.8	22 41.7	22 27.5	29 52.5	18 05.8	19 30.4	5 55.0	14 12.1	19 48.5
30 F	8 33 51	7 39 00	12♑30 46	20 02 09	6 39.6	4 25.7	23 27.5	23 05.4	0♍19.5	18 16.9	19 38.0	5 53.0	14 10.4	19 47.6
31 Sa	8 37 47	8 36 22	27 33 29	5♒03 32	6 29.0	5 10.1	24 14.2	23 43.3	0 46.4	18 28.2	19 45.5	5 50.9	14 08.8	19 46.7

August 2004

LONGITUDE

Day	Sid.Time	☉	0 hr ☽	Noon ☽	True ☊	☿	♀	♂	⚳	♃	♄	♅	♆	♇
1 Su	8 41 44	9♌33 45	12♒31 05	19♒54 56	6♉17.9	5♍50.9	25♊01.7	24♌21.2	1♍13.4	18♍39.5	19♋53.0	5♓48.9	14♒07.2	19♐45.8
2 M	8 45 40	10 31 08	27 14 05	4♓27 37	6R 07.8	6 27.9	25 50.0	24 59.1	1 40.4	18 50.8	20 00.5	5R 46.8	14R 05.6	19R 45.0
3 Tu	8 49 37	11 28 33	11♓34 52	18 35 20	5 59.6	7 01.0	26 39.0	25 37.0	2 07.5	19 02.2	20 08.0	5 44.7	14 03.9	19 44.1
4 W	8 53 33	12 25 59	25 28 44	2♈15 00	5 53.8	7 29.9	27 28.8	26 15.0	2 34.5	19 13.7	20 15.4	5 42.6	14 02.3	19 43.3
5 Th	8 57 30	13 23 25	8♈54 11	15 26 34	5 50.6	7 54.5	28 19.2	26 52.9	3 01.6	19 25.3	20 22.8	5 40.4	14 00.7	19 42.5
6 F	9 01 27	14 20 54	21 52 30	28 12 28	5D 49.4	8 14.6	29 10.3	27 30.9	3 28.7	19 36.9	20 30.2	5 38.3	13 59.0	19 41.8
7 Sa	9 05 23	15 18 23	4♉27 02	10♉36 49	5R 49.3	8 29.9	0♋02.1	28 08.8	3 55.9	19 48.5	20 37.5	5 36.1	13 57.4	19 41.1
8 Su	9 09 20	16 15 54	16 42 27	22 44 38	5 49.2	8 40.4	0 54.5	28 46.8	4 23.1	20 00.3	20 44.8	5 33.9	13 55.8	19 40.4
9 M	9 13 16	17 13 26	28 44 00	4♊41 15	5 48.1	8R 45.7	1 47.5	29 24.8	4 50.3	20 12.0	20 52.1	5 31.7	13 54.1	19 39.7
10 Tu	9 17 13	18 11 00	10♊37 00	16 31 53	5 45.0	8 45.9	2 41.1	0♍02.8	5 17.5	20 23.9	20 59.4	5 29.4	13 52.5	19 39.1
11 W	9 21 09	19 08 35	22 26 28	28 21 16	5 39.3	8 40.6	3 35.2	0 40.8	5 44.8	20 35.7	21 06.6	5 27.2	13 50.9	19 38.4
12 Th	9 25 06	20 06 11	4♋16 49	10♋13 30	5 31.1	8 29.9	4 29.9	1 18.8	6 12.0	20 47.7	21 13.7	5 24.9	13 49.3	19 37.9
13 F	9 29 02	21 03 49	16 11 44	22 11 50	5 20.5	8 13.7	5 25.1	1 56.9	6 39.3	20 59.7	21 20.9	5 22.6	13 47.6	19 37.3
14 Sa	9 32 59	22 01 28	28 14 04	4♌18 37	5 08.4	7 52.0	6 20.9	2 34.9	7 06.7	21 11.7	21 28.0	5 20.3	13 46.0	19 36.8
15 Su	9 36 56	22 59 08	10♌25 42	16 35 23	4 55.6	7 24.9	7 17.1	3 13.0	7 34.0	21 23.8	21 35.1	5 18.0	13 44.4	19 36.3
16 M	9 40 52	23 56 50	22 47 46	29 02 54	4 43.4	6 52.7	8 13.8	3 51.0	8 01.4	21 35.9	21 42.1	5 15.7	13 42.8	19 35.8
17 Tu	9 44 49	24 54 32	5♍20 47	11♍41 27	4 32.8	6 15.5	9 10.9	4 29.1	8 28.8	21 48.1	21 49.1	5 13.3	13 41.2	19 35.4
18 W	9 48 45	25 52 16	18 04 52	24 31 04	4 24.6	5 33.9	10 08.5	5 07.2	8 56.2	22 00.3	21 56.0	5 11.0	13 39.6	19 35.0
19 Th	9 52 42	26 50 02	1♎00 03	7♎31 53	4 19.1	4 48.4	11 06.5	5 45.3	9 23.6	22 12.5	22 02.9	5 08.6	13 38.0	19 34.6
20 F	9 56 38	27 47 48	14 06 36	20 44 19	4 16.3	3 59.6	12 05.0	6 23.4	9 51.0	22 24.8	22 09.7	5 06.3	13 36.5	19 34.3
21 Sa	10 00 35	28 45 36	27 25 07	4♏09 08	4D 15.6	3 08.4	13 03.8	7 01.6	10 18.5	22 37.2	22 16.6	5 03.9	13 34.9	19 34.0
22 Su	10 04 31	29 43 24	10♏56 31	17 47 22	4R 15.9	2 15.6	14 03.0	7 39.7	10 45.9	22 49.6	22 23.3	5 01.5	13 33.3	19 33.7
23 M	10 08 28	0♍41 14	24 41 50	1♐39 57	4 16.2	1 22.2	15 02.6	8 17.9	11 13.4	23 02.0	22 30.0	4 59.1	13 31.8	19 33.4
24 Tu	10 12 25	1 39 05	8♐41 45	15 47 10	4 15.4	0 29.2	16 02.6	8 56.0	11 40.9	23 14.4	22 36.7	4 56.7	13 30.2	19 33.2
25 W	10 16 21	2 36 58	22 56 02	0♑08 06	4 12.6	29♌37.9	17 03.0	9 34.2	12 08.4	23 26.9	22 43.3	4 54.3	13 28.7	19 33.1
26 Th	10 20 18	3 34 51	7♑22 57	14 40 05	4 07.5	28 49.3	18 03.7	10 12.4	12 35.9	23 39.4	22 49.9	4 51.9	13 27.2	19 32.9
27 F	10 24 14	4 32 46	21 58 50	29 18 27	4 00.3	28 04.4	19 04.7	10 50.6	13 03.4	23 52.0	22 56.4	4 49.6	13 25.7	19 32.8
28 Sa	10 28 11	5 30 43	6♒38 06	13♒56 53	3 51.6	27 24.4	20 06.1	11 28.8	13 31.0	24 04.5	23 02.8	4 47.2	13 24.2	19 32.7
29 Su	10 32 07	6 28 40	21 13 51	28 28 06	3 42.6	26 50.0	21 07.8	12 07.0	13 58.5	24 17.2	23 09.2	4 44.8	13 22.7	19 32.6
30 M	10 36 04	7 26 39	5♓38 47	12♓45 07	3 34.3	26 22.2	22 09.8	12 45.3	14 26.1	24 29.8	23 15.6	4 42.4	13 21.3	19D 32.6
31 Tu	10 40 00	8 24 40	19 46 28	26 42 19	3 27.5	26 01.6	23 12.2	13 23.5	14 53.6	24 42.4	23 21.9	4 40.0	13 19.8	19 32.6

Astro Data	Planet Ingress	Last Aspect	☽ Ingress	Last Aspect	☽ Ingress	☽ Phases & Eclipses	Astro Data
Dy Hr Mn	Dy Hr Mn	Dy Hr Mn	Dy Hr Mn	Dy Hr Mn	Dy Hr Mn	Dy Hr Mn	1 July 2004
☽0N 8 10:39	☿ ♌ 4 14:52	1 2:53 ♇ ☌	♑ 1 18:01	1 20:51 ♀ △	♓ 2 4:34	2 11:09 ○ 10♑54	Julian Day # 38168
♃⊼♆ 9 21:10	☉ ♌ 22 11:50	3 14:25 ☿ ☍	♒ 3 17:22	4 2:58 ♀ □	♈ 4 7:59	9 7:34 ☾ 17♈25	SVP 5♓11'59"
☽0S 23 3:47	☿ ♍ 25 13:58	5 2:15 ♇ ⚹	♓ 5 18:26	6 13:59 ♀ ⚹	♉ 6 15:26	17 11:24 ● 25♋13	GC 26♐54.1 ⚴ 9♋44.8
♄⊼♇ 31 15:20	⚳ ♍ 29 18:39	7 5:30 ♇ □	♈ 7 23:03	9 0:46 ♂ □	♊ 9 2:33	25 3:37 ☽ 2♏32	Eris 20♈50.6 ⚵ 19♑04.7R
		9 12:52 ♇ △	♉ 10 7:51	10 19:59 ♃ □	♋ 11 15:20	31 18:05 ○ 8♒51	⚷ 24♑06.6R ⚶ 25♓49.2
☽0N 4 18:27	♀ ♋ 7 11:02	11 23:29 ☉ ⚹	♊ 12 19:45	13 10:17 ♄ ☌	♌ 14 3:30		☽ Mean ☊ 8♉02.2
♃□♇ 6 21:31	♂ ♍ 10 10:14	14 12:33 ♇ ☍	♋ 15 8:40	16 1:24 ☉ ☌	♍ 16 13:49	7 22:01 ☾ 15♉42	
♄⚻♅ 7 8:26	☉ ♍ 22 18:53	17 11:24 ☉ ☌	♌ 17 20:56	18 7:15 ♃ ☌	♎ 18 22:09	16 1:24 ● 23♌31	1 August 2004
☿R 10 0:32	☿ ♌R 25 1:33	19 18:50 ☿ ☌	♍ 20 7:44	21 1:39 ☉ ⚹	♏ 21 4:37	23 10:12 ☽ 0♐37	Julian Day # 38199
♃⚹♄ 17 16:33		21 21:48 ♇ □	♎ 22 16:39	22 20:54 ♃ ⚹	♐ 23 9:08	30 2:22 ○ 7♓03	SVP 5♓11'53"
☽0S 19 8:30		24 21:54 ☿ ⚹	♏ 24 23:08	25 11:13 ☿ △	♑ 25 11:47		GC 26♐54.2 ⚴ 28♋09.1
♇D 30 19:38		26 10:48 ♂ □	♐ 27 2:48	27 2:58 ♃ △	♒ 27 13:08		Eris 20♈50.6R ⚵ 12♑10.1R
		28 15:06 ♀ ☍	♑ 29 3:57	29 9:23 ☿ ☍	♓ 29 14:33		⚷ 22♑17.1R ⚶ 28♓18.5R
		30 11:21 ♄ ☍	♒ 31 3:54	31 8:28 ♃ ☍	♈ 31 17:46		☽ Mean ☊ 6♉23.8

LONGITUDE — September 2004

Day	Sid.Time	☉	0 hr ☽	Noon ☽	True ☊	☿	♀	♂	⚳	♃	♄	♅	♆	♇
1 W	10 43 57	9♍22 42	3♈32 19	10♈16 14	3♉22.9	25♌48.8	24♋14.9	14♍01.8	15♍21.2	24♍55.1	23♋28.1	4♓37.6	13♒18.4	19♐32.7
2 Th	10 47 54	10 20 46	16 54 02	23 25 47	3D 20.5	25D 44.2	25 17.8	14 40.1	15 48.8	25 07.8	23 34.3	4R 35.2	13R 17.0	19 32.7
3 F	10 51 50	11 18 52	29 51 42	6♉12 07	3 20.1	25 48.1	26 21.1	15 18.4	16 16.4	25 20.6	23 40.4	4 32.8	13 15.6	19 32.8
4 Sa	10 55 47	12 17 01	12♉27 26	18 38 09	3 20.9	26 00.6	27 24.6	15 56.7	16 44.0	25 33.4	23 46.5	4 30.5	13 14.2	19 33.0
5 Su	10 59 43	13 15 11	24 44 49	0♊48 02	3 22.1	26 21.7	28 28.4	16 35.0	17 11.6	25 46.1	23 52.4	4 28.1	13 12.8	19 33.1
6 M	11 03 40	14 13 23	6♊48 24	12 46 35	3R 22.8	26 51.5	29 32.5	17 13.4	17 39.2	25 58.9	23 58.4	4 25.8	13 11.5	19 33.3
7 Tu	11 07 36	15 11 37	18 43 13	24 38 57	3 22.2	27 29.7	0♌36.9	17 51.8	18 06.8	26 11.8	24 04.3	4 23.4	13 10.2	19 33.6
8 W	11 11 33	16 09 53	0♋34 24	6♋30 11	3 19.9	28 16.0	1 41.5	18 30.2	18 34.4	26 24.6	24 10.1	4 21.1	13 08.9	19 33.8
9 Th	11 15 29	17 08 11	12 26 51	18 24 59	3 15.7	29 10.2	2 46.4	19 08.6	19 02.1	26 37.5	24 15.8	4 18.8	13 07.6	19 34.1
10 F	11 19 26	18 06 31	24 25 02	0♌27 27	3 09.7	0♍11.7	3 51.5	19 47.0	19 29.7	26 50.4	24 21.5	4 16.4	13 06.3	19 34.5
11 Sa	11 23 23	19 04 54	6♌32 38	12 40 53	3 02.4	1 20.2	4 56.8	20 25.5	19 57.3	27 03.3	24 27.1	4 14.1	13 05.0	19 34.8
12 Su	11 27 19	20 03 18	18 52 29	25 07 37	2 54.6	2 35.0	6 02.4	21 03.9	20 25.0	27 16.2	24 32.6	4 11.9	13 03.8	19 35.2
13 M	11 31 16	21 01 44	1♍26 25	7♍48 56	2 47.0	3 55.6	7 08.2	21 42.4	20 52.6	27 29.1	24 38.1	4 09.6	13 02.6	19 35.7
14 Tu	11 35 12	22 00 12	14 15 10	20 45 05	2 40.5	5 21.6	8 14.2	22 20.9	21 20.3	27 42.0	24 43.5	4 07.3	13 01.4	19 36.1
15 W	11 39 09	22 58 41	27 18 34	3♎55 29	2 35.6	6 52.1	9 20.4	22 59.5	21 47.9	27 55.0	24 48.8	4 05.1	13 00.2	19 36.6
16 Th	11 43 05	23 57 13	10♎35 41	17 18 58	2 32.7	8 26.8	10 26.9	23 38.0	22 15.5	28 07.9	24 54.0	4 02.9	12 59.1	19 37.1
17 F	11 47 02	24 55 47	24 05 08	0♏54 00	2D 31.7	10 05.0	11 33.5	24 16.6	22 43.2	28 20.9	24 59.2	4 00.7	12 58.0	19 37.7
18 Sa	11 50 58	25 54 22	7♏45 23	14 39 06	2 32.2	11 46.2	12 40.3	24 55.1	23 10.8	28 33.8	25 04.3	3 58.5	12 56.9	19 38.3
19 Su	11 54 55	26 52 59	21 35 00	28 32 55	2 33.5	13 29.8	13 47.4	25 33.7	23 38.4	28 46.8	25 09.3	3 56.4	12 55.8	19 38.9
20 M	11 58 52	27 51 37	5♐32 43	12♐34 15	2 34.9	15 15.5	14 54.6	26 12.3	24 06.1	28 59.8	25 14.2	3 54.2	12 54.8	19 39.6
21 Tu	12 02 48	28 50 18	19 37 20	26 41 50	2R 35.7	17 02.7	16 02.0	26 51.0	24 33.7	29 12.8	25 19.1	3 52.1	12 53.8	19 40.3
22 W	12 06 45	29 49 00	3♑47 32	10♑54 11	2 35.2	18 51.1	17 09.6	27 29.6	25 01.3	29 25.7	25 23.8	3 50.1	12 52.8	19 41.0
23 Th	12 10 41	0♎47 44	18 01 30	25 09 11	2 33.3	20 40.3	18 17.4	28 08.3	25 28.9	29 38.7	25 28.5	3 48.0	12 51.8	19 41.7
24 F	12 14 38	1 46 29	2♒16 49	9♒23 59	2 30.1	22 30.0	19 25.4	28 47.0	25 56.5	29 51.7	25 33.1	3 46.0	12 50.9	19 42.5
25 Sa	12 18 34	2 45 16	16 30 13	23 35 01	2 25.9	24 20.1	20 33.5	29 25.7	26 24.1	0♎04.7	25 37.7	3 44.0	12 49.9	19 43.3
26 Su	12 22 31	3 44 05	0♓37 52	7♓38 16	2 21.5	26 10.2	21 41.8	0♎04.4	26 51.7	0 17.6	25 42.1	3 42.0	12 49.1	19 44.2
27 M	12 26 27	4 42 55	14 35 41	21 29 41	2 17.4	28 00.2	22 50.3	0 43.2	27 19.3	0 30.6	25 46.5	3 40.0	12 48.2	19 45.1
28 Tu	12 30 24	5 41 48	28 19 50	5♈05 48	2 14.2	29 49.9	23 58.9	1 21.9	27 46.8	0 43.5	25 50.7	3 38.1	12 47.4	19 46.0
29 W	12 34 20	6 40 42	11♈47 18	18 24 09	2 12.3	1♎39.2	25 07.7	2 00.7	28 14.4	0 56.5	25 54.9	3 36.2	12 46.5	19 46.9
30 Th	12 38 17	7 39 39	24 56 16	1♉23 38	2D 11.6	3 28.0	26 16.7	2 39.5	28 41.9	1 09.4	25 59.0	3 34.3	12 45.8	19 47.9

LONGITUDE — October 2004

Day	Sid.Time	☉	0 hr ☽	Noon ☽	True ☊	☿	♀	♂	⚳	♃	♄	♅	♆	♇
1 F	12 42 14	8♎38 37	7♉46 20	14♉04 32	2♉12.0	5♎16.3	27♌25.8	3♎18.4	29♍09.4	1♎22.3	26♋03.0	3♓32.5	12♒45.0	19♐48.9
2 Sa	12 46 10	9 37 38	20 18 29	26 28 31	2 13.3	7 03.9	28 35.1	3 57.2	29 37.0	1 35.3	26 06.9	3R 30.7	12R 44.3	19 49.9
3 Su	12 50 07	10 36 42	2♊35 00	8♊38 22	2 14.9	8 50.9	29 44.5	4 36.1	0♎04.5	1 48.2	26 10.8	3 28.9	12 43.6	19 50.9
4 M	12 54 03	11 35 47	14 39 08	20 37 49	2 16.5	10 37.1	0♍54.1	5 15.0	0 32.0	2 01.1	26 14.5	3 27.2	12 43.0	19 52.0
5 Tu	12 58 00	12 34 55	26 34 59	2♋31 12	2R 17.6	12 22.5	2 03.9	5 53.9	0 59.4	2 13.9	26 18.1	3 25.5	12 42.3	19 53.1
6 W	13 01 56	13 34 05	8♋27 04	14 23 11	2 18.0	14 07.2	3 13.8	6 32.9	1 26.9	2 26.8	26 21.7	3 23.9	12 41.7	19 54.3
7 Th	13 05 53	14 33 18	20 20 10	26 18 35	2 17.5	15 51.2	4 23.8	7 11.8	1 54.4	2 39.7	26 25.1	3 22.2	12 41.2	19 55.5
8 F	13 09 49	15 32 32	2♌19 02	8♌22 03	2 16.2	17 34.3	5 34.0	7 50.8	2 21.8	2 52.5	26 28.5	3 20.6	12 40.6	19 56.7
9 Sa	13 13 46	16 31 49	14 28 10	20 37 49	2 14.4	19 16.7	6 44.3	8 29.9	2 49.2	3 05.3	26 31.7	3 19.1	12 40.1	19 57.9
10 Su	13 17 43	17 31 08	26 51 27	3♍09 24	2 12.2	20 58.4	7 54.7	9 08.9	3 16.6	3 18.1	26 34.9	3 17.6	12 39.6	19 59.2
11 M	13 21 39	18 30 30	9♍31 58	15 59 20	2 10.2	22 39.2	9 05.3	9 48.0	3 44.0	3 30.9	26 37.9	3 16.1	12 39.2	20 00.4
12 Tu	13 25 36	19 29 53	22 31 38	29 08 53	2 08.4	24 19.4	10 16.0	10 27.1	4 11.4	3 43.6	26 40.9	3 14.6	12 38.8	20 01.8
13 W	13 29 32	20 29 19	5♎51 02	12♎37 54	2 07.2	25 58.8	11 26.8	11 06.2	4 38.7	3 56.3	26 43.8	3 13.2	12 38.4	20 03.1
14 Th	13 33 29	21 28 47	19 29 15	26 24 46	2D 06.7	27 37.5	12 37.7	11 45.3	5 06.0	4 09.0	26 46.5	3 11.9	12 38.0	20 04.5
15 F	13 37 25	22 28 17	3♏24 01	10♏26 34	2 06.7	29 15.5	13 48.7	12 24.5	5 33.3	4 21.7	26 49.2	3 10.6	12 37.7	20 05.9
16 Sa	13 41 22	23 27 48	17 31 54	24 39 29	2 07.2	0♏52.8	14 59.9	13 03.7	6 00.6	4 34.3	26 51.7	3 09.3	12 37.4	20 07.3
17 Su	13 45 18	24 27 22	1♐48 44	8♐59 08	2 07.9	2 29.5	16 11.2	13 42.9	6 27.8	4 46.9	26 54.2	3 08.1	12 37.2	20 08.7
18 M	13 49 15	25 26 58	16 10 07	23 21 11	2 08.5	4 05.5	17 22.6	14 22.2	6 55.0	4 59.5	26 56.5	3 06.9	12 37.0	20 10.2
19 Tu	13 53 12	26 26 35	0♑31 51	7♑41 41	2 09.0	5 40.9	18 34.0	15 01.4	7 22.2	5 12.0	26 58.7	3 05.7	12 36.8	20 11.7
20 W	13 57 08	27 26 14	14 50 18	21 57 21	2R 09.3	7 15.7	19 45.6	15 40.7	7 49.4	5 24.5	27 00.9	3 04.6	12 36.7	20 13.3
21 Th	14 01 05	28 25 55	29 02 33	6♒05 38	2 09.3	8 49.9	20 57.3	16 20.0	8 16.5	5 37.0	27 02.9	3 03.6	12 36.5	20 14.8
22 F	14 05 01	29 25 37	13♒06 22	20 04 35	2 09.1	10 23.5	22 09.1	16 59.3	8 43.6	5 49.4	27 04.8	3 02.6	12 36.5	20 16.4
23 Sa	14 08 58	0♏25 21	27 00 07	3♓52 49	2 08.9	11 56.5	23 21.0	17 38.7	9 10.7	6 01.8	27 06.6	3 01.6	12D 36.4	20 18.0
24 Su	14 12 54	1 25 07	10♓42 33	17 29 13	2D 08.7	13 29.0	24 33.0	18 18.1	9 37.7	6 14.2	27 08.3	3 00.7	12 36.4	20 19.6
25 M	14 16 51	2 24 54	24 12 43	0♈52 57	2 08.7	15 00.9	25 45.0	18 57.4	10 04.7	6 26.5	27 09.9	2 59.8	12 36.4	20 21.3
26 Tu	14 20 47	3 24 44	7♈29 51	14 03 21	2 08.8	16 32.3	26 57.2	19 36.9	10 31.7	6 38.7	27 11.4	2 59.0	12 36.5	20 22.9
27 W	14 24 44	4 24 35	20 33 25	27 00 01	2R 08.9	18 03.1	28 09.5	20 16.3	10 58.6	6 51.0	27 12.8	2 58.2	12 36.6	20 24.6
28 Th	14 28 41	5 24 28	3♉23 10	9♉42 53	2 08.8	19 33.4	29 21.8	20 55.8	11 25.5	7 03.1	27 14.0	2 57.5	12 36.7	20 26.3
29 F	14 32 37	6 24 22	15 59 15	22 12 23	2 08.6	21 03.2	0♎34.3	21 35.3	11 52.4	7 15.3	27 15.2	2 56.8	12 36.8	20 28.1
30 Sa	14 36 34	7 24 19	28 22 24	4♊29 30	2 08.1	22 32.5	1 46.8	22 14.8	12 19.2	7 27.3	27 16.2	2 56.1	12 37.0	20 29.8
31 Su	14 40 30	8 24 19	10♊33 56	16 35 57	2 07.3	24 01.2	2 59.4	22 54.4	12 46.0	7 39.4	27 17.2	2 55.6	12 37.2	20 31.6

Astro Data (Dy Hr Mn)

☽0N	1 3:32
☿D	2 13:09
☽0S	15 14:46
♃⚼♆	15 20:59
☉0S	22 16:29
☽0N	28 12:38
♂0S	29 13:26
☿0S	30 14:53
♃0S	6 19:13
♃⚻♅	10 11:07
☽0S	12 23:20
♆D	24 11:56
☽0N	25 20:21

Planet Ingress (Dy Hr Mn)

♀	♌	6 22:16
☿	♍	10 7:38
☉	♎	22 16:30
♃	♎	25 3:23
♂	♎	26 9:15
☿	♎	28 14:13
⚳	♎	3 8:06
♀	♍	3 17:20
☿	♏	15 22:57
☉	♏	23 1:49
♀	♎	29 0:39

Last Aspect / ☽ Ingress (Dy Hr Mn)

Last Aspect		☽ Ingress	
2 16:17	♀ △	♉	3 0:16
5 6:56	♀ ⚹	♊	5 10:24
7 18:08	♀ ⚹	♋	7 22:50
10 4:42	♃ ⚹	♌	10 11:06
12 1:22	♇ △	♍	12 21:16
15 0:55	♃ ☌	♎	15 4:54
17 1:31	♄ □	♏	17 10:25
19 12:24	♃ ⚹	♐	19 14:30
21 16:19	♃ □	♑	21 17:35
23 19:41	♃ △	♒	23 20:10
25 6:25	♀ ☍	♓	25 22:55
28 1:12	☿ ☍	♈	28 2:57
30 1:53	♄ □	♉	30 9:24

Last Aspect / ☽ Ingress (Dy Hr Mn)

Last Aspect		☽ Ingress	
2 16:34	♀ □	♊	2 18:55
4 10:28	♇ ☍	♋	5 6:54
7 12:13	♄ ☌	♌	7 19:23
9 10:42	♇ △	♍	10 6:00
12 7:32	♄ ⚹	♎	12 13:32
14 14:22	☿ ☌	♏	14 18:10
16 15:43	♄ △	♐	16 20:58
18 15:46	☉ ⚹	♑	18 23:07
20 21:59	☉ □	♒	21 1:38
22 12:20	♇ ⚹	♓	23 5:13
25 5:17	♄ △	♈	25 10:24
27 12:24	♄ □	♉	27 17:37
29 21:50	♄ ⚹	♊	30 3:11

☽ Phases & Eclipses (Dy Hr Mn)

6 15:11	☾	14♊21
14 14:29	●	22♍06
21 15:54	☽	29♐00
28 13:09	○	5♈45
6 10:12	☾	13♋30
14 2:48	●	21♎06
14 2:59:18	•	P 0.928
20 21:59	☽	27♑51
28 3:07	○	5♉02
28 3:04	•	T 1.308

Astro Data

1 September 2004
Julian Day # 38230
SVP 5♓11'49"
GC 26♐54.3 ⚴ 15♌54.8
Eris 20♈41.1R ⚵ 9♑09.7R
⚷ 20♑53.9R ⚶ 23♓46.0R
☽ Mean ☊ 4♉45.3

1 October 2004
Julian Day # 38260
SVP 5♓11'46"
GC 26♐54.3 ⚴ 2♍02.4
Eris 20♈25.4R ⚵ 11♑47.7
⚷ 20♑31.0 ⚶ 16♓35.3R
☽ Mean ☊ 3♉09.9

November 2004 LONGITUDE

Day	Sid.Time	☉	0 hr ☽	Noon ☽	True ☊	☿	♀	♂	⚳	♃	♄	♅	♆	♇
1 M	14 44 27	9♏24 20	22♊35 54	28♊34 07	2♉06.4	25♏29.4	4♎12.1	23♎34.0	13♎12.8	7♎51.3	27♋18.0	2♓55.0	12♒37.5	20♐33.4
2 Tu	14 48 23	10 24 23	4♋31 02	10♋27 04	2R 05.3	26 57.0	5 24.9	24 13.6	13 39.5	8 03.3	27 18.7	2R 54.5	12 37.8	20 35.3
3 W	14 52 20	11 24 28	16 22 44	22 18 31	2 04.4	28 24.0	6 37.8	24 53.2	14 06.2	8 15.1	27 19.3	2 54.1	12 38.1	20 37.1
4 Th	14 56 16	12 24 35	28 14 58	4♌12 39	2D 03.8	29 50.4	7 50.8	25 32.9	14 32.8	8 27.0	27 19.8	2 53.7	12 38.5	20 39.0
5 F	15 00 13	13 24 45	10♌12 08	16 14 00	2 03.7	1♐16.2	9 03.8	26 12.6	14 59.4	8 38.7	27 20.2	2 53.3	12 38.9	20 40.8
6 Sa	15 04 10	14 24 56	22 18 51	28 27 15	2 04.1	2 41.4	10 16.9	26 52.3	15 25.9	8 50.4	27 20.4	2 53.0	12 39.3	20 42.7
7 Su	15 08 06	15 25 09	4♍39 46	10♍56 53	2 05.0	4 05.8	11 30.1	27 32.1	15 52.4	9 02.1	27R 20.6	2 52.8	12 39.7	20 44.7
8 M	15 12 03	16 25 25	17 19 07	23 46 51	2 06.2	5 29.4	12 43.4	28 11.8	16 18.9	9 13.6	27 20.6	2 52.6	12 40.2	20 46.6
9 Tu	15 15 59	17 25 42	0♎20 26	7♎00 06	2 07.5	6 52.2	13 56.7	28 51.6	16 45.3	9 25.2	27 20.5	2 52.5	12 40.8	20 48.6
10 W	15 19 56	18 26 02	13 45 59	20 38 05	2R 08.4	8 14.1	15 10.1	29 31.5	17 11.7	9 36.6	27 20.3	2 52.4	12 41.3	20 50.5
11 Th	15 23 52	19 26 23	27 36 16	4♏40 14	2 08.6	9 35.0	16 23.6	0♏11.3	17 38.0	9 48.0	27 20.0	2D 52.3	12 41.9	20 52.5
12 F	15 27 49	20 26 46	11♏49 34	19 03 40	2 08.0	10 54.8	17 37.1	0 51.2	18 04.2	9 59.3	27 19.6	2 52.3	12 42.5	20 54.5
13 Sa	15 31 45	21 27 10	26 21 51	3♐43 14	2 06.4	12 13.3	18 50.7	1 31.2	18 30.5	10 10.5	27 19.1	2 52.4	12 43.2	20 56.5
14 Su	15 35 42	22 27 37	11♐06 56	18 31 57	2 03.9	13 30.5	20 04.3	2 11.1	18 56.6	10 21.7	27 18.4	2 52.5	12 43.9	20 58.6
15 M	15 39 39	23 28 05	25 57 17	3♑21 58	2 01.0	14 46.1	21 18.0	2 51.1	19 22.7	10 32.8	27 17.7	2 52.7	12 44.6	21 00.6
16 Tu	15 43 35	24 28 34	10♑45 03	18 05 43	1 58.1	16 00.0	22 31.8	3 31.1	19 48.7	10 43.8	27 16.8	2 52.9	12 45.4	21 02.7
17 W	15 47 32	25 29 05	25 23 14	2♒36 59	1 55.7	17 11.9	23 45.6	4 11.1	20 14.7	10 54.8	27 15.8	2 53.2	12 46.2	21 04.8
18 Th	15 51 28	26 29 37	9♒46 33	16 51 33	1D 54.3	18 21.5	24 59.4	4 51.1	20 40.6	11 05.7	27 14.7	2 53.5	12 47.0	21 06.9
19 F	15 55 25	27 30 09	23 51 50	0♓47 18	1 54.0	19 28.7	26 13.3	5 31.2	21 06.5	11 16.4	27 13.5	2 53.9	12 47.9	21 09.0
20 Sa	15 59 21	28 30 44	7♓37 59	14 23 57	1 54.8	20 32.9	27 27.3	6 11.3	21 32.3	11 27.1	27 12.2	2 54.3	12 48.8	21 11.1
21 Su	16 03 18	29 31 19	21 05 23	27 42 30	1 56.3	21 33.9	28 41.3	6 51.4	21 58.0	11 37.8	27 10.8	2 54.8	12 49.7	21 13.2
22 M	16 07 14	0♐31 55	4♈15 32	10♈44 43	1 58.0	22 31.3	29 55.3	7 31.6	22 23.7	11 48.3	27 09.3	2 55.3	12 50.7	21 15.4
23 Tu	16 11 11	1 32 33	17 10 19	23 32 35	1R 59.2	23 24.4	1♏09.4	8 11.8	22 49.3	11 58.7	27 07.6	2 55.9	12 51.6	21 17.5
24 W	16 15 08	2 33 12	29 51 44	6♉08 01	1 59.4	24 12.8	2 23.5	8 52.0	23 14.8	12 09.1	27 05.9	2 56.5	12 52.7	21 19.7
25 Th	16 19 04	3 33 52	12♉21 37	18 32 44	1 58.2	24 55.8	3 37.7	9 32.2	23 40.3	12 19.4	27 04.0	2 57.2	12 53.7	21 21.8
26 F	16 23 01	4 34 33	24 41 31	0♊48 08	1 55.2	25 32.7	4 51.9	10 12.5	24 05.7	12 29.5	27 02.1	2 57.9	12 54.8	21 24.0
27 Sa	16 26 57	5 35 16	6♊52 45	12 55 31	1 50.5	26 02.9	6 06.2	10 52.8	24 31.0	12 39.6	27 00.0	2 58.7	12 55.9	21 26.2
28 Su	16 30 54	6 36 00	18 56 36	24 56 10	1 44.4	26 25.5	7 20.5	11 33.1	24 56.2	12 49.6	26 57.9	2 59.5	12 57.0	21 28.4
29 M	16 34 50	7 36 46	0♋54 25	6♋51 34	1 37.5	26 39.7	8 34.8	12 13.5	25 21.4	12 59.5	26 55.6	3 00.4	12 58.2	21 30.6
30 Tu	16 38 47	8 37 33	12 47 52	18 43 37	1 30.5	26R 44.6	9 49.2	12 53.9	25 46.5	13 09.3	26 53.3	3 01.3	12 59.4	21 32.8

December 2004 LONGITUDE

Day	Sid.Time	☉	0 hr ☽	Noon ☽	True ☊	☿	♀	♂	⚳	♃	♄	♅	♆	♇
1 W	16 42 44	9♐38 21	24♋39 07	0♌34 45	1♉24.0	26♐39.7	11♏03.7	13♏34.3	26♎11.5	13♎19.0	26♋50.8	3♓02.3	13♒00.7	21♐35.1
2 Th	16 46 40	10 39 10	6♌30 55	12 28 03	1R 18.7	26R 24.1	12 18.1	14 14.7	26 36.5	13 28.6	26R 48.2	3 03.3	13 01.9	21 37.3
3 F	16 50 37	11 40 01	18 26 38	24 27 11	1 15.1	25 57.5	13 32.6	14 55.2	27 01.4	13 38.1	26 45.6	3 04.4	13 03.2	21 39.5
4 Sa	16 54 33	12 40 54	0♍30 16	6♍36 27	1D 13.4	25 19.6	14 47.2	15 35.7	27 26.2	13 47.5	26 42.8	3 05.5	13 04.5	21 41.8
5 Su	16 58 30	13 41 47	12 46 19	19 00 28	1 13.3	24 30.8	16 01.7	16 16.2	27 50.9	13 56.8	26 40.0	3 06.7	13 05.9	21 44.0
6 M	17 02 26	14 42 42	25 19 30	1♎43 58	1 14.3	23 31.7	17 16.3	16 56.8	28 15.5	14 05.9	26 37.0	3 07.9	13 07.3	21 46.3
7 Tu	17 06 23	15 43 38	8♎14 24	14 51 16	1 15.8	22 23.5	18 31.0	17 37.4	28 40.0	14 15.0	26 34.0	3 09.2	13 08.7	21 48.5
8 W	17 10 19	16 44 35	21 34 56	28 25 41	1R 16.7	21 08.0	19 45.6	18 18.0	29 04.5	14 23.9	26 30.8	3 10.5	13 10.1	21 50.8
9 Th	17 14 16	17 45 34	5♏23 37	12♏28 42	1 16.1	19 47.5	21 00.3	18 58.7	29 28.8	14 32.8	26 27.6	3 11.9	13 11.5	21 53.0
10 F	17 18 13	18 46 34	19 40 41	26 59 08	1 13.6	18 24.7	22 15.1	19 39.4	29 53.1	14 41.5	26 24.3	3 13.3	13 13.0	21 55.3
11 Sa	17 22 09	19 47 34	4♐23 23	11♐52 35	1 08.7	17 02.2	23 29.8	20 20.1	0♏17.3	14 50.1	26 20.9	3 14.8	13 14.6	21 57.5
12 Su	17 26 06	20 48 36	19 25 38	27 01 21	1 01.9	15 43.0	24 44.6	21 00.8	0 41.3	14 58.6	26 17.4	3 16.3	13 16.1	21 59.8
13 M	17 30 02	21 49 39	4♑38 23	12♑15 21	0 53.8	14 29.5	25 59.4	21 41.6	1 05.3	15 06.9	26 13.9	3 17.9	13 17.7	22 02.1
14 Tu	17 33 59	22 50 42	19 50 55	27 23 45	0 45.6	13 23.8	27 14.2	22 22.4	1 29.2	15 15.2	26 10.2	3 19.5	13 19.3	22 04.3
15 W	17 37 55	23 51 46	4♒52 44	12♒16 52	0 38.3	12 27.5	28 29.0	23 03.2	1 52.9	15 23.3	26 06.5	3 21.1	13 20.9	22 06.6
16 Th	17 41 52	24 52 50	19 35 22	26 47 38	0 32.8	11 41.7	29 43.9	23 44.1	2 16.6	15 31.2	26 02.7	3 22.8	13 22.5	22 08.9
17 F	17 45 48	25 53 54	3♓53 28	10♓52 33	0 29.6	11 06.9	0♐58.8	24 25.0	2 40.2	15 39.1	25 58.9	3 24.6	13 24.2	22 11.1
18 Sa	17 49 45	26 54 59	17 44 58	24 30 53	0D 28.4	10 43.1	2 13.6	25 05.9	3 03.6	15 46.8	25 54.9	3 26.4	13 25.9	22 13.4
19 Su	17 53 42	27 56 04	1♈10 37	7♈44 31	0 28.7	10D 30.1	3 28.5	25 46.8	3 26.9	15 54.4	25 50.9	3 28.2	13 27.6	22 15.7
20 M	17 57 38	28 57 09	14 13 03	20 36 41	0R 29.6	10 27.4	4 43.5	26 27.8	3 50.2	16 01.8	25 46.8	3 30.1	13 29.3	22 17.9
21 Tu	18 01 35	29 58 14	26 55 56	3♉11 17	0 29.9	10 34.3	5 58.4	27 08.8	4 13.3	16 09.1	25 42.7	3 32.0	13 31.1	22 20.2
22 W	18 05 31	0♑59 20	9♉23 12	15 32 09	0 28.7	10 50.1	7 13.3	27 49.8	4 36.3	16 16.3	25 38.5	3 34.0	13 32.9	22 22.4
23 Th	18 09 28	2 00 26	21 38 34	27 42 49	0 25.0	11 14.0	8 28.3	28 30.8	4 59.2	16 23.3	25 34.2	3 36.0	13 34.7	22 24.6
24 F	18 13 24	3 01 32	3♊45 14	9♊46 08	0 18.5	11 45.1	9 43.3	29 11.9	5 21.9	16 30.2	25 29.9	3 38.0	13 36.5	22 26.9
25 Sa	18 17 21	4 02 39	15 45 47	21 44 24	0 09.3	12 22.8	10 58.3	29 53.0	5 44.5	16 37.0	25 25.5	3 40.1	13 38.3	22 29.1
26 Su	18 21 17	5 03 46	27 42 12	3♋39 20	29♈57.7	13 06.4	12 13.3	0♐34.2	6 07.1	16 43.6	25 21.1	3 42.3	13 40.2	22 31.3
27 M	18 25 14	6 04 53	9♋35 59	15 32 18	29 44.6	13 55.1	13 28.3	1 15.3	6 29.5	16 50.1	25 16.6	3 44.4	13 42.1	22 33.6
28 Tu	18 29 11	7 06 00	21 28 28	27 24 37	29 31.1	14 48.4	14 43.3	1 56.5	6 51.7	16 56.4	25 12.0	3 46.7	13 44.0	22 35.8
29 W	18 33 07	8 07 08	3♌20 58	9♌17 43	29 18.3	15 45.8	15 58.4	2 37.8	7 13.8	17 02.5	25 07.5	3 48.9	13 45.9	22 38.0
30 Th	18 37 04	9 08 16	15 15 07	21 13 28	29 07.2	16 46.7	17 13.4	3 19.0	7 35.8	17 08.5	25 02.8	3 51.2	13 47.9	22 40.2
31 F	18 41 00	10 09 24	27 13 05	3♍14 20	28 58.7	17 50.9	18 28.5	4 00.3	7 57.7	17 14.4	24 58.2	3 53.5	13 49.8	22 42.4

Astro Data Dy Hr Mn	Planet Ingress Dy Hr Mn	Last Aspect Dy Hr Mn	☽ Ingress Dy Hr Mn	Last Aspect Dy Hr Mn	☽ Ingress Dy Hr Mn	☽ Phases & Eclipses Dy Hr Mn
♀0S 1 1:20	☿ ♐ 4 14:40	1 1:21 ♂ △	♋ 1 14:53	1 4:28 ♄ ☌	♌ 1 10:50	5 5:53 ☾ 13♌09
♄R 8 6:54	♂ ♏ 11 5:11	4 2:00 ☿ △	♌ 4 3:32	3 14:52 ☿ △	♍ 3 23:00	12 14:27 ● 20♏33
☽0S 9 9:15	☉ ♐ 21 23:22	6 8:45 ♂ ⚹	♍ 6 15:00	6 2:28 ♄ ⚹	♎ 6 8:46	19 5:50 ☽ 27♒15
♅D 11 19:12	♀ ♏ 22 13:31	8 18:32 ♄ ⚹	♎ 8 23:23	8 8:41 ♄ □	♏ 8 14:44	26 20:07 ○ 4♊55
⚳0S 13 13:10		11 4:02 ♂ ☌	♏ 11 4:05	10 11:03 ♄ △	♐ 10 16:54	
☽0N 22 2:08	⚳ ♏ 10 18:52	13 1:34 ♄ △	♐ 13 5:56	12 4:03 ♇ ☌	♑ 12 16:42	5 0:53 ☾ 13♍14
♃△♆ 29 8:26	♀ ♐ 16 17:10	14 15:58 ♇ ☌	♑ 15 6:33	14 11:43 ♀ ⚹	♒ 14 16:10	12 1:29 ● 20♐22
☿R 30 12:17	☉ ♑ 21 12:42	17 3:07 ♄ ☍	♒ 17 7:39	16 8:33 ☉ ⚹	♓ 16 17:24	18 16:40 ☽ 27♓07
	♂ ♐ 25 16:04	19 5:50 ☉ □	♓ 19 10:38	18 16:40 ☉ □	♈ 18 21:52	26 15:06 ○ 5♋12
☽0S 6 18:30	☊ ♈R 26 7:29	21 15:35 ☉ △	♈ 21 16:11	21 5:16 ☉ △	♉ 21 5:52	
☽0N 19 7:06		23 18:47 ♄ □	♉ 24 0:16	23 13:41 ♂ ☍	♊ 23 16:32	
☿D 20 6:28		26 4:37 ♄ ⚹	♊ 26 10:25	25 13:30 ♇ ☍	♋ 26 4:38	
		28 15:04 ☿ ☍	♋ 28 22:10	28 7:34 ♄ ☌	♌ 28 17:14	
				30 14:54 ♇ △	♍ 31 5:33	

Astro Data

1 November 2004
Julian Day # 38291
SVP 5♓11'42"
GC 26♐54.4 ⚴ 17♍07.4
Eris 20♈07.1R ⚵ 19♑04.4
⚷ 21♑18.6 ⚶ 13♓57.4
☽ Mean ☊ 1♉31.4

1 December 2004
Julian Day # 38321
SVP 5♓11'37"
GC 26♐54.5 ⚴ 29♍32.1
Eris 19♈52.6R ⚵ 29♑06.1
⚷ 23♑04.9 ⚶ 17♓52.8
☽ Mean ☊ 29♈56.1

LONGITUDE — January 2005

Day	Sid.Time	☉	0 hr ☽	Noon☽	True☊	☿	♀	♂	⚳	♃	♄	♅	♆	♇
1 Sa	18 44 57	11♑10 33	9♍17 40	15♍23 30	28♈53.0	18♐57.9	19♐43.6	4♐41.6	8♏19.4	17♎20.1	24♋53.5	3♓55.9	13♒51.8	22♐44.5
2 Su	18 48 53	12 11 42	21 32 23	27 44 49	28R50.0	20 07.4	20 58.6	5 23.0	8 41.0	17 25.6	24R48.7	3 58.3	13 53.8	22 46.7
3 M	18 52 50	13 12 51	4♎01 23	10♎22 38	28D49.0	21 19.2	22 13.7	6 04.4	9 02.5	17 31.0	24 44.0	4 00.7	13 55.8	22 48.8
4 Tu	18 56 47	14 14 00	16 49 11	23 21 32	28R49.1	22 32.9	23 28.9	6 45.8	9 23.8	17 36.3	24 39.2	4 03.2	13 57.8	22 51.0
5 W	19 00 43	15 15 10	0♏00 14	6♏45 43	28 49.0	23 48.4	24 44.0	7 27.2	9 44.9	17 41.3	24 34.3	4 05.7	13 59.9	22 53.1
6 Th	19 04 40	16 16 20	13 38 18	20 38 12	28 47.4	25 05.5	25 59.1	8 08.7	10 05.9	17 46.2	24 29.5	4 08.3	14 01.9	22 55.3
7 F	19 08 36	17 17 30	27 45 28	4♐59 55	28 43.4	26 24.0	27 14.3	8 50.2	10 26.8	17 51.0	24 24.6	4 10.9	14 04.0	22 57.4
8 Sa	19 12 33	18 18 40	12♐21 10	19 48 36	28 36.5	27 43.9	28 29.4	9 31.8	10 47.5	17 55.5	24 19.7	4 13.5	14 06.1	22 59.5
9 Su	19 16 29	19 19 51	27 21 19	4♑58 15	28 27.0	29 04.9	29 44.6	10 13.3	11 08.0	17 59.9	24 14.8	4 16.1	14 08.2	23 01.6
10 M	19 20 26	20 21 01	12♑38 04	20 19 20	28 15.8	0♑27.0	0♑59.7	10 54.9	11 28.4	18 04.2	24 09.9	4 18.8	14 10.3	23 03.6
11 Tu	19 24 22	21 22 11	28 00 31	5♒40 05	28 04.0	1 50.1	2 14.9	11 36.6	11 48.6	18 08.2	24 04.9	4 21.5	14 12.5	23 05.7
12 W	19 28 19	22 23 20	13♒16 36	20 48 44	27 53.2	3 14.1	3 30.1	12 18.2	12 08.6	18 12.1	24 00.0	4 24.3	14 14.6	23 07.7
13 Th	19 32 16	23 24 29	28 15 21	5♓35 35	27 44.4	4 38.9	4 45.2	12 59.9	12 28.5	18 15.8	23 55.0	4 27.1	14 16.7	23 09.8
14 F	19 36 12	24 25 37	12♓48 46	19 54 32	27 38.5	6 04.6	6 00.4	13 41.6	12 48.2	18 19.3	23 50.1	4 29.9	14 18.9	23 11.8
15 Sa	19 40 09	25 26 44	26 52 42	3♈43 20	27 35.3	7 31.0	7 15.6	14 23.3	13 07.7	18 22.7	23 45.1	4 32.7	14 21.1	23 13.8
16 Su	19 44 05	26 27 51	10♈26 38	17 02 59	27 34.1	8 58.1	8 30.7	15 05.1	13 27.0	18 25.9	23 40.2	4 35.6	14 23.3	23 15.7
17 M	19 48 02	27 28 57	23 32 50	29 56 43	27 34.0	10 26.0	9 45.9	15 46.8	13 46.2	18 28.9	23 35.3	4 38.5	14 25.5	23 17.7
18 Tu	19 51 58	28 30 02	6♉15 16	12♉29 04	27 33.7	11 54.5	11 01.0	16 28.6	14 05.1	18 31.7	23 30.3	4 41.4	14 27.7	23 19.6
19 W	19 55 55	29 31 06	18 38 46	24 44 57	27 31.8	13 23.6	12 16.2	17 10.5	14 23.9	18 34.3	23 25.4	4 44.4	14 29.9	23 21.6
20 Th	19 59 51	0♒32 09	0♊48 13	6♊49 06	27 27.5	14 53.4	13 31.4	17 52.3	14 42.5	18 36.8	23 20.5	4 47.3	14 32.1	23 23.5
21 F	20 03 48	1 33 12	12 48 09	18 45 48	27 20.3	16 23.8	14 46.5	18 34.2	15 00.9	18 39.0	23 15.7	4 50.3	14 34.3	23 25.4
22 Sa	20 07 45	2 34 14	24 42 28	0♋38 32	27 10.0	17 54.8	16 01.7	19 16.2	15 19.0	18 41.1	23 10.8	4 53.4	14 36.6	23 27.2
23 Su	20 11 41	3 35 15	6♋34 18	12 30 04	26 57.2	19 26.5	17 16.8	19 58.1	15 37.0	18 43.0	23 06.0	4 56.4	14 38.8	23 29.1
24 M	20 15 38	4 36 15	18 26 02	24 22 26	26 42.8	20 58.7	18 32.0	20 40.1	15 54.8	18 44.7	23 01.2	4 59.5	14 41.1	23 30.9
25 Tu	20 19 34	5 37 14	0♌19 24	6♌17 07	26 27.8	22 31.6	19 47.2	21 22.1	16 12.4	18 46.3	22 56.4	5 02.6	14 43.3	23 32.7
26 W	20 23 31	6 38 12	12 15 42	18 15 18	26 13.5	24 05.1	21 02.3	22 04.1	16 29.8	18 47.6	22 51.7	5 05.7	14 45.6	23 34.5
27 Th	20 27 27	7 39 10	24 16 03	0♍18 07	26 01.0	25 39.3	22 17.5	22 46.2	16 46.9	18 48.8	22 47.0	5 08.8	14 47.8	23 36.3
28 F	20 31 24	8 40 06	6♍21 40	12 26 56	25 51.2	27 14.1	23 32.6	23 28.3	17 03.9	18 49.7	22 42.3	5 12.0	14 50.1	23 38.0
29 Sa	20 35 20	9 41 02	18 34 09	24 43 36	25 44.4	28 49.5	24 47.8	24 10.4	17 20.6	18 50.5	22 37.7	5 15.2	14 52.4	23 39.7
30 Su	20 39 17	10 41 57	0♎55 38	7♎10 36	25 40.6	0♒25.6	26 02.9	24 52.6	17 37.1	18 51.1	22 33.1	5 18.4	14 54.7	23 41.4
31 M	20 43 14	11 42 52	13 28 54	19 50 59	25D39.2	2 02.4	27 18.1	25 34.7	17 53.3	18 51.5	22 28.6	5 21.6	14 56.9	23 43.1

LONGITUDE — February 2005

Day	Sid.Time	☉	0 hr ☽	Noon☽	True☊	☿	♀	♂	⚳	♃	♄	♅	♆	♇
1 Tu	20 47 10	12♒43 45	26♎17 18	2♏48 18	25♈39.2	3♒39.9	28♑33.2	26♐17.0	18♏09.4	18♎51.7	22♋24.1	5♓24.8	14♒59.2	23♐44.7
2 W	20 51 07	13 44 38	9♏24 27	16 06 11	25R39.4	5 18.1	29 48.4	26 59.2	18 25.1	18R51.7	22R19.6	5 28.1	15 01.5	23 46.4
3 Th	20 55 03	14 45 30	22 53 51	29 47 44	25 38.5	6 57.0	1♒03.5	27 41.5	18 40.7	18 51.6	22 15.3	5 31.4	15 03.8	23 48.0
4 F	20 59 00	15 46 21	6♐48 01	13♐54 42	25 35.5	8 36.7	2 18.7	28 23.8	18 56.0	18 51.2	22 10.9	5 34.7	15 06.0	23 49.6
5 Sa	21 02 56	16 47 12	21 07 41	28 26 35	25 30.0	10 17.1	3 33.9	29 06.1	19 11.1	18 50.7	22 06.7	5 38.0	15 08.3	23 51.1
6 Su	21 06 53	17 48 02	5♑50 52	13♑19 46	25 22.0	11 58.2	4 49.0	29 48.5	19 25.9	18 49.9	22 02.4	5 41.3	15 10.6	23 52.6
7 M	21 10 49	18 48 50	20 52 18	28 27 20	25 12.2	13 40.2	6 04.1	0♑30.9	19 40.4	18 49.0	21 58.3	5 44.6	15 12.9	23 54.1
8 Tu	21 14 46	19 49 38	6♒03 32	13♒39 35	25 01.7	15 22.9	7 19.3	1 13.3	19 54.7	18 47.8	21 54.2	5 48.0	15 15.2	23 55.6
9 W	21 18 43	20 50 24	21 14 03	28 45 38	24 52.0	17 06.4	8 34.4	1 55.7	20 08.7	18 46.5	21 50.2	5 51.3	15 17.4	23 57.1
10 Th	21 22 39	21 51 09	6♓13 05	13♓35 22	24 44.0	18 50.7	9 49.5	2 38.2	20 22.5	18 45.0	21 46.3	5 54.7	15 19.7	23 58.5
11 F	21 26 36	22 51 52	20 51 36	28 01 09	24 38.5	20 35.9	11 04.7	3 20.6	20 36.0	18 43.3	21 42.4	5 58.1	15 22.0	23 59.9
12 Sa	21 30 32	23 52 33	5♈03 36	11♈58 43	24D35.7	22 21.8	12 19.8	4 03.2	20 49.2	18 41.4	21 38.6	6 01.4	15 24.3	24 01.2
13 Su	21 34 29	24 53 13	18 46 32	25 27 10	24 34.9	24 08.6	13 34.9	4 45.7	21 02.1	18 39.3	21 34.8	6 04.8	15 26.5	24 02.6
14 M	21 38 25	25 53 52	2♉00 58	8♉28 19	24 35.5	25 56.2	14 50.0	5 28.2	21 14.7	18 37.1	21 31.2	6 08.2	15 28.8	24 03.9
15 Tu	21 42 22	26 54 28	14 49 46	21 05 52	24R36.3	27 44.5	16 05.0	6 10.8	21 27.0	18 34.6	21 27.6	6 11.7	15 31.0	24 05.2
16 W	21 46 18	27 55 03	27 17 14	3♊24 31	24 36.3	29 33.7	17 20.1	6 53.4	21 39.1	18 32.0	21 24.2	6 15.1	15 33.3	24 06.4
17 Th	21 50 15	28 55 37	9♊28 20	15 29 20	24 34.5	1♓23.6	18 35.2	7 36.0	21 50.8	18 29.2	21 20.8	6 18.5	15 35.5	24 07.7
18 F	21 54 12	29 56 08	21 28 07	27 25 17	24 30.6	3 14.1	19 50.2	8 18.7	22 02.3	18 26.2	21 17.4	6 21.9	15 37.7	24 08.9
19 Sa	21 58 08	0♓56 38	3♋21 21	9♋16 50	24 24.4	5 05.4	21 05.3	9 01.4	22 13.4	18 23.1	21 14.2	6 25.4	15 39.9	24 10.0
20 Su	22 02 05	1 57 06	15 12 13	21 07 53	24 16.1	6 57.2	22 20.3	9 44.1	22 24.2	18 19.7	21 11.1	6 28.8	15 42.2	24 11.2
21 M	22 06 01	2 57 32	27 04 13	3♌01 32	24 06.5	8 49.4	23 35.3	10 26.8	22 34.8	18 16.2	21 08.0	6 32.3	15 44.4	24 12.3
22 Tu	22 09 58	3 57 57	9♌00 07	15 00 11	23 56.3	10 42.1	24 50.3	11 09.5	22 45.0	18 12.5	21 05.1	6 35.7	15 46.6	24 13.3
23 W	22 13 54	4 58 19	21 01 55	27 05 31	23 46.6	12 35.0	26 05.3	11 52.3	22 54.8	18 08.7	21 02.2	6 39.2	15 48.7	24 14.4
24 Th	22 17 51	5 58 40	3♍11 05	9♍18 44	23 38.2	14 27.9	27 20.3	12 35.1	23 04.4	18 04.6	20 59.4	6 42.6	15 50.9	24 15.4
25 F	22 21 47	6 58 59	15 28 36	21 40 45	23 31.7	16 20.7	28 35.3	13 17.9	23 13.6	18 00.4	20 56.8	6 46.1	15 53.1	24 16.4
26 Sa	22 25 44	7 59 17	27 55 18	4♎12 23	23 27.6	18 13.2	29 50.3	14 00.8	23 22.5	17 56.1	20 54.2	6 49.5	15 55.2	24 17.3
27 Su	22 29 41	8 59 33	10♎32 06	16 54 39	23D25.7	20 05.1	1♓05.2	14 43.7	23 31.1	17 51.5	20 51.7	6 53.0	15 57.4	24 18.3
28 M	22 33 37	9 59 47	23 20 10	29 48 51	23 25.6	21 56.0	2 20.2	15 26.6	23 39.3	17 46.9	20 49.3	6 56.4	15 59.5	24 19.2

Astro Data Dy Hr Mn	Planet Ingress Dy Hr Mn	Last Aspect Dy Hr Mn	☽ Ingress Dy Hr Mn	Last Aspect Dy Hr Mn	☽ Ingress Dy Hr Mn	☽ Phases & Eclipses Dy Hr Mn
☽0S 3 1:24	♀ ♑ 9 16:56	2 6:23 ♄ ✱	♎ 2 16:19	1 3:21 ♀ □	♏ 1 6:51	3 17:46 ☾ 13♎28
☽0N 15 13:29	☿ ♑ 10 4:09	4 14:20 ♄ □	♏ 4 24:00	2 22:56 ♄ △	♐ 3 12:21	10 12:03 ● 20♑21
♄⚻♇ 20 1:37	☉ ♒ 19 23:22	6 18:29 ♄ △	♐ 7 3:44	5 13:08 ♂ ☌	♑ 5 14:32	17 6:57 ☽ 27♈16
☽0S 30 6:25	☿ ♒ 30 5:37	9 3:02 ♀ ☌	♑ 9 4:11	7 1:47 ♄ ☍	♒ 7 14:26	25 10:32 ○ 5♌34
		10 17:58 ♄ ☍	♒ 11 3:07	9 4:19 ♇ ✱	♓ 9 13:59	
♃R 2 2:26	♀ ♒ 2 15:42	12 15:44 ♇ ✱	♓ 13 2:50	11 5:14 ♇ □	♈ 11 15:21	2 7:27 ☾ 13♏33
☽0N 11 22:23	♂ ♑ 6 18:32	14 20:22 ☉ ✱	♈ 15 5:27	13 10:54 ☉ ✱	♉ 13 20:18	8 22:28 ● 20♒16
♄⚼♅ 17 19:59	☿ ♓ 16 17:46	17 6:57 ☉ □	♉ 17 12:06	16 3:07 ☿ □	♊ 16 5:18	16 0:16 ☽ 27♉25
☽0S 26 11:33	☉ ♓ 18 13:32	19 22:19 ☉ △	♊ 19 22:24	18 5:23 ♇ ☍	♋ 18 17:13	24 4:54 ○ 5♍41
	♀ ♓ 26 15:07	21 21:26 ♇ ☍	♋ 22 10:42	20 12:06 ♄ ☌	♌ 21 5:54	
		24 9:17 ♄ ☌	♌ 24 23:21	23 9:47 ♀ ☍	♍ 23 17:44	
		26 22:39 ♇ △	♍ 27 11:24	25 17:00 ♇ □	♎ 26 3:59	
		29 21:07 ☿ △	♎ 29 22:13	28 1:49 ♇ ✱	♏ 28 12:21	

Astro Data

1 January 2005
Julian Day # 38352
SVP 5♓11'31"
GC 26♐54.5 ⚴ 8♎53.7
Eris 19♈45.5R ✱ 11♒29.7
⚷ 25♑35.5 ⚵ 26♓34.7
☽ Mean ☊ 28♈17.7

1 February 2005
Julian Day # 38383
SVP 5♓11'26"
GC 26♐54.6 ⚴ 12♎36.5R
Eris 19♈48.9 ✱ 25♒15.9
⚷ 28♑19.6 ⚵ 7♈59.0
☽ Mean ☊ 26♈39.2

March 2005 LONGITUDE

Day	Sid.Time	☉	0 hr ☽	Noon ☽	True ☊	☿	♀	♂	⚳	♃	♄	♅	♆	♇
1 Tu	22 37 34	11♓00 00	6♏20 57	12♏56 40	23♈26.7	23♓45.7	3♓35.1	16♑09.5	23♏47.2	17♎42.0	20♋47.0	6♓59.8	16♒01.6	24♐20.0
2 W	22 41 30	12 00 11	19 36 14	26 19 53	23 28.2	25 33.7	4 50.1	16 52.4	23 54.7	17R37.0	20R44.9	7 03.3	16 03.7	24 20.8
3 Th	22 45 27	13 00 21	3♐07 49	10♐00 10	23R29.1	27 19.6	6 05.0	17 35.4	24 01.8	17 31.9	20 42.8	7 06.7	16 05.8	24 21.6
4 F	22 49 23	14 00 30	16 57 04	23 58 30	23 28.6	29 02.9	7 19.9	18 18.4	24 08.6	17 26.6	20 40.8	7 10.2	16 07.9	24 22.4
5 Sa	22 53 20	15 00 37	1♑04 24	8♑14 34	23 26.6	0♈43.2	8 34.8	19 01.5	24 15.1	17 21.2	20 38.9	7 13.6	16 09.9	24 23.1
6 Su	22 57 16	16 00 43	15 28 40	22 46 13	23 22.9	2 19.9	9 49.7	19 44.5	24 21.1	17 15.6	20 37.2	7 17.0	16 12.0	24 23.8
7 M	23 01 13	17 00 47	0♒06 36	7♒29 04	23 17.9	3 52.5	11 04.6	20 27.6	24 26.8	17 09.9	20 35.5	7 20.4	16 14.0	24 24.5
8 Tu	23 05 10	18 00 49	14 52 47	22 16 47	23 12.4	5 20.4	12 19.5	21 10.7	24 32.1	17 04.0	20 33.9	7 23.9	16 16.0	24 25.1
9 W	23 09 06	19 00 49	29 40 06	7♓01 41	23 07.2	6 43.1	13 34.4	21 53.8	24 37.1	16 58.0	20 32.5	7 27.3	16 18.0	24 25.7
10 Th	23 13 03	20 00 47	14♓20 36	21 35 56	23 02.9	8 00.0	14 49.2	22 36.9	24 41.6	16 51.9	20 31.1	7 30.7	16 20.0	24 26.3
11 F	23 16 59	21 00 44	28 46 52	5♈52 44	23 00.2	9 10.6	16 04.1	23 20.1	24 45.8	16 45.7	20 29.9	7 34.0	16 22.0	24 26.8
12 Sa	23 20 56	22 00 38	12♈53 01	19 47 20	22D59.1	10 14.5	17 18.9	24 03.2	24 49.5	16 39.3	20 28.8	7 37.4	16 23.9	24 27.3
13 Su	23 24 52	23 00 31	26 35 27	3♉17 20	22 59.4	11 11.3	18 33.7	24 46.4	24 52.9	16 32.9	20 27.8	7 40.8	16 25.9	24 27.8
14 M	23 28 49	24 00 21	9♉53 03	16 22 47	23 00.7	12 00.5	19 48.5	25 29.6	24 55.9	16 26.3	20 26.9	7 44.1	16 27.8	24 28.2
15 Tu	23 32 45	25 00 09	22 46 50	29 05 37	23 02.4	12 41.8	21 03.3	26 12.8	24 58.5	16 19.6	20 26.1	7 47.5	16 29.7	24 28.6
16 W	23 36 42	25 59 55	5♊19 34	11♊29 14	23 04.0	13 15.1	22 18.0	26 56.0	25 00.7	16 12.8	20 25.4	7 50.8	16 31.5	24 29.0
17 Th	23 40 39	26 59 39	17 35 10	23 37 56	23R04.8	13 40.0	23 32.8	27 39.3	25 02.4	16 05.9	20 24.8	7 54.1	16 33.4	24 29.4
18 F	23 44 35	27 59 21	29 38 09	5♋36 26	23 04.5	13 56.7	24 47.5	28 22.5	25 03.8	15 59.0	20 24.4	7 57.4	16 35.2	24 29.7
19 Sa	23 48 32	28 59 00	11♋33 21	17 29 31	23 03.2	14R05.0	26 02.2	29 05.8	25 04.8	15 51.9	20 24.0	8 00.7	16 37.0	24 29.9
20 Su	23 52 28	29 58 37	23 25 28	29 21 45	23 00.8	14 05.1	27 16.9	29 49.1	25R05.4	15 44.8	20 23.8	8 04.0	16 38.8	24 30.2
21 M	23 56 25	0♈58 12	5♌18 51	11♌17 16	22 57.6	13 57.2	28 31.6	0♒32.4	25 05.5	15 37.6	20D23.7	8 07.2	16 40.6	24 30.4
22 Tu	0 00 21	1 57 44	17 17 23	23 19 36	22 54.1	13 41.6	29 46.3	1 15.8	25 05.3	15 30.3	20 23.7	8 10.4	16 42.4	24 30.5
23 W	0 04 18	2 57 14	29 24 14	5♍31 35	22 50.8	13 18.9	1♈00.9	1 59.1	25 04.6	15 23.0	20 23.8	8 13.7	16 44.1	24 30.7
24 Th	0 08 14	3 56 43	11♍41 51	17 55 15	22 47.9	12 49.6	2 15.5	2 42.5	25 03.6	15 15.6	20 24.0	8 16.9	16 45.8	24 30.8
25 F	0 12 11	4 56 08	24 11 55	0♎31 55	22 45.8	12 14.4	3 30.1	3 25.8	25 02.1	15 08.1	20 24.3	8 20.0	16 47.5	24 30.8
26 Sa	0 16 08	5 55 32	6♎55 19	13 22 09	22D44.7	11 34.2	4 44.7	4 09.2	25 00.2	15 00.6	20 24.7	8 23.2	16 49.1	24R30.9
27 Su	0 20 04	6 54 54	19 52 23	26 25 59	22 44.5	10 49.8	5 59.3	4 52.6	24 57.9	14 53.1	20 25.2	8 26.3	16 50.7	24 30.9
28 M	0 24 01	7 54 14	3♏02 53	9♏43 02	22 45.1	10 02.3	7 13.9	5 36.1	24 55.2	14 45.5	20 25.9	8 29.4	16 52.3	24 30.9
29 Tu	0 27 57	8 53 32	16 26 20	23 12 41	22 46.1	9 12.7	8 28.4	6 19.5	24 52.1	14 37.8	20 26.7	8 32.5	16 53.9	24 30.8
30 W	0 31 54	9 52 49	0♐02 00	6♐54 11	22 47.2	8 21.9	9 43.0	7 03.0	24 48.6	14 30.2	20 27.5	8 35.6	16 55.5	24 30.7
31 Th	0 35 50	10 52 03	13 49 05	20 46 36	22 48.1	7 31.2	10 57.5	7 46.4	24 44.6	14 22.5	20 28.5	8 38.7	16 57.0	24 30.6

April 2005 LONGITUDE

Day	Sid.Time	☉	0 hr ☽	Noon ☽	True ☊	☿	♀	♂	⚳	♃	♄	♅	♆	♇
1 F	0 39 47	11♈51 16	27♐46 34	4♑48 49	22♈48.7	6♈41.4	12♈12.0	8♒29.9	24♏40.3	14♎14.8	20♋29.6	8♓41.7	16♒58.5	24♐30.4
2 Sa	0 43 43	12 50 27	11♑53 10	18 59 21	22R48.7	5R53.5	13 26.5	9 13.4	24R35.6	14R07.1	20 30.8	8 44.7	17 00.0	24R30.2
3 Su	0 47 40	13 49 37	26 07 06	3♒16 05	22 48.3	5 08.3	14 40.9	9 57.0	24 30.4	13 59.4	20 32.1	8 47.7	17 01.5	24 30.0
4 M	0 51 37	14 48 45	10♒25 55	17 36 12	22 47.5	4 26.5	15 55.4	10 40.5	24 24.9	13 51.6	20 33.5	8 50.7	17 02.9	24 29.8
5 Tu	0 55 33	15 47 50	24 46 26	1♓56 09	22 46.7	3 48.8	17 09.9	11 24.0	24 19.0	13 43.9	20 35.0	8 53.6	17 04.3	24 29.5
6 W	0 59 30	16 46 54	9♓04 47	16 11 47	22 45.9	3 15.6	18 24.3	12 07.6	24 12.6	13 36.2	20 36.7	8 56.5	17 05.7	24 29.2
7 Th	1 03 26	17 45 56	23 16 38	0♈18 47	22 45.4	2 47.2	19 38.7	12 51.1	24 05.9	13 28.5	20 38.4	8 59.4	17 07.0	24 28.8
8 F	1 07 23	18 44 56	7♈17 44	14 13 02	22D45.1	2 24.0	20 53.1	13 34.6	23 58.8	13 20.8	20 40.3	9 02.2	17 08.4	24 28.4
9 Sa	1 11 19	19 43 54	21 04 16	27 51 09	22 45.1	2 06.1	22 07.5	14 18.2	23 51.4	13 13.1	20 42.2	9 05.0	17 09.7	24 28.0
10 Su	1 15 16	20 42 51	4♉33 26	11♉10 56	22 45.2	1 53.6	23 21.8	15 01.8	23 43.6	13 05.5	20 44.3	9 07.8	17 10.9	24 27.6
11 M	1 19 12	21 41 45	17 43 37	24 11 29	22 45.3	1D46.5	24 36.2	15 45.3	23 35.4	12 57.9	20 46.4	9 10.6	17 12.2	24 27.1
12 Tu	1 23 09	22 40 37	0♊34 39	6♊53 18	22R45.4	1 44.8	25 50.5	16 28.9	23 26.8	12 50.4	20 48.7	9 13.3	17 13.4	24 26.6
13 W	1 27 05	23 39 26	13 07 43	19 18 12	22 45.3	1 48.4	27 04.8	17 12.4	23 18.0	12 42.9	20 51.1	9 16.0	17 14.5	24 26.0
14 Th	1 31 02	24 38 14	25 25 11	1♋29 05	22 45.2	1 57.1	28 19.1	17 56.0	23 08.7	12 35.4	20 53.5	9 18.7	17 15.7	24 25.5
15 F	1 34 59	25 36 59	7♋30 23	13 29 38	22 45.0	2 10.7	29 33.3	18 39.6	22 59.2	12 28.0	20 56.1	9 21.3	17 16.8	24 24.9
16 Sa	1 38 55	26 35 42	19 27 22	25 24 10	22D45.0	2 29.2	0♉47.6	19 23.1	22 49.4	12 20.7	20 58.9	9 23.9	17 17.9	24 24.3
17 Su	1 42 52	27 34 23	1♌20 35	7♌17 14	22 45.0	2 52.3	2 01.8	20 06.7	22 39.2	12 13.5	21 01.6	9 26.5	17 19.0	24 23.6
18 M	1 46 48	28 33 02	13 14 41	19 13 29	22 45.4	3 19.9	3 16.0	20 50.3	22 28.8	12 06.3	21 04.4	9 29.1	17 20.0	24 22.9
19 Tu	1 50 45	29 31 38	25 14 13	1♍17 23	22 45.9	3 51.7	4 30.2	21 33.8	22 18.0	11 59.2	21 07.4	9 31.6	17 21.0	24 22.2
20 W	1 54 41	0♉30 12	7♍23 28	13 32 56	22 46.7	4 27.6	5 44.4	22 17.4	22 07.0	11 52.1	21 10.5	9 34.0	17 22.0	24 21.5
21 Th	1 58 38	1 28 44	19 46 10	26 03 30	22 47.5	5 07.4	6 58.5	23 00.9	21 55.8	11 45.2	21 13.7	9 36.5	17 22.9	24 20.7
22 F	2 02 34	2 27 14	2♎25 14	8♎51 31	22 48.1	5 50.8	8 12.6	23 44.5	21 44.3	11 38.3	21 16.9	9 38.9	17 23.8	24 19.9
23 Sa	2 06 31	3 25 42	15 22 31	21 58 16	22R48.4	6 37.8	9 26.7	24 28.0	21 32.5	11 31.6	21 20.3	9 41.2	17 24.7	24 19.1
24 Su	2 10 28	4 24 08	28 38 42	5♏23 41	22 48.2	7 28.2	10 40.8	25 11.6	21 20.6	11 24.9	21 23.7	9 43.6	17 25.5	24 18.3
25 M	2 14 24	5 22 33	12♏13 01	19 06 25	22 47.3	8 21.9	11 54.9	25 55.2	21 08.4	11 18.4	21 27.3	9 45.9	17 26.3	24 17.4
26 Tu	2 18 21	6 20 55	26 03 29	3♐03 48	22 45.9	9 18.6	13 08.9	26 38.7	20 56.1	11 11.9	21 30.9	9 48.1	17 27.1	24 16.5
27 W	2 22 17	7 19 16	10♐06 55	17 11 32	22 44.1	10 18.3	14 22.9	27 22.3	20 43.5	11 05.6	21 34.6	9 50.4	17 27.9	24 15.6
28 Th	2 26 14	8 17 35	24 19 26	1♑27 48	22 42.2	11 20.8	15 36.9	28 05.8	20 30.8	10 59.4	21 38.5	9 52.5	17 28.6	24 14.6
29 F	2 30 10	9 15 53	8♑36 53	15 46 12	22 40.6	12 26.1	16 50.9	28 49.3	20 18.0	10 53.3	21 42.4	9 54.7	17 29.3	24 13.6
30 Sa	2 34 07	10 14 09	22 55 18	0♒03 46	22D39.6	13 34.1	18 04.9	29 32.9	20 04.9	10 47.3	21 46.4	9 56.8	17 30.0	24 12.7

Astro Data	Dy Hr Mn
☿0N	4 17:04
☽0N	11 8:42
♃△♆	14 7:46
☿R	20 0:13
☉0N	20 12:33
⚳R	21 9:29
♄D	22 2:54
♀0N	25 6:09
☽0S	25 18:23
♇R	27 2:29
☽0N	7 18:13
☿D	12 7:45
☿0S	14 4:21
☿0N	21 0:01
☽0S	22 2:51

Planet Ingress		Dy Hr Mn
☿	♈	5 1:34
☉	♈	20 12:33
♂	♒	20 18:02
♀	♈	22 16:25
♀	♉	15 20:37
☉	♉	19 23:37

Last Aspect Dy Hr Mn		☽ Ingress	Dy Hr Mn
2 10:25	☿ △	♐	2 18:29
4 21:45	☿ □	♑	4 22:12
6 8:29	♄ ☍	♒	6 23:49
8 15:28	♇ ⚹	♓	9 0:32
10 16:44	♇ □	♈	11 2:03
12 20:13	♇ △	♉	13 6:05
15 6:10	♂ △	♊	15 13:44
17 19:19	☉ □	♋	18 0:44
20 12:59	♂ ☍	♌	20 13:17
22 14:20	♇ △	♍	23 1:10
25 0:36	♇ □	♎	25 11:00
27 8:30	♇ ⚹	♏	27 18:29
29 7:06	♄ △	♐	29 23:56

Last Aspect Dy Hr Mn		☽ Ingress	Dy Hr Mn
31 18:24	♇ ☌	♑	1 3:48
2 14:34	♄ ☍	♒	3 6:31
4 23:32	♇ ⚹	♓	5 8:45
7 2:03	♇ □	♈	7 11:28
9 6:00	♇ △	♉	9 15:50
11 5:37	♄ ⚹	♊	11 22:55
14 5:01	♀ ⚹	♋	14 9:03
16 14:37	☉ □	♌	16 21:17
19 8:13	☉ △	♍	19 9:27
21 8:45	♇ □	♎	21 19:27
23 16:46	♂ △	♏	24 2:25
26 0:24	♂ □	♐	26 6:46
28 6:03	♂ ⚹	♑	28 9:33
29 22:00	♄ ☍	♒	30 11:54

☽ Phases & Eclipses Dy Hr Mn		
3 17:36	☾	13♐14
10 9:10	●	19♓54
17 19:19	☽	27♊18
25 20:59	○	5♎18
2 0:50	☾	12♑23
8 20:32	●	19♈06
8 20:35:46	●	AT00'42"
16 14:37	☽	26♋42
24 10:06	○	4♏20
24 9:55	●	A 0.865

Astro Data

1 March 2005
Julian Day # 38411
SVP 5♓11'22"
GC 26♐54.7 ⚵ 9♎08.4R
Eris 20♈00.2 ✱ 8♓29.7
⚷ 0♒35.0 ⚶ 19♈32.3
☽ Mean ☊ 25♈10.2

1 April 2005
Julian Day # 38442
SVP 5♓11'18"
GC 26♐54.8 ⚵ 29♍53.2R
Eris 20♈18.8 ✱ 23♓43.6
⚷ 2♒25.9 ⚶ 3♉00.6
☽ Mean ☊ 23♈31.7

LONGITUDE — May 2005

Day	Sid.Time	☉	0 hr ☽	Noon ☽	True ☊	☿	♀	♂	⚳	♃	♄	♅	♆	♇
1 Su	2 38 04	11♉12 24	7♒11 15	14♒17 25	22♈39.4	14♈44.6	19♉18.9	0♓16.4	19♍51.8	10♎41.5	21♋50.5	9♓58.9	17♒30.6	24♐11.6
2 M	2 42 00	12 10 37	21 21 59	28 24 44	22 40.0	15 57.5	20 32.8	0 59.9	19R 38.6	10R 35.7	21 54.6	10 00.9	17 31.2	24R 10.6
3 Tu	2 45 57	13 08 49	5♓25 28	12♓23 59	22 41.1	17 12.9	21 46.8	1 43.4	19 25.2	10 30.1	21 58.9	10 02.9	17 31.7	24 09.5
4 W	2 49 53	14 06 59	19 20 08	26 13 45	22 42.5	18 30.6	23 00.7	2 26.9	19 11.8	10 24.7	22 03.2	10 04.8	17 32.3	24 08.4
5 Th	2 53 50	15 05 08	3♈04 44	9♈52 55	22R 43.7	19 50.6	24 14.6	3 10.3	18 58.4	10 19.4	22 07.7	10 06.7	17 32.7	24 07.3
6 F	2 57 46	16 03 15	16 38 10	23 20 22	22 44.1	21 12.8	25 28.5	3 53.8	18 44.8	10 14.2	22 12.2	10 08.6	17 33.2	24 06.2
7 Sa	3 01 43	17 01 21	29 59 23	6♉35 06	22 43.5	22 37.2	26 42.4	4 37.2	18 31.3	10 09.2	22 16.8	10 10.4	17 33.6	24 05.0
8 Su	3 05 39	17 59 25	13♉07 27	19 36 19	22 41.6	24 03.8	27 56.2	5 20.6	18 17.7	10 04.3	22 21.5	10 12.2	17 34.0	24 03.8
9 M	3 09 36	18 57 28	26 01 41	2♊23 31	22 38.4	25 32.5	29 10.1	6 04.0	18 04.2	9 59.6	22 26.2	10 13.9	17 34.4	24 02.6
10 Tu	3 13 32	19 55 29	8♊41 52	14 56 48	22 34.2	27 03.3	0♊23.9	6 47.3	17 50.7	9 55.0	22 31.1	10 15.6	17 34.7	24 01.4
11 W	3 17 29	20 53 28	21 08 26	27 16 57	22 29.5	28 36.1	1 37.7	7 30.6	17 37.2	9 50.6	22 36.0	10 17.3	17 35.0	24 00.2
12 Th	3 21 26	21 51 26	3♋22 36	9♋25 39	22 24.8	0♉11.1	2 51.5	8 13.9	17 23.8	9 46.4	22 41.0	10 18.9	17 35.3	23 58.9
13 F	3 25 22	22 49 21	15 26 27	21 25 23	22 20.6	1 48.1	4 05.2	8 57.2	17 10.4	9 42.3	22 46.0	10 20.5	17 35.5	23 57.6
14 Sa	3 29 19	23 47 16	27 22 54	3♌19 27	22 17.4	3 27.2	5 19.0	9 40.5	16 57.2	9 38.3	22 51.2	10 22.0	17 35.7	23 56.3
15 Su	3 33 15	24 45 08	9♌15 35	15 11 50	22D 15.6	5 08.3	6 32.7	10 23.7	16 44.0	9 34.6	22 56.4	10 23.4	17 35.9	23 55.0
16 M	3 37 12	25 42 58	21 08 47	27 07 01	22 15.1	6 51.5	7 46.4	11 06.8	16 31.0	9 31.0	23 01.7	10 24.9	17 36.0	23 53.7
17 Tu	3 41 08	26 40 47	3♍07 10	9♍09 49	22 15.8	8 36.8	9 00.1	11 50.0	16 18.1	9 27.6	23 07.1	10 26.3	17 36.1	23 52.3
18 W	3 45 05	27 38 34	15 15 34	21 25 01	22 17.2	10 24.1	10 13.7	12 33.1	16 05.4	9 24.3	23 12.5	10 27.6	17 36.2	23 51.0
19 Th	3 49 02	28 36 20	27 38 43	3♎57 10	22 18.8	12 13.5	11 27.4	13 16.2	15 52.8	9 21.2	23 18.0	10 28.9	17R 36.2	23 49.6
20 F	3 52 58	29 34 03	10♎20 50	16 50 05	22R 19.9	14 04.9	12 41.0	13 59.2	15 40.4	9 18.3	23 23.6	10 30.1	17 36.2	23 48.2
21 Sa	3 56 55	0♊31 46	23 25 13	0♏06 23	22 19.7	15 58.4	13 54.6	14 42.2	15 28.2	9 15.6	23 29.2	10 31.3	17 36.2	23 46.8
22 Su	4 00 51	1 29 26	6♏53 39	13 46 56	22 18.0	17 53.9	15 08.2	15 25.2	15 16.2	9 13.0	23 34.9	10 32.5	17 36.1	23 45.4
23 M	4 04 48	2 27 06	20 46 00	27 50 28	22 14.4	19 51.4	16 21.8	16 08.2	15 04.4	9 10.6	23 40.7	10 33.6	17 36.0	23 43.9
24 Tu	4 08 44	3 24 44	4♐59 48	12♐13 21	22 09.3	21 50.8	17 35.3	16 51.1	14 52.9	9 08.4	23 46.5	10 34.7	17 35.9	23 42.5
25 W	4 12 41	4 22 21	19 30 19	26 49 50	22 03.1	23 52.2	18 48.9	17 34.0	14 41.5	9 06.4	23 52.4	10 35.7	17 35.7	23 41.0
26 Th	4 16 37	5 19 57	4♑10 58	11♑32 45	21 56.7	25 55.4	20 02.4	18 16.8	14 30.5	9 04.5	23 58.4	10 36.6	17 35.5	23 39.6
27 F	4 20 34	6 17 32	18 54 17	26 14 40	21 51.0	28 00.2	21 15.9	18 59.6	14 19.7	9 02.9	24 04.4	10 37.6	17 35.3	23 38.1
28 Sa	4 24 31	7 15 06	3♒33 07	10♒48 58	21 46.7	0♊06.7	22 29.3	19 42.3	14 09.1	9 01.4	24 10.5	10 38.4	17 35.1	23 36.6
29 Su	4 28 27	8 12 39	18 01 39	25 10 44	21D 44.1	2 14.6	23 42.8	20 25.0	13 58.9	9 00.0	24 16.6	10 39.3	17 34.8	23 35.1
30 M	4 32 24	9 10 11	2♓15 56	9♓17 04	21 43.4	4 23.8	24 56.3	21 07.7	13 48.9	8 58.9	24 22.8	10 40.0	17 34.5	23 33.6
31 Tu	4 36 20	10 07 43	16 14 03	23 06 55	21 43.9	6 34.1	26 09.7	21 50.3	13 39.2	8 57.9	24 29.0	10 40.8	17 34.1	23 32.0

LONGITUDE — June 2005

Day	Sid.Time	☉	0 hr ☽	Noon ☽	True ☊	☿	♀	♂	⚳	♃	♄	♅	♆	♇
1 W	4 40 17	11♊05 13	29♓55 45	6♈40 38	21♈45.0	8♊45.2	27♊23.1	22♓32.8	13♍29.9	8♎57.2	24♋35.3	10♓41.4	17♒33.7	23♐30.5
2 Th	4 44 13	12 02 43	13♈21 47	19 59 20	21R 45.7	10 56.9	28 36.5	23 15.3	13R 20.8	8R 56.6	24 41.7	10 42.1	17R 33.3	23R 29.0
3 F	4 48 10	13 00 12	26 33 29	3♉04 23	21 45.1	13 08.9	29 49.9	23 57.7	13 12.1	8 56.1	24 48.1	10 42.7	17 32.9	23 27.4
4 Sa	4 52 06	13 57 41	9♉32 12	15 57 04	21 42.5	15 21.1	1♋03.3	24 40.1	13 03.7	8D 55.9	24 54.6	10 43.2	17 32.4	23 25.9
5 Su	4 56 03	14 55 08	22 19 05	28 38 23	21 37.5	17 33.0	2 16.7	25 22.4	12 55.7	8 55.8	25 01.1	10 43.7	17 31.9	23 24.3
6 M	5 00 00	15 52 35	4♊55 00	11♊09 03	21 30.2	19 44.4	3 30.0	26 04.6	12 48.0	8 56.0	25 07.7	10 44.1	17 31.4	23 22.8
7 Tu	5 03 56	16 50 01	17 20 36	23 29 42	21 21.0	21 55.1	4 43.3	26 46.8	12 40.6	8 56.3	25 14.3	10 44.5	17 30.8	23 21.2
8 W	5 07 53	17 47 26	29 36 29	5♋41 02	21 10.7	24 04.8	5 56.7	27 28.9	12 33.6	8 56.8	25 21.0	10 44.9	17 30.2	23 19.6
9 Th	5 11 49	18 44 50	11♋43 30	17 44 04	21 00.1	26 13.3	7 10.0	28 10.9	12 27.0	8 57.4	25 27.7	10 45.1	17 29.6	23 18.1
10 F	5 15 46	19 42 13	23 42 58	29 40 27	20 50.3	28 20.3	8 23.2	28 52.9	12 20.7	8 58.3	25 34.5	10 45.4	17 28.9	23 16.5
11 Sa	5 19 42	20 39 36	5♌36 50	11♌32 30	20 42.1	0♋25.8	9 36.5	29 34.8	12 14.9	8 59.3	25 41.3	10 45.6	17 28.2	23 14.9
12 Su	5 23 39	21 36 57	17 27 50	23 23 18	20 36.0	2 29.4	10 49.7	0♈16.5	12 09.3	9 00.5	25 48.1	10 45.7	17 27.5	23 13.3
13 M	5 27 35	22 34 17	29 19 25	5♍16 43	20 32.3	4 31.2	12 02.9	0 58.2	12 04.2	9 01.9	25 55.0	10 45.8	17 26.8	23 11.7
14 Tu	5 31 32	23 31 36	11♍15 47	17 17 13	20D 30.7	6 30.9	13 16.1	1 39.9	11 59.4	9 03.5	26 02.0	10R 45.9	17 26.0	23 10.1
15 W	5 35 29	24 28 55	23 21 41	29 29 47	20 30.6	8 28.5	14 29.3	2 21.4	11 55.1	9 05.2	26 09.0	10 45.9	17 25.2	23 08.6
16 Th	5 39 25	25 26 12	5♎42 11	11♎59 29	20R 31.1	10 24.0	15 42.5	3 02.9	11 51.1	9 07.1	26 16.0	10 45.8	17 24.4	23 07.0
17 F	5 43 22	26 23 29	18 22 18	24 51 08	20 31.3	12 17.2	16 55.6	3 44.2	11 47.4	9 09.2	26 23.0	10 45.7	17 23.5	23 05.4
18 Sa	5 47 18	27 20 45	1♏26 28	8♏08 39	20 30.0	14 08.1	18 08.7	4 25.5	11 44.2	9 11.4	26 30.1	10 45.6	17 22.7	23 03.8
19 Su	5 51 15	28 18 00	14 57 54	21 54 19	20 26.6	15 56.8	19 21.8	5 06.7	11 41.4	9 13.9	26 37.3	10 45.4	17 21.8	23 02.3
20 M	5 55 11	29 15 14	28 57 46	6♐07 57	20 20.7	17 43.1	20 34.8	5 47.8	11 38.9	9 16.5	26 44.4	10 45.1	17 20.8	23 00.7
21 Tu	5 59 08	0♋12 29	13♐24 22	20 46 19	20 12.6	19 27.1	21 47.9	6 28.8	11 36.8	9 19.2	26 51.6	10 44.9	17 19.9	22 59.1
22 W	6 03 04	1 09 42	28 12 51	5♑42 55	20 03.0	21 08.8	23 00.9	7 09.7	11 35.1	9 22.2	26 58.9	10 44.5	17 18.9	22 57.6
23 Th	6 07 01	2 06 55	13♑15 18	20 48 43	19 52.9	22 48.1	24 13.9	7 50.6	11 33.8	9 25.3	27 06.1	10 44.1	17 17.9	22 56.0
24 F	6 10 58	3 04 08	28 21 54	5♒53 34	19 43.6	24 25.0	25 26.9	8 31.3	11 32.9	9 28.6	27 13.4	10 43.7	17 16.9	22 54.5
25 Sa	6 14 54	4 01 21	13♒22 36	20 47 59	19 36.1	25 59.5	26 39.8	9 11.9	11 32.3	9 32.0	27 20.8	10 43.2	17 15.8	22 52.9
26 Su	6 18 51	4 58 33	28 08 53	5♓24 41	19 31.0	27 31.7	27 52.8	9 52.4	11D 32.1	9 35.6	27 28.1	10 42.7	17 14.7	22 51.4
27 M	6 22 47	5 55 46	12♓34 56	19 39 24	19 28.4	29 01.4	29 05.7	10 32.8	11 32.3	9 39.3	27 35.5	10 42.1	17 13.6	22 49.8
28 Tu	6 26 44	6 52 58	26 37 58	3♈30 43	19D 27.5	0♌28.8	0♌18.6	11 13.1	11 32.8	9 43.3	27 42.9	10 41.5	17 12.5	22 48.3
29 W	6 30 40	7 50 11	10♈17 49	16 59 33	19R 27.6	1 53.6	1 31.4	11 53.2	11 33.8	9 47.3	27 50.3	10 40.9	17 11.3	22 46.8
30 Th	6 34 37	8 47 24	23 36 13	0♉08 13	19 27.3	3 16.0	2 44.3	12 33.3	11 35.0	9 51.6	27 57.8	10 40.1	17 10.2	22 45.3

Astro Data	Planet Ingress	Last Aspect ☽ Ingress	Last Aspect ☽ Ingress	☽ Phases & Eclipses	Astro Data
Dy Hr Mn	Dy Hr Mn	Dy Hr Mn Dy Hr Mn	Dy Hr Mn Dy Hr Mn	Dy Hr Mn	1 May 2005
☽0N 5 1:28	♂ ♓ 1 2:58	2 4:47 ♇ ⚹ ♓ 2 14:43	31 17:53 ♀ □ ♈ 1 0:08	1 6:24 ☾ 10♒59	Julian Day # 38472
♃⚻♅ 7 7:37	♀ ♊ 10 4:14	4 8:22 ♇ □ ♈ 4 18:36	3 5:24 ♀ ⚹ ♉ 3 6:20	8 8:45 ● 17♉52	SVP 5♓11'14"
☽0S 19 11:44	☿ ♉ 12 9:14	6 13:22 ♇ △ ♉ 7 0:01	5 5:25 ♂ ⚹ ♊ 5 14:36	16 8:57 ☽ 25♌36	GC 26♐54.8 ⚳ 23♍50.0R
♆ R 19 23:36	☉ ♊ 20 22:47	9 5:15 ♀ ☌ ♊ 9 7:29	7 18:50 ♂ □ ♋ 8 0:46	23 20:18 ○ 2♐47	Eris 20♈38.3 ⚵ 8♈50.0
♄⚻♇ 23 22:47	☿ ♊ 28 10:44	11 14:58 ☿ ⚹ ♋ 11 17:20	10 10:18 ♂ △ ♌ 10 12:39	30 11:47 ☾ 9♓10	⚷ 3♒15.3 ⚶ 16♉17.0
		13 15:04 ☉ ⚹ ♌ 14 5:17	12 11:40 ♇ △ ♍ 13 1:22		☽ Mean ☊ 21♈56.4
☽0N 1 6:40	♀ ♋ 3 15:18	16 8:57 ☉ □ ♍ 16 17:46	15 5:24 ♄ ⚹ ♎ 15 12:59	6 21:55 ● 16♊16	
♃ D 5 7:20	☿ ♋ 11 7:03	19 1:00 ☉ △ ♎ 19 4:30	17 15:02 ☉ △ ♏ 17 21:24	15 1:22 ☽ 24♍04	1 June 2005
♄Q♅ 12 3:24	♂ ♈ 12 2:30	21 0:40 ♇ ⚹ ♏ 21 11:49	19 20:06 ♄ △ ♐ 20 1:45	22 4:14 ○ 0♑51	Julian Day # 38503
♅ R 14 22:38	☉ ♋ 21 6:46	23 4:54 ♄ △ ♐ 23 15:38	21 15:34 ♇ ☌ ♑ 22 2:52	28 18:23 ☾ 7♈08	SVP 5♓11'09"
☽0S 15 19:40	☿ ♌ 28 4:01	25 6:52 ♇ ☌ ♑ 25 17:11	23 22:04 ♄ ☍ ♒ 24 2:36		GC 26♐54.9 ⚳ 24♍51.8
♂0N 20 3:21	♀ ♌ 28 5:53	27 15:22 ☿ △ ♒ 27 18:10	25 15:23 ♇ ⚹ ♓ 26 3:03		Eris 20♈55.2 ⚵ 24♈36.6
⚳ D 26 12:27		29 9:19 ♇ ⚹ ♓ 29 20:09	28 5:51 ♀ △ ♈ 28 5:51		⚷ 2♒57.7R ⚶ 29♉55.1
☽0N 28 11:33			30 7:57 ♄ □ ♉ 30 11:45		☽ Mean ☊ 20♈17.9

July 2005 — LONGITUDE

Day	Sid.Time	☉	0 hr ☽	Noon ☽	True ☊	☿	♀	♂	⚳	♃	♄	♅	♆	♇
1 F	6 38 34	9♋44 37	6♉35 54	12♉59 41	19♈25.5	4♌35.9	3♌57.1	13♈13.2	11♏36.7	9♎56.0	28♋05.3	10♓39.4	17♒09.0	22♐43.8
2 Sa	6 42 30	10 41 50	19 19 55	25 36 56	19R 21.4	5 53.2	5 10.0	13 53.0	11 38.7	10 00.5	28 12.8	10R 38.6	17R 07.8	22R 42.3
3 Su	6 46 27	11 39 03	1♊51 06	8♊02 39	19 14.5	7 07.9	6 22.7	14 32.6	11 41.1	10 05.2	28 20.3	10 37.7	17 06.5	22 40.8
4 M	6 50 23	12 36 17	14 11 52	20 18 58	19 04.7	8 19.9	7 35.5	15 12.1	11 43.9	10 10.1	28 27.9	10 36.9	17 05.3	22 39.3
5 Tu	6 54 20	13 33 30	26 24 07	2♋27 31	18 52.6	9 29.2	8 48.3	15 51.5	11 47.0	10 15.1	28 35.5	10 35.9	17 04.0	22 37.9
6 W	6 58 16	14 30 44	8♋29 17	14 29 35	18 39.1	10 35.7	10 01.0	16 30.7	11 50.4	10 20.3	28 43.1	10 34.9	17 02.7	22 36.5
7 Th	7 02 13	15 27 57	20 28 33	26 26 20	18 25.3	11 39.3	11 13.7	17 09.8	11 54.3	10 25.6	28 50.7	10 33.9	17 01.4	22 35.0
8 F	7 06 09	16 25 11	2♌23 07	8♌19 05	18 12.2	12 39.9	12 26.4	17 48.7	11 58.4	10 31.1	28 58.3	10 32.9	17 00.1	22 33.6
9 Sa	7 10 06	17 22 25	14 14 27	20 09 30	18 01.0	13 37.5	13 39.0	18 27.5	12 02.9	10 36.7	29 06.0	10 31.8	16 58.7	22 32.2
10 Su	7 14 03	18 19 38	26 04 31	1♍59 52	17 52.3	14 31.8	14 51.7	19 06.1	12 07.8	10 42.5	29 13.6	10 30.6	16 57.3	22 30.8
11 M	7 17 59	19 16 52	7♍55 57	13 53 11	17 46.4	15 22.9	16 04.3	19 44.6	12 13.0	10 48.4	29 21.3	10 29.4	16 56.0	22 29.4
12 Tu	7 21 56	20 14 05	19 52 05	25 53 11	17 43.2	16 10.5	17 16.8	20 22.8	12 18.5	10 54.4	29 29.0	10 28.2	16 54.5	22 28.1
13 W	7 25 52	21 11 19	1♎57 02	8♎04 15	17D 41.9	16 54.6	18 29.4	21 00.9	12 24.3	11 00.6	29 36.7	10 26.9	16 53.1	22 26.7
14 Th	7 29 49	22 08 32	14 15 27	20 31 15	17R 41.8	17 35.0	19 41.9	21 38.9	12 30.5	11 07.0	29 44.4	10 25.6	16 51.7	22 25.4
15 F	7 33 45	23 05 46	26 52 18	3♏19 10	17 41.6	18 11.5	20 54.4	22 16.6	12 37.0	11 13.4	29 52.1	10 24.2	16 50.2	22 24.1
16 Sa	7 37 42	24 03 00	9♏52 25	16 32 31	17 40.2	18 44.0	22 06.8	22 54.2	12 43.8	11 20.0	29 59.8	10 22.8	16 48.8	22 22.8
17 Su	7 41 38	25 00 13	23 19 50	0♐14 36	17 36.8	19 12.5	23 19.2	23 31.6	12 50.9	11 26.8	0♌07.6	10 21.4	16 47.3	22 21.6
18 M	7 45 35	25 57 27	7♐16 54	14 26 36	17 30.9	19 36.6	24 31.6	24 08.8	12 58.4	11 33.6	0 15.3	10 19.9	16 45.8	22 20.3
19 Tu	7 49 32	26 54 42	21 43 21	29 06 35	17 22.7	19 56.2	25 44.0	24 45.8	13 06.1	11 40.6	0 23.1	10 18.4	16 44.3	22 19.1
20 W	7 53 28	27 51 56	6♑35 29	14♑09 01	17 12.7	20 11.3	26 56.3	25 22.7	13 14.1	11 47.8	0 30.8	10 16.9	16 42.8	22 17.9
21 Th	7 57 25	28 49 12	21 45 58	29 24 57	17 02.3	20 21.7	28 08.6	25 59.3	13 22.5	11 55.0	0 38.6	10 15.3	16 41.3	22 16.7
22 F	8 01 21	29 46 27	7♒04 33	14♒43 18	16 52.5	20R 27.2	29 20.8	26 35.8	13 31.1	12 02.4	0 46.3	10 13.7	16 39.7	22 15.5
23 Sa	8 05 18	0♌43 43	22 19 50	29 52 51	16 44.5	20 27.8	0♍33.0	27 12.0	13 40.0	12 09.9	0 54.1	10 12.1	16 38.2	22 14.4
24 Su	8 09 14	1 41 00	7♓21 16	14♓44 11	16 38.9	20 23.5	1 45.2	27 48.0	13 49.2	12 17.6	1 01.8	10 10.4	16 36.6	22 13.2
25 M	8 13 11	2 38 18	22 00 58	29 11 08	16 35.9	20 14.1	2 57.4	28 23.9	13 58.6	12 25.3	1 09.6	10 08.7	16 35.1	22 12.1
26 Tu	8 17 07	3 35 36	6♈14 28	13♈10 55	16D 34.9	19 59.8	4 09.5	28 59.4	14 08.4	12 33.2	1 17.3	10 06.9	16 33.5	22 11.0
27 W	8 21 04	4 32 56	20 00 37	26 43 49	16R 35.1	19 40.6	5 21.6	29 34.8	14 18.4	12 41.2	1 25.1	10 05.1	16 31.9	22 10.0
28 Th	8 25 01	5 30 16	3♉20 51	9♉52 10	16 35.1	19 16.6	6 33.6	0♉09.9	14 28.6	12 49.3	1 32.8	10 03.3	16 30.3	22 08.9
29 F	8 28 57	6 27 38	16 18 12	22 39 28	16 34.0	18 48.2	7 45.6	0 44.8	14 39.2	12 57.5	1 40.5	10 01.5	16 28.7	22 07.9
30 Sa	8 32 54	7 25 01	28 56 27	5♊09 40	16 30.8	18 15.5	8 57.6	1 19.4	14 50.0	13 05.9	1 48.3	9 59.6	16 27.1	22 06.9
31 Su	8 36 50	8 22 25	11♊19 35	17 26 37	16 25.1	17 39.1	10 09.5	1 53.8	15 01.0	13 14.3	1 56.0	9 57.7	16 25.5	22 05.9

August 2005 — LONGITUDE

Day	Sid.Time	☉	0 hr ☽	Noon ☽	True ☊	☿	♀	♂	⚳	♃	♄	♅	♆	♇
1 M	8 40 47	9♌19 49	23♊31 12	29♊33 43	16♈16.8	16♌59.3	11♍21.5	2♉28.0	15♏12.4	13♎22.9	2♌03.7	9♓55.7	16♒23.9	22♐05.0
2 Tu	8 44 43	10 17 15	5♋34 28	11♋33 46	16R 06.5	16R 16.8	12 33.3	3 01.8	15 23.9	13 31.6	2 11.5	9R 53.8	16R 22.3	22R 04.1
3 W	8 48 40	11 14 42	17 31 54	23 29 05	15 54.7	15 32.2	13 45.2	3 35.4	15 35.7	13 40.4	2 19.2	9 51.8	16 20.7	22 03.2
4 Th	8 52 36	12 12 10	29 25 33	5♌21 29	15 42.7	14 46.3	14 57.0	4 08.7	15 47.8	13 49.3	2 26.8	9 49.8	16 19.0	22 02.3
5 F	8 56 33	13 09 39	11♌17 04	17 12 31	15 31.3	13 59.8	16 08.7	4 41.7	16 00.1	13 58.3	2 34.5	9 47.7	16 17.4	22 01.4
6 Sa	9 00 30	14 07 09	23 08 00	29 03 45	15 21.6	13 13.7	17 20.5	5 14.4	16 12.6	14 07.4	2 42.2	9 45.7	16 15.8	22 00.6
7 Su	9 04 26	15 04 40	4♍59 58	10♍56 56	15 14.1	12 28.7	18 32.2	5 46.8	16 25.4	14 16.6	2 49.8	9 43.6	16 14.1	21 59.8
8 M	9 08 23	16 02 11	16 54 56	22 54 17	15 09.2	11 45.7	19 43.8	6 18.9	16 38.4	14 25.9	2 57.5	9 41.4	16 12.5	21 59.1
9 Tu	9 12 19	16 59 44	28 55 21	4♎58 33	15D 06.7	11 05.7	20 55.4	6 50.7	16 51.6	14 35.4	3 05.1	9 39.3	16 10.9	21 58.3
10 W	9 16 16	17 57 17	11♎04 17	17 13 04	15 06.2	10 29.3	22 06.9	7 22.1	17 05.0	14 44.9	3 12.7	9 37.1	16 09.2	21 57.6
11 Th	9 20 12	18 54 51	23 25 23	29 41 45	15 06.8	9 57.4	23 18.5	7 53.2	17 18.7	14 54.5	3 20.3	9 35.0	16 07.6	21 56.9
12 F	9 24 09	19 52 27	6♏02 43	12♏28 49	15R 07.7	9 30.7	24 29.9	8 24.0	17 32.6	15 04.2	3 27.8	9 32.8	16 06.0	21 56.3
13 Sa	9 28 05	20 50 03	19 00 32	25 38 20	15 07.8	9 09.6	25 41.3	8 54.5	17 46.6	15 14.0	3 35.4	9 30.5	16 04.3	21 55.7
14 Su	9 32 02	21 47 40	2♐22 37	9♐13 41	15 06.3	8 54.8	26 52.7	9 24.6	18 00.9	15 23.9	3 42.9	9 28.3	16 02.7	21 55.1
15 M	9 35 59	22 45 18	16 11 43	23 16 42	15 03.0	8D 46.7	28 04.0	9 54.4	18 15.4	15 33.9	3 50.4	9 26.1	16 01.1	21 54.5
16 Tu	9 39 55	23 42 57	0♑28 31	7♑46 47	14 57.7	8 45.6	29 15.3	10 23.8	18 30.1	15 43.9	3 57.9	9 23.8	15 59.5	21 54.0
17 W	9 43 52	24 40 37	15 10 56	22 40 10	14 50.9	8 51.7	0♎26.5	10 52.8	18 45.0	15 54.1	4 05.3	9 21.5	15 57.9	21 53.5
18 Th	9 47 48	25 38 19	0♒13 29	7♒49 45	14 43.6	9 05.2	1 37.6	11 21.5	19 00.1	16 04.4	4 12.7	9 19.2	15 56.2	21 53.0
19 F	9 51 45	26 36 01	15 27 39	23 05 51	14 36.7	9 26.2	2 48.7	11 49.8	19 15.3	16 14.7	4 20.1	9 16.9	15 54.6	21 52.5
20 Sa	9 55 41	27 33 45	0♓42 57	8♓17 38	14 31.1	9 54.7	3 59.7	12 17.7	19 30.8	16 25.1	4 27.5	9 14.6	15 53.1	21 52.1
21 Su	9 59 38	28 31 30	15 48 41	23 15 03	14 27.3	10 30.6	5 10.7	12 45.1	19 46.4	16 35.6	4 34.8	9 12.3	15 51.5	21 51.7
22 M	10 03 34	29 29 17	0♈35 50	7♈50 24	14D 25.7	11 13.9	6 21.7	13 12.2	20 02.2	16 46.2	4 42.1	9 09.9	15 49.9	21 51.4
23 Tu	10 07 31	0♍27 05	14 58 16	21 59 11	14 25.7	12 04.5	7 32.5	13 38.9	20 18.2	16 56.8	4 49.4	9 07.6	15 48.3	21 51.0
24 W	10 11 28	1 24 55	28 53 05	5♉40 02	14 26.8	13 02.0	8 43.3	14 05.1	20 34.3	17 07.6	4 56.6	9 05.2	15 46.7	21 50.7
25 Th	10 15 24	2 22 47	12♉20 20	18 54 06	14 28.1	14 06.2	9 54.1	14 30.9	20 50.7	17 18.4	5 03.8	9 02.8	15 45.2	21 50.5
26 F	10 19 21	3 20 40	25 21 58	1♊44 21	14R 28.8	15 16.9	11 04.8	14 56.2	21 07.2	17 29.3	5 11.0	9 00.4	15 43.6	21 50.2
27 Sa	10 23 17	4 18 36	8♊01 46	14 14 44	14 28.3	16 33.6	12 15.5	15 21.0	21 23.8	17 40.2	5 18.1	8 58.1	15 42.1	21 50.0
28 Su	10 27 14	5 16 33	20 23 49	26 29 33	14 26.1	17 56.0	13 26.1	15 45.4	21 40.7	17 51.3	5 25.2	8 55.7	15 40.6	21 49.9
29 M	10 31 10	6 14 32	2♋32 27	8♋33 02	14 22.3	19 23.6	14 36.6	16 09.3	21 57.6	18 02.4	5 32.3	8 53.3	15 39.1	21 49.7
30 Tu	10 35 07	7 12 33	14 31 46	20 29 05	14 17.0	20 56.0	15 47.1	16 32.7	22 14.8	18 13.6	5 39.3	8 50.9	15 37.6	21 49.6
31 W	10 39 03	8 10 36	26 25 25	2♌21 06	14 10.7	22 32.7	16 57.5	16 55.5	22 32.1	18 24.8	5 46.3	8 48.5	15 36.1	21 49.5

Astro Data (Dy Hr Mn)	Planet Ingress (Dy Hr Mn)	Last Aspect (Dy Hr Mn)	☽ Ingress (Dy Hr Mn)	Last Aspect (Dy Hr Mn)	☽ Ingress (Dy Hr Mn)	☽ Phases & Eclipses (Dy Hr Mn)	Astro Data
♃⚻♅ 8 18:21	♄ ♌ 16 12:31	2 17:02 ♄ ⚹	♊ 2 20:26	31 21:10 ♇ ☍	♋ 1 12:52	6 12:03 ● 14♋31	1 July 2005
☽0S 13 2:00	☉ ♌ 22 17:41	4 16:36 ♇ ☍	♋ 5 7:07	2 16:00 ♃ □	♌ 4 1:10	14 15:20 ☽ 22♎16	Julian Day # 38533
☿R 23 2:59	♀ ♍ 23 1:01	7 16:54 ♄ ☌	♌ 7 19:11	5 21:45 ♇ △	♍ 6 13:54	21 11:00 ○ 28♑47	SVP 5♓11'04"
☽0N 25 18:06	♂ ♉ 28 5:12	9 16:49 ♇ △	♍ 10 7:57	8 10:10 ♇ □	♎ 9 2:08	28 3:19 ☾ 5♉10	GC 26♐55.0 ⚴ 1♎12.0
		12 19:12 ♄ ⚹	♎ 12 20:09	10 21:10 ♇ ⚹	♏ 11 12:35		Eris 21♈04.5 ⚵ 9♉46.5
☽0S 9 7:13	♀ ♎ 17 3:05	15 5:32 ♄ □	♏ 15 5:51	13 12:06 ♀ ⚹	♐ 13 19:47	5 3:05 ● 12♌48	⚷ 1♒43.8R ⚶ 12♊46.6
☿D 16 3:50	☉ ♍ 23 0:45	17 2:15 ☉ △	♐ 17 11:35	15 20:43 ♀ □	♑ 15 23:13	13 2:39 ☽ 20♏28	☽ Mean ☊ 18♈42.6
♃△♆ 17 19:36		19 6:03 ♀ △	♑ 19 13:26	17 1:02 ♃ □	♒ 17 23:39	19 17:53 ○ 26♒50	
♀0S 18 10:56		21 11:00 ☉ ☍	♒ 21 12:55	19 17:53 ☉ ☍	♓ 19 22:52	26 15:18 ☾ 3♊29	1 August 2005
☽0N 22 3:05		23 7:33 ♂ ⚹	♓ 23 12:11	21 9:45 ♇ □	♈ 21 23:01		Julian Day # 38564
		25 0:19 ♇ □	♈ 25 13:23	23 11:46 ♇ △	♉ 24 1:58		SVP 5♓10'58"
		27 17:23 ♂ ☌	♉ 27 17:54	25 6:14 ♆ □	♊ 26 8:43		GC 26♐55.0 ⚴ 11♎00.6
		29 4:59 ☿ □	♊ 30 2:02	28 2:49 ♇ ☍	♋ 28 18:57		Eris 21♈04.6R ⚵ 24♉52.2
				30 7:22 ♃ □	♌ 31 7:14		⚷ 29♑58.8R ⚶ 25♊24.3
							☽ Mean ☊ 17♈04.2

LONGITUDE September 2005

Day	Sid.Time	☉	0 hr ☽	Noon☽	True☊	☿	♀	♂	⚳	♃	♄	♅	♆	♇
1 Th	10 43 00	9♍08 40	8♌16 31	14♌11 57	14♈04.1	24♌13.3	18♎07.9	17♉17.8	22♏49.6	18♎36.1	5♌53.3	8♓46.1	15♒34.6	21♐49.5
2 F	10 46 57	10 06 47	20 07 41	26 03 58	13R58.0	25 57.2	19 18.2	17 39.6	23 07.2	18 47.5	6 00.2	8R43.7	15R33.2	21D49.5
3 Sa	10 50 53	11 04 54	2♍01 02	7♍59 07	13 52.8	27 43.9	20 28.4	18 00.9	23 25.0	18 59.0	6 07.0	8 41.3	15 31.7	21 49.5
4 Su	10 54 50	12 03 04	13 58 26	19 59 10	13 49.0	29 33.0	21 38.6	18 21.5	23 42.9	19 10.5	6 13.8	8 38.9	15 30.3	21 49.5
5 M	10 58 46	13 01 15	26 01 34	2♎05 49	13D46.8	1♍24.0	22 48.7	18 41.6	24 00.9	19 22.0	6 20.6	8 36.5	15 28.9	21 49.6
6 Tu	11 02 43	13 59 28	8♎12 10	14 20 52	13 46.2	3 16.5	23 58.7	19 01.1	24 19.1	19 33.7	6 27.3	8 34.1	15 27.5	21 49.7
7 W	11 06 39	14 57 42	20 32 11	26 46 25	13 46.8	5 10.2	25 08.6	19 20.0	24 37.5	19 45.4	6 34.0	8 31.7	15 26.1	21 49.9
8 Th	11 10 36	15 55 59	3♏03 51	9♏24 50	13 48.2	7 04.6	26 18.5	19 38.3	24 55.9	19 57.1	6 40.6	8 29.4	15 24.8	21 50.1
9 F	11 14 32	16 54 16	15 49 42	22 18 47	13 49.8	8 59.5	27 28.3	19 55.9	25 14.6	20 08.9	6 47.2	8 27.0	15 23.4	21 50.3
10 Sa	11 18 29	17 52 36	28 52 23	5♐30 51	13R51.1	10 54.5	28 38.1	20 13.0	25 33.3	20 20.8	6 53.7	8 24.7	15 22.1	21 50.5
11 Su	11 22 26	18 50 56	12♐14 26	19 03 21	13 51.6	12 49.6	29 47.7	20 29.3	25 52.2	20 32.7	7 00.1	8 22.3	15 20.8	21 50.8
12 M	11 26 22	19 49 19	25 57 44	2♑57 38	13 51.0	14 44.4	0♏57.3	20 45.1	26 11.2	20 44.7	7 06.6	8 20.0	15 19.5	21 51.1
13 Tu	11 30 19	20 47 43	10♑02 59	17 13 34	13 49.4	16 38.7	2 06.8	21 00.1	26 30.3	20 56.7	7 12.9	8 17.6	15 18.3	21 51.5
14 W	11 34 15	21 46 08	24 29 03	1♒48 56	13 47.0	18 32.5	3 16.2	21 14.5	26 49.5	21 08.8	7 19.2	8 15.3	15 17.0	21 51.8
15 Th	11 38 12	22 44 35	9♒12 33	16 39 06	13 44.2	20 25.7	4 25.5	21 28.2	27 08.9	21 20.9	7 25.4	8 13.0	15 15.8	21 52.2
16 F	11 42 08	23 43 04	24 07 40	1♓37 15	13 41.6	22 18.1	5 34.7	21 41.2	27 28.4	21 33.1	7 31.6	8 10.7	15 14.6	21 52.7
17 Sa	11 46 05	24 41 34	9♓06 45	16 35 06	13 39.5	24 09.7	6 43.8	21 53.5	27 48.0	21 45.3	7 37.8	8 08.5	15 13.4	21 53.1
18 Su	11 50 01	25 40 06	24 01 12	1♈24 05	13D38.3	26 00.4	7 52.8	22 05.0	28 07.7	21 57.6	7 43.8	8 06.2	15 12.3	21 53.6
19 M	11 53 58	26 38 41	8♈42 50	15 56 41	13 38.0	27 50.1	9 01.7	22 15.8	28 27.5	22 09.9	7 49.8	8 04.0	15 11.2	21 54.2
20 Tu	11 57 55	27 37 17	23 05 01	0♉07 20	13 38.5	29 39.0	10 10.6	22 25.8	28 47.4	22 22.2	7 55.8	8 01.8	15 10.0	21 54.7
21 W	12 01 51	28 35 55	7♉03 22	13 52 57	13 39.5	1♎26.8	11 19.3	22 35.1	29 07.5	22 34.6	8 01.6	7 59.6	15 09.0	21 55.3
22 Th	12 05 48	29 34 36	20 36 05	27 12 54	13 40.7	3 13.8	12 27.9	22 43.6	29 27.6	22 47.1	8 07.4	7 57.4	15 07.9	21 56.0
23 F	12 09 44	0♎33 19	3♊43 37	10♊08 35	13 41.7	4 59.7	13 36.5	22 51.3	29 47.9	22 59.5	8 13.2	7 55.2	15 06.9	21 56.6
24 Sa	12 13 41	1 32 04	16 28 12	22 42 57	13R42.4	6 44.7	14 44.9	22 58.1	0♐08.2	23 12.1	8 18.9	7 53.1	15 05.9	21 57.3
25 Su	12 17 37	2 30 51	28 53 20	4♋59 55	13 42.6	8 28.7	15 53.2	23 04.1	0 28.7	23 24.6	8 24.5	7 51.0	15 04.9	21 58.1
26 M	12 21 34	3 29 41	11♋03 14	17 03 52	13 42.2	10 11.7	17 01.4	23 09.3	0 49.2	23 37.2	8 30.0	7 48.9	15 03.9	21 58.8
27 Tu	12 25 30	4 28 33	23 02 23	28 59 20	13 41.4	11 53.9	18 09.5	23 13.7	1 09.9	23 49.8	8 35.5	7 46.8	15 03.0	21 59.6
28 W	12 29 27	5 27 27	4♌55 16	10♌50 40	13 40.4	13 35.1	19 17.5	23 17.1	1 30.7	24 02.5	8 40.9	7 44.8	15 02.1	22 00.4
29 Th	12 33 24	6 26 23	16 46 02	22 41 50	13 39.3	15 15.3	20 25.4	23 19.7	1 51.5	24 15.1	8 46.3	7 42.7	15 01.2	22 01.3
30 F	12 37 20	7 25 21	28 38 29	4♍36 22	13 38.4	16 54.7	21 33.2	23 21.4	2 12.5	24 27.9	8 51.5	7 40.8	15 00.4	22 02.2

LONGITUDE October 2005

Day	Sid.Time	☉	0 hr ☽	Noon☽	True☊	☿	♀	♂	⚳	♃	♄	♅	♆	♇
1 Sa	12 41 17	8♎24 22	10♍35 49	16♍37 09	13♈37.7	18♎33.3	22♏40.8	23♉22.3	2♐33.5	24♎40.6	8♌56.7	7♓38.8	14♒59.5	22♐03.1
2 Su	12 45 13	9 23 25	22 40 39	28 46 34	13R37.3	20 10.9	23 48.3	23R22.2	2 54.6	24 53.4	9 01.8	7R36.9	14R58.8	22 04.0
3 M	12 49 10	10 22 29	4♎55 05	11♎06 23	13D37.1	21 47.8	24 55.7	23 21.2	3 15.8	25 06.2	9 06.8	7 34.9	14 58.0	22 05.0
4 Tu	12 53 06	11 21 36	17 20 36	23 37 54	13 37.2	23 23.8	26 02.9	23 19.3	3 37.1	25 19.0	9 11.8	7 33.1	14 57.3	22 06.0
5 W	12 57 03	12 20 45	29 58 20	6♏22 02	13 37.3	24 58.9	27 10.1	23 16.6	3 58.5	25 31.8	9 16.6	7 31.2	14 56.5	22 07.0
6 Th	13 00 59	13 19 56	12♏49 03	19 19 26	13R37.3	26 33.4	28 17.0	23 12.9	4 20.0	25 44.7	9 21.4	7 29.4	14 55.9	22 08.1
7 F	13 04 56	14 19 08	25 53 16	2♐30 34	13 37.3	28 07.0	29 23.9	23 08.3	4 41.6	25 57.6	9 26.1	7 27.6	14 55.2	22 09.2
8 Sa	13 08 53	15 18 23	9♐11 22	15 55 43	13 37.2	29 39.8	0♐30.5	23 02.8	5 03.2	26 10.5	9 30.7	7 25.9	14 54.6	22 10.3
9 Su	13 12 49	16 17 39	22 43 37	29 35 02	13 37.0	1♏11.9	1 37.1	22 56.5	5 24.9	26 23.5	9 35.3	7 24.2	14 54.0	22 11.4
10 M	13 16 46	17 16 57	6♑29 57	13♑28 16	13D36.9	2 43.2	2 43.4	22 49.3	5 46.7	26 36.4	9 39.7	7 22.5	14 53.5	22 12.6
11 Tu	13 20 42	18 16 17	20 29 53	27 34 38	13 37.0	4 13.8	3 49.6	22 41.2	6 08.6	26 49.4	9 44.1	7 20.9	14 53.0	22 13.8
12 W	13 24 39	19 15 39	4♒42 16	11♒52 30	13 37.2	5 43.6	4 55.6	22 32.2	6 30.6	27 02.4	9 48.4	7 19.3	14 52.5	22 15.1
13 Th	13 28 35	20 15 02	19 04 57	26 19 12	13 37.8	7 12.7	6 01.4	22 22.4	6 52.6	27 15.3	9 52.6	7 17.7	14 52.0	22 16.3
14 F	13 32 32	21 14 27	3♓34 43	10♓50 56	13 38.4	8 41.0	7 07.0	22 11.7	7 14.7	27 28.4	9 56.7	7 16.2	14 51.6	22 17.6
15 Sa	13 36 28	22 13 54	18 07 12	25 22 51	13 39.0	10 08.6	8 12.5	22 00.3	7 36.8	27 41.4	10 00.7	7 14.7	14 51.2	22 18.9
16 Su	13 40 25	23 13 22	2♈37 12	9♈49 31	13R39.3	11 35.4	9 17.7	21 48.0	7 59.1	27 54.4	10 04.6	7 13.3	14 50.8	22 20.3
17 M	13 44 21	24 12 53	16 59 08	24 05 25	13 39.2	13 01.4	10 22.7	21 35.0	8 21.3	28 07.4	10 08.5	7 11.9	14 50.5	22 21.7
18 Tu	13 48 18	25 12 25	1♉07 45	8♉05 38	13 38.5	14 26.6	11 27.5	21 21.2	8 43.7	28 20.5	10 12.2	7 10.5	14 50.2	22 23.1
19 W	13 52 15	26 12 00	14 58 40	21 46 32	13 37.2	15 50.9	12 32.1	21 06.6	9 06.1	28 33.5	10 15.9	7 09.2	14 49.9	22 24.5
20 Th	13 56 11	27 11 37	28 29 01	5♊06 01	13 35.4	17 14.4	13 36.5	20 51.4	9 28.6	28 46.6	10 19.4	7 07.9	14 49.7	22 25.9
21 F	14 00 08	28 11 16	11♊37 34	18 03 46	13 33.4	18 37.0	14 40.7	20 35.4	9 51.2	28 59.6	10 22.9	7 06.6	14 49.5	22 27.4
22 Sa	14 04 04	29 10 58	24 24 51	0♋41 07	13 31.4	19 58.7	15 44.6	20 18.8	10 13.8	29 12.7	10 26.2	7 05.4	14 49.3	22 28.9
23 Su	14 08 01	0♏10 41	6♋52 56	13 00 45	13 29.9	21 19.3	16 48.2	20 01.6	10 36.4	29 25.8	10 29.5	7 04.3	14 49.2	22 30.4
24 M	14 11 57	1 10 27	19 05 05	25 06 26	13D29.0	22 38.9	17 51.6	19 43.7	10 59.2	29 38.8	10 32.7	7 03.2	14 49.1	22 32.0
25 Tu	14 15 54	2 10 15	1♌05 25	7♌02 35	13 29.0	23 57.4	18 54.8	19 25.4	11 22.0	29 51.9	10 35.8	7 02.1	14 49.0	22 33.6
26 W	14 19 51	3 10 06	12 58 34	18 53 58	13 29.7	25 14.6	19 57.7	19 06.5	11 44.8	0♏05.0	10 38.7	7 01.1	14D49.0	22 35.2
27 Th	14 23 47	4 09 58	24 49 24	0♍45 26	13 31.1	26 30.4	21 00.3	18 47.1	12 07.7	0 18.0	10 41.6	7 00.1	14 49.0	22 36.8
28 F	14 27 44	5 09 52	6♍42 39	12 41 37	13 32.8	27 44.8	22 02.6	18 27.3	12 30.7	0 31.1	10 44.4	6 59.1	14 49.1	22 38.4
29 Sa	14 31 40	6 09 49	18 42 48	24 46 42	13 34.4	28 57.6	23 04.6	18 07.1	12 53.7	0 44.1	10 47.0	6 58.3	14 49.1	22 40.1
30 Su	14 35 37	7 09 48	0♎53 43	7♎04 14	13R35.4	0♐08.7	24 06.3	17 46.6	13 16.8	0 57.2	10 49.6	6 57.4	14 49.2	22 41.8
31 M	14 39 33	8 09 49	13 18 32	19 36 51	13 35.4	1 17.8	25 07.7	17 25.8	13 39.9	1 10.2	10 52.0	6 56.6	14 49.4	22 43.5

Astro Data Dy Hr Mn	Planet Ingress Dy Hr Mn	Last Aspect Dy Hr Mn	☽ Ingress Dy Hr Mn	Last Aspect Dy Hr Mn	☽ Ingress Dy Hr Mn	☽ Phases & Eclipses Dy Hr Mn	Astro Data
♇ D 2 10:52	☿ ♍ 4 17:52	2 11:44 ☿ ☌	♍ 2 19:56	2 1:22 ♂ △	♎ 2 14:24	3 18:45 ● 11♍21	1 September 2005
☽ 0S 5 12:34	♀ ♏ 11 16:14	4 15:40 ♇ □	♎ 5 7:52	4 15:15 ♃ ☌	♏ 5 0:03	11 11:37 ☽ 18♐50	Julian Day # 38595
♄⚼♇ 9 23:53	☿ ♎ 20 16:40	7 8:33 ♀ ☌	♏ 7 18:10	7 5:51 ♀ ☌	♐ 7 7:28	18 2:01 ○ 25♓16	SVP 5♓10'54"
♃⚹♇ 18 3:57	☉ ♎ 22 22:23	9 7:31 ♂ ☍	♐ 10 2:03	9 6:20 ♃ ⚹	♑ 9 12:43	25 6:41 ☾ 2♋18	GC 26♐55.1 ⚴ 22♎44.5
☽ 0N 18 13:36	⚳ ♐ 24 2:19	11 16:52 ♇ ☌	♑ 12 6:57	11 10:42 ♃ □	♒ 11 16:05		Eris 20♈55.3R ⚵ 8♊28.4
♄⚻♅ 21 5:49		13 18:22 ♂ △	♒ 14 9:02	13 13:34 ♃ △	♓ 13 18:05	3 10:28 ● 10♎19	⚷ 28♑27.9R ⚶ 6♋52.7
☿0S 22 6:19	♀ ♐ 8 1:00	15 20:23 ♇ ⚹	♓ 16 9:24	15 6:55 ♇ □	♈ 15 19:39	3 10:31:43 • A 04'31"	☽ Mean ☊ 15♈25.7
☉0S 22 22:23	☿ ♏ 8 17:15	18 2:01 ☉ ☍	♈ 18 9:43	17 18:58 ♃ ☍	♉ 17 22:04	10 19:01 ☽ 17♑34	
♃⚼♅ 23 4:55	☉ ♏ 23 7:42	19 22:36 ♃ ☍	♉ 20 11:47	19 10:50 ♂ ☌	♊ 20 2:44	17 12:14 ○ 24♈13	1 October 2005
	♃ ♏ 26 2:52	22 16:41 ☉ △	♊ 22 17:07	22 9:07 ♃ △	♋ 22 10:41	17 12:03 • P 0.062	Julian Day # 38625
♂ R 1 22:04	☿ ♐ 30 9:02	24 12:57 ♃ △	♋ 25 2:10	24 21:16 ♃ □	♌ 24 21:49	25 1:17 ☾ 1♌44	SVP 5♓10'50"
☽ 0S 2 19:03		27 1:24 ♃ □	♌ 27 14:03	27 2:23 ☿ □	♍ 27 10:28		GC 26♐55.2 ⚴ 5♏09.5
☽ 0N 15 23:37		29 15:12 ♃ ⚹	♍ 30 2:44	29 21:06 ☿ ⚹	♎ 29 22:15		Eris 20♈39.6R ⚵ 18♊33.4
♆ D 26 23:24							⚷ 27♑48.6R ⚶ 16♋04.8
☽ 0S 30 2:52							☽ Mean ☊ 13♈50.3

November 2005 — LONGITUDE

Day	Sid.Time	☉	0 hr ☽	Noon ☽	True ☊	☿	♀	♂	⚳	♃	♄	♅	♆	♇
1 Tu	14 43 30	9♏09 51	25♎59 21	2♏26 08	13♈34.1	2♐24.8	26♐08.8	17♉04.8	14♐03.0	1♏23.3	10♌54.4	6♓55.9	14♒49.5	22♐45.3
2 W	14 47 26	10 09 56	8♏57 12	15 32 29	13R31.6	3 29.4	27 09.5	16R43.6	14 26.3	1 36.3	10 56.6	6R55.2	14 49.7	22 47.0
3 Th	14 51 23	11 10 03	22 11 52	28 55 08	13 27.8	4 31.3	28 09.9	16 22.3	14 49.5	1 49.3	10 58.8	6 54.5	14 50.0	22 48.8
4 F	14 55 19	12 10 11	5♐42 03	12♐32 18	13 23.3	5 30.3	29 09.9	16 01.0	15 12.9	2 02.3	11 00.8	6 53.9	14 50.3	22 50.6
5 Sa	14 59 16	13 10 21	19 25 33	26 21 27	13 18.7	6 25.9	0♑09.5	15 39.6	15 36.2	2 15.2	11 02.8	6 53.4	14 50.6	22 52.4
6 Su	15 03 13	14 10 33	3♑19 36	10♑19 40	13 14.6	7 17.9	1 08.7	15 18.3	15 59.6	2 28.2	11 04.6	6 52.9	14 50.9	22 54.3
7 M	15 07 09	15 10 46	17 21 16	24 24 06	13 11.5	8 05.7	2 07.5	14 57.1	16 23.1	2 41.1	11 06.3	6 52.4	14 51.3	22 56.1
8 Tu	15 11 06	16 11 01	1♒27 51	8♒32 13	13D10.0	8 48.8	3 05.8	14 36.0	16 46.6	2 54.1	11 07.9	6 52.0	14 51.7	22 58.0
9 W	15 15 02	17 11 17	15 36 58	22 41 53	13 09.8	9 26.8	4 03.7	14 15.1	17 10.1	3 07.0	11 09.4	6 51.7	14 52.1	22 59.9
10 Th	15 18 59	18 11 35	29 46 44	6♓51 20	13 10.8	9 58.9	5 01.2	13 54.5	17 33.6	3 19.8	11 10.8	6 51.4	14 52.6	23 01.8
11 F	15 22 55	19 11 53	13♓55 27	20 58 54	13 12.4	10 24.6	5 58.1	13 34.2	17 57.2	3 32.7	11 12.0	6 51.1	14 53.1	23 03.7
12 Sa	15 26 52	20 12 14	28 01 26	5♈02 48	13R13.6	10 43.1	6 54.5	13 14.2	18 20.9	3 45.5	11 13.2	6 50.9	14 53.7	23 05.7
13 Su	15 30 48	21 12 35	12♈02 44	19 00 55	13 13.7	10R53.8	7 50.4	12 54.6	18 44.6	3 58.3	11 14.2	6 50.7	14 54.3	23 07.7
14 M	15 34 45	22 12 58	25 57 02	2♉50 44	13 12.0	10 55.9	8 45.7	12 35.5	19 08.3	4 11.1	11 15.2	6 50.6	14 54.9	23 09.6
15 Tu	15 38 42	23 13 23	9♉41 39	16 29 29	13 08.4	10 48.8	9 40.4	12 16.8	19 32.0	4 23.8	11 16.0	6 50.6	14 55.5	23 11.6
16 W	15 42 38	24 13 50	23 13 52	29 54 31	13 02.8	10 31.8	10 34.6	11 58.6	19 55.8	4 36.5	11 16.7	6D50.6	14 56.2	23 13.6
17 Th	15 46 35	25 14 18	6♊31 11	13♊03 41	12 55.6	10 04.6	11 28.1	11 40.9	20 19.6	4 49.2	11 17.3	6 50.6	14 56.9	23 15.7
18 F	15 50 31	26 14 47	19 31 53	25 55 45	12 47.7	9 27.0	12 20.9	11 23.9	20 43.4	5 01.9	11 17.8	6 50.7	14 57.7	23 17.7
19 Sa	15 54 28	27 15 19	2♋15 18	8♋30 41	12 39.7	8 39.0	13 13.1	11 07.4	21 07.3	5 14.5	11 18.2	6 50.9	14 58.5	23 19.8
20 Su	15 58 24	28 15 52	14 42 05	20 49 46	12 32.7	7 41.3	14 04.6	10 51.5	21 31.2	5 27.0	11 18.5	6 51.1	14 59.3	23 21.8
21 M	16 02 21	29 16 27	26 54 06	2♌55 30	12 27.1	6 34.8	14 55.4	10 36.3	21 55.1	5 39.6	11R18.6	6 51.3	15 00.1	23 23.9
22 Tu	16 06 18	0♐17 03	8♌54 27	14 51 29	12 23.6	5 21.0	15 45.4	10 21.8	22 19.1	5 52.1	11 18.7	6 51.7	15 01.0	23 26.0
23 W	16 10 14	1 17 41	20 47 11	26 42 09	12D22.0	4 02.1	16 34.7	10 08.0	22 43.1	6 04.6	11 18.6	6 52.0	15 01.9	23 28.1
24 Th	16 14 11	2 18 21	2♍37 03	8♍32 31	12 22.1	2 40.4	17 23.1	9 54.9	23 07.1	6 17.0	11 18.4	6 52.4	15 02.8	23 30.3
25 F	16 18 07	3 19 02	14 29 14	20 27 50	12 23.1	1 18.7	18 10.7	9 42.6	23 31.1	6 29.4	11 18.1	6 52.9	15 03.8	23 32.4
26 Sa	16 22 04	4 19 45	26 29 01	2♎33 22	12R24.3	29♏59.6	18 57.4	9 31.0	23 55.2	6 41.7	11 17.7	6 53.4	15 04.8	23 34.5
27 Su	16 26 00	5 20 29	8♎41 30	14 53 57	12 24.7	28 45.9	19 43.1	9 20.2	24 19.2	6 54.0	11 17.2	6 53.9	15 05.9	23 36.7
28 M	16 29 57	6 21 15	21 11 12	27 33 39	12 23.4	27 39.7	20 28.0	9 10.1	24 43.3	7 06.2	11 16.5	6 54.6	15 06.9	23 38.8
29 Tu	16 33 53	7 22 03	4♏01 35	10♏35 13	12 19.9	26 42.8	21 11.8	9 00.9	25 07.5	7 18.4	11 15.8	6 55.2	15 08.0	23 41.0
30 W	16 37 50	8 22 52	17 14 37	23 59 43	12 13.8	25 56.5	21 54.6	8 52.5	25 31.6	7 30.6	11 14.9	6 55.9	15 09.1	23 43.2

December 2005 — LONGITUDE

Day	Sid.Time	☉	0 hr ☽	Noon ☽	True ☊	☿	♀	♂	⚳	♃	♄	♅	♆	♇
1 Th	16 41 47	9♐23 42	0♐50 20	7♐46 06	12♈05.6	25♏21.6	22♑36.3	8♉45.0	25♐55.8	7♏42.6	11♌14.0	6♓56.7	15♒10.3	23♐45.4
2 F	16 45 43	10 24 33	14 46 34	21 51 09	11R55.9	24R58.2	23 16.9	8R38.2	26 20.0	7 54.7	11R12.9	6 57.5	15 11.5	23 47.6
3 Sa	16 49 40	11 25 26	28 59 09	6♑09 49	11 45.8	24D46.2	23 56.3	8 32.3	26 44.2	8 06.7	11 11.7	6 58.4	15 12.7	23 49.8
4 Su	16 53 36	12 26 20	13♑22 21	20 35 58	11 36.4	24 45.1	24 34.5	8 27.2	27 08.4	8 18.6	11 10.4	6 59.3	15 14.0	23 52.0
5 M	16 57 33	13 27 14	27 49 53	5♒03 23	11 28.9	24 54.3	25 11.4	8 23.0	27 32.7	8 30.5	11 09.0	7 00.3	15 15.3	23 54.2
6 Tu	17 01 29	14 28 09	12♒15 52	19 26 46	11 23.8	25 12.9	25 47.0	8 19.6	27 56.9	8 42.3	11 07.5	7 01.3	15 16.6	23 56.4
7 W	17 05 26	15 29 05	26 35 42	3♓42 19	11D21.2	25 40.1	26 21.1	8 17.0	28 21.2	8 54.0	11 05.8	7 02.4	15 17.9	23 58.7
8 Th	17 09 22	16 30 01	10♓46 25	17 47 52	11 20.7	26 15.1	26 53.8	8 15.3	28 45.4	9 05.7	11 04.1	7 03.5	15 19.3	24 00.9
9 F	17 13 19	17 30 58	24 46 37	1♈42 39	11R21.1	26 56.9	27 25.0	8D14.3	29 09.7	9 17.3	11 02.2	7 04.7	15 20.7	24 03.1
10 Sa	17 17 16	18 31 56	8♈36 01	15 26 46	11 21.2	27 44.9	27 54.6	8 14.2	29 34.0	9 28.8	11 00.3	7 05.9	15 22.1	24 05.4
11 Su	17 21 12	19 32 54	22 14 58	29 00 00	11 19.9	28 38.2	28 22.6	8 14.8	29 58.3	9 40.3	10 58.2	7 07.1	15 23.5	24 07.6
12 M	17 25 09	20 33 53	5♉43 48	12♉24 29	11 16.1	29 36.3	28 48.9	8 16.3	0♑22.6	9 51.7	10 56.1	7 08.5	15 25.0	24 09.8
13 Tu	17 29 05	21 34 53	19 02 36	25 38 08	11 09.4	0♐38.5	29 13.3	8 18.5	0 46.9	10 03.1	10 53.8	7 09.8	15 26.5	24 12.1
14 W	17 33 02	22 35 53	2♊10 57	8♊40 59	10 59.7	1 44.3	29 36.0	8 21.5	1 11.2	10 14.3	10 51.5	7 11.2	15 28.0	24 14.3
15 Th	17 36 58	23 36 54	15 08 05	21 32 10	10 47.7	2 53.3	29 56.8	8 25.2	1 35.6	10 25.5	10 49.0	7 12.7	15 29.6	24 16.6
16 F	17 40 55	24 37 56	27 53 07	4♋10 53	10 34.3	4 05.1	0♒15.6	8 29.7	1 59.9	10 36.6	10 46.5	7 14.2	15 31.2	24 18.8
17 Sa	17 44 52	25 38 58	10♋25 26	16 36 48	10 20.7	5 19.2	0 32.3	8 34.9	2 24.2	10 47.7	10 43.8	7 15.8	15 32.8	24 21.1
18 Su	17 48 48	26 40 01	22 45 03	28 50 20	10 08.1	6 35.4	0 47.0	8 40.8	2 48.6	10 58.6	10 41.1	7 17.3	15 34.4	24 23.3
19 M	17 52 45	27 41 05	4♌52 51	10♌52 54	9 57.5	7 53.5	0 59.5	8 47.5	3 12.9	11 09.5	10 38.2	7 19.0	15 36.1	24 25.6
20 Tu	17 56 41	28 42 09	16 50 48	22 46 58	9 49.6	9 13.1	1 09.9	8 54.8	3 37.2	11 20.3	10 35.3	7 20.7	15 37.8	24 27.8
21 W	18 00 38	29 43 15	28 41 51	4♍36 00	9 44.4	10 34.2	1 17.9	9 02.7	4 01.6	11 31.0	10 32.3	7 22.4	15 39.5	24 30.1
22 Th	18 04 34	0♑44 21	10♍29 59	16 24 24	9 41.9	11 56.5	1 23.7	9 11.4	4 25.9	11 41.7	10 29.2	7 24.2	15 41.2	24 32.3
23 F	18 08 31	1 45 27	22 19 56	28 17 14	9 41.1	13 19.9	1R27.0	9 20.7	4 50.2	11 52.2	10 26.0	7 26.0	15 42.9	24 34.5
24 Sa	18 12 27	2 46 34	4♎17 00	10♎19 57	9 41.1	14 44.2	1 28.0	9 30.6	5 14.6	12 02.7	10 22.7	7 27.9	15 44.7	24 36.8
25 Su	18 16 24	3 47 42	16 26 47	22 38 10	9 40.7	16 09.5	1 26.5	9 41.2	5 38.9	12 13.0	10 19.3	7 29.8	15 46.5	24 39.0
26 M	18 20 21	4 48 51	28 54 45	5♏17 05	9 38.6	17 35.4	1 22.6	9 52.4	6 03.2	12 23.3	10 15.8	7 31.7	15 48.3	24 41.2
27 Tu	18 24 17	5 50 00	11♏45 42	18 20 57	9 34.2	19 02.1	1 16.2	10 04.2	6 27.6	12 33.5	10 12.3	7 33.7	15 50.1	24 43.4
28 W	18 28 14	6 51 10	25 03 08	1♐52 20	9 26.9	20 29.5	1 07.3	10 16.6	6 51.9	12 43.6	10 08.6	7 35.8	15 52.0	24 45.6
29 Th	18 32 10	7 52 20	8♐48 29	15 51 20	9 17.0	21 57.4	0 55.9	10 29.6	7 16.2	12 53.6	10 04.9	7 37.9	15 53.9	24 47.9
30 F	18 36 07	8 53 31	23 00 25	0♑15 06	9 05.1	23 25.8	0 42.0	10 43.2	7 40.5	13 03.4	10 01.2	7 40.0	15 55.8	24 50.1
31 Sa	18 40 03	9 54 41	7♑34 32	14 57 45	8 52.7	24 54.8	0 25.7	10 57.3	8 04.8	13 13.2	9 57.3	7 42.1	15 57.7	24 52.2

Astro Data (Dy Hr Mn)

☽0N 12 7:16
☿R 14 5:42
♅D 16 0:07
♄R 22 9:01
☽0S 26 11:08
♃△♅ 27 11:56

☿D 4 2:22
♃∠♇ 7 23:48
☽0N 9 12:22
♂D 10 4:03
♃□♄ 17 5:16
☽0S 23 18:43
♀R 24 9:36

Planet Ingress (Dy Hr Mn)

♀ ♑ 5 8:10
☉ ♐ 22 5:15
☿ ♏R 26 11:53

⚳ ♑ 11 13:41
☿ ♐ 12 21:19
♀ ♒ 15 15:57
☉ ♑ 21 18:35

Last Aspect Dy Hr Mn	☽ Ingress Dy Hr Mn
31 23:17 ♀ ⚹	♏ 1 7:29
2 14:05 ♂ ☍	♐ 3 13:55
5 5:58 ♇ ☌	♑ 5 18:17
6 20:18 ♂ △	♒ 7 21:31
9 12:31 ♇ ⚹	♓ 10 0:22
11 15:33 ♇ □	♈ 12 3:22
13 19:07 ♇ △	♉ 14 7:02
16 0:58 ☉ ☍	♊ 16 12:10
18 7:02 ♇ ☍	♋ 18 19:42
21 4:03 ☉ △	♌ 21 6:10
23 5:25 ♇ △	♍ 23 18:41
25 18:10 ♇ □	♎ 26 6:58
28 4:38 ♇ ⚹	♏ 28 16:33
30 15:16 ☿ ☌	♐ 30 22:32

Last Aspect Dy Hr Mn	☽ Ingress Dy Hr Mn
2 15:17 ♇ ☌	♑ 3 1:42
4 18:56 ☿ ⚹	♒ 5 3:36
6 21:58 ☿ □	♓ 7 5:44
9 4:17 ♀ ⚹	♈ 9 9:02
11 10:50 ♀ □	♉ 11 13:46
13 18:46 ♀ △	♊ 13 19:59
15 17:11 ♇ ☍	♋ 16 4:01
17 0:33 ♃ △	♌ 18 14:18
21 1:09 ☉ △	♍ 21 2:39
23 4:30 ♇ □	♎ 23 15:26
25 15:53 ♇ ⚹	♏ 26 2:04
27 7:26 ♆ □	♐ 28 8:44
30 3:01 ♇ ☌	♑ 30 11:35

☽ Phases & Eclipses (Dy Hr Mn)

2 1:25 ● 9♏43
9 1:57 ☽ 16♒46
16 0:58 ○ 23♉46
23 22:11 ☾ 1♍43

1 15:01 ● 9♐31
8 9:36 ☽ 16♓24
15 16:16 ○ 23♊48
23 19:36 ☾ 2♎05
31 3:12 ● 9♑32

Astro Data

1 November 2005
Julian Day # 38656
SVP 5♓10'47"
GC 26♐55.2 ⚴ 18♏34.2
Eris 20♈21.3R ⚵ 22♊52.8
⚷ 28♑15.3 ⚶ 22♋09.0
☽ Mean ☊ 12♈11.8

1 December 2005
Julian Day # 38686
SVP 5♓10'42"
GC 26♐55.3 ⚴ 1♐41.9
Eris 20♈06.7R ⚵ 19♊08.9R
⚷ 29♑42.5 ⚶ 22♋37.0R
☽ Mean ☊ 10♈36.5

LONGITUDE — January 2006

Day	Sid.Time	☉	0 hr ☽	Noon☽	True☊	☿	♀	♂	⚳	♃	♄	♅	♆	♇
1 Su	18 44 00	10♑55 52	22♑23 38	29♑51 03	8♈40.9	26♐24.2	0♒07.0	11♉11.9	8♑29.1	13♏22.9	9♌53.4	7♓44.4	15♒59.6	24♐54.4
2 M	18 47 56	11 57 03	7♒18 48	14♒45 46	8R 31.2	27 54.1	29♑46.0	11 27.1	8 53.4	13 32.5	9R 49.4	7 46.6	16 01.6	24 56.6
3 Tu	18 51 53	12 58 13	22 10 56	29 33 22	8 24.3	29 24.4	29R 22.7	11 42.9	9 17.7	13 42.0	9 45.3	7 48.9	16 03.6	24 58.8
4 W	18 55 50	13 59 23	6♓52 21	14♓07 17	8 20.4	0♑55.1	28 57.3	11 59.1	9 41.9	13 51.3	9 41.2	7 51.2	16 05.6	25 00.9
5 Th	18 59 46	15 00 33	21 17 46	28 23 33	8D 18.8	2 26.2	28 29.8	12 15.9	10 06.2	14 00.6	9 37.0	7 53.6	16 07.6	25 03.1
6 F	19 03 43	16 01 43	5♈24 33	12♈20 46	8R 18.7	3 57.8	28 00.4	12 33.1	10 30.4	14 09.7	9 32.7	7 56.0	16 09.6	25 05.2
7 Sa	19 07 39	17 02 52	19 12 20	25 59 25	8 18.5	5 29.8	27 29.4	12 50.8	10 54.6	14 18.7	9 28.4	7 58.4	16 11.6	25 07.3
8 Su	19 11 36	18 04 00	2♉42 15	9♉21 07	8 17.0	7 02.1	26 56.8	13 09.0	11 18.8	14 27.6	9 24.1	8 00.9	16 13.7	25 09.4
9 M	19 15 32	19 05 08	15 56 16	22 27 56	8 13.1	8 34.9	26 22.9	13 27.6	11 43.0	14 36.4	9 19.6	8 03.4	16 15.7	25 11.5
10 Tu	19 19 29	20 06 16	28 56 23	5♊21 48	8 06.2	10 08.1	25 47.8	13 46.6	12 07.1	14 45.1	9 15.2	8 05.9	16 17.8	25 13.6
11 W	19 23 25	21 07 23	11♊44 23	18 04 16	7 56.4	11 41.8	25 11.9	14 06.1	12 31.2	14 53.6	9 10.7	8 08.5	16 19.9	25 15.7
12 Th	19 27 22	22 08 30	24 21 34	0♋36 22	7 44.2	13 15.9	24 35.4	14 26.0	12 55.3	15 02.1	9 06.1	8 11.1	16 22.0	25 17.8
13 F	19 31 19	23 09 37	6♋48 44	12 58 44	7 30.5	14 50.4	23 58.6	14 46.3	13 19.4	15 10.4	9 01.5	8 13.7	16 24.2	25 19.8
14 Sa	19 35 15	24 10 43	19 06 26	25 11 53	7 16.6	16 25.4	23 21.6	15 07.0	13 43.5	15 18.6	8 56.9	8 16.4	16 26.3	25 21.9
15 Su	19 39 12	25 11 48	1♌15 12	7♌16 27	7 03.5	18 00.9	22 44.8	15 28.0	14 07.5	15 26.6	8 52.2	8 19.1	16 28.5	25 23.9
16 M	19 43 08	26 12 53	13 15 49	19 13 28	6 52.4	19 36.9	22 08.4	15 49.4	14 31.6	15 34.5	8 47.5	8 21.9	16 30.6	25 25.9
17 Tu	19 47 05	27 13 58	25 09 38	1♍04 37	6 44.0	21 13.4	21 32.7	16 11.2	14 55.6	15 42.3	8 42.7	8 24.6	16 32.8	25 27.9
18 W	19 51 01	28 15 02	6♍58 44	12 52 22	6 38.4	22 50.4	20 58.0	16 33.4	15 19.5	15 50.0	8 37.9	8 27.4	16 35.0	25 29.8
19 Th	19 54 58	29 16 06	18 45 59	24 40 04	6 35.5	24 27.9	20 24.4	16 55.9	15 43.5	15 57.5	8 33.1	8 30.3	16 37.2	25 31.8
20 F	19 58 54	0♒17 10	0♎35 09	6♎31 50	6D 34.8	26 06.0	19 52.2	17 18.7	16 07.4	16 04.9	8 28.3	8 33.1	16 39.4	25 33.7
21 Sa	20 02 51	1 18 13	12 30 43	18 32 28	6 35.2	27 44.7	19 21.5	17 41.8	16 31.3	16 12.2	8 23.5	8 36.0	16 41.6	25 35.6
22 Su	20 06 48	2 19 15	24 37 44	0♏47 13	6R 35.7	29 23.9	18 52.6	18 05.3	16 55.1	16 19.3	8 18.6	8 38.9	16 43.8	25 37.5
23 M	20 10 44	3 20 18	7♏01 35	13 21 28	6 35.1	1♒03.8	18 25.7	18 29.1	17 19.0	16 26.3	8 13.7	8 41.8	16 46.0	25 39.4
24 Tu	20 14 41	4 21 19	19 47 28	26 20 08	6 32.8	2 44.2	18 00.8	18 53.2	17 42.8	16 33.1	8 08.8	8 44.8	16 48.2	25 41.3
25 W	20 18 37	5 22 21	2♐59 52	9♐47 01	6 28.1	4 25.3	17 38.1	19 17.6	18 06.5	16 39.8	8 03.9	8 47.8	16 50.5	25 43.1
26 Th	20 22 34	6 23 22	16 41 42	23 43 55	6 21.0	6 07.0	17 17.6	19 42.3	18 30.3	16 46.3	7 59.0	8 50.8	16 52.7	25 45.0
27 F	20 26 30	7 24 22	0♑53 24	8♑09 44	6 12.3	7 49.3	16 59.5	20 07.3	18 54.0	16 52.7	7 54.0	8 53.9	16 55.0	25 46.8
28 Sa	20 30 27	8 25 22	15 32 13	22 59 58	6 02.7	9 32.3	16 43.8	20 32.5	19 17.6	16 59.0	7 49.1	8 56.9	16 57.2	25 48.6
29 Su	20 34 24	9 26 21	0♒31 53	8♒06 46	5 53.6	11 15.8	16 30.6	20 58.1	19 41.3	17 05.1	7 44.2	9 00.0	16 59.5	25 50.3
30 M	20 38 20	10 27 18	15 43 16	23 20 02	5 46.0	13 00.1	16 19.8	21 23.9	20 04.9	17 11.0	7 39.3	9 03.1	17 01.8	25 52.1
31 Tu	20 42 17	11 28 15	0♓55 44	8♓29 06	5 40.7	14 44.9	16 11.5	21 50.0	20 28.4	17 16.8	7 34.4	9 06.3	17 04.1	25 53.8

LONGITUDE — February 2006

Day	Sid.Time	☉	0 hr ☽	Noon☽	True☊	☿	♀	♂	⚳	♃	♄	♅	♆	♇
1 W	20 46 13	12♒29 10	15♓59 03	23♓24 38	5♈37.9	16♒30.2	16♑05.6	22♉16.3	20♑51.9	17♏22.4	7♌29.5	9♓09.4	17♒06.3	25♐55.5
2 Th	20 50 10	13 30 04	0♈45 06	7♈59 54	5D 37.3	18 16.2	16D 02.3	22 42.8	21 15.4	17 27.9	7R 24.6	9 12.6	17 08.6	25 57.1
3 F	20 54 06	14 30 57	15 08 42	22 11 19	5 38.1	20 02.6	16 01.3	23 09.7	21 38.8	17 33.2	7 19.7	9 15.8	17 10.9	25 58.8
4 Sa	20 58 03	15 31 49	29 07 45	5♉58 05	5R 39.1	21 49.5	16 02.8	23 36.7	22 02.2	17 38.3	7 14.9	9 19.0	17 13.2	26 00.4
5 Su	21 01 59	16 32 39	12♉42 34	19 21 28	5 39.4	23 36.8	16 06.6	24 04.0	22 25.5	17 43.3	7 10.0	9 22.2	17 15.4	26 02.0
6 M	21 05 56	17 33 27	25 55 10	2♊24 02	5 38.2	25 24.4	16 12.8	24 31.5	22 48.8	17 48.1	7 05.2	9 25.5	17 17.7	26 03.6
7 Tu	21 09 53	18 34 14	8♊48 27	15 08 50	5 34.8	27 12.2	16 21.2	24 59.2	23 12.0	17 52.8	7 00.4	9 28.8	17 20.0	26 05.1
8 W	21 13 49	19 35 00	21 25 33	27 38 59	5 29.4	29 00.0	16 31.9	25 27.1	23 35.2	17 57.2	6 55.7	9 32.0	17 22.3	26 06.7
9 Th	21 17 46	20 35 44	3♋49 28	9♋57 19	5 22.2	0♓47.7	16 44.8	25 55.2	23 58.3	18 01.6	6 51.0	9 35.3	17 24.6	26 08.2
10 F	21 21 42	21 36 27	16 02 50	22 06 14	5 13.8	2 35.2	16 59.7	26 23.5	24 21.4	18 05.7	6 46.3	9 38.6	17 26.8	26 09.6
11 Sa	21 25 39	22 37 08	28 07 48	4♌07 44	5 05.2	4 22.2	17 16.7	26 52.0	24 44.5	18 09.7	6 41.7	9 42.0	17 29.1	26 11.1
12 Su	21 29 35	23 37 48	10♌06 14	16 03 29	4 57.2	6 08.4	17 35.7	27 20.7	25 07.5	18 13.5	6 37.1	9 45.3	17 31.4	26 12.5
13 M	21 33 32	24 38 26	21 59 42	27 55 05	4 50.4	7 53.5	17 56.6	27 49.6	25 30.4	18 17.1	6 32.5	9 48.6	17 33.7	26 13.9
14 Tu	21 37 28	25 39 03	3♍49 50	9♍44 11	4 45.5	9 37.3	18 19.4	28 18.6	25 53.3	18 20.6	6 28.0	9 52.0	17 35.9	26 15.3
15 W	21 41 25	26 39 38	15 38 24	21 32 45	4 42.5	11 19.2	18 43.9	28 47.8	26 16.1	18 23.8	6 23.5	9 55.4	17 38.2	26 16.6
16 Th	21 45 22	27 40 12	27 27 34	3♎23 11	4D 41.5	12 58.9	19 10.2	29 17.2	26 38.9	18 26.9	6 19.1	9 58.7	17 40.4	26 17.9
17 F	21 49 18	28 40 45	9♎20 00	15 18 26	4 42.0	14 35.8	19 38.2	29 46.7	27 01.6	18 29.9	6 14.7	10 02.1	17 42.7	26 19.2
18 Sa	21 53 15	29 41 17	21 18 58	27 22 04	4 43.5	16 09.4	20 07.8	0♊16.4	27 24.2	18 32.6	6 10.4	10 05.5	17 44.9	26 20.5
19 Su	21 57 11	0♓41 47	3♏28 16	9♏38 07	4 45.3	17 39.2	20 38.9	0 46.3	27 46.8	18 35.2	6 06.2	10 08.9	17 47.2	26 21.7
20 M	22 01 08	1 42 16	15 52 10	22 10 58	4R 46.7	19 04.5	21 11.6	1 16.3	28 09.3	18 37.6	6 02.0	10 12.3	17 49.4	26 22.9
21 Tu	22 05 04	2 42 43	28 35 04	5♐04 58	4 47.0	20 24.7	21 45.6	1 46.5	28 31.8	18 39.8	5 57.8	10 15.8	17 51.6	26 24.1
22 W	22 09 01	3 43 10	11♐41 08	18 23 55	4 46.1	21 39.1	22 21.0	2 16.8	28 54.2	18 41.8	5 53.8	10 19.2	17 53.8	26 25.2
23 Th	22 12 57	4 43 35	25 13 38	2♑10 25	4 43.8	22 47.0	22 57.8	2 47.3	29 16.6	18 43.6	5 49.8	10 22.6	17 56.1	26 26.3
24 F	22 16 54	5 43 59	9♑14 14	16 24 57	4 40.3	23 47.8	23 35.8	3 17.9	29 38.9	18 45.3	5 45.8	10 26.1	17 58.3	26 27.4
25 Sa	22 20 51	6 44 21	23 42 10	1♒05 18	4 36.3	24 40.9	24 15.0	3 48.6	0♒01.1	18 46.7	5 42.0	10 29.5	18 00.4	26 28.5
26 Su	22 24 47	7 44 42	8♒33 35	16 06 03	4 32.3	25 25.8	24 55.4	4 19.5	0 23.2	18 48.0	5 38.2	10 33.0	18 02.6	26 29.5
27 M	22 28 44	8 45 01	23 41 36	1♓18 59	4 29.0	26 02.0	25 36.9	4 50.5	0 45.3	18 49.1	5 34.5	10 36.4	18 04.8	26 30.5
28 Tu	22 32 40	9 45 19	8♓56 53	16 34 02	4 26.8	26 29.1	26 19.4	5 21.6	1 07.3	18 50.0	5 30.8	10 39.8	18 07.0	26 31.5

Astro Data
Dy Hr Mn
♄♇♇ 1 7:53
☽0N 5 17:08
♄⚻♅ 19 21:02
☽0S 20 1:05
♃□♆ 28 1:24

☽0N 2 0:21
♀D 3 9:19
☽0S 16 6:48
☿0N 26 13:11

Planet Ingress
Dy Hr Mn
♀ ♑R 1 20:18
☿ ♑ 3 21:26
☉ ♒ 20 5:15
☿ ♒ 22 20:41

☿ ♓ 9 1:22
♂ ♊ 17 22:44
☉ ♓ 18 19:26
⚳ ♒ 25 10:50

Last Aspect ☽ Ingress
Dy Hr Mn — Dy Hr Mn
31 9:09 ♃ ⚹ ♒ 1 12:14
3 11:44 ☿ ⚹ ♓ 3 12:44
5 12:10 ♀ ⚹ ♈ 5 14:44
7 14:34 ♀ □ ♉ 7 19:09
9 18:56 ♀ △ ♊ 10 1:58
12 1:46 ♇ ☍ ♋ 12 10:50
14 9:48 ☉ ☍ ♌ 14 21:31
17 0:35 ♇ △ ♍ 17 9:49
19 22:13 ☉ △ ♎ 19 22:49
22 8:53 ☿ □ ♏ 22 10:28
23 21:53 ♂ ☍ ♐ 24 18:38
26 15:24 ♇ ☌ ♑ 26 22:31
28 7:57 ♂ △ ♒ 28 23:09
30 16:00 ♇ ⚹ ♓ 30 22:32

Last Aspect ☽ Ingress
Dy Hr Mn — Dy Hr Mn
1 16:06 ♇ □ ♈ 1 22:46
3 18:33 ♇ △ ♉ 4 1:31
5 21:00 ☿ □ ♊ 6 7:32
8 15:04 ☿ △ ♋ 8 16:33
10 20:53 ♂ ⚹ ♌ 11 3:44
13 11:48 ♂ □ ♍ 13 16:13
16 3:21 ♂ △ ♎ 16 5:09
18 16:59 ☉ △ ♏ 18 17:11
20 10:03 ♀ ⚹ ♐ 21 2:38
23 2:06 ♇ ☌ ♑ 23 8:16
25 0:58 ☿ ⚹ ♒ 25 10:14
27 4:26 ♇ ⚹ ♓ 27 9:56

☽ Phases & Eclipses
Dy Hr Mn
6 18:57 ☽ 16♈19
14 9:48 ○ 24♋05
22 15:14 ☾ 2♏27
29 14:15 ● 9♒32

5 6:29 ☽ 16♉19
13 4:44 ○ 24♌20
21 7:17 ☾ 2♐31
28 0:31 ● 9♓16

Astro Data
1 January 2006
Julian Day # 38717
SVP 5♓10'35"
GC 26♐55.4 ⚴ 14♐58.3
Eris 19♈59.5R ⚵ 12♊59.0R
⚷ 1♒57.6 ⚶ 16♋38.9R
☽ Mean ☊ 8♈58.1

1 February 2006
Julian Day # 38748
SVP 5♓10'30"
GC 26♐55.5 ⚴ 27♐23.3
Eris 20♈02.7 ⚵ 13♊37.8
⚷ 4♒32.3 ⚶ 9♋21.0R
☽ Mean ☊ 7♈19.6

March 2006 LONGITUDE

Day	Sid.Time	☉	0 hr ☽	Noon ☽	True ☊	☿	♀	♂	⚳	♃	♄	♅	♆	♇
1 W	22 36 37	10♓45 34	24♓09 07	1♈41 00	4♈25.9	26♓46.7	27♑03.0	5♊52.9	1♒29.2	18♏50.7	5♌27.2	10♓43.3	18♒09.1	26♐32.4
2 Th	22 40 33	11 45 48	9♈08 37	16 31 07	4D 26.3	26R 54.9	27 47.5	6 24.3	1 51.1	18 51.2	5R 23.8	10 46.7	18 11.2	26 33.3
3 F	22 44 30	12 45 59	23 47 47	0♉58 08	4 27.4	26 53.5	28 33.0	6 55.8	2 12.8	18 51.6	5 20.4	10 50.2	18 13.4	26 34.1
4 Sa	22 48 26	13 46 09	8♉01 51	14 58 48	4 28.9	26 42.8	29 19.4	7 27.4	2 34.5	18R 51.7	5 17.0	10 53.6	18 15.5	26 35.0
5 Su	22 52 23	14 46 17	21 48 59	28 32 33	4 30.1	26 23.0	0♒06.6	7 59.2	2 56.2	18 51.6	5 13.8	10 57.1	18 17.6	26 35.8
6 M	22 56 19	15 46 23	5♊09 46	11♊40 58	4R 30.8	25 54.9	0 54.7	8 31.0	3 17.7	18 51.4	5 10.7	11 00.5	18 19.7	26 36.6
7 Tu	23 00 16	16 46 26	18 06 34	24 27 00	4 30.7	25 19.0	1 43.6	9 03.0	3 39.1	18 51.0	5 07.6	11 03.9	18 21.7	26 37.3
8 W	23 04 13	17 46 27	0♋42 45	6♋54 20	4 29.7	24 36.3	2 33.3	9 35.0	4 00.5	18 50.4	5 04.7	11 07.4	18 23.8	26 38.0
9 Th	23 08 09	18 46 27	13 02 15	19 06 57	4 28.0	23 47.8	3 23.7	10 07.2	4 21.8	18 49.6	5 01.8	11 10.8	18 25.8	26 38.7
10 F	23 12 06	19 46 24	25 08 56	1♌08 40	4 25.9	22 54.8	4 14.8	10 39.5	4 43.0	18 48.6	4 59.0	11 14.2	18 27.8	26 39.3
11 Sa	23 16 02	20 46 19	7♌06 34	13 03 01	4 23.7	21 58.6	5 06.6	11 11.8	5 04.1	18 47.4	4 56.3	11 17.6	18 29.8	26 39.9
12 Su	23 19 59	21 46 11	18 58 26	24 53 08	4 21.6	21 00.5	5 59.0	11 44.3	5 25.1	18 46.1	4 53.8	11 21.0	18 31.8	26 40.5
13 M	23 23 55	22 46 02	0♍47 28	6♍41 43	4 20.0	20 01.8	6 52.1	12 16.8	5 46.1	18 44.5	4 51.3	11 24.4	18 33.8	26 41.1
14 Tu	23 27 52	23 45 51	12 36 12	18 31 10	4 19.0	19 03.8	7 45.8	12 49.4	6 06.9	18 42.8	4 48.9	11 27.8	18 35.8	26 41.6
15 W	23 31 48	24 45 37	24 26 52	0♎23 34	4D 18.5	18 07.7	8 40.1	13 22.1	6 27.7	18 40.9	4 46.6	11 31.2	18 37.7	26 42.0
16 Th	23 35 45	25 45 22	6♎21 32	12 21 00	4 18.6	17 14.7	9 35.0	13 54.9	6 48.3	18 38.8	4 44.4	11 34.6	18 39.6	26 42.5
17 F	23 39 42	26 45 05	18 22 14	24 25 30	4 19.0	16 25.5	10 30.4	14 27.8	7 08.9	18 36.5	4 42.3	11 37.9	18 41.5	26 42.9
18 Sa	23 43 38	27 44 46	0♏31 06	6♏39 19	4 19.7	15 41.0	11 26.4	15 00.7	7 29.3	18 34.0	4 40.3	11 41.3	18 43.4	26 43.3
19 Su	23 47 35	28 44 25	12 50 28	19 04 53	4 20.3	15 01.8	12 22.9	15 33.8	7 49.7	18 31.4	4 38.4	11 44.6	18 45.3	26 43.6
20 M	23 51 31	29 44 02	25 22 54	1♐44 51	4 20.9	14 28.2	13 19.8	16 06.9	8 10.0	18 28.6	4 36.6	11 47.9	18 47.1	26 43.9
21 Tu	23 55 28	0♈43 38	8♐11 05	14 41 56	4 21.2	14 00.5	14 17.3	16 40.0	8 30.1	18 25.6	4 34.9	11 51.2	18 48.9	26 44.2
22 W	23 59 24	1 43 12	21 17 42	27 58 40	4R 21.3	13 39.0	15 15.2	17 13.3	8 50.2	18 22.4	4 33.3	11 54.5	18 50.7	26 44.5
23 Th	0 03 21	2 42 45	4♑45 04	11♑37 04	4 21.3	13 23.6	16 13.5	17 46.6	9 10.2	18 19.1	4 31.9	11 57.8	18 52.5	26 44.7
24 F	0 07 17	3 42 15	18 34 43	25 38 00	4D 21.3	13 14.2	17 12.3	18 20.0	9 30.0	18 15.5	4 30.5	12 01.1	18 54.3	26 44.9
25 Sa	0 11 14	4 41 44	2♒46 47	10♒00 45	4 21.3	13D 10.9	18 11.4	18 53.5	9 49.8	18 11.9	4 29.2	12 04.3	18 56.0	26 45.0
26 Su	0 15 11	5 41 11	17 19 30	24 42 27	4 21.3	13 13.3	19 11.0	19 27.1	10 09.4	18 08.0	4 28.1	12 07.6	18 57.7	26 45.2
27 M	0 19 07	6 40 36	2♓08 52	9♓37 55	4 21.5	13 21.4	20 10.9	20 00.7	10 28.9	18 04.0	4 27.0	12 10.8	18 59.4	26 45.2
28 Tu	0 23 04	7 40 00	17 08 39	24 40 01	4R 21.7	13 34.8	21 11.2	20 34.4	10 48.3	17 59.8	4 26.1	12 14.0	19 01.1	26 45.3
29 W	0 27 00	8 39 21	2♈10 55	9♈40 16	4 21.7	13 53.4	22 11.9	21 08.1	11 07.6	17 55.4	4 25.3	12 17.2	19 02.7	26R 45.3
30 Th	0 30 57	9 38 40	17 07 01	24 30 11	4 21.5	14 16.8	23 12.8	21 41.9	11 26.8	17 50.9	4 24.5	12 20.3	19 04.3	26 45.3
31 F	0 34 53	10 37 57	1♉48 51	9♉02 19	4 20.9	14 44.9	24 14.1	22 15.8	11 45.8	17 46.2	4 23.9	12 23.5	19 05.9	26 45.3

April 2006 LONGITUDE

Day	Sid.Time	☉	0 hr ☽	Noon ☽	True ☊	☿	♀	♂	⚳	♃	♄	♅	♆	♇
1 Sa	0 38 50	11♈37 12	16♉09 57	23♉11 20	4♈20.1	15♓17.3	25♒15.7	22♊49.8	12♒04.7	17♏41.4	4♌23.4	12♓26.6	19♒07.5	26♐45.2
2 Su	0 42 46	12 36 25	0♊06 10	6♊54 22	4R 19.2	15 53.9	26 17.6	23 23.8	12 23.5	17R 36.4	4R 23.0	12 29.7	19 09.1	26R 45.1
3 M	0 46 43	13 35 36	13 35 56	20 11 02	4 18.3	16 34.4	27 19.8	23 57.8	12 42.2	17 31.3	4 22.8	12 32.8	19 10.6	26 44.9
4 Tu	0 50 40	14 34 44	26 39 57	3♋03 02	4D 17.6	17 18.6	28 22.3	24 32.0	13 00.7	17 26.0	4 22.6	12 35.8	19 12.1	26 44.7
5 W	0 54 36	15 33 50	9♋20 43	15 33 31	4 17.3	18 06.4	29 25.0	25 06.1	13 19.1	17 20.6	4D 22.5	12 38.9	19 13.5	26 44.5
6 Th	0 58 33	16 32 54	21 41 58	27 46 37	4 17.6	18 57.4	0♓28.0	25 40.4	13 37.4	17 15.0	4 22.6	12 41.9	19 15.0	26 44.3
7 F	1 02 29	17 31 55	3♌48 04	9♌46 54	4 18.4	19 51.6	1 31.2	26 14.6	13 55.6	17 09.3	4 22.7	12 44.8	19 16.4	26 44.0
8 Sa	1 06 26	18 30 54	15 43 40	21 38 57	4 19.6	20 48.8	2 34.7	26 49.0	14 13.6	17 03.5	4 23.0	12 47.8	19 17.8	26 43.7
9 Su	1 10 22	19 29 51	27 33 17	3♍27 11	4 21.0	21 48.8	3 38.5	27 23.3	14 31.4	16 57.6	4 23.4	12 50.7	19 19.2	26 43.4
10 M	1 14 19	20 28 45	9♍21 09	15 15 37	4 22.3	22 51.6	4 42.4	27 57.8	14 49.1	16 51.5	4 23.9	12 53.6	19 20.5	26 43.0
11 Tu	1 18 15	21 27 38	21 11 00	27 07 43	4R 23.1	23 56.9	5 46.6	28 32.2	15 06.7	16 45.3	4 24.5	12 56.5	19 21.8	26 42.6
12 W	1 22 12	22 26 28	3♎06 04	9♎06 24	4 23.2	25 04.7	6 51.1	29 06.7	15 24.1	16 39.0	4 25.2	12 59.4	19 23.1	26 42.2
13 Th	1 26 09	23 25 16	15 08 57	21 13 58	4 22.3	26 14.9	7 55.7	29 41.3	15 41.4	16 32.6	4 26.0	13 02.2	19 24.3	26 41.7
14 F	1 30 05	24 24 02	27 21 40	3♏32 13	4 20.5	27 27.4	9 00.5	0♋15.9	15 58.6	16 26.1	4 26.9	13 05.0	19 25.5	26 41.3
15 Sa	1 34 02	25 22 46	9♏45 45	16 02 23	4 17.8	28 42.1	10 05.6	0 50.5	16 15.6	16 19.5	4 27.9	13 07.7	19 26.7	26 40.7
16 Su	1 37 58	26 21 29	22 22 15	28 45 25	4 14.5	29 58.9	11 10.8	1 25.2	16 32.4	16 12.8	4 29.1	13 10.5	19 27.9	26 40.2
17 M	1 41 55	27 20 10	5♐11 57	11♐41 57	4 11.0	1♈17.8	12 16.2	1 59.9	16 49.1	16 06.0	4 30.3	13 13.2	19 29.0	26 39.6
18 Tu	1 45 51	28 18 49	18 15 27	24 52 31	4 07.8	2 38.7	13 21.8	2 34.7	17 05.6	15 59.1	4 31.7	13 15.9	19 30.1	26 39.0
19 W	1 49 48	29 17 26	1♑33 12	8♑17 33	4 05.3	4 01.6	14 27.6	3 09.5	17 22.0	15 52.1	4 33.1	13 18.5	19 31.2	26 38.4
20 Th	1 53 44	0♉16 02	15 05 36	21 57 22	4D 04.0	5 26.4	15 33.6	3 44.4	17 38.2	15 45.0	4 34.7	13 21.1	19 32.3	26 37.7
21 F	1 57 41	1 14 36	28 52 50	5♒51 57	4 03.8	6 53.1	16 39.7	4 19.2	17 54.2	15 37.9	4 36.3	13 23.7	19 33.3	26 37.0
22 Sa	2 01 38	2 13 08	12♒54 40	20 00 49	4 04.6	8 21.7	17 46.0	4 54.2	18 10.1	15 30.7	4 38.1	13 26.3	19 34.3	26 36.3
23 Su	2 05 34	3 11 39	27 10 12	4♓22 31	4 06.0	9 52.1	18 52.5	5 29.1	18 25.7	15 23.4	4 40.0	13 28.8	19 35.2	26 35.6
24 M	2 09 31	4 10 08	11♓37 26	18 54 27	4 07.4	11 24.3	19 59.1	6 04.1	18 41.3	15 16.1	4 42.0	13 31.3	19 36.2	26 34.8
25 Tu	2 13 27	5 08 35	26 13 03	3♈32 35	4R 08.0	12 58.3	21 05.8	6 39.2	18 56.6	15 08.7	4 44.1	13 33.7	19 37.0	26 34.0
26 W	2 17 24	6 07 01	10♈52 20	18 11 32	4 07.3	14 34.1	22 12.7	7 14.3	19 11.8	15 01.2	4 46.2	13 36.1	19 37.9	26 33.2
27 Th	2 21 20	7 05 25	25 29 22	2♉45 03	4 05.0	16 11.7	23 19.8	7 49.4	19 26.7	14 53.7	4 48.5	13 38.5	19 38.7	26 32.3
28 F	2 25 17	8 03 47	9♉57 45	17 06 44	4 01.2	17 51.0	24 26.9	8 24.6	19 41.5	14 46.2	4 50.9	13 40.8	19 39.5	26 31.4
29 Sa	2 29 13	9 02 08	24 11 19	1♊10 56	3 56.1	19 32.2	25 34.2	8 59.8	19 56.1	14 38.6	4 53.4	13 43.1	19 40.3	26 30.5
30 Su	2 33 10	10 00 26	8♊05 07	14 53 32	3 50.3	21 15.1	26 41.6	9 35.0	20 10.5	14 31.0	4 56.0	13 45.4	19 41.0	26 29.6

Astro Data (Dy Hr Mn)

☽0N 1 10:33
☿ R 2 20:31
♃ R 4 18:02
☿0S 11 18:50
☽0S 15 12:44
♃□♆ 16 7:05
☉0N 20 18:26
☿ D 25 13:42
☽0N 28 21:44
♇ R 29 12:40

♄ D 5 12:54
☽0S 11 19:19
☿0N 21 1:10
☽0N 25 7:23

Planet Ingress (Dy Hr Mn)

♀ ♒ 5 8:39
☉ ♈ 20 18:26

♀ ♓ 6 1:21
♂ ♋ 14 0:59
☿ ♈ 16 12:20
☉ ♉ 20 5:26

Last Aspect / ☽ Ingress (Dy Hr Mn / Dy Hr Mn)

1 4:14 ♀ ⚹ ♈ 1 9:19
3 7:42 ♀ □ ♉ 3 10:22
5 8:14 ☿ ⚹ ♊ 5 14:38
7 16:09 ♇ ☍ ♋ 7 22:38
9 20:41 ☿ △ ♌ 10 9:42
12 15:38 ♇ △ ♍ 12 22:24
15 4:33 ♇ □ ♎ 15 11:12
17 16:31 ♇ ⚹ ♏ 17 22:59
20 7:54 ☉ △ ♐ 20 8:43
22 9:47 ♇ ☌ ♑ 22 15:36
23 23:30 ♃ ⚹ ♒ 24 19:21
26 15:18 ♇ ⚹ ♓ 26 20:33
28 15:20 ♇ □ ♈ 28 20:31
30 15:41 ♇ △ ♉ 30 21:01

Last Aspect / ☽ Ingress (Dy Hr Mn / Dy Hr Mn)

1 15:52 ♀ □ ♊ 1 23:49
4 2:24 ♀ △ ♋ 4 6:15
5 17:19 ☿ △ ♌ 6 16:25
8 23:02 ♂ ⚹ ♍ 9 4:58
11 14:59 ♂ □ ♎ 11 17:47
13 22:42 ♇ ⚹ ♏ 14 5:08
15 18:29 ♆ □ ♐ 16 14:19
18 18:41 ☉ △ ♑ 18 21:13
20 1:15 ♃ ⚹ ♒ 21 1:56
22 23:03 ♇ ⚹ ♓ 23 4:43
25 0:35 ♇ □ ♈ 25 6:12
27 1:44 ♇ △ ♉ 27 7:27
29 1:31 ♀ ⚹ ♊ 29 9:58

☽ Phases & Eclipses (Dy Hr Mn)

6 20:16 ☽ 16♊07
14 23:35 ○ 24♍15
14 23:47 A 1.030
22 19:10 ☾ 2♑01
29 10:15 ● 8♈35
29 10:11:18 T 04'07"

5 12:01 ☽ 15♋34
13 16:40 ○ 23♎37
21 3:28 ☾ 0♒54
27 19:44 ● 7♉24

Astro Data

1 March 2006
Julian Day # 38776
SVP 5♓10'26"
GC 26♐55.5 ⚳ 7♑13.8
Eris 20♈13.9 ⚵ 20♊19.9
⚷ 6♒45.2 ⚶ 7♋38.7
☽ Mean ☊ 5♈50.6

1 April 2006
Julian Day # 38807
SVP 5♓10'23"
GC 26♐55.6 ⚳ 15♑33.5
Eris 20♈32.4 ⚵ 1♋35.7
⚷ 8♒40.1 ⚶ 12♋01.8
☽ Mean ☊ 4♈12.1

LONGITUDE — May 2006

Day	Sid.Time	☉	0 hr ☽	Noon ☽	True ☊	☿	♀	♂	⚳	♃	♄	♅	♆	♇
1 M	2 37 07	10♉58 43	21♊36 00	28♊12 27	3♈44.7	22♈59.8	27♓49.1	10♋10.3	20♒24.7	14♏23.4	4♌58.7	13♓47.6	19♒41.7	26♐28.6
2 Tu	2 41 03	11 56 58	4♋42 58	11♋07 43	3R39.9	24 46.3	28 56.7	10 45.6	20 38.7	14R15.8	5 01.5	13 49.8	19 42.4	26R27.7
3 W	2 45 00	12 55 11	17 27 01	23 41 16	3 36.4	26 34.6	0♈04.5	11 20.9	20 52.5	14 08.1	5 04.4	13 52.0	19 43.1	26 26.7
4 Th	2 48 56	13 53 21	29 50 55	5♌56 29	3D34.5	28 24.7	1 12.3	11 56.3	21 06.1	14 00.5	5 07.4	13 54.1	19 43.7	26 25.6
5 F	2 52 53	14 51 30	11♌58 35	17 57 48	3 34.2	0♉16.6	2 20.3	12 31.7	21 19.5	13 52.8	5 10.5	13 56.2	19 44.2	26 24.6
6 Sa	2 56 49	15 49 37	23 54 46	29 50 09	3 35.1	2 10.3	3 28.4	13 07.1	21 32.7	13 45.2	5 13.7	13 58.2	19 44.8	26 23.5
7 Su	3 00 46	16 47 41	5♍44 35	11♍38 41	3 36.6	4 05.8	4 36.5	13 42.6	21 45.7	13 37.6	5 16.9	14 00.2	19 45.3	26 22.4
8 M	3 04 42	17 45 44	17 33 06	23 28 24	3R37.9	6 03.1	5 44.8	14 18.0	21 58.5	13 29.9	5 20.3	14 02.1	19 45.8	26 21.3
9 Tu	3 08 39	18 43 45	29 25 09	5♎23 53	3 38.4	8 02.1	6 53.1	14 53.5	22 11.0	13 22.3	5 23.8	14 04.1	19 46.2	26 20.1
10 W	3 12 36	19 41 44	11♎25 05	17 29 08	3 37.3	10 02.9	8 01.6	15 29.1	22 23.3	13 14.7	5 27.3	14 05.9	19 46.6	26 19.0
11 Th	3 16 32	20 39 42	23 36 26	29 47 16	3 34.3	12 05.3	9 10.1	16 04.6	22 35.4	13 07.2	5 30.9	14 07.8	19 47.0	26 17.8
12 F	3 20 29	21 37 38	6♏01 51	12♏20 22	3 29.1	14 09.3	10 18.8	16 40.2	22 47.3	12 59.7	5 34.7	14 09.5	19 47.3	26 16.6
13 Sa	3 24 25	22 35 32	18 42 54	25 09 28	3 22.1	16 14.8	11 27.5	17 15.8	22 58.9	12 52.2	5 38.5	14 11.3	19 47.7	26 15.4
14 Su	3 28 22	23 33 25	1♐40 01	8♐14 26	3 13.9	18 21.7	12 36.3	17 51.5	23 10.4	12 44.8	5 42.4	14 13.0	19 47.9	26 14.1
15 M	3 32 18	24 31 16	14 52 33	21 34 10	3 05.2	20 29.9	13 45.2	18 27.1	23 21.5	12 37.4	5 46.4	14 14.7	19 48.2	26 12.9
16 Tu	3 36 15	25 29 06	28 19 02	5♑06 53	2 57.1	22 39.1	14 54.2	19 02.8	23 32.5	12 30.1	5 50.5	14 16.3	19 48.4	26 11.6
17 W	3 40 11	26 26 55	11♑57 28	18 50 30	2 50.4	24 49.3	16 03.3	19 38.6	23 43.2	12 22.8	5 54.7	14 17.9	19 48.6	26 10.3
18 Th	3 44 08	27 24 43	25 45 44	2♒42 57	2 45.7	27 00.1	17 12.5	20 14.3	23 53.6	12 15.6	5 58.9	14 19.4	19 48.8	26 09.0
19 F	3 48 05	28 22 29	9♒41 55	16 42 28	2D43.2	29 11.4	18 21.7	20 50.1	24 03.8	12 08.5	6 03.3	14 20.9	19 48.9	26 07.6
20 Sa	3 52 01	29 20 15	23 44 26	0♓47 41	2 42.6	1♊22.9	19 31.0	21 25.9	24 13.8	12 01.4	6 07.7	14 22.3	19 49.0	26 06.3
21 Su	3 55 58	0♊17 59	7♓52 03	14 57 24	2 43.1	3 34.3	20 40.4	22 01.7	24 23.4	11 54.4	6 12.2	14 23.7	19 49.0	26 04.9
22 M	3 59 54	1 15 42	22 03 33	29 10 19	2R43.8	5 45.4	21 49.9	22 37.6	24 32.9	11 47.5	6 16.8	14 25.1	19R49.0	26 03.6
23 Tu	4 03 51	2 13 24	6♈17 27	13♈24 40	2 43.4	7 55.8	22 59.4	23 13.4	24 42.0	11 40.7	6 21.4	14 26.4	19 49.0	26 02.2
24 W	4 07 47	3 11 05	20 31 36	27 37 51	2 41.0	10 05.4	24 09.0	23 49.3	24 50.9	11 34.0	6 26.2	14 27.6	19 49.0	26 00.8
25 Th	4 11 44	4 08 45	4♉42 58	11♉46 26	2 36.2	12 13.7	25 18.7	24 25.3	24 59.5	11 27.4	6 31.0	14 28.8	19 48.9	25 59.3
26 F	4 15 40	5 06 24	18 47 43	25 46 17	2 28.8	14 20.6	26 28.4	25 01.3	25 07.9	11 20.9	6 35.9	14 30.0	19 48.8	25 57.9
27 Sa	4 19 37	6 04 02	2♊41 37	9♊33 13	2 19.3	16 25.9	27 38.2	25 37.2	25 15.9	11 14.5	6 40.9	14 31.1	19 48.6	25 56.5
28 Su	4 23 34	7 01 39	16 20 38	23 03 31	2 08.7	18 29.4	28 48.1	26 13.3	25 23.7	11 08.2	6 45.9	14 32.2	19 48.5	25 55.0
29 M	4 27 30	7 59 14	29 41 35	6♋14 40	1 58.0	20 30.8	29 58.0	26 49.3	25 31.2	11 02.0	6 51.0	14 33.2	19 48.3	25 53.5
30 Tu	4 31 27	8 56 49	12♋42 41	19 05 41	1 48.3	22 30.0	1♉08.0	27 25.4	25 38.4	10 55.9	6 56.2	14 34.2	19 48.0	25 52.1
31 W	4 35 23	9 54 22	25 23 50	1♌37 21	1 40.4	24 26.9	2 18.0	28 01.5	25 45.3	10 50.0	7 01.5	14 35.2	19 47.7	25 50.6

LONGITUDE — June 2006

Day	Sid.Time	☉	0 hr ☽	Noon ☽	True ☊	☿	♀	♂	⚳	♃	♄	♅	♆	♇
1 Th	4 39 20	10♊51 53	7♌46 36	13♌51 59	1♈34.8	26♊21.5	3♉28.1	28♋37.6	25♒51.9	10♏44.1	7♌06.8	14♓36.0	19♒47.4	25♐49.1
2 F	4 43 16	11 49 23	19 54 01	25 53 13	1R31.6	28 13.5	4 38.2	29 13.7	25 58.2	10R38.5	7 12.2	14 36.9	19R47.1	25R47.6
3 Sa	4 47 13	12 46 52	1♍50 13	7♍45 38	1D30.4	0♋02.9	5 48.4	29 49.9	26 04.2	10 32.9	7 17.7	14 37.7	19 46.7	25 46.0
4 Su	4 51 09	13 44 20	13 40 08	19 34 24	1 30.4	1 49.8	6 58.6	0♌26.1	26 09.9	10 27.5	7 23.3	14 38.4	19 46.3	25 44.5
5 M	4 55 06	14 41 47	25 29 06	1♎24 56	1R30.6	3 33.9	8 08.9	1 02.3	26 15.3	10 22.2	7 28.9	14 39.1	19 45.9	25 43.0
6 Tu	4 59 03	15 39 12	7♎22 32	13 22 34	1 30.1	5 15.4	9 19.3	1 38.5	26 20.3	10 17.0	7 34.6	14 39.7	19 45.4	25 41.4
7 W	5 02 59	16 36 36	19 25 36	25 32 13	1 27.8	6 54.2	10 29.7	2 14.7	26 25.1	10 12.0	7 40.3	14 40.3	19 45.0	25 39.9
8 Th	5 06 56	17 33 59	1♏42 53	7♏58 01	1 23.2	8 30.2	11 40.1	2 51.0	26 29.5	10 07.2	7 46.1	14 40.9	19 44.4	25 38.4
9 F	5 10 52	18 31 21	14 17 58	20 42 57	1 16.0	10 03.4	12 50.6	3 27.3	26 33.7	10 02.5	7 52.0	14 41.4	19 43.9	25 36.8
10 Sa	5 14 49	19 28 42	27 13 08	3♐48 30	1 06.4	11 33.9	14 01.2	4 03.6	26 37.5	9 58.0	7 57.9	14 41.8	19 43.3	25 35.2
11 Su	5 18 45	20 26 03	10♐28 58	17 14 19	0 55.3	13 01.5	15 11.8	4 39.9	26 40.9	9 53.6	8 03.9	14 42.3	19 42.7	25 33.7
12 M	5 22 42	21 23 23	24 04 14	0♑58 19	0 43.5	14 26.3	16 22.4	5 16.3	26 44.1	9 49.3	8 09.9	14 42.6	19 42.1	25 32.1
13 Tu	5 26 39	22 20 42	7♑56 03	14 56 52	0 32.4	15 48.2	17 33.1	5 52.6	26 46.9	9 45.3	8 16.0	14 42.9	19 41.4	25 30.6
14 W	5 30 35	23 18 00	22 00 13	29 05 27	0 22.9	17 07.2	18 43.9	6 29.0	26 49.4	9 41.3	8 22.2	14 43.2	19 40.7	25 29.0
15 Th	5 34 32	24 15 18	6♒12 01	13♒19 21	0 16.0	18 23.2	19 54.7	7 05.4	26 51.5	9 37.6	8 28.4	14 43.4	19 40.0	25 27.4
16 F	5 38 28	25 12 35	20 26 59	27 34 27	0 11.8	19 36.2	21 05.5	7 41.9	26 53.3	9 34.0	8 34.7	14 43.6	19 39.2	25 25.8
17 Sa	5 42 25	26 09 52	4♓41 25	11♓47 37	0 10.0	20 46.2	22 16.4	8 18.3	26 54.8	9 30.6	8 41.0	14 43.7	19 38.5	25 24.3
18 Su	5 46 21	27 07 09	18 52 48	25 56 50	0 09.6	21 53.0	23 27.4	8 54.8	26 55.9	9 27.3	8 47.4	14R43.7	19 37.6	25 22.7
19 M	5 50 18	28 04 26	2♈59 36	10♈01 00	0 09.5	22 56.7	24 38.4	9 31.3	26 56.7	9 24.2	8 53.8	14 43.8	19 36.8	25 21.1
20 Tu	5 54 14	29 01 42	17 00 58	23 59 25	0 08.3	23 57.1	25 49.4	10 07.9	26R57.1	9 21.3	9 00.3	14 43.7	19 35.9	25 19.6
21 W	5 58 11	29 58 58	0♉56 14	7♉51 19	0 05.1	24 54.1	27 00.5	10 44.4	26 57.1	9 18.5	9 06.8	14 43.6	19 35.1	25 18.0
22 Th	6 02 08	0♋56 14	14 44 30	21 35 36	29♓59.1	25 47.7	28 11.7	11 21.0	26 56.9	9 16.0	9 13.4	14 43.5	19 34.1	25 16.4
23 F	6 06 04	1 53 30	28 24 23	5♊10 37	29 50.4	26 37.7	29 22.9	11 57.6	26 56.2	9 13.6	9 20.0	14 43.3	19 33.2	25 14.9
24 Sa	6 10 01	2 50 46	11♊54 01	18 34 19	29 39.3	27 24.1	0♊34.1	12 34.2	26 55.2	9 11.3	9 26.7	14 43.1	19 32.2	25 13.3
25 Su	6 13 57	3 48 01	25 11 16	1♋44 38	29 26.8	28 06.7	1 45.4	13 10.9	26 53.8	9 09.3	9 33.5	14 42.8	19 31.2	25 11.8
26 M	6 17 54	4 45 17	8♋14 13	14 39 54	29 14.2	28 45.4	2 56.7	13 47.6	26 52.1	9 07.4	9 40.2	14 42.5	19 30.2	25 10.2
27 Tu	6 21 50	5 42 31	21 01 35	27 19 16	29 02.5	29 20.2	4 08.0	14 24.3	26 50.0	9 05.7	9 47.0	14 42.2	19 29.2	25 08.7
28 W	6 25 47	6 39 46	3♌33 02	9♌43 02	28 52.7	29 50.8	5 19.4	15 01.0	26 47.6	9 04.2	9 53.9	14 41.7	19 28.1	25 07.1
29 Th	6 29 43	7 37 00	15 49 30	21 52 43	28 45.5	0♌17.2	6 30.9	15 37.8	26 44.8	9 02.9	10 00.8	14 41.3	19 27.0	25 05.6
30 F	6 33 40	8 34 13	27 53 06	3♍51 04	28 40.9	0 39.2	7 42.3	16 14.6	26 41.6	9 01.8	10 07.7	14 40.8	19 25.9	25 04.1

Astro Data Dy Hr Mn	Planet Ingress Dy Hr Mn	Last Aspect Dy Hr Mn	☽ Ingress Dy Hr Mn	Last Aspect Dy Hr Mn	☽ Ingress Dy Hr Mn	☽ Phases & Eclipses Dy Hr Mn	Astro Data
♃△♅ 5 3:48	♀ ♈ 3 10:25	1 11:13 ♀ □	♋ 1 15:17	2 17:34 ☿ ⚹	♍ 2 20:17	5 5:13 ☽ 14♌35	1 May 2006
♀0N 6 11:52	☿ ♉ 5 8:28	3 18:35 ☿ □	♌ 4 0:18	5 0:30 ♇ □	♎ 5 9:08	13 6:51 ○ 22♏23	Julian Day # 38837
☽0S 9 2:26	☿ ♊ 19 20:52	6 5:02 ♇ △	♍ 6 12:20	7 12:15 ♇ ⚹	♏ 7 20:41	20 9:21 ☾ 29♒14	SVP 5♓10'19"
♆R 22 13:06	☉ ♊ 21 4:32	8 17:49 ♇ □	♎ 9 1:10	9 10:10 ♆ □	♐ 10 5:05	27 5:26 ● 5♊48	GC 26♐55.7 ⚴ 19♑29.3
☽0N 22 14:11	♀ ♉ 29 12:41	11 5:15 ♇ ⚹	♏ 11 12:25	12 2:34 ♇ ☌	♑ 12 10:19		Eris 20♈51.9 ⚵ 14♋19.7
♃∠♇ 31 8:41		13 6:51 ☉ ☍	♐ 13 20:56	13 16:50 ♀ △	♒ 14 13:32	3 23:06 ☽ 13♍13	⚷ 9♒39.4 ⚶ 20♋33.2
	☿ ♋ 3 11:21	15 20:15 ♇ ☌	♑ 16 2:59	16 8:24 ♇ ⚹	♓ 16 16:05	11 18:03 ○ 20♐41	☽ Mean ☊ 2♈36.8
☽0S 5 9:39	♂ ♌ 3 18:43	18 2:10 ☉ △	♒ 18 7:19	18 14:08 ☉ □	♈ 18 18:54	18 14:08 ☾ 27♓12	
☽0N 18 18:57	☉ ♋ 21 12:26	20 9:21 ☉ □	♓ 20 10:39	20 21:20 ☉ ⚹	♉ 20 22:23	25 16:05 ● 3♋58	1 June 2006
♅R 19 7:40	☊ ♓R 22 9:03	22 6:46 ♇ □	♈ 22 13:24	23 0:44 ♀ ☌	♊ 23 2:49		Julian Day # 38868
⚳R 21 4:07	♀ ♊ 24 0:31	24 9:16 ♇ △	♉ 24 16:00	25 0:02 ♇ ☍	♋ 25 8:48		SVP 5♓10'13"
♃□♄ 22 18:44	☿ ♌ 28 19:57	26 10:39 ♂ ⚹	♊ 26 19:19	27 16:03 ☿ ☌	♌ 27 17:09		GC 26♐55.7 ⚴ 17♑23.0R
♄⚼♇ 30 1:39		28 23:23 ♀ ⚹	♋ 29 0:34	29 18:24 ♇ △	♍ 30 4:15		Eris 21♈08.9 ⚵ 28♋13.9
		31 4:42 ♂ ☌	♌ 31 8:52				⚷ 9♒35.9R ⚶ 2♌00.1
							☽ Mean ☊ 0♈58.3

July 2006

LONGITUDE

Day	Sid.Time	☉	0 hr ☽	Noon ☽	True ☊	☿	♀	♂	⚳	♃	♄	♅	♆	♇
1 Sa	6 37 37	9♋31 26	9♍47 08	15♍41 51	28♓38.7	0♌56.8	8♊53.8	16♌51.3	26♒38.1	9♏00.8	10♌14.7	14♓40.2	19♒24.8	25♐02.6
2 Su	6 41 33	10 28 39	21 35 49	27 29 40	28D 38.2	1 09.9	10 05.4	17 28.2	26R 34.2	9R 00.0	10 21.7	14R 39.6	19R 23.6	25R 01.1
3 M	6 45 30	11 25 51	3♎24 04	9♎19 42	28R 38.3	1 18.4	11 17.0	18 05.0	26 30.0	8 59.4	10 28.8	14 39.0	19 22.4	24 59.6
4 Tu	6 49 26	12 23 03	15 17 14	21 17 22	28 38.0	1R 22.2	12 28.6	18 41.9	26 25.4	8 59.0	10 35.9	14 38.3	19 21.2	24 58.1
5 W	6 53 23	13 20 15	27 20 46	3♏28 05	28 36.4	1 21.3	13 40.3	19 18.7	26 20.5	8D 58.8	10 43.0	14 37.5	19 20.0	24 56.6
6 Th	6 57 19	14 17 27	9♏39 54	15 56 45	28 32.6	1 15.8	14 52.0	19 55.7	26 15.2	8 58.7	10 50.1	14 36.7	19 18.7	24 55.1
7 F	7 01 16	15 14 38	22 19 06	28 47 20	28 26.6	1 05.7	16 03.7	20 32.6	26 09.6	8 58.8	10 57.3	14 35.9	19 17.5	24 53.7
8 Sa	7 05 12	16 11 50	5♐21 41	12♐02 17	28 18.2	0 51.0	17 15.5	21 09.5	26 03.7	8 59.1	11 04.5	14 35.0	19 16.2	24 52.2
9 Su	7 09 09	17 09 01	18 49 07	25 42 01	28 08.2	0 32.0	18 27.4	21 46.5	25 57.4	8 59.6	11 11.8	14 34.1	19 14.9	24 50.8
10 M	7 13 06	18 06 12	2♑40 39	9♑44 33	27 57.6	0 08.9	19 39.2	22 23.5	25 50.7	9 00.3	11 19.1	14 33.1	19 13.6	24 49.4
11 Tu	7 17 02	19 03 24	16 53 07	24 05 35	27 47.4	29♋42.0	20 51.1	23 00.5	25 43.8	9 01.2	11 26.4	14 32.1	19 12.2	24 48.0
12 W	7 20 59	20 00 36	1♒21 10	8♒38 58	27 38.9	29 11.5	22 03.1	23 37.5	25 36.5	9 02.2	11 33.7	14 31.1	19 10.9	24 46.6
13 Th	7 24 55	20 57 47	15 58 06	23 17 41	27 32.6	28 38.0	23 15.1	24 14.6	25 28.9	9 03.4	11 41.1	14 30.0	19 09.5	24 45.2
14 F	7 28 52	21 55 00	0♓36 53	7♓55 00	27 29.0	28 02.0	24 27.2	24 51.7	25 20.9	9 04.7	11 48.5	14 28.9	19 08.1	24 43.9
15 Sa	7 32 48	22 52 13	15 11 21	22 25 25	27D 27.6	27 23.9	25 39.2	25 28.8	25 12.7	9 06.3	11 55.9	14 27.7	19 06.7	24 42.5
16 Su	7 36 45	23 49 26	29 36 47	6♈45 08	27 27.7	26 44.5	26 51.4	26 05.9	25 04.1	9 08.0	12 03.3	14 26.5	19 05.3	24 41.2
17 M	7 40 41	24 46 40	13♈50 17	20 52 05	27R 28.2	26 04.3	28 03.6	26 43.1	24 55.3	9 09.9	12 10.8	14 25.2	19 03.8	24 39.9
18 Tu	7 44 38	25 43 55	27 50 30	4♉45 31	27 27.9	25 24.1	29 15.8	27 20.3	24 46.1	9 12.0	12 18.3	14 23.9	19 02.4	24 38.6
19 W	7 48 35	26 41 10	11♉37 10	18 25 30	27 25.9	24 44.6	0♋28.0	27 57.5	24 36.7	9 14.3	12 25.8	14 22.6	19 00.9	24 37.3
20 Th	7 52 31	27 38 27	25 10 34	1♊52 25	27 21.6	24 06.4	1 40.4	28 34.7	24 26.9	9 16.7	12 33.3	14 21.2	18 59.4	24 36.1
21 F	7 56 28	28 35 44	8♊31 06	15 06 38	27 15.0	23 30.3	2 52.7	29 12.0	24 16.9	9 19.3	12 40.9	14 19.8	18 57.9	24 34.8
22 Sa	8 00 24	29 33 02	21 39 02	28 08 17	27 06.4	22 56.9	4 05.1	29 49.3	24 06.6	9 22.1	12 48.4	14 18.3	18 56.4	24 33.6
23 Su	8 04 21	0♌30 20	4♋34 24	10♋57 22	26 56.7	22 26.9	5 17.6	0♍26.6	23 56.1	9 25.0	12 56.0	14 16.8	18 54.9	24 32.4
24 M	8 08 17	1 27 40	17 17 10	23 33 49	26 46.7	22 00.7	6 30.0	1 04.0	23 45.3	9 28.1	13 03.6	14 15.3	18 53.4	24 31.2
25 Tu	8 12 14	2 24 59	29 47 21	5♌57 50	26 37.5	21 39.0	7 42.6	1 41.4	23 34.3	9 31.4	13 11.2	14 13.7	18 51.8	24 30.1
26 W	8 16 11	3 22 20	12♌05 22	18 10 05	26 29.9	21 22.2	8 55.1	2 18.8	23 23.1	9 34.9	13 18.8	14 12.1	18 50.3	24 29.0
27 Th	8 20 07	4 19 41	24 12 10	0♍11 53	26 24.3	21 10.6	10 07.7	2 56.2	23 11.6	9 38.5	13 26.5	14 10.5	18 48.7	24 27.8
28 F	8 24 04	5 17 02	6♍09 30	12 05 22	26 21.1	21D 04.6	11 20.3	3 33.7	22 59.9	9 42.3	13 34.1	14 08.8	18 47.1	24 26.7
29 Sa	8 28 00	6 14 24	17 59 52	23 53 28	26D 19.9	21 04.4	12 33.0	4 11.1	22 48.0	9 46.2	13 41.8	14 07.1	18 45.6	24 25.7
30 Su	8 31 57	7 11 47	29 46 39	5♎39 55	26 20.2	21 10.3	13 45.7	4 48.6	22 36.0	9 50.3	13 49.4	14 05.4	18 44.0	24 24.6
31 M	8 35 53	8 09 10	11♎33 53	17 29 07	26 21.4	21 22.4	14 58.5	5 26.2	22 23.8	9 54.6	13 57.1	14 03.6	18 42.4	24 23.6

August 2006

LONGITUDE

Day	Sid.Time	☉	0 hr ☽	Noon ☽	True ☊	☿	♀	♂	⚳	♃	♄	♅	♆	♇
1 Tu	8 39 50	9♌06 34	23♎26 16	29♎25 57	26♓22.6	21♋40.8	16♋11.3	6♍03.7	22♒11.4	9♏59.1	14♌04.8	14♓01.8	18♒40.8	24♐22.6
2 W	8 43 46	10 03 58	5♏28 50	11♏35 34	26R 23.0	22 05.5	17 24.1	6 41.3	21R 58.9	10 03.7	14 12.5	13R 59.9	18R 39.2	24R 21.6
3 Th	8 47 43	11 01 24	17 46 46	24 03 02	26 22.1	22 36.5	18 37.0	7 18.9	21 46.2	10 08.4	14 20.2	13 58.1	18 37.5	24 20.6
4 F	8 51 40	11 58 49	0♐24 55	6♐52 53	26 19.4	23 14.0	19 49.9	7 56.6	21 33.4	10 13.3	14 27.9	13 56.2	18 35.9	24 19.7
5 Sa	8 55 36	12 56 16	13 27 21	20 08 34	26 15.0	23 57.7	21 02.8	8 34.2	21 20.6	10 18.4	14 35.6	13 54.3	18 34.3	24 18.8
6 Su	8 59 33	13 53 43	26 56 41	3♑51 43	26 09.4	24 47.6	22 15.8	9 11.9	21 07.6	10 23.6	14 43.3	13 52.3	18 32.7	24 17.9
7 M	9 03 29	14 51 11	10♑53 27	18 01 33	26 03.1	25 43.7	23 28.8	9 49.6	20 54.5	10 29.0	14 51.0	13 50.3	18 31.1	24 17.1
8 Tu	9 07 26	15 48 40	25 15 29	2♒34 34	25 57.0	26 45.8	24 41.9	10 27.4	20 41.4	10 34.5	14 58.7	13 48.3	18 29.4	24 16.3
9 W	9 11 22	16 46 10	9♒57 56	17 24 36	25 51.9	27 53.7	25 55.0	11 05.1	20 28.2	10 40.2	15 06.4	13 46.3	18 27.8	24 15.5
10 Th	9 15 19	17 43 41	24 53 32	2♓23 37	25 48.3	29 07.4	27 08.1	11 42.9	20 15.0	10 46.0	15 14.1	13 44.2	18 26.2	24 14.7
11 F	9 19 15	18 41 13	9♓53 45	17 22 54	25D 46.6	0♌26.4	28 21.3	12 20.8	20 01.8	10 52.0	15 21.8	13 42.1	18 24.5	24 13.9
12 Sa	9 23 12	19 38 46	24 50 04	2♈14 25	25 46.5	1 50.7	29 34.5	12 58.6	19 48.5	10 58.1	15 29.5	13 40.0	18 22.9	24 13.2
13 Su	9 27 09	20 36 21	9♈35 12	16 51 51	25 47.5	3 19.9	0♌47.8	13 36.5	19 35.3	11 04.3	15 37.1	13 37.9	18 21.3	24 12.5
14 M	9 31 05	21 33 57	24 03 54	1♉11 04	25 48.9	4 53.8	2 01.1	14 14.4	19 22.0	11 10.7	15 44.8	13 35.8	18 19.6	24 11.8
15 Tu	9 35 02	22 31 35	8♉13 09	15 10 06	25R 50.0	6 31.9	3 14.5	14 52.3	19 08.8	11 17.2	15 52.5	13 33.6	18 18.0	24 11.2
16 W	9 38 58	23 29 14	22 01 56	28 48 45	25 50.0	8 14.0	4 27.9	15 30.3	18 55.6	11 23.9	16 00.2	13 31.4	18 16.4	24 10.6
17 Th	9 42 55	24 26 55	5♊30 43	12♊08 00	25 48.8	9 59.7	5 41.3	16 08.3	18 42.5	11 30.7	16 07.8	13 29.2	18 14.7	24 10.0
18 F	9 46 51	25 24 38	18 40 52	25 09 32	25 46.2	11 48.4	6 54.8	16 46.4	18 29.4	11 37.7	16 15.5	13 27.0	18 13.1	24 09.4
19 Sa	9 50 48	26 22 22	1♋34 14	7♋55 15	25 42.4	13 39.9	8 08.3	17 24.4	18 16.5	11 44.8	16 23.1	13 24.7	18 11.5	24 08.9
20 Su	9 54 44	27 20 07	14 12 47	20 27 06	25 37.9	15 33.7	9 21.9	18 02.5	18 03.6	11 52.0	16 30.7	13 22.4	18 09.9	24 08.4
21 M	9 58 41	28 17 55	26 38 24	2♌46 54	25 33.2	17 29.4	10 35.5	18 40.7	17 50.8	11 59.3	16 38.3	13 20.2	18 08.3	24 08.0
22 Tu	10 02 38	29 15 43	8♌52 49	14 56 21	25 28.9	19 26.6	11 49.1	19 18.8	17 38.2	12 06.8	16 45.9	13 17.9	18 06.7	24 07.5
23 W	10 06 34	0♍13 33	20 57 43	26 57 07	25 25.5	21 24.9	13 02.8	19 57.0	17 25.7	12 14.4	16 53.5	13 15.6	18 05.1	24 07.1
24 Th	10 10 31	1 11 25	2♍54 48	8♍51 00	25 23.2	23 23.9	14 16.5	20 35.2	17 13.3	12 22.2	17 01.1	13 13.2	18 03.5	24 06.7
25 F	10 14 27	2 09 18	14 45 57	20 39 58	25D 22.2	25 23.4	15 30.2	21 13.5	17 01.1	12 30.0	17 08.6	13 10.9	18 01.9	24 06.4
26 Sa	10 18 24	3 07 12	26 33 21	2♎26 26	25 22.3	27 23.1	16 44.0	21 51.8	16 49.1	12 38.0	17 16.1	13 08.6	18 00.4	24 06.1
27 Su	10 22 20	4 05 08	8♎19 35	14 13 12	25 23.2	29 22.6	17 57.8	22 30.1	16 37.3	12 46.1	17 23.6	13 06.2	17 58.8	24 05.8
28 M	10 26 17	5 03 05	20 07 44	26 03 39	25 24.7	1♍21.9	19 11.7	23 08.5	16 25.6	12 54.4	17 31.1	13 03.8	17 57.2	24 05.5
29 Tu	10 30 13	6 01 03	2♏01 25	8♏01 34	25 26.3	3 20.7	20 25.5	23 46.9	16 14.2	13 02.7	17 38.6	13 01.5	17 55.7	24 05.3
30 W	10 34 10	6 59 03	14 04 39	20 11 12	25 27.6	5 18.7	21 39.5	24 25.3	16 03.0	13 11.2	17 46.0	12 59.1	17 54.2	24 05.1
31 Th	10 38 07	7 57 04	26 21 48	2♐36 59	25R 28.3	7 16.1	22 53.4	25 03.7	15 52.1	13 19.8	17 53.4	12 56.7	17 52.7	24 05.0

Astro Data

	Dy Hr Mn
☽ 0S	2 16:37
☿ R	4 19:34
♃ D	6 7:18
☽ 0N	15 23:55
♃∠♇	25 4:54
☿ D	29 0:38
☽ 0S	29 23:10
♄⚻♅	1 4:22
☽ 0N	12 7:10
☽ 0S	26 5:22
♃△♅	29 9:13
♄☍♆	31 9:54

Planet Ingress

	Dy Hr Mn
☿ ♋R	10 20:18
♀ ♋	19 2:41
♂ ♍	22 18:53
☉ ♌	22 23:18
☿ ♌	11 4:09
♀ ♌	12 20:21
☉ ♍	23 6:23
☿ ♍	27 19:31

Last Aspect / ☽ Ingress

Last Aspect Dy Hr Mn		☽ Ingress Dy Hr Mn
2 6:58 ♇ □	♎	2 17:06
4 19:17 ♇ ⚹	♏	5 5:13
6 19:54 ♂ □	♐	7 14:14
9 10:31 ♇ ☌	♑	9 19:25
11 20:58 ☿ ☍	♒	11 21:46
13 14:23 ♇ ⚹	♓	13 22:59
15 19:56 ☿ △	♈	16 0:39
18 1:33 ♀ ⚹	♉	18 3:44
20 5:48 ♂ □	♊	20 8:38
22 15:17 ♂ ⚹	♋	22 15:28
24 9:07 ☿ ☌	♌	25 0:24
27 0:32 ♇ △	♍	27 11:36
29 13:06 ♇ □	♎	30 0:27

Last Aspect / ☽ Ingress

Last Aspect Dy Hr Mn		☽ Ingress Dy Hr Mn
1 1:54 ♇ ⚹	♏	1 13:08
3 9:08 ☿ △	♐	3 23:13
5 19:22 ♇ ☌	♑	6 5:19
8 1:44 ☿ ☍	♒	8 7:47
9 22:58 ♇ ⚹	♓	10 8:10
12 7:17 ♀ △	♈	12 8:22
14 0:14 ♇ △	♉	14 10:00
16 1:51 ☉ □	♊	16 14:07
18 12:30 ☉ ⚹	♋	18 21:03
20 7:06 ♂ ⚹	♌	21 6:33
23 6:19 ♇ △	♍	23 18:08
25 19:00 ♇ □	♎	26 7:01
28 8:02 ♇ ⚹	♏	28 19:56
30 20:41 ♂ ⚹	♐	31 7:00

☽ Phases & Eclipses

Dy Hr Mn	
3 16:37	☽ 11♎37
11 3:02	○ 18♑42
17 19:13	☾ 25♈04
25 4:31	● 2♌07
2 8:46	☽ 9♏56
9 10:54	○ 16♒44
16 1:51	☾ 23♉05
23 19:10	● 0♍31
31 22:57	☽ 8♐24

Astro Data

1 July 2006
Julian Day # 38898
SVP 5♓10'08"
GC 26♐55.8 ⚴ 9♑54.8R
Eris 21♈18.3 ⚵ 11♌50.9
⚷ 8♒34.6R ⚶ 14♌38.3
☽ Mean ☊ 29♓23.0

1 August 2006
Julian Day # 38929
SVP 5♓10'03"
GC 26♐55.9 ⚴ 2♑36.0R
Eris 21♈18.6R ⚵ 25♌46.1
⚷ 6♒56.1R ⚶ 28♌43.7
☽ Mean ☊ 27♓44.6

LONGITUDE — September 2006

Day	Sid.Time	☉	0 hr ☽	Noon☽	True☊	☿	♀	♂	⚷	♃	♄	♅	♆	♇
1 F	10 42 03	8♍55 07	8♐57 17	15♐23 12	25♓28.2	9♍12.5	24♌07.4	25♍42.2	15♒41.4	13♏28.5	18♌00.8	12♓54.3	17♒51.2	24♐04.8
2 Sa	10 46 00	9 53 11	21 55 12	28 33 39	25R 27.5	11 07.9	25 21.4	26 20.7	15R 30.9	13 37.3	18 08.2	12R 51.9	17R 49.7	24R 04.8
3 Su	10 49 56	10 51 16	5♑18 50	12♑10 55	25 26.1	13 02.3	26 35.5	26 59.2	15 20.7	13 46.2	18 15.5	12 49.5	17 48.2	24 04.7
4 M	10 53 53	11 49 23	19 09 56	26 15 47	25 24.5	14 55.6	27 49.5	27 37.8	15 10.8	13 55.3	18 22.8	12 47.1	17 46.7	24D 04.7
5 Tu	10 57 49	12 47 31	3♒28 10	10♒46 36	25 22.9	16 47.8	29 03.6	28 16.4	15 01.1	14 04.4	18 30.1	12 44.8	17 45.3	24 04.7
6 W	11 01 46	13 45 41	18 10 27	25 38 54	25 21.6	18 38.8	0♍17.8	28 55.0	14 51.8	14 13.7	18 37.3	12 42.4	17 43.8	24 04.7
7 Th	11 05 42	14 43 52	3♓10 59	10♓45 35	25D 20.8	20 28.7	1 31.9	29 33.7	14 42.7	14 23.0	18 44.5	12 40.0	17 42.4	24 04.8
8 F	11 09 39	15 42 05	18 21 34	25 57 42	25 20.5	22 17.4	2 46.1	0♎12.4	14 33.9	14 32.5	18 51.7	12 37.6	17 41.0	24 04.8
9 Sa	11 13 36	16 40 20	3♈32 48	11♈05 41	25 20.8	24 05.0	4 00.4	0 51.1	14 25.4	14 42.1	18 58.8	12 35.2	17 39.6	24 05.0
10 Su	11 17 32	17 38 37	18 35 20	26 00 48	25 21.3	25 51.3	5 14.6	1 29.9	14 17.3	14 51.7	19 05.9	12 32.8	17 38.3	24 05.1
11 M	11 21 29	18 36 56	3♉21 18	10♉36 15	25 21.9	27 36.6	6 28.9	2 08.7	14 09.5	15 01.5	19 13.0	12 30.4	17 36.9	24 05.3
12 Tu	11 25 25	19 35 17	17 45 10	24 47 48	25 22.5	29 20.7	7 43.3	2 47.5	14 01.9	15 11.4	19 20.0	12 28.0	17 35.6	24 05.5
13 W	11 29 22	20 33 40	1♊44 00	8♊33 48	25R 22.8	1♎03.7	8 57.7	3 26.4	13 54.7	15 21.3	19 27.0	12 25.7	17 34.3	24 05.8
14 Th	11 33 18	21 32 05	15 17 18	21 54 45	25 22.9	2 45.6	10 12.1	4 05.3	13 47.9	15 31.4	19 34.0	12 23.3	17 33.0	24 06.1
15 F	11 37 15	22 30 32	28 26 26	4♋52 43	25 22.8	4 26.4	11 26.5	4 44.3	13 41.4	15 41.5	19 40.9	12 21.0	17 31.7	24 06.4
16 Sa	11 41 11	23 29 02	11♋14 01	17 30 45	25 22.7	6 06.1	12 41.0	5 23.3	13 35.2	15 51.8	19 47.8	12 18.6	17 30.5	24 06.8
17 Su	11 45 08	24 27 34	23 43 22	29 52 18	25D 22.5	7 44.8	13 55.4	6 02.3	13 29.4	16 02.1	19 54.6	12 16.3	17 29.2	24 07.1
18 M	11 49 05	25 26 07	5♌57 59	12♌00 52	25 22.5	9 22.5	15 10.0	6 41.4	13 23.9	16 12.6	20 01.4	12 14.0	17 28.0	24 07.6
19 Tu	11 53 01	26 24 43	18 01 20	23 59 48	25 22.5	10 59.1	16 24.5	7 20.5	13 18.8	16 23.1	20 08.1	12 11.7	17 26.8	24 08.0
20 W	11 56 58	27 23 21	29 56 36	5♍52 06	25 22.7	12 34.7	17 39.1	7 59.6	13 14.0	16 33.7	20 14.8	12 09.4	17 25.7	24 08.5
21 Th	12 00 54	28 22 01	11♍46 38	17 40 30	25R 22.8	14 09.3	18 53.7	8 38.8	13 09.6	16 44.4	20 21.5	12 07.1	17 24.5	24 09.0
22 F	12 04 51	29 20 43	23 34 01	29 27 26	25 22.8	15 43.0	20 08.3	9 18.0	13 05.5	16 55.1	20 28.1	12 04.8	17 23.4	24 09.5
23 Sa	12 08 47	0♎19 27	5♎21 04	11♎15 10	25 22.6	17 15.6	21 23.0	9 57.2	13 01.8	17 06.0	20 34.6	12 02.6	17 22.3	24 10.1
24 Su	12 12 44	1 18 12	17 10 02	23 05 57	25 22.1	18 47.3	22 37.6	10 36.5	12 58.5	17 17.0	20 41.1	12 00.3	17 21.2	24 10.7
25 M	12 16 40	2 17 00	29 03 11	5♏02 05	25 21.3	20 18.0	23 52.3	11 15.8	12 55.6	17 28.0	20 47.5	11 58.1	17 20.2	24 11.4
26 Tu	12 20 37	3 15 50	11♏02 56	17 06 06	25 20.3	21 47.8	25 07.1	11 55.2	12 53.0	17 39.1	20 53.9	11 55.9	17 19.2	24 12.0
27 W	12 24 33	4 14 41	23 11 56	29 20 49	25 19.1	23 16.6	26 21.8	12 34.6	12 50.8	17 50.3	21 00.3	11 53.8	17 18.2	24 12.7
28 Th	12 28 30	5 13 34	5♐33 07	11♐49 16	25 18.1	24 44.4	27 36.6	13 14.0	12 48.9	18 01.5	21 06.5	11 51.6	17 17.2	24 13.5
29 F	12 32 27	6 12 29	18 09 39	24 34 40	25D 17.4	26 11.2	28 51.3	13 53.5	12 47.4	18 12.8	21 12.8	11 49.5	17 16.3	24 14.2
30 Sa	12 36 23	7 11 26	1♑04 44	7♑40 10	25 17.1	27 37.0	0♎06.1	14 33.0	12 46.3	18 24.2	21 18.9	11 47.4	17 15.3	24 15.0

LONGITUDE — October 2006

Day	Sid.Time	☉	0 hr ☽	Noon☽	True☊	☿	♀	♂	⚷	♃	♄	♅	♆	♇
1 Su	12 40 20	8♎10 24	14♑21 19	21♑08 27	25♓17.4	29♎01.8	1♎21.0	15♎12.5	12♒45.6	18♏35.7	21♌25.0	11♓45.3	17♒14.5	24♐15.9
2 M	12 44 16	9 09 25	28 01 43	5♒01 13	25 18.2	0♏25.6	2 35.8	15 52.1	12D 45.2	18 47.3	21 31.1	11R 43.3	17R 13.6	24 16.7
3 Tu	12 48 13	10 08 26	12♒06 54	19 18 36	25 19.3	1 48.3	3 50.6	16 31.7	12 45.1	18 58.9	21 37.0	11 41.3	17 12.8	24 17.6
4 W	12 52 09	11 07 30	26 36 00	3♓58 35	25 20.4	3 09.9	5 05.5	17 11.3	12 45.5	19 10.5	21 43.0	11 39.3	17 12.0	24 18.5
5 Th	12 56 06	12 06 35	11♓25 43	18 56 34	25R 21.1	4 30.3	6 20.4	17 51.0	12 46.1	19 22.3	21 48.8	11 37.3	17 11.2	24 19.5
6 F	13 00 02	13 05 43	26 30 10	4♈05 27	25 21.0	5 49.6	7 35.3	18 30.7	12 47.2	19 34.1	21 54.6	11 35.3	17 10.4	24 20.5
7 Sa	13 03 59	14 04 52	11♈41 13	19 16 16	25 20.0	7 07.6	8 50.2	19 10.5	12 48.6	19 45.9	22 00.3	11 33.4	17 09.7	24 21.5
8 Su	13 07 56	15 04 03	26 49 24	4♉19 27	25 18.0	8 24.3	10 05.2	19 50.3	12 50.3	19 57.9	22 06.0	11 31.5	17 09.0	24 22.5
9 M	13 11 52	16 03 17	11♉45 22	19 06 12	25 15.4	9 39.6	11 20.1	20 30.1	12 52.4	20 09.9	22 11.6	11 29.7	17 08.4	24 23.6
10 Tu	13 15 49	17 02 33	26 21 12	3♊29 47	25 12.4	10 53.4	12 35.1	21 10.0	12 54.8	20 21.9	22 17.1	11 27.9	17 07.7	24 24.7
11 W	13 19 45	18 01 51	10♊31 33	17 26 17	25 09.7	12 05.6	13 50.1	21 49.9	12 57.6	20 34.0	22 22.5	11 26.1	17 07.1	24 25.8
12 Th	13 23 42	19 01 12	24 13 56	0♋54 38	25 07.6	13 16.1	15 05.1	22 29.9	13 00.8	20 46.2	22 27.9	11 24.3	17 06.6	24 27.0
13 F	13 27 38	20 00 34	7♋28 36	13 56 12	25D 06.4	14 24.8	16 20.1	23 09.9	13 04.2	20 58.4	22 33.2	11 22.6	17 06.0	24 28.1
14 Sa	13 31 35	21 00 00	20 17 52	26 34 08	25 06.4	15 31.5	17 35.2	23 49.9	13 08.0	21 10.7	22 38.5	11 20.9	17 05.5	24 29.3
15 Su	13 35 31	21 59 27	2♌45 31	8♌52 37	25 07.4	16 36.1	18 50.2	24 30.0	13 12.1	21 23.0	22 43.6	11 19.3	17 05.1	24 30.6
16 M	13 39 28	22 58 57	14 56 02	20 56 21	25 09.0	17 38.2	20 05.3	25 10.1	13 16.6	21 35.4	22 48.7	11 17.7	17 04.6	24 31.9
17 Tu	13 43 25	23 58 28	26 54 09	2♍50 01	25 10.8	18 37.8	21 20.4	25 50.3	13 21.4	21 47.8	22 53.7	11 16.1	17 04.2	24 33.1
18 W	13 47 21	24 58 03	8♍44 28	14 38 02	25R 12.2	19 34.6	22 35.5	26 30.5	13 26.5	22 00.3	22 58.6	11 14.6	17 03.8	24 34.5
19 Th	13 51 18	25 57 39	20 31 10	26 24 19	25 12.7	20 28.2	23 50.6	27 10.8	13 32.0	22 12.8	23 03.5	11 13.1	17 03.5	24 35.8
20 F	13 55 14	26 57 17	2♎17 52	8♎12 12	25 11.8	21 18.4	25 05.8	27 51.1	13 37.7	22 25.4	23 08.2	11 11.6	17 03.2	24 37.2
21 Sa	13 59 11	27 56 58	14 07 38	20 04 27	25 09.3	22 04.8	26 20.9	28 31.4	13 43.8	22 38.0	23 12.9	11 10.2	17 02.9	24 38.6
22 Su	14 03 07	28 56 40	26 02 55	2♏03 13	25 05.1	22 46.9	27 36.0	29 11.8	13 50.2	22 50.7	23 17.5	11 08.8	17 02.6	24 40.0
23 M	14 07 04	29 56 25	8♏05 35	14 10 11	24 59.5	23 24.5	28 51.2	29 52.2	13 56.9	23 03.4	23 22.0	11 07.5	17 02.4	24 41.5
24 Tu	14 11 00	0♏56 11	20 17 11	26 26 43	24 53.0	23 56.9	0♏06.4	0♏32.7	14 03.9	23 16.1	23 26.5	11 06.2	17 02.2	24 42.9
25 W	14 14 57	1 56 00	2♐38 57	8♐54 02	24 46.3	24 23.6	1 21.6	1 13.2	14 11.2	23 28.9	23 30.8	11 04.9	17 02.1	24 44.4
26 Th	14 18 54	2 55 50	15 12 07	21 33 22	24 40.0	24 44.2	2 36.8	1 53.7	14 18.8	23 41.7	23 35.1	11 03.7	17 02.0	24 46.0
27 F	14 22 50	3 55 42	27 57 58	4♑26 07	24 35.0	24 58.0	3 52.0	2 34.3	14 26.7	23 54.6	23 39.2	11 02.5	17 01.9	24 47.5
28 Sa	14 26 47	4 55 36	10♑58 01	17 33 52	24 31.7	25R 04.3	5 07.2	3 14.9	14 34.9	24 07.5	23 43.3	11 01.4	17D 01.8	24 49.1
29 Su	14 30 43	5 55 31	24 13 54	0♒58 19	24D 30.3	25 02.7	6 22.4	3 55.6	14 43.4	24 20.4	23 47.3	11 00.3	17 01.8	24 50.7
30 M	14 34 40	6 55 28	7♒47 16	14 40 57	24 30.4	24 52.5	7 37.6	4 36.3	14 52.2	24 33.3	23 51.2	10 59.3	17 01.9	24 52.3
31 Tu	14 38 36	7 55 27	21 39 25	28 42 42	24 31.5	24 33.2	8 52.8	5 17.0	15 01.2	24 46.3	23 55.0	10 58.3	17 01.9	24 54.0

Astro Data	Dy Hr Mn
♇ D	4 23:21
☽ 0N	8 17:05
♂ 0S	10 19:53
☿ 0S	13 21:56
☽ 0S	22 11:27
☉ 0S	23 4:03
♃□♆	24 20:31
♀ 0S	3 1:06
⚷ D	3 2:02
☽ 0N	6 4:15
☽ 0S	19 17:38
♃□♄	25 17:26
☿ R	28 19:16
♆ D	29 7:56

Planet Ingress	Dy Hr Mn
♀ ♍	6 6:15
♂ ♎	8 4:18
☿ ♎	12 21:08
☉ ♎	23 4:03
♀ ♎	30 10:02
☿ ♏	2 4:38
☉ ♏	23 13:26
♂ ♏	23 16:38
♀ ♏	24 9:58

Last Aspect Dy Hr Mn		☽ Ingress Dy Hr Mn
2 7:49	♂ □	♑ 2 14:34
4 14:24	♂ △	♒ 4 18:15
6 9:29	♇ ✶	♓ 6 18:56
8 9:02	♇ □	♈ 8 18:23
10 8:52	♇ △	♉ 10 18:30
12 20:58	☿ △	♊ 12 20:59
14 16:00	♇ ☍	♋ 15 2:54
17 0:31	☉ ✶	♌ 17 12:15
19 12:17	♇ △	♍ 20 0:07
22 11:45	☉ ☌	♎ 22 13:06
24 14:11	♇ ✶	♏ 25 1:54
27 5:32	♀ ✶	♐ 27 13:16
29 20:45	♀ □	♑ 29 22:01

Last Aspect Dy Hr Mn		☽ Ingress Dy Hr Mn
2 3:16	☿ □	♒ 2 3:24
3 20:14	♇ ✶	♓ 4 5:33
5 20:33	♇ □	♈ 6 5:32
7 20:05	♇ △	♉ 8 5:04
9 17:08	♄ □	♊ 10 6:06
12 0:22	♇ ☍	♋ 12 10:21
14 6:27	♂ □	♌ 14 18:38
16 21:01	♂ ✶	♍ 17 6:16
19 8:18	♇ □	♎ 19 19:19
22 5:58	♂ ☌	♏ 22 7:54
24 6:56	☿ ☌	♐ 24 18:53
26 18:02	♇ ☌	♑ 27 3:47
29 1:30	☿ ✶	♒ 29 10:17
31 5:31	♇ ✶	♓ 31 14:11

☽ Phases & Eclipses Dy Hr Mn	
7 18:42	○ 15♓00
7 18:51	• P 0.184
14 11:15	☾ 21♊30
22 11:45	● 29♍20
22 11:40:11	• A 07'09"
30 11:04	☽ 7♑09
7 3:13	○ 13♈43
14 0:26	☾ 20♋31
22 5:14	● 28♎40
29 21:25	☽ 6♒19

Astro Data

1 September 2006
Julian Day # 38960
SVP 5♓09'58"
GC 26♐55.9 ⚴ 1♑00.7
Eris 21♈09.4R ⚵ 9♍19.1
⚳ 5♒21.3R ⚶ 13♍31.2
☽ Mean ☊ 26♓06.1

1 October 2006
Julian Day # 38990
SVP 5♓09'55"
GC 26♐56.0 ⚴ 4♑45.4
Eris 20♈53.8R ⚵ 21♍52.1
⚳ 4♒29.5R ⚶ 28♍15.8
☽ Mean ☊ 24♓30.8

November 2006 LONGITUDE

Day	Sid.Time	☉	0 hr ☽	Noon ☽	True ☊	☿	♀	♂	⚳	♃	♄	♅	♆	♇
1 W	14 42 33	8♏55 27	5♓50 44	13♓03 19	24♓32.7	24♏04.6	10♏08.1	5♏57.8	15♒10.6	24♏59.3	23♌58.7	10♓57.4	17♒02.0	24♐55.7
2 Th	14 46 29	9 55 28	20 20 10	27 40 50	24R 33.1	23R 26.4	11 23.3	6 38.6	15 20.1	25 12.4	24 02.4	10R 56.5	17 02.1	24 57.3
3 F	14 50 26	10 55 31	5♈04 42	12♈31 02	24 31.8	22 38.9	12 38.5	7 19.5	15 30.0	25 25.5	24 05.9	10 55.6	17 02.3	24 59.1
4 Sa	14 54 23	11 55 36	19 58 57	27 27 30	24 28.3	21 42.4	13 53.8	8 00.4	15 40.1	25 38.6	24 09.3	10 54.8	17 02.5	25 00.8
5 Su	14 58 19	12 55 43	4♉55 35	12♉22 07	24 22.6	20 37.9	15 09.0	8 41.3	15 50.5	25 51.7	24 12.7	10 54.0	17 02.7	25 02.5
6 M	15 02 16	13 55 52	19 46 01	27 06 13	24 15.1	19 26.7	16 24.3	9 22.3	16 01.2	26 04.8	24 15.9	10 53.3	17 03.0	25 04.3
7 Tu	15 06 12	14 56 02	4♊21 48	11♊31 57	24 06.8	18 10.6	17 39.5	10 03.4	16 12.1	26 18.0	24 19.0	10 52.7	17 03.2	25 06.1
8 W	15 10 09	15 56 15	18 36 01	25 33 31	23 58.5	16 51.6	18 54.8	10 44.4	16 23.2	26 31.2	24 22.1	10 52.1	17 03.6	25 07.9
9 Th	15 14 05	16 56 29	2♋24 11	9♋07 54	23 51.3	15 32.3	20 10.1	11 25.6	16 34.6	26 44.4	24 25.0	10 51.5	17 03.9	25 09.8
10 F	15 18 02	17 56 46	15 44 44	22 14 53	23 46.0	14 15.2	21 25.3	12 06.7	16 46.2	26 57.6	24 27.9	10 51.0	17 04.3	25 11.6
11 Sa	15 21 58	18 57 04	28 38 41	4♌56 36	23 42.7	13 02.9	22 40.6	12 47.9	16 58.1	27 10.9	24 30.6	10 50.5	17 04.8	25 13.5
12 Su	15 25 55	19 57 24	11♌09 10	17 16 58	23D 41.5	11 57.5	23 55.9	13 29.2	17 10.2	27 24.1	24 33.3	10 50.1	17 05.2	25 15.4
13 M	15 29 52	20 57 46	23 20 39	29 20 53	23 41.8	11 01.0	25 11.2	14 10.5	17 22.6	27 37.4	24 35.8	10 49.7	17 05.7	25 17.3
14 Tu	15 33 48	21 58 11	5♍18 22	11♍13 46	23 42.7	10 14.9	26 26.5	14 51.8	17 35.1	27 50.7	24 38.2	10 49.4	17 06.3	25 19.2
15 W	15 37 45	22 58 37	17 07 45	23 00 59	23R 43.3	9 40.0	27 41.8	15 33.2	17 47.9	28 04.0	24 40.6	10 49.1	17 06.8	25 21.2
16 Th	15 41 41	23 59 04	28 54 05	4♎47 38	23 42.6	9 16.7	28 57.1	16 14.7	18 00.9	28 17.3	24 42.8	10 48.9	17 07.4	25 23.1
17 F	15 45 38	24 59 34	10♎42 10	16 38 11	23 39.7	9D 05.1	0♐12.4	16 56.1	18 14.2	28 30.6	24 44.9	10 48.7	17 08.1	25 25.1
18 Sa	15 49 34	26 00 05	22 36 07	28 36 20	23 34.3	9 04.9	1 27.8	17 37.7	18 27.7	28 44.0	24 46.9	10 48.6	17 08.7	25 27.1
19 Su	15 53 31	27 00 38	4♏39 09	10♏44 49	23 26.1	9 15.5	2 43.1	18 19.2	18 41.3	28 57.3	24 48.8	10D 48.6	17 09.4	25 29.1
20 M	15 57 27	28 01 13	16 53 32	23 05 26	23 15.7	9 36.0	3 58.4	19 00.8	18 55.2	29 10.6	24 50.6	10 48.6	17 10.1	25 31.1
21 Tu	16 01 24	29 01 49	29 20 34	5♐38 58	23 03.6	10 05.7	5 13.8	19 42.5	19 09.3	29 24.0	24 52.3	10 48.6	17 10.9	25 33.2
22 W	16 05 21	0♐02 27	12♐00 37	18 25 26	22 51.0	10 43.7	6 29.1	20 24.2	19 23.6	29 37.3	24 53.9	10 48.7	17 11.7	25 35.2
23 Th	16 09 17	1 03 06	24 53 21	1♑24 16	22 39.4	11 29.0	7 44.4	21 05.9	19 38.1	29 50.7	24 55.3	10 48.8	17 12.5	25 37.3
24 F	16 13 14	2 03 47	7♑58 06	14 34 44	22 29.4	12 20.9	8 59.8	21 47.7	19 52.8	0♐04.1	24 56.7	10 49.0	17 13.4	25 39.4
25 Sa	16 17 10	3 04 28	21 14 06	27 56 10	22 22.0	13 18.4	10 15.1	22 29.5	20 07.7	0 17.4	24 57.9	10 49.3	17 14.3	25 41.4
26 Su	16 21 07	4 05 11	4♒40 54	11♒28 19	22 17.4	14 21.0	11 30.4	23 11.4	20 22.8	0 30.8	24 59.1	10 49.6	17 15.2	25 43.5
27 M	16 25 03	5 05 55	18 18 26	25 11 17	22D 15.4	15 27.9	12 45.8	23 53.3	20 38.1	0 44.1	25 00.1	10 49.9	17 16.2	25 45.7
28 Tu	16 29 00	6 06 39	2♓06 57	9♓05 27	22R 15.1	16 38.5	14 01.1	24 35.3	20 53.5	0 57.4	25 01.0	10 50.3	17 17.2	25 47.8
29 W	16 32 56	7 07 25	16 06 49	23 11 00	22 15.3	17 52.3	15 16.4	25 17.3	21 09.2	1 10.8	25 01.8	10 50.8	17 18.2	25 49.9
30 Th	16 36 53	8 08 11	0♈17 55	7♈27 24	22 14.5	19 08.8	16 31.8	25 59.3	21 25.0	1 24.1	25 02.5	10 51.3	17 19.3	25 52.0

December 2006 LONGITUDE

Day	Sid.Time	☉	0 hr ☽	Noon ☽	True ☊	☿	♀	♂	⚳	♃	♄	♅	♆	♇
1 F	16 40 50	9♐08 59	14♈39 09	21♈52 48	22♓11.7	20♏27.7	17♐47.1	26♏41.4	21♒41.0	1♐37.4	25♌03.0	10♓51.8	17♒20.4	25♐54.2
2 Sa	16 44 46	10 09 47	29 07 52	6♉23 44	22R 06.1	21 48.7	19 02.4	27 23.5	21 57.1	1 50.7	25 03.5	10 52.4	17 21.5	25 56.4
3 Su	16 48 43	11 10 37	13♉39 42	20 54 58	21 57.6	23 11.3	20 17.7	28 05.6	22 13.5	2 04.0	25 03.9	10 53.1	17 22.6	25 58.5
4 M	16 52 39	12 11 27	28 08 42	5♊20 05	21 46.6	24 35.4	21 33.0	28 47.8	22 30.0	2 17.2	25 04.1	10 53.8	17 23.8	26 00.7
5 Tu	16 56 36	13 12 19	12♊28 14	19 32 25	21 34.2	26 00.8	22 48.4	29 30.1	22 46.6	2 30.5	25R 04.2	10 54.5	17 25.0	26 02.9
6 W	17 00 32	14 13 12	26 31 55	3♋26 11	21 21.7	27 27.2	24 03.7	0♐12.4	23 03.4	2 43.7	25 04.3	10 55.3	17 26.3	26 05.1
7 Th	17 04 29	15 14 06	10♋14 46	16 57 24	21 10.3	28 54.5	25 19.0	0 54.7	23 20.4	2 57.0	25 04.2	10 56.2	17 27.5	26 07.3
8 F	17 08 26	16 15 01	23 33 56	0♌04 24	21 01.1	0♐22.6	26 34.3	1 37.1	23 37.5	3 10.2	25 04.0	10 57.1	17 28.8	26 09.5
9 Sa	17 12 22	17 15 57	6♌28 56	12 47 51	20 54.6	1 51.4	27 49.6	2 19.5	23 54.8	3 23.4	25 03.6	10 58.1	17 30.1	26 11.7
10 Su	17 16 19	18 16 54	19 01 31	25 10 25	20 50.9	3 20.7	29 04.9	3 02.0	24 12.3	3 36.5	25 03.2	10 59.1	17 31.5	26 13.9
11 M	17 20 15	19 17 52	1♍15 08	7♍16 17	20 49.3	4 50.5	0♑20.2	3 44.5	24 29.8	3 49.7	25 02.7	11 00.1	17 32.9	26 16.1
12 Tu	17 24 12	20 18 52	13 14 30	19 10 30	20 49.0	6 20.7	1 35.5	4 27.1	24 47.6	4 02.8	25 02.0	11 01.2	17 34.3	26 18.3
13 W	17 28 08	21 19 52	25 05 00	0♎58 41	20 48.9	7 51.3	2 50.9	5 09.7	25 05.4	4 15.9	25 01.2	11 02.4	17 35.7	26 20.6
14 Th	17 32 05	22 20 54	6♎52 16	12 46 26	20 47.7	9 22.2	4 06.2	5 52.4	25 23.5	4 28.9	25 00.4	11 03.6	17 37.2	26 22.8
15 F	17 36 01	23 21 56	18 41 51	24 39 07	20 44.5	10 53.4	5 21.5	6 35.1	25 41.6	4 42.0	24 59.4	11 04.8	17 38.7	26 25.0
16 Sa	17 39 58	24 23 00	0♏38 50	6♏41 30	20 38.7	12 24.9	6 36.8	7 17.8	25 59.9	4 55.0	24 58.3	11 06.1	17 40.2	26 27.2
17 Su	17 43 55	25 24 04	12 47 35	18 57 26	20 29.9	13 56.5	7 52.1	8 00.6	26 18.3	5 08.0	24 57.1	11 07.5	17 41.7	26 29.5
18 M	17 47 51	26 25 10	25 11 21	1♐29 32	20 18.6	15 28.5	9 07.4	8 43.4	26 36.9	5 20.9	24 55.7	11 08.9	17 43.3	26 31.7
19 Tu	17 51 48	27 26 16	7♐52 06	14 19 04	20 05.4	17 00.6	10 22.7	9 26.3	26 55.6	5 33.8	24 54.3	11 10.3	17 44.9	26 33.9
20 W	17 55 44	28 27 23	20 50 20	27 25 47	19 51.7	18 32.9	11 38.0	10 09.2	27 14.4	5 46.7	24 52.8	11 11.8	17 46.5	26 36.2
21 Th	17 59 41	29 28 30	4♑05 08	10♑48 07	19 38.6	20 05.5	12 53.3	10 52.2	27 33.4	5 59.5	24 51.1	11 13.4	17 48.2	26 38.4
22 F	18 03 37	0♑29 38	17 34 22	24 23 30	19 27.4	21 38.2	14 08.6	11 35.2	27 52.4	6 12.3	24 49.4	11 15.0	17 49.9	26 40.6
23 Sa	18 07 34	1 30 46	1♒15 10	8♒08 59	19 19.0	23 11.2	15 23.9	12 18.2	28 11.6	6 25.1	24 47.5	11 16.6	17 51.6	26 42.9
24 Su	18 11 30	2 31 54	15 04 35	22 01 41	19 13.6	24 44.3	16 39.2	13 01.3	28 30.9	6 37.8	24 45.6	11 18.3	17 53.3	26 45.1
25 M	18 15 27	3 33 02	29 00 00	5♓59 19	19D 11.1	26 17.7	17 54.4	13 44.4	28 50.4	6 50.5	24 43.5	11 20.0	17 55.0	26 47.3
26 Tu	18 19 24	4 34 11	12♓59 30	20 00 24	19 10.6	27 51.3	19 09.7	14 27.6	29 09.9	7 03.1	24 41.3	11 21.8	17 56.8	26 49.5
27 W	18 23 20	5 35 19	27 01 55	4♈04 01	19R 10.8	29 25.1	20 24.9	15 10.8	29 29.6	7 15.7	24 39.1	11 23.6	17 58.6	26 51.7
28 Th	18 27 17	6 36 28	11♈06 35	18 09 34	19 10.3	0♑59.2	21 40.2	15 54.1	29 49.3	7 28.2	24 36.7	11 25.5	18 00.4	26 53.9
29 F	18 31 13	7 37 36	25 12 49	2♉16 12	19 08.0	2 33.5	22 55.4	16 37.3	0♓09.2	7 40.7	24 34.2	11 27.4	18 02.2	26 56.1
30 Sa	18 35 10	8 38 44	9♉19 30	16 22 25	19 03.1	4 08.1	24 10.6	17 20.7	0 29.2	7 53.1	24 31.7	11 29.3	18 04.0	26 58.3
31 Su	18 39 06	9 39 53	23 24 39	0♊25 46	18 55.4	5 43.0	25 25.8	18 04.0	0 49.2	8 05.5	24 29.0	11 31.3	18 05.9	27 00.5

Astro Data

	Dy Hr Mn
♃⚺♇	1 4:11
☽0N	2 14:15
☽0S	16 0:03
☿D	18 0:23
♅D	20 6:08
☽0N	29 21:18
♄R	6 4:06
☽0S	13 6:51
☽0N	27 1:57

Planet Ingress

	Dy Hr Mn
♀ ♐	17 8:02
☉ ♐	22 11:02
♃ ♐	24 4:43
♂ ♐	6 4:58
☿ ♐	8 5:52
♀ ♑	11 5:33
☉ ♑	22 0:22
☿ ♑	27 20:55
⚳ ♓	29 0:55

Last Aspect / ☽ Ingress

Last Aspect Dy Hr Mn		☽ Ingress Dy Hr Mn
2 7:54	♃ △	♈ 2 15:46
4 8:04	♇ △	♉ 4 16:05
6 10:18	♃ ☍	♊ 6 16:46
8 11:16	♇ ☍	♋ 8 19:46
10 20:59	♃ △	♌ 11 2:34
13 8:29	♃ □	♍ 13 13:19
15 22:41	♀ ⚹	♎ 16 2:14
18 5:41	♇ ⚹	♏ 18 14:47
20 23:54	♃ ☌	♐ 21 1:15
23 1:19	♇ ☌	♑ 23 9:25
25 1:43	♂ ⚹	♒ 25 15:41
27 13:00	♇ ⚹	♓ 27 20:21
29 16:29	♇ □	♈ 29 23:30

Last Aspect / ☽ Ingress

Last Aspect Dy Hr Mn		☽ Ingress Dy Hr Mn
1 18:41	♇ △	♉ 2 1:26
4 0:32	♂ ☍	♊ 4 3:05
5 23:12	♇ ☍	♋ 6 6:00
7 1:13	♅ △	♌ 8 11:52
10 20:35	♀ △	♍ 10 21:31
13 2:32	♇ □	♎ 13 10:00
15 15:33	♇ ⚹	♏ 15 22:43
17 23:31	♄ □	♐ 18 9:10
20 14:01	☉ ☌	♑ 20 16:39
21 16:05	♀ ☌	♒ 22 21:49
24 20:09	♇ ⚹	♓ 25 1:43
27 3:05	☿ □	♈ 27 5:04
29 2:54	♇ △	♉ 29 8:08
31 2:37	♀ △	♊ 31 11:16

☽ Phases & Eclipses

Dy Hr Mn	
5 12:58	○ 12♉58
12 17:45	☾ 20♌12
20 22:18	● 28♏27
28 6:29	☽ 5♓53
5 0:25	○ 12♊43
12 14:32	☾ 20♍25
20 14:01	● 28♐32
27 14:48	☽ 5♈42

Astro Data

1 November 2006
Julian Day # 39021
SVP 5♓09'51"
GC 26♐56.1 ⚴ 12♑09.2
Eris 20♈35.5R ⚵ 3♎56.4
⚷ 4♒38.5 ⚶ 13♎41.8
☽ Mean ☊ 22♓52.2

1 December 2006
Julian Day # 39051
SVP 5♓09'46"
GC 26♐56.2 ⚴ 21♑16.3
Eris 20♈20.8R ⚵ 14♎15.4
⚷ 5♒48.5 ⚶ 28♎31.6
☽ Mean ☊ 21♓16.9

LONGITUDE — January 2007

Day	Sid.Time	☉	0 hr ☽	Noon ☽	True ☊	☿	♀	♂	⚳	♃	♄	♅	♆	♇
1 M	18 43 03	10♑41 01	7♊25 19	14♊22 50	18♓45.4	7♑18.2	26♑41.0	18♐47.4	1♓09.4	8♐17.8	24♌26.3	11♓33.3	18♒07.8	27♐02.7
2 Tu	18 46 59	11 42 09	21 17 49	28 09 46	18R33.9	8 53.8	27 56.2	19 30.9	1 29.7	8 30.1	24R23.4	11 35.4	18 09.7	27 04.9
3 W	18 50 56	12 43 17	4♋58 13	11♋42 43	18 22.2	10 29.7	29 11.4	20 14.4	1 50.0	8 42.3	24 20.5	11 37.5	18 11.6	27 07.1
4 Th	18 54 53	13 44 25	18 22 57	24 58 38	18 11.5	12 05.9	0♒26.6	20 57.9	2 10.5	8 54.4	24 17.4	11 39.7	18 13.6	27 09.2
5 F	18 58 49	14 45 34	1♌29 35	7♌55 44	18 02.7	13 42.5	1 41.7	21 41.5	2 31.1	9 06.5	24 14.3	11 41.9	18 15.6	27 11.4
6 Sa	19 02 46	15 46 42	14 17 05	20 33 48	17 56.5	15 19.4	2 56.8	22 25.1	2 51.7	9 18.6	24 11.1	11 44.1	18 17.5	27 13.5
7 Su	19 06 42	16 47 50	26 46 05	2♍54 17	17 52.9	16 56.8	4 12.0	23 08.8	3 12.5	9 30.5	24 07.8	11 46.4	18 19.5	27 15.7
8 M	19 10 39	17 48 58	8♍58 45	15 00 00	17D51.6	18 34.6	5 27.1	23 52.5	3 33.3	9 42.5	24 04.5	11 48.7	18 21.5	27 17.8
9 Tu	19 14 35	18 50 06	20 58 32	26 54 57	17 51.9	20 12.7	6 42.2	24 36.2	3 54.2	9 54.3	24 01.0	11 51.0	18 23.6	27 19.9
10 W	19 18 32	19 51 14	2♎49 52	8♎43 57	17 52.8	21 51.4	7 57.3	25 20.0	4 15.2	10 06.1	23 57.5	11 53.4	18 25.6	27 22.0
11 Th	19 22 29	20 52 23	14 37 52	20 32 18	17R53.3	23 30.4	9 12.4	26 03.9	4 36.3	10 17.8	23 53.8	11 55.8	18 27.7	27 24.1
12 F	19 26 25	21 53 31	26 27 55	2♏25 26	17 52.6	25 09.9	10 27.4	26 47.7	4 57.4	10 29.4	23 50.1	11 58.3	18 29.8	27 26.2
13 Sa	19 30 22	22 54 39	8♏25 29	14 28 41	17 49.9	26 49.8	11 42.5	27 31.7	5 18.7	10 41.0	23 46.4	12 00.8	18 31.9	27 28.2
14 Su	19 34 18	23 55 47	20 35 38	26 46 50	17 45.0	28 30.1	12 57.6	28 15.6	5 40.0	10 52.5	23 42.5	12 03.3	18 34.0	27 30.3
15 M	19 38 15	24 56 56	3♐02 45	9♐23 43	17 38.0	0♒10.9	14 12.6	28 59.6	6 01.4	11 03.9	23 38.6	12 05.9	18 36.1	27 32.3
16 Tu	19 42 11	25 58 03	15 50 03	22 21 52	17 29.4	1 52.1	15 27.6	29 43.7	6 22.9	11 15.2	23 34.6	12 08.5	18 38.2	27 34.4
17 W	19 46 08	26 59 11	28 59 14	5♑42 03	17 20.1	3 33.6	16 42.6	0♑27.7	6 44.5	11 26.5	23 30.6	12 11.1	18 40.4	27 36.4
18 Th	19 50 04	28 00 18	12♑30 07	19 23 07	17 11.2	5 15.5	17 57.6	1 11.9	7 06.1	11 37.7	23 26.5	12 13.8	18 42.5	27 38.4
19 F	19 54 01	29 01 25	26 20 36	3♒22 03	17 03.5	6 57.7	19 12.6	1 56.0	7 27.8	11 48.8	23 22.3	12 16.5	18 44.7	27 40.3
20 Sa	19 57 58	0♒02 31	10♒26 52	17 34 23	16 58.0	8 40.1	20 27.5	2 40.2	7 49.6	11 59.8	23 18.1	12 19.2	18 46.9	27 42.3
21 Su	20 01 54	1 03 36	24 43 58	1♓54 55	16 54.8	10 22.7	21 42.5	3 24.4	8 11.4	12 10.7	23 13.8	12 22.0	18 49.1	27 44.3
22 M	20 05 51	2 04 40	9♓06 37	16 18 27	16D53.7	12 05.4	22 57.4	4 08.7	8 33.3	12 21.6	23 09.4	12 24.8	18 51.3	27 46.2
23 Tu	20 09 47	3 05 43	23 29 55	0♈40 33	16 54.4	13 48.1	24 12.3	4 53.0	8 55.3	12 32.3	23 05.0	12 27.6	18 53.5	27 48.1
24 W	20 13 44	4 06 46	7♈49 58	14 57 50	16 55.7	15 30.6	25 27.1	5 37.3	9 17.4	12 43.0	23 00.6	12 30.4	18 55.7	27 50.0
25 Th	20 17 40	5 07 47	22 03 56	29 08 03	16R56.7	17 12.9	26 42.0	6 21.7	9 39.5	12 53.5	22 56.1	12 33.3	18 57.9	27 51.9
26 F	20 21 37	6 08 47	6♉10 03	13♉09 49	16 56.6	18 54.6	27 56.8	7 06.1	10 01.6	13 04.0	22 51.5	12 36.2	19 00.1	27 53.7
27 Sa	20 25 33	7 09 46	20 07 15	27 02 15	16 54.8	20 35.7	29 11.6	7 50.6	10 23.8	13 14.4	22 46.9	12 39.2	19 02.4	27 55.6
28 Su	20 29 30	8 10 44	3♊54 45	10♊44 39	16 51.2	22 15.8	0♓26.4	8 35.0	10 46.1	13 24.7	22 42.3	12 42.1	19 04.6	27 57.4
29 M	20 33 27	9 11 41	17 31 50	24 16 13	16 46.0	23 54.7	1 41.1	9 19.6	11 08.4	13 34.8	22 37.7	12 45.1	19 06.9	27 59.2
30 Tu	20 37 23	10 12 37	0♋57 38	7♋35 59	16 39.9	25 31.9	2 55.8	10 04.1	11 30.8	13 44.9	22 33.0	12 48.1	19 09.1	28 01.0
31 W	20 41 20	11 13 31	14 11 08	20 42 59	16 33.4	27 07.2	4 10.5	10 48.7	11 53.2	13 54.9	22 28.3	12 51.2	19 11.4	28 02.7

LONGITUDE — February 2007

Day	Sid.Time	☉	0 hr ☽	Noon ☽	True ☊	☿	♀	♂	⚳	♃	♄	♅	♆	♇
1 Th	20 45 16	12♒14 25	27♋11 24	3♌36 21	16♓27.6	28♒40.0	5♓25.1	11♑33.3	12♓15.7	14♐04.8	22♌23.5	12♓54.2	19♒13.7	28♐04.5
2 F	20 49 13	13 15 17	9♌57 47	16 15 41	16R22.8	0♓09.8	6 39.7	12 18.0	12 38.3	14 14.6	22R18.8	12 57.3	19 15.9	28 06.2
3 Sa	20 53 09	14 16 08	22 30 06	28 41 10	16 19.7	1 36.1	7 54.3	13 02.7	13 00.8	14 24.2	22 14.0	13 00.4	19 18.2	28 07.9
4 Su	20 57 06	15 16 58	4♍49 00	10♍53 49	16D18.2	2 58.2	9 08.9	13 47.4	13 23.5	14 33.8	22 09.1	13 03.5	19 20.5	28 09.5
5 M	21 01 02	16 17 47	16 55 54	22 55 33	16 18.3	4 15.5	10 23.4	14 32.2	13 46.2	14 43.2	22 04.3	13 06.7	19 22.7	28 11.2
6 Tu	21 04 59	17 18 35	28 53 08	4♎49 06	16 19.5	5 27.2	11 37.9	15 17.0	14 08.9	14 52.6	21 59.4	13 09.8	19 25.0	28 12.8
7 W	21 08 56	18 19 22	10♎43 54	16 38 02	16 21.3	6 32.6	12 52.4	16 01.8	14 31.6	15 01.8	21 54.6	13 13.0	19 27.3	28 14.4
8 Th	21 12 52	19 20 09	22 32 04	28 26 33	16 23.1	7 30.9	14 06.8	16 46.7	14 54.5	15 10.9	21 49.7	13 16.2	19 29.6	28 16.0
9 F	21 16 49	20 20 54	4♏22 07	10♏19 20	16R24.5	8 21.4	15 21.2	17 31.6	15 17.3	15 19.9	21 44.8	13 19.4	19 31.8	28 17.5
10 Sa	21 20 45	21 21 38	16 18 53	22 21 21	16 24.9	9 03.2	16 35.6	18 16.5	15 40.2	15 28.8	21 39.9	13 22.7	19 34.1	28 19.0
11 Su	21 24 42	22 22 21	28 27 22	4♐37 31	16 24.3	9 35.8	17 49.9	19 01.5	16 03.1	15 37.5	21 35.1	13 25.9	19 36.4	28 20.5
12 M	21 28 38	23 23 03	10♐52 21	17 12 24	16 22.5	9 58.6	19 04.2	19 46.5	16 26.1	15 46.2	21 30.2	13 29.2	19 38.7	28 22.0
13 Tu	21 32 35	24 23 44	23 38 04	0♑09 44	16 19.9	10R11.2	20 18.5	20 31.6	16 49.1	15 54.7	21 25.3	13 32.5	19 41.0	28 23.5
14 W	21 36 31	25 24 24	6♑47 38	13 31 56	16 16.8	10 13.2	21 32.7	21 16.6	17 12.2	16 03.0	21 20.4	13 35.8	19 43.3	28 24.9
15 Th	21 40 28	26 25 02	20 22 36	27 19 30	16 13.7	10 04.7	22 46.9	22 01.8	17 35.3	16 11.3	21 15.6	13 39.1	19 45.5	28 26.3
16 F	21 44 25	27 25 40	4♒22 22	11♒30 44	16 11.1	9 45.8	24 01.0	22 46.9	17 58.4	16 19.4	21 10.7	13 42.5	19 47.8	28 27.7
17 Sa	21 48 21	28 26 15	18 44 02	26 01 34	16 09.4	9 16.9	25 15.2	23 32.1	18 21.6	16 27.4	21 05.9	13 45.8	19 50.1	28 29.0
18 Su	21 52 18	29 26 50	3♓22 30	10♓45 56	16D08.6	8 38.7	26 29.2	24 17.3	18 44.8	16 35.3	21 01.1	13 49.1	19 52.3	28 30.3
19 M	21 56 14	0♓27 22	18 10 55	25 36 31	16 08.7	7 52.2	27 43.3	25 02.5	19 08.0	16 43.0	20 56.3	13 52.5	19 54.6	28 31.6
20 Tu	22 00 11	1 27 53	3♈01 47	10♈25 49	16 09.4	6 58.8	28 57.3	25 47.7	19 31.3	16 50.6	20 51.5	13 55.9	19 56.8	28 32.9
21 W	22 04 07	2 28 22	17 47 49	25 07 04	16 10.5	5 59.7	0♈11.2	26 33.0	19 54.5	16 58.0	20 46.8	13 59.3	19 59.1	28 34.1
22 Th	22 08 04	3 28 50	2♉22 59	9♉35 04	16 11.6	4 56.6	1 25.1	27 18.3	20 17.8	17 05.3	20 42.0	14 02.7	20 01.3	28 35.3
23 F	22 12 00	4 29 15	16 42 57	23 46 22	16R12.2	3 51.1	2 39.0	28 03.7	20 41.2	17 12.5	20 37.4	14 06.1	20 03.5	28 36.5
24 Sa	22 15 57	5 29 39	0♊45 12	7♊39 22	16 12.4	2 45.1	3 52.8	28 49.0	21 04.5	17 19.5	20 32.7	14 09.5	20 05.7	28 37.6
25 Su	22 19 54	6 30 00	14 28 53	21 13 49	16 12.1	1 40.0	5 06.5	29 34.4	21 27.9	17 26.4	20 28.1	14 12.9	20 08.0	28 38.7
26 M	22 23 50	7 30 20	27 54 17	4♋30 29	16 11.3	0 37.3	6 20.2	0♒19.8	21 51.3	17 33.1	20 23.6	14 16.3	20 10.2	28 39.8
27 Tu	22 27 47	8 30 38	11♋02 33	17 30 42	16 10.4	29♒38.5	7 33.9	1 05.2	22 14.8	17 39.7	20 19.0	14 19.7	20 12.4	28 40.9
28 W	22 31 43	9 30 53	23 55 09	0♌16 05	16 09.4	28 44.4	8 47.5	1 50.7	22 38.2	17 46.2	20 14.6	14 23.2	20 14.5	28 41.9

Astro Data (Dy Hr Mn)

☽0S 9 14:04
♃□♅ 22 21:42
☽0N 23 7:06

☽0S 5 21:27
☿R 14 4:36
☽0N 19 15:11
♀0N 23 4:06
♄☍♆ 28 12:01

Planet Ingress (Dy Hr Mn)

♀ ♒ 4 3:31
☿ ♒ 15 9:25
♂ ♑ 16 20:54
☉ ♒ 20 11:01
♀ ♓ 28 3:32

☿ ♓ 2 9:20
☉ ♓ 19 1:09
♀ ♈ 21 8:21
♂ ♒ 26 1:32
☿ ♒R 27 3:01

Last Aspect Dy Hr Mn		☽ Ingress Dy Hr Mn
2 10:06	♇ ☍	♋ 2 15:14
3 13:57	☉ ☍	♌ 4 21:14
7 0:56	♇ △	♍ 7 6:18
9 12:51	♇ □	♎ 9 18:15
12 1:56	♇ ⚹	♏ 12 7:08
14 15:50	☿ ⚹	♐ 14 18:11
16 21:28	♇ ☌	♑ 17 1:49
19 4:01	☉ ☌	♒ 19 6:16
21 5:01	♇ ⚹	♓ 21 8:48
23 7:11	♇ □	♈ 23 10:52
25 9:50	♇ △	♉ 25 13:28
27 16:08	♀ □	♊ 27 17:10
29 18:40	♇ ☍	♋ 29 22:16

Last Aspect Dy Hr Mn		☽ Ingress Dy Hr Mn
30 21:30	♅ △	♌ 1 5:15
3 10:55	♇ △	♍ 3 14:34
5 22:37	♇ □	♎ 6 2:15
8 11:38	♇ ⚹	♏ 8 15:09
10 10:39	♄ □	♐ 11 3:01
13 8:45	♇ ☌	♑ 13 11:42
15 3:24	♀ ⚹	♒ 15 16:34
17 16:14	☉ ☌	♓ 17 18:30
19 16:43	♇ □	♈ 19 19:06
21 17:42	♇ □	♉ 21 20:03
23 19:47	♂ △	♊ 23 22:42
26 1:21	♇ ☍	♋ 26 3:48
27 6:03	♅ △	♌ 28 11:29

☽ Phases & Eclipses (Dy Hr Mn)

3 13:57 ○ 12♋48
11 12:45 ☾ 20♎54
19 4:01 ● 28♑41
25 23:01 ☽ 5♉36

2 5:45 ○ 12♌59
10 9:51 ☾ 21♏16
17 16:14 ● 28♒37
24 7:56 ☽ 5♊19

Astro Data

1 January 2007
Julian Day # 39082
SVP 5♓09'40"
GC 26♐56.2 ⚴ 1♒43.8
Eris 20♈13.5R ⚵ 22♎39.3
⚷ 7♒49.1 ⚶ 13♏17.3
☽ Mean ☊ 19♓38.5

1 February 2007
Julian Day # 39113
SVP 5♓09'34"
GC 26♐56.3 ⚴ 12♒31.9
Eris 20♈16.5 ⚵ 27♎24.0
⚷ 10♒14.5 ⚶ 26♏45.6
☽ Mean ☊ 18♓00.0

March 2007 LONGITUDE

Day	Sid.Time	☉	0 hr ☽	Noon ☽	True ☊	☿	♀	♂	⚳	♃	♄	♅	♆	♇
1 Th	22 35 40	10♓31 07	6♌33 43	12♌48 14	16♓08.6	27♒56.0	10♈01.0	2♒36.2	23♓01.7	17♐52.5	20♌10.1	14♓26.6	20♒16.7	28♐42.9
2 F	22 39 36	11 31 19	18 59 52	25 08 47	16R 08.1	27R 13.9	11 14.5	3 21.7	23 25.1	17 58.6	20R 05.7	14 30.0	20 18.9	28 43.9
3 Sa	22 43 33	12 31 29	1♍15 11	7♍19 17	16D 07.8	26 38.5	12 27.9	4 07.2	23 48.6	18 04.6	20 01.4	14 33.5	20 21.0	28 44.8
4 Su	22 47 29	13 31 37	13 21 16	19 21 21	16 07.7	26 10.0	13 41.3	4 52.7	24 12.2	18 10.4	19 57.1	14 36.9	20 23.2	28 45.7
5 M	22 51 26	14 31 43	25 19 47	1♎16 47	16 07.8	25 48.6	14 54.6	5 38.3	24 35.7	18 16.1	19 52.9	14 40.3	20 25.3	28 46.6
6 Tu	22 55 23	15 31 47	7♎12 39	13 07 40	16R 07.9	25 34.0	16 07.9	6 23.9	24 59.2	18 21.6	19 48.8	14 43.8	20 27.4	28 47.4
7 W	22 59 19	16 31 50	19 02 09	24 56 27	16 07.9	25D 26.2	17 21.1	7 09.6	25 22.8	18 26.9	19 44.7	14 47.2	20 29.5	28 48.2
8 Th	23 03 16	17 31 51	0♏50 58	6♏46 04	16 07.8	25 24.9	18 34.2	7 55.2	25 46.4	18 32.1	19 40.6	14 50.7	20 31.6	28 49.0
9 F	23 07 12	18 31 50	12 42 15	18 39 56	16 07.6	25 29.9	19 47.3	8 40.9	26 10.0	18 37.1	19 36.7	14 54.1	20 33.7	28 49.7
10 Sa	23 11 09	19 31 48	24 39 38	0♐41 53	16 07.3	25 40.8	21 00.3	9 26.6	26 33.6	18 42.0	19 32.7	14 57.5	20 35.7	28 50.5
11 Su	23 15 05	20 31 44	6♐47 11	12 56 06	16D 07.0	25 57.4	22 13.3	10 12.3	26 57.2	18 46.7	19 28.9	15 01.0	20 37.8	28 51.1
12 M	23 19 02	21 31 39	19 09 09	25 26 53	16 07.0	26 19.3	23 26.2	10 58.1	27 20.8	18 51.2	19 25.2	15 04.4	20 39.8	28 51.8
13 Tu	23 22 58	22 31 32	1♑49 49	8♑18 23	16 07.3	26 46.2	24 39.0	11 43.8	27 44.5	18 55.6	19 21.5	15 07.8	20 41.8	28 52.4
14 W	23 26 55	23 31 23	14 53 01	21 34 02	16 07.8	27 17.7	25 51.8	12 29.6	28 08.1	18 59.8	19 17.8	15 11.2	20 43.8	28 53.0
15 Th	23 30 52	24 31 13	28 21 42	5♒16 08	16 08.5	27 53.6	27 04.5	13 15.4	28 31.8	19 03.8	19 14.3	15 14.6	20 45.8	28 53.6
16 F	23 34 48	25 31 00	12♒17 18	19 25 03	16 09.3	28 33.7	28 17.2	14 01.2	28 55.4	19 07.7	19 10.8	15 18.0	20 47.8	28 54.1
17 Sa	23 38 45	26 30 46	26 39 03	3♓58 47	16R 09.9	29 17.5	29 29.8	14 47.1	29 19.1	19 11.3	19 07.5	15 21.4	20 49.7	28 54.6
18 Su	23 42 41	27 30 30	11♓23 33	18 52 31	16 10.1	0♓04.9	0♉42.3	15 32.9	29 42.8	19 14.8	19 04.2	15 24.8	20 51.7	28 55.0
19 M	23 46 38	28 30 12	26 24 41	3♈58 56	16 09.6	0 55.7	1 54.7	16 18.8	0♈06.5	19 18.2	19 01.0	15 28.2	20 53.6	28 55.5
20 Tu	23 50 34	29 29 52	11♈34 05	19 08 56	16 08.5	1 49.7	3 07.1	17 04.7	0 30.1	19 21.3	18 57.8	15 31.6	20 55.5	28 55.9
21 W	23 54 31	0♈29 30	26 42 17	4♉12 59	16 06.9	2 46.6	4 19.4	17 50.6	0 53.8	19 24.3	18 54.8	15 34.9	20 57.3	28 56.2
22 Th	23 58 27	1 29 06	11♉40 01	19 02 31	16 05.0	3 46.4	5 31.6	18 36.5	1 17.5	19 27.0	18 51.8	15 38.3	20 59.2	28 56.5
23 F	0 02 24	2 28 40	26 19 44	3♊31 08	16 03.2	4 48.7	6 43.8	19 22.4	1 41.2	19 29.6	18 49.0	15 41.6	21 01.0	28 56.8
24 Sa	0 06 21	3 28 11	10♊36 21	17 35 10	16 01.8	5 53.6	7 55.9	20 08.3	2 04.9	19 32.1	18 46.2	15 44.9	21 02.8	28 57.1
25 Su	0 10 17	4 27 40	24 27 32	1♋13 34	16D 01.2	7 00.8	9 07.9	20 54.2	2 28.6	19 34.3	18 43.5	15 48.3	21 04.6	28 57.3
26 M	0 14 14	5 27 07	7♋53 26	14 27 26	16 01.4	8 10.3	10 19.8	21 40.2	2 52.2	19 36.3	18 41.0	15 51.5	21 06.4	28 57.5
27 Tu	0 18 10	6 26 31	20 55 57	27 19 22	16 02.4	9 21.9	11 31.7	22 26.1	3 15.9	19 38.2	18 38.5	15 54.8	21 08.1	28 57.7
28 W	0 22 07	7 25 53	3♌38 08	9♌52 42	16 03.9	10 35.6	12 43.4	23 12.1	3 39.6	19 39.9	18 36.1	15 58.1	21 09.9	28 57.8
29 Th	0 26 03	8 25 13	16 03 31	22 11 03	16 05.5	11 51.3	13 55.1	23 58.1	4 03.2	19 41.4	18 33.8	16 01.3	21 11.6	28 57.9
30 F	0 30 00	9 24 30	28 15 43	4♍17 57	16R 06.8	13 08.9	15 06.6	24 44.0	4 26.9	19 42.7	18 31.6	16 04.6	21 13.2	28 58.0
31 Sa	0 33 56	10 23 45	10♍18 07	16 16 36	16 07.3	14 28.3	16 18.1	25 30.0	4 50.5	19 43.8	18 29.5	16 07.8	21 14.9	28R 58.0

April 2007 LONGITUDE

Day	Sid.Time	☉	0 hr ☽	Noon ☽	True ☊	☿	♀	♂	⚳	♃	♄	♅	♆	♇
1 Su	0 37 53	11♈22 58	22♍13 43	28♍09 47	16♓06.6	15♓49.6	17♉29.5	26♒16.0	5♈14.2	19♐44.8	18♌27.5	16♓11.0	21♒16.5	28♐58.0
2 M	0 41 49	12 22 09	4♎05 06	9♎59 56	16R 04.7	17 12.5	18 40.8	27 02.0	5 37.8	19 45.5	18R 25.6	16 14.2	21 18.1	28R 58.0
3 Tu	0 45 46	13 21 18	15 54 32	21 49 09	16 01.4	18 37.2	19 52.0	27 48.0	6 01.4	19 46.1	18 23.8	16 17.3	21 19.7	28 57.9
4 W	0 49 43	14 20 25	27 44 12	3♏39 25	15 56.9	20 03.5	21 03.1	28 34.0	6 25.0	19 46.5	18 22.1	16 20.5	21 21.3	28 57.8
5 Th	0 53 39	15 19 30	9♏35 33	15 32 42	15 51.8	21 31.5	22 14.2	29 20.1	6 48.6	19R 46.7	18 20.5	16 23.6	21 22.8	28 57.7
6 F	0 57 36	16 18 33	21 31 08	27 31 10	15 46.4	23 01.1	23 25.1	0♓06.1	7 12.2	19 46.7	18 19.0	16 26.7	21 24.3	28 57.5
7 Sa	1 01 32	17 17 34	3♐33 06	9♐37 18	15 41.5	24 32.2	24 35.9	0 52.1	7 35.8	19 46.5	18 17.7	16 29.8	21 25.8	28 57.3
8 Su	1 05 29	18 16 34	15 44 07	21 53 57	15 37.5	26 04.9	25 46.6	1 38.2	7 59.3	19 46.2	18 16.4	16 32.8	21 27.2	28 57.1
9 M	1 09 25	19 15 32	28 07 14	4♑24 22	15 34.9	27 39.2	26 57.3	2 24.2	8 22.9	19 45.6	18 15.2	16 35.8	21 28.7	28 56.9
10 Tu	1 13 22	20 14 28	10♑45 50	17 12 03	15D 33.8	29 15.1	28 07.8	3 10.3	8 46.4	19 44.9	18 14.2	16 38.9	21 30.1	28 56.6
11 W	1 17 18	21 13 22	23 43 28	0♒20 28	15 34.1	0♈52.5	29 18.2	3 56.3	9 10.0	19 44.0	18 13.2	16 41.8	21 31.5	28 56.3
12 Th	1 21 15	22 12 15	7♒03 26	13 52 39	15 35.3	2 31.4	0♊28.6	4 42.4	9 33.5	19 42.8	18 12.3	16 44.8	21 32.8	28 55.9
13 F	1 25 12	23 11 05	20 48 18	27 50 30	15 36.7	4 11.9	1 38.8	5 28.4	9 57.0	19 41.5	18 11.6	16 47.7	21 34.1	28 55.5
14 Sa	1 29 08	24 09 54	4♓59 12	12♓14 09	15R 37.6	5 54.0	2 48.9	6 14.5	10 20.4	19 40.0	18 10.9	16 50.6	21 35.4	28 55.1
15 Su	1 33 05	25 08 42	19 35 00	27 01 09	15 37.2	7 37.6	3 58.9	7 00.5	10 43.9	19 38.4	18 10.4	16 53.5	21 36.7	28 54.7
16 M	1 37 01	26 07 27	4♈31 48	12♈06 01	15 34.9	9 22.7	5 08.8	7 46.5	11 07.3	19 36.5	18 10.0	16 56.4	21 37.9	28 54.2
17 Tu	1 40 58	27 06 10	19 42 39	27 20 27	15 30.8	11 09.5	6 18.6	8 32.6	11 30.7	19 34.4	18 09.7	16 59.2	21 39.1	28 53.7
18 W	1 44 54	28 04 52	4♉58 07	12♉34 17	15 25.0	12 57.8	7 28.3	9 18.6	11 54.1	19 32.2	18 09.5	17 02.0	21 40.3	28 53.2
19 Th	1 48 51	29 03 32	20 07 39	27 37 01	15 18.4	14 47.8	8 37.8	10 04.6	12 17.5	19 29.8	18D 09.4	17 04.8	21 41.5	28 52.6
20 F	1 52 47	0♉02 09	5♊01 19	12♊19 42	15 11.9	16 39.3	9 47.3	10 50.6	12 40.9	19 27.2	18 09.4	17 07.5	21 42.6	28 52.0
21 Sa	1 56 44	1 00 45	19 31 29	26 36 12	15 06.3	18 32.4	10 56.6	11 36.6	13 04.2	19 24.4	18 09.5	17 10.2	21 43.7	28 51.4
22 Su	2 00 41	1 59 18	3♋33 38	10♋23 43	15 02.3	20 27.2	12 05.8	12 22.6	13 27.5	19 21.5	18 09.7	17 12.9	21 44.7	28 50.8
23 M	2 04 37	2 57 49	17 06 35	23 42 31	15D 00.1	22 23.5	13 14.8	13 08.6	13 50.8	19 18.4	18 10.1	17 15.6	21 45.8	28 50.1
24 Tu	2 08 34	3 56 18	0♌11 52	6♌35 09	14 59.7	24 21.4	14 23.7	13 54.6	14 14.0	19 15.1	18 10.5	17 18.2	21 46.8	28 49.4
25 W	2 12 30	4 54 45	12 52 53	19 05 40	15 00.5	26 20.8	15 32.5	14 40.5	14 37.2	19 11.6	18 11.1	17 20.8	21 47.8	28 48.7
26 Th	2 16 27	5 53 10	25 14 06	1♍18 48	15 01.7	28 21.8	16 41.2	15 26.4	15 00.4	19 08.0	18 11.7	17 23.3	21 48.7	28 47.9
27 F	2 20 23	6 51 32	7♍20 22	13 19 24	15R 02.5	0♉24.3	17 49.6	16 12.4	15 23.5	19 04.1	18 12.5	17 25.9	21 49.6	28 47.1
28 Sa	2 24 20	7 49 52	19 16 26	25 12 01	15 01.9	2 28.1	18 58.0	16 58.3	15 46.7	19 00.2	18 13.3	17 28.3	21 50.5	28 46.3
29 Su	2 28 16	8 48 11	1♎06 37	7♎00 42	14 59.3	4 33.3	20 06.2	17 44.2	16 09.7	18 56.0	18 14.3	17 30.8	21 51.3	28 45.5
30 M	2 32 13	9 46 27	12 54 38	18 48 48	14 54.4	6 39.6	21 14.2	18 30.0	16 32.8	18 51.7	18 15.4	17 33.2	21 52.1	28 44.6

Astro Data

	Dy Hr Mn
☽0S	5 4:31
☿D	8 4:44
♃△♄	16 22:42
☽0N	19 1:51
⊙0N	21 0:07
♇R	31 22:45
☽0S	1 10:50
♃R	6 1:22
☿0N	14 6:37
☽0N	15 12:49
♄D	19 21:24
☽0S	28 16:34

Planet Ingress

	Dy Hr Mn
♀ ♉	17 22:00
☿ ♓	18 9:35
⚳ ♈	19 5:27
⊙ ♈	21 0:07
♂ ♓	6 8:49
☿ ♈	10 23:07
♀ ♊	12 2:15
⊙ ♉	20 11:07
☿ ♉	27 7:16

Last Aspect / ☽ Ingress

Last Aspect Dy Hr Mn		☽ Ingress Dy Hr Mn
2 19:03 ♇ △	♍	2 21:32
5 6:56 ♇ □	♎	5 9:25
7 19:51 ♇ ⚹	♏	7 22:17
10 1:51 ☿ □	♐	10 10:37
12 18:27 ♇ ☌	♑	12 20:35
14 20:21 ♀ □	♒	15 2:52
17 4:01 ♀ ⚹	♓	17 5:30
19 3:59 ♇ □	♈	19 5:42
21 3:33 ♇ △	♉	21 5:15
22 15:12 ♆ □	♊	23 6:06
25 7:57 ♇ ☍	♋	25 9:49
26 14:36 ♅ △	♌	27 17:04
30 1:24 ♇ △	♍	30 3:27

Last Aspect / ☽ Ingress

Last Aspect Dy Hr Mn		☽ Ingress Dy Hr Mn
1 13:38 ♇ □	♎	1 15:43
4 2:30 ♇ ⚹	♏	4 4:36
6 2:54 ♀ ☍	♐	6 16:57
9 1:35 ♇ ☌	♑	9 3:36
11 9:57 ♀ △	♒	11 11:23
13 13:50 ♇ ⚹	♓	13 15:39
15 15:02 ♇ □	♈	15 16:47
17 14:27 ♇ △	♉	17 16:11
19 2:29 ♆ □	♊	19 15:51
21 15:52 ♇ ☍	♋	21 17:50
23 9:10 ♀ □	♌	23 23:38
26 7:02 ♇ △	♍	26 9:24
28 19:14 ♇ □	♎	28 21:45

☽ Phases & Eclipses

Dy Hr Mn	
3 23:17	○ 13♍00
3 23:21	• T 1.233
12 3:54	☾ 21♐11
19 2:43	● 28♓07
19 2:31:52	• P 0.876
25 18:16	☽ 4♋43
2 17:15	○ 12♎35
10 18:04	☾ 20♑29
17 11:36	● 27♈05
24 6:36	☽ 3♌43

Astro Data

1 March 2007
Julian Day # 39141
SVP 5♓09'30"
GC 26♐56.4 ⚴ 22♒06.3
Eris 20♈27.6 ⚵ 27♎11.4R
⚷ 12♒24.1 ⚶ 6♐50.7
☽ Mean ☊ 16♓31.1

1 April 2007
Julian Day # 39172
SVP 5♓09'27"
GC 26♐56.4 ⚴ 1♓59.5
Eris 20♈46.0 ⚵ 21♎50.2R
⚷ 14♒21.3 ⚶ 13♐56.3
☽ Mean ☊ 14♓52.5

LONGITUDE — May 2007

Day	Sid.Time	☉	0 hr ☽	Noon ☽	True ☊	☿	♀	♂	⚳	♃	♄	♅	♆	♇
1 Tu	2 36 10	10♉44 42	24♎43 30	0♏39 02	14♓47.1	8♉47.1	22♊22.1	19♓15.9	16♈55.8	18♐47.3	18♌16.6	17♓35.6	21♒52.9	28♐43.7
2 W	2 40 06	11 42 55	6♏35 38	12 33 30	14R37.7	10 55.4	23 29.8	20 01.7	17 18.8	18R42.7	18 17.9	17 37.9	21 53.7	28R42.8
3 Th	2 44 03	12 41 06	18 32 50	24 33 47	14 27.1	13 04.5	24 37.4	20 47.6	17 41.8	18 37.9	18 19.3	17 40.2	21 54.4	28 41.9
4 F	2 47 59	13 39 15	0♐36 33	6♐41 14	14 16.0	15 14.2	25 44.7	21 33.4	18 04.7	18 33.0	18 20.8	17 42.5	21 55.1	28 40.9
5 Sa	2 51 56	14 37 23	12 48 03	18 57 07	14 05.6	17 24.1	26 52.0	22 19.2	18 27.6	18 27.9	18 22.4	17 44.8	21 55.7	28 39.9
6 Su	2 55 52	15 35 29	25 08 39	1♑22 51	13 56.6	19 34.0	27 59.0	23 05.0	18 50.4	18 22.7	18 24.1	17 47.0	21 56.4	28 38.9
7 M	2 59 49	16 33 34	7♑39 57	14 00 13	13 49.9	21 43.7	29 05.9	23 50.7	19 13.3	18 17.4	18 25.9	17 49.1	21 57.0	28 37.9
8 Tu	3 03 45	17 31 38	20 23 55	26 51 23	13 45.6	23 52.8	0♋12.6	24 36.5	19 36.0	18 11.9	18 27.8	17 51.2	21 57.5	28 36.8
9 W	3 07 42	18 29 40	3♒22 55	9♒58 52	13D43.7	26 01.2	1 19.1	25 22.2	19 58.8	18 06.2	18 29.9	17 53.3	21 58.1	28 35.7
10 Th	3 11 39	19 27 41	16 39 34	23 25 17	13 43.4	28 08.4	2 25.4	26 07.9	20 21.5	18 00.5	18 32.0	17 55.4	21 58.5	28 34.6
11 F	3 15 35	20 25 40	0♓16 19	7♓12 51	13R43.8	0♊14.2	3 31.6	26 53.6	20 44.1	17 54.6	18 34.2	17 57.4	21 59.0	28 33.5
12 Sa	3 19 32	21 23 38	14 15 00	21 22 45	13 43.7	2 18.3	4 37.5	27 39.2	21 06.7	17 48.6	18 36.5	17 59.3	21 59.4	28 32.4
13 Su	3 23 28	22 21 35	28 35 57	5♈54 18	13 42.0	4 20.5	5 43.2	28 24.8	21 29.3	17 42.4	18 38.9	18 01.3	21 59.8	28 31.2
14 M	3 27 25	23 19 30	13♈17 18	20 44 17	13 37.9	6 20.6	6 48.8	29 10.4	21 51.8	17 36.2	18 41.4	18 03.2	22 00.2	28 30.0
15 Tu	3 31 21	24 17 25	28 14 24	5♉46 37	13 31.2	8 18.3	7 54.1	29 56.0	22 14.3	17 29.8	18 44.1	18 05.0	22 00.5	28 28.8
16 W	3 35 18	25 15 18	13♉19 47	20 52 40	13 22.2	10 13.5	8 59.3	0♈41.5	22 36.8	17 23.3	18 46.8	18 06.8	22 00.8	28 27.6
17 Th	3 39 14	26 13 09	28 23 59	5♊52 29	13 11.8	12 05.9	10 04.2	1 27.0	22 59.1	17 16.7	18 49.6	18 08.6	22 01.1	28 26.3
18 F	3 43 11	27 10 59	13♊17 00	20 36 29	13 01.3	13 55.6	11 08.8	2 12.5	23 21.5	17 10.0	18 52.5	18 10.3	22 01.3	28 25.1
19 Sa	3 47 08	28 08 48	27 50 06	4♋57 10	12 51.8	15 42.3	12 13.3	2 57.9	23 43.8	17 03.3	18 55.5	18 12.0	22 01.5	28 23.8
20 Su	3 51 04	29 06 35	11♋57 14	18 50 03	12 44.3	17 26.0	13 17.5	3 43.3	24 06.0	16 56.4	18 58.6	18 13.6	22 01.7	28 22.5
21 M	3 55 01	0♊04 20	25 35 34	2♌13 55	12 39.3	19 06.6	14 21.5	4 28.7	24 28.2	16 49.4	19 01.8	18 15.2	22 01.8	28 21.2
22 Tu	3 58 57	1 02 04	8♌45 24	15 10 24	12 36.6	20 44.1	15 25.2	5 14.0	24 50.3	16 42.4	19 05.1	18 16.7	22 01.9	28 19.9
23 W	4 02 54	1 59 46	21 29 27	27 43 07	12D35.8	22 18.3	16 28.6	5 59.3	25 12.4	16 35.3	19 08.5	18 18.2	22 02.0	28 18.5
24 Th	4 06 50	2 57 26	3♍52 01	9♍56 51	12R35.8	23 49.3	17 31.8	6 44.5	25 34.4	16 28.1	19 11.9	18 19.7	22R02.0	28 17.1
25 F	4 10 47	3 55 05	15 58 15	21 56 55	12 35.6	25 16.9	18 34.7	7 29.7	25 56.4	16 20.9	19 15.5	18 21.1	22 02.0	28 15.8
26 Sa	4 14 44	4 52 42	27 53 31	3♎48 40	12 34.0	26 41.2	19 37.2	8 14.9	26 18.2	16 13.5	19 19.2	18 22.4	22 02.0	28 14.4
27 Su	4 18 40	5 50 18	9♎42 58	15 36 59	12 30.4	28 02.2	20 39.5	9 00.0	26 40.1	16 06.2	19 22.9	18 23.7	22 02.0	28 13.0
28 M	4 22 37	6 47 53	21 31 15	27 26 14	12 24.1	29 19.7	21 41.5	9 45.1	27 01.9	15 58.8	19 26.7	18 25.0	22 01.9	28 11.6
29 Tu	4 26 33	7 45 26	3♏22 20	9♏19 55	12 15.0	0♋33.7	22 43.2	10 30.1	27 23.6	15 51.3	19 30.6	18 26.2	22 01.7	28 10.1
30 W	4 30 30	8 42 58	15 19 18	21 20 43	12 03.7	1 44.2	23 44.5	11 15.1	27 45.2	15 43.8	19 34.6	18 27.4	22 01.6	28 08.7
31 Th	4 34 26	9 40 29	27 24 24	3♐30 28	11 50.7	2 51.1	24 45.6	12 00.0	28 06.8	15 36.3	19 38.7	18 28.6	22 01.4	28 07.2

LONGITUDE — June 2007

Day	Sid.Time	☉	0 hr ☽	Noon ☽	True ☊	☿	♀	♂	⚳	♃	♄	♅	♆	♇
1 F	4 38 23	10♊37 59	9♐39 04	15♐50 15	11♓37.3	3♋54.4	25♋46.2	12♈44.9	28♈28.4	15♐28.7	19♌42.9	18♓29.7	22♒01.2	28♐05.8
2 Sa	4 42 19	11 35 28	22 04 05	28 20 36	11R24.4	4 54.0	26 46.6	13 29.8	28 49.8	15R21.1	19 47.1	18 30.7	22R00.9	28R04.3
3 Su	4 46 16	12 32 56	4♑39 49	11♑01 45	11 13.3	5 49.7	27 46.5	14 14.6	29 11.2	15 13.5	19 51.5	18 31.7	22 00.6	28 02.8
4 M	4 50 13	13 30 23	17 26 27	23 53 59	11 04.7	6 41.7	28 46.1	14 59.4	29 32.6	15 05.8	19 55.9	18 32.6	22 00.3	28 01.3
5 Tu	4 54 09	14 27 49	0♒24 24	6♒57 48	10 59.0	7 29.6	29 45.3	15 44.1	29 53.8	14 58.2	20 00.4	18 33.6	22 00.0	27 59.8
6 W	4 58 06	15 25 14	13 34 20	20 14 08	10 56.0	8 13.6	0♌44.1	16 28.8	0♉15.0	14 50.6	20 04.9	18 34.4	21 59.6	27 58.3
7 Th	5 02 02	16 22 39	26 57 22	3♓44 13	10 54.9	8 53.5	1 42.5	17 13.4	0 36.2	14 42.9	20 09.6	18 35.2	21 59.2	27 56.8
8 F	5 05 59	17 20 03	10♓34 51	17 29 24	10 54.9	9 29.1	2 40.5	17 58.0	0 57.2	14 35.3	20 14.3	18 36.0	21 58.7	27 55.3
9 Sa	5 09 55	18 17 27	24 27 58	1♈30 35	10 54.5	10 00.5	3 38.0	18 42.5	1 18.2	14 27.6	20 19.1	18 36.7	21 58.3	27 53.7
10 Su	5 13 52	19 14 50	8♈37 13	15 47 41	10 52.6	10 27.5	4 35.1	19 27.0	1 39.1	14 20.0	20 24.0	18 37.3	21 57.8	27 52.2
11 M	5 17 48	20 12 12	23 01 43	0♉18 52	10 48.4	10 50.2	5 31.8	20 11.4	1 59.9	14 12.4	20 28.9	18 38.0	21 57.2	27 50.6
12 Tu	5 21 45	21 09 35	7♉38 35	15 00 09	10 41.6	11 08.3	6 28.0	20 55.7	2 20.7	14 04.9	20 34.0	18 38.5	21 56.7	27 49.1
13 W	5 25 42	22 06 56	22 22 45	29 45 27	10 32.4	11 21.9	7 23.6	21 40.0	2 41.3	13 57.3	20 39.1	18 39.0	21 56.1	27 47.5
14 Th	5 29 38	23 04 17	7♊07 14	14♊27 06	10 21.7	11 30.9	8 18.8	22 24.2	3 01.9	13 49.8	20 44.2	18 39.5	21 55.4	27 46.0
15 F	5 33 35	24 01 38	21 44 03	28 57 09	10 10.8	11R35.4	9 13.5	23 08.4	3 22.4	13 42.4	20 49.5	18 39.9	21 54.8	27 44.4
16 Sa	5 37 31	24 58 58	6♋05 35	13♋08 39	10 00.7	11 35.3	10 07.6	23 52.5	3 42.8	13 35.0	20 54.8	18 40.3	21 54.1	27 42.9
17 Su	5 41 28	25 56 17	20 05 48	26 56 42	9 52.7	11 30.8	11 01.2	24 36.6	4 03.2	13 27.6	21 00.2	18 40.6	21 53.4	27 41.3
18 M	5 45 24	26 53 35	3♌41 09	10♌19 08	9 47.0	11 21.9	11 54.2	25 20.5	4 23.4	13 20.3	21 05.6	18 40.9	21 52.7	27 39.8
19 Tu	5 49 21	27 50 53	16 50 46	23 16 18	9 43.9	11 08.8	12 46.5	26 04.4	4 43.6	13 13.1	21 11.2	18 41.1	21 51.9	27 38.2
20 W	5 53 17	28 48 10	29 36 08	5♍50 43	9D42.8	10 51.6	13 38.3	26 48.3	5 03.6	13 06.0	21 16.7	18 41.3	21 51.1	27 36.6
21 Th	5 57 14	29 45 26	12♍00 36	18 06 23	9 42.9	10 30.7	14 29.4	27 32.0	5 23.6	12 58.9	21 22.4	18 41.4	21 50.3	27 35.1
22 F	6 01 11	0♋42 41	24 08 42	0♎08 13	9R43.2	10 06.3	15 19.8	28 15.7	5 43.4	12 51.9	21 28.1	18 41.5	21 49.4	27 33.5
23 Sa	6 05 07	1 39 56	6♎05 36	12 01 32	9 42.7	9 38.8	16 09.5	28 59.3	6 03.2	12 45.0	21 33.9	18R41.5	21 48.6	27 31.9
24 Su	6 09 04	2 37 10	17 56 38	23 51 34	9 40.4	9 08.7	16 58.4	29 42.9	6 22.9	12 38.1	21 39.7	18 41.5	21 47.7	27 30.4
25 M	6 13 00	3 34 23	29 46 55	5♏43 15	9 36.0	8 36.4	17 46.6	0♉26.4	6 42.4	12 31.4	21 45.6	18 41.5	21 46.7	27 28.8
26 Tu	6 16 57	4 31 36	11♏41 06	17 40 54	9 29.2	8 02.4	18 34.0	1 09.8	7 01.9	12 24.8	21 51.6	18 41.3	21 45.8	27 27.3
27 W	6 20 53	5 28 48	23 43 06	29 48 01	9 20.3	7 27.3	19 20.6	1 53.1	7 21.3	12 18.2	21 57.6	18 41.2	21 44.8	27 25.7
28 Th	6 24 50	6 26 00	5♐55 58	12♐07 08	9 09.9	6 51.8	20 06.4	2 36.3	7 40.5	12 11.8	22 03.6	18 41.0	21 43.8	27 24.2
29 F	6 28 46	7 23 12	18 21 41	24 39 43	8 59.1	6 16.3	20 51.3	3 19.5	7 59.7	12 05.5	22 09.8	18 40.7	21 42.8	27 22.7
30 Sa	6 32 43	8 20 24	1♑01 15	7♑26 17	8 48.7	5 41.5	21 35.2	4 02.6	8 18.8	11 59.3	22 16.0	18 40.4	21 41.7	27 21.1

Astro Data

	Dy Hr Mn
⚳0N	4 22:13
♃△♄	6 7:11
♃□♅	11 3:32
☽0N	12 21:47
♂0N	20 4:36
♆R	25 1:08
☽0S	25 22:21
☽0N	9 4:00
☿R	15 23:41
☽0S	22 4:54
♅R	23 14:43
♄☍♆	25 15:54

Planet Ingress

		Dy Hr Mn
♀	♋	8 7:28
☿	♊	11 9:17
♂	♈	15 14:06
☉	♊	21 10:12
☿	♋	29 0:56
♀	♌	5 17:59
⚳	♉	5 18:59
☉	♋	21 18:06
♂	♉	24 21:27

Last Aspect / ☽ Ingress

Last Aspect Dy Hr Mn			☽ Ingress	Dy Hr Mn
1 8:07	♇	⚹	♏	1 10:41
3 6:42	♆	□	♐	3 22:48
6 6:46	♇	☌	♑	6 9:21
8 7:35	♂	⚹	♒	8 17:48
10 21:47	☿	□	♓	10 23:32
12 23:53	♇	□	♈	13 2:19
15 0:24	♇	△	♉	15 2:48
16 19:27	☉	☌	♊	17 2:34
19 0:57	♇	☍	♋	19 3:38
21 7:46	☉	⚹	♌	21 7:57
23 13:09	♇	△	♍	23 16:26
26 0:44	♇	□	♎	26 4:16
28 16:17	☿	△	♏	28 17:11
30 17:11	♀	△	♐	31 5:07

Last Aspect / ☽ Ingress

Last Aspect Dy Hr Mn			☽ Ingress	Dy Hr Mn
2 11:29	♇	☌	♑	2 15:09
4 21:43	♀	☍	♒	4 23:15
7 1:47	♇	⚹	♓	7 5:24
9 5:52	♇	□	♈	9 9:26
11 7:57	♇	△	♉	11 11:29
12 23:17	♆	□	♊	13 12:24
15 9:59	♇	☍	♋	15 13:45
17 7:39	♂	□	♌	17 17:25
19 21:22	☉	⚹	♍	20 0:46
22 6:50	♇	□	♎	22 11:43
24 19:23	♇	⚹	♏	25 0:26
26 20:23	♄	□	♐	27 12:24
29 17:08	♇	☌	♑	29 22:05

☽ Phases & Eclipses

Dy Hr Mn		
2 10:09	○	11♏38
10 4:27	☾	19♒09
16 19:27	●	25♉33
23 21:03	☽	2♍21
1 1:04	○	10♐12
8 11:43	☾	17♓19
15 3:13	●	23♊41
22 13:15	☽	0♎46
30 13:49	○	8♑25

Astro Data

1 May 2007
Julian Day # 39202
SVP 5♓09'23"
GC 26♐56.5 ⚴ 10♓15.4
Eris 21♈05.6 ⚵ 15♎12.4R
⚷ 15♒28.4 ⚶ 14♐25.4R
☽ Mean ☊ 13♓17.2

1 June 2007
Julian Day # 39233
SVP 5♓09'18"
GC 26♐56.6 ⚴ 16♓34.9
Eris 21♈22.6 ⚵ 12♎04.4R
⚷ 15♒37.0R ⚶ 8♐20.3R
☽ Mean ☊ 11♓38.7

July 2007 LONGITUDE

Day	Sid.Time	☉	0 hr ☽	Noon ☽	True ☊	☿	♀	♂	⚳	♃	♄	♅	♆	♇
1 Su	6 36 40	9♋17 35	13♑54 43	20♑26 27	8♓39.8	5♋08.0	22♌18.2	4♉45.7	8♉37.7	11♐53.2	22♌22.2	18♓40.1	21♒40.6	27♐19.6
2 M	6 40 36	10 14 46	27 01 22	3♒39 19	8R 33.0	4R 36.5	23 00.2	5 28.6	8 56.5	11R 47.2	22 28.5	18R 39.7	21R 39.5	27R 18.1
3 Tu	6 44 33	11 11 57	10♒20 10	17 03 45	8 28.7	4 07.3	23 41.2	6 11.5	9 15.3	11 41.4	22 34.8	18 39.2	21 38.4	27 16.6
4 W	6 48 29	12 09 09	23 49 58	0♓38 41	8D 26.7	3 41.2	24 21.2	6 54.3	9 33.9	11 35.6	22 41.2	18 38.7	21 37.3	27 15.1
5 Th	6 52 26	13 06 20	7♓29 50	14 23 19	8 26.6	3 18.5	25 00.0	7 37.0	9 52.3	11 30.1	22 47.6	18 38.2	21 36.1	27 13.6
6 F	6 56 22	14 03 32	21 19 06	28 17 07	8 27.4	2 59.6	25 37.7	8 19.6	10 10.7	11 24.6	22 54.1	18 37.6	21 34.9	27 12.1
7 Sa	7 00 19	15 00 44	5♈17 19	12♈19 36	8R 28.0	2 44.9	26 14.2	9 02.2	10 29.0	11 19.3	23 00.7	18 37.0	21 33.7	27 10.6
8 Su	7 04 16	15 57 56	19 23 53	26 29 59	8 27.6	2 34.7	26 49.6	9 44.6	10 47.1	11 14.1	23 07.3	18 36.3	21 32.5	27 09.2
9 M	7 08 12	16 55 09	3♉37 41	10♉46 42	8 25.4	2D 29.3	27 23.6	10 27.0	11 05.1	11 09.1	23 13.9	18 35.6	21 31.2	27 07.7
10 Tu	7 12 09	17 52 22	17 56 41	25 07 09	8 21.1	2 28.8	27 56.3	11 09.3	11 22.9	11 04.2	23 20.6	18 34.8	21 29.9	27 06.3
11 W	7 16 05	18 49 36	2♊17 38	9♊27 32	8 15.0	2 33.5	28 27.7	11 51.5	11 40.7	10 59.5	23 27.3	18 34.0	21 28.6	27 04.8
12 Th	7 20 02	19 46 50	16 36 13	23 43 03	8 07.7	2 43.3	28 57.6	12 33.6	11 58.3	10 54.9	23 34.1	18 33.1	21 27.3	27 03.4
13 F	7 23 58	20 44 04	0♋47 22	7♋48 34	8 00.1	2 58.5	29 26.1	13 15.5	12 15.8	10 50.4	23 40.9	18 32.2	21 26.0	27 02.0
14 Sa	7 27 55	21 41 19	14 46 03	21 39 19	7 53.1	3 19.0	29 53.1	13 57.4	12 33.1	10 46.2	23 47.7	18 31.3	21 24.6	27 00.6
15 Su	7 31 51	22 38 34	28 27 57	5♌11 37	7 47.6	3 44.9	0♍18.5	14 39.2	12 50.3	10 42.1	23 54.6	18 30.3	21 23.3	26 59.3
16 M	7 35 48	23 35 50	11♌50 09	18 23 26	7 43.9	4 16.1	0 42.2	15 20.9	13 07.3	10 38.1	24 01.5	18 29.3	21 21.9	26 57.9
17 Tu	7 39 45	24 33 05	24 51 29	1♍14 27	7D 42.2	4 52.7	1 04.2	16 02.5	13 24.2	10 34.4	24 08.5	18 28.2	21 20.5	26 56.6
18 W	7 43 41	25 30 21	7♍32 34	13 46 08	7 42.1	5 34.6	1 24.5	16 44.0	13 40.9	10 30.8	24 15.5	18 27.1	21 19.1	26 55.2
19 Th	7 47 38	26 27 36	19 55 33	26 01 17	7 43.2	6 21.8	1 42.9	17 25.4	13 57.5	10 27.3	24 22.5	18 25.9	21 17.6	26 53.9
20 F	7 51 34	27 24 52	2♎03 51	8♎03 49	7 44.8	7 14.2	1 59.4	18 06.6	14 14.0	10 24.0	24 29.6	18 24.7	21 16.2	26 52.6
21 Sa	7 55 31	28 22 09	14 01 46	19 58 19	7R 46.0	8 11.7	2 14.0	18 47.8	14 30.2	10 21.0	24 36.7	18 23.4	21 14.7	26 51.4
22 Su	7 59 27	29 19 25	25 54 06	1♏49 43	7 46.3	9 14.4	2 26.6	19 28.8	14 46.3	10 18.0	24 43.9	18 22.1	21 13.2	26 50.1
23 M	8 03 24	0♌16 42	7♏45 49	13 43 00	7 45.3	10 22.0	2 37.1	20 09.8	15 02.3	10 15.3	24 51.0	18 20.8	21 11.7	26 48.9
24 Tu	8 07 20	1 13 59	19 41 50	25 42 54	7 42.7	11 34.6	2 45.5	20 50.6	15 18.1	10 12.7	24 58.2	18 19.5	21 10.2	26 47.6
25 W	8 11 17	2 11 17	1♐46 42	7♐53 42	7 38.7	12 52.0	2 51.7	21 31.3	15 33.7	10 10.3	25 05.5	18 18.1	21 08.7	26 46.4
26 Th	8 15 14	3 08 35	14 04 18	20 18 51	7 33.7	14 14.1	2 55.6	22 11.9	15 49.2	10 08.1	25 12.7	18 16.6	21 07.2	26 45.2
27 F	8 19 10	4 05 53	26 37 37	3♑00 48	7 28.2	15 40.8	2R 57.3	22 52.4	16 04.5	10 06.1	25 20.0	18 15.1	21 05.7	26 44.1
28 Sa	8 23 07	5 03 12	9♑28 31	16 00 47	7 22.9	17 11.8	2 56.7	23 32.8	16 19.6	10 04.3	25 27.3	18 13.6	21 04.1	26 42.9
29 Su	8 27 03	6 00 32	22 37 34	29 18 45	7 18.4	18 47.2	2 53.7	24 13.0	16 34.5	10 02.6	25 34.7	18 12.1	21 02.6	26 41.8
30 M	8 31 00	6 57 53	6♒04 05	12♒53 20	7 15.2	20 26.5	2 48.3	24 53.1	16 49.3	10 01.1	25 42.0	18 10.5	21 01.0	26 40.7
31 Tu	8 34 56	7 55 14	19 46 11	26 42 15	7D 13.4	22 09.6	2 40.6	25 33.2	17 03.8	9 59.8	25 49.4	18 08.8	20 59.4	26 39.6

August 2007 LONGITUDE

Day	Sid.Time	☉	0 hr ☽	Noon ☽	True ☊	☿	♀	♂	⚳	♃	♄	♅	♆	♇
1 W	8 38 53	8♌52 36	3♓41 08	10♓42 27	7♓13.1	23♋56.3	2♍30.5	26♉13.1	17♉18.2	9♐58.7	25♌56.8	18♓07.2	20♒57.8	26♐38.6
2 Th	8 42 49	9 49 59	17 45 46	24 50 41	7 13.9	25 46.2	2R 17.9	26 52.8	17 32.4	9R 57.8	26 04.2	18R 05.5	20R 56.3	26R 37.5
3 F	8 46 46	10 47 23	1♈56 48	9♈03 45	7 15.2	27 39.0	2 03.0	27 32.5	17 46.4	9 57.0	26 11.7	18 03.8	20 54.7	26 36.5
4 Sa	8 50 43	11 44 48	16 11 11	23 18 47	7 16.6	29 34.5	1 45.8	28 12.0	18 00.2	9 56.4	26 19.1	18 02.0	20 53.0	26 35.5
5 Su	8 54 39	12 42 14	0♉26 12	7♉33 11	7R 17.4	1♌32.1	1 26.4	28 51.4	18 13.8	9 56.0	26 26.6	18 00.2	20 51.4	26 34.6
6 M	8 58 36	13 39 42	14 39 26	21 44 42	7 17.3	3 31.6	1 04.7	29 30.6	18 27.2	9D 55.8	26 34.1	17 58.4	20 49.8	26 33.6
7 Tu	9 02 32	14 37 11	28 48 41	5♊51 09	7 16.1	5 32.7	0 40.9	0♊09.7	18 40.4	9 55.8	26 41.7	17 56.5	20 48.2	26 32.7
8 W	9 06 29	15 34 42	12♊51 48	19 50 23	7 14.0	7 34.9	0 15.0	0 48.7	18 53.3	9 56.0	26 49.2	17 54.6	20 46.6	26 31.8
9 Th	9 10 25	16 32 14	26 46 37	3♋40 14	7 11.4	9 37.9	29♌47.2	1 27.6	19 06.1	9 56.3	26 56.7	17 52.7	20 45.0	26 31.0
10 F	9 14 22	17 29 47	10♋30 57	17 18 32	7 08.5	11 41.4	29 17.7	2 06.2	19 18.6	9 56.9	27 04.3	17 50.8	20 43.3	26 30.1
11 Sa	9 18 18	18 27 21	24 02 45	0♌43 23	7 06.0	13 45.1	28 46.5	2 44.8	19 31.0	9 57.6	27 11.9	17 48.8	20 41.7	26 29.3
12 Su	9 22 15	19 24 57	7♌20 17	13 53 18	7 04.0	15 48.7	28 13.8	3 23.2	19 43.0	9 58.5	27 19.5	17 46.8	20 40.1	26 28.5
13 M	9 26 12	20 22 33	20 22 22	26 47 28	7D 02.9	17 52.0	27 39.9	4 01.4	19 54.9	9 59.6	27 27.1	17 44.8	20 38.4	26 27.8
14 Tu	9 30 08	21 20 11	3♍08 36	9♍25 54	7 02.7	19 54.7	27 04.8	4 39.5	20 06.5	10 00.9	27 34.7	17 42.7	20 36.8	26 27.0
15 W	9 34 05	22 17 50	15 39 29	21 49 34	7 03.2	21 56.7	26 28.9	5 17.4	20 17.9	10 02.3	27 42.3	17 40.6	20 35.1	26 26.3
16 Th	9 38 01	23 15 30	27 56 25	4♎00 21	7 04.1	23 57.9	25 52.3	5 55.2	20 29.0	10 04.0	27 49.9	17 38.5	20 33.5	26 25.6
17 F	9 41 58	24 13 11	10♎01 43	16 00 58	7 05.3	25 58.1	25 15.2	6 32.8	20 39.9	10 05.8	27 57.5	17 36.4	20 31.9	26 25.0
18 Sa	9 45 54	25 10 53	21 58 31	27 54 53	7 06.5	27 57.1	24 37.9	7 10.2	20 50.6	10 07.8	28 05.2	17 34.3	20 30.2	26 24.4
19 Su	9 49 51	26 08 36	3♏50 35	9♏46 09	7 07.4	29 55.1	24 00.7	7 47.5	21 00.9	10 10.0	28 12.8	17 32.1	20 28.6	26 23.8
20 M	9 53 47	27 06 21	15 42 10	21 39 13	7R 07.8	1♍51.7	23 23.7	8 24.6	21 11.1	10 12.4	28 20.4	17 29.9	20 27.0	26 23.2
21 Tu	9 57 44	28 04 06	27 37 53	3♐38 44	7 07.8	3 47.1	22 47.3	9 01.6	21 20.9	10 14.9	28 28.1	17 27.7	20 25.4	26 22.7
22 W	10 01 41	29 01 53	9♐42 21	15 49 16	7 07.4	5 41.2	22 11.6	9 38.3	21 30.5	10 17.7	28 35.7	17 25.5	20 23.8	26 22.1
23 Th	10 05 37	29 59 41	22 00 02	28 15 07	7 06.8	7 34.0	21 36.8	10 14.9	21 39.9	10 20.6	28 43.3	17 23.2	20 22.1	26 21.7
24 F	10 09 34	0♍57 30	4♑34 57	10♑59 52	7 06.0	9 25.4	21 03.2	10 51.3	21 48.9	10 23.6	28 51.0	17 21.0	20 20.5	26 21.2
25 Sa	10 13 30	1 55 20	17 30 11	24 06 06	7 05.3	11 15.4	20 31.0	11 27.6	21 57.7	10 26.9	28 58.6	17 18.7	20 18.9	26 20.8
26 Su	10 17 27	2 53 12	0♒47 40	7♒34 55	7 04.8	13 04.1	20 00.4	12 03.6	22 06.2	10 30.3	29 06.2	17 16.4	20 17.4	26 20.4
27 M	10 21 23	3 51 05	14 27 42	21 25 46	7 04.5	14 51.5	19 31.4	12 39.5	22 14.5	10 33.9	29 13.9	17 14.1	20 15.8	26 20.1
28 Tu	10 25 20	4 48 59	28 28 45	5♓36 11	7D 04.4	16 37.5	19 04.4	13 15.2	22 22.4	10 37.7	29 21.5	17 11.8	20 14.2	26 19.7
29 W	10 29 16	5 46 55	12♓47 29	20 01 59	7 04.5	18 22.3	18 39.3	13 50.7	22 30.1	10 41.6	29 29.1	17 09.5	20 12.6	26 19.4
30 Th	10 33 13	6 44 52	27 18 56	4♈37 36	7R 04.5	20 05.7	18 16.4	14 26.0	22 37.4	10 45.7	29 36.7	17 07.1	20 11.1	26 19.1
31 F	10 37 10	7 42 52	11♈57 10	19 16 51	7 04.5	21 47.8	17 55.7	15 01.1	22 44.5	10 50.0	29 44.3	17 04.8	20 09.5	26 18.9

Astro Data	Dy Hr Mn
☽ 0N	6 8:41
☿ D	10 2:14
☽ 0S	19 12:21
♀ R	27 17:28
☽ 0N	2 14:06
♄△♇	6 10:35
♃ D	7 2:04
☽ 0S	15 20:15
☽ 0N	29 21:53

Planet Ingress		Dy Hr Mn
♀	♍	14 18:23
☉	♌	23 5:00
☿	♌	4 17:15
♂	♊	7 6:01
♀	♌R	9 1:10
☿	♍	19 13:01
☉	♍	23 12:08

Last Aspect Dy Hr Mn			☽ Ingress	Dy Hr Mn
1 8:45	♅	✶	♒	2 5:24
4 6:03	♇	✶	♓	4 10:52
6 10:08	♇	□	♈	6 14:57
8 13:06	♇	△	♉	8 17:54
10 16:54	♀	□	♊	10 20:10
12 21:12	♀	✶	♋	12 22:39
14 12:04	☉	☌	♌	15 2:43
17 3:55	♇	△	♍	17 9:39
19 13:44	♇	□	♎	19 19:53
22 6:29	☉	□	♏	22 8:18
24 10:30	♄	□	♐	24 20:29
27 0:13	♇	☌	♑	27 6:21
29 2:23	♂	△	♒	29 13:14
31 11:56	♇	✶	♓	31 17:40

Last Aspect Dy Hr Mn			☽ Ingress	Dy Hr Mn
2 15:37	♂	✶	♈	2 20:43
4 17:31	♇	△	♉	4 23:16
7 1:50	♂	☌	♊	7 2:01
9 5:27	♀	✶	♋	9 5:36
10 12:57	♅	△	♌	11 10:42
13 13:34	♀	☌	♍	13 18:03
15 21:02	♇	□	♎	16 4:04
18 12:21	♄	✶	♏	18 16:13
21 1:34	♄	□	♐	21 4:44
23 12:54	♄	△	♑	23 15:20
24 23:41	♅	✶	♒	25 22:35
28 1:23	♄	☍	♓	28 2:34
29 22:22	♇	□	♈	30 4:25

☽ Phases & Eclipses Dy Hr Mn		
7 16:54	☾	15♈12
14 12:04	●	21♋41
22 6:29	☽	29♎06
30 0:48	○	6♒31
5 21:20	☾	13♉05
12 23:03	●	19♌51
20 23:54	☽	27♏35
28 10:35	○	4♓46
28 10:37	☍	T 1.476

Astro Data

1 July 2007
Julian Day # 39263
SVP 5♓09'12"
GC 26♐56.6 ⚴ 19♓20.8
Eris 21♈32.1 ⚵ 13♎55.1
⚷ 14♒47.5R ⚶ 2♐50.3R
☽ Mean ☊ 10♓03.5

1 August 2007
Julian Day # 39294
SVP 5♓09'06"
GC 26♐56.7 ⚴ 17♓18.4R
Eris 21♈32.6R ⚵ 19♎36.9
⚷ 13♒16.4R ⚶ 3♐56.9
☽ Mean ☊ 8♓25.0

LONGITUDE — September 2007

Day	Sid.Time	☉	0 hr ☽	Noon ☽	True ☊	☿	♀	♂	⯲	♃	♄	♅	♆	♇
1 Sa	10 41 06	8♍40 53	26♈35 54	3♉53 37	7♓04.4	23♍28.7	17♌37.3	15♊36.0	22♉51.2	10♐54.4	29♌51.9	17♓02.4	20♒08.0	26♐18.7
2 Su	10 45 03	9 38 56	11♉09 22	18 22 37	7R04.2	25 08.3	17R21.2	16 10.7	22 57.6	10 59.0	29 59.4	17R00.0	20R06.5	26R18.5
3 M	10 48 59	10 37 01	25 32 53	2♊39 48	7D04.0	26 46.7	17 07.5	16 45.2	23 03.8	11 03.8	0♍07.0	16 57.7	20 05.0	26 18.4
4 Tu	10 52 56	11 35 08	9♊43 07	16 42 36	7 04.0	28 23.9	16 56.3	17 19.5	23 09.6	11 08.7	0 14.5	16 55.3	20 03.5	26 18.3
5 W	10 56 52	12 33 17	23 38 09	0♋29 43	7 04.2	29 59.8	16 47.5	17 53.5	23 15.1	11 13.8	0 22.1	16 52.9	20 02.0	26 18.2
6 Th	11 00 49	13 31 28	7♋17 17	14 00 53	7 04.7	1♎34.6	16 41.1	18 27.4	23 20.2	11 19.1	0 29.6	16 50.5	20 00.5	26 18.1
7 F	11 04 45	14 29 41	20 40 36	27 16 32	7 05.4	3 08.1	16 37.1	19 01.0	23 25.0	11 24.5	0 37.1	16 48.1	19 59.1	26D18.1
8 Sa	11 08 42	15 27 56	3♌48 47	10♌17 28	7 06.1	4 40.5	16D35.5	19 34.4	23 29.5	11 30.0	0 44.6	16 45.7	19 57.6	26 18.1
9 Su	11 12 39	16 26 13	16 42 43	23 04 39	7 06.7	6 11.7	16 36.2	20 07.6	23 33.7	11 35.8	0 52.1	16 43.3	19 56.2	26 18.2
10 M	11 16 35	17 24 32	29 23 25	5♍39 08	7R07.0	7 41.7	16 39.3	20 40.5	23 37.5	11 41.6	0 59.5	16 40.9	19 54.8	26 18.2
11 Tu	11 20 32	18 22 52	11♍51 57	18 02 01	7 06.8	9 10.5	16 44.7	21 13.1	23 40.9	11 47.7	1 06.9	16 38.5	19 53.4	26 18.3
12 W	11 24 28	19 21 15	24 09 30	0♎14 33	7 06.0	10 38.0	16 52.2	21 45.6	23 44.0	11 53.8	1 14.3	16 36.1	19 52.0	26 18.5
13 Th	11 28 25	20 19 39	6♎17 24	12 18 15	7 04.5	12 04.4	17 02.0	22 17.7	23 46.8	12 00.2	1 21.7	16 33.7	19 50.6	26 18.6
14 F	11 32 21	21 18 05	18 17 21	24 14 59	7 02.5	13 29.6	17 13.8	22 49.6	23 49.2	12 06.7	1 29.1	16 31.3	19 49.3	26 18.9
15 Sa	11 36 18	22 16 32	0♏11 28	6♏07 07	7 00.2	14 53.5	17 27.7	23 21.2	23 51.2	12 13.3	1 36.4	16 28.9	19 48.0	26 19.1
16 Su	11 40 14	23 15 02	12 02 21	17 57 33	6 57.8	16 16.1	17 43.7	23 52.6	23 52.9	12 20.1	1 43.7	16 26.6	19 46.7	26 19.4
17 M	11 44 11	24 13 33	23 53 10	29 49 42	6 55.8	17 37.4	18 01.5	24 23.7	23 54.2	12 27.0	1 51.0	16 24.2	19 45.4	26 19.7
18 Tu	11 48 08	25 12 06	5♐47 38	11♐47 31	6 54.4	18 57.4	18 21.3	24 54.5	23 55.2	12 34.1	1 58.2	16 21.8	19 44.1	26 20.0
19 W	11 52 04	26 10 40	17 49 52	23 55 17	6D53.8	20 15.9	18 42.9	25 25.1	23 55.7	12 41.3	2 05.4	16 19.5	19 42.9	26 20.4
20 Th	11 56 01	27 09 16	0♑04 19	6♑17 31	6 54.1	21 33.1	19 06.2	25 55.3	23R55.9	12 48.6	2 12.6	16 17.1	19 41.7	26 20.7
21 F	11 59 57	28 07 54	12 35 27	18 58 35	6 55.1	22 48.7	19 31.3	26 25.3	23 55.8	12 56.1	2 19.8	16 14.8	19 40.5	26 21.2
22 Sa	12 03 54	29 06 34	25 27 26	2♒02 21	6 56.5	24 02.7	19 58.0	26 54.9	23 55.2	13 03.7	2 26.9	16 12.5	19 39.3	26 21.6
23 Su	12 07 50	0♎05 15	8♒43 41	15 31 37	6 58.0	25 15.1	20 26.3	27 24.3	23 54.3	13 11.5	2 34.0	16 10.2	19 38.1	26 22.1
24 M	12 11 47	1 03 58	22 26 14	29 27 29	6R58.9	26 25.8	20 56.2	27 53.3	23 53.0	13 19.4	2 41.0	16 07.9	19 37.0	26 22.7
25 Tu	12 15 43	2 02 42	6♓35 08	13♓48 48	6 58.9	27 34.5	21 27.6	28 22.1	23 51.3	13 27.4	2 48.0	16 05.6	19 35.9	26 23.2
26 W	12 19 40	3 01 29	21 07 54	28 31 41	6 57.7	28 41.3	22 00.4	28 50.5	23 49.3	13 35.5	2 55.0	16 03.3	19 34.8	26 23.8
27 Th	12 23 37	4 00 17	5♈59 17	13♈29 38	6 55.2	29 46.0	22 34.6	29 18.6	23 46.8	13 43.8	3 01.9	16 01.1	19 33.7	26 24.4
28 F	12 27 33	4 59 08	21 01 38	28 34 06	6 51.7	0♏48.5	23 10.2	29 46.3	23 44.0	13 52.2	3 08.8	15 58.8	19 32.7	26 25.1
29 Sa	12 31 30	5 58 01	6♉05 51	13♉35 45	6 47.6	1 48.5	23 47.0	0♋13.8	23 40.8	14 00.7	3 15.7	15 56.6	19 31.7	26 25.7
30 Su	12 35 26	6 56 56	21 02 45	28 25 56	6 43.7	2 45.9	24 25.1	0 40.9	23 37.2	14 09.4	3 22.5	15 54.4	19 30.7	26 26.4

LONGITUDE — October 2007

Day	Sid.Time	☉	0 hr ☽	Noon ☽	True ☊	☿	♀	♂	⯲	♃	♄	♅	♆	♇
1 M	12 39 23	7♎55 53	5♊44 32	12♊57 58	6♓40.5	3♏40.4	25♌04.5	1♋07.6	23♉33.2	14♐18.2	3♍29.3	15♓52.2	19♒29.8	26♐27.2
2 Tu	12 43 19	8 54 53	20 05 47	27 07 45	6D38.5	4 31.9	25 45.0	1 34.0	23R28.9	14 27.0	3 36.0	15R50.1	19R28.8	26 28.0
3 W	12 47 16	9 53 55	4♋03 46	10♋53 51	6 37.9	5 20.1	26 26.6	2 00.0	23 24.1	14 36.1	3 42.7	15 48.0	19 27.9	26 28.8
4 Th	12 51 12	10 52 59	17 38 11	24 17 00	6 38.6	6 04.6	27 09.3	2 25.6	23 19.0	14 45.2	3 49.3	15 45.8	19 27.1	26 29.6
5 F	12 55 09	11 52 06	0♌50 36	7♌19 20	6 40.1	6 45.2	27 53.0	2 50.8	23 13.5	14 54.4	3 55.9	15 43.8	19 26.2	26 30.5
6 Sa	12 59 06	12 51 15	13 43 37	20 03 49	6 41.7	7 21.4	28 37.7	3 15.7	23 07.6	15 03.8	4 02.5	15 41.7	19 25.4	26 31.4
7 Su	13 03 02	13 50 26	26 20 20	2♍33 32	6R42.7	7 53.0	29 23.4	3 40.1	23 01.4	15 13.3	4 09.0	15 39.7	19 24.6	26 32.3
8 M	13 06 59	14 49 39	8♍43 49	14 51 29	6 42.4	8 19.4	0♍10.0	4 04.1	22 54.7	15 22.9	4 15.4	15 37.7	19 23.8	26 33.2
9 Tu	13 10 55	15 48 55	20 56 52	27 00 14	6 40.3	8 40.2	0 57.5	4 27.7	22 47.7	15 32.6	4 21.8	15 35.7	19 23.1	26 34.2
10 W	13 14 52	16 48 12	3♎01 51	9♎01 57	6 36.3	8 55.0	1 45.9	4 50.8	22 40.4	15 42.4	4 28.1	15 33.7	19 22.4	26 35.2
11 Th	13 18 48	17 47 32	15 00 45	20 58 28	6 30.3	9R03.2	2 35.0	5 13.5	22 32.6	15 52.3	4 34.4	15 31.8	19 21.7	26 36.3
12 F	13 22 45	18 46 54	26 55 17	2♏51 23	6 22.8	9 04.4	3 25.0	5 35.8	22 24.5	16 02.3	4 40.6	15 29.9	19 21.1	26 37.4
13 Sa	13 26 41	19 46 18	8♏47 01	14 42 22	6 14.3	8 58.1	4 15.7	5 57.6	22 16.1	16 12.4	4 46.8	15 28.0	19 20.5	26 38.5
14 Su	13 30 38	20 45 43	20 37 41	26 33 14	6 05.7	8 43.9	5 07.2	6 18.9	22 07.3	16 22.6	4 52.9	15 26.2	19 19.9	26 39.6
15 M	13 34 34	21 45 11	2♐29 20	8♐26 17	5 57.8	8 21.4	5 59.4	6 39.7	21 58.2	16 33.0	4 58.9	15 24.4	19 19.3	26 40.7
16 Tu	13 38 31	22 44 41	14 24 28	20 24 17	5 51.3	7 50.5	6 52.3	7 00.0	21 48.8	16 43.4	5 04.9	15 22.7	19 18.8	26 41.9
17 W	13 42 28	23 44 12	26 26 10	2♑30 38	5 46.8	7 11.0	7 45.8	7 19.9	21 39.0	16 53.9	5 10.8	15 20.9	19 18.3	26 43.2
18 Th	13 46 24	24 43 45	8♑38 09	14 49 16	5D44.4	6 23.3	8 40.0	7 39.2	21 29.0	17 04.5	5 16.7	15 19.2	19 17.9	26 44.4
19 F	13 50 21	25 43 20	21 04 33	27 24 33	5 43.8	5 27.7	9 34.8	7 58.0	21 18.6	17 15.2	5 22.5	15 17.6	19 17.4	26 45.7
20 Sa	13 54 17	26 42 57	3♒49 48	10♒20 51	5 44.5	4 25.1	10 30.2	8 16.3	21 08.0	17 26.1	5 28.2	15 16.0	19 17.0	26 47.0
21 Su	13 58 14	27 42 35	16 58 10	23 42 09	5R45.6	3 16.7	11 26.2	8 34.0	20 57.0	17 36.9	5 33.9	15 14.4	19 16.7	26 48.3
22 M	14 02 10	28 42 15	0♓33 09	7♓31 19	5 46.1	2 04.1	12 22.7	8 51.2	20 45.8	17 47.9	5 39.5	15 12.8	19 16.4	26 49.6
23 Tu	14 06 07	29 41 57	14 36 42	21 49 09	5 44.9	0 49.1	13 19.8	9 07.9	20 34.3	17 59.0	5 45.0	15 11.3	19 16.1	26 51.0
24 W	14 10 03	0♏41 40	29 08 20	6♈33 38	5 41.6	29♎33.8	14 17.4	9 23.9	20 22.6	18 10.2	5 50.5	15 09.8	19 15.8	26 52.4
25 Th	14 14 00	1 41 26	14♈04 17	21 39 16	5 35.9	28 20.6	15 15.5	9 39.4	20 10.6	18 21.4	5 55.9	15 08.4	19 15.6	26 53.9
26 F	14 17 57	2 41 13	29 17 21	6♉57 13	5 28.1	27 11.6	16 14.2	9 54.3	19 58.4	18 32.7	6 01.2	15 07.0	19 15.4	26 55.3
27 Sa	14 21 53	3 41 02	14♉37 24	22 16 27	5 19.2	26 09.0	17 13.3	10 08.6	19 46.0	18 44.1	6 06.4	15 05.7	19 15.2	26 56.8
28 Su	14 25 50	4 40 54	29 52 58	7♊25 38	5 10.3	25 14.7	18 12.9	10 22.3	19 33.4	18 55.6	6 11.6	15 04.4	19 15.1	26 58.3
29 M	14 29 46	5 40 47	14♊53 20	22 15 09	5 02.4	24 30.1	19 13.0	10 35.3	19 20.6	19 07.2	6 16.7	15 03.1	19 15.0	26 59.8
30 Tu	14 33 43	6 40 43	29 30 21	6♋38 31	4 56.6	23 56.2	20 13.5	10 47.7	19 07.6	19 18.8	6 21.7	15 01.9	19 14.9	27 01.4
31 W	14 37 39	7 40 41	13♋39 23	20 32 56	4 53.0	23 33.7	21 14.4	10 59.4	18 54.4	19 30.6	6 26.7	15 00.7	19D14.9	27 03.0

Astro Data

	Dy Hr Mn
☿0S	5 19:15
♇ D	7 14:55
♀ D	8 16:14
☽0S	12 3:43
⯲ R	20 13:05
☉0S	23 9:51
☽0N	26 7:59
☽0S	9 10:04
♃□♅	9 18:23
☿ R	12 3:59
☽0N	23 18:45
♃⚹♆	30 3:59
♆ D	31 20:06

Planet Ingress

	Dy Hr Mn
♄ ♍	2 13:49
☿ ♎	5 12:02
☉ ♎	23 9:51
☿ ♏	27 17:17
♂ ♋	28 23:55
♀ ♍	8 6:53
☉ ♏	23 19:15
☿ ♎R	24 3:36

Last Aspect / ☽ Ingress

Last Aspect Dy Hr Mn		☽ Ingress Dy Hr Mn
1 5:19	♄ △	♉ 1 5:35
3 0:47	☿ △	♊ 3 7:30
5 11:01	☿ □	♋ 5 11:08
6 17:04	♅ △	♌ 7 16:59
9 18:07	♇ △	♍ 10 1:10
12 4:14	♇ □	♎ 12 11:31
14 16:10	♇ ⚹	♏ 14 23:37
16 23:40	☉ ⚹	♐ 17 12:21
19 16:48	☉ □	♑ 19 23:52
22 6:15	☉ △	♒ 22 8:18
24 9:14	♂ △	♓ 24 12:55
26 12:31	♂ □	♈ 26 14:22
28 13:59	♂ ⚹	♉ 28 14:17
30 5:10	♀ □	♊ 30 14:34

Last Aspect / ☽ Ingress

Last Aspect Dy Hr Mn		☽ Ingress Dy Hr Mn
2 10:52	♇ ☍	♋ 2 16:57
3 20:41	♅ △	♌ 4 22:27
7 5:28	♀ ☌	♍ 7 7:03
9 11:08	♇ □	♎ 9 17:58
11 23:23	♇ ⚹	♏ 12 6:13
13 21:23	♆ □	♐ 14 18:58
17 0:33	♇ ☌	♑ 17 7:03
19 8:33	☉ □	♒ 19 16:52
21 19:36	☉ △	♓ 21 23:02
23 20:17	♇ □	♈ 24 1:24
25 21:46	☿ ☍	♉ 26 1:07
27 7:15	♆ □	♊ 28 0:11
29 19:51	♇ ☍	♋ 30 0:49

☽ Phases & Eclipses

Dy Hr Mn		
4 2:32	☾	11♊12
11 12:44	●	18♍25
11 12:31:19	●	P 0.751
19 16:48	☽	26♐22
26 19:45	○	3♈20
3 10:06	☾	9♋49
11 5:01	●	17♎30
19 8:33	☽	25♑35
26 4:52	○	2♉23

Astro Data

1 September 2007
Julian Day # 39325
SVP 5♓09'02"
GC 26♐56.8 ⚳ 10♓31.1R
Eris 21♈23.5R ⚵ 27♎44.6
⚷ 11♒40.3R ⚶ 11♐24.5
☽ Mean ☊ 6♓46.5

1 October 2007
Julian Day # 39355
SVP 5♓08'59"
GC 26♐56.9 ⚳ 3♓34.0R
Eris 21♈08.0R ⚵ 6♏59.4
⚷ 10♒39.0R ⚶ 22♐23.5
☽ Mean ☊ 5♓11.2

November 2007 — LONGITUDE

Day	Sid.Time	☉	0 hr ☽	Noon ☽	True ☊	☿	♀	♂	⚳	♃	♄	♅	♆	♇
1 Th	14 41 36	8♏40 41	27♋19 17	3♌58 45	4♓51.6	23♎22.7	22♍15.8	11♋10.5	18♉41.1	19♐42.4	6♍31.5	14♓59.6	19♒14.9	27♐04.6
2 F	14 45 33	9 40 43	10♌31 44	16 58 42	4D51.7	23D23.2	23 17.5	11 20.8	18R27.7	19 54.2	6 36.3	14R58.5	19 14.9	27 06.2
3 Sa	14 49 29	10 40 48	23 20 13	29 36 50	4R52.2	23 34.6	24 19.7	11 30.5	18 14.1	20 06.2	6 41.0	14 57.4	19 15.0	27 07.8
4 Su	14 53 26	11 40 54	5♍49 08	11♍57 43	4 52.1	23 56.5	25 22.2	11 39.4	18 00.4	20 18.2	6 45.6	14 56.4	19 15.1	27 09.5
5 M	14 57 22	12 41 03	18 03 07	24 05 51	4 50.2	24 27.9	26 25.0	11 47.6	17 46.7	20 30.3	6 50.2	14 55.5	19 15.2	27 11.2
6 Tu	15 01 19	13 41 13	0♎06 26	6♎05 19	4 45.8	25 08.1	27 28.3	11 55.1	17 32.8	20 42.4	6 54.6	14 54.5	19 15.4	27 12.9
7 W	15 05 15	14 41 26	12 02 52	17 59 29	4 38.6	25 56.2	28 31.8	12 01.8	17 18.9	20 54.6	6 59.0	14 53.7	19 15.6	27 14.6
8 Th	15 09 12	15 41 40	23 55 27	29 51 03	4 28.4	26 51.2	29 35.7	12 07.8	17 05.0	21 06.9	7 03.3	14 52.9	19 15.9	27 16.4
9 F	15 13 08	16 41 56	5♏46 31	11♏42 03	4 15.9	27 52.4	0♎39.9	12 12.9	16 51.0	21 19.3	7 07.5	14 52.1	19 16.1	27 18.1
10 Sa	15 17 05	17 42 15	17 37 51	23 34 04	4 02.0	28 58.9	1 44.5	12 17.3	16 37.0	21 31.7	7 11.6	14 51.4	19 16.5	27 19.9
11 Su	15 21 01	18 42 34	29 30 51	5♐28 23	3 47.7	0♏10.1	2 49.3	12 20.9	16 23.0	21 44.1	7 15.6	14 50.7	19 16.8	27 21.8
12 M	15 24 58	19 42 56	11♐26 48	17 26 19	3 34.3	1 25.2	3 54.4	12 23.7	16 09.1	21 56.7	7 19.5	14 50.1	19 17.2	27 23.6
13 Tu	15 28 55	20 43 19	23 27 09	29 29 31	3 22.9	2 43.8	4 59.8	12 25.6	15 55.2	22 09.3	7 23.4	14 49.5	19 17.6	27 25.4
14 W	15 32 51	21 43 44	5♑33 42	11♑40 03	3 14.1	4 05.1	6 05.4	12R26.8	15 41.4	22 21.9	7 27.1	14 49.0	19 18.1	27 27.3
15 Th	15 36 48	22 44 10	17 48 55	24 00 42	3 08.3	5 28.9	7 11.4	12 27.0	15 27.6	22 34.6	7 30.8	14 48.5	19 18.5	27 29.2
16 F	15 40 44	23 44 37	0♒15 50	6♒34 49	3 05.3	6 54.8	8 17.5	12 26.5	15 13.9	22 47.4	7 34.3	14 48.1	19 19.1	27 31.1
17 Sa	15 44 41	24 45 06	12 58 08	19 26 16	3D04.3	8 22.2	9 23.9	12 25.1	15 00.4	23 00.2	7 37.8	14 47.7	19 19.6	27 33.0
18 Su	15 48 37	25 45 36	25 59 46	2♓39 03	3R04.3	9 51.1	10 30.6	12 22.9	14 46.9	23 13.0	7 41.2	14 47.4	19 20.2	27 35.0
19 M	15 52 34	26 46 07	9♓24 35	16 16 40	3 03.9	11 21.1	11 37.5	12 19.8	14 33.6	23 25.9	7 44.4	14 47.1	19 20.8	27 36.9
20 Tu	15 56 30	27 46 40	23 15 33	0♈21 20	3 01.9	12 52.1	12 44.6	12 15.8	14 20.5	23 38.9	7 47.6	14 46.8	19 21.5	27 38.9
21 W	16 00 27	28 47 13	7♈33 54	14 52 59	2 57.4	14 23.8	13 52.0	12 11.0	14 07.5	23 51.9	7 50.7	14 46.7	19 22.1	27 40.9
22 Th	16 04 24	29 47 48	22 18 03	29 48 22	2 50.1	15 56.1	14 59.6	12 05.3	13 54.7	24 04.9	7 53.6	14 46.5	19 22.9	27 42.9
23 F	16 08 20	0♐48 24	7♉22 58	15♉00 38	2 40.3	17 28.8	16 07.4	11 58.8	13 42.1	24 18.0	7 56.5	14D46.5	19 23.6	27 44.9
24 Sa	16 12 17	1 49 02	22 40 04	0♊19 47	2 28.9	19 02.0	17 15.4	11 51.4	13 29.7	24 31.1	7 59.3	14 46.4	19 24.4	27 46.9
25 Su	16 16 13	2 49 41	7♊58 18	15 34 11	2 17.2	20 35.4	18 23.6	11 43.1	13 17.6	24 44.3	8 02.0	14 46.5	19 25.2	27 49.0
26 M	16 20 10	3 50 22	23 06 05	0♋32 47	2 06.6	22 09.0	19 32.0	11 34.0	13 05.6	24 57.5	8 04.5	14 46.6	19 26.1	27 51.0
27 Tu	16 24 06	4 51 04	7♋53 22	15 07 02	1 58.2	23 42.8	20 40.6	11 24.0	12 54.0	25 10.7	8 07.0	14 46.7	19 27.0	27 53.1
28 W	16 28 03	5 51 47	22 13 21	29 12 01	1 52.6	25 16.7	21 49.3	11 13.2	12 42.5	25 24.0	8 09.4	14 46.9	19 27.9	27 55.2
29 Th	16 32 00	6 52 32	6♌03 01	12♌46 29	1 49.7	26 50.6	22 58.3	11 01.5	12 31.4	25 37.3	8 11.7	14 47.1	19 28.8	27 57.3
30 F	16 35 56	7 53 19	19 22 44	25 52 13	1D48.7	28 24.6	24 07.5	10 49.0	12 20.5	25 50.7	8 13.8	14 47.4	19 29.8	27 59.4

December 2007 — LONGITUDE

Day	Sid.Time	☉	0 hr ☽	Noon ☽	True ☊	☿	♀	♂	⚳	♃	♄	♅	♆	♇
1 Sa	16 39 53	8♐54 07	2♍15 27	8♍33 03	1♓48.6	29♏58.6	25♎16.8	10♋35.7	12♉09.9	26♐04.1	8♍15.9	14♓47.7	19♒30.8	28♐01.5
2 Su	16 43 49	9 54 56	14 45 38	20 53 52	1R48.3	1♐32.7	26 26.3	10R21.5	11R59.6	26 17.5	8 17.8	14 48.1	19 31.8	28 03.6
3 M	16 47 46	10 55 47	26 58 24	2♎59 54	1 46.4	3 06.7	27 35.9	10 06.6	11 49.7	26 30.9	8 19.6	14 48.5	19 32.9	28 05.7
4 Tu	16 51 42	11 56 40	8♎59 00	14 56 15	1 42.2	4 40.7	28 45.7	9 50.9	11 40.0	26 44.4	8 21.4	14 49.0	19 34.0	28 07.9
5 W	16 55 39	12 57 33	20 52 14	26 47 26	1 35.1	6 14.7	29 55.7	9 34.4	11 30.7	26 57.9	8 23.0	14 49.6	19 35.2	28 10.0
6 Th	16 59 35	13 58 28	2♏42 18	8♏37 15	1 25.0	7 48.7	1♏05.8	9 17.2	11 21.7	27 11.4	8 24.5	14 50.2	19 36.3	28 12.2
7 F	17 03 32	14 59 24	14 32 36	20 28 41	1 12.6	9 22.7	2 16.0	8 59.3	11 13.1	27 25.0	8 25.9	14 50.8	19 37.5	28 14.3
8 Sa	17 07 29	16 00 22	26 25 43	2♐23 56	0 58.5	10 56.8	3 26.4	8 40.7	11 04.8	27 38.6	8 27.2	14 51.5	19 38.7	28 16.5
9 Su	17 11 25	17 01 20	8♐23 29	14 24 30	0 44.1	12 30.8	4 36.9	8 21.5	10 56.9	27 52.2	8 28.4	14 52.2	19 40.0	28 18.7
10 M	17 15 22	18 02 19	20 27 08	26 31 28	0 30.5	14 04.8	5 47.5	8 01.7	10 49.4	28 05.8	8 29.4	14 53.0	19 41.3	28 20.9
11 Tu	17 19 18	19 03 20	2♑37 36	8♑45 38	0 18.8	15 38.9	6 58.3	7 41.3	10 42.2	28 19.4	8 30.4	14 53.9	19 42.6	28 23.0
12 W	17 23 15	20 04 21	14 55 42	21 07 57	0 09.8	17 13.0	8 09.2	7 20.4	10 35.4	28 33.1	8 31.3	14 54.8	19 43.9	28 25.2
13 Th	17 27 11	21 05 22	27 22 33	3♒39 41	0 03.9	18 47.2	9 20.2	6 59.0	10 29.0	28 46.8	8 32.0	14 55.7	19 45.3	28 27.4
14 F	17 31 08	22 06 24	9♒59 38	16 22 39	0 00.8	20 21.4	10 31.3	6 37.1	10 23.0	29 00.4	8 32.6	14 56.7	19 46.7	28 29.6
15 Sa	17 35 04	23 07 27	22 49 02	29 19 09	29♒59.9	21 55.8	11 42.5	6 14.9	10 17.4	29 14.1	8 33.1	14 57.8	19 48.1	28 31.9
16 Su	17 39 01	24 08 30	5♓53 20	12♓31 55	0♓00.3	23 30.2	12 53.8	5 52.3	10 12.2	29 27.9	8 33.5	14 58.9	19 49.6	28 34.1
17 M	17 42 58	25 09 34	19 15 16	26 03 40	0 00.6	25 04.7	14 05.2	5 29.4	10 07.3	29 41.6	8 33.8	15 00.0	19 51.1	28 36.3
18 Tu	17 46 54	26 10 38	2♈57 21	9♈56 28	29♒59.7	26 39.4	15 16.7	5 06.2	10 02.9	29 55.3	8 34.0	15 01.2	19 52.6	28 38.5
19 W	17 50 51	27 11 42	17 01 05	24 11 03	29 56.8	28 14.3	16 28.3	4 42.8	9 58.9	0♑09.1	8R34.1	15 02.5	19 54.1	28 40.7
20 Th	17 54 47	28 12 46	1♉26 09	8♉45 55	29 51.4	29 49.3	17 40.0	4 19.3	9 55.3	0 22.8	8 34.0	15 03.8	19 55.7	28 42.9
21 F	17 58 44	29 13 51	16 09 45	23 36 48	29 43.7	1♑24.4	18 51.8	3 55.7	9 52.1	0 36.6	8 33.9	15 05.1	19 57.3	28 45.1
22 Sa	18 02 40	0♑14 57	1♊06 08	8♊36 38	29 34.5	2 59.8	20 03.7	3 32.0	9 49.3	0 50.3	8 33.6	15 06.5	19 58.9	28 47.3
23 Su	18 06 37	1 16 02	16 07 06	23 36 20	29 24.9	4 35.3	21 15.6	3 08.3	9 46.9	1 04.0	8 33.2	15 07.9	20 00.5	28 49.6
24 M	18 10 34	2 17 08	1♋03 05	8♋26 14	29 16.1	6 11.1	22 27.7	2 44.6	9 44.9	1 17.8	8 32.7	15 09.4	20 02.2	28 51.8
25 Tu	18 14 30	3 18 15	15 44 46	22 57 49	29 09.1	7 47.1	23 39.8	2 21.0	9 43.3	1 31.6	8 32.1	15 11.0	20 03.9	28 54.0
26 W	18 18 27	4 19 22	0♌04 44	7♌05 01	29 04.5	9 23.3	24 52.1	1 57.5	9 42.2	1 45.3	8 31.4	15 12.5	20 05.6	28 56.2
27 Th	18 22 23	5 20 29	13 58 25	20 44 49	29D02.2	10 59.8	26 04.4	1 34.2	9 41.4	1 59.1	8 30.6	15 14.2	20 07.3	28 58.4
28 F	18 26 20	6 21 37	27 24 20	3♍57 10	29 02.0	12 36.4	27 16.8	1 11.1	9D41.0	2 12.9	8 29.7	15 15.8	20 09.0	29 00.6
29 Sa	18 30 16	7 22 45	10♍23 41	16 44 20	29 03.0	14 13.3	28 29.2	0 48.3	9 41.0	2 26.6	8 28.6	15 17.5	20 10.8	29 02.8
30 Su	18 34 13	8 23 54	22 59 40	29 10 15	29R04.1	15 50.4	29 41.8	0 25.8	9 41.4	2 40.3	8 27.5	15 19.3	20 12.6	29 05.0
31 M	18 38 09	9 25 03	5♎16 44	11♎19 45	29 04.5	17 27.8	0♐54.4	0 03.7	9 42.2	2 54.1	8 26.2	15 21.1	20 14.4	29 07.2

Astro Data

	Dy Hr Mn
☿ D	1 23:01
☽0S	5 15:25
♀0S	11 15:19
♂ R	15 8:24
☽0N	20 3:53
♅ D	24 10:15
☽0S	2 20:46
♃☌♇	11 19:36
☽0N	17 10:11
♄ R	19 14:10
⚳ D	28 23:24
☽0S	30 3:33

Planet Ingress

		Dy Hr Mn
♀	♎	8 21:05
☿	♏	11 8:41
☉	♐	22 16:50
☿	♐	1 12:21
♀	♏	5 13:29
☊	♒R	15 6:01
☊	♓	15 21:28
☊	♒R	18 8:05
♃	♑	18 20:11
☿	♑	20 14:43
☉	♑	22 6:08
♀	♐	30 18:02
♂	♊R	31 16:00

Last Aspect / ☽ Ingress

Last Aspect Dy Hr Mn			☽ Ingress	Dy Hr Mn
31 17:13	☿	□	♌	1 4:48
3 7:13	♇	△	♍	3 12:45
5 18:10	♇	□	♎	5 23:47
8 6:46	♇	✶	♏	8 12:18
10 3:19	♆	□	♐	11 0:59
13 7:53	♇	☌	♑	13 13:00
15 9:19	☉	✶	♒	15 23:30
18 2:51	♇	✶	♓	18 7:14
20 7:26	♇	□	♈	20 11:24
22 8:40	♇	△	♉	22 12:18
23 18:53	♆	□	♊	24 11:29
26 7:38	♇	☍	♋	26 11:07
28 4:22	☿	△	♌	28 13:23
30 17:25	☿	□	♍	30 19:44

Last Aspect Dy Hr Mn			☽ Ingress	Dy Hr Mn
3 2:12	♇	□	♎	3 6:01
5 14:48	♇	✶	♏	5 18:31
7 10:16	♆	□	♐	8 7:11
10 15:36	♇	☌	♑	10 18:51
11 23:57	♅	✶	♒	13 5:01
15 11:51	♃	✶	♓	15 13:15
17 18:27	♃	□	♈	17 18:52
19 19:33	☿	△	♉	19 21:38
21 6:06	♆	□	♊	21 22:14
23 20:26	♇	☍	♋	23 22:18
25 13:17	♀	△	♌	25 23:52
28 2:54	♇	△	♍	28 4:44
30 13:08	♀	✶	♎	30 13:37

☽ Phases & Eclipses

Dy Hr Mn		
1 21:18	☾	9♌04
9 23:03	●	17♏10
17 22:33	☽	25♒12
24 14:30	○	1♊55
1 12:44	☾	8♍56
9 17:40	●	17♐16
17 10:17	☽	25♓05
24 1:16	○	1♋50
31 7:51	☾	9♎14

Astro Data

1 November 2007
Julian Day # 39386
SVP 5♓08'55"
GC 26♐56.9 ⚴ 0♓52.1
Eris 20♈49.7R ⚵ 17♏18.4
⚷ 10♒33.1 ⚶ 5♑59.0
☽ Mean ☊ 3♓32.7

1 December 2007
Julian Day # 39416
SVP 5♓08'50"
GC 26♐57.0 ⚴ 3♓24.9
Eris 20♈34.9R ⚵ 27♏31.3
⚷ 11♒27.9 ⚶ 20♑22.5
☽ Mean ☊ 1♓57.4

LONGITUDE — January 2008

Day	Sid.Time	☉	0 hr ☽	Noon ☽	True ☊	☿	♀	♂	⚳	♃	♄	♅	♆	♇
1 Tu	18 42 06	10♑26 13	17♎19 57	23♎17 59	29♒03.4	19♑05.3	2♐07.0	29♊41.9	9♉43.4	3♑07.8	8♍24.9	15♓23.0	20♒16.3	29♐09.4
2 W	18 46 03	11 27 22	29 14 29	5♏10 02	29R 00.3	20 42.9	3 19.8	29R 20.6	9 45.0	3 21.5	8R 23.4	15 24.8	20 18.1	29 11.5
3 Th	18 49 59	12 28 33	11♏05 14	17 00 35	28 55.0	22 20.7	4 32.6	28 59.8	9 47.0	3 35.2	8 21.8	15 26.8	20 20.0	29 13.7
4 F	18 53 56	13 29 43	22 56 36	28 53 42	28 48.0	23 58.6	5 45.4	28 39.4	9 49.3	3 48.9	8 20.1	15 28.8	20 21.9	29 15.9
5 Sa	18 57 52	14 30 54	4♐52 17	10♐52 40	28 39.6	25 36.4	6 58.3	28 19.7	9 52.1	4 02.6	8 18.4	15 30.8	20 23.8	29 18.0
6 Su	19 01 49	15 32 05	16 55 09	22 59 58	28 30.9	27 14.3	8 11.3	28 00.5	9 55.2	4 16.3	8 16.5	15 32.8	20 25.8	29 20.2
7 M	19 05 45	16 33 16	29 07 17	5♑17 15	28 22.6	28 51.9	9 24.3	27 41.9	9 58.8	4 29.9	8 14.5	15 35.0	20 27.7	29 22.3
8 Tu	19 09 42	17 34 27	11♑29 56	17 45 26	28 15.5	0♒29.3	10 37.4	27 24.0	10 02.7	4 43.5	8 12.4	15 37.1	20 29.7	29 24.5
9 W	19 13 38	18 35 38	24 03 45	0♒24 56	28 10.3	2 06.4	11 50.5	27 06.8	10 06.9	4 57.1	8 10.2	15 39.3	20 31.7	29 26.6
10 Th	19 17 35	19 36 48	6♒48 58	13 15 52	28 07.1	3 42.9	13 03.7	26 50.3	10 11.6	5 10.7	8 07.9	15 41.5	20 33.7	29 28.7
11 F	19 21 32	20 37 58	19 45 39	26 18 19	28D 06.0	5 18.7	14 16.9	26 34.5	10 16.6	5 24.3	8 05.5	15 43.8	20 35.7	29 30.8
12 Sa	19 25 28	21 39 07	2♓53 55	9♓32 30	28 06.5	6 53.5	15 30.2	26 19.4	10 21.9	5 37.8	8 03.0	15 46.1	20 37.8	29 32.9
13 Su	19 29 25	22 40 16	16 14 08	22 58 52	28 08.0	8 27.2	16 43.5	26 05.1	10 27.7	5 51.3	8 00.4	15 48.4	20 39.8	29 35.0
14 M	19 33 21	23 41 24	29 46 48	6♈38 00	28 09.5	9 59.3	17 56.8	25 51.6	10 33.8	6 04.8	7 57.7	15 50.8	20 41.9	29 37.0
15 Tu	19 37 18	24 42 32	13♈32 30	20 30 19	28R 10.5	11 29.6	19 10.1	25 38.9	10 40.2	6 18.3	7 54.9	15 53.2	20 44.0	29 39.1
16 W	19 41 14	25 43 39	27 31 24	4♉35 39	28 10.2	12 57.7	20 23.5	25 26.9	10 47.0	6 31.7	7 52.0	15 55.7	20 46.1	29 41.1
17 Th	19 45 11	26 44 45	11♉42 54	18 52 51	28 08.5	14 23.0	21 37.0	25 15.8	10 54.1	6 45.1	7 49.1	15 58.2	20 48.2	29 43.2
18 F	19 49 07	27 45 50	26 05 09	3♊19 19	28 05.4	15 45.2	22 50.5	25 05.5	11 01.5	6 58.4	7 46.0	16 00.7	20 50.3	29 45.2
19 Sa	19 53 04	28 46 55	10♊34 47	17 50 52	28 01.3	17 03.5	24 04.0	24 56.0	11 09.3	7 11.8	7 42.9	16 03.2	20 52.5	29 47.2
20 Su	19 57 01	29 47 59	25 06 53	2♋22 03	27 56.9	18 17.3	25 17.5	24 47.3	11 17.4	7 25.0	7 39.7	16 05.8	20 54.6	29 49.2
21 M	20 00 57	0♒49 02	9♋35 34	16 46 39	27 52.8	19 25.9	26 31.1	24 39.5	11 25.9	7 38.3	7 36.4	16 08.5	20 56.8	29 51.1
22 Tu	20 04 54	1 50 04	23 54 33	0♌58 38	27 49.6	20 28.5	27 44.7	24 32.4	11 34.6	7 51.5	7 33.0	16 11.1	20 59.0	29 53.1
23 W	20 08 50	2 51 06	7♌58 16	14 53 01	27D 47.7	21 24.3	28 58.3	24 26.2	11 43.7	8 04.7	7 29.5	16 13.8	21 01.2	29 55.0
24 Th	20 12 47	3 52 06	21 42 29	28 26 28	27 47.2	22 12.4	0♑12.0	24 20.7	11 53.1	8 17.8	7 26.0	16 16.5	21 03.4	29 56.9
25 F	20 16 43	4 53 06	5♍04 51	11♍37 38	27 47.7	22 52.1	1 25.7	24 16.1	12 02.7	8 30.9	7 22.4	16 19.3	21 05.6	29 58.8
26 Sa	20 20 40	5 54 06	18 04 58	24 27 04	27 49.1	23 22.3	2 39.4	24 12.3	12 12.7	8 43.9	7 18.7	16 22.1	21 07.8	0♑00.7
27 Su	20 24 36	6 55 05	0♎44 15	6♎56 55	27 50.8	23 42.5	3 53.1	24 09.2	12 23.0	8 56.9	7 14.9	16 24.9	21 10.0	0 02.6
28 M	20 28 33	7 56 03	13 05 31	19 10 35	27 52.3	23R 52.1	5 06.9	24 06.9	12 33.5	9 09.9	7 11.1	16 27.7	21 12.2	0 04.4
29 Tu	20 32 30	8 57 00	25 12 39	1♏12 19	27R 53.3	23 50.4	6 20.7	24 05.5	12 44.4	9 22.8	7 07.1	16 30.6	21 14.4	0 06.3
30 W	20 36 26	9 57 57	7♏10 10	13 06 48	27 53.5	23 37.4	7 34.6	24D 04.7	12 55.5	9 35.6	7 03.2	16 33.5	21 16.7	0 08.1
31 Th	20 40 23	10 58 54	19 02 50	24 58 52	27 52.8	23 13.1	8 48.4	24 04.8	13 06.9	9 48.4	6 59.1	16 36.4	21 18.9	0 09.9

LONGITUDE — February 2008

Day	Sid.Time	☉	0 hr ☽	Noon ☽	True ☊	☿	♀	♂	⚳	♃	♄	♅	♆	♇
1 F	20 44 19	11♒59 49	0♐55 29	6♐53 13	27♒51.4	22♒38.0	10♑02.3	24♊05.6	13♉18.6	10♑01.2	6♍55.0	16♓39.4	21♒21.2	0♑11.7
2 Sa	20 48 16	13 00 44	12 52 38	18 54 12	27R 49.4	21R 52.8	11 16.2	24 07.1	13 30.6	10 13.9	6R 50.9	16 42.3	21 23.5	0 13.4
3 Su	20 52 12	14 01 38	24 58 21	1♑05 31	27 47.3	20 58.7	12 30.2	24 09.4	13 42.8	10 26.5	6 46.6	16 45.3	21 25.7	0 15.1
4 M	20 56 09	15 02 31	7♑16 01	13 30 08	27 45.2	19 57.2	13 44.1	24 12.4	13 55.3	10 39.1	6 42.4	16 48.4	21 28.0	0 16.9
5 Tu	21 00 06	16 03 23	19 48 06	26 10 03	27 43.5	18 50.0	14 58.1	24 16.1	14 08.1	10 51.7	6 38.0	16 51.4	21 30.3	0 18.5
6 W	21 04 02	17 04 14	2♒36 05	9♒06 13	27 42.4	17 39.2	16 12.0	24 20.6	14 21.1	11 04.1	6 33.7	16 54.5	21 32.5	0 20.2
7 Th	21 07 59	18 05 04	15 40 24	22 18 33	27D 41.9	16 26.8	17 26.0	24 25.7	14 34.3	11 16.5	6 29.2	16 57.6	21 34.8	0 21.9
8 F	21 11 55	19 05 52	29 00 30	5♓46 02	27 41.9	15 14.8	18 40.0	24 31.5	14 47.9	11 28.9	6 24.8	17 00.7	21 37.1	0 23.5
9 Sa	21 15 52	20 06 40	12♓34 56	19 26 54	27 42.4	14 05.1	19 54.0	24 38.0	15 01.6	11 41.1	6 20.2	17 03.9	21 39.4	0 25.1
10 Su	21 19 48	21 07 25	26 21 38	3♈18 52	27 43.0	12 59.4	21 08.1	24 45.1	15 15.6	11 53.3	6 15.7	17 07.0	21 41.7	0 26.6
11 M	21 23 45	22 08 09	10♈18 15	17 19 28	27 43.6	11 58.9	22 22.1	24 52.9	15 29.9	12 05.5	6 11.1	17 10.2	21 43.9	0 28.2
12 Tu	21 27 41	23 08 52	24 22 13	1♉26 12	27 44.0	11 05.0	23 36.2	25 01.3	15 44.3	12 17.5	6 06.5	17 13.4	21 46.2	0 29.7
13 W	21 31 38	24 09 33	8♉31 07	15 36 40	27R 44.3	10 18.1	24 50.2	25 10.4	15 59.0	12 29.5	6 01.8	17 16.6	21 48.5	0 31.2
14 Th	21 35 34	25 10 12	22 42 34	29 48 33	27 44.3	9 39.0	26 04.3	25 20.0	16 13.9	12 41.5	5 57.1	17 19.8	21 50.8	0 32.7
15 F	21 39 31	26 10 50	6♊54 19	13♊59 35	27 44.2	9 07.7	27 18.3	25 30.2	16 29.1	12 53.3	5 52.4	17 23.1	21 53.1	0 34.1
16 Sa	21 43 28	27 11 26	21 04 03	28 07 26	27D 44.1	8 44.3	28 32.4	25 41.1	16 44.4	13 05.1	5 47.7	17 26.4	21 55.3	0 35.5
17 Su	21 47 24	28 12 00	5♋09 24	12♋09 39	27 44.1	8 28.7	29 46.5	25 52.5	17 00.0	13 16.8	5 42.9	17 29.6	21 57.6	0 36.9
18 M	21 51 21	29 12 32	19 07 50	26 03 38	27 44.2	8D 20.6	1♒00.6	26 04.4	17 15.8	13 28.4	5 38.1	17 32.9	21 59.9	0 38.3
19 Tu	21 55 17	0♓13 03	2♌56 44	9♌46 51	27 44.4	8 19.7	2 14.7	26 16.9	17 31.8	13 39.9	5 33.3	17 36.3	22 02.1	0 39.7
20 W	21 59 14	1 13 31	16 33 40	23 16 58	27R 44.5	8 25.7	3 28.8	26 29.9	17 47.9	13 51.4	5 28.5	17 39.6	22 04.4	0 41.0
21 Th	22 03 10	2 13 59	29 56 31	6♍32 08	27 44.5	8 38.0	4 42.9	26 43.4	18 04.3	14 02.8	5 23.7	17 42.9	22 06.7	0 42.3
22 F	22 07 07	3 14 24	13♍03 45	19 31 16	27 44.2	8 56.4	5 57.1	26 57.4	18 20.9	14 14.1	5 18.9	17 46.3	22 08.9	0 43.5
23 Sa	22 11 03	4 14 48	25 54 43	2♎14 09	27 43.5	9 20.3	7 11.2	27 11.9	18 37.6	14 25.3	5 14.0	17 49.6	22 11.2	0 44.7
24 Su	22 15 00	5 15 11	8♎29 43	14 41 37	27 42.6	9 49.4	8 25.3	27 26.9	18 54.6	14 36.4	5 09.2	17 53.0	22 13.4	0 46.0
25 M	22 18 57	6 15 32	20 50 07	26 55 31	27 41.4	10 23.4	9 39.5	27 42.3	19 11.7	14 47.4	5 04.4	17 56.3	22 15.6	0 47.1
26 Tu	22 22 53	7 15 51	2♏58 12	8♏58 36	27 40.2	11 01.7	10 53.6	27 58.2	19 29.0	14 58.3	4 59.5	17 59.7	22 17.8	0 48.3
27 W	22 26 50	8 16 10	14 57 10	20 54 25	27 39.2	11 44.2	12 07.8	28 14.6	19 46.5	15 09.2	4 54.7	18 03.1	22 20.1	0 49.4
28 Th	22 30 46	9 16 26	26 50 53	2♐47 09	27D 38.6	12 30.5	13 22.0	28 31.4	20 04.1	15 19.9	4 49.9	18 06.5	22 22.3	0 50.5
29 F	22 34 43	10 16 42	8♐43 45	14 41 20	27 38.6	13 20.4	14 36.2	28 48.6	20 22.0	15 30.6	4 45.1	18 09.9	22 24.5	0 51.5

Astro Data

	Dy Hr Mn
♃∠♆	12 11:55
☽0N	13 14:55
♃△♄	21 9:14
☽0S	26 12:10
☿R	28 20:33
♂D	30 22:33
☽0N	9 20:45
☿D	19 2:57
☽0S	22 21:20

Planet Ingress

	Dy Hr Mn
☿ ♒	8 4:46
☉ ♒	20 16:44
♀ ♑	24 8:06
♇ ♑	26 2:37
♀ ♒	17 16:22
☉ ♓	19 6:50

Last Aspect / ☽ Ingress

Last Aspect Dy Hr Mn		☽ Ingress	Dy Hr Mn
2 0:33	♂ △	♏	2 1:32
4 0:30	☿ ⚹	♐	4 14:13
7 0:27	♇ ☌	♑	7 1:43
8 11:37	☉ ☌	♒	9 11:13
11 17:52	♇ ⚹	♓	11 18:44
13 23:41	♇ □	♈	14 0:23
16 3:39	♇ △	♉	16 4:13
18 2:05	☉ △	♊	18 6:30
20 7:46	♇ ☍	♋	20 8:05
21 10:56	♅ △	♌	22 10:20
24 14:43	♇ △	♍	24 14:48
26 11:32	♂ □	♎	26 22:35
28 21:48	♂ △	♏	29 9:35
31 8:35	☿ □	♐	31 22:08

Last Aspect / ☽ Ingress

Last Aspect Dy Hr Mn		☽ Ingress	Dy Hr Mn
2 22:21	♂ ☍	♑	3 9:52
4 18:20	♅ ⚹	♒	5 19:10
7 15:50	♂ △	♓	8 1:46
9 21:05	♂ □	♈	10 6:17
12 1:00	♂ ⚹	♉	12 9:34
14 5:05	♀ △	♊	14 12:19
16 10:17	☉ △	♋	16 15:12
17 21:13	♅ △	♌	18 18:51
20 17:53	♂ ⚹	♍	21 0:06
23 2:15	♂ □	♎	23 7:45
25 13:35	♂ △	♏	25 18:06
27 14:53	♆ □	♐	28 6:22

☽ Phases & Eclipses

Dy Hr Mn	
8 11:37	● 17♑33
15 19:46	☽ 25♈02
22 13:35	○ 1♌54
30 5:03	☾ 9♏40
7 3:44	● 17♒44
7 3:55:03	● A 02'12"
14 3:33	☽ 24♉49
21 3:31	○ 1♍53
21 3:26	● T 1.106
29 2:18	☾ 9♐52

Astro Data

1 January 2008
Julian Day # 39447
SVP 5♓08'44"
GC 26♐57.1 ⚵ 9♓58.8
Eris 20♈27.5R ⚶ 7♐47.4
⚷ 13♒15.0 ⚴ 5♒54.6
☽ Mean ☊ 0♓18.9

1 February 2008
Julian Day # 39478
SVP 5♓08'39"
GC 26♐57.1 ⚵ 19♓06.0
Eris 20♈30.4 ⚶ 17♐07.1
⚷ 15♒31.2 ⚴ 21♒40.5
☽ Mean ☊ 28♒40.4

March 2008 — LONGITUDE

Day	Sid.Time	☉	0 hr ☽	Noon ☽	True ☊	☿	♀	♂	⚳	♃	♄	♅	♆	♇
1 Sa	22 38 39	11♓16 56	20♐40 27	26♐41 42	27♒39.1	14♒13.5	15♒50.3	29♊06.2	20♉40.0	15♑41.2	4♍40.3	18♓13.4	22♒26.7	0♑52.6
2 Su	22 42 36	12 17 08	2♑45 40	8♑52 55	27 40.1	15 09.7	17 04.5	29 24.3	20 58.2	15 51.6	4R 35.5	18 16.8	22 28.8	0 53.6
3 M	22 46 32	13 17 19	15 03 56	21 19 13	27 41.5	16 08.7	18 18.7	29 42.7	21 16.5	16 02.0	4 30.7	18 20.2	22 31.0	0 54.5
4 Tu	22 50 29	14 17 28	27 39 11	4♒04 09	27 42.8	17 10.4	19 32.9	0♋01.6	21 35.0	16 12.2	4 26.0	18 23.6	22 33.2	0 55.5
5 W	22 54 26	15 17 35	10♒34 26	17 10 09	27R 43.8	18 14.5	20 47.1	0 20.8	21 53.7	16 22.4	4 21.3	18 27.1	22 35.3	0 56.4
6 Th	22 58 22	16 17 41	23 51 25	0♓38 10	27 44.1	19 21.0	22 01.3	0 40.4	22 12.5	16 32.4	4 16.6	18 30.5	22 37.5	0 57.3
7 F	23 02 19	17 17 44	7♓30 14	14 27 20	27 43.3	20 29.7	23 15.5	1 00.4	22 31.5	16 42.4	4 11.9	18 33.9	22 39.6	0 58.1
8 Sa	23 06 15	18 17 46	21 29 04	28 34 56	27 41.6	21 40.4	24 29.7	1 20.7	22 50.6	16 52.2	4 07.3	18 37.4	22 41.7	0 58.9
9 Su	23 10 12	19 17 46	5♈44 18	12♈56 30	27 38.9	22 53.1	25 43.9	1 41.4	23 09.8	17 01.9	4 02.7	18 40.8	22 43.8	0 59.7
10 M	23 14 08	20 17 44	20 10 48	27 26 25	27 35.8	24 07.7	26 58.1	2 02.4	23 29.3	17 11.5	3 58.1	18 44.2	22 45.9	1 00.5
11 Tu	23 18 05	21 17 40	4♉42 36	11♉58 36	27 32.6	25 24.0	28 12.3	2 23.8	23 48.8	17 21.0	3 53.6	18 47.7	22 47.9	1 01.2
12 W	23 22 01	22 17 34	19 13 44	26 27 22	27 29.9	26 42.1	29 26.5	2 45.5	24 08.5	17 30.4	3 49.2	18 51.1	22 50.0	1 01.9
13 Th	23 25 58	23 17 25	3♊38 59	10♊48 09	27D 28.2	28 01.8	0♓40.6	3 07.5	24 28.4	17 39.6	3 44.7	18 54.6	22 52.0	1 02.5
14 F	23 29 55	24 17 15	17 54 29	24 57 45	27 27.6	29 23.0	1 54.8	3 29.8	24 48.3	17 48.8	3 40.4	18 58.0	22 54.0	1 03.2
15 Sa	23 33 51	25 17 02	1♋57 47	8♋54 28	27 28.2	0♓45.8	3 09.0	3 52.5	25 08.4	17 57.8	3 36.0	19 01.4	22 56.1	1 03.8
16 Su	23 37 48	26 16 47	15 47 45	22 37 40	27 29.6	2 10.1	4 23.2	4 15.4	25 28.7	18 06.7	3 31.8	19 04.8	22 58.0	1 04.3
17 M	23 41 44	27 16 29	29 24 13	6♌07 28	27 31.2	3 35.9	5 37.3	4 38.6	25 49.0	18 15.4	3 27.5	19 08.2	23 00.0	1 04.9
18 Tu	23 45 41	28 16 09	12♌47 30	19 24 22	27R 32.4	5 03.1	6 51.5	5 02.1	26 09.5	18 24.1	3 23.4	19 11.6	23 02.0	1 05.4
19 W	23 49 37	29 15 47	25 58 08	2♍28 51	27 32.5	6 31.7	8 05.6	5 25.8	26 30.1	18 32.6	3 19.3	19 15.0	23 03.9	1 05.8
20 Th	23 53 34	0♈15 23	8♍56 35	15 21 21	27 31.2	8 01.6	9 19.8	5 49.8	26 50.8	18 41.0	3 15.2	19 18.4	23 05.8	1 06.3
21 F	23 57 30	1 14 56	21 43 13	28 02 11	27 28.1	9 32.9	10 33.9	6 14.1	27 11.7	18 49.2	3 11.2	19 21.8	23 07.7	1 06.7
22 Sa	0 01 27	2 14 28	4♎18 20	10♎31 42	27 23.3	11 05.6	11 48.1	6 38.6	27 32.6	18 57.3	3 07.3	19 25.2	23 09.6	1 07.0
23 Su	0 05 24	3 13 58	16 42 23	22 50 28	27 17.3	12 39.6	13 02.2	7 03.4	27 53.7	19 05.3	3 03.5	19 28.6	23 11.5	1 07.4
24 M	0 09 20	4 13 25	28 56 06	4♏59 27	27 10.5	14 15.0	14 16.3	7 28.4	28 14.9	19 13.2	2 59.7	19 31.9	23 13.3	1 07.7
25 Tu	0 13 17	5 12 51	11♏00 46	17 00 17	27 03.6	15 51.7	15 30.5	7 53.6	28 36.2	19 20.9	2 56.0	19 35.3	23 15.1	1 07.9
26 W	0 17 13	6 12 15	22 58 19	28 55 14	26 57.4	17 29.7	16 44.6	8 19.1	28 57.6	19 28.5	2 52.3	19 38.6	23 16.9	1 08.2
27 Th	0 21 10	7 11 37	4♐51 26	10♐47 22	26 52.4	19 09.1	17 58.7	8 44.8	29 19.1	19 35.9	2 48.7	19 41.9	23 18.7	1 08.4
28 F	0 25 06	8 10 58	16 43 32	22 40 27	26 49.2	20 49.8	19 12.8	9 10.7	29 40.7	19 43.2	2 45.3	19 45.2	23 20.5	1 08.6
29 Sa	0 29 03	9 10 17	28 38 42	4♑38 51	26D 47.7	22 31.9	20 27.0	9 36.8	0♊02.4	19 50.4	2 41.8	19 48.5	23 22.2	1 08.7
30 Su	0 32 59	10 09 33	10♑41 31	16 47 19	26 47.8	24 15.4	21 41.1	10 03.2	0 24.2	19 57.4	2 38.5	19 51.8	23 23.9	1 08.8
31 M	0 36 56	11 08 49	22 56 53	29 10 49	26 48.9	26 00.2	22 55.2	10 29.7	0 46.1	20 04.3	2 35.2	19 55.1	23 25.6	1 08.9

April 2008 — LONGITUDE

Day	Sid.Time	☉	0 hr ☽	Noon ☽	True ☊	☿	♀	♂	⚳	♃	♄	♅	♆	♇
1 Tu	0 40 53	12♈08 02	5♒29 42	11♒54 02	26♒50.3	27♓46.4	24♓09.3	10♋56.5	1♊08.1	20♑11.0	2♍32.1	19♓58.3	23♒27.3	1♑08.9
2 W	0 44 49	13 07 13	18 24 20	25 00 57	26R 51.1	29 34.0	25 23.4	11 23.4	1 30.2	20 17.5	2R 29.0	20 01.5	23 28.9	1R 09.0
3 Th	0 48 46	14 06 23	1♓44 11	8♓34 10	26 50.5	1♈23.1	26 37.5	11 50.6	1 52.4	20 24.0	2 26.0	20 04.8	23 30.5	1 08.9
4 F	0 52 42	15 05 30	15 30 53	22 34 12	26 47.9	3 13.5	27 51.6	12 17.9	2 14.7	20 30.2	2 23.1	20 08.0	23 32.1	1 08.9
5 Sa	0 56 39	16 04 36	29 43 43	6♈58 54	26 43.1	5 05.4	29 05.7	12 45.5	2 37.1	20 36.3	2 20.2	20 11.1	23 33.7	1 08.8
6 Su	1 00 35	17 03 40	14♈19 02	21 43 13	26 36.4	6 58.7	0♈19.8	13 13.2	2 59.6	20 42.3	2 17.5	20 14.3	23 35.2	1 08.7
7 M	1 04 32	18 02 42	29 10 24	6♉39 28	26 28.5	8 53.4	1 33.9	13 41.1	3 22.2	20 48.1	2 14.8	20 17.4	23 36.8	1 08.5
8 Tu	1 08 28	19 01 41	14♉09 14	21 38 32	26 20.4	10 49.6	2 47.9	14 09.2	3 44.8	20 53.7	2 12.3	20 20.6	23 38.3	1 08.4
9 W	1 12 25	20 00 39	29 06 14	6♊31 19	26 13.2	12 47.1	4 02.0	14 37.4	4 07.6	20 59.1	2 09.8	20 23.7	23 39.7	1 08.1
10 Th	1 16 22	20 59 34	13♊52 53	21 10 13	26 07.8	14 46.0	5 16.0	15 05.9	4 30.4	21 04.4	2 07.5	20 26.8	23 41.2	1 07.9
11 F	1 20 18	21 58 27	28 22 47	5♋30 12	26 04.5	16 46.3	6 30.1	15 34.5	4 53.3	21 09.6	2 05.2	20 29.8	23 42.6	1 07.6
12 Sa	1 24 15	22 57 18	12♋32 15	19 28 53	26D 03.2	18 47.8	7 44.1	16 03.2	5 16.3	21 14.6	2 03.0	20 32.9	23 44.0	1 07.3
13 Su	1 28 11	23 56 07	26 20 09	3♌06 15	26 03.5	20 50.6	8 58.1	16 32.1	5 39.3	21 19.4	2 00.9	20 35.9	23 45.3	1 07.0
14 M	1 32 08	24 54 53	9♌47 24	16 23 55	26R 04.2	22 54.5	10 12.1	17 01.2	6 02.4	21 24.0	1 59.0	20 38.9	23 46.7	1 06.6
15 Tu	1 36 04	25 53 36	22 56 06	29 24 18	26 04.5	24 59.4	11 26.1	17 30.4	6 25.6	21 28.5	1 57.1	20 41.8	23 48.0	1 06.2
16 W	1 40 01	26 52 18	5♍48 52	12♍10 07	26 03.2	27 05.2	12 40.1	17 59.7	6 48.9	21 32.8	1 55.3	20 44.8	23 49.3	1 05.8
17 Th	1 43 57	27 50 57	18 28 21	24 43 50	25 59.6	29 11.8	13 54.1	18 29.2	7 12.3	21 36.9	1 53.6	20 47.7	23 50.5	1 05.4
18 F	1 47 54	28 49 34	0♎56 48	7♎07 28	25 53.3	1♉18.9	15 08.1	18 58.8	7 35.7	21 40.8	1 52.0	20 50.5	23 51.7	1 04.9
19 Sa	1 51 50	29 48 10	13 16 01	19 22 37	25 44.5	3 26.3	16 22.0	19 28.6	7 59.2	21 44.6	1 50.6	20 53.4	23 52.9	1 04.3
20 Su	1 55 47	0♉46 43	25 27 24	1♏30 30	25 33.5	5 33.8	17 36.0	19 58.4	8 22.7	21 48.2	1 49.2	20 56.2	23 54.1	1 03.8
21 M	1 59 44	1 45 14	7♏32 02	13 32 09	25 21.3	7 41.2	18 49.9	20 28.5	8 46.3	21 51.7	1 47.9	20 59.0	23 55.2	1 03.2
22 Tu	2 03 40	2 43 44	19 31 00	25 28 44	25 08.8	9 48.1	20 03.8	20 58.6	9 10.0	21 54.9	1 46.8	21 01.8	23 56.3	1 02.6
23 W	2 07 37	3 42 12	1♐25 35	7♐21 47	24 57.1	11 54.3	21 17.8	21 28.9	9 33.8	21 58.0	1 45.7	21 04.6	23 57.4	1 02.0
24 Th	2 11 33	4 40 38	13 17 35	19 13 19	24 47.2	13 59.3	22 31.7	21 59.3	9 57.6	22 00.9	1 44.7	21 07.3	23 58.5	1 01.3
25 F	2 15 30	5 39 02	25 09 22	1♑06 09	24 39.6	16 03.0	23 45.6	22 29.8	10 21.5	22 03.6	1 43.9	21 10.0	23 59.5	1 00.7
26 Sa	2 19 26	6 37 25	7♑04 06	13 03 45	24 34.8	18 05.0	24 59.6	23 00.4	10 45.4	22 06.1	1 43.1	21 12.6	24 00.5	1 00.0
27 Su	2 23 23	7 35 46	19 05 38	25 10 20	24 32.3	20 05.0	26 13.5	23 31.2	11 09.4	22 08.5	1 42.5	21 15.2	24 01.4	0 59.2
28 M	2 27 20	8 34 06	1♒18 28	7♒30 39	24D 31.6	22 02.6	27 27.4	24 02.1	11 33.4	22 10.6	1 41.9	21 17.8	24 02.4	0 58.4
29 Tu	2 31 16	9 32 24	13 47 30	20 09 39	24R 31.8	23 57.8	28 41.3	24 33.0	11 57.6	22 12.6	1 41.5	21 20.4	24 03.2	0 57.7
30 W	2 35 13	10 30 40	26 37 40	3♓12 05	24 31.6	25 50.1	29 55.2	25 04.1	12 21.7	22 14.4	1 41.2	21 22.9	24 04.1	0 56.8

Astro Data

	Dy Hr Mn
☽0N	8 5:09
♃□♄	18 10:41
☉0N	20 5:48
☽0S	21 5:20
♃⚹♅	29 0:17
♇ R	2 9:23
☽0N	4 15:13
☿0N	5 5:38
♀0N	9 1:02
☽0S	17 11:23

Planet Ingress

	Dy Hr Mn
♂ ♋	4 10:01
♀ ♓	12 22:51
☿ ♓	14 22:46
☉ ♈	20 5:48
⚳ ♊	29 9:22
☿ ♈	2 17:45
♀ ♈	6 5:35
☿ ♉	17 21:07
☉ ♉	19 16:51
♀ ♉	30 13:34

Last Aspect / ☽ Ingress

Last Aspect Dy Hr Mn		☽ Ingress Dy Hr Mn
1 16:54	♂ ☍	♑ 1 18:33
3 6:16	♅ ⚹	♒ 4 4:24
5 21:46	♆ ☌	♓ 6 10:53
7 19:04	♅ ☌	♈ 8 14:23
10 11:09	♀ ⚹	♉ 10 16:14
12 17:26	♀ □	♊ 12 17:54
14 20:24	☿ △	♋ 14 20:38
16 18:58	☉ △	♌ 17 1:04
18 18:38	♆ ☍	♍ 19 7:25
20 19:28	♅ ☍	♎ 21 15:45
23 12:41	♆ △	♏ 24 2:06
26 0:36	♆ □	♐ 26 14:11
28 13:21	♆ ⚹	♑ 29 2:43
31 4:54	☿ ⚹	♒ 31 13:34

Last Aspect / ☽ Ingress

Last Aspect Dy Hr Mn		☽ Ingress Dy Hr Mn
2 9:14	♆ ☌	♓ 2 20:55
4 21:43	♀ ☌	♈ 5 0:27
6 15:01	♆ ⚹	♉ 7 1:20
8 15:13	♆ □	♊ 9 1:27
10 16:11	♆ △	♋ 11 2:43
12 18:32	☉ □	♌ 13 6:29
15 4:56	☉ △	♍ 15 13:07
17 5:59	♃ △	♎ 17 22:10
19 20:54	♆ △	♏ 20 9:00
22 8:54	♆ □	♐ 22 21:07
24 21:38	♆ ⚹	♑ 25 9:47
27 14:18	♀ □	♒ 27 21:27
30 5:25	♀ ⚹	♓ 30 6:11

☽ Phases & Eclipses

Dy Hr Mn	
7 17:14	● 17♓31
14 10:46	☽ 24♊14
21 18:40	○ 1♎31
29 21:47	☾ 9♑34
6 3:55	● 16♈44
12 18:32	☽ 23♋13
20 10:25	○ 0♏43
28 14:12	☾ 8♒39

Astro Data

1 March 2008
Julian Day # 39507
SVP 5♓08'34"
GC 26♐57.2 ⚴ 29♓03.6
Eris 20♈41.9 ⚵ 24♐13.2
⚷ 17♒41.4 ⚶ 6♓18.7
☽ Mean ☊ 27♒08.3

1 April 2008
Julian Day # 39538
SVP 5♓08'31"
GC 26♐57.3 ⚴ 10♈38.0
Eris 21♈00.3 ⚵ 28♐54.5
⚷ 19♒38.8 ⚶ 21♓32.6
☽ Mean ☊ 25♒29.8

LONGITUDE — May 2008

Day	Sid.Time	☉	0 hr ☽	Noon ☽	True ☊	☿	♀	♂	⚳	♃	♄	♅	♆	♇
1 Th	2 39 09	11♉28 55	9♓53 21	16♓41 49	24♒30.0	27♉39.3	1♉09.1	25♋35.4	12♊46.0	22♑16.0	1♍40.9	21♓25.4	24♒04.9	0♑56.0
2 F	2 43 06	12 27 09	23 37 39	0♈40 54	24R 26.1	29 25.4	2 22.9	26 06.7	13 10.2	22 17.5	1D 40.8	21 27.9	24 05.7	0R 55.1
3 Sa	2 47 02	13 25 21	7♈51 24	15 08 44	24 19.6	1♊08.1	3 36.8	26 38.1	13 34.6	22 18.7	1 40.8	21 30.3	24 06.5	0 54.2
4 Su	2 50 59	14 23 31	22 32 18	0♉01 15	24 10.6	2 47.2	4 50.7	27 09.6	13 59.0	22 19.7	1 40.9	21 32.7	24 07.2	0 53.3
5 M	2 54 55	15 21 40	7♉34 30	15 10 49	24 00.1	4 22.7	6 04.6	27 41.3	14 23.4	22 20.6	1 41.1	21 35.1	24 08.0	0 52.3
6 Tu	2 58 52	16 19 47	22 48 51	0♊27 08	23 49.2	5 54.4	7 18.4	28 13.0	14 47.9	22 21.2	1 41.4	21 37.4	24 08.6	0 51.4
7 W	3 02 48	17 17 53	8♊04 16	15 38 52	23 39.1	7 22.3	8 32.3	28 44.9	15 12.5	22 21.7	1 41.8	21 39.7	24 09.3	0 50.4
8 Th	3 06 45	18 15 57	23 09 45	0♋35 52	23 31.1	8 46.3	9 46.1	29 16.8	15 37.1	22 22.0	1 42.3	21 41.9	24 09.9	0 49.4
9 F	3 10 42	19 13 58	7♋56 23	15 10 43	23 25.7	10 06.2	11 00.0	29 48.9	16 01.7	22R 22.1	1 43.0	21 44.1	24 10.5	0 48.3
10 Sa	3 14 38	20 11 59	22 18 27	29 19 27	23 22.8	11 22.1	12 13.8	0♌21.0	16 26.4	22 22.0	1 43.7	21 46.3	24 11.0	0 47.3
11 Su	3 18 35	21 09 57	6♌13 42	13♌01 23	23 21.9	12 33.8	13 27.6	0 53.2	16 51.1	22 21.7	1 44.6	21 48.4	24 11.5	0 46.2
12 M	3 22 31	22 07 53	19 42 47	26 18 16	23 21.8	13 41.3	14 41.4	1 25.5	17 15.9	22 21.3	1 45.5	21 50.5	24 12.0	0 45.1
13 Tu	3 26 28	23 05 47	2♍48 17	9♍13 19	23 21.4	14 44.6	15 55.2	1 57.9	17 40.7	22 20.6	1 46.5	21 52.6	24 12.4	0 43.9
14 W	3 30 24	24 03 40	15 33 51	21 50 23	23 19.4	15 43.5	17 09.0	2 30.4	18 05.6	22 19.7	1 47.7	21 54.6	24 12.9	0 42.8
15 Th	3 34 21	25 01 30	28 03 24	4♎13 22	23 15.1	16 38.0	18 22.8	3 03.0	18 30.5	22 18.7	1 48.9	21 56.6	24 13.2	0 41.6
16 F	3 38 18	25 59 20	10♎20 40	16 25 42	23 08.0	17 28.1	19 36.6	3 35.7	18 55.4	22 17.5	1 50.3	21 58.5	24 13.6	0 40.4
17 Sa	3 42 14	26 57 07	22 28 49	28 30 19	22 58.1	18 13.7	20 50.3	4 08.4	19 20.4	22 16.1	1 51.8	22 00.4	24 13.9	0 39.2
18 Su	3 46 11	27 54 53	4♏30 27	10♏29 28	22 45.9	18 54.6	22 04.1	4 41.2	19 45.4	22 14.5	1 53.3	22 02.2	24 14.2	0 38.0
19 M	3 50 07	28 52 38	16 27 33	22 24 55	22 32.3	19 31.0	23 17.9	5 14.1	20 10.5	22 12.7	1 55.0	22 04.1	24 14.4	0 36.7
20 Tu	3 54 04	29 50 21	28 21 42	4♐18 06	22 18.4	20 02.6	24 31.6	5 47.1	20 35.6	22 10.7	1 56.8	22 05.8	24 14.6	0 35.5
21 W	3 58 00	0♊48 03	10♐14 16	16 10 22	22 05.3	20 29.5	25 45.4	6 20.2	21 00.7	22 08.6	1 58.6	22 07.6	24 14.8	0 34.2
22 Th	4 01 57	1 45 43	22 06 38	28 03 17	21 54.1	20 51.6	26 59.1	6 53.3	21 25.9	22 06.2	2 00.6	22 09.2	24 15.0	0 32.9
23 F	4 05 53	2 43 23	4♑00 34	9♑58 47	21 45.4	21 08.9	28 12.9	7 26.5	21 51.1	22 03.7	2 02.7	22 10.9	24 15.1	0 31.6
24 Sa	4 09 50	3 41 01	15 58 17	21 59 26	21 39.5	21 21.5	29 26.6	7 59.8	22 16.3	22 01.0	2 04.8	22 12.5	24 15.2	0 30.3
25 Su	4 13 47	4 38 39	28 02 40	4♒08 26	21 36.3	21 29.2	0♊40.4	8 33.1	22 41.6	21 58.1	2 07.1	22 14.0	24 15.3	0 28.9
26 M	4 17 43	5 36 15	10♒17 16	16 29 41	21D 35.2	21R 32.3	1 54.1	9 06.6	23 06.9	21 55.1	2 09.5	22 15.6	24R 15.3	0 27.6
27 Tu	4 21 40	6 33 50	22 46 14	29 07 30	21R 35.2	21 30.7	3 07.8	9 40.1	23 32.2	21 51.9	2 11.9	22 17.0	24 15.3	0 26.2
28 W	4 25 36	7 31 25	5♓34 01	12♓06 21	21 35.2	21 24.7	4 21.6	10 13.7	23 57.6	21 48.4	2 14.5	22 18.4	24 15.2	0 24.8
29 Th	4 29 33	8 28 58	18 44 57	25 30 15	21 34.2	21 14.3	5 35.3	10 47.3	24 23.0	21 44.9	2 17.1	22 19.8	24 15.1	0 23.4
30 F	4 33 29	9 26 31	2♈22 32	9♈22 00	21 31.2	20 59.8	6 49.0	11 21.0	24 48.4	21 41.1	2 19.9	22 21.2	24 15.0	0 22.0
31 Sa	4 37 26	10 24 03	16 28 38	23 42 15	21 25.8	20 41.5	8 02.8	11 54.8	25 13.9	21 37.2	2 22.7	22 22.4	24 14.9	0 20.5

LONGITUDE — June 2008

Day	Sid.Time	☉	0 hr ☽	Noon ☽	True ☊	☿	♀	♂	⚳	♃	♄	♅	♆	♇
1 Su	4 41 22	11♊21 34	1♉02 25	8♉28 32	21♒18.1	20♊19.7	9♊16.5	12♌28.7	25♊39.4	21♑33.1	2♍25.7	22♓23.7	24♒14.7	0♑19.1
2 M	4 45 19	12 19 04	15 59 42	23 34 50	21R 08.8	19R 54.8	10 30.3	13 02.6	26 04.9	21R 28.8	2 28.7	22 24.9	24R 14.5	0R 17.6
3 Tu	4 49 16	13 16 34	1♊12 42	8♊51 55	20 59.0	19 27.2	11 44.0	13 36.6	26 30.4	21 24.4	2 31.8	22 26.0	24 14.3	0 16.2
4 W	4 53 12	14 14 02	16 31 02	24 08 38	20 49.9	18 57.3	12 57.7	14 10.7	26 56.0	21 19.8	2 35.0	22 27.1	24 14.0	0 14.7
5 Th	4 57 09	15 11 30	1♋43 20	9♋13 56	20 42.6	18 25.7	14 11.5	14 44.9	27 21.6	21 15.1	2 38.3	22 28.2	24 13.7	0 13.2
6 F	5 01 05	16 08 57	16 39 22	23 58 49	20 37.6	17 52.9	15 25.2	15 19.1	27 47.3	21 10.2	2 41.7	22 29.2	24 13.4	0 11.7
7 Sa	5 05 02	17 06 22	1♌11 41	8♌17 34	20D 35.1	17 19.4	16 38.9	15 53.3	28 12.9	21 05.1	2 45.2	22 30.2	24 13.0	0 10.2
8 Su	5 08 58	18 03 46	15 16 19	22 07 55	20 34.6	16 45.9	17 52.7	16 27.7	28 38.6	20 59.9	2 48.8	22 31.1	24 12.6	0 08.7
9 M	5 12 55	19 01 10	28 52 34	5♍30 34	20 35.0	16 12.9	19 06.4	17 02.1	29 04.3	20 54.6	2 52.5	22 32.0	24 12.2	0 07.2
10 Tu	5 16 51	19 58 32	12♍02 19	18 28 17	20R 35.5	15 41.0	20 20.1	17 36.5	29 30.0	20 49.1	2 56.2	22 32.8	24 11.8	0 05.7
11 W	5 20 48	20 55 53	24 49 30	1♎05 00	20 35.0	15 10.7	21 33.8	18 11.1	29 55.7	20 43.5	3 00.1	22 33.6	24 11.3	0 04.2
12 Th	5 24 45	21 53 13	7♎16 52	13 25 08	20 32.7	14 42.6	22 47.5	18 45.7	0♋21.5	20 37.7	3 04.0	22 34.3	24 10.7	0 02.6
13 F	5 28 41	22 50 32	19 30 20	25 33 00	20 28.1	14 17.0	24 01.3	19 20.3	0 47.3	20 31.9	3 08.0	22 35.0	24 10.2	0 01.1
14 Sa	5 32 38	23 47 50	1♏33 34	7♏32 31	20 21.3	13 54.5	25 15.0	19 55.0	1 13.1	20 25.8	3 12.1	22 35.6	24 09.6	29♐59.6
15 Su	5 36 34	24 45 07	13 30 13	19 27 04	20 12.6	13 35.4	26 28.7	20 29.8	1 38.9	20 19.7	3 16.3	22 36.2	24 09.0	29 58.0
16 M	5 40 31	25 42 24	25 23 21	1♐19 23	20 02.8	13 20.0	27 42.4	21 04.6	2 04.7	20 13.4	3 20.5	22 36.7	24 08.4	29 56.5
17 Tu	5 44 27	26 39 40	7♐15 25	13 11 41	19 52.6	13 08.7	28 56.1	21 39.4	2 30.6	20 07.1	3 24.9	22 37.2	24 07.7	29 54.9
18 W	5 48 24	27 36 55	19 08 24	25 05 46	19 43.1	13 01.5	0♋09.8	22 14.4	2 56.5	20 00.6	3 29.3	22 37.6	24 07.0	29 53.4
19 Th	5 52 20	28 34 10	1♑03 58	7♑03 11	19 35.0	12D 58.8	1 23.5	22 49.4	3 22.3	19 54.0	3 33.8	22 38.0	24 06.3	29 51.8
20 F	5 56 17	29 31 24	13 03 38	19 05 31	19 28.9	13 00.6	2 37.2	23 24.4	3 48.2	19 47.3	3 38.3	22 38.4	24 05.6	29 50.3
21 Sa	6 00 14	0♋28 39	25 09 04	1♒14 32	19 25.0	13 07.0	3 50.9	23 59.5	4 14.2	19 40.5	3 43.0	22 38.6	24 04.8	29 48.7
22 Su	6 04 10	1 25 52	7♒22 13	13 32 25	19D 23.3	13 18.2	5 04.6	24 34.6	4 40.1	19 33.7	3 47.7	22 38.9	24 04.0	29 47.2
23 M	6 08 07	2 23 06	19 45 29	26 01 47	19 23.3	13 34.0	6 18.4	25 09.8	5 06.0	19 26.7	3 52.5	22 39.1	24 03.1	29 45.6
24 Tu	6 12 03	3 20 19	2♓21 42	8♓45 38	19 24.4	13 54.5	7 32.1	25 45.1	5 32.0	19 19.6	3 57.4	22 39.2	24 02.3	29 44.1
25 W	6 16 00	4 17 32	15 14 01	21 47 13	19 25.6	14 19.8	8 45.8	26 20.4	5 58.0	19 12.5	4 02.3	22 39.3	24 01.4	29 42.5
26 Th	6 19 56	5 14 45	28 25 39	5♈09 37	19R 26.2	14 49.7	9 59.5	26 55.8	6 24.0	19 05.3	4 07.3	22R 39.4	24 00.5	29 41.0
27 F	6 23 53	6 11 59	11♈59 23	18 55 09	19 25.5	15 24.2	11 13.3	27 31.2	6 50.0	18 58.0	4 12.4	22 39.4	23 59.5	29 39.4
28 Sa	6 27 49	7 09 12	25 56 56	3♉04 40	19 23.1	16 03.4	12 27.0	28 06.7	7 16.0	18 50.6	4 17.6	22 39.3	23 58.6	29 37.9
29 Su	6 31 46	8 06 25	10♉18 07	17 36 51	19 19.0	16 47.0	13 40.7	28 42.3	7 42.0	18 43.2	4 22.8	22 39.2	23 57.6	29 36.3
30 M	6 35 43	9 03 39	25 00 15	2♊27 34	19 13.8	17 35.1	14 54.5	29 17.9	8 08.1	18 35.7	4 28.1	22 39.1	23 56.6	29 34.8

Astro Data

	Dy Hr Mn
☽ 0N	2 1:00
♄ D	3 3:07
♃ R	9 12:11
☽ 0S	14 16:15
♃⚹♅	21 18:05
☿ R	26 15:48
♆ R	26 16:15
☽ 0N	29 8:55
☽ 0S	10 21:39
☿ D	19 14:31
☽ 0N	25 14:48
♃⚼♄	26 7:57
♅ R	27 0:01

Planet Ingress

		Dy Hr Mn
☿	♊	2 20:00
♂	♌	9 20:20
☉	♊	20 16:01
♀	♊	24 22:52
⚳	♋	11 15:58
♇	♐R	14 5:13
♀	♋	18 8:48
☉	♋	20 23:59

Last Aspect / ☽ Ingress (May)

Last Aspect Dy Hr Mn			☽ Ingress	Dy Hr Mn
2 9:34	☿	⚹	♈	2 10:51
4 7:16	♂	□	♉	4 11:58
6 8:22	♂	⚹	♊	6 11:17
8 1:36	♆	△	♋	8 11:02
10 0:06	♃	☍	♌	10 13:10
12 8:09	♆	☍	♍	12 18:48
14 16:38	☉	△	♎	15 3:46
17 3:29	♆	△	♏	17 14:59
20 2:11	☉	☍	♐	20 3:19
22 4:19	♆	⚹	♑	22 15:55
24 12:26	♅	⚹	♒	25 3:52
27 2:49	♆	☌	♓	27 13:38
29 6:23	♅	☌	♈	29 19:52
31 12:54	♆	⚹	♉	31 22:19

Last Aspect / ☽ Ingress (June)

Last Aspect Dy Hr Mn			☽ Ingress	Dy Hr Mn
2 13:02	♆	□	♊	2 22:06
4 12:09	♆	△	♋	4 21:16
6 9:32	♅	△	♌	6 22:00
8 15:41	♆	☍	♍	9 2:01
10 19:42	♅	☍	♎	11 9:55
13 9:15	♆	△	♏	13 20:53
15 21:29	♆	□	♐	16 9:19
18 21:37	♇	☌	♑	18 21:52
20 19:02	♅	⚹	♒	21 9:33
23 19:04	♇	⚹	♓	23 19:32
26 2:16	♇	□	♈	26 2:49
28 6:14	♇	△	♉	28 6:50
30 6:43	♂	□	♊	30 8:03

☽ Phases & Eclipses

Dy Hr Mn		
5 12:18	●	15♉22
12 3:47	☽	21♌48
20 2:11	○	29♏27
28 2:57	☾	7♓10
3 19:23	●	13♊34
10 15:04	☽	20♍06
18 17:30	○	27♐50
26 12:10	☾	5♈15

Astro Data

1 May 2008
Julian Day # 39568
SVP 5♓08'27"
GC 26♐57.3 ⚴ 22♈22.6
Eris 21♈19.8 ⚵ 29♐12.2R
⚷ 20♒50.6 ⚶ 5♈35.6
☽ Mean ☊ 23♒54.4

1 June 2008
Julian Day # 39599
SVP 5♓08'23"
GC 26♐57.4 ⚴ 4♉47.6
Eris 21♈36.7 ⚵ 24♐33.1R
⚷ 21♒07.4R ⚶ 19♈01.6
☽ Mean ☊ 22♒16.0

July 2008

LONGITUDE

Day	Sid.Time	☉	0 hr ☽	Noon ☽	True ☊	☿	♀	♂	⚳	♃	♄	♅	♆	♇
1 Tu	6 39 39	10♋00 53	9♊57 50	17♊29 58	19♒08.1	18♊27.6	16♋08.2	29♌53.5	8♋34.1	18♑28.2	4♍33.5	22♓38.9	23♒55.5	29♐33.3
2 W	6 43 36	10 58 07	25 02 49	2♋35 10	19R 02.7	19 24.4	17 22.0	0♍29.2	9 00.2	18R 20.6	4 38.9	22R 38.7	23R 54.5	29R 31.8
3 Th	6 47 32	11 55 20	10♋05 48	17 33 33	18 58.5	20 25.5	18 35.8	1 05.0	9 26.3	18 13.0	4 44.4	22 38.4	23 53.4	29 30.3
4 F	6 51 29	12 52 34	24 57 23	2♌16 24	18 55.8	21 30.8	19 49.5	1 40.8	9 52.4	18 05.4	4 50.0	22 38.0	23 52.3	29 28.8
5 Sa	6 55 25	13 49 48	9♌29 51	16 37 11	18D 54.8	22 40.3	21 03.3	2 16.7	10 18.4	17 57.7	4 55.6	22 37.7	23 51.1	29 27.3
6 Su	6 59 22	14 47 01	23 38 00	0♍32 09	18 55.2	23 53.9	22 17.0	2 52.6	10 44.5	17 50.0	5 01.3	22 37.2	23 50.0	29 25.8
7 M	7 03 19	15 44 14	7♍19 34	14 00 22	18 56.5	25 11.6	23 30.8	3 28.6	11 10.6	17 42.3	5 07.0	22 36.7	23 48.8	29 24.3
8 Tu	7 07 15	16 41 27	20 34 49	27 03 14	18 58.0	26 33.2	24 44.5	4 04.7	11 36.7	17 34.6	5 12.9	22 36.2	23 47.6	29 22.8
9 W	7 11 12	17 38 39	3♎26 03	9♎43 45	18R 59.2	27 58.8	25 58.3	4 40.7	12 02.8	17 26.9	5 18.7	22 35.6	23 46.4	29 21.4
10 Th	7 15 08	18 35 52	15 56 51	22 05 55	18 59.4	29 28.3	27 12.1	5 16.9	12 28.9	17 19.2	5 24.7	22 35.0	23 45.1	29 19.9
11 F	7 19 05	19 33 05	28 11 29	4♏14 09	18 58.4	1♋01.5	28 25.8	5 53.1	12 55.1	17 11.5	5 30.6	22 34.4	23 43.8	29 18.5
12 Sa	7 23 01	20 30 17	10♏14 27	16 12 55	18 56.1	2 38.4	29 39.6	6 29.3	13 21.2	17 03.8	5 36.7	22 33.7	23 42.6	29 17.0
13 Su	7 26 58	21 27 30	22 10 05	28 06 25	18 52.7	4 19.0	0♌53.3	7 05.6	13 47.3	16 56.1	5 42.8	22 32.9	23 41.3	29 15.6
14 M	7 30 54	22 24 43	4♐02 22	9♐58 23	18 48.6	6 03.0	2 07.1	7 41.9	14 13.4	16 48.4	5 48.9	22 32.1	23 39.9	29 14.2
15 Tu	7 34 51	23 21 55	15 54 49	21 52 02	18 44.3	7 50.3	3 20.8	8 18.3	14 39.5	16 40.8	5 55.1	22 31.3	23 38.6	29 12.8
16 W	7 38 48	24 19 09	27 50 20	3♑50 02	18 40.3	9 40.8	4 34.6	8 54.7	15 05.6	16 33.2	6 01.4	22 30.4	23 37.2	29 11.5
17 Th	7 42 44	25 16 22	9♑51 21	15 54 32	18 37.0	11 34.1	5 48.3	9 31.2	15 31.8	16 25.6	6 07.7	22 29.4	23 35.9	29 10.1
18 F	7 46 41	26 13 36	21 59 46	28 07 15	18 34.6	13 30.2	7 02.1	10 07.7	15 57.9	16 18.1	6 14.1	22 28.5	23 34.5	29 08.8
19 Sa	7 50 37	27 10 50	4♒17 08	10♒29 37	18D 33.4	15 28.7	8 15.8	10 44.3	16 24.0	16 10.6	6 20.5	22 27.4	23 33.1	29 07.4
20 Su	7 54 34	28 08 05	16 44 49	23 02 54	18 33.2	17 29.4	9 29.6	11 20.9	16 50.1	16 03.2	6 26.9	22 26.4	23 31.6	29 06.1
21 M	7 58 30	29 05 20	29 24 02	5♓48 22	18 33.9	19 31.9	10 43.3	11 57.6	17 16.2	15 55.9	6 33.4	22 25.3	23 30.2	29 04.8
22 Tu	8 02 27	0♌02 36	12♓16 04	18 47 18	18 35.2	21 35.9	11 57.1	12 34.3	17 42.3	15 48.6	6 40.0	22 24.1	23 28.7	29 03.6
23 W	8 06 23	0 59 52	25 22 14	2♈01 01	18 36.5	23 41.2	13 10.9	13 11.1	18 08.5	15 41.3	6 46.5	22 22.9	23 27.3	29 02.3
24 Th	8 10 20	1 57 10	8♈43 47	15 30 40	18 37.5	25 47.3	14 24.6	13 47.9	18 34.6	15 34.2	6 53.2	22 21.7	23 25.8	29 01.0
25 F	8 14 17	2 54 28	22 21 44	29 17 01	18R 38.1	27 54.0	15 38.4	14 24.8	19 00.7	15 27.1	6 59.9	22 20.4	23 24.3	28 59.8
26 Sa	8 18 13	3 51 48	6♉16 29	13♉20 03	18 37.9	0♌01.0	16 52.1	15 01.7	19 26.8	15 20.1	7 06.6	22 19.1	23 22.8	28 58.6
27 Su	8 22 10	4 49 08	20 27 30	27 38 32	18 37.1	2 08.0	18 05.9	15 38.7	19 52.9	15 13.2	7 13.3	22 17.8	23 21.3	28 57.4
28 M	8 26 06	5 46 30	4♊52 46	12♊09 43	18 35.9	4 14.7	19 19.7	16 15.7	20 19.0	15 06.4	7 20.2	22 16.4	23 19.7	28 56.2
29 Tu	8 30 03	6 43 53	19 28 45	26 49 11	18 34.5	6 20.9	20 33.4	16 52.8	20 45.1	14 59.7	7 27.0	22 14.9	23 18.2	28 55.1
30 W	8 33 59	7 41 16	4♋10 15	11♋31 08	18 33.2	8 26.4	21 47.2	17 30.0	21 11.1	14 53.1	7 33.9	22 13.5	23 16.6	28 54.0
31 Th	8 37 56	8 38 41	18 50 58	26 08 56	18 32.2	10 30.9	23 01.0	18 07.1	21 37.2	14 46.6	7 40.8	22 12.0	23 15.1	28 52.9

August 2008

LONGITUDE

Day	Sid.Time	☉	0 hr ☽	Noon ☽	True ☊	☿	♀	♂	⚳	♃	♄	♅	♆	♇
1 F	8 41 52	9♌36 06	3♌24 12	10♌36 01	18♒31.8	12♌34.5	24♌14.8	18♍44.4	22♋03.3	14♑40.2	7♍47.8	22♓10.4	23♒13.5	28♐51.8
2 Sa	8 45 49	10 33 33	17 43 42	24 46 41	18D 31.7	14 36.8	25 28.5	19 21.7	22 29.3	14R 33.9	7 54.8	22R 08.9	23R 11.9	28R 50.7
3 Su	8 49 46	11 31 00	1♍44 31	8♍36 52	18 32.1	16 37.9	26 42.3	19 59.0	22 55.4	14 27.8	8 01.8	22 07.2	23 10.3	28 49.7
4 M	8 53 42	12 28 27	15 23 31	22 04 24	18 32.6	18 37.7	27 56.1	20 36.4	23 21.4	14 21.8	8 08.8	22 05.6	23 08.7	28 48.7
5 Tu	8 57 39	13 25 56	28 39 32	5♎09 05	18 33.1	20 36.0	29 09.8	21 13.8	23 47.4	14 15.9	8 15.9	22 03.9	23 07.1	28 47.7
6 W	9 01 35	14 23 25	11♎33 16	17 52 25	18 33.6	22 32.9	0♍23.6	21 51.3	24 13.4	14 10.1	8 23.0	22 02.2	23 05.5	28 46.7
7 Th	9 05 32	15 20 55	24 06 57	0♏17 17	18 33.9	24 28.2	1 37.3	22 28.9	24 39.4	14 04.5	8 30.2	22 00.4	23 03.9	28 45.7
8 F	9 09 28	16 18 26	6♏23 56	12 27 26	18R 34.0	26 22.1	2 51.1	23 06.5	25 05.4	13 59.0	8 37.4	21 58.6	23 02.3	28 44.8
9 Sa	9 13 25	17 15 58	18 28 20	24 27 12	18 34.0	28 14.5	4 04.8	23 44.1	25 31.3	13 53.6	8 44.6	21 56.8	23 00.7	28 43.9
10 Su	9 17 21	18 13 30	0♐24 36	6♐21 07	18D 33.9	0♍05.3	5 18.5	24 21.8	25 57.3	13 48.4	8 51.8	21 55.0	22 59.0	28 43.0
11 M	9 21 18	19 11 04	12 17 17	18 13 39	18 34.0	1 54.6	6 32.3	24 59.5	26 23.2	13 43.4	8 59.1	21 53.1	22 57.4	28 42.2
12 Tu	9 25 15	20 08 38	24 10 44	0♑09 01	18 34.1	3 42.4	7 46.0	25 37.3	26 49.1	13 38.5	9 06.4	21 51.2	22 55.8	28 41.4
13 W	9 29 11	21 06 14	6♑08 58	12 10 59	18 34.3	5 28.7	8 59.7	26 15.1	27 15.0	13 33.8	9 13.7	21 49.2	22 54.1	28 40.6
14 Th	9 33 08	22 03 50	18 15 27	24 22 43	18 34.6	7 13.4	10 13.4	26 53.0	27 40.8	13 29.2	9 21.0	21 47.3	22 52.5	28 39.8
15 F	9 37 04	23 01 28	0♒33 03	6♒46 41	18R 34.9	8 56.7	11 27.1	27 30.9	28 06.7	13 24.8	9 28.3	21 45.3	22 50.9	28 39.1
16 Sa	9 41 01	23 59 07	13 03 49	19 24 34	18 35.0	10 38.6	12 40.8	28 08.9	28 32.5	13 20.5	9 35.7	21 43.3	22 49.2	28 38.3
17 Su	9 44 57	24 56 46	25 49 03	2♓17 17	18 34.8	12 18.9	13 54.5	28 46.9	28 58.3	13 16.5	9 43.1	21 41.2	22 47.6	28 37.6
18 M	9 48 54	25 54 28	8♓49 16	15 24 56	18 34.3	13 57.8	15 08.1	29 25.0	29 24.1	13 12.5	9 50.5	21 39.2	22 46.0	28 37.0
19 Tu	9 52 50	26 52 10	22 04 13	28 47 00	18 33.5	15 35.3	16 21.8	0♎03.1	29 49.9	13 08.8	9 57.9	21 37.1	22 44.3	28 36.3
20 W	9 56 47	27 49 54	5♈33 06	12♈22 23	18 32.4	17 11.3	17 35.5	0 41.3	0♌15.6	13 05.2	10 05.4	21 34.9	22 42.7	28 35.7
21 Th	10 00 44	28 47 40	19 14 37	26 09 37	18 31.2	18 46.0	18 49.1	1 19.5	0 41.3	13 01.8	10 12.8	21 32.8	22 41.1	28 35.1
22 F	10 04 40	29 45 27	3♉07 10	10♉07 01	18 30.3	20 19.2	20 02.8	1 57.7	1 07.0	12 58.6	10 20.3	21 30.6	22 39.4	28 34.6
23 Sa	10 08 37	0♍43 17	17 08 56	24 12 40	18D 29.7	21 51.0	21 16.4	2 36.1	1 32.7	12 55.5	10 27.8	21 28.5	22 37.8	28 34.1
24 Su	10 12 33	1 41 08	1♊17 58	8♊24 33	18 29.7	23 21.3	22 30.0	3 14.4	1 58.4	12 52.6	10 35.3	21 26.3	22 36.2	28 33.6
25 M	10 16 30	2 39 01	15 32 07	22 40 22	18 30.3	24 50.3	23 43.7	3 52.9	2 24.0	12 50.0	10 42.8	21 24.0	22 34.6	28 33.1
26 Tu	10 20 26	3 36 55	29 48 58	6♋57 32	18 31.3	26 17.8	24 57.3	4 31.4	2 49.6	12 47.4	10 50.3	21 21.8	22 33.0	28 32.7
27 W	10 24 23	4 34 52	14♋05 43	21 13 05	18 32.5	27 43.9	26 10.9	5 09.9	3 15.1	12 45.1	10 57.8	21 19.6	22 31.4	28 32.3
28 Th	10 28 19	5 32 50	28 19 13	5♌23 40	18R 33.4	29 08.5	27 24.5	5 48.5	3 40.7	12 43.0	11 05.4	21 17.3	22 29.8	28 31.9
29 F	10 32 16	6 30 50	12♌25 59	19 25 43	18 33.7	0♎31.6	28 38.2	6 27.1	4 06.2	12 41.0	11 12.9	21 15.0	22 28.2	28 31.5
30 Sa	10 36 13	7 28 51	26 22 27	3♍15 46	18 33.2	1 53.2	29 51.8	7 05.8	4 31.7	12 39.3	11 20.5	21 12.7	22 26.7	28 31.2
31 Su	10 40 09	8 26 55	10♍05 19	16 50 47	18 31.7	3 13.2	1♎05.3	7 44.6	4 57.1	12 37.7	11 28.0	21 10.4	22 25.1	28 30.9

Astro Data	Dy Hr Mn
☽0S	8 4:51
☽0N	22 19:51
☽0S	4 13:48
☽0N	19 1:48
♂0S	21 14:29
☿0S	28 5:13
☽0S	31 23:13

Planet Ingress		Dy Hr Mn
♂	♍	1 16:21
☿	♋	10 20:17
♀	♌	12 18:39
☉	♌	22 10:55
☿	♌	26 11:48
♀	♍	6 4:20
☿	♍	10 10:51
♂	♎	19 10:03
⚳	♌	19 21:26
☉	♍	22 18:02
☿	♎	29 2:50
♀	♎	30 14:41

Last Aspect Dy Hr Mn			☽ Ingress	Dy Hr Mn
2 7:08	♇	☍	♋	2 7:53
3 20:14	♅	△	♌	4 8:15
6 10:04	♇	△	♍	6 11:04
8 16:21	♇	□	♎	8 17:31
11 2:14	♇	⚹	♏	11 3:35
13 3:05	♆	□	♐	13 15:50
16 2:44	♇	☌	♑	16 4:20
18 7:59	☉	☍	♒	18 15:40
20 23:25	♇	⚹	♓	21 1:08
23 6:39	♇	□	♈	23 8:22
25 11:30	♇	△	♉	25 13:14
27 4:52	♆	□	♊	27 15:55
29 15:25	♇	☍	♋	29 17:12
31 5:31	♅	△	♌	31 18:22

Last Aspect Dy Hr Mn			☽ Ingress	Dy Hr Mn
2 18:59	♇	△	♍	2 20:59
5 0:16	♇	□	♎	5 2:28
7 9:02	♇	⚹	♏	7 11:26
9 21:02	☿	□	♐	9 23:10
12 9:04	♇	☌	♑	12 11:42
14 17:09	♂	△	♒	14 22:56
17 5:14	♇	⚹	♓	17 7:46
19 11:41	♇	□	♈	19 14:10
21 16:53	☉	△	♉	21 18:38
23 9:19	♆	□	♊	23 21:48
25 21:52	♇	☍	♋	26 0:19
28 0:13	☿	⚹	♌	28 2:51
30 3:44	♇	△	♍	30 6:18

☽ Phases & Eclipses Dy Hr Mn		
3 2:19	●	11♋32
10 4:35	☽	18♎18
18 7:59	○	26♑04
25 18:42	☾	3♉10
1 10:13	●	9♌32
1 10:21:05	•	T 02'27"
8 20:20	☽	16♏38
16 21:16	○	24♒21
16 21:10	•	P 0.807
23 23:50	☾	1♊12
30 19:58	●	7♍48

Astro Data

1 July 2008
Julian Day # 39629
SVP 5♓08'17"
GC 26♐57.5 ⚴ 16♉50.3
Eris 21♈46.2 ⚵ 17♐57.9R
⚷ 20♒27.1R ⚶ 0♉27.0
☽ Mean ☊ 20♒40.7

1 August 2008
Julian Day # 39660
SVP 5♓08'11"
GC 26♐57.6 ⚴ 28♉56.4
Eris 21♈46.5R ⚵ 14♐07.8R
⚷ 19♒02.7R ⚶ 9♉40.8
☽ Mean ☊ 19♒02.2

LONGITUDE — September 2008

Day	Sid.Time	☉	0 hr ☽	Noon☽	True☊	☿	♀	♂	⚳	♃	♄	♅	♆	♇
1 M	10 44 06	9♍24 59	23♍31 55	0♎08 32	18♒29.2	4♎31.6	2♎18.9	8♎23.4	5♌22.5	12♑36.3	11♍35.6	21♓08.0	22♒23.6	28♐30.7
2 Tu	10 48 02	10 23 05	6♎40 33	13 07 56	18R 26.0	5 48.4	3 32.5	9 02.2	5 47.9	12R 35.1	11 43.2	21R 05.7	22R 22.0	28R 30.5
3 W	10 51 59	11 21 13	19 30 45	25 49 09	18 22.5	7 03.4	4 46.1	9 41.1	6 13.2	12 34.1	11 50.7	21 03.3	22 20.5	28 30.3
4 Th	10 55 55	12 19 22	2♏03 21	8♏13 39	18 19.1	8 16.7	5 59.6	10 20.0	6 38.5	12 33.3	11 58.3	21 01.0	22 19.0	28 30.1
5 F	10 59 52	13 17 33	14 20 26	20 24 05	18 16.4	9 28.1	7 13.1	10 59.0	7 03.7	12 32.7	12 05.8	20 58.6	22 17.5	28 30.0
6 Sa	11 03 48	14 15 45	26 25 06	2♐24 00	18 14.6	10 37.6	8 26.7	11 38.1	7 28.9	12 32.3	12 13.4	20 56.2	22 16.0	28 29.9
7 Su	11 07 45	15 13 59	8♐21 19	14 17 39	18D 13.9	11 45.1	9 40.2	12 17.2	7 54.1	12D 32.1	12 21.0	20 53.9	22 14.5	28 29.8
8 M	11 11 42	16 12 15	20 13 35	26 09 44	18 14.4	12 50.4	10 53.7	12 56.3	8 19.2	12 32.0	12 28.5	20 51.5	22 13.0	28D 29.8
9 Tu	11 15 38	17 10 32	2♑06 43	8♑05 08	18 15.7	13 53.5	12 07.2	13 35.6	8 44.3	12 32.2	12 36.1	20 49.1	22 11.6	28 29.8
10 W	11 19 35	18 08 50	14 05 33	20 08 34	18 17.4	14 54.1	13 20.6	14 14.8	9 09.3	12 32.5	12 43.6	20 46.7	22 10.1	28 29.8
11 Th	11 23 31	19 07 10	26 14 42	2♒24 26	18 19.0	15 52.2	14 34.1	14 54.1	9 34.3	12 33.1	12 51.1	20 44.3	22 08.7	28 29.8
12 F	11 27 28	20 05 31	8♒38 13	14 56 25	18R 19.9	16 47.6	15 47.5	15 33.5	9 59.3	12 33.8	12 58.7	20 41.9	22 07.3	28 29.9
13 Sa	11 31 24	21 03 55	21 19 20	27 47 10	18 19.5	17 40.1	17 00.9	16 12.9	10 24.2	12 34.7	13 06.2	20 39.5	22 05.9	28 30.1
14 Su	11 35 21	22 02 20	4♓20 04	10♓58 03	18 17.6	18 29.4	18 14.3	16 52.3	10 49.0	12 35.8	13 13.7	20 37.1	22 04.6	28 30.2
15 M	11 39 17	23 00 46	17 41 01	24 28 47	18 14.2	19 15.4	19 27.7	17 31.8	11 13.8	12 37.1	13 21.2	20 34.7	22 03.2	28 30.4
16 Tu	11 43 14	23 59 15	1♈21 04	8♈17 29	18 09.3	19 57.8	20 41.1	18 11.4	11 38.6	12 38.6	13 28.7	20 32.3	22 01.9	28 30.6
17 W	11 47 11	24 57 45	15 17 33	22 20 45	18 03.7	20 36.4	21 54.4	18 51.0	12 03.3	12 40.3	13 36.1	20 29.9	22 00.6	28 30.9
18 Th	11 51 07	25 56 18	29 26 28	6♉34 07	17 57.9	21 10.7	23 07.8	19 30.6	12 27.9	12 42.2	13 43.6	20 27.5	21 59.3	28 31.1
19 F	11 55 04	26 54 53	13♉43 04	20 52 45	17 52.9	21 40.6	24 21.1	20 10.3	12 52.5	12 44.2	13 51.0	20 25.1	21 58.0	28 31.4
20 Sa	11 59 00	27 53 30	28 02 34	5♊12 03	17 49.2	22 05.6	25 34.4	20 50.1	13 17.0	12 46.5	13 58.5	20 22.7	21 56.7	28 31.8
21 Su	12 02 57	28 52 09	12♊20 44	19 28 15	17D 47.2	22 25.5	26 47.7	21 29.9	13 41.5	12 48.9	14 05.9	20 20.4	21 55.5	28 32.2
22 M	12 06 53	29 50 51	26 34 18	3♋38 40	17 46.9	22 39.7	28 01.0	22 09.8	14 06.0	12 51.5	14 13.3	20 18.0	21 54.3	28 32.6
23 Tu	12 10 50	0♎49 35	10♋41 08	17 41 35	17 47.8	22R 48.1	29 14.3	22 49.7	14 30.3	12 54.3	14 20.7	20 15.7	21 53.1	28 33.0
24 W	12 14 46	1 48 21	24 39 55	1♌36 03	17 49.1	22 50.0	0♏27.5	23 29.7	14 54.6	12 57.3	14 28.0	20 13.3	21 51.9	28 33.5
25 Th	12 18 43	2 47 09	8♌29 54	15 21 24	17R 49.9	22 45.3	1 40.8	24 09.8	15 18.9	13 00.5	14 35.3	20 11.0	21 50.8	28 34.0
26 F	12 22 40	3 46 00	22 10 28	28 57 01	17 49.3	22 33.6	2 54.0	24 49.8	15 43.0	13 03.9	14 42.6	20 08.7	21 49.7	28 34.5
27 Sa	12 26 36	4 44 52	5♍40 54	12♍22 02	17 46.8	22 14.5	4 07.2	25 30.0	16 07.2	13 07.4	14 49.9	20 06.4	21 48.6	28 35.1
28 Su	12 30 33	5 43 47	19 00 14	25 35 23	17 41.9	21 48.0	5 20.4	26 10.2	16 31.2	13 11.1	14 57.2	20 04.1	21 47.5	28 35.7
29 M	12 34 29	6 42 44	2♎07 21	8♎35 58	17 34.9	21 14.0	6 33.6	26 50.5	16 55.2	13 15.0	15 04.4	20 01.8	21 46.4	28 36.3
30 Tu	12 38 26	7 41 43	15 01 11	21 22 54	17 26.2	20 32.5	7 46.8	27 30.8	17 19.1	13 19.1	15 11.6	19 59.5	21 45.4	28 36.9

LONGITUDE — October 2008

Day	Sid.Time	☉	0 hr ☽	Noon☽	True☊	☿	♀	♂	⚳	♃	♄	♅	♆	♇
1 W	12 42 22	8♎40 43	27♎41 06	3♏55 50	17♒16.6	19♎43.9	8♏59.9	28♎11.1	17♌42.9	13♑23.3	15♍18.8	19♓57.3	21♒44.4	28♐37.6
2 Th	12 46 19	9 39 46	10♏07 10	16 15 16	17R 07.2	18R 48.9	10 13.1	28 51.6	18 06.6	13 27.7	15 25.9	19R 55.1	21R 43.4	28 38.4
3 F	12 50 15	10 38 51	22 20 21	28 22 41	16 58.7	17 48.1	11 26.2	29 32.0	18 30.3	13 32.4	15 33.0	19 52.9	21 42.5	28 39.1
4 Sa	12 54 12	11 37 57	4♐22 38	10♐20 35	16 51.9	16 42.7	12 39.3	0♏12.6	18 53.9	13 37.1	15 40.1	19 50.7	21 41.6	28 39.9
5 Su	12 58 08	12 37 06	16 17 01	22 12 25	16 47.3	15 34.2	13 52.4	0 53.1	19 17.4	13 42.1	15 47.2	19 48.5	21 40.7	28 40.7
6 M	13 02 05	13 36 16	28 07 23	4♑02 29	16D 44.9	14 24.1	15 05.4	1 33.8	19 40.8	13 47.2	15 54.2	19 46.4	21 39.8	28 41.6
7 Tu	13 06 02	14 35 28	9♑58 21	15 55 38	16 44.4	13 14.4	16 18.5	2 14.5	20 04.2	13 52.5	16 01.1	19 44.3	21 39.0	28 42.4
8 W	13 09 58	15 34 42	21 55 00	27 57 07	16 44.9	12 06.8	17 31.5	2 55.2	20 27.4	13 58.0	16 08.1	19 42.2	21 38.2	28 43.3
9 Th	13 13 55	16 33 57	4♒02 38	10♒12 11	16R 45.7	11 03.4	18 44.5	3 36.0	20 50.6	14 03.6	16 15.0	19 40.1	21 37.4	28 44.3
10 F	13 17 51	17 33 14	16 26 24	22 45 47	16 45.7	10 05.9	19 57.5	4 16.8	21 13.7	14 09.4	16 21.8	19 38.1	21 36.7	28 45.2
11 Sa	13 21 48	18 32 33	29 10 51	5♓41 57	16 44.0	9 16.0	21 10.4	4 57.7	21 36.7	14 15.3	16 28.7	19 36.1	21 36.0	28 46.2
12 Su	13 25 44	19 31 54	12♓19 24	19 03 18	16 40.0	8 35.1	22 23.3	5 38.7	21 59.6	14 21.4	16 35.4	19 34.1	21 35.3	28 47.2
13 M	13 29 41	20 31 17	25 53 40	2♈50 20	16 33.4	8 04.2	23 36.2	6 19.7	22 22.4	14 27.7	16 42.2	19 32.1	21 34.6	28 48.3
14 Tu	13 33 37	21 30 41	9♈52 58	17 01 02	16 24.7	7 43.9	24 49.1	7 00.7	22 45.1	14 34.1	16 48.8	19 30.2	21 34.0	28 49.4
15 W	13 37 34	22 30 08	24 13 53	1♉30 42	16 14.5	7D 34.6	26 01.9	7 41.8	23 07.7	14 40.7	16 55.5	19 28.3	21 33.4	28 50.5
16 Th	13 41 31	23 29 37	8♉50 33	16 12 25	16 04.1	7 36.4	27 14.7	8 23.0	23 30.2	14 47.4	17 02.1	19 26.4	21 32.8	28 51.6
17 F	13 45 27	24 29 08	23 35 18	0♊58 10	15 54.6	7 49.0	28 27.5	9 04.2	23 52.6	14 54.3	17 08.6	19 24.6	21 32.3	28 52.8
18 Sa	13 49 24	25 28 41	8♊20 03	15 40 07	15 47.1	8 12.0	29 40.3	9 45.5	24 14.9	15 01.3	17 15.1	19 22.8	21 31.8	28 54.0
19 Su	13 53 20	26 28 17	22 57 36	0♋11 54	15 42.1	8 44.8	0♐53.0	10 26.8	24 37.1	15 08.5	17 21.6	19 21.0	21 31.3	28 55.2
20 M	13 57 17	27 27 55	7♋22 35	14 29 20	15 39.6	9 26.6	2 05.7	11 08.2	24 59.2	15 15.9	17 28.0	19 19.2	21 30.9	28 56.4
21 Tu	14 01 13	28 27 35	21 31 59	28 30 28	15D 39.0	10 16.7	3 18.4	11 49.6	25 21.2	15 23.4	17 34.4	19 17.5	21 30.5	28 57.7
22 W	14 05 10	29 27 17	5♌24 50	12♌15 11	15R 39.2	11 14.1	4 31.1	12 31.1	25 43.0	15 31.0	17 40.7	19 15.9	21 30.1	28 59.0
23 Th	14 09 06	0♏27 02	19 01 41	25 44 31	15 38.9	12 18.2	5 43.7	13 12.7	26 04.8	15 38.8	17 46.9	19 14.2	21 29.7	29 00.3
24 F	14 13 03	1 26 49	2♍23 53	8♍59 59	15 36.9	13 28.1	6 56.3	13 54.3	26 26.4	15 46.7	17 53.1	19 12.6	21 29.4	29 01.7
25 Sa	14 17 00	2 26 38	15 32 59	22 03 02	15 32.4	14 43.0	8 08.9	14 36.0	26 47.9	15 54.7	17 59.3	19 11.1	21 29.1	29 03.1
26 Su	14 20 56	3 26 29	28 30 17	4♎54 48	15 24.7	16 02.2	9 21.5	15 17.7	27 09.3	16 02.9	18 05.3	19 09.6	21 28.9	29 04.5
27 M	14 24 53	4 26 22	11♎16 39	17 35 53	15 14.2	17 25.1	10 34.0	15 59.5	27 30.5	16 11.3	18 11.4	19 08.1	21 28.7	29 05.9
28 Tu	14 28 49	5 26 17	23 52 31	0♏06 35	15 01.3	18 51.1	11 46.6	16 41.3	27 51.7	16 19.7	18 17.3	19 06.6	21 28.5	29 07.4
29 W	14 32 46	6 26 15	6♏18 05	12 27 03	14 47.2	20 19.7	12 59.0	17 23.2	28 12.6	16 28.3	18 23.2	19 05.2	21 28.3	29 08.8
30 Th	14 36 42	7 26 14	18 33 34	24 37 41	14 33.0	21 50.4	14 11.5	18 05.1	28 33.5	16 37.1	18 29.0	19 03.9	21 28.2	29 10.4
31 F	14 40 39	8 26 15	0♐39 33	6♐39 21	14 19.9	23 22.8	15 23.9	18 47.1	28 54.2	16 45.9	18 34.8	19 02.5	21 28.1	29 11.9

Astro Data

	Dy Hr Mn
♀0S	1 14:22
♃ D	8 4:16
♃△♄	8 23:18
♇ D	9 3:14
☽0N	15 9:37
☉0S	22 15:45
☿ R	24 7:17
☽0S	28 7:30
☽0N	12 19:00
☿ D	15 20:08
☽0S	25 13:37

Planet Ingress

	Dy Hr Mn
☉ ♎	22 15:44
♀ ♏	24 2:59
♂ ♏	4 4:34
♀ ♐	18 18:31
☉ ♏	23 1:09

Last Aspect / ☽ Ingress

Last Aspect Dy Hr Mn		☽ Ingress Dy Hr Mn
1 9:02	♇ □	♎ 1 11:44
3 17:09	♇ ✶	♏ 3 20:02
5 15:45	♆ □	♐ 6 7:11
8 16:43	♇ ☌	♑ 8 19:45
10 13:15	♅ ✶	♒ 11 7:20
13 13:19	♇ ✶	♓ 13 16:04
15 19:03	♇ □	♈ 15 21:39
17 22:26	♇ △	♉ 18 0:57
19 22:51	☉ △	♊ 20 3:17
22 5:04	☉ □	♋ 22 5:49
23 21:17	♂ □	♌ 24 9:13
26 11:20	♇ △	♍ 26 13:52
28 17:31	♇ □	♎ 28 20:05

Last Aspect / ☽ Ingress

Last Aspect Dy Hr Mn		☽ Ingress Dy Hr Mn
1 1:48	♇ ✶	♏ 1 4:26
2 22:46	♆ □	♐ 3 15:14
6 1:09	♇ ☌	♑ 6 3:48
7 19:37	♅ ✶	♒ 8 16:03
10 23:13	♇ ✶	♓ 11 1:31
13 5:02	♇ □	♈ 13 7:07
15 7:36	♇ △	♉ 15 9:31
17 7:33	♀ ☍	♊ 17 10:25
19 9:52	♇ ☍	♋ 19 11:40
21 11:55	☉ □	♌ 21 14:35
23 17:53	♇ △	♍ 23 19:40
26 1:03	♇ □	♎ 26 2:48
28 10:05	♇ ✶	♏ 28 11:47
30 5:45	♆ □	♐ 30 22:41

☽ Phases & Eclipses

Dy Hr Mn	
7 14:04	☽ 15♐19
15 9:13	○ 22♓54
22 5:04	☾ 29♊34
29 8:12	● 6♎33
7 9:04	☽ 14♑28
14 20:02	○ 21♈51
21 11:55	☾ 28♋27
28 23:14	● 5♏54

Astro Data

1 September 2008
Julian Day # 39691
SVP 5♓08'07"
GC 26♐57.6 ⚴ 9♊56.4
Eris 21♈37.3R ⚵ 15♐32.7
⚷ 17♒27.4R ⚶ 14♉38.8
☽ Mean ☊ 17♒23.7

1 October 2008
Julian Day # 39721
SVP 5♓08'04"
GC 26♐57.7 ⚴ 17♊59.9
Eris 21♈21.7R ⚵ 21♐06.9
⚷ 16♒20.3R ⚶ 13♉24.1R
☽ Mean ☊ 15♒48.4

November 2008 — LONGITUDE

Day	Sid.Time	☉	0 hr ☽	Noon ☽	True ☊	☿	♀	♂	⚳	♃	♄	♅	♆	♇
1 Sa	14 44 35	9♏26 18	12♐37 16	18♐33 37	14♒08.9	24♎56.7	16♐36.3	19♏29.2	29♌14.8	16♑54.9	18♍40.5	19♓01.3	21♒28.1	29♐13.4
2 Su	14 48 32	10 26 23	24 28 44	0♑23 01	14R 00.7	26 31.6	17 48.6	20 11.3	29 35.2	17 04.1	18 46.2	19R 00.0	21D 28.1	29 15.0
3 M	14 52 29	11 26 29	6♑16 53	12 10 52	13 55.4	28 07.4	19 01.0	20 53.4	29 55.4	17 13.3	18 51.7	18 58.8	21 28.1	29 16.6
4 Tu	14 56 25	12 26 37	18 05 32	24 01 27	13 52.7	29 43.9	20 13.2	21 35.7	0♍15.6	17 22.7	18 57.3	18 57.7	21 28.2	29 18.3
5 W	15 00 22	13 26 46	29 59 15	5♒59 38	13 51.9	1♏20.8	21 25.5	22 17.9	0 35.5	17 32.2	19 02.7	18 56.6	21 28.3	29 19.9
6 Th	15 04 18	14 26 57	12♒03 15	18 10 49	13 51.8	2 58.1	22 37.7	23 00.3	0 55.3	17 41.8	19 08.1	18 55.5	21 28.4	29 21.6
7 F	15 08 15	15 27 09	24 23 01	0♓40 30	13 51.3	4 35.5	23 49.8	23 42.6	1 15.0	17 51.6	19 13.4	18 54.5	21 28.6	29 23.3
8 Sa	15 12 11	16 27 23	7♓03 53	13 33 44	13 49.3	6 13.0	25 01.9	24 25.0	1 34.5	18 01.4	19 18.6	18 53.5	21 28.7	29 25.0
9 Su	15 16 08	17 27 39	20 10 31	26 54 34	13 44.9	7 50.6	26 13.9	25 07.5	1 53.8	18 11.4	19 23.7	18 52.6	21 29.0	29 26.7
10 M	15 20 04	18 27 55	3♈46 04	10♈45 02	13 37.8	9 28.1	27 25.9	25 50.0	2 12.9	18 21.5	19 28.8	18 51.8	21 29.2	29 28.4
11 Tu	15 24 01	19 28 14	17 51 17	25 04 25	13 28.2	11 05.5	28 37.9	26 32.6	2 31.9	18 31.6	19 33.8	18 50.9	21 29.5	29 30.2
12 W	15 27 58	20 28 34	2♉23 49	9♉48 38	13 16.9	12 42.8	29 49.8	27 15.3	2 50.7	18 41.9	19 38.7	18 50.1	21 29.9	29 32.0
13 Th	15 31 54	21 28 55	17 17 49	24 50 10	13 05.2	14 19.9	1♑01.6	27 58.0	3 09.3	18 52.4	19 43.6	18 49.4	21 30.2	29 33.8
14 F	15 35 51	22 29 19	2♊24 25	9♊59 13	12 54.4	15 56.8	2 13.4	28 40.7	3 27.8	19 02.9	19 48.3	18 48.7	21 30.6	29 35.6
15 Sa	15 39 47	23 29 44	17 33 13	25 05 12	12 45.7	17 33.5	3 25.2	29 23.5	3 46.0	19 13.5	19 53.0	18 48.1	21 31.1	29 37.5
16 Su	15 43 44	24 30 11	2♋34 03	9♋58 50	12 39.7	19 10.0	4 36.8	0♐06.4	4 04.1	19 24.2	19 57.6	18 47.5	21 31.5	29 39.4
17 M	15 47 40	25 30 40	17 18 46	24 33 21	12 36.5	20 46.2	5 48.5	0 49.3	4 22.0	19 35.0	20 02.1	18 47.0	21 32.0	29 41.2
18 Tu	15 51 37	26 31 10	1♌42 13	8♌45 12	12D 35.5	22 22.2	7 00.0	1 32.2	4 39.7	19 46.0	20 06.6	18 46.5	21 32.6	29 43.1
19 W	15 55 34	27 31 43	15 42 18	22 33 37	12R 35.6	23 58.0	8 11.5	2 15.3	4 57.2	19 57.0	20 10.9	18 46.0	21 33.1	29 45.1
20 Th	15 59 30	28 32 17	29 19 24	5♍59 56	12 35.5	25 33.6	9 23.0	2 58.3	5 14.4	20 08.1	20 15.2	18 45.6	21 33.7	29 47.0
21 F	16 03 27	29 32 53	12♍35 34	19 06 41	12 33.9	27 09.0	10 34.4	3 41.5	5 31.5	20 19.3	20 19.4	18 45.3	21 34.4	29 48.9
22 Sa	16 07 23	0♐33 30	25 33 38	1♎56 49	12 29.9	28 44.2	11 45.7	4 24.6	5 48.4	20 30.6	20 23.5	18 45.0	21 35.0	29 50.9
23 Su	16 11 20	1 34 09	8♎16 34	14 33 12	12 23.1	0♐19.2	12 56.9	5 07.9	6 05.0	20 42.0	20 27.5	18 44.8	21 35.7	29 52.9
24 M	16 15 16	2 34 50	20 47 02	26 58 18	12 13.4	1 54.0	14 08.1	5 51.2	6 21.4	20 53.5	20 31.4	18 44.6	21 36.5	29 54.9
25 Tu	16 19 13	3 35 33	3♏07 13	9♏14 00	12 01.6	3 28.7	15 19.3	6 34.5	6 37.6	21 05.1	20 35.2	18 44.4	21 37.3	29 56.9
26 W	16 23 09	4 36 17	15 18 48	21 21 46	11 48.4	5 03.2	16 30.3	7 17.9	6 53.5	21 16.8	20 39.0	18 44.4	21 38.1	29 58.9
27 Th	16 27 06	5 37 02	27 23 02	3♐22 43	11 35.2	6 37.6	17 41.3	8 01.4	7 09.2	21 28.6	20 42.6	18D 44.3	21 38.9	0♑00.9
28 F	16 31 03	6 37 49	9♐20 59	15 17 58	11 22.9	8 11.9	18 52.2	8 44.9	7 24.7	21 40.4	20 46.2	18 44.3	21 39.8	0 03.0
29 Sa	16 34 59	7 38 37	21 13 51	27 08 50	11 12.6	9 46.0	20 03.0	9 28.5	7 40.0	21 52.3	20 49.6	18 44.4	21 40.7	0 05.0
30 Su	16 38 56	8 39 26	3♑03 09	8♑57 05	11 04.9	11 20.1	21 13.7	10 12.1	7 54.9	22 04.4	20 53.0	18 44.5	21 41.6	0 07.1

December 2008 — LONGITUDE

Day	Sid.Time	☉	0 hr ☽	Noon ☽	True ☊	☿	♀	♂	⚳	♃	♄	♅	♆	♇
1 M	16 42 52	9♐40 16	14♑50 57	20♑45 08	11♒00.0	12♐54.1	22♑24.4	10♐55.7	8♍09.7	22♑16.4	20♍56.2	18♓44.7	21♒42.6	0♑09.2
2 Tu	16 46 49	10 41 07	26 40 03	2♒36 09	10D 57.6	14 28.1	23 34.9	11 39.5	8 24.1	22 28.6	20 59.4	18 44.9	21 43.6	0 11.3
3 W	16 50 45	11 41 59	8♒33 58	14 34 03	10 57.3	16 02.0	24 45.4	12 23.2	8 38.3	22 40.9	21 02.5	18 45.2	21 44.6	0 13.4
4 Th	16 54 42	12 42 52	20 36 59	26 43 24	10 58.0	17 35.9	25 55.7	13 07.0	8 52.3	22 53.2	21 05.4	18 45.5	21 45.7	0 15.5
5 F	16 58 38	13 43 46	2♓53 54	9♓09 10	10R 58.8	19 09.8	27 06.0	13 50.9	9 05.9	23 05.6	21 08.3	18 45.9	21 46.7	0 17.6
6 Sa	17 02 35	14 44 40	15 29 47	21 56 23	10 58.6	20 43.6	28 16.1	14 34.8	9 19.3	23 18.0	21 11.1	18 46.3	21 47.9	0 19.7
7 Su	17 06 32	15 45 36	28 29 30	5♈09 36	10 56.7	22 17.5	29 26.2	15 18.8	9 32.4	23 30.6	21 13.7	18 46.8	21 49.0	0 21.9
8 M	17 10 28	16 46 31	11♈57 03	18 52 02	10 52.6	23 51.4	0♒36.1	16 02.8	9 45.2	23 43.2	21 16.3	18 47.3	21 50.2	0 24.0
9 Tu	17 14 25	17 47 28	25 54 38	3♉04 41	10 46.4	25 25.2	1 45.9	16 46.8	9 57.7	23 55.8	21 18.8	18 47.9	21 51.4	0 26.2
10 W	17 18 21	18 48 25	10♉21 48	17 45 25	10 38.6	26 59.2	2 55.5	17 30.9	10 10.0	24 08.6	21 21.1	18 48.5	21 52.6	0 28.3
11 Th	17 22 18	19 49 23	25 14 40	2♊48 32	10 30.3	28 33.1	4 05.1	18 15.1	10 21.9	24 21.4	21 23.4	18 49.2	21 53.9	0 30.5
12 F	17 26 14	20 50 22	10♊25 47	18 05 05	10 22.6	0♑07.0	5 14.5	18 59.3	10 33.5	24 34.2	21 25.6	18 50.0	21 55.2	0 32.7
13 Sa	17 30 11	21 51 22	25 44 59	3♋24 06	10 16.3	1 41.0	6 23.7	19 43.6	10 44.9	24 47.1	21 27.6	18 50.8	21 56.6	0 34.8
14 Su	17 34 07	22 52 23	11♋01 02	18 34 33	10 12.2	3 14.9	7 32.9	20 27.9	10 55.9	25 00.1	21 29.6	18 51.6	21 57.9	0 37.0
15 M	17 38 04	23 53 24	26 03 35	3♌27 14	10D 10.4	4 48.8	8 41.8	21 12.3	11 06.6	25 13.2	21 31.4	18 52.5	21 59.3	0 39.2
16 Tu	17 42 01	24 54 26	10♌44 51	17 55 57	10 10.4	6 22.7	9 50.7	21 56.7	11 17.0	25 26.3	21 33.1	18 53.4	22 00.7	0 41.4
17 W	17 45 57	25 55 29	25 00 18	1♍57 49	10 11.6	7 56.5	10 59.3	22 41.1	11 27.0	25 39.4	21 34.7	18 54.4	22 02.2	0 43.6
18 Th	17 49 54	26 56 33	8♍48 34	15 32 47	10R 12.9	9 30.1	12 07.9	23 25.6	11 36.7	25 52.6	21 36.3	18 55.5	22 03.6	0 45.8
19 F	17 53 50	27 57 38	22 10 46	28 42 54	10 13.4	11 03.6	13 16.2	24 10.2	11 46.1	26 05.9	21 37.7	18 56.5	22 05.1	0 48.0
20 Sa	17 57 47	28 58 44	5♎09 39	11♎31 26	10 12.5	12 36.9	14 24.4	24 54.8	11 55.1	26 19.2	21 39.0	18 57.7	22 06.6	0 50.2
21 Su	18 01 43	29 59 50	17 48 47	24 02 09	10 09.7	14 09.8	15 32.4	25 39.5	12 03.7	26 32.5	21 40.2	18 58.9	22 08.2	0 52.4
22 M	18 05 40	1♑00 58	0♏12 01	6♏18 50	10 05.1	15 42.3	16 40.3	26 24.2	12 12.0	26 45.9	21 41.2	19 00.1	22 09.8	0 54.6
23 Tu	18 09 36	2 02 06	12 23 00	18 24 56	9 58.9	17 14.4	17 48.0	27 08.9	12 20.0	26 59.4	21 42.2	19 01.4	22 11.4	0 56.8
24 W	18 13 33	3 03 14	24 24 58	0♐23 27	9 51.9	18 45.7	18 55.5	27 53.7	12 27.6	27 12.9	21 43.1	19 02.7	22 13.0	0 59.0
25 Th	18 17 30	4 04 24	6♐20 40	12 16 53	9 44.6	20 16.3	20 02.7	28 38.6	12 34.8	27 26.4	21 43.8	19 04.1	22 14.6	1 01.2
26 F	18 21 26	5 05 33	18 12 22	24 07 21	9 37.9	21 45.8	21 09.8	29 23.5	12 41.6	27 40.0	21 44.5	19 05.5	22 16.3	1 03.4
27 Sa	18 25 23	6 06 43	0♑02 02	5♑56 39	9 32.4	23 14.2	22 16.7	0♑08.4	12 48.0	27 53.6	21 45.0	19 07.0	22 18.0	1 05.5
28 Su	18 29 19	7 07 54	11 51 25	17 46 33	9 28.5	24 41.0	23 23.4	0 53.4	12 54.1	28 07.3	21 45.4	19 08.5	22 19.7	1 07.7
29 M	18 33 16	8 09 04	23 42 18	29 38 56	9D 26.3	26 06.1	24 29.8	1 38.4	12 59.7	28 21.0	21 45.7	19 10.1	22 21.5	1 09.9
30 Tu	18 37 12	9 10 15	5♒36 43	11♒35 59	9 25.9	27 29.0	25 36.1	2 23.5	13 05.0	28 34.7	21 45.9	19 11.7	22 23.3	1 12.1
31 W	18 41 09	10 11 25	17 37 03	23 40 19	9 26.7	28 49.4	26 42.0	3 08.6	13 09.8	28 48.5	21R 46.0	19 13.4	22 25.0	1 14.3

Astro Data

	Dy Hr Mn
♆ D	2 6:39
♄☍♅	4 13:36
☽ 0N	9 4:29
♃✶♅	13 5:40
♃△♄	21 12:13
☽ 0S	21 18:16
♅ D	27 16:08
♃⚺♆	28 10:35
☽ 0N	6 12:26
☽ 0S	18 23:41
♄ R	31 18:08

Planet Ingress

		Dy Hr Mn
⚳	♍	3 17:25
☿	♏	4 16:00
♀	♑	12 15:25
♂	♐	16 8:27
☉	♐	21 22:44
☿	♐	23 7:09
♇	♑	27 1:03
♀	♒	7 23:37
☿	♑	12 10:13
☉	♑	21 12:04
♂	♑	27 7:30

Last Aspect / ☽ Ingress

Last Aspect Dy Hr Mn			☽ Ingress	Dy Hr Mn
2 9:41	♇	☌	♑	2 11:13
4 6:47	♂	✶	♒	5 0:01
7 9:33	♇	✶	♓	7 10:43
9 16:28	♇	□	♈	9 17:26
11 19:17	♇	△	♉	11 20:05
13 17:13	♂	☍	♊	13 20:11
15 19:17	♇	☍	♋	15 19:52
17 13:43	☉	△	♌	17 21:08
20 0:48	♇	△	♍	20 1:13
22 8:02	♇	□	♎	22 8:20
24 17:45	♇	✶	♏	24 17:54
26 12:32	♆	□	♐	27 5:14
29 0:53	♆	✶	♑	29 17:48

Last Aspect / ☽ Ingress

Last Aspect Dy Hr Mn			☽ Ingress	Dy Hr Mn
1 15:44	♀	☌	♒	2 6:45
4 2:15	♆	☌	♓	4 18:23
7 0:43	♀	✶	♈	7 2:44
8 21:35	☿	△	♉	9 6:52
10 22:23	♃	△	♊	11 7:33
12 18:01	♆	△	♋	13 6:40
14 22:27	♃	☍	♌	15 6:23
17 0:46	☉	△	♍	17 8:36
19 10:29	☉	□	♎	19 14:23
21 16:57	♃	□	♏	21 23:37
24 5:30	♃	✶	♐	24 11:13
26 23:25	♂	☌	♑	26 23:56
29 9:20	♃	☌	♒	29 12:42

☽ Phases & Eclipses

Dy Hr Mn	
6 4:03	☽ 14♒07
13 6:17	○ 21♉15
19 21:31	☾ 27♌56
27 16:55	● 5♐49
5 21:26	☽ 14♓08
12 16:37	○ 21♊02
19 10:29	☾ 27♍54
27 12:22	● 6♑08

Astro Data

1 November 2008
Julian Day # 39752
SVP 5♓08'00"
GC 26♐57.8 ⚵ 20♊27.0R
Eris 21♈03.4R ⚶ 29♐49.9
⚷ 16♒03.9 ⚴ 6♉22.4R
☽ Mean ☊ 14♒09.9

1 December 2008
Julian Day # 39782
SVP 5♓07'55"
GC 26♐57.8 ⚵ 14♊00.9R
Eris 20♈48.7R ⚶ 10♑07.7
⚷ 16♒46.9 ⚴ 0♉21.3R
☽ Mean ☊ 12♒34.6

LONGITUDE — January 2009

Day	Sid.Time	☉	0 hr ☽	Noon☽	True☊	☿	♀	♂	⚳	♃	♄	♅	♆	♇
1 Th	18 45 06	11♑12 35	29♒46 11	5♓55 04	9♒28.3	0♒06.8	27♒47.7	3♑53.8	13♍14.3	29♑02.3	21♍46.0	19♓15.1	22♒26.9	1♑16.5
2 F	18 49 02	12 13 45	12♓07 26	18 23 45	9 30.1	1 20.6	28 53.2	4 39.0	13 18.3	29 16.2	21R45.8	19 16.8	22 28.7	1 18.6
3 Sa	18 52 59	13 14 55	24 44 31	1♈10 11	9R31.5	2 30.3	29 58.4	5 24.3	13 21.9	29 30.0	21 45.6	19 18.6	22 30.5	1 20.8
4 Su	18 56 55	14 16 05	7♈41 13	14 18 01	9 32.0	3 35.1	1♓03.3	6 09.5	13 25.2	29 43.9	21 45.2	19 20.5	22 32.4	1 22.9
5 M	19 00 52	15 17 14	21 00 58	27 50 19	9 31.5	4 34.4	2 07.9	6 54.9	13 28.0	29 57.9	21 44.8	19 22.3	22 34.3	1 25.1
6 Tu	19 04 48	16 18 23	4♉46 15	11♉48 48	9 29.8	5 27.3	3 12.3	7 40.2	13 30.3	0♒11.8	21 44.2	19 24.3	22 36.2	1 27.2
7 W	19 08 45	17 19 32	18 57 50	26 13 04	9 27.2	6 12.9	4 16.3	8 25.6	13 32.3	0 25.8	21 43.5	19 26.2	22 38.1	1 29.4
8 Th	19 12 41	18 20 40	3♊34 02	11♊00 04	9 24.3	6 50.4	5 19.9	9 11.1	13 33.8	0 39.8	21 42.7	19 28.3	22 40.1	1 31.5
9 F	19 16 38	19 21 48	18 30 19	26 03 46	9 21.4	7 18.8	6 23.3	9 56.6	13 34.9	0 53.8	21 41.8	19 30.3	22 42.1	1 33.6
10 Sa	19 20 35	20 22 56	3♋39 17	11♋15 39	9 19.2	7 37.4	7 26.3	10 42.1	13 35.6	1 07.9	21 40.8	19 32.4	22 44.1	1 35.7
11 Su	19 24 31	21 24 03	18 51 35	26 25 51	9D17.9	7R45.2	8 28.9	11 27.7	13R35.8	1 21.9	21 39.7	19 34.6	22 46.1	1 37.8
12 M	19 28 28	22 25 10	3♌57 16	11♌24 44	9 17.5	7 41.7	9 31.2	12 13.3	13 35.6	1 36.0	21 38.5	19 36.7	22 48.1	1 39.9
13 Tu	19 32 24	23 26 16	18 47 19	26 04 16	9 18.1	7 26.4	10 33.1	12 58.9	13 35.0	1 50.1	21 37.1	19 38.9	22 50.1	1 42.0
14 W	19 36 21	24 27 22	3♍14 58	10♍19 03	9 19.1	6 59.4	11 34.6	13 44.6	13 33.9	2 04.2	21 35.7	19 41.2	22 52.2	1 44.1
15 Th	19 40 17	25 28 28	17 16 17	24 06 35	9 20.3	6 20.9	12 35.7	14 30.4	13 32.4	2 18.3	21 34.2	19 43.5	22 54.2	1 46.1
16 F	19 44 14	26 29 34	0♎50 05	7♎26 59	9 21.4	5 31.7	13 36.4	15 16.1	13 30.4	2 32.5	21 32.5	19 45.8	22 56.3	1 48.2
17 Sa	19 48 10	27 30 40	13 57 35	20 22 19	9R22.0	4 32.8	14 36.6	16 01.9	13 28.0	2 46.6	21 30.8	19 48.2	22 58.4	1 50.2
18 Su	19 52 07	28 31 45	26 41 39	2♏56 04	9 22.1	3 26.0	15 36.4	16 47.8	13 25.2	3 00.8	21 28.9	19 50.6	23 00.5	1 52.2
19 M	19 56 04	29 32 50	9♏06 08	15 12 23	9 21.6	2 13.3	16 35.7	17 33.7	13 21.9	3 15.0	21 27.0	19 53.0	23 02.6	1 54.2
20 Tu	20 00 00	0♒33 55	21 15 22	27 15 39	9 20.8	0 57.0	17 34.6	18 19.6	13 18.1	3 29.2	21 24.9	19 55.5	23 04.8	1 56.2
21 W	20 03 57	1 35 00	3♐13 44	9♐10 09	9 19.7	29♑39.3	18 33.0	19 05.6	13 13.9	3 43.3	21 22.8	19 58.0	23 06.9	1 58.2
22 Th	20 07 53	2 36 04	15 05 22	20 59 51	9 18.6	28 22.8	19 30.8	19 51.6	13 09.3	3 57.5	21 20.5	20 00.6	23 09.1	2 00.1
23 F	20 11 50	3 37 07	26 54 00	2♑48 13	9 17.7	27 09.5	20 28.2	20 37.6	13 04.3	4 11.7	21 18.2	20 03.2	23 11.2	2 02.1
24 Sa	20 15 46	4 38 10	8♑42 51	14 38 14	9 17.1	26 01.4	21 24.9	21 23.7	12 58.8	4 25.9	21 15.7	20 05.8	23 13.4	2 04.0
25 Su	20 19 43	5 39 12	20 34 40	26 32 24	9 16.7	24 59.8	22 21.1	22 09.8	12 52.9	4 40.1	21 13.2	20 08.4	23 15.6	2 05.9
26 M	20 23 39	6 40 13	2♒31 42	8♒32 48	9D16.6	24 06.0	23 16.7	22 55.9	12 46.5	4 54.3	21 10.5	20 11.1	23 17.8	2 07.8
27 Tu	20 27 36	7 41 14	14 35 54	20 41 13	9 16.7	23 20.7	24 11.7	23 42.1	12 39.8	5 08.5	21 07.8	20 13.8	23 20.0	2 09.7
28 W	20 31 33	8 42 13	26 48 56	2♓59 15	9R16.8	22 44.2	25 06.1	24 28.3	12 32.6	5 22.7	21 05.0	20 16.6	23 22.2	2 11.6
29 Th	20 35 29	9 43 12	9♓12 21	15 28 28	9 16.8	22 16.5	25 59.8	25 14.5	12 25.0	5 36.9	21 02.1	20 19.4	23 24.5	2 13.4
30 F	20 39 26	10 44 09	21 47 47	28 10 30	9 16.6	21 57.7	26 52.8	26 00.7	12 17.0	5 51.1	20 59.1	20 22.2	23 26.7	2 15.2
31 Sa	20 43 22	11 45 05	4♈36 51	11♈07 02	9 16.4	21D47.3	27 45.0	26 47.0	12 08.6	6 05.3	20 56.0	20 25.0	23 28.9	2 17.0

LONGITUDE — February 2009

Day	Sid.Time	☉	0 hr ☽	Noon☽	True☊	☿	♀	♂	⚳	♃	♄	♅	♆	♇
1 Su	20 47 19	12♒46 00	17♈41 17	24♈19 46	9♒16.1	21♑44.9	28♓36.5	27♑33.3	11♍59.9	6♒19.5	20♍52.8	20♓27.9	23♒31.2	2♑18.8
2 M	20 51 15	13 46 53	1♉02 41	7♉50 10	9D15.9	21 50.2	29 27.3	28 19.7	11R50.8	6 33.6	20R49.5	20 30.8	23 33.4	2 20.6
3 Tu	20 55 12	14 47 45	14 42 20	21 39 12	9 16.0	22 02.5	0♈17.2	29 06.0	11 41.3	6 47.8	20 46.2	20 33.7	23 35.7	2 22.3
4 W	20 59 08	15 48 36	28 40 46	5♊46 53	9 16.3	22 21.3	1 06.3	29 52.4	11 31.4	7 01.9	20 42.8	20 36.6	23 38.0	2 24.1
5 Th	21 03 05	16 49 25	12♊57 21	20 11 50	9 16.8	22 46.2	1 54.5	0♒38.8	11 21.2	7 16.0	20 39.3	20 39.6	23 40.2	2 25.8
6 F	21 07 02	17 50 13	27 29 53	4♋50 55	9 17.6	23 16.6	2 41.8	1 25.3	11 10.7	7 30.1	20 35.7	20 42.6	23 42.5	2 27.4
7 Sa	21 10 58	18 51 00	12♋14 17	19 39 11	9 18.3	23 52.0	3 28.1	2 11.8	10 59.9	7 44.2	20 32.1	20 45.6	23 44.8	2 29.1
8 Su	21 14 55	19 51 45	27 04 45	4♌30 04	9R18.7	24 32.1	4 13.4	2 58.2	10 48.8	7 58.3	20 28.4	20 48.7	23 47.0	2 30.7
9 M	21 18 51	20 52 28	11♌54 12	19 16 10	9 18.6	25 16.5	4 57.7	3 44.8	10 37.3	8 12.3	20 24.6	20 51.7	23 49.3	2 32.4
10 Tu	21 22 48	21 53 10	26 35 06	3♍50 08	9 17.8	26 04.7	5 40.9	4 31.3	10 25.6	8 26.4	20 20.8	20 54.8	23 51.6	2 33.9
11 W	21 26 44	22 53 51	11♍00 32	18 05 40	9 16.4	26 56.5	6 23.0	5 17.9	10 13.6	8 40.4	20 16.9	20 57.9	23 53.9	2 35.5
12 Th	21 30 41	23 54 31	25 05 04	1♎58 23	9 14.4	27 51.6	7 04.0	6 04.5	10 01.4	8 54.3	20 12.9	21 01.1	23 56.2	2 37.1
13 F	21 34 37	24 55 09	8♎45 24	15 26 05	9 12.3	28 49.7	7 43.8	6 51.1	9 48.9	9 08.3	20 08.8	21 04.2	23 58.4	2 38.6
14 Sa	21 38 34	25 55 46	22 00 31	28 28 53	9 10.2	29 50.5	8 22.3	7 37.7	9 36.2	9 22.2	20 04.7	21 07.4	24 00.7	2 40.1
15 Su	21 42 31	26 56 23	4♏51 29	11♏08 43	9 08.7	0♒53.9	8 59.5	8 24.4	9 23.3	9 36.1	20 00.6	21 10.6	24 03.0	2 41.5
16 M	21 46 27	27 56 57	17 21 04	23 29 03	9D07.9	1 59.7	9 35.4	9 11.1	9 10.2	9 50.0	19 56.4	21 13.8	24 05.3	2 43.0
17 Tu	21 50 24	28 57 31	29 33 12	5♐34 09	9 08.0	3 07.6	10 10.0	9 57.8	8 56.9	10 03.9	19 52.1	21 17.0	24 07.6	2 44.4
18 W	21 54 20	29 58 04	11♐32 30	17 28 52	9 08.9	4 17.6	10 43.0	10 44.5	8 43.5	10 17.7	19 47.8	21 20.2	24 09.8	2 45.8
19 Th	21 58 17	0♓58 35	23 23 51	29 18 04	9 10.4	5 29.5	11 14.6	11 31.3	8 29.9	10 31.5	19 43.4	21 23.5	24 12.1	2 47.2
20 F	22 02 13	1 59 05	5♑12 06	11♑06 30	9 12.2	6 43.3	11 44.6	12 18.0	8 16.2	10 45.3	19 39.0	21 26.8	24 14.4	2 48.5
21 Sa	22 06 10	2 59 33	17 01 47	22 58 27	9 13.8	7 58.7	12 13.1	13 04.8	8 02.4	10 59.0	19 34.6	21 30.1	24 16.6	2 49.8
22 Su	22 10 06	4 00 00	28 56 57	4♒57 40	9R14.7	9 15.7	12 39.8	13 51.6	7 48.5	11 12.7	19 30.1	21 33.4	24 18.9	2 51.1
23 M	22 14 03	5 00 26	11♒00 57	17 07 07	9 14.5	10 34.2	13 04.8	14 38.5	7 34.5	11 26.3	19 25.6	21 36.7	24 21.2	2 52.4
24 Tu	22 18 00	6 00 50	23 16 25	29 29 01	9 13.0	11 54.2	13 28.1	15 25.3	7 20.5	11 39.9	19 21.0	21 40.0	24 23.4	2 53.6
25 W	22 21 56	7 01 12	5♓45 05	12♓04 42	9 10.0	13 15.6	13 49.4	16 12.1	7 06.4	11 53.5	19 16.4	21 43.4	24 25.6	2 54.8
26 Th	22 25 53	8 01 32	18 27 54	24 54 41	9 05.9	14 38.3	14 08.9	16 59.0	6 52.4	12 07.0	19 11.8	21 46.7	24 27.9	2 56.0
27 F	22 29 49	9 01 51	1♈25 00	7♈58 47	9 00.9	16 02.4	14 26.3	17 45.9	6 38.4	12 20.5	19 07.1	21 50.1	24 30.1	2 57.1
28 Sa	22 33 46	10 02 08	14 35 57	21 16 22	8 55.8	17 27.6	14 41.7	18 32.8	6 24.4	12 33.9	19 02.4	21 53.5	24 32.3	2 58.3

Astro Data

	Dy Hr Mn
☽0N	2 18:27
⚳R	11 13:04
☿R	11 16:45
♃⊻♇	12 19:51
☽0S	15 7:49
♃∠♅	27 23:05
☽0N	29 23:50
♀0N	30 9:31
♃⚼♄	30 23:03
☿D	1 7:10
♄☍♅	5 10:56
☽0S	11 18:14
☽0N	26 6:13

Planet Ingress

		Dy Hr Mn
☿	♒	1 9:51
♀	♓	3 12:35
♃	♒	5 15:41
☉	♒	19 22:40
☿	♑R	21 5:36
♀	♈	3 3:41
♂	♒	4 15:55
☿	♒	14 15:39
☉	♓	18 12:46

Last Aspect / ☽ Ingress

Dy Hr Mn	Last Aspect	☽ Ingress	Dy Hr Mn
31 18:34	♀ ☌	♓	1 0:27
3 8:51	♃ ⚹	♈	3 9:50
5 2:44	♆ ⚹	♉	5 15:46
7 6:05	♆ □	♊	7 18:12
9 6:40	♆ △	♋	9 18:14
11 4:27	♄ ⚹	♌	11 17:41
13 6:38	♆ ☍	♍	13 18:33
15 14:37	☉ △	♎	15 22:30
18 2:46	☉ □	♏	18 6:20
20 3:37	♆ □	♐	20 17:30
22 16:23	♆ ⚹	♑	23 6:18
25 9:08	☿ ☌	♒	25 18:56
27 17:13	♆ ☌	♓	28 6:12
30 9:24	♀ ☌	♈	30 15:25

Last Aspect / ☽ Ingress

Dy Hr Mn	Last Aspect	☽ Ingress	Dy Hr Mn
1 18:08	♂ □	♉	1 22:09
4 1:27	♂ △	♊	4 2:14
5 17:44	♆ △	♋	6 4:06
7 19:07	☿ ☍	♌	8 4:43
9 19:29	♆ ☍	♍	10 5:38
12 4:18	☿ △	♎	12 8:33
14 14:46	☿ □	♏	14 14:51
16 21:37	☉ □	♐	17 0:53
19 1:36	♆ ⚹	♑	19 13:25
21 9:01	♅ ⚹	♒	22 2:06
24 2:08	♆ ☌	♓	24 13:00
26 6:09	♅ ☌	♈	26 21:24

☽ Phases & Eclipses

Dy Hr Mn		
4 11:56	☽	14♈16
11 3:27	○	21♋02
18 2:46	☾	28♎08
26 7:55	●	6♒30
26 7:58:38	●	A 07'54"
2 23:13	☽	14♉15
9 14:49	○	21♌00
9 14:38	●	A 0.900
16 21:37	☾	28♏21
25 1:35	●	6♓35

Astro Data

1 January 2009
Julian Day # 39813
SVP 5♓07'49"
GC 26♐57.9 ⚵ 5♊05.0R
Eris 20♈41.4R ⚴ 21♑58.2
⚷ 18♒23.0 ⚶ 0♉29.1
☽ Mean ☊ 10♒56.1

1 February 2009
Julian Day # 39844
SVP 5♓07'44"
GC 26♐58.0 ⚵ 5♊45.5
Eris 20♈44.5 ⚴ 4♒29.7
⚷ 20♒31.0 ⚶ 6♉30.2
☽ Mean ☊ 9♒17.6

March 2009 LONGITUDE

Day	Sid.Time	☉	0 hr ☽	Noon ☽	True ☊	☿	♀	♂	⚳	♃	♄	♅	♆	♇
1 Su	22 37 42	11♓02 22	27♈59 54	4♉46 26	8♒51.2	18♒54.2	14♈55.0	19♒19.7	6♍10.4	12♒47.3	18♍57.7	21♓56.8	24♒34.5	2♑59.3
2 M	22 41 39	12 02 35	11♉35 50	18 27 58	8R47.7	20 21.9	15 06.1	20 06.6	5R56.6	13 00.6	18R53.0	22 00.2	24 36.7	3 00.4
3 Tu	22 45 35	13 02 46	25 22 44	2♊19 59	8D45.6	21 50.8	15 14.9	20 53.5	5 42.8	13 13.9	18 48.3	22 03.6	24 38.9	3 01.4
4 W	22 49 32	14 02 55	9♊19 36	16 21 29	8 45.2	23 20.8	15 21.5	21 40.4	5 29.1	13 27.2	18 43.5	22 07.0	24 41.1	3 02.4
5 Th	22 53 29	15 03 01	23 25 28	0♋31 22	8 46.0	24 52.0	15 25.6	22 27.3	5 15.6	13 40.4	18 38.7	22 10.5	24 43.3	3 03.4
6 F	22 57 25	16 03 06	7♋39 01	14 48 08	8 47.4	26 24.4	15R27.4	23 14.3	5 02.2	13 53.5	18 34.0	22 13.9	24 45.5	3 04.4
7 Sa	23 01 22	17 03 08	21 58 26	29 09 32	8R48.6	27 57.8	15 26.7	24 01.2	4 49.0	14 06.6	18 29.2	22 17.3	24 47.6	3 05.3
8 Su	23 05 18	18 03 08	6♌21 01	13♌32 24	8 48.9	29 32.5	15 23.5	24 48.2	4 36.0	14 19.6	18 24.4	22 20.7	24 49.7	3 06.2
9 M	23 09 15	19 03 06	20 43 08	27 52 38	8 47.4	1♓08.2	15 17.8	25 35.1	4 23.1	14 32.6	18 19.6	22 24.1	24 51.9	3 07.0
10 Tu	23 13 11	20 03 02	5♍00 18	12♍05 28	8 43.9	2 45.1	15 09.6	26 22.1	4 10.5	14 45.5	18 14.8	22 27.6	24 54.0	3 07.8
11 W	23 17 08	21 02 56	19 07 33	26 05 58	8 38.4	4 23.1	14 58.9	27 09.1	3 58.1	14 58.3	18 10.1	22 31.0	24 56.1	3 08.6
12 Th	23 21 04	22 02 48	3♎00 11	9♎49 47	8 31.4	6 02.3	14 45.7	27 56.0	3 45.9	15 11.1	18 05.3	22 34.4	24 58.2	3 09.4
13 F	23 25 01	23 02 38	16 34 23	23 13 46	8 23.7	7 42.7	14 29.9	28 43.0	3 34.0	15 23.8	18 00.5	22 37.9	25 00.2	3 10.1
14 Sa	23 28 58	24 02 27	29 47 48	6♏16 28	8 16.0	9 24.2	14 11.8	29 30.0	3 22.3	15 36.5	17 55.8	22 41.3	25 02.3	3 10.8
15 Su	23 32 54	25 02 13	12♏39 52	18 58 12	8 09.3	11 06.9	13 51.3	0♓17.0	3 11.0	15 49.1	17 51.1	22 44.7	25 04.4	3 11.5
16 M	23 36 51	26 01 58	25 11 46	1♐20 57	8 04.2	12 50.8	13 28.5	1 04.0	2 59.9	16 01.6	17 46.3	22 48.2	25 06.4	3 12.1
17 Tu	23 40 47	27 01 41	7♐26 15	13 28 09	8 01.1	14 36.0	13 03.5	1 50.9	2 49.1	16 14.0	17 41.7	22 51.6	25 08.4	3 12.7
18 W	23 44 44	28 01 23	19 27 15	25 24 11	7D59.9	16 22.3	12 36.4	2 37.9	2 38.7	16 26.4	17 37.0	22 55.0	25 10.4	3 13.3
19 Th	23 48 40	29 01 03	1♑19 33	7♑14 03	8 00.2	18 09.9	12 07.4	3 24.9	2 28.6	16 38.8	17 32.3	22 58.4	25 12.4	3 13.8
20 F	23 52 37	0♈00 41	13 08 21	19 03 05	8 01.3	19 58.7	11 36.6	4 11.9	2 18.8	16 51.0	17 27.7	23 01.9	25 14.3	3 14.3
21 Sa	23 56 33	1 00 17	24 58 56	0♒56 31	8R02.4	21 48.8	11 04.1	4 58.9	2 09.4	17 03.2	17 23.1	23 05.3	25 16.3	3 14.8
22 Su	0 00 30	1 59 51	6♒56 26	12 59 15	8 02.5	23 40.1	10 30.3	5 45.9	2 00.3	17 15.3	17 18.6	23 08.7	25 18.2	3 15.2
23 M	0 04 27	2 59 24	19 05 28	25 15 30	8 00.8	25 32.8	9 55.2	6 32.9	1 51.6	17 27.3	17 14.0	23 12.1	25 20.1	3 15.6
24 Tu	0 08 23	3 58 55	1♓29 46	7♓48 31	7 56.9	27 26.6	9 19.1	7 19.9	1 43.3	17 39.2	17 09.6	23 15.5	25 22.0	3 16.0
25 W	0 12 20	4 58 23	14 11 59	20 40 14	7 50.5	29 21.7	8 42.2	8 06.9	1 35.4	17 51.1	17 05.1	23 18.8	25 23.9	3 16.4
26 Th	0 16 16	5 57 50	27 13 18	3♈51 05	7 42.0	1♈18.1	8 04.9	8 53.8	1 27.9	18 02.9	17 00.7	23 22.2	25 25.7	3 16.7
27 F	0 20 13	6 57 15	10♈33 22	17 19 52	7 32.0	3 15.6	7 27.2	9 40.8	1 20.7	18 14.6	16 56.3	23 25.6	25 27.6	3 16.9
28 Sa	0 24 09	7 56 37	24 10 14	1♉04 01	7 21.7	5 14.3	6 49.5	10 27.7	1 14.0	18 26.2	16 52.0	23 28.9	25 29.4	3 17.2
29 Su	0 28 06	8 55 58	8♉00 46	14 59 58	7 12.1	7 14.2	6 11.9	11 14.7	1 07.7	18 37.7	16 47.8	23 32.3	25 31.2	3 17.4
30 M	0 32 02	9 55 16	22 01 07	29 03 44	7 04.3	9 15.0	5 34.9	12 01.6	1 01.8	18 49.1	16 43.6	23 35.6	25 32.9	3 17.6
31 Tu	0 35 59	10 54 32	6♊07 23	13♊11 39	6 58.8	11 16.8	4 58.5	12 48.5	0 56.4	19 00.5	16 39.4	23 38.9	25 34.7	3 17.7

April 2009 LONGITUDE

Day	Sid.Time	☉	0 hr ☽	Noon ☽	True ☊	☿	♀	♂	⚳	♃	♄	♅	♆	♇
1 W	0 39 55	11♈53 46	20♊16 11	27♊20 43	6♒55.9	13♈19.5	4♈23.1	13♓35.4	0♍51.3	19♒11.7	16♍35.3	23♓42.3	25♒36.4	3♑17.9
2 Th	0 43 52	12 52 58	4♋25 00	11♋28 52	6D55.0	15 22.8	3R48.8	14 22.3	0R46.7	19 22.9	16R31.3	23 45.6	25 38.1	3 18.0
3 F	0 47 49	13 52 07	18 32 10	25 34 48	6R55.3	17 26.6	3 15.8	15 09.2	0 42.6	19 33.9	16 27.3	23 48.8	25 39.8	3 18.0
4 Sa	0 51 45	14 51 14	2♌36 40	9♌37 38	6 55.5	19 30.8	2 44.4	15 56.1	0 38.8	19 44.9	16 23.4	23 52.1	25 41.4	3R18.0
5 Su	0 55 42	15 50 18	16 37 37	23 36 27	6 54.4	21 35.1	2 14.8	16 42.9	0 35.5	19 55.8	16 19.5	23 55.4	25 43.1	3 18.0
6 M	0 59 38	16 49 20	0♍33 57	7♍29 54	6 51.1	23 39.3	1 47.0	17 29.8	0 32.6	20 06.5	16 15.7	23 58.6	25 44.7	3 18.0
7 Tu	1 03 35	17 48 20	14 24 01	21 16 02	6 45.0	25 43.1	1 21.2	18 16.6	0 30.1	20 17.2	16 12.0	24 01.8	25 46.3	3 17.9
8 W	1 07 31	18 47 17	28 05 35	4♎52 22	6 36.2	27 46.1	0 57.6	19 03.4	0 28.1	20 27.8	16 08.4	24 05.0	25 47.8	3 17.8
9 Th	1 11 28	19 46 13	11♎36 02	18 16 14	6 25.1	29 48.1	0 36.2	19 50.1	0 26.5	20 38.2	16 04.8	24 08.2	25 49.4	3 17.7
10 F	1 15 24	20 45 06	24 52 43	1♏25 15	6 12.8	1♉48.7	0 17.2	20 36.9	0 25.4	20 48.6	16 01.3	24 11.3	25 50.9	3 17.5
11 Sa	1 19 21	21 43 58	7♏53 37	14 17 46	6 00.4	3 47.5	0 00.5	21 23.7	0 24.6	20 58.8	15 57.9	24 14.5	25 52.3	3 17.3
12 Su	1 23 18	22 42 48	20 37 39	26 53 22	5 49.1	5 44.3	29♓46.3	22 10.4	0D24.3	21 09.0	15 54.5	24 17.6	25 53.8	3 17.1
13 M	1 27 14	23 41 36	3♐05 03	9♐12 57	5 39.8	7 38.6	29 34.5	22 57.1	0 24.4	21 19.0	15 51.2	24 20.7	25 55.2	3 16.8
14 Tu	1 31 11	24 40 22	15 17 24	21 18 48	5 33.0	9 30.1	29 25.2	23 43.8	0 25.0	21 28.9	15 48.0	24 23.8	25 56.6	3 16.5
15 W	1 35 07	25 39 06	27 17 36	3♑14 21	5 28.9	11 18.5	29 18.4	24 30.5	0 25.9	21 38.8	15 44.9	24 26.9	25 58.0	3 16.2
16 Th	1 39 04	26 37 49	9♑09 37	15 04 01	5 27.0	13 03.4	29 14.0	25 17.2	0 27.3	21 48.5	15 41.9	24 29.9	25 59.4	3 15.9
17 F	1 43 00	27 36 30	20 58 13	26 52 53	5 26.5	14 44.7	29D12.1	26 03.8	0 29.1	21 58.1	15 38.9	24 32.9	26 00.7	3 15.5
18 Sa	1 46 57	28 35 09	2♒48 43	8♒46 24	5 26.6	16 22.1	29 12.5	26 50.4	0 31.3	22 07.5	15 36.1	24 35.9	26 02.0	3 15.1
19 Su	1 50 53	29 33 46	14 46 38	20 50 03	5 25.9	17 55.3	29 15.3	27 37.0	0 33.9	22 16.9	15 33.3	24 38.9	26 03.2	3 14.6
20 M	1 54 50	0♉32 22	26 57 19	3♓09 00	5 23.5	19 24.1	29 20.4	28 23.6	0 36.9	22 26.1	15 30.6	24 41.8	26 04.5	3 14.2
21 Tu	1 58 47	1 30 56	9♓25 38	15 47 37	5 18.8	20 48.5	29 27.8	29 10.1	0 40.3	22 35.2	15 28.0	24 44.7	26 05.7	3 13.7
22 W	2 02 43	2 29 29	22 15 20	28 48 58	5 11.4	22 08.2	29 37.4	29 56.6	0 44.1	22 44.2	15 25.5	24 47.6	26 06.9	3 13.1
23 Th	2 06 40	3 27 59	5♈28 38	12♈14 18	5 01.5	23 23.0	29 49.1	0♈43.1	0 48.3	22 53.0	15 23.1	24 50.5	26 08.0	3 12.6
24 F	2 10 36	4 26 28	19 05 44	26 02 37	4 49.9	24 33.0	0♈02.9	1 29.6	0 52.9	23 01.8	15 20.8	24 53.3	26 09.1	3 12.0
25 Sa	2 14 33	5 24 55	3♉04 27	10♉10 37	4 37.7	25 38.0	0 18.6	2 16.0	0 57.9	23 10.4	15 18.5	24 56.1	26 10.2	3 11.4
26 Su	2 18 29	6 23 21	17 20 23	24 32 59	4 26.3	26 37.8	0 36.4	3 02.4	1 03.3	23 18.8	15 16.4	24 58.9	26 11.3	3 10.7
27 M	2 22 26	7 21 44	1♊47 33	9♊03 15	4 16.8	27 32.5	0 56.0	3 48.8	1 09.1	23 27.1	15 14.4	25 01.7	26 12.3	3 10.1
28 Tu	2 26 22	8 20 06	16 19 17	23 34 54	4 10.0	28 22.0	1 17.4	4 35.1	1 15.2	23 35.3	15 12.4	25 04.4	26 13.3	3 09.4
29 W	2 30 19	9 18 25	0♋49 25	8♋02 18	4 06.0	29 06.1	1 40.5	5 21.4	1 21.7	23 43.4	15 10.6	25 07.1	26 14.3	3 08.6
30 Th	2 34 16	10 16 43	15 13 05	22 21 27	4D04.3	29 44.8	2 05.4	6 07.7	1 28.6	23 51.3	15 08.8	25 09.8	26 15.3	3 07.9

Astro Data Dy Hr Mn	Planet Ingress Dy Hr Mn	Last Aspect Dy Hr Mn	☽ Ingress Dy Hr Mn	Last Aspect Dy Hr Mn	☽ Ingress Dy Hr Mn	☽ Phases & Eclipses Dy Hr Mn	Astro Data
♀R 6 17:17	☿ ♓ 8 18:56	28 17:51 ♆ ⚹	♉ 1 3:33	1 9:03 ♆ △	♋ 1 16:30	4 7:46 ☽ 13♊52	1 March 2009
☽0S 11 4:37	♂ ♓ 15 3:20	2 22:42 ♆ □	♊ 3 7:59	3 8:59 ♅ △	♌ 3 19:32	11 2:38 ○ 20♍40	Julian Day # 39872
☉0N 20 11:44	☉ ♈ 20 11:44	5 2:10 ♆ △	♋ 5 11:07	5 15:39 ♆ ☍	♍ 5 23:01	18 17:47 ☾ 28♐16	SVP 5♓07'40"
♃⊼♄ 22 16:46	☿ ♈ 25 19:55	7 0:29 ♅ △	♌ 7 13:24	7 16:52 ♅ ☍	♎ 8 3:22	26 16:06 ● 6♈08	GC 26♐58.0 ⚴ 14♊05.4
☽0N 25 14:05		9 7:56 ♂ ☍	♍ 9 15:34	10 1:45 ♆ △	♏ 10 9:23		Eris 20♈55.6 ⚵ 16♒01.7
☿0N 27 15:28	☿ ♉ 9 14:21	11 5:48 ♅ ☍	♎ 11 18:46	12 17:28 ♀ △	♐ 12 18:01	2 14:34 ☽ 12♋59	⚷ 22♒32.8 ⚶ 15♉06.5
♃∠♇ 27 17:03	♀ ♓R 11 12:47	13 22:39 ♂ △	♏ 14 0:22	15 4:07 ♀ □	♑ 15 5:27	9 14:56 ○ 19♎53	☽ Mean ☊ 7♒48.6
	☉ ♉ 19 22:44	16 0:43 ☉ △	♐ 16 9:21	17 16:42 ♀ ⚹	♒ 17 18:19	17 13:36 ☾ 27♑40	
♇R 4 17:36	♂ ♈ 22 13:44	18 17:47 ☉ □	♑ 18 21:19	19 22:16 ♆ ☌	♓ 20 5:55	25 3:23 ● 5♉04	1 April 2009
☽0S 7 12:49	♀ ♈ 24 7:18	20 20:06 ♅ ⚹	♒ 21 10:06	22 13:29 ♀ ☌	♈ 22 14:09		Julian Day # 39903
⚳D 12 17:40	☿ ♊ 30 22:29	23 12:09 ♆ ☌	♓ 23 21:08	24 12:11 ♆ ⚹	♉ 24 18:46		SVP 5♓07'37"
♀D 17 19:24		25 16:53 ♅ ☌	♈ 26 5:03	26 15:42 ☿ ☌	♊ 26 21:02		GC 26♐58.1 ⚴ 27♊41.5
☽0N 21 22:44		28 2:17 ♆ ⚹	♉ 28 10:09	28 16:23 ♆ △	♋ 28 22:38		Eris 21♈14.0 ⚵ 28♒40.0
♂0N 25 23:29		30 6:00 ♆ □	♊ 30 13:36				⚷ 24♒30.8 ⚶ 26♉37.4
							☽ Mean ☊ 6♒10.1

LONGITUDE May 2009

Day	Sid.Time	☉	0 hr ☽	Noon ☽	True ☊	☿	♀	♂	⚳	♃	♄	♅	♆	♇
1 F	2 38 12	11♉14 58	29♋27 09	6♌30 03	4♒04.1	0♊18.1	2♈31.8	6♈54.0	1♍35.9	23♒59.1	15♍07.2	25♓12.4	26♒16.2	3♑07.1
2 Sa	2 42 09	12 13 11	13♌30 05	20 27 14	4R 04.0	0 46.0	2 59.9	7 40.2	1 43.5	24 06.7	15R 05.7	25 15.0	26 17.0	3R 06.3
3 Su	2 46 05	13 11 22	27 21 32	4♍13 00	4 02.7	1 08.4	3 29.4	8 26.3	1 51.4	24 14.2	15 04.2	25 17.6	26 17.9	3 05.5
4 M	2 50 02	14 09 31	11♍01 42	17 47 39	3 59.3	1 25.4	4 00.4	9 12.4	1 59.7	24 21.6	15 02.9	25 20.1	26 18.7	3 04.6
5 Tu	2 53 58	15 07 38	24 30 54	1♎11 25	3 53.1	1 37.0	4 32.8	9 58.5	2 08.4	24 28.8	15 01.6	25 22.6	26 19.5	3 03.7
6 W	2 57 55	16 05 43	7♎49 11	14 24 08	3 44.2	1R 43.2	5 06.6	10 44.6	2 17.3	24 35.8	15 00.5	25 25.1	26 20.2	3 02.8
7 Th	3 01 51	17 03 46	20 56 12	27 25 18	3 33.1	1 44.3	5 41.7	11 30.6	2 26.6	24 42.8	14 59.4	25 27.5	26 21.0	3 01.9
8 F	3 05 48	18 01 48	3♏51 20	10♏14 14	3 20.7	1 40.3	6 18.0	12 16.6	2 36.2	24 49.5	14 58.5	25 29.9	26 21.6	3 00.9
9 Sa	3 09 45	18 59 48	16 33 56	22 50 25	3 08.1	1 31.5	6 55.5	13 02.5	2 46.2	24 56.1	14 57.7	25 32.3	26 22.3	3 00.0
10 Su	3 13 41	19 57 47	29 03 41	5♐13 46	2 56.6	1 18.1	7 34.2	13 48.4	2 56.5	25 02.6	14 56.9	25 34.6	26 22.9	2 59.0
11 M	3 17 38	20 55 44	11♐20 49	17 24 59	2 46.9	1 00.4	8 14.0	14 34.3	3 07.0	25 08.9	14 56.3	25 36.9	26 23.5	2 57.9
12 Tu	3 21 34	21 53 39	23 26 30	29 25 40	2 39.8	0 38.8	8 54.9	15 20.1	3 17.9	25 15.0	14 55.8	25 39.1	26 24.1	2 56.9
13 W	3 25 31	22 51 34	5♑22 49	11♑18 22	2 35.3	0 13.6	9 36.8	16 05.9	3 29.1	25 21.0	14 55.4	25 41.4	26 24.6	2 55.8
14 Th	3 29 27	23 49 26	17 12 47	23 06 36	2D 33.2	29♉45.4	10 19.7	16 51.7	3 40.5	25 26.9	14 55.0	25 43.6	26 25.1	2 54.7
15 F	3 33 24	24 47 18	29 00 22	4♒54 42	2 32.8	29 14.7	11 03.6	17 37.4	3 52.3	25 32.5	14 54.8	25 45.7	26 25.6	2 53.6
16 Sa	3 37 20	25 45 08	10♒50 13	16 47 34	2R 33.2	28 42.0	11 48.3	18 23.1	4 04.4	25 38.1	14D 54.7	25 47.8	26 26.0	2 52.5
17 Su	3 41 17	26 42 57	22 47 27	28 50 32	2 33.5	28 08.0	12 34.0	19 08.7	4 16.7	25 43.4	14 54.7	25 49.9	26 26.4	2 51.3
18 M	3 45 14	27 40 45	4♓57 30	11♓08 58	2 32.5	27 33.1	13 20.5	19 54.3	4 29.3	25 48.6	14 54.8	25 51.9	26 26.8	2 50.1
19 Tu	3 49 10	28 38 32	17 25 33	23 47 49	2 29.7	26 58.2	14 07.8	20 39.8	4 42.2	25 53.6	14 55.0	25 53.9	26 27.1	2 49.0
20 W	3 53 07	29 36 18	0♈16 14	6♈51 09	2 24.7	26 23.6	14 55.9	21 25.3	4 55.3	25 58.4	14 55.3	25 55.8	26 27.4	2 47.7
21 Th	3 57 03	0♊34 02	13 32 49	20 21 21	2 17.5	25 50.1	15 44.7	22 10.8	5 08.7	26 03.1	14 55.7	25 57.7	26 27.7	2 46.5
22 F	4 01 00	1 31 46	27 16 42	4♉18 36	2 08.7	25 18.3	16 34.2	22 56.2	5 22.4	26 07.6	14 56.2	25 59.6	26 27.9	2 45.3
23 Sa	4 04 56	2 29 28	11♉26 38	18 40 13	1 59.4	24 48.5	17 24.5	23 41.5	5 36.4	26 11.9	14 56.8	26 01.4	26 28.1	2 44.0
24 Su	4 08 53	3 27 09	25 58 35	3♊20 49	1 50.5	24 21.4	18 15.4	24 26.9	5 50.5	26 16.1	14 57.6	26 03.2	26 28.3	2 42.7
25 M	4 12 49	4 24 49	10♊45 55	18 12 48	1 43.1	23 57.2	19 06.9	25 12.1	6 05.0	26 20.0	14 58.4	26 05.0	26 28.4	2 41.4
26 Tu	4 16 46	5 22 28	25 40 23	3♋07 36	1 37.9	23 36.5	19 59.0	25 57.3	6 19.7	26 23.8	14 59.3	26 06.7	26 28.5	2 40.1
27 W	4 20 43	6 20 05	10♋33 27	17 57 04	1D 35.1	23 19.5	20 51.8	26 42.5	6 34.6	26 27.5	15 00.3	26 08.3	26 28.6	2 38.8
28 Th	4 24 39	7 17 41	25 17 42	2♌34 42	1 34.4	23 06.4	21 45.0	27 27.6	6 49.8	26 30.9	15 01.5	26 09.9	26R 28.7	2 37.4
29 F	4 28 36	8 15 16	9♌47 39	16 56 11	1 35.0	22 57.4	22 38.9	28 12.7	7 05.2	26 34.2	15 02.7	26 11.5	26 28.7	2 36.1
30 Sa	4 32 32	9 12 49	24 00 08	0♍59 25	1R 35.9	22D 52.8	23 33.2	28 57.6	7 20.8	26 37.2	15 04.1	26 13.0	26 28.6	2 34.7
31 Su	4 36 29	10 10 20	7♍54 03	14 44 06	1 36.0	22 52.5	24 28.1	29 42.6	7 36.7	26 40.1	15 05.5	26 14.5	26 28.6	2 33.3

LONGITUDE June 2009

Day	Sid.Time	☉	0 hr ☽	Noon ☽	True ☊	☿	♀	♂	⚳	♃	♄	♅	♆	♇
1 M	4 40 25	11♊07 50	21♍29 42	28♍11 02	1♒34.6	22♉56.7	25♈23.4	0♉27.5	7♍52.7	26♒42.8	15♍07.0	26♓15.9	26♒28.5	2♑31.9
2 Tu	4 44 22	12 05 19	4♎48 18	11♎21 41	1R 31.1	23 05.4	26 19.2	1 12.3	8 09.0	26 45.3	15 08.7	26 17.3	26R 28.4	2R 30.5
3 W	4 48 18	13 02 47	17 51 24	24 17 37	1 25.7	23 18.6	27 15.5	1 57.1	8 25.5	26 47.7	15 10.4	26 18.7	26 28.2	2 29.0
4 Th	4 52 15	14 00 13	0♏40 31	7♏00 16	1 18.6	23 36.3	28 12.2	2 41.8	8 42.2	26 49.8	15 12.3	26 20.0	26 28.0	2 27.6
5 F	4 56 12	14 57 39	13 17 00	19 30 52	1 10.5	23 58.3	29 09.4	3 26.5	8 59.1	26 51.8	15 14.2	26 21.2	26 27.8	2 26.2
6 Sa	5 00 08	15 55 03	25 42 00	1♐50 32	1 02.3	24 24.7	0♉06.9	4 11.1	9 16.2	26 53.6	15 16.2	26 22.4	26 27.5	2 24.7
7 Su	5 04 05	16 52 27	7♐56 35	14 00 19	0 54.7	24 55.4	1 04.9	4 55.7	9 33.5	26 55.2	15 18.4	26 23.6	26 27.3	2 23.2
8 M	5 08 01	17 49 49	20 01 54	26 01 30	0 48.5	25 30.2	2 03.3	5 40.2	9 50.9	26 56.6	15 20.6	26 24.7	26 27.0	2 21.8
9 Tu	5 11 58	18 47 11	1♑59 20	7♑55 39	0 44.1	26 09.2	3 02.0	6 24.6	10 08.6	26 57.8	15 23.0	26 25.8	26 26.6	2 20.3
10 W	5 15 54	19 44 32	13 50 45	19 44 57	0D 41.6	26 52.2	4 01.1	7 09.0	10 26.5	26 58.8	15 25.4	26 26.8	26 26.2	2 18.8
11 Th	5 19 51	20 41 53	25 38 35	1♒32 05	0 41.0	27 39.2	5 00.6	7 53.3	10 44.5	26 59.6	15 27.9	26 27.8	26 25.8	2 17.3
12 F	5 23 48	21 39 13	7♒25 53	13 20 28	0 41.7	28 30.0	6 00.4	8 37.6	11 02.7	27 00.3	15 30.5	26 28.7	26 25.4	2 15.8
13 Sa	5 27 44	22 36 32	19 16 21	25 14 04	0 43.2	29 24.5	7 00.6	9 21.8	11 21.1	27 00.7	15 33.2	26 29.6	26 24.9	2 14.3
14 Su	5 31 41	23 33 51	1♓14 13	7♓17 22	0 44.7	0♊22.8	8 01.1	10 06.0	11 39.7	27R 01.0	15 36.0	26 30.5	26 24.4	2 12.7
15 M	5 35 37	24 31 09	13 24 09	19 35 09	0R 45.7	1 24.7	9 01.8	10 50.1	11 58.4	27 01.0	15 38.9	26 31.3	26 23.9	2 11.2
16 Tu	5 39 34	25 28 27	25 50 57	2♈12 08	0 45.6	2 30.2	10 02.9	11 34.2	12 17.3	27 00.9	15 41.9	26 32.0	26 23.3	2 09.7
17 W	5 43 30	26 25 45	8♈39 13	15 12 38	0 44.2	3 39.1	11 04.3	12 18.1	12 36.3	27 00.6	15 45.0	26 32.7	26 22.7	2 08.1
18 Th	5 47 27	27 23 02	21 52 45	28 39 49	0 41.3	4 51.6	12 06.0	13 02.1	12 55.6	27 00.1	15 48.1	26 33.3	26 22.1	2 06.6
19 F	5 51 23	28 20 20	5♉33 56	12♉35 03	0 37.4	6 07.4	13 07.9	13 45.9	13 15.0	26 59.4	15 51.4	26 33.9	26 21.5	2 05.1
20 Sa	5 55 20	29 17 37	19 42 57	26 57 13	0 32.9	7 26.6	14 10.1	14 29.7	13 34.5	26 58.5	15 54.8	26 34.5	26 20.8	2 03.5
21 Su	5 59 17	0♋14 54	4♊17 17	11♊42 20	0 28.6	8 49.2	15 12.6	15 13.5	13 54.2	26 57.4	15 58.2	26 35.0	26 20.1	2 02.0
22 M	6 03 13	1 12 10	19 11 27	26 43 34	0 25.1	10 15.0	16 15.3	15 57.2	14 14.0	26 56.1	16 01.7	26 35.4	26 19.4	2 00.4
23 Tu	6 07 10	2 09 27	4♋17 31	11♋52 06	0 22.7	11 44.1	17 18.2	16 40.8	14 34.0	26 54.6	16 05.3	26 35.9	26 18.6	1 58.9
24 W	6 11 06	3 06 42	19 26 09	26 58 29	0D 21.8	13 16.4	18 21.4	17 24.3	14 54.2	26 52.9	16 09.0	26 36.2	26 17.8	1 57.3
25 Th	6 15 03	4 03 58	4♌28 05	11♌54 00	0 22.1	14 51.9	19 24.8	18 07.8	15 14.5	26 51.1	16 12.8	26 36.5	26 17.0	1 55.8
26 F	6 18 59	5 01 12	19 15 28	26 31 53	0 23.2	16 30.6	20 28.4	18 51.2	15 34.9	26 49.0	16 16.7	26 36.8	26 16.1	1 54.3
27 Sa	6 22 56	5 58 26	3♍42 47	10♍47 54	0 24.6	18 12.3	21 32.2	19 34.5	15 55.4	26 46.8	16 20.7	26 37.0	26 15.3	1 52.7
28 Su	6 26 52	6 55 40	17 47 03	24 40 14	0R 25.8	19 57.1	22 36.3	20 17.8	16 16.1	26 44.3	16 24.7	26 37.1	26 14.4	1 51.2
29 M	6 30 49	7 52 53	1♎27 32	8♎09 08	0 26.2	21 44.9	23 40.5	21 00.9	16 37.0	26 41.7	16 28.8	26 37.3	26 13.4	1 49.6
30 Tu	6 34 46	8 50 06	14 45 17	21 16 16	0 25.7	23 35.5	24 44.9	21 44.1	16 57.9	26 38.9	16 33.0	26R 37.3	26 12.5	1 48.1

Astro Data

	Dy Hr Mn
☽0S	4 18:26
☿R	7 5:00
♄D	17 2:06
☽0N	19 7:01
♃⚺♅	19 14:25
♃☌♆	27 20:06
♆R	29 4:29
☿D	31 1:21
☽0S	31 23:02
♅⚺♆	10 1:44
♃R	15 7:50
☽0N	15 14:12
☽0S	28 4:56

Planet Ingress

	Dy Hr Mn
☿ ♉R	13 23:53
☉ ♊	20 21:51
♂ ♉	31 21:18
♀ ♉	6 9:07
☿ ♊	14 2:47
☉ ♋	21 5:46

Last Aspect / ☽ Ingress

Last Aspect Dy Hr Mn		☽ Ingress Dy Hr Mn
30 16:45 ♅ △	♌	1 0:56
2 22:08 ♆ ☍	♍	3 4:37
5 1:31 ♅ ☍	♎	5 9:51
7 10:00 ♆ △	♏	7 16:48
9 18:48 ♆ □	♐	10 1:49
12 5:55 ♆ ⚹	♑	12 13:09
15 0:58 ♅ △	♒	15 2:01
17 10:40 ♅ □	♓	17 14:17
19 21:43 ☉ ⚹	♈	19 23:30
21 22:36 ♆ ⚹	♉	22 4:40
24 0:48 ♆ □	♊	24 6:34
26 1:17 ♆ △	♋	26 6:58
28 3:06 ♂ □	♌	28 7:44
30 8:18 ♂ △	♍	30 10:17

Last Aspect / ☽ Ingress

Last Aspect Dy Hr Mn		☽ Ingress Dy Hr Mn
1 8:32 ♅ ☍	♎	1 15:17
3 18:00 ♀ ☍	♏	3 22:44
6 2:18 ♃ □	♐	6 8:24
8 13:51 ♃ ⚹	♑	8 20:00
11 3:31 ♅ △	♒	11 8:52
13 21:04 ♅ □	♓	13 21:32
16 1:17 ♅ ☌	♈	16 7:52
18 9:35 ☉ ⚹	♉	18 14:20
20 12:02 ♃ △	♊	20 17:00
22 12:20 ♃ △	♋	22 17:12
24 11:25 ♅ △	♌	24 16:50
26 12:28 ♃ ☍	♍	26 17:47
28 15:26 ♅ ☍	♎	28 21:24

☽ Phases & Eclipses

Dy Hr Mn	
1 20:44	☽ 11♌36
9 4:01	○ 18♏41
17 7:26	☾ 26♒32
24 12:11	● 3♊28
31 3:22	☽ 9♍50
7 18:12	○ 17♐07
15 22:15	☾ 24♓56
22 19:35	● 1♋30
29 11:28	☽ 7♎52

Astro Data

1 May 2009
Julian Day # 39933
SVP 5♓07'33"
GC 26♐58.2 ⚴ 12♋40.0
Eris 21♈33.5 ✱ 10♓21.1
⚷ 25♒47.8 ⚶ 8♊51.8
☽ Mean ☊ 4♒34.8

1 June 2009
Julian Day # 39964
SVP 5♓07'28"
GC 26♐58.2 ⚴ 28♋39.4
Eris 21♈50.5 ✱ 21♓14.5
⚷ 26♒13.7R ⚶ 22♊05.2
☽ Mean ☊ 2♒56.3

July 2009 LONGITUDE

Day	Sid.Time	☉	0 hr ☽	Noon ☽	True ☊	☿	♀	♂	⚳	♃	♄	♅	♆	♇
1 W	6 38 42	9♋47 18	27♎42 27	4♏04 09	0♒24.2	25♊28.9	25♉49.5	22♉27.1	17♍19.0	26♒36.0	16♍37.3	26♓37.3	26♒11.5	1♑46.6
2 Th	6 42 39	10 44 30	10♏21 46	16 35 38	0R 22.0	27 24.9	26 54.3	23 10.1	17 40.2	26R 32.8	16 41.6	26R 37.3	26R 10.5	1R 45.0
3 F	6 46 35	11 41 41	22 46 09	28 53 37	0 19.3	29 23.4	27 59.3	23 53.0	18 01.5	26 29.5	16 46.1	26 37.2	26 09.5	1 43.5
4 Sa	6 50 32	12 38 53	4♐58 25	11♐00 51	0 16.5	1♋24.1	29 04.5	24 35.8	18 23.0	26 25.9	16 50.6	26 37.1	26 08.4	1 42.0
5 Su	6 54 28	13 36 04	17 01 13	22 59 49	0 14.0	3 26.9	0♊09.9	25 18.6	18 44.5	26 22.2	16 55.2	26 36.9	26 07.3	1 40.5
6 M	6 58 25	14 33 15	28 56 56	4♑52 51	0 12.1	5 31.5	1 15.4	26 01.3	19 06.2	26 18.4	16 59.8	26 36.7	26 06.2	1 39.0
7 Tu	7 02 21	15 30 26	10♑47 50	16 42 08	0 10.9	7 37.7	2 21.1	26 43.9	19 28.0	26 14.3	17 04.6	26 36.4	26 05.1	1 37.5
8 W	7 06 18	16 27 38	22 36 04	28 29 53	0D 10.4	9 45.1	3 27.0	27 26.5	19 49.9	26 10.1	17 09.4	26 36.1	26 04.0	1 36.0
9 Th	7 10 15	17 24 49	4♒23 53	10♒18 24	0 10.6	11 53.5	4 33.0	28 09.0	20 11.9	26 05.8	17 14.3	26 35.7	26 02.8	1 34.6
10 F	7 14 11	18 22 01	16 13 45	22 10 17	0 11.4	14 02.6	5 39.2	28 51.4	20 34.0	26 01.2	17 19.2	26 35.3	26 01.6	1 33.1
11 Sa	7 18 08	19 19 13	28 08 22	4♓08 25	0 12.3	16 12.1	6 45.6	29 33.7	20 56.2	25 56.5	17 24.2	26 34.9	26 00.4	1 31.6
12 Su	7 22 04	20 16 25	10♓10 51	16 16 06	0 13.3	18 21.6	7 52.1	0♊16.0	21 18.5	25 51.6	17 29.3	26 34.4	25 59.2	1 30.2
13 M	7 26 01	21 13 38	22 24 37	28 36 52	0 14.2	20 31.0	8 58.8	0 58.1	21 40.9	25 46.6	17 34.5	26 33.8	25 57.9	1 28.8
14 Tu	7 29 57	22 10 51	4♈53 19	11♈14 27	0R 14.7	22 39.9	10 05.6	1 40.3	22 03.4	25 41.4	17 39.7	26 33.2	25 56.6	1 27.3
15 W	7 33 54	23 08 05	17 40 42	24 12 29	0 14.8	24 48.1	11 12.5	2 22.3	22 26.1	25 36.1	17 45.0	26 32.6	25 55.3	1 25.9
16 Th	7 37 50	24 05 19	0♉50 09	7♉34 01	0 14.7	26 55.5	12 19.7	3 04.3	22 48.8	25 30.6	17 50.4	26 31.9	25 54.0	1 24.5
17 F	7 41 47	25 02 35	14 24 17	21 21 02	0 14.3	29 01.8	13 26.9	3 46.2	23 11.6	25 25.0	17 55.8	26 31.1	25 52.7	1 23.1
18 Sa	7 45 44	25 59 51	28 24 16	5♊33 48	0 13.8	1♌07.0	14 34.3	4 28.0	23 34.5	25 19.2	18 01.3	26 30.3	25 51.4	1 21.8
19 Su	7 49 40	26 57 08	12♊49 19	20 10 17	0 13.4	3 10.8	15 41.8	5 09.7	23 57.5	25 13.3	18 06.9	26 29.5	25 50.0	1 20.4
20 M	7 53 37	27 54 25	27 36 04	5♋05 49	0 13.2	5 13.1	16 49.5	5 51.4	24 20.6	25 07.3	18 12.5	26 28.6	25 48.6	1 19.1
21 Tu	7 57 33	28 51 43	12♋38 35	20 13 16	0D 13.1	7 13.9	17 57.2	6 32.9	24 43.8	25 01.1	18 18.2	26 27.7	25 47.2	1 17.7
22 W	8 01 30	29 49 02	27 48 45	5♌23 48	0R 13.1	9 13.2	19 05.1	7 14.4	25 07.0	24 54.8	18 23.9	26 26.8	25 45.8	1 16.4
23 Th	8 05 26	0♌46 21	12♌57 16	20 28 02	0 13.1	11 10.8	20 13.1	7 55.8	25 30.4	24 48.4	18 29.7	26 25.8	25 44.4	1 15.1
24 F	8 09 23	1 43 40	27 55 03	5♍17 26	0 13.0	13 06.8	21 21.3	8 37.2	25 53.8	24 41.9	18 35.6	26 24.7	25 42.9	1 13.8
25 Sa	8 13 20	2 41 00	12♍34 27	19 45 30	0 12.8	15 01.0	22 29.5	9 18.4	26 17.3	24 35.2	18 41.5	26 23.6	25 41.4	1 12.6
26 Su	8 17 16	3 38 20	26 50 11	3♎48 15	0 12.5	16 53.6	23 37.9	9 59.5	26 40.9	24 28.4	18 47.5	26 22.5	25 40.0	1 11.3
27 M	8 21 13	4 35 41	10♎39 38	17 24 22	0 12.2	18 44.5	24 46.3	10 40.6	27 04.6	24 21.6	18 53.5	26 21.3	25 38.5	1 10.1
28 Tu	8 25 09	5 33 02	24 02 39	0♏34 45	0D 12.0	20 33.6	25 54.9	11 21.6	27 28.3	24 14.6	18 59.6	26 20.1	25 37.0	1 08.9
29 W	8 29 06	6 30 24	7♏01 02	13 21 56	0 12.0	22 21.0	27 03.6	12 02.4	27 52.2	24 07.6	19 05.7	26 18.8	25 35.5	1 07.7
30 Th	8 33 02	7 27 46	19 37 54	25 49 26	0 12.3	24 06.8	28 12.4	12 43.2	28 16.1	24 00.4	19 11.9	26 17.5	25 33.9	1 06.5
31 F	8 36 59	8 25 09	1♐57 04	8♐01 19	0 13.0	25 50.8	29 21.3	13 24.0	28 40.0	23 53.2	19 18.1	26 16.2	25 32.4	1 05.4

August 2009 LONGITUDE

Day	Sid.Time	☉	0 hr ☽	Noon ☽	True ☊	☿	♀	♂	⚳	♃	♄	♅	♆	♇
1 Sa	8 40 55	9♌22 32	14♐02 40	20♐01 37	0♒13.9	27♌33.2	0♋30.3	14♊04.6	29♍04.1	23♒45.9	19♍24.4	26♓14.8	25♒30.8	1♑04.2
2 Su	8 44 52	10 19 56	25 58 41	1♑54 17	0 14.8	29 13.9	1 39.4	14 45.1	29 28.2	23R 38.5	19 30.7	26R 13.4	25R 29.3	1R 03.1
3 M	8 48 49	11 17 21	7♑48 53	13 42 51	0 15.6	0♍53.0	2 48.7	15 25.6	29 52.4	23 31.0	19 37.1	26 11.9	25 27.7	1 02.0
4 Tu	8 52 45	12 14 46	19 36 36	25 30 28	0R 16.1	2 30.3	3 58.0	16 05.9	0♎16.6	23 23.5	19 43.6	26 10.4	25 26.1	1 01.0
5 W	8 56 42	13 12 13	1♒24 46	7♒19 50	0 16.0	4 06.0	5 07.4	16 46.2	0 40.9	23 16.0	19 50.0	26 08.9	25 24.6	0 59.9
6 Th	9 00 38	14 09 40	13 15 57	19 13 21	0 15.3	5 40.1	6 16.9	17 26.4	1 05.3	23 08.3	19 56.6	26 07.3	25 23.0	0 58.9
7 F	9 04 35	15 07 08	25 12 20	1♓13 08	0 13.9	7 12.5	7 26.6	18 06.5	1 29.7	23 00.7	20 03.1	26 05.7	25 21.4	0 57.9
8 Sa	9 08 31	16 04 38	7♓15 59	13 21 08	0 11.8	8 43.2	8 36.3	18 46.5	1 54.2	22 53.0	20 09.7	26 04.1	25 19.8	0 56.9
9 Su	9 12 28	17 02 08	19 28 49	25 39 18	0 09.4	10 12.3	9 46.1	19 26.4	2 18.8	22 45.2	20 16.4	26 02.4	25 18.1	0 55.9
10 M	9 16 24	17 59 40	1♈52 49	8♈09 39	0 06.9	11 39.7	10 56.1	20 06.2	2 43.4	22 37.4	20 23.1	26 00.7	25 16.5	0 55.0
11 Tu	9 20 21	18 57 13	14 30 02	20 54 15	0 04.7	13 05.3	12 06.1	20 45.9	3 08.1	22 29.6	20 29.8	25 59.0	25 14.9	0 54.1
12 W	9 24 18	19 54 48	27 22 35	3♉55 18	0 03.1	14 29.3	13 16.2	21 25.5	3 32.8	22 21.8	20 36.6	25 57.2	25 13.3	0 53.2
13 Th	9 28 14	20 52 24	10♉32 38	17 14 49	0D 02.3	15 51.5	14 26.5	22 05.1	3 57.6	22 13.9	20 43.4	25 55.4	25 11.6	0 52.4
14 F	9 32 11	21 50 02	24 02 02	0♊54 26	0 02.5	17 11.9	15 36.8	22 44.5	4 22.4	22 06.1	20 50.2	25 53.5	25 10.0	0 51.5
15 Sa	9 36 07	22 47 41	7♊52 05	14 54 59	0 03.5	18 30.5	16 47.2	23 23.9	4 47.3	21 58.2	20 57.1	25 51.7	25 08.4	0 50.7
16 Su	9 40 04	23 45 22	22 02 59	29 15 54	0 04.8	19 47.2	17 57.7	24 03.1	5 12.3	21 50.4	21 04.0	25 49.8	25 06.7	0 49.9
17 M	9 44 00	24 43 04	6♋33 21	13♋54 51	0 06.1	21 02.0	19 08.3	24 42.3	5 37.3	21 42.5	21 11.0	25 47.8	25 05.1	0 49.2
18 Tu	9 47 57	25 40 48	21 19 47	28 47 21	0R 06.7	22 14.8	20 19.0	25 21.3	6 02.4	21 34.7	21 17.9	25 45.9	25 03.5	0 48.4
19 W	9 51 53	26 38 33	6♌16 41	13♌46 49	0 06.2	23 25.5	21 29.8	26 00.3	6 27.5	21 26.9	21 25.0	25 43.9	25 01.8	0 47.7
20 Th	9 55 50	27 36 20	21 16 41	28 45 12	0 04.3	24 34.1	22 40.7	26 39.1	6 52.7	21 19.1	21 32.0	25 41.9	25 00.2	0 47.1
21 F	9 59 47	28 34 07	6♍11 19	13♍34 01	0 01.2	25 40.4	23 51.6	27 17.8	7 17.9	21 11.4	21 39.1	25 39.8	24 58.6	0 46.4
22 Sa	10 03 43	29 31 57	20 52 22	28 05 34	29♑57.1	26 44.4	25 02.6	27 56.4	7 43.1	21 03.6	21 46.2	25 37.8	24 56.9	0 45.8
23 Su	10 07 40	0♍29 47	5♎12 57	12♎14 03	29 52.7	27 46.0	26 13.7	28 34.9	8 08.4	20 56.0	21 53.3	25 35.7	24 55.3	0 45.2
24 M	10 11 36	1 27 39	19 08 32	25 56 15	29 48.5	28 45.0	27 24.9	29 13.3	8 33.8	20 48.4	22 00.5	25 33.6	24 53.7	0 44.6
25 Tu	10 15 33	2 25 32	2♏37 13	9♏11 35	29 45.2	29 41.2	28 36.2	29 51.6	8 59.2	20 40.8	22 07.7	25 31.4	24 52.0	0 44.1
26 W	10 19 29	3 23 26	15 39 36	22 01 41	29D 43.1	0♎34.6	29 47.5	0♋29.8	9 24.6	20 33.3	22 14.9	25 29.3	24 50.4	0 43.6
27 Th	10 23 26	4 21 22	28 18 16	4♐29 53	29 42.5	1 24.9	0♌59.0	1 07.9	9 50.1	20 25.9	22 22.1	25 27.1	24 48.8	0 43.1
28 F	10 27 22	5 19 19	10♐37 08	16 40 35	29 43.1	2 12.0	2 10.4	1 45.8	10 15.6	20 18.5	22 29.4	25 24.9	24 47.2	0 42.7
29 Sa	10 31 19	6 17 17	22 40 53	28 38 39	29 44.5	2 55.7	3 22.0	2 23.7	10 41.2	20 11.2	22 36.6	25 22.7	24 45.6	0 42.3
30 Su	10 35 16	7 15 16	4♑34 30	10♑29 02	29 46.2	3 35.7	4 33.7	3 01.4	11 06.8	20 04.1	22 43.9	25 20.4	24 44.0	0 41.9
31 M	10 39 12	8 13 17	16 22 49	22 16 25	29R 47.5	4 11.8	5 45.4	3 39.0	11 32.4	19 57.0	22 51.3	25 18.2	24 42.4	0 41.5

Astro Data	Dy Hr Mn
♃⊻♅	1 1:03
♅R	1 7:38
♃☌♆	10 9:13
☽0N	12 20:21
☽0S	25 13:18
☽0N	9 2:08
♃⚻♄	19 15:07
☿0S	21 21:06
☽0S	21 23:35

Planet Ingress		Dy Hr Mn
☿	♋	3 19:20
♀	♊	5 8:23
♂	♊	12 2:56
☿	♌	17 23:08
☉	♌	22 16:36
♀	♋	1 1:28
☿	♍	2 23:07
⚳	♎	3 19:33
☊	♑R	21 19:26
☉	♍	22 23:39
♂	♋	25 17:15
☿	♎	25 20:18
♀	♌	26 16:12

Last Aspect Dy Hr Mn		☽ Ingress	Dy Hr Mn
30 21:59	♃ △	♏	1 4:19
3 10:03	♀ ☍	♐	3 14:11
5 19:17	♅ □	♑	6 2:07
8 9:43	♂ △	♒	8 15:03
11 2:17	♂ □	♓	11 3:44
13 8:03	♅ ☌	♈	13 14:40
15 15:07	♆ ⚹	♉	15 22:30
17 20:48	♅ ⚹	♊	18 2:41
19 22:12	♅ □	♋	20 3:51
22 2:35	☉ ☌	♌	22 3:28
23 20:28	♆ ☍	♍	24 3:23
25 23:14	♅ ☍	♎	26 5:25
28 2:53	♆ △	♏	28 10:56
30 12:55	♅ △	♐	30 20:10

Last Aspect Dy Hr Mn		☽ Ingress	Dy Hr Mn
2 5:42	☿ △	♑	2 8:08
4 13:21	♅ ⚹	♒	4 21:08
7 0:20	♆ ☌	♓	7 9:34
9 12:45	♅ ☌	♈	9 20:23
11 20:03	♆ ⚹	♉	12 4:50
14 3:17	♅ ⚹	♊	14 10:25
16 6:19	♅ □	♋	16 13:13
18 7:09	♅ △	♌	18 13:57
20 10:02	☉ ☌	♍	20 14:00
22 11:44	♂ □	♎	22 15:12
24 18:10	♂ △	♏	24 19:16
26 18:35	♅ △	♐	27 3:16
29 5:26	♅ □	♑	29 14:44

☽ Phases & Eclipses Dy Hr Mn	
7 9:21	○ 15♑24
7 9:39	☍ A 0.156
15 9:53	☾ 23♈03
22 2:35	● 29♋27
22 2:35:18	☌ T 06'39"
28 22:00	☽ 5♏57
6 0:55	○ 13♒43
6 0:39	☍ A 0.402
13 18:55	☾ 21♉09
20 10:02	● 27♌32
27 11:42	☽ 4♐21

Astro Data

1 July 2009
Julian Day # 39994
SVP 5♓07'23"
GC 26♐58.3 ⚳ 14♌03.0
Eris 22♈00.1 ⚵ 29♓38.7
⚷ 25♒43.2R ⚶ 5♋06.4
☽ Mean ☊ 1♒21.0

1 August 2009
Julian Day # 40025
SVP 5♓07'17"
GC 26♐58.4 ⚳ 29♌38.3
Eris 22♈00.5R ⚵ 4♈20.7
⚷ 24♒26.5R ⚶ 18♋31.9
☽ Mean ☊ 29♑42.6

LONGITUDE — September 2009

Day	Sid.Time	☉	0 hr ☽	Noon ☽	True ☊	☿	♀	♂	⚳	♃	♄	♅	♆	♇
1 Tu	10 43 09	9♍11 19	28♑10 21	4♒05 04	29♑47.7	4♎43.8	6♌57.2	4♋16.5	11♎58.1	19♒49.9	22♍58.6	25♓15.9	24♒40.9	0♑41.2
2 W	10 47 05	10 09 23	10♒01 02	15 58 36	29R 46.2	5 11.4	8 09.1	4 53.9	12 23.8	19R 43.0	23 05.9	25R 13.6	24R 39.3	0R 40.9
3 Th	10 51 02	11 07 28	21 58 07	27 59 53	29 42.9	5 34.2	9 21.0	5 31.1	12 49.6	19 36.2	23 13.3	25 11.3	24 37.7	0 40.6
4 F	10 54 58	12 05 35	4♓04 09	10♓11 06	29 37.7	5 52.1	10 33.1	6 08.3	13 15.3	19 29.5	23 20.7	25 09.0	24 36.2	0 40.4
5 Sa	10 58 55	13 03 44	16 20 55	22 33 41	29 30.9	6 04.7	11 45.2	6 45.3	13 41.1	19 22.9	23 28.1	25 06.7	24 34.6	0 40.2
6 Su	11 02 51	14 01 54	28 49 31	5♈08 28	29 23.2	6R 11.8	12 57.3	7 22.2	14 07.0	19 16.5	23 35.5	25 04.4	24 33.1	0 40.0
7 M	11 06 48	15 00 06	11♈30 33	17 55 49	29 15.2	6 13.0	14 09.6	7 59.0	14 32.8	19 10.1	23 42.9	25 02.0	24 31.6	0 39.8
8 Tu	11 10 44	15 58 20	24 24 16	0♉55 55	29 07.9	6 08.0	15 21.9	8 35.6	14 58.7	19 03.9	23 50.3	24 59.6	24 30.1	0 39.7
9 W	11 14 41	16 56 36	7♉30 46	14 08 52	29 02.0	5 56.7	16 34.3	9 12.2	15 24.7	18 57.8	23 57.8	24 57.3	24 28.6	0 39.6
10 Th	11 18 38	17 54 54	20 50 14	27 34 55	28 58.0	5 38.9	17 46.8	9 48.6	15 50.7	18 51.8	24 05.2	24 54.9	24 27.1	0 39.6
11 F	11 22 34	18 53 14	4♊22 58	11♊14 25	28D 56.1	5 14.5	18 59.3	10 24.8	16 16.6	18 46.0	24 12.7	24 52.5	24 25.7	0D 39.5
12 Sa	11 26 31	19 51 37	18 09 19	25 07 42	28 56.0	4 43.4	20 12.0	11 01.0	16 42.7	18 40.3	24 20.2	24 50.1	24 24.2	0 39.5
13 Su	11 30 27	20 50 01	2♋09 31	9♋14 43	28 56.8	4 05.9	21 24.7	11 37.0	17 08.7	18 34.7	24 27.6	24 47.7	24 22.8	0 39.6
14 M	11 34 24	21 48 28	16 23 09	23 34 37	28R 57.6	3 22.1	22 37.4	12 12.9	17 34.8	18 29.4	24 35.1	24 45.3	24 21.4	0 39.7
15 Tu	11 38 20	22 46 57	0♌48 47	8♌05 15	28 57.4	2 32.7	23 50.2	12 48.6	18 00.9	18 24.1	24 42.6	24 42.9	24 20.0	0 39.8
16 W	11 42 17	23 45 28	15 23 27	22 42 47	28 55.2	1 38.2	25 03.1	13 24.2	18 27.1	18 19.0	24 50.1	24 40.5	24 18.6	0 39.9
17 Th	11 46 13	24 44 00	0♍02 30	7♍21 47	28 50.7	0 39.5	26 16.1	13 59.7	18 53.2	18 14.1	24 57.6	24 38.1	24 17.2	0 40.1
18 F	11 50 10	25 42 35	14 39 47	21 55 36	28 43.7	29♍37.7	27 29.1	14 35.0	19 19.4	18 09.3	25 05.0	24 35.7	24 15.9	0 40.3
19 Sa	11 54 07	26 41 12	29 08 22	6♎17 16	28 34.9	28 34.0	28 42.2	15 10.1	19 45.6	18 04.7	25 12.5	24 33.3	24 14.6	0 40.5
20 Su	11 58 03	27 39 51	13♎21 34	20 20 39	28 25.2	27 30.0	29 55.3	15 45.2	20 11.9	18 00.3	25 20.0	24 30.9	24 13.3	0 40.7
21 M	12 02 00	28 38 31	27 14 03	4♏01 24	28 15.6	26 27.2	1♍08.5	16 20.0	20 38.1	17 56.1	25 27.5	24 28.5	24 12.0	0 41.0
22 Tu	12 05 56	29 37 13	10♏42 32	17 17 26	28 07.3	25 27.1	2 21.8	16 54.7	21 04.4	17 52.0	25 35.0	24 26.1	24 10.7	0 41.4
23 W	12 09 53	0♎35 57	23 46 12	0♐09 05	28 01.0	24 31.3	3 35.1	17 29.2	21 30.7	17 48.1	25 42.4	24 23.7	24 09.5	0 41.7
24 Th	12 13 49	1 34 43	6♐26 25	12 38 40	27 56.9	23 41.3	4 48.4	18 03.6	21 57.0	17 44.4	25 49.9	24 21.4	24 08.2	0 42.1
25 F	12 17 46	2 33 31	18 46 23	24 50 07	27D 55.1	22 58.4	6 01.9	18 37.9	22 23.3	17 40.8	25 57.4	24 19.0	24 07.0	0 42.5
26 Sa	12 21 42	3 32 20	0♑50 32	6♑48 17	27 54.8	22 23.7	7 15.3	19 11.9	22 49.7	17 37.5	26 04.8	24 16.6	24 05.9	0 43.0
27 Su	12 25 39	4 31 11	12 44 03	18 38 31	27R 55.3	21 58.1	8 28.9	19 45.8	23 16.0	17 34.3	26 12.3	24 14.3	24 04.7	0 43.5
28 M	12 29 36	5 30 04	24 32 22	0♒26 16	27 55.5	21 42.3	9 42.5	20 19.6	23 42.4	17 31.3	26 19.7	24 11.9	24 03.6	0 44.0
29 Tu	12 33 32	6 28 58	6♒20 51	12 16 43	27 54.5	21D 36.6	10 56.1	20 53.1	24 08.8	17 28.6	26 27.1	24 09.6	24 02.5	0 44.5
30 W	12 37 29	7 27 54	18 14 25	24 14 29	27 51.3	21 41.3	12 09.8	21 26.5	24 35.2	17 26.0	26 34.5	24 07.3	24 01.4	0 45.1

LONGITUDE — October 2009

Day	Sid.Time	☉	0 hr ☽	Noon ☽	True ☊	☿	♀	♂	⚳	♃	♄	♅	♆	♇
1 Th	12 41 25	8♎26 52	0♓17 22	6♓23 26	27♑45.6	21♍56.1	13♍23.5	21♋59.7	25♎01.6	17♒23.6	26♍41.9	24♓04.9	24♒00.3	0♑45.7
2 F	12 45 22	9 25 52	12 33 00	18 46 20	27R 37.2	22 20.9	14 37.3	22 32.8	25 28.0	17R 21.3	26 49.3	24R 02.6	23R 59.3	0 46.3
3 Sa	12 49 18	10 24 54	25 03 34	1♈24 48	27 26.6	22 55.3	15 51.1	23 05.7	25 54.4	17 19.3	26 56.6	24 00.4	23 58.3	0 47.0
4 Su	12 53 15	11 23 57	7♈50 01	14 19 10	27 14.5	23 38.6	17 05.0	23 38.4	26 20.9	17 17.5	27 03.9	23 58.1	23 57.3	0 47.7
5 M	12 57 11	12 23 03	20 52 06	27 28 39	27 02.0	24 30.3	18 19.0	24 10.9	26 47.4	17 15.9	27 11.3	23 55.8	23 56.3	0 48.4
6 Tu	13 01 08	13 22 11	4♉08 33	10♉51 32	26 50.4	25 29.6	19 32.9	24 43.2	27 13.8	17 14.4	27 18.6	23 53.6	23 55.4	0 49.2
7 W	13 05 05	14 21 21	17 37 21	24 25 42	26 40.7	26 35.9	20 47.0	25 15.3	27 40.3	17 13.2	27 25.9	23 51.4	23 54.5	0 50.0
8 Th	13 09 01	15 20 34	1♊16 20	8♊09 00	26 33.6	27 48.4	22 01.1	25 47.3	28 06.8	17 12.2	27 33.1	23 49.2	23 53.6	0 50.8
9 F	13 12 58	16 19 48	15 03 30	21 59 40	26 29.4	29 06.2	23 15.2	26 19.1	28 33.3	17 11.3	27 40.4	23 47.1	23 52.8	0 51.7
10 Sa	13 16 54	17 19 06	28 57 22	5♋56 31	26D 27.6	0♎28.9	24 29.4	26 50.6	28 59.8	17 10.7	27 47.6	23 44.9	23 51.9	0 52.5
11 Su	13 20 51	18 18 25	12♋57 02	19 58 51	26R 27.3	1 55.5	25 43.6	27 22.0	29 26.3	17 10.3	27 54.8	23 42.8	23 51.2	0 53.5
12 M	13 24 47	19 17 47	27 01 55	4♌06 07	26 27.2	3 25.6	26 57.9	27 53.1	29 52.8	17D 10.0	28 01.9	23 40.7	23 50.4	0 54.4
13 Tu	13 28 44	20 17 11	11♌11 21	18 17 26	26 26.0	4 58.6	28 12.2	28 24.1	0♏19.3	17 10.0	28 09.1	23 38.6	23 49.7	0 55.4
14 W	13 32 40	21 16 37	25 24 07	2♍31 06	26 22.6	6 34.0	29 26.6	28 54.8	0 45.9	17 10.1	28 16.2	23 36.5	23 49.0	0 56.4
15 Th	13 36 37	22 16 06	9♍38 00	16 44 20	26 16.3	8 11.3	0♎41.0	29 25.3	1 12.4	17 10.5	28 23.3	23 34.5	23 48.3	0 57.4
16 F	13 40 34	23 15 36	23 49 36	0♎53 12	26 07.1	9 50.0	1 55.5	29 55.6	1 38.9	17 11.1	28 30.3	23 32.5	23 47.6	0 58.4
17 Sa	13 44 30	24 15 09	7♎54 32	14 53 01	25 55.6	11 30.0	3 09.9	0♌25.6	2 05.5	17 11.8	28 37.3	23 30.5	23 47.0	0 59.5
18 Su	13 48 27	25 14 44	21 48 03	28 39 06	25 42.8	13 10.8	4 24.5	0 55.4	2 32.0	17 12.8	28 44.3	23 28.6	23 46.4	1 00.6
19 M	13 52 23	26 14 21	5♏25 42	12♏07 29	25 30.0	14 52.3	5 39.0	1 25.0	2 58.6	17 14.0	28 51.3	23 26.7	23 45.9	1 01.8
20 Tu	13 56 20	27 14 00	18 44 12	25 15 43	25 18.5	16 34.2	6 53.6	1 54.3	3 25.1	17 15.3	28 58.2	23 24.8	23 45.4	1 03.0
21 W	14 00 16	28 13 41	1♐41 58	8♐03 04	25 09.3	18 16.3	8 08.3	2 23.4	3 51.6	17 16.9	29 05.0	23 23.0	23 44.9	1 04.2
22 Th	14 04 13	29 13 24	14 19 14	20 30 45	25 02.8	19 58.5	9 22.9	2 52.2	4 18.2	17 18.7	29 11.9	23 21.1	23 44.4	1 05.4
23 F	14 08 09	0♏13 08	26 38 03	2♑41 34	24 59.0	21 40.6	10 37.6	3 20.8	4 44.7	17 20.7	29 18.7	23 19.4	23 44.0	1 06.6
24 Sa	14 12 06	1 12 54	8♑41 53	14 39 35	24D 57.4	23 22.6	11 52.3	3 49.1	5 11.2	17 22.8	29 25.5	23 17.6	23 43.6	1 07.9
25 Su	14 16 03	2 12 42	20 35 20	26 29 46	24R 57.1	25 04.4	13 07.1	4 17.1	5 37.8	17 25.2	29 32.2	23 15.9	23 43.2	1 09.2
26 M	14 19 59	3 12 32	2♒23 37	8♒17 34	24 57.1	26 45.9	14 21.9	4 44.9	6 04.3	17 27.7	29 38.8	23 14.2	23 42.9	1 10.6
27 Tu	14 23 56	4 12 23	14 12 20	20 08 34	24 56.1	28 27.0	15 36.7	5 12.4	6 30.8	17 30.5	29 45.5	23 12.6	23 42.6	1 11.9
28 W	14 27 52	5 12 16	26 06 58	2♓08 09	24 53.3	0♏07.8	16 51.5	5 39.6	6 57.3	17 33.4	29 52.1	23 11.0	23 42.3	1 13.3
29 Th	14 31 49	6 12 10	8♓12 41	14 21 07	24 48.1	1 48.1	18 06.3	6 06.6	7 23.8	17 36.6	29 58.6	23 09.4	23 42.1	1 14.7
30 F	14 35 45	7 12 06	20 33 52	26 51 20	24 40.1	3 28.1	19 21.2	6 33.2	7 50.3	17 39.9	0♎05.1	23 07.9	23 41.9	1 16.2
31 Sa	14 39 42	8 12 04	3♈13 46	9♈41 21	24 29.7	5 07.6	20 36.1	6 59.6	8 16.8	17 43.4	0 11.5	23 06.4	23 41.8	1 17.6

Astro Data	Planet Ingress	Last Aspect	☽ Ingress	Last Aspect	☽ Ingress	☽ Phases & Eclipses	Astro Data
Dy Hr Mn	Dy Hr Mn	Dy Hr Mn	Dy Hr Mn	Dy Hr Mn	Dy Hr Mn	Dy Hr Mn	1 September 2009
☽0N 5 8:24	☿ ♍R 18 3:26	31 18:09 ♅ ⚹	♒ 1 3:43	3 3:29 ♄ ☍	♈ 3 9:21	4 16:03 ○ 12♓15	Julian Day # 40056
☿R 7 4:44	♀ ♍ 20 13:32	3 5:19 ♆ ☌	♓ 3 15:58	5 5:46 ♂ □	♉ 5 16:33	12 2:16 ☾ 19♊28	SVP 5♓07'13"
⚳0S 9 9:22	☉ ♎ 22 21:19	5 16:53 ♅ ☌	♈ 6 2:14	7 17:19 ♄ △	♊ 7 21:46	18 18:44 ● 25♍59	GC 26♐58.5 ♀ 14♍49.2
♇D 11 16:58		8 0:12 ♆ ⚹	♉ 8 10:18	10 1:35 ☿ □	♋ 10 1:48	26 4:50 ☽ 3♑15	Eris 21♈51.4R ⚵ 2♈42.8R
♄⊼♆ 12 22:58	☿ ♎ 10 3:46	10 7:17 ♅ ⚹	♊ 10 16:17	12 1:37 ♅ △	♌ 12 5:02		⚷ 22♒52.7R ⚶ 1♌38.9
♄☍♅ 15 12:51	⚳ ♏ 12 18:30	12 11:30 ♅ □	♋ 12 20:20	13 21:20 ♆ ☍	♍ 14 7:45	4 6:10 ○ 11♈10	☽ Mean ☊ 28♑04.1
☽0S 18 9:57	♀ ♎ 14 22:46	14 13:57 ♅ △	♌ 14 22:39	16 10:18 ♂ ⚹	♎ 16 10:29	11 8:56 ☾ 18♋11	
☉0S 22 21:18	♂ ♌ 16 15:32	16 16:11 ♀ ☌	♍ 16 23:56	18 5:33 ☉ ☌	♏ 18 14:23	18 5:33 ● 24♎59	1 October 2009
☿0N 23 2:03	☉ ♏ 23 6:43	18 23:56 ☿ ☌	♎ 19 1:26	20 18:57 ♄ ⚹	♐ 20 20:49	26 0:42 ☽ 2♒44	Julian Day # 40086
☿D 29 13:14	☿ ♏ 28 10:09	20 18:43 ♆ △	♏ 21 4:52	23 6:39 ☉ ⚹	♑ 23 6:39		SVP 5♓07'10"
☽0N 2 15:36	♄ ♎ 29 17:09	23 3:33 ♄ ⚹	♐ 23 11:43	25 18:15 ♄ △	♒ 25 19:08		GC 26♐58.5 ♀ 29♍04.3
♅⊻♆ 5 3:08		25 14:15 ♄ □	♑ 25 22:19	28 7:22 ☿ △	♓ 28 7:45		Eris 21♈35.9R ⚵ 26♓00.5R
♃D 13 4:34		28 3:33 ♄ △	♒ 28 11:07	30 4:56 ♅ ☌	♈ 30 17:56		⚷ 21♒40.2R ⚶ 13♌39.6
☿0S 13 5:44	♀0S17 19:03	30 11:34 ♆ ☌	♓ 30 23:26				☽ Mean ☊ 26♑28.7
☽0S 15 18:26	☽0N29 23:35						

November 2009 LONGITUDE

Day	Sid.Time	☉	0 hr ☽	Noon ☽	True ☊	☿	♀	♂	⚳	♃	♄	♅	♆	♇
1 Su	14 43 38	9♏12 04	16♈14 08	22♈52 03	24♑17.8	6♏46.6	21♎51.1	7♌25.6	8♏43.2	17♒47.1	0♎17.9	23♓04.9	23♒41.6	1♑19.1
2 M	14 47 35	10 12 05	29 34 56	6♉22 29	24R 05.4	8 25.2	23 06.0	7 51.4	9 09.7	17 51.0	0 24.3	23R 03.5	23R 41.5	1 20.6
3 Tu	14 51 31	11 12 09	13♉14 19	20 09 58	23 53.8	10 03.4	24 21.0	8 16.8	9 36.1	17 55.1	0 30.6	23 02.1	23 41.5	1 22.1
4 W	14 55 28	12 12 14	27 08 54	4♊10 32	23 44.1	11 41.1	25 36.0	8 41.9	10 02.6	17 59.4	0 36.8	23 00.8	23D 41.4	1 23.7
5 Th	14 59 25	13 12 21	11♊14 17	18 19 35	23 37.0	13 18.5	26 51.1	9 06.7	10 29.0	18 03.8	0 43.0	22 59.5	23 41.5	1 25.3
6 F	15 03 21	14 12 31	25 25 53	2♋32 41	23 32.9	14 55.4	28 06.1	9 31.2	10 55.4	18 08.4	0 49.1	22 58.3	23 41.5	1 26.9
7 Sa	15 07 18	15 12 42	9♋39 34	16 46 09	23D 31.2	16 31.9	29 21.2	9 55.4	11 21.8	18 13.3	0 55.2	22 57.1	23 41.6	1 28.5
8 Su	15 11 14	16 12 55	23 52 09	0♌57 22	23 31.2	18 08.0	0♏36.3	10 19.1	11 48.2	18 18.2	1 01.3	22 55.9	23 41.7	1 30.1
9 M	15 15 11	17 13 11	8♌01 36	15 04 44	23R 31.6	19 43.7	1 51.5	10 42.6	12 14.5	18 23.4	1 07.2	22 54.8	23 41.8	1 31.8
10 Tu	15 19 07	18 13 28	22 06 40	29 07 19	23 31.1	21 19.1	3 06.6	11 05.6	12 40.9	18 28.7	1 13.1	22 53.7	23 42.0	1 33.5
11 W	15 23 04	19 13 47	6♍06 36	13♍04 26	23 28.7	22 54.2	4 21.8	11 28.3	13 07.2	18 34.3	1 19.0	22 52.7	23 42.2	1 35.2
12 Th	15 27 01	20 14 09	20 00 39	26 55 07	23 23.8	24 28.9	5 37.0	11 50.7	13 33.6	18 39.9	1 24.7	22 51.7	23 42.5	1 36.9
13 F	15 30 57	21 14 32	3♎47 39	10♎38 01	23 16.3	26 03.3	6 52.2	12 12.6	13 59.9	18 45.8	1 30.5	22 50.8	23 42.7	1 38.7
14 Sa	15 34 54	22 14 57	17 25 58	24 11 13	23 06.7	27 37.5	8 07.5	12 34.1	14 26.1	18 51.8	1 36.1	22 49.9	23 43.0	1 40.4
15 Su	15 38 50	23 15 24	0♏53 30	7♏32 32	22 55.9	29 11.3	9 22.7	12 55.2	14 52.4	18 58.0	1 41.7	22 49.0	23 43.4	1 42.2
16 M	15 42 47	24 15 52	14 08 05	20 39 55	22 45.0	0♐44.9	10 38.0	13 15.9	15 18.6	19 04.4	1 47.2	22 48.2	23 43.8	1 44.0
17 Tu	15 46 43	25 16 23	27 07 53	3♐31 51	22 35.2	2 18.3	11 53.3	13 36.2	15 44.9	19 11.0	1 52.7	22 47.5	23 44.2	1 45.9
18 W	15 50 40	26 16 55	9♐51 48	16 07 45	22 27.3	3 51.4	13 08.6	13 56.0	16 11.1	19 17.7	1 58.1	22 46.8	23 44.6	1 47.7
19 Th	15 54 36	27 17 28	22 19 48	28 28 10	22 21.8	5 24.3	14 23.9	14 15.4	16 37.2	19 24.5	2 03.4	22 46.2	23 45.1	1 49.6
20 F	15 58 33	28 18 02	4♑33 06	10♑34 56	22D 18.8	6 57.0	15 39.2	14 34.4	17 03.4	19 31.6	2 08.6	22 45.6	23 45.7	1 51.5
21 Sa	16 02 30	29 18 38	16 34 04	22 30 57	22 18.0	8 29.5	16 54.6	14 52.9	17 29.5	19 38.7	2 13.8	22 45.0	23 46.2	1 53.4
22 Su	16 06 26	0♐19 16	28 26 08	4♒20 10	22 18.6	10 01.8	18 09.9	15 10.9	17 55.6	19 46.1	2 18.9	22 44.5	23 46.8	1 55.3
23 M	16 10 23	1 19 54	10♒13 39	16 07 13	22 19.9	11 33.8	19 25.3	15 28.4	18 21.6	19 53.6	2 23.9	22 44.1	23 47.4	1 57.2
24 Tu	16 14 19	2 20 33	22 01 32	27 57 17	22R 20.8	13 05.7	20 40.6	15 45.4	18 47.7	20 01.2	2 28.9	22 43.7	23 48.1	1 59.1
25 W	16 18 16	3 21 14	3♓55 07	9♓55 44	22 20.7	14 37.4	21 56.0	16 02.0	19 13.7	20 09.0	2 33.7	22 43.3	23 48.8	2 01.1
26 Th	16 22 12	4 21 55	15 59 46	22 07 51	22 18.8	16 08.9	23 11.4	16 18.0	19 39.6	20 17.0	2 38.5	22 43.0	23 49.5	2 03.1
27 F	16 26 09	5 22 38	28 20 33	4♈38 23	22 14.9	17 40.2	24 26.8	16 33.5	20 05.6	20 25.1	2 43.2	22 42.8	23 50.2	2 05.0
28 Sa	16 30 05	6 23 22	11♈01 47	17 31 07	22 09.1	19 11.3	25 42.2	16 48.5	20 31.5	20 33.3	2 47.9	22 42.6	23 51.0	2 07.0
29 Su	16 34 02	7 24 07	24 06 35	0♉48 18	22 02.0	20 42.1	26 57.6	17 03.0	20 57.3	20 41.7	2 52.4	22 42.4	23 51.9	2 09.1
30 M	16 37 59	8 24 52	7♉36 15	14 30 13	21 54.4	22 12.6	28 13.0	17 16.9	21 23.2	20 50.3	2 56.9	22 42.3	23 52.7	2 11.1

December 2009 LONGITUDE

Day	Sid.Time	☉	0 hr ☽	Noon ☽	True ☊	☿	♀	♂	⚳	♃	♄	♅	♆	♇
1 Tu	16 41 55	9♐25 40	21♉29 54	28♉34 48	21♑47.2	23♐42.9	29♏28.4	17♌30.3	21♏49.0	20♒58.9	3♎01.3	22♓42.3	23♒53.6	2♑13.1
2 W	16 45 52	10 26 28	5♊44 20	12♊57 45	21R 41.2	25 12.9	0♐43.8	17 43.1	22 14.7	21 07.7	3 05.6	22D 42.3	23 54.5	2 15.2
3 Th	16 49 48	11 27 17	20 14 17	27 33 04	21 37.0	26 42.4	1 59.2	17 55.3	22 40.5	21 16.7	3 09.8	22 42.3	23 55.5	2 17.2
4 F	16 53 45	12 28 08	4♋53 12	12♋13 50	21D 34.9	28 11.5	3 14.7	18 06.9	23 06.1	21 25.8	3 13.9	22 42.5	23 56.4	2 19.3
5 Sa	16 57 41	13 29 00	19 34 09	26 53 23	21 34.7	29 40.1	4 30.1	18 17.9	23 31.8	21 35.0	3 18.0	22 42.6	23 57.5	2 21.4
6 Su	17 01 38	14 29 53	4♌10 53	11♌26 05	21 35.7	1♑08.1	5 45.6	18 28.3	23 57.4	21 44.3	3 21.9	22 42.8	23 58.5	2 23.5
7 M	17 05 34	15 30 47	18 38 32	25 47 52	21 37.2	2 35.5	7 01.1	18 38.1	24 23.0	21 53.8	3 25.8	22 43.1	23 59.6	2 25.6
8 Tu	17 09 31	16 31 43	2♍53 50	9♍56 15	21R 38.3	4 02.0	8 16.5	18 47.2	24 48.5	22 03.4	3 29.6	22 43.4	24 00.7	2 27.7
9 W	17 13 28	17 32 39	16 55 02	23 50 07	21 38.3	5 27.5	9 32.0	18 55.6	25 14.0	22 13.1	3 33.3	22 43.8	24 01.8	2 29.8
10 Th	17 17 24	18 33 37	0♎41 32	7♎29 17	21 36.8	6 51.9	10 47.5	19 03.4	25 39.4	22 23.0	3 36.9	22 44.2	24 03.0	2 31.9
11 F	17 21 21	19 34 37	14 13 26	20 54 03	21 33.8	8 15.0	12 03.0	19 10.5	26 04.8	22 32.9	3 40.4	22 44.6	24 04.2	2 34.0
12 Sa	17 25 17	20 35 37	27 31 12	4♏04 55	21 29.4	9 36.6	13 18.5	19 16.9	26 30.2	22 43.0	3 43.8	22 45.2	24 05.4	2 36.2
13 Su	17 29 14	21 36 38	10♏35 18	17 02 22	21 24.3	10 56.3	14 34.0	19 22.6	26 55.5	22 53.2	3 47.1	22 45.7	24 06.7	2 38.3
14 M	17 33 10	22 37 41	23 26 12	29 46 50	21 19.1	12 14.0	15 49.5	19 27.6	27 20.8	23 03.6	3 50.3	22 46.4	24 08.0	2 40.5
15 Tu	17 37 07	23 38 44	6♐04 20	12♐18 46	21 14.4	13 29.1	17 05.0	19 31.8	27 46.0	23 14.0	3 53.5	22 47.0	24 09.3	2 42.6
16 W	17 41 03	24 39 48	18 30 14	24 38 50	21 10.8	14 41.4	18 20.6	19 35.3	28 11.1	23 24.6	3 56.5	22 47.8	24 10.6	2 44.8
17 Th	17 45 00	25 40 53	0♑44 41	6♑47 59	21 08.5	15 50.3	19 36.1	19 38.1	28 36.3	23 35.3	3 59.4	22 48.5	24 12.0	2 47.0
18 F	17 48 57	26 41 58	12 48 54	18 47 43	21D 07.6	16 55.2	20 51.6	19 40.1	29 01.3	23 46.1	4 02.2	22 49.4	24 13.4	2 49.1
19 Sa	17 52 53	27 43 04	24 44 40	0♒40 07	21 07.9	17 55.7	22 07.1	19 41.3	29 26.3	23 57.0	4 05.0	22 50.2	24 14.9	2 51.3
20 Su	17 56 50	28 44 10	6♒34 25	12 27 58	21 09.1	18 51.0	23 22.6	19R 41.7	29 51.2	24 08.0	4 07.6	22 51.2	24 16.3	2 53.5
21 M	18 00 46	29 45 17	18 21 13	24 14 40	21 10.9	19 40.3	24 38.2	19 41.4	0♐16.1	24 19.1	4 10.1	22 52.2	24 17.8	2 55.7
22 Tu	18 04 43	0♑46 24	0♓08 50	6♓04 16	21 12.6	20 22.8	25 53.7	19 40.2	0 41.0	24 30.3	4 12.5	22 53.2	24 19.3	2 57.8
23 W	18 08 39	1 47 31	12 01 33	18 01 17	21 13.9	20 57.7	27 09.2	19 38.3	1 05.7	24 41.6	4 14.9	22 54.3	24 20.8	3 00.0
24 Th	18 12 36	2 48 38	24 04 03	0♈10 30	21R 14.6	21 24.1	28 24.7	19 35.5	1 30.4	24 53.0	4 17.1	22 55.4	24 22.4	3 02.2
25 F	18 16 32	3 49 45	6♈21 11	12 36 43	21 14.3	21 41.0	29 40.2	19 32.0	1 55.1	25 04.5	4 19.2	22 56.6	24 24.0	3 04.4
26 Sa	18 20 29	4 50 52	18 57 38	25 24 24	21 13.3	21R 47.7	0♑55.7	19 27.6	2 19.6	25 16.1	4 21.2	22 57.8	24 25.6	3 06.6
27 Su	18 24 26	5 52 00	1♉57 27	8♉37 04	21 11.6	21 43.2	2 11.2	19 22.5	2 44.2	25 27.8	4 23.1	22 59.1	24 27.2	3 08.7
28 M	18 28 22	6 53 07	15 23 30	22 16 48	21 09.7	21 27.2	3 26.7	19 16.5	3 08.6	25 39.6	4 24.9	23 00.4	24 28.9	3 10.9
29 Tu	18 32 19	7 54 15	29 16 53	6♊23 31	21 07.8	20 59.4	4 42.3	19 09.6	3 33.0	25 51.5	4 26.6	23 01.8	24 30.6	3 13.1
30 W	18 36 15	8 55 23	13♊36 16	20 54 35	21 06.3	20 19.8	5 57.8	19 02.0	3 57.3	26 03.4	4 28.2	23 03.2	24 32.3	3 15.3
31 Th	18 40 12	9 56 30	28 17 42	5♋44 44	21 05.3	19 29.0	7 13.3	18 53.6	4 21.5	26 15.5	4 29.7	23 04.7	24 34.0	3 17.4

Astro Data

	Dy Hr Mn
♆ D	4 18:10
☽ 0S	12 0:14
♄□♇	15 15:20
☽ 0N	26 7:38
♅ D	1 20:28
☽ 0S	9 4:51
♃⚺♅	12 17:19
♂ R	20 13:26
♃☌♆	21 8:51
☽ 0N	23 15:03
☿ R	26 14:39

Planet Ingress

		Dy Hr Mn
♀	♏	8 0:23
☿	♐	16 0:28
☉	♐	22 4:23
♀	♐	1 22:04
☿	♑	5 17:24
⚳	♐	20 20:26
☉	♑	21 17:47
♀	♑	25 18:17

Last Aspect / ☽ Ingress

Last Aspect Dy Hr Mn			☽ Ingress	Dy Hr Mn
1 13:29	♆	⚹	♉	2 0:45
3 18:04	♆	□	♊	4 4:53
6 3:47	♀	△	♋	6 7:42
7 22:26	♅	△	♌	8 10:23
10 2:43	♆	☍	♍	10 13:30
12 7:13	☿	⚹	♎	12 17:22
14 11:10	♆	△	♏	14 22:24
16 19:14	☉	☌	♐	17 5:22
19 2:46	♆	⚹	♑	19 15:01
22 3:04	☉	⚹	♒	22 3:11
24 3:36	♆	☌	♓	24 16:07
26 14:17	♀	△	♈	27 3:11
28 23:33	♆	⚹	♉	29 10:34

Last Aspect / ☽ Ingress

Last Aspect Dy Hr Mn			☽ Ingress	Dy Hr Mn
1 13:39	♀	☍	♊	1 14:23
3 10:28	☿	☍	♋	3 16:01
5 5:09	♅	△	♌	5 17:07
7 8:58	♆	☍	♍	7 19:05
9 10:04	♅	☍	♎	9 22:47
11 17:44	♆	△	♏	12 4:31
14 1:18	♆	□	♐	14 12:25
16 12:02	☉	☌	♑	16 22:32
18 20:08	♅	⚹	♒	19 10:39
21 12:54	♀	⚹	♓	21 23:42
24 8:09	♀	□	♈	24 11:39
26 11:44	♃	⚹	♉	26 20:26
28 17:54	♃	□	♊	29 1:13
30 20:29	♃	△	♋	31 2:45

☽ Phases & Eclipses

Dy Hr Mn	
2 19:14	○ 10♉30
9 15:56	☾ 17♌23
16 19:14	● 24♏34
24 21:39	☽ 2♓45
2 7:30	○ 10♊15
9 0:13	☾ 17♍03
16 12:02	● 24♐40
24 17:36	☽ 3♈03
31 19:13	○ 10♋15
31 19:23	• P 0.076

Astro Data

1 November 2009
Julian Day # 40117
SVP 5♓07'07"
GC 26♐58.6 ⚴ 13♎13.0
Eris 21♈17.6R ⚵ 21♓33.8R
⚷ 21♒13.1 ⚶ 24♌41.0
☽ Mean ☊ 24♑50.2

1 December 2009
Julian Day # 40147
SVP 5♓07'02"
GC 26♐58.7 ⚴ 26♎04.4
Eris 21♈02.9R ⚵ 24♓46.4
⚷ 21♒43.9 ⚶ 2♍50.5
☽ Mean ☊ 23♑14.9

LONGITUDE — January 2010

Day	Sid.Time	☉	0 hr ☽	Noon ☽	True ☊	☿	♀	♂	⚳	♃	♄	♅	♆	♇
1 F	18 44 08	10♑57 38	13♋14 40	20♋46 26	21♑05.0	18♑28.1	8♑28.7	18♌44.3	4♐45.7	26♒27.6	4♎31.1	23♓06.2	24♒35.8	3♑19.6
2 Sa	18 48 05	11 58 46	28 18 54	5♌50 56	21D 05.3	17R 18.7	9 44.2	18R 34.2	5 09.8	26 39.8	4 32.3	23 07.7	24 37.6	3 21.8
3 Su	18 52 02	12 59 54	13♌21 28	20 49 29	21 05.9	16 02.9	10 59.7	18 23.3	5 33.9	26 52.1	4 33.5	23 09.3	24 39.4	3 23.9
4 M	18 55 58	14 01 02	28 14 07	5♍34 35	21 06.6	14 43.1	12 15.2	18 11.7	5 57.8	27 04.5	4 34.6	23 11.0	24 41.2	3 26.1
5 Tu	18 59 55	15 02 11	12♍50 17	20 00 47	21 07.2	13 21.9	13 30.7	17 59.1	6 21.7	27 17.0	4 35.5	23 12.7	24 43.1	3 28.2
6 W	19 03 51	16 03 19	27 05 45	4♎05 01	21R 07.5	12 02.1	14 46.2	17 45.9	6 45.5	27 29.5	4 36.3	23 14.4	24 44.9	3 30.4
7 Th	19 07 48	17 04 28	10♎58 32	17 46 23	21 07.6	10 45.9	16 01.7	17 31.8	7 09.3	27 42.1	4 37.1	23 16.2	24 46.8	3 32.5
8 F	19 11 44	18 05 37	24 28 43	1♏05 44	21 07.5	9 35.6	17 17.2	17 16.9	7 32.9	27 54.8	4 37.7	23 18.0	24 48.7	3 34.6
9 Sa	19 15 41	19 06 46	7♏37 44	14 05 01	21 07.3	8 32.9	18 32.7	17 01.3	7 56.5	28 07.6	4 38.2	23 19.9	24 50.6	3 36.8
10 Su	19 19 37	20 07 55	20 27 55	26 46 46	21D 07.2	7 38.9	19 48.2	16 45.0	8 20.0	28 20.4	4 38.6	23 21.8	24 52.6	3 38.9
11 M	19 23 34	21 09 04	3♐01 56	9♐13 45	21 07.1	6 54.4	21 03.6	16 28.0	8 43.4	28 33.3	4 38.9	23 23.8	24 54.5	3 41.0
12 Tu	19 27 31	22 10 13	15 22 32	21 28 36	21 07.2	6 19.7	22 19.1	16 10.2	9 06.7	28 46.3	4 39.1	23 25.8	24 56.5	3 43.1
13 W	19 31 27	23 11 22	27 32 16	3♑33 47	21 07.4	5 54.8	23 34.6	15 51.8	9 29.9	28 59.3	4R 39.2	23 27.8	24 58.5	3 45.2
14 Th	19 35 24	24 12 31	9♑33 27	15 31 31	21R 07.5	5 39.6	24 50.1	15 32.8	9 53.1	29 12.4	4 39.1	23 29.9	25 00.5	3 47.2
15 F	19 39 20	25 13 39	21 28 14	27 23 50	21 07.5	5D 33.4	26 05.5	15 13.1	10 16.1	29 25.6	4 39.0	23 32.1	25 02.5	3 49.3
16 Sa	19 43 17	26 14 47	3♒18 36	9♒12 46	21 07.2	5 35.9	27 21.0	14 52.9	10 39.1	29 38.8	4 38.7	23 34.2	25 04.6	3 51.4
17 Su	19 47 13	27 15 54	15 06 35	21 00 22	21 06.6	5 46.4	28 36.5	14 32.2	11 02.0	29 52.1	4 38.3	23 36.4	25 06.7	3 53.4
18 M	19 51 10	28 17 00	26 54 24	2♓49 00	21 05.7	6 04.2	29 51.9	14 10.9	11 24.7	0♓05.5	4 37.9	23 38.7	25 08.7	3 55.4
19 Tu	19 55 06	29 18 06	8♓44 31	14 41 19	21 04.5	6 28.7	1♒07.3	13 49.1	11 47.4	0 18.9	4 37.3	23 41.0	25 10.8	3 57.5
20 W	19 59 03	0♒19 11	20 39 49	26 40 26	21 03.3	6 59.3	2 22.8	13 27.0	12 10.0	0 32.3	4 36.6	23 43.3	25 12.9	3 59.5
21 Th	20 03 00	1 20 15	2♈43 38	8♈49 52	21 02.1	7 35.5	3 38.2	13 04.4	12 32.4	0 45.8	4 35.8	23 45.7	25 15.0	4 01.5
22 F	20 06 56	2 21 18	14 59 39	21 13 28	21D 01.3	8 16.7	4 53.6	12 41.5	12 54.8	0 59.4	4 34.9	23 48.1	25 17.2	4 03.4
23 Sa	20 10 53	3 22 21	27 31 50	3♉55 13	21 01.1	9 02.4	6 09.0	12 18.4	13 17.1	1 13.0	4 33.9	23 50.5	25 19.3	4 05.4
24 Su	20 14 49	4 23 22	10♉24 07	16 58 57	21 01.4	9 52.2	7 24.4	11 54.9	13 39.2	1 26.7	4 32.7	23 53.0	25 21.5	4 07.3
25 M	20 18 46	5 24 22	23 40 04	0♊27 47	21 02.3	10 45.7	8 39.8	11 31.3	14 01.3	1 40.4	4 31.5	23 55.5	25 23.6	4 09.3
26 Tu	20 22 42	6 25 21	7♊22 15	14 23 34	21 03.5	11 42.6	9 55.1	11 07.5	14 23.2	1 54.2	4 30.2	23 58.0	25 25.8	4 11.2
27 W	20 26 39	7 26 20	21 31 36	28 46 08	21 04.7	12 42.5	11 10.5	10 43.5	14 45.0	2 08.0	4 28.8	24 00.6	25 28.0	4 13.1
28 Th	20 30 35	8 27 17	6♋06 43	13♋32 44	21R 05.5	13 45.2	12 25.8	10 19.5	15 06.7	2 21.8	4 27.2	24 03.2	25 30.2	4 15.0
29 F	20 34 32	9 28 13	21 03 23	28 37 40	21 05.5	14 50.3	13 41.2	9 55.5	15 28.3	2 35.7	4 25.6	24 05.9	25 32.4	4 16.9
30 Sa	20 38 29	10 29 08	6♌14 29	13♌52 36	21 04.4	15 57.8	14 56.5	9 31.5	15 49.8	2 49.6	4 23.9	24 08.5	25 34.6	4 18.7
31 Su	20 42 25	11 30 01	21 30 43	29 07 32	21 02.4	17 07.4	16 11.8	9 07.6	16 11.2	3 03.6	4 22.0	24 11.3	25 36.8	4 20.5

LONGITUDE — February 2010

Day	Sid.Time	☉	0 hr ☽	Noon ☽	True ☊	☿	♀	♂	⚳	♃	♄	♅	♆	♇
1 M	20 46 22	12♒30 54	6♍41 48	14♍12 20	20♑59.6	18♑18.9	17♒27.1	8♌43.7	16♐32.4	3♓17.6	4♎20.1	24♓14.0	25♒39.0	4♑22.4
2 Tu	20 50 18	13 31 46	21 38 07	28 58 18	20R 56.5	19 32.1	18 42.4	8R 20.1	16 53.6	3 31.6	4R 18.0	24 16.8	25 41.3	4 24.2
3 W	20 54 15	14 32 38	6♎12 12	13♎19 22	20 53.6	20 47.1	19 57.6	7 56.6	17 14.6	3 45.7	4 15.9	24 19.5	25 43.5	4 25.9
4 Th	20 58 11	15 33 28	20 19 31	27 12 33	20 51.3	22 03.6	21 12.9	7 33.3	17 35.4	3 59.8	4 13.7	24 22.4	25 45.8	4 27.7
5 F	21 02 08	16 34 18	3♏58 34	10♏37 46	20D 50.1	23 21.5	22 28.2	7 10.4	17 56.2	4 13.9	4 11.3	24 25.2	25 48.0	4 29.4
6 Sa	21 06 04	17 35 06	17 10 29	23 37 07	20 50.1	24 40.8	23 43.4	6 47.7	18 16.8	4 28.1	4 08.9	24 28.1	25 50.3	4 31.1
7 Su	21 10 01	18 35 54	29 58 09	6♐14 07	20 51.2	26 01.4	24 58.7	6 25.5	18 37.3	4 42.3	4 06.4	24 31.0	25 52.6	4 32.8
8 M	21 13 58	19 36 41	12♐25 33	18 33 02	20 52.9	27 23.2	26 13.9	6 03.6	18 57.6	4 56.5	4 03.8	24 34.0	25 54.8	4 34.5
9 Tu	21 17 54	20 37 27	24 37 05	0♑38 15	20 54.7	28 46.2	27 29.1	5 42.2	19 17.9	5 10.8	4 01.1	24 36.9	25 57.1	4 36.2
10 W	21 21 51	21 38 12	6♑37 04	12 34 00	20R 56.0	0♒10.2	28 44.3	5 21.3	19 37.9	5 25.1	3 58.3	24 39.9	25 59.4	4 37.8
11 Th	21 25 47	22 38 56	18 29 30	24 23 59	20 56.3	1 35.4	29 59.5	5 00.9	19 57.9	5 39.4	3 55.4	24 42.9	26 01.7	4 39.4
12 F	21 29 44	23 39 38	0♒17 50	6♒11 25	20 55.1	3 01.6	1♓14.7	4 41.0	20 17.7	5 53.7	3 52.5	24 46.0	26 03.9	4 41.0
13 Sa	21 33 40	24 40 19	12 05 01	17 58 56	20 52.1	4 28.7	2 29.8	4 21.7	20 37.3	6 08.0	3 49.4	24 49.0	26 06.2	4 42.6
14 Su	21 37 37	25 40 59	23 53 25	29 48 43	20 47.3	5 56.9	3 45.0	4 03.1	20 56.8	6 22.4	3 46.3	24 52.1	26 08.5	4 44.1
15 M	21 41 33	26 41 37	5♓45 02	11♓42 35	20 41.1	7 26.1	5 00.1	3 45.0	21 16.1	6 36.8	3 43.0	24 55.2	26 10.8	4 45.6
16 Tu	21 45 30	27 42 14	17 41 35	23 42 14	20 34.0	8 56.2	6 15.2	3 27.7	21 35.3	6 51.2	3 39.7	24 58.4	26 13.0	4 47.1
17 W	21 49 27	28 42 49	29 44 44	5♈49 20	20 26.8	10 27.2	7 30.3	3 11.0	21 54.3	7 05.6	3 36.4	25 01.5	26 15.3	4 48.6
18 Th	21 53 23	29 43 22	11♈56 17	18 05 51	20 20.0	11 59.2	8 45.4	2 55.1	22 13.2	7 20.1	3 32.9	25 04.7	26 17.6	4 50.0
19 F	21 57 20	0♓43 54	24 18 20	0♉34 02	20 14.6	13 32.1	10 00.4	2 39.8	22 31.9	7 34.5	3 29.4	25 07.9	26 19.9	4 51.4
20 Sa	22 01 16	1 44 24	6♉53 18	13 16 29	20 10.9	15 06.0	11 15.5	2 25.3	22 50.4	7 49.0	3 25.8	25 11.1	26 22.2	4 52.8
21 Su	22 05 13	2 44 52	19 43 59	26 16 08	20D 09.2	16 40.7	12 30.5	2 11.6	23 08.8	8 03.4	3 22.1	25 14.3	26 24.4	4 54.2
22 M	22 09 09	3 45 18	2♊53 20	9♊35 54	20 09.1	18 16.5	13 45.5	1 58.6	23 27.0	8 17.9	3 18.4	25 17.5	26 26.7	4 55.5
23 Tu	22 13 06	4 45 43	16 24 08	23 18 15	20 10.1	19 53.2	15 00.4	1 46.5	23 45.0	8 32.4	3 14.6	25 20.8	26 29.0	4 56.8
24 W	22 17 02	5 46 05	0♋18 25	7♋24 38	20R 11.4	21 30.8	16 15.4	1 35.1	24 02.9	8 46.9	3 10.7	25 24.0	26 31.2	4 58.1
25 Th	22 20 59	6 46 25	14 36 49	21 54 40	20 11.9	23 09.4	17 30.3	1 24.4	24 20.6	9 01.4	3 06.8	25 27.3	26 33.5	4 59.4
26 F	22 24 56	7 46 44	29 17 44	6♌45 24	20 10.8	24 49.0	18 45.2	1 14.6	24 38.1	9 15.9	3 02.8	25 30.6	26 35.7	5 00.6
27 Sa	22 28 52	8 47 01	14♌16 50	21 51 02	20 07.5	26 29.5	20 00.1	1 05.6	24 55.4	9 30.4	2 58.7	25 33.9	26 38.0	5 01.8
28 Su	22 32 49	9 47 15	29 26 50	7♍03 01	20 01.9	28 11.1	21 14.9	0 57.3	25 12.5	9 44.8	2 54.6	25 37.3	26 40.2	5 03.0

Astro Data

	Dy Hr Mn
☽0S	5 11:09
♄R	13 15:56
☿D	15 16:52
☽0N	19 21:42
♄□♇	31 21:27
☽0S	1 20:39
♃⚻♄	5 8:14
♃✱♇	6 17:51
☽0N	16 3:58

Planet Ingress

		Dy Hr Mn
♃	♓	18 2:10
♀	♒	18 14:35
☉	♒	20 4:28
☿	♒	10 9:06
♀	♓	11 12:10
☉	♓	18 18:36

Last Aspect / ☽ Ingress

Last Aspect Dy Hr Mn			☽ Ingress	Dy Hr Mn
1 15:43	♅	△	♌	2 2:41
3 21:55	♃	☍	♍	4 2:52
5 17:25	♅	☍	♎	6 4:58
8 6:07	♃	△	♏	8 10:00
10 15:02	♃	□	♐	10 18:10
13 2:43	♃	✱	♑	13 4:54
15 9:02	♀	☌	♒	15 17:17
17 20:22	♆	☌	♓	18 6:17
20 6:06	♅	☌	♈	20 18:36
22 19:46	♆	✱	♉	23 4:39
25 3:03	♆	□	♊	25 11:11
27 6:32	♆	△	♋	27 14:01
29 4:49	♅	△	♌	29 14:10
31 6:27	♆	☍	♍	31 13:23

Last Aspect / ☽ Ingress

Last Aspect Dy Hr Mn			☽ Ingress	Dy Hr Mn
2 4:17	♅	☍	♎	2 13:42
4 9:27	♆	△	♏	4 16:55
6 16:11	♆	□	♐	7 0:04
9 4:58	♀	✱	♑	9 10:43
11 12:39	♅	✱	♒	11 23:24
14 4:33	♆	☌	♓	14 12:23
16 14:32	♅	☌	♈	17 0:30
19 3:52	♆	✱	♉	19 10:55
21 12:15	♆	□	♊	21 18:47
23 17:29	♆	△	♋	23 23:29
25 17:48	♅	△	♌	26 1:08
27 20:15	☿	☍	♍	28 0:52

☽ Phases & Eclipses

Dy Hr Mn		
7 10:40	☾	17♎01
15 7:11	●	25♑01
15 7:06:33	●	A 11'07"
23 10:53	☽	3♉20
30 6:18	○	10♌15
5 23:48	☾	17♏04
14 2:51	●	25♒18
22 0:42	☽	3♊17
28 16:38	○	9♍59

Astro Data

1 January 2010
Julian Day # 40178
SVP 5♓06'56"
GC 26♐58.7 ⚴ 7♏57.5
Eris 20♈55.4R ⚵ 4♈37.6
⚷ 23♒08.6 ⚶ 6♍38.3
☽ Mean ☊ 21♑36.5

1 February 2010
Julian Day # 40209
SVP 5♓06'50"
GC 26♐58.8 ⚴ 17♏24.5
Eris 20♈58.4 ⚵ 18♈36.0
⚷ 25♒08.4 ⚶ 3♍32.6R
☽ Mean ☊ 19♑58.0

March 2010

LONGITUDE

Day	Sid.Time	☉	0 hr ☽	Noon ☽	True ☊	☿	♀	♂	⚳	♃	♄	♅	♆	♇
1 M	22 36 45	10♓47 28	14♍38 14	22♍11 12	19♑54.6	29♒53.7	22♓29.8	0♌49.9	25♐29.5	9♓59.3	2♎50.5	25♓40.6	26♒42.5	5♑04.1
2 Tu	22 40 42	11 47 39	29 40 39	7♎05 28	19R 46.2	1♓37.4	23 44.6	0R 43.2	25 46.2	10 13.8	2R 46.3	25 43.9	26 44.7	5 05.3
3 W	22 44 38	12 47 49	14♎24 39	21 37 27	19 38.0	3 22.0	24 59.4	0 37.3	26 02.8	10 28.3	2 42.0	25 47.3	26 46.9	5 06.3
4 Th	22 48 35	13 47 57	28 43 16	5♏41 45	19 31.0	5 07.8	26 14.1	0 32.2	26 19.2	10 42.8	2 37.7	25 50.7	26 49.1	5 07.4
5 F	22 52 31	14 48 03	12♏32 45	19 16 20	19 25.8	6 54.6	27 28.9	0 27.9	26 35.3	10 57.3	2 33.4	25 54.0	26 51.3	5 08.4
6 Sa	22 56 28	15 48 08	25 52 40	2♐22 08	19 22.7	8 42.5	28 43.6	0 24.3	26 51.3	11 11.8	2 29.0	25 57.4	26 53.5	5 09.4
7 Su	23 00 25	16 48 11	8♐45 11	15 02 21	19D 21.7	10 31.6	29 58.3	0 21.5	27 07.1	11 26.2	2 24.5	26 00.8	26 55.7	5 10.4
8 M	23 04 21	17 48 13	21 14 16	27 21 33	19 22.0	12 21.7	1♈12.9	0 19.5	27 22.7	11 40.7	2 20.1	26 04.2	26 57.8	5 11.4
9 Tu	23 08 18	18 48 13	3♑24 54	9♑24 58	19R 22.9	14 12.9	2 27.6	0 18.2	27 38.0	11 55.2	2 15.6	26 07.6	27 00.0	5 12.3
10 W	23 12 14	19 48 12	15 22 25	21 17 53	19 23.2	16 05.2	3 42.2	0D 17.7	27 53.1	12 09.6	2 11.0	26 11.1	27 02.1	5 13.2
11 Th	23 16 11	20 48 09	27 11 59	3♒05 17	19 22.1	17 58.5	4 56.8	0 17.9	28 08.1	12 24.0	2 06.5	26 14.5	27 04.3	5 14.0
12 F	23 20 07	21 48 04	8♒58 20	14 51 36	19 18.8	19 52.9	6 11.4	0 18.9	28 22.7	12 38.5	2 01.9	26 17.9	27 06.4	5 14.8
13 Sa	23 24 04	22 47 57	20 45 31	26 40 29	19 12.8	21 48.4	7 26.0	0 20.5	28 37.2	12 52.9	1 57.2	26 21.3	27 08.5	5 15.6
14 Su	23 28 00	23 47 48	2♓36 49	8♓34 48	19 04.1	23 44.8	8 40.5	0 22.9	28 51.4	13 07.2	1 52.6	26 24.7	27 10.6	5 16.4
15 M	23 31 57	24 47 38	14 34 41	20 36 38	18 53.1	25 42.1	9 55.0	0 26.0	29 05.4	13 21.6	1 47.9	26 28.2	27 12.7	5 17.1
16 Tu	23 35 54	25 47 25	26 40 49	2♈47 20	18 40.7	27 40.3	11 09.5	0 29.8	29 19.2	13 36.0	1 43.2	26 31.6	27 14.7	5 17.8
17 W	23 39 50	26 47 11	8♈56 17	15 07 45	18 27.9	29 39.2	12 23.9	0 34.2	29 32.7	13 50.3	1 38.6	26 35.0	27 16.8	5 18.5
18 Th	23 43 47	27 46 54	21 21 47	27 38 26	18 15.8	1♈38.7	13 38.3	0 39.3	29 46.0	14 04.6	1 33.8	26 38.5	27 18.8	5 19.1
19 F	23 47 43	28 46 35	3♉57 49	10♉20 00	18 05.5	3 38.6	14 52.7	0 45.1	29 59.0	14 18.9	1 29.1	26 41.9	27 20.9	5 19.7
20 Sa	23 51 40	29 46 15	16 45 05	23 13 13	17 57.8	5 38.9	16 07.1	0 51.6	0♑11.8	14 33.1	1 24.4	26 45.3	27 22.9	5 20.3
21 Su	23 55 36	0♈45 52	29 44 35	6♊19 21	17 52.9	7 39.3	17 21.4	0 58.7	0 24.4	14 47.4	1 19.7	26 48.8	27 24.8	5 20.9
22 M	23 59 33	1 45 26	12♊57 45	19 39 59	17D 50.6	9 39.5	18 35.7	1 06.4	0 36.6	15 01.6	1 15.0	26 52.2	27 26.8	5 21.4
23 Tu	0 03 29	2 44 59	26 26 17	3♋16 51	17 50.1	11 39.3	19 50.0	1 14.7	0 48.6	15 15.7	1 10.2	26 55.6	27 28.8	5 21.8
24 W	0 07 26	3 44 29	10♋11 53	17 11 28	17R 50.3	13 38.4	21 04.2	1 23.6	1 00.4	15 29.9	1 05.5	26 59.0	27 30.7	5 22.3
25 Th	0 11 23	4 43 57	24 15 41	1♌24 25	17 49.8	15 36.4	22 18.4	1 33.2	1 11.9	15 44.0	1 00.8	27 02.4	27 32.6	5 22.7
26 F	0 15 19	5 43 22	8♌37 32	15 54 39	17 47.4	17 33.0	23 32.5	1 43.2	1 23.1	15 58.1	0 56.1	27 05.8	27 34.5	5 23.1
27 Sa	0 19 16	6 42 45	23 15 19	0♍38 52	17 42.4	19 27.8	24 46.7	1 53.9	1 34.0	16 12.1	0 51.4	27 09.2	27 36.4	5 23.4
28 Su	0 23 12	7 42 06	8♍04 30	15 31 17	17 34.7	21 20.3	26 00.8	2 05.1	1 44.7	16 26.1	0 46.7	27 12.6	27 38.3	5 23.8
29 M	0 27 09	8 41 25	22 58 10	0♎24 03	17 24.5	23 10.3	27 14.8	2 16.8	1 55.1	16 40.1	0 42.1	27 16.0	27 40.1	5 24.1
30 Tu	0 31 05	9 40 41	7♎47 47	15 08 17	17 13.0	24 57.2	28 28.8	2 29.1	2 05.2	16 54.1	0 37.4	27 19.4	27 41.9	5 24.3
31 W	0 35 02	10 39 56	22 24 34	29 35 43	17 01.4	26 40.7	29 42.8	2 41.8	2 15.0	17 08.0	0 32.8	27 22.7	27 43.7	5 24.5

April 2010

LONGITUDE

Day	Sid.Time	☉	0 hr ☽	Noon ☽	True ☊	☿	♀	♂	⚳	♃	♄	♅	♆	♇
1 Th	0 38 58	11♈39 08	6♏41 01	13♏39 56	16♑50.9	28♈20.3	0♉56.8	2♌55.1	2♑24.5	17♓21.8	0♎28.2	27♓26.1	27♒45.5	5♑24.7
2 F	0 42 55	12 38 19	20 32 06	27 17 22	16R 42.6	29 55.7	2 10.7	3 08.9	2 33.8	17 35.6	0R 23.6	27 29.4	27 47.3	5 24.9
3 Sa	0 46 51	13 37 28	3♐55 44	10♐27 22	16 37.0	1♉26.6	3 24.6	3 23.1	2 42.7	17 49.4	0 19.1	27 32.8	27 49.0	5 25.0
4 Su	0 50 48	14 36 35	16 52 36	23 11 51	16 33.8	2 52.6	4 38.4	3 37.8	2 51.3	18 03.2	0 14.6	27 36.1	27 50.7	5 25.1
5 M	0 54 45	15 35 41	29 25 38	5♑34 34	16 32.7	4 13.5	5 52.2	3 53.0	2 59.6	18 16.9	0 10.1	27 39.4	27 52.4	5 25.2
6 Tu	0 58 41	16 34 44	11♑39 17	17 40 27	16 32.5	5 28.9	7 06.0	4 08.6	3 07.7	18 30.5	0 05.7	27 42.7	27 54.1	5R 25.2
7 W	1 02 38	17 33 46	23 38 46	29 34 57	16 32.3	6 38.7	8 19.8	4 24.7	3 15.4	18 44.1	0 01.2	27 46.0	27 55.7	5 25.2
8 Th	1 06 34	18 32 46	5♒29 40	11♒23 35	16 30.8	7 42.7	9 33.5	4 41.2	3 22.7	18 57.7	29♍56.9	27 49.3	27 57.3	5 25.2
9 F	1 10 31	19 31 45	17 17 21	23 11 34	16 27.2	8 40.6	10 47.2	4 58.2	3 29.8	19 11.2	29 52.6	27 52.5	27 58.9	5 25.1
10 Sa	1 14 27	20 30 41	29 06 47	5♓03 30	16 20.9	9 32.4	12 00.8	5 15.5	3 36.5	19 24.7	29 48.3	27 55.7	28 00.5	5 25.0
11 Su	1 18 24	21 29 36	11♓02 11	17 03 12	16 11.9	10 17.9	13 14.4	5 33.3	3 42.9	19 38.1	29 44.1	27 59.0	28 02.0	5 24.9
12 M	1 22 20	22 28 28	23 06 53	29 13 30	16 00.4	10 57.0	14 28.0	5 51.5	3 49.0	19 51.4	29 39.9	28 02.2	28 03.6	5 24.8
13 Tu	1 26 17	23 27 19	5♈23 13	11♈36 10	15 47.3	11 29.7	15 41.6	6 10.0	3 54.7	20 04.7	29 35.7	28 05.4	28 05.1	5 24.6
14 W	1 30 14	24 26 08	17 52 26	24 12 01	15 33.8	11 56.0	16 55.1	6 29.0	4 00.1	20 17.9	29 31.7	28 08.5	28 06.5	5 24.4
15 Th	1 34 10	25 24 55	0♉34 51	7♉00 54	15 21.0	12 15.9	18 08.5	6 48.3	4 05.1	20 31.1	29 27.7	28 11.7	28 08.0	5 24.1
16 F	1 38 07	26 23 40	13 30 03	20 02 10	15 10.0	12 29.4	19 22.0	7 08.0	4 09.8	20 44.2	29 23.7	28 14.8	28 09.4	5 23.8
17 Sa	1 42 03	27 22 23	26 37 10	3♊14 55	15 01.6	12R 36.5	20 35.4	7 28.0	4 14.2	20 57.3	29 19.8	28 17.9	28 10.8	5 23.5
18 Su	1 46 00	28 21 04	9♊55 20	16 38 21	14 56.3	12 37.6	21 48.7	7 48.5	4 18.2	21 10.3	29 16.0	28 21.0	28 12.1	5 23.2
19 M	1 49 56	29 19 43	23 23 55	0♋12 03	14 53.6	12 32.7	23 02.1	8 09.2	4 21.8	21 23.2	29 12.2	28 24.1	28 13.5	5 22.8
20 Tu	1 53 53	0♉18 19	7♋02 44	13 56 01	14D 52.9	12 22.1	24 15.3	8 30.3	4 25.1	21 36.1	29 08.5	28 27.1	28 14.8	5 22.4
21 W	1 57 49	1 16 54	20 51 56	27 50 30	14R 53.1	12 06.1	25 28.6	8 51.7	4 28.0	21 48.9	29 04.9	28 30.1	28 16.1	5 22.0
22 Th	2 01 46	2 15 26	4♌51 43	11♌55 32	14 52.8	11 45.2	26 41.7	9 13.5	4 30.6	22 01.7	29 01.3	28 33.1	28 17.3	5 21.5
23 F	2 05 43	3 13 55	19 01 50	26 10 27	14 51.0	11 19.7	27 54.9	9 35.5	4 32.8	22 14.3	28 57.8	28 36.1	28 18.5	5 21.0
24 Sa	2 09 39	4 12 23	3♍21 05	10♍33 22	14 46.8	10 50.3	29 08.0	9 57.9	4 34.6	22 26.9	28 54.4	28 39.1	28 19.7	5 20.5
25 Su	2 13 36	5 10 48	17 46 48	25 00 47	14 40.0	10 17.4	0♊21.0	10 20.6	4 36.1	22 39.4	28 51.0	28 42.0	28 20.9	5 20.0
26 M	2 17 32	6 09 11	2♎14 41	9♎27 43	14 31.0	9 41.8	1 34.0	10 43.5	4 37.2	22 51.9	28 47.8	28 44.9	28 22.0	5 19.4
27 Tu	2 21 29	7 07 33	16 39 07	23 48 07	14 20.7	9 04.2	2 47.0	11 06.7	4 37.9	23 04.3	28 44.6	28 47.7	28 23.1	5 18.8
28 W	2 25 25	8 05 52	0♏53 56	7♏55 52	14 10.2	8 25.1	3 59.9	11 30.3	4R 38.3	23 16.6	28 41.4	28 50.6	28 24.2	5 18.2
29 Th	2 29 22	9 04 10	14 53 17	21 45 42	14 00.7	7 45.5	5 12.8	11 54.0	4 38.2	23 28.8	28 38.4	28 53.4	28 25.3	5 17.5
30 F	2 33 18	10 02 26	28 32 43	5♐14 06	13 53.1	7 05.9	6 25.6	12 18.1	4 37.8	23 41.0	28 35.5	28 56.2	28 26.3	5 16.8

Astro Data	Planet Ingress	Last Aspect	☽ Ingress	Last Aspect	☽ Ingress	☽ Phases & Eclipses	Astro Data
Dy Hr Mn	Dy Hr Mn	Dy Hr Mn	Dy Hr Mn	Dy Hr Mn	Dy Hr Mn	Dy Hr Mn	
☽0S 1 8:04	☿ ♓ 1 13:28	1 17:36 ♅ ☍	♎ 2 0:31	2 12:54 ♆ □	♐ 2 16:52	7 15:42 ☾ 16♐57	1 March 2010
♀0N 9 18:56	♀ ♈ 7 12:33	3 20:43 ♆ △	♏ 4 2:11	4 20:57 ♆ ⚹	♑ 5 1:07	15 21:01 ● 25♓10	Julian Day # 40237
♂ D 10 17:09	☿ ♈ 17 16:12	6 4:32 ♀ △	♐ 6 7:36	7 8:18 ♅ ⚹	♒ 7 12:51	23 11:00 ☽ 2♋43	SVP 5♓06'47"
☽0N 15 10:18	⚳ ♑ 19 13:47	8 11:13 ♆ ⚹	♑ 8 17:13	9 21:44 ♆ ☌	♓ 10 1:48	30 2:25 ○ 9♎17	GC 26♐58.9 ⚴ 22♏23.6
☿0N 18 19:57	☉ ♈ 20 17:32	10 21:59 ♅ ⚹	♒ 11 5:42	12 12:51 ♄ ☍	♈ 12 13:31		Eris 21♈09.3 ⚵ 3♉15.4
☉0N 20 17:32	♀ ♉ 31 17:35	13 12:57 ♆ ☌	♓ 13 18:44	14 19:23 ♆ ⚹	♉ 14 22:55		⚷ 27♒06.2 ⚶ 26♌31.8R
☽0S 28 18:42		16 0:01 ☿ ☌	♈ 16 6:32	17 4:57 ♄ △	♊ 17 6:08	6 9:37 ☾ 16♑29	☽ Mean ☊ 18♑29.0
	☿ ♉ 2 13:06	18 11:23 ♆ ⚹	♉ 18 16:29	19 10:21 ☉ ⚹	♋ 19 11:39	14 12:29 ● 24♈27	
♇ R 7 2:34	♄ ♍R 7 18:51	20 19:41 ♆ □	♊ 21 0:28	21 14:07 ♄ ⚹	♌ 21 15:42	21 18:20 ☽ 1♌32	1 April 2010
☽0N 11 17:01	☉ ♉ 20 4:30	23 1:49 ♆ △	♋ 23 6:16	23 15:35 ♆ ☍	♍ 23 18:24	28 12:19 ○ 8♏07	Julian Day # 40268
♅⚺♆ 13 7:43	♀ ♊ 25 5:05	25 4:39 ♅ △	♌ 25 9:39	25 18:20 ♄ ☌	♎ 25 20:16		SVP 5♓06'44"
☿ R 18 4:05		27 7:04 ♆ ☍	♍ 27 10:57	27 19:45 ♆ △	♏ 27 22:28		GC 26♐58.9 ⚴ 21♏43.7R
☽0S 25 2:41		29 6:55 ♅ ☍	♎ 29 11:21	30 0:39 ♅ △	♐ 30 2:36		Eris 21♈27.7 ⚵ 20♉39.9
♄☍♅ 26 23:23		31 12:13 ♀ ☍	♏ 31 12:41				⚷ 29♒04.2 ⚶ 21♌42.8R
⚳ R 28 23:01							☽ Mean ☊ 16♑50.5

LONGITUDE — May 2010

Day	Sid.Time	☉	0 hr ☽	Noon ☽	True ☊	☿	♀	♂	⚳	♃	♄	♅	♆	♇
1 Sa	2 37 15	11♉00 41	11♐49 43	18♐19 37	13♑47.8	6♉27.2	7♊38.4	12♌42.4	4♑37.1	23♓53.0	28♍32.6	28♓58.9	28♒27.3	5♑16.1
2 Su	2 41 12	11 58 53	24 43 56	1♑02 57	13R45.0	5R49.9	8 51.2	13 06.9	4R35.9	24 05.0	28R29.8	29 01.7	28 28.2	5R15.4
3 M	2 45 08	12 57 05	7♑17 02	13 26 37	13D44.2	5 14.7	10 03.9	13 31.8	4 34.4	24 16.9	28 27.1	29 04.4	28 29.2	5 14.6
4 Tu	2 49 05	13 55 15	19 32 13	25 34 26	13 44.6	4 42.1	11 16.5	13 56.8	4 32.5	24 28.8	28 24.5	29 07.1	28 30.1	5 13.8
5 W	2 53 01	14 53 23	1♒33 52	7♒31 10	13R45.4	4 12.6	12 29.1	14 22.1	4 30.2	24 40.5	28 22.0	29 09.7	28 30.9	5 13.0
6 Th	2 56 58	15 51 30	13 26 59	19 22 00	13 45.6	3 46.7	13 41.7	14 47.7	4 27.6	24 52.1	28 19.5	29 12.3	28 31.8	5 12.2
7 F	3 00 54	16 49 35	25 16 52	1♓12 14	13 44.3	3 24.7	14 54.2	15 13.4	4 24.5	25 03.7	28 17.2	29 14.9	28 32.6	5 11.3
8 Sa	3 04 51	17 47 39	7♓08 43	13 06 56	13 41.1	3 06.8	16 06.7	15 39.4	4 21.1	25 15.2	28 14.9	29 17.4	28 33.3	5 10.4
9 Su	3 08 47	18 45 42	19 07 24	25 10 39	13 35.7	2 53.3	17 19.1	16 05.7	4 17.3	25 26.6	28 12.8	29 19.9	28 34.1	5 09.5
10 M	3 12 44	19 43 43	1♈17 06	7♈27 09	13 28.3	2 44.4	18 31.5	16 32.1	4 13.1	25 37.9	28 10.7	29 22.4	28 34.8	5 08.6
11 Tu	3 16 41	20 41 42	13 41 05	19 59 08	13 19.6	2D40.0	19 43.8	16 58.8	4 08.6	25 49.1	28 08.7	29 24.9	28 35.4	5 07.6
12 W	3 20 37	21 39 41	26 21 27	2♉48 05	13 10.4	2 40.3	20 56.1	17 25.7	4 03.7	26 00.2	28 06.8	29 27.3	28 36.1	5 06.6
13 Th	3 24 34	22 37 38	9♉19 01	15 54 09	13 01.6	2 45.3	22 08.4	17 52.7	3 58.4	26 11.2	28 05.0	29 29.6	28 36.7	5 05.6
14 F	3 28 30	23 35 33	22 33 18	29 16 16	12 54.1	2 54.8	23 20.6	18 20.0	3 52.7	26 22.1	28 03.4	29 32.0	28 37.3	5 04.6
15 Sa	3 32 27	24 33 27	6♊02 44	12♊52 25	12 48.7	3 09.0	24 32.7	18 47.5	3 46.7	26 32.9	28 01.8	29 34.3	28 37.8	5 03.5
16 Su	3 36 23	25 31 20	19 44 58	26 40 02	12 45.4	3 27.6	25 44.8	19 15.3	3 40.3	26 43.6	28 00.3	29 36.6	28 38.3	5 02.4
17 M	3 40 20	26 29 11	3♋37 17	10♋36 25	12D44.3	3 50.5	26 56.9	19 43.2	3 33.6	26 54.2	27 58.9	29 38.8	28 38.8	5 01.3
18 Tu	3 44 16	27 27 00	17 37 07	24 39 07	12 44.7	4 17.8	28 08.9	20 11.2	3 26.5	27 04.7	27 57.6	29 41.0	28 39.3	5 00.2
19 W	3 48 13	28 24 48	1♌42 12	8♌46 07	12 45.9	4 49.1	29 20.8	20 39.5	3 19.1	27 15.1	27 56.4	29 43.1	28 39.7	4 59.1
20 Th	3 52 10	29 22 33	15 50 41	22 55 42	12R46.9	5 24.5	0♋32.7	21 08.0	3 11.4	27 25.3	27 55.3	29 45.3	28 40.1	4 57.9
21 F	3 56 06	0♊20 17	0♍00 59	7♍06 19	12 46.8	6 03.8	1 44.5	21 36.6	3 03.3	27 35.5	27 54.3	29 47.3	28 40.4	4 56.7
22 Sa	4 00 03	1 18 00	14 11 28	21 16 12	12 45.2	6 46.9	2 56.3	22 05.4	2 54.9	27 45.5	27 53.4	29 49.4	28 40.7	4 55.5
23 Su	4 03 59	2 15 40	28 20 13	5♎23 12	12 41.8	7 33.6	4 08.0	22 34.4	2 46.2	27 55.5	27 52.6	29 51.4	28 41.0	4 54.3
24 M	4 07 56	3 13 20	12♎24 49	19 24 39	12 36.9	8 23.9	5 19.6	23 03.5	2 37.1	28 05.3	27 51.9	29 53.3	28 41.3	4 53.1
25 Tu	4 11 52	4 10 57	26 22 19	3♏17 26	12 31.1	9 17.6	6 31.2	23 32.8	2 27.8	28 15.0	27 51.4	29 55.3	28 41.5	4 51.8
26 W	4 15 49	5 08 34	10♏09 35	16 58 24	12 25.1	10 14.7	7 42.7	24 02.3	2 18.2	28 24.6	27 50.9	29 57.1	28 41.7	4 50.5
27 Th	4 19 45	6 06 09	23 43 33	0♐24 44	12 19.7	11 15.0	8 54.2	24 31.9	2 08.3	28 34.1	27 50.5	29 59.0	28 41.8	4 49.3
28 F	4 23 42	7 03 43	7♐01 45	13 34 25	12 15.4	12 18.5	10 05.6	25 01.7	1 58.1	28 43.4	27 50.2	0♈00.8	28 42.0	4 48.0
29 Sa	4 27 39	8 01 16	20 02 40	26 26 31	12 12.7	13 25.1	11 16.9	25 31.6	1 47.7	28 52.6	27 50.0	0 02.5	28 42.1	4 46.6
30 Su	4 31 35	8 58 48	2♑46 01	9♑01 22	12D11.6	14 34.7	12 28.2	26 01.7	1 37.0	29 01.7	27D50.0	0 04.2	28 42.1	4 45.3
31 M	4 35 32	9 56 19	15 12 46	21 20 33	12 11.9	15 47.2	13 39.4	26 32.0	1 26.0	29 10.7	27 50.0	0 05.9	28R42.1	4 44.0

LONGITUDE — June 2010

Day	Sid.Time	☉	0 hr ☽	Noon ☽	True ☊	☿	♀	♂	⚳	♃	♄	♅	♆	♇
1 Tu	4 39 28	10♊53 49	27♑25 05	3♒26 47	12♑13.2	17♉02.7	14♋50.5	27♌02.3	1♑14.9	29♓19.6	27♍50.1	0♈07.5	28♒42.1	4♑42.6
2 W	4 43 25	11 51 18	9♒26 07	15 23 38	12 14.9	18 21.0	16 01.6	27 32.9	1R03.4	29 28.3	27 50.3	0 09.1	28R42.1	4R41.2
3 Th	4 47 21	12 48 46	21 19 52	27 15 23	12 16.5	19 42.1	17 12.6	28 03.5	0 51.8	29 36.9	27 50.7	0 10.7	28 42.0	4 39.8
4 F	4 51 18	13 46 13	3♓10 49	9♓06 44	12R17.4	21 06.0	18 23.6	28 34.3	0 40.0	29 45.4	27 51.1	0 12.2	28 41.9	4 38.4
5 Sa	4 55 14	14 43 40	15 03 47	21 02 34	12 17.3	22 32.7	19 34.5	29 05.3	0 27.9	29 53.7	27 51.6	0 13.6	28 41.8	4 37.0
6 Su	4 59 11	15 41 06	27 03 39	3♈07 37	12 16.1	24 02.1	20 45.3	29 36.4	0 15.7	0♈01.9	27 52.3	0 15.0	28 41.6	4 35.6
7 M	5 03 08	16 38 32	9♈15 01	15 26 20	12 13.7	25 34.2	21 56.0	0♍07.6	0 03.3	0 09.9	27 53.0	0 16.4	28 41.4	4 34.2
8 Tu	5 07 04	17 35 57	21 42 00	28 02 22	12 10.6	27 09.0	23 06.7	0 38.9	29♐50.8	0 17.8	27 53.8	0 17.7	28 41.2	4 32.7
9 W	5 11 01	18 33 21	4♉27 46	10♉58 22	12 07.1	28 46.5	24 17.3	1 10.4	29 38.1	0 25.6	27 54.8	0 19.0	28 40.9	4 31.3
10 Th	5 14 57	19 30 45	17 34 18	24 15 33	12 03.7	0♊26.6	25 27.8	1 42.0	29 25.3	0 33.2	27 55.8	0 20.2	28 40.6	4 29.8
11 F	5 18 54	20 28 08	1♊02 03	7♊53 34	12 00.9	2 09.4	26 38.3	2 13.8	29 12.4	0 40.7	27 57.0	0 21.4	28 40.3	4 28.3
12 Sa	5 22 50	21 25 30	14 49 48	21 50 21	11 58.9	3 54.8	27 48.7	2 45.7	28 59.3	0 48.1	27 58.2	0 22.5	28 39.9	4 26.8
13 Su	5 26 47	22 22 52	28 54 44	6♋02 23	11D58.0	5 42.8	28 59.0	3 17.7	28 46.2	0 55.3	27 59.6	0 23.6	28 39.5	4 25.4
14 M	5 30 43	23 20 13	13♋12 43	20 25 04	11 58.1	7 33.3	0♌09.3	3 49.8	28 33.1	1 02.3	28 01.0	0 24.6	28 39.1	4 23.9
15 Tu	5 34 40	24 17 33	27 38 50	4♌53 20	11 58.9	9 26.4	1 19.4	4 22.1	28 19.8	1 09.2	28 02.6	0 25.6	28 38.7	4 22.4
16 W	5 38 37	25 14 52	12♌07 59	19 22 12	12 00.0	11 21.8	2 29.5	4 54.4	28 06.6	1 15.9	28 04.2	0 26.6	28 38.2	4 20.8
17 Th	5 42 33	26 12 11	26 35 27	3♍47 17	12 01.1	13 19.6	3 39.5	5 26.9	27 53.3	1 22.5	28 05.9	0 27.5	28 37.7	4 19.3
18 F	5 46 30	27 09 28	10♍57 16	18 05 03	12R01.8	15 19.7	4 49.4	5 59.5	27 40.0	1 28.9	28 07.8	0 28.3	28 37.1	4 17.8
19 Sa	5 50 26	28 06 45	25 10 21	2♎12 54	12 01.9	17 21.8	5 59.2	6 32.3	27 26.7	1 35.2	28 09.7	0 29.1	28 36.5	4 16.3
20 Su	5 54 23	29 04 00	9♎12 31	16 09 02	12 01.4	19 25.9	7 08.9	7 05.1	27 13.4	1 41.3	28 11.8	0 29.9	28 35.9	4 14.8
21 M	5 58 19	0♋01 15	23 02 20	29 52 19	12 00.4	21 31.7	8 18.6	7 38.0	27 00.1	1 47.2	28 13.9	0 30.6	28 35.3	4 13.2
22 Tu	6 02 16	0 58 30	6♏38 55	13♏22 03	11 59.1	23 39.1	9 28.1	8 11.1	26 46.9	1 53.0	28 16.1	0 31.3	28 34.6	4 11.7
23 W	6 06 13	1 55 44	20 01 42	26 37 50	11 57.8	25 47.8	10 37.5	8 44.2	26 33.8	1 58.6	28 18.4	0 31.9	28 33.9	4 10.2
24 Th	6 10 09	2 52 57	3♐10 26	9♐39 32	11 56.6	27 57.5	11 46.9	9 17.5	26 20.8	2 04.1	28 20.9	0 32.5	28 33.2	4 08.6
25 F	6 14 06	3 50 10	16 05 08	22 27 18	11 55.8	0♋08.0	12 56.1	9 50.9	26 07.8	2 09.4	28 23.4	0 33.0	28 32.5	4 07.1
26 Sa	6 18 02	4 47 22	28 46 05	5♑01 36	11D55.4	2 19.0	14 05.2	10 24.4	25 54.9	2 14.5	28 26.0	0 33.4	28 31.7	4 05.6
27 Su	6 21 59	5 44 34	11♑13 57	17 23 19	11 55.4	4 30.3	15 14.3	10 57.9	25 42.2	2 19.4	28 28.7	0 33.9	28 30.9	4 04.0
28 M	6 25 55	6 41 46	23 29 52	29 33 51	11 55.7	6 41.4	16 23.2	11 31.6	25 29.6	2 24.2	28 31.5	0 34.2	28 30.1	4 02.5
29 Tu	6 29 52	7 38 58	5♒35 31	11♒35 11	11 56.1	8 52.3	17 32.0	12 05.4	25 17.1	2 28.8	28 34.4	0 34.6	28 29.2	4 00.9
30 W	6 33 48	8 36 10	17 33 10	23 29 52	11 56.5	11 02.5	18 40.7	12 39.2	25 04.8	2 33.3	28 37.3	0 34.8	28 28.3	3 59.4

Astro Data Dy Hr Mn	Planet Ingress Dy Hr Mn	Last Aspect Dy Hr Mn	☽ Ingress Dy Hr Mn	Last Aspect Dy Hr Mn	☽ Ingress Dy Hr Mn	☽ Phases & Eclipses Dy Hr Mn	Astro Data
♄⚻♆ 2 22:22	♀ ♋ 20 1:05	2 8:08 ♅ □	♑ 2 10:00	1 3:41 ♃ ⚹	♒ 1 5:08	6 4:15 ☾ 15♒33	1 May 2010
☽ 0N 9 0:08	☉ ♊ 21 3:34	4 19:07 ♅ ⚹	♒ 4 20:52	3 14:56 ♆ ☌	♓ 3 17:34	14 1:04 ● 23♉09	Julian Day # 40298
☿ D 11 22:28	♅ ♈ 28 1:44	7 6:36 ♆ ☌	♓ 7 9:34	6 5:49 ♃ ☌	♈ 6 5:50	20 23:43 ☽ 29♌51	SVP 5♓06'40"
☽ 0S 22 8:09		9 20:12 ♅ ☌	♈ 9 21:29	8 13:13 ♆ ⚹	♉ 8 15:41	27 23:07 ○ 6♐33	GC 26♐59.0 ⚴ 14♏25.8R
♃☍♄ 23 5:36	♃ ♈ 6 6:28	12 4:11 ♆ ⚹	♉ 12 6:48	10 19:50 ♆ □	♊ 10 22:11		Eris 21♈47.2 ⚵ 7♊58.5
♃⚺♆ 28 8:14	♂ ♍ 7 6:11	14 12:28 ♅ ⚹	♊ 14 13:18	12 23:35 ♆ △	♋ 13 1:50	4 22:13 ☾ 14♓11	⚷ 0♓25.4 ⚶ 23♌55.2
♄ D 30 18:08	⚳ ♐R 7 18:24	16 17:06 ♅ □	♋ 16 17:46	15 0:38 ♄ ⚹	♌ 15 3:54	12 11:15 ● 21♊24	☽ Mean ☊ 15♑15.2
♆ R 31 18:48	☿ ♊ 10 5:41	18 20:35 ♅ △	♌ 18 21:06	17 3:24 ♆ ☍	♍ 17 5:41	19 4:29 ☽ 27♍49	
	♀ ♌ 14 8:50	20 23:43 ☉ □	♍ 20 23:58	19 5:04 ♄ ☌	♎ 19 8:13	26 11:30 ○ 4♑46	1 June 2010
☽ 0N 5 7:34	☉ ♋ 21 11:28	23 2:34 ♅ ☍	♎ 23 2:50	21 9:44 ♆ △	♏ 21 12:14	26 11:38 ☊ P 0.537	Julian Day # 40329
♃☌♅ 8 11:27	☿ ♋ 25 10:32	25 4:01 ♆ △	♏ 25 6:17	23 15:32 ♆ □	♐ 23 18:10		SVP 5♓06'35"
☽ 0S 18 13:06		27 11:13 ♅ △	♐ 27 11:15	25 23:33 ♆ ⚹	♑ 26 2:21		GC 26♐59.1 ⚴ 6♏13.3R
♄⚻♆ 28 2:46		29 16:40 ♃ □	♑ 29 18:44	28 9:56 ♄ △	♒ 28 12:52		Eris 22♈04.3 ⚵ 25♊48.4
							⚷ 0♓59.2 ⚶ 1♍49.7
							☽ Mean ☊ 13♑36.7

July 2010 — LONGITUDE

Day	Sid.Time	☉	0 hr ☽	Noon ☽	True ☊	☿	♀	♂	⚳	♃	♄	♅	♆	♇
1 Th	6 37 45	9♋33 22	29♒25 40	5♓21 03	11♑56.8	13♋12.0	19♌49.3	13♍13.2	24♐52.6	2♈37.5	28♍40.4	0♈35.1	28♒27.4	3♑57.9
2 F	6 41 42	10 30 33	11♓16 27	17 12 24	11 57.0	15 20.4	20 57.8	13 47.3	24R40.7	2 41.6	28 43.5	0 35.2	28R26.5	3R56.4
3 Sa	6 45 38	11 27 45	23 09 25	29 08 02	11R57.1	17 27.6	22 06.1	14 21.5	24 28.9	2 45.5	28 46.8	0 35.4	28 25.5	3 54.8
4 Su	6 49 35	12 24 57	5♈08 50	11♈12 21	11D57.1	19 33.4	23 14.4	14 55.7	24 17.3	2 49.2	28 50.1	0 35.5	28 24.5	3 53.3
5 M	6 53 31	13 22 10	17 19 09	23 29 48	11 57.1	21 37.8	24 22.5	15 30.1	24 05.9	2 52.8	28 53.5	0R35.5	28 23.5	3 51.8
6 Tu	6 57 28	14 19 23	29 44 48	6♉04 39	11 57.2	23 40.5	25 30.5	16 04.5	23 54.8	2 56.1	28 57.0	0 35.5	28 22.5	3 50.3
7 W	7 01 24	15 16 36	12♉29 47	19 00 35	11 57.5	25 41.5	26 38.4	16 39.1	23 43.9	2 59.3	29 00.6	0 35.4	28 21.4	3 48.8
8 Th	7 05 21	16 13 49	25 37 20	2♊20 14	11 57.9	27 40.8	27 46.2	17 13.8	23 33.2	3 02.3	29 04.3	0 35.3	28 20.3	3 47.3
9 F	7 09 17	17 11 03	9♊09 22	16 04 42	11 58.3	29 38.3	28 53.8	17 48.5	23 22.8	3 05.1	29 08.0	0 35.2	28 19.2	3 45.8
10 Sa	7 13 14	18 08 17	23 06 03	0♋13 07	11R58.7	1♌33.9	0♍01.3	18 23.4	23 12.6	3 07.7	29 11.9	0 34.9	28 18.1	3 44.3
11 Su	7 17 11	19 05 31	7♋25 24	14 42 19	11 58.8	3 27.6	1 08.7	18 58.3	23 02.8	3 10.1	29 15.8	0 34.7	28 16.9	3 42.9
12 M	7 21 07	20 02 46	22 03 08	29 26 59	11 58.5	5 19.4	2 16.0	19 33.3	22 53.2	3 12.3	29 19.8	0 34.4	28 15.7	3 41.4
13 Tu	7 25 04	21 00 01	6♌52 57	14♌20 03	11 57.8	7 09.3	3 23.1	20 08.5	22 43.9	3 14.4	29 23.9	0 34.0	28 14.5	3 39.9
14 W	7 29 00	21 57 15	21 47 17	29 13 40	11 56.8	8 57.3	4 30.0	20 43.7	22 34.9	3 16.2	29 28.0	0 33.6	28 13.3	3 38.5
15 Th	7 32 57	22 54 30	6♍38 17	14♍00 16	11 55.6	10 43.4	5 36.8	21 19.0	22 26.2	3 17.9	29 32.3	0 33.2	28 12.1	3 37.1
16 F	7 36 53	23 51 45	21 18 54	28 33 33	11 54.5	12 27.6	6 43.5	21 54.4	22 17.9	3 19.3	29 36.6	0 32.7	28 10.8	3 35.6
17 Sa	7 40 50	24 49 00	5♎43 44	12♎49 07	11D53.7	14 09.9	7 50.0	22 29.9	22 09.8	3 20.6	29 41.0	0 32.2	28 09.5	3 34.2
18 Su	7 44 46	25 46 15	19 49 29	26 44 42	11 53.5	15 50.2	8 56.3	23 05.4	22 02.1	3 21.7	29 45.5	0 31.6	28 08.2	3 32.8
19 M	7 48 43	26 43 30	3♏34 46	10♏19 47	11 53.8	17 28.7	10 02.5	23 41.1	21 54.7	3 22.6	29 50.0	0 30.9	28 06.9	3 31.4
20 Tu	7 52 40	27 40 46	16 59 54	23 35 19	11 54.7	19 05.2	11 08.5	24 16.8	21 47.7	3 23.2	29 54.7	0 30.3	28 05.5	3 30.1
21 W	7 56 36	28 38 02	0♐06 16	6♐33 03	11 56.0	20 39.9	12 14.3	24 52.6	21 41.0	3 23.7	29 59.4	0 29.5	28 04.2	3 28.7
22 Th	8 00 33	29 35 18	12 55 55	19 15 10	11 57.3	22 12.6	13 19.9	25 28.5	21 34.6	3 24.0	0♎04.1	0 28.8	28 02.8	3 27.4
23 F	8 04 29	0♌32 34	25 31 06	1♑43 57	11R58.2	23 43.4	14 25.3	26 04.5	21 28.6	3R24.1	0 09.0	0 27.9	28 01.4	3 26.0
24 Sa	8 08 26	1 29 51	7♑54 01	14 01 33	11 58.5	25 12.3	15 30.6	26 40.6	21 22.9	3 24.0	0 13.9	0 27.1	28 00.0	3 24.7
25 Su	8 12 22	2 27 08	20 06 47	26 09 58	11 57.9	26 39.2	16 35.6	27 16.7	21 17.6	3 23.7	0 18.9	0 26.2	27 58.6	3 23.4
26 M	8 16 19	3 24 26	2♒11 18	8♒11 03	11 56.2	28 04.1	17 40.5	27 52.9	21 12.6	3 23.2	0 23.9	0 25.2	27 57.2	3 22.1
27 Tu	8 20 15	4 21 45	14 09 25	20 06 38	11 53.4	29 27.0	18 45.1	28 29.2	21 08.0	3 22.5	0 29.1	0 24.2	27 55.7	3 20.9
28 W	8 24 12	5 19 04	26 02 58	1♓58 40	11 49.9	0♍47.9	19 49.6	29 05.6	21 03.8	3 21.7	0 34.3	0 23.2	27 54.2	3 19.6
29 Th	8 28 09	6 16 24	7♓54 02	13 49 22	11 45.9	2 06.7	20 53.8	29 42.1	20 59.9	3 20.6	0 39.5	0 22.1	27 52.7	3 18.4
30 F	8 32 05	7 13 45	19 44 59	25 41 16	11 41.9	3 23.4	21 57.8	0♎18.6	20 56.3	3 19.3	0 44.8	0 21.0	27 51.2	3 17.2
31 Sa	8 36 02	8 11 07	1♈38 37	7♈37 26	11 38.3	4 37.9	23 01.5	0 55.3	20 53.2	3 17.8	0 50.2	0 19.8	27 49.7	3 16.0

August 2010 — LONGITUDE

Day	Sid.Time	☉	0 hr ☽	Noon ☽	True ☊	☿	♀	♂	⚳	♃	♄	♅	♆	♇
1 Su	8 39 58	9♌08 31	13♈38 11	19♈41 21	11♑35.7	5♍50.1	24♍05.1	1♎32.0	20♐50.4	3♈16.2	0♎55.6	0♈18.6	27♒48.2	3♑14.8
2 M	8 43 55	10 05 55	25 47 25	1♉56 55	11D34.2	7 00.1	25 08.4	2 08.7	20R47.9	3R14.3	1 01.2	0R17.4	27R46.7	3R13.6
3 Tu	8 47 51	11 03 20	8♉10 22	14 28 18	11 33.9	8 07.7	26 11.5	2 45.6	20 45.8	3 12.2	1 06.7	0 16.1	27 45.1	3 12.5
4 W	8 51 48	12 00 47	20 51 13	27 19 37	11 34.7	9 12.8	27 14.3	3 22.5	20 44.1	3 10.0	1 12.4	0 14.8	27 43.6	3 11.4
5 Th	8 55 44	12 58 15	3♊53 56	10♊34 33	11 36.2	10 15.3	28 16.8	3 59.6	20 42.7	3 07.5	1 18.0	0 13.4	27 42.0	3 10.3
6 F	8 59 41	13 55 44	17 21 45	24 15 43	11 37.6	11 15.1	29 19.1	4 36.7	20 41.7	3 04.9	1 23.8	0 12.0	27 40.4	3 09.2
7 Sa	9 03 38	14 53 15	1♋16 30	8♋24 00	11R38.4	12 12.2	0♎21.2	5 13.9	20 41.1	3 02.1	1 29.6	0 10.6	27 38.9	3 08.2
8 Su	9 07 34	15 50 46	15 37 56	22 57 50	11 38.0	13 06.3	1 23.0	5 51.1	20D40.8	2 59.1	1 35.5	0 09.1	27 37.3	3 07.1
9 M	9 11 31	16 48 19	0♌23 02	7♌52 42	11 36.1	13 57.3	2 24.4	6 28.5	20 40.9	2 55.9	1 41.4	0 07.6	27 35.7	3 06.1
10 Tu	9 15 27	17 45 53	15 25 48	23 01 11	11 32.5	14 45.1	3 25.6	7 05.9	20 41.3	2 52.5	1 47.4	0 06.0	27 34.1	3 05.1
11 W	9 19 24	18 43 28	0♍37 35	8♍13 43	11 27.6	15 29.6	4 26.5	7 43.4	20 42.1	2 48.9	1 53.4	0 04.4	27 32.5	3 04.2
12 Th	9 23 20	19 41 04	15 48 17	23 20 04	11 22.1	16 10.4	5 27.1	8 21.0	20 43.3	2 45.1	1 59.5	0 02.8	27 30.8	3 03.2
13 F	9 27 17	20 38 41	0♎47 59	8♎11 03	11 16.8	16 47.5	6 27.3	8 58.6	20 44.8	2 41.2	2 05.6	0 01.1	27 29.2	3 02.3
14 Sa	9 31 13	21 36 19	15 28 31	22 39 50	11 12.5	17 20.6	7 27.2	9 36.4	20 46.6	2 37.1	2 11.8	29♓59.4	27 27.6	3 01.4
15 Su	9 35 10	22 33 58	29 44 37	6♏42 41	11 09.7	17 49.5	8 26.8	10 14.2	20 48.9	2 32.8	2 18.0	29 57.7	27 26.0	3 00.6
16 M	9 39 07	23 31 37	13♏34 03	20 18 50	11D08.5	18 14.0	9 26.0	10 52.1	20 51.4	2 28.3	2 24.3	29 55.9	27 24.3	2 59.7
17 Tu	9 43 03	24 29 18	26 57 19	3♐29 50	11 08.8	18 33.8	10 24.8	11 30.0	20 54.3	2 23.7	2 30.7	29 54.1	27 22.7	2 58.9
18 W	9 47 00	25 27 00	9♐56 49	16 18 44	11 10.0	18 48.8	11 23.3	12 08.1	20 57.5	2 18.8	2 37.0	29 52.3	27 21.1	2 58.1
19 Th	9 50 56	26 24 43	22 36 05	28 49 22	11 11.4	18 58.7	12 21.3	12 46.2	21 01.1	2 13.9	2 43.5	29 50.4	27 19.4	2 57.4
20 F	9 54 53	27 22 27	4♑59 05	11♑05 42	11R12.0	19R03.2	13 18.9	13 24.3	21 05.0	2 08.8	2 49.9	29 48.5	27 17.8	2 56.6
21 Sa	9 58 49	28 20 13	17 09 41	23 11 28	11 11.2	19 02.3	14 16.1	14 02.6	21 09.3	2 03.5	2 56.4	29 46.6	27 16.1	2 55.9
22 Su	10 02 46	29 17 59	29 11 26	5♒09 57	11 08.4	18 55.7	15 12.8	14 40.9	21 13.8	1 58.0	3 03.0	29 44.6	27 14.5	2 55.2
23 M	10 06 42	0♍15 47	11♒07 19	17 03 51	11 03.3	18 43.2	16 09.1	15 19.3	21 18.7	1 52.4	3 09.6	29 42.7	27 12.9	2 54.6
24 Tu	10 10 39	1 13 36	22 59 49	28 55 27	10 56.2	18 24.9	17 04.9	15 57.8	21 23.9	1 46.7	3 16.2	29 40.7	27 11.2	2 53.9
25 W	10 14 36	2 11 26	4♓50 58	10♓46 34	10 47.3	18 00.8	18 00.3	16 36.3	21 29.4	1 40.8	3 22.9	29 38.6	27 09.6	2 53.3
26 Th	10 18 32	3 09 18	16 42 28	22 38 52	10 37.4	17 30.8	18 55.1	17 14.9	21 35.2	1 34.7	3 29.6	29 36.6	27 08.0	2 52.8
27 F	10 22 29	4 07 12	28 35 59	4♈34 02	10 27.4	16 55.3	19 49.4	17 53.6	21 41.3	1 28.6	3 36.3	29 34.5	27 06.3	2 52.2
28 Sa	10 26 25	5 05 07	10♈33 17	16 33 59	10 18.2	16 14.5	20 43.1	18 32.3	21 47.8	1 22.3	3 43.1	29 32.4	27 04.7	2 51.7
29 Su	10 30 22	6 03 04	22 36 28	28 41 04	10 10.6	15 28.9	21 36.3	19 11.1	21 54.5	1 15.8	3 49.9	29 30.2	27 03.1	2 51.2
30 M	10 34 18	7 01 03	4♉48 08	10♉58 05	10 05.1	14 39.2	22 28.9	19 50.0	22 01.5	1 09.3	3 56.8	29 28.1	27 01.5	2 50.7
31 Tu	10 38 15	7 59 04	17 11 22	23 28 27	10 01.9	13 46.1	23 20.9	20 29.0	22 08.9	1 02.6	4 03.7	29 25.9	26 59.9	2 50.3

Astro Data	Dy Hr Mn
☽0N	2 15:00
♅R	5 16:49
♃0N	8 17:51
☽0S	15 19:43
♃R	23 12:03
♃□♇	25 4:20
♄☍♅	26 17:07
☽0N	29 22:05
♃0S	31 2:22
♂0S	31 17:45
♃□♇	3 5:32
♀0S	6 10:15
⚳D	8 18:31
☽0S	12 4:53
♃☍♄	16 20:45

Planet Ingress	Dy Hr Mn
☿ ♌	9 16:29
♀ ♍	10 11:32
♄ ♎	21 15:10
☉ ♌	22 22:21
☿ ♍	27 21:43
♂ ♎	29 23:46
♀ ♎	7 3:47
♅ ♓R	14 3:36
☉ ♍	23 5:27
☿ R	20 19:59
♄□□	21 10:16
☽0N	26 4:37

Last Aspect Dy Hr Mn		☽ Ingress Dy Hr Mn
30 22:03	♆ ☌	♓ 1 1:10
3 11:17	♄ ☍	♈ 3 13:44
5 21:24	♆ ⚹	♉ 6 0:29
8 6:10	♄ △	♊ 8 7:51
10 10:17	♄ □	♋ 10 11:38
12 11:48	♄ ⚹	♌ 12 12:53
14 10:23	♆ ☍	♍ 14 13:15
16 13:46	♄ ☌	♎ 16 14:24
18 14:26	♆ △	♏ 18 17:42
20 23:43	♄ ⚹	♐ 20 23:48
23 4:50	♆ ⚹	♑ 23 8:39
25 14:20	♂ △	♒ 25 19:38
28 3:46	♆ ☌	♓ 28 8:00
30 3:44	♀ ☍	♈ 30 20:42

Last Aspect Dy Hr Mn		☽ Ingress Dy Hr Mn
2 3:54	♆ ⚹	♉ 2 8:13
4 12:44	♆ □	♊ 4 16:54
6 21:22	♀ □	♋ 6 21:50
7 18:46	☿ ⚹	♌ 8 23:23
10 19:10	♆ ☍	♍ 10 23:01
12 0:04	☿ ☌	♎ 12 22:43
14 20:06	♆ △	♏ 15 0:26
17 5:24	♅ △	♐ 17 5:34
19 13:58	♅ □	♑ 19 14:17
22 1:08	♅ ⚹	♒ 22 1:37
24 8:29	♆ ☌	♓ 24 14:11
27 2:00	♅ ☌	♈ 27 2:49
29 8:47	♆ ⚹	♉ 29 14:35

☽ Phases & Eclipses Dy Hr Mn	
4 14:35	☾ 12♈31
11 19:40	● 19♋24
11 19:33:32	◐ T 05'20"
18 10:11	☽ 25♎42
26 1:37	○ 3♒00
3 4:59	☾ 10♉47
10 3:08	● 17♌25
16 18:14	☽ 23♏47
24 17:05	○ 1♓26

Astro Data

1 July 2010
Julian Day # 40359
SVP 5♓06'30"
GC 26♐59.2 ⚴ 4♏18.8
Eris 22♈13.9 ⚵ 12♋39.2
⚷ 0♓37.8R ⚶ 12♍51.5
☽ Mean ☊ 12♑01.4

1 August 2010
Julian Day # 40390
SVP 5♓06'25"
GC 26♐59.2 ⚴ 8♏42.8
Eris 22♈14.6R ⚵ 29♋22.0
⚷ 29♒28.6R ⚶ 26♍22.7
☽ Mean ☊ 10♑22.9

LONGITUDE — September 2010

Day	Sid.Time	☉	0 hr ☽	Noon ☽	True ☊	☿	♀	♂	⚳	♃	♄	♅	♆	♇
1 W	10 42 11	8♍57 06	29♉49 47	6♊15 53	10♑00.7	12♍50.5	24♎12.3	21♎08.0	22♐16.5	0♈55.8	4♎10.6	29♓23.7	26♒58.3	2♑49.9
2 Th	10 46 08	9 55 11	12♊47 12	19 24 13	10D 01.0	11R 53.4	25 03.1	21 47.2	22 24.4	0R 48.9	4 17.5	29R 21.5	26R 56.7	2R 49.5
3 F	10 50 05	10 53 18	26 07 20	2♋56 53	10R 01.7	10 56.1	25 53.2	22 26.3	22 32.6	0 41.9	4 24.5	29 19.3	26 55.1	2 49.2
4 Sa	10 54 01	11 51 26	9♋53 06	16 56 08	10 01.6	9 59.7	26 42.6	23 05.6	22 41.1	0 34.7	4 31.5	29 17.0	26 53.5	2 48.9
5 Su	10 57 58	12 49 37	24 05 54	1♌22 12	9 59.9	9 05.5	27 31.3	23 45.0	22 49.8	0 27.5	4 38.6	29 14.8	26 52.0	2 48.6
6 M	11 01 54	13 47 49	8♌44 36	16 12 26	9 55.8	8 14.8	28 19.3	24 24.4	22 58.8	0 20.2	4 45.7	29 12.5	26 50.4	2 48.3
7 Tu	11 05 51	14 46 03	23 44 52	1♍20 49	9 49.2	7 28.8	29 06.5	25 03.8	23 08.1	0 12.8	4 52.8	29 10.2	26 48.9	2 48.1
8 W	11 09 47	15 44 19	8♍59 03	16 38 11	9 40.5	6 48.6	29 52.8	25 43.4	23 17.7	0 05.3	4 59.9	29 07.9	26 47.3	2 47.9
9 Th	11 13 44	16 42 37	24 16 49	1♎53 29	9 30.7	6 15.1	0♏38.4	26 23.0	23 27.5	29♓57.7	5 07.0	29 05.5	26 45.8	2 47.7
10 F	11 17 40	17 40 57	9♎26 52	16 55 43	9 21.0	5 49.3	1 23.1	27 02.7	23 37.6	29 50.1	5 14.2	29 03.2	26 44.3	2 47.6
11 Sa	11 21 37	18 39 18	24 19 01	1♏35 55	9 12.5	5 31.7	2 06.9	27 42.5	23 48.0	29 42.4	5 21.4	29 00.8	26 42.8	2 47.5
12 Su	11 25 34	19 37 40	8♏45 49	15 48 22	9 06.1	5D 23.0	2 49.7	28 22.4	23 58.6	29 34.6	5 28.6	28 58.5	26 41.3	2 47.4
13 M	11 29 30	20 36 05	22 43 25	29 31 02	9 02.1	5 23.3	3 31.6	29 02.3	24 09.5	29 26.8	5 35.8	28 56.1	26 39.8	2D 47.4
14 Tu	11 33 27	21 34 31	6♐11 25	12♐44 56	9D 00.4	5 32.9	4 12.4	29 42.3	24 20.6	29 19.0	5 43.1	28 53.7	26 38.4	2 47.4
15 W	11 37 23	22 32 58	19 12 03	25 33 19	9 00.1	5 51.8	4 52.1	0♏22.3	24 31.9	29 11.1	5 50.3	28 51.3	26 37.0	2 47.4
16 Th	11 41 20	23 31 28	1♑49 19	8♑00 40	9R 00.3	6 19.8	5 30.8	1 02.5	24 43.5	29 03.1	5 57.6	28 49.0	26 35.5	2 47.5
17 F	11 45 16	24 29 58	14 08 01	20 11 58	8 59.9	6 56.8	6 08.3	1 42.6	24 55.3	28 55.2	6 04.9	28 46.6	26 34.1	2 47.6
18 Sa	11 49 13	25 28 31	26 13 08	2♒12 06	8 57.7	7 42.2	6 44.6	2 22.9	25 07.4	28 47.2	6 12.2	28 44.2	26 32.7	2 47.7
19 Su	11 53 09	26 27 05	8♒09 24	14 05 31	8 53.1	8 35.8	7 19.6	3 03.2	25 19.6	28 39.2	6 19.6	28 41.8	26 31.4	2 47.8
20 M	11 57 06	27 25 41	20 00 55	25 55 59	8 45.6	9 36.9	7 53.3	3 43.6	25 32.1	28 31.2	6 26.9	28 39.4	26 30.0	2 48.0
21 Tu	12 01 03	28 24 18	1♓51 04	7♓46 30	8 35.4	10 45.0	8 25.7	4 24.1	25 44.9	28 23.2	6 34.2	28 36.9	26 28.7	2 48.2
22 W	12 04 59	29 22 57	13 42 32	19 39 23	8 22.9	11 59.4	8 56.6	5 04.6	25 57.8	28 15.2	6 41.6	28 34.5	26 27.4	2 48.5
23 Th	12 08 56	0♎21 39	25 37 15	1♈36 18	8 09.1	13 19.6	9 26.1	5 45.2	26 10.9	28 07.2	6 49.0	28 32.1	26 26.1	2 48.7
24 F	12 12 52	1 20 22	7♈36 40	13 38 30	7 55.0	14 44.8	9 54.1	6 25.9	26 24.3	27 59.2	6 56.3	28 29.7	26 24.8	2 49.0
25 Sa	12 16 49	2 19 07	19 41 55	25 47 04	7 41.9	16 14.5	10 20.5	7 06.6	26 37.9	27 51.2	7 03.7	28 27.3	26 23.5	2 49.4
26 Su	12 20 45	3 17 55	1♉54 06	8♉03 12	7 30.7	17 48.0	10 45.2	7 47.4	26 51.6	27 43.2	7 11.1	28 24.9	26 22.3	2 49.7
27 M	12 24 42	4 16 44	14 14 33	20 28 25	7 22.3	19 24.7	11 08.3	8 28.3	27 05.6	27 35.3	7 18.5	28 22.5	26 21.1	2 50.1
28 Tu	12 28 38	5 15 36	26 45 02	3♊04 45	7 16.8	21 04.2	11 29.6	9 09.2	27 19.8	27 27.4	7 25.9	28 20.1	26 19.9	2 50.6
29 W	12 32 35	6 14 30	9♊27 53	15 54 48	7 13.9	22 45.8	11 49.1	9 50.3	27 34.1	27 19.6	7 33.3	28 17.8	26 18.7	2 51.0
30 Th	12 36 31	7 13 26	22 25 54	29 01 34	7 13.1	24 29.3	12 06.8	10 31.4	27 48.7	27 11.8	7 40.7	28 15.4	26 17.6	2 51.5

LONGITUDE — October 2010

Day	Sid.Time	☉	0 hr ☽	Noon ☽	True ☊	☿	♀	♂	⚳	♃	♄	♅	♆	♇
1 F	12 40 28	8♎12 25	5♋42 10	12♋28 05	7♑13.0	26♍14.1	12♏22.5	11♏12.5	28♐03.4	27♓04.1	7♎48.1	28♓13.0	26♒16.4	2♑52.1
2 Sa	12 44 25	9 11 26	19 19 35	26 16 53	7R 12.5	27 59.9	12 36.3	11 53.7	28 18.4	26R 56.4	7 55.5	28R 10.7	26R 15.3	2 52.6
3 Su	12 48 21	10 10 30	3♌20 06	10♌29 12	7 10.3	29 46.4	12 48.0	12 35.0	28 33.5	26 48.8	8 02.9	28 08.3	26 14.3	2 53.2
4 M	12 52 18	11 09 35	17 43 59	25 04 03	7 05.6	1♎33.3	12 57.6	13 16.4	28 48.8	26 41.2	8 10.3	28 06.0	26 13.2	2 53.8
5 Tu	12 56 14	12 08 43	2♍28 50	9♍57 32	6 58.1	3 20.5	13 05.0	13 57.8	29 04.3	26 33.8	8 17.7	28 03.7	26 12.2	2 54.5
6 W	13 00 11	13 07 53	17 29 11	25 02 39	6 48.2	5 07.7	13 10.2	14 39.3	29 19.9	26 26.4	8 25.1	28 01.4	26 11.2	2 55.1
7 Th	13 04 07	14 07 05	2♎36 40	10♎09 56	6 37.0	6 54.8	13R 13.2	15 20.9	29 35.7	26 19.1	8 32.5	27 59.1	26 10.2	2 55.8
8 F	13 08 04	15 06 19	17 41 06	25 08 55	6 25.7	8 41.6	13 13.9	16 02.6	29 51.7	26 11.9	8 39.9	27 56.8	26 09.3	2 56.6
9 Sa	13 12 00	16 05 35	2♏32 15	9♏50 06	6 15.5	10 28.1	13 12.3	16 44.3	0♑07.9	26 04.8	8 47.3	27 54.5	26 08.3	2 57.4
10 Su	13 15 57	17 04 53	17 01 42	24 06 28	6 07.7	12 14.1	13 08.2	17 26.1	0 24.3	25 57.8	8 54.6	27 52.3	26 07.5	2 58.2
11 M	13 19 54	18 04 14	1♐04 04	7♐54 21	6 02.4	13 59.6	13 01.8	18 07.9	0 40.8	25 51.0	9 02.0	27 50.1	26 06.6	2 59.0
12 Tu	13 23 50	19 03 35	14 37 23	21 13 22	5 59.8	15 44.6	12 52.9	18 49.8	0 57.4	25 44.2	9 09.3	27 47.9	26 05.8	2 59.9
13 W	13 27 47	20 02 59	27 42 40	4♑05 46	5D 59.0	17 29.0	12 41.7	19 31.8	1 14.2	25 37.6	9 16.7	27 45.7	26 05.0	3 00.8
14 Th	13 31 43	21 02 25	10♑23 11	16 35 32	5R 59.2	19 12.7	12 28.0	20 13.9	1 31.2	25 31.1	9 24.0	27 43.6	26 04.2	3 01.7
15 F	13 35 40	22 01 52	22 43 29	28 47 42	5 59.0	20 55.8	12 11.9	20 56.0	1 48.3	25 24.7	9 31.3	27 41.4	26 03.4	3 02.6
16 Sa	13 39 36	23 01 21	4♒48 50	10♒47 33	5 57.6	22 38.2	11 53.5	21 38.2	2 05.6	25 18.4	9 38.6	27 39.3	26 02.7	3 03.6
17 Su	13 43 33	24 00 51	16 44 29	22 40 15	5 53.9	24 20.0	11 32.8	22 20.4	2 23.0	25 12.3	9 45.8	27 37.2	26 02.0	3 04.6
18 M	13 47 29	25 00 23	28 35 24	4♓30 27	5 47.6	26 01.1	11 09.9	23 02.7	2 40.6	25 06.4	9 53.1	27 35.2	26 01.4	3 05.6
19 Tu	13 51 26	25 59 58	10♓25 54	16 22 10	5 38.7	27 41.6	10 44.9	23 45.1	2 58.3	25 00.6	10 00.3	27 33.1	26 00.7	3 06.7
20 W	13 55 23	26 59 34	22 19 36	28 18 32	5 27.6	29 21.4	10 17.9	24 27.5	3 16.1	24 54.9	10 07.5	27 31.1	26 00.1	3 07.8
21 Th	13 59 19	27 59 11	4♈19 13	10♈21 51	5 15.2	1♏00.6	9 49.0	25 10.0	3 34.1	24 49.4	10 14.7	27 29.1	25 59.6	3 08.9
22 F	14 03 16	28 58 51	16 26 37	22 33 39	5 02.5	2 39.2	9 18.5	25 52.6	3 52.2	24 44.1	10 21.8	27 27.2	25 59.0	3 10.1
23 Sa	14 07 12	29 58 33	28 43 00	4♉54 46	4 50.6	4 17.2	8 46.4	26 35.2	4 10.5	24 38.9	10 29.0	27 25.3	25 58.5	3 11.3
24 Su	14 11 09	0♏58 17	11♉08 59	17 25 41	4 40.6	5 54.6	8 13.0	27 17.9	4 28.8	24 33.9	10 36.1	27 23.4	25 58.0	3 12.5
25 M	14 15 05	1 58 03	23 44 54	0♊06 42	4 33.1	7 31.4	7 38.5	28 00.7	4 47.3	24 29.0	10 43.2	27 21.5	25 57.6	3 13.7
26 Tu	14 19 02	2 57 51	6♊31 09	12 58 20	4 28.3	9 07.7	7 03.1	28 43.5	5 06.0	24 24.4	10 50.2	27 19.7	25 57.2	3 14.9
27 W	14 22 58	3 57 41	19 28 22	26 01 25	4D 26.2	10 43.4	6 27.0	29 26.4	5 24.7	24 19.9	10 57.3	27 17.9	25 56.8	3 16.2
28 Th	14 26 55	4 57 33	2♋37 37	9♋17 10	4 25.9	12 18.7	5 50.5	0♐09.3	5 43.6	24 15.6	11 04.3	27 16.1	25 56.5	3 17.5
29 F	14 30 52	5 57 28	16 00 17	22 47 08	4 26.7	13 53.4	5 13.9	0 52.3	6 02.6	24 11.4	11 11.2	27 14.4	25 56.2	3 18.9
30 Sa	14 34 48	6 57 24	29 37 55	6♌32 45	4R 27.2	15 27.6	4 37.3	1 35.4	6 21.7	24 07.5	11 18.2	27 12.7	25 55.9	3 20.2
31 Su	14 38 45	7 57 23	13♌31 44	20 34 51	4 26.4	17 01.4	4 01.1	2 18.6	6 40.9	24 03.7	11 25.1	27 11.1	25 55.6	3 21.6

Astro Data

	Dy Hr Mn
♄0S	8 13:57
☽0S	8 15:43
☿D	12 23:11
♇D	14 4:36
♃☌♅	19 1:03
☽0N	22 10:44
☉0S	23 3:10
☿0S	5 22:27
☽0S	6 2:16
♀R	8 7:05
♃⚺♆	8 22:14
☽0N	19 16:53
♄⚼♆	27 10:30

Planet Ingress

		Dy Hr Mn
♀	♏	8 15:44
♃	♓R	9 4:50
♂	♏	14 22:38
☉	♎	23 3:09
☿	♎	3 15:04
⚳	♑	9 0:17
☿	♏	20 21:19
☉	♏	23 12:35
♂	♐	28 6:47

Last Aspect / ☽ Ingress

Last Aspect Dy Hr Mn			☽ Ingress	Dy Hr Mn
31 23:13	♅	⚹	♊	1 0:19
3 5:40	♅	□	♋	3 6:50
5 8:31	♅	△	♌	5 9:45
7 8:17	♀	⚹	♍	7 9:53
9 8:59	♃	☍	♎	9 9:01
11 5:16	♂	☌	♏	11 9:21
13 11:53	♃	△	♐	13 12:52
15 18:52	♃	□	♑	15 20:30
18 5:13	♃	⚹	♒	18 7:35
20 13:09	♆	☌	♓	20 20:15
23 5:52	♅	☌	♈	23 8:47
25 13:12	♆	⚹	♉	25 20:17
28 3:03	♅	⚹	♊	28 6:10
30 10:37	♅	□	♋	30 13:46

Last Aspect / ☽ Ingress

Last Aspect Dy Hr Mn			☽ Ingress	Dy Hr Mn
2 15:21	☿	⚹	♌	2 18:21
4 13:52	♆	☍	♍	4 20:00
6 16:43	♅	☍	♎	6 19:52
8 13:38	♆	△	♏	8 19:52
10 18:27	♅	△	♐	10 22:09
13 0:08	♅	□	♑	13 4:17
15 9:49	♅	⚹	♒	15 14:24
17 18:49	♆	☌	♓	18 2:52
20 10:25	♅	☌	♈	20 15:23
23 1:37	☉	☍	♉	23 2:30
25 7:49	♂	☍	♊	25 11:47
27 14:19	♅	□	♋	27 19:14
29 19:48	♅	△	♌	30 0:39

☽ Phases & Eclipses

Dy Hr Mn		
1 17:22	☾	9♊10
8 10:30	●	15♍41
15 5:50	☽	22♐18
23 9:17	○	0♈15
1 3:52	☾	7♋52
7 18:44	●	14♎24
14 21:27	☽	21♑26
23 1:37	○	29♈33
30 12:46	☾	6♌59

Astro Data

1 September 2010
Julian Day # 40421
SVP 5♓06'21"
GC 26♐59.3 ⚴ 17♏13.7
Eris 22♈05.6R ⚵ 15♌08.0
⚷ 27♒57.2R ⚶ 11♎16.7
☽ Mean ☊ 8♑44.4

1 October 2010
Julian Day # 40451
SVP 5♓06'18"
GC 26♐59.4 ⚴ 27♏42.2
Eris 21♈50.2R ⚵ 29♌12.6
⚷ 26♒41.0R ⚶ 26♎33.9
☽ Mean ☊ 7♑09.1

November 2010 — LONGITUDE

Day	Sid.Time	☉	0 hr ☽	Noon ☽	True ☊	☿	♀	♂	⚳	♃	♄	♅	♆	♇
1 M	14 42 41	8♏57 24	27♌42 02	4♍53 01	4♑23.7	18♏34.7	3♏25.5	3♐01.8	7♑00.3	24♓00.1	11♎32.0	27♓09.4	25♒55.4	3♑23.0
2 Tu	14 46 38	9 57 27	12♍07 30	19 24 57	4R 18.7	20 07.6	2R 50.7	3 45.1	7 19.7	23R 56.7	11 38.8	27R 07.8	25R 55.2	3 24.5
3 W	14 50 34	10 57 32	26 44 46	4♎06 11	4 11.7	21 40.0	2 17.0	4 28.4	7 39.3	23 53.5	11 45.6	27 06.3	25 55.1	3 25.9
4 Th	14 54 31	11 57 40	11♎28 20	18 50 15	4 03.4	23 12.0	1 44.5	5 11.8	7 58.9	23 50.5	11 52.4	27 04.8	25 55.0	3 27.4
5 F	14 58 27	12 57 49	26 10 58	3♏29 28	3 54.9	24 43.6	1 13.4	5 55.3	8 18.7	23 47.7	11 59.1	27 03.3	25 54.9	3 28.9
6 Sa	15 02 24	13 58 00	10♏44 48	17 56 06	3 47.2	26 14.8	0 44.0	6 38.9	8 38.6	23 45.1	12 05.8	27 01.9	25D 54.8	3 30.5
7 Su	15 06 21	14 58 13	25 02 37	2♐03 43	3 41.3	27 45.6	0 16.4	7 22.5	8 58.6	23 42.7	12 12.4	27 00.5	25 54.8	3 32.0
8 M	15 10 17	15 58 28	8♐58 58	15 48 03	3 37.6	29 16.0	29♎50.7	8 06.1	9 18.7	23 40.5	12 19.0	26 59.2	25 54.9	3 33.6
9 Tu	15 14 14	16 58 45	22 30 50	29 07 21	3D 36.0	0♐46.0	29 27.1	8 49.9	9 38.9	23 38.4	12 25.6	26 57.9	25 54.9	3 35.2
10 W	15 18 10	17 59 03	5♑37 44	12♑02 17	3 36.2	2 15.6	29 05.6	9 33.7	9 59.2	23 36.7	12 32.1	26 56.6	25 55.0	3 36.8
11 Th	15 22 07	18 59 22	18 21 22	24 35 27	3 37.5	3 44.7	28 46.4	10 17.5	10 19.6	23 35.1	12 38.6	26 55.4	25 55.2	3 38.5
12 F	15 26 03	19 59 43	0♒45 05	6♒50 49	3 38.9	5 13.4	28 29.6	11 01.4	10 40.1	23 33.7	12 45.0	26 54.2	25 55.3	3 40.2
13 Sa	15 30 00	21 00 05	12 53 17	18 53 07	3R 39.8	6 41.7	28 15.1	11 45.4	11 00.7	23 32.5	12 51.4	26 53.1	25 55.5	3 41.8
14 Su	15 33 56	22 00 28	24 50 58	0♓47 27	3 39.3	8 09.4	28 03.1	12 29.4	11 21.3	23 31.5	12 57.7	26 52.0	25 55.7	3 43.6
15 M	15 37 53	23 00 53	6♓43 13	12 38 52	3 37.1	9 36.7	27 53.5	13 13.5	11 42.1	23 30.7	13 04.0	26 51.0	25 56.0	3 45.3
16 Tu	15 41 50	24 01 19	18 34 58	24 32 04	3 33.1	11 03.4	27 46.4	13 57.6	12 02.9	23 30.2	13 10.2	26 50.0	25 56.3	3 47.0
17 W	15 45 46	25 01 47	0♈30 40	6♈31 13	3 27.5	12 29.5	27 41.8	14 41.8	12 23.8	23 29.8	13 16.3	26 49.1	25 56.6	3 48.8
18 Th	15 49 43	26 02 16	12 34 07	18 39 41	3 21.0	13 54.9	27D 39.6	15 26.1	12 44.8	23D 29.7	13 22.4	26 48.2	25 57.0	3 50.6
19 F	15 53 39	27 02 46	24 48 14	0♉59 59	3 14.1	15 19.7	27 39.9	16 10.4	13 05.9	23 29.7	13 28.5	26 47.3	25 57.4	3 52.4
20 Sa	15 57 36	28 03 18	7♉15 05	13 33 37	3 07.6	16 43.6	27 42.6	16 54.7	13 27.1	23 30.0	13 34.5	26 46.5	25 57.8	3 54.2
21 Su	16 01 32	29 03 51	19 55 40	26 21 12	3 02.3	18 06.6	27 47.6	17 39.2	13 48.3	23 30.5	13 40.4	26 45.7	25 58.3	3 56.0
22 M	16 05 29	0♐04 26	2♊50 12	9♊22 33	2 58.4	19 28.6	27 55.0	18 23.7	14 09.7	23 31.2	13 46.3	26 45.0	25 58.8	3 57.9
23 Tu	16 09 25	1 05 03	15 58 09	22 36 52	2D 56.4	20 49.5	28 04.7	19 08.2	14 31.0	23 32.1	13 52.1	26 44.4	25 59.4	3 59.8
24 W	16 13 22	2 05 40	29 18 34	6♋03 06	2 56.0	22 09.1	28 16.6	19 52.8	14 52.5	23 33.2	13 57.9	26 43.8	25 59.9	4 01.7
25 Th	16 17 19	3 06 20	12♋50 20	19 40 08	2 56.8	23 27.2	28 30.7	20 37.4	15 14.1	23 34.5	14 03.6	26 43.2	26 00.5	4 03.6
26 F	16 21 15	4 07 01	26 32 22	3♌26 56	2 58.4	24 43.6	28 47.0	21 22.2	15 35.7	23 36.0	14 09.3	26 42.7	26 01.2	4 05.5
27 Sa	16 25 12	5 07 43	10♌23 42	17 22 34	2 59.9	25 58.1	29 05.2	22 06.9	15 57.4	23 37.7	14 14.8	26 42.2	26 01.8	4 07.4
28 Su	16 29 08	6 08 27	24 23 24	1♍26 04	3R 00.8	27 10.5	29 25.5	22 51.7	16 19.1	23 39.6	14 20.3	26 41.8	26 02.5	4 09.4
29 M	16 33 05	7 09 13	8♍30 23	15 36 09	3 00.6	28 20.3	29 47.7	23 36.6	16 40.9	23 41.7	14 25.8	26 41.5	26 03.3	4 11.3
30 Tu	16 37 01	8 10 00	22 43 06	29 50 57	2 59.2	29 27.3	0♏11.7	24 21.6	17 02.8	23 44.0	14 31.2	26 41.1	26 04.1	4 13.3

December 2010 — LONGITUDE

Day	Sid.Time	☉	0 hr ☽	Noon ☽	True ☊	☿	♀	♂	⚳	♃	♄	♅	♆	♇
1 W	16 40 58	9♐10 49	6♎59 19	14♎07 48	2♑56.8	0♑30.9	0♏37.5	25♐06.6	17♑24.8	23♓46.5	14♎36.5	26♓40.9	26♒04.9	4♑15.3
2 Th	16 44 54	10 11 39	21 15 54	28 23 09	2R 53.6	1 30.8	1 05.1	25 51.6	17 46.8	23 49.2	14 41.7	26R 40.7	26 05.7	4 17.3
3 F	16 48 51	11 12 31	5♏29 00	12♏32 53	2 50.3	2 26.4	1 34.3	26 36.7	18 08.9	23 52.2	14 46.9	26 40.5	26 06.6	4 19.3
4 Sa	16 52 48	12 13 23	19 34 16	26 32 37	2 47.3	3 17.1	2 05.1	27 21.9	18 31.0	23 55.3	14 52.0	26 40.4	26 07.5	4 21.4
5 Su	16 56 44	13 14 18	3♐27 27	10♐18 22	2 45.1	4 02.2	2 37.5	28 07.1	18 53.3	23 58.6	14 57.0	26D 40.3	26 08.4	4 23.4
6 M	17 00 41	14 15 13	17 04 58	23 47 01	2D 43.9	4 40.9	3 11.3	28 52.4	19 15.5	24 02.1	15 01.9	26 40.3	26 09.4	4 25.5
7 Tu	17 04 37	15 16 09	0♑24 19	6♑56 46	2 43.8	5 12.6	3 46.6	29 37.7	19 37.8	24 05.8	15 06.8	26 40.4	26 10.4	4 27.5
8 W	17 08 34	16 17 06	13 24 22	19 47 15	2 44.4	5 36.2	4 23.2	0♑23.0	20 00.2	24 09.7	15 11.6	26 40.5	26 11.4	4 29.6
9 Th	17 12 30	17 18 04	26 05 33	2♒19 34	2 45.7	5 51.0	5 01.2	1 08.5	20 22.7	24 13.8	15 16.3	26 40.6	26 12.5	4 31.7
10 F	17 16 27	18 19 03	8♒29 37	14 36 06	2 47.1	5R 56.2	5 40.4	1 53.9	20 45.1	24 18.1	15 20.9	26 40.8	26 13.6	4 33.8
11 Sa	17 20 23	19 20 02	20 39 29	26 40 15	2 48.4	5 50.8	6 20.8	2 39.4	21 07.7	24 22.6	15 25.5	26 41.1	26 14.7	4 35.9
12 Su	17 24 20	20 21 02	2♓38 56	8♓36 08	2 49.2	5 34.5	7 02.4	3 25.0	21 30.3	24 27.2	15 30.0	26 41.4	26 15.9	4 38.0
13 M	17 28 17	21 22 02	14 32 25	20 28 22	2R 49.6	5 06.6	7 45.1	4 10.6	21 52.9	24 32.1	15 34.3	26 41.7	26 17.0	4 40.1
14 Tu	17 32 13	22 23 03	26 24 37	2♈21 45	2 49.3	4 27.2	8 28.9	4 56.3	22 15.6	24 37.1	15 38.7	26 42.1	26 18.3	4 42.2
15 W	17 36 10	23 24 04	8♈20 21	14 20 59	2 48.6	3 36.7	9 13.7	5 42.0	22 38.3	24 42.3	15 42.9	26 42.6	26 19.5	4 44.3
16 Th	17 40 06	24 25 06	20 24 13	26 30 31	2 47.7	2 35.9	9 59.5	6 27.7	23 01.1	24 47.7	15 47.0	26 43.1	26 20.8	4 46.5
17 F	17 44 03	25 26 08	2♉40 21	8♉54 08	2 46.6	1 26.2	10 46.3	7 13.5	23 23.9	24 53.3	15 51.1	26 43.7	26 22.1	4 48.6
18 Sa	17 47 59	26 27 11	15 12 11	21 34 48	2 45.7	0 09.6	11 34.1	7 59.3	23 46.7	24 59.1	15 55.0	26 44.3	26 23.4	4 50.7
19 Su	17 51 56	27 28 14	28 02 08	4♊34 19	2 45.0	28♐48.5	12 22.7	8 45.2	24 09.6	25 05.0	15 58.9	26 45.0	26 24.8	4 52.9
20 M	17 55 52	28 29 18	11♊11 22	17 53 12	2 44.6	27 25.6	13 12.2	9 31.1	24 32.6	25 11.1	16 02.7	26 45.7	26 26.2	4 55.0
21 Tu	17 59 49	29 30 23	24 39 39	1♋30 30	2D 44.4	26 03.7	14 02.5	10 17.1	24 55.6	25 17.4	16 06.4	26 46.4	26 27.6	4 57.2
22 W	18 03 46	0♑31 27	8♋25 23	15 23 56	2 44.5	24 45.5	14 53.6	11 03.1	25 18.6	25 23.8	16 10.0	26 47.3	26 29.0	4 59.3
23 Th	18 07 42	1 32 33	22 25 41	29 30 08	2 44.6	23 33.4	15 45.5	11 49.2	25 41.6	25 30.4	16 13.5	26 48.1	26 30.5	5 01.5
24 F	18 11 39	2 33 39	6♌36 45	13♌44 59	2R 44.7	22 29.4	16 38.1	12 35.3	26 04.7	25 37.2	16 17.0	26 49.1	26 32.0	5 03.7
25 Sa	18 15 35	3 34 45	20 54 18	28 04 11	2 44.7	21 34.7	17 31.5	13 21.4	26 27.8	25 44.1	16 20.3	26 50.0	26 33.5	5 05.8
26 Su	18 19 32	4 35 52	5♍14 08	12♍23 41	2 44.5	20 50.2	18 25.5	14 07.6	26 51.0	25 51.2	16 23.5	26 51.0	26 35.1	5 08.0
27 M	18 23 28	5 37 00	19 32 25	26 39 59	2D 44.4	20 16.4	19 20.2	14 53.8	27 14.2	25 58.5	16 26.7	26 52.1	26 36.7	5 10.1
28 Tu	18 27 25	6 38 08	3♎46 02	10♎50 19	2 44.4	19 53.3	20 15.6	15 40.1	27 37.4	26 05.9	16 29.7	26 53.2	26 38.3	5 12.3
29 W	18 31 22	7 39 17	17 52 35	24 52 38	2 44.6	19D 40.6	21 11.5	16 26.4	28 00.6	26 13.5	16 32.7	26 54.4	26 39.9	5 14.5
30 Th	18 35 18	8 40 26	1♏50 19	8♏45 28	2 45.0	19 37.7	22 08.0	17 12.7	28 23.9	26 21.2	16 35.5	26 55.6	26 41.5	5 16.6
31 F	18 39 15	9 41 36	15 37 56	22 27 38	2 45.7	19 43.9	23 05.1	17 59.1	28 47.2	26 29.1	16 38.3	26 56.9	26 43.2	5 18.8

Astro Data	Dy Hr Mn
☽0S	2 10:37
♆D	7 6:04
☽0N	15 23:36
♃D	18 16:53
♀D	18 21:18
☽0S	29 16:24
♅D	6 1:50
☿R	10 12:04
☽0N	13 7:13
☽0S	26 21:33
☿D	30 7:20

Planet Ingress		Dy Hr Mn
♀	♎R	8 3:06
☿	♐	8 23:43
☉	♐	22 10:15
♀	♏	30 0:33
☿	♑	1 0:10
♂	♑	7 23:49
☿	♐R	18 14:53
☉	♑	21 23:38

Last Aspect Dy Hr Mn		☽ Ingress Dy Hr Mn
31 21:01	♆ ☍	♍ 1 3:51
3 0:36	♅ ☍	♎ 3 5:19
4 23:34	♆ △	♏ 5 6:16
7 3:44	♅ ☌	♐ 7 8:27
9 12:35	♀ ⚹	♑ 9 13:36
11 19:57	♀ □	♒ 11 22:32
14 6:33	♀ △	♓ 14 10:24
16 16:37	♅ ☌	♈ 16 22:59
19 5:33	♀ ☍	♉ 19 10:04
21 17:27	☉ ☍	♊ 21 18:46
23 21:56	♀ △	♋ 24 1:14
26 3:44	♀ □	♌ 26 6:01
28 8:30	♀ ⚹	♍ 28 9:34
30 11:17	☿ □	♎ 30 12:15

Last Aspect Dy Hr Mn		☽ Ingress Dy Hr Mn
2 8:08	♆ △	♏ 2 14:44
4 12:13	♅ △	♐ 4 17:59
6 21:46	♂ ☌	♑ 6 23:16
9 1:07	♅ ⚹	♒ 9 7:30
11 11:09	♆ ☌	♓ 11 18:41
14 0:35	♅ ☌	♈ 14 7:15
16 11:41	♅ ⚹	♉ 16 18:49
18 21:36	♅ ⚹	♊ 19 3:37
21 8:13	☉ ☍	♋ 21 9:22
23 7:25	♅ △	♌ 23 12:51
25 9:28	♅ △	♍ 25 15:14
27 12:21	♅ ☍	♎ 27 17:38
29 15:05	♆ △	♏ 29 20:49

☽ Phases & Eclipses Dy Hr Mn	
6 4:52	● 13♏40
13 16:39	☽ 21♒12
21 17:27	○ 29♉18
28 20:36	☾ 6♍30
5 17:36	● 13♐28
13 13:59	☽ 21♓27
21 8:13	○ 29♊21
21 8:17	• T 1.256
28 4:18	☾ 6♎19

Astro Data

1 November 2010
Julian Day # 40482
SVP 5♓06'15"
GC 26♐59.4 ⚴ 9♐46.7
Eris 21♈31.9R ⚵ 12♍03.8
⚷ 26♒04.7R ⚶ 12♍55.5
☽ Mean ☊ 5♑30.6

1 December 2010
Julian Day # 40512
SVP 5♓06'10"
GC 26♐59.5 ⚴ 22♐01.1
Eris 21♈17.0R ⚵ 22♍04.8
⚷ 26♒24.6 ⚶ 29♏01.5
☽ Mean ☊ 3♑55.3

LONGITUDE — January 2011

Day	Sid.Time	☉	0 hr ☽	Noon ☽	True ☊	☿	♀	♂	⚳	♃	♄	♅	♆	♇
1 Sa	18 43 11	10♑42 46	29♏14 26	5♐58 14	2♑46.4	19♐58.7	24♏02.7	18♑45.5	29♑10.6	26♓37.1	16♎40.9	26♓58.2	26♒44.9	5♑21.0
2 Su	18 47 08	11 43 57	12♐38 55	19 16 25	2 47.0	20 21.2	25 00.9	19 32.0	29 34.0	26 45.3	16 43.5	26 59.5	26 46.7	5 23.1
3 M	18 51 04	12 45 08	25 50 39	2♑21 31	2R47.3	20 50.6	25 59.5	20 18.5	29 57.4	26 53.7	16 46.0	27 01.0	26 48.4	5 25.3
4 Tu	18 55 01	13 46 18	8♑49 01	15 13 05	2 47.0	21 26.4	26 58.7	21 05.1	0♒20.8	27 02.2	16 48.3	27 02.4	26 50.2	5 27.4
5 W	18 58 57	14 47 29	21 33 45	27 51 02	2 46.1	22 07.8	27 58.2	21 51.6	0 44.2	27 10.8	16 50.6	27 03.9	26 52.0	5 29.6
6 Th	19 02 54	15 48 40	4♒05 02	10♒15 53	2 44.5	22 54.3	28 58.3	22 38.2	1 07.7	27 19.6	16 52.7	27 05.5	26 53.8	5 31.7
7 F	19 06 51	16 49 50	16 23 44	22 28 48	2 42.4	23 45.2	29 58.7	23 24.9	1 31.2	27 28.5	16 54.8	27 07.1	26 55.6	5 33.8
8 Sa	19 10 47	17 51 00	28 31 23	4♓31 46	2 40.0	24 40.2	0♐59.6	24 11.6	1 54.7	27 37.5	16 56.7	27 08.7	26 57.5	5 36.0
9 Su	19 14 44	18 52 09	10♓30 20	16 27 29	2 37.6	25 38.8	2 00.8	24 58.3	2 18.2	27 46.7	16 58.5	27 10.4	26 59.3	5 38.1
10 M	19 18 40	19 53 19	22 23 42	28 19 26	2 35.6	26 40.5	3 02.5	25 45.0	2 41.8	27 56.0	17 00.3	27 12.1	27 01.2	5 40.2
11 Tu	19 22 37	20 54 27	4♈15 14	10♈11 40	2D34.3	27 45.1	4 04.5	26 31.8	3 05.3	28 05.5	17 01.9	27 13.9	27 03.2	5 42.3
12 W	19 26 33	21 55 35	16 09 17	22 08 41	2 33.9	28 52.3	5 06.8	27 18.6	3 28.9	28 15.1	17 03.4	27 15.7	27 05.1	5 44.4
13 Th	19 30 30	22 56 43	28 10 29	4♉15 16	2 34.4	0♑01.7	6 09.5	28 05.4	3 52.5	28 24.8	17 04.8	27 17.6	27 07.0	5 46.5
14 F	19 34 26	23 57 50	10♉23 38	16 36 09	2 35.6	1 13.3	7 12.5	28 52.2	4 16.1	28 34.6	17 06.2	27 19.5	27 09.0	5 48.6
15 Sa	19 38 23	24 58 56	22 53 21	29 15 42	2 37.2	2 26.6	8 15.9	29 39.1	4 39.7	28 44.6	17 07.4	27 21.5	27 11.0	5 50.6
16 Su	19 42 20	26 00 02	5♊43 37	12♊17 27	2 38.8	3 41.7	9 19.6	0♒26.0	5 03.3	28 54.7	17 08.5	27 23.5	27 13.0	5 52.7
17 M	19 46 16	27 01 07	18 57 26	25 43 41	2R39.8	4 58.4	10 23.5	1 12.9	5 26.9	29 04.9	17 09.5	27 25.5	27 15.0	5 54.8
18 Tu	19 50 13	28 02 11	2♋36 10	9♋34 44	2 39.8	6 16.4	11 27.8	1 59.9	5 50.6	29 15.2	17 10.4	27 27.6	27 17.1	5 56.8
19 W	19 54 09	29 03 15	16 39 05	23 48 45	2 38.5	7 35.8	12 32.4	2 46.9	6 14.2	29 25.7	17 11.1	27 29.7	27 19.1	5 58.8
20 Th	19 58 06	0♒04 18	1♌03 06	8♌21 23	2 35.8	8 56.3	13 37.2	3 33.9	6 37.9	29 36.2	17 11.8	27 31.9	27 21.2	6 00.8
21 F	20 02 02	1 05 21	15 42 44	23 06 13	2 32.0	10 18.0	14 42.3	4 20.9	7 01.5	29 46.9	17 12.4	27 34.1	27 23.3	6 02.9
22 Sa	20 05 59	2 06 22	0♍30 48	7♍55 29	2 27.5	11 40.7	15 47.6	5 08.0	7 25.2	29 57.7	17 12.8	27 36.3	27 25.4	6 04.8
23 Su	20 09 55	3 07 24	15 19 18	22 41 19	2 23.2	13 04.4	16 53.2	5 55.0	7 48.9	0♈08.5	17 13.2	27 38.6	27 27.5	6 06.8
24 M	20 13 52	4 08 25	0♎00 45	7♎16 54	2 19.6	14 29.1	17 59.1	6 42.1	8 12.6	0 19.5	17 13.4	27 40.9	27 29.6	6 08.8
25 Tu	20 17 49	5 09 25	14 29 13	21 37 18	2 17.3	15 54.6	19 05.2	7 29.2	8 36.2	0 30.6	17R13.6	27 43.3	27 31.7	6 10.7
26 W	20 21 45	6 10 25	28 40 51	5♏39 45	2D16.5	17 21.0	20 11.5	8 16.4	8 59.9	0 41.8	17 13.6	27 45.7	27 33.9	6 12.7
27 Th	20 25 42	7 11 24	12♏33 57	19 23 32	2 17.1	18 48.2	21 18.0	9 03.6	9 23.6	0 53.1	17 13.5	27 48.1	27 36.0	6 14.6
28 F	20 29 38	8 12 23	26 08 36	2♐49 21	2 18.5	20 16.2	22 24.7	9 50.7	9 47.3	1 04.5	17 13.3	27 50.6	27 38.2	6 16.5
29 Sa	20 33 35	9 13 22	9♐26 01	15 58 50	2 20.1	21 44.9	23 31.7	10 37.9	10 11.0	1 16.0	17 13.0	27 53.1	27 40.4	6 18.4
30 Su	20 37 31	10 14 19	22 28 03	28 53 54	2R21.1	23 14.5	24 38.8	11 25.2	10 34.7	1 27.6	17 12.6	27 55.6	27 42.6	6 20.3
31 M	20 41 28	11 15 16	5♑16 37	11♑36 25	2 20.7	24 44.8	25 46.1	12 12.4	10 58.4	1 39.3	17 12.1	27 58.2	27 44.8	6 22.1

LONGITUDE — February 2011

Day	Sid.Time	☉	0 hr ☽	Noon ☽	True ☊	☿	♀	♂	⚳	♃	♄	♅	♆	♇
1 Tu	20 45 24	12♒16 12	17♑53 28	24♑07 56	2♑18.4	26♑15.8	26♐53.6	12♒59.7	11♒22.1	1♈51.1	17♎11.5	28♓00.8	27♒47.0	6♑24.0
2 W	20 49 21	13 17 07	0♒19 59	6♒29 44	2R14.0	27 47.5	28 01.3	13 46.9	11 45.7	2 03.0	17R10.8	28 03.4	27 49.2	6 25.8
3 Th	20 53 18	14 18 01	12 37 18	18 42 49	2 07.5	29 20.0	29 09.1	14 34.2	12 09.4	2 15.0	17 09.9	28 06.1	27 51.4	6 27.6
4 F	20 57 14	15 18 54	24 46 25	0♓48 12	1 59.5	0♒53.3	0♑17.1	15 21.5	12 33.1	2 27.0	17 09.0	28 08.8	27 53.7	6 29.4
5 Sa	21 01 11	16 19 45	6♓48 22	12 47 04	1 50.6	2 27.2	1 25.2	16 08.8	12 56.7	2 39.2	17 08.0	28 11.5	27 55.9	6 31.2
6 Su	21 05 07	17 20 36	18 44 32	24 41 01	1 41.6	4 01.9	2 33.5	16 56.2	13 20.4	2 51.4	17 06.8	28 14.3	27 58.2	6 32.9
7 M	21 09 04	18 21 25	0♈36 49	6♈32 15	1 33.4	5 37.4	3 42.0	17 43.5	13 44.0	3 03.7	17 05.6	28 17.1	28 00.4	6 34.6
8 Tu	21 13 00	19 22 12	12 27 42	18 23 37	1 26.9	7 13.6	4 50.5	18 30.8	14 07.7	3 16.1	17 04.2	28 19.9	28 02.7	6 36.4
9 W	21 16 57	20 22 58	24 20 28	0♉18 45	1 22.3	8 50.6	5 59.3	19 18.2	14 31.3	3 28.6	17 02.8	28 22.7	28 04.9	6 38.0
10 Th	21 20 53	21 23 43	6♉19 02	12 21 54	1D19.9	10 28.4	7 08.1	20 05.6	14 54.9	3 41.2	17 01.2	28 25.6	28 07.2	6 39.7
11 F	21 24 50	22 24 26	18 27 56	24 37 46	1 19.5	12 07.0	8 17.1	20 52.9	15 18.5	3 53.8	16 59.5	28 28.5	28 09.5	6 41.3
12 Sa	21 28 47	23 25 07	0♊52 02	7♊11 20	1 20.2	13 46.4	9 26.1	21 40.3	15 42.1	4 06.5	16 57.8	28 31.5	28 11.7	6 43.0
13 Su	21 32 43	24 25 47	13 36 16	20 07 20	1R21.3	15 26.7	10 35.4	22 27.7	16 05.6	4 19.3	16 55.9	28 34.4	28 14.0	6 44.6
14 M	21 36 40	25 26 25	26 45 02	3♋29 42	1 21.8	17 07.7	11 44.7	23 15.0	16 29.2	4 32.1	16 54.0	28 37.4	28 16.3	6 46.2
15 Tu	21 40 36	26 27 02	10♋21 35	17 20 46	1 20.6	18 49.7	12 54.1	24 02.4	16 52.7	4 45.0	16 51.9	28 40.4	28 18.6	6 47.7
16 W	21 44 33	27 27 36	24 27 09	1♌40 27	1 17.1	20 32.5	14 03.7	24 49.8	17 16.2	4 58.0	16 49.8	28 43.4	28 20.9	6 49.2
17 Th	21 48 29	28 28 10	9♌00 08	16 25 28	1 11.2	22 16.2	15 13.3	25 37.2	17 39.7	5 11.0	16 47.5	28 46.5	28 23.1	6 50.8
18 F	21 52 26	29 28 41	23 55 31	1♍29 08	1 03.2	24 00.8	16 23.1	26 24.6	18 03.1	5 24.1	16 45.2	28 49.6	28 25.4	6 52.2
19 Sa	21 56 22	0♓29 11	9♍05 04	16 41 57	0 54.0	25 46.3	17 33.0	27 12.0	18 26.6	5 37.3	16 42.8	28 52.7	28 27.7	6 53.7
20 Su	22 00 19	1 29 39	24 18 24	1♎53 03	0 44.6	27 32.7	18 42.9	27 59.4	18 50.0	5 50.5	16 40.3	28 55.8	28 30.0	6 55.1
21 M	22 04 16	2 30 07	9♎24 40	16 52 09	0 36.4	29 20.0	19 53.0	28 46.7	19 13.4	6 03.8	16 37.7	28 58.9	28 32.2	6 56.5
22 Tu	22 08 12	3 30 32	24 14 36	1♏31 18	0 30.1	1♓08.3	21 03.2	29 34.1	19 36.8	6 17.1	16 35.0	29 02.1	28 34.5	6 57.9
23 W	22 12 09	4 30 57	8♏41 48	15 45 48	0 26.3	2 57.5	22 13.4	0♓21.5	20 00.1	6 30.5	16 32.2	29 05.3	28 36.8	6 59.3
24 Th	22 16 05	5 31 20	22 43 15	29 34 12	0D24.7	4 47.5	23 23.8	1 08.9	20 23.5	6 44.0	16 29.3	29 08.5	28 39.1	7 00.6
25 F	22 20 02	6 31 42	6♐18 54	12♐57 39	0 24.7	6 38.5	24 34.2	1 56.3	20 46.8	6 57.5	16 26.4	29 11.7	28 41.3	7 01.9
26 Sa	22 23 58	7 32 02	19 30 51	25 58 58	0R25.2	8 30.3	25 44.7	2 43.7	21 10.1	7 11.1	16 23.3	29 14.9	28 43.6	7 03.2
27 Su	22 27 55	8 32 21	2♑22 27	8♑41 47	0 24.9	10 23.0	26 55.4	3 31.1	21 33.3	7 24.7	16 20.2	29 18.2	28 45.9	7 04.5
28 M	22 31 51	9 32 39	14 57 26	21 09 51	0 22.9	12 16.4	28 06.0	4 18.5	21 56.6	7 38.4	16 17.0	29 21.4	28 48.1	7 05.7

Astro Data

	Dy Hr Mn
♃⚺♆	2 16:51
♃☌♅	4 12:53
☽0N	9 15:24
☽0S	23 4:45
♄ R	26 6:10
♃0N	5 13:48
☽0N	5 23:17
☽0S	19 14:48
♃□♇	25 20:40

Planet Ingress

		Dy Hr Mn
⚳	♒	3 14:42
♀	♐	7 12:30
☿	♑	13 11:25
♂	♒	15 22:41
☉	♒	20 10:19
♃	♈	22 17:11
☿	♒	3 22:19
♀	♑	4 5:58
☉	♓	19 0:25
☿	♓	21 20:53
♂	♓	23 1:06

Last Aspect / ☽ Ingress

Last Aspect Dy Hr Mn		☽ Ingress	Dy Hr Mn
31 19:57	♅ △	♐	1 1:21
3 2:08	♅ □	♑	3 7:39
5 12:15	♀ ⚹	♒	5 16:08
7 20:51	♆ ☌	♓	8 2:57
10 11:12	♃ ☌	♈	10 15:24
13 2:47	☿ △	♉	13 3:37
15 12:47	♂ △	♊	15 13:23
17 17:57	♃ □	♋	17 19:29
19 21:26	♃ △	♌	19 22:16
21 18:57	♆ ☍	♍	21 23:10
23 20:08	♅ ☍	♎	23 23:59
25 22:04	♆ △	♏	26 2:15
28 3:01	♅ △	♐	28 6:55
30 10:10	♅ □	♑	30 14:04

Last Aspect / ☽ Ingress

Last Aspect Dy Hr Mn		☽ Ingress	Dy Hr Mn
1 19:32	♅ ⚹	♒	1 23:21
4 6:11	♆ ☌	♓	4 10:24
6 19:13	♅ ☌	♈	6 22:45
9 7:31	♆ ⚹	♉	9 11:22
11 19:27	♅ ⚹	♊	11 22:20
14 3:19	♅ □	♋	14 5:48
16 7:06	♅ △	♌	16 9:14
18 8:36	☉ ☍	♍	18 9:39
20 7:18	♅ ☍	♎	20 9:01
22 8:35	♂ △	♏	22 9:29
24 11:14	♅ △	♐	24 12:46
26 18:08	♅ □	♑	26 19:32

☽ Phases & Eclipses

Dy Hr Mn		
4 9:03	●	13♑39
4 8:50:36	◐	P 0.858
12 11:31	☽	21♈54
19 21:21	○	29♋27
26 12:57	☾	6♏13
3 2:31	●	13♒54
11 7:18	☽	22♉13
18 8:36	○	29♌20
24 23:26	☾	6♐00

Astro Data

1 January 2011
Julian Day # 40543
SVP 5♓06'04"
GC 26♐59.6 ⚴ 4♑42.3
Eris 21♈09.5R ⚵ 28♍32.0
⚷ 27♒38.7 ⚶ 15♐37.5
☽ Mean ☊ 2♑16.8

1 February 2011
Julian Day # 40574
SVP 5♓05'59"
GC 26♐59.6 ⚴ 16♑55.0
Eris 21♈12.2 ⚵ 29♍07.1R
⚷ 29♒30.5 ⚶ 1♑48.5
☽ Mean ☊ 0♑38.3

March 2011 LONGITUDE

Day	Sid.Time	☉	0 hr ☽	Noon ☽	True ☊	☿	♀	♂	⚳	♃	♄	♅	♆	♇
1 Tu	22 35 48	10♓32 55	27♑19 27	3♒26 36	0♑18.3	14♓10.5	29♑16.8	5♓05.9	22♒19.8	7♈52.1	16♎13.8	29♓24.7	28♒50.4	7♑06.9
2 W	22 39 45	11 33 09	9♒31 39	15 34 53	0R10.7	16 05.2	0♒27.6	5 53.2	22 42.9	8 05.8	16R10.4	29 28.0	28 52.6	7 08.1
3 Th	22 43 41	12 33 22	21 36 34	27 36 55	0 00.3	18 00.4	1 38.5	6 40.6	23 06.1	8 19.6	16 07.0	29 31.3	28 54.8	7 09.2
4 F	22 47 38	13 33 33	3♓36 08	9♓34 23	29♐47.6	19 56.0	2 49.5	7 28.0	23 29.1	8 33.5	16 03.5	29 34.6	28 57.1	7 10.4
5 Sa	22 51 34	14 33 42	15 31 50	21 28 37	29 33.5	21 51.8	4 00.5	8 15.3	23 52.2	8 47.4	15 59.9	29 38.0	28 59.3	7 11.4
6 Su	22 55 31	15 33 49	27 24 54	3♈20 50	29 19.2	23 47.6	5 11.6	9 02.6	24 15.2	9 01.3	15 56.2	29 41.3	29 01.5	7 12.5
7 M	22 59 27	16 33 54	9♈16 37	15 12 28	29 05.9	25 43.2	6 22.7	9 50.0	24 38.2	9 15.3	15 52.5	29 44.7	29 03.7	7 13.5
8 Tu	23 03 24	17 33 57	21 08 36	27 05 19	28 54.5	27 38.3	7 33.9	10 37.3	25 01.2	9 29.3	15 48.8	29 48.0	29 05.9	7 14.5
9 W	23 07 20	18 33 59	3♉02 58	9♉01 54	28 45.9	29 32.6	8 45.1	11 24.6	25 24.1	9 43.3	15 44.9	29 51.4	29 08.1	7 15.5
10 Th	23 11 17	19 33 58	15 02 32	21 05 22	28 40.3	1♈25.8	9 56.4	12 11.8	25 47.0	9 57.4	15 41.0	29 54.8	29 10.2	7 16.5
11 F	23 15 14	20 33 55	27 10 53	3♊19 38	28 37.3	3 17.6	11 07.8	12 59.1	26 09.8	10 11.5	15 37.1	29 58.2	29 12.4	7 17.4
12 Sa	23 19 10	21 33 50	9♊32 13	15 49 12	28 36.3	5 07.4	12 19.2	13 46.4	26 32.6	10 25.7	15 33.1	0♈01.6	29 14.6	7 18.3
13 Su	23 23 07	22 33 43	22 11 11	28 38 47	28 36.3	6 54.9	13 30.6	14 33.6	26 55.3	10 39.8	15 29.0	0 05.0	29 16.7	7 19.1
14 M	23 27 03	23 33 33	5♋12 33	11♋52 57	28 35.9	8 39.6	14 42.1	15 20.8	27 18.1	10 54.1	15 24.9	0 08.4	29 18.8	7 19.9
15 Tu	23 31 00	24 33 22	18 40 25	25 35 14	28 34.0	10 21.1	15 53.6	16 08.0	27 40.7	11 08.3	15 20.7	0 11.8	29 20.9	7 20.7
16 W	23 34 56	25 33 08	2♌37 33	9♌47 17	28 29.8	11 58.7	17 05.2	16 55.2	28 03.3	11 22.5	15 16.5	0 15.2	29 23.0	7 21.5
17 Th	23 38 53	26 32 51	17 04 11	24 27 46	28 22.8	13 32.1	18 16.8	17 42.4	28 25.9	11 36.8	15 12.2	0 18.7	29 25.1	7 22.2
18 F	23 42 49	27 32 33	1♍57 16	9♍31 42	28 13.3	15 00.8	19 28.5	18 29.5	28 48.4	11 51.1	15 07.9	0 22.1	29 27.2	7 22.9
19 Sa	23 46 46	28 32 12	17 09 52	24 50 24	28 02.2	16 24.2	20 40.2	19 16.6	29 10.9	12 05.4	15 03.6	0 25.5	29 29.3	7 23.6
20 Su	23 50 42	29 31 50	2♎31 49	10♎12 35	27 50.9	17 41.9	21 52.0	20 03.7	29 33.3	12 19.8	14 59.2	0 28.9	29 31.3	7 24.2
21 M	23 54 39	0♈31 25	17 51 12	25 26 17	27 40.6	18 53.6	23 03.8	20 50.8	29 55.6	12 34.1	14 54.8	0 32.4	29 33.3	7 24.8
22 Tu	23 58 36	1 30 59	2♏56 38	10♏21 14	27 32.4	19 58.9	24 15.6	21 37.8	0♓18.0	12 48.5	14 50.3	0 35.8	29 35.3	7 25.4
23 W	0 02 32	2 30 31	17 39 17	24 50 18	27 27.0	20 57.4	25 27.5	22 24.9	0 40.2	13 02.9	14 45.9	0 39.2	29 37.3	7 26.0
24 Th	0 06 29	3 30 01	1♐53 57	8♐50 12	27 24.2	21 48.9	26 39.4	23 11.9	1 02.4	13 17.3	14 41.3	0 42.6	29 39.3	7 26.5
25 F	0 10 25	4 29 29	15 39 08	22 21 01	27D23.3	22 33.1	27 51.4	23 58.9	1 24.6	13 31.8	14 36.8	0 46.1	29 41.3	7 27.0
26 Sa	0 14 22	5 28 56	28 56 15	5♑25 18	27R23.3	23 09.8	29 03.3	24 45.9	1 46.7	13 46.2	14 32.2	0 49.5	29 43.2	7 27.4
27 Su	0 18 18	6 28 21	11♑48 43	18 07 04	27 22.9	23 39.0	0♓15.4	25 32.8	2 08.8	14 00.7	14 27.7	0 52.9	29 45.2	7 27.9
28 M	0 22 15	7 27 44	24 20 56	0♒30 53	27 21.0	24 00.5	1 27.4	26 19.7	2 30.7	14 15.2	14 23.1	0 56.3	29 47.1	7 28.3
29 Tu	0 26 11	8 27 05	6♒37 30	12 41 19	27 16.6	24 14.5	2 39.5	27 06.6	2 52.7	14 29.6	14 18.4	0 59.7	29 49.0	7 28.6
30 W	0 30 08	9 26 25	18 42 50	24 42 30	27 09.5	24R20.9	3 51.7	27 53.5	3 14.5	14 44.1	14 13.8	1 03.1	29 50.8	7 28.9
31 Th	0 34 05	10 25 42	0♓40 44	6♓37 55	26 59.5	24 19.9	5 03.8	28 40.3	3 36.3	14 58.6	14 09.1	1 06.5	29 52.7	7 29.2

April 2011 LONGITUDE

Day	Sid.Time	☉	0 hr ☽	Noon ☽	True ☊	☿	♀	♂	⚳	♃	♄	♅	♆	♇
1 F	0 38 01	11♈24 58	12♓34 21	18♓30 20	26♐47.3	24♈11.8	6♓16.0	29♓27.1	3♓58.1	15♈13.1	14♎04.5	1♈09.9	29♒54.5	7♑29.5
2 Sa	0 41 58	12 24 12	24 26 07	0♈21 54	26R33.7	23R57.0	7 28.2	0♈13.9	4 19.8	15 27.7	13R59.8	1 13.3	29 56.3	7 29.7
3 Su	0 45 54	13 23 23	6♈17 52	12 14 12	26 19.8	23 35.8	8 40.4	1 00.7	4 41.4	15 42.2	13 55.1	1 16.7	29 58.1	7 29.9
4 M	0 49 51	14 22 33	18 11 05	24 08 38	26 06.8	23 08.8	9 52.7	1 47.4	5 02.9	15 56.7	13 50.5	1 20.1	29 59.9	7 30.1
5 Tu	0 53 47	15 21 41	0♉07 04	6♉06 32	25 55.8	22 36.5	11 05.0	2 34.1	5 24.4	16 11.2	13 45.8	1 23.4	0♓01.6	7 30.2
6 W	0 57 44	16 20 46	12 07 17	18 09 31	25 47.3	21 59.9	12 17.3	3 20.8	5 45.8	16 25.7	13 41.1	1 26.8	0 03.3	7 30.3
7 Th	1 01 40	17 19 50	24 13 32	0♊19 38	25 41.7	21 19.5	13 29.6	4 07.4	6 07.1	16 40.2	13 36.5	1 30.1	0 05.0	7 30.4
8 F	1 05 37	18 18 51	6♊28 12	12 39 35	25 38.8	20 36.3	14 41.9	4 54.0	6 28.4	16 54.8	13 31.8	1 33.4	0 06.7	7R30.4
9 Sa	1 09 34	19 17 50	18 54 14	25 12 37	25D38.1	19 51.1	15 54.3	5 40.5	6 49.6	17 09.3	13 27.2	1 36.7	0 08.4	7 30.5
10 Su	1 13 30	20 16 47	1♋35 11	8♋02 27	25 38.4	19 04.9	17 06.7	6 27.1	7 10.7	17 23.8	13 22.6	1 40.0	0 10.0	7 30.4
11 M	1 17 27	21 15 41	14 34 52	21 12 55	25R38.8	18 18.5	18 19.1	7 13.6	7 31.7	17 38.3	13 18.0	1 43.3	0 11.6	7 30.4
12 Tu	1 21 23	22 14 33	27 56 58	4♌47 22	25 38.1	17 32.8	19 31.5	8 00.0	7 52.7	17 52.8	13 13.4	1 46.6	0 13.2	7 30.3
13 W	1 25 20	23 13 23	11♌44 19	18 47 55	25 35.5	16 48.7	20 43.9	8 46.4	8 13.5	18 07.3	13 08.8	1 49.9	0 14.8	7 30.2
14 Th	1 29 16	24 12 10	25 58 05	3♍14 32	25 30.6	16 06.9	21 56.3	9 32.8	8 34.3	18 21.7	13 04.3	1 53.1	0 16.3	7 30.0
15 F	1 33 13	25 10 55	10♍36 48	18 04 11	25 23.5	15 28.0	23 08.8	10 19.1	8 55.0	18 36.2	12 59.8	1 56.3	0 17.8	7 29.9
16 Sa	1 37 09	26 09 38	25 35 48	3♎10 32	25 15.1	14 52.6	24 21.2	11 05.4	9 15.7	18 50.6	12 55.3	1 59.5	0 19.3	7 29.7
17 Su	1 41 06	27 08 19	10♎47 09	18 24 20	25 06.2	14 21.3	25 33.7	11 51.7	9 36.2	19 05.1	12 50.8	2 02.7	0 20.7	7 29.4
18 M	1 45 03	28 06 58	26 00 40	3♏34 48	24 58.0	13 54.4	26 46.2	12 37.9	9 56.6	19 19.5	12 46.4	2 05.9	0 22.1	7 29.2
19 Tu	1 48 59	29 05 35	11♏05 29	18 31 36	24 51.6	13 32.2	27 58.8	13 24.0	10 17.0	19 33.9	12 42.0	2 09.0	0 23.6	7 28.9
20 W	1 52 56	0♉04 10	25 52 10	3♐06 28	24 47.4	13 14.8	29 11.3	14 10.2	10 37.3	19 48.3	12 37.6	2 12.2	0 24.9	7 28.5
21 Th	1 56 52	1 02 44	10♐13 58	17 14 21	24D45.5	13 02.5	0♈23.9	14 56.3	10 57.5	20 02.6	12 33.3	2 15.3	0 26.3	7 28.2
22 F	2 00 49	2 01 16	24 07 32	0♑53 34	24 45.4	12D55.3	1 36.4	15 42.4	11 17.6	20 17.0	12 29.1	2 18.4	0 27.6	7 27.8
23 Sa	2 04 45	2 59 46	7♑32 39	14 05 10	24 46.3	12 53.2	2 49.0	16 28.4	11 37.6	20 31.3	12 24.8	2 21.4	0 28.9	7 27.4
24 Su	2 08 42	3 58 15	20 31 31	26 52 13	24R47.3	12 56.1	4 01.7	17 14.4	11 57.5	20 45.6	12 20.7	2 24.5	0 30.2	7 26.9
25 M	2 12 38	4 56 42	3♒07 51	9♒18 59	24 47.4	13 04.0	5 14.3	18 00.3	12 17.3	20 59.9	12 16.5	2 27.5	0 31.4	7 26.5
26 Tu	2 16 35	5 55 07	15 26 14	21 30 11	24 46.0	13 16.7	6 26.9	18 46.2	12 37.1	21 14.2	12 12.4	2 30.5	0 32.6	7 26.0
27 W	2 20 32	6 53 31	27 31 25	3♓30 30	24 42.6	13 34.1	7 39.6	19 32.1	12 56.7	21 28.4	12 08.4	2 33.5	0 33.8	7 25.4
28 Th	2 24 28	7 51 53	9♓27 58	15 24 19	24 37.2	13 56.1	8 52.3	20 17.9	13 16.2	21 42.6	12 04.4	2 36.5	0 35.0	7 24.9
29 F	2 28 25	8 50 13	21 20 00	27 15 26	24 30.1	14 22.5	10 04.9	21 03.7	13 35.6	21 56.8	12 00.5	2 39.4	0 36.1	7 24.3
30 Sa	2 32 21	9 48 32	3♈11 00	9♈07 03	24 21.9	14 53.1	11 17.6	21 49.4	13 54.9	22 11.0	11 56.7	2 42.3	0 37.2	7 23.6

Astro Data

	Dy Hr Mn
☽0N	5 6:08
☿0N	10 2:34
☽0S	19 2:07
☉0N	20 23:21
♄⚼♆	24 19:30
♃☍♄	28 21:55
☿R	30 20:49
♃∠♆	31 0:41
☽0N	1 11:55
♂0N	4 21:48
♇R	9 8:51
♅0N	9 19:30
☽0S	15 12:20
☿D	23 10:04
♀0N	24 4:24

Planet Ingress

		Dy Hr Mn
♀	♒	2 2:39
☊	♐R	3 12:37
☿	♈	9 17:47
♅	♈	12 0:49
☉	♈	20 23:21
⚳	♓	21 16:41
♀	♓	27 6:53
♂	♈	2 4:51
♆	♓	4 13:50
☉	♉	20 10:17
♀	♈	21 4:06
☽0N28 17:32		

Last Aspect / ☽ Ingress

Dy Hr Mn	Last Aspect	☽ Ingress	Dy Hr Mn
1 4:03	♅ ⚹	♒	1 5:14
3 14:36	♆ ☌	♓	3 16:47
6 4:34	♅ ☌	♈	6 5:14
8 16:04	♆ ⚹	♉	8 17:52
11 5:26	♅ ⚹	♊	11 5:31
13 13:10	♆ △	♋	13 14:29
15 10:05	☉ △	♌	15 19:33
17 19:58	♆ ☍	♍	17 20:53
19 18:10	☉ ☍	♎	19 20:03
21 18:35	♆ △	♏	21 19:17
23 20:08	♆ □	♐	23 20:45
26 1:25	♆ ⚹	♑	26 1:57
28 3:17	♂ ⚹	♒	28 11:00
30 22:21	♆ ☌	♓	30 22:38

Last Aspect / ☽ Ingress

Dy Hr Mn	Last Aspect	☽ Ingress	Dy Hr Mn
31 13:44	♇ ⚹	♈	2 11:16
4 10:04	☿ ☌	♉	4 23:46
5 23:02	♀ ⚹	♊	7 11:21
9 2:24	☿ ⚹	♋	9 21:02
11 12:05	☉ □	♌	12 3:37
13 19:58	☉ △	♍	14 6:40
15 20:49	♀ ☍	♎	16 6:59
18 2:44	☉ ☍	♏	18 6:19
20 4:53	♀ △	♐	20 6:50
21 16:57	♃ △	♑	22 10:24
24 0:13	♃ □	♒	24 17:59
26 11:28	♃ ⚹	♓	27 4:57
27 19:52	♇ ⚹	♈	29 17:33

☽ Phases & Eclipses

Dy Hr Mn	
4 20:46	● 13♓56
12 23:45	☽ 22♊03
19 18:10	○ 28♍48
26 12:07	☾ 5♑29
3 14:32	● 13♈30
11 12:05	☽ 21♋16
18 2:44	○ 27♎44
25 2:47	☾ 4♒34

Astro Data

1 March 2011
Julian Day # 40602
SVP 5♓05'55"
GC 26♐59.7 ⚴ 27♑03.3
Eris 21♈23.1 ⚵ 24♍10.6R
⚷ 1♓24.5 ⚶ 15♑40.4
☽ Mean ☊ 29♐09.3

1 April 2011
Julian Day # 40633
SVP 5♓05'53"
GC 26♐59.8 ⚴ 6♒36.7
Eris 21♈41.3 ⚵ 16♍56.2R
⚷ 3♓22.1 ⚶ 29♑35.0
☽ Mean ☊ 27♐30.8

LONGITUDE — May 2011

Day	Sid.Time	☉	0 hr ☽	Noon ☽	True ☊	☿	♀	♂	⚳	♃	♄	♅	♆	♇
1 Su	2 36 18	10♉46 49	15♈03 51	21♈01 40	24♐13.5	15♈27.8	12♈30.3	22♈35.1	14♓14.1	22♈25.1	11♎52.9	2♈45.2	0♓38.2	7♑23.0
2 M	2 40 14	11 45 04	27 00 44	3♉01 16	24R 05.6	16 06.4	13 43.0	23 20.7	14 33.2	22 39.2	11R 49.1	2 48.0	0 39.3	7R 22.3
3 Tu	2 44 11	12 43 18	9♉03 26	15 07 23	23 58.9	16 48.8	14 55.8	24 06.3	14 52.2	22 53.3	11 45.4	2 50.8	0 40.3	7 21.6
4 W	2 48 07	13 41 30	21 13 19	27 21 21	23 54.0	17 34.8	16 08.5	24 51.8	15 11.1	23 07.3	11 41.8	2 53.6	0 41.2	7 20.9
5 Th	2 52 04	14 39 41	3♊31 39	9♊44 25	23 51.1	18 24.2	17 21.3	25 37.3	15 29.8	23 21.3	11 38.3	2 56.4	0 42.2	7 20.2
6 F	2 56 01	15 37 49	15 59 48	22 18 03	23D 50.1	19 16.9	18 34.0	26 22.8	15 48.5	23 35.3	11 34.8	2 59.2	0 43.1	7 19.4
7 Sa	2 59 57	16 35 56	28 39 21	5♋03 58	23 50.6	20 12.8	19 46.8	27 08.2	16 07.0	23 49.2	11 31.4	3 01.9	0 44.0	7 18.6
8 Su	3 03 54	17 34 01	11♋32 10	18 04 12	23 52.0	21 11.8	20 59.5	27 53.6	16 25.4	24 03.1	11 28.1	3 04.5	0 44.8	7 17.7
9 M	3 07 50	18 32 04	24 40 20	1♌20 50	23 53.5	22 13.7	22 12.3	28 38.9	16 43.7	24 16.9	11 24.9	3 07.2	0 45.6	7 16.9
10 Tu	3 11 47	19 30 05	8♌05 55	14 55 47	23R 54.4	23 18.5	23 25.1	29 24.1	17 01.8	24 30.7	11 21.7	3 09.8	0 46.4	7 16.0
11 W	3 15 43	20 28 04	21 50 33	28 50 16	23 54.2	24 26.1	24 37.9	0♉09.3	17 19.8	24 44.5	11 18.6	3 12.4	0 47.2	7 15.1
12 Th	3 19 40	21 26 01	5♍54 52	13♍04 10	23 52.6	25 36.3	25 50.6	0 54.4	17 37.7	24 58.2	11 15.6	3 15.0	0 47.9	7 14.2
13 F	3 23 36	22 23 56	20 17 53	27 35 32	23 49.7	26 49.2	27 03.4	1 39.5	17 55.5	25 11.9	11 12.6	3 17.5	0 48.6	7 13.2
14 Sa	3 27 33	23 21 50	4♎56 32	12♎20 09	23 45.8	28 04.6	28 16.2	2 24.6	18 13.1	25 25.5	11 09.8	3 20.0	0 49.3	7 12.2
15 Su	3 31 30	24 19 42	19 45 33	27 11 45	23 41.7	29 22.5	29 29.0	3 09.6	18 30.6	25 39.1	11 07.0	3 22.4	0 49.9	7 11.2
16 M	3 35 26	25 17 32	4♏37 46	12♏02 34	23 37.8	0♉42.8	0♉41.9	3 54.5	18 48.0	25 52.6	11 04.3	3 24.8	0 50.5	7 10.2
17 Tu	3 39 23	26 15 20	19 25 08	26 44 30	23 34.8	2 05.5	1 54.7	4 39.4	19 05.2	26 06.1	11 01.7	3 27.2	0 51.0	7 09.2
18 W	3 43 19	27 13 08	3♐59 50	11♐10 23	23D 33.1	3 30.6	3 07.5	5 24.2	19 22.3	26 19.5	10 59.2	3 29.6	0 51.6	7 08.1
19 Th	3 47 16	28 10 54	18 15 33	25 14 53	23 32.6	4 58.0	4 20.4	6 09.0	19 39.2	26 32.9	10 56.8	3 31.9	0 52.1	7 07.0
20 F	3 51 12	29 08 39	2♑08 05	8♑55 02	23 33.3	6 27.8	5 33.3	6 53.8	19 56.0	26 46.3	10 54.4	3 34.2	0 52.5	7 05.9
21 Sa	3 55 09	0♊06 22	15 35 43	22 10 16	23 34.6	7 59.8	6 46.1	7 38.5	20 12.7	26 59.5	10 52.2	3 36.4	0 53.0	7 04.8
22 Su	3 59 05	1 04 04	28 38 56	5♒02 03	23 36.1	9 34.1	7 59.0	8 23.1	20 29.2	27 12.8	10 50.0	3 38.6	0 53.4	7 03.7
23 M	4 03 02	2 01 46	11♒20 01	17 33 20	23 37.4	11 10.7	9 11.9	9 07.7	20 45.6	27 25.9	10 47.9	3 40.8	0 53.8	7 02.5
24 Tu	4 06 59	2 59 26	23 42 30	29 48 04	23R 38.1	12 49.6	10 24.8	9 52.2	21 01.8	27 39.0	10 46.0	3 42.9	0 54.1	7 01.3
25 W	4 10 55	3 57 05	5♓50 37	11♓50 43	23 37.9	14 30.7	11 37.7	10 36.7	21 17.8	27 52.1	10 44.1	3 45.0	0 54.4	7 00.1
26 Th	4 14 52	4 54 43	17 48 57	23 45 53	23 36.9	16 14.0	12 50.7	11 21.1	21 33.7	28 05.1	10 42.3	3 47.1	0 54.7	6 58.9
27 F	4 18 48	5 52 20	29 42 03	5♈38 00	23 35.1	17 59.6	14 03.6	12 05.5	21 49.4	28 18.0	10 40.6	3 49.1	0 54.9	6 57.7
28 Sa	4 22 45	6 49 56	11♈34 14	17 31 12	23 32.8	19 47.5	15 16.6	12 49.8	22 05.0	28 30.8	10 38.9	3 51.0	0 55.1	6 56.4
29 Su	4 26 41	7 47 32	23 29 20	29 29 02	23 30.3	21 37.6	16 29.5	13 34.1	22 20.4	28 43.6	10 37.4	3 53.0	0 55.3	6 55.1
30 M	4 30 38	8 45 06	5♉30 40	11♉34 32	23 28.1	23 29.9	17 42.5	14 18.3	22 35.6	28 56.4	10 36.0	3 54.9	0 55.4	6 53.8
31 Tu	4 34 34	9 42 39	17 40 53	23 49 59	23 26.2	25 24.4	18 55.5	15 02.5	22 50.6	29 09.0	10 34.7	3 56.7	0 55.5	6 52.5

LONGITUDE — June 2011

Day	Sid.Time	☉	0 hr ☽	Noon ☽	True ☊	☿	♀	♂	⚳	♃	♄	♅	♆	♇
1 W	4 38 31	10♊40 12	0♊02 00	6♊17 06	23♐25.0	27♉21.0	20♉08.5	15♉46.6	23♓05.5	29♈21.6	10♎33.5	3♈58.5	0♓55.6	6♑51.2
2 Th	4 42 28	11 37 43	12 35 23	18 56 57	23D 24.5	29 19.8	21 21.5	16 30.6	23 20.2	29 34.2	10R 32.4	4 00.3	0R 55.6	6R 49.9
3 F	4 46 24	12 35 14	25 21 52	1♋50 09	23 24.6	1♊20.5	22 34.5	17 14.6	23 34.7	29 46.6	10 31.4	4 02.0	0 55.6	6 48.5
4 Sa	4 50 21	13 32 43	8♋21 51	14 56 56	23 25.1	3 23.2	23 47.5	17 58.5	23 49.0	29 59.0	10 30.4	4 03.7	0 55.6	6 47.2
5 Su	4 54 17	14 30 11	21 35 25	28 17 16	23 25.9	5 27.7	25 00.5	18 42.4	24 03.2	0♉11.3	10 29.6	4 05.4	0 55.6	6 45.8
6 M	4 58 14	15 27 38	5♌02 27	11♌50 54	23 26.7	7 33.9	26 13.6	19 26.2	24 17.1	0 23.5	10 28.9	4 07.0	0 55.5	6 44.4
7 Tu	5 02 10	16 25 04	18 42 35	25 37 23	23 27.3	9 41.6	27 26.6	20 10.0	24 30.8	0 35.7	10 28.3	4 08.5	0 55.4	6 43.0
8 W	5 06 07	17 22 28	2♍35 13	9♍35 55	23R 27.6	11 50.6	28 39.7	20 53.7	24 44.4	0 47.8	10 27.7	4 10.0	0 55.2	6 41.6
9 Th	5 10 03	18 19 51	16 39 19	23 45 12	23 27.6	14 00.8	29 52.7	21 37.3	24 57.7	0 59.7	10 27.3	4 11.5	0 55.0	6 40.2
10 F	5 14 00	19 17 14	0♎53 16	8♎03 12	23 27.4	16 11.8	1♊05.8	22 20.9	25 10.9	1 11.7	10 27.0	4 12.9	0 54.8	6 38.7
11 Sa	5 17 57	20 14 35	15 14 37	22 27 03	23 27.1	18 23.4	2 18.9	23 04.4	25 23.8	1 23.5	10 26.8	4 14.3	0 54.5	6 37.3
12 Su	5 21 53	21 11 55	29 40 02	6♏52 59	23 26.8	20 35.4	3 32.0	23 47.9	25 36.6	1 35.2	10D 26.7	4 15.6	0 54.3	6 35.8
13 M	5 25 50	22 09 14	14♏05 21	21 16 32	23 26.7	22 47.4	4 45.1	24 31.3	25 49.1	1 46.9	10 26.7	4 16.9	0 54.0	6 34.4
14 Tu	5 29 46	23 06 33	28 25 55	5♐32 54	23D 26.6	24 59.3	5 58.2	25 14.6	26 01.4	1 58.4	10 26.7	4 18.1	0 53.6	6 32.9
15 W	5 33 43	24 03 50	12♐36 55	19 37 27	23R 26.6	27 10.6	7 11.3	25 57.9	26 13.5	2 09.9	10 26.9	4 19.3	0 53.2	6 31.4
16 Th	5 37 39	25 01 07	26 34 02	3♑26 16	23 26.6	29 21.3	8 24.4	26 41.1	26 25.4	2 21.3	10 27.2	4 20.5	0 52.8	6 29.9
17 F	5 41 36	25 58 24	10♑13 51	16 56 33	23 26.5	1♋31.0	9 37.6	27 24.3	26 37.0	2 32.6	10 27.6	4 21.6	0 52.4	6 28.4
18 Sa	5 45 32	26 55 40	23 34 16	0♒06 56	23 26.2	3 39.5	10 50.7	28 07.4	26 48.5	2 43.8	10 28.1	4 22.7	0 51.9	6 26.9
19 Su	5 49 29	27 52 55	6♒34 38	12 57 30	23 25.7	5 46.6	12 03.9	28 50.5	26 59.7	2 55.0	10 28.7	4 23.7	0 51.4	6 25.4
20 M	5 53 26	28 50 10	19 15 46	25 29 44	23 25.1	7 52.2	13 17.1	29 33.5	27 10.6	3 06.0	10 29.3	4 24.6	0 50.9	6 23.9
21 Tu	5 57 22	29 47 25	1♓39 47	7♓46 18	23 24.5	9 56.1	14 30.3	0♊16.4	27 21.4	3 16.9	10 30.1	4 25.6	0 50.3	6 22.4
22 W	6 01 19	0♋44 40	13 49 48	19 50 45	23D 24.1	11 58.2	15 43.6	0 59.3	27 31.9	3 27.7	10 31.0	4 26.4	0 49.8	6 20.9
23 Th	6 05 15	1 41 54	25 49 44	1♈47 16	23 23.9	13 58.4	16 56.8	1 42.1	27 42.1	3 38.4	10 32.0	4 27.2	0 49.1	6 19.4
24 F	6 09 12	2 39 09	7♈43 57	13 40 21	23 24.1	15 56.6	18 10.1	2 24.9	27 52.1	3 49.1	10 33.1	4 28.0	0 48.5	6 17.9
25 Sa	6 13 08	3 36 23	19 37 02	25 34 36	23 24.7	17 52.8	19 23.3	3 07.6	28 01.8	3 59.6	10 34.3	4 28.7	0 47.8	6 16.3
26 Su	6 17 05	4 33 37	1♉33 35	7♉34 30	23 25.6	19 46.9	20 36.6	3 50.2	28 11.3	4 10.0	10 35.5	4 29.4	0 47.1	6 14.8
27 M	6 21 01	5 30 51	13 37 52	19 44 08	23 26.7	21 38.9	21 50.0	4 32.8	28 20.6	4 20.3	10 36.9	4 30.1	0 46.4	6 13.3
28 Tu	6 24 58	6 28 05	25 53 43	2♊06 58	23 27.8	23 28.8	23 03.3	5 15.3	28 29.5	4 30.5	10 38.4	4 30.6	0 45.6	6 11.7
29 W	6 28 55	7 25 19	8♊24 13	14 45 40	23R 28.5	25 16.5	24 16.6	5 57.8	28 38.2	4 40.6	10 40.0	4 31.2	0 44.8	6 10.2
30 Th	6 32 51	8 22 33	21 11 32	27 41 52	23 28.6	27 02.0	25 30.0	6 40.2	28 46.7	4 50.6	10 41.7	4 31.7	0 44.0	6 08.7

Astro Data (Dy Hr Mn)

☽0S 12 20:06
☽0N 26 0:01

♆R 3 7:27
☽0S 9 1:52
♃✶♆ 9 2:39
♄D 13 3:51
☽0N 22 7:50
♃⚺♅ 28 12:20

Planet Ingress (Dy Hr Mn)

♂ ♉ 11 7:03
♀ ♉ 15 22:12
☿ ♉ 15 23:18
☉ ♊ 21 9:21

☿ ♊ 2 20:02
♃ ♉ 4 13:56
♀ ♊ 9 14:23
☿ ♋ 16 19:09
♂ ♊ 21 2:50
☉ ♋ 21 17:16

Last Aspect Dy Hr Mn		☽ Ingress Dy Hr Mn	
1 15:20	♂ ☌	♉	2 5:58
3 6:51	☉ ☌	♊	4 17:09
6 20:12	♂ ✶	♋	7 2:32
9 6:52	♂ □	♌	9 9:35
11 4:52	♃ △	♍	11 13:59
13 2:52	☉ △	♎	13 15:56
15 16:01	☿ ☍	♏	15 16:31
17 11:09	☉ ☍	♐	17 17:22
19 14:17	♃ △	♑	19 20:16
21 21:04	♃ □	♒	22 2:32
24 7:40	♃ ✶	♓	24 12:24
25 18:15	☿ ✶	♈	27 0:36
29 10:28	♃ ☌	♉	29 13:02
31 15:37	☿ ☌	♊	31 23:56

Last Aspect Dy Hr Mn		☽ Ingress Dy Hr Mn	
3 8:08	♃ ✶	♋	3 8:36
5 5:33	♀ ✶	♌	5 15:03
7 15:27	♀ □	♍	7 19:33
9 8:13	☉ △	♎	9 22:31
11 8:04	☉ △	♏	12 0:33
13 17:43	♂ ☍	♐	14 2:38
16 3:31	☿ ☍	♑	16 5:59
18 8:07	☉ △	♒	18 11:47
20 20:23	♂ □	♓	20 20:45
22 2:51	☉ □	♈	23 8:24
24 22:07	♀ ✶	♉	25 20:53
27 16:24	☿ ✶	♊	28 7:56
30 7:33	♀ ☌	♋	30 16:13

☽ Phases & Eclipses (Dy Hr Mn)

3 6:51 ● 12♉31
10 20:33 ☽ 19♌51
17 11:09 ○ 26♏13
24 18:52 ☾ 3♓16

1 21:03 ● 11♊02
1 21:16:07 ● P 0.601
9 2:11 ☽ 17♍56
15 20:14 ○ 24♐23
15 20:13 ● T 1.700
23 11:48 ☾ 1♈41

Astro Data

1 May 2011
Julian Day # 40663
SVP 5♓05'50"
GC 26♐59.9 ⚴ 13♒13.0
Eris 22♈00.9 ⚵ 14♍00.1R
⚷ 4♓46.8 ⚶ 10♒41.2
☽ Mean ☊ 25♐55.5

1 June 2011
Julian Day # 40694
SVP 5♓05'45"
GC 26♐59.9 ⚴ 15♒49.7R
Eris 22♈18.0 ⚵ 16♍29.5
⚷ 5♓27.5 ⚶ 18♒07.6
☽ Mean ☊ 24♐17.0

July 2011 LONGITUDE

Day	Sid.Time	☉	0 hr ☽	Noon ☽	True ☊	☿	♀	♂	⚳	♃	♄	♅	♆	♇
1 F	6 36 48	9♋19 47	4♋16 43	10♋56 01	23♐28.0	28♋45.4	26♊43.4	7♊22.5	28♓54.8	5♉00.4	10♎43.4	4♈32.1	0♓43.2	6♑07.2
2 Sa	6 40 44	10 17 01	17 39 37	24 27 18	23R 26.5	0♌26.7	27 56.8	8 04.8	29 02.7	5 10.2	10 45.3	4 32.5	0R 42.3	6R 05.6
3 Su	6 44 41	11 14 15	1♌18 49	8♌13 49	23 24.5	2 05.7	29 10.2	8 47.0	29 10.3	5 19.8	10 47.3	4 32.8	0 41.4	6 04.1
4 M	6 48 37	12 11 28	15 11 55	22 12 41	23 22.0	3 42.6	0♋23.6	9 29.2	29 17.6	5 29.3	10 49.3	4 33.1	0 40.5	6 02.6
5 Tu	6 52 34	13 08 41	29 15 42	6♍20 30	23 19.6	5 17.2	1 37.1	10 11.3	29 24.6	5 38.7	10 51.5	4 33.4	0 39.5	6 01.1
6 W	6 56 30	14 05 54	13♍26 39	20 33 42	23 17.6	6 49.7	2 50.5	10 53.3	29 31.3	5 48.0	10 53.7	4 33.6	0 38.5	5 59.6
7 Th	7 00 27	15 03 06	27 41 14	4♎48 52	23D 16.4	8 19.9	4 04.0	11 35.3	29 37.7	5 57.1	10 56.1	4 33.7	0 37.5	5 58.1
8 F	7 04 24	16 00 18	11♎56 15	19 03 05	23 16.2	9 47.9	5 17.4	12 17.2	29 43.9	6 06.1	10 58.5	4 33.8	0 36.5	5 56.5
9 Sa	7 08 20	16 57 30	26 09 02	3♏13 52	23 16.8	11 13.7	6 30.9	12 59.0	29 49.7	6 15.0	11 01.1	4R 33.9	0 35.5	5 55.1
10 Su	7 12 17	17 54 42	10♏17 20	17 19 12	23 18.1	12 37.1	7 44.5	13 40.8	29 55.2	6 23.8	11 03.7	4 33.9	0 34.4	5 53.6
11 M	7 16 13	18 51 54	24 19 15	1♐17 16	23 19.5	13 58.3	8 58.0	14 22.5	0♈00.4	6 32.4	11 06.4	4 33.8	0 33.3	5 52.1
12 Tu	7 20 10	19 49 06	8♐13 02	15 06 20	23R 20.5	15 17.1	10 11.5	15 04.1	0 05.3	6 40.9	11 09.2	4 33.7	0 32.2	5 50.6
13 W	7 24 06	20 46 18	21 56 58	28 44 44	23 20.6	16 33.4	11 25.1	15 45.7	0 09.9	6 49.3	11 12.1	4 33.6	0 31.0	5 49.1
14 Th	7 28 03	21 43 30	5♑29 23	12♑10 46	23 19.4	17 47.3	12 38.7	16 27.2	0 14.2	6 57.5	11 15.1	4 33.4	0 29.8	5 47.7
15 F	7 32 00	22 40 42	18 48 41	25 22 59	23 16.8	18 58.7	13 52.3	17 08.7	0 18.1	7 05.6	11 18.2	4 33.2	0 28.7	5 46.2
16 Sa	7 35 56	23 37 55	1♒53 35	8♒20 22	23 12.9	20 07.5	15 05.9	17 50.1	0 21.8	7 13.6	11 21.3	4 32.9	0 27.4	5 44.8
17 Su	7 39 53	24 35 07	14 43 21	21 02 33	23 08.0	21 13.6	16 19.5	18 31.4	0 25.1	7 21.4	11 24.6	4 32.5	0 26.2	5 43.4
18 M	7 43 49	25 32 21	27 18 03	3♓30 01	23 02.7	22 16.9	17 33.2	19 12.7	0 28.1	7 29.1	11 27.9	4 32.2	0 25.0	5 41.9
19 Tu	7 47 46	26 29 35	9♓38 40	15 44 15	22 57.5	23 17.4	18 46.8	19 53.9	0 30.7	7 36.6	11 31.3	4 31.7	0 23.7	5 40.5
20 W	7 51 42	27 26 49	21 47 08	27 47 41	22 53.1	24 15.0	20 00.5	20 35.0	0 33.0	7 44.0	11 34.8	4 31.2	0 22.4	5 39.1
21 Th	7 55 39	28 24 05	3♈46 20	9♈43 35	22 49.8	25 09.4	21 14.2	21 16.1	0 35.0	7 51.2	11 38.4	4 30.7	0 21.1	5 37.8
22 F	7 59 35	29 21 21	15 39 58	21 36 01	22D 48.1	26 00.7	22 28.0	21 57.1	0 36.6	7 58.3	11 42.1	4 30.1	0 19.7	5 36.4
23 Sa	8 03 32	0♌18 38	27 32 21	3♉29 32	22 47.8	26 48.7	23 41.7	22 38.1	0 37.8	8 05.3	11 45.9	4 29.5	0 18.4	5 35.0
24 Su	8 07 29	1 15 55	9♉28 13	15 29 00	22 48.7	27 33.2	24 55.5	23 19.0	0 38.8	8 12.0	11 49.7	4 28.9	0 17.0	5 33.7
25 M	8 11 25	2 13 14	21 32 30	27 39 18	22 50.1	28 14.1	26 09.3	23 59.8	0 39.3	8 18.7	11 53.6	4 28.2	0 15.6	5 32.3
26 Tu	8 15 22	3 10 33	3♊49 59	10♊05 03	22 51.6	28 51.2	27 23.1	24 40.6	0R 39.6	8 25.2	11 57.6	4 27.4	0 14.2	5 31.0
27 W	8 19 18	4 07 54	16 24 59	22 50 11	22R 52.2	29 24.4	28 37.0	25 21.3	0 39.4	8 31.5	12 01.7	4 26.6	0 12.8	5 29.7
28 Th	8 23 15	5 05 15	29 20 56	5♋57 27	22 51.4	29 53.4	29 50.8	26 02.0	0 38.9	8 37.6	12 05.9	4 25.8	0 11.4	5 28.5
29 F	8 27 11	6 02 38	12♋39 50	19 28 02	22 48.8	0♍18.2	1♌04.7	26 42.5	0 38.1	8 43.6	12 10.1	4 24.9	0 09.9	5 27.2
30 Sa	8 31 08	7 00 01	26 21 53	3♌21 03	22 44.2	0 38.5	2 18.6	27 23.1	0 36.9	8 49.5	12 14.4	4 23.9	0 08.5	5 25.9
31 Su	8 35 04	7 57 24	10♌25 06	17 33 26	22 38.1	0 54.2	3 32.5	28 03.5	0 35.3	8 55.1	12 18.8	4 23.0	0 07.0	5 24.7

August 2011 LONGITUDE

Day	Sid.Time	☉	0 hr ☽	Noon ☽	True ☊	☿	♀	♂	⚳	♃	♄	♅	♆	♇
1 M	8 39 01	8♌54 49	24♌45 22	2♍00 07	22♐31.1	1♍05.0	4♌46.5	28♊43.9	0♈33.3	9♉00.6	12♎23.3	4♈21.9	0♓05.5	5♑23.5
2 Tu	8 42 58	9 52 14	9♍16 49	16 34 39	22R 24.0	1R 11.0	6 00.4	29 24.2	0R 31.0	9 06.0	12 27.8	4R 20.9	0R 04.0	5R 22.3
3 W	8 46 54	10 49 40	23 52 44	1♎10 16	22 17.8	1 11.8	7 14.4	0♋04.4	0 28.4	9 11.1	12 32.4	4 19.8	0 02.5	5 21.1
4 Th	8 50 51	11 47 06	8♎26 32	15 40 53	22 13.3	1 07.4	8 28.4	0 44.6	0 25.4	9 16.1	12 37.1	4 18.6	0 01.0	5 19.9
5 F	8 54 47	12 44 34	22 52 47	0♏01 49	22D 10.8	0 57.8	9 42.4	1 24.7	0 22.0	9 20.9	12 41.9	4 17.4	29♒59.4	5 18.8
6 Sa	8 58 44	13 42 02	7♏07 41	14 10 12	22 10.1	0 42.9	10 56.4	2 04.7	0 18.2	9 25.6	12 46.7	4 16.2	29 57.9	5 17.7
7 Su	9 02 40	14 39 30	21 09 14	28 04 45	22 10.6	0 22.7	12 10.4	2 44.7	0 14.1	9 30.0	12 51.6	4 14.9	29 56.3	5 16.6
8 M	9 06 37	15 37 00	4♐56 49	11♐45 27	22R 11.6	29♌57.4	13 24.5	3 24.6	0 09.7	9 34.3	12 56.6	4 13.6	29 54.7	5 15.5
9 Tu	9 10 33	16 34 30	18 30 47	25 12 54	22 11.9	29 27.3	14 38.5	4 04.4	0 04.9	9 38.4	13 01.6	4 12.2	29 53.2	5 14.5
10 W	9 14 30	17 32 01	1♑51 54	8♑27 52	22 10.6	28 52.4	15 52.6	4 44.2	29♓59.7	9 42.4	13 06.8	4 10.8	29 51.6	5 13.4
11 Th	9 18 27	18 29 33	15 00 53	21 31 01	22 07.2	28 13.4	17 06.7	5 23.9	29 54.2	9 46.1	13 11.9	4 09.4	29 50.0	5 12.4
12 F	9 22 23	19 27 06	27 58 16	4♒22 41	22 01.2	27 30.6	18 20.8	6 03.5	29 48.3	9 49.7	13 17.2	4 07.9	29 48.4	5 11.4
13 Sa	9 26 20	20 24 40	10♒44 16	17 03 01	21 52.9	26 44.8	19 34.9	6 43.0	29 42.1	9 53.1	13 22.5	4 06.4	29 46.8	5 10.4
14 Su	9 30 16	21 22 15	23 18 58	29 32 08	21 42.9	25 56.5	20 49.1	7 22.5	29 35.6	9 56.3	13 27.8	4 04.9	29 45.2	5 09.5
15 M	9 34 13	22 19 51	5♓42 34	11♓50 22	21 31.9	25 06.7	22 03.2	8 01.9	29 28.7	9 59.3	13 33.2	4 03.3	29 43.5	5 08.6
16 Tu	9 38 09	23 17 29	17 55 37	23 58 32	21 21.0	24 16.3	23 17.4	8 41.3	29 21.4	10 02.1	13 38.7	4 01.7	29 41.9	5 07.7
17 W	9 42 06	24 15 08	29 59 17	5♈58 10	21 11.1	23 26.1	24 31.6	9 20.6	29 13.9	10 04.8	13 44.3	4 00.0	29 40.3	5 06.8
18 Th	9 46 02	25 12 48	11♈55 29	17 51 38	21 03.1	22 37.2	25 45.8	9 59.8	29 06.0	10 07.2	13 49.9	3 58.3	29 38.6	5 06.0
19 F	9 49 59	26 10 30	23 47 01	29 42 08	20 57.4	21 50.7	27 00.0	10 39.0	28 57.8	10 09.5	13 55.5	3 56.6	29 37.0	5 05.1
20 Sa	9 53 55	27 08 14	5♉37 29	11♉33 40	20 54.0	21 07.4	28 14.2	11 18.0	28 49.2	10 11.5	14 01.3	3 54.8	29 35.4	5 04.3
21 Su	9 57 52	28 05 59	17 31 16	23 30 54	20D 52.7	20 28.3	29 28.5	11 57.0	28 40.4	10 13.4	14 07.1	3 53.0	29 33.7	5 03.6
22 M	10 01 49	29 03 46	29 33 14	5♊38 56	20 52.8	19 54.2	0♍42.8	12 36.0	28 31.2	10 15.1	14 12.9	3 51.2	29 32.1	5 02.8
23 Tu	10 05 45	0♍01 35	11♊48 39	18 03 01	20R 53.1	19 26.0	1 57.1	13 14.9	28 21.8	10 16.6	14 18.8	3 49.4	29 30.4	5 02.1
24 W	10 09 42	0 59 25	24 22 39	0♋48 06	20 52.8	19 04.3	3 11.4	13 53.7	28 12.0	10 17.8	14 24.7	3 47.5	29 28.8	5 01.4
25 Th	10 13 38	1 57 17	7♋19 49	13 58 13	20 50.8	18 49.7	4 25.7	14 32.4	28 02.0	10 18.9	14 30.7	3 45.6	29 27.2	5 00.7
26 F	10 17 35	2 55 11	20 43 32	27 35 52	20 46.3	18D 42.5	5 40.0	15 11.1	27 51.7	10 19.8	14 36.8	3 43.6	29 25.5	5 00.1
27 Sa	10 21 31	3 53 07	4♌35 10	11♌41 09	20 39.4	18 43.2	6 54.4	15 49.7	27 41.1	10 20.5	14 42.9	3 41.6	29 23.9	4 59.5
28 Su	10 25 28	4 51 04	18 53 22	26 11 10	20 30.2	18 51.8	8 08.8	16 28.2	27 30.3	10 21.0	14 49.0	3 39.6	29 22.3	4 58.9
29 M	10 29 25	5 49 03	3♍33 41	10♍59 56	20 19.6	19 08.7	9 23.2	17 06.6	27 19.2	10R 21.2	14 55.2	3 37.6	29 20.6	4 58.3
30 Tu	10 33 21	6 47 03	18 28 46	25 59 00	20 08.9	19 33.7	10 37.5	17 45.0	27 07.8	10 21.3	15 01.5	3 35.6	29 19.0	4 57.8
31 W	10 37 18	7 45 04	3♎29 22	10♎58 44	19 59.2	20 06.8	11 52.0	18 23.2	26 56.3	10 21.2	15 07.8	3 33.5	29 17.4	4 57.3

Astro Data	Dy Hr Mn
☽0S	6 7:24
♃△♇	7 14:06
♅R	10 0:35
☽0N	19 16:24
⚳R	26 14:54
☽0S	2 14:30
☿R	3 3:49
☽0N	16 0:38
♄⚼♆	25 0:49
☿D	26 22:04
☽0S	29 23:45
♃R	30 9:17

Planet Ingress	Dy Hr Mn
☿ ♌	2 5:38
♀ ♋	4 4:17
⚳ ♈	11 10:00
☉ ♌	23 4:12
♀ ♌	28 14:59
☿ ♍	28 17:59
♂ ♋	3 9:22
♆ ♒R	5 2:54
☿ ♌R	8 9:46
⚳ ♓R	10 10:38
♀ ♍	21 22:11
☉ ♍	23 11:21

Last Aspect Dy Hr Mn		☽ Ingress	Dy Hr Mn
1 11:37	♄ □	♌	2 21:43
3 16:25	♄ ⚹	♍	5 1:15
6 0:19	☉ ⚹	♎	7 3:54
8 6:29	☉ □	♏	9 6:31
10 13:05	☉ △	♐	11 9:47
12 12:21	☿ △	♑	13 14:14
15 6:40	☉ ☍	♒	15 20:30
17 12:23	☿ ☍	♓	18 5:13
20 11:15	☉ △	♈	20 16:25
22 21:34	☿ △	♉	23 4:58
25 13:12	☿ □	♊	25 16:34
28 0:35	☿ ⚹	♋	28 1:11
28 23:03	♄ □	♌	30 6:16

Last Aspect Dy Hr Mn		☽ Ingress	Dy Hr Mn
1 6:20	♂ ⚹	♍	1 8:41
1 23:38	♃ △	♎	3 10:04
5 11:56	♆ △	♏	5 11:57
7 15:14	♆ □	♐	7 15:21
9 20:24	♆ ⚹	♑	9 20:38
10 20:34	♄ □	♒	12 3:47
14 12:25	♆ ☌	♓	14 12:54
15 8:21	♃ ⚹	♈	17 0:01
19 11:50	♆ ⚹	♉	19 12:36
21 23:59	♆ □	♊	22 0:53
24 9:33	♆ △	♋	24 10:31
25 13:04	♂ ☌	♌	26 16:09
28 17:11	♆ ☍	♍	28 18:13
29 22:15	♂ ⚹	♎	30 18:25

☽ Phases & Eclipses Dy Hr Mn		
1 8:54	●	9♋12
1 8:38:24	●	P 0.097
8 6:29	☽	15♎47
15 6:40	○	22♑28
23 5:02	☾	0♉02
30 18:40	●	7♌16
6 11:08	☽	13♏40
13 18:57	○	20♒41
21 21:54	☾	28♉30
29 3:04	●	5♍27

Astro Data

1 July 2011
Julian Day # 40724
SVP 5♓05'39"
GC 27♐00.0 ⚴ 12♒53.7R
Eris 22♈27.8 ⚵ 22♍40.3
⚷ 5♓14.4R ⚶ 19♒16.2R
☽ Mean ☊ 22♐41.7

1 August 2011
Julian Day # 40755
SVP 5♓05'34"
GC 27♐00.1 ⚴ 5♒20.3R
Eris 22♈28.6R ⚵ 1♎22.2
⚷ 4♓12.6R ⚶ 13♒39.1R
☽ Mean ☊ 21♐03.2

LONGITUDE — September 2011

Day	Sid.Time	☉	0 hr ☽	Noon ☽	True ☊	☿	♀	♂	⚳	♃	♄	♅	♆	♇
1 Th	10 41 14	8♍43 07	18♎25 57	25♎50 06	19♐51.7	20♌47.9	13♍06.4	19♋01.4	26♓44.5	10♉20.9	15♎14.1	3♈31.4	29♒15.8	4♑56.8
2 F	10 45 11	9 41 12	3♏10 20	10♏26 04	19R 46.8	21 36.6	14 20.8	19 39.6	26R 32.6	10R 20.4	15 20.5	3R 29.2	29R 14.1	4R 56.4
3 Sa	10 49 07	10 39 18	17 36 49	24 42 21	19 44.4	22 32.9	15 35.2	20 17.6	26 20.4	10 19.6	15 27.0	3 27.1	29 12.5	4 56.0
4 Su	10 53 04	11 37 25	1♐42 33	8♐37 25	19 43.7	23 36.2	16 49.7	20 55.6	26 08.1	10 18.7	15 33.4	3 24.9	29 10.9	4 55.6
5 M	10 57 00	12 35 34	15 27 07	22 11 51	19 43.7	24 46.2	18 04.1	21 33.5	25 55.6	10 17.6	15 40.0	3 22.7	29 09.4	4 55.2
6 Tu	11 00 57	13 33 45	28 51 53	5♑27 33	19 43.1	26 02.4	19 18.6	22 11.3	25 42.9	10 16.3	15 46.5	3 20.5	29 07.8	4 54.9
7 W	11 04 53	14 31 56	11♑59 09	18 27 02	19 40.8	27 24.4	20 33.0	22 49.0	25 30.1	10 14.7	15 53.1	3 18.3	29 06.2	4 54.6
8 Th	11 08 50	15 30 09	24 51 28	1♒12 46	19 35.8	28 51.6	21 47.5	23 26.7	25 17.2	10 13.0	15 59.7	3 16.0	29 04.6	4 54.3
9 F	11 12 47	16 28 24	7♒31 11	13 46 55	19 28.0	0♍23.5	23 02.0	24 04.2	25 04.1	10 11.1	16 06.4	3 13.8	29 03.1	4 54.1
10 Sa	11 16 43	17 26 40	20 00 11	26 11 08	19 17.3	1 59.5	24 16.5	24 41.7	24 51.0	10 09.0	16 13.1	3 11.5	29 01.6	4 53.9
11 Su	11 20 40	18 24 58	2♓19 53	8♓26 35	19 04.6	3 39.2	25 31.0	25 19.1	24 37.8	10 06.7	16 19.9	3 09.2	29 00.0	4 53.7
12 M	11 24 36	19 23 18	14 31 20	20 34 14	18 50.6	5 21.9	26 45.4	25 56.5	24 24.5	10 04.1	16 26.6	3 06.9	28 58.5	4 53.6
13 Tu	11 28 33	20 21 40	26 35 24	2♈34 58	18 36.7	7 07.2	28 00.0	26 33.7	24 11.1	10 01.4	16 33.4	3 04.5	28 57.0	4 53.5
14 W	11 32 29	21 20 03	8♈33 06	14 29 58	18 23.9	8 54.6	29 14.5	27 10.9	23 57.7	9 58.5	16 40.3	3 02.2	28 55.5	4 53.4
15 Th	11 36 26	22 18 28	20 25 49	26 20 55	18 13.2	10 43.7	0♎29.0	27 48.0	23 44.2	9 55.5	16 47.2	2 59.9	28 54.0	4 53.3
16 F	11 40 22	23 16 56	2♉15 34	8♉10 09	18 05.2	12 34.0	1 43.5	28 25.0	23 30.8	9 52.2	16 54.1	2 57.5	28 52.6	4D 53.3
17 Sa	11 44 19	24 15 26	14 05 04	20 00 48	18 00.0	14 25.3	2 58.0	29 01.9	23 17.3	9 48.7	17 01.0	2 55.1	28 51.1	4 53.3
18 Su	11 48 16	25 13 57	25 57 52	1♊56 49	17 57.4	16 17.2	4 12.6	29 38.8	23 03.8	9 45.0	17 08.0	2 52.7	28 49.7	4 53.3
19 M	11 52 12	26 12 31	7♊58 14	14 02 46	17D 56.6	18 09.3	5 27.1	0♌15.5	22 50.4	9 41.2	17 15.0	2 50.4	28 48.3	4 53.4
20 Tu	11 56 09	27 11 07	20 11 03	26 23 44	17R 56.7	20 01.6	6 41.7	0 52.2	22 37.0	9 37.2	17 22.0	2 48.0	28 46.9	4 53.5
21 W	12 00 05	28 09 46	2♋41 29	9♋04 54	17 56.3	21 53.7	7 56.3	1 28.8	22 23.7	9 33.0	17 29.0	2 45.6	28 45.5	4 53.6
22 Th	12 04 02	29 08 26	15 34 36	22 11 03	17 54.5	23 45.6	9 10.8	2 05.3	22 10.4	9 28.6	17 36.1	2 43.2	28 44.1	4 53.8
23 F	12 07 58	0♎07 09	28 54 41	5♌45 46	17 50.5	25 37.0	10 25.4	2 41.7	21 57.2	9 24.0	17 43.2	2 40.8	28 42.8	4 54.0
24 Sa	12 11 55	1 05 54	12♌44 26	19 50 35	17 43.9	27 27.9	11 40.0	3 18.1	21 44.1	9 19.3	17 50.3	2 38.3	28 41.4	4 54.2
25 Su	12 15 51	2 04 41	27 03 57	4♍24 00	17 35.0	29 18.2	12 54.6	3 54.3	21 31.1	9 14.3	17 57.4	2 35.9	28 40.1	4 54.5
26 M	12 19 48	3 03 31	11♍49 59	19 20 57	17 24.6	1♎07.7	14 09.2	4 30.4	21 18.3	9 09.2	18 04.6	2 33.5	28 38.8	4 54.8
27 Tu	12 23 45	4 02 22	26 55 42	4♎32 55	17 13.9	2 56.5	15 23.8	5 06.5	21 05.5	9 04.0	18 11.8	2 31.1	28 37.6	4 55.1
28 W	12 27 41	5 01 15	12♎11 14	19 49 11	17 04.2	4 44.5	16 38.4	5 42.4	20 53.0	8 58.6	18 19.0	2 28.7	28 36.3	4 55.4
29 Th	12 31 38	6 00 10	27 25 25	4♏58 39	16 56.5	6 31.7	17 53.0	6 18.3	20 40.6	8 53.0	18 26.2	2 26.3	28 35.1	4 55.8
30 F	12 35 34	6 59 08	12♏27 46	19 51 52	16 51.4	8 18.1	19 07.7	6 54.0	20 28.4	8 47.2	18 33.4	2 23.9	28 33.9	4 56.2

LONGITUDE — October 2011

Day	Sid.Time	☉	0 hr ☽	Noon ☽	True ☊	☿	♀	♂	⚳	♃	♄	♅	♆	♇
1 Sa	12 39 31	7♎58 07	27♏10 14	4♐22 23	16♐49.0	10♎03.5	20♎22.3	7♌29.7	20♓16.3	8♉41.3	18♎40.6	2♈21.5	28♒32.7	4♑56.7
2 Su	12 43 27	8 57 08	11♐28 03	18 27 08	16D 48.4	11 48.1	21 36.9	8 05.2	20R 04.5	8R 35.3	18 47.9	2R 19.1	28R 31.5	4 57.2
3 M	12 47 24	9 56 10	25 19 43	2♑05 59	16R 48.8	13 31.9	22 51.5	8 40.7	19 52.9	8 29.1	18 55.2	2 16.7	28 30.4	4 57.7
4 Tu	12 51 20	10 55 14	8♑46 14	15 20 53	16 48.9	15 14.8	24 06.1	9 16.0	19 41.6	8 22.8	19 02.4	2 14.3	28 29.3	4 58.2
5 W	12 55 17	11 54 20	21 50 19	28 15 00	16 47.6	16 56.8	25 20.7	9 51.3	19 30.5	8 16.3	19 09.7	2 11.9	28 28.2	4 58.8
6 Th	12 59 14	12 53 28	4♒35 24	10♒51 58	16 44.1	18 38.1	26 35.4	10 26.4	19 19.6	8 09.8	19 17.0	2 09.6	28 27.1	4 59.4
7 F	13 03 10	13 52 38	17 05 07	23 15 16	16 38.0	20 18.4	27 50.0	11 01.4	19 09.0	8 03.0	19 24.3	2 07.2	28 26.1	5 00.0
8 Sa	13 07 07	14 51 49	29 22 47	5♓28 01	16 29.5	21 58.0	29 04.6	11 36.4	18 58.6	7 56.2	19 31.6	2 04.9	28 25.1	5 00.7
9 Su	13 11 03	15 51 02	11♓31 15	17 32 47	16 19.0	23 36.8	0♏19.2	12 11.2	18 48.6	7 49.3	19 38.9	2 02.6	28 24.1	5 01.4
10 M	13 15 00	16 50 17	23 32 50	29 31 37	16 07.5	25 14.9	1 33.8	12 45.9	18 38.8	7 42.2	19 46.3	2 00.3	28 23.1	5 02.1
11 Tu	13 18 56	17 49 34	5♈29 19	11♈26 09	15 56.0	26 52.2	2 48.4	13 20.5	18 29.3	7 35.0	19 53.6	1 58.0	28 22.2	5 02.8
12 W	13 22 53	18 48 53	17 22 17	23 17 53	15 45.4	28 28.7	4 03.0	13 55.0	18 20.1	7 27.7	20 00.9	1 55.7	28 21.3	5 03.6
13 Th	13 26 49	19 48 14	29 13 10	5♉08 19	15 36.7	0♏04.5	5 17.6	14 29.4	18 11.3	7 20.4	20 08.2	1 53.4	28 20.4	5 04.4
14 F	13 30 46	20 47 38	11♉03 35	16 59 14	15 30.2	1 39.7	6 32.2	15 03.7	18 02.7	7 12.9	20 15.6	1 51.2	28 19.6	5 05.3
15 Sa	13 34 42	21 47 03	22 55 34	28 52 55	15 26.3	3 14.1	7 46.8	15 37.8	17 54.5	7 05.3	20 22.9	1 48.9	28 18.7	5 06.1
16 Su	13 38 39	22 46 31	4♊51 40	10♊52 14	15D 24.7	4 47.9	9 01.4	16 11.9	17 46.6	6 57.7	20 30.2	1 46.7	28 17.9	5 07.0
17 M	13 42 36	23 46 01	16 55 05	23 00 41	15 24.9	6 21.0	10 16.0	16 45.8	17 39.0	6 50.0	20 37.5	1 44.5	28 17.2	5 08.0
18 Tu	13 46 32	24 45 33	29 09 36	5♋22 21	15 26.0	7 53.5	11 30.6	17 19.7	17 31.8	6 42.2	20 44.9	1 42.4	28 16.4	5 08.9
19 W	13 50 29	25 45 08	11♋39 30	18 01 38	15R 27.0	9 25.4	12 45.2	17 53.4	17 24.9	6 34.4	20 52.2	1 40.2	28 15.7	5 09.9
20 Th	13 54 25	26 44 44	24 29 16	1♌02 55	15 27.2	10 56.6	13 59.9	18 26.9	17 18.4	6 26.5	20 59.5	1 38.1	28 15.1	5 10.9
21 F	13 58 22	27 44 24	7♌43 02	14 29 58	15 25.8	12 27.2	15 14.5	19 00.4	17 12.3	6 18.5	21 06.8	1 36.0	28 14.4	5 12.0
22 Sa	14 02 18	28 44 05	21 23 58	28 25 07	15 22.5	13 57.2	16 29.1	19 33.7	17 06.4	6 10.5	21 14.1	1 33.9	28 13.8	5 13.1
23 Su	14 06 15	29 43 48	5♍33 22	12♍48 25	15 17.3	15 26.6	17 43.7	20 06.9	17 01.0	6 02.5	21 21.4	1 31.9	28 13.2	5 14.2
24 M	14 10 11	0♏43 34	20 09 47	27 36 46	15 10.8	16 55.3	18 58.3	20 40.0	16 55.9	5 54.4	21 28.6	1 29.9	28 12.7	5 15.3
25 Tu	14 14 08	1 43 22	5♎08 28	12♎43 45	15 04.0	18 23.4	20 12.9	21 12.9	16 51.2	5 46.3	21 35.9	1 27.9	28 12.1	5 16.4
26 W	14 18 05	2 43 12	20 21 24	28 00 02	14 57.7	19 50.9	21 27.5	21 45.7	16 46.9	5 38.1	21 43.2	1 25.9	28 11.6	5 17.6
27 Th	14 22 01	3 43 04	5♏38 18	13♏14 49	14 52.8	21 17.7	22 42.1	22 18.3	16 42.9	5 30.0	21 50.4	1 24.0	28 11.2	5 18.8
28 F	14 25 58	4 42 58	20 48 19	28 17 39	14 49.8	22 43.9	23 56.8	22 50.8	16 39.3	5 21.8	21 57.6	1 22.1	28 10.8	5 20.1
29 Sa	14 29 54	5 42 54	5♐41 53	13♐00 14	14D 48.7	24 09.3	25 11.4	23 23.2	16 36.1	5 13.7	22 04.8	1 20.2	28 10.4	5 21.3
30 Su	14 33 51	6 42 52	20 12 09	27 17 16	14 49.2	25 34.0	26 26.0	23 55.4	16 33.3	5 05.5	22 12.0	1 18.3	28 10.0	5 22.6
31 M	14 37 47	7 42 51	4♑15 25	11♑06 38	14 50.6	26 58.0	27 40.6	24 27.5	16 30.8	4 57.4	22 19.2	1 16.5	28 09.7	5 23.9

Astro Data	Planet Ingress	Last Aspect	☽ Ingress	Last Aspect	☽ Ingress	☽ Phases & Eclipses	Astro Data
Dy Hr Mn	Dy Hr Mn	Dy Hr Mn	Dy Hr Mn	Dy Hr Mn	Dy Hr Mn	Dy Hr Mn	1 September 2011
☽0N 12 7:38	☿ ♍ 9 5:58	1 17:35 ♆ △	♏ 1 18:48	1 2:17 ♆ □	♐ 1 4:42	4 17:39 ☽ 11♐51	Julian Day # 40786
♇D 16 18:25	♀ ♎ 15 2:40	3 19:41 ♆ □	♐ 3 21:03	3 5:37 ♆ ✶	♑ 3 8:16	12 9:27 ○ 19♓17	SVP 5♓05'31"
♀0S 17 11:15	♂ ♌ 19 1:51	6 0:30 ♆ ✶	♑ 6 2:03	5 5:58 ♀ □	♒ 5 15:18	20 13:39 ☾ 27♊15	GC 27♐00.1 ⚴ 28♑43.6R
☉0S 23 9:04	☉ ♎ 23 9:05	7 20:35 ♂ ☍	♒ 8 9:42	7 22:08 ♆ ☌	♓ 8 1:13	27 11:09 ● 4♎00	Eris 22♈19.8R ⚵ 11♎23.4
☽0S 26 10:19	☿ ♎ 25 21:09	10 17:32 ♆ ☌	♓ 10 19:26	8 16:51 ♃ ✶	♈ 10 12:57		⚷ 2♓44.3R ⚶ 7♒11.0R
☿0S 27 17:17		13 1:45 ♀ ☍	♈ 13 6:49	13 0:08 ☿ ☍	♉ 13 1:35	4 3:15 ☽ 10♑34	☽ Mean ☊ 19♐24.7
	♀ ♏ 9 5:50	15 17:10 ♆ ✶	♉ 15 19:25	15 10:51 ♆ □	♊ 15 14:15	12 2:06 ○ 18♈24	
☽0N 9 13:21	☿ ♏ 13 10:52	18 7:09 ♂ ✶	♊ 18 8:06	17 22:18 ♆ △	♋ 18 1:38	20 3:30 ☾ 26♋24	1 October 2011
♅0S 16 17:53	☉ ♏ 23 18:30	20 16:33 ♆ △	♋ 20 18:53	20 3:30 ☉ □	♌ 20 10:06	26 19:56 ● 3♏03	Julian Day # 40816
☽0S 23 20:32		23 1:22 ☉ ✶	♌ 23 1:55	22 12:34 ☉ ✶	♍ 22 14:41		SVP 5♓05'28"
♃△♇ 28 16:29		25 2:39 ♆ ☍	♍ 25 4:49	23 20:47 ♀ ✶	♎ 24 15:49		GC 27♐00.2 ⚴ 27♑20.4
		25 19:47 ♃ △	♎ 27 4:51	26 12:18 ♆ △	♏ 26 15:08		Eris 22♈04.4R ⚵ 21♎43.6
		29 1:51 ♆ △	♏ 29 4:05	28 11:49 ♆ □	♐ 28 14:45		⚷ 1♓25.3R ⚶ 6♒49.9
				30 13:30 ♆ ✶	♑ 30 16:39		☽ Mean ☊ 17♐49.4

November 2011

LONGITUDE

Day	Sid.Time	☉	0 hr ☽	Noon ☽	True ☊	☿	♀	♂	⚳	♃	♄	♅	♆	♇
1 Tu	14 41 44	8♏42 52	17♑51 04	24♑28 59	14♐52.1	28♏21.1	28♏55.2	24♌59.4	16♓28.8	4♉49.3	22♎26.3	1♈14.8	28♒09.4	5♑25.3
2 W	14 45 40	9 42 54	1♒00 44	7♒26 48	14R 52.9	29 43.3	0♐09.8	25 31.2	16R 27.1	4R 41.2	22 33.5	1R 13.0	28R 09.1	5 26.7
3 Th	14 49 37	10 42 58	13 47 38	20 03 45	14 52.4	1♐04.6	1 24.4	26 02.8	16 25.8	4 33.1	22 40.6	1 11.3	28 08.9	5 28.1
4 F	14 53 34	11 43 04	26 15 41	2♓23 58	14 50.4	2 24.8	2 38.9	26 34.2	16 24.8	4 25.1	22 47.7	1 09.7	28 08.7	5 29.5
5 Sa	14 57 30	12 43 11	8♓29 07	14 31 36	14 46.9	3 44.0	3 53.5	27 05.5	16D 24.3	4 17.1	22 54.7	1 08.0	28 08.5	5 30.9
6 Su	15 01 27	13 43 19	20 31 55	26 30 29	14 42.3	5 01.9	5 08.1	27 36.6	16 24.1	4 09.1	23 01.7	1 06.4	28 08.4	5 32.4
7 M	15 05 23	14 43 30	2♈27 42	8♈23 59	14 36.9	6 18.4	6 22.6	28 07.6	16 24.3	4 01.3	23 08.7	1 04.9	28 08.3	5 33.9
8 Tu	15 09 20	15 43 42	14 19 38	20 14 58	14 31.4	7 33.5	7 37.2	28 38.4	16 24.9	3 53.4	23 15.7	1 03.4	28 08.3	5 35.4
9 W	15 13 16	16 43 55	26 10 17	2♉05 50	14 26.4	8 46.9	8 51.7	29 09.0	16 25.8	3 45.7	23 22.7	1 01.9	28D 08.2	5 36.9
10 Th	15 17 13	17 44 10	8♉01 52	13 58 37	14 22.4	9 58.5	10 06.2	29 39.5	16 27.1	3 38.0	23 29.6	1 00.5	28 08.2	5 38.5
11 F	15 21 09	18 44 27	19 56 17	25 55 05	14 19.7	11 08.0	11 20.8	0♍09.8	16 28.8	3 30.4	23 36.5	0 59.1	28 08.3	5 40.1
12 Sa	15 25 06	19 44 46	1♊55 16	7♊57 03	14D 18.3	12 15.1	12 35.3	0 39.9	16 30.8	3 22.9	23 43.3	0 57.7	28 08.4	5 41.7
13 Su	15 29 03	20 45 07	14 00 39	20 06 22	14 18.3	13 19.7	13 49.8	1 09.8	16 33.2	3 15.5	23 50.1	0 56.4	28 08.5	5 43.3
14 M	15 32 59	21 45 29	26 14 27	2♋25 12	14 19.2	14 21.3	15 04.3	1 39.5	16 35.9	3 08.1	23 56.9	0 55.1	28 08.6	5 44.9
15 Tu	15 36 56	22 45 54	8♋38 57	14 56 02	14 20.8	15 19.7	16 18.9	2 09.1	16 39.0	3 00.9	24 03.7	0 53.9	28 08.8	5 46.6
16 W	15 40 52	23 46 20	21 16 48	27 41 36	14 22.4	16 14.2	17 33.4	2 38.5	16 42.5	2 53.8	24 10.4	0 52.7	28 09.0	5 48.3
17 Th	15 44 49	24 46 47	4♌10 49	10♌44 46	14 23.6	17 04.6	18 47.9	3 07.7	16 46.2	2 46.8	24 17.1	0 51.6	28 09.2	5 50.0
18 F	15 48 45	25 47 17	17 23 48	24 08 09	14R 24.2	17 50.2	20 02.4	3 36.6	16 50.4	2 39.9	24 23.7	0 50.5	28 09.5	5 51.7
19 Sa	15 52 42	26 47 49	0♍58 03	7♍53 38	14 23.8	18 30.5	21 16.8	4 05.4	16 54.9	2 33.1	24 30.3	0 49.4	28 09.8	5 53.5
20 Su	15 56 38	27 48 22	14 54 54	22 01 46	14 22.7	19 04.7	22 31.3	4 34.0	16 59.7	2 26.4	24 36.9	0 48.4	28 10.2	5 55.2
21 M	16 00 35	28 48 57	29 13 59	6♎31 10	14 21.0	19 32.3	23 45.8	5 02.3	17 04.9	2 19.9	24 43.4	0 47.5	28 10.6	5 57.0
22 Tu	16 04 32	29 49 34	13♎52 46	21 18 04	14 19.1	19 52.4	25 00.3	5 30.4	17 10.4	2 13.5	24 49.8	0 46.5	28 11.0	5 58.8
23 W	16 08 28	0♐50 13	28 46 14	6♏16 18	14 17.3	20R 04.2	26 14.8	5 58.3	17 16.2	2 07.3	24 56.3	0 45.7	28 11.4	6 00.6
24 Th	16 12 25	1 50 53	13♏47 11	21 17 49	14 16.0	20 07.1	27 29.2	6 26.0	17 22.3	2 01.2	25 02.6	0 44.9	28 11.9	6 02.5
25 F	16 16 21	2 51 35	28 47 03	6♐13 49	14D 15.4	20 00.2	28 43.7	6 53.5	17 28.8	1 55.3	25 09.0	0 44.1	28 12.5	6 04.3
26 Sa	16 20 18	3 52 18	13♐37 06	20 56 00	14 15.3	19 43.0	29 58.1	7 20.7	17 35.6	1 49.5	25 15.3	0 43.4	28 13.0	6 06.2
27 Su	16 24 14	4 53 02	28 09 46	5♑17 47	14 15.8	19 15.1	1♑12.6	7 47.6	17 42.8	1 43.8	25 21.5	0 42.7	28 13.6	6 08.1
28 M	16 28 11	5 53 48	12♑19 37	19 14 58	14 16.6	18 36.2	2 27.0	8 14.4	17 50.2	1 38.4	25 27.7	0 42.1	28 14.2	6 10.0
29 Tu	16 32 07	6 54 34	26 03 44	2♒45 56	14 17.4	17 46.7	3 41.4	8 40.8	17 58.0	1 33.1	25 33.8	0 41.5	28 14.9	6 11.9
30 W	16 36 04	7 55 22	9♒21 44	15 51 24	14 18.0	16 47.1	4 55.8	9 07.0	18 06.0	1 27.9	25 39.9	0 41.0	28 15.6	6 13.8

December 2011

LONGITUDE

Day	Sid.Time	☉	0 hr ☽	Noon ☽	True ☊	☿	♀	♂	⚳	♃	♄	♅	♆	♇
1 Th	16 40 01	8♐56 10	22♒15 16	28♒33 48	14♐18.4	15♐38.6	6♑10.2	9♍33.0	18♓14.4	1♉23.0	25♎45.9	0♈40.5	28♒16.3	6♑15.8
2 F	16 43 57	9 56 59	4♓47 29	10♓56 51	14R 18.5	14R 23.1	7 24.6	9 58.7	18 23.0	1R 18.2	25 51.9	0R 40.1	28 17.1	6 17.7
3 Sa	16 47 54	10 57 49	17 02 27	23 04 52	14 18.4	13 02.6	8 39.0	10 24.1	18 32.0	1 13.6	25 57.8	0 39.7	28 17.9	6 19.7
4 Su	16 51 50	11 58 40	29 04 40	5♈02 26	14 18.2	11 39.9	9 53.3	10 49.2	18 41.2	1 09.2	26 03.6	0 39.4	28 18.7	6 21.7
5 M	16 55 47	12 59 32	10♈58 42	16 54 01	14 18.0	10 17.7	11 07.6	11 14.1	18 50.7	1 05.0	26 09.4	0 39.1	28 19.5	6 23.7
6 Tu	16 59 43	14 00 25	22 48 54	28 43 49	14D 17.9	8 58.8	12 21.9	11 38.6	19 00.5	1 00.9	26 15.1	0 38.9	28 20.4	6 25.7
7 W	17 03 40	15 01 19	4♉39 12	10♉35 30	14 17.9	7 45.7	13 36.2	12 02.9	19 10.6	0 57.1	26 20.8	0 38.7	28 21.3	6 27.7
8 Th	17 07 36	16 02 13	16 33 03	22 32 13	14 18.0	6 40.6	14 50.5	12 26.9	19 21.0	0 53.4	26 26.4	0 38.6	28 22.3	6 29.7
9 F	17 11 33	17 03 09	28 33 17	4♊36 31	14R 18.2	5 45.1	16 04.7	12 50.6	19 31.6	0 49.9	26 31.9	0D 38.5	28 23.3	6 31.8
10 Sa	17 15 30	18 04 05	10♊42 09	16 50 22	14 18.2	5 00.2	17 19.0	13 13.9	19 42.5	0 46.7	26 37.4	0 38.5	28 24.3	6 33.8
11 Su	17 19 26	19 05 02	23 01 22	29 15 15	14 18.1	4 26.6	18 33.2	13 37.0	19 53.6	0 43.6	26 42.8	0 38.6	28 25.4	6 35.9
12 M	17 23 23	20 06 00	5♋32 09	11♋52 11	14 17.6	4 04.3	19 47.4	13 59.7	20 05.0	0 40.7	26 48.1	0 38.6	28 26.4	6 38.0
13 Tu	17 27 19	21 07 00	18 15 24	24 41 54	14 16.8	3D 53.0	21 01.6	14 22.1	20 16.7	0 38.0	26 53.4	0 38.8	28 27.5	6 40.1
14 W	17 31 16	22 08 00	1♌11 44	7♌44 58	14 15.8	3 52.3	22 15.7	14 44.2	20 28.6	0 35.5	26 58.6	0 39.0	28 28.7	6 42.1
15 Th	17 35 12	23 09 00	14 21 38	21 01 49	14 14.8	4 01.3	23 29.8	15 06.0	20 40.7	0 33.3	27 03.8	0 39.2	28 29.9	6 44.2
16 F	17 39 09	24 10 02	27 45 31	4♍32 47	14 13.9	4 19.4	24 43.9	15 27.3	20 53.1	0 31.2	27 08.8	0 39.5	28 31.1	6 46.3
17 Sa	17 43 05	25 11 05	11♍23 36	18 17 59	14D 13.3	4 45.7	25 58.0	15 48.3	21 05.7	0 29.3	27 13.8	0 39.8	28 32.3	6 48.4
18 Su	17 47 02	26 12 09	25 15 52	2♎17 09	14 13.3	5 19.4	27 12.1	16 09.0	21 18.6	0 27.7	27 18.7	0 40.2	28 33.6	6 50.5
19 M	17 50 59	27 13 14	9♎21 42	16 29 19	14 13.8	5 59.7	28 26.1	16 29.2	21 31.7	0 26.2	27 23.6	0 40.7	28 34.8	6 52.7
20 Tu	17 54 55	28 14 19	23 39 43	0♏52 33	14 14.8	6 45.9	29 40.2	16 49.1	21 45.0	0 25.0	27 28.3	0 41.2	28 36.2	6 54.8
21 W	17 58 52	29 15 26	8♏07 24	15 23 43	14 16.0	7 37.2	0♒54.2	17 08.6	21 58.6	0 23.9	27 33.0	0 41.7	28 37.5	6 56.9
22 Th	18 02 48	0♑16 33	22 40 57	29 58 25	14R 17.0	8 33.1	2 08.1	17 27.7	22 12.3	0 23.1	27 37.6	0 42.3	28 38.9	6 59.1
23 F	18 06 45	1 17 41	7♐15 26	14♐31 15	14 17.4	9 33.0	3 22.1	17 46.3	22 26.3	0 22.5	27 42.2	0 43.0	28 40.3	7 01.2
24 Sa	18 10 41	2 18 50	21 45 06	28 56 15	14 16.9	10 36.5	4 36.0	18 04.6	22 40.5	0 22.1	27 46.6	0 43.7	28 41.7	7 03.3
25 Su	18 14 38	3 19 59	6♑04 01	13♑07 45	14 15.4	11 43.1	5 49.9	18 22.4	22 55.0	0D 21.9	27 51.0	0 44.5	28 43.2	7 05.5
26 M	18 18 35	4 21 08	20 06 53	27 00 58	14 12.9	12 52.4	7 03.8	18 39.7	23 09.6	0 21.9	27 55.3	0 45.3	28 44.7	7 07.6
27 Tu	18 22 31	5 22 18	3♒49 40	10♒32 44	14 09.7	14 04.2	8 17.6	18 56.6	23 24.4	0 22.1	27 59.5	0 46.1	28 46.2	7 09.8
28 W	18 26 28	6 23 27	17 10 06	23 41 46	14 06.2	15 18.0	9 31.4	19 13.0	23 39.5	0 22.6	28 03.6	0 47.0	28 47.7	7 11.9
29 Th	18 30 24	7 24 37	0♓07 52	6♓28 39	14 03.0	16 33.8	10 45.1	19 29.0	23 54.7	0 23.2	28 07.7	0 48.0	28 49.3	7 14.1
30 F	18 34 21	8 25 46	12 44 27	18 55 39	14 00.5	17 51.2	11 58.9	19 44.5	24 10.2	0 24.1	28 11.6	0 49.0	28 50.9	7 16.2
31 Sa	18 38 17	9 26 55	25 02 46	1♈06 18	13D 59.0	19 10.1	13 12.5	19 59.5	24 25.8	0 25.1	28 15.5	0 50.1	28 52.5	7 18.3

Astro Data	Dy Hr Mn
☽0N	5 18:43
⚳D	6 11:39
♆D	9 18:54
☽0S	20 4:46
☿R	24 7:19
☽0N	3 1:16
♅D	10 7:04
♃⚺♅	13 5:23
☿D	14 1:42
☽0S	17 10:58
♃D	25 22:08
☽0N	30 9:49

Planet Ingress	Dy Hr Mn
♀ ♐	2 8:51
☿ ♐	2 16:54
♂ ♍	11 4:15
☉ ♐	22 16:08
♀ ♑	26 12:36
♀ ♒	20 18:26
☉ ♑	22 5:30

Last Aspect Dy Hr Mn		☽ Ingress Dy Hr Mn
1 21:00 ♀ ⚹	♒	1 22:08
4 3:40 ♆ ☌	♓	4 7:18
5 8:05 ☉ △	♈	6 19:02
9 5:46 ♂ △	♉	9 7:45
11 16:27 ♆ □	♊	11 20:10
14 3:42 ♆ △	♋	14 7:19
16 5:22 ♄ □	♌	16 16:17
18 19:05 ♆ ☍	♍	18 22:19
20 22:21 ☉ ⚹	♎	21 1:16
22 23:04 ♆ △	♏	23 1:58
24 23:04 ♆ □	♐	25 1:57
27 0:06 ♆ ⚹	♑	27 3:04
28 23:01 ♄ □	♒	29 7:02

Last Aspect Dy Hr Mn		☽ Ingress Dy Hr Mn
1 11:27 ♆ ☌	♓	1 14:45
2 18:06 ♆ □	♈	4 1:51
6 11:12 ♆ ⚹	♉	6 14:34
8 23:39 ♆ □	♊	9 2:52
11 10:24 ♆ △	♋	11 13:26
13 16:05 ♄ □	♌	13 21:48
16 1:20 ♆ ☍	♍	16 3:58
18 2:29 ♀ △	♎	18 8:06
20 9:49 ☉ □	♏	20 10:33
22 9:49 ♆ □	♐	22 12:03
24 11:36 ♆ ⚹	♑	24 13:47
26 13:36 ♄ □	♒	26 17:14
28 21:31 ♆ ☌	♓	28 23:45
30 13:37 ♂ ☍	♈	31 9:48

☽ Phases & Eclipses Dy Hr Mn	
2 16:38	☽ 9♒55
10 20:16	○ 18♉05
18 15:09	☾ 25♌55
25 6:10	● 2♐37
25 6:20:14	● P 0.905
2 9:52	☽ 9♓52
10 14:36	○ 18♊11
10 14:32	● T 1.106
18 0:48	☾ 25♍44
24 18:06	● 2♑34

Astro Data

1 November 2011
Julian Day # 40847
SVP 5♓05'24"
GC 27♐00.3 ⚴ 0♒54.4
Eris 21♈46.1R ⚵ 2♏35.6
⚷ 0♓41.2R ⚶ 12♒50.4
☽ Mean ☊ 16♐10.9

1 December 2011
Julian Day # 40877
SVP 5♓05'20"
GC 27♐00.3 ⚴ 7♒36.3
Eris 21♈31.2R ⚵ 12♏50.4
⚷ 0♓51.3 ⚶ 22♒38.2
☽ Mean ☊ 14♐35.6

LONGITUDE — January 2012

Day	Sid.Time	☉	0 hr ☽	Noon ☽	True ☊	☿	♀	♂	⚳	♃	♄	♅	♆	♇
1 Su	18 42 14	10♑28 05	7♈06 50	13♈04 58	13♐58.7	20♐30.3	14♒26.2	20♍14.0	24♓41.6	0♉26.4	28♎19.2	0♈51.2	28♒54.2	7♑20.5
2 M	18 46 10	11 29 14	19 01 20	24 56 34	13 59.5	21 51.7	15 39.8	20 28.0	24 57.6	0 27.9	28 22.9	0 52.3	28 55.8	7 22.6
3 Tu	18 50 07	12 30 22	0♉51 17	6♉46 06	14 01.1	23 14.2	16 53.3	20 41.5	25 13.8	0 29.6	28 26.5	0 53.5	28 57.5	7 24.8
4 W	18 54 04	13 31 31	12 41 38	18 38 27	14 03.0	24 37.7	18 06.8	20 54.4	25 30.1	0 31.4	28 30.0	0 54.8	28 59.2	7 26.9
5 Th	18 58 00	14 32 40	24 37 07	0♊38 07	14 04.6	26 02.0	19 20.3	21 06.8	25 46.7	0 33.5	28 33.4	0 56.1	29 01.0	7 29.0
6 F	19 01 57	15 33 48	6♊41 55	12 48 56	14R 05.4	27 27.2	20 33.7	21 18.7	26 03.4	0 35.8	28 36.8	0 57.5	29 02.7	7 31.2
7 Sa	19 05 53	16 34 56	18 59 30	25 13 54	14 04.8	28 53.1	21 47.0	21 30.0	26 20.2	0 38.3	28 40.0	0 58.9	29 04.5	7 33.3
8 Su	19 09 50	17 36 04	1♋32 20	7♋54 57	14 02.5	0♑19.7	23 00.3	21 40.7	26 37.3	0 41.0	28 43.1	1 00.3	29 06.3	7 35.4
9 M	19 13 46	18 37 12	14 21 47	20 52 49	13 58.5	1 47.0	24 13.5	21 50.9	26 54.5	0 43.9	28 46.2	1 01.8	29 08.1	7 37.5
10 Tu	19 17 43	19 38 19	27 27 59	4♌07 06	13 53.1	3 14.9	25 26.7	22 00.5	27 11.8	0 47.0	28 49.1	1 03.4	29 10.0	7 39.7
11 W	19 21 39	20 39 26	10♌49 57	17 36 16	13 46.9	4 43.4	26 39.8	22 09.4	27 29.3	0 50.3	28 52.0	1 04.9	29 11.9	7 41.8
12 Th	19 25 36	21 40 33	24 25 44	1♍18 01	13 40.5	6 12.5	27 52.9	22 17.8	27 47.0	0 53.8	28 54.7	1 06.6	29 13.7	7 43.9
13 F	19 29 33	22 41 40	8♍12 46	15 09 39	13 34.8	7 42.1	29 05.9	22 25.5	28 04.8	0 57.5	28 57.4	1 08.3	29 15.6	7 45.9
14 Sa	19 33 29	23 42 47	22 08 20	29 08 30	13 30.6	9 12.3	0♓18.9	22 32.6	28 22.8	1 01.3	28 59.9	1 10.0	29 17.6	7 48.0
15 Su	19 37 26	24 43 53	6♎09 53	13♎12 14	13D 28.1	10 43.0	1 31.8	22 39.0	28 40.9	1 05.4	29 02.4	1 11.8	29 19.5	7 50.1
16 M	19 41 22	25 45 00	20 15 21	27 19 00	13 27.5	12 14.3	2 44.6	22 44.8	28 59.2	1 09.6	29 04.7	1 13.6	29 21.5	7 52.2
17 Tu	19 45 19	26 46 06	4♏23 03	11♏27 18	13 28.2	13 46.1	3 57.4	22 49.8	29 17.6	1 14.1	29 07.0	1 15.4	29 23.4	7 54.2
18 W	19 49 15	27 47 12	18 31 37	25 35 48	13 29.6	15 18.5	5 10.1	22 54.2	29 36.1	1 18.7	29 09.2	1 17.3	29 25.4	7 56.3
19 Th	19 53 12	28 48 18	2♐39 39	9♐42 56	13R 30.5	16 51.4	6 22.7	22 57.9	29 54.8	1 23.5	29 11.2	1 19.3	29 27.5	7 58.3
20 F	19 57 08	29 49 24	16 45 22	23 46 38	13 30.1	18 24.8	7 35.3	23 00.9	0♈13.7	1 28.5	29 13.2	1 21.3	29 29.5	8 00.4
21 Sa	20 01 05	0♒50 29	0♑46 23	7♑44 13	13 27.6	19 58.8	8 47.8	23 03.2	0 32.6	1 33.6	29 15.0	1 23.3	29 31.5	8 02.4
22 Su	20 05 02	1 51 34	14 39 44	21 32 31	13 22.7	21 33.3	10 00.2	23 04.7	0 51.7	1 39.0	29 16.8	1 25.4	29 33.6	8 04.4
23 M	20 08 58	2 52 38	28 22 08	5♒08 12	13 15.5	23 08.4	11 12.6	23R 05.5	1 10.9	1 44.5	29 18.4	1 27.5	29 35.7	8 06.4
24 Tu	20 12 55	3 53 42	11♒50 22	18 28 20	13 06.6	24 44.1	12 24.8	23 05.5	1 30.3	1 50.2	29 20.0	1 29.6	29 37.8	8 08.4
25 W	20 16 51	4 54 44	25 01 53	1♓30 52	12 56.8	26 20.4	13 37.0	23 04.8	1 49.7	1 56.1	29 21.4	1 31.8	29 39.9	8 10.3
26 Th	20 20 48	5 55 45	7♓55 15	14 15 05	12 47.2	27 57.2	14 49.2	23 03.3	2 09.3	2 02.2	29 22.7	1 34.1	29 42.0	8 12.3
27 F	20 24 44	6 56 46	20 30 29	26 41 41	12 38.7	29 34.7	16 01.2	23 01.0	2 29.0	2 08.4	29 24.0	1 36.3	29 44.1	8 14.2
28 Sa	20 28 41	7 57 45	2♈49 00	8♈52 50	12 32.2	1♒12.9	17 13.1	22 58.0	2 48.9	2 14.8	29 25.1	1 38.6	29 46.3	8 16.1
29 Su	20 32 37	8 58 43	14 53 39	20 51 58	12 27.9	2 51.7	18 25.0	22 54.1	3 08.8	2 21.4	29 26.1	1 41.0	29 48.4	8 18.1
30 M	20 36 34	9 59 41	26 48 21	2♉43 26	12D 25.9	4 31.1	19 36.7	22 49.5	3 28.9	2 28.1	29 27.0	1 43.4	29 50.6	8 19.9
31 Tu	20 40 31	11 00 36	8♉37 52	14 32 18	12 25.6	6 11.2	20 48.4	22 44.2	3 49.0	2 35.0	29 27.8	1 45.8	29 52.8	8 21.8

LONGITUDE — February 2012

Day	Sid.Time	☉	0 hr ☽	Noon ☽	True ☊	☿	♀	♂	⚳	♃	♄	♅	♆	♇
1 W	20 44 27	12♒01 31	20♉27 26	26♉23 56	12♐26.4	7♒52.0	21♓59.9	22♍38.0	4♈09.3	2♉42.0	29♎28.5	1♈48.3	29♒54.9	8♑23.7
2 Th	20 48 24	13 02 25	2♊22 29	8♊22 45	12R 27.1	9 33.6	23 11.3	22R 31.0	4 29.7	2 49.2	29 29.1	1 50.8	29 57.1	8 25.5
3 F	20 52 20	14 03 17	14 28 21	20 36 51	12 26.8	11 15.8	24 22.7	22 23.3	4 50.1	2 56.6	29 29.6	1 53.3	29 59.4	8 27.4
4 Sa	20 56 17	15 04 07	26 49 46	3♋07 34	12 24.6	12 58.8	25 33.9	22 14.8	5 10.7	3 04.1	29 30.0	1 55.8	0♓01.6	8 29.2
5 Su	21 00 13	16 04 57	9♋30 37	15 59 09	12 20.0	14 42.5	26 45.0	22 05.4	5 31.4	3 11.8	29 30.2	1 58.4	0 03.8	8 31.0
6 M	21 04 10	17 05 45	22 33 20	29 13 10	12 12.7	16 26.9	27 56.0	21 55.3	5 52.2	3 19.6	29 30.4	2 01.1	0 06.0	8 32.8
7 Tu	21 08 06	18 06 32	5♌58 33	12♌49 13	12 03.2	18 12.0	29 06.9	21 44.5	6 13.0	3 27.6	29R 30.5	2 03.7	0 08.3	8 34.5
8 W	21 12 03	19 07 18	19 44 48	26 44 48	11 52.1	19 57.9	0♈17.6	21 32.8	6 34.0	3 35.7	29 30.4	2 06.4	0 10.5	8 36.3
9 Th	21 16 00	20 08 02	3♍48 36	10♍55 31	11 40.8	21 44.6	1 28.3	21 20.4	6 55.0	3 43.9	29 30.3	2 09.2	0 12.7	8 38.0
10 F	21 19 56	21 08 45	18 04 48	25 15 43	11 30.5	23 31.9	2 38.8	21 07.2	7 16.2	3 52.3	29 30.0	2 11.9	0 15.0	8 39.7
11 Sa	21 23 53	22 09 27	2♎27 31	9♎39 30	11 22.1	25 19.9	3 49.1	20 53.3	7 37.4	4 00.9	29 29.7	2 14.7	0 17.3	8 41.3
12 Su	21 27 49	23 10 08	16 51 02	24 01 35	11 16.4	27 08.5	4 59.4	20 38.6	7 58.7	4 09.5	29 29.2	2 17.5	0 19.5	8 43.0
13 M	21 31 46	24 10 48	1♏10 41	8♏18 00	11 13.4	28 57.7	6 09.5	20 23.3	8 20.1	4 18.3	29 28.6	2 20.3	0 21.8	8 44.6
14 Tu	21 35 42	25 11 27	15 23 17	22 26 23	11D 12.5	0♓47.5	7 19.4	20 07.2	8 41.6	4 27.3	29 28.0	2 23.2	0 24.1	8 46.3
15 W	21 39 39	26 12 04	29 27 11	6♐25 40	11R 12.6	2 37.7	8 29.3	19 50.4	9 03.2	4 36.4	29 27.2	2 26.1	0 26.3	8 47.9
16 Th	21 43 35	27 12 41	13♐21 50	20 15 43	11 12.4	4 28.2	9 39.0	19 32.9	9 24.8	4 45.6	29 26.3	2 29.0	0 28.6	8 49.4
17 F	21 47 32	28 13 17	27 07 20	3♑56 41	11 10.6	6 19.0	10 48.5	19 14.8	9 46.6	4 54.9	29 25.3	2 32.0	0 30.9	8 51.0
18 Sa	21 51 29	29 13 51	10♑43 46	17 28 32	11 06.3	8 09.8	11 57.9	18 56.1	10 08.4	5 04.4	29 24.2	2 35.0	0 33.2	8 52.5
19 Su	21 55 25	0♓14 24	24 10 55	0♒50 48	10 58.9	10 00.5	13 07.2	18 36.8	10 30.3	5 14.0	29 23.0	2 38.0	0 35.5	8 54.0
20 M	21 59 22	1 14 55	7♒28 03	14 02 31	10 48.5	11 50.8	14 16.3	18 16.9	10 52.2	5 23.7	29 21.7	2 41.0	0 37.7	8 55.5
21 Tu	22 03 18	2 15 25	20 34 02	27 02 27	10 35.8	13 40.6	15 25.2	17 56.5	11 14.3	5 33.6	29 20.3	2 44.1	0 40.0	8 57.0
22 W	22 07 15	3 15 53	3♓27 36	9♓49 22	10 21.9	15 29.5	16 34.0	17 35.5	11 36.4	5 43.5	29 18.8	2 47.1	0 42.3	8 58.4
23 Th	22 11 11	4 16 20	16 07 42	22 22 33	10 08.0	17 17.2	17 42.6	17 14.1	11 58.5	5 53.6	29 17.2	2 50.2	0 44.6	8 59.8
24 F	22 15 08	5 16 45	28 34 00	4♈42 07	9 55.3	19 03.4	18 51.0	16 52.3	12 20.8	6 03.8	29 15.5	2 53.3	0 46.9	9 01.2
25 Sa	22 19 04	6 17 08	10♈47 06	16 49 12	9 44.9	20 47.4	19 59.3	16 30.1	12 43.1	6 14.1	29 13.8	2 56.5	0 49.1	9 02.5
26 Su	22 23 01	7 17 29	22 48 44	28 46 05	9 37.2	22 29.1	21 07.3	16 07.6	13 05.5	6 24.5	29 11.9	2 59.6	0 51.4	9 03.9
27 M	22 26 58	8 17 49	4♉41 43	10♉36 08	9 32.5	24 07.7	22 15.2	15 44.7	13 27.9	6 35.0	29 09.9	3 02.8	0 53.7	9 05.2
28 Tu	22 30 54	9 18 06	16 29 55	22 23 39	9 30.2	25 42.8	23 22.8	15 21.6	13 50.4	6 45.7	29 07.8	3 06.0	0 55.9	9 06.4
29 W	22 34 51	10 18 22	28 18 00	4♊13 39	9 29.5	27 13.8	24 30.3	14 58.3	14 13.0	6 56.4	29 05.6	3 09.2	0 58.2	9 07.7

Astro Data	Planet Ingress	Last Aspect	☽ Ingress	Last Aspect	☽ Ingress	☽ Phases & Eclipses
Dy Hr Mn	Dy Hr Mn	Dy Hr Mn	Dy Hr Mn	Dy Hr Mn	Dy Hr Mn	Dy Hr Mn
☽0S 13 16:52	☿ ♑ 8 6:34	2 20:07 ♆ ⚹	♉ 2 22:16	1 19:06 ♆ □	♊ 1 19:14	1 6:15 ☽ 10♈13
♃⚹♅ 18 0:12	♀ ♓ 14 5:47	5 8:46 ☿ △	♊ 5 10:44	4 5:06 ♄ △	♋ 4 6:04	9 7:30 ○ 18♋26
♂R 24 0:53	⚳ ♈ 19 18:37	7 19:52 ☿ ☍	♋ 7 21:05	6 12:31 ♄ □	♌ 6 13:24	16 9:08 ☾ 25♎38
☽0N 26 19:30	☉ ♒ 20 16:10	10 2:25 ♄ □	♌ 10 4:35	8 16:42 ♄ ⚹	♍ 8 17:32	23 7:39 ● 2♒42
♅0N 28 3:36	☿ ♒ 27 18:12	12 8:23 ♆ ☍	♍ 12 9:44	10 5:11 ♂ ☌	♎ 10 19:54	31 4:10 ☽ 10♉41
		14 1:58 ☉ △	♎ 14 13:28	12 21:09 ♄ ☌	♏ 12 22:01	
♄R 7 14:03	♆ ♓ 3 19:03	16 15:28 ♆ △	♏ 16 16:33	14 17:04 ☉ □	♐ 15 0:56	7 21:54 ○ 18♌32
♀0N 9 3:27	♀ ♈ 8 6:01	18 18:31 ♆ □	♐ 18 19:29	17 4:03 ♄ ⚹	♑ 17 5:03	14 17:04 ☾ 25♏24
☽0S 10 0:27	☿ ♓ 14 1:38	20 21:49 ♆ ⚹	♑ 20 22:40	19 9:22 ♄ □	♒ 19 10:28	21 22:35 ● 2♓42
☽0N 23 4:30	☉ ♓ 19 6:18	23 1:38 ♄ □	♒ 23 2:53	21 16:17 ♄ △	♓ 21 17:31	
		25 8:33 ♆ ☌	♓ 25 9:11	23 2:24 ♂ ☍	♈ 24 2:48	
		27 4:53 ♂ ☍	♈ 27 18:28	26 12:52 ♄ ☍	♉ 26 14:29	
		30 6:08 ♆ ⚹	♉ 30 6:28	28 19:46 ♆ ⚹	♊ 29 3:27	

Astro Data

1 January 2012
Julian Day # 40908
SVP 5♓05'15"
GC 27♐00.4 ⚴ 16♒30.3
Eris 21♈23.5R ⚵ 22♏34.9
⚷ 1♓55.5 ⚶ 5♓05.7
☽ Mean ☊ 12♐57.1

1 February 2012
Julian Day # 40939
SVP 5♓05'10"
GC 27♐00.5 ⚴ 26♒27.0
Eris 21♈26.1 ⚵ 0♐39.5
⚷ 3♓39.8 ⚶ 18♓49.2
☽ Mean ☊ 11♐18.6

March 2012 LONGITUDE

Day	Sid.Time	☉	0 hr ☽	Noon ☽	True ☊	☿	♀	♂	⚳	♃	♄	♅	♆	♇
1 Th	22 38 47	11♓18 35	10♊11 16	16♊11 35	9♐29.5	28♓40.1	25♈37.6	14♍34.8	14♈35.6	7♉07.3	29♎03.4	3♈12.4	1♓00.4	9♑08.9
2 F	22 42 44	12 18 47	22 15 17	28 23 03	9R 28.8	0♈01.1	26 44.6	14R 11.2	14 58.3	7 18.2	29R 01.0	3 15.7	1 02.7	9 10.1
3 Sa	22 46 40	13 18 56	4♋35 33	10♋53 22	9 26.5	1 16.2	27 51.4	13 47.5	15 21.0	7 29.3	28 58.6	3 19.0	1 04.9	9 11.3
4 Su	22 50 37	14 19 04	17 17 03	23 47 01	9 21.9	2 24.8	28 58.0	13 23.8	15 43.8	7 40.4	28 56.0	3 22.2	1 07.2	9 12.4
5 M	22 54 33	15 19 09	0♌23 37	7♌07 00	9 14.5	3 26.5	0♉04.4	13 00.0	16 06.7	7 51.7	28 53.4	3 25.5	1 09.4	9 13.5
6 Tu	22 58 30	16 19 12	13 57 13	20 54 07	9 04.6	4 20.7	1 10.5	12 36.3	16 29.5	8 03.0	28 50.7	3 28.8	1 11.6	9 14.6
7 W	23 02 27	17 19 13	27 57 22	5♍06 28	8 53.1	5 06.9	2 16.4	12 12.8	16 52.5	8 14.4	28 47.9	3 32.1	1 13.8	9 15.7
8 Th	23 06 23	18 19 12	12♍20 42	19 39 15	8 41.2	5 44.8	3 22.0	11 49.3	17 15.5	8 25.9	28 45.0	3 35.5	1 16.0	9 16.7
9 F	23 10 20	19 19 10	27 01 07	4♎25 16	8 30.1	6 14.1	4 27.3	11 26.0	17 38.5	8 37.5	28 42.1	3 38.8	1 18.2	9 17.7
10 Sa	23 14 16	20 19 05	11♎50 36	19 16 02	8 21.1	6 34.7	5 32.4	11 03.0	18 01.6	8 49.2	28 39.0	3 42.2	1 20.4	9 18.7
11 Su	23 18 13	21 18 59	26 40 33	4♏03 14	8 14.8	6R 46.4	6 37.2	10 40.2	18 24.7	9 01.0	28 35.9	3 45.5	1 22.6	9 19.6
12 M	23 22 09	22 18 51	11♏23 19	18 40 07	8 11.3	6 49.2	7 41.8	10 17.7	18 47.9	9 12.9	28 32.7	3 48.9	1 24.8	9 20.6
13 Tu	23 26 06	23 18 42	25 53 10	3♐02 08	8D 10.1	6 43.4	8 46.0	9 55.6	19 11.1	9 24.8	28 29.4	3 52.3	1 26.9	9 21.4
14 W	23 30 02	24 18 30	10♐06 48	17 07 06	8R 10.1	6 29.2	9 50.0	9 33.8	19 34.4	9 36.8	28 26.1	3 55.7	1 29.1	9 22.3
15 Th	23 33 59	25 18 18	24 03 03	0♑54 45	8 10.1	6 07.2	10 53.6	9 12.5	19 57.7	9 48.9	28 22.7	3 59.1	1 31.2	9 23.1
16 F	23 37 56	26 18 03	7♑42 20	14 26 00	8 08.8	5 37.7	11 57.0	8 51.6	20 21.1	10 01.1	28 19.2	4 02.5	1 33.3	9 23.9
17 Sa	23 41 52	27 17 47	21 05 57	27 42 22	8 05.2	5 01.8	13 00.0	8 31.2	20 44.5	10 13.4	28 15.6	4 05.9	1 35.4	9 24.7
18 Su	23 45 49	28 17 29	4♒15 27	10♒45 21	7 58.9	4 20.1	14 02.8	8 11.3	21 07.9	10 25.7	28 12.0	4 09.3	1 37.5	9 25.4
19 M	23 49 45	29 17 09	17 12 13	23 36 10	7 49.9	3 33.6	15 05.1	7 51.9	21 31.4	10 38.1	28 08.3	4 12.7	1 39.6	9 26.1
20 Tu	23 53 42	0♈16 48	29 57 18	6♓15 39	7 38.8	2 43.6	16 07.2	7 33.2	21 54.9	10 50.6	28 04.6	4 16.1	1 41.7	9 26.8
21 W	23 57 38	1 16 24	12♓31 18	18 44 18	7 26.4	1 51.0	17 08.9	7 15.0	22 18.5	11 03.2	28 00.8	4 19.5	1 43.7	9 27.4
22 Th	0 01 35	2 15 59	24 54 42	1♈02 33	7 14.0	0 57.1	18 10.2	6 57.5	22 42.0	11 15.8	27 56.9	4 23.0	1 45.8	9 28.1
23 F	0 05 31	3 15 31	7♈07 56	13 10 58	7 02.7	0 03.1	19 11.1	6 40.7	23 05.7	11 28.5	27 52.9	4 26.4	1 47.8	9 28.6
24 Sa	0 09 28	4 15 01	19 11 48	25 10 37	6 53.3	29♓09.9	20 11.7	6 24.6	23 29.3	11 41.2	27 49.0	4 29.8	1 49.8	9 29.2
25 Su	0 13 24	5 14 30	1♉07 39	7♉03 10	6 46.4	28 18.7	21 11.8	6 09.1	23 53.0	11 54.0	27 44.9	4 33.2	1 51.8	9 29.7
26 M	0 17 21	6 13 56	12 57 32	18 51 07	6 42.2	27 30.3	22 11.5	5 54.4	24 16.7	12 06.9	27 40.8	4 36.7	1 53.7	9 30.2
27 Tu	0 21 18	7 13 20	24 44 21	0♊37 44	6D 40.4	26 45.6	23 10.8	5 40.4	24 40.5	12 19.8	27 36.7	4 40.1	1 55.7	9 30.7
28 W	0 25 14	8 12 42	6♊31 47	12 27 05	6 40.3	26 05.2	24 09.7	5 27.2	25 04.2	12 32.8	27 32.5	4 43.5	1 57.6	9 31.1
29 Th	0 29 11	9 12 01	18 24 15	24 23 55	6 41.2	25 29.6	25 08.0	5 14.7	25 28.0	12 45.9	27 28.3	4 47.0	1 59.5	9 31.5
30 F	0 33 07	10 11 18	0♋26 45	6♋33 23	6R 41.9	24 59.1	26 05.9	5 03.0	25 51.9	12 59.0	27 24.0	4 50.4	2 01.4	9 31.8
31 Sa	0 37 04	11 10 33	12 44 30	19 00 45	6 41.6	24 34.2	27 03.3	4 52.1	26 15.7	13 12.2	27 19.7	4 53.8	2 03.3	9 32.2

April 2012 LONGITUDE

Day	Sid.Time	☉	0 hr ☽	Noon ☽	True ☊	☿	♀	♂	⚳	♃	♄	♅	♆	♇
1 Su	0 41 00	12♈09 46	25♋22 44	1♌50 58	6♐39.6	24♓14.9	28♉00.2	4♍41.9	26♈39.6	13♉25.4	27♎15.4	4♈57.2	2♓05.2	9♑32.5
2 M	0 44 57	13 08 56	8♌25 56	15 07 59	6R 35.5	24R 01.2	28 56.6	4R 32.6	27 03.5	13 38.6	27R 11.0	5 00.6	2 07.0	9 32.7
3 Tu	0 48 53	14 08 04	21 57 19	28 54 00	6 29.5	23D 53.3	29 52.4	4 24.0	27 27.4	13 52.0	27 06.6	5 04.0	2 08.8	9 33.0
4 W	0 52 50	15 07 09	5♍57 54	13♍08 42	6 22.0	23 50.9	0♊47.6	4 16.2	27 51.3	14 05.3	27 02.1	5 07.4	2 10.6	9 33.2
5 Th	0 56 47	16 06 13	20 25 50	27 48 36	6 14.0	23 54.0	1 42.2	4 09.2	28 15.3	14 18.7	26 57.7	5 10.8	2 12.4	9 33.4
6 F	1 00 43	17 05 14	5♎16 03	12♎47 08	6 06.5	24 02.5	2 36.3	4 03.0	28 39.3	14 32.2	26 53.2	5 14.2	2 14.2	9 33.5
7 Sa	1 04 40	18 04 13	20 20 37	27 55 16	6 00.4	24 16.1	3 29.7	3 57.6	29 03.3	14 45.7	26 48.7	5 17.5	2 15.9	9 33.6
8 Su	1 08 36	19 03 10	5♏29 50	13♏03 04	5 56.3	24 34.7	4 22.4	3 52.9	29 27.3	14 59.2	26 44.1	5 20.9	2 17.6	9 33.7
9 M	1 12 33	20 02 06	20 33 53	28 01 16	5D 54.4	24 58.0	5 14.5	3 49.0	29 51.3	15 12.8	26 39.6	5 24.2	2 19.3	9 33.7
10 Tu	1 16 29	21 00 59	5♐24 24	12♐42 39	5 54.3	25 25.8	6 05.8	3 45.9	0♉15.4	15 26.4	26 35.0	5 27.6	2 21.0	9R 33.8
11 W	1 20 26	21 59 51	19 55 32	27 02 46	5 55.3	25 58.0	6 56.5	3 43.6	0 39.5	15 40.1	26 30.4	5 30.9	2 22.6	9 33.8
12 Th	1 24 22	22 58 42	4♑04 10	10♑59 45	5R 56.6	26 34.2	7 46.4	3 41.9	1 03.5	15 53.7	26 25.8	5 34.2	2 24.2	9 33.7
13 F	1 28 19	23 57 30	17 49 37	24 33 56	5 57.1	27 14.4	8 35.5	3D 41.1	1 27.6	16 07.5	26 21.2	5 37.5	2 25.8	9 33.6
14 Sa	1 32 16	24 56 17	1♒12 58	7♒47 01	5 56.3	27 58.2	9 23.8	3 41.0	1 51.8	16 21.2	26 16.6	5 40.8	2 27.4	9 33.5
15 Su	1 36 12	25 55 02	14 16 24	20 41 27	5 53.7	28 45.6	10 11.3	3 41.6	2 15.9	16 35.0	26 12.0	5 44.1	2 28.9	9 33.4
16 M	1 40 09	26 53 45	27 02 32	3♓19 57	5 49.3	29 36.3	10 58.0	3 42.9	2 40.0	16 48.9	26 07.4	5 47.3	2 30.5	9 33.2
17 Tu	1 44 05	27 52 27	9♓34 03	15 45 06	5 43.6	0♈30.3	11 43.7	3 45.0	3 04.2	17 02.7	26 02.8	5 50.6	2 32.0	9 33.0
18 W	1 48 02	28 51 06	21 53 24	27 59 12	5 37.0	1 27.3	12 28.5	3 47.8	3 28.4	17 16.6	25 58.2	5 53.8	2 33.4	9 32.8
19 Th	1 51 58	29 49 44	4♈02 45	10♈04 16	5 30.2	2 27.1	13 12.4	3 51.2	3 52.5	17 30.6	25 53.6	5 57.0	2 34.9	9 32.5
20 F	1 55 55	0♉48 21	16 03 59	22 02 06	5 24.1	3 29.8	13 55.3	3 55.4	4 16.7	17 44.5	25 49.0	6 00.2	2 36.3	9 32.3
21 Sa	1 59 51	1 46 55	27 58 50	3♉54 25	5 19.2	4 35.2	14 37.1	4 00.3	4 40.9	17 58.5	25 44.4	6 03.4	2 37.7	9 31.9
22 Su	2 03 48	2 45 27	9♉49 05	15 43 04	5 15.8	5 43.1	15 17.9	4 05.8	5 05.1	18 12.5	25 39.8	6 06.5	2 39.0	9 31.6
23 M	2 07 44	3 43 58	21 36 39	27 30 08	5D 14.1	6 53.4	15 57.5	4 12.0	5 29.4	18 26.5	25 35.3	6 09.7	2 40.4	9 31.2
24 Tu	2 11 41	4 42 26	3♊23 52	9♊18 11	5 13.8	8 06.2	16 36.0	4 18.8	5 53.6	18 40.6	25 30.8	6 12.8	2 41.7	9 30.8
25 W	2 15 38	5 40 53	15 13 29	21 10 13	5 14.8	9 21.3	17 13.2	4 26.3	6 17.8	18 54.6	25 26.3	6 15.9	2 43.0	9 30.4
26 Th	2 19 34	6 39 17	27 08 50	3♋09 49	5 16.4	10 38.6	17 49.2	4 34.4	6 42.0	19 08.7	25 21.8	6 19.0	2 44.2	9 29.9
27 F	2 23 31	7 37 40	9♋13 42	15 21 01	5 18.1	11 58.0	18 23.9	4 43.2	7 06.3	19 22.8	25 17.3	6 22.0	2 45.4	9 29.4
28 Sa	2 27 27	8 36 00	21 32 19	27 48 09	5R 19.4	13 19.6	18 57.2	4 52.5	7 30.5	19 36.9	25 12.9	6 25.1	2 46.6	9 28.9
29 Su	2 31 24	9 34 18	4♌09 03	10♌35 32	5 19.8	14 43.3	19 29.1	5 02.5	7 54.7	19 51.1	25 08.5	6 28.1	2 47.8	9 28.3
30 M	2 35 20	10 32 34	17 08 04	23 47 02	5 19.2	16 09.1	19 59.6	5 13.0	8 18.9	20 05.2	25 04.1	6 31.1	2 48.9	9 27.8

Astro Data	Dy Hr Mn
☿0N	1 3:45
⚳0N	4 20:20
☽0S	8 10:06
☿ R	12 7:48
♃△♇	13 4:43
☉0N	20 5:14
☽0N	21 11:30
☿0S	28 21:18
☿ D	4 10:11
☽0S	4 20:34
♇ R	10 16:24
♂ D	14 3:53
☽0N	17 16:51
☿0N	22 22:51

Planet Ingress		Dy Hr Mn
☿	♈	2 11:41
♀	♉	5 10:25
☉	♈	20 5:14
☿	♓R	23 13:22
♀	♊	3 15:18
⚳	♉	9 20:39
☿	♈	16 22:42
☉	♉	19 16:12

Last Aspect Dy Hr Mn			☽ Ingress	Dy Hr Mn
2 13:14	♄	△	♋	2 15:08
4 22:17	♀	□	♌	4 23:17
7 1:27	♄	✶	♍	7 3:27
8 9:39	☉	☍	♎	9 4:50
11 3:09	♄	☌	♏	11 5:24
12 18:30	☉	△	♐	13 6:53
15 7:34	♄	✶	♑	15 10:24
17 13:00	♄	□	♒	17 16:11
19 20:31	♄	△	♓	20 0:05
21 8:39	♀	✶	♈	22 9:57
24 17:17	♄	☍	♉	24 21:43
27 4:35	☿	✶	♊	27 10:43
29 18:05	♄	△	♋	29 23:07

Last Aspect Dy Hr Mn			☽ Ingress	Dy Hr Mn
1 4:20	♀	✶	♌	1 8:35
3 13:47	♀	□	♍	3 13:53
5 5:37	☿	☍	♎	5 15:32
7 10:15	♄	☌	♏	7 15:17
9 6:56	☿	△	♐	9 15:12
11 11:06	♄	✶	♑	11 17:02
13 17:05	☿	✶	♒	13 21:48
15 22:42	☉	✶	♓	16 5:38
17 14:34	♃	✶	♈	18 15:59
20 19:35	♄	☍	♉	21 4:05
22 17:10	♃	☌	♊	23 17:05
25 20:31	♄	△	♋	26 5:42
28 7:05	♄	□	♌	28 16:10
30 14:17	♄	✶	♍	30 23:02

☽ Phases & Eclipses Dy Hr Mn		
1 1:21	☽	10♊52
8 9:39	○	18♍13
15 1:25	☾	24♐52
22 14:37	●	2♈22
30 19:41	☽	10♋30
6 19:19	○	17♎23
13 10:50	☾	23♑55
21 7:18	●	1♉35
29 9:57	☽	9♌29

Astro Data

1 March 2012
Julian Day # 40968
SVP 5♓05'06"
GC 27♐00.6 ⚵ 6♓05.5
Eris 21♈37.3 ⚶ 5♐41.1
⚷ 5♓33.8 ⚴ 2♈11.1
☽ Mean ☊ 9♐46.5

1 April 2012
Julian Day # 40999
SVP 5♓05'03"
GC 27♐00.6 ⚵ 16♓14.0
Eris 21♈55.6 ⚶ 6♐57.2R
⚷ 7♓30.2 ⚴ 16♈35.9
☽ Mean ☊ 8♐07.9

LONGITUDE — May 2012

Day	Sid.Time	☉	0 hr ☽	Noon ☽	True ☊	☿	♀	♂	⚳	♃	♄	♅	♆	♇
1 Tu	2 39 17	11♉30 49	0♍32 46	7♍25 27	5♐17.5	17♈36.8	20♊28.5	5♍24.1	8♉43.2	20♉19.4	24♎59.8	6♈34.0	2♓50.0	9♑27.2
2 W	2 43 13	12 29 00	14 25 08	21 31 43	5R15.0	19 06.5	20 55.8	5 35.7	9 07.4	20 33.5	24R55.5	6 37.0	2 51.1	9R26.5
3 Th	2 47 10	13 27 10	28 44 55	6♎04 17	5 12.1	20 38.2	21 21.4	5 47.9	9 31.6	20 47.7	24 51.2	6 39.9	2 52.2	9 25.9
4 F	2 51 07	14 25 19	13♎29 08	20 58 39	5 09.3	22 11.9	21 45.4	6 00.7	9 55.9	21 01.9	24 47.0	6 42.8	2 53.2	9 25.2
5 Sa	2 55 03	15 23 25	28 31 50	6♏07 32	5 07.1	23 47.5	22 07.5	6 13.9	10 20.1	21 16.1	24 42.8	6 45.6	2 54.2	9 24.5
6 Su	2 59 00	16 21 29	13♏44 33	21 21 38	5D05.8	25 25.0	22 27.9	6 27.7	10 44.3	21 30.3	24 38.7	6 48.5	2 55.1	9 23.7
7 M	3 02 56	17 19 33	28 57 31	6♐31 02	5 05.4	27 04.5	22 46.3	6 41.9	11 08.5	21 44.5	24 34.7	6 51.3	2 56.1	9 23.0
8 Tu	3 06 53	18 17 34	14♐01 05	21 26 43	5 05.9	28 45.9	23 02.9	6 56.7	11 32.7	21 58.7	24 30.6	6 54.0	2 57.0	9 22.2
9 W	3 10 49	19 15 34	28 47 11	6♑01 50	5 06.9	0♉29.3	23 17.4	7 11.9	11 56.9	22 13.0	24 26.7	6 56.8	2 57.8	9 21.4
10 Th	3 14 46	20 13 33	13♑10 14	20 12 09	5 08.0	2 14.6	23 29.9	7 27.6	12 21.1	22 27.2	24 22.7	6 59.5	2 58.7	9 20.5
11 F	3 18 42	21 11 30	27 07 26	3♒56 09	5 09.0	4 01.9	23 40.2	7 43.8	12 45.3	22 41.4	24 18.9	7 02.2	2 59.5	9 19.7
12 Sa	3 22 39	22 09 26	10♒38 27	17 14 35	5R09.5	5 51.1	23 48.4	8 00.4	13 09.5	22 55.6	24 15.1	7 04.9	3 00.2	9 18.8
13 Su	3 26 36	23 07 21	23 44 52	0♓09 43	5 09.5	7 42.2	23 54.4	8 17.5	13 33.7	23 09.9	24 11.3	7 07.5	3 01.0	9 17.8
14 M	3 30 32	24 05 15	6♓29 32	12 44 47	5 08.9	9 35.3	23 58.1	8 35.0	13 57.9	23 24.1	24 07.6	7 10.1	3 01.7	9 16.9
15 Tu	3 34 29	25 03 07	18 55 57	25 03 30	5 07.9	11 30.4	23R59.5	8 53.0	14 22.1	23 38.3	24 04.0	7 12.6	3 02.4	9 15.9
16 W	3 38 25	26 00 58	1♈07 53	7♈09 33	5 06.7	13 27.3	23 58.6	9 11.3	14 46.2	23 52.5	24 00.4	7 15.2	3 03.0	9 15.0
17 Th	3 42 22	26 58 48	13 08 56	19 06 28	5 05.4	15 26.1	23 55.3	9 30.1	15 10.4	24 06.7	23 56.9	7 17.7	3 03.6	9 14.0
18 F	3 46 18	27 56 36	25 02 31	0♉57 27	5 04.4	17 26.8	23 49.6	9 49.3	15 34.5	24 20.9	23 53.5	7 20.1	3 04.2	9 12.9
19 Sa	3 50 15	28 54 24	6♉51 37	12 45 21	5 03.7	19 29.2	23 41.5	10 08.9	15 58.7	24 35.1	23 50.1	7 22.6	3 04.7	9 11.9
20 Su	3 54 11	29 52 10	18 38 57	24 32 42	5D03.3	21 33.3	23 30.9	10 28.9	16 22.8	24 49.3	23 46.8	7 25.0	3 05.3	9 10.8
21 M	3 58 08	0♊49 54	0♊26 55	6♊21 51	5 03.2	23 39.1	23 18.0	10 49.2	16 46.9	25 03.5	23 43.6	7 27.3	3 05.7	9 09.7
22 Tu	4 02 05	1 47 38	12 17 47	18 15 01	5 03.3	25 46.2	23 02.7	11 10.0	17 11.0	25 17.7	23 40.5	7 29.7	3 06.2	9 08.6
23 W	4 06 01	2 45 20	24 13 48	0♋14 27	5 03.5	27 54.7	22 45.0	11 31.1	17 35.0	25 31.9	23 37.4	7 32.0	3 06.6	9 07.5
24 Th	4 09 58	3 43 00	6♋17 17	12 22 35	5 03.7	0♊04.4	22 24.9	11 52.6	17 59.1	25 46.0	23 34.5	7 34.2	3 07.0	9 06.3
25 F	4 13 54	4 40 40	18 30 43	24 42 00	5R03.8	2 14.9	22 02.7	12 14.4	18 23.1	26 00.1	23 31.5	7 36.4	3 07.4	9 05.1
26 Sa	4 17 51	5 38 17	0♌56 48	7♌15 30	5 03.8	4 26.2	21 38.2	12 36.6	18 47.2	26 14.2	23 28.7	7 38.6	3 07.7	9 04.0
27 Su	4 21 47	6 35 54	13 38 26	20 05 58	5 03.7	6 38.0	21 11.7	12 59.1	19 11.2	26 28.3	23 26.0	7 40.8	3 08.0	9 02.7
28 M	4 25 44	7 33 28	26 38 26	3♍16 08	5D03.7	8 50.0	20 43.2	13 21.9	19 35.1	26 42.4	23 23.3	7 42.9	3 08.2	9 01.5
29 Tu	4 29 40	8 31 02	9♍59 21	16 48 17	5 03.7	11 01.8	20 12.9	13 45.1	19 59.1	26 56.5	23 20.7	7 44.9	3 08.4	9 00.3
30 W	4 33 37	9 28 34	23 43 02	0♎43 39	5 03.9	13 13.4	19 41.0	14 08.6	20 23.0	27 10.5	23 18.2	7 46.9	3 08.6	8 59.0
31 Th	4 37 34	10 26 04	7♎50 02	15 01 57	5 04.3	15 24.3	19 07.5	14 32.4	20 46.9	27 24.5	23 15.8	7 48.9	3 08.8	8 57.7

LONGITUDE — June 2012

Day	Sid.Time	☉	0 hr ☽	Noon ☽	True ☊	☿	♀	♂	⚳	♃	♄	♅	♆	♇
1 F	4 41 30	11♊23 33	22♎19 04	29♎40 51	5♐04.8	17♊34.4	18♊32.8	14♍56.5	21♉10.8	27♉38.5	23♎13.5	7♈50.9	3♓08.9	8♑56.4
2 Sa	4 45 27	12 21 01	7♏06 40	14♏35 42	5 05.3	19 43.3	17R57.0	15 20.9	21 34.7	27 52.5	23R11.3	7 52.8	3 09.0	8R55.1
3 Su	4 49 23	13 18 28	22 07 02	29 39 39	5R05.6	21 50.9	17 20.4	15 45.6	21 58.6	28 06.4	23 09.1	7 54.7	3 09.1	8 53.8
4 M	4 53 20	14 15 54	7♐12 27	14♐44 20	5 05.6	23 56.8	16 43.1	16 10.5	22 22.4	28 20.3	23 07.1	7 56.5	3R09.1	8 52.5
5 Tu	4 57 16	15 13 19	22 14 11	29 40 57	5 05.0	26 01.1	16 05.5	16 35.8	22 46.2	28 34.2	23 05.1	7 58.3	3 09.1	8 51.1
6 W	5 01 13	16 10 43	7♑03 40	14♑21 30	5 04.0	28 03.4	15 27.7	17 01.3	23 09.9	28 48.1	23 03.3	8 00.0	3 09.0	8 49.8
7 Th	5 05 10	17 08 07	21 33 45	28 39 53	5 02.6	0♋03.7	14 50.1	17 27.1	23 33.7	29 01.9	23 01.5	8 01.7	3 09.0	8 48.4
8 F	5 09 06	18 05 30	5♒39 31	12♒32 27	5 01.1	2 01.8	14 12.8	17 53.1	23 57.4	29 15.7	22 59.8	8 03.4	3 08.9	8 47.0
9 Sa	5 13 03	19 02 52	19 18 37	25 58 08	4 59.8	3 57.7	13 36.1	18 19.4	24 21.1	29 29.5	22 58.2	8 05.0	3 08.7	8 45.6
10 Su	5 16 59	20 00 13	2♓31 12	8♓58 08	4D58.8	5 51.2	13 00.3	18 46.0	24 44.8	29 43.2	22 56.7	8 06.6	3 08.6	8 44.2
11 M	5 20 56	20 57 34	15 19 20	21 35 16	4 58.5	7 42.4	12 25.6	19 12.8	25 08.4	29 56.9	22 55.3	8 08.1	3 08.4	8 42.8
12 Tu	5 24 52	21 54 55	27 46 28	3♈53 28	4 58.9	9 31.2	11 52.1	19 39.9	25 32.0	0♊10.6	22 54.0	8 09.6	3 08.1	8 41.3
13 W	5 28 49	22 52 15	9♈56 51	15 57 11	4 59.9	11 17.6	11 20.1	20 07.2	25 55.6	0 24.2	22 52.8	8 11.0	3 07.9	8 39.9
14 Th	5 32 45	23 49 34	21 55 03	27 51 01	5 01.3	13 01.5	10 49.7	20 34.7	26 19.2	0 37.8	22 51.6	8 12.4	3 07.6	8 38.4
15 F	5 36 42	24 46 54	3♉45 37	9♉39 23	5 02.9	14 42.9	10 21.1	21 02.5	26 42.7	0 51.4	22 50.6	8 13.7	3 07.2	8 37.0
16 Sa	5 40 39	25 44 13	15 32 48	21 26 20	5 04.1	16 21.8	9 54.5	21 30.6	27 06.2	1 04.9	22 49.7	8 15.0	3 06.9	8 35.5
17 Su	5 44 35	26 41 31	27 20 24	3♊15 25	5R04.7	17 58.1	9 29.9	21 58.8	27 29.6	1 18.4	22 48.9	8 16.3	3 06.5	8 34.0
18 M	5 48 32	27 38 49	9♊11 43	15 09 38	5 04.3	19 32.0	9 07.4	22 27.3	27 53.0	1 31.8	22 48.1	8 17.5	3 06.1	8 32.6
19 Tu	5 52 28	28 36 07	21 09 27	27 11 26	5 02.8	21 03.3	8 47.1	22 56.0	28 16.4	1 45.2	22 47.5	8 18.7	3 05.6	8 31.1
20 W	5 56 25	29 33 24	3♋15 49	9♋22 46	5 00.2	22 32.0	8 29.1	23 24.9	28 39.7	1 58.6	22 47.0	8 19.8	3 05.1	8 29.6
21 Th	6 00 21	0♋30 40	15 32 29	21 45 07	4 56.6	23 58.2	8 13.5	23 54.1	29 03.0	2 11.9	22 46.5	8 20.9	3 04.6	8 28.1
22 F	6 04 18	1 27 57	28 00 49	4♌19 43	4 52.5	25 21.7	8 00.2	24 23.4	29 26.3	2 25.1	22 46.2	8 21.9	3 04.1	8 26.6
23 Sa	6 08 14	2 25 12	10♌41 56	17 07 34	4 48.3	26 42.5	7 49.2	24 53.0	29 49.5	2 38.4	22 46.0	8 22.9	3 03.5	8 25.1
24 Su	6 12 11	3 22 27	23 36 46	0♍09 38	4 44.6	28 00.7	7 40.7	25 22.8	0♊12.7	2 51.5	22D45.8	8 23.8	3 02.9	8 23.6
25 M	6 16 08	4 19 41	6♍46 16	13 26 47	4 41.8	29 16.1	7 34.5	25 52.8	0 35.8	3 04.6	22 45.8	8 24.7	3 02.3	8 22.0
26 Tu	6 20 04	5 16 55	20 11 17	26 59 51	4D40.3	0♌28.7	7 30.7	26 22.9	0 58.9	3 17.7	22 45.9	8 25.6	3 01.6	8 20.5
27 W	6 24 01	6 14 08	3♎52 32	10♎49 21	4 40.1	1 38.4	7D29.3	26 53.3	1 21.9	3 30.6	22 46.0	8 26.3	3 00.9	8 19.0
28 Th	6 27 57	7 11 21	17 55 10	24 55 15	4 41.0	2 45.2	7 30.1	27 23.8	1 44.9	3 43.6	22 46.3	8 27.1	3 00.2	8 17.5
29 F	6 31 54	8 08 33	2♏04 04	9♏16 29	4 42.4	3 49.0	7 33.3	27 54.6	2 07.9	3 56.5	22 46.7	8 27.8	2 59.5	8 16.0
30 Sa	6 35 50	9 05 45	16 32 11	23 50 41	4R43.6	4 49.7	7 38.6	28 25.5	2 30.8	4 09.3	22 47.1	8 28.4	2 58.7	8 14.4

Astro Data Dy Hr Mn	Planet Ingress Dy Hr Mn	Last Aspect Dy Hr Mn	☽ Ingress Dy Hr Mn	Last Aspect Dy Hr Mn	☽ Ingress Dy Hr Mn	☽ Phases & Eclipses Dy Hr Mn	Astro Data
☽0S 2 6:11	☿ ♉ 9 5:14	2 10:58 ♀ □	♎ 3 2:04	1 1:31 ♄ ☌	♏ 1 12:31	6 3:35 ○ 16♏01	1 May 2012
♃∠♅ 8 2:09	☉ ♊ 20 15:15	4 18:02 ♄ ☌	♏ 5 2:20	3 9:29 ♃ ☍	♐ 3 12:32	12 21:47 ☾ 22♒33	Julian Day # 41029
☽0N 14 22:10	☿ ♊ 24 11:12	6 12:14 ♃ ☍	♐ 7 1:39	5 5:08 ☿ ☍	♑ 5 12:31	20 23:47 ● 0♊21	SVP 5♓05'00"
♀R 15 14:33		9 1:34 ☿ △	♑ 9 2:00	7 12:38 ♃ △	♒ 7 14:17	20 23:52:45 ✔ A 05'36"	GC 27♐00.7 ⚴ 25♓23.7
♃⊼♄ 16 22:42	☿ ♋ 7 11:16	10 19:11 ♄ □	♒ 11 5:03	9 18:33 ♃ □	♓ 9 19:22	28 20:16 ☽ 7♍53	Eris 22♈15.1 ✱ 3♐19.6R
♃□♇ 17 23:22	♃ ♊ 11 17:22	13 0:52 ♄ △	♓ 13 11:42	11 10:41 ☉ □	♈ 12 4:21		⚷ 8♓56.6 ⚶ 0♉21.7
☽0S 29 14:01	☉ ♋ 20 23:09	15 11:59 ☉ ⚹	♈ 15 21:45	14 3:08 ☉ ⚹	♉ 14 16:22	4 11:12 ○ 14♐14	☽ Mean ☊ 6♐32.6
	⚳ ♊ 23 22:52	17 21:44 ♄ ☍	♉ 18 10:03	16 12:09 ♂ △	♊ 17 5:24	4 11:03 • P 0.370	
♆R 4 21:04	☿ ♌ 26 2:24	20 12:35 ♃ ☌	♊ 20 23:05	19 15:02 ☿ ☌	♋ 19 17:34	11 10:41 ☾ 20♓54	1 June 2012
☽0N 11 5:08		22 22:51 ♄ △	♋ 23 11:31	21 16:48 ☿ ☌	♌ 22 3:47	19 15:02 ● 28♊43	Julian Day # 41060
♅□♇ 24 9:12		25 14:34 ♃ ⚹	♌ 25 22:11	23 22:26 ♄ ⚹	♍ 24 11:42	27 3:30 ☽ 5♎54	SVP 5♓04'56"
♃□♆ 25 7:56		27 23:54 ♃ □	♍ 28 6:06	26 10:53 ♂ ☌	♎ 26 17:15		GC 27♐00.8 ⚴ 3♈33.1
♄D 25 8:00		30 5:50 ♃ △	♎ 30 10:46	28 8:22 ♄ ☌	♏ 28 20:32		Eris 22♈32.2 ⚵ 26♏37.5R
☽0S 25 20:25				30 19:46 ♂ ⚹	♐ 30 22:04		⚷ 9♓41.9 ⚶ 14♉06.9
♀D 27 15:07							☽ Mean ☊ 4♐54.1

July 2012 LONGITUDE

Day	Sid.Time	☉	0 hr ☽	Noon ☽	True ☊	☿	♀	♂	⚳	♃	♄	♅	♆	♇
1 Su	6 39 47	10♋02 56	1♐11 26	8♐33 46	4♐43.9	5♌47.3	7♊46.2	28♍56.6	2♊53.6	4♊22.1	22♎47.7	8♈29.0	2♓57.9	8♑12.9
2 M	6 43 43	11 00 07	15 56 56	23 20 06	4R 42.7	6 41.5	7 55.9	29 27.9	3 16.4	4 34.8	22 48.4	8 29.6	2R 57.0	8R 11.4
3 Tu	6 47 40	11 57 18	0♑42 22	8♑02 51	4 39.8	7 32.3	8 07.6	29 59.3	3 39.2	4 47.4	22 49.1	8 30.1	2 56.2	8 09.9
4 W	6 51 37	12 54 29	15 20 38	22 34 51	4 35.3	8 19.6	8 21.4	0♎30.9	4 01.9	5 00.0	22 50.0	8 30.5	2 55.3	8 08.4
5 Th	6 55 33	13 51 40	29 44 45	6♒49 38	4 29.6	9 03.3	8 37.2	1 02.7	4 24.6	5 12.5	22 51.0	8 31.0	2 54.4	8 06.9
6 F	6 59 30	14 48 51	13♒48 58	20 42 21	4 23.4	9 43.2	8 54.9	1 34.7	4 47.2	5 25.0	22 52.0	8 31.3	2 53.5	8 05.4
7 Sa	7 03 26	15 46 02	27 29 30	4♓10 19	4 17.5	10 19.3	9 14.5	2 06.8	5 09.7	5 37.4	22 53.2	8 31.6	2 52.5	8 03.8
8 Su	7 07 23	16 43 14	10♓44 51	17 13 15	4 12.6	10 51.3	9 35.8	2 39.1	5 32.2	5 49.7	22 54.4	8 31.9	2 51.5	8 02.3
9 M	7 11 19	17 40 26	23 35 48	29 52 53	4 09.2	11 19.1	9 58.9	3 11.5	5 54.6	6 01.9	22 55.8	8 32.1	2 50.5	8 00.8
10 Tu	7 15 16	18 37 38	6♈04 59	12♈12 36	4D 07.5	11 42.7	10 23.7	3 44.1	6 17.0	6 14.1	22 57.2	8 32.3	2 49.5	7 59.4
11 W	7 19 12	19 34 51	18 16 20	24 16 49	4 07.4	12 01.9	10 50.1	4 16.9	6 39.3	6 26.2	22 58.8	8 32.4	2 48.4	7 57.9
12 Th	7 23 09	20 32 04	0♉14 39	6♉10 31	4 08.3	12 16.5	11 18.0	4 49.8	7 01.6	6 38.3	23 00.4	8R 32.4	2 47.3	7 56.4
13 F	7 27 06	21 29 18	12 05 04	17 58 54	4 09.7	12 26.5	11 47.4	5 22.9	7 23.8	6 50.2	23 02.1	8 32.5	2 46.2	7 54.9
14 Sa	7 31 02	22 26 32	23 52 41	29 46 58	4R 10.7	12R 31.7	12 18.3	5 56.1	7 45.9	7 02.1	23 04.0	8 32.4	2 45.1	7 53.5
15 Su	7 34 59	23 23 47	5♊42 20	11♊39 18	4 10.4	12 32.2	12 50.6	6 29.5	8 08.0	7 13.9	23 05.9	8 32.4	2 43.9	7 52.0
16 M	7 38 55	24 21 02	17 38 19	23 39 50	4 08.4	12 27.8	13 24.2	7 03.0	8 30.0	7 25.7	23 07.9	8 32.2	2 42.7	7 50.6
17 Tu	7 42 52	25 18 18	29 44 11	5♋51 41	4 04.3	12 18.6	13 59.0	7 36.7	8 52.0	7 37.3	23 10.0	8 32.1	2 41.5	7 49.1
18 W	7 46 48	26 15 35	12♋02 34	18 17 01	3 58.0	12 04.6	14 35.1	8 10.6	9 13.8	7 48.9	23 12.2	8 31.8	2 40.3	7 47.7
19 Th	7 50 45	27 12 52	24 35 08	0♌56 59	3 49.8	11 46.0	15 12.4	8 44.6	9 35.7	8 00.4	23 14.6	8 31.6	2 39.1	7 46.3
20 F	7 54 41	28 10 09	7♌22 32	13 51 44	3 40.6	11 22.9	15 50.9	9 18.7	9 57.4	8 11.8	23 16.9	8 31.3	2 37.8	7 44.9
21 Sa	7 58 38	29 07 26	20 24 29	27 00 39	3 31.2	10 55.6	16 30.4	9 53.0	10 19.0	8 23.1	23 19.4	8 30.9	2 36.5	7 43.5
22 Su	8 02 35	0♌04 45	3♍40 04	10♍22 34	3 22.7	10 24.3	17 10.9	10 27.4	10 40.6	8 34.3	23 22.0	8 30.5	2 35.2	7 42.1
23 M	8 06 31	1 02 03	17 07 57	23 56 05	3 15.8	9 49.5	17 52.5	11 01.9	11 02.1	8 45.4	23 24.7	8 30.0	2 33.9	7 40.7
24 Tu	8 10 28	1 59 22	0♎46 46	7♎39 54	3 11.1	9 11.7	18 35.1	11 36.6	11 23.6	8 56.5	23 27.5	8 29.5	2 32.5	7 39.4
25 W	8 14 24	2 56 41	14 35 21	21 33 00	3D 08.7	8 31.4	19 18.6	12 11.5	11 44.9	9 07.4	23 30.3	8 28.9	2 31.2	7 38.0
26 Th	8 18 21	3 54 00	28 32 46	5♏34 34	3 08.2	7 49.2	20 03.0	12 46.4	12 06.2	9 18.3	23 33.2	8 28.3	2 29.8	7 36.7
27 F	8 22 17	4 51 20	12♏38 18	19 43 50	3R 08.7	7 05.9	20 48.3	13 21.5	12 27.4	9 29.0	23 36.3	8 27.7	2 28.4	7 35.4
28 Sa	8 26 14	5 48 41	26 51 00	3♐59 37	3 09.0	6 22.1	21 34.4	13 56.8	12 48.5	9 39.7	23 39.4	8 27.0	2 27.0	7 34.1
29 Su	8 30 10	6 46 02	11♐09 23	18 19 59	3 08.2	5 38.8	22 21.3	14 32.1	13 09.5	9 50.2	23 42.6	8 26.3	2 25.6	7 32.8
30 M	8 34 07	7 43 23	25 31 00	2♑41 56	3 05.2	4 56.5	23 09.0	15 07.6	13 30.4	10 00.7	23 45.9	8 25.5	2 24.1	7 31.5
31 Tu	8 38 04	8 40 45	9♑52 14	17 01 16	2 59.6	4 16.3	23 57.5	15 43.2	13 51.3	10 11.0	23 49.3	8 24.6	2 22.7	7 30.3

August 2012 LONGITUDE

Day	Sid.Time	☉	0 hr ☽	Noon ☽	True ☊	☿	♀	♂	⚳	♃	♄	♅	♆	♇
1 W	8 42 00	9♌38 08	24♑08 25	1♒13 00	2♐51.6	3♌38.7	24♊46.7	16♎18.9	14♊12.0	10♊21.3	23♎52.7	8♈23.8	2♓21.2	7♑29.1
2 Th	8 45 57	10 35 31	8♒14 22	15 11 56	2R 41.6	3R 04.6	25 36.7	16 54.7	14 32.7	10 31.4	23 56.3	8R 22.8	2R 19.7	7R 27.8
3 F	8 49 53	11 32 56	22 05 09	28 53 34	2 30.8	2 34.7	26 27.3	17 30.7	14 53.3	10 41.5	23 59.9	8 21.9	2 18.2	7 26.6
4 Sa	8 53 50	12 30 21	5♓36 50	12♓14 44	2 20.1	2 09.5	27 18.6	18 06.8	15 13.7	10 51.4	24 03.6	8 20.9	2 16.7	7 25.5
5 Su	8 57 46	13 27 48	18 47 08	25 14 06	2 10.7	1 49.6	28 10.5	18 43.0	15 34.1	11 01.2	24 07.4	8 19.8	2 15.2	7 24.3
6 M	9 01 43	14 25 15	1♈35 44	7♈52 17	2 03.3	1 35.4	29 03.0	19 19.3	15 54.4	11 10.9	24 11.3	8 18.7	2 13.6	7 23.2
7 Tu	9 05 39	15 22 44	14 04 06	20 11 38	1 58.4	1D 27.4	29 56.2	19 55.8	16 14.6	11 20.5	24 15.2	8 17.6	2 12.1	7 22.0
8 W	9 09 36	16 20 14	26 15 23	2♉15 55	1 55.8	1 25.8	0♋49.9	20 32.3	16 34.7	11 30.0	24 19.2	8 16.4	2 10.5	7 20.9
9 Th	9 13 33	17 17 46	8♉13 50	14 09 48	1D 54.9	1 31.0	1 44.2	21 09.0	16 54.7	11 39.4	24 23.3	8 15.2	2 09.0	7 19.8
10 F	9 17 29	18 15 19	20 04 30	25 58 35	1R 55.0	1 43.0	2 39.0	21 45.8	17 14.6	11 48.6	24 27.5	8 13.9	2 07.4	7 18.8
11 Sa	9 21 26	19 12 53	1♊52 46	7♊47 43	1 54.9	2 01.9	3 34.4	22 22.7	17 34.3	11 57.8	24 31.8	8 12.6	2 05.8	7 17.7
12 Su	9 25 22	20 10 29	13 44 06	19 42 32	1 53.7	2 27.9	4 30.2	22 59.7	17 54.0	12 06.8	24 36.1	8 11.3	2 04.2	7 16.7
13 M	9 29 19	21 08 06	25 43 37	1♋47 53	1 50.5	3 00.9	5 26.6	23 36.9	18 13.6	12 15.6	24 40.5	8 09.9	2 02.6	7 15.7
14 Tu	9 33 15	22 05 45	7♋55 48	14 07 49	1 44.8	3 40.8	6 23.4	24 14.2	18 33.0	12 24.4	24 45.0	8 08.5	2 01.0	7 14.8
15 W	9 37 12	23 03 25	20 24 13	26 45 15	1 36.4	4 27.6	7 20.7	24 51.5	18 52.3	12 33.0	24 49.6	8 07.0	1 59.4	7 13.8
16 Th	9 41 08	24 01 06	3♌11 04	9♌41 42	1 25.8	5 21.2	8 18.4	25 29.0	19 11.5	12 41.5	24 54.2	8 05.5	1 57.8	7 12.9
17 F	9 45 05	24 58 49	16 17 05	22 57 03	1 13.7	6 21.2	9 16.5	26 06.6	19 30.6	12 49.9	24 58.9	8 04.0	1 56.1	7 12.0
18 Sa	9 49 02	25 56 33	29 41 19	6♍29 35	1 01.3	7 27.7	10 15.1	26 44.3	19 49.6	12 58.1	25 03.7	8 02.4	1 54.5	7 11.1
19 Su	9 52 58	26 54 18	13♍21 25	20 16 21	0 49.9	8 40.2	11 14.0	27 22.2	20 08.4	13 06.2	25 08.6	8 00.8	1 52.9	7 10.2
20 M	9 56 55	27 52 04	27 13 55	4♎13 38	0 40.6	9 58.5	12 13.3	28 00.1	20 27.1	13 14.2	25 13.5	7 59.1	1 51.2	7 09.4
21 Tu	10 00 51	28 49 52	11♎15 01	18 17 38	0 33.9	11 22.2	13 13.0	28 38.2	20 45.6	13 22.0	25 18.5	7 57.4	1 49.6	7 08.6
22 W	10 04 48	29 47 41	25 21 05	2♏25 03	0 30.0	12 51.1	14 13.1	29 16.3	21 04.1	13 29.6	25 23.5	7 55.7	1 48.0	7 07.8
23 Th	10 08 44	0♍45 31	9♏29 14	16 33 25	0D 28.4	14 24.6	15 13.5	29 54.6	21 22.4	13 37.2	25 28.6	7 53.9	1 46.3	7 07.1
24 F	10 12 41	1 43 22	23 37 26	0♐41 09	0R 28.2	16 02.4	16 14.3	0♏32.9	21 40.5	13 44.6	25 33.8	7 52.2	1 44.7	7 06.3
25 Sa	10 16 37	2 41 15	7♐44 27	14 47 13	0 28.0	17 44.1	17 15.4	1 11.4	21 58.5	13 51.8	25 39.1	7 50.3	1 43.0	7 05.6
26 Su	10 20 34	3 39 08	21 49 23	28 50 47	0 26.6	19 29.2	18 16.9	1 50.0	22 16.4	13 58.9	25 44.4	7 48.5	1 41.4	7 05.0
27 M	10 24 31	4 37 03	5♑51 16	12♑50 38	0 22.9	21 17.2	19 18.6	2 28.6	22 34.1	14 05.8	25 49.8	7 46.6	1 39.8	7 04.3
28 Tu	10 28 27	5 34 59	19 48 38	26 45 00	0 16.4	23 07.7	20 20.7	3 07.4	22 51.7	14 12.6	25 55.2	7 44.7	1 38.1	7 03.7
29 W	10 32 24	6 32 57	3♒39 22	10♒31 23	0 07.2	25 00.2	21 23.1	3 46.3	23 09.1	14 19.3	26 00.7	7 42.8	1 36.5	7 03.1
30 Th	10 36 20	7 30 56	17 20 41	24 06 54	29♏55.9	26 54.3	22 25.8	4 25.2	23 26.4	14 25.8	26 06.3	7 40.8	1 34.8	7 02.5
31 F	10 40 17	8 28 56	0♓49 39	7♓28 38	29 43.5	28 49.7	23 28.8	5 04.3	23 43.5	14 32.1	26 11.9	7 38.8	1 33.2	7 02.0

Astro Data

	Dy Hr Mn
♂0S	5 0:42
☽0N	8 14:04
♅R	13 9:49
☿R	15 2:15
♃⚻♇	18 9:46
♃⚼♄	21 2:00
♃✶♅	22 4:04
☽0S	23 2:32
☽0N	4 23:54
☿D	8 5:39
☽0S	19 9:38

Planet Ingress

	Dy Hr Mn
♂ ♎	3 12:31
☉ ♌	22 10:01
♀ ♋	7 13:43
☉ ♍	22 17:07
♂ ♏	23 15:24
☊ ♏R	30 3:40

Last Aspect / ☽ Ingress

Last Aspect Dy Hr Mn		☽ Ingress	Dy Hr Mn
2 22:21	♂ □	♑	2 22:51
4 12:25	♄ □	♒	5 0:26
6 15:49	♄ △	♓	7 4:29
8 11:00	☉ △	♈	9 12:14
11 9:23	♄ ☍	♉	11 23:30
13 19:46	☉ ✶	♊	14 12:26
16 10:56	♄ △	♋	17 0:31
19 4:24	☉ ☌	♌	19 10:13
21 5:17	♄ ✶	♍	21 17:24
23 0:44	♀ □	♎	23 22:38
25 15:22	♄ ☌	♏	26 2:29
26 15:38	☿ □	♐	28 5:18
29 21:01	♄ ✶	♑	30 7:29

Last Aspect / ☽ Ingress

Last Aspect Dy Hr Mn		☽ Ingress	Dy Hr Mn
31 23:30	♄ □	♒	1 9:56
3 7:24	♀ △	♓	3 13:58
5 17:56	♀ □	♈	5 20:58
7 20:04	♄ ☍	♉	8 7:28
9 18:55	☉ □	♊	10 20:11
12 21:49	♄ △	♋	13 8:27
15 8:21	♄ □	♌	15 18:05
17 17:55	♂ ✶	♍	18 0:33
18 23:26	♃ □	♎	20 4:45
22 7:13	☉ ✶	♏	22 7:54
23 9:34	♀ △	♐	24 10:50
26 6:39	♄ ✶	♑	26 13:58
28 10:33	♄ □	♒	28 17:38
30 17:48	☿ ☍	♓	30 22:31

☽ Phases & Eclipses

Dy Hr Mn		
3 18:52	○	12♑14
11 1:48	☾	19♈11
19 4:24	●	26♋55
26 8:56	☽	3♏47
2 3:27	○	10♒15
9 18:55	☾	17♉34
17 15:54	●	25♌08
24 13:54	☽	1♐48
31 13:58	○	8♓34

Astro Data

1 July 2012
Julian Day # 41090
SVP 5♓04'51"
GC 27♐00.8 ⚴ 9♈16.2
Eris 22♈41.8 ⚵ 22♏01.3R
⚷ 9♓34.7R ⚶ 26♉40.3
☽ Mean ☊ 3♐18.8

1 August 2012
Julian Day # 41121
SVP 5♓04'46"
GC 27♐00.9 ⚴ 11♈28.8R
Eris 22♈42.5R ⚵ 22♏04.8
⚷ 8♓38.8R ⚶ 8♊25.1
☽ Mean ☊ 1♐40.3

LONGITUDE — September 2012

Day	Sid.Time	☉	0 hr ☽	Noon☽	True☊	☿	♀	♂	⚳	♃	♄	♅	♆	♇
1 Sa	10 44 13	9♍26 58	14♓03 34	20♓34 16	29♏31.3	0♍45.9	24♋32.0	5♏43.5	24♊00.4	14♊38.3	26♎17.5	7♈36.8	1♓31.6	7♑01.5
2 Su	10 48 10	10 25 02	27 00 36	3♈22 31	29R 20.3	2 42.7	25 35.6	6 22.7	24 17.2	14 44.3	26 23.3	7R 34.7	1R 30.0	7R 01.0
3 M	10 52 06	11 23 07	9♈40 04	15 53 24	29 11.4	4 39.7	26 39.4	7 02.1	24 33.8	14 50.2	26 29.0	7 32.7	1 28.3	7 00.5
4 Tu	10 56 03	12 21 15	22 02 45	28 08 24	29 05.2	6 36.8	27 43.5	7 41.5	24 50.3	14 55.8	26 34.9	7 30.6	1 26.7	7 00.1
5 W	11 00 00	13 19 24	4♉10 46	10♉10 18	29 01.6	8 33.6	28 47.8	8 21.1	25 06.6	15 01.4	26 40.8	7 28.4	1 25.1	6 59.7
6 Th	11 03 56	14 17 35	16 07 31	22 02 59	29D 00.1	10 30.0	29 52.5	9 00.7	25 22.7	15 06.7	26 46.7	7 26.3	1 23.5	6 59.3
7 F	11 07 53	15 15 49	27 57 19	3♊51 09	29 00.0	12 25.9	0♌57.3	9 40.4	25 38.6	15 11.9	26 52.7	7 24.1	1 22.0	6 59.0
8 Sa	11 11 49	16 14 04	9♊45 10	15 40 03	29R 00.2	14 21.1	2 02.4	10 20.3	25 54.4	15 17.0	26 58.7	7 21.9	1 20.4	6 58.7
9 Su	11 15 46	17 12 22	21 36 30	27 35 11	28 59.7	16 15.5	3 07.8	11 00.2	26 10.0	15 21.8	27 04.8	7 19.7	1 18.8	6 58.4
10 M	11 19 42	18 10 41	3♋36 46	9♋41 54	28 57.6	18 09.0	4 13.4	11 40.3	26 25.3	15 26.5	27 11.0	7 17.5	1 17.2	6 58.2
11 Tu	11 23 39	19 09 03	15 51 09	22 05 05	28 53.3	20 01.6	5 19.2	12 20.4	26 40.5	15 31.0	27 17.2	7 15.2	1 15.7	6 57.9
12 W	11 27 35	20 07 26	28 24 08	4♌48 41	28 46.5	21 53.3	6 25.2	13 00.6	26 55.5	15 35.3	27 23.4	7 13.0	1 14.2	6 57.8
13 Th	11 31 32	21 05 52	11♌18 59	17 55 11	28 37.5	23 43.9	7 31.4	13 40.9	27 10.3	15 39.5	27 29.7	7 10.7	1 12.6	6 57.6
14 F	11 35 28	22 04 19	24 37 18	1♍25 11	28 27.1	25 33.5	8 37.9	14 21.4	27 24.9	15 43.4	27 36.0	7 08.4	1 11.1	6 57.5
15 Sa	11 39 25	23 02 49	8♍18 35	15 17 06	28 16.3	27 22.0	9 44.5	15 01.9	27 39.2	15 47.2	27 42.4	7 06.1	1 09.6	6 57.4
16 Su	11 43 22	24 01 20	22 20 11	29 27 12	28 06.3	29 09.5	10 51.4	15 42.5	27 53.4	15 50.8	27 48.8	7 03.7	1 08.1	6 57.3
17 M	11 47 18	24 59 53	6♎37 27	13♎50 08	27 58.1	0♎55.9	11 58.4	16 23.2	28 07.3	15 54.2	27 55.3	7 01.4	1 06.6	6D 57.3
18 Tu	11 51 15	25 58 29	21 04 29	28 19 44	27 52.4	2 41.3	13 05.7	17 04.0	28 21.1	15 57.5	28 01.8	6 59.0	1 05.2	6 57.3
19 W	11 55 11	26 57 06	5♏35 08	12♏50 01	27 49.3	4 25.6	14 13.1	17 44.8	28 34.6	16 00.5	28 08.3	6 56.7	1 03.7	6 57.3
20 Th	11 59 08	27 55 44	20 03 49	27 16 02	27D 48.4	6 08.9	15 20.7	18 25.8	28 47.8	16 03.4	28 14.9	6 54.3	1 02.3	6 57.3
21 F	12 03 04	28 54 25	4♐26 18	11♐34 17	27 48.8	7 51.2	16 28.4	19 06.9	29 00.9	16 06.0	28 21.5	6 51.9	1 00.9	6 57.4
22 Sa	12 07 01	29 53 07	18 39 48	25 42 41	27R 49.5	9 32.5	17 36.4	19 48.0	29 13.7	16 08.5	28 28.2	6 49.5	0 59.5	6 57.5
23 Su	12 10 57	0♎51 50	2♑42 51	9♑40 14	27 49.2	11 12.8	18 44.5	20 29.3	29 26.2	16 10.8	28 34.9	6 47.1	0 58.1	6 57.7
24 M	12 14 54	1 50 36	16 34 51	23 26 38	27 47.1	12 52.1	19 52.8	21 10.6	29 38.5	16 12.8	28 41.6	6 44.7	0 56.8	6 57.9
25 Tu	12 18 51	2 49 23	0♒15 36	7♒01 43	27 42.7	14 30.5	21 01.3	21 52.0	29 50.6	16 14.7	28 48.4	6 42.3	0 55.4	6 58.1
26 W	12 22 47	3 48 11	13 44 57	20 25 14	27 36.2	16 07.9	22 09.9	22 33.5	0♋02.4	16 16.4	28 55.1	6 39.9	0 54.1	6 58.3
27 Th	12 26 44	4 47 02	27 02 31	3♓36 42	27 27.8	17 44.4	23 18.7	23 15.0	0 14.0	16 17.9	29 02.0	6 37.5	0 52.8	6 58.6
28 F	12 30 40	5 45 54	10♓07 44	16 35 30	27 18.6	19 20.1	24 27.6	23 56.7	0 25.3	16 19.2	29 08.8	6 35.1	0 51.5	6 58.9
29 Sa	12 34 37	6 44 48	22 59 58	29 21 04	27 09.4	20 54.8	25 36.7	24 38.4	0 36.4	16 20.3	29 15.7	6 32.7	0 50.3	6 59.2
30 Su	12 38 33	7 43 45	5♈38 48	11♈53 11	27 01.1	22 28.7	26 45.9	25 20.2	0 47.1	16 21.2	29 22.6	6 30.2	0 49.0	6 59.6

LONGITUDE — October 2012

Day	Sid.Time	☉	0 hr ☽	Noon☽	True☊	☿	♀	♂	⚳	♃	♄	♅	♆	♇
1 M	12 42 30	8♎42 43	18♈04 16	24♈12 11	26♏54.6	24♎01.7	27♌55.3	26♏02.1	0♋57.7	16♊22.0	29♎29.5	6♈27.8	0♓47.8	7♑00.0
2 Tu	12 46 26	9 41 43	0♉17 07	6♉19 16	26R 50.2	25 33.8	29 04.9	26 44.1	1 07.9	16 22.5	29 36.5	6R 25.4	0R 46.6	7 00.4
3 W	12 50 23	10 40 46	12 18 56	18 16 26	26D 47.9	27 05.2	0♍14.6	27 26.2	1 17.8	16 22.8	29 43.4	6 23.0	0 45.4	7 00.9
4 Th	12 54 20	11 39 51	24 12 11	0♊06 37	26 47.6	28 35.6	1 24.4	28 08.3	1 27.5	16R 22.9	29 50.5	6 20.6	0 44.3	7 01.4
5 F	12 58 16	12 38 58	6♊00 13	11 53 32	26 48.5	0♏05.3	2 34.4	28 50.6	1 36.9	16 22.8	29 57.5	6 18.2	0 43.2	7 01.9
6 Sa	13 02 13	13 38 07	17 47 07	23 41 36	26 50.1	1 34.0	3 44.6	29 32.9	1 46.0	16 22.5	0♏04.5	6 15.8	0 42.1	7 02.5
7 Su	13 06 09	14 37 19	29 37 34	5♋35 42	26R 51.4	3 02.0	4 54.8	0♐15.3	1 54.8	16 22.0	0 11.6	6 13.4	0 41.0	7 03.0
8 M	13 10 06	15 36 33	11♋36 37	17 41 00	26 51.8	4 29.1	6 05.2	0 57.8	2 03.2	16 21.3	0 18.7	6 11.0	0 39.9	7 03.7
9 Tu	13 14 02	16 35 49	23 49 28	0♌02 38	26 50.8	5 55.3	7 15.7	1 40.3	2 11.4	16 20.4	0 25.8	6 08.7	0 38.9	7 04.3
10 W	13 17 59	17 35 07	6♌21 03	12 45 12	26 48.1	7 20.7	8 26.4	2 23.0	2 19.3	16 19.3	0 32.9	6 06.3	0 37.9	7 05.0
11 Th	13 21 55	18 34 28	19 15 31	25 52 19	26 43.8	8 45.1	9 37.2	3 05.7	2 26.8	16 18.0	0 40.1	6 04.0	0 36.9	7 05.7
12 F	13 25 52	19 33 51	2♍35 47	9♍25 58	26 38.4	10 08.7	10 48.1	3 48.5	2 34.0	16 16.5	0 47.3	6 01.6	0 36.0	7 06.4
13 Sa	13 29 48	20 33 17	16 22 45	23 25 53	26 32.5	11 31.2	11 59.1	4 31.4	2 40.9	16 14.8	0 54.4	5 59.3	0 35.1	7 07.2
14 Su	13 33 45	21 32 44	0♎34 56	7♎49 17	26 27.0	12 52.8	13 10.2	5 14.4	2 47.4	16 12.9	1 01.6	5 57.0	0 34.2	7 08.0
15 M	13 37 42	22 32 14	15 08 12	22 30 47	26 22.6	14 13.3	14 21.5	5 57.4	2 53.6	16 10.8	1 08.8	5 54.7	0 33.3	7 08.8
16 Tu	13 41 38	23 31 45	29 56 06	7♏23 06	26 19.7	15 32.7	15 32.8	6 40.5	2 59.5	16 08.5	1 16.0	5 52.4	0 32.4	7 09.6
17 W	13 45 35	24 31 19	14♏50 46	22 18 05	26D 18.5	16 50.9	16 44.3	7 23.8	3 05.0	16 05.9	1 23.3	5 50.2	0 31.6	7 10.5
18 Th	13 49 31	25 30 55	29 44 05	7♐07 55	26 18.8	18 07.8	17 55.9	8 07.0	3 10.1	16 03.2	1 30.5	5 47.9	0 30.9	7 11.4
19 F	13 53 28	26 30 32	14♐28 50	21 46 13	26 20.0	19 23.4	19 07.5	8 50.4	3 14.9	16 00.3	1 37.7	5 45.7	0 30.1	7 12.4
20 Sa	13 57 24	27 30 11	28 59 35	6♑08 33	26 21.5	20 37.6	20 19.3	9 33.8	3 19.4	15 57.2	1 45.0	5 43.5	0 29.4	7 13.4
21 Su	14 01 21	28 29 52	13♑12 54	20 12 30	26R 22.6	21 50.1	21 31.2	10 17.3	3 23.4	15 53.9	1 52.2	5 41.3	0 28.7	7 14.4
22 M	14 05 17	29 29 34	27 07 18	3♒57 21	26 22.8	23 01.0	22 43.1	11 00.9	3 27.1	15 50.5	1 59.5	5 39.2	0 28.0	7 15.4
23 Tu	14 09 14	0♏29 19	10♒42 45	17 23 38	26 21.7	24 10.0	23 55.2	11 44.6	3 30.5	15 46.8	2 06.8	5 37.0	0 27.4	7 16.4
24 W	14 13 11	1 29 04	24 00 11	0♓32 35	26 19.5	25 16.9	25 07.3	12 28.3	3 33.5	15 42.9	2 14.0	5 34.9	0 26.8	7 17.5
25 Th	14 17 07	2 28 52	7♓01 04	13 25 48	26 16.3	26 21.5	26 19.5	13 12.1	3 36.0	15 38.9	2 21.3	5 32.8	0 26.2	7 18.6
26 F	14 21 04	3 28 41	19 47 02	26 04 55	26 12.6	27 23.6	27 31.9	13 55.9	3 38.2	15 34.7	2 28.5	5 30.8	0 25.7	7 19.8
27 Sa	14 25 00	4 28 32	2♈19 41	8♈31 30	26 08.9	28 23.0	28 44.3	14 39.8	3 40.1	15 30.3	2 35.8	5 28.7	0 25.2	7 20.9
28 Su	14 28 57	5 28 25	14 40 33	20 47 02	26 05.7	29 19.3	29 56.8	15 23.8	3 41.5	15 25.7	2 43.0	5 26.7	0 24.7	7 22.1
29 M	14 32 53	6 28 20	26 51 07	2♉53 00	26 03.3	0♐12.2	1♎09.4	16 07.9	3 42.6	15 20.9	2 50.3	5 24.8	0 24.3	7 23.3
30 Tu	14 36 50	7 28 16	8♉52 54	14 51 01	26D 01.9	1 01.3	2 22.0	16 52.0	3 43.2	15 16.0	2 57.5	5 22.8	0 23.9	7 24.6
31 W	14 40 46	8 28 15	20 47 36	26 42 55	26 01.5	1 46.2	3 34.8	17 36.2	3R 43.5	15 10.9	3 04.8	5 20.9	0 23.5	7 25.9

Astro Data

	Dy Hr Mn
☽0N	1 9:05
☽0S	15 18:19
♇D	18 5:06
☿0S	18 8:03
♅□♇	19 5:57
☉0S	22 14:49
☽0N	28 16:24
♃R	4 13:18
♄△♆	11 2:38
☽0S	13 4:09
♃⚻♄	15 16:56
☽0N	25 21:59
♀0S	31 13:36
⚳R	31 15:46

Planet Ingress

	Dy Hr Mn
☿ ♍	1 2:32
♀ ♌	6 14:48
☿ ♎	16 23:22
☉ ♎	22 14:49
⚳ ♋	26 7:00
♀ ♍	3 6:59
☿ ♏	5 10:35
♄ ♏	5 20:34
♂ ♐	7 3:21
☉ ♏	23 0:14
♀ ♎	28 13:04
☿ ♐	29 6:18

Last Aspect / ☽ Ingress (September)

Last Aspect Dy Hr Mn		☽ Ingress Dy Hr Mn
1 20:02	♀ △	♈ 2 5:37
4 11:06	♀ □	♉ 4 15:41
5 18:54	☉ △	♊ 7 4:10
9 10:59	♄ △	♋ 9 16:49
11 21:58	♄ □	♌ 12 3:00
14 5:14	♄ ⚹	♍ 14 9:30
16 11:26	☿ ☌	♎ 16 12:55
18 11:30	♄ ☌	♏ 18 14:46
20 13:11	☉ ⚹	♐ 20 16:34
22 16:45	♄ ⚹	♑ 22 19:20
24 21:19	♄ □	♒ 24 23:32
27 3:33	♄ △	♓ 27 5:23
29 2:34	♂ △	♈ 29 13:14

Last Aspect / ☽ Ingress (October)

Last Aspect Dy Hr Mn		☽ Ingress Dy Hr Mn
1 22:32	♄ ☍	♉ 1 23:26
4 7:44	♂ ☍	♊ 4 11:47
5 21:08	♃ ☌	♋ 7 0:45
8 7:33	☉ □	♌ 9 11:55
10 21:40	☉ ⚹	♍ 11 19:23
12 23:48	♃ □	♎ 13 23:02
15 12:02	☉ ☌	♏ 16 0:06
17 2:23	☿ ☌	♐ 18 0:26
19 20:27	☉ ⚹	♑ 20 1:41
22 3:32	☉ □	♒ 22 5:02
24 1:27	☿ □	♓ 24 11:00
26 15:04	♀ ☍	♈ 26 19:31
28 1:32	♃ ⚹	♉ 29 6:15
29 21:01	♇ △	♊ 31 18:40

☽ Phases & Eclipses

Dy Hr Mn	
8 13:15	☾ 16♊17
16 2:11	● 23♍37
22 19:41	☽ 0♑12
30 3:19	○ 7♈22
8 7:33	☾ 15♋26
15 12:02	● 22♎32
22 3:32	☽ 29♑09
29 19:49	○ 6♉48

Astro Data

1 September 2012
Julian Day # 41152
SVP 5♓04'42"
GC 27♐01.0 ⚴ 8♈16.1R
Eris 22♈33.5R ⚵ 26♏35.0
⚷ 7♓13.5R ⚶ 18♊07.4
☽ Mean ☊ 0♐01.8

1 October 2012
Julian Day # 41182
SVP 5♓04'40"
GC 27♐01.0 ⚴ 0♈40.0R
Eris 22♈18.1R ⚵ 3♐52.4
⚷ 5♓53.3R ⚶ 24♊14.5
☽ Mean ☊ 28♏26.5

November 2012 LONGITUDE

Day	Sid.Time	☉	0 hr ☽	Noon ☽	True ☊	☿	♀	♂	⚳	♃	♄	♅	♆	♇
1 Th	14 44 43	9♏28 15	2♊37 16	8♊30 58	26♏01.9	2♐26.4	4♎47.6	18♐20.5	3♋43.3	15♊05.6	3♏12.0	5♈19.0	0♓23.1	7♑27.2
2 F	14 48 40	10 28 18	14 24 21	20 17 50	26 03.0	3 01.4	6 00.6	19 04.8	3R42.8	15R00.2	3 19.3	5R17.2	0R22.8	7 28.5
3 Sa	14 52 36	11 28 23	26 11 49	2♋06 46	26 04.4	3 30.6	7 13.6	19 49.2	3 41.9	14 54.6	3 26.5	5 15.4	0 22.6	7 29.8
4 Su	14 56 33	12 28 29	8♋03 10	14 01 30	26 05.7	3 53.4	8 26.6	20 33.7	3 40.5	14 48.9	3 33.7	5 13.6	0 22.3	7 31.2
5 M	15 00 29	13 28 38	20 02 20	26 06 12	26 06.8	4 09.1	9 39.8	21 18.2	3 38.8	14 43.0	3 40.9	5 11.8	0 22.1	7 32.6
6 Tu	15 04 26	14 28 49	2♌13 40	8♌25 18	26R07.4	4R17.1	10 53.0	22 02.8	3 36.6	14 36.9	3 48.1	5 10.1	0 21.9	7 34.0
7 W	15 08 22	15 29 02	14 41 39	21 03 14	26 07.4	4 16.8	12 06.3	22 47.5	3 34.0	14 30.7	3 55.2	5 08.4	0 21.8	7 35.5
8 Th	15 12 19	16 29 16	27 30 34	4♍04 05	26 06.9	4 07.4	13 19.7	23 32.2	3 31.0	14 24.4	4 02.4	5 06.8	0 21.7	7 36.9
9 F	15 16 15	17 29 33	10♍44 06	17 30 55	26 06.1	3 48.5	14 33.1	24 17.0	3 27.6	14 17.9	4 09.5	5 05.2	0 21.6	7 38.4
10 Sa	15 20 12	18 29 52	24 24 38	1♎25 16	26 05.2	3 19.7	15 46.6	25 01.9	3 23.8	14 11.3	4 16.7	5 03.6	0D21.5	7 39.9
11 Su	15 24 09	19 30 13	8♎32 39	15 46 26	26 04.3	2 40.9	17 00.2	25 46.8	3 19.6	14 04.5	4 23.8	5 02.1	0 21.5	7 41.5
12 M	15 28 05	20 30 36	23 06 06	0♏30 57	26 03.7	1 52.1	18 13.8	26 31.8	3 14.9	13 57.6	4 30.9	5 00.6	0 21.5	7 43.0
13 Tu	15 32 02	21 31 00	8♏00 08	15 32 39	26D03.4	0 54.0	19 27.5	27 16.9	3 09.9	13 50.7	4 37.9	4 59.1	0 21.6	7 44.6
14 W	15 35 58	22 31 26	23 07 21	0♐43 05	26 03.3	29♏47.6	20 41.2	28 02.0	3 04.5	13 43.5	4 45.0	4 57.7	0 21.7	7 46.2
15 Th	15 39 55	23 31 54	8♐18 37	15 52 45	26 03.4	28 34.2	21 55.0	28 47.2	2 58.6	13 36.3	4 52.0	4 56.4	0 21.8	7 47.9
16 F	15 43 51	24 32 24	23 24 23	0♑52 27	26 03.6	27 16.0	23 08.9	29 32.4	2 52.3	13 29.0	4 59.0	4 55.0	0 22.0	7 49.5
17 Sa	15 47 48	25 32 55	8♑16 06	15 34 36	26R03.7	25 55.2	24 22.8	0♑17.7	2 45.7	13 21.6	5 06.0	4 53.7	0 22.2	7 51.2
18 Su	15 51 44	26 33 27	22 47 22	29 54 02	26 03.7	24 34.5	25 36.7	1 03.1	2 38.7	13 14.1	5 13.0	4 52.5	0 22.4	7 52.9
19 M	15 55 41	27 34 00	6♒54 22	13♒48 18	26 03.7	23 16.5	26 50.7	1 48.5	2 31.2	13 06.5	5 19.9	4 51.3	0 22.7	7 54.6
20 Tu	15 59 38	28 34 34	20 35 53	27 17 17	26D03.6	22 03.8	28 04.8	2 34.0	2 23.4	12 58.8	5 26.8	4 50.2	0 23.0	7 56.3
21 W	16 03 34	29 35 10	3♓52 47	10♓22 41	26 03.7	20 58.7	29 18.8	3 19.5	2 15.3	12 51.1	5 33.6	4 49.1	0 23.3	7 58.0
22 Th	16 07 31	0♐35 46	16 47 24	23 07 20	26 04.0	20 02.9	0♏33.0	4 05.1	2 06.7	12 43.2	5 40.5	4 48.0	0 23.7	7 59.8
23 F	16 11 27	1 36 24	29 22 55	5♈34 35	26 04.5	19 17.8	1 47.1	4 50.7	1 57.8	12 35.4	5 47.2	4 47.0	0 24.1	8 01.6
24 Sa	16 15 24	2 37 03	11♈42 49	17 48 00	26 05.2	18 44.0	3 01.3	5 36.4	1 48.5	12 27.4	5 54.0	4 46.0	0 24.5	8 03.4
25 Su	16 19 20	3 37 44	23 50 34	29 50 54	26 05.9	18 21.9	4 15.6	6 22.1	1 38.9	12 19.4	6 00.7	4 45.1	0 25.0	8 05.2
26 M	16 23 17	4 38 25	5♉49 23	11♉46 21	26 06.5	18D11.3	5 29.9	7 07.9	1 29.0	12 11.4	6 07.4	4 44.2	0 25.5	8 07.0
27 Tu	16 27 13	5 39 08	17 42 08	23 37 02	26R06.9	18 11.9	6 44.2	7 53.7	1 18.7	12 03.3	6 14.1	4 43.4	0 26.0	8 08.9
28 W	16 31 10	6 39 52	29 31 20	5♊25 19	26 06.7	18 22.8	7 58.6	8 39.6	1 08.1	11 55.2	6 20.7	4 42.6	0 26.6	8 10.8
29 Th	16 35 07	7 40 37	11♊19 14	17 13 22	26 05.9	18 43.3	9 13.0	9 25.5	0 57.3	11 47.1	6 27.3	4 41.9	0 27.2	8 12.6
30 F	16 39 03	8 41 24	23 07 57	29 03 15	26 04.5	19 12.6	10 27.5	10 11.5	0 46.1	11 38.9	6 33.8	4 41.2	0 27.9	8 14.5

December 2012 LONGITUDE

Day	Sid.Time	☉	0 hr ☽	Noon ☽	True ☊	☿	♀	♂	⚳	♃	♄	♅	♆	♇
1 Sa	16 43 00	9♐42 12	4♋59 34	10♋57 09	26♏02.6	19♏49.8	11♏41.9	10♑57.5	0♋34.6	11♊30.7	6♏40.3	4♈40.5	0♓28.6	8♑16.4
2 Su	16 46 56	10 43 01	16 56 20	22 57 24	26R00.3	20 34.0	12 56.5	11 43.6	0R22.8	11R22.6	6 46.8	4R40.0	0 29.3	8 18.4
3 M	16 50 53	11 43 51	29 00 44	5♌06 41	25 58.0	21 24.3	14 11.0	12 29.7	0 10.8	11 14.4	6 53.2	4 39.4	0 30.0	8 20.3
4 Tu	16 54 49	12 44 43	11♌15 38	17 27 59	25 55.9	22 20.1	15 25.6	13 15.9	29♊58.5	11 06.2	6 59.6	4 38.9	0 30.8	8 22.3
5 W	16 58 46	13 45 36	23 44 09	0♍04 35	25 54.5	23 20.6	16 40.3	14 02.1	29 46.0	10 58.0	7 05.9	4 38.5	0 31.6	8 24.2
6 Th	17 02 42	14 46 31	6♍29 40	12 59 51	25D53.9	24 25.3	17 54.9	14 48.4	29 33.2	10 49.9	7 12.2	4 38.1	0 32.4	8 26.2
7 F	17 06 39	15 47 26	19 35 31	26 16 59	25 54.2	25 33.6	19 09.6	15 34.7	29 20.3	10 41.7	7 18.4	4 37.8	0 33.3	8 28.2
8 Sa	17 10 36	16 48 23	3♎04 34	9♎58 27	25 55.3	26 45.0	20 24.3	16 21.0	29 07.1	10 33.6	7 24.6	4 37.5	0 34.2	8 30.2
9 Su	17 14 32	17 49 21	16 58 44	24 05 23	25 56.7	27 59.1	21 39.1	17 07.4	28 53.7	10 25.6	7 30.7	4 37.3	0 35.1	8 32.2
10 M	17 18 29	18 50 21	1♏18 13	8♏36 55	25 58.1	29 15.6	22 53.8	17 53.8	28 40.2	10 17.5	7 36.8	4 37.1	0 36.1	8 34.2
11 Tu	17 22 25	19 51 21	16 00 57	23 29 37	25R58.7	0♐34.0	24 08.6	18 40.3	28 26.6	10 09.6	7 42.8	4 36.9	0 37.1	8 36.3
12 W	17 26 22	20 52 23	1♐02 02	8♐37 10	25 58.3	1 54.2	25 23.5	19 26.8	28 12.8	10 01.6	7 48.8	4 36.9	0 38.2	8 38.3
13 Th	17 30 18	21 53 25	16 13 53	23 50 54	25 56.5	3 15.9	26 38.3	20 13.4	27 58.9	9 53.8	7 54.7	4D36.8	0 39.2	8 40.4
14 F	17 34 15	22 54 28	1♑26 58	9♑00 48	25 53.4	4 38.9	27 53.2	21 00.0	27 44.9	9 46.0	8 00.5	4 36.9	0 40.3	8 42.4
15 Sa	17 38 12	23 55 32	16 31 11	23 57 03	25 49.4	6 03.1	29 08.1	21 46.7	27 30.8	9 38.3	8 06.3	4 36.9	0 41.4	8 44.5
16 Su	17 42 08	24 56 37	1♒17 27	8♒31 39	25 45.1	7 28.2	0♐23.0	22 33.4	27 16.6	9 30.6	8 12.1	4 37.1	0 42.6	8 46.6
17 M	17 46 05	25 57 41	15 39 05	22 39 26	25 41.0	8 54.2	1 37.9	23 20.1	27 02.4	9 23.1	8 17.8	4 37.2	0 43.8	8 48.7
18 Tu	17 50 01	26 58 46	29 32 31	6♓18 22	25 37.9	10 21.0	2 52.8	24 06.8	26 48.2	9 15.6	8 23.4	4 37.5	0 45.0	8 50.7
19 W	17 53 58	27 59 52	12♓57 10	19 29 12	25D36.2	11 48.4	4 07.8	24 53.6	26 34.0	9 08.2	8 28.9	4 37.8	0 46.3	8 52.8
20 Th	17 57 54	29 00 57	25 54 55	2♈14 48	25 35.9	13 16.4	5 22.7	25 40.4	26 19.8	9 01.0	8 34.4	4 38.1	0 47.5	8 54.9
21 F	18 01 51	0♑02 03	8♈29 24	14 39 18	25 36.8	14 44.9	6 37.7	26 27.3	26 05.6	8 53.8	8 39.8	4 38.5	0 48.9	8 57.0
22 Sa	18 05 47	1 03 09	20 45 07	26 47 27	25 38.5	16 13.9	7 52.7	27 14.1	25 51.5	8 46.8	8 45.2	4 38.9	0 50.2	8 59.1
23 Su	18 09 44	2 04 16	2♉46 55	8♉44 06	25 40.3	17 43.4	9 07.7	28 01.0	25 37.4	8 39.8	8 50.5	4 39.4	0 51.6	9 01.3
24 M	18 13 41	3 05 22	14 39 33	20 33 49	25R41.4	19 13.3	10 22.7	28 48.0	25 23.4	8 33.0	8 55.7	4 39.9	0 52.9	9 03.4
25 Tu	18 17 37	4 06 29	26 27 22	2♊20 39	25 41.3	20 43.5	11 37.8	29 34.9	25 09.5	8 26.4	9 00.9	4 40.5	0 54.4	9 05.5
26 W	18 21 34	5 07 36	8♊14 06	14 08 03	25 39.4	22 14.1	12 52.8	0♒21.9	24 55.8	8 19.8	9 06.0	4 41.2	0 55.8	9 07.6
27 Th	18 25 30	6 08 43	20 02 52	25 58 48	25 35.5	23 45.1	14 07.8	1 08.9	24 42.1	8 13.4	9 11.0	4 41.9	0 57.3	9 09.8
28 F	18 29 27	7 09 50	1♋56 06	7♋55 01	25 29.5	25 16.3	15 22.9	1 56.0	24 28.6	8 07.2	9 15.9	4 42.6	0 58.8	9 11.9
29 Sa	18 33 23	8 10 58	13 55 43	19 58 21	25 22.0	26 47.9	16 38.0	2 43.0	24 15.3	8 01.0	9 20.8	4 43.4	1 00.3	9 14.0
30 Su	18 37 20	9 12 06	26 03 07	2♌10 07	25 13.4	28 19.9	17 53.1	3 30.1	24 02.2	7 55.1	9 25.6	4 44.3	1 01.9	9 16.1
31 M	18 41 16	10 13 14	8♌19 30	14 31 25	25 04.7	29 52.1	19 08.2	4 17.2	23 49.2	7 49.2	9 30.3	4 45.2	1 03.5	9 18.3

Astro Data	Dy Hr Mn	Planet Ingress	Dy Hr Mn	Last Aspect Dy Hr Mn		☽ Ingress Dy Hr Mn	Last Aspect Dy Hr Mn		☽ Ingress Dy Hr Mn	☽ Phases & Eclipses Dy Hr Mn	
☿ R	6 23:04	☿ ♏R	14 7:42	2 9:21	♂ ☍	♋ 3 7:43	2 6:55	☿ △	♌ 3 1:57	7 0:36	☾ 15♌00
☽ 0S	9 13:54	♂ ♑	17 2:36	4 8:37	☉ △	♌ 5 19:39	4 22:07	☿ □	♍ 5 11:51	13 22:08	● 21♏57
♆ D	11 7:52	☉ ♐	21 21:50	7 15:27	♂ △	♍ 8 4:35	7 10:35	☿ ⚹	♎ 7 18:35	13 22:11:47	● T 04'02"
♄⚻♅	16 0:27	♀ ♏	22 1:20	10 0:27	♂ □	♎ 10 9:35	9 0:37	☉ ⚹	♏ 9 21:51	20 14:31	☽ 28♒41
☽ 0N	22 3:24			12 5:13	♂ ⚹	♏ 12 11:10	11 13:08	♀ ☌	♐ 11 22:22	28 14:46	○ 6♊47
☿ D	26 22:50	⚳ ♊R	4 9:05	14 10:39	☿ ☌	♐ 14 10:52	13 8:42	☉ ☌	♑ 13 21:42	28 14:33	● A 0.915
		☿ ♐	11 1:40	16 9:44	♂ ☌	♑ 16 10:35	15 21:15	♀ ⚹	♒ 15 21:53		
☽ 0S	6 22:21	♀ ♐	16 4:38	18 5:54	☉ ⚹	♒ 18 12:10	17 18:12	☉ ⚹	♓ 18 0:48	6 15:31	☾ 14♍55
♅ D	13 12:02	☉ ♑	21 11:12	20 14:31	☉ □	♓ 20 16:55	20 5:19	☉ □	♈ 20 7:43	13 8:42	● 21♐45
☽ 0N	19 10:46	♂ ♒	26 0:49	22 6:32	☿ △	♈ 23 1:12	22 12:57	♂ □	♉ 22 18:25	20 5:19	☽ 28♓44
♃⚻♇	21 3:35	☿ ♑	31 14:03	24 1:34	♃ ⚹	♉ 25 12:18	25 5:58	♂ △	♊ 25 7:13	28 10:21	○ 7♋06
♃⚻♄	22 15:02			27 0:57	☿ ☍	♊ 28 0:58	27 6:50	☿ ☍	♋ 27 20:06		
♄⚹♇	27 1:41			29 1:04	♃ ☌	♋ 30 13:55	28 14:43	♄ △	♌ 30 7:45		

Astro Data

1 November 2012
Julian Day # 41213
SVP 5♓04'37"
GC 27♐01.1 ⚴ 23♓47.1R
Eris 21♈59.7R ⚵ 13♐20.5
⚷ 5♓04.1R ⚶ 25♊06.7R
☽ Mean ☊ 26♏48.0

1 December 2012
Julian Day # 41243
SVP 5♓04'32"
GC 27♐01.2 ⚴ 22♓48.2
Eris 21♈44.9R ⚵ 23♐38.6
⚷ 5♓07.0 ⚶ 19♊41.5R
☽ Mean ☊ 25♏12.7

LONGITUDE — January 2013

Day	Sid.Time	☉	0 hr ☽	Noon ☽	True ☊	☿	♀	♂	⚳	♃	♄	♅	♆	♇
1 Tu	18 45 13	11♑14 22	20♌46 02	27♌03 29	24♏56.8	1♑24.7	20♐23.3	5♒04.4	23♊36.5	7♊43.6	9♏35.0	4♈46.1	1♓05.1	9♑20.4
2 W	18 49 10	12 15 31	3♍24 00	9♍47 47	24R50.3	2 57.6	21 38.4	5 51.5	23R24.0	7R38.1	9 39.5	4 47.1	1 06.7	9 22.5
3 Th	18 53 06	13 16 39	16 15 02	22 46 02	24 46.0	4 30.9	22 53.5	6 38.7	23 11.7	7 32.7	9 44.0	4 48.2	1 08.4	9 24.6
4 F	18 57 03	14 17 48	29 21 03	6♎00 19	24D43.8	6 04.5	24 08.7	7 25.9	22 59.7	7 27.6	9 48.4	4 49.3	1 10.0	9 26.8
5 Sa	19 00 59	15 18 57	12♎44 06	19 32 40	24 43.5	7 38.5	25 23.8	8 13.1	22 47.9	7 22.5	9 52.8	4 50.4	1 11.7	9 28.9
6 Su	19 04 56	16 20 07	26 26 11	3♏24 47	24 44.4	9 12.8	26 39.0	9 00.4	22 36.4	7 17.7	9 57.0	4 51.6	1 13.5	9 31.0
7 M	19 08 52	17 21 17	10♏28 32	17 37 22	24R45.3	10 47.5	27 54.1	9 47.6	22 25.3	7 13.1	10 01.2	4 52.9	1 15.2	9 33.1
8 Tu	19 12 49	18 22 27	24 51 07	2♐09 26	24 45.3	12 22.7	29 09.3	10 34.9	22 14.4	7 08.6	10 05.3	4 54.2	1 17.0	9 35.2
9 W	19 16 45	19 23 37	9♐31 50	16 57 40	24 43.3	13 58.2	0♑24.5	11 22.2	22 03.8	7 04.3	10 09.3	4 55.5	1 18.8	9 37.3
10 Th	19 20 42	20 24 47	24 26 06	1♑56 09	24 38.7	15 34.2	1 39.7	12 09.6	21 53.6	7 00.2	10 13.2	4 56.9	1 20.6	9 39.4
11 F	19 24 39	21 25 56	9♑26 46	16 56 46	24 31.7	17 10.6	2 54.9	12 56.9	21 43.7	6 56.3	10 17.0	4 58.3	1 22.4	9 41.5
12 Sa	19 28 35	22 27 06	24 24 57	1♒50 10	24 22.7	18 47.4	4 10.1	13 44.2	21 34.2	6 52.6	10 20.8	4 59.8	1 24.3	9 43.6
13 Su	19 32 32	23 28 15	9♒11 18	16 27 23	24 12.8	20 24.7	5 25.3	14 31.6	21 25.0	6 49.0	10 24.4	5 01.4	1 26.2	9 45.7
14 M	19 36 28	24 29 23	23 37 38	0♓41 23	24 03.1	22 02.5	6 40.5	15 19.0	21 16.1	6 45.7	10 28.0	5 02.9	1 28.1	9 47.8
15 Tu	19 40 25	25 30 31	7♓38 14	14 27 56	23 54.8	23 40.8	7 55.7	16 06.4	21 07.7	6 42.5	10 31.5	5 04.6	1 30.0	9 49.9
16 W	19 44 21	26 31 38	21 10 27	27 45 56	23 48.6	25 19.6	9 10.9	16 53.8	20 59.6	6 39.6	10 34.9	5 06.2	1 31.9	9 51.9
17 Th	19 48 18	27 32 44	4♈14 38	10♈36 59	23 44.8	26 59.0	10 26.0	17 41.2	20 52.0	6 36.8	10 38.2	5 08.0	1 33.9	9 54.0
18 F	19 52 14	28 33 50	16 53 29	23 04 43	23D43.2	28 38.8	11 41.2	18 28.6	20 44.7	6 34.3	10 41.4	5 09.7	1 35.8	9 56.0
19 Sa	19 56 11	29 34 54	29 11 19	5♉13 59	23 43.2	0♒19.2	12 56.4	19 16.0	20 37.8	6 32.0	10 44.5	5 11.5	1 37.8	9 58.1
20 Su	20 00 08	0♒35 58	11♉13 23	17 10 14	23R43.8	2 00.1	14 11.6	20 03.4	20 31.4	6 29.8	10 47.5	5 13.4	1 39.8	10 00.1
21 M	20 04 04	1 37 01	23 05 13	28 58 59	23 43.8	3 41.6	15 26.8	20 50.8	20 25.3	6 27.9	10 50.4	5 15.3	1 41.9	10 02.1
22 Tu	20 08 01	2 38 03	4♊52 11	10♊45 25	23 42.2	5 23.6	16 42.0	21 38.3	20 19.7	6 26.1	10 53.2	5 17.2	1 43.9	10 04.1
23 W	20 11 57	3 39 04	16 39 15	22 34 10	23 38.3	7 06.2	17 57.2	22 25.7	20 14.5	6 24.6	10 55.9	5 19.2	1 46.0	10 06.1
24 Th	20 15 54	4 40 05	28 30 38	4♋29 02	23 31.6	8 49.2	19 12.3	23 13.1	20 09.7	6 23.3	10 58.6	5 21.2	1 48.0	10 08.1
25 F	20 19 50	5 41 04	10♋29 43	16 32 57	23 22.1	10 32.8	20 27.5	24 00.6	20 05.3	6 22.2	11 01.1	5 23.3	1 50.1	10 10.0
26 Sa	20 23 47	6 42 02	22 38 56	28 47 49	23 10.2	12 16.8	21 42.7	24 48.0	20 01.3	6 21.3	11 03.6	5 25.4	1 52.2	10 12.0
27 Su	20 27 43	7 43 00	4♌59 43	11♌14 39	22 56.9	14 01.3	22 57.9	25 35.4	19 57.8	6 20.5	11 05.9	5 27.5	1 54.3	10 13.9
28 M	20 31 40	8 43 56	17 32 37	23 53 37	22 43.3	15 46.2	24 13.0	26 22.8	19 54.7	6 20.0	11 08.1	5 29.7	1 56.4	10 15.9
29 Tu	20 35 37	9 44 52	0♍17 34	6♍44 25	22 30.6	17 31.4	25 28.2	27 10.3	19 52.0	6D19.7	11 10.3	5 32.0	1 58.6	10 17.8
30 W	20 39 33	10 45 46	13 14 05	19 46 32	22 19.9	19 16.8	26 43.4	27 57.7	19 49.7	6 19.6	11 12.3	5 34.2	2 00.7	10 19.7
31 Th	20 43 30	11 46 40	26 21 43	2♎59 37	22 12.0	21 02.4	27 58.6	28 45.1	19 47.9	6 19.7	11 14.3	5 36.5	2 02.9	10 21.5

LONGITUDE — February 2013

Day	Sid.Time	☉	0 hr ☽	Noon ☽	True ☊	☿	♀	♂	⚳	♃	♄	♅	♆	♇
1 F	20 47 26	12♒47 33	9♎40 14	16♎23 39	22♏07.1	22♒48.0	29♑13.7	29♒32.5	19♊46.4	6♊20.1	11♏16.1	5♈38.9	2♓05.1	10♑23.4
2 Sa	20 51 23	13 48 26	23 09 55	29 59 08	22R04.8	24 33.5	0♒28.9	0♓20.0	19R45.4	6 20.6	11 17.8	5 41.2	2 07.2	10 25.3
3 Su	20 55 19	14 49 17	6♏51 24	13♏46 49	22 04.3	26 18.7	1 44.1	1 07.4	19D44.9	6 21.3	11 19.5	5 43.6	2 09.4	10 27.1
4 M	20 59 16	15 50 08	20 45 27	27 47 20	22 04.3	28 03.4	2 59.2	1 54.8	19 44.7	6 22.2	11 21.0	5 46.1	2 11.6	10 28.9
5 Tu	21 03 12	16 50 58	4♐52 26	12♐00 40	22 03.3	29 47.4	4 14.4	2 42.2	19 45.0	6 23.3	11 22.5	5 48.6	2 13.8	10 30.7
6 W	21 07 09	17 51 48	19 11 46	26 25 27	22 00.3	1♓30.3	5 29.5	3 29.6	19 45.7	6 24.7	11 23.8	5 51.1	2 16.1	10 32.5
7 Th	21 11 06	18 52 36	3♑41 13	10♑58 31	21 54.3	3 11.9	6 44.7	4 17.0	19 46.8	6 26.2	11 25.0	5 53.7	2 18.3	10 34.3
8 F	21 15 02	19 53 23	18 16 38	25 34 45	21 45.4	4 51.7	7 59.9	5 04.4	19 48.3	6 27.9	11 26.1	5 56.3	2 20.5	10 36.0
9 Sa	21 18 59	20 54 09	2♒52 01	10♒07 30	21 34.2	6 29.3	9 15.0	5 51.8	19 50.2	6 29.8	11 27.2	5 58.9	2 22.8	10 37.8
10 Su	21 22 55	21 54 54	17 20 16	24 29 28	21 21.6	8 04.3	10 30.1	6 39.1	19 52.5	6 32.0	11 28.1	6 01.5	2 25.0	10 39.5
11 M	21 26 52	22 55 37	1♓34 18	8♓34 05	21 09.0	9 36.1	11 45.3	7 26.5	19 55.3	6 34.3	11 28.9	6 04.2	2 27.3	10 41.2
12 Tu	21 30 48	23 56 19	15 28 16	22 16 28	20 57.8	11 04.0	13 00.4	8 13.8	19 58.4	6 36.8	11 29.6	6 06.9	2 29.5	10 42.8
13 W	21 34 45	24 56 59	28 58 27	5♈34 09	20 49.0	12 27.6	14 15.5	9 01.1	20 02.0	6 39.5	11 30.2	6 09.7	2 31.8	10 44.5
14 Th	21 38 41	25 57 38	12♈03 39	18 27 11	20 42.9	13 46.0	15 30.6	9 48.5	20 05.9	6 42.4	11 30.7	6 12.5	2 34.0	10 46.1
15 F	21 42 38	26 58 15	24 45 05	0♉57 48	20 39.6	14 58.6	16 45.7	10 35.8	20 10.3	6 45.5	11 31.0	6 15.3	2 36.3	10 47.7
16 Sa	21 46 35	27 58 51	7♉05 52	13 09 53	20D38.3	16 04.7	18 00.8	11 23.0	20 15.0	6 48.8	11 31.3	6 18.1	2 38.6	10 49.3
17 Su	21 50 31	28 59 24	19 10 29	25 08 22	20R38.2	17 03.6	19 15.9	12 10.3	20 20.2	6 52.3	11 31.5	6 21.0	2 40.9	10 50.9
18 M	21 54 28	29 59 56	1♊04 12	6♊58 44	20 38.1	17 54.5	20 31.0	12 57.5	20 25.7	6 56.0	11R31.6	6 23.9	2 43.1	10 52.4
19 Tu	21 58 24	1♓00 26	12 52 38	18 46 35	20 36.8	18 37.0	21 46.0	13 44.8	20 31.5	6 59.9	11 31.5	6 26.8	2 45.4	10 53.9
20 W	22 02 21	2 00 54	24 41 16	0♋37 17	20 33.5	19 10.4	23 01.1	14 32.0	20 37.8	7 03.9	11 31.4	6 29.8	2 47.7	10 55.4
21 Th	22 06 17	3 01 21	6♋35 13	12 35 37	20 27.5	19 34.3	24 16.1	15 19.1	20 44.4	7 08.1	11 31.2	6 32.7	2 50.0	10 56.9
22 F	22 10 14	4 01 46	18 38 55	24 45 32	20 18.9	19R48.4	25 31.1	16 06.3	20 51.4	7 12.5	11 30.8	6 35.7	2 52.3	10 58.4
23 Sa	22 14 10	5 02 08	0♌55 48	7♌09 57	20 07.9	19 52.4	26 46.1	16 53.4	20 58.7	7 17.1	11 30.4	6 38.7	2 54.5	10 59.8
24 Su	22 18 07	6 02 29	13 28 08	19 50 26	19 55.4	19 46.5	28 01.1	17 40.5	21 06.4	7 21.9	11 29.8	6 41.8	2 56.8	11 01.2
25 M	22 22 04	7 02 48	26 16 50	2♍47 16	19 42.4	19 30.7	29 16.1	18 27.6	21 14.4	7 26.8	11 29.2	6 44.9	2 59.1	11 02.6
26 Tu	22 26 00	8 03 06	9♍21 33	15 59 30	19 30.3	19 05.7	0♓31.1	19 14.7	21 22.8	7 31.9	11 28.4	6 47.9	3 01.4	11 03.9
27 W	22 29 57	9 03 22	22 40 49	29 25 14	19 20.2	18 31.8	1 46.1	20 01.7	21 31.5	7 37.2	11 27.6	6 51.1	3 03.6	11 05.2
28 Th	22 33 53	10 03 36	6♎12 26	13♎02 07	19 12.6	17 50.2	3 01.0	20 48.7	21 40.5	7 42.7	11 26.6	6 54.2	3 05.9	11 06.5

Astro Data

	Dy Hr Mn
☽ 0S	3 5:16
☽ 0N	15 20:40
♃ D	30 11:37
☽ 0S	30 11:43
⚳ D	4 8:48
☽ 0N	12 7:36
♄ R	18 17:02
☿ R	23 9:40
☽ 0S	26 19:03

Planet Ingress

	Dy Hr Mn
♀ ♑	9 4:11
☿ ♒	19 7:25
☉ ♒	19 21:52
♂ ♓	2 1:54
♀ ♒	2 2:47
☿ ♓	5 14:55
☉ ♓	18 12:02
♀ ♓	26 2:03

Last Aspect / ☽ Ingress

Last Aspect Dy Hr Mn		☽ Ingress Dy Hr Mn
31 21:52	♀ △	♍ 1 17:35
3 12:15	♀ □	♎ 4 1:11
5 23:13	♀ ⚹	♏ 6 6:09
7 11:31	☉ ⚹	♐ 8 8:28
9 2:28	♂ ⚹	♑ 10 8:54
11 19:44	☉ ☌	♒ 12 9:01
13 8:37	♂ ☌	♓ 14 10:49
16 9:32	☉ ⚹	♈ 16 16:07
19 0:40	☿ □	♉ 19 1:36
20 18:16	♂ □	♊ 21 14:04
23 11:42	♂ △	♋ 24 3:00
25 20:35	♀ ☍	♌ 26 14:20
28 16:59	♂ ☍	♍ 28 23:27
31 1:59	♀ △	♎ 31 6:36

Last Aspect / ☽ Ingress

Last Aspect Dy Hr Mn		☽ Ingress Dy Hr Mn
2 1:03	☿ △	♏ 2 12:02
4 12:31	☿ □	♐ 4 15:45
5 20:42	☉ ⚹	♑ 6 17:55
7 12:44	♄ ⚹	♒ 8 19:16
10 7:20	☉ ☌	♓ 10 21:19
11 17:03	♄ △	♈ 13 1:51
15 3:35	☉ ⚹	♉ 15 10:08
17 20:31	☉ □	♊ 17 21:50
19 18:48	♀ △	♋ 20 10:45
22 2:08	☿ △	♌ 22 22:12
25 4:50	♀ ☍	♍ 25 6:52
26 18:13	♂ ☍	♎ 27 13:02

☽ Phases & Eclipses

Dy Hr Mn	
5 3:58	☾ 14♎58
11 19:44	● 21♑46
18 23:45	☽ 29♈04
27 4:38	○ 7♌24
3 13:56	☾ 14♏54
10 7:20	● 21♒43
17 20:31	☽ 29♉21
25 20:26	○ 7♍24

Astro Data

1 January 2013
Julian Day # 41274
SVP 5♓04'27"
GC 27♐01.3 ⚴ 27♓40.1
Eris 21♈37.3R ⚵ 4♑53.0
⚷ 6♓03.7 ⚶ 12♊12.0R
☽ Mean ☊ 23♏34.2

1 February 2013
Julian Day # 41305
SVP 5♓04'22"
GC 27♐01.3 ⚴ 6♈43.8
Eris 21♈40.1 ⚵ 16♑12.5
⚷ 7♓41.8 ⚶ 9♊58.0
☽ Mean ☊ 21♏55.7

March 2013 — LONGITUDE

Day	Sid.Time	☉	0 hr ☽	Noon ☽	True ☊	☿	♀	♂	⚳	♃	♄	♅	♆	♇
1 F	22 37 50	11♓03 48	19♎54 00	26♎47 48	19♏08.0	17♓01.8	4♓16.0	21♓35.7	21♊49.9	7♊48.3	11♏25.6	6♈57.3	3♓08.2	11♑07.8
2 Sa	22 41 46	12 03 59	3♏43 19	10♏40 20	19D 06.1	16R 07.9	5 30.9	22 22.7	21 59.5	7 54.1	11R 24.4	7 00.5	3 10.4	11 09.0
3 Su	22 45 43	13 04 09	17 38 43	24 38 21	19 05.9	15 09.9	6 45.8	23 09.6	22 09.6	8 00.0	11 23.2	7 03.7	3 12.7	11 10.3
4 M	22 49 39	14 04 17	1♐39 07	8♐40 58	19R 06.4	14 09.2	8 00.8	23 56.5	22 19.9	8 06.1	11 21.8	7 06.9	3 14.9	11 11.5
5 Tu	22 53 36	15 04 23	15 43 48	22 47 32	19 06.2	13 07.3	9 15.7	24 43.4	22 30.5	8 12.4	11 20.3	7 10.1	3 17.2	11 12.6
6 W	22 57 33	16 04 28	29 52 00	6♑57 03	19 04.4	12 05.8	10 30.6	25 30.3	22 41.4	8 18.8	11 18.8	7 13.4	3 19.4	11 13.8
7 Th	23 01 29	17 04 32	14♑02 26	21 07 52	19 00.1	11 05.9	11 45.5	26 17.1	22 52.7	8 25.4	11 17.1	7 16.6	3 21.7	11 14.9
8 F	23 05 26	18 04 34	28 12 57	5♒17 18	18 53.4	10 08.8	13 00.4	27 03.9	23 04.2	8 32.2	11 15.4	7 19.9	3 23.9	11 16.0
9 Sa	23 09 22	19 04 34	12♒20 24	19 21 44	18 44.6	9 15.7	14 15.2	27 50.7	23 16.0	8 39.1	11 13.6	7 23.2	3 26.1	11 17.0
10 Su	23 13 19	20 04 32	26 20 47	3♓16 58	18 34.6	8 27.4	15 30.1	28 37.4	23 28.2	8 46.1	11 11.6	7 26.5	3 28.3	11 18.1
11 M	23 17 15	21 04 29	10♓09 48	16 58 48	18 24.5	7 44.5	16 44.9	29 24.1	23 40.6	8 53.3	11 09.6	7 29.8	3 30.5	11 19.1
12 Tu	23 21 12	22 04 23	23 43 33	0♈23 45	18 15.4	7 07.6	17 59.8	0♈10.8	23 53.2	9 00.7	11 07.5	7 33.1	3 32.7	11 20.0
13 W	23 25 08	23 04 16	6♈59 08	13 29 37	18 08.3	6 36.9	19 14.6	0 57.5	24 06.2	9 08.2	11 05.2	7 36.5	3 34.9	11 21.0
14 Th	23 29 05	24 04 06	19 55 09	26 15 50	18 03.4	6 12.6	20 29.4	1 44.1	24 19.4	9 15.8	11 02.9	7 39.8	3 37.1	11 21.9
15 F	23 33 01	25 03 55	2♉31 51	8♉43 29	18D 01.0	5 54.8	21 44.2	2 30.7	24 32.9	9 23.6	11 00.5	7 43.2	3 39.2	11 22.8
16 Sa	23 36 58	26 03 41	14 51 05	20 55 07	18 00.6	5 43.4	22 59.0	3 17.2	24 46.7	9 31.6	10 58.0	7 46.5	3 41.4	11 23.6
17 Su	23 40 55	27 03 25	26 56 04	2♊54 30	18 01.4	5D 38.3	24 13.7	4 03.7	25 00.7	9 39.6	10 55.5	7 49.9	3 43.5	11 24.5
18 M	23 44 51	28 03 07	8♊51 00	14 46 12	18 02.7	5 39.3	25 28.4	4 50.2	25 15.0	9 47.8	10 52.8	7 53.3	3 45.6	11 25.3
19 Tu	23 48 48	29 02 47	20 40 45	26 35 19	18R 03.5	5 46.1	26 43.2	5 36.6	25 29.5	9 56.2	10 50.1	7 56.7	3 47.7	11 26.0
20 W	23 52 44	0♈02 24	2♋30 33	8♋27 08	18 03.1	5 58.6	27 57.9	6 23.0	25 44.3	10 04.7	10 47.3	8 00.1	3 49.8	11 26.8
21 Th	23 56 41	1 01 59	14 25 40	20 26 48	18 00.9	6 16.3	29 12.5	7 09.4	25 59.3	10 13.3	10 44.4	8 03.5	3 51.9	11 27.5
22 F	0 00 37	2 01 32	26 31 06	2♌39 05	17 56.8	6 39.1	0♈27.2	7 55.7	26 14.5	10 22.0	10 41.4	8 06.9	3 54.0	11 28.1
23 Sa	0 04 34	3 01 03	8♌51 12	15 07 52	17 50.9	7 06.6	1 41.9	8 42.0	26 30.0	10 30.8	10 38.3	8 10.3	3 56.1	11 28.8
24 Su	0 08 30	4 00 31	21 29 23	27 55 58	17 43.8	7 38.6	2 56.5	9 28.2	26 45.7	10 39.8	10 35.2	8 13.8	3 58.1	11 29.4
25 M	0 12 27	4 59 57	4♍27 43	11♍04 41	17 36.3	8 14.9	4 11.1	10 14.4	27 01.6	10 48.9	10 32.0	8 17.2	4 00.1	11 30.0
26 Tu	0 16 24	5 59 21	17 46 44	24 33 40	17 29.1	8 55.2	5 25.7	11 00.5	27 17.8	10 58.1	10 28.7	8 20.6	4 02.1	11 30.5
27 W	0 20 20	6 58 43	1♎25 12	8♎20 55	17 23.2	9 39.2	6 40.3	11 46.6	27 34.1	11 07.5	10 25.3	8 24.0	4 04.1	11 31.0
28 Th	0 24 17	7 58 03	15 20 22	22 23 02	17 19.0	10 26.7	7 54.8	12 32.7	27 50.7	11 16.9	10 21.9	8 27.5	4 06.1	11 31.5
29 F	0 28 13	8 57 21	29 28 19	6♏35 41	17D 16.8	11 17.6	9 09.4	13 18.7	28 07.4	11 26.5	10 18.4	8 30.9	4 08.1	11 32.0
30 Sa	0 32 10	9 56 37	13♏44 32	20 54 21	17 16.4	12 11.7	10 23.9	14 04.7	28 24.4	11 36.2	10 14.9	8 34.3	4 10.0	11 32.4
31 Su	0 36 06	10 55 51	28 04 35	5♐14 46	17 17.3	13 08.7	11 38.4	14 50.7	28 41.6	11 46.0	10 11.2	8 37.7	4 11.9	11 32.8

April 2013 — LONGITUDE

Day	Sid.Time	☉	0 hr ☽	Noon ☽	True ☊	☿	♀	♂	⚳	♃	♄	♅	♆	♇
1 M	0 40 03	11♈55 04	12♐24 31	19♐33 27	17♏18.7	14♓08.6	12♈52.9	15♈36.6	28♊59.0	11♊55.9	10♏07.6	8♈41.2	4♓13.8	11♑33.2
2 Tu	0 43 59	12 54 14	26 41 16	3♑47 41	17R 19.9	15 11.2	14 07.4	16 22.4	29 16.5	12 05.9	10R 03.8	8 44.6	4 15.7	11 33.5
3 W	0 47 56	13 53 23	10♑52 29	17 55 29	17 20.2	16 16.3	15 21.9	17 08.3	29 34.3	12 16.0	10 00.0	8 48.0	4 17.6	11 33.8
4 Th	0 51 53	14 52 31	24 56 29	1♒55 19	17 19.0	17 23.9	16 36.3	17 54.1	29 52.2	12 26.2	9 56.2	8 51.4	4 19.5	11 34.1
5 F	0 55 49	15 51 36	8♒51 52	15 45 56	17 16.4	18 33.7	17 50.8	18 39.8	0♋10.4	12 36.6	9 52.2	8 54.8	4 21.3	11 34.4
6 Sa	0 59 46	16 50 40	22 37 22	29 26 01	17 12.6	19 45.9	19 05.2	19 25.5	0 28.7	12 47.0	9 48.3	8 58.2	4 23.1	11 34.6
7 Su	1 03 42	17 49 42	6♓11 42	12♓54 16	17 08.0	21 00.1	20 19.6	20 11.1	0 47.2	12 57.5	9 44.3	9 01.6	4 24.9	11 34.8
8 M	1 07 39	18 48 42	19 33 35	26 09 28	17 03.3	22 16.4	21 34.0	20 56.8	1 05.9	13 08.1	9 40.2	9 05.0	4 26.6	11 34.9
9 Tu	1 11 35	19 47 40	2♈41 50	9♈10 35	16 59.2	23 34.8	22 48.3	21 42.3	1 24.7	13 18.9	9 36.1	9 08.4	4 28.4	11 35.0
10 W	1 15 32	20 46 36	15 35 39	21 57 02	16 56.0	24 55.0	24 02.7	22 27.8	1 43.8	13 29.7	9 31.9	9 11.8	4 30.1	11 35.1
11 Th	1 19 28	21 45 30	28 14 47	4♉28 58	16 54.1	26 17.1	25 17.0	23 13.3	2 02.9	13 40.6	9 27.7	9 15.2	4 31.8	11 35.2
12 F	1 23 25	22 44 22	10♉39 43	16 47 14	16D 53.5	27 41.1	26 31.4	23 58.7	2 22.3	13 51.6	9 23.5	9 18.5	4 33.5	11R 35.2
13 Sa	1 27 21	23 43 12	22 51 46	28 53 38	16 54.0	29 06.9	27 45.7	24 44.1	2 41.8	14 02.7	9 19.2	9 21.9	4 35.1	11 35.2
14 Su	1 31 18	24 42 00	4♊53 10	10♊50 46	16 55.3	0♈34.4	28 59.9	25 29.4	3 01.5	14 13.8	9 14.9	9 25.2	4 36.8	11 35.1
15 M	1 35 15	25 40 46	16 46 53	22 42 00	16 56.9	2 03.7	0♉14.2	26 14.7	3 21.3	14 25.1	9 10.5	9 28.6	4 38.4	11 35.1
16 Tu	1 39 11	26 39 30	28 36 38	4♋31 21	16 58.5	3 34.7	1 28.4	27 00.0	3 41.3	14 36.5	9 06.1	9 31.9	4 40.0	11 35.0
17 W	1 43 08	27 38 11	10♋26 42	16 23 17	16 59.7	5 07.4	2 42.7	27 45.1	4 01.5	14 47.9	9 01.7	9 35.2	4 41.5	11 34.9
18 Th	1 47 04	28 36 50	22 21 42	28 22 34	17R 00.1	6 41.8	3 56.9	28 30.3	4 21.7	14 59.4	8 57.3	9 38.5	4 43.0	11 34.7
19 F	1 51 01	29 35 27	4♌26 28	10♌33 59	16 59.7	8 17.8	5 11.0	29 15.3	4 42.2	15 11.0	8 52.9	9 41.8	4 44.6	11 34.5
20 Sa	1 54 57	0♉34 02	16 45 39	23 02 00	16 58.5	9 55.6	6 25.2	0♉00.4	5 02.7	15 22.6	8 48.4	9 45.0	4 46.0	11 34.3
21 Su	1 58 54	1 32 35	29 23 28	5♍50 27	16 56.8	11 35.0	7 39.3	0 45.3	5 23.4	15 34.4	8 43.9	9 48.3	4 47.5	11 34.0
22 M	2 02 50	2 31 05	12♍23 14	19 02 02	16 54.9	13 16.1	8 53.4	1 30.3	5 44.3	15 46.2	8 39.4	9 51.5	4 48.9	11 33.8
23 Tu	2 06 47	3 29 33	25 46 56	2♎37 54	16 53.0	14 58.8	10 07.5	2 15.1	6 05.2	15 58.0	8 34.9	9 54.7	4 50.3	11 33.4
24 W	2 10 44	4 27 59	9♎34 46	16 37 14	16 51.5	16 43.3	11 21.6	3 00.0	6 26.3	16 10.0	8 30.3	9 57.9	4 51.7	11 33.1
25 Th	2 14 40	5 26 24	23 44 52	0♏57 07	16 50.6	18 29.4	12 35.7	3 44.7	6 47.6	16 22.0	8 25.8	10 01.1	4 53.0	11 32.7
26 F	2 18 37	6 24 46	8♏13 17	15 32 37	16D 50.3	20 17.3	13 49.7	4 29.5	7 08.9	16 34.1	8 21.2	10 04.3	4 54.4	11 32.3
27 Sa	2 22 33	7 23 07	22 54 17	0♐17 25	16 50.5	22 06.9	15 03.7	5 14.1	7 30.4	16 46.2	8 16.7	10 07.4	4 55.7	11 31.9
28 Su	2 26 30	8 21 26	7♐41 06	15 04 29	16 51.0	23 58.1	16 17.7	5 58.8	7 52.0	16 58.5	8 12.1	10 10.5	4 56.9	11 31.5
29 M	2 30 26	9 19 44	22 26 44	29 47 06	16 51.7	25 51.2	17 31.7	6 43.4	8 13.7	17 10.7	8 07.6	10 13.6	4 58.2	11 31.0
30 Tu	2 34 23	10 18 00	7♑04 54	14♑19 34	16 52.3	27 45.9	18 45.7	7 27.9	8 35.6	17 23.1	8 03.0	10 16.7	4 59.4	11 30.5

Astro Data	Dy Hr Mn
♄⚹♇	8 7:06
☽0N	11 17:15
♂0N	14 10:49
☿ D	17 20:03
☉0N	20 11:02
♃⚻♄	24 2:51
♀0N	24 16:50
☽0S	26 3:43
♃⚻♇	30 2:19
☽0N	8 0:26
♇ R	12 19:34
♄⚻♅	13 3:29
☿0N	18 1:04
☽0S	22 13:10

Planet Ingress		Dy Hr Mn
♂	♈	12 6:26
☉	♈	20 11:02
♀	♈	22 3:15
⚳	♋	4 22:17
☿	♈	14 2:37
♀	♉	15 7:25
☉	♉	19 22:03
♂	♉	20 11:48

Last Aspect Dy Hr Mn			☽ Ingress	Dy Hr Mn
28 8:37	♇	□	♏	1 17:33
3 9:19	♂	△	♐	3 21:11
5 15:28	♂	□	♑	6 0:14
7 21:14	♂	⚹	♒	8 3:01
8 22:08	♄	□	♓	10 6:19
11 19:51	☉	☌	♈	12 11:17
13 8:02	♇	□	♉	14 19:08
16 23:11	☉	⚹	♊	17 6:09
19 17:27	☉	□	♋	19 18:55
20 18:02	♇	☍	♌	22 6:50
23 3:28	♄	□	♍	24 15:49
25 12:46	♇	△	♎	26 21:32
27 18:14	♂	☍	♏	29 0:53
29 20:25	☿	△	♐	31 3:13

Last Aspect Dy Hr Mn			☽ Ingress	Dy Hr Mn
1 5:00	♂	△	♑	2 5:35
3 10:35	♂	□	♒	4 8:41
5 17:22	♂	⚹	♓	6 13:00
8 4:10	☿	☌	♈	8 19:02
10 16:25	♀	☌	♉	11 3:22
13 12:30	☿	⚹	♊	13 14:13
15 19:41	♂	⚹	♋	16 2:49
18 12:31	☉	□	♌	18 15:13
19 21:06	♃	⚹	♍	21 1:08
22 6:02	♃	□	♎	23 7:25
24 12:12	☿	☍	♏	25 10:25
26 8:56	♀	☍	♐	27 11:32
29 4:37	☿	△	♑	29 12:21

☽ Phases & Eclipses Dy Hr Mn	
4 21:53	☾ 14♐29
11 19:51	● 21♓24
19 17:27	☽ 29♊16
27 9:27	○ 6♎52
3 4:37	☾ 13♑35
10 9:35	● 20♈41
18 12:31	☽ 28♋38
25 19:57	○ 5♏46
25 20:07	☍ P 0.015

Astro Data

1 March 2013
Julian Day # 41333
SVP 5♓04'19"
GC 27♐01.4 ⚴ 17♈19.6
Eris 21♈51.0 ⚵ 26♑04.0
⚷ 9♓28.2 ⚶ 13♊34.7
☽ Mean ☊ 20♏26.7

1 April 2013
Julian Day # 41364
SVP 5♓04'16"
GC 27♐01.5 ⚴ 0♉56.0
Eris 22♈09.2 ⚵ 5♒58.1
⚷ 11♓23.8 ⚶ 21♊51.5
☽ Mean ☊ 18♏48.2

LONGITUDE — May 2013

Day	Sid.Time	☉	0 hr ☽	Noon ☽	True ☊	☿	♀	♂	⚳	♃	♄	♅	♆	♇
1 W	2 38 19	11♉16 14	21♑30 38	28♑37 45	16♏52.7	29♈42.3	19♉59.6	8♉12.4	8♋57.5	17♊35.5	7♏58.5	10♈19.8	5♓00.6	11♑29.9
2 Th	2 42 16	12 14 27	5♒40 38	12♒39 07	16R52.8	1♉40.4	21 13.5	8 56.8	9 19.6	17 48.0	7R53.9	10 22.8	5 01.7	11R29.4
3 F	2 46 13	13 12 39	19 33 08	26 22 39	16 52.7	3 40.2	22 27.5	9 41.2	9 41.8	18 00.5	7 49.4	10 25.8	5 02.8	11 28.8
4 Sa	2 50 09	14 10 49	3♓07 45	9♓48 29	16 52.5	5 41.6	23 41.4	10 25.5	10 04.1	18 13.0	7 44.9	10 28.8	5 03.9	11 28.2
5 Su	2 54 06	15 08 57	16 25 01	22 57 29	16 52.3	7 44.6	24 55.2	11 09.8	10 26.5	18 25.7	7 40.4	10 31.8	5 05.0	11 27.5
6 M	2 58 02	16 07 05	29 26 04	5♈50 57	16D52.1	9 49.0	26 09.1	11 54.0	10 49.0	18 38.4	7 35.9	10 34.7	5 06.0	11 26.8
7 Tu	3 01 59	17 05 10	12♈12 18	18 30 19	16 52.1	11 54.9	27 23.0	12 38.2	11 11.7	18 51.1	7 31.4	10 37.7	5 07.0	11 26.1
8 W	3 05 55	18 03 14	24 45 12	0♉57 07	16 52.1	14 02.1	28 36.8	13 22.3	11 34.4	19 03.9	7 26.9	10 40.6	5 08.0	11 25.4
9 Th	3 09 52	19 01 17	7♉06 17	13 12 53	16R52.2	16 10.3	29 50.6	14 06.4	11 57.2	19 16.7	7 22.5	10 43.4	5 08.9	11 24.6
10 F	3 13 48	19 59 18	19 17 08	25 19 14	16 52.2	18 19.6	1♊04.4	14 50.4	12 20.2	19 29.6	7 18.1	10 46.3	5 09.9	11 23.9
11 Sa	3 17 45	20 57 18	1♊19 24	7♊17 54	16 51.9	20 29.6	2 18.2	15 34.4	12 43.2	19 42.5	7 13.7	10 49.1	5 10.7	11 23.1
12 Su	3 21 42	21 55 16	13 14 59	19 10 56	16 51.5	22 40.2	3 32.0	16 18.3	13 06.3	19 55.5	7 09.4	10 51.9	5 11.6	11 22.2
13 M	3 25 38	22 53 12	25 06 05	1♋00 46	16 50.8	24 51.1	4 45.7	17 02.1	13 29.6	20 08.6	7 05.1	10 54.6	5 12.4	11 21.4
14 Tu	3 29 35	23 51 07	6♋55 21	12 50 14	16 49.9	27 02.1	5 59.4	17 46.0	13 52.9	20 21.6	7 00.8	10 57.4	5 13.2	11 20.5
15 W	3 33 31	24 49 00	18 45 51	24 42 40	16 48.9	29 12.8	7 13.2	18 29.7	14 16.3	20 34.7	6 56.6	11 00.1	5 14.0	11 19.6
16 Th	3 37 28	25 46 51	0♌41 09	6♌41 49	16 48.1	1♊23.0	8 26.8	19 13.4	14 39.8	20 47.9	6 52.4	11 02.7	5 14.7	11 18.7
17 F	3 41 24	26 44 40	12 45 13	18 51 50	16D47.6	3 32.5	9 40.5	19 57.1	15 03.4	21 01.1	6 48.2	11 05.4	5 15.4	11 17.7
18 Sa	3 45 21	27 42 28	25 02 15	1♍16 59	16 47.5	5 40.8	10 54.2	20 40.6	15 27.1	21 14.3	6 44.1	11 08.0	5 16.0	11 16.8
19 Su	3 49 17	28 40 14	7♍36 33	14 01 27	16 47.9	7 47.9	12 07.8	21 24.2	15 50.8	21 27.5	6 40.0	11 10.6	5 16.7	11 15.8
20 M	3 53 14	29 37 58	20 32 05	27 08 51	16 48.7	9 53.3	13 21.4	22 07.7	16 14.6	21 40.8	6 36.0	11 13.1	5 17.3	11 14.7
21 Tu	3 57 11	0♊35 41	3♎52 03	10♎41 52	16 49.8	11 56.9	14 35.0	22 51.1	16 38.6	21 54.1	6 32.1	11 15.6	5 17.8	11 13.7
22 W	4 01 07	1 33 23	17 38 21	24 41 26	16 50.8	13 58.5	15 48.5	23 34.5	17 02.6	22 07.5	6 28.1	11 18.1	5 18.4	11 12.6
23 Th	4 05 04	2 31 02	1♏50 54	9♏06 21	16R51.5	15 57.9	17 02.1	24 17.8	17 26.6	22 20.9	6 24.3	11 20.5	5 18.9	11 11.6
24 F	4 09 00	3 28 41	16 27 12	23 52 44	16 51.5	17 55.0	18 15.6	25 01.0	17 50.8	22 34.3	6 20.5	11 22.9	5 19.3	11 10.5
25 Sa	4 12 57	4 26 18	1♐22 02	8♐54 05	16 50.7	19 49.5	19 29.1	25 44.2	18 15.0	22 47.7	6 16.7	11 25.3	5 19.8	11 09.3
26 Su	4 16 53	5 23 54	16 27 47	24 01 56	16 49.0	21 41.5	20 42.6	26 27.4	18 39.3	23 01.2	6 13.0	11 27.7	5 20.2	11 08.2
27 M	4 20 50	6 21 29	1♑35 22	9♑06 56	16 46.8	23 30.7	21 56.1	27 10.5	19 03.7	23 14.7	6 09.4	11 30.0	5 20.5	11 07.0
28 Tu	4 24 46	7 19 03	16 35 32	24 00 14	16 44.2	25 17.2	23 09.5	27 53.6	19 28.2	23 28.2	6 05.8	11 32.2	5 20.9	11 05.9
29 W	4 28 43	8 16 36	1♒20 13	8♒34 51	16 41.9	27 00.9	24 23.0	28 36.6	19 52.7	23 41.8	6 02.3	11 34.5	5 21.2	11 04.7
30 Th	4 32 40	9 14 08	15 43 40	22 46 22	16 40.2	28 41.8	25 36.4	29 19.5	20 17.3	23 55.3	5 58.9	11 36.7	5 21.5	11 03.5
31 F	4 36 36	10 11 39	29 42 48	6♓32 59	16D39.4	0♋19.7	26 49.8	0♊02.4	20 41.9	24 08.9	5 55.5	11 38.8	5 21.7	11 02.2

LONGITUDE — June 2013

Day	Sid.Time	☉	0 hr ☽	Noon ☽	True ☊	☿	♀	♂	⚳	♃	♄	♅	♆	♇
1 Sa	4 40 33	11♊09 10	13♓17 02	19♓55 11	16♏39.6	1♋54.7	28♊03.2	0♊45.3	21♋06.7	24♊22.5	5♏52.2	11♈40.9	5♓21.9	11♑01.0
2 Su	4 44 29	12 06 39	26 27 45	2♈55 06	16 40.6	3 26.7	29 16.6	1 28.1	21 31.4	24 36.1	5R49.0	11 43.0	5 22.1	10R59.7
3 M	4 48 26	13 04 08	9♈17 37	15 35 45	16 42.2	4 55.8	0♋29.9	2 10.8	21 56.3	24 49.8	5 45.8	11 45.1	5 22.2	10 58.4
4 Tu	4 52 22	14 01 37	21 49 55	28 00 33	16 43.7	6 21.8	1 43.3	2 53.5	22 21.2	25 03.5	5 42.7	11 47.1	5 22.3	10 57.1
5 W	4 56 19	14 59 04	4♉08 04	10♉12 53	16R44.8	7 44.8	2 56.6	3 36.1	22 46.2	25 17.1	5 39.7	11 49.0	5 22.4	10 55.8
6 Th	5 00 15	15 56 31	16 15 21	22 15 50	16 44.8	9 04.7	4 09.9	4 18.7	23 11.3	25 30.8	5 36.8	11 50.9	5R22.5	10 54.5
7 F	5 04 12	16 53 57	28 14 41	4♊12 10	16 43.5	10 21.4	5 23.2	5 01.3	23 36.4	25 44.5	5 33.9	11 52.8	5 22.5	10 53.2
8 Sa	5 08 09	17 51 22	10♊08 35	16 04 12	16 40.6	11 35.0	6 36.5	5 43.8	24 01.6	25 58.3	5 31.1	11 54.7	5 22.4	10 51.8
9 Su	5 12 05	18 48 47	21 59 16	27 54 03	16 36.3	12 45.3	7 49.7	6 26.2	24 26.8	26 12.0	5 28.4	11 56.5	5 22.4	10 50.5
10 M	5 16 02	19 46 10	3♋48 45	9♋43 39	16 30.9	13 52.3	9 03.0	7 08.6	24 52.1	26 25.7	5 25.8	11 58.2	5 22.3	10 49.1
11 Tu	5 19 58	20 43 33	15 38 58	21 35 00	16 24.8	14 56.0	10 16.2	7 50.9	25 17.5	26 39.5	5 23.3	11 59.9	5 22.2	10 47.7
12 W	5 23 55	21 40 55	27 32 02	3♌30 21	16 18.7	15 56.2	11 29.4	8 33.2	25 42.9	26 53.2	5 20.8	12 01.6	5 22.0	10 46.3
13 Th	5 27 51	22 38 16	9♌30 19	15 32 16	16 13.3	16 52.9	12 42.6	9 15.4	26 08.4	27 07.0	5 18.5	12 03.2	5 21.8	10 44.9
14 F	5 31 48	23 35 36	21 36 36	27 43 44	16 09.0	17 46.0	13 55.7	9 57.5	26 33.9	27 20.8	5 16.2	12 04.8	5 21.6	10 43.5
15 Sa	5 35 44	24 32 55	3♍54 06	10♍08 10	16 06.3	18 35.4	15 08.9	10 39.7	26 59.4	27 34.5	5 14.0	12 06.4	5 21.4	10 42.0
16 Su	5 39 41	25 30 13	16 26 25	22 49 19	16D05.3	19 21.1	16 22.0	11 21.7	27 25.1	27 48.3	5 11.9	12 07.9	5 21.1	10 40.6
17 M	5 43 38	26 27 31	29 17 21	5♎50 56	16 05.6	20 02.8	17 35.1	12 03.7	27 50.7	28 02.1	5 09.9	12 09.3	5 20.8	10 39.1
18 Tu	5 47 34	27 24 47	12♎30 30	19 16 23	16 06.8	20 40.5	18 48.1	12 45.6	28 16.4	28 15.9	5 07.9	12 10.7	5 20.4	10 37.7
19 W	5 51 31	28 22 03	26 08 50	3♏08 01	16R08.0	21 14.1	20 01.2	13 27.5	28 42.2	28 29.6	5 06.1	12 12.1	5 20.1	10 36.2
20 Th	5 55 27	29 19 18	10♏13 56	17 26 26	16 08.5	21 43.5	21 14.2	14 09.4	29 08.0	28 43.4	5 04.4	12 13.4	5 19.7	10 34.7
21 F	5 59 24	0♋16 32	24 45 12	2♐09 41	16 07.6	22 08.6	22 27.2	14 51.2	29 33.9	28 57.2	5 02.7	12 14.7	5 19.2	10 33.3
22 Sa	6 03 20	1 13 46	9♐39 11	17 12 45	16 04.7	22 29.3	23 40.1	15 32.9	29 59.8	29 10.9	5 01.1	12 15.9	5 18.8	10 31.8
23 Su	6 07 17	2 11 00	24 49 18	2♑27 35	15 59.9	22 45.5	24 53.1	16 14.6	0♌25.7	29 24.7	4 59.7	12 17.1	5 18.3	10 30.3
24 M	6 11 13	3 08 13	10♑06 16	17 43 58	15 53.6	22 57.2	26 06.0	16 56.2	0 51.7	29 38.4	4 58.3	12 18.3	5 17.7	10 28.8
25 Tu	6 15 10	4 05 25	25 19 22	2♒51 11	15 46.5	23 04.3	27 18.9	17 37.8	1 17.7	29 52.2	4 57.0	12 19.3	5 17.2	10 27.3
26 W	6 19 07	5 02 38	10♒18 18	17 39 46	15 39.8	23R06.8	28 31.8	18 19.3	1 43.8	0♋05.9	4 55.8	12 20.4	5 16.6	10 25.8
27 Th	6 23 03	5 59 50	24 54 51	2♓03 02	15 34.1	23 04.8	29 44.7	19 00.8	2 09.9	0 19.6	4 54.7	12 21.4	5 16.0	10 24.3
28 F	6 27 00	6 57 03	9♓04 00	15 57 40	15 30.2	22 58.2	0♌57.5	19 42.2	2 36.1	0 33.4	4 53.7	12 22.3	5 15.3	10 22.8
29 Sa	6 30 56	7 54 15	22 44 05	29 23 29	15D28.2	22 47.1	2 10.3	20 23.6	3 02.3	0 47.1	4 52.8	12 23.3	5 14.7	10 21.3
30 Su	6 34 53	8 51 28	5♈56 13	12♈22 45	15 27.9	22 31.8	3 23.1	21 04.9	3 28.5	1 00.8	4 52.0	12 24.1	5 14.0	10 19.8

Astro Data

	Dy Hr Mn
☽0N	5 5:55
☽0S	19 22:26
♃⚼♄	20 5:21
♅□♇	20 23:02
☽0N	1 11:43
♆R	7 8:25
♄△♆	11 23:26
☽0S	16 6:42
☿R	26 13:08
☽0N	28 19:28

Planet Ingress

	Dy Hr Mn
☿ ♉	1 15:37
♀ ♊	9 15:03
☉ ♊	20 21:09
☿ ♋	31 7:07
♂ ♊	31 10:39
♀ ♋	3 2:13
☉ ♋	21 5:04
⚳ ♌	22 12:12
♃ ♋	26 1:40
♀ ♌	27 17:03

Last Aspect / ☽ Ingress (May)

Last Aspect Dy Hr Mn		☽ Ingress Dy Hr Mn
1 14:07 ♀ □	♒	1 14:19
3 4:24 ♀ □	♓	3 18:25
5 16:00 ♀ ⚹	♈	6 1:03
7 12:40 ♃ ⚹	♉	8 10:09
10 0:28 ☉ ☌	♊	10 21:21
12 13:32 ♃ ☌	♋	13 9:57
15 12:14 ☉ ⚹	♌	15 22:38
18 4:34 ☉ □	♍	18 9:33
20 16:48 ☉ △	♎	20 17:07
22 7:35 ♃ △	♏	22 20:55
24 13:55 ♂ ☍	♐	24 21:49
26 10:22 ♃ ☍	♑	26 21:28
28 18:40 ♂ △	♒	28 21:48
30 23:57 ♂ □	♓	31 0:30

Last Aspect / ☽ Ingress (June)

Last Aspect Dy Hr Mn		☽ Ingress Dy Hr Mn
2 4:30 ♀ □	♈	2 6:33
4 6:09 ♃ ⚹	♉	4 15:53
5 13:25 ♇ △	♊	7 3:32
9 8:29 ♃ ☌	♋	9 16:16
10 21:15 ☿ ☌	♌	12 4:58
14 11:14 ♃ ⚹	♍	14 16:26
16 21:26 ♃ □	♎	17 1:19
19 3:55 ♃ △	♏	19 6:38
20 19:16 ☿ △	♐	21 8:31
23 7:08 ♃ ☍	♑	23 8:08
25 2:24 ♀ ☍	♒	25 7:26
26 13:08 ♂ △	♓	27 8:32
29 0:16 ☿ △	♈	29 13:06

☽ Phases & Eclipses

Dy Hr Mn	
2 11:14	☾ 12♒13
10 0:28	● 19♉31
10 0:25:12	● A 06'03"
18 4:34	☽ 27♌25
25 4:25	○ 4♐08
25 4:10	◐ A 0.015
31 18:58	☾ 10♓28
8 15:56	● 18♊01
16 17:24	☽ 25♍43
23 11:32	○ 2♑10
30 4:54	☾ 8♈35

Astro Data

1 May 2013
Julian Day # 41394
SVP 5♓04'13"
GC 27♐01.5 ⚴ 15♉32.2
Eris 22♈28.7 ⚵ 13♒42.3
⚷ 12♓52.9 ⚶ 2♋25.7
☽ Mean ☊ 17♏12.9

1 June 2013
Julian Day # 41425
SVP 5♓04'09"
GC 27♐01.6 ⚴ 1♊49.3
Eris 22♈45.8 ⚵ 18♒26.5
⚷ 13♓43.8 ⚶ 14♋52.9
☽ Mean ☊ 15♏34.4

July 2013 LONGITUDE

Day	Sid.Time	☉	0 hr ☽	Noon ☽	True ☊	☿	♀	♂	⚳	♃	♄	♅	♆	♇
1 M	6 38 49	9♋48 40	18♈43 36	24♈59 18	15♏28.7	22♋12.4	4♌35.9	21♊46.2	3♌54.8	1♋14.4	4♏51.3	12♈24.9	5♓13.2	10♑18.3
2 Tu	6 42 46	10 45 53	1♉10 28	7♉17 42	15R 29.6	21R 49.1	5 48.6	22 27.4	4 21.1	1 28.1	4R 50.7	12 25.7	5R 12.5	10R 16.7
3 W	6 46 42	11 43 06	13 21 33	19 22 37	15 29.8	21 22.3	7 01.3	23 08.6	4 47.5	1 41.7	4 50.2	12 26.4	5 11.7	10 15.2
4 Th	6 50 39	12 40 20	25 21 25	1♊18 29	15 28.4	20 52.4	8 14.0	23 49.8	5 13.9	1 55.4	4 49.8	12 27.1	5 10.9	10 13.7
5 F	6 54 36	13 37 33	7♊14 15	13 09 10	15 24.8	20 19.8	9 26.7	24 30.8	5 40.3	2 09.0	4 49.5	12 27.7	5 10.0	10 12.2
6 Sa	6 58 32	14 34 47	19 03 37	24 57 56	15 18.7	19 45.0	10 39.4	25 11.9	6 06.8	2 22.6	4 49.2	12 28.3	5 09.1	10 10.7
7 Su	7 02 29	15 32 01	0♋52 26	6♋47 22	15 10.3	19 08.5	11 52.0	25 52.9	6 33.3	2 36.2	4D 49.1	12 28.8	5 08.2	10 09.2
8 M	7 06 25	16 29 14	12 42 59	18 39 29	14 59.9	18 30.9	13 04.6	26 33.8	6 59.8	2 49.7	4 49.1	12 29.3	5 07.3	10 07.7
9 Tu	7 10 22	17 26 28	24 37 04	0♌35 55	14 48.5	17 53.0	14 17.2	27 14.7	7 26.4	3 03.3	4 49.2	12 29.7	5 06.4	10 06.2
10 W	7 14 18	18 23 42	6♌36 12	12 38 06	14 36.9	17 15.2	15 29.8	27 55.5	7 53.0	3 16.8	4 49.3	12 30.1	5 05.4	10 04.7
11 Th	7 18 15	19 20 57	18 41 48	24 47 31	14 26.2	16 38.4	16 42.3	28 36.3	8 19.7	3 30.2	4 49.6	12 30.4	5 04.4	10 03.2
12 F	7 22 12	20 18 11	0♍55 28	7♍05 54	14 17.3	16 03.0	17 54.8	29 17.0	8 46.3	3 43.7	4 50.0	12 30.7	5 03.4	10 01.7
13 Sa	7 26 08	21 15 25	13 19 07	19 35 25	14 10.8	15 29.8	19 07.3	29 57.7	9 13.0	3 57.1	4 50.5	12 30.9	5 02.3	10 00.3
14 Su	7 30 05	22 12 39	25 55 09	2♎18 41	14 06.9	14 59.4	20 19.7	0♋38.3	9 39.7	4 10.5	4 51.0	12 31.1	5 01.2	9 58.8
15 M	7 34 01	23 09 53	8♎46 25	15 18 45	14D 05.2	14 32.3	21 32.1	1 18.9	10 06.5	4 23.9	4 51.7	12 31.2	5 00.1	9 57.3
16 Tu	7 37 58	24 07 07	21 56 03	28 38 41	14 05.0	14 09.0	22 44.5	1 59.4	10 33.3	4 37.2	4 52.5	12 31.3	4 59.0	9 55.9
17 W	7 41 54	25 04 22	5♏27 00	12♏21 14	14R 05.3	13 49.9	23 56.8	2 39.9	11 00.1	4 50.5	4 53.3	12R 31.3	4 57.9	9 54.4
18 Th	7 45 51	26 01 36	19 21 34	26 28 01	14 04.8	13 35.5	25 09.1	3 20.3	11 26.9	5 03.8	4 54.3	12 31.3	4 56.7	9 53.0
19 F	7 49 47	26 58 51	3♐40 29	10♐58 41	14 02.6	13 26.1	26 21.4	4 00.6	11 53.8	5 17.0	4 55.4	12 31.2	4 55.5	9 51.5
20 Sa	7 53 44	27 56 06	18 22 09	25 50 12	13 57.9	13D 21.9	27 33.6	4 41.0	12 20.6	5 30.2	4 56.5	12 31.1	4 54.3	9 50.1
21 Su	7 57 41	28 53 21	3♑21 56	10♑56 20	13 50.6	13 23.2	28 45.8	5 21.2	12 47.5	5 43.3	4 57.8	12 31.0	4 53.1	9 48.7
22 M	8 01 37	29 50 37	18 32 10	26 08 08	13 41.3	13 30.2	29 57.9	6 01.5	13 14.5	5 56.5	4 59.1	12 30.8	4 51.8	9 47.3
23 Tu	8 05 34	0♌47 53	3♒42 53	11♒15 05	13 30.9	13 42.9	1♍10.1	6 41.6	13 41.4	6 09.5	5 00.6	12 30.5	4 50.5	9 45.9
24 W	8 09 30	1 45 10	18 43 29	26 06 57	13 20.5	14 01.5	2 22.2	7 21.7	14 08.4	6 22.6	5 02.1	12 30.2	4 49.2	9 44.5
25 Th	8 13 27	2 42 27	3♓24 34	10♓35 36	13 11.5	14 26.0	3 34.2	8 01.8	14 35.4	6 35.6	5 03.8	12 29.9	4 47.9	9 43.2
26 F	8 17 23	3 39 46	17 39 33	24 36 07	13 04.7	14 56.4	4 46.2	8 41.8	15 02.4	6 48.5	5 05.5	12 29.5	4 46.6	9 41.8
27 Sa	8 21 20	4 37 05	1♈25 14	8♈07 01	13 00.3	15 32.7	5 58.2	9 21.8	15 29.4	7 01.4	5 07.3	12 29.0	4 45.2	9 40.5
28 Su	8 25 16	5 34 25	14 41 44	21 09 45	12 58.2	16 14.9	7 10.1	10 01.8	15 56.5	7 14.3	5 09.2	12 28.5	4 43.9	9 39.1
29 M	8 29 13	6 31 46	27 31 36	3♉47 50	12 57.6	17 03.0	8 22.0	10 41.6	16 23.6	7 27.1	5 11.3	12 28.0	4 42.5	9 37.8
30 Tu	8 33 10	7 29 09	9♉59 06	16 06 01	12 57.6	17 56.8	9 33.9	11 21.5	16 50.6	7 39.9	5 13.4	12 27.4	4 41.1	9 36.5
31 W	8 37 06	8 26 32	22 09 17	28 09 33	12 57.0	18 56.3	10 45.7	12 01.3	17 17.8	7 52.6	5 15.6	12 26.8	4 39.7	9 35.2

August 2013 LONGITUDE

Day	Sid.Time	☉	0 hr ☽	Noon ☽	True ☊	☿	♀	♂	⚳	♃	♄	♅	♆	♇
1 Th	8 41 03	9♌23 57	4♊07 27	10♊03 38	12♏54.8	20♋01.4	11♍57.5	12♋41.0	17♌44.9	8♋05.3	5♏17.9	12♈26.1	4♓38.2	9♑34.0
2 F	8 44 59	10 21 22	15 58 39	21 53 03	12R 50.2	21 11.9	13 09.3	13 20.7	18 12.1	8 17.9	5 20.2	12R 25.4	4R 36.8	9R 32.7
3 Sa	8 48 56	11 18 49	27 47 20	3♋41 57	12 42.9	22 27.6	14 21.0	14 00.4	18 39.2	8 30.4	5 22.7	12 24.6	4 35.3	9 31.5
4 Su	8 52 52	12 16 17	9♋37 18	15 33 44	12 32.9	23 48.6	15 32.7	14 40.0	19 06.4	8 43.0	5 25.3	12 23.8	4 33.8	9 30.3
5 M	8 56 49	13 13 46	21 31 31	27 30 56	12 20.7	25 14.4	16 44.3	15 19.5	19 33.6	8 55.4	5 27.9	12 22.9	4 32.3	9 29.1
6 Tu	9 00 45	14 11 16	3♌32 09	9♌35 20	12 07.1	26 44.9	17 55.9	15 59.1	20 00.8	9 07.8	5 30.7	12 22.0	4 30.8	9 27.9
7 W	9 04 42	15 08 47	15 40 37	21 48 06	11 53.4	28 19.9	19 07.4	16 38.5	20 28.1	9 20.1	5 33.5	12 21.1	4 29.3	9 26.7
8 Th	9 08 39	16 06 18	27 57 52	4♍10 00	11 40.7	29 59.1	20 19.0	17 17.9	20 55.3	9 32.4	5 36.5	12 20.1	4 27.8	9 25.6
9 F	9 12 35	17 03 51	10♍24 33	16 41 38	11 30.0	1♌42.1	21 30.4	17 57.3	21 22.6	9 44.6	5 39.5	12 19.0	4 26.2	9 24.5
10 Sa	9 16 32	18 01 25	23 01 20	29 23 48	11 22.0	3 28.7	22 41.8	18 36.6	21 49.8	9 56.8	5 42.6	12 17.9	4 24.7	9 23.4
11 Su	9 20 28	18 59 00	5♎49 09	12♎17 36	11 16.9	5 18.4	23 53.2	19 15.9	22 17.1	10 08.9	5 45.8	12 16.8	4 23.1	9 22.3
12 M	9 24 25	19 56 35	18 49 21	25 24 33	11 14.4	7 10.8	25 04.5	19 55.1	22 44.4	10 20.9	5 49.0	12 15.6	4 21.5	9 21.2
13 Tu	9 28 21	20 54 12	2♏03 42	8♏46 48	11 13.7	9 05.7	26 15.8	20 34.2	23 11.7	10 32.8	5 52.4	12 14.4	4 19.9	9 20.2
14 W	9 32 18	21 51 49	15 34 11	22 26 03	11 13.8	11 02.6	27 27.0	21 13.3	23 39.0	10 44.7	5 55.8	12 13.2	4 18.4	9 19.1
15 Th	9 36 14	22 49 28	29 22 35	6♐23 51	11 13.3	13 01.1	28 38.2	21 52.4	24 06.3	10 56.5	5 59.4	12 11.9	4 16.8	9 18.1
16 F	9 40 11	23 47 07	13♐29 51	20 40 26	11 11.1	15 00.8	29 49.3	22 31.4	24 33.7	11 08.3	6 03.0	12 10.5	4 15.2	9 17.2
17 Sa	9 44 07	24 44 47	27 55 20	5♑14 08	11 06.6	17 01.4	1♎00.4	23 10.4	25 01.0	11 19.9	6 06.7	12 09.2	4 13.5	9 16.2
18 Su	9 48 04	25 42 29	12♑36 12	20 00 48	10 59.4	19 02.6	2 11.4	23 49.3	25 28.3	11 31.5	6 10.5	12 07.7	4 11.9	9 15.3
19 M	9 52 01	26 40 12	27 27 02	4♒53 53	10 50.2	21 04.0	3 22.3	24 28.2	25 55.7	11 43.0	6 14.3	12 06.3	4 10.3	9 14.4
20 Tu	9 55 57	27 37 55	12♒20 15	19 45 00	10 39.8	23 05.4	4 33.2	25 07.0	26 23.0	11 54.5	6 18.2	12 04.8	4 08.7	9 13.5
21 W	9 59 54	28 35 40	27 07 04	4♓25 22	10 29.4	25 06.5	5 44.0	25 45.8	26 50.4	12 05.8	6 22.3	12 03.3	4 07.0	9 12.6
22 Th	10 03 50	29 33 27	11♓39 00	18 47 12	10 20.2	27 07.2	6 54.8	26 24.5	27 17.7	12 17.1	6 26.3	12 01.7	4 05.4	9 11.8
23 F	10 07 47	0♍31 15	25 49 20	2♈45 01	10 13.0	29 07.2	8 05.5	27 03.2	27 45.1	12 28.3	6 30.5	12 00.1	4 03.8	9 11.0
24 Sa	10 11 43	1 29 04	9♈33 59	16 16 11	10 08.4	1♍06.4	9 16.1	27 41.8	28 12.4	12 39.4	6 34.7	11 58.5	4 02.1	9 10.2
25 Su	10 15 40	2 26 55	22 51 44	29 20 52	10D 06.1	3 04.8	10 26.7	28 20.4	28 39.8	12 50.4	6 39.1	11 56.8	4 00.5	9 09.4
26 M	10 19 36	3 24 48	5♉43 58	12♉01 29	10 05.6	5 02.1	11 37.2	28 58.9	29 07.2	13 01.4	6 43.5	11 55.1	3 58.8	9 08.7
27 Tu	10 23 33	4 22 43	18 13 58	24 22 01	10R 06.1	6 58.4	12 47.7	29 37.4	29 34.5	13 12.2	6 47.9	11 53.3	3 57.2	9 08.0
28 W	10 27 30	5 20 40	0♊26 16	6♊27 22	10 06.4	8 53.5	13 58.1	0♌15.9	0♍01.9	13 23.0	6 52.5	11 51.5	3 55.5	9 07.3
29 Th	10 31 26	6 18 39	12 25 59	18 22 48	10 05.6	10 47.5	15 08.4	0 54.3	0 29.3	13 33.7	6 57.1	11 49.7	3 53.9	9 06.7
30 F	10 35 23	7 16 39	24 18 25	0♋13 30	10 02.9	12 40.3	16 18.7	1 32.6	0 56.7	13 44.2	7 01.8	11 47.9	3 52.3	9 06.0
31 Sa	10 39 19	8 14 41	6♋08 37	12 04 19	9 57.9	14 31.8	17 28.9	2 11.0	1 24.0	13 54.7	7 06.5	11 46.0	3 50.6	9 05.4

Astro Data Dy Hr Mn	Planet Ingress Dy Hr Mn	Last Aspect Dy Hr Mn	☽ Ingress Dy Hr Mn	Last Aspect Dy Hr Mn	☽ Ingress Dy Hr Mn	☽ Phases & Eclipses Dy Hr Mn	Astro Data
♄ D 8 5:12	♂ ♋ 13 13:22	1 6:48 ☿ □	♉ 1 21:43	1 16:48 ♅ ⚹	♋ 3 4:29	8 7:14 ● 16♋18	1 July 2013
☽ 0S 13 13:47	♀ ♍ 22 12:41	3 15:51 ☿ ⚹	♊ 4 9:21	5 6:49 ☿ ☌	♌ 5 16:58	16 3:18 ☽ 23♎46	Julian Day # 41455
♅ R 17 17:19	☉ ♌ 22 15:56	6 12:30 ♂ ☌	♋ 6 22:14	6 21:51 ☉ ☌	♍ 8 3:57	22 18:16 ○ 0♒06	SVP 5♓04'04"
♃△♄ 17 17:31		8 11:44 ☿ ☌	♌ 9 10:48	9 22:05 ♀ ☌	♎ 10 13:08	29 17:43 ☾ 6♉45	GC 27♐01.7 ⚴ 18♊30.1
♃△♆ 18 0:14	☿ ♌ 8 12:13	11 19:54 ♂ ⚹	♍ 11 22:12	12 1:29 ♂ □	♏ 12 20:18		Eris 22♈55.6 ⚵ 18♒10.8R
♄△♆ 19 13:20	♀ ♎ 16 15:37	13 15:26 ☉ ⚹	♎ 14 7:41	14 21:30 ♀ ⚹	♐ 15 1:04	6 21:51 ● 14♌35	⚷ 13♓43.8R ⚶ 27♋49.3
☿ D 20 18:23	☉ ♍ 22 23:02	16 3:18 ☉ □	♏ 16 14:24	16 17:32 ☉ △	♑ 17 3:25	14 10:56 ☽ 21♏49	☽ Mean ☊ 13♏59.1
☽ 0N 26 5:18	☿ ♍ 23 22:36	18 11:12 ☉ △	♐ 18 17:54	18 18:26 ♂ ☍	♒ 19 4:06	21 1:45 ○ 28♒11	
	♂ ♌ 28 2:05	20 15:00 ♀ △	♑ 20 18:39	21 1:45 ☉ ☍	♓ 21 4:43	28 9:35 ☾ 5♊15	1 August 2013
♃☍♇ 7 23:46	⚳ ♍ 28 10:20	21 15:53 ☿ ☍	♒ 22 18:07	23 1:38 ♂ △	♈ 23 7:13		Julian Day # 41486
☽ 0S 9 20:13		23 14:01 ♅ ⚹	♓ 24 18:22	25 10:02 ♂ □	♉ 25 13:13		SVP 5♓03'59"
♀0S 17 22:50		25 18:43 ☿ △	♈ 26 21:29	27 22:58 ♂ ⚹	♊ 27 23:08		GC 27♐01.7 ⚴ 6♋21.1
♃□♅ 21 7:15		28 2:19 ☿ □	♉ 29 4:43	29 4:44 ♀ △	♋ 30 11:33		Eris 22♈56.4R ⚵ 12♒27.6R
☽ 0N 22 16:00		30 15:58 ☿ ⚹	♊ 31 15:42				⚷ 12♓54.7R ⚶ 11♌44.8
							☽ Mean ☊ 12♏20.6

LONGITUDE — September 2013

Day	Sid.Time	☉	0 hr ☽	Noon ☽	True ☊	☿	♀	♂	⚳	♃	♄	♅	♆	♇
1 Su	10 43 16	9♍12 45	18♋01 06	23♋59 25	9♏50.5	16♍22.1	18♎39.0	2♌49.2	1♍51.4	14♋05.1	7♏11.3	11♈44.1	3♓49.0	9♑04.8
2 M	10 47 12	10 10 51	29 59 41	6♌02 13	9R41.2	18 11.1	19 49.1	3 27.4	2 18.8	14 15.4	7 16.2	11R42.2	3R47.3	9R04.3
3 Tu	10 51 09	11 08 59	12♌07 19	18 15 12	9 30.8	19 58.9	20 59.1	4 05.6	2 46.2	14 25.6	7 21.2	11 40.2	3 45.7	9 03.8
4 W	10 55 05	12 07 08	24 26 01	0♍39 54	9 20.0	21 45.5	22 09.1	4 43.7	3 13.5	14 35.7	7 26.2	11 38.2	3 44.1	9 03.3
5 Th	10 59 02	13 05 19	6♍56 53	13 17 00	9 10.1	23 30.9	23 19.0	5 21.8	3 40.9	14 45.7	7 31.3	11 36.2	3 42.5	9 02.8
6 F	11 02 59	14 03 32	19 40 14	26 06 32	9 01.8	25 15.0	24 28.8	5 59.8	4 08.2	14 55.6	7 36.5	11 34.2	3 40.8	9 02.4
7 Sa	11 06 55	15 01 46	2♎35 51	9♎08 05	8 55.7	26 58.0	25 38.5	6 37.8	4 35.6	15 05.4	7 41.7	11 32.1	3 39.2	9 02.0
8 Su	11 10 52	16 00 02	15 43 13	22 21 10	8 52.2	28 39.8	26 48.1	7 15.7	5 02.9	15 15.0	7 47.0	11 30.0	3 37.6	9 01.6
9 M	11 14 48	16 58 20	29 01 54	5♏45 24	8D50.9	0♎20.4	27 57.7	7 53.5	5 30.3	15 24.6	7 52.3	11 27.9	3 36.0	9 01.2
10 Tu	11 18 45	17 56 40	12♏31 40	19 20 43	8 51.2	1 59.8	29 07.2	8 31.3	5 57.6	15 34.0	7 57.7	11 25.7	3 34.5	9 00.9
11 W	11 22 41	18 55 00	26 12 34	3♐07 14	8 52.2	3 38.2	0♏16.6	9 09.1	6 24.9	15 43.4	8 03.2	11 23.5	3 32.9	9 00.6
12 Th	11 26 38	19 53 23	10♐04 44	17 05 02	8R53.0	5 15.4	1 25.9	9 46.8	6 52.2	15 52.6	8 08.7	11 21.3	3 31.3	9 00.4
13 F	11 30 34	20 51 47	24 08 03	1♑13 41	8 52.5	6 51.5	2 35.1	10 24.5	7 19.5	16 01.7	8 14.3	11 19.1	3 29.8	9 00.2
14 Sa	11 34 31	21 50 13	8♑21 42	15 31 51	8 50.3	8 26.6	3 44.3	11 02.1	7 46.8	16 10.6	8 20.0	11 16.9	3 28.2	9 00.0
15 Su	11 38 28	22 48 40	22 43 43	29 56 50	8 46.1	10 00.5	4 53.3	11 39.6	8 14.0	16 19.5	8 25.7	11 14.7	3 26.7	8 59.8
16 M	11 42 24	23 47 08	7♒10 38	14♒24 29	8 40.3	11 33.4	6 02.3	12 17.1	8 41.3	16 28.2	8 31.4	11 12.4	3 25.2	8 59.7
17 Tu	11 46 21	24 45 39	21 37 41	28 49 28	8 33.5	13 05.2	7 11.1	12 54.6	9 08.5	16 36.9	8 37.2	11 10.1	3 23.6	8 59.5
18 W	11 50 17	25 44 11	5♓59 07	13♓05 53	8 26.7	14 35.9	8 19.8	13 32.0	9 35.8	16 45.3	8 43.1	11 07.8	3 22.2	8 59.5
19 Th	11 54 14	26 42 45	20 09 06	27 08 09	8 20.6	16 05.6	9 28.5	14 09.3	10 03.0	16 53.7	8 49.0	11 05.5	3 20.7	8 59.4
20 F	11 58 10	27 41 21	4♈02 31	10♈51 49	8 16.0	17 34.2	10 37.0	14 46.6	10 30.2	17 01.9	8 55.0	11 03.2	3 19.2	8D59.4
21 Sa	12 02 07	28 39 58	17 35 47	24 14 14	8 13.3	19 01.7	11 45.4	15 23.9	10 57.3	17 10.0	9 01.0	11 00.8	3 17.7	8 59.4
22 Su	12 06 03	29 38 38	0♉47 10	7♉14 40	8D12.3	20 28.2	12 53.7	16 01.0	11 24.5	17 18.0	9 07.0	10 58.5	3 16.3	8 59.4
23 M	12 10 00	0♎37 20	13 36 56	19 54 15	8 12.9	21 53.5	14 01.9	16 38.2	11 51.6	17 25.8	9 13.1	10 56.1	3 14.9	8 59.5
24 Tu	12 13 56	1 36 05	26 07 00	2♊15 39	8 14.3	23 17.7	15 10.0	17 15.3	12 18.8	17 33.5	9 19.3	10 53.7	3 13.5	8 59.6
25 W	12 17 53	2 34 51	8♊20 42	14 22 41	8 16.0	24 40.9	16 18.0	17 52.3	12 45.9	17 41.1	9 25.5	10 51.3	3 12.1	8 59.8
26 Th	12 21 50	3 33 40	20 22 13	26 19 53	8R17.2	26 02.8	17 25.8	18 29.3	13 13.0	17 48.5	9 31.8	10 48.9	3 10.7	8 59.9
27 F	12 25 46	4 32 31	2♋16 19	8♋12 08	8 17.4	27 23.5	18 33.6	19 06.3	13 40.0	17 55.8	9 38.1	10 46.5	3 09.4	9 00.1
28 Sa	12 29 43	5 31 25	14 07 59	20 04 26	8 16.3	28 43.0	19 41.2	19 43.2	14 07.1	18 03.0	9 44.4	10 44.1	3 08.0	9 00.4
29 Su	12 33 39	6 30 20	26 02 05	2♌01 29	8 13.7	0♏01.2	20 48.7	20 20.0	14 34.1	18 09.9	9 50.8	10 41.7	3 06.7	9 00.6
30 M	12 37 36	7 29 18	8♌03 09	14 07 33	8 09.9	1 18.0	21 56.0	20 56.8	15 01.1	18 16.8	9 57.2	10 39.3	3 05.4	9 00.9

LONGITUDE — October 2013

Day	Sid.Time	☉	0 hr ☽	Noon ☽	True ☊	☿	♀	♂	⚳	♃	♄	♅	♆	♇
1 Tu	12 41 32	8♎28 18	20♌15 06	26♌26 09	8♏05.2	2♏33.4	23♏03.3	21♌33.5	15♍28.1	18♋23.5	10♏03.7	10♈36.9	3♓04.2	9♑01.2
2 W	12 45 29	9 27 20	2♍41 00	8♍59 53	8R00.3	3 47.3	24 10.4	22 10.2	15 55.0	18 30.0	10 10.2	10R34.5	3R02.9	9 01.6
3 Th	12 49 25	10 26 24	15 22 56	21 50 14	7 55.7	4 59.6	25 17.3	22 46.8	16 22.0	18 36.4	10 16.7	10 32.0	3 01.7	9 02.0
4 F	12 53 22	11 25 31	28 21 46	4♎57 29	7 51.9	6 10.2	26 24.2	23 23.3	16 48.9	18 42.6	10 23.3	10 29.6	3 00.5	9 02.4
5 Sa	12 57 19	12 24 39	11♎37 15	18 20 51	7 49.4	7 18.9	27 30.8	23 59.8	17 15.7	18 48.7	10 29.9	10 27.2	2 59.3	9 02.8
6 Su	13 01 15	13 23 50	25 08 03	1♏58 35	7D48.2	8 25.7	28 37.4	24 36.2	17 42.6	18 54.6	10 36.6	10 24.8	2 58.1	9 03.3
7 M	13 05 12	14 23 02	8♏52 07	15 48 20	7 48.3	9 30.4	29 43.7	25 12.6	18 09.4	19 00.4	10 43.3	10 22.3	2 57.0	9 03.8
8 Tu	13 09 08	15 22 17	22 46 53	29 47 27	7 49.3	10 32.8	0♐49.9	25 48.9	18 36.2	19 06.0	10 50.0	10 19.9	2 55.8	9 04.3
9 W	13 13 05	16 21 33	6♐49 42	13♐53 19	7 50.7	11 32.6	1 56.0	26 25.2	19 02.9	19 11.4	10 56.7	10 17.5	2 54.8	9 04.9
10 Th	13 17 01	17 20 51	20 57 59	28 03 26	7 52.0	12 29.8	3 01.8	27 01.4	19 29.6	19 16.7	11 03.5	10 15.1	2 53.7	9 05.5
11 F	13 20 58	18 20 11	5♑09 22	12♑15 31	7R52.8	13 24.0	4 07.5	27 37.5	19 56.3	19 21.8	11 10.3	10 12.7	2 52.6	9 06.1
12 Sa	13 24 54	19 19 33	19 21 38	26 27 25	7 52.7	14 15.0	5 13.0	28 13.6	20 22.9	19 26.7	11 17.2	10 10.3	2 51.6	9 06.8
13 Su	13 28 51	20 18 56	3♒32 37	10♒36 56	7 51.8	15 02.3	6 18.2	28 49.6	20 49.5	19 31.4	11 24.0	10 08.0	2 50.6	9 07.5
14 M	13 32 48	21 18 21	17 40 04	24 41 43	7 50.2	15 45.8	7 23.3	29 25.5	21 16.1	19 36.0	11 30.9	10 05.6	2 49.7	9 08.2
15 Tu	13 36 44	22 17 48	1♓41 32	8♓39 13	7 48.2	16 25.0	8 28.2	0♍01.4	21 42.6	19 40.4	11 37.8	10 03.2	2 48.7	9 08.9
16 W	13 40 41	23 17 16	15 34 25	22 26 50	7 46.1	16 59.4	9 32.8	0 37.2	22 09.0	19 44.7	11 44.8	10 00.9	2 47.8	9 09.7
17 Th	13 44 37	24 16 47	29 16 09	6♈02 05	7 44.4	17 28.7	10 37.3	1 12.9	22 35.5	19 48.7	11 51.7	9 58.6	2 47.0	9 10.5
18 F	13 48 34	25 16 19	12♈44 23	19 22 52	7 43.2	17 52.3	11 41.5	1 48.6	23 01.9	19 52.6	11 58.7	9 56.2	2 46.1	9 11.4
19 Sa	13 52 30	26 15 53	25 57 22	2♉27 46	7D42.6	18 09.7	12 45.4	2 24.2	23 28.2	19 56.3	12 05.7	9 53.9	2 45.3	9 12.2
20 Su	13 56 27	27 15 30	8♉54 04	15 16 16	7 42.6	18R20.3	13 49.1	2 59.8	23 54.5	19 59.8	12 12.8	9 51.6	2 44.5	9 13.1
21 M	14 00 23	28 15 08	21 34 29	27 48 50	7 43.2	18 23.6	14 52.6	3 35.3	24 20.8	20 03.1	12 19.8	9 49.4	2 43.7	9 14.0
22 Tu	14 04 20	29 14 49	3♊59 34	10♊06 58	7 44.0	18 19.1	15 55.8	4 10.7	24 47.0	20 06.3	12 26.9	9 47.1	2 43.0	9 15.0
23 W	14 08 17	0♏14 32	16 11 20	22 13 05	7 44.8	18 06.3	16 58.7	4 46.1	25 13.2	20 09.3	12 34.0	9 44.9	2 42.3	9 16.0
24 Th	14 12 13	1 14 17	28 12 39	4♋10 30	7 45.6	17 44.7	18 01.4	5 21.4	25 39.3	20 12.1	12 41.1	9 42.7	2 41.6	9 17.0
25 F	14 16 10	2 14 04	10♋07 08	16 03 06	7 46.1	17 14.2	19 03.8	5 56.6	26 05.4	20 14.6	12 48.2	9 40.5	2 40.9	9 18.0
26 Sa	14 20 06	3 13 53	21 58 58	27 55 19	7R46.3	16 34.5	20 05.8	6 31.8	26 31.4	20 17.0	12 55.3	9 38.3	2 40.3	9 19.1
27 Su	14 24 03	4 13 45	3♌52 43	9♌51 47	7 46.4	15 46.0	21 07.6	7 06.8	26 57.4	20 19.3	13 02.4	9 36.2	2 39.7	9 20.2
28 M	14 27 59	5 13 39	15 53 04	21 57 11	7 46.2	14 49.0	22 09.1	7 41.9	27 23.3	20 21.3	13 09.6	9 34.1	2 39.2	9 21.3
29 Tu	14 31 56	6 13 35	28 04 38	4♍15 57	7 46.0	13 44.6	23 10.2	8 16.8	27 49.2	20 23.1	13 16.7	9 32.0	2 38.7	9 22.4
30 W	14 35 52	7 13 33	10♍31 36	16 51 59	7D45.9	12 34.0	24 11.0	8 51.7	28 15.0	20 24.7	13 23.9	9 29.9	2 38.2	9 23.6
31 Th	14 39 49	8 13 33	23 17 26	29 48 12	7 45.9	11 18.9	25 11.4	9 26.5	28 40.7	20 26.2	13 31.1	9 27.9	2 37.7	9 24.8

Astro Data

	Dy Hr Mn
☽0S	6 2:56
☿0S	10 1:24
☽0N	19 1:51
♇ D	20 15:29
♄✱♇	21 5:45
☉0S	22 20:44
♃⊼♆	29 2:38
☽0S	3 10:46
♄⊼♅	5 4:45
☽0N	16 9:39
☿ R	21 10:29
☽0S	30 19:51

Planet Ingress

		Dy Hr Mn
☿	♎	9 7:07
♀	♏	11 6:16
☉	♎	22 20:44
☿	♏	29 11:38
♀	♐	7 17:54
♂	♍	15 11:05
☉	♏	23 6:10

Last Aspect / ☽ Ingress

Last Aspect Dy Hr Mn		☽ Ingress	Dy Hr Mn
1 0:06	♀ □	♌	2 0:01
3 17:52	♀ ✱	♍	4 10:43
6 10:10	☿ ☌	♎	6 19:12
8 20:46	♀ ☌	♏	9 1:44
10 9:21	☉ ✱	♐	11 6:36
12 17:08	☉ □	♑	13 9:56
14 23:17	☉ △	♒	15 12:05
16 8:19	♂ ☍	♓	17 13:58
19 11:13	☉ ☍	♈	19 16:58
21 1:25	☿ ☍	♉	21 22:33
23 7:13	♃ ✱	♊	24 7:34
26 11:21	☿ △	♋	26 19:24
29 7:30	☿ □	♌	29 7:57

Last Aspect / ☽ Ingress

Last Aspect Dy Hr Mn		☽ Ingress	Dy Hr Mn
1 4:48	♀ □	♍	1 18:52
3 18:57	♀ ✱	♎	4 2:59
5 22:28	♂ ✱	♏	6 8:33
8 4:54	♂ □	♐	8 12:21
10 10:10	♂ △	♑	10 15:17
12 0:04	♃ ☍	♒	12 18:00
14 20:28	♂ ☍	♓	14 21:06
16 7:15	♃ △	♈	17 1:17
18 23:38	☉ ☍	♉	19 7:27
20 21:02	♃ ✱	♊	21 16:14
23 0:35	♀ ☍	♋	24 3:36
25 20:31	♃ ☌	♌	26 16:11
28 12:25	♀ △	♍	29 3:45
31 2:48	♀ □	♎	31 12:22

☽ Phases & Eclipses

Dy Hr Mn	
5 11:36	● 13♍04
12 17:08	☽ 20♐06
19 11:13	○ 26♓41
27 3:55	☾ 4♋13
5 0:35	● 11♎56
11 23:02	☽ 18♑47
18 23:38	○ 25♈45
18 23:50	☊ A 0.765
26 23:40	☾ 3♌43

Astro Data

1 September 2013
Julian Day # 41517
SVP 5♓03'56"
GC 27♐01.8 ⚴ 24♋16.9
Eris 22♈47.5R ⚵ 5♒41.0R
⚷ 11♓33.1R ⚶ 25♌58.6
☽ Mean ☊ 10♏42.1

1 October 2013
Julian Day # 41547
SVP 5♓03'53"
GC 27♐01.9 ⚴ 10♌56.4
Eris 22♈32.2R ⚵ 4♒01.7
⚷ 10♓11.7R ⚶ 9♍48.4
☽ Mean ☊ 9♏06.7

November 2013 LONGITUDE

Day	Sid.Time	☉	0 hr ☽	Noon ☽	True ☊	☿	♀	♂	⚳	♃	♄	♅	♆	♇
1 F	14 43 45	9♏13 35	6♎24 28	13♎06 17	7♏46.0	10♏01.4	26♐11.5	10♍01.2	29♍06.4	20♋27.4	13♏38.3	9♈25.8	2♓37.3	9♑26.0
2 Sa	14 47 42	10 13 39	19 53 37	26 46 16	7R46.1	8R43.8	27 11.2	10 35.8	29 32.0	20 28.4	13 45.5	9R23.8	2R36.9	9 27.3
3 Su	14 51 39	11 13 46	3♏44 00	10♏46 23	7 46.2	7 28.6	28 10.6	11 10.4	29 57.6	20 29.3	13 52.7	9 21.9	2 36.5	9 28.6
4 M	14 55 35	12 13 54	17 52 57	25 03 05	7 46.0	6 18.2	29 09.5	11 44.8	0♎23.1	20 29.9	13 59.9	9 20.0	2 36.2	9 29.9
5 Tu	14 59 32	13 14 04	2♐16 08	9♐31 22	7 45.6	5 14.7	0♑08.0	12 19.2	0 48.5	20 30.4	14 07.1	9 18.1	2 35.9	9 31.2
6 W	15 03 28	14 14 15	16 48 03	24 05 24	7 44.9	4 20.0	1 06.1	12 53.5	1 13.9	20R30.6	14 14.3	9 16.2	2 35.6	9 32.6
7 Th	15 07 25	15 14 29	1♑22 40	8♑39 11	7 44.1	3 35.5	2 03.7	13 27.8	1 39.2	20 30.6	14 21.5	9 14.4	2 35.4	9 33.9
8 F	15 11 21	16 14 43	15 54 18	23 07 26	7 43.3	3 02.2	3 00.8	14 01.9	2 04.4	20 30.5	14 28.7	9 12.6	2 35.2	9 35.4
9 Sa	15 15 18	17 15 00	0♒18 08	7♒25 58	7D42.8	2 40.4	3 57.4	14 35.9	2 29.6	20 30.1	14 35.9	9 10.8	2 35.1	9 36.8
10 Su	15 19 14	18 15 17	14 30 40	21 31 59	7 42.7	2D30.3	4 53.5	15 09.9	2 54.7	20 29.6	14 43.1	9 09.1	2 34.9	9 38.2
11 M	15 23 11	19 15 36	28 29 46	5♓23 57	7 43.1	2 31.6	5 49.1	15 43.8	3 19.7	20 28.8	14 50.3	9 07.4	2 34.8	9 39.7
12 Tu	15 27 08	20 15 56	12♓14 28	19 01 22	7 43.9	2 43.7	6 44.1	16 17.6	3 44.6	20 27.8	14 57.5	9 05.7	2 34.8	9 41.2
13 W	15 31 04	21 16 18	25 44 40	2♈24 26	7 45.1	3 05.9	7 38.5	16 51.2	4 09.4	20 26.7	15 04.6	9 04.1	2D34.7	9 42.7
14 Th	15 35 01	22 16 41	9♈00 44	15 33 40	7 46.2	3 37.4	8 32.3	17 24.8	4 34.2	20 25.3	15 11.8	9 02.5	2 34.8	9 44.3
15 F	15 38 57	23 17 06	22 03 18	28 29 43	7R47.1	4 17.3	9 25.5	17 58.3	4 58.9	20 23.8	15 19.0	9 01.0	2 34.8	9 45.8
16 Sa	15 42 54	24 17 32	4♉53 00	11♉13 14	7 47.3	5 04.6	10 18.0	18 31.7	5 23.5	20 22.0	15 26.1	8 59.5	2 34.9	9 47.4
17 Su	15 46 50	25 18 00	17 30 31	23 44 55	7 46.5	5 58.6	11 09.8	19 05.1	5 48.0	20 20.1	15 33.3	8 58.0	2 35.0	9 49.0
18 M	15 50 47	26 18 29	29 56 35	6♊05 35	7 44.8	6 58.4	12 00.9	19 38.3	6 12.5	20 17.9	15 40.4	8 56.6	2 35.1	9 50.6
19 Tu	15 54 43	27 19 00	12♊12 06	18 16 17	7 42.2	8 03.2	12 51.3	20 11.4	6 36.8	20 15.6	15 47.5	8 55.2	2 35.3	9 52.3
20 W	15 58 40	28 19 32	24 18 21	0♋18 31	7 38.9	9 12.4	13 40.9	20 44.4	7 01.1	20 13.0	15 54.6	8 53.9	2 35.5	9 54.0
21 Th	16 02 37	29 20 06	6♋17 04	12 14 17	7 35.2	10 25.3	14 29.6	21 17.4	7 25.2	20 10.3	16 01.7	8 52.6	2 35.8	9 55.7
22 F	16 06 33	0♐20 42	18 10 33	24 06 13	7 31.6	11 41.5	15 17.6	21 50.2	7 49.3	20 07.4	16 08.7	8 51.3	2 36.1	9 57.4
23 Sa	16 10 30	1 21 20	0♌01 45	5♌57 36	7 28.5	13 00.4	16 04.7	22 22.9	8 13.3	20 04.3	16 15.8	8 50.1	2 36.4	9 59.1
24 Su	16 14 26	2 21 59	11 54 17	17 52 18	7 26.4	14 21.7	16 50.9	22 55.5	8 37.2	20 00.9	16 22.8	8 49.0	2 36.7	10 00.8
25 M	16 18 23	3 22 39	23 52 14	29 54 39	7D25.4	15 44.9	17 36.1	23 28.0	9 01.0	19 57.4	16 29.8	8 47.8	2 37.1	10 02.6
26 Tu	16 22 19	4 23 21	6♍00 19	12♍09 19	7 25.6	17 09.8	18 20.4	24 00.4	9 24.7	19 53.8	16 36.8	8 46.8	2 37.5	10 04.4
27 W	16 26 16	5 24 05	18 22 45	24 41 00	7 26.8	18 36.0	19 03.6	24 32.7	9 48.3	19 49.9	16 43.8	8 45.7	2 38.0	10 06.2
28 Th	16 30 12	6 24 51	1♎04 35	7♎33 59	7 28.4	20 03.5	19 45.8	25 04.9	10 11.7	19 45.8	16 50.7	8 44.8	2 38.5	10 08.0
29 F	16 34 09	7 25 37	14 09 37	20 51 45	7 30.0	21 31.9	20 26.9	25 36.9	10 35.1	19 41.6	16 57.6	8 43.8	2 39.0	10 09.8
30 Sa	16 38 06	8 26 26	27 40 36	4♏36 12	7R30.9	23 01.2	21 06.8	26 08.9	10 58.4	19 37.2	17 04.5	8 42.9	2 39.6	10 11.7

December 2013 LONGITUDE

Day	Sid.Time	☉	0 hr ☽	Noon ☽	True ☊	☿	♀	♂	⚳	♃	♄	♅	♆	♇
1 Su	16 42 02	9♐27 16	11♏38 27	18♏47 04	7♏30.4	24♏31.1	21♑45.6	26♍40.7	11♎21.5	19♋32.6	17♏11.4	8♈42.1	2♓40.1	10♑13.5
2 M	16 45 59	10 28 07	26 01 36	3♐21 24	7R28.4	26 01.6	22 23.1	27 12.4	11 44.6	19R27.8	17 18.2	8R41.3	2 40.8	10 15.4
3 Tu	16 49 55	11 28 59	10♐45 39	18 13 22	7 24.6	27 32.5	22 59.3	27 43.9	12 07.5	19 22.8	17 25.0	8 40.5	2 41.4	10 17.3
4 W	16 53 52	12 29 53	25 43 29	3♑14 48	7 19.6	29 03.9	23 34.2	28 15.4	12 30.3	19 17.7	17 31.8	8 39.8	2 42.1	10 19.2
5 Th	16 57 48	13 30 47	10♑46 09	18 16 21	7 14.0	0♐35.5	24 07.6	28 46.6	12 53.0	19 12.5	17 38.6	8 39.2	2 42.9	10 21.1
6 F	17 01 45	14 31 43	25 44 17	3♒08 58	7 08.7	2 07.5	24 39.6	29 17.8	13 15.5	19 07.0	17 45.3	8 38.6	2 43.6	10 23.1
7 Sa	17 05 42	15 32 39	10♒29 33	17 45 22	7 04.4	3 39.6	25 10.1	29 48.8	13 37.9	19 01.4	17 52.0	8 38.1	2 44.4	10 25.0
8 Su	17 09 38	16 33 36	24 55 55	2♓00 53	7 01.6	5 11.9	25 38.9	0♎19.7	14 00.2	18 55.7	17 58.6	8 37.6	2 45.2	10 27.0
9 M	17 13 35	17 34 33	9♓00 05	15 53 32	7D00.6	6 44.4	26 06.1	0 50.4	14 22.4	18 49.8	18 05.2	8 37.1	2 46.1	10 28.9
10 Tu	17 17 31	18 35 31	22 41 20	29 23 41	7 01.1	8 17.0	26 31.5	1 21.0	14 44.4	18 43.7	18 11.7	8 36.7	2 47.0	10 30.9
11 W	17 21 28	19 36 29	6♈00 53	12♈33 15	7 02.4	9 49.8	26 55.2	1 51.4	15 06.3	18 37.5	18 18.3	8 36.4	2 47.9	10 32.9
12 Th	17 25 24	20 37 28	19 01 11	25 25 02	7R03.8	11 22.6	27 17.0	2 21.7	15 28.0	18 31.2	18 24.7	8 36.1	2 48.9	10 34.9
13 F	17 29 21	21 38 28	1♉45 11	8♉02 01	7 04.4	12 55.6	27 36.8	2 51.9	15 49.6	18 24.7	18 31.2	8 35.8	2 49.9	10 36.9
14 Sa	17 33 17	22 39 28	14 15 51	20 27 01	7 03.4	14 28.7	27 54.7	3 21.9	16 11.1	18 18.1	18 37.6	8 35.6	2 50.9	10 39.0
15 Su	17 37 14	23 40 29	26 35 48	2♊42 28	7 00.1	16 01.9	28 10.5	3 51.7	16 32.4	18 11.4	18 43.9	8 35.5	2 51.9	10 41.0
16 M	17 41 11	24 41 31	8♊47 13	14 50 17	6 54.5	17 35.2	28 24.2	4 21.4	16 53.6	18 04.6	18 50.2	8 35.4	2 53.0	10 43.0
17 Tu	17 45 07	25 42 33	20 51 50	26 52 01	6 46.7	19 08.6	28 35.7	4 50.9	17 14.6	17 57.6	18 56.5	8D35.4	2 54.1	10 45.1
18 W	17 49 04	26 43 36	2♋51 02	8♋49 01	6 37.2	20 42.2	28 45.0	5 20.3	17 35.5	17 50.6	19 02.7	8 35.4	2 55.3	10 47.1
19 Th	17 53 00	27 44 39	14 46 08	20 42 35	6 26.7	22 15.9	28 51.9	5 49.5	17 56.2	17 43.4	19 08.9	8 35.4	2 56.5	10 49.2
20 F	17 56 57	28 45 44	26 38 34	2♌34 20	6 16.2	23 49.8	28 56.5	6 18.5	18 16.7	17 36.2	19 15.0	8 35.6	2 57.7	10 51.3
21 Sa	18 00 53	29 46 48	8♌30 07	14 26 17	6 06.7	25 23.8	28R58.7	6 47.3	18 37.1	17 28.8	19 21.1	8 35.7	2 58.9	10 53.3
22 Su	18 04 50	0♑47 54	20 23 08	26 21 06	5 59.0	26 58.0	28 58.5	7 16.0	18 57.3	17 21.3	19 27.1	8 35.9	3 00.2	10 55.4
23 M	18 08 46	1 49 00	2♍20 36	8♍22 07	5 53.5	28 32.5	28 55.8	7 44.5	19 17.4	17 13.8	19 33.1	8 36.2	3 01.5	10 57.5
24 Tu	18 12 43	2 50 07	14 26 11	20 33 21	5 50.5	0♑07.1	28 50.7	8 12.8	19 37.2	17 06.2	19 39.0	8 36.5	3 02.8	10 59.6
25 W	18 16 40	3 51 14	26 44 12	2♎59 19	5D49.5	1 41.9	28 43.0	8 40.9	19 57.0	16 58.5	19 44.8	8 36.9	3 04.1	11 01.7
26 Th	18 20 36	4 52 22	9♎19 19	15 44 46	5 50.0	3 17.0	28 32.9	9 08.8	20 16.5	16 50.7	19 50.6	8 37.3	3 05.5	11 03.8
27 F	18 24 33	5 53 31	22 16 14	28 54 12	5R50.7	4 52.4	28 20.3	9 36.5	20 35.8	16 42.9	19 56.4	8 37.8	3 06.9	11 05.9
28 Sa	18 28 29	6 54 40	5♏39 07	12♏31 15	5 50.7	6 28.0	28 05.2	10 04.0	20 55.0	16 35.0	20 02.0	8 38.3	3 08.4	11 08.0
29 Su	18 32 26	7 55 50	19 30 48	26 37 44	5 48.9	8 03.9	27 47.7	10 31.3	21 13.9	16 27.1	20 07.7	8 38.9	3 09.8	11 10.1
30 M	18 36 22	8 57 00	3♐51 50	11♐12 41	5 44.5	9 40.1	27 27.9	10 58.4	21 32.7	16 19.1	20 13.2	8 39.6	3 11.3	11 12.2
31 Tu	18 40 19	9 58 11	18 39 37	26 11 42	5 37.5	11 16.6	27 05.8	11 25.3	21 51.3	16 11.1	20 18.7	8 40.2	3 12.8	11 14.3

Astro Data

	Dy Hr Mn
♅□♇	1 10:30
♃ R	7 5:03
☿ D	10 21:14
☽0N	12 15:40
♆ D	13 18:42
☽0S	27 5:26
☽0N	9 21:43
♃△♄	13 0:01
♂0S	17 1:57
♅ D	17 17:39
♃⚻♆	17 22:19
♀ R	21 21:54
☽0S	24 14:21

Planet Ingress

	Dy Hr Mn
⚳ ♎	3 14:15
♀ ♑	5 8:43
☉ ♐	22 3:48
☿ ♐	5 2:42
♂ ♎	7 20:41
☉ ♑	21 17:11
☿ ♑	24 10:12

Last Aspect / ☽ Ingress

Last Aspect Dy Hr Mn		☽ Ingress Dy Hr Mn
2 12:47	♀ ⚹	♏ 2 17:35
4 4:23	♃ △	♐ 4 20:14
5 16:48	♂ □	♑ 6 21:44
8 7:39	♃ ☍	♒ 8 23:30
10 5:57	☉ □	♓ 11 2:36
12 14:34	♃ △	♈ 13 7:39
14 20:57	♃ □	♉ 15 14:49
17 15:16	☉ ☍	♊ 18 0:07
19 15:59	♂ □	♋ 20 11:23
22 7:11	♂ ⚹	♌ 22 23:56
24 8:59	♄ □	♍ 25 12:11
27 11:44	♂ ☌	♎ 27 22:00
29 11:13	♀ □	♏ 30 4:03

Last Aspect / ☽ Ingress

Last Aspect Dy Hr Mn		☽ Ingress Dy Hr Mn
2 1:34	♂ ⚹	♐ 2 6:31
4 3:45	♂ □	♑ 4 6:49
6 5:31	♂ △	♒ 6 6:53
7 12:11	♄ □	♓ 8 8:34
10 6:41	♀ ⚹	♈ 10 13:05
12 15:37	♀ □	♉ 12 20:40
15 2:54	♀ △	♊ 15 6:40
17 9:28	☉ ☍	♋ 17 18:17
20 4:37	♀ ☍	♌ 20 6:48
22 13:25	☿ △	♍ 22 19:19
25 3:55	♀ △	♎ 25 6:17
27 11:00	♀ □	♏ 27 13:58
29 13:54	♀ ⚹	♐ 29 17:37
30 11:36	♂ ⚹	♑ 31 18:01

☽ Phases & Eclipses

Dy Hr Mn	
3 12:50	● 11♏16
3 12:46:28	✔ AT01'40"
10 5:57	☽ 18♒00
17 15:16	○ 25♉26
25 19:28	☾ 3♍42
3 0:22	● 10♐59
9 15:12	☽ 17♓43
17 9:28	○ 25♊36
25 13:48	☾ 3♎56

Astro Data

1 November 2013
Julian Day # 41578
SVP 5♓03'50"
GC 27♐02.0 ⚵ 26♌18.7
Eris 22♈13.8R ⚶ 8♒38.1
⚷ 9♓16.6R ⚴ 23♍50.5
☽ Mean ☊ 7♏28.2

1 December 2013
Julian Day # 41608
SVP 5♓03'46"
GC 27♐02.0 ⚵ 7♍49.1
Eris 21♈58.9R ⚶ 17♒39.3
⚷ 9♓11.4 ⚴ 6♎41.8
☽ Mean ☊ 5♏52.9

LONGITUDE — January 2014

Day	Sid.Time	☉	0 hr ☽	Noon ☽	True ☊	☿	♀	♂	⚳	♃	♄	♅	♆	♇
1 W	18 44 15	10♑59 22	3♑47 49	11♑26 42	5♏28.3	12♑53.4	26♑41.5	11♎51.9	22♎09.7	16♋03.0	20♏24.2	8♈41.0	3♓14.4	11♑16.5
2 Th	18 48 12	12 00 33	19 06 53	26 46 53	5R17.9	14 30.6	26R15.1	12 18.4	22 27.8	15R54.9	20 29.6	8 41.8	3 15.9	11 18.6
3 F	18 52 09	13 01 43	4♒25 15	12♒00 33	5 07.6	16 08.1	25 46.8	12 44.5	22 45.8	15 46.8	20 34.9	8 42.6	3 17.5	11 20.7
4 Sa	18 56 05	14 02 54	19 31 35	26 57 15	4 58.6	17 45.9	25 16.8	13 10.5	23 03.5	15 38.7	20 40.1	8 43.5	3 19.2	11 22.8
5 Su	19 00 02	15 04 04	4♓16 45	11♓29 29	4 51.9	19 24.1	24 45.0	13 36.2	23 21.1	15 30.6	20 45.3	8 44.4	3 20.8	11 24.9
6 M	19 03 58	16 05 14	18 35 06	25 33 28	4 47.9	21 02.6	24 11.9	14 01.6	23 38.4	15 22.5	20 50.4	8 45.4	3 22.5	11 27.0
7 Tu	19 07 55	17 06 24	2♈24 39	9♈08 52	4D46.1	22 41.5	23 37.5	14 26.8	23 55.5	15 14.4	20 55.4	8 46.5	3 24.2	11 29.1
8 W	19 11 51	18 07 33	15 46 27	22 17 52	4R46.0	24 20.7	23 02.2	14 51.8	24 12.3	15 06.3	21 00.4	8 47.6	3 25.9	11 31.2
9 Th	19 15 48	19 08 41	28 43 37	5♉04 16	4 46.2	26 00.2	22 26.1	15 16.4	24 28.9	14 58.2	21 05.3	8 48.7	3 27.6	11 33.3
10 F	19 19 44	20 09 49	11♉20 22	17 32 29	4 45.5	27 40.0	21 49.5	15 40.9	24 45.3	14 50.1	21 10.1	8 49.9	3 29.4	11 35.4
11 Sa	19 23 41	21 10 57	23 41 10	29 46 57	4 42.9	29 20.0	21 12.6	16 05.0	25 01.5	14 42.1	21 14.8	8 51.1	3 31.2	11 37.5
12 Su	19 27 38	22 12 04	5♊50 19	11♊51 42	4 37.6	1♒00.3	20 35.8	16 28.9	25 17.4	14 34.1	21 19.5	8 52.4	3 33.0	11 39.6
13 M	19 31 34	23 13 11	17 51 30	23 50 04	4 29.2	2 40.7	19 59.2	16 52.5	25 33.1	14 26.2	21 24.1	8 53.8	3 34.8	11 41.7
14 Tu	19 35 31	24 14 17	29 47 42	5♋44 41	4 17.8	4 21.2	19 23.1	17 15.8	25 48.5	14 18.3	21 28.6	8 55.2	3 36.7	11 43.7
15 W	19 39 27	25 15 23	11♋41 13	17 37 31	4 04.2	6 01.8	18 47.9	17 38.8	26 03.7	14 10.4	21 33.0	8 56.6	3 38.5	11 45.8
16 Th	19 43 24	26 16 28	23 33 45	29 30 04	3 49.3	7 42.3	18 13.7	18 01.5	26 18.6	14 02.6	21 37.4	8 58.1	3 40.4	11 47.9
17 F	19 47 20	27 17 32	5♌26 37	11♌23 33	3 34.3	9 22.5	17 40.7	18 23.9	26 33.2	13 54.9	21 41.7	8 59.6	3 42.3	11 49.9
18 Sa	19 51 17	28 18 36	17 21 02	23 19 13	3 20.4	11 02.5	17 09.2	18 46.0	26 47.6	13 47.3	21 45.9	9 01.2	3 44.2	11 52.0
19 Su	19 55 13	29 19 40	29 18 21	5♍18 39	3 08.7	12 41.9	16 39.3	19 07.7	27 01.7	13 39.7	21 50.0	9 02.8	3 46.2	11 54.0
20 M	19 59 10	0♒20 43	11♍20 23	17 23 54	2 59.8	14 20.6	16 11.3	19 29.2	27 15.6	13 32.2	21 54.0	9 04.4	3 48.2	11 56.0
21 Tu	20 03 07	1 21 46	23 29 34	29 37 46	2 54.0	15 58.3	15 45.3	19 50.3	27 29.2	13 24.8	21 58.0	9 06.1	3 50.1	11 58.1
22 W	20 07 03	2 22 48	5♎48 59	12♎03 42	2 51.0	17 34.8	15 21.4	20 11.0	27 42.4	13 17.5	22 01.8	9 07.9	3 52.1	12 00.1
23 Th	20 11 00	3 23 50	18 22 25	24 45 42	2 50.1	19 09.7	14 59.7	20 31.4	27 55.4	13 10.3	22 05.6	9 09.7	3 54.1	12 02.1
24 F	20 14 56	4 24 52	1♏14 04	7♏48 03	2 50.0	20 42.7	14 40.3	20 51.5	28 08.1	13 03.2	22 09.3	9 11.5	3 56.2	12 04.1
25 Sa	20 18 53	5 25 53	14 28 08	21 14 45	2 49.5	22 13.2	14 23.4	21 11.1	28 20.5	12 56.2	22 12.9	9 13.4	3 58.2	12 06.0
26 Su	20 22 49	6 26 53	28 08 12	5♐08 42	2 47.3	23 40.8	14 08.9	21 30.4	28 32.6	12 49.3	22 16.5	9 15.4	4 00.3	12 08.0
27 M	20 26 46	7 27 54	12♐16 17	19 30 47	2 42.6	25 05.0	13 56.8	21 49.3	28 44.4	12 42.5	22 19.9	9 17.3	4 02.4	12 10.0
28 Tu	20 30 42	8 28 53	26 51 49	4♑18 47	2 35.1	26 25.1	13 47.3	22 07.8	28 55.9	12 35.9	22 23.2	9 19.3	4 04.5	12 11.9
29 W	20 34 39	9 29 52	11♑50 49	19 26 52	2 25.1	27 40.4	13 40.2	22 25.9	29 07.1	12 29.4	22 26.5	9 21.4	4 06.6	12 13.8
30 Th	20 38 36	10 30 50	27 05 38	4♒45 42	2 13.7	28 50.3	13 35.7	22 43.6	29 17.9	12 23.0	22 29.7	9 23.5	4 08.7	12 15.7
31 F	20 42 32	11 31 46	12♒25 36	20 03 50	2 02.1	29 53.8	13D33.5	23 00.9	29 28.4	12 16.7	22 32.7	9 25.6	4 10.8	12 17.7

LONGITUDE — February 2014

Day	Sid.Time	☉	0 hr ☽	Noon ☽	True ☊	☿	♀	♂	⚳	♃	♄	♅	♆	♇
1 Sa	20 46 29	12♒32 42	27♒38 57	5♓09 39	1♏51.7	0♓50.3	13♑33.9	23♎17.7	29♎38.6	12♋10.6	22♏35.7	9♈27.8	4♓13.0	12♑19.5
2 Su	20 50 25	13 33 37	12♓34 52	19 53 42	1R43.7	1 38.8	13 36.6	23 34.0	29 48.4	12R04.7	22 38.6	9 30.0	4 15.1	12 21.4
3 M	20 54 22	14 34 30	27 05 29	4♈09 52	1 38.5	2 18.7	13 41.6	23 49.9	29 57.9	11 58.8	22 41.4	9 32.3	4 17.3	12 23.3
4 Tu	20 58 18	15 35 22	11♈06 40	17 55 54	1 36.0	2 49.1	13 49.0	24 05.4	0♏07.0	11 53.2	22 44.1	9 34.6	4 19.5	12 25.1
5 W	21 02 15	16 36 12	24 37 49	1♉12 44	1D35.3	3 09.5	13 58.6	24 20.4	0 15.8	11 47.7	22 46.6	9 36.9	4 21.6	12 26.9
6 Th	21 06 11	17 37 01	7♉41 09	14 03 36	1R35.5	3R19.4	14 10.4	24 34.9	0 24.3	11 42.3	22 49.1	9 39.3	4 23.8	12 28.7
7 F	21 10 08	18 37 49	20 20 40	26 33 00	1 35.3	3 18.3	14 24.3	24 48.9	0 32.4	11 37.2	22 51.6	9 41.7	4 26.0	12 30.5
8 Sa	21 14 05	19 38 35	2♊41 14	8♊45 59	1 33.5	3 06.3	14 40.3	25 02.4	0 40.1	11 32.1	22 53.9	9 44.2	4 28.3	12 32.3
9 Su	21 18 01	20 39 20	14 47 53	20 47 30	1 29.4	2 43.5	14 58.3	25 15.4	0 47.4	11 27.3	22 56.1	9 46.6	4 30.5	12 34.1
10 M	21 21 58	21 40 03	26 45 23	2♋42 02	1 22.5	2 10.4	15 18.3	25 27.9	0 54.4	11 22.6	22 58.2	9 49.2	4 32.7	12 35.8
11 Tu	21 25 54	22 40 45	8♋37 54	14 33 25	1 13.0	1 27.8	15 40.1	25 39.8	1 01.1	11 18.1	23 00.2	9 51.7	4 35.0	12 37.5
12 W	21 29 51	23 41 25	20 28 54	26 24 42	1 01.3	0 36.8	16 03.8	25 51.3	1 07.3	11 13.8	23 02.1	9 54.3	4 37.2	12 39.2
13 Th	21 33 47	24 42 03	2♌21 03	8♌18 12	0 48.4	29♒38.7	16 29.2	26 02.1	1 13.2	11 09.7	23 03.9	9 56.9	4 39.4	12 40.9
14 F	21 37 44	25 42 40	14 16 20	20 15 37	0 35.4	28 35.3	16 56.3	26 12.5	1 18.6	11 05.7	23 05.6	9 59.6	4 41.7	12 42.6
15 Sa	21 41 40	26 43 16	26 16 11	2♍18 11	0 23.2	27 28.2	17 25.1	26 22.2	1 23.7	11 01.9	23 07.2	10 02.2	4 44.0	12 44.2
16 Su	21 45 37	27 43 50	8♍21 44	14 26 57	0 13.0	26 19.4	17 55.4	26 31.4	1 28.4	10 58.3	23 08.7	10 05.0	4 46.2	12 45.8
17 M	21 49 34	28 44 22	20 34 01	26 43 04	0 05.4	25 10.6	18 27.3	26 39.9	1 32.7	10 54.9	23 10.2	10 07.7	4 48.5	12 47.4
18 Tu	21 53 30	29 44 54	2♎54 19	9♎07 59	0 00.6	24 03.7	19 00.6	26 47.9	1 36.6	10 51.7	23 11.5	10 10.5	4 50.8	12 49.0
19 W	21 57 27	0♓45 24	15 24 19	21 43 38	29♎58.3	23 00.0	19 35.3	26 55.2	1 40.1	10 48.7	23 12.7	10 13.3	4 53.0	12 50.5
20 Th	22 01 23	1 45 52	28 06 15	4♏32 29	29D58.1	22 00.9	20 11.4	27 01.9	1 43.2	10 45.8	23 13.8	10 16.1	4 55.3	12 52.1
21 F	22 05 20	2 46 20	11♏02 45	17 37 24	29 58.9	21 07.5	20 48.8	27 08.0	1 45.9	10 43.2	23 14.8	10 19.0	4 57.6	12 53.6
22 Sa	22 09 16	3 46 46	24 16 47	1♐01 14	29R59.5	20 20.6	21 27.4	27 13.4	1 48.1	10 40.7	23 15.7	10 21.8	4 59.9	12 55.1
23 Su	22 13 13	4 47 11	7♐51 03	14 46 26	29 59.1	19 40.6	22 07.2	27 18.1	1 50.0	10 38.4	23 16.5	10 24.8	5 02.1	12 56.5
24 M	22 17 09	5 47 34	21 47 27	28 54 07	29 56.8	19 07.9	22 48.2	27 22.2	1 51.4	10 36.4	23 17.2	10 27.7	5 04.4	12 58.0
25 Tu	22 21 06	6 47 56	6♑06 15	13♑23 28	29 52.2	18 42.5	23 30.3	27 25.6	1 52.4	10 34.5	23 17.8	10 30.7	5 06.7	12 59.4
26 W	22 25 03	7 48 17	20 45 16	28 10 54	29 45.7	18 24.5	24 13.4	27 28.3	1R53.0	10 32.8	23 18.3	10 33.7	5 09.0	13 00.8
27 Th	22 28 59	8 48 36	5♒39 31	13♒10 02	29 37.9	18 13.6	24 57.5	27 30.2	1 53.1	10 31.3	23 18.6	10 36.7	5 11.3	13 02.2
28 F	22 32 56	9 48 53	20 41 20	28 12 12	29 29.8	18D09.7	25 42.6	27 31.5	1 52.8	10 30.0	23 18.9	10 39.7	5 13.5	13 03.5

Astro Data Dy Hr Mn	Planet Ingress Dy Hr Mn	Last Aspect Dy Hr Mn	☽ Ingress Dy Hr Mn	Last Aspect Dy Hr Mn	☽ Ingress Dy Hr Mn	☽ Phases & Eclipses Dy Hr Mn
☽0N 6 5:55	☿ ♒ 11 21:35	2 11:12 ♀ ☌	♒ 2 17:03	31 16:45 ♂ △	♓ 1 3:44	1 11:14 ● 10♑57
☽0S 20 21:56	☉ ♒ 20 3:51	4 1:47 ♄ □	♓ 4 16:58	2 16:35 ♄ △	♈ 3 4:55	8 3:39 ☽ 17♈46
⚳0S 26 6:42	☿ ♓ 31 14:29	6 9:44 ♀ ⚹	♈ 6 19:45	4 23:14 ♂ ☍	♉ 5 9:46	16 4:52 ○ 25♋58
♃☍♇ 31 9:16		8 16:22 ☿ □	♉ 9 2:24	7 4:49 ♄ ☍	♊ 7 18:44	24 5:19 ☾ 4♏08
♀ D 31 20:49	⚳ ♏ 3 17:29	11 10:58 ☿ △	♊ 11 12:26	9 21:08 ♂ △	♋ 10 6:33	30 21:39 ● 10♒55
	☿ ♒R 13 3:30	12 21:33 ♂ △	♋ 14 0:25	12 10:51 ♂ □	♌ 12 19:15	
☽0N 2 16:35	☊ ♎R 18 16:19	16 4:52 ☉ ☍	♌ 16 13:00	15 3:13 ☿ ☍	♍ 15 7:26	6 19:22 ☽ 17♉56
☿ R 6 21:46	☉ ♓ 18 17:59	18 8:51 ♄ □	♍ 19 1:23	17 5:04 ♄ ⚹	♎ 17 18:22	14 23:53 ○ 26♌13
⚳0N 12 10:37		20 20:55 ♄ ⚹	♎ 21 12:43	19 21:52 ♂ ☌	♏ 20 3:33	22 17:15 ☾ 4♐00
☽0S 17 4:33		23 3:50 ♂ ☌	♏ 23 21:43	21 22:10 ♄ ☌	♐ 22 10:12	
♃□♅ 26 7:29		25 13:55 ☿ □	♐ 26 3:13	24 9:25 ♂ ⚹	♑ 24 13:50	
⚳ R 27 8:07		27 22:02 ☿ ⚹	♑ 28 5:04	26 10:51 ♂ □	♒ 26 14:55	
☿ D 28 14:00		29 16:47 ♂ □	♒ 30 4:33	28 10:55 ♂ △	♓ 28 14:52	

Astro Data

1 January 2014
Julian Day # 41639
SVP 5♓03'41"
GC 27♐02.1 ⚴ 13♍37.6
Eris 21♈51.2R ⚵ 0♓05.2
⚷ 9♓59.5 ⚶ 18♎22.8
☽ Mean ☊ 4♏14.4

1 February 2014
Julian Day # 41670
SVP 5♓03'36"
GC 27♐02.2 ⚴ 10♍13.3R
Eris 21♈53.8 ⚵ 14♓37.2
⚷ 11♓30.8 ⚶ 26♎56.1
☽ Mean ☊ 2♏35.9

March 2014

LONGITUDE

Day	Sid.Time	☉	0 hr ☽	Noon ☽	True ☊	☿	♀	♂	⚳	♃	♄	♅	♆	♇
1 Sa	22 36 52	10♓49 09	5♓41 23	13♓07 43	29♎22.4	18♒12.4	26♑28.6	27♎32.0	1♏52.1	10♋29.0	23♏19.1	10♈42.8	5♓15.8	13♑04.8
2 Su	22 40 49	11 49 23	20 30 06	27 47 36	29R 16.8	18 21.4	27 15.5	27R 31.7	1R 51.0	10R 28.1	23R 19.2	10 45.9	5 18.1	13 06.1
3 M	22 44 45	12 49 35	4♈59 27	12♈05 02	29 13.3	18 36.3	28 03.3	27 30.7	1 49.4	10 27.4	23 19.1	10 49.0	5 20.3	13 07.4
4 Tu	22 48 42	13 49 45	19 03 58	25 56 03	29D 12.0	18 56.8	28 51.8	27 29.0	1 47.4	10 26.9	23 19.0	10 52.1	5 22.6	13 08.6
5 W	22 52 38	14 49 53	2♉41 14	9♉19 40	29 12.3	19 22.5	29 41.2	27 26.5	1 45.0	10D 26.6	23 18.8	10 55.3	5 24.9	13 09.9
6 Th	22 56 35	15 49 59	15 51 37	22 17 27	29 13.6	19 53.0	0♒31.3	27 23.3	1 42.1	10 26.5	23 18.4	10 58.4	5 27.1	13 11.1
7 F	23 00 31	16 50 03	28 37 38	4♊52 41	29 15.0	20 28.1	1 22.1	27 19.3	1 38.8	10 26.6	23 18.0	11 01.6	5 29.4	13 12.2
8 Sa	23 04 28	17 50 05	11♊03 12	17 09 47	29R 15.7	21 07.4	2 13.6	27 14.5	1 35.1	10 26.9	23 17.4	11 04.8	5 31.6	13 13.4
9 Su	23 08 25	18 50 05	23 13 02	29 13 36	29 15.0	21 50.6	3 05.8	27 09.0	1 31.0	10 27.4	23 16.8	11 08.0	5 33.8	13 14.5
10 M	23 12 21	19 50 02	5♋12 04	11♋09 03	29 12.6	22 37.5	3 58.6	27 02.7	1 26.5	10 28.1	23 16.0	11 11.3	5 36.1	13 15.5
11 Tu	23 16 18	20 49 58	17 05 05	23 00 43	29 08.5	23 27.8	4 52.1	26 55.6	1 21.5	10 29.0	23 15.2	11 14.5	5 38.3	13 16.6
12 W	23 20 14	21 49 51	28 56 26	4♌52 42	29 02.9	24 21.3	5 46.1	26 47.7	1 16.2	10 30.1	23 14.3	11 17.8	5 40.5	13 17.6
13 Th	23 24 11	22 49 42	10♌49 55	16 48 27	28 56.4	25 17.8	6 40.8	26 39.1	1 10.4	10 31.4	23 13.2	11 21.1	5 42.7	13 18.6
14 F	23 28 07	23 49 31	22 48 37	28 50 40	28 49.7	26 17.1	7 36.0	26 29.7	1 04.2	10 32.9	23 12.1	11 24.4	5 44.9	13 19.6
15 Sa	23 32 04	24 49 18	4♍54 51	11♍01 22	28 43.5	27 19.1	8 31.7	26 19.6	0 57.6	10 34.5	23 10.8	11 27.7	5 47.1	13 20.5
16 Su	23 36 00	25 49 03	17 10 20	23 21 54	28 38.3	28 23.6	9 27.9	26 08.7	0 50.7	10 36.4	23 09.5	11 31.0	5 49.3	13 21.4
17 M	23 39 57	26 48 45	29 36 09	5♎53 11	28 34.7	29 30.4	10 24.7	25 57.0	0 43.3	10 38.4	23 08.0	11 34.4	5 51.4	13 22.3
18 Tu	23 43 54	27 48 26	12♎13 03	18 35 49	28D 32.7	0♓39.4	11 21.9	25 44.6	0 35.6	10 40.7	23 06.5	11 37.7	5 53.6	13 23.2
19 W	23 47 50	28 48 05	25 01 33	1♏30 19	28 32.3	1 50.6	12 19.6	25 31.5	0 27.5	10 43.1	23 04.9	11 41.1	5 55.7	13 24.0
20 Th	23 51 47	29 47 42	8♏02 10	14 37 13	28 33.1	3 03.8	13 17.7	25 17.7	0 19.0	10 45.7	23 03.2	11 44.4	5 57.8	13 24.8
21 F	23 55 43	0♈47 18	21 15 32	27 57 12	28 34.6	4 18.9	14 16.3	25 03.1	0 10.2	10 48.5	23 01.4	11 47.8	6 00.0	13 25.6
22 Sa	23 59 40	1 46 51	4♐42 20	11♐30 59	28 36.2	5 35.9	15 15.3	24 47.8	0 01.0	10 51.5	22 59.4	11 51.2	6 02.1	13 26.3
23 Su	0 03 36	2 46 23	18 23 13	25 19 03	28R 37.2	6 54.7	16 14.7	24 31.8	29♎51.5	10 54.6	22 57.4	11 54.6	6 04.2	13 27.0
24 M	0 07 33	3 45 54	2♑18 27	9♑21 20	28 37.3	8 15.2	17 14.5	24 15.2	29 41.7	10 58.0	22 55.4	11 58.0	6 06.2	13 27.7
25 Tu	0 11 29	4 45 22	16 27 33	23 36 49	28 36.3	9 37.4	18 14.7	23 58.0	29 31.5	11 01.5	22 53.2	12 01.4	6 08.3	13 28.3
26 W	0 15 26	5 44 49	0♒48 49	8♒03 05	28 34.2	11 01.2	19 15.2	23 40.1	29 21.0	11 05.2	22 50.9	12 04.8	6 10.4	13 29.0
27 Th	0 19 23	6 44 14	15 19 05	22 36 12	28 31.5	12 26.6	20 16.1	23 21.6	29 10.2	11 09.0	22 48.6	12 08.2	6 12.4	13 29.5
28 F	0 23 19	7 43 37	29 53 42	7♓10 52	28 28.5	13 53.6	21 17.3	23 02.5	28 59.1	11 13.1	22 46.1	12 11.6	6 14.4	13 30.1
29 Sa	0 27 16	8 42 58	14♓26 52	21 40 55	28 25.8	15 22.0	22 18.8	22 42.9	28 47.8	11 17.3	22 43.6	12 15.1	6 16.4	13 30.6
30 Su	0 31 12	9 42 18	28 52 16	6♈00 12	28 23.9	16 52.0	23 20.7	22 22.8	28 36.2	11 21.7	22 41.0	12 18.5	6 18.4	13 31.1
31 M	0 35 09	10 41 35	13♈04 04	20 03 19	28D 22.9	18 23.5	24 22.8	22 02.2	28 24.3	11 26.2	22 38.3	12 21.9	6 20.4	13 31.6

April 2014

LONGITUDE

Day	Sid.Time	☉	0 hr ☽	Noon ☽	True ☊	☿	♀	♂	⚳	♃	♄	♅	♆	♇
1 Tu	0 39 05	11♈40 50	26♈57 33	3♉46 25	28♎22.8	19♓56.5	25♒25.2	21♎41.2	28♎12.2	11♋31.0	22♏35.5	12♈25.3	6♓22.3	13♑32.0
2 W	0 43 02	12 40 03	10♉29 46	17 07 31	28 23.4	21 30.9	26 27.9	21R 19.8	27R 59.9	11 35.9	22R 32.6	12 28.8	6 24.3	13 32.4
3 Th	0 46 58	13 39 14	23 39 42	0♊06 30	28 24.6	23 06.7	27 30.8	20 58.1	27 47.3	11 40.9	22 29.7	12 32.2	6 26.2	13 32.8
4 F	0 50 55	14 38 23	6♊28 09	12 44 59	28 25.8	24 44.0	28 34.0	20 36.0	27 34.6	11 46.2	22 26.7	12 35.6	6 28.1	13 33.1
5 Sa	0 54 51	15 37 29	18 57 25	25 05 54	28 26.9	26 22.8	29 37.4	20 13.7	27 21.7	11 51.6	22 23.6	12 39.0	6 30.0	13 33.4
6 Su	0 58 48	16 36 33	1♋10 56	7♋13 06	28R 27.6	28 03.0	0♓41.1	19 51.1	27 08.7	11 57.1	22 20.4	12 42.5	6 31.8	13 33.7
7 M	1 02 45	17 35 35	13 12 55	19 11 00	28 27.8	29 44.7	1 45.0	19 28.4	26 55.5	12 02.8	22 17.2	12 45.9	6 33.6	13 34.0
8 Tu	1 06 41	18 34 35	25 07 55	1♌04 15	28 27.5	1♈27.9	2 49.2	19 05.5	26 42.2	12 08.7	22 13.9	12 49.3	6 35.5	13 34.2
9 W	1 10 38	19 33 32	7♌00 36	12 57 29	28 26.8	3 12.5	3 53.5	18 42.5	26 28.8	12 14.7	22 10.5	12 52.7	6 37.3	13 34.4
10 Th	1 14 34	20 32 27	18 55 28	24 55 02	28 25.9	4 58.6	4 58.1	18 19.5	26 15.4	12 20.9	22 07.0	12 56.1	6 39.0	13 34.5
11 F	1 18 31	21 31 20	0♍56 39	7♍00 44	28 24.9	6 46.2	6 02.9	17 56.5	26 01.8	12 27.2	22 03.5	12 59.5	6 40.8	13 34.6
12 Sa	1 22 27	22 30 10	13 07 42	19 17 50	28 24.0	8 35.3	7 07.9	17 33.5	25 48.2	12 33.7	22 00.0	13 02.9	6 42.5	13 34.7
13 Su	1 26 24	23 28 58	25 31 27	1♎48 45	28 23.4	10 26.0	8 13.1	17 10.6	25 34.5	12 40.3	21 56.3	13 06.3	6 44.2	13 34.8
14 M	1 30 20	24 27 45	8♎09 53	14 34 59	28 23.0	12 18.1	9 18.4	16 47.8	25 20.9	12 47.1	21 52.6	13 09.7	6 45.9	13R 34.8
15 Tu	1 34 17	25 26 29	21 04 04	27 37 07	28D 22.9	14 11.8	10 24.0	16 25.1	25 07.2	12 54.0	21 48.9	13 13.1	6 47.6	13 34.8
16 W	1 38 14	26 25 11	4♏14 05	10♏54 51	28 23.0	16 07.1	11 29.7	16 02.7	24 53.5	13 01.0	21 45.1	13 16.4	6 49.2	13 34.8
17 Th	1 42 10	27 23 52	17 39 14	24 27 02	28 23.1	18 03.8	12 35.6	15 40.6	24 39.9	13 08.2	21 41.2	13 19.8	6 50.8	13 34.7
18 F	1 46 07	28 22 30	1♐18 02	8♐11 58	28R 23.1	20 02.0	13 41.7	15 18.7	24 26.3	13 15.6	21 37.3	13 23.1	6 52.4	13 34.6
19 Sa	1 50 03	29 21 07	15 08 34	22 07 31	28 23.1	22 01.7	14 48.0	14 57.2	24 12.8	13 23.0	21 33.3	13 26.5	6 54.0	13 34.5
20 Su	1 54 00	0♉19 43	29 08 32	6♑11 18	28 22.9	24 02.9	15 54.4	14 36.0	23 59.4	13 30.6	21 29.3	13 29.8	6 55.6	13 34.4
21 M	1 57 56	1 18 16	13♑15 32	20 20 56	28D 22.8	26 05.4	17 01.0	14 15.2	23 46.0	13 38.3	21 25.3	13 33.1	6 57.1	13 34.2
22 Tu	2 01 53	2 16 48	27 27 10	4♒33 57	28 22.8	28 09.2	18 07.7	13 54.9	23 32.9	13 46.2	21 21.2	13 36.4	6 58.6	13 34.0
23 W	2 05 49	3 15 19	11♒40 58	18 47 54	28 22.9	0♉14.3	19 14.5	13 35.0	23 19.7	13 54.2	21 17.0	13 39.7	7 00.0	13 33.7
24 Th	2 09 46	4 13 47	25 54 26	3♓00 15	28 23.3	2 20.5	20 21.6	13 15.7	23 06.7	14 02.3	21 12.8	13 43.0	7 01.5	13 33.5
25 F	2 13 43	5 12 15	10♓05 00	17 08 20	28 23.9	4 27.6	21 28.7	12 56.9	22 53.9	14 10.5	21 08.6	13 46.2	7 02.9	13 33.2
26 Sa	2 17 39	6 10 40	24 09 55	1♈09 22	28 24.5	6 35.5	22 36.0	12 38.7	22 41.3	14 18.9	21 04.4	13 49.5	7 04.3	13 32.8
27 Su	2 21 36	7 09 04	8♈06 22	15 00 34	28R 25.0	8 44.0	23 43.4	12 21.1	22 28.8	14 27.4	21 00.1	13 52.7	7 05.7	13 32.5
28 M	2 25 32	8 07 26	21 51 39	28 39 18	28 25.2	10 52.9	24 50.9	12 04.1	22 16.6	14 36.0	20 55.7	13 55.9	7 07.0	13 32.1
29 Tu	2 29 29	9 05 47	5♉23 17	12♉03 22	28 25.0	13 02.0	25 58.5	11 47.8	22 04.6	14 44.7	20 51.4	13 59.1	7 08.3	13 31.7
30 W	2 33 25	10 04 05	18 39 23	25 11 15	28 24.1	15 10.9	27 06.3	11 32.2	21 52.8	14 53.6	20 47.0	14 02.2	7 09.6	13 31.2

Astro Data

	Dy Hr Mn
♂ R	1 16:24
☽ 0N	2 4:02
♄ R	2 16:19
♃ D	6 10:42
☽ 0S	16 11:16
☉ 0N	20 16:57
☽ 0N	29 14:05
☿ 0N	10 14:18
☽ 0S	12 18:56
♇ R	14 23:47
♃□♅	20 7:29
♃☍♇	20 23:26
♅□♇	21 19:21
☽ 0N	25 21:48

Planet Ingress

		Dy Hr Mn
♀	♒	5 21:03
☿	♓	17 22:24
☉	♈	20 16:57
⚳	♎R	22 14:41
♀	♓	5 20:31
☿	♈	7 15:35
☉	♉	20 3:56
☿	♉	23 9:16

Last Aspect / ☽ Ingress (March)

Last Aspect Dy Hr Mn		☽ Ingress	Dy Hr Mn
2 11:04	♀ ⚹	♈	2 15:40
4 17:31	♀ □	♉	4 19:12
6 13:55	♄ ☍	♊	7 2:37
9 7:53	♂ △	♋	9 13:33
11 19:50	♂ □	♌	12 2:09
14 7:24	♂ ⚹	♍	14 14:17
16 17:08	☉ ☍	♎	17 0:46
19 1:07	♂ ☌	♏	19 9:13
21 3:11	♄ ☌	♐	21 15:39
23 10:40	♂ ⚹	♑	23 20:03
25 12:35	♂ □	♒	25 22:39
27 13:13	♂ △	♓	28 0:10
29 13:44	♄ △	♈	30 1:54

Last Aspect / ☽ Ingress (April)

Last Aspect Dy Hr Mn		☽ Ingress	Dy Hr Mn
31 20:07	♀ ⚹	♉	1 5:20
3 6:43	♀ □	♊	3 11:48
5 14:55	☿ □	♋	5 21:40
7 18:14	♄ △	♌	8 9:50
10 6:26	♄ □	♍	10 22:08
12 17:12	♄ ⚹	♎	13 8:33
15 7:42	☉ ☍	♏	15 16:20
17 7:09	♄ ☌	♐	17 21:44
20 1:17	☉ △	♑	20 1:28
21 23:21	☿ □	♒	22 4:18
23 16:10	♄ □	♓	24 6:55
25 20:03	♀ ☌	♈	26 10:01
27 11:02	♃ □	♉	28 14:23
30 15:53	♀ ⚹	♊	30 20:56

☽ Phases & Eclipses

Dy Hr Mn	
1 8:00	● 10♓39
8 13:27	☽ 17♊54
16 17:08	○ 26♍02
24 1:46	☾ 3♑21
30 18:45	● 9♈59
7 8:31	☽ 17♋27
15 7:42	○ 25♎16
15 7:46	• T 1.290
22 7:52	☾ 2♒07
29 6:14	● 8♉52
29 6:03:25	• A non-C

Astro Data

1 March 2014
Julian Day # 41698
SVP 5♓03'33"
GC 27♐02.2 ⚴ 1♍20.6R
Eris 22♈04.5 ⚵ 28♓59.0
⚷ 13♓13.5 ⚶ 29♎59.6
☽ Mean ☊ 1♏07.0

1 April 2014
Julian Day # 41729
SVP 5♓03'30"
GC 27♐02.3 ⚴ 25♌11.5R
Eris 22♈22.7 ⚵ 15♈50.5
⚷ 15♓08.1 ⚶ 26♎22.3R
☽ Mean ☊ 29♎28.4

LONGITUDE — May 2014

Day	Sid.Time	☉	0 hr ☽	Noon☽	True☊	☿	♀	♂	⚳	♃	♄	♅	♆	♇
1 Th	2 37 22	11♉02 22	1♊38 54	8♊02 22	28♎22.7	17♉19.5	28♓14.2	11♎17.3	21♎41.3	15♋02.6	20♏42.6	14♈05.4	7♓10.8	13♑30.7
2 F	2 41 18	12 00 37	14 21 44	20 37 10	28R20.8	19 27.3	29 22.1	11R03.1	21R30.0	15 11.6	20R38.2	14 08.5	7 12.1	13R30.2
3 Sa	2 45 15	12 58 50	26 48 52	2♋57 08	28 18.7	21 34.1	0♈30.2	10 49.6	21 19.0	15 20.8	20 33.7	14 11.6	7 13.3	13 29.7
4 Su	2 49 12	13 57 02	9♋02 19	15 04 48	28 16.8	23 39.6	1 38.4	10 37.0	21 08.3	15 30.1	20 29.3	14 14.7	7 14.4	13 29.2
5 M	2 53 08	14 55 11	21 05 03	27 03 31	28 15.3	25 43.5	2 46.7	10 25.0	20 57.9	15 39.5	20 24.8	14 17.8	7 15.6	13 28.6
6 Tu	2 57 05	15 53 18	3♌00 45	8♌57 17	28D14.4	27 45.6	3 55.0	10 13.9	20 47.8	15 49.0	20 20.3	14 20.9	7 16.7	13 28.0
7 W	3 01 01	16 51 23	14 53 42	20 50 34	28 14.3	29 45.5	5 03.5	10 03.6	20 38.0	15 58.7	20 15.8	14 23.9	7 17.7	13 27.3
8 Th	3 04 58	17 49 27	26 48 30	2♍48 04	28 14.9	1♊43.0	6 12.0	9 54.0	20 28.5	16 08.4	20 11.3	14 26.9	7 18.8	13 26.7
9 F	3 08 54	18 47 28	8♍49 51	14 54 25	28 16.2	3 37.9	7 20.7	9 45.3	20 19.4	16 18.2	20 06.8	14 29.9	7 19.8	13 26.0
10 Sa	3 12 51	19 45 28	21 02 18	27 14 00	28 17.8	5 30.0	8 29.4	9 37.3	20 10.6	16 28.1	20 02.3	14 32.8	7 20.8	13 25.2
11 Su	3 16 47	20 43 25	3♎29 57	9♎50 33	28 19.2	7 19.2	9 38.2	9 30.2	20 02.1	16 38.1	19 57.8	14 35.7	7 21.8	13 24.5
12 M	3 20 44	21 41 21	16 16 06	22 46 51	28R20.0	9 05.3	10 47.1	9 23.8	19 54.0	16 48.2	19 53.3	14 38.6	7 22.7	13 23.7
13 Tu	3 24 41	22 39 16	29 22 56	6♏04 23	28 19.9	10 48.2	11 56.1	9 18.3	19 46.3	16 58.4	19 48.8	14 41.5	7 23.6	13 22.9
14 W	3 28 37	23 37 09	12♏51 07	19 42 58	28 18.7	12 27.9	13 05.1	9 13.5	19 38.9	17 08.7	19 44.3	14 44.4	7 24.4	13 22.1
15 Th	3 32 34	24 35 00	26 39 37	3♐40 40	28 16.2	14 04.1	14 14.3	9 09.6	19 31.9	17 19.1	19 39.8	14 47.2	7 25.3	13 21.3
16 F	3 36 30	25 32 50	10♐45 35	17 53 47	28 12.7	15 36.9	15 23.5	9 06.4	19 25.3	17 29.6	19 35.3	14 50.0	7 26.1	13 20.4
17 Sa	3 40 27	26 30 39	25 04 37	2♑17 22	28 08.8	17 06.2	16 32.8	9 04.1	19 19.1	17 40.1	19 30.8	14 52.8	7 26.9	13 19.5
18 Su	3 44 23	27 28 26	9♑31 19	16 45 46	28 04.9	18 32.0	17 42.2	9 02.5	19 13.2	17 50.8	19 26.4	14 55.5	7 27.6	13 18.6
19 M	3 48 20	28 26 12	24 00 02	1♒13 28	28 01.7	19 54.1	18 51.7	9D01.6	19 07.7	18 01.5	19 22.0	14 58.2	7 28.3	13 17.7
20 Tu	3 52 16	29 23 57	8♒25 33	15 35 47	27 59.6	21 12.5	20 01.2	9 01.6	19 02.6	18 12.3	19 17.5	15 00.9	7 29.0	13 16.7
21 W	3 56 13	0♊21 41	22 43 46	29 49 13	27D58.9	22 27.3	21 10.8	9 02.3	18 57.9	18 23.2	19 13.2	15 03.6	7 29.6	13 15.7
22 Th	4 00 10	1 19 24	6♓51 55	13♓51 40	27 59.4	23 38.3	22 20.5	9 03.8	18 53.6	18 34.2	19 08.8	15 06.2	7 30.3	13 14.7
23 F	4 04 06	2 17 06	20 48 24	27 42 04	28 00.7	24 45.5	23 30.2	9 06.0	18 49.7	18 45.3	19 04.4	15 08.8	7 30.8	13 13.7
24 Sa	4 08 03	3 14 47	4♈32 38	11♈20 06	28 02.1	25 48.8	24 40.0	9 09.0	18 46.1	18 56.4	19 00.1	15 11.3	7 31.4	13 12.7
25 Su	4 11 59	4 12 27	18 04 29	24 45 49	28R03.0	26 48.1	25 49.9	9 12.7	18 43.0	19 07.6	18 55.8	15 13.9	7 31.9	13 11.6
26 M	4 15 56	5 10 06	1♉24 06	7♉59 20	28 02.6	27 43.5	26 59.8	9 17.1	18 40.3	19 18.9	18 51.6	15 16.3	7 32.4	13 10.5
27 Tu	4 19 52	6 07 43	14 31 32	21 00 40	28 00.5	28 34.8	28 09.8	9 22.2	18 37.9	19 30.2	18 47.4	15 18.8	7 32.8	13 09.4
28 W	4 23 49	7 05 20	27 26 45	3♊49 46	27 56.5	29 21.9	29 19.8	9 28.1	18 36.0	19 41.7	18 43.2	15 21.2	7 33.3	13 08.3
29 Th	4 27 45	8 02 56	10♊09 44	16 26 39	27 50.8	0♋04.8	0♉29.9	9 34.7	18 34.5	19 53.2	18 39.1	15 23.6	7 33.6	13 07.1
30 F	4 31 42	9 00 30	22 40 36	28 51 37	27 43.8	0 43.4	1 40.1	9 41.9	18 33.3	20 04.8	18 35.0	15 26.0	7 34.0	13 06.0
31 Sa	4 35 39	9 58 03	4♋59 51	11♋05 27	27 36.2	1 17.6	2 50.3	9 49.9	18 32.6	20 16.4	18 30.9	15 28.3	7 34.3	13 04.8

LONGITUDE — June 2014

Day	Sid.Time	☉	0 hr ☽	Noon☽	True☊	☿	♀	♂	⚳	♃	♄	♅	♆	♇
1 Su	4 39 35	10♊55 35	17♋08 38	23♋09 38	27♎28.7	1♋47.4	4♉00.6	9♎58.5	18♎32.3	20♋28.1	18♏26.9	15♈30.6	7♓34.6	13♑03.6
2 M	4 43 32	11 53 06	29 08 46	5♌06 25	27R22.2	2 12.7	5 10.9	10 07.7	18D32.3	20 39.9	18R23.0	15 32.8	7 34.9	13R02.4
3 Tu	4 47 28	12 50 36	11♌02 57	16 58 51	27 17.2	2 33.4	6 21.2	10 17.6	18 32.8	20 51.7	18 19.1	15 35.0	7 35.1	13 01.1
4 W	4 51 25	13 48 04	22 54 36	28 50 44	27 14.0	2 49.5	7 31.6	10 28.2	18 33.6	21 03.6	18 15.2	15 37.2	7 35.3	12 59.9
5 Th	4 55 21	14 45 31	4♍47 50	10♍46 29	27D12.6	3 00.9	8 42.1	10 39.4	18 34.9	21 15.5	18 11.4	15 39.3	7 35.4	12 58.6
6 F	4 59 18	15 42 57	16 47 19	22 50 57	27 12.8	3R07.8	9 52.6	10 51.1	18 36.5	21 27.5	18 07.6	15 41.4	7 35.6	12 57.3
7 Sa	5 03 14	16 40 22	28 58 00	5♎09 06	27 13.8	3 10.1	11 03.1	11 03.5	18 38.5	21 39.6	18 04.0	15 43.5	7 35.7	12 56.0
8 Su	5 07 11	17 37 45	11♎24 50	17 45 45	27R14.9	3 07.8	12 13.7	11 16.5	18 40.9	21 51.7	18 00.3	15 45.5	7 35.7	12 54.7
9 M	5 11 08	18 35 08	24 12 20	0♏45 00	27 15.2	3 01.1	13 24.4	11 30.0	18 43.6	22 03.9	17 56.8	15 47.5	7R35.7	12 53.4
10 Tu	5 15 04	19 32 29	7♏24 03	14 09 42	27 13.9	2 50.2	14 35.1	11 44.2	18 46.7	22 16.1	17 53.3	15 49.4	7 35.7	12 52.0
11 W	5 19 01	20 29 50	21 01 58	28 00 46	27 10.5	2 35.2	15 45.8	11 58.8	18 50.2	22 28.4	17 49.8	15 51.3	7 35.7	12 50.7
12 Th	5 22 57	21 27 10	5♐05 47	12♐16 35	27 05.0	2 16.3	16 56.6	12 14.0	18 54.1	22 40.7	17 46.4	15 53.2	7 35.6	12 49.3
13 F	5 26 54	22 24 29	19 32 31	26 52 46	26 57.6	1 54.0	18 07.4	12 29.8	18 58.3	22 53.1	17 43.1	15 55.0	7 35.5	12 47.9
14 Sa	5 30 50	23 21 47	4♑16 25	11♑42 23	26 49.3	1 28.5	19 18.3	12 46.0	19 02.9	23 05.5	17 39.9	15 56.8	7 35.4	12 46.6
15 Su	5 34 47	24 19 05	19 09 36	26 36 56	26 41.0	1 00.2	20 29.2	13 02.8	19 07.8	23 18.0	17 36.7	15 58.5	7 35.2	12 45.2
16 M	5 38 43	25 16 22	4♒03 17	11♒27 40	26 33.7	0 29.7	21 40.2	13 20.0	19 13.0	23 30.5	17 33.6	16 00.2	7 35.0	12 43.8
17 Tu	5 42 40	26 13 39	18 49 13	26 07 10	26 28.3	29♊57.4	22 51.2	13 37.8	19 18.6	23 43.0	17 30.6	16 01.8	7 34.8	12 42.3
18 W	5 46 37	27 10 56	3♓20 57	10♓30 09	26 25.1	29 23.8	24 02.3	13 56.0	19 24.6	23 55.6	17 27.7	16 03.4	7 34.5	12 40.9
19 Th	5 50 33	28 08 12	17 34 31	24 33 56	26D23.9	28 49.6	25 13.4	14 14.7	19 30.9	24 08.3	17 24.8	16 05.0	7 34.2	12 39.5
20 F	5 54 30	29 05 28	1♈28 24	8♈18 01	26 24.1	28 15.3	26 24.6	14 33.9	19 37.5	24 20.9	17 22.0	16 06.5	7 33.9	12 38.0
21 Sa	5 58 26	0♋02 44	15 02 59	21 43 30	26R24.6	27 41.5	27 35.8	14 53.5	19 44.4	24 33.7	17 19.2	16 08.0	7 33.6	12 36.6
22 Su	6 02 23	1 00 00	28 19 51	4♉52 20	26 24.4	27 08.7	28 47.0	15 13.6	19 51.7	24 46.4	17 16.6	16 09.4	7 33.2	12 35.1
23 M	6 06 19	1 57 16	11♉21 11	17 46 42	26 22.4	26 37.7	29 58.3	15 34.1	19 59.3	24 59.2	17 14.0	16 10.8	7 32.8	12 33.6
24 Tu	6 10 16	2 54 31	24 09 07	0♊28 40	26 18.0	26 08.8	1♊09.7	15 55.1	20 07.2	25 12.1	17 11.6	16 12.1	7 32.3	12 32.2
25 W	6 14 12	3 51 47	6♊45 30	12 59 49	26 10.9	25 42.5	2 21.1	16 16.4	20 15.4	25 24.9	17 09.2	16 13.4	7 31.8	12 30.7
26 Th	6 18 09	4 49 02	19 11 45	25 21 25	26 01.2	25 19.4	3 32.5	16 38.3	20 23.9	25 37.8	17 06.9	16 14.7	7 31.3	12 29.2
27 F	6 22 06	5 46 17	1♋28 56	7♋34 23	25 49.6	24 59.8	4 44.0	17 00.5	20 32.7	25 50.8	17 04.6	16 15.9	7 30.8	12 27.7
28 Sa	6 26 02	6 43 31	13 37 54	19 39 36	25 37.0	24 44.1	5 55.5	17 23.1	20 41.9	26 03.7	17 02.5	16 17.0	7 30.2	12 26.2
29 Su	6 29 59	7 40 46	25 39 38	1♌38 10	25 24.5	24 32.6	7 07.0	17 46.1	20 51.3	26 16.7	17 00.4	16 18.1	7 29.6	12 24.7
30 M	6 33 55	8 38 00	7♌35 25	13 31 37	25 13.1	24 25.4	8 18.6	18 09.5	21 01.0	26 29.7	16 58.5	16 19.2	7 29.0	12 23.2

Astro Data

	Dy Hr Mn
♀0N	6 2:53
☽0S	10 3:43
♂ D	20 1:31
☽0N	23 3:58
♃△♄	24 17:47
⚳ D	1 20:15
☽0S	6 12:59
☿ R	7 11:56
♆ R	9 19:50
♃⚻♆	12 2:11
☽0N	19 10:21
⚳0S	22 8:55

Planet Ingress

	Dy Hr Mn
♀ ♈	3 1:21
☿ ♊	7 14:57
☉ ♊	21 2:59
♀ ♉	29 1:45
☿ ♋	29 9:12
☿ ♊R	17 10:04
☉ ♋	21 10:51
♀ ♊	23 12:33

Last Aspect / ☽ Ingress

Last Aspect Dy Hr Mn		☽ Ingress Dy Hr Mn
1 23:32 ♅ ⚹	♋	3 6:13
5 8:46 ☿ ⚹	♌	5 17:55
7 10:50 ♄ □	♍	8 6:24
9 22:08 ♄ ⚹	♎	10 17:19
12 0:51 ♃ □	♏	13 1:07
14 19:16 ☉ ☍	♐	15 5:44
16 7:43 ☿ ☍	♑	17 8:12
19 7:02 ☉ △	♒	19 9:58
20 22:21 ☿ △	♓	21 12:18
23 6:25 ☿ □	♈	23 16:01
25 15:57 ☿ ⚹	♉	25 21:28
27 9:10 ♃ ⚹	♊	28 4:47
29 9:59 ♅ ⚹	♋	30 14:13

Last Aspect / ☽ Ingress

Last Aspect Dy Hr Mn		☽ Ingress Dy Hr Mn
1 6:32 ♃ ☌	♌	2 1:43
3 14:41 ♄ □	♍	4 14:20
6 9:13 ♃ ⚹	♎	7 2:01
8 19:47 ♃ □	♏	9 10:38
11 2:21 ♃ △	♐	11 15:23
13 4:11 ☉ ☍	♑	13 17:04
15 6:35 ♃ ☍	♒	15 17:27
17 18:07 ☿ △	♓	17 18:26
19 19:05 ☿ □	♈	19 21:26
21 22:24 ☿ ⚹	♉	22 3:03
24 1:49 ♃ ⚹	♊	24 11:05
26 11:56 ☿ ☌	♋	26 21:05
29 1:02 ♃ ☌	♌	29 8:43

☽ Phases & Eclipses

Dy Hr Mn	
7 3:15	☽ 16♌30
14 19:16	○ 23♏55
21 12:59	☾ 0♓24
28 18:40	● 7♊21
5 20:39	☽ 15♍06
13 4:11	○ 22♐06
19 18:39	☾ 28♓24
27 8:08	● 5♋37

Astro Data

1 May 2014
Julian Day # 41759
SVP 5♓03'28"
GC 27♐02.4 ⚵ 26♌55.0
Eris 22♈42.2 ⚶ 2♉48.5
⚷ 16♓39.5 ⚴ 19♎13.1R
☽ Mean ☊ 27♎53.1

1 June 2014
Julian Day # 41790
SVP 5♓03'23"
GC 27♐02.4 ⚵ 4♍10.2
Eris 22♈59.4 ⚶ 20♉43.6
⚷ 17♓35.6 ⚴ 16♎30.0
☽ Mean ☊ 26♎14.6

July 2014 LONGITUDE

Day	Sid.Time	☉	0 hr ☽	Noon ☽	True ☊	☿	♀	♂	⚳	♃	♄	♅	♆	♇
1 Tu	6 37 52	9♋35 13	19♌27 05	25♌22 09	25♎03.7	24♊22.9	9♊30.2	18♎33.3	21♎11.0	26♋42.8	16♏56.6	16♈20.2	7♓28.3	12♑21.7
2 W	6 41 48	10 32 27	1♍17 12	7♍12 41	24R 56.8	24D 25.1	10 41.9	18 57.5	21 21.3	26 55.8	16R 54.8	16 21.2	7R 27.6	12R 20.2
3 Th	6 45 45	11 29 40	13 09 05	19 06 55	24 52.6	24 32.2	11 53.6	19 22.0	21 31.9	27 08.9	16 53.1	16 22.1	7 26.9	12 18.7
4 F	6 49 41	12 26 52	25 06 47	1♎09 17	24D 50.6	24 44.3	13 05.3	19 46.9	21 42.7	27 22.1	16 51.5	16 23.0	7 26.2	12 17.2
5 Sa	6 53 38	13 24 05	7♎15 01	13 24 39	24R 50.2	25 01.4	14 17.1	20 12.2	21 53.8	27 35.2	16 50.0	16 23.8	7 25.4	12 15.7
6 Su	6 57 35	14 21 17	19 38 50	25 58 11	24 50.3	25 23.5	15 28.9	20 37.7	22 05.2	27 48.4	16 48.6	16 24.6	7 24.6	12 14.2
7 M	7 01 31	15 18 29	2♏23 18	8♏54 45	24 49.7	25 50.7	16 40.7	21 03.7	22 16.8	28 01.5	16 47.2	16 25.3	7 23.7	12 12.7
8 Tu	7 05 28	16 15 41	15 32 59	22 18 21	24 47.5	26 22.8	17 52.6	21 29.9	22 28.7	28 14.7	16 46.0	16 26.0	7 22.9	12 11.2
9 W	7 09 24	17 12 52	29 11 05	6♐11 15	24 43.0	27 00.0	19 04.5	21 56.5	22 40.9	28 27.9	16 44.9	16 26.6	7 22.0	12 09.7
10 Th	7 13 21	18 10 04	13♐18 42	20 33 05	24 35.9	27 42.1	20 16.5	22 23.4	22 53.3	28 41.2	16 43.8	16 27.2	7 21.1	12 08.2
11 F	7 17 17	19 07 16	27 53 50	5♑20 09	24 26.7	28 29.1	21 28.5	22 50.6	23 05.9	28 54.4	16 42.9	16 27.8	7 20.2	12 06.7
12 Sa	7 21 14	20 04 28	12♑51 02	20 25 17	24 16.1	29 21.0	22 40.5	23 18.1	23 18.8	29 07.7	16 42.0	16 28.3	7 19.2	12 05.2
13 Su	7 25 10	21 01 40	28 01 35	5♒38 35	24 05.4	0♋17.6	23 52.6	23 45.9	23 31.9	29 21.0	16 41.3	16 28.7	7 18.2	12 03.8
14 M	7 29 07	21 58 52	13♒14 52	20 49 08	23 55.9	1 19.1	25 04.7	24 14.0	23 45.2	29 34.2	16 40.6	16 29.1	7 17.2	12 02.3
15 Tu	7 33 04	22 56 05	28 20 10	5♓46 55	23 48.5	2 25.1	26 16.9	24 42.4	23 58.8	29 47.5	16 40.0	16 29.4	7 16.2	12 00.8
16 W	7 37 00	23 53 18	13♓08 34	20 24 29	23 43.7	3 35.9	27 29.1	25 11.1	24 12.6	0♌00.8	16 39.6	16 29.7	7 15.1	11 59.3
17 Th	7 40 57	24 50 32	27 34 15	4♈37 39	23 41.4	4 51.1	28 41.4	25 40.0	24 26.6	0 14.1	16 39.2	16 30.0	7 14.0	11 57.9
18 F	7 44 53	25 47 46	11♈34 39	18 25 21	23 40.7	6 10.8	29 53.7	26 09.2	24 40.8	0 27.5	16 38.9	16 30.2	7 12.9	11 56.4
19 Sa	7 48 50	26 45 01	25 09 59	1♉48 54	23 40.7	7 34.9	1♋06.0	26 38.7	24 55.2	0 40.8	16 38.7	16 30.3	7 11.8	11 55.0
20 Su	7 52 46	27 42 18	8♉22 27	14 51 05	23 40.0	9 03.2	2 18.4	27 08.5	25 09.9	0 54.1	16D 38.6	16 30.4	7 10.6	11 53.6
21 M	7 56 43	28 39 34	21 15 14	27 35 20	23 37.6	10 35.7	3 30.8	27 38.5	25 24.8	1 07.5	16 38.7	16R 30.5	7 09.4	11 52.1
22 Tu	8 00 39	29 36 52	3♊51 50	10♊05 07	23 32.7	12 12.2	4 43.3	28 08.8	25 39.8	1 20.8	16 38.8	16 30.5	7 08.2	11 50.7
23 W	8 04 36	0♌34 10	16 15 33	22 23 30	23 25.0	13 52.5	5 55.8	28 39.4	25 55.1	1 34.1	16 39.0	16 30.5	7 07.0	11 49.3
24 Th	8 08 33	1 31 30	28 29 15	4♋33 04	23 14.6	15 36.5	7 08.4	29 10.2	26 10.6	1 47.5	16 39.3	16 30.4	7 05.7	11 47.9
25 F	8 12 29	2 28 49	10♋35 11	16 35 49	23 02.1	17 23.9	8 20.9	29 41.2	26 26.2	2 00.8	16 39.7	16 30.2	7 04.5	11 46.5
26 Sa	8 16 26	3 26 10	22 35 08	28 33 18	22 48.6	19 14.4	9 33.6	0♏12.5	26 42.1	2 14.2	16 40.2	16 30.0	7 03.2	11 45.1
27 Su	8 20 22	4 23 31	4♌30 30	10♌26 54	22 35.1	21 07.9	10 46.2	0 44.1	26 58.1	2 27.5	16 40.8	16 29.8	7 01.9	11 43.8
28 M	8 24 19	5 20 53	16 22 39	22 17 59	22 22.7	23 04.1	11 59.0	1 15.9	27 14.3	2 40.8	16 41.5	16 29.5	7 00.6	11 42.4
29 Tu	8 28 15	6 18 16	28 13 05	4♍08 13	22 12.4	25 02.5	13 11.7	1 47.9	27 30.8	2 54.2	16 42.3	16 29.2	6 59.2	11 41.1
30 W	8 32 12	7 15 39	10♍03 40	15 59 47	22 04.8	27 02.9	14 24.5	2 20.1	27 47.3	3 07.5	16 43.2	16 28.8	6 57.9	11 39.8
31 Th	8 36 08	8 13 02	21 56 55	27 55 30	21 59.9	29 04.9	15 37.3	2 52.6	28 04.1	3 20.8	16 44.2	16 28.4	6 56.5	11 38.5

August 2014 LONGITUDE

Day	Sid.Time	☉	0 hr ☽	Noon ☽	True ☊	☿	♀	♂	⚳	♃	♄	♅	♆	♇
1 F	8 40 05	9♌10 27	3♎55 59	9♎58 53	21♎57.5	1♌08.1	16♋50.2	3♏25.3	28♎21.0	3♌34.1	16♏45.3	16♈27.9	6♓55.1	11♑37.2
2 Sa	8 44 02	10 07 52	16 04 44	22 14 07	21D 56.9	3 12.4	18 03.1	3 58.3	28 38.2	3 47.4	16 46.5	16R 27.4	6R 53.7	11R 35.9
3 Su	8 47 58	11 05 17	28 27 36	4♏45 49	21R 57.2	5 17.2	19 16.0	4 31.4	28 55.4	4 00.7	16 47.7	16 26.8	6 52.2	11 34.6
4 M	8 51 55	12 02 44	11♏09 20	17 38 43	21 57.2	7 22.3	20 29.0	5 04.8	29 12.9	4 14.0	16 49.1	16 26.2	6 50.8	11 33.4
5 Tu	8 55 51	13 00 11	24 14 30	0♐57 07	21 55.9	9 27.5	21 42.0	5 38.3	29 30.5	4 27.2	16 50.6	16 25.5	6 49.3	11 32.1
6 W	8 59 48	13 57 38	7♐46 54	14 44 04	21 52.5	11 32.4	22 55.0	6 12.1	29 48.2	4 40.5	16 52.2	16 24.8	6 47.9	11 30.9
7 Th	9 03 44	14 55 07	21 48 37	29 00 26	21 46.9	13 36.9	24 08.1	6 46.1	0♏06.1	4 53.7	16 53.8	16 24.0	6 46.4	11 29.7
8 F	9 07 41	15 52 36	6♑19 06	13♑44 01	21 39.1	15 40.7	25 21.2	7 20.2	0 24.2	5 06.9	16 55.6	16 23.2	6 44.9	11 28.5
9 Sa	9 11 37	16 50 06	21 14 21	28 49 03	21 30.1	17 43.6	26 34.4	7 54.6	0 42.4	5 20.1	16 57.4	16 22.4	6 43.4	11 27.4
10 Su	9 15 34	17 47 37	6♒26 51	14♒06 25	21 20.8	19 45.6	27 47.6	8 29.1	1 00.8	5 33.3	16 59.4	16 21.5	6 41.8	11 26.2
11 M	9 19 31	18 45 09	21 46 17	29 25 02	21 12.5	21 46.5	29 00.8	9 03.9	1 19.3	5 46.4	17 01.4	16 20.5	6 40.3	11 25.1
12 Tu	9 23 27	19 42 42	7♓01 17	14♓33 46	21 06.1	23 46.1	0♌14.1	9 38.8	1 37.9	5 59.5	17 03.6	16 19.6	6 38.8	11 24.0
13 W	9 27 24	20 40 17	22 01 26	29 23 25	21 02.0	25 44.5	1 27.4	10 13.9	1 56.7	6 12.7	17 05.8	16 18.5	6 37.2	11 22.9
14 Th	9 31 20	21 37 53	6♈39 02	13♈47 54	21D 00.2	27 41.6	2 40.7	10 49.2	2 15.6	6 25.7	17 08.1	16 17.5	6 35.6	11 21.9
15 F	9 35 17	22 35 30	20 49 45	27 44 35	21 00.1	29 37.4	3 54.1	11 24.6	2 34.6	6 38.8	17 10.5	16 16.3	6 34.0	11 20.8
16 Sa	9 39 13	23 33 09	4♉32 32	11♉13 50	21 00.9	1♍31.7	5 07.6	12 00.3	2 53.8	6 51.8	17 13.0	16 15.2	6 32.5	11 19.8
17 Su	9 43 10	24 30 50	17 48 51	24 18 02	21R 01.4	3 24.6	6 21.1	12 36.1	3 13.1	7 04.8	17 15.6	16 14.0	6 30.9	11 18.8
18 M	9 47 06	25 28 32	0♊41 52	7♊00 50	21 00.7	5 16.1	7 34.6	13 12.1	3 32.6	7 17.8	17 18.3	16 12.8	6 29.3	11 17.8
19 Tu	9 51 03	26 26 15	13 15 30	19 26 21	20 58.0	7 06.2	8 48.2	13 48.3	3 52.1	7 30.8	17 21.0	16 11.5	6 27.6	11 16.8
20 W	9 55 00	27 24 01	25 33 54	1♋38 38	20 53.2	8 54.9	10 01.8	14 24.6	4 11.8	7 43.7	17 23.9	16 10.1	6 26.0	11 15.9
21 Th	9 58 56	28 21 48	7♋40 59	13 41 23	20 46.3	10 42.2	11 15.4	15 01.1	4 31.6	7 56.6	17 26.8	16 08.8	6 24.4	11 15.0
22 F	10 02 53	29 19 36	19 40 13	25 37 48	20 37.6	12 28.1	12 29.1	15 37.8	4 51.6	8 09.5	17 29.9	16 07.4	6 22.8	11 14.1
23 Sa	10 06 49	0♍17 26	1♌34 28	7♌30 30	20 28.1	14 12.6	13 42.8	16 14.7	5 11.6	8 22.3	17 33.0	16 05.9	6 21.1	11 13.2
24 Su	10 10 46	1 15 18	13 26 07	19 21 35	20 18.6	15 55.7	14 56.6	16 51.7	5 31.8	8 35.1	17 36.2	16 04.5	6 19.5	11 12.4
25 M	10 14 42	2 13 11	25 17 06	1♍12 53	20 09.8	17 37.5	16 10.3	17 28.9	5 52.1	8 47.8	17 39.5	16 02.9	6 17.9	11 11.6
26 Tu	10 18 39	3 11 05	7♍09 07	13 06 02	20 02.7	19 17.9	17 24.2	18 06.2	6 12.5	9 00.5	17 42.8	16 01.4	6 16.2	11 10.8
27 W	10 22 35	4 09 01	19 03 50	25 02 47	19 57.6	20 57.0	18 38.0	18 43.7	6 33.0	9 13.2	17 46.3	15 59.8	6 14.6	11 10.0
28 Th	10 26 32	5 06 58	1♎03 07	7♎05 10	19 54.7	22 34.8	19 51.9	19 21.4	6 53.6	9 25.8	17 49.8	15 58.1	6 12.9	11 09.3
29 F	10 30 29	6 04 57	13 09 13	19 15 38	19D 53.7	24 11.2	21 05.8	19 59.2	7 14.3	9 38.4	17 53.5	15 56.5	6 11.3	11 08.6
30 Sa	10 34 25	7 02 57	25 24 48	1♏37 07	19 54.3	25 46.4	22 19.8	20 37.2	7 35.2	9 50.9	17 57.2	15 54.8	6 09.6	11 07.9
31 Su	10 38 22	8 00 59	7♏53 04	14 13 03	19 55.7	27 20.2	23 33.8	21 15.3	7 56.1	10 03.4	18 01.0	15 53.0	6 08.0	11 07.2

Astro Data	Dy Hr Mn
☿ D	1 12:50
☽ 0S	3 21:47
☽ 0N	16 18:27
♄ D	20 20:35
♅ R	22 2:53
☽ 0S	31 5:22
☽ 0N	13 4:29
♃⚻♆	15 4:12
☽ 0S	27 11:50

Planet Ingress		Dy Hr Mn
☿	♋	13 4:45
♃	♌	16 10:30
♀	♋	18 14:06
☉	♌	22 21:41
♂	♏	26 2:25
☿	♌	31 22:46
⚳	♏	7 3:47
♀	♌	12 7:24
☿	♍	15 16:44
☉	♍	23 4:46

Last Aspect Dy Hr Mn			☽ Ingress	Dy Hr Mn
1 10:00	☿	⚹	♍	1 21:23
4 4:21	♃	⚹	♎	4 9:43
6 15:31	♃	☐	♏	6 19:33
8 22:32	♃	△	♐	9 1:24
11 0:19	☿	☍	♑	11 3:24
13 1:56	♃	☍	♒	13 3:07
14 19:23	♀	△	♓	15 2:40
17 0:57	♀	☐	♈	17 4:07
19 2:18	♂	☍	♉	19 8:42
21 14:12	☉	⚹	♊	21 16:36
24 0:53	♂	△	♋	24 2:59
25 13:53	☿	☌	♌	26 14:55
28 0:37	♄	☐	♍	29 3:37
31 14:47	☿	⚹	♎	31 16:09

Last Aspect Dy Hr Mn			☽ Ingress	Dy Hr Mn
2 2:58	♀	☐	♏	3 2:57
4 17:43	♀	△	♐	5 10:19
6 14:52	♅	△	♑	7 13:38
9 8:09	♀	☍	♒	9 13:52
10 22:12	☿	☍	♓	11 12:55
12 16:01	♄	△	♈	13 13:00
15 15:50	☿	△	♉	15 15:58
17 12:26	☉	☐	♊	17 22:41
20 2:54	☉	⚹	♋	20 8:45
21 19:34	♄	△	♌	22 20:49
24 8:26	♄	☐	♍	25 9:33
27 2:29	☿	☌	♎	27 21:54
29 16:00	♀	⚹	♏	30 8:53

☽ Phases & Eclipses Dy Hr Mn	
5 11:59	☽ 13♎24
12 11:25	○ 20♑03
19 2:08	☾ 26♈21
26 22:42	● 3♌52
4 0:50	☽ 11♏36
10 18:09	○ 18♒02
17 12:26	☾ 24♉32
25 14:13	● 2♍19

Astro Data

1 July 2014
Julian Day # 41820
SVP 5♓03'18"
GC 27♐02.5 ⚴ 14♍06.9
Eris 23♈09.3 ⚵ 8♊08.2
⚷ 17♓42.2R ⚶ 20♎53.2
☽ Mean ☊ 24♎39.3

1 August 2014
Julian Day # 41851
SVP 5♓03'14"
GC 27♐02.6 ⚴ 26♍03.6
Eris 23♈10.2R ⚵ 25♊48.0
⚷ 16♓59.8R ⚶ 0♏33.5
☽ Mean ☊ 23♎00.8

LONGITUDE — September 2014

Day	Sid.Time	☉	0 hr ☽	Noon ☽	True ☊	☿	♀	♂	⚳	♃	♄	♅	♆	♇
1 M	10 42 18	8♍59 02	20♏37 33	27♏07 01	19♎57.0	28♍52.8	24♌47.8	21♏53.5	8♏17.1	10♌15.9	18♏04.8	15♈51.2	6♓06.3	11♑06.6
2 Tu	10 46 15	9 57 06	3♐41 52	10♐22 30	19R57.5	0♎24.1	26 01.9	22 31.9	8 38.3	10 28.3	18 08.8	15R49.4	6R04.7	11R06.0
3 W	10 50 11	10 55 12	17 09 14	24 02 17	19 56.7	1 54.1	27 15.9	23 10.5	8 59.5	10 40.6	18 12.8	15 47.6	6 03.0	11 05.4
4 Th	10 54 08	11 53 19	1♑01 45	8♑07 38	19 54.4	3 22.8	28 30.1	23 49.2	9 20.8	10 52.9	18 16.9	15 45.7	6 01.4	11 04.8
5 F	10 58 04	12 51 28	15 19 43	22 37 38	19 50.5	4 50.2	29 44.2	24 28.0	9 42.2	11 05.2	18 21.1	15 43.8	5 59.8	11 04.3
6 Sa	11 02 01	13 49 38	0♒00 48	7♒28 28	19 45.7	6 16.3	0♍58.4	25 07.0	10 03.7	11 17.4	18 25.3	15 41.9	5 58.2	11 03.8
7 Su	11 05 58	14 47 49	14 59 43	22 33 27	19 40.6	7 41.0	2 12.6	25 46.1	10 25.3	11 29.5	18 29.7	15 39.9	5 56.5	11 03.3
8 M	11 09 54	15 46 02	0♓08 29	7♓43 34	19 35.9	9 04.4	3 26.8	26 25.3	10 47.0	11 41.6	18 34.1	15 38.0	5 54.9	11 02.9
9 Tu	11 13 51	16 44 17	15 17 25	22 48 49	19 32.5	10 26.3	4 41.1	27 04.7	11 08.8	11 53.6	18 38.5	15 35.9	5 53.3	11 02.5
10 W	11 17 47	17 42 33	0♈16 40	7♈39 57	19D30.5	11 46.9	5 55.3	27 44.2	11 30.6	12 05.6	18 43.1	15 33.9	5 51.7	11 02.1
11 Th	11 21 44	18 40 52	14 57 51	22 09 43	19 30.1	13 06.0	7 09.7	28 23.8	11 52.5	12 17.5	18 47.7	15 31.8	5 50.1	11 01.7
12 F	11 25 40	19 39 12	29 15 07	6♉13 45	19 30.8	14 23.6	8 24.0	29 03.6	12 14.5	12 29.3	18 52.4	15 29.7	5 48.5	11 01.4
13 Sa	11 29 37	20 37 35	13♉05 34	19 50 35	19 32.3	15 39.6	9 38.4	29 43.4	12 36.6	12 41.1	18 57.1	15 27.6	5 46.9	11 01.1
14 Su	11 33 33	21 35 59	26 29 00	3♊01 08	19 33.8	16 54.1	10 52.8	0♐23.4	12 58.8	12 52.8	19 02.0	15 25.5	5 45.3	11 00.8
15 M	11 37 30	22 34 26	9♊27 22	15 48 10	19R34.8	18 06.8	12 07.3	1 03.6	13 21.1	13 04.5	19 06.9	15 23.3	5 43.8	11 00.6
16 Tu	11 41 26	23 32 55	22 04 01	28 15 28	19 34.9	19 17.7	13 21.8	1 43.8	13 43.4	13 16.1	19 11.8	15 21.1	5 42.2	11 00.4
17 W	11 45 23	24 31 26	4♋23 04	10♋27 22	19 33.9	20 26.8	14 36.3	2 24.2	14 05.8	13 27.6	19 16.9	15 18.9	5 40.7	11 00.2
18 Th	11 49 20	25 30 00	16 28 55	22 28 16	19 31.7	21 33.9	15 50.8	3 04.7	14 28.3	13 39.0	19 21.9	15 16.7	5 39.1	11 00.1
19 F	11 53 16	26 28 35	28 25 53	4♌22 18	19 28.7	22 38.9	17 05.4	3 45.3	14 50.8	13 50.4	19 27.1	15 14.4	5 37.6	10 59.9
20 Sa	11 57 13	27 27 13	10♌17 56	16 13 14	19 25.1	23 41.7	18 20.0	4 26.1	15 13.4	14 01.7	19 32.3	15 12.2	5 36.1	10 59.9
21 Su	12 01 09	28 25 52	22 08 34	28 04 18	19 21.5	24 42.0	19 34.6	5 07.0	15 36.1	14 13.0	19 37.6	15 09.9	5 34.6	10 59.8
22 M	12 05 06	29 24 34	4♍00 45	9♍58 14	19 18.2	25 39.8	20 49.2	5 47.9	15 58.9	14 24.1	19 43.0	15 07.6	5 33.2	10D59.8
23 Tu	12 09 02	0♎23 17	15 56 59	21 57 15	19 15.7	26 34.9	22 03.9	6 29.0	16 21.7	14 35.2	19 48.4	15 05.3	5 31.7	10 59.8
24 W	12 12 59	1 22 03	27 59 15	4♎03 12	19 14.0	27 26.9	23 18.6	7 10.3	16 44.6	14 46.2	19 53.8	15 02.9	5 30.2	10 59.8
25 Th	12 16 55	2 20 51	10♎09 17	16 17 43	19D13.4	28 15.8	24 33.3	7 51.6	17 07.6	14 57.1	19 59.4	15 00.6	5 28.8	10 59.9
26 F	12 20 52	3 19 40	22 28 39	28 42 17	19 13.6	29 01.2	25 48.0	8 33.1	17 30.6	15 07.9	20 05.0	14 58.2	5 27.4	10 59.9
27 Sa	12 24 49	4 18 32	4♏58 49	11♏18 27	19 14.4	29 42.8	27 02.8	9 14.6	17 53.7	15 18.7	20 10.6	14 55.8	5 26.0	11 00.1
28 Su	12 28 45	5 17 25	17 41 22	24 07 49	19 15.6	0♏20.4	28 17.6	9 56.3	18 16.9	15 29.3	20 16.3	14 53.5	5 24.6	11 00.2
29 M	12 32 42	6 16 20	0♐38 00	7♐12 08	19 16.8	0 53.5	29 32.3	10 38.1	18 40.1	15 39.9	20 22.1	14 51.1	5 23.2	11 00.4
30 Tu	12 36 38	7 15 17	13 50 24	20 33 00	19 17.6	1 21.8	0♎47.2	11 20.0	19 03.4	15 50.4	20 27.9	14 48.7	5 21.9	11 00.6

LONGITUDE — October 2014

Day	Sid.Time	☉	0 hr ☽	Noon ☽	True ☊	☿	♀	♂	⚳	♃	♄	♅	♆	♇
1 W	12 40 35	8♎14 16	27♐20 04	4♑11 42	19♎18.1	1♏44.9	2♎02.0	12♐02.0	19♏26.7	16♌00.8	20♏33.7	14♈46.3	5♓20.6	11♑00.9
2 Th	12 44 31	9 13 16	11♑07 58	18 08 49	19R18.0	2 02.3	3 16.8	12 44.1	19 50.1	16 11.1	20 39.6	14R43.9	5R19.3	11 01.2
3 F	12 48 28	10 12 18	25 14 08	2♒23 42	19 17.5	2 13.7	4 31.7	13 26.3	20 13.5	16 21.3	20 45.6	14 41.4	5 18.0	11 01.5
4 Sa	12 52 24	11 11 22	9♒37 10	16 54 05	19 16.7	2R18.6	5 46.6	14 08.6	20 37.0	16 31.4	20 51.6	14 39.0	5 16.7	11 01.8
5 Su	12 56 21	12 10 27	24 13 53	1♓35 53	19 15.8	2 16.5	7 01.5	14 51.0	21 00.6	16 41.4	20 57.7	14 36.6	5 15.5	11 02.2
6 M	13 00 18	13 09 35	8♓59 19	16 23 20	19 15.1	2 07.1	8 16.4	15 33.5	21 24.2	16 51.3	21 03.8	14 34.2	5 14.3	11 02.6
7 Tu	13 04 14	14 08 44	23 47 02	1♈09 29	19 14.6	1 49.9	9 31.3	16 16.1	21 47.8	17 01.1	21 09.9	14 31.7	5 13.1	11 03.0
8 W	13 08 11	15 07 55	8♈29 47	15 47 04	19D14.4	1 24.8	10 46.2	16 58.7	22 11.5	17 10.8	21 16.1	14 29.3	5 11.9	11 03.5
9 Th	13 12 07	16 07 08	23 00 33	0♉09 32	19 14.5	0 51.7	12 01.2	17 41.5	22 35.2	17 20.4	21 22.4	14 26.9	5 10.7	11 04.0
10 F	13 16 04	17 06 23	7♉13 27	14 11 50	19 14.6	0 10.4	13 16.2	18 24.4	22 59.0	17 29.8	21 28.7	14 24.4	5 09.6	11 04.5
11 Sa	13 20 00	18 05 41	21 04 22	27 50 53	19 14.8	29♎21.5	14 31.2	19 07.3	23 22.8	17 39.2	21 35.0	14 22.0	5 08.5	11 05.0
12 Su	13 23 57	19 05 01	4♊31 20	11♊05 48	19R14.9	28 25.3	15 46.2	19 50.4	23 46.7	17 48.5	21 41.4	14 19.6	5 07.4	11 05.6
13 M	13 27 53	20 04 23	17 34 28	23 57 37	19 14.8	27 22.8	17 01.2	20 33.5	24 10.6	17 57.7	21 47.8	14 17.2	5 06.4	11 06.2
14 Tu	13 31 50	21 03 47	0♋15 38	6♋28 55	19 14.7	26 15.1	18 16.2	21 16.8	24 34.6	18 06.7	21 54.2	14 14.8	5 05.3	11 06.9
15 W	13 35 46	22 03 14	12 38 00	18 43 22	19D14.7	25 03.8	19 31.3	22 00.1	24 58.6	18 15.7	22 00.7	14 12.4	5 04.3	11 07.5
16 Th	13 39 43	23 02 43	24 45 38	0♌45 19	19 14.7	23 50.7	20 46.4	22 43.5	25 22.7	18 24.5	22 07.2	14 10.0	5 03.3	11 08.2
17 F	13 43 40	24 02 14	6♌43 03	12 39 24	19 15.0	22 37.7	22 01.4	23 27.0	25 46.7	18 33.2	22 13.8	14 07.6	5 02.4	11 09.0
18 Sa	13 47 36	25 01 48	18 34 56	24 30 13	19 15.4	21 27.1	23 16.5	24 10.6	26 10.9	18 41.8	22 20.4	14 05.2	5 01.5	11 09.7
19 Su	13 51 33	26 01 23	0♍25 47	6♍22 09	19 16.1	20 20.9	24 31.7	24 54.3	26 35.0	18 50.2	22 27.0	14 02.8	5 00.6	11 10.5
20 M	13 55 29	27 01 01	12 19 48	18 19 09	19 16.9	19 21.1	25 46.8	25 38.0	26 59.3	18 58.6	22 33.7	14 00.5	4 59.7	11 11.3
21 Tu	13 59 26	28 00 41	24 20 36	0♎24 32	19 17.7	18 29.5	27 01.9	26 21.9	27 23.5	19 06.8	22 40.4	13 58.1	4 58.9	11 12.2
22 W	14 03 22	29 00 23	6♎31 14	12 40 58	19R18.1	17 47.3	28 17.1	27 05.8	27 47.8	19 14.9	22 47.1	13 55.8	4 58.0	11 13.1
23 Th	14 07 19	0♏00 07	18 53 56	25 10 19	19 18.1	17 15.7	29 32.2	27 49.8	28 12.1	19 22.8	22 53.9	13 53.5	4 57.3	11 14.0
24 F	14 11 15	0 59 54	1♏30 14	7♏53 44	19 17.6	16 55.2	0♏47.4	28 33.9	28 36.5	19 30.6	23 00.7	13 51.2	4 56.5	11 14.9
25 Sa	14 15 12	1 59 42	14 20 50	20 51 32	19 16.4	16D46.1	2 02.6	29 18.1	29 00.8	19 38.3	23 07.5	13 48.9	4 55.8	11 15.9
26 Su	14 19 09	2 59 32	27 25 47	4♐03 30	19 14.6	16 48.3	3 17.8	0♑02.4	29 25.3	19 45.8	23 14.4	13 46.6	4 55.1	11 16.9
27 M	14 23 05	3 59 24	10♐44 35	17 28 54	19 12.6	17 01.4	4 33.0	0 46.7	29 49.7	19 53.3	23 21.2	13 44.4	4 54.4	11 17.9
28 Tu	14 27 02	4 59 18	24 16 19	1♑06 41	19 10.6	17 24.9	5 48.2	1 31.1	0♐14.2	20 00.5	23 28.1	13 42.2	4 53.8	11 18.9
29 W	14 30 58	5 59 13	7♑59 51	14 55 39	19 09.0	17 57.9	7 03.4	2 15.6	0 38.7	20 07.6	23 35.0	13 40.0	4 53.2	11 20.0
30 Th	14 34 55	6 59 10	21 53 54	28 54 27	19D08.1	18 39.8	8 18.6	3 00.2	1 03.2	20 14.6	23 42.0	13 37.8	4 52.6	11 21.1
31 F	14 38 51	7 59 09	5♒57 06	13♒01 38	19 08.0	19 29.6	9 33.8	3 44.8	1 27.8	20 21.5	23 49.0	13 35.7	4 52.1	11 22.3

Astro Data

	Dy Hr Mn
☿0S	2 2:53
♃⚻♇	5 10:23
☽0N	9 15:30
♇ D	23 0:36
☉0S	23 2:29
☽0S	23 18:04
♃△♅	25 18:19
♀0S	2 11:48
☿ R	4 17:02
☽0N	7 1:55
☽0S	21 1:13
☿ D	25 19:19

Planet Ingress

		Dy Hr Mn
☿	♎	2 5:38
♀	♍	5 17:07
♂	♐	13 21:57
☉	♎	23 2:29
☿	♏	27 22:39
♀	♎	29 20:52
☿	♎R	10 17:26
☉	♏	23 11:57
♀	♏	23 20:52
♂	♑	26 10:43
⚳	♐	27 22:06

Last Aspect / ☽ Ingress (September)

Last Aspect Dy Hr Mn			☽ Ingress	Dy Hr Mn
1 15:40	☿	✶	♐	1 17:17
3 18:06	♀	△	♑	3 22:15
5 15:08	♂	✶	♒	5 23:59
7 17:19	♂	□	♓	7 23:47
9 19:10	♂	△	♈	9 23:33
11 0:58	♅	☌	♉	12 1:17
13 13:31	☉	△	♊	14 6:26
16 2:05	☉	□	♋	16 15:24
18 18:38	☉	✶	♌	19 3:10
21 4:33	☿	✶	♍	21 15:54
23 12:15	♀	☌	♎	24 3:59
26 12:39	☿	☌	♏	26 14:29
28 20:30	♀	✶	♐	28 22:50

Last Aspect / ☽ Ingress (October)

Last Aspect Dy Hr Mn			☽ Ingress	Dy Hr Mn
30 3:29	♃	△	♑	1 4:41
2 16:18	♄	✶	♒	3 8:00
4 18:32	♄	□	♓	5 9:24
6 19:38	♄	△	♈	7 10:07
8 14:20	♃	△	♉	9 11:44
11 0:49	♄	☍	♊	11 15:51
13 17:58	☿	△	♋	13 23:30
15 23:27	☿	□	♌	16 10:29
18 13:10	☉	✶	♍	18 23:08
21 3:30	♂	□	♎	21 11:12
23 17:22	♂	✶	♏	23 21:10
25 16:11	♄	☌	♐	26 4:40
27 16:18	♃	△	♑	28 10:03
30 3:01	♄	✶	♒	30 13:52

☽ Phases & Eclipses

Dy Hr Mn		
2 11:11	☽	9♐55
9 1:38	○	16♓19
16 2:05	☾	23♊09
24 6:14	●	1♎08
1 19:33	☽	8♑33
8 10:51	○	15♈05
8 10:55		T 1.166
15 19:12	☾	22♋21
23 21:57	●	0♏25
23 21:44:30		P 0.811
31 2:48	☽	7♒36

Astro Data

1 September 2014
Julian Day # 41882
SVP 5♓03'11"
GC 27♐02.6 ⚴ 8♎59.1
Eris 23♈01.5R ⚵ 12♋34.7
⚷ 15♓42.1R ⚶ 13♏20.7
☽ Mean ☊ 21♎22.3

1 October 2014
Julian Day # 41912
SVP 5♓03'08"
GC 27♐02.7 ⚴ 22♎01.6
Eris 22♈46.2R ⚵ 27♋11.9
⚷ 14♓20.2R ⚶ 27♏28.6
☽ Mean ☊ 19♎47.0

November 2014 LONGITUDE

Day	Sid.Time	☉	0 hr ☽	Noon ☽	True ☊	☿	♀	♂	⚳	♃	♄	♅	♆	♇
1 Sa	14 42 48	8♏59 09	20♒07 50	27♒15 26	19♎08.7	20♎26.5	10♏49.0	4♑29.5	1♐52.4	20♌28.2	23♏55.9	13♈33.5	4♓51.6	11♑23.4
2 Su	14 46 44	9 59 11	4♓24 08	11♓33 38	19 09.9	21 29.6	12 04.2	5 14.3	2 17.0	20 34.7	24 02.9	13R 31.4	4R 51.1	11 24.6
3 M	14 50 41	10 59 14	18 43 33	25 53 28	19 11.3	22 38.2	13 19.5	5 59.1	2 41.6	20 41.1	24 09.9	13 29.3	4 50.7	11 25.8
4 Tu	14 54 38	11 59 19	3♈02 55	10♈11 25	19R 12.4	23 51.5	14 34.7	6 44.0	3 06.2	20 47.3	24 17.0	13 27.3	4 50.3	11 27.0
5 W	14 58 34	12 59 25	17 18 28	24 23 31	19 12.5	25 08.8	15 49.9	7 29.0	3 30.9	20 53.4	24 24.0	13 25.2	4 49.9	11 28.3
6 Th	15 02 31	13 59 33	1♉26 03	8♉25 33	19 11.4	26 29.6	17 05.2	8 14.0	3 55.6	20 59.3	24 31.1	13 23.2	4 49.5	11 29.6
7 F	15 06 27	14 59 43	15 21 30	22 13 30	19 09.0	27 53.2	18 20.4	8 59.1	4 20.3	21 05.1	24 38.2	13 21.3	4 49.2	11 30.9
8 Sa	15 10 24	15 59 55	29 01 09	5♊44 11	19 05.3	29 19.3	19 35.7	9 44.2	4 45.0	21 10.7	24 45.3	13 19.3	4 48.9	11 32.2
9 Su	15 14 20	17 00 09	12♊22 21	18 55 34	19 00.8	0♏47.4	20 50.9	10 29.4	5 09.8	21 16.2	24 52.4	13 17.4	4 48.7	11 33.6
10 M	15 18 17	18 00 25	25 23 47	1♋47 06	18 56.0	2 17.2	22 06.2	11 14.7	5 34.6	21 21.5	24 59.5	13 15.6	4 48.5	11 35.0
11 Tu	15 22 13	19 00 42	8♋05 40	14 19 45	18 51.6	3 48.3	23 21.4	12 00.0	5 59.3	21 26.6	25 06.6	13 13.7	4 48.3	11 36.4
12 W	15 26 10	20 01 02	20 29 42	26 35 53	18 47.9	5 20.5	24 36.7	12 45.4	6 24.1	21 31.6	25 13.7	13 11.9	4 48.2	11 37.8
13 Th	15 30 07	21 01 23	2♌38 49	8♌39 00	18 45.6	6 53.5	25 52.0	13 30.8	6 49.0	21 36.4	25 20.9	13 10.1	4 48.1	11 39.3
14 F	15 34 03	22 01 47	14 37 00	20 33 24	18D 44.7	8 27.3	27 07.3	14 16.3	7 13.8	21 41.0	25 28.0	13 08.4	4 48.0	11 40.8
15 Sa	15 38 00	23 02 12	26 28 51	2♍23 57	18 45.1	10 01.6	28 22.6	15 01.9	7 38.6	21 45.5	25 35.2	13 06.7	4D 47.9	11 42.3
16 Su	15 41 56	24 02 39	8♍19 21	14 15 42	18 46.5	11 36.2	29 37.9	15 47.5	8 03.5	21 49.8	25 42.3	13 05.0	4 47.9	11 43.8
17 M	15 45 53	25 03 08	20 13 37	26 13 41	18 48.3	13 11.2	0♐53.2	16 33.2	8 28.4	21 53.9	25 49.5	13 03.4	4 47.9	11 45.3
18 Tu	15 49 49	26 03 38	2♎16 28	8♎22 31	18R 49.8	14 46.3	2 08.5	17 18.9	8 53.3	21 57.8	25 56.6	13 01.8	4 48.0	11 46.9
19 W	15 53 46	27 04 11	14 32 17	20 46 11	18 50.3	16 21.6	3 23.8	18 04.7	9 18.2	22 01.6	26 03.8	13 00.2	4 48.1	11 48.5
20 Th	15 57 42	28 04 45	27 04 34	3♏27 41	18 49.2	17 56.9	4 39.1	18 50.5	9 43.1	22 05.2	26 10.9	12 58.7	4 48.2	11 50.1
21 F	16 01 39	29 05 21	9♏55 41	16 28 38	18 46.1	19 32.3	5 54.4	19 36.4	10 08.0	22 08.6	26 18.1	12 57.2	4 48.4	11 51.7
22 Sa	16 05 36	0♐05 58	23 06 32	29 49 12	18 41.1	21 07.6	7 09.7	20 22.3	10 32.9	22 11.8	26 25.2	12 55.8	4 48.6	11 53.4
23 Su	16 09 32	1 06 37	6♐36 24	13♐27 49	18 34.6	22 42.8	8 25.0	21 08.3	10 57.9	22 14.8	26 32.4	12 54.4	4 48.8	11 55.1
24 M	16 13 29	2 07 18	20 23 01	27 21 31	18 27.1	24 18.0	9 40.4	21 54.3	11 22.8	22 17.7	26 39.5	12 53.0	4 49.1	11 56.7
25 Tu	16 17 25	3 07 59	4♑22 47	11♑26 15	18 19.7	25 53.1	10 55.7	22 40.4	11 47.8	22 20.3	26 46.6	12 51.7	4 49.4	11 58.5
26 W	16 21 22	4 08 42	18 31 22	25 37 34	18 13.3	27 28.1	12 11.0	23 26.5	12 12.7	22 22.8	26 53.8	12 50.5	4 49.7	12 00.2
27 Th	16 25 18	5 09 26	2♒44 21	9♒51 15	18 08.6	29 03.0	13 26.3	24 12.7	12 37.7	22 25.1	27 00.9	12 49.3	4 50.1	12 01.9
28 F	16 29 15	6 10 10	16 57 53	24 03 53	18D 05.9	0♐37.8	14 41.6	24 58.9	13 02.6	22 27.2	27 08.0	12 48.1	4 50.5	12 03.7
29 Sa	16 33 11	7 10 56	1♓09 00	8♓13 01	18 05.2	2 12.5	15 57.0	25 45.1	13 27.6	22 29.1	27 15.1	12 46.9	4 51.0	12 05.5
30 Su	16 37 08	8 11 43	15 15 47	22 17 10	18 05.9	3 47.0	17 12.3	26 31.4	13 52.5	22 30.8	27 22.1	12 45.9	4 51.4	12 07.3

December 2014 LONGITUDE

Day	Sid.Time	☉	0 hr ☽	Noon ☽	True ☊	☿	♀	♂	⚳	♃	♄	♅	♆	♇
1 M	16 41 05	9♐12 30	29♓17 04	6♈15 23	18♎07.0	5♐21.5	18♐27.6	27♑17.7	14♐17.4	22♌32.3	27♏29.2	12♈44.8	4♓51.9	12♑09.1
2 Tu	16 45 01	10 13 19	13♈12 04	20 06 59	18R 07.4	6 55.9	19 42.9	28 04.1	14 42.4	22 33.7	27 36.2	12R 43.8	4 52.5	12 10.9
3 W	16 48 58	11 14 08	27 00 02	3♉51 03	18 06.2	8 30.3	20 58.2	28 50.5	15 07.3	22 34.8	27 43.3	12 42.9	4 53.1	12 12.8
4 Th	16 52 54	12 14 58	10♉39 51	17 26 16	18 02.7	10 04.6	22 13.5	29 36.9	15 32.3	22 35.8	27 50.3	12 42.0	4 53.7	12 14.6
5 F	16 56 51	13 15 50	24 10 02	0♊50 57	17 56.5	11 38.8	23 28.8	0♒23.3	15 57.2	22 36.5	27 57.3	12 41.1	4 54.3	12 16.5
6 Sa	17 00 47	14 16 42	7♊28 46	14 03 15	17 47.9	13 13.0	24 44.1	1 09.8	16 22.1	22 37.1	28 04.3	12 40.3	4 55.0	12 18.4
7 Su	17 04 44	15 17 35	20 34 13	27 01 31	17 37.5	14 47.3	25 59.4	1 56.3	16 47.1	22 37.4	28 11.2	12 39.6	4 55.7	12 20.3
8 M	17 08 40	16 18 30	3♋25 01	9♋44 40	17 26.3	16 21.5	27 14.7	2 42.9	17 12.0	22R 37.6	28 18.2	12 38.9	4 56.5	12 22.2
9 Tu	17 12 37	17 19 25	16 00 31	22 12 39	17 15.4	17 55.7	28 30.0	3 29.4	17 36.9	22 37.6	28 25.1	12 38.2	4 57.2	12 24.1
10 W	17 16 34	18 20 22	28 21 14	4♌26 31	17 05.7	19 30.0	29 45.3	4 16.0	18 01.8	22 37.4	28 32.0	12 37.6	4 58.0	12 26.1
11 Th	17 20 30	19 21 20	10♌28 49	16 28 30	16 58.1	21 04.3	1♑00.6	5 02.7	18 26.7	22 36.9	28 38.8	12 37.0	4 58.9	12 28.0
12 F	17 24 27	20 22 18	22 26 04	28 22 00	16 53.0	22 38.7	2 15.8	5 49.3	18 51.6	22 36.3	28 45.7	12 36.5	4 59.8	12 30.0
13 Sa	17 28 23	21 23 18	4♍16 52	10♍11 16	16 50.3	24 13.2	3 31.1	6 36.0	19 16.5	22 35.5	28 52.5	12 36.0	5 00.7	12 32.0
14 Su	17 32 20	22 24 19	16 05 51	22 01 17	16D 49.5	25 47.7	4 46.4	7 22.7	19 41.3	22 34.5	28 59.2	12 35.6	5 01.6	12 33.9
15 M	17 36 16	23 25 21	27 58 15	3♎57 27	16 49.8	27 22.4	6 01.7	8 09.4	20 06.2	22 33.3	29 06.0	12 35.3	5 02.6	12 35.9
16 Tu	17 40 13	24 26 24	9♎59 34	16 05 15	16R 50.2	28 57.2	7 17.0	8 56.2	20 31.0	22 31.9	29 12.7	12 35.0	5 03.6	12 37.9
17 W	17 44 09	25 27 28	22 15 10	28 29 54	16 49.6	0♑32.1	8 32.3	9 42.9	20 55.9	22 30.3	29 19.4	12 34.7	5 04.6	12 40.0
18 Th	17 48 06	26 28 32	4♏49 57	11♏15 47	16 47.0	2 07.2	9 47.5	10 29.7	21 20.7	22 28.5	29 26.0	12 34.5	5 05.7	12 42.0
19 F	17 52 03	27 29 38	17 47 44	24 26 01	16 41.7	3 42.4	11 02.8	11 16.5	21 45.5	22 26.5	29 32.7	12 34.3	5 06.8	12 44.0
20 Sa	17 55 59	28 30 44	1♐10 41	8♐01 41	16 33.7	5 17.7	12 18.1	12 03.4	22 10.3	22 24.3	29 39.2	12 34.2	5 07.9	12 46.0
21 Su	17 59 56	29 31 51	14 58 44	22 01 26	16 23.3	6 53.2	13 33.4	12 50.2	22 35.0	22 21.9	29 45.8	12D 34.2	5 09.1	12 48.1
22 M	18 03 52	0♑32 59	29 09 13	6♑21 19	16 11.6	8 28.8	14 48.7	13 37.1	22 59.8	22 19.3	29 52.3	12 34.2	5 10.3	12 50.2
23 Tu	18 07 49	1 34 07	13♑36 55	20 55 05	15 59.7	10 04.5	16 03.9	14 24.0	23 24.5	22 16.5	29 58.8	12 34.2	5 11.5	12 52.2
24 W	18 11 45	2 35 16	28 14 49	5♒35 09	15 49.1	11 40.4	17 19.2	15 10.9	23 49.2	22 13.6	0♐05.2	12 34.4	5 12.8	12 54.3
25 Th	18 15 42	3 36 24	12♒55 10	20 13 58	15 40.7	13 16.3	18 34.4	15 57.9	24 13.9	22 10.4	0 11.6	12 34.5	5 14.0	12 56.4
26 F	18 19 38	4 37 33	27 30 51	4♓45 10	15 35.2	14 52.3	19 49.7	16 44.8	24 38.6	22 07.1	0 17.9	12 34.7	5 15.4	12 58.4
27 Sa	18 23 35	5 38 42	11♓56 27	19 04 22	15 32.4	16 28.4	21 04.9	17 31.7	25 03.2	22 03.6	0 24.2	12 35.0	5 16.7	13 00.5
28 Su	18 27 32	6 39 50	26 08 42	3♈09 21	15 31.6	18 04.4	22 20.1	18 18.7	25 27.8	21 59.9	0 30.5	12 35.3	5 18.1	13 02.6
29 M	18 31 28	7 40 59	10♈06 19	16 59 40	15 31.6	19 40.3	23 35.3	19 05.6	25 52.4	21 56.0	0 36.7	12 35.7	5 19.5	13 04.7
30 Tu	18 35 25	8 42 07	23 49 31	0♉36 02	15 31.1	21 16.1	24 50.5	19 52.6	26 16.9	21 51.9	0 42.8	12 36.1	5 20.9	13 06.8
31 W	18 39 21	9 43 16	7♉19 21	13 59 39	15 28.6	22 51.7	26 05.7	20 39.6	26 41.5	21 47.7	0 48.9	12 36.6	5 22.3	13 08.9

Astro Data

	Dy Hr Mn
☽ 0N	3 10:32
♆ D	16 7:06
☽ 0S	17 9:53
♄∠♇	27 16:47
☽ 0N	30 17:21
♄⚼♅	3 10:46
♃ R	8 20:41
☽ 0S	14 19:34
♅□♇	15 5:14
♅ D	21 22:45
☽ 0N	27 23:57

Planet Ingress

	Dy Hr Mn
☿ ♏	8 23:09
♀ ♐	16 19:03
☉ ♐	22 9:38
☿ ♐	28 2:26
♂ ♒	4 23:57
♀ ♑	10 16:42
☿ ♑	17 3:53
☉ ♑	21 23:03
♄ ♐	23 16:34

Last Aspect / ☽ Ingress (November)

Last Aspect Dy Hr Mn		☽ Ingress Dy Hr Mn
1 6:22	♄ □	♓ 1 16:37
3 9:05	♄ △	♈ 3 18:53
5 13:25	☿ ☍	♉ 5 21:33
7 16:17	♄ ☍	♊ 8 1:45
9 16:22	♃ ⚹	♋ 10 8:38
12 9:16	♄ △	♌ 12 18:44
15 2:53	♀ □	♍ 15 7:08
17 11:11	♄ ⚹	♎ 17 19:30
19 14:25	♃ ⚹	♏ 20 5:31
22 5:53	♄ ☌	♐ 22 12:19
24 3:16	♃ △	♑ 24 16:31
26 15:30	☿ ⚹	♒ 26 19:23
28 17:14	♄ □	♓ 28 22:03

Last Aspect / ☽ Ingress (December)

Last Aspect Dy Hr Mn		☽ Ingress Dy Hr Mn
30 20:47	♄ △	♈ 1 1:14
3 2:42	♂ □	♉ 3 5:15
5 6:45	♄ ☍	♊ 5 10:28
7 9:52	♀ ☍	♋ 7 17:34
10 0:14	♄ △	♌ 10 3:14
12 12:48	♄ □	♍ 12 15:19
15 2:11	♄ ⚹	♎ 15 4:05
17 5:40	☉ ⚹	♏ 17 14:52
19 21:11	♄ ☌	♐ 19 21:55
21 12:34	♃ △	♑ 22 1:25
23 3:17	♀ ☌	♒ 24 2:52
25 15:11	♃ ☍	♓ 26 4:07
27 15:44	♀ ⚹	♈ 28 6:35
30 0:46	♀ □	♉ 30 10:56

☽ Phases & Eclipses

Dy Hr Mn	
6 22:23	○ 14♉26
14 15:16	☾ 22♌10
22 12:32	● 0♐07
29 10:06	☽ 7♓06
6 12:27	○ 14♊18
14 12:51	☾ 22♍26
22 1:36	● 0♑06
28 18:31	☽ 6♈56

Astro Data

1 November 2014
Julian Day # 41943
SVP 5♓03'05"
GC 27♐02.8 ⚴ 5♏44.2
Eris 22♈27.9R ⚵ 9♌22.5
⚷ 13♓20.1R ⚶ 13♐10.0
☽ Mean ☊ 18♎08.4

1 December 2014
Julian Day # 41973
SVP 5♓03'01"
GC 27♐02.9 ⚴ 18♏54.7
Eris 22♈12.9R ⚵ 16♌21.5
⚷ 13♓07.4 ⚶ 28♐56.5
☽ Mean ☊ 16♎33.1

LONGITUDE — January 2015

Day	Sid.Time	☉	0 hr ☽	Noon ☽	True ☊	☿	♀	♂	⚳	♃	♄	♅	♆	♇
1 Th	18 43 18	10♑44 24	20♉37 02	27♉11 38	15♎23.4	24♑26.9	27♑20.9	21♒26.5	27♐06.0	21♌43.3	0♐55.0	12♈37.1	5♓23.8	13♑10.9
2 F	18 47 14	11 45 32	3♊43 32	10♊12 45	15R 15.1	26 01.7	28 36.1	22 13.5	27 30.4	21R 38.7	1 01.0	12 37.6	5 25.3	13 13.0
3 Sa	18 51 11	12 46 40	16 39 18	23 03 12	15 03.9	27 35.9	29 51.2	23 00.5	27 54.9	21 34.0	1 07.0	12 38.3	5 26.9	13 15.1
4 Su	18 55 07	13 47 48	29 24 24	5♋42 53	14 50.4	29 09.3	1♒06.4	23 47.5	28 19.3	21 29.1	1 12.9	12 39.0	5 28.4	13 17.2
5 M	18 59 04	14 48 56	11♋58 36	18 11 32	14 35.9	0♒41.7	2 21.5	24 34.5	28 43.6	21 24.0	1 18.7	12 39.7	5 30.0	13 19.3
6 Tu	19 03 01	15 50 04	24 21 43	0♌29 11	14 21.4	2 12.9	3 36.6	25 21.4	29 08.0	21 18.8	1 24.5	12 40.5	5 31.6	13 21.4
7 W	19 06 57	16 51 12	6♌34 01	12 36 22	14 08.4	3 42.6	4 51.7	26 08.4	29 32.3	21 13.4	1 30.2	12 41.3	5 33.2	13 23.5
8 Th	19 10 54	17 52 20	18 36 25	24 34 27	13 57.7	5 10.4	6 06.8	26 55.4	29 56.6	21 07.9	1 35.9	12 42.2	5 34.9	13 25.6
9 F	19 14 50	18 53 28	0♍30 45	6♍25 43	13 49.8	6 36.0	7 21.9	27 42.4	0♑20.8	21 02.2	1 41.5	12 43.1	5 36.6	13 27.7
10 Sa	19 18 47	19 54 36	12 19 46	18 13 25	13 44.9	7 58.9	8 37.0	28 29.3	0 45.0	20 56.3	1 47.1	12 44.1	5 38.3	13 29.8
11 Su	19 22 43	20 55 43	24 07 12	0♎01 43	13 42.6	9 18.7	9 52.0	29 16.3	1 09.2	20 50.4	1 52.6	12 45.1	5 40.0	13 31.9
12 M	19 26 40	21 56 51	5♎57 36	11 55 30	13 42.0	10 34.6	11 07.0	0♓03.3	1 33.3	20 44.2	1 58.0	12 46.2	5 41.8	13 33.9
13 Tu	19 30 36	22 57 59	17 56 06	24 00 08	13 42.0	11 46.2	12 22.1	0 50.2	1 57.4	20 38.0	2 03.4	12 47.3	5 43.5	13 36.0
14 W	19 34 33	23 59 07	0♏08 17	6♏21 13	13 41.5	12 52.6	13 37.1	1 37.2	2 21.4	20 31.6	2 08.7	12 48.5	5 45.3	13 38.1
15 Th	19 38 30	25 00 14	12 39 37	19 04 03	13 39.3	13 53.2	14 52.1	2 24.1	2 45.4	20 25.1	2 14.0	12 49.7	5 47.1	13 40.1
16 F	19 42 26	26 01 21	25 35 02	2♐13 00	13 34.7	14 47.0	16 07.1	3 11.1	3 09.4	20 18.4	2 19.2	12 51.0	5 49.0	13 42.2
17 Sa	19 46 23	27 02 29	8♐58 13	15 50 48	13 27.4	15 33.2	17 22.0	3 58.0	3 33.3	20 11.7	2 24.3	12 52.3	5 50.8	13 44.3
18 Su	19 50 19	28 03 36	22 50 41	29 57 36	13 17.8	16 11.0	18 37.0	4 44.9	3 57.2	20 04.8	2 29.3	12 53.7	5 52.7	13 46.3
19 M	19 54 16	29 04 42	7♑11 04	14♑30 24	13 06.5	16 39.4	19 51.9	5 31.9	4 21.0	19 57.9	2 34.3	12 55.1	5 54.6	13 48.3
20 Tu	19 58 12	0♒05 48	21 54 42	29 22 54	12 54.9	16 57.7	21 06.9	6 18.8	4 44.8	19 50.8	2 39.2	12 56.6	5 56.6	13 50.4
21 W	20 02 09	1 06 54	6♒53 48	14♒26 10	12 44.4	17R 05.1	22 21.8	7 05.7	5 08.5	19 43.6	2 44.1	12 58.1	5 58.5	13 52.4
22 Th	20 06 06	2 07 58	21 58 42	29 30 10	12 36.1	17 01.2	23 36.6	7 52.6	5 32.2	19 36.3	2 48.8	12 59.7	6 00.4	13 54.4
23 F	20 10 02	3 09 02	6♓59 26	14♓25 30	12 30.5	16 45.8	24 51.5	8 39.4	5 55.8	19 29.0	2 53.5	13 01.3	6 02.4	13 56.4
24 Sa	20 13 59	4 10 05	21 47 33	29 04 56	12D 27.7	16 18.8	26 06.3	9 26.3	6 19.4	19 21.6	2 58.1	13 02.9	6 04.4	13 58.4
25 Su	20 17 55	5 11 06	6♈17 12	13♈24 05	12 27.1	15 40.7	27 21.1	10 13.1	6 42.9	19 14.0	3 02.6	13 04.6	6 06.4	14 00.4
26 M	20 21 52	6 12 07	20 25 27	27 21 20	12R 27.5	14 52.3	28 35.9	11 00.0	7 06.3	19 06.5	3 07.1	13 06.4	6 08.4	14 02.4
27 Tu	20 25 48	7 13 06	4♉11 52	10♉57 15	12 27.6	13 54.9	29 50.7	11 46.8	7 29.7	18 58.8	3 11.5	13 08.2	6 10.5	14 04.3
28 W	20 29 45	8 14 05	17 37 47	24 13 45	12 26.3	12 50.0	1♓05.4	12 33.6	7 53.1	18 51.1	3 15.8	13 10.0	6 12.5	14 06.3
29 Th	20 33 41	9 15 02	0♊45 29	7♊13 19	12 22.8	11 39.6	2 20.1	13 20.3	8 16.4	18 43.4	3 20.0	13 11.9	6 14.6	14 08.2
30 F	20 37 38	10 15 58	13 37 34	19 58 30	12 16.6	10 25.9	3 34.8	14 07.1	8 39.6	18 35.6	3 24.1	13 13.8	6 16.7	14 10.2
31 Sa	20 41 35	11 16 53	26 16 24	2♋31 30	12 07.8	9 11.0	4 49.4	14 53.8	9 02.7	18 27.7	3 28.2	13 15.8	6 18.8	14 12.1

LONGITUDE — February 2015

Day	Sid.Time	☉	0 hr ☽	Noon ☽	True ☊	☿	♀	♂	⚳	♃	♄	♅	♆	♇
1 Su	20 45 31	12♒17 47	8♋44 00	14♋54 05	11♎57.2	7♒57.0	6♓04.0	15♓40.5	9♑25.8	18♌19.8	3♐32.2	13♈17.8	6♓20.9	14♑14.0
2 M	20 49 28	13 18 39	21 01 54	27 07 36	11R 45.6	6R 46.1	7 18.6	16 27.2	9 48.9	18R 11.9	3 36.1	13 19.9	6 23.0	14 15.9
3 Tu	20 53 24	14 19 30	3♌11 19	9♌13 09	11 34.0	5 39.8	8 33.1	17 13.8	10 11.9	18 04.0	3 39.9	13 21.9	6 25.2	14 17.7
4 W	20 57 21	15 20 21	15 13 16	21 11 48	11 23.5	4 39.6	9 47.7	18 00.4	10 34.8	17 56.0	3 43.6	13 24.1	6 27.3	14 19.6
5 Th	21 01 17	16 21 10	27 08 55	3♍04 49	11 14.9	3 46.5	11 02.1	18 47.0	10 57.6	17 48.1	3 47.3	13 26.3	6 29.5	14 21.5
6 F	21 05 14	17 21 58	8♍59 45	14 53 57	11 08.8	3 01.2	12 16.6	19 33.6	11 20.4	17 40.1	3 50.8	13 28.5	6 31.6	14 23.3
7 Sa	21 09 10	18 22 44	20 47 46	26 41 33	11 05.1	2 24.2	13 31.0	20 20.1	11 43.1	17 32.1	3 54.3	13 30.7	6 33.8	14 25.1
8 Su	21 13 07	19 23 30	2♎35 42	8♎30 40	11D 03.8	1 55.5	14 45.4	21 06.7	12 05.7	17 24.2	3 57.7	13 33.0	6 36.0	14 26.9
9 M	21 17 03	20 24 15	14 26 57	20 25 06	11 04.2	1 35.1	15 59.7	21 53.1	12 28.3	17 16.2	4 01.0	13 35.3	6 38.2	14 28.7
10 Tu	21 21 00	21 24 59	26 25 47	2♏29 15	11 05.4	1 22.7	17 14.0	22 39.6	12 50.8	17 08.2	4 04.2	13 37.7	6 40.4	14 30.4
11 W	21 24 57	22 25 41	8♏36 30	14 48 01	11R 06.6	1D 18.1	18 28.3	23 26.1	13 13.2	17 00.3	4 07.3	13 40.1	6 42.6	14 32.2
12 Th	21 28 53	23 26 23	21 04 27	27 26 23	11 06.8	1 20.8	19 42.5	24 12.5	13 35.5	16 52.4	4 10.3	13 42.5	6 44.9	14 33.9
13 F	21 32 50	24 27 04	3♐54 25	10♐29 01	11 05.4	1 30.3	20 56.7	24 58.8	13 57.8	16 44.6	4 13.2	13 45.0	6 47.1	14 35.6
14 Sa	21 36 46	25 27 43	17 10 37	23 59 30	11 02.0	1 46.3	22 10.9	25 45.2	14 20.0	16 36.7	4 16.1	13 47.5	6 49.3	14 37.3
15 Su	21 40 43	26 28 22	0♑55 49	7♑59 32	10 56.9	2 08.3	23 25.0	26 31.5	14 42.1	16 29.0	4 18.8	13 50.1	6 51.6	14 39.0
16 M	21 44 39	27 28 59	15 10 27	22 28 07	10 50.5	2 35.7	24 39.1	27 17.8	15 04.1	16 21.2	4 21.5	13 52.6	6 53.8	14 40.6
17 Tu	21 48 36	28 29 35	29 51 53	7♒20 52	10 43.6	3 08.2	25 53.2	28 04.1	15 26.1	16 13.6	4 24.0	13 55.2	6 56.1	14 42.3
18 W	21 52 32	29 30 09	14♒54 03	22 30 12	10 37.2	3 45.4	27 07.2	28 50.3	15 47.9	16 05.9	4 26.5	13 57.9	6 58.4	14 43.9
19 Th	21 56 29	0♓30 42	0♓08 01	7♓46 09	10 32.2	4 27.0	28 21.2	29 36.5	16 09.7	15 58.4	4 28.8	14 00.6	7 00.6	14 45.5
20 F	22 00 26	1 31 13	15 23 14	22 58 02	10 29.1	5 12.5	29 35.1	0♈22.7	16 31.4	15 50.9	4 31.1	14 03.3	7 02.9	14 47.0
21 Sa	22 04 22	2 31 43	0♈29 22	7♈56 17	10D 27.9	6 01.6	0♈49.0	1 08.9	16 53.0	15 43.5	4 33.3	14 06.0	7 05.2	14 48.6
22 Su	22 08 19	3 32 11	15 17 57	22 33 47	10 28.4	6 54.1	2 02.8	1 55.0	17 14.5	15 36.2	4 35.3	14 08.8	7 07.5	14 50.1
23 M	22 12 15	4 32 37	29 43 22	6♉46 28	10 29.7	7 49.8	3 16.6	2 41.0	17 35.9	15 29.0	4 37.3	14 11.6	7 09.7	14 51.6
24 Tu	22 16 12	5 33 01	13♉43 02	20 33 08	10 31.2	8 48.3	4 30.3	3 27.1	17 57.2	15 21.9	4 39.2	14 14.4	7 12.0	14 53.1
25 W	22 20 08	6 33 23	27 16 58	3♊54 50	10R 32.0	9 49.5	5 44.0	4 13.0	18 18.4	15 14.9	4 41.0	14 17.3	7 14.3	14 54.5
26 Th	22 24 05	7 33 43	10♊27 04	16 54 04	10 31.6	10 53.2	6 57.6	4 59.0	18 39.5	15 08.0	4 42.6	14 20.2	7 16.6	14 56.0
27 F	22 28 01	8 34 01	23 16 17	29 34 08	10 29.7	11 59.3	8 11.2	5 44.9	19 00.6	15 01.2	4 44.2	14 23.1	7 18.8	14 57.4
28 Sa	22 31 58	9 34 17	5♋48 05	11♋58 32	10 26.4	13 07.5	9 24.7	6 30.8	19 21.5	14 54.5	4 45.7	14 26.0	7 21.1	14 58.8

Astro Data (Dy Hr Mn)

	Dy Hr Mn
☽0S	11 4:57
☿R	21 15:55
☽0N	24 8:18
☽0S	7 12:55
☿D	11 14:57
☽0N	20 18:50
♂0N	21 17:29
♀0N	22 15:28
♃⚻♇	27 23:11

Planet Ingress (Dy Hr Mn)

		Dy Hr Mn
♀	♒	3 14:48
☿	♒	5 1:08
⚳	♑	8 15:24
♂	♓	12 10:20
☉	♒	20 9:43
♀	♓	27 15:00
☉	♓	18 23:50
♂	♈	20 0:11
♀	♈	20 20:05

Last Aspect / ☽ Ingress (Dy Hr Mn)

Last Aspect		☽ Ingress	
1 12:19	♀ △	♊	1 17:09
3 11:55	♂ △	♋	4 1:07
5 4:53	☉ ☍	♌	6 11:03
8 17:05	♂ ☍	♍	8 22:58
10 15:46	☉ △	♎	11 11:57
13 9:46	☉ □	♏	13 23:44
15 23:52	☉ ⚹	♐	16 8:01
17 19:25	♃ △	♑	18 12:04
19 10:51	♇ ☌	♒	20 12:59
22 1:45	♀ ☌	♓	22 12:48
23 11:13	♇ ⚹	♈	24 13:31
26 14:23	♀ ⚹	♉	26 16:37
28 2:18	♃ □	♊	28 22:36
30 9:24	♃ ⚹	♋	31 7:09

Last Aspect / ☽ Ingress (Dy Hr Mn)

Last Aspect		☽ Ingress	
1 13:37	♂ △	♌	2 17:41
4 5:31	♃ ☌	♍	5 5:46
6 22:09	♂ ☍	♎	7 18:44
9 11:58	☉ △	♏	10 7:05
12 5:32	♂ △	♐	12 16:46
14 15:15	♂ □	♑	14 22:24
16 20:17	♂ ⚹	♒	17 0:13
18 23:47	☉ ☌	♓	18 23:47
19 23:02	♇ ⚹	♈	20 23:13
22 0:36	♃ △	♉	23 0:28
24 2:57	♃ □	♊	25 4:54
26 8:43	♃ ⚹	♋	27 12:50

☽ Phases & Eclipses (Dy Hr Mn)

Dy Hr Mn		
5 4:53	○	14♋31
13 9:46	☾	22♎52
20 13:14	●	0♒09
27 4:48	☽	6♉55
3 23:09	○	14♌48
12 3:50	☾	23♏06
18 23:47	●	0♓00
25 17:14	☽	6♊47

Astro Data

1 January 2015
Julian Day # 42004
SVP 5♓02'56"
GC 27♐02.9 ⚴ 1♐59.5
Eris 22♈05.0R ⚵ 16♌04.2R
⚷ 13♓47.5 ⚶ 15♑29.0
☽ Mean ☊ 14♎54.6

1 February 2015
Julian Day # 42035
SVP 5♓02'51"
GC 27♐03.0 ⚴ 13♐53.6
Eris 22♈07.5 ⚵ 9♌03.0R
⚷ 15♓12.2 ⚶ 1♒56.2
☽ Mean ☊ 13♎16.2

March 2015 LONGITUDE

Day	Sid.Time	☉	0 hr ☽	Noon ☽	True ☊	☿	♀	♂	⚳	♃	♄	♅	♆	♇
1 Su	22 35 55	10♓34 32	18♋05 54	24♋10 36	10♎21.9	14♒17.8	10♈38.2	7♈16.6	19♑42.3	14♌47.9	4♐47.1	14♈29.0	7♓23.4	15♑00.1
2 M	22 39 51	11 34 44	0♌12 59	6♌13 23	10R16.7	15 30.0	11 51.6	8 02.4	20 03.0	14R41.5	4 48.4	14 32.0	7 25.7	15 01.5
3 Tu	22 43 48	12 34 54	12 12 08	18 09 30	10 11.5	16 44.1	13 05.0	8 48.2	20 23.6	14 35.1	4 49.5	14 35.0	7 28.0	15 02.8
4 W	22 47 44	13 35 02	24 05 47	0♍01 13	10 06.9	17 59.9	14 18.2	9 33.9	20 44.1	14 28.9	4 50.6	14 38.0	7 30.2	15 04.1
5 Th	22 51 41	14 35 09	5♍56 04	11 50 34	10 03.2	19 17.4	15 31.5	10 19.5	21 04.5	14 22.9	4 51.6	14 41.1	7 32.5	15 05.3
6 F	22 55 37	15 35 13	17 44 56	23 39 27	10 00.8	20 36.4	16 44.6	11 05.2	21 24.8	14 17.0	4 52.5	14 44.1	7 34.8	15 06.6
7 Sa	22 59 34	16 35 16	29 34 21	5♎29 54	9D59.7	21 57.0	17 57.7	11 50.7	21 44.9	14 11.2	4 53.2	14 47.2	7 37.0	15 07.8
8 Su	23 03 30	17 35 17	11♎26 24	17 24 10	9 59.9	23 19.1	19 10.8	12 36.3	22 05.0	14 05.5	4 53.9	14 50.4	7 39.3	15 09.0
9 M	23 07 27	18 35 16	23 23 32	29 24 53	10 00.9	24 42.6	20 23.8	13 21.8	22 24.9	14 00.0	4 54.5	14 53.5	7 41.5	15 10.1
10 Tu	23 11 24	19 35 14	5♏28 35	11♏35 03	10 02.4	26 07.5	21 36.7	14 07.2	22 44.8	13 54.7	4 54.9	14 56.7	7 43.8	15 11.3
11 W	23 15 20	20 35 10	17 44 45	23 58 07	10 04.0	27 33.8	22 49.5	14 52.7	23 04.5	13 49.5	4 55.3	14 59.9	7 46.0	15 12.4
12 Th	23 19 17	21 35 04	0♐15 38	6♐37 45	10 05.3	29 01.4	24 02.3	15 38.0	23 24.0	13 44.5	4 55.6	15 03.1	7 48.2	15 13.4
13 F	23 23 13	22 34 56	13 04 56	19 37 36	10R05.9	0♓30.3	25 15.0	16 23.4	23 43.5	13 39.6	4 55.7	15 06.3	7 50.5	15 14.5
14 Sa	23 27 10	23 34 47	26 16 07	3♑00 49	10 05.7	2 00.5	26 27.7	17 08.7	24 02.9	13 34.9	4R55.8	15 09.5	7 52.7	15 15.5
15 Su	23 31 06	24 34 37	9♑51 54	16 49 29	10 04.7	3 31.9	27 40.3	17 53.9	24 22.1	13 30.4	4 55.8	15 12.8	7 54.9	15 16.5
16 M	23 35 03	25 34 24	23 53 33	1♒03 56	10 03.2	5 04.7	28 52.8	18 39.1	24 41.1	13 26.0	4 55.6	15 16.0	7 57.1	15 17.5
17 Tu	23 38 59	26 34 10	8♒20 17	15 42 05	10 01.5	6 38.7	0♉05.3	19 24.3	25 00.1	13 21.8	4 55.4	15 19.3	7 59.3	15 18.4
18 W	23 42 56	27 33 54	23 08 38	0♓39 04	9 59.9	8 13.9	1 17.7	20 09.4	25 18.9	13 17.7	4 55.0	15 22.6	8 01.5	15 19.3
19 Th	23 46 52	28 33 37	8♓12 24	15 47 28	9 58.7	9 50.4	2 30.0	20 54.5	25 37.6	13 13.9	4 54.6	15 25.9	8 03.6	15 20.2
20 F	23 50 49	29 33 17	23 23 07	0♈58 07	9D58.1	11 28.1	3 42.3	21 39.5	25 56.1	13 10.2	4 54.0	15 29.3	8 05.8	15 21.1
21 Sa	23 54 46	0♈32 55	8♈31 14	16 01 23	9 58.0	13 07.1	4 54.5	22 24.5	26 14.5	13 06.7	4 53.4	15 32.6	8 07.9	15 21.9
22 Su	23 58 42	1 32 31	23 27 31	0♉48 44	9 58.4	14 47.4	6 06.6	23 09.4	26 32.8	13 03.4	4 52.6	15 35.9	8 10.1	15 22.7
23 M	0 02 39	2 32 05	8♉04 20	15 13 46	9 59.0	16 28.9	7 18.6	23 54.3	26 50.9	13 00.2	4 51.8	15 39.3	8 12.2	15 23.5
24 Tu	0 06 35	3 31 37	22 16 40	29 12 48	9 59.7	18 11.7	8 30.5	24 39.2	27 08.8	12 57.3	4 50.9	15 42.7	8 14.3	15 24.2
25 W	0 10 32	4 31 06	6♊02 10	12♊44 50	10 00.2	19 55.8	9 42.4	25 24.0	27 26.6	12 54.5	4 49.8	15 46.0	8 16.4	15 24.9
26 Th	0 14 28	5 30 34	19 21 01	25 51 03	10R00.5	21 41.2	10 54.2	26 08.7	27 44.3	12 51.9	4 48.7	15 49.4	8 18.5	15 25.6
27 F	0 18 25	6 29 59	2♋15 19	8♋34 16	10 00.6	23 27.9	12 05.9	26 53.5	28 01.8	12 49.5	4 47.4	15 52.8	8 20.6	15 26.2
28 Sa	0 22 21	7 29 21	14 48 24	20 58 15	10 00.5	25 16.0	13 17.5	27 38.1	28 19.1	12 47.3	4 46.1	15 56.2	8 22.6	15 26.8
29 Su	0 26 18	8 28 41	27 04 20	3♌07 12	10 00.4	27 05.3	14 29.0	28 22.7	28 36.3	12 45.3	4 44.7	15 59.6	8 24.7	15 27.4
30 M	0 30 15	9 27 59	9♌07 23	15 05 23	10D00.3	28 56.1	15 40.4	29 07.3	28 53.3	12 43.4	4 43.1	16 03.0	8 26.7	15 28.0
31 Tu	0 34 11	10 27 15	21 01 42	26 56 48	10 00.2	0♈48.1	16 51.7	29 51.8	29 10.2	12 41.8	4 41.5	16 06.4	8 28.7	15 28.5

April 2015 LONGITUDE

Day	Sid.Time	☉	0 hr ☽	Noon ☽	True ☊	☿	♀	♂	⚳	♃	♄	♅	♆	♇
1 W	0 38 08	11♈26 28	2♍51 08	8♍45 08	10♎00.4	2♈41.6	18♉03.0	0♉36.2	29♑26.9	12♌40.3	4♐39.8	16♈09.9	8♓30.7	15♑29.0
2 Th	0 42 04	12 25 40	14 39 09	20 33 34	10 00.5	4 36.4	19 14.1	1 20.6	29 43.4	12R39.1	4R38.0	16 13.3	8 32.7	15 29.5
3 F	0 46 01	13 24 49	26 28 42	2♎24 52	10R00.7	6 32.5	20 25.2	2 05.0	29 59.8	12 38.0	4 36.1	16 16.7	8 34.6	15 29.9
4 Sa	0 49 57	14 23 56	8♎22 21	14 21 23	10 00.7	8 29.9	21 36.1	2 49.3	0♒15.9	12 37.1	4 34.1	16 20.1	8 36.6	15 30.3
5 Su	0 53 54	15 23 01	20 22 14	26 25 08	10 00.5	10 28.7	22 46.9	3 33.5	0 32.0	12 36.4	4 32.1	16 23.6	8 38.5	15 30.7
6 M	0 57 50	16 22 04	2♏30 18	8♏37 57	10 00.0	12 28.7	23 57.7	4 17.8	0 47.8	12 35.9	4 29.9	16 27.0	8 40.4	15 31.0
7 Tu	1 01 47	17 21 05	14 48 17	21 01 32	9 59.1	14 29.9	25 08.3	5 01.9	1 03.4	12 35.6	4 27.7	16 30.4	8 42.3	15 31.3
8 W	1 05 44	18 20 04	27 17 54	3♐37 36	9 58.1	16 32.2	26 18.9	5 46.0	1 18.9	12D35.4	4 25.3	16 33.8	8 44.1	15 31.6
9 Th	1 09 40	19 19 01	10♐00 52	16 27 55	9 56.9	18 35.5	27 29.3	6 30.1	1 34.2	12 35.5	4 22.9	16 37.3	8 46.0	15 31.9
10 F	1 13 37	20 17 57	22 58 58	29 34 13	9 56.0	20 39.8	28 39.6	7 14.1	1 49.3	12 35.7	4 20.4	16 40.7	8 47.8	15 32.1
11 Sa	1 17 33	21 16 51	6♑13 52	12♑58 06	9D55.4	22 44.9	29 49.8	7 58.1	2 04.2	12 36.2	4 17.8	16 44.1	8 49.6	15 32.3
12 Su	1 21 30	22 15 43	19 47 01	26 40 44	9 55.3	24 50.5	1♊00.0	8 42.0	2 18.9	12 36.8	4 15.1	16 47.6	8 51.4	15 32.4
13 M	1 25 26	23 14 34	3♒39 14	10♒42 30	9 55.8	26 56.6	2 10.0	9 25.9	2 33.4	12 37.6	4 12.4	16 51.0	8 53.2	15 32.6
14 Tu	1 29 23	24 13 23	17 50 21	25 02 32	9 56.7	29 02.9	3 19.9	10 09.7	2 47.7	12 38.6	4 09.6	16 54.4	8 54.9	15 32.7
15 W	1 33 19	25 12 10	2♓18 43	9♓38 23	9 57.8	1♉09.1	4 29.6	10 53.5	3 01.8	12 39.8	4 06.7	16 57.8	8 56.6	15 32.7
16 Th	1 37 16	26 10 55	17 00 56	24 25 40	9 58.7	3 15.0	5 39.3	11 37.2	3 15.7	12 41.1	4 03.7	17 01.2	8 58.3	15R32.8
17 F	1 41 12	27 09 38	1♈51 45	9♈18 18	9R59.2	5 20.2	6 48.8	12 20.9	3 29.3	12 42.7	4 00.6	17 04.6	9 00.0	15 32.8
18 Sa	1 45 09	28 08 20	16 44 22	24 08 58	9 58.7	7 24.5	7 58.3	13 04.5	3 42.8	12 44.4	3 57.5	17 08.0	9 01.7	15 32.7
19 Su	1 49 06	29 07 00	1♉31 09	8♉50 01	9 57.4	9 27.4	9 07.6	13 48.1	3 56.0	12 46.3	3 54.3	17 11.4	9 03.3	15 32.7
20 M	1 53 02	0♉05 37	16 04 43	23 14 31	9 55.1	11 28.8	10 16.7	14 31.6	4 09.0	12 48.4	3 51.0	17 14.7	9 04.9	15 32.6
21 Tu	1 56 59	1 04 13	0♊18 51	7♊17 13	9 52.2	13 28.2	11 25.8	15 15.1	4 21.8	12 50.7	3 47.7	17 18.1	9 06.5	15 32.5
22 W	2 00 55	2 02 47	14 09 21	20 55 05	9 49.1	15 25.4	12 34.7	15 58.5	4 34.4	12 53.2	3 44.3	17 21.4	9 08.0	15 32.3
23 Th	2 04 52	3 01 19	27 34 24	4♋07 25	9 46.3	17 20.0	13 43.5	16 41.9	4 46.7	12 55.8	3 40.8	17 24.8	9 09.6	15 32.2
24 F	2 08 48	3 59 48	10♋34 24	16 55 39	9 44.2	19 11.7	14 52.1	17 25.2	4 58.8	12 58.6	3 37.3	17 28.1	9 11.1	15 32.0
25 Sa	2 12 45	4 58 15	23 11 38	29 22 48	9D43.1	21 00.3	16 00.6	18 08.5	5 10.7	13 01.6	3 33.7	17 31.4	9 12.6	15 31.7
26 Su	2 16 41	5 56 40	5♌29 44	11♌33 00	9 43.1	22 45.6	17 09.0	18 51.7	5 22.3	13 04.8	3 30.0	17 34.7	9 14.0	15 31.5
27 M	2 20 38	6 55 03	17 33 12	23 30 56	9 44.1	24 27.3	18 17.2	19 34.9	5 33.7	13 08.1	3 26.3	17 38.0	9 15.5	15 31.2
28 Tu	2 24 35	7 53 24	29 26 50	5♍21 30	9 45.7	26 05.3	19 25.2	20 18.0	5 44.8	13 11.6	3 22.5	17 41.3	9 16.9	15 30.8
29 W	2 28 31	8 51 43	11♍15 32	17 09 28	9 47.5	27 39.3	20 33.1	21 01.1	5 55.7	13 15.3	3 18.7	17 44.6	9 18.2	15 30.5
30 Th	2 32 28	9 50 00	23 03 53	28 59 15	9R48.9	29 09.4	21 40.8	21 44.1	6 06.3	13 19.1	3 14.8	17 47.8	9 19.6	15 30.1

Astro Data	Dy Hr Mn
♃△♅	3 12:25
☽0S	6 19:28
♄ R	14 15:02
♅□♇	17 2:54
☽0N	20 6:13
☉0N	20 22:45
☿0N	2 6:37
☽0S	3 1:40
♃ D	8 16:57
☽0N	16 16:40
♇ R	17 3:54
☽0S	30 8:46

Planet Ingress		Dy Hr Mn
☿	♓	13 3:52
♀	♉	17 10:15
☉	♈	20 22:45
☿	♈	31 1:44
♂	♉	31 16:26
⚳	♒	3 12:21
♀	♊	11 15:28
☿	♉	14 22:51
☉	♉	20 9:42

Last Aspect Dy Hr Mn			☽ Ingress	Dy Hr Mn
28 17:53	♇	☍	♌	1 23:34
3 8:47	☿	☍	♍	4 11:58
5 18:36	♇	△	♎	7 0:52
9 1:24	☿	△	♏	9 13:10
11 19:46	☿	□	♐	11 23:30
13 23:11	♀	△	♑	14 6:40
16 8:02	♀	□	♒	16 10:14
17 18:18	♂	⚹	♓	18 10:58
20 9:36	☉	☌	♈	20 10:28
21 22:51	♂	☌	♉	22 10:40
23 14:25	☿	⚹	♊	24 13:22
26 12:35	♂	⚹	♋	26 19:45
29 1:58	♂	□	♌	29 5:48
30 13:57	♅	△	♍	31 18:12

Last Aspect Dy Hr Mn			☽ Ingress	Dy Hr Mn
2 9:01	♀	△	♎	3 7:07
4 15:58	♅	☍	♏	5 19:04
7 20:42	♀	☍	♐	8 5:08
9 17:42	☉	△	♑	10 12:47
12 8:15	☿	□	♒	12 17:44
14 19:45	☿	⚹	♓	14 20:12
15 21:37	♇	⚹	♈	16 21:00
18 18:57	☉	☌	♉	18 21:31
19 23:07	♇	△	♊	20 23:28
22 5:38	♅	⚹	♋	23 4:25
24 17:04	☿	⚹	♌	25 13:13
27 14:12	☿	□	♍	28 1:07
30 12:23	☿	△	♎	30 14:03

☽ Phases & Eclipses Dy Hr Mn		
5 18:05	○	14♍50
13 17:48	☾	22♐49
20 9:36	●	29♓27
20 9:45:37	●	T 02'47"
27 7:43	☽	6♋19
4 12:06	○	14♎24
4 12:00	●	T 1.001
12 3:44	☾	21♑55
18 18:57	●	28♈25
25 23:55	☽	5♌27

Astro Data

1 March 2015
Julian Day # 42063
SVP 5♓02'48"
GC 27♐03.1 ⚴ 22♐48.7
Eris 22♈18.1 ⚵ 3♌47.9R
⚷ 16♓51.3 ⚶ 16♒26.9
☽ Mean ☊ 11♎47.2

1 April 2015
Julian Day # 42094
SVP 5♓02'46"
GC 27♐03.1 ⚴ 29♐13.2
Eris 22♈36.2 ⚵ 4♌26.4
⚷ 18♓44.8 ⚶ 1♓48.5
☽ Mean ☊ 10♎08.7

LONGITUDE — May 2015

Day	Sid.Time	☉	0 hr ☽	Noon ☽	True ☊	☿	♀	♂	⚳	♃	♄	♅	♆	♇
1 F	2 36 24	10♉48 15	4♎56 02	10♎54 41	9♎49.4	0♊35.3	22♊48.4	22♉27.1	6♒16.7	13♌23.2	3♐10.9	17♈51.0	9♓20.9	15♑29.7
2 Sa	2 40 21	11 46 28	16 55 33	22 58 59	9R 48.5	1 56.9	23 55.7	23 10.0	6 26.8	13 27.3	3R 06.9	17 54.2	9 22.2	15R 29.3
3 Su	2 44 17	12 44 39	29 05 14	5♏14 34	9 46.1	3 14.2	25 02.9	23 52.9	6 36.6	13 31.7	3 02.9	17 57.4	9 23.5	15 28.8
4 M	2 48 14	13 42 48	11♏27 07	17 43 03	9 42.2	4 27.1	26 10.0	24 35.7	6 46.2	13 36.2	2 58.9	18 00.6	9 24.7	15 28.3
5 Tu	2 52 10	14 40 56	24 02 26	0♐25 18	9 37.0	5 35.5	27 16.8	25 18.5	6 55.5	13 40.8	2 54.8	18 03.8	9 25.9	15 27.8
6 W	2 56 07	15 39 02	6♐51 41	13 21 32	9 31.1	6 39.3	28 23.5	26 01.2	7 04.6	13 45.7	2 50.6	18 06.9	9 27.1	15 27.2
7 Th	3 00 04	16 37 07	19 54 48	26 31 25	9 25.1	7 38.4	29 30.0	26 43.8	7 13.4	13 50.6	2 46.4	18 10.0	9 28.2	15 26.7
8 F	3 04 00	17 35 10	3♑11 18	9♑54 23	9 19.8	8 32.9	0♋36.3	27 26.5	7 21.9	13 55.8	2 42.2	18 13.1	9 29.4	15 26.1
9 Sa	3 07 57	18 33 12	16 40 33	23 29 44	9 15.7	9 22.6	1 42.4	28 09.0	7 30.1	14 01.1	2 38.0	18 16.2	9 30.5	15 25.4
10 Su	3 11 53	19 31 12	0♒21 51	7♒16 48	9D 13.4	10 07.4	2 48.2	28 51.6	7 38.0	14 06.5	2 33.7	18 19.3	9 31.5	15 24.8
11 M	3 15 50	20 29 11	14 14 32	21 14 55	9 12.7	10 47.4	3 53.9	29 34.1	7 45.6	14 12.1	2 29.4	18 22.3	9 32.6	15 24.1
12 Tu	3 19 46	21 27 09	28 17 52	5♓23 14	9 13.4	11 22.5	4 59.4	0♊16.5	7 52.9	14 17.9	2 25.1	18 25.3	9 33.6	15 23.4
13 W	3 23 43	22 25 05	12♓30 51	19 40 28	9 14.6	11 52.5	6 04.7	0 58.9	8 00.0	14 23.7	2 20.7	18 28.3	9 34.5	15 22.7
14 Th	3 27 39	23 23 00	26 51 47	4♈04 28	9R 15.5	12 17.6	7 09.8	1 41.2	8 06.7	14 29.8	2 16.3	18 31.3	9 35.5	15 21.9
15 F	3 31 36	24 20 54	11♈18 05	18 32 06	9 15.3	12 37.7	8 14.6	2 23.5	8 13.1	14 36.0	2 11.9	18 34.2	9 36.4	15 21.1
16 Sa	3 35 33	25 18 47	25 45 57	2♉59 00	9 13.2	12 52.8	9 19.2	3 05.8	8 19.2	14 42.3	2 07.5	18 37.1	9 37.3	15 20.3
17 Su	3 39 29	26 16 38	10♉10 34	17 19 59	9 08.9	13 02.9	10 23.6	3 48.0	8 25.0	14 48.8	2 03.1	18 40.0	9 38.1	15 19.5
18 M	3 43 26	27 14 28	24 26 32	1♊29 33	9 02.6	13R 08.1	11 27.8	4 30.1	8 30.5	14 55.4	1 58.6	18 42.9	9 39.0	15 18.6
19 Tu	3 47 22	28 12 17	8♊28 27	15 22 42	8 54.9	13 08.5	12 31.7	5 12.2	8 35.7	15 02.1	1 54.2	18 45.7	9 39.7	15 17.8
20 W	3 51 19	29 10 04	22 11 53	28 55 41	8 46.6	13 04.1	13 35.3	5 54.3	8 40.5	15 09.0	1 49.7	18 48.5	9 40.5	15 16.9
21 Th	3 55 15	0♊07 50	5♋33 55	12♋06 31	8 38.5	12 55.3	14 38.7	6 36.3	8 45.0	15 16.0	1 45.2	18 51.3	9 41.2	15 15.9
22 F	3 59 12	1 05 34	18 33 33	24 55 12	8 31.7	12 42.1	15 41.8	7 18.3	8 49.2	15 23.2	1 40.8	18 54.1	9 41.9	15 15.0
23 Sa	4 03 08	2 03 16	1♌11 44	7♌23 32	8 26.7	12 24.9	16 44.6	8 00.2	8 53.0	15 30.5	1 36.3	18 56.8	9 42.6	15 14.0
24 Su	4 07 05	3 00 57	13 31 04	19 34 51	8 23.7	12 04.0	17 47.2	8 42.0	8 56.6	15 37.9	1 31.8	18 59.5	9 43.2	15 13.0
25 M	4 11 02	3 58 37	25 35 27	1♍33 29	8D 22.6	11 39.8	18 49.4	9 23.8	8 59.7	15 45.5	1 27.3	19 02.2	9 43.8	15 12.0
26 Tu	4 14 58	4 56 15	7♍29 36	13 24 28	8 22.9	11 12.7	19 51.3	10 05.6	9 02.6	15 53.1	1 22.9	19 04.8	9 44.4	15 11.0
27 W	4 18 55	5 53 51	19 18 44	25 13 05	8 23.8	10 43.1	20 52.9	10 47.3	9 05.1	16 00.9	1 18.4	19 07.4	9 44.9	15 09.9
28 Th	4 22 51	6 51 26	1♎08 08	7♎04 33	8R 24.4	10 11.7	21 54.2	11 29.0	9 07.2	16 08.8	1 14.0	19 10.0	9 45.4	15 08.8
29 F	4 26 48	7 48 59	13 02 54	19 03 46	8 23.8	9 38.9	22 55.2	12 10.6	9 09.0	16 16.9	1 09.5	19 12.5	9 45.9	15 07.7
30 Sa	4 30 44	8 46 32	25 07 37	1♏14 55	8 21.3	9 05.3	23 55.8	12 52.2	9 10.5	16 25.0	1 05.1	19 15.0	9 46.3	15 06.6
31 Su	4 34 41	9 44 03	7♏26 03	13 41 20	8 16.4	8 31.5	24 56.0	13 33.7	9 11.6	16 33.3	1 00.7	19 17.5	9 46.7	15 05.5

LONGITUDE — June 2015

Day	Sid.Time	☉	0 hr ☽	Noon ☽	True ☊	☿	♀	♂	⚳	♃	♄	♅	♆	♇
1 M	4 38 37	10♊41 33	20♏00 57	26♏25 04	8♎09.2	7♊58.1	25♋55.9	14♊15.2	9♒12.4	16♌41.7	0♐56.3	19♈19.9	9♓47.1	15♑04.3
2 Tu	4 42 34	11 39 01	2♐53 43	9♐26 52	8R 00.0	7R 25.6	26 55.4	14 56.6	9R 12.8	16 50.2	0R 52.0	19 22.3	9 47.4	15R 03.2
3 W	4 46 31	12 36 29	16 04 21	22 46 00	7 49.6	6 54.7	27 54.5	15 38.0	9 12.9	16 58.8	0 47.6	19 24.7	9 47.7	15 02.0
4 Th	4 50 27	13 33 56	29 31 29	6♑20 28	7 39.1	6 25.8	28 53.1	16 19.4	9 12.6	17 07.5	0 43.3	19 27.0	9 48.0	15 00.8
5 F	4 54 24	14 31 22	13♑12 36	20 07 25	7 29.5	5 59.4	29 51.4	17 00.7	9 11.9	17 16.4	0 39.0	19 29.3	9 48.3	14 59.5
6 Sa	4 58 20	15 28 47	27 04 33	4♒03 35	7 21.8	5 36.0	0♌49.3	17 41.9	9 10.9	17 25.3	0 34.8	19 31.6	9 48.5	14 58.3
7 Su	5 02 17	16 26 11	11♒04 07	18 05 50	7 16.5	5 15.9	1 46.7	18 23.2	9 09.6	17 34.4	0 30.6	19 33.8	9 48.7	14 57.0
8 M	5 06 13	17 23 35	25 08 26	2♓11 40	7 13.7	4 59.4	2 43.6	19 04.3	9 07.8	17 43.5	0 26.4	19 36.0	9 48.8	14 55.8
9 Tu	5 10 10	18 20 58	9♓15 19	16 19 14	7D 12.9	4 46.8	3 40.1	19 45.5	9 05.7	17 52.8	0 22.2	19 38.1	9 48.9	14 54.5
10 W	5 14 06	19 18 21	23 23 15	0♈27 15	7R 13.0	4 38.4	4 36.1	20 26.5	9 03.3	18 02.1	0 18.1	19 40.3	9 49.0	14 53.2
11 Th	5 18 03	20 15 43	7♈31 07	14 34 41	7 13.0	4D 34.2	5 31.6	21 07.6	9 00.5	18 11.6	0 14.0	19 42.3	9R 49.0	14 51.9
12 F	5 22 00	21 13 05	21 37 48	28 40 16	7 11.5	4 34.5	6 26.6	21 48.6	8 57.3	18 21.1	0 10.0	19 44.4	9 49.0	14 50.5
13 Sa	5 25 56	22 10 26	5♉41 48	12♉42 08	7 07.6	4 39.3	7 21.1	22 29.6	8 53.7	18 30.8	0 06.0	19 46.4	9 49.0	14 49.2
14 Su	5 29 53	23 07 47	19 40 55	26 37 45	7 01.0	4 48.6	8 15.0	23 10.5	8 49.8	18 40.5	0 02.1	19 48.3	9 49.0	14 47.9
15 M	5 33 49	24 05 08	3♊32 13	10♊23 56	6 51.8	5 02.5	9 08.4	23 51.4	8 45.6	18 50.4	29♏58.2	19 50.2	9 48.9	14 46.5
16 Tu	5 37 46	25 02 28	17 12 26	23 57 22	6 40.6	5 20.9	10 01.2	24 32.2	8 40.9	19 00.3	29 54.3	19 52.1	9 48.8	14 45.1
17 W	5 41 42	25 59 47	0♋38 21	7♋15 07	6 28.4	5 43.9	10 53.3	25 13.0	8 36.0	19 10.4	29 50.5	19 53.9	9 48.6	14 43.7
18 Th	5 45 39	26 57 05	13 47 26	20 15 10	6 16.4	6 11.3	11 44.9	25 53.8	8 30.6	19 20.5	29 46.8	19 55.7	9 48.4	14 42.3
19 F	5 49 35	27 54 23	26 38 19	2♌56 55	6 05.8	6 43.2	12 35.7	26 34.5	8 25.0	19 30.7	29 43.1	19 57.5	9 48.2	14 40.9
20 Sa	5 53 32	28 51 40	9♌11 07	15 21 11	5 57.3	7 19.5	13 25.9	27 15.1	8 18.9	19 41.0	29 39.5	19 59.2	9 48.0	14 39.5
21 Su	5 57 29	29 48 57	21 27 27	27 30 19	5 51.5	8 00.0	14 15.4	27 55.8	8 12.6	19 51.4	29 35.9	20 00.9	9 47.7	14 38.1
22 M	6 01 25	0♋46 13	3♍30 16	9♍27 51	5 48.1	8 44.8	15 04.1	28 36.4	8 05.9	20 01.8	29 32.4	20 02.5	9 47.4	14 36.6
23 Tu	6 05 22	1 43 28	15 23 38	21 18 16	5D 46.7	9 33.8	15 52.1	29 16.9	7 58.8	20 12.4	29 29.0	20 04.0	9 47.1	14 35.2
24 W	6 09 18	2 40 42	27 12 24	3♎06 44	5R 46.5	10 26.8	16 39.3	29 57.4	7 51.4	20 23.0	29 25.6	20 05.6	9 46.7	14 33.7
25 Th	6 13 15	3 37 56	9♎01 55	14 58 40	5 46.4	11 23.9	17 25.6	0♋37.8	7 43.7	20 33.7	29 22.3	20 07.1	9 46.3	14 32.3
26 F	6 17 11	4 35 09	20 57 38	26 59 30	5 45.3	12 25.0	18 11.1	1 18.3	7 35.7	20 44.5	29 19.0	20 08.5	9 45.8	14 30.8
27 Sa	6 21 08	5 32 22	3♏04 51	9♏14 17	5 42.3	13 30.0	18 55.7	1 58.6	7 27.4	20 55.3	29 15.9	20 09.9	9 45.4	14 29.4
28 Su	6 25 04	6 29 34	15 28 18	21 47 18	5 37.0	14 38.9	19 39.4	2 39.0	7 18.8	21 06.2	29 12.8	20 11.3	9 44.9	14 27.9
29 M	6 29 01	7 26 46	28 11 39	4♐41 34	5 29.0	15 51.5	20 22.1	3 19.3	7 09.9	21 17.2	29 09.7	20 12.6	9 44.4	14 26.4
30 Tu	6 32 58	8 23 58	11♐17 09	17 58 25	5 18.9	17 08.0	21 03.8	3 59.5	7 00.7	21 28.3	29 06.8	20 13.8	9 43.8	14 24.9

Astro Data

	Dy Hr Mn
♄⚼♅	4 6:12
☽0N	14 1:11
☿R	19 1:48
♃⊼♇	21 11:39
☽0S	27 17:17
⚳R	3 4:20
☽0N	10 8:05
☿D	11 22:34
♆R	12 9:08
♄∠♇	20 11:45
♃△♅	22 13:46
☽0S	24 2:41

Planet Ingress

	Dy Hr Mn
☿ ♊	1 2:00
♀ ♋	7 22:52
♂ ♊	12 2:40
☉ ♊	21 8:45
♀ ♌	5 15:33
♄ ♏R	15 0:36
☉ ♋	21 16:38
♂ ♋	24 13:33

Last Aspect / ☽ Ingress (May)

Last Aspect Dy Hr Mn		☽ Ingress Dy Hr Mn
2 14:03	♀ △	♏ 3 1:47
5 1:49	♂ ☍	♐ 5 11:13
7 17:51	♀ ☍	♑ 7 18:16
9 20:35	♂ △	♒ 9 23:22
11 10:36	☉ □	♓ 12 2:53
13 16:55	☉ ⚹	♈ 14 5:13
15 12:03	♅ ☌	♉ 16 7:02
18 4:13	☉ ☌	♊ 18 9:27
19 17:57	♅ ⚹	♋ 20 13:56
22 0:36	♅ □	♌ 22 21:42
24 10:50	♅ △	♍ 25 8:52
27 2:21	♀ ⚹	♎ 27 21:42
29 20:20	♀ □	♏ 30 9:34

Last Aspect / ☽ Ingress (June)

Last Aspect Dy Hr Mn		☽ Ingress Dy Hr Mn
1 11:01	♀ △	♐ 1 18:39
3 5:59	♅ △	♑ 4 0:50
5 10:54	♅ □	♒ 6 5:02
7 14:30	♅ ⚹	♓ 8 8:16
9 18:08	♂ □	♈ 10 11:14
11 23:43	♂ ⚹	♉ 12 14:16
13 22:06	♃ □	♊ 14 17:51
16 14:05	☉ ☌	♋ 16 22:51
19 5:52	♄ △	♌ 19 6:22
21 16:09	♄ □	♍ 21 16:59
24 5:12	♂ □	♎ 24 5:41
25 23:22	♃ ⚹	♏ 26 17:57
29 1:50	♄ ☌	♐ 29 3:21

☽ Phases & Eclipses

Dy Hr Mn	
4 3:42	○ 13♏23
11 10:36	☾ 20♒26
18 4:13	● 26♉56
25 17:19	☽ 4♍11
2 16:19	○ 11♐49
9 15:42	☾ 18♓30
16 14:05	● 25♊07
24 11:03	☽ 2♎38

Astro Data

1 May 2015
Julian Day # 42124
SVP 5♓02'43"
GC 27♐03.2 ⚴ 29♐56.2R
Eris 22♈55.7 ⚵ 10♌23.2
⚷ 20♓18.2 ⚶ 15♓34.6
☽ Mean ☊ 8♎33.3

1 June 2015
Julian Day # 42155
SVP 5♓02'39"
GC 27♐03.3 ⚴ 23♐51.0R
Eris 23♈12.9 ⚵ 19♌39.5
⚷ 21♓19.0 ⚶ 28♓04.5
☽ Mean ☊ 6♎54.8

July 2015 LONGITUDE

Day	Sid.Time	☉	0 hr ☽	Noon ☽	True ☊	☿	♀	♂	⚳	♃	♄	♅	♆	♇
1 W	6 36 54	9♋21 09	24♐45 11	1♑37 10	5♎07.4	18♊28.2	21♌44.5	4♋39.7	6♒51.2	21♌39.4	29♏03.9	20♈15.1	9♓43.2	14♑23.4
2 Th	6 40 51	10 18 21	8♑33 59	15 35 05	4R 55.7	19 52.0	22 24.0	5 19.9	6R 41.4	21 50.6	29R 01.1	20 16.2	9R 42.6	14R 22.0
3 F	6 44 47	11 15 32	22 39 52	29 47 38	4 44.9	21 19.5	23 02.5	6 00.0	6 31.3	22 01.9	28 58.4	20 17.4	9 42.0	14 20.5
4 Sa	6 48 44	12 12 43	6♒57 40	14♒09 14	4 36.2	22 50.6	23 39.8	6 40.1	6 21.0	22 13.3	28 55.7	20 18.5	9 41.3	14 19.0
5 Su	6 52 40	13 09 54	21 21 37	28 34 11	4 30.1	24 25.2	24 15.9	7 20.2	6 10.5	22 24.7	28 53.1	20 19.5	9 40.6	14 17.5
6 M	6 56 37	14 07 05	5♓46 19	12♓57 30	4 26.7	26 03.3	24 50.8	8 00.2	5 59.7	22 36.1	28 50.6	20 20.5	9 39.8	14 16.0
7 Tu	7 00 33	15 04 17	20 07 21	27 15 31	4D 25.5	27 44.7	25 24.3	8 40.2	5 48.6	22 47.6	28 48.2	20 21.4	9 39.1	14 14.5
8 W	7 04 30	16 01 29	4♈21 46	11♈25 56	4R 25.5	29 29.5	25 56.6	9 20.1	5 37.3	22 59.2	28 45.9	20 22.3	9 38.3	14 13.0
9 Th	7 08 27	16 58 41	18 27 54	25 27 36	4 25.3	1♋17.4	26 27.4	10 00.1	5 25.9	23 10.9	28 43.6	20 23.2	9 37.5	14 11.5
10 F	7 12 23	17 55 54	2♉25 00	9♉20 05	4 23.9	3 08.3	26 56.8	10 39.9	5 14.2	23 22.6	28 41.5	20 24.0	9 36.6	14 10.0
11 Sa	7 16 20	18 53 08	16 12 47	23 03 05	4 20.2	5 02.1	27 24.7	11 19.8	5 02.3	23 34.4	28 39.4	20 24.7	9 35.8	14 08.5
12 Su	7 20 16	19 50 21	29 50 53	6♊36 08	4 13.8	6 58.5	27 51.1	11 59.6	4 50.2	23 46.2	28 37.4	20 25.4	9 34.9	14 07.0
13 M	7 24 13	20 47 36	13♊18 41	19 58 24	4 04.9	8 57.4	28 15.9	12 39.4	4 38.0	23 58.1	28 35.5	20 26.1	9 34.0	14 05.6
14 Tu	7 28 09	21 44 50	26 35 08	3♋08 45	3 54.1	10 58.5	28 39.0	13 19.1	4 25.6	24 10.0	28 33.7	20 26.7	9 33.0	14 04.1
15 W	7 32 06	22 42 06	9♋39 05	16 06 00	3 42.2	13 01.5	29 00.4	13 58.8	4 13.0	24 22.0	28 32.0	20 27.3	9 32.0	14 02.6
16 Th	7 36 03	23 39 21	22 29 24	28 49 14	3 30.6	15 06.1	29 20.0	14 38.5	4 00.4	24 34.0	28 30.4	20 27.8	9 31.0	14 01.1
17 F	7 39 59	24 36 37	5♌05 29	11♌18 12	3 20.1	17 12.1	29 37.7	15 18.1	3 47.6	24 46.1	28 28.8	20 28.2	9 30.0	13 59.7
18 Sa	7 43 56	25 33 53	17 27 29	23 33 31	3 11.7	19 19.1	29 53.6	15 57.7	3 34.7	24 58.2	28 27.4	20 28.6	9 28.9	13 58.2
19 Su	7 47 52	26 31 09	29 36 32	5♍36 52	3 05.8	21 26.8	0♍07.5	16 37.3	3 21.7	25 10.4	28 26.0	20 29.0	9 27.9	13 56.7
20 M	7 51 49	27 28 25	11♍34 51	17 30 56	3 02.5	23 34.9	0 19.4	17 16.8	3 08.7	25 22.6	28 24.7	20 29.3	9 26.8	13 55.3
21 Tu	7 55 45	28 25 42	23 25 36	29 19 24	3D 01.2	25 43.1	0 29.2	17 56.3	2 55.5	25 34.9	28 23.6	20 29.6	9 25.6	13 53.9
22 W	7 59 42	29 22 59	5♎12 53	11♎06 41	3 01.4	27 51.1	0 36.8	18 35.7	2 42.4	25 47.2	28 22.5	20 29.8	9 24.5	13 52.4
23 Th	8 03 38	0♌20 16	17 01 26	22 57 48	3R 02.0	29 58.7	0 42.3	19 15.2	2 29.2	25 59.6	28 21.5	20 30.0	9 23.3	13 51.0
24 F	8 07 35	1 17 34	28 56 28	4♏58 05	3 02.2	2♌05.7	0R 45.5	19 54.5	2 16.0	26 11.9	28 20.6	20 30.1	9 22.1	13 49.6
25 Sa	8 11 31	2 14 52	11♏03 21	17 12 52	3 00.9	4 11.8	0 46.4	20 33.9	2 02.7	26 24.4	28 19.8	20R 30.1	9 20.9	13 48.2
26 Su	8 15 28	3 12 11	23 27 15	29 47 03	2 57.8	6 17.0	0 45.0	21 13.2	1 49.5	26 36.8	28 19.1	20 30.2	9 19.7	13 46.8
27 M	8 19 25	4 09 30	6♐12 42	12♐44 35	2 52.5	8 20.9	0 41.2	21 52.5	1 36.3	26 49.3	28 18.5	20 30.1	9 18.4	13 45.4
28 Tu	8 23 21	5 06 49	19 22 58	26 07 55	2 45.3	10 23.6	0 35.0	22 31.7	1 23.2	27 01.9	28 18.0	20 30.1	9 17.2	13 44.0
29 W	8 27 18	6 04 09	2♑59 27	9♑57 20	2 36.8	12 25.0	0 26.5	23 10.9	1 10.1	27 14.4	28 17.6	20 29.9	9 15.9	13 42.7
30 Th	8 31 14	7 01 29	17 01 14	24 10 35	2 28.0	14 24.9	0 15.5	23 50.1	0 57.1	27 27.0	28 17.3	20 29.8	9 14.6	13 41.3
31 F	8 35 11	7 58 51	1♒24 44	8♒42 52	2 19.9	16 23.3	0 02.1	24 29.3	0 44.1	27 39.7	28 17.1	20 29.5	9 13.2	13 40.0

August 2015 LONGITUDE

Day	Sid.Time	☉	0 hr ☽	Noon ☽	True ☊	☿	♀	♂	⚳	♃	♄	♅	♆	♇
1 Sa	8 39 07	8♌56 13	16♒04 04	23♒27 22	2♎13.5	18♌20.1	29♌46.4	25♋08.4	0♒31.2	27♌52.3	28♏17.0	20♈29.3	9♓11.9	13♑38.7
2 Su	8 43 04	9 53 35	0♓51 46	8♓16 19	2R 09.1	20 15.4	29R 28.3	25 47.4	0R 18.5	28 05.0	28D 17.0	20R 29.0	9R 10.5	13R 37.4
3 M	8 47 01	10 50 59	15 40 04	23 02 11	2D 07.1	22 09.1	29 08.0	26 26.5	0 05.8	28 17.8	28 17.0	20 28.6	9 09.1	13 36.1
4 Tu	8 50 57	11 48 24	0♈21 58	7♈38 49	2 06.8	24 01.2	28 45.5	27 05.5	29♑53.3	28 30.5	28 17.2	20 28.2	9 07.7	13 34.8
5 W	8 54 54	12 45 51	14 52 13	22 01 52	2 07.7	25 51.7	28 20.9	27 44.5	29 40.9	28 43.3	28 17.5	20 27.7	9 06.3	13 33.6
6 Th	8 58 50	13 43 18	29 07 29	6♉08 58	2R 08.7	27 40.6	27 54.2	28 23.5	29 28.7	28 56.1	28 17.8	20 27.2	9 04.8	13 32.3
7 F	9 02 47	14 40 47	13♉06 15	19 59 21	2 08.7	29 27.9	27 25.8	29 02.4	29 16.6	29 08.9	28 18.3	20 26.7	9 03.4	13 31.1
8 Sa	9 06 43	15 38 17	26 48 21	3♊33 19	2 07.3	1♍13.7	26 55.5	29 41.3	29 04.7	29 21.8	28 18.8	20 26.1	9 01.9	13 29.9
9 Su	9 10 40	16 35 49	10♊14 23	16 51 42	2 03.8	2 57.8	26 23.7	0♌20.2	28 53.0	29 34.6	28 19.5	20 25.4	9 00.4	13 28.7
10 M	9 14 36	17 33 21	23 25 22	29 55 31	1 58.5	4 40.4	25 50.5	0 59.0	28 41.5	29 47.5	28 20.3	20 24.7	8 59.0	13 27.5
11 Tu	9 18 33	18 30 56	6♋22 16	12♋45 44	1 51.8	6 21.5	25 16.1	1 37.9	28 30.2	0♍00.4	28 21.1	20 24.0	8 57.4	13 26.3
12 W	9 22 30	19 28 31	19 06 00	25 23 11	1 44.3	8 01.0	24 40.7	2 16.6	28 19.2	0 13.4	28 22.1	20 23.2	8 55.9	13 25.2
13 Th	9 26 26	20 26 08	1♌37 21	7♌48 38	1 36.9	9 39.1	24 04.5	2 55.4	28 08.3	0 26.3	28 23.1	20 22.3	8 54.4	13 24.1
14 F	9 30 23	21 23 46	13 57 08	20 02 59	1 30.4	11 15.5	23 27.7	3 34.1	27 57.7	0 39.3	28 24.2	20 21.5	8 52.8	13 22.9
15 Sa	9 34 19	22 21 25	26 06 20	2♍07 22	1 25.2	12 50.5	22 50.5	4 12.8	27 47.4	0 52.3	28 25.5	20 20.5	8 51.3	13 21.9
16 Su	9 38 16	23 19 05	8♍06 19	14 03 24	1 21.9	14 23.9	22 13.3	4 51.5	27 37.3	1 05.2	28 26.8	20 19.6	8 49.7	13 20.8
17 M	9 42 12	24 16 47	19 58 57	25 53 16	1D 20.3	15 55.9	21 36.1	5 30.1	27 27.5	1 18.3	28 28.2	20 18.6	8 48.1	13 19.7
18 Tu	9 46 09	25 14 29	1♎46 44	7♎39 46	1 20.3	17 26.2	20 59.4	6 08.7	27 18.0	1 31.3	28 29.8	20 17.5	8 46.6	13 18.7
19 W	9 50 05	26 12 13	13 32 50	19 26 25	1 21.5	18 55.1	20 23.2	6 47.3	27 08.8	1 44.3	28 31.4	20 16.4	8 45.0	13 17.7
20 Th	9 54 02	27 09 58	25 21 03	1♏17 18	1 23.2	20 22.4	19 47.8	7 25.9	26 59.9	1 57.3	28 33.1	20 15.2	8 43.4	13 16.7
21 F	9 57 58	28 07 44	7♏15 45	13 17 00	1 24.8	21 48.2	19 13.5	8 04.4	26 51.2	2 10.4	28 34.9	20 14.0	8 41.7	13 15.8
22 Sa	10 01 55	29 05 31	19 21 40	25 30 21	1R 25.6	23 12.4	18 40.4	8 42.9	26 42.9	2 23.4	28 36.8	20 12.8	8 40.1	13 14.8
23 Su	10 05 52	0♍03 19	1♐43 41	8♐02 13	1 25.4	24 34.9	18 08.8	9 21.3	26 34.9	2 36.4	28 38.8	20 11.5	8 38.5	13 13.9
24 M	10 09 48	1 01 09	14 26 28	20 56 55	1 23.8	25 55.9	17 38.7	9 59.7	26 27.2	2 49.5	28 40.9	20 10.2	8 36.9	13 13.0
25 Tu	10 13 45	1 59 00	27 33 57	4♑17 49	1 21.1	27 15.1	17 10.4	10 38.1	26 19.9	3 02.6	28 43.1	20 08.9	8 35.3	13 12.2
26 W	10 17 41	2 56 52	11♑08 41	18 06 32	1 17.5	28 32.6	16 44.1	11 16.5	26 12.9	3 15.6	28 45.4	20 07.5	8 33.6	13 11.3
27 Th	10 21 38	3 54 45	25 11 12	2♒22 20	1 13.6	29 48.4	16 19.7	11 54.8	26 06.2	3 28.7	28 47.7	20 06.1	8 32.0	13 10.5
28 F	10 25 34	4 52 40	9♒39 24	17 01 43	1 09.9	1♎02.3	15 57.5	12 33.2	25 59.9	3 41.7	28 50.2	20 04.6	8 30.3	13 09.7
29 Sa	10 29 31	5 50 36	24 28 23	1♓58 26	1 07.0	2 14.2	15 37.5	13 11.4	25 53.9	3 54.8	28 52.7	20 03.1	8 28.7	13 09.0
30 Su	10 33 27	6 48 33	9♓30 46	17 04 14	1D 05.3	3 24.2	15 19.8	13 49.7	25 48.2	4 07.8	28 55.4	20 01.5	8 27.0	13 08.2
31 M	10 37 24	7 46 32	24 37 39	2♈09 55	1 04.8	4 32.2	15 04.5	14 27.9	25 42.9	4 20.8	28 58.1	19 59.9	8 25.4	13 07.5

Astro Data	Dy Hr Mn
☽0N	7 14:43
☽0S	21 11:47
♀R	25 9:29
♅R	26 10:38
♄D	2 5:53
♃□♄	3 10:36
☽0N	3 22:29
♃⚻♇	4 19:22
♄∠♇	13 22:17
☽0S	17 19:39
☿0S	25 22:03
☽0N	31 8:05

Planet Ingress		Dy Hr Mn
☿	♋	8 18:52
♀	♍	18 22:38
☉	♌	23 3:30
☿	♌	23 12:14
♀	♌R	31 15:27
⚳	♑R	3 23:08
☿	♍	7 19:15
♂	♌	8 23:32
♃	♍	11 11:11
☉	♍	23 10:37
☿	♎	27 15:44

Last Aspect Dy Hr Mn			☽ Ingress	Dy Hr Mn
30 18:18	♃	△	♑	1 9:11
3 10:38	♄	⚹	♒	3 12:21
5 12:32	♄	□	♓	5 14:23
7 14:36	♄	△	♈	7 16:37
9 13:47	♀	△	♉	9 19:49
11 21:52	♄	☍	♊	12 0:16
14 3:31	♀	⚹	♋	14 6:14
16 11:24	♄	△	♌	16 14:15
18 21:41	♄	□	♍	19 0:47
21 10:07	♄	⚹	♎	21 13:23
23 18:12	♃	⚹	♏	24 2:07
26 9:14	♄	☌	♐	26 12:24
28 13:36	♃	△	♑	28 18:47
30 18:50	♄	⚹	♒	30 21:40

Last Aspect Dy Hr Mn			☽ Ingress	Dy Hr Mn
1 22:02	♀	☍	♓	1 22:36
3 20:35	♄	△	♈	3 23:24
5 23:29	♃	△	♉	6 1:29
8 4:46	♂	⚹	♊	8 5:40
10 11:45	♃	⚹	♋	10 12:08
12 17:44	♄	△	♌	12 20:52
15 4:36	♄	□	♍	15 7:45
17 17:16	♄	⚹	♎	17 20:22
20 2:56	☉	⚹	♏	20 9:24
22 19:31	☉	□	♐	22 20:41
24 22:04	☿	□	♑	25 4:22
27 7:20	☿	△	♒	27 8:03
29 7:03	♄	□	♓	29 8:51
31 6:53	♄	△	♈	31 8:33

☽ Phases & Eclipses Dy Hr Mn		
2 2:20	○	9♑55
8 20:24	☾	16♈22
16 1:24	●	23♋14
24 4:04	☽	0♏59
31 10:43	○	7♒56
7 2:03	☾	14♉17
14 14:53	●	21♌31
22 19:31	☽	29♏24
29 18:35	○	6♓06

Astro Data

1 July 2015
Julian Day # 42185
SVP 5♓02'34"
GC 27♐03.3 ⚴ 15♐31.2R
Eris 23♈23.0 ⚵ 0♍11.9
⚷ 21♓32.0R ⚶ 7♈33.2
☽ Mean ☊ 5♎19.5

1 August 2015
Julian Day # 42216
SVP 5♓02'29"
GC 27♐03.4 ⚴ 11♐39.8R
Eris 23♈24.0R ⚵ 11♍52.5
⚷ 20♓56.1R ⚶ 12♈58.6
☽ Mean ☊ 3♎41.0

LONGITUDE — September 2015

Day	Sid.Time	☉	0 hr ☽	Noon ☽	True ☊	☿	♀	♂	⚳	♃	♄	♅	♆	♇
1 Tu	10 41 21	8♍44 33	9♈39 59	17♈06 53	1♎05.3	5♎37.9	14♌51.6	15♌06.1	25♑37.9	4♍33.9	29♏00.9	19♈58.3	8♓23.7	13♑06.8
2 W	10 45 17	9 42 36	24 29 48	1♉48 06	1 06.5	6 41.4	14R41.1	15 44.3	25R33.3	4 46.9	29 03.8	19R56.6	8R22.1	13R06.1
3 Th	10 49 14	10 40 41	9♉01 16	16 08 56	1 07.9	7 42.4	14 33.0	16 22.4	25 29.1	4 59.9	29 06.8	19 54.9	8 20.4	13 05.5
4 F	10 53 10	11 38 47	23 10 54	0♊07 05	1R08.9	8 41.0	14 27.4	17 00.6	25 25.2	5 13.0	29 09.9	19 53.2	8 18.8	13 04.9
5 Sa	10 57 07	12 36 56	6♊57 30	13 42 16	1 09.2	9 36.8	14D24.2	17 38.7	25 21.6	5 26.0	29 13.0	19 51.5	8 17.2	13 04.3
6 Su	11 01 03	13 35 07	20 21 37	26 55 46	1 08.7	10 29.7	14 23.3	18 16.8	25 18.5	5 39.0	29 16.3	19 49.7	8 15.5	13 03.7
7 M	11 05 00	14 33 20	3♋25 01	9♋49 43	1 07.5	11 19.6	14 24.8	18 54.8	25 15.6	5 52.0	29 19.6	19 47.8	8 13.9	13 03.2
8 Tu	11 08 56	15 31 34	16 10 10	22 26 43	1 05.6	12 06.3	14 28.7	19 32.8	25 13.2	6 04.9	29 23.0	19 46.0	8 12.2	13 02.7
9 W	11 12 53	16 29 51	28 39 43	4♌49 29	1 03.5	12 49.4	14 34.8	20 10.9	25 11.1	6 17.9	29 26.5	19 44.1	8 10.6	13 02.2
10 Th	11 16 50	17 28 10	10♌56 20	17 00 35	1 01.3	13 28.8	14 43.1	20 48.8	25 09.4	6 30.8	29 30.1	19 42.1	8 09.0	13 01.8
11 F	11 20 46	18 26 30	23 02 32	29 02 27	0 59.6	14 04.2	14 53.5	21 26.8	25 08.0	6 43.8	29 33.8	19 40.2	8 07.4	13 01.3
12 Sa	11 24 43	19 24 53	5♍00 36	10♍57 16	0 58.3	14 35.3	15 06.1	22 04.7	25 07.0	6 56.7	29 37.5	19 38.2	8 05.8	13 00.9
13 Su	11 28 39	20 23 17	16 52 42	22 47 11	0D57.6	15 01.8	15 20.7	22 42.6	25 06.3	7 09.5	29 41.3	19 36.2	8 04.2	13 00.6
14 M	11 32 36	21 21 43	28 40 59	4♎34 21	0 57.5	15 23.4	15 37.3	23 20.5	25D06.0	7 22.4	29 45.2	19 34.1	8 02.6	13 00.2
15 Tu	11 36 32	22 20 11	10♎27 38	16 21 06	0 57.8	15 39.7	15 55.8	23 58.3	25 06.1	7 35.2	29 49.2	19 32.1	8 01.0	12 59.9
16 W	11 40 29	23 18 41	22 15 06	28 09 59	0 58.5	15 50.3	16 16.2	24 36.1	25 06.5	7 48.1	29 53.3	19 30.0	7 59.4	12 59.6
17 Th	11 44 25	24 17 12	4♏06 09	10♏03 59	0 59.2	15R55.1	16 38.4	25 13.9	25 07.3	8 00.9	29 57.4	19 27.9	7 57.8	12 59.4
18 F	11 48 22	25 15 45	16 03 56	22 06 26	0 59.9	15 53.5	17 02.3	25 51.7	25 08.5	8 13.6	0♐01.6	19 25.7	7 56.2	12 59.2
19 Sa	11 52 18	26 14 20	28 11 58	4♐21 02	1 00.4	15 45.3	17 28.0	26 29.4	25 10.0	8 26.4	0 05.9	19 23.5	7 54.7	12 59.0
20 Su	11 56 15	27 12 57	10♐34 06	16 51 41	1R00.7	15 30.3	17 55.2	27 07.1	25 11.8	8 39.1	0 10.3	19 21.4	7 53.2	12 58.8
21 M	12 00 12	28 11 35	23 14 15	29 42 16	1 00.7	15 08.2	18 24.0	27 44.8	25 14.0	8 51.7	0 14.7	19 19.1	7 51.6	12 58.7
22 Tu	12 04 08	29 10 15	6♑16 09	12♑56 15	1 00.7	14 38.9	18 54.4	28 22.4	25 16.5	9 04.4	0 19.2	19 16.9	7 50.1	12 58.6
23 W	12 08 05	0♎08 57	19 42 50	26 36 05	1D00.6	14 02.6	19 26.2	29 00.0	25 19.4	9 17.0	0 23.8	19 14.7	7 48.6	12 58.5
24 Th	12 12 01	1 07 40	3♒36 03	10♒42 38	1 00.6	13 19.4	19 59.4	29 37.6	25 22.7	9 29.6	0 28.5	19 12.4	7 47.1	12D58.5
25 F	12 15 58	2 06 25	17 55 37	25 14 33	1 00.6	12 29.6	20 34.0	0♍15.2	25 26.2	9 42.1	0 33.2	19 10.1	7 45.7	12 58.5
26 Sa	12 19 54	3 05 12	2♓38 51	10♓07 45	1 00.8	11 34.0	21 09.9	0 52.7	25 30.1	9 54.6	0 38.0	19 07.8	7 44.2	12 58.5
27 Su	12 23 51	4 04 00	17 40 19	25 15 31	1R00.9	10 33.5	21 47.1	1 30.2	25 34.3	10 07.1	0 42.9	19 05.5	7 42.8	12 58.6
28 M	12 27 47	5 02 51	2♈52 11	10♈29 05	1 00.8	9 29.1	22 25.6	2 07.7	25 38.9	10 19.5	0 47.8	19 03.2	7 41.3	12 58.6
29 Tu	12 31 44	6 01 43	18 05 00	25 38 43	1 00.6	8 22.2	23 05.2	2 45.2	25 43.7	10 31.9	0 52.8	19 00.8	7 39.9	12 58.8
30 W	12 35 41	7 00 38	3♉09 09	10♉35 17	1 00.0	7 14.5	23 46.0	3 22.6	25 48.9	10 44.2	0 57.8	18 58.5	7 38.5	12 58.9

LONGITUDE — October 2015

Day	Sid.Time	☉	0 hr ☽	Noon ☽	True ☊	☿	♀	♂	⚳	♃	♄	♅	♆	♇
1 Th	12 39 37	7♎59 35	17♉56 15	25♉11 23	0♎59.3	6♎07.6	24♌27.8	4♍00.0	25♑54.4	10♍56.5	1♐03.0	18♈56.1	7♓37.2	12♑59.1
2 F	12 43 34	8 58 34	2♊20 11	9♊22 20	0R58.5	5R03.4	25 10.8	4 37.4	26 00.2	11 08.8	1 08.1	18R53.7	7R35.8	12 59.3
3 Sa	12 47 30	9 57 36	16 17 39	23 06 08	0 57.8	4 03.5	25 54.8	5 14.8	26 06.4	11 21.0	1 13.4	18 51.3	7 34.5	12 59.5
4 Su	12 51 27	10 56 40	29 47 56	6♋23 19	0D57.4	3 09.7	26 39.7	5 52.1	26 12.8	11 33.2	1 18.7	18 48.9	7 33.2	12 59.8
5 M	12 55 23	11 55 46	12♋52 35	19 16 10	0 57.5	2 23.5	27 25.7	6 29.4	26 19.5	11 45.3	1 24.1	18 46.5	7 31.9	13 00.1
6 Tu	12 59 20	12 54 54	25 34 33	1♌48 12	0 58.0	1 46.0	28 12.5	7 06.7	26 26.6	11 57.4	1 29.5	18 44.1	7 30.6	13 00.4
7 W	13 03 16	13 54 05	7♌57 40	14 03 26	0 59.1	1 18.2	29 00.2	7 44.0	26 33.9	12 09.4	1 35.0	18 41.7	7 29.3	13 00.8
8 Th	13 07 13	14 53 18	20 06 04	26 06 02	1 00.3	1 00.8	29 48.8	8 21.2	26 41.5	12 21.4	1 40.6	18 39.2	7 28.1	13 01.1
9 F	13 11 10	15 52 33	2♍03 50	7♍59 55	1 01.6	0D54.0	0♍38.2	8 58.4	26 49.5	12 33.3	1 46.2	18 36.8	7 26.9	13 01.6
10 Sa	13 15 06	16 51 51	13 54 44	19 48 41	1R02.6	0 58.1	1 28.3	9 35.6	26 57.7	12 45.1	1 51.8	18 34.4	7 25.7	13 02.0
11 Su	13 19 03	17 51 10	25 42 09	1♎35 28	1 02.9	1 12.7	2 19.3	10 12.7	27 06.2	12 56.9	1 57.6	18 31.9	7 24.5	13 02.5
12 M	13 22 59	18 50 32	7♎28 58	13 22 56	1 02.4	1 37.5	3 10.9	10 49.9	27 14.9	13 08.7	2 03.3	18 29.5	7 23.4	13 03.0
13 Tu	13 26 56	19 49 56	19 17 39	25 13 24	1 01.0	2 12.0	4 03.3	11 27.0	27 24.0	13 20.3	2 09.2	18 27.0	7 22.3	13 03.5
14 W	13 30 52	20 49 22	1♏10 23	7♏08 54	0 58.5	2 55.5	4 56.4	12 04.0	27 33.3	13 32.0	2 15.0	18 24.6	7 21.2	13 04.1
15 Th	13 34 49	21 48 49	13 09 08	19 11 22	0 55.4	3 47.2	5 50.1	12 41.1	27 42.9	13 43.5	2 21.0	18 22.2	7 20.1	13 04.7
16 F	13 38 45	22 48 19	25 15 49	1♐22 45	0 51.8	4 46.3	6 44.4	13 18.1	27 52.8	13 55.0	2 27.0	18 19.7	7 19.0	13 05.3
17 Sa	13 42 42	23 47 51	7♐32 27	13 45 10	0 48.2	5 52.2	7 39.4	13 55.0	28 02.9	14 06.4	2 33.0	18 17.3	7 18.0	13 06.0
18 Su	13 46 38	24 47 24	20 01 13	26 20 54	0 45.1	7 03.8	8 34.9	14 32.0	28 13.3	14 17.7	2 39.1	18 14.9	7 17.0	13 06.7
19 M	13 50 35	25 46 59	2♑44 33	9♑12 29	0 42.9	8 20.6	9 31.0	15 08.9	28 24.0	14 29.0	2 45.2	18 12.5	7 16.1	13 07.4
20 Tu	13 54 32	26 46 36	15 45 00	22 22 25	0D41.9	9 41.8	10 27.7	15 45.8	28 34.9	14 40.2	2 51.4	18 10.1	7 15.1	13 08.1
21 W	13 58 28	27 46 15	29 05 01	5♒53 01	0 42.1	11 06.8	11 24.9	16 22.6	28 46.0	14 51.4	2 57.6	18 07.7	7 14.2	13 08.9
22 Th	14 02 25	28 45 55	12♒46 36	19 45 52	0 43.2	12 34.9	12 22.6	16 59.4	28 57.4	15 02.4	3 03.8	18 05.3	7 13.3	13 09.7
23 F	14 06 21	29 45 37	26 50 48	4♓01 18	0 44.7	14 05.7	13 20.9	17 36.2	29 09.1	15 13.4	3 10.1	18 02.9	7 12.5	13 10.6
24 Sa	14 10 18	0♏45 21	11♓17 04	18 37 43	0R46.0	15 38.6	14 19.6	18 13.0	29 20.9	15 24.3	3 16.5	18 00.5	7 11.7	13 11.4
25 Su	14 14 14	1 45 06	26 02 41	3♈31 13	0 46.3	17 13.3	15 18.8	18 49.7	29 33.0	15 35.1	3 22.9	17 58.2	7 10.9	13 12.3
26 M	14 18 11	2 44 54	11♈02 27	18 35 22	0 45.3	18 49.4	16 18.4	19 26.4	29 45.4	15 45.9	3 29.3	17 55.9	7 10.1	13 13.2
27 Tu	14 22 07	3 44 43	26 08 51	3♉41 43	0 42.6	20 26.5	17 18.5	20 03.1	29 57.9	15 56.5	3 35.8	17 53.5	7 09.4	13 14.2
28 W	14 26 04	4 44 34	11♉12 48	18 40 56	0 38.4	22 04.5	18 19.1	20 39.7	0♒10.7	16 07.1	3 42.2	17 51.2	7 08.7	13 15.2
29 Th	14 30 01	5 44 27	26 05 01	3♊24 07	0 33.2	23 43.1	19 20.1	21 16.3	0 23.7	16 17.6	3 48.8	17 48.9	7 08.0	13 16.2
30 F	14 33 57	6 44 22	10♊37 26	17 44 20	0 27.6	25 22.1	20 21.4	21 52.9	0 36.9	16 28.0	3 55.4	17 46.7	7 07.3	13 17.2
31 Sa	14 37 54	7 44 20	24 44 24	1♋37 22	0 22.5	27 01.4	21 23.2	22 29.4	0 50.3	16 38.3	4 02.0	17 44.4	7 06.7	13 18.3

Astro Data

	Dy Hr Mn
♃□♅	3 3:52
♀ D	6 8:29
☽ 0S	14 2:09
⚳ D	14 19:14
♃☍♆	17 6:54
☿ R	17 18:10
☉ 0S	23 8:21
♇ D	25 6:58
☽ 0N	27 19:02
☿ 0N	9 10:23
☿ D	9 14:58
☽ 0S	11 8:11
♃△♇	11 23:51
☿ 0S	15 12:31
♄□♅	22 15:59

Planet Ingress

	Dy Hr Mn
♄ ♐	18 2:49
☉ ♎	23 8:21
♂ ♍	25 2:18
♀ ♍	8 17:29
☉ ♏	23 17:47
⚳ ♒	27 15:56
☽ 0N	25 6:02

Last Aspect / ☽ Ingress

Last Aspect Dy Hr Mn		☽ Ingress Dy Hr Mn
1 16:37	♅ ☌	♉ 2 9:02
4 10:20	♄ ☍	♊ 4 11:48
5 23:04	♅ ⚹	♋ 6 17:40
9 1:28	♄ △	♌ 9 2:36
11 13:03	♄ □	♍ 11 13:55
14 2:08	♄ ⚹	♎ 14 2:41
16 4:22	♂ ⚹	♏ 16 15:43
18 19:49	♂ □	♐ 19 3:32
21 8:59	☉ □	♑ 21 12:33
22 23:13	♅ □	♒ 23 17:51
25 4:02	♀ ☍	♓ 25 19:44
26 16:32	♇ ⚹	♈ 27 19:29
29 7:45	♀ △	♉ 29 18:57

Last Aspect / ☽ Ingress

Last Aspect Dy Hr Mn		☽ Ingress Dy Hr Mn
1 10:44	♀ □	♊ 1 20:03
3 17:18	♀ ⚹	♋ 4 0:22
5 11:04	♅ □	♌ 6 8:31
7 21:10	♅ △	♍ 8 19:50
9 22:12	♇ △	♎ 11 8:45
13 0:06	☉ ☌	♏ 13 21:38
15 0:58	♃ ⚹	♐ 16 9:18
18 8:48	☉ ⚹	♑ 18 18:52
20 20:31	☉ □	♒ 21 1:38
23 4:22	☉ △	♓ 23 5:18
24 11:18	♂ ☍	♈ 25 6:22
26 12:25	☿ ☍	♉ 27 6:07
28 15:20	♂ △	♊ 29 6:24
31 2:52	☿ △	♋ 31 9:09

☽ Phases & Eclipses

Dy Hr Mn	
5 9:54	☾ 12♊32
13 6:41	● 20♍10
13 6:54:09	◐ P 0.788
21 8:59	☽ 28♐04
28 2:50	○ 4♈40
28 2:47	◑ T 1.276
4 21:06	☾ 11♋19
13 0:06	● 19♎20
20 20:31	☽ 27♑08
27 12:05	○ 3♉45

Astro Data

1 September 2015
Julian Day # 42247
SVP 5♓02'26"
GC 27♐03.5 ⚴ 14♐13.2
Eris 23♈15.4R ⚵ 23♍51.2
⚷ 19♓42.5R ⚶ 11♈50.0R
☽ Mean ☊ 2♎02.5

1 October 2015
Julian Day # 42277
SVP 5♓02'24"
GC 27♐03.6 ⚴ 20♐54.6
Eris 23♈00.2R ⚵ 5♎23.4
⚷ 18♓20.6R ⚶ 5♈04.4R
☽ Mean ☊ 0♎27.2

November 2015 — LONGITUDE

Day	Sid.Time	☉	0 hr ☽	Noon ☽	True ☊	☿	♀	♂	⚳	♃	♄	♅	♆	♇
1 Su	14 41 50	8♏44 19	8♋23 11	15♋01 57	0♎18.5	28♎40.8	22♍25.4	23♍06.0	1♒04.0	16♍48.5	4♐08.6	17♈42.2	7♓06.1	13♑19.4
2 M	14 45 47	9 44 21	21 33 55	27 59 26	0R16.0	0♏20.3	23 28.0	23 42.4	1 17.8	16 58.7	4 15.3	17R40.0	7R05.6	13 20.5
3 Tu	14 49 43	10 44 24	4♌18 59	10♌33 06	0D15.2	1 59.7	24 30.9	24 18.9	1 31.9	17 08.7	4 22.0	17 37.8	7 05.1	13 21.6
4 W	14 53 40	11 44 30	16 42 22	22 47 25	0 15.8	3 38.9	25 34.2	24 55.3	1 46.1	17 18.7	4 28.7	17 35.6	7 04.6	13 22.8
5 Th	14 57 36	12 44 38	28 48 54	4♍47 27	0 17.3	5 18.0	26 37.8	25 31.7	2 00.6	17 28.5	4 35.5	17 33.5	7 04.1	13 24.0
6 F	15 01 33	13 44 48	10♍43 42	16 38 18	0 18.8	6 56.9	27 41.7	26 08.1	2 15.2	17 38.2	4 42.2	17 31.3	7 03.7	13 25.2
7 Sa	15 05 30	14 45 00	22 31 50	28 24 51	0R19.7	8 35.4	28 46.0	26 44.4	2 30.0	17 47.9	4 49.1	17 29.2	7 03.3	13 26.4
8 Su	15 09 26	15 45 14	4♎17 54	10♎11 27	0 19.1	10 13.7	29 50.5	27 20.7	2 45.1	17 57.4	4 55.9	17 27.2	7 02.9	13 27.7
9 M	15 13 23	16 45 30	16 05 55	22 01 44	0 16.5	11 51.7	0♎55.4	27 56.9	3 00.3	18 06.9	5 02.8	17 25.1	7 02.6	13 29.0
10 Tu	15 17 19	17 45 48	27 59 12	3♏58 38	0 11.6	13 29.4	2 00.5	28 33.1	3 15.7	18 16.2	5 09.7	17 23.1	7 02.3	13 30.3
11 W	15 21 16	18 46 07	10♏00 15	16 04 16	0 04.6	15 06.8	3 06.0	29 09.3	3 31.3	18 25.4	5 16.6	17 21.1	7 02.0	13 31.7
12 Th	15 25 12	19 46 29	22 10 50	28 20 05	29♍55.8	16 43.8	4 11.7	29 45.4	3 47.0	18 34.5	5 23.5	17 19.2	7 01.8	13 33.0
13 F	15 29 09	20 46 52	4♐32 04	10♐46 53	29 46.0	18 20.5	5 17.6	0♎21.5	4 03.0	18 43.5	5 30.5	17 17.3	7 01.6	13 34.4
14 Sa	15 33 05	21 47 16	17 04 35	23 25 11	29 36.2	19 57.0	6 23.9	0 57.6	4 19.1	18 52.4	5 37.4	17 15.4	7 01.4	13 35.8
15 Su	15 37 02	22 47 43	29 48 46	6♑15 20	29 27.3	21 33.1	7 30.3	1 33.6	4 35.4	19 01.2	5 44.4	17 13.5	7 01.3	13 37.3
16 M	15 40 59	23 48 10	12♑45 00	19 17 49	29 20.2	23 08.9	8 37.0	2 09.6	4 51.8	19 09.8	5 51.4	17 11.7	7 01.2	13 38.8
17 Tu	15 44 55	24 48 39	25 53 54	2♒33 21	29 15.5	24 44.5	9 44.0	2 45.5	5 08.4	19 18.4	5 58.4	17 09.9	7 01.2	13 40.2
18 W	15 48 52	25 49 09	9♒16 19	16 02 55	29D13.1	26 19.7	10 51.2	3 21.4	5 25.2	19 26.8	6 05.5	17 08.2	7D01.1	13 41.8
19 Th	15 52 48	26 49 41	22 53 18	29 47 36	29 12.7	27 54.8	11 58.5	3 57.3	5 42.1	19 35.0	6 12.5	17 06.4	7 01.2	13 43.3
20 F	15 56 45	27 50 13	6♓45 52	13♓48 09	29 13.3	29 29.6	13 06.1	4 33.1	5 59.2	19 43.2	6 19.6	17 04.8	7 01.2	13 44.8
21 Sa	16 00 41	28 50 47	20 54 24	28 04 30	29R13.9	1♐04.1	14 13.9	5 08.8	6 16.4	19 51.2	6 26.7	17 03.1	7 01.3	13 46.4
22 Su	16 04 38	29 51 22	5♈18 12	12♈35 07	29 13.2	2 38.5	15 22.0	5 44.6	6 33.8	19 59.1	6 33.7	17 01.5	7 01.4	13 48.0
23 M	16 08 34	0♐51 58	19 54 45	27 16 29	29 10.2	4 12.6	16 30.2	6 20.2	6 51.4	20 06.9	6 40.8	16 59.9	7 01.5	13 49.6
24 Tu	16 12 31	1 52 35	4♉39 33	12♉03 02	29 04.6	5 46.6	17 38.6	6 55.9	7 09.0	20 14.5	6 47.9	16 58.4	7 01.7	13 51.2
25 W	16 16 28	2 53 14	19 26 01	26 47 29	28 56.4	7 20.5	18 47.2	7 31.5	7 26.9	20 22.0	6 55.0	16 56.9	7 01.9	13 52.9
26 Th	16 20 24	3 53 54	4♊06 25	11♊21 51	28 46.3	8 54.2	19 56.0	8 07.0	7 44.8	20 29.4	7 02.1	16 55.5	7 02.2	13 54.6
27 F	16 24 21	4 54 36	18 32 53	25 38 45	28 35.3	10 27.8	21 04.9	8 42.5	8 02.9	20 36.7	7 09.2	16 54.1	7 02.5	13 56.3
28 Sa	16 28 17	5 55 19	2♋38 49	9♋32 38	28 24.8	12 01.2	22 14.1	9 18.0	8 21.1	20 43.8	7 16.3	16 52.7	7 02.8	13 58.0
29 Su	16 32 14	6 56 03	16 19 54	23 00 30	28 15.7	13 34.6	23 23.4	9 53.4	8 39.5	20 50.7	7 23.5	16 51.4	7 03.2	13 59.7
30 M	16 36 10	7 56 49	29 34 28	6♌02 02	28 08.8	15 07.8	24 32.9	10 28.8	8 58.0	20 57.5	7 30.6	16 50.1	7 03.5	14 01.4

December 2015 — LONGITUDE

Day	Sid.Time	☉	0 hr ☽	Noon ☽	True ☊	☿	♀	♂	⚳	♃	♄	♅	♆	♇
1 Tu	16 40 07	8♐57 36	12♌23 30	18♌39 18	28♍04.6	16♐41.0	25♎42.6	11♎04.1	9♒16.6	21♍04.2	7♐37.7	16♈48.9	7♓04.0	14♑03.2
2 W	16 44 03	9 58 25	24 49 59	0♍56 08	28D02.6	18 14.1	26 52.4	11 39.4	9 35.4	21 10.7	7 44.8	16R47.7	7 04.4	14 05.0
3 Th	16 48 00	10 59 15	6♍58 24	12 57 27	28 02.2	19 47.2	28 02.3	12 14.6	9 54.2	21 17.1	7 51.9	16 46.5	7 04.9	14 06.8
4 F	16 51 57	12 00 07	18 54 01	24 48 47	28R02.5	21 20.2	29 12.4	12 49.8	10 13.2	21 23.3	7 59.0	16 45.4	7 05.4	14 08.6
5 Sa	16 55 53	13 01 00	0♎42 27	6♎35 42	28 02.2	22 53.1	0♏22.7	13 24.9	10 32.3	21 29.4	8 06.1	16 44.4	7 06.0	14 10.4
6 Su	16 59 50	14 01 54	12 29 12	18 23 34	28 00.3	24 25.9	1 33.1	14 00.0	10 51.6	21 35.3	8 13.2	16 43.4	7 06.6	14 12.2
7 M	17 03 46	15 02 49	24 19 23	0♏17 09	27 56.1	25 58.7	2 43.6	14 35.0	11 10.9	21 41.1	8 20.3	16 42.4	7 07.2	14 14.1
8 Tu	17 07 43	16 03 46	6♏17 21	12 20 23	27 48.9	27 31.3	3 54.3	15 10.0	11 30.4	21 46.7	8 27.4	16 41.5	7 07.9	14 16.0
9 W	17 11 39	17 04 44	18 26 35	24 36 13	27 38.9	29 03.9	5 05.1	15 44.9	11 50.0	21 52.1	8 34.5	16 40.6	7 08.6	14 17.9
10 Th	17 15 36	18 05 43	0♐49 27	7♐06 23	27 26.6	0♑36.3	6 16.0	16 19.8	12 09.7	21 57.4	8 41.5	16 39.8	7 09.3	14 19.8
11 F	17 19 32	19 06 43	13 27 04	19 51 27	27 12.8	2 08.5	7 27.0	16 54.6	12 29.5	22 02.6	8 48.6	16 39.0	7 10.1	14 21.7
12 Sa	17 23 29	20 07 44	26 19 26	2♑50 52	26 58.9	3 40.6	8 38.1	17 29.3	12 49.4	22 07.5	8 55.6	16 38.3	7 10.9	14 23.6
13 Su	17 27 26	21 08 45	9♑25 34	16 03 18	26 46.2	5 12.3	9 49.4	18 04.0	13 09.4	22 12.3	9 02.7	16 37.6	7 11.7	14 25.5
14 M	17 31 22	22 09 47	22 43 52	29 27 02	26 35.7	6 43.7	11 00.7	18 38.6	13 29.5	22 16.9	9 09.7	16 37.0	7 12.6	14 27.5
15 Tu	17 35 19	23 10 50	6♒12 37	13♒00 25	26 28.2	8 14.8	12 12.2	19 13.1	13 49.8	22 21.4	9 16.7	16 36.4	7 13.5	14 29.4
16 W	17 39 15	24 11 53	19 50 19	26 42 12	26 23.7	9 45.3	13 23.7	19 47.6	14 10.1	22 25.7	9 23.6	16 35.9	7 14.4	14 31.4
17 Th	17 43 12	25 12 57	3♓36 00	10♓31 42	26 21.8	11 15.2	14 35.4	20 22.0	14 30.5	22 29.8	9 30.6	16 35.4	7 15.4	14 33.4
18 F	17 47 08	26 14 01	17 29 17	24 28 45	26 21.5	12 44.4	15 47.1	20 56.4	14 51.0	22 33.7	9 37.5	16 35.0	7 16.4	14 35.4
19 Sa	17 51 05	27 15 05	1♈30 04	8♈33 13	26 21.3	14 12.6	16 58.9	21 30.7	15 11.6	22 37.5	9 44.4	16 34.7	7 17.4	14 37.4
20 Su	17 55 01	28 16 10	15 38 06	22 44 36	26 19.9	15 39.9	18 10.8	22 04.9	15 32.3	22 41.1	9 51.3	16 34.3	7 18.4	14 39.4
21 M	17 58 58	29 17 15	29 52 27	7♉01 24	26 16.3	17 05.8	19 22.8	22 39.1	15 53.1	22 44.5	9 58.2	16 34.1	7 19.5	14 41.4
22 Tu	18 02 55	0♑18 20	14♉11 00	21 20 46	26 09.6	18 30.2	20 34.9	23 13.1	16 13.9	22 47.7	10 05.0	16 33.8	7 20.6	14 43.4
23 W	18 06 51	1 19 25	28 30 09	5♊38 29	26 00.1	19 52.7	21 47.0	23 47.2	16 34.9	22 50.7	10 11.8	16 33.7	7 21.8	14 45.4
24 Th	18 10 48	2 20 31	12♊45 06	19 49 16	25 48.4	21 13.1	22 59.3	24 21.1	16 55.9	22 53.6	10 18.6	16 33.6	7 23.0	14 47.5
25 F	18 14 44	3 21 37	26 50 18	3♋47 34	25 35.5	22 30.9	24 11.6	24 55.0	17 17.1	22 56.3	10 25.4	16D33.5	7 24.2	14 49.5
26 Sa	18 18 41	4 22 44	10♋40 28	17 28 33	25 22.9	23 45.7	25 24.0	25 28.8	17 38.2	22 58.8	10 32.1	16 33.5	7 25.4	14 51.6
27 Su	18 22 37	5 23 51	24 11 25	0♌48 51	25 11.8	24 57.0	26 36.5	26 02.5	17 59.5	23 01.1	10 38.8	16 33.5	7 26.7	14 53.6
28 M	18 26 34	6 24 58	7♌20 44	13 47 05	25 03.1	26 04.2	27 49.0	26 36.2	18 20.9	23 03.3	10 45.5	16 33.6	7 28.0	14 55.7
29 Tu	18 30 31	7 26 06	20 08 04	26 23 55	24 57.1	27 06.7	29 01.6	27 09.8	18 42.3	23 05.2	10 52.1	16 33.8	7 29.3	14 57.7
30 W	18 34 27	8 27 14	2♍35 02	8♍41 50	24 53.9	28 03.6	0♐14.3	27 43.3	19 03.8	23 07.0	10 58.7	16 34.0	7 30.7	14 59.8
31 Th	18 38 24	9 28 22	14 44 53	20 44 44	24D52.8	28 54.3	1 27.1	28 16.7	19 25.4	23 08.6	11 05.3	16 34.2	7 32.0	15 01.9

Astro Data

	Dy Hr Mn
♃⊼♅	5 22:01
☽0S	7 15:03
♀0S	11 10:39
♂0S	18 9:58
♆D	18 16:31
☽0N	21 15:32
♄□♆	26 12:15
☽0S	4 23:35
☽0N	18 23:01
♅D	26 3:53

Planet Ingress

	Dy Hr Mn
☿ ♏	2 7:06
♀ ♎	8 15:31
☊ ♍R	12 0:57
♂ ♎	12 21:41
☿ ♐	20 19:43
☉ ♐	22 15:25
♀ ♏	5 4:15
☿ ♑	10 2:34
☉ ♑	22 4:48
♀ ♐	30 7:16

Last Aspect / ☽ Ingress (November)

Last Aspect Dy Hr Mn		☽ Ingress Dy Hr Mn
2 3:35 ♂ ⚹	♌	2 15:48
4 1:46 ♅ △	♍	5 2:22
7 12:47 ♀ ☌	♎	7 15:14
9 2:42 ♅ ☍	♏	10 4:02
12 14:54 ♂ ⚹	♐	12 15:14
14 3:18 ♃ □	♑	15 0:21
16 20:53 ☉ ⚹	♒	17 7:24
19 8:19 ☿ □	♓	19 12:21
21 13:23 ☉ △	♈	21 15:12
22 19:16 ♅ ☌	♉	23 16:26
25 1:26 ♃ △	♊	25 17:15
27 3:35 ♀ △	♋	27 19:27
29 12:46 ♀ □	♌	30 0:47

Last Aspect / ☽ Ingress (December)

Last Aspect Dy Hr Mn		☽ Ingress Dy Hr Mn
2 3:09 ♀ ⚹	♍	2 10:09
4 4:59 ♃ ☌	♎	4 22:34
7 2:03 ☿ ⚹	♏	7 11:26
9 6:39 ♃ ⚹	♐	9 22:25
11 16:06 ♃ □	♑	12 6:46
13 23:07 ♃ △	♒	14 12:59
16 7:17 ☉ ⚹	♓	16 17:45
18 15:14 ☉ □	♈	18 21:26
20 22:01 ☉ △	♉	21 0:13
22 14:26 ♃ △	♊	23 2:31
24 20:04 ♂ △	♋	25 5:26
27 3:36 ♀ △	♌	27 10:31
29 17:38 ♀ □	♍	29 18:58

☽ Phases & Eclipses

Dy Hr Mn	
3 12:24	☾ 10♌45
11 17:47	● 19♏01
19 6:27	☽ 26♒36
25 22:44	○ 3♊20
3 7:40	☾ 10♍48
11 10:29	● 19♐03
18 15:14	☽ 26♓22
25 11:12	○ 3♋20

Astro Data

1 November 2015
Julian Day # 42308
SVP 5♓02'21"
GC 27♐03.6 ⚴ 0♑20.6
Eris 22♈41.9R ⚵ 16♎54.1
⚷ 17♓16.2R ⚶ 29♓09.1R
☽ Mean ☊ 28♍48.7

1 December 2015
Julian Day # 42338
SVP 5♓02'16"
GC 27♐03.7 ⚴ 10♑47.0
Eris 22♈26.8R ⚵ 27♎12.6
⚷ 16♓56.6 ⚶ 29♓42.5
☽ Mean ☊ 27♍13.3

LONGITUDE — January 2016

Day	Sid.Time	☉	0 hr ☽	Noon ☽	True ☊	☿	♀	♂	⚳	♃	♄	♅	♆	♇
1 F	18 42 20	10♑29 31	26♍42 03	2♎37 30	24♍52.9	29♑37.8	2♐39.9	28♎50.0	19♒47.0	23♍09.9	11♐11.8	16♈34.5	7♓33.5	15♑03.9
2 Sa	18 46 17	11 30 40	8♎31 45	14 25 32	24R 53.0	0♒13.3	3 52.8	29 23.3	20 08.7	23 11.1	11 18.3	16 34.9	7 34.9	15 06.0
3 Su	18 50 13	12 31 50	20 19 33	26 14 28	24 52.0	0 39.8	5 05.7	29 56.5	20 30.5	23 12.1	11 24.8	16 35.3	7 36.4	15 08.1
4 M	18 54 10	13 32 59	2♏10 59	8♏09 43	24 49.1	0 56.5	6 18.7	0♏29.6	20 52.4	23 13.0	11 31.2	16 35.7	7 37.9	15 10.2
5 Tu	18 58 06	14 34 09	14 11 17	20 16 13	24 43.6	1R 02.6	7 31.8	1 02.6	21 14.3	23 13.6	11 37.6	16 36.3	7 39.4	15 12.2
6 W	19 02 03	15 35 20	26 25 00	2♐38 02	24 35.5	0 57.4	8 44.9	1 35.5	21 36.3	23 14.0	11 43.9	16 36.8	7 40.9	15 14.3
7 Th	19 06 00	16 36 30	8♐55 37	15 17 59	24 25.1	0 40.4	9 58.0	2 08.3	21 58.4	23R 14.2	11 50.2	16 37.4	7 42.5	15 16.4
8 F	19 09 56	17 37 41	21 45 16	28 17 26	24 13.4	0 11.6	11 11.2	2 41.1	22 20.5	23 14.3	11 56.4	16 38.1	7 44.1	15 18.5
9 Sa	19 13 53	18 38 51	4♑54 26	11♑36 02	24 01.3	29♑31.2	12 24.5	3 13.7	22 42.6	23 14.1	12 02.6	16 38.8	7 45.7	15 20.6
10 Su	19 17 49	19 40 01	18 21 58	25 11 50	23 50.2	28 39.9	13 37.8	3 46.2	23 04.9	23 13.8	12 08.8	16 39.6	7 47.4	15 22.6
11 M	19 21 46	20 41 11	2♒05 13	9♒01 36	23 41.0	27 38.9	14 51.1	4 18.7	23 27.2	23 13.2	12 14.9	16 40.4	7 49.0	15 24.7
12 Tu	19 25 42	21 42 21	16 00 31	23 01 26	23 34.6	26 29.9	16 04.5	4 51.0	23 49.5	23 12.5	12 20.9	16 41.3	7 50.7	15 26.8
13 W	19 29 39	22 43 30	0♓03 53	7♓07 25	23 30.9	25 15.1	17 17.9	5 23.2	24 11.9	23 11.5	12 27.0	16 42.2	7 52.5	15 28.9
14 Th	19 33 35	23 44 38	14 11 37	21 16 10	23D 29.8	23 56.8	18 31.4	5 55.3	24 34.4	23 10.4	12 32.9	16 43.2	7 54.2	15 30.9
15 F	19 37 32	24 45 46	28 20 46	5♈25 11	23 30.1	22 37.5	19 44.8	6 27.3	24 56.9	23 09.1	12 38.8	16 44.2	7 56.0	15 33.0
16 Sa	19 41 29	25 46 53	12♈29 15	19 32 49	23R 30.9	21 19.6	20 58.3	6 59.2	25 19.5	23 07.6	12 44.6	16 45.3	7 57.7	15 35.0
17 Su	19 45 25	26 47 59	26 35 46	3♉38 00	23 30.8	20 05.6	22 11.9	7 30.9	25 42.1	23 05.9	12 50.4	16 46.4	7 59.6	15 37.1
18 M	19 49 22	27 49 05	10♉39 22	17 39 46	23 28.9	18 57.2	23 25.5	8 02.6	26 04.7	23 04.0	12 56.2	16 47.6	8 01.4	15 39.1
19 Tu	19 53 18	28 50 09	24 39 01	1♊36 56	23 24.7	17 56.0	24 39.1	8 34.1	26 27.4	23 01.9	13 01.9	16 48.8	8 03.2	15 41.2
20 W	19 57 15	29 51 13	8♊33 18	15 27 49	23 18.2	17 03.1	25 52.7	9 05.6	26 50.2	22 59.6	13 07.5	16 50.1	8 05.1	15 43.2
21 Th	20 01 11	0♒52 16	22 20 12	29 10 08	23 09.9	16 19.1	27 06.4	9 36.9	27 12.9	22 57.2	13 13.0	16 51.4	8 07.0	15 45.2
22 F	20 05 08	1 53 19	5♋57 17	12♋41 20	23 00.6	15 44.5	28 20.1	10 08.1	27 35.8	22 54.5	13 18.5	16 52.7	8 08.9	15 47.2
23 Sa	20 09 04	2 54 20	19 21 58	25 58 55	22 51.4	15 19.2	29 33.8	10 39.1	27 58.6	22 51.7	13 24.0	16 54.2	8 10.8	15 49.2
24 Su	20 13 01	3 55 21	2♌31 57	9♌00 55	22 43.3	15 02.9	0♑47.6	11 10.1	28 21.6	22 48.7	13 29.4	16 55.6	8 12.8	15 51.2
25 M	20 16 58	4 56 20	15 25 42	21 46 19	22 37.0	14D 55.4	2 01.3	11 40.9	28 44.5	22 45.5	13 34.7	16 57.1	8 14.8	15 53.2
26 Tu	20 20 54	5 57 20	28 02 48	4♍15 18	22 32.9	14 56.1	3 15.2	12 11.6	29 07.5	22 42.1	13 39.9	16 58.7	8 16.7	15 55.2
27 W	20 24 51	6 58 18	10♍24 01	16 29 17	22D 31.0	15 04.5	4 29.0	12 42.1	29 30.5	22 38.6	13 45.1	17 00.3	8 18.7	15 57.2
28 Th	20 28 47	7 59 16	22 31 26	28 30 55	22 30.9	15 20.0	5 42.8	13 12.5	29 53.6	22 34.8	13 50.2	17 01.9	8 20.8	15 59.1
29 F	20 32 44	9 00 13	4♎28 11	10♎23 48	22 32.1	15 42.1	6 56.7	13 42.8	0♓16.7	22 30.9	13 55.3	17 03.6	8 22.8	16 01.1
30 Sa	20 36 40	10 01 09	16 18 20	22 12 23	22 33.8	16 10.1	8 10.6	14 12.9	0 39.8	22 26.9	14 00.3	17 05.4	8 24.8	16 03.0
31 Su	20 40 37	11 02 05	28 06 35	4♏01 36	22R 35.1	16 43.7	9 24.6	14 42.9	1 02.9	22 22.6	14 05.2	17 07.1	8 26.9	16 05.0

LONGITUDE — February 2016

Day	Sid.Time	☉	0 hr ☽	Noon ☽	True ☊	☿	♀	♂	⚳	♃	♄	♅	♆	♇
1 M	20 44 33	12♒03 00	9♏58 05	15♏56 41	22♍35.3	17♑22.2	10♑38.5	15♏12.7	1♓26.1	22♍18.2	14♐10.0	17♈09.0	8♓29.0	16♑06.9
2 Tu	20 48 30	13 03 54	21 58 04	28 02 50	22R 33.9	18 05.3	11 52.5	15 42.4	1 49.4	22R 13.6	14 14.8	17 10.8	8 31.1	16 08.8
3 W	20 52 27	14 04 47	4♐11 35	10♐24 51	22 30.8	18 52.5	13 06.5	16 11.9	2 12.6	22 08.9	14 19.5	17 12.8	8 33.2	16 10.7
4 Th	20 56 23	15 05 40	16 43 06	23 06 45	22 26.2	19 43.5	14 20.5	16 41.3	2 35.9	22 04.0	14 24.2	17 14.7	8 35.3	16 12.5
5 F	21 00 20	16 06 32	29 36 04	6♑11 17	22 20.6	20 37.9	15 34.6	17 10.5	2 59.2	21 58.9	14 28.7	17 16.7	8 37.4	16 14.4
6 Sa	21 04 16	17 07 22	12♑52 26	19 39 29	22 14.3	21 35.5	16 48.6	17 39.5	3 22.6	21 53.7	14 33.2	17 18.8	8 39.6	16 16.3
7 Su	21 08 13	18 08 12	26 32 15	3♒30 23	22 08.6	22 35.9	18 02.7	18 08.4	3 45.9	21 48.3	14 37.6	17 20.9	8 41.7	16 18.1
8 M	21 12 09	19 09 01	10♒33 27	17 40 52	22 03.9	23 38.9	19 16.8	18 37.0	4 09.3	21 42.8	14 41.9	17 23.0	8 43.9	16 19.9
9 Tu	21 16 06	20 09 48	24 51 59	2♓06 04	22 00.8	24 44.3	20 30.8	19 05.5	4 32.7	21 37.1	14 46.2	17 25.1	8 46.1	16 21.7
10 W	21 20 02	21 10 34	9♓22 19	16 39 58	21D 59.5	25 52.0	21 44.9	19 33.8	4 56.2	21 31.3	14 50.3	17 27.3	8 48.3	16 23.5
11 Th	21 23 59	22 11 18	23 58 12	1♈16 18	21 59.6	27 01.7	22 59.1	20 01.9	5 19.6	21 25.4	14 54.4	17 29.6	8 50.5	16 25.3
12 F	21 27 56	23 12 01	8♈33 34	15 49 23	22 00.8	28 13.3	24 13.2	20 29.9	5 43.1	21 19.3	14 58.4	17 31.9	8 52.7	16 27.0
13 Sa	21 31 52	24 12 42	23 03 14	0♉14 41	22 02.3	29 26.7	25 27.3	20 57.6	6 06.6	21 13.1	15 02.4	17 34.2	8 54.9	16 28.7
14 Su	21 35 49	25 13 22	7♉23 22	14 29 01	22R 03.6	0♒41.8	26 41.4	21 25.1	6 30.1	21 06.7	15 06.2	17 36.6	8 57.1	16 30.5
15 M	21 39 45	26 14 00	21 31 27	28 30 31	22 03.9	1 58.4	27 55.6	21 52.4	6 53.6	21 00.3	15 10.0	17 39.0	8 59.3	16 32.2
16 Tu	21 43 42	27 14 36	5♊26 08	12♊18 17	22 03.1	3 16.5	29 09.7	22 19.5	7 17.2	20 53.7	15 13.6	17 41.4	9 01.6	16 33.8
17 W	21 47 38	28 15 10	19 06 56	25 52 05	22 01.1	4 36.1	0♒23.8	22 46.4	7 40.7	20 47.1	15 17.2	17 43.9	9 03.8	16 35.5
18 Th	21 51 35	29 15 43	2♋33 46	9♋12 00	21 58.2	5 57.0	1 38.0	23 13.1	8 04.3	20 40.3	15 20.7	17 46.4	9 06.1	16 37.1
19 F	21 55 31	0♓16 14	15 46 50	22 18 16	21 54.8	7 19.1	2 52.2	23 39.6	8 27.8	20 33.4	15 24.1	17 48.9	9 08.3	16 38.8
20 Sa	21 59 28	1 16 43	28 46 22	5♌11 09	21 51.4	8 42.5	4 06.3	24 05.8	8 51.4	20 26.4	15 27.5	17 51.5	9 10.6	16 40.4
21 Su	22 03 24	2 17 10	11♌32 40	17 51 00	21 48.5	10 07.1	5 20.5	24 31.8	9 15.0	20 19.4	15 30.7	17 54.1	9 12.8	16 41.9
22 M	22 07 21	3 17 36	24 06 12	0♍18 23	21 46.3	11 32.9	6 34.7	24 57.6	9 38.6	20 12.2	15 33.8	17 56.7	9 15.1	16 43.5
23 Tu	22 11 18	4 18 00	6♍27 39	12 34 09	21D 45.1	12 59.8	7 48.9	25 23.1	10 02.2	20 05.0	15 36.9	17 59.4	9 17.4	16 45.0
24 W	22 15 14	5 18 23	18 38 05	24 39 39	21 44.9	14 27.8	9 03.1	25 48.4	10 25.9	19 57.7	15 39.9	18 02.1	9 19.6	16 46.5
25 Th	22 19 11	6 18 44	0♎39 08	6♎36 48	21 45.5	15 56.9	10 17.3	26 13.5	10 49.5	19 50.3	15 42.8	18 04.8	9 21.9	16 48.0
26 F	22 23 07	7 19 03	12 33 00	18 28 06	21 46.6	17 27.1	11 31.5	26 38.3	11 13.1	19 42.8	15 45.5	18 07.6	9 24.2	16 49.5
27 Sa	22 27 04	8 19 21	24 22 30	0♏16 41	21 47.9	18 58.3	12 45.7	27 02.8	11 36.8	19 35.3	15 48.2	18 10.4	9 26.5	16 51.0
28 Su	22 31 00	9 19 37	6♏11 08	12 06 20	21 49.2	20 30.6	13 59.9	27 27.1	12 00.4	19 27.7	15 50.8	18 13.2	9 28.8	16 52.4
29 M	22 34 57	10 19 52	18 02 50	24 01 13	21 50.2	22 04.0	15 14.1	27 51.0	12 24.1	19 20.1	15 53.3	18 16.1	9 31.0	16 53.8

Astro Data (Dy Hr Mn)

☽0S 1 9:21
☿R 5 13:06
♃R 8 4:40
☽0N 15 5:40
☿D 25 21:50
☽0S 28 18:57

☽0N 11 13:25
☽0S 25 3:09

Planet Ingress (Dy Hr Mn)

☿ ♒ 2 2:20
♂ ♏ 3 14:32
☿ ♑R 8 19:36
☉ ♒ 20 15:27
♀ ♑ 23 20:31
⚳ ♓ 28 18:42

☿ ♒ 13 22:43
♀ ♒ 17 4:17
☉ ♓ 19 5:34

Last Aspect (Dy Hr Mn) / **☽ Ingress** (Dy Hr Mn)

1 5:33 ☿ △ ♎ 1 6:41
2 16:23 ♅ ☍ ♏ 3 19:36
5 17:47 ♃ ⚹ ♐ 6 6:56
8 2:44 ♃ □ ♑ 8 15:07
10 17:39 ☿ ☌ ♒ 10 20:23
12 1:09 ♅ ⚹ ♓ 12 23:53
14 16:31 ☉ ⚹ ♈ 15 2:48
16 23:26 ☉ □ ♉ 17 5:48
19 6:50 ☉ △ ♊ 19 9:13
21 8:01 ♀ ☍ ♋ 21 13:28
23 6:21 ♃ ⚹ ♌ 23 19:21
25 2:51 ♅ △ ♍ 26 3:46
28 0:11 ♃ ☌ ♎ 28 14:59
30 1:34 ♅ ☍ ♏ 31 3:50

Last Aspect (Dy Hr Mn) / **☽ Ingress** (Dy Hr Mn)

2 0:35 ♃ ⚹ ♐ 2 15:50
4 10:04 ♃ □ ♑ 5 0:44
6 15:54 ♃ △ ♒ 7 5:59
8 14:39 ☉ ☌ ♓ 9 8:31
11 4:25 ☿ ⚹ ♈ 11 9:55
13 10:32 ☿ □ ♉ 13 11:35
15 10:54 ♀ △ ♊ 15 14:35
17 16:37 ☉ △ ♋ 17 19:24
19 14:36 ♂ △ ♌ 20 2:17
22 1:17 ♂ □ ♍ 22 11:24
24 14:22 ♂ ⚹ ♎ 24 22:41
26 11:18 ♅ ☍ ♏ 27 11:26
29 19:55 ♂ ☌ ♐ 29 23:56

☽ Phases & Eclipses (Dy Hr Mn)

2 5:30 ☾ 11♎14
10 1:31 ● 19♑13
16 23:26 ☽ 26♈16
24 1:46 ○ 3♌29

1 3:28 ☾ 11♏41
8 14:39 ● 19♒16
15 7:46 ☽ 26♉03
22 18:20 ○ 3♍34

Astro Data

1 January 2016
Julian Day # 42369
SVP 5♓02'11"
GC 27♐03.8 ⚴ 22♑09.4
Eris 22♈18.8R ⚵ 6♏18.9
⚷ 17♓29.0 ⚶ 6♈06.0
☽ Mean ☊ 25♍34.9

1 February 2016
Julian Day # 42400
SVP 5♓02'07"
GC 27♐03.8 ⚴ 3♒31.6
Eris 22♈21.0 ⚵ 12♏47.8
⚷ 18♓47.4 ⚶ 16♈07.5
☽ Mean ☊ 23♍56.4

March 2016

LONGITUDE

Day	Sid.Time	☉	0 hr ☽	Noon☽	True☊	☿	♀	♂	⚳	♃	♄	♅	♆	♇
1 Tu	22 38 53	11♓20 05	0♐02 04	6♐05 56	21♍50.7	23♒38.4	16♒28.3	28♏14.7	12♓47.7	19♍12.5	15♐55.8	18♈18.9	9♓33.3	16♑55.2
2 W	22 42 50	12 20 17	12 13 26	18 25 08	21R 50.7	25 13.9	17 42.6	28 38.2	13 11.4	19R 04.7	15 58.1	18 21.8	9 35.6	16 56.5
3 Th	22 46 47	13 20 27	24 41 35	1♑03 16	21 50.2	26 50.4	18 56.8	29 01.3	13 35.0	18 57.0	16 00.3	18 24.8	9 37.9	16 57.9
4 F	22 50 43	14 20 36	7♑30 40	14 04 10	21 49.5	28 28.0	20 11.0	29 24.1	13 58.7	18 49.2	16 02.4	18 27.7	9 40.1	16 59.2
5 Sa	22 54 40	15 20 44	20 44 02	27 30 27	21 48.7	0♓06.7	21 25.3	29 46.6	14 22.3	18 41.4	16 04.5	18 30.7	9 42.4	17 00.5
6 Su	22 58 36	16 20 49	4♒23 29	11♒23 02	21 47.9	1 46.4	22 39.5	0♐08.8	14 46.0	18 33.6	16 06.4	18 33.7	9 44.7	17 01.7
7 M	23 02 33	17 20 53	18 28 52	25 40 35	21 47.4	3 27.2	23 53.8	0 30.6	15 09.7	18 25.8	16 08.3	18 36.8	9 47.0	17 02.9
8 Tu	23 06 29	18 20 55	2♓57 36	10♓19 14	21D 47.2	5 09.2	25 08.0	0 52.1	15 33.3	18 17.9	16 10.0	18 39.8	9 49.2	17 04.2
9 W	23 10 26	19 20 55	17 44 36	25 12 46	21 47.1	6 52.3	26 22.3	1 13.3	15 57.0	18 10.1	16 11.6	18 42.9	9 51.5	17 05.3
10 Th	23 14 22	20 20 54	2♈42 41	10♈13 17	21 47.2	8 36.5	27 36.5	1 34.1	16 20.6	18 02.3	16 13.2	18 46.0	9 53.7	17 06.5
11 F	23 18 19	21 20 50	17 43 29	25 12 15	21R 47.2	10 21.8	28 50.7	1 54.5	16 44.2	17 54.5	16 14.6	18 49.1	9 56.0	17 07.6
12 Sa	23 22 16	22 20 44	2♉38 37	10♉01 43	21 47.2	12 08.3	0♓05.0	2 14.6	17 07.9	17 46.7	16 16.0	18 52.3	9 58.2	17 08.7
13 Su	23 26 12	23 20 36	17 20 50	24 35 21	21 47.1	13 55.9	1 19.2	2 34.3	17 31.5	17 38.9	16 17.2	18 55.4	10 00.4	17 09.8
14 M	23 30 09	24 20 26	1♊44 51	8♊48 59	21 47.0	15 44.8	2 33.4	2 53.6	17 55.1	17 31.1	16 18.3	18 58.6	10 02.7	17 10.8
15 Tu	23 34 05	25 20 13	15 47 37	22 40 41	21D 46.9	17 34.8	3 47.6	3 12.6	18 18.7	17 23.4	16 19.4	19 01.8	10 04.9	17 11.8
16 W	23 38 02	26 19 59	29 28 14	6♋10 25	21 47.0	19 26.0	5 01.8	3 31.1	18 42.2	17 15.7	16 20.3	19 05.0	10 07.1	17 12.8
17 Th	23 41 58	27 19 42	12♋47 26	19 19 33	21 47.3	21 18.4	6 16.0	3 49.2	19 05.8	17 08.1	16 21.2	19 08.3	10 09.3	17 13.8
18 F	23 45 55	28 19 22	25 47 04	2♌10 17	21 47.8	23 11.9	7 30.2	4 07.0	19 29.4	17 00.5	16 21.9	19 11.5	10 11.5	17 14.7
19 Sa	23 49 51	29 19 01	8♌29 34	14 45 13	21 48.6	25 06.7	8 44.4	4 24.3	19 52.9	16 53.0	16 22.6	19 14.8	10 13.7	17 15.6
20 Su	23 53 48	0♈18 37	20 57 34	27 06 57	21 49.4	27 02.5	9 58.6	4 41.1	20 16.4	16 45.6	16 23.1	19 18.1	10 15.9	17 16.5
21 M	23 57 45	1 18 11	3♍13 39	9♍17 59	21 50.0	28 59.5	11 12.8	4 57.6	20 39.9	16 38.2	16 23.5	19 21.4	10 18.0	17 17.4
22 Tu	0 01 41	2 17 43	15 20 12	21 20 35	21R 50.3	0♈57.6	12 27.0	5 13.5	21 03.4	16 30.8	16 23.9	19 24.7	10 20.2	17 18.2
23 W	0 05 38	3 17 13	27 19 23	3♎16 50	21 50.0	2 56.7	13 41.1	5 29.0	21 26.9	16 23.6	16 24.1	19 28.0	10 22.3	17 19.0
24 Th	0 09 34	4 16 40	9♎13 13	15 08 45	21 49.1	4 56.7	14 55.3	5 44.1	21 50.3	16 16.4	16R 24.3	19 31.3	10 24.4	17 19.7
25 F	0 13 31	5 16 06	21 03 42	26 58 21	21 47.5	6 57.5	16 09.5	5 58.7	22 13.8	16 09.3	16 24.3	19 34.7	10 26.6	17 20.5
26 Sa	0 17 27	6 15 30	2♏52 58	8♏47 51	21 45.4	8 59.1	17 23.6	6 12.7	22 37.2	16 02.3	16 24.3	19 38.0	10 28.7	17 21.2
27 Su	0 21 24	7 14 52	14 43 19	20 39 45	21 43.0	11 01.2	18 37.8	6 26.3	23 00.6	15 55.4	16 24.1	19 41.4	10 30.8	17 21.9
28 M	0 25 20	8 14 12	26 37 30	2♐36 58	21 40.6	13 03.7	19 51.9	6 39.4	23 24.0	15 48.6	16 23.8	19 44.7	10 32.8	17 22.5
29 Tu	0 29 17	9 13 31	8♐38 36	14 42 50	21 38.6	15 06.4	21 06.1	6 51.9	23 47.3	15 42.0	16 23.5	19 48.1	10 34.9	17 23.1
30 W	0 33 13	10 12 47	20 50 09	27 01 03	21 37.1	17 09.0	22 20.2	7 03.9	24 10.7	15 35.4	16 23.0	19 51.5	10 36.9	17 23.7
31 Th	0 37 10	11 12 02	3♑16 00	9♑35 31	21D 36.6	19 11.3	23 34.4	7 15.3	24 34.0	15 28.9	16 22.5	19 54.9	10 39.0	17 24.3

April 2016

LONGITUDE

Day	Sid.Time	☉	0 hr ☽	Noon☽	True☊	☿	♀	♂	⚳	♃	♄	♅	♆	♇
1 F	0 41 07	12♈11 15	16♑00 05	22♑30 10	21♍36.9	21♈13.1	24♓48.5	7♐26.2	24♓57.3	15♍22.5	16♐21.8	19♈58.3	10♓41.0	17♑24.8
2 Sa	0 45 03	13 10 26	29 06 10	5♒48 26	21 37.9	23 13.8	26 02.7	7 36.5	25 20.5	15R 16.3	16R 21.1	20 01.7	10 43.0	17 25.3
3 Su	0 49 00	14 09 36	12♒37 15	19 32 46	21 39.4	25 13.3	27 16.8	7 46.2	25 43.8	15 10.2	16 20.2	20 05.2	10 45.0	17 25.8
4 M	0 52 56	15 08 43	26 35 01	3♓43 54	21 40.7	27 11.2	28 30.9	7 55.3	26 07.0	15 04.2	16 19.3	20 08.6	10 47.0	17 26.2
5 Tu	0 56 53	16 07 49	10♓59 06	18 20 11	21R 41.4	29 07.0	29 45.1	8 03.8	26 30.1	14 58.3	16 18.2	20 12.0	10 48.9	17 26.6
6 W	1 00 49	17 06 53	25 46 29	3♈17 10	21 41.1	1♉00.4	0♈59.2	8 11.6	26 53.3	14 52.6	16 17.1	20 15.4	10 50.8	17 27.0
7 Th	1 04 46	18 05 55	10♈51 13	18 27 30	21 39.4	2 51.0	2 13.3	8 18.8	27 16.4	14 47.0	16 15.8	20 18.9	10 52.8	17 27.3
8 F	1 08 42	19 04 55	26 04 47	3♉41 46	21 36.5	4 38.5	3 27.4	8 25.4	27 39.5	14 41.5	16 14.5	20 22.3	10 54.6	17 27.6
9 Sa	1 12 39	20 03 53	11♉17 10	18 49 44	21 32.7	6 22.5	4 41.5	8 31.3	28 02.5	14 36.2	16 13.1	20 25.7	10 56.5	17 27.9
10 Su	1 16 36	21 02 49	26 18 23	3♊42 06	21 28.6	8 02.8	5 55.5	8 36.6	28 25.6	14 31.1	16 11.6	20 29.2	10 58.4	17 28.2
11 M	1 20 32	22 01 42	11♊00 06	18 11 48	21 24.7	9 38.9	7 09.6	8 41.2	28 48.5	14 26.1	16 09.9	20 32.6	11 00.2	17 28.4
12 Tu	1 24 29	23 00 34	25 16 47	2♋14 49	21 21.9	11 10.6	8 23.7	8 45.1	29 11.5	14 21.3	16 08.2	20 36.0	11 02.0	17 28.6
13 W	1 28 25	23 59 23	9♋05 54	15 50 08	21D 20.3	12 37.7	9 37.7	8 48.3	29 34.4	14 16.6	16 06.4	20 39.5	11 03.8	17 28.7
14 Th	1 32 22	24 58 09	22 27 47	28 59 10	21 20.0	14 00.0	10 51.7	8 50.8	29 57.3	14 12.1	16 04.6	20 42.9	11 05.6	17 28.9
15 F	1 36 18	25 56 54	5♌24 45	11♌44 59	21 21.0	15 17.3	12 05.8	8 52.6	0♈20.1	14 07.7	16 02.6	20 46.3	11 07.4	17 29.0
16 Sa	1 40 15	26 55 36	18 00 25	24 11 35	21 22.6	16 29.3	13 19.8	8 53.7	0 42.9	14 03.5	16 00.5	20 49.7	11 09.1	17 29.1
17 Su	1 44 11	27 54 16	0♍19 01	6♍23 14	21 24.2	17 36.1	14 33.8	8R 54.0	1 05.6	13 59.5	15 58.4	20 53.2	11 10.8	17R 29.1
18 M	1 48 08	28 52 53	12 24 46	18 24 06	21R 25.1	18 37.4	15 47.8	8 53.7	1 28.4	13 55.6	15 56.1	20 56.6	11 12.5	17 29.1
19 Tu	1 52 05	29 51 29	24 21 40	0♎17 54	21 24.7	19 33.2	17 01.8	8 52.6	1 51.0	13 51.9	15 53.8	21 00.0	11 14.2	17 29.1
20 W	1 56 01	0♉50 02	6♎13 11	12 07 53	21 22.5	20 23.3	18 15.7	8 50.8	2 13.6	13 48.4	15 51.4	21 03.4	11 15.8	17 29.0
21 Th	1 59 58	1 48 34	18 02 17	23 56 43	21 18.5	21 07.6	19 29.7	8 48.2	2 36.2	13 45.0	15 48.9	21 06.8	11 17.4	17 29.0
22 F	2 03 54	2 47 04	29 51 24	5♏46 37	21 12.6	21 46.2	20 43.7	8 44.8	2 58.8	13 41.9	15 46.3	21 10.1	11 19.0	17 28.8
23 Sa	2 07 51	3 45 31	11♏42 33	17 39 27	21 05.2	22 19.0	21 57.6	8 40.8	3 21.2	13 38.9	15 43.7	21 13.5	11 20.6	17 28.7
24 Su	2 11 47	4 43 57	23 37 30	29 36 55	20 57.0	22 46.0	23 11.6	8 35.9	3 43.7	13 36.0	15 40.9	21 16.9	11 22.1	17 28.5
25 M	2 15 44	5 42 22	5♐37 56	11♐40 46	20 48.8	23 07.1	24 25.5	8 30.3	4 06.1	13 33.4	15 38.1	21 20.2	11 23.6	17 28.3
26 Tu	2 19 40	6 40 44	17 45 42	23 52 58	20 41.4	23 22.4	25 39.4	8 23.9	4 28.4	13 30.9	15 35.3	21 23.6	11 25.1	17 28.1
27 W	2 23 37	7 39 05	0♑02 55	6♑15 50	20 35.5	23 32.0	26 53.4	8 16.8	4 50.7	13 28.6	15 32.3	21 26.9	11 26.6	17 27.9
28 Th	2 27 33	8 37 24	12 32 06	18 52 05	20 31.4	23R 36.0	28 07.3	8 08.9	5 13.0	13 26.5	15 29.3	21 30.2	11 28.1	17 27.6
29 F	2 31 30	9 35 42	25 16 10	1♒44 46	20D 29.5	23 34.5	29 21.2	8 00.2	5 35.2	13 24.6	15 26.2	21 33.6	11 29.5	17 27.3
30 Sa	2 35 27	10 33 59	8♒18 16	14 57 02	20 29.2	23 27.7	0♉35.1	7 50.8	5 57.3	13 22.8	15 23.0	21 36.9	11 30.9	17 26.9

Astro Data	Dy Hr Mn
♃⚻♅	6 11:45
☽0N	9 23:13
♃△♇	16 20:06
☉0N	20 4:31
☽0S	23 9:49
♃□♄	23 10:15
☿0N	23 13:24
♄ R	25 10:01
☽0N	6 10:18
♀0N	8 12:08
♂ R	17 12:14
♇ R	18 7:26
☽0S	19 15:59
☿ R	28 17:20

Planet Ingress		Dy Hr Mn
☿	♓	5 10:23
♂	♐	6 2:29
♀	♓	12 10:24
☉	♈	20 4:30
☿	♈	22 0:19
♀	♈	5 16:50
☿	♉	5 23:09
⚳	♈	14 14:52
☉	♉	19 15:29
♀	♉	30 0:36

Last Aspect Dy Hr Mn			☽ Ingress	Dy Hr Mn
3 2:55	☿	⚹	♑	3 10:01
5 16:05	♂	⚹	♒	5 16:22
7 8:46	♀	☌	♓	7 19:08
9 1:54	☉	☌	♈	9 19:40
11 18:24	♀	⚹	♉	11 19:44
13 9:46	☉	⚹	♊	13 21:03
15 17:03	☉	□	♋	16 0:57
18 4:09	☉	△	♌	18 7:54
19 20:43	♅	△	♍	20 17:39
22 3:55	♇	△	♎	23 5:23
24 20:55	♅	☍	♏	25 18:09
27 7:25	♀	△	♐	28 6:46
30 1:55	♀	□	♑	30 17:45

Last Aspect Dy Hr Mn			☽ Ingress	Dy Hr Mn
1 16:39	♀	⚹	♒	2 1:37
3 23:16	☿	⚹	♓	4 5:45
5 10:33	♇	⚹	♈	6 6:46
7 14:56	♅	☌	♉	8 6:10
9 9:49	♇	△	♊	10 5:59
11 18:57	☉	⚹	♋	12 8:06
14 3:59	☉	□	♌	14 13:53
16 17:48	☉	△	♍	16 23:23
18 12:29	☿	△	♎	19 11:24
21 6:13	♅	☍	♏	22 0:17
23 21:46	☿	☍	♐	24 12:46
26 15:51	♀	△	♑	26 23:54
29 7:07	♀	□	♒	29 8:47

☽ Phases & Eclipses Dy Hr Mn	
1 23:11	☾ 11♐48
9 1:54	● 18♓56
9 1:57:10	● T 04'10"
15 17:03	☽ 25♊33
23 12:01	○ 3♎17
23 11:47	● A 0.775
31 15:17	☾ 11♑20
7 11:24	● 18♈04
14 3:59	☽ 24♋39
22 5:24	○ 2♏31
30 3:29	☾ 10♒13

Astro Data

1 March 2016
Julian Day # 42429
SVP 5♓02'04"
GC 27♐03.9 ⚴ 13♒40.7
Eris 22♈32.0 ⚵ 15♏10.3
⚷ 20♓26.6 ⚶ 27♈19.6
☽ Mean ☊ 22♍24.2

1 April 2016
Julian Day # 42460
SVP 5♓02'01"
GC 27♐04.0 ⚴ 23♒27.5
Eris 22♈50.2 ⚵ 12♏35.7R
⚷ 22♓18.8 ⚶ 10♉18.6
☽ Mean ☊ 20♍45.7

LONGITUDE

May 2016

Day	Sid.Time	☉	0 hr ☽	Noon☽	True☊	☿	♀	♂	⚳	♃	♄	♅	♆	♇
1 Su	2 39 23	11♉32 13	21♒41 27	28♒31 46	20♍30.0	23♉15.9	1♉49.0	7♐40.6	6♈19.4	13♍21.3	15♐19.7	21♈40.1	11♓32.2	17♑26.5
2 M	2 43 20	12 30 27	5♓28 12	12♓30 52	20R 31.0	22R 59.4	3 02.9	7R 29.7	6 41.5	13R 19.9	15R 16.4	21 43.4	11 33.6	17R 26.1
3 Tu	2 47 16	13 28 38	19 39 43	26 54 35	20 31.0	22 38.6	4 16.8	7 18.0	7 03.5	13 18.7	15 13.0	21 46.7	11 34.9	17 25.7
4 W	2 51 13	14 26 49	4♈15 05	11♈40 41	20 29.3	22 13.9	5 30.7	7 05.6	7 25.4	13 17.6	15 09.6	21 49.9	11 36.1	17 25.3
5 Th	2 55 09	15 24 57	19 10 36	26 43 56	20 25.3	21 45.7	6 44.6	6 52.5	7 47.3	13 16.8	15 06.1	21 53.1	11 37.4	17 24.8
6 F	2 59 06	16 23 05	4♉19 32	11♉56 11	20 19.0	21 14.6	7 58.5	6 38.8	8 09.1	13 16.2	15 02.5	21 56.3	11 38.6	17 24.3
7 Sa	3 03 02	17 21 10	19 32 34	27 07 21	20 11.0	20 41.2	9 12.4	6 24.3	8 30.8	13 15.7	14 58.9	21 59.5	11 39.8	17 23.7
8 Su	3 06 59	18 19 14	4♊39 12	12♊06 56	20 02.2	20 06.1	10 26.2	6 09.2	8 52.5	13 15.4	14 55.2	22 02.7	11 41.0	17 23.2
9 M	3 10 56	19 17 17	19 29 29	26 45 58	19 53.7	19 29.9	11 40.1	5 53.5	9 14.1	13D 15.3	14 51.5	22 05.8	11 42.1	17 22.6
10 Tu	3 14 52	20 15 17	3♋55 44	10♋58 20	19 46.5	18 53.3	12 53.9	5 37.2	9 35.7	13 15.4	14 47.7	22 09.0	11 43.2	17 22.0
11 W	3 18 49	21 13 16	17 53 32	24 41 19	19 41.3	18 16.9	14 07.8	5 20.3	9 57.2	13 15.7	14 43.8	22 12.1	11 44.3	17 21.3
12 Th	3 22 45	22 11 13	1♌21 48	7♌55 19	19 38.4	17 41.4	15 21.6	5 02.8	10 18.6	13 16.1	14 39.9	22 15.2	11 45.4	17 20.6
13 F	3 26 42	23 09 08	14 22 15	20 43 08	19D 37.4	17 07.3	16 35.4	4 44.9	10 39.9	13 16.8	14 36.0	22 18.2	11 46.4	17 19.9
14 Sa	3 30 38	24 07 01	26 58 31	3♍09 03	19 37.6	16 35.2	17 49.2	4 26.5	11 01.2	13 17.6	14 32.0	22 21.3	11 47.4	17 19.2
15 Su	3 34 35	25 04 52	9♍15 22	15 18 07	19R 38.1	16 05.7	19 03.0	4 07.7	11 22.4	13 18.6	14 28.0	22 24.3	11 48.3	17 18.5
16 M	3 38 31	26 02 42	21 17 57	27 15 29	19 37.9	15 39.1	20 16.8	3 48.5	11 43.5	13 19.8	14 23.9	22 27.3	11 49.3	17 17.7
17 Tu	3 42 28	27 00 29	3♎11 18	9♎06 00	19 36.1	15 16.0	21 30.6	3 28.9	12 04.6	13 21.1	14 19.8	22 30.3	11 50.2	17 16.9
18 W	3 46 25	27 58 16	15 00 03	20 53 58	19 31.9	14 56.5	22 44.4	3 08.9	12 25.6	13 22.7	14 15.6	22 33.2	11 51.0	17 16.1
19 Th	3 50 21	28 56 01	26 48 10	2♏43 01	19 25.0	14 41.0	23 58.1	2 48.7	12 46.5	13 24.4	14 11.5	22 36.2	11 51.9	17 15.2
20 F	3 54 18	29 53 44	8♏38 51	14 35 58	19 15.6	14 29.7	25 11.9	2 28.3	13 07.3	13 26.3	14 07.2	22 39.1	11 52.7	17 14.4
21 Sa	3 58 14	0♊51 26	20 34 35	26 34 55	19 04.2	14 22.8	26 25.7	2 07.6	13 28.1	13 28.3	14 03.0	22 41.9	11 53.5	17 13.5
22 Su	4 02 11	1 49 06	2♐37 07	8♐41 21	18 51.6	14D 20.3	27 39.4	1 46.8	13 48.8	13 30.6	13 58.7	22 44.8	11 54.2	17 12.5
23 M	4 06 07	2 46 46	14 47 42	20 56 17	18 38.9	14 22.3	28 53.2	1 25.8	14 09.3	13 33.0	13 54.4	22 47.6	11 54.9	17 11.6
24 Tu	4 10 04	3 44 24	27 07 13	3♑20 36	18 27.1	14 28.8	0♊06.9	1 04.8	14 29.9	13 35.6	13 50.1	22 50.4	11 55.6	17 10.7
25 W	4 14 00	4 42 01	9♑36 32	15 55 11	18 17.3	14 39.9	1 20.7	0 43.7	14 50.3	13 38.3	13 45.8	22 53.2	11 56.2	17 09.7
26 Th	4 17 57	5 39 37	22 16 41	28 41 14	18 10.1	14 55.4	2 34.4	0 22.6	15 10.6	13 41.3	13 41.4	22 55.9	11 56.9	17 08.7
27 F	4 21 54	6 37 12	5♒09 03	11♒40 22	18 05.7	15 15.4	3 48.2	0 01.6	15 30.9	13 44.4	13 37.0	22 58.6	11 57.4	17 07.6
28 Sa	4 25 50	7 34 46	18 15 27	24 54 34	18 03.6	15 39.7	5 01.9	29♏40.7	15 51.1	13 47.6	13 32.6	23 01.3	11 58.0	17 06.6
29 Su	4 29 47	8 32 19	1♓38 00	8♓25 59	18 03.2	16 08.3	6 15.7	29 19.9	16 11.2	13 51.0	13 28.2	23 03.9	11 58.5	17 05.5
30 M	4 33 43	9 29 52	15 18 45	22 16 27	18 03.2	16 41.0	7 29.4	28 59.4	16 31.1	13 54.6	13 23.8	23 06.6	11 59.0	17 04.5
31 Tu	4 37 40	10 27 23	29 19 10	6♈26 52	18 02.4	17 17.8	8 43.1	28 39.0	16 51.0	13 58.4	13 19.3	23 09.2	11 59.5	17 03.3

LONGITUDE

June 2016

Day	Sid.Time	☉	0 hr ☽	Noon☽	True☊	☿	♀	♂	⚳	♃	♄	♅	♆	♇
1 W	4 41 36	11♊24 54	13♈39 24	20♈56 27	17♍59.7	17♉58.5	9♊56.9	28♏18.9	17♈10.8	14♍02.3	13♐14.9	23♈11.7	11♓59.9	17♑02.2
2 Th	4 45 33	12 22 24	28 17 32	5♉42 01	17R 54.4	18 43.1	11 10.6	27R 59.2	17 30.6	14 06.4	13R 10.5	23 14.2	12 00.3	17R 01.1
3 F	4 49 29	13 19 53	13♉09 04	20 37 44	17 46.4	19 31.5	12 24.4	27 39.8	17 50.2	14 10.6	13 06.0	23 16.7	12 00.6	16 59.9
4 Sa	4 53 26	14 17 22	28 06 56	5♊35 30	17 36.3	20 23.5	13 38.1	27 20.8	18 09.7	14 15.0	13 01.6	23 19.2	12 00.9	16 58.7
5 Su	4 57 23	15 14 49	13♊02 16	20 26 03	17 25.1	21 19.0	14 51.8	27 02.3	18 29.1	14 19.6	12 57.1	23 21.6	12 01.2	16 57.5
6 M	5 01 19	16 12 16	27 45 48	5♋00 33	17 14.0	22 18.1	16 05.6	26 44.3	18 48.4	14 24.3	12 52.7	23 24.0	12 01.5	16 56.3
7 Tu	5 05 16	17 09 42	12♋09 32	19 12 09	17 04.4	23 20.6	17 19.4	26 26.8	19 07.6	14 29.2	12 48.2	23 26.3	12 01.7	16 55.1
8 W	5 09 12	18 07 07	26 07 59	2♌56 51	16 57.0	24 26.3	18 33.1	26 09.9	19 26.7	14 34.2	12 43.8	23 28.6	12 01.9	16 53.9
9 Th	5 13 09	19 04 30	9♌38 42	16 13 43	16 52.2	25 35.4	19 46.8	25 53.6	19 45.6	14 39.4	12 39.4	23 30.9	12 02.1	16 52.6
10 F	5 17 05	20 01 53	22 42 10	29 04 28	16 49.8	26 47.7	21 00.5	25 37.9	20 04.5	14 44.8	12 35.0	23 33.2	12 02.2	16 51.3
11 Sa	5 21 02	20 59 14	5♍21 07	11♍32 42	16 49.1	28 03.1	22 14.2	25 22.9	20 23.2	14 50.2	12 30.6	23 35.4	12 02.3	16 50.0
12 Su	5 24 58	21 56 35	17 39 51	23 43 14	16 49.0	29 21.7	23 28.0	25 08.5	20 41.9	14 55.9	12 26.3	23 37.5	12 02.4	16 48.7
13 M	5 28 55	22 53 54	29 43 30	5♎41 22	16 48.6	0♊43.3	24 41.7	24 54.9	21 00.4	15 01.6	12 21.9	23 39.7	12R 02.4	16 47.4
14 Tu	5 32 52	23 51 12	11♎37 28	17 32 27	16 46.7	2 08.1	25 55.4	24 42.0	21 18.8	15 07.5	12 17.6	23 41.7	12 02.4	16 46.1
15 W	5 36 48	24 48 30	23 26 57	29 21 32	16 42.6	3 35.8	27 09.1	24 29.8	21 37.0	15 13.6	12 13.3	23 43.8	12 02.4	16 44.7
16 Th	5 40 45	25 45 47	5♏16 44	11♏13 02	16 35.9	5 06.6	28 22.8	24 18.4	21 55.2	15 19.8	12 09.1	23 45.8	12 02.3	16 43.4
17 F	5 44 41	26 43 03	17 10 52	23 10 36	16 26.7	6 40.3	29 36.5	24 07.8	22 13.2	15 26.1	12 04.8	23 47.8	12 02.2	16 42.0
18 Sa	5 48 38	27 40 19	29 12 34	5♐17 00	16 15.4	8 17.0	0♋50.2	23 57.9	22 31.1	15 32.6	12 00.6	23 49.7	12 02.1	16 40.6
19 Su	5 52 34	28 37 33	11♐24 07	17 34 04	16 02.8	9 56.6	2 03.9	23 48.9	22 48.9	15 39.2	11 56.4	23 51.6	12 01.9	16 39.3
20 M	5 56 31	29 34 48	23 46 55	0♑02 44	15 50.1	11 39.1	3 17.6	23 40.7	23 06.5	15 46.0	11 52.3	23 53.5	12 01.7	16 37.9
21 Tu	6 00 27	0♋32 02	6♑21 31	12 43 16	15 38.4	13 24.5	4 31.3	23 33.3	23 24.0	15 52.8	11 48.2	23 55.3	12 01.5	16 36.5
22 W	6 04 24	1 29 15	19 07 56	25 35 30	15 28.6	15 12.7	5 45.1	23 26.7	23 41.4	15 59.8	11 44.2	23 57.0	12 01.2	16 35.0
23 Th	6 08 21	2 26 28	2♒05 54	8♒39 07	15 21.4	17 03.6	6 58.8	23 20.9	23 58.6	16 07.0	11 40.1	23 58.8	12 00.9	16 33.6
24 F	6 12 17	3 23 41	15 15 10	21 54 01	15 16.9	18 57.2	8 12.5	23 15.9	24 15.7	16 14.2	11 36.2	24 00.4	12 00.6	16 32.2
25 Sa	6 16 14	4 20 54	28 35 44	5♓20 23	15D 15.0	20 53.3	9 26.2	23 11.8	24 32.7	16 21.6	11 32.2	24 02.1	12 00.2	16 30.8
26 Su	6 20 10	5 18 07	12♓08 01	18 58 44	15 14.7	22 51.8	10 39.9	23 08.5	24 49.5	16 29.1	11 28.4	24 03.7	11 59.9	16 29.3
27 M	6 24 07	6 15 20	25 52 37	2♈49 44	15R 15.0	24 52.6	11 53.6	23 06.0	25 06.2	16 36.8	11 24.5	24 05.2	11 59.4	16 27.9
28 Tu	6 28 03	7 12 33	9♈50 05	16 53 38	15 14.7	26 55.4	13 07.4	23 04.4	25 22.7	16 44.5	11 20.7	24 06.8	11 59.0	16 26.4
29 W	6 32 00	8 09 46	24 00 19	1♉09 53	15 12.8	29 00.2	14 21.1	23D 03.6	25 39.1	16 52.4	11 17.0	24 08.2	11 58.5	16 24.9
30 Th	6 35 56	9 06 59	8♉22 04	15 36 27	15 08.6	1♋06.5	15 34.8	23 03.6	25 55.3	17 00.4	11 13.3	24 09.6	11 58.0	16 23.5

Astro Data

	Dy Hr Mn
☽0N	3 21:04
♃ D	9 12:14
☽0S	16 22:54
☿ D	22 13:20
♃□♄	26 12:28
☽0N	31 6:14
☽0S	13 7:14
♆ R	13 20:42
♄□♆	18 3:29
⚳0N	18 12:27
♃△♇	26 12:30
☽0N	27 13:32
♂ D	29 23:38

Planet Ingress

	Dy Hr Mn
☉ ♊	20 14:36
♀ ♊	24 9:44
♂ ♏R	27 13:51
☿ ♊	12 23:22
♀ ♋	17 19:39
☉ ♋	20 22:34
☿ ♋	29 23:24

Last Aspect / ☽ Ingress

Last Aspect Dy Hr Mn		☽ Ingress Dy Hr Mn
1 2:56 ☿ □	♓	1 14:33
3 5:08 ☿ ✶	♈	3 17:04
5 4:17 ♅ ☌	♉	5 17:10
7 2:10 ☿ ☌	♊	7 16:34
9 4:15 ♅ ✶	♋	9 17:24
11 7:34 ♅ □	♌	11 21:32
13 17:02 ☉ □	♍	14 5:52
16 9:20 ☉ △	♎	16 17:33
18 15:23 ♅ ☍	♏	19 6:29
21 11:39 ♀ ☍	♐	21 18:48
23 15:37 ♅ △	♑	24 5:34
26 1:11 ♅ □	♒	26 14:27
28 20:19 ♂ □	♓	28 21:06
30 23:10 ♂ △	♈	31 1:09

Last Aspect / ☽ Ingress

Last Aspect Dy Hr Mn		☽ Ingress Dy Hr Mn
1 15:42 ♅ ☌	♉	2 2:46
3 23:02 ♂ ☍	♊	4 3:01
5 16:47 ♅ ✶	♋	6 3:41
8 0:18 ♂ △	♌	8 6:47
10 7:14 ☿ □	♍	10 13:46
12 14:47 ♂ ✶	♎	13 0:33
15 7:00 ♀ △	♏	15 13:18
17 13:52 ♂ ☌	♐	18 1:34
20 11:02 ☉ ☍	♑	20 11:55
22 8:57 ♅ □	♒	22 20:08
24 15:48 ♅ ✶	♓	25 2:30
26 19:55 ☿ □	♈	27 7:08
29 7:46 ☿ ✶	♉	29 10:03

☽ Phases & Eclipses

Dy Hr Mn	
6 19:29	● 16♉41
13 17:02	☽ 23♌21
21 21:14	○ 1♐14
29 12:12	☾ 8♓33
5 3:00	● 14♊53
12 8:10	☽ 21♍47
20 11:02	○ 29♐33
27 18:19	☾ 6♈30

Astro Data

1 May 2016
Julian Day # 42490
SVP 5♓01'58"
GC 27♐04.0 ⚴ 1♓10.1
Eris 23♈09.7 ⚵ 6♏16.6R
⚷ 23♓53.1 ⚶ 23♉19.4
☽ Mean ☊ 19♍10.4

1 June 2016
Julian Day # 42521
SVP 5♓01'54"
GC 27♐04.1 ⚴ 6♓15.8
Eris 23♈26.9 ⚵ 0♏38.1R
⚷ 24♓57.2 ⚶ 6♊51.8
☽ Mean ☊ 17♍31.9

July 2016 — LONGITUDE

Day	Sid.Time	☉	0 hr ☽	Noon ☽	True ☊	☿	♀	♂	⚳	♃	♄	♅	♆	♇
1 F	6 39 53	10♋04 12	22♉52 29	0♊09 32	15♍02.0	3♋14.2	16♋48.6	23♏04.4	26♈11.3	17♍08.5	11♐09.7	24♈11.0	11♓57.5	16♑22.0
2 Sa	6 43 50	11 01 26	7♊26 51	14 43 37	14R53.5	5 23.1	18 02.3	23 06.1	26 27.2	17 16.7	11R06.2	24 12.4	11R56.9	16R20.5
3 Su	6 47 46	11 58 39	21 59 00	29 12 08	14 43.9	7 32.7	19 16.0	23 08.6	26 43.0	17 25.1	11 02.7	24 13.6	11 56.3	16 19.0
4 M	6 51 43	12 55 53	6♋22 09	13♋28 18	14 34.4	9 42.9	20 29.8	23 11.9	26 58.5	17 33.5	10 59.2	24 14.9	11 55.7	16 17.6
5 Tu	6 55 39	13 53 06	20 29 54	27 26 23	14 26.0	11 53.2	21 43.5	23 16.0	27 13.9	17 42.1	10 55.8	24 16.1	11 55.0	16 16.1
6 W	6 59 36	14 50 20	4♌17 20	11♌02 27	14 19.6	14 03.6	22 57.3	23 20.9	27 29.1	17 50.8	10 52.5	24 17.2	11 54.3	16 14.6
7 Th	7 03 32	15 47 33	17 41 38	24 14 52	14 15.5	16 13.6	24 11.0	23 26.6	27 44.2	17 59.6	10 49.3	24 18.3	11 53.6	16 13.1
8 F	7 07 29	16 44 46	0♍42 18	7♍04 11	14D13.6	18 23.0	25 24.8	23 33.0	27 59.0	18 08.5	10 46.1	24 19.4	11 52.9	16 11.6
9 Sa	7 11 26	17 42 00	13 20 54	19 32 53	14 13.5	20 31.7	26 38.5	23 40.3	28 13.7	18 17.5	10 43.0	24 20.4	11 52.1	16 10.1
10 Su	7 15 22	18 39 13	25 40 39	1♎44 46	14 14.3	22 39.3	27 52.3	23 48.3	28 28.2	18 26.6	10 40.0	24 21.4	11 51.3	16 08.7
11 M	7 19 19	19 36 26	7♎45 51	13 44 32	14R15.2	24 45.8	29 06.0	23 57.0	28 42.5	18 35.8	10 37.0	24 22.3	11 50.5	16 07.2
12 Tu	7 23 15	20 33 38	19 41 28	25 37 18	14 15.2	26 51.0	0♌19.8	24 06.5	28 56.6	18 45.1	10 34.1	24 23.1	11 49.6	16 05.7
13 W	7 27 12	21 30 51	1♏32 41	7♏28 14	14 13.6	28 54.7	1 33.5	24 16.7	29 10.5	18 54.5	10 31.3	24 23.9	11 48.7	16 04.2
14 Th	7 31 08	22 28 04	13 24 33	19 22 13	14 10.2	0♌56.9	2 47.2	24 27.7	29 24.3	19 04.0	10 28.6	24 24.7	11 47.8	16 02.7
15 F	7 35 05	23 25 18	25 21 46	1♐23 39	14 04.7	2 57.5	4 01.0	24 39.3	29 37.8	19 13.6	10 25.9	24 25.4	11 46.9	16 01.3
16 Sa	7 39 01	24 22 31	7♐28 20	13 36 09	13 57.6	4 56.4	5 14.7	24 51.6	29 51.1	19 23.2	10 23.4	24 26.1	11 45.9	15 59.8
17 Su	7 42 58	25 19 44	19 47 24	26 02 20	13 49.4	6 53.6	6 28.5	25 04.6	0♉04.3	19 33.0	10 20.9	24 26.7	11 44.9	15 58.3
18 M	7 46 55	26 16 58	2♑21 06	8♑43 46	13 41.0	8 49.1	7 42.2	25 18.3	0 17.2	19 42.9	10 18.4	24 27.3	11 43.9	15 56.9
19 Tu	7 50 51	27 14 12	15 10 23	21 40 54	13 33.3	10 42.7	8 55.9	25 32.6	0 29.9	19 52.8	10 16.1	24 27.9	11 42.9	15 55.4
20 W	7 54 48	28 11 27	28 15 12	4♒53 08	13 26.9	12 34.6	10 09.7	25 47.5	0 42.4	20 02.9	10 13.9	24 28.3	11 41.8	15 54.0
21 Th	7 58 44	29 08 42	11♒34 30	18 19 05	13 22.5	14 24.7	11 23.4	26 03.0	0 54.7	20 13.0	10 11.7	24 28.8	11 40.7	15 52.5
22 F	8 02 41	0♌05 58	25 06 39	1♓56 58	13D20.1	16 13.0	12 37.1	26 19.2	1 06.7	20 23.2	10 09.6	24 29.1	11 39.6	15 51.1
23 Sa	8 06 37	1 03 14	8♓49 46	15 44 50	13 19.5	17 59.5	13 50.9	26 36.0	1 18.6	20 33.5	10 07.6	24 29.5	11 38.5	15 49.7
24 Su	8 10 34	2 00 31	22 41 57	29 40 55	13 20.3	19 44.2	15 04.6	26 53.3	1 30.2	20 43.9	10 05.7	24 29.8	11 37.3	15 48.3
25 M	8 14 30	2 57 49	6♈41 32	13♈43 39	13 21.6	21 27.2	16 18.3	27 11.3	1 41.5	20 54.4	10 03.9	24 30.0	11 36.1	15 46.9
26 Tu	8 18 27	3 55 08	20 47 04	27 51 37	13R22.6	23 08.4	17 32.1	27 29.8	1 52.7	21 04.9	10 02.1	24 30.2	11 34.9	15 45.5
27 W	8 22 24	4 52 28	4♉57 06	12♉03 17	13 22.5	24 47.8	18 45.8	27 48.8	2 03.6	21 15.5	10 00.5	24 30.3	11 33.7	15 44.1
28 Th	8 26 20	5 49 49	19 09 57	26 16 46	13 21.0	26 25.5	19 59.5	28 08.5	2 14.2	21 26.2	9 58.9	24 30.4	11 32.5	15 42.7
29 F	8 30 17	6 47 11	3♊23 26	10♊29 33	13 17.8	28 01.4	21 13.3	28 28.6	2 24.6	21 37.0	9 57.5	24R30.5	11 31.2	15 41.3
30 Sa	8 34 13	7 44 35	17 34 41	24 38 25	13 13.4	29 35.6	22 27.0	28 49.3	2 34.8	21 47.8	9 56.1	24 30.5	11 29.9	15 40.0
31 Su	8 38 10	8 41 59	1♋40 15	8♋39 44	13 08.2	1♍08.0	23 40.7	29 10.5	2 44.7	21 58.8	9 54.8	24 30.4	11 28.6	15 38.6

August 2016 — LONGITUDE

Day	Sid.Time	☉	0 hr ☽	Noon ☽	True ☊	☿	♀	♂	⚳	♃	♄	♅	♆	♇
1 M	8 42 06	9♌39 24	15♋36 21	22♋29 42	13♍03.0	2♍38.6	24♌54.5	29♏32.3	2♉54.3	22♍09.8	9♐53.6	24♈30.3	11♓27.3	15♑37.3
2 Tu	8 46 03	10 36 51	29 19 22	6♌04 59	12R58.5	4 07.5	26 08.2	29 54.5	3 03.7	22 20.8	9R52.5	24R30.1	11R26.0	15R36.0
3 W	8 49 59	11 34 18	12♌46 17	19 23 04	12 55.1	5 34.5	27 22.0	0♐17.3	3 12.8	22 32.0	9 51.5	24 29.9	11 24.6	15 34.7
4 Th	8 53 56	12 31 46	25 55 14	2♍22 44	12D53.2	6 59.8	28 35.7	0 40.5	3 21.6	22 43.2	9 50.6	24 29.7	11 23.2	15 33.4
5 F	8 57 53	13 29 15	8♍45 38	15 04 05	12 52.8	8 23.2	29 49.4	1 04.2	3 30.2	22 54.4	9 49.8	24 29.4	11 21.8	15 32.1
6 Sa	9 01 49	14 26 44	21 18 18	27 28 36	12 53.5	9 44.7	1♍03.1	1 28.4	3 38.5	23 05.8	9 49.1	24 29.0	11 20.4	15 30.9
7 Su	9 05 46	15 24 15	3♎35 19	9♎38 54	12 55.0	11 04.3	2 16.9	1 53.1	3 46.4	23 17.2	9 48.4	24 28.6	11 19.0	15 29.6
8 M	9 09 42	16 21 46	15 39 49	21 38 36	12 56.7	12 22.0	3 30.6	2 18.1	3 54.1	23 28.6	9 47.9	24 28.2	11 17.5	15 28.4
9 Tu	9 13 39	17 19 18	27 35 46	3♏31 56	12 58.2	13 37.6	4 44.3	2 43.7	4 01.5	23 40.1	9 47.5	24 27.7	11 16.1	15 27.2
10 W	9 17 35	18 16 51	9♏27 39	15 23 33	12R58.9	14 51.2	5 58.0	3 09.6	4 08.7	23 51.7	9 47.2	24 27.2	11 14.6	15 26.0
11 Th	9 21 32	19 14 25	21 20 14	27 18 18	12 58.6	16 02.6	7 11.7	3 36.0	4 15.5	24 03.4	9 46.9	24 26.6	11 13.1	15 24.8
12 F	9 25 28	20 12 00	3♐18 20	9♐20 53	12 57.4	17 11.8	8 25.4	4 02.8	4 22.0	24 15.0	9D46.8	24 25.9	11 11.6	15 23.6
13 Sa	9 29 25	21 09 36	15 26 29	21 35 38	12 55.2	18 18.8	9 39.0	4 30.0	4 28.2	24 26.8	9 46.7	24 25.3	11 10.1	15 22.5
14 Su	9 33 21	22 07 12	27 48 45	4♑06 12	12 52.4	19 23.3	10 52.7	4 57.6	4 34.1	24 38.6	9 46.8	24 24.5	11 08.5	15 21.4
15 M	9 37 18	23 04 50	10♑28 19	16 55 17	12 49.5	20 25.3	12 06.4	5 25.6	4 39.7	24 50.5	9 47.0	24 23.8	11 07.0	15 20.3
16 Tu	9 41 15	24 02 29	23 27 16	0♒04 19	12 46.8	21 24.7	13 20.0	5 54.0	4 45.0	25 02.4	9 47.2	24 22.9	11 05.5	15 19.2
17 W	9 45 11	25 00 09	6♒46 22	13 33 17	12 44.6	22 21.4	14 33.7	6 22.7	4 49.9	25 14.3	9 47.6	24 22.1	11 03.9	15 18.1
18 Th	9 49 08	25 57 50	20 24 49	27 20 40	12 43.2	23 15.2	15 47.3	6 51.8	4 54.6	25 26.3	9 48.0	24 21.2	11 02.3	15 17.1
19 F	9 53 04	26 55 33	4♓20 25	11♓23 36	12D42.7	24 05.9	17 00.9	7 21.2	4 58.9	25 38.4	9 48.5	24 20.2	11 00.7	15 16.1
20 Sa	9 57 01	27 53 17	18 29 43	25 38 12	12 43.0	24 53.4	18 14.5	7 51.0	5 02.9	25 50.5	9 49.2	24 19.2	10 59.2	15 15.1
21 Su	10 00 57	28 51 02	2♈48 29	10♈00 00	12 43.8	25 37.5	19 28.1	8 21.1	5 06.5	26 02.6	9 49.9	24 18.2	10 57.6	15 14.1
22 M	10 04 54	29 48 49	17 12 11	24 24 30	12 44.8	26 18.0	20 41.7	8 51.5	5 09.8	26 14.8	9 50.7	24 17.1	10 55.9	15 13.1
23 Tu	10 08 50	0♍46 38	1♉36 27	8♉47 33	12 45.7	26 54.7	21 55.3	9 22.3	5 12.8	26 27.0	9 51.7	24 15.9	10 54.3	15 12.2
24 W	10 12 47	1 44 29	15 57 25	23 05 40	12R46.3	27 27.4	23 08.9	9 53.4	5 15.4	26 39.3	9 52.7	24 14.8	10 52.7	15 11.3
25 Th	10 16 44	2 42 21	0♊11 59	7♊16 05	12 46.4	27 55.8	24 22.5	10 24.8	5 17.7	26 51.6	9 53.8	24 13.5	10 51.1	15 10.4
26 F	10 20 40	3 40 16	14 17 44	21 16 43	12 46.0	28 19.7	25 36.1	10 56.5	5 19.6	27 03.9	9 55.0	24 12.3	10 49.5	15 09.5
27 Sa	10 24 37	4 38 12	28 12 53	5♋06 04	12 45.3	28 38.8	26 49.6	11 28.5	5 21.2	27 16.3	9 56.3	24 11.0	10 47.8	15 08.7
28 Su	10 28 33	5 36 10	11♋56 08	18 43 00	12 44.5	28 52.8	28 03.2	12 00.9	5 22.4	27 28.8	9 57.7	24 09.6	10 46.2	15 07.8
29 M	10 32 30	6 34 10	25 26 32	2♌06 40	12 43.7	29 01.5	29 16.8	12 33.5	5 23.2	27 41.2	9 59.2	24 08.3	10 44.5	15 07.0
30 Tu	10 36 26	7 32 11	8♌43 21	15 16 32	12 43.0	29R04.6	0♎30.3	13 06.4	5R23.7	27 53.7	10 00.8	24 06.8	10 42.9	15 06.3
31 W	10 40 23	8 30 14	21 46 11	28 12 17	12 42.7	29 02.0	1 43.8	13 39.6	5 23.8	28 06.3	10 02.5	24 05.4	10 41.2	15 05.5

Astro Data

	Dy Hr Mn
☽0S	10 16:31
☽0N	24 19:53
♅R	29 21:06
☽0S	7 1:42
♃⊼♅	13 9:02
♄D	13 9:50
☿0S	19 19:17
☽0N	21 2:53
☿R	30 13:04
⚳R	31 7:09

Planet Ingress

	Dy Hr Mn
♀ ♌	12 5:34
☿ ♌	14 0:47
⚳ ♉	17 4:10
☉ ♌	22 9:30
☿ ♍	30 18:18
♂ ♐	2 17:49
♀ ♍	5 15:27
☉ ♍	22 16:38
♀ ♎	30 2:07

Last Aspect / ☽ Ingress

Last Aspect Dy Hr Mn		☽ Ingress Dy Hr Mn
1 0:19 ♂ ☍	♊	1 11:44
3 3:43 ♅ ⚹	♋	3 13:20
5 6:29 ♅ □	♌	5 16:28
7 12:06 ♅ △	♍	7 22:41
10 3:28 ♀ ⚹	♎	10 8:32
12 15:01 ☿ □	♏	12 20:52
14 22:22 ♂ ☌	♐	15 9:14
17 8:57 ♅ △	♑	17 19:33
19 22:57 ☉ ☍	♒	20 3:10
22 1:56 ♂ □	♓	22 8:35
24 7:06 ♂ △	♈	24 12:33
26 6:19 ♅ ☌	♉	26 15:37
28 15:13 ♂ ☍	♊	28 18:17
30 11:46 ♅ ⚹	♋	30 21:09

Last Aspect / ☽ Ingress

Last Aspect Dy Hr Mn		☽ Ingress Dy Hr Mn
2 0:44 ♂ △	♌	2 1:12
4 4:13 ♀ ☌	♍	4 7:34
6 3:20 ♃ ☌	♎	6 16:56
8 17:41 ♅ ☍	♏	9 4:51
11 5:22 ♃ ⚹	♐	11 17:24
13 17:37 ♃ □	♑	14 4:11
16 2:45 ♃ △	♒	16 11:52
18 9:27 ☉ ☍	♓	18 16:34
20 12:21 ♃ ☍	♈	20 19:18
22 11:48 ♅ ☌	♉	22 21:19
24 19:38 ☿ △	♊	24 23:40
27 0:30 ☿ □	♋	27 3:06
29 6:23 ☿ ⚹	♌	29 8:11
31 4:20 ♅ △	♍	31 15:22

☽ Phases & Eclipses

Dy Hr Mn	
4 11:01	● 12♋54
12 0:52	☽ 20♎07
19 22:57	○ 27♑40
26 23:00	☾ 4♉21
2 20:45	● 10♌58
10 18:21	☽ 18♏32
18 9:27	○ 25♒52
25 3:41	☾ 2♊22

Astro Data

1 July 2016
Julian Day # 42551
SVP 5♓01'49"
GC 27♐04.2 ⚴ 7♓02.3R
Eris 23♈36.8 ⚵ 29♎35.8
⚷ 25♓14.6R ⚶ 19♊47.7
☽ Mean ☊ 15♍56.6

1 August 2016
Julian Day # 42582
SVP 5♓01'45"
GC 27♐04.3 ⚴ 2♓34.0R
Eris 23♈37.7R ⚵ 3♏05.9
⚷ 24♓43.5R ⚶ 2♋41.7
☽ Mean ☊ 14♍18.1

LONGITUDE — September 2016

Day	Sid.Time	☉	0 hr ☽	Noon ☽	True ☊	☿	♀	♂	⚳	♃	♄	♅	♆	♇
1 Th	10 44 19	9♍28 19	4♍34 53	10♍54 02	12♍42.5	28♍53.2	2♎57.4	14♐13.1	5♉23.5	28♍18.8	10♐04.3	24♈03.9	10♓39.6	15♑04.8
2 F	10 48 16	10 26 25	17 09 47	23 22 18	12D42.6	28R38.4	4 10.9	14 46.9	5R22.9	28 31.4	10 06.2	24R02.3	10R37.9	15R04.1
3 Sa	10 52 13	11 24 33	29 31 43	5♎38 15	12 42.7	28 17.2	5 24.4	15 20.9	5 21.9	28 44.1	10 08.2	24 00.7	10 36.3	15 03.4
4 Su	10 56 09	12 22 43	11♎42 09	17 43 40	12R42.8	27 49.7	6 37.9	15 55.3	5 20.5	28 56.7	10 10.2	23 59.1	10 34.6	15 02.8
5 M	11 00 06	13 20 54	23 43 10	29 40 59	12 42.7	27 16.1	7 51.4	16 29.8	5 18.8	29 09.4	10 12.4	23 57.5	10 33.0	15 02.1
6 Tu	11 04 02	14 19 07	5♏37 33	11♏33 18	12 42.6	26 36.5	9 04.8	17 04.7	5 16.7	29 22.1	10 14.7	23 55.8	10 31.3	15 01.6
7 W	11 07 59	15 17 21	17 28 42	23 24 16	12 42.4	25 51.3	10 18.3	17 39.7	5 14.2	29 34.8	10 17.0	23 54.1	10 29.7	15 01.0
8 Th	11 11 55	16 15 37	29 20 32	5♐18 03	12D42.2	25 01.0	11 31.7	18 15.1	5 11.3	29 47.6	10 19.4	23 52.3	10 28.1	15 00.5
9 F	11 15 52	17 13 54	11♐17 22	17 19 05	12 42.1	24 06.5	12 45.2	18 50.6	5 08.1	0♎00.4	10 22.0	23 50.5	10 26.4	14 59.9
10 Sa	11 19 48	18 12 13	23 23 45	29 31 56	12 42.2	23 08.5	13 58.6	19 26.4	5 04.4	0 13.2	10 24.6	23 48.7	10 24.8	14 59.5
11 Su	11 23 45	19 10 34	5♑44 11	12♑01 00	12 42.6	22 08.3	15 12.0	20 02.5	5 00.5	0 26.0	10 27.3	23 46.8	10 23.2	14 59.0
12 M	11 27 42	20 08 56	18 22 51	24 50 09	12 43.3	21 07.1	16 25.3	20 38.7	4 56.1	0 38.8	10 30.1	23 44.9	10 21.5	14 58.6
13 Tu	11 31 38	21 07 19	1♒23 13	8♒02 19	12 44.0	20 06.1	17 38.7	21 15.2	4 51.4	0 51.7	10 33.0	23 43.0	10 19.9	14 58.2
14 W	11 35 35	22 05 45	14 47 34	21 38 59	12 44.7	19 06.9	18 52.0	21 51.9	4 46.3	1 04.5	10 36.0	23 41.1	10 18.3	14 57.8
15 Th	11 39 31	23 04 12	28 36 28	5♓39 44	12R45.2	18 10.9	20 05.4	22 28.7	4 40.8	1 17.4	10 39.0	23 39.1	10 16.7	14 57.5
16 F	11 43 28	24 02 40	12♓48 25	20 01 58	12 45.2	17 19.6	21 18.7	23 05.8	4 35.0	1 30.3	10 42.2	23 37.1	10 15.1	14 57.2
17 Sa	11 47 24	25 01 11	27 19 42	4♈40 51	12 44.6	16 34.1	22 31.9	23 43.1	4 28.8	1 43.2	10 45.4	23 35.0	10 13.5	14 56.9
18 Su	11 51 21	25 59 43	12♈04 30	19 29 43	12 43.4	15 55.7	23 45.2	24 20.6	4 22.2	1 56.2	10 48.7	23 33.0	10 11.9	14 56.6
19 M	11 55 17	26 58 18	26 55 32	4♉20 59	12 41.7	15 25.4	24 58.5	24 58.3	4 15.3	2 09.1	10 52.1	23 30.9	10 10.4	14 56.4
20 Tu	11 59 14	27 56 55	11♉45 07	19 07 05	12 39.9	15 04.0	26 11.7	25 36.2	4 08.1	2 22.0	10 55.6	23 28.8	10 08.8	14 56.2
21 W	12 03 10	28 55 34	26 26 07	3♊41 36	12 38.3	14D52.0	27 24.9	26 14.2	4 00.5	2 35.0	10 59.1	23 26.6	10 07.3	14 56.0
22 Th	12 07 07	29 54 15	10♊52 59	17 59 54	12D37.2	14 49.7	28 38.1	26 52.5	3 52.5	2 47.9	11 02.8	23 24.5	10 05.7	14 55.9
23 F	12 11 04	0♎52 58	25 02 06	1♋59 25	12 36.9	14 57.4	29 51.3	27 30.9	3 44.2	3 00.9	11 06.5	23 22.3	10 04.2	14 55.8
24 Sa	12 15 00	1 51 44	8♋51 51	15 39 25	12 37.3	15 14.8	1♏04.5	28 09.5	3 35.6	3 13.9	11 10.3	23 20.1	10 02.7	14 55.7
25 Su	12 18 57	2 50 32	22 22 16	29 00 34	12 38.5	15 41.9	2 17.7	28 48.3	3 26.6	3 26.8	11 14.2	23 17.8	10 01.2	14 55.7
26 M	12 22 53	3 49 23	5♌34 33	12♌04 25	12 40.0	16 18.3	3 30.8	29 27.2	3 17.3	3 39.8	11 18.2	23 15.6	9 59.7	14D55.6
27 Tu	12 26 50	4 48 15	18 30 28	24 52 55	12 41.4	17 03.5	4 44.0	0♑06.4	3 07.7	3 52.8	11 22.2	23 13.3	9 58.3	14 55.6
28 W	12 30 46	5 47 10	1♍12 02	7♍28 03	12R42.2	17 56.9	5 57.1	0 45.7	2 57.8	4 05.8	11 26.3	23 11.0	9 56.8	14 55.7
29 Th	12 34 43	6 46 07	13 41 13	19 51 43	12 42.1	18 57.8	7 10.2	1 25.1	2 47.6	4 18.7	11 30.5	23 08.7	9 55.4	14 55.8
30 F	12 38 39	7 45 06	25 59 47	2♎05 36	12 40.8	20 05.7	8 23.3	2 04.8	2 37.1	4 31.7	11 34.8	23 06.4	9 54.0	14 55.9

LONGITUDE — October 2016

Day	Sid.Time	☉	0 hr ☽	Noon ☽	True ☊	☿	♀	♂	⚳	♃	♄	♅	♆	♇
1 Sa	12 42 36	8♎44 07	8♎09 21	14♎11 14	12♍38.1	21♍19.8	9♏36.4	2♑44.5	2♉26.3	4♎44.7	11♐39.2	23♈04.1	9♓52.6	14♑56.0
2 Su	12 46 33	9 43 09	20 11 26	26 10 10	12R34.2	22 39.3	10 49.4	3 24.5	2R15.3	4 57.6	11 43.6	23R01.7	9R51.2	14 56.2
3 M	12 50 29	10 42 14	2♏07 39	8♏04 07	12 29.4	24 03.7	12 02.4	4 04.6	2 04.0	5 10.6	11 48.1	22 59.3	9 49.8	14 56.3
4 Tu	12 54 26	11 41 21	13 59 50	19 55 06	12 24.1	25 32.2	13 15.5	4 44.9	1 52.4	5 23.5	11 52.7	22 57.0	9 48.5	14 56.6
5 W	12 58 22	12 40 30	25 50 15	1♐45 39	12 19.0	27 04.3	14 28.4	5 25.3	1 40.6	5 36.5	11 57.3	22 54.6	9 47.1	14 56.8
6 Th	13 02 19	13 39 41	7♐41 40	13 38 46	12 14.7	28 39.3	15 41.4	6 05.8	1 28.6	5 49.4	12 02.0	22 52.2	9 45.8	14 57.1
7 F	13 06 15	14 38 53	19 37 24	25 38 03	12 11.5	0♎16.7	16 54.4	6 46.5	1 16.4	6 02.3	12 06.8	22 49.8	9 44.5	14 57.4
8 Sa	13 10 12	15 38 07	1♑41 17	7♑47 37	12D09.8	1 56.1	18 07.3	7 27.4	1 04.0	6 15.2	12 11.7	22 47.4	9 43.3	14 57.8
9 Su	13 14 08	16 37 24	13 57 38	20 11 53	12 09.6	3 37.1	19 20.2	8 08.3	0 51.3	6 28.1	12 16.6	22 44.9	9 42.0	14 58.2
10 M	13 18 05	17 36 41	26 30 56	2♒55 20	12 10.5	5 19.2	20 33.1	8 49.4	0 38.5	6 41.0	12 21.6	22 42.5	9 40.8	14 58.6
11 Tu	13 22 02	18 36 01	9♒25 34	16 02 05	12 12.0	7 02.3	21 45.9	9 30.7	0 25.6	6 53.8	12 26.6	22 40.1	9 39.6	14 59.0
12 W	13 25 58	19 35 22	22 45 15	29 35 20	12R13.4	8 45.9	22 58.8	10 12.0	0 12.5	7 06.7	12 31.7	22 37.6	9 38.4	14 59.5
13 Th	13 29 55	20 34 45	6♓32 26	13♓36 33	12 13.9	10 30.0	24 11.5	10 53.5	29♈59.3	7 19.5	12 36.9	22 35.2	9 37.3	15 00.0
14 F	13 33 51	21 34 10	20 47 29	28 04 48	12 12.9	12 14.2	25 24.3	11 35.1	29 45.9	7 32.3	12 42.2	22 32.8	9 36.1	15 00.5
15 Sa	13 37 48	22 33 37	5♈27 56	12♈56 05	12 10.1	13 58.5	26 37.1	12 16.8	29 32.5	7 45.0	12 47.5	22 30.3	9 35.0	15 01.0
16 Su	13 41 44	23 33 06	20 28 14	28 03 15	12 05.4	15 42.7	27 49.8	12 58.6	29 18.9	7 57.8	12 52.8	22 27.9	9 33.9	15 01.6
17 M	13 45 41	24 32 36	5♉39 53	13♉16 47	11 59.3	17 26.6	29 02.4	13 40.5	29 05.3	8 10.5	12 58.3	22 25.4	9 32.9	15 02.2
18 Tu	13 49 37	25 32 09	20 52 37	28 26 07	11 52.7	19 10.3	0♐15.1	14 22.5	28 51.6	8 23.2	13 03.7	22 23.0	9 31.9	15 02.9
19 W	13 53 34	26 31 45	5♊56 05	13♊21 31	11 46.4	20 53.6	1 27.7	15 04.6	28 37.9	8 35.9	13 09.3	22 20.5	9 30.9	15 03.6
20 Th	13 57 31	27 31 22	20 41 34	27 55 38	11 41.4	22 36.5	2 40.3	15 46.9	28 24.1	8 48.5	13 14.9	22 18.1	9 29.9	15 04.3
21 F	14 01 27	28 31 02	5♋03 15	12♋04 14	11 38.2	24 18.9	3 52.9	16 29.2	28 10.4	9 01.1	13 20.5	22 15.7	9 28.9	15 05.0
22 Sa	14 05 24	29 30 44	18 58 31	25 46 12	11D36.8	26 00.9	5 05.5	17 11.7	27 56.6	9 13.7	13 26.3	22 13.3	9 28.0	15 05.8
23 Su	14 09 20	0♏30 29	2♌27 33	9♌02 53	11 37.1	27 42.3	6 18.0	17 54.2	27 42.8	9 26.2	13 32.0	22 10.9	9 27.1	15 06.6
24 M	14 13 17	1 30 15	15 32 38	21 57 15	11 38.2	29 23.3	7 30.5	18 36.9	27 29.1	9 38.8	13 37.8	22 08.4	9 26.2	15 07.4
25 Tu	14 17 13	2 30 04	28 17 14	4♍33 03	11R39.3	1♏03.6	8 42.9	19 19.6	27 15.4	9 51.2	13 43.7	22 06.0	9 25.4	15 08.2
26 W	14 21 10	3 29 55	10♍45 12	16 54 10	11 39.3	2 43.5	9 55.4	20 02.5	27 01.8	10 03.7	13 49.6	22 03.7	9 24.6	15 09.1
27 Th	14 25 06	4 29 48	23 00 23	29 04 15	11 37.6	4 22.8	11 07.8	20 45.4	26 48.2	10 16.1	13 55.6	22 01.3	9 23.8	15 10.0
28 F	14 29 03	5 29 43	5♎06 09	11♎06 24	11 33.4	6 01.6	12 20.2	21 28.4	26 34.8	10 28.4	14 01.6	21 58.9	9 23.0	15 11.0
29 Sa	14 32 59	6 29 40	17 05 20	23 03 10	11 26.7	7 39.9	13 32.5	22 11.6	26 21.4	10 40.8	14 07.7	21 56.6	9 22.3	15 11.9
30 Su	14 36 56	7 29 40	29 00 11	4♏56 33	11 17.6	9 17.7	14 44.8	22 54.8	26 08.2	10 53.0	14 13.8	21 54.2	9 21.6	15 12.9
31 M	14 40 53	8 29 41	10♏52 28	16 48 09	11 06.7	10 55.0	15 57.1	23 38.1	25 55.1	11 05.3	14 20.0	21 51.9	9 20.9	15 13.9

Astro Data

	Dy Hr Mn
♀0S	1 1:30
☽0S	3 9:52
♄□♆	10 13:04
☿0N	12 0:24
☽0N	17 11:45
♃0S	21 4:59
☿ D	22 5:29
☉0S	22 14:21
♇ D	26 15:02
☽0S	30 16:46
⚳0S	1 18:15
☿0S	9 23:51
☽0N	14 22:31
♃⚻♆	23 13:33
☽0S	27 23:03

Planet Ingress

		Dy Hr Mn
♃	♎	9 11:18
☉	♎	22 14:21
♀	♏	23 14:51
♂	♑	27 8:07
☿	♎	7 7:56
⚳	♈R	13 10:41
♀	♐	18 7:01
☉	♏	22 23:46
☿	♏	24 20:46

Last Aspect / ☽ Ingress

Last Aspect Dy Hr Mn			☽ Ingress	Dy Hr Mn
2 22:13	♃	☌	♎	3 0:55
5 0:30	♅	☍	♏	5 12:38
8 0:42	♃	⚹	♐	8 1:20
10 0:51	♅	△	♑	10 12:55
12 10:00	♅	□	♒	12 21:28
14 15:31	♅	⚹	♓	15 2:23
16 19:05	☉	☍	♈	17 4:22
18 20:10	♂	△	♉	19 4:58
21 3:32	☉	△	♊	21 5:53
23 7:57	♀	△	♋	23 8:33
25 1:42	♅	□	♌	25 13:48
27 8:52	♅	△	♍	27 21:43
29 10:05	☿	☌	♎	30 7:52

Last Aspect / ☽ Ingress

Last Aspect Dy Hr Mn			☽ Ingress	Dy Hr Mn
2 5:43	♅	☍	♏	2 19:43
5 1:04	☿	⚹	♐	5 8:26
7 6:26	♅	△	♑	7 20:40
9 16:51	♅	□	♒	10 6:33
11 23:49	♅	⚹	♓	12 12:43
14 7:13	♀	△	♈	14 15:08
16 4:23	☉	☍	♉	16 15:04
17 14:47	♇	△	♊	18 14:30
20 11:17	☉	△	♋	20 15:28
22 19:14	☉	□	♌	22 19:34
24 12:21	♅	△	♍	25 3:16
26 18:33	♂	△	♎	27 13:51
29 10:09	♂	□	♏	30 2:01

☽ Phases & Eclipses

Dy Hr Mn		
1 9:03	●	9♍21
1 9:06:52	●	A 03'05"
9 11:49	☽	17♐13
16 19:05	○	24♓20
16 18:54	●	A 0.908
23 9:56	☾	0♋48
1 0:11	●	8♎15
9 4:33	☽	16♑19
16 4:23	○	23♈14
22 19:14	☾	29♋49
30 17:38	●	7♏44

Astro Data

1 September 2016
Julian Day # 42613
SVP 5♓01'41"
GC 27♐04.3 ⚵ 24♒53.7R
Eris 23♈28.9R ⚴ 9♏51.6
⚷ 23♓33.3R ⚶ 14♋43.6
☽ Mean ☊ 12♍39.6

1 October 2016
Julian Day # 42643
SVP 5♓01'39"
GC 27♐04.4 ⚵ 19♒37.9R
Eris 23♈13.6R ⚴ 18♏21.7
⚷ 22♓11.8R ⚶ 24♋53.9
☽ Mean ☊ 11♍04.2

November 2016 — LONGITUDE

Day	Sid.Time	☉	0 hr ☽	Noon☽	True☊	☿	♀	♂	⚳	♃	♄	♅	♆	♇
1 Tu	14 44 49	9♏29 44	22♏43 44	28♏39 26	10♍54.9	12♏31.8	17♐09.4	24♑21.4	25♈42.2	11♎17.5	14♐26.2	21♈49.6	9♓20.3	15♑15.0
2 W	14 48 46	10 29 49	4♐35 26	10♐31 57	10R 43.2	14 08.2	18 21.6	25 04.9	25R 29.4	11 29.6	14 32.4	21R 47.3	9R 19.7	15 16.0
3 Th	14 52 42	11 29 55	16 29 14	22 27 34	10 32.6	15 44.1	19 33.7	25 48.5	25 16.9	11 41.7	14 38.7	21 45.1	9 19.1	15 17.1
4 F	14 56 39	12 30 03	28 27 16	4♑28 40	10 24.0	17 19.6	20 45.9	26 32.1	25 04.5	11 53.8	14 45.1	21 42.8	9 18.6	15 18.3
5 Sa	15 00 35	13 30 13	10♑32 12	16 38 17	10 18.0	18 54.6	21 58.0	27 15.8	24 52.3	12 05.8	14 51.4	21 40.6	9 18.1	15 19.4
6 Su	15 04 32	14 30 25	22 47 23	29 00 02	10 14.5	20 29.3	23 10.0	27 59.5	24 40.4	12 17.7	14 57.9	21 38.4	9 17.6	15 20.6
7 M	15 08 28	15 30 38	5♒16 45	11♒38 04	10D 13.2	22 03.6	24 22.0	28 43.4	24 28.7	12 29.6	15 04.3	21 36.2	9 17.2	15 21.8
8 Tu	15 12 25	16 30 52	18 04 34	24 36 45	10 13.3	23 37.5	25 33.9	29 27.3	24 17.2	12 41.4	15 10.8	21 34.1	9 16.8	15 23.0
9 W	15 16 22	17 31 08	1♓15 07	8♓00 06	10R 13.8	25 11.1	26 45.8	0♒11.3	24 06.0	12 53.2	15 17.3	21 31.9	9 16.4	15 24.3
10 Th	15 20 18	18 31 25	14 52 03	21 51 10	10 13.3	26 44.3	27 57.7	0 55.3	23 55.1	13 04.9	15 23.9	21 29.8	9 16.1	15 25.6
11 F	15 24 15	19 31 44	28 57 30	6♈10 57	10 10.8	28 17.2	29 09.5	1 39.4	23 44.5	13 16.5	15 30.5	21 27.7	9 15.7	15 26.9
12 Sa	15 28 11	20 32 04	13♈31 09	20 57 33	10 05.8	29 49.8	0♑21.2	2 23.5	23 34.1	13 28.1	15 37.1	21 25.7	9 15.5	15 28.2
13 Su	15 32 08	21 32 25	28 29 21	6♉05 30	9 58.1	1♐22.0	1 32.9	3 07.7	23 24.1	13 39.6	15 43.8	21 23.7	9 15.2	15 29.6
14 M	15 36 04	22 32 49	13♉44 45	21 25 44	9 48.2	2 54.0	2 44.5	3 52.0	23 14.4	13 51.1	15 50.5	21 21.7	9 15.0	15 30.9
15 Tu	15 40 01	23 33 14	29 06 56	6♊46 50	9 37.3	4 25.7	3 56.0	4 36.3	23 04.9	14 02.5	15 57.2	21 19.7	9 14.8	15 32.3
16 W	15 43 57	24 33 40	14♊24 00	21 57 04	9 26.7	5 57.2	5 07.5	5 20.7	22 55.8	14 13.8	16 03.9	21 17.8	9 14.7	15 33.8
17 Th	15 47 54	25 34 09	29 24 51	6♋46 26	9 17.6	7 28.3	6 19.0	6 05.1	22 47.1	14 25.1	16 10.7	21 15.9	9 14.6	15 35.2
18 F	15 51 51	26 34 39	14♋01 05	21 08 21	9 10.9	8 59.1	7 30.3	6 49.5	22 38.6	14 36.3	16 17.5	21 14.0	9 14.5	15 36.7
19 Sa	15 55 47	27 35 11	28 08 00	5♌00 02	9 06.8	10 29.7	8 41.6	7 34.0	22 30.5	14 47.4	16 24.3	21 12.2	9D 14.5	15 38.2
20 Su	15 59 44	28 35 44	11♌44 38	18 22 06	9D 05.0	12 00.0	9 52.9	8 18.6	22 22.8	14 58.4	16 31.2	21 10.4	9 14.5	15 39.7
21 M	16 03 40	29 36 20	24 52 53	1♍17 31	9R 04.7	13 29.9	11 04.1	9 03.2	22 15.4	15 09.4	16 38.1	21 08.6	9 14.5	15 41.2
22 Tu	16 07 37	0♐36 57	7♍36 36	13 50 45	9 04.7	14 59.6	12 15.2	9 47.8	22 08.4	15 20.3	16 45.0	21 06.9	9 14.6	15 42.8
23 W	16 11 33	1 37 36	20 00 35	26 06 44	9 03.8	16 28.9	13 26.2	10 32.5	22 01.8	15 31.1	16 51.9	21 05.2	9 14.6	15 44.4
24 Th	16 15 30	2 38 16	2♎09 49	8♎10 23	9 00.8	17 57.8	14 37.2	11 17.2	21 55.5	15 41.8	16 58.8	21 03.5	9 14.8	15 45.9
25 F	16 19 26	3 38 58	14 09 00	20 06 09	8 55.1	19 26.2	15 48.0	12 02.0	21 49.6	15 52.4	17 05.8	21 01.9	9 14.9	15 47.6
26 Sa	16 23 23	4 39 42	26 02 16	1♏57 45	8 46.2	20 54.2	16 58.9	12 46.8	21 44.1	16 03.0	17 12.7	21 00.3	9 15.1	15 49.2
27 Su	16 27 20	5 40 27	7♏52 58	13 48 11	8 34.5	22 21.7	18 09.6	13 31.7	21 38.9	16 13.5	17 19.7	20 58.7	9 15.4	15 50.9
28 M	16 31 16	6 41 13	19 43 40	25 39 39	8 20.5	23 48.5	19 20.2	14 16.6	21 34.2	16 23.8	17 26.7	20 57.2	9 15.6	15 52.5
29 Tu	16 35 13	7 42 01	1♐36 17	7♐33 45	8 05.4	25 14.7	20 30.8	15 01.5	21 29.8	16 34.1	17 33.7	20 55.8	9 16.0	15 54.2
30 W	16 39 09	8 42 50	13 32 10	19 31 42	7 50.2	26 40.1	21 41.3	15 46.5	21 25.9	16 44.3	17 40.8	20 54.4	9 16.3	15 55.9

December 2016 — LONGITUDE

Day	Sid.Time	☉	0 hr ☽	Noon☽	True☊	☿	♀	♂	⚳	♃	♄	♅	♆	♇
1 Th	16 43 06	9♐43 41	25♐32 27	1♑34 34	7♍36.4	28♐04.6	22♑51.6	16♒31.5	21♈22.3	16♎54.5	17♐47.8	20♈53.0	9♓16.7	15♑57.7
2 F	16 47 02	10 44 32	7♑38 14	13 43 38	7R 24.9	29 28.0	24 01.9	17 16.5	21R 19.1	17 04.5	17 54.9	20R 51.7	9 17.1	15 59.4
3 Sa	16 50 59	11 45 24	19 50 59	26 00 34	7 16.3	0♑50.2	25 12.1	18 01.5	21 16.3	17 14.4	18 01.9	20 50.4	9 17.5	16 01.2
4 Su	16 54 55	12 46 18	2♒12 39	8♒27 36	7 10.9	2 11.0	26 22.2	18 46.6	21 14.0	17 24.2	18 09.0	20 49.1	9 18.0	16 03.0
5 M	16 58 52	13 47 12	14 45 48	21 07 40	7 08.2	3 30.2	27 32.2	19 31.7	21 12.0	17 33.9	18 16.1	20 47.9	9 18.5	16 04.7
6 Tu	17 02 49	14 48 07	27 33 38	4♓04 09	7 07.5	4 47.5	28 42.0	20 16.9	21 10.4	17 43.5	18 23.2	20 46.8	9 19.1	16 06.6
7 W	17 06 45	15 49 02	10♓39 41	17 20 39	7 07.5	6 02.6	29 51.7	21 02.0	21 09.2	17 53.0	18 30.3	20 45.6	9 19.6	16 08.4
8 Th	17 10 42	16 49 58	24 07 25	1♈00 19	7 07.0	7 15.2	1♒01.3	21 47.2	21 08.4	18 02.4	18 37.4	20 44.6	9 20.3	16 10.2
9 F	17 14 38	17 50 55	7♈59 33	15 05 10	7 04.6	8 24.9	2 10.8	22 32.4	21D 08.0	18 11.7	18 44.5	20 43.5	9 20.9	16 12.1
10 Sa	17 18 35	18 51 52	22 17 06	29 35 02	6 59.7	9 31.1	3 20.1	23 17.6	21 08.0	18 20.9	18 51.5	20 42.6	9 21.6	16 13.9
11 Su	17 22 31	19 52 50	6♉58 30	14♉26 46	6 52.0	10 33.5	4 29.3	24 02.8	21 08.4	18 30.0	18 58.6	20 41.6	9 22.3	16 15.8
12 M	17 26 28	20 53 49	21 58 55	29 33 51	6 42.1	11 31.4	5 38.4	24 48.0	21 09.2	18 38.9	19 05.7	20 40.8	9 23.0	16 17.7
13 Tu	17 30 24	21 54 49	7♊10 15	14♊46 48	6 31.0	12 24.1	6 47.3	25 33.3	21 10.3	18 47.8	19 12.8	20 39.9	9 23.8	16 19.6
14 W	17 34 21	22 55 49	22 22 04	29 54 41	6 19.9	13 10.9	7 56.1	26 18.5	21 11.9	18 56.5	19 19.9	20 39.2	9 24.7	16 21.5
15 Th	17 38 18	23 56 50	7♋23 22	14♋47 00	6 10.2	13 51.1	9 04.7	27 03.8	21 13.8	19 05.1	19 27.0	20 38.4	9 25.5	16 23.5
16 F	17 42 14	24 57 52	22 04 40	29 15 39	6 02.9	14 23.8	10 13.1	27 49.1	21 16.1	19 13.6	19 34.1	20 37.7	9 26.4	16 25.4
17 Sa	17 46 11	25 58 54	6♌19 28	13♌15 52	5 58.2	14 48.0	11 21.4	28 34.4	21 18.7	19 22.0	19 41.1	20 37.1	9 27.3	16 27.4
18 Su	17 50 07	26 59 58	20 04 47	26 46 23	5D 56.1	15R 03.0	12 29.5	29 19.6	21 21.8	19 30.3	19 48.2	20 36.5	9 28.2	16 29.3
19 M	17 54 04	28 01 02	3♍20 55	9♍48 51	5 55.9	15 07.8	13 37.4	0♓04.9	21 25.2	19 38.4	19 55.3	20 36.0	9 29.2	16 31.3
20 Tu	17 58 00	29 02 07	16 10 39	22 26 56	5R 56.3	15 01.8	14 45.2	0 50.2	21 28.9	19 46.4	20 02.3	20 35.5	9 30.2	16 33.3
21 W	18 01 57	0♑03 13	28 38 19	4♎45 27	5 56.4	14 44.3	15 52.7	1 35.5	21 33.1	19 54.3	20 09.3	20 35.1	9 31.3	16 35.3
22 Th	18 05 54	1 04 20	10♎49 01	16 49 39	5 54.9	14 15.1	17 00.1	2 20.9	21 37.5	20 02.0	20 16.4	20 34.7	9 32.3	16 37.3
23 F	18 09 50	2 05 27	22 48 00	28 44 41	5 51.3	13 34.2	18 07.3	3 06.2	21 42.4	20 09.6	20 23.4	20 34.3	9 33.4	16 39.3
24 Sa	18 13 47	3 06 35	4♏40 16	10♏35 18	5 45.0	12 42.2	19 14.3	3 51.5	21 47.6	20 17.1	20 30.3	20 34.1	9 34.6	16 41.3
25 Su	18 17 43	4 07 44	16 30 14	22 25 32	5 36.1	11 40.1	20 21.1	4 36.8	21 53.1	20 24.5	20 37.3	20 33.8	9 35.7	16 43.3
26 M	18 21 40	5 08 53	28 21 34	4♐18 40	5 25.3	10 29.5	21 27.6	5 22.2	21 59.0	20 31.7	20 44.3	20 33.7	9 36.9	16 45.3
27 Tu	18 25 36	6 10 03	10♐17 08	16 17 10	5 13.4	9 12.6	22 33.9	6 07.5	22 05.2	20 38.7	20 51.2	20 33.5	9 38.2	16 47.3
28 W	18 29 33	7 11 13	22 18 59	28 22 43	5 01.4	7 51.7	23 40.1	6 52.8	22 11.8	20 45.7	20 58.2	20D 33.5	9 39.4	16 49.4
29 Th	18 33 29	8 12 23	4♑28 30	10♑36 24	4 50.4	6 29.7	24 45.9	7 38.1	22 18.7	20 52.4	21 05.1	20 33.4	9 40.7	16 51.4
30 F	18 37 26	9 13 33	16 46 31	22 58 55	4 41.3	5 09.1	25 51.5	8 23.5	22 26.0	20 59.1	21 11.9	20 33.5	9 42.0	16 53.5
31 Sa	18 41 23	10 14 44	29 13 41	5♒30 53	4 34.8	3 52.6	26 56.9	9 08.8	22 33.5	21 05.6	21 18.8	20 33.6	9 43.4	16 55.5

Astro Data	Dy Hr Mn
♄⚺♇	10 19:39
☽0N	11 9:52
♆D	20 4:39
☽0S	24 5:54
♃□♇	24 23:00
☽0N	8 19:50
⚳D	10 0:26
⚳0N	14 21:23
☿R	19 10:55
☽0S	21 14:12
♄△♅	25 0:21
♃☍♅	26 18:35
♅D	29 9:29

Planet Ingress		Dy Hr Mn
♂	♒	9 5:51
♀	♑	12 4:54
☿	♐	12 14:39
☉	♐	21 21:22
☿	♑	2 21:18
♀	♒	7 14:51
♂	♓	19 9:23
☉	♑	21 10:44

Last Aspect Dy Hr Mn			☽ Ingress	Dy Hr Mn
1 2:44	♂	⚹	♐	1 14:43
3 10:35	♅	△	♑	4 3:05
6 9:56	♂	☌	♒	6 13:55
8 13:54	♀	⚹	♓	8 21:45
10 23:16	♀	□	♈	11 1:45
12 12:45	♅	☌	♉	13 2:24
14 13:52	☉	☍	♊	15 1:23
16 10:58	♅	⚹	♋	17 0:57
18 22:02	☉	△	♌	19 3:14
21 8:33	☉	□	♍	21 9:34
22 17:41	♄	□	♎	23 19:42
25 13:52	♅	☍	♏	26 8:01
27 21:48	♀	⚹	♐	28 20:46

Last Aspect Dy Hr Mn			☽ Ingress	Dy Hr Mn
1 4:08	☿	☌	♑	1 8:52
3 10:16	♀	☌	♒	3 19:44
5 11:23	♅	⚹	♓	6 4:31
7 14:05	♄	□	♈	8 10:15
10 1:06	♂	⚹	♉	10 12:41
12 4:04	♂	□	♊	12 12:41
14 5:57	♂	△	♋	14 12:09
15 21:37	♅	□	♌	16 13:15
18 16:55	♂	☍	♍	18 17:52
21 1:56	☉	□	♎	21 2:40
22 19:31	♅	☍	♏	23 14:32
25 7:22	♀	□	♐	26 3:19
28 1:45	♀	⚹	♑	28 15:12
30 8:07	♃	□	♒	31 1:29

☽ Phases & Eclipses Dy Hr Mn	
7 19:51	☽ 15♒50
14 13:52	○ 22♉38
21 8:33	☾ 29♌28
29 12:18	● 7♐43
7 9:03	☽ 15♓42
14 0:06	○ 22♊26
21 1:56	☾ 29♍38
29 6:53	● 7♑59

Astro Data

1 November 2016
Julian Day # 42674
SVP 5♓01'36"
GC 27♐04.5 ⚴ 19♒26.6
Eris 22♈55.3R ⚵ 28♏21.0
⚷ 21♓04.6R ⚶ 2♌41.5
☽ Mean ☊ 9♍25.7

1 December 2016
Julian Day # 42704
SVP 5♓01'32"
GC 27♐04.5 ⚴ 23♒43.7
Eris 22♈40.3R ⚵ 8♐36.1
⚷ 20♓40.2 ⚶ 5♌42.5
☽ Mean ☊ 7♍50.4

LONGITUDE January 2017

Day	Sid.Time	☉	0 hr ☽	Noon ☽	True ☊	☿	♀	♂	⚳	♃	♄	♅	♆	♇
1 Su	18 45 19	11♑15 54	11♒50 37	18♒13 02	4♍30.9	2♑42.3	28♒02.0	9♓54.1	22♈41.4	21♎11.9	21♐25.6	20♈33.7	9♓44.7	16♑57.6
2 M	18 49 16	12 17 05	24 38 16	1♓06 31	4D 29.4	1R 40.0	29 06.8	10 39.4	22 49.6	21 18.1	21 32.4	20 33.9	9 46.1	16 59.6
3 Tu	18 53 12	13 18 15	7♓37 58	14 12 51	4 29.7	0 46.8	0♓11.3	11 24.7	22 58.2	21 24.1	21 39.2	20 34.1	9 47.6	17 01.7
4 W	18 57 09	14 19 25	20 51 25	27 33 54	4 30.9	0 03.6	1 15.6	12 10.0	23 07.0	21 30.0	21 46.0	20 34.4	9 49.0	17 03.8
5 Th	19 01 05	15 20 34	4♈20 31	11♈11 29	4R 31.7	29♐30.5	2 19.5	12 55.3	23 16.1	21 35.7	21 52.7	20 34.8	9 50.5	17 05.8
6 F	19 05 02	16 21 43	18 06 55	25 06 54	4 31.4	29 07.6	3 23.1	13 40.6	23 25.6	21 41.3	21 59.4	20 35.1	9 52.0	17 07.9
7 Sa	19 08 58	17 22 52	2♉11 25	9♉20 18	4 29.3	28D 54.6	4 26.3	14 25.8	23 35.3	21 46.7	22 06.0	20 35.6	9 53.5	17 09.9
8 Su	19 12 55	18 24 00	16 33 17	23 49 58	4 25.1	28 51.0	5 29.2	15 11.1	23 45.3	21 51.9	22 12.7	20 36.1	9 55.1	17 12.0
9 M	19 16 52	19 25 08	1♊09 44	8♊31 55	4 19.2	28 56.1	6 31.8	15 56.3	23 55.7	21 57.0	22 19.2	20 36.7	9 56.7	17 14.1
10 Tu	19 20 48	20 26 15	15 55 40	23 20 00	4 12.2	29 09.3	7 33.9	16 41.5	24 06.3	22 01.9	22 25.8	20 37.3	9 58.3	17 16.1
11 W	19 24 45	21 27 22	0♋43 57	8♋06 27	4 05.2	29 30.0	8 35.7	17 26.7	24 17.1	22 06.7	22 32.3	20 37.9	9 59.9	17 18.2
12 Th	19 28 41	22 28 29	15 26 30	22 43 07	3 58.9	29 57.4	9 37.1	18 11.9	24 28.3	22 11.3	22 38.8	20 38.6	10 01.6	17 20.2
13 F	19 32 38	23 29 35	29 55 26	7♌02 43	3 54.3	0♑30.9	10 38.1	18 57.0	24 39.7	22 15.7	22 45.3	20 39.4	10 03.3	17 22.3
14 Sa	19 36 34	24 30 41	14♌04 23	21 00 01	3D 51.6	1 09.9	11 38.6	19 42.2	24 51.4	22 20.0	22 51.7	20 40.2	10 05.0	17 24.3
15 Su	19 40 31	25 31 47	27 49 21	4♍32 17	3 50.9	1 53.9	12 38.7	20 27.3	25 03.3	22 24.1	22 58.0	20 41.1	10 06.7	17 26.4
16 M	19 44 27	26 32 52	11♍08 53	17 39 20	3 51.6	2 42.4	13 38.4	21 12.4	25 15.5	22 28.0	23 04.4	20 42.0	10 08.5	17 28.4
17 Tu	19 48 24	27 33 57	24 03 55	0♎23 03	3 53.2	3 34.8	14 37.5	21 57.4	25 28.0	22 31.7	23 10.7	20 42.9	10 10.3	17 30.5
18 W	19 52 21	28 35 02	6♎37 12	12 46 54	3 54.9	4 30.9	15 36.2	22 42.5	25 40.7	22 35.3	23 16.9	20 43.9	10 12.1	17 32.5
19 Th	19 56 17	29 36 06	18 52 44	24 55 19	3R 56.0	5 30.2	16 34.4	23 27.5	25 53.6	22 38.7	23 23.1	20 45.0	10 13.9	17 34.5
20 F	20 00 14	0♒37 10	0♏55 16	6♏53 12	3 55.9	6 32.5	17 32.1	24 12.5	26 06.8	22 41.9	23 29.2	20 46.1	10 15.7	17 36.5
21 Sa	20 04 10	1 38 14	12 49 46	18 45 33	3 54.3	7 37.4	18 29.2	24 57.5	26 20.3	22 45.0	23 35.4	20 47.3	10 17.6	17 38.6
22 Su	20 08 07	2 39 17	24 41 08	0♐37 06	3 51.2	8 44.7	19 25.7	25 42.5	26 33.9	22 47.8	23 41.4	20 48.5	10 19.5	17 40.6
23 M	20 12 03	3 40 20	6♐33 56	12 32 09	3 46.9	9 54.1	20 21.7	26 27.5	26 47.8	22 50.5	23 47.4	20 49.7	10 21.4	17 42.6
24 Tu	20 16 00	4 41 22	18 32 09	24 34 20	3 41.9	11 05.6	21 17.1	27 12.4	27 02.0	22 53.0	23 53.4	20 51.1	10 23.3	17 44.6
25 W	20 19 56	5 42 24	0♑39 01	6♑46 29	3 36.6	12 18.8	22 11.9	27 57.3	27 16.3	22 55.3	23 59.3	20 52.4	10 25.2	17 46.6
26 Th	20 23 53	6 43 25	12 56 57	19 10 36	3 31.8	13 33.7	23 06.0	28 42.2	27 30.9	22 57.4	24 05.1	20 53.8	10 27.2	17 48.5
27 F	20 27 50	7 44 25	25 27 32	1♒47 49	3 28.0	14 50.2	23 59.5	29 27.0	27 45.7	22 59.4	24 10.9	20 55.3	10 29.2	17 50.5
28 Sa	20 31 46	8 45 25	8♒11 28	14 38 29	3 25.4	16 08.0	24 52.2	0♈11.9	28 00.7	23 01.1	24 16.7	20 56.8	10 31.2	17 52.5
29 Su	20 35 43	9 46 23	21 08 49	27 42 25	3D 24.2	17 27.2	25 44.2	0 56.7	28 15.9	23 02.7	24 22.4	20 58.3	10 33.2	17 54.4
30 M	20 39 39	10 47 20	4♓19 10	10♓59 00	3 24.2	18 47.7	26 35.5	1 41.4	28 31.4	23 04.1	24 28.0	20 59.9	10 35.2	17 56.3
31 Tu	20 43 36	11 48 17	17 41 49	24 27 30	3 25.2	20 09.3	27 26.0	2 26.2	28 47.0	23 05.3	24 33.6	21 01.6	10 37.2	17 58.3

LONGITUDE February 2017

Day	Sid.Time	☉	0 hr ☽	Noon ☽	True ☊	☿	♀	♂	⚳	♃	♄	♅	♆	♇
1 W	20 47 32	12♒49 11	1♈15 59	8♈07 09	3♍26.7	21♑32.0	28♓15.7	3♈10.9	29♈02.9	23♎06.3	24♐39.1	21♈03.2	10♓39.3	18♑00.2
2 Th	20 51 29	13 50 05	15 00 55	21 57 10	3 28.1	22 55.7	29 04.5	3 55.6	29 18.9	23 07.1	24 44.5	21 05.0	10 41.4	18 02.1
3 F	20 55 25	14 50 57	28 55 50	5♉56 45	3R 29.0	24 20.5	29 52.4	4 40.3	29 35.1	23 07.7	24 49.9	21 06.7	10 43.4	18 04.0
4 Sa	20 59 22	15 51 48	12♉59 46	20 04 41	3 29.2	25 46.2	0♈39.4	5 24.9	29 51.5	23 08.1	24 55.3	21 08.6	10 45.5	18 05.8
5 Su	21 03 19	16 52 38	27 11 17	4♊19 16	3 28.5	27 12.9	1 25.4	6 09.5	0♉08.1	23R 08.4	25 00.5	21 10.4	10 47.7	18 07.7
6 M	21 07 15	17 53 26	11♊28 18	18 37 58	3 27.1	28 40.5	2 10.5	6 54.1	0 24.9	23 08.4	25 05.7	21 12.3	10 49.8	18 09.6
7 Tu	21 11 12	18 54 12	25 47 50	2♋57 23	3 25.2	0♒08.9	2 54.4	7 38.6	0 41.9	23 08.3	25 10.9	21 14.3	10 51.9	18 11.4
8 W	21 15 08	19 54 57	10♋06 05	17 13 22	3 23.3	1 38.3	3 37.3	8 23.1	0 59.0	23 08.0	25 15.9	21 16.3	10 54.1	18 13.2
9 Th	21 19 05	20 55 41	24 18 41	1♌21 26	3 21.7	3 08.5	4 19.1	9 07.5	1 16.3	23 07.4	25 20.9	21 18.3	10 56.2	18 15.0
10 F	21 23 01	21 56 23	8♌21 08	15 17 16	3 20.6	4 39.6	4 59.7	9 51.9	1 33.8	23 06.7	25 25.9	21 20.4	10 58.4	18 16.8
11 Sa	21 26 58	22 57 04	22 09 24	28 57 12	3D 20.2	6 11.5	5 39.1	10 36.3	1 51.4	23 05.8	25 30.7	21 22.5	11 00.6	18 18.6
12 Su	21 30 54	23 57 43	5♍40 22	12♍18 46	3 20.2	7 44.3	6 17.2	11 20.7	2 09.2	23 04.8	25 35.5	21 24.7	11 02.8	18 20.3
13 M	21 34 51	24 58 21	18 52 16	25 20 53	3 20.7	9 17.9	6 54.0	12 05.0	2 27.2	23 03.5	25 40.2	21 26.9	11 05.0	18 22.1
14 Tu	21 38 48	25 58 58	1♎44 43	8♎03 57	3 21.5	10 52.4	7 29.4	12 49.2	2 45.3	23 02.0	25 44.9	21 29.1	11 07.2	18 23.8
15 W	21 42 44	26 59 33	14 18 50	20 29 43	3 22.2	12 27.8	8 03.4	13 33.5	3 03.6	23 00.4	25 49.5	21 31.4	11 09.4	18 25.5
16 Th	21 46 41	28 00 07	26 36 58	2♏41 04	3 22.9	14 04.0	8 36.0	14 17.7	3 22.0	22 58.6	25 54.0	21 33.7	11 11.6	18 27.2
17 F	21 50 37	29 00 41	8♏42 28	14 41 44	3 23.3	15 41.1	9 07.0	15 01.8	3 40.6	22 56.5	25 58.4	21 36.1	11 13.9	18 28.9
18 Sa	21 54 34	0♓01 12	20 39 24	26 36 03	3R 23.4	17 19.1	9 36.4	15 46.0	3 59.3	22 54.3	26 02.7	21 38.4	11 16.1	18 30.5
19 Su	21 58 30	1 01 43	2♐32 17	8♐28 42	3 23.4	18 58.0	10 04.2	16 30.1	4 18.2	22 51.9	26 07.0	21 40.9	11 18.4	18 32.1
20 M	22 02 27	2 02 12	14 25 52	20 24 22	3 23.3	20 37.8	10 30.4	17 14.1	4 37.2	22 49.4	26 11.2	21 43.3	11 20.6	18 33.7
21 Tu	22 06 23	3 02 40	26 24 46	2♑27 36	3D 23.2	22 18.6	10 54.7	17 58.2	4 56.4	22 46.6	26 15.3	21 45.8	11 22.9	18 35.3
22 W	22 10 20	4 03 07	8♑33 22	14 42 30	3 23.3	24 00.3	11 17.3	18 42.1	5 15.7	22 43.7	26 19.4	21 48.4	11 25.1	18 36.9
23 Th	22 14 17	5 03 32	20 55 25	27 12 28	3 23.4	25 42.9	11 37.9	19 26.1	5 35.1	22 40.6	26 23.3	21 50.9	11 27.4	18 38.5
24 F	22 18 13	6 03 56	3♒33 54	9♒59 56	3 23.6	27 26.6	11 56.6	20 10.0	5 54.7	22 37.3	26 27.2	21 53.5	11 29.7	18 40.0
25 Sa	22 22 10	7 04 18	16 30 41	23 06 11	3R 23.8	29 11.2	12 13.3	20 53.9	6 14.4	22 33.8	26 31.0	21 56.2	11 31.9	18 41.5
26 Su	22 26 06	8 04 38	29 46 24	6♓31 10	3 23.9	0♓56.8	12 28.0	21 37.7	6 34.2	22 30.1	26 34.7	21 58.8	11 34.2	18 43.0
27 M	22 30 03	9 04 57	13♓20 16	20 13 25	3 23.7	2 43.4	12 40.5	22 21.5	6 54.2	22 26.3	26 38.3	22 01.5	11 36.5	18 44.4
28 Tu	22 33 59	10 05 14	27 10 15	4♈10 19	3 23.1	4 31.0	12 50.8	23 05.3	7 14.3	22 22.3	26 41.9	22 04.3	11 38.8	18 45.9

Astro Data Dy Hr Mn	Planet Ingress Dy Hr Mn	Last Aspect Dy Hr Mn	☽ Ingress Dy Hr Mn	Last Aspect Dy Hr Mn	☽ Ingress Dy Hr Mn	☽ Phases & Eclipses Dy Hr Mn	Astro Data
☽0N 5 3:23	♀ ♓ 3 7:47	2 7:59 ♀ ☌	♓ 2 9:57	2 16:50 ♄ △	♉ 3 1:50	5 19:47 ☽ 15♈40	1 January 2017
☿D 8 9:43	☿ ♐R 4 14:17	4 16:14 ☿ □	♈ 4 16:20	4 22:42 ♄ △	♊ 5 4:44	12 11:34 ○ 22♋27	Julian Day # 42735
☽0S 17 23:46	☿ ♑ 12 14:03	6 18:41 ☿ △	♉ 6 20:18	6 22:53 ♄ ☍	♋ 7 7:03	19 22:13 ☾ 0♏02	SVP 5♓01'27"
♂0N 29 12:07	☉ ♒ 19 21:24	8 2:23 ☉ △	♊ 8 22:06	8 22:00 ♃ □	♌ 9 9:41	28 0:07 ● 8♒15	GC 27♐04.6 ⚴ 1♓13.5
♀0N 30 8:02	♂ ♈ 28 5:39	10 21:38 ☿ ☍	♋ 10 22:49	11 5:52 ♄ △	♍ 11 13:52		Eris 22♈32.4R ⚵ 19♐16.2
		12 11:34 ☉ ☍	♌ 13 0:08	13 12:36 ♄ □	♎ 13 20:43	4 4:19 ☽ 15♉32	⚷ 21♓07.0 ⚶ 2♌12.2R
☽0N 1 9:29	♀ ♈ 3 15:51	14 15:17 ♄ △	♍ 15 3:52	16 1:54 ☉ △	♏ 16 6:41	11 0:33 ○ 22♌28	☽ Mean ☊ 6♍11.9
♃R 6 6:52	⚳ ♉ 5 0:17	17 6:09 ☉ △	♎ 17 11:16	17 19:38 ♇ ⚹	♐ 18 18:52	11 0:44 A 0.988	
☽0S 14 9:29	☿ ♒ 7 9:35	19 8:55 ♄ ⚹	♏ 19 22:09	20 23:37 ♄ ☌	♑ 21 7:08	18 19:33 ☾ 0♐20	1 February 2017
☽0N 28 16:22	☉ ♓ 18 11:31	22 1:24 ♂ △	♐ 22 10:45	23 3:24 ♃ □	♒ 23 17:17	26 14:58 ● 8♓12	Julian Day # 42766
	☿ ♓ 25 23:07	24 17:33 ♂ □	♑ 24 22:43	25 18:11 ♄ ⚹	♓ 26 0:24	26 14:53:22 A 00'44"	SVP 5♓01'22"
		27 7:18 ♂ ⚹	♒ 27 8:37	27 23:08 ♄ □	♈ 28 4:52		GC 27♐04.7 ⚴ 10♓36.0
		29 5:52 ♄ ⚹	♓ 29 16:10				Eris 22♈34.9 ⚵ 29♐26.6
		31 17:36 ♀ ☌	♈ 31 21:46				⚷ 22♓20.7 ⚶ 24♋23.7R
							☽ Mean ☊ 4♍33.4

March 2017 — LONGITUDE

Day	Sid.Time	☉	0 hr ☽	Noon ☽	True ☊	☿	♀	♂	⚳	♃	♄	♅	♆	♇
1 W	22 37 56	11♓05 29	11♈13 09	18♈18 16	3♍22.3	6♓19.7	12♈58.8	23♈49.0	7♉34.5	22♎18.2	26♐45.3	22♈07.0	11♓41.1	18♑47.3
2 Th	22 41 52	12 05 42	25 25 07	2♉33 12	3R 21.3	8 09.3	13 04.5	24 32.7	7 54.8	22R 13.8	26 48.7	22 09.8	11 43.3	18 48.7
3 F	22 45 49	13 05 53	9♉42 01	16 51 03	3 20.3	10 00.0	13R 07.9	25 16.3	8 15.2	22 09.3	26 52.0	22 12.6	11 45.6	18 50.1
4 Sa	22 49 45	14 06 02	23 59 54	1♊08 07	3D 19.5	11 51.7	13 08.8	25 59.9	8 35.8	22 04.7	26 55.2	22 15.5	11 47.9	18 51.4
5 Su	22 53 42	15 06 09	8♊15 22	15 21 20	3 19.3	13 44.4	13 07.3	26 43.5	8 56.4	21 59.9	26 58.3	22 18.4	11 50.2	18 52.7
6 M	22 57 39	16 06 14	22 25 43	29 28 18	3 19.6	15 38.0	13 03.3	27 27.0	9 17.2	21 54.9	27 01.3	22 21.3	11 52.4	18 54.0
7 Tu	23 01 35	17 06 16	6♋28 53	13♋27 16	3 20.4	17 32.6	12 56.7	28 10.5	9 38.1	21 49.8	27 04.2	22 24.2	11 54.7	18 55.3
8 W	23 05 32	18 06 17	20 23 18	27 16 49	3 21.6	19 28.0	12 47.6	28 53.9	9 59.1	21 44.6	27 07.1	22 27.2	11 57.0	18 56.6
9 Th	23 09 28	19 06 15	4♌07 43	10♌55 51	3 22.8	21 24.2	12 36.1	29 37.3	10 20.2	21 39.2	27 09.8	22 30.1	11 59.3	18 57.8
10 F	23 13 25	20 06 11	17 41 05	24 23 17	3R 23.6	23 21.1	12 21.9	0♉20.7	10 41.4	21 33.7	27 12.4	22 33.1	12 01.5	18 59.0
11 Sa	23 17 21	21 06 05	1♍02 22	7♍38 12	3 23.8	25 18.7	12 05.4	1 04.0	11 02.6	21 28.0	27 15.0	22 36.2	12 03.8	19 00.2
12 Su	23 21 18	22 05 57	14 10 42	20 39 47	3 23.0	27 16.7	11 46.3	1 47.2	11 24.0	21 22.2	27 17.5	22 39.2	12 06.0	19 01.3
13 M	23 25 14	23 05 47	27 05 26	3♎27 36	3 21.1	29 15.0	11 25.0	2 30.4	11 45.5	21 16.2	27 19.8	22 42.3	12 08.3	19 02.4
14 Tu	23 29 11	24 05 35	9♎46 20	16 01 42	3 18.4	1♈13.5	11 01.3	3 13.6	12 07.1	21 10.2	27 22.1	22 45.4	12 10.5	19 03.5
15 W	23 33 08	25 05 22	22 13 48	28 22 49	3 14.9	3 11.8	10 35.5	3 56.7	12 28.7	21 04.0	27 24.3	22 48.5	12 12.8	19 04.6
16 Th	23 37 04	26 05 06	4♏28 57	10♏32 28	3 11.1	5 09.8	10 07.6	4 39.8	12 50.5	20 57.7	27 26.4	22 51.6	12 15.0	19 05.6
17 F	23 41 01	27 04 49	16 33 43	22 33 02	3 07.5	7 07.2	9 37.9	5 22.8	13 12.3	20 51.3	27 28.4	22 54.8	12 17.2	19 06.6
18 Sa	23 44 57	28 04 30	28 30 52	4♐27 39	3 04.5	9 03.6	9 06.4	6 05.8	13 34.3	20 44.7	27 30.3	22 58.0	12 19.4	19 07.6
19 Su	23 48 54	29 04 09	10♐23 54	16 20 08	3 02.6	10 58.7	8 33.3	6 48.8	13 56.3	20 38.1	27 32.1	23 01.2	12 21.6	19 08.6
20 M	23 52 50	0♈03 47	22 16 56	28 14 53	3D 01.8	12 52.1	7 58.9	7 31.7	14 18.4	20 31.4	27 33.8	23 04.4	12 23.8	19 09.5
21 Tu	23 56 47	1 03 23	4♑14 33	10♑16 35	3 02.1	14 43.4	7 23.4	8 14.6	14 40.6	20 24.5	27 35.4	23 07.6	12 26.0	19 10.4
22 W	0 00 43	2 02 57	16 21 34	22 30 04	3 03.4	16 32.1	6 46.9	8 57.4	15 02.9	20 17.6	27 36.9	23 10.9	12 28.2	19 11.3
23 Th	0 04 40	3 02 29	28 42 41	4♒59 56	3 05.1	18 17.8	6 09.8	9 40.2	15 25.2	20 10.6	27 38.3	23 14.1	12 30.4	19 12.2
24 F	0 08 37	4 02 00	11♒22 16	17 50 07	3 06.7	20 00.1	5 32.3	10 22.9	15 47.7	20 03.5	27 39.7	23 17.4	12 32.5	19 13.0
25 Sa	0 12 33	5 01 28	24 23 47	1♓03 30	3R 07.4	21 38.5	4 54.5	11 05.6	16 10.2	19 56.3	27 40.9	23 20.7	12 34.7	19 13.8
26 Su	0 16 30	6 00 55	7♓49 21	14 41 17	3 06.9	23 12.6	4 16.9	11 48.3	16 32.8	19 49.1	27 42.0	23 24.0	12 36.8	19 14.5
27 M	0 20 26	7 00 20	21 39 09	28 42 36	3 04.8	24 42.0	3 39.5	12 30.9	16 55.4	19 41.7	27 43.0	23 27.3	12 38.9	19 15.3
28 Tu	0 24 23	7 59 43	5♈51 09	13♈04 11	3 01.0	26 06.4	3 02.8	13 13.5	17 18.2	19 34.4	27 43.9	23 30.7	12 41.0	19 16.0
29 W	0 28 19	8 59 04	20 20 56	27 40 32	2 56.0	27 25.2	2 26.8	13 56.1	17 41.0	19 26.9	27 44.7	23 34.0	12 43.1	19 16.6
30 Th	0 32 16	9 58 22	5♉02 03	12♉24 33	2 50.3	28 38.4	1 51.8	14 38.6	18 03.8	19 19.4	27 45.4	23 37.4	12 45.2	19 17.3
31 F	0 36 12	10 57 39	19 47 02	27 08 35	2 44.9	29 45.5	1 18.1	15 21.0	18 26.8	19 11.9	27 46.1	23 40.7	12 47.3	19 17.9

April 2017 — LONGITUDE

Day	Sid.Time	☉	0 hr ☽	Noon ☽	True ☊	☿	♀	♂	⚳	♃	♄	♅	♆	♇
1 Sa	0 40 09	11♈56 53	4♊28 22	11♊45 39	2♍40.4	0♉46.3	0♈45.8	16♉03.4	18♉49.8	19♎04.3	27♐46.6	23♈44.1	12♓49.3	19♑18.5
2 Su	0 44 05	12 56 05	18 59 47	26 10 19	2R 37.4	1 40.6	0R 15.2	16 45.8	19 12.9	18R 56.7	27 47.0	23 47.5	12 51.4	19 19.0
3 M	0 48 02	13 55 15	3♋16 52	10♋19 13	2D 36.2	2 28.3	29♓46.3	17 28.1	19 36.0	18 49.1	27 47.3	23 50.9	12 53.4	19 19.6
4 Tu	0 51 59	14 54 22	17 17 15	24 10 58	2 36.5	3 09.2	29 19.4	18 10.4	19 59.2	18 41.4	27 47.5	23 54.3	12 55.4	19 20.1
5 W	0 55 55	15 53 27	1♌00 26	7♌45 46	2 37.7	3 43.2	28 54.5	18 52.7	20 22.5	18 33.7	27R 47.7	23 57.7	12 57.4	19 20.5
6 Th	0 59 52	16 52 29	14 27 08	21 04 44	2R 39.0	4 10.3	28 31.7	19 34.9	20 45.8	18 26.0	27 47.7	24 01.1	12 59.4	19 21.0
7 F	1 03 48	17 51 30	27 38 46	4♍09 26	2 39.5	4 30.5	28 11.3	20 17.0	21 09.2	18 18.3	27 47.6	24 04.6	13 01.4	19 21.4
8 Sa	1 07 45	18 50 28	10♍36 56	17 01 27	2 38.4	4 43.7	27 53.2	20 59.1	21 32.6	18 10.6	27 47.4	24 08.0	13 03.3	19 21.7
9 Su	1 11 41	19 49 23	23 23 06	29 42 03	2 35.2	4R 50.1	27 37.4	21 41.2	21 56.1	18 02.9	27 47.2	24 11.4	13 05.2	19 22.1
10 M	1 15 38	20 48 17	5♎58 25	12♎12 17	2 29.8	4 49.9	27 24.2	22 23.2	22 19.7	17 55.2	27 46.8	24 14.8	13 07.1	19 22.4
11 Tu	1 19 34	21 47 09	18 23 45	24 32 56	2 22.2	4 43.3	27 13.3	23 05.1	22 43.3	17 47.5	27 46.3	24 18.3	13 09.0	19 22.7
12 W	1 23 31	22 45 58	0♏39 53	6♏44 45	2 13.1	4 30.6	27 05.0	23 47.1	23 06.9	17 39.8	27 45.7	24 21.7	13 10.9	19 22.9
13 Th	1 27 28	23 44 46	12 47 39	18 48 45	2 03.2	4 12.2	26 59.1	24 29.0	23 30.6	17 32.2	27 45.1	24 25.1	13 12.7	19 23.2
14 F	1 31 24	24 43 32	24 48 14	0♐46 20	1 53.5	3 48.5	26D 55.6	25 10.8	23 54.4	17 24.6	27 44.3	24 28.6	13 14.5	19 23.4
15 Sa	1 35 21	25 42 16	6♐43 20	12 39 34	1 44.9	3 20.0	26 54.6	25 52.6	24 18.2	17 17.0	27 43.5	24 32.0	13 16.3	19 23.5
16 Su	1 39 17	26 40 59	18 35 23	24 31 12	1 38.0	2 47.4	26 55.9	26 34.4	24 42.0	17 09.5	27 42.5	24 35.4	13 18.1	19 23.7
17 M	1 43 14	27 39 39	0♑27 30	6♑24 46	1 33.2	2 11.4	26 59.6	27 16.1	25 06.0	17 02.0	27 41.5	24 38.9	13 19.9	19 23.8
18 Tu	1 47 10	28 38 18	12 23 34	18 24 28	1D 30.8	1 32.6	27 05.6	27 57.8	25 29.9	16 54.5	27 40.3	24 42.3	13 21.6	19 23.9
19 W	1 51 07	29 36 56	24 28 04	0♒35 00	1 30.1	0 51.8	27 13.9	28 39.4	25 53.9	16 47.1	27 39.1	24 45.7	13 23.4	19 23.9
20 Th	1 55 03	0♉35 31	6♒45 53	13 01 22	1 30.7	0 09.9	27 24.3	29 21.0	26 17.9	16 39.8	27 37.7	24 49.2	13 25.1	19R 23.9
21 F	1 59 00	1 34 05	19 22 03	25 48 28	1R 31.4	29♈27.6	27 36.8	0♊02.5	26 42.0	16 32.5	27 36.3	24 52.6	13 26.7	19 23.9
22 Sa	2 02 57	2 32 37	2♓21 09	9♓00 30	1 31.3	28 45.6	27 51.5	0 44.1	27 06.2	16 25.3	27 34.8	24 56.0	13 28.4	19 23.9
23 Su	2 06 53	3 31 08	15 46 50	22 40 17	1 29.4	28 04.8	28 08.1	1 25.5	27 30.3	16 18.2	27 33.2	24 59.4	13 30.0	19 23.8
24 M	2 10 50	4 29 37	29 40 53	6♈48 26	1 25.1	27 25.8	28 26.6	2 07.0	27 54.6	16 11.1	27 31.5	25 02.8	13 31.6	19 23.7
25 Tu	2 14 46	5 28 04	14♈02 32	21 22 35	1 18.4	26 49.3	28 47.0	2 48.4	28 18.8	16 04.2	27 29.7	25 06.2	13 33.2	19 23.5
26 W	2 18 43	6 26 29	28 47 45	6♉17 03	1 09.7	26 15.7	29 09.2	3 29.7	28 43.1	15 57.3	27 27.8	25 09.6	13 34.8	19 23.4
27 Th	2 22 39	7 24 53	13♉49 19	21 23 17	0 59.9	25 45.7	29 33.1	4 11.1	29 07.4	15 50.5	27 25.8	25 13.0	13 36.3	19 23.2
28 F	2 26 36	8 23 15	28 57 37	6♊31 01	0 50.2	25 19.6	29 58.7	4 52.3	29 31.8	15 43.8	27 23.7	25 16.4	13 37.8	19 23.0
29 Sa	2 30 32	9 21 35	14♊02 15	21 30 12	0 41.8	24 57.6	0♈25.8	5 33.6	29 56.2	15 37.2	27 21.6	25 19.7	13 39.3	19 22.7
30 Su	2 34 29	10 19 53	28 53 54	6♋12 37	0 35.5	24 40.2	0 54.6	6 14.8	0♊20.7	15 30.8	27 19.4	25 23.1	13 40.8	19 22.4

Astro Data

	Dy Hr Mn
♃☍♅	3 1:15
♀ R	4 9:09
☽ 0S	13 18:07
☿ 0N	14 17:44
☉ 0N	20 10:28
☽ 0N	28 1:21
♃□♇	30 18:19
♄ R	6 5:06
☿ R	9 23:16
☽ 0S	10 1:20
♀ D	15 10:18
♇ R	20 12:49
☽ 0N	24 11:59

Planet Ingress

		Dy Hr Mn
♂	♉	10 0:34
☿	♈	13 21:07
☉	♈	20 10:29
☿	♉	31 17:30
♀	♓R	3 0:25
☉	♉	19 21:27
☿	♈R	20 17:37
♂	♊	21 10:32
♀	♈	28 13:13
⚳	♊	29 15:42

Last Aspect / ☽ Ingress (March)

Last Aspect Dy Hr Mn			☽ Ingress	Dy Hr Mn
2 2:18	♄	△	♉	2 7:43
3 15:20	♇	△	♊	4 10:05
6 8:22	♂	⚹	♋	6 12:54
8 14:59	♂	□	♌	8 16:45
10 17:05	♄	△	♍	10 22:07
13 2:36	☿	☍	♎	13 5:28
15 10:05	♄	⚹	♏	15 15:11
17 21:56	☉	△	♐	18 3:00
20 10:37	♄	☌	♑	20 15:31
22 13:20	♅	□	♒	23 2:28
25 5:56	♄	⚹	♓	25 10:06
27 10:19	♄	□	♈	27 14:11
29 12:07	♄	△	♉	29 15:48
30 23:12	♇	△	♊	31 16:40

Last Aspect / ☽ Ingress (April)

Last Aspect Dy Hr Mn			☽ Ingress	Dy Hr Mn
2 14:43	♄	☍	♋	2 18:27
4 20:45	♀	△	♌	4 22:13
7 0:16	♄	△	♍	7 4:20
9 8:21	♄	□	♎	9 12:34
11 18:19	♄	⚹	♏	11 22:42
14 4:18	♀	△	♐	14 10:27
16 18:26	♄	☌	♑	16 23:04
19 9:57	☉	□	♒	19 10:52
21 18:23	☿	⚹	♓	21 19:43
23 21:34	♀	☌	♈	24 0:32
25 21:53	♄	△	♉	26 1:56
28 1:18	♀	⚹	♊	28 1:39
29 21:28	♄	☍	♋	30 1:48

☽ Phases & Eclipses

Dy Hr Mn		
5 11:32	☽	15♊05
12 14:54	○	22♍13
20 15:58	☾	0♑14
28 2:57	●	7♈37
3 18:39	☽	14♋12
11 6:08	○	21♎33
19 9:57	☾	29♑32
26 12:16	●	6♉27

Astro Data

1 March 2017
Julian Day # 42794
SVP 5♓01'19"
GC 27♐04.7 ⚴ 19♓58.3
Eris 22♈45.5 ⚵ 7♑37.0
⚷ 23♓53.2 ⚶ 20♋15.2R
☽ Mean ☊ 3♍04.4

1 April 2017
Julian Day # 42825
SVP 5♓01'17"
GC 27♐04.8 ⚴ 0♈48.7
Eris 23♈03.6 ⚵ 14♑38.3
⚷ 25♓44.4 ⚶ 22♋19.5
☽ Mean ☊ 1♍25.9

LONGITUDE — May 2017

Day	Sid.Time	☉	0 hr ☽	Noon☽	True☊	☿	♀	♂	⚳	♃	♄	♅	♆	♇
1 M	2 38 26	11♉18 09	13♋25 46	20♋32 59	0♍31.8	24♈27.3	1♈24.8	6♊56.0	0♊45.2	15♎24.4	27♐17.0	25♈26.4	13♓42.2	19♑22.1
2 Tu	2 42 22	12 16 22	27 34 08	4♌29 10	0D 30.2	24R 19.2	1 56.4	7 37.1	1 09.7	15R 18.2	27R 14.6	25 29.8	13 43.6	19R 21.8
3 W	2 46 19	13 14 34	11♌18 15	18 01 37	0R 30.0	24D 15.9	2 29.4	8 18.2	1 34.2	15 12.0	27 12.2	25 33.1	13 45.0	19 21.4
4 Th	2 50 15	14 12 44	24 39 34	1♍12 30	0 30.2	24 17.4	3 03.7	8 59.2	1 58.8	15 06.0	27 09.6	25 36.4	13 46.3	19 21.0
5 F	2 54 12	15 10 51	7♍40 49	14 04 57	0 29.6	24 23.6	3 39.3	9 40.2	2 23.4	15 00.2	27 07.0	25 39.7	13 47.6	19 20.6
6 Sa	2 58 08	16 08 57	20 25 17	26 42 15	0 27.0	24 34.6	4 16.2	10 21.1	2 48.0	14 54.4	27 04.2	25 43.0	13 48.9	19 20.2
7 Su	3 02 05	17 07 01	2♎56 13	9♎07 30	0 21.8	24 50.2	4 54.2	11 02.1	3 12.7	14 48.8	27 01.4	25 46.2	13 50.2	19 19.7
8 M	3 06 01	18 05 03	15 16 25	21 23 14	0 13.8	25 10.2	5 33.4	11 42.9	3 37.4	14 43.3	26 58.6	25 49.5	13 51.4	19 19.2
9 Tu	3 09 58	19 03 03	27 28 11	3♏31 28	0 03.1	25 34.7	6 13.6	12 23.8	4 02.1	14 38.0	26 55.6	25 52.7	13 52.7	19 18.7
10 W	3 13 54	20 01 02	9♏33 15	15 33 44	29♌50.4	26 03.4	6 54.9	13 04.6	4 26.8	14 32.8	26 52.6	25 55.9	13 53.8	19 18.1
11 Th	3 17 51	20 58 59	21 33 01	27 31 17	29 36.6	26 36.2	7 37.2	13 45.3	4 51.6	14 27.7	26 49.5	25 59.1	13 55.0	19 17.5
12 F	3 21 48	21 56 54	3♐28 40	9♐25 20	29 23.0	27 13.0	8 20.5	14 26.0	5 16.4	14 22.8	26 46.3	26 02.3	13 56.1	19 16.9
13 Sa	3 25 44	22 54 48	15 21 30	21 17 22	29 10.5	27 53.7	9 04.8	15 06.7	5 41.2	14 18.1	26 43.1	26 05.4	13 57.2	19 16.3
14 Su	3 29 41	23 52 41	27 13 11	3♑09 17	29 00.2	28 38.0	9 49.9	15 47.4	6 06.0	14 13.5	26 39.8	26 08.6	13 58.3	19 15.6
15 M	3 33 37	24 50 32	9♑05 58	15 03 39	28 52.5	29 25.9	10 35.9	16 28.0	6 30.9	14 09.0	26 36.4	26 11.7	13 59.3	19 14.9
16 Tu	3 37 34	25 48 22	21 02 46	27 03 46	28 47.7	0♉17.2	11 22.7	17 08.5	6 55.8	14 04.7	26 33.0	26 14.8	14 00.3	19 14.2
17 W	3 41 30	26 46 11	3♒07 13	9♒13 39	28 45.3	1 11.9	12 10.4	17 49.1	7 20.7	14 00.6	26 29.5	26 17.9	14 01.3	19 13.5
18 Th	3 45 27	27 43 59	15 23 39	21 37 50	28 44.6	2 09.8	12 58.8	18 29.6	7 45.6	13 56.6	26 26.0	26 20.9	14 02.2	19 12.7
19 F	3 49 24	28 41 45	27 56 49	4♓21 10	28 44.5	3 10.9	13 47.9	19 10.0	8 10.6	13 52.8	26 22.4	26 24.0	14 03.2	19 11.9
20 Sa	3 53 20	29 39 31	10♓51 30	17 28 18	28 43.9	4 14.9	14 37.8	19 50.5	8 35.6	13 49.2	26 18.7	26 27.0	14 04.0	19 11.1
21 Su	3 57 17	0♊37 15	24 12 01	1♈02 57	28 41.7	5 21.9	15 28.3	20 30.9	9 00.6	13 45.7	26 15.0	26 30.0	14 04.9	19 10.3
22 M	4 01 13	1 34 58	8♈01 19	15 07 05	28 37.2	6 31.8	16 19.5	21 11.2	9 25.6	13 42.4	26 11.2	26 33.0	14 05.7	19 09.4
23 Tu	4 05 10	2 32 40	22 20 05	29 39 52	28 30.0	7 44.4	17 11.4	21 51.6	9 50.6	13 39.2	26 07.4	26 35.9	14 06.5	19 08.5
24 W	4 09 06	3 30 22	7♉05 46	14♉36 55	28 20.6	8 59.8	18 03.8	22 31.9	10 15.7	13 36.3	26 03.5	26 38.8	14 07.3	19 07.6
25 Th	4 13 03	4 28 02	22 12 11	29 50 17	28 09.9	10 17.9	18 56.8	23 12.1	10 40.7	13 33.5	25 59.6	26 41.7	14 08.0	19 06.7
26 F	4 16 59	5 25 41	7♊29 48	15♊09 17	27 59.2	11 38.6	19 50.4	23 52.4	11 05.8	13 30.8	25 55.6	26 44.6	14 08.7	19 05.7
27 Sa	4 20 56	6 23 18	22 47 17	0♋22 25	27 49.7	13 01.9	20 44.5	24 32.6	11 30.9	13 28.4	25 51.6	26 47.4	14 09.4	19 04.8
28 Su	4 24 53	7 20 55	7♋53 27	15 19 23	27 42.4	14 27.8	21 39.1	25 12.7	11 56.0	13 26.1	25 47.6	26 50.2	14 10.0	19 03.8
29 M	4 28 49	8 18 30	22 39 23	29 52 51	27 37.8	15 56.2	22 34.2	25 52.9	12 21.2	13 24.1	25 43.5	26 53.0	14 10.6	19 02.8
30 Tu	4 32 46	9 16 03	6♌59 27	13♌59 02	27D 35.6	17 27.1	23 29.8	26 33.0	12 46.3	13 22.1	25 39.4	26 55.8	14 11.2	19 01.7
31 W	4 36 42	10 13 35	20 51 37	27 37 25	27 35.1	19 00.5	24 25.9	27 13.0	13 11.5	13 20.4	25 35.2	26 58.5	14 11.7	19 00.7

LONGITUDE — June 2017

Day	Sid.Time	☉	0 hr ☽	Noon☽	True☊	☿	♀	♂	⚳	♃	♄	♅	♆	♇
1 Th	4 40 39	11♊11 06	4♍16 44	10♍49 58	27♌35.2	20♉36.4	25♈22.4	27♊53.0	13♊36.6	13♎18.9	25♐31.0	27♈01.2	14♓12.2	18♑59.6
2 F	4 44 35	12 08 35	17 17 36	23 40 09	27R 34.7	22 14.8	26 19.3	28 33.0	14 01.8	13R 17.5	25R 26.8	27 03.8	14 12.7	18R 58.5
3 Sa	4 48 32	13 06 03	29 58 07	6♎12 03	27 32.6	23 55.7	27 16.7	29 13.0	14 27.0	13 16.3	25 22.5	27 06.5	14 13.1	18 57.4
4 Su	4 52 28	14 03 30	12♎22 27	18 29 49	27 28.2	25 39.0	28 14.5	29 52.9	14 52.2	13 15.3	25 18.2	27 09.1	14 13.5	18 56.3
5 M	4 56 25	15 00 56	24 34 37	0♏37 15	27 21.1	27 24.8	29 12.6	0♋32.8	15 17.3	13 14.5	25 13.9	27 11.6	14 13.9	18 55.1
6 Tu	5 00 22	15 58 21	6♏38 06	12 37 32	27 11.5	29 13.0	0♉11.1	1 12.7	15 42.6	13 13.8	25 09.6	27 14.2	14 14.2	18 53.9
7 W	5 04 18	16 55 44	18 35 50	24 33 16	27 00.0	1♊03.7	1 10.1	1 52.5	16 07.8	13 13.4	25 05.3	27 16.7	14 14.6	18 52.8
8 Th	5 08 15	17 53 07	0♐30 05	6♐26 29	26 47.5	2 56.7	2 09.3	2 32.3	16 33.0	13 13.1	25 00.9	27 19.1	14 14.8	18 51.6
9 F	5 12 11	18 50 29	12 22 41	18 18 50	26 35.1	4 52.0	3 09.0	3 12.0	16 58.2	13D 13.0	24 56.5	27 21.6	14 15.1	18 50.3
10 Sa	5 16 08	19 47 50	24 15 09	0♑11 47	26 23.8	6 49.6	4 08.9	3 51.8	17 23.4	13 13.0	24 52.1	27 24.0	14 15.3	18 49.1
11 Su	5 20 04	20 45 10	6♑08 58	12 06 53	26 14.4	8 49.4	5 09.2	4 31.5	17 48.7	13 13.3	24 47.7	27 26.4	14 15.5	18 47.9
12 M	5 24 01	21 42 30	18 05 49	24 06 00	26 07.5	10 51.2	6 09.8	5 11.1	18 13.9	13 13.7	24 43.3	27 28.7	14 15.6	18 46.6
13 Tu	5 27 57	22 39 49	0♒07 46	6♒11 28	26 03.2	12 55.0	7 10.7	5 50.8	18 39.2	13 14.3	24 38.9	27 31.0	14 15.7	18 45.3
14 W	5 31 54	23 37 08	12 17 28	18 26 13	26D 01.3	15 00.5	8 11.9	6 30.4	19 04.4	13 15.1	24 34.5	27 33.2	14 15.8	18 44.0
15 Th	5 35 51	24 34 26	24 38 09	0♓53 46	26 01.1	17 07.7	9 13.4	7 10.0	19 29.7	13 16.1	24 30.0	27 35.5	14R 15.9	18 42.7
16 F	5 39 47	25 31 43	7♓13 34	13 38 02	26R 01.8	19 16.2	10 15.2	7 49.5	19 54.9	13 17.2	24 25.6	27 37.7	14 15.9	18 41.4
17 Sa	5 43 44	26 29 01	20 07 42	26 43 02	26 02.2	21 26.0	11 17.3	8 29.1	20 20.2	13 18.6	24 21.2	27 39.8	14 15.9	18 40.1
18 Su	5 47 40	27 26 18	3♈24 26	10♈12 16	26 01.5	23 36.6	12 19.6	9 08.6	20 45.4	13 20.1	24 16.8	27 41.9	14 15.8	18 38.7
19 M	5 51 37	28 23 35	17 06 46	24 08 04	25 58.9	25 47.9	13 22.2	9 48.0	21 10.7	13 21.7	24 12.4	27 44.0	14 15.7	18 37.4
20 Tu	5 55 33	29 20 51	1♉16 05	8♉30 35	25 54.1	27 59.5	14 25.0	10 27.5	21 36.0	13 23.6	24 07.9	27 46.0	14 15.6	18 36.0
21 W	5 59 30	0♋18 08	15 51 09	23 17 07	25 47.5	0♋11.2	15 28.1	11 06.9	22 01.2	13 25.6	24 03.6	27 48.0	14 15.5	18 34.6
22 Th	6 03 26	1 15 24	0♊47 37	8♊21 36	25 39.8	2 22.7	16 31.4	11 46.3	22 26.5	13 27.8	23 59.2	27 50.0	14 15.3	18 33.2
23 F	6 07 23	2 12 40	15 57 51	23 35 04	25 31.8	4 33.8	17 34.9	12 25.7	22 51.8	13 30.2	23 54.8	27 51.9	14 15.1	18 31.9
24 Sa	6 11 20	3 09 56	1♋11 52	8♋46 56	25 24.8	6 44.2	18 38.6	13 05.0	23 17.0	13 32.7	23 50.5	27 53.7	14 14.8	18 30.5
25 Su	6 15 16	4 07 12	16 18 57	23 46 48	25 19.4	8 53.6	19 42.6	13 44.4	23 42.3	13 35.4	23 46.1	27 55.6	14 14.6	18 29.0
26 M	6 19 13	5 04 27	1♌09 31	8♌26 17	25 16.2	11 01.9	20 46.7	14 23.7	24 07.6	13 38.3	23 41.8	27 57.4	14 14.3	18 27.6
27 Tu	6 23 09	6 01 41	15 36 34	22 39 59	25D 15.0	13 08.9	21 51.1	15 02.9	24 32.8	13 41.4	23 37.5	27 59.1	14 13.9	18 26.2
28 W	6 27 06	6 58 55	29 36 23	6♍25 47	25 15.4	15 14.3	22 55.6	15 42.2	24 58.0	13 44.6	23 33.3	28 00.8	14 13.6	18 24.8
29 Th	6 31 02	7 56 09	13♍08 21	19 44 21	25 16.5	17 18.2	24 00.3	16 21.4	25 23.3	13 48.0	23 29.1	28 02.5	14 13.2	18 23.3
30 F	6 34 59	8 53 22	26 14 12	2♎38 20	25R 17.5	19 20.4	25 05.2	17 00.6	25 48.5	13 51.5	23 24.9	28 04.1	14 12.7	18 21.9

Astro Data	Planet Ingress	Last Aspect	☽ Ingress	Last Aspect	☽ Ingress	☽ Phases & Eclipses	Astro Data
Dy Hr Mn	Dy Hr Mn	Dy Hr Mn	Dy Hr Mn	Dy Hr Mn	Dy Hr Mn	Dy Hr Mn	1 May 2017
☿ D 3 16:33	☊ ♌R 9 18:06	1 20:23 ♅ □	♌ 2 4:12	2 21:48 ♂ □	♎ 3 0:04	3 2:47 ☽ 12♌52	Julian Day # 42855
☽ 0S 7 7:46	☿ ♉ 16 4:07	4 4:35 ♄ △	♍ 4 9:46	5 8:57 ♀ ☍	♏ 5 10:46	10 21:42 ○ 20♏24	SVP 5♓01'13"
♃⚻♆ 17 8:37	☉ ♊ 20 20:31	6 12:42 ♄ □	♎ 6 18:20	7 0:35 ♇ ⚹	♐ 7 22:59	19 0:33 ☾ 28♒14	GC 27♐04.9 ⚴ 11♈21.6
♄△♅ 19 6:14		8 22:59 ♄ ⚹	♏ 9 5:01	10 6:20 ♅ △	♑ 10 11:36	25 19:44 ● 4♊47	Eris 23♈23.1 ⚵ 18♑08.7
☽ 0N 21 22:43	♂ ♋ 4 16:16	10 21:42 ☉ ☍	♐ 11 16:59	12 18:45 ♅ □	♒ 12 23:45		⚷ 27♓20.4 ⚶ 29♋32.6
	♀ ♉ 6 7:26	14 2:14 ☿ △	♑ 14 5:37	15 5:40 ♅ ⚹	♓ 15 10:17	1 12:42 ☽ 11♍13	☽ Mean ☊ 29♌50.6
☽ 0S 3 14:33	☿ ♊ 6 22:15	16 10:22 ♅ □	♒ 16 17:50	17 11:33 ☉ □	♈ 17 17:55	9 13:10 ○ 18♐53	
♃ D 9 14:03	☉ ♋ 21 4:24	19 0:33 ☉ □	♓ 19 3:52	19 19:42 ☉ ⚹	♉ 19 21:53	17 11:33 ☾ 26♓28	1 June 2017
♆ R 16 11:09	☿ ♋ 21 9:57	21 3:39 ♄ □	♈ 21 10:11	21 4:26 ♇ △	♊ 21 22:44	24 2:31 ● 2♋47	Julian Day # 42886
☽ 0N 18 7:57		23 6:59 ♅ ☌	♉ 23 12:33	23 18:45 ♅ ⚹	♋ 23 22:07		SVP 5♓01'09"
☽ 0S 30 22:26		24 19:08 ♇ △	♊ 25 12:15	25 18:44 ♅ □	♌ 25 22:06		GC 27♐05.0 ⚴ 21♈54.8
		27 6:18 ♅ ⚹	♋ 27 11:24	27 21:12 ♅ △	♍ 28 0:41		Eris 23♈40.4 ⚵ 16♑52.9R
		29 6:59 ♅ □	♌ 29 12:12	29 20:34 ♀ △	♎ 30 7:02		⚷ 28♓28.7 ⚶ 10♌18.4
		31 11:14 ♂ ⚹	♍ 31 16:16				☽ Mean ☊ 28♌12.1

July 2017 — LONGITUDE

Day	Sid.Time	☉	0 hr ☽	Noon ☽	True ☊	☿	♀	♂	⚳	♃	♄	♅	♆	♇
1 Sa	6 38 55	9♋50 34	8♎57 18	15♎11 37	25♌17.5	21♋20.7	26♉10.3	17♋39.7	26♊13.7	13♎55.2	23♐20.7	28♈05.7	14♓12.3	18♑20.4
2 Su	6 42 52	10 47 46	21 21 51	27 28 34	25R 16.0	23 19.2	27 15.6	18 18.9	26 38.9	13 59.1	23R 16.6	28 07.2	14R 11.8	18R 18.9
3 M	6 46 49	11 44 58	3♏32 18	9♏33 35	25 12.6	25 15.7	28 21.0	18 58.0	27 04.1	14 03.1	23 12.5	28 08.7	14 11.2	18 17.5
4 Tu	6 50 45	12 42 10	15 32 56	21 30 48	25 07.5	27 10.3	29 26.6	19 37.1	27 29.3	14 07.3	23 08.4	28 10.1	14 10.7	18 16.0
5 W	6 54 42	13 39 21	27 27 38	3♐23 50	25 01.0	29 02.9	0♊32.4	20 16.1	27 54.5	14 11.7	23 04.4	28 11.5	14 10.1	18 14.5
6 Th	6 58 38	14 36 33	9♐19 45	15 15 42	24 53.8	0♌53.5	1 38.3	20 55.2	28 19.7	14 16.2	23 00.5	28 12.9	14 09.5	18 13.1
7 F	7 02 35	15 33 44	21 12 01	27 08 56	24 46.5	2 42.2	2 44.4	21 34.2	28 44.8	14 20.9	22 56.6	28 14.2	14 08.8	18 11.6
8 Sa	7 06 31	16 30 55	3♑06 42	9♑05 33	24 40.0	4 28.7	3 50.7	22 13.2	29 10.0	14 25.7	22 52.7	28 15.4	14 08.2	18 10.1
9 Su	7 10 28	17 28 06	15 05 40	21 07 15	24 34.6	6 13.3	4 57.1	22 52.2	29 35.1	14 30.7	22 48.9	28 16.7	14 07.5	18 08.7
10 M	7 14 24	18 25 18	27 10 30	3♒15 36	24 30.9	7 55.9	6 03.6	23 31.1	0♋00.2	14 35.8	22 45.1	28 17.8	14 06.7	18 07.2
11 Tu	7 18 21	19 22 30	9♒22 47	15 32 14	24D 29.0	9 36.4	7 10.3	24 10.0	0 25.3	14 41.1	22 41.4	28 19.0	14 06.0	18 05.7
12 W	7 22 18	20 19 42	21 44 13	27 58 58	24 28.7	11 14.9	8 17.2	24 48.9	0 50.4	14 46.5	22 37.7	28 20.0	14 05.2	18 04.2
13 Th	7 26 14	21 16 54	4♓16 45	10♓37 53	24 29.6	12 51.4	9 24.2	25 27.8	1 15.5	14 52.1	22 34.1	28 21.1	14 04.4	18 02.8
14 F	7 30 11	22 14 07	17 02 39	23 31 22	24 31.1	14 25.9	10 31.3	26 06.7	1 40.6	14 57.8	22 30.5	28 22.0	14 03.5	18 01.3
15 Sa	7 34 07	23 11 20	0♈04 20	6♈41 51	24 32.5	15 58.4	11 38.6	26 45.5	2 05.6	15 03.6	22 27.0	28 23.0	14 02.7	17 59.8
16 Su	7 38 04	24 08 34	13 24 11	20 11 33	24R 33.4	17 28.8	12 46.0	27 24.3	2 30.7	15 09.6	22 23.6	28 23.9	14 01.8	17 58.3
17 M	7 42 00	25 05 49	27 04 08	4♉01 59	24 33.1	18 57.2	13 53.6	28 03.2	2 55.7	15 15.8	22 20.2	28 24.7	14 00.9	17 56.9
18 Tu	7 45 57	26 03 04	11♉05 05	18 13 17	24 31.7	20 23.4	15 01.2	28 41.9	3 20.7	15 22.1	22 16.9	28 25.5	13 59.9	17 55.4
19 W	7 49 53	27 00 20	25 26 18	2♊43 42	24 29.1	21 47.6	16 09.0	29 20.7	3 45.7	15 28.5	22 13.7	28 26.2	13 58.9	17 54.0
20 Th	7 53 50	27 57 37	10♊04 55	17 29 12	24 25.8	23 09.7	17 17.0	29 59.5	4 10.6	15 35.1	22 10.5	28 26.9	13 57.9	17 52.5
21 F	7 57 47	28 54 55	24 55 43	2♋23 31	24 22.3	24 29.6	18 25.0	0♌38.2	4 35.6	15 41.8	22 07.4	28 27.6	13 56.9	17 51.1
22 Sa	8 01 43	29 52 14	9♋51 32	17 18 45	24 19.2	25 47.3	19 33.2	1 16.9	5 00.5	15 48.6	22 04.4	28 28.2	13 55.9	17 49.6
23 Su	8 05 40	0♌49 33	24 44 05	2♌06 33	24 17.0	27 02.7	20 41.5	1 55.6	5 25.4	15 55.6	22 01.4	28 28.7	13 54.8	17 48.2
24 M	8 09 36	1 46 52	9♌25 13	16 39 18	24D 15.8	28 15.8	21 49.9	2 34.3	5 50.3	16 02.7	21 58.5	28 29.2	13 53.7	17 46.8
25 Tu	8 13 33	2 44 12	23 48 08	0♍51 12	24 15.8	29 26.5	22 58.4	3 13.0	6 15.2	16 09.9	21 55.7	28 29.7	13 52.6	17 45.4
26 W	8 17 29	3 41 33	7♍48 10	14 38 51	24 16.6	0♍34.7	24 07.0	3 51.6	6 40.0	16 17.2	21 52.9	28 30.1	13 51.4	17 43.9
27 Th	8 21 26	4 38 54	21 23 11	28 01 17	24 17.9	1 40.4	25 15.7	4 30.3	7 04.8	16 24.7	21 50.3	28 30.5	13 50.3	17 42.5
28 F	8 25 22	5 36 15	4♎33 19	10♎59 37	24 19.3	2 43.4	26 24.6	5 08.9	7 29.5	16 32.3	21 47.7	28 30.8	13 49.1	17 41.2
29 Sa	8 29 19	6 33 37	17 20 34	23 36 36	24 20.3	3 43.7	27 33.5	5 47.5	7 54.3	16 40.1	21 45.2	28 31.0	13 47.9	17 39.8
30 Su	8 33 16	7 30 59	29 48 14	5♏55 59	24R 20.8	4 41.2	28 42.5	6 26.0	8 19.0	16 47.9	21 42.8	28 31.2	13 46.6	17 38.4
31 M	8 37 12	8 28 22	12♏00 25	18 02 05	24 20.5	5 35.6	29 51.7	7 04.6	8 43.7	16 55.9	21 40.4	28 31.4	13 45.4	17 37.0

August 2017 — LONGITUDE

Day	Sid.Time	☉	0 hr ☽	Noon ☽	True ☊	☿	♀	♂	⚳	♃	♄	♅	♆	♇
1 Tu	8 41 09	9♌25 46	24♏01 34	29♏59 23	24♌19.6	6♍26.9	1♋00.9	7♌43.1	9♋08.3	17♎04.0	21♐38.2	28♈31.5	13♓44.1	17♑35.7
2 W	8 45 05	10 23 10	5♐56 06	11♐52 14	24R 18.1	7 15.0	2 10.2	8 21.7	9 33.0	17 12.2	21R 36.0	28R 31.5	13R 42.8	17R 34.4
3 Th	8 49 02	11 20 35	17 48 16	23 44 39	24 16.3	7 59.7	3 19.7	9 00.2	9 57.5	17 20.5	21 33.9	28 31.6	13 41.5	17 33.0
4 F	8 52 58	12 18 01	29 41 50	5♑40 13	24 14.5	8 40.7	4 29.2	9 38.6	10 22.1	17 28.9	21 31.9	28 31.5	13 40.1	17 31.7
5 Sa	8 56 55	13 15 27	11♑40 07	17 41 53	24 12.9	9 18.1	5 38.8	10 17.1	10 46.6	17 37.5	21 30.0	28 31.4	13 38.8	17 30.4
6 Su	9 00 51	14 12 55	23 45 48	29 52 06	24 11.7	9 51.4	6 48.5	10 55.6	11 11.1	17 46.1	21 28.2	28 31.3	13 37.4	17 29.1
7 M	9 04 48	15 10 23	6♒01 01	12♒12 43	24D 11.1	10 20.6	7 58.4	11 34.0	11 35.6	17 54.9	21 26.4	28 31.1	13 36.0	17 27.9
8 Tu	9 08 45	16 07 52	18 27 21	24 45 04	24 10.8	10 45.5	9 08.3	12 12.4	12 00.0	18 03.8	21 24.8	28 30.9	13 34.6	17 26.6
9 W	9 12 41	17 05 22	1♓05 56	7♓30 04	24 11.0	11 05.9	10 18.3	12 50.9	12 24.4	18 12.8	21 23.2	28 30.6	13 33.2	17 25.4
10 Th	9 16 38	18 02 54	13 57 32	20 28 22	24 11.5	11 21.4	11 28.4	13 29.3	12 48.7	18 21.9	21 21.8	28 30.3	13 31.8	17 24.1
11 F	9 20 34	19 00 26	27 02 39	3♈40 22	24 12.0	11 32.1	12 38.6	14 07.6	13 13.0	18 31.0	21 20.4	28 29.9	13 30.3	17 22.9
12 Sa	9 24 31	19 58 00	10♈21 35	17 06 17	24 12.5	11R 37.6	13 48.9	14 46.0	13 37.3	18 40.3	21 19.1	28 29.5	13 28.8	17 21.7
13 Su	9 28 27	20 55 36	23 54 28	0♉46 05	24 12.8	11 37.8	14 59.3	15 24.4	14 01.5	18 49.7	21 17.9	28 29.0	13 27.4	17 20.6
14 M	9 32 24	21 53 13	7♉41 07	14 39 26	24R 12.9	11 32.6	16 09.8	16 02.7	14 25.7	18 59.2	21 16.8	28 28.5	13 25.9	17 19.4
15 Tu	9 36 20	22 50 52	21 40 56	28 45 25	24 12.9	11 21.9	17 20.4	16 41.1	14 49.9	19 08.8	21 15.8	28 27.9	13 24.4	17 18.3
16 W	9 40 17	23 48 32	5♊52 39	13♊02 19	24D 12.9	11 05.5	18 31.1	17 19.4	15 14.0	19 18.5	21 14.9	28 27.3	13 22.8	17 17.1
17 Th	9 44 14	24 46 14	20 14 04	27 27 27	24 12.9	10 43.6	19 41.8	17 57.7	15 38.0	19 28.3	21 14.0	28 26.6	13 21.3	17 16.0
18 F	9 48 10	25 43 57	4♋41 59	11♋57 05	24 13.0	10 16.2	20 52.7	18 36.1	16 02.1	19 38.1	21 13.3	28 25.9	13 19.8	17 15.0
19 Sa	9 52 07	26 41 42	19 12 09	26 26 32	24 13.2	9 43.5	22 03.6	19 14.4	16 26.0	19 48.1	21 12.7	28 25.1	13 18.2	17 13.9
20 Su	9 56 03	27 39 28	3♌39 35	10♌50 38	24R 13.4	9 05.9	23 14.6	19 52.7	16 49.9	19 58.2	21 12.2	28 24.3	13 16.6	17 12.8
21 M	10 00 00	28 37 16	17 59 01	25 04 08	24 13.5	8 23.6	24 25.7	20 30.9	17 13.8	20 08.3	21 11.7	28 23.5	13 15.1	17 11.8
22 Tu	10 03 56	29 35 05	2♍05 26	9♍02 27	24 13.3	7 37.3	25 36.9	21 09.2	17 37.6	20 18.6	21 11.4	28 22.6	13 13.5	17 10.8
23 W	10 07 53	0♍32 56	15 54 46	22 42 06	24 12.9	6 47.7	26 48.1	21 47.5	18 01.4	20 28.9	21 11.1	28 21.7	13 11.9	17 09.8
24 Th	10 11 49	1 30 48	29 24 15	6♎01 07	24 12.1	5 55.5	27 59.5	22 25.7	18 25.1	20 39.3	21 11.0	28 20.7	13 10.3	17 08.9
25 F	10 15 46	2 28 41	12♎32 44	18 59 12	24 11.1	5 01.7	29 10.9	23 04.0	18 48.7	20 49.8	21D 10.9	28 19.6	13 08.7	17 07.9
26 Sa	10 19 43	3 26 36	25 20 43	1♏37 33	24 10.0	4 07.3	0♌22.4	23 42.2	19 12.3	21 00.4	21 11.0	28 18.6	13 07.0	17 07.0
27 Su	10 23 39	4 24 31	7♏50 03	13 58 40	24 09.1	3 13.4	1 33.9	24 20.4	19 35.9	21 11.0	21 11.1	28 17.4	13 05.4	17 06.1
28 M	10 27 36	5 22 29	20 03 51	26 06 06	24D 08.4	2 21.1	2 45.6	24 58.6	19 59.3	21 21.8	21 11.4	28 16.3	13 03.8	17 05.3
29 Tu	10 31 32	6 20 27	2♐05 59	8♐04 03	24 08.2	1 31.6	3 57.3	25 36.8	20 22.8	21 32.6	21 11.7	28 15.1	13 02.1	17 04.4
30 W	10 35 29	7 18 27	14 00 54	19 57 06	24 08.6	0 46.0	5 09.0	26 15.0	20 46.1	21 43.5	21 12.2	28 13.8	13 00.5	17 03.6
31 Th	10 39 25	8 16 28	25 53 14	1♑49 53	24 09.5	0 05.4	6 20.9	26 53.1	21 09.4	21 54.4	21 12.7	28 12.5	12 58.9	17 02.8

Astro Data

	Dy Hr Mn
♃⊼♆	5 4:19
☽0N	15 15:03
☽0S	28 7:22
♅R	3 5:31
♃□♇	4 18:48
☽0N	11 20:49
♅∠♆	11 21:49
☿R	13 1:00
☽0S	24 16:41
♄D	25 12:08
♃✶♄	27 12:15

Planet Ingress

	Dy Hr Mn
♀ ♊	5 0:11
☿ ♌	6 0:20
⚳ ♋	10 11:47
♂ ♌	20 12:19
☉ ♌	22 15:15
☿ ♍	25 23:41
♀ ♋	31 14:54
☉ ♍	22 22:20
♀ ♌	26 4:30
☿ ♌R	31 15:28

Last Aspect / ☽ Ingress

Last Aspect Dy Hr Mn	☽ Ingress Dy Hr Mn
2 13:16 ♅ ☍	♏ 2 16:59
5 1:34 ♅ △	♐ 5 5:08
7 14:12 ♅ △	♑ 7 17:45
10 2:12 ♅ □	♒ 10 5:35
12 12:40 ♅ ✶	♓ 12 15:51
14 17:00 ♂ △	♈ 14 23:52
17 2:19 ♅ ☌	♉ 17 5:04
19 6:11 ♂ ✶	♊ 19 7:31
21 5:41 ♅ ✶	♋ 21 8:09
23 6:05 ♅ □	♌ 23 8:34
25 9:22 ☿ ☌	♍ 25 10:32
27 6:31 ♀ □	♎ 27 15:37
29 21:30 ♅ ☍	♏ 30 0:23

Last Aspect / ☽ Ingress

Last Aspect Dy Hr Mn	☽ Ingress Dy Hr Mn
31 11:10 ♇ ✶	♐ 1 12:01
3 21:38 ♅ △	♑ 4 0:37
6 9:22 ♅ □	♒ 6 12:15
8 19:07 ♅ ✶	♓ 8 21:56
10 13:38 ♄ □	♈ 11 5:22
13 8:01 ♅ ☌	♉ 13 10:40
15 1:15 ☉ □	♊ 15 14:06
17 13:38 ♅ ✶	♋ 17 16:13
19 15:17 ♅ □	♌ 19 17:55
21 18:30 ☉ ☌	♍ 21 20:25
23 20:02 ☿ ✶	♎ 24 1:04
26 5:39 ♅ ☍	♏ 26 8:53
28 9:38 ♂ □	♐ 28 19:47
31 4:42 ♅ △	♑ 31 8:18

☽ Phases & Eclipses

Dy Hr Mn	
1 0:51	☽ 9♎24
9 4:07	○ 17♑09
16 19:26	☾ 24♈26
23 9:46	● 0♌44
30 15:23	☽ 7♏39
7 18:11	○ 15♒25
7 18:20	• P 0.246
15 1:15	☾ 22♉25
21 18:30	● 28♌53
21 18:25:30	• T 02'40"
29 8:13	☽ 6♐11

Astro Data

1 July 2017
Julian Day # 42916
SVP 5♓01'04"
GC 27♐05.0 ⚴ 1♉17.8
Eris 23♈50.4 ⚵ 11♑05.4R
⚷ 28♓51.9R ⚶ 22♌40.0
☽ Mean ☊ 26♌36.8

1 August 2017
Julian Day # 42947
SVP 5♓01'00"
GC 27♐05.1 ⚴ 9♉16.7
Eris 23♈51.4R ⚵ 4♑39.6R
⚷ 28♓27.0R ⚶ 6♍43.0
☽ Mean ☊ 24♌58.3

LONGITUDE — September 2017

Day	Sid.Time	☉	0 hr ☽	Noon☽	True☊	☿	♀	♂	⚳	♃	♄	♅	♆	♇
1 F	10 43 22	9♍14 31	7♑47 37	13♑46 57	24♌10.8	29♌30.7	7♌32.8	27♌31.3	21♋32.6	22♎05.5	21♐13.3	28♈11.2	12♓57.2	17♑02.0
2 Sa	10 47 18	10 12 35	19 48 24	25 52 27	24 12.1	29R 02.7	8 44.8	28 09.5	21 55.8	22 16.6	21 14.1	28R 09.8	12R 55.6	17R 01.3
3 Su	10 51 15	11 10 40	1♒59 29	8♒09 54	24 13.3	28 42.1	9 56.9	28 47.6	22 18.9	22 27.8	21 14.9	28 08.4	12 53.9	17 00.5
4 M	10 55 12	12 08 47	14 24 02	20 42 06	24R 13.9	28D 29.6	11 09.0	29 25.7	22 41.9	22 39.0	21 15.8	28 07.0	12 52.3	16 59.8
5 Tu	10 59 08	13 06 56	27 04 20	3♓30 49	24 13.7	28 25.5	12 21.2	0♍03.8	23 04.8	22 50.3	21 16.8	28 05.5	12 50.6	16 59.2
6 W	11 03 05	14 05 06	10♓01 37	16 36 42	24 12.5	28 30.0	13 33.5	0 42.0	23 27.7	23 01.7	21 18.0	28 03.9	12 49.0	16 58.5
7 Th	11 07 01	15 03 18	23 15 58	29 59 16	24 10.4	28 43.4	14 45.9	1 20.1	23 50.5	23 13.1	21 19.2	28 02.4	12 47.3	16 57.9
8 F	11 10 58	16 01 31	6♈46 22	13♈36 59	24 07.5	29 05.6	15 58.3	1 58.2	24 13.3	23 24.6	21 20.5	28 00.8	12 45.7	16 57.3
9 Sa	11 14 54	16 59 47	20 30 48	27 27 27	24 04.3	29 36.6	17 10.8	2 36.3	24 35.9	23 36.2	21 21.9	27 59.1	12 44.0	16 56.7
10 Su	11 18 51	17 58 05	4♉26 34	11♉27 45	24 01.2	0♍16.0	18 23.4	3 14.4	24 58.5	23 47.9	21 23.4	27 57.4	12 42.4	16 56.2
11 M	11 22 47	18 56 24	18 30 37	25 34 48	23 58.7	1 03.6	19 36.0	3 52.4	25 21.0	23 59.5	21 25.0	27 55.7	12 40.7	16 55.7
12 Tu	11 26 44	19 54 46	2♊39 56	9♊45 41	23D 57.2	1 59.1	20 48.7	4 30.5	25 43.4	24 11.3	21 26.7	27 54.0	12 39.1	16 55.2
13 W	11 30 40	20 53 10	16 51 44	23 57 49	23 56.9	3 01.9	22 01.5	5 08.6	26 05.8	24 23.1	21 28.5	27 52.2	12 37.5	16 54.7
14 Th	11 34 37	21 51 37	1♋03 40	8♋09 01	23 57.6	4 11.5	23 14.4	5 46.7	26 28.1	24 35.0	21 30.3	27 50.4	12 35.8	16 54.3
15 F	11 38 34	22 50 05	15 13 38	22 17 17	23 59.0	5 27.4	24 27.3	6 24.7	26 50.2	24 46.9	21 32.3	27 48.5	12 34.2	16 53.9
16 Sa	11 42 30	23 48 36	29 19 43	6♌20 43	24 00.5	6 49.1	25 40.3	7 02.8	27 12.3	24 58.9	21 34.4	27 46.6	12 32.6	16 53.5
17 Su	11 46 27	24 47 08	13♌19 59	20 17 16	24R 01.3	8 15.8	26 53.3	7 40.9	27 34.3	25 10.9	21 36.5	27 44.7	12 31.0	16 53.2
18 M	11 50 23	25 45 43	27 12 16	4♍04 42	24 01.0	9 47.0	28 06.4	8 18.9	27 56.2	25 23.0	21 38.8	27 42.8	12 29.4	16 52.8
19 Tu	11 54 20	26 44 20	10♍54 16	17 40 41	23 59.1	11 22.2	29 19.6	8 57.0	28 18.0	25 35.2	21 41.1	27 40.8	12 27.8	16 52.6
20 W	11 58 16	27 42 58	24 23 40	1♎03 00	23 55.5	13 00.6	0♍32.8	9 35.0	28 39.7	25 47.3	21 43.6	27 38.8	12 26.2	16 52.3
21 Th	12 02 13	28 41 39	7♎38 29	14 09 56	23 50.4	14 41.9	1 46.1	10 13.0	29 01.3	25 59.6	21 46.1	27 36.7	12 24.6	16 52.1
22 F	12 06 09	29 40 21	20 37 17	27 00 30	23 44.3	16 25.5	2 59.4	10 51.1	29 22.8	26 11.9	21 48.7	27 34.7	12 23.1	16 51.8
23 Sa	12 10 06	0♎39 05	3♏19 38	9♏34 47	23 37.9	18 10.9	4 12.8	11 29.1	29 44.2	26 24.2	21 51.4	27 32.6	12 21.5	16 51.7
24 Su	12 14 03	1 37 52	15 46 10	21 54 01	23 31.9	19 57.8	5 26.2	12 07.1	0♌05.5	26 36.6	21 54.2	27 30.5	12 20.0	16 51.5
25 M	12 17 59	2 36 39	27 58 40	4♐00 32	23 26.9	21 45.7	6 39.7	12 45.1	0 26.7	26 49.0	21 57.1	27 28.3	12 18.5	16 51.4
26 Tu	12 21 56	3 35 29	10♐00 02	15 57 41	23 23.4	23 34.4	7 53.3	13 23.1	0 47.8	27 01.4	22 00.1	27 26.2	12 16.9	16 51.3
27 W	12 25 52	4 34 21	21 54 02	27 49 40	23D 21.7	25 23.5	9 06.9	14 01.1	1 08.8	27 13.9	22 03.2	27 24.0	12 15.4	16 51.3
28 Th	12 29 49	5 33 14	3♑45 10	9♑41 10	23 21.5	27 12.8	10 20.6	14 39.1	1 29.6	27 26.4	22 06.3	27 21.8	12 13.9	16D 51.2
29 F	12 33 45	6 32 09	15 38 20	21 37 16	23 22.5	29 02.2	11 34.3	15 17.1	1 50.3	27 39.0	22 09.6	27 19.5	12 12.5	16 51.3
30 Sa	12 37 42	7 31 06	27 38 37	3♒43 01	23 24.0	0♎51.4	12 48.0	15 55.1	2 11.0	27 51.6	22 12.9	27 17.3	12 11.0	16 51.3

LONGITUDE — October 2017

Day	Sid.Time	☉	0 hr ☽	Noon☽	True☊	☿	♀	♂	⚳	♃	♄	♅	♆	♇
1 Su	12 41 38	8♎30 04	9♒51 01	16♒03 10	23♌25.2	2♎40.3	14♍01.8	16♍33.0	2♌31.5	28♎04.2	22♐16.3	27♈15.0	12♓09.6	16♑51.4
2 M	12 45 35	9 29 04	22 19 58	28 41 49	23R 25.3	4 28.8	15 15.7	17 11.0	2 51.8	28 16.9	22 19.8	27R 12.7	12R 08.1	16 51.4
3 Tu	12 49 32	10 28 06	5♓09 03	11♓41 54	23 23.6	6 16.7	16 29.6	17 49.0	3 12.1	28 29.6	22 23.4	27 10.4	12 06.7	16 51.6
4 W	12 53 28	11 27 10	18 20 28	25 04 46	23 19.9	8 04.1	17 43.5	18 26.9	3 32.2	28 42.3	22 27.0	27 08.1	12 05.3	16 51.7
5 Th	12 57 25	12 26 16	1♈54 39	8♈49 50	23 14.1	9 50.9	18 57.5	19 04.9	3 52.2	28 55.1	22 30.7	27 05.8	12 04.0	16 51.9
6 F	13 01 21	13 25 24	15 49 55	22 54 20	23 06.6	11 37.0	20 11.6	19 42.8	4 12.0	29 07.9	22 34.6	27 03.4	12 02.6	16 52.1
7 Sa	13 05 18	14 24 34	0♉02 28	7♉13 35	22 58.3	13 22.4	21 25.7	20 20.8	4 31.7	29 20.7	22 38.5	27 01.1	12 01.3	16 52.4
8 Su	13 09 14	15 23 46	14 26 54	21 41 36	22 50.2	15 07.1	22 39.8	20 58.7	4 51.3	29 33.5	22 42.4	26 58.7	11 59.9	16 52.6
9 M	13 13 11	16 23 00	28 56 53	6♊12 00	22 43.2	16 51.1	23 54.0	21 36.7	5 10.7	29 46.4	22 46.5	26 56.3	11 58.6	16 52.9
10 Tu	13 17 07	17 22 17	13♊26 15	20 39 03	22 38.1	18 34.3	25 08.2	22 14.6	5 30.0	29 59.3	22 50.6	26 53.9	11 57.4	16 53.3
11 W	13 21 04	18 21 36	27 49 52	4♋58 20	22 35.3	20 16.7	26 22.5	22 52.5	5 49.2	0♏12.2	22 54.8	26 51.5	11 56.1	16 53.6
12 Th	13 25 00	19 20 58	12♋04 10	19 07 08	22D 34.5	21 58.5	27 36.8	23 30.5	6 08.2	0 25.1	22 59.1	26 49.1	11 54.9	16 54.0
13 F	13 28 57	20 20 22	26 07 10	3♌04 13	22 35.0	23 39.5	28 51.2	24 08.4	6 27.0	0 38.1	23 03.5	26 46.6	11 53.7	16 54.5
14 Sa	13 32 54	21 19 48	9♌58 17	16 49 25	22R 35.7	25 19.7	0♎05.6	24 46.4	6 45.7	0 51.1	23 07.9	26 44.2	11 52.5	16 54.9
15 Su	13 36 50	22 19 16	23 37 41	0♍23 07	22 35.5	26 59.3	1 20.1	25 24.3	7 04.3	1 04.0	23 12.4	26 41.8	11 51.3	16 55.4
16 M	13 40 47	23 18 47	7♍05 48	13 45 45	22 33.5	28 38.2	2 34.6	26 02.2	7 22.6	1 17.1	23 17.0	26 39.3	11 50.2	16 55.9
17 Tu	13 44 43	24 18 19	20 22 58	26 57 27	22 28.9	0♏16.4	3 49.1	26 40.2	7 40.8	1 30.1	23 21.6	26 36.9	11 49.0	16 56.5
18 W	13 48 40	25 17 54	3♎29 10	9♎58 03	22 21.5	1 54.0	5 03.7	27 18.1	7 58.8	1 43.1	23 26.4	26 34.4	11 47.9	16 57.0
19 Th	13 52 36	26 17 31	16 24 01	22 47 02	22 11.6	3 30.9	6 18.3	27 56.0	8 16.7	1 56.2	23 31.2	26 32.0	11 46.9	16 57.6
20 F	13 56 33	27 17 10	29 07 02	5♏23 59	21 59.9	5 07.2	7 32.9	28 33.9	8 34.3	2 09.2	23 36.0	26 29.5	11 45.8	16 58.3
21 Sa	14 00 29	28 16 52	11♏37 51	17 48 42	21 47.4	6 42.9	8 47.6	29 11.8	8 51.8	2 22.3	23 41.0	26 27.1	11 44.8	16 58.9
22 Su	14 04 26	29 16 35	23 56 36	0♐01 42	21 35.3	8 18.0	10 02.3	29 49.8	9 09.1	2 35.4	23 45.9	26 24.6	11 43.8	16 59.6
23 M	14 08 23	0♏16 19	6♐04 11	12 04 18	21 24.7	9 52.5	11 17.0	0♎27.7	9 26.2	2 48.5	23 51.0	26 22.2	11 42.8	17 00.4
24 Tu	14 12 19	1 16 06	18 02 24	23 58 50	21 16.2	11 26.4	12 31.8	1 05.6	9 43.2	3 01.6	23 56.1	26 19.7	11 41.9	17 01.1
25 W	14 16 16	2 15 55	29 54 03	5♑48 32	21 10.3	12 59.9	13 46.6	1 43.5	9 59.9	3 14.6	24 01.3	26 17.3	11 41.0	17 01.9
26 Th	14 20 12	3 15 45	11♑42 51	17 37 34	21 07.1	14 32.7	15 01.4	2 21.4	10 16.4	3 27.7	24 06.6	26 14.9	11 40.1	17 02.7
27 F	14 24 09	4 15 37	23 33 20	29 30 47	21D 05.9	16 05.1	16 16.2	2 59.3	10 32.7	3 40.8	24 11.9	26 12.4	11 39.3	17 03.5
28 Sa	14 28 05	5 15 30	5♒30 36	11♒33 29	21R 05.9	17 36.9	17 31.1	3 37.1	10 48.8	3 53.9	24 17.3	26 10.0	11 38.4	17 04.4
29 Su	14 32 02	6 15 25	17 40 06	23 51 08	21 06.0	19 08.2	18 46.0	4 15.0	11 04.7	4 07.0	24 22.7	26 07.6	11 37.6	17 05.3
30 M	14 35 58	7 15 22	0♓07 13	6♓28 57	21 05.1	20 39.0	20 00.9	4 52.9	11 20.4	4 20.1	24 28.2	26 05.2	11 36.9	17 06.2
31 Tu	14 39 55	8 15 21	12 56 49	19 31 16	21 02.2	22 09.4	21 15.9	5 30.8	11 35.9	4 33.2	24 33.8	26 02.8	11 36.1	17 07.2

Astro Data	Dy Hr Mn	Planet Ingress	Dy Hr Mn	Last Aspect Dy Hr Mn		☽ Ingress	Dy Hr Mn	Last Aspect Dy Hr Mn		☽ Ingress	Dy Hr Mn	☽ Phases & Eclipses Dy Hr Mn	
☿ D	5 11:29	♂ ♍	5 9:35	2 16:30	♅ □	♒	2 20:06	2 11:12	♃ △	♓	2 14:26	6 7:03	○ 13♓53
☽ 0N	8 3:03	☿ ♍	10 2:52	5 5:15	♂ ☍	♓	5 5:28	4 7:19	♄ □	♈	4 20:40	13 6:25	☾ 20♊40
☽ 0S	21 1:29	♀ ♍	20 1:15	6 20:29	♄ □	♈	7 12:01	6 22:38	♃ ☍	♉	6 23:56	20 5:30	● 27♍27
☉0S	22 20:02	☉ ♎	22 20:02	9 15:52	☿ △	♉	9 16:23	8 13:45	♀ △	♊	9 1:44	28 2:53	☽ 5♑11
♃⚼♆	27 14:37	⚳ ♌	24 5:45	11 0:54	♀ □	♊	11 19:29	10 22:25	♅ ⚹	♋	11 3:38		
♃☍♅	28 4:25	☿ ♎	30 0:42	13 18:35	♅ ⚹	♋	13 22:12	13 4:00	♀ ⚹	♌	13 6:41	5 18:40	○ 12♈43
♇ D	28 19:36			15 21:23	♅ □	♌	16 1:09	15 5:27	♅ △	♍	15 11:19	12 12:25	☾ 19♋22
		♃ ♏	10 13:20	18 0:55	♅ △	♍	18 4:52	17 11:27	♂ ☌	♎	17 17:35	19 19:12	● 26♎35
☿0S	2 3:12	♀ ♎	14 10:11	20 5:30	☉ ☌	♎	20 10:06	19 19:12	☉ ☌	♏	20 1:41	27 22:22	☽ 4♒41
☽ 0N	5 11:18	☿ ♏	17 7:58	22 13:04	♅ ☍	♏	22 17:40	22 11:35	♂ ⚹	♐	22 11:57		
♅∠♆	7 7:14	♂ ♎	22 18:29	24 7:33	☿ ⚹	♐	25 4:01	24 16:44	♅ △	♑	25 0:12		
♀0S	17 6:19	☉ ♏	23 5:27	27 11:08	♅ △	♑	27 16:24	27 5:22	♅ □	♒	27 12:59		
☽ 0S	18 9:12			30 0:13	♃ □	♒	30 4:40	29 16:22	♅ ⚹	♓	29 23:46		
♂0S	26 23:00												

Astro Data

1 September 2017
Julian Day # 42978
SVP 5♓00'56"
GC 27♐05.2 ⚴ 13♉54.7
Eris 23♈42.8R ⚵ 2♑49.2
⚷ 27♓21.2R ⚶ 21♍38.4
☽ Mean ☊ 23♌19.8

1 October 2017
Julian Day # 43008
SVP 5♓00'54"
GC 27♐05.2 ⚴ 12♉44.7R
Eris 23♈27.6R ⚵ 6♑18.6
⚷ 26♓00.4R ⚶ 6♎38.4
☽ Mean ☊ 21♌44.4

November 2017 LONGITUDE

Day	Sid.Time	☉	0 hr ☽	Noon ☽	True ☊	☿	♀	♂	⚳	♃	♄	♅	♆	♇
1 W	14 43 52	9♏15 21	26♓12 34	3♈00 53	20♌56.7	23♏39.2	22♎30.8	6♎08.6	11♌51.1	4♏46.3	24♐39.4	26♈00.5	11♓35.4	17♑08.2
2 Th	14 47 48	10 15 22	9♈56 13	16 58 20	20R48.5	25 08.5	23 45.8	6 46.5	12 06.2	4 59.4	24 45.1	25R58.1	11R34.7	17 09.2
3 F	14 51 45	11 15 26	24 06 52	1♉21 12	20 38.1	26 37.3	25 00.8	7 24.3	12 20.9	5 12.5	24 50.8	25 55.8	11 34.1	17 10.2
4 Sa	14 55 41	12 15 31	8♉40 32	16 03 57	20 26.5	28 05.6	26 15.9	8 02.2	12 35.5	5 25.5	24 56.6	25 53.4	11 33.5	17 11.3
5 Su	14 59 38	13 15 38	23 30 21	0♊58 35	20 14.9	29 33.4	27 30.9	8 40.0	12 49.8	5 38.6	25 02.4	25 51.1	11 32.9	17 12.3
6 M	15 03 34	14 15 48	8♊27 25	15 55 44	20 04.7	1♐00.6	28 46.0	9 17.9	13 03.9	5 51.6	25 08.3	25 48.8	11 32.3	17 13.5
7 Tu	15 07 31	15 15 59	23 22 24	0♋46 28	19 56.9	2 27.2	0♏01.1	9 55.8	13 17.7	6 04.6	25 14.2	25 46.5	11 31.8	17 14.6
8 W	15 11 27	16 16 12	8♋07 06	15 23 40	19 51.9	3 53.2	1 16.3	10 33.6	13 31.3	6 17.7	25 20.2	25 44.3	11 31.3	17 15.8
9 Th	15 15 24	17 16 27	22 35 41	29 42 51	19 49.5	5 18.6	2 31.4	11 11.5	13 44.6	6 30.7	25 26.2	25 42.1	11 30.9	17 16.9
10 F	15 19 21	18 16 44	6♌45 02	13♌42 12	19 48.9	6 43.3	3 46.6	11 49.3	13 57.7	6 43.7	25 32.3	25 39.8	11 30.4	17 18.2
11 Sa	15 23 17	19 17 03	20 34 28	27 22 01	19 48.9	8 07.2	5 01.8	12 27.2	14 10.5	6 56.6	25 38.4	25 37.7	11 30.1	17 19.4
12 Su	15 27 14	20 17 25	4♍05 05	10♍43 56	19 48.0	9 30.4	6 17.0	13 05.0	14 23.0	7 09.6	25 44.6	25 35.5	11 29.7	17 20.7
13 M	15 31 10	21 17 48	17 18 51	23 50 09	19 45.1	10 52.6	7 32.2	13 42.8	14 35.3	7 22.5	25 50.8	25 33.3	11 29.4	17 22.0
14 Tu	15 35 07	22 18 13	0♎18 05	6♎42 54	19 39.4	12 13.8	8 47.5	14 20.7	14 47.2	7 35.4	25 57.1	25 31.2	11 29.1	17 23.3
15 W	15 39 03	23 18 39	13 04 48	19 24 00	19 30.6	13 33.9	10 02.8	14 58.5	14 58.9	7 48.3	26 03.4	25 29.1	11 28.8	17 24.6
16 Th	15 43 00	24 19 08	25 40 36	1♏54 45	19 19.0	14 52.8	11 18.1	15 36.3	15 10.3	8 01.2	26 09.7	25 27.1	11 28.6	17 26.0
17 F	15 46 56	25 19 38	8♏06 32	14 16 02	19 05.3	16 10.3	12 33.4	16 14.2	15 21.3	8 14.0	26 16.1	25 25.0	11 28.4	17 27.4
18 Sa	15 50 53	26 20 10	20 23 20	26 28 28	18 50.6	17 26.2	13 48.7	16 52.0	15 32.1	8 26.8	26 22.5	25 23.0	11 28.2	17 28.8
19 Su	15 54 50	27 20 44	2♐31 33	8♐32 41	18 36.2	18 40.4	15 04.0	17 29.8	15 42.6	8 39.6	26 29.0	25 21.0	11 28.1	17 30.2
20 M	15 58 46	28 21 19	14 31 59	20 29 39	18 23.3	19 52.5	16 19.4	18 07.6	15 52.8	8 52.4	26 35.5	25 19.1	11 28.0	17 31.7
21 Tu	16 02 43	29 21 55	26 25 52	2♑20 55	18 12.8	21 02.4	17 34.7	18 45.4	16 02.6	9 05.1	26 42.0	25 17.2	11 28.0	17 33.1
22 W	16 06 39	0♐22 33	8♑15 06	14 08 49	18 05.2	22 09.7	18 50.1	19 23.2	16 12.1	9 17.8	26 48.6	25 15.3	11D27.9	17 34.6
23 Th	16 10 36	1 23 12	20 02 26	25 56 29	18 00.6	23 14.1	20 05.4	20 01.0	16 21.3	9 30.5	26 55.2	25 13.4	11 27.9	17 36.1
24 F	16 14 32	2 23 52	1♒51 27	7♒47 55	17D58.5	24 15.1	21 20.8	20 38.8	16 30.1	9 43.1	27 01.9	25 11.6	11 28.0	17 37.7
25 Sa	16 18 29	3 24 33	13 46 30	19 47 50	17 58.1	25 12.4	22 36.2	21 16.6	16 38.7	9 55.7	27 08.5	25 09.8	11 28.1	17 39.3
26 Su	16 22 25	4 25 15	25 52 35	2♓01 27	17R58.3	26 05.3	23 51.6	21 54.3	16 46.8	10 08.2	27 15.2	25 08.1	11 28.2	17 40.8
27 M	16 26 22	5 25 59	8♓15 06	14 34 12	17 58.0	26 53.3	25 07.0	22 32.1	16 54.7	10 20.7	27 22.0	25 06.4	11 28.3	17 42.4
28 Tu	16 30 19	6 26 43	20 59 22	27 31 09	17 56.0	27 35.7	26 22.4	23 09.8	17 02.1	10 33.1	27 28.7	25 04.7	11 28.5	17 44.1
29 W	16 34 15	7 27 28	4♈10 02	10♈56 21	17 51.8	28 11.9	27 37.8	23 47.6	17 09.3	10 45.6	27 35.5	25 03.1	11 28.7	17 45.7
30 Th	16 38 12	8 28 14	17 50 19	24 51 56	17 45.0	28 41.0	28 53.3	24 25.3	17 16.0	10 57.9	27 42.3	25 01.5	11 29.0	17 47.3

December 2017 LONGITUDE

Day	Sid.Time	☉	0 hr ☽	Noon ☽	True ☊	☿	♀	♂	⚳	♃	♄	♅	♆	♇
1 F	16 42 08	9♐29 02	2♉01 02	9♉17 10	17♌36.0	29♐02.3	0♐08.7	25♎03.1	17♌22.4	11♏10.2	27♐49.1	24♈59.9	11♓29.3	17♑49.0
2 Sa	16 46 05	10 29 50	16 39 44	24 07 49	17R25.7	29R14.9	1 24.1	25 40.8	17 28.5	11 22.5	27 56.0	24R58.4	11 29.6	17 50.7
3 Su	16 50 01	11 30 39	1♊40 22	9♊16 08	17 15.2	29 18.0	2 39.6	26 18.5	17 34.1	11 34.8	28 02.9	24 56.9	11 30.0	17 52.4
4 M	16 53 58	12 31 30	16 53 45	24 31 49	17 06.0	29 10.9	3 55.0	26 56.2	17 39.4	11 46.9	28 09.8	24 55.5	11 30.4	17 54.2
5 Tu	16 57 54	13 32 22	2♋08 55	9♋43 46	16 58.8	28 52.9	5 10.5	27 33.9	17 44.3	11 59.1	28 16.7	24 54.1	11 30.8	17 55.9
6 W	17 01 51	14 33 15	17 15 10	24 42 08	16 54.3	28 23.8	6 25.9	28 11.6	17 48.8	12 11.1	28 23.6	24 52.8	11 31.3	17 57.7
7 Th	17 05 48	15 34 09	2♌03 51	9♌19 44	16D52.4	27 43.3	7 41.4	28 49.3	17 53.0	12 23.2	28 30.6	24 51.5	11 31.8	17 59.4
8 F	17 09 44	16 35 04	16 29 25	23 32 43	16 52.3	26 51.9	8 56.9	29 27.0	17 56.7	12 35.1	28 37.5	24 50.2	11 32.3	18 01.2
9 Sa	17 13 41	17 36 01	0♍29 36	7♍20 12	16R53.0	25 50.4	10 12.4	0♏04.7	18 00.0	12 47.0	28 44.5	24 49.0	11 32.9	18 03.0
10 Su	17 17 37	18 36 59	14 04 45	20 43 34	16 53.4	24 40.2	11 27.9	0 42.4	18 02.9	12 58.9	28 51.5	24 47.8	11 33.5	18 04.9
11 M	17 21 34	19 37 58	27 17 03	3♎45 35	16 52.3	23 23.2	12 43.4	1 20.1	18 05.4	13 10.7	28 58.6	24 46.7	11 34.1	18 06.7
12 Tu	17 25 30	20 38 58	10♎09 37	16 29 34	16 48.9	22 01.8	13 58.9	1 57.8	18 07.5	13 22.4	29 05.6	24 45.6	11 34.7	18 08.6
13 W	17 29 27	21 39 59	22 45 51	28 58 52	16 43.2	20 38.8	15 14.4	2 35.4	18 09.2	13 34.0	29 12.6	24 44.6	11 35.4	18 10.4
14 Th	17 33 23	22 41 01	5♏08 58	11♏16 29	16 35.1	19 16.9	16 29.9	3 13.1	18 10.5	13 45.6	29 19.7	24 43.6	11 36.2	18 12.3
15 F	17 37 20	23 42 04	17 21 44	23 24 58	16 25.2	17 58.8	17 45.4	3 50.7	18 11.3	13 57.2	29 26.7	24 42.6	11 36.9	18 14.2
16 Sa	17 41 17	24 43 08	29 26 25	5♐26 18	16 14.6	16 47.1	19 00.9	4 28.4	18R11.7	14 08.6	29 33.8	24 41.7	11 37.7	18 16.1
17 Su	17 45 13	25 44 13	11♐24 49	17 22 09	16 04.1	15 43.6	20 16.5	5 06.0	18 11.7	14 20.0	29 40.9	24 40.9	11 38.6	18 18.0
18 M	17 49 10	26 45 18	23 18 29	29 13 58	15 54.7	14 49.7	21 32.0	5 43.6	18 11.2	14 31.3	29 48.0	24 40.1	11 39.4	18 19.9
19 Tu	17 53 06	27 46 24	5♑08 49	11♑03 14	15 47.2	14 06.4	22 47.5	6 21.2	18 10.3	14 42.6	29 55.0	24 39.4	11 40.4	18 21.9
20 W	17 57 03	28 47 31	16 57 28	22 51 45	15 41.9	13 34.0	24 03.0	6 58.8	18 09.0	14 53.7	0♑02.1	24 38.7	11 41.3	18 23.8
21 Th	18 00 59	29 48 38	28 46 24	4♒41 45	15D39.1	13 12.6	25 18.6	7 36.4	18 07.2	15 04.8	0 09.2	24 38.0	11 42.2	18 25.8
22 F	18 04 56	0♑49 45	10♒38 10	16 36 05	15 38.3	13D01.8	26 34.1	8 13.9	18 05.0	15 15.8	0 16.3	24 37.4	11 43.2	18 27.7
23 Sa	18 08 52	1 50 53	22 35 56	28 38 15	15 39.1	13 01.0	27 49.6	8 51.5	18 02.4	15 26.7	0 23.4	24 36.9	11 44.3	18 29.7
24 Su	18 12 49	2 52 00	4♓43 32	10♓52 20	15 40.6	13 09.6	29 05.1	9 29.0	17 59.3	15 37.6	0 30.5	24 36.4	11 45.3	18 31.7
25 M	18 16 46	3 53 08	17 05 15	23 22 50	15R42.0	13 26.8	0♑20.7	10 06.5	17 55.8	15 48.3	0 37.5	24 35.9	11 46.4	18 33.7
26 Tu	18 20 42	4 54 16	29 45 41	6♈14 19	15 42.5	13 51.8	1 36.2	10 44.0	17 51.9	15 59.0	0 44.6	24 35.5	11 47.5	18 35.7
27 W	18 24 39	5 55 24	12♈49 15	19 30 54	15 41.5	14 23.9	2 51.7	11 21.5	17 47.6	16 09.6	0 51.7	24 35.2	11 48.7	18 37.7
28 Th	18 28 35	6 56 31	26 19 35	3♉15 30	15 38.8	15 02.3	4 07.2	11 59.0	17 42.8	16 20.1	0 58.8	24 34.9	11 49.9	18 39.7
29 F	18 32 32	7 57 39	10♉18 41	17 29 00	15 34.5	15 46.3	5 22.7	12 36.4	17 37.6	16 30.5	1 05.8	24 34.7	11 51.1	18 41.7
30 Sa	18 36 28	8 58 47	24 46 06	2♊09 26	15 29.2	16 35.4	6 38.2	13 13.9	17 31.9	16 40.8	1 12.9	24 34.5	11 52.3	18 43.7
31 Su	18 40 25	9 59 55	9♊38 12	17 11 26	15 23.6	17 28.9	7 53.7	13 51.3	17 25.9	16 51.0	1 19.9	24 34.3	11 53.6	18 45.7

Astro Data

	Dy Hr Mn
☽0N	1 21:45
♄△♅	11 9:45
☽0S	14 15:56
♆ D	22 14:21
☽0N	29 8:52
♃△♆	3 2:19
☿ R	3 7:33
☽0S	11 22:35
⚳ R	16 22:28
♃∠♄	22 14:55
☿ D	23 1:50
☽0N	26 18:27

Planet Ingress

		Dy Hr Mn
☿	♐	5 19:19
♀	♏	7 11:38
☉	♐	22 3:05
♀	♐	1 9:14
♂	♏	9 8:59
♄	♑	20 4:49
☉	♑	21 16:28
♀	♑	25 5:26

Last Aspect / ☽ Ingress

Last Aspect Dy Hr Mn			☽ Ingress	Dy Hr Mn
31 21:08	♄	□	♈	1 6:43
3 3:03	♅	☌	♉	3 9:46
5 9:29	☿	☍	♊	5 10:26
7 10:40	♀	△	♋	7 10:44
9 5:14	♅	□	♌	9 12:29
11 8:55	♅	△	♍	11 16:41
13 15:45	♄	□	♎	13 23:26
16 0:50	♄	⚹	♏	16 8:19
18 11:42	☉	☌	♐	18 18:59
21 0:26	♄	☌	♑	21 7:14
23 10:33	♅	□	♒	23 20:14
26 2:37	♄	⚹	♓	26 8:04
28 12:09	☿	□	♈	28 16:30
30 18:37	☿	△	♉	30 20:38

Last Aspect / ☽ Ingress

Last Aspect Dy Hr Mn			☽ Ingress	Dy Hr Mn
2 1:53	♇	△	♊	2 21:21
4 19:13	☿	☍	♋	4 20:37
6 17:56	♂	□	♌	6 20:37
8 22:40	♂	⚹	♍	8 23:09
11 3:02	♄	□	♎	11 5:01
13 12:27	♄	⚹	♏	13 13:59
15 1:42	♇	⚹	♐	16 1:07
18 13:10	♄	☌	♑	18 13:33
20 15:37	♅	□	♒	21 2:29
23 10:13	♀	⚹	♓	23 14:42
25 2:48	♇	⚹	♈	26 0:27
27 20:57	♅	☌	♉	28 6:23
29 14:01	♇	△	♊	30 8:31

☽ Phases & Eclipses

Dy Hr Mn		
4 5:23	○	11♉59
10 20:36	☾	18♌38
18 11:42	●	26♏19
26 17:03	☽	4♓38
3 15:47	○	11♊40
10 7:51	☾	18♍26
18 6:30	●	26♐31
26 9:20	☽	4♈47

Astro Data

1 November 2017
Julian Day # 43039
SVP 5♓00'51"
GC 27♐05.3 ⚴ 4♉35.8R
Eris 23♈09.2R ⚵ 14♑01.2
⚷ 24♓49.9R ⚶ 22♎28.1
☽ Mean ☊ 20♌05.9

1 December 2017
Julian Day # 43069
SVP 5♓00'47"
GC 27♐05.4 ⚴ 26♈27.3R
Eris 22♈54.2R ⚵ 24♑08.2
⚷ 24♓19.4R ⚶ 7♏50.0
☽ Mean ☊ 18♌30.6

LONGITUDE

January 2018

Day	Sid.Time	☉	0 hr ☽	Noon ☽	True ☊	☿	♀	♂	⚳	♃	♄	♅	♆	♇
1 M	18 44 21	11♑01 03	24♊48 00	2♋26 35	15♌18.6	18♐26.4	9♑09.2	14♏28.7	17♌19.4	17♏01.2	1♑26.9	24♈34.3	11♓54.9	18♑47.8
2 Tu	18 48 18	12 02 11	10♋05 52	17 44 27	15R14.8	19 27.4	10 24.7	15 06.2	17R12.6	17 11.2	1 33.9	24D34.2	11 56.2	18 49.8
3 W	18 52 15	13 03 18	25 21 01	2♌54 18	15D12.6	20 31.5	11 40.2	15 43.6	17 05.3	17 21.1	1 40.9	24 34.2	11 57.6	18 51.8
4 Th	18 56 11	14 04 26	10♌23 15	17 46 56	15 12.1	21 38.4	12 55.7	16 20.9	16 57.6	17 31.0	1 47.9	24 34.3	11 59.0	18 53.9
5 F	19 00 08	15 05 34	25 04 38	2♍15 50	15 12.9	22 47.7	14 11.2	16 58.3	16 49.6	17 40.7	1 54.9	24 34.4	12 00.4	18 55.9
6 Sa	19 04 04	16 06 43	9♍20 13	16 17 40	15 14.5	23 59.3	15 26.7	17 35.7	16 41.1	17 50.3	2 01.9	24 34.6	12 01.8	18 58.0
7 Su	19 08 01	17 07 51	23 08 11	29 51 57	15 16.0	25 12.8	16 42.1	18 13.0	16 32.3	17 59.8	2 08.8	24 34.8	12 03.3	19 00.0
8 M	19 11 57	18 08 59	6♎29 15	13♎00 27	15R17.0	26 28.1	17 57.6	18 50.3	16 23.0	18 09.2	2 15.7	24 35.1	12 04.8	19 02.0
9 Tu	19 15 54	19 10 08	19 25 59	25 46 19	15 16.9	27 44.9	19 13.1	19 27.6	16 13.5	18 18.5	2 22.6	24 35.4	12 06.3	19 04.1
10 W	19 19 51	20 11 17	2♏01 57	8♏13 25	15 15.6	29 03.2	20 28.6	20 04.9	16 03.5	18 27.7	2 29.5	24 35.8	12 07.9	19 06.1
11 Th	19 23 47	21 12 25	14 21 13	20 25 51	15 13.1	0♑22.8	21 44.1	20 42.2	15 53.2	18 36.8	2 36.3	24 36.3	12 09.5	19 08.2
12 F	19 27 44	22 13 34	26 27 48	2♐27 32	15 09.7	1 43.6	22 59.5	21 19.5	15 42.6	18 45.8	2 43.2	24 36.8	12 11.1	19 10.2
13 Sa	19 31 40	23 14 42	8♐25 29	14 22 02	15 05.9	3 05.5	24 15.0	21 56.7	15 31.7	18 54.6	2 50.0	24 37.3	12 12.7	19 12.3
14 Su	19 35 37	24 15 51	20 17 34	26 12 25	15 02.0	4 28.5	25 30.5	22 33.9	15 20.4	19 03.4	2 56.8	24 37.9	12 14.3	19 14.3
15 M	19 39 33	25 16 59	2♑06 53	8♑01 17	14 58.7	5 52.3	26 45.9	23 11.1	15 08.9	19 12.0	3 03.5	24 38.5	12 16.0	19 16.3
16 Tu	19 43 30	26 18 06	13 55 53	19 50 54	14 56.1	7 17.0	28 01.4	23 48.3	14 57.0	19 20.5	3 10.3	24 39.2	12 17.7	19 18.4
17 W	19 47 26	27 19 14	25 46 36	1♒43 14	14 54.5	8 42.6	29 16.9	24 25.4	14 44.9	19 28.8	3 16.9	24 40.0	12 19.4	19 20.4
18 Th	19 51 23	28 20 20	7♒41 00	13 40 09	14D53.9	10 08.9	0♒32.3	25 02.5	14 32.5	19 37.1	3 23.6	24 40.8	12 21.2	19 22.4
19 F	19 55 20	29 21 26	19 40 56	25 43 38	14 54.3	11 36.0	1 47.7	25 39.6	14 19.9	19 45.2	3 30.2	24 41.6	12 23.0	19 24.5
20 Sa	19 59 16	0♒22 32	1♓48 29	7♓55 50	14 55.2	13 03.8	3 03.2	26 16.7	14 07.1	19 53.2	3 36.8	24 42.5	12 24.7	19 26.5
21 Su	20 03 13	1 23 36	14 05 57	20 19 12	14 56.5	14 32.3	4 18.6	26 53.7	13 54.0	20 01.0	3 43.4	24 43.5	12 26.6	19 28.5
22 M	20 07 09	2 24 39	26 35 56	2♈56 31	14 57.7	16 01.4	5 34.0	27 30.8	13 40.8	20 08.7	3 49.9	24 44.5	12 28.4	19 30.5
23 Tu	20 11 06	3 25 42	9♈21 18	15 50 39	14 58.7	17 31.3	6 49.4	28 07.8	13 27.4	20 16.3	3 56.4	24 45.5	12 30.2	19 32.5
24 W	20 15 02	4 26 43	22 24 55	29 04 25	14R59.2	19 01.8	8 04.8	28 44.7	13 13.8	20 23.7	4 02.9	24 46.6	12 32.1	19 34.5
25 Th	20 18 59	5 27 44	5♉49 24	12♉40 05	14 59.1	20 32.9	9 20.1	29 21.7	13 00.1	20 31.0	4 09.3	24 47.8	12 34.0	19 36.5
26 F	20 22 55	6 28 43	19 36 34	26 38 52	14 58.7	22 04.7	10 35.5	29 58.6	12 46.2	20 38.2	4 15.7	24 49.0	12 35.9	19 38.5
27 Sa	20 26 52	7 29 42	3♊46 50	11♊00 14	14 57.9	23 37.1	11 50.9	0♐35.4	12 32.3	20 45.2	4 22.0	24 50.3	12 37.8	19 40.4
28 Su	20 30 49	8 30 39	18 18 39	25 41 31	14 57.1	25 10.2	13 06.2	1 12.3	12 18.3	20 52.1	4 28.3	24 51.6	12 39.8	19 42.4
29 M	20 34 45	9 31 35	3♋08 05	10♋37 30	14 56.5	26 44.0	14 21.5	1 49.1	12 04.2	20 58.9	4 34.6	24 52.9	12 41.8	19 44.4
30 Tu	20 38 42	10 32 30	18 08 47	25 40 53	14 56.0	28 18.4	15 36.8	2 25.9	11 50.1	21 05.5	4 40.8	24 54.3	12 43.8	19 46.3
31 W	20 42 38	11 33 24	3♌12 39	10♌42 59	14D55.9	29 53.4	16 52.1	3 02.7	11 35.9	21 11.9	4 46.9	24 55.8	12 45.8	19 48.2

LONGITUDE

February 2018

Day	Sid.Time	☉	0 hr ☽	Noon ☽	True ☊	☿	♀	♂	⚳	♃	♄	♅	♆	♇
1 Th	20 46 35	12♒34 17	18♌10 47	25♌35 01	14♌55.9	1♒29.2	18♒07.4	3♐39.4	11♌21.8	21♏18.2	4♑53.0	24♈57.3	12♓47.8	19♑50.2
2 F	20 50 31	13 35 08	2♍54 48	10♍09 21	14 56.0	3 05.7	19 22.7	4 16.2	11R07.6	21 24.4	4 59.1	24 58.8	12 49.8	19 52.1
3 Sa	20 54 28	14 35 59	17 18 03	24 20 27	14R56.1	4 42.8	20 38.0	4 52.9	10 53.5	21 30.3	5 05.1	25 00.4	12 51.9	19 54.0
4 Su	20 58 24	15 36 49	1♎16 17	8♎05 24	14 56.1	6 20.7	21 53.2	5 29.5	10 39.4	21 36.2	5 11.1	25 02.0	12 53.9	19 55.8
5 M	21 02 21	16 37 38	14 47 50	21 23 44	14 56.0	7 59.3	23 08.5	6 06.1	10 25.3	21 41.9	5 17.0	25 03.7	12 56.0	19 57.7
6 Tu	21 06 18	17 38 26	27 53 23	4♏17 08	14 55.8	9 38.7	24 23.7	6 42.7	10 11.4	21 47.4	5 22.9	25 05.4	12 58.1	19 59.6
7 W	21 10 14	18 39 13	10♏35 26	16 48 47	14D55.7	11 18.9	25 38.9	7 19.3	9 57.5	21 52.8	5 28.7	25 07.2	13 00.2	20 01.4
8 Th	21 14 11	19 39 59	22 57 43	29 02 47	14 55.8	12 59.8	26 54.1	7 55.8	9 43.8	21 58.0	5 34.5	25 09.0	13 02.3	20 03.3
9 F	21 18 07	20 40 45	5♐04 36	11♐03 44	14 56.1	14 41.5	28 09.3	8 32.3	9 30.2	22 03.0	5 40.2	25 10.8	13 04.4	20 05.1
10 Sa	21 22 04	21 41 29	17 00 45	22 56 13	14 56.7	16 24.1	29 24.5	9 08.8	9 16.7	22 07.9	5 45.8	25 12.7	13 06.6	20 06.9
11 Su	21 26 00	22 42 12	28 50 41	4♑44 40	14 57.6	18 07.4	0♓39.7	9 45.2	9 03.4	22 12.7	5 51.4	25 14.7	13 08.8	20 08.7
12 M	21 29 57	23 42 54	10♑38 39	16 33 06	14 58.5	19 51.6	1 54.9	10 21.6	8 50.3	22 17.2	5 56.9	25 16.7	13 10.9	20 10.5
13 Tu	21 33 53	24 43 35	22 28 24	28 24 58	14 59.3	21 36.6	3 10.0	10 57.9	8 37.5	22 21.6	6 02.4	25 18.7	13 13.1	20 12.2
14 W	21 37 50	25 44 15	4♒23 07	10♒23 10	14R59.7	23 22.5	4 25.1	11 34.2	8 24.8	22 25.8	6 07.8	25 20.8	13 15.3	20 14.0
15 Th	21 41 47	26 44 53	16 25 24	22 30 01	14 59.7	25 09.2	5 40.3	12 10.5	8 12.4	22 29.9	6 13.2	25 22.9	13 17.5	20 15.7
16 F	21 45 43	27 45 29	28 37 15	4♓47 14	14 58.9	26 56.8	6 55.4	12 46.7	8 00.2	22 33.7	6 18.5	25 25.0	13 19.7	20 17.4
17 Sa	21 49 40	28 46 04	11♓00 10	17 16 07	14 57.5	28 45.2	8 10.4	13 22.9	7 48.3	22 37.4	6 23.7	25 27.2	13 21.9	20 19.1
18 Su	21 53 36	29 46 38	23 35 14	29 57 34	14 55.5	0♓34.4	9 25.5	13 59.0	7 36.7	22 40.9	6 28.9	25 29.5	13 24.1	20 20.8
19 M	21 57 33	0♓47 10	6♈23 14	12♈52 18	14 53.1	2 24.4	10 40.5	14 35.0	7 25.3	22 44.3	6 34.0	25 31.7	13 26.4	20 22.4
20 Tu	22 01 29	1 47 40	19 24 49	26 00 51	14 50.8	4 15.1	11 55.6	15 11.0	7 14.3	22 47.4	6 39.0	25 34.0	13 28.6	20 24.1
21 W	22 05 26	2 48 08	2♉40 29	9♉23 45	14 48.8	6 06.5	13 10.6	15 47.0	7 03.6	22 50.4	6 43.9	25 36.4	13 30.8	20 25.7
22 Th	22 09 22	3 48 34	16 10 42	23 01 21	14D47.6	7 58.6	14 25.5	16 22.9	6 53.3	22 53.2	6 48.8	25 38.8	13 33.1	20 27.3
23 F	22 13 19	4 48 59	29 55 43	6♊53 45	14 47.3	9 51.3	15 40.5	16 58.8	6 43.3	22 55.9	6 53.7	25 41.2	13 35.3	20 28.9
24 Sa	22 17 15	5 49 22	13♊55 23	21 00 29	14 47.9	11 44.4	16 55.4	17 34.6	6 33.6	22 58.3	6 58.4	25 43.6	13 37.6	20 30.4
25 Su	22 21 12	6 49 42	28 08 51	5♋20 14	14 49.1	13 37.9	18 10.3	18 10.4	6 24.3	23 00.6	7 03.1	25 46.1	13 39.9	20 32.0
26 M	22 25 09	7 50 01	12♋34 15	19 50 29	14 50.6	15 31.6	19 25.2	18 46.1	6 15.4	23 02.7	7 07.7	25 48.7	13 42.1	20 33.5
27 Tu	22 29 05	8 50 18	27 08 23	4♌27 20	14R51.7	17 25.2	20 40.1	19 21.8	6 06.9	23 04.6	7 12.2	25 51.2	13 44.4	20 35.0
28 W	22 33 02	9 50 33	11♌46 40	19 05 36	14 51.9	19 18.7	21 54.9	19 57.4	5 58.7	23 06.3	7 16.7	25 53.8	13 46.7	20 36.5

Astro Data

	Dy Hr Mn
♅ D	2 14:11
☽ 0S	8 6:20
♃✶♇	16 4:13
☽ 0N	23 1:22
☽ 0S	4 15:37
☽ 0N	19 6:48

Planet Ingress

	Dy Hr Mn
☿ ♑	11 5:09
♀ ♒	18 1:44
☉ ♒	20 3:09
♂ ♐	26 12:56
☿ ♒	31 13:39
♀ ♓	10 23:19
☿ ♓	18 4:28
☉ ♓	18 17:18

Last Aspect / ☽ Ingress (January)

Last Aspect Dy Hr Mn		☽ Ingress Dy Hr Mn
31 23:38 ♅ ✶	♋	1 8:10
2 22:46 ♅ □	♌	3 7:22
4 23:10 ♅ △	♍	5 8:12
7 2:51 ☿ □	♎	7 12:14
9 16:13 ☿ ✶	♏	9 20:05
11 14:53 ♀ ✶	♐	12 7:04
14 8:48 ♅ △	♑	14 19:42
17 6:30 ♀ ☌	♒	17 8:32
19 11:52 ♂ □	♓	19 20:26
22 1:13 ♂ △	♈	22 6:27
24 4:16 ♅ ☌	♉	24 13:39
26 3:16 ☿ △	♊	26 17:40
28 10:39 ♅ ✶	♋	28 18:57
30 16:40 ☿ ☍	♌	30 18:53

Last Aspect / ☽ Ingress (February)

Last Aspect Dy Hr Mn		☽ Ingress Dy Hr Mn
1 10:59 ♅ △	♍	1 19:13
3 7:07 ♃ ✶	♎	3 21:47
5 18:46 ♅ ☍	♏	6 3:56
8 7:16 ♀ □	♐	8 13:53
10 16:38 ♅ △	♑	11 2:21
13 5:43 ♅ □	♒	13 15:11
15 21:05 ☉ ☌	♓	16 2:42
17 22:13 ♃ △	♈	18 12:05
20 11:11 ♅ ☌	♉	20 19:12
22 11:46 ♃ ☍	♊	23 0:07
24 19:58 ♅ ✶	♋	25 3:06
26 21:51 ♅ □	♌	27 4:42

☽ Phases & Eclipses

Dy Hr Mn	
2 2:24	○ 11♋38
8 22:25	☾ 18♎36
17 2:17	● 26♑54
24 22:20	☽ 4♉53
31 13:27	○ 11♌37
31 13:30	• T 1.316
7 15:54	☾ 18♏49
15 21:05	● 27♒08
15 20:51:22	• P 0.599
23 8:09	☽ 4♊39

Astro Data

1 January 2018
Julian Day # 43100
SVP 5♓00'41"
GC 27♐05.4 ⚵ 26♈06.1
Eris 22♈46.2R ⚶ 6♒23.2
⚷ 24♓39.3 ⚴ 23♏22.5
☽ Mean ☊ 16♌52.1

1 February 2018
Julian Day # 43131
SVP 5♓00'36"
GC 27♐05.5 ⚵ 3♉54.2
Eris 22♈48.5 ⚶ 19♒49.7
⚷ 25♓47.0 ⚴ 8♐01.2
☽ Mean ☊ 15♌13.7

March 2018 — LONGITUDE

Day	Sid.Time	☉	0 hr ☽	Noon ☽	True ☊	☿	♀	♂	⚳	♃	♄	♅	♆	♇
1 Th	22 36 58	10♓50 45	26♌23 23	3♍39 12	14♌50.9	21♓11.8	23♓09.7	20♐32.9	5♌51.0	23♏07.8	7♑21.1	25♈56.5	13♓49.0	20♑37.9
2 F	22 40 55	11 50 56	10♍52 16	18 01 49	14R48.4	23 04.2	24 24.5	21 08.4	5R43.6	23 09.2	7 25.4	25 59.1	13 51.2	20 39.4
3 Sa	22 44 51	12 51 06	25 07 10	2♎07 46	14 44.7	24 55.5	25 39.3	21 43.9	5 36.7	23 10.3	7 29.6	26 01.8	13 53.5	20 40.8
4 Su	22 48 48	13 51 13	9♎03 05	15 52 48	14 40.2	26 45.4	26 54.0	22 19.2	5 30.1	23 11.3	7 33.8	26 04.5	13 55.8	20 42.1
5 M	22 52 44	14 51 19	22 36 39	29 14 34	14 35.4	28 33.5	28 08.7	22 54.6	5 24.0	23 12.1	7 37.8	26 07.3	13 58.1	20 43.5
6 Tu	22 56 41	15 51 23	5♏46 35	12♏12 50	14 31.0	0♈19.3	29 23.4	23 29.8	5 18.3	23 12.7	7 41.8	26 10.1	14 00.3	20 44.9
7 W	23 00 38	16 51 26	18 33 34	24 49 11	14 27.5	2 02.5	0♈38.1	24 05.1	5 13.0	23 13.1	7 45.8	26 12.9	14 02.6	20 46.2
8 Th	23 04 34	17 51 27	1♐00 04	7♐06 46	14D25.4	3 42.4	1 52.7	24 40.2	5 08.1	23R13.3	7 49.6	26 15.7	14 04.9	20 47.5
9 F	23 08 31	18 51 27	13 09 49	19 09 49	14 24.7	5 18.6	3 07.4	25 15.3	5 03.7	23 13.4	7 53.3	26 18.6	14 07.2	20 48.7
10 Sa	23 12 27	19 51 24	25 07 23	1♑03 10	14 25.3	6 50.5	4 22.0	25 50.3	4 59.7	23 13.2	7 57.0	26 21.5	14 09.4	20 50.0
11 Su	23 16 24	20 51 21	6♑57 49	12 51 57	14 26.9	8 17.6	5 36.5	26 25.2	4 56.2	23 12.9	8 00.6	26 24.4	14 11.7	20 51.2
12 M	23 20 20	21 51 15	18 46 12	24 41 12	14 28.6	9 39.4	6 51.1	27 00.1	4 53.0	23 12.3	8 04.1	26 27.4	14 14.0	20 52.4
13 Tu	23 24 17	22 51 08	0♒37 29	6♒35 37	14R30.0	10 55.3	8 05.6	27 34.9	4 50.3	23 11.6	8 07.5	26 30.4	14 16.2	20 53.6
14 W	23 28 13	23 50 59	12 36 06	18 39 22	14 30.2	12 04.9	9 20.1	28 09.6	4 48.1	23 10.7	8 10.9	26 33.4	14 18.5	20 54.7
15 Th	23 32 10	24 50 48	24 45 49	0♓55 46	14 28.7	13 07.7	10 34.6	28 44.3	4 46.2	23 09.6	8 14.1	26 36.4	14 20.8	20 55.8
16 F	23 36 07	25 50 36	7♓09 29	13 27 10	14 25.3	14 03.4	11 49.0	29 18.8	4 44.9	23 08.3	8 17.3	26 39.4	14 23.0	20 56.9
17 Sa	23 40 03	26 50 21	19 48 54	26 14 46	14 19.9	14 51.7	13 03.4	29 53.3	4 43.9	23 06.8	8 20.3	26 42.5	14 25.2	20 58.0
18 Su	23 44 00	27 50 05	2♈44 41	9♈18 36	14 13.0	15 32.2	14 17.8	0♑27.7	4D43.4	23 05.2	8 23.3	26 45.6	14 27.5	20 59.0
19 M	23 47 56	28 49 46	15 56 21	22 37 42	14 05.2	16 04.7	15 32.2	1 02.0	4 43.3	23 03.3	8 26.2	26 48.7	14 29.7	21 00.0
20 Tu	23 51 53	29 49 25	29 22 24	6♉10 12	13 57.5	16 29.1	16 46.5	1 36.2	4 43.7	23 01.3	8 29.0	26 51.9	14 31.9	21 01.0
21 W	23 55 49	0♈49 03	13♉00 47	19 53 51	13 50.6	16 45.3	18 00.8	2 10.3	4 44.5	22 59.1	8 31.7	26 55.0	14 34.1	21 01.9
22 Th	23 59 46	1 48 38	26 49 08	3♊46 21	13 45.4	16R53.4	19 15.1	2 44.3	4 45.7	22 56.7	8 34.3	26 58.2	14 36.3	21 02.9
23 F	0 03 42	2 48 10	10♊45 15	17 45 38	13 42.3	16 53.5	20 29.3	3 18.3	4 47.3	22 54.1	8 36.9	27 01.4	14 38.5	21 03.8
24 Sa	0 07 39	3 47 41	24 47 17	1♋50 03	13D41.3	16 45.9	21 43.5	3 52.1	4 49.4	22 51.4	8 39.3	27 04.6	14 40.7	21 04.6
25 Su	0 11 36	4 47 09	8♋53 46	15 58 17	13 41.7	16 30.8	22 57.7	4 25.8	4 51.9	22 48.4	8 41.6	27 07.8	14 42.9	21 05.5
26 M	0 15 32	5 46 35	23 03 27	0♌09 05	13R42.7	16 08.7	24 11.8	4 59.5	4 54.8	22 45.3	8 43.9	27 11.1	14 45.0	21 06.3
27 Tu	0 19 29	6 45 58	7♌14 59	14 20 53	13 43.2	15 40.2	25 25.9	5 33.0	4 58.1	22 42.1	8 46.0	27 14.4	14 47.2	21 07.1
28 W	0 23 25	7 45 19	21 26 31	28 31 30	13 42.3	15 06.0	26 39.9	6 06.5	5 01.8	22 38.6	8 48.1	27 17.6	14 49.3	21 07.8
29 Th	0 27 22	8 44 38	5♍35 29	12♍37 59	13 39.1	14 26.9	27 54.0	6 39.8	5 06.0	22 35.0	8 50.1	27 20.9	14 51.5	21 08.6
30 F	0 31 18	9 43 54	19 38 33	26 36 42	13 33.4	13 43.7	29 07.9	7 13.0	5 10.5	22 31.2	8 51.9	27 24.2	14 53.6	21 09.3
31 Sa	0 35 15	10 43 09	3♎31 54	10♎23 42	13 25.3	12 57.4	0♉21.9	7 46.1	5 15.4	22 27.2	8 53.7	27 27.6	14 55.7	21 09.9

April 2018 — LONGITUDE

Day	Sid.Time	☉	0 hr ☽	Noon ☽	True ☊	☿	♀	♂	⚳	♃	♄	♅	♆	♇
1 Su	0 39 11	11♈42 21	17♎11 39	23♎55 23	13♌15.6	12♈08.9	1♉35.8	8♑19.2	5♌20.7	22♏23.1	8♑55.4	27♈30.9	14♓57.8	21♑10.6
2 M	0 43 08	12 41 31	0♏34 35	7♏09 02	13R05.2	11R19.4	2 49.7	8 52.1	5 26.4	22R18.8	8 56.9	27 34.2	14 59.8	21 11.2
3 Tu	0 47 04	13 40 40	13 38 37	20 03 18	12 55.1	10 29.8	4 03.5	9 24.9	5 32.4	22 14.4	8 58.4	27 37.6	15 01.9	21 11.8
4 W	0 51 01	14 39 47	26 23 12	2♐38 28	12 46.4	9 41.0	5 17.3	9 57.5	5 38.8	22 09.8	8 59.8	27 41.0	15 04.0	21 12.3
5 Th	0 54 58	15 38 52	8♐49 23	14 56 21	12 39.7	8 54.0	6 31.1	10 30.1	5 45.6	22 05.0	9 01.1	27 44.3	15 06.0	21 12.9
6 F	0 58 54	16 37 55	20 59 46	27 00 09	12 35.4	8 09.5	7 44.8	11 02.5	5 52.8	22 00.1	9 02.3	27 47.7	15 08.0	21 13.4
7 Sa	1 02 51	17 36 56	2♑58 05	8♑54 10	12D33.3	7 28.3	8 58.5	11 34.8	6 00.3	21 55.1	9 03.4	27 51.1	15 10.0	21 13.8
8 Su	1 06 47	18 35 56	14 49 02	20 43 21	12 32.9	6 51.0	10 12.2	12 07.0	6 08.2	21 49.8	9 04.4	27 54.5	15 12.0	21 14.3
9 M	1 10 44	19 34 54	26 37 49	2♒33 05	12R33.4	6 18.1	11 25.8	12 39.0	6 16.5	21 44.5	9 05.3	27 57.9	15 14.0	21 14.7
10 Tu	1 14 40	20 33 50	8♒29 52	14 28 48	12 33.6	5 49.9	12 39.4	13 10.9	6 25.1	21 39.0	9 06.1	28 01.3	15 15.9	21 15.1
11 W	1 18 37	21 32 44	20 30 31	26 35 37	12 32.7	5 26.7	13 53.0	13 42.6	6 34.0	21 33.4	9 06.8	28 04.8	15 17.8	21 15.4
12 Th	1 22 33	22 31 37	2♓44 38	8♓58 03	12 29.7	5 08.7	15 06.5	14 14.2	6 43.3	21 27.6	9 07.4	28 08.2	15 19.8	21 15.7
13 F	1 26 30	23 30 27	15 16 15	21 39 32	12 24.1	4 56.1	16 20.0	14 45.6	6 52.9	21 21.7	9 07.9	28 11.6	15 21.7	21 16.0
14 Sa	1 30 27	24 29 16	28 08 06	4♈42 04	12 16.0	4D48.7	17 33.5	15 16.9	7 02.8	21 15.7	9 08.3	28 15.1	15 23.5	21 16.3
15 Su	1 34 23	25 28 03	11♈21 21	18 05 49	12 05.7	4 46.7	18 46.9	15 48.0	7 13.1	21 09.6	9 08.6	28 18.5	15 25.4	21 16.5
16 M	1 38 20	26 26 48	24 55 11	1♉49 04	11 54.1	4 49.9	20 00.3	16 18.9	7 23.6	21 03.3	9 08.8	28 21.9	15 27.2	21 16.7
17 Tu	1 42 16	27 25 31	8♉46 57	15 48 17	11 42.4	4 58.1	21 13.6	16 49.7	7 34.5	20 57.0	9R08.9	28 25.4	15 29.0	21 16.8
18 W	1 46 13	28 24 12	22 52 25	29 58 43	11 31.9	5 11.3	22 26.9	17 20.3	7 45.7	20 50.5	9 08.9	28 28.8	15 30.8	21 17.0
19 Th	1 50 09	29 22 51	7♊06 31	14♊15 11	11 23.5	5 29.3	23 40.2	17 50.7	7 57.3	20 43.9	9 08.8	28 32.2	15 32.6	21 17.1
20 F	1 54 06	0♉21 28	21 24 09	28 32 55	11 17.9	5 52.0	24 53.4	18 20.9	8 09.1	20 37.2	9 08.6	28 35.7	15 34.4	21 17.2
21 Sa	1 58 02	1 20 03	5♋41 01	12♋48 08	11 14.9	6 19.0	26 06.6	18 50.9	8 21.2	20 30.5	9 08.4	28 39.1	15 36.1	21 17.2
22 Su	2 01 59	2 18 35	19 53 59	26 58 24	11D14.0	6 50.3	27 19.7	19 20.8	8 33.6	20 23.6	9 08.0	28 42.6	15 37.8	21R17.2
23 M	2 05 56	3 17 06	4♌01 13	11♌02 21	11R14.0	7 25.7	28 32.8	19 50.5	8 46.3	20 16.6	9 07.5	28 46.0	15 39.5	21 17.2
24 Tu	2 09 52	4 15 34	18 01 47	24 59 26	11 13.5	8 05.0	29 45.8	20 19.9	8 59.3	20 09.6	9 06.9	28 49.4	15 41.2	21 17.2
25 W	2 13 49	5 13 59	1♍55 17	8♍49 15	11 11.5	8 48.0	0♊58.8	20 49.2	9 12.5	20 02.5	9 06.2	28 52.9	15 42.8	21 17.1
26 Th	2 17 45	6 12 23	15 41 17	22 31 14	11 07.0	9 34.6	2 11.7	21 18.2	9 26.0	19 55.3	9 05.5	28 56.3	15 44.4	21 17.0
27 F	2 21 42	7 10 45	29 18 59	6♎04 19	10 59.5	10 24.5	3 24.6	21 47.1	9 39.8	19 48.1	9 04.6	28 59.7	15 46.0	21 16.9
28 Sa	2 25 38	8 09 04	12♎47 03	19 26 58	10 49.3	11 17.7	4 37.5	22 15.7	9 53.9	19 40.8	9 03.6	29 03.1	15 47.6	21 16.7
29 Su	2 29 35	9 07 22	26 03 49	2♏37 24	10 37.2	12 14.1	5 50.3	22 44.1	10 08.2	19 33.4	9 02.6	29 06.5	15 49.1	21 16.5
30 M	2 33 31	10 05 38	9♏07 30	15 33 59	10 24.1	13 13.4	7 03.1	23 12.3	10 22.7	19 26.0	9 01.4	29 09.9	15 50.7	21 16.3

Astro Data

	Dy Hr Mn
☽0S	4 1:37
☿0N	6 4:58
♃ R	9 4:45
♀0N	9 5:55
♃∠♄	14 11:03
☽0N	18 13:02
⚳ D	19 4:12
☉0N	20 16:16
☿ R	23 0:17
☽0S	31 11:03
♃✶♇	14 9:58
☽0N	14 21:22
☿ D	15 9:21
♄ R	18 1:47
♇ R	22 15:26

Planet Ingress

	Dy Hr Mn
☿ ♈	6 7:34
♀ ♈	6 23:45
♂ ♑	17 16:40
☉ ♈	20 16:15
♀ ♉	31 4:54
☉ ♉	20 3:12
♀ ♊	24 16:40

☽0S27 19:00

Last Aspect / ☽ Ingress

Last Aspect Dy Hr Mn		☽ Ingress Dy Hr Mn
28 23:13 ♅ △	♍	1 5:57
2 23:50 ♀ ☍	♎	3 8:20
5 6:19 ♅ ☍	♏	5 13:23
7 8:55 ♃ ☌	♐	7 22:03
10 2:27 ♅ △	♑	10 9:52
12 15:36 ♅ □	♒	12 22:44
15 7:32 ♂ ✶	♓	15 10:12
17 13:11 ☉ ☌	♈	17 18:57
19 19:29 ♅ ☌	♉	20 1:07
21 17:21 ♃ ☍	♊	22 5:30
24 3:52 ♅ ✶	♋	24 8:53
26 6:58 ♅ □	♌	26 11:45
28 9:54 ♅ △	♍	28 14:30
30 4:59 ♃ ✶	♎	30 17:52

Last Aspect / ☽ Ingress

Last Aspect Dy Hr Mn		☽ Ingress Dy Hr Mn
1 18:29 ♅ ☍	♏	1 22:57
3 16:06 ♃ ☌	♐	4 6:55
6 13:36 ♅ △	♑	6 18:01
9 2:40 ♅ □	♒	9 6:50
11 14:55 ♅ ✶	♓	11 18:40
13 11:27 ♃ △	♈	14 3:25
16 5:59 ♅ ☌	♉	16 8:51
17 22:05 ♀ ☌	♊	18 12:02
20 12:05 ♅ ✶	♋	20 14:26
22 14:58 ♅ □	♌	22 17:09
24 18:39 ♅ △	♍	24 20:40
26 9:49 ♇ △	♎	27 1:13
29 5:32 ♅ ☍	♏	29 7:11

☽ Phases & Eclipses

Dy Hr Mn	
2 0:51	○ 11♍23
9 11:20	☾ 18♐50
17 13:11	● 26♓53
24 15:35	☽ 3♋57
31 12:37	○ 10♎45
8 7:18	☾ 18♑24
16 1:57	● 26♈02
22 21:46	☽ 2♌42
30 0:58	○ 9♏39

Astro Data

1 March 2018
Julian Day # 43159
SVP 5♓00'33"
GC 27♐05.6 ⚵ 15♉30.0
Eris 22♈59.0 ⚴ 2♓37.3
⚷ 27♓16.2 ⚶ 19♐45.8
☽ Mean ☊ 13♌44.7

1 April 2018
Julian Day # 43190
SVP 5♓00'31"
GC 27♐05.6 ⚵ 1♊19.2
Eris 23♈17.0 ⚴ 17♓12.7
⚷ 29♓06.2 ⚶ 29♐51.2
☽ Mean ☊ 12♌06.2

LONGITUDE May 2018

Day	Sid.Time	☉	0 hr ☽	Noon ☽	True ☊	☿	♀	♂	⚳	♃	♄	♅	♆	♇
1 Tu	2 37 28	11♉03 52	21♏56 44	28♏15 41	10♌11.3	14♈15.7	8♊15.8	23♑40.3	10♌37.5	19♏18.5	9♑00.2	29♈13.3	15♓52.2	21♑16.1
2 W	2 41 25	12 02 05	4♐30 53	10♐42 24	9R59.9	15 20.7	9 28.4	24 08.0	10 52.5	19R11.0	8R58.8	29 16.7	15 53.6	21R15.8
3 Th	2 45 21	13 00 16	16 50 25	22 55 09	9 50.7	16 28.4	10 41.1	24 35.5	11 07.8	19 03.5	8 57.4	29 20.1	15 55.1	21 15.5
4 F	2 49 18	13 58 25	28 56 57	4♑56 10	9 44.2	17 38.7	11 53.6	25 02.7	11 23.3	18 55.9	8 55.9	29 23.4	15 56.5	21 15.2
5 Sa	2 53 14	14 56 33	10♑53 17	16 48 46	9 40.4	18 51.5	13 06.2	25 29.7	11 39.1	18 48.3	8 54.3	29 26.8	15 57.9	21 14.8
6 Su	2 57 11	15 54 40	22 43 13	28 37 13	9D38.7	20 06.7	14 18.6	25 56.4	11 55.0	18 40.7	8 52.6	29 30.1	15 59.3	21 14.4
7 M	3 01 07	16 52 45	4♒31 25	10♒26 28	9R38.4	21 24.3	15 31.1	26 22.8	12 11.2	18 33.1	8 50.8	29 33.4	16 00.6	21 14.0
8 Tu	3 05 04	17 50 49	16 23 04	22 21 54	9 38.4	22 44.3	16 43.4	26 48.9	12 27.7	18 25.4	8 48.9	29 36.8	16 01.9	21 13.6
9 W	3 09 00	18 48 51	28 23 39	4♓29 00	9 37.6	24 06.5	17 55.8	27 14.8	12 44.3	18 17.8	8 46.9	29 40.1	16 03.2	21 13.1
10 Th	3 12 57	19 46 52	10♓38 34	16 52 58	9 35.0	25 31.0	19 08.1	27 40.4	13 01.1	18 10.1	8 44.9	29 43.4	16 04.4	21 12.6
11 F	3 16 54	20 44 51	23 12 44	29 38 17	9 30.1	26 57.6	20 20.3	28 05.6	13 18.2	18 02.5	8 42.7	29 46.6	16 05.7	21 12.1
12 Sa	3 20 50	21 42 49	6♈09 59	12♈48 03	9 22.7	28 26.5	21 32.5	28 30.5	13 35.4	17 54.9	8 40.5	29 49.9	16 06.9	21 11.5
13 Su	3 24 47	22 40 46	19 32 34	26 23 27	9 13.0	29 57.4	22 44.7	28 55.1	13 52.9	17 47.2	8 38.2	29 53.1	16 08.0	21 11.0
14 M	3 28 43	23 38 42	3♉20 28	10♉23 12	9 02.0	1♉30.6	23 56.8	29 19.4	14 10.6	17 39.6	8 35.8	29 56.4	16 09.2	21 10.4
15 Tu	3 32 40	24 36 36	17 31 07	24 43 30	8 50.9	3 05.8	25 08.8	29 43.3	14 28.4	17 32.1	8 33.3	29 59.6	16 10.3	21 09.7
16 W	3 36 36	25 34 29	1♊59 30	9♊18 15	8 40.7	4 43.2	26 20.8	0♒06.9	14 46.5	17 24.5	8 30.7	0♉02.8	16 11.4	21 09.1
17 Th	3 40 33	26 32 20	16 38 45	24 00 05	8 32.6	6 22.6	27 32.8	0 30.1	15 04.7	17 17.0	8 28.1	0 05.9	16 12.4	21 08.4
18 F	3 44 29	27 30 09	1♋21 18	8♋41 33	8 27.2	8 04.2	28 44.6	0 53.0	15 23.2	17 09.6	8 25.4	0 09.1	16 13.4	21 07.7
19 Sa	3 48 26	28 27 57	16 00 07	23 16 19	8 24.4	9 47.9	29 56.5	1 15.5	15 41.8	17 02.2	8 22.6	0 12.2	16 14.4	21 07.0
20 Su	3 52 23	29 25 44	0♌29 41	7♌39 50	8D23.6	11 33.7	1♋08.3	1 37.6	16 00.6	16 54.8	8 19.7	0 15.3	16 15.4	21 06.2
21 M	3 56 19	0♊23 28	14 46 30	21 49 31	8R23.9	13 21.6	2 20.0	1 59.3	16 19.6	16 47.5	8 16.8	0 18.4	16 16.3	21 05.4
22 Tu	4 00 16	1 21 11	28 48 51	5♍44 29	8 24.0	15 11.6	3 31.6	2 20.6	16 38.7	16 40.3	8 13.8	0 21.5	16 17.2	21 04.6
23 W	4 04 12	2 18 52	12♍36 29	19 24 55	8 22.7	17 03.7	4 43.2	2 41.5	16 58.0	16 33.2	8 10.7	0 24.6	16 18.1	21 03.8
24 Th	4 08 09	3 16 32	26 09 55	2♎51 35	8 19.4	18 57.8	5 54.7	3 02.0	17 17.5	16 26.1	8 07.5	0 27.6	16 18.9	21 02.9
25 F	4 12 05	4 14 10	9♎30 00	16 05 15	8 13.5	20 54.0	7 06.2	3 22.1	17 37.1	16 19.1	8 04.3	0 30.6	16 19.8	21 02.1
26 Sa	4 16 02	5 11 47	22 37 24	29 06 31	8 05.3	22 52.3	8 17.6	3 41.7	17 56.9	16 12.1	8 01.0	0 33.6	16 20.5	21 01.2
27 Su	4 19 58	6 09 22	5♏32 36	11♏55 41	7 55.3	24 52.4	9 28.9	4 00.9	18 16.8	16 05.3	7 57.7	0 36.5	16 21.3	21 00.3
28 M	4 23 55	7 06 56	18 15 48	24 32 56	7 44.5	26 54.5	10 40.2	4 19.7	18 36.9	15 58.6	7 54.2	0 39.4	16 22.0	20 59.3
29 Tu	4 27 52	8 04 29	0♐47 08	6♐58 26	7 33.9	28 58.4	11 51.4	4 38.0	18 57.2	15 51.9	7 50.8	0 42.4	16 22.7	20 58.4
30 W	4 31 48	9 02 01	13 06 55	19 12 42	7 24.5	1♊03.9	13 02.6	4 55.8	19 17.6	15 45.4	7 47.2	0 45.2	16 23.3	20 57.4
31 Th	4 35 45	9 59 32	25 15 55	1♑16 47	7 17.0	3 11.1	14 13.6	5 13.1	19 38.1	15 38.9	7 43.6	0 48.1	16 23.9	20 56.4

LONGITUDE June 2018

Day	Sid.Time	☉	0 hr ☽	Noon ☽	True ☊	☿	♀	♂	⚳	♃	♄	♅	♆	♇
1 F	4 39 41	10♊57 02	7♑15 31	13♑12 25	7♌11.8	5♊19.6	15♋24.6	5♒30.0	19♌58.8	15♏32.6	7♑40.0	0♉50.9	16♓24.5	20♑55.3
2 Sa	4 43 38	11 54 31	19 07 50	25 02 10	7R08.9	7 29.2	16 35.6	5 46.3	20 19.6	15R26.4	7R36.3	0 53.7	16 25.1	20R54.3
3 Su	4 47 34	12 51 59	0♒55 52	6♒49 24	7D08.0	9 39.9	17 46.4	6 02.1	20 40.6	15 20.3	7 32.5	0 56.5	16 25.6	20 53.2
4 M	4 51 31	13 49 26	12 43 20	18 38 13	7 08.6	11 51.3	18 57.2	6 17.4	21 01.7	15 14.3	7 28.7	0 59.2	16 26.1	20 52.2
5 Tu	4 55 27	14 46 52	24 34 39	0♓33 17	7 09.7	14 03.2	20 07.9	6 32.1	21 22.9	15 08.4	7 24.9	1 01.9	16 26.6	20 51.1
6 W	4 59 24	15 44 18	6♓34 45	12 39 42	7R10.4	16 15.3	21 18.6	6 46.2	21 44.2	15 02.6	7 21.0	1 04.6	16 27.0	20 49.9
7 Th	5 03 21	16 41 43	18 48 47	25 02 37	7 10.1	18 27.4	22 29.2	6 59.8	22 05.7	14 57.0	7 17.0	1 07.3	16 27.4	20 48.8
8 F	5 07 17	17 39 08	1♈21 48	7♈46 51	7 08.1	20 39.2	23 39.7	7 12.7	22 27.3	14 51.5	7 13.0	1 09.9	16 27.7	20 47.6
9 Sa	5 11 14	18 36 32	14 18 15	20 56 20	7 04.2	22 50.3	24 50.1	7 25.1	22 49.0	14 46.2	7 09.0	1 12.5	16 28.1	20 46.5
10 Su	5 15 10	19 33 55	27 41 20	4♉33 21	6 58.6	25 00.6	26 00.5	7 36.9	23 10.9	14 41.0	7 04.9	1 15.0	16 28.4	20 45.3
11 M	5 19 07	20 31 18	11♉32 18	18 37 57	6 51.9	27 09.8	27 10.7	7 48.0	23 32.9	14 35.9	7 00.8	1 17.5	16 28.6	20 44.1
12 Tu	5 23 03	21 28 40	25 49 50	3♊07 21	6 44.8	29 17.7	28 21.0	7 58.5	23 55.0	14 31.0	6 56.6	1 20.0	16 28.8	20 42.8
13 W	5 27 00	22 26 02	10♊29 40	17 55 52	6 38.4	1♋24.1	29 31.1	8 08.3	24 17.2	14 26.2	6 52.4	1 22.5	16 29.0	20 41.6
14 Th	5 30 56	23 23 23	25 24 53	2♋55 35	6 33.3	3 28.9	0♌41.1	8 17.5	24 39.5	14 21.6	6 48.2	1 24.9	16 29.2	20 40.4
15 F	5 34 53	24 20 44	10♋26 50	17 57 30	6 30.2	5 31.8	1 51.1	8 26.0	25 02.0	14 17.2	6 44.0	1 27.3	16 29.3	20 39.1
16 Sa	5 38 50	25 18 04	25 26 30	2♌52 56	6D28.9	7 32.8	3 01.0	8 33.8	25 24.5	14 12.9	6 39.7	1 29.7	16 29.4	20 37.8
17 Su	5 42 46	26 15 22	10♌15 56	17 34 51	6 29.3	9 31.8	4 10.8	8 40.9	25 47.2	14 08.7	6 35.4	1 32.0	16 29.5	20 36.5
18 M	5 46 43	27 12 40	24 49 10	1♍58 30	6 30.4	11 28.6	5 20.5	8 47.3	26 09.9	14 04.7	6 31.1	1 34.3	16R29.5	20 35.2
19 Tu	5 50 39	28 09 57	9♍02 40	16 01 31	6R31.7	13 23.3	6 30.1	8 53.1	26 32.8	14 00.9	6 26.7	1 36.5	16 29.5	20 33.9
20 W	5 54 36	29 07 14	22 55 06	29 43 29	6 32.2	15 15.8	7 39.6	8 58.1	26 55.8	13 57.3	6 22.4	1 38.7	16 29.5	20 32.5
21 Th	5 58 32	0♋04 29	6♎26 50	13♎05 22	6 31.4	17 06.1	8 49.0	9 02.4	27 18.8	13 53.8	6 18.0	1 40.9	16 29.4	20 31.2
22 F	6 02 29	1 01 44	19 39 19	26 08 58	6 29.1	18 54.1	9 58.3	9 06.0	27 42.0	13 50.4	6 13.6	1 43.0	16 29.3	20 29.8
23 Sa	6 06 25	1 58 58	2♏34 33	8♏56 22	6 25.2	20 39.8	11 07.5	9 08.8	28 05.3	13 47.3	6 09.2	1 45.1	16 29.2	20 28.5
24 Su	6 10 22	2 56 11	15 14 39	21 29 41	6 20.3	22 23.2	12 16.7	9 11.0	28 28.6	13 44.3	6 04.8	1 47.1	16 29.1	20 27.1
25 M	6 14 19	3 53 24	27 41 42	3♐50 55	6 14.8	24 04.3	13 25.7	9 12.4	28 52.0	13 41.5	6 00.4	1 49.2	16 28.9	20 25.7
26 Tu	6 18 15	4 50 37	9♐57 34	16 01 51	6 09.4	25 43.1	14 34.5	9R13.0	29 15.6	13 38.9	5 56.0	1 51.1	16 28.6	20 24.3
27 W	6 22 12	5 47 49	22 03 59	28 04 10	6 04.7	27 19.6	15 43.3	9 12.9	29 39.2	13 36.4	5 51.6	1 53.1	16 28.4	20 22.9
28 Th	6 26 08	6 45 01	4♑02 39	9♑59 37	6 01.1	28 53.7	16 52.0	9 12.1	0♍02.9	13 34.1	5 47.2	1 55.0	16 28.1	20 21.5
29 F	6 30 05	7 42 13	15 55 21	21 50 05	5 58.8	0♌25.5	18 00.5	9 10.5	0 26.7	13 32.0	5 42.8	1 56.8	16 27.8	20 20.1
30 Sa	6 34 01	8 39 24	27 44 07	3♒37 46	5D57.9	1 54.9	19 09.0	9 08.2	0 50.6	13 30.1	5 38.3	1 58.6	16 27.4	20 18.7

Astro Data	Dy Hr Mn
☽0N	12 7:21
☽0S	25 1:41
♃△♆	25 9:52
☽0N	8 17:26
♅∠♆	16 9:41
♆ R	18 23:27
☽0S	21 8:03
♂ R	26 21:05

Planet Ingress	Dy Hr Mn
☿ ♉	13 12:40
♅ ♉	15 15:16
♂ ♒	16 4:55
♀ ♋	19 13:11
☉ ♊	21 2:15
☿ ♊	29 23:49
☿ ♋	12 20:00
♀ ♌	13 21:54
☉ ♋	21 10:07
⚳ ♍	28 9:04
☿ ♌	29 5:16

Last Aspect Dy Hr Mn		☽ Ingress Dy Hr Mn
1 2:56	♂ ⚹	♐ 1 15:19
4 0:50	♅ △	♑ 4 2:06
6 13:48	♅ □	♒ 6 14:48
9 2:29	♅ ⚹	♓ 9 3:11
11 9:02	♂ ⚹	♈ 11 12:40
13 18:05	♅ ☌	♉ 13 18:15
15 20:30	♂ △	♊ 15 20:43
17 18:18	♀ ☌	♋ 17 21:47
19 21:14	☉ ⚹	♌ 19 23:11
21 3:30	♃ □	♍ 22 2:03
23 14:55	♇ △	♎ 24 6:52
25 21:04	♇ □	♏ 26 13:39
28 17:25	☿ ☍	♐ 28 22:29
30 6:26	♆ □	♑ 31 9:26

Last Aspect Dy Hr Mn		☽ Ingress Dy Hr Mn
2 3:37	♇ ☌	♒ 2 22:06
4 5:10	♃ □	♓ 5 10:53
7 6:35	♀ △	♈ 7 21:26
9 19:37	♀ □	♉ 10 4:04
12 3:29	♀ ⚹	♊ 12 6:53
13 19:43	☉ ☌	♋ 14 7:20
15 16:18	♇ ☍	♌ 16 7:21
18 3:26	☉ ⚹	♍ 18 8:40
20 10:51	☉ □	♎ 20 12:29
22 1:34	♇ □	♏ 22 19:11
24 14:00	☿ △	♐ 25 4:29
26 12:53	♆ □	♑ 27 15:52
29 8:58	♇ ☌	♒ 30 4:37

☽ Phases & Eclipses Dy Hr Mn	
8 2:09	☾ 17♒27
15 11:48	● 24♉36
22 3:49	☽ 1♍02
29 14:20	○ 8♐10
6 18:32	☾ 16♓00
13 19:43	● 22♊44
20 10:51	☽ 29♍04
28 4:53	○ 6♑28

Astro Data

1 May 2018
Julian Day # 43220
SVP 5♓00'28"
GC 27♐05.7 ⚵ 18♊16.0
Eris 23♈36.5 ⚶ 1♈31.0
⚷ 0♈43.7 ⚴ 4♑43.4
☽ Mean ☊ 10♌30.8

1 June 2018
Julian Day # 43251
SVP 5♓00'23"
GC 27♐05.8 ⚵ 6♋27.0
Eris 23♈53.8 ⚶ 16♈13.9
⚷ 1♈56.1 ⚴ 2♑34.3R
☽ Mean ☊ 8♌52.3

July 2018 — LONGITUDE

Day	Sid.Time	☉	0 hr ☽	Noon ☽	True ☊	☿	♀	♂	⚳	♃	♄	♅	♆	♇
1 Su	6 37 58	9♋36 36	9♒31 23	15♒25 20	5♌58.2	3♌22.0	20♌17.3	9♒05.0	1♍14.5	13♏28.4	5♑33.9	2♉00.4	16♓27.0	20♑17.2
2 M	6 41 54	10 33 48	21 20 01	27 15 53	5 59.4	4 46.6	21 25.5	9R 01.2	1 38.5	13R 26.8	5R 29.5	2 02.1	16R 26.6	20R 15.8
3 Tu	6 45 51	11 30 59	3♓13 24	9♓13 05	6 01.0	6 08.8	22 33.6	8 56.6	2 02.7	13 25.4	5 25.2	2 03.8	16 26.2	20 14.4
4 W	6 49 48	12 28 11	15 15 25	21 20 59	6 02.6	7 28.6	23 41.5	8 51.2	2 26.8	13 24.2	5 20.8	2 05.4	16 25.7	20 12.9
5 Th	6 53 44	13 25 23	27 30 17	3♈43 55	6R 03.7	8 45.8	24 49.3	8 45.1	2 51.1	13 23.1	5 16.4	2 07.0	16 25.2	20 11.5
6 F	6 57 41	14 22 35	10♈02 24	16 26 14	6 04.0	10 00.4	25 57.0	8 38.3	3 15.5	13 22.3	5 12.1	2 08.6	16 24.7	20 10.0
7 Sa	7 01 37	15 19 48	22 55 55	29 31 50	6 03.4	11 12.5	27 04.6	8 30.7	3 39.9	13 21.6	5 07.7	2 10.1	16 24.1	20 08.5
8 Su	7 05 34	16 17 00	6♉14 19	13♉03 36	6 01.9	12 21.8	28 12.0	8 22.4	4 04.4	13 21.1	5 03.4	2 11.6	16 23.5	20 07.1
9 M	7 09 30	17 14 14	19 59 47	27 02 47	5 59.9	13 28.4	29 19.3	8 13.5	4 28.9	13 20.8	4 59.2	2 13.0	16 22.9	20 05.6
10 Tu	7 13 27	18 11 28	4♊12 25	11♊28 16	5 57.6	14 32.1	0♍26.5	8 03.8	4 53.6	13D 20.7	4 54.9	2 14.4	16 22.2	20 04.1
11 W	7 17 23	19 08 42	18 49 46	26 16 10	5 55.5	15 32.9	1 33.5	7 53.5	5 18.3	13 20.7	4 50.7	2 15.7	16 21.5	20 02.7
12 Th	7 21 20	20 05 56	3♋46 33	11♋19 53	5 53.9	16 30.7	2 40.4	7 42.5	5 43.1	13 21.0	4 46.5	2 17.0	16 20.8	20 01.2
13 F	7 25 17	21 03 11	18 55 00	26 30 44	5D 53.0	17 25.3	3 47.1	7 30.9	6 07.9	13 21.4	4 42.3	2 18.2	16 20.1	19 59.7
14 Sa	7 29 13	22 00 26	4♌05 52	11♌39 13	5 53.0	18 16.7	4 53.7	7 18.8	6 32.8	13 22.0	4 38.2	2 19.4	16 19.3	19 58.3
15 Su	7 33 10	22 57 41	19 09 43	26 36 24	5 53.5	19 04.7	6 00.1	7 06.1	6 57.8	13 22.7	4 34.1	2 20.6	16 18.5	19 56.8
16 M	7 37 06	23 54 57	3♍58 25	11♍15 07	5 54.3	19 49.1	7 06.4	6 52.9	7 22.9	13 23.7	4 30.1	2 21.7	16 17.7	19 55.4
17 Tu	7 41 03	24 52 12	18 26 00	25 30 44	5 55.3	20 29.9	8 12.5	6 39.2	7 48.0	13 24.8	4 26.1	2 22.7	16 16.8	19 53.9
18 W	7 44 59	25 49 27	2♎29 08	9♎21 10	5 56.0	21 06.9	9 18.4	6 25.0	8 13.1	13 26.2	4 22.1	2 23.7	16 16.0	19 52.4
19 Th	7 48 56	26 46 43	16 06 55	22 46 34	5R 56.3	21 39.9	10 24.1	6 10.5	8 38.4	13 27.7	4 18.2	2 24.7	16 15.0	19 51.0
20 F	7 52 52	27 43 58	29 20 24	5♏48 44	5 56.2	22 08.8	11 29.7	5 55.5	9 03.6	13 29.3	4 14.3	2 25.6	16 14.1	19 49.5
21 Sa	7 56 49	28 41 14	12♏11 58	18 30 31	5 55.8	22 33.5	12 35.0	5 40.3	9 29.0	13 31.2	4 10.5	2 26.4	16 13.1	19 48.1
22 Su	8 00 46	29 38 31	24 44 48	0♐55 16	5 55.2	22 53.6	13 40.2	5 24.7	9 54.4	13 33.2	4 06.7	2 27.2	16 12.2	19 46.6
23 M	8 04 42	0♌35 47	7♐02 21	13 06 29	5 54.5	23 09.2	14 45.2	5 09.0	10 19.8	13 35.4	4 03.0	2 28.0	16 11.1	19 45.2
24 Tu	8 08 39	1 33 04	19 08 05	25 07 31	5 53.9	23 20.1	15 49.9	4 53.0	10 45.3	13 37.8	3 59.3	2 28.7	16 10.1	19 43.8
25 W	8 12 35	2 30 22	1♑05 12	7♑01 27	5 53.4	23R 26.1	16 54.5	4 36.8	11 10.8	13 40.4	3 55.7	2 29.4	16 09.0	19 42.3
26 Th	8 16 32	3 27 40	12 56 39	18 51 05	5 53.2	23 27.2	17 58.8	4 20.5	11 36.4	13 43.1	3 52.2	2 30.0	16 08.0	19 40.9
27 F	8 20 28	4 24 58	24 45 05	0♒38 56	5D 53.1	23 23.2	19 02.9	4 04.2	12 02.1	13 46.0	3 48.7	2 30.6	16 06.9	19 39.5
28 Sa	8 24 25	5 22 17	6♒32 55	12 27 21	5R 53.1	23 14.1	20 06.8	3 47.8	12 27.8	13 49.1	3 45.2	2 31.1	16 05.7	19 38.1
29 Su	8 28 21	6 19 37	18 22 28	24 18 36	5 53.1	23 00.0	21 10.5	3 31.4	12 53.5	13 52.3	3 41.9	2 31.6	16 04.6	19 36.7
30 M	8 32 18	7 16 58	0♓16 02	6♓15 04	5 53.0	22 40.9	22 13.9	3 15.0	13 19.3	13 55.7	3 38.5	2 32.0	16 03.4	19 35.3
31 Tu	8 36 15	8 14 20	12 16 00	18 19 12	5 52.8	22 17.0	23 17.1	2 58.8	13 45.2	13 59.3	3 35.3	2 32.4	16 02.2	19 34.0

August 2018 — LONGITUDE

Day	Sid.Time	☉	0 hr ☽	Noon ☽	True ☊	☿	♀	♂	⚳	♃	♄	♅	♆	♇
1 W	8 40 11	9♌11 42	24♓25 00	0♈33 46	5♌52.4	21♌48.4	24♍20.0	2♒42.6	14♍11.0	14♏03.0	3♑32.1	2♉32.7	16♓01.0	19♑32.6
2 Th	8 44 08	10 09 06	6♈45 51	13 01 40	5R 52.0	21R 15.5	25 22.7	2R 26.7	14 37.0	14 06.9	3R 29.0	2 33.0	15R 59.7	19R 31.2
3 F	8 48 04	11 06 31	19 21 36	25 46 00	5 51.6	20 38.7	26 25.1	2 11.0	15 02.9	14 10.9	3 26.0	2 33.2	15 58.5	19 29.9
4 Sa	8 52 01	12 03 57	2♉15 17	8♉49 45	5D 51.4	19 58.4	27 27.2	1 55.6	15 28.9	14 15.2	3 23.0	2 33.4	15 57.2	19 28.6
5 Su	8 55 57	13 01 24	15 29 45	22 15 30	5 51.5	19 15.2	28 29.1	1 40.4	15 55.0	14 19.6	3 20.1	2 33.5	15 55.9	19 27.2
6 M	8 59 54	13 58 53	29 07 12	6♊04 54	5 51.9	18 29.8	29 30.7	1 25.7	16 21.1	14 24.1	3 17.3	2 33.6	15 54.5	19 25.9
7 Tu	9 03 50	14 56 23	13♊08 37	20 18 11	5 52.6	17 43.0	0♎32.0	1 11.3	16 47.3	14 28.8	3 14.6	2R 33.7	15 53.2	19 24.6
8 W	9 07 47	15 53 54	27 33 18	4♋53 31	5 53.4	16 55.5	1 33.0	0 57.3	17 13.4	14 33.7	3 11.9	2 33.6	15 51.8	19 23.3
9 Th	9 11 44	16 51 27	12♋18 15	19 46 43	5 54.0	16 08.3	2 33.7	0 43.9	17 39.7	14 38.7	3 09.3	2 33.6	15 50.5	19 22.1
10 F	9 15 40	17 49 00	27 18 03	4♌51 13	5R 54.3	15 22.2	3 34.1	0 30.9	18 05.9	14 43.9	3 06.8	2 33.5	15 49.1	19 20.8
11 Sa	9 19 37	18 46 35	12♌25 08	19 58 39	5 54.1	14 38.1	4 34.1	0 18.5	18 32.2	14 49.2	3 04.4	2 33.3	15 47.7	19 19.6
12 Su	9 23 33	19 44 11	27 30 37	4♍59 55	5 53.1	13 57.0	5 33.9	0 06.7	18 58.6	14 54.7	3 02.0	2 33.1	15 46.2	19 18.4
13 M	9 27 30	20 41 48	12♍25 30	19 46 28	5 51.6	13 19.6	6 33.2	29♑55.5	19 25.0	15 00.3	2 59.8	2 32.8	15 44.8	19 17.2
14 Tu	9 31 26	21 39 26	27 02 02	4♎11 35	5 49.6	12 46.7	7 32.2	29 45.0	19 51.4	15 06.1	2 57.6	2 32.5	15 43.3	19 16.0
15 W	9 35 23	22 37 05	11♎14 41	18 11 03	5 47.6	12 19.1	8 30.8	29 35.2	20 17.8	15 12.0	2 55.5	2 32.1	15 41.8	19 14.8
16 Th	9 39 19	23 34 45	25 00 35	1♏43 20	5 45.9	11 57.4	9 29.1	29 26.0	20 44.3	15 18.1	2 53.5	2 31.7	15 40.3	19 13.6
17 F	9 43 16	24 32 26	8♏19 29	14 49 19	5D 44.8	11 42.0	10 26.9	29 17.6	21 10.8	15 24.4	2 51.6	2 31.3	15 38.8	19 12.5
18 Sa	9 47 13	25 30 08	21 13 14	27 31 40	5 44.6	11D 33.5	11 24.3	29 10.0	21 37.3	15 30.7	2 49.7	2 30.8	15 37.3	19 11.4
19 Su	9 51 09	26 27 52	3♐45 08	9♐54 11	5 45.1	11 32.2	12 21.3	29 03.1	22 03.9	15 37.2	2 48.0	2 30.2	15 35.8	19 10.3
20 M	9 55 06	27 25 36	15 59 24	22 01 20	5 46.4	11 38.3	13 17.8	28 57.0	22 30.5	15 43.9	2 46.3	2 29.6	15 34.3	19 09.2
21 Tu	9 59 02	28 23 21	28 00 33	3♑57 38	5 48.0	11 51.9	14 13.9	28 51.6	22 57.1	15 50.7	2 44.8	2 29.0	15 32.7	19 08.1
22 W	10 02 59	29 21 08	9♑53 06	15 47 28	5 49.6	12 13.3	15 09.5	28 47.1	23 23.7	15 57.6	2 43.3	2 28.3	15 31.1	19 07.1
23 Th	10 06 55	0♍18 56	21 41 13	27 34 50	5R 50.7	12 42.3	16 04.5	28 43.4	23 50.4	16 04.7	2 41.9	2 27.5	15 29.6	19 06.1
24 F	10 10 52	1 16 45	3♒28 41	9♒23 12	5 50.9	13 18.9	16 59.1	28 40.5	24 17.1	16 11.9	2 40.7	2 26.7	15 28.0	19 05.1
25 Sa	10 14 48	2 14 35	15 18 43	21 15 32	5 49.9	14 03.0	17 53.1	28 38.4	24 43.8	16 19.2	2 39.5	2 25.9	15 26.4	19 04.1
26 Su	10 18 45	3 12 27	27 13 58	3♓14 14	5 47.6	14 54.4	18 46.6	28 37.1	25 10.6	16 26.7	2 38.4	2 25.0	15 24.8	19 03.1
27 M	10 22 42	4 10 20	9♓16 34	15 21 12	5 44.0	15 52.9	19 39.5	28D 36.6	25 37.3	16 34.3	2 37.4	2 24.1	15 23.2	19 02.2
28 Tu	10 26 38	5 08 15	21 28 16	27 37 59	5 39.5	16 58.1	20 31.8	28 36.9	26 04.1	16 42.0	2 36.4	2 23.1	15 21.6	19 01.3
29 W	10 30 35	6 06 12	3♈50 30	10♈05 57	5 34.4	18 09.8	21 23.5	28 38.1	26 31.0	16 49.8	2 35.6	2 22.1	15 20.0	19 00.4
30 Th	10 34 31	7 04 10	16 24 29	22 46 17	5 29.5	19 27.5	22 14.5	28 40.0	26 57.8	16 57.8	2 34.9	2 21.1	15 18.3	18 59.5
31 F	10 38 28	8 02 10	29 11 30	5♉40 17	5 25.2	20 50.8	23 04.9	28 42.8	27 24.7	17 05.9	2 34.3	2 19.9	15 16.7	18 58.7

Astro Data

	Dy Hr Mn
☽0N	6 2:01
♃D	10 17:03
☽0S	18 15:15
☿R	26 5:02
☽0N	2 8:31
♀0S	6 2:32
♅R	7 16:49
☽0S	14 23:51
☿D	19 4:24
♃△♆	19 7:44
♂D	27 14:05
☽0N	29 13:46

Planet Ingress

	Dy Hr Mn
♀ ♍	10 2:32
☉ ♌	22 21:00
♀ ♎	6 23:27
♂ ♑R	13 2:14
☉ ♍	23 4:09

Last Aspect / ☽ Ingress

Last Aspect Dy Hr Mn		☽ Ingress Dy Hr Mn
1 22:56	♀ ☍	♓ 2 17:31
4 9:47	♇ ⚹	♈ 5 4:50
7 7:09	♀ △	♉ 7 12:51
9 16:09	♀ □	♊ 9 16:58
10 20:00	♆ □	♋ 11 17:59
13 2:48	☉ ☌	♌ 13 17:31
14 23:12	☿ ☌	♍ 15 17:31
17 10:50	☉ ⚹	♎ 17 19:42
19 19:52	☉ □	♏ 20 1:13
22 9:18	☉ △	♐ 22 10:12
24 8:22	☿ △	♑ 24 21:49
26 13:41	♇ ☌	♒ 27 10:41
29 9:25	☿ ☍	♓ 29 23:28

Last Aspect / ☽ Ingress

Last Aspect Dy Hr Mn		☽ Ingress Dy Hr Mn
31 22:42	♀ ☍	♈ 1 10:54
3 2:52	☿ △	♉ 3 19:51
5 23:46	♀ △	♊ 6 1:32
7 7:54	☿ ⚹	♋ 8 4:01
9 11:21	♇ ☍	♌ 10 4:18
11 9:58	☉ ☌	♍ 12 3:59
14 4:37	♂ △	♎ 14 4:57
16 7:56	♂ □	♏ 16 8:54
18 15:07	♂ ⚹	♐ 18 16:45
20 23:47	☉ △	♑ 21 4:00
23 14:19	♂ ☌	♒ 23 16:55
25 4:39	♀ △	♓ 26 5:32
28 13:54	♂ ⚹	♈ 28 16:35
30 23:04	♂ □	♉ 31 1:30

☽ Phases & Eclipses

Dy Hr Mn	
6 7:51	☾ 14♈13
13 2:48	● 20♋41
13 3:01:07	● P 0.337
19 19:52	☽ 27♎05
27 20:20	○ 4♒45
27 20:22	◐ T 1.609
4 18:18	☾ 12♉19
11 9:58	● 18♌42
11 9:46:16	● P 0.737
18 7:49	☽ 25♏20
26 11:56	○ 3♓12

Astro Data

1 July 2018
Julian Day # 43281
SVP 5♓00'18"
GC 27♐05.9 ⚴ 24♋00.4
Eris 24♈04.0 ⚵ 0♉03.6
⚷ 2♈25.0 ⚶ 25♐46.8R
☽ Mean ☊ 7♌17.0

1 August 2018
Julian Day # 43312
SVP 5♓00'14"
GC 27♐05.9 ⚴ 11♌37.9
Eris 24♈05.2R ⚵ 13♉16.8
⚷ 2♈06.2R ⚶ 22♐08.2
☽ Mean ☊ 5♌38.5

LONGITUDE — September 2018

Day	Sid.Time	☉	0 hr ☽	Noon ☽	True ☊	☿	♀	♂	⚳	♃	♄	♅	♆	♇
1 Sa	10 42 24	9♍00 12	12♉12 49	18♉49 15	5♌22.1	22♌19.3	23♎54.6	28♑46.4	27♍51.5	17♏14.1	2♑33.7	2♉18.8	15♓15.1	18♑57.8
2 Su	10 46 21	9 58 16	25 29 46	2♊14 31	5D 20.5	23 52.5	24 43.6	28 50.8	28 18.4	17 22.4	2R 33.3	2R 17.6	15R 13.4	18R 57.0
3 M	10 50 17	10 56 22	9♊03 38	15 57 14	5 20.3	25 29.8	25 31.9	28 55.9	28 45.4	17 30.9	2 33.0	2 16.4	15 11.8	18 56.3
4 Tu	10 54 14	11 54 30	22 55 20	29 57 57	5 21.2	27 10.9	26 19.4	29 01.9	29 12.3	17 39.4	2 32.7	2 15.1	15 10.1	18 55.5
5 W	10 58 11	12 52 40	7♋04 59	14♋16 15	5 22.6	28 55.1	27 06.2	29 08.6	29 39.3	17 48.1	2D 32.6	2 13.8	15 08.5	18 54.8
6 Th	11 02 07	13 50 52	21 31 28	28 50 12	5R 23.7	0♍42.0	27 52.1	29 16.2	0♎06.3	17 56.9	2 32.5	2 12.4	15 06.8	18 54.1
7 F	11 06 04	14 49 06	6♌11 55	13♌35 56	5 23.6	2 31.1	28 37.1	29 24.5	0 33.3	18 05.9	2 32.6	2 11.0	15 05.2	18 53.4
8 Sa	11 10 00	15 47 21	21 01 28	28 27 38	5 21.7	4 22.0	29 21.3	29 33.6	1 00.3	18 14.9	2 32.7	2 09.6	15 03.5	18 52.8
9 Su	11 13 57	16 45 39	5♍53 29	13♍17 58	5 17.9	6 14.2	0♏04.6	29 43.4	1 27.3	18 24.0	2 33.0	2 08.1	15 01.9	18 52.1
10 M	11 17 53	17 43 58	20 40 07	27 58 57	5 12.4	8 07.4	0 46.9	29 54.0	1 54.4	18 33.3	2 33.3	2 06.6	15 00.2	18 51.5
11 Tu	11 21 50	18 42 19	5♎13 33	12♎23 10	5 05.7	10 01.3	1 28.2	0♒05.3	2 21.4	18 42.7	2 33.8	2 05.0	14 58.6	18 51.0
12 W	11 25 46	19 40 42	19 27 07	26 24 56	4 58.6	11 55.6	2 08.5	0 17.4	2 48.5	18 52.1	2 34.3	2 03.4	14 56.9	18 50.4
13 Th	11 29 43	20 39 06	3♏16 17	10♏01 00	4 52.1	13 49.9	2 47.7	0 30.2	3 15.6	19 01.7	2 35.0	2 01.8	14 55.3	18 49.9
14 F	11 33 39	21 37 33	16 39 06	23 10 43	4 46.9	15 44.2	3 25.8	0 43.7	3 42.7	19 11.4	2 35.7	2 00.1	14 53.6	18 49.4
15 Sa	11 37 36	22 36 00	29 36 07	5♐55 43	4 43.4	17 38.2	4 02.7	0 57.9	4 09.8	19 21.1	2 36.5	1 58.4	14 52.0	18 48.9
16 Su	11 41 33	23 34 30	12♐09 58	18 19 25	4D 41.9	19 31.7	4 38.4	1 12.8	4 36.9	19 31.0	2 37.5	1 56.7	14 50.4	18 48.5
17 M	11 45 29	24 33 01	24 24 40	0♑26 21	4 41.9	21 24.6	5 12.8	1 28.3	5 04.0	19 41.0	2 38.5	1 54.9	14 48.7	18 48.1
18 Tu	11 49 26	25 31 33	6♑25 07	12 21 38	4 42.9	23 16.9	5 45.9	1 44.6	5 31.2	19 51.1	2 39.6	1 53.1	14 47.1	18 47.7
19 W	11 53 22	26 30 08	18 16 33	24 10 31	4R 44.1	25 08.4	6 17.6	2 01.4	5 58.3	20 01.2	2 40.9	1 51.2	14 45.5	18 47.4
20 Th	11 57 19	27 28 44	0♒04 08	5♒58 02	4 44.6	26 59.0	6 47.9	2 18.9	6 25.4	20 11.5	2 42.2	1 49.3	14 43.9	18 47.0
21 F	12 01 15	28 27 21	11 52 44	17 48 45	4 43.5	28 48.9	7 16.6	2 37.0	6 52.6	20 21.8	2 43.6	1 47.4	14 42.3	18 46.7
22 Sa	12 05 12	29 26 01	23 46 33	29 46 32	4 40.4	0♎37.8	7 43.9	2 55.7	7 19.8	20 32.3	2 45.1	1 45.5	14 40.7	18 46.5
23 Su	12 09 08	0♎24 42	5♓49 04	11♓54 26	4 34.9	2 25.7	8 09.5	3 14.9	7 46.9	20 42.8	2 46.7	1 43.5	14 39.1	18 46.2
24 M	12 13 05	1 23 25	18 02 52	24 14 31	4 27.1	4 12.8	8 33.4	3 34.8	8 14.1	20 53.4	2 48.4	1 41.5	14 37.6	18 46.0
25 Tu	12 17 02	2 22 10	0♈29 32	6♈47 57	4 17.5	5 58.9	8 55.7	3 55.2	8 41.2	21 04.1	2 50.2	1 39.5	14 36.0	18 45.8
26 W	12 20 58	3 20 57	13 09 46	19 34 57	4 07.0	7 44.0	9 16.1	4 16.1	9 08.4	21 14.9	2 52.1	1 37.4	14 34.5	18 45.7
27 Th	12 24 55	4 19 46	26 03 27	2♉35 08	3 56.5	9 28.3	9 34.7	4 37.6	9 35.6	21 25.8	2 54.1	1 35.3	14 32.9	18 45.6
28 F	12 28 51	5 18 37	9♉09 55	15 47 41	3 47.1	11 11.5	9 51.4	4 59.6	10 02.8	21 36.7	2 56.2	1 33.2	14 31.4	18 45.5
29 Sa	12 32 48	6 17 31	22 28 19	29 11 43	3 39.7	12 53.9	10 06.1	5 22.1	10 29.9	21 47.8	2 58.4	1 31.1	14 29.9	18 45.4
30 Su	12 36 44	7 16 27	5♊57 49	12♊46 34	3 34.8	14 35.4	10 18.9	5 45.1	10 57.1	21 58.9	3 00.7	1 28.9	14 28.4	18D 45.4

LONGITUDE — October 2018

Day	Sid.Time	☉	0 hr ☽	Noon ☽	True ☊	☿	♀	♂	⚳	♃	♄	♅	♆	♇
1 M	12 40 41	8♎15 25	19♊37 55	26♊31 51	3♌32.3	16♎16.0	10♏29.5	6♒08.6	11♎24.3	22♏10.1	3♑03.0	1♉26.8	14♓26.9	18♑45.4
2 Tu	12 44 37	9 14 25	3♋28 22	10♋27 27	3D 31.7	17 55.7	10 38.0	6 32.5	11 51.5	22 21.3	3 05.5	1R 24.6	14R 25.4	18 45.4
3 W	12 48 34	10 13 28	17 29 04	24 33 11	3R 32.1	19 34.5	10 44.3	6 57.0	12 18.7	22 32.7	3 08.0	1 22.3	14 24.0	18 45.5
4 Th	12 52 31	11 12 33	1♌39 40	8♌48 21	3 32.1	21 12.5	10 48.4	7 21.8	12 45.8	22 44.1	3 10.7	1 20.1	14 22.6	18 45.5
5 F	12 56 27	12 11 41	15 58 59	23 11 14	3 30.7	22 49.7	10R 50.3	7 47.2	13 13.0	22 55.6	3 13.4	1 17.8	14 21.1	18 45.7
6 Sa	13 00 24	13 10 50	0♍24 39	7♍38 42	3 26.9	24 26.1	10 49.8	8 12.9	13 40.2	23 07.1	3 16.2	1 15.5	14 19.7	18 45.8
7 Su	13 04 20	14 10 02	14 52 46	22 06 09	3 20.3	26 01.7	10 47.0	8 39.1	14 07.4	23 18.8	3 19.1	1 13.2	14 18.3	18 46.0
8 M	13 08 17	15 09 16	29 18 06	6♎27 49	3 11.0	27 36.6	10 41.8	9 05.8	14 34.5	23 30.5	3 22.1	1 10.9	14 17.0	18 46.2
9 Tu	13 12 13	16 08 32	13♎34 33	20 37 34	2 59.9	29 10.6	10 34.2	9 32.8	15 01.7	23 42.3	3 25.2	1 08.5	14 15.6	18 46.4
10 W	13 16 10	17 07 50	27 36 12	4♏29 54	2 48.0	0♏44.0	10 24.2	10 00.2	15 28.8	23 54.1	3 28.4	1 06.2	14 14.3	18 46.7
11 Th	13 20 06	18 07 11	11♏18 14	18 00 53	2 36.7	2 16.6	10 11.8	10 28.1	15 56.0	24 06.0	3 31.6	1 03.8	14 13.0	18 47.0
12 F	13 24 03	19 06 33	24 37 41	1♐08 37	2 26.9	3 48.4	9 57.0	10 56.3	16 23.1	24 18.0	3 35.0	1 01.4	14 11.7	18 47.3
13 Sa	13 28 00	20 05 57	7♐33 49	13 53 29	2 19.5	5 19.6	9 39.9	11 24.9	16 50.3	24 30.0	3 38.4	0 59.0	14 10.4	18 47.7
14 Su	13 31 56	21 05 22	20 07 59	26 17 45	2 14.8	6 50.0	9 20.5	11 53.9	17 17.4	24 42.1	3 41.9	0 56.6	14 09.2	18 48.1
15 M	13 35 53	22 04 50	2♑23 18	8♑25 14	2 12.4	8 19.7	8 58.8	12 23.2	17 44.5	24 54.2	3 45.5	0 54.2	14 07.9	18 48.5
16 Tu	13 39 49	23 04 19	14 24 11	20 20 48	2D 11.8	9 48.7	8 35.0	12 52.9	18 11.6	25 06.4	3 49.2	0 51.8	14 06.7	18 48.9
17 W	13 43 46	24 03 50	26 15 48	2♒09 51	2R 11.8	11 17.0	8 09.1	13 22.9	18 38.6	25 18.7	3 53.0	0 49.4	14 05.6	18 49.4
18 Th	13 47 42	25 03 23	8♒03 41	13 57 57	2 11.4	12 44.6	7 41.2	13 53.2	19 05.7	25 31.0	3 56.8	0 46.9	14 04.4	18 49.9
19 F	13 51 39	26 02 58	19 53 21	25 50 29	2 09.5	14 11.4	7 11.6	14 23.8	19 32.8	25 43.3	4 00.7	0 44.5	14 03.3	18 50.4
20 Sa	13 55 35	27 02 34	1♓49 58	7♓52 19	2 05.3	15 37.4	6 40.4	14 54.8	19 59.8	25 55.7	4 04.7	0 42.0	14 02.2	18 51.0
21 Su	13 59 32	28 02 12	13 58 01	20 07 30	1 58.3	17 02.7	6 07.7	15 26.0	20 26.8	26 08.2	4 08.8	0 39.6	14 01.1	18 51.6
22 M	14 03 28	29 01 52	26 21 03	2♈38 56	1 48.7	18 27.1	5 33.7	15 57.5	20 53.8	26 20.7	4 13.0	0 37.1	14 00.0	18 52.2
23 Tu	14 07 25	0♏01 34	9♈01 18	15 28 11	1 36.8	19 50.8	4 58.8	16 29.4	21 20.8	26 33.3	4 17.2	0 34.7	13 59.0	18 52.9
24 W	14 11 22	1 01 17	21 59 33	28 35 15	1 23.7	21 13.5	4 23.0	17 01.4	21 47.8	26 45.9	4 21.5	0 32.2	13 58.0	18 53.6
25 Th	14 15 18	2 01 03	5♉15 05	11♉58 44	1 10.6	22 35.3	3 46.6	17 33.8	22 14.7	26 58.5	4 25.9	0 29.8	13 57.0	18 54.3
26 F	14 19 15	3 00 51	18 45 52	25 36 05	0 58.8	23 56.2	3 10.0	18 06.4	22 41.6	27 11.2	4 30.4	0 27.3	13 56.1	18 55.0
27 Sa	14 23 11	4 00 41	2♊28 58	9♊24 06	0 49.2	25 15.9	2 33.3	18 39.2	23 08.6	27 23.9	4 34.9	0 24.8	13 55.1	18 55.8
28 Su	14 27 08	5 00 33	16 21 05	23 19 35	0 42.6	26 34.6	1 56.7	19 12.3	23 35.5	27 36.7	4 39.5	0 22.4	13 54.2	18 56.6
29 M	14 31 04	6 00 27	0♋19 15	7♋19 49	0 38.9	27 52.0	1 20.7	19 45.7	24 02.3	27 49.5	4 44.2	0 20.0	13 53.4	18 57.4
30 Tu	14 35 01	7 00 23	14 21 05	21 22 51	0D 37.5	29 08.1	0 45.3	20 19.2	24 29.2	28 02.4	4 49.0	0 17.5	13 52.5	18 58.3
31 W	14 38 57	8 00 22	28 25 02	5♌27 31	0R 37.4	0♐22.7	0 10.8	20 53.0	24 56.0	28 15.3	4 53.8	0 15.1	13 51.7	18 59.1

Astro Data Dy Hr Mn	Planet Ingress Dy Hr Mn	Last Aspect Dy Hr Mn	☽ Ingress Dy Hr Mn	Last Aspect Dy Hr Mn	☽ Ingress Dy Hr Mn	☽ Phases & Eclipses Dy Hr Mn
♃∠♄ 3 17:42	☿ ♍ 6 2:39	2 5:56 ♂ △	♊ 2 8:02	30 15:38 ☿ △	♋ 1 18:00	3 2:37 ☾ 10♊34
♄ D 6 11:08	⚳ ♎ 6 6:26	4 6:37 ☿ ✶	♋ 4 12:03	3 8:33 ♃ △	♌ 3 21:12	9 18:01 ● 17♍00
☽0S 11 9:35	♀ ♏ 9 9:25	6 12:43 ♂ ☍	♌ 6 13:54	5 11:34 ♃ □	♍ 5 23:19	16 23:15 ☽ 24♐02
♃✶♇ 12 7:55	♂ ♒ 11 0:56	8 13:31 ♀ ✶	♍ 8 14:29	7 14:02 ♃ ✶	♎ 8 1:10	25 2:52 ○ 2♈00
☉0S 23 1:54	☿ ♎ 22 3:39	10 15:12 ♂ △	♎ 10 15:20	9 8:50 ♇ □	♏ 10 4:09	
☿0S 23 19:13	☉ ♎ 23 1:54	11 22:58 ♇ □	♏ 12 18:15	11 23:12 ♃ ☌	♐ 12 9:53	2 9:45 ☾ 9♋09
☽0N 25 19:37		14 8:54 ☉ ✶	♐ 15 0:45	14 0:58 ☉ ✶	♑ 14 19:17	9 3:47 ● 15♎48
	☿ ♏ 10 0:40	16 23:15 ☉ □	♑ 17 11:07	16 21:49 ♃ ✶	♒ 17 7:36	16 18:02 ☽ 23♑19
♇ D 1 2:03	☉ ♏ 23 11:22	19 17:10 ☉ △	♒ 19 23:52	19 12:27 ☉ △	♓ 19 20:20	24 16:45 ○ 1♉13
♀ R 5 19:05	☿ ♐ 31 4:38	21 17:13 ♃ □	♓ 22 12:27	21 23:47 ♃ △	♈ 22 6:58	31 16:40 ☾ 8♌12
☽0S 8 19:22	♀ ♎R 31 19:42	24 5:26 ♃ △	♈ 24 23:04	23 18:18 ♇ □	♉ 24 14:33	
⚳0S 12 12:16		26 10:28 ♇ □	♉ 27 7:16	26 14:49 ♃ ☍	♊ 26 19:41	
☽0N 23 3:30		28 22:36 ♃ ☍	♊ 29 13:26	28 4:37 ♂ △	♋ 28 23:27	
				31 2:31 ☿ △	♌ 31 2:42	

Astro Data

1 September 2018
Julian Day # 43343
SVP 5♓00'10"
GC 27♐06.0 ⚴ 28♌26.8
Eris 23♈56.7R ⚵ 24♉08.4
⚷ 1♈04.9R ⚶ 25♐41.6
☽ Mean ☊ 4♌00.0

1 October 2018
Julian Day # 43373
SVP 5♓00'08"
GC 27♐06.1 ⚴ 13♍46.4
Eris 23♈41.6R ⚵ 0♊09.1
⚷ 29♓45.1R ⚶ 4♑18.4
☽ Mean ☊ 2♌24.7

November 2018 LONGITUDE

Day	Sid.Time	☉	0 hr ☽	Noon ☽	True ☊	☿	♀	♂	⚳	♃	♄	♅	♆	♇
1 Th	14 42 54	9♏00 23	12♌30 13	19♌33 02	0♌37.1	1♐35.8	29♎37.5	21♒27.0	25♎22.8	28♏28.2	4♑58.7	0♉12.7	13♓50.9	19♑00.0
2 F	14 46 51	10 00 26	26 35 54	3♍38 40	0R 35.5	2 47.1	29R 05.6	22 01.3	25 49.6	28 41.2	5 03.6	0R 10.2	13R 50.2	19 01.0
3 Sa	14 50 47	11 00 31	10♍41 09	17 43 08	0 31.4	3 56.4	28 35.2	22 35.7	26 16.4	28 54.2	5 08.6	0 07.8	13 49.5	19 01.9
4 Su	14 54 44	12 00 38	24 44 19	1♎44 22	0 24.4	5 03.6	28 06.5	23 10.4	26 43.1	29 07.2	5 13.7	0 05.4	13 48.8	19 02.9
5 M	14 58 40	13 00 47	8♎42 51	15 39 22	0 14.7	6 08.3	27 39.7	23 45.2	27 09.8	29 20.3	5 18.9	0 03.1	13 48.1	19 04.0
6 Tu	15 02 37	14 00 58	22 33 26	29 24 36	0 02.9	7 10.4	27 14.9	24 20.3	27 36.5	29 33.4	5 24.1	0 00.7	13 47.5	19 05.0
7 W	15 06 33	15 01 11	6♏12 24	12♏56 25	29♋50.3	8 09.4	26 52.2	24 55.6	28 03.1	29 46.5	5 29.4	29♈58.3	13 46.9	19 06.1
8 Th	15 10 30	16 01 26	19 36 18	26 11 47	29 38.0	9 05.1	26 31.8	25 31.0	28 29.7	29 59.6	5 34.8	29 56.0	13 46.3	19 07.2
9 F	15 14 26	17 01 42	2♐42 39	9♐08 49	29 27.3	9 56.9	26 13.7	26 06.7	28 56.3	0♐12.8	5 40.2	29 53.7	13 45.7	19 08.3
10 Sa	15 18 23	18 02 01	15 30 17	21 47 08	29 19.1	10 44.5	25 57.9	26 42.5	29 22.9	0 26.0	5 45.6	29 51.4	13 45.2	19 09.4
11 Su	15 22 20	19 02 21	27 59 36	4♑07 57	29 13.5	11 27.4	25 44.5	27 18.5	29 49.4	0 39.2	5 51.2	29 49.1	13 44.8	19 10.6
12 M	15 26 16	20 02 42	10♑12 34	16 13 54	29 10.6	12 04.8	25 33.6	27 54.7	0♏15.9	0 52.5	5 56.8	29 46.8	13 44.3	19 11.8
13 Tu	15 30 13	21 03 05	22 12 29	28 08 53	29D 09.8	12 36.3	25 25.2	28 31.0	0 42.3	1 05.8	6 02.4	29 44.6	13 43.9	19 13.1
14 W	15 34 09	22 03 29	4♒03 43	9♒57 37	29 10.1	13 01.2	25 19.2	29 07.5	1 08.7	1 19.0	6 08.1	29 42.3	13 43.5	19 14.3
15 Th	15 38 06	23 03 55	15 51 18	21 45 25	29R 10.5	13 18.7	25D 15.6	29 44.2	1 35.1	1 32.3	6 13.9	29 40.1	13 43.2	19 15.6
16 F	15 42 02	24 04 22	27 40 42	3♓37 48	29 10.0	13R 28.1	25 14.5	0♓21.0	2 01.4	1 45.6	6 19.7	29 37.9	13 42.9	19 16.9
17 Sa	15 45 59	25 04 50	9♓37 26	15 40 12	29 07.7	13 28.6	25 15.9	0 57.9	2 27.7	1 59.0	6 25.5	29 35.8	13 42.6	19 18.2
18 Su	15 49 55	26 05 19	21 46 44	27 57 34	29 03.0	13 19.7	25 19.6	1 35.0	2 54.0	2 12.3	6 31.4	29 33.7	13 42.4	19 19.6
19 M	15 53 52	27 05 50	4♈13 10	10♈33 56	28 56.0	13 00.7	25 25.6	2 12.2	3 20.2	2 25.7	6 37.4	29 31.6	13 42.2	19 20.9
20 Tu	15 57 49	28 06 22	17 00 10	23 32 02	28 47.0	12 31.3	25 34.0	2 49.5	3 46.3	2 39.0	6 43.4	29 29.5	13 42.0	19 22.3
21 W	16 01 45	29 06 56	0♉09 36	6♉52 49	28 36.7	11 51.2	25 44.6	3 27.0	4 12.5	2 52.4	6 49.5	29 27.4	13 41.9	19 23.7
22 Th	16 05 42	0♐07 31	13 41 26	20 35 10	28 26.3	11 00.9	25 57.4	4 04.6	4 38.5	3 05.8	6 55.6	29 25.4	13 41.7	19 25.2
23 F	16 09 38	1 08 07	27 33 33	4♊36 01	28 16.8	10 00.8	26 12.3	4 42.3	5 04.6	3 19.2	7 01.7	29 23.4	13 41.7	19 26.6
24 Sa	16 13 35	2 08 45	11♊41 58	18 50 40	28 09.3	8 52.2	26 29.3	5 20.1	5 30.5	3 32.6	7 07.9	29 21.5	13D 41.6	19 28.1
25 Su	16 17 31	3 09 24	26 01 27	3♋13 34	28 04.3	7 36.7	26 48.4	5 58.0	5 56.5	3 46.0	7 14.2	29 19.5	13 41.6	19 29.6
26 M	16 21 28	4 10 05	10♋26 20	17 39 08	28D 01.8	6 16.6	27 09.4	6 36.0	6 22.4	3 59.4	7 20.5	29 17.6	13 41.7	19 31.2
27 Tu	16 25 24	5 10 48	24 51 25	2♌02 40	28 01.4	4 54.4	27 32.3	7 14.2	6 48.2	4 12.8	7 26.8	29 15.8	13 41.7	19 32.7
28 W	16 29 21	6 11 32	9♌12 31	16 20 38	28 02.2	3 32.8	27 57.1	7 52.4	7 14.0	4 26.2	7 33.2	29 13.9	13 41.8	19 34.3
29 Th	16 33 18	7 12 17	23 26 46	0♍30 46	28R 03.1	2 14.5	28 23.6	8 30.8	7 39.8	4 39.6	7 39.6	29 12.2	13 42.0	19 35.9
30 F	16 37 14	8 13 04	7♍32 30	14 31 52	28 03.1	1 02.2	28 51.9	9 09.2	8 05.5	4 53.0	7 46.0	29 10.4	13 42.1	19 37.5

December 2018 LONGITUDE

Day	Sid.Time	☉	0 hr ☽	Noon ☽	True ☊	☿	♀	♂	⚳	♃	♄	♅	♆	♇
1 Sa	16 41 11	9♐13 53	21♍28 49	28♍23 18	28♋01.4	29♏58.0	29♎21.7	9♓47.7	8♏31.1	5♐06.4	7♑52.5	29♈08.7	13♓42.3	19♑39.1
2 Su	16 45 07	10 14 43	5♎15 15	12♎04 36	27R 57.4	29R 03.5	29 53.2	10 26.3	8 56.7	5 19.8	7 59.0	29R 07.0	13 42.6	19 40.7
3 M	16 49 04	11 15 34	18 51 18	25 35 14	27 51.4	28 19.8	0♏26.2	11 05.0	9 22.2	5 33.1	8 05.6	29 05.3	13 42.8	19 42.4
4 Tu	16 53 00	12 16 27	2♏16 18	8♏54 23	27 43.8	27 47.5	1 00.7	11 43.8	9 47.7	5 46.5	8 12.2	29 03.7	13 43.2	19 44.1
5 W	16 56 57	13 17 21	15 29 20	22 01 04	27 35.5	27 26.6	1 36.5	12 22.7	10 13.1	5 59.9	8 18.8	29 02.1	13 43.5	19 45.8
6 Th	17 00 53	14 18 17	28 29 27	4♐54 23	27 27.4	27D 17.0	2 13.7	13 01.7	10 38.4	6 13.3	8 25.5	29 00.6	13 43.9	19 47.5
7 F	17 04 50	15 19 13	11♐15 50	17 33 46	27 20.4	27 18.1	2 52.2	13 40.8	11 03.7	6 26.6	8 32.2	28 59.1	13 44.3	19 49.2
8 Sa	17 08 47	16 20 11	23 48 14	29 59 16	27 15.0	27 29.3	3 32.0	14 19.9	11 28.9	6 40.0	8 38.9	28 57.7	13 44.7	19 51.0
9 Su	17 12 43	17 21 09	6♑07 03	12♑11 45	27 11.7	27 49.5	4 12.9	14 59.1	11 54.1	6 53.3	8 45.7	28 56.3	13 45.2	19 52.7
10 M	17 16 40	18 22 08	18 13 37	24 12 59	27D 10.4	28 18.1	4 55.0	15 38.4	12 19.2	7 06.6	8 52.4	28 54.9	13 45.7	19 54.5
11 Tu	17 20 36	19 23 08	0♒10 12	6♒05 41	27 10.8	28 54.2	5 38.2	16 17.8	12 44.2	7 19.9	8 59.2	28 53.6	13 46.3	19 56.3
12 W	17 24 33	20 24 09	11 59 56	17 53 27	27 12.2	29 37.0	6 22.5	16 57.2	13 09.2	7 33.2	9 06.1	28 52.3	13 46.9	19 58.1
13 Th	17 28 29	21 25 10	23 46 47	29 40 31	27 14.1	0♐25.6	7 07.8	17 36.7	13 34.0	7 46.4	9 12.9	28 51.1	13 47.5	19 59.9
14 F	17 32 26	22 26 12	5♓35 18	11♓31 44	27R 15.6	1 19.4	7 54.1	18 16.3	13 58.9	7 59.6	9 19.8	28 49.9	13 48.1	20 01.8
15 Sa	17 36 23	23 27 14	17 30 30	23 32 13	27 16.2	2 17.8	8 41.3	18 55.9	14 23.6	8 12.8	9 26.7	28 48.8	13 48.8	20 03.6
16 Su	17 40 19	24 28 16	29 37 32	5♈47 05	27 15.5	3 20.2	9 29.4	19 35.6	14 48.2	8 26.0	9 33.6	28 47.7	13 49.5	20 05.5
17 M	17 44 16	25 29 19	12♈01 25	18 21 06	27 13.3	4 26.1	10 18.4	20 15.3	15 12.8	8 39.2	9 40.5	28 46.6	13 50.3	20 07.3
18 Tu	17 48 12	26 30 23	24 46 33	1♉18 11	27 09.8	5 35.0	11 08.2	20 55.1	15 37.3	8 52.3	9 47.5	28 45.6	13 51.1	20 09.2
19 W	17 52 09	27 31 26	7♉56 14	14 40 51	27 05.4	6 46.6	11 58.8	21 34.9	16 01.7	9 05.4	9 54.5	28 44.7	13 51.9	20 11.1
20 Th	17 56 05	28 32 31	21 32 03	28 29 39	27 00.7	8 00.5	12 50.3	22 14.8	16 26.1	9 18.5	10 01.5	28 43.8	13 52.8	20 13.0
21 F	18 00 02	29 33 35	5♊33 23	12♊42 45	26 56.4	9 16.5	13 42.5	22 54.7	16 50.4	9 31.5	10 08.5	28 42.9	13 53.6	20 14.9
22 Sa	18 03 58	0♑34 40	19 57 09	27 15 49	26 53.1	10 34.3	14 35.4	23 34.7	17 14.5	9 44.5	10 15.5	28 42.1	13 54.6	20 16.9
23 Su	18 07 55	1 35 46	4♋37 54	12♋02 27	26D 51.1	11 53.6	15 29.0	24 14.7	17 38.6	9 57.5	10 22.5	28 41.3	13 55.5	20 18.8
24 M	18 11 52	2 36 52	19 28 29	26 55 00	26 50.4	13 14.4	16 23.3	24 54.7	18 02.7	10 10.4	10 29.6	28 40.6	13 56.5	20 20.8
25 Tu	18 15 48	3 37 59	4♌21 03	11♌45 43	26 51.0	14 36.3	17 18.2	25 34.8	18 26.6	10 23.3	10 36.6	28 40.0	13 57.5	20 22.7
26 W	18 19 45	4 39 06	19 08 11	26 27 45	26 52.2	15 59.4	18 13.8	26 14.9	18 50.4	10 36.2	10 43.7	28 39.4	13 58.6	20 24.7
27 Th	18 23 41	5 40 13	3♍43 50	10♍55 57	26 53.7	17 23.4	19 10.0	26 55.0	19 14.2	10 49.0	10 50.7	28 38.8	13 59.6	20 26.7
28 F	18 27 38	6 41 21	18 03 47	25 07 06	26R 54.8	18 48.3	20 06.7	27 35.2	19 37.8	11 01.8	10 57.8	28 38.3	14 00.7	20 28.6
29 Sa	18 31 34	7 42 30	2♎05 45	8♎59 43	26 55.1	20 14.0	21 04.1	28 15.4	20 01.4	11 14.5	11 04.9	28 37.8	14 01.9	20 30.6
30 Su	18 35 31	8 43 39	15 49 03	22 33 48	26 54.6	21 40.4	22 01.9	28 55.7	20 24.9	11 27.2	11 12.0	28 37.4	14 03.0	20 32.6
31 M	18 39 27	9 44 49	29 14 08	5♏50 13	26 53.2	23 07.5	23 00.3	29 35.9	20 48.2	11 39.9	11 19.1	28 37.1	14 04.2	20 34.6

Astro Data	Dy Hr Mn	Planet Ingress	Dy Hr Mn
☽ 0S	5 4:00	☊ ♋R	6 17:37
♃⚻♅	8 6:20	♅ ♈R	6 19:00
♀ D	16 10:51	♃ ♐	8 12:38
☿ R	17 1:32	⚳ ♏	11 21:37
☽ 0N	19 13:18	♂ ♓	15 22:21
♆ D	25 1:08	☉ ♐	22 9:01
♃∠♇	29 4:28		
		☿ ♏R	1 11:12
☽ 0S	2 10:56	♀ ♏	2 17:02
☿ D	6 21:24	☿ ♐	12 23:43
♅∠♆	15 11:11	☉ ♑	21 22:23
☽ 0N	16 23:26		
♃⚺♄	27 19:18		
☽ 0S	29 17:01		

Last Aspect Dy Hr Mn		☽ Ingress Dy Hr Mn	
2 4:32	♀ ⚹	♍	2 5:48
4 7:26	♃ ⚹	♎	4 9:01
6 8:19	♀ ☌	♏	6 13:02
8 10:42	♂ □	♐	8 18:59
11 3:35	♅ △	♑	11 3:55
13 15:13	♅ □	♒	13 15:45
16 3:58	♅ ⚹	♓	16 4:41
18 8:04	☉ △	♈	18 15:56
20 22:46	♅ ☌	♉	20 23:43
22 9:59	♇ △	♊	23 4:10
25 5:31	♅ ⚹	♋	25 6:38
27 7:22	♅ □	♌	27 8:35
29 9:47	♅ △	♍	29 11:08

Last Aspect Dy Hr Mn		☽ Ingress Dy Hr Mn	
1 14:34	☿ ⚹	♎	1 14:49
3 18:16	♅ ☍	♏	3 19:55
5 21:53	☿ ☌	♐	6 2:49
8 10:00	♅ △	♑	8 12:01
10 21:27	♅ □	♒	10 23:39
13 10:20	♅ ⚹	♓	13 12:40
15 11:49	☉ □	♈	16 0:44
18 7:21	♅ ☌	♉	18 9:37
20 0:42	♂ ⚹	♊	20 14:34
22 14:21	♅ ⚹	♋	22 16:28
24 14:50	♅ □	♌	24 16:58
26 15:37	♅ △	♍	26 17:50
28 16:27	♂ ☍	♎	28 20:23
30 22:53	♅ ☍	♏	31 1:23

☽ Phases & Eclipses Dy Hr Mn	
7 16:02	● 15♏11
15 14:54	☽ 23♒11
23 5:39	○ 0♊52
30 0:19	☾ 7♍43
7 7:20	● 15♐07
15 11:49	☽ 23♓27
22 17:49	○ 0♋49
29 9:34	☾ 7♎36

Astro Data

1 November 2018
Julian Day # 43404
SVP 5♓00'04"
GC 27♐06.1 ⚵ 28♍24.7
Eris 23♈23.2R ⚶ 28♉52.3R
⚷ 28♓31.7R ⚴ 16♑23.1
☽ Mean ☊ 0♌46.2

1 December 2018
Julian Day # 43434
SVP 5♓00'00"
GC 27♐06.2 ⚵ 11♎01.8
Eris 23♈08.1R ⚶ 22♉35.6R
⚷ 27♓55.6R ⚴ 29♑49.8
☽ Mean ☊ 29♋10.9

LONGITUDE — January 2019

Day	Sid.Time	☉	0 hr ☽	Noon ☽	True ☊	☿	♀	♂	⚳	♃	♄	♅	♆	♇
1 Tu	18 43 24	10♑45 59	12♏22 14	18♏50 22	26♋51.1	24♐35.2	23♏59.2	0♈16.2	21♏11.5	11♐52.5	11♑26.2	28♈36.8	14♓05.5	20♑36.6
2 W	18 47 21	11 47 09	25 14 49	1♐35 48	26R48.8	26 03.4	24 58.5	0 56.6	21 34.7	12 05.0	11 33.2	28R36.5	14 06.7	20 38.6
3 Th	18 51 17	12 48 20	7♐53 29	14 08 04	26 46.5	27 32.2	25 58.3	1 37.0	21 57.7	12 17.5	11 40.3	28 36.3	14 08.0	20 40.6
4 F	18 55 14	13 49 31	20 19 45	26 28 41	26 44.6	29 01.5	26 58.6	2 17.4	22 20.7	12 30.0	11 47.4	28 36.1	14 09.3	20 42.6
5 Sa	18 59 10	14 50 42	2♑35 03	8♑39 03	26 43.3	0♑31.2	27 59.3	2 57.8	22 43.6	12 42.4	11 54.5	28 36.1	14 10.7	20 44.7
6 Su	19 03 07	15 51 53	14 40 52	20 40 43	26D42.7	2 01.5	29 00.3	3 38.2	23 06.3	12 54.7	12 01.6	28D36.0	14 12.1	20 46.7
7 M	19 07 03	16 53 04	26 38 49	2♒35 23	26 42.7	3 32.1	0♐01.8	4 18.7	23 28.9	13 07.0	12 08.7	28 36.0	14 13.5	20 48.7
8 Tu	19 11 00	17 54 14	8♒30 43	14 25 06	26 43.2	5 03.3	1 03.6	4 59.2	23 51.4	13 19.2	12 15.8	28 36.1	14 14.9	20 50.7
9 W	19 14 56	18 55 24	20 18 52	26 12 22	26 43.9	6 34.8	2 05.9	5 39.7	24 13.8	13 31.4	12 22.8	28 36.2	14 16.4	20 52.8
10 Th	19 18 53	19 56 34	2♓05 58	8♓00 08	26 44.8	8 06.8	3 08.4	6 20.3	24 36.1	13 43.5	12 29.9	28 36.4	14 17.8	20 54.8
11 F	19 22 50	20 57 44	13 55 18	19 51 57	26 45.5	9 39.3	4 11.3	7 00.8	24 58.3	13 55.6	12 36.9	28 36.6	14 19.4	20 56.8
12 Sa	19 26 46	21 58 52	25 50 36	1♈51 47	26 46.0	11 12.2	5 14.5	7 41.4	25 20.3	14 07.6	12 44.0	28 36.8	14 20.9	20 58.9
13 Su	19 30 43	23 00 01	7♈56 04	14 04 00	26R46.3	12 45.5	6 18.1	8 22.0	25 42.2	14 19.5	12 51.0	28 37.2	14 22.5	21 00.9
14 M	19 34 39	24 01 08	20 16 08	26 33 03	26 46.3	14 19.3	7 21.9	9 02.6	26 04.0	14 31.3	12 58.0	28 37.5	14 24.0	21 02.9
15 Tu	19 38 36	25 02 15	2♉55 15	9♉23 13	26 46.3	15 53.6	8 26.0	9 43.2	26 25.7	14 43.1	13 05.0	28 38.0	14 25.7	21 04.9
16 W	19 42 32	26 03 21	15 57 23	22 38 05	26D46.2	17 28.4	9 30.4	10 23.8	26 47.2	14 54.8	13 12.0	28 38.4	14 27.3	21 07.0
17 Th	19 46 29	27 04 27	29 25 35	6♊20 00	26 46.2	19 03.7	10 35.1	11 04.4	27 08.6	15 06.4	13 19.0	28 39.0	14 29.0	21 09.0
18 F	19 50 25	28 05 32	13♊21 19	20 29 21	26 46.3	20 39.4	11 40.1	11 45.0	27 29.9	15 18.0	13 25.9	28 39.6	14 30.7	21 11.0
19 Sa	19 54 22	29 06 36	27 43 45	5♋04 01	26 46.4	22 15.7	12 45.3	12 25.7	27 51.0	15 29.5	13 32.8	28 40.2	14 32.4	21 13.0
20 Su	19 58 19	0♒07 39	12♋29 25	19 59 05	26R46.6	23 52.6	13 50.8	13 06.3	28 12.0	15 40.9	13 39.8	28 40.9	14 34.1	21 15.0
21 M	20 02 15	1 08 42	27 32 01	5♌07 05	26 46.6	25 29.9	14 56.5	13 46.9	28 32.9	15 52.2	13 46.6	28 41.6	14 35.9	21 17.1
22 Tu	20 06 12	2 09 44	12♌43 04	20 18 46	26 46.3	27 07.9	16 02.5	14 27.6	28 53.6	16 03.5	13 53.5	28 42.4	14 37.6	21 19.1
23 W	20 10 08	3 10 45	27 52 59	5♍24 33	26 45.7	28 46.4	17 08.7	15 08.2	29 14.1	16 14.7	14 00.4	28 43.3	14 39.4	21 21.1
24 Th	20 14 05	4 11 46	12♍52 26	20 15 47	26 44.9	0♒25.6	18 15.1	15 48.8	29 34.6	16 25.8	14 07.2	28 44.1	14 41.3	21 23.0
25 F	20 18 01	5 12 46	27 33 50	4♎46 03	26 44.0	2 05.3	19 21.8	16 29.5	29 54.8	16 36.8	14 14.0	28 45.1	14 43.1	21 25.0
26 Sa	20 21 58	6 13 46	11♎52 04	18 51 38	26 43.2	3 45.7	20 28.6	17 10.1	0♐15.0	16 47.7	14 20.7	28 46.1	14 45.0	21 27.0
27 Su	20 25 54	7 14 45	25 44 44	2♏31 25	26D42.7	5 26.7	21 35.7	17 50.8	0 34.9	16 58.5	14 27.5	28 47.1	14 46.9	21 29.0
28 M	20 29 51	8 15 44	9♏11 54	15 46 27	26 42.8	7 08.4	22 42.9	18 31.4	0 54.7	17 09.3	14 34.2	28 48.2	14 48.8	21 30.9
29 Tu	20 33 48	9 16 42	22 15 25	28 39 14	26 43.4	8 50.7	23 50.4	19 12.0	1 14.4	17 19.9	14 40.9	28 49.3	14 50.7	21 32.9
30 W	20 37 44	10 17 39	4♐58 18	11♐13 05	26 44.5	10 33.7	24 58.0	19 52.7	1 33.9	17 30.5	14 47.5	28 50.5	14 52.6	21 34.8
31 Th	20 41 41	11 18 36	17 24 03	23 31 37	26 45.9	12 17.4	26 05.8	20 33.3	1 53.2	17 41.0	14 54.1	28 51.8	14 54.6	21 36.8

LONGITUDE — February 2019

Day	Sid.Time	☉	0 hr ☽	Noon ☽	True ☊	☿	♀	♂	⚳	♃	♄	♅	♆	♇
1 F	20 45 37	12♒19 32	29♐36 15	5♑38 22	26♋47.2	14♒01.7	27♐13.7	21♈14.0	2♐12.3	17♐51.3	15♑00.7	28♈53.1	14♓56.6	21♑38.7
2 Sa	20 49 34	13 20 27	11♑38 19	17 36 31	26R48.2	15 46.6	28 21.8	21 54.6	2 31.3	18 01.6	15 07.3	28 54.4	14 58.6	21 40.6
3 Su	20 53 30	14 21 21	23 33 16	29 28 54	26 48.4	17 32.2	29 30.1	22 35.3	2 50.1	18 11.8	15 13.8	28 55.8	15 00.6	21 42.5
4 M	20 57 27	15 22 14	5♒23 42	11♒17 58	26 47.7	19 18.4	0♑38.5	23 15.9	3 08.8	18 21.9	15 20.3	28 57.2	15 02.6	21 44.4
5 Tu	21 01 23	16 23 05	17 11 56	23 05 52	26 45.9	21 05.1	1 47.1	23 56.5	3 27.2	18 31.8	15 26.7	28 58.7	15 04.6	21 46.3
6 W	21 05 20	17 23 56	29 00 01	4♓54 38	26 43.1	22 52.4	2 55.8	24 37.2	3 45.4	18 41.7	15 33.1	29 00.3	15 06.7	21 48.2
7 Th	21 09 17	18 24 45	10♓49 57	16 46 15	26 39.5	24 40.1	4 04.6	25 17.8	4 03.5	18 51.5	15 39.5	29 01.8	15 08.8	21 50.1
8 F	21 13 13	19 25 33	22 43 48	28 42 55	26 35.6	26 28.2	5 13.6	25 58.4	4 21.4	19 01.1	15 45.8	29 03.5	15 10.9	21 51.9
9 Sa	21 17 10	20 26 20	4♈43 55	10♈47 09	26 31.6	28 16.7	6 22.7	26 39.0	4 39.1	19 10.7	15 52.1	29 05.1	15 13.0	21 53.8
10 Su	21 21 06	21 27 05	16 52 59	23 01 49	26 28.2	0♓05.2	7 31.9	27 19.6	4 56.9	19 20.1	15 58.3	29 06.8	15 15.1	21 55.6
11 M	21 25 03	22 27 48	29 14 05	5♉30 11	26 25.8	1 53.9	8 41.2	28 00.2	5 13.9	19 29.4	16 04.5	29 08.6	15 17.2	21 57.4
12 Tu	21 28 59	23 28 30	11♉50 35	18 15 43	26D24.7	3 42.4	9 50.7	28 40.8	5 30.9	19 38.6	16 10.6	29 10.4	15 19.3	21 59.2
13 W	21 32 56	24 29 10	24 46 03	1♊21 57	26 24.7	5 30.5	11 00.2	29 21.4	5 47.8	19 47.7	16 16.7	29 12.3	15 21.5	22 01.0
14 Th	21 36 52	25 29 49	8♊03 48	14 51 54	26 25.8	7 18.1	12 09.9	0♉01.9	6 04.5	19 56.6	16 22.8	29 14.2	15 23.7	22 02.7
15 F	21 40 49	26 30 26	21 46 28	28 47 36	26 27.4	9 04.9	13 19.6	0 42.5	6 21.0	20 05.5	16 28.8	29 16.1	15 25.8	22 04.5
16 Sa	21 44 46	27 31 01	5♋55 17	13♋09 18	26R28.8	10 50.4	14 29.5	1 23.0	6 37.2	20 14.2	16 34.7	29 18.1	15 28.0	22 06.2
17 Su	21 48 42	28 31 34	20 29 20	27 54 48	26 29.3	12 34.5	15 39.4	2 03.5	6 53.2	20 22.8	16 40.6	29 20.1	15 30.2	22 07.9
18 M	21 52 39	29 32 06	5♌24 59	12♌58 57	26 28.3	14 16.6	16 49.5	2 44.0	7 09.1	20 31.3	16 46.5	29 22.2	15 32.4	22 09.6
19 Tu	21 56 35	0♓32 36	20 35 36	28 13 43	26 25.7	15 56.3	17 59.6	3 24.5	7 24.6	20 39.6	16 52.2	29 24.3	15 34.6	22 11.3
20 W	22 00 32	1 33 05	5♍52 00	13♍29 06	26 21.5	17 33.1	19 09.9	4 05.0	7 40.0	20 47.8	16 58.0	29 26.4	15 36.8	22 13.0
21 Th	22 04 28	2 33 32	21 03 43	28 34 36	26 16.1	19 06.4	20 20.2	4 45.4	7 55.1	20 55.9	17 03.7	29 28.6	15 39.1	22 14.6
22 F	22 08 25	3 33 57	6♎00 40	13♎20 59	26 10.4	20 35.6	21 30.7	5 25.9	8 10.0	21 03.9	17 09.3	29 30.8	15 41.3	22 16.2
23 Sa	22 12 21	4 34 21	20 34 49	27 41 39	26 05.2	22 00.2	22 41.2	6 06.3	8 24.7	21 11.7	17 14.8	29 33.1	15 43.5	22 17.8
24 Su	22 16 18	5 34 44	4♏41 10	11♏33 17	26 01.1	23 19.5	23 51.8	6 46.7	8 39.1	21 19.4	17 20.4	29 35.4	15 45.8	22 19.4
25 M	22 20 15	6 35 05	18 18 03	24 55 43	25D58.6	24 32.8	25 02.4	7 27.1	8 53.3	21 27.0	17 25.8	29 37.7	15 48.0	22 21.0
26 Tu	22 24 11	7 35 25	1♐26 37	7♐51 12	25 57.9	25 39.6	26 13.2	8 07.5	9 07.2	21 34.4	17 31.2	29 40.1	15 50.3	22 22.5
27 W	22 28 08	8 35 44	14 10 01	20 23 38	25 58.5	26 39.1	27 24.0	8 47.8	9 20.9	21 41.7	17 36.5	29 42.5	15 52.6	22 24.1
28 Th	22 32 04	9 36 01	26 32 39	2♑37 42	26 00.0	27 30.9	28 35.0	9 28.2	9 34.3	21 48.8	17 41.8	29 45.0	15 54.8	22 25.6

Astro Data

	Dy Hr Mn
♂0N	2 0:57
♅D	6 20:26
♃⚼♅	9 21:33
☽0N	13 7:51
♃□♆	13 18:58
☽0S	26 0:06
♄✶♆	31 14:15
☽0N	9 14:01
☽0S	22 9:18
☿0N	27 6:27

Planet Ingress

	Dy Hr Mn
♂ ♈	1 2:20
☿ ♑	5 3:40
♀ ♐	7 11:18
☉ ♒	20 8:59
☿ ♒	24 5:49
⚳ ♐	25 18:08
♀ ♑	3 22:29
☿ ♓	10 10:51
♂ ♉	14 10:51
☉ ♓	18 23:04

Last Aspect / ☽ Ingress

Last Aspect Dy Hr Mn		☽ Ingress Dy Hr Mn
1 22:26 ♀ ☌	♐	2 8:58
4 17:41 ☿ ☌	♑	4 18:55
7 6:20 ♀ ✶	♒	7 6:46
9 16:53 ♅ ✶	♓	9 19:44
11 14:25 ☉ ✶	♈	12 8:18
14 15:56 ♅ ☌	♉	14 18:31
16 18:34 ☉ △	♊	17 1:00
19 1:32 ♅ ✶	♋	19 3:44
21 1:50 ♅ □	♌	21 3:54
23 1:19 ♅ △	♍	23 3:22
24 13:50 ♇ △	♎	25 4:02
27 5:21 ♅ ☍	♏	27 7:31
28 22:39 ♇ ✶	♐	29 14:33

Last Aspect / ☽ Ingress

Last Aspect Dy Hr Mn		☽ Ingress Dy Hr Mn
31 22:33 ♅ △	♑	1 0:47
3 10:53 ♅ □	♒	3 13:03
5 23:59 ♅ ✶	♓	6 2:02
7 22:14 ♇ ✶	♈	8 14:34
10 23:48 ♅ ☌	♉	11 1:28
12 22:26 ☉ □	♊	13 9:32
15 12:48 ♅ ✶	♋	15 14:03
17 14:17 ♅ □	♌	17 15:21
19 13:51 ♅ △	♍	19 14:47
21 1:52 ♇ △	♎	21 14:17
23 15:11 ♅ ☍	♏	23 15:56
25 12:14 ♀ ✶	♐	25 21:19
28 6:17 ♅ △	♑	28 6:48

☽ Phases & Eclipses

Dy Hr Mn	
6 1:28	● 15♑25
6 1:41:29	● P 0.715
14 6:45	☽ 23♈48
21 5:16	○ 0♌52
21 5:12	● T 1.195
27 21:10	☾ 7♏38
4 21:04	● 15♒45
12 22:26	☽ 23♉55
19 15:54	○ 0♍42
26 11:28	☾ 7♐34

Astro Data

1 January 2019
Julian Day # 43465
SVP 4♓59'55"
GC 27♐06.3 ⚵ 21♎40.4
Eris 22♈59.9R ⚶ 20♉38.9
⚷ 28♓08.7 ⚴ 14♒42.3
☽ Mean ☊ 27♋32.4

1 February 2019
Julian Day # 43496
SVP 4♓59'50"
GC 27♐06.4 ⚵ 28♎21.5
Eris 23♈02.1 ⚶ 26♉50.2
⚷ 29♓10.6 ⚴ 0♓01.2
☽ Mean ☊ 25♋53.9

March 2019 LONGITUDE

Day	Sid.Time	☉	0 hr ☽	Noon ☽	True ☊	☿	♀	♂	⚳	♃	♄	♅	♆	♇
1 F	22 36 01	10♓36 17	8♑39 25	14♑38 22	26♋01.4	28♓14.4	29♑45.9	10♉08.5	9♐47.5	21♐55.8	17♑47.0	29♈47.4	15♓57.1	22♑27.1
2 Sa	22 39 57	11 36 31	20 35 09	26 30 20	26R02.0	28 49.2	0♒57.0	10 48.8	10 00.4	22 02.7	17 52.1	29 50.0	15 59.4	22 28.5
3 Su	22 43 54	12 36 43	2♒24 23	8♒17 49	26 01.1	29 15.0	2 08.1	11 29.1	10 13.0	22 09.4	17 57.2	29 52.5	16 01.6	22 30.0
4 M	22 47 50	13 36 54	14 11 02	20 04 26	25 58.0	29 31.5	3 19.3	12 09.4	10 25.4	22 15.9	18 02.2	29 55.1	16 03.9	22 31.4
5 Tu	22 51 47	14 37 03	25 58 21	1♓53 05	25 52.6	29R38.6	4 30.5	12 49.7	10 37.4	22 22.3	18 07.1	29 57.7	16 06.2	22 32.8
6 W	22 55 44	15 37 10	7♓48 54	13 46 01	25 45.0	29 36.5	5 41.8	13 29.9	10 49.2	22 28.6	18 12.0	0♉00.4	16 08.5	22 34.2
7 Th	22 59 40	16 37 15	19 44 39	25 44 59	25 35.7	29 25.1	6 53.1	14 10.1	11 00.7	22 34.7	18 16.8	0 03.1	16 10.8	22 35.5
8 F	23 03 37	17 37 19	1♈47 08	7♈51 18	25 25.4	29 05.1	8 04.5	14 50.4	11 11.9	22 40.6	18 21.5	0 05.8	16 13.0	22 36.9
9 Sa	23 07 33	18 37 20	13 57 36	20 06 12	25 15.1	28 36.9	9 15.9	15 30.6	11 22.9	22 46.4	18 26.2	0 08.6	16 15.3	22 38.2
10 Su	23 11 30	19 37 20	26 17 16	2♉30 59	25 05.8	28 01.2	10 27.4	16 10.7	11 33.5	22 52.0	18 30.8	0 11.3	16 17.6	22 39.5
11 M	23 15 26	20 37 17	8♉47 33	15 07 11	24 58.4	27 19.0	11 38.9	16 50.9	11 43.8	22 57.5	18 35.3	0 14.1	16 19.9	22 40.7
12 Tu	23 19 23	21 37 12	21 30 11	27 56 47	24 53.3	26 31.2	12 50.5	17 31.1	11 53.8	23 02.8	18 39.7	0 17.0	16 22.1	22 42.0
13 W	23 23 19	22 37 05	4♊27 19	11♊02 05	24D50.6	25 39.1	14 02.1	18 11.2	12 03.5	23 07.9	18 44.1	0 19.9	16 24.4	22 43.2
14 Th	23 27 16	23 36 56	17 41 23	24 25 32	24 49.9	24 43.9	15 13.8	18 51.3	12 12.9	23 12.9	18 48.4	0 22.8	16 26.7	22 44.3
15 F	23 31 12	24 36 45	1♋14 47	8♋09 21	24 50.5	23 46.9	16 25.5	19 31.4	12 22.0	23 17.7	18 52.6	0 25.7	16 28.9	22 45.5
16 Sa	23 35 09	25 36 31	15 09 24	22 14 56	24R51.0	22 49.4	17 37.3	20 11.4	12 30.8	23 22.3	18 56.7	0 28.6	16 31.2	22 46.6
17 Su	23 39 06	26 36 15	29 25 53	6♌42 02	24 50.5	21 52.6	18 49.0	20 51.5	12 39.2	23 26.8	19 00.7	0 31.6	16 33.5	22 47.8
18 M	23 43 02	27 35 57	14♌02 58	21 28 06	24 48.0	20 57.7	20 00.9	21 31.5	12 47.3	23 31.1	19 04.7	0 34.6	16 35.7	22 48.8
19 Tu	23 46 59	28 35 37	28 56 41	6♍27 47	24 42.8	20 05.7	21 12.7	22 11.5	12 55.1	23 35.3	19 08.6	0 37.6	16 37.9	22 49.9
20 W	23 50 55	29 35 14	14♍00 19	21 33 07	24 35.1	19 17.5	22 24.6	22 51.4	13 02.6	23 39.2	19 12.4	0 40.7	16 40.2	22 50.9
21 Th	23 54 52	0♈34 49	29 04 55	6♎34 28	24 25.5	18 33.8	23 36.6	23 31.4	13 09.7	23 43.0	19 16.1	0 43.7	16 42.4	22 51.9
22 F	23 58 48	1 34 23	14♎00 34	21 22 08	24 15.1	17 55.2	24 48.5	24 11.3	13 16.5	23 46.6	19 19.8	0 46.8	16 44.6	22 52.9
23 Sa	0 02 45	2 33 54	28 38 11	5♏47 58	24 05.1	17 22.2	26 00.5	24 51.2	13 22.9	23 50.1	19 23.3	0 49.9	16 46.8	22 53.8
24 Su	0 06 41	3 33 24	12♏50 55	19 46 42	23 56.5	16 54.9	27 12.6	25 31.1	13 29.0	23 53.4	19 26.8	0 53.1	16 49.0	22 54.8
25 M	0 10 38	4 32 52	26 35 08	3♐16 18	23 50.3	16 33.6	28 24.7	26 10.9	13 34.7	23 56.5	19 30.2	0 56.2	16 51.2	22 55.7
26 Tu	0 14 35	5 32 18	9♐50 22	16 17 43	23 46.5	16 18.4	29 36.8	26 50.7	13 40.1	23 59.4	19 33.5	0 59.4	16 53.4	22 56.5
27 W	0 18 31	6 31 42	22 38 47	28 54 08	23D44.8	16 09.1	0♓48.9	27 30.6	13 45.2	24 02.1	19 36.8	1 02.6	16 55.6	22 57.4
28 Th	0 22 28	7 31 05	5♑04 23	11♑10 11	23 44.6	16D05.8	2 01.1	28 10.3	13 49.8	24 04.7	19 39.9	1 05.8	16 57.8	22 58.2
29 F	0 26 24	8 30 26	17 12 14	23 11 12	23R44.8	16 08.1	3 13.4	28 50.1	13 54.1	24 07.0	19 42.9	1 09.1	16 59.9	22 59.0
30 Sa	0 30 21	9 29 45	29 07 47	5♒02 40	23 44.3	16 16.0	4 25.6	29 29.9	13 58.0	24 09.2	19 45.9	1 12.3	17 02.1	22 59.7
31 Su	0 34 17	10 29 02	10♒56 28	16 49 47	23 42.1	16 29.3	5 37.9	0♊09.6	14 01.6	24 11.2	19 48.8	1 15.6	17 04.2	23 00.5

April 2019 LONGITUDE

Day	Sid.Time	☉	0 hr ☽	Noon ☽	True ☊	☿	♀	♂	⚳	♃	♄	♅	♆	♇
1 M	0 38 14	11♈28 17	22♒43 12	28♒37 14	23♋37.4	16♓47.6	6♓50.2	0♊49.3	14♐04.8	24♐13.1	19♑51.6	1♉18.8	17♓06.3	23♑01.2
2 Tu	0 42 10	12 27 31	4♓32 20	10♓28 55	23R29.8	17 10.8	8 02.5	1 29.0	14 07.5	24 14.7	19 54.3	1 22.1	17 08.5	23 01.8
3 W	0 46 07	13 26 42	16 27 19	22 27 51	23 19.5	17 38.6	9 14.8	2 08.7	14 10.0	24 16.1	19 56.9	1 25.5	17 10.6	23 02.5
4 Th	0 50 04	14 25 52	28 30 44	4♈36 10	23 07.1	18 10.7	10 27.2	2 48.3	14 12.0	24 17.4	19 59.4	1 28.8	17 12.6	23 03.1
5 F	0 54 00	15 24 59	10♈44 16	16 55 07	22 53.3	18 47.0	11 39.6	3 27.9	14 13.6	24 18.5	20 01.8	1 32.1	17 14.7	23 03.7
6 Sa	0 57 57	16 24 05	23 08 45	29 25 13	22 39.6	19 27.3	12 52.0	4 07.6	14 14.9	24 19.4	20 04.1	1 35.5	17 16.8	23 04.2
7 Su	1 01 53	17 23 08	5♉44 31	12♉06 36	22 26.9	20 11.2	14 04.4	4 47.1	14 15.7	24 20.0	20 06.3	1 38.8	17 18.8	23 04.7
8 M	1 05 50	18 22 09	18 31 30	24 59 11	22 16.5	20 58.7	15 16.9	5 26.7	14R16.2	24 20.6	20 08.5	1 42.2	17 20.8	23 05.2
9 Tu	1 09 46	19 21 09	1♊29 43	8♊03 06	22 08.9	21 49.5	16 29.3	6 06.3	14 16.3	24 20.9	20 10.5	1 45.6	17 22.8	23 05.7
10 W	1 13 43	20 20 06	14 39 25	21 18 47	22 04.3	22 43.5	17 41.8	6 45.8	14 15.9	24R21.0	20 12.5	1 49.0	17 24.8	23 06.1
11 Th	1 17 39	21 19 00	28 01 19	4♋47 09	22 02.2	23 40.5	18 54.3	7 25.3	14 15.2	24 21.0	20 14.3	1 52.4	17 26.8	23 06.5
12 F	1 21 36	22 17 53	11♋36 27	18 29 20	22 01.8	24 40.3	20 06.8	8 04.8	14 14.1	24 20.7	20 16.1	1 55.8	17 28.8	23 06.9
13 Sa	1 25 33	23 16 43	25 25 56	2♌26 19	22 01.7	25 42.9	21 19.3	8 44.2	14 12.6	24 20.3	20 17.7	1 59.2	17 30.7	23 07.3
14 Su	1 29 29	24 15 31	9♌30 29	16 38 21	22 00.7	26 48.1	22 31.9	9 23.7	14 10.7	24 19.7	20 19.3	2 02.6	17 32.6	23 07.6
15 M	1 33 26	25 14 16	23 49 43	1♍04 17	21 57.6	27 55.8	23 44.4	10 03.1	14 08.5	24 18.9	20 20.8	2 06.0	17 34.5	23 07.9
16 Tu	1 37 22	26 12 59	8♍21 34	15 41 00	21 51.8	29 05.9	24 57.0	10 42.5	14 05.8	24 17.9	20 22.1	2 09.4	17 36.4	23 08.1
17 W	1 41 19	27 11 40	23 01 51	0♎23 16	21 43.3	0♈18.3	26 09.6	11 21.8	14 02.7	24 16.7	20 23.4	2 12.9	17 38.3	23 08.3
18 Th	1 45 15	28 10 19	7♎44 21	15 04 07	21 32.7	1 32.9	27 22.1	12 01.1	13 59.3	24 15.3	20 24.6	2 16.3	17 40.1	23 08.5
19 F	1 49 12	29 08 56	22 21 33	29 35 44	21 21.1	2 49.7	28 34.7	12 40.5	13 55.4	24 13.8	20 25.7	2 19.8	17 42.0	23 08.7
20 Sa	1 53 08	0♉07 31	6♏45 45	13♏50 52	21 09.7	4 08.7	29 47.4	13 19.7	13 51.2	24 12.0	20 26.6	2 23.2	17 43.8	23 08.8
21 Su	1 57 05	1 06 04	20 50 27	27 44 01	20 59.8	5 29.6	1♈00.0	13 59.0	13 46.6	24 10.1	20 27.5	2 26.6	17 45.6	23 09.0
22 M	2 01 01	2 04 36	4♐31 16	11♐12 05	20 52.3	6 52.6	2 12.7	14 38.3	13 41.6	24 08.0	20 28.3	2 30.1	17 47.3	23 09.0
23 Tu	2 04 58	3 03 05	17 46 29	24 14 39	20 47.3	8 17.5	3 25.3	15 17.5	13 36.2	24 05.8	20 29.0	2 33.5	17 49.1	23 09.1
24 W	2 08 55	4 01 33	0♑36 53	6♑53 36	20 44.8	9 44.3	4 38.0	15 56.7	13 30.5	24 03.3	20 29.6	2 37.0	17 50.8	23R09.1
25 Th	2 12 51	5 00 00	13 05 17	19 12 31	20D44.1	11 13.1	5 50.7	16 35.9	13 24.4	24 00.7	20 30.1	2 40.4	17 52.5	23 09.1
26 F	2 16 48	5 58 25	25 15 56	1♒16 10	20R44.2	12 43.7	7 03.4	17 15.0	13 17.9	23 57.8	20 30.5	2 43.9	17 54.2	23 09.1
27 Sa	2 20 44	6 56 48	7♒13 54	13 09 50	20 44.2	14 16.2	8 16.1	17 54.2	13 11.0	23 54.8	20 30.8	2 47.3	17 55.8	23 09.0
28 Su	2 24 41	7 55 09	19 04 39	24 59 00	20 42.8	15 50.5	9 28.9	18 33.3	13 03.8	23 51.7	20 31.0	2 50.8	17 57.5	23 08.9
29 M	2 28 37	8 53 29	0♓53 32	6♓48 52	20 39.4	17 26.6	10 41.6	19 12.4	12 56.2	23 48.3	20R31.1	2 54.2	17 59.1	23 08.8
30 Tu	2 32 34	9 51 48	12 45 34	18 44 09	20 33.5	19 04.5	11 54.4	19 51.5	12 48.3	23 44.8	20 31.1	2 57.6	18 00.6	23 08.6

Astro Data	Dy Hr Mn
☿ R	5 18:20
♃⚺♇	7 16:33
☽ 0N	8 19:13
☿ 0S	16 21:55
☉ 0N	20 21:58
☽ 0S	21 19:53
☿ D	28 13:59
☽ 0N	5 1:18
⚳ R	9 4:35
♃ R	10 17:01
☽ 0S	18 6:08
☿ 0N	22 1:51
♀ 0N	23 16:19
♇ R	24 18:48
♄ R	30 0:54

Planet Ingress		Dy Hr Mn
♀	♒	1 16:45
♅	♉	6 8:26
☉	♈	20 21:58
♀	♓	26 19:43
♂	♊	31 6:12
☿	♈	17 6:01
☉	♉	20 8:55
♀	♈	20 16:10

Last Aspect Dy Hr Mn			☽ Ingress	Dy Hr Mn
2 18:47	♅	□	♒	2 19:06
5 8:05	♅	⚹	♓	5 8:11
7 19:08	☿	☌	♈	7 20:27
9 17:14	♃	△	♉	10 7:10
12 9:31	☿	⚹	♊	12 15:48
14 12:30	☿	□	♋	14 21:49
16 18:03	☉	△	♌	17 0:57
18 15:19	♃	△	♍	19 1:41
20 15:22	♃	□	♎	21 1:28
22 18:10	♀	△	♏	23 2:16
25 2:24	♀	□	♐	25 6:06
27 2:37	♃	☌	♑	27 14:07
30 0:05	♂	△	♒	30 1:46

Last Aspect Dy Hr Mn			☽ Ingress	Dy Hr Mn
1 3:02	♃	⚹	♓	1 14:48
3 15:36	♃	□	♈	4 2:56
6 2:15	♃	△	♉	6 13:06
8 8:29	♇	△	♊	8 21:15
10 17:27	♃	☍	♋	11 3:31
12 23:33	☿	△	♌	13 7:50
15 1:38	☉	△	♍	15 10:14
17 4:29	♀	☍	♎	17 11:22
19 11:12	☉	☍	♏	19 12:40
21 4:00	♇	⚹	♐	21 15:59
23 11:43	♃	☌	♑	23 22:50
25 19:48	♇	☌	♒	26 9:27
28 9:44	♃	⚹	♓	28 22:11

☽ Phases & Eclipses Dy Hr Mn		
6 16:04	●	15♓47
14 10:27	☽	23♊33
21 1:43	○	0♎09
28 4:10	☾	7♑12
5 8:50	●	15♈17
12 19:06	☽	22♋35
19 11:12	○	29♎07
26 22:18	☾	6♒23

Astro Data

1 March 2019
Julian Day # 43524
SVP 4♓59'46"
GC 27♐06.4 ⚴ 29♎00.3R
Eris 23♈12.5 ⚵ 7♊01.5
⚷ 0♈36.5 ⚶ 13♓53.2
☽ Mean ☊ 24♋24.9

1 April 2019
Julian Day # 43555
SVP 4♓59'43"
GC 27♐06.5 ⚴ 22♎31.7R
Eris 23♈30.4 ⚵ 20♊49.8
⚷ 2♈25.2 ⚶ 28♓58.4
☽ Mean ☊ 22♋46.4

LONGITUDE — May 2019

Day	Sid.Time	☉	0 hr ☽	Noon ☽	True ☊	☿	♀	♂	⚳	♃	♄	♅	♆	♇
1 W	2 36 30	10♉50 05	24♓45 05	0♈48 46	20♋25.1	20♈44.3	13♈07.2	20♊30.6	12♐40.0	23♐41.1	20♑31.0	3♉01.0	18♓02.2	23♑08.4
2 Th	2 40 27	11 48 20	6♈55 34	13 05 42	20R 14.6	22 25.9	14 20.0	21 09.6	12R 31.4	23R 37.2	20R 30.8	3 04.5	18 03.7	23R 08.2
3 F	2 44 24	12 46 33	19 19 25	25 36 48	20 03.0	24 09.3	15 32.7	21 48.6	12 22.5	23 33.2	20 30.5	3 07.9	18 05.2	23 08.0
4 Sa	2 48 20	13 44 45	1♉57 55	8♉22 45	19 51.2	25 54.6	16 45.5	22 27.6	12 13.2	23 29.0	20 30.2	3 11.3	18 06.7	23 07.7
5 Su	2 52 17	14 42 56	14 51 13	21 23 13	19 40.4	27 41.6	17 58.4	23 06.6	12 03.7	23 24.6	20 29.7	3 14.7	18 08.2	23 07.4
6 M	2 56 13	15 41 04	27 58 34	4♊37 05	19 31.5	29 30.6	19 11.2	23 45.6	11 53.8	23 20.1	20 29.1	3 18.1	18 09.6	23 07.1
7 Tu	3 00 10	16 39 11	11♊18 34	18 02 50	19 25.2	1♉21.3	20 24.0	24 24.6	11 43.7	23 15.5	20 28.4	3 21.5	18 11.0	23 06.7
8 W	3 04 06	17 37 16	24 49 39	1♋38 53	19 21.5	3 13.9	21 36.8	25 03.5	11 33.2	23 10.6	20 27.6	3 24.8	18 12.4	23 06.4
9 Th	3 08 03	18 35 20	8♋30 21	15 23 56	19D 20.2	5 08.3	22 49.7	25 42.4	11 22.5	23 05.7	20 26.8	3 28.2	18 13.8	23 06.0
10 F	3 11 59	19 33 21	22 19 33	29 17 07	19 20.4	7 04.6	24 02.5	26 21.3	11 11.6	23 00.5	20 25.8	3 31.5	18 15.1	23 05.5
11 Sa	3 15 56	20 31 21	6♌16 33	13♌17 47	19R 21.0	9 02.6	25 15.4	27 00.2	11 00.3	22 55.3	20 24.7	3 34.9	18 16.4	23 05.1
12 Su	3 19 53	21 29 18	20 20 44	27 25 17	19 21.0	11 02.5	26 28.2	27 39.1	10 48.9	22 49.9	20 23.6	3 38.2	18 17.7	23 04.6
13 M	3 23 49	22 27 14	4♍31 16	11♍38 29	19 19.5	13 04.0	27 41.1	28 17.9	10 37.2	22 44.3	20 22.3	3 41.5	18 18.9	23 04.0
14 Tu	3 27 46	23 25 08	18 46 38	25 55 22	19 15.8	15 07.2	28 53.9	28 56.7	10 25.4	22 38.6	20 21.0	3 44.8	18 20.1	23 03.5
15 W	3 31 42	24 23 00	3♎04 15	10♎12 48	19 09.9	17 12.0	0♉06.8	29 35.5	10 13.3	22 32.8	20 19.6	3 48.1	18 21.3	23 02.9
16 Th	3 35 39	25 20 50	17 20 28	24 26 38	19 02.3	19 18.2	1 19.7	0♋14.3	10 01.0	22 26.9	20 18.0	3 51.4	18 22.4	23 02.3
17 F	3 39 35	26 18 39	1♏30 41	8♏32 02	18 53.8	21 25.8	2 32.5	0 53.0	9 48.6	22 20.8	20 16.4	3 54.6	18 23.6	23 01.7
18 Sa	3 43 32	27 16 26	15 30 04	22 24 16	18 45.5	23 34.6	3 45.4	1 31.8	9 36.0	22 14.7	20 14.7	3 57.9	18 24.7	23 01.1
19 Su	3 47 28	28 14 12	29 14 10	5♐59 24	18 38.2	25 44.4	4 58.3	2 10.5	9 23.3	22 08.4	20 12.9	4 01.1	18 25.7	23 00.4
20 M	3 51 25	29 11 56	12♐39 41	19 14 52	18 32.7	27 55.0	6 11.2	2 49.2	9 10.4	22 02.0	20 11.1	4 04.3	18 26.8	22 59.7
21 Tu	3 55 22	0♊09 39	25 44 53	2♑09 49	18 29.3	0♊06.2	7 24.2	3 27.9	8 57.4	21 55.5	20 09.1	4 07.5	18 27.8	22 59.0
22 W	3 59 18	1 07 21	8♑29 49	14 45 09	18D 28.0	2 17.8	8 37.1	4 06.5	8 44.3	21 48.9	20 07.0	4 10.6	18 28.8	22 58.2
23 Th	4 03 15	2 05 02	20 56 09	27 03 15	18 28.2	4 29.4	9 50.0	4 45.2	8 31.2	21 42.2	20 04.9	4 13.8	18 29.7	22 57.5
24 F	4 07 11	3 02 42	3♒06 55	9♒07 42	18 29.4	6 40.9	11 03.0	5 23.8	8 17.9	21 35.4	20 02.7	4 16.9	18 30.6	22 56.7
25 Sa	4 11 08	4 00 21	15 06 11	21 02 58	18 30.8	8 51.8	12 16.0	6 02.4	8 04.6	21 28.5	20 00.4	4 20.0	18 31.5	22 55.8
26 Su	4 15 04	4 57 59	26 58 40	2♓53 56	18R 31.6	11 02.0	13 28.9	6 41.0	7 51.3	21 21.5	19 58.0	4 23.1	18 32.4	22 55.0
27 M	4 19 01	5 55 35	8♓49 24	14 45 42	18 31.2	13 11.2	14 41.9	7 19.6	7 37.9	21 14.4	19 55.5	4 26.2	18 33.2	22 54.1
28 Tu	4 22 57	6 53 11	20 43 27	26 43 14	18 29.1	15 19.1	15 54.9	7 58.2	7 24.5	21 07.3	19 53.0	4 29.2	18 34.0	22 53.3
29 W	4 26 54	7 50 46	2♈45 38	8♈51 08	18 25.4	17 25.5	17 07.9	8 36.8	7 11.1	21 00.1	19 50.3	4 32.2	18 34.8	22 52.3
30 Th	4 30 51	8 48 20	15 00 11	21 13 13	18 20.2	19 30.2	18 20.9	9 15.3	6 57.7	20 52.8	19 47.6	4 35.2	18 35.5	22 51.4
31 F	4 34 47	9 45 53	27 30 31	3♉52 21	18 14.0	21 33.0	19 34.0	9 53.8	6 44.3	20 45.4	19 44.8	4 38.2	18 36.2	22 50.5

LONGITUDE — June 2019

Day	Sid.Time	☉	0 hr ☽	Noon ☽	True ☊	☿	♀	♂	⚳	♃	♄	♅	♆	♇
1 Sa	4 38 44	10♊43 25	10♉18 53	16♉50 10	18♋07.7	23♊33.7	20♉47.0	10♋32.3	6♐31.0	20♐38.0	19♑42.0	4♉41.2	18♓36.9	22♑49.5
2 Su	4 42 40	11 40 56	23 26 11	0♊06 49	18R 01.8	25 32.2	22 00.1	11 10.9	6R 17.8	20R 30.6	19R 39.0	4 44.1	18 37.5	22R 48.5
3 M	4 46 37	12 38 27	6♊51 54	13 41 07	17 57.1	27 28.4	23 13.1	11 49.3	6 04.6	20 23.1	19 36.0	4 47.0	18 38.1	22 47.5
4 Tu	4 50 33	13 35 56	20 34 10	27 30 37	17 53.9	29 22.3	24 26.2	12 27.8	5 51.6	20 15.6	19 32.9	4 49.9	18 38.7	22 46.4
5 W	4 54 30	14 33 25	4♋30 05	11♋32 04	17D 52.4	1♋13.6	25 39.3	13 06.3	5 38.6	20 08.0	19 29.8	4 52.7	18 39.2	22 45.4
6 Th	4 58 27	15 30 52	18 36 08	25 41 49	17 52.5	3 02.4	26 52.3	13 44.8	5 25.8	20 00.4	19 26.6	4 55.5	18 39.7	22 44.3
7 F	5 02 23	16 28 18	2♌48 41	9♌56 19	17 53.6	4 48.6	28 05.4	14 23.2	5 13.1	19 52.8	19 23.3	4 58.3	18 40.2	22 43.2
8 Sa	5 06 20	17 25 43	17 04 21	24 12 25	17 55.0	6 32.3	29 18.5	15 01.6	5 00.6	19 45.2	19 19.9	5 01.1	18 40.7	22 42.1
9 Su	5 10 16	18 23 07	1♍20 12	8♍27 24	17R 56.1	8 13.2	0♊31.6	15 40.0	4 48.2	19 37.5	19 16.5	5 03.8	18 41.1	22 41.0
10 M	5 14 13	19 20 29	15 33 46	22 39 02	17 56.4	9 51.5	1 44.7	16 18.4	4 36.0	19 29.9	19 13.1	5 06.5	18 41.4	22 39.8
11 Tu	5 18 09	20 17 51	29 42 58	6♎45 18	17 55.5	11 27.1	2 57.9	16 56.8	4 24.0	19 22.2	19 09.5	5 09.2	18 41.8	22 38.7
12 W	5 22 06	21 15 11	13♎45 51	20 44 18	17 53.4	13 00.0	4 11.0	17 35.2	4 12.2	19 14.6	19 05.9	5 11.8	18 42.1	22 37.5
13 Th	5 26 02	22 12 31	27 40 27	4♏34 03	17 50.3	14 30.2	5 24.1	18 13.5	4 00.7	19 06.9	19 02.3	5 14.4	18 42.4	22 36.3
14 F	5 29 59	23 09 49	11♏24 52	18 12 39	17 46.8	15 57.6	6 37.3	18 51.8	3 49.3	18 59.3	18 58.6	5 17.0	18 42.6	22 35.1
15 Sa	5 33 56	24 07 07	24 57 10	1♐38 15	17 43.3	17 22.2	7 50.4	19 30.2	3 38.2	18 51.7	18 54.8	5 19.5	18 42.8	22 33.8
16 Su	5 37 52	25 04 24	8♐15 42	14 49 24	17 40.3	18 44.0	9 03.6	20 08.5	3 27.4	18 44.1	18 51.0	5 22.0	18 43.0	22 32.6
17 M	5 41 49	26 01 41	21 19 14	27 45 11	17 38.2	20 02.9	10 16.8	20 46.8	3 16.8	18 36.6	18 47.2	5 24.5	18 43.2	22 31.3
18 Tu	5 45 45	26 58 57	4♑07 14	10♑25 29	17D 37.1	21 19.0	11 30.0	21 25.1	3 06.4	18 29.0	18 43.3	5 26.9	18 43.3	22 30.1
19 W	5 49 42	27 56 12	16 40 01	22 51 02	17 37.0	22 32.0	12 43.2	22 03.3	2 56.4	18 21.6	18 39.3	5 29.3	18 43.4	22 28.8
20 Th	5 53 38	28 53 27	28 58 45	5♒03 29	17 37.7	23 42.1	13 56.4	22 41.6	2 46.6	18 14.1	18 35.3	5 31.7	18 43.4	22 27.5
21 F	5 57 35	29 50 41	11♒05 34	17 05 23	17 39.0	24 49.2	15 09.7	23 19.9	2 37.1	18 06.7	18 31.3	5 34.1	18R 43.5	22 26.2
22 Sa	6 01 31	0♋47 56	23 03 22	29 00 00	17 40.5	25 53.0	16 22.9	23 58.1	2 28.0	17 59.4	18 27.2	5 36.4	18 43.4	22 24.9
23 Su	6 05 28	1 45 10	4♓55 47	10♓51 14	17 41.7	26 53.7	17 36.2	24 36.4	2 19.1	17 52.1	18 23.1	5 38.6	18 43.4	22 23.5
24 M	6 09 25	2 42 24	16 46 57	22 43 28	17R 42.6	27 51.1	18 49.5	25 14.6	2 10.5	17 44.9	18 19.0	5 40.8	18 43.3	22 22.2
25 Tu	6 13 21	3 39 37	28 41 23	4♈41 18	17 42.9	28 45.0	20 02.8	25 52.8	2 02.3	17 37.8	18 14.8	5 43.0	18 43.2	22 20.8
26 W	6 17 18	4 36 51	10♈43 46	16 49 22	17 42.5	29 35.5	21 16.1	26 31.0	1 54.4	17 30.7	18 10.6	5 45.2	18 43.1	22 19.5
27 Th	6 21 14	5 34 05	22 58 39	29 12 06	17 41.6	0♌22.3	22 29.5	27 09.2	1 46.8	17 23.8	18 06.3	5 47.3	18 42.9	22 18.1
28 F	6 25 11	6 31 18	5♉30 11	11♉53 18	17 40.4	1 05.5	23 42.8	27 47.4	1 39.5	17 16.9	18 02.0	5 49.4	18 42.7	22 16.7
29 Sa	6 29 07	7 28 32	18 21 45	24 55 48	17 39.1	1 44.8	24 56.2	28 25.6	1 32.6	17 10.0	17 57.7	5 51.4	18 42.4	22 15.3
30 Su	6 33 04	8 25 46	1♊35 34	8♊21 05	17 37.9	2 20.2	26 09.6	29 03.8	1 26.1	17 03.3	17 53.4	5 53.4	18 42.2	22 13.9

Astro Data	Dy Hr Mn
♅∠♆	2 2:49
☽0N	2 9:06
♃⚻♇	9 10:30
☽0S	15 14:37
☽0N	29 18:05
♃⚼♅	6 23:19
☽0S	11 21:10
♃⚻♄	14 16:28
♃□♆	16 15:22
♄⚹♆	18 11:47
♆ R	21 14:36
☽0N	26 2:59

Planet Ingress		Dy Hr Mn
☿	♉	6 18:25
♀	♉	15 9:46
♂	♋	16 3:09
☉	♊	21 7:59
☿	♊	21 10:52
☿	♋	4 20:04
♀	♊	9 1:37
☉	♋	21 15:54
☿	♌	27 0:19

Last Aspect Dy Hr Mn			☽ Ingress	Dy Hr Mn
30 21:57	♃	□	♈	1 10:24
3 8:47	☿	☌	♉	3 20:18
5 15:10	♇	△	♊	6 3:40
7 23:50	♂	☌	♋	8 9:06
10 2:06	♀	□	♌	10 13:14
12 12:24	♂	⚹	♍	12 16:22
14 17:19	♂	□	♎	14 18:51
16 9:37	♇	□	♏	16 21:26
18 21:11	☉	☍	♐	19 1:21
20 17:05	♃	☌	♑	21 7:56
23 3:58	♇	☌	♒	23 17:49
25 12:51	♃	⚹	♓	26 6:07
28 4:21	♇	⚹	♈	28 18:32
30 15:08	♇	□	♉	31 4:43

Last Aspect Dy Hr Mn			☽ Ingress	Dy Hr Mn
1 22:53	♇	△	♊	2 11:48
4 15:42	☿	☌	♋	4 16:17
6 14:10	♀	⚹	♌	6 19:16
8 21:23	♀	□	♍	8 21:45
10 12:01	♇	△	♎	11 0:29
12 15:15	♇	□	♏	13 4:02
14 19:46	♇	⚹	♐	15 9:03
17 8:31	☉	☍	♑	17 16:13
19 11:19	☿	☍	♒	20 2:01
21 14:02	♃	⚹	♓	22 14:01
24 23:10	☿	△	♈	25 2:38
27 7:51	♂	□	♉	27 13:32
29 18:38	♂	⚹	♊	29 21:09

☽ Phases & Eclipses Dy Hr Mn	
4 22:45	● 14♉11
12 1:12	☽ 21♌03
18 21:11	○ 27♏39
26 16:34	☾ 5♓09
3 10:02	● 12♊34
10 5:59	☽ 19♍06
17 8:31	○ 25♐53
25 9:46	☾ 3♈34

Astro Data

1 May 2019
Julian Day # 43585
SVP 4♓59'40"
GC 27♐06.6 ⚵ 13♎49.9R
Eris 23♈49.9 ⚴ 5♋15.4
⚷ 4♈04.2 ⚶ 13♈02.3
☽ Mean ☊ 21♋11.1

1 June 2019
Julian Day # 43616
SVP 4♓59'36"
GC 27♐06.6 ⚵ 10♎23.0
Eris 24♈07.4 ⚴ 20♋26.9
⚷ 5♈20.6 ⚶ 26♈42.2
☽ Mean ☊ 19♋32.6

July 2019 LONGITUDE

Day	Sid.Time	☉	0 hr ☽	Noon ☽	True ☊	☿	♀	♂	⚳	♃	♄	♅	♆	♇
1 M	6 37 00	9♋23 00	15♊12 16	22♊08 55	17♋37.0	2♌51.5	27♊23.0	29♋42.0	1♐19.9	16♐56.7	17♑49.1	5♉55.4	18♓41.9	22♑12.5
2 Tu	6 40 57	10 20 14	29 10 41	6♋17 09	17D 36.5	3 18.6	28 36.5	0♌20.2	1R 14.1	16R 50.2	17R 44.7	5 57.3	18R 41.5	22R 11.1
3 W	6 44 54	11 17 27	13♋27 46	20 41 51	17 36.4	3 41.4	29 49.9	0 58.3	1 08.6	16 43.8	17 40.4	5 59.2	18 41.2	22 09.7
4 Th	6 48 50	12 14 41	27 58 43	5♌17 35	17 36.6	3 59.7	1♋03.4	1 36.5	1 03.5	16 37.5	17 36.0	6 01.0	18 40.8	22 08.2
5 F	6 52 47	13 11 54	12♌37 38	19 58 06	17 36.9	4 13.6	2 16.8	2 14.7	0 58.7	16 31.3	17 31.6	6 02.8	18 40.3	22 06.8
6 Sa	6 56 43	14 09 07	27 18 11	4♍37 09	17 37.3	4 22.8	3 30.3	2 52.8	0 54.4	16 25.3	17 27.2	6 04.5	18 39.9	22 05.4
7 Su	7 00 40	15 06 20	11♍54 21	19 09 11	17 37.6	4R 27.4	4 43.8	3 31.0	0 50.4	16 19.3	17 22.7	6 06.2	18 39.4	22 03.9
8 M	7 04 36	16 03 33	26 21 08	3♎29 49	17 37.7	4 27.2	5 57.3	4 09.1	0 46.8	16 13.5	17 18.3	6 07.9	18 38.9	22 02.5
9 Tu	7 08 33	17 00 45	10♎34 54	17 36 08	17 37.7	4 22.4	7 10.8	4 47.2	0 43.5	16 07.8	17 13.9	6 09.5	18 38.3	22 01.0
10 W	7 12 29	17 57 57	24 33 23	1♏26 34	17 37.7	4 12.8	8 24.4	5 25.3	0 40.6	16 02.3	17 09.5	6 11.1	18 37.7	21 59.6
11 Th	7 16 26	18 55 10	8♏15 38	15 00 37	17 37.8	3 58.7	9 37.9	6 03.4	0 38.1	15 56.9	17 05.1	6 12.6	18 37.1	21 58.1
12 F	7 20 23	19 52 22	21 41 35	28 18 37	17 38.0	3 40.2	10 51.5	6 41.6	0 36.0	15 51.6	17 00.6	6 14.1	18 36.5	21 56.7
13 Sa	7 24 19	20 49 34	4♐51 49	11♐21 20	17 38.2	3 17.4	12 05.1	7 19.7	0 34.2	15 46.5	16 56.2	6 15.6	18 35.8	21 55.2
14 Su	7 28 16	21 46 46	17 47 16	24 09 48	17 38.6	2 50.6	13 18.7	7 57.8	0 32.8	15 41.6	16 51.8	6 17.0	18 35.1	21 53.7
15 M	7 32 12	22 43 58	0♑29 02	6♑45 09	17R 38.9	2 20.2	14 32.3	8 35.8	0 31.8	15 36.7	16 47.4	6 18.3	18 34.4	21 52.3
16 Tu	7 36 09	23 41 11	12 58 18	19 08 39	17 39.0	1 46.6	15 46.0	9 13.9	0 31.2	15 32.1	16 43.1	6 19.6	18 33.6	21 50.8
17 W	7 40 05	24 38 24	25 16 23	1♒21 41	17 38.8	1 10.3	16 59.6	9 52.0	0D 30.9	15 27.5	16 38.7	6 20.9	18 32.9	21 49.4
18 Th	7 44 02	25 35 37	7♒24 45	13 25 49	17 38.2	0 31.8	18 13.3	10 30.1	0 30.9	15 23.2	16 34.4	6 22.1	18 32.1	21 47.9
19 F	7 47 58	26 32 51	19 25 09	25 23 00	17 37.2	29♋51.7	19 27.0	11 08.2	0 31.4	15 19.0	16 30.0	6 23.3	18 31.2	21 46.5
20 Sa	7 51 55	27 30 05	1♓19 41	7♓15 33	17 35.9	29 10.8	20 40.7	11 46.2	0 32.2	15 14.9	16 25.7	6 24.4	18 30.4	21 45.0
21 Su	7 55 52	28 27 20	13 10 56	19 06 15	17 34.4	28 29.6	21 54.4	12 24.3	0 33.3	15 11.1	16 21.4	6 25.5	18 29.5	21 43.6
22 M	7 59 48	29 24 36	25 01 56	0♈58 26	17 33.0	27 49.0	23 08.2	13 02.4	0 34.8	15 07.4	16 17.2	6 26.5	18 28.5	21 42.1
23 Tu	8 03 45	0♌21 52	6♈56 13	12 55 49	17 31.9	27 09.7	24 21.9	13 40.4	0 36.7	15 03.8	16 13.0	6 27.5	18 27.6	21 40.7
24 W	8 07 41	1 19 09	18 57 45	25 02 34	17D 31.2	26 32.3	25 35.7	14 18.5	0 38.9	15 00.4	16 08.8	6 28.4	18 26.6	21 39.2
25 Th	8 11 38	2 16 27	1♉10 47	7♉22 59	17 31.2	25 57.6	26 49.5	14 56.6	0 41.5	14 57.2	16 04.6	6 29.3	18 25.6	21 37.8
26 F	8 15 34	3 13 46	13 39 39	20 01 20	17 31.8	25 26.3	28 03.4	15 34.7	0 44.4	14 54.2	16 00.4	6 30.1	18 24.6	21 36.4
27 Sa	8 19 31	4 11 06	26 28 28	3♊01 27	17 32.9	24 58.8	29 17.2	16 12.7	0 47.6	14 51.3	15 56.4	6 30.9	18 23.5	21 35.0
28 Su	8 23 27	5 08 27	9♊40 39	16 26 16	17 34.1	24 35.9	0♌31.1	16 50.8	0 51.2	14 48.7	15 52.3	6 31.7	18 22.5	21 33.6
29 M	8 27 24	6 05 49	23 18 26	0♋17 08	17 35.3	24 17.8	1 45.0	17 28.9	0 55.2	14 46.2	15 48.3	6 32.4	18 21.4	21 32.1
30 Tu	8 31 21	7 03 12	7♋22 14	14 33 24	17R 35.9	24 05.2	2 58.9	18 07.0	0 59.4	14 43.8	15 44.3	6 33.0	18 20.3	21 30.8
31 W	8 35 17	8 00 36	21 50 08	29 11 48	17 35.6	23D 58.2	4 12.8	18 45.0	1 04.0	14 41.7	15 40.4	6 33.6	18 19.1	21 29.4

August 2019 LONGITUDE

Day	Sid.Time	☉	0 hr ☽	Noon ☽	True ☊	☿	♀	♂	⚳	♃	♄	♅	♆	♇
1 Th	8 39 14	8♌58 00	6♌37 34	14♌06 30	17♋34.3	23♋57.2	5♌26.8	19♌23.1	1♐09.0	14♐39.7	15♑36.5	6♉34.2	18♓18.0	21♑28.0
2 F	8 43 10	9 55 26	21 37 32	29 09 33	17R 32.0	24 02.4	6 40.8	20 01.2	1 14.2	14R 38.0	15R 32.6	6 34.7	18R 16.8	21R 26.6
3 Sa	8 47 07	10 52 52	6♍41 23	14♍11 55	17 29.1	24 13.9	7 54.7	20 39.3	1 19.8	14 36.4	15 28.9	6 35.1	18 15.6	21 25.3
4 Su	8 51 03	11 50 18	21 40 04	29 04 53	17 26.0	24 31.9	9 08.7	21 17.4	1 25.7	14 35.0	15 25.1	6 35.5	18 14.3	21 23.9
5 M	8 55 00	12 47 46	6♎25 31	13♎41 18	17 23.2	24 56.3	10 22.8	21 55.4	1 32.0	14 33.7	15 21.4	6 35.8	18 13.1	21 22.6
6 Tu	8 58 56	13 45 14	20 51 43	27 56 26	17 21.3	25 27.3	11 36.8	22 33.5	1 38.5	14 32.7	15 17.8	6 36.1	18 11.8	21 21.2
7 W	9 02 53	14 42 43	4♏55 15	11♏48 08	17D 20.4	26 04.8	12 50.8	23 11.6	1 45.3	14 31.8	15 14.3	6 36.4	18 10.5	21 19.9
8 Th	9 06 50	15 40 12	18 35 09	25 16 30	17 20.7	26 48.8	14 04.9	23 49.7	1 52.5	14 31.2	15 10.7	6 36.6	18 09.2	21 18.6
9 F	9 10 46	16 37 43	1♐52 25	8♐23 15	17 21.9	27 39.1	15 19.0	24 27.8	1 59.9	14 30.7	15 07.3	6 36.7	18 07.8	21 17.3
10 Sa	9 14 43	17 35 14	14 49 20	21 11 05	17 23.5	28 35.7	16 33.0	25 05.9	2 07.7	14 30.4	15 03.9	6 36.9	18 06.5	21 16.1
11 Su	9 18 39	18 32 46	27 28 52	3♑43 05	17 25.0	29 38.4	17 47.1	25 43.9	2 15.7	14D 30.3	15 00.6	6R 36.9	18 05.1	21 14.8
12 M	9 22 36	19 30 19	9♑54 07	16 02 19	17R 25.7	0♌47.1	19 01.3	26 22.0	2 24.0	14 30.4	14 57.4	6 36.9	18 03.7	21 13.5
13 Tu	9 26 32	20 27 53	22 08 03	28 11 36	17 25.1	2 01.5	20 15.4	27 00.1	2 32.7	14 30.6	14 54.2	6 36.9	18 02.3	21 12.3
14 W	9 30 29	21 25 28	4♒13 18	10♒13 23	17 23.0	3 21.4	21 29.5	27 38.2	2 41.5	14 31.1	14 51.1	6 36.8	18 00.9	21 11.1
15 Th	9 34 25	22 23 05	16 12 07	22 09 45	17 19.2	4 46.5	22 43.7	28 16.3	2 50.7	14 31.7	14 48.0	6 36.6	17 59.5	21 09.9
16 F	9 38 22	23 20 42	28 06 31	4♓02 37	17 13.8	6 16.6	23 57.9	28 54.4	3 00.1	14 32.5	14 45.1	6 36.4	17 58.0	21 08.7
17 Sa	9 42 19	24 18 21	9♓58 17	15 53 45	17 07.4	7 51.2	25 12.0	29 32.5	3 09.8	14 33.5	14 42.2	6 36.2	17 56.6	21 07.5
18 Su	9 46 15	25 16 01	21 49 17	27 45 07	17 00.5	9 30.1	26 26.3	0♍10.6	3 19.8	14 34.7	14 39.3	6 35.9	17 55.1	21 06.4
19 M	9 50 12	26 13 42	3♈41 33	9♈38 54	16 53.7	11 12.8	27 40.5	0 48.8	3 30.0	14 36.1	14 36.6	6 35.6	17 53.6	21 05.3
20 Tu	9 54 08	27 11 25	15 37 30	21 37 44	16 47.8	12 58.9	28 54.7	1 26.9	3 40.5	14 37.6	14 33.9	6 35.2	17 52.1	21 04.1
21 W	9 58 05	28 09 10	27 40 01	3♉44 46	16 43.3	14 48.1	0♍09.0	2 05.0	3 51.2	14 39.4	14 31.3	6 34.7	17 50.5	21 03.0
22 Th	10 02 01	29 06 56	9♉52 28	16 03 37	16 40.6	16 39.8	1 23.2	2 43.1	4 02.2	14 41.3	14 28.8	6 34.3	17 49.0	21 02.0
23 F	10 05 58	0♍04 44	22 18 42	28 38 15	16D 39.7	18 33.7	2 37.5	3 21.3	4 13.4	14 43.4	14 26.4	6 33.7	17 47.5	21 00.9
24 Sa	10 09 54	1 02 34	5♊02 47	11♊32 47	16 40.1	20 29.3	3 51.8	3 59.5	4 24.9	14 45.7	14 24.0	6 33.1	17 45.9	20 59.8
25 Su	10 13 51	2 00 26	18 08 43	24 50 59	16 41.3	22 26.3	5 06.1	4 37.6	4 36.6	14 48.1	14 21.8	6 32.5	17 44.3	20 58.8
26 M	10 17 48	2 58 19	1♋39 54	8♋35 40	16R 42.4	24 24.3	6 20.5	5 15.8	4 48.6	14 50.8	14 19.6	6 31.8	17 42.8	20 57.8
27 Tu	10 21 44	3 56 14	15 38 22	22 47 55	16 42.5	26 22.9	7 34.8	5 54.0	5 00.7	14 53.6	14 17.5	6 31.1	17 41.2	20 56.9
28 W	10 25 41	4 54 11	0♌04 02	7♌26 16	16 40.8	28 21.8	8 49.2	6 32.2	5 13.2	14 56.6	14 15.5	6 30.3	17 39.6	20 55.9
29 Th	10 29 37	5 52 10	14 53 56	22 26 07	16 37.0	0♍20.8	10 03.5	7 10.4	5 25.8	14 59.7	14 13.5	6 29.5	17 38.0	20 55.0
30 F	10 33 34	6 50 10	0♍01 45	7♍39 36	16 31.2	2 19.7	11 17.9	7 48.6	5 38.7	15 03.1	14 11.7	6 28.7	17 36.4	20 54.0
31 Sa	10 37 30	7 48 11	15 18 20	22 56 32	16 23.9	4 18.1	12 32.3	8 26.8	5 51.7	15 06.6	14 10.0	6 27.8	17 34.7	20 53.1

Astro Data Dy Hr Mn	Planet Ingress Dy Hr Mn	Last Aspect Dy Hr Mn	☽ Ingress Dy Hr Mn	Last Aspect Dy Hr Mn	☽ Ingress Dy Hr Mn	☽ Phases & Eclipses Dy Hr Mn	Astro Data
☿R 7 23:15	♂ ♌ 1 23:19	1 21:48 ♀ ☌	♋ 2 1:24	1 20:48 ♂ ☌	♍ 2 13:20	2 19:16 ● 10♋38	1 July 2019
☽0S 9 2:53	♀ ♋ 3 15:18	3 14:25 ♇ ☍	♌ 4 3:19	4 4:27 ☿ ⚹	♎ 4 13:30	2 19:22:57 ◐ T 04'33"	Julian Day # 43646
⚳D 17 19:06	☿ ♋R 19 7:06	5 6:24 ♃ △	♍ 6 4:25	6 7:36 ☿ □	♏ 6 15:31	9 10:55 ☽ 16♎58	SVP 4♓59'31"
☽0N 23 10:36	☉ ♌ 23 2:50	7 16:50 ♇ △	♎ 8 6:07	8 14:58 ☿ △	♐ 8 20:35	16 21:38 ○ 24♑04	GC 27♐06.7 ⚴ 13♎39.6
	♀ ♌ 28 1:54	9 19:35 ♇ □	♏ 10 9:29	10 19:50 ♂ △	♑ 11 4:50	16 21:31 • P 0.653	Eris 24♈17.7 ⚵ 5♌00.8
☿D 1 3:57		12 0:28 ♇ ⚹	♐ 12 15:05	12 22:11 ♇ ☌	♒ 13 15:35	25 1:18 ☾ 1♉51	⚷ 5♈54.9 ⚶ 8♉39.6
☽0S 5 9:27	☿ ♌ 11 19:46	14 1:30 ♆ □	♑ 14 23:05	16 1:02 ♂ ☍	♓ 16 3:49		☽ Mean ☊ 17♋57.3
♃D 11 13:37	♂ ♍ 18 5:18	16 21:38 ☉ ☍	♒ 17 9:19	17 22:34 ♇ ⚹	♈ 18 16:33	1 3:12 ● 8♌37	
♅R 12 2:27	♀ ♍ 21 9:06	18 15:53 ♃ ⚹	♓ 19 21:19	21 4:06 ♀ △	♉ 21 4:37	7 17:31 ☽ 14♏56	1 August 2019
♃⚺♄ 19 14:47	☉ ♍ 23 10:02	22 8:34 ☉ △	♈ 22 10:02	22 21:33 ♇ △	♊ 23 14:34	15 12:29 ○ 22♒24	Julian Day # 43677
☽0N 19 16:41	☿ ♍ 29 7:48	24 14:48 ☿ □	♉ 24 21:42	25 6:58 ☿ ⚹	♋ 25 21:05	23 14:56 ☾ 0♊12	SVP 4♓59'26"
		27 4:28 ♀ ⚹	♊ 27 6:29	27 8:55 ♇ ☍	♌ 27 23:53	30 10:37 ● 6♍47	GC 27♐06.8 ⚴ 21♎36.4
		28 15:24 ♆ □	♋ 29 11:31	29 0:07 ♃ △	♍ 29 23:57		Eris 24♈19.0R ⚵ 19♌41.3
		31 3:32 ☿ ☌	♌ 31 13:18	31 8:46 ♇ △	♎ 31 23:08		⚷ 5♈42.3R ⚶ 18♉58.6
							☽ Mean ☊ 16♋18.8

LONGITUDE — September 2019

Day	Sid.Time	☉	0 hr ☽	Noon ☽	True ☊	☿	♀	♂	⚳	♃	♄	♅	♆	♇
1 Su	10 41 27	8♍46 14	0♎32 50	8♎05 55	16♋16.0	6♍16.0	13♍46.7	9♍05.0	6♐05.1	15♐10.3	14♑08.3	6♉26.8	17♓33.1	20♑52.3
2 M	10 45 23	9 44 19	15 34 38	22 57 59	16R 08.7	8 13.2	15 01.1	9 43.2	6 18.6	15 14.2	14R 06.7	6R 25.8	17R 31.5	20R 51.4
3 Tu	10 49 20	10 42 25	0♏15 10	7♏25 39	16 02.8	10 09.6	16 15.6	10 21.5	6 32.3	15 18.2	14 05.3	6 24.7	17 29.8	20 50.6
4 W	10 53 17	11 40 33	14 29 04	21 25 16	15 58.8	12 05.1	17 30.0	10 59.7	6 46.2	15 22.4	14 03.9	6 23.7	17 28.2	20 49.8
5 Th	10 57 13	12 38 42	28 14 20	4♐56 27	15D 57.0	13 59.6	18 44.4	11 38.0	7 00.4	15 26.8	14 02.6	6 22.5	17 26.6	20 49.0
6 F	11 01 10	13 36 52	11♐31 56	18 01 15	15 56.8	15 53.1	19 58.9	12 16.2	7 14.7	15 31.3	14 01.4	6 21.3	17 24.9	20 48.3
7 Sa	11 05 06	14 35 04	24 24 52	0♑43 20	15 57.5	17 45.5	21 13.3	12 54.5	7 29.3	15 36.0	14 00.3	6 20.1	17 23.3	20 47.5
8 Su	11 09 03	15 33 17	6♑57 13	13 07 06	15R 58.1	19 36.8	22 27.8	13 32.8	7 44.0	15 40.9	13 59.3	6 18.9	17 21.6	20 46.8
9 M	11 12 59	16 31 32	19 13 32	25 17 05	15 57.7	21 26.9	23 42.3	14 11.1	7 58.9	15 46.0	13 58.4	6 17.6	17 20.0	20 46.2
10 Tu	11 16 56	17 29 49	1♒18 14	7♒17 28	15 55.4	23 15.9	24 56.7	14 49.4	8 14.0	15 51.2	13 57.6	6 16.2	17 18.3	20 45.5
11 W	11 20 52	18 28 07	13 15 14	19 11 55	15 50.6	25 03.8	26 11.2	15 27.7	8 29.3	15 56.5	13 56.9	6 14.8	17 16.7	20 44.9
12 Th	11 24 49	19 26 26	25 07 52	1♓03 24	15 43.2	26 50.5	27 25.7	16 06.0	8 44.8	16 02.0	13 56.3	6 13.4	17 15.0	20 44.3
13 F	11 28 46	20 24 48	6♓58 49	12 54 19	15 33.3	28 36.1	28 40.2	16 44.3	9 00.4	16 07.7	13 55.7	6 11.9	17 13.4	20 43.7
14 Sa	11 32 42	21 23 11	18 50 08	24 46 28	15 21.6	0♎20.6	29 54.7	17 22.7	9 16.2	16 13.5	13 55.3	6 10.4	17 11.7	20 43.2
15 Su	11 36 39	22 21 36	0♈43 29	6♈41 21	15 09.1	2 04.0	1♎09.2	18 01.0	9 32.2	16 19.5	13 55.0	6 08.9	17 10.1	20 42.6
16 M	11 40 35	23 20 03	12 40 15	18 40 23	14 56.7	3 46.3	2 23.7	18 39.4	9 48.4	16 25.7	13 54.8	6 07.3	17 08.4	20 42.1
17 Tu	11 44 32	24 18 32	24 41 55	0♉45 05	14 45.5	5 27.6	3 38.2	19 17.7	10 04.7	16 31.9	13D 54.6	6 05.6	17 06.8	20 41.7
18 W	11 48 28	25 17 03	6♉50 08	12 57 22	14 36.5	7 07.8	4 52.7	19 56.1	10 21.2	16 38.4	13 54.6	6 04.0	17 05.1	20 41.2
19 Th	11 52 25	26 15 36	19 07 06	25 19 42	14 30.0	8 46.9	6 07.2	20 34.5	10 37.8	16 45.0	13 54.6	6 02.3	17 03.5	20 40.8
20 F	11 56 21	27 14 12	1♊35 32	7♊55 03	14 26.2	10 25.1	7 21.8	21 12.9	10 54.6	16 51.7	13 54.8	6 00.6	17 01.9	20 40.4
21 Sa	12 00 18	28 12 49	14 18 40	20 46 52	14D 24.7	12 02.2	8 36.3	21 51.4	11 11.6	16 58.6	13 55.1	5 58.8	17 00.3	20 40.1
22 Su	12 04 14	29 11 29	27 20 07	3♋58 49	14R 24.5	13 38.3	9 50.9	22 29.8	11 28.7	17 05.6	13 55.4	5 57.0	16 58.7	20 39.7
23 M	12 08 11	0♎10 11	10♋43 24	17 34 10	14 24.6	15 13.5	11 05.4	23 08.3	11 46.0	17 12.8	13 55.9	5 55.2	16 57.1	20 39.4
24 Tu	12 12 08	1 08 56	24 31 23	1♌35 08	14 23.7	16 47.7	12 20.0	23 46.8	12 03.4	17 20.1	13 56.4	5 53.3	16 55.5	20 39.2
25 W	12 16 04	2 07 43	8♌45 25	16 01 58	14 20.8	18 21.0	13 34.5	24 25.2	12 21.0	17 27.5	13 57.1	5 51.4	16 53.9	20 38.9
26 Th	12 20 01	3 06 31	23 24 23	0♍52 00	14 15.2	19 53.3	14 49.1	25 03.7	12 38.7	17 35.1	13 57.9	5 49.4	16 52.3	20 38.7
27 F	12 23 57	4 05 22	8♍23 59	15 59 14	14 06.9	21 24.7	16 03.7	25 42.3	12 56.6	17 42.8	13 58.7	5 47.5	16 50.7	20 38.5
28 Sa	12 27 54	5 04 15	23 36 32	1♎14 32	13 56.6	22 55.2	17 18.3	26 20.8	13 14.6	17 50.7	13 59.7	5 45.5	16 49.2	20 38.4
29 Su	12 31 50	6 03 11	8♎51 47	16 26 54	13 45.3	24 24.7	18 32.9	26 59.3	13 32.7	17 58.7	14 00.7	5 43.5	16 47.6	20 38.2
30 M	12 35 47	7 02 08	23 58 31	1♏25 26	13 34.5	25 53.3	19 47.4	27 37.9	13 51.0	18 06.8	14 01.8	5 41.4	16 46.1	20 38.1

LONGITUDE — October 2019

Day	Sid.Time	☉	0 hr ☽	Noon ☽	True ☊	☿	♀	♂	⚳	♃	♄	♅	♆	♇
1 Tu	12 39 43	8♎01 07	8♏46 39	16♏01 20	13♋25.3	27♎20.9	21♎02.0	28♍16.5	14♐09.4	18♐15.1	14♑03.1	5♉39.3	16♓44.6	20♑38.1
2 W	12 43 40	9 00 07	23 08 55	0♐09 05	13R 18.6	28 47.6	22 16.6	28 55.1	14 28.0	18 23.4	14 04.4	5R 37.2	16R 43.1	20D 38.0
3 Th	12 47 37	9 59 10	7♐01 42	13 46 51	13 14.6	0♏13.4	23 31.2	29 33.7	14 46.6	18 32.0	14 05.9	5 35.1	16 41.6	20 38.0
4 F	12 51 33	10 58 15	20 24 46	26 55 51	13 12.8	1 38.1	24 45.8	0♎12.3	15 05.4	18 40.6	14 07.4	5 32.9	16 40.1	20 38.0
5 Sa	12 55 30	11 57 21	3♑20 35	9♑39 32	13 12.4	3 01.9	26 00.4	0 50.9	15 24.4	18 49.4	14 09.1	5 30.7	16 38.6	20 38.1
6 Su	12 59 26	12 56 29	15 53 18	22 02 34	13 12.3	4 24.6	27 15.0	1 29.6	15 43.4	18 58.3	14 10.8	5 28.5	16 37.2	20 38.2
7 M	13 03 23	13 55 39	28 07 58	4♒10 10	13 11.3	5 46.2	28 29.6	2 08.2	16 02.6	19 07.3	14 12.6	5 26.3	16 35.8	20 38.3
8 Tu	13 07 19	14 54 50	10♒09 48	16 07 27	13 08.4	7 06.7	29 44.2	2 46.9	16 21.8	19 16.4	14 14.6	5 24.1	16 34.4	20 38.4
9 W	13 11 16	15 54 04	22 03 43	27 59 07	13 02.8	8 26.0	0♏58.7	3 25.6	16 41.2	19 25.6	14 16.6	5 21.8	16 33.0	20 38.6
10 Th	13 15 12	16 53 19	3♓54 07	9♓49 08	12 54.4	9 44.1	2 13.3	4 04.3	17 00.7	19 35.0	14 18.7	5 19.5	16 31.6	20 38.8
11 F	13 19 09	17 52 36	15 44 35	21 40 46	12 43.3	11 00.9	3 27.9	4 43.0	17 20.4	19 44.4	14 20.9	5 17.2	16 30.2	20 39.0
12 Sa	13 23 06	18 51 55	27 37 57	3♈36 23	12 30.1	12 16.3	4 42.5	5 21.7	17 40.1	19 54.0	14 23.2	5 14.9	16 28.9	20 39.3
13 Su	13 27 02	19 51 15	9♈36 14	15 37 41	12 16.0	13 30.3	5 57.0	6 00.4	17 59.9	20 03.7	14 25.6	5 12.5	16 27.6	20 39.6
14 M	13 30 59	20 50 38	21 40 51	27 45 49	12 01.9	14 42.7	7 11.6	6 39.2	18 19.9	20 13.5	14 28.1	5 10.2	16 26.3	20 39.9
15 Tu	13 34 55	21 50 03	3♉52 42	10♉01 36	11 49.2	15 53.4	8 26.2	7 18.0	18 39.9	20 23.4	14 30.6	5 07.8	16 25.0	20 40.2
16 W	13 38 52	22 49 31	16 12 36	22 25 50	11 38.7	17 02.2	9 40.7	7 56.8	19 00.1	20 33.4	14 33.3	5 05.4	16 23.7	20 40.6
17 Th	13 42 48	23 49 00	28 41 27	4♊59 35	11 31.1	18 09.1	10 55.3	8 35.6	19 20.3	20 43.6	14 36.1	5 03.0	16 22.5	20 41.0
18 F	13 46 45	24 48 32	11♊20 29	17 44 21	11 26.5	19 13.8	12 09.9	9 14.4	19 40.7	20 53.8	14 38.9	5 00.6	16 21.3	20 41.5
19 Sa	13 50 41	25 48 06	24 11 28	0♋42 08	11D 24.4	20 16.1	13 24.5	9 53.3	20 01.1	21 04.1	14 41.9	4 58.2	16 20.1	20 41.9
20 Su	13 54 38	26 47 42	7♋16 40	13 55 22	11 24.1	21 15.7	14 39.0	10 32.2	20 21.6	21 14.5	14 44.9	4 55.8	16 18.9	20 42.4
21 M	13 58 35	27 47 20	20 38 35	27 26 34	11R 24.3	22 12.6	15 53.6	11 11.1	20 42.3	21 25.0	14 48.0	4 53.3	16 17.8	20 42.9
22 Tu	14 02 31	28 47 01	4♌19 35	11♌17 47	11 23.7	23 06.2	17 08.2	11 50.0	21 03.0	21 35.7	14 51.2	4 50.9	16 16.7	20 43.5
23 W	14 06 28	29 46 44	18 21 14	25 29 52	11 21.4	23 56.4	18 22.7	12 28.9	21 23.8	21 46.4	14 54.5	4 48.5	16 15.6	20 44.1
24 Th	14 10 24	0♏46 30	2♍43 28	10♍01 38	11 16.5	24 42.7	19 37.3	13 07.9	21 44.7	21 57.2	14 57.9	4 46.0	16 14.5	20 44.7
25 F	14 14 21	1 46 17	17 23 51	24 49 20	11 09.1	25 24.7	20 51.9	13 46.8	22 05.7	22 08.1	15 01.4	4 43.5	16 13.4	20 45.3
26 Sa	14 18 17	2 46 07	2♎17 12	9♎46 23	10 59.6	26 01.9	22 06.5	14 25.8	22 26.8	22 19.1	15 04.9	4 41.1	16 12.4	20 46.0
27 Su	14 22 14	3 45 59	17 15 46	24 44 08	10 49.1	26 33.9	23 21.0	15 04.8	22 48.0	22 30.2	15 08.5	4 38.6	16 11.4	20 46.7
28 M	14 26 10	4 45 52	2♏10 16	9♏33 04	10 38.8	27 00.2	24 35.6	15 43.9	23 09.3	22 41.4	15 12.3	4 36.1	16 10.4	20 47.4
29 Tu	14 30 07	5 45 48	16 51 28	24 04 35	10 30.0	27 20.0	25 50.2	16 22.9	23 30.6	22 52.6	15 16.1	4 33.7	16 09.5	20 48.2
30 W	14 34 03	6 45 46	1♐11 43	8♐12 21	10 23.5	27 32.9	27 04.7	17 02.0	23 52.0	23 04.0	15 20.0	4 31.2	16 08.6	20 49.0
31 Th	14 38 00	7 45 45	15 06 10	21 53 03	10 19.6	27R 38.2	28 19.3	17 41.1	24 13.5	23 15.4	15 23.9	4 28.7	16 07.7	20 49.8

Astro Data (Dy Hr Mn)	Planet Ingress (Dy Hr Mn)	Last Aspect (Dy Hr Mn)	☽ Ingress (Dy Hr Mn)	Last Aspect (Dy Hr Mn)	☽ Ingress (Dy Hr Mn)	☽ Phases & Eclipses (Dy Hr Mn)
☽0S 1 18:01	☿ ♎ 14 7:14	2 8:34 ♇ □	♏ 2 23:35	2 9:46 ♂ ⚹	♐ 2 11:44	6 3:10 ☽ 13♐15
☿0S 15 10:26	♀ ♎ 14 13:43	4 10:58 ♇ ⚹	♐ 5 3:08	4 7:34 ♀ ⚹	♑ 4 17:43	14 4:33 ○ 21♓05
☽0N 15 22:02	⊙ ♎ 23 7:50	6 16:03 ♀ □	♑ 7 10:37	6 23:25 ♀ □	♒ 7 3:42	22 2:41 ☾ 28♊49
♀0S 16 22:06		9 8:30 ♀ △	♒ 9 21:24	8 18:27 ♃ ⚹	♓ 9 16:05	28 18:26 ● 5♎20
♄ D 18 8:47	☿ ♏ 3 8:14	11 5:22 ♃ ⚹	♓ 12 9:52	11 9:55 ♇ ⚹	♈ 12 4:46	
♃□♆ 21 16:44	♂ ♎ 4 4:22	14 4:33 ⊙ ☍	♈ 14 22:32	13 21:59 ♇ □	♉ 14 16:24	5 16:47 ☽ 12♑09
⊙0S 23 7:50	♀ ♏ 8 17:06	16 16:03 ♇ □	♉ 17 10:31	16 8:37 ♇ △	♊ 17 2:30	13 21:08 ○ 20♈14
☽0S 29 4:25	⊙ ♏ 23 17:20	19 13:57 ⊙ △	♊ 19 20:58	19 2:14 ⊙ △	♋ 19 10:43	21 12:39 ☾ 27♋49
♇ D 3 6:39		22 2:41 ⊙ □	♋ 22 4:50	21 12:39 ⊙ □	♌ 21 16:29	28 3:38 ● 4♏25
♂0S 7 14:18		23 22:05 ♂ ⚹	♌ 24 9:19	23 9:14 ♀ □	♍ 23 19:29	
☽0N 13 4:02		25 16:14 ☿ ⚹	♍ 26 10:37	25 12:59 ☿ ⚹	♎ 25 20:20	
♃⚻♅ 14 5:26		28 3:58 ♂ ☌	♎ 28 10:03	27 8:22 ♃ ⚹	♏ 27 20:29	
♃×♇ 17 5:45		30 2:06 ☿ ☌	♏ 30 9:42	29 17:34 ☿ ☌	♐ 29 21:58	
☽0S 26 15:08						
☿ R 31 15:42						

Astro Data

1 September 2019
Julian Day # 43708
SVP 4♓59'22"
GC 27♐06.8 ⚴ 2♏15.4
Eris 24♈10.7R ⚵ 3♍48.3
⚷ 4♈45.6R ⚶ 25♉54.3
☽ Mean ☊ 14♋40.3

1 October 2019
Julian Day # 43738
SVP 4♓59'20"
GC 27♐06.9 ⚴ 14♏02.2
Eris 23♈55.7R ⚵ 16♍44.4
⚷ 3♈27.2R ⚶ 27♉27.2R
☽ Mean ☊ 13♋05.0

November 2019 LONGITUDE

Day	Sid.Time	☉	0 hr ☽	Noon ☽	True ☊	☿	♀	♂	⚳	♃	♄	♅	♆	♇
1 F	14 41 57	8♏45 46	28♐33 02	5♑06 20	10♋18.0	27♏35.2	29♏33.9	18♎20.2	24♐35.1	23♐26.9	15♑28.0	4♉26.3	16♓06.9	20♑50.6
2 Sa	14 45 53	9 45 49	11♑33 16	17 54 18	10D 18.1	27R 23.5	0♐48.4	18 59.3	24 56.8	23 38.5	15 32.1	4R 23.8	16R 06.0	20 51.5
3 Su	14 49 50	10 45 54	24 09 57	0♒20 48	10R 18.8	27 02.6	2 03.0	19 38.4	25 18.5	23 50.2	15 36.3	4 21.4	16 05.2	20 52.4
4 M	14 53 46	11 46 00	6♒27 30	12 30 40	10 19.3	26 32.1	3 17.5	20 17.6	25 40.3	24 02.0	15 40.6	4 18.9	16 04.5	20 53.3
5 Tu	14 57 43	12 46 07	18 31 00	24 29 08	10 18.4	25 51.9	4 32.1	20 56.7	26 02.2	24 13.8	15 44.9	4 16.5	16 03.7	20 54.3
6 W	15 01 39	13 46 16	0♓25 42	6♓21 21	10 15.5	25 02.2	5 46.6	21 35.9	26 24.1	24 25.7	15 49.4	4 14.1	16 03.0	20 55.3
7 Th	15 05 36	14 46 27	12 16 39	18 12 08	10 10.3	24 03.7	7 01.1	22 15.1	26 46.1	24 37.7	15 53.9	4 11.7	16 02.3	20 56.3
8 F	15 09 33	15 46 39	24 08 20	0♈05 40	10 02.9	22 57.2	8 15.6	22 54.3	27 08.2	24 49.7	15 58.5	4 09.3	16 01.7	20 57.3
9 Sa	15 13 29	16 46 52	6♈04 33	12 05 20	9 53.7	21 44.3	9 30.1	23 33.6	27 30.3	25 01.8	16 03.1	4 06.9	16 01.1	20 58.4
10 Su	15 17 26	17 47 08	18 08 18	24 13 40	9 43.6	20 26.8	10 44.6	24 12.8	27 52.5	25 14.0	16 07.8	4 04.5	16 00.5	20 59.5
11 M	15 21 22	18 47 25	0♉21 38	6♉32 19	9 33.6	19 07.1	11 59.1	24 52.1	28 14.8	25 26.2	16 12.6	4 02.1	15 59.9	21 00.6
12 Tu	15 25 19	19 47 43	12 45 48	19 02 08	9 24.4	17 47.6	13 13.6	25 31.4	28 37.1	25 38.5	16 17.5	3 59.8	15 59.4	21 01.7
13 W	15 29 15	20 48 04	25 21 21	1♊43 25	9 17.1	16 30.9	14 28.1	26 10.7	28 59.5	25 50.9	16 22.4	3 57.4	15 58.9	21 02.9
14 Th	15 33 12	21 48 26	8♊08 20	14 36 05	9 12.0	15 19.6	15 42.5	26 50.1	29 21.9	26 03.4	16 27.4	3 55.1	15 58.5	21 04.1
15 F	15 37 08	22 48 50	21 06 38	27 39 59	9D 09.2	14 15.9	16 57.0	27 29.4	29 44.4	26 15.9	16 32.5	3 52.8	15 58.1	21 05.3
16 Sa	15 41 05	23 49 16	4♋16 10	10♋55 12	9 08.6	13 21.5	18 11.5	28 08.8	0♑07.0	26 28.4	16 37.6	3 50.6	15 57.7	21 06.5
17 Su	15 45 02	24 49 43	17 37 07	24 22 00	9 09.4	12 37.7	19 25.9	28 48.2	0 29.6	26 41.0	16 42.9	3 48.3	15 57.3	21 07.8
18 M	15 48 58	25 50 13	1♌09 54	8♌00 55	9 10.7	12 05.4	20 40.4	29 27.7	0 52.2	26 53.7	16 48.1	3 46.1	15 57.0	21 09.1
19 Tu	15 52 55	26 50 44	14 55 04	21 52 25	9R 11.7	11 44.7	21 54.8	0♏07.1	1 15.0	27 06.5	16 53.4	3 43.8	15 56.7	21 10.4
20 W	15 56 51	27 51 17	28 52 56	5♍56 33	9 11.6	11D 35.7	23 09.2	0 46.6	1 37.7	27 19.2	16 58.8	3 41.7	15 56.4	21 11.7
21 Th	16 00 48	28 51 52	13♍03 05	20 12 20	9 09.7	11 37.9	24 23.7	1 26.1	2 00.5	27 32.1	17 04.3	3 39.5	15 56.2	21 13.1
22 F	16 04 44	29 52 28	27 23 56	4♎37 26	9 06.0	11 50.6	25 38.1	2 05.6	2 23.4	27 45.0	17 09.8	3 37.3	15 56.0	21 14.4
23 Sa	16 08 41	0♐53 06	11♎52 19	19 07 55	9 00.8	12 13.0	26 52.5	2 45.1	2 46.3	27 57.9	17 15.4	3 35.2	15 55.9	21 15.8
24 Su	16 12 37	1 53 46	26 23 31	3♏38 22	8 54.9	12 44.4	28 06.9	3 24.7	3 09.3	28 10.9	17 21.0	3 33.1	15 55.7	21 17.3
25 M	16 16 34	2 54 28	10♏51 40	18 02 36	8 49.0	13 23.7	29 21.3	4 04.3	3 32.3	28 24.0	17 26.7	3 31.1	15 55.6	21 18.7
26 Tu	16 20 31	3 55 11	25 10 26	2♐14 26	8 43.9	14 10.1	0♑35.7	4 43.9	3 55.4	28 37.0	17 32.4	3 29.0	15 55.6	21 20.2
27 W	16 24 27	4 55 56	9♐14 01	16 08 42	8 40.3	15 02.8	1 50.1	5 23.5	4 18.5	28 50.2	17 38.2	3 27.0	15D 55.6	21 21.7
28 Th	16 28 24	5 56 41	22 58 04	29 41 54	8D 38.4	16 01.0	3 04.5	6 03.2	4 41.7	29 03.4	17 44.1	3 25.0	15 55.6	21 23.2
29 F	16 32 20	6 57 28	6♑20 05	12♑52 37	8 38.1	17 04.0	4 18.9	6 42.8	5 04.9	29 16.6	17 50.0	3 23.1	15 55.6	21 24.7
30 Sa	16 36 17	7 58 16	19 19 38	25 41 22	8 39.1	18 11.1	5 33.2	7 22.5	5 28.1	29 29.8	17 56.0	3 21.2	15 55.7	21 26.3

December 2019 LONGITUDE

Day	Sid.Time	☉	0 hr ☽	Noon ☽	True ☊	☿	♀	♂	⚳	♃	♄	♅	♆	♇
1 Su	16 40 13	8♐59 05	1♒58 09	8♒10 24	8♋40.9	19♏21.8	6♑47.6	8♏02.2	5♑51.4	29♐43.1	18♑02.0	3♉19.3	15♓55.8	21♑27.9
2 M	16 44 10	9 59 55	14 18 35	20 23 14	8 42.6	20 35.5	8 01.9	8 41.9	6 14.7	29 56.5	18 08.0	3R 17.5	15 56.0	21 29.4
3 Tu	16 48 06	11 00 46	26 24 55	2♓24 13	8R 43.9	21 51.9	9 16.2	9 21.7	6 38.0	0♑09.8	18 14.1	3 15.7	15 56.2	21 31.1
4 W	16 52 03	12 01 38	8♓21 46	14 18 11	8 44.2	23 10.6	10 30.5	10 01.4	7 01.4	0 23.2	18 20.3	3 13.9	15 56.4	21 32.7
5 Th	16 56 00	13 02 30	20 14 05	26 10 04	8 43.4	24 31.3	11 44.8	10 41.2	7 24.8	0 36.7	18 26.5	3 12.1	15 56.7	21 34.3
6 F	16 59 56	14 03 24	2♈06 44	8♈04 38	8 41.3	25 53.6	12 59.0	11 21.0	7 48.3	0 50.2	18 32.7	3 10.4	15 57.0	21 36.0
7 Sa	17 03 53	15 04 18	14 04 19	20 06 16	8 38.3	27 17.3	14 13.3	12 00.8	8 11.8	1 03.6	18 39.0	3 08.8	15 57.3	21 37.7
8 Su	17 07 49	16 05 13	26 10 56	2♉18 41	8 34.7	28 42.3	15 27.5	12 40.6	8 35.3	1 17.2	18 45.4	3 07.2	15 57.6	21 39.4
9 M	17 11 46	17 06 08	8♉29 52	14 44 45	8 31.0	0♐08.3	16 41.7	13 20.5	8 58.8	1 30.7	18 51.7	3 05.6	15 58.0	21 41.1
10 Tu	17 15 42	18 07 05	21 03 32	27 26 20	8 27.6	1 35.2	17 55.9	14 00.4	9 22.4	1 44.3	18 58.1	3 04.0	15 58.5	21 42.8
11 W	17 19 39	19 08 03	3♊53 14	10♊24 13	8 25.0	3 02.9	19 10.0	14 40.3	9 46.0	1 57.9	19 04.6	3 02.5	15 58.9	21 44.6
12 Th	17 23 35	20 09 01	16 59 14	23 38 08	8 23.4	4 31.2	20 24.1	15 20.2	10 09.6	2 11.5	19 11.1	3 01.1	15 59.4	21 46.3
13 F	17 27 32	21 10 00	0♋20 45	7♋06 51	8D 22.8	6 00.1	21 38.2	16 00.1	10 33.2	2 25.2	19 17.6	2 59.7	16 00.0	21 48.1
14 Sa	17 31 29	22 11 00	13 56 12	20 48 29	8 23.2	7 29.5	22 52.3	16 40.1	10 56.9	2 38.9	19 24.2	2 58.3	16 00.5	21 49.9
15 Su	17 35 25	23 12 01	27 43 26	4♌40 43	8 24.1	8 59.4	24 06.4	17 20.1	11 20.6	2 52.6	19 30.8	2 57.0	16 01.1	21 51.7
16 M	17 39 22	24 13 03	11♌40 03	18 41 07	8 25.3	10 29.6	25 20.4	18 00.1	11 44.3	3 06.3	19 37.4	2 55.7	16 01.8	21 53.5
17 Tu	17 43 18	25 14 06	25 43 39	2♍47 20	8 26.4	12 00.2	26 34.5	18 40.1	12 08.1	3 20.0	19 44.1	2 54.4	16 02.5	21 55.4
18 W	17 47 15	26 15 09	9♍51 55	16 57 07	8R 27.1	13 31.1	27 48.4	19 20.2	12 31.8	3 33.7	19 50.8	2 53.2	16 03.2	21 57.2
19 Th	17 51 11	27 16 14	24 02 41	1♎08 20	8 27.2	15 02.3	29 02.4	20 00.3	12 55.6	3 47.5	19 57.5	2 52.1	16 03.9	21 59.1
20 F	17 55 08	28 17 20	8♎13 50	15 18 52	8 26.8	16 33.7	0♒16.4	20 40.4	13 19.4	4 01.3	20 04.2	2 50.9	16 04.7	22 00.9
21 Sa	17 59 04	29 18 26	22 23 10	29 26 25	8 26.0	18 05.4	1 30.3	21 20.5	13 43.2	4 15.1	20 11.0	2 49.9	16 05.5	22 02.8
22 Su	18 03 01	0♑19 33	6♏28 18	13♏28 29	8 24.9	19 37.4	2 44.2	22 00.6	14 07.1	4 28.9	20 17.8	2 48.9	16 06.3	22 04.7
23 M	18 06 58	1 20 41	20 26 37	27 22 23	8 24.0	21 09.5	3 58.0	22 40.8	14 31.0	4 42.7	20 24.7	2 47.9	16 07.2	22 06.6
24 Tu	18 10 54	2 21 50	4♐15 26	11♐05 27	8 23.2	22 42.0	5 11.9	23 21.0	14 54.8	4 56.5	20 31.5	2 47.0	16 08.1	22 08.5
25 W	18 14 51	3 22 59	17 52 07	24 35 13	8 22.8	24 14.6	6 25.7	24 01.2	15 18.7	5 10.3	20 38.4	2 46.1	16 09.0	22 10.4
26 Th	18 18 47	4 24 09	1♑14 29	7♑49 45	8D 22.6	25 47.5	7 39.5	24 41.5	15 42.6	5 24.2	20 45.3	2 45.3	16 10.0	22 12.4
27 F	18 22 44	5 25 19	14 20 56	20 47 58	8 22.7	27 20.6	8 53.2	25 21.7	16 06.6	5 38.0	20 52.3	2 44.5	16 11.0	22 14.3
28 Sa	18 26 40	6 26 29	27 10 52	3♒29 42	8 22.9	28 54.0	10 06.9	26 02.0	16 30.5	5 51.8	20 59.2	2 43.8	16 12.0	22 16.3
29 Su	18 30 37	7 27 39	9♒44 38	15 55 52	8R 23.1	0♑27.7	11 20.6	26 42.3	16 54.4	6 05.6	21 06.2	2 43.1	16 13.1	22 18.2
30 M	18 34 33	8 28 49	22 03 41	28 08 26	8 23.1	2 01.6	12 34.2	27 22.6	17 18.4	6 19.5	21 13.2	2 42.5	16 14.2	22 20.2
31 Tu	18 38 30	9 29 59	4♓10 29	10♓10 17	8 23.1	3 35.8	13 47.8	28 02.9	17 42.4	6 33.3	21 20.2	2 41.9	16 15.3	22 22.2

Astro Data

	Dy Hr Mn
♄⚹♆	9 2:45
☽0N	9 11:31
☿D	20 19:13
☽0S	23 0:15
♆D	27 12:32
☽0N	6 20:12
♃△♅	15 19:01
☽0S	20 6:51

Planet Ingress

	Dy Hr Mn
♀ ♐	1 20:25
⚳ ♑	16 4:36
♂ ♏	19 7:40
☉ ♐	22 14:59
♀ ♑	26 0:28
♃ ♑	2 18:20
☿ ♐	9 9:42
♀ ♒	20 6:41
☉ ♑	22 4:19
☿ ♑	29 4:55

Last Aspect / ☽ Ingress

Last Aspect Dy Hr Mn		☽ Ingress Dy Hr Mn
31 14:29 ♃☌	♑	1 2:38
3 5:46 ☿⚹	♒	3 11:19
5 14:37 ☿□	♓	5 23:08
8 1:13 ♃□	♈	8 11:49
10 14:00 ♃△	♉	10 23:18
12 15:48 ♇△	♊	13 8:46
15 11:40 ♂△	♋	15 16:15
17 20:14 ♂□	♌	17 21:57
19 21:11 ☉□	♍	20 1:54
22 3:31 ☉⚹	♎	22 4:20
24 2:49 ♃⚹	♏	24 5:58
25 17:30 ♇⚹	♐	26 8:11
28 10:50 ♃☌	♑	28 12:33
30 3:57 ♇☌	♒	30 20:13

Last Aspect / ☽ Ingress

Last Aspect Dy Hr Mn		☽ Ingress Dy Hr Mn
2 12:27 ☿□	♓	3 7:11
5 8:15 ☿△	♈	5 19:44
7 15:01 ♇□	♉	8 7:29
10 1:13 ♇△	♊	10 16:47
12 5:12 ☉☍	♋	12 23:23
14 15:56 ♀☍	♌	15 3:56
16 22:10 ☉△	♍	17 7:16
19 8:07 ♀△	♎	19 10:04
21 11:45 ☉⚹	♏	21 12:57
23 3:27 ♂☌	♐	23 16:34
25 11:18 ☿☌	♑	25 21:45
27 21:03 ♂⚹	♒	28 5:21
30 10:24 ♂□	♓	30 15:41

☽ Phases & Eclipses

Dy Hr Mn	
4 10:23	☽ 11♒42
12 13:34	○ 19♉52
19 21:11	☾ 27♌14
26 15:06	● 4♐03
4 6:58	☽ 11♓49
12 5:12	○ 19♊52
19 4:57	☾ 26♍58
26 5:13	● 4♑07
26 5:17:42	A 03'39"

Astro Data

1 November 2019
Julian Day # 43769
SVP 4♓59'16"
GC 27♐07.0 ⚴ 27♏02.1
Eris 23♈37.3R ⚵ 29♍02.0
⚷ 2♈11.2R ⚶ 22♉27.5R
☽ Mean ☊ 11♋26.5

1 December 2019
Julian Day # 43799
SVP 4♓59'11"
GC 27♐07.0 ⚴ 9♐55.0
Eris 23♈22.1R ⚵ 9♎21.5
⚷ 1♈29.8R ⚶ 15♉03.8R
☽ Mean ☊ 9♋51.1

LONGITUDE — January 2020

Day	Sid.Time	☉	0 hr ☽	Noon ☽	True ☊	☿	♀	♂	⚳	♃	♄	♅	♆	♇
1 W	18 42 27	10♑31 09	16♓08 19	22♓05 06	8♋22.9	5♑10.3	15♒01.3	28♏43.3	18♑06.3	6♑47.1	21♑27.2	2♉41.4	16♓16.5	22♑24.1
2 Th	18 46 23	11 32 19	28 01 11	3♈57 07	8D 22.8	6 45.1	16 14.8	29 23.6	18 30.3	7 01.0	21 34.2	2R 40.9	16 17.6	22 26.1
3 F	18 50 20	12 33 29	9♈53 31	15 50 57	8 22.7	8 20.2	17 28.3	0♐04.0	18 54.3	7 14.8	21 41.3	2 40.5	16 18.9	22 28.1
4 Sa	18 54 16	13 34 38	21 50 02	27 51 21	8 22.9	9 55.7	18 41.7	0 44.4	19 18.2	7 28.6	21 48.3	2 40.1	16 20.1	22 30.1
5 Su	18 58 13	14 35 48	3♉55 28	10♉02 56	8 23.4	11 31.5	19 55.0	1 24.8	19 42.2	7 42.4	21 55.4	2 39.8	16 21.4	22 32.1
6 M	19 02 09	15 36 57	16 14 16	22 29 56	8 24.1	13 07.7	21 08.3	2 05.3	20 06.2	7 56.2	22 02.5	2 39.5	16 22.7	22 34.1
7 Tu	19 06 06	16 38 05	28 50 19	5♊15 47	8 24.9	14 44.2	22 21.6	2 45.7	20 30.2	8 09.9	22 09.6	2 39.3	16 24.0	22 36.1
8 W	19 10 02	17 39 14	11♊46 33	18 22 49	8 25.7	16 21.2	23 34.8	3 26.2	20 54.2	8 23.7	22 16.7	2 39.2	16 25.4	22 38.1
9 Th	19 13 59	18 40 22	25 04 36	1♋51 51	8R 26.2	17 58.6	24 47.9	4 06.7	21 18.2	8 37.4	22 23.8	2 39.1	16 26.8	22 40.1
10 F	19 17 56	19 41 30	8♋44 25	15 42 00	8 26.2	19 36.4	26 01.0	4 47.2	21 42.1	8 51.2	22 30.9	2D 39.0	16 28.2	22 42.1
11 Sa	19 21 52	20 42 37	22 44 11	29 50 27	8 25.5	21 14.6	27 14.0	5 27.8	22 06.1	9 04.9	22 38.0	2 39.0	16 29.6	22 44.1
12 Su	19 25 49	21 43 44	7♌00 13	14♌12 48	8 24.2	22 53.3	28 26.9	6 08.4	22 30.1	9 18.6	22 45.1	2 39.0	16 31.1	22 46.2
13 M	19 29 45	22 44 51	21 27 27	28 43 25	8 22.4	24 32.4	29 39.8	6 49.0	22 54.1	9 32.3	22 52.2	2 39.1	16 32.6	22 48.2
14 Tu	19 33 42	23 45 58	5♍59 57	13♍16 19	8 20.4	26 12.0	0♓52.6	7 29.6	23 18.0	9 45.9	22 59.3	2 39.3	16 34.1	22 50.2
15 W	19 37 38	24 47 05	20 31 49	27 45 50	8 18.6	27 52.1	2 05.4	8 10.2	23 42.0	9 59.6	23 06.4	2 39.5	16 35.7	22 52.2
16 Th	19 41 35	25 48 11	4♎57 49	12♎07 20	8 17.3	29 32.6	3 18.1	8 50.9	24 05.9	10 13.2	23 13.5	2 39.8	16 37.3	22 54.2
17 F	19 45 32	26 49 18	19 14 00	26 17 34	8D 16.8	1♒13.6	4 30.7	9 31.6	24 29.9	10 26.8	23 20.6	2 40.1	16 38.9	22 56.2
18 Sa	19 49 28	27 50 24	3♏17 51	10♏14 42	8 17.2	2 55.1	5 43.3	10 12.3	24 53.8	10 40.3	23 27.7	2 40.4	16 40.5	22 58.2
19 Su	19 53 25	28 51 30	17 08 06	23 58 01	8 18.4	4 36.9	6 55.8	10 53.0	25 17.8	10 53.9	23 34.8	2 40.8	16 42.1	23 00.2
20 M	19 57 21	29 52 36	0♐44 29	7♐27 34	8 19.9	6 19.2	8 08.2	11 33.7	25 41.7	11 07.4	23 41.9	2 41.3	16 43.8	23 02.2
21 Tu	20 01 18	0♒53 41	14 07 19	20 43 48	8 21.4	8 01.8	9 20.5	12 14.5	26 05.6	11 20.9	23 49.0	2 41.8	16 45.5	23 04.2
22 W	20 05 14	1 54 46	27 17 06	3♑47 17	8R 22.2	9 44.7	10 32.8	12 55.3	26 29.5	11 34.3	23 56.1	2 42.4	16 47.3	23 06.2
23 Th	20 09 11	2 55 50	10♑14 25	16 38 31	8 22.0	11 27.9	11 45.0	13 36.1	26 53.4	11 47.7	24 03.1	2 43.0	16 49.0	23 08.2
24 F	20 13 07	3 56 54	22 59 41	29 17 56	8 20.5	13 11.3	12 57.1	14 16.9	27 17.3	12 01.1	24 10.2	2 43.7	16 50.8	23 10.2
25 Sa	20 17 04	4 57 57	5♒33 20	11♒45 58	8 17.5	14 54.8	14 09.1	14 57.8	27 41.2	12 14.4	24 17.2	2 44.4	16 52.6	23 12.2
26 Su	20 21 01	5 58 59	17 55 55	24 03 19	8 13.3	16 38.2	15 21.0	15 38.6	28 05.0	12 27.7	24 24.3	2 45.2	16 54.4	23 14.2
27 M	20 24 57	7 00 00	0♓08 17	6♓11 01	8 08.1	18 21.5	16 32.9	16 19.5	28 28.8	12 41.0	24 31.3	2 46.0	16 56.2	23 16.2
28 Tu	20 28 54	8 01 00	12 11 44	18 10 42	8 02.6	20 04.4	17 44.6	17 00.4	28 52.6	12 54.2	24 38.3	2 46.9	16 58.1	23 18.1
29 W	20 32 50	9 01 59	24 08 14	0♈04 41	7 57.3	21 46.8	18 56.3	17 41.3	29 16.4	13 07.4	24 45.3	2 47.8	16 59.9	23 20.1
30 Th	20 36 47	10 02 57	6♈00 27	11 55 59	7 52.8	23 28.5	20 07.9	18 22.2	29 40.2	13 20.5	24 52.2	2 48.8	17 01.8	23 22.0
31 F	20 40 43	11 03 54	17 51 45	23 48 18	7 49.7	25 09.2	21 19.3	19 03.2	0♒03.9	13 33.6	24 59.2	2 49.8	17 03.8	23 24.0

LONGITUDE — February 2020

Day	Sid.Time	☉	0 hr ☽	Noon ☽	True ☊	☿	♀	♂	⚳	♃	♄	♅	♆	♇
1 Sa	20 44 40	12♒04 49	29♈46 10	5♉45 56	7♋48.1	26♒48.4	22♓30.7	19♐44.1	0♒27.7	13♑46.7	25♑06.1	2♉50.9	17♓05.7	23♑25.9
2 Su	20 48 36	13 05 44	11♉48 12	17 53 36	7D 48.0	28 26.0	23 41.9	20 25.1	0 51.4	13 59.7	25 13.0	2 52.1	17 07.6	23 27.8
3 M	20 52 33	14 06 37	24 02 44	0♊16 12	7 49.0	0♓01.5	24 53.0	21 06.1	1 15.0	14 12.6	25 19.8	2 53.2	17 09.6	23 29.7
4 Tu	20 56 30	15 07 28	6♊34 35	12 58 25	7 50.7	1 34.3	26 04.1	21 47.1	1 38.7	14 25.5	25 26.7	2 54.5	17 11.6	23 31.6
5 W	21 00 26	16 08 18	19 28 11	26 04 16	7R 52.1	3 04.0	27 14.9	22 28.2	2 02.3	14 38.3	25 33.5	2 55.8	17 13.6	23 33.5
6 Th	21 04 23	17 09 07	2♋46 59	9♋36 29	7 52.7	4 30.0	28 25.7	23 09.2	2 25.9	14 51.1	25 40.3	2 57.1	17 15.6	23 35.4
7 F	21 08 19	18 09 55	16 32 49	23 35 49	7 51.6	5 51.6	29 36.4	23 50.3	2 49.5	15 03.9	25 47.1	2 58.5	17 17.7	23 37.3
8 Sa	21 12 16	19 10 41	0♌45 10	8♌00 22	7 48.5	7 08.1	0♈46.9	24 31.4	3 13.0	15 16.5	25 53.8	2 59.9	17 19.7	23 39.1
9 Su	21 16 12	20 11 25	15 20 43	22 45 21	7 43.6	8 18.9	1 57.3	25 12.5	3 36.5	15 29.2	26 00.6	3 01.4	17 21.8	23 41.0
10 M	21 20 09	21 12 09	0♍13 14	7♍43 15	7 37.1	9 23.1	3 07.5	25 53.6	4 00.0	15 41.7	26 07.2	3 02.9	17 23.9	23 42.8
11 Tu	21 24 05	22 12 51	15 14 13	22 44 55	7 30.0	10 20.1	4 17.6	26 34.7	4 23.4	15 54.2	26 13.9	3 04.5	17 26.0	23 44.7
12 W	21 28 02	23 13 32	0♎14 13	7♎40 59	7 23.3	11 09.0	5 27.6	27 15.9	4 46.8	16 06.7	26 20.5	3 06.1	17 28.1	23 46.5
13 Th	21 31 59	24 14 12	15 04 18	22 23 24	7 17.8	11 49.2	6 37.4	27 57.1	5 10.2	16 19.0	26 27.1	3 07.7	17 30.2	23 48.3
14 F	21 35 55	25 14 50	29 37 38	6♏46 36	7 14.1	12 20.0	7 47.1	28 38.3	5 33.5	16 31.3	26 33.6	3 09.4	17 32.3	23 50.0
15 Sa	21 39 52	26 15 28	13♏50 01	20 47 48	7D 12.5	12 41.1	8 56.6	29 19.5	5 56.9	16 43.6	26 40.2	3 11.2	17 34.5	23 51.8
16 Su	21 43 48	27 16 05	27 39 59	4♐26 42	7 12.6	12R 51.9	10 06.0	0♑00.8	6 20.1	16 55.8	26 46.6	3 13.0	17 36.6	23 53.5
17 M	21 47 45	28 16 40	11♐08 13	17 44 50	7 13.6	12 52.3	11 15.3	0 42.0	6 43.4	17 07.9	26 53.1	3 14.8	17 38.8	23 55.3
18 Tu	21 51 41	29 17 14	24 16 53	0♑44 43	7R 14.6	12 42.2	12 24.3	1 23.3	7 06.6	17 19.9	26 59.5	3 16.7	17 41.0	23 57.0
19 W	21 55 38	0♓17 47	7♑08 43	13 29 14	7 14.6	12 22.0	13 33.3	2 04.6	7 29.7	17 31.9	27 05.8	3 18.6	17 43.2	23 58.7
20 Th	21 59 34	1 18 19	19 46 37	26 01 09	7 12.7	11 52.2	14 42.0	2 45.9	7 52.9	17 43.8	27 12.2	3 20.6	17 45.4	24 00.4
21 F	22 03 31	2 18 49	2♒13 08	8♒22 49	7 08.3	11 13.3	15 50.6	3 27.3	8 15.9	17 55.6	27 18.4	3 22.6	17 47.6	24 02.1
22 Sa	22 07 28	3 19 18	14 30 23	20 36 02	7 01.2	10 26.6	16 59.0	4 08.6	8 39.0	18 07.3	27 24.7	3 24.7	17 49.8	24 03.7
23 Su	22 11 24	4 19 45	26 39 57	2♓42 15	6 51.7	9 33.1	18 07.3	4 50.0	9 02.0	18 19.0	27 30.9	3 26.8	17 52.0	24 05.4
24 M	22 15 21	5 20 10	8♓43 06	14 42 38	6 40.4	8 34.4	19 15.3	5 31.3	9 24.9	18 30.6	27 37.0	3 28.9	17 54.2	24 07.0
25 Tu	22 19 17	6 20 33	20 40 59	26 38 19	6 28.3	7 31.9	20 23.2	6 12.7	9 47.8	18 42.1	27 43.1	3 31.1	17 56.5	24 08.6
26 W	22 23 14	7 20 55	2♈34 49	8♈30 43	6 16.4	6 27.4	21 30.8	6 54.1	10 10.7	18 53.5	27 49.1	3 33.3	17 58.7	24 10.1
27 Th	22 27 10	8 21 15	14 26 16	20 21 45	6 05.8	5 22.5	22 38.3	7 35.5	10 33.5	19 04.8	27 55.1	3 35.6	18 01.0	24 11.7
28 F	22 31 07	9 21 33	26 17 31	2♉13 57	5 57.2	4 18.6	23 45.5	8 16.9	10 56.2	19 16.0	28 01.1	3 37.9	18 03.2	24 13.2
29 Sa	22 35 03	10 21 49	8♉11 29	14 10 36	5 51.2	3 17.3	24 52.6	8 58.4	11 18.9	19 27.2	28 07.0	3 40.2	18 05.5	24 14.8

Astro Data

Astro Data	Dy Hr Mn
☽0N	3 4:51
♅D	11 1:49
♄☌♇	12 16:58
☽0S	16 12:11
☽0N	30 12:18
♀0N	8 16:24
☽0S	12 18:53
☿R	17 0:51
♃✶♆	20 15:56
☽0N	26 18:29

Planet Ingress

Planet Ingress	Dy Hr Mn
♂ ♐	3 9:37
♀ ♓	13 18:39
☿ ♒	16 18:31
☉ ♒	20 14:55
⚳ ♒	31 8:01
☿ ♓	3 11:37
♀ ♈	7 20:02
♂ ♑	16 11:33
☉ ♓	19 4:57

Last Aspect / ☽ Ingress

Last Aspect Dy Hr Mn		☽ Ingress Dy Hr Mn
2 2:14 ♂ △	♈	2 4:00
4 1:18 ♇ □	♉	4 16:15
6 12:08 ♇ △	♊	7 2:11
8 22:16 ♇ △	♋	9 8:43
10 23:58 ♇ ☍	♌	11 12:16
13 13:42 ♀ ☍	♍	13 14:06
15 12:12 ☿ △	♎	15 15:43
17 12:58 ☉ □	♏	17 18:20
19 21:22 ☉ ✶	♐	19 22:41
21 4:46 ♆ □	♑	22 5:00
24 2:08 ♄ ☌	♒	24 13:20
25 19:06 ☿ ☌	♓	26 23:44
29 1:08 ♄ ✶	♈	29 11:51

Last Aspect Dy Hr Mn		☽ Ingress Dy Hr Mn
31 15:09 ☿ ✶	♉	1 0:28
3 11:28 ☿ □	♊	3 11:29
5 14:19 ☿ □	♋	5 19:03
7 15:43 ♄ ☍	♌	7 22:45
9 16:08 ♂ △	♍	9 23:39
11 18:26 ♂ □	♎	11 23:37
13 21:40 ♂ ✶	♏	14 0:37
15 22:20 ♀ ✶	♐	16 4:07
18 9:03 ☉ ✶	♑	18 10:37
20 14:18 ♄ ☌	♒	20 19:42
22 4:08 ♀ ✶	♓	23 6:37
25 14:12 ☿ ✶	♈	25 18:47
28 3:25 ♄ □	♉	28 7:30

☽ Phases & Eclipses

Dy Hr Mn	
3 4:45	☽ 12♈15
10 19:21	○ 20♋00
10 19:10	• A 0.895
17 12:58	☾ 26♎52
24 21:42	● 4♒22
2 1:42	☽ 12♉40
9 7:33	○ 20♌00
15 22:17	☾ 26♏41
23 15:32	● 4♓29

Astro Data

1 January 2020
Julian Day # 43830
SVP 4♓59'06"
GC 27♐07.1 ⚴ 23♐04.1
Eris 23♈13.8R ⚵ 17♎28.0
⚷ 1♈36.3 ⚶ 12♉06.9
☽ Mean ☊ 8♋12.7

1 February 2020
Julian Day # 43861
SVP 4♓59'01"
GC 27♐07.2 ⚴ 5♑31.7
Eris 23♈15.8 ⚵ 21♎29.5
⚷ 2♈32.6 ⚶ 15♉46.7
☽ Mean ☊ 6♋34.2

March 2020 LONGITUDE

Day	Sid.Time	☉	0 hr ☽	Noon ☽	True ☊	☿	♀	♂	⚳	♃	♄	♅	♆	♇
1 Su	22 39 00	11♓22 04	20♉11 49	26♉15 41	5♋47.8	2♓19.7	25♈59.4	9♑39.8	11♒41.5	19♑38.2	28♑12.8	3♉42.6	18♓07.7	24♑16.3
2 M	22 42 56	12 22 16	2♊22 49	8♊33 49	5D 46.6	1R 26.9	27 06.0	10 21.3	12 04.1	19 49.2	28 18.6	3 45.0	18 10.0	24 17.7
3 Tu	22 46 53	13 22 26	14 49 18	21 09 54	5 46.7	0 39.7	28 12.4	11 02.7	12 26.7	20 00.1	28 24.3	3 47.4	18 12.3	24 19.2
4 W	22 50 50	14 22 34	27 36 12	4♋08 47	5R 47.1	29♒58.6	29 18.5	11 44.2	12 49.1	20 10.8	28 30.0	3 49.9	18 14.6	24 20.6
5 Th	22 54 46	15 22 40	10♋48 06	17 34 34	5 46.6	29 24.1	0♉24.3	12 25.7	13 11.6	20 21.5	28 35.6	3 52.4	18 16.8	24 22.0
6 F	22 58 43	16 22 44	24 28 27	1♌29 50	5 44.1	28 56.4	1 30.0	13 07.2	13 33.9	20 32.1	28 41.2	3 55.0	18 19.1	24 23.4
7 Sa	23 02 39	17 22 45	8♌38 39	15 54 36	5 39.1	28 35.6	2 35.3	13 48.7	13 56.2	20 42.6	28 46.7	3 57.6	18 21.4	24 24.8
8 Su	23 06 36	18 22 45	23 17 09	0♍45 33	5 31.5	28 21.5	3 40.4	14 30.3	14 18.5	20 52.9	28 52.1	4 00.2	18 23.7	24 26.1
9 M	23 10 32	19 22 43	8♍18 47	15 55 39	5 21.7	28D 14.1	4 45.2	15 11.8	14 40.7	21 03.2	28 57.5	4 02.8	18 25.9	24 27.5
10 Tu	23 14 29	20 22 38	23 34 48	1♎14 46	5 10.8	28 13.1	5 49.7	15 53.4	15 02.8	21 13.4	29 02.8	4 05.5	18 28.2	24 28.8
11 W	23 18 25	21 22 32	8♎54 05	16 31 18	5 00.2	28 18.2	6 53.9	16 34.9	15 24.8	21 23.5	29 08.1	4 08.2	18 30.5	24 30.0
12 Th	23 22 22	22 22 24	24 05 06	1♏34 18	4 51.0	28 29.3	7 57.8	17 16.5	15 46.8	21 33.4	29 13.2	4 11.0	18 32.8	24 31.3
13 F	23 26 19	23 22 14	8♏57 57	16 15 21	4 44.2	28 45.9	9 01.5	17 58.1	16 08.8	21 43.3	29 18.4	4 13.7	18 35.0	24 32.5
14 Sa	23 30 15	24 22 02	23 26 00	0♐29 38	4 40.1	29 07.7	10 04.8	18 39.7	16 30.6	21 53.0	29 23.4	4 16.6	18 37.3	24 33.7
15 Su	23 34 12	25 21 49	7♐26 13	14 15 50	4D 38.4	29 34.5	11 07.7	19 21.4	16 52.4	22 02.7	29 28.4	4 19.4	18 39.6	24 34.9
16 M	23 38 08	26 21 35	20 58 46	27 35 23	4R 38.0	0♓06.0	12 10.4	20 03.0	17 14.2	22 12.2	29 33.4	4 22.3	18 41.9	24 36.0
17 Tu	23 42 05	27 21 18	4♑06 08	10♑31 31	4 38.0	0 41.8	13 12.7	20 44.6	17 35.8	22 21.6	29 38.2	4 25.1	18 44.1	24 37.2
18 W	23 46 01	28 21 00	16 52 05	23 08 22	4 37.0	1 21.6	14 14.7	21 26.3	17 57.4	22 30.9	29 43.0	4 28.1	18 46.4	24 38.3
19 Th	23 49 58	29 20 40	29 20 52	5♒30 07	4 33.9	2 05.3	15 16.3	22 08.0	18 18.9	22 40.0	29 47.8	4 31.0	18 48.6	24 39.4
20 F	23 53 54	0♈20 19	11♒36 35	17 40 41	4 28.1	2 52.6	16 17.5	22 49.6	18 40.4	22 49.1	29 52.4	4 34.0	18 50.9	24 40.4
21 Sa	23 57 51	1 19 55	23 42 50	29 43 23	4 19.2	3 43.3	17 18.4	23 31.3	19 01.7	22 58.0	29 57.0	4 37.0	18 53.1	24 41.4
22 Su	0 01 48	2 19 29	5♓42 36	11♓40 48	4 07.5	4 37.1	18 18.8	24 13.0	19 23.0	23 06.8	0♒01.5	4 40.0	18 55.3	24 42.4
23 M	0 05 44	3 19 02	17 38 11	23 34 57	3 53.8	5 33.9	19 18.9	24 54.7	19 44.2	23 15.5	0 05.9	4 43.0	18 57.6	24 43.4
24 Tu	0 09 41	4 18 32	29 31 16	5♈27 20	3 39.0	6 33.6	20 18.5	25 36.4	20 05.3	23 24.0	0 10.3	4 46.1	18 59.8	24 44.3
25 W	0 13 37	5 18 01	11♈23 17	17 19 16	3 24.3	7 35.9	21 17.7	26 18.1	20 26.4	23 32.4	0 14.6	4 49.2	19 02.0	24 45.3
26 Th	0 17 34	6 17 27	23 15 29	29 12 07	3 11.0	8 40.7	22 16.5	26 59.8	20 47.3	23 40.7	0 18.8	4 52.3	19 04.2	24 46.1
27 F	0 21 30	7 16 51	5♉09 22	11♉07 31	3 00.0	9 47.8	23 14.8	27 41.5	21 08.2	23 48.8	0 22.9	4 55.5	19 06.4	24 47.0
28 Sa	0 25 27	8 16 14	17 06 50	23 07 41	2 51.9	10 57.3	24 12.6	28 23.2	21 29.0	23 56.8	0 26.9	4 58.6	19 08.6	24 47.8
29 Su	0 29 23	9 15 33	29 10 25	5♊15 29	2 46.8	12 09.0	25 09.9	29 04.9	21 49.7	24 04.7	0 30.9	5 01.8	19 10.7	24 48.6
30 M	0 33 20	10 14 51	11♊23 21	17 34 31	2 44.3	13 22.7	26 06.7	29 46.6	22 10.3	24 12.5	0 34.8	5 05.0	19 12.9	24 49.4
31 Tu	0 37 17	11 14 07	23 49 31	0♋08 54	2 43.6	14 38.4	27 02.9	0♒28.3	22 30.8	24 20.1	0 38.6	5 08.2	19 15.1	24 50.2

April 2020 LONGITUDE

Day	Sid.Time	☉	0 hr ☽	Noon ☽	True ☊	☿	♀	♂	⚳	♃	♄	♅	♆	♇
1 W	0 41 13	12♈13 20	6♋33 15	13♋03 06	2♋43.6	15♓56.1	27♉58.7	1♒10.0	22♒51.2	24♑27.5	0♒42.3	5♉11.4	19♓17.2	24♑50.9
2 Th	0 45 10	13 12 30	19 38 59	26 21 20	2R 43.1	17 15.6	28 53.8	1 51.7	23 11.5	24 34.8	0 46.0	5 14.7	19 19.3	24 51.6
3 F	0 49 06	14 11 39	3♌10 34	10♌06 55	2 41.0	18 37.0	29 48.3	2 33.4	23 31.8	24 42.0	0 49.5	5 17.9	19 21.5	24 52.3
4 Sa	0 53 03	15 10 45	17 10 30	24 21 14	2 36.5	20 00.1	0♊42.2	3 15.1	23 51.9	24 49.0	0 53.0	5 21.2	19 23.6	24 52.9
5 Su	0 56 59	16 09 48	1♍38 51	9♍02 50	2 29.4	21 24.9	1 35.5	3 56.8	24 11.9	24 55.9	0 56.4	5 24.5	19 25.6	24 53.5
6 M	1 00 56	17 08 50	16 32 25	24 06 39	2 20.1	22 51.4	2 28.1	4 38.5	24 31.9	25 02.6	0 59.7	5 27.8	19 27.7	24 54.1
7 Tu	1 04 52	18 07 49	1♎44 20	9♎24 07	2 09.6	24 19.6	3 20.0	5 20.2	24 51.7	25 09.2	1 02.9	5 31.1	19 29.8	24 54.6
8 W	1 08 49	19 06 46	17 04 33	24 44 09	1 59.2	25 49.4	4 11.2	6 01.9	25 11.4	25 15.6	1 06.0	5 34.5	19 31.8	24 55.1
9 Th	1 12 45	20 05 41	2♏21 27	9♏55 06	1 50.1	27 20.9	5 01.7	6 43.6	25 31.0	25 21.9	1 09.1	5 37.8	19 33.9	24 55.6
10 F	1 16 42	21 04 34	17 23 57	24 46 59	1 43.3	28 53.9	5 51.4	7 25.3	25 50.6	25 28.0	1 12.1	5 41.2	19 35.9	24 56.1
11 Sa	1 20 39	22 03 26	2♐03 29	9♐12 55	1 39.0	0♈28.5	6 40.3	8 07.0	26 10.0	25 34.0	1 14.9	5 44.6	19 37.9	24 56.5
12 Su	1 24 35	23 02 16	16 15 00	23 09 40	1D 37.2	2 04.8	7 28.5	8 48.7	26 29.3	25 39.8	1 17.7	5 47.9	19 39.9	24 56.9
13 M	1 28 32	24 01 04	29 57 02	6♑37 21	1 37.0	3 42.6	8 15.7	9 30.4	26 48.5	25 45.5	1 20.4	5 51.3	19 41.8	24 57.3
14 Tu	1 32 28	24 59 50	13♑11 00	19 38 28	1R 37.4	5 22.0	9 02.1	10 12.1	27 07.5	25 51.0	1 23.0	5 54.7	19 43.8	24 57.7
15 W	1 36 25	25 58 35	26 00 17	2♒17 01	1 37.3	7 02.9	9 47.6	10 53.8	27 26.5	25 56.3	1 25.5	5 58.1	19 45.7	24 58.0
16 Th	1 40 21	26 57 18	8♒29 16	14 37 38	1 35.7	8 45.5	10 32.2	11 35.5	27 45.4	26 01.5	1 27.9	6 01.6	19 47.6	24 58.3
17 F	1 44 18	27 55 59	20 42 41	26 45 00	1 31.9	10 29.7	11 15.7	12 17.2	28 04.1	26 06.5	1 30.3	6 05.0	19 49.5	24 58.5
18 Sa	1 48 14	28 54 38	2♓45 06	8♓43 28	1 25.5	12 15.4	11 58.3	12 58.8	28 22.7	26 11.3	1 32.5	6 08.4	19 51.4	24 58.8
19 Su	1 52 11	29 53 16	14 40 33	20 36 46	1 16.8	14 02.8	12 39.8	13 40.5	28 41.2	26 16.0	1 34.6	6 11.8	19 53.3	24 59.0
20 M	1 56 08	0♉51 52	26 32 29	2♈27 59	1 06.3	15 51.8	13 20.3	14 22.1	28 59.5	26 20.4	1 36.7	6 15.3	19 55.1	24 59.1
21 Tu	2 00 04	1 50 26	8♈23 36	14 19 33	0 54.8	17 42.4	13 59.6	15 03.7	29 17.7	26 24.8	1 38.6	6 18.7	19 56.9	24 59.3
22 W	2 04 01	2 48 58	20 16 03	26 13 18	0 43.4	19 34.6	14 37.7	15 45.3	29 35.8	26 28.9	1 40.5	6 22.2	19 58.7	24 59.4
23 Th	2 07 57	3 47 29	2♉11 29	8♉10 46	0 33.1	21 28.5	15 14.6	16 26.9	29 53.8	26 32.9	1 42.3	6 25.6	20 00.5	24 59.5
24 F	2 11 54	4 45 57	14 11 19	20 13 19	0 24.6	23 24.0	15 50.2	17 08.4	0♓11.6	26 36.7	1 43.9	6 29.1	20 02.3	24 59.5
25 Sa	2 15 50	5 44 24	26 16 56	2♊22 25	0 18.5	25 21.1	16 24.5	17 50.0	0 29.3	26 40.3	1 45.5	6 32.5	20 04.0	24R 59.5
26 Su	2 19 47	6 42 48	8♊29 58	14 39 52	0 15.0	27 19.9	16 57.4	18 31.5	0 46.9	26 43.7	1 47.0	6 36.0	20 05.7	24 59.5
27 M	2 23 43	7 41 11	20 52 25	27 07 57	0D 13.6	29 20.2	17 28.9	19 13.0	1 04.3	26 47.0	1 48.3	6 39.4	20 07.4	24 59.5
28 Tu	2 27 40	8 39 32	3♋26 49	9♋49 23	0 14.0	1♉22.0	17 59.0	19 54.5	1 21.5	26 50.1	1 49.6	6 42.9	20 09.1	24 59.4
29 W	2 31 37	9 37 51	16 16 05	22 47 17	0 15.0	3 25.2	18 27.4	20 35.9	1 38.7	26 53.0	1 50.8	6 46.3	20 10.7	24 59.3
30 Th	2 35 33	10 36 07	29 23 22	6♌04 44	0R 15.9	5 29.9	18 54.3	21 17.3	1 55.6	26 55.7	1 51.9	6 49.8	20 12.3	24 59.2

Astro Data	Dy Hr Mn
☿ D	10 3:48
☽ 0S	11 4:15
☉ 0N	20 3:50
☽ 0N	25 0:13
♃ ☌ ♇	5 2:45
☽ 0S	7 15:20
☿ 0N	14 16:07
☽ 0N	21 6:26
♇ R	25 18:54

Planet Ingress		Dy Hr Mn
☿	♒R	4 11:08
♀	♉	5 3:07
☿	♓	16 7:42
☉	♈	20 3:50
♄	♒	22 3:58
♂	♒	30 19:43
♀	♊	3 17:11
☿	♈	11 4:48
☉	♉	19 14:45
⚳	♓	23 20:20
☿	♉	27 19:53

Last Aspect Dy Hr Mn		☽ Ingress	Dy Hr Mn
1 15:52	♄ △	♊	1 19:21
4 2:20	♀ ⚹	♋	4 4:25
6 7:11	♄ ☍	♌	6 9:28
8 8:12	☿ ☍	♍	8 10:47
10 8:32	♄ △	♎	10 10:03
12 8:12	♄ □	♏	12 9:28
14 10:06	♄ ⚹	♐	14 11:09
16 9:34	☉ □	♑	16 16:25
19 0:48	♄ ☌	♒	19 1:16
20 9:00	♀ □	♓	21 12:33
23 14:51	♂ ⚹	♈	24 0:58
26 7:16	♂ □	♉	26 13:37
28 23:05	♂ △	♊	29 1:38
30 15:10	♆ □	♋	31 11:43

Last Aspect Dy Hr Mn		☽ Ingress	Dy Hr Mn
2 16:49	♀ ⚹	♌	2 18:26
3 19:29	☉ △	♍	4 21:18
6 13:29	♃ △	♎	6 21:16
8 12:50	♃ □	♏	8 20:17
10 19:35	☿ △	♐	10 20:35
12 11:46	☉ △	♑	13 0:05
14 23:47	♃ ☌	♒	15 7:37
17 14:34	☉ ⚹	♓	17 18:29
19 23:31	♃ ⚹	♈	20 7:00
22 12:32	♃ □	♉	22 19:36
25 0:43	♃ △	♊	25 7:20
27 17:00	☿ ⚹	♋	27 17:28
29 19:29	♃ ☍	♌	30 1:06

☽ Phases & Eclipses Dy Hr Mn	
2 19:57	☽ 12♊42
9 17:48	○ 19♍37
16 9:34	☾ 26♐16
24 9:28	● 4♈12
1 10:21	☽ 12♋09
8 2:35	○ 18♎44
14 22:56	☾ 25♑27
23 2:26	● 3♉24
30 20:38	☽ 10♌57

Astro Data

1 March 2020
Julian Day # 43890
SVP 4♓58'58"
GC 27♐07.3 ⚵ 15♑58.1
Eris 23♈26.5 ⚶ 20♎09.0R
⚷ 3♈58.3 ⚴ 23♉23.5
☽ Mean ☊ 5♋02.0

1 April 2020
Julian Day # 43921
SVP 4♓58'54"
GC 27♐07.3 ⚵ 24♑56.0
Eris 23♈44.6 ⚶ 13♎51.4R
⚷ 5♈46.1 ⚴ 4♊08.1
☽ Mean ☊ 3♋23.5

LONGITUDE — May 2020

Day	Sid.Time	☉	0 hr ☽	Noon☽	True☊	☿	♀	♂	⚳	♃	♄	♅	♆	♇
1 F	2 39 30	11♉34 22	12♌51 39	19♌44 22	0♋15.6	7♉35.8	19♊19.5	21♒58.7	2♓12.5	26♑58.3	1♒52.9	6♉53.2	20♓13.9	24♑59.1
2 Sa	2 43 26	12 32 34	26 43 02	3♍47 39	0R 13.7	9 43.0	19 43.0	22 40.1	2 29.1	27 00.6	1 53.8	6 56.7	20 15.5	24R 58.9
3 Su	2 47 23	13 30 44	10♍58 04	18 14 00	0 09.9	11 51.1	20 04.7	23 21.4	2 45.6	27 02.8	1 54.6	7 00.1	20 17.0	24 58.7
4 M	2 51 19	14 28 52	25 34 57	3♎00 14	0 04.4	14 00.1	20 24.6	24 02.7	3 02.0	27 04.8	1 55.3	7 03.5	20 18.6	24 58.4
5 Tu	2 55 16	15 26 59	10♎29 00	18 00 16	29♊58.0	16 09.7	20 42.5	24 44.0	3 18.2	27 06.6	1 55.9	7 07.0	20 20.1	24 58.2
6 W	2 59 12	16 25 03	25 32 52	3♏05 37	29 51.4	18 19.7	20 58.4	25 25.3	3 34.2	27 08.2	1 56.4	7 10.4	20 21.5	24 57.9
7 Th	3 03 09	17 23 06	10♏37 17	18 06 38	29 45.7	20 30.0	21 12.4	26 06.5	3 50.1	27 09.6	1 56.8	7 13.8	20 23.0	24 57.6
8 F	3 07 06	18 21 07	25 32 34	2♐54 03	29 41.4	22 40.1	21 24.2	26 47.7	4 05.8	27 10.9	1 57.1	7 17.2	20 24.4	24 57.2
9 Sa	3 11 02	19 19 07	10♐10 16	17 20 31	29D 39.1	24 49.9	21 33.9	27 28.9	4 21.4	27 11.9	1 57.3	7 20.6	20 25.8	24 56.8
10 Su	3 14 59	20 17 05	24 24 21	1♑21 27	29 38.5	26 59.0	21 41.4	28 10.0	4 36.7	27 12.8	1R 57.4	7 24.0	20 27.2	24 56.4
11 M	3 18 55	21 15 02	8♑11 43	14 55 11	29 39.2	29 07.1	21 46.7	28 51.1	4 52.0	27 13.5	1 57.4	7 27.4	20 28.5	24 56.0
12 Tu	3 22 52	22 12 58	21 32 04	28 02 39	29 40.7	1♊14.1	21R 49.7	29 32.2	5 07.0	27 14.0	1 57.3	7 30.8	20 29.8	24 55.5
13 W	3 26 48	23 10 52	4♒27 20	10♒46 36	29 42.1	3 19.5	21 50.4	0♓13.2	5 21.8	27 14.3	1 57.2	7 34.1	20 31.1	24 55.1
14 Th	3 30 45	24 08 45	17 00 59	23 11 02	29R 42.8	5 23.2	21 48.7	0 54.2	5 36.5	27R 14.4	1 56.9	7 37.5	20 32.4	24 54.6
15 F	3 34 41	25 06 37	29 17 19	5♓20 27	29 42.2	7 24.8	21 44.6	1 35.1	5 51.0	27 14.3	1 56.5	7 40.8	20 33.6	24 54.0
16 Sa	3 38 38	26 04 27	11♓21 01	17 19 33	29 40.2	9 24.3	21 38.1	2 16.0	6 05.3	27 14.1	1 56.0	7 44.1	20 34.8	24 53.4
17 Su	3 42 35	27 02 17	23 16 38	29 12 45	29 36.7	11 21.3	21 29.2	2 56.8	6 19.4	27 13.6	1 55.5	7 47.4	20 36.0	24 52.9
18 M	3 46 31	28 00 05	5♈08 26	11♈04 06	29 32.1	13 15.8	21 17.8	3 37.6	6 33.3	27 13.0	1 54.8	7 50.7	20 37.1	24 52.2
19 Tu	3 50 28	28 57 52	17 00 10	22 57 02	29 26.9	15 07.6	21 04.1	4 18.3	6 47.0	27 12.1	1 54.0	7 54.0	20 38.2	24 51.6
20 W	3 54 24	29 55 37	28 55 01	4♉54 24	29 21.6	16 56.6	20 48.0	4 59.0	7 00.5	27 11.1	1 53.2	7 57.3	20 39.3	24 50.9
21 Th	3 58 21	0♊53 22	10♉55 29	16 58 28	29 16.9	18 42.7	20 29.5	5 39.6	7 13.8	27 09.9	1 52.2	8 00.5	20 40.4	24 50.2
22 F	4 02 17	1 51 05	23 03 34	29 10 57	29 13.1	20 25.9	20 08.8	6 20.2	7 26.9	27 08.5	1 51.2	8 03.8	20 41.4	24 49.5
23 Sa	4 06 14	2 48 47	5♊20 46	11♊33 10	29 10.6	22 05.9	19 45.8	7 00.7	7 39.8	27 06.9	1 50.0	8 07.0	20 42.4	24 48.8
24 Su	4 10 10	3 46 28	17 48 17	24 06 15	29D 09.5	23 42.9	19 20.7	7 41.1	7 52.5	27 05.1	1 48.8	8 10.2	20 43.3	24 48.0
25 M	4 14 07	4 44 07	0♋27 11	6♋51 12	29 09.6	25 16.7	18 53.6	8 21.4	8 04.9	27 03.1	1 47.5	8 13.4	20 44.3	24 47.2
26 Tu	4 18 04	5 41 45	13 18 28	19 49 07	29 10.6	26 47.4	18 24.6	9 01.7	8 17.2	27 01.0	1 46.0	8 16.6	20 45.2	24 46.4
27 W	4 22 00	6 39 22	26 23 17	3♌01 07	29 12.0	28 14.8	17 53.8	9 41.9	8 29.2	26 58.7	1 44.5	8 19.7	20 46.1	24 45.6
28 Th	4 25 57	7 36 57	9♌42 45	16 28 18	29 13.4	29 39.0	17 21.5	10 22.1	8 41.0	26 56.1	1 42.9	8 22.8	20 46.9	24 44.7
29 F	4 29 53	8 34 30	23 17 51	0♍11 28	29R 14.3	0♋59.8	16 47.7	11 02.1	8 52.5	26 53.4	1 41.2	8 25.9	20 47.7	24 43.9
30 Sa	4 33 50	9 32 03	7♍09 09	14 10 50	29 14.4	2 17.3	16 12.6	11 42.1	9 03.9	26 50.5	1 39.4	8 29.0	20 48.5	24 43.0
31 Su	4 37 46	10 29 33	21 16 23	28 25 32	29 13.7	3 31.4	15 36.6	12 22.0	9 15.0	26 47.5	1 37.6	8 32.1	20 49.2	24 42.0

LONGITUDE — June 2020

Day	Sid.Time	☉	0 hr ☽	Noon☽	True☊	☿	♀	♂	⚳	♃	♄	♅	♆	♇
1 M	4 41 43	11♊27 03	5♎37 57	12♎53 13	29♊12.2	4♋42.1	14♊59.8	13♓01.8	9♓25.8	26♑44.2	1♒35.6	8♉35.1	20♓50.0	24♑41.1
2 Tu	4 45 39	12 24 31	20 10 46	27 29 58	29R 10.3	5 49.2	14R 22.4	13 41.5	9 36.4	26R 40.8	1R 33.6	8 38.1	20 50.6	24R 40.1
3 W	4 49 36	13 21 58	4♏50 05	12♏10 21	29 08.2	6 52.8	13 44.7	14 21.2	9 46.8	26 37.3	1 31.4	8 41.1	20 51.3	24 39.1
4 Th	4 53 33	14 19 24	19 29 54	26 47 55	29 06.5	7 52.7	13 06.9	15 00.7	9 56.9	26 33.5	1 29.2	8 44.1	20 51.9	24 38.1
5 F	4 57 29	15 16 49	4♐03 35	11♐16 07	29 05.3	8 49.0	12 29.3	15 40.2	10 06.8	26 29.6	1 26.9	8 47.0	20 52.5	24 37.1
6 Sa	5 01 26	16 14 13	18 24 49	25 29 04	29D 04.8	9 41.4	11 52.2	16 19.6	10 16.4	26 25.5	1 24.5	8 49.9	20 53.1	24 36.1
7 Su	5 05 22	17 11 36	2♑28 23	9♑22 22	29 05.0	10 30.0	11 15.7	16 58.9	10 25.8	26 21.2	1 22.1	8 52.8	20 53.6	24 35.0
8 M	5 09 19	18 08 58	16 10 46	22 53 28	29 05.6	11 14.7	10 40.2	17 38.1	10 34.9	26 16.8	1 19.5	8 55.7	20 54.1	24 33.9
9 Tu	5 13 15	19 06 20	29 30 27	6♒01 48	29 06.5	11 55.3	10 05.7	18 17.2	10 43.7	26 12.3	1 16.9	8 58.5	20 54.6	24 32.8
10 W	5 17 12	20 03 41	12♒27 45	18 48 34	29 07.4	12 31.7	9 32.6	18 56.2	10 52.3	26 07.5	1 14.2	9 01.3	20 55.0	24 31.7
11 Th	5 21 09	21 01 01	25 04 37	1♓16 20	29 08.1	13 04.0	9 01.1	19 35.1	11 00.6	26 02.6	1 11.4	9 04.1	20 55.4	24 30.6
12 F	5 25 05	21 58 21	7♓24 13	13 28 45	29R 08.5	13 31.9	8 31.2	20 13.9	11 08.6	25 57.6	1 08.6	9 06.8	20 55.7	24 29.4
13 Sa	5 29 02	22 55 41	19 30 29	25 30 00	29 08.6	13 55.5	8 03.1	20 52.5	11 16.4	25 52.4	1 05.7	9 09.6	20 56.1	24 28.2
14 Su	5 32 58	23 53 00	1♈27 52	7♈24 39	29 08.4	14 14.6	7 37.0	21 31.1	11 23.8	25 47.1	1 02.7	9 12.2	20 56.4	24 27.0
15 M	5 36 55	24 50 19	13 20 54	19 17 11	29 08.0	14 29.2	7 13.0	22 09.5	11 31.0	25 41.6	0 59.6	9 14.9	20 56.6	24 25.8
16 Tu	5 40 51	25 47 37	25 14 02	1♉11 57	29 07.6	14 39.2	6 51.2	22 47.8	11 37.9	25 35.9	0 56.4	9 17.5	20 56.9	24 24.6
17 W	5 44 48	26 44 55	7♉11 24	13 12 50	29 07.3	14R 44.7	6 31.7	23 25.9	11 44.5	25 30.2	0 53.2	9 20.1	20 57.1	24 23.4
18 Th	5 48 44	27 42 13	19 16 38	25 23 10	29 07.0	14 45.6	6 14.5	24 03.9	11 50.8	25 24.3	0 49.9	9 22.7	20 57.2	24 22.1
19 F	5 52 41	28 39 30	1♊32 44	7♊45 36	29D 07.0	14 42.1	5 59.6	24 41.8	11 56.7	25 18.3	0 46.6	9 25.2	20 57.4	24 20.9
20 Sa	5 56 38	29 36 47	14 01 58	20 21 59	29R 07.0	14 34.1	5 47.1	25 19.5	12 02.4	25 12.1	0 43.2	9 27.7	20 57.5	24 19.6
21 Su	6 00 34	0♋34 04	26 45 46	3♋13 22	29 07.0	14 21.9	5 37.0	25 57.1	12 07.8	25 05.8	0 39.7	9 30.2	20 57.6	24 18.3
22 M	6 04 31	1 31 20	9♋44 47	16 19 58	29 06.9	14 05.5	5 29.2	26 34.5	12 12.8	24 59.5	0 36.2	9 32.6	20R 57.6	24 17.0
23 Tu	6 08 27	2 28 36	22 58 51	29 41 19	29 06.7	13 45.3	5 23.9	27 11.8	12 17.6	24 53.0	0 32.6	9 35.0	20 57.6	24 15.7
24 W	6 12 24	3 25 51	6♌27 12	13♌16 20	29 06.2	13 21.5	5D 20.9	27 48.9	12 22.0	24 46.4	0 28.9	9 37.4	20 57.6	24 14.4
25 Th	6 16 20	4 23 05	20 08 31	27 03 31	29 05.7	12 54.5	5 20.2	28 25.8	12 26.1	24 39.6	0 25.2	9 39.7	20 57.5	24 13.0
26 F	6 20 17	5 20 19	4♍01 07	11♍01 03	29 05.2	12 24.6	5 21.9	29 02.6	12 29.9	24 32.8	0 21.5	9 42.0	20 57.4	24 11.7
27 Sa	6 24 13	6 17 33	18 03 04	25 06 54	29D 04.7	11 52.4	5 25.8	29 39.1	12 33.3	24 25.9	0 17.7	9 44.2	20 57.3	24 10.3
28 Su	6 28 10	7 14 46	2♎12 17	9♎18 54	29 04.6	11 18.4	5 31.9	0♈15.5	12 36.4	24 18.9	0 13.8	9 46.4	20 57.1	24 09.0
29 M	6 32 07	8 11 58	16 26 28	23 34 39	29 04.9	10 43.1	5 40.1	0 51.7	12 39.2	24 11.8	0 09.9	9 48.6	20 56.9	24 07.6
30 Tu	6 36 03	9 09 10	0♏43 06	7♏51 29	29 05.5	10 07.0	5 50.5	1 27.8	12 41.7	24 04.7	0 05.9	9 50.8	20 56.7	24 06.2

Astro Data	Planet Ingress	Last Aspect ☽ Ingress	Last Aspect ☽ Ingress	☽ Phases & Eclipses	Astro Data
Dy Hr Mn	Dy Hr Mn	Dy Hr Mn / Dy Hr Mn	Dy Hr Mn / Dy Hr Mn	Dy Hr Mn	1 May 2020
☽0S 5 1:58	☊ ♊R 5 4:39	1 16:04 ♂ ☍ ♍ 2 5:35	2 10:40 ♃ □ ♏ 2 16:06	7 10:45 ○ 17♏20	Julian Day # 43951
♄ R 11 4:09	☿ ♊ 11 21:58	4 2:24 ♃ △ ♎ 4 7:09	4 11:36 ♃ ✶ ♐ 4 17:17	14 14:03 ☾ 24♒14	SVP 4♓58'51"
♀ R 13 6:45	♂ ♓ 13 4:17	6 2:31 ♃ □ ♏ 6 7:05	6 4:10 ♆ □ ♑ 6 19:44	22 17:39 ● 2♊05	GC 27♐07.4 ⚴ 0♒09.1
♃ R 14 14:32	☉ ♊ 20 13:49	8 2:39 ♃ ✶ ♐ 8 7:15	8 18:06 ♃ ☌ ♒ 9 0:54	30 3:30 ☽ 9♍12	Eris 24♈04.1 ⚵ 7♎41.1R
☽0N 18 13:31	☿ ♋ 28 18:09	10 6:11 ♂ ✶ ♑ 10 9:38	10 14:35 ☉ △ ♓ 11 9:31		⚷ 7♈26.0 ⚶ 15♊58.4
		12 10:30 ♃ ☌ ♒ 12 15:39	13 12:45 ♃ ✶ ♈ 13 21:03	5 19:12 ○ 15♐34	☽ Mean ☊ 1♋48.2
☽0S 1 10:26	☉ ♋ 20 21:44	14 14:03 ☉ □ ♓ 15 1:24	16 0:49 ♃ □ ♉ 16 9:35	5 19:25 ☍ A 0.568	
☽0N 14 21:16	♂ ♈ 28 1:45	17 7:59 ♃ ✶ ♈ 17 13:36	18 12:02 ♃ △ ♊ 18 21:00	13 6:24 ☾ 22♓42	1 June 2020
☿ R 18 4:58		19 20:33 ♃ □ ♉ 20 2:10	20 21:48 ♂ □ ♋ 21 6:02	21 6:41 ● 0♋21	Julian Day # 43982
♆ R 23 4:31		22 8:01 ♃ △ ♊ 22 13:36	23 7:20 ♂ △ ♌ 23 12:33	21 6:40:03 ● A 00'38"	SVP 4♓58'46"
♀ D 25 6:48		24 11:09 ☿ ☌ ♋ 24 23:09	24 5:34 ♅ □ ♍ 25 17:05	28 8:16 ☽ 7♎06	GC 27♐07.5 ⚴ 0♒10.1R
☽0S 28 16:30		27 1:06 ♃ ☍ ♌ 27 6:33	27 20:02 ♂ ☍ ♎ 27 20:16		Eris 24♈21.5 ⚵ 5♎53.1
♃☌♇ 30 5:46		28 13:30 ♀ ✶ ♍ 29 11:40	29 13:02 ♃ □ ♏ 29 22:48		⚷ 8♈45.1 ⚶ 29♊01.0
		31 9:17 ♃ △ ♎ 31 14:38			☽ Mean ☊ 0♋09.7

July 2020 LONGITUDE

Day	Sid.Time	☉	0 hr ☽	Noon ☽	True ☊	☿	♀	♂	⚳	♃	♄	♅	♆	♇
1 W	6 40 00	10♋06 22	14♏59 24	22♏06 27	29♊06.4	9♋30.9	6♊03.0	2♈03.6	12♓43.8	23♑57.5	0♒01.9	9♉52.9	20♓56.5	24♑04.8
2 Th	6 43 56	11 03 33	29 12 15	6♐16 20	29 07.2	8R55.3	6 17.4	2 39.3	12 45.6	23R50.2	29♑57.9	9 54.9	20R56.2	24R03.4
3 F	6 47 53	12 00 44	13♐18 20	20 17 47	29R07.8	8 20.9	6 33.8	3 14.7	12 47.0	23 42.8	29R53.8	9 56.9	20 55.9	24 02.0
4 Sa	6 51 49	12 57 55	27 14 19	4♑07 32	29 07.9	7 48.2	6 52.0	3 50.0	12 48.1	23 35.4	29 49.7	9 58.9	20 55.5	24 00.6
5 Su	6 55 46	13 55 06	10♑57 06	17 42 45	29 07.3	7 17.9	7 12.2	4 25.0	12 48.9	23 27.9	29 45.6	10 00.9	20 55.1	23 59.2
6 M	6 59 42	14 52 17	24 24 13	1♒01 20	29 05.9	6 50.4	7 34.0	4 59.8	12R49.3	23 20.4	29 41.4	10 02.8	20 54.7	23 57.8
7 Tu	7 03 39	15 49 28	7♒34 00	14 02 11	29 03.9	6 26.3	7 57.6	5 34.5	12 49.4	23 12.8	29 37.2	10 04.6	20 54.3	23 56.3
8 W	7 07 36	16 46 39	20 25 56	26 45 22	29 01.4	6 06.0	8 22.9	6 08.8	12 49.1	23 05.2	29 32.9	10 06.4	20 53.8	23 54.9
9 Th	7 11 32	17 43 50	3♓00 40	9♓12 08	28 58.8	5 49.8	8 49.7	6 43.0	12 48.4	22 57.6	29 28.7	10 08.2	20 53.3	23 53.5
10 F	7 15 29	18 41 02	15 20 03	21 24 49	28 56.4	5 38.2	9 18.1	7 16.9	12 47.4	22 49.9	29 24.4	10 09.9	20 52.8	23 52.0
11 Sa	7 19 25	19 38 14	27 26 53	3♈26 43	28 54.7	5D31.4	9 48.0	7 50.6	12 46.1	22 42.2	29 20.0	10 11.6	20 52.2	23 50.6
12 Su	7 23 22	20 35 27	9♈24 50	15 21 48	28D53.8	5 29.6	10 19.3	8 24.0	12 44.3	22 34.5	29 15.7	10 13.3	20 51.6	23 49.1
13 M	7 27 18	21 32 40	21 18 11	27 14 34	28 53.8	5 33.0	10 52.0	8 57.1	12 42.3	22 26.7	29 11.3	10 14.9	20 51.0	23 47.7
14 Tu	7 31 15	22 29 54	3♉11 33	9♉09 43	28 54.6	5 41.7	11 26.0	9 30.0	12 39.8	22 19.0	29 06.9	10 16.4	20 50.4	23 46.2
15 W	7 35 11	23 27 08	15 09 39	21 11 56	28 56.1	5 55.8	12 01.3	10 02.6	12 37.0	22 11.3	29 02.5	10 17.9	20 49.7	23 44.8
16 Th	7 39 08	24 24 23	27 17 07	3♊25 40	28 57.7	6 15.4	12 37.8	10 34.9	12 33.9	22 03.5	28 58.1	10 19.4	20 49.0	23 43.3
17 F	7 43 05	25 21 39	9♊38 05	15 54 45	28 59.1	6 40.5	13 15.4	11 06.9	12 30.4	21 55.8	28 53.7	10 20.8	20 48.2	23 41.9
18 Sa	7 47 01	26 18 55	22 16 01	28 42 08	28R59.6	7 11.1	13 54.2	11 38.6	12 26.5	21 48.1	28 49.3	10 22.2	20 47.5	23 40.4
19 Su	7 50 58	27 16 12	5♋13 17	11♋49 33	28 59.0	7 47.2	14 34.1	12 10.0	12 22.3	21 40.4	28 44.8	10 23.6	20 46.7	23 39.0
20 M	7 54 54	28 13 29	18 30 55	25 17 14	28 57.1	8 28.8	15 15.1	12 41.1	12 17.7	21 32.8	28 40.4	10 24.8	20 45.8	23 37.5
21 Tu	7 58 51	29 10 47	2♌08 18	9♌03 46	28 53.8	9 15.7	15 57.0	13 11.9	12 12.7	21 25.1	28 36.0	10 26.1	20 45.0	23 36.1
22 W	8 02 47	0♌08 05	16 03 13	23 06 08	28 49.5	10 08.1	16 39.9	13 42.3	12 07.4	21 17.6	28 31.5	10 27.3	20 44.1	23 34.6
23 Th	8 06 44	1 05 24	0♍11 58	7♍20 06	28 44.8	11 05.7	17 23.7	14 12.3	12 01.8	21 10.0	28 27.1	10 28.4	20 43.2	23 33.2
24 F	8 10 40	2 02 43	14 29 53	21 40 43	28 40.4	12 08.5	18 08.4	14 42.0	11 55.8	21 02.5	28 22.6	10 29.5	20 42.3	23 31.8
25 Sa	8 14 37	3 00 02	28 51 58	6♎03 04	28 36.8	13 16.5	18 54.0	15 11.4	11 49.5	20 55.1	28 18.2	10 30.6	20 41.3	23 30.3
26 Su	8 18 34	3 57 22	13♎13 31	20 22 52	28 34.6	14 29.5	19 40.4	15 40.4	11 42.8	20 47.7	28 13.8	10 31.6	20 40.3	23 28.9
27 M	8 22 30	4 54 42	27 30 44	4♏36 48	28D33.8	15 47.4	20 27.6	16 09.0	11 35.8	20 40.4	28 09.4	10 32.5	20 39.3	23 27.5
28 Tu	8 26 27	5 52 03	11♏40 51	18 42 40	28 34.4	17 10.1	21 15.5	16 37.2	11 28.4	20 33.2	28 05.0	10 33.5	20 38.3	23 26.1
29 W	8 30 23	6 49 24	25 42 07	2♐39 07	28 35.7	18 37.5	22 04.2	17 05.1	11 20.8	20 26.0	28 00.7	10 34.3	20 37.2	23 24.7
30 Th	8 34 20	7 46 46	9♐33 35	16 25 26	28R37.0	20 09.3	22 53.7	17 32.5	11 12.8	20 18.9	27 56.3	10 35.1	20 36.1	23 23.3
31 F	8 38 16	8 44 08	23 14 36	0♑01 03	28 37.5	21 45.3	23 43.8	17 59.5	11 04.5	20 11.9	27 52.0	10 35.9	20 35.0	23 21.9

August 2020 LONGITUDE

Day	Sid.Time	☉	0 hr ☽	Noon ☽	True ☊	☿	♀	♂	⚳	♃	♄	♅	♆	♇
1 Sa	8 42 13	9♌41 31	6♑44 41	13♑25 26	28♊36.5	23♋25.4	24♊34.6	18♈26.2	10♓55.9	20♑05.0	27♑47.7	10♉36.6	20♓33.9	23♑20.5
2 Su	8 46 10	10 38 54	20 03 12	26 37 55	28R33.6	25 09.2	25 26.0	18 52.4	10R47.0	19R58.2	27R43.4	10 37.3	20R32.8	23R19.1
3 M	8 50 06	11 36 19	3♒09 29	9♒37 48	28 28.7	26 56.5	26 18.1	19 18.1	10 37.8	19 51.5	27 39.2	10 37.9	20 31.6	23 17.8
4 Tu	8 54 03	12 33 44	16 02 50	22 24 32	28 22.1	28 47.0	27 10.8	19 43.4	10 28.3	19 44.9	27 35.0	10 38.5	20 30.4	23 16.4
5 W	8 57 59	13 31 10	28 42 53	4♓57 56	28 14.3	0♌40.3	28 04.1	20 08.3	10 18.6	19 38.4	27 30.8	10 39.0	20 29.2	23 15.1
6 Th	9 01 56	14 28 38	11♓09 46	17 18 30	28 06.1	2 36.0	28 57.9	20 32.7	10 08.5	19 32.0	27 26.6	10 39.5	20 27.9	23 13.8
7 F	9 05 52	15 26 06	23 24 21	29 27 34	27 58.3	4 33.9	29 52.4	20 56.6	9 58.2	19 25.7	27 22.5	10 39.9	20 26.7	23 12.4
8 Sa	9 09 49	16 23 36	5♈28 26	11♈27 20	27 51.7	6 33.5	0♋47.3	21 20.0	9 47.6	19 19.6	27 18.4	10 40.3	20 25.4	23 11.1
9 Su	9 13 45	17 21 07	17 24 40	23 20 55	27 46.7	8 34.5	1 42.8	21 42.9	9 36.8	19 13.6	27 14.4	10 40.6	20 24.1	23 09.8
10 M	9 17 42	18 18 39	29 16 35	5♉12 13	27 43.8	10 36.5	2 38.7	22 05.2	9 25.8	19 07.7	27 10.4	10 40.9	20 22.7	23 08.5
11 Tu	9 21 38	19 16 13	11♉08 25	17 05 48	27D42.7	12 39.2	3 35.2	22 27.1	9 14.5	19 01.9	27 06.4	10 41.1	20 21.4	23 07.3
12 W	9 25 35	20 13 48	23 04 59	29 06 36	27 43.0	14 42.2	4 32.1	22 48.4	9 03.0	18 56.3	27 02.5	10 41.3	20 20.0	23 06.0
13 Th	9 29 32	21 11 24	5♊11 20	11♊19 46	27 44.0	16 45.3	5 29.5	23 09.1	8 51.2	18 50.8	26 58.7	10 41.4	20 18.7	23 04.8
14 F	9 33 28	22 09 03	17 32 31	23 50 09	27R44.8	18 48.3	6 27.3	23 29.2	8 39.3	18 45.4	26 54.9	10 41.5	20 17.3	23 03.5
15 Sa	9 37 25	23 06 42	0♋13 11	6♋42 02	27 44.5	20 50.8	7 25.6	23 48.8	8 27.2	18 40.2	26 51.1	10R41.5	20 15.9	23 02.3
16 Su	9 41 21	24 04 23	13 17 01	19 58 22	27 42.4	22 52.7	8 24.2	24 07.7	8 14.9	18 35.2	26 47.4	10 41.5	20 14.4	23 01.1
17 M	9 45 18	25 02 06	26 46 10	3♌40 19	27 37.9	24 53.9	9 23.3	24 26.0	8 02.5	18 30.3	26 43.8	10 41.4	20 13.0	22 59.9
18 Tu	9 49 14	25 59 50	10♌40 36	17 46 37	27 31.2	26 54.2	10 22.7	24 43.7	7 49.9	18 25.6	26 40.2	10 41.3	20 11.5	22 58.8
19 W	9 53 11	26 57 35	24 57 46	2♍13 20	27 22.8	28 53.4	11 22.5	25 00.7	7 37.1	18 21.0	26 36.7	10 41.1	20 10.0	22 57.6
20 Th	9 57 07	27 55 21	9♍32 28	16 54 11	27 13.5	0♍51.6	12 22.7	25 17.1	7 24.3	18 16.6	26 33.2	10 40.9	20 08.6	22 56.5
21 F	10 01 04	28 53 09	24 17 28	1♎41 17	27 04.5	2 48.5	13 23.2	25 32.8	7 11.3	18 12.3	26 29.8	10 40.6	20 07.0	22 55.4
22 Sa	10 05 01	29 50 58	9♎04 38	16 26 33	26 56.9	4 44.3	14 24.0	25 47.8	6 58.2	18 08.2	26 26.5	10 40.3	20 05.5	22 54.3
23 Su	10 08 57	0♍48 48	23 46 15	1♏02 59	26 51.4	6 38.7	15 25.2	26 02.1	6 45.1	18 04.3	26 23.2	10 39.9	20 04.0	22 53.2
24 M	10 12 54	1 46 40	8♏16 14	15 25 33	26 48.3	8 31.9	16 26.7	26 15.7	6 31.8	18 00.6	26 20.0	10 39.5	20 02.5	22 52.1
25 Tu	10 16 50	2 44 32	22 30 42	29 31 32	26D47.2	10 23.7	17 28.6	26 28.6	6 18.6	17 57.0	26 16.8	10 39.1	20 00.9	22 51.1
26 W	10 20 47	3 42 26	6♐28 01	13♐20 13	26R47.4	12 14.3	18 30.7	26 40.7	6 05.3	17 53.6	26 13.8	10 38.6	19 59.3	22 50.1
27 Th	10 24 43	4 40 22	20 08 16	26 52 20	26 47.7	14 03.5	19 33.1	26 52.2	5 51.9	17 50.4	26 10.8	10 38.0	19 57.8	22 49.1
28 F	10 28 40	5 38 18	3♑32 38	10♑09 22	26 47.0	15 51.4	20 35.9	27 02.8	5 38.6	17 47.4	26 07.9	10 37.4	19 56.2	22 48.1
29 Sa	10 32 36	6 36 16	16 42 45	23 12 58	26 44.3	17 38.0	21 38.9	27 12.8	5 25.3	17 44.6	26 05.1	10 36.7	19 54.6	22 47.2
30 Su	10 36 33	7 34 15	29 40 11	6♒04 33	26 38.9	19 23.3	22 42.2	27 21.9	5 12.0	17 41.9	26 02.3	10 36.0	19 53.0	22 46.2
31 M	10 40 30	8 32 15	12♒26 11	18 45 10	26 30.8	21 07.3	23 45.7	27 30.3	4 58.7	17 39.4	25 59.6	10 35.3	19 51.4	22 45.3

Astro Data

	Dy Hr Mn
⚳R	7 4:01
♂0N	11 12:17
☽0N	12 5:02
☿D	12 8:26
☽0S	25 21:34
♃✶♆	27 16:07
☽0N	8 12:16
♅R	15 14:26
☽0S	22 3:48

Planet Ingress

	Dy Hr Mn
♄ ♑R	1 23:37
☉ ♌	22 8:37
☿ ♌	5 3:32
♀ ♋	7 15:21
☿ ♍	20 1:30
☉ ♍	22 15:45

Last Aspect / ☽ Ingress

Last Aspect Dy Hr Mn		☽ Ingress Dy Hr Mn
2 1:20	♄ ✶	♐ 2 1:21
3 13:06	♆ □	♑ 4 4:48
6 9:35	♄ ☌	♒ 6 10:08
7 4:37	♅ □	♓ 8 18:12
11 3:49	♄ ✶	♈ 11 5:06
13 15:54	♄ □	♉ 13 17:34
16 3:21	♄ △	♊ 16 5:19
17 21:14	♆ □	♋ 18 14:24
20 17:55	♄ ☍	♌ 20 20:16
22 0:27	♀ ✶	♍ 22 23:40
24 23:08	♄ △	♎ 25 1:54
27 1:09	♄ □	♏ 27 4:12
29 4:01	♄ ✶	♐ 29 7:25
31 0:08	♀ ☍	♑ 31 11:58

Last Aspect / ☽ Ingress

Last Aspect Dy Hr Mn		☽ Ingress Dy Hr Mn
2 13:59	♄ ☌	♒ 2 18:11
4 21:45	♀ △	♓ 5 2:28
7 12:53	♀ □	♈ 7 13:05
9 19:50	♄ □	♉ 10 1:28
12 7:55	♄ △	♊ 12 13:46
14 11:19	♂ ✶	♋ 14 23:35
16 23:59	♄ ☍	♌ 17 5:38
19 5:38	☿ ☌	♍ 19 8:20
21 3:37	♄ △	♎ 21 9:16
23 4:20	♄ □	♏ 23 10:16
25 6:27	♄ ✶	♐ 25 12:49
27 12:00	♂ △	♑ 27 17:37
29 19:31	♂ □	♒ 30 0:37

☽ Phases & Eclipses

Dy Hr Mn	
5 4:44	○ 13♑38
5 4:30	• A 0.354
12 23:29	☾ 21♈03
20 17:33	● 28♋27
27 12:33	☽ 4♏56
3 15:59	○ 11♒46
11 16:45	☾ 19♉28
19 2:42	● 26♌35
25 17:58	☽ 2♐59

Astro Data

1 July 2020
Julian Day # 44012
SVP 4♓58'41"
GC 27♐07.5 ⚴ 24♑19.4R
Eris 24♈31.6 ⚵ 8♎53.8
⚷ 9♈23.4 ⚶ 12♋02.4
☽ Mean ☊ 28♊34.4

1 August 2020
Julian Day # 44043
SVP 4♓58'36"
GC 27♐07.6 ⚴ 16♑12.2R
Eris 24♈32.8R ⚵ 15♎25.1
⚷ 9♈15.3R ⚶ 25♋38.3
☽ Mean ☊ 26♊55.9

LONGITUDE — September 2020

Day	Sid.Time	☉	0 hr ☽	Noon ☽	True ☊	☿	♀	♂	⚳	♃	♄	♅	♆	♇
1 Tu	10 44 26	9♍30 17	25♒01 35	1♓15 30	26♊20.1	22♍50.0	24♋49.6	27♈37.8	4♓45.4	17♑37.2	25♑57.0	10♉34.5	19♓49.8	22♑44.4
2 W	10 48 23	10 28 21	7♓26 57	13 36 00	26R 07.7	24 31.5	25 53.7	27 44.6	4R 32.2	17R 35.1	25R 54.5	10R 33.6	19R 48.1	22R 43.5
3 Th	10 52 19	11 26 26	19 42 43	25 47 12	25 54.5	26 11.7	26 58.0	27 50.5	4 19.1	17 33.1	25 52.0	10 32.7	19 46.5	22 42.7
4 F	10 56 16	12 24 33	1♈49 34	7♈49 59	25 41.8	27 50.8	28 02.6	27 55.7	4 06.1	17 31.4	25 49.7	10 31.8	19 44.9	22 41.9
5 Sa	11 00 12	13 22 42	13 48 39	19 45 49	25 30.5	29 28.6	29 07.5	27 59.9	3 53.2	17 29.9	25 47.4	10 30.8	19 43.2	22 41.1
6 Su	11 04 09	14 20 52	25 41 47	1♉36 55	25 21.4	1♎05.2	0♌12.6	28 03.3	3 40.4	17 28.5	25 45.2	10 29.8	19 41.6	22 40.3
7 M	11 08 05	15 19 05	7♉31 37	13 26 21	25 15.1	2 40.7	1 17.9	28 05.9	3 27.7	17 27.3	25 43.1	10 28.7	19 40.0	22 39.5
8 Tu	11 12 02	16 17 20	19 21 36	25 17 58	25 11.3	4 15.0	2 23.5	28 07.6	3 15.1	17 26.4	25 41.1	10 27.6	19 38.3	22 38.8
9 W	11 15 59	17 15 36	1♊16 01	7♊16 22	25D 09.8	5 48.1	3 29.3	28R 08.4	3 02.7	17 25.6	25 39.2	10 26.4	19 36.7	22 38.1
10 Th	11 19 55	18 13 55	13 19 42	19 26 40	25R 09.5	7 20.1	4 35.3	28 08.4	2 50.5	17 25.0	25 37.3	10 25.2	19 35.0	22 37.4
11 F	11 23 52	19 12 16	25 37 56	1♋54 09	25 09.4	8 50.9	5 41.6	28 07.4	2 38.4	17 24.6	25 35.6	10 24.0	19 33.3	22 36.8
12 Sa	11 27 48	20 10 39	8♋15 58	14 43 56	25 08.4	10 20.5	6 48.0	28 05.6	2 26.5	17D 24.4	25 33.9	10 22.7	19 31.7	22 36.1
13 Su	11 31 45	21 09 04	21 18 32	28 00 11	25 05.5	11 49.0	7 54.7	28 02.9	2 14.9	17 24.4	25 32.3	10 21.4	19 30.0	22 35.5
14 M	11 35 41	22 07 32	4♌49 06	11♌45 25	25 00.0	13 16.4	9 01.5	27 59.2	2 03.4	17 24.6	25 30.9	10 20.0	19 28.4	22 35.0
15 Tu	11 39 38	23 06 01	18 49 01	25 59 37	24 51.9	14 42.5	10 08.6	27 54.7	1 52.2	17 25.0	25 29.5	10 18.6	19 26.7	22 34.4
16 W	11 43 34	24 04 32	3♍16 40	10♍39 28	24 41.7	16 07.5	11 15.8	27 49.4	1 41.2	17 25.6	25 28.2	10 17.1	19 25.1	22 33.9
17 Th	11 47 31	25 03 05	18 07 02	25 38 16	24 30.4	17 31.2	12 23.3	27 43.1	1 30.4	17 26.3	25 27.0	10 15.6	19 23.4	22 33.4
18 F	11 51 28	26 01 40	3♎11 54	10♎46 37	24 19.2	18 53.7	13 30.9	27 36.0	1 19.9	17 27.3	25 25.9	10 14.1	19 21.8	22 32.9
19 Sa	11 55 24	27 00 17	18 21 04	25 53 59	24 09.6	20 14.9	14 38.6	27 28.0	1 09.7	17 28.4	25 24.9	10 12.5	19 20.2	22 32.5
20 Su	11 59 21	27 58 56	3♏24 10	10♏50 36	24 02.3	21 34.8	15 46.6	27 19.2	0 59.7	17 29.8	25 24.0	10 10.9	19 18.5	22 32.0
21 M	12 03 17	28 57 36	18 12 26	25 29 03	23 57.9	22 53.4	16 54.7	27 09.6	0 50.0	17 31.3	25 23.2	10 09.2	19 16.9	22 31.7
22 Tu	12 07 14	29 56 18	2♐39 59	9♐45 02	23 55.9	24 10.5	18 03.0	26 59.3	0 40.7	17 33.1	25 22.4	10 07.5	19 15.3	22 31.3
23 W	12 11 10	0♎55 02	16 44 05	23 37 13	23 55.4	25 26.1	19 11.4	26 48.1	0 31.6	17 35.0	25 21.8	10 05.8	19 13.7	22 31.0
24 Th	12 15 07	1 53 48	0♑24 38	7♑06 37	23 55.4	26 40.2	20 20.1	26 36.2	0 22.8	17 37.1	25 21.3	10 04.1	19 12.0	22 30.7
25 F	12 19 03	2 52 35	13 43 28	20 15 36	23 54.5	27 52.7	21 28.8	26 23.6	0 14.4	17 39.4	25 20.9	10 02.3	19 10.5	22 30.4
26 Sa	12 23 00	3 51 24	26 43 23	3♒07 14	23 51.6	29 03.4	22 37.7	26 10.3	0 06.2	17 41.9	25 20.6	10 00.4	19 08.9	22 30.1
27 Su	12 26 57	4 50 15	9♒27 29	15 44 31	23 46.0	0♏12.3	23 46.8	25 56.4	29♒58.4	17 44.6	25 20.4	9 58.6	19 07.3	22 29.9
28 M	12 30 53	5 49 07	21 58 39	28 10 11	23 37.6	1 19.2	24 56.0	25 41.8	29 51.0	17 47.5	25D 20.3	9 56.7	19 05.7	22 29.7
29 Tu	12 34 50	6 48 01	4♓19 20	10♓26 20	23 26.6	2 24.0	26 05.4	25 26.6	29 43.8	17 50.5	25 20.2	9 54.7	19 04.1	22 29.6
30 W	12 38 46	7 46 57	16 31 24	22 34 40	23 13.8	3 26.5	27 14.9	25 10.9	29 37.0	17 53.7	25 20.3	9 52.8	19 02.6	22 29.4

LONGITUDE — October 2020

Day	Sid.Time	☉	0 hr ☽	Noon ☽	True ☊	☿	♀	♂	⚳	♃	♄	♅	♆	♇
1 Th	12 42 43	8♎45 55	28♓36 18	4♈36 27	23♊00.2	4♏26.7	28♌24.6	24♈54.6	29♒30.6	17♑57.2	25♑20.5	9♉50.8	19♓01.1	22♑29.3
2 F	12 46 39	9 44 55	10♈35 14	16 32 50	22R 46.9	5 24.2	29 34.4	24R 37.9	29R 24.5	18 00.8	25 20.8	9R 48.8	18R 59.5	22R 29.3
3 Sa	12 50 36	10 43 57	22 29 23	28 25 05	22 35.2	6 18.8	0♍44.3	24 20.7	29 18.7	18 04.5	25 21.1	9 46.7	18 58.0	22 29.2
4 Su	12 54 32	11 43 02	4♉20 09	10♉14 52	22 25.6	7 10.3	1 54.4	24 03.1	29 13.3	18 08.5	25 21.6	9 44.6	18 56.5	22D 29.2
5 M	12 58 29	12 42 08	16 09 30	22 04 24	22 18.8	7 58.5	3 04.6	23 45.1	29 08.3	18 12.6	25 22.2	9 42.5	18 55.0	22 29.2
6 Tu	13 02 25	13 41 17	27 59 58	3♊56 38	22 14.8	8 43.0	4 15.0	23 26.8	29 03.6	18 16.9	25 22.9	9 40.4	18 53.6	22 29.3
7 W	13 06 22	14 40 28	9♊54 53	15 55 14	22D 13.2	9 23.5	5 25.5	23 08.3	28 59.3	18 21.4	25 23.6	9 38.3	18 52.1	22 29.3
8 Th	13 10 19	15 39 41	21 58 16	28 04 33	22 13.1	9 59.6	6 36.1	22 49.5	28 55.3	18 26.1	25 24.5	9 36.1	18 50.7	22 29.4
9 F	13 14 15	16 38 57	4♋14 43	10♋29 24	22R 13.6	10 30.9	7 46.8	22 30.5	28 51.8	18 30.9	25 25.5	9 33.9	18 49.2	22 29.6
10 Sa	13 18 12	17 38 14	16 49 13	23 14 47	22 13.6	10 57.0	8 57.7	22 11.4	28 48.5	18 35.9	25 26.6	9 31.7	18 47.8	22 29.7
11 Su	13 22 08	18 37 35	29 46 37	6♌25 15	22 12.1	11 17.4	10 08.7	21 52.2	28 45.7	18 41.1	25 27.7	9 29.4	18 46.5	22 29.9
12 M	13 26 05	19 36 57	13♌11 03	20 04 16	22 08.5	11 31.6	11 19.8	21 33.0	28 43.2	18 46.5	25 29.0	9 27.2	18 45.1	22 30.1
13 Tu	13 30 01	20 36 22	27 05 01	4♍13 12	22 02.5	11R 39.1	12 31.0	21 13.8	28 41.1	18 52.0	25 30.4	9 24.9	18 43.7	22 30.4
14 W	13 33 58	21 35 49	11♍28 31	18 50 26	21 54.5	11 39.4	13 42.3	20 54.7	28 39.3	18 57.7	25 31.8	9 22.6	18 42.4	22 30.7
15 Th	13 37 54	22 35 18	26 18 11	3♎50 47	21 45.4	11 32.0	14 53.8	20 35.7	28 38.0	19 03.5	25 33.4	9 20.2	18 41.1	22 31.0
16 F	13 41 51	23 34 49	11♎27 03	19 05 39	21 36.3	11 16.6	16 05.3	20 16.9	28 37.0	19 09.5	25 35.1	9 17.9	18 39.8	22 31.3
17 Sa	13 45 48	24 34 23	26 45 10	4♏24 11	21 28.4	10 52.7	17 17.0	19 58.3	28 36.3	19 15.7	25 36.8	9 15.5	18 38.5	22 31.7
18 Su	13 49 44	25 33 58	12♏01 18	19 35 13	21 22.5	10 20.2	18 28.7	19 40.0	28D 36.1	19 22.0	25 38.7	9 13.2	18 37.3	22 32.1
19 M	13 53 41	26 33 36	27 04 49	4♐29 11	21 19.1	9 39.1	19 40.6	19 22.1	28 36.2	19 28.5	25 40.6	9 10.8	18 36.0	22 32.5
20 Tu	13 57 37	27 33 15	11♐47 35	18 59 31	21D 17.9	8 49.5	20 52.5	19 04.5	28 36.6	19 35.2	25 42.7	9 08.4	18 34.8	22 33.0
21 W	14 01 34	28 32 56	26 04 42	3♑03 01	21 18.3	7 52.2	22 04.5	18 47.4	28 37.5	19 42.0	25 44.9	9 06.0	18 33.7	22 33.5
22 Th	14 05 30	29 32 39	9♑54 33	16 39 30	21 19.3	6 47.9	23 16.7	18 30.7	28 38.7	19 49.0	25 47.1	9 03.5	18 32.5	22 34.0
23 F	14 09 27	0♏32 23	23 18 11	29 50 58	21R 19.9	5 37.9	24 28.9	18 14.5	28 40.3	19 56.1	25 49.4	9 01.1	18 31.4	22 34.5
24 Sa	14 13 23	1 32 09	6♒18 18	12♒40 41	21 19.2	4 24.0	25 41.2	17 58.9	28 42.2	20 03.4	25 51.9	8 58.7	18 30.3	22 35.1
25 Su	14 17 20	2 31 57	18 58 35	25 12 30	21 16.5	3 08.1	26 53.6	17 43.9	28 44.5	20 10.8	25 54.4	8 56.2	18 29.2	22 35.7
26 M	14 21 17	3 31 46	1♓22 55	7♓30 16	21 11.7	1 52.4	28 06.0	17 29.4	28 47.1	20 18.4	25 57.0	8 53.8	18 28.1	22 36.3
27 Tu	14 25 13	4 31 37	13 35 01	19 37 32	21 05.0	0 39.3	29 18.6	17 15.6	28 50.1	20 26.1	25 59.7	8 51.3	18 27.1	22 37.0
28 W	14 29 10	5 31 30	25 38 12	1♈37 20	20 56.8	29♎31.0	0♎31.2	17 02.5	28 53.4	20 33.9	26 02.5	8 48.8	18 26.1	22 37.7
29 Th	14 33 06	6 31 24	7♈35 14	13 32 10	20 48.0	28 29.6	1 44.0	16 50.0	28 57.1	20 41.9	26 05.4	8 46.4	18 25.1	22 38.4
30 F	14 37 03	7 31 21	19 28 23	25 24 06	20 39.3	27 37.0	2 56.8	16 38.3	29 01.1	20 50.1	26 08.4	8 43.9	18 24.1	22 39.2
31 Sa	14 40 59	8 31 19	1♉19 32	7♉14 53	20 31.7	26 54.4	4 09.6	16 27.2	29 05.4	20 58.3	26 11.5	8 41.4	18 23.2	22 39.9

Astro Data

	Dy Hr Mn
☽ 0N	4 18:49
☿ 0S	6 6:26
♂ R	9 22:23
♃ D	13 0:41
☽ 0S	18 12:35
☉ 0S	22 13:30
♄ D	29 5:11
☽ 0N	2 1:00
♇ D	4 13:32
♃✶♆	12 7:06
☿ R	14 1:04
☽ 0S	15 23:31
⚳ D	18 16:59
☽ 0N	29 7:17
♀ 0S	31 2:04

Planet Ingress

	Dy Hr Mn
☿ ♎	5 19:46
♀ ♌	6 7:22
☉ ♎	22 13:31
⚳ ♒R	27 7:08
☿ ♏	27 7:41
♀ ♍	2 20:48
☉ ♏	22 22:59
☿ ♎R	28 1:33
♀ ♎	28 1:41

Last Aspect / ☽ Ingress (September)

Last Aspect Dy Hr Mn		☽ Ingress Dy Hr Mn
1 4:56 ♂ ✶	♓	1 9:34
3 14:34 ♀ △	♈	3 20:22
6 4:45 ♂ ☌	♉	6 8:43
8 12:46 ♄ △	♊	8 21:27
11 4:48 ♂ ✶	♋	11 8:23
13 12:05 ♂ □	♌	13 15:32
15 15:09 ♂ △	♍	15 18:37
17 11:42 ♄ △	♎	17 18:56
19 14:29 ♂ ☍	♏	19 18:33
21 18:13 ☉ ✶	♐	21 19:32
23 17:31 ♂ △	♑	23 23:16
26 3:36 ☿ □	♒	26 6:08
28 7:18 ♂ ✶	♓	28 15:34

Last Aspect / ☽ Ingress (October)

Last Aspect Dy Hr Mn		☽ Ingress Dy Hr Mn
30 17:29 ♄ ✶	♈	1 2:47
3 5:47 ♄ □	♉	3 15:12
5 18:41 ♄ △	♊	6 4:03
8 1:57 ♂ ✶	♋	8 15:45
10 16:04 ♄ ☍	♌	11 0:24
12 14:29 ♂ △	♍	13 4:56
14 22:47 ♄ △	♎	15 5:54
16 22:11 ♄ □	♏	17 5:05
18 21:43 ♄ ✶	♐	19 4:43
21 3:38 ☉ ✶	♑	21 6:44
23 4:35 ♄ ☌	♒	23 12:17
24 21:54 ♂ ✶	♓	25 21:18
28 0:46 ♄ ✶	♈	28 8:45
30 16:12 ☿ ☍	♉	30 21:19

☽ Phases & Eclipses

Dy Hr Mn	
2 5:22	○ 10♓12
10 9:26	☾ 18♊08
17 11:00	● 25♍01
24 1:55	☽ 1♑29
1 21:05	○ 9♈08
10 0:39	☾ 17♋10
16 19:31	● 23♎53
23 13:23	☽ 0♒36
31 14:49	○ 8♉38

Astro Data

1 September 2020
Julian Day # 44074
SVP 4♓58'32"
GC 27♐07.7 ⚴ 12♑16.2R
Eris 24♈24.3R ⚵ 24♎03.8
⚷ 8♈22.2R ⚶ 9♌07.3
☽ Mean ☊ 25♊17.4

1 October 2020
Julian Day # 44104
SVP 4♓58'29"
GC 27♐07.7 ⚴ 14♑00.5
Eris 24♈09.2R ⚵ 3♏36.0
⚷ 7♈05.0R ⚶ 21♌44.5
☽ Mean ☊ 23♊42.1

November 2020 LONGITUDE

Day	Sid.Time	☉	0 hr ☽	Noon ☽	True ☊	☿	♀	♂	⚳	♃	♄	♅	♆	♇
1 Su	14 44 56	9♏31 19	13♉10 23	19♉06 12	20♊25.7	26♎22.8	5♎22.6	16♈16.9	29♒10.1	21♑06.8	26♑14.7	8♉39.0	18♓22.3	22♑40.7
2 M	14 48 52	10 31 21	25 02 36	0♊59 49	20R 21.7	26R 02.7	6 35.6	16R 07.3	29 15.1	21 15.3	26 17.9	8R 36.5	18R 21.5	22 41.6
3 Tu	14 52 49	11 31 25	6♊58 07	12 57 48	20D 19.8	25D 54.2	7 48.8	15 58.6	29 20.4	21 24.0	26 21.2	8 34.0	18 20.6	22 42.4
4 W	14 56 46	12 31 32	18 59 12	25 02 41	20 19.6	25 57.0	9 01.9	15 50.5	29 26.1	21 32.8	26 24.7	8 31.6	18 19.8	22 43.3
5 Th	15 00 42	13 31 40	1♋08 39	7♋17 31	20 20.7	26 10.8	10 15.2	15 43.3	29 32.1	21 41.7	26 28.2	8 29.1	18 19.0	22 44.2
6 F	15 04 39	14 31 50	13 29 44	19 45 47	20 22.3	26 34.6	11 28.5	15 36.8	29 38.4	21 50.8	26 31.8	8 26.6	18 18.3	22 45.2
7 Sa	15 08 35	15 32 02	26 06 09	2♌31 19	20 23.8	27 07.9	12 42.0	15 31.2	29 45.0	22 00.0	26 35.5	8 24.2	18 17.5	22 46.2
8 Su	15 12 32	16 32 16	9♌01 45	15 37 52	20R 24.5	27 49.7	13 55.4	15 26.3	29 51.9	22 09.3	26 39.2	8 21.8	18 16.9	22 47.1
9 M	15 16 28	17 32 33	22 20 03	29 08 36	20 24.0	28 39.0	15 09.0	15 22.3	29 59.1	22 18.8	26 43.1	8 19.3	18 16.2	22 48.2
10 Tu	15 20 25	18 32 51	6♍03 42	13♍05 25	20 21.9	29 35.1	16 22.6	15 19.0	0♓06.7	22 28.4	26 47.0	8 16.9	18 15.6	22 49.2
11 W	15 24 21	19 33 11	20 13 40	27 28 09	20 18.5	0♏37.0	17 36.2	15 16.6	0 14.5	22 38.1	26 51.0	8 14.5	18 15.0	22 50.3
12 Th	15 28 18	20 33 33	4♎48 27	12♎13 53	20 14.4	1 44.1	18 49.9	15 14.9	0 22.6	22 47.9	26 55.1	8 12.1	18 14.4	22 51.4
13 F	15 32 15	21 33 57	19 43 37	27 16 38	20 10.0	2 55.6	20 03.7	15D 14.1	0 31.0	22 57.8	26 59.3	8 09.7	18 13.8	22 52.5
14 Sa	15 36 11	22 34 23	4♏51 48	12♏27 52	20 06.3	4 10.9	21 17.6	15 14.1	0 39.8	23 07.8	27 03.5	8 07.3	18 13.3	22 53.7
15 Su	15 40 08	23 34 51	20 03 33	27 37 35	20 03.6	5 29.4	22 31.5	15 14.9	0 48.8	23 18.0	27 07.9	8 04.9	18 12.9	22 54.8
16 M	15 44 04	24 35 20	5♐08 47	12♐36 01	20D 02.2	6 50.7	23 45.4	15 16.5	0 58.1	23 28.3	27 12.3	8 02.6	18 12.4	22 56.0
17 Tu	15 48 01	25 35 51	19 58 23	27 15 05	20 02.2	8 14.3	24 59.4	15 18.8	1 07.6	23 38.7	27 16.8	8 00.3	18 12.0	22 57.3
18 W	15 51 57	26 36 23	4♑25 33	11♑29 23	20 03.2	9 39.8	26 13.4	15 22.0	1 17.5	23 49.2	27 21.3	7 58.0	18 11.7	22 58.5
19 Th	15 55 54	27 36 57	18 26 23	25 16 31	20 04.7	11 06.9	27 27.5	15 26.0	1 27.6	23 59.8	27 26.0	7 55.7	18 11.3	22 59.8
20 F	15 59 50	28 37 32	1♒59 52	8♒36 40	20 06.2	12 35.3	28 41.6	15 30.7	1 38.0	24 10.5	27 30.7	7 53.4	18 11.0	23 01.1
21 Sa	16 03 47	29 38 08	15 07 17	21 32 06	20R 07.2	14 04.9	29 55.8	15 36.1	1 48.6	24 21.3	27 35.5	7 51.1	18 10.7	23 02.4
22 Su	16 07 44	0♐38 45	27 51 35	4♓06 16	20 07.3	15 35.3	1♏10.0	15 42.3	1 59.5	24 32.2	27 40.3	7 48.9	18 10.5	23 03.8
23 M	16 11 40	1 39 23	10♓16 41	16 23 23	20 06.6	17 06.5	2 24.2	15 49.3	2 10.7	24 43.2	27 45.3	7 46.7	18 10.3	23 05.1
24 Tu	16 15 37	2 40 02	22 26 55	28 27 49	20 05.0	18 38.3	3 38.5	15 56.9	2 22.1	24 54.3	27 50.2	7 44.5	18 10.1	23 06.5
25 W	16 19 33	3 40 42	4♈26 35	10♈23 45	20 02.8	20 10.5	4 52.9	16 05.3	2 33.8	25 05.5	27 55.3	7 42.4	18 10.0	23 07.9
26 Th	16 23 30	4 41 24	16 19 45	22 15 03	20 00.3	21 43.1	6 07.2	16 14.3	2 45.7	25 16.8	28 00.4	7 40.2	18 09.9	23 09.4
27 F	16 27 26	5 42 07	28 10 02	4♉05 04	19 57.8	23 16.0	7 21.6	16 24.1	2 57.8	25 28.2	28 05.6	7 38.1	18 09.8	23 10.8
28 Sa	16 31 23	6 42 51	10♉00 31	15 56 40	19 55.8	24 49.1	8 36.1	16 34.4	3 10.2	25 39.7	28 10.9	7 36.0	18D 09.8	23 12.3
29 Su	16 35 19	7 43 36	21 53 49	27 52 13	19 54.3	26 22.4	9 50.5	16 45.5	3 22.8	25 51.3	28 16.2	7 34.0	18 09.8	23 13.8
30 M	16 39 16	8 44 22	3♊52 06	9♊53 41	19D 53.4	27 55.9	11 05.0	16 57.1	3 35.7	26 02.9	28 21.6	7 32.0	18 09.8	23 15.3

December 2020 LONGITUDE

Day	Sid.Time	☉	0 hr ☽	Noon ☽	True ☊	☿	♀	♂	⚳	♃	♄	♅	♆	♇
1 Tu	16 43 13	9♐45 10	15♊57 11	22♊02 48	19♊53.2	29♏29.4	12♏19.6	17♈09.4	3♓48.7	26♑14.7	28♑27.0	7♉30.0	18♓09.9	23♑16.9
2 W	16 47 09	10 45 59	28 10 43	4♋21 08	19 53.6	1♐03.0	13 34.2	17 22.3	4 02.0	26 26.5	28 32.6	7R 28.0	18 10.0	23 18.4
3 Th	16 51 06	11 46 49	10♋34 15	16 50 16	19 54.2	2 36.6	14 48.8	17 35.8	4 15.5	26 38.5	28 38.1	7 26.1	18 10.1	23 20.0
4 F	16 55 02	12 47 40	23 09 25	29 31 54	19 55.0	4 10.3	16 03.4	17 49.9	4 29.3	26 50.5	28 43.8	7 24.2	18 10.3	23 21.6
5 Sa	16 58 59	13 48 33	5♌57 58	12♌27 49	19 55.7	5 44.0	17 18.1	18 04.5	4 43.2	27 02.5	28 49.4	7 22.4	18 10.5	23 23.2
6 Su	17 02 55	14 49 27	19 01 42	25 39 49	19 56.2	7 17.7	18 32.8	18 19.7	4 57.3	27 14.7	28 55.2	7 20.6	18 10.7	23 24.8
7 M	17 06 52	15 50 22	2♍22 22	9♍09 30	19R 56.5	8 51.5	19 47.6	18 35.4	5 11.7	27 26.9	29 01.0	7 18.8	18 11.0	23 26.5
8 Tu	17 10 48	16 51 19	16 01 21	22 57 56	19 56.5	10 25.3	21 02.3	18 51.7	5 26.2	27 39.3	29 06.8	7 17.0	18 11.3	23 28.1
9 W	17 14 45	17 52 16	29 59 14	7♎05 09	19 56.4	11 59.1	22 17.1	19 08.4	5 41.0	27 51.6	29 12.7	7 15.3	18 11.7	23 29.8
10 Th	17 18 42	18 53 15	14♎15 26	21 29 45	19D 56.2	13 32.9	23 31.9	19 25.7	5 56.0	28 04.1	29 18.7	7 13.6	18 12.0	23 31.5
11 F	17 22 38	19 54 15	28 47 38	6♏08 30	19 56.2	15 06.8	24 46.8	19 43.5	6 11.1	28 16.7	29 24.7	7 12.0	18 12.4	23 33.2
12 Sa	17 26 35	20 55 16	13♏31 39	20 56 19	19 56.2	16 40.8	26 01.7	20 01.8	6 26.4	28 29.3	29 30.8	7 10.4	18 12.9	23 35.0
13 Su	17 30 31	21 56 19	28 21 35	5♐46 31	19R 56.3	18 14.8	27 16.6	20 20.6	6 42.0	28 41.9	29 36.9	7 08.8	18 13.4	23 36.7
14 M	17 34 28	22 57 22	13♐10 12	20 31 40	19 56.4	19 48.9	28 31.5	20 39.8	6 57.7	28 54.7	29 43.1	7 07.3	18 13.9	23 38.5
15 Tu	17 38 24	23 58 26	27 50 00	5♑04 25	19 56.3	21 23.1	29 46.4	20 59.5	7 13.6	29 07.5	29 49.3	7 05.8	18 14.5	23 40.3
16 W	17 42 21	24 59 31	12♑14 10	19 18 40	19 55.9	22 57.4	1♐01.4	21 19.7	7 29.7	29 20.4	29 55.5	7 04.4	18 15.0	23 42.1
17 Th	17 46 18	26 00 36	26 17 26	3♒10 11	19 55.3	24 31.8	2 16.3	21 40.3	7 45.9	29 33.3	0♒01.8	7 03.0	18 15.7	23 43.9
18 F	17 50 14	27 01 41	9♒56 42	16 36 58	19 54.4	26 06.4	3 31.3	22 01.3	8 02.4	29 46.3	0 08.2	7 01.7	18 16.3	23 45.7
19 Sa	17 54 11	28 02 47	23 11 05	29 39 14	19 53.5	27 41.1	4 46.3	22 22.7	8 19.0	29 59.4	0 14.6	7 00.3	18 17.0	23 47.5
20 Su	17 58 07	29 03 53	6♓01 45	12♓19 02	19 52.7	29 16.0	6 01.3	22 44.6	8 35.7	0♒12.5	0 21.0	6 59.1	18 17.7	23 49.4
21 M	18 02 04	0♑05 00	18 31 31	24 39 44	19D 52.2	0♑51.0	7 16.3	23 06.8	8 52.7	0 25.7	0 27.5	6 57.9	18 18.5	23 51.2
22 Tu	18 06 00	1 06 06	0♈44 14	6♈45 37	19 52.2	2 26.3	8 31.3	23 29.4	9 09.7	0 38.9	0 34.0	6 56.7	18 19.3	23 53.1
23 W	18 09 57	2 07 13	12 44 28	18 41 23	19 52.8	4 01.7	9 46.4	23 52.4	9 27.0	0 52.2	0 40.5	6 55.6	18 20.1	23 55.0
24 Th	18 13 53	3 08 20	24 36 59	0♉31 49	19 53.8	5 37.4	11 01.4	24 15.8	9 44.4	1 05.5	0 47.1	6 54.5	18 21.0	23 56.8
25 F	18 17 50	4 09 27	6♉26 29	12 21 31	19 55.2	7 13.3	12 16.5	24 39.5	10 01.9	1 18.9	0 53.7	6 53.5	18 21.8	23 58.7
26 Sa	18 21 47	5 10 34	18 17 26	24 14 41	19 56.6	8 49.5	13 31.6	25 03.5	10 19.6	1 32.3	1 00.3	6 52.5	18 22.8	24 00.6
27 Su	18 25 43	6 11 42	0♊13 44	6♊14 56	19 57.7	10 25.9	14 46.7	25 27.9	10 37.5	1 45.8	1 07.0	6 51.6	18 23.7	24 02.6
28 M	18 29 40	7 12 49	12 18 40	18 25 13	19R 58.2	12 02.6	16 01.8	25 52.6	10 55.5	1 59.3	1 13.7	6 50.7	18 24.7	24 04.5
29 Tu	18 33 36	8 13 57	24 34 49	0♋47 41	19 57.9	13 39.5	17 16.9	26 17.6	11 13.6	2 12.9	1 20.5	6 49.8	18 25.7	24 06.4
30 W	18 37 33	9 15 05	7♋03 56	13 23 40	19 56.5	15 16.7	18 32.0	26 42.9	11 31.9	2 26.5	1 27.3	6 49.0	18 26.8	24 08.4
31 Th	18 41 29	10 16 13	19 46 57	26 13 47	19 54.2	16 54.1	19 47.1	27 08.5	11 50.3	2 40.1	1 34.1	6 48.3	18 27.9	24 10.3

Astro Data	Planet Ingress	Last Aspect	☽ Ingress	Last Aspect	☽ Ingress	☽ Phases & Eclipses	Astro Data
Dy Hr Mn	Dy Hr Mn	Dy Hr Mn	Dy Hr Mn	Dy Hr Mn	Dy Hr Mn	Dy Hr Mn	1 November 2020
☿ D 3 17:51	⚳ ♓ 9 14:48	2 2:29 ♄ △	♊ 2 10:00	1 4:22 ♆ □	♋ 2 3:33	8 13:46 ☾ 16♌37	Julian Day # 44135
☽ 0S 12 10:33	☿ ♏ 10 21:55	4 13:49 ☿ △	♋ 4 21:45	4 10:29 ♄ ☍	♌ 4 12:53	15 5:07 ● 23♏18	SVP 4♓58'26"
♃☌♇ 12 21:39	♀ ♏ 21 13:22	7 1:27 ☿ □	♌ 7 7:18	5 22:28 ♂ △	♍ 6 19:46	22 4:45 ☽ 0♓20	GC 27♐07.8 ⚴ 19♑58.2
♂ D 14 0:35	☉ ♐ 21 20:40	9 11:05 ☿ ⚹	♍ 9 13:30	8 22:35 ♄ △	♎ 9 0:01	30 9:30 ○ 8♊38	Eris 23♈50.9R ⚵ 14♏03.5
☽ 0N 25 14:03		11 10:58 ♄ △	♎ 11 16:09	11 0:56 ♄ □	♏ 11 1:58	30 9:43 • A 0.828	⚷ 5♈47.4R ⚶ 3♍48.2
♆ D 29 0:36	☿ ♐ 1 19:51	13 11:32 ♄ □	♏ 13 16:19	13 1:58 ♄ ⚹	♐ 13 2:39		☽ Mean ☊ 22♊03.6
	♀ ♐ 15 16:21	15 11:13 ♄ ⚹	♐ 15 15:47	14 16:17 ☉ ☌	♑ 15 3:35	8 0:37 ☾ 16♍22	
☽ 0S 9 19:21	♄ ♒ 17 5:04	17 7:54 ♀ ⚹	♑ 17 16:35	17 5:34 ♃ ☌	♒ 17 6:27	14 16:17 ● 23♐08	1 December 2020
♃☌♄ 21 18:20	♃ ♒ 19 13:07	19 16:30 ☉ ⚹	♒ 19 20:25	19 8:45 ☉ ⚹	♓ 19 12:39	14 16:13:27 • T 02'10"	Julian Day # 44165
☽ 0N 22 21:24	☿ ♑ 20 23:07	21 0:49 ♂ ⚹	♓ 22 4:06	21 10:24 ♇ ⚹	♈ 21 22:32	21 23:41 ☽ 0♈35	SVP 4♓58'21"
	☉ ♑ 21 10:02	24 10:44 ♄ ⚹	♈ 24 15:05	23 22:51 ♂ ☌	♉ 24 10:55	30 3:28 ○ 8♋53	GC 27♐07.9 ⚴ 28♑10.3
		26 23:46 ♄ □	♉ 27 3:43	26 11:32 ♇ △	♊ 26 23:33		Eris 23♈35.7R ⚵ 24♏16.7
		29 12:48 ♄ △	♊ 29 16:16	29 3:01 ♂ ⚹	♋ 29 10:28		⚷ 5♈02.2R ⚶ 13♍37.6
				31 13:45 ♂ □	♌ 31 18:58		☽ Mean ☊ 20♊28.3

LONGITUDE — January 2021

Day	Sid.Time	☉	0 hr ☽	Noon ☽	True ☊	☿	♀	♂	⚳	♃	♄	♅	♆	♇
1 F	18 45 26	11♑17 22	2♌44 08	9♌17 56	19♊51.0	18♑31.8	21♐02.2	27♈34.5	12♓08.9	2♒53.8	1♒40.9	6♉47.6	18♓29.0	24♑12.3
2 Sa	18 49 22	12 18 30	15 55 06	22 35 31	19R47.5	20 09.7	22 17.4	28 00.6	12 27.5	3 07.6	1 47.8	6R47.0	18 30.1	24 14.2
3 Su	18 53 19	13 19 39	29 19 05	6♍05 39	19 44.1	21 47.8	23 32.5	28 27.1	12 46.3	3 21.3	1 54.6	6 46.4	18 31.3	24 16.2
4 M	18 57 16	14 20 47	12♍55 06	19 47 18	19 41.3	23 26.1	24 47.7	28 53.8	13 05.3	3 35.1	2 01.6	6 45.9	18 32.5	24 18.2
5 Tu	19 01 12	15 21 56	26 42 06	3♎39 24	19D39.6	25 04.5	26 02.9	29 20.8	13 24.3	3 49.0	2 08.5	6 45.4	18 33.7	24 20.1
6 W	19 05 09	16 23 06	10♎39 02	17 40 52	19 39.1	26 43.0	27 18.1	29 48.1	13 43.5	4 02.8	2 15.4	6 44.9	18 35.0	24 22.1
7 Th	19 09 05	17 24 15	24 44 45	1♏50 29	19 39.7	28 21.5	28 33.3	0♉15.6	14 02.8	4 16.7	2 22.4	6 44.5	18 36.3	24 24.1
8 F	19 13 02	18 25 25	8♏57 51	16 06 35	19 41.1	0♒00.0	29 48.5	0 43.3	14 22.2	4 30.7	2 29.4	6 44.2	18 37.6	24 26.1
9 Sa	19 16 58	19 26 35	23 16 22	0♐26 52	19 42.7	1 38.4	1♑03.7	1 11.3	14 41.8	4 44.6	2 36.4	6 43.9	18 38.9	24 28.1
10 Su	19 20 55	20 27 45	7♐37 39	14 48 13	19R43.7	3 16.5	2 18.9	1 39.5	15 01.4	4 58.6	2 43.4	6 43.7	18 40.3	24 30.1
11 M	19 24 51	21 28 54	21 58 05	29 06 40	19 43.4	4 54.2	3 34.1	2 08.0	15 21.2	5 12.6	2 50.5	6 43.5	18 41.7	24 32.1
12 Tu	19 28 48	22 30 04	6♑13 23	13♑17 38	19 41.5	6 31.3	4 49.3	2 36.6	15 41.1	5 26.7	2 57.6	6 43.4	18 43.2	24 34.1
13 W	19 32 45	23 31 14	20 18 51	27 16 27	19 37.8	8 07.7	6 04.5	3 05.5	16 01.1	5 40.8	3 04.6	6D43.3	18 44.6	24 36.1
14 Th	19 36 41	24 32 22	4♒09 58	10♒58 58	19 32.6	9 43.1	7 19.8	3 34.6	16 21.2	5 54.9	3 11.7	6 43.3	18 46.1	24 38.1
15 F	19 40 38	25 33 31	17 43 07	24 22 10	19 26.3	11 17.2	8 35.0	4 04.0	16 41.4	6 09.0	3 18.8	6 43.3	18 47.6	24 40.1
16 Sa	19 44 34	26 34 39	0♓56 00	7♓24 35	19 19.8	12 49.7	9 50.2	4 33.5	17 01.7	6 23.1	3 25.9	6 43.4	18 49.2	24 42.1
17 Su	19 48 31	27 35 46	13 48 01	20 06 30	19 13.8	14 20.3	11 05.4	5 03.2	17 22.1	6 37.3	3 33.1	6 43.6	18 50.7	24 44.1
18 M	19 52 27	28 36 52	26 20 17	2♈29 45	19 08.9	15 48.6	12 20.7	5 33.1	17 42.7	6 51.4	3 40.2	6 43.8	18 52.3	24 46.1
19 Tu	19 56 24	29 37 57	8♈35 22	14 37 37	19 05.7	17 13.9	13 35.9	6 03.2	18 03.3	7 05.6	3 47.3	6 44.0	18 53.9	24 48.1
20 W	20 00 20	0♒39 02	20 37 05	26 34 20	19D04.3	18 35.9	14 51.1	6 33.5	18 24.0	7 19.8	3 54.5	6 44.3	18 55.6	24 50.0
21 Th	20 04 17	1 40 05	2♉30 02	8♉24 49	19 04.4	19 53.8	16 06.3	7 03.9	18 44.8	7 34.0	4 01.6	6 44.6	18 57.3	24 52.0
22 F	20 08 14	2 41 08	14 19 20	20 14 15	19 05.7	21 07.1	17 21.5	7 34.5	19 05.6	7 48.2	4 08.7	6 45.0	18 58.9	24 54.0
23 Sa	20 12 10	3 42 10	26 10 13	2♊07 52	19 07.3	22 14.9	18 36.7	8 05.3	19 26.6	8 02.4	4 15.9	6 45.5	19 00.7	24 56.0
24 Su	20 16 07	4 43 11	8♊07 48	14 10 34	19R08.4	23 16.5	19 51.9	8 36.3	19 47.7	8 16.7	4 23.0	6 46.0	19 02.4	24 58.0
25 M	20 20 03	5 44 11	20 16 42	26 26 38	19 08.2	24 11.0	21 07.1	9 07.4	20 08.8	8 30.9	4 30.2	6 46.6	19 04.2	25 00.0
26 Tu	20 24 00	6 45 10	2♋40 47	8♋59 27	19 06.1	24 57.6	22 22.3	9 38.6	20 30.0	8 45.1	4 37.3	6 47.2	19 05.9	25 01.9
27 W	20 27 56	7 46 08	15 22 50	21 51 06	19 01.8	25 35.5	23 37.5	10 10.0	20 51.4	8 59.4	4 44.5	6 47.8	19 07.7	25 03.9
28 Th	20 31 53	8 47 05	28 24 14	5♌02 11	18 55.3	26 03.9	24 52.7	10 41.5	21 12.7	9 13.7	4 51.6	6 48.6	19 09.6	25 05.8
29 F	20 35 50	9 48 01	11♌44 46	18 31 42	18 47.0	26 22.0	26 07.9	11 13.2	21 34.2	9 27.9	4 58.7	6 49.3	19 11.4	25 07.8
30 Sa	20 39 46	10 48 56	25 22 38	2♍17 07	18 37.9	26R29.3	27 23.1	11 45.0	21 55.7	9 42.1	5 05.9	6 50.1	19 13.3	25 09.7
31 Su	20 43 43	11 49 50	9♍14 40	16 14 46	18 28.9	26 25.5	28 38.3	12 16.9	22 17.4	9 56.4	5 13.0	6 51.0	19 15.2	25 11.7

LONGITUDE — February 2021

Day	Sid.Time	☉	0 hr ☽	Noon ☽	True ☊	☿	♀	♂	⚳	♃	♄	♅	♆	♇
1 M	20 47 39	12♒50 43	23♍16 54	0♎20 30	18♊21.0	26♒10.4	29♑53.5	12♉49.0	22♓39.0	10♒10.6	5♒20.1	6♉51.9	19♓17.1	25♑13.6
2 Tu	20 51 36	13 51 35	7♎25 06	14 30 15	18R15.2	25R44.2	1♒08.6	13 21.2	23 00.8	10 24.9	5 27.2	6 52.9	19 19.0	25 15.5
3 W	20 55 32	14 52 27	21 35 32	28 40 39	18 11.7	25 07.4	2 23.8	13 53.5	23 22.6	10 39.1	5 34.3	6 53.9	19 20.9	25 17.4
4 Th	20 59 29	15 53 18	5♏45 19	12♏49 19	18D10.5	24 20.9	3 39.0	14 25.9	23 44.5	10 53.4	5 41.4	6 55.0	19 22.9	25 19.3
5 F	21 03 25	16 54 08	19 52 30	26 54 45	18 10.7	23 25.9	4 54.2	14 58.4	24 06.5	11 07.6	5 48.4	6 56.1	19 24.9	25 21.2
6 Sa	21 07 22	17 54 57	3♐55 58	10♐56 04	18R11.5	22 24.0	6 09.4	15 31.1	24 28.6	11 21.8	5 55.5	6 57.3	19 26.9	25 23.1
7 Su	21 11 18	18 55 45	17 54 58	24 52 32	18 11.4	21 16.8	7 24.5	16 03.9	24 50.7	11 36.0	6 02.5	6 58.5	19 28.9	25 25.0
8 M	21 15 15	19 56 33	1♑48 39	8♑43 09	18 09.6	20 06.4	8 39.7	16 36.7	25 12.8	11 50.3	6 09.6	6 59.8	19 30.9	25 26.8
9 Tu	21 19 12	20 57 19	15 35 49	22 26 24	18 05.1	18 54.8	9 54.9	17 09.7	25 35.1	12 04.4	6 16.6	7 01.1	19 33.0	25 28.7
10 W	21 23 08	21 58 04	29 14 38	6♒00 14	17 57.8	17 43.9	11 10.0	17 42.8	25 57.4	12 18.6	6 23.6	7 02.5	19 35.0	25 30.5
11 Th	21 27 05	22 58 48	12♒42 53	19 22 17	17 47.9	16 35.6	12 25.2	18 16.0	26 19.7	12 32.8	6 30.5	7 03.9	19 37.1	25 32.3
12 F	21 31 01	23 59 30	25 58 10	2♓30 18	17 36.1	15 31.3	13 40.3	18 49.3	26 42.2	12 46.9	6 37.5	7 05.3	19 39.2	25 34.1
13 Sa	21 34 58	25 00 11	8♓58 29	15 22 38	17 23.7	14 32.4	14 55.5	19 22.7	27 04.6	13 01.1	6 44.4	7 06.8	19 41.3	25 35.9
14 Su	21 38 54	26 00 51	21 42 41	27 58 40	17 11.7	13 40.0	16 10.6	19 56.2	27 27.2	13 15.2	6 51.3	7 08.4	19 43.4	25 37.7
15 M	21 42 51	27 01 29	4♈10 43	10♈19 02	17 01.3	12 54.6	17 25.7	20 29.8	27 49.8	13 29.2	6 58.2	7 10.0	19 45.5	25 39.5
16 Tu	21 46 47	28 02 05	16 23 54	22 25 41	16 53.2	12 16.8	18 40.8	21 03.5	28 12.4	13 43.3	7 05.0	7 11.7	19 47.7	25 41.2
17 W	21 50 44	29 02 39	28 24 49	4♉21 48	16 47.7	11 46.7	19 55.9	21 37.2	28 35.1	13 57.3	7 11.8	7 13.4	19 49.8	25 43.0
18 Th	21 54 41	0♓03 12	10♉17 11	16 11 35	16 44.9	11 24.4	21 11.0	22 11.1	28 57.8	14 11.4	7 18.6	7 15.1	19 52.0	25 44.7
19 F	21 58 37	1 03 43	22 05 37	27 59 59	16D43.9	11 09.7	22 26.1	22 45.0	29 20.6	14 25.3	7 25.4	7 16.9	19 54.2	25 46.4
20 Sa	22 02 34	2 04 12	3♊55 20	9♊52 24	16R44.0	11D02.4	23 41.1	23 19.0	29 43.4	14 39.3	7 32.1	7 18.7	19 56.3	25 48.1
21 Su	22 06 30	3 04 39	15 51 52	21 54 25	16 44.0	11 02.1	24 56.2	23 53.1	0♈06.3	14 53.2	7 38.9	7 20.6	19 58.5	25 49.8
22 M	22 10 27	4 05 05	28 00 43	4♋11 22	16 42.8	11 08.5	26 11.2	24 27.2	0 29.2	15 07.1	7 45.5	7 22.5	20 00.7	25 51.4
23 Tu	22 14 23	5 05 29	10♋26 56	16 47 55	16 39.5	11 21.2	27 26.3	25 01.5	0 52.2	15 21.0	7 52.2	7 24.5	20 03.0	25 53.1
24 W	22 18 20	6 05 50	23 14 40	29 47 31	16 33.5	11 39.9	28 41.3	25 35.8	1 15.2	15 34.8	7 58.8	7 26.5	20 05.2	25 54.7
25 Th	22 22 16	7 06 10	6♌26 34	13♌11 52	16 24.8	12 04.0	29 56.3	26 10.1	1 38.3	15 48.6	8 05.3	7 28.5	20 07.4	25 56.3
26 F	22 26 13	8 06 28	20 03 14	27 00 23	16 13.9	12 33.2	1♓11.3	26 44.6	2 01.3	16 02.4	8 11.9	7 30.6	20 09.6	25 57.9
27 Sa	22 30 10	9 06 44	4♍02 51	11♍10 01	16 01.7	13 07.2	2 26.3	27 19.0	2 24.5	16 16.1	8 18.4	7 32.8	20 11.9	25 59.4
28 Su	22 34 06	10 06 59	18 21 08	25 35 23	15 49.6	13 45.5	3 41.2	27 53.6	2 47.6	16 29.8	8 24.8	7 34.9	20 14.1	26 01.0

Astro Data

	Dy Hr Mn
♃∠♆	4 6:58
☽0S	6 1:10
♅D	14 8:36
♃□♅	17 22:50
☽0N	19 5:07
♄∠♆	20 16:57
☿R	30 15:53
☽0S	2 5:59
☽0N	15 12:50
♄□♅	17 19:08
☿D	21 0:52

Planet Ingress

	Dy Hr Mn
♂ ♉	6 22:27
☿ ♒	8 12:00
♀ ♑	8 15:41
☉ ♒	19 20:40
♀ ♒	1 14:05
☉ ♓	18 10:44
⚳ ♈	21 5:23
♀ ♓	25 13:11

Last Aspect / ☽ Ingress

Last Aspect Dy Hr Mn		☽ Ingress Dy Hr Mn
2 22:00 ♂ △	♍	3 1:13
4 21:34 ♀ □	♎	5 5:42
7 5:55 ♀ ⚹	♏	7 8:53
9 1:59 ♇ ⚹	♐	9 11:15
10 18:29 ♆ □	♑	11 13:30
13 7:22 ♇ ☌	♒	13 16:44
14 9:28 ☿ ☌	♓	15 22:17
18 3:44 ☉ ⚹	♈	18 7:07
20 8:29 ♇ □	♉	20 18:56
22 21:28 ♇ △	♊	23 7:43
25 7:17 ☿ △	♋	25 18:52
27 17:55 ♇ ☍	♌	28 2:54
30 1:53 ☿ ☍	♍	30 8:02

Last Aspect / ☽ Ingress

Last Aspect Dy Hr Mn		☽ Ingress Dy Hr Mn
1 11:10 ♀ △	♎	1 11:25
3 6:15 ☿ △	♏	3 14:14
5 9:20 ♇ ⚹	♐	5 17:16
7 6:16 ☿ ⚹	♑	7 20:52
9 17:22 ♇ ☌	♒	10 1:20
11 19:06 ☉ ☌	♓	12 7:23
14 7:29 ♇ ⚹	♈	14 15:54
17 0:17 ☉ ⚹	♉	17 3:12
19 7:28 ♇ △	♊	19 16:03
21 18:39 ♀ △	♋	22 3:53
24 4:54 ♇ ☍	♌	24 12:23
26 11:32 ♂ □	♍	26 17:07
28 15:58 ♂ △	♎	28 19:17

☽ Phases & Eclipses

Dy Hr Mn		
6 9:37	☾	16♎17
13 5:00	●	23♑13
20 21:02	☽	1♉02
28 19:16	○	9♌06
4 17:37	☾	16♏08
11 19:06	●	23♒17
19 18:47	☽	1♊21
27 8:17	○	8♍57

Astro Data

1 January 2021
Julian Day # 44196
SVP 4♓58'15"
GC 27♐08.0 ⚵ 8♒01.1
Eris 23♈27.6R ⚶ 4♐24.4
⚷ 5♈04.0 ⚴ 20♍12.4
☽ Mean ☊ 18♊49.8

1 February 2021
Julian Day # 44227
SVP 4♓58'10"
GC 27♐08.0 ⚵ 18♒27.6
Eris 23♈29.8 ⚶ 13♐24.7
⚷ 5♈56.1 ⚴ 20♍42.9R
☽ Mean ☊ 17♊11.3

March 2021 — LONGITUDE

Day	Sid.Time	☉	0 hr ☽	Noon ☽	True ☊	☿	♀	♂	⚳	♃	♄	♅	♆	♇
1 M	22 38 03	11♓07 11	2♎51 51	10♎09 39	15♊38.8	14♒28.0	4♓56.2	28♉28.2	3♈10.8	16♒43.4	8♒31.2	7♉37.1	20♓16.4	26♑02.5
2 Tu	22 41 59	12 07 23	17 27 51	24 45 38	15R30.4	15 14.2	6 11.1	29 02.8	3 34.0	16 57.1	8 37.6	7 39.4	20 18.6	26 04.0
3 W	22 45 56	13 07 32	2♏02 13	9♏16 59	15 24.9	16 04.0	7 26.1	29 37.6	3 57.3	17 10.6	8 43.9	7 41.7	20 20.9	26 05.5
4 Th	22 49 52	14 07 40	16 29 23	23 39 01	15 22.1	16 57.1	8 41.0	0♊12.3	4 20.6	17 24.1	8 50.2	7 44.0	20 23.2	26 07.0
5 F	22 53 49	15 07 47	0♐45 38	7♐49 03	15 21.3	17 53.1	9 55.9	0 47.2	4 44.0	17 37.6	8 56.5	7 46.3	20 25.4	26 08.4
6 Sa	22 57 45	16 07 52	14 49 12	21 46 05	15 21.2	18 52.1	11 10.8	1 22.1	5 07.3	17 51.1	9 02.7	7 48.8	20 27.7	26 09.8
7 Su	23 01 42	17 07 55	28 39 46	5♑30 19	15 20.5	19 53.7	12 25.7	1 57.0	5 30.7	18 04.5	9 08.9	7 51.2	20 30.0	26 11.2
8 M	23 05 39	18 07 57	12♑17 51	19 02 29	15 18.0	20 57.8	13 40.6	2 32.0	5 54.2	18 17.8	9 15.0	7 53.7	20 32.3	26 12.6
9 Tu	23 09 35	19 07 58	25 44 16	2♒23 18	15 12.8	22 04.2	14 55.5	3 07.0	6 17.6	18 31.1	9 21.0	7 56.2	20 34.5	26 14.0
10 W	23 13 32	20 07 56	8♒59 36	15 33 11	15 04.5	23 12.9	16 10.4	3 42.1	6 41.1	18 44.3	9 27.1	7 58.7	20 36.8	26 15.3
11 Th	23 17 28	21 07 53	22 04 01	28 32 03	14 53.4	24 23.6	17 25.2	4 17.3	7 04.6	18 57.5	9 33.0	8 01.3	20 39.1	26 16.6
12 F	23 21 25	22 07 48	4♓57 14	11♓19 30	14 40.3	25 36.3	18 40.1	4 52.5	7 28.2	19 10.7	9 38.9	8 03.9	20 41.4	26 17.9
13 Sa	23 25 21	23 07 41	17 38 48	23 55 04	14 26.4	26 50.9	19 54.9	5 27.7	7 51.7	19 23.7	9 44.8	8 06.6	20 43.6	26 19.2
14 Su	23 29 18	24 07 32	0♈08 19	6♈18 34	14 12.8	28 07.3	21 09.7	6 03.0	8 15.3	19 36.7	9 50.6	8 09.2	20 45.9	26 20.4
15 M	23 33 14	25 07 21	12 25 52	18 30 22	14 00.7	29 25.5	22 24.5	6 38.4	8 39.0	19 49.7	9 56.3	8 11.9	20 48.2	26 21.6
16 Tu	23 37 11	26 07 08	24 32 14	0♉31 44	13 51.1	0♓45.3	23 39.3	7 13.7	9 02.6	20 02.6	10 02.0	8 14.7	20 50.5	26 22.8
17 W	23 41 08	27 06 53	6♉29 09	12 24 53	13 44.3	2 06.7	24 54.1	7 49.2	9 26.2	20 15.4	10 07.7	8 17.5	20 52.7	26 24.0
18 Th	23 45 04	28 06 35	18 19 19	24 12 58	13 40.3	3 29.7	26 08.8	8 24.6	9 49.9	20 28.2	10 13.2	8 20.3	20 55.0	26 25.1
19 F	23 49 01	29 06 16	0♊06 22	6♊00 05	13D38.7	4 54.2	27 23.5	9 00.1	10 13.6	20 40.9	10 18.8	8 23.1	20 57.3	26 26.3
20 Sa	23 52 57	0♈05 54	11 54 46	17 51 02	13 38.5	6 20.1	28 38.2	9 35.7	10 37.3	20 53.6	10 24.2	8 26.0	20 59.5	26 27.4
21 Su	23 56 54	1 05 30	23 49 36	29 51 08	13R38.7	7 47.6	29 52.9	10 11.2	11 01.1	21 06.1	10 29.6	8 28.8	21 01.8	26 28.4
22 M	0 00 50	2 05 04	5♋56 21	12♋05 54	13 38.3	9 16.4	1♈07.6	10 46.9	11 24.8	21 18.6	10 35.0	8 31.8	21 04.0	26 29.5
23 Tu	0 04 47	3 04 36	18 20 27	24 40 37	13 36.2	10 46.7	2 22.3	11 22.5	11 48.6	21 31.1	10 40.2	8 34.7	21 06.3	26 30.5
24 W	0 08 43	4 04 05	1♌06 55	7♌39 49	13 31.8	12 18.3	3 36.9	11 58.2	12 12.3	21 43.4	10 45.4	8 37.7	21 08.5	26 31.5
25 Th	0 12 40	5 03 31	14 19 37	21 06 32	13 25.0	13 51.3	4 51.5	12 33.9	12 36.1	21 55.7	10 50.6	8 40.7	21 10.7	26 32.4
26 F	0 16 37	6 02 56	28 00 35	5♍01 36	13 16.1	15 25.7	6 06.1	13 09.6	12 59.9	22 07.9	10 55.7	8 43.7	21 13.0	26 33.4
27 Sa	0 20 33	7 02 18	12♍09 15	19 22 58	13 06.0	17 01.5	7 20.7	13 45.4	13 23.7	22 20.1	11 00.7	8 46.7	21 15.2	26 34.3
28 Su	0 24 30	8 01 38	26 42 01	4♎05 30	12 55.7	18 38.6	8 35.3	14 21.2	13 47.5	22 32.1	11 05.6	8 49.8	21 17.4	26 35.2
29 M	0 28 26	9 00 56	11♎32 21	19 01 27	12 46.5	20 17.1	9 49.8	14 57.0	14 11.3	22 44.1	11 10.5	8 52.9	21 19.6	26 36.0
30 Tu	0 32 23	10 00 12	26 31 36	4♏01 38	12 39.3	21 56.9	11 04.3	15 32.8	14 35.2	22 56.0	11 15.3	8 56.0	21 21.8	26 36.9
31 W	0 36 19	10 59 27	11♏30 27	18 57 02	12 34.7	23 38.2	12 18.8	16 08.7	14 59.0	23 07.8	11 20.1	8 59.1	21 23.9	26 37.7

April 2021 — LONGITUDE

Day	Sid.Time	☉	0 hr ☽	Noon ☽	True ☊	☿	♀	♂	⚳	♃	♄	♅	♆	♇
1 Th	0 40 16	11♈58 39	26♏20 30	3♐40 10	12♊32.7	25♓20.8	13♈33.3	16♊44.6	15♈22.8	23♒19.6	11♒24.7	9♉02.3	21♓26.1	26♑38.4
2 F	0 44 12	12 57 50	10♐55 28	18 06 01	12D32.5	27 04.9	14 47.8	17 20.5	15 46.7	23 31.2	11 29.3	9 05.5	21 28.3	26 39.2
3 Sa	0 48 09	13 56 59	25 11 35	2♑12 04	12R33.2	28 50.3	16 02.3	17 56.5	16 10.6	23 42.8	11 33.9	9 08.6	21 30.4	26 39.9
4 Su	0 52 06	14 56 06	9♑07 30	15 57 59	12 33.6	0♈37.2	17 16.7	18 32.4	16 34.4	23 54.3	11 38.3	9 11.9	21 32.5	26 40.6
5 M	0 56 02	15 55 11	22 43 41	29 24 50	12 32.7	2 25.5	18 31.2	19 08.4	16 58.3	24 05.7	11 42.7	9 15.1	21 34.7	26 41.3
6 Tu	0 59 59	16 54 15	6♒01 39	12♒34 26	12 29.7	4 15.2	19 45.6	19 44.5	17 22.2	24 17.0	11 47.0	9 18.3	21 36.8	26 41.9
7 W	1 03 55	17 53 17	19 03 25	25 28 50	12 24.3	6 06.4	21 00.0	20 20.5	17 46.1	24 28.2	11 51.2	9 21.6	21 38.9	26 42.5
8 Th	1 07 52	18 52 17	1♓50 56	8♓09 56	12 16.8	7 59.1	22 14.4	20 56.6	18 09.9	24 39.3	11 55.4	9 24.9	21 41.0	26 43.1
9 F	1 11 48	19 51 15	14 25 59	20 39 16	12 07.7	9 53.1	23 28.7	21 32.7	18 33.8	24 50.4	11 59.4	9 28.2	21 43.0	26 43.6
10 Sa	1 15 45	20 50 11	26 49 56	2♈58 08	11 57.9	11 48.7	24 43.1	22 08.8	18 57.7	25 01.3	12 03.4	9 31.5	21 45.1	26 44.1
11 Su	1 19 41	21 49 06	9♈03 59	15 07 38	11 48.3	13 45.7	25 57.4	22 44.9	19 21.6	25 12.1	12 07.3	9 34.8	21 47.1	26 44.6
12 M	1 23 38	22 47 58	21 09 13	27 08 54	11 39.8	15 44.1	27 11.7	23 21.1	19 45.5	25 22.8	12 11.2	9 38.1	21 49.1	26 45.1
13 Tu	1 27 34	23 46 48	3♉06 51	9♉03 18	11 33.1	17 43.9	28 26.0	23 57.3	20 09.3	25 33.5	12 14.9	9 41.5	21 51.2	26 45.5
14 W	1 31 31	24 45 37	14 58 29	20 52 42	11 28.6	19 45.0	29 40.3	24 33.5	20 33.2	25 44.0	12 18.6	9 44.9	21 53.2	26 45.9
15 Th	1 35 28	25 44 23	26 46 15	2♊39 30	11D26.3	21 47.4	0♉54.6	25 09.8	20 57.1	25 54.4	12 22.2	9 48.2	21 55.1	26 46.3
16 F	1 39 24	26 43 07	8♊32 52	14 26 49	11 25.9	23 51.0	2 08.8	25 46.0	21 21.0	26 04.7	12 25.7	9 51.6	21 57.1	26 46.6
17 Sa	1 43 21	27 41 49	20 21 49	26 18 25	11 26.8	25 55.7	3 23.0	26 22.3	21 44.8	26 14.9	12 29.1	9 55.0	21 59.0	26 46.9
18 Su	1 47 17	28 40 29	2♋17 10	8♋18 41	11 28.3	28 01.5	4 37.2	26 58.6	22 08.7	26 25.0	12 32.4	9 58.4	22 01.0	26 47.2
19 M	1 51 14	29 39 07	14 23 32	20 32 23	11R29.6	0♉08.0	5 51.4	27 34.9	22 32.5	26 35.0	12 35.6	10 01.8	22 02.9	26 47.5
20 Tu	1 55 10	0♉37 42	26 45 50	3♌04 28	11 29.9	2 15.2	7 05.5	28 11.2	22 56.3	26 44.9	12 38.8	10 05.3	22 04.8	26 47.7
21 W	1 59 07	1 36 15	9♌28 53	15 59 33	11 28.8	4 22.9	8 19.7	28 47.6	23 20.2	26 54.6	12 41.9	10 08.7	22 06.6	26 47.9
22 Th	2 03 03	2 34 46	22 36 56	29 21 20	11 26.1	6 30.8	9 33.8	29 23.9	23 44.0	27 04.2	12 44.9	10 12.1	22 08.5	26 48.1
23 F	2 07 00	3 33 15	6♍12 58	13♍11 52	11 22.0	8 38.8	10 47.9	0♋00.3	24 07.8	27 13.8	12 47.7	10 15.6	22 10.3	26 48.2
24 Sa	2 10 57	4 31 42	20 17 54	27 30 45	11 16.8	10 46.4	12 01.9	0 36.7	24 31.6	27 23.2	12 50.5	10 19.0	22 12.1	26 48.3
25 Su	2 14 53	5 30 06	4♎49 54	12♎14 35	11 11.4	12 53.4	13 16.0	1 13.1	24 55.3	27 32.4	12 53.3	10 22.4	22 13.9	26 48.4
26 M	2 18 50	6 28 29	19 43 56	27 16 52	11 06.5	14 59.6	14 30.0	1 49.5	25 19.1	27 41.6	12 55.9	10 25.9	22 15.7	26 48.5
27 Tu	2 22 46	7 26 49	4♏52 12	12♏28 40	11 02.8	17 04.5	15 44.0	2 25.9	25 42.9	27 50.6	12 58.4	10 29.3	22 17.4	26R48.5
28 W	2 26 43	8 25 08	20 05 00	27 39 58	11D00.7	19 08.0	16 58.0	3 02.3	26 06.6	27 59.5	13 00.9	10 32.8	22 19.1	26 48.5
29 Th	2 30 39	9 23 26	5♐12 25	12♐41 18	11 00.1	21 09.6	18 12.0	3 38.8	26 30.3	28 08.3	13 03.2	10 36.3	22 20.8	26 48.4
30 F	2 34 36	10 21 41	20 05 46	27 25 06	11 00.8	23 09.2	19 25.9	4 15.2	26 54.0	28 17.0	13 05.5	10 39.7	22 22.5	26 48.4

Astro Data

	Dy Hr Mn
☽0S	1 12:40
☽0N	14 20:06
⊙0N	20 9:37
♃⊻♆	21 1:51
♀0N	24 3:39
☽0S	28 22:13
⚳0N	4 14:59
☿0N	6 18:31
☽0N	11 2:42
♃⊻♇	20 19:09
☽0S	25 9:14
♇R	27 20:02

Planet Ingress

		Dy Hr Mn
♂	♊	4 3:29
☿	♓	15 22:26
⊙	♈	20 9:37
♀	♈	21 14:16
☿	♈	4 3:41
♀	♉	14 18:22
☿	♉	19 10:29
⊙	♉	19 20:33
♂	♋	23 11:49

Last Aspect / ☽ Ingress

Last Aspect Dy Hr Mn			☽ Ingress	Dy Hr Mn
2 14:09	♇	□	♏	2 20:38
4 16:10	♇	⚹	♐	4 22:43
6 9:44	♆	□	♑	7 2:20
9 0:52	♇	☌	♒	9 7:41
11 3:32	☿	☌	♓	11 14:44
13 16:38	♇	⚹	♈	13 23:44
16 3:40	♇	□	♉	16 10:56
18 20:40	⊙	⚹	♊	18 23:47
21 12:04	♀	□	♋	21 12:18
23 15:26	♇	☍	♌	23 21:56
25 13:27	♃	☍	♍	26 3:25
27 23:48	♇	△	♎	28 5:22
30 0:08	♇	□	♏	30 5:33

Last Aspect / ☽ Ingress

Last Aspect Dy Hr Mn			☽ Ingress	Dy Hr Mn
1 0:29	♇	⚹	♐	1 5:59
3 5:24	☿	□	♑	3 8:13
5 7:05	♇	☌	♒	5 13:04
7 10:05	♃	☌	♓	7 20:30
9 23:48	♇	⚹	♈	10 6:11
12 12:06	♀	☌	♉	12 17:44
14 24:00	♇	△	♊	15 6:35
17 15:03	⊙	⚹	♋	17 19:25
20 0:03	♇	☍	♌	20 6:11
22 12:05	♂	⚹	♍	22 13:08
24 10:50	♇	△	♎	24 16:06
26 12:40	♃	△	♏	26 16:18
28 12:31	♃	□	♐	28 15:42
30 13:27	♃	⚹	♑	30 16:16

☽ Phases & Eclipses

Dy Hr Mn		
6 1:30	☾	15♐42
13 10:21	●	23♓04
21 14:40	☽	1♋12
28 18:48	○	8♎18
4 10:02	☾	14♑51
12 2:31	●	22♈25
20 6:59	☽	0♌25
27 3:32	○	7♏06

Astro Data

1 March 2021
Julian Day # 44255
SVP 4♓58'07"
GC 27♐08.1 ⚴ 27♒53.7
Eris 23♈40.2 ⚵ 19♐47.7
⚷ 7♈16.0 ⚶ 15♍13.8R
☽ Mean ☊ 15♊42.4

1 April 2021
Julian Day # 44286
SVP 4♓58'04"
GC 27♐08.2 ⚴ 7♓50.2
Eris 23♈58.2 ⚵ 23♐43.0
⚷ 9♈02.5 ⚶ 8♍07.9R
☽ Mean ☊ 14♊03.8

LONGITUDE — May 2021

Day	Sid.Time	☉	0 hr ☽	Noon ☽	True ☊	☿	♀	♂	⚳	♃	♄	♅	♆	♇
1 Sa	2 38 32	11♉19 56	4♑38 46	11♑46 26	11♊02.2	25♉06.3	20♉39.8	4♋51.7	27♈17.7	28♒25.5	13♒07.6	10♉43.2	22♓24.2	26♑48.3
2 Su	2 42 29	12 18 09	18 47 55	25 43 08	11 03.6	27 00.9	21 53.8	5 28.2	27 41.4	28 33.9	13 09.7	10 46.6	22 25.8	26R48.2
3 M	2 46 26	13 16 20	2♒32 12	9♒15 17	11R04.5	28 52.6	23 07.7	6 04.7	28 05.0	28 42.2	13 11.7	10 50.1	22 27.4	26 48.0
4 Tu	2 50 22	14 14 30	15 52 38	22 24 34	11 04.3	0♊41.2	24 21.5	6 41.2	28 28.7	28 50.3	13 13.6	10 53.6	22 29.0	26 47.9
5 W	2 54 19	15 12 38	28 51 28	5♓13 42	11 02.9	2 26.6	25 35.4	7 17.7	28 52.3	28 58.3	13 15.4	10 57.0	22 30.6	26 47.7
6 Th	2 58 15	16 10 45	11♓31 40	17 45 45	11 00.3	4 08.7	26 49.2	7 54.3	29 15.9	29 06.1	13 17.1	11 00.5	22 32.1	26 47.4
7 F	3 02 12	17 08 50	23 56 22	0♈03 52	10 57.0	5 47.2	28 03.1	8 30.8	29 39.5	29 13.8	13 18.7	11 03.9	22 33.6	26 47.2
8 Sa	3 06 08	18 06 54	6♈08 37	12 10 59	10 53.2	7 22.2	29 16.9	9 07.4	0♉03.0	29 21.4	13 20.2	11 07.4	22 35.1	26 46.9
9 Su	3 10 05	19 04 56	18 11 15	24 09 45	10 49.5	8 53.5	0♊30.7	9 44.0	0 26.6	29 28.8	13 21.6	11 10.8	22 36.5	26 46.5
10 M	3 14 01	20 02 57	0♉06 46	6♉02 34	10 46.4	10 21.0	1 44.5	10 20.6	0 50.1	29 36.1	13 22.9	11 14.2	22 38.0	26 46.2
11 Tu	3 17 58	21 00 57	11 57 25	17 51 35	10 44.0	11 44.7	2 58.2	10 57.2	1 13.6	29 43.2	13 24.1	11 17.6	22 39.4	26 45.8
12 W	3 21 55	21 58 55	23 45 20	29 38 56	10D42.6	13 04.4	4 12.0	11 33.8	1 37.1	29 50.2	13 25.2	11 21.1	22 40.8	26 45.4
13 Th	3 25 51	22 56 51	5♊32 40	11♊26 50	10 42.2	14 20.2	5 25.7	12 10.5	2 00.5	29 57.0	13 26.2	11 24.5	22 42.1	26 45.0
14 F	3 29 48	23 54 46	17 21 43	23 17 40	10 42.6	15 31.9	6 39.4	12 47.1	2 23.9	0♓03.7	13 27.2	11 27.9	22 43.5	26 44.5
15 Sa	3 33 44	24 52 40	29 15 03	5♋14 13	10 43.7	16 39.6	7 53.1	13 23.8	2 47.3	0 10.2	13 28.0	11 31.3	22 44.8	26 44.1
16 Su	3 37 41	25 50 31	11♋15 35	17 19 36	10 45.0	17 43.1	9 06.8	14 00.5	3 10.6	0 16.6	13 28.7	11 34.7	22 46.0	26 43.6
17 M	3 41 37	26 48 21	23 26 41	29 37 18	10 46.2	18 42.4	10 20.4	14 37.1	3 34.0	0 22.8	13 29.3	11 38.0	22 47.3	26 43.0
18 Tu	3 45 34	27 46 09	5♌51 56	12♌11 03	10 47.2	19 37.4	11 34.1	15 13.8	3 57.2	0 28.9	13 29.9	11 41.4	22 48.5	26 42.5
19 W	3 49 30	28 43 56	18 35 06	25 04 33	10R47.6	20 28.0	12 47.7	15 50.6	4 20.5	0 34.8	13 30.3	11 44.8	22 49.7	26 41.9
20 Th	3 53 27	29 41 41	1♍39 46	8♍21 06	10 47.5	21 14.2	14 01.2	16 27.3	4 43.7	0 40.5	13 30.6	11 48.1	22 50.8	26 41.3
21 F	3 57 24	0♊39 24	15 08 47	22 03 01	10 46.9	21 56.0	15 14.8	17 04.0	5 06.9	0 46.0	13 30.9	11 51.4	22 52.0	26 40.6
22 Sa	4 01 20	1 37 05	29 03 48	6♎11 02	10 46.1	22 33.2	16 28.3	17 40.7	5 30.1	0 51.4	13R31.0	11 54.7	22 53.1	26 40.0
23 Su	4 05 17	2 34 45	13♎24 27	20 43 38	10 45.1	23 05.8	17 41.9	18 17.5	5 53.2	0 56.7	13 31.0	11 58.0	22 54.1	26 39.3
24 M	4 09 13	3 32 24	28 07 57	5♏36 39	10 44.3	23 33.7	18 55.4	18 54.2	6 16.3	1 01.8	13 31.0	12 01.3	22 55.2	26 38.6
25 Tu	4 13 10	4 30 01	13♏08 48	20 43 20	10 43.7	23 56.9	20 08.8	19 31.0	6 39.3	1 06.7	13 30.8	12 04.6	22 56.2	26 37.8
26 W	4 17 06	5 27 37	28 19 08	5♐54 58	10D43.5	24 15.4	21 22.3	20 07.8	7 02.3	1 11.4	13 30.6	12 07.8	22 57.2	26 37.1
27 Th	4 21 03	6 25 11	13♐29 41	21 02 05	10 43.5	24 29.4	22 35.7	20 44.5	7 25.3	1 16.0	13 30.2	12 11.1	22 58.1	26 36.3
28 F	4 24 59	7 22 45	28 31 06	5♑55 47	10 43.7	24 38.2	23 49.2	21 21.3	7 48.2	1 20.4	13 29.8	12 14.3	22 59.1	26 35.5
29 Sa	4 28 56	8 20 18	13♑15 18	20 29 02	10 44.0	24R42.6	25 02.6	21 58.1	8 11.1	1 24.6	13 29.2	12 17.5	22 59.9	26 34.7
30 Su	4 32 53	9 17 50	27 36 28	4♒37 19	10 44.2	24 42.3	26 16.0	22 34.9	8 34.0	1 28.6	13 28.6	12 20.7	23 00.8	26 33.8
31 M	4 36 49	10 15 20	11♒31 26	18 18 49	10R44.3	24 37.5	27 29.3	23 11.8	8 56.8	1 32.5	13 27.9	12 23.8	23 01.6	26 33.0

LONGITUDE — June 2021

Day	Sid.Time	☉	0 hr ☽	Noon ☽	True ☊	☿	♀	♂	⚳	♃	♄	♅	♆	♇
1 Tu	4 40 46	11♊12 50	24♒59 36	1♓34 02	10♊44.3	24♊28.4	28♊42.7	23♋48.6	9♉19.6	1♓36.2	13♒27.0	12♉27.0	23♓02.4	26♑32.1
2 W	4 44 42	12 10 20	8♓02 27	14 25 14	10D44.3	24R15.1	29 56.0	24 25.4	9 42.3	1 39.7	13R26.1	12 30.1	23 03.2	26R31.2
3 Th	4 48 39	13 07 48	20 42 52	26 55 50	10 44.3	23 58.0	1♋09.3	25 02.3	10 05.0	1 43.0	13 25.1	12 33.2	23 03.9	26 30.2
4 F	4 52 35	14 05 16	3♈04 39	9♈09 50	10 44.5	23 37.2	2 22.6	25 39.2	10 27.6	1 46.2	13 24.0	12 36.3	23 04.6	26 29.3
5 Sa	4 56 32	15 02 43	15 11 54	21 11 23	10 44.9	23 13.2	3 35.9	26 16.0	10 50.2	1 49.2	13 22.8	12 39.3	23 05.3	26 28.3
6 Su	5 00 28	16 00 09	27 08 45	3♉04 29	10 45.5	22 46.3	4 49.2	26 52.9	11 12.8	1 51.9	13 21.5	12 42.3	23 06.0	26 27.3
7 M	5 04 25	16 57 35	8♉59 04	14 52 53	10 46.1	22 17.0	6 02.4	27 29.8	11 35.3	1 54.5	13 20.1	12 45.3	23 06.6	26 26.3
8 Tu	5 08 22	17 55 00	20 46 21	26 39 50	10 46.6	21 45.8	7 15.6	28 06.8	11 57.7	1 57.0	13 18.6	12 48.3	23 07.1	26 25.2
9 W	5 12 18	18 52 24	2♊33 41	8♊28 14	10R46.8	21 13.3	8 28.9	28 43.7	12 20.1	1 59.2	13 17.0	12 51.3	23 07.7	26 24.2
10 Th	5 16 15	19 49 47	14 23 46	20 20 34	10 46.7	20 39.9	9 42.0	29 20.6	12 42.5	2 01.2	13 15.3	12 54.2	23 08.2	26 23.1
11 F	5 20 11	20 47 10	26 18 55	2♋19 03	10 46.1	20 06.3	10 55.2	29 57.6	13 04.8	2 03.1	13 13.6	12 57.1	23 08.7	26 22.0
12 Sa	5 24 08	21 44 32	8♋21 14	14 25 41	10 45.0	19 33.0	12 08.4	0♌34.6	13 27.0	2 04.7	13 11.7	13 00.0	23 09.1	26 20.9
13 Su	5 28 04	22 41 53	20 32 40	26 42 25	10 43.4	19 00.6	13 21.5	1 11.6	13 49.2	2 06.2	13 09.8	13 02.9	23 09.6	26 19.8
14 M	5 32 01	23 39 14	2♌55 11	9♌11 13	10 41.7	18 29.6	14 34.6	1 48.5	14 11.3	2 07.5	13 07.8	13 05.7	23 09.9	26 18.6
15 Tu	5 35 58	24 36 33	15 30 46	21 54 05	10 40.0	18 00.6	15 47.7	2 25.6	14 33.4	2 08.5	13 05.6	13 08.5	23 10.3	26 17.4
16 W	5 39 54	25 33 52	28 21 27	4♍53 05	10 38.6	17 34.1	17 00.8	3 02.6	14 55.4	2 09.4	13 03.4	13 11.3	23 10.6	26 16.3
17 Th	5 43 51	26 31 09	11♍29 16	18 10 10	10D37.8	17 10.5	18 13.8	3 39.6	15 17.4	2 10.1	13 01.2	13 14.0	23 10.9	26 15.1
18 F	5 47 47	27 28 26	24 56 00	1♎46 53	10 37.6	16 50.1	19 26.9	4 16.6	15 39.2	2 10.6	12 58.8	13 16.7	23 11.1	26 13.9
19 Sa	5 51 44	28 25 42	8♎42 55	15 44 04	10 38.2	16 33.4	20 39.8	4 53.7	16 01.1	2 10.9	12 56.3	13 19.4	23 11.4	26 12.6
20 Su	5 55 40	29 22 57	22 50 16	0♏01 18	10 39.3	16 20.7	21 52.8	5 30.7	16 22.8	2R11.1	12 53.8	13 22.0	23 11.5	26 11.4
21 M	5 59 37	0♋20 11	7♏16 51	14 36 29	10 40.5	16 12.2	23 05.8	6 07.8	16 44.5	2 11.0	12 51.2	13 24.7	23 11.7	26 10.1
22 Tu	6 03 33	1 17 25	21 59 38	29 25 35	10R41.5	16D08.0	24 18.7	6 44.9	17 06.1	2 10.7	12 48.5	13 27.3	23 11.8	26 08.9
23 W	6 07 30	2 14 39	6♐53 31	14♐22 31	10 41.7	16 08.4	25 31.6	7 22.0	17 27.7	2 10.3	12 45.7	13 29.8	23 11.9	26 07.6
24 Th	6 11 27	3 11 51	21 51 37	29 19 46	10 40.9	16 13.4	26 44.4	7 59.1	17 49.2	2 09.6	12 42.9	13 32.3	23 12.0	26 06.3
25 F	6 15 23	4 09 04	6♑45 57	14♑09 09	10 39.0	16 23.2	27 57.3	8 36.2	18 10.6	2 08.8	12 40.0	13 34.8	23R12.0	26 05.0
26 Sa	6 19 20	5 06 16	21 28 28	28 43 03	10 36.1	16 37.7	29 10.1	9 13.3	18 32.0	2 07.8	12 37.0	13 37.3	23 12.0	26 03.7
27 Su	6 23 16	6 03 28	5♒52 14	12♒55 26	10 32.7	16 57.1	0♌22.9	9 50.4	18 53.3	2 06.6	12 33.9	13 39.7	23 11.9	26 02.4
28 M	6 27 13	7 00 40	19 52 18	26 42 35	10 29.1	17 21.2	1 35.7	10 27.6	19 14.5	2 05.1	12 30.8	13 42.1	23 11.9	26 01.0
29 Tu	6 31 09	7 57 52	3♓26 14	10♓03 18	10 26.0	17 50.0	2 48.4	11 04.7	19 35.6	2 03.5	12 27.6	13 44.4	23 11.8	25 59.7
30 W	6 35 06	8 55 04	16 34 00	22 58 38	10 23.7	18 23.6	4 01.1	11 41.9	19 56.7	2 01.7	12 24.3	13 46.7	23 11.6	25 58.3

Astro Data

	Dy Hr Mn
☽0N	8 8:49
☽0S	22 19:28
♄R	23 9:19
☿R	29 22:35
☽0N	4 15:00
♄□♅	14 22:01
☽0S	19 3:16
♃R	20 15:05
☿D	22 22:01
♆R	25 19:21

Planet Ingress

	Dy Hr Mn
☿ ♊	4 2:49
⚳ ♉	8 8:54
♀ ♊	9 2:01
♃ ♓	13 22:36
☉ ♊	20 19:37
♀ ♋	2 13:19
♂ ♌	11 13:34
☉ ♋	21 3:32
♀ ♌	27 4:27

Last Aspect / ☽ Ingress

Last Aspect Dy Hr Mn	☽ Ingress Dy Hr Mn
2 14:38 ☿ △	♒ 2 19:31
5 0:05 ♃ ☌	♓ 5 2:08
7 7:36 ♀ ⚹	♈ 7 11:52
9 22:50 ♃ ⚹	♉ 9 23:46
12 12:23 ♃ □	♊ 12 12:43
14 10:51 ♆ □	♋ 15 1:30
17 6:23 ♇ ☍	♌ 17 12:44
19 19:13 ☉ □	♍ 19 20:59
21 19:56 ♇ △	♎ 22 1:35
23 21:36 ♇ □	♏ 24 3:00
25 21:20 ♇ ⚹	♐ 26 2:39
27 17:35 ☿ ☍	♑ 28 2:23
29 22:15 ♇ ☌	♒ 30 4:04

Last Aspect / ☽ Ingress

Last Aspect Dy Hr Mn	☽ Ingress Dy Hr Mn
1 6:14 ♀ △	♓ 1 9:07
3 11:10 ♇ ⚹	♈ 3 17:59
5 22:47 ♂ □	♉ 6 5:46
8 15:07 ♂ ⚹	♊ 8 18:47
10 17:37 ♆ □	♋ 11 7:22
13 11:16 ♇ ☍	♌ 13 18:22
15 17:27 ☉ ⚹	♍ 16 3:02
18 3:54 ☉ □	♎ 18 8:54
20 10:52 ☉ △	♏ 20 11:58
22 6:43 ♇ ⚹	♐ 22 12:55
24 2:09 ♆ □	♑ 24 13:05
26 12:49 ♆ ☍	♒ 26 14:08
27 19:08 ☿ △	♓ 28 17:51

☽ Phases & Eclipses

Dy Hr Mn	
3 19:50	☾ 13♒35
11 19:00	● 21♉18
19 19:13	☽ 29♌01
26 11:14	○ 5♐26
26 11:19	• T 1.009
2 7:24	☾ 11♓59
10 10:53	● 19♊47
10 10:41:53	• A 03'51"
18 3:54	☽ 27♍09
24 18:40	○ 3♑28

Astro Data

1 May 2021
Julian Day # 44316
SVP 4♓58'00"
GC 27♐08.2 ⚴ 16♓24.7
Eris 24♈17.7 ⚵ 23♐01.8R
⚷ 10♈43.9 ⚶ 7♍11.1
☽ Mean ☊ 12♊28.5

1 June 2021
Julian Day # 44347
SVP 4♓57'55"
GC 27♐08.3 ⚴ 23♓24.9
Eris 24♈35.2 ⚵ 17♐37.0R
⚷ 12♈06.8 ⚶ 12♍56.9
☽ Mean ☊ 10♊50.0

July 2021 LONGITUDE

Day	Sid.Time	☉	0 hr ☽	Noon ☽	True ☊	☿	♀	♂	⚳	♃	♄	♅	♆	♇
1 Th	6 39 02	9♋52 16	29♓17 37	5♈31 26	10♊22.7	19♊01.9	5♌13.8	12♌19.1	20♉17.7	1♓59.8	12♒21.0	13♉49.0	23♓11.4	25♑56.9
2 F	6 42 59	10 49 28	11♈40 37	17 45 45	10D 22.8	19 44.8	6 26.5	12 56.3	20 38.6	1R 57.6	12R 17.6	13 51.2	23R 11.2	25R 55.6
3 Sa	6 46 56	11 46 41	23 47 25	29 46 15	10 23.9	20 32.2	7 39.2	13 33.5	20 59.4	1 55.2	12 14.1	13 53.4	23 11.0	25 54.2
4 Su	6 50 52	12 43 54	5♉42 52	11♉37 51	10 25.5	21 24.2	8 51.8	14 10.7	21 20.1	1 52.7	12 10.6	13 55.6	23 10.7	25 52.8
5 M	6 54 49	13 41 06	17 31 49	23 25 19	10 27.2	22 20.7	10 04.4	14 48.0	21 40.8	1 49.9	12 07.0	13 57.7	23 10.4	25 51.4
6 Tu	6 58 45	14 38 20	29 18 55	5♊13 05	10R 28.3	23 21.5	11 17.0	15 25.2	22 01.4	1 47.0	12 03.4	13 59.8	23 10.1	25 50.0
7 W	7 02 42	15 35 33	11♊08 18	17 04 59	10 28.2	24 26.7	12 29.5	16 02.5	22 21.9	1 43.9	11 59.7	14 01.9	23 09.8	25 48.6
8 Th	7 06 38	16 32 47	23 03 32	29 04 17	10 26.5	25 36.2	13 42.1	16 39.8	22 42.3	1 40.6	11 55.9	14 03.9	23 09.4	25 47.2
9 F	7 10 35	17 30 01	5♋07 29	11♋13 25	10 23.2	26 49.9	14 54.6	17 17.1	23 02.6	1 37.1	11 52.1	14 05.8	23 08.9	25 45.7
10 Sa	7 14 31	18 27 15	17 22 16	23 34 11	10 18.2	28 07.7	16 07.0	17 54.5	23 22.8	1 33.5	11 48.2	14 07.8	23 08.5	25 44.3
11 Su	7 18 28	19 24 29	29 49 16	6♌07 38	10 12.0	29 29.7	17 19.5	18 31.8	23 42.9	1 29.6	11 44.3	14 09.7	23 08.0	25 42.9
12 M	7 22 25	20 21 43	12♌29 18	18 54 18	10 05.2	0♋55.7	18 31.9	19 09.2	24 03.0	1 25.6	11 40.3	14 11.5	23 07.5	25 41.5
13 Tu	7 26 21	21 18 57	25 22 39	1♍54 21	9 58.6	2 25.6	19 44.3	19 46.5	24 22.9	1 21.5	11 36.3	14 13.3	23 06.9	25 40.0
14 W	7 30 18	22 16 12	8♍29 22	15 07 43	9 52.8	3 59.4	20 56.6	20 23.9	24 42.7	1 17.1	11 32.3	14 15.0	23 06.4	25 38.6
15 Th	7 34 14	23 13 26	21 49 23	28 34 22	9 48.6	5 37.0	22 09.0	21 01.3	25 02.4	1 12.6	11 28.2	14 16.8	23 05.8	25 37.1
16 F	7 38 11	24 10 40	5♎22 39	12♎14 15	9D 46.2	7 18.2	23 21.2	21 38.8	25 22.1	1 07.9	11 24.1	14 18.4	23 05.1	25 35.7
17 Sa	7 42 07	25 07 55	19 09 09	26 07 19	9 45.6	9 02.9	24 33.5	22 16.2	25 41.6	1 03.1	11 19.9	14 20.1	23 04.4	25 34.3
18 Su	7 46 04	26 05 10	3♏08 42	10♏13 13	9 46.2	10 50.9	25 45.7	22 53.6	26 01.0	0 58.1	11 15.7	14 21.6	23 03.8	25 32.8
19 M	7 50 00	27 02 25	17 20 43	24 31 00	9 47.3	12 42.0	26 57.9	23 31.1	26 20.3	0 53.0	11 11.5	14 23.2	23 03.0	25 31.4
20 Tu	7 53 57	27 59 40	1♐43 47	8♐58 41	9R 47.9	14 35.9	28 10.0	24 08.6	26 39.5	0 47.7	11 07.2	14 24.7	23 02.3	25 29.9
21 W	7 57 54	28 56 55	16 15 14	23 32 52	9 47.2	16 32.5	29 22.1	24 46.1	26 58.6	0 42.2	11 02.9	14 26.1	23 01.5	25 28.5
22 Th	8 01 50	29 54 11	0♑50 57	8♑08 45	9 44.5	18 31.5	0♍34.2	25 23.6	27 17.5	0 36.6	10 58.6	14 27.5	23 00.7	25 27.1
23 F	8 05 47	0♌51 27	15 25 30	22 40 23	9 39.5	20 32.5	1 46.2	26 01.1	27 36.4	0 30.9	10 54.3	14 28.9	22 59.9	25 25.6
24 Sa	8 09 43	1 48 44	29 52 36	7♒01 22	9 32.5	22 35.2	2 58.2	26 38.6	27 55.1	0 25.0	10 49.9	14 30.2	22 59.0	25 24.2
25 Su	8 13 40	2 46 01	14♒05 58	21 05 48	9 24.3	24 39.4	4 10.1	27 16.2	28 13.7	0 19.0	10 45.5	14 31.5	22 58.1	25 22.8
26 M	8 17 36	3 43 19	28 00 20	4♓49 11	9 15.6	26 44.6	5 22.0	27 53.8	28 32.2	0 12.9	10 41.1	14 32.7	22 57.2	25 21.3
27 Tu	8 21 33	4 40 38	11♓32 07	18 09 03	9 07.5	28 50.6	6 33.9	28 31.4	28 50.6	0 06.6	10 36.7	14 33.9	22 56.2	25 19.9
28 W	8 25 30	5 37 57	24 39 59	1♈05 05	9 00.9	0♌57.0	7 45.7	29 09.0	29 08.9	0 00.2	10 32.3	14 35.0	22 55.3	25 18.5
29 Th	8 29 26	6 35 18	7♈24 40	13 39 04	8 56.1	3 03.5	8 57.5	29 46.6	29 27.0	29♒53.7	10 27.8	14 36.1	22 54.3	25 17.1
30 F	8 33 23	7 32 40	19 48 47	25 54 20	8 53.5	5 09.9	10 09.3	0♍24.3	29 45.0	29 47.0	10 23.4	14 37.1	22 53.3	25 15.7
31 Sa	8 37 19	8 30 02	1♉56 18	7♉55 20	8D 52.7	7 16.0	11 21.0	1 01.9	0♊02.8	29 40.3	10 18.9	14 38.1	22 52.2	25 14.3

August 2021 LONGITUDE

Day	Sid.Time	☉	0 hr ☽	Noon ☽	True ☊	☿	♀	♂	⚳	♃	♄	♅	♆	♇
1 Su	8 41 16	9♌27 26	13♉52 05	19♉47 12	8♊53.1	9♌21.4	12♍32.6	1♍39.6	0♊20.5	29♒33.5	10♒14.5	14♉39.1	22♓51.1	25♑12.9
2 M	8 45 12	10 24 51	25 41 22	1♊35 15	8R 53.9	11 26.1	13 44.3	2 17.3	0 38.1	29R 26.5	10R 10.0	14 39.9	22R 50.0	25R 11.5
3 Tu	8 49 09	11 22 17	7♊29 31	13 24 45	8 54.0	13 29.8	14 55.8	2 55.1	0 55.5	29 19.5	10 05.5	14 40.8	22 48.9	25 10.1
4 W	8 53 05	12 19 45	19 21 35	25 20 32	8 52.5	15 32.5	16 07.4	3 32.8	1 12.8	29 12.3	10 01.1	14 41.6	22 47.8	25 08.8
5 Th	8 57 02	13 17 13	1♋22 06	7♋26 44	8 49.0	17 33.9	17 18.9	4 10.6	1 30.0	29 05.1	9 56.6	14 42.3	22 46.6	25 07.4
6 F	9 00 59	14 14 43	13 34 48	19 46 36	8 42.9	19 34.1	18 30.4	4 48.4	1 47.0	28 57.8	9 52.2	14 43.0	22 45.4	25 06.1
7 Sa	9 04 55	15 12 14	26 02 22	2♌22 14	8 34.4	21 32.9	19 41.8	5 26.2	2 03.8	28 50.4	9 47.7	14 43.7	22 44.2	25 04.7
8 Su	9 08 52	16 09 45	8♌46 16	15 14 27	8 24.0	23 30.2	20 53.2	6 04.1	2 20.5	28 42.9	9 43.3	14 44.3	22 43.0	25 03.4
9 M	9 12 48	17 07 18	21 46 41	28 22 50	8 12.7	25 26.2	22 04.5	6 41.9	2 37.1	28 35.4	9 38.9	14 44.8	22 41.7	25 02.1
10 Tu	9 16 45	18 04 52	5♍02 39	11♍45 53	8 01.5	27 20.6	23 15.8	7 19.8	2 53.4	28 27.8	9 34.5	14 45.3	22 40.5	25 00.8
11 W	9 20 41	19 02 27	18 32 15	25 21 25	7 51.5	29 13.6	24 27.0	7 57.7	3 09.6	28 20.2	9 30.1	14 45.8	22 39.2	24 59.5
12 Th	9 24 38	20 00 03	2♎13 05	9♎06 58	7 43.8	1♍05.1	25 38.2	8 35.6	3 25.6	28 12.5	9 25.7	14 46.2	22 37.9	24 58.2
13 F	9 28 34	20 57 39	16 02 47	23 00 17	7 38.6	2 55.1	26 49.3	9 13.6	3 41.5	28 04.7	9 21.4	14 46.5	22 36.5	24 56.9
14 Sa	9 32 31	21 55 17	29 59 16	6♏59 35	7 36.0	4 43.6	28 00.4	9 51.5	3 57.2	27 57.0	9 17.1	14 46.8	22 35.2	24 55.7
15 Su	9 36 27	22 52 56	14♏01 05	21 03 38	7D 35.3	6 30.6	29 11.4	10 29.5	4 12.7	27 49.2	9 12.8	14 47.1	22 33.8	24 54.4
16 M	9 40 24	23 50 35	28 07 09	5♐11 31	7R 35.4	8 16.1	0♎22.3	11 07.5	4 28.0	27 41.3	9 08.6	14 47.3	22 32.4	24 53.2
17 Tu	9 44 21	24 48 16	12♐16 36	19 22 14	7 35.1	10 00.2	1 33.2	11 45.5	4 43.2	27 33.5	9 04.3	14 47.4	22 31.0	24 52.0
18 W	9 48 17	25 45 58	26 28 14	3♑34 19	7 33.1	11 42.8	2 44.1	12 23.6	4 58.2	27 25.6	9 00.2	14 47.5	22 29.6	24 50.8
19 Th	9 52 14	26 43 40	10♑40 09	17 45 22	7 28.7	13 24.0	3 54.9	13 01.7	5 12.9	27 17.8	8 56.0	14R 47.6	22 28.2	24 49.6
20 F	9 56 10	27 41 24	24 49 31	1♒52 04	7 21.4	15 03.7	5 05.6	13 39.8	5 27.5	27 09.9	8 51.9	14 47.6	22 26.7	24 48.5
21 Sa	10 00 07	28 39 09	8♒52 32	15 50 21	7 11.6	16 42.0	6 16.2	14 17.9	5 41.9	27 02.0	8 47.8	14 47.5	22 25.2	24 47.3
22 Su	10 04 03	29 36 56	22 44 59	29 35 55	7 00.0	18 19.0	7 26.8	14 56.0	5 56.1	26 54.2	8 43.8	14 47.4	22 23.8	24 46.2
23 M	10 08 00	0♍34 43	6♓22 44	13♓05 01	6 47.7	19 54.5	8 37.3	15 34.2	6 10.1	26 46.3	8 39.8	14 47.3	22 22.3	24 45.1
24 Tu	10 11 57	1 32 33	19 42 32	26 15 04	6 36.0	21 28.6	9 47.8	16 12.3	6 23.9	26 38.5	8 35.9	14 47.1	22 20.8	24 44.0
25 W	10 15 53	2 30 23	2♈42 34	9♈05 03	6 25.9	23 01.4	10 58.2	16 50.5	6 37.5	26 30.7	8 32.0	14 46.8	22 19.2	24 42.9
26 Th	10 19 50	3 28 16	15 22 41	21 35 42	6 18.2	24 32.7	12 08.5	17 28.8	6 50.9	26 22.9	8 28.2	14 46.5	22 17.7	24 41.9
27 F	10 23 46	4 26 10	27 44 28	3♉49 22	6 13.1	26 02.7	13 18.8	18 07.0	7 04.1	26 15.2	8 24.4	14 46.2	22 16.1	24 40.8
28 Sa	10 27 43	5 24 06	9♉50 56	15 49 43	6 10.4	27 31.3	14 29.0	18 45.3	7 17.0	26 07.5	8 20.6	14 45.8	22 14.6	24 39.8
29 Su	10 31 39	6 22 04	21 46 18	27 41 21	6 09.5	28 58.5	15 39.1	19 23.6	7 29.7	25 59.9	8 17.0	14 45.4	22 13.0	24 38.8
30 M	10 35 36	7 20 04	3♊35 33	9♊29 33	6 09.4	0♎24.3	16 49.2	20 01.9	7 42.2	25 52.3	8 13.4	14 44.9	22 11.4	24 37.8
31 Tu	10 39 32	8 18 05	15 24 04	21 19 48	6 09.1	1 48.6	17 59.2	20 40.3	7 54.5	25 44.7	8 09.8	14 44.3	22 09.8	24 36.9

Astro Data

	Dy Hr Mn
☽0N	1 21:45
☽0S	16 8:41
☽0N	29 5:16
☽0S	12 13:24
♀0S	17 10:59
♅ R	20 1:39
☽0N	25 13:16
☿0S	29 13:40

Planet Ingress

	Dy Hr Mn
☿ ♋	11 20:35
♀ ♍	22 0:37
☉ ♌	22 14:26
☿ ♌	28 1:12
♃ ♒R	28 12:43
♂ ♍	29 20:32
⚳ ♊	31 8:13
☿ ♍	11 21:57
♀ ♎	16 4:27
☉ ♍	22 21:35
☿ ♎	30 5:10

Last Aspect / ☽ Ingress

Last Aspect Dy Hr Mn	☽ Ingress Dy Hr Mn
30 17:40 ♇ ⚹	♈ 1 1:21
3 4:15 ♇ □	♉ 3 12:28
5 16:57 ♇ △	♊ 6 1:24
8 4:20 ☿ ☌	♋ 8 13:51
10 16:10 ♇ ☍	♌ 11 0:20
12 12:29 ♂ ☌	♍ 13 8:30
15 6:46 ♇ △	♎ 15 14:31
17 11:03 ♇ □	♏ 17 18:38
19 16:30 ☉ △	♐ 19 21:08
21 22:25 ♀ △	♑ 21 22:36
23 16:34 ♇ ☌	♒ 24 0:12
25 23:14 ♂ ☍	♓ 26 3:30
28 1:13 ♇ ⚹	♈ 28 9:58
30 19:38 ♃ ⚹	♉ 30 20:08

Last Aspect Dy Hr Mn	☽ Ingress Dy Hr Mn
2 7:41 ♃ □	♊ 2 8:46
4 19:38 ♃ △	♋ 4 21:17
6 22:12 ♇ ☍	♌ 7 7:31
9 12:22 ♃ ☍	♍ 9 14:56
11 11:22 ♇ △	♎ 11 20:08
13 20:39 ♃ △	♏ 14 0:01
16 3:05 ♀ ⚹	♐ 16 3:12
18 1:43 ♃ ⚹	♑ 18 5:58
19 23:59 ♇ ☌	♒ 20 8:49
22 12:02 ☉ ☍	♓ 22 12:42
24 9:12 ♇ ⚹	♈ 24 18:57
26 21:14 ♃ ⚹	♉ 27 4:27
29 14:59 ☿ △	♊ 29 16:42

☽ Phases & Eclipses

Dy Hr Mn	
1 21:11	☾ 10♈14
10 1:17	● 18♋02
17 10:11	☽ 25♎04
24 2:37	○ 1♒26
31 13:16	☾ 8♉33
8 13:50	● 16♌14
15 15:20	☽ 23♏01
22 12:02	○ 29♒37
30 7:13	☾ 7♊09

Astro Data

1 July 2021
Julian Day # 44377
SVP 4♓57'50"
GC 27♐08.4 ⚵ 27♓17.7
Eris 24♈45.4 ⚶ 11♐15.1R
⚷ 12♈50.5 ⚴ 22♍50.9
☽ Mean ☊ 9♊14.7

1 August 2021
Julian Day # 44408
SVP 4♓57'45"
GC 27♐08.4 ⚵ 26♓47.6R
Eris 24♈46.8R ⚶ 8♐20.8R
⚷ 12♈48.6R ⚴ 5♎46.0
☽ Mean ☊ 7♊36.3

LONGITUDE — September 2021

Day	Sid.Time	☉	0 hr ☽	Noon ☽	True ☊	☿	♀	♂	⚳	♃	♄	♅	♆	♇
1 W	10 43 29	9♍16 09	27♊17 24	3♋17 32	6♊07.4	3♎11.5	19♎09.1	21♍18.7	8♊06.5	25♒37.3	8♒06.3	14♉43.8	22♓08.3	24♑35.9
2 Th	10 47 25	10 14 14	9♋20 47	15 27 45	6R 03.6	4 32.9	20 19.0	21 57.1	8 18.3	25R 29.9	8R 02.9	14R 43.1	22R 06.6	24R 35.0
3 F	10 51 22	11 12 21	21 38 53	27 54 39	5 57.2	5 52.7	21 28.7	22 35.6	8 29.9	25 22.6	7 59.5	14 42.4	22 05.0	24 34.1
4 Sa	10 55 19	12 10 31	4♌15 21	10♌41 14	5 48.2	7 11.0	22 38.4	23 14.0	8 41.2	25 15.3	7 56.2	14 41.7	22 03.4	24 33.3
5 Su	10 59 15	13 08 41	17 12 25	23 48 54	5 37.2	8 27.7	23 48.1	23 52.5	8 52.2	25 08.2	7 53.0	14 40.9	22 01.8	24 32.4
6 M	11 03 12	14 06 54	0♍30 34	7♍17 11	5 25.0	9 42.7	24 57.6	24 31.1	9 03.0	25 01.1	7 49.8	14 40.1	22 00.2	24 31.6
7 Tu	11 07 08	15 05 09	14 08 24	21 03 47	5 12.9	10 55.9	26 07.1	25 09.6	9 13.5	24 54.1	7 46.7	14 39.2	21 58.5	24 30.8
8 W	11 11 05	16 03 25	28 02 48	5♎04 52	5 02.1	12 07.3	27 16.5	25 48.2	9 23.8	24 47.3	7 43.7	14 38.3	21 56.9	24 30.0
9 Th	11 15 01	17 01 43	12♎09 22	19 15 41	4 53.6	13 16.8	28 25.8	26 26.8	9 33.8	24 40.5	7 40.7	14 37.3	21 55.2	24 29.3
10 F	11 18 58	18 00 02	26 23 12	3♏31 22	4 47.9	14 24.3	29 35.1	27 05.4	9 43.5	24 33.9	7 37.9	14 36.3	21 53.6	24 28.5
11 Sa	11 22 54	18 58 23	10♏39 42	17 47 45	4 45.0	15 29.7	0♏44.2	27 44.1	9 52.9	24 27.4	7 35.1	14 35.3	21 51.9	24 27.8
12 Su	11 26 51	19 56 46	24 55 11	2♐01 42	4D 44.1	16 32.8	1 53.3	28 22.8	10 02.1	24 21.0	7 32.4	14 34.2	21 50.3	24 27.1
13 M	11 30 48	20 55 10	9♐07 05	16 11 12	4R 44.2	17 33.5	3 02.2	29 01.5	10 11.0	24 14.7	7 29.7	14 33.0	21 48.6	24 26.5
14 Tu	11 34 44	21 53 36	23 13 55	0♑15 09	4 44.0	18 31.7	4 11.1	29 40.2	10 19.6	24 08.6	7 27.2	14 31.8	21 47.0	24 25.9
15 W	11 38 41	22 52 03	7♑14 49	14 12 50	4 42.4	19 27.2	5 19.8	0♎19.0	10 27.9	24 02.6	7 24.7	14 30.6	21 45.3	24 25.3
16 Th	11 42 37	23 50 32	21 09 06	28 03 31	4 38.4	20 19.8	6 28.5	0 57.8	10 35.8	23 56.7	7 22.4	14 29.3	21 43.7	24 24.7
17 F	11 46 34	24 49 03	4♒55 55	11♒46 07	4 31.7	21 09.2	7 37.0	1 36.6	10 43.5	23 51.0	7 20.1	14 28.0	21 42.0	24 24.1
18 Sa	11 50 30	25 47 35	18 33 54	25 19 02	4 22.6	21 55.3	8 45.5	2 15.5	10 50.9	23 45.4	7 17.8	14 26.6	21 40.3	24 23.6
19 Su	11 54 27	26 46 09	2♓01 17	8♓40 24	4 11.8	22 37.7	9 53.8	2 54.4	10 58.0	23 40.0	7 15.7	14 25.2	21 38.7	24 23.1
20 M	11 58 23	27 44 45	15 16 08	21 48 18	4 00.3	23 16.3	11 02.0	3 33.3	11 04.8	23 34.7	7 13.7	14 23.8	21 37.1	24 22.6
21 Tu	12 02 20	28 43 22	28 16 42	4♈41 15	3 49.3	23 50.6	12 10.1	4 12.2	11 11.2	23 29.6	7 11.7	14 22.3	21 35.4	24 22.2
22 W	12 06 17	29 42 02	11♈01 52	17 18 34	3 39.7	24 20.4	13 18.1	4 51.2	11 17.4	23 24.6	7 09.9	14 20.8	21 33.8	24 21.8
23 Th	12 10 13	0♎40 43	23 31 26	29 40 38	3 32.4	24 45.3	14 25.9	5 30.2	11 23.2	23 19.8	7 08.1	14 19.2	21 32.1	24 21.4
24 F	12 14 10	1 39 27	5♉46 23	11♉49 00	3 27.6	25 04.9	15 33.7	6 09.2	11 28.6	23 15.2	7 06.5	14 17.6	21 30.5	24 21.0
25 Sa	12 18 06	2 38 13	17 48 51	23 46 23	3D 25.1	25 18.8	16 41.3	6 48.2	11 33.8	23 10.8	7 04.9	14 16.0	21 28.9	24 20.7
26 Su	12 22 03	3 37 01	29 42 04	5♊36 28	3 24.7	25R 26.7	17 48.7	7 27.3	11 38.6	23 06.5	7 03.4	14 14.3	21 27.3	24 20.4
27 M	12 25 59	4 35 52	11♊30 10	17 23 46	3 25.3	25 28.2	18 56.1	8 06.5	11 43.0	23 02.4	7 02.0	14 12.6	21 25.7	24 20.1
28 Tu	12 29 56	5 34 44	23 17 56	29 13 20	3R 26.1	25 22.7	20 03.3	8 45.6	11 47.2	22 58.4	7 00.7	14 10.8	21 24.1	24 19.8
29 W	12 33 52	6 33 39	5♋10 39	11♋10 32	3 26.2	25 10.2	21 10.4	9 24.8	11 50.9	22 54.7	6 59.5	14 09.1	21 22.5	24 19.6
30 Th	12 37 49	7 32 36	17 13 41	23 20 43	3 24.8	24 50.1	22 17.4	10 04.0	11 54.3	22 51.1	6 58.4	14 07.2	21 20.9	24 19.4

LONGITUDE — October 2021

Day	Sid.Time	☉	0 hr ☽	Noon ☽	True ☊	☿	♀	♂	⚳	♃	♄	♅	♆	♇
1 F	12 41 46	8♎31 36	29♋32 13	5♌48 46	3♊21.3	24♎22.5	23♏24.2	10♎43.3	11♊57.3	22♒47.7	6♒57.4	14♉05.4	21♓19.3	24♑19.3
2 Sa	12 45 42	9 30 38	12♌10 49	18 38 45	3R 15.6	23R 47.2	24 30.8	11 22.6	12 00.0	22R 44.5	6R 56.5	14R 03.5	21R 17.8	24R 19.1
3 Su	12 49 39	10 29 42	25 12 50	1♍53 13	3 08.2	23 04.3	25 37.3	12 01.9	12 02.3	22 41.5	6 55.7	14 01.6	21 16.2	24 19.0
4 M	12 53 35	11 28 48	8♍39 55	15 32 47	2 59.8	22 14.3	26 43.7	12 41.2	12 04.3	22 38.6	6 54.9	13 59.6	21 14.7	24 18.9
5 Tu	12 57 32	12 27 56	22 31 32	29 35 42	2 51.2	21 17.8	27 49.9	13 20.6	12 05.8	22 36.0	6 54.3	13 57.6	21 13.2	24 18.9
6 W	13 01 28	13 27 06	6♎44 43	13♎57 52	2 43.5	20 15.5	28 55.9	14 00.0	12 07.0	22 33.6	6 53.8	13 55.6	21 11.7	24D 18.9
7 Th	13 05 25	14 26 19	21 14 20	28 33 14	2 37.6	19 08.8	0♐01.8	14 39.5	12 07.8	22 31.3	6 53.4	13 53.6	21 10.2	24 18.9
8 F	13 09 21	15 25 33	5♏53 41	13♏14 47	2 33.9	17 59.1	1 07.5	15 19.0	12R 08.2	22 29.3	6 53.1	13 51.5	21 08.7	24 18.9
9 Sa	13 13 18	16 24 50	20 35 41	27 55 35	2D 32.4	16 48.2	2 13.0	15 58.5	12 08.2	22 27.4	6 52.9	13 49.4	21 07.2	24 19.0
10 Su	13 17 14	17 24 08	5♐13 48	12♐29 44	2 32.6	15 37.8	3 18.3	16 38.0	12 07.8	22 25.8	6D 52.7	13 47.3	21 05.8	24 19.1
11 M	13 21 11	18 23 28	19 42 55	26 52 59	2 33.8	14 30.1	4 23.4	17 17.6	12 07.1	22 24.3	6 52.7	13 45.1	21 04.4	24 19.2
12 Tu	13 25 08	19 22 50	3♑59 39	11♑02 45	2R 34.9	13 27.0	5 28.4	17 57.2	12 05.9	22 23.1	6 52.8	13 43.0	21 02.9	24 19.4
13 W	13 29 04	20 22 13	18 02 11	24 57 55	2 35.0	12 30.3	6 33.1	18 36.9	12 04.4	22 22.0	6 53.0	13 40.8	21 01.5	24 19.5
14 Th	13 33 01	21 21 38	1♒49 57	8♒38 20	2 33.6	11 41.5	7 37.6	19 16.6	12 02.5	22 21.2	6 53.3	13 38.5	21 00.2	24 19.8
15 F	13 36 57	22 21 05	15 23 07	22 04 22	2 30.4	11 02.1	8 41.8	19 56.3	12 00.2	22 20.5	6 53.7	13 36.3	20 58.8	24 20.0
16 Sa	13 40 54	23 20 34	28 42 09	5♓16 33	2 25.4	10 33.0	9 45.9	20 36.0	11 57.5	22 20.1	6 54.2	13 34.0	20 57.5	24 20.3
17 Su	13 44 50	24 20 04	11♓47 36	18 15 22	2 19.2	10 14.8	10 49.6	21 15.8	11 54.4	22D 19.8	6 54.8	13 31.7	20 56.1	24 20.6
18 M	13 48 47	25 19 37	24 39 54	1♈01 15	2 12.6	10D 07.7	11 53.2	21 55.6	11 50.9	22 19.8	6 55.5	13 29.4	20 54.8	24 20.9
19 Tu	13 52 43	26 19 11	7♈19 27	13 34 35	2 06.2	10 11.7	12 56.4	22 35.4	11 47.0	22 19.9	6 56.3	13 27.1	20 53.6	24 21.3
20 W	13 56 40	27 18 47	19 46 43	25 55 56	2 00.7	10 26.5	13 59.4	23 15.3	11 42.7	22 20.3	6 57.2	13 24.8	20 52.3	24 21.7
21 Th	14 00 37	28 18 25	2♉02 23	8♉06 13	1 56.6	10 51.5	15 02.2	23 55.2	11 38.0	22 20.8	6 58.2	13 22.4	20 51.1	24 22.1
22 F	14 04 33	29 18 05	14 07 37	20 06 50	1D 54.3	11 26.2	16 04.6	24 35.2	11 33.0	22 21.6	6 59.3	13 20.0	20 49.8	24 22.5
23 Sa	14 08 30	0♏17 47	26 04 08	1♊59 50	1 53.5	12 09.7	17 06.8	25 15.1	11 27.5	22 22.6	7 00.5	13 17.7	20 48.6	24 23.0
24 Su	14 12 26	1 17 32	7♊54 18	13 47 56	1 54.2	13 01.3	18 08.6	25 55.2	11 21.7	22 23.7	7 01.8	13 15.3	20 47.5	24 23.5
25 M	14 16 23	2 17 18	19 41 12	25 34 33	1 55.7	14 00.0	19 10.1	26 35.2	11 15.5	22 25.1	7 03.2	13 12.8	20 46.3	24 24.1
26 Tu	14 20 19	3 17 07	1♋28 33	7♋23 43	1 57.5	15 05.0	20 11.3	27 15.3	11 08.9	22 26.6	7 04.7	13 10.4	20 45.2	24 24.6
27 W	14 24 16	4 16 58	13 20 40	19 19 59	1 59.2	16 15.6	21 12.2	27 55.4	11 01.9	22 28.4	7 06.2	13 08.0	20 44.1	24 25.2
28 Th	14 28 12	5 16 51	25 22 16	1♌28 10	2R 00.0	17 31.0	22 12.8	28 35.6	10 54.5	22 30.4	7 07.9	13 05.5	20 43.0	24 25.8
29 F	14 32 09	6 16 47	7♌38 16	13 53 10	1 59.9	18 50.5	23 12.9	29 15.8	10 46.8	22 32.5	7 09.7	13 03.1	20 42.0	24 26.5
30 Sa	14 36 06	7 16 44	20 13 25	26 39 31	1 58.5	20 13.5	24 12.7	29 56.1	10 38.7	22 34.9	7 11.6	13 00.6	20 41.0	24 27.2
31 Su	14 40 02	8 16 44	3♍11 53	9♍50 51	1 56.1	21 39.4	25 12.1	0♏36.3	10 30.2	22 37.4	7 13.6	12 58.2	20 40.0	24 27.9

Astro Data

	Dy Hr Mn
☽ 0S	8 19:41
♃×♇	11 10:06
♂ 0S	17 20:32
☽ 0N	21 21:09
☉ 0S	22 19:20
☿ R	27 5:10
☽ 0S	6 4:39
♇ D	6 18:29
⚳ R	9 1:31
♄ D	11 2:17
♃ D	18 5:30
☿ D	18 15:18
☽ 0N	19 4:17

Planet Ingress

	Dy Hr Mn
♀ ♏	10 20:39
♂ ♎	15 0:14
☉ ♎	22 19:21
♀ ♐	7 11:21
☉ ♏	23 4:51
♂ ♏	30 14:21

Last Aspect / ☽ Ingress

Last Aspect Dy Hr Mn		☽ Ingress Dy Hr Mn
31 20:48 ♃ △	♋	1 5:26
3 5:37 ♇ ☍	♌	3 15:58
5 14:21 ♃ ☍	♍	5 23:06
7 19:23 ♂ ☌	♎	8 3:20
10 4:48 ♀ ☌	♏	10 6:05
12 5:33 ♂ ✶	♐	12 8:34
14 10:57 ♂ □	♑	14 11:34
16 5:40 ♇ ☌	♒	16 15:23
18 9:14 ♃ ☌	♓	18 20:22
20 23:55 ☉ ☍	♈	21 3:13
23 2:05 ☿ ☍	♉	23 12:38
25 13:09 ♇ △	♊	26 0:36
28 4:18 ☿ △	♋	28 13:34

Last Aspect / ☽ Ingress

Last Aspect Dy Hr Mn		☽ Ingress Dy Hr Mn
30 14:49 ☿ □	♌	1 0:53
2 23:43 ♀ □	♍	3 8:38
5 8:46 ♀ ✶	♎	5 12:41
7 5:03 ♇ □	♏	7 14:22
9 6:05 ♇ ✶	♐	9 15:24
11 4:30 ♃ ✶	♑	11 17:15
13 10:53 ♇ ☌	♒	13 20:47
15 12:33 ☉ △	♓	16 2:22
17 23:24 ♇ ✶	♈	18 10:04
20 14:57 ☉ ☍	♉	20 19:59
22 20:35 ♇ △	♊	23 7:57
25 14:11 ♂ △	♋	25 21:00
28 6:02 ♂ □	♌	28 9:07
30 7:05 ♀ △	♍	30 18:09

☽ Phases & Eclipses

Dy Hr Mn	
7 0:52	● 14♍38
13 20:39	☽ 21♐16
20 23:55	○ 28♓14
29 1:57	☾ 6♋09
6 11:05	● 13♎25
13 3:25	☽ 20♑01
20 14:57	○ 27♈26
28 20:05	☾ 5♌37

Astro Data

1 September 2021
Julian Day # 44439
SVP 4♓57'40"
GC 27♐08.5 ⚵ 21♓01.9R
Eris 24♈38.5R ⚴ 10♐35.6
⚷ 12♈00.4R ⚶ 20♎22.6
☽ Mean ☊ 5♊57.8

1 October 2021
Julian Day # 44469
SVP 4♓57'37"
GC 27♐08.6 ⚵ 13♓27.7R
Eris 24♈23.4R ⚴ 16♐38.5
⚷ 10♈45.0R ⚶ 5♏32.9
☽ Mean ☊ 4♊22.4

November 2021 — LONGITUDE

Day	Sid.Time	☉	0 hr ☽	Noon ☽	True ☊	☿	♀	♂	⚳	♃	♄	♅	♆	♇
1 M	14 43 59	9♏16 45	16♍36 38	23♍29 18	1♊53.1	23♎07.8	26♐11.2	1♏16.7	10♊21.4	22♒40.1	7♒15.7	12♉55.7	20♓39.0	24♑28.6
2 Tu	14 47 55	10 16 49	0♎28 48	7♎34 52	1R49.9	24 38.2	27 09.8	1 57.0	10R12.3	22 43.1	7 17.9	12R53.2	20R38.1	24 29.4
3 W	14 51 52	11 16 55	14 47 07	22 04 56	1 47.0	26 10.3	28 08.0	2 37.4	10 02.8	22 46.2	7 20.2	12 50.7	20 37.2	24 30.2
4 Th	14 55 48	12 17 03	29 27 36	6♏54 11	1 44.8	27 43.7	29 05.7	3 17.8	9 52.9	22 49.5	7 22.5	12 48.3	20 36.3	24 31.0
5 F	14 59 45	13 17 12	14♏23 42	21 55 04	1D43.7	29 18.1	0♑03.0	3 58.3	9 42.8	22 53.1	7 25.0	12 45.8	20 35.4	24 31.9
6 Sa	15 03 41	14 17 24	29 27 08	6♐58 48	1 43.5	0♏53.4	0 59.8	4 38.8	9 32.3	22 56.8	7 27.6	12 43.3	20 34.6	24 32.7
7 Su	15 07 38	15 17 37	14♐29 00	21 56 43	1 44.2	2 29.2	1 56.1	5 19.3	9 21.5	23 00.7	7 30.2	12 40.8	20 33.8	24 33.6
8 M	15 11 35	16 17 52	29 21 07	6♑41 26	1 45.3	4 05.5	2 51.9	5 59.9	9 10.5	23 04.8	7 33.0	12 38.4	20 33.0	24 34.6
9 Tu	15 15 31	17 18 09	13♑57 06	21 07 39	1 46.4	5 42.1	3 47.2	6 40.5	8 59.1	23 09.0	7 35.8	12 35.9	20 32.3	24 35.5
10 W	15 19 28	18 18 26	28 12 48	5♒12 23	1 47.3	7 19.0	4 41.9	7 21.2	8 47.5	23 13.5	7 38.8	12 33.4	20 31.6	24 36.5
11 Th	15 23 24	19 18 46	12♒06 22	18 54 47	1R47.6	8 55.9	5 35.9	8 01.8	8 35.6	23 18.1	7 41.8	12 31.0	20 30.9	24 37.5
12 F	15 27 21	20 19 06	25 37 48	2♓15 37	1 47.3	10 32.8	6 29.4	8 42.6	8 23.5	23 23.0	7 45.0	12 28.5	20 30.3	24 38.6
13 Sa	15 31 17	21 19 28	8♓48 30	15 16 43	1 46.5	12 09.7	7 22.2	9 23.3	8 11.1	23 28.0	7 48.2	12 26.1	20 29.6	24 39.6
14 Su	15 35 14	22 19 51	21 40 36	28 00 28	1 45.4	13 46.6	8 14.3	10 04.1	7 58.6	23 33.2	7 51.5	12 23.6	20 29.1	24 40.7
15 M	15 39 10	23 20 16	4♈16 38	10♈29 25	1 44.2	15 23.3	9 05.8	10 44.9	7 45.8	23 38.5	7 54.9	12 21.2	20 28.5	24 41.8
16 Tu	15 43 07	24 20 42	16 39 08	22 46 05	1 43.0	16 59.8	9 56.5	11 25.8	7 32.8	23 44.0	7 58.3	12 18.8	20 28.0	24 43.0
17 W	15 47 04	25 21 09	28 50 32	4♉52 46	1 42.2	18 36.2	10 46.4	12 06.7	7 19.6	23 49.8	8 01.9	12 16.4	20 27.5	24 44.2
18 Th	15 51 00	26 21 38	10♉53 03	16 51 37	1 41.7	20 12.5	11 35.6	12 47.6	7 06.3	23 55.6	8 05.5	12 14.0	20 27.0	24 45.3
19 F	15 54 57	27 22 09	22 48 44	28 44 38	1D41.5	21 48.5	12 24.0	13 28.6	6 52.9	24 01.7	8 09.3	12 11.6	20 26.6	24 46.6
20 Sa	15 58 53	28 22 41	4♊39 35	10♊33 50	1 41.5	23 24.3	13 11.4	14 09.6	6 39.3	24 07.9	8 13.1	12 09.3	20 26.2	24 47.8
21 Su	16 02 50	29 23 15	16 27 41	22 21 24	1 41.7	24 59.9	13 58.0	14 50.6	6 25.5	24 14.3	8 17.0	12 06.9	20 25.9	24 49.1
22 M	16 06 46	0♐23 50	28 15 17	4♋09 42	1 41.9	26 35.4	14 43.7	15 31.7	6 11.7	24 20.9	8 21.0	12 04.6	20 25.5	24 50.3
23 Tu	16 10 43	1 24 27	10♋05 00	16 01 33	1R42.0	28 10.6	15 28.4	16 12.9	5 57.8	24 27.6	8 25.1	12 02.3	20 25.3	24 51.7
24 W	16 14 40	2 25 05	21 59 47	28 00 07	1 41.9	29 45.7	16 12.1	16 54.0	5 43.8	24 34.5	8 29.2	12 00.0	20 25.0	24 53.0
25 Th	16 18 36	3 25 45	4♌03 02	10♌09 01	1 41.8	1♐20.7	16 54.8	17 35.2	5 29.8	24 41.5	8 33.5	11 57.8	20 24.8	24 54.3
26 F	16 22 33	4 26 27	16 18 33	22 32 09	1 41.7	2 55.4	17 36.4	18 16.5	5 15.7	24 48.7	8 37.8	11 55.5	20 24.6	24 55.7
27 Sa	16 26 29	5 27 10	28 50 18	5♍13 31	1D41.6	4 30.1	18 16.9	18 57.8	5 01.6	24 56.0	8 42.2	11 53.3	20 24.4	24 57.1
28 Su	16 30 26	6 27 55	11♍42 16	18 16 57	1 41.7	6 04.6	18 56.2	19 39.1	4 47.5	25 03.6	8 46.6	11 51.1	20 24.3	24 58.5
29 M	16 34 22	7 28 41	24 57 56	1♎45 29	1 42.0	7 39.0	19 34.2	20 20.5	4 33.4	25 11.2	8 51.2	11 48.9	20 24.2	25 00.0
30 Tu	16 38 19	8 29 29	8♎39 47	15 40 52	1 42.6	9 13.3	20 11.0	21 01.9	4 19.3	25 19.0	8 55.8	11 46.8	20 24.2	25 01.4

December 2021 — LONGITUDE

Day	Sid.Time	☉	0 hr ☽	Noon ☽	True ☊	☿	♀	♂	⚳	♃	♄	♅	♆	♇
1 W	16 42 15	9♐30 18	22♎48 38	0♏02 49	1♊43.3	10♐47.5	20♑46.5	21♏43.3	4♊05.3	25♒27.0	9♒00.5	11♉44.7	20♓24.1	25♑02.9
2 Th	16 46 12	10 31 09	7♏22 58	14 48 27	1 43.9	12 21.6	21 20.6	22 24.8	3R51.3	25 35.1	9 05.2	11R42.6	20D24.2	25 04.4
3 F	16 50 09	11 32 01	22 18 28	29 52 02	1R44.2	13 55.8	21 53.3	23 06.3	3 37.4	25 43.4	9 10.1	11 40.5	20 24.2	25 06.0
4 Sa	16 54 05	12 32 54	7♐28 04	15♐05 20	1 44.0	15 29.8	22 24.5	23 47.9	3 23.6	25 51.8	9 15.0	11 38.5	20 24.3	25 07.5
5 Su	16 58 02	13 33 49	22 42 37	0♑18 36	1 43.2	17 03.9	22 54.2	24 29.5	3 10.0	26 00.4	9 20.0	11 36.5	20 24.4	25 09.1
6 M	17 01 58	14 34 44	7♑52 06	15 21 58	1 41.8	18 38.0	23 22.2	25 11.2	2 56.4	26 09.1	9 25.0	11 34.5	20 24.6	25 10.7
7 Tu	17 05 55	15 35 41	22 47 13	0♒07 02	1 40.0	20 12.0	23 48.6	25 52.9	2 43.0	26 17.9	9 30.2	11 32.6	20 24.8	25 12.3
8 W	17 09 51	16 36 38	7♒20 44	14 27 53	1 38.2	21 46.1	24 13.2	26 34.6	2 29.8	26 26.9	9 35.4	11 30.7	20 25.0	25 13.9
9 Th	17 13 48	17 37 35	21 28 12	28 21 35	1 36.8	23 20.2	24 36.0	27 16.3	2 16.8	26 36.0	9 40.6	11 28.8	20 25.3	25 15.5
10 F	17 17 44	18 38 33	5♓08 06	11♓47 55	1D35.9	24 54.3	24 56.9	27 58.1	2 03.9	26 45.2	9 45.9	11 26.9	20 25.6	25 17.2
11 Sa	17 21 41	19 39 32	18 21 22	24 48 48	1 35.8	26 28.5	25 15.8	28 39.9	1 51.3	26 54.6	9 51.3	11 25.1	20 25.9	25 18.8
12 Su	17 25 38	20 40 31	1♈10 42	7♈27 33	1 36.6	28 02.7	25 32.8	29 21.8	1 38.9	27 04.1	9 56.8	11 23.4	20 26.3	25 20.5
13 M	17 29 34	21 41 31	13 39 52	19 48 12	1 38.0	29 37.0	25 47.6	0♐03.7	1 26.7	27 13.7	10 02.3	11 21.6	20 26.7	25 22.2
14 Tu	17 33 31	22 42 32	25 53 04	1♉54 59	1 39.7	1♑11.3	26 00.3	0 45.6	1 14.8	27 23.5	10 07.9	11 20.0	20 27.1	25 23.9
15 W	17 37 27	23 43 33	7♉54 28	13 52 00	1 41.3	2 45.6	26 10.8	1 27.6	1 03.2	27 33.4	10 13.5	11 18.3	20 27.6	25 25.7
16 Th	17 41 24	24 44 34	19 47 59	25 42 53	1R42.3	4 20.0	26 19.0	2 09.6	0 51.8	27 43.4	10 19.2	11 16.7	20 28.1	25 27.4
17 F	17 45 20	25 45 36	1♊37 03	7♊30 51	1 42.3	5 54.4	26 24.8	2 51.7	0 40.7	27 53.5	10 24.9	11 15.1	20 28.6	25 29.2
18 Sa	17 49 17	26 46 39	13 24 35	19 18 34	1 41.0	7 28.8	26R28.3	3 33.8	0 29.9	28 03.8	10 30.8	11 13.6	20 29.2	25 31.0
19 Su	17 53 13	27 47 43	25 13 03	1♋08 18	1 38.3	9 03.2	26 29.4	4 15.9	0 19.4	28 14.1	10 36.6	11 12.1	20 29.8	25 32.7
20 M	17 57 10	28 48 47	7♋04 32	13 01 58	1 34.4	10 37.5	26 28.0	4 58.1	0 09.3	28 24.6	10 42.5	11 10.6	20 30.4	25 34.6
21 Tu	18 01 07	29 49 51	19 00 51	25 01 23	1 29.5	12 11.8	26 24.2	5 40.3	29♉59.5	28 35.2	10 48.5	11 09.2	20 31.1	25 36.4
22 W	18 05 03	0♑50 56	1♌03 47	7♌08 19	1 24.1	13 45.8	26 17.8	6 22.5	29 50.0	28 45.9	10 54.5	11 07.9	20 31.8	25 38.2
23 Th	18 09 00	1 52 02	13 15 12	19 24 44	1 18.9	15 19.7	26 09.0	7 04.8	29 40.8	28 56.7	11 00.6	11 06.6	20 32.5	25 40.0
24 F	18 12 56	2 53 08	25 37 13	1♍52 56	1 14.4	16 53.2	25 57.6	7 47.2	29 32.0	29 07.6	11 06.7	11 05.3	20 33.3	25 41.9
25 Sa	18 16 53	3 54 15	8♍12 13	14 35 26	1 11.1	18 26.3	25 43.8	8 29.5	29 23.5	29 18.6	11 12.9	11 04.0	20 34.1	25 43.7
26 Su	18 20 49	4 55 23	21 02 56	27 35 04	1D09.4	19 58.9	25 27.5	9 12.0	29 15.5	29 29.8	11 19.1	11 02.9	20 34.9	25 45.6
27 M	18 24 46	5 56 31	4♎12 10	10♎54 34	1 09.3	21 30.8	25 08.8	9 54.4	29 07.8	29 41.0	11 25.4	11 01.7	20 35.8	25 47.5
28 Tu	18 28 42	6 57 40	17 42 33	24 36 18	1 10.3	23 01.9	24 47.9	10 36.9	29 00.4	29 52.3	11 31.7	11 00.6	20 36.7	25 49.4
29 W	18 32 39	7 58 49	1♏35 58	8♏41 33	1 11.8	24 32.0	24 24.7	11 19.4	28 53.5	0♓03.7	11 38.1	10 59.6	20 37.7	25 51.3
30 Th	18 36 36	8 59 59	15 52 57	23 09 54	1R13.0	26 00.8	23 59.3	12 02.0	28 46.9	0 15.3	11 44.5	10 58.6	20 38.6	25 53.2
31 F	18 40 32	10 01 09	0♐31 58	7♐58 33	1 13.0	27 28.0	23 32.0	12 44.6	28 40.8	0 26.9	11 50.9	10 57.6	20 39.6	25 55.1

Astro Data

	Dy Hr Mn
☽0S	2 15:27
☽0N	15 10:27
♃⊻♇	27 16:16
☽0S	30 1:47
♆D	1 13:22
☽0N	12 16:15
♀R	19 10:36
♄□♅	24 7:17
☽0S	27 9:29

Planet Ingress

		Dy Hr Mn
♀	♑	5 10:44
☿	♏	5 22:35
☉	♐	22 2:34
☿	♐	24 15:36
♂	♐	13 9:53
☿	♑	13 17:52
⚳	♉R	21 10:38
☉	♑	21 15:59
♃	♓	29 4:09

Last Aspect / ☽ Ingress

Last Aspect Dy Hr Mn			☽ Ingress	Dy Hr Mn
1 17:00	♀	□	♎	1 23:11
3 22:32	♀	⚹	♏	4 0:52
5 16:10	♇	⚹	♐	6 0:52
7 13:44	♃	⚹	♑	8 1:03
9 17:51	♇	☌	♒	10 3:03
11 19:52	♃	☌	♓	12 7:54
14 5:40	♇	⚹	♈	14 15:48
16 15:51	♇	□	♉	17 2:18
19 8:57	☉	☍	♊	19 14:33
21 15:52	♃	△	♋	22 3:33
24 5:46	♇	☍	♌	24 15:58
26 16:24	♃	☍	♍	27 2:12
29 0:02	♇	△	♎	29 8:55

Last Aspect / ☽ Ingress

Last Aspect Dy Hr Mn			☽ Ingress	Dy Hr Mn
1 4:19	♃	△	♏	1 11:55
3 5:22	♃	□	♐	3 12:13
5 5:08	♃	⚹	♑	5 11:31
7 4:42	♂	⚹	♒	7 11:48
9 9:59	♂	□	♓	9 14:53
11 19:40	♂	△	♈	11 21:46
14 2:52	♃	⚹	♉	14 8:11
16 16:08	♃	□	♊	16 20:43
19 6:02	♃	△	♋	19 9:42
21 14:44	♀	☍	♌	21 21:54
24 6:39	♃	☍	♍	24 8:24
26 8:39	♇	△	♎	26 16:24
28 21:11	♃	△	♏	28 21:16
30 17:10	☿	⚹	♐	30 23:08

☽ Phases & Eclipses

Dy Hr Mn		
4 21:15	●	12♏40
11 12:46	☽	19♒21
19 8:57	○	27♉14
19 9:03	•	P 0.974
27 12:28	☾	5♍28
4 7:43	●	12♐22
4 7:33:24	•	T 01'55"
11 1:36	☽	19♓13
19 4:35	○	27♊29
27 2:24	☾	5♎32

Astro Data

1 November 2021
Julian Day # 44500
SVP 4♓57'34"
GC 27♐08.7 ⚴ 9♓12.3R
Eris 24♈05.1R ⚵ 25♐34.3
⚷ 9♈25.4R ⚶ 21♏53.7
☽ Mean ☊ 2♊43.9

1 December 2021
Julian Day # 44530
SVP 4♓57'29"
GC 27♐08.7 ⚴ 10♓35.2
Eris 23♈49.9R ⚵ 5♑52.8
⚷ 8♈35.2R ⚶ 8♐03.3
☽ Mean ☊ 1♊08.6

LONGITUDE — January 2022

Day	Sid.Time	☉	0 hr ☽	Noon ☽	True ☊	☿	♀	♂	⚳	♃	♄	♅	♆	♇
1 Sa	18 44 29	11♑02 20	15♐28 50	23♐01 53	1♊11.3	28♑53.4	23♑02.9	13♐27.3	28♉35.0	0♓38.6	11♒57.4	10♉56.7	20♓40.7	25♑57.0
2 Su	18 48 25	12 03 31	0♑36 35	8♑11 45	1R 07.5	0♒16.6	22R 32.1	14 10.0	28R 29.7	0 50.5	12 04.0	10R 55.9	20 41.7	25 59.0
3 M	18 52 22	13 04 42	15 46 07	23 18 24	1 01.9	1 37.1	21 59.7	14 52.7	28 24.8	1 02.4	12 10.5	10 55.1	20 42.8	26 00.9
4 Tu	18 56 18	14 05 53	0♒47 23	8♒11 57	0 55.0	2 54.4	21 26.0	15 35.5	28 20.2	1 14.4	12 17.1	10 54.3	20 44.0	26 02.9
5 W	19 00 15	15 07 03	15 31 08	22 44 07	0 47.7	4 08.0	20 51.3	16 18.3	28 16.1	1 26.4	12 23.8	10 53.6	20 45.1	26 04.8
6 Th	19 04 12	16 08 14	29 50 19	6♓49 22	0 41.2	5 17.3	20 15.7	17 01.1	28 12.4	1 38.6	12 30.5	10 53.0	20 46.3	26 06.8
7 F	19 08 08	17 09 23	13♓41 03	20 25 23	0 36.0	6 21.5	19 39.4	17 44.0	28 09.1	1 50.9	12 37.2	10 52.3	20 47.5	26 08.7
8 Sa	19 12 05	18 10 33	27 02 33	3♈32 52	0 32.8	7 20.0	19 02.7	18 26.9	28 06.3	2 03.2	12 43.9	10 51.8	20 48.8	26 10.7
9 Su	19 16 01	19 11 42	9♈56 44	16 14 42	0D 31.5	8 11.7	18 26.0	19 09.8	28 03.8	2 15.6	12 50.7	10 51.3	20 50.1	26 12.7
10 M	19 19 58	20 12 50	22 27 21	28 35 18	0 31.8	8 56.0	17 49.3	19 52.8	28 01.8	2 28.1	12 57.5	10 50.8	20 51.4	26 14.6
11 Tu	19 23 54	21 13 59	4♉39 13	10♉39 45	0 33.0	9 31.8	17 13.1	20 35.8	28 00.2	2 40.7	13 04.3	10 50.4	20 52.7	26 16.6
12 W	19 27 51	22 15 06	16 37 35	22 33 20	0R 34.2	9 58.4	16 37.4	21 18.9	27 59.0	2 53.3	13 11.2	10 50.1	20 54.1	26 18.6
13 Th	19 31 47	23 16 13	28 27 38	4♊21 03	0 34.4	10R 14.8	16 02.7	22 02.0	27 58.2	3 06.0	13 18.1	10 49.8	20 55.5	26 20.6
14 F	19 35 44	24 17 20	10♊14 08	16 07 24	0 32.9	10 20.2	15 29.1	22 45.1	27D 57.9	3 18.8	13 25.0	10 49.6	20 56.9	26 22.6
15 Sa	19 39 41	25 18 26	22 01 16	27 56 10	0 29.0	10 14.3	14 56.8	23 28.3	27 57.9	3 31.7	13 32.0	10 49.4	20 58.3	26 24.5
16 Su	19 43 37	26 19 31	3♋52 27	9♋50 23	0 22.6	9 56.6	14 26.1	24 11.5	27 58.4	3 44.6	13 38.9	10 49.2	20 59.8	26 26.5
17 M	19 47 34	27 20 36	15 50 15	21 52 15	0 13.7	9 27.2	13 57.1	24 54.7	27 59.2	3 57.6	13 45.9	10 49.1	21 01.3	26 28.5
18 Tu	19 51 30	28 21 40	27 56 32	4♌03 14	0 03.0	8 46.6	13 30.0	25 38.0	28 00.5	4 10.7	13 52.9	10D 49.1	21 02.9	26 30.5
19 W	19 55 27	29 22 44	10♌12 27	16 24 14	29♉51.4	7 55.4	13 05.0	26 21.3	28 02.1	4 23.8	13 59.9	10 49.1	21 04.4	26 32.5
20 Th	19 59 23	0♒23 47	22 38 40	28 55 47	29 39.9	6 55.1	12 42.1	27 04.6	28 04.2	4 37.0	14 07.0	10 49.2	21 06.0	26 34.4
21 F	20 03 20	1 24 50	5♍15 39	11♍38 19	29 29.5	5 47.4	12 21.4	27 48.0	28 06.7	4 50.3	14 14.1	10 49.3	21 07.6	26 36.4
22 Sa	20 07 16	2 25 52	18 03 53	24 32 26	29 21.3	4 34.3	12 03.2	28 31.4	28 09.5	5 03.6	14 21.1	10 49.5	21 09.2	26 38.4
23 Su	20 11 13	3 26 53	1♎04 08	7♎39 05	29 15.7	3 18.1	11 47.3	29 14.9	28 12.7	5 16.9	14 28.2	10 49.7	21 10.9	26 40.4
24 M	20 15 10	4 27 55	14 17 31	20 59 35	29 12.7	2 01.1	11 34.0	29 58.4	28 16.3	5 30.3	14 35.4	10 50.0	21 12.5	26 42.3
25 Tu	20 19 06	5 28 55	27 45 29	4♏35 26	29D 11.8	0 45.7	11 23.1	0♑41.9	28 20.3	5 43.8	14 42.5	10 50.3	21 14.3	26 44.3
26 W	20 23 03	6 29 56	11♏29 35	18 28 02	29R 12.1	29♑33.8	11 14.7	1 25.5	28 24.7	5 57.4	14 49.6	10 50.7	21 16.0	26 46.3
27 Th	20 26 59	7 30 55	25 30 53	2♐38 03	29 12.3	28 27.4	11 08.9	2 09.1	28 29.5	6 10.9	14 56.8	10 51.2	21 17.7	26 48.2
28 F	20 30 56	8 31 55	9♐49 25	17 04 42	29 11.1	27 27.6	11D 05.5	2 52.8	28 34.6	6 24.6	15 03.9	10 51.6	21 19.5	26 50.2
29 Sa	20 34 52	9 32 54	24 23 29	1♑45 12	29 07.5	26 35.7	11 04.6	3 36.5	28 40.1	6 38.3	15 11.1	10 52.2	21 21.3	26 52.1
30 Su	20 38 49	10 33 52	9♑09 07	16 34 21	29 01.1	25 52.1	11 06.2	4 20.2	28 46.0	6 52.0	15 18.3	10 52.8	21 23.1	26 54.1
31 M	20 42 45	11 34 49	23 59 57	1♒24 51	28 51.9	25 17.2	11 10.1	5 04.0	28 52.2	7 05.8	15 25.5	10 53.4	21 25.0	26 56.0

LONGITUDE — February 2022

Day	Sid.Time	☉	0 hr ☽	Noon ☽	True ☊	☿	♀	♂	⚳	♃	♄	♅	♆	♇
1 Tu	20 46 42	12♒35 45	8♒47 58	16♒08 12	28♉40.7	24♑51.1	11♑16.3	5♑47.8	28♉58.8	7♓19.6	15♒32.7	10♉54.1	21♓26.8	26♑57.9
2 W	20 50 39	13 36 40	23 24 33	0♓36 06	28R 28.8	24R 33.6	11 24.9	6 31.6	29 05.7	7 33.5	15 39.9	10 54.9	21 28.7	26 59.9
3 Th	20 54 35	14 37 34	7♓42 04	14 41 52	28 17.5	24D 24.3	11 35.6	7 15.5	29 13.0	7 47.4	15 47.1	10 55.7	21 30.6	27 01.8
4 F	20 58 32	15 38 26	21 35 06	28 21 30	28 07.9	24 23.0	11 48.5	7 59.3	29 20.7	8 01.4	15 54.3	10 56.6	21 32.5	27 03.7
5 Sa	21 02 28	16 39 17	5♈01 02	11♈33 50	28 00.7	24 29.0	12 03.6	8 43.3	29 28.6	8 15.4	16 01.5	10 57.5	21 34.4	27 05.6
6 Su	21 06 25	17 40 07	18 00 09	24 20 22	27 56.3	24 42.0	12 20.6	9 27.2	29 36.9	8 29.4	16 08.7	10 58.4	21 36.4	27 07.5
7 M	21 10 21	18 40 55	0♉35 00	6♉44 37	27 54.3	25 01.3	12 39.6	10 11.2	29 45.6	8 43.4	16 15.8	10 59.4	21 38.4	27 09.3
8 Tu	21 14 18	19 41 42	12 49 51	18 51 22	27 53.8	25 26.6	13 00.6	10 55.2	29 54.5	8 57.5	16 23.0	11 00.5	21 40.3	27 11.2
9 W	21 18 14	20 42 28	24 49 53	0♊46 05	27 53.8	25 57.3	13 23.3	11 39.2	0♊03.8	9 11.7	16 30.2	11 01.6	21 42.3	27 13.0
10 Th	21 22 11	21 43 12	6♊40 42	12 34 23	27 53.2	26 33.0	13 47.9	12 23.3	0 13.4	9 25.8	16 37.4	11 02.8	21 44.4	27 14.9
11 F	21 26 08	22 43 54	18 27 51	24 21 41	27 50.7	27 13.2	14 14.2	13 07.4	0 23.3	9 40.0	16 44.6	11 04.0	21 46.4	27 16.7
12 Sa	21 30 04	23 44 35	0♋16 29	6♋12 48	27 45.8	27 57.6	14 42.2	13 51.6	0 33.6	9 54.3	16 51.8	11 05.2	21 48.5	27 18.5
13 Su	21 34 01	24 45 14	12 11 07	18 11 51	27 38.0	28 45.9	15 11.7	14 35.7	0 44.1	10 08.5	16 58.9	11 06.5	21 50.5	27 20.4
14 M	21 37 57	25 45 52	24 15 21	0♌21 55	27 27.3	29 37.7	15 42.8	15 20.0	0 54.9	10 22.8	17 06.1	11 07.9	21 52.6	27 22.1
15 Tu	21 41 54	26 46 28	6♌31 44	12 44 59	27 14.6	0♒32.7	16 15.4	16 04.2	1 06.0	10 37.1	17 13.2	11 09.3	21 54.7	27 23.9
16 W	21 45 50	27 47 02	19 01 43	25 21 56	27 00.6	1 30.7	16 49.4	16 48.5	1 17.4	10 51.4	17 20.3	11 10.8	21 56.8	27 25.7
17 Th	21 49 47	28 47 35	1♍45 37	8♍12 38	26 46.7	2 31.5	17 24.8	17 32.8	1 29.1	11 05.7	17 27.4	11 12.3	21 58.9	27 27.4
18 F	21 53 43	29 48 07	14 42 52	21 16 10	26 34.1	3 34.8	18 01.6	18 17.1	1 41.1	11 20.1	17 34.5	11 13.8	22 01.1	27 29.2
19 Sa	21 57 40	0♓48 37	27 52 22	4♎31 17	26 23.8	4 40.5	18 39.6	19 01.4	1 53.3	11 34.5	17 41.6	11 15.4	22 03.2	27 30.9
20 Su	22 01 37	1 49 05	11♎12 46	17 56 41	26 16.6	5 48.4	19 18.8	19 45.8	2 05.8	11 48.9	17 48.7	11 17.0	22 05.4	27 32.6
21 M	22 05 33	2 49 33	24 42 58	1♏31 31	26 12.3	6 58.3	19 59.2	20 30.3	2 18.6	12 03.3	17 55.7	11 18.7	22 07.5	27 34.3
22 Tu	22 09 30	3 49 59	8♏22 19	15 15 21	26D 10.6	8 10.2	20 40.7	21 14.7	2 31.6	12 17.7	18 02.8	11 20.4	22 09.7	27 36.0
23 W	22 13 26	4 50 23	22 10 40	29 08 15	26R 10.3	9 23.9	21 23.3	21 59.2	2 44.9	12 32.2	18 09.8	11 22.2	22 11.9	27 37.6
24 Th	22 17 23	5 50 47	6♐08 08	13♐10 18	26 10.3	10 39.3	22 07.0	22 43.7	2 58.4	12 46.6	18 16.8	11 24.0	22 14.1	27 39.3
25 F	22 21 19	6 51 09	20 14 41	27 21 10	26 09.0	11 56.3	22 51.6	23 28.3	3 12.2	13 01.1	18 23.7	11 25.9	22 16.3	27 40.9
26 Sa	22 25 16	7 51 30	4♑29 33	11♑39 32	26 05.5	13 14.9	23 37.2	24 12.9	3 26.3	13 15.6	18 30.7	11 27.8	22 18.5	27 42.5
27 Su	22 29 12	8 51 49	18 50 44	26 02 38	25 59.1	14 34.9	24 23.8	24 57.5	3 40.6	13 30.1	18 37.6	11 29.8	22 20.8	27 44.1
28 M	22 33 09	9 52 07	3♒14 40	10♒26 09	25 50.1	15 56.4	25 11.2	25 42.1	3 55.1	13 44.6	18 44.5	11 31.8	22 23.0	27 45.7

Astro Data

Astro Data	Dy Hr Mn
☽0N	8 22:51
☿R	14 11:41
⚳D	14 21:20
♅D	18 15:26
☽0S	23 14:32
♀D	29 8:46
☿D	4 4:13
☽0N	5 7:00
♃✶♅	18 0:13
☽0S	19 19:21
♃∠♇	23 22:16

Planet Ingress

Planet Ingress	Dy Hr Mn
☿ ♒	2 7:10
☊ ♉R	18 18:20
☉ ♒	20 2:39
♂ ♑	24 12:53
☿ ♑R	26 3:05
⚳ ♊	9 2:13
☿ ♒	14 21:54
☉ ♓	18 16:43

Last Aspect / ☽ Ingress

Last Aspect Dy Hr Mn		☽ Ingress Dy Hr Mn
1 8:16 ♆ □	♑	1 23:02
3 16:21 ♇ ☌	♒	3 22:44
5 0:45 ♂ ✶	♓	6 0:16
7 22:23 ♇ ✶	♈	8 5:26
10 7:23 ♇ □	♉	10 14:47
12 19:39 ♇ △	♊	13 3:08
15 2:21 ♂ ☍	♋	15 16:11
17 23:48 ☉ ☍	♌	18 4:03
20 8:15 ♂ △	♍	20 14:02
22 19:46 ♂ □	♎	22 22:03
24 22:10 ♇ □	♏	25 3:57
27 5:28 ♆ ✶	♐	27 7:34
28 19:00 ♆ □	♑	29 9:09
31 4:44 ♇ ☌	♒	31 9:43

Last Aspect Dy Hr Mn		☽ Ingress Dy Hr Mn
1 11:01 ♄ ☌	♓	2 10:59
4 9:41 ♇ ✶	♈	4 14:56
6 17:21 ♇ □	♉	6 22:52
9 4:48 ♇ △	♊	9 10:27
11 8:23 ☉ △	♋	11 23:27
14 10:27 ☿ ☍	♌	14 11:17
16 16:56 ☉ ☍	♍	16 20:42
18 23:19 ♇ △	♎	19 3:51
21 5:02 ♇ □	♏	21 9:19
23 9:24 ♇ □	♐	23 13:29
25 3:24 ♆ □	♑	25 16:27
27 14:49 ♇ ☌	♒	27 18:36

☽ Phases & Eclipses

Dy Hr Mn		
2 18:33	●	12♑20
9 18:11	☽	19♈27
17 23:48	○	27♋51
25 13:41	☾	5♏33
1 5:46	●	12♒20
8 13:50	☽	19♉46
16 16:56	○	28♌00
23 22:32	☾	5♐17

Astro Data

1 January 2022
Julian Day # 44561
SVP 4♓57'23"
GC 27♐08.8 ⚴ 16♓35.0
Eris 23♈41.6R ⚵ 17♑34.7
⚷ 8♈30.7 ⚶ 24♐47.7
☽ Mean ☊ 29♉30.2

1 February 2022
Julian Day # 44592
SVP 4♓57'17"
GC 27♐08.9 ⚴ 25♓39.3
Eris 23♈43.7 ⚵ 29♑49.0
⚷ 9♈17.2 ⚶ 11♑13.8
☽ Mean ☊ 27♉51.7

March 2022 — LONGITUDE

Day	Sid.Time	☉	0 hr ☽	Noon ☽	True ☊	☿	♀	♂	⚳	♃	♄	♅	♆	♇
1 Tu	22 37 06	10♓52 23	17♒36 22	24♒44 33	25♉39.0	17♒19.3	25♑59.4	26♑26.8	4♊09.9	13♓59.1	18♒51.4	11♉33.8	22♓25.2	27♑47.3
2 W	22 41 02	11 52 38	1♓49 58	8♓51 52	25R 27.0	18 43.4	26 48.4	27 11.5	4 24.9	14 13.6	18 58.2	11 35.9	22 27.5	27 48.8
3 Th	22 44 59	12 52 50	15 49 37	22 42 39	25 15.4	20 08.9	27 38.2	27 56.2	4 40.1	14 28.1	19 05.0	11 38.0	22 29.7	27 50.3
4 F	22 48 55	13 53 01	29 30 31	6♈12 55	25 05.4	21 35.6	28 28.8	28 40.9	4 55.5	14 42.7	19 11.8	11 40.2	22 32.0	27 51.8
5 Sa	22 52 52	14 53 10	12♈49 40	19 20 43	24 57.7	23 03.5	29 20.0	29 25.7	5 11.2	14 57.2	19 18.5	11 42.4	22 34.2	27 53.3
6 Su	22 56 48	15 53 17	25 46 09	2♉06 12	24 52.8	24 32.7	0♒12.0	0♒10.5	5 27.1	15 11.7	19 25.3	11 44.6	22 36.5	27 54.7
7 M	23 00 45	16 53 22	8♉21 10	14 31 29	24D 50.4	26 03.0	1 04.6	0 55.3	5 43.2	15 26.2	19 31.9	11 46.9	22 38.8	27 56.2
8 Tu	23 04 41	17 53 24	20 37 37	26 40 10	24 50.0	27 34.5	1 57.8	1 40.1	5 59.5	15 40.7	19 38.6	11 49.2	22 41.0	27 57.6
9 W	23 08 38	18 53 25	2♊39 43	8♊36 56	24R 50.4	29 07.2	2 51.6	2 25.0	6 16.0	15 55.2	19 45.2	11 51.6	22 43.3	27 59.0
10 Th	23 12 35	19 53 24	14 32 28	20 27 01	24 50.8	0♓41.1	3 46.0	3 09.9	6 32.7	16 09.7	19 51.8	11 54.0	22 45.6	28 00.3
11 F	23 16 31	20 53 20	26 21 17	2♋15 55	24 50.0	2 16.1	4 41.0	3 54.8	6 49.7	16 24.2	19 58.3	11 56.4	22 47.9	28 01.7
12 Sa	23 20 28	21 53 14	8♋11 36	14 08 58	24 47.3	3 52.2	5 36.5	4 39.7	7 06.8	16 38.7	20 04.8	11 58.9	22 50.1	28 03.0
13 Su	23 24 24	22 53 06	20 08 35	26 11 02	24 42.3	5 29.6	6 32.5	5 24.6	7 24.1	16 53.2	20 11.3	12 01.4	22 52.4	28 04.3
14 M	23 28 21	23 52 56	2♌16 47	8♌26 15	24 34.9	7 08.1	7 29.1	6 09.6	7 41.5	17 07.7	20 17.7	12 03.9	22 54.7	28 05.6
15 Tu	23 32 17	24 52 44	14 39 48	20 57 40	24 25.6	8 47.8	8 26.1	6 54.5	7 59.2	17 22.1	20 24.1	12 06.5	22 57.0	28 06.8
16 W	23 36 14	25 52 29	27 20 04	3♍47 03	24 15.2	10 28.7	9 23.6	7 39.5	8 17.1	17 36.6	20 30.4	12 09.1	22 59.2	28 08.1
17 Th	23 40 10	26 52 12	10♍18 36	16 54 38	24 04.8	12 10.8	10 21.6	8 24.6	8 35.1	17 51.0	20 36.7	12 11.7	23 01.5	28 09.3
18 F	23 44 07	27 51 54	23 34 57	0♎19 17	23 55.3	13 54.1	11 20.0	9 09.6	8 53.3	18 05.4	20 42.9	12 14.4	23 03.8	28 10.5
19 Sa	23 48 04	28 51 33	7♎07 18	13 58 38	23 47.6	15 38.6	12 18.8	9 54.7	9 11.6	18 19.8	20 49.1	12 17.1	23 06.1	28 11.6
20 Su	23 52 00	29 51 10	20 52 53	27 49 37	23 42.4	17 24.4	13 18.0	10 39.8	9 30.2	18 34.2	20 55.3	12 19.8	23 08.3	28 12.8
21 M	23 55 57	0♈50 46	4♏48 27	11♏48 58	23D 39.7	19 11.4	14 17.7	11 24.9	9 48.9	18 48.5	21 01.4	12 22.6	23 10.6	28 13.9
22 Tu	23 59 53	1 50 20	18 50 48	25 53 39	23 39.1	20 59.7	15 17.7	12 10.0	10 07.7	19 02.9	21 07.4	12 25.4	23 12.9	28 15.0
23 W	0 03 50	2 49 52	2♐57 13	10♐01 16	23 39.8	22 49.3	16 18.1	12 55.1	10 26.7	19 17.2	21 13.4	12 28.2	23 15.1	28 16.0
24 Th	0 07 46	3 49 22	17 05 36	24 10 01	23R 40.8	24 40.2	17 18.8	13 40.3	10 45.9	19 31.5	21 19.4	12 31.1	23 17.4	28 17.1
25 F	0 11 43	4 48 51	1♑14 22	8♑18 29	23 41.1	26 32.3	18 19.9	14 25.5	11 05.3	19 45.8	21 25.3	12 34.0	23 19.6	28 18.1
26 Sa	0 15 39	5 48 18	15 22 11	22 25 19	23 39.8	28 25.7	19 21.3	15 10.7	11 24.8	20 00.0	21 31.2	12 36.9	23 21.9	28 19.1
27 Su	0 19 36	6 47 43	29 27 39	6♒28 56	23 36.6	0♈20.5	20 23.1	15 55.9	11 44.4	20 14.3	21 37.0	12 39.8	23 24.1	28 20.0
28 M	0 23 33	7 47 07	13♒28 54	20 27 13	23 31.3	2 16.4	21 25.1	16 41.2	12 04.2	20 28.5	21 42.7	12 42.8	23 26.3	28 20.9
29 Tu	0 27 29	8 46 28	27 23 34	4♓17 35	23 24.5	4 13.7	22 27.5	17 26.4	12 24.1	20 42.6	21 48.4	12 45.8	23 28.5	28 21.8
30 W	0 31 26	9 45 48	11♓08 53	17 57 07	23 17.0	6 12.1	23 30.1	18 11.7	12 44.2	20 56.8	21 54.0	12 48.8	23 30.7	28 22.7
31 Th	0 35 22	10 45 05	24 41 57	1♈23 04	23 09.7	8 11.7	24 33.0	18 56.9	13 04.4	21 10.9	21 59.6	12 51.8	23 32.9	28 23.6

April 2022 — LONGITUDE

Day	Sid.Time	☉	0 hr ☽	Noon ☽	True ☊	☿	♀	♂	⚳	♃	♄	♅	♆	♇
1 F	0 39 19	11♈44 21	8♈00 13	14♈33 13	23♉03.4	10♈12.4	25♒36.1	19♒42.2	13♊24.7	21♓25.0	22♒05.1	12♉54.9	23♓35.1	28♑24.4
2 Sa	0 43 15	12 43 35	21 01 55	27 26 18	22R 58.7	12 14.1	26 39.5	20 27.5	13 45.2	21 39.0	22 10.5	12 58.0	23 37.3	28 25.2
3 Su	0 47 12	13 42 46	3♉46 24	10♉02 18	22 56.0	14 16.8	27 43.2	21 12.8	14 05.8	21 53.0	22 15.9	13 01.1	23 39.5	28 26.0
4 M	0 51 08	14 41 55	16 14 13	22 22 25	22D 55.1	16 20.2	28 47.1	21 58.1	14 26.6	22 07.0	22 21.2	13 04.2	23 41.7	28 26.7
5 Tu	0 55 05	15 41 03	28 27 14	4♊29 04	22 55.7	18 24.3	29 51.2	22 43.4	14 47.5	22 20.9	22 26.5	13 07.4	23 43.8	28 27.4
6 W	0 59 01	16 40 08	10♊28 23	16 25 41	22 57.2	20 28.9	0♓55.5	23 28.7	15 08.5	22 34.8	22 31.7	13 10.5	23 45.9	28 28.1
7 Th	1 02 58	17 39 11	22 21 31	28 16 28	22 58.9	22 33.7	2 00.1	24 14.1	15 29.6	22 48.6	22 36.8	13 13.7	23 48.1	28 28.7
8 F	1 06 55	18 38 11	4♋11 09	10♋06 10	23R 00.2	24 38.5	3 04.8	24 59.4	15 50.9	23 02.4	22 41.9	13 17.0	23 50.2	28 29.4
9 Sa	1 10 51	19 37 09	16 02 10	21 59 47	23 00.6	26 43.1	4 09.8	25 44.7	16 12.2	23 16.2	22 46.9	13 20.2	23 52.3	28 30.0
10 Su	1 14 48	20 36 05	27 59 38	4♌02 20	22 59.6	28 47.2	5 14.9	26 30.1	16 33.7	23 29.9	22 51.8	13 23.4	23 54.4	28 30.5
11 M	1 18 44	21 34 59	10♌08 27	16 18 31	22 57.2	0♉50.4	6 20.2	27 15.4	16 55.3	23 43.6	22 56.6	13 26.7	23 56.5	28 31.1
12 Tu	1 22 41	22 33 50	22 33 01	28 52 22	22 53.6	2 52.5	7 25.8	28 00.8	17 17.0	23 57.2	23 01.4	13 30.0	23 58.5	28 31.6
13 W	1 26 37	23 32 39	5♍16 54	11♍46 52	22 49.3	4 53.0	8 31.5	28 46.1	17 38.8	24 10.8	23 06.1	13 33.3	24 00.6	28 32.1
14 Th	1 30 34	24 31 26	18 22 25	25 03 34	22 44.7	6 51.6	9 37.3	29 31.5	18 00.8	24 24.3	23 10.8	13 36.6	24 02.6	28 32.5
15 F	1 34 30	25 30 11	1♎50 15	8♎42 15	22 40.5	8 48.0	10 43.4	0♓16.8	18 22.8	24 37.8	23 15.3	13 39.9	24 04.6	28 33.0
16 Sa	1 38 27	26 28 53	15 39 17	22 40 54	22 37.3	10 41.9	11 49.6	1 02.2	18 44.9	24 51.2	23 19.8	13 43.2	24 06.6	28 33.4
17 Su	1 42 24	27 27 34	29 46 36	6♏55 46	22 35.3	12 32.9	12 55.9	1 47.6	19 07.1	25 04.6	23 24.3	13 46.6	24 08.6	28 33.7
18 M	1 46 20	28 26 13	14♏07 45	21 21 52	22D 34.6	14 20.7	14 02.5	2 32.9	19 29.5	25 17.9	23 28.6	13 50.0	24 10.6	28 34.1
19 Tu	1 50 17	29 24 50	28 37 24	5♐53 39	22 35.0	16 05.1	15 09.2	3 18.3	19 51.9	25 31.2	23 32.9	13 53.3	24 12.5	28 34.4
20 W	1 54 13	0♉23 25	13♐09 57	20 25 40	22 36.1	17 45.7	16 16.0	4 03.7	20 14.4	25 44.4	23 37.1	13 56.7	24 14.5	28 34.7
21 Th	1 58 10	1 21 59	27 40 15	4♑53 12	22 37.5	19 22.4	17 23.0	4 49.0	20 37.0	25 57.5	23 41.2	14 00.1	24 16.4	28 34.9
22 F	2 02 06	2 20 31	12♑04 05	19 12 32	22 38.6	20 55.0	18 30.1	5 34.4	20 59.8	26 10.6	23 45.2	14 03.5	24 18.3	28 35.2
23 Sa	2 06 03	3 19 02	26 18 16	3♒21 03	22R 39.0	22 23.3	19 37.4	6 19.8	21 22.6	26 23.7	23 49.2	14 06.9	24 20.2	28 35.4
24 Su	2 09 59	4 17 31	10♒20 43	17 17 07	22 38.6	23 47.2	20 44.8	7 05.2	21 45.5	26 36.6	23 53.1	14 10.4	24 22.0	28 35.5
25 M	2 13 56	5 15 58	24 10 10	0♓59 48	22 37.3	25 06.5	21 52.3	7 50.5	22 08.5	26 49.5	23 56.9	14 13.8	24 23.9	28 35.7
26 Tu	2 17 53	6 14 24	7♓45 59	14 28 40	22 35.4	26 21.0	22 59.9	8 35.9	22 31.5	27 02.4	24 00.6	14 17.2	24 25.7	28 35.8
27 W	2 21 49	7 12 48	21 07 51	27 43 32	22 33.3	27 30.8	24 07.7	9 21.2	22 54.7	27 15.1	24 04.3	14 20.7	24 27.5	28 35.9
28 Th	2 25 46	8 11 10	4♈15 44	10♈44 27	22 31.2	28 35.7	25 15.6	10 06.6	23 18.0	27 27.8	24 07.8	14 24.1	24 29.3	28 35.9
29 F	2 29 42	9 09 30	17 09 43	23 31 36	22 29.4	29 35.6	26 23.5	10 51.9	23 41.3	27 40.5	24 11.3	14 27.6	24 31.0	28R 35.9
30 Sa	2 33 39	10 07 49	29 50 09	6♉05 27	22 28.3	0♊30.5	27 31.6	11 37.2	24 04.7	27 53.0	24 14.7	14 31.0	24 32.7	28 35.9

Astro Data

	Dy Hr Mn
☽0N	4 16:07
☽0S	19 2:16
☉0N	20 15:33
☿0N	29 5:55
☽0N	1 0:44
♃×♄	6 3:24
♃☌♆	12 14:42
☽0S	15 11:34
☽0N	28 7:50
♇ R	29 18:36

Planet Ingress

	Dy Hr Mn
♂ ♒	6 6:23
♀ ♒	6 6:30
☿ ♓	10 1:32
☉ ♈	20 15:33
☿ ♈	27 7:44
♀ ♓	5 15:18
☿ ♉	11 2:09
♂ ♓	15 3:06
☉ ♉	20 2:24
☿ ♊	29 22:23

Last Aspect / ☽ Ingress

Last Aspect Dy Hr Mn		☽ Ingress Dy Hr Mn
1 2:01	♄ ☌	♓ 1 20:53
3 21:45	♂ ⚹	♈ 4 0:52
6 4:02	♇ □	♉ 6 8:00
8 14:35	♇ △	♊ 8 18:40
10 16:43	♆ □	♋ 11 7:24
13 15:44	♇ ☍	♌ 13 19:32
15 10:56	♄ ☍	♍ 16 4:59
18 8:11	♇ △	♎ 18 11:26
20 12:40	♇ □	♏ 20 15:44
22 16:01	♇ ⚹	♐ 22 18:59
24 12:59	☿ □	♑ 24 21:54
26 23:51	☿ ⚹	♒ 27 0:55
28 14:11	♄ ☌	♓ 29 4:32
31 6:37	♇ ⚹	♈ 31 9:30

Last Aspect / ☽ Ingress

Last Aspect Dy Hr Mn		☽ Ingress Dy Hr Mn
2 13:51	♇ □	♉ 2 16:50
5 1:53	♀ □	♊ 5 3:04
7 3:15	♂ △	♋ 7 15:30
10 1:01	♇ ☍	♌ 10 4:00
12 10:16	♂ ☍	♍ 12 14:07
14 18:11	♇ △	♎ 14 20:46
16 21:57	♇ □	♏ 17 0:23
18 23:55	♇ ⚹	♐ 19 2:16
20 20:56	♃ □	♑ 21 3:52
23 3:53	♇ ☌	♒ 23 6:17
25 0:33	☿ □	♓ 25 10:15
27 13:36	♇ ⚹	♈ 27 16:10
29 21:38	♇ □	♉ 30 0:19

☽ Phases & Eclipses

Dy Hr Mn	
2 17:35	● 12♓07
10 10:45	☽ 19♊50
18 7:17	○ 27♍40
25 5:37	☾ 4♑33
1 6:24	● 11♈31
9 6:48	☽ 19♋24
16 18:55	○ 26♎46
23 11:56	☾ 3♒19
30 20:28	● 10♉28
30 20:41:25	P 0.640

Astro Data

1 March 2022
Julian Day # 44620
SVP 4♓57'14"
GC 27♐08.9 ⚴ 5♈33.3
Eris 23♈54.0 ⚵ 10♒57.4
⚷ 10♈33.7 ⚶ 25♑28.5
☽ Mean ☊ 26♉22.7

1 April 2022
Julian Day # 44651
SVP 4♓57'11"
GC 27♐09.0 ⚴ 17♈46.4
Eris 24♈11.9 ⚵ 22♒58.1
⚷ 12♈19.0 ⚶ 10♒06.4
☽ Mean ☊ 24♉44.2

LONGITUDE — May 2022

Day	Sid.Time	☉	0 hr ☽	Noon ☽	True ☊	☿	♀	♂	⚳	♃	♄	♅	♆	♇
1 Su	2 37 35	11♉06 07	12♉17 38	18♉26 51	22♉27.8	1♊20.3	28♓39.8	12♓22.5	24♊28.2	28♓05.5	24♒17.9	14♉34.5	24♓34.5	28♑35.9
2 M	2 41 32	12 04 22	24 33 15	0♊37 03	22D 27.9	2 04.8	29 48.1	13 07.8	24 51.8	28 17.9	24 21.2	14 38.0	24 36.1	28R 35.8
3 Tu	2 45 28	13 02 36	6♊38 30	12 37 53	22 28.4	2 44.2	0♈56.5	13 53.1	25 15.5	28 30.3	24 24.3	14 41.4	24 37.8	28 35.7
4 W	2 49 25	14 00 47	18 35 32	24 31 49	22 29.2	3 18.2	2 05.0	14 38.3	25 39.2	28 42.6	24 27.3	14 44.9	24 39.5	28 35.6
5 Th	2 53 22	14 58 57	0♋27 06	6♋21 51	22 30.1	3 47.0	3 13.6	15 23.6	26 03.0	28 54.7	24 30.3	14 48.4	24 41.1	28 35.5
6 F	2 57 18	15 57 05	12 16 31	18 11 36	22 30.8	4 10.4	4 22.2	16 08.8	26 26.9	29 06.9	24 33.1	14 51.8	24 42.7	28 35.3
7 Sa	3 01 15	16 55 11	24 07 38	0♌05 09	22 31.3	4 28.6	5 31.0	16 54.0	26 50.9	29 18.9	24 35.9	14 55.3	24 44.3	28 35.1
8 Su	3 05 11	17 53 16	6♌04 42	12 06 53	22R 31.6	4 41.4	6 39.8	17 39.2	27 14.9	29 30.8	24 38.6	14 58.8	24 45.8	28 34.9
9 M	3 09 08	18 51 18	18 12 16	24 21 23	22 31.6	4R 49.0	7 48.7	18 24.4	27 39.0	29 42.7	24 41.2	15 02.2	24 47.3	28 34.6
10 Tu	3 13 04	19 49 18	0♍34 48	6♍53 02	22 31.4	4 51.5	8 57.7	19 09.5	28 03.2	29 54.5	24 43.7	15 05.7	24 48.8	28 34.3
11 W	3 17 01	20 47 16	13 16 32	19 45 44	22 31.2	4 49.0	10 06.8	19 54.6	28 27.4	0♈06.1	24 46.1	15 09.2	24 50.3	28 34.0
12 Th	3 20 57	21 45 13	26 20 56	3♎02 24	22D 31.1	4 41.7	11 15.9	20 39.7	28 51.7	0 17.7	24 48.4	15 12.6	24 51.8	28 33.7
13 F	3 24 54	22 43 08	9♎50 14	16 44 27	22 31.1	4 29.7	12 25.1	21 24.8	29 16.0	0 29.2	24 50.6	15 16.1	24 53.2	28 33.3
14 Sa	3 28 51	23 41 01	23 44 56	0♏51 22	22 31.1	4 13.5	13 34.4	22 09.8	29 40.4	0 40.7	24 52.7	15 19.5	24 54.6	28 32.9
15 Su	3 32 47	24 38 52	8♏03 21	15 20 17	22R 31.2	3 53.2	14 43.8	22 54.9	0♋04.9	0 52.0	24 54.7	15 22.9	24 55.9	28 32.5
16 M	3 36 44	25 36 42	22 41 27	0♐06 01	22 31.2	3 29.4	15 53.2	23 39.9	0 29.5	1 03.2	24 56.7	15 26.4	24 57.3	28 32.0
17 Tu	3 40 40	26 34 31	7♐33 03	15 01 33	22 31.0	3 02.5	17 02.8	24 24.8	0 54.1	1 14.4	24 58.5	15 29.8	24 58.6	28 31.5
18 W	3 44 37	27 32 18	22 30 30	29 58 51	22 30.6	2 32.9	18 12.4	25 09.8	1 18.7	1 25.4	25 00.3	15 33.2	24 59.9	28 31.0
19 Th	3 48 33	28 30 05	7♑25 38	14♑49 58	22 30.0	2 01.1	19 22.0	25 54.7	1 43.4	1 36.4	25 01.9	15 36.6	25 01.1	28 30.5
20 F	3 52 30	29 27 50	22 11 01	29 28 08	22 29.4	1 27.9	20 31.8	26 39.6	2 08.2	1 47.2	25 03.5	15 40.0	25 02.4	28 30.0
21 Sa	3 56 26	0♊25 33	6♒40 45	13♒48 27	22 28.8	0 53.6	21 41.6	27 24.5	2 33.0	1 58.0	25 05.0	15 43.4	25 03.6	28 29.4
22 Su	4 00 23	1 23 16	20 51 00	27 48 12	22D 28.5	0 19.0	22 51.4	28 09.4	2 57.9	2 08.6	25 06.3	15 46.8	25 04.8	28 28.8
23 M	4 04 20	2 20 58	4♓40 04	11♓26 37	22 28.6	29♉44.7	24 01.4	28 54.2	3 22.9	2 19.1	25 07.6	15 50.1	25 05.9	28 28.1
24 Tu	4 08 16	3 18 38	18 08 00	24 44 26	22 29.2	29 11.2	25 11.4	29 39.0	3 47.8	2 29.6	25 08.8	15 53.5	25 07.0	28 27.5
25 W	4 12 13	4 16 18	1♈16 09	7♈43 27	22 30.1	28 39.1	26 21.4	0♈23.7	4 12.9	2 39.9	25 09.8	15 56.8	25 08.1	28 26.8
26 Th	4 16 09	5 13 56	14 06 36	20 25 56	22 31.2	28 09.0	27 31.5	1 08.4	4 38.0	2 50.1	25 10.8	16 00.2	25 09.2	28 26.1
27 F	4 20 06	6 11 34	26 41 45	2♉54 20	22 32.2	27 41.3	28 41.7	1 53.1	5 03.1	3 00.2	25 11.7	16 03.5	25 10.2	28 25.4
28 Sa	4 24 02	7 09 11	9♉04 01	15 11 02	22R 32.9	27 16.4	29 51.9	2 37.7	5 28.3	3 10.2	25 12.5	16 06.8	25 11.2	28 24.6
29 Su	4 27 59	8 06 46	21 15 42	27 18 14	22 32.9	26 54.8	1♉02.2	3 22.3	5 53.6	3 20.1	25 13.2	16 10.1	25 12.2	28 23.8
30 M	4 31 55	9 04 21	3♊18 55	9♊17 58	22 32.2	26 36.8	2 12.5	4 06.8	6 18.9	3 29.9	25 13.7	16 13.3	25 13.1	28 23.0
31 Tu	4 35 52	10 01 54	15 15 39	21 12 12	22 30.6	26 22.7	3 22.9	4 51.3	6 44.2	3 39.5	25 14.2	16 16.6	25 14.0	28 22.2

LONGITUDE — June 2022

Day	Sid.Time	☉	0 hr ☽	Noon ☽	True ☊	☿	♀	♂	⚳	♃	♄	♅	♆	♇
1 W	4 39 49	10♊59 26	27♊07 53	3♋02 57	22♉28.2	26♉12.6	4♉33.3	5♈35.7	7♋09.6	3♈49.1	25♒14.6	16♉19.8	25♓14.9	28♑21.4
2 Th	4 43 45	11 56 58	8♋57 41	14 52 24	22R 25.3	26D 06.8	5 43.8	6 20.1	7 35.1	3 58.5	25 14.9	16 23.0	25 15.7	28R 20.5
3 F	4 47 42	12 54 28	20 47 24	26 43 03	22 22.0	26 05.3	6 54.3	7 04.5	8 00.6	4 07.7	25 15.1	16 26.2	25 16.6	28 19.6
4 Sa	4 51 38	13 51 56	2♌39 43	8♌37 49	22 19.0	26 08.3	8 04.9	7 48.8	8 26.1	4 16.9	25R 15.2	16 29.4	25 17.4	28 18.7
5 Su	4 55 35	14 49 24	14 37 47	20 40 03	22 16.4	26 15.7	9 15.5	8 33.0	8 51.6	4 25.9	25 15.2	16 32.6	25 18.1	28 17.8
6 M	4 59 31	15 46 50	26 45 08	2♍53 31	22 14.7	26 27.7	10 26.1	9 17.2	9 17.2	4 34.8	25 15.1	16 35.7	25 18.8	28 16.8
7 Tu	5 03 28	16 44 15	9♍05 42	15 22 13	22D 14.1	26 44.1	11 36.8	10 01.3	9 42.9	4 43.6	25 14.8	16 38.8	25 19.5	28 15.9
8 W	5 07 25	17 41 39	21 43 33	28 10 11	22 14.4	27 04.9	12 47.6	10 45.4	10 08.6	4 52.3	25 14.5	16 41.9	25 20.2	28 14.9
9 Th	5 11 21	18 39 02	4♎42 36	11♎21 09	22 15.6	27 30.2	13 58.4	11 29.4	10 34.3	5 00.8	25 14.1	16 45.0	25 20.8	28 13.9
10 F	5 15 18	19 36 24	18 06 10	24 57 52	22 17.1	27 59.7	15 09.2	12 13.4	11 00.0	5 09.1	25 13.6	16 48.0	25 21.4	28 12.8
11 Sa	5 19 14	20 33 45	1♏56 22	9♏01 36	22R 18.3	28 33.5	16 20.1	12 57.3	11 25.8	5 17.4	25 13.0	16 51.1	25 21.9	28 11.8
12 Su	5 23 11	21 31 05	16 13 24	23 31 20	22 18.8	29 11.5	17 31.0	13 41.2	11 51.7	5 25.5	25 12.4	16 54.1	25 22.5	28 10.7
13 M	5 27 07	22 28 24	0♐54 53	8♐23 15	22 18.0	29 53.6	18 41.9	14 24.9	12 17.5	5 33.5	25 11.6	16 57.0	25 23.0	28 09.6
14 Tu	5 31 04	23 25 42	15 55 32	23 30 38	22 15.8	0♊39.7	19 52.9	15 08.7	12 43.4	5 41.3	25 10.7	17 00.0	25 23.4	28 08.5
15 W	5 35 00	24 23 00	1♑07 20	8♑44 22	22 12.3	1 29.8	21 04.0	15 52.4	13 09.4	5 49.0	25 09.7	17 02.9	25 23.9	28 07.4
16 Th	5 38 57	25 20 17	16 20 27	23 54 19	22 07.8	2 23.7	22 15.1	16 36.0	13 35.3	5 56.5	25 08.7	17 05.8	25 24.3	28 06.3
17 F	5 42 54	26 17 34	1♒24 48	8♒50 51	22 03.2	3 21.4	23 26.2	17 19.5	14 01.3	6 03.9	25 07.5	17 08.7	25 24.7	28 05.1
18 Sa	5 46 50	27 14 50	16 11 36	23 26 23	21 59.0	4 22.8	24 37.4	18 03.0	14 27.3	6 11.2	25 06.2	17 11.6	25 25.0	28 03.9
19 Su	5 50 47	28 12 06	0♓34 43	7♓36 18	21 55.9	5 27.8	25 48.7	18 46.4	14 53.4	6 18.3	25 04.9	17 14.4	25 25.3	28 02.7
20 M	5 54 43	29 09 21	14 31 01	21 18 58	21D 54.3	6 36.5	26 59.9	19 29.8	15 19.5	6 25.3	25 03.4	17 17.2	25 25.6	28 01.5
21 Tu	5 58 40	0♋06 37	28 00 18	4♈35 20	21 54.1	7 48.7	28 11.2	20 13.1	15 45.6	6 32.1	25 01.9	17 19.9	25 25.8	28 00.3
22 W	6 02 36	1 03 52	11♈04 29	17 28 10	21 55.0	9 04.5	29 22.6	20 56.3	16 11.8	6 38.7	25 00.3	17 22.7	25 26.0	27 59.1
23 Th	6 06 33	2 01 07	23 46 53	0♉01 09	21 56.5	10 23.6	0♊34.0	21 39.4	16 38.0	6 45.2	24 58.5	17 25.4	25 26.2	27 57.8
24 F	6 10 29	2 58 22	6♉11 29	12 18 23	21R 57.8	11 46.2	1 45.5	22 22.5	17 04.2	6 51.6	24 56.7	17 28.1	25 26.3	27 56.6
25 Sa	6 14 26	3 55 37	18 22 21	24 23 52	21 58.2	13 12.2	2 56.9	23 05.4	17 30.4	6 57.7	24 54.8	17 30.7	25 26.4	27 55.3
26 Su	6 18 23	4 52 52	0♊23 21	6♊21 12	21 57.0	14 41.6	4 08.5	23 48.3	17 56.7	7 03.8	24 52.8	17 33.3	25 26.5	27 54.0
27 M	6 22 19	5 50 06	12 17 48	18 13 29	21 53.9	16 14.2	5 20.0	24 31.1	18 23.0	7 09.6	24 50.7	17 35.9	25R 26.5	27 52.7
28 Tu	6 26 16	6 47 21	24 08 33	0♋03 18	21 48.7	17 50.2	6 31.6	25 13.9	18 49.3	7 15.3	24 48.6	17 38.4	25 26.6	27 51.4
29 W	6 30 12	7 44 35	5♋57 58	11 52 47	21 41.7	19 29.3	7 43.3	25 56.5	19 15.7	7 20.8	24 46.3	17 41.0	25 26.5	27 50.1
30 Th	6 34 09	8 41 49	17 47 59	23 43 47	21 33.4	21 11.6	8 55.0	26 39.1	19 42.1	7 26.2	24 44.0	17 43.4	25 26.5	27 48.8

Astro Data

	Dy Hr Mn
♃⚹♇	3 22:33
♀0N	5 17:43
☿R	10 11:47
♃∠♅	11 20:52
☽0S	12 21:42
♄⊻♆	17 15:39
♃0N	25 8:19
☽0N	25 13:29
♂0N	30 9:19
♄⊻♆	31 22:03
☿D	3 8:00
♄R	4 21:47
☽0S	9 6:44
☽0N	21 18:53
♆R	28 7:55

Planet Ingress

	Dy Hr Mn
♀ ♈	2 16:10
♃ ♈	10 23:22
⚳ ♋	15 7:11
☉ ♊	21 1:22
☿ ♉R	23 1:15
♂ ♈	24 23:17
♀ ♉	28 14:46
☿ ♊	13 15:27
☉ ♋	21 9:14
♀ ♊	23 0:34

Last Aspect / ☽ Ingress

Last Aspect Dy Hr Mn		☽ Ingress Dy Hr Mn
2 10:13 ♀ ⚹	♊	2 10:46
4 20:37 ♃ □	♋	4 23:05
7 10:25 ♃ △	♌	7 11:50
9 12:38 ♄ ☍	♍	9 22:53
12 3:59 ♇ △	♎	12 6:34
14 8:07 ♇ □	♏	14 10:34
16 9:28 ♇ ⚹	♐	16 11:50
18 3:59 ♄ ⚹	♑	18 12:02
20 12:00 ☉ △	♒	20 12:53
22 7:19 ♄ ☌	♓	22 15:49
24 21:33 ♂ ☌	♈	24 21:39
27 3:20 ♇ □	♉	27 6:22
29 14:11 ♇ △	♊	29 17:22

Last Aspect / ☽ Ingress

Last Aspect Dy Hr Mn		☽ Ingress Dy Hr Mn
31 20:10 ♄ △	♋	1 5:49
3 15:15 ♇ ☍	♌	3 18:38
5 23:12 ☿ □	♍	6 6:22
8 12:09 ♇ △	♎	8 15:23
10 17:36 ♇ □	♏	10 20:41
12 21:40 ☿ ☍	♐	12 22:31
14 14:58 ♆ □	♑	14 22:14
16 18:41 ♇ ☌	♒	16 21:44
18 18:50 ☉ △	♓	18 23:01
21 3:11 ☉ □	♈	21 3:37
23 8:02 ♇ □	♉	23 11:58
25 19:02 ♇ △	♊	25 23:13
28 2:38 ♆ □	♋	28 11:53

☽ Phases & Eclipses

Dy Hr Mn	
9 0:21	☽ 18♌23
16 4:14	○ 25♏18
16 4:11	☍ T 1.413
22 18:43	☾ 1♓39
30 11:30	● 9♊03
7 14:48	☽ 16♍51
14 11:52	○ 23♐25
21 3:11	☾ 29♓46
29 2:52	● 7♋23

Astro Data

1 May 2022
Julian Day # 44681
SVP 4♓57'07"
GC 27♐09.1 ⚴ 0♉29.6
Eris 24♈31.4 ⚵ 3♓46.3
⚷ 14♈01.7 ⚶ 22♒26.7
☽ Mean ☊ 23♉08.9

1 June 2022
Julian Day # 44712
SVP 4♓57'02"
GC 27♐09.1 ⚴ 14♉20.5
Eris 24♈48.9 ⚵ 13♓18.2
⚷ 15♈28.4 ⚶ 2♓08.3
☽ Mean ☊ 21♉30.4

July 2022 LONGITUDE

Day	Sid.Time	☉	0 hr ☽	Noon ☽	True ☊	☿	♀	♂	⚳	♃	♄	♅	♆	♇
1 F	6 38 05	9♋39 03	29♋40 24	5♌38 04	21♉24.4	22♊57.0	10♊06.7	27♈21.5	20♋08.5	7♈31.4	24♒41.6	17♉45.9	25♓26.4	27♑47.4
2 Sa	6 42 02	10 36 16	11♌37 00	17 37 28	21R 15.6	24 45.4	11 18.4	28 03.9	20 34.9	7 36.4	24R 39.1	17 48.3	25R 26.3	27R 46.1
3 Su	6 45 58	11 33 30	23 39 44	29 44 08	21 07.9	26 36.7	12 30.2	28 46.2	21 01.3	7 41.3	24 36.5	17 50.7	25 26.1	27 44.7
4 M	6 49 55	12 30 43	5♍50 59	12♍00 39	21 01.9	28 30.7	13 42.1	29 28.3	21 27.8	7 45.9	24 33.8	17 53.0	25 25.9	27 43.4
5 Tu	6 53 52	13 27 55	18 13 32	24 30 03	20 58.0	0♋27.4	14 53.9	0♉10.4	21 54.3	7 50.4	24 31.1	17 55.3	25 25.7	27 42.0
6 W	6 57 48	14 25 08	0♎50 38	7♎15 45	20D 56.1	2 26.4	16 05.8	0 52.4	22 20.8	7 54.7	24 28.2	17 57.6	25 25.5	27 40.6
7 Th	7 01 45	15 22 20	13 45 49	20 21 18	20 56.0	4 27.7	17 17.8	1 34.2	22 47.3	7 58.9	24 25.3	17 59.8	25 25.2	27 39.2
8 F	7 05 41	16 19 32	27 02 34	3♏49 59	20 56.7	6 31.0	18 29.7	2 16.0	23 13.9	8 02.9	24 22.3	18 02.0	25 24.9	27 37.8
9 Sa	7 09 38	17 16 43	10♏43 48	17 44 10	20R 57.4	8 35.9	19 41.7	2 57.7	23 40.4	8 06.6	24 19.3	18 04.1	25 24.5	27 36.4
10 Su	7 13 34	18 13 55	24 51 08	2♐04 32	20 57.0	10 42.3	20 53.8	3 39.2	24 07.0	8 10.3	24 16.2	18 06.2	25 24.1	27 35.0
11 M	7 17 31	19 11 07	9♐24 04	16 49 11	20 54.6	12 49.9	22 05.9	4 20.7	24 33.6	8 13.7	24 13.0	18 08.3	25 23.7	27 33.6
12 Tu	7 21 27	20 08 19	24 19 10	1♑53 05	20 50.0	14 58.3	23 18.0	5 02.1	25 00.2	8 16.9	24 09.7	18 10.3	25 23.3	27 32.2
13 W	7 25 24	21 05 31	9♑29 49	17 08 05	20 43.1	17 07.3	24 30.1	5 43.3	25 26.8	8 20.0	24 06.4	18 12.3	25 22.8	27 30.8
14 Th	7 29 21	22 02 43	24 46 32	2♒23 47	20 34.6	19 16.4	25 42.3	6 24.5	25 53.5	8 22.9	24 03.0	18 14.3	25 22.3	27 29.3
15 F	7 33 17	22 59 55	9♒58 26	17 29 15	20 25.6	21 25.6	26 54.6	7 05.5	26 20.1	8 25.6	23 59.6	18 16.2	25 21.8	27 27.9
16 Sa	7 37 14	23 57 08	24 55 04	2♓14 58	20 17.1	23 34.5	28 06.9	7 46.4	26 46.8	8 28.1	23 56.0	18 18.1	25 21.3	27 26.5
17 Su	7 41 10	24 54 21	9♓28 13	16 34 18	20 10.1	25 42.8	29 19.2	8 27.2	27 13.5	8 30.4	23 52.5	18 19.9	25 20.7	27 25.1
18 M	7 45 07	25 51 35	23 32 59	0♈24 10	20 05.3	27 50.3	0♋31.6	9 07.9	27 40.2	8 32.5	23 48.8	18 21.7	25 20.0	27 23.6
19 Tu	7 49 03	26 48 49	7♈07 58	13 44 39	20 02.7	29 57.0	1 44.0	9 48.5	28 06.9	8 34.4	23 45.1	18 23.4	25 19.4	27 22.2
20 W	7 53 00	27 46 05	20 14 38	26 38 24	20D 02.0	2♌02.5	2 56.4	10 28.9	28 33.6	8 36.2	23 41.4	18 25.1	25 18.7	27 20.7
21 Th	7 56 56	28 43 21	2♉56 30	9♉09 34	20R 02.2	4 06.7	4 08.9	11 09.2	29 00.4	8 37.7	23 37.5	18 26.8	25 18.0	27 19.3
22 F	8 00 53	29 40 38	15 18 12	21 23 04	20 02.5	6 09.6	5 21.4	11 49.4	29 27.1	8 39.1	23 33.7	18 28.4	25 17.3	27 17.9
23 Sa	8 04 50	0♌37 55	27 24 46	3♊23 55	20 01.7	8 11.0	6 34.0	12 29.5	29 53.9	8 40.2	23 29.8	18 30.0	25 16.5	27 16.4
24 Su	8 08 46	1 35 14	9♊21 06	15 16 51	19 58.9	10 10.9	7 46.6	13 09.4	0♌20.7	8 41.2	23 25.8	18 31.5	25 15.7	27 15.0
25 M	8 12 43	2 32 33	21 11 40	27 06 00	19 53.6	12 09.2	8 59.3	13 49.2	0 47.5	8 41.9	23 21.8	18 33.0	25 14.9	27 13.6
26 Tu	8 16 39	3 29 54	3♋00 16	8♋54 49	19 45.6	14 05.9	10 12.0	14 28.8	1 14.2	8 42.5	23 17.7	18 34.4	25 14.0	27 12.2
27 W	8 20 36	4 27 15	14 49 57	20 45 58	19 35.1	16 01.0	11 24.7	15 08.3	1 41.1	8 42.9	23 13.6	18 35.8	25 13.2	27 10.7
28 Th	8 24 32	5 24 36	26 43 06	2♌41 31	19 22.7	17 54.3	12 37.5	15 47.6	2 07.9	8R 43.1	23 09.5	18 37.1	25 12.3	27 09.3
29 F	8 28 29	6 21 59	8♌41 24	14 42 54	19 09.4	19 46.1	13 50.3	16 26.8	2 34.7	8 43.0	23 05.3	18 38.4	25 11.3	27 07.9
30 Sa	8 32 26	7 19 22	20 46 10	26 51 19	18 56.3	21 36.1	15 03.1	17 05.9	3 01.5	8 42.8	23 01.1	18 39.7	25 10.4	27 06.5
31 Su	8 36 22	8 16 45	2♍58 29	9♍07 50	18 44.6	23 24.4	16 16.0	17 44.8	3 28.3	8 42.4	22 56.8	18 40.9	25 09.4	27 05.1

August 2022 LONGITUDE

Day	Sid.Time	☉	0 hr ☽	Noon ☽	True ☊	☿	♀	♂	⚳	♃	♄	♅	♆	♇
1 M	8 40 19	9♌14 10	15♍19 33	21♍33 47	18♉35.1	25♌11.1	17♋28.9	18♉23.5	3♌55.2	8♈41.7	22♒52.6	18♉42.1	25♓08.4	27♑03.7
2 Tu	8 44 15	10 11 35	27 50 48	4♎10 50	18R 28.3	26 56.1	18 41.9	19 02.0	4 22.0	8R 40.9	22R 48.2	18 43.2	25R 07.4	27R 02.3
3 W	8 48 12	11 09 01	10♎34 11	17 01 09	18 24.3	28 39.5	19 54.9	19 40.4	4 48.9	8 39.9	22 43.9	18 44.2	25 06.3	27 00.9
4 Th	8 52 08	12 06 27	23 32 04	0♏07 18	18D 22.6	0♍21.2	21 07.9	20 18.7	5 15.7	8 38.7	22 39.5	18 45.2	25 05.2	26 59.5
5 F	8 56 05	13 03 54	6♏47 11	13 32 02	18R 22.3	2 01.3	22 21.0	20 56.8	5 42.5	8 37.3	22 35.1	18 46.2	25 04.1	26 58.2
6 Sa	9 00 01	14 01 22	20 22 08	27 17 44	18 22.2	3 39.7	23 34.1	21 34.7	6 09.4	8 35.7	22 30.7	18 47.1	25 03.0	26 56.8
7 Su	9 03 58	14 58 50	4♐18 56	11♐25 46	18 21.0	5 16.6	24 47.2	22 12.4	6 36.2	8 33.9	22 26.3	18 48.0	25 01.8	26 55.4
8 M	9 07 55	15 56 20	18 38 06	25 55 38	18 17.8	6 51.8	26 00.4	22 49.9	7 03.1	8 31.9	22 21.9	18 48.8	25 00.7	26 54.1
9 Tu	9 11 51	16 53 50	3♑17 53	10♑44 13	18 12.0	8 25.3	27 13.6	23 27.3	7 29.9	8 29.7	22 17.4	18 49.6	24 59.5	26 52.8
10 W	9 15 48	17 51 21	18 13 44	25 45 27	18 03.6	9 57.3	28 26.9	24 04.5	7 56.8	8 27.3	22 12.9	18 50.3	24 58.2	26 51.5
11 Th	9 19 44	18 48 53	3♒18 11	10♒50 42	17 53.3	11 27.6	29 40.1	24 41.5	8 23.6	8 24.7	22 08.5	18 51.0	24 57.0	26 50.2
12 F	9 23 41	19 46 26	18 21 43	25 49 59	17 42.2	12 56.3	0♌53.5	25 18.4	8 50.5	8 22.0	22 04.0	18 51.6	24 55.7	26 48.9
13 Sa	9 27 37	20 44 00	3♓14 19	10♓33 42	17 31.6	14 23.3	2 06.8	25 55.0	9 17.3	8 19.0	21 59.5	18 52.2	24 54.5	26 47.6
14 Su	9 31 34	21 41 35	17 47 15	24 54 18	17 22.7	15 48.7	3 20.2	26 31.5	9 44.1	8 15.9	21 55.0	18 52.7	24 53.2	26 46.3
15 M	9 35 30	22 39 12	1♈54 26	8♈47 21	17 16.1	17 12.3	4 33.7	27 07.7	10 11.0	8 12.5	21 50.5	18 53.2	24 51.8	26 45.0
16 Tu	9 39 27	23 36 50	15 33 03	22 11 39	17 12.1	18 34.3	5 47.1	27 43.8	10 37.8	8 09.0	21 46.0	18 53.6	24 50.5	26 43.8
17 W	9 43 24	24 34 30	28 43 25	5♉08 45	17D 10.3	19 54.5	7 00.7	28 19.6	11 04.6	8 05.3	21 41.5	18 54.0	24 49.1	26 42.5
18 Th	9 47 20	25 32 11	11♉28 10	17 42 15	17R 09.9	21 12.9	8 14.2	28 55.3	11 31.5	8 01.5	21 37.0	18 54.3	24 47.7	26 41.3
19 F	9 51 17	26 29 54	23 51 37	29 56 55	17 09.9	22 29.4	9 27.8	29 30.7	11 58.3	7 57.4	21 32.5	18 54.6	24 46.4	26 40.1
20 Sa	9 55 13	27 27 39	5♊58 49	11♊58 01	17 09.2	23 44.0	10 41.5	0♊05.9	12 25.1	7 53.2	21 28.1	18 54.8	24 44.9	26 38.9
21 Su	9 59 10	28 25 25	17 55 09	23 50 51	17 06.7	24 56.7	11 55.1	0 40.9	12 51.9	7 48.8	21 23.6	18 55.0	24 43.5	26 37.7
22 M	10 03 06	29 23 13	29 45 43	5♋40 19	17 01.9	26 07.4	13 08.9	1 15.7	13 18.7	7 44.2	21 19.2	18 55.1	24 42.1	26 36.6
23 Tu	10 07 03	0♍21 03	11♋35 09	17 30 42	16 54.3	27 15.9	14 22.6	1 50.2	13 45.5	7 39.4	21 14.7	18 55.2	24 40.6	26 35.4
24 W	10 10 59	1 18 54	23 27 22	29 25 32	16 44.3	28 22.2	15 36.4	2 24.5	14 12.3	7 34.5	21 10.3	18R 55.3	24 39.1	26 34.3
25 Th	10 14 56	2 16 46	5♌25 28	11♌27 27	16 32.3	29 26.2	16 50.2	2 58.6	14 39.1	7 29.4	21 06.0	18 55.2	24 37.6	26 33.2
26 F	10 18 53	3 14 41	17 31 39	23 38 15	16 19.4	0♎27.8	18 04.1	3 32.4	15 05.8	7 24.2	21 01.6	18 55.2	24 36.1	26 32.1
27 Sa	10 22 49	4 12 36	29 47 20	5♍58 59	16 06.7	1 26.8	19 18.0	4 05.9	15 32.6	7 18.7	20 57.3	18 55.0	24 34.6	26 31.1
28 Su	10 26 46	5 10 34	12♍13 15	18 30 10	15 55.3	2 23.1	20 31.9	4 39.2	15 59.3	7 13.2	20 53.0	18 54.9	24 33.1	26 30.0
29 M	10 30 42	6 08 32	24 49 45	1♎12 01	15 46.0	3 16.6	21 45.9	5 12.2	16 26.0	7 07.5	20 48.7	18 54.6	24 31.5	26 29.0
30 Tu	10 34 39	7 06 32	7♎37 01	14 04 47	15 39.5	4 07.0	22 59.9	5 45.0	16 52.7	7 01.6	20 44.5	18 54.4	24 30.0	26 27.9
31 W	10 38 35	8 04 34	20 35 25	27 09 00	15 35.7	4 54.2	24 13.9	6 17.5	17 19.4	6 55.6	20 40.3	18 54.0	24 28.4	26 26.9

Astro Data

	Dy Hr Mn
☽0S	6 13:31
☽0N	19 1:23
♃∠♄	21 11:17
♃R	28 20:38
☽0S	2 18:29
☽0N	15 9:40
☿0S	22 22:26
♅R	24 13:54
☽0S	29 23:21

Planet Ingress

	Dy Hr Mn
♂ ♉	5 6:04
☿ ♋	5 6:25
♀ ♋	18 1:32
☿ ♌	19 12:35
☉ ♌	22 20:07
⚳ ♌	23 17:29
☿ ♍	4 6:58
♀ ♌	11 18:30
♂ ♊	20 7:56
☉ ♍	23 3:16
☿ ♎	26 1:03

Last Aspect / ☽ Ingress

Last Aspect Dy Hr Mn		☽ Ingress Dy Hr Mn
30 20:14 ♇ ☍	♌	1 0:40
3 9:59 ♂ △	♍	3 12:31
5 18:03 ♇ △	♎	5 22:25
8 1:04 ♇ □	♏	8 5:15
10 4:34 ♇ ⚹	♐	10 8:34
12 1:42 ♆ □	♑	12 9:01
14 4:17 ♇ ☌	♒	14 8:13
16 4:36 ♀ △	♓	16 8:18
18 6:43 ♇ ⚹	♈	18 11:17
20 14:19 ☉ □	♉	20 18:23
22 23:45 ♇ △	♊	23 5:11
25 8:14 ♆ □	♋	25 17:54
28 0:54 ♇ ☍	♌	28 6:36
30 4:29 ♄ ☍	♍	30 18:11

Last Aspect / ☽ Ingress

Last Aspect Dy Hr Mn		☽ Ingress Dy Hr Mn
1 22:29 ♇ △	♎	2 4:05
4 6:20 ♇ □	♏	4 11:47
6 11:24 ♇ ⚹	♐	6 16:39
8 10:30 ♆ □	♑	8 18:39
10 16:39 ♀ ☍	♒	10 18:45
12 11:07 ♂ □	♓	12 18:44
14 15:11 ♇ ⚹	♈	14 20:43
16 20:18 ♇ □	♉	17 2:22
19 11:06 ♂ ☌	♊	19 12:06
21 22:06 ☉ ⚹	♋	22 0:29
24 9:40 ☿ ⚹	♌	24 13:09
26 6:55 ♄ ☍	♍	27 0:25
29 3:08 ♇ △	♎	29 9:45
31 10:43 ♇ □	♏	31 17:11

☽ Phases & Eclipses

Dy Hr Mn	
7 2:14	☽ 14♎59
13 18:38	○ 21♑21
20 14:19	☾ 27♈52
28 17:55	● 5♌39
5 11:06	☽ 13♏02
12 1:36	○ 19♒21
19 4:36	☾ 26♉12
27 8:17	● 4♍04

Astro Data

1 July 2022
Julian Day # 44742
SVP 4♓56'56"
GC 27♐09.2 ⚴ 28♉16.9
Eris 24♈59.4 ⚵ 19♓41.6
⚷ 16♈17.5 ⚶ 6♓44.2
☽ Mean ☊ 19♉55.1

1 August 2022
Julian Day # 44773
SVP 4♓56'51"
GC 27♐09.3 ⚴ 13♊03.3
Eris 25♈00.9R ⚵ 21♓20.3R
⚷ 16♈21.7R ⚶ 4♓32.4R
☽ Mean ☊ 18♉16.6

LONGITUDE — September 2022

Day	Sid.Time	☉	0 hr ☽	Noon ☽	True ☊	☿	♀	♂	⚳	♃	♄	♅	♆	♇
1 Th	10 42 32	9♍02 37	3♏45 40	10♏25 33	15♉34.3	5♎38.0	25♌28.0	6♊49.7	17♌46.1	6♈49.4	20♒36.1	18♉53.7	24♓26.8	26♑26.0
2 F	10 46 28	10 00 42	17 08 49	23 55 38	15D34.4	6 18.1	26 42.0	7 21.6	18 12.8	6R43.1	20R32.0	18R53.2	24R25.3	26R25.0
3 Sa	10 50 25	10 58 48	0♐46 09	7♐40 31	15R34.8	6 54.3	27 56.2	7 53.2	18 39.4	6 36.7	20 27.9	18 52.8	24 23.7	26 24.1
4 Su	10 54 21	11 56 55	14 38 48	21 41 02	15 34.5	7 26.4	29 10.3	8 24.5	19 06.0	6 30.2	20 23.9	18 52.3	24 22.1	26 23.2
5 M	10 58 18	12 55 04	28 47 08	5♑56 56	15 32.4	7 54.0	0♍24.5	8 55.6	19 32.6	6 23.5	20 19.9	18 51.7	24 20.4	26 22.3
6 Tu	11 02 15	13 53 14	13♑10 08	20 26 18	15 28.0	8 16.9	1 38.7	9 26.3	19 59.2	6 16.8	20 16.0	18 51.1	24 18.8	26 21.4
7 W	11 06 11	14 51 25	27 44 54	5♒05 12	15 21.4	8 34.8	2 52.9	9 56.7	20 25.8	6 09.9	20 12.1	18 50.4	24 17.2	26 20.6
8 Th	11 10 08	15 49 38	12♒26 24	19 47 38	15 13.1	8 47.3	4 07.2	10 26.8	20 52.3	6 02.9	20 08.3	18 49.7	24 15.6	26 19.8
9 F	11 14 04	16 47 53	27 07 54	4♓26 16	15 03.9	8R54.2	5 21.4	10 56.6	21 18.8	5 55.8	20 04.5	18 49.0	24 13.9	26 19.0
10 Sa	11 18 01	17 46 09	11♓41 46	18 53 31	14 55.1	8 55.1	6 35.8	11 26.1	21 45.3	5 48.6	20 00.8	18 48.1	24 12.3	26 18.2
11 Su	11 21 57	18 44 27	26 00 45	3♈02 48	14 47.6	8 49.8	7 50.1	11 55.3	22 11.8	5 41.3	19 57.1	18 47.3	24 10.7	26 17.4
12 M	11 25 54	19 42 47	9♈59 09	16 49 29	14 42.2	8 38.0	9 04.5	12 24.1	22 38.2	5 33.9	19 53.5	18 46.4	24 09.0	26 16.7
13 Tu	11 29 50	20 41 09	23 33 35	0♉11 26	14 39.0	8 19.6	10 18.9	12 52.5	23 04.6	5 26.4	19 49.9	18 45.4	24 07.4	26 16.0
14 W	11 33 47	21 39 33	6♉43 08	13 08 56	14D38.0	7 54.4	11 33.3	13 20.6	23 31.0	5 18.9	19 46.5	18 44.5	24 05.7	26 15.3
15 Th	11 37 44	22 37 59	19 29 11	25 44 18	14 38.5	7 22.5	12 47.8	13 48.4	23 57.4	5 11.2	19 43.1	18 43.4	24 04.0	26 14.7
16 F	11 41 40	23 36 28	1♊54 48	8♊01 16	14 39.6	6 44.0	14 02.3	14 15.7	24 23.8	5 03.5	19 39.7	18 42.3	24 02.4	26 14.0
17 Sa	11 45 37	24 34 58	14 04 18	20 04 31	14R40.5	5 59.1	15 16.8	14 42.7	24 50.1	4 55.8	19 36.4	18 41.2	24 00.7	26 13.4
18 Su	11 49 33	25 33 31	26 02 35	1♋59 09	14 40.4	5 08.5	16 31.3	15 09.3	25 16.4	4 48.0	19 33.2	18 40.0	23 59.1	26 12.8
19 M	11 53 30	26 32 06	7♋54 50	13 50 16	14 38.6	4 12.7	17 45.9	15 35.5	25 42.6	4 40.1	19 30.1	18 38.8	23 57.4	26 12.3
20 Tu	11 57 26	27 30 43	19 46 03	25 42 44	14 34.8	3 12.8	19 00.5	16 01.3	26 08.8	4 32.2	19 27.0	18 37.6	23 55.8	26 11.8
21 W	12 01 23	28 29 22	1♌40 51	7♌40 52	14 29.2	2 09.8	20 15.2	16 26.7	26 35.0	4 24.3	19 24.0	18 36.3	23 54.1	26 11.3
22 Th	12 05 19	29 28 03	13 43 13	19 48 16	14 22.0	1 05.1	21 29.8	16 51.6	27 01.2	4 16.3	19 21.1	18 34.9	23 52.5	26 10.8
23 F	12 09 16	0♎26 46	25 56 18	2♍07 35	14 14.1	0 00.2	22 44.5	17 16.1	27 27.3	4 08.3	19 18.3	18 33.5	23 50.8	26 10.3
24 Sa	12 13 13	1 25 32	8♍22 16	14 40 30	14 06.1	28♍56.7	23 59.2	17 40.1	27 53.4	4 00.3	19 15.5	18 32.1	23 49.2	26 09.9
25 Su	12 17 09	2 24 19	21 02 19	27 27 43	13 59.0	27 56.2	25 13.9	18 03.7	28 19.5	3 52.2	19 12.9	18 30.6	23 47.5	26 09.5
26 M	12 21 06	3 23 08	3♎56 38	10♎29 01	13 53.3	27 00.3	26 28.7	18 26.9	28 45.5	3 44.2	19 10.3	18 29.1	23 45.9	26 09.2
27 Tu	12 25 02	4 22 00	17 04 43	23 43 35	13 49.6	26 10.6	27 43.4	18 49.5	29 11.4	3 36.1	19 07.8	18 27.6	23 44.3	26 08.8
28 W	12 28 59	5 20 53	0♏25 29	7♏10 14	13D47.9	25 28.3	28 58.2	19 11.6	29 37.4	3 28.1	19 05.4	18 26.0	23 42.7	26 08.5
29 Th	12 32 55	6 19 48	13 57 41	20 47 41	13 47.9	24 54.6	0♎13.0	19 33.3	0♍03.3	3 20.1	19 03.0	18 24.3	23 41.1	26 08.2
30 F	12 36 52	7 18 45	27 40 07	4♐34 49	13 49.0	24 30.3	1 27.9	19 54.5	0 29.1	3 12.1	19 00.8	18 22.7	23 39.4	26 08.0

LONGITUDE — October 2022

Day	Sid.Time	☉	0 hr ☽	Noon ☽	True ☊	☿	♀	♂	⚳	♃	♄	♅	♆	♇
1 Sa	12 40 48	8♎17 44	11♐31 43	18♐30 40	13♉50.5	24♍16.0	2♎42.7	20♊15.1	0♍54.9	3♈04.1	18♒58.6	18♉21.0	23♓37.9	26♑07.7
2 Su	12 44 45	9 16 45	25 31 33	2♑34 15	13R51.6	24D12.0	3 57.6	20 35.2	1 20.7	2R56.1	18R56.6	18R19.2	23R36.3	26R07.6
3 M	12 48 42	10 15 47	9♑38 35	16 44 22	13 51.5	24 18.5	5 12.4	20 54.8	1 46.4	2 48.2	18 54.6	18 17.5	23 34.7	26 07.4
4 Tu	12 52 38	11 14 51	23 51 22	0♒59 16	13 50.1	24 35.2	6 27.3	21 13.8	2 12.0	2 40.3	18 52.7	18 15.7	23 33.1	26 07.2
5 W	12 56 35	12 13 57	8♒07 44	15 16 22	13 47.3	25 01.9	7 42.2	21 32.3	2 37.6	2 32.5	18 50.9	18 13.8	23 31.6	26 07.1
6 Th	13 00 31	13 13 05	22 24 41	29 32 11	13 43.3	25 38.1	8 57.1	21 50.2	3 03.2	2 24.8	18 49.2	18 11.9	23 30.0	26 07.1
7 F	13 04 28	14 12 14	6♓38 20	13♓42 35	13 38.8	26 23.1	10 12.1	22 07.5	3 28.7	2 17.0	18 47.6	18 10.0	23 28.5	26 07.0
8 Sa	13 08 24	15 11 25	20 44 22	27 43 09	13 34.5	27 16.4	11 27.0	22 24.3	3 54.1	2 09.4	18 46.1	18 08.1	23 27.0	26D07.0
9 Su	13 12 21	16 10 38	4♈38 26	11♈29 47	13 30.8	28 17.1	12 42.0	22 40.4	4 19.5	2 01.8	18 44.7	18 06.1	23 25.5	26 07.0
10 M	13 16 17	17 09 53	18 16 51	24 59 19	13 28.3	29 24.5	13 57.0	22 55.9	4 44.8	1 54.3	18 43.4	18 04.1	23 24.0	26 07.0
11 Tu	13 20 14	18 09 10	1♉37 01	8♉09 50	13D27.2	0♎37.9	15 11.9	23 10.8	5 10.1	1 46.9	18 42.2	18 02.1	23 22.5	26 07.1
12 W	13 24 11	19 08 29	14 37 47	21 00 57	13 27.3	1 56.4	16 26.9	23 25.1	5 35.3	1 39.6	18 41.1	18 00.0	23 21.1	26 07.2
13 Th	13 28 07	20 07 51	27 19 30	3♊33 44	13 28.3	3 19.5	17 42.0	23 38.7	6 00.5	1 32.4	18 40.0	17 57.9	23 19.6	26 07.3
14 F	13 32 04	21 07 15	9♊43 57	15 50 34	13 29.9	4 46.5	18 57.0	23 51.7	6 25.6	1 25.2	18 39.1	17 55.8	23 18.2	26 07.4
15 Sa	13 36 00	22 06 41	21 54 02	27 54 52	13 31.6	6 16.7	20 12.1	24 03.9	6 50.7	1 18.2	18 38.3	17 53.6	23 16.8	26 07.6
16 Su	13 39 57	23 06 09	3♋53 35	9♋50 46	13 32.9	7 49.6	21 27.1	24 15.5	7 15.7	1 11.3	18 37.6	17 51.5	23 15.4	26 07.8
17 M	13 43 53	24 05 40	15 47 01	21 42 55	13R33.5	9 24.8	22 42.2	24 26.3	7 40.6	1 04.5	18 36.9	17 49.3	23 14.0	26 08.1
18 Tu	13 47 50	25 05 12	27 39 04	3♌36 05	13 33.3	11 01.7	23 57.3	24 36.5	8 05.4	0 57.8	18 36.4	17 47.1	23 12.7	26 08.3
19 W	13 51 46	26 04 48	9♌34 33	15 35 03	13 32.2	12 40.0	25 12.4	24 45.9	8 30.2	0 51.3	18 36.0	17 44.8	23 11.4	26 08.6
20 Th	13 55 43	27 04 25	21 38 05	27 44 12	13 30.4	14 19.5	26 27.5	24 54.5	8 54.9	0 44.8	18 35.7	17 42.5	23 10.0	26 09.0
21 F	13 59 40	28 04 05	3♍53 50	10♍07 23	13 28.2	15 59.7	27 42.7	25 02.4	9 19.6	0 38.5	18 35.5	17 40.3	23 08.8	26 09.3
22 Sa	14 03 36	29 03 46	16 25 11	22 47 31	13 26.0	17 40.5	28 57.8	25 09.5	9 44.2	0 32.4	18D35.3	17 38.0	23 07.5	26 09.7
23 Su	14 07 33	0♏03 30	29 14 33	5♎46 25	13 24.0	19 21.7	0♏13.0	25 15.8	10 08.7	0 26.3	18 35.3	17 35.6	23 06.2	26 10.1
24 M	14 11 29	1 03 16	12♎23 06	19 04 32	13 22.6	21 03.1	1 28.1	25 21.3	10 33.1	0 20.5	18 35.4	17 33.3	23 05.0	26 10.5
25 Tu	14 15 26	2 03 04	25 50 35	2♏40 58	13D21.8	22 44.6	2 43.3	25 26.0	10 57.4	0 14.7	18 35.6	17 30.9	23 03.8	26 11.0
26 W	14 19 22	3 02 54	9♏35 23	16 33 26	13 21.6	24 26.0	3 58.5	25 29.8	11 21.7	0 09.2	18 35.9	17 28.5	23 02.6	26 11.5
27 Th	14 23 19	4 02 46	23 34 42	0♐38 40	13 22.0	26 07.3	5 13.7	25 32.8	11 45.8	0 03.8	18 36.3	17 26.2	23 01.4	26 12.1
28 F	14 27 15	5 02 40	7♐44 51	14 52 43	13 22.6	27 48.3	6 28.9	25 35.0	12 09.9	29♓58.5	18 36.8	17 23.8	23 00.3	26 12.6
29 Sa	14 31 12	6 02 36	22 01 45	29 11 27	13 23.3	29 29.1	7 44.1	25 36.4	12 33.9	29 53.5	18 37.4	17 21.3	22 59.2	26 13.2
30 Su	14 35 09	7 02 33	6♑21 21	13♑30 59	13 23.9	1♏09.6	8 59.3	25R36.8	12 57.8	29 48.6	18 38.1	17 18.9	22 58.1	26 13.8
31 M	14 39 05	8 02 32	20 39 58	27 47 55	13R24.3	2 49.7	10 14.5	25 36.5	13 21.7	29 43.8	18 38.9	17 16.5	22 57.1	26 14.5

Astro Data

	Dy Hr Mn
☿R	10 3:37
☽0N	11 19:10
♃∠♄	21 13:08
⊙0S	23 1:04
☽0S	26 5:54
♃0S	26 10:57
☿0N	27 7:36
♃∠♅	28 19:57
♀0S	1 22:33
☿D	2 9:07
♇D	8 21:56
☽0N	9 4:25
☿0S	14 8:11
♄D	23 4:07
☽0S	23 14:37

Planet Ingress

	Dy Hr Mn
♀ ♍	5 4:05
⊙ ♎	23 1:04
☿ ♍R	23 12:04
♀ ♎	29 7:49
⚳ ♍	29 8:59
☿ ♎	10 23:51
♀ ♏	23 7:52
⊙ ♏	23 10:36
♃ ♓R	28 5:10
☿ ♏	29 19:22
♂ R	30 13:26

Last Aspect / ☽ Ingress

Last Aspect Dy Hr Mn		☽ Ingress Dy Hr Mn
2 17:22	♀ □	♐ 2 22:39
5 1:51	♀ △	♑ 5 2:02
6 21:43	♇ ☌	♒ 7 3:41
8 12:34	♄ ☌	♓ 9 4:42
11 0:29	♇ ✶	♈ 11 6:47
13 4:53	♇ □	♉ 13 11:39
15 12:59	♇ △	♊ 15 20:16
17 21:52	⊙ □	♋ 18 7:59
20 15:57	⊙ ✶	♌ 20 20:38
22 11:07	♄ ☍	♍ 23 7:53
25 12:49	☿ ☌	♎ 25 16:43
27 16:21	♇ □	♏ 27 23:15
29 21:20	♇ ✶	♐ 30 4:03

Last Aspect / ☽ Ingress

Last Aspect Dy Hr Mn		☽ Ingress Dy Hr Mn
1 21:46	☿ □	♑ 2 7:38
4 3:49	♇ ☌	♒ 4 10:20
5 22:45	♂ △	♓ 6 12:47
8 11:10	☿ ☍	♈ 8 15:57
10 14:02	♇ □	♉ 10 21:04
12 21:42	♇ △	♊ 13 5:08
15 4:11	♂ ☌	♋ 15 16:11
17 20:56	♇ ☍	♌ 18 4:44
20 10:35	⊙ ✶	♍ 20 16:25
22 18:17	♇ △	♎ 23 1:24
25 0:36	♇ □	♏ 25 7:18
27 4:27	♇ ✶	♐ 27 10:55
29 13:10	♃ □	♑ 29 13:21
31 15:14	♃ ✶	♒ 31 15:43

☽ Phases & Eclipses

Dy Hr Mn	
3 18:08	☽ 11♐14
10 9:59	○ 17♓41
17 21:52	☾ 24♊59
25 21:54	● 2♎49
3 0:14	☽ 9♑47
9 20:55	○ 16♈33
17 17:15	☾ 24♋19
25 10:49	● 2♏00
25 11:00:07	● P 0.862

Astro Data

1 September 2022
Julian Day # 44804
SVP 4♓56'47"
GC 27♐09.4 ⚴ 27♊48.4
Eris 24♈52.7R ⚵ 16♓33.2R
⚷ 15♈38.6R ⚶ 27♒18.0R
☽ Mean ☊ 16♉38.1

1 October 2022
Julian Day # 44834
SVP 4♓56'44"
GC 27♐09.4 ⚴ 11♋12.8
Eris 24♈37.7R ⚵ 9♓41.2R
⚷ 14♈25.4R ⚶ 23♒02.4R
☽ Mean ☊ 15♉02.8

November 2022 LONGITUDE

Day	Sid.Time	☉	0 hr ☽	Noon ☽	True ☊	☿	♀	♂	⚳	♃	♄	♅	♆	♇
1 Tu	14 43 02	9♏02 32	4♒54 31	11♒59 28	13♉24.4	4♏29.4	11♏29.7	25♊35.2	13♍45.4	29♓39.3	18♒39.8	17♉14.0	22♓56.0	26♑15.1
2 W	14 46 58	10 02 34	19 02 32	26 03 28	13R 24.2	6 08.8	12 44.9	25R 33.1	14 09.0	29R 34.9	18 40.8	17R 11.6	22R 55.0	26 15.9
3 Th	14 50 55	11 02 38	3♓02 05	9♓58 12	13 24.0	7 47.7	14 00.1	25 30.1	14 32.6	29 30.7	18 42.0	17 09.1	22 54.0	26 16.6
4 F	14 54 51	12 02 42	16 51 39	23 42 17	13 23.8	9 26.2	15 15.4	25 26.2	14 56.0	29 26.7	18 43.2	17 06.6	22 53.1	26 17.3
5 Sa	14 58 48	13 02 49	0♈29 57	7♈14 32	13D 23.7	11 04.3	16 30.6	25 21.5	15 19.3	29 22.9	18 44.5	17 04.2	22 52.2	26 18.1
6 Su	15 02 44	14 02 57	13 55 55	20 33 59	13 23.7	12 42.0	17 45.8	25 15.9	15 42.6	29 19.3	18 45.9	17 01.7	22 51.3	26 18.9
7 M	15 06 41	15 03 07	27 08 38	3♉39 50	13R 23.8	14 19.3	19 01.1	25 09.4	16 05.7	29 15.8	18 47.4	16 59.2	22 50.4	26 19.8
8 Tu	15 10 38	16 03 19	10♉07 31	16 31 40	13 23.8	15 56.1	20 16.3	25 02.0	16 28.7	29 12.6	18 49.0	16 56.7	22 49.5	26 20.6
9 W	15 14 34	17 03 32	22 52 18	29 09 30	13 23.7	17 32.7	21 31.5	24 53.7	16 51.6	29 09.5	18 50.8	16 54.2	22 48.7	26 21.5
10 Th	15 18 31	18 03 47	5♊23 22	11♊34 01	13 23.3	19 08.8	22 46.8	24 44.6	17 14.4	29 06.7	18 52.6	16 51.7	22 47.9	26 22.5
11 F	15 22 27	19 04 05	17 41 39	23 46 30	13 22.6	20 44.6	24 02.0	24 34.6	17 37.1	29 04.0	18 54.5	16 49.3	22 47.2	26 23.4
12 Sa	15 26 24	20 04 24	29 48 53	5♋49 05	13 21.8	22 20.1	25 17.3	24 23.8	17 59.7	29 01.6	18 56.5	16 46.8	22 46.5	26 24.4
13 Su	15 30 20	21 04 45	11♋47 31	17 44 35	13 20.8	23 55.2	26 32.6	24 12.1	18 22.2	28 59.3	18 58.6	16 44.3	22 45.8	26 25.4
14 M	15 34 17	22 05 07	23 40 44	29 36 27	13 19.8	25 30.1	27 47.8	23 59.6	18 44.6	28 57.2	19 00.9	16 41.8	22 45.1	26 26.4
15 Tu	15 38 13	23 05 32	5♌32 18	11♌28 47	13 19.1	27 04.6	29 03.1	23 46.2	19 06.8	28 55.4	19 03.2	16 39.4	22 44.5	26 27.5
16 W	15 42 10	24 05 58	17 26 30	23 26 02	13D 18.8	28 38.9	0♐18.4	23 32.0	19 28.9	28 53.7	19 05.6	16 36.9	22 43.9	26 28.6
17 Th	15 46 07	25 06 27	29 27 57	5♍32 52	13 19.1	0♐12.9	1 33.7	23 17.0	19 50.9	28 52.3	19 08.1	16 34.4	22 43.3	26 29.7
18 F	15 50 03	26 06 57	11♍41 20	17 53 54	13 19.8	1 46.7	2 48.9	23 01.3	20 12.7	28 51.0	19 10.7	16 32.0	22 42.8	26 30.8
19 Sa	15 54 00	27 07 29	24 11 06	0♎33 23	13 20.9	3 20.3	4 04.2	22 44.8	20 34.4	28 50.0	19 13.4	16 29.6	22 42.3	26 31.9
20 Su	15 57 56	28 08 02	7♎01 09	13 34 44	13 22.2	4 53.6	5 19.5	22 27.6	20 56.0	28 49.2	19 16.2	16 27.1	22 41.8	26 33.1
21 M	16 01 53	29 08 38	20 14 21	27 00 06	13 23.3	6 26.8	6 34.8	22 09.7	21 17.4	28 48.5	19 19.1	16 24.7	22 41.4	26 34.3
22 Tu	16 05 49	0♐09 15	3♏51 59	10♏49 51	13R 23.8	7 59.7	7 50.1	21 51.2	21 38.7	28 48.1	19 22.0	16 22.3	22 40.9	26 35.5
23 W	16 09 46	1 09 53	17 53 23	25 02 09	13 23.5	9 32.5	9 05.4	21 32.0	21 59.9	28D 47.9	19 25.1	16 19.9	22 40.6	26 36.8
24 Th	16 13 42	2 10 34	2♐15 34	9♐32 55	13 22.3	11 05.1	10 20.7	21 12.2	22 20.9	28 47.9	19 28.3	16 17.6	22 40.2	26 38.1
25 F	16 17 39	3 11 15	16 53 21	24 16 00	13 20.1	12 37.6	11 36.0	20 51.9	22 41.7	28 48.2	19 31.5	16 15.2	22 39.9	26 39.4
26 Sa	16 21 36	4 11 58	1♑39 52	9♑04 00	13 17.3	14 09.9	12 51.4	20 31.1	23 02.4	28 48.6	19 34.9	16 12.9	22 39.7	26 40.7
27 Su	16 25 32	5 12 42	16 27 27	23 49 20	13 14.3	15 42.0	14 06.7	20 09.8	23 23.0	28 49.2	19 38.3	16 10.6	22 39.4	26 42.0
28 M	16 29 29	6 13 27	1♒08 50	8♒25 16	13 11.7	17 14.0	15 22.0	19 48.2	23 43.3	28 50.1	19 41.9	16 08.3	22 39.2	26 43.4
29 Tu	16 33 25	7 14 13	15 38 04	22 46 49	13 09.9	18 45.8	16 37.3	19 26.1	24 03.5	28 51.1	19 45.5	16 06.0	22 39.0	26 44.8
30 W	16 37 22	8 15 00	29 51 10	6♓50 59	13D 09.2	20 17.4	17 52.6	19 03.8	24 23.6	28 52.4	19 49.2	16 03.7	22 38.9	26 46.2

December 2022 LONGITUDE

Day	Sid.Time	☉	0 hr ☽	Noon ☽	True ☊	☿	♀	♂	⚳	♃	♄	♅	♆	♇
1 Th	16 41 18	9♐15 48	13♓46 09	20♓36 44	13♉09.6	21♐48.8	19♐07.9	18♊41.2	24♍43.4	28♓53.8	19♒53.0	16♉01.5	22♓38.8	26♑47.6
2 F	16 45 15	10 16 36	27 22 47	4♈04 29	13 10.9	23 20.0	20 23.2	18R 18.4	25 03.1	28 55.5	19 56.9	15R 59.3	22R 38.7	26 49.1
3 Sa	16 49 11	11 17 26	10♈42 01	17 15 36	13 12.6	24 51.0	21 38.5	17 55.4	25 22.7	28 57.4	20 00.8	15 57.1	22D 38.7	26 50.6
4 Su	16 53 08	12 18 16	23 45 28	0♉11 50	13 14.1	26 21.7	22 53.7	17 32.3	25 42.0	28 59.5	20 04.9	15 54.9	22 38.7	26 52.0
5 M	16 57 05	13 19 07	6♉34 57	12 55 00	13R 14.7	27 52.1	24 09.0	17 09.1	26 01.2	29 01.7	20 09.0	15 52.8	22 38.7	26 53.6
6 Tu	17 01 01	14 20 00	19 12 11	25 26 42	13 14.0	29 22.1	25 24.3	16 45.9	26 20.1	29 04.2	20 13.2	15 50.7	22 38.8	26 55.1
7 W	17 04 58	15 20 53	1♊38 41	7♊48 19	13 11.6	0♑51.7	26 39.6	16 22.8	26 38.9	29 06.9	20 17.5	15 48.6	22 38.9	26 56.6
8 Th	17 08 54	16 21 47	13 55 43	20 01 02	13 07.5	2 20.8	27 54.9	15 59.7	26 57.5	29 09.8	20 21.8	15 46.6	22 39.0	26 58.2
9 F	17 12 51	17 22 43	26 04 25	2♋06 01	13 01.9	3 49.3	29 10.1	15 36.8	27 15.9	29 12.9	20 26.3	15 44.6	22 39.2	26 59.8
10 Sa	17 16 47	18 23 39	8♋06 01	14 04 36	12 55.2	5 17.1	0♑25.4	15 14.1	27 34.1	29 16.2	20 30.8	15 42.6	22 39.4	27 01.4
11 Su	17 20 44	19 24 36	20 01 59	25 58 28	12 48.2	6 44.1	1 40.7	14 51.5	27 52.2	29 19.6	20 35.4	15 40.6	22 39.7	27 03.0
12 M	17 24 40	20 25 34	1♌54 18	7♌49 50	12 41.4	8 10.2	2 55.9	14 29.3	28 10.0	29 23.3	20 40.1	15 38.7	22 40.0	27 04.7
13 Tu	17 28 37	21 26 34	13 45 27	19 41 33	12 35.7	9 35.0	4 11.2	14 07.3	28 27.5	29 27.2	20 44.9	15 36.8	22 40.3	27 06.3
14 W	17 32 34	22 27 34	25 38 37	1♍37 07	12 31.5	10 58.6	5 26.5	13 45.8	28 44.9	29 31.2	20 49.7	15 35.0	22 40.6	27 08.0
15 Th	17 36 30	23 28 35	7♍37 37	13 40 39	12D 29.1	12 20.5	6 41.7	13 24.6	29 02.1	29 35.4	20 54.6	15 33.1	22 41.0	27 09.7
16 F	17 40 27	24 29 37	19 46 49	25 56 43	12 28.5	13 40.6	7 57.0	13 03.9	29 19.0	29 39.9	20 59.6	15 31.3	22 41.4	27 11.4
17 Sa	17 44 23	25 30 40	2♎10 57	8♎30 07	12 29.2	14 58.4	9 12.2	12 43.6	29 35.7	29 44.5	21 04.6	15 29.6	22 41.9	27 13.1
18 Su	17 48 20	26 31 45	14 54 46	21 25 27	12 30.7	16 13.7	10 27.5	12 23.9	29 52.2	29 49.3	21 09.7	15 27.9	22 42.3	27 14.8
19 M	17 52 16	27 32 50	28 02 35	4♏46 34	12R 31.9	17 26.0	11 42.7	12 04.7	0♎08.4	29 54.3	21 14.9	15 26.2	22 42.9	27 16.6
20 Tu	17 56 13	28 33 55	11♏37 37	18 35 51	12 31.9	18 34.8	12 58.0	11 46.2	0 24.4	29 59.4	21 20.1	15 24.6	22 43.4	27 18.3
21 W	18 00 09	29 35 02	25 41 11	2♐53 22	12 30.1	19 39.5	14 13.2	11 28.2	0 40.1	0♈04.8	21 25.5	15 23.0	22 44.0	27 20.1
22 Th	18 04 06	0♑36 10	10♐11 56	17 36 11	12 26.1	20 39.5	15 28.5	11 11.0	0 55.6	0 10.3	21 30.9	15 21.4	22 44.6	27 21.9
23 F	18 08 03	1 37 18	25 05 13	2♑37 59	12 19.9	21 34.1	16 43.7	10 54.4	1 10.8	0 16.1	21 36.3	15 19.9	22 45.3	27 23.7
24 Sa	18 11 59	2 38 26	10♑13 15	17 49 40	12 12.2	22 22.6	17 59.0	10 38.5	1 25.8	0 21.9	21 41.8	15 18.5	22 46.0	27 25.5
25 Su	18 15 56	3 39 35	25 25 54	3♒00 36	12 03.9	23 03.9	19 14.2	10 23.3	1 40.5	0 28.0	21 47.4	15 17.0	22 46.7	27 27.4
26 M	18 19 52	4 40 44	10♒32 29	18 00 28	11 56.1	23 37.4	20 29.4	10 08.9	1 55.0	0 34.3	21 53.1	15 15.7	22 47.5	27 29.2
27 Tu	18 23 49	5 41 53	25 23 36	2♓41 07	11 49.9	24 02.1	21 44.6	9 55.3	2 09.1	0 40.7	21 58.8	15 14.3	22 48.3	27 31.0
28 W	18 27 45	6 43 02	9♓52 31	16 57 28	11 45.8	24R 17.0	22 59.8	9 42.5	2 23.0	0 47.2	22 04.5	15 13.0	22 49.1	27 32.9
29 Th	18 31 42	7 44 11	23 55 51	0♈47 42	11D 43.9	24 21.3	24 15.0	9 30.5	2 36.6	0 54.0	22 10.3	15 11.8	22 49.9	27 34.8
30 F	18 35 39	8 45 19	7♈33 13	14 12 42	11 43.8	24 14.5	25 30.2	9 19.2	2 49.9	1 00.9	22 16.2	15 10.6	22 50.8	27 36.6
31 Sa	18 39 35	9 46 28	20 46 30	27 15 05	11 44.6	23 55.9	26 45.4	9 08.8	3 02.9	1 08.0	22 22.1	15 09.4	22 51.8	27 38.5

Astro Data	Planet Ingress	Last Aspect	☽ Ingress	Last Aspect	☽ Ingress	☽ Phases & Eclipses	Astro Data
Dy Hr Mn	Dy Hr Mn	Dy Hr Mn	Dy Hr Mn	Dy Hr Mn	Dy Hr Mn	Dy Hr Mn	1 November 2022
☽0N 5 11:59	♀ ♐ 16 6:08	2 11:08 ♂ △	♓ 2 18:46	2 2:44 ♃ ☌	♈ 2 4:41	1 6:37 ☽ 8♒49	Julian Day # 44865
☽0S 20 0:21	☿ ♐ 17 8:42	4 22:05 ♃ ☌	♈ 4 23:07	4 5:46 ♇ □	♉ 4 11:38	8 11:02 ○ 16♉01	SVP 4♓56'40"
♃ D 23 23:02	☉ ♐ 22 8:20	6 22:30 ♇ □	♉ 7 5:15	6 19:02 ♃ ⚹	♊ 6 20:49	8 10:59 ☍ T 1.359	GC 27♐09.5 ⚵ 22♋14.0
		9 12:00 ♃ ⚹	♊ 9 13:37	9 6:13 ♃ □	♋ 9 7:49	16 13:27 ☾ 24♌10	Eris 24♈19.4R ⚶ 8♓01.9
☽0N 2 17:33	☿ ♑ 6 22:08	11 22:28 ♃ □	♋ 12 0:22	11 18:49 ♃ △	♌ 11 20:09	23 22:57 ● 1♐38	⚷ 13♈04.1R ⚴ 25♒31.1
♆ D 4 0:14	♀ ♑ 10 3:54	14 10:41 ♃ △	♌ 14 12:48	13 15:52 ☉ △	♍ 14 8:45	30 14:37 ☽ 8♓22	☽ Mean ☊ 13♉24.3
☽0S 17 9:05	⚳ ♎ 18 23:34	16 23:55 ☿ □	♍ 17 1:03	16 19:13 ♃ ☍	♎ 16 19:49		
♃∠♅ 24 0:43	♃ ♈ 20 14:32	19 8:46 ♃ ☍	♎ 19 10:58	18 22:35 ♇ □	♏ 19 3:31	8 4:08 ○ 16♊02	1 December 2022
☿ R 29 9:31	☉ ♑ 21 21:48	21 11:14 ♇ □	♏ 21 17:16	21 2:45 ♇ ⚹	♐ 21 7:12	16 8:56 ☾ 24♍22	Julian Day # 44895
☽0N 29 22:38		23 18:16 ♃ △	♐ 23 20:16	22 20:16 ♆ □	♑ 23 7:49	23 10:17 ● 1♑33	SVP 4♓56'35"
		25 19:22 ♃ □	♑ 25 21:18	25 3:11 ♇ ☌	♒ 25 7:14	30 1:20 ☽ 8♈18	GC 27♐09.6 ⚵ 26♋32.5R
		27 20:11 ♃ ⚹	♒ 27 22:07	26 18:19 ♄ ☌	♓ 27 7:34		Eris 24♈04.1R ⚶ 13♓37.2
		29 6:53 ♄ ☌	♓ 30 0:15	29 6:21 ♇ ⚹	♈ 29 10:36		⚷ 12♈09.2R ⚴ 3♓08.2
				31 12:44 ♇ □	♉ 31 17:08		☽ Mean ☊ 11♉49.0

LONGITUDE — January 2023

Day	Sid.Time	☉	0 hr ☽	Noon ☽	True ☊	☿	♀	♂	⚳	♃	♄	♅	♆	♇
1 Su	18 43 32	10♑47 36	3♉38 55	9♉58 28	11♉45.2	23♑25.4	28♑00.5	8♊59.3	3♎15.7	1♈15.2	22♒28.1	15♉08.3	22♓52.7	27♑40.4
2 M	18 47 28	11 48 45	16 14 14	22 26 39	11R44.6	22R43.3	29 15.7	8R50.5	3 28.1	1 22.6	22 34.2	15R07.2	22 53.7	27 42.3
3 Tu	18 51 25	12 49 53	28 36 10	4♊43 11	11 41.9	21 50.2	0♒30.8	8 42.6	3 40.2	1 30.2	22 40.3	15 06.2	22 54.7	27 44.2
4 W	18 55 21	13 51 01	10♊48 03	16 51 05	11 36.4	20 47.4	1 45.9	8 35.5	3 52.0	1 37.9	22 46.4	15 05.3	22 55.8	27 46.2
5 Th	18 59 18	14 52 09	22 52 34	28 52 46	11 28.1	19 36.6	3 01.0	8 29.2	4 03.5	1 45.7	22 52.6	15 04.4	22 56.9	27 48.1
6 F	19 03 14	15 53 17	4♋51 52	10♋50 03	11 17.3	18 20.0	4 16.1	8 23.7	4 14.7	1 53.8	22 58.8	15 03.5	22 58.0	27 50.0
7 Sa	19 07 11	16 54 25	16 47 31	22 44 24	11 04.6	17 00.0	5 31.2	8 19.1	4 25.6	2 01.9	23 05.1	15 02.7	22 59.1	27 51.9
8 Su	19 11 08	17 55 33	28 40 51	4♌37 03	10 51.1	15 39.3	6 46.3	8 15.2	4 36.1	2 10.2	23 11.5	15 01.9	23 00.3	27 53.9
9 M	19 15 04	18 56 40	10♌33 09	16 29 22	10 38.0	14 20.5	8 01.3	8 12.2	4 46.3	2 18.7	23 17.9	15 01.2	23 01.5	27 55.8
10 Tu	19 19 01	19 57 48	22 25 55	28 23 03	10 26.2	13 05.8	9 16.3	8 09.9	4 56.1	2 27.3	23 24.3	15 00.5	23 02.7	27 57.8
11 W	19 22 57	20 58 55	4♍21 06	10♍20 24	10 16.8	11 57.3	10 31.4	8 08.5	5 05.7	2 36.0	23 30.8	14 59.9	23 04.0	27 59.7
12 Th	19 26 54	22 00 02	16 21 21	22 24 23	10 10.1	10 56.6	11 46.4	8D07.8	5 14.8	2 44.9	23 37.3	14 59.3	23 05.3	28 01.7
13 F	19 30 50	23 01 09	28 29 58	4♎38 39	10 06.2	10 04.7	13 01.4	8 07.9	5 23.6	2 53.9	23 43.8	14 58.8	23 06.6	28 03.7
14 Sa	19 34 47	24 02 17	10♎50 57	17 07 29	10D04.6	9 22.3	14 16.3	8 08.8	5 32.1	3 03.0	23 50.4	14 58.3	23 08.0	28 05.6
15 Su	19 38 43	25 03 23	23 28 49	29 55 32	10R04.5	8 49.6	15 31.3	8 10.4	5 40.2	3 12.3	23 57.0	14 57.9	23 09.3	28 07.6
16 M	19 42 40	26 04 30	6♏28 11	13♏07 18	10 04.6	8 26.5	16 46.2	8 12.7	5 47.9	3 21.7	24 03.7	14 57.5	23 10.7	28 09.5
17 Tu	19 46 37	27 05 37	19 53 17	26 46 28	10 03.7	8 12.9	18 01.2	8 15.8	5 55.2	3 31.3	24 10.4	14 57.2	23 12.2	28 11.5
18 W	19 50 33	28 06 44	3♐47 03	10♐55 02	10 00.6	8D08.2	19 16.1	8 19.7	6 02.2	3 41.0	24 17.2	14 56.9	23 13.6	28 13.5
19 Th	19 54 30	29 07 50	18 10 14	25 32 12	9 54.8	8 11.8	20 31.0	8 24.2	6 08.7	3 50.8	24 23.9	14 56.7	23 15.1	28 15.4
20 F	19 58 26	0♒08 56	3♑00 18	10♑33 35	9 46.2	8 23.3	21 45.9	8 29.5	6 14.9	4 00.7	24 30.8	14 56.6	23 16.7	28 17.4
21 Sa	20 02 23	1 10 01	18 10 56	25 51 02	9 35.5	8 41.9	23 00.7	8 35.4	6 20.7	4 10.8	24 37.6	14 56.5	23 18.2	28 19.4
22 Su	20 06 19	2 11 06	3♒32 23	11♒13 28	9 23.7	9 07.1	24 15.6	8 42.0	6 26.1	4 20.9	24 44.5	14D56.4	23 19.8	28 21.4
23 M	20 10 16	3 12 10	18 52 47	26 28 51	9 12.4	9 38.3	25 30.4	8 49.3	6 31.1	4 31.2	24 51.4	14 56.4	23 21.4	28 23.3
24 Tu	20 14 13	4 13 13	4♓00 25	11♓26 23	9 02.9	10 14.8	26 45.2	8 57.3	6 35.6	4 41.7	24 58.3	14 56.5	23 23.0	28 25.3
25 W	20 18 09	5 14 15	18 45 53	25 58 20	8 55.9	10 56.3	28 00.0	9 05.9	6 39.8	4 52.2	25 05.3	14 56.6	23 24.6	28 27.2
26 Th	20 22 06	6 15 16	3♈03 22	10♈00 52	8 51.8	11 42.2	29 14.7	9 15.1	6 43.6	5 02.8	25 12.3	14 56.8	23 26.3	28 29.2
27 F	20 26 02	7 16 16	16 50 54	23 33 42	8 50.0	12 32.1	0♓29.4	9 25.0	6 46.9	5 13.6	25 19.3	14 57.0	23 28.0	28 31.1
28 Sa	20 29 59	8 17 15	0♉09 38	6♉39 12	8 49.7	13 25.7	1 44.1	9 35.5	6 49.8	5 24.4	25 26.3	14 57.2	23 29.7	28 33.1
29 Su	20 33 55	9 18 13	13 02 56	19 21 25	8 49.5	14 22.5	2 58.8	9 46.5	6 52.3	5 35.4	25 33.4	14 57.6	23 31.4	28 35.0
30 M	20 37 52	10 19 09	25 35 16	1♊45 06	8 48.3	15 22.4	4 13.4	9 58.2	6 54.3	5 46.5	25 40.4	14 57.9	23 33.2	28 37.0
31 Tu	20 41 48	11 20 04	7♊51 30	13 55 02	8 45.0	16 25.0	5 28.0	10 10.4	6 56.0	5 57.7	25 47.5	14 58.4	23 35.0	28 38.9

LONGITUDE — February 2023

Day	Sid.Time	☉	0 hr ☽	Noon ☽	True ☊	☿	♀	♂	⚳	♃	♄	♅	♆	♇
1 W	20 45 45	12♒20 58	19♊56 14	25♊55 37	8♉38.8	17♑30.0	6♓42.6	10♊23.1	6♎57.2	6♈08.9	25♒54.6	14♉58.8	23♓36.8	28♑40.8
2 Th	20 49 42	13 21 51	1♋53 35	7♋50 34	8R29.6	18 37.4	7 57.1	10 36.4	6 58.0	6 20.3	26 01.8	14 59.4	23 38.6	28 42.7
3 F	20 53 38	14 22 43	13 46 54	19 42 53	8 17.6	19 46.9	9 11.6	10 50.2	6R58.3	6 31.8	26 08.9	14 59.9	23 40.5	28 44.7
4 Sa	20 57 35	15 23 33	25 38 46	1♌34 48	8 03.7	20 58.3	10 26.1	11 04.6	6 58.2	6 43.4	26 16.1	15 00.6	23 42.3	28 46.6
5 Su	21 01 31	16 24 22	7♌31 09	13 27 59	7 48.8	22 11.5	11 40.5	11 19.4	6 57.7	6 55.0	26 23.3	15 01.3	23 44.2	28 48.5
6 M	21 05 28	17 25 10	19 25 27	25 23 42	7 34.1	23 26.3	12 54.9	11 34.7	6 56.8	7 06.8	26 30.5	15 02.0	23 46.1	28 50.3
7 Tu	21 09 24	18 25 57	1♍22 52	7♍23 07	7 20.9	24 42.7	14 09.3	11 50.5	6 55.4	7 18.6	26 37.7	15 02.8	23 48.1	28 52.2
8 W	21 13 21	19 26 43	13 24 36	19 27 32	7 10.1	26 00.6	15 23.6	12 06.7	6 53.5	7 30.5	26 44.9	15 03.6	23 50.0	28 54.1
9 Th	21 17 17	20 27 27	25 32 09	1♎38 44	7 02.3	27 19.8	16 37.9	12 23.4	6 51.2	7 42.6	26 52.1	15 04.5	23 52.0	28 56.0
10 F	21 21 14	21 28 11	7♎47 34	13 59 01	6 57.5	28 40.4	17 52.1	12 40.6	6 48.5	7 54.7	26 59.3	15 05.5	23 53.9	28 57.8
11 Sa	21 25 11	22 28 53	20 13 28	26 31 22	6D55.4	0♒02.2	19 06.3	12 58.2	6 45.4	8 06.9	27 06.6	15 06.5	23 55.9	28 59.6
12 Su	21 29 07	23 29 34	2♏53 09	9♏19 19	6 55.0	1 25.1	20 20.5	13 16.2	6 41.8	8 19.1	27 13.8	15 07.5	23 57.9	29 01.5
13 M	21 33 04	24 30 15	15 50 20	22 26 39	6R55.2	2 49.2	21 34.6	13 34.6	6 37.7	8 31.5	27 21.1	15 08.6	24 00.0	29 03.3
14 Tu	21 37 00	25 30 54	29 08 43	5♐56 53	6 54.8	4 14.5	22 48.8	13 53.4	6 33.3	8 43.9	27 28.3	15 09.7	24 02.0	29 05.1
15 W	21 40 57	26 31 32	12♐51 26	19 52 32	6 52.7	5 40.7	24 02.8	14 12.6	6 28.4	8 56.4	27 35.6	15 10.9	24 04.1	29 06.9
16 Th	21 44 53	27 32 09	27 00 10	4♑14 11	6 48.2	7 08.1	25 16.8	14 32.2	6 23.0	9 09.0	27 42.8	15 12.2	24 06.2	29 08.7
17 F	21 48 50	28 32 45	11♑34 12	18 59 36	6 41.0	8 36.4	26 30.8	14 52.2	6 17.3	9 21.7	27 50.1	15 13.5	24 08.2	29 10.4
18 Sa	21 52 46	29 33 20	26 29 36	4♒03 10	6 31.8	10 05.7	27 44.8	15 12.6	6 11.1	9 34.4	27 57.4	15 14.8	24 10.4	29 12.2
19 Su	21 56 43	0♓33 53	11♒39 06	19 16 06	6 21.6	11 36.1	28 58.7	15 33.3	6 04.5	9 47.2	28 04.6	15 16.2	24 12.5	29 13.9
20 M	22 00 40	1 34 24	26 52 44	4♓27 38	6 11.5	13 07.4	0♈12.5	15 54.3	5 57.5	10 00.1	28 11.9	15 17.7	24 14.6	29 15.7
21 Tu	22 04 36	2 34 54	11♓59 28	19 26 59	6 02.8	14 39.6	1 26.3	16 15.8	5 50.1	10 13.1	28 19.1	15 19.1	24 16.7	29 17.4
22 W	22 08 33	3 35 23	26 49 11	4♈05 13	5 56.4	16 12.9	2 40.1	16 37.5	5 42.3	10 26.1	28 26.4	15 20.7	24 18.9	29 19.1
23 Th	22 12 29	4 35 49	11♈14 27	18 16 32	5 52.7	17 47.1	3 53.8	16 59.6	5 34.1	10 39.2	28 33.6	15 22.3	24 21.1	29 20.7
24 F	22 16 26	5 36 14	25 11 15	1♉58 39	5D51.3	19 22.2	5 07.5	17 22.0	5 25.5	10 52.3	28 40.8	15 23.9	24 23.2	29 22.4
25 Sa	22 20 22	6 36 36	8♉38 54	15 12 21	5 51.5	20 58.3	6 21.1	17 44.7	5 16.5	11 05.5	28 48.1	15 25.6	24 25.4	29 24.1
26 Su	22 24 19	7 36 57	21 39 26	28 00 39	5R52.3	22 35.4	7 34.7	18 07.7	5 07.2	11 18.8	28 55.3	15 27.3	24 27.6	29 25.7
27 M	22 28 15	8 37 16	4♊16 36	10♊27 52	5 52.7	24 13.5	8 48.2	18 31.1	4 57.6	11 32.1	29 02.5	15 29.0	24 29.8	29 27.3
28 Tu	22 32 12	9 37 33	16 35 07	22 38 58	5 51.6	25 52.6	10 01.6	18 54.7	4 47.6	11 45.4	29 09.7	15 30.9	24 32.0	29 28.9

Astro Data

	Dy Hr Mn
♄⚺♆	6 7:56
♂ D	12 20:56
♃0N	13 5:56
☽0S	13 15:33
☿ D	18 13:12
♅ D	22 22:58
☽0N	26 5:32
⚳ R	3 19:13
☽0S	9 20:31
♀0N	22 2:55
☽0N	22 15:00

Planet Ingress

	Dy Hr Mn
♀ ♒	3 2:09
☉ ♒	20 8:29
♀ ♓	27 2:33
☿ ♒	11 11:22
☉ ♓	18 22:34
♀ ♈	20 7:56

Last Aspect / ☽ Ingress

Last Aspect Dy Hr Mn		☽ Ingress Dy Hr Mn
2 22:16	♇ △	♊ 3 2:44
5 0:07	♆ □	♋ 5 14:15
7 22:23	♇ ☍	♌ 8 2:40
10 1:52	♄ ☍	♍ 10 15:15
12 23:06	♇ △	♎ 13 2:56
15 8:40	♇ □	♏ 15 12:08
17 14:27	♇ ⚹	♐ 17 17:33
19 10:08	♄ ⚹	♑ 19 19:11
21 15:52	♇ ☌	♒ 21 18:29
23 10:19	♀ ☌	♓ 23 17:36
25 16:11	♇ ⚹	♈ 25 18:48
27 21:01	♇ □	♉ 27 23:42
30 5:52	♇ △	♊ 30 8:35

Last Aspect / ☽ Ingress

Last Aspect Dy Hr Mn		☽ Ingress Dy Hr Mn
1 11:58	♄ △	♋ 1 20:11
4 6:19	♇ ☍	♌ 4 8:48
6 14:15	♄ ☍	♍ 6 21:14
9 6:40	♇ △	♎ 9 8:46
11 16:41	♇ □	♏ 11 18:34
13 23:52	♇ ⚹	♐ 14 1:31
16 1:06	♄ ⚹	♑ 16 5:00
18 4:18	♇ ☌	♒ 18 5:35
20 2:00	♄ ☌	♓ 20 4:56
22 4:05	♇ ⚹	♈ 22 5:14
24 7:22	♇ □	♉ 24 8:29
26 14:42	♇ △	♊ 26 15:48

☽ Phases & Eclipses

Dy Hr Mn		
6 23:08	○	16♋22
15 2:10	☾	24♎38
21 20:53	●	1♒33
28 15:19	☽	8♉26
5 18:28	○	16♌41
13 16:01	☾	24♏40
20 7:06	●	1♓22
27 8:06	☽	8♊27

Astro Data

1 January 2023
Julian Day # 44926
SVP 4♓56'29"
GC 27♐09.6 ⚵ 20♋39.7R
Eris 23♈55.7R ⚴ 24♓46.9
⚷ 11♈58.4 ⚶ 14♓13.0
☽ Mean ☊ 10♉10.5

1 February 2023
Julian Day # 44957
SVP 4♓56'23"
GC 27♐09.7 ⚵ 11♋42.0R
Eris 23♈57.6 ⚴ 9♈21.2
⚷ 12♈39.2 ⚶ 27♓04.8
☽ Mean ☊ 8♉32.1

March 2023

LONGITUDE

Day	Sid.Time	☉	0 hr ☽	Noon ☽	True ☊	☿	♀	♂	⚳	♃	♄	♅	♆	♇
1 W	22 36 09	10♓37 48	28♊40 02	4♋38 55	5♉48.4	27♒32.7	11♈15.0	19♊18.6	4♎37.2	11♈58.9	29♒16.8	15♉32.7	24♓34.2	29♑30.5
2 Th	22 40 05	11 38 01	10♋36 11	16 32 22	5R43.0	29 13.9	12 28.3	19 42.7	4R26.6	12 12.4	29 24.0	15 34.6	24 36.5	29 32.0
3 F	22 44 02	12 38 12	22 27 57	28 23 23	5 35.3	0♓56.0	13 41.6	20 07.2	4 15.7	12 25.9	29 31.1	15 36.6	24 38.7	29 33.6
4 Sa	22 47 58	13 38 21	4♌19 04	10♌15 20	5 26.1	2 39.3	14 54.8	20 31.8	4 04.4	12 39.5	29 38.3	15 38.5	24 40.9	29 35.1
5 Su	22 51 55	14 38 28	16 12 30	22 10 50	5 16.0	4 23.5	16 07.9	20 56.8	3 52.9	12 53.1	29 45.4	15 40.6	24 43.2	29 36.6
6 M	22 55 51	15 38 33	28 10 34	4♍11 52	5 06.0	6 08.9	17 21.0	21 22.0	3 41.1	13 06.8	29 52.5	15 42.6	24 45.4	29 38.1
7 Tu	22 59 48	16 38 36	10♍14 53	16 19 48	4 57.0	7 55.3	18 34.0	21 47.4	3 29.1	13 20.5	29 59.5	15 44.8	24 47.7	29 39.5
8 W	23 03 44	17 38 37	22 26 42	28 35 42	4 49.8	9 42.9	19 47.0	22 13.0	3 16.8	13 34.3	0♓06.6	15 46.9	24 50.0	29 41.0
9 Th	23 07 41	18 38 36	4♎46 57	11♎00 33	4 44.8	11 31.6	20 59.8	22 38.9	3 04.3	13 48.1	0 13.6	15 49.1	24 52.2	29 42.4
10 F	23 11 37	19 38 34	17 16 39	23 35 25	4D42.1	13 21.3	22 12.6	23 05.0	2 51.6	14 01.9	0 20.6	15 51.3	24 54.5	29 43.8
11 Sa	23 15 34	20 38 29	29 57 00	6♏21 38	4 41.5	15 12.2	23 25.4	23 31.3	2 38.7	14 15.8	0 27.6	15 53.6	24 56.8	29 45.2
12 Su	23 19 31	21 38 24	12♏49 33	19 20 58	4 42.3	17 04.3	24 38.1	23 57.9	2 25.6	14 29.7	0 34.5	15 55.9	24 59.0	29 46.5
13 M	23 23 27	22 38 16	25 56 09	2♐35 22	4 43.7	18 57.4	25 50.7	24 24.6	2 12.4	14 43.7	0 41.5	15 58.2	25 01.3	29 47.9
14 Tu	23 27 24	23 38 07	9♐18 51	16 06 48	4R44.9	20 51.6	27 03.2	24 51.5	1 59.0	14 57.7	0 48.4	16 00.6	25 03.6	29 49.2
15 W	23 31 20	24 37 56	22 59 23	29 56 44	4 45.0	22 46.9	28 15.7	25 18.7	1 45.5	15 11.7	0 55.3	16 03.1	25 05.9	29 50.5
16 Th	23 35 17	25 37 44	6♑58 49	14♑05 33	4 43.5	24 43.2	29 28.1	25 46.0	1 31.9	15 25.8	1 02.1	16 05.5	25 08.1	29 51.8
17 F	23 39 13	26 37 30	21 16 44	28 31 58	4 40.4	26 40.5	0♉40.5	26 13.6	1 18.2	15 39.9	1 08.9	16 08.0	25 10.4	29 53.0
18 Sa	23 43 10	27 37 14	5♒50 46	13♒12 27	4 35.8	28 38.7	1 52.7	26 41.3	1 04.5	15 54.1	1 15.7	16 10.5	25 12.7	29 54.2
19 Su	23 47 06	28 36 57	20 36 16	28 01 18	4 30.4	0♈37.8	3 04.9	27 09.2	0 50.6	16 08.2	1 22.4	16 13.1	25 15.0	29 55.4
20 M	23 51 03	29 36 37	5♓26 34	12♓51 01	4 25.0	2 37.5	4 17.1	27 37.3	0 36.8	16 22.4	1 29.2	16 15.7	25 17.2	29 56.6
21 Tu	23 55 00	0♈36 16	20 13 39	27 33 28	4 20.3	4 37.8	5 29.1	28 05.5	0 22.9	16 36.6	1 35.8	16 18.3	25 19.5	29 57.8
22 W	23 58 56	1 35 52	4♈49 31	12♈01 02	4 17.0	6 38.6	6 41.1	28 34.0	0 09.0	16 50.9	1 42.5	16 21.0	25 21.8	29 58.9
23 Th	0 02 53	2 35 27	19 07 20	26 07 54	4D15.4	8 39.5	7 53.0	29 02.6	29♍55.2	17 05.2	1 49.1	16 23.7	25 24.1	29 60.0
24 F	0 06 49	3 34 59	3♉02 23	9♉50 35	4 15.2	10 40.5	9 04.8	29 31.4	29 41.4	17 19.5	1 55.6	16 26.4	25 26.3	0♒01.1
25 Sa	0 10 46	4 34 30	16 32 28	23 08 07	4 16.2	12 41.3	10 16.5	0♋00.3	29 27.6	17 33.8	2 02.2	16 29.2	25 28.6	0 02.1
26 Su	0 14 42	5 33 58	29 37 44	6♊01 41	4 17.9	14 41.5	11 28.1	0 29.4	29 14.0	17 48.1	2 08.7	16 32.0	25 30.8	0 03.1
27 M	0 18 39	6 33 24	12♊20 21	18 34 12	4 19.5	16 40.9	12 39.7	0 58.6	29 00.4	18 02.5	2 15.1	16 34.8	25 33.1	0 04.1
28 Tu	0 22 35	7 32 47	24 43 46	0♋49 38	4R20.6	18 39.0	13 51.2	1 28.0	28 47.0	18 16.8	2 21.5	16 37.7	25 35.3	0 05.1
29 W	0 26 32	8 32 08	6♋52 22	12 52 34	4 20.7	20 35.7	15 02.5	1 57.6	28 33.7	18 31.2	2 27.9	16 40.5	25 37.6	0 06.1
30 Th	0 30 29	9 31 27	18 50 50	24 47 46	4 19.6	22 30.4	16 13.8	2 27.3	28 20.6	18 45.6	2 34.2	16 43.5	25 39.8	0 07.0
31 F	0 34 25	10 30 44	0♌43 56	6♌39 53	4 17.5	24 22.7	17 25.0	2 57.1	28 07.6	19 00.1	2 40.4	16 46.4	25 42.0	0 07.9

April 2023

LONGITUDE

Day	Sid.Time	☉	0 hr ☽	Noon ☽	True ☊	☿	♀	♂	⚳	♃	♄	♅	♆	♇
1 Sa	0 38 22	11♈29 58	12♌36 09	18♌33 12	4♉14.5	26♈12.3	18♉36.0	3♋27.0	27♍54.8	19♈14.5	2♓46.7	16♉49.4	25♓44.2	0♒08.8
2 Su	0 42 18	12 29 10	24 31 30	0♍31 26	4R11.0	27 58.8	19 47.0	3 57.1	27R42.2	19 28.9	2 52.8	16 52.3	25 46.4	0 09.6
3 M	0 46 15	13 28 20	6♍33 24	12 37 41	4 07.5	29 41.7	20 57.9	4 27.3	27 29.8	19 43.4	2 58.9	16 55.4	25 48.6	0 10.4
4 Tu	0 50 11	14 27 27	18 44 34	24 54 17	4 04.3	1♉20.7	22 08.7	4 57.7	27 17.7	19 57.8	3 05.0	16 58.4	25 50.8	0 11.2
5 W	0 54 08	15 26 33	1♎07 00	7♎22 52	4 01.9	2 55.4	23 19.3	5 28.1	27 05.8	20 12.3	3 11.0	17 01.4	25 53.0	0 12.0
6 Th	0 58 04	16 25 36	13 41 58	20 04 22	4 00.5	4 25.6	24 29.9	5 58.7	26 54.1	20 26.7	3 17.0	17 04.5	25 55.1	0 12.7
7 F	1 02 01	17 24 37	26 30 06	2♏59 10	4D00.0	5 50.9	25 40.3	6 29.4	26 42.7	20 41.2	3 22.9	17 07.6	25 57.3	0 13.4
8 Sa	1 05 58	18 23 37	9♏31 33	16 07 14	4 00.3	7 11.1	26 50.7	7 00.2	26 31.6	20 55.7	3 28.8	17 10.8	25 59.4	0 14.1
9 Su	1 09 54	19 22 34	22 46 10	29 28 18	4 01.2	8 25.9	28 00.9	7 31.1	26 20.8	21 10.2	3 34.6	17 13.9	26 01.6	0 14.7
10 M	1 13 51	20 21 30	6♐13 34	13♐01 54	4 02.3	9 35.1	29 11.0	8 02.1	26 10.3	21 24.6	3 40.3	17 17.1	26 03.7	0 15.4
11 Tu	1 17 47	21 20 24	19 53 13	26 47 27	4 03.4	10 38.6	0♊21.0	8 33.3	26 00.1	21 39.1	3 46.0	17 20.3	26 05.8	0 15.9
12 W	1 21 44	22 19 17	3♑44 28	10♑44 10	4R04.1	11 36.2	1 30.9	9 04.5	25 50.3	21 53.6	3 51.7	17 23.5	26 07.9	0 16.5
13 Th	1 25 40	23 18 08	17 46 22	24 50 53	4 04.3	12 27.8	2 40.7	9 35.9	25 40.8	22 08.1	3 57.2	17 26.7	26 10.0	0 17.1
14 F	1 29 37	24 16 57	1♒57 28	9♒05 50	4 04.0	13 13.3	3 50.4	10 07.3	25 31.6	22 22.6	4 02.8	17 30.0	26 12.1	0 17.6
15 Sa	1 33 33	25 15 44	16 15 39	23 26 30	4 03.3	13 52.5	4 59.9	10 38.9	25 22.7	22 37.0	4 08.2	17 33.2	26 14.1	0 18.1
16 Su	1 37 30	26 14 29	0♓37 56	7♓49 27	4 02.4	14 25.5	6 09.3	11 10.5	25 14.3	22 51.5	4 13.6	17 36.5	26 16.2	0 18.5
17 M	1 41 27	27 13 13	15 00 31	22 10 32	4 01.5	14 52.3	7 18.6	11 42.3	25 06.2	23 06.0	4 18.9	17 39.8	26 18.2	0 18.9
18 Tu	1 45 23	28 11 55	29 18 57	6♈25 09	4 00.9	15 12.7	8 27.8	12 14.1	24 58.4	23 20.4	4 24.2	17 43.1	26 20.2	0 19.3
19 W	1 49 20	29 10 35	13♈28 36	20 28 45	4D00.5	15 27.0	9 36.8	12 46.1	24 51.1	23 34.9	4 29.4	17 46.4	26 22.2	0 19.7
20 Th	1 53 16	0♉09 13	27 25 09	4♉17 22	4 00.4	15R35.1	10 45.8	13 18.1	24 44.1	23 49.3	4 34.6	17 49.8	26 24.2	0 20.0
21 F	1 57 13	1 07 50	11♉05 05	17 48 04	4 00.5	15 37.2	11 54.5	13 50.3	24 37.6	24 03.7	4 39.6	17 53.1	26 26.1	0 20.3
22 Sa	2 01 09	2 06 24	24 26 09	0♊59 16	4 00.6	15 33.5	13 03.2	14 22.5	24 31.4	24 18.1	4 44.6	17 56.5	26 28.1	0 20.6
23 Su	2 05 06	3 04 56	7♊27 29	13 50 53	4R00.8	15 24.2	14 11.7	14 54.8	24 25.7	24 32.5	4 49.6	17 59.9	26 30.0	0 20.9
24 M	2 09 02	4 03 27	20 09 43	26 24 13	4 00.8	15 09.6	15 20.0	15 27.2	24 20.4	24 46.9	4 54.4	18 03.3	26 31.9	0 21.1
25 Tu	2 12 59	5 01 55	2♋34 46	8♋41 46	4 00.8	14 50.2	16 28.2	15 59.7	24 15.5	25 01.3	4 59.2	18 06.7	26 33.8	0 21.3
26 W	2 16 56	6 00 21	14 45 40	20 46 59	4 00.7	14 26.2	17 36.3	16 32.3	24 11.0	25 15.6	5 03.9	18 10.1	26 35.7	0 21.5
27 Th	2 20 52	6 58 45	26 46 13	2♌43 57	4D00.6	13 58.2	18 44.2	17 05.0	24 06.9	25 30.0	5 08.6	18 13.5	26 37.5	0 21.6
28 F	2 24 49	7 57 07	8♌40 45	14 37 12	4 00.6	13 26.8	19 51.9	17 37.7	24 03.2	25 44.3	5 13.2	18 17.0	26 39.4	0 21.7
29 Sa	2 28 45	8 55 27	20 33 52	26 31 20	4 00.8	12 52.5	20 59.4	18 10.5	24 00.0	25 58.5	5 17.7	18 20.4	26 41.2	0 21.8
30 Su	2 32 42	9 53 44	2♍30 09	8♍30 53	4 01.3	12 16.1	22 06.8	18 43.4	23 57.1	26 12.8	5 22.1	18 23.8	26 42.9	0 21.8

Astro Data	Planet Ingress	Last Aspect	☽ Ingress	Last Aspect	☽ Ingress	☽ Phases & Eclipses	Astro Data
Dy Hr Mn	Dy Hr Mn	Dy Hr Mn	Dy Hr Mn	Dy Hr Mn	Dy Hr Mn	Dy Hr Mn	1 March 2023
♄⚺♇ 3 22:26	☿ ♓ 2 22:52	1 1:07 ♄ △	♋ 1 2:40	2 6:03 ☿ △	♍ 2 10:57	7 12:40 ○ 16♍40	Julian Day # 44985
☽0S 9 1:53	♄ ♓ 7 13:34	3 14:22 ♇ ☍	♌ 3 15:16	4 13:50 ♆ ☍	♎ 4 21:51	15 2:08 ☾ 24♐13	SVP 4♓56'20"
♃⚺♅ 19 22:06	♀ ♉ 16 22:34	6 3:18 ♄ ☍	♍ 6 3:38	6 12:43 ♃ ☍	♏ 7 6:29	21 17:23 ● 0♈50	GC 27♐09.8 ⚵ 11♋16.6
☿0N 20 10:53	☿ ♈ 19 4:24	8 14:07 ♇ △	♎ 8 14:44	9 9:09 ♀ ☍	♐ 9 12:57	29 2:32 ☽ 8♋09	Eris 24♈07.8 ⚴ 24♈17.8
☉0N 20 21:25	☉ ♈ 20 21:24	10 23:36 ♇ □	♏ 11 0:06	11 10:48 ♆ □	♑ 11 17:33		⚷ 13♈52.3 ⚶ 9♈28.8
♃∠♄ 21 9:26	⚳ ♍R 23 3:37	13 6:58 ♇ ⚹	♐ 13 7:21	13 14:14 ♆ ⚹	♒ 13 20:42	6 4:34 ○ 16♎07	☽ Mean ☊ 7♉03.1
☽0N 22 1:32	♇ ♒ 23 12:13	15 8:50 ♀ △	♑ 15 12:06	15 15:16 ☉ ⚹	♓ 15 22:57	13 9:11 ☾ 23♑11	
	♂ ♋ 25 11:45	17 14:14 ♇ ☌	♒ 17 14:25	17 18:57 ♆ ☌	♈ 18 1:09	20 4:12 ● 29♈50	1 April 2023
☽0S 5 8:54		19 10:33 ♂ △	♓ 19 15:12	20 4:12 ☉ ☌	♉ 20 4:30	20 4:16:43 ● AT01'16"	Julian Day # 45016
☽0N 18 10:55	☿ ♉ 3 16:22	21 15:58 ♇ ⚹	♈ 21 16:01	22 3:41 ♆ ⚹	♊ 22 10:11	27 21:20 ☽ 7♌21	SVP 4♓56'16"
☿R 21 8:34	♀ ♊ 11 4:47	23 17:13 ♂ ⚹	♉ 23 18:42	24 12:15 ♆ □	♋ 24 18:58		GC 27♐09.8 ⚵ 18♋32.8
	☉ ♉ 20 8:14	25 16:19 ♆ ⚹	♊ 26 0:41	26 23:41 ♆ △	♌ 27 6:30		Eris 24♈25.6 ⚴ 11♉58.0
		28 1:39 ♆ □	♋ 28 10:22	29 10:53 ♃ △	♍ 29 18:59		⚷ 15♈36.3 ⚶ 23♈32.5
		30 13:45 ♆ △	♌ 30 22:31				☽ Mean ☊ 5♉24.6

LONGITUDE — May 2023

Day	Sid.Time	☉	0 hr ☽	Noon ☽	True ☊	☿	♀	♂	⚳	♃	♄	♅	♆	♇
1 M	2 36 38	10♉52 00	14♍34 01	20♍40 02	4♉01.9	11♉38.2	23♊14.0	19♋16.3	23♍54.7	26♈27.0	5♓26.4	18♉27.3	26♓44.7	0♒21.9
2 Tu	2 40 35	11 50 13	26 49 21	3♎02 23	4 02.7	10R 59.5	24 21.1	19 49.3	23R 52.7	26 41.2	5 30.7	18 30.7	26 46.5	0R 21.8
3 W	2 44 31	12 48 25	9♎19 25	15 40 44	4 03.4	10 20.7	25 27.9	20 22.4	23 51.1	26 55.4	5 34.9	18 34.2	26 48.2	0 21.8
4 Th	2 48 28	13 46 35	22 06 31	28 36 52	4R 03.8	9 42.6	26 34.6	20 55.6	23 50.0	27 09.6	5 39.0	18 37.7	26 49.9	0 21.7
5 F	2 52 25	14 44 43	5♏11 50	11♏51 21	4 03.7	9 05.6	27 41.0	21 28.8	23 49.2	27 23.7	5 43.1	18 41.1	26 51.6	0 21.7
6 Sa	2 56 21	15 42 49	18 35 19	25 23 30	4 03.1	8 30.6	28 47.3	22 02.1	23D 48.9	27 37.8	5 47.0	18 44.6	26 53.2	0 21.5
7 Su	3 00 18	16 40 54	2♐15 37	9♐11 21	4 01.9	7 58.0	29 53.4	22 35.5	23 49.0	27 51.9	5 50.9	18 48.1	26 54.9	0 21.4
8 M	3 04 14	17 38 58	16 10 18	23 12 01	4 00.3	7 28.4	0♋59.2	23 08.9	23 49.5	28 05.9	5 54.7	18 51.5	26 56.5	0 21.2
9 Tu	3 08 11	18 37 00	0♑16 01	7♑21 51	3 58.5	7 02.1	2 04.9	23 42.4	23 50.4	28 19.9	5 58.4	18 55.0	26 58.1	0 21.0
10 W	3 12 07	19 35 00	14 29 01	21 37 02	3 56.9	6 39.6	3 10.4	24 16.0	23 51.7	28 33.9	6 02.1	18 58.5	26 59.6	0 20.8
11 Th	3 16 04	20 32 59	28 45 27	5♒53 51	3 55.7	6 21.1	4 15.6	24 49.6	23 53.4	28 47.8	6 05.6	19 02.0	27 01.2	0 20.5
12 F	3 20 00	21 30 57	13♒01 51	20 09 05	3D 55.2	6 06.9	5 20.6	25 23.3	23 55.4	29 01.7	6 09.1	19 05.4	27 02.7	0 20.2
13 Sa	3 23 57	22 28 54	27 15 16	4♓20 05	3 55.5	5 57.2	6 25.4	25 57.0	23 57.9	29 15.6	6 12.5	19 08.9	27 04.2	0 19.9
14 Su	3 27 54	23 26 49	11♓23 20	18 24 45	3 56.5	5D 51.9	7 30.0	26 30.8	24 00.8	29 29.4	6 15.8	19 12.4	27 05.6	0 19.6
15 M	3 31 50	24 24 43	25 24 09	2♈21 21	3 57.8	5 51.3	8 34.3	27 04.7	24 04.1	29 43.2	6 19.0	19 15.9	27 07.1	0 19.2
16 Tu	3 35 47	25 22 36	9♈16 10	16 08 25	3 59.1	5 55.3	9 38.4	27 38.6	24 07.7	29 57.0	6 22.1	19 19.3	27 08.5	0 18.8
17 W	3 39 43	26 20 27	22 57 56	29 44 32	3R 59.8	6 03.9	10 42.2	28 12.6	24 11.8	0♉10.7	6 25.1	19 22.8	27 09.9	0 18.4
18 Th	3 43 40	27 18 17	6♉28 04	13♉08 23	3 59.6	6 17.0	11 45.8	28 46.7	24 16.2	0 24.3	6 28.1	19 26.2	27 11.2	0 18.0
19 F	3 47 36	28 16 06	19 45 20	26 18 47	3 58.2	6 34.6	12 49.1	29 20.8	24 21.0	0 37.9	6 30.9	19 29.7	27 12.5	0 17.5
20 Sa	3 51 33	29 13 54	2♊48 41	9♊14 56	3 55.6	6 56.6	13 52.1	29 55.0	24 26.1	0 51.5	6 33.7	19 33.1	27 13.8	0 17.0
21 Su	3 55 29	0♊11 40	15 37 32	21 56 31	3 51.9	7 22.9	14 54.9	0♌29.2	24 31.7	1 05.0	6 36.4	19 36.6	27 15.1	0 16.5
22 M	3 59 26	1 09 25	28 11 58	4♋24 00	3 47.5	7 53.4	15 57.4	1 03.5	24 37.6	1 18.5	6 39.0	19 40.0	27 16.4	0 15.9
23 Tu	4 03 23	2 07 08	10♋32 49	16 38 41	3 42.9	8 27.9	16 59.5	1 37.8	24 43.8	1 31.9	6 41.5	19 43.4	27 17.6	0 15.3
24 W	4 07 19	3 04 50	22 41 52	28 42 45	3 38.6	9 06.3	18 01.4	2 12.2	24 50.5	1 45.3	6 43.9	19 46.8	27 18.8	0 14.7
25 Th	4 11 16	4 02 30	4♌41 44	10♌39 17	3 35.3	9 48.6	19 03.0	2 46.7	24 57.4	1 58.6	6 46.2	19 50.2	27 20.0	0 14.1
26 F	4 15 12	5 00 09	16 35 52	22 32 02	3 33.1	10 34.6	20 04.2	3 21.2	25 04.7	2 11.9	6 48.4	19 53.6	27 21.1	0 13.4
27 Sa	4 19 09	5 57 46	28 28 20	4♍25 22	3D 32.3	11 24.2	21 05.1	3 55.7	25 12.4	2 25.1	6 50.5	19 57.0	27 22.2	0 12.8
28 Su	4 23 05	6 55 22	10♍23 43	16 24 00	3 32.7	12 17.3	22 05.6	4 30.3	25 20.4	2 38.2	6 52.5	20 00.4	27 23.3	0 12.1
29 M	4 27 02	7 52 56	22 26 49	28 32 47	3 34.0	13 13.7	23 05.8	5 05.0	25 28.7	2 51.3	6 54.4	20 03.7	27 24.3	0 11.3
30 Tu	4 30 58	8 50 29	4♎42 26	10♎56 21	3 35.6	14 13.5	24 05.6	5 39.7	25 37.3	3 04.3	6 56.3	20 07.1	27 25.3	0 10.6
31 W	4 34 55	9 48 00	17 15 00	23 38 49	3R 36.9	15 16.5	25 05.0	6 14.4	25 46.3	3 17.3	6 58.0	20 10.4	27 26.3	0 09.8

LONGITUDE — June 2023

Day	Sid.Time	☉	0 hr ☽	Noon ☽	True ☊	☿	♀	♂	⚳	♃	♄	♅	♆	♇
1 Th	4 38 52	10♊45 31	0♏08 10	6♏43 18	3♉37.2	16♉22.7	26♋04.0	6♌49.2	25♍55.6	3♉30.2	6♓59.6	20♉13.7	27♓27.3	0♒09.0
2 F	4 42 48	11 43 00	13 24 23	20 11 26	3R 36.1	17 32.0	27 02.6	7 24.1	26 05.2	3 43.0	7 01.2	20 17.0	27 28.2	0R 08.2
3 Sa	4 46 45	12 40 28	27 04 20	4♐02 52	3 33.2	18 44.2	28 00.8	7 58.9	26 15.1	3 55.8	7 02.6	20 20.3	27 29.1	0 07.4
4 Su	4 50 41	13 37 55	11♐06 36	18 15 02	3 28.7	19 59.5	28 58.5	8 33.9	26 25.3	4 08.5	7 04.0	20 23.6	27 29.9	0 06.5
5 M	4 54 38	14 35 21	25 27 29	2♑43 12	3 22.9	21 17.6	29 55.8	9 08.9	26 35.8	4 21.2	7 05.2	20 26.8	27 30.8	0 05.6
6 Tu	4 58 34	15 32 46	10♑01 20	17 20 59	3 16.6	22 38.7	0♌52.6	9 43.9	26 46.5	4 33.8	7 06.4	20 30.0	27 31.6	0 04.7
7 W	5 02 31	16 30 10	24 41 15	2♒01 14	3 10.7	24 02.6	1 49.0	10 18.9	26 57.6	4 46.3	7 07.5	20 33.3	27 32.4	0 03.8
8 Th	5 06 27	17 27 34	9♒20 07	16 37 10	3 05.9	25 29.3	2 44.8	10 54.1	27 08.9	4 58.7	7 08.4	20 36.5	27 33.1	0 02.9
9 F	5 10 24	18 24 57	23 51 45	1♓03 21	3 02.8	26 58.9	3 40.2	11 29.2	27 20.6	5 11.1	7 09.3	20 39.6	27 33.8	0 01.9
10 Sa	5 14 21	19 22 20	8♓11 34	15 16 08	3D 01.5	28 31.2	4 35.0	12 04.4	27 32.5	5 23.4	7 10.1	20 42.8	27 34.5	0 00.9
11 Su	5 18 17	20 19 42	22 16 52	29 13 43	3 01.7	0♊06.3	5 29.3	12 39.7	27 44.6	5 35.6	7 10.7	20 45.9	27 35.1	29♑59.9
12 M	5 22 14	21 17 03	6♈06 41	12♈55 50	3 02.7	1 44.1	6 23.0	13 14.9	27 57.1	5 47.8	7 11.3	20 49.1	27 35.7	29 58.9
13 Tu	5 26 10	22 14 24	19 41 17	26 23 08	3R 03.7	3 24.6	7 16.2	13 50.3	28 09.8	5 59.9	7 11.8	20 52.1	27 36.3	29 57.8
14 W	5 30 07	23 11 45	3♉01 34	9♉36 43	3 03.7	5 07.9	8 08.7	14 25.7	28 22.7	6 11.9	7 12.1	20 55.2	27 36.9	29 56.8
15 Th	5 34 03	24 09 05	16 08 42	22 37 39	3 01.9	6 53.8	9 00.7	15 01.1	28 35.9	6 23.8	7 12.4	20 58.3	27 37.4	29 55.7
16 F	5 38 00	25 06 25	29 03 40	5♊26 50	2 57.8	8 42.4	9 52.0	15 36.6	28 49.4	6 35.6	7 12.6	21 01.3	27 37.9	29 54.6
17 Sa	5 41 57	26 03 44	11♊47 12	18 04 51	2 51.4	10 33.5	10 42.6	16 12.1	29 03.1	6 47.4	7R 12.6	21 04.3	27 38.3	29 53.5
18 Su	5 45 53	27 01 03	24 19 49	0♋32 11	2 42.9	12 27.2	11 32.6	16 47.7	29 17.0	6 59.0	7 12.6	21 07.3	27 38.7	29 52.3
19 M	5 49 50	27 58 21	6♋41 59	12 49 20	2 33.1	14 23.4	12 21.8	17 23.3	29 31.2	7 10.6	7 12.5	21 10.2	27 39.1	29 51.2
20 Tu	5 53 46	28 55 39	18 54 20	24 57 09	2 22.7	16 21.8	13 10.3	17 59.0	29 45.7	7 22.1	7 12.3	21 13.2	27 39.5	29 50.0
21 W	5 57 43	29 52 56	0♌57 58	6♌57 01	2 12.8	18 22.5	13 58.0	18 34.7	0♎00.3	7 33.5	7 11.9	21 16.1	27 39.8	29 48.9
22 Th	6 01 39	0♋50 12	12 54 34	18 50 59	2 04.2	20 25.3	14 45.0	19 10.4	0 15.2	7 44.8	7 11.5	21 18.9	27 40.1	29 47.7
23 F	6 05 36	1 47 28	24 46 38	0♍41 57	1 57.5	22 29.9	15 31.1	19 46.2	0 30.3	7 56.0	7 11.0	21 21.8	27 40.4	29 46.4
24 Sa	6 09 32	2 44 43	6♍37 25	12 33 32	1 53.2	24 36.2	16 16.3	20 22.0	0 45.6	8 07.1	7 10.4	21 24.6	27 40.6	29 45.2
25 Su	6 13 29	3 41 57	18 30 54	24 30 05	1D 51.0	26 44.0	17 00.6	20 57.9	1 01.1	8 18.1	7 09.6	21 27.4	27 40.8	29 44.0
26 M	6 17 26	4 39 11	0♎31 43	6♎36 26	1 50.6	28 53.0	17 44.0	21 33.8	1 16.9	8 29.0	7 08.8	21 30.1	27 40.9	29 42.7
27 Tu	6 21 22	5 36 24	12 44 53	18 57 41	1 51.1	1♋02.9	18 26.4	22 09.7	1 32.8	8 39.9	7 07.9	21 32.9	27 41.0	29 41.5
28 W	6 25 19	6 33 37	25 15 29	1♏38 50	1R 51.5	3 13.5	19 07.8	22 45.7	1 49.0	8 50.6	7 06.9	21 35.6	27 41.1	29 40.2
29 Th	6 29 15	7 30 49	8♏08 16	14 44 13	1 50.8	5 24.5	19 48.1	23 21.7	2 05.3	9 01.2	7 05.8	21 38.2	27 41.2	29 38.9
30 F	6 33 12	8 28 01	21 26 59	28 16 48	1 48.2	7 35.5	20 27.4	23 57.8	2 21.9	9 11.7	7 04.6	21 40.9	27R 41.2	29 37.6

Astro Data	Dy Hr Mn
♇ R	1 17:09
☽ 0S	2 17:16
♃⊻♆	2 22:03
⚳ D	6 19:24
☿ D	15 3:16
☽ 0N	15 17:53
♃□♇	18 1:11
☽ 0S	30 1:49
☽ 0N	11 22:57
♄ R	17 17:27
♃✱♄	19 15:53
☽ 0S	26 9:22
♆ R	30 21:06

Planet Ingress	Dy Hr Mn
♀ ♋	7 14:25
♃ ♉	16 17:20
♂ ♌	20 15:31
☉ ♊	21 7:09
♀ ♌	5 13:46
♇ ♑R	11 9:47
☿ ♊	11 10:27
⚳ ♎	21 11:30
☉ ♋	21 14:58
☿ ♋	27 0:24

Last Aspect Dy Hr Mn	☽ Ingress Dy Hr Mn
1 23:53 ♆ ☍	♎ 2 6:09
4 9:17 ♃ ☍	♏ 4 14:32
6 14:38 ♆ △	♐ 6 20:04
8 20:28 ♃ △	♑ 8 23:33
10 23:52 ♃ □	♒ 11 2:05
13 3:15 ♃ ✱	♓ 13 4:39
15 2:56 ♆ ☌	♈ 15 7:56
17 9:10 ♂ □	♉ 17 12:27
19 17:51 ♂ ✱	♊ 19 18:48
21 22:12 ♆ □	♋ 22 3:28
24 9:12 ♆ △	♌ 24 14:35
26 6:38 ♅ □	♍ 27 3:05
29 9:46 ♆ ☍	♎ 29 14:51
31 14:53 ♀ □	♏ 31 23:45

Last Aspect Dy Hr Mn	☽ Ingress Dy Hr Mn
3 0:51 ♀ △	♐ 3 5:03
5 3:24 ♆ □	♑ 5 7:31
7 4:40 ♆ ✱	♒ 7 8:41
9 4:24 ♆ □	♓ 9 10:14
11 13:20 ♇ ✱	♈ 11 13:20
13 18:27 ♇ □	♉ 13 18:31
16 1:36 ♇ △	♊ 16 1:46
18 6:24 ♆ □	♋ 18 10:58
20 21:43 ♇ ☍	♌ 20 22:04
22 17:01 ♅ □	♍ 23 10:35
25 22:24 ♇ △	♎ 25 22:57
28 8:19 ♇ □	♏ 28 8:55
30 14:20 ♇ ✱	♐ 30 14:59

☽ Phases & Eclipses Dy Hr Mn	
5 17:34	○ 14♏58
5 17:23	A 0.963
12 14:28	☾ 21♒37
19 15:53	● 28♉25
27 15:22	☽ 6♍06
4 3:42	○ 13♐18
10 19:31	☾ 19♓40
18 4:37	● 26♊43
26 7:50	☽ 4♎29

Astro Data

1 May 2023
Julian Day # 45046
SVP 4♓56'12"
GC 27♐09.9 ⚴ 29♋30.8
Eris 24♈45.2 ⚵ 29♉35.2
⚷ 17♈20.2 ⚶ 7♉08.2
☽ Mean ☊ 3♉49.3

1 June 2023
Julian Day # 45077
SVP 4♓56'08"
GC 27♐10.0 ⚴ 12♌36.6
Eris 25♈02.8 ⚵ 17♊49.9
⚷ 18♈50.7 ⚶ 20♉52.8
☽ Mean ☊ 2♉10.8

July 2023 — LONGITUDE

Day	Sid.Time	☉	0 hr ☽	Noon ☽	True ☊	☿	♀	♂	⚳	♃	♄	♅	♆	♇
1 Sa	6 37 08	9♋25 12	5♐13 40	12♐17 28	1♉43.2	9♋46.4	21♌05.5	24♌33.9	2♎38.6	9♉22.1	7♓03.3	21♉43.5	27♓41.2	29♑36.3
2 Su	6 41 05	10 22 23	19 27 50	26 44 15	1R 35.8	11 56.8	21 42.5	25 10.0	2 55.5	9 32.5	7R 01.9	21 46.0	27R 41.2	29R 35.0
3 M	6 45 01	11 19 35	4♑05 57	11♑32 01	1 26.7	14 06.5	22 18.2	25 46.2	3 12.6	9 42.7	7 00.4	21 48.6	27 41.1	29 33.6
4 Tu	6 48 58	12 16 46	19 01 22	26 32 48	1 16.7	16 15.3	22 52.6	26 22.4	3 29.9	9 52.8	6 58.9	21 51.1	27 41.0	29 32.3
5 W	6 52 55	13 13 57	4♒05 04	11♒36 54	1 07.0	18 23.0	23 25.7	26 58.7	3 47.4	10 02.7	6 57.2	21 53.6	27 40.9	29 31.0
6 Th	6 56 51	14 11 08	19 07 06	26 34 36	0 58.9	20 29.5	23 57.5	27 34.9	4 05.0	10 12.6	6 55.5	21 56.0	27 40.7	29 29.6
7 F	7 00 48	15 08 19	3♓58 26	11♓17 50	0 52.9	22 34.5	24 27.8	28 11.3	4 22.8	10 22.4	6 53.6	21 58.4	27 40.5	29 28.2
8 Sa	7 04 44	16 05 31	18 32 13	25 41 12	0 49.5	24 38.0	24 56.7	28 47.6	4 40.8	10 32.0	6 51.7	22 00.8	27 40.3	29 26.9
9 Su	7 08 41	17 02 42	2♈44 34	9♈42 16	0D 48.2	26 39.8	25 24.0	29 24.1	4 58.9	10 41.5	6 49.6	22 03.1	27 40.0	29 25.5
10 M	7 12 37	17 59 55	16 34 21	23 21 01	0R 48.1	28 40.0	25 49.8	0♍00.5	5 17.2	10 50.9	6 47.5	22 05.4	27 39.7	29 24.1
11 Tu	7 16 34	18 57 08	0♉02 32	6♉39 13	0 48.0	0♌38.4	26 14.0	0 37.0	5 35.6	11 00.2	6 45.3	22 07.6	27 39.4	29 22.7
12 W	7 20 30	19 54 21	13 11 25	19 39 28	0 46.9	2 34.9	26 36.4	1 13.5	5 54.3	11 09.4	6 43.0	22 09.9	27 39.0	29 21.3
13 Th	7 24 27	20 51 35	26 03 46	2♊24 38	0 43.7	4 29.7	26 57.2	1 50.1	6 13.0	11 18.4	6 40.7	22 12.0	27 38.6	29 19.9
14 F	7 28 24	21 48 49	8♊42 23	14 57 19	0 37.7	6 22.6	27 16.1	2 26.7	6 32.0	11 27.3	6 38.2	22 14.2	27 38.2	29 18.5
15 Sa	7 32 20	22 46 04	21 09 40	27 19 41	0 28.9	8 13.6	27 33.2	3 03.4	6 51.1	11 36.1	6 35.7	22 16.3	27 37.8	29 17.1
16 Su	7 36 17	23 43 19	3♋27 31	9♋33 23	0 17.6	10 02.7	27 48.4	3 40.1	7 10.3	11 44.8	6 33.0	22 18.3	27 37.3	29 15.6
17 M	7 40 13	24 40 35	15 37 24	21 39 42	0 04.5	11 50.0	28 01.6	4 16.9	7 29.7	11 53.3	6 30.3	22 20.4	27 36.8	29 14.2
18 Tu	7 44 10	25 37 51	27 40 25	3♌39 42	29♈50.6	13 35.4	28 12.7	4 53.6	7 49.2	12 01.7	6 27.5	22 22.4	27 36.2	29 12.8
19 W	7 48 06	26 35 07	9♌37 42	15 34 36	29 37.2	15 18.9	28 21.8	5 30.5	8 08.8	12 09.9	6 24.7	22 24.3	27 35.7	29 11.4
20 Th	7 52 03	27 32 24	21 30 34	27 25 53	29 25.4	17 00.5	28 28.7	6 07.3	8 28.6	12 18.0	6 21.7	22 26.2	27 35.1	29 09.9
21 F	7 55 59	28 29 41	3♍20 48	9♍15 39	29 15.8	18 40.3	28 33.4	6 44.2	8 48.6	12 26.0	6 18.7	22 28.0	27 34.4	29 08.5
22 Sa	7 59 56	29 26 58	15 10 49	21 06 42	29 09.0	20 18.2	28R 35.8	7 21.2	9 08.6	12 33.8	6 15.6	22 29.9	27 33.8	29 07.1
23 Su	8 03 53	0♌24 15	27 03 47	3♎02 34	29 05.0	21 54.2	28 36.0	7 58.2	9 28.8	12 41.5	6 12.4	22 31.6	27 33.1	29 05.7
24 M	8 07 49	1 21 33	9♎03 37	15 07 31	29 03.2	23 28.4	28 33.8	8 35.2	9 49.1	12 49.1	6 09.2	22 33.4	27 32.4	29 04.2
25 Tu	8 11 46	2 18 51	21 14 52	27 26 20	29 02.8	25 00.7	28 29.2	9 12.2	10 09.6	12 56.5	6 05.9	22 35.0	27 31.6	29 02.8
26 W	8 15 42	3 16 10	3♏42 32	10♏04 05	29 02.7	26 31.1	28 22.3	9 49.3	10 30.1	13 03.7	6 02.5	22 36.7	27 30.8	29 01.4
27 Th	8 19 39	4 13 29	16 31 36	23 05 36	29 01.8	27 59.6	28 12.9	10 26.5	10 50.8	13 10.8	5 59.0	22 38.3	27 30.0	29 00.0
28 F	8 23 35	5 10 49	29 46 34	6♐34 49	28 59.2	29 26.2	28 01.2	11 03.7	11 11.6	13 17.8	5 55.5	22 39.8	27 29.2	28 58.5
29 Sa	8 27 32	6 08 09	13♐30 35	20 33 52	28 54.1	0♍50.8	27 47.1	11 40.9	11 32.6	13 24.6	5 52.0	22 41.4	27 28.3	28 57.1
30 Su	8 31 29	7 05 29	27 44 31	5♑02 08	28 46.5	2 13.5	27 30.6	12 18.1	11 53.6	13 31.3	5 48.3	22 42.8	27 27.4	28 55.7
31 M	8 35 25	8 02 50	12♑26 05	19 55 32	28 36.9	3 34.2	27 11.7	12 55.4	12 14.7	13 37.8	5 44.6	22 44.2	27 26.5	28 54.3

August 2023 — LONGITUDE

Day	Sid.Time	☉	0 hr ☽	Noon ☽	True ☊	☿	♀	♂	⚳	♃	♄	♅	♆	♇
1 Tu	8 39 22	9♌00 12	27♑29 23	5♒06 24	28♈26.4	4♍52.8	26♌50.6	13♍32.8	12♎36.0	13♉44.1	5♓40.9	22♉45.6	27♓25.6	28♑52.9
2 W	8 43 18	9 57 35	12♒45 12	20 24 21	28R 16.1	6 09.3	26R 27.4	14 10.1	12 57.3	13 50.3	5R 37.1	22 46.9	27R 24.6	28R 51.5
3 Th	8 47 15	10 54 58	28 02 24	5♓38 01	28 07.3	7 23.7	26 02.0	14 47.5	13 18.8	13 56.3	5 33.2	22 48.2	27 23.6	28 50.1
4 F	8 51 11	11 52 23	13♓09 57	20 37 11	28 00.9	8 35.9	25 34.7	15 25.0	13 40.4	14 02.2	5 29.3	22 49.5	27 22.6	28 48.7
5 Sa	8 55 08	12 49 48	27 58 51	5♈14 21	27 57.0	9 45.7	25 05.5	16 02.5	14 02.0	14 07.9	5 25.3	22 50.6	27 21.6	28 47.4
6 Su	8 59 04	13 47 15	12♈23 18	19 25 29	27D 55.4	10 53.3	24 34.6	16 40.0	14 23.8	14 13.4	5 21.3	22 51.8	27 20.5	28 46.0
7 M	9 03 01	14 44 43	26 20 55	3♉09 45	27R 55.2	11 58.4	24 02.2	17 17.6	14 45.6	14 18.7	5 17.3	22 52.9	27 19.4	28 44.6
8 Tu	9 06 57	15 42 13	9♉52 13	16 28 42	27 55.4	13 00.9	23 28.5	17 55.2	15 07.6	14 23.9	5 13.2	22 53.9	27 18.3	28 43.3
9 W	9 10 54	16 39 43	22 59 37	29 25 25	27 54.7	14 00.8	22 53.6	18 32.8	15 29.6	14 29.0	5 09.0	22 54.9	27 17.1	28 41.9
10 Th	9 14 51	17 37 16	5♊46 37	12♊03 40	27 52.3	14 57.9	22 17.8	19 10.5	15 51.8	14 33.8	5 04.8	22 55.9	27 16.0	28 40.6
11 F	9 18 47	18 34 49	18 17 03	24 27 13	27 47.3	15 52.1	21 41.3	19 48.3	16 14.0	14 38.5	5 00.6	22 56.8	27 14.8	28 39.3
12 Sa	9 22 44	19 32 24	0♋34 36	6♋39 33	27 39.8	16 43.3	21 04.3	20 26.0	16 36.4	14 43.0	4 56.3	22 57.6	27 13.6	28 37.9
13 Su	9 26 40	20 30 00	12 42 27	18 43 36	27 29.9	17 31.2	20 27.1	21 03.9	16 58.8	14 47.3	4 52.0	22 58.4	27 12.4	28 36.6
14 M	9 30 37	21 27 38	24 43 15	0♌41 41	27 18.3	18 15.8	19 49.8	21 41.7	17 21.3	14 51.5	4 47.7	22 59.2	27 11.1	28 35.3
15 Tu	9 34 33	22 25 17	6♌39 07	12 35 44	27 06.1	18 56.8	19 12.8	22 19.7	17 43.9	14 55.4	4 43.3	22 59.9	27 09.8	28 34.1
16 W	9 38 30	23 22 57	18 31 44	24 27 18	26 54.2	19 34.1	18 36.2	22 57.6	18 06.6	14 59.2	4 38.9	23 00.6	27 08.5	28 32.8
17 Th	9 42 27	24 20 38	0♍22 38	6♍17 55	26 43.7	20 07.3	18 00.3	23 35.6	18 29.4	15 02.8	4 34.5	23 01.2	27 07.2	28 31.5
18 F	9 46 23	25 18 20	12 13 22	18 09 14	26 35.3	20 36.4	17 25.3	24 13.6	18 52.2	15 06.2	4 30.1	23 01.7	27 05.9	28 30.3
19 Sa	9 50 20	26 16 04	24 05 47	0♎03 20	26 29.4	21 01.1	16 51.4	24 51.7	19 15.2	15 09.5	4 25.6	23 02.2	27 04.5	28 29.1
20 Su	9 54 16	27 13 49	6♎02 13	12 02 50	26 26.1	21 21.1	16 18.9	25 29.8	19 38.2	15 12.5	4 21.1	23 02.7	27 03.2	28 27.8
21 M	9 58 13	28 11 35	18 05 36	24 10 59	26D 25.0	21 36.2	15 47.8	26 08.0	20 01.2	15 15.3	4 16.6	23 03.1	27 01.8	28 26.6
22 Tu	10 02 09	29 09 22	0♏19 28	6♏31 36	26 25.3	21 46.2	15 18.3	26 46.2	20 24.4	15 18.0	4 12.1	23 03.4	27 00.4	28 25.4
23 W	10 06 06	0♍07 11	12 47 55	19 08 58	26R 26.2	21R 50.8	14 50.7	27 24.5	20 47.6	15 20.5	4 07.6	23 03.7	26 58.9	28 24.3
24 Th	10 10 02	1 05 00	25 35 17	2♐07 23	26 26.6	21 49.9	14 25.1	28 02.8	21 10.9	15 22.7	4 03.0	23 04.0	26 57.5	28 23.1
25 F	10 13 59	2 02 51	8♐45 45	15 30 45	26 25.7	21 43.2	14 01.4	28 41.1	21 34.3	15 24.8	3 58.5	23 04.2	26 56.0	28 22.0
26 Sa	10 17 55	3 00 43	22 22 42	29 21 43	26 22.9	21 30.6	13 40.0	29 19.5	21 57.8	15 26.7	3 54.0	23 04.3	26 54.6	28 20.9
27 Su	10 21 52	3 58 37	6♑27 49	13♑40 48	26 18.1	21 12.0	13 20.8	29 57.9	22 21.3	15 28.4	3 49.4	23 04.5	26 53.1	28 19.8
28 M	10 25 49	4 56 31	21 00 15	28 25 34	26 11.7	20 47.4	13 03.9	0♎36.3	22 44.8	15 29.9	3 44.9	23R 04.5	26 51.6	28 18.7
29 Tu	10 29 45	5 54 27	5♒55 54	13♒30 13	26 04.3	20 17.0	12 49.3	1 14.8	23 08.5	15 31.2	3 40.3	23 04.5	26 50.1	28 17.6
30 W	10 33 42	6 52 24	21 07 18	28 45 50	25 56.9	19 40.8	12 37.1	1 53.3	23 32.2	15 32.3	3 35.8	23 04.5	26 48.6	28 16.6
31 Th	10 37 38	7 50 23	6♓24 27	14♓01 44	25 50.7	18 59.3	12 27.4	2 31.9	23 55.9	15 33.3	3 31.3	23 04.4	26 47.0	28 15.5

Astro Data

	Dy Hr Mn
☽0N	9 4:00
♃∠♆	22 11:46
♀R	23 1:32
☽0S	23 15:30
☽0N	5 10:59
⚳0S	9 20:30
☽0S	19 20:46
☿0S	21 3:27
☿R	23 20:00
♅R	29 2:38
♂0S	29 22:08
☿0N	30 18:50

Planet Ingress

	Dy Hr Mn
♂ ♍	10 11:40
☿ ♌	11 4:11
☊ ♈R	17 19:46
☉ ♌	23 1:50
☿ ♍	28 21:31
☉ ♍	23 9:01
♂ ♎	27 13:20

Last Aspect / ☽ Ingress

Last Aspect Dy Hr Mn		☽ Ingress Dy Hr Mn
2 13:33 ♆ □	♑	2 17:20
4 16:45 ♇ ☌	♒	4 17:30
6 13:42 ♂ ☍	♓	6 17:32
8 18:22 ♇ ⚹	♈	8 19:19
10 23:11 ☿ □	♉	10 23:55
13 6:11 ♇ △	♊	13 7:26
15 12:35 ♆ □	♋	15 17:13
18 3:06 ♇ ☍	♌	18 4:39
20 14:08 ♀ ☌	♍	20 17:13
23 4:06 ♇ △	♎	23 5:54
25 15:05 ♇ □	♏	25 16:55
27 22:36 ♇ ⚹	♐	28 0:24
29 23:51 ♀ △	♑	30 3:44

Last Aspect / ☽ Ingress

Last Aspect Dy Hr Mn		☽ Ingress Dy Hr Mn
1 2:13 ♇ ☌	♒	1 3:58
2 21:15 ♀ ☍	♓	3 3:05
5 1:21 ♇ ⚹	♈	5 3:19
7 4:13 ♇ □	♉	7 6:24
9 10:39 ♇ △	♊	9 13:05
11 17:27 ♆ □	♋	11 22:52
14 7:46 ♇ ☍	♌	14 10:36
16 9:38 ☉ ☌	♍	16 23:14
19 8:51 ♇ △	♎	19 11:53
21 20:31 ☉ ⚹	♏	21 23:22
24 5:10 ♇ ⚹	♐	24 8:07
26 11:56 ♂ □	♑	26 13:05
28 11:49 ♇ ☌	♒	28 14:32
30 3:04 ♅ □	♓	30 13:56

☽ Phases & Eclipses

Dy Hr Mn		
3 11:39	○	11♑19
10 1:48	☾	17♈36
17 18:32	●	24♋56
25 22:07	☽	2♏43
1 18:32	○	9♒16
8 10:28	☾	15♉39
16 9:38	●	23♌17
24 9:57	☽	1♐00
31 1:36	○	7♓25

Astro Data

1 July 2023
Julian Day # 45107
SVP 4♓56'02"
GC 27♐10.0 ⚴ 26♌00.6
Eris 25♈13.3 ⚵ 5♋08.9
⚷ 19♈45.2 ⚶ 3♊37.0
☽ Mean ☊ 0♉35.5

1 August 2023
Julian Day # 45138
SVP 4♓55'56"
GC 27♐10.1 ⚴ 10♍09.5
Eris 25♈15.0R ⚵ 22♋22.0
⚷ 19♈55.7R ⚶ 15♊49.1
☽ Mean ☊ 28♈57.0

LONGITUDE — September 2023

Day	Sid.Time	☉	0 hr ☽	Noon☽	True☊	☿	♀	♂	⚳	♃	♄	♅	♆	♇
1 F	10 41 35	8♍48 24	21♓36 24	29♓07 13	25♈46.1	18♍12.8	12♌20.0	3♎10.5	24♎19.7	15♉34.0	3♓26.8	23♉04.2	26♓45.5	28♑14.5
2 Sa	10 45 31	9 46 26	6♈33 11	13♈53 26	25D43.7	17R22.1	12R15.1	3 49.2	24 43.6	15 34.5	3R22.3	23R04.0	26R43.9	28R13.5
3 Su	10 49 28	10 44 30	21 07 20	28 14 29	25 43.2	16 28.0	12D12.6	4 27.9	25 07.6	15 34.8	3 17.8	23 03.8	26 42.3	28 12.5
4 M	10 53 24	11 42 35	5♉14 39	12♉07 48	25 44.0	15 31.3	12 12.5	5 06.7	25 31.6	15R34.9	3 13.3	23 03.5	26 40.8	28 11.6
5 Tu	10 57 21	12 40 43	18 54 02	25 33 36	25 45.3	14 33.1	12 14.7	5 45.5	25 55.6	15 34.8	3 08.8	23 03.1	26 39.2	28 10.7
6 W	11 01 18	13 38 53	2♊06 51	8♊34 13	25R46.3	13 34.8	12 19.2	6 24.3	26 19.7	15 34.6	3 04.4	23 02.8	26 37.6	28 09.8
7 Th	11 05 14	14 37 05	14 56 12	21 13 17	25 46.2	12 37.5	12 26.0	7 03.2	26 43.9	15 34.1	3 00.0	23 02.3	26 36.0	28 08.9
8 F	11 09 11	15 35 19	27 26 01	3♋34 57	25 44.5	11 42.5	12 34.9	7 42.1	27 08.1	15 33.4	2 55.6	23 01.8	26 34.4	28 08.0
9 Sa	11 13 07	16 33 36	9♋40 36	15 43 29	25 41.0	10 51.2	12 46.1	8 21.1	27 32.4	15 32.5	2 51.2	23 01.3	26 32.7	28 07.2
10 Su	11 17 04	17 31 54	21 44 05	27 42 51	25 36.0	10 04.7	12 59.3	9 00.1	27 56.7	15 31.4	2 46.9	23 00.7	26 31.1	28 06.3
11 M	11 21 00	18 30 14	3♌40 13	9♌36 35	25 29.8	9 24.4	13 14.5	9 39.2	28 21.1	15 30.1	2 42.6	23 00.1	26 29.5	28 05.5
12 Tu	11 24 57	19 28 36	15 32 17	21 27 40	25 23.1	8 51.0	13 31.8	10 18.3	28 45.6	15 28.6	2 38.4	22 59.4	26 27.8	28 04.8
13 W	11 28 53	20 26 59	27 23 00	3♍18 35	25 16.5	8 25.6	13 50.9	10 57.5	29 10.0	15 26.9	2 34.1	22 58.6	26 26.2	28 04.0
14 Th	11 32 50	21 25 25	9♍14 38	15 11 23	25 10.7	8 08.6	14 11.9	11 36.7	29 34.6	15 25.0	2 29.9	22 57.8	26 24.5	28 03.3
15 F	11 36 47	22 23 53	21 09 04	27 07 53	25 06.3	8D00.8	14 34.6	12 16.0	29 59.1	15 22.9	2 25.8	22 57.0	26 22.9	28 02.6
16 Sa	11 40 43	23 22 22	3♎08 03	9♎09 48	25 03.5	8 02.2	14 59.1	12 55.3	0♏23.8	15 20.6	2 21.7	22 56.1	26 21.2	28 01.9
17 Su	11 44 40	24 20 54	15 13 21	21 18 58	25D02.3	8 13.1	15 25.3	13 34.6	0 48.4	15 18.1	2 17.6	22 55.2	26 19.6	28 01.2
18 M	11 48 36	25 19 27	27 26 54	3♏37 27	25 02.6	8 33.4	15 53.0	14 14.0	1 13.1	15 15.5	2 13.6	22 54.2	26 17.9	28 00.6
19 Tu	11 52 33	26 18 02	9♏50 56	16 07 41	25 03.8	9 02.9	16 22.4	14 53.5	1 37.9	15 12.6	2 09.7	22 53.2	26 16.2	28 00.0
20 W	11 56 29	27 16 38	22 28 02	28 52 22	25 05.4	9 41.4	16 53.2	15 33.0	2 02.7	15 09.5	2 05.8	22 52.1	26 14.6	27 59.4
21 Th	12 00 26	28 15 17	5♐21 01	11♐54 21	25 06.9	10 28.4	17 25.4	16 12.5	2 27.5	15 06.2	2 01.9	22 51.0	26 12.9	27 58.9
22 F	12 04 22	29 13 57	18 32 41	25 16 19	25R07.7	11 23.4	17 59.1	16 52.1	2 52.4	15 02.8	1 58.2	22 49.9	26 11.3	27 58.3
23 Sa	12 08 19	0♎12 39	2♑05 28	9♑00 16	25 07.5	12 25.9	18 34.1	17 31.7	3 17.3	14 59.1	1 54.4	22 48.7	26 09.6	27 57.8
24 Su	12 12 16	1 11 22	16 00 47	23 06 55	25 06.2	13 35.2	19 10.4	18 11.4	3 42.3	14 55.3	1 50.8	22 47.4	26 08.0	27 57.4
25 M	12 16 12	2 10 07	0♒18 27	7♒35 00	25 03.9	14 50.7	19 47.9	18 51.1	4 07.3	14 51.3	1 47.2	22 46.1	26 06.3	27 56.9
26 Tu	12 20 09	3 08 54	14 56 04	22 20 55	25 01.1	16 11.8	20 26.7	19 30.8	4 32.3	14 47.1	1 43.6	22 44.8	26 04.7	27 56.5
27 W	12 24 05	4 07 42	29 48 45	7♓18 34	24 58.3	17 37.7	21 06.6	20 10.6	4 57.3	14 42.7	1 40.2	22 43.4	26 03.0	27 56.1
28 Th	12 28 02	5 06 33	14♓49 21	22 19 58	24 55.9	19 07.9	21 47.6	20 50.5	5 22.4	14 38.2	1 36.8	22 42.0	26 01.4	27 55.7
29 F	12 31 58	6 05 25	29 49 18	7♈16 15	24 54.2	20 41.7	22 29.7	21 30.4	5 47.5	14 33.5	1 33.4	22 40.6	25 59.8	27 55.4
30 Sa	12 35 55	7 04 19	14♈39 49	21 59 05	24D53.6	22 18.6	23 12.9	22 10.3	6 12.7	14 28.6	1 30.1	22 39.1	25 58.1	27 55.1

LONGITUDE — October 2023

Day	Sid.Time	☉	0 hr ☽	Noon☽	True☊	☿	♀	♂	⚳	♃	♄	♅	♆	♇
1 Su	12 39 51	8♎03 15	29♈13 18	6♉21 49	24♈53.8	23♍58.0	23♌57.1	22♎50.3	6♏37.9	14♉23.5	1♓27.0	22♉37.5	25♓56.5	27♑54.8
2 M	12 43 48	9 02 14	13♉24 13	20 20 11	24 54.7	25 39.4	24 42.3	23 30.3	7 03.1	14R18.3	1R23.8	22R36.0	25R54.9	27R54.6
3 Tu	12 47 45	10 01 15	27 09 37	3♊52 32	24 55.9	27 22.5	25 28.4	24 10.4	7 28.3	14 12.9	1 20.8	22 34.4	25 53.3	27 54.3
4 W	12 51 41	11 00 18	10♊29 03	16 59 28	24 57.1	29 06.9	26 15.5	24 50.5	7 53.6	14 07.3	1 17.8	22 32.7	25 51.7	27 54.1
5 Th	12 55 38	11 59 23	23 24 07	29 43 24	24 57.9	0♎52.1	27 03.4	25 30.7	8 18.9	14 01.6	1 14.9	22 31.0	25 50.2	27 54.0
6 F	12 59 34	12 58 31	5♋57 51	12♋07 57	24R58.3	2 38.0	27 52.1	26 11.0	8 44.2	13 55.7	1 12.1	22 29.3	25 48.6	27 53.8
7 Sa	13 03 31	13 57 41	18 14 16	24 17 21	24 58.1	4 24.2	28 41.7	26 51.2	9 09.5	13 49.7	1 09.4	22 27.5	25 47.0	27 53.7
8 Su	13 07 27	14 56 54	0♌17 47	6♌16 08	24 57.3	6 10.7	29 32.0	27 31.6	9 34.9	13 43.6	1 06.8	22 25.7	25 45.5	27 53.6
9 M	13 11 24	15 56 08	12 12 55	18 08 42	24 56.3	7 57.1	0♍23.1	28 12.0	10 00.3	13 37.3	1 04.2	22 23.9	25 43.9	27 53.6
10 Tu	13 15 20	16 55 25	24 03 57	29 59 10	24 55.1	9 43.4	1 15.0	28 52.4	10 25.8	13 30.8	1 01.7	22 22.0	25 42.4	27D53.5
11 W	13 19 17	17 54 44	5♍54 47	11♍51 13	24 54.0	11 29.4	2 07.5	29 32.9	10 51.2	13 24.2	0 59.4	22 20.1	25 40.9	27 53.5
12 Th	13 23 14	18 54 06	17 48 50	23 47 58	24 53.2	13 15.0	3 00.7	0♏13.4	11 16.7	13 17.5	0 57.1	22 18.2	25 39.4	27 53.5
13 F	13 27 10	19 53 29	29 48 55	5♎51 57	24 52.6	15 00.3	3 54.6	0 54.0	11 42.2	13 10.7	0 54.8	22 16.2	25 37.9	27 53.6
14 Sa	13 31 07	20 52 54	11♎57 18	18 05 10	24D52.4	16 45.0	4 49.1	1 34.6	12 07.7	13 03.7	0 52.7	22 14.2	25 36.4	27 53.7
15 Su	13 35 03	21 52 22	24 15 44	0♏29 08	24 52.3	18 29.2	5 44.2	2 15.3	12 33.2	12 56.7	0 50.7	22 12.2	25 35.0	27 53.8
16 M	13 39 00	22 51 52	6♏45 32	13 05 01	24 52.5	20 12.8	6 39.8	2 56.0	12 58.8	12 49.5	0 48.8	22 10.1	25 33.6	27 54.0
17 Tu	13 42 56	23 51 23	19 27 41	25 53 39	24 52.6	21 55.8	7 36.1	3 36.8	13 24.4	12 42.2	0 46.9	22 08.0	25 32.1	27 54.1
18 W	13 46 53	24 50 57	2♐22 58	8♐55 45	24R52.6	23 38.2	8 32.9	4 17.6	13 50.0	12 34.8	0 45.2	22 05.9	25 30.7	27 54.3
19 Th	13 50 49	25 50 32	15 32 02	22 11 55	24 52.6	25 20.0	9 30.2	4 58.5	14 15.6	12 27.3	0 43.6	22 03.8	25 29.4	27 54.6
20 F	13 54 46	26 50 09	28 55 25	5♑42 35	24 52.5	27 01.1	10 28.0	5 39.4	14 41.2	12 19.8	0 42.0	22 01.6	25 28.0	27 54.8
21 Sa	13 58 43	27 49 48	12♑33 26	19 27 57	24D52.3	28 41.6	11 26.4	6 20.4	15 06.9	12 12.2	0 40.6	21 59.4	25 26.6	27 55.1
22 Su	14 02 39	28 49 29	26 26 04	3♒27 41	24 52.3	0♏21.5	12 25.2	7 01.4	15 32.5	12 04.4	0 39.2	21 57.2	25 25.3	27 55.5
23 M	14 06 36	29 49 11	10♒32 39	17 40 44	24 52.5	2 00.8	13 24.5	7 42.5	15 58.2	11 56.7	0 38.0	21 55.0	25 24.0	27 55.8
24 Tu	14 10 32	0♏48 55	24 51 36	2♓04 55	24 52.9	3 39.5	14 24.2	8 23.6	16 23.9	11 48.8	0 36.8	21 52.7	25 22.7	27 56.2
25 W	14 14 29	1 48 40	9♓20 11	16 36 52	24 53.5	5 17.6	15 24.4	9 04.8	16 49.5	11 40.9	0 35.8	21 50.4	25 21.5	27 56.6
26 Th	14 18 25	2 48 28	23 54 23	1♈12 01	24 54.1	6 55.2	16 25.0	9 46.0	17 15.2	11 32.9	0 34.8	21 48.1	25 20.2	27 57.0
27 F	14 22 22	3 48 17	8♈29 05	15 44 50	24R54.6	8 32.2	17 26.0	10 27.2	17 40.9	11 24.9	0 33.9	21 45.8	25 19.0	27 57.5
28 Sa	14 26 18	4 48 07	22 58 32	0♉09 28	24 54.6	10 08.6	18 27.4	11 08.6	18 06.6	11 16.9	0 33.2	21 43.4	25 17.8	27 58.0
29 Su	14 30 15	5 48 00	7♉16 56	14 20 21	24 54.2	11 44.6	19 29.2	11 49.9	18 32.4	11 08.8	0 32.5	21 41.1	25 16.6	27 58.5
30 M	14 34 12	6 47 55	21 19 11	28 13 01	24 53.1	13 20.0	20 31.4	12 31.3	18 58.1	11 00.7	0 32.0	21 38.7	25 15.5	27 59.1
31 Tu	14 38 08	7 47 52	5♊01 30	11♊44 28	24 51.5	14 55.0	21 34.0	13 12.8	19 23.8	10 52.6	0 31.6	21 36.3	25 14.4	27 59.6

Astro Data

	Dy Hr Mn
☽0N	1 20:25
♀D	4 1:20
♃R	4 14:11
☿D	15 20:23
☽0S	16 2:17
☉0S	23 6:50
☽0N	29 7:11
☿0S	7 9:36
♇D	11 1:11
☽0S	13 8:54
☽0N	26 17:07

Planet Ingress

		Dy Hr Mn
⚳	♏	15 12:50
☉	♎	23 6:50
☿	♎	5 0:09
♀	♍	9 1:11
♂	♏	12 4:04
☿	♏	22 6:49
☉	♏	23 16:21

Last Aspect / ☽ Ingress (September)

Last Aspect Dy Hr Mn			☽ Ingress	Dy Hr Mn
1 10:36	♇	⚹	♈	1 13:25
3 11:57	♇	□	♉	3 15:00
5 16:46	♇	△	♊	5 20:07
7 22:22	♆	□	♋	8 5:00
10 12:47	♇	☍	♌	10 16:36
12 15:06	♅	□	♍	13 5:18
15 13:49	♇	△	♎	15 17:44
18 1:06	♇	□	♏	18 4:58
20 10:21	♇	⚹	♐	20 14:06
22 19:32	☉	□	♑	22 20:20
24 20:05	♇	☌	♒	24 23:29
26 12:38	♅	□	♓	27 0:18
28 20:58	♇	⚹	♈	29 0:17

Last Aspect / ☽ Ingress (October)

Last Aspect Dy Hr Mn			☽ Ingress	Dy Hr Mn
30 21:49	♇	□	♉	1 1:18
3 1:20	♇	△	♊	3 5:03
5 6:34	♀	⚹	♋	5 12:32
7 19:12	♇	☍	♌	7 23:24
10 9:36	♂	⚹	♍	10 12:02
12 20:10	♇	△	♎	13 0:22
15 7:01	♇	□	♏	15 11:04
17 15:44	♇	⚹	♐	17 19:36
19 19:02	☉	⚹	♑	20 1:55
22 6:00	☿	□	♒	22 6:06
23 19:04	♅	□	♓	24 8:33
26 6:39	♇	⚹	♈	26 10:01
28 8:20	♇	□	♉	28 11:44
30 11:36	♇	△	♊	30 15:08

☽ Phases & Eclipses

Dy Hr Mn		
6 22:21	☾	14♊04
15 1:40	●	21♍59
22 19:32	☽	29♐32
29 9:58	○	6♈00
6 13:48	☾	13♋03
14 17:55	●	21♎08
14 17:59:27	●	A 05'17"
22 3:29	☽	28♑28
28 20:24	○	5♉09
28 20:14	●	P 0.122

Astro Data

1 September 2023
Julian Day # 45169
SVP 4♓55'52"
GC 27♐10.2 ⚴ 24♍24.1
Eris 25♈07.0R ⚵ 8♌35.3
⚷ 19♈18.0R ⚶ 26♊25.0
☽ Mean ☊ 27♈18.5

1 October 2023
Julian Day # 45199
SVP 4♓55'49"
GC 27♐10.3 ⚴ 8♎08.7
Eris 24♈52.1R ⚵ 22♌59.3
⚷ 18♈07.2R ⚶ 4♋05.1
☽ Mean ☊ 25♈43.2

November 2023 LONGITUDE

Day	Sid.Time	☉	0 hr ☽	Noon ☽	True ☊	☿	♀	♂	⚳	♃	♄	♅	♆	♇
1 W	14 42 05	8♏47 51	18♊21 50	24♊53 36	24♈49.5	16♏29.4	22♍36.9	13♏54.3	19♍49.6	10♉44.4	0♓31.2	21♉33.9	25♓13.3	28♑00.3
2 Th	14 46 01	9 47 52	1♋19 55	7♋41 01	24R47.6	18 03.5	23 40.2	14 35.9	20 15.3	10R36.3	0R31.0	21R31.5	25R12.2	28 00.9
3 F	14 49 58	10 47 55	13 57 14	20 08 57	24 45.9	19 37.1	24 43.9	15 17.5	20 41.1	10 28.1	0D30.9	21 29.1	25 11.2	28 01.6
4 Sa	14 53 54	11 48 01	26 16 37	2♌20 46	24D44.9	21 10.3	25 47.8	15 59.1	21 06.8	10 20.0	0 30.8	21 26.6	25 10.1	28 02.3
5 Su	14 57 51	12 48 08	8♌21 57	14 20 43	24 44.6	22 43.0	26 52.1	16 40.9	21 32.6	10 11.8	0 30.9	21 24.2	25 09.1	28 03.0
6 M	15 01 47	13 48 17	20 17 43	26 13 31	24 45.1	24 15.4	27 56.7	17 22.6	21 58.3	10 03.7	0 31.1	21 21.7	25 08.2	28 03.7
7 Tu	15 05 44	14 48 29	2♍08 45	8♍04 00	24 46.3	25 47.4	29 01.6	18 04.4	22 24.1	9 55.6	0 31.4	21 19.2	25 07.2	28 04.5
8 W	15 09 41	15 48 42	13 59 53	19 56 56	24 47.9	27 19.0	0♎06.8	18 46.3	22 49.9	9 47.5	0 31.7	21 16.8	25 06.3	28 05.3
9 Th	15 13 37	16 48 58	25 55 42	1♎56 41	24 49.6	28 50.2	1 12.3	19 28.2	23 15.6	9 39.5	0 32.2	21 14.3	25 05.4	28 06.1
10 F	15 17 34	17 49 15	8♎00 20	14 07 04	24R50.9	0♐21.1	2 18.0	20 10.2	23 41.4	9 31.4	0 32.8	21 11.8	25 04.6	28 07.0
11 Sa	15 21 30	18 49 34	20 17 13	26 31 04	24 51.3	1 51.6	3 24.0	20 52.2	24 07.2	9 23.5	0 33.5	21 09.3	25 03.7	28 07.9
12 Su	15 25 27	19 49 55	2♏48 52	9♏10 44	24 50.5	3 21.7	4 30.3	21 34.3	24 32.9	9 15.6	0 34.3	21 06.8	25 02.9	28 08.8
13 M	15 29 23	20 50 18	15 36 47	22 06 59	24 48.3	4 51.5	5 36.8	22 16.4	24 58.7	9 07.7	0 35.2	21 04.3	25 02.2	28 09.7
14 Tu	15 33 20	21 50 43	28 41 19	5♐19 37	24 44.9	6 20.8	6 43.5	22 58.6	25 24.5	9 00.0	0 36.2	21 01.8	25 01.4	28 10.7
15 W	15 37 16	22 51 09	12♐01 44	18 47 24	24 40.6	7 49.8	7 50.5	23 40.9	25 50.2	8 52.2	0 37.4	20 59.3	25 00.7	28 11.7
16 Th	15 41 13	23 51 37	25 36 21	2♑28 16	24 36.0	9 18.3	8 57.7	24 23.1	26 16.0	8 44.6	0 38.6	20 56.8	25 00.0	28 12.7
17 F	15 45 10	24 52 06	9♑22 49	16 19 41	24 31.6	10 46.4	10 05.1	25 05.5	26 41.7	8 37.1	0 39.9	20 54.3	24 59.4	28 13.8
18 Sa	15 49 06	25 52 37	23 18 32	0♒19 03	24 28.1	12 13.9	11 12.8	25 47.8	27 07.4	8 29.6	0 41.3	20 51.9	24 58.8	28 14.8
19 Su	15 53 03	26 53 08	7♒20 56	14 23 54	24D25.9	13 41.0	12 20.6	26 30.3	27 33.2	8 22.3	0 42.9	20 49.4	24 58.2	28 15.9
20 M	15 56 59	27 53 41	21 27 42	28 32 08	24 25.3	15 07.5	13 28.6	27 12.7	27 58.9	8 15.0	0 44.5	20 46.9	24 57.6	28 17.1
21 Tu	16 00 56	28 54 15	5♓36 57	12♓41 57	24 25.9	16 33.3	14 36.9	27 55.3	28 24.6	8 07.9	0 46.2	20 44.4	24 57.1	28 18.2
22 W	16 04 52	29 54 50	19 46 56	26 51 42	24 27.4	17 58.4	15 45.3	28 37.8	28 50.3	8 00.8	0 48.1	20 42.0	24 56.6	28 19.4
23 Th	16 08 49	0♐55 27	3♈56 00	10♈59 35	24R28.8	19 22.7	16 53.9	29 20.5	29 15.9	7 53.9	0 50.0	20 39.5	24 56.2	28 20.6
24 F	16 12 45	1 56 04	18 02 10	25 03 26	24 29.4	20 46.2	18 02.7	0♐03.1	29 41.6	7 47.1	0 52.1	20 37.1	24 55.7	28 21.8
25 Sa	16 16 42	2 56 43	2♉03 03	9♉00 39	24 28.5	22 08.6	19 11.7	0 45.8	0♐07.2	7 40.5	0 54.2	20 34.7	24 55.4	28 23.0
26 Su	16 20 39	3 57 23	15 55 50	22 48 14	24 25.6	23 29.9	20 20.8	1 28.6	0 32.9	7 33.9	0 56.4	20 32.3	24 55.0	28 24.3
27 M	16 24 35	4 58 05	29 37 26	6♊23 07	24 20.7	24 49.8	21 30.2	2 11.4	0 58.5	7 27.5	0 58.8	20 29.9	24 54.7	28 25.6
28 Tu	16 28 32	5 58 47	13♊04 57	19 42 39	24 14.0	26 08.3	22 39.7	2 54.3	1 24.1	7 21.3	1 01.2	20 27.5	24 54.4	28 26.9
29 W	16 32 28	6 59 31	26 16 03	2♋45 00	24 06.3	27 25.1	23 49.3	3 37.2	1 49.7	7 15.2	1 03.7	20 25.1	24 54.1	28 28.2
30 Th	16 36 25	8 00 17	9♋09 28	15 29 29	23 58.3	28 39.9	24 59.1	4 20.2	2 15.2	7 09.2	1 06.4	20 22.8	24 53.9	28 29.6

December 2023 LONGITUDE

Day	Sid.Time	☉	0 hr ☽	Noon ☽	True ☊	☿	♀	♂	⚳	♃	♄	♅	♆	♇
1 F	16 40 21	9♐01 04	21♋45 11	27♋56 48	23♈50.8	29♐52.5	26♎09.1	5♐03.2	2♐40.8	7♉03.4	1♓09.1	20♉20.4	24♓53.7	28♑31.0
2 Sa	16 44 18	10 01 52	4♌04 36	10♌08 59	23R44.8	1♑02.5	27 19.2	5 46.2	3 06.3	6R57.8	1 11.9	20R18.1	24R53.6	28 32.4
3 Su	16 48 14	11 02 42	16 10 22	22 09 16	23 40.5	2 09.5	28 29.5	6 29.4	3 31.8	6 52.3	1 14.8	20 15.8	24 53.5	28 33.8
4 M	16 52 11	12 03 33	28 06 13	4♍01 49	23D38.3	3 13.2	29 39.9	7 12.5	3 57.3	6 46.9	1 17.9	20 13.6	24 53.4	28 35.2
5 Tu	16 56 08	13 04 25	9♍56 42	15 51 30	23 37.9	4 12.9	0♏50.4	7 55.7	4 22.8	6 41.8	1 21.0	20 11.3	24 53.3	28 36.7
6 W	17 00 04	14 05 19	21 46 54	27 43 32	23 38.8	5 08.1	2 01.1	8 39.0	4 48.2	6 36.8	1 24.2	20 09.1	24D53.3	28 38.1
7 Th	17 04 01	15 06 14	3♎42 07	9♎43 15	23 40.0	5 58.3	3 11.9	9 22.3	5 13.7	6 32.0	1 27.4	20 06.9	24 53.3	28 39.6
8 F	17 07 57	16 07 10	15 47 34	21 55 39	23R40.8	6 42.7	4 22.8	10 05.7	5 39.1	6 27.3	1 30.8	20 04.7	24 53.4	28 41.2
9 Sa	17 11 54	17 08 07	28 08 03	4♏25 11	23 40.2	7 20.4	5 33.9	10 49.1	6 04.4	6 22.9	1 34.3	20 02.6	24 53.4	28 42.7
10 Su	17 15 50	18 09 06	10♏47 28	17 15 10	23 37.4	7 50.8	6 45.0	11 32.6	6 29.8	6 18.6	1 37.9	20 00.4	24 53.6	28 44.3
11 M	17 19 47	19 10 05	23 48 28	0♐27 24	23 32.2	8 13.0	7 56.3	12 16.1	6 55.1	6 14.5	1 41.5	19 58.3	24 53.7	28 45.8
12 Tu	17 23 43	20 11 06	7♐11 55	14 01 47	23 24.7	8R26.0	9 07.7	12 59.7	7 20.4	6 10.6	1 45.3	19 56.3	24 53.9	28 47.4
13 W	17 27 40	21 12 08	20 56 40	27 56 06	23 15.3	8 29.1	10 19.2	13 43.3	7 45.7	6 06.9	1 49.1	19 54.2	24 54.1	28 49.0
14 Th	17 31 37	22 13 10	4♑59 30	12♑06 11	23 05.1	8 21.5	11 30.8	14 27.0	8 10.9	6 03.4	1 53.0	19 52.2	24 54.4	28 50.7
15 F	17 35 33	23 14 13	19 15 27	26 26 31	22 55.3	8 02.6	12 42.4	15 10.7	8 36.1	6 00.1	1 57.0	19 50.3	24 54.7	28 52.3
16 Sa	17 39 30	24 15 17	3♒38 38	10♒51 05	22 46.9	7 32.2	13 54.2	15 54.5	9 01.3	5 57.0	2 01.1	19 48.3	24 55.0	28 54.0
17 Su	17 43 26	25 16 21	18 03 11	25 14 22	22 40.8	6 50.2	15 06.1	16 38.3	9 26.5	5 54.1	2 05.3	19 46.4	24 55.4	28 55.6
18 M	17 47 23	26 17 25	2♓24 09	9♓32 08	22 37.3	5 57.1	16 18.0	17 22.1	9 51.6	5 51.4	2 09.6	19 44.5	24 55.8	28 57.3
19 Tu	17 51 19	27 18 30	16 38 01	23 41 37	22D36.1	4 54.1	17 30.0	18 06.0	10 16.6	5 48.9	2 13.9	19 42.7	24 56.2	28 59.0
20 W	17 55 16	28 19 35	0♈42 49	7♈41 34	22 36.3	3 42.6	18 42.1	18 49.9	10 41.7	5 46.6	2 18.3	19 40.9	24 56.7	29 00.8
21 Th	17 59 13	29 20 40	14 37 52	21 31 44	22R36.7	2 24.8	19 54.3	19 33.9	11 06.6	5 44.5	2 22.8	19 39.1	24 57.2	29 02.5
22 F	18 03 09	0♑21 45	28 23 11	5♉12 16	22 36.0	1 03.1	21 06.6	20 18.0	11 31.6	5 42.6	2 27.4	19 37.4	24 57.8	29 04.2
23 Sa	18 07 06	1 22 51	11♉59 00	18 43 21	22 33.2	29♐40.4	22 18.9	21 02.0	11 56.5	5 40.9	2 32.0	19 35.7	24 58.3	29 06.0
24 Su	18 11 02	2 23 57	25 25 18	2♊04 45	22 27.6	28 19.3	23 31.4	21 46.1	12 21.4	5 39.4	2 36.8	19 34.1	24 58.9	29 07.8
25 M	18 14 59	3 25 03	8♊41 36	15 15 45	22 19.0	27 02.6	24 43.9	22 30.3	12 46.2	5 38.1	2 41.6	19 32.5	24 59.6	29 09.6
26 Tu	18 18 55	4 26 09	21 47 02	28 15 19	22 07.8	25 52.3	25 56.4	23 14.5	13 11.0	5 37.1	2 46.5	19 30.9	25 00.3	29 11.4
27 W	18 22 52	5 27 16	4♋40 28	11♋02 23	21 54.8	24 50.4	27 09.1	23 58.8	13 35.7	5 36.2	2 51.4	19 29.4	25 01.0	29 13.2
28 Th	18 26 48	6 28 23	17 20 59	23 36 14	21 41.2	23 58.1	28 21.8	24 43.1	14 00.4	5 35.6	2 56.5	19 27.9	25 01.7	29 15.0
29 F	18 30 45	7 29 31	29 48 10	5♌56 51	21 28.1	23 16.0	29 34.5	25 27.4	14 25.1	5 35.1	3 01.6	19 26.5	25 02.5	29 16.8
30 Sa	18 34 42	8 30 38	12♌02 28	18 05 13	21 16.8	22 44.5	0♐47.4	26 11.8	14 49.7	5D34.9	3 06.7	19 25.1	25 03.3	29 18.7
31 Su	18 38 38	9 31 47	24 05 24	0♍03 23	21 07.9	22 23.6	2 00.3	26 56.3	15 14.3	5 34.9	3 12.0	19 23.7	25 04.1	29 20.5

Astro Data

	Dy Hr Mn
♄ D	4 7:03
♃∠♆	5 21:04
☽ 0S	9 16:37
♀0S	11 5:21
☽ 0N	23 0:25
♆ D	6 13:22
☽ 0S	7 0:36
☿ R	13 7:08
☽ 0N	20 5:17
♃ D	31 2:40

Planet Ingress

		Dy Hr Mn
♀	♎	8 9:30
☿	♐	10 6:25
☉	♐	22 14:03
♂	♐	24 10:15
⚳	♐	25 5:14
☿	♑	1 14:31
♀	♏	4 18:51
☉	♑	22 3:27
☿	♐R	23 6:17
♀	♐	29 20:24

Last Aspect / ☽ Ingress

Dy Hr Mn				Dy Hr Mn
1 12:36	♆	□	♋	1 21:30
4 3:28	♇	☍	♌	4 7:21
6 7:25	☿	□	♍	6 19:39
9 4:55	☿	⚹	♎	9 8:08
11 15:05	♇	□	♏	11 18:39
13 23:03	♇	⚹	♐	14 2:23
15 22:57	♆	□	♑	16 7:41
18 8:27	♇	☌	♒	18 11:27
20 10:50	☉	□	♓	20 14:29
22 15:10	♂	△	♈	22 17:19
24 17:40	♇	□	♉	24 20:29
26 21:52	♇	△	♊	27 0:40
29 1:03	☿	☍	♋	29 6:54

Last Aspect / ☽ Ingress

Dy Hr Mn				Dy Hr Mn
1 13:07	♇	☍	♌	1 16:00
4 2:11	♀	⚹	♍	4 3:50
6 13:50	♇	△	♎	6 16:35
9 1:05	♇	□	♏	9 3:35
11 8:57	♇	⚹	♐	11 11:11
13 6:48	♆	□	♑	13 15:31
15 16:04	♇	☌	♒	15 17:56
17 12:04	☉	⚹	♓	17 19:58
19 21:03	♇	⚹	♈	19 22:47
22 2:47	☉	△	♉	22 2:50
24 6:40	♇	△	♊	24 8:15
26 7:55	☿	☍	♋	26 15:15
28 22:57	♇	☍	♌	29 0:23
31 5:18	♂	△	♍	31 11:53

☽ Phases & Eclipses

Dy Hr Mn		
5 8:37	☾	12♌40
13 9:27	●	20♏44
20 10:50	☽	27♒51
27 9:16	○	4♊51
5 5:49	☾	12♍49
12 23:32	●	20♐40
19 18:39	☽	27♓35
27 0:33	○	4♋58

Astro Data

1 November 2023
Julian Day # 45230
SVP 4♓55'45"
GC 27♐10.3 ⚴ 22♎07.9
Eris 24♈33.8R ⚵ 5♍57.5
⚷ 16♈44.6R ⚶ 7♋29.6
☽ Mean ☊ 24♈04.7

1 December 2023
Julian Day # 45260
SVP 4♓55'40"
GC 27♐10.4 ⚴ 5♏12.1
Eris 24♈18.4R ⚵ 15♍44.2
⚷ 15♈45.0R ⚶ 4♋33.3R
☽ Mean ☊ 22♈29.4

LONGITUDE — January 2024

Day	Sid.Time	☉	0 hr ☽	Noon ☽	True☊	☿	♀	♂	⚳	♃	♄	♅	♆	♇
1 M	18 42 35	10♑32 55	5♍59 34	11♍54 28	21♈01.9	22♐12.7	3♐13.2	27♐40.8	15♐38.8	5♉35.1	3♓17.3	19♉22.4	25♓05.0	29♑22.4
2 Tu	18 46 31	11 34 03	17 48 36	23 42 33	20R58.5	22D11.5	4 26.2	28 25.3	16 03.2	5 35.5	3 22.7	19R21.1	25 05.9	29 24.3
3 W	18 50 28	12 35 12	29 36 58	5♎32 31	20D57.3	22 19.2	5 39.3	29 09.9	16 27.7	5 36.1	3 28.1	19 19.9	25 06.9	29 26.1
4 Th	18 54 24	13 36 22	11♎29 52	17 29 44	20R57.2	22 35.2	6 52.5	29 54.5	16 52.0	5 36.9	3 33.6	19 18.7	25 07.8	29 28.0
5 F	18 58 21	14 37 31	23 32 48	29 39 48	20 57.0	22 58.6	8 05.6	0♑39.1	17 16.3	5 37.9	3 39.2	19 17.6	25 08.8	29 29.9
6 Sa	19 02 17	15 38 41	5♏51 22	12♏08 09	20 55.6	23 28.9	9 18.9	1 23.9	17 40.6	5 39.1	3 44.8	19 16.5	25 09.9	29 31.8
7 Su	19 06 14	16 39 51	18 30 41	24 59 29	20 52.1	24 05.2	10 32.2	2 08.6	18 04.8	5 40.5	3 50.5	19 15.5	25 10.9	29 33.7
8 M	19 10 11	17 41 01	1♐34 52	8♐17 07	20 45.7	24 47.1	11 45.5	2 53.4	18 29.0	5 42.2	3 56.3	19 14.5	25 12.0	29 35.7
9 Tu	19 14 07	18 42 11	15 06 16	22 02 16	20 36.6	25 33.9	12 58.9	3 38.3	18 53.1	5 44.0	4 02.1	19 13.5	25 13.2	29 37.6
10 W	19 18 04	19 43 22	29 04 48	6♑13 25	20 25.3	26 25.0	14 12.3	4 23.2	19 17.1	5 46.1	4 08.0	19 12.7	25 14.3	29 39.5
11 Th	19 22 00	20 44 32	13♑27 27	20 46 03	20 12.9	27 20.1	15 25.8	5 08.1	19 41.1	5 48.3	4 13.9	19 11.8	25 15.5	29 41.4
12 F	19 25 57	21 45 41	28 08 15	5♒32 58	20 00.7	28 18.7	16 39.3	5 53.1	20 05.0	5 50.8	4 19.9	19 11.0	25 16.7	29 43.4
13 Sa	19 29 53	22 46 51	12♒59 04	20 25 27	19 50.0	29 20.5	17 52.8	6 38.1	20 28.8	5 53.4	4 26.0	19 10.3	25 18.0	29 45.3
14 Su	19 33 50	23 47 59	27 50 59	5♓14 44	19 42.0	0♑25.0	19 06.4	7 23.1	20 52.6	5 56.3	4 32.1	19 09.6	25 19.3	29 47.3
15 M	19 37 47	24 49 08	12♓35 49	19 53 32	19 37.0	1 32.0	20 20.0	8 08.2	21 16.3	5 59.3	4 38.2	19 08.9	25 20.6	29 49.2
16 Tu	19 41 43	25 50 15	27 07 22	4♈16 55	19 34.6	2 41.4	21 33.6	8 53.3	21 40.0	6 02.6	4 44.4	19 08.4	25 21.9	29 51.2
17 W	19 45 40	26 51 21	11♈21 59	18 22 28	19 34.1	3 52.7	22 47.2	9 38.5	22 03.6	6 06.0	4 50.7	19 07.8	25 23.3	29 53.1
18 Th	19 49 36	27 52 27	25 18 24	2♉09 54	19 34.1	5 06.0	24 00.9	10 23.7	22 27.1	6 09.6	4 57.0	19 07.3	25 24.7	29 55.1
19 F	19 53 33	28 53 32	8♉57 08	15 40 19	19 33.2	6 20.9	25 14.6	11 08.9	22 50.5	6 13.5	5 03.4	19 06.9	25 26.1	29 57.0
20 Sa	19 57 29	29 54 36	22 19 42	28 55 31	19 30.3	7 37.4	26 28.4	11 54.2	23 13.9	6 17.5	5 09.8	19 06.5	25 27.6	29 59.0
21 Su	20 01 26	0♒55 40	5♊28 00	11♊57 21	19 24.6	8 55.3	27 42.1	12 39.5	23 37.2	6 21.7	5 16.2	19 06.2	25 29.0	0♒00.9
22 M	20 05 22	1 56 42	18 23 44	24 47 18	19 15.9	10 14.5	28 55.9	13 24.8	24 00.4	6 26.1	5 22.7	19 05.9	25 30.5	0 02.9
23 Tu	20 09 19	2 57 44	1♋08 11	7♋26 27	19 04.5	11 34.9	0♑09.7	14 10.2	24 23.5	6 30.7	5 29.3	19 05.7	25 32.1	0 04.8
24 W	20 13 16	3 58 45	13 42 10	19 55 23	18 51.3	12 56.4	1 23.6	14 55.7	24 46.6	6 35.4	5 35.8	19 05.5	25 33.6	0 06.8
25 Th	20 17 12	4 59 44	26 06 09	2♌14 31	18 37.4	14 19.0	2 37.4	15 41.1	25 09.6	6 40.4	5 42.5	19 05.4	25 35.2	0 08.7
26 F	20 21 09	6 00 44	8♌20 32	14 24 18	18 24.0	15 42.7	3 51.3	16 26.6	25 32.5	6 45.5	5 49.1	19D05.3	25 36.8	0 10.7
27 Sa	20 25 05	7 01 42	20 25 54	26 25 31	18 12.2	17 07.2	5 05.3	17 12.1	25 55.3	6 50.8	5 55.8	19 05.3	25 38.4	0 12.6
28 Su	20 29 02	8 02 39	2♍23 20	8♍19 35	18 02.8	18 32.7	6 19.2	17 57.7	26 18.1	6 56.3	6 02.6	19 05.3	25 40.1	0 14.5
29 M	20 32 58	9 03 36	14 14 35	20 08 41	17 56.3	19 59.1	7 33.2	18 43.3	26 40.7	7 02.0	6 09.3	19 05.4	25 41.8	0 16.5
30 Tu	20 36 55	10 04 32	26 02 18	1♎55 51	17 52.5	21 26.3	8 47.1	19 28.9	27 03.3	7 07.8	6 16.1	19 05.6	25 43.5	0 18.4
31 W	20 40 51	11 05 27	7♎49 54	13 44 57	17D51.2	22 54.3	10 01.2	20 14.6	27 25.8	7 13.8	6 23.0	19 05.8	25 45.2	0 20.3

LONGITUDE — February 2024

Day	Sid.Time	☉	0 hr ☽	Noon ☽	True☊	☿	♀	♂	⚳	♃	♄	♅	♆	♇
1 Th	20 44 48	12♒06 21	19♎41 39	25♎40 36	17♈51.3	24♑23.1	11♑15.2	21♑00.3	27♐48.2	7♉19.9	6♓29.9	19♉06.0	25♓47.0	0♒22.2
2 F	20 48 45	13 07 15	1♏42 28	7♏47 56	17R51.9	25 52.7	12 29.2	21 46.1	28 10.5	7 26.3	6 36.8	19 06.3	25 48.7	0 24.2
3 Sa	20 52 41	14 08 08	13 57 40	20 12 20	17 51.8	27 23.1	13 43.3	22 31.8	28 32.8	7 32.8	6 43.7	19 06.7	25 50.5	0 26.1
4 Su	20 56 38	15 09 00	26 32 36	2♐59 02	17 50.1	28 54.3	14 57.4	23 17.6	28 54.9	7 39.5	6 50.7	19 07.1	25 52.3	0 28.0
5 M	21 00 34	16 09 52	9♐32 08	16 12 21	17 46.3	0♒26.3	16 11.5	24 03.5	29 16.9	7 46.3	6 57.7	19 07.5	25 54.2	0 29.9
6 Tu	21 04 31	17 10 42	22 59 57	29 55 02	17 40.0	1 59.0	17 25.6	24 49.4	29 38.9	7 53.3	7 04.7	19 08.0	25 56.0	0 31.8
7 W	21 08 27	18 11 32	6♑57 35	14♑07 19	17 31.8	3 32.5	18 39.7	25 35.3	0♑00.7	8 00.4	7 11.8	19 08.6	25 57.9	0 33.7
8 Th	21 12 24	19 12 20	21 23 44	28 46 09	17 22.3	5 06.7	19 53.9	26 21.2	0 22.5	8 07.7	7 18.8	19 09.2	25 59.8	0 35.5
9 F	21 16 20	20 13 08	6♒13 40	13♒45 10	17 12.9	6 41.8	21 08.1	27 07.2	0 44.1	8 15.2	7 25.9	19 09.9	26 01.7	0 37.4
10 Sa	21 20 17	21 13 54	21 19 26	28 55 10	17 04.6	8 17.6	22 22.2	27 53.2	1 05.7	8 22.8	7 33.1	19 10.6	26 03.7	0 39.3
11 Su	21 24 14	22 14 38	6♓31 01	14♓05 42	16 58.5	9 54.2	23 36.4	28 39.2	1 27.1	8 30.6	7 40.2	19 11.4	26 05.6	0 41.1
12 M	21 28 10	23 15 21	21 37 59	29 06 50	16 54.8	11 31.6	24 50.6	29 25.3	1 48.4	8 38.5	7 47.4	19 12.2	26 07.6	0 42.9
13 Tu	21 32 07	24 16 03	6♈31 20	13♈50 46	16D53.4	13 09.8	26 04.8	0♒11.4	2 09.6	8 46.5	7 54.6	19 13.1	26 09.6	0 44.8
14 W	21 36 03	25 16 43	21 04 39	28 12 39	16 53.8	14 48.9	27 19.0	0 57.5	2 30.7	8 54.8	8 01.8	19 14.0	26 11.6	0 46.6
15 Th	21 40 00	26 17 21	5♉14 37	12♉10 33	16 54.8	16 28.8	28 33.2	1 43.6	2 51.7	9 03.1	8 09.0	19 15.0	26 13.6	0 48.4
16 F	21 43 56	27 17 58	19 00 34	25 44 53	16R55.5	18 09.6	29 47.4	2 29.7	3 12.6	9 11.6	8 16.2	19 16.0	26 15.6	0 50.2
17 Sa	21 47 53	28 18 33	2♊23 47	8♊57 36	16 54.9	19 51.3	1♒01.6	3 15.9	3 33.4	9 20.2	8 23.5	19 17.1	26 17.7	0 51.9
18 Su	21 51 49	29 19 06	15 26 44	21 51 31	16 52.3	21 33.8	2 15.8	4 02.1	3 54.0	9 29.0	8 30.7	19 18.3	26 19.8	0 53.7
19 M	21 55 46	0♓19 37	28 12 22	4♋29 36	16 47.6	23 17.2	3 30.0	4 48.4	4 14.5	9 37.9	8 38.0	19 19.4	26 21.8	0 55.5
20 Tu	21 59 43	1 20 07	10♋43 36	16 54 40	16 41.0	25 01.6	4 44.2	5 34.6	4 34.9	9 46.9	8 45.3	19 20.7	26 23.9	0 57.2
21 W	22 03 39	2 20 35	23 03 06	29 09 09	16 33.0	26 46.9	5 58.5	6 20.9	4 55.2	9 56.1	8 52.6	19 22.0	26 26.1	0 58.9
22 Th	22 07 36	3 21 01	5♌13 05	11♌15 06	16 24.4	28 33.1	7 12.7	7 07.2	5 15.4	10 05.4	8 59.9	19 23.3	26 28.2	1 00.6
23 F	22 11 32	4 21 25	17 15 24	23 14 13	16 16.1	0♓20.3	8 26.9	7 53.5	5 35.4	10 14.8	9 07.2	19 24.7	26 30.3	1 02.3
24 Sa	22 15 29	5 21 48	29 11 42	5♍08 04	16 08.9	2 08.4	9 41.2	8 39.8	5 55.3	10 24.3	9 14.5	19 26.1	26 32.5	1 04.0
25 Su	22 19 25	6 22 08	11♍03 30	16 58 14	16 03.3	3 57.4	10 55.4	9 26.2	6 15.0	10 34.0	9 21.8	19 27.6	26 34.6	1 05.7
26 M	22 23 22	7 22 28	22 52 31	28 46 35	15 59.7	5 47.4	12 09.7	10 12.5	6 34.7	10 43.7	9 29.2	19 29.1	26 36.8	1 07.3
27 Tu	22 27 18	8 22 45	4♎40 45	10♎35 21	15D58.0	7 38.3	13 23.9	10 58.9	6 54.2	10 53.6	9 36.5	19 30.6	26 38.9	1 09.0
28 W	22 31 15	9 23 01	16 30 45	22 27 21	15 58.1	9 30.1	14 38.2	11 45.4	7 13.5	11 03.6	9 43.8	19 32.3	26 41.1	1 10.6
29 Th	22 35 12	10 23 16	28 25 36	4♏25 58	15 59.3	11 22.8	15 52.5	12 31.8	7 32.8	11 13.7	9 51.1	19 33.9	26 43.3	1 12.2

Astro Data

	Dy Hr Mn
☿ D	2 3:07
☽ 0S	3 7:53
☽ 0N	16 10:18
♅ D	27 7:36
☽ 0S	30 14:12
☽ 0N	12 18:04
☽ 0S	26 20:04

Planet Ingress

	Dy Hr Mn
♂ ♑	4 14:58
☿ ♑	14 2:49
☉ ♒	20 14:07
♇ ♒	21 0:50
♀ ♑	23 8:50
☿ ♒	5 5:10
⚳ ♑	7 11:11
♂ ♒	13 6:05
♀ ♒	16 16:05
☉ ♓	19 4:13
☿ ♓	23 7:29

Last Aspect / ☽ Ingress (January)

Last Aspect Dy Hr Mn		☽ Ingress Dy Hr Mn
2 23:36	♇ △	♎ 3 0:47
5 11:41	♇ □	♏ 5 12:39
7 20:22	♇ ⚹	♐ 7 21:08
9 18:24	☿ ☌	♑ 10 1:33
12 2:33	♇ ☌	♒ 12 3:01
13 9:59	♅ □	♓ 14 3:29
16 4:33	♇ ⚹	♈ 16 4:48
18 8:03	♇ □	♉ 18 8:12
20 13:57	☉ △	♊ 20 13:58
22 20:40	♀ ☍	♋ 22 21:51
24 22:58	♆ △	♌ 25 7:37
26 21:19	♅ □	♍ 27 19:11
29 23:20	♆ ☍	♎ 30 8:04

Last Aspect / ☽ Ingress (February)

Last Aspect Dy Hr Mn		☽ Ingress Dy Hr Mn
1 9:03	☿ □	♏ 1 20:37
4 3:24	☿ ⚹	♐ 4 6:28
6 5:06	♆ □	♑ 6 12:09
8 7:52	♂ ☌	♒ 8 13:59
9 22:59	☉ ☌	♓ 10 13:42
12 12:31	♂ ⚹	♈ 12 13:26
14 10:21	♀ □	♉ 14 15:02
16 15:01	☉ □	♊ 16 19:39
19 3:21	☉ △	♋ 19 3:25
21 6:38	♆ △	♌ 21 13:40
23 4:18	♅ □	♍ 24 1:37
26 7:35	♆ ☍	♎ 26 14:29
27 18:22	♀ △	♏ 29 3:09

☽ Phases & Eclipses

Dy Hr Mn	
4 3:30	☾ 13♎15
11 11:57	● 20♑44
18 3:53	☽ 27♈32
25 17:54	○ 5♌15
2 23:18	☾ 13♏36
9 22:59	● 20♒41
16 15:01	☽ 27♉26
24 12:30	○ 5♍23

Astro Data

1 January 2024
Julian Day # 45291
SVP 4♓55'34"
GC 27♐10.5 ⚴ 17♏45.6
Eris 24♈09.9R ⚵ 21♍21.7
⚷ 15♈27.9 ⚶ 26♊52.3R
☽ Mean ☊ 20♈50.9

1 February 2024
Julian Day # 45322
SVP 4♓55'28"
GC 27♐10.5 ⚴ 28♏33.2
Eris 24♈11.6 ⚵ 20♍28.4R
⚷ 16♈02.9 ⚶ 21♊55.4R
☽ Mean ☊ 19♈12.5

March 2024

LONGITUDE

Day	Sid.Time	☉	0 hr ☽	Noon ☽	True ☊	☿	♀	♂	⚳	♃	♄	♅	♆	♇
1 F	22 39 08	11♓23 29	10♏28 58	16♏35 09	16♈01.1	13♓16.3	17♒06.7	13♒18.3	7♑51.8	11♉24.0	9♓58.5	19♉35.6	26♓45.5	1♒13.8
2 Sa	22 43 05	12 23 40	22 45 02	28 59 13	16 02.6	15 10.6	18 21.0	14 04.7	8 10.8	11 34.3	10 05.8	19 37.4	26 47.8	1 15.3
3 Su	22 47 01	13 23 50	5♐18 15	11♐42 41	16R 03.4	17 05.6	19 35.3	14 51.3	8 29.6	11 44.8	10 13.1	19 39.2	26 50.0	1 16.9
4 M	22 50 58	14 23 59	18 13 00	24 49 41	16 02.9	19 01.1	20 49.6	15 37.8	8 48.2	11 55.4	10 20.4	19 41.0	26 52.2	1 18.4
5 Tu	22 54 54	15 24 06	1♑33 04	8♑23 26	16 01.0	20 57.1	22 03.8	16 24.3	9 06.7	12 06.0	10 27.8	19 42.9	26 54.4	1 19.9
6 W	22 58 51	16 24 12	15 20 55	22 25 27	15 57.9	22 53.5	23 18.1	17 10.9	9 25.1	12 16.8	10 35.1	19 44.8	26 56.7	1 21.4
7 Th	23 02 47	17 24 15	29 36 52	6♒54 44	15 54.0	24 50.0	24 32.4	17 57.4	9 43.3	12 27.7	10 42.4	19 46.8	26 58.9	1 22.9
8 F	23 06 44	18 24 18	14♒18 27	21 47 12	15 49.9	26 46.5	25 46.7	18 44.0	10 01.3	12 38.7	10 49.7	19 48.8	27 01.2	1 24.3
9 Sa	23 10 41	19 24 18	29 20 01	6♓55 46	15 46.2	28 42.6	27 01.0	19 30.6	10 19.1	12 49.8	10 57.0	19 50.9	27 03.5	1 25.8
10 Su	23 14 37	20 24 16	14♓33 11	22 10 59	15 43.6	0♈38.2	28 15.3	20 17.2	10 36.8	13 00.9	11 04.2	19 53.0	27 05.7	1 27.2
11 M	23 18 34	21 24 13	29 47 51	7♈22 33	15D 42.3	2 32.9	29 29.5	21 03.8	10 54.4	13 12.2	11 11.5	19 55.1	27 08.0	1 28.6
12 Tu	23 22 30	22 24 07	14♈53 55	22 20 57	15 42.2	4 26.4	0♓43.8	21 50.5	11 11.7	13 23.6	11 18.8	19 57.3	27 10.2	1 29.9
13 W	23 26 27	23 24 00	29 42 49	6♉58 50	15 43.1	6 18.3	1 58.1	22 37.1	11 28.9	13 35.0	11 26.0	19 59.5	27 12.5	1 31.3
14 Th	23 30 23	24 23 50	14♉08 33	21 11 40	15 44.5	8 08.1	3 12.4	23 23.7	11 45.9	13 46.6	11 33.2	20 01.8	27 14.8	1 32.6
15 F	23 34 20	25 23 38	28 08 04	4♊57 47	15 45.8	9 55.4	4 26.6	24 10.4	12 02.8	13 58.2	11 40.4	20 04.1	27 17.1	1 33.9
16 Sa	23 38 16	26 23 24	11♊40 58	18 17 53	15R 46.8	11 39.8	5 40.9	24 57.0	12 19.4	14 09.9	11 47.6	20 06.4	27 19.4	1 35.2
17 Su	23 42 13	27 23 08	24 48 53	1♋14 21	15 46.9	13 20.8	6 55.1	25 43.7	12 35.9	14 21.7	11 54.8	20 08.8	27 21.6	1 36.5
18 M	23 46 10	28 22 49	7♋34 45	13 50 33	15 46.2	14 57.9	8 09.3	26 30.4	12 52.2	14 33.6	12 01.9	20 11.2	27 23.9	1 37.7
19 Tu	23 50 06	29 22 29	20 02 13	26 10 16	15 44.7	16 30.6	9 23.6	27 17.0	13 08.3	14 45.6	12 09.1	20 13.7	27 26.2	1 38.9
20 W	23 54 03	0♈22 05	2♌15 09	8♌17 20	15 42.7	17 58.4	10 37.8	28 03.7	13 24.2	14 57.6	12 16.2	20 16.2	27 28.5	1 40.1
21 Th	23 57 59	1 21 40	14 17 15	20 15 19	15 40.4	19 21.0	11 52.0	28 50.4	13 39.9	15 09.7	12 23.2	20 18.7	27 30.7	1 41.3
22 F	0 01 56	2 21 12	26 11 56	2♍07 28	15 38.2	20 37.9	13 06.2	29 37.1	13 55.4	15 21.9	12 30.3	20 21.2	27 33.0	1 42.4
23 Sa	0 05 52	3 20 43	8♍02 14	13 56 34	15 36.4	21 48.7	14 20.4	0♓23.8	14 10.8	15 34.2	12 37.3	20 23.8	27 35.3	1 43.5
24 Su	0 09 49	4 20 11	19 50 46	25 45 07	15 35.1	22 53.1	15 34.6	1 10.4	14 25.9	15 46.5	12 44.3	20 26.4	27 37.5	1 44.6
25 M	0 13 45	5 19 37	1♎39 53	7♎35 19	15D 34.5	23 50.8	16 48.8	1 57.1	14 40.8	15 58.9	12 51.3	20 29.1	27 39.8	1 45.7
26 Tu	0 17 42	6 19 01	13 31 41	19 29 15	15 34.4	24 41.6	18 03.0	2 43.8	14 55.5	16 11.4	12 58.3	20 31.8	27 42.1	1 46.7
27 W	0 21 38	7 18 23	25 28 17	1♏29 03	15 34.7	25 25.2	19 17.2	3 30.5	15 10.0	16 24.0	13 05.2	20 34.5	27 44.3	1 47.7
28 Th	0 25 35	8 17 43	7♏31 50	13 36 56	15 35.3	26 01.5	20 31.4	4 17.2	15 24.3	16 36.6	13 12.1	20 37.3	27 46.6	1 48.7
29 F	0 29 32	9 17 01	19 44 41	25 55 23	15 36.0	26 30.4	21 45.6	5 03.9	15 38.4	16 49.2	13 18.9	20 40.1	27 48.8	1 49.7
30 Sa	0 33 28	10 16 17	2♐09 25	8♐27 06	15 36.7	26 51.8	22 59.7	5 50.6	15 52.2	17 02.0	13 25.8	20 42.9	27 51.0	1 50.6
31 Su	0 37 25	11 15 32	14 48 50	21 14 56	15 37.1	27 05.8	24 13.9	6 37.3	16 05.9	17 14.8	13 32.6	20 45.7	27 53.3	1 51.5

April 2024

LONGITUDE

Day	Sid.Time	☉	0 hr ☽	Noon ☽	True ☊	☿	♀	♂	⚳	♃	♄	♅	♆	♇
1 M	0 41 21	12♈14 45	27♐45 47	4♑21 41	15♈37.3	27♈12.5	25♓28.1	7♓24.0	16♑19.3	17♉27.6	13♓39.3	20♉48.6	27♓55.5	1♒52.4
2 Tu	0 45 18	13 13 56	11♑02 56	17 49 44	15R 37.3	27R 12.0	26 42.3	8 10.7	16 32.5	17 40.6	13 46.1	20 51.5	27 57.7	1 53.3
3 W	0 49 14	14 13 06	24 42 17	1♒40 37	15 37.3	27 04.5	27 56.4	8 57.4	16 45.4	17 53.5	13 52.7	20 54.4	27 59.9	1 54.1
4 Th	0 53 11	15 12 14	8♒44 43	15 54 23	15D 37.2	26 50.5	29 10.6	9 44.1	16 58.1	18 06.6	13 59.4	20 57.4	28 02.1	1 54.9
5 F	0 57 07	16 11 19	23 09 20	0♓29 07	15 37.2	26 30.2	0♈24.7	10 30.8	17 10.6	18 19.7	14 06.0	21 00.4	28 04.3	1 55.7
6 Sa	1 01 04	17 10 23	7♓53 06	15 20 32	15 37.3	26 04.3	1 38.9	11 17.4	17 22.8	18 32.8	14 12.6	21 03.4	28 06.5	1 56.5
7 Su	1 05 01	18 09 26	22 50 34	0♈22 10	15 37.5	25 33.3	2 53.0	12 04.1	17 34.8	18 46.0	14 19.1	21 06.4	28 08.7	1 57.2
8 M	1 08 57	19 08 26	7♈54 18	15 25 51	15R 37.5	24 57.9	4 07.1	12 50.8	17 46.5	18 59.2	14 25.6	21 09.5	28 10.8	1 57.9
9 Tu	1 12 54	20 07 24	22 55 41	0♉22 46	15 37.4	24 18.8	5 21.2	13 37.4	17 58.0	19 12.5	14 32.1	21 12.5	28 13.0	1 58.6
10 W	1 16 50	21 06 20	7♉46 06	15 04 49	15 37.0	23 36.9	6 35.3	14 24.0	18 09.2	19 25.9	14 38.5	21 15.6	28 15.1	1 59.2
11 Th	1 20 47	22 05 15	22 18 11	29 25 38	15 36.4	22 53.0	7 49.4	15 10.7	18 20.1	19 39.3	14 44.8	21 18.8	28 17.3	1 59.8
12 F	1 24 43	23 04 07	6♊26 43	13♊21 13	15 35.5	22 08.0	9 03.5	15 57.3	18 30.8	19 52.7	14 51.1	21 21.9	28 19.4	2 00.4
13 Sa	1 28 40	24 02 56	20 09 01	26 50 11	15 34.7	21 22.7	10 17.6	16 43.9	18 41.2	20 06.2	14 57.4	21 25.1	28 21.5	2 01.0
14 Su	1 32 36	25 01 44	3♋24 53	9♋53 25	15 34.0	20 38.0	11 31.7	17 30.4	18 51.3	20 19.7	15 03.6	21 28.3	28 23.6	2 01.5
15 M	1 36 33	26 00 29	16 16 09	22 33 32	15D 33.6	19 54.6	12 45.7	18 17.0	19 01.2	20 33.2	15 09.8	21 31.5	28 25.7	2 02.0
16 Tu	1 40 30	26 59 12	28 46 05	4♌54 19	15 33.7	19 13.5	13 59.8	19 03.5	19 10.8	20 46.8	15 15.9	21 34.7	28 27.7	2 02.5
17 W	1 44 26	27 57 53	10♌58 49	17 00 09	15 34.3	18 35.1	15 13.8	19 50.1	19 20.1	21 00.5	15 21.9	21 38.0	28 29.8	2 02.9
18 Th	1 48 23	28 56 32	22 58 53	28 55 36	15 35.4	18 00.0	16 27.8	20 36.6	19 29.1	21 14.1	15 28.0	21 41.2	28 31.8	2 03.4
19 F	1 52 19	29 55 08	4♍50 51	10♍45 08	15 36.7	17 28.9	17 41.8	21 23.1	19 37.8	21 27.8	15 33.9	21 44.5	28 33.8	2 03.7
20 Sa	1 56 16	0♉53 42	16 39 00	22 32 53	15 38.0	17 01.9	18 55.8	22 09.5	19 46.3	21 41.5	15 39.8	21 47.8	28 35.8	2 04.1
21 Su	2 00 12	1 52 14	28 27 15	4♎22 29	15R 38.9	16 39.6	20 09.8	22 56.0	19 54.4	21 55.3	15 45.7	21 51.1	28 37.8	2 04.4
22 M	2 04 09	2 50 44	10♎18 59	16 17 03	15 39.3	16 22.0	21 23.8	23 42.4	20 02.2	22 09.1	15 51.4	21 54.5	28 39.8	2 04.7
23 Tu	2 08 05	3 49 12	22 17 01	28 19 07	15 38.8	16 09.3	22 37.8	24 28.8	20 09.8	22 22.9	15 57.2	21 57.8	28 41.7	2 05.0
24 W	2 12 02	4 47 39	4♏23 37	10♏30 42	15 37.3	16 01.6	23 51.7	25 15.2	20 17.0	22 36.7	16 02.8	22 01.2	28 43.6	2 05.3
25 Th	2 15 59	5 46 03	16 40 33	22 53 20	15 35.0	15D 58.9	25 05.7	26 01.6	20 24.0	22 50.6	16 08.5	22 04.5	28 45.6	2 05.5
26 F	2 19 55	6 44 26	29 09 10	5♐28 11	15 32.0	16 01.2	26 19.7	26 48.0	20 30.6	23 04.5	16 14.0	22 07.9	28 47.5	2 05.7
27 Sa	2 23 52	7 42 47	11♐50 29	18 16 10	15 28.6	16 08.4	27 33.6	27 34.3	20 36.9	23 18.4	16 19.5	22 11.3	28 49.3	2 05.8
28 Su	2 27 48	8 41 06	24 45 20	1♑18 05	15 25.4	16 20.4	28 47.5	28 20.6	20 42.9	23 32.4	16 25.0	22 14.7	28 51.2	2 06.0
29 M	2 31 45	9 39 24	7♑54 28	14 34 36	15 22.7	16 37.1	0♉01.5	29 06.9	20 48.5	23 46.4	16 30.3	22 18.1	28 53.0	2 06.1
30 Tu	2 35 41	10 37 41	21 18 32	28 06 20	15D 21.0	16 58.4	1 15.4	29 53.2	20 53.9	24 00.4	16 35.6	22 21.5	28 54.9	2 06.2

Astro Data

	Dy Hr Mn
♃∠♆	4 2:57
☿0N	10 16:33
☽0N	11 4:38
☉0N	20 3:06
☽0S	25 2:08
☿ R	1 22:16
☽0N	7 15:46
♀0N	7 23:06
♃☌♅	21 2:27
☽0S	21 8:40
☿ D	25 12:54

Planet Ingress

		Dy Hr Mn
☿	♈	10 4:03
♀	♓	11 21:50
☉	♈	20 3:06
♂	♓	22 23:47
♀	♈	5 4:00
☉	♉	19 14:00
♀	♉	29 11:31
♂	♈	30 15:33

Last Aspect / ☽ Ingress

Last Aspect Dy Hr Mn			☽ Ingress	Dy Hr Mn
2 7:47	♆	△	♐	2 13:56
4 15:41	♆	□	♑	4 21:15
6 19:35	♆	⚹	♒	7 0:38
8 18:56	♀	☌	♓	9 1:03
10 19:45	♆	☌	♈	11 0:19
12 11:08	♂	⚹	♉	13 0:28
14 22:29	♆	⚹	♊	15 3:16
17 4:43	♆	□	♋	17 9:40
19 18:52	☉	△	♌	19 19:33
22 6:34	♂	☍	♍	22 7:42
24 15:49	♆	☍	♎	24 20:37
26 23:09	☿	☍	♏	27 9:03
29 15:40	♆	△	♐	29 19:52

Last Aspect / ☽ Ingress

Last Aspect Dy Hr Mn			☽ Ingress	Dy Hr Mn
1 0:16	♆	□	♑	1 4:05
3 5:40	♆	⚹	♒	3 9:08
5 5:39	☿	⚹	♓	5 11:13
7 8:27	♆	☌	♈	7 11:25
9 2:39	☿	☌	♉	9 11:23
11 10:04	♆	⚹	♊	11 12:58
13 14:46	♆	□	♋	13 17:45
15 23:22	♆	△	♌	16 2:24
18 12:02	☉	△	♍	18 14:10
21 0:19	♆	☍	♎	21 3:08
22 23:24	♀	☍	♏	23 15:20
25 23:17	♆	△	♐	26 1:37
28 7:31	♆	□	♑	28 9:37
30 15:19	♂	⚹	♒	30 15:19

☽ Phases & Eclipses

Dy Hr Mn	
3 15:23	☾ 13♐32
10 9:00	● 20♓17
17 4:11	☽ 27♊04
25 7:00	○ 5♎07
25 7:13	☍ A 0.956
2 3:15	☾ 12♑52
8 18:21	● 19♈24
8 18:17:15	☌ T 04'28"
15 19:13	☽ 26♋18
23 23:49	○ 4♏18

Astro Data

1 March 2024
Julian Day # 45351
SVP 4♓55'25"
GC 27♐10.6 ⚵ 5♐50.3
Eris 24♈22.1 ⚶ 14♍13.2R
⚷ 17♈15.5 ⚴ 23♊25.8
☽ Mean ☊ 17♈40.3

1 April 2024
Julian Day # 45382
SVP 4♓55'21"
GC 27♐10.7 ⚵ 8♐33.7R
Eris 24♈40.0 ⚶ 7♍40.9R
⚷ 18♈58.6 ⚴ 0♋17.7
☽ Mean ☊ 16♈01.8

LONGITUDE — May 2024

Day	Sid.Time	☉	0 hr ☽	Noon☽	True☊	☿	♀	♂	⚳	♃	♄	♅	♆	♇
1 W	2 39 38	11♉35 56	4♒58 01	11♒53 37	15♈20.5	17♈24.1	2♉29.3	0♈39.4	20♑58.9	24♉14.4	16♓40.9	22♉25.0	28♓56.7	2♒06.2
2 Th	2 43 34	12 34 09	18 53 06	25 56 21	15 21.0	17 54.0	3 43.2	1 25.6	21 03.5	24 28.4	16 46.1	22 28.4	28 58.4	2R 06.2
3 F	2 47 31	13 32 21	3♓03 16	10♓13 36	15 22.2	18 28.1	4 57.2	2 11.8	21 07.9	24 42.4	16 51.2	22 31.9	29 00.2	2 06.2
4 Sa	2 51 28	14 30 31	17 27 02	24 43 12	15 23.7	19 06.1	6 11.1	2 58.0	21 11.9	24 56.5	16 56.2	22 35.3	29 01.9	2 06.2
5 Su	2 55 24	15 28 40	2♈01 35	9♈21 36	15R 24.6	19 47.8	7 25.0	3 44.1	21 15.5	25 10.6	17 01.2	22 38.8	29 03.6	2 06.1
6 M	2 59 21	16 26 48	16 42 34	24 03 44	15 24.5	20 33.2	8 38.9	4 30.2	21 18.8	25 24.7	17 06.1	22 42.2	29 05.3	2 06.0
7 Tu	3 03 17	17 24 54	1♉24 17	8♉43 22	15 22.8	21 22.1	9 52.7	5 16.3	21 21.8	25 38.8	17 10.9	22 45.7	29 07.0	2 05.9
8 W	3 07 14	18 22 58	16 00 09	23 13 47	15 19.6	22 14.3	11 06.6	6 02.3	21 24.4	25 52.9	17 15.7	22 49.2	29 08.7	2 05.8
9 Th	3 11 10	19 21 01	0♊23 32	7♊28 41	15 15.0	23 09.7	12 20.5	6 48.3	21 26.6	26 07.0	17 20.4	22 52.7	29 10.3	2 05.6
10 F	3 15 07	20 19 02	14 28 41	21 23 05	15 09.6	24 08.3	13 34.4	7 34.3	21 28.5	26 21.2	17 25.0	22 56.2	29 11.9	2 05.4
11 Sa	3 19 03	21 17 02	28 11 34	4♋53 58	15 04.1	25 09.9	14 48.2	8 20.2	21 30.0	26 35.3	17 29.5	22 59.7	29 13.5	2 05.2
12 Su	3 23 00	22 14 59	11♋30 14	18 00 30	14 59.1	26 14.3	16 02.1	9 06.1	21 31.2	26 49.5	17 34.0	23 03.1	29 15.0	2 04.9
13 M	3 26 57	23 12 55	24 24 57	0♌43 55	14 55.3	27 21.6	17 15.9	9 52.0	21 32.0	27 03.6	17 38.4	23 06.6	29 16.5	2 04.6
14 Tu	3 30 53	24 10 49	6♌57 49	13 07 09	14D 53.0	28 31.6	18 29.8	10 37.8	21R 32.5	27 17.8	17 42.7	23 10.1	29 18.0	2 04.3
15 W	3 34 50	25 08 41	19 12 25	25 14 15	14 52.3	29 44.3	19 43.6	11 23.6	21 32.6	27 31.9	17 46.9	23 13.6	29 19.5	2 04.0
16 Th	3 38 46	26 06 32	1♍13 15	7♍10 03	14 52.9	0♉59.5	20 57.4	12 09.3	21 32.3	27 46.1	17 51.1	23 17.1	29 21.0	2 03.6
17 F	3 42 43	27 04 21	13 05 17	18 59 37	14 54.3	2 17.3	22 11.2	12 55.0	21 31.6	28 00.3	17 55.1	23 20.6	29 22.4	2 03.2
18 Sa	3 46 39	28 02 08	24 53 40	0♎48 02	14 55.8	3 37.6	23 25.0	13 40.6	21 30.6	28 14.4	17 59.1	23 24.0	29 23.8	2 02.8
19 Su	3 50 36	28 59 53	6♎43 17	12 40 00	14R 56.7	5 00.3	24 38.8	14 26.3	21 29.3	28 28.6	18 03.0	23 27.5	29 25.2	2 02.3
20 M	3 54 32	29 57 37	18 38 39	24 39 43	14 56.2	6 25.4	25 52.6	15 11.8	21 27.5	28 42.7	18 06.9	23 31.0	29 26.5	2 01.9
21 Tu	3 58 29	0♊55 20	0♏43 35	6♏50 37	14 53.8	7 52.9	27 06.3	15 57.4	21 25.4	28 56.9	18 10.6	23 34.4	29 27.8	2 01.4
22 W	4 02 26	1 53 01	13 01 04	19 15 11	14 49.4	9 22.8	28 20.1	16 42.8	21 22.9	29 11.0	18 14.3	23 37.9	29 29.1	2 00.8
23 Th	4 06 22	2 50 40	25 33 06	1♐54 53	14 43.1	10 55.0	29 33.9	17 28.3	21 20.1	29 25.1	18 17.9	23 41.4	29 30.4	2 00.3
24 F	4 10 19	3 48 19	8♐20 35	14 50 09	14 35.3	12 29.6	0♊47.6	18 13.7	21 16.9	29 39.3	18 21.4	23 44.8	29 31.6	1 59.7
25 Sa	4 14 15	4 45 56	21 23 28	28 00 23	14 26.8	14 06.4	2 01.4	18 59.1	21 13.3	29 53.4	18 24.8	23 48.2	29 32.8	1 59.1
26 Su	4 18 12	5 43 32	4♑40 44	11♑24 18	14 18.6	15 45.6	3 15.1	19 44.4	21 09.4	0♊07.5	18 28.1	23 51.7	29 34.0	1 58.5
27 M	4 22 08	6 41 08	18 10 52	25 00 11	14 11.4	17 27.2	4 28.9	20 29.7	21 05.1	0 21.6	18 31.3	23 55.1	29 35.1	1 57.9
28 Tu	4 26 05	7 38 42	1♒52 03	8♒46 14	14 06.1	19 11.0	5 42.7	21 14.9	21 00.5	0 35.7	18 34.5	23 58.5	29 36.3	1 57.2
29 W	4 30 01	8 36 15	15 42 33	22 40 50	14 02.9	20 57.1	6 56.4	22 00.1	20 55.4	0 49.8	18 37.6	24 01.9	29 37.4	1 56.5
30 Th	4 33 58	9 33 47	29 40 55	6♓42 41	14D 01.7	22 45.5	8 10.1	22 45.2	20 50.1	1 03.8	18 40.5	24 05.3	29 38.4	1 55.8
31 F	4 37 55	10 31 19	13♓45 59	20 50 41	14 02.0	24 36.2	9 23.9	23 30.3	20 44.3	1 17.9	18 43.4	24 08.7	29 39.4	1 55.0

LONGITUDE — June 2024

Day	Sid.Time	☉	0 hr ☽	Noon☽	True☊	☿	♀	♂	⚳	♃	♄	♅	♆	♇
1 Sa	4 41 51	11♊28 50	27♓56 37	5♈03 38	14♈02.7	26♉29.1	10♊37.6	24♈15.4	20♑38.2	1♊31.9	18♓46.2	24♉12.1	29♓40.4	1♒54.3
2 Su	4 45 48	12 26 20	12♈11 29	19 19 54	14R 02.9	28 24.3	11 51.4	25 00.3	20R 31.8	1 45.9	18 48.9	24 15.4	29 41.4	1R 53.5
3 M	4 49 44	13 23 49	26 28 33	3♉37 02	14 01.3	0♊21.6	13 05.1	25 45.3	20 25.0	1 59.9	18 51.5	24 18.8	29 42.4	1 52.7
4 Tu	4 53 41	14 21 18	10♉44 54	17 51 39	13 57.5	2 21.1	14 18.9	26 30.2	20 17.9	2 13.9	18 54.0	24 22.1	29 43.3	1 51.8
5 W	4 57 37	15 18 46	24 56 42	1♊59 30	13 51.1	4 22.5	15 32.6	27 15.0	20 10.5	2 27.9	18 56.5	24 25.4	29 44.2	1 51.0
6 Th	5 01 34	16 16 13	8♊59 28	15 56 02	13 42.4	6 25.9	16 46.4	27 59.8	20 02.7	2 41.8	18 58.8	24 28.7	29 45.0	1 50.1
7 F	5 05 31	17 13 39	22 48 41	29 36 59	13 32.3	8 31.1	18 00.1	28 44.5	19 54.6	2 55.7	19 01.0	24 32.0	29 45.8	1 49.2
8 Sa	5 09 27	18 11 04	6♋20 32	12♋59 06	13 21.7	10 37.9	19 13.9	29 29.2	19 46.1	3 09.6	19 03.2	24 35.3	29 46.6	1 48.3
9 Su	5 13 24	19 08 29	19 32 30	26 00 41	13 11.8	12 46.1	20 27.6	0♉13.8	19 37.4	3 23.5	19 05.2	24 38.6	29 47.4	1 47.3
10 M	5 17 20	20 05 52	2♌23 44	8♌41 49	13 03.4	14 55.6	21 41.3	0 58.3	19 28.4	3 37.3	19 07.2	24 41.8	29 48.1	1 46.4
11 Tu	5 21 17	21 03 14	14 55 12	21 04 16	12 57.2	17 06.1	22 55.1	1 42.8	19 19.0	3 51.1	19 09.0	24 45.0	29 48.8	1 45.4
12 W	5 25 13	22 00 36	27 09 28	3♍11 17	12 53.4	19 17.4	24 08.8	2 27.2	19 09.4	4 04.9	19 10.8	24 48.2	29 49.5	1 44.4
13 Th	5 29 10	22 57 56	9♍10 19	15 07 09	12D 51.7	21 29.1	25 22.5	3 11.6	18 59.5	4 18.6	19 12.5	24 51.4	29 50.1	1 43.4
14 F	5 33 06	23 55 15	21 02 28	26 56 55	12 51.5	23 41.1	26 36.3	3 55.9	18 49.3	4 32.3	19 14.0	24 54.5	29 50.7	1 42.3
15 Sa	5 37 03	24 52 34	2♎51 11	8♎45 56	12R 51.8	25 53.1	27 50.0	4 40.1	18 38.9	4 46.0	19 15.5	24 57.7	29 51.2	1 41.3
16 Su	5 41 00	25 49 51	14 41 51	20 39 35	12 51.6	28 04.7	29 03.7	5 24.3	18 28.2	4 59.7	19 16.9	25 00.8	29 51.8	1 40.2
17 M	5 44 56	26 47 08	26 39 45	2♏42 57	12 50.0	0♋15.7	0♋17.4	6 08.4	18 17.3	5 13.3	19 18.1	25 03.9	29 52.3	1 39.1
18 Tu	5 48 53	27 44 24	8♏49 41	15 00 26	12 46.2	2 25.9	1 31.1	6 52.5	18 06.2	5 26.8	19 19.3	25 07.0	29 52.7	1 38.0
19 W	5 52 49	28 41 39	21 15 35	27 35 27	12 39.8	4 35.1	2 44.8	7 36.5	17 54.8	5 40.4	19 20.4	25 10.0	29 53.2	1 36.9
20 Th	5 56 46	29 38 54	4♐00 14	10♐30 03	12 31.0	6 42.9	3 58.5	8 20.4	17 43.2	5 53.9	19 21.4	25 13.0	29 53.6	1 35.7
21 F	6 00 42	0♋36 08	17 04 54	23 44 40	12 20.3	8 49.4	5 12.2	9 04.3	17 31.4	6 07.3	19 22.2	25 16.0	29 54.0	1 34.6
22 Sa	6 04 39	1 33 22	0♑29 08	7♑17 59	12 08.6	10 54.2	6 25.9	9 48.1	17 19.5	6 20.8	19 23.0	25 19.0	29 54.3	1 33.4
23 Su	6 08 35	2 30 35	14 10 48	21 07 08	11 57.1	12 57.3	7 39.7	10 31.8	17 07.3	6 34.1	19 23.7	25 22.0	29 54.6	1 32.2
24 M	6 12 32	3 27 48	28 06 26	5♒08 10	11 47.0	14 58.6	8 53.4	11 15.5	16 55.0	6 47.5	19 24.3	25 24.9	29 54.9	1 31.0
25 Tu	6 16 29	4 25 01	12♒11 46	19 16 43	11 39.1	16 58.0	10 07.1	11 59.1	16 42.6	7 00.8	19 24.8	25 27.8	29 55.1	1 29.8
26 W	6 20 25	5 22 14	26 22 30	3♓28 42	11 34.0	18 55.4	11 20.8	12 42.6	16 30.0	7 14.0	19 25.1	25 30.7	29 55.3	1 28.6
27 Th	6 24 22	6 19 27	10♓34 55	17 40 50	11 31.4	20 50.8	12 34.5	13 26.1	16 17.3	7 27.2	19 25.4	25 33.5	29 55.5	1 27.3
28 F	6 28 18	7 16 39	24 46 14	1♈50 55	11 30.6	22 44.1	13 48.2	14 09.5	16 04.4	7 40.4	19 25.6	25 36.3	29 55.7	1 26.1
29 Sa	6 32 15	8 13 52	8♈54 43	15 57 33	11 30.6	24 35.3	15 01.9	14 52.8	15 51.5	7 53.5	19R 25.7	25 39.1	29 55.8	1 24.8
30 Su	6 36 11	9 11 05	22 59 18	29 59 53	11 30.0	26 24.5	16 15.7	15 36.1	15 38.5	8 06.5	19 25.7	25 41.9	29 55.9	1 23.5

Astro Data

	Dy Hr Mn
♇ R	2 17:47
♂0N	4 10:17
☽0N	5 1:03
♄∠♇	6 11:50
⚳ R	15 5:34
☽0S	18 15:35
♃⚹♆	23 21:44
☽0N	1 7:30
♃△♇	3 0:13
☽0S	14 22:38
☽0N	28 12:09
♄ R	29 19:06

Planet Ingress

		Dy Hr Mn
☿	♉	15 17:05
☉	♊	20 12:59
♀	♊	23 20:30
♃	♊	25 23:15
☿	♊	3 7:37
♂	♉	9 4:35
♀	♋	17 6:20
☿	♋	17 9:07
☉	♋	20 20:51

Last Aspect / ☽ Ingress

Last Aspect Dy Hr Mn			☽ Ingress	Dy Hr Mn
2 9:28	♃	□	♓	2 18:52
4 19:06	♆	☌	♈	4 20:41
6 5:57	☿	☌	♉	6 21:42
8 21:55	♆	⚹	♊	8 23:20
11 1:49	♆	□	♋	11 3:13
13 9:13	♆	△	♌	13 10:36
15 16:41	♃	□	♍	15 21:33
18 9:09	♆	☍	♎	18 10:22
19 15:48	♂	☍	♏	20 22:34
23 7:28	♆	△	♐	23 8:24
25 14:47	♆	□	♑	25 15:36
27 20:02	♆	⚹	♒	27 20:45
29 14:20	♅	□	♓	30 0:33

Last Aspect / ☽ Ingress

Last Aspect Dy Hr Mn			☽ Ingress	Dy Hr Mn
1 2:55	♆	☌	♈	1 3:28
2 22:03	♂	☌	♉	3 5:55
5 8:09	♆	⚹	♊	5 8:36
7 12:16	♆	□	♋	7 12:41
9 19:05	♆	△	♌	9 19:29
11 19:16	♅	□	♍	12 5:39
14 17:53	♆	☍	♎	14 18:12
17 6:05	☿	△	♏	17 6:38
19 16:19	♆	△	♐	19 16:32
21 22:58	♆	□	♑	21 23:08
24 3:05	♆	⚹	♒	24 3:14
25 22:30	♅	□	♓	26 6:07
28 8:44	♆	☌	♈	28 8:52
30 4:56	☿	□	♉	30 12:00

☽ Phases & Eclipses

Dy Hr Mn		
1 11:27	☾	11♒35
8 3:22	●	18♉02
15 11:48	☽	25♌08
23 13:53	○	2♐55
30 17:13	☾	9♓46
6 12:38	●	16♊18
14 5:18	☽	23♍39
22 1:08	○	1♑07
28 21:53	☾	7♈40

Astro Data

1 May 2024
Julian Day # 45412
SVP 4♓55'17"
GC 27♐10.7 ⚴ 4♐18.0R
Eris 24♈59.6 ⚵ 6♍33.9
⚷ 20♈43.6 ⚶ 10♋07.6
☽ Mean ☊ 14♈26.5

1 June 2024
Julian Day # 45443
SVP 4♓55'12"
GC 27♐10.8 ⚴ 25♏21.5R
Eris 25♈17.1 ⚵ 10♍40.3
⚷ 22♈17.0 ⚶ 22♋13.0
☽ Mean ☊ 12♈48.0

July 2024

LONGITUDE

Day	Sid.Time	☉	0 hr ☽	Noon ☽	True ☊	☿	♀	♂	⚳	♃	♄	♅	♆	♇
1 M	6 40 08	10♋08 18	6♉59 12	13♉57 06	11♈27.6	28♋11.5	17♋29.4	16♉19.3	15♑25.4	8♊19.5	19♓25.5	25♉44.6	29♓55.9	1♒22.2
2 Tu	6 44 04	11 05 32	20 53 26	27 47 59	11R 22.6	29 56.4	18 43.1	17 02.4	15R 12.2	8 32.5	19R 25.3	25 47.3	29R 55.9	1R 20.9
3 W	6 48 01	12 02 45	4♊40 32	11♊30 48	11 14.8	1♌39.2	19 56.8	17 45.5	14 59.0	8 45.3	19 25.0	25 49.9	29 55.9	1 19.6
4 Th	6 51 58	12 59 59	18 18 30	25 03 19	11 04.5	3 19.8	21 10.6	18 28.4	14 45.8	8 58.2	19 24.6	25 52.6	29 55.8	1 18.3
5 F	6 55 54	13 57 13	1♋44 56	8♋23 05	10 52.4	4 58.3	22 24.3	19 11.3	14 32.5	9 11.0	19 24.1	25 55.2	29 55.8	1 16.9
6 Sa	6 59 51	14 54 26	14 57 31	21 28 00	10 39.8	6 34.7	23 38.1	19 54.2	14 19.3	9 23.7	19 23.4	25 57.7	29 55.6	1 15.6
7 Su	7 03 47	15 51 40	27 54 25	4♌16 41	10 27.7	8 08.9	24 51.8	20 36.9	14 06.1	9 36.4	19 22.7	26 00.3	29 55.5	1 14.2
8 M	7 07 44	16 48 54	10♌34 48	16 48 52	10 17.3	9 41.0	26 05.5	21 19.5	13 52.9	9 49.0	19 21.9	26 02.8	29 55.3	1 12.9
9 Tu	7 11 40	17 46 07	22 59 03	29 05 37	10 09.3	11 10.9	27 19.3	22 02.1	13 39.7	10 01.5	19 21.0	26 05.2	29 55.1	1 11.5
10 W	7 15 37	18 43 21	5♍08 52	11♍09 13	10 03.9	12 38.6	28 33.0	22 44.6	13 26.6	10 14.0	19 20.0	26 07.7	29 54.9	1 10.1
11 Th	7 19 34	19 40 34	17 07 09	23 03 10	10 01.0	14 04.1	29 46.8	23 27.0	13 13.6	10 26.4	19 18.9	26 10.1	29 54.6	1 08.8
12 F	7 23 30	20 37 48	28 57 52	4♎51 51	10D 00.0	15 27.4	1♌00.5	24 09.3	13 00.6	10 38.7	19 17.7	26 12.4	29 54.3	1 07.4
13 Sa	7 27 27	21 35 01	10♎45 46	16 40 17	10R 00.0	16 48.3	2 14.2	24 51.6	12 47.8	10 51.0	19 16.4	26 14.7	29 53.9	1 06.0
14 Su	7 31 23	22 32 15	22 36 06	28 33 53	9 59.9	18 07.0	3 27.9	25 33.7	12 35.0	11 03.2	19 15.0	26 17.0	29 53.5	1 04.6
15 M	7 35 20	23 29 28	4♏34 20	10♏38 05	9 58.8	19 23.2	4 41.7	26 15.8	12 22.4	11 15.3	19 13.5	26 19.3	29 53.1	1 03.2
16 Tu	7 39 16	24 26 42	16 45 47	22 58 01	9 55.7	20 37.1	5 55.4	26 57.8	12 10.0	11 27.4	19 11.9	26 21.5	29 52.7	1 01.8
17 W	7 43 13	25 23 56	29 15 16	5♐38 00	9 50.3	21 48.5	7 09.1	27 39.7	11 57.7	11 39.3	19 10.2	26 23.6	29 52.2	1 00.3
18 Th	7 47 09	26 21 10	12♐06 32	18 41 06	9 42.5	22 57.3	8 22.8	28 21.5	11 45.5	11 51.3	19 08.4	26 25.8	29 51.7	0 58.9
19 F	7 51 06	27 18 25	25 21 47	2♑08 33	9 32.8	24 03.5	9 36.6	29 03.2	11 33.6	12 03.1	19 06.6	26 27.9	29 51.2	0 57.5
20 Sa	7 55 03	28 15 39	9♑01 11	15 59 21	9 22.1	25 06.9	10 50.3	29 44.9	11 21.8	12 14.9	19 04.6	26 29.9	29 50.7	0 56.1
21 Su	7 58 59	29 12 54	23 02 33	0♒10 12	9 11.5	26 07.5	12 04.0	0♊26.5	11 10.2	12 26.5	19 02.6	26 31.9	29 50.1	0 54.7
22 M	8 02 56	0♌10 10	7♒21 32	14 35 47	9 02.1	27 05.2	13 17.7	1 07.9	10 58.8	12 38.1	19 00.4	26 33.9	29 49.5	0 53.3
23 Tu	8 06 52	1 07 26	21 52 05	29 09 36	8 54.9	27 59.9	14 31.4	1 49.3	10 47.7	12 49.6	18 58.2	26 35.8	29 48.8	0 51.9
24 W	8 10 49	2 04 43	6♓27 30	13♓45 02	8 50.3	28 51.4	15 45.1	2 30.6	10 36.7	13 01.1	18 55.9	26 37.7	29 48.1	0 50.4
25 Th	8 14 45	3 02 01	21 01 29	28 16 18	8D 48.1	29 39.6	16 58.8	3 11.8	10 26.0	13 12.4	18 53.5	26 39.6	29 47.4	0 49.0
26 F	8 18 42	3 59 19	5♈28 58	12♈39 08	8 47.8	0♍24.4	18 12.5	3 52.9	10 15.6	13 23.7	18 51.0	26 41.4	29 46.7	0 47.6
27 Sa	8 22 38	4 56 39	19 46 31	26 50 56	8R 48.2	1 05.6	19 26.2	4 34.0	10 05.4	13 34.9	18 48.4	26 43.1	29 45.9	0 46.2
28 Su	8 26 35	5 54 00	3♉52 16	10♉50 28	8 48.3	1 43.0	20 39.9	5 14.9	9 55.5	13 46.0	18 45.8	26 44.8	29 45.1	0 44.8
29 M	8 30 32	6 51 21	17 45 31	24 37 27	8 47.0	2 16.5	21 53.6	5 55.7	9 45.8	13 57.0	18 43.1	26 46.5	29 44.3	0 43.3
30 Tu	8 34 28	7 48 44	1♊26 17	8♊12 02	8 43.4	2 45.9	23 07.3	6 36.5	9 36.4	14 07.9	18 40.2	26 48.2	29 43.5	0 41.9
31 W	8 38 25	8 46 08	14 54 44	21 34 22	8 37.5	3 11.0	24 21.0	7 17.1	9 27.4	14 18.7	18 37.3	26 49.7	29 42.6	0 40.5

August 2024

LONGITUDE

Day	Sid.Time	☉	0 hr ☽	Noon ☽	True ☊	☿	♀	♂	⚳	♃	♄	♅	♆	♇
1 Th	8 42 21	9♌43 33	28♊10 56	4♋44 25	8♈29.4	3♍31.6	25♌34.7	7♊57.7	9♑18.6	14♊29.4	18♓34.4	26♉51.3	29♓41.7	0♒39.1
2 F	8 46 18	10 40 59	11♋14 46	17 41 56	8R 19.9	3 47.6	26 48.4	8 38.1	9R 10.1	14 40.0	18R 31.3	26 52.8	29R 40.8	0R 37.7
3 Sa	8 50 14	11 38 26	24 05 54	0♌26 38	8 09.7	3 58.8	28 02.1	9 18.4	9 01.9	14 50.5	18 28.2	26 54.2	29 39.8	0 36.4
4 Su	8 54 11	12 35 54	6♌44 07	12 58 22	8 00.0	4R 05.0	29 15.8	9 58.7	8 54.1	15 01.0	18 25.0	26 55.6	29 38.8	0 35.0
5 M	8 58 07	13 33 23	19 09 28	25 17 29	7 51.7	4 06.1	0♍29.5	10 38.8	8 46.6	15 11.3	18 21.7	26 57.0	29 37.8	0 33.6
6 Tu	9 02 04	14 30 53	1♍22 36	7♍24 59	7 45.4	4 01.9	1 43.2	11 18.8	8 39.4	15 21.5	18 18.4	26 58.3	29 36.8	0 32.2
7 W	9 06 01	15 28 23	13 24 53	19 22 38	7 41.3	3 52.4	2 56.9	11 58.7	8 32.5	15 31.6	18 14.9	26 59.6	29 35.7	0 30.8
8 Th	9 09 57	16 25 55	25 18 35	1♎13 08	7D 39.4	3 37.5	4 10.6	12 38.5	8 26.0	15 41.6	18 11.4	27 00.8	29 34.7	0 29.5
9 F	9 13 54	17 23 27	7♎06 45	12 59 57	7 39.3	3 17.3	5 24.3	13 18.2	8 19.8	15 51.5	18 07.9	27 02.0	29 33.6	0 28.1
10 Sa	9 17 50	18 21 01	18 53 17	24 47 20	7 40.3	2 51.9	6 37.9	13 57.8	8 14.0	16 01.2	18 04.3	27 03.1	29 32.4	0 26.8
11 Su	9 21 47	19 18 35	0♏42 42	6♏40 02	7 41.6	2 21.5	7 51.6	14 37.3	8 08.6	16 10.9	18 00.6	27 04.2	29 31.3	0 25.5
12 M	9 25 43	20 16 10	12 39 59	18 43 12	7R 42.3	1 46.3	9 05.2	15 16.6	8 03.4	16 20.4	17 56.9	27 05.2	29 30.1	0 24.1
13 Tu	9 29 40	21 13 46	24 50 20	1♐02 01	7 41.7	1 06.8	10 18.9	15 55.9	7 58.7	16 29.9	17 53.1	27 06.2	29 28.9	0 22.8
14 W	9 33 36	22 11 23	7♐18 49	13 41 17	7 39.5	0 23.4	11 32.5	16 35.0	7 54.3	16 39.2	17 49.2	27 07.1	29 27.7	0 21.5
15 Th	9 37 33	23 09 01	20 09 51	26 44 55	7 35.5	29♌36.8	12 46.1	17 14.0	7 50.2	16 48.4	17 45.3	27 08.0	29 26.4	0 20.2
16 F	9 41 30	24 06 40	3♑26 43	10♑15 21	7 30.0	28 47.7	13 59.7	17 52.9	7 46.5	16 57.5	17 41.3	27 08.8	29 25.2	0 19.0
17 Sa	9 45 26	25 04 20	17 10 47	24 12 48	7 23.7	27 57.0	15 13.3	18 31.7	7 43.2	17 06.4	17 37.3	27 09.6	29 23.9	0 17.7
18 Su	9 49 23	26 02 01	1♒21 02	8♒34 54	7 17.2	27 05.5	16 26.9	19 10.4	7 40.2	17 15.2	17 33.3	27 10.3	29 22.6	0 16.5
19 M	9 53 19	26 59 44	15 53 43	23 16 35	7 11.5	26 14.3	17 40.5	19 48.9	7 37.6	17 23.9	17 29.1	27 11.0	29 21.3	0 15.2
20 Tu	9 57 16	27 57 27	0♓42 33	8♓10 35	7 07.3	25 24.3	18 54.1	20 27.3	7 35.4	17 32.5	17 25.0	27 11.7	29 19.9	0 14.0
21 W	10 01 12	28 55 12	15 39 35	23 08 30	7D 04.8	24 36.7	20 07.6	21 05.6	7 33.5	17 41.0	17 20.8	27 12.3	29 18.6	0 12.8
22 Th	10 05 09	29 52 59	0♈36 19	8♈02 06	7 04.1	23 52.5	21 21.2	21 43.8	7 31.9	17 49.3	17 16.5	27 12.8	29 17.2	0 11.6
23 F	10 09 05	0♍50 47	15 25 03	22 44 29	7 04.8	23 12.5	22 34.7	22 21.9	7 30.7	17 57.5	17 12.3	27 13.3	29 15.8	0 10.4
24 Sa	10 13 02	1 48 37	29 59 52	7♉10 46	7 06.2	22 37.8	23 48.2	22 59.8	7 29.9	18 05.5	17 07.9	27 13.7	29 14.4	0 09.2
25 Su	10 16 59	2 46 29	14♉16 56	21 18 12	7R 07.4	22 09.0	25 01.8	23 37.6	7D 29.4	18 13.4	17 03.6	27 14.1	29 12.9	0 08.1
26 M	10 20 55	3 44 22	28 14 30	5♊05 53	7 07.9	21 47.0	26 15.3	24 15.3	7 29.3	18 21.2	16 59.2	27 14.4	29 11.5	0 07.0
27 Tu	10 24 52	4 42 18	11♊52 26	18 34 18	7 07.0	21 32.2	27 28.8	24 52.9	7 29.6	18 28.9	16 54.8	27 14.7	29 10.0	0 05.8
28 W	10 28 48	5 40 15	25 11 40	1♋44 45	7 04.8	21D 25.1	28 42.3	25 30.3	7 30.2	18 36.4	16 50.3	27 15.0	29 08.6	0 04.7
29 Th	10 32 45	6 38 14	8♋13 46	14 38 56	7 01.2	21 26.1	29 55.8	26 07.6	7 31.1	18 43.7	16 45.9	27 15.2	29 07.1	0 03.7
30 F	10 36 41	7 36 15	21 00 28	27 18 35	6 56.7	21 35.3	1♎09.3	26 44.7	7 32.4	18 50.9	16 41.4	27 15.3	29 05.6	0 02.6
31 Sa	10 40 38	8 34 18	3♌33 31	9♌45 25	6 51.9	21 52.8	2 22.7	27 21.7	7 34.1	18 58.0	16 36.9	27 15.4	29 04.0	0 01.5

Astro Data	Dy Hr Mn	Planet Ingress	Dy Hr Mn
♆R	2 10:41	☿ ♌	2 12:50
☽0S	12 5:33	♀ ♌	11 16:19
☽0N	25 17:21	♂ ♊	20 20:43
		☉ ♌	22 7:44
☿R	5 4:55	☿ ♍	25 22:42
♃⚼♇	7 10:28		
☽0S	8 12:12	♀ ♍	5 2:23
♃□♄	19 21:46	☿ ♌R	15 0:15
☽0N	22 1:00	☉ ♍	22 14:55
⚳D	26 7:36	♀ ♎	29 13:23
☿D	28 21:15		
♀0S	31 12:29		

Last Aspect Dy Hr Mn		☽ Ingress Dy Hr Mn	
2 15:43	♆ ⚹	♊	2 15:50
4 20:44	♆ □	♋	4 20:51
7 3:47	♆ △	♌	7 3:56
9 6:04	♅ □	♍	9 13:47
12 1:55	♆ ☍	♎	12 2:06
13 22:49	☉ □	♏	14 14:53
17 1:10	♆ △	♐	17 1:25
19 7:58	♆ □	♑	19 8:14
21 11:26	♆ ⚹	♒	21 11:43
23 9:58	☿ ☍	♓	23 13:23
25 14:31	♆ ☌	♈	25 14:52
26 22:14	♀ △	♉	27 17:22
29 20:59	♆ ⚹	♊	29 21:28

Last Aspect Dy Hr Mn		☽ Ingress Dy Hr Mn	
1 2:46	♆ □	♋	1 3:19
3 10:31	♆ △	♌	3 11:09
5 15:16	♅ □	♍	5 21:17
8 8:40	♆ ☍	♎	8 9:31
9 21:45	☉ ⚹	♏	10 22:34
13 9:01	♆ △	♐	13 10:01
15 16:52	☿ △	♑	15 17:51
17 20:43	♆ ⚹	♒	17 21:45
19 18:26	☉ ☍	♓	19 22:51
21 21:54	♆ ☌	♈	21 23:02
23 12:44	☿ △	♉	24 0:00
26 1:40	♆ ⚹	♊	26 3:04
28 7:14	♆ □	♋	28 8:47
30 15:24	♆ △	♌	30 17:09

☽ Phases & Eclipses Dy Hr Mn	
5 22:57	● 14♋23
13 22:49	☽ 22♎01
21 10:17	○ 29♑09
28 2:51	☾ 5♉32
4 11:13	● 12♌34
12 15:19	☽ 20♏24
19 18:26	○ 27♒15
26 9:26	☾ 3♊38

Astro Data

1 July 2024
Julian Day # 45473
SVP 4♓55'06"
GC 27♐10.9 ⚴ 20♏03.1R
Eris 25♈27.5 ⚵ 17♍54.6
⚷ 23♈15.7 ⚶ 5♌03.2
☽ Mean ☊ 11♈12.7

1 August 2024
Julian Day # 45504
SVP 4♓55'00"
GC 27♐11.0 ⚴ 21♏27.1
Eris 25♈29.0R ⚵ 27♍18.6
⚷ 23♈31.2R ⚶ 19♌03.7
☽ Mean ☊ 9♈34.2

LONGITUDE — September 2024

Day	Sid.Time	☉	0 hr ☽	Noon ☽	True ☊	☿	♀	♂	⚳	♃	♄	♅	♆	♇
1 Su	10 44 34	9♍32 22	15♌54 31	22♌01 00	6♈47.3	22♌18.6	3♎36.2	27♊58.6	7♑36.1	19♊04.9	16♓32.3	27♉15.4	29♓02.5	0♒00.5
2 M	10 48 31	10 30 28	28 05 03	4♍06 52	6R43.4	22 52.7	4 49.7	28 35.3	7 38.4	19 11.7	16R27.8	27R15.4	29R01.0	29♑59.5
3 Tu	10 52 28	11 28 36	10♍06 39	16 04 38	6 40.6	23 34.9	6 03.1	29 11.8	7 41.1	19 18.3	16 23.2	27 15.3	28 59.4	29R58.5
4 W	10 56 24	12 26 45	22 01 03	27 56 10	6D39.1	24 24.9	7 16.5	29 48.2	7 44.1	19 24.7	16 18.6	27 15.2	28 57.8	29 57.5
5 Th	11 00 21	13 24 56	3♎50 17	9♎43 41	6 38.9	25 22.3	8 29.9	0♋24.5	7 47.4	19 31.0	16 14.0	27 15.0	28 56.3	29 56.6
6 F	11 04 17	14 23 09	15 36 45	21 29 51	6 39.6	26 26.8	9 43.4	1 00.6	7 51.1	19 37.1	16 09.4	27 14.8	28 54.7	29 55.7
7 Sa	11 08 14	15 21 23	27 23 24	3♏17 51	6 41.0	27 38.0	10 56.7	1 36.5	7 55.2	19 43.1	16 04.8	27 14.5	28 53.1	29 54.8
8 Su	11 12 10	16 19 39	9♏13 41	15 11 25	6 42.6	28 55.3	12 10.1	2 12.3	7 59.5	19 48.9	16 00.2	27 14.2	28 51.5	29 53.9
9 M	11 16 07	17 17 57	21 11 34	27 14 43	6 44.0	0♍18.3	13 23.5	2 48.0	8 04.2	19 54.5	15 55.6	27 13.8	28 49.8	29 53.0
10 Tu	11 20 03	18 16 16	3♐21 23	9♐32 11	6R45.0	1 46.4	14 36.8	3 23.4	8 09.2	20 00.0	15 51.0	27 13.4	28 48.2	29 52.2
11 W	11 24 00	19 14 36	15 47 38	22 08 19	6 45.2	3 19.0	15 50.2	3 58.7	8 14.5	20 05.3	15 46.4	27 13.0	28 46.6	29 51.3
12 Th	11 27 57	20 12 58	28 34 41	5♑07 13	6 44.6	4 55.6	17 03.5	4 33.9	8 20.2	20 10.5	15 41.9	27 12.4	28 45.0	29 50.5
13 F	11 31 53	21 11 22	11♑46 16	18 32 06	6 43.3	6 35.6	18 16.8	5 08.8	8 26.1	20 15.5	15 37.3	27 11.9	28 43.3	29 49.8
14 Sa	11 35 50	22 09 47	25 24 53	2♒24 37	6 41.7	8 18.5	19 30.0	5 43.6	8 32.4	20 20.3	15 32.7	27 11.3	28 41.7	29 49.0
15 Su	11 39 46	23 08 14	9♒31 09	16 44 10	6 39.9	10 03.8	20 43.3	6 18.3	8 38.9	20 24.9	15 28.2	27 10.6	28 40.0	29 48.3
16 M	11 43 43	24 06 43	24 03 10	1♓27 28	6 38.4	11 51.1	21 56.5	6 52.7	8 45.8	20 29.3	15 23.7	27 09.9	28 38.4	29 47.6
17 Tu	11 47 39	25 05 13	8♓56 14	16 28 28	6 37.3	13 39.9	23 09.7	7 27.0	8 52.9	20 33.6	15 19.2	27 09.1	28 36.7	29 46.9
18 W	11 51 36	26 03 45	24 03 05	1♈38 52	6D36.8	15 29.8	24 22.9	8 01.1	9 00.4	20 37.7	15 14.7	27 08.3	28 35.1	29 46.3
19 Th	11 55 32	27 02 19	9♈14 39	16 49 13	6 36.9	17 20.5	25 36.1	8 35.0	9 08.1	20 41.6	15 10.2	27 07.4	28 33.4	29 45.6
20 F	11 59 29	28 00 55	24 21 27	1♉50 19	6 37.4	19 11.8	26 49.3	9 08.7	9 16.1	20 45.4	15 05.8	27 06.5	28 31.8	29 45.0
21 Sa	12 03 25	28 59 33	9♉14 56	16 34 32	6 38.0	21 03.2	28 02.4	9 42.3	9 24.4	20 48.9	15 01.4	27 05.6	28 30.1	29 44.5
22 Su	12 07 22	29 58 14	23 48 34	0♊56 35	6 38.7	22 54.7	29 15.5	10 15.6	9 33.0	20 52.3	14 57.0	27 04.6	28 28.4	29 43.9
23 M	12 11 19	0♎56 56	7♊58 21	14 53 46	6 39.1	24 46.0	0♏28.6	10 48.8	9 41.8	20 55.5	14 52.7	27 03.6	28 26.8	29 43.4
24 Tu	12 15 15	1 55 41	21 42 52	28 25 46	6R39.3	26 37.1	1 41.7	11 21.8	9 51.0	20 58.5	14 48.4	27 02.5	28 25.1	29 42.9
25 W	12 19 12	2 54 29	5♋02 44	11♋34 03	6 39.3	28 27.6	2 54.8	11 54.6	10 00.4	21 01.3	14 44.2	27 01.3	28 23.5	29 42.4
26 Th	12 23 08	3 53 18	18 00 04	24 21 13	6 39.1	0♎17.6	4 07.9	12 27.1	10 10.0	21 04.0	14 39.9	27 00.2	28 21.8	29 42.0
27 F	12 27 05	4 52 10	0♌37 54	6♌50 33	6 38.9	2 07.0	5 20.9	12 59.5	10 19.9	21 06.4	14 35.8	26 58.9	28 20.2	29 41.5
28 Sa	12 31 01	5 51 04	12 59 35	19 05 26	6D38.7	3 55.7	6 33.9	13 31.6	10 30.1	21 08.6	14 31.6	26 57.7	28 18.5	29 41.1
29 Su	12 34 58	6 50 00	25 08 31	1♍09 13	6 38.7	5 43.6	7 47.0	14 03.5	10 40.5	21 10.7	14 27.5	26 56.4	28 16.9	29 40.8
30 M	12 38 54	7 48 58	7♍07 55	13 04 57	6 38.8	7 30.8	8 59.9	14 35.2	10 51.2	21 12.5	14 23.5	26 55.0	28 15.2	29 40.4

LONGITUDE — October 2024

Day	Sid.Time	☉	0 hr ☽	Noon ☽	True ☊	☿	♀	♂	⚳	♃	♄	♅	♆	♇
1 Tu	12 42 51	8♎47 59	19♍00 40	24♍55 22	6♈38.9	9♎17.2	10♏12.9	15♋06.7	11♑02.1	21♊14.2	14♓19.5	26♉53.6	28♓13.6	29♑40.1
2 W	12 46 48	9 47 01	0♎49 22	6♎42 56	6R38.9	11 02.7	11 25.9	15 37.9	11 13.3	21 15.6	14R15.6	26R52.2	28R12.0	29R39.8
3 Th	12 50 44	10 46 06	12 36 23	18 29 57	6 38.8	12 47.4	12 38.8	16 08.9	11 24.7	21 16.9	14 11.7	26 50.7	28 10.4	29 39.6
4 F	12 54 41	11 45 12	24 23 56	0♏18 37	6 38.5	14 31.3	13 51.7	16 39.7	11 36.4	21 18.0	14 07.9	26 49.1	28 08.8	29 39.3
5 Sa	12 58 37	12 44 21	6♏14 17	12 11 14	6 37.8	16 14.4	15 04.6	17 10.2	11 48.3	21 18.8	14 04.2	26 47.6	28 07.2	29 39.1
6 Su	13 02 34	13 43 31	18 09 48	24 10 18	6 36.9	17 56.6	16 17.5	17 40.5	12 00.4	21 19.5	14 00.5	26 46.0	28 05.6	29 39.0
7 M	13 06 30	14 42 44	0♐13 06	6♐18 34	6 35.8	19 38.0	17 30.4	18 10.5	12 12.8	21 19.9	13 56.8	26 44.3	28 04.0	29 38.8
8 Tu	13 10 27	15 41 58	12 27 06	18 39 07	6 34.8	21 18.6	18 43.2	18 40.2	12 25.4	21R20.2	13 53.3	26 42.7	28 02.4	29 38.7
9 W	13 14 23	16 41 14	24 55 01	1♑15 14	6 34.0	22 58.5	19 56.0	19 09.7	12 38.2	21 20.3	13 49.8	26 40.9	28 00.9	29 38.6
10 Th	13 18 20	17 40 32	7♑40 11	14 10 17	6D33.6	24 37.5	21 08.8	19 39.0	12 51.2	21 20.1	13 46.4	26 39.2	27 59.3	29 38.6
11 F	13 22 17	18 39 52	20 45 53	27 27 19	6 33.7	26 15.9	22 21.5	20 07.9	13 04.4	21 19.8	13 43.0	26 37.4	27 57.8	29D38.5
12 Sa	13 26 13	19 39 13	4♒14 50	11♒08 39	6 34.4	27 53.5	23 34.3	20 36.6	13 17.9	21 19.2	13 39.8	26 35.6	27 56.3	29 38.5
13 Su	13 30 10	20 38 36	18 08 48	25 15 15	6 35.4	29 30.3	24 46.9	21 05.0	13 31.5	21 18.5	13 36.6	26 33.7	27 54.8	29 38.6
14 M	13 34 06	21 38 01	2♓27 49	9♓46 08	6 36.5	1♏06.5	25 59.6	21 33.1	13 45.4	21 17.5	13 33.5	26 31.8	27 53.3	29 38.6
15 Tu	13 38 03	22 37 28	17 09 40	24 37 46	6R37.3	2 42.0	27 12.2	22 00.9	13 59.4	21 16.4	13 30.4	26 29.9	27 51.8	29 38.7
16 W	13 41 59	23 36 56	2♈09 32	9♈43 59	6 37.5	4 16.8	28 24.8	22 28.5	14 13.7	21 15.0	13 27.4	26 27.9	27 50.3	29 38.8
17 Th	13 45 56	24 36 26	17 20 00	24 56 23	6 36.9	5 51.0	29 37.4	22 55.7	14 28.1	21 13.5	13 24.6	26 25.9	27 48.9	29 38.9
18 F	13 49 52	25 35 59	2♉31 54	10♉05 19	6 35.3	7 24.5	0♐50.0	23 22.6	14 42.7	21 11.7	13 21.8	26 23.9	27 47.5	29 39.1
19 Sa	13 53 49	26 35 33	17 35 29	25 01 20	6 32.9	8 57.4	2 02.5	23 49.3	14 57.5	21 09.8	13 19.0	26 21.9	27 46.0	29 39.3
20 Su	13 57 46	27 35 10	2♊21 58	9♊36 38	6 30.1	10 29.7	3 15.0	24 15.6	15 12.5	21 07.7	13 16.4	26 19.8	27 44.7	29 39.5
21 M	14 01 42	28 34 49	16 44 46	23 46 01	6 27.2	12 01.4	4 27.4	24 41.6	15 27.7	21 05.3	13 13.9	26 17.7	27 43.3	29 39.8
22 Tu	14 05 39	29 34 31	0♋40 11	7♋27 14	6 24.9	13 32.5	5 39.8	25 07.2	15 43.1	21 02.8	13 11.4	26 15.5	27 41.9	29 40.1
23 W	14 09 35	0♏34 14	14 07 20	20 40 44	6D23.4	15 03.0	6 52.2	25 32.5	15 58.6	21 00.0	13 09.1	26 13.4	27 40.6	29 40.4
24 Th	14 13 32	1 34 00	27 07 49	3♌29 01	6 23.1	16 32.9	8 04.6	25 57.5	16 14.4	20 57.1	13 06.8	26 11.2	27 39.3	29 40.8
25 F	14 17 28	2 33 48	9♌44 53	15 55 56	6 23.7	18 02.3	9 16.9	26 22.1	16 30.3	20 54.0	13 04.6	26 09.0	27 38.0	29 41.1
26 Sa	14 21 25	3 33 38	22 02 47	28 06 00	6 25.2	19 31.0	10 29.2	26 46.3	16 46.3	20 50.7	13 02.5	26 06.7	27 36.7	29 41.5
27 Su	14 25 21	4 33 31	4♍06 11	10♍03 55	6 27.0	20 59.2	11 41.5	27 10.2	17 02.5	20 47.1	13 00.5	26 04.5	27 35.4	29 42.0
28 M	14 29 18	5 33 25	15 59 44	21 54 11	6 28.6	22 26.7	12 53.7	27 33.7	17 18.9	20 43.4	12 58.6	26 02.2	27 34.2	29 42.4
29 Tu	14 33 15	6 33 22	27 47 45	3♎40 54	6R29.5	23 53.7	14 05.9	27 56.8	17 35.5	20 39.5	12 56.8	25 59.9	27 33.0	29 42.9
30 W	14 37 11	7 33 21	9♎34 02	15 27 34	6 29.1	25 19.9	15 18.1	28 19.5	17 52.2	20 35.5	12 55.1	25 57.6	27 31.8	29 43.4
31 Th	14 41 08	8 33 21	21 21 49	27 17 07	6 27.2	26 45.5	16 30.2	28 41.8	18 09.1	20 31.2	12 53.5	25 55.2	27 30.6	29 44.0

Astro Data

	Dy Hr Mn
♅R	1 15:18
☽0S	4 18:33
☽0N	18 11:14
⊙0S	22 12:44
♄∠♇	25 23:09
☿0S	28 6:04
☽0S	2 0:42
♃R	9 7:05
♇D	12 0:34
☽0N	15 22:25
☽0S	29 6:48

Planet Ingress

	Dy Hr Mn
♇ ♑R	2 0:10
♂ ♋	4 19:46
☿ ♍	9 6:50
⊙ ♎	22 12:44
♀ ♏	23 2:36
☿ ♎	26 8:09
☿ ♏	13 19:23
♀ ♐	17 19:28
⊙ ♏	22 22:15

Last Aspect / ☽ Ingress

Last Aspect Dy Hr Mn		☽ Ingress Dy Hr Mn
2 0:25	♂ ✱	♍ 2 3:48
4 16:06	♇ △	♎ 4 16:12
7 5:08	♇ □	♏ 7 5:18
9 17:11	♇ ✱	♐ 9 17:25
12 0:20	♆ □	♑ 12 2:37
14 7:35	♇ ☌	♒ 14 7:53
16 5:04	♅ □	♓ 16 9:39
18 9:02	♇ ✱	♈ 18 9:24
20 8:39	♇ □	♉ 20 9:02
22 10:14	⊙ △	♊ 22 10:24
24 11:59	♆ □	♋ 24 14:50
26 22:12	♇ ☍	♌ 26 22:47
29 3:36	♅ □	♍ 29 9:41

Last Aspect / ☽ Ingress

Last Aspect Dy Hr Mn		☽ Ingress Dy Hr Mn
1 21:39	♇ △	♎ 1 22:20
4 10:40	♇ □	♏ 4 11:22
6 22:52	♇ ✱	♐ 6 23:34
9 5:54	♆ □	♑ 9 9:38
11 15:53	♇ ☌	♒ 11 16:31
13 14:11	♅ □	♓ 13 19:55
15 20:00	♇ ✱	♈ 15 20:34
17 19:26	♇ □	♉ 17 20:00
19 19:33	♇ △	♊ 19 20:07
21 21:00	⊙ △	♋ 21 22:50
24 4:47	♇ ☍	♌ 24 5:24
26 8:04	♅ □	♍ 26 15:47
29 3:54	♇ △	♎ 29 4:30
31 16:57	♇ □	♏ 31 17:29

☽ Phases & Eclipses

Dy Hr Mn	
3 1:56	● 11♍04
11 6:06	☽ 19♐00
18 2:34	○ 25♓41
18 2:44	• P 0.085
24 18:50	☾ 2♋12
2 18:49	● 10♎04
2 18:44:59	• A 07'25"
10 18:55	☽ 17♑58
17 11:26	○ 24♈35
24 8:03	☾ 1♌24

Astro Data

1 September 2024
Julian Day # 45535
SVP 4♓54'56"
GC 27♐11.0 ⚴ 28♍02.9
Eris 25♈20.9R ⚵ 7♎46.4
⚷ 22♈57.5R ⚶ 3♏32.5
☽ Mean ☊ 7♈55.8

1 October 2024
Julian Day # 45565
SVP 4♓54'53"
GC 27♐11.1 ⚴ 7♐19.9
Eris 25♈05.9R ⚵ 18♎21.9
⚷ 21♈48.7R ⚶ 17♏46.8
☽ Mean ☊ 6♈20.4

November 2024 LONGITUDE

Day	Sid.Time	☉	0 hr ☽	Noon ☽	True ☊	☿	♀	♂	⚳	♃	♄	♅	♆	♇
1 F	14 45 04	9♏33 24	3♏13 44	9♏11 54	6♈23.5	28♏10.4	17♐42.3	29♋03.6	18♑26.1	20♊26.8	12♓52.0	25♉52.9	27♓29.5	29♑44.5
2 Sa	14 49 01	10 33 28	15 11 50	21 13 45	6R 18.3	29 34.6	18 54.4	29 25.1	18 43.3	20R 22.1	12R 50.5	25R 50.5	27R 28.4	29 45.1
3 Su	14 52 57	11 33 35	27 17 48	3♐24 11	6 12.1	0♐57.9	20 06.4	29 46.1	19 00.6	20 17.3	12 49.2	25 48.1	27 27.3	29 45.8
4 M	14 56 54	12 33 43	9♐33 02	15 44 32	6 05.3	2 20.4	21 18.4	0♌06.7	19 18.1	20 12.4	12 48.0	25 45.7	27 26.2	29 46.4
5 Tu	15 00 50	13 33 53	21 58 50	28 16 07	5 58.8	3 42.0	22 30.3	0 26.8	19 35.7	20 07.2	12 46.9	25 43.3	27 25.2	29 47.1
6 W	15 04 47	14 34 05	4♑36 34	11♑00 25	5 53.3	5 02.5	23 42.2	0 46.4	19 53.5	20 01.9	12 45.9	25 40.8	27 24.2	29 47.9
7 Th	15 08 44	15 34 18	17 27 51	23 59 07	5 49.4	6 22.0	24 54.0	1 05.6	20 11.4	19 56.5	12 45.0	25 38.4	27 23.2	29 48.6
8 F	15 12 40	16 34 32	0♒34 28	7♒14 07	5D 47.2	7 40.2	26 05.8	1 24.3	20 29.4	19 50.8	12 44.2	25 35.9	27 22.3	29 49.4
9 Sa	15 16 37	17 34 48	13 58 18	20 47 14	5 46.8	8 57.1	27 17.5	1 42.6	20 47.6	19 45.0	12 43.5	25 33.5	27 21.3	29 50.2
10 Su	15 20 33	18 35 06	27 41 03	4♓39 52	5 47.7	10 12.5	28 29.2	2 00.3	21 05.9	19 39.1	12 42.9	25 31.0	27 20.4	29 51.0
11 M	15 24 30	19 35 24	11♓43 42	18 52 30	5 49.0	11 26.2	29 40.8	2 17.5	21 24.3	19 33.0	12 42.4	25 28.5	27 19.6	29 51.8
12 Tu	15 28 26	20 35 45	26 06 01	3♈23 58	5R 49.9	12 38.0	0♑52.4	2 34.2	21 42.9	19 26.8	12 42.1	25 26.0	27 18.7	29 52.7
13 W	15 32 23	21 36 06	10♈45 51	18 11 02	5 49.3	13 47.8	2 03.9	2 50.4	22 01.6	19 20.4	12 41.8	25 23.5	27 17.9	29 53.6
14 Th	15 36 19	22 36 29	25 38 43	3♉08 01	5 46.6	14 55.1	3 15.3	3 06.0	22 20.4	19 13.9	12 41.6	25 21.0	27 17.1	29 54.6
15 F	15 40 16	23 36 54	10♉37 51	18 07 10	5 41.7	15 59.9	4 26.7	3 21.2	22 39.3	19 07.3	12D 41.6	25 18.5	27 16.4	29 55.5
16 Sa	15 44 13	24 37 20	25 34 47	2♊59 36	5 34.8	17 01.6	5 38.0	3 35.7	22 58.3	19 00.5	12 41.6	25 16.0	27 15.6	29 56.5
17 Su	15 48 09	25 37 48	10♊20 33	17 36 42	5 26.7	17 59.9	6 49.2	3 49.7	23 17.5	18 53.7	12 41.8	25 13.5	27 14.9	29 57.5
18 M	15 52 06	26 38 18	24 47 12	1♋51 27	5 18.2	18 54.3	8 00.4	4 03.1	23 36.8	18 46.7	12 42.0	25 11.0	27 14.3	29 58.6
19 Tu	15 56 02	27 38 49	8♋48 59	15 39 33	5 10.6	19 44.4	9 11.5	4 15.9	23 56.2	18 39.5	12 42.4	25 08.5	27 13.7	29 59.6
20 W	15 59 59	28 39 22	22 23 03	28 59 35	5 04.6	20 29.6	10 22.5	4 28.1	24 15.7	18 32.3	12 42.8	25 06.0	27 13.1	0♒00.7
21 Th	16 03 55	29 39 57	5♌29 23	11♌52 49	5 00.6	21 09.3	11 33.4	4 39.7	24 35.3	18 25.0	12 43.4	25 03.5	27 12.5	0 01.8
22 F	16 07 52	0♐40 34	18 10 22	24 22 34	4D 58.8	21 42.8	12 44.3	4 50.6	24 55.0	18 17.6	12 44.1	25 01.0	27 11.9	0 03.0
23 Sa	16 11 48	1 41 12	0♍30 02	6♍33 25	4 58.7	22 09.3	13 55.1	5 00.9	25 14.8	18 10.1	12 44.9	24 58.6	27 11.4	0 04.1
24 Su	16 15 45	2 41 52	12 33 25	18 30 41	4 59.5	22 28.2	15 05.8	5 10.5	25 34.7	18 02.5	12 45.7	24 56.1	27 11.0	0 05.3
25 M	16 19 42	3 42 33	24 25 56	0♎19 48	5R 00.3	22R 38.5	16 16.5	5 19.5	25 54.7	17 54.8	12 46.7	24 53.6	27 10.5	0 06.5
26 Tu	16 23 38	4 43 16	6♎12 57	12 05 59	5 00.1	22 39.6	17 27.0	5 27.8	26 14.9	17 47.0	12 47.8	24 51.1	27 10.1	0 07.7
27 W	16 27 35	5 44 01	17 59 28	23 53 56	4 58.1	22 30.7	18 37.5	5 35.3	26 35.1	17 39.2	12 49.0	24 48.7	27 09.7	0 09.0
28 Th	16 31 31	6 44 47	29 49 50	5♏47 37	4 53.5	22 11.2	19 47.9	5 42.2	26 55.4	17 31.3	12 50.3	24 46.3	27 09.4	0 10.3
29 F	16 35 28	7 45 34	11♏47 38	17 50 10	4 46.2	21 40.8	20 58.2	5 48.3	27 15.8	17 23.3	12 51.8	24 43.8	27 09.1	0 11.6
30 Sa	16 39 24	8 46 23	23 55 28	0♐03 42	4 36.4	20 59.3	22 08.4	5 53.7	27 36.3	17 15.3	12 53.3	24 41.4	27 08.8	0 12.9

December 2024 LONGITUDE

Day	Sid.Time	☉	0 hr ☽	Noon ☽	True ☊	☿	♀	♂	⚳	♃	♄	♅	♆	♇
1 Su	16 43 21	9♐47 13	6♐15 00	12♐29 25	4♈24.7	20♐07.3	23♑18.5	5♌58.4	27♑56.9	17♊07.3	12♓54.9	24♉39.0	27♓08.6	0♒14.2
2 M	16 47 18	10 48 05	18 46 59	25 07 41	4R 12.1	19R 05.3	24 28.4	6 02.3	28 17.6	16R 59.2	12 56.6	24R 36.6	27R 08.4	0 15.6
3 Tu	16 51 14	11 48 57	1♑31 28	7♑58 15	3 59.8	17 54.9	25 38.3	6 05.4	28 38.4	16 51.1	12 58.5	24 34.3	27 08.2	0 17.0
4 W	16 55 11	12 49 51	14 27 59	21 00 35	3 49.0	16 37.8	26 48.1	6 07.8	28 59.3	16 42.9	13 00.4	24 31.9	27 08.1	0 18.4
5 Th	16 59 07	13 50 45	27 36 00	4♒14 11	3 40.5	15 16.4	27 57.8	6 09.4	29 20.3	16 34.8	13 02.4	24 29.6	27 08.0	0 19.8
6 F	17 03 04	14 51 40	10♒55 07	17 38 51	3 34.9	13 53.5	29 07.3	6R 10.2	29 41.3	16 26.6	13 04.6	24 27.3	27 07.9	0 21.3
7 Sa	17 07 00	15 52 36	24 25 23	1♓14 48	3 31.9	12 31.8	0♒16.7	6 10.2	0♒02.4	16 18.4	13 06.8	24 25.0	27D 07.9	0 22.7
8 Su	17 10 57	16 53 32	8♓07 10	15 02 33	3D 31.1	11 14.0	1 26.0	6 09.3	0 23.6	16 10.2	13 09.2	24 22.7	27 07.9	0 24.2
9 M	17 14 53	17 54 29	22 01 02	29 02 37	3R 31.3	10 02.7	2 35.1	6 07.7	0 44.9	16 02.1	13 11.6	24 20.5	27 07.9	0 25.7
10 Tu	17 18 50	18 55 27	6♈07 17	13♈14 56	3 31.0	8 59.8	3 44.1	6 05.2	1 06.2	15 53.9	13 14.2	24 18.3	27 08.0	0 27.3
11 W	17 22 47	19 56 25	20 25 22	27 38 17	3 29.1	8 06.7	4 52.9	6 02.0	1 27.6	15 45.8	13 16.8	24 16.1	27 08.1	0 28.8
12 Th	17 26 43	20 57 24	4♉53 16	12♉09 47	3 24.7	7 24.4	6 01.6	5 57.9	1 49.1	15 37.6	13 19.5	24 13.9	27 08.2	0 30.4
13 F	17 30 40	21 58 24	19 27 11	26 44 43	3 17.2	6 53.4	7 10.2	5 53.0	2 10.7	15 29.6	13 22.4	24 11.8	27 08.4	0 32.0
14 Sa	17 34 36	22 59 24	4♊01 32	11♊16 45	3 07.0	6 33.5	8 18.5	5 47.2	2 32.3	15 21.5	13 25.3	24 09.7	27 08.6	0 33.6
15 Su	17 38 33	24 00 25	18 29 30	25 38 54	2 55.0	6D 24.5	9 26.7	5 40.6	2 54.0	15 13.5	13 28.3	24 07.6	27 08.8	0 35.2
16 M	17 42 29	25 01 27	2♋44 08	9♋44 32	2 42.4	6 25.7	10 34.8	5 33.2	3 15.8	15 05.6	13 31.5	24 05.5	27 09.1	0 36.8
17 Tu	17 46 26	26 02 29	16 39 31	23 28 38	2 30.5	6 36.5	11 42.6	5 24.9	3 37.6	14 57.7	13 34.7	24 03.5	27 09.4	0 38.4
18 W	17 50 22	27 03 32	0♌11 38	6♌48 24	2 20.5	6 56.1	12 50.3	5 15.8	3 59.5	14 49.8	13 38.0	24 01.5	27 09.8	0 40.1
19 Th	17 54 19	28 04 36	13 18 59	19 43 33	2 13.1	7 23.6	13 57.8	5 05.9	4 21.5	14 42.1	13 41.4	23 59.6	27 10.2	0 41.8
20 F	17 58 16	29 05 41	26 02 24	2♍15 58	2 08.4	7 58.2	15 05.0	4 55.1	4 43.5	14 34.4	13 44.9	23 57.6	27 10.6	0 43.5
21 Sa	18 02 12	0♑06 46	8♍24 45	14 29 20	2 06.2	8 39.2	16 12.1	4 43.5	5 05.6	14 26.8	13 48.5	23 55.8	27 11.0	0 45.2
22 Su	18 06 09	1 07 52	20 30 21	26 28 27	2 05.6	9 25.9	17 19.0	4 31.1	5 27.7	14 19.2	13 52.2	23 53.9	27 11.5	0 46.9
23 M	18 10 05	2 08 59	2♎24 22	8♎18 47	2 05.5	10 17.6	18 25.7	4 17.8	5 49.9	14 11.8	13 55.9	23 52.1	27 12.1	0 48.6
24 Tu	18 14 02	3 10 07	14 12 26	20 06 00	2 04.8	11 13.8	19 32.1	4 03.8	6 12.1	14 04.4	13 59.8	23 50.3	27 12.6	0 50.4
25 W	18 17 58	4 11 15	26 00 10	1♏55 35	2 02.4	12 13.8	20 38.3	3 49.0	6 34.5	13 57.2	14 03.7	23 48.5	27 13.2	0 52.2
26 Th	18 21 55	5 12 23	7♏52 51	13 52 32	1 57.5	13 17.3	21 44.3	3 33.4	6 56.8	13 50.0	14 07.7	23 46.8	27 13.8	0 53.9
27 F	18 25 51	6 13 33	19 55 07	26 01 03	1 49.6	14 23.8	22 50.1	3 17.1	7 19.2	13 43.0	14 11.9	23 45.2	27 14.5	0 55.7
28 Sa	18 29 48	7 14 43	2♐10 40	8♐24 15	1 39.0	15 33.0	23 55.6	3 00.1	7 41.7	13 36.1	14 16.1	23 43.5	27 15.2	0 57.5
29 Su	18 33 45	8 15 53	14 41 59	21 03 58	1 26.3	16 44.6	25 00.8	2 42.3	8 04.2	13 29.3	14 20.4	23 41.9	27 15.9	0 59.3
30 M	18 37 41	9 17 03	27 30 12	4♑00 36	1 12.5	17 58.3	26 05.8	2 23.9	8 26.8	13 22.7	14 24.7	23 40.4	27 16.7	1 01.1
31 Tu	18 41 38	10 18 14	10♑35 00	17 13 11	0 58.9	19 13.8	27 10.5	2 04.8	8 49.4	13 16.1	14 29.2	23 38.9	27 17.5	1 03.0

Astro Data

	Dy Hr Mn
☽ 0N	12 8:04
♄ D	15 14:20
☽ 0S	25 13:04
☿ R	26 2:41
♂ R	6 23:33
♆ D	7 23:43
☽ 0N	9 14:38
♃☍♇	13 6:03
☿ D	15 20:58
☽ 0S	22 19:51
♃□♄	24 21:59

Planet Ingress

		Dy Hr Mn
☿	♐	2 19:18
♂	♌	4 4:10
♀	♑	11 18:26
♇	♒	19 20:29
☉	♐	21 19:56
♀	♒	7 6:13
⚳	♒	7 9:16
☉	♑	21 9:20

Last Aspect / ☽ Ingress

Last Aspect Dy Hr Mn			☽ Ingress	Dy Hr Mn
3 4:51	♇	⚹	♐	3 5:19
5 10:23	♆	□	♑	5 15:17
7 22:37	♇	☌	♒	7 22:58
10 0:23	♀	⚹	♓	10 4:00
12 6:13	♇	⚹	♈	12 6:26
14 6:50	♇	□	♉	14 6:59
16 7:03	♇	△	♊	16 7:09
18 4:09	♆	□	♋	18 8:50
20 11:20	☉	△	♌	20 13:51
22 13:15	♅	□	♍	22 23:01
25 5:35	♆	☍	♎	25 11:20
27 9:14	☿	⚹	♏	28 0:21
30 6:19	♆	△	♐	30 11:53

Last Aspect / ☽ Ingress

Last Aspect Dy Hr Mn			☽ Ingress	Dy Hr Mn
2 15:47	♆	□	♑	2 21:09
4 23:34	♀	☌	♒	5 4:21
7 0:01	♅	□	♓	7 9:49
9 8:45	♆	☌	♈	9 13:38
10 22:13	☉	△	♉	11 15:55
13 12:39	♆	⚹	♊	13 17:22
15 14:32	♆	□	♋	15 19:21
17 18:33	♆	△	♌	17 23:39
20 5:19	☉	△	♍	20 7:37
22 13:27	♆	☍	♎	22 19:08
24 10:44	♀	△	♏	25 8:06
27 14:24	♆	△	♐	27 19:46
29 23:34	♆	□	♑	30 4:37

☽ Phases & Eclipses

Dy Hr Mn		
1 12:47	●	9♏35
9 5:55	☽	17♒20
15 21:28	○	24♉01
23 1:28	☾	1♍15
1 6:21	●	9♐33
8 15:27	☽	17♓02
15 9:02	○	23♊53
22 22:18	☾	1♎34
30 22:27	●	9♑44

Astro Data

1 November 2024
Julian Day # 45596
SVP 4♓54'49"
GC 27♐11.2 ⚳ 18♐34.0
Eris 24♈47.5R ⚵ 29♎21.0
⚷ 20♈25.0R ⚶ 2♎27.4
☽ Mean ☊ 4♈41.9

1 December 2024
Julian Day # 45626
SVP 4♓54'44"
GC 27♐11.2 ⚳ 0♑13.2
Eris 24♈32.3R ⚵ 9♏34.6
⚷ 19♈22.1R ⚶ 16♎14.6
☽ Mean ☊ 3♈06.6

LONGITUDE — January 2025

Day	Sid.Time	☉	0 hr ☽	Noon ☽	True ☊	☿	♀	♂	⚳	♃	♄	♅	♆	♇
1 W	18 45 34	11♑19 25	23♑54 52	0♒39 43	0♈46.9	20♐31.0	28♒14.9	1♌45.2	9♒12.1	13♊09.8	14♓33.7	23♉37.4	27♓18.3	1♒04.8
2 Th	18 49 31	12 20 35	7♒27 24	14 17 34	0R 37.3	21 49.6	29 19.0	1R 24.9	9 34.8	13R 03.5	14 38.3	23R 36.0	27 19.1	1 06.7
3 F	18 53 27	13 21 46	21 09 53	28 04 02	0 30.8	23 09.6	0♓22.8	1 04.1	9 57.6	12 57.4	14 43.0	23 34.6	27 20.0	1 08.5
4 Sa	18 57 24	14 22 56	4♓59 46	11♓56 52	0 27.2	24 30.8	1 26.3	0 42.8	10 20.4	12 51.5	14 47.8	23 33.3	27 21.0	1 10.4
5 Su	19 01 21	15 24 06	18 55 08	25 54 28	0D 26.1	25 53.0	2 29.5	0 21.0	10 43.2	12 45.7	14 52.7	23 32.0	27 21.9	1 12.3
6 M	19 05 17	16 25 15	2♈54 45	9♈55 55	0R 26.1	27 16.3	3 32.3	29♋58.8	11 06.1	12 40.0	14 57.6	23 30.8	27 22.9	1 14.1
7 Tu	19 09 14	17 26 24	16 57 54	24 00 38	0 26.1	28 40.4	4 34.7	29 36.2	11 29.0	12 34.5	15 02.6	23 29.6	27 23.9	1 16.0
8 W	19 13 10	18 27 33	1♉04 02	8♉07 58	0 24.6	0♑05.3	5 36.8	29 13.3	11 51.9	12 29.2	15 07.7	23 28.4	27 25.0	1 17.9
9 Th	19 17 07	19 28 41	15 12 15	22 16 38	0 20.7	1 31.1	6 38.4	28 50.1	12 14.9	12 24.1	15 12.8	23 27.3	27 26.1	1 19.8
10 F	19 21 03	20 29 49	29 20 49	6♊24 25	0 14.1	2 57.5	7 39.7	28 26.7	12 37.9	12 19.1	15 18.0	23 26.3	27 27.2	1 21.7
11 Sa	19 25 00	21 30 56	13♊26 58	20 28 01	0 04.9	4 24.7	8 40.6	28 03.0	13 01.0	12 14.3	15 23.3	23 25.3	27 28.3	1 23.6
12 Su	19 28 56	22 32 03	27 27 01	4♋23 25	29♓53.9	5 52.5	9 41.0	27 39.2	13 24.1	12 09.7	15 28.7	23 24.3	27 29.5	1 25.6
13 M	19 32 53	23 33 09	11♋16 42	18 06 23	29 42.2	7 20.9	10 41.0	27 15.3	13 47.2	12 05.3	15 34.1	23 23.4	27 30.7	1 27.5
14 Tu	19 36 50	24 34 15	24 52 00	1♌33 12	29 31.1	8 49.9	11 40.5	26 51.3	14 10.3	12 01.0	15 39.6	23 22.5	27 32.0	1 29.4
15 W	19 40 46	25 35 21	8♌09 43	14 41 21	29 21.6	10 19.5	12 39.5	26 27.3	14 33.5	11 57.0	15 45.2	23 21.7	27 33.2	1 31.3
16 Th	19 44 43	26 36 26	21 08 02	27 29 50	29 14.4	11 49.7	13 38.0	26 03.3	14 56.7	11 53.1	15 50.8	23 21.0	27 34.5	1 33.3
17 F	19 48 39	27 37 31	3♍46 53	9♍59 25	29 10.0	13 20.5	14 36.0	25 39.3	15 19.9	11 49.4	15 56.5	23 20.3	27 35.8	1 35.2
18 Sa	19 52 36	28 38 35	16 07 47	22 12 23	29D 08.0	14 51.8	15 33.5	25 15.5	15 43.2	11 45.9	16 02.2	23 19.6	27 37.2	1 37.1
19 Su	19 56 32	29 39 39	28 13 43	4♎12 20	29 07.8	16 23.7	16 30.4	24 51.9	16 06.4	11 42.6	16 08.0	23 19.0	27 38.6	1 39.1
20 M	20 00 29	0♒40 42	10♎08 50	16 03 50	29 08.6	17 56.2	17 26.8	24 28.5	16 29.7	11 39.4	16 13.9	23 18.4	27 40.0	1 41.0
21 Tu	20 04 25	1 41 46	21 58 00	27 52 01	29R 09.4	19 29.2	18 22.6	24 05.3	16 53.1	11 36.5	16 19.8	23 17.9	27 41.4	1 42.9
22 W	20 08 22	2 42 48	3♏46 34	9♏42 20	29 09.2	21 02.8	19 17.7	23 42.4	17 16.4	11 33.8	16 25.8	23 17.5	27 42.9	1 44.9
23 Th	20 12 19	3 43 51	15 39 59	21 40 10	29 07.2	22 37.0	20 12.3	23 19.9	17 39.8	11 31.2	16 31.8	23 17.0	27 44.4	1 46.8
24 F	20 16 15	4 44 53	27 43 30	3♐50 32	29 03.0	24 11.8	21 06.1	22 57.8	18 03.2	11 28.9	16 38.0	23 16.7	27 45.9	1 48.7
25 Sa	20 20 12	5 45 54	10♐01 46	16 17 39	28 56.6	25 47.2	21 59.3	22 36.0	18 26.6	11 26.8	16 44.1	23 16.4	27 47.4	1 50.7
26 Su	20 24 08	6 46 55	22 38 30	29 04 35	28 48.5	27 23.2	22 51.8	22 14.8	18 50.0	11 24.9	16 50.3	23 16.2	27 49.0	1 52.6
27 M	20 28 05	7 47 55	5♑36 02	12♑12 53	28 39.3	28 59.8	23 43.6	21 54.0	19 13.5	11 23.1	16 56.6	23 16.0	27 50.6	1 54.6
28 Tu	20 32 01	8 48 55	18 55 01	25 42 15	28 30.1	0♒37.1	24 34.6	21 33.8	19 37.0	11 21.6	17 02.9	23 15.8	27 52.2	1 56.5
29 W	20 35 58	9 49 54	2♒34 14	9♒30 33	28 21.8	2 15.0	25 24.8	21 14.2	20 00.4	11 20.3	17 09.3	23 15.7	27 53.9	1 58.4
30 Th	20 39 54	10 50 51	16 30 42	23 34 06	28 15.4	3 53.6	26 14.2	20 55.1	20 23.9	11 19.2	17 15.7	23D 15.7	27 55.5	2 00.3
31 F	20 43 51	11 51 48	0♓40 08	7♓48 10	28 11.3	5 32.8	27 02.7	20 36.7	20 47.4	11 18.3	17 22.2	23 15.7	27 57.2	2 02.3

LONGITUDE — February 2025

Day	Sid.Time	☉	0 hr ☽	Noon ☽	True ☊	☿	♀	♂	⚳	♃	♄	♅	♆	♇
1 Sa	20 47 48	12♒52 43	14♓57 36	22♓07 48	28♓09.5	7♒12.8	27♓50.3	20♋19.0	21♒11.0	11♊17.6	17♓28.7	23♉15.8	27♓58.9	2♒04.2
2 Su	20 51 44	13 53 37	29 18 16	6♈28 28	28D 09.6	8 53.5	28 37.0	20R 01.9	21 34.5	11R 17.1	17 35.2	23 15.9	28 00.7	2 06.1
3 M	20 55 41	14 54 29	13♈38 01	20 46 32	28 10.8	10 34.9	29 22.8	19 45.6	21 58.0	11D 16.8	17 41.8	23 16.1	28 02.4	2 08.0
4 Tu	20 59 37	15 55 21	27 53 44	4♉59 24	28R 12.0	12 17.0	0♈07.5	19 30.0	22 21.6	11 16.7	17 48.5	23 16.3	28 04.2	2 09.9
5 W	21 03 34	16 56 11	12♉03 20	19 05 23	28 12.4	13 59.9	0 51.1	19 15.1	22 45.1	11 16.8	17 55.1	23 16.6	28 06.0	2 11.8
6 Th	21 07 30	17 56 59	26 05 26	3♊03 22	28 11.3	15 43.5	1 33.7	19 01.0	23 08.7	11 17.2	18 01.9	23 16.9	28 07.9	2 13.6
7 F	21 11 27	18 57 46	9♊59 04	16 52 25	28 08.4	17 27.9	2 15.1	18 47.6	23 32.3	11 17.7	18 08.6	23 17.3	28 09.7	2 15.5
8 Sa	21 15 23	19 58 31	23 43 18	0♋31 35	28 03.8	19 13.1	2 55.4	18 35.0	23 55.8	11 18.4	18 15.4	23 17.8	28 11.6	2 17.4
9 Su	21 19 20	20 59 15	7♋17 06	13 59 43	27 57.9	20 59.0	3 34.3	18 23.2	24 19.4	11 19.4	18 22.3	23 18.3	28 13.5	2 19.2
10 M	21 23 17	21 59 58	20 39 16	27 15 36	27 51.5	22 45.7	4 12.0	18 12.2	24 43.0	11 20.5	18 29.1	23 18.8	28 15.4	2 21.1
11 Tu	21 27 13	23 00 39	3♌48 33	10♌18 02	27 45.4	24 33.1	4 48.4	18 02.0	25 06.6	11 21.8	18 36.1	23 19.4	28 17.3	2 22.9
12 W	21 31 10	24 01 18	16 43 57	23 06 15	27 40.2	26 21.2	5 23.4	17 52.6	25 30.1	11 23.4	18 43.0	23 20.1	28 19.2	2 24.8
13 Th	21 35 06	25 01 56	29 24 55	5♍40 01	27 36.5	28 10.1	5 56.9	17 44.0	25 53.7	11 25.1	18 50.0	23 20.8	28 21.2	2 26.6
14 F	21 39 03	26 02 33	11♍51 38	17 59 57	27D 34.5	29 59.5	6 28.9	17 36.1	26 17.3	11 27.0	18 57.0	23 21.5	28 23.2	2 28.4
15 Sa	21 42 59	27 03 08	24 05 11	0♎07 35	27 34.1	1♓49.6	6 59.4	17 29.1	26 40.8	11 29.2	19 04.0	23 22.3	28 25.2	2 30.2
16 Su	21 46 56	28 03 42	6♎07 31	12 05 20	27 34.9	3 40.2	7 28.3	17 22.9	27 04.4	11 31.5	19 11.1	23 23.2	28 27.2	2 32.0
17 M	21 50 52	29 04 15	18 01 30	23 56 29	27 36.6	5 31.2	7 55.5	17 17.4	27 28.0	11 34.0	19 18.2	23 24.1	28 29.2	2 33.7
18 Tu	21 54 49	0♓04 46	29 50 47	5♏45 00	27 38.5	7 22.5	8 21.0	17 12.7	27 51.5	11 36.7	19 25.3	23 25.1	28 31.3	2 35.5
19 W	21 58 46	1 05 16	11♏39 40	17 35 25	27 40.0	9 14.0	8 44.7	17 08.9	28 15.1	11 39.6	19 32.4	23 26.1	28 33.3	2 37.3
20 Th	22 02 42	2 05 45	23 32 52	29 32 38	27R 40.8	11 05.6	9 06.5	17 05.8	28 38.7	11 42.7	19 39.6	23 27.1	28 35.4	2 39.0
21 F	22 06 39	3 06 13	5♐35 21	11♐41 37	27 40.5	12 57.0	9 26.4	17 03.4	29 02.2	11 46.0	19 46.8	23 28.2	28 37.5	2 40.7
22 Sa	22 10 35	4 06 39	17 52 02	24 07 07	27 39.1	14 47.9	9 44.4	17 01.9	29 25.8	11 49.4	19 54.0	23 29.4	28 39.6	2 42.4
23 Su	22 14 32	5 07 04	0♑27 22	6♑53 13	27 36.7	16 38.3	10 00.3	17D 01.0	29 49.3	11 53.1	20 01.2	23 30.6	28 41.7	2 44.1
24 M	22 18 28	6 07 28	13 24 59	20 02 55	27 33.7	18 27.6	10 14.1	17 01.0	0♓12.8	11 56.9	20 08.5	23 31.9	28 43.8	2 45.8
25 Tu	22 22 25	7 07 50	26 47 07	3♒37 34	27 30.5	20 15.6	10 25.8	17 01.7	0 36.3	12 00.9	20 15.8	23 33.2	28 46.0	2 47.5
26 W	22 26 21	8 08 10	10♒34 08	17 36 29	27 27.7	22 01.9	10 35.3	17 03.1	0 59.8	12 05.1	20 23.0	23 34.6	28 48.1	2 49.1
27 Th	22 30 18	9 08 29	24 44 12	1♓56 42	27 25.6	23 46.0	10 42.5	17 05.2	1 23.3	12 09.5	20 30.4	23 36.0	28 50.3	2 50.8
28 F	22 34 15	10 08 46	9♓13 16	16 33 06	27D 24.4	25 27.5	10 47.3	17 08.1	1 46.8	12 14.1	20 37.7	23 37.4	28 52.5	2 52.4

Astro Data

	Dy Hr Mn
☽0N	5 19:08
☽0S	19 3:15
♄∠♇	27 0:46
♀0N	30 7:31
♅ D	30 16:22
☽0N	2 0:38
♃ D	4 9:40
☽0S	15 10:54
♂ D	24 2:00

Planet Ingress

	Dy Hr Mn
♀ ♓	3 3:24
♂ ♋R	6 10:44
☿ ♑	8 10:30
☊ ♓R	11 23:02
☉ ♒	19 20:00
☿ ♒	28 2:53
♀ ♈	4 7:57
☿ ♓	14 12:06
☉ ♓	18 10:06
⚳ ♓	23 22:55

Last Aspect / ☽ Ingress

Last Aspect Dy Hr Mn		☽ Ingress Dy Hr Mn
1 6:02	♆ ⚹	♒ 1 10:50
3 4:13	♅ □	♓ 3 15:21
5 14:30	♆ ☌	♈ 5 19:01
7 21:16	♂ □	♉ 7 22:11
9 22:50	♂ ⚹	♊ 10 1:07
12 0:03	♆ □	♋ 12 4:24
14 4:45	♆ △	♌ 14 9:12
16 4:10	♅ □	♍ 16 16:46
19 2:01	☉ △	♎ 19 3:33
21 4:33	♂ □	♏ 21 16:20
24 0:03	♆ △	♐ 24 4:29
26 9:39	♆ □	♑ 26 13:43
28 15:48	♆ ⚹	♒ 28 19:31
30 11:29	♅ □	♓ 30 22:52

Last Aspect / ☽ Ingress

Last Aspect Dy Hr Mn		☽ Ingress Dy Hr Mn
1 22:06	♀ ☌	♈ 2 1:10
3 10:19	♂ □	♉ 4 3:33
6 3:29	♆ ⚹	♊ 6 6:44
8 7:52	♆ □	♋ 8 11:04
10 13:49	♆ △	♌ 10 17:00
12 19:12	☿ ☍	♍ 13 1:07
15 8:35	♆ ☍	♎ 15 11:45
17 23:24	☉ △	♏ 18 0:19
20 10:05	♆ △	♐ 20 12:55
22 20:38	♆ □	♑ 22 23:09
25 3:28	♆ ⚹	♒ 25 5:40
26 22:04	♅ □	♓ 27 8:46

☽ Phases & Eclipses

Dy Hr Mn		
6 23:56	☽	16♈56
13 22:27	○	24♋00
21 20:31	☾	2♏03
29 12:36	●	9♒51
5 8:02	☽	16♉46
12 13:53	○	24♌06
20 17:32	☾	2♐20
28 0:45	●	9♓41

Astro Data

1 January 2025
Julian Day # 45657
SVP 4♓54'38"
GC 27♐11.3 ⚴ 12♑28.0
Eris 24♈23.9R ⚵ 19♏08.0
⚷ 19♈00.2 ⚶ 29♎25.1
☽ Mean ☊ 1♈28.2

1 February 2025
Julian Day # 45688
SVP 4♓54'32"
GC 27♐11.4 ⚴ 24♑23.6
Eris 24♈25.8 ⚵ 26♏48.1
⚷ 19♈31.0 ⚶ 10♏24.5
☽ Mean ☊ 29♓49.7

March 2025 LONGITUDE

Day	Sid.Time	☉	0 hr ☽	Noon ☽	True ☊	☿	♀	♂	⚳	♃	♄	♅	♆	♇
1 Sa	22 38 11	11♓09 02	23♓55 21	1♈19 05	27♓24.2	27♓05.8	10♈49.8	17♋11.6	2♓10.3	12♊18.8	20♓45.0	23♉38.9	28♓54.6	2♒54.0
2 Su	22 42 08	12 09 15	8♈43 22	16 07 20	27 24.7	28 40.5	10R 49.9	17 15.9	2 33.7	12 23.8	20 52.4	23 40.5	28 56.8	2 55.6
3 M	22 46 04	13 09 26	23 30 07	0♉50 56	27 25.7	0♈10.8	10 47.5	17 20.8	2 57.1	12 28.8	20 59.7	23 42.1	28 59.0	2 57.2
4 Tu	22 50 01	14 09 36	8♉09 08	15 24 07	27 26.8	1 36.3	10 42.6	17 26.4	3 20.6	12 34.1	21 07.1	23 43.7	29 01.2	2 58.7
5 W	22 53 57	15 09 43	22 35 26	29 42 45	27 27.7	2 56.4	10 35.2	17 32.7	3 43.9	12 39.5	21 14.5	23 45.4	29 03.5	3 00.2
6 Th	22 57 54	16 09 48	6♊45 47	13♊44 25	27R 28.1	4 10.5	10 25.2	17 39.6	4 07.3	12 45.1	21 21.8	23 47.2	29 05.7	3 01.8
7 F	23 01 50	17 09 52	20 38 34	27 28 14	27 27.9	5 18.1	10 12.8	17 47.1	4 30.7	12 50.9	21 29.2	23 49.0	29 07.9	3 03.3
8 Sa	23 05 47	18 09 53	4♋13 30	10♋54 26	27 27.3	6 18.6	9 57.8	17 55.3	4 54.0	12 56.9	21 36.6	23 50.8	29 10.2	3 04.7
9 Su	23 09 44	19 09 51	17 31 13	24 03 58	27 26.3	7 11.6	9 40.4	18 04.1	5 17.3	13 02.9	21 44.0	23 52.7	29 12.4	3 06.2
10 M	23 13 40	20 09 48	0♌32 52	6♌58 07	27 25.3	7 56.7	9 20.5	18 13.4	5 40.6	13 09.2	21 51.5	23 54.6	29 14.7	3 07.6
11 Tu	23 17 37	21 09 42	13 19 53	19 38 21	27 24.4	8 33.5	8 58.3	18 23.3	6 03.8	13 15.6	21 58.9	23 56.5	29 16.9	3 09.1
12 W	23 21 33	22 09 35	25 53 42	2♍06 06	27 23.8	9 01.9	8 33.9	18 33.8	6 27.1	13 22.2	22 06.3	23 58.5	29 19.2	3 10.5
13 Th	23 25 30	23 09 25	8♍15 46	14 22 51	27 23.4	9 21.7	8 07.3	18 44.9	6 50.3	13 28.9	22 13.7	24 00.6	29 21.4	3 11.8
14 F	23 29 26	24 09 13	20 27 33	26 30 04	27D 23.2	9R 32.7	7 38.7	18 56.5	7 13.4	13 35.8	22 21.1	24 02.7	29 23.7	3 13.2
15 Sa	23 33 23	25 09 00	2♎30 38	8♎29 27	27 23.3	9 35.1	7 08.3	19 08.6	7 36.6	13 42.8	22 28.5	24 04.8	29 26.0	3 14.5
16 Su	23 37 19	26 08 44	14 26 47	20 22 55	27 23.4	9 29.1	6 36.2	19 21.3	7 59.7	13 50.0	22 35.9	24 07.0	29 28.2	3 15.8
17 M	23 41 16	27 08 27	26 18 08	2♏12 46	27R 23.5	9 14.9	6 02.5	19 34.4	8 22.8	13 57.3	22 43.3	24 09.2	29 30.5	3 17.1
18 Tu	23 45 13	28 08 07	8♏07 12	14 01 48	27 23.5	8 53.1	5 27.6	19 48.1	8 45.9	14 04.7	22 50.7	24 11.4	29 32.8	3 18.4
19 W	23 49 09	29 07 46	19 57 01	25 53 16	27 23.3	8 24.1	4 51.7	20 02.2	9 08.9	14 12.3	22 58.0	24 13.7	29 35.1	3 19.6
20 Th	23 53 06	0♈07 24	1♐51 04	7♐50 54	27 23.1	7 48.7	4 14.9	20 16.8	9 31.9	14 20.1	23 05.4	24 16.0	29 37.3	3 20.9
21 F	23 57 02	1 06 59	13 53 17	19 58 47	27D 22.8	7 07.8	3 37.5	20 31.9	9 54.9	14 28.0	23 12.8	24 18.4	29 39.6	3 22.1
22 Sa	0 00 59	2 06 33	26 07 56	2♑21 16	27 22.7	6 22.4	2 59.8	20 47.4	10 17.8	14 36.0	23 20.2	24 20.8	29 41.9	3 23.2
23 Su	0 04 55	3 06 05	8♑39 19	15 02 36	27 22.9	5 33.4	2 22.0	21 03.4	10 40.7	14 44.1	23 27.5	24 23.2	29 44.2	3 24.4
24 M	0 08 52	4 05 35	21 31 34	28 06 36	27 23.3	4 42.0	1 44.4	21 19.8	11 03.6	14 52.4	23 34.8	24 25.7	29 46.4	3 25.5
25 Tu	0 12 48	5 05 04	4♒48 03	11♒36 06	27 23.9	3 49.3	1 07.2	21 36.7	11 26.4	15 00.8	23 42.2	24 28.2	29 48.7	3 26.6
26 W	0 16 45	6 04 31	18 30 54	25 32 23	27 24.7	2 56.3	0 30.7	21 53.9	11 49.2	15 09.4	23 49.5	24 30.8	29 51.0	3 27.7
27 Th	0 20 42	7 03 56	2♓40 21	9♓54 29	27 25.4	2 04.3	29♓55.1	22 11.6	12 11.9	15 18.1	23 56.8	24 33.4	29 53.2	3 28.8
28 F	0 24 38	8 03 18	17 14 12	24 38 50	27R 25.7	1 14.1	29 20.7	22 29.7	12 34.7	15 26.9	24 04.0	24 36.0	29 55.5	3 29.8
29 Sa	0 28 35	9 02 39	2♈07 31	9♈39 15	27 25.5	0 26.6	28 47.5	22 48.2	12 57.3	15 35.8	24 11.3	24 38.6	29 57.8	3 30.8
30 Su	0 32 31	10 01 58	17 12 55	24 47 21	27 24.7	29♓42.7	28 15.9	23 07.0	13 20.0	15 44.9	24 18.5	24 41.3	0♈00.0	3 31.8
31 M	0 36 28	11 01 15	2♉21 21	9♉53 46	27 23.3	29 02.9	27 46.0	23 26.3	13 42.5	15 54.0	24 25.8	24 44.0	0 02.2	3 32.8

April 2025 LONGITUDE

Day	Sid.Time	☉	0 hr ☽	Noon ☽	True ☊	☿	♀	♂	⚳	♃	♄	♅	♆	♇
1 Tu	0 40 24	12♈00 30	17♉23 29	24♉49 31	27♓21.5	28♓27.8	27♓18.0	23♋45.9	14♓05.1	16♊03.3	24♓33.0	24♉46.8	0♈04.5	3♒33.7
2 W	0 44 21	12 59 42	2♊11 01	9♊27 17	27R 19.7	27R 57.8	26R 51.9	24 05.9	14 27.6	16 12.8	24 40.2	24 49.6	0 06.7	3 34.6
3 Th	0 48 17	13 58 53	16 37 49	23 42 15	27 18.2	27 33.0	26 27.9	24 26.2	14 50.0	16 22.3	24 47.3	24 52.4	0 09.0	3 35.5
4 F	0 52 14	14 58 01	0♋40 25	7♋32 17	27D 17.3	27 13.8	26 06.2	24 46.9	15 12.4	16 31.9	24 54.4	24 55.2	0 11.2	3 36.3
5 Sa	0 56 11	15 57 06	14 17 56	20 57 34	27 17.3	27 00.2	25 46.7	25 07.9	15 34.8	16 41.7	25 01.5	24 58.1	0 13.4	3 37.2
6 Su	1 00 07	16 56 09	27 31 29	4♌00 02	27 18.0	26D 52.1	25 29.6	25 29.2	15 57.1	16 51.5	25 08.6	25 01.0	0 15.6	3 38.0
7 M	1 04 04	17 55 10	10♌23 36	16 42 38	27 19.3	26 49.6	25 14.8	25 50.9	16 19.3	17 01.5	25 15.7	25 03.9	0 17.8	3 38.7
8 Tu	1 08 00	18 54 09	22 57 32	29 08 47	27 20.9	26 52.5	25 02.5	26 12.8	16 41.5	17 11.6	25 22.7	25 06.9	0 20.0	3 39.5
9 W	1 11 57	19 53 05	5♍16 47	11♍21 57	27 22.3	27 00.6	24 52.7	26 35.1	17 03.6	17 21.7	25 29.7	25 09.8	0 22.2	3 40.2
10 Th	1 15 53	20 51 59	17 24 41	23 25 22	27R 23.1	27 13.9	24 45.3	26 57.6	17 25.7	17 32.0	25 36.6	25 12.8	0 24.3	3 40.9
11 F	1 19 50	21 50 51	29 24 19	5♎21 52	27 22.9	27 32.1	24 40.4	27 20.5	17 47.7	17 42.4	25 43.6	25 15.9	0 26.5	3 41.5
12 Sa	1 23 46	22 49 41	11♎18 20	17 13 59	27 21.5	27 54.9	24D 37.8	27 43.6	18 09.7	17 52.8	25 50.5	25 18.9	0 28.6	3 42.2
13 Su	1 27 43	23 48 29	23 09 04	29 03 51	27 18.7	28 22.3	24 37.7	28 07.0	18 31.6	18 03.4	25 57.3	25 22.0	0 30.7	3 42.8
14 M	1 31 39	24 47 15	4♏58 35	10♏53 30	27 14.7	28 54.0	24 40.0	28 30.7	18 53.5	18 14.1	26 04.2	25 25.1	0 32.9	3 43.4
15 Tu	1 35 36	25 45 59	16 48 51	22 44 54	27 09.9	29 29.9	24 44.6	28 54.6	19 15.3	18 24.8	26 10.9	25 28.2	0 35.0	3 43.9
16 W	1 39 33	26 44 41	28 41 55	4♐40 11	27 04.7	0♈09.6	24 51.5	29 18.8	19 37.0	18 35.7	26 17.7	25 31.4	0 37.1	3 44.5
17 Th	1 43 29	27 43 22	10♐40 02	16 41 47	26 59.7	0 53.0	25 00.6	29 43.2	19 58.7	18 46.6	26 24.4	25 34.5	0 39.2	3 45.0
18 F	1 47 26	28 42 01	22 45 48	28 52 28	26 55.4	1 40.0	25 11.8	0♌07.9	20 20.3	18 57.6	26 31.1	25 37.7	0 41.2	3 45.4
19 Sa	1 51 22	29 40 38	5♑02 13	11♑15 28	26 52.4	2 30.4	25 25.2	0 32.8	20 41.9	19 08.7	26 37.7	25 40.9	0 43.3	3 45.9
20 Su	1 55 19	0♉39 13	17 32 40	23 54 16	26D 50.9	3 24.0	25 40.6	0 58.0	21 03.4	19 19.9	26 44.3	25 44.2	0 45.3	3 46.3
21 M	1 59 15	1 37 47	0♒20 45	6♒52 32	26 50.8	4 20.7	25 58.0	1 23.4	21 24.8	19 31.2	26 50.9	25 47.4	0 47.3	3 46.7
22 Tu	2 03 12	2 36 19	13 30 01	20 13 34	26 51.8	5 20.3	26 17.3	1 49.0	21 46.2	19 42.5	26 57.4	25 50.7	0 49.4	3 47.0
23 W	2 07 09	3 34 50	27 03 28	3♓59 55	26 53.2	6 22.7	26 38.4	2 14.9	22 07.5	19 54.0	27 03.9	25 53.9	0 51.4	3 47.4
24 Th	2 11 05	4 33 19	11♓02 57	18 12 31	26R 54.4	7 27.9	27 01.4	2 41.0	22 28.7	20 05.5	27 10.3	25 57.2	0 53.3	3 47.7
25 F	2 15 02	5 31 46	25 28 21	2♈50 03	26 54.5	8 35.6	27 26.0	3 07.2	22 49.9	20 17.1	27 16.7	26 00.6	0 55.3	3 47.9
26 Sa	2 18 58	6 30 12	10♈16 58	17 48 17	26 53.0	9 45.8	27 52.3	3 33.8	23 10.9	20 28.8	27 23.0	26 03.9	0 57.2	3 48.2
27 Su	2 22 55	7 28 35	25 23 01	3♉00 00	26 49.6	10 58.5	28 20.2	4 00.5	23 31.9	20 40.5	27 29.3	26 07.2	0 59.2	3 48.4
28 M	2 26 51	8 26 58	10♉37 58	18 15 35	26 44.4	12 13.5	28 49.6	4 27.4	23 52.9	20 52.3	27 35.5	26 10.6	1 01.1	3 48.6
29 Tu	2 30 48	9 25 18	25 51 30	3♊24 25	26 38.2	13 30.8	29 20.5	4 54.5	24 13.7	21 04.2	27 41.7	26 14.0	1 03.0	3 48.7
30 W	2 34 44	10 23 37	10♊53 12	18 16 47	26 31.7	14 50.2	29 52.7	5 21.9	24 34.5	21 16.2	27 47.9	26 17.4	1 04.8	3 48.9

Astro Data	Planet Ingress	Last Aspect	☽ Ingress	Last Aspect	☽ Ingress	☽ Phases & Eclipses
Dy Hr Mn	Dy Hr Mn	Dy Hr Mn	Dy Hr Mn	Dy Hr Mn	Dy Hr Mn	Dy Hr Mn
☽0N 1 9:07	☿ ♈ 3 9:04	1 8:05 ♆ ☌	♈ 1 9:52	1 17:43 ♆ ✶	♊ 1 20:26	6 16:32 ☽ 16♊21
♀R 2 0:36	☉ ♈ 20 9:01	2 13:52 ♂ □	♉ 3 10:37	3 18:26 ♆ □	♋ 3 22:50	14 6:55 ○ 23♍57
☿0N 2 12:30	♀ ♓R 27 8:41	5 10:53 ♆ ✶	♊ 5 12:29	5 22:54 ♆ △	♌ 6 4:34	14 6:59 • T 1.179
☽0S 14 18:04	☿ ♓R 30 2:18	7 14:57 ♆ □	♋ 7 16:29	8 4:08 ♅ □	♍ 8 13:40	22 11:29 ☾ 2♑05
☿R 15 6:45	♆ ♈ 30 11:59	9 21:32 ♆ △	♌ 9 22:59	10 19:49 ♆ ☍	♎ 11 1:12	29 10:58 ● 9♈00
☉0N 20 9:02		11 20:16 ♅ □	♍ 12 7:56	13 10:01 ♂ □	♏ 13 13:54	29 10:47:21 • P 0.938
☽0N 28 19:52	☿ ♈ 16 6:25	14 17:47 ♆ ☍	♎ 14 18:59	16 2:24 ♆ △	♐ 16 2:37	
☿0S 3 5:48	♂ ♌ 18 4:21	16 9:53 ♂ □	♏ 17 7:30	18 11:38 ☉ △	♑ 18 14:12	5 2:15 ☽ 15♋33
♄✶♆ 4 16:21	☉ ♉ 19 19:56	19 19:28 ♆ △	♐ 19 20:17	20 17:21 ♄ ✶	♒ 20 23:22	13 0:22 ○ 23♎20
☿D 7 11:07	♀ ♈ 30 17:16	22 6:53 ♆ □	♑ 22 7:29	22 21:55 ♅ □	♓ 23 5:07	21 1:35 ☾ 1♒12
☽0S 11 0:17		24 15:01 ♆ ✶	♒ 24 15:25	25 2:57 ♀ ☌	♈ 25 7:24	27 19:31 ● 7♉47
♀D 13 1:02		26 10:15 ♅ □	♓ 26 19:31	26 16:18 ♃ ✶	♉ 27 7:17	
♃□♇ 17 8:16		28 20:30 ♆ ☌	♈ 28 20:36	29 5:18 ♀ ✶	♊ 29 6:34	
☿0N 23 4:14		30 9:18 ♂ □	♉ 30 20:16			
☽0N 25 6:31						

Astro Data

1 March 2025
Julian Day # 45716
SVP 4♓54'28"
GC 27♐11.4 ⚴ 4♒26.2
Eris 24♈35.9 ✻ 1♐04.5
⚷ 20♈38.1 ⚵ 16♏54.8
☽ Mean ☊ 28♓20.7

1 April 2025
Julian Day # 45747
SVP 4♓54'25"
GC 27♐11.5 ⚴ 14♒08.4
Eris 24♈53.8 ✻ 1♐29.7R
⚷ 22♈19.7 ⚵ 17♏57.2R
☽ Mean ☊ 26♓42.2

LONGITUDE — May 2025

Day	Sid.Time	☉	0 hr ☽	Noon ☽	True ☊	☿	♀	♂	⚳	♃	♄	♅	♆	♇
1 Th	2 38 41	11♉21 53	25♊34 20	2♋45 15	26♓25.9	16♈11.9	0♈26.4	5♌49.4	24♓55.2	21♊28.2	27♓53.9	26♉20.8	1♈06.7	3♒49.0
2 F	2 42 38	12 20 08	9♋49 05	16 45 40	26R 21.4	17 35.7	1 01.3	6 17.1	25 15.8	21 40.3	28 00.0	26 24.2	1 08.5	3 49.1
3 Sa	2 46 34	13 18 20	23 34 57	0♌17 06	26 18.7	19 01.5	1 37.5	6 45.0	25 36.3	21 52.5	28 05.9	26 27.6	1 10.3	3 49.1
4 Su	2 50 31	14 16 31	6♌52 24	13 21 15	26D 17.8	20 29.4	2 14.8	7 13.0	25 56.7	22 04.7	28 11.9	26 31.0	1 12.1	3R49.1
5 M	2 54 27	15 14 39	19 44 09	26 01 37	26 18.3	21 59.4	2 53.4	7 41.3	26 17.1	22 17.0	28 17.7	26 34.4	1 13.9	3 49.1
6 Tu	2 58 24	16 12 45	2♍14 15	8♍22 38	26 19.5	23 31.3	3 33.0	8 09.7	26 37.4	22 29.3	28 23.5	26 37.9	1 15.6	3 49.1
7 W	3 02 20	17 10 50	14 27 23	20 29 05	26R 20.5	25 05.2	4 13.7	8 38.3	26 57.5	22 41.7	28 29.3	26 41.3	1 17.3	3 49.0
8 Th	3 06 17	18 08 52	26 28 18	2♎25 35	26 20.5	26 41.2	4 55.5	9 07.0	27 17.6	22 54.1	28 34.9	26 44.8	1 19.0	3 48.9
9 F	3 10 13	19 06 53	8♎21 25	14 16 16	26 18.7	28 19.1	5 38.2	9 35.9	27 37.6	23 06.6	28 40.6	26 48.3	1 20.7	3 48.8
10 Sa	3 14 10	20 04 52	20 10 34	26 04 43	26 14.6	29 58.9	6 21.9	10 05.0	27 57.5	23 19.2	28 46.1	26 51.7	1 22.4	3 48.6
11 Su	3 18 06	21 02 50	1♏59 02	7♏53 49	26 08.2	1♉40.8	7 06.5	10 34.2	28 17.3	23 31.8	28 51.6	26 55.2	1 24.0	3 48.5
12 M	3 22 03	22 00 45	13 49 20	19 45 50	25 59.6	3 24.7	7 52.0	11 03.6	28 37.0	23 44.5	28 57.0	26 58.7	1 25.6	3 48.3
13 Tu	3 26 00	22 58 40	25 43 31	1♐42 34	25 49.4	5 10.5	8 38.4	11 33.1	28 56.6	23 57.2	29 02.4	27 02.2	1 27.2	3 48.0
14 W	3 29 56	23 56 33	7♐43 10	13 45 28	25 38.6	6 58.3	9 25.6	12 02.8	29 16.1	24 10.0	29 07.7	27 05.7	1 28.8	3 47.8
15 Th	3 33 53	24 54 24	19 49 38	25 55 52	25 28.0	8 48.1	10 13.5	12 32.6	29 35.6	24 22.8	29 13.0	27 09.2	1 30.3	3 47.5
16 F	3 37 49	25 52 14	2♑04 20	8♑15 15	25 18.6	10 39.9	11 02.3	13 02.5	29 54.9	24 35.6	29 18.2	27 12.7	1 31.8	3 47.2
17 Sa	3 41 46	26 50 03	14 28 51	20 45 23	25 11.2	12 33.7	11 51.7	13 32.6	0♈14.1	24 48.5	29 23.3	27 16.2	1 33.3	3 46.8
18 Su	3 45 42	27 47 51	27 05 10	3♒28 29	25 06.1	14 29.4	12 41.9	14 02.8	0 33.2	25 01.5	29 28.3	27 19.6	1 34.8	3 46.5
19 M	3 49 39	28 45 37	9♒55 41	16 27 07	25 03.5	16 27.1	13 32.7	14 33.2	0 52.2	25 14.5	29 33.3	27 23.1	1 36.2	3 46.1
20 Tu	3 53 36	29 43 23	23 03 08	29 44 04	25D 02.8	18 26.6	14 24.2	15 03.7	1 11.1	25 27.5	29 38.2	27 26.6	1 37.6	3 45.7
21 W	3 57 32	0♊41 07	6♓30 14	13♓21 55	25R 03.2	20 28.0	15 16.3	15 34.3	1 29.9	25 40.6	29 43.0	27 30.1	1 39.0	3 45.2
22 Th	4 01 29	1 38 50	20 19 17	27 22 27	25 03.4	22 31.2	16 09.0	16 05.1	1 48.5	25 53.7	29 47.8	27 33.6	1 40.4	3 44.8
23 F	4 05 25	2 36 32	4♈31 22	11♈45 52	25 02.4	24 36.0	17 02.3	16 35.9	2 07.1	26 06.8	29 52.4	27 37.1	1 41.7	3 44.3
24 Sa	4 09 22	3 34 13	19 05 35	26 30 00	24 59.3	26 42.5	17 56.2	17 07.0	2 25.5	26 20.0	29 57.0	27 40.6	1 43.0	3 43.7
25 Su	4 13 18	4 31 54	3♉58 22	11♉29 48	24 53.5	28 50.3	18 50.6	17 38.1	2 43.8	26 33.3	0♈01.6	27 44.1	1 44.3	3 43.2
26 M	4 17 15	5 29 33	19 03 12	26 37 22	24 45.4	0♊59.4	19 45.4	18 09.4	3 02.0	26 46.5	0 06.0	27 47.5	1 45.6	3 42.6
27 Tu	4 21 11	6 27 11	4♊11 03	11♊42 56	24 35.5	3 09.5	20 40.8	18 40.8	3 20.1	26 59.8	0 10.4	27 51.0	1 46.8	3 42.0
28 W	4 25 08	7 24 48	19 11 45	26 36 21	24 25.1	5 20.5	21 36.7	19 12.3	3 38.0	27 13.1	0 14.7	27 54.5	1 48.0	3 41.4
29 Th	4 29 05	8 22 24	3♋55 42	11♋08 59	24 15.3	7 32.2	22 33.0	19 43.9	3 55.9	27 26.5	0 18.9	27 57.9	1 49.1	3 40.8
30 F	4 33 01	9 19 58	18 15 34	25 15 01	24 07.2	9 44.1	23 29.7	20 15.7	4 13.5	27 39.9	0 23.1	28 01.4	1 50.3	3 40.1
31 Sa	4 36 58	10 17 31	2♌07 10	8♌51 59	24 01.4	11 56.2	24 26.9	20 47.5	4 31.1	27 53.3	0 27.2	28 04.8	1 51.4	3 39.4

LONGITUDE — June 2025

Day	Sid.Time	☉	0 hr ☽	Noon ☽	True ☊	☿	♀	♂	⚳	♃	♄	♅	♆	♇
1 Su	4 40 54	11♊15 02	15♌29 38	22♌00 27	23♓58.1	14♊08.1	25♈24.5	21♌19.5	4♈48.5	28♊06.7	0♈31.1	28♉08.3	1♈52.5	3♒38.7
2 M	4 44 51	12 12 33	28 24 51	4♍43 21	23D 56.8	16 19.5	26 22.5	21 51.6	5 05.8	28 20.1	0 35.0	28 11.7	1 53.5	3R 37.9
3 Tu	4 48 47	13 10 02	10♍56 35	17 05 08	23R 56.7	18 30.1	27 20.8	22 23.8	5 22.9	28 33.6	0 38.8	28 15.1	1 54.5	3 37.2
4 W	4 52 44	14 07 29	23 09 43	29 10 58	23 56.6	20 39.8	28 19.6	22 56.1	5 39.9	28 47.1	0 42.6	28 18.5	1 55.5	3 36.4
5 Th	4 56 40	15 04 56	5♎09 33	11♎06 08	23 55.6	22 48.2	29 18.7	23 28.5	5 56.8	29 00.6	0 46.2	28 21.9	1 56.5	3 35.6
6 F	5 00 37	16 02 21	17 01 20	22 55 43	23 52.8	24 55.3	0♉18.1	24 01.0	6 13.5	29 14.2	0 49.8	28 25.3	1 57.4	3 34.7
7 Sa	5 04 34	16 59 45	28 49 51	4♏44 13	23 47.3	27 00.6	1 17.9	24 33.5	6 30.0	29 27.7	0 53.2	28 28.6	1 58.3	3 33.9
8 Su	5 08 30	17 57 09	10♏39 15	16 35 23	23 39.2	29 04.2	2 18.0	25 06.2	6 46.4	29 41.3	0 56.6	28 32.0	1 59.2	3 33.0
9 M	5 12 27	18 54 31	22 32 55	28 32 09	23 28.5	1♋05.8	3 18.4	25 39.0	7 02.7	29 54.9	0 59.9	28 35.3	2 00.0	3 32.1
10 Tu	5 16 23	19 51 52	4♐33 21	10♐36 40	23 16.0	3 05.3	4 19.2	26 11.9	7 18.8	0♋08.5	1 03.2	28 38.6	2 00.8	3 31.2
11 W	5 20 20	20 49 13	16 42 16	22 50 16	23 02.6	5 02.7	5 20.2	26 44.9	7 34.8	0 22.1	1 06.3	28 41.9	2 01.6	3 30.3
12 Th	5 24 16	21 46 33	29 00 44	5♑13 44	22 49.4	6 57.9	6 21.6	27 18.0	7 50.6	0 35.7	1 09.3	28 45.2	2 02.3	3 29.3
13 F	5 28 13	22 43 52	11♑29 19	17 47 31	22 37.6	8 50.7	7 23.2	27 51.2	8 06.2	0 49.4	1 12.3	28 48.5	2 03.0	3 28.3
14 Sa	5 32 09	23 41 11	24 08 24	0♒32 02	22 28.1	10 41.2	8 25.1	28 24.4	8 21.7	1 03.0	1 15.1	28 51.8	2 03.7	3 27.3
15 Su	5 36 06	24 38 29	6♒58 30	13 27 55	22 21.4	12 29.3	9 27.3	28 57.8	8 37.0	1 16.7	1 17.9	28 55.0	2 04.4	3 26.3
16 M	5 40 03	25 35 47	20 00 24	26 36 08	22 17.5	14 15.0	10 29.7	29 31.2	8 52.1	1 30.4	1 20.6	28 58.2	2 05.0	3 25.3
17 Tu	5 43 59	26 33 04	3♓15 18	9♓58 06	22D 15.9	15 58.3	11 32.4	0♍04.8	9 07.1	1 44.1	1 23.1	29 01.4	2 05.6	3 24.2
18 W	5 47 56	27 30 21	16 44 44	23 35 23	22R 15.6	17 39.2	12 35.3	0 38.4	9 21.8	1 57.7	1 25.6	29 04.6	2 06.1	3 23.2
19 Th	5 51 52	28 27 38	0♈30 13	7♈29 19	22 15.5	19 17.6	13 38.5	1 12.1	9 36.5	2 11.4	1 28.0	29 07.8	2 06.6	3 22.1
20 F	5 55 49	29 24 55	14 32 44	21 40 23	22 14.2	20 53.5	14 41.9	1 45.9	9 50.9	2 25.1	1 30.3	29 10.9	2 07.1	3 21.0
21 Sa	5 59 45	0♋22 11	28 52 05	6♉07 32	22 10.9	22 27.0	15 45.6	2 19.8	10 05.1	2 38.8	1 32.5	29 14.0	2 07.6	3 19.9
22 Su	6 03 42	1 19 28	13♉26 14	20 47 34	22 05.0	23 58.0	16 49.4	2 53.8	10 19.2	2 52.5	1 34.6	29 17.1	2 08.0	3 18.7
23 M	6 07 38	2 16 44	28 10 47	5♊35 00	21 56.5	25 26.4	17 53.5	3 27.9	10 33.0	3 06.3	1 36.6	29 20.2	2 08.4	3 17.6
24 Tu	6 11 35	3 14 00	12♊59 12	20 22 22	21 46.3	26 52.4	18 57.8	4 02.0	10 46.7	3 20.0	1 38.6	29 23.2	2 08.8	3 16.4
25 W	6 15 32	4 11 16	27 43 26	5♋01 22	21 35.3	28 15.7	20 02.2	4 36.3	11 00.2	3 33.7	1 40.4	29 26.3	2 09.1	3 15.2
26 Th	6 19 28	5 08 32	12♋15 13	19 24 10	21 24.8	29 36.5	21 06.9	5 10.6	11 13.4	3 47.4	1 42.1	29 29.3	2 09.4	3 14.0
27 F	6 23 25	6 05 47	26 27 33	3♌24 50	21 16.0	0♌54.6	22 11.7	5 45.0	11 26.5	4 01.1	1 43.7	29 32.3	2 09.6	3 12.8
28 Sa	6 27 21	7 03 01	10♌15 41	16 59 57	21 09.6	2 10.0	23 16.7	6 19.5	11 39.4	4 14.8	1 45.2	29 35.2	2 09.9	3 11.6
29 Su	6 31 18	8 00 16	23 37 39	0♍08 56	21 05.7	3 22.6	24 21.9	6 54.1	11 52.0	4 28.5	1 46.7	29 38.1	2 10.1	3 10.4
30 M	6 35 14	8 57 29	6♍34 05	12 53 32	21D 04.0	4 32.5	25 27.3	7 28.8	12 04.4	4 42.1	1 48.0	29 41.0	2 10.2	3 09.1

Astro Data

	Dy Hr Mn
♇ R	4 15:27
☽ 0S	8 5:50
☽ 0N	22 15:00
♃⊻♅	1 15:48
☽ 0S	4 11:35
♃□♄	15 14:36
☽ 0N	18 20:52
♃□♆	19 3:16
♃⊼♇	24 6:16

Planet Ingress

		Dy Hr Mn
☿	♉	10 12:15
⚳	♈	16 18:23
☉	♊	20 18:55
♄	♈	25 3:35
☿	♊	26 0:59
♀	♉	6 4:43
☿	♋	8 22:58
♃	♋	9 21:02
♂	♍	17 8:35
☉	♋	21 2:42
☿	♌	26 19:09

Last Aspect / ☽ Ingress

Last Aspect Dy Hr Mn		☽ Ingress	Dy Hr Mn
1 3:49	♄ □	♋	1 7:23
3 8:02	♄ △	♌	3 11:29
5 13:03	♅ □	♍	5 19:40
8 4:11	♄ ☍	♎	8 7:06
10 6:17	♃ △	♏	10 19:58
13 6:37	♄ △	♐	13 8:35
15 18:28	♄ □	♑	15 19:58
18 4:27	♄ ⚹	♒	18 5:29
20 11:59	☉ □	♓	20 12:28
22 16:06	♄ ☌	♈	22 16:26
24 11:44	♃ ⚹	♉	24 17:38
26 13:52	♅ ☌	♊	26 17:21
28 13:01	♃ ☌	♋	28 17:33
30 16:50	♅ ⚹	♌	30 20:16

Last Aspect / ☽ Ingress

Last Aspect Dy Hr Mn		☽ Ingress	Dy Hr Mn
1 23:38	♃ ⚹	♍	2 3:00
4 11:11	♃ □	♎	4 13:38
7 1:04	♃ △	♏	7 2:23
9 12:06	♅ ☍	♐	9 14:55
11 19:58	♂ △	♑	12 1:55
14 8:52	♅ △	♒	14 11:00
16 17:31	♂ ☍	♓	16 18:09
18 21:34	♅ ⚹	♈	18 23:08
21 1:49	☉ ⚹	♉	21 1:53
23 1:50	♅ ☌	♊	23 2:57
23 8:26	♂ □	♋	25 3:44
27 5:16	♅ ⚹	♌	27 6:05
29 11:03	♅ □	♍	29 11:43

☽ Phases & Eclipses

Dy Hr Mn	
4 13:52	☽ 14♌21
12 16:56	○ 22♏13
20 11:59	☾ 29♒43
27 3:02	● 6♊06
3 3:41	☽ 12♍50
11 7:44	○ 20♐39
18 19:19	☾ 27♓48
25 10:32	● 4♋08

Astro Data

1 May 2025
Julian Day # 45777
SVP 4♓54'21"
GC 27♐11.6 ⚵ 21♒16.9
Eris 25♈13.4 ⚶ 27♏05.9R
⚷ 24♈06.0 ⚴ 12♏17.9R
☽ Mean ☊ 25♓06.9

1 June 2025
Julian Day # 45808
SVP 4♓54'16"
GC 27♐11.7 ⚵ 25♒03.1
Eris 25♈31.0 ⚶ 20♏21.9R
⚷ 25♈43.3 ⚴ 6♏04.7R
☽ Mean ☊ 23♓28.4

July 2025

LONGITUDE

Day	Sid.Time	☉	0 hr ☽	Noon ☽	True ☊	☿	♀	♂	⚳	♃	♄	♅	♆	♇
1 Tu	6 39 11	9♋54 43	19♍07 44	25♍17 17	21♓03.8	5♌39.4	26♉32.8	8♍03.5	12♈16.6	4♋55.8	1♈49.2	29♉43.9	2♈10.3	3♒07.8
2 W	6 43 08	10 51 56	1♎22 47	7♎24 53	21R 04.1	6 43.4	27 38.5	8 38.3	12 28.6	5 09.5	1 50.3	29 46.7	2 10.4	3R 06.6
3 Th	6 47 04	11 49 08	13 24 14	19 21 32	21 03.9	7 44.4	28 44.3	9 13.2	12 40.4	5 23.1	1 51.4	29 49.5	2 10.5	3 05.3
4 F	6 51 01	12 46 20	25 17 24	1♏12 32	21 02.2	8 42.2	29 50.3	9 48.2	12 51.9	5 36.7	1 52.3	29 52.3	2R 10.5	3 04.0
5 Sa	6 54 57	13 43 33	7♏07 30	13 02 56	20 58.4	9 36.8	0♊56.5	10 23.2	13 03.2	5 50.4	1 53.1	29 55.1	2 10.5	3 02.7
6 Su	6 58 54	14 40 44	18 59 20	24 57 14	20 52.2	10 28.0	2 02.8	10 58.3	13 14.3	6 04.0	1 53.8	29 57.8	2 10.5	3 01.3
7 M	7 02 50	15 37 56	0♐57 04	6♐59 13	20 43.7	11 15.8	3 09.3	11 33.5	13 25.2	6 17.6	1 54.4	0♊00.5	2 10.4	3 00.0
8 Tu	7 06 47	16 35 08	13 04 01	19 11 43	20 33.6	11 59.9	4 15.9	12 08.8	13 35.8	6 31.1	1 55.0	0 03.1	2 10.3	2 58.7
9 W	7 10 43	17 32 20	25 22 32	1♑36 36	20 22.6	12 40.3	5 22.6	12 44.1	13 46.1	6 44.7	1 55.4	0 05.8	2 10.2	2 57.3
10 Th	7 14 40	18 29 32	7♑54 00	14 14 45	20 11.8	13 16.9	6 29.5	13 19.5	13 56.3	6 58.2	1 55.7	0 08.4	2 10.0	2 56.0
11 F	7 18 37	19 26 44	20 38 50	27 06 11	20 02.1	13 49.5	7 36.6	13 55.0	14 06.1	7 11.8	1 55.9	0 10.9	2 09.8	2 54.6
12 Sa	7 22 33	20 23 56	3♒36 44	10♒10 21	19 54.4	14 17.9	8 43.8	14 30.6	14 15.8	7 25.3	1R 56.0	0 13.4	2 09.6	2 53.3
13 Su	7 26 30	21 21 08	16 46 56	23 26 22	19 49.1	14 42.1	9 51.1	15 06.2	14 25.1	7 38.7	1 56.1	0 15.9	2 09.3	2 51.9
14 M	7 30 26	22 18 21	0♓08 33	6♓53 24	19D 46.4	15 01.8	10 58.5	15 41.9	14 34.2	7 52.2	1 56.0	0 18.4	2 09.1	2 50.5
15 Tu	7 34 23	23 15 34	13 40 51	20 30 51	19 45.6	15 17.0	12 06.1	16 17.6	14 43.1	8 05.6	1 55.8	0 20.8	2 08.7	2 49.1
16 W	7 38 19	24 12 48	27 23 22	4♈18 23	19 46.2	15 27.5	13 13.8	16 53.5	14 51.6	8 19.0	1 55.5	0 23.2	2 08.4	2 47.7
17 Th	7 42 16	25 10 02	11♈15 52	18 15 47	19R 47.0	15R 33.3	14 21.6	17 29.4	14 59.9	8 32.4	1 55.1	0 25.6	2 08.0	2 46.3
18 F	7 46 12	26 07 18	25 18 04	2♉22 36	19 47.0	15 34.3	15 29.6	18 05.4	15 07.9	8 45.8	1 54.6	0 27.9	2 07.6	2 44.9
19 Sa	7 50 09	27 04 34	9♉29 14	16 37 44	19 45.4	15 30.4	16 37.7	18 41.4	15 15.7	8 59.1	1 54.0	0 30.2	2 07.1	2 43.5
20 Su	7 54 06	28 01 51	23 47 46	0♊58 57	19 41.7	15 21.6	17 45.9	19 17.5	15 23.1	9 12.4	1 53.4	0 32.4	2 06.6	2 42.1
21 M	7 58 02	28 59 08	8♊10 48	15 22 45	19 36.1	15 08.0	18 54.2	19 53.7	15 30.3	9 25.7	1 52.6	0 34.6	2 06.1	2 40.7
22 Tu	8 01 59	29 56 27	22 34 11	29 44 25	19 29.0	14 49.6	20 02.7	20 30.0	15 37.2	9 38.9	1 51.7	0 36.8	2 05.6	2 39.3
23 W	8 05 55	0♌53 46	6♋52 45	13♋58 30	19 21.3	14 26.7	21 11.2	21 06.3	15 43.7	9 52.1	1 50.7	0 38.9	2 05.0	2 37.9
24 Th	8 09 52	1 51 06	21 01 00	27 59 39	19 13.9	13 59.4	22 19.9	21 42.8	15 50.0	10 05.3	1 49.6	0 41.0	2 04.4	2 36.5
25 F	8 13 48	2 48 26	4♌53 56	11♌43 24	19 07.8	13 28.0	23 28.6	22 19.2	15 56.0	10 18.4	1 48.4	0 43.0	2 03.8	2 35.1
26 Sa	8 17 45	3 45 47	18 27 45	25 06 47	19 03.3	12 53.0	24 37.5	22 55.8	16 01.6	10 31.5	1 47.1	0 45.0	2 03.1	2 33.7
27 Su	8 21 41	4 43 08	1♍40 26	8♍08 44	19D 00.9	12 14.8	25 46.4	23 32.4	16 07.0	10 44.5	1 45.8	0 47.0	2 02.4	2 32.3
28 M	8 25 38	5 40 30	14 31 50	20 50 00	19 00.4	11 33.9	26 55.5	24 09.1	16 12.0	10 57.6	1 44.3	0 48.9	2 01.7	2 30.8
29 Tu	8 29 35	6 37 53	27 03 33	3♎12 56	19 01.1	10 51.1	28 04.7	24 45.9	16 16.7	11 10.5	1 42.7	0 50.8	2 01.0	2 29.4
30 W	8 33 31	7 35 16	9♎18 37	15 21 07	19 02.6	10 07.0	29 13.9	25 22.7	16 21.1	11 23.5	1 41.0	0 52.6	2 00.2	2 28.0
31 Th	8 37 28	8 32 39	21 21 02	27 18 58	19 04.0	9 22.3	0♋23.3	25 59.6	16 25.2	11 36.3	1 39.2	0 54.4	1 59.4	2 26.6

August 2025

LONGITUDE

Day	Sid.Time	☉	0 hr ☽	Noon ☽	True ☊	☿	♀	♂	⚳	♃	♄	♅	♆	♇
1 F	8 41 24	9♌30 03	3♏15 31	9♏11 20	19♓04.6	8♌37.9	1♋32.7	26♍36.5	16♈28.9	11♋49.2	1♈37.4	0♊56.2	1♈58.6	2♒25.2
2 Sa	8 45 21	10 27 28	15 07 02	21 03 14	19R 03.9	7R 54.6	2 42.3	27 13.6	16 32.3	12 02.0	1R 35.4	0 57.9	1R 57.7	2R 23.8
3 Su	8 49 17	11 24 53	27 00 32	2♐59 32	19 01.7	7 13.2	3 51.9	27 50.6	16 35.4	12 14.7	1 33.4	0 59.5	1 56.8	2 22.4
4 M	8 53 14	12 22 20	9♐00 44	15 04 39	18 57.9	6 34.4	5 01.6	28 27.8	16 38.1	12 27.4	1 31.3	1 01.1	1 55.9	2 21.0
5 Tu	8 57 10	13 19 46	21 11 43	27 22 20	18 53.0	5 59.2	6 11.5	29 05.0	16 40.6	12 40.1	1 29.0	1 02.7	1 54.9	2 19.6
6 W	9 01 07	14 17 14	3♑36 50	9♑55 26	18 47.4	5 28.1	7 21.4	29 42.3	16 42.6	12 52.6	1 26.7	1 04.3	1 54.0	2 18.3
7 Th	9 05 04	15 14 43	16 18 20	22 45 38	18 41.8	5 01.8	8 31.4	0♎19.6	16 44.3	13 05.2	1 24.3	1 05.7	1 53.0	2 16.9
8 F	9 09 00	16 12 12	29 17 20	5♒53 23	18 36.8	4 40.9	9 41.5	0 57.0	16 45.7	13 17.7	1 21.8	1 07.2	1 52.0	2 15.5
9 Sa	9 12 57	17 09 42	12♒33 39	19 17 56	18 32.9	4 25.9	10 51.7	1 34.5	16 46.7	13 30.1	1 19.3	1 08.6	1 50.9	2 14.2
10 Su	9 16 53	18 07 14	26 05 59	2♓57 30	18 30.5	4D 17.2	12 02.0	2 12.0	16 47.4	13 42.5	1 16.6	1 09.9	1 49.9	2 12.8
11 M	9 20 50	19 04 46	9♓52 08	16 49 32	18D 29.7	4 15.1	13 12.4	2 49.6	16R 47.7	13 54.8	1 13.8	1 11.2	1 48.8	2 11.5
12 Tu	9 24 46	20 02 20	23 49 20	0♈51 08	18 30.1	4 19.8	14 22.8	3 27.3	16 47.7	14 07.1	1 11.0	1 12.5	1 47.6	2 10.1
13 W	9 28 43	20 59 55	7♈54 36	14 59 22	18 31.3	4 31.6	15 33.4	4 05.0	16 47.3	14 19.3	1 08.1	1 13.7	1 46.5	2 08.8
14 Th	9 32 39	21 57 32	22 05 06	29 11 30	18 32.8	4 50.6	16 44.0	4 42.8	16 46.6	14 31.4	1 05.1	1 14.8	1 45.3	2 07.5
15 F	9 36 36	22 55 10	6♉18 14	13♉25 04	18R 33.8	5 16.7	17 54.8	5 20.7	16 45.4	14 43.5	1 02.0	1 15.9	1 44.2	2 06.2
16 Sa	9 40 33	23 52 50	20 31 41	27 37 49	18 34.0	5 50.0	19 05.6	5 58.6	16 44.0	14 55.5	0 58.9	1 17.0	1 42.9	2 04.9
17 Su	9 44 29	24 50 31	4♊43 12	11♊47 34	18 33.2	6 30.4	20 16.5	6 36.6	16 42.1	15 07.4	0 55.7	1 18.0	1 41.7	2 03.6
18 M	9 48 26	25 48 14	18 50 38	25 52 05	18 31.3	7 17.8	21 27.5	7 14.6	16 39.9	15 19.3	0 52.4	1 19.0	1 40.5	2 02.4
19 Tu	9 52 22	26 45 59	2♋51 37	9♋48 57	18 28.7	8 12.1	22 38.6	7 52.8	16 37.3	15 31.1	0 49.0	1 19.9	1 39.2	2 01.1
20 W	9 56 19	27 43 45	16 43 45	23 35 43	18 25.8	9 13.0	23 49.8	8 31.0	16 34.4	15 42.9	0 45.6	1 20.8	1 37.9	1 59.9
21 Th	10 00 15	28 41 33	0♌24 34	7♌10 02	18 23.0	10 20.4	25 01.0	9 09.2	16 31.1	15 54.6	0 42.1	1 21.6	1 36.6	1 58.6
22 F	10 04 12	29 39 22	13 51 53	20 29 55	18 20.7	11 33.8	26 12.3	9 47.5	16 27.4	16 06.2	0 38.5	1 22.4	1 35.3	1 57.4
23 Sa	10 08 09	0♍37 13	27 03 59	3♍34 01	18 19.2	12 53.1	27 23.7	10 25.9	16 23.3	16 17.7	0 34.8	1 23.1	1 33.9	1 56.2
24 Su	10 12 05	1 35 04	9♍59 57	16 21 49	18D 18.7	14 17.8	28 35.2	11 04.4	16 18.9	16 29.1	0 31.1	1 23.7	1 32.5	1 55.0
25 M	10 16 02	2 32 58	22 39 44	28 53 50	18 18.9	15 47.5	29 46.7	11 42.9	16 14.1	16 40.5	0 27.3	1 24.4	1 31.1	1 53.8
26 Tu	10 19 58	3 30 52	5♎04 19	11♎11 30	18 19.8	17 21.9	0♌58.3	12 21.5	16 08.9	16 51.8	0 23.5	1 24.9	1 29.7	1 52.7
27 W	10 23 55	4 28 48	17 15 40	23 17 15	18 21.0	19 00.4	2 10.0	13 00.1	16 03.4	17 03.0	0 19.6	1 25.4	1 28.3	1 51.5
28 Th	10 27 51	5 26 46	29 16 38	5♏14 19	18 22.2	20 42.6	3 21.8	13 38.8	15 57.6	17 14.1	0 15.7	1 25.9	1 26.9	1 50.4
29 F	10 31 48	6 24 45	11♏10 47	17 06 35	18 23.3	22 28.1	4 33.6	14 17.6	15 51.3	17 25.1	0 11.6	1 26.3	1 25.4	1 49.3
30 Sa	10 35 44	7 22 45	23 02 16	28 58 24	18R 23.9	24 16.4	5 45.5	14 56.4	15 44.8	17 36.1	0 07.6	1 26.7	1 23.9	1 48.2
31 Su	10 39 41	8 20 46	4♐55 35	10♐54 25	18 24.0	26 07.0	6 57.5	15 35.3	15 37.9	17 46.9	0 03.5	1 27.0	1 22.4	1 47.1

Astro Data	Dy Hr Mn
☽ 0S	1 18:17
♆ R	4 21:33
♄ R	13 4:06
☽ 0N	16 1:30
☿ R	18 4:44
☽ 0S	29 2:02
♂ 0S	8 21:32
☿ D	11 7:29
⚳ R	11 21:36
♄ ⚹ ♅	12 3:32
☽ 0N	12 7:09
♃ ∠ ♅	24 0:01
☽ 0S	25 10:11
♅ ⚹ ♆	29 0:09

Planet Ingress		Dy Hr Mn
♀	♊	4 15:31
♅	♊	7 7:45
☉	♌	22 13:29
♀	♋	31 3:57
♂	♎	6 23:23
☉	♍	22 20:34
♀	♌	25 16:27

Last Aspect Dy Hr Mn			☽ Ingress	Dy Hr Mn
1 20:47	♅	△	♎	1 21:16
2 19:30	☉	□	♏	4 9:33
6 22:04	♅	☍	♐	6 22:06
7 21:29	♂	□	♑	9 8:55
10 20:37	☉	☍	♒	11 17:21
12 19:45	☿	☍	♓	13 23:45
15 17:10	☉	△	♈	16 4:32
18 0:38	☉	□	♉	18 7:59
20 6:43	☉	⚹	♊	20 10:22
21 19:52	♂	□	♋	22 12:26
24 0:42	♂	⚹	♌	24 15:28
26 11:02	♀	⚹	♍	26 20:55
29 0:57	♀	□	♎	29 5:43
30 3:59	♃	□	♏	31 17:25

Last Aspect Dy Hr Mn			☽ Ingress	Dy Hr Mn
3 1:07	♂	⚹	♐	3 6:00
5 15:29	♂	□	♑	5 17:04
6 17:40	♃	☍	♒	8 1:18
9 7:55	☉	☍	♓	10 6:50
11 6:55	♃	△	♈	12 10:33
13 22:54	☉	△	♉	14 13:22
16 5:12	☉	□	♊	16 16:00
18 11:53	☉	⚹	♋	18 19:05
20 12:27	♀	☌	♌	20 23:17
21 18:13	☿	☌	♍	23 5:24
25 13:53	♀	⚹	♎	25 14:08
27 2:06	☿	⚹	♏	28 1:27
30 0:47	☿	□	♐	30 14:04

☽ Phases & Eclipses Dy Hr Mn	
2 19:30	☽ 11♎10
10 20:37	○ 18♑50
18 0:38	☾ 25♈40
24 19:11	● 2♌08
1 12:41	☽ 9♏32
9 7:55	○ 17♒00
16 5:12	☾ 23♉36
23 6:06	● 0♍23
31 6:25	☽ 8♐07

Astro Data

1 July 2025
Julian Day # 45838
SVP 4♓54'10"
GC 27♐11.7 ⚴ 23♒45.2R
Eris 25♈41.5 ⚵ 16♏29.5R
⚷ 26♈47.6 ⚶ 6♏28.1
☽ Mean ☊ 21♓53.1

1 August 2025
Julian Day # 45869
SVP 4♓54'05"
GC 27♐11.8 ⚴ 17♒16.7R
Eris 25♈43.2R ⚵ 17♏23.0
⚷ 27♈09.7R ⚶ 13♏26.6
☽ Mean ☊ 20♓14.6

LONGITUDE — September 2025

Day	Sid.Time	☉	0 hr ☽	Noon ☽	True ☊	☿	♀	♂	⚳	♃	♄	♅	♆	♇
1 M	10 43 37	9♍18 49	16♐55 27	22♐59 16	18♓23.7	27♌59.5	8♌09.6	16♎14.3	15♈30.6	17♋57.7	29♓59.3	1♊27.3	1♈20.9	1♒46.0
2 Tu	10 47 34	10 16 53	29 06 24	5♑17 23	18R 23.0	29 53.4	9 21.7	16 53.3	15R 23.0	18 08.4	29R 55.1	1 27.5	1R 19.4	1R 45.0
3 W	10 51 31	11 14 59	11♑32 40	17 52 39	18 22.2	1♍48.4	10 33.9	17 32.4	15 15.1	18 19.0	29 50.9	1 27.6	1 17.9	1 44.0
4 Th	10 55 27	12 13 06	24 17 42	0♒48 05	18 21.4	3 44.2	11 46.1	18 11.5	15 06.8	18 29.5	29 46.6	1 27.8	1 16.4	1 43.0
5 F	10 59 24	13 11 15	7♒23 57	14 05 24	18 20.7	5 40.4	12 58.4	18 50.7	14 58.3	18 39.9	29 42.3	1R 27.8	1 14.8	1 42.0
6 Sa	11 03 20	14 09 25	20 52 22	27 44 45	18 20.3	7 36.8	14 10.8	19 30.0	14 49.4	18 50.2	29 37.9	1 27.8	1 13.2	1 41.0
7 Su	11 07 17	15 07 36	4♓42 15	11♓44 31	18D 20.1	9 33.1	15 23.3	20 09.3	14 40.2	19 00.4	29 33.5	1 27.8	1 11.7	1 40.1
8 M	11 11 13	16 05 50	18 51 05	26 01 21	18 20.1	11 29.1	16 35.8	20 48.7	14 30.7	19 10.5	29 29.0	1 27.7	1 10.1	1 39.1
9 Tu	11 15 10	17 04 05	3♈14 40	10♈30 21	18 20.2	13 24.7	17 48.4	21 28.2	14 20.9	19 20.5	29 24.6	1 27.5	1 08.5	1 38.2
10 W	11 19 06	18 02 22	17 47 39	25 05 48	18R 20.2	15 19.6	19 01.1	22 07.7	14 10.8	19 30.4	29 20.1	1 27.4	1 06.9	1 37.4
11 Th	11 23 03	19 00 41	2♉24 04	9♉41 44	18 20.2	17 13.9	20 13.8	22 47.2	14 00.4	19 40.2	29 15.5	1 27.1	1 05.3	1 36.5
12 F	11 27 00	19 59 02	16 58 09	24 12 42	18 20.1	19 07.4	21 26.6	23 26.9	13 49.8	19 49.9	29 11.0	1 26.8	1 03.7	1 35.7
13 Sa	11 30 56	20 57 26	1♊24 53	8♊34 15	18D 20.0	21 00.0	22 39.5	24 06.6	13 38.9	19 59.5	29 06.4	1 26.5	1 02.0	1 34.8
14 Su	11 34 53	21 55 51	15 40 29	22 43 18	18 19.9	22 51.7	23 52.4	24 46.4	13 27.7	20 09.0	29 01.8	1 26.1	1 00.4	1 34.0
15 M	11 38 49	22 54 19	29 42 31	6♋38 00	18 20.0	24 42.4	25 05.4	25 26.2	13 16.3	20 18.3	28 57.2	1 25.7	0 58.8	1 33.3
16 Tu	11 42 46	23 52 49	13♋29 42	20 17 35	18 20.4	26 32.1	26 18.5	26 06.1	13 04.7	20 27.6	28 52.6	1 25.2	0 57.1	1 32.5
17 W	11 46 42	24 51 21	27 01 42	3♌42 04	18 20.9	28 20.8	27 31.6	26 46.1	12 52.9	20 36.7	28 48.0	1 24.6	0 55.5	1 31.8
18 Th	11 50 39	25 49 56	10♌18 45	16 51 52	18 21.6	0♎08.5	28 44.8	27 26.1	12 40.8	20 45.8	28 43.3	1 24.0	0 53.8	1 31.1
19 F	11 54 35	26 48 32	23 21 29	29 47 42	18 22.3	1 55.2	29 58.0	28 06.2	12 28.5	20 54.7	28 38.7	1 23.4	0 52.2	1 30.4
20 Sa	11 58 32	27 47 10	6♍10 37	12♍30 20	18R 22.7	3 40.8	1♍11.3	28 46.4	12 16.0	21 03.4	28 34.0	1 22.7	0 50.5	1 29.8
21 Su	12 02 29	28 45 50	18 46 59	25 00 40	18 22.6	5 25.4	2 24.7	29 26.6	12 03.4	21 12.1	28 29.4	1 22.0	0 48.8	1 29.1
22 M	12 06 25	29 44 32	1♎11 32	7♎19 44	18 22.0	7 09.0	3 38.1	0♏06.9	11 50.6	21 20.6	28 24.7	1 21.2	0 47.2	1 28.5
23 Tu	12 10 22	0♎43 16	13 25 26	19 28 49	18 20.8	8 51.7	4 51.6	0 47.2	11 37.7	21 29.0	28 20.0	1 20.3	0 45.5	1 28.0
24 W	12 14 18	1 42 02	25 30 07	1♏29 35	18 19.1	10 33.3	6 05.1	1 27.6	11 24.6	21 37.3	28 15.4	1 19.5	0 43.8	1 27.4
25 Th	12 18 15	2 40 50	7♏27 30	13 24 11	18 16.9	12 14.0	7 18.7	2 08.1	11 11.4	21 45.4	28 10.7	1 18.5	0 42.2	1 26.9
26 F	12 22 11	3 39 40	19 20 00	25 15 19	18 14.6	13 53.7	8 32.3	2 48.7	10 58.1	21 53.4	28 06.1	1 17.5	0 40.5	1 26.4
27 Sa	12 26 08	4 38 31	1♐10 35	7♐06 15	18 12.5	15 32.5	9 46.0	3 29.3	10 44.7	22 01.3	28 01.5	1 16.5	0 38.9	1 25.9
28 Su	12 30 04	5 37 24	13 02 49	19 00 48	18 11.0	17 10.4	10 59.7	4 09.9	10 31.3	22 09.1	27 56.9	1 15.4	0 37.2	1 25.5
29 M	12 34 01	6 36 20	25 00 44	1♑03 12	18D 10.1	18 47.4	12 13.5	4 50.7	10 17.7	22 16.7	27 52.3	1 14.3	0 35.6	1 25.0
30 Tu	12 37 58	7 35 16	7♑08 44	13 17 56	18 10.1	20 23.5	13 27.3	5 31.5	10 04.2	22 24.1	27 47.8	1 13.2	0 33.9	1 24.7

LONGITUDE — October 2025

Day	Sid.Time	☉	0 hr ☽	Noon ☽	True ☊	☿	♀	♂	⚳	♃	♄	♅	♆	♇
1 W	12 41 54	8♎34 15	19♑31 21	25♑49 32	18♓10.9	21♎58.7	14♍41.1	6♏12.3	9♈50.6	22♋31.4	27♓43.2	1♊12.0	0♈32.3	1♒24.3
2 Th	12 45 51	9 33 15	2♒12 58	8♒42 08	18 12.3	23 33.1	15 55.1	6 53.2	9R 37.0	22 38.6	27R 38.7	1R 10.7	0R 30.6	1R 23.9
3 F	12 49 47	10 32 17	15 17 24	21 59 04	18 13.8	25 06.7	17 09.0	7 34.2	9 23.4	22 45.7	27 34.2	1 09.4	0 29.0	1 23.6
4 Sa	12 53 44	11 31 21	28 47 19	5♓42 13	18R 15.0	26 39.4	18 23.0	8 15.2	9 09.8	22 52.5	27 29.8	1 08.1	0 27.4	1 23.3
5 Su	12 57 40	12 30 26	12♓43 40	19 51 26	18 15.4	28 11.3	19 37.1	8 56.3	8 56.2	22 59.3	27 25.3	1 06.7	0 25.7	1 23.1
6 M	13 01 37	13 29 34	27 05 06	4♈24 03	18 14.6	29 42.3	20 51.2	9 37.5	8 42.7	23 05.9	27 21.0	1 05.3	0 24.1	1 22.9
7 Tu	13 05 33	14 28 43	11♈47 32	19 14 39	18 12.6	1♏12.6	22 05.3	10 18.7	8 29.2	23 12.3	27 16.6	1 03.8	0 22.5	1 22.7
8 W	13 09 30	15 27 55	26 44 22	4♉15 34	18 09.4	2 42.1	23 19.5	11 00.0	8 15.9	23 18.6	27 12.3	1 02.3	0 20.9	1 22.5
9 Th	13 13 27	16 27 08	11♉47 04	19 17 45	18 05.5	4 10.7	24 33.7	11 41.3	8 02.6	23 24.7	27 08.0	1 00.8	0 19.3	1 22.3
10 F	13 17 23	17 26 24	26 46 29	4♊12 16	18 01.5	5 38.6	25 48.0	12 22.7	7 49.4	23 30.7	27 03.8	0 59.2	0 17.8	1 22.2
11 Sa	13 21 20	18 25 43	11♊34 14	18 51 39	17 58.0	7 05.6	27 02.3	13 04.2	7 36.3	23 36.5	26 59.6	0 57.5	0 16.2	1 22.1
12 Su	13 25 16	19 25 04	26 03 57	3♋10 46	17 55.6	8 31.8	28 16.7	13 45.7	7 23.3	23 42.2	26 55.5	0 55.9	0 14.7	1 22.1
13 M	13 29 13	20 24 27	10♋11 52	17 07 10	17D 54.5	9 57.1	29 31.1	14 27.3	7 10.5	23 47.7	26 51.4	0 54.2	0 13.1	1D 22.0
14 Tu	13 33 09	21 23 52	23 56 43	0♌40 40	17 54.8	11 21.6	0♎45.6	15 09.0	6 57.9	23 53.0	26 47.4	0 52.4	0 11.6	1 22.0
15 W	13 37 06	22 23 19	7♌19 18	13 52 52	17 56.1	12 45.2	2 00.1	15 50.7	6 45.4	23 58.2	26 43.5	0 50.7	0 10.1	1 22.1
16 Th	13 41 02	23 22 49	20 21 45	26 46 18	17 57.7	14 07.8	3 14.6	16 32.5	6 33.1	24 03.2	26 39.5	0 48.8	0 08.6	1 22.1
17 F	13 44 59	24 22 21	3♍06 54	9♍23 56	17R 59.0	15 29.4	4 29.2	17 14.3	6 20.9	24 08.0	26 35.7	0 47.0	0 07.1	1 22.2
18 Sa	13 48 56	25 21 55	15 37 44	21 48 40	17 59.3	16 50.0	5 43.8	17 56.2	6 09.0	24 12.7	26 31.9	0 45.1	0 05.6	1 22.3
19 Su	13 52 52	26 21 32	27 57 01	4♎03 05	17 57.9	18 09.6	6 58.4	18 38.2	5 57.4	24 17.1	26 28.2	0 43.2	0 04.1	1 22.4
20 M	13 56 49	27 21 10	10♎07 08	16 09 23	17 54.5	19 27.9	8 13.1	19 20.3	5 45.9	24 21.4	26 24.5	0 41.2	0 02.7	1 22.6
21 Tu	14 00 45	28 20 51	22 10 04	28 09 24	17 49.2	20 45.1	9 27.8	20 02.4	5 34.7	24 25.6	26 20.9	0 39.2	0 01.3	1 22.8
22 W	14 04 42	29 20 33	4♏07 32	10♏04 42	17 42.1	22 00.8	10 42.5	20 44.5	5 23.8	24 29.5	26 17.4	0 37.2	29♓59.9	1 23.0
23 Th	14 08 38	0♏20 18	16 01 05	21 56 52	17 33.9	23 15.2	11 57.3	21 26.7	5 13.1	24 33.3	26 13.9	0 35.2	29 58.5	1 23.3
24 F	14 12 35	1 20 04	27 52 18	3♐47 37	17 25.3	24 28.0	13 12.1	22 09.0	5 02.7	24 36.9	26 10.6	0 33.1	29 57.1	1 23.6
25 Sa	14 16 31	2 19 53	9♐43 06	15 39 03	17 17.1	25 39.0	14 26.9	22 51.4	4 52.6	24 40.3	26 07.3	0 31.0	29 55.8	1 23.9
26 Su	14 20 28	3 19 43	21 35 50	27 33 49	17 10.0	26 48.2	15 41.7	23 33.8	4 42.8	24 43.5	26 04.0	0 28.9	29 54.4	1 24.2
27 M	14 24 25	4 19 35	3♑33 26	9♑35 08	17 04.8	27 55.3	16 56.6	24 16.3	4 33.3	24 46.5	26 00.9	0 26.7	29 53.1	1 24.6
28 Tu	14 28 21	5 19 28	15 39 25	21 46 49	17 01.7	29 00.2	18 11.5	24 58.8	4 24.1	24 49.4	25 57.8	0 24.5	29 51.8	1 25.0
29 W	14 32 18	6 19 24	27 57 53	4♒13 11	17D 00.6	0♐02.5	19 26.5	25 41.4	4 15.2	24 52.1	25 54.9	0 22.3	29 50.6	1 25.4
30 Th	14 36 14	7 19 20	10♒33 18	16 58 45	17 01.0	1 02.0	20 41.4	26 24.1	4 06.7	24 54.5	25 52.0	0 20.1	29 49.3	1 25.9
31 F	14 40 11	8 19 19	23 30 07	0♓07 50	17 02.1	1 58.3	21 56.4	27 06.8	3 58.5	24 56.8	25 49.2	0 17.8	29 48.1	1 26.4

Astro Data

	Dy Hr Mn
♅ R	6 4:51
☽ 0N	8 15:13
☿ 0S	19 20:50
☽ 0S	21 17:44
☉ 0S	22 18:19
☽ 0N	6 1:26
♇ D	14 2:54
♀ 0S	16 17:16
☽ 0S	18 23:58

Planet Ingress

	Dy Hr Mn
♄ ♓R	1 8:06
☿ ♍	2 13:23
☿ ♎	18 10:06
♀ ♍	19 12:39
♂ ♏	22 7:54
☉ ♎	22 18:19
☿ ♏	6 16:41
♀ ♎	13 21:19
♆ ♓R	22 9:48
☉ ♏	23 3:51
☿ ♐	29 11:02

Last Aspect / ☽ Ingress

Last Aspect Dy Hr Mn		☽ Ingress Dy Hr Mn
2 1:39	♄ □	♑ 2 1:45
4 10:08	♄ ⚹	♒ 4 10:32
5 20:51	♂ △	♓ 6 15:54
8 17:44	♄ ☌	♈ 8 18:37
10 6:54	♂ ☍	♉ 10 20:03
12 20:14	♄ ⚹	♊ 12 21:38
14 22:46	♄ □	♋ 15 0:30
17 3:14	♄ △	♌ 17 5:20
19 12:21	♀ ☌	♍ 19 12:23
21 19:54	☉ ☌	♎ 21 21:41
23 16:02	♃ □	♏ 24 9:00
26 17:44	♄ △	♐ 26 21:37
29 5:44	♄ □	♑ 29 9:55

Last Aspect / ☽ Ingress

Last Aspect Dy Hr Mn		☽ Ingress Dy Hr Mn
1 15:33	♄ ⚹	♒ 1 19:51
3 18:15	☿ △	♓ 4 2:07
6 0:30	♄ ☌	♈ 6 4:48
7 18:24	♃ □	♉ 8 5:12
10 0:31	♄ ⚹	♊ 10 5:12
12 2:56	♀ □	♋ 12 6:37
14 5:05	♄ △	♌ 14 10:47
16 5:06	☉ ⚹	♍ 16 18:06
18 21:10	♄ ☍	♎ 19 4:01
21 12:25	☉ ☌	♏ 21 15:42
24 4:14	♆ △	♐ 24 4:19
26 16:42	♆ □	♑ 26 16:53
29 3:38	♆ ⚹	♒ 29 3:55
31 6:15	♂ □	♓ 31 11:46

☽ Phases & Eclipses

Dy Hr Mn	
7 18:09	○ 15♓23
7 18:12	• T 1.362
14 10:33	☾ 21♊52
21 19:54	● 29♍05
21 19:41:49	• P 0.855
29 23:54	☽ 7♑06
7 3:47	○ 14♈08
13 18:13	☾ 20♋40
21 12:25	● 28♎22
29 16:21	☽ 6♒30

Astro Data

1 September 2025
Julian Day # 45900
SVP 4♓54'00"
GC 27♐11.9 ⚴ 9♒49.3R
Eris 25♈35.1R ⚵ 22♏27.3
⚷ 26♈41.9R ⚶ 24♏39.3
☽ Mean ☊ 18♓36.2

1 October 2025
Julian Day # 45930
SVP 4♓53'57"
GC 27♐11.9 ⚴ 6♒41.0R
Eris 25♈20.2R ⚵ 0♐02.9
⚷ 25♈36.1R ⚶ 7♐51.7
☽ Mean ☊ 17♓00.8

November 2025 — LONGITUDE

Day	Sid.Time	☉	0 hr ☽	Noon ☽	True ☊	☿	♀	♂	⚳	♃	♄	♅	♆	♇
1 Sa	14 44 07	9♏19 19	6♓52 20	13♓43 54	17♓02.9	2♐51.2	23♎11.4	27♏49.5	3♈50.6	24♋58.9	25♓46.4	0♊15.5	29♓46.9	1♒26.9
2 Su	14 48 04	10 19 20	20 42 43	27 48 47	17R 02.4	3 40.3	24 26.4	28 32.4	3R 43.1	25 00.8	25R 43.8	0R 13.2	29R 45.7	1 27.4
3 M	14 52 00	11 19 23	5♈01 55	12♈21 45	16 59.9	4 25.0	25 41.4	29 15.2	3 35.9	25 02.5	25 41.2	0 10.9	29 44.6	1 28.0
4 Tu	14 55 57	12 19 28	19 47 39	27 18 46	16 55.0	5 04.8	26 56.5	29 58.2	3 29.1	25 04.0	25 38.8	0 08.6	29 43.5	1 28.6
5 W	14 59 53	13 19 35	4♉54 05	12♉32 21	16 47.9	5 39.4	28 11.5	0♐41.2	3 22.7	25 05.3	25 36.4	0 06.2	29 42.4	1 29.2
6 Th	15 03 50	14 19 43	20 12 11	27 52 10	16 39.3	6 07.9	29 26.6	1 24.2	3 16.6	25 06.5	25 34.1	0 03.8	29 41.3	1 29.9
7 F	15 07 47	15 19 54	5♊30 49	13♊06 45	16 30.2	6 29.9	0♏41.8	2 07.4	3 10.9	25 07.4	25 32.0	0 01.4	29 40.2	1 30.6
8 Sa	15 11 43	16 20 06	20 38 42	28 05 34	16 21.8	6 44.6	1 56.9	2 50.5	3 05.5	25 08.1	25 29.9	29♉59.0	29 39.2	1 31.3
9 Su	15 15 40	17 20 21	5♋26 27	12♋40 44	16 15.1	6R 51.3	3 12.1	3 33.8	3 00.6	25 08.7	25 27.9	29 56.6	29 38.2	1 32.0
10 M	15 19 36	18 20 37	19 47 58	26 47 57	16 10.7	6 49.5	4 27.3	4 17.1	2 56.0	25 09.0	25 26.0	29 54.2	29 37.2	1 32.8
11 Tu	15 23 33	19 20 55	3♌40 41	10♌26 21	16D 08.6	6 38.4	5 42.5	5 00.5	2 51.7	25R 09.2	25 24.2	29 51.7	29 36.3	1 33.6
12 W	15 27 29	20 21 16	17 05 14	23 37 45	16 08.3	6 17.5	6 57.7	5 43.9	2 47.9	25 09.1	25 22.5	29 49.3	29 35.4	1 34.4
13 Th	15 31 26	21 21 38	0♍04 25	6♍25 45	16R 08.8	5 46.6	8 13.0	6 27.4	2 44.4	25 08.8	25 20.9	29 46.8	29 34.5	1 35.2
14 F	15 35 23	22 22 02	12 42 18	18 54 40	16 09.1	5 05.4	9 28.2	7 10.9	2 41.4	25 08.4	25 19.4	29 44.3	29 33.6	1 36.1
15 Sa	15 39 19	23 22 28	25 03 25	1♎09 03	16 07.9	4 14.3	10 43.5	7 54.5	2 38.7	25 07.7	25 18.0	29 41.8	29 32.8	1 37.0
16 Su	15 43 16	24 22 56	7♎12 07	13 13 04	16 04.4	3 14.0	11 58.8	8 38.2	2 36.3	25 06.8	25 16.7	29 39.3	29 32.0	1 37.9
17 M	15 47 12	25 23 25	19 12 19	25 10 16	15 58.1	2 05.4	13 14.1	9 21.9	2 34.4	25 05.8	25 15.5	29 36.8	29 31.2	1 38.9
18 Tu	15 51 09	26 23 57	1♏07 14	7♏03 32	15 48.9	0 50.4	14 29.4	10 05.7	2 32.9	25 04.5	25 14.5	29 34.3	29 30.5	1 39.8
19 W	15 55 05	27 24 30	12 59 24	18 55 04	15 37.1	29♏31.0	15 44.8	10 49.5	2 31.7	25 03.0	25 13.5	29 31.8	29 29.8	1 40.8
20 Th	15 59 02	28 25 04	24 50 43	0♐46 32	15 23.4	28 09.6	17 00.1	11 33.4	2 31.0	25 01.4	25 12.6	29 29.3	29 29.1	1 41.9
21 F	16 02 58	29 25 40	6♐42 40	12 39 17	15 09.0	26 49.0	18 15.5	12 17.4	2D 30.6	24 59.5	25 11.8	29 26.8	29 28.4	1 42.9
22 Sa	16 06 55	0♐26 18	18 36 32	24 34 37	14 55.1	25 31.8	19 30.9	13 01.4	2 30.6	24 57.4	25 11.2	29 24.3	29 27.8	1 44.0
23 Su	16 10 52	1 26 57	0♑33 42	6♑34 02	14 42.8	24 20.5	20 46.3	13 45.4	2 31.0	24 55.2	25 10.6	29 21.8	29 27.2	1 45.1
24 M	16 14 48	2 27 37	12 35 52	18 39 30	14 33.0	23 17.3	22 01.7	14 29.6	2 31.7	24 52.7	25 10.2	29 19.3	29 26.7	1 46.2
25 Tu	16 18 45	3 28 18	24 45 18	0♒53 38	14 26.1	22 23.9	23 17.1	15 13.8	2 32.9	24 50.1	25 09.8	29 16.7	29 26.2	1 47.4
26 W	16 22 41	4 29 01	7♒04 57	13 19 41	14 22.1	21 41.3	24 32.5	15 58.0	2 34.4	24 47.2	25 09.6	29 14.2	29 25.7	1 48.6
27 Th	16 26 38	5 29 44	19 38 22	26 01 29	14D 20.5	21 10.2	25 47.9	16 42.3	2 36.3	24 44.2	25D 09.5	29 11.8	29 25.2	1 49.8
28 F	16 30 34	6 30 28	2♓29 35	9♓03 10	14R 20.3	20 50.8	27 03.3	17 26.6	2 38.5	24 41.0	25 09.5	29 09.3	29 24.8	1 51.0
29 Sa	16 34 31	7 31 14	15 42 42	22 28 38	14 20.2	20D 42.7	28 18.7	18 11.0	2 41.2	24 37.5	25 09.6	29 06.8	29 24.4	1 52.2
30 Su	16 38 27	8 32 00	29 21 18	6♈20 54	14 18.9	20 45.5	29 34.1	18 55.4	2 44.1	24 33.9	25 09.7	29 04.3	29 24.1	1 53.5

December 2025 — LONGITUDE

Day	Sid.Time	☉	0 hr ☽	Noon ☽	True ☊	☿	♀	♂	⚳	♃	♄	♅	♆	♇
1 M	16 42 24	9♐32 47	13♈27 31	20♈41 03	14♓15.4	20♏58.4	0♐49.6	19♐39.9	2♈47.5	24♋30.2	25♓10.1	29♉01.8	29♓23.7	1♒54.8
2 Tu	16 46 21	10 33 35	28 01 08	5♉27 16	14R 09.1	21 20.7	2 05.0	20 24.5	2 51.2	24R 26.2	25 10.5	28R 59.4	29R 23.4	1 56.1
3 W	16 50 17	11 34 24	12♉58 36	20 34 10	14 00.1	21 51.5	3 20.5	21 09.1	2 55.3	24 22.0	25 11.0	28 57.0	29 23.2	1 57.4
4 Th	16 54 14	12 35 15	28 12 42	5♊52 51	13 49.1	22 29.8	4 35.9	21 53.7	2 59.7	24 17.7	25 11.6	28 54.5	29 23.0	1 58.8
5 F	16 58 10	13 36 06	13♊33 07	21 12 01	13 37.3	23 14.9	5 51.4	22 38.4	3 04.4	24 13.2	25 12.4	28 52.1	29 22.8	2 00.2
6 Sa	17 02 07	14 36 59	28 48 03	6♋19 56	13 26.1	24 05.9	7 06.8	23 23.2	3 09.5	24 08.5	25 13.2	28 49.7	29 22.6	2 01.6
7 Su	17 06 03	15 37 52	13♋46 28	21 06 42	13 16.8	25 02.2	8 22.3	24 08.0	3 15.0	24 03.7	25 14.2	28 47.4	29 22.5	2 03.0
8 M	17 10 00	16 38 47	28 19 57	5♌25 45	13 10.2	26 03.0	9 37.8	24 52.9	3 20.8	23 58.7	25 15.2	28 45.0	29 22.4	2 04.4
9 Tu	17 13 56	17 39 43	12♌23 53	19 14 20	13 06.3	27 07.8	10 53.3	25 37.8	3 26.9	23 53.5	25 16.4	28 42.7	29 22.4	2 05.9
10 W	17 17 53	18 40 40	25 57 18	2♍33 05	13D 04.8	28 16.1	12 08.8	26 22.8	3 33.3	23 48.1	25 17.7	28 40.3	29D 22.4	2 07.4
11 Th	17 21 50	19 41 38	9♍02 09	15 25 03	13R 04.5	29 27.5	13 24.3	27 07.8	3 40.1	23 42.6	25 19.0	28 38.0	29 22.4	2 08.9
12 F	17 25 46	20 42 38	21 42 23	27 54 48	13 04.4	0♐41.4	14 39.8	27 52.8	3 47.1	23 37.0	25 20.5	28 35.7	29 22.4	2 10.4
13 Sa	17 29 43	21 43 38	4♎02 56	10♎07 28	13 03.2	1 57.6	15 55.3	28 38.0	3 54.5	23 31.2	25 22.1	28 33.5	29 22.5	2 11.9
14 Su	17 33 39	22 44 39	16 09 00	22 08 11	12 59.8	3 15.8	17 10.8	29 23.1	4 02.2	23 25.2	25 23.8	28 31.2	29 22.6	2 13.5
15 M	17 37 36	23 45 42	28 05 34	4♏01 41	12 53.7	4 35.6	18 26.3	0♑08.4	4 10.3	23 19.1	25 25.6	28 29.0	29 22.8	2 15.0
16 Tu	17 41 32	24 46 45	9♏57 01	15 52 01	12 44.5	5 57.0	19 41.8	0 53.6	4 18.6	23 12.8	25 27.5	28 26.8	29 23.0	2 16.6
17 W	17 45 29	25 47 50	21 47 02	27 42 24	12 32.8	7 19.7	20 57.3	1 39.0	4 27.2	23 06.4	25 29.5	28 24.7	29 23.2	2 18.2
18 Th	17 49 25	26 48 55	3♐38 26	9♐35 20	12 19.1	8 43.4	22 12.9	2 24.3	4 36.2	22 59.9	25 31.6	28 22.6	29 23.5	2 19.9
19 F	17 53 22	27 50 01	15 33 19	21 32 32	12 04.6	10 08.2	23 28.4	3 09.8	4 45.4	22 53.3	25 33.9	28 20.4	29 23.8	2 21.5
20 Sa	17 57 19	28 51 07	27 33 07	3♑35 12	11 50.5	11 33.9	24 43.9	3 55.2	4 54.9	22 46.5	25 36.2	28 18.4	29 24.1	2 23.1
21 Su	18 01 15	29 52 14	9♑38 53	15 44 17	11 37.9	13 00.3	25 59.5	4 40.8	5 04.8	22 39.6	25 38.6	28 16.3	29 24.5	2 24.8
22 M	18 05 12	0♑53 21	21 51 31	28 00 43	11 27.8	14 27.4	27 15.0	5 26.3	5 14.9	22 32.6	25 41.1	28 14.3	29 24.9	2 26.5
23 Tu	18 09 08	1 54 29	4♒12 04	10♒25 45	11 20.8	15 55.1	28 30.5	6 11.9	5 25.2	22 25.5	25 43.8	28 12.3	29 25.3	2 28.2
24 W	18 13 05	2 55 37	16 42 00	23 01 06	11 16.7	17 23.3	29 46.1	6 57.6	5 35.9	22 18.3	25 46.5	28 10.4	29 25.8	2 29.9
25 Th	18 17 01	3 56 45	29 23 20	5♓49 03	11D 15.1	18 52.1	1♑01.6	7 43.3	5 46.8	22 11.0	25 49.3	28 08.5	29 26.3	2 31.6
26 F	18 20 58	4 57 53	12♓18 37	18 52 24	11 15.1	20 21.3	2 17.1	8 29.0	5 58.0	22 03.6	25 52.2	28 06.6	29 26.8	2 33.4
27 Sa	18 24 55	5 59 01	25 30 46	2♈14 03	11R 15.6	21 50.9	3 32.6	9 14.8	6 09.5	21 56.1	25 55.3	28 04.8	29 27.4	2 35.1
28 Su	18 28 51	7 00 09	9♈02 36	15 56 38	11 15.3	23 21.0	4 48.1	10 00.6	6 21.2	21 48.5	25 58.4	28 03.0	29 28.0	2 36.9
29 M	18 32 48	8 01 17	22 56 19	0♉01 39	11 13.2	24 51.4	6 03.6	10 46.5	6 33.2	21 40.9	26 01.6	28 01.2	29 28.7	2 38.6
30 Tu	18 36 44	9 02 25	7♉12 32	14 28 41	11 08.7	26 22.2	7 19.1	11 32.4	6 45.4	21 33.1	26 04.9	27 59.5	29 29.3	2 40.4
31 W	18 40 41	10 03 33	21 49 37	29 14 41	11 01.8	27 53.4	8 34.6	12 18.3	6 57.9	21 25.4	26 08.3	27 57.8	29 30.0	2 42.2

Astro Data

	Dy Hr Mn
☽ 0N	2 11:58
☿ R	9 19:02
♃ R	11 16:41
☽ 0S	15 5:07
♅⚹♆	20 14:39
⚳ D	21 23:57
♄ D	28 3:52
☿ D	29 17:40
☽ 0N	29 20:34
♆ D	10 12:24
☽ 0S	12 10:33
☽ 0N	27 2:23

Planet Ingress

		Dy Hr Mn
♂	♐	4 13:01
♀	♏	6 22:39
♅	♉R	8 2:22
☿	♏R	19 3:20
☉	♐	22 1:35
♀	♐	30 20:13
☿	♐	11 22:40
♂	♑	15 7:34
☉	♑	21 15:03
♀	♑	24 16:26

Last Aspect / ☽ Ingress (November)

Last Aspect Dy Hr Mn			☽ Ingress	Dy Hr Mn
2 15:15	♆	☌	♈	2 15:39
4 11:21	♀	☍	♉	4 16:16
6 14:51	♆	⚹	♊	6 15:20
8 14:32	♆	□	♋	8 15:06
10 17:22	♅	⚹	♌	10 17:33
12 23:29	♅	□	♍	12 23:52
15 9:08	♅	△	♎	15 9:44
17 11:51	♃	□	♏	17 21:44
20 9:24	♅	☍	♐	20 10:26
22 21:48	♆	□	♑	22 22:53
25 9:10	♆	⚹	♒	25 10:15
27 17:53	♅	□	♓	27 19:24
30 0:05	♆	☌	♈	30 1:07

Last Aspect / ☽ Ingress (December)

Last Aspect Dy Hr Mn			☽ Ingress	Dy Hr Mn
1 18:14	♃	□	♉	2 3:13
4 1:50	♆	⚹	♊	4 2:48
6 0:55	♆	□	♋	6 1:54
8 1:45	♆	△	♌	8 2:48
10 4:56	♅	□	♍	10 7:20
12 14:51	♆	☍	♎	12 16:04
15 3:36	♂	⚹	♏	15 3:51
17 15:24	♆	△	♐	17 16:38
20 3:41	♆	□	♑	20 4:52
22 14:44	♆	⚹	♒	22 15:52
24 21:42	♅	□	♓	25 1:09
27 7:03	♆	☌	♈	27 8:02
29 2:13	☿	△	♉	29 11:57
31 12:25	♆	⚹	♊	31 13:13

☽ Phases & Eclipses

Dy Hr Mn		
5 13:19	○	13♉23
12 5:28	☾	20♌05
20 6:47	●	28♏12
28 6:59	☽	6♓18
4 23:14	○	13♊04
11 20:52	☾	20♍04
20 1:43	●	28♐25
27 19:10	☽	6♈17

Astro Data

1 November 2025
Julian Day # 45961
SVP 4♓53'53"
GC 27♐12.0 ⚴ 8♒42.9
Eris 25♈01.9R ⚵ 9♐38.8
⚷ 24♈11.6R ⚶ 22♐55.9
☽ Mean ☊ 15♓22.3

1 December 2025
Julian Day # 45991
SVP 4♓53'48"
GC 27♐12.1 ⚴ 14♒26.1
Eris 24♈46.5R ⚵ 19♐56.2
⚷ 23♈04.2R ⚶ 8♑17.9
☽ Mean ☊ 13♓47.0

LONGITUDE — January 2026

Day	Sid.Time	☉	0 hr ☽	Noon ☽	True ☊	☿	♀	♂	⚳	♃	♄	♅	♆	♇
1 Th	18 44 37	11♑04 41	6♊43 00	14♊13 35	10♓53.1	29♐24.9	9♑50.1	13♑04.3	7♈10.6	21♋17.5	26♓11.8	27♉56.1	29♓30.8	2♒44.0
2 F	18 48 34	12 05 49	21 45 16	29 16 50	10R43.5	0♑56.8	11 05.6	13 50.3	7 23.5	21R09.6	26 15.4	27R54.5	29 31.6	2 45.9
3 Sa	18 52 30	13 06 57	6♋47 01	14♋14 36	10 34.3	2 29.0	12 21.1	14 36.4	7 36.7	21 01.7	26 19.1	27 53.0	29 32.4	2 47.7
4 Su	18 56 27	14 08 05	21 38 24	28 57 26	10 26.5	4 01.6	13 36.6	15 22.5	7 50.1	20 53.7	26 22.8	27 51.4	29 33.2	2 49.5
5 M	19 00 24	15 09 13	6♌10 50	13♌17 57	10 21.0	5 34.6	14 52.1	16 08.6	8 03.8	20 45.7	26 26.7	27 50.0	29 34.1	2 51.4
6 Tu	19 04 20	16 10 20	20 18 20	27 11 44	10D18.0	7 07.9	16 07.6	16 54.8	8 17.6	20 37.7	26 30.7	27 48.5	29 35.0	2 53.2
7 W	19 08 17	17 11 28	3♍58 04	10♍37 27	10 17.1	8 41.6	17 23.1	17 41.0	8 31.7	20 29.6	26 34.7	27 47.1	29 36.0	2 55.1
8 Th	19 12 13	18 12 36	17 10 08	23 36 30	10 17.8	10 15.7	18 38.6	18 27.3	8 46.0	20 21.6	26 38.8	27 45.8	29 36.9	2 56.9
9 F	19 16 10	19 13 44	29 57 01	6♎12 14	10 19.0	11 50.2	19 54.0	19 13.5	9 00.5	20 13.5	26 43.0	27 44.5	29 37.9	2 58.8
10 Sa	19 20 06	20 14 52	12♎22 43	18 29 08	10R19.7	13 25.1	21 09.5	19 59.9	9 15.2	20 05.4	26 47.3	27 43.2	29 39.0	3 00.7
11 Su	19 24 03	21 16 01	24 32 07	0♏32 18	10 19.2	15 00.5	22 25.0	20 46.2	9 30.2	19 57.3	26 51.7	27 42.0	29 40.0	3 02.6
12 M	19 27 59	22 17 09	6♏30 21	12 26 52	10 16.7	16 36.3	23 40.4	21 32.6	9 45.3	19 49.2	26 56.2	27 40.8	29 41.1	3 04.5
13 Tu	19 31 56	23 18 17	18 22 26	24 17 39	10 12.2	18 12.6	24 55.9	22 19.1	10 00.6	19 41.1	27 00.7	27 39.7	29 42.3	3 06.4
14 W	19 35 53	24 19 25	0♐12 59	6♐08 56	10 05.6	19 49.3	26 11.4	23 05.6	10 16.2	19 33.0	27 05.3	27 38.6	29 43.4	3 08.3
15 Th	19 39 49	25 20 33	12 05 55	18 04 18	9 57.6	21 26.5	27 26.8	23 52.1	10 31.9	19 25.0	27 10.1	27 37.6	29 44.6	3 10.2
16 F	19 43 46	26 21 40	24 04 25	0♑06 32	9 48.9	23 04.2	28 42.3	24 38.6	10 47.8	19 17.0	27 14.9	27 36.6	29 45.8	3 12.1
17 Sa	19 47 42	27 22 47	6♑10 52	12 17 36	9 40.3	24 42.5	29 57.7	25 25.2	11 04.0	19 09.1	27 19.7	27 35.7	29 47.1	3 14.0
18 Su	19 51 39	28 23 54	18 26 52	24 38 44	9 32.7	26 21.3	1♒13.2	26 11.8	11 20.3	19 01.1	27 24.7	27 34.8	29 48.4	3 15.9
19 M	19 55 35	29 25 00	0♒53 19	7♒10 38	9 26.8	28 00.6	2 28.6	26 58.5	11 36.7	18 53.3	27 29.7	27 33.9	29 49.7	3 17.8
20 Tu	19 59 32	0♒26 06	13 30 43	19 53 36	9 22.8	29 40.4	3 44.0	27 45.1	11 53.4	18 45.5	27 34.8	27 33.2	29 51.0	3 19.8
21 W	20 03 29	1 27 11	26 19 19	2♓47 54	9D21.0	1♒20.9	4 59.5	28 31.8	12 10.2	18 37.7	27 40.0	27 32.4	29 52.4	3 21.7
22 Th	20 07 25	2 28 14	9♓19 24	15 53 53	9 21.0	3 01.9	6 14.9	29 18.6	12 27.2	18 30.0	27 45.2	27 31.7	29 53.8	3 23.6
23 F	20 11 22	3 29 17	22 31 26	29 12 09	9 22.2	4 43.4	7 30.3	0♒05.3	12 44.4	18 22.4	27 50.5	27 31.1	29 55.2	3 25.5
24 Sa	20 15 18	4 30 19	5♈56 07	12♈43 27	9 23.8	6 25.6	8 45.6	0 52.1	13 01.8	18 14.9	27 55.9	27 30.5	29 56.7	3 27.4
25 Su	20 19 15	5 31 20	19 34 13	26 28 30	9R25.0	8 08.3	10 01.0	1 38.9	13 19.3	18 07.5	28 01.4	27 30.0	29 58.1	3 29.4
26 M	20 23 11	6 32 20	3♉26 19	10♉27 37	9 25.3	9 51.6	11 16.4	2 25.7	13 36.9	18 00.1	28 06.9	27 29.5	29 59.6	3 31.3
27 Tu	20 27 08	7 33 19	17 32 19	24 40 13	9 24.1	11 35.4	12 31.7	3 12.6	13 54.8	17 52.9	28 12.5	27 29.1	0♈01.2	3 33.2
28 W	20 31 04	8 34 17	1♊51 00	9♊04 18	9 21.5	13 19.7	13 47.1	3 59.4	14 12.7	17 45.8	28 18.1	27 28.7	0 02.7	3 35.1
29 Th	20 35 01	9 35 13	16 19 37	23 36 20	9 17.7	15 04.5	15 02.4	4 46.3	14 30.9	17 38.7	28 23.9	27 28.4	0 04.3	3 37.0
30 F	20 38 58	10 36 08	0♋53 45	8♋11 06	9 13.4	16 49.8	16 17.7	5 33.3	14 49.1	17 31.8	28 29.6	27 28.1	0 05.9	3 39.0
31 Sa	20 42 54	11 37 03	15 27 36	22 42 24	9 09.1	18 35.5	17 33.0	6 20.2	15 07.6	17 25.0	28 35.5	27 27.9	0 07.6	3 40.9

LONGITUDE — February 2026

Day	Sid.Time	☉	0 hr ☽	Noon ☽	True ☊	☿	♀	♂	⚳	♃	♄	♅	♆	♇
1 Su	20 46 51	12♒37 56	29♋54 43	7♌03 45	9♓05.6	20♒21.5	18♒48.3	7♒07.2	15♈26.1	17♋18.3	28♓41.4	27♉27.8	0♈09.2	3♒42.8
2 M	20 50 47	13 38 47	14♌08 50	21 09 23	9R03.2	22 07.7	20 03.6	7 54.1	15 44.8	17R11.7	28 47.4	27R27.7	0 10.9	3 44.7
3 Tu	20 54 44	14 39 38	28 04 53	4♍55 00	9D02.2	23 54.1	21 18.8	8 41.1	16 03.7	17 05.3	28 53.4	27D27.6	0 12.6	3 46.6
4 W	20 58 40	15 40 28	11♍39 30	18 18 18	9 02.4	25 40.4	22 34.1	9 28.2	16 22.6	16 59.0	28 59.5	27 27.6	0 14.3	3 48.5
5 Th	21 02 37	16 41 17	24 51 25	1♎18 59	9 03.5	27 26.7	23 49.3	10 15.2	16 41.7	16 52.8	29 05.6	27 27.6	0 16.1	3 50.4
6 F	21 06 33	17 42 04	7♎41 16	13 58 35	9 05.1	29 12.5	25 04.5	11 02.3	17 01.0	16 46.8	29 11.8	27 27.7	0 17.9	3 52.2
7 Sa	21 10 30	18 42 51	20 11 21	26 20 02	9 06.7	0♓57.8	26 19.7	11 49.3	17 20.4	16 40.9	29 18.1	27 27.9	0 19.6	3 54.1
8 Su	21 14 27	19 43 37	2♏25 09	8♏27 16	9 07.9	2 42.3	27 34.9	12 36.4	17 39.8	16 35.2	29 24.4	27 28.1	0 21.5	3 56.0
9 M	21 18 23	20 44 22	14 26 58	20 24 51	9R08.4	4 25.7	28 50.1	13 23.6	17 59.5	16 29.6	29 30.7	27 28.4	0 23.3	3 57.8
10 Tu	21 22 20	21 45 06	26 21 31	2♐17 34	9 08.0	6 07.6	0♓05.3	14 10.7	18 19.2	16 24.2	29 37.1	27 28.7	0 25.2	3 59.7
11 W	21 26 16	22 45 49	8♐13 37	14 10 12	9 06.8	7 47.6	1 20.5	14 57.9	18 39.1	16 18.9	29 43.6	27 29.0	0 27.0	4 01.5
12 Th	21 30 13	23 46 31	20 07 54	26 07 12	9 04.9	9 25.3	2 35.6	15 45.0	18 59.1	16 13.8	29 50.1	27 29.5	0 28.9	4 03.4
13 F	21 34 09	24 47 12	2♑08 37	8♑12 34	9 02.8	11 00.1	3 50.7	16 32.2	19 19.2	16 08.9	29 56.7	27 29.9	0 30.8	4 05.2
14 Sa	21 38 06	25 47 51	14 19 25	20 29 31	9 00.6	12 31.6	5 05.9	17 19.4	19 39.4	16 04.1	0♈03.3	27 30.5	0 32.8	4 07.0
15 Su	21 42 02	26 48 29	26 43 08	3♒00 29	8 58.8	13 59.1	6 21.0	18 06.6	19 59.7	15 59.5	0 09.9	27 31.0	0 34.7	4 08.8
16 M	21 45 59	27 49 06	9♒21 42	15 46 53	8 57.4	15 21.9	7 36.0	18 53.8	20 20.1	15 55.1	0 16.6	27 31.7	0 36.7	4 10.6
17 Tu	21 49 56	28 49 41	22 16 03	28 49 09	8D56.7	16 39.5	8 51.1	19 41.1	20 40.7	15 50.8	0 23.3	27 32.4	0 38.7	4 12.4
18 W	21 53 52	29 50 15	5♓26 08	12♓06 49	8 56.5	17 51.1	10 06.2	20 28.3	21 01.3	15 46.8	0 30.1	27 33.1	0 40.7	4 14.2
19 Th	21 57 49	0♓50 47	18 51 02	25 38 35	8 56.9	18 55.9	11 21.2	21 15.6	21 22.1	15 42.9	0 36.9	27 33.9	0 42.7	4 15.9
20 F	22 01 45	1 51 18	2♈29 13	9♈22 39	8 57.4	19 53.5	12 36.2	22 02.8	21 42.9	15 39.2	0 43.8	27 34.7	0 44.8	4 17.7
21 Sa	22 05 42	2 51 47	16 18 37	23 16 51	8 58.1	20 43.0	13 51.2	22 50.1	22 03.9	15 35.6	0 50.7	27 35.6	0 46.8	4 19.4
22 Su	22 09 38	3 52 14	0♉17 03	7♉18 57	8 58.6	21 24.0	15 06.2	23 37.3	22 25.0	15 32.3	0 57.6	27 36.6	0 48.9	4 21.1
23 M	22 13 35	4 52 39	14 22 16	21 26 43	8 58.9	21 55.8	16 21.1	24 24.6	22 46.1	15 29.2	1 04.6	27 37.6	0 51.0	4 22.9
24 Tu	22 17 31	5 53 02	28 32 01	5♊37 54	8R59.0	22 18.2	17 36.0	25 11.9	23 07.4	15 26.2	1 11.6	27 38.6	0 53.0	4 24.6
25 W	22 21 28	6 53 23	12♊44 06	19 50 18	8 59.0	22R30.9	18 50.9	25 59.2	23 28.7	15 23.5	1 18.6	27 39.7	0 55.2	4 26.2
26 Th	22 25 25	7 53 42	26 56 49	4♋01 30	8 58.9	22 33.7	20 05.8	26 46.4	23 50.1	15 20.9	1 25.7	27 40.9	0 57.3	4 27.9
27 F	22 29 21	8 54 00	11♋05 53	18 08 58	8D58.8	22 26.7	21 20.6	27 33.7	24 11.6	15 18.5	1 32.8	27 42.1	0 59.4	4 29.6
28 Sa	22 33 18	9 54 15	25 10 27	2♌09 56	8 58.9	22 10.1	22 35.5	28 21.0	24 33.2	15 16.4	1 39.9	27 43.3	1 01.6	4 31.2

Astro Data

	Dy Hr Mn
☽0S	8 17:45
♄✱♅	20 5:19
☽0N	23 7:05
⚳0N	4 1:57
♅D	4 2:33
☽0S	5 2:49
☽0N	19 13:14
♄☌♆	20 16:53
☿R	26 6:47

Planet Ingress

	Dy Hr Mn
☿ ♑	1 21:11
♀ ♒	17 12:43
☉ ♒	20 1:45
☿ ♒	20 16:41
♂ ♒	23 9:17
♆ ♈	26 17:37
☿ ♓	6 22:48
♀ ♓	10 10:19
♄ ♈	14 0:11
☉ ♓	18 15:52

Last Aspect / ☽ Ingress

Last Aspect Dy Hr Mn		☽ Ingress Dy Hr Mn
2 12:24	♆ □	♋ 2 13:09
4 12:59	♆ △	♌ 4 13:43
6 13:05	♅ □	♍ 6 16:57
8 23:23	♆ ☍	♎ 9 0:06
10 17:54	♀ □	♏ 11 10:55
13 22:59	♆ △	♐ 13 23:34
16 11:19	♆ □	♑ 16 11:47
18 21:57	♆ ✱	♒ 18 22:18
21 2:16	♅ □	♓ 21 6:50
23 13:17	♆ ☌	♈ 23 13:26
24 21:36	♃ □	♉ 25 18:05
27 17:58	♄ ✱	♊ 27 20:55
29 19:56	♄ □	♋ 29 22:32

Last Aspect / ☽ Ingress

Last Aspect Dy Hr Mn		☽ Ingress Dy Hr Mn
31 21:52	♄ △	♌ 1 0:09
2 22:55	♅ □	♍ 3 3:21
5 7:49	♄ ☍	♎ 5 9:32
7 11:59	♀ △	♏ 7 19:13
10 7:01	♀ □	♐ 10 7:22
12 19:29	♄ □	♑ 12 19:44
15 1:31	♅ △	♒ 15 6:17
17 12:01	☉ ☌	♓ 17 14:09
19 15:23	♅ ✱	♈ 19 19:39
21 11:11	♂ ✱	♉ 21 23:31
23 22:29	♅ ☌	♊ 24 2:29
25 23:00	♂ △	♋ 26 5:11
28 4:21	♅ ✱	♌ 28 8:17

☽ Phases & Eclipses

Dy Hr Mn		
3 10:03	○	13♋02
10 15:48	☾	20♎25
18 19:52	●	28♑44
26 4:47	☽	6♉14
1 22:09	○	13♌04
9 12:43	☾	20♏46
17 12:01	●	28♒50
17 12:11:49	✓	A 02'20"
24 12:28	☽	5♊54

Astro Data

1 January 2026
Julian Day # 46022
SVP 4♓53'42"
GC 27♐12.1 ⚴ 22♒44.2
Eris 24♈38.0R ⚵ 1♑02.6
⚷ 22♈36.0R ⚶ 24♑32.9
☽ Mean ☊ 12♓08.6

1 February 2026
Julian Day # 46053
SVP 4♓53'36"
GC 27♐12.2 ⚴ 2♓23.8
Eris 24♈39.7 ⚵ 12♑06.4
⚷ 23♈00.7 ⚶ 10♒49.0
☽ Mean ☊ 10♓30.1

March 2026

LONGITUDE

Day	Sid.Time	☉	0 hr ☽	Noon ☽	True ☊	☿	♀	♂	⚳	♃	♄	♅	♆	♇
1 Su	22 37 14	10♓54 28	9♌07 05	16♌01 32	8♓59.0	21♓44.5	23♓50.3	29♒08.3	24♈54.9	15♋14.4	1♈47.0	27♉44.6	1♈03.7	4♒32.8
2 M	22 41 11	11 54 40	22 52 57	29 41 03	8R 59.1	21R 10.4	25 05.0	29 55.5	25 16.7	15R 12.6	1 54.2	27 45.9	1 05.9	4 34.4
3 Tu	22 45 07	12 54 49	6♍25 32	13♍06 11	8 59.2	20 28.8	26 19.8	0♓42.8	25 38.5	15 11.0	2 01.4	27 47.3	1 08.1	4 36.0
4 W	22 49 04	13 54 57	19 42 49	26 15 19	8 59.0	19 40.6	27 34.5	1 30.1	26 00.4	15 09.6	2 08.6	27 48.8	1 10.2	4 37.6
5 Th	22 53 00	14 55 02	2♎43 36	9♎07 43	8 58.5	18 47.3	28 49.2	2 17.4	26 22.4	15 08.4	2 15.9	27 50.3	1 12.4	4 39.1
6 F	22 56 57	15 55 07	15 27 43	21 43 44	8 57.7	17 50.0	0♈03.9	3 04.6	26 44.5	15 07.4	2 23.2	27 51.8	1 14.6	4 40.7
7 Sa	23 00 53	16 55 09	27 56 00	4♏04 47	8 56.6	16 50.3	1 18.5	3 51.9	27 06.6	15 06.5	2 30.5	27 53.4	1 16.9	4 42.2
8 Su	23 04 50	17 55 10	10♏10 25	16 13 16	8 55.4	15 49.5	2 33.1	4 39.2	27 28.9	15 05.9	2 37.8	27 55.0	1 19.1	4 43.7
9 M	23 08 47	18 55 09	22 13 48	28 12 28	8 54.4	14 49.1	3 47.7	5 26.4	27 51.1	15 05.5	2 45.1	27 56.7	1 21.3	4 45.2
10 Tu	23 12 43	19 55 07	4♐09 49	10♐06 21	8D 53.7	13 50.3	5 02.3	6 13.7	28 13.5	15D 05.3	2 52.5	27 58.4	1 23.5	4 46.7
11 W	23 16 40	20 55 03	16 02 40	21 59 21	8 53.5	12 54.4	6 16.8	7 01.0	28 35.9	15 05.3	2 59.8	28 00.2	1 25.8	4 48.1
12 Th	23 20 36	21 54 57	27 56 59	3♑56 09	8 53.8	12 02.4	7 31.3	7 48.2	28 58.5	15 05.4	3 07.2	28 02.0	1 28.0	4 49.5
13 F	23 24 33	22 54 50	9♑57 27	16 01 26	8 54.7	11 15.1	8 45.8	8 35.5	29 21.0	15 05.8	3 14.6	28 03.8	1 30.3	4 50.9
14 Sa	23 28 29	23 54 41	22 08 40	28 19 39	8 56.0	10 33.1	10 00.3	9 22.7	29 43.7	15 06.3	3 22.1	28 05.7	1 32.5	4 52.3
15 Su	23 32 26	24 54 30	4♒34 50	10♒54 38	8 57.3	9 56.9	11 14.8	10 09.9	0♉06.4	15 07.1	3 29.5	28 07.7	1 34.8	4 53.7
16 M	23 36 23	25 54 17	17 19 22	23 49 17	8 58.4	9 26.9	12 29.2	10 57.2	0 29.1	15 08.0	3 36.9	28 09.7	1 37.1	4 55.0
17 Tu	23 40 19	26 54 03	0♓24 34	7♓05 14	8R 59.0	9 03.1	13 43.6	11 44.4	0 52.0	15 09.2	3 44.4	28 11.7	1 39.3	4 56.4
18 W	23 44 16	27 53 47	13 51 16	20 42 29	8 58.6	8 45.7	14 57.9	12 31.6	1 14.9	15 10.5	3 51.8	28 13.8	1 41.6	4 57.7
19 Th	23 48 12	28 53 28	27 38 36	4♈39 13	8 57.3	8 34.6	16 12.2	13 18.7	1 37.8	15 12.0	3 59.3	28 15.9	1 43.9	4 58.9
20 F	23 52 09	29 53 08	11♈43 51	18 51 54	8 55.0	8D 29.7	17 26.5	14 05.9	2 00.8	15 13.7	4 06.8	28 18.1	1 46.1	5 00.2
21 Sa	23 56 05	0♈52 45	26 02 43	3♉15 36	8 52.0	8 30.8	18 40.8	14 53.1	2 23.9	15 15.6	4 14.3	28 20.3	1 48.4	5 01.4
22 Su	0 00 02	1 52 21	10♉29 49	17 44 38	8 48.8	8 37.7	19 55.0	15 40.2	2 47.0	15 17.7	4 21.8	28 22.5	1 50.7	5 02.6
23 M	0 03 58	2 51 54	24 59 22	2♊13 22	8 45.9	8 50.1	21 09.2	16 27.3	3 10.2	15 20.0	4 29.2	28 24.8	1 53.0	5 03.8
24 Tu	0 07 55	3 51 25	9♊26 02	16 36 51	8 43.9	9 07.7	22 23.4	17 14.4	3 33.4	15 22.5	4 36.7	28 27.1	1 55.2	5 05.0
25 W	0 11 51	4 50 54	23 45 26	0♋51 26	8D 42.9	9 30.4	23 37.5	18 01.5	3 56.7	15 25.2	4 44.2	28 29.4	1 57.5	5 06.1
26 Th	0 15 48	5 50 20	7♋54 35	14 54 43	8 43.2	9 57.8	24 51.6	18 48.6	4 20.0	15 28.0	4 51.7	28 31.8	1 59.8	5 07.3
27 F	0 19 45	6 49 44	21 51 44	28 45 34	8 44.3	10 29.6	26 05.7	19 35.6	4 43.4	15 31.0	4 59.2	28 34.3	2 02.1	5 08.4
28 Sa	0 23 41	7 49 06	5♌36 12	12♌23 38	8 45.9	11 05.7	27 19.7	20 22.7	5 06.8	15 34.2	5 06.7	28 36.7	2 04.3	5 09.4
29 Su	0 27 38	8 48 25	19 07 55	25 49 04	8R 47.3	11 45.7	28 33.7	21 09.7	5 30.3	15 37.6	5 14.2	28 39.2	2 06.6	5 10.5
30 M	0 31 34	9 47 42	2♍27 08	9♍02 07	8 47.8	12 29.6	29 47.6	21 56.6	5 53.8	15 41.2	5 21.7	28 41.8	2 08.9	5 11.5
31 Tu	0 35 31	10 46 57	15 34 05	22 03 01	8 47.1	13 16.9	1♉01.5	22 43.6	6 17.3	15 44.9	5 29.1	28 44.4	2 11.1	5 12.5

April 2026

LONGITUDE

Day	Sid.Time	☉	0 hr ☽	Noon ☽	True ☊	☿	♀	♂	⚳	♃	♄	♅	♆	♇
1 W	0 39 27	11♈46 10	28♍28 58	4♎51 55	8♓44.6	14♓07.6	2♉15.4	23♓30.5	6♉40.9	15♋48.8	5♈36.6	28♉47.0	2♈13.4	5♒13.5
2 Th	0 43 24	12 45 20	11♎11 54	17 28 57	8R 40.6	15 01.5	3 29.2	24 17.5	7 04.5	15 52.9	5 44.1	28 49.6	2 15.6	5 14.4
3 F	0 47 20	13 44 29	23 43 07	29 54 28	8 35.0	15 58.3	4 43.0	25 04.3	7 28.2	15 57.2	5 51.5	28 52.3	2 17.9	5 15.3
4 Sa	0 51 17	14 43 35	6♏03 07	12♏09 13	8 28.6	16 58.1	5 56.8	25 51.2	7 51.9	16 01.6	5 58.9	28 55.0	2 20.1	5 16.2
5 Su	0 55 14	15 42 40	18 12 56	24 14 31	8 21.8	18 00.5	7 10.5	26 38.1	8 15.7	16 06.2	6 06.4	28 57.7	2 22.3	5 17.1
6 M	0 59 10	16 41 43	0♐14 14	6♐12 25	8 15.5	19 05.5	8 24.2	27 24.9	8 39.4	16 10.9	6 13.8	29 00.5	2 24.5	5 17.9
7 Tu	1 03 07	17 40 44	12 09 26	18 05 42	8 10.2	20 12.9	9 37.9	28 11.7	9 03.3	16 15.8	6 21.2	29 03.3	2 26.8	5 18.8
8 W	1 07 03	18 39 44	24 01 41	29 57 54	8 06.5	21 22.7	10 51.5	28 58.5	9 27.1	16 20.9	6 28.6	29 06.1	2 29.0	5 19.6
9 Th	1 11 00	19 38 41	5♑54 54	11♑53 14	8D 04.5	22 34.8	12 05.1	29 45.2	9 51.0	16 26.2	6 36.0	29 09.0	2 31.2	5 20.3
10 F	1 14 56	20 37 37	17 53 31	23 56 21	8 04.2	23 49.1	13 18.6	0♈31.9	10 15.0	16 31.6	6 43.3	29 11.9	2 33.4	5 21.1
11 Sa	1 18 53	21 36 31	0♒02 21	6♒12 09	8 05.1	25 05.4	14 32.1	1 18.6	10 38.9	16 37.1	6 50.7	29 14.8	2 35.5	5 21.8
12 Su	1 22 49	22 35 24	12 26 21	18 45 30	8 06.5	26 23.8	15 45.6	2 05.3	11 02.9	16 42.9	6 58.0	29 17.7	2 37.7	5 22.5
13 M	1 26 46	23 34 14	25 10 08	1♓40 42	8R 07.6	27 44.1	16 59.0	2 51.9	11 27.0	16 48.7	7 05.3	29 20.7	2 39.9	5 23.1
14 Tu	1 30 43	24 33 03	8♓17 33	15 00 56	8 07.6	29 06.4	18 12.4	3 38.5	11 51.0	16 54.8	7 12.6	29 23.7	2 42.0	5 23.8
15 W	1 34 39	25 31 50	21 51 00	28 47 41	8 05.7	0♈30.5	19 25.8	4 25.1	12 15.1	17 01.0	7 19.8	29 26.7	2 44.2	5 24.4
16 Th	1 38 36	26 30 35	5♈50 49	12♈59 59	8 01.7	1 56.5	20 39.1	5 11.6	12 39.3	17 07.3	7 27.1	29 29.8	2 46.3	5 24.9
17 F	1 42 32	27 29 18	20 14 39	27 34 03	7 55.7	3 24.2	21 52.4	5 58.2	13 03.4	17 13.8	7 34.3	29 32.8	2 48.4	5 25.5
18 Sa	1 46 29	28 28 00	4♉57 19	12♉23 26	7 48.3	4 53.8	23 05.6	6 44.6	13 27.6	17 20.4	7 41.5	29 35.9	2 50.5	5 26.0
19 Su	1 50 25	29 26 39	19 51 16	27 19 41	7 40.3	6 25.0	24 18.8	7 31.1	13 51.8	17 27.2	7 48.6	29 39.1	2 52.6	5 26.5
20 M	1 54 22	0♉25 17	4♊47 33	12♊13 48	7 32.8	7 58.1	25 32.0	8 17.5	14 16.1	17 34.1	7 55.8	29 42.2	2 54.7	5 27.0
21 Tu	1 58 18	1 23 52	19 37 27	26 57 40	7 26.8	9 32.8	26 45.1	9 03.9	14 40.3	17 41.2	8 02.9	29 45.4	2 56.7	5 27.4
22 W	2 02 15	2 22 25	4♋13 46	11♋25 15	7 22.8	11 09.3	27 58.2	9 50.2	15 04.6	17 48.4	8 10.0	29 48.6	2 58.8	5 27.8
23 Th	2 06 12	3 20 56	18 31 47	25 33 09	7D 20.9	12 47.4	29 11.2	10 36.5	15 28.9	17 55.7	8 17.0	29 51.8	3 00.8	5 28.2
24 F	2 10 08	4 19 25	2♌29 20	9♌20 23	7 20.7	14 27.3	0♊24.2	11 22.7	15 53.2	18 03.2	8 24.0	29 55.0	3 02.8	5 28.5
25 Sa	2 14 05	5 17 51	16 06 29	22 47 50	7 21.4	16 08.9	1 37.1	12 09.0	16 17.6	18 10.8	8 31.0	29 58.3	3 04.8	5 28.9
26 Su	2 18 01	6 16 15	29 24 44	5♍57 30	7R 22.0	17 52.1	2 50.0	12 55.1	16 41.9	18 18.5	8 38.0	0♊01.5	3 06.8	5 29.2
27 M	2 21 58	7 14 38	12♍26 25	18 51 48	7 21.4	19 37.2	4 02.8	13 41.3	17 06.3	18 26.4	8 44.9	0 04.8	3 08.8	5 29.4
28 Tu	2 25 54	8 12 58	25 13 57	1♎33 08	7 18.7	21 23.9	5 15.6	14 27.4	17 30.7	18 34.4	8 51.8	0 08.1	3 10.7	5 29.7
29 W	2 29 51	9 11 16	7♎49 35	14 03 32	7 13.5	23 12.4	6 28.3	15 13.4	17 55.1	18 42.5	8 58.6	0 11.4	3 12.7	5 29.9
30 Th	2 33 47	10 09 32	20 15 08	26 24 33	7 05.6	25 02.6	7 41.0	15 59.4	18 19.6	18 50.7	9 05.4	0 14.7	3 14.6	5 30.1

Astro Data Dy Hr Mn	Planet Ingress Dy Hr Mn
☽0S 4 12:11	♂ ♓ 2 14:16
♀0N 8 16:42	♀ ♈ 6 10:46
♃ D 11 3:30	⚳ ♉ 15 5:16
☽0N 18 21:48	⊙ ♈ 20 14:46
⊙0N 20 14:46	♀ ♉ 30 16:01
☿ D 20 19:33	
♄0N 26 21:26	♂ ♈ 9 19:36
♄✶♇ 28 22:13	☿ ♈ 15 3:21
☽0S 31 20:02	⊙ ♉ 20 1:39
	♀ ♊ 24 4:03
♂0N 12 18:22	♅ ♊ 26 0:50
☽0N 15 7:41	
☿0N 19 6:43	
♆0N 24 4:40	
☽0S 28 1:50	

Last Aspect Dy Hr Mn	☽ Ingress Dy Hr Mn
2 12:27 ♂ ☍	♍ 2 12:34
4 14:53 ♅ △	♎ 4 18:56
5 23:22 ♃ □	♏ 7 4:01
9 11:28 ♅ ☍	♐ 9 15:36
11 9:38 ⊙ □	♑ 12 4:07
14 11:33 ♅ △	♒ 14 15:13
16 19:57 ♅ □	♓ 16 23:16
19 1:23 ⊙ ☌	♈ 19 4:03
20 9:23 ♀ ☌	♉ 21 6:35
23 5:40 ♅ ☌	♊ 23 8:19
24 22:37 ♀ ✶	♋ 25 10:33
27 11:40 ♅ ✶	♌ 27 14:10
29 17:28 ♀ △	♍ 29 19:33

Last Aspect Dy Hr Mn	☽ Ingress Dy Hr Mn
1 0:31 ♅ △	♎ 1 2:51
2 8:55 ♃ □	♏ 3 12:11
5 21:29 ♅ ☍	♐ 5 23:31
8 9:51 ♂ □	♑ 8 12:04
10 22:24 ♅ △	♒ 10 23:55
13 7:42 ♅ □	♓ 13 8:55
15 13:07 ♅ ✶	♈ 15 14:04
17 11:52 ⊙ ☌	♉ 17 15:58
19 15:45 ♅ ☌	♊ 19 16:18
20 5:17 ♂ ✶	♋ 21 17:00
23 19:28 ♅ ✶	♌ 23 19:41
24 22:21 ☿ △	♍ 26 1:04
27 11:12 ♃ ✶	♎ 28 9:03
30 8:52 ☿ ☍	♏ 30 19:02

☽ Phases & Eclipses Dy Hr Mn	
3 11:38	○ 12♍54
3 11:34	• T 1.151
11 9:38	☾ 20♐49
19 1:23	● 28♓27
25 19:18	☽ 5♋09
2 2:12	○ 12♎21
10 4:52	☾ 20♑20
17 11:52	● 27♈29
24 2:32	☽ 3♌56

Astro Data

1 March 2026
Julian Day # 46081
SVP 4♓53'32"
GC 27♐12.3 ⚴ 11♓40.0
Eris 24♈49.8 ⚵ 21♑35.2
⚷ 24♈04.1 ⚶ 25♒15.3
☽ Mean ☊ 9♓01.1

1 April 2026
Julian Day # 46112
SVP 4♓53'29"
GC 27♐12.4 ⚴ 22♓00.6
Eris 25♈07.5 ⚵ 0♒51.1
⚷ 25♈44.1 ⚶ 10♓39.6
☽ Mean ☊ 7♓22.6

LONGITUDE — May 2026

Day	Sid.Time	☉	0 hr ☽	Noon ☽	True ☊	☿	♀	♂	⚳	♃	♄	♅	♆	♇
1 F	2 37 44	11♉07 46	2♏31 57	8♏37 26	6♓55.4	26♈54.6	8♊53.6	16♈45.4	18♉44.0	18♋59.1	9♈12.2	0♊18.1	3♈16.5	5♒30.2
2 Sa	2 41 41	12 05 59	14 41 07	20 43 09	6R 43.7	28 48.3	10 06.2	17 31.3	19 08.5	19 07.5	9 18.9	0 21.4	3 18.4	5 30.3
3 Su	2 45 37	13 04 10	26 43 38	2♐42 45	6 31.4	0♉43.8	11 18.8	18 17.2	19 32.9	19 16.1	9 25.6	0 24.8	3 20.2	5 30.4
4 M	2 49 34	14 02 20	8♐40 40	14 37 36	6 19.6	2 41.0	12 31.2	19 03.1	19 57.4	19 24.9	9 32.2	0 28.2	3 22.1	5 30.5
5 Tu	2 53 30	15 00 28	20 33 48	26 29 34	6 09.2	4 39.9	13 43.7	19 48.9	20 21.9	19 33.7	9 38.8	0 31.6	3 23.9	5 30.6
6 W	2 57 27	15 58 34	2♑25 14	8♑21 12	6 01.0	6 40.4	14 56.1	20 34.6	20 46.5	19 42.6	9 45.4	0 35.0	3 25.7	5R 30.6
7 Th	3 01 23	16 56 39	14 17 54	20 15 48	5 55.4	8 42.6	16 08.4	21 20.4	21 11.0	19 51.7	9 51.9	0 38.4	3 27.5	5 30.6
8 F	3 05 20	17 54 42	26 15 27	2♒17 23	5 52.3	10 46.4	17 20.7	22 06.0	21 35.5	20 00.9	9 58.4	0 41.9	3 29.2	5 30.5
9 Sa	3 09 16	18 52 44	8♒22 14	14 30 35	5D 51.1	12 51.6	18 33.0	22 51.7	22 00.1	20 10.1	10 04.8	0 45.3	3 31.0	5 30.5
10 Su	3 13 13	19 50 45	20 43 05	27 00 22	5R 51.2	14 58.2	19 45.2	23 37.3	22 24.7	20 19.5	10 11.2	0 48.8	3 32.7	5 30.4
11 M	3 17 10	20 48 45	3♓23 01	9♓51 39	5 51.2	17 06.0	20 57.3	24 22.8	22 49.2	20 29.0	10 17.5	0 52.2	3 34.4	5 30.2
12 Tu	3 21 06	21 46 43	16 26 45	23 08 45	5 50.2	19 15.0	22 09.4	25 08.3	23 13.8	20 38.6	10 23.8	0 55.7	3 36.0	5 30.1
13 W	3 25 03	22 44 39	29 57 57	6♈54 32	5 47.2	21 24.8	23 21.4	25 53.8	23 38.4	20 48.3	10 30.0	0 59.2	3 37.7	5 29.9
14 Th	3 28 59	23 42 35	13♈58 29	21 09 34	5 41.6	23 35.3	24 33.4	26 39.2	24 03.0	20 58.1	10 36.1	1 02.6	3 39.3	5 29.7
15 F	3 32 56	24 40 29	28 27 23	5♉51 15	5 33.5	25 46.2	25 45.4	27 24.6	24 27.6	21 08.0	10 42.3	1 06.1	3 40.9	5 29.5
16 Sa	3 36 52	25 38 22	13♉20 16	20 53 22	5 23.5	27 57.4	26 57.3	28 09.9	24 52.3	21 18.0	10 48.3	1 09.6	3 42.5	5 29.2
17 Su	3 40 49	26 36 13	28 29 18	6♊06 40	5 12.6	0♊08.5	28 09.1	28 55.2	25 16.9	21 28.1	10 54.3	1 13.1	3 44.0	5 28.9
18 M	3 44 45	27 34 03	13♊44 06	21 20 10	5 02.2	2 19.3	29 20.9	29 40.4	25 41.5	21 38.2	11 00.3	1 16.6	3 45.6	5 28.6
19 Tu	3 48 42	28 31 52	28 53 34	6♋23 08	4 53.5	4 29.4	0♋32.6	0♉25.5	26 06.2	21 48.5	11 06.2	1 20.1	3 47.1	5 28.3
20 W	3 52 39	29 29 39	13♋47 54	21 07 05	4 47.2	6 38.7	1 44.3	1 10.7	26 30.8	21 58.9	11 12.0	1 23.6	3 48.6	5 27.9
21 Th	3 56 35	0♊27 24	28 20 08	5♌26 43	4 43.5	8 46.7	2 55.9	1 55.7	26 55.4	22 09.4	11 17.8	1 27.1	3 50.0	5 27.5
22 F	4 00 32	1 25 08	12♌26 41	19 20 06	4D 42.0	10 53.4	4 07.4	2 40.7	27 20.1	22 19.9	11 23.5	1 30.7	3 51.4	5 27.1
23 Sa	4 04 28	2 22 50	26 07 07	2♍48 03	4R 41.8	12 58.3	5 18.9	3 25.7	27 44.7	22 30.5	11 29.2	1 34.1	3 52.8	5 26.7
24 Su	4 08 25	3 20 30	9♍23 15	15 53 11	4 41.6	15 01.4	6 30.3	4 10.6	28 09.3	22 41.2	11 34.8	1 37.6	3 54.2	5 26.2
25 M	4 12 21	4 18 09	22 18 17	28 39 03	4 40.3	17 02.4	7 41.7	4 55.4	28 34.0	22 52.0	11 40.3	1 41.1	3 55.6	5 25.7
26 Tu	4 16 18	5 15 46	4♎55 57	11♎09 26	4 36.9	19 01.1	8 52.9	5 40.2	28 58.6	23 02.9	11 45.8	1 44.6	3 56.9	5 25.2
27 W	4 20 14	6 13 22	17 19 55	23 27 48	4 30.7	20 57.5	10 04.1	6 24.9	29 23.2	23 13.8	11 51.2	1 48.1	3 58.2	5 24.6
28 Th	4 24 11	7 10 57	29 33 27	5♏37 10	4 21.7	22 51.3	11 15.3	7 09.6	29 47.8	23 24.9	11 56.5	1 51.6	3 59.4	5 24.1
29 F	4 28 08	8 08 30	11♏39 13	17 39 52	4 10.3	24 42.6	12 26.4	7 54.3	0♊12.5	23 36.0	12 01.8	1 55.1	4 00.7	5 23.5
30 Sa	4 32 04	9 06 02	23 39 19	29 37 46	3 57.1	26 31.3	13 37.4	8 38.8	0 37.1	23 47.2	12 07.0	1 58.6	4 01.9	5 22.8
31 Su	4 36 01	10 03 33	5♐35 23	11♐32 20	3 43.2	28 17.2	14 48.3	9 23.3	1 01.7	23 58.4	12 12.1	2 02.1	4 03.1	5 22.2

LONGITUDE — June 2026

Day	Sid.Time	☉	0 hr ☽	Noon ☽	True ☊	☿	♀	♂	⚳	♃	♄	♅	♆	♇
1 M	4 39 57	11♊01 03	17♐28 47	23♐24 53	3♓29.9	0♋00.3	15♋59.1	10♉07.8	1♊26.3	24♋09.7	12♈17.2	2♊05.6	4♈04.2	5♒21.5
2 Tu	4 43 54	11 58 32	29 20 52	5♑16 54	3R 18.0	1 40.6	17 09.9	10 52.2	1 50.9	24 21.1	12 22.2	2 09.1	4 05.3	5R 20.8
3 W	4 47 50	12 56 00	11♑13 16	17 10 14	3 08.4	3 18.1	18 20.6	11 36.6	2 15.5	24 32.6	12 27.1	2 12.5	4 06.4	5 20.1
4 Th	4 51 47	13 53 27	23 08 06	29 07 15	3 01.6	4 52.7	19 31.3	12 20.9	2 40.1	24 44.1	12 32.0	2 16.0	4 07.5	5 19.4
5 F	4 55 43	14 50 54	5♒08 05	11♒11 03	2 57.6	6 24.4	20 41.8	13 05.1	3 04.7	24 55.7	12 36.8	2 19.4	4 08.5	5 18.6
6 Sa	4 59 40	15 48 19	17 16 38	23 25 22	2D 55.9	7 53.2	21 52.3	13 49.3	3 29.2	25 07.4	12 41.5	2 22.9	4 09.5	5 17.9
7 Su	5 03 37	16 45 44	29 37 48	5♓54 30	2R 55.6	9 19.0	23 02.7	14 33.5	3 53.8	25 19.1	12 46.1	2 26.3	4 10.5	5 17.0
8 M	5 07 33	17 43 09	12♓16 04	18 43 03	2 55.7	10 41.8	24 13.1	15 17.6	4 18.4	25 30.9	12 50.6	2 29.7	4 11.4	5 16.2
9 Tu	5 11 30	18 40 33	25 15 59	1♈55 21	2 55.1	12 01.7	25 23.3	16 01.6	4 42.9	25 42.7	12 55.1	2 33.1	4 12.4	5 15.4
10 W	5 15 26	19 37 56	8♈41 32	15 34 51	2 52.8	13 18.4	26 33.5	16 45.6	5 07.5	25 54.6	12 59.5	2 36.5	4 13.2	5 14.5
11 Th	5 19 23	20 35 19	22 35 25	29 43 12	2 48.2	14 32.0	27 43.6	17 29.5	5 32.0	26 06.6	13 03.8	2 39.9	4 14.1	5 13.6
12 F	5 23 19	21 32 41	6♉57 58	14♉19 15	2 41.2	15 42.5	28 53.6	18 13.3	5 56.5	26 18.6	13 08.1	2 43.3	4 14.9	5 12.7
13 Sa	5 27 16	22 30 03	21 46 22	29 18 24	2 32.3	16 49.7	0♌03.6	18 57.1	6 21.0	26 30.7	13 12.3	2 46.6	4 15.7	5 11.8
14 Su	5 31 13	23 27 24	6♊54 13	14♊32 32	2 22.5	17 53.7	1 13.4	19 40.9	6 45.5	26 42.8	13 16.3	2 50.0	4 16.5	5 10.8
15 M	5 35 09	24 24 45	22 11 57	29 51 00	2 13.0	18 54.3	2 23.2	20 24.6	7 10.0	26 55.0	13 20.3	2 53.3	4 17.2	5 09.8
16 Tu	5 39 06	25 22 06	7♋28 18	15♋02 28	2 04.9	19 51.4	3 32.9	21 08.2	7 34.5	27 07.3	13 24.3	2 56.6	4 17.9	5 08.9
17 W	5 43 02	26 19 25	22 32 21	29 56 56	1 59.1	20 45.0	4 42.5	21 51.7	7 58.9	27 19.6	13 28.1	2 59.9	4 18.6	5 07.8
18 Th	5 46 59	27 16 44	7♌15 26	14♌27 18	1 55.7	21 35.0	5 52.0	22 35.2	8 23.3	27 31.9	13 31.8	3 03.2	4 19.2	5 06.8
19 F	5 50 55	28 14 01	21 32 11	28 29 57	1D 54.6	22 21.2	7 01.4	23 18.7	8 47.7	27 44.3	13 35.5	3 06.4	4 19.8	5 05.8
20 Sa	5 54 52	29 11 18	5♍20 41	12♍04 33	1 54.8	23 03.6	8 10.6	24 02.0	9 12.1	27 56.7	13 39.1	3 09.7	4 20.4	5 04.7
21 Su	5 58 48	0♋08 34	18 41 52	25 13 05	1R 55.4	23 42.1	9 19.8	24 45.3	9 36.5	28 09.2	13 42.6	3 12.9	4 20.9	5 03.6
22 M	6 02 45	1 05 50	1♎38 38	7♎59 05	1 55.2	24 16.4	10 28.9	25 28.6	10 00.9	28 21.7	13 46.0	3 16.1	4 21.4	5 02.5
23 Tu	6 06 42	2 03 05	14 14 56	20 26 45	1 53.5	24 46.7	11 37.9	26 11.7	10 25.2	28 34.3	13 49.3	3 19.3	4 21.9	5 01.4
24 W	6 10 38	3 00 19	26 35 05	2♏40 25	1 49.6	25 12.6	12 46.8	26 54.8	10 49.5	28 46.9	13 52.5	3 22.4	4 22.3	5 00.3
25 Th	6 14 35	3 57 32	8♏43 15	14 44 03	1 43.3	25 34.2	13 55.5	27 37.9	11 13.8	28 59.5	13 55.6	3 25.6	4 22.7	4 59.1
26 F	6 18 31	4 54 46	20 43 14	26 41 10	1 35.1	25 51.3	15 04.2	28 20.9	11 38.0	29 12.2	13 58.7	3 28.7	4 23.1	4 58.0
27 Sa	6 22 28	5 51 58	2♐38 12	8♐34 38	1 25.4	26 03.9	16 12.7	29 03.8	12 02.3	29 24.9	14 01.6	3 31.8	4 23.4	4 56.8
28 Su	6 26 24	6 49 11	14 30 44	20 26 46	1 15.1	26 11.9	17 21.1	29 46.6	12 26.5	29 37.7	14 04.5	3 34.9	4 23.8	4 55.6
29 M	6 30 21	7 46 23	26 22 57	2♑19 28	1 05.1	26R 15.3	18 29.4	0♊29.4	12 50.7	29 50.5	14 07.2	3 37.9	4 24.0	4 54.4
30 Tu	6 34 17	8 43 35	8♑16 32	14 14 21	0 56.4	26 14.1	19 37.6	1 12.2	13 14.8	0♌03.3	14 09.9	3 41.0	4 24.3	4 53.2

Astro Data

	Dy Hr Mn
♇R	6 15:34
☽0N	12 17:00
☽0S	25 6:36
☽0N	9 0:26
☽0S	21 12:12
☿R	29 17:36

Planet Ingress

		Dy Hr Mn
☿	♉	3 2:57
☿	♊	17 10:26
♂	♉	18 22:25
♀	♋	19 1:05
☉	♊	21 0:37
⚳	♊	28 23:52
☿	♋	1 11:56
♀	♌	13 10:47
☉	♋	21 8:24
♂	♊	28 19:29
♃	♌	30 5:52

Last Aspect / ☽ Ingress

Last Aspect Dy Hr Mn			☽ Ingress	Dy Hr Mn
2 8:47	♃	△	♐	3 6:33
4 21:33	♂	△	♑	5 19:06
7 14:18	♂	□	♒	8 7:27
10 5:09	♂	✶	♓	10 17:39
12 10:04	♀	□	♈	13 0:04
14 21:33	♂	☌	♉	15 2:31
17 1:02	☿	☌	♊	17 2:23
17 19:36	♄	✶	♋	19 1:46
20 13:27	♃	☌	♌	21 2:48
21 22:05	♄	△	♍	23 6:57
25 0:54	♃	✶	♎	25 14:34
27 11:32	♃	□	♏	28 0:52
30 0:05	♃	△	♐	30 12:45

Last Aspect / ☽ Ingress

Last Aspect Dy Hr Mn			☽ Ingress	Dy Hr Mn
31 13:21	♄	△	♑	2 1:19
4 3:04	♃	☍	♒	4 13:45
5 19:51	☉	△	♓	7 0:43
9 0:38	♃	△	♈	9 8:33
11 8:22	♀	□	♉	11 12:28
13 7:30	♃	✶	♊	13 13:06
15 2:54	☉	☌	♋	15 12:14
17 7:41	♃	☌	♌	17 12:05
19 11:30	☉	✶	♍	19 14:37
21 17:33	♃	✶	♎	21 20:55
24 4:11	♃	□	♏	24 6:43
26 17:10	♃	△	♐	26 18:41
28 5:05	♀	△	♑	29 7:18

☽ Phases & Eclipses

Dy Hr Mn		
1 17:23	○	11♏21
9 21:10	☾	19♒15
16 20:01	●	25♉58
23 11:11	☽	2♍21
31 8:45	○	9♐56
8 10:00	☾	17♓38
15 2:54	●	24♊03
21 21:55	☽	0♎32
29 23:57	○	8♑15

Astro Data

1 May 2026
Julian Day # 46142
SVP 4♓53'26"
GC 27♐12.4 ⚴ 1♈39.0
Eris 25♈27.1 ⚵ 7♒38.8
⚷ 27♈31.7 ⚶ 24♓39.8
☽ Mean ☊ 5♓47.3

1 June 2026
Julian Day # 46173
SVP 4♓53'20"
GC 27♐12.5 ⚴ 10♈41.2
Eris 25♈44.8 ⚵ 10♒56.6
⚷ 29♈12.8 ⚶ 7♈43.6
☽ Mean ☊ 4♓08.8

July 2026

LONGITUDE

Day	Sid.Time	☉	0 hr ☽	Noon ☽	True ☊	☿	♀	♂	⚳	♃	♄	♅	♆	♇
1 W	6 38 14	9♋40 46	20♑13 06	26♑13 00	0♓49.5	26♋08.3	20♌45.6	1♊54.8	13♊39.0	0♌16.1	14♈12.5	3♊44.0	4♈24.5	4♒52.0
2 Th	6 42 11	10 37 58	2♒14 17	8♒17 11	0R 44.8	25R 57.9	21 53.5	2 37.4	14 03.1	0 29.0	14 15.0	3 46.9	4 24.7	4R 50.7
3 F	6 46 07	11 35 10	14 21 59	20 29 00	0D 42.3	25 43.2	23 01.3	3 20.0	14 27.2	0 41.9	14 17.4	3 49.9	4 24.8	4 49.5
4 Sa	6 50 04	12 32 21	26 38 34	2♓51 04	0 41.8	25 24.3	24 08.9	4 02.5	14 51.2	0 54.9	14 19.7	3 52.8	4 24.9	4 48.2
5 Su	6 54 00	13 29 33	9♓06 52	15 26 23	0 42.5	25 01.5	25 16.4	4 44.9	15 15.3	1 07.8	14 21.9	3 55.7	4 25.0	4 46.9
6 M	6 57 57	14 26 45	21 50 05	28 18 22	0 43.8	24 34.9	26 23.8	5 27.2	15 39.3	1 20.8	14 24.0	3 58.6	4R 25.1	4 45.6
7 Tu	7 01 53	15 23 58	4♈51 39	11♈30 21	0R 44.6	24 05.1	27 31.0	6 09.5	16 03.2	1 33.8	14 26.0	4 01.4	4 25.1	4 44.3
8 W	7 05 50	16 21 11	18 14 46	25 05 12	0 44.4	23 32.4	28 38.1	6 51.7	16 27.2	1 46.9	14 27.9	4 04.2	4 25.1	4 43.0
9 Th	7 09 46	17 18 24	2♉01 47	9♉04 35	0 42.5	22 57.4	29 45.1	7 33.9	16 51.1	2 00.0	14 29.7	4 07.0	4 25.0	4 41.7
10 F	7 13 43	18 15 38	16 13 28	23 28 10	0 38.9	22 20.5	0♍51.9	8 16.0	17 15.0	2 13.1	14 31.4	4 09.7	4 24.9	4 40.3
11 Sa	7 17 40	19 12 52	0♊48 13	8♊12 58	0 33.8	21 42.5	1 58.5	8 58.0	17 38.8	2 26.2	14 33.0	4 12.5	4 24.8	4 39.0
12 Su	7 21 36	20 10 06	15 41 36	23 13 07	0 28.1	21 03.8	3 05.0	9 40.0	18 02.6	2 39.3	14 34.5	4 15.2	4 24.7	4 37.7
13 M	7 25 33	21 07 22	0♋46 23	8♋20 12	0 22.4	20 25.2	4 11.3	10 21.9	18 26.4	2 52.5	14 35.9	4 17.8	4 24.5	4 36.3
14 Tu	7 29 29	22 04 37	15 53 19	23 24 31	0 17.6	19 47.3	5 17.5	11 03.7	18 50.1	3 05.7	14 37.2	4 20.4	4 24.3	4 35.0
15 W	7 33 26	23 01 53	0♌52 38	8♌16 38	0 14.2	19 10.9	6 23.5	11 45.5	19 13.8	3 18.8	14 38.5	4 23.0	4 24.1	4 33.6
16 Th	7 37 22	23 59 08	15 35 37	22 48 52	0D 12.6	18 36.5	7 29.4	12 27.2	19 37.5	3 32.0	14 39.6	4 25.6	4 23.8	4 32.2
17 F	7 41 19	24 56 24	29 55 52	6♍56 16	0 12.6	18 04.8	8 35.0	13 08.8	20 01.1	3 45.3	14 40.6	4 28.1	4 23.5	4 30.8
18 Sa	7 45 16	25 53 40	13♍49 54	20 36 48	0 13.6	17 36.3	9 40.5	13 50.3	20 24.6	3 58.5	14 41.5	4 30.6	4 23.1	4 29.4
19 Su	7 49 12	26 50 57	27 17 04	3♎50 59	0 15.2	17 11.7	10 45.8	14 31.8	20 48.2	4 11.7	14 42.3	4 33.1	4 22.8	4 28.1
20 M	7 53 09	27 48 13	10♎18 55	16 41 17	0R 16.5	16 51.3	11 50.9	15 13.2	21 11.6	4 25.0	14 43.0	4 35.5	4 22.3	4 26.7
21 Tu	7 57 05	28 45 30	22 58 37	29 11 24	0 17.0	16 35.6	12 55.8	15 54.5	21 35.1	4 38.2	14 43.5	4 37.9	4 21.9	4 25.3
22 W	8 01 02	29 42 47	5♏20 13	11♏25 36	0 16.3	16 24.9	14 00.5	16 35.8	21 58.5	4 51.5	14 44.0	4 40.2	4 21.5	4 23.9
23 Th	8 04 58	0♌40 04	17 28 08	23 28 21	0 14.3	16D 19.6	15 05.0	17 16.9	22 21.8	5 04.8	14 44.4	4 42.5	4 21.0	4 22.5
24 F	8 08 55	1 37 21	29 26 47	5♐23 54	0 11.1	16 19.8	16 09.2	17 58.1	22 45.1	5 18.1	14 44.7	4 44.8	4 20.4	4 21.1
25 Sa	8 12 51	2 34 40	11♐20 13	17 16 08	0 07.0	16 25.9	17 13.3	18 39.1	23 08.3	5 31.3	14 44.9	4 47.0	4 19.9	4 19.7
26 Su	8 16 48	3 31 58	23 12 04	29 08 24	0 02.5	16 37.8	18 17.1	19 20.1	23 31.5	5 44.6	14R 45.0	4 49.2	4 19.3	4 18.3
27 M	8 20 45	4 29 17	5♑05 26	11♑03 30	29♒58.2	16 55.7	19 20.6	20 01.0	23 54.7	5 57.9	14 45.0	4 51.4	4 18.7	4 16.9
28 Tu	8 24 41	5 26 37	17 02 52	23 03 46	29 54.4	17 19.6	20 24.0	20 41.8	24 17.8	6 11.2	14 44.9	4 53.5	4 18.0	4 15.4
29 W	8 28 38	6 23 57	29 06 26	5♒11 04	29 51.6	17 49.7	21 27.0	21 22.5	24 40.8	6 24.5	14 44.6	4 55.6	4 17.4	4 14.0
30 Th	8 32 34	7 21 18	11♒17 50	17 26 56	29D 49.9	18 25.8	22 29.8	22 03.2	25 03.8	6 37.8	14 44.3	4 57.6	4 16.7	4 12.6
31 F	8 36 31	8 18 40	23 38 33	29 52 49	29 49.4	19 07.9	23 32.4	22 43.8	25 26.7	6 51.1	14 43.9	4 59.6	4 15.9	4 11.2

August 2026

LONGITUDE

Day	Sid.Time	☉	0 hr ☽	Noon ☽	True ☊	☿	♀	♂	⚳	♃	♄	♅	♆	♇
1 Sa	8 40 27	9♌16 02	6♓09 57	12♓30 06	29♒49.8	19♋56.0	24♍34.7	23♊24.4	25♊49.6	7♌04.3	14♈43.4	5♊01.6	4♈15.2	4♒09.8
2 Su	8 44 24	10 13 26	18 53 28	25 20 14	29 50.9	20 50.0	25 36.7	24 04.8	26 12.4	7 17.6	14R 42.7	5 03.5	4R 14.4	4R 08.4
3 M	8 48 20	11 10 51	1♈50 36	8♈24 46	29 52.3	21 49.9	26 38.4	24 45.2	26 35.2	7 30.9	14 42.0	5 05.3	4 13.5	4 07.0
4 Tu	8 52 17	12 08 16	15 02 53	21 45 10	29 53.6	22 55.4	27 39.8	25 25.6	26 57.9	7 44.2	14 41.2	5 07.2	4 12.7	4 05.6
5 W	8 56 14	13 05 43	28 31 43	5♉22 39	29R 54.3	24 06.5	28 41.0	26 05.8	27 20.6	7 57.4	14 40.2	5 08.9	4 11.8	4 04.3
6 Th	9 00 10	14 03 12	12♉18 01	19 17 47	29 54.4	25 22.9	29 41.8	26 46.0	27 43.1	8 10.7	14 39.2	5 10.7	4 10.9	4 02.9
7 F	9 04 07	15 00 42	26 21 51	3♊30 01	29 53.8	26 44.5	0♎42.3	27 26.1	28 05.7	8 23.9	14 38.0	5 12.4	4 10.0	4 01.5
8 Sa	9 08 03	15 58 13	10♊41 58	17 57 18	29 52.6	28 11.2	1 42.5	28 06.1	28 28.1	8 37.2	14 36.8	5 14.0	4 09.0	4 00.1
9 Su	9 12 00	16 55 45	25 15 28	2♋35 49	29 51.1	29 42.5	2 42.4	28 46.1	28 50.5	8 50.4	14 35.5	5 15.7	4 08.1	3 58.8
10 M	9 15 56	17 53 19	9♋57 39	17 20 08	29 49.6	1♌18.3	3 41.9	29 26.0	29 12.8	9 03.6	14 34.0	5 17.2	4 07.1	3 57.4
11 Tu	9 19 53	18 50 54	24 42 24	2♌03 34	29 48.4	2 58.2	4 41.0	0♋05.8	29 35.1	9 16.8	14 32.5	5 18.7	4 06.0	3 56.1
12 W	9 23 49	19 48 30	9♌22 46	16 39 08	29D 47.7	4 41.9	5 39.8	0 45.5	29 57.3	9 30.0	14 30.9	5 20.2	4 05.0	3 54.7
13 Th	9 27 46	20 46 08	23 51 54	1♍00 23	29 47.5	6 29.0	6 38.3	1 25.2	0♋19.4	9 43.1	14 29.2	5 21.6	4 03.9	3 53.4
14 F	9 31 43	21 43 46	8♍04 00	15 02 18	29 47.7	8 19.2	7 36.3	2 04.7	0 41.4	9 56.3	14 27.3	5 23.0	4 02.8	3 52.0
15 Sa	9 35 39	22 41 26	21 54 58	28 41 47	29 48.3	10 12.0	8 33.9	2 44.2	1 03.3	10 09.4	14 25.4	5 24.4	4 01.7	3 50.7
16 Su	9 39 36	23 39 06	5♎22 43	11♎57 49	29 48.9	12 07.1	9 31.1	3 23.6	1 25.2	10 22.5	14 23.4	5 25.6	4 00.5	3 49.4
17 M	9 43 32	24 36 48	18 27 14	24 51 15	29 49.4	14 04.0	10 27.9	4 02.9	1 47.0	10 35.6	14 21.3	5 26.9	3 59.3	3 48.1
18 Tu	9 47 29	25 34 30	1♏10 11	7♏24 29	29 49.8	16 02.4	11 24.2	4 42.1	2 08.7	10 48.6	14 19.1	5 28.1	3 58.1	3 46.8
19 W	9 51 25	26 32 14	13 34 34	19 41 00	29R 50.0	18 01.9	12 20.0	5 21.3	2 30.3	11 01.7	14 16.8	5 29.2	3 56.9	3 45.6
20 Th	9 55 22	27 29 59	25 44 17	1♐44 59	29 50.0	20 02.2	13 15.4	6 00.4	2 51.9	11 14.7	14 14.4	5 30.3	3 55.7	3 44.3
21 F	9 59 18	28 27 45	7♐43 41	13 40 56	29 50.0	22 02.9	14 10.2	6 39.3	3 13.3	11 27.6	14 11.9	5 31.3	3 54.4	3 43.0
22 Sa	10 03 15	29 25 32	19 37 19	25 33 22	29D 49.9	24 03.7	15 04.5	7 18.2	3 34.7	11 40.6	14 09.4	5 32.3	3 53.1	3 41.8
23 Su	10 07 12	0♍23 20	1♑29 37	7♑26 35	29 49.9	26 04.4	15 58.3	7 57.1	3 56.0	11 53.5	14 06.7	5 33.3	3 51.8	3 40.6
24 M	10 11 08	1 21 10	13 24 44	19 24 30	29 50.1	28 04.8	16 51.5	8 35.8	4 17.2	12 06.4	14 04.0	5 34.2	3 50.5	3 39.4
25 Tu	10 15 05	2 19 01	25 26 18	1♒30 29	29 50.3	0♍04.6	17 44.1	9 14.5	4 38.3	12 19.3	14 01.1	5 35.0	3 49.1	3 38.2
26 W	10 19 01	3 16 53	7♒37 24	13 47 17	29 50.5	2 03.8	18 36.1	9 53.0	4 59.3	12 32.1	13 58.2	5 35.8	3 47.8	3 37.0
27 Th	10 22 58	4 14 46	20 00 22	26 16 51	29R 50.7	4 02.1	19 27.5	10 31.5	5 20.2	12 44.9	13 55.3	5 36.6	3 46.4	3 35.8
28 F	10 26 54	5 12 41	2♓36 51	9♓00 27	29 50.6	5 59.6	20 18.2	11 09.9	5 41.0	12 57.6	13 52.2	5 37.3	3 45.0	3 34.6
29 Sa	10 30 51	6 10 38	15 27 43	21 58 37	29 50.2	7 55.9	21 08.3	11 48.2	6 01.7	13 10.4	13 49.0	5 37.9	3 43.6	3 33.5
30 Su	10 34 47	7 08 36	28 33 08	5♈11 12	29 49.6	9 51.3	21 57.7	12 26.4	6 22.3	13 23.0	13 45.8	5 38.5	3 42.1	3 32.4
31 M	10 38 44	8 06 35	11♈52 43	18 37 34	29 48.6	11 45.4	22 46.3	13 04.6	6 42.8	13 35.7	13 42.5	5 39.1	3 40.7	3 31.3

Astro Data	Dy Hr Mn
☽ 0N	6 6:02
♆ R	7 10:55
♅⚹♆	15 20:32
♅△♇	18 4:45
☽ 0S	18 19:48
♃△♆	20 7:23
♃☍♇	20 14:45
♃⚹♅	21 11:11
☿ D	23 22:59
♆⚹♇	25 5:49
♄ R	26 19:56
☽ 0N	2 11:06
♀0S	5 18:46
☽ 0S	15 5:08
☽ 0N	29 17:14

Planet Ingress		Dy Hr Mn
♀	♍	9 17:22
☉	♌	22 19:13
☊	♒R	27 1:42
♀	♎	6 19:13
☿	♌	9 16:28
♂	♋	11 8:30
⚳	♋	12 14:58
☉	♍	23 2:19
☿	♍	25 11:04
♃△△		31 22:17

Last Aspect Dy Hr Mn			☽ Ingress	Dy Hr Mn
1 11:51	☿	☍	♒	1 19:33
3 17:27	♀	☍	♓	4 6:30
6 5:21	☿	△	♈	6 15:07
8 18:42	♀	△	♉	8 20:31
10 10:13	☿	⚹	♊	10 22:42
11 22:11	♄	⚹	♋	12 22:46
14 9:44	☉	☌	♌	14 22:35
15 22:27	♄	△	♍	17 0:07
18 22:13	☉	⚹	♎	19 4:56
21 11:06	☉	□	♏	21 13:34
22 21:48	☿	△	♐	24 1:07
25 14:58	♂	☍	♑	26 13:44
28 6:11	♀	△	♒	29 1:46
30 21:27	♂	△	♓	31 12:14

Last Aspect Dy Hr Mn			☽ Ingress	Dy Hr Mn
2 12:33	♀	☍	♈	2 20:37
4 18:52	♂	⚹	♉	5 2:35
6 23:25	☿	⚹	♊	7 6:08
9 5:27	♂	☌	♋	9 7:46
10 7:30	♄	□	♌	11 8:38
12 17:37	☉	☌	♍	13 10:18
13 19:24	♅	□	♎	15 14:20
17 11:31	☉	⚹	♏	17 21:46
20 2:46	☉	□	♐	20 8:30
22 20:31	☉	△	♑	22 20:59
24 6:30	♀	□	♒	25 9:02
26 21:59	♀	△	♓	27 19:04
28 16:14	♂	△	♈	30 2:38

☽ Phases & Eclipses Dy Hr Mn	
7 19:29	☾ 15♈42
14 9:44	● 21♋59
21 11:06	☽ 28♎43
29 14:36	○ 6♒30
6 2:21	☾ 13♉40
12 17:37	● 20♌02
12 17:45:48	● T 02'18"
20 2:46	☽ 27♏08
28 4:18	○ 4♓54
28 4:13	● P 0.930

Astro Data

1 July 2026
Julian Day # 46203
SVP 4♓53'14"
GC 27♐12.6 ⚴ 17♈47.4
Eris 25♈55.5 ⚵ 8♒59.4R
⚷ 0♉22.8 ⚶ 18♈17.1
☽ Mean ☊ 2♓33.5

1 August 2026
Julian Day # 46234
SVP 4♓53'09"
GC 27♐12.6 ⚴ 22♈09.7
Eris 25♈57.3R ⚵ 2♒20.1R
⚷ 0♉51.9 ⚶ 25♈44.4
☽ Mean ☊ 0♓55.1

LONGITUDE — September 2026

Day	Sid.Time	☉	0 hr ☽	Noon ☽	True ☊	☿	♀	♂	⚳	♃	♄	♅	♆	♇
1 Tu	10 42 40	9♍04 37	25♈25 36	2♉16 40	29♒47.5	13♍38.4	23♎34.2	13♋42.6	7♋03.2	13♌48.3	13♈39.1	5♊39.6	3♈39.2	3♒30.2
2 W	10 46 37	10 02 41	9♉10 35	16 07 10	29R46.6	15 30.3	24 21.3	14 20.6	7 23.5	14 00.8	13R35.7	5 40.0	3R37.7	3R29.1
3 Th	10 50 34	11 00 46	23 06 13	0♊07 31	29D45.9	17 20.9	25 07.6	14 58.5	7 43.7	14 13.4	13 32.2	5 40.4	3 36.3	3 28.0
4 F	10 54 30	11 58 54	7♊10 51	14 15 59	29 45.7	19 10.3	25 53.0	15 36.3	8 03.7	14 25.8	13 28.6	5 40.8	3 34.7	3 27.0
5 Sa	10 58 27	12 57 04	21 22 38	28 30 32	29 46.1	20 58.5	26 37.6	16 14.0	8 23.7	14 38.3	13 24.9	5 41.1	3 33.2	3 26.0
6 Su	11 02 23	13 55 15	5♋39 20	12♋48 43	29 47.0	22 45.5	27 21.3	16 51.6	8 43.5	14 50.7	13 21.2	5 41.3	3 31.7	3 25.0
7 M	11 06 20	14 53 29	19 58 17	27 07 37	29 48.1	24 31.3	28 04.1	17 29.1	9 03.2	15 03.0	13 17.4	5 41.5	3 30.1	3 24.0
8 Tu	11 10 16	15 51 44	4♌16 17	11♌23 49	29 49.1	26 15.9	28 45.9	18 06.6	9 22.8	15 15.3	13 13.6	5 41.7	3 28.6	3 23.1
9 W	11 14 13	16 50 02	18 29 43	25 33 31	29R49.7	27 59.3	29 26.6	18 43.9	9 42.3	15 27.5	13 09.6	5 41.8	3 27.0	3 22.1
10 Th	11 18 10	17 48 21	2♍34 43	9♍32 50	29 49.5	29 41.6	0♏06.4	19 21.1	10 01.6	15 39.7	13 05.7	5R41.8	3 25.4	3 21.2
11 F	11 22 06	18 46 42	16 27 28	23 18 12	29 48.4	1♎22.8	0 45.0	19 58.3	10 20.9	15 51.9	13 01.6	5 41.8	3 23.8	3 20.3
12 Sa	11 26 03	19 45 05	0♎04 43	6♎46 45	29 46.3	3 02.8	1 22.5	20 35.3	10 39.9	16 03.9	12 57.5	5 41.7	3 22.2	3 19.4
13 Su	11 29 59	20 43 30	13 24 08	19 56 45	29 43.4	4 41.7	1 58.8	21 12.2	10 58.9	16 15.9	12 53.4	5 41.6	3 20.6	3 18.5
14 M	11 33 56	21 41 56	26 24 35	2♏47 43	29 40.0	6 19.5	2 33.9	21 49.1	11 17.7	16 27.9	12 49.2	5 41.5	3 19.0	3 17.7
15 Tu	11 37 52	22 40 24	9♏06 19	15 20 38	29 36.7	7 56.2	3 07.6	22 25.8	11 36.3	16 39.8	12 44.9	5 41.3	3 17.4	3 16.9
16 W	11 41 49	23 38 54	21 30 57	27 37 41	29 33.8	9 31.9	3 40.1	23 02.4	11 54.8	16 51.6	12 40.7	5 41.0	3 15.7	3 16.1
17 Th	11 45 45	24 37 25	3♐41 15	9♐42 09	29 31.7	11 06.5	4 11.1	23 38.9	12 13.2	17 03.4	12 36.3	5 40.7	3 14.1	3 15.3
18 F	11 49 42	25 35 58	15 40 56	21 38 07	29D30.7	12 40.0	4 40.7	24 15.3	12 31.4	17 15.1	12 31.9	5 40.3	3 12.5	3 14.6
19 Sa	11 53 38	26 34 33	27 34 20	3♑30 10	29 30.9	14 12.6	5 08.8	24 51.6	12 49.5	17 26.8	12 27.5	5 39.9	3 10.8	3 13.9
20 Su	11 57 35	27 33 09	9♑26 15	15 23 10	29 32.0	15 44.0	5 35.3	25 27.8	13 07.4	17 38.3	12 23.1	5 39.4	3 09.2	3 13.2
21 M	12 01 32	28 31 47	21 21 31	27 21 55	29 33.7	17 14.5	6 00.2	26 03.9	13 25.1	17 49.9	12 18.6	5 38.9	3 07.5	3 12.5
22 Tu	12 05 28	29 30 27	3♒24 54	9♒30 58	29 35.4	18 43.9	6 23.3	26 39.9	13 42.7	18 01.3	12 14.1	5 38.3	3 05.9	3 11.9
23 W	12 09 25	0♎29 08	15 40 38	21 54 18	29R36.6	20 12.3	6 44.8	27 15.8	14 00.1	18 12.7	12 09.5	5 37.7	3 04.2	3 11.2
24 Th	12 13 21	1 27 52	28 12 19	4♓34 58	29 36.7	21 39.6	7 04.4	27 51.6	14 17.4	18 24.0	12 05.0	5 37.1	3 02.5	3 10.6
25 F	12 17 18	2 26 37	11♓02 28	17 34 53	29 35.4	23 05.9	7 22.1	28 27.2	14 34.5	18 35.2	12 00.4	5 36.3	3 00.9	3 10.1
26 Sa	12 21 14	3 25 23	24 12 15	0♈54 27	29 32.4	24 31.1	7 37.9	29 02.8	14 51.4	18 46.3	11 55.7	5 35.6	2 59.2	3 09.5
27 Su	12 25 11	4 24 12	7♈41 20	14 32 34	29 28.0	25 55.3	7 51.7	29 38.2	15 08.1	18 57.4	11 51.1	5 34.8	2 57.5	3 09.0
28 M	12 29 07	5 23 03	21 27 47	28 26 33	29 22.6	27 18.3	8 03.4	0♌13.5	15 24.7	19 08.4	11 46.4	5 33.9	2 55.9	3 08.5
29 Tu	12 33 04	6 21 56	5♉28 20	12♉32 35	29 16.8	28 40.2	8 13.0	0 48.7	15 41.0	19 19.3	11 41.7	5 33.0	2 54.2	3 08.0
30 W	12 37 01	7 20 51	19 38 44	26 46 13	29 11.5	0♏00.9	8 20.5	1 23.8	15 57.2	19 30.1	11 37.1	5 32.0	2 52.5	3 07.6

LONGITUDE — October 2026

Day	Sid.Time	☉	0 hr ☽	Noon ☽	True ☊	☿	♀	♂	⚳	♃	♄	♅	♆	♇
1 Th	12 40 57	8♎19 49	3♊54 27	11♊02 58	29♒07.2	1♏20.4	8♏25.7	1♌58.8	16♋13.2	19♌40.8	11♈32.4	5♊31.1	2♈50.9	3♒07.1
2 F	12 44 54	9 18 49	18 11 16	25 18 57	29R04.7	2 38.6	8R28.7	2 33.6	16 29.1	19 51.5	11R27.6	5R30.0	2R49.2	3R06.8
3 Sa	12 48 50	10 17 51	2♋25 42	9♋31 13	29D03.8	3 55.4	8 29.4	3 08.4	16 44.7	20 02.1	11 22.9	5 28.9	2 47.6	3 06.4
4 Su	12 52 47	11 16 56	16 35 18	23 37 45	29 04.3	5 10.9	8 27.8	3 43.0	17 00.1	20 12.6	11 18.2	5 27.8	2 46.0	3 06.1
5 M	12 56 43	12 16 03	0♌38 26	7♌37 15	29 05.6	6 24.9	8 23.8	4 17.4	17 15.3	20 23.0	11 13.5	5 26.6	2 44.3	3 05.7
6 Tu	13 00 40	13 15 12	14 34 06	21 28 53	29R06.7	7 37.2	8 17.4	4 51.8	17 30.3	20 33.3	11 08.8	5 25.4	2 42.7	3 05.5
7 W	13 04 36	14 14 23	28 21 29	5♍11 47	29 06.7	8 47.9	8 08.7	5 26.0	17 45.1	20 43.5	11 04.1	5 24.1	2 41.0	3 05.2
8 Th	13 08 33	15 13 37	11♍59 39	18 44 57	29 05.0	9 56.8	7 57.6	6 00.1	17 59.6	20 53.6	10 59.4	5 22.8	2 39.4	3 05.0
9 F	13 12 30	16 12 52	25 27 29	2♎07 05	29 01.0	11 03.7	7 44.0	6 34.0	18 13.9	21 03.6	10 54.7	5 21.4	2 37.8	3 04.8
10 Sa	13 16 26	17 12 10	8♎43 34	15 16 46	28 54.7	12 08.5	7 28.2	7 07.9	18 28.1	21 13.5	10 50.0	5 20.0	2 36.2	3 04.6
11 Su	13 20 23	18 11 30	21 46 32	28 12 45	28 46.5	13 11.0	7 10.0	7 41.5	18 41.9	21 23.3	10 45.3	5 18.5	2 34.6	3 04.4
12 M	13 24 19	19 10 52	4♏35 21	10♏54 17	28 37.2	14 11.0	6 49.5	8 15.0	18 55.6	21 33.0	10 40.7	5 17.0	2 33.0	3 04.3
13 Tu	13 28 16	20 10 16	17 09 36	23 21 23	28 27.7	15 08.3	6 26.9	8 48.4	19 09.0	21 42.7	10 36.0	5 15.5	2 31.5	3 04.2
14 W	13 32 12	21 09 42	29 29 48	5♐35 06	28 18.8	16 02.6	6 02.1	9 21.7	19 22.1	21 52.2	10 31.4	5 13.9	2 29.9	3 04.2
15 Th	13 36 09	22 09 09	11♐37 33	17 37 33	28 11.4	16 53.6	5 35.4	9 54.8	19 35.0	22 01.6	10 26.8	5 12.3	2 28.3	3D04.1
16 F	13 40 05	23 08 39	23 35 30	29 31 53	28 06.2	17 41.0	5 06.8	10 27.7	19 47.7	22 10.8	10 22.3	5 10.7	2 26.8	3 04.1
17 Sa	13 44 02	24 08 10	5♑27 14	11♑22 08	28 03.1	18 24.4	4 36.5	11 00.5	20 00.1	22 20.0	10 17.8	5 09.0	2 25.3	3 04.2
18 Su	13 47 59	25 07 43	17 17 11	23 13 01	28D02.1	19 03.4	4 04.6	11 33.1	20 12.2	22 29.1	10 13.3	5 07.3	2 23.8	3 04.2
19 M	13 51 55	26 07 18	29 10 19	5♒09 44	28 02.4	19 37.6	3 31.4	12 05.6	20 24.1	22 38.0	10 08.8	5 05.5	2 22.3	3 04.3
20 Tu	13 55 52	27 06 54	11♒11 56	17 17 34	28R03.3	20 06.6	2 57.0	12 37.9	20 35.7	22 46.8	10 04.4	5 03.7	2 20.8	3 04.4
21 W	13 59 48	28 06 32	23 27 17	29 41 39	28 03.7	20 29.7	2 21.7	13 10.0	20 47.0	22 55.5	10 00.1	5 01.8	2 19.3	3 04.5
22 Th	14 03 45	29 06 12	6♓01 13	12♓26 26	28 02.6	20 46.4	1 45.6	13 42.0	20 58.1	23 04.1	9 55.7	5 00.0	2 17.9	3 04.7
23 F	14 07 41	0♏05 54	18 57 40	25 35 09	27 59.4	20R56.2	1 09.1	14 13.8	21 08.8	23 12.6	9 51.4	4 58.1	2 16.5	3 04.9
24 Sa	14 11 38	1 05 37	2♈19 01	9♈09 14	27 53.6	20 58.6	0 32.4	14 45.5	21 19.3	23 20.9	9 47.2	4 56.1	2 15.0	3 05.1
25 Su	14 15 34	2 05 22	16 05 36	23 07 45	27 45.5	20 52.9	29♎55.7	15 17.0	21 29.5	23 29.1	9 43.0	4 54.1	2 13.6	3 05.4
26 M	14 19 31	3 05 10	0♉15 10	7♉27 11	27 35.6	20 38.6	29 19.2	15 48.3	21 39.4	23 37.2	9 38.9	4 52.1	2 12.3	3 05.7
27 Tu	14 23 28	4 04 59	14 42 58	22 01 36	27 25.0	20 15.5	28 43.4	16 19.4	21 49.0	23 45.2	9 34.8	4 50.1	2 10.9	3 06.0
28 W	14 27 24	5 04 50	29 22 08	6♊43 34	27 15.0	19 43.1	28 08.3	16 50.4	21 58.3	23 53.0	9 30.8	4 48.0	2 09.6	3 06.3
29 Th	14 31 21	6 04 44	14♊04 55	21 25 16	27 06.6	19 01.5	27 34.2	17 21.2	22 07.2	24 00.7	9 26.8	4 45.9	2 08.2	3 06.7
30 F	14 35 17	7 04 40	28 43 49	5♋59 53	27 00.6	18 10.9	27 01.3	17 51.8	22 15.9	24 08.3	9 22.9	4 43.8	2 06.9	3 07.1
31 Sa	14 39 14	8 04 37	13♋12 54	20 22 28	26 57.3	17 12.0	26 29.9	18 22.2	22 24.3	24 15.7	9 19.1	4 41.7	2 05.7	3 07.5

Astro Data

	Dy Hr Mn
♅ R	10 18:27
☿0S	11 13:23
☽0S	11 14:44
♆✶♇	16 1:47
♆0S	16 2:35
♃⚼♆	22 20:23
☉0S	23 0:05
☽0N	26 1:11
♀ R	3 7:16
☽0S	8 22:53
♇ D	16 2:40
☽0N	23 10:26
☿ R	24 7:12
♃⚼♄	31 19:13

Planet Ingress

	Dy Hr Mn
♀ ♏	10 8:07
☿ ♎	10 16:21
☉ ♎	23 0:05
♂ ♌	28 2:49
☿ ♏	30 11:44
☉ ♏	23 9:38
♀ ♎R	25 9:10

Last Aspect / ☽ Ingress (September)

Last Aspect Dy Hr Mn		☽ Ingress	Dy Hr Mn
31 19:47	♀ ☍	♉	1 8:01
2 10:47	☿ △	♊	3 11:47
5 8:40	♀ △	♋	5 14:30
7 13:40	♀ □	♌	7 16:49
9 18:58	♀ ✶	♍	9 19:35
11 5:52	♂ ✶	♎	11 23:52
13 14:26	♂ □	♏	14 6:44
16 3:30	☉ ✶	♐	16 16:41
18 20:44	☉ □	♑	19 4:55
21 14:31	☉ △	♒	21 17:14
23 8:18	☿ △	♓	24 3:24
26 8:32	♂ △	♈	26 10:23
28 9:50	☿ ☍	♉	28 14:40
29 23:36	♃ □	♊	30 17:26

Last Aspect / ☽ Ingress (October)

Last Aspect Dy Hr Mn		☽ Ingress	Dy Hr Mn
2 2:42	♃ ✶	♋	2 19:54
3 15:08	♄ □	♌	4 22:54
6 10:22	♃ ☌	♍	7 2:53
7 18:57	☿ ✶	♎	9 8:10
10 23:07	♃ ✶	♏	11 15:21
13 8:46	♃ □	♐	14 0:59
15 21:56	☉ ✶	♑	16 12:57
18 16:13	☉ □	♒	19 1:40
21 8:42	☉ △	♓	21 12:35
23 3:31	☿ △	♈	23 19:53
25 22:59	♀ ☍	♉	25 23:35
27 14:51	♃ □	♊	28 1:02
29 21:43	♀ △	♋	30 2:05

☽ Phases & Eclipses

Dy Hr Mn		
4 7:51	☾	11♊49
11 3:27	●	18♍26
18 20:44	☽	25♐57
26 16:49	○	3♈37
3 13:25	☾	10♋21
10 15:50	●	17♎22
18 16:13	☽	25♑18
26 4:12	○	2♉46

Astro Data

1 September 2026
Julian Day # 46265
SVP 4♓53'05"
GC 27♐12.7 ⚴ 21♈35.7R
Eris 25♈49.3R ⚵ 26♑30.3R
⚷ 0♉30.4R ⚶ 27♈38.0R
☽ Mean ☊ 29♒16.6

1 October 2026
Julian Day # 46295
SVP 4♓53'02"
GC 27♐12.8 ⚴ 15♈16.5R
Eris 25♈34.5R ⚵ 26♑22.1
⚷ 29♈28.1R ⚶ 22♈55.7R
☽ Mean ☊ 27♒41.2

November 2026 LONGITUDE

Day	Sid.Time	☉	0 hr ☽	Noon ☽	True ☊	☿	♀	♂	⚳	♃	♄	♅	♆	♇
1 Su	14 43 10	9♏04 37	27♋28 18	4♌30 16	26♒56.1	16♏05.7	26♎00.2	18♌52.4	22♋32.3	24♌23.0	9♈15.3	4♊39.5	2♈04.4	3♒08.0
2 M	14 47 07	10 04 40	11♌28 18	18 22 27	26R 56.1	14R 53.4	25R 32.2	19 22.4	22 39.9	24 30.2	9R 11.6	4R 37.3	2R 03.2	3 08.4
3 Tu	14 51 03	11 04 44	25 12 50	1♍59 36	26 56.2	13 37.0	25 06.2	19 52.2	22 47.3	24 37.2	9 08.0	4 35.0	2 02.0	3 08.9
4 W	14 55 00	12 04 50	8♍42 55	15 22 57	26 54.9	12 18.7	24 42.2	20 21.8	22 54.3	24 44.1	9 04.4	4 32.8	2 00.8	3 09.5
5 Th	14 58 57	13 04 59	21 59 52	28 33 50	26 51.3	11 00.9	24 20.5	20 51.3	23 00.9	24 50.8	9 00.9	4 30.5	1 59.6	3 10.0
6 F	15 02 53	14 05 09	5♎04 56	11♎33 17	26 44.8	9 46.0	24 01.0	21 20.4	23 07.2	24 57.3	8 57.5	4 28.2	1 58.5	3 10.6
7 Sa	15 06 50	15 05 21	17 58 55	24 21 54	26 35.2	8 36.6	23 43.8	21 49.4	23 13.2	25 03.8	8 54.1	4 25.9	1 57.3	3 11.3
8 Su	15 10 46	16 05 36	0♏42 12	6♏59 51	26 23.0	7 34.6	23 29.1	22 18.2	23 18.7	25 10.0	8 50.8	4 23.5	1 56.2	3 11.9
9 M	15 14 43	17 05 52	13 14 50	19 27 10	26 09.2	6 41.9	23 16.8	22 46.7	23 24.0	25 16.1	8 47.7	4 21.2	1 55.2	3 12.6
10 Tu	15 18 39	18 06 10	25 36 51	1♐43 56	25 54.8	5 59.7	23 06.9	23 15.0	23 28.8	25 22.1	8 44.5	4 18.8	1 54.1	3 13.3
11 W	15 22 36	19 06 29	7♐48 31	13 50 43	25 41.2	5 28.8	22 59.5	23 43.0	23 33.3	25 27.9	8 41.5	4 16.4	1 53.1	3 14.0
12 Th	15 26 32	20 06 51	19 50 45	25 48 49	25 29.3	5 09.7	22 54.6	24 10.8	23 37.3	25 33.6	8 38.6	4 14.0	1 52.1	3 14.8
13 F	15 30 29	21 07 13	1♑45 13	7♑40 20	25 20.1	5D 02.2	22D 52.1	24 38.4	23 41.0	25 39.0	8 35.7	4 11.5	1 51.2	3 15.6
14 Sa	15 34 26	22 07 38	13 34 33	19 28 21	25 13.9	5 05.9	22 52.1	25 05.7	23 44.4	25 44.4	8 33.0	4 09.1	1 50.3	3 16.4
15 Su	15 38 22	23 08 03	25 22 16	1♒16 51	25 10.4	5 20.2	22 54.4	25 32.8	23 47.3	25 49.5	8 30.3	4 06.6	1 49.4	3 17.2
16 M	15 42 19	24 08 30	7♒12 43	13 10 32	25 09.0	5 44.4	22 59.2	25 59.6	23 49.8	25 54.5	8 27.7	4 04.2	1 48.5	3 18.1
17 Tu	15 46 15	25 08 59	19 10 58	25 14 42	25 08.8	6 17.6	23 06.2	26 26.1	23 51.9	25 59.3	8 25.3	4 01.7	1 47.6	3 19.0
18 W	15 50 12	26 09 28	1♓22 26	7♓34 52	25 08.6	6 58.9	23 15.5	26 52.4	23 53.7	26 04.0	8 22.9	3 59.2	1 46.8	3 19.9
19 Th	15 54 08	27 09 59	13 52 39	20 16 24	25 07.2	7 47.4	23 27.0	27 18.4	23 55.0	26 08.5	8 20.6	3 56.7	1 46.0	3 20.9
20 F	15 58 05	28 10 31	26 46 38	3♈23 49	25 03.6	8 42.2	23 40.6	27 44.1	23 55.9	26 12.8	8 18.4	3 54.2	1 45.3	3 21.8
21 Sa	16 02 01	29 11 04	10♈08 16	17 00 08	24 57.4	9 42.6	23 56.4	28 09.5	23R 56.4	26 16.9	8 16.3	3 51.7	1 44.5	3 22.8
22 Su	16 05 58	0♐11 39	23 59 24	1♉05 51	24 48.5	10 47.8	24 14.2	28 34.7	23 56.5	26 20.9	8 14.3	3 49.2	1 43.9	3 23.8
23 M	16 09 55	1 12 15	8♉19 03	15 38 21	24 37.6	11 57.3	24 34.0	28 59.6	23 56.2	26 24.6	8 12.4	3 46.7	1 43.2	3 24.9
24 Tu	16 13 51	2 12 52	23 02 52	0♊31 35	24 25.8	13 10.3	24 55.8	29 24.1	23 55.5	26 28.3	8 10.6	3 44.2	1 42.6	3 26.0
25 W	16 17 48	3 13 31	8♊03 16	15 36 40	24 14.4	14 26.4	25 19.4	29 48.4	23 54.3	26 31.7	8 08.8	3 41.7	1 42.0	3 27.1
26 Th	16 21 44	4 14 11	23 10 26	0♋43 18	24 04.7	15 45.1	25 44.8	0♍12.3	23 52.8	26 35.0	8 07.2	3 39.1	1 41.4	3 28.2
27 F	16 25 41	5 14 53	8♋14 04	15 41 39	23 57.6	17 06.1	26 12.0	0 36.0	23 50.8	26 38.0	8 05.8	3 36.6	1 40.9	3 29.3
28 Sa	16 29 37	6 15 36	23 05 10	0♌23 55	23 53.4	18 29.0	26 40.8	0 59.3	23 48.4	26 40.9	8 04.4	3 34.1	1 40.4	3 30.5
29 Su	16 33 34	7 16 21	7♌37 24	14 45 18	23D 51.7	19 53.5	27 11.3	1 22.2	23 45.6	26 43.6	8 03.1	3 31.6	1 39.9	3 31.7
30 M	16 37 30	8 17 07	21 47 29	28 43 57	23R 51.5	21 19.3	27 43.4	1 44.9	23 42.3	26 46.1	8 01.9	3 29.1	1 39.4	3 32.9

December 2026 LONGITUDE

Day	Sid.Time	☉	0 hr ☽	Noon ☽	True ☊	☿	♀	♂	⚳	♃	♄	♅	♆	♇
1 Tu	16 41 27	9♐17 55	5♍34 50	12♍20 22	23♒51.6	22♏46.3	28♎16.9	2♍07.1	23♋38.7	26♌48.5	8♈00.8	3♊26.6	1♈39.0	3♒34.1
2 W	16 45 24	10 18 44	19 00 50	25 36 34	23R 50.6	24 14.3	28 51.9	2 29.1	23R 34.6	26 50.6	7R 59.8	3R 24.1	1R 38.7	3 35.4
3 Th	16 49 20	11 19 34	2♎07 57	8♎35 18	23 47.6	25 43.1	29 28.3	2 50.6	23 30.0	26 52.6	7 58.9	3 21.6	1 38.3	3 36.7
4 F	16 53 17	12 20 27	14 59 00	21 19 21	23 41.8	27 12.5	0♏06.0	3 11.8	23 25.1	26 54.3	7 58.2	3 19.1	1 38.0	3 38.0
5 Sa	16 57 13	13 21 20	27 36 40	3♏51 12	23 33.0	28 42.5	0 45.1	3 32.6	23 19.7	26 55.9	7 57.5	3 16.6	1 37.7	3 39.3
6 Su	17 01 10	14 22 15	10♏03 12	16 12 50	23 21.8	0♐13.0	1 25.3	3 53.0	23 14.0	26 57.3	7 57.0	3 14.1	1 37.5	3 40.6
7 M	17 05 06	15 23 10	22 20 17	28 25 41	23 09.0	1 43.9	2 06.7	4 13.0	23 07.8	26 58.5	7 56.5	3 11.7	1 37.3	3 42.0
8 Tu	17 09 03	16 24 07	4♐29 12	10♐30 55	22 55.6	3 15.2	2 49.3	4 32.6	23 01.2	26 59.4	7 56.2	3 09.2	1 37.1	3 43.4
9 W	17 12 59	17 25 05	16 30 59	22 29 31	22 42.8	4 46.7	3 33.0	4 51.7	22 54.2	27 00.2	7 56.0	3 06.8	1 37.0	3 44.8
10 Th	17 16 56	18 26 04	28 26 40	4♑22 38	22 31.7	6 18.4	4 17.7	5 10.5	22 46.8	27 00.8	7D 55.9	3 04.4	1 36.9	3 46.2
11 F	17 20 53	19 27 04	10♑17 37	16 11 52	22 23.0	7 50.4	5 03.4	5 28.8	22 39.0	27 01.2	7 55.9	3 02.0	1 36.8	3 47.7
12 Sa	17 24 49	20 28 05	22 05 39	27 59 21	22 17.1	9 22.6	5 50.0	5 46.7	22 30.8	27R 01.4	7 56.0	2 59.6	1D 36.8	3 49.2
13 Su	17 28 46	21 29 06	3♒53 20	9♒48 02	22 13.9	10 54.9	6 37.6	6 04.1	22 22.2	27 01.5	7 56.2	2 57.3	1 36.8	3 50.7
14 M	17 32 42	22 30 07	15 43 56	21 41 35	22D 13.0	12 27.4	7 26.1	6 21.0	22 13.3	27 01.3	7 56.5	2 54.9	1 36.8	3 52.2
15 Tu	17 36 39	23 31 10	27 41 31	3♓44 23	22 13.5	14 00.1	8 15.5	6 37.5	22 03.9	27 00.9	7 57.0	2 52.6	1 36.9	3 53.7
16 W	17 40 35	24 32 12	9♓50 46	16 01 21	22R 14.4	15 32.8	9 05.7	6 53.5	21 54.3	27 00.3	7 57.5	2 50.3	1 37.0	3 55.2
17 Th	17 44 32	25 33 15	22 16 45	28 37 38	22 14.6	17 05.8	9 56.6	7 09.0	21 44.3	26 59.5	7 58.2	2 48.0	1 37.1	3 56.8
18 F	17 48 29	26 34 19	5♈04 34	11♈38 06	22 13.3	18 38.8	10 48.4	7 24.0	21 33.9	26 58.5	7 59.0	2 45.8	1 37.3	3 58.4
19 Sa	17 52 25	27 35 22	18 18 41	25 06 40	22 10.0	20 12.0	11 40.8	7 38.5	21 23.3	26 57.4	7 59.8	2 43.5	1 37.5	4 00.0
20 Su	17 56 22	28 36 26	2♉02 14	9♉05 25	22 04.4	21 45.4	12 34.0	7 52.4	21 12.3	26 56.0	8 00.8	2 41.3	1 37.8	4 01.6
21 M	18 00 18	29 37 31	16 16 02	23 33 40	21 57.1	23 18.9	13 27.9	8 05.9	21 01.0	26 54.4	8 01.9	2 39.2	1 38.0	4 03.2
22 Tu	18 04 15	0♑38 36	0♊57 41	8♊27 15	21 48.9	24 52.6	14 22.4	8 18.8	20 49.4	26 52.7	8 03.1	2 37.0	1 38.4	4 04.8
23 W	18 08 11	1 39 41	16 01 18	23 38 34	21 40.7	26 26.5	15 17.6	8 31.1	20 37.6	26 50.7	8 04.5	2 34.9	1 38.7	4 06.5
24 Th	18 12 08	2 40 47	1♋17 43	8♋57 19	21 33.8	28 00.6	16 13.4	8 42.9	20 25.4	26 48.6	8 05.9	2 32.8	1 39.1	4 08.2
25 F	18 16 04	3 41 53	16 35 58	24 12 20	21 28.8	29 34.9	17 09.8	8 54.1	20 13.1	26 46.3	8 07.4	2 30.7	1 39.5	4 09.8
26 Sa	18 20 01	4 42 59	1♌45 12	9♌13 31	21D 26.1	1♑09.5	18 06.7	9 04.8	20 00.4	26 43.8	8 09.0	2 28.7	1 40.0	4 11.5
27 Su	18 23 58	5 44 06	16 36 25	23 53 17	21 25.5	2 44.2	19 04.3	9 14.8	19 47.6	26 41.1	8 10.8	2 26.7	1 40.5	4 13.3
28 M	18 27 54	6 45 14	1♍03 42	8♍07 25	21 26.4	4 19.3	20 02.3	9 24.3	19 34.5	26 38.2	8 12.6	2 24.8	1 41.0	4 15.0
29 Tu	18 31 51	7 46 22	15 04 22	21 54 41	21 27.8	5 54.6	21 00.9	9 33.1	19 21.3	26 35.1	8 14.6	2 22.8	1 41.5	4 16.7
30 W	18 35 47	8 47 30	28 38 33	5♎16 18	21R 28.7	7 30.2	21 59.9	9 41.2	19 07.9	26 31.8	8 16.6	2 20.9	1 42.1	4 18.5
31 Th	18 39 44	9 48 39	11♎48 19	18 15 01	21 28.4	9 06.1	22 59.5	9 48.7	18 54.2	26 28.3	8 18.8	2 19.1	1 42.8	4 20.2

Astro Data (Dy Hr Mn)

	Dy Hr Mn
☽0S	5 4:42
☿D	13 15:55
♀D	14 0:27
☽0N	19 19:28
⚳R	22 5:58
♅△♇	29 11:21
☽0S	2 9:15
♄D	10 23:31
♆D	12 22:18
♃R	13 0:56
☽0N	17 2:53
☽0S	29 15:02

Planet Ingress (Dy Hr Mn)

		Dy Hr Mn
☉	♐	22 7:23
♂	♍	25 23:37
♀	♏	4 8:13
☿	♐	6 8:33
☉	♑	21 20:50
☿	♑	25 18:22

Last Aspect / ☽ Ingress

Last Aspect Dy Hr Mn		☽ Ingress Dy Hr Mn	
31 22:00	♀ □	♌	1 4:18
3 0:10	♀ ⚹	♍	3 8:28
4 6:57	☿ ⚹	♎	5 14:38
7 13:20	♃ ⚹	♏	7 22:40
9 23:25	♃ □	♐	10 8:36
12 11:29	♃ △	♑	12 20:27
14 18:56	♀ □	♒	15 9:24
17 14:26	♂ ☍	♓	17 21:19
20 1:46	☉ △	♈	20 5:52
22 7:38	♂ △	♉	22 10:10
24 10:09	♂ □	♊	24 11:10
26 5:24	♃ ⚹	♋	26 10:51
28 5:40	♀ □	♌	28 11:21
30 10:10	♀ ⚹	♍	30 14:13

Last Aspect / ☽ Ingress

Last Aspect Dy Hr Mn		☽ Ingress Dy Hr Mn	
2 9:11	☿ ⚹	♎	2 20:04
4 22:40	♃ ⚹	♏	5 4:35
7 9:08	♃ □	♐	7 15:06
9 21:06	♃ △	♑	10 3:09
10 19:12	♄ □	♒	12 16:06
14 22:39	♃ ☍	♓	15 4:36
17 5:43	☉ □	♈	17 14:34
19 16:40	☉ △	♉	19 20:30
21 17:26	♃ □	♊	21 22:27
23 17:01	♃ ⚹	♋	23 21:58
25 0:09	♀ △	♌	25 21:12
27 16:39	♃ ☌	♍	27 22:13
29 10:18	♀ ⚹	♎	30 2:27

☽ Phases & Eclipses

Dy Hr Mn		
1 20:28	☾	9♌26
9 7:02	●	16♏53
17 11:48	☽	25♒08
24 14:53	○	2♊20
1 6:09	☾	9♍03
9 0:52	●	16♐57
17 5:43	☽	25♓17
24 1:28	○	2♋14
30 18:59	☾	9♎05

Astro Data

1 November 2026
Julian Day # 46326
SVP 4♓52'57"
GC 27♐12.8 ⚴ 6♈42.8R
Eris 25♈16.2R ⚵ 2♒00.7
⚷ 28♈03.1R ⚶ 15♈24.2R
☽ Mean ☊ 26♒02.7

1 December 2026
Julian Day # 46356
SVP 4♓52'53"
GC 27♐12.9 ⚴ 3♈17.6
Eris 25♈00.7R ⚵ 11♒27.6
⚷ 26♈51.4R ⚶ 12♈42.6
☽ Mean ☊ 24♒27.4

LONGITUDE — January 2027

Day	Sid.Time	☉	0 hr ☽	Noon ☽	True ☊	☿	♀	♂	⚳	♃	♄	♅	♆	♇
1 F	18 43 40	10♑49 48	24♎36 54	0♏54 23	21♒26.3	10♑42.3	23♏59.5	9♍55.6	18♋40.5	26♌24.7	8♈21.1	2♊17.2	1♈43.4	4♒22.0
2 Sa	18 47 37	11 50 58	7♏07 59	13 18 07	21R 22.2	12 18.8	24 59.9	10 01.8	18R 26.6	26R 20.9	8 23.4	2R 15.4	1 44.1	4 23.8
3 Su	18 51 33	12 52 08	19 25 13	25 29 42	21 16.5	13 55.7	26 00.8	10 07.3	18 12.6	26 16.9	8 25.9	2 13.7	1 44.8	4 25.6
4 M	18 55 30	13 53 19	1♐31 57	7♐32 17	21 09.7	15 33.0	27 02.0	10 12.1	17 58.5	26 12.7	8 28.5	2 12.0	1 45.6	4 27.4
5 Tu	18 59 27	14 54 29	13 31 01	19 28 26	21 02.4	17 10.6	28 03.7	10 16.2	17 44.4	26 08.3	8 31.2	2 10.3	1 46.4	4 29.2
6 W	19 03 23	15 55 40	25 24 49	1♑20 23	20 55.4	18 48.6	29 05.7	10 19.6	17 30.1	26 03.8	8 34.0	2 08.7	1 47.2	4 31.0
7 Th	19 07 20	16 56 50	7♑15 22	13 09 59	20 49.4	20 26.9	0♐08.1	10 22.2	17 15.9	25 59.1	8 36.8	2 07.1	1 48.1	4 32.8
8 F	19 11 16	17 58 01	19 04 28	24 59 01	20 44.9	22 05.7	1 10.8	10 24.2	17 01.6	25 54.2	8 39.8	2 05.5	1 49.0	4 34.7
9 Sa	19 15 13	18 59 11	0♒53 52	6♒49 16	20 42.2	23 44.8	2 13.9	10 25.3	16 47.3	25 49.2	8 42.9	2 04.0	1 49.9	4 36.5
10 Su	19 19 09	20 00 21	12 45 31	18 42 53	20D 41.1	25 24.3	3 17.3	10R 25.7	16 33.1	25 44.0	8 46.1	2 02.6	1 50.9	4 38.4
11 M	19 23 06	21 01 30	24 41 42	0♓42 20	20 41.6	27 04.1	4 21.0	10 25.4	16 18.9	25 38.7	8 49.4	2 01.1	1 51.9	4 40.3
12 Tu	19 27 03	22 02 39	6♓45 10	12 50 38	20 43.0	28 44.3	5 25.0	10 24.3	16 04.7	25 33.2	8 52.7	1 59.8	1 52.9	4 42.1
13 W	19 30 59	23 03 48	18 59 10	25 11 15	20 44.8	0♒24.7	6 29.3	10 22.4	15 50.6	25 27.5	8 56.2	1 58.4	1 53.9	4 44.0
14 Th	19 34 56	24 04 55	1♈27 23	7♈48 02	20 46.4	2 05.5	7 33.9	10 19.7	15 36.6	25 21.7	8 59.8	1 57.1	1 55.0	4 45.9
15 F	19 38 52	25 06 03	14 13 42	20 44 50	20R 47.3	3 46.5	8 38.7	10 16.2	15 22.8	25 15.8	9 03.4	1 55.9	1 56.1	4 47.8
16 Sa	19 42 49	26 07 09	27 21 52	4♉05 09	20 47.1	5 27.7	9 43.9	10 12.0	15 09.0	25 09.7	9 07.2	1 54.7	1 57.3	4 49.6
17 Su	19 46 45	27 08 15	10♉54 58	17 51 27	20 45.8	7 08.9	10 49.2	10 06.9	14 55.4	25 03.5	9 11.0	1 53.6	1 58.5	4 51.5
18 M	19 50 42	28 09 20	24 54 39	2♊04 24	20 43.5	8 50.2	11 54.8	10 01.1	14 42.0	24 57.2	9 14.9	1 52.5	1 59.7	4 53.4
19 Tu	19 54 38	29 10 24	9♊20 24	16 42 09	20 40.6	10 31.4	13 00.7	9 54.4	14 28.8	24 50.7	9 19.0	1 51.4	2 00.9	4 55.3
20 W	19 58 35	0♒11 28	24 08 58	1♋39 57	20 37.7	12 12.4	14 06.8	9 47.0	14 15.7	24 44.1	9 23.1	1 50.4	2 02.2	4 57.2
21 Th	20 02 32	1 12 30	9♋14 04	16 50 11	20 35.2	13 53.1	15 13.1	9 38.8	14 02.9	24 37.4	9 27.3	1 49.5	2 03.5	4 59.1
22 F	20 06 28	2 13 32	24 27 02	2♌03 20	20 33.5	15 33.1	16 19.6	9 29.8	13 50.3	24 30.6	9 31.5	1 48.6	2 04.8	5 01.1
23 Sa	20 10 25	3 14 33	9♌37 51	17 09 24	20D 32.8	17 12.4	17 26.3	9 19.9	13 38.0	24 23.7	9 35.9	1 47.7	2 06.2	5 03.0
24 Su	20 14 21	4 15 34	24 36 53	1♍59 24	20 33.0	18 50.7	18 33.3	9 09.3	13 25.9	24 16.7	9 40.4	1 46.9	2 07.5	5 04.9
25 M	20 18 18	5 16 34	9♍16 11	16 26 41	20 33.9	20 27.6	19 40.4	8 57.9	13 14.1	24 09.6	9 44.9	1 46.1	2 09.0	5 06.8
26 Tu	20 22 14	6 17 33	23 30 31	0♎27 28	20 35.1	22 02.8	20 47.8	8 45.7	13 02.5	24 02.3	9 49.5	1 45.4	2 10.4	5 08.7
27 W	20 26 11	7 18 31	7♎17 30	14 00 44	20 36.3	23 36.0	21 55.3	8 32.8	12 51.3	23 55.0	9 54.2	1 44.8	2 11.9	5 10.6
28 Th	20 30 07	8 19 30	20 37 23	27 07 47	20R 37.1	25 06.6	23 03.0	8 19.0	12 40.3	23 47.7	9 59.0	1 44.2	2 13.3	5 12.5
29 F	20 34 04	9 20 27	3♏32 21	9♏51 33	20 37.3	26 34.1	24 10.9	8 04.6	12 29.7	23 40.2	10 03.8	1 43.6	2 14.9	5 14.4
30 Sa	20 38 01	10 21 24	16 05 53	22 15 53	20 37.0	27 58.0	25 19.0	7 49.3	12 19.4	23 32.7	10 08.8	1 43.1	2 16.4	5 16.3
31 Su	20 41 57	11 22 20	28 22 07	4♐25 06	20 36.3	29 17.6	26 27.2	7 33.4	12 09.5	23 25.0	10 13.8	1 42.7	2 18.0	5 18.2

LONGITUDE — February 2027

Day	Sid.Time	☉	0 hr ☽	Noon ☽	True ☊	☿	♀	♂	⚳	♃	♄	♅	♆	♇
1 M	20 45 54	12♒23 16	10♐25 24	16♐23 30	20♒35.3	0♓32.2	27♐35.6	7♍16.7	11♋59.9	23♌17.4	10♈18.9	1♊42.3	2♈19.6	5♒20.1
2 Tu	20 49 50	13 24 10	22 19 56	28 15 09	20R 34.2	1 41.1	28 44.1	6R 59.4	11R 50.7	23R 09.7	10 24.1	1R 41.9	2 21.2	5 22.0
3 W	20 53 47	14 25 04	4♑09 35	10♑03 40	20 33.2	2 43.5	29 52.8	6 41.4	11 41.8	23 01.9	10 29.3	1 41.6	2 22.8	5 23.9
4 Th	20 57 43	15 25 57	15 57 45	21 52 12	20 32.4	3 38.5	1♑01.6	6 22.7	11 33.3	22 54.1	10 34.6	1 41.4	2 24.5	5 25.8
5 F	21 01 40	16 26 49	27 47 20	3♒43 27	20 32.0	4 25.5	2 10.6	6 03.5	11 25.2	22 46.2	10 40.0	1 41.2	2 26.2	5 27.7
6 Sa	21 05 36	17 27 39	9♒40 48	15 39 38	20D 31.8	5 03.6	3 19.7	5 43.6	11 17.5	22 38.3	10 45.5	1 41.1	2 27.9	5 29.5
7 Su	21 09 33	18 28 29	21 40 12	27 42 42	20 31.8	5 32.2	4 28.9	5 23.3	11 10.3	22 30.4	10 51.0	1 41.0	2 29.7	5 31.4
8 M	21 13 30	19 29 17	3♓47 21	9♓54 22	20 31.9	5 50.7	5 38.2	5 02.4	11 03.4	22 22.5	10 56.6	1D 41.0	2 31.4	5 33.3
9 Tu	21 17 26	20 30 04	16 03 57	22 16 20	20R 31.9	5R 58.6	6 47.6	4 41.0	10 56.9	22 14.5	11 02.3	1 41.0	2 33.2	5 35.1
10 W	21 21 23	21 30 49	28 31 42	4♈50 17	20 31.9	5 55.7	7 57.2	4 19.2	10 50.9	22 06.5	11 08.0	1 41.1	2 35.0	5 37.0
11 Th	21 25 19	22 31 33	11♈12 20	17 38 05	20 31.7	5 42.0	9 06.8	3 56.9	10 45.3	21 58.6	11 13.8	1 41.2	2 36.8	5 38.8
12 F	21 29 16	23 32 15	24 07 44	0♉41 34	20 31.4	5 17.7	10 16.6	3 34.4	10 40.1	21 50.6	11 19.7	1 41.4	2 38.7	5 40.7
13 Sa	21 33 12	24 32 56	7♉19 45	14 02 31	20D 31.2	4 43.4	11 26.5	3 11.5	10 35.3	21 42.7	11 25.6	1 41.6	2 40.5	5 42.5
14 Su	21 37 09	25 33 35	20 50 00	27 42 19	20 31.1	4 00.0	12 36.4	2 48.3	10 31.0	21 34.7	11 31.6	1 41.9	2 42.4	5 44.3
15 M	21 41 05	26 34 13	4♊39 31	11♊41 34	20 31.3	3 08.5	13 46.5	2 24.9	10 27.1	21 26.8	11 37.6	1 42.3	2 44.3	5 46.1
16 Tu	21 45 02	27 34 48	18 48 21	25 59 37	20 31.8	2 10.3	14 56.6	2 01.3	10 23.7	21 19.0	11 43.7	1 42.7	2 46.3	5 47.9
17 W	21 48 59	28 35 22	3♋15 01	10♋34 05	20 32.5	1 07.2	16 06.9	1 37.6	10 20.7	21 11.1	11 49.9	1 43.1	2 48.2	5 49.7
18 Th	21 52 55	29 35 54	17 56 14	25 20 45	20 33.2	0 00.7	17 17.2	1 13.8	10 18.1	21 03.3	11 56.1	1 43.6	2 50.2	5 51.5
19 F	21 56 52	0♓36 25	2♌46 48	10♌13 31	20R 33.7	28♒52.8	18 27.6	0 49.9	10 15.9	20 55.5	12 02.4	1 44.2	2 52.2	5 53.3
20 Sa	22 00 48	1 36 53	17 39 56	25 05 04	20 33.8	27 45.1	19 38.1	0 26.1	10 14.2	20 47.8	12 08.7	1 44.8	2 54.2	5 55.0
21 Su	22 04 45	2 37 20	2♍27 57	9♍47 39	20 33.3	26 39.4	20 48.7	0 02.2	10 13.0	20 40.2	12 15.1	1 45.5	2 56.2	5 56.8
22 M	22 08 41	3 37 46	17 03 20	24 14 14	20 32.2	25 37.1	21 59.4	29♌38.4	10 12.1	20 32.6	12 21.5	1 46.2	2 58.2	5 58.5
23 Tu	22 12 38	4 38 10	1♎19 45	8♎19 23	20 30.4	24 39.4	23 10.1	29 14.8	10D 11.7	20 25.0	12 28.0	1 47.0	3 00.2	6 00.2
24 W	22 16 34	5 38 32	15 12 50	21 59 53	20 28.4	23 47.3	24 21.0	28 51.3	10 11.7	20 17.6	12 34.5	1 47.8	3 02.3	6 02.0
25 Th	22 20 31	6 38 53	28 40 32	5♏14 51	20 26.3	23 01.6	25 31.9	28 28.0	10 12.1	20 10.2	12 41.1	1 48.6	3 04.4	6 03.7
26 F	22 24 28	7 39 13	11♏43 04	18 05 30	20 24.6	22 22.7	26 42.9	28 05.0	10 13.0	20 02.9	12 47.7	1 49.6	3 06.5	6 05.3
27 Sa	22 28 24	8 39 31	24 22 34	0♐34 43	20D 23.5	21 50.9	27 53.9	27 42.3	10 14.3	19 55.6	12 54.4	1 50.5	3 08.6	6 07.0
28 Su	22 32 21	9 39 48	6♐42 31	12 46 31	20 23.4	21 26.4	29 05.0	27 19.8	10 16.0	19 48.5	13 01.1	1 51.6	3 10.7	6 08.7

Astro Data

	Dy Hr Mn
♂ R	10 12:59
☽ 0N	13 8:37
♅⚹♆	15 9:31
♃ꝑ♄	22 10:01
☽ 0S	25 23:46
♅ D	8 12:29
☽ 0N	9 14:04
☿ R	9 17:37
☽ 0S	22 10:33
⚳ D	23 23:24
♆ 0N	26 17:34

Planet Ingress

		Dy Hr Mn
♀	♐	7 8:53
☿	♒	13 6:06
☉	♒	20 7:30
☿	♓	1 1:26
♀	♑	3 14:30
☿	♒R	18 12:15
☉	♓	18 21:33
♂	♌R	21 14:13

Last Aspect / ☽ Ingress (January)

Dy Hr Mn	Aspect	☽ Ingress	Dy Hr Mn
1 3:27	♃ ⚹	♏	1 10:16
3 13:33	♃ □	♐	3 20:57
6 1:23	♃ △	♑	6 9:17
8 5:11	☿ ☌	♒	8 22:11
11 1:59	♃ ☍	♓	11 10:36
13 7:32	☉ ⚹	♈	13 21:13
15 20:34	☉ □	♉	16 4:44
18 4:57	☉ △	♊	18 8:33
20 1:01	♃ ⚹	♋	20 9:21
21 0:45	♂ ⚹	♌	22 8:45
23 23:33	♃ ☌	♍	24 8:45
25 17:56	♀ □	♎	26 11:12
28 7:46	☿ △	♏	28 17:21
31 0:36	☿ □	♐	31 3:14

Last Aspect / ☽ Ingress (February)

Dy Hr Mn	Aspect	☽ Ingress	Dy Hr Mn
2 13:05	♀ ☌	♑	2 15:33
3 12:53	♄ □	♒	5 4:28
7 1:47	♃ ☍	♓	7 16:32
8 3:52	☿ ☌	♈	10 2:49
11 21:49	☉ ⚹	♉	12 10:44
14 7:58	☉ □	♊	14 15:59
16 14:50	☉ △	♋	16 18:38
17 21:49	♀ ☍	♌	18 19:31
20 16:02	☿ ☍	♍	20 19:59
22 7:54	♀ △	♎	22 21:44
24 23:58	♂ ⚹	♏	25 2:24
27 6:35	♂ □	♐	27 10:52

☽ Phases & Eclipses

Dy Hr Mn	
7 20:24	● 17♑18
15 20:34	☽ 25♈28
22 12:17	○ 2♌14
29 10:55	☾ 9♏18
6 15:56	● 17♒38
6 15:59:32	● A 07'51"
14 7:58	☽ 25♉23
20 23:24	○ 2♍06
20 23:13	● A 0.927
28 5:16	☾ 9♐23

Astro Data

1 January 2027
Julian Day # 46387
SVP 4♓52'47"
GC 27♐13.0 ⚴ 6♈46.8
Eris 24♈52.0R ⚵ 23♒56.6
⚷ 26♈16.6R ⚶ 16♈30.7
☽ Mean ☊ 22♒49.0

1 February 2027
Julian Day # 46418
SVP 4♓52'41"
GC 27♐13.1 ⚴ 15♈37.8
Eris 24♈53.6 ⚵ 8♓16.6
⚷ 26♈35.1 ⚶ 24♈56.6
☽ Mean ☊ 21♒10.5

March 2027 — LONGITUDE

Day	Sid.Time	☉	0 hr ☽	Noon ☽	True ☊	☿	♀	♂	⚳	♃	♄	♅	♆	♇
1 M	22 36 17	10♓40 03	18♐47 19	24♐45 32	20♒24.0	21♒09.1	0♒16.2	26♌57.8	10♋18.1	19♌41.5	13♈07.9	1♊52.6	3♈12.8	6♒10.3
2 Tu	22 40 14	11 40 17	0♑41 46	6♑36 39	20 25.4	20R58.8	1 27.5	26R36.2	10 20.7	19R34.5	13 14.7	1 53.8	3 14.9	6 11.9
3 W	22 44 10	12 40 29	12 30 45	18 24 40	20 27.1	20D55.4	2 38.8	26 15.0	10 23.6	19 27.7	13 21.5	1 54.9	3 17.1	6 13.5
4 Th	22 48 07	13 40 40	24 18 56	0♒14 03	20 28.8	20 58.5	3 50.1	25 54.3	10 27.0	19 21.0	13 28.4	1 56.2	3 19.2	6 15.1
5 F	22 52 03	14 40 49	6♒10 30	12 08 44	20R30.0	21 07.7	5 01.6	25 34.2	10 30.8	19 14.4	13 35.4	1 57.4	3 21.4	6 16.7
6 Sa	22 56 00	15 40 56	18 09 07	24 12 00	20 30.2	21 22.8	6 13.0	25 14.5	10 34.9	19 07.9	13 42.3	1 58.8	3 23.6	6 18.3
7 Su	22 59 57	16 41 02	0♓17 41	6♓26 23	20 29.1	21 43.4	7 24.6	24 55.5	10 39.5	19 01.5	13 49.3	2 00.1	3 25.8	6 19.8
8 M	23 03 53	17 41 05	12 38 19	18 53 36	20 26.7	22 09.1	8 36.2	24 37.1	10 44.5	18 55.3	13 56.4	2 01.6	3 28.0	6 21.3
9 Tu	23 07 50	18 41 07	25 12 21	1♈34 36	20 22.9	22 39.7	9 47.8	24 19.3	10 49.8	18 49.2	14 03.4	2 03.0	3 30.2	6 22.8
10 W	23 11 46	19 41 07	8♈00 21	14 29 36	20 18.3	23 14.7	10 59.4	24 02.1	10 55.6	18 43.2	14 10.6	2 04.6	3 32.4	6 24.3
11 Th	23 15 43	20 41 05	21 02 17	27 38 20	20 13.2	23 54.0	12 11.2	23 45.7	11 01.7	18 37.4	14 17.7	2 06.1	3 34.6	6 25.8
12 F	23 19 39	21 41 01	4♉17 39	11♉00 09	20 08.4	24 37.1	13 22.9	23 30.0	11 08.2	18 31.7	14 24.9	2 07.7	3 36.9	6 27.3
13 Sa	23 23 36	22 40 54	17 45 44	24 34 18	20 04.5	25 24.0	14 34.7	23 14.9	11 15.1	18 26.2	14 32.1	2 09.4	3 39.1	6 28.7
14 Su	23 27 32	23 40 46	1♊25 46	8♊20 01	20 01.9	26 14.2	15 46.5	23 00.7	11 22.4	18 20.8	14 39.3	2 11.1	3 41.4	6 30.1
15 M	23 31 29	24 40 35	15 16 57	22 16 30	20D00.9	27 07.6	16 58.4	22 47.1	11 30.0	18 15.6	14 46.6	2 12.9	3 43.6	6 31.5
16 Tu	23 35 26	25 40 22	29 18 30	6♋22 51	20 01.3	28 04.0	18 10.3	22 34.4	11 38.0	18 10.5	14 53.8	2 14.7	3 45.9	6 32.9
17 W	23 39 22	26 40 07	13♋29 22	20 37 49	20 02.6	29 03.3	19 22.2	22 22.4	11 46.3	18 05.6	15 01.2	2 16.5	3 48.1	6 34.2
18 Th	23 43 19	27 39 49	27 47 57	4♌59 26	20 04.0	0♓05.2	20 34.2	22 11.2	11 55.0	18 00.9	15 08.5	2 18.4	3 50.4	6 35.6
19 F	23 47 15	28 39 28	12♌11 52	19 24 48	20R04.7	1 09.6	21 46.2	22 00.7	12 04.0	17 56.3	15 15.8	2 20.3	3 52.6	6 36.9
20 Sa	23 51 12	29 39 07	26 37 41	3♍49 56	20 03.9	2 16.3	22 58.3	21 51.0	12 13.4	17 51.9	15 23.2	2 22.3	3 54.9	6 38.2
21 Su	23 55 08	0♈38 43	11♍00 56	18 10 01	20 01.2	3 25.3	24 10.3	21 42.2	12 23.1	17 47.6	15 30.6	2 24.3	3 57.2	6 39.4
22 M	23 59 05	1 38 16	25 16 31	2♎19 48	19 56.5	4 36.5	25 22.4	21 34.1	12 33.1	17 43.6	15 38.0	2 26.4	3 59.5	6 40.7
23 Tu	0 03 01	2 37 48	9♎19 16	16 14 23	19 50.2	5 49.7	26 34.6	21 26.7	12 43.4	17 39.6	15 45.4	2 28.5	4 01.7	6 41.9
24 W	0 06 58	3 37 17	23 04 41	29 49 51	19 42.7	7 04.9	27 46.8	21 20.2	12 54.1	17 35.9	15 52.9	2 30.6	4 04.0	6 43.1
25 Th	0 10 54	4 36 45	6♏29 38	13♏03 55	19 35.1	8 21.9	28 59.0	21 14.5	13 05.1	17 32.4	16 00.4	2 32.8	4 06.3	6 44.3
26 F	0 14 51	5 36 11	19 32 43	25 56 08	19 28.2	9 40.8	0♓11.2	21 09.5	13 16.3	17 29.0	16 07.8	2 35.0	4 08.5	6 45.4
27 Sa	0 18 48	6 35 35	2♐14 25	8♐27 53	19 22.6	11 01.4	1 23.5	21 05.3	13 27.9	17 25.8	16 15.3	2 37.3	4 10.8	6 46.6
28 Su	0 22 44	7 34 57	14 36 56	20 42 04	19 19.0	12 23.7	2 35.8	21 01.8	13 39.8	17 22.8	16 22.8	2 39.6	4 13.1	6 47.7
29 M	0 26 41	8 34 18	26 43 49	2♑42 47	19D17.2	13 47.7	3 48.1	20 59.1	13 52.0	17 19.9	16 30.4	2 41.9	4 15.4	6 48.8
30 Tu	0 30 37	9 33 37	8♑39 34	14 34 50	19 17.1	15 13.3	5 00.5	20 57.2	14 04.4	17 17.3	16 37.9	2 44.3	4 17.6	6 49.8
31 W	0 34 34	10 32 54	20 29 16	26 23 30	19 18.1	16 40.5	6 12.9	20 56.0	14 17.2	17 14.8	16 45.4	2 46.7	4 19.9	6 50.9

April 2027 — LONGITUDE

Day	Sid.Time	☉	0 hr ☽	Noon ☽	True ☊	☿	♀	♂	⚳	♃	♄	♅	♆	♇
1 Th	0 38 30	11♈32 09	2♒18 12	8♒14 01	19♒19.3	18♓09.2	7♓25.3	20♌55.6	14♋30.2	17♌12.5	16♈53.0	2♊49.2	4♈22.2	6♒51.9
2 F	0 42 27	12 31 22	14 11 34	20 11 27	19R19.8	19 39.5	8 37.7	20D55.9	14 43.5	17R10.4	17 00.5	2 51.7	4 24.4	6 52.9
3 Sa	0 46 23	13 30 34	26 14 11	2♓20 16	19 18.8	21 11.3	9 50.2	20 56.9	14 57.1	17 08.5	17 08.1	2 54.2	4 26.7	6 53.8
4 Su	0 50 20	14 29 43	8♓30 07	14 44 05	19 15.7	22 44.5	11 02.7	20 58.7	15 10.9	17 06.8	17 15.7	2 56.8	4 28.9	6 54.8
5 M	0 54 17	15 28 51	21 02 27	27 25 23	19 10.2	24 19.3	12 15.2	21 01.1	15 25.0	17 05.2	17 23.2	2 59.4	4 31.2	6 55.7
6 Tu	0 58 13	16 27 57	3♈52 59	10♈25 15	19 02.4	25 55.6	13 27.7	21 04.3	15 39.4	17 03.9	17 30.8	3 02.0	4 33.4	6 56.5
7 W	1 02 10	17 27 00	17 02 04	23 43 15	18 53.0	27 33.4	14 40.2	21 08.2	15 54.0	17 02.7	17 38.4	3 04.7	4 35.6	6 57.4
8 Th	1 06 06	18 26 02	0♉28 32	7♉17 34	18 42.8	29 12.6	15 52.8	21 12.7	16 08.9	17 01.7	17 45.9	3 07.3	4 37.9	6 58.2
9 F	1 10 03	19 25 02	14 09 56	21 05 12	18 32.9	0♈53.3	17 05.3	21 17.9	16 24.1	17 01.0	17 53.5	3 10.1	4 40.1	6 59.1
10 Sa	1 13 59	20 23 59	28 02 56	5♊02 38	18 24.4	2 35.6	18 17.9	21 23.8	16 39.4	17 00.4	18 01.1	3 12.8	4 42.3	6 59.8
11 Su	1 17 56	21 22 54	12♊03 54	19 06 18	18 18.1	4 19.3	19 30.5	21 30.3	16 55.1	17 00.0	18 08.7	3 15.6	4 44.5	7 00.6
12 M	1 21 52	22 21 48	26 09 30	3♋13 11	18 14.3	6 04.5	20 43.1	21 37.5	17 10.9	16D59.8	18 16.2	3 18.5	4 46.7	7 01.3
13 Tu	1 25 49	23 20 38	10♋17 05	17 21 01	18D12.8	7 51.3	21 55.7	21 45.3	17 27.0	16 59.7	18 23.8	3 21.3	4 48.9	7 02.0
14 W	1 29 46	24 19 27	24 24 48	1♌28 17	18 12.8	9 39.6	23 08.4	21 53.7	17 43.3	16 59.9	18 31.3	3 24.2	4 51.1	7 02.7
15 Th	1 33 42	25 18 13	8♌31 23	15 33 58	18R13.2	11 29.4	24 21.0	22 02.7	17 59.8	17 00.3	18 38.9	3 27.1	4 53.2	7 03.4
16 F	1 37 39	26 16 57	22 35 55	29 37 04	18 12.8	13 20.8	25 33.7	22 12.3	18 16.6	17 00.8	18 46.4	3 30.1	4 55.4	7 04.0
17 Sa	1 41 35	27 15 38	6♍37 14	13♍36 12	18 10.4	15 13.7	26 46.3	22 22.5	18 33.5	17 01.5	18 54.0	3 33.0	4 57.5	7 04.6
18 Su	1 45 32	28 14 17	20 33 42	27 29 24	18 05.5	17 08.2	27 59.0	22 33.2	18 50.7	17 02.5	19 01.5	3 36.0	4 59.7	7 05.1
19 M	1 49 28	29 12 54	4♎22 59	11♎14 03	17 57.7	19 04.2	29 11.7	22 44.5	19 08.1	17 03.6	19 09.0	3 39.0	5 01.8	7 05.7
20 Tu	1 53 25	0♉11 29	18 02 16	24 47 13	17 47.5	21 01.7	0♈24.4	22 56.3	19 25.6	17 04.8	19 16.5	3 42.1	5 03.9	7 06.2
21 W	1 57 21	1 10 03	1♏28 36	8♏06 05	17 35.7	23 00.8	1 37.1	23 08.7	19 43.4	17 06.3	19 23.9	3 45.1	5 06.0	7 06.7
22 Th	2 01 18	2 08 34	14 39 26	21 08 28	17 23.5	25 01.3	2 49.8	23 21.6	20 01.4	17 08.0	19 31.4	3 48.2	5 08.1	7 07.1
23 F	2 05 15	3 07 04	27 33 07	3♐53 22	17 11.9	27 03.3	4 02.6	23 35.0	20 19.5	17 09.8	19 38.8	3 51.4	5 10.1	7 07.6
24 Sa	2 09 11	4 05 32	10♐09 18	16 21 07	17 02.0	29 06.7	5 15.3	23 48.9	20 37.8	17 11.8	19 46.3	3 54.5	5 12.2	7 08.0
25 Su	2 13 08	5 03 58	22 29 04	28 33 30	16 54.6	1♉11.3	6 28.1	24 03.2	20 56.4	17 14.0	19 53.7	3 57.7	5 14.2	7 08.3
26 M	2 17 04	6 02 22	4♑34 51	10♑33 35	16 49.7	3 17.1	7 40.9	24 18.1	21 15.1	17 16.4	20 01.1	4 00.8	5 16.2	7 08.7
27 Tu	2 21 01	7 00 45	16 30 16	22 25 30	16 47.2	5 24.0	8 53.7	24 33.4	21 34.0	17 18.9	20 08.4	4 04.0	5 18.3	7 09.0
28 W	2 24 57	7 59 07	28 19 54	4♒14 08	16D46.4	7 31.8	10 06.5	24 49.2	21 53.0	17 21.6	20 15.8	4 07.3	5 20.3	7 09.3
29 Th	2 28 54	8 57 27	10♒08 52	16 04 50	16R46.4	9 40.3	11 19.3	25 05.4	22 12.3	17 24.5	20 23.1	4 10.5	5 22.2	7 09.6
30 F	2 32 50	9 55 45	22 02 41	28 03 07	16 46.1	11 49.4	12 32.1	25 22.1	22 31.7	17 27.6	20 30.4	4 13.8	5 24.2	7 09.8

Astro Data Dy Hr Mn	Planet Ingress Dy Hr Mn	Last Aspect Dy Hr Mn	☽ Ingress Dy Hr Mn	Last Aspect Dy Hr Mn	☽ Ingress Dy Hr Mn	☽ Phases & Eclipses Dy Hr Mn
☿ D 3 12:32	♀ ♒ 1 6:32	1 16:19 ♂ △	♑ 1 22:35	2 13:29 ♂ ☍	♓ 3 7:25	8 9:29 ● 17♓35
☽ 0N 8 20:36	☿ ♓ 18 10:02	3 1:37 ♄ □	♒ 4 11:32	5 5:22 ☿ ☌	♈ 5 16:48	15 16:25 ☽ 24♊52
♃☐♆ 11 20:24	☉ ♈ 20 20:25	6 14:00 ♂ ☍	♓ 6 23:25	7 7:21 ♂ △	♉ 7 23:10	22 10:44 ○ 1♎35
☉0N 20 20:25	♀ ♓ 26 8:16	8 9:29 ☉ ☌	♈ 9 9:02	9 12:22 ♂ □	♊ 10 3:21	30 0:54 ☾ 9♑06
☽ 0S 21 20:50		11 5:06 ♂ △	♉ 11 16:16	11 16:10 ☉ ⚹	♋ 12 6:32	
	☿ ♈ 8 23:20	13 13:33 ☿ □	♊ 13 21:30	13 22:57 ☉ □	♌ 14 9:30	6 23:51 ● 16♈57
♂ D 1 14:08	♀ ♈ 20 3:57	15 20:52 ☿ △	♋ 16 1:11	16 5:52 ☉ △	♍ 16 12:39	13 22:57 ☽ 23♋47
♃△♄ 3 12:59	☉ ♉ 20 7:17	17 22:52 ☉ △	♌ 18 3:41	18 12:56 ♀ ☍	♎ 18 16:22	20 22:27 ○ 0♏37
☽ 0N 5 4:23	☿ ♉ 24 22:18	19 16:16 ♀ ☍	♍ 20 5:37	20 8:39 ♂ ⚹	♏ 20 21:20	28 20:18 ☾ 8♒19
☿0N 12 1:21		20 9:34 ♅ □	♎ 22 8:02	22 16:13 ♂ □	♐ 23 4:37	
♄∠♅ 12 23:22		24 7:59 ♀ △	♏ 24 12:18	25 2:55 ♂ △	♑ 25 14:52	
♃ D 13 2:11		26 3:04 ♂ □	♐ 26 19:43	27 7:19 ♄ □	♒ 28 3:23	
☽ 0S 18 4:40		28 12:39 ♂ △	♑ 29 6:33	30 6:31 ♂ ☍	♓ 30 15:52	
♀0N 23 3:54		30 16:13 ♄ □	♒ 31 19:20			

Astro Data

1 March 2027
Julian Day # 46446
SVP 4♓52'37"
GC 27♐13.1 ⚴ 26♈42.1
Eris 25♈03.5 ⚵ 22♓19.5
⚷ 27♈34.4 ⚶ 4♉51.6
☽ Mean ☊ 19♒41.5

1 April 2027
Julian Day # 46477
SVP 4♓52'34"
GC 27♐13.2 ⚴ 11♉17.9
Eris 25♈21.2 ⚵ 8♈44.4
⚷ 29♈12.8 ⚶ 17♉13.7
☽ Mean ☊ 18♒03.0

LONGITUDE — May 2027

Day	Sid.Time	☉	0 hr ☽	Noon ☽	True ☊	☿	♀	♂	⚳	♃	♄	♅	♆	♇
1 Sa	2 36 47	10♉54 01	4♓06 46	10♓14 15	16♒44.4	13♉58.7	13♈45.0	25♌39.2	22♋51.2	17♌30.8	20♈37.7	4♊17.1	5♈26.1	7♒10.0
2 Su	2 40 44	11 52 16	16 26 09	22 42 57	16R40.5	16 08.1	14 57.8	25 56.7	23 11.0	17 34.2	20 45.0	4 20.4	5 28.1	7 10.2
3 M	2 44 40	12 50 30	29 05 03	5♈32 47	16 34.0	18 17.2	16 10.7	26 14.6	23 30.9	17 37.8	20 52.2	4 23.7	5 30.0	7 10.4
4 Tu	2 48 37	13 48 42	12♈06 19	18 45 44	16 24.8	20 25.8	17 23.6	26 33.0	23 50.9	17 41.6	20 59.4	4 27.0	5 31.8	7 10.5
5 W	2 52 33	14 46 52	25 30 57	2♉21 47	16 13.8	22 33.6	18 36.4	26 51.8	24 11.2	17 45.5	21 06.6	4 30.3	5 33.7	7 10.6
6 Th	2 56 30	15 45 01	9♉17 50	16 18 38	16 01.7	24 40.2	19 49.3	27 10.9	24 31.5	17 49.6	21 13.7	4 33.7	5 35.6	7 10.6
7 F	3 00 26	16 43 08	23 23 35	0♊31 58	15 49.9	26 45.5	21 02.2	27 30.5	24 52.1	17 53.8	21 20.9	4 37.1	5 37.4	7 10.7
8 Sa	3 04 23	17 41 14	7♊43 02	14 55 58	15 39.7	28 49.0	22 15.1	27 50.4	25 12.7	17 58.2	21 27.9	4 40.5	5 39.2	7R10.7
9 Su	3 08 19	18 39 18	22 10 00	29 24 22	15 31.8	0♊50.6	23 28.0	28 10.7	25 33.6	18 02.8	21 35.0	4 43.9	5 41.0	7 10.7
10 M	3 12 16	19 37 20	6♋38 22	13♋51 25	15 26.9	2 50.0	24 40.9	28 31.3	25 54.5	18 07.6	21 42.0	4 47.3	5 42.8	7 10.6
11 Tu	3 16 13	20 35 20	21 02 58	28 12 39	15 24.5	4 46.9	25 53.8	28 52.3	26 15.6	18 12.5	21 49.0	4 50.7	5 44.5	7 10.6
12 W	3 20 09	21 33 18	5♌20 09	12♌25 15	15 23.8	6 41.2	27 06.7	29 13.7	26 36.9	18 17.5	21 55.9	4 54.2	5 46.3	7 10.5
13 Th	3 24 06	22 31 14	19 27 50	26 27 50	15 23.8	8 32.7	28 19.7	29 35.4	26 58.2	18 22.7	22 02.8	4 57.6	5 48.0	7 10.3
14 F	3 28 02	23 29 09	3♍25 13	10♍19 59	15 23.1	10 21.3	29 32.6	29 57.4	27 19.8	18 28.1	22 09.7	5 01.1	5 49.6	7 10.2
15 Sa	3 31 59	24 27 01	17 12 11	24 01 47	15 20.5	12 06.8	0♉45.5	0♍19.8	27 41.4	18 33.6	22 16.5	5 04.5	5 51.3	7 10.0
16 Su	3 35 55	25 24 52	0♎48 50	7♎33 17	15 15.4	13 49.1	1 58.4	0 42.4	28 03.1	18 39.3	22 23.3	5 08.0	5 52.9	7 09.8
17 M	3 39 52	26 22 41	14 15 04	20 54 09	15 07.4	15 28.3	3 11.4	1 05.4	28 25.0	18 45.1	22 30.1	5 11.5	5 54.5	7 09.6
18 Tu	3 43 48	27 20 28	27 30 26	4♏03 46	14 57.0	17 04.0	4 24.3	1 28.7	28 47.0	18 51.0	22 36.8	5 15.0	5 56.1	7 09.3
19 W	3 47 45	28 18 14	10♏34 05	17 01 14	14 45.1	18 36.4	5 37.3	1 52.2	29 09.2	18 57.1	22 43.4	5 18.5	5 57.7	7 09.0
20 Th	3 51 42	29 15 59	23 25 07	29 45 41	14 32.5	20 05.4	6 50.2	2 16.1	29 31.4	19 03.4	22 50.1	5 22.0	5 59.2	7 08.7
21 F	3 55 38	0♊13 42	6♐02 53	12♐16 44	14 20.6	21 30.9	8 03.2	2 40.2	29 53.8	19 09.8	22 56.6	5 25.5	6 00.7	7 08.4
22 Sa	3 59 35	1 11 24	18 27 18	24 34 41	14 10.4	22 52.9	9 16.2	3 04.6	0♌16.2	19 16.3	23 03.2	5 29.0	6 02.2	7 08.0
23 Su	4 03 31	2 09 05	0♑39 05	6♑40 44	14 02.4	24 11.3	10 29.2	3 29.3	0 38.8	19 22.9	23 09.6	5 32.5	6 03.7	7 07.6
24 M	4 07 28	3 06 45	12 39 58	18 37 09	13 57.1	25 26.0	11 42.2	3 54.2	1 01.5	19 29.7	23 16.1	5 36.0	6 05.1	7 07.2
25 Tu	4 11 24	4 04 23	24 32 43	0♒27 09	13 54.3	26 37.1	12 55.2	4 19.5	1 24.3	19 36.7	23 22.5	5 39.5	6 06.6	7 06.8
26 W	4 15 21	5 02 01	6♒20 59	12 14 49	13D53.4	27 44.5	14 08.2	4 44.9	1 47.2	19 43.7	23 28.8	5 43.0	6 08.0	7 06.3
27 Th	4 19 17	5 59 37	18 09 14	24 04 55	13 53.7	28 48.1	15 21.2	5 10.6	2 10.2	19 50.9	23 35.1	5 46.5	6 09.3	7 05.8
28 F	4 23 14	6 57 13	0♓02 30	6♓02 41	13R54.0	29 47.8	16 34.3	5 36.6	2 33.3	19 58.3	23 41.3	5 50.0	6 10.6	7 05.3
29 Sa	4 27 11	7 54 47	12 06 08	18 13 31	13 53.5	0♋43.6	17 47.3	6 02.8	2 56.6	20 05.7	23 47.5	5 53.6	6 12.0	7 04.7
30 Su	4 31 07	8 52 21	24 25 28	0♈42 35	13 51.3	1 35.4	19 00.4	6 29.3	3 19.9	20 13.3	23 53.6	5 57.1	6 13.2	7 04.2
31 M	4 35 04	9 49 54	7♈05 22	13 34 18	13 46.9	2 23.2	20 13.4	6 56.0	3 43.3	20 21.0	23 59.7	6 00.6	6 14.5	7 03.6

LONGITUDE — June 2027

Day	Sid.Time	☉	0 hr ☽	Noon ☽	True ☊	☿	♀	♂	⚳	♃	♄	♅	♆	♇
1 Tu	4 39 00	10♊47 26	20♈09 42	26♈51 47	13♒40.3	3♋06.8	21♉26.5	7♍22.9	4♌06.8	20♌28.8	24♈05.7	6♊04.1	6♈15.7	7♒02.9
2 W	4 42 57	11 44 57	3♉40 37	10♉36 06	13R31.9	3 46.2	22 39.6	7 50.1	4 30.4	20 36.8	24 11.6	6 07.6	6 16.9	7R02.3
3 Th	4 46 53	12 42 27	17 37 58	24 45 47	13 22.5	4 21.3	23 52.7	8 17.4	4 54.1	20 44.8	24 17.5	6 11.1	6 18.1	7 01.6
4 F	4 50 50	13 39 57	1♊58 54	9♊16 35	13 13.2	4 52.1	25 05.8	8 45.1	5 17.9	20 53.0	24 23.4	6 14.6	6 19.2	7 00.9
5 Sa	4 54 46	14 37 26	16 37 54	24 01 52	13 05.1	5 18.4	26 18.9	9 12.9	5 41.8	21 01.4	24 29.2	6 18.1	6 20.3	7 00.2
6 Su	4 58 43	15 34 53	1♋27 27	8♋53 35	12 59.0	5 40.1	27 32.1	9 40.9	6 05.8	21 09.8	24 34.9	6 21.6	6 21.4	6 59.5
7 M	5 02 40	16 32 20	16 19 16	23 43 34	12 55.4	5 57.4	28 45.2	10 09.2	6 29.9	21 18.3	24 40.5	6 25.1	6 22.5	6 58.7
8 Tu	5 06 36	17 29 45	1♌05 38	8♌24 47	12D53.9	6 10.0	29 58.4	10 37.7	6 54.0	21 27.0	24 46.1	6 28.6	6 23.5	6 58.0
9 W	5 10 33	18 27 10	15 40 27	22 52 12	12 54.1	6 18.1	1♊11.5	11 06.3	7 18.3	21 35.7	24 51.7	6 32.0	6 24.5	6 57.2
10 Th	5 14 29	19 24 33	29 59 46	7♍02 57	12R55.0	6R21.5	2 24.7	11 35.2	7 42.6	21 44.6	24 57.1	6 35.5	6 25.4	6 56.3
11 F	5 18 26	20 21 55	14♍01 41	20 56 00	12 55.5	6 20.4	3 37.8	12 04.3	8 07.0	21 53.6	25 02.5	6 38.9	6 26.4	6 55.5
12 Sa	5 22 22	21 19 16	27 45 58	4♎31 42	12 54.6	6 14.9	4 51.0	12 33.5	8 31.5	22 02.7	25 07.8	6 42.3	6 27.3	6 54.6
13 Su	5 26 19	22 16 36	11♎13 22	17 51 07	12 51.8	6 05.1	6 04.2	13 03.0	8 56.0	22 11.9	25 13.1	6 45.8	6 28.1	6 53.7
14 M	5 30 15	23 13 55	24 25 08	0♏55 34	12 47.0	5 51.1	7 17.4	13 32.6	9 20.6	22 21.1	25 18.3	6 49.2	6 29.0	6 52.8
15 Tu	5 34 12	24 11 13	7♏22 35	13 46 20	12 40.3	5 33.2	8 30.6	14 02.4	9 45.3	22 30.5	25 23.4	6 52.6	6 29.8	6 51.9
16 W	5 38 09	25 08 30	20 06 57	26 24 32	12 32.4	5 11.6	9 43.8	14 32.4	10 10.1	22 40.0	25 28.4	6 56.0	6 30.5	6 50.9
17 Th	5 42 05	26 05 47	2♐39 13	8♐51 06	12 24.0	4 46.8	10 57.0	15 02.5	10 34.9	22 49.6	25 33.4	6 59.3	6 31.3	6 50.0
18 F	5 46 02	27 03 03	15 00 17	21 06 55	12 16.0	4 19.1	12 10.2	15 32.8	10 59.9	22 59.3	25 38.3	7 02.7	6 32.0	6 49.0
19 Sa	5 49 58	28 00 19	27 11 08	3♑13 06	12 09.2	3 48.9	13 23.5	16 03.3	11 24.8	23 09.1	25 43.1	7 06.1	6 32.7	6 48.0
20 Su	5 53 55	28 57 34	9♑12 59	15 11 01	12 04.2	3 16.7	14 36.7	16 34.0	11 49.9	23 18.9	25 47.9	7 09.4	6 33.3	6 47.0
21 M	5 57 51	29 54 48	21 07 28	27 02 37	12 01.0	2 43.1	15 50.0	17 04.8	12 15.0	23 28.9	25 52.6	7 12.7	6 34.0	6 45.9
22 Tu	6 01 48	0♋52 02	2♒56 49	8♒50 26	11D59.8	2 08.7	17 03.3	17 35.8	12 40.2	23 38.9	25 57.2	7 16.0	6 34.6	6 44.9
23 W	6 05 45	1 49 16	14 43 54	20 37 39	12 00.1	1 33.9	18 16.6	18 06.9	13 05.4	23 49.0	26 01.7	7 19.3	6 35.1	6 43.8
24 Th	6 09 41	2 46 30	26 32 13	2♓28 07	12 01.3	0 59.5	19 29.9	18 38.2	13 30.7	23 59.3	26 06.2	7 22.5	6 35.6	6 42.7
25 F	6 13 38	3 43 44	8♓25 56	14 26 13	12 02.9	0 25.9	20 43.3	19 09.7	13 56.1	24 09.6	26 10.5	7 25.8	6 36.1	6 41.6
26 Sa	6 17 34	4 40 57	20 29 36	26 36 41	12R04.2	29♊53.9	21 56.6	19 41.3	14 21.5	24 20.0	26 14.8	7 29.0	6 36.6	6 40.5
27 Su	6 21 31	5 38 10	2♈48 06	9♈04 24	12 04.4	29 23.9	23 10.0	20 13.0	14 47.0	24 30.4	26 19.0	7 32.2	6 37.0	6 39.3
28 M	6 25 27	6 35 24	15 26 10	21 53 54	12 03.3	28 56.4	24 23.4	20 44.9	15 12.6	24 41.0	26 23.1	7 35.4	6 37.4	6 38.2
29 Tu	6 29 24	7 32 37	28 28 02	5♉08 54	12 00.8	28 32.0	25 36.8	21 17.0	15 38.2	24 51.6	26 27.2	7 38.6	6 37.8	6 37.0
30 W	6 33 20	8 29 51	11♉56 43	18 51 34	11 57.0	28 11.0	26 50.2	21 49.2	16 03.8	25 02.3	26 31.2	7 41.7	6 38.1	6 35.8

Astro Data (Dy Hr Mn)	Planet Ingress (Dy Hr Mn)	Last Aspect (Dy Hr Mn)	☽ Ingress (Dy Hr Mn)	Last Aspect (Dy Hr Mn)	☽ Ingress (Dy Hr Mn)	☽ Phases & Eclipses (Dy Hr Mn)	Astro Data
☽0N 2 12:41	☿ ♊ 9 1:58	1 20:47 ☿ ✱	♈ 3 1:43	1 7:02 ♄ ☌	♉ 1 17:33	6 10:58 ● 15♉43	1 May 2027
♇R 8 12:56	♂ ♍ 14 14:47	5 2:09 ☿ ☌	♉ 5 7:53	3 10:23 ♀ ☌	♊ 3 20:43	13 4:44 ☽ 22♌14	Julian Day # 46507
☽0S 15 9:59	♀ ♉ 14 21:01	7 6:48 ♂ □	♊ 7 11:06	5 12:44 ♀ ✱	♋ 5 21:39	20 10:59 ○ 29♏14	SVP 4♓52'30"
☽0N 29 20:31	☉ ♊ 21 6:18	9 9:55 ♂ ✱	♋ 9 12:59	7 20:55 ♀ ✱	♌ 7 22:13	28 13:58 ☾ 7♓02	GC 27♐13.3 ♀ 27♉06.9
	⚳ ♌ 21 18:41	11 7:45 ♀ □	♌ 11 15:00	9 15:22 ♄ △	♍ 10 0:00		Eris 25♈40.8 ✱ 25♈13.8
♅✱♆ 6 10:08	☿ ♋ 28 17:06	13 17:32 ♂ ☌	♍ 13 18:05	11 10:56 ☉ □	♎ 12 3:57	4 19:40 ● 13♊58	⚷ 1♉01.6 ⚶ 29♉54.6
♃⚼♆ 8 1:02		15 12:48 ☉ △	♎ 15 22:33	14 1:33 ♄ ☍	♏ 14 10:17	11 10:56 ☽ 20♍19	☽ Mean ☊ 16♒27.7
☿R 10 18:16	♀ ♊ 8 12:32	17 14:55 ♄ ☍	♏ 18 4:33	16 4:46 ♃ □	♐ 16 18:53	19 0:44 ○ 27♐33	
☽0S 11 14:37	☉ ♋ 21 14:11	20 10:59 ☉ ☍	♐ 20 12:27	19 0:44 ☉ ☍	♑ 19 5:35	27 4:54 ☾ 5♈21	1 June 2027
♅△♇ 15 8:12	☿ ♊R 26 7:19	22 8:59 ♄ △	♑ 22 22:43	21 9:37 ♄ □	♒ 21 18:00		Julian Day # 46538
☽0N 26 3:23		24 21:30 ♄ □	♒ 25 11:05	23 23:02 ♄ ✱	♓ 24 7:01		SVP 4♓52'26"
♆✱♇ 29 0:09		27 22:23 ☿ △	♓ 27 23:55	26 18:08 ☿ □	♈ 26 18:35		GC 27♐13.3 ♀ 14♊41.4
		29 11:03 ♀ ✱	♈ 30 10:39	29 0:28 ☿ ✱	♉ 29 2:46		Eris 25♈58.5 ✱ 12♉39.4
							⚷ 2♉46.6 ⚶ 13♊18.6
							☽ Mean ☊ 14♒49.2

July 2027 LONGITUDE

Day	Sid.Time	☉	0 hr ☽	Noon ☽	True ☊	☿	♀	♂	⚳	♃	♄	♅	♆	♇
1 Th	6 37 17	9♋27 05	25♉53 22	3♊01 51	11♒52.5	27♊53.9	28♊03.6	22♍21.6	16♌29.6	25♌13.1	26♈35.0	7♊44.8	6♈38.4	6♒34.6
2 F	6 41 14	10 24 19	10♊16 35	17 36 56	11R47.9	27R40.9	29 17.1	22 54.1	16 55.4	25 24.0	26 38.8	7 48.0	6 38.6	6R33.4
3 Sa	6 45 10	11 21 33	25 02 05	2♋31 06	11 43.9	27 32.3	0♋30.5	23 26.7	17 21.2	25 34.9	26 42.5	7 51.0	6 38.9	6 32.2
4 Su	6 49 07	12 18 46	10♋02 54	17 36 19	11 41.1	27D28.4	1 44.0	23 59.5	17 47.1	25 45.9	26 46.2	7 54.1	6 39.1	6 30.9
5 M	6 53 03	13 16 00	25 10 12	2♌43 20	11D39.6	27 29.3	2 57.5	24 32.5	18 13.0	25 57.0	26 49.7	7 57.1	6 39.2	6 29.7
6 Tu	6 57 00	14 13 14	10♌14 39	17 43 08	11 39.4	27 35.1	4 11.1	25 05.5	18 39.0	26 08.2	26 53.1	8 00.1	6 39.4	6 28.4
7 W	7 00 56	15 10 27	25 07 53	2♍28 11	11 40.3	27 46.0	5 24.6	25 38.7	19 05.1	26 19.4	26 56.5	8 03.1	6 39.5	6 27.2
8 Th	7 04 53	16 07 40	9♍43 27	16 53 18	11 41.7	28 01.9	6 38.1	26 12.1	19 31.2	26 30.7	26 59.7	8 06.1	6 39.5	6 25.9
9 F	7 08 49	17 04 53	23 57 26	0♎55 45	11 43.0	28 23.0	7 51.7	26 45.5	19 57.3	26 42.0	27 02.9	8 09.0	6R39.6	6 24.6
10 Sa	7 12 46	18 02 06	7♎48 14	14 35 00	11R43.7	28 49.2	9 05.2	27 19.1	20 23.5	26 53.4	27 06.0	8 11.9	6 39.6	6 23.3
11 Su	7 16 43	18 59 19	21 16 12	27 52 07	11 43.4	29 20.6	10 18.8	27 52.9	20 49.8	27 04.9	27 09.0	8 14.7	6 39.5	6 22.0
12 M	7 20 39	19 56 31	4♏23 00	10♏49 12	11 42.2	29 57.1	11 32.4	28 26.7	21 16.0	27 16.5	27 11.8	8 17.6	6 39.5	6 20.6
13 Tu	7 24 36	20 53 44	17 11 03	23 28 54	11 40.1	0♋38.6	12 46.0	29 00.7	21 42.4	27 28.1	27 14.6	8 20.4	6 39.4	6 19.3
14 W	7 28 32	21 50 57	29 43 04	5♐53 56	11 37.4	1 25.2	13 59.7	29 34.8	22 08.7	27 39.7	27 17.3	8 23.2	6 39.2	6 18.0
15 Th	7 32 29	22 48 10	12♐01 48	18 06 59	11 34.4	2 16.8	15 13.3	0♎09.0	22 35.1	27 51.4	27 20.0	8 25.9	6 39.1	6 16.6
16 F	7 36 25	23 45 23	24 09 48	0♑10 31	11 31.7	3 13.2	16 27.0	0 43.4	23 01.6	28 03.2	27 22.5	8 28.6	6 38.9	6 15.3
17 Sa	7 40 22	24 42 36	6♑09 26	12 06 49	11 29.4	4 14.6	17 40.6	1 17.8	23 28.1	28 15.0	27 24.9	8 31.3	6 38.7	6 13.9
18 Su	7 44 19	25 39 49	18 02 56	23 58 03	11 27.9	5 20.8	18 54.3	1 52.4	23 54.6	28 26.9	27 27.2	8 34.0	6 38.4	6 12.5
19 M	7 48 15	26 37 03	29 52 25	5♒46 20	11D27.2	6 31.7	20 08.1	2 27.1	24 21.2	28 38.8	27 29.4	8 36.6	6 38.1	6 11.2
20 Tu	7 52 12	27 34 18	11♒40 04	17 33 57	11 27.2	7 47.2	21 21.8	3 01.9	24 47.8	28 50.8	27 31.6	8 39.2	6 37.8	6 09.8
21 W	7 56 08	28 31 33	23 28 17	29 23 25	11 27.8	9 07.3	22 35.5	3 36.8	25 14.4	29 02.8	27 33.6	8 41.7	6 37.4	6 08.4
22 Th	8 00 05	29 28 48	5♓19 43	11♓17 34	11 28.7	10 31.9	23 49.3	4 11.9	25 41.1	29 14.9	27 35.5	8 44.3	6 37.1	6 07.0
23 F	8 04 01	0♌26 04	17 17 23	23 19 37	11 29.8	12 00.8	25 03.1	4 47.0	26 07.8	29 27.0	27 37.4	8 46.8	6 36.6	6 05.6
24 Sa	8 07 58	1 23 21	29 24 42	5♈33 08	11 30.8	13 33.9	26 16.9	5 22.2	26 34.5	29 39.2	27 39.1	8 49.2	6 36.2	6 04.2
25 Su	8 11 54	2 20 39	11♈45 23	18 01 56	11 31.5	15 11.0	27 30.7	5 57.6	27 01.3	29 51.4	27 40.7	8 51.6	6 35.7	6 02.8
26 M	8 15 51	3 17 58	24 23 15	0♉49 49	11R31.7	16 52.0	28 44.6	6 33.1	27 28.1	0♍03.7	27 42.2	8 54.0	6 35.2	6 01.5
27 Tu	8 19 47	4 15 17	7♉22 01	14 00 14	11 31.6	18 36.6	29 58.4	7 08.7	27 55.0	0 16.0	27 43.7	8 56.3	6 34.7	6 00.1
28 W	8 23 44	5 12 38	20 44 46	27 35 47	11 31.3	20 24.7	1♌12.3	7 44.4	28 21.9	0 28.3	27 45.0	8 58.6	6 34.1	5 58.7
29 Th	8 27 41	6 10 00	4♊33 24	11♊37 33	11 30.7	22 15.8	2 26.2	8 20.2	28 48.8	0 40.7	27 46.2	9 00.9	6 33.5	5 57.3
30 F	8 31 37	7 07 23	18 48 02	26 04 29	11 30.2	24 09.9	3 40.1	8 56.1	29 15.8	0 53.1	27 47.3	9 03.2	6 32.9	5 55.9
31 Sa	8 35 34	8 04 47	3♋26 23	10♋53 00	11 29.8	26 06.4	4 54.1	9 32.2	29 42.7	1 05.6	27 48.4	9 05.3	6 32.2	5 54.5

August 2027 LONGITUDE

Day	Sid.Time	☉	0 hr ☽	Noon ☽	True ☊	☿	♀	♂	⚳	♃	♄	♅	♆	♇
1 Su	8 39 30	9♌02 12	18♋23 30	25♋56 52	11♒29.6	28♋05.1	6♌08.1	10♎08.3	0♍09.8	1♍18.1	27♈49.3	9♊07.5	6♈31.5	5♒53.1
2 M	8 43 27	9 59 38	3♌32 01	11♌07 45	11D29.6	0♌05.7	7 22.0	10 44.6	0 36.8	1 30.6	27 50.1	9 09.6	6R30.8	5R51.7
3 Tu	8 47 23	10 57 04	18 42 53	26 16 14	11R29.6	2 07.8	8 36.0	11 20.9	1 03.9	1 43.2	27 50.8	9 11.7	6 30.1	5 50.3
4 W	8 51 20	11 54 31	3♍46 43	11♍13 18	11 29.6	4 11.0	9 50.0	11 57.4	1 31.0	1 55.8	27 51.4	9 13.7	6 29.3	5 48.9
5 Th	8 55 17	12 51 59	18 35 06	25 51 26	11 29.5	6 15.0	11 04.1	12 33.9	1 58.1	2 08.5	27 51.9	9 15.7	6 28.5	5 47.5
6 F	8 59 13	13 49 28	3♎01 45	10♎05 39	11 29.3	8 19.5	12 18.1	13 10.6	2 25.2	2 21.1	27 52.3	9 17.6	6 27.6	5 46.1
7 Sa	9 03 10	14 46 57	17 02 56	23 53 33	11 29.1	10 24.2	13 32.2	13 47.4	2 52.4	2 33.8	27 52.6	9 19.5	6 26.8	5 44.7
8 Su	9 07 06	15 44 28	0♏37 34	7♏15 12	11D28.9	12 28.7	14 46.2	14 24.2	3 19.6	2 46.5	27 52.7	9 21.4	6 25.9	5 43.4
9 M	9 11 03	16 41 59	13 46 44	20 12 32	11 28.8	14 33.0	16 00.3	15 01.2	3 46.8	2 59.3	27R52.8	9 23.2	6 25.0	5 42.0
10 Tu	9 14 59	17 39 31	26 33 02	2♐48 42	11 29.0	16 36.7	17 14.4	15 38.3	4 14.1	3 12.0	27 52.8	9 25.0	6 24.0	5 40.6
11 W	9 18 56	18 37 03	9♐00 02	15 07 32	11 29.5	18 39.7	18 28.5	16 15.4	4 41.4	3 24.8	27 52.7	9 26.7	6 23.1	5 39.3
12 Th	9 22 52	19 34 37	21 11 42	27 13 03	11 30.3	20 41.8	19 42.7	16 52.7	5 08.6	3 37.7	27 52.4	9 28.4	6 22.1	5 37.9
13 F	9 26 49	20 32 12	3♑12 03	9♑09 10	11 31.2	22 42.8	20 56.8	17 30.0	5 35.9	3 50.5	27 52.1	9 30.1	6 21.1	5 36.6
14 Sa	9 30 46	21 29 47	15 04 50	20 59 30	11 32.0	24 42.8	22 11.0	18 07.5	6 03.3	4 03.4	27 51.7	9 31.7	6 20.0	5 35.2
15 Su	9 34 42	22 27 24	26 53 31	2♒47 16	11R32.6	26 41.5	23 25.1	18 45.0	6 30.6	4 16.2	27 51.1	9 33.2	6 18.9	5 33.9
16 M	9 38 39	23 25 02	8♒41 06	14 35 19	11 32.7	28 38.9	24 39.3	19 22.7	6 58.0	4 29.1	27 50.5	9 34.7	6 17.9	5 32.6
17 Tu	9 42 35	24 22 41	20 30 13	26 26 06	11 32.2	0♍35.1	25 53.5	20 00.4	7 25.3	4 42.1	27 49.7	9 36.2	6 16.7	5 31.3
18 W	9 46 32	25 20 21	2♓23 12	8♓21 49	11 31.1	2 29.9	27 07.7	20 38.2	7 52.7	4 55.0	27 48.9	9 37.6	6 15.6	5 30.0
19 Th	9 50 28	26 18 03	14 22 10	20 24 31	11 29.3	4 23.3	28 21.9	21 16.1	8 20.1	5 07.9	27 47.9	9 39.0	6 14.4	5 28.7
20 F	9 54 25	27 15 46	26 29 07	2♈36 13	11 27.1	6 15.3	29 36.1	21 54.1	8 47.6	5 20.9	27 46.8	9 40.3	6 13.2	5 27.4
21 Sa	9 58 21	28 13 30	8♈46 05	14 59 01	11 24.7	8 05.9	0♍50.4	22 32.2	9 15.0	5 33.8	27 45.7	9 41.6	6 12.0	5 26.1
22 Su	10 02 18	29 11 16	21 15 16	27 35 07	11 22.4	9 55.2	2 04.7	23 10.4	9 42.5	5 46.8	27 44.4	9 42.8	6 10.8	5 24.9
23 M	10 06 14	0♍09 04	3♉58 54	10♉26 53	11 20.7	11 43.0	3 18.9	23 48.7	10 10.0	5 59.8	27 43.1	9 44.0	6 09.5	5 23.6
24 Tu	10 10 11	1 06 54	16 59 21	23 36 35	11D19.7	13 29.5	4 33.2	24 27.0	10 37.4	6 12.8	27 41.6	9 45.1	6 08.3	5 22.4
25 W	10 14 08	2 04 45	0♊18 50	7♊06 17	11 19.6	15 14.6	5 47.5	25 05.5	11 05.0	6 25.8	27 40.0	9 46.2	6 07.0	5 21.2
26 Th	10 18 04	3 02 38	13 59 06	20 57 20	11 20.3	16 58.4	7 01.9	25 44.1	11 32.5	6 38.9	27 38.4	9 47.2	6 05.7	5 20.0
27 F	10 22 01	4 00 33	28 01 00	5♋09 56	11 21.6	18 40.8	8 16.2	26 22.7	12 00.0	6 51.9	27 36.6	9 48.2	6 04.3	5 18.8
28 Sa	10 25 57	4 58 30	12♋23 55	19 42 33	11 22.9	20 21.9	9 30.6	27 01.5	12 27.6	7 04.9	27 34.8	9 49.2	6 03.0	5 17.6
29 Su	10 29 54	5 56 29	27 05 19	4♌31 32	11R23.8	22 01.7	10 44.9	27 40.3	12 55.1	7 18.0	27 32.8	9 50.0	6 01.6	5 16.4
30 M	10 33 50	6 54 29	12♌00 24	19 30 59	11 23.7	23 40.2	11 59.3	28 19.2	13 22.7	7 31.0	27 30.7	9 50.9	6 00.2	5 15.3
31 Tu	10 37 47	7 52 31	27 02 15	4♍33 08	11 22.4	25 17.4	13 13.7	28 58.3	13 50.3	7 44.1	27 28.6	9 51.7	5 58.8	5 14.1

Astro Data Dy Hr Mn	Planet Ingress Dy Hr Mn	Last Aspect Dy Hr Mn	☽ Ingress Dy Hr Mn	Last Aspect Dy Hr Mn	☽ Ingress Dy Hr Mn	☽ Phases & Eclipses Dy Hr Mn
☿ D 4 19:40	♀ ♋ 3 2:01	30 22:42 ♃ □	♊ 1 6:56	1 15:54 ☿ ☌	♌ 1 18:25	4 3:02 ● 11♋57
☽ 0S 8 20:50	☿ ♋ 12 13:48	3 4:05 ☿ ☌	♋ 3 7:58	3 14:31 ♄ △	♍ 3 17:57	10 18:39 ☽ 18♎18
♆ R 9 22:41	♂ ♎ 15 5:40	5 2:36 ♄ □	♌ 5 7:40	4 8:46 ♅ □	♎ 5 18:55	18 15:45 ○ 25♑49
♃△♄ 11 23:16	☉ ♌ 23 1:05	7 4:11 ☿ ⚹	♍ 7 7:57	7 19:05 ♄ ☍	♏ 7 22:53	18 16:03 ☍ A 0.001
♂ 0S 16 18:49	♃ ♍ 26 4:49	9 7:28 ☿ □	♎ 9 10:23	9 4:54 ☉ □	♐ 10 6:36	26 16:55 ☾ 3♉30
☽ 0N 23 9:25	♀ ♌ 27 12:31	11 14:50 ☿ △	♏ 11 15:55	12 13:19 ♄ △	♑ 12 17:34	
		13 23:09 ♂ ⚹	♐ 14 0:33	15 1:58 ♄ □	♒ 15 6:20	2 10:05 ● 9♌55
☽ 0S 5 5:39	⚳ ♍ 1 3:20	16 7:41 ♃ △	♑ 16 11:39	17 14:49 ♄ ⚹	♓ 17 19:12	2 10:06:34 ☌ T 06'23"
♄ R 9 18:06	☿ ♌ 2 10:52	18 19:06 ♄ □	♒ 19 0:15	18 14:32 ♅ □	♈ 20 6:54	9 4:54 ☽ 16♏25
☽ 0N 19 15:15	☿ ♍ 17 4:43	21 11:18 ♃ ☍	♓ 21 13:14	22 15:16 ☉ △	♉ 22 16:33	17 7:29 ○ 24♒12
♃⚻♇ 20 22:59	♀ ♍ 20 19:43	23 15:48 ♀ △	♈ 24 1:09	23 14:43 ☿ △	♊ 24 23:26	17 7:14 ☍ A 0.545
♃⚻♆ 24 4:20	☉ ♍ 23 8:14	26 7:43 ♀ □	♉ 26 10:28	26 23:20 ♄ ⚹	♋ 27 3:21	25 2:27 ☾ 1♊42
		27 21:28 ☿ ⚹	♊ 28 16:10	29 0:46 ♄ □	♌ 29 4:42	31 17:41 ● 8♍06
		30 14:48 ♄ ⚹	♋ 30 18:25	31 2:41 ♂ ⚹	♍ 31 4:44	

Astro Data

1 July 2027
Julian Day # 46568
SVP 4♓52'20"
GC 27♐13.4 ⚴ 2♋25.0
Eris 26♈09.3 ⚵ 29♉37.9
⚷ 4♉02.6 ⚶ 26♊16.7
☽ Mean ☊ 13♒13.9

1 August 2027
Julian Day # 46599
SVP 4♓52'14"
GC 27♐13.5 ⚴ 20♋55.4
Eris 26♈11.3R ⚵ 16♊54.0
⚷ 4♉38.9 ⚶ 9♋24.8
☽ Mean ☊ 11♒35.4

LONGITUDE — September 2027

Day	Sid.Time	☉	0 hr ☽	Noon ☽	True ☊	☿	♀	♂	⚳	♃	♄	♅	♆	♇
1 W	10 41 44	8♍50 34	12♍02 30	19♍29 17	11♒19.8	26♍53.4	14♍28.1	29♎37.4	14♍17.8	7♍57.1	27♈26.3	9♊52.4	5♈57.4	5♒13.0
2 Th	10 45 40	9 48 39	26 52 26	4♎11 02	11R16.1	28 28.1	15 42.5	0♏16.6	14 45.4	8 10.1	27R24.0	9 53.1	5R55.9	5R11.9
3 F	10 49 37	10 46 46	11♎24 17	18 31 34	11 11.8	0♎01.5	16 56.9	0 55.8	15 13.0	8 23.2	27 21.6	9 53.7	5 54.5	5 10.8
4 Sa	10 53 33	11 44 54	25 32 24	2♏26 30	11 07.6	1 33.7	18 11.4	1 35.2	15 40.6	8 36.2	27 19.0	9 54.3	5 53.0	5 09.8
5 Su	10 57 30	12 43 03	9♏13 45	15 54 10	11 04.0	3 04.6	19 25.8	2 14.7	16 08.3	8 49.2	27 16.4	9 54.8	5 51.5	5 08.7
6 M	11 01 26	13 41 14	22 27 58	28 55 25	11 01.6	4 34.3	20 40.2	2 54.2	16 35.9	9 02.2	27 13.7	9 55.3	5 50.0	5 07.7
7 Tu	11 05 23	14 39 27	5♐16 57	11♐33 01	11D00.6	6 02.7	21 54.7	3 33.9	17 03.5	9 15.3	27 10.9	9 55.7	5 48.5	5 06.7
8 W	11 09 19	15 37 41	17 44 11	23 51 02	11 00.9	7 29.8	23 09.2	4 13.6	17 31.1	9 28.3	27 08.1	9 56.1	5 47.0	5 05.7
9 Th	11 13 16	16 35 56	29 54 09	5♑54 11	11 02.1	8 55.6	24 23.6	4 53.4	17 58.7	9 41.3	27 05.1	9 56.5	5 45.4	5 04.7
10 F	11 17 12	17 34 13	11♑51 44	17 47 25	11 03.8	10 20.2	25 38.1	5 33.3	18 26.4	9 54.2	27 02.1	9 56.7	5 43.9	5 03.7
11 Sa	11 21 09	18 32 32	23 41 50	29 35 33	11R05.3	11 43.4	26 52.5	6 13.2	18 54.0	10 07.2	26 58.9	9 57.0	5 42.3	5 02.8
12 Su	11 25 06	19 30 52	5♒29 05	11♒22 57	11 05.9	13 05.2	28 07.0	6 53.3	19 21.6	10 20.2	26 55.7	9 57.1	5 40.7	5 01.9
13 M	11 29 02	20 29 14	17 17 35	23 13 26	11 05.1	14 25.7	29 21.5	7 33.4	19 49.2	10 33.1	26 52.4	9 57.3	5 39.1	5 01.0
14 Tu	11 32 59	21 27 37	29 10 50	5♓10 07	11 02.4	15 44.7	0♎36.0	8 13.6	20 16.9	10 46.0	26 49.1	9R57.3	5 37.5	5 00.1
15 W	11 36 55	22 26 03	11♓11 34	17 15 25	10 57.9	17 02.2	1 50.5	8 53.9	20 44.5	10 58.9	26 45.6	9 57.3	5 35.9	4 59.3
16 Th	11 40 52	23 24 30	23 21 52	29 31 04	10 51.6	18 18.2	3 04.9	9 34.3	21 12.1	11 11.8	26 42.1	9 57.3	5 34.3	4 58.4
17 F	11 44 48	24 22 59	5♈43 07	11♈58 08	10 44.1	19 32.6	4 19.4	10 14.7	21 39.7	11 24.7	26 38.5	9 57.2	5 32.7	4 57.6
18 Sa	11 48 45	25 21 30	18 16 10	24 37 16	10 36.1	20 45.3	5 33.9	10 55.3	22 07.3	11 37.5	26 34.9	9 57.1	5 31.0	4 56.8
19 Su	11 52 41	26 20 03	1♉01 29	7♉28 52	10 28.5	21 56.3	6 48.4	11 35.9	22 34.9	11 50.4	26 31.2	9 56.9	5 29.4	4 56.1
20 M	11 56 38	27 18 38	13 59 27	20 33 16	10 22.0	23 05.4	8 03.0	12 16.6	23 02.5	12 03.2	26 27.4	9 56.7	5 27.8	4 55.3
21 Tu	12 00 35	28 17 15	27 10 24	3♊50 53	10 17.4	24 12.6	9 17.5	12 57.4	23 30.2	12 16.0	26 23.5	9 56.4	5 26.1	4 54.6
22 W	12 04 31	29 15 55	10♊34 50	17 22 19	10D14.8	25 17.6	10 32.0	13 38.2	23 57.8	12 28.7	26 19.6	9 56.1	5 24.5	4 53.9
23 Th	12 08 28	0♎14 37	24 13 25	1♋08 10	10 14.1	26 20.4	11 46.5	14 19.2	24 25.4	12 41.5	26 15.6	9 55.7	5 22.8	4 53.3
24 F	12 12 24	1 13 21	8♋06 38	15 08 48	10 14.7	27 20.9	13 01.1	15 00.2	24 53.0	12 54.2	26 11.6	9 55.2	5 21.2	4 52.6
25 Sa	12 16 21	2 12 08	22 14 35	29 23 52	10R15.7	28 18.8	14 15.6	15 41.3	25 20.5	13 06.8	26 07.5	9 54.8	5 19.5	4 52.0
26 Su	12 20 17	3 10 56	6♌36 23	13♌51 48	10 16.0	29 13.9	15 30.2	16 22.5	25 48.1	13 19.5	26 03.3	9 54.2	5 17.8	4 51.4
27 M	12 24 14	4 09 47	21 09 40	28 29 25	10 14.6	0♏06.0	16 44.7	17 03.8	26 15.7	13 32.1	25 59.1	9 53.6	5 16.2	4 50.8
28 Tu	12 28 10	5 08 40	5♍50 21	13♍11 40	10 11.0	0 54.9	17 59.3	17 45.1	26 43.3	13 44.7	25 54.8	9 53.0	5 14.5	4 50.3
29 W	12 32 07	6 07 35	20 32 31	27 51 59	10 04.8	1 40.3	19 13.8	18 26.6	27 10.8	13 57.2	25 50.5	9 52.3	5 12.8	4 49.7
30 Th	12 36 04	7 06 32	5♎09 08	12♎23 05	9 56.6	2 21.9	20 28.4	19 08.1	27 38.3	14 09.7	25 46.1	9 51.6	5 11.2	4 49.2

LONGITUDE — October 2027

Day	Sid.Time	☉	0 hr ☽	Noon ☽	True ☊	☿	♀	♂	⚳	♃	♄	♅	♆	♇
1 F	12 40 00	8♎05 32	19♎32 57	26♎38 02	9♒47.1	2♏59.4	21♎43.0	19♏49.7	28♍05.9	14♍22.2	25♈41.7	9♊50.8	5♈09.5	4♒48.8
2 Sa	12 43 57	9 04 33	3♏37 41	10♏31 26	9R37.5	3 32.4	22 57.5	20 31.4	28 33.4	14 34.6	25R37.3	9R49.9	5R07.8	4R48.3
3 Su	12 47 53	10 03 36	17 18 58	24 00 08	9 28.7	4 00.6	24 12.1	21 13.1	29 00.9	14 47.0	25 32.8	9 49.1	5 06.2	4 47.9
4 M	12 51 50	11 02 41	0♐34 55	7♐03 29	9 21.7	4 23.4	25 26.7	21 55.0	29 28.4	14 59.4	25 28.3	9 48.1	5 04.5	4 47.5
5 Tu	12 55 46	12 01 47	13 26 05	19 43 06	9 16.9	4 40.5	26 41.2	22 36.9	29 55.8	15 11.7	25 23.7	9 47.1	5 02.9	4 47.2
6 W	12 59 43	13 00 56	25 55 00	2♑02 22	9D14.4	4 51.4	27 55.8	23 18.9	0♎23.3	15 23.9	25 19.1	9 46.1	5 01.2	4 46.8
7 Th	13 03 39	14 00 06	8♑05 47	14 05 55	9 13.8	4R55.6	29 10.3	24 00.9	0 50.7	15 36.1	25 14.5	9 45.0	4 59.6	4 46.5
8 F	13 07 36	14 59 18	20 03 25	25 58 59	9 14.2	4 52.8	0♏24.9	24 43.0	1 18.1	15 48.3	25 09.8	9 43.9	4 57.9	4 46.2
9 Sa	13 11 33	15 58 32	1♒53 18	7♒47 02	9R14.6	4 42.4	1 39.5	25 25.3	1 45.5	16 00.4	25 05.2	9 42.8	4 56.3	4 46.0
10 Su	13 15 29	16 57 48	13 40 52	19 35 23	9 14.1	4 24.2	2 54.0	26 07.5	2 12.9	16 12.5	25 00.5	9 41.5	4 54.7	4 45.7
11 M	13 19 26	17 57 05	25 31 13	1♓28 53	9 11.7	3 57.8	4 08.6	26 49.9	2 40.2	16 24.5	24 55.8	9 40.3	4 53.1	4 45.5
12 Tu	13 23 22	18 56 24	7♓28 52	13 31 38	9 06.8	3 23.2	5 23.1	27 32.3	3 07.6	16 36.5	24 51.0	9 39.0	4 51.4	4 45.4
13 W	13 27 19	19 55 45	19 37 31	25 46 49	8 59.2	2 40.5	6 37.7	28 14.8	3 34.9	16 48.4	24 46.3	9 37.6	4 49.8	4 45.2
14 Th	13 31 15	20 55 08	1♈59 46	8♈16 31	8 49.1	1 49.8	7 52.2	28 57.4	4 02.1	17 00.2	24 41.5	9 36.3	4 48.3	4 45.1
15 F	13 35 12	21 54 33	14 37 07	21 01 33	8 37.3	0 52.0	9 06.7	29 40.0	4 29.4	17 12.0	24 36.8	9 34.8	4 46.7	4 45.0
16 Sa	13 39 08	22 54 00	27 29 47	4♉01 39	8 24.7	29♎47.8	10 21.3	0♐22.7	4 56.6	17 23.7	24 32.0	9 33.3	4 45.1	4 44.9
17 Su	13 43 05	23 53 29	10♉37 00	17 15 35	8 12.5	28 38.7	11 35.8	1 05.5	5 23.8	17 35.4	24 27.2	9 31.8	4 43.5	4D44.9
18 M	13 47 01	24 53 00	23 57 11	0♊41 32	8 01.9	27 26.1	12 50.3	1 48.4	5 51.0	17 47.0	24 22.4	9 30.3	4 42.0	4 44.9
19 Tu	13 50 58	25 52 34	7♊28 26	14 17 37	7 53.7	26 12.1	14 04.9	2 31.3	6 18.2	17 58.6	24 17.7	9 28.7	4 40.5	4 44.9
20 W	13 54 55	26 52 10	21 08 55	28 02 09	7 48.4	24 58.7	15 19.4	3 14.3	6 45.3	18 10.1	24 12.9	9 27.0	4 39.0	4 45.0
21 Th	13 58 51	27 51 48	4♋57 13	11♋54 02	7 45.8	23 48.1	16 33.9	3 57.4	7 12.4	18 21.5	24 08.1	9 25.4	4 37.4	4 45.1
22 F	14 02 48	28 51 28	18 52 30	25 52 36	7 45.1	22 42.4	17 48.5	4 40.6	7 39.5	18 32.8	24 03.4	9 23.7	4 36.0	4 45.2
23 Sa	14 06 44	29 51 11	2♌54 16	9♌57 27	7 45.1	21 43.6	19 03.0	5 23.8	8 06.6	18 44.1	23 58.6	9 21.9	4 34.5	4 45.3
24 Su	14 10 41	0♏50 55	17 02 04	24 07 59	7 44.4	20 53.4	20 17.5	6 07.1	8 33.6	18 55.3	23 53.9	9 20.1	4 33.0	4 45.5
25 M	14 14 37	1 50 42	1♍15 00	8♍22 50	7 41.9	20 13.1	21 32.1	6 50.5	9 00.6	19 06.5	23 49.2	9 18.3	4 31.6	4 45.7
26 Tu	14 18 34	2 50 32	15 31 10	22 39 33	7 36.7	19 43.6	22 46.6	7 33.9	9 27.5	19 17.6	23 44.5	9 16.4	4 30.2	4 45.9
27 W	14 22 30	3 50 23	29 47 28	6♎54 20	7 28.5	19 25.5	24 01.1	8 17.4	9 54.4	19 28.5	23 39.8	9 14.5	4 28.7	4 46.1
28 Th	14 26 27	4 50 17	13♎59 33	21 02 27	7 17.6	19D18.8	25 15.6	9 01.0	10 21.3	19 39.5	23 35.1	9 12.6	4 27.3	4 46.4
29 F	14 30 24	5 50 12	28 02 23	4♏58 45	7 05.1	19 23.3	26 30.2	9 44.6	10 48.2	19 50.3	23 30.5	9 10.6	4 26.0	4 46.7
30 Sa	14 34 20	6 50 10	11♏50 58	18 38 34	6 52.2	19 38.7	27 44.7	10 28.4	11 15.0	20 01.1	23 25.9	9 08.6	4 24.6	4 47.1
31 Su	14 38 17	7 50 09	25 21 11	1♐58 33	6 40.1	20 04.2	28 59.2	11 12.2	11 41.7	20 11.7	23 21.3	9 06.6	4 23.3	4 47.4

Astro Data

Astro Data	Dy Hr Mn
☽0S	1 16:12
☿0S	3 13:07
♃□♅	10 16:41
♅ R	15 9:09
☽0N	15 21:34
♀0S	16 8:37
♃⚼♄	18 8:08
☉0S	23 6:02
☽0S	29 2:32
☿ R	7 14:37
☽0N	13 4:41
♄∠♅	16 2:04
♆⚹♇	16 14:28
♇ D	18 3:50
☽0S	26 10:40

Planet Ingress

Planet Ingress	Dy Hr Mn
♂ ♏	2 1:52
☿ ♎	3 11:37
♀ ♎	14 0:25
☉ ♎	23 6:02
☿ ♏	27 9:10
⚳ ♎	5 15:39
♀ ♏	8 3:59
♂ ♐	15 23:14
☿ ♎R	16 7:36
☉ ♏	23 15:33
☿ D	28 14:11
♃⚼⚼	29 3:49

Last Aspect / ☽ Ingress

Last Aspect Dy Hr Mn		☽ Ingress Dy Hr Mn
2 1:29	☿ ☌	♎ 2 5:07
4 3:06	♄ ☍	♏ 4 7:44
5 19:06	♀ ⚹	♐ 6 14:01
8 18:28	♄ △	♑ 9 0:12
11 6:42	♄ □	♒ 11 12:50
13 19:20	♄ ⚹	♓ 14 1:39
15 23:03	☉ ☍	♈ 16 12:56
18 15:40	♄ ☌	♉ 18 22:05
21 1:13	☉ △	♊ 21 5:06
23 3:35	♄ ⚹	♋ 23 10:02
25 10:03	☿ □	♌ 25 13:00
27 7:55	♄ △	♍ 27 14:28
28 19:48	♂ ⚹	♎ 29 15:30

Last Aspect Dy Hr Mn		☽ Ingress Dy Hr Mn
1 10:25	♄ ☍	♏ 1 17:45
3 6:42	♂ ☌	♐ 3 22:56
6 3:01	♀ ⚹	♑ 6 7:59
8 10:21	♄ □	♒ 8 20:10
11 2:03	♂ □	♓ 11 9:01
13 17:04	♂ △	♈ 13 20:10
15 18:37	♄ ☌	♉ 16 4:37
17 12:36	♃ △	♊ 18 10:46
20 9:49	☉ △	♋ 20 15:25
22 17:29	☉ □	♌ 22 19:03
24 11:36	♄ △	♍ 24 21:54
26 12:13	♀ ⚹	♎ 27 0:21
28 16:20	♄ ☍	♏ 29 3:23
31 6:00	♀ ☌	♐ 31 8:24

☽ Phases & Eclipses

Dy Hr Mn	
7 18:31	☽ 14♐55
15 23:03	○ 22♓53
23 10:20	☾ 0♋11
30 2:36	● 6♎43
7 11:47	☽ 14♑00
15 13:47	○ 21♈59
22 17:29	☾ 29♋05
29 13:37	● 5♏54

Astro Data

1 September 2027
Julian Day # 46630
SVP 4♓52'10"
GC 27♐13.5 ⚳ 9♌00.8
Eris 26♈03.5R ⚵ 3♋16.6
⚷ 4♉24.1R ⚶ 21♋56.6
☽ Mean ☊ 9♒56.9

1 October 2027
Julian Day # 46660
SVP 4♓52'07"
GC 27♐13.6 ⚳ 25♌31.6
Eris 25♈48.8R ⚵ 17♋20.1
⚷ 3♉25.9R ⚶ 2♌59.1
☽ Mean ☊ 8♒21.6

November 2027 — LONGITUDE

Day	Sid.Time	☉	0 hr ☽	Noon ☽	True ☊	☿	♀	♂	⚳	♃	♄	♅	♆	♇
1 M	14 42 13	8♏50 10	8♐30 32	14♐57 07	6♒30.0	20♎39.2	0♐13.7	11♐56.0	12♎08.5	20♍22.3	23♈16.8	9♊04.5	4♈22.0	4♒47.8
2 Tu	14 46 10	9 50 13	21 18 26	27 34 41	6R 22.5	21 22.7	1 28.3	12 40.0	12 35.1	20 32.8	23R 12.3	9R 02.4	4R 20.7	4 48.2
3 W	14 50 06	10 50 18	3♑46 14	9♑53 29	6 17.8	22 13.9	2 42.8	13 24.0	13 01.8	20 43.2	23 07.9	9 00.3	4 19.4	4 48.7
4 Th	14 54 03	11 50 24	15 56 56	21 57 09	6 15.6	23 11.9	3 57.3	14 08.0	13 28.4	20 53.6	23 03.5	8 58.2	4 18.2	4 49.2
5 F	14 58 00	12 50 32	27 54 45	3♒50 25	6 15.0	24 15.8	5 11.8	14 52.1	13 54.9	21 03.8	22 59.1	8 56.0	4 17.0	4 49.7
6 Sa	15 01 56	13 50 41	9♒44 48	15 38 38	6 15.0	25 25.0	6 26.3	15 36.3	14 21.4	21 13.9	22 54.8	8 53.8	4 15.7	4 50.2
7 Su	15 05 53	14 50 52	21 32 35	27 27 22	6 14.5	26 38.7	7 40.7	16 20.6	14 47.9	21 24.0	22 50.6	8 51.6	4 14.6	4 50.8
8 M	15 09 49	15 51 04	3♓23 40	9♓22 08	6 12.3	27 56.2	8 55.2	17 04.9	15 14.3	21 33.9	22 46.4	8 49.3	4 13.4	4 51.4
9 Tu	15 13 46	16 51 18	15 23 23	21 27 59	6 07.8	29 17.0	10 09.7	17 49.3	15 40.7	21 43.8	22 42.2	8 47.0	4 12.3	4 52.0
10 W	15 17 42	17 51 34	27 36 27	3♈49 11	6 00.6	0♏40.6	11 24.1	18 33.7	16 07.0	21 53.5	22 38.1	8 44.7	4 11.2	4 52.6
11 Th	15 21 39	18 51 50	10♈06 32	16 28 46	5 50.9	2 06.4	12 38.6	19 18.2	16 33.2	22 03.2	22 34.1	8 42.4	4 10.1	4 53.3
12 F	15 25 35	19 52 09	22 56 02	29 28 20	5 39.2	3 34.2	13 53.0	20 02.7	16 59.4	22 12.7	22 30.1	8 40.1	4 09.0	4 54.0
13 Sa	15 29 32	20 52 29	6♉05 38	12♉47 42	5 26.6	5 03.5	15 07.4	20 47.4	17 25.6	22 22.1	22 26.2	8 37.7	4 08.0	4 54.7
14 Su	15 33 28	21 52 51	19 34 17	26 24 59	5 14.4	6 34.1	16 21.9	21 32.0	17 51.7	22 31.5	22 22.3	8 35.3	4 07.0	4 55.5
15 M	15 37 25	22 53 14	3♊19 21	10♊16 51	5 03.7	8 05.8	17 36.3	22 16.8	18 17.7	22 40.7	22 18.6	8 32.9	4 06.0	4 56.3
16 Tu	15 41 22	23 53 39	17 16 59	24 19 09	4 55.5	9 38.3	18 50.7	23 01.6	18 43.7	22 49.8	22 14.9	8 30.5	4 05.1	4 57.1
17 W	15 45 18	24 54 06	1♋22 51	8♋27 35	4 50.3	11 11.5	20 05.1	23 46.4	19 09.7	22 58.8	22 11.2	8 28.1	4 04.2	4 57.9
18 Th	15 49 15	25 54 35	15 32 53	22 38 23	4D 47.7	12 45.2	21 19.5	24 31.4	19 35.5	23 07.7	22 07.7	8 25.6	4 03.3	4 58.8
19 F	15 53 11	26 55 06	29 43 45	6♌48 45	4 47.2	14 19.3	22 33.9	25 16.3	20 01.3	23 16.5	22 04.2	8 23.2	4 02.4	4 59.7
20 Sa	15 57 08	27 55 38	13♌53 10	20 56 52	4R 47.6	15 53.7	23 48.2	26 01.4	20 27.1	23 25.2	22 00.8	8 20.7	4 01.6	5 00.6
21 Su	16 01 04	28 56 12	27 59 43	5♍01 39	4 47.6	17 28.3	25 02.6	26 46.5	20 52.8	23 33.7	21 57.5	8 18.2	4 00.8	5 01.5
22 M	16 05 01	29 56 48	12♍02 33	19 02 20	4 46.0	19 03.0	26 17.0	27 31.6	21 18.4	23 42.2	21 54.2	8 15.7	4 00.0	5 02.5
23 Tu	16 08 58	0♐57 25	26 00 53	2♎58 01	4 42.0	20 37.8	27 31.3	28 16.9	21 44.0	23 50.5	21 51.0	8 13.2	3 59.3	5 03.5
24 W	16 12 54	1 58 05	9♎53 35	16 47 19	4 35.4	22 12.6	28 45.7	29 02.1	22 09.5	23 58.6	21 48.0	8 10.7	3 58.6	5 04.5
25 Th	16 16 51	2 58 46	23 38 59	0♏28 16	4 26.4	23 47.4	0♑00.0	29 47.5	22 34.9	24 06.7	21 45.0	8 08.2	3 57.9	5 05.5
26 F	16 20 47	3 59 28	7♏14 52	13 58 29	4 15.9	25 22.2	1 14.4	0♑32.9	23 00.2	24 14.6	21 42.1	8 05.7	3 57.2	5 06.6
27 Sa	16 24 44	5 00 12	20 38 47	27 15 31	4 04.9	26 57.0	2 28.7	1 18.3	23 25.5	24 22.4	21 39.2	8 03.2	3 56.6	5 07.7
28 Su	16 28 40	6 00 58	3♐48 25	10♐17 20	3 54.6	28 31.7	3 43.0	2 03.8	23 50.7	24 30.1	21 36.5	8 00.6	3 56.0	5 08.8
29 M	16 32 37	7 01 44	16 42 08	23 02 47	3 45.9	0♐06.3	4 57.3	2 49.4	24 15.9	24 37.6	21 33.9	7 58.1	3 55.5	5 09.9
30 Tu	16 36 33	8 02 32	29 19 18	5♑31 50	3 39.5	1 40.9	6 11.6	3 35.0	24 40.9	24 45.0	21 31.3	7 55.6	3 55.0	5 11.1

December 2027 — LONGITUDE

Day	Sid.Time	☉	0 hr ☽	Noon ☽	True ☊	☿	♀	♂	⚳	♃	♄	♅	♆	♇
1 W	16 40 30	9♐03 21	11♑40 34	17♑45 46	3♒35.7	3♐15.4	7♑25.9	4♑20.6	25♎05.9	24♍52.2	21♈28.9	7♊53.1	3♈54.5	5♒12.3
2 Th	16 44 27	10 04 11	23 47 48	29 47 05	3D 34.2	4 49.8	8 40.2	5 06.4	25 30.8	24 59.4	21R 26.6	7R 50.5	3R 54.0	5 13.5
3 F	16 48 23	11 05 02	5♒44 06	11♒39 22	3 34.4	6 24.2	9 54.4	5 52.1	25 55.6	25 06.3	21 24.3	7 48.0	3 53.6	5 14.7
4 Sa	16 52 20	12 05 54	17 33 29	23 27 03	3 35.6	7 58.5	11 08.7	6 37.9	26 20.3	25 13.2	21 22.2	7 45.5	3 53.2	5 16.0
5 Su	16 56 16	13 06 46	29 20 43	5♓15 09	3R 36.7	9 32.7	12 22.9	7 23.8	26 44.9	25 19.8	21 20.1	7 42.9	3 52.8	5 17.3
6 M	17 00 13	14 07 40	11♓11 01	17 09 01	3 37.0	11 07.0	13 37.1	8 09.7	27 09.5	25 26.4	21 18.2	7 40.4	3 52.5	5 18.6
7 Tu	17 04 09	15 08 34	23 09 48	29 14 01	3 35.7	12 41.2	14 51.2	8 55.6	27 33.9	25 32.7	21 16.3	7 37.9	3 52.2	5 19.9
8 W	17 08 06	16 09 29	5♈22 16	11♈35 08	3 32.4	14 15.4	16 05.4	9 41.6	27 58.3	25 39.0	21 14.6	7 35.4	3 52.0	5 21.2
9 Th	17 12 02	17 10 24	17 53 07	24 16 37	3 27.2	15 49.6	17 19.5	10 27.7	28 22.6	25 45.1	21 12.9	7 32.9	3 51.8	5 22.6
10 F	17 15 59	18 11 21	0♉45 58	7♉21 23	3 20.4	17 23.8	18 33.6	11 13.8	28 46.8	25 51.0	21 11.4	7 30.5	3 51.6	5 24.0
11 Sa	17 19 56	19 12 18	14 02 55	20 50 33	3 12.8	18 58.0	19 47.7	11 59.9	29 10.8	25 56.8	21 10.0	7 28.0	3 51.4	5 25.4
12 Su	17 23 52	20 13 16	27 44 04	4♊43 08	3 05.2	20 32.3	21 01.8	12 46.1	29 34.8	26 02.4	21 08.7	7 25.5	3 51.3	5 26.8
13 M	17 27 49	21 14 14	11♊47 15	18 55 50	2 58.6	22 06.7	22 15.8	13 32.3	29 58.7	26 07.9	21 07.5	7 23.1	3 51.2	5 28.2
14 Tu	17 31 45	22 15 14	26 08 10	3♋23 29	2 53.6	23 41.2	23 29.8	14 18.6	0♏22.5	26 13.2	21 06.3	7 20.7	3D 51.2	5 29.7
15 W	17 35 42	23 16 14	10♋40 56	17 59 41	2 50.8	25 15.7	24 43.8	15 04.9	0 46.2	26 18.3	21 05.3	7 18.3	3 51.2	5 31.2
16 Th	17 39 38	24 17 16	25 18 55	2♌37 50	2D 49.9	26 50.4	25 57.8	15 51.2	1 09.8	26 23.3	21 04.5	7 15.9	3 51.2	5 32.7
17 F	17 43 35	25 18 18	9♌55 45	17 12 01	2 50.5	28 25.2	27 11.7	16 37.6	1 33.3	26 28.1	21 03.7	7 13.5	3 51.2	5 34.2
18 Sa	17 47 31	26 19 20	24 26 08	1♍37 39	2 51.9	0♑00.1	28 25.6	17 24.0	1 56.7	26 32.8	21 03.0	7 11.1	3 51.3	5 35.7
19 Su	17 51 28	27 20 24	8♍46 14	15 51 39	2R 53.3	1 35.2	29 39.5	18 10.5	2 19.9	26 37.2	21 02.4	7 08.8	3 51.4	5 37.2
20 M	17 55 25	28 21 29	22 53 44	29 52 23	2 53.8	3 10.5	0♒53.3	18 57.0	2 43.1	26 41.6	21 02.0	7 06.5	3 51.6	5 38.8
21 Tu	17 59 21	29 22 34	6♎47 33	13♎39 13	2 52.9	4 45.9	2 07.2	19 43.6	3 06.1	26 45.7	21 01.6	7 04.2	3 51.8	5 40.4
22 W	18 03 18	0♑23 41	20 27 24	27 12 09	2 50.3	6 21.5	3 21.0	20 30.2	3 29.1	26 49.7	21 01.4	7 01.9	3 52.0	5 42.0
23 Th	18 07 14	1 24 48	3♏53 28	10♏31 25	2 46.4	7 57.2	4 34.7	21 16.8	3 51.9	26 53.5	21D 01.3	6 59.6	3 52.3	5 43.6
24 F	18 11 11	2 25 56	17 06 02	23 37 21	2 41.5	9 33.2	5 48.5	22 03.5	4 14.5	26 57.1	21 01.2	6 57.4	3 52.6	5 45.2
25 Sa	18 15 07	3 27 04	0♐05 22	6♐30 09	2 36.2	11 09.3	7 02.2	22 50.2	4 37.1	27 00.5	21 01.3	6 55.2	3 52.9	5 46.9
26 Su	18 19 04	4 28 13	12 51 42	19 10 05	2 31.3	12 45.5	8 15.9	23 37.0	4 59.5	27 03.8	21 01.6	6 53.1	3 53.3	5 48.5
27 M	18 23 01	5 29 23	25 25 20	1♑37 32	2 27.2	14 21.9	9 29.5	24 23.7	5 21.9	27 06.8	21 01.9	6 50.9	3 53.7	5 50.2
28 Tu	18 26 57	6 30 33	7♑46 48	13 53 14	2 24.5	15 58.5	10 43.1	25 10.6	5 44.0	27 09.7	21 02.3	6 48.8	3 54.1	5 51.9
29 W	18 30 54	7 31 43	19 57 02	25 58 23	2D 23.1	17 35.1	11 56.7	25 57.4	6 06.1	27 12.5	21 02.9	6 46.7	3 54.6	5 53.6
30 Th	18 34 50	8 32 53	1♒57 31	7♒54 46	2 23.0	19 11.7	13 10.2	26 44.3	6 28.0	27 15.0	21 03.5	6 44.7	3 55.1	5 55.3
31 F	18 38 47	9 34 03	13 50 25	19 44 53	2 24.0	20 48.4	14 23.7	27 31.2	6 49.7	27 17.3	21 04.3	6 42.6	3 55.6	5 57.1

Astro Data

	Dy Hr Mn
☽ 0N	9 12:22
♃⊼♄	13 19:20
⚳ 0S	16 13:41
☽ 0S	22 16:07
☽ 0N	6 20:02
♆ D	15 9:07
☽ 0S	19 20:45
♄ D	24 2:46

Planet Ingress

		Dy Hr Mn
♀	♐	1 7:34
☿	♏	10 0:26
☉	♐	22 13:16
♀	♑	25 11:59
♂	♑	25 18:38
☿	♐	29 10:23
⚳	♏	13 13:17
☿	♑	18 11:58
♀	♒	19 18:40
☉	♑	22 2:42

Last Aspect / ☽ Ingress (November)

Last Aspect Dy Hr Mn			☽ Ingress	Dy Hr Mn
2 3:40	♄	△	♑	2 16:41
4 14:44	☿	□	♒	5 4:13
7 10:10	☿	△	♓	7 17:09
9 12:31	♃	☍	♈	10 4:38
11 23:16	♄	☌	♉	12 12:58
14 5:07	♃	△	♊	14 18:14
16 9:41	♂	☍	♋	16 21:39
18 17:57	☉	△	♌	19 0:28
21 0:48	☉	□	♍	21 3:25
23 3:27	♂	□	♎	23 6:52
25 11:05	♀	⚹	♏	25 11:10
27 11:22	☿	☌	♐	27 17:01
29 15:02	♃	□	♑	30 1:18

Last Aspect / ☽ Ingress (December)

Last Aspect Dy Hr Mn			☽ Ingress	Dy Hr Mn
2 2:17	♃	△	♒	2 12:26
4 7:46	♄	⚹	♓	5 1:20
7 4:40	♃	☍	♈	7 13:30
9 6:17	♄	☌	♉	9 22:36
11 20:58	♃	△	♊	12 3:55
14 0:04	♃	□	♋	14 6:24
16 1:42	♃	⚹	♌	16 7:41
18 8:57	☿	△	♍	18 9:17
20 9:11	☉	□	♎	20 12:13
22 1:00	♄	☍	♏	22 17:00
24 18:12	♃	⚹	♐	24 23:50
27 3:14	♃	□	♑	27 8:51
29 14:29	♃	△	♒	29 20:04

☽ Phases & Eclipses

Dy Hr Mn		
6 8:00	☽	13♒41
14 3:26	○	21♉31
21 0:48	☾	28♌28
28 3:24	●	5♐39
6 5:22	☽	13♓51
13 16:09	○	21♊25
20 9:11	☾	28♍14
27 20:12	●	5♑50

Astro Data

1 November 2027
Julian Day # 46691
SVP 4♓52'03"
GC 27♐13.7 ⚴ 10♍53.8
Eris 25♈30.4R ⚵ 28♋22.8
⚷ 2♉00.7R ⚶ 12♌20.1
☽ Mean ☊ 6♒43.1

1 December 2027
Julian Day # 46721
SVP 4♓51'58"
GC 27♐13.8 ⚴ 23♍16.0
Eris 25♈14.9R ⚵ 3♌13.2
⚷ 0♉44.9R ⚶ 17♌49.2
☽ Mean ☊ 5♒07.8

LONGITUDE — January 2028

Day	Sid.Time	☉	0 hr ☽	Noon ☽	True ☊	☿	♀	♂	⚳	♃	♄	♅	♆	♇
1 Sa	18 42 43	10♑35 13	25♒38 35	1♓31 57	2♒25.6	22♑25.0	15♒37.1	28♑18.1	7♏11.4	27♍19.5	21♈05.2	6♊40.7	3♈56.2	5♒58.8
2 Su	18 46 40	11 36 23	7♓25 30	13 19 46	2 27.4	24 01.4	16 50.5	29 05.1	7 32.8	27 21.5	21 06.2	6R 38.7	3 56.8	6 00.5
3 M	18 50 36	12 37 32	19 15 18	25 12 42	2 28.9	25 37.7	18 03.8	29 52.1	7 54.2	27 23.2	21 07.3	6 36.8	3 57.5	6 02.3
4 Tu	18 54 33	13 38 42	1♈12 33	7♈15 29	2R 29.8	27 13.6	19 17.1	0♒39.1	8 15.3	27 24.8	21 08.5	6 34.9	3 58.2	6 04.1
5 W	18 58 30	14 39 51	13 22 07	19 33 01	2 29.9	28 49.0	20 30.4	1 26.2	8 36.4	27 26.2	21 09.8	6 33.0	3 58.9	6 05.8
6 Th	19 02 26	15 41 00	25 48 46	2♉09 54	2 29.1	0♒23.8	21 43.6	2 13.3	8 57.2	27 27.4	21 11.2	6 31.2	3 59.6	6 07.6
7 F	19 06 23	16 42 09	8♉36 55	15 10 11	2 27.6	1 57.8	22 56.7	3 00.4	9 18.0	27 28.5	21 12.8	6 29.5	4 00.4	6 09.4
8 Sa	19 10 19	17 43 17	21 50 00	28 36 35	2 25.7	3 30.8	24 09.7	3 47.5	9 38.5	27 29.3	21 14.4	6 27.7	4 01.2	6 11.3
9 Su	19 14 16	18 44 25	5♊29 57	12♊30 02	2 23.7	5 02.4	25 22.8	4 34.6	9 58.9	27 29.9	21 16.2	6 26.0	4 02.0	6 13.1
10 M	19 18 12	19 45 32	19 36 34	26 49 07	2 22.0	6 32.5	26 35.7	5 21.8	10 19.2	27 30.4	21 18.0	6 24.4	4 02.9	6 14.9
11 Tu	19 22 09	20 46 40	4♋07 06	11♋29 45	2 20.9	8 00.7	27 48.6	6 09.0	10 39.3	27R 30.7	21 20.0	6 22.8	4 03.8	6 16.7
12 W	19 26 05	21 47 46	18 56 12	26 25 25	2D 20.3	9 26.4	29 01.4	6 56.2	10 59.2	27 30.7	21 22.1	6 21.2	4 04.8	6 18.6
13 Th	19 30 02	22 48 53	3♌56 23	11♌27 57	2 20.4	10 49.4	0♓14.1	7 43.4	11 18.9	27 30.6	21 24.3	6 19.7	4 05.8	6 20.4
14 F	19 33 59	23 49 59	18 59 02	26 28 36	2 20.9	12 09.0	1 26.8	8 30.7	11 38.5	27 30.3	21 26.5	6 18.2	4 06.8	6 22.3
15 Sa	19 37 55	24 51 05	3♍55 39	11♍19 20	2 21.5	13 24.7	2 39.4	9 17.9	11 57.8	27 29.8	21 28.9	6 16.7	4 07.8	6 24.1
16 Su	19 41 52	25 52 11	18 38 56	25 53 51	2 22.2	14 35.7	3 52.0	10 05.2	12 17.1	27 29.1	21 31.4	6 15.3	4 08.9	6 26.0
17 M	19 45 48	26 53 16	3♎03 39	10♎08 04	2 22.7	15 41.4	5 04.4	10 52.5	12 36.1	27 28.2	21 34.0	6 14.0	4 10.0	6 27.9
18 Tu	19 49 45	27 54 22	17 06 55	24 00 09	2R 22.9	16 40.9	6 16.8	11 39.8	12 54.9	27 27.1	21 36.7	6 12.7	4 11.1	6 29.7
19 W	19 53 41	28 55 27	0♏47 52	7♏30 11	2 22.8	17 33.5	7 29.1	12 27.2	13 13.6	27 25.8	21 39.5	6 11.4	4 12.3	6 31.6
20 Th	19 57 38	29 56 32	14 07 19	20 39 32	2 22.7	18 18.2	8 41.4	13 14.5	13 32.0	27 24.4	21 42.4	6 10.2	4 13.5	6 33.5
21 F	20 01 34	0♒57 37	27 07 09	3♐30 28	2 22.5	18 54.2	9 53.5	14 01.9	13 50.3	27 22.7	21 45.4	6 09.0	4 14.7	6 35.4
22 Sa	20 05 31	1 58 41	9♐49 48	16 05 29	2D 22.4	19 20.6	11 05.6	14 49.3	14 08.3	27 20.8	21 48.5	6 07.9	4 15.9	6 37.3
23 Su	20 09 28	2 59 45	22 17 52	28 27 13	2 22.4	19R 36.7	12 17.6	15 36.7	14 26.2	27 18.8	21 51.7	6 06.8	4 17.2	6 39.2
24 M	20 13 24	4 00 48	4♑33 51	10♑38 04	2 22.5	19 41.9	13 29.6	16 24.1	14 43.8	27 16.6	21 55.0	6 05.8	4 18.5	6 41.1
25 Tu	20 17 21	5 01 51	16 40 07	22 40 15	2R 22.7	19 35.7	14 41.4	17 11.5	15 01.2	27 14.1	21 58.4	6 04.8	4 19.9	6 43.0
26 W	20 21 17	6 02 52	28 38 44	4♒35 49	2 22.7	19 18.0	15 53.1	17 59.0	15 18.4	27 11.5	22 01.9	6 03.9	4 21.2	6 44.9
27 Th	20 25 14	7 03 53	10♒31 44	16 26 43	2 22.5	18 48.9	17 04.8	18 46.4	15 35.4	27 08.7	22 05.5	6 03.0	4 22.6	6 46.8
28 F	20 29 10	8 04 53	22 21 03	28 15 00	2 22.1	18 09.0	18 16.3	19 33.9	15 52.2	27 05.8	22 09.2	6 02.2	4 24.1	6 48.7
29 Sa	20 33 07	9 05 52	4♓08 50	10♓02 52	2 21.3	17 19.2	19 27.8	20 21.3	16 08.7	27 02.6	22 13.0	6 01.4	4 25.5	6 50.5
30 Su	20 37 03	10 06 50	15 57 26	21 52 53	2 20.2	16 20.7	20 39.1	21 08.8	16 25.0	26 59.2	22 16.9	6 00.6	4 27.0	6 52.4
31 M	20 41 00	11 07 47	27 49 37	3♈48 02	2 18.9	15 15.3	21 50.4	21 56.3	16 41.1	26 55.7	22 20.8	6 00.0	4 28.5	6 54.3

LONGITUDE — February 2028

Day	Sid.Time	☉	0 hr ☽	Noon ☽	True ☊	☿	♀	♂	⚳	♃	♄	♅	♆	♇
1 Tu	20 44 57	12♒08 43	9♈48 34	15♈51 42	2♒17.8	14♒04.9	23♓01.5	22♒43.8	16♏57.0	26♍52.0	22♈24.9	5♊59.3	4♈30.0	6♒56.2
2 W	20 48 53	13 09 37	21 57 55	28 07 42	2R 16.8	12R 51.6	24 12.5	23 31.2	17 12.5	26R 48.1	22 29.0	5R 58.7	4 31.6	6 58.1
3 Th	20 52 50	14 10 30	4♉21 35	10♉40 03	2D 16.4	11 37.5	25 23.4	24 18.7	17 27.9	26 44.1	22 33.3	5 58.2	4 33.2	7 00.0
4 F	20 56 46	15 11 22	17 03 37	23 32 45	2 16.5	10 24.7	26 34.2	25 06.2	17 43.0	26 39.9	22 37.6	5 57.8	4 34.8	7 01.9
5 Sa	21 00 43	16 12 12	0♊07 52	6♊49 21	2 17.2	9 15.2	27 44.9	25 53.7	17 57.9	26 35.5	22 42.0	5 57.3	4 36.4	7 03.7
6 Su	21 04 39	17 13 01	13 37 27	20 32 22	2 18.3	8 10.5	28 55.4	26 41.2	18 12.4	26 30.9	22 46.5	5 57.0	4 38.1	7 05.6
7 M	21 08 36	18 13 49	27 34 07	4♋42 37	2 19.6	7 12.0	0♈05.8	27 28.6	18 26.8	26 26.2	22 51.1	5 56.7	4 39.8	7 07.5
8 Tu	21 12 32	19 14 35	11♋57 35	19 18 33	2R 20.5	6 20.5	1 16.1	28 16.1	18 40.9	26 21.4	22 55.7	5 56.4	4 41.5	7 09.4
9 W	21 16 29	20 15 20	26 44 54	4♌15 46	2 20.8	5 36.8	2 26.2	29 03.6	18 54.7	26 16.3	23 00.5	5 56.2	4 43.2	7 11.2
10 Th	21 20 26	21 16 03	11♌50 12	19 27 02	2 20.2	5 01.1	3 36.2	29 51.0	19 08.2	26 11.2	23 05.3	5 56.0	4 45.0	7 13.1
11 F	21 24 22	22 16 45	27 05 02	4♍42 55	2 18.6	4 33.7	4 46.0	0♓38.5	19 21.5	26 05.8	23 10.2	5 55.9	4 46.7	7 14.9
12 Sa	21 28 19	23 17 25	12♍19 22	19 53 10	2 16.1	4 14.4	5 55.7	1 26.0	19 34.5	26 00.4	23 15.2	5D 55.9	4 48.5	7 16.7
13 Su	21 32 15	24 18 05	27 23 10	4♎48 20	2 13.0	4 03.0	7 05.2	2 13.4	19 47.2	25 54.7	23 20.2	5 55.9	4 50.3	7 18.6
14 M	21 36 12	25 18 43	12♎07 53	19 21 08	2 10.0	3D 59.1	8 14.6	3 00.9	19 59.6	25 49.0	23 25.3	5 55.9	4 52.2	7 20.4
15 Tu	21 40 08	26 19 20	26 27 40	3♏27 13	2 07.5	4 02.5	9 23.8	3 48.3	20 11.7	25 43.1	23 30.5	5 56.0	4 54.0	7 22.2
16 W	21 44 05	27 19 56	10♏19 45	17 05 19	2D 05.9	4 12.5	10 32.9	4 35.7	20 23.5	25 37.1	23 35.8	5 56.2	4 55.9	7 24.0
17 Th	21 48 01	28 20 31	23 44 09	0♐16 35	2 05.5	4 28.9	11 41.8	5 23.2	20 35.1	25 30.9	23 41.2	5 56.4	4 57.8	7 25.8
18 F	21 51 58	29 21 04	6♐43 03	13 04 01	2 06.2	4 51.1	12 50.5	6 10.6	20 46.3	25 24.6	23 46.6	5 56.7	4 59.7	7 27.6
19 Sa	21 55 55	0♓21 37	19 19 59	25 31 31	2 07.8	5 18.8	13 59.1	6 58.0	20 57.2	25 18.2	23 52.1	5 57.0	5 01.6	7 29.4
20 Su	21 59 51	1 22 08	1♑39 09	7♑43 25	2 09.6	5 51.5	15 07.4	7 45.4	21 07.8	25 11.7	23 57.7	5 57.4	5 03.6	7 31.2
21 M	22 03 48	2 22 38	13 44 50	19 43 55	2 11.1	6 28.7	16 15.7	8 32.8	21 18.1	25 05.1	24 03.3	5 57.8	5 05.6	7 32.9
22 Tu	22 07 44	3 23 06	25 41 08	1♒36 55	2R 11.8	7 10.3	17 23.7	9 20.2	21 28.0	24 58.3	24 09.0	5 58.3	5 07.6	7 34.7
23 W	22 11 41	4 23 33	7♒31 40	13 25 44	2 11.1	7 55.8	18 31.5	10 07.6	21 37.7	24 51.5	24 14.8	5 58.8	5 09.6	7 36.4
24 Th	22 15 37	5 23 58	19 19 29	25 13 13	2 08.8	8 44.9	19 39.2	10 54.9	21 46.9	24 44.5	24 20.7	5 59.4	5 11.6	7 38.1
25 F	22 19 34	6 24 22	1♓07 10	7♓01 38	2 04.7	9 37.4	20 46.6	11 42.3	21 55.9	24 37.5	24 26.6	6 00.1	5 13.6	7 39.8
26 Sa	22 23 30	7 24 44	12 56 50	18 52 59	1 59.0	10 33.0	21 53.8	12 29.6	22 04.5	24 30.3	24 32.5	6 00.8	5 15.7	7 41.5
27 Su	22 27 27	8 25 04	24 50 17	0♈48 58	1 52.2	11 31.5	23 00.8	13 16.9	22 12.8	24 23.1	24 38.6	6 01.5	5 17.7	7 43.2
28 M	22 31 24	9 25 22	6♈49 15	12 51 21	1 45.0	12 32.6	24 07.7	14 04.2	22 20.7	24 15.8	24 44.7	6 02.3	5 19.8	7 44.9
29 Tu	22 35 20	10 25 38	18 55 32	25 02 02	1 38.0	13 36.3	25 14.2	14 51.5	22 28.2	24 08.5	24 50.8	6 03.1	5 21.9	7 46.5

Astro Data

	Dy Hr Mn
☽ 0N	3 3:12
♄∠♅	12 6:18
♃ R	12 8:53
♅△♇	13 6:39
☽ 0S	16 3:32
☿ R	24 11:02
☽ 0N	30 9:49
♀0N	8 5:18
☽ 0S	12 13:32
♅ D	12 23:49
☿ D	14 12:38
♃⚻♄	26 7:59
☽ 0N	26 16:07

Planet Ingress

		Dy Hr Mn
♂	♒	3 16:01
☿	♒	6 5:58
♀	♓	13 7:20
☉	♒	20 13:22
♀	♈	7 10:01
♂	♓	10 16:32
☉	♓	19 3:26

Last Aspect / ☽ Ingress (January)

Last Aspect Dy Hr Mn		☽ Ingress	Dy Hr Mn
31 14:42	♄ ✶	♓	1 8:53
3 16:22	♃ ☍	♈	3 21:35
5 15:07	♄ ☌	♉	6 7:56
8 10:01	♃ △	♊	8 14:26
10 13:08	♃ □	♋	10 17:15
12 13:44	♃ ✶	♌	12 17:43
14 3:55	♄ △	♍	14 17:40
16 14:39	♃ ☌	♎	16 18:51
18 19:26	☉ □	♏	18 22:35
21 0:31	♃ ✶	♐	21 5:24
23 9:47	♃ □	♑	23 15:02
25 21:08	♃ △	♒	26 2:44
27 23:32	♄ ✶	♓	28 15:34
30 22:16	♃ ☍	♈	31 4:22

Last Aspect / ☽ Ingress (February)

Last Aspect Dy Hr Mn		☽ Ingress	Dy Hr Mn
2 2:25	♂ ✶	♉	2 15:37
4 18:05	♀ ✶	♊	4 23:46
7 3:35	♀ □	♋	7 4:06
8 23:18	♃ ✶	♌	9 5:12
10 17:45	♄ △	♍	11 4:35
12 21:43	♃ ☌	♎	13 4:13
14 22:49	☉ △	♏	15 6:03
17 8:08	☉ □	♐	17 11:29
19 11:34	♃ □	♑	19 20:45
21 22:41	♃ △	♒	22 8:44
24 10:12	♄ ✶	♓	24 21:43
26 23:13	♃ ☍	♈	27 10:22
29 12:26	♀ ☌	♉	29 21:42

☽ Phases & Eclipses

Dy Hr Mn	
5 1:40	☽ 14♈14
12 4:03	○ 21♋28
12 4:13	☍ P 0.066
18 19:26	☾ 28♎13
26 15:12	● 6♒11
26 15:07:43	● A 10'27"
3 19:10	☽ 14♉29
10 15:04	○ 21♌24
17 8:08	☾ 28♏11
25 10:37	● 6♓21

Astro Data

1 January 2028
Julian Day # 46752
SVP 4♓51'52"
GC 27♐13.8 ⚵ 1♎57.8
Eris 25♈06.0R ⚴ 29♋57.9R
⚷ 0♉03.4R ⚶ 17♌30.7R
☽ Mean ☊ 3♒29.3

1 February 2028
Julian Day # 46783
SVP 4♓51'47"
GC 27♐13.9 ⚵ 4♎02.5R
Eris 25♈07.4 ⚴ 22♋35.0R
⚷ 0♉15.3 ⚶ 10♌49.4R
☽ Mean ☊ 1♒50.9

March 2028 LONGITUDE

Day	Sid.Time	☉	0 hr ☽	Noon ☽	True ☊	☿	♀	♂	⚳	♃	♄	♅	♆	♇
1 W	22 39 17	11♓25 53	1♉11 10	7♉23 15	1♒32.1	14♒42.3	26♈20.6	15♓38.7	22♏35.5	24♍01.0	24♈57.0	6♊04.0	5♈24.0	7♒48.2
2 Th	22 43 13	12 26 05	13 38 36	19 57 35	1R 27.9	15 50.5	27 26.7	16 26.0	22 42.3	23R 53.5	25 03.3	6 05.0	5 26.1	7 49.8
3 F	22 47 10	13 26 16	26 20 35	2♊48 00	1D 25.5	17 00.8	28 32.5	17 13.2	22 48.8	23 46.0	25 09.6	6 06.0	5 28.3	7 51.4
4 Sa	22 51 06	14 26 25	9♊20 12	15 57 34	1 24.9	18 13.0	29 38.2	18 00.4	22 54.9	23 38.4	25 16.0	6 07.1	5 30.4	7 53.0
5 Su	22 55 03	15 26 31	22 40 27	29 29 08	1 25.6	19 27.1	0♉43.5	18 47.6	23 00.6	23 30.8	25 22.4	6 08.2	5 32.6	7 54.6
6 M	22 58 59	16 26 35	6♋23 52	13♋24 45	1 26.9	20 43.0	1 48.6	19 34.7	23 06.0	23 23.1	25 28.9	6 09.3	5 34.7	7 56.1
7 Tu	23 02 56	17 26 37	20 31 50	27 44 56	1R 27.8	22 00.5	2 53.4	20 21.8	23 11.0	23 15.4	25 35.5	6 10.5	5 36.9	7 57.7
8 W	23 06 53	18 26 37	5♌03 48	12♌27 54	1 27.4	23 19.6	3 57.9	21 08.9	23 15.6	23 07.6	25 42.0	6 11.8	5 39.1	7 59.2
9 Th	23 10 49	19 26 35	19 56 35	27 28 59	1 24.9	24 40.3	5 02.1	21 56.0	23 19.8	22 59.8	25 48.7	6 13.1	5 41.3	8 00.7
10 F	23 14 46	20 26 31	5♍04 04	12♍40 37	1 20.3	26 02.5	6 06.0	22 43.0	23 23.7	22 52.1	25 55.4	6 14.5	5 43.5	8 02.2
11 Sa	23 18 42	21 26 24	20 17 23	27 53 02	1 13.6	27 26.2	7 09.5	23 30.0	23 27.1	22 44.3	26 02.1	6 15.9	5 45.7	8 03.7
12 Su	23 22 39	22 26 16	5♎26 14	12♎55 44	1 05.6	28 51.2	8 12.8	24 17.0	23 30.2	22 36.4	26 08.8	6 17.3	5 47.9	8 05.2
13 M	23 26 35	23 26 06	20 20 26	27 39 22	0 57.4	0♓17.7	9 15.7	25 04.0	23 32.9	22 28.6	26 15.7	6 18.8	5 50.1	8 06.6
14 Tu	23 30 32	24 25 54	4♏51 46	11♏57 06	0 49.9	1 45.5	10 18.3	25 50.9	23 35.1	22 20.8	26 22.5	6 20.4	5 52.4	8 08.0
15 W	23 34 28	25 25 41	18 55 03	25 45 30	0 44.1	3 14.6	11 20.6	26 37.8	23 37.0	22 13.0	26 29.4	6 21.9	5 54.6	8 09.4
16 Th	23 38 25	26 25 26	2♐28 31	9♐04 21	0 40.4	4 45.1	12 22.5	27 24.7	23 38.5	22 05.3	26 36.4	6 23.6	5 56.9	8 10.8
17 F	23 42 22	27 25 09	15 33 20	21 55 59	0D 38.8	6 16.9	13 24.0	28 11.6	23 39.5	21 57.5	26 43.3	6 25.3	5 59.1	8 12.2
18 Sa	23 46 18	28 24 51	28 12 49	4♑24 29	0 38.8	7 49.9	14 25.2	28 58.4	23 40.2	21 49.8	26 50.4	6 27.0	6 01.4	8 13.5
19 Su	23 50 15	29 24 30	10♑31 36	16 34 51	0 39.6	9 24.3	15 25.9	29 45.2	23R 40.4	21 42.1	26 57.4	6 28.8	6 03.6	8 14.8
20 M	23 54 11	0♈24 08	22 34 53	28 32 22	0R 40.3	10 59.9	16 26.3	0♈32.0	23 40.2	21 34.4	27 04.5	6 30.6	6 05.9	8 16.1
21 Tu	23 58 08	1 23 45	4♒27 54	10♒22 06	0 39.7	12 36.8	17 26.3	1 18.7	23 39.7	21 26.8	27 11.7	6 32.5	6 08.2	8 17.4
22 W	0 02 04	2 23 19	16 15 30	22 08 39	0 37.2	14 15.0	18 25.8	2 05.4	23 38.6	21 19.2	27 18.8	6 34.4	6 10.4	8 18.7
23 Th	0 06 01	3 22 51	28 01 59	3♓55 56	0 32.2	15 54.5	19 24.9	2 52.1	23 37.2	21 11.7	27 26.0	6 36.4	6 12.7	8 19.9
24 F	0 09 57	4 22 22	9♓50 52	15 47 06	0 24.4	17 35.3	20 23.6	3 38.7	23 35.4	21 04.2	27 33.2	6 38.4	6 15.0	8 21.1
25 Sa	0 13 54	5 21 51	21 44 53	27 44 28	0 14.3	19 17.4	21 21.7	4 25.3	23 33.1	20 56.8	27 40.5	6 40.4	6 17.2	8 22.3
26 Su	0 17 51	6 21 17	3♈46 02	9♈49 42	0 02.4	21 00.8	22 19.4	5 11.9	23 30.5	20 49.5	27 47.8	6 42.5	6 19.5	8 23.5
27 M	0 21 47	7 20 42	15 55 38	22 03 53	29♑49.7	22 45.5	23 16.6	5 58.4	23 27.4	20 42.2	27 55.1	6 44.6	6 21.8	8 24.6
28 Tu	0 25 44	8 20 04	28 14 34	4♉27 46	29 37.3	24 31.6	24 13.3	6 44.9	23 23.9	20 35.0	28 02.5	6 46.8	6 24.1	8 25.7
29 W	0 29 40	9 19 24	10♉43 33	17 02 02	29 26.4	26 19.0	25 09.5	7 31.4	23 20.0	20 27.9	28 09.8	6 49.0	6 26.3	8 26.8
30 Th	0 33 37	10 18 43	23 23 20	29 47 35	29 17.8	28 07.8	26 05.0	8 17.8	23 15.7	20 20.9	28 17.2	6 51.2	6 28.6	8 27.9
31 F	0 37 33	11 17 59	6♊14 58	12♊45 41	29 12.0	29 57.9	27 00.1	9 04.2	23 11.0	20 14.0	28 24.6	6 53.5	6 30.9	8 28.9

April 2028 LONGITUDE

Day	Sid.Time	☉	0 hr ☽	Noon ☽	True ☊	☿	♀	♂	⚳	♃	♄	♅	♆	♇
1 Sa	0 41 30	12♈17 12	19♊19 56	25♊57 58	29♑08.9	1♈49.4	27♉54.5	9♈50.6	23♏05.9	20♍07.2	28♈32.1	6♊55.9	6♈33.1	8♒30.0
2 Su	0 45 26	13 16 24	2♋40 03	9♋26 24	29D 07.9	3 42.3	28 48.3	10 36.9	23R 00.4	20R 00.5	28 39.5	6 58.2	6 35.4	8 31.0
3 M	0 49 23	14 15 33	16 17 15	23 12 46	29R 08.0	5 36.5	29 41.4	11 23.1	22 54.5	19 53.9	28 47.0	7 00.6	6 37.7	8 31.9
4 Tu	0 53 20	15 14 39	0♌13 05	7♌18 13	29 07.8	7 32.2	0♊33.9	12 09.3	22 48.2	19 47.4	28 54.5	7 03.1	6 39.9	8 32.9
5 W	0 57 16	16 13 43	14 28 05	21 42 29	29 06.3	9 29.1	1 25.7	12 55.5	22 41.5	19 41.0	29 02.0	7 05.6	6 42.2	8 33.8
6 Th	1 01 13	17 12 45	29 01 01	6♍23 10	29 02.4	11 27.5	2 16.8	13 41.7	22 34.5	19 34.8	29 09.6	7 08.1	6 44.4	8 34.7
7 F	1 05 09	18 11 45	13♍48 14	21 15 22	28 55.7	13 27.1	3 07.1	14 27.8	22 27.1	19 28.7	29 17.1	7 10.6	6 46.7	8 35.6
8 Sa	1 09 06	19 10 42	28 43 33	6♎11 43	28 46.4	15 27.9	3 56.6	15 13.8	22 19.3	19 22.6	29 24.7	7 13.2	6 48.9	8 36.5
9 Su	1 13 02	20 09 37	13♎38 43	21 03 22	28 35.4	17 30.0	4 45.3	15 59.8	22 11.2	19 16.8	29 32.2	7 15.8	6 51.1	8 37.3
10 M	1 16 59	21 08 31	28 24 35	5♏41 20	28 23.9	19 33.2	5 33.2	16 45.8	22 02.7	19 11.0	29 39.8	7 18.5	6 53.3	8 38.1
11 Tu	1 20 55	22 07 22	12♏52 46	19 58 10	28 13.1	21 37.3	6 20.3	17 31.7	21 53.9	19 05.4	29 47.4	7 21.2	6 55.6	8 38.8
12 W	1 24 52	23 06 12	26 57 00	3♐48 58	28 04.1	23 42.4	7 06.4	18 17.6	21 44.7	19 00.0	29 55.0	7 23.9	6 57.8	8 39.6
13 Th	1 28 48	24 05 00	10♐33 55	17 11 54	27 57.7	25 48.1	7 51.7	19 03.4	21 35.3	18 54.7	0♉02.6	7 26.6	7 00.0	8 40.3
14 F	1 32 45	25 03 46	23 43 08	0♑07 57	27 53.8	27 54.4	8 36.0	19 49.2	21 25.5	18 49.5	0 10.3	7 29.4	7 02.2	8 41.0
15 Sa	1 36 42	26 02 30	6♑26 48	12 40 15	27 52.1	0♉01.1	9 19.2	20 35.0	21 15.4	18 44.5	0 17.9	7 32.2	7 04.3	8 41.7
16 Su	1 40 38	27 01 13	18 48 52	24 53 20	27 51.7	2 07.8	10 01.5	21 20.7	21 04.9	18 39.6	0 25.5	7 35.1	7 06.5	8 42.3
17 M	1 44 35	27 59 54	0♒54 20	6♒52 32	27 51.7	4 14.3	10 42.7	22 06.4	20 54.2	18 34.9	0 33.2	7 38.0	7 08.7	8 42.9
18 Tu	1 48 31	28 58 33	12 48 39	18 43 22	27 50.7	6 20.4	11 22.8	22 52.0	20 43.3	18 30.3	0 40.8	7 40.9	7 10.8	8 43.5
19 W	1 52 28	29 57 11	24 37 19	0♓31 07	27 47.9	8 25.8	12 01.7	23 37.6	20 32.0	18 25.9	0 48.5	7 43.8	7 13.0	8 44.1
20 Th	1 56 24	0♉55 46	6♓25 23	12 20 38	27 42.5	10 30.0	12 39.5	24 23.1	20 20.5	18 21.7	0 56.1	7 46.8	7 15.1	8 44.6
21 F	2 00 21	1 54 20	18 17 21	24 15 58	27 34.3	12 32.9	13 16.0	25 08.6	20 08.8	18 17.6	1 03.8	7 49.7	7 17.2	8 45.1
22 Sa	2 04 17	2 52 53	0♈16 51	6♈20 18	27 23.6	14 34.0	13 51.2	25 54.0	19 56.8	18 13.7	1 11.4	7 52.8	7 19.3	8 45.6
23 Su	2 08 14	3 51 23	12 26 36	18 35 48	27 11.0	16 33.0	14 25.1	26 39.4	19 44.6	18 09.9	1 19.1	7 55.8	7 21.4	8 46.1
24 M	2 12 11	4 49 52	24 48 09	1♉03 39	26 57.5	18 29.7	14 57.6	27 24.8	19 32.3	18 06.4	1 26.7	7 58.9	7 23.5	8 46.5
25 Tu	2 16 07	5 48 19	7♉22 20	13 44 10	26 44.3	20 23.8	15 28.7	28 10.1	19 19.7	18 03.0	1 34.4	8 01.9	7 25.5	8 46.9
26 W	2 20 04	6 46 44	20 09 05	26 37 01	26 32.6	22 15.0	15 58.2	28 55.3	19 07.0	17 59.7	1 42.0	8 05.1	7 27.6	8 47.3
27 Th	2 24 00	7 45 07	3♊07 52	9♊41 33	26 23.3	24 03.0	16 26.3	29 40.5	18 54.1	17 56.7	1 49.6	8 08.2	7 29.6	8 47.6
28 F	2 27 57	8 43 28	16 18 00	22 57 11	26 16.9	25 47.6	16 52.7	0♉25.7	18 41.0	17 53.8	1 57.2	8 11.4	7 31.6	8 47.9
29 Sa	2 31 53	9 41 48	29 39 03	6♋23 37	26 13.3	27 28.7	17 17.4	1 10.8	18 27.9	17 51.1	2 04.9	8 14.5	7 33.6	8 48.2
30 Su	2 35 50	10 40 05	13♋10 54	20 00 57	26D 12.0	29 06.1	17 40.4	1 55.8	18 14.6	17 48.6	2 12.5	8 17.7	7 35.6	8 48.5

Astro Data Dy Hr Mn	Planet Ingress Dy Hr Mn
♃☍♇ 9 9:43	♀ ♉ 4 20:01
☽0S 11 1:01	☿ ♓ 13 7:07
⚳R 19 13:46	♂ ♈ 19 19:36
☉0N 20 2:17	☉ ♈ 20 2:17
♂0N 22 4:39	☊ ♑R 26 16:31
☽0N 24 22:22	☿ ♈ 31 12:28
☿0N 2 20:06	♀ ♊ 3 20:27
☽0S 7 11:18	♄ ♉ 13 3:39
☽0N 21 4:49	☿ ♉ 15 11:48
	☉ ♉ 19 13:09
	♂ ♉ 27 22:21

Last Aspect Dy Hr Mn	☽ Ingress Dy Hr Mn	Last Aspect Dy Hr Mn	☽ Ingress Dy Hr Mn
2 19:20 ♃ △	♊ 3 6:49	1 16:39 ♄ ✶	♋ 1 19:14
5 4:43 ♄ ✶	♋ 5 12:54	3 21:38 ♄ □	♌ 3 23:38
7 8:24 ♄ □	♌ 7 15:43	6 0:08 ♄ △	♍ 6 1:36
9 9:20 ♄ △	♍ 9 15:59	7 9:09 ♃ ☌	♎ 8 2:03
11 4:41 ♂ ☍	♎ 11 15:21	10 1:58 ♄ ☍	♏ 10 2:37
13 9:41 ♄ ☍	♏ 13 15:53	11 10:31 ♃ ✶	♐ 12 5:18
15 13:39 ♂ △	♐ 15 19:33	14 6:59 ☿ △	♑ 14 11:45
18 0:46 ♂ □	♑ 18 3:27	16 16:37 ☉ □	♒ 16 22:11
20 9:01 ♄ □	♒ 20 14:57	19 10:45 ☉ ✶	♓ 19 10:57
22 22:39 ♄ ✶	♓ 23 4:00	21 0:05 ♃ ☍	♈ 21 23:26
24 22:32 ♃ ☍	♈ 25 16:30	24 4:34 ♂ ☌	♉ 24 9:58
27 23:29 ♄ ☌	♉ 28 3:24	26 2:34 ☿ ☌	♊ 26 18:15
30 8:23 ☿ ✶	♊ 30 12:23	28 2:55 ♃ □	♋ 29 0:37

☽ Phases & Eclipses Dy Hr Mn	
4 9:02	☽ 14♊19
11 1:06	○ 20♍59
17 23:23	☾ 27♐53
26 4:31	● 6♈03
2 19:15	☽ 13♋34
9 10:27	○ 20♎06
16 16:37	☾ 27♑13
24 19:47	● 5♉09

Astro Data

1 March 2028
Julian Day # 46812
SVP 4♓51'44"
GC 27♐14.0 ⚴ 28♍21.1R
Eris 25♈17.7 ⚵ 20♋11.2
⚷ 1♉13.1 ⚶ 4♌24.3R
☽ Mean ☊ 0♒18.7

1 April 2028
Julian Day # 46843
SVP 4♓51'40"
GC 27♐14.0 ⚴ 18♍53.9R
Eris 25♈35.5 ⚵ 24♋21.6
⚷ 2♉50.5 ⚶ 3♌45.3
☽ Mean ☊ 28♑40.2

LONGITUDE — May 2028

Day	Sid.Time	☉	0 hr ☽	Noon☽	True☊	☿	♀	♂	⚳	♃	♄	♅	♆	♇
1 M	2 39 46	11♉38 20	26♋53 50	3♌49 36	26♑12.0	0♊39.7	18♊01.6	2♉40.8	18♏01.3	17♍46.3	2♉20.1	8♊21.0	7♈37.6	8♒48.7
2 Tu	2 43 43	12 36 33	10♌48 17	17 49 54	26R12.0	2 09.3	18 20.9	3 25.8	17R47.9	17R44.1	2 27.6	8 24.2	7 39.5	8 48.9
3 W	2 47 40	13 34 44	24 54 22	2♍01 36	26 10.8	3 34.8	18 38.3	4 10.7	17 34.4	17 42.1	2 35.2	8 27.5	7 41.5	8 49.1
4 Th	2 51 36	14 32 53	9♍11 22	16 23 20	26 07.6	4 56.1	18 53.7	4 55.5	17 20.9	17 40.4	2 42.8	8 30.8	7 43.4	8 49.2
5 F	2 55 33	15 30 59	23 37 07	0♎52 08	26 01.7	6 13.2	19 07.0	5 40.3	17 07.4	17 38.7	2 50.3	8 34.0	7 45.3	8 49.3
6 Sa	2 59 29	16 29 04	8♎07 46	15 23 18	25 53.5	7 26.0	19 18.2	6 25.0	16 53.8	17 37.3	2 57.8	8 37.4	7 47.2	8 49.4
7 Su	3 03 26	17 27 07	22 37 56	29 50 49	25 43.6	8 34.4	19 27.3	7 09.7	16 40.3	17 36.1	3 05.3	8 40.7	7 49.0	8 49.5
8 M	3 07 22	18 25 09	7♏01 09	14♏08 09	25 33.1	9 38.3	19 34.1	7 54.3	16 26.8	17 35.0	3 12.8	8 44.0	7 50.8	8R49.5
9 Tu	3 11 19	19 23 09	21 11 04	28 09 17	25 23.2	10 37.7	19 38.7	8 38.9	16 13.3	17 34.1	3 20.3	8 47.4	7 52.7	8 49.5
10 W	3 15 15	20 21 07	5♐02 17	11♐49 43	25 14.9	11 32.5	19R41.0	9 23.4	15 59.9	17 33.4	3 27.7	8 50.8	7 54.5	8 49.5
11 Th	3 19 12	21 19 04	18 31 21	25 07 06	25 08.8	12 22.7	19 40.9	10 07.9	15 46.6	17 32.9	3 35.1	8 54.2	7 56.3	8 49.5
12 F	3 23 09	22 16 59	1♑37 00	8♑01 15	25 05.2	13 08.1	19 38.4	10 52.3	15 33.3	17 32.6	3 42.5	8 57.6	7 58.0	8 49.4
13 Sa	3 27 05	23 14 53	14 20 08	20 34 03	25D03.8	13 48.8	19 33.5	11 36.7	15 20.2	17D32.4	3 49.9	9 01.0	7 59.8	8 49.3
14 Su	3 31 02	24 12 46	26 43 27	2♒48 54	25 03.9	14 24.7	19 26.2	12 21.0	15 07.1	17 32.5	3 57.3	9 04.4	8 01.5	8 49.2
15 M	3 34 58	25 10 38	8♒50 59	14 50 19	25R04.7	14 55.7	19 16.5	13 05.3	14 54.2	17 32.7	4 04.6	9 07.9	8 03.2	8 49.0
16 Tu	3 38 55	26 08 28	20 47 34	26 43 23	25 05.1	15 21.8	19 04.3	13 49.5	14 41.4	17 33.1	4 11.9	9 11.3	8 04.8	8 48.8
17 W	3 42 51	27 06 17	2♓38 26	8♓33 22	25 04.3	15 43.0	18 49.7	14 33.7	14 28.8	17 33.6	4 19.2	9 14.8	8 06.5	8 48.6
18 Th	3 46 48	28 04 05	14 28 50	20 25 26	25 01.7	15 59.3	18 32.8	15 17.8	14 16.4	17 34.4	4 26.4	9 18.2	8 08.1	8 48.4
19 F	3 50 44	29 01 51	26 23 45	2♈24 20	24 56.9	16 10.6	18 13.6	16 01.9	14 04.1	17 35.3	4 33.6	9 21.7	8 09.7	8 48.1
20 Sa	3 54 41	29 59 37	8♈27 37	14 34 04	24 50.0	16R17.1	17 52.0	16 45.9	13 52.0	17 36.4	4 40.8	9 25.2	8 11.3	8 47.8
21 Su	3 58 38	0♊57 21	20 44 01	26 57 44	24 41.5	16 18.8	17 28.4	17 29.8	13 40.2	17 37.7	4 48.0	9 28.7	8 12.8	8 47.5
22 M	4 02 34	1 55 04	3♉15 27	9♉37 17	24 32.2	16 15.9	17 02.6	18 13.7	13 28.6	17 39.2	4 55.1	9 32.2	8 14.4	8 47.2
23 Tu	4 06 31	2 52 46	16 03 17	22 33 25	24 23.1	16 08.4	16 34.8	18 57.6	13 17.2	17 40.9	5 02.2	9 35.7	8 15.9	8 46.8
24 W	4 10 27	3 50 27	29 07 35	5♊45 37	24 15.0	15 56.6	16 05.2	19 41.4	13 06.1	17 42.7	5 09.3	9 39.2	8 17.4	8 46.4
25 Th	4 14 24	4 48 07	12♊27 19	19 12 24	24 08.7	15 40.8	15 33.9	20 25.1	12 55.2	17 44.7	5 16.3	9 42.7	8 18.8	8 46.0
26 F	4 18 20	5 45 46	26 00 37	2♋51 38	24 04.6	15 21.1	15 01.1	21 08.8	12 44.7	17 46.9	5 23.3	9 46.3	8 20.2	8 45.6
27 Sa	4 22 17	6 43 23	9♋45 11	16 40 57	24D02.7	14 58.1	14 26.9	21 52.4	12 34.4	17 49.2	5 30.2	9 49.8	8 21.6	8 45.1
28 Su	4 26 14	7 40 58	23 38 40	0♌38 05	24 02.6	14 32.0	13 51.6	22 36.0	12 24.4	17 51.8	5 37.1	9 53.3	8 23.0	8 44.6
29 M	4 30 10	8 38 33	7♌38 59	14 41 09	24 03.6	14 03.4	13 15.3	23 19.5	12 14.7	17 54.5	5 44.0	9 56.8	8 24.4	8 44.1
30 Tu	4 34 07	9 36 05	21 44 24	28 48 33	24R04.7	13 32.7	12 38.3	24 03.0	12 05.3	17 57.4	5 50.8	10 00.4	8 25.7	8 43.5
31 W	4 38 03	10 33 37	5♍53 25	12♍58 49	24 05.1	13 00.4	12 00.9	24 46.4	11 56.2	18 00.4	5 57.6	10 03.9	8 27.0	8 43.0

LONGITUDE — June 2028

Day	Sid.Time	☉	0 hr ☽	Noon☽	True☊	☿	♀	♂	⚳	♃	♄	♅	♆	♇
1 Th	4 42 00	11♊31 07	20♍04 33	27♍10 21	24♑04.0	12♊27.2	11♊23.2	25♉29.8	11♏47.5	18♍03.6	6♉04.3	10♊07.4	8♈28.2	8♒42.4
2 F	4 45 56	12 28 35	4♎15 57	11♎21 03	24R01.2	11R53.5	10R45.5	26 13.0	11R39.1	18 07.0	6 11.0	10 10.9	8 29.5	8R41.8
3 Sa	4 49 53	13 26 03	18 25 16	25 28 13	23 56.7	11 20.1	10 08.1	26 56.3	11 31.0	18 10.5	6 17.7	10 14.5	8 30.7	8 41.1
4 Su	4 53 49	14 23 29	2♏29 28	9♏28 36	23 51.1	10 47.4	9 31.1	27 39.5	11 23.3	18 14.2	6 24.3	10 18.0	8 31.9	8 40.5
5 M	4 57 46	15 20 54	16 25 08	23 18 40	23 45.0	10 16.0	8 54.9	28 22.6	11 16.0	18 18.1	6 30.8	10 21.5	8 33.0	8 39.8
6 Tu	5 01 43	16 18 18	0♐08 47	6♐55 07	23 39.2	9 46.4	8 19.7	29 05.6	11 09.0	18 22.1	6 37.3	10 25.0	8 34.2	8 39.1
7 W	5 05 39	17 15 41	13 37 22	20 15 18	23 34.4	9 19.2	7 45.6	29 48.7	11 02.3	18 26.3	6 43.8	10 28.5	8 35.3	8 38.3
8 Th	5 09 36	18 13 04	26 48 44	3♑17 38	23 31.1	8 54.8	7 12.9	0♊31.6	10 56.1	18 30.7	6 50.2	10 32.0	8 36.3	8 37.6
9 F	5 13 32	19 10 25	9♑41 59	16 01 53	23D29.5	8 33.6	6 41.8	1 14.5	10 50.1	18 35.2	6 56.6	10 35.5	8 37.4	8 36.8
10 Sa	5 17 29	20 07 46	22 17 31	28 29 07	23 29.3	8 15.9	6 12.5	1 57.4	10 44.6	18 39.9	7 02.9	10 39.0	8 38.4	8 36.0
11 Su	5 21 25	21 05 07	4♒37 02	10♒41 39	23 30.3	8 02.0	5 45.0	2 40.2	10 39.4	18 44.7	7 09.1	10 42.5	8 39.3	8 35.2
12 M	5 25 22	22 02 26	16 43 25	22 42 49	23 32.0	7 52.2	5 19.5	3 22.9	10 34.6	18 49.6	7 15.3	10 46.0	8 40.3	8 34.3
13 Tu	5 29 18	22 59 46	28 40 22	4♓36 40	23 33.6	7D46.7	4 56.2	4 05.6	10 30.2	18 54.8	7 21.5	10 49.5	8 41.2	8 33.5
14 W	5 33 15	23 57 04	10♓32 17	16 27 50	23R34.8	7 45.5	4 35.1	4 48.2	10 26.2	19 00.0	7 27.6	10 52.9	8 42.1	8 32.6
15 Th	5 37 12	24 54 23	22 23 55	28 21 08	23 35.0	7 48.9	4 16.2	5 30.8	10 22.5	19 05.5	7 33.6	10 56.4	8 43.0	8 31.7
16 F	5 41 08	25 51 41	4♈20 07	10♈21 27	23 34.0	7 56.9	3 59.7	6 13.3	10 19.2	19 11.0	7 39.6	10 59.8	8 43.8	8 30.8
17 Sa	5 45 05	26 48 58	16 25 39	22 33 17	23 31.9	8 09.4	3 45.6	6 55.8	10 16.3	19 16.7	7 45.5	11 03.3	8 44.6	8 29.8
18 Su	5 49 01	27 46 16	28 44 48	5♉00 37	23 28.8	8 26.6	3 33.9	7 38.2	10 13.8	19 22.6	7 51.3	11 06.7	8 45.3	8 28.9
19 M	5 52 58	28 43 33	11♉21 05	17 46 29	23 25.3	8 48.3	3 24.6	8 20.6	10 11.7	19 28.6	7 57.1	11 10.1	8 46.1	8 27.9
20 Tu	5 56 54	29 40 50	24 16 58	0♊52 39	23 21.6	9 14.6	3 17.7	9 02.9	10 09.9	19 34.7	8 02.8	11 13.5	8 46.8	8 26.9
21 W	6 00 51	0♋38 07	7♊33 31	14 19 27	23 18.4	9 45.5	3 13.2	9 45.1	10 08.6	19 41.0	8 08.5	11 16.9	8 47.4	8 25.9
22 Th	6 04 47	1 35 23	21 10 14	28 05 33	23 16.0	10 20.8	3D11.0	10 27.3	10 07.6	19 47.4	8 14.1	11 20.3	8 48.1	8 24.8
23 F	6 08 44	2 32 39	5♋05 02	12♋08 12	23D14.7	11 00.4	3 11.2	11 09.5	10 07.0	19 54.0	8 19.7	11 23.6	8 48.7	8 23.8
24 Sa	6 12 41	3 29 55	19 14 30	26 23 23	23 14.4	11 44.5	3 13.6	11 51.6	10D06.8	20 00.7	8 25.1	11 27.0	8 49.3	8 22.7
25 Su	6 16 37	4 27 10	3♌34 16	10♌46 31	23 15.0	12 32.7	3 18.3	12 33.6	10 07.0	20 07.5	8 30.5	11 30.3	8 49.8	8 21.6
26 M	6 20 34	5 24 24	17 59 33	25 12 48	23 16.1	13 25.2	3 25.2	13 15.6	10 07.5	20 14.5	8 35.9	11 33.6	8 50.3	8 20.5
27 Tu	6 24 30	6 21 38	2♍25 44	9♍37 51	23 17.3	14 21.8	3 34.2	13 57.5	10 08.4	20 21.6	8 41.1	11 36.9	8 50.8	8 19.4
28 W	6 28 27	7 18 51	16 48 44	23 58 00	23 18.2	15 22.5	3 45.4	14 39.4	10 09.7	20 28.8	8 46.3	11 40.1	8 51.2	8 18.2
29 Th	6 32 23	8 16 04	1♎05 17	8♎10 18	23R18.5	16 27.3	3 58.5	15 21.1	10 11.4	20 36.1	8 51.4	11 43.4	8 51.6	8 17.1
30 F	6 36 20	9 13 17	15 12 49	22 12 38	23 18.1	17 36.0	4 13.6	16 02.9	10 13.4	20 43.6	8 56.5	11 46.6	8 52.0	8 15.9

Astro Data

	Dy Hr Mn
♃⊼♄	4 5:47
☽0S	4 18:47
♇ R	9 9:33
♅△♇	10 3:06
♀ R	10 23:03
♃ D	13 20:00
☽0N	18 11:40
☿ R	21 8:43
☽0S	31 23:58
♆✶♇	9 4:37
☿ D	14 6:05
☽0N	14 18:55
♀ D	22 22:13
♄□♇	24 3:02
⚳ D	24 13:29

Planet Ingress

		Dy Hr Mn
☿	♊	1 1:42
☉	♊	20 12:10
♂	♊	7 18:20
☉	♋	20 20:02
☽0S		28 4:59
♄⊻⊻		29 12:58

Last Aspect / ☽ Ingress

Last Aspect Dy Hr Mn			☽ Ingress	Dy Hr Mn
30 8:09	♃	✶	♌	1 5:23
2 12:54	♀	✶	♍	3 8:36
4 16:14	♀	□	♎	5 10:34
6 18:33	♀	△	♏	7 12:15
8 19:49	☉	☍	♐	9 15:12
11 2:06	♀	☍	♑	11 21:00
13 17:39	☉	△	♒	14 6:26
16 10:43	☉	□	♓	16 18:39
19 4:41	☉	✶	♈	19 7:12
20 18:15	♀	✶	♉	21 17:48
23 4:59	♂	☌	♊	24 1:35
25 9:24	♃	□	♋	26 7:00
27 21:27	♂	✶	♌	28 10:55
30 3:29	♂	□	♍	30 14:01

Last Aspect / ☽ Ingress

Last Aspect Dy Hr Mn			☽ Ingress	Dy Hr Mn
1 9:01	♂	△	♎	1 16:47
2 14:03	☉	△	♏	3 19:44
5 21:23	♂	☍	♐	5 23:45
7 8:41	♃	□	♑	8 5:53
9 16:55	♃	△	♒	10 14:57
12 10:32	☉	△	♓	13 2:41
15 4:27	☉	□	♈	15 15:19
17 20:58	☉	✶	♉	18 2:25
19 15:11	♃	△	♊	20 10:25
21 21:29	♃	□	♋	22 15:17
24 1:13	♃	✶	♌	24 18:02
25 15:08	☿	✶	♍	26 19:58
28 6:06	♃	☌	♎	28 22:10

☽ Phases & Eclipses

Dy Hr Mn		
2 2:26	☽	12♌13
8 19:49	○	18♏44
16 10:43	☾	26♒05
24 8:16	●	3♊41
31 7:36	☽	10♍23
7 6:09	○	17♐02
15 4:27	☾	24♓36
22 18:27	●	1♋51
29 12:11	☽	8♎16

Astro Data

1 May 2028
Julian Day # 46873
SVP 4♓51'36"
GC 27♐14.1 ⚵ 15♍02.4R
Eris 25♈55.1 ⚶ 2♌38.3
⚷ 4♉40.6 ⚴ 9♌16.8
☽ Mean ☊ 27♑04.9

1 June 2028
Julian Day # 46904
SVP 4♓51'32"
GC 27♐14.2 ⚵ 18♍13.1
Eris 26♈12.7 ⚶ 13♌27.3
⚷ 6♉29.2 ⚴ 19♌07.9
☽ Mean ☊ 25♑26.4

July 2028

LONGITUDE

Day	Sid.Time	☉	0 hr ☽	Noon☽	True☊	☿	♀	♂	⚳	♃	♄	♅	♆	♇
1 Sa	6 40 16	10♋10 29	29♎09 34	6♏03 27	23♑17.2	18♊48.6	4♊30.7	16♊44.6	10♏15.8	20♍51.2	9♉01.5	11♊49.8	8♈52.4	8♒14.7
2 Su	6 44 13	11 07 40	12♏54 11	19 41 40	23R15.9	20 05.1	4 49.6	17 26.2	10 18.6	20 58.9	9 06.4	11 53.0	8 52.7	8R13.5
3 M	6 48 10	12 04 52	26 25 47	3♐06 29	23 14.4	21 25.4	5 10.3	18 07.8	10 21.7	21 06.8	9 11.2	11 56.2	8 52.9	8 12.3
4 Tu	6 52 06	13 02 03	9♐43 42	16 17 24	23 13.1	22 49.5	5 32.7	18 49.3	10 25.1	21 14.7	9 15.9	11 59.3	8 53.2	8 11.1
5 W	6 56 03	13 59 14	22 47 34	29 14 12	23 12.1	24 17.3	5 56.8	19 30.7	10 28.9	21 22.8	9 20.6	12 02.5	8 53.4	8 09.9
6 Th	6 59 59	14 56 25	5♑37 19	11♑56 59	23D11.5	25 48.8	6 22.6	20 12.2	10 33.1	21 31.0	9 25.2	12 05.6	8 53.6	8 08.6
7 F	7 03 56	15 53 36	18 13 17	24 26 20	23 11.4	27 23.9	6 49.9	20 53.5	10 37.6	21 39.3	9 29.7	12 08.7	8 53.7	8 07.4
8 Sa	7 07 52	16 50 47	0♒36 17	6♒43 20	23 11.6	29 02.5	7 18.8	21 34.8	10 42.4	21 47.7	9 34.2	12 11.7	8 53.9	8 06.1
9 Su	7 11 49	17 47 59	12 47 43	18 49 43	23 12.0	0♋44.5	7 49.1	22 16.0	10 47.6	21 56.2	9 38.5	12 14.7	8 53.9	8 04.8
10 M	7 15 46	18 45 10	24 49 37	0♓47 48	23 12.5	2 29.9	8 20.9	22 57.2	10 53.1	22 04.9	9 42.8	12 17.8	8 54.0	8 03.6
11 Tu	7 19 42	19 42 22	6♓44 39	12 40 35	23 12.9	4 18.4	8 54.0	23 38.4	10 58.9	22 13.6	9 47.0	12 20.7	8R54.0	8 02.3
12 W	7 23 39	20 39 35	18 36 04	24 31 34	23 13.2	6 10.0	9 28.4	24 19.4	11 05.1	22 22.4	9 51.1	12 23.7	8 54.0	8 01.0
13 Th	7 27 35	21 36 47	0♈27 38	6♈24 48	23 13.4	8 04.3	10 04.0	25 00.5	11 11.5	22 31.4	9 55.2	12 26.6	8 54.0	7 59.6
14 F	7 31 32	22 34 01	12 23 35	18 24 35	23 13.5	10 01.3	10 40.9	25 41.4	11 18.3	22 40.4	9 59.1	12 29.5	8 53.9	7 58.3
15 Sa	7 35 28	23 31 15	24 28 21	0♉35 27	23 13.5	12 00.7	11 19.0	26 22.4	11 25.4	22 49.6	10 03.0	12 32.4	8 53.8	7 57.0
16 Su	7 39 25	24 28 29	6♉46 25	13 01 47	23 13.5	14 02.2	11 58.1	27 03.2	11 32.8	22 58.9	10 06.7	12 35.2	8 53.6	7 55.6
17 M	7 43 21	25 25 45	19 22 00	25 47 31	23 13.7	16 05.5	12 38.4	27 44.1	11 40.5	23 08.2	10 10.4	12 38.0	8 53.4	7 54.3
18 Tu	7 47 18	26 23 01	2♊18 40	8♊55 44	23 13.9	18 10.4	13 19.7	28 24.8	11 48.5	23 17.7	10 14.0	12 40.8	8 53.2	7 52.9
19 W	7 51 15	27 20 17	15 38 54	22 28 14	23 14.3	20 16.4	14 01.9	29 05.5	11 56.8	23 27.2	10 17.5	12 43.6	8 53.0	7 51.6
20 Th	7 55 11	28 17 35	29 23 38	6♋24 57	23 14.6	22 23.4	14 45.2	29 46.2	12 05.4	23 36.9	10 20.9	12 46.3	8 52.7	7 50.2
21 F	7 59 08	29 14 53	13♋31 48	20 43 43	23R14.8	24 30.9	15 29.3	0♋26.8	12 14.3	23 46.7	10 24.3	12 49.0	8 52.4	7 48.8
22 Sa	8 03 04	0♌12 11	28 00 05	5♌20 10	23 14.7	26 38.7	16 14.3	1 07.3	12 23.5	23 56.5	10 27.5	12 51.6	8 52.1	7 47.5
23 Su	8 07 01	1 09 30	12♌43 07	20 08 02	23 14.2	28 46.4	17 00.2	1 47.8	12 33.0	24 06.4	10 30.6	12 54.3	8 51.7	7 46.1
24 M	8 10 57	2 06 50	27 33 58	4♍59 55	23 13.4	0♌53.9	17 46.9	2 28.2	12 42.7	24 16.4	10 33.7	12 56.9	8 51.3	7 44.7
25 Tu	8 14 54	3 04 09	12♍24 59	19 48 14	23 12.3	3 00.9	18 34.4	3 08.6	12 52.7	24 26.5	10 36.6	12 59.4	8 50.9	7 43.3
26 W	8 18 50	4 01 30	27 08 55	4♎26 17	23 11.3	5 07.2	19 22.6	3 48.9	13 03.0	24 36.7	10 39.5	13 01.9	8 50.4	7 41.9
27 Th	8 22 47	4 58 50	11♎39 48	18 49 00	23 10.4	7 12.5	20 11.6	4 29.2	13 13.6	24 47.0	10 42.3	13 04.4	8 49.9	7 40.5
28 F	8 26 44	5 56 11	25 53 32	2♏53 14	23D10.0	9 16.8	21 01.2	5 09.4	13 24.4	24 57.4	10 44.9	13 06.9	8 49.4	7 39.2
29 Sa	8 30 40	6 53 33	9♏47 59	16 37 48	23 10.2	11 19.9	21 51.6	5 49.5	13 35.4	25 07.8	10 47.5	13 09.3	8 48.9	7 37.8
30 Su	8 34 37	7 50 55	23 22 44	0♐02 56	23 10.9	13 21.7	22 42.6	6 29.6	13 46.8	25 18.3	10 50.0	13 11.7	8 48.3	7 36.4
31 M	8 38 33	8 48 18	6♐38 37	13 09 59	23 12.0	15 22.1	23 34.2	7 09.6	13 58.3	25 28.9	10 52.3	13 14.0	8 47.7	7 35.0

August 2028

LONGITUDE

Day	Sid.Time	☉	0 hr ☽	Noon☽	True☊	☿	♀	♂	⚳	♃	♄	♅	♆	♇
1 Tu	8 42 30	9♌45 41	19♐37 17	26♐00 46	23♑13.3	17♌21.1	24♊26.5	7♋49.6	14♏10.2	25♍39.6	10♉54.6	13♊16.3	8♈47.0	7♒33.6
2 W	8 46 26	10 43 05	2♑20 43	8♑37 23	23 14.4	19 18.5	25 19.4	8 29.5	14 22.2	25 50.4	10 56.8	13 18.6	8R46.3	7R32.2
3 Th	8 50 23	11 40 30	14 51 01	21 01 50	23R14.9	21 14.5	26 12.8	9 09.4	14 34.5	26 01.2	10 58.9	13 20.8	8 45.6	7 30.8
4 F	8 54 19	12 37 56	27 10 06	3♒16 02	23 14.6	23 08.8	27 06.8	9 49.2	14 47.1	26 12.1	11 00.9	13 23.0	8 44.9	7 29.4
5 Sa	8 58 16	13 35 22	9♒19 50	15 21 45	23 13.3	25 01.7	28 01.3	10 29.0	14 59.8	26 23.1	11 02.7	13 25.1	8 44.1	7 28.1
6 Su	9 02 13	14 32 49	21 21 58	27 20 43	23 11.0	26 52.9	28 56.4	11 08.7	15 12.8	26 34.1	11 04.5	13 27.2	8 43.4	7 26.7
7 M	9 06 09	15 30 18	3♓18 16	9♓14 49	23 07.8	28 42.6	29 52.0	11 48.3	15 26.0	26 45.2	11 06.2	13 29.3	8 42.5	7 25.3
8 Tu	9 10 06	16 27 47	15 10 41	21 06 07	23 04.1	0♍30.6	0♋48.1	12 27.9	15 39.4	26 56.4	11 07.7	13 31.3	8 41.7	7 23.9
9 W	9 14 02	17 25 18	27 01 29	2♈57 05	23 00.1	2 17.2	1 44.6	13 07.4	15 53.1	27 07.6	11 09.2	13 33.3	8 40.8	7 22.6
10 Th	9 17 59	18 22 50	8♈53 20	14 50 37	22 56.5	4 02.2	2 41.7	13 46.9	16 06.9	27 18.9	11 10.6	13 35.2	8 39.9	7 21.2
11 F	9 21 55	19 20 23	20 49 23	26 50 07	22 53.7	5 45.6	3 39.1	14 26.4	16 21.0	27 30.3	11 11.8	13 37.1	8 39.0	7 19.8
12 Sa	9 25 52	20 17 58	2♉53 17	8♉59 25	22D51.9	7 27.6	4 37.1	15 05.7	16 35.2	27 41.7	11 13.0	13 39.0	8 38.0	7 18.5
13 Su	9 29 48	21 15 35	15 09 03	21 22 42	22 51.3	9 08.0	5 35.4	15 45.1	16 49.7	27 53.2	11 14.1	13 40.8	8 37.1	7 17.1
14 M	9 33 45	22 13 12	27 40 55	4♊04 13	22 51.8	10 46.9	6 34.1	16 24.3	17 04.4	28 04.8	11 15.0	13 42.6	8 36.1	7 15.8
15 Tu	9 37 42	23 10 52	10♊33 05	17 07 56	22 53.1	12 24.3	7 33.3	17 03.6	17 19.2	28 16.4	11 15.9	13 44.3	8 35.0	7 14.5
16 W	9 41 38	24 08 33	23 49 09	0♋37 00	22 54.6	14 00.3	8 32.8	17 42.7	17 34.3	28 28.1	11 16.6	13 46.0	8 34.0	7 13.1
17 Th	9 45 35	25 06 15	7♋31 39	14 33 07	22R55.8	15 34.7	9 32.7	18 21.8	17 49.6	28 39.8	11 17.2	13 47.6	8 32.9	7 11.8
18 F	9 49 31	26 03 59	21 41 16	28 55 47	22 55.9	17 07.7	10 33.0	19 00.9	18 05.0	28 51.6	11 17.8	13 49.2	8 31.8	7 10.5
19 Sa	9 53 28	27 01 45	6♌16 09	13♌41 41	22 54.5	18 39.2	11 33.6	19 39.9	18 20.6	29 03.5	11 18.2	13 50.8	8 30.7	7 09.2
20 Su	9 57 24	27 59 31	21 11 30	28 44 34	22 51.5	20 09.2	12 34.6	20 18.8	18 36.4	29 15.4	11 18.5	13 52.3	8 29.5	7 08.0
21 M	10 01 21	28 57 20	6♍19 42	13♍55 40	22 47.1	21 37.7	13 35.8	20 57.7	18 52.4	29 27.3	11 18.7	13 53.7	8 28.3	7 06.7
22 Tu	10 05 17	29 55 09	21 31 08	29 04 52	22 41.8	23 04.7	14 37.4	21 36.5	19 08.6	29 39.3	11R18.8	13 55.1	8 27.1	7 05.4
23 W	10 09 14	0♍53 00	6♎35 41	14♎02 29	22 36.4	24 30.2	15 39.3	22 15.3	19 24.9	29 51.4	11 18.8	13 56.5	8 25.9	7 04.2
24 Th	10 13 11	1 50 52	21 24 24	28 40 41	22 31.8	25 54.1	16 41.5	22 54.0	19 41.4	0♎03.5	11 18.7	13 57.8	8 24.6	7 02.9
25 F	10 17 07	2 48 45	5♏50 51	12♏54 32	22 28.5	27 16.5	17 44.0	23 32.6	19 58.1	0 15.6	11 18.5	13 59.1	8 23.4	7 01.7
26 Sa	10 21 04	3 46 39	19 51 37	26 42 07	22D26.9	28 37.2	18 46.8	24 11.2	20 15.0	0 27.8	11 18.1	14 00.3	8 22.1	7 00.5
27 Su	10 25 00	4 44 35	3♐26 12	10♐04 07	22 26.8	29 56.3	19 49.9	24 49.8	20 32.0	0 40.0	11 17.7	14 01.4	8 20.8	6 59.3
28 M	10 28 57	5 42 32	16 36 14	23 02 58	22 27.8	1♎13.7	20 53.2	25 28.2	20 49.1	0 52.3	11 17.2	14 02.6	8 19.5	6 58.1
29 Tu	10 32 53	6 40 30	29 24 48	5♑42 12	22 29.2	2 29.4	21 56.8	26 06.6	21 06.5	1 04.6	11 16.5	14 03.6	8 18.1	6 56.9
30 W	10 36 50	7 38 30	11♑55 39	18 05 38	22R30.1	3 43.2	23 00.7	26 45.0	21 23.9	1 17.0	11 15.8	14 04.6	8 16.8	6 55.8
31 Th	10 40 46	8 36 31	24 12 37	0♒17 01	22 29.9	4 55.1	24 04.8	27 23.3	21 41.6	1 29.3	11 14.9	14 05.6	8 15.4	6 54.6

Astro Data

	Dy Hr Mn
♆ R	11 13:04
☽0N	12 2:19
♃⚼♇	16 4:43
☽0S	25 11:56
♃⚼♄	3 5:40
☽0N	8 9:25
☽0S	21 21:25
♄ R	22 22:17
☿0S	26 4:20

Planet Ingress

		Dy Hr Mn
☿	♋	9 1:37
♂	♋	20 20:10
☉	♌	22 6:54
☿	♌	24 1:50
♀	♋	7 15:26
☿	♍	8 5:10
☉	♍	22 14:01
♃	♎	24 5:08
☿	♎	27 13:08

Last Aspect / ☽ Ingress

Last Aspect Dy Hr Mn			☽ Ingress	Dy Hr Mn
30 3:22	☿	△	♏	1 1:27
2 14:19	♃	⚹	♐	3 6:24
5 1:35	☿	☍	♑	5 13:26
7 6:33	♃	△	♒	7 22:49
9 19:17	♂	△	♓	10 10:24
12 11:34	♂	□	♈	12 23:04
15 3:15	♂	⚹	♉	15 10:51
17 11:16	☉	⚹	♊	17 19:46
20 0:04	♂	☌	♋	20 1:03
22 3:02	☉	☌	♌	22 3:17
23 6:40	♀	⚹	♍	24 3:56
25 19:39	♃	☌	♎	26 4:41
27 14:28	♀	△	♏	28 7:02
30 3:20	♃	⚹	♐	30 11:55

Last Aspect / ☽ Ingress

Last Aspect Dy Hr Mn			☽ Ingress	Dy Hr Mn
1 11:20	♃	□	♑	1 19:33
3 21:54	♃	△	♒	4 5:34
6 15:29	♀	△	♓	6 17:20
9 0:01	♃	☍	♈	9 6:02
10 19:43	☉	△	♉	11 18:17
14 0:35	♃	△	♊	14 4:22
16 8:10	♃	□	♋	16 10:55
18 11:53	♃	⚹	♌	18 13:46
20 10:44	☉	☌	♍	20 13:59
22 12:56	♃	☌	♎	22 13:28
24 2:01	♂	□	♏	24 14:12
26 15:46	☿	⚹	♐	26 17:51
27 19:15	♅	☍	♑	29 1:07
31 5:57	♂	☍	♒	31 11:26

☽ Phases & Eclipses

Dy Hr Mn		
6 18:11	○	15♑11
6 18:20	◐	P 0.389
14 20:56	☾	22♈55
22 3:02	●	29♋51
22 2:55:23	◑	T 05'10"
28 17:40	☽	6♏10
5 8:10	○	13♒26
13 11:45	☾	21♉15
20 10:44	●	27♌56
27 1:36	☽	4♐19

Astro Data

1 July 2028
Julian Day # 46934
SVP 4♓51'26"
GC 27♐14.2 ⚳ 25♍51.5
Eris 26♈23.4 ⚵ 24♌58.7
⚷ 7♉50.2 ⚶ 1♍05.7
☽ Mean ☊ 23♑51.1

1 August 2028
Julian Day # 46965
SVP 4♓51'21"
GC 27♐14.3 ⚳ 6♎27.3
Eris 26♈25.2R ⚵ 7♍20.6
⚷ 8♉32.5 ⚶ 15♍01.9
☽ Mean ☊ 22♑12.6

LONGITUDE — September 2028

Day	Sid.Time	☉	0 hr ☽	Noon ☽	True ☊	☿	♀	♂	⚳	♃	♄	♅	♆	♇
1 F	10 44 43	9♍34 34	6♒19 14	12♒19 40	22♑27.8	6♎05.1	25♋09.2	28♋01.5	21♍59.3	1♎41.8	11♉14.0	14♊06.5	8♈14.0	6♒53.5
2 Sa	10 48 40	10 32 38	18 18 38	24 16 25	22R 23.6	7 13.1	26 13.8	28 39.7	22 17.2	1 54.2	11R 12.9	14 07.4	8R 12.6	6R 52.4
3 Su	10 52 36	11 30 43	0♓13 20	6♓09 36	22 17.1	8 18.8	27 18.7	29 17.8	22 35.3	2 06.7	11 11.8	14 08.2	8 11.1	6 51.3
4 M	10 56 33	12 28 50	12 05 27	18 01 06	22 08.8	9 22.3	28 23.8	29 55.9	22 53.5	2 19.2	11 10.5	14 09.0	8 09.7	6 50.2
5 Tu	11 00 29	13 26 59	23 56 45	29 52 37	21 59.2	10 23.5	29 29.2	0♌33.9	23 11.8	2 31.8	11 09.1	14 09.7	8 08.2	6 49.1
6 W	11 04 26	14 25 10	5♈48 53	11♈45 47	21 49.2	11 22.0	0♌34.7	1 11.8	23 30.3	2 44.4	11 07.7	14 10.4	8 06.7	6 48.1
7 Th	11 08 22	15 23 22	17 43 33	23 42 27	21 39.7	12 17.9	1 40.5	1 49.7	23 48.9	2 57.0	11 06.1	14 11.0	8 05.2	6 47.1
8 F	11 12 19	16 21 37	29 42 47	5♉44 52	21 31.5	13 11.0	2 46.5	2 27.5	24 07.6	3 09.7	11 04.4	14 11.6	8 03.7	6 46.1
9 Sa	11 16 15	17 19 53	11♉49 03	17 55 46	21 25.3	14 00.9	3 52.8	3 05.3	24 26.4	3 22.3	11 02.7	14 12.1	8 02.2	6 45.1
10 Su	11 20 12	18 18 12	24 05 25	0♊18 27	21 21.4	14 47.6	4 59.2	3 43.0	24 45.4	3 35.0	11 00.8	14 12.6	8 00.6	6 44.1
11 M	11 24 08	19 16 32	6♊35 23	12 56 42	21D 19.6	15 30.8	6 05.9	4 20.7	25 04.5	3 47.8	10 58.8	14 13.0	7 59.1	6 43.1
12 Tu	11 28 05	20 14 55	19 22 55	25 54 30	21 19.6	16 10.3	7 12.7	4 58.3	25 23.8	4 00.5	10 56.7	14 13.4	7 57.5	6 42.2
13 W	11 32 02	21 13 20	2♋31 55	9♋15 36	21R 20.2	16 45.7	8 19.8	5 35.8	25 43.1	4 13.3	10 54.6	14 13.7	7 56.0	6 41.3
14 Th	11 35 58	22 11 47	16 05 52	23 02 58	21 20.6	17 16.8	9 27.0	6 13.3	26 02.6	4 26.1	10 52.3	14 13.9	7 54.4	6 40.4
15 F	11 39 55	23 10 17	0♌06 57	7♌17 47	21 19.6	17 43.2	10 34.4	6 50.7	26 22.2	4 39.0	10 50.0	14 14.1	7 52.8	6 39.5
16 Sa	11 43 51	24 08 48	14 35 12	21 58 42	21 16.4	18 04.6	11 42.0	7 28.1	26 41.9	4 51.8	10 47.5	14 14.3	7 51.2	6 38.7
17 Su	11 47 48	25 07 21	29 27 37	7♍01 01	21 10.6	18 20.7	12 49.8	8 05.4	27 01.7	5 04.7	10 45.0	14 14.4	7 49.6	6 37.9
18 M	11 51 44	26 05 56	14♍37 48	22 16 41	21 02.6	18 31.2	13 57.8	8 42.6	27 21.7	5 17.5	10 42.3	14R 14.5	7 47.9	6 37.1
19 Tu	11 55 41	27 04 34	29 56 15	7♎35 04	20 53.0	18R 35.5	15 05.9	9 19.8	27 41.7	5 30.4	10 39.6	14 14.5	7 46.3	6 36.3
20 W	11 59 37	28 03 13	15♎11 42	22 44 49	20 43.1	18 33.5	16 14.2	9 56.9	28 01.9	5 43.3	10 36.8	14 14.4	7 44.7	6 35.5
21 Th	12 03 34	29 01 54	0♏13 12	7♏35 50	20 34.1	18 24.7	17 22.7	10 33.9	28 22.1	5 56.3	10 33.8	14 14.3	7 43.0	6 34.8
22 F	12 07 31	0♎00 36	14 51 58	22 01 01	20 26.9	18 09.0	18 31.3	11 10.8	28 42.5	6 09.2	10 30.8	14 14.1	7 41.4	6 34.1
23 Sa	12 11 27	0 59 21	29 02 41	5♐56 50	20 22.2	17 46.1	19 40.0	11 47.7	29 03.0	6 22.2	10 27.8	14 13.9	7 39.7	6 33.4
24 Su	12 15 24	1 58 07	12♐43 36	19 23 12	20 19.7	17 15.9	20 48.9	12 24.6	29 23.5	6 35.1	10 24.6	14 13.7	7 38.1	6 32.7
25 M	12 19 20	2 56 55	25 56 01	2♑22 33	20D 19.1	16 38.4	21 58.0	13 01.3	29 44.2	6 48.1	10 21.3	14 13.4	7 36.4	6 32.1
26 Tu	12 23 17	3 55 45	8♑43 21	14 58 59	20R 19.3	15 54.0	23 07.2	13 38.0	0♐05.0	7 01.0	10 18.0	14 13.0	7 34.8	6 31.5
27 W	12 27 13	4 54 36	21 10 07	27 17 20	20 19.2	15 03.0	24 16.6	14 14.6	0 25.8	7 14.0	10 14.6	14 12.6	7 33.1	6 30.9
28 Th	12 31 10	5 53 29	3♒21 16	9♒22 29	20 17.7	14 06.1	25 26.1	14 51.2	0 46.8	7 27.0	10 11.1	14 12.2	7 31.4	6 30.3
29 F	12 35 06	6 52 24	15 21 34	21 19 02	20 13.9	13 04.2	26 35.7	15 27.6	1 07.8	7 40.0	10 07.6	14 11.6	7 29.8	6 29.8
30 Sa	12 39 03	7 51 20	27 15 20	3♓10 55	20 07.3	11 58.6	27 45.5	16 04.1	1 28.9	7 53.0	10 03.9	14 11.1	7 28.1	6 29.2

LONGITUDE — October 2028

Day	Sid.Time	☉	0 hr ☽	Noon ☽	True ☊	☿	♀	♂	⚳	♃	♄	♅	♆	♇
1 Su	12 43 00	8♎50 19	9♓06 10	15♓01 24	19♑57.9	10♎50.6	28♌55.4	16♌40.4	1♐50.2	8♎05.9	10♉00.2	14♊10.5	7♈26.4	6♒28.7
2 M	12 46 56	9 49 19	20 56 54	26 52 56	19R 46.0	9R 42.0	0♍05.5	17 16.7	2 11.5	8 18.9	9R 56.4	14R 09.8	7R 24.8	6R 28.3
3 Tu	12 50 53	10 48 21	2♈49 42	8♈47 22	19 32.4	8 34.5	1 15.6	17 52.9	2 32.8	8 31.9	9 52.6	14 09.1	7 23.1	6 27.8
4 W	12 54 49	11 47 26	14 46 08	20 46 06	19 18.1	7 30.0	2 26.0	18 29.0	2 54.3	8 44.9	9 48.7	14 08.3	7 21.4	6 27.4
5 Th	12 58 46	12 46 32	26 47 25	2♉50 15	19 04.4	6 30.3	3 36.4	19 05.1	3 15.8	8 57.9	9 44.7	14 07.5	7 19.8	6 27.0
6 F	13 02 42	13 45 41	8♉54 43	15 01 00	18 52.4	5 37.0	4 47.0	19 41.0	3 37.5	9 10.8	9 40.7	14 06.7	7 18.1	6 26.7
7 Sa	13 06 39	14 44 51	21 09 18	27 19 50	18 42.9	4 51.6	5 57.7	20 17.0	3 59.2	9 23.8	9 36.6	14 05.8	7 16.5	6 26.3
8 Su	13 10 35	15 44 04	3♊32 53	9♊48 45	18 36.3	4 15.4	7 08.5	20 52.8	4 21.0	9 36.8	9 32.4	14 04.8	7 14.8	6 26.0
9 M	13 14 32	16 43 20	16 07 46	22 30 17	18 32.5	3 49.2	8 19.5	21 28.6	4 42.8	9 49.7	9 28.2	14 03.8	7 13.2	6 25.7
10 Tu	13 18 29	17 42 37	28 56 44	5♋27 30	18D 31.1	3D 33.6	9 30.5	22 04.3	5 04.8	10 02.6	9 23.9	14 02.8	7 11.5	6 25.5
11 W	13 22 25	18 41 57	12♋03 00	18 43 39	18R 30.9	3 28.9	10 41.7	22 39.9	5 26.8	10 15.6	9 19.6	14 01.7	7 09.9	6 25.3
12 Th	13 26 22	19 41 20	25 29 48	2♌21 45	18 30.6	3 35.0	11 53.0	23 15.5	5 48.9	10 28.5	9 15.2	14 00.5	7 08.3	6 25.1
13 F	13 30 18	20 40 44	9♌19 44	16 23 49	18 29.1	3 51.6	13 04.4	23 50.9	6 11.0	10 41.4	9 10.8	13 59.3	7 06.7	6 24.9
14 Sa	13 34 15	21 40 11	23 33 58	0♍49 56	18 25.4	4 18.5	14 15.9	24 26.3	6 33.2	10 54.3	9 06.4	13 58.1	7 05.1	6 24.7
15 Su	13 38 11	22 39 40	8♍11 19	15 37 29	18 18.8	4 54.8	15 27.6	25 01.6	6 55.5	11 07.2	9 01.8	13 56.8	7 03.5	6 24.6
16 M	13 42 08	23 39 12	23 07 35	0♎40 36	18 09.7	5 40.0	16 39.3	25 36.9	7 17.9	11 20.0	8 57.3	13 55.5	7 01.9	6 24.5
17 Tu	13 46 04	24 38 45	8♎15 20	15 50 29	17 58.7	6 33.2	17 51.1	26 12.0	7 40.3	11 32.9	8 52.7	13 54.1	7 00.3	6 24.5
18 W	13 50 01	25 38 21	23 24 42	0♏56 37	17 47.1	7 33.6	19 03.0	26 47.1	8 02.8	11 45.7	8 48.1	13 52.7	6 58.7	6D 24.4
19 Th	13 53 57	26 37 59	8♏24 58	15 48 37	17 36.4	8 40.5	20 15.1	27 22.0	8 25.4	11 58.5	8 43.4	13 51.3	6 57.2	6 24.4
20 F	13 57 54	27 37 38	23 06 35	0♐18 07	17 27.6	9 53.0	21 27.2	27 56.9	8 48.0	12 11.2	8 38.7	13 49.8	6 55.6	6 24.4
21 Sa	14 01 51	28 37 20	7♐22 41	14 19 57	17 21.4	11 10.4	22 39.4	28 31.7	9 10.7	12 24.0	8 34.0	13 48.2	6 54.1	6 24.5
22 Su	14 05 47	29 37 03	21 09 50	27 52 24	17 17.9	12 31.9	23 51.7	29 06.4	9 33.4	12 36.7	8 29.3	13 46.6	6 52.6	6 24.6
23 M	14 09 44	0♏36 48	4♑27 55	10♑56 46	17D 16.6	13 57.1	25 04.0	29 41.0	9 56.2	12 49.4	8 24.5	13 45.0	6 51.1	6 24.7
24 Tu	14 13 40	1 36 35	17 19 25	23 36 28	17R 16.5	15 25.2	26 16.5	0♍15.6	10 19.1	13 02.1	8 19.8	13 43.4	6 49.6	6 24.8
25 W	14 17 37	2 36 23	29 48 30	5♒56 11	17 16.6	16 55.8	27 29.0	0 50.0	10 42.0	13 14.7	8 15.0	13 41.7	6 48.1	6 25.0
26 Th	14 21 33	3 36 13	12♒00 12	18 01 12	17 15.6	18 28.5	28 41.7	1 24.3	11 05.0	13 27.3	8 10.1	13 39.9	6 46.7	6 25.2
27 F	14 25 30	4 36 04	23 59 51	29 56 45	17 12.7	20 02.8	29 54.4	1 58.6	11 28.0	13 39.9	8 05.3	13 38.1	6 45.2	6 25.4
28 Sa	14 29 26	5 35 58	5♓52 31	11♓47 41	17 07.2	21 38.4	1♎07.1	2 32.7	11 51.1	13 52.4	8 00.5	13 36.3	6 43.8	6 25.7
29 Su	14 33 23	6 35 53	17 42 45	23 38 12	16 59.0	23 15.0	2 20.0	3 06.8	12 14.2	14 04.9	7 55.7	13 34.5	6 42.4	6 25.9
30 M	14 37 20	7 35 49	29 34 25	5♈31 45	16 48.4	24 52.4	3 32.9	3 40.7	12 37.3	14 17.3	7 50.8	13 32.6	6 41.0	6 26.3
31 Tu	14 41 16	8 35 48	11♈30 31	17 30 56	16 36.1	26 30.4	4 45.9	4 14.6	13 00.5	14 29.8	7 46.0	13 30.7	6 39.7	6 26.6

Astro Data (Dy Hr Mn)

	Dy Hr Mn
☽0N	4 15:56
♃0S	5 14:46
☽0S	18 8:21
♅R	19 0:02
☿R	19 16:34
⊙0S	22 11:45
♃△♇	24 7:46
♃☍♆	28 19:15
☽0N	1 21:55
♃⚻♄	8 5:55
☿D	11 10:27
☽0S	15 18:38
♇D	19 3:42
♃△♅	27 9:06
☽0N	29 3:50

Planet Ingress (Dy Hr Mn)

	Dy Hr Mn
♂ ♌	4 14:36
♀ ♌	5 23:18
⊙ ♎	22 11:45
⚳ ♐	26 6:16
♀ ♍	2 10:08
⊙ ♏	22 21:13
♂ ♍	24 1:10
♀ ♎	27 13:52

♀0S30 14:05

Last Aspect / ☽ Ingress (September)

Last Aspect Dy Hr Mn		☽ Ingress Dy Hr Mn
1 15:34 ♅ △	♓	2 23:33
5 11:08 ♀ △	♈	5 12:15
6 16:52 ♅ ⚹	♉	8 0:34
9 10:44 ⊙ △	♊	10 11:25
12 0:46 ⊙ □	♋	12 19:26
14 10:26 ⊙ ⚹	♌	14 23:48
16 5:33 ☿ ⚹	♍	17 0:52
18 18:24 ⊙ ☌	♎	19 0:06
20 5:22 ☿ ☌	♏	20 23:39
22 5:36 ♀ □	♐	23 1:39
24 14:51 ♀ △	♑	25 7:33
26 13:40 ☿ □	♒	27 17:21
29 23:49 ♀ ☍	♓	30 5:33

Last Aspect / ☽ Ingress (October)

Last Aspect Dy Hr Mn		☽ Ingress Dy Hr Mn
1 10:17 ♅ □	♈	2 18:18
4 7:12 ♂ △	♉	5 6:23
6 21:36 ♂ □	♊	7 17:10
9 9:59 ♂ ⚹	♋	10 1:57
11 11:57 ⊙ □	♌	12 7:53
14 1:00 ♂ ☌	♍	14 10:38
15 11:43 ♀ ☌	♎	16 10:56
18 5:06 ♂ ⚹	♏	18 10:30
20 7:53 ♂ □	♐	20 11:30
22 15:25 ⊙ ⚹	♑	22 15:51
24 17:42 ♀ △	♒	25 0:22
26 13:03 ☿ △	♓	27 12:07
28 15:40 ♅ □	♈	30 0:52

☽ Phases & Eclipses (Dy Hr Mn)

Dy Hr Mn	
3 23:47	○ 11♓59
12 0:46	☾ 19♊48
18 18:24	● 26♍22
25 13:10	☽ 3♑00
3 16:25	○ 10♈59
11 11:57	☾ 18♋42
18 2:57	● 25♎16
25 4:53	☽ 2♒19

Astro Data

1 September 2028
Julian Day # 46996
SVP 4♓51'17"
GC 27♐14.4 ⚴ 18♎39.0
Eris 26♈17.2R ⚵ 19♍47.1
⚷ 8♉23.4R ⚶ 0♎01.9
☽ Mean ☊ 20♑34.1

1 October 2028
Julian Day # 47026
SVP 4♓51'14"
GC 27♐14.5 ⚴ 1♏20.3
Eris 26♈02.4R ⚵ 1♎36.2
⚷ 7♉28.4R ⚶ 15♎13.9
☽ Mean ☊ 18♑58.8

November 2028 — LONGITUDE

Day	Sid.Time	☉	0 hr ☽	Noon ☽	True ☊	☿	♀	♂	⚳	♃	♄	♅	♆	♇
1 W	14 45 13	9♏35 48	23♈33 12	29♈37 30	16♑23.2	28♎08.8	5♎59.0	4♍48.3	13♐23.8	14♎42.1	7♉41.2	13♊28.7	6♈38.3	6♒26.9
2 Th	14 49 09	10 35 50	5♉43 56	11♉52 35	16R 10.7	29 47.4	7 12.2	5 22.0	13 47.1	14 54.5	7R 36.3	13R 26.7	6R 37.0	6 27.3
3 F	14 53 06	11 35 54	18 03 31	24 16 48	15 59.8	1♏26.1	8 25.4	5 55.5	14 10.4	15 06.8	7 31.5	13 24.7	6 35.7	6 27.8
4 Sa	14 57 02	12 36 00	0♊32 29	6♊50 36	15 51.2	3 04.9	9 38.7	6 29.0	14 33.8	15 19.0	7 26.7	13 22.6	6 34.4	6 28.2
5 Su	15 00 59	13 36 08	13 11 16	19 34 34	15 45.4	4 43.6	10 52.1	7 02.3	14 57.3	15 31.3	7 21.9	13 20.6	6 33.2	6 28.7
6 M	15 04 55	14 36 18	26 00 36	2♋29 31	15 42.3	6 22.2	12 05.5	7 35.6	15 20.8	15 43.4	7 17.1	13 18.4	6 31.9	6 29.2
7 Tu	15 08 52	15 36 30	9♋01 32	15 36 48	15D 41.5	8 00.6	13 19.0	8 08.7	15 44.3	15 55.5	7 12.3	13 16.3	6 30.7	6 29.7
8 W	15 12 49	16 36 44	22 15 34	28 58 04	15 42.0	9 38.9	14 32.6	8 41.8	16 07.8	16 07.6	7 07.6	13 14.1	6 29.5	6 30.3
9 Th	15 16 45	17 36 59	5♌44 30	12♌35 04	15R 42.7	11 16.8	15 46.2	9 14.7	16 31.4	16 19.6	7 02.9	13 11.9	6 28.4	6 30.9
10 F	15 20 42	18 37 17	19 29 55	26 29 09	15 42.5	12 54.6	16 59.9	9 47.5	16 55.1	16 31.6	6 58.2	13 09.7	6 27.2	6 31.5
11 Sa	15 24 38	19 37 37	3♍32 45	10♍40 38	15 40.6	14 32.0	18 13.7	10 20.2	17 18.7	16 43.5	6 53.5	13 07.5	6 26.1	6 32.1
12 Su	15 28 35	20 37 59	17 52 33	25 08 08	15 36.3	16 09.2	19 27.5	10 52.8	17 42.5	16 55.4	6 48.9	13 05.2	6 25.0	6 32.8
13 M	15 32 31	21 38 23	2♎26 51	9♎48 02	15 29.9	17 46.1	20 41.4	11 25.2	18 06.2	17 07.2	6 44.3	13 02.9	6 23.9	6 33.5
14 Tu	15 36 28	22 38 48	17 10 53	24 34 28	15 21.9	19 22.7	21 55.3	11 57.5	18 30.0	17 18.9	6 39.7	13 00.6	6 22.9	6 34.2
15 W	15 40 24	23 39 16	1♏57 48	9♏19 52	15 13.3	20 59.0	23 09.3	12 29.7	18 53.8	17 30.6	6 35.2	12 58.2	6 21.9	6 35.0
16 Th	15 44 21	24 39 45	16 39 36	23 56 02	15 05.2	22 35.1	24 23.3	13 01.8	19 17.7	17 42.2	6 30.7	12 55.9	6 20.9	6 35.8
17 F	15 48 18	25 40 16	1♐08 18	8♐15 36	14 58.5	24 10.9	25 37.4	13 33.8	19 41.5	17 53.8	6 26.3	12 53.5	6 19.9	6 36.6
18 Sa	15 52 14	26 40 49	15 17 21	22 13 04	14 53.9	25 46.4	26 51.5	14 05.6	20 05.5	18 05.3	6 21.9	12 51.1	6 19.0	6 37.4
19 Su	15 56 11	27 41 22	29 02 30	5♑45 30	14D 51.6	27 21.7	28 05.7	14 37.2	20 29.4	18 16.7	6 17.5	12 48.7	6 18.1	6 38.3
20 M	16 00 07	28 41 57	12♑22 09	18 52 35	14 51.3	28 56.8	29 19.9	15 08.8	20 53.4	18 28.0	6 13.2	12 46.2	6 17.2	6 39.1
21 Tu	16 04 04	29 42 34	25 17 07	1♒36 09	14 52.3	0♐31.6	0♏34.1	15 40.2	21 17.4	18 39.3	6 09.0	12 43.8	6 16.4	6 40.1
22 W	16 08 00	0♐43 11	7♒50 09	13 59 42	14 53.8	2 06.3	1 48.4	16 11.4	21 41.4	18 50.5	6 04.8	12 41.3	6 15.6	6 41.0
23 Th	16 11 57	1 43 50	20 05 21	26 07 45	14R 54.9	3 40.7	3 02.8	16 42.5	22 05.4	19 01.7	6 00.7	12 38.9	6 14.8	6 41.9
24 F	16 15 54	2 44 30	2♓07 32	8♓05 20	14 54.9	5 15.0	4 17.1	17 13.5	22 29.5	19 12.7	5 56.6	12 36.4	6 14.0	6 42.9
25 Sa	16 19 50	3 45 10	14 01 47	19 57 32	14 53.2	6 49.1	5 31.5	17 44.3	22 53.6	19 23.7	5 52.7	12 33.9	6 13.3	6 43.9
26 Su	16 23 47	4 45 52	25 53 09	1♈49 13	14 49.8	8 23.1	6 46.0	18 14.9	23 17.7	19 34.6	5 48.7	12 31.4	6 12.6	6 45.0
27 M	16 27 43	5 46 35	7♈46 15	13 44 45	14 44.6	9 56.9	8 00.4	18 45.4	23 41.8	19 45.4	5 44.9	12 28.9	6 11.9	6 46.0
28 Tu	16 31 40	6 47 19	19 45 09	25 47 50	14 38.2	11 30.7	9 14.9	19 15.8	24 05.9	19 56.2	5 41.1	12 26.3	6 11.3	6 47.1
29 W	16 35 36	7 48 04	1♉53 06	8♉01 16	14 31.3	13 04.4	10 29.5	19 46.0	24 30.1	20 06.8	5 37.4	12 23.8	6 10.7	6 48.2
30 Th	16 39 33	8 48 51	14 12 30	20 26 58	14 24.5	14 37.9	11 44.0	20 16.0	24 54.3	20 17.4	5 33.7	12 21.3	6 10.1	6 49.4

December 2028 — LONGITUDE

Day	Sid.Time	☉	0 hr ☽	Noon ☽	True ☊	☿	♀	♂	⚳	♃	♄	♅	♆	♇
1 F	16 43 29	9♐49 38	26♉44 47	3♊05 58	14♑18.6	16♐11.4	12♏58.6	20♍45.9	25♐18.5	20♎27.9	5♉30.2	12♊18.7	6♈09.6	6♒50.5
2 Sa	16 47 26	10 50 27	9♊30 32	15 58 26	14R 14.1	17 44.9	14 13.3	21 15.6	25 42.7	20 38.3	5R 26.7	12R 16.2	6R 09.1	6 51.7
3 Su	16 51 23	11 51 17	22 29 35	29 03 56	14 11.4	19 18.3	15 27.9	21 45.1	26 06.9	20 48.6	5 23.3	12 13.7	6 08.6	6 52.9
4 M	16 55 19	12 52 08	5♋41 20	12♋21 42	14D 10.4	20 51.6	16 42.6	22 14.5	26 31.2	20 58.9	5 20.0	12 11.1	6 08.2	6 54.1
5 Tu	16 59 16	13 53 00	19 04 54	25 50 50	14 10.8	22 24.9	17 57.4	22 43.7	26 55.4	21 09.0	5 16.7	12 08.6	6 07.8	6 55.4
6 W	17 03 12	14 53 53	2♌39 24	9♌30 30	14 12.2	23 58.2	19 12.1	23 12.7	27 19.7	21 19.0	5 13.6	12 06.1	6 07.4	6 56.6
7 Th	17 07 09	15 54 48	16 24 04	23 20 01	14 13.8	25 31.5	20 26.9	23 41.5	27 44.0	21 29.0	5 10.5	12 03.5	6 07.0	6 57.9
8 F	17 11 05	16 55 44	0♍18 14	7♍18 38	14R 15.0	27 04.7	21 41.7	24 10.2	28 08.3	21 38.8	5 07.5	12 01.0	6 06.7	6 59.2
9 Sa	17 15 02	17 56 41	14 21 05	21 25 25	14 15.3	28 37.8	22 56.6	24 38.6	28 32.6	21 48.6	5 04.6	11 58.5	6 06.5	7 00.6
10 Su	17 18 58	18 57 39	28 31 26	5♎38 52	14 14.4	0♑10.9	24 11.4	25 06.9	28 56.9	21 58.2	5 01.8	11 55.9	6 06.2	7 01.9
11 M	17 22 55	19 58 39	12♎47 24	19 56 38	14 12.3	1 43.9	25 26.3	25 35.0	29 21.2	22 07.8	4 59.1	11 53.4	6 06.0	7 03.3
12 Tu	17 26 52	20 59 39	27 06 09	4♏15 26	14 09.3	3 16.7	26 41.2	26 02.8	29 45.6	22 17.2	4 56.5	11 50.9	6 05.8	7 04.7
13 W	17 30 48	22 00 41	11♏23 57	18 31 07	14 06.0	4 49.5	27 56.2	26 30.4	0♑09.9	22 26.5	4 54.0	11 48.4	6 05.7	7 06.1
14 Th	17 34 45	23 01 44	25 36 21	2♐39 05	14 02.8	6 22.0	29 11.1	26 57.9	0 34.2	22 35.8	4 51.6	11 45.9	6 05.6	7 07.5
15 F	17 38 41	24 02 48	9♐38 45	16 34 50	14 00.3	7 54.3	0♐26.1	27 25.1	0 58.6	22 44.9	4 49.2	11 43.5	6 05.5	7 09.0
16 Sa	17 42 38	25 03 52	23 26 54	0♑14 34	13 58.7	9 26.3	1 41.1	27 52.1	1 23.0	22 53.9	4 47.0	11 41.0	6D 05.5	7 10.4
17 Su	17 46 34	26 04 57	6♑57 33	13 35 40	13D 58.2	10 57.9	2 56.1	28 18.8	1 47.3	23 02.8	4 44.9	11 38.6	6 05.5	7 11.9
18 M	17 50 31	27 06 03	20 08 50	26 37 03	13 58.6	12 28.9	4 11.1	28 45.3	2 11.7	23 11.5	4 42.9	11 36.1	6 05.6	7 13.4
19 Tu	17 54 27	28 07 09	3♒00 25	9♒19 08	13 59.7	13 59.4	5 26.2	29 11.6	2 36.0	23 20.2	4 41.0	11 33.7	6 05.6	7 15.0
20 W	17 58 24	29 08 15	15 33 28	21 43 47	14 01.1	15 29.2	6 41.2	29 37.7	3 00.4	23 28.7	4 39.2	11 31.3	6 05.7	7 16.5
21 Th	18 02 21	0♑09 21	27 50 28	3♓53 59	14 02.4	16 58.0	7 56.3	0♎03.5	3 24.7	23 37.1	4 37.5	11 28.9	6 05.9	7 18.1
22 F	18 06 17	1 10 28	9♓54 52	15 53 39	14 03.5	18 25.7	9 11.3	0 29.0	3 49.1	23 45.4	4 35.9	11 26.6	6 06.1	7 19.6
23 Sa	18 10 14	2 11 35	21 50 55	27 47 15	14R 04.0	19 52.1	10 26.4	0 54.3	4 13.4	23 53.5	4 34.4	11 24.3	6 06.3	7 21.2
24 Su	18 14 10	3 12 42	3♈43 14	9♈39 30	14 03.9	21 16.9	11 41.5	1 19.3	4 37.8	24 01.6	4 33.0	11 21.9	6 06.5	7 22.8
25 M	18 18 07	4 13 49	15 36 38	21 35 13	14 03.4	22 39.8	12 56.6	1 44.0	5 02.1	24 09.5	4 31.7	11 19.6	6 06.8	7 24.4
26 Tu	18 22 03	5 14 57	27 35 49	3♉38 57	14 02.5	24 00.4	14 11.7	2 08.5	5 26.4	24 17.2	4 30.6	11 17.4	6 07.1	7 26.1
27 W	18 26 00	6 16 04	9♉45 08	15 54 47	14 01.4	25 18.4	15 26.8	2 32.7	5 50.8	24 24.9	4 29.5	11 15.1	6 07.5	7 27.7
28 Th	18 29 56	7 17 12	22 08 18	28 26 01	14 00.4	26 33.2	16 41.9	2 56.7	6 15.1	24 32.4	4 28.6	11 12.9	6 07.9	7 29.4
29 F	18 33 53	8 18 19	4♊48 11	11♊14 59	13 59.6	27 44.4	17 57.1	3 20.3	6 39.4	24 39.7	4 27.7	11 10.7	6 08.3	7 31.1
30 Sa	18 37 50	9 19 27	17 46 31	24 22 48	13 59.0	28 51.2	19 12.2	3 43.7	7 03.7	24 47.0	4 27.0	11 08.6	6 08.7	7 32.8
31 Su	18 41 46	10 20 35	1♋03 44	7♋49 12	13D 58.8	29 53.1	20 27.4	4 06.7	7 28.0	24 54.1	4 26.4	11 06.4	6 09.2	7 34.5

Astro Data

	Dy Hr Mn
♆⚹♇	8 1:33
☽0S	12 2:28
♄□♇	15 12:54
♄⚺♆	19 7:59
☽0N	25 10:24
☽0S	9 7:52
♆ D	16 20:43
☽0N	22 18:01

Planet Ingress

	Dy Hr Mn
☿ ♏	2 15:04
♀ ♏	21 0:58
☿ ♐	21 4:00
☉ ♐	21 18:54
☿ ♑	10 9:12
⚳ ♑	13 2:14
♀ ♐	15 3:39
☉ ♑	21 8:20
♂ ♎	21 8:46
☿ ♒	31 14:49

Last Aspect / ☽ Ingress

Last Aspect Dy Hr Mn	☽ Ingress Dy Hr Mn
1 8:38 ☿ ☍	♉ 1 12:44
2 9:17 ☉ ☍	♊ 3 22:58
5 4:16 ♃ △	♋ 6 7:24
7 12:35 ♃ □	♌ 8 13:50
9 21:26 ☉ □	♍ 10 17:59
12 4:01 ☉ ⚹	♎ 12 19:59
14 7:18 ♀ ☌	♏ 14 20:49
16 13:18 ☉ ☌	♐ 16 22:06
18 20:57 ♀ ⚹	♑ 19 1:42
21 8:04 ☉ ⚹	♒ 21 8:56
22 21:41 ♃ △	♓ 23 19:44
25 7:18 ♂ ☍	♈ 26 8:19
28 0:11 ♃ ☍	♉ 28 20:18

Last Aspect / ☽ Ingress

Last Aspect Dy Hr Mn	☽ Ingress Dy Hr Mn
30 11:38 ♂ △	♊ 1 6:10
2 22:07 ♂ □	♋ 3 13:42
5 6:16 ♂ ⚹	♌ 5 19:20
7 16:15 ☿ △	♍ 7 23:29
10 1:40 ☿ □	♎ 10 2:29
11 15:42 ♃ ☌	♏ 12 4:51
14 5:31 ♀ ☌	♐ 14 7:28
16 7:39 ♂ □	♑ 16 11:34
18 16:09 ♂ △	♒ 18 18:20
21 3:54 ☉ ⚹	♓ 21 4:16
22 17:48 ☿ ⚹	♈ 23 16:28
25 17:12 ♃ ☍	♉ 26 4:47
28 8:03 ☿ △	♊ 28 14:58
30 12:44 ♃ △	♋ 30 22:06

☽ Phases & Eclipses

Dy Hr Mn	
2 9:17	○ 10♉29
9 21:26	☾ 18♌01
16 13:18	● 24♏43
24 0:15	☽ 2♓15
2 1:40	○ 10♊24
9 5:39	☾ 17♍41
16 2:06	● 24♐39
23 21:45	☽ 2♈36
31 16:48	○ 10♋33
31 16:52	• T 1.246

Astro Data

1 November 2028
Julian Day # 47057
SVP 4♓51'11"
GC 27♐14.5 ⚴ 14♏55.4
Eris 25♈44.0R ⚵ 13♎15.3
⚷ 6♉03.2R ⚶ 1♏22.6
☽ Mean ☊ 17♑20.3

1 December 2028
Julian Day # 47087
SVP 4♓51'06"
GC 27♐14.6 ⚴ 28♏08.9
Eris 25♈28.5R ⚵ 23♎31.7
⚷ 4♉44.0R ⚶ 17♏09.5
☽ Mean ☊ 15♑45.0

LONGITUDE — January 2029

Day	Sid.Time	☉	0 hr ☽	Noon ☽	True ☊	☿	♀	♂	⚳	♃	♄	♅	♆	♇
1 M	18 45 43	11♑21 43	14♋38 56	21♋32 37	13♑58.8	0♒49.3	21♐42.5	4♎29.4	7♑52.2	25♎01.0	4♉25.9	11♊04.3	6♈09.8	7♒36.2
2 Tu	18 49 39	12 22 50	28 29 54	5♌30 19	13 58.9	1 38.9	22 57.7	4 51.9	8 16.5	25 07.8	4R 25.5	11R 02.3	6 10.3	7 37.9
3 W	18 53 36	13 23 59	12♌33 25	19 38 41	13R 59.0	2 21.1	24 12.9	5 14.0	8 40.7	25 14.5	4 25.2	11 00.2	6 10.9	7 39.6
4 Th	18 57 32	14 25 07	26 45 37	3♍53 43	13 59.1	2 54.9	25 28.1	5 35.8	9 05.0	25 21.0	4 25.1	10 58.2	6 11.5	7 41.4
5 F	19 01 29	15 26 15	11♍02 29	18 11 27	13 59.0	3 19.6	26 43.3	5 57.2	9 29.2	25 27.4	4D 25.0	10 56.2	6 12.2	7 43.2
6 Sa	19 05 26	16 27 23	25 20 12	2♎28 18	13 58.8	3R 34.2	27 58.5	6 18.3	9 53.4	25 33.6	4 25.0	10 54.3	6 12.9	7 44.9
7 Su	19 09 22	17 28 32	9♎35 26	16 41 17	13D 58.7	3 37.9	29 13.7	6 39.1	10 17.6	25 39.7	4 25.2	10 52.4	6 13.6	7 46.7
8 M	19 13 19	18 29 41	23 45 34	0♏48 03	13 58.8	3 30.1	0♑28.9	6 59.5	10 41.7	25 45.6	4 25.5	10 50.5	6 14.4	7 48.5
9 Tu	19 17 15	19 30 50	7♏48 31	14 46 48	13 59.2	3 10.6	1 44.1	7 19.5	11 05.9	25 51.4	4 25.9	10 48.7	6 15.2	7 50.3
10 W	19 21 12	20 31 59	21 42 43	28 36 07	13 59.8	2 39.3	2 59.3	7 39.2	11 30.0	25 57.0	4 26.4	10 46.9	6 16.0	7 52.1
11 Th	19 25 08	21 33 09	5♐26 51	12♐14 47	14 00.5	1 56.5	4 14.6	7 58.4	11 54.1	26 02.5	4 27.0	10 45.1	6 16.9	7 53.9
12 F	19 29 05	22 34 18	18 59 46	25 41 40	14 01.2	1 03.2	5 29.8	8 17.3	12 18.2	26 07.7	4 27.7	10 43.4	6 17.8	7 55.7
13 Sa	19 33 01	23 35 27	2♑20 24	8♑55 49	14R 01.6	0 00.6	6 45.1	8 35.8	12 42.3	26 12.9	4 28.6	10 41.7	6 18.7	7 57.6
14 Su	19 36 58	24 36 35	15 27 51	21 56 26	14 01.5	28♑50.6	8 00.3	8 53.8	13 06.4	26 17.8	4 29.5	10 40.1	6 19.7	7 59.4
15 M	19 40 55	25 37 43	28 21 30	4♒43 05	14 00.8	27 35.3	9 15.6	9 11.5	13 30.4	26 22.6	4 30.6	10 38.5	6 20.6	8 01.3
16 Tu	19 44 51	26 38 51	11♒01 12	17 15 56	13 59.5	26 17.1	10 30.8	9 28.6	13 54.4	26 27.3	4 31.8	10 36.9	6 21.7	8 03.1
17 W	19 48 48	27 39 58	23 27 23	29 35 45	13 57.5	24 58.5	11 46.0	9 45.4	14 18.3	26 31.7	4 33.1	10 35.4	6 22.7	8 05.0
18 Th	19 52 44	28 41 04	5♓41 16	11♓44 11	13 55.2	23 41.9	13 01.3	10 01.7	14 42.3	26 36.0	4 34.5	10 33.9	6 23.8	8 06.8
19 F	19 56 41	29 42 09	17 44 51	23 43 38	13 52.8	22 29.3	14 16.5	10 17.5	15 06.2	26 40.1	4 36.0	10 32.5	6 24.9	8 08.7
20 Sa	20 00 37	0♒43 14	29 40 57	5♈37 17	13 50.7	21 22.7	15 31.7	10 32.9	15 30.1	26 44.1	4 37.6	10 31.1	6 26.1	8 10.5
21 Su	20 04 34	1 44 18	11♈33 07	17 29 00	13 49.2	20 23.5	16 47.0	10 47.8	15 53.9	26 47.9	4 39.3	10 29.8	6 27.3	8 12.4
22 M	20 08 30	2 45 20	23 25 29	29 23 09	13D 48.4	19 32.6	18 02.2	11 02.2	16 17.7	26 51.5	4 41.2	10 28.5	6 28.5	8 14.3
23 Tu	20 12 27	3 46 22	5♉22 36	11♉24 27	13 48.6	18 50.5	19 17.4	11 16.1	16 41.5	26 54.9	4 43.1	10 27.3	6 29.7	8 16.2
24 W	20 16 24	4 47 23	17 29 17	23 37 41	13 49.6	18 17.7	20 32.7	11 29.5	17 05.3	26 58.2	4 45.2	10 26.1	6 31.0	8 18.0
25 Th	20 20 20	5 48 23	29 50 14	6♊07 25	13 51.1	17 53.9	21 47.9	11 42.4	17 29.0	27 01.2	4 47.3	10 24.9	6 32.3	8 19.9
26 F	20 24 17	6 49 22	12♊29 45	18 57 36	13 52.8	17 39.1	23 03.1	11 54.8	17 52.6	27 04.1	4 49.6	10 23.8	6 33.6	8 21.8
27 Sa	20 28 13	7 50 20	25 31 18	2♋11 04	13R 54.1	17D 32.8	24 18.3	12 06.6	18 16.3	27 06.8	4 52.0	10 22.8	6 35.0	8 23.7
28 Su	20 32 10	8 51 17	8♋57 01	15 49 06	13 54.5	17 34.5	25 33.5	12 17.9	18 39.9	27 09.4	4 54.5	10 21.8	6 36.3	8 25.6
29 M	20 36 06	9 52 12	22 47 09	29 50 51	13 53.6	17 43.7	26 48.7	12 28.7	19 03.4	27 11.7	4 57.1	10 20.8	6 37.8	8 27.4
30 Tu	20 40 03	10 53 07	6♌59 44	14♌13 11	13 51.4	17 59.9	28 03.9	12 38.9	19 27.0	27 13.9	4 59.7	10 19.9	6 39.2	8 29.3
31 W	20 43 59	11 54 00	21 30 26	28 50 40	13 48.0	18 22.5	29 19.1	12 48.5	19 50.4	27 15.9	5 02.5	10 19.0	6 40.7	8 31.2

LONGITUDE — February 2029

Day	Sid.Time	☉	0 hr ☽	Noon ☽	True ☊	☿	♀	♂	⚳	♃	♄	♅	♆	♇
1 Th	20 47 56	12♒54 53	6♍12 56	13♍36 15	13♑43.7	18♑50.9	0♒34.3	12♎57.5	20♑13.9	27♎17.7	5♉05.4	10♊18.2	6♈42.2	8♒33.1
2 F	20 51 53	13 55 45	20 59 40	28 22 14	13R 39.3	19 24.8	1 49.5	13 05.9	20 37.3	27 19.3	5 08.4	10R 17.5	6 43.7	8 34.9
3 Sa	20 55 49	14 56 36	5♎43 04	13♎01 24	13 35.4	20 03.5	3 04.7	13 13.7	21 00.6	27 20.7	5 11.5	10 16.8	6 45.2	8 36.8
4 Su	20 59 46	15 57 26	20 16 35	27 28 05	13 32.6	20 46.7	4 19.9	13 20.8	21 23.9	27 22.0	5 14.7	10 16.1	6 46.8	8 38.7
5 M	21 03 42	16 58 15	4♏35 31	11♏38 38	13D 31.2	21 34.0	5 35.0	13 27.3	21 47.2	27 23.0	5 18.0	10 15.5	6 48.4	8 40.6
6 Tu	21 07 39	17 59 03	18 37 18	25 31 28	13 31.3	22 25.0	6 50.2	13 33.2	22 10.4	27 23.9	5 21.4	10 15.0	6 50.0	8 42.4
7 W	21 11 35	18 59 51	2♐21 11	9♐06 36	13 32.5	23 19.3	8 05.4	13 38.4	22 33.6	27 24.5	5 24.8	10 14.5	6 51.6	8 44.3
8 Th	21 15 32	20 00 38	15 47 52	22 25 12	13 34.1	24 16.8	9 20.6	13 43.0	22 56.7	27 25.0	5 28.4	10 14.0	6 53.3	8 46.1
9 F	21 19 28	21 01 23	28 58 48	5♑28 54	13R 35.4	25 17.2	10 35.8	13 46.8	23 19.8	27 25.3	5 32.1	10 13.6	6 55.0	8 48.0
10 Sa	21 23 25	22 02 08	11♑55 42	18 19 25	13 35.6	26 20.1	11 50.9	13 49.9	23 42.8	27R 25.4	5 35.9	10 13.3	6 56.7	8 49.8
11 Su	21 27 22	23 02 51	24 40 14	0♒58 18	13 34.0	27 25.5	13 06.1	13 52.4	24 05.8	27 25.3	5 39.7	10 13.0	6 58.5	8 51.7
12 M	21 31 18	24 03 33	7♒13 45	13 26 44	13 30.4	28 33.0	14 21.2	13 54.1	24 28.7	27 25.1	5 43.7	10 12.7	7 00.2	8 53.5
13 Tu	21 35 15	25 04 14	19 37 21	25 45 43	13 24.7	29 42.7	15 36.4	13R 55.1	24 51.5	27 24.6	5 47.8	10 12.6	7 02.0	8 55.3
14 W	21 39 11	26 04 53	1♓51 55	7♓56 07	13 17.2	0♒54.2	16 51.5	13 55.3	25 14.3	27 23.9	5 51.9	10 12.4	7 03.8	8 57.1
15 Th	21 43 08	27 05 31	13 58 24	19 58 57	13 08.6	2 07.6	18 06.7	13 54.9	25 37.1	27 23.1	5 56.1	10D 12.4	7 05.6	8 58.9
16 F	21 47 04	28 06 07	25 57 58	1♈55 39	12 59.6	3 22.6	19 21.8	13 53.6	25 59.8	27 22.0	6 00.4	10 12.3	7 07.5	9 00.7
17 Sa	21 51 01	29 06 42	7♈52 17	13 48 10	12 51.2	4 39.3	20 36.9	13 51.6	26 22.4	27 20.8	6 04.8	10 12.4	7 09.4	9 02.5
18 Su	21 54 57	0♓07 14	19 43 38	25 39 06	12 44.1	5 57.4	21 52.0	13 48.9	26 44.9	27 19.4	6 09.3	10 12.4	7 11.2	9 04.3
19 M	21 58 54	1 07 46	1♉35 01	7♉31 51	12 38.9	7 17.0	23 07.1	13 45.4	27 07.4	27 17.8	6 13.9	10 12.6	7 13.2	9 06.1
20 Tu	22 02 51	2 08 15	13 30 09	19 30 28	12 35.9	8 37.9	24 22.1	13 41.1	27 29.9	27 16.0	6 18.6	10 12.8	7 15.1	9 07.9
21 W	22 06 47	3 08 42	25 33 23	1♊39 33	12D 34.8	10 00.1	25 37.2	13 36.0	27 52.2	27 14.0	6 23.3	10 13.0	7 17.0	9 09.6
22 Th	22 10 44	4 09 08	7♊49 33	14 04 01	12 35.3	11 23.6	26 52.3	13 30.2	28 14.5	27 11.8	6 28.2	10 13.3	7 19.0	9 11.3
23 F	22 14 40	5 09 32	20 23 35	26 48 49	12 36.4	12 48.3	28 07.3	13 23.6	28 36.8	27 09.5	6 33.1	10 13.7	7 21.0	9 13.1
24 Sa	22 18 37	6 09 54	3♋20 13	9♋58 15	12R 37.2	14 14.2	29 22.3	13 16.2	28 58.9	27 07.0	6 38.0	10 14.1	7 23.0	9 14.8
25 Su	22 22 33	7 10 14	16 43 16	23 35 28	12 36.6	15 41.3	0♓37.3	13 08.0	29 21.0	27 04.2	6 43.1	10 14.5	7 25.0	9 16.5
26 M	22 26 30	8 10 32	0♌34 55	7♌41 29	12 34.0	17 09.5	1 52.3	12 59.1	29 43.0	27 01.4	6 48.3	10 15.1	7 27.0	9 18.2
27 Tu	22 30 26	9 10 48	14 54 50	22 14 27	12 29.0	18 38.8	3 07.3	12 49.4	0♒05.0	26 58.3	6 53.5	10 15.6	7 29.0	9 19.9
28 W	22 34 23	10 11 02	29 39 34	7♍09 12	12 21.8	20 09.2	4 22.3	12 38.9	0 26.9	26 55.0	6 58.8	10 16.2	7 31.1	9 21.6

Astro Data

	Dy Hr Mn
♂0S	5 6:09
♄ D	5 12:39
☽0S	5 13:07
☿ R	7 7:55
♃☐♅	9 3:22
☽0N	19 2:19
☿ D	27 18:41
☽0S	1 20:45
♃ R	10 13:07
♂ R	14 8:16
☽0N	15 10:14
♅ D	16 10:52

Planet Ingress

		Dy Hr Mn
♀	♑	8 2:47
☿	♑R	13 12:13
☉	♒	19 19:01
♀	♒	1 1:03
☿	♒	13 17:52
☉	♓	18 9:08
♀	♓	25 0:03
⚳	♒	27 6:32

Last Aspect / ☽ Ingress

Last Aspect Dy Hr Mn			☽ Ingress	Dy Hr Mn
1 18:03	♃	☐	♌	2 2:35
3 21:31	♃	⚹	♍	4 5:27
6 3:42	♀	☐	♎	6 7:50
8 3:21	♃	☌	♏	8 10:38
9 20:50	☉	⚹	♐	10 14:27
12 12:47	♃	⚹	♑	12 19:46
14 23:46	☿	☌	♒	15 3:05
17 5:57	♃	△	♓	17 12:48
19 9:44	☿	⚹	♈	20 0:38
22 6:54	♃	☍	♉	22 13:14
24 5:18	♀	△	♊	25 0:19
27 2:51	♃	△	♋	27 8:05
29 7:30	♃	☐	♌	29 12:15
31 9:25	♃	⚹	♍	31 13:53

Last Aspect / ☽ Ingress

Last Aspect Dy Hr Mn			☽ Ingress	Dy Hr Mn
1 20:50	☿	△	♎	2 14:39
4 11:50	♃	☌	♏	4 16:15
6 6:13	☿	⚹	♐	6 19:51
8 21:08	♃	⚹	♑	9 1:53
11 5:14	♃	☐	♒	11 10:09
13 15:14	♃	△	♓	13 20:20
14 16:30	♅	☐	♈	16 8:07
18 15:23	♃	☍	♉	18 20:48
20 22:46	♀	☐	♊	21 8:45
23 14:41	♀	△	♋	23 17:53
25 17:59	♃	☐	♌	25 23:01
27 19:38	♃	⚹	♍	28 0:33

☽ Phases & Eclipses

Dy Hr Mn		
7 13:26	☾	17♎32
14 17:24	●	24♑50
14 17:12:31	●	P 0.871
22 19:23	☽	3♉04
30 6:03	○	10♌38
5 21:52	☾	17♏23
13 10:31	●	25♒01
21 15:10	☽	3♊17
28 17:10	○	10♍24

Astro Data

1 January 2029
Julian Day # 47118
SVP 4♓50'59"
GC 27♐14.7 ⚵ 11♐27.2
Eris 25♈19.9R ⚴ 2♏22.6
⚷ 3♉57.2R ⚶ 3♐17.6
☽ Mean ☊ 14♑06.5

1 February 2029
Julian Day # 47149
SVP 4♓50'54"
GC 27♐14.7 ⚵ 23♐49.0
Eris 25♈21.4 ⚴ 8♏16.6
⚷ 4♉04.0 ⚶ 18♐47.5
☽ Mean ☊ 12♑28.0

March 2029 LONGITUDE

Day	Sid.Time	☉	0 hr ☽	Noon ☽	True ☊	☿	♀	♂	⚳	♃	♄	♅	♆	♇
1 Th	22 38 20	11♓11 14	14♍42 15	22♍17 26	12♑12.9	21♒40.7	5♓37.3	12♎27.7	0♒48.7	26♎51.6	7♉04.1	10♊16.9	7♈33.2	9♒23.2
2 F	22 42 16	12 11 25	29 53 24	7♎28 48	12R 03.5	23 13.3	6 52.2	12R 15.7	1 10.4	26R 48.0	7 09.6	10 17.6	7 35.3	9 24.8
3 Sa	22 46 13	13 11 34	15♎02 19	22 32 45	11 54.9	24 47.0	8 07.2	12 03.0	1 32.0	26 44.3	7 15.1	10 18.4	7 37.4	9 26.5
4 Su	22 50 09	14 11 41	29 59 03	7♏20 20	11 47.9	26 21.8	9 22.1	11 49.5	1 53.6	26 40.3	7 20.7	10 19.2	7 39.5	9 28.1
5 M	22 54 06	15 11 47	14♏35 59	21 45 32	11 43.2	27 57.6	10 37.0	11 35.3	2 15.1	26 36.2	7 26.3	10 20.1	7 41.6	9 29.7
6 Tu	22 58 02	16 11 52	28 48 44	5♐45 33	11D 40.9	29 34.6	11 51.9	11 20.4	2 36.5	26 32.0	7 32.0	10 21.0	7 43.7	9 31.3
7 W	23 01 59	17 11 55	12♐36 03	19 20 28	11 40.5	1♓12.6	13 06.8	11 04.8	2 57.8	26 27.5	7 37.8	10 22.0	7 45.9	9 32.8
8 Th	23 05 55	18 11 56	25 59 08	2♑32 25	11R 40.9	2 51.8	14 21.7	10 48.4	3 19.1	26 22.9	7 43.7	10 23.0	7 48.0	9 34.4
9 F	23 09 52	19 11 56	9♑00 47	15 24 38	11 41.0	4 32.0	15 36.6	10 31.4	3 40.2	26 18.2	7 49.6	10 24.1	7 50.2	9 35.9
10 Sa	23 13 49	20 11 54	21 44 29	28 00 44	11 39.8	6 13.4	16 51.5	10 13.8	4 01.3	26 13.3	7 55.6	10 25.3	7 52.4	9 37.4
11 Su	23 17 45	21 11 51	4♒13 49	10♒24 07	11 36.2	7 55.9	18 06.3	9 55.5	4 22.3	26 08.2	8 01.6	10 26.4	7 54.6	9 38.9
12 M	23 21 42	22 11 45	16 32 00	22 37 46	11 29.8	9 39.6	19 21.2	9 36.7	4 43.1	26 03.0	8 07.7	10 27.7	7 56.8	9 40.4
13 Tu	23 25 38	23 11 38	28 41 42	4♓44 01	11 20.4	11 24.4	20 36.0	9 17.3	5 03.9	25 57.7	8 13.9	10 29.0	7 59.0	9 41.9
14 W	23 29 35	24 11 29	10♓44 57	16 44 39	11 08.5	13 10.4	21 50.8	8 57.3	5 24.6	25 52.2	8 20.1	10 30.3	8 01.2	9 43.3
15 Th	23 33 31	25 11 18	22 43 18	28 41 03	10 54.9	14 57.6	23 05.6	8 36.9	5 45.2	25 46.5	8 26.4	10 31.7	8 03.4	9 44.7
16 F	23 37 28	26 11 05	4♈38 02	10♈34 25	10 40.7	16 46.0	24 20.4	8 15.9	6 05.7	25 40.8	8 32.7	10 33.1	8 05.7	9 46.2
17 Sa	23 41 24	27 10 50	16 30 22	22 26 05	10 27.1	18 35.6	25 35.2	7 54.6	6 26.1	25 34.8	8 39.1	10 34.6	8 07.9	9 47.5
18 Su	23 45 21	28 10 32	28 21 47	4♉17 44	10 15.1	20 26.4	26 49.9	7 32.8	6 46.4	25 28.8	8 45.6	10 36.1	8 10.1	9 48.9
19 M	23 49 17	29 10 13	10♉14 14	16 11 39	10 05.7	22 18.4	28 04.6	7 10.7	7 06.6	25 22.7	8 52.1	10 37.7	8 12.4	9 50.3
20 Tu	23 53 14	0♈09 52	22 10 21	28 10 49	9 59.1	24 11.7	29 19.4	6 48.3	7 26.7	25 16.4	8 58.7	10 39.3	8 14.6	9 51.6
21 W	23 57 11	1 09 28	4♊13 30	10♊18 56	9 55.3	26 06.1	0♈34.1	6 25.6	7 46.7	25 10.0	9 05.3	10 41.0	8 16.9	9 52.9
22 Th	0 01 07	2 09 02	16 27 42	22 40 24	9D 53.8	28 01.7	1 48.7	6 02.7	8 06.6	25 03.5	9 11.9	10 42.7	8 19.2	9 54.2
23 F	0 05 04	3 08 34	28 57 36	5♋19 57	9R 53.6	29 58.5	3 03.4	5 39.6	8 26.4	24 56.9	9 18.6	10 44.5	8 21.4	9 55.4
24 Sa	0 09 00	4 08 04	11♋48 01	18 22 21	9 53.5	1♈56.4	4 18.0	5 16.4	8 46.0	24 50.2	9 25.4	10 46.3	8 23.7	9 56.7
25 Su	0 12 57	5 07 31	25 03 26	1♌51 40	9 52.2	3 55.3	5 32.7	4 53.1	9 05.6	24 43.4	9 32.2	10 48.1	8 26.0	9 57.9
26 M	0 16 53	6 06 56	8♌47 19	15 50 28	9 48.9	5 55.3	6 47.3	4 29.7	9 25.0	24 36.5	9 39.0	10 50.0	8 28.2	9 59.1
27 Tu	0 20 50	7 06 18	23 01 04	0♍18 47	9 42.9	7 56.2	8 01.8	4 06.3	9 44.3	24 29.5	9 45.9	10 52.0	8 30.5	10 00.3
28 W	0 24 46	8 05 39	7♍43 04	15 13 09	9 34.3	9 57.8	9 16.4	3 43.0	10 03.5	24 22.5	9 52.9	10 53.9	8 32.8	10 01.4
29 Th	0 28 43	9 04 57	22 48 00	0♎26 23	9 23.7	12 00.2	10 30.9	3 19.8	10 22.6	24 15.3	9 59.8	10 56.0	8 35.0	10 02.6
30 F	0 32 40	10 04 13	8♎06 54	15 48 05	9 12.4	14 03.0	11 45.5	2 56.6	10 41.5	24 08.1	10 06.8	10 58.0	8 37.3	10 03.7
31 Sa	0 36 36	11 03 27	23 28 23	1♏06 22	9 01.7	16 06.2	13 00.0	2 33.7	11 00.4	24 00.8	10 13.9	11 00.1	8 39.6	10 04.8

April 2029 LONGITUDE

Day	Sid.Time	☉	0 hr ☽	Noon ☽	True ☊	☿	♀	♂	⚳	♃	♄	♅	♆	♇
1 Su	0 40 33	12♈02 39	8♏40 39	16♏10 04	8♑52.8	18♈09.5	14♈14.5	2♎10.9	11♒19.1	23♎53.5	10♉21.0	11♊02.3	8♈41.8	10♒05.8
2 M	0 44 29	13 01 49	23 33 40	0♐50 43	8R 46.5	20 12.6	15 28.9	1R 48.4	11 37.6	23R 46.1	10 28.1	11 04.5	8 44.1	10 06.9
3 Tu	0 48 26	14 00 58	8♐00 45	15 03 29	8 42.8	22 15.3	16 43.4	1 26.2	11 56.1	23 38.6	10 35.3	11 06.7	8 46.4	10 07.9
4 W	0 52 22	15 00 04	21 58 54	28 47 08	8D 41.4	24 17.2	17 57.8	1 04.3	12 14.4	23 31.1	10 42.5	11 09.0	8 48.7	10 08.9
5 Th	0 56 19	15 59 10	5♑28 27	12♑03 16	8R 41.2	26 18.1	19 12.3	0 42.8	12 32.6	23 23.6	10 49.7	11 11.3	8 50.9	10 09.8
6 F	1 00 15	16 58 13	18 32 02	24 55 19	8 41.1	28 17.6	20 26.7	0 21.7	12 50.7	23 16.0	10 57.0	11 13.7	8 53.2	10 10.8
7 Sa	1 04 12	17 57 14	1♒13 39	7♒27 38	8 39.8	0♉15.3	21 41.1	0 01.0	13 08.6	23 08.4	11 04.2	11 16.0	8 55.4	10 11.7
8 Su	1 08 09	18 56 14	13 37 48	19 44 42	8 36.3	2 10.9	22 55.5	29♍40.8	13 26.4	23 00.7	11 11.6	11 18.5	8 57.7	10 12.6
9 M	1 12 05	19 55 12	25 48 52	1♓50 46	8 30.2	4 03.9	24 09.8	29 21.1	13 44.0	22 53.0	11 18.9	11 20.9	8 59.9	10 13.5
10 Tu	1 16 02	20 54 08	7♓50 49	13 49 26	8 21.1	5 54.0	25 24.2	29 01.9	14 01.5	22 45.4	11 26.3	11 23.4	9 02.2	10 14.3
11 W	1 19 58	21 53 02	19 46 57	25 43 41	8 09.6	7 41.0	26 38.5	28 43.4	14 18.8	22 37.6	11 33.7	11 26.0	9 04.4	10 15.1
12 Th	1 23 55	22 51 54	1♈39 53	7♈35 47	7 56.5	9 24.4	27 52.8	28 25.4	14 36.0	22 29.9	11 41.1	11 28.5	9 06.6	10 15.9
13 F	1 27 51	23 50 45	13 31 36	19 27 31	7 42.6	11 03.9	29 07.1	28 08.1	14 53.0	22 22.2	11 48.6	11 31.2	9 08.8	10 16.7
14 Sa	1 31 48	24 49 33	25 23 42	1♉20 19	7 29.3	12 39.3	0♉21.3	27 51.4	15 09.9	22 14.5	11 56.1	11 33.8	9 11.0	10 17.4
15 Su	1 35 44	25 48 20	7♉17 31	13 15 31	7 17.5	14 10.4	1 35.6	27 35.4	15 26.6	22 06.8	12 03.6	11 36.5	9 13.2	10 18.1
16 M	1 39 41	26 47 04	19 14 30	25 14 43	7 08.2	15 36.9	2 49.8	27 20.1	15 43.2	21 59.2	12 11.1	11 39.2	9 15.4	10 18.8
17 Tu	1 43 38	27 45 47	1♊16 24	7♊19 52	7 01.6	16 58.6	4 04.0	27 05.6	15 59.6	21 51.5	12 18.7	11 41.9	9 17.6	10 19.5
18 W	1 47 34	28 44 27	13 25 27	19 33 32	6 57.9	18 15.4	5 18.2	26 51.7	16 15.8	21 43.9	12 26.2	11 44.7	9 19.8	10 20.1
19 Th	1 51 31	29 43 05	25 44 32	1♋58 55	6D 56.5	19 27.1	6 32.4	26 38.7	16 31.9	21 36.3	12 33.8	11 47.5	9 22.0	10 20.7
20 F	1 55 27	0♉41 41	8♋17 08	14 39 42	6 56.6	20 33.7	7 46.5	26 26.4	16 47.8	21 28.8	12 41.4	11 50.4	9 24.1	10 21.3
21 Sa	1 59 24	1 40 15	21 07 07	27 39 52	6R 57.0	21 34.8	9 00.7	26 14.8	17 03.5	21 21.3	12 49.0	11 53.2	9 26.3	10 21.9
22 Su	2 03 20	2 38 47	4♌18 24	11♌03 09	6 56.8	22 30.6	10 14.8	26 04.1	17 19.1	21 13.8	12 56.7	11 56.1	9 28.4	10 22.4
23 M	2 07 17	3 37 16	17 54 23	24 52 20	6 54.9	23 20.8	11 28.9	25 54.1	17 34.4	21 06.4	13 04.3	11 59.0	9 30.5	10 22.9
24 Tu	2 11 13	4 35 43	1♍57 04	9♍08 26	6 50.8	24 05.5	12 42.9	25 44.9	17 49.6	20 59.1	13 12.0	12 02.0	9 32.6	10 23.3
25 W	2 15 10	5 34 08	16 26 09	23 49 41	6 44.4	24 44.6	13 56.9	25 36.5	18 04.6	20 51.8	13 19.6	12 05.0	9 34.7	10 23.8
26 Th	2 19 07	6 32 31	1♎18 17	8♎51 00	6 36.4	25 17.9	15 11.0	25 28.9	18 19.4	20 44.6	13 27.3	12 08.0	9 36.8	10 24.2
27 F	2 23 03	7 30 52	16 26 43	24 04 07	6 27.5	25 45.6	16 25.0	25 22.1	18 34.1	20 37.5	13 35.0	12 11.0	9 38.9	10 24.6
28 Sa	2 27 00	8 29 11	1♏41 52	9♏18 33	6 19.0	26 07.6	17 38.9	25 16.1	18 48.5	20 30.4	13 42.7	12 14.1	9 40.9	10 25.0
29 Su	2 30 56	9 27 28	16 52 50	24 23 26	6 11.9	26 23.9	18 52.9	25 10.9	19 02.8	20 23.5	13 50.4	12 17.1	9 42.9	10 25.3
30 M	2 34 53	10 25 44	1♐49 16	9♐09 24	6 06.9	26 34.6	20 06.8	25 06.4	19 16.9	20 16.6	13 58.1	12 20.3	9 45.0	10 25.6

Astro Data (Dy Hr Mn)

☽0S 1 7:02
♄⊻♆ 9 15:57
☽0N 14 16:54
♂0N 17 7:12
♃□♅ 17 12:51
☉0N 20 8:01
♀0N 23 14:15
☿0N 25 4:01
☽0S 28 18:08
♄□♇ 29 23:11

♄⊻♅ 9 21:54
☽0N 10 22:25
☽0S 25 3:49

Planet Ingress (Dy Hr Mn)

☿ ♓ 6 18:15
☉ ♈ 20 8:02
♀ ♈ 21 1:03
☿ ♈ 23 12:18

☿ ♉ 7 8:51
♂ ♍R 7 13:09
♀ ♉ 14 5:06
☉ ♉ 19 18:56

Last Aspect Dy Hr Mn		☽ Ingress Dy Hr Mn
28 17:10	☉ ☍	♎ 2 0:10
3 18:43	♃ ☌	♏ 4 0:02
5 23:55	☿ □	♐ 6 2:02
8 0:47	♃ ⚹	♑ 8 7:20
10 8:35	♃ □	♒ 10 15:50
12 18:43	♃ △	♓ 13 2:35
15 4:19	☉ ☌	♈ 15 14:39
17 18:19	♃ ☍	♉ 18 3:19
20 14:32	♀ ⚹	♊ 20 15:37
23 0:05	♀ □	♋ 23 1:58
24 23:31	♃ □	♌ 25 8:44
27 2:31	♃ ⚹	♍ 27 11:29
28 5:05	♅ ☍	♎ 29 11:19
31 0:56	♃ ☌	♏ 31 10:15

Last Aspect Dy Hr Mn		☽ Ingress Dy Hr Mn
1 2:36	♄ ☍	♐ 2 10:36
4 2:47	♃ ⚹	♑ 4 14:10
6 19:35	☿ □	♒ 6 21:39
8 18:59	♀ ⚹	♓ 9 8:19
11 17:54	♂ ☍	♈ 11 20:38
13 21:40	☉ ☌	♉ 14 9:18
16 16:05	♂ △	♊ 16 21:28
19 7:18	☉ ⚹	♋ 19 8:12
21 9:27	☿ ⚹	♌ 21 16:14
23 9:14	☿ □	♍ 23 20:43
25 14:51	♂ ☌	♎ 25 21:55
27 6:37	♃ ☌	♏ 27 21:20
29 15:17	☿ ☍	♐ 29 21:03

☽ Phases & Eclipses (Dy Hr Mn)

7 7:52 ☾ 17♐02
15 4:19 ● 24♓52
23 7:33 ☽ 2♋58
30 2:26 ○ 9♎41

5 19:52 ☾ 16♑18
13 21:40 ● 24♈14
21 19:50 ☽ 1♌59
28 10:37 ○ 8♏26

Astro Data

1 March 2029
Julian Day # 47177
SVP 4♓50'51"
GC 27♐14.8 ⚵ 3♑29.2
Eris 25♈31.4 ⚶ 9♏47.0R
⚷ 4♉56.0 ⚴ 1♑42.4
☽ Mean ☊ 10♑59.1

1 April 2029
Julian Day # 47208
SVP 4♓50'48"
GC 27♐14.9 ⚵ 11♑23.1
Eris 25♈49.1 ⚶ 6♏17.5R
⚷ 6♉31.4 ⚴ 13♑54.0
☽ Mean ☊ 9♑20.5

LONGITUDE — May 2029

Day	Sid.Time	☉	0 hr ☽	Noon ☽	True ☊	☿	♀	♂	⚳	♃	♄	♅	♆	♇
1 Tu	2 38 49	11♉23 58	16♐23 09	23♐30 02	6♑04.2	26♉39.8	21♉20.7	25♍02.7	19♒30.7	20♎09.8	14♉05.8	12♊23.4	9♈47.0	10♒25.9
2 W	2 42 46	12 22 10	0♑29 46	7♑22 16	6D 03.5	26R 39.6	22 34.6	24R 59.9	19 44.4	20R 03.1	14 13.5	12 26.5	9 49.0	10 26.1
3 Th	2 46 42	13 20 21	14 07 39	20 46 10	6 04.2	26 34.2	23 48.5	24 57.7	19 57.8	19 56.5	14 21.2	12 29.7	9 51.0	10 26.4
4 F	2 50 39	14 18 31	27 18 09	3♒44 04	6R 05.2	26 23.8	25 02.4	24 56.4	20 11.1	19 50.0	14 28.9	12 32.9	9 52.9	10 26.6
5 Sa	2 54 36	15 16 39	10♒04 25	16 19 48	6 05.7	26 08.8	26 16.2	24D 55.8	20 24.1	19 43.6	14 36.6	12 36.1	9 54.9	10 26.7
6 Su	2 58 32	16 14 45	22 30 46	28 37 55	6 04.8	25 49.4	27 30.0	24 55.9	20 37.0	19 37.4	14 44.3	12 39.4	9 56.8	10 26.9
7 M	3 02 29	17 12 51	4♓41 50	10♓43 06	6 02.0	25 26.0	28 43.8	24 56.8	20 49.6	19 31.2	14 52.1	12 42.6	9 58.7	10 27.0
8 Tu	3 06 25	18 10 54	16 42 16	22 39 49	5 57.1	24 59.2	29 57.6	24 58.5	21 02.0	19 25.2	14 59.8	12 45.9	10 00.6	10 27.1
9 W	3 10 22	19 08 57	28 36 16	4♈32 01	5 50.4	24 29.4	1♊11.4	25 00.9	21 14.1	19 19.2	15 07.5	12 49.2	10 02.4	10 27.1
10 Th	3 14 18	20 06 57	10♈27 30	16 23 03	5 42.4	23 57.1	2 25.2	25 04.0	21 26.1	19 13.5	15 15.2	12 52.5	10 04.3	10R 27.2
11 F	3 18 15	21 04 57	22 19 00	28 15 38	5 33.9	23 23.0	3 38.9	25 07.8	21 37.8	19 07.8	15 22.9	12 55.9	10 06.1	10 27.2
12 Sa	3 22 11	22 02 55	4♉13 12	10♉11 55	5 25.6	22 47.7	4 52.6	25 12.3	21 49.2	19 02.3	15 30.6	12 59.2	10 07.9	10 27.2
13 Su	3 26 08	23 00 52	16 11 59	22 13 35	5 18.4	22 11.8	6 06.3	25 17.5	22 00.5	18 56.9	15 38.2	13 02.6	10 09.7	10 27.1
14 M	3 30 05	23 58 47	28 16 54	4♊22 05	5 12.9	21 35.9	7 20.0	25 23.5	22 11.4	18 51.7	15 45.9	13 06.0	10 11.5	10 27.0
15 Tu	3 34 01	24 56 40	10♊29 19	16 38 46	5 09.2	21 00.7	8 33.7	25 30.1	22 22.2	18 46.6	15 53.6	13 09.3	10 13.3	10 26.9
16 W	3 37 58	25 54 32	22 50 39	29 05 10	5D 07.6	20 26.8	9 47.3	25 37.3	22 32.7	18 41.6	16 01.2	13 12.8	10 15.0	10 26.8
17 Th	3 41 54	26 52 23	5♋22 33	11♋43 04	5 07.6	19 54.6	11 01.0	25 45.3	22 42.9	18 36.8	16 08.9	13 16.2	10 16.7	10 26.6
18 F	3 45 51	27 50 12	18 06 59	24 34 35	5 08.7	19 24.9	12 14.6	25 53.8	22 52.9	18 32.2	16 16.5	13 19.6	10 18.4	10 26.5
19 Sa	3 49 47	28 47 59	1♌06 10	7♌42 01	5 10.2	18 57.9	13 28.2	26 03.1	23 02.6	18 27.7	16 24.1	13 23.1	10 20.0	10 26.3
20 Su	3 53 44	29 45 44	14 22 25	21 07 36	5R 11.4	18 34.2	14 41.7	26 12.9	23 12.1	18 23.4	16 31.7	13 26.5	10 21.7	10 26.0
21 M	3 57 40	0♊43 28	27 57 47	4♍53 05	5 11.6	18 14.0	15 55.3	26 23.3	23 21.3	18 19.2	16 39.3	13 30.0	10 23.3	10 25.7
22 Tu	4 01 37	1 41 10	11♍53 32	18 59 03	5 10.4	17 57.7	17 08.8	26 34.4	23 30.2	18 15.2	16 46.8	13 33.5	10 24.9	10 25.5
23 W	4 05 34	2 38 50	26 09 28	3♎24 26	5 07.9	17 45.4	18 22.3	26 46.0	23 38.9	18 11.3	16 54.4	13 36.9	10 26.4	10 25.1
24 Th	4 09 30	3 36 29	10♎43 26	18 05 52	5 04.2	17 37.5	19 35.8	26 58.2	23 47.3	18 07.6	17 01.9	13 40.4	10 28.0	10 24.8
25 F	4 13 27	4 34 07	25 30 55	2♏57 43	5 00.0	17D 33.9	20 49.2	27 11.0	23 55.4	18 04.1	17 09.4	13 43.9	10 29.5	10 24.4
26 Sa	4 17 23	5 31 43	10♏25 15	17 52 29	4 55.9	17 34.7	22 02.6	27 24.3	24 03.2	18 00.8	17 16.8	13 47.4	10 31.0	10 24.0
27 Su	4 21 20	6 29 18	25 18 21	2♐41 49	4 52.5	17 40.1	23 16.1	27 38.2	24 10.8	17 57.6	17 24.3	13 50.9	10 32.5	10 23.6
28 M	4 25 16	7 26 51	10♐01 54	17 17 46	4 50.3	17 50.0	24 29.4	27 52.6	24 18.0	17 54.6	17 31.7	13 54.5	10 33.9	10 23.2
29 Tu	4 29 13	8 24 24	24 28 39	1♑34 00	4D 49.4	18 04.4	25 42.8	28 07.5	24 25.0	17 51.8	17 39.1	13 58.0	10 35.3	10 22.7
30 W	4 33 09	9 21 56	8♑33 21	15 26 28	4 49.7	18 23.2	26 56.2	28 22.9	24 31.7	17 49.1	17 46.5	14 01.5	10 36.7	10 22.2
31 Th	4 37 06	10 19 26	22 13 14	28 53 39	4 50.8	18 46.4	28 09.5	28 38.8	24 38.1	17 46.6	17 53.9	14 05.1	10 38.1	10 21.7

LONGITUDE — June 2029

Day	Sid.Time	☉	0 hr ☽	Noon ☽	True ☊	☿	♀	♂	⚳	♃	♄	♅	♆	♇
1 F	4 41 03	11♊16 56	5♒27 54	11♒56 15	4♑52.3	19♉13.8	29♊22.8	28♍55.2	24♒44.2	17♎44.3	18♉01.2	14♊08.6	10♈39.4	10♒21.2
2 Sa	4 44 59	12 14 25	18 19 02	24 36 42	4 53.7	19 45.5	0♋36.1	29 12.1	24 50.0	17R 42.2	18 08.5	14 12.1	10 40.7	10R 20.6
3 Su	4 48 56	13 11 53	0♓49 43	6♓58 38	4R 54.6	20 21.3	1 49.4	29 29.4	24 55.4	17 40.2	18 15.7	14 15.7	10 42.0	10 20.0
4 M	4 52 52	14 09 21	13 04 00	19 06 22	4 54.7	21 01.1	3 02.6	29 47.2	25 00.6	17 38.4	18 23.0	14 19.2	10 43.3	10 19.4
5 Tu	4 56 49	15 06 47	25 06 20	1♈04 28	4 53.8	21 44.9	4 15.9	0♎05.5	25 05.4	17 36.8	18 30.2	14 22.7	10 44.5	10 18.7
6 W	5 00 45	16 04 13	7♈01 19	12 57 26	4 52.1	22 32.4	5 29.1	0 24.2	25 09.9	17 35.4	18 37.3	14 26.3	10 45.7	10 18.1
7 Th	5 04 42	17 01 39	18 53 19	24 49 28	4 49.8	23 23.7	6 42.3	0 43.4	25 14.1	17 34.1	18 44.5	14 29.8	10 46.8	10 17.4
8 F	5 08 38	17 59 04	0♉46 19	6♉44 18	4 47.3	24 18.6	7 55.5	1 03.0	25 18.0	17 33.0	18 51.6	14 33.3	10 48.0	10 16.7
9 Sa	5 12 35	18 56 28	12 43 47	18 45 08	4 44.8	25 17.1	9 08.6	1 23.0	25 21.6	17 32.2	18 58.6	14 36.9	10 49.1	10 15.9
10 Su	5 16 32	19 53 51	24 48 37	0♊54 30	4 42.7	26 19.1	10 21.8	1 43.4	25 24.8	17 31.5	19 05.7	14 40.4	10 50.2	10 15.2
11 M	5 20 28	20 51 14	7♊03 01	13 14 21	4 41.2	27 24.5	11 34.9	2 04.3	25 27.6	17 30.9	19 12.7	14 43.9	10 51.2	10 14.4
12 Tu	5 24 25	21 48 36	19 28 40	25 46 04	4D 40.4	28 33.2	12 48.0	2 25.5	25 30.2	17 30.6	19 19.6	14 47.5	10 52.3	10 13.6
13 W	5 28 21	22 45 58	2♋06 39	8♋30 31	4 40.2	29 45.3	14 01.1	2 47.2	25 32.4	17D 30.4	19 26.5	14 51.0	10 53.3	10 12.8
14 Th	5 32 18	23 43 18	14 57 41	21 28 14	4 40.7	1♊00.6	15 14.2	3 09.2	25 34.2	17 30.5	19 33.4	14 54.5	10 54.2	10 12.0
15 F	5 36 14	24 40 38	28 02 11	4♌39 33	4 41.4	2 19.1	16 27.2	3 31.6	25 35.8	17 30.7	19 40.2	14 58.0	10 55.2	10 11.1
16 Sa	5 40 11	25 37 57	11♌20 20	18 04 32	4 42.3	3 40.8	17 40.2	3 54.4	25 36.9	17 31.0	19 47.0	15 01.5	10 56.1	10 10.2
17 Su	5 44 07	26 35 15	24 52 09	1♍43 08	4 43.0	5 05.6	18 53.2	4 17.5	25 37.7	17 31.6	19 53.7	15 05.0	10 56.9	10 09.3
18 M	5 48 04	27 32 33	8♍37 26	15 34 57	4R 43.4	6 33.5	20 06.2	4 41.0	25R 38.2	17 32.3	20 00.4	15 08.5	10 57.8	10 08.4
19 Tu	5 52 01	28 29 49	22 35 34	29 39 08	4 43.6	8 04.5	21 19.2	5 04.9	25 38.3	17 33.3	20 07.0	15 12.0	10 58.6	10 07.5
20 W	5 55 57	29 27 05	6♎45 23	13♎54 04	4 43.4	9 38.6	22 32.1	5 29.1	25 38.1	17 34.4	20 13.6	15 15.4	10 59.4	10 06.5
21 Th	5 59 54	0♋24 19	21 04 50	28 17 16	4 43.1	11 15.7	23 45.0	5 53.6	25 37.5	17 35.6	20 20.2	15 18.9	11 00.1	10 05.5
22 F	6 03 50	1 21 34	5♏30 53	12♏45 10	4 42.7	12 55.8	24 57.8	6 18.4	25 36.6	17 37.1	20 26.7	15 22.3	11 00.8	10 04.5
23 Sa	6 07 47	2 18 47	19 59 33	27 13 22	4 42.4	14 38.8	26 10.7	6 43.6	25 35.3	17 38.7	20 33.1	15 25.7	11 01.5	10 03.5
24 Su	6 11 43	3 16 00	4♐26 01	11♐36 50	4 42.3	16 24.7	27 23.5	7 09.1	25 33.6	17 40.5	20 39.5	15 29.2	11 02.2	10 02.5
25 M	6 15 40	4 13 13	18 45 11	25 50 28	4 42.2	18 13.5	28 36.3	7 34.9	25 31.6	17 42.5	20 45.8	15 32.6	11 02.8	10 01.4
26 Tu	6 19 36	5 10 25	2♑52 08	9♑49 43	4 42.2	20 05.1	29 49.0	8 01.0	25 29.3	17 44.7	20 52.1	15 36.0	11 03.4	10 00.4
27 W	6 23 33	6 07 37	16 42 48	23 31 04	4 42.2	21 59.3	1♌01.8	8 27.3	25 26.6	17 47.0	20 58.4	15 39.3	11 03.9	9 59.3
28 Th	6 27 30	7 04 49	0♒14 18	6♒52 24	4 42.0	23 56.0	2 14.5	8 54.0	25 23.5	17 49.5	21 04.5	15 42.7	11 04.5	9 58.2
29 F	6 31 26	8 02 01	13 25 19	19 53 10	4 41.7	25 55.2	3 27.1	9 20.9	25 20.1	17 52.2	21 10.6	15 46.0	11 05.0	9 57.1
30 Sa	6 35 23	8 59 13	26 16 04	2♓34 18	4 41.2	27 56.5	4 39.8	9 48.2	25 16.3	17 55.0	21 16.7	15 49.4	11 05.4	9 55.9

Astro Data	Planet Ingress	Last Aspect	☽ Ingress	Last Aspect	☽ Ingress	☽ Phases & Eclipses	Astro Data
Dy Hr Mn	Dy Hr Mn	Dy Hr Mn	Dy Hr Mn	Dy Hr Mn	Dy Hr Mn	Dy Hr Mn	1 May 2029
☿ R 1 23:06	♀ ♊ 8 12:46	1 14:37 ♂ □	♑ 1 23:09	2 2:19 ☿ □	♓ 2 22:24	5 9:48 ☾ 15♒11	Julian Day # 47238
♂ D 5 19:00	☉ ♊ 20 17:56	3 22:31 ☿ △	♒ 4 5:01	4 16:03 ☿ ✶	♈ 5 9:50	13 13:42 ● 23♉05	SVP 4♓50'44"
☽ 0N 8 3:51		6 9:31 ♀ □	♓ 6 14:42	6 21:21 ♃ ☍	♉ 7 22:27	21 4:16 ☽ 0♍25	GC 27♐14.9 ⚴ 14♑30.6
♇ R 11 4:18	♀ ♋ 2 0:11	8 16:41 ♂ ☍	♈ 9 2:49	10 2:07 ☿ ☌	♊ 10 10:13	27 18:37 ○ 6♐45	Eris 26♈08.6 ⚵ 29♎41.3R
☽ 0S 22 11:01	♂ ♎ 5 4:49	10 17:42 ♃ ☍	♉ 11 15:30	12 3:50 ☉ ☌	♋ 12 20:01		⚷ 8♉22.6 ⚶ 22♑08.3
♆ ✶ ♇ 22 19:27	☿ ♊ 13 16:46	13 18:08 ♂ △	♊ 14 3:24	14 8:27 ♄ ✶	♌ 15 3:34	4 1:19 ☾ 13♓44	☽ Mean ☊ 7♑45.2
☿ D 25 19:21	☉ ♋ 21 1:48	16 5:17 ♂ □	♋ 16 13:45	17 2:21 ☉ ✶	♍ 17 9:00	12 3:50 ● 21♊29	
♃ ⊼ ♄ 30 18:15	♀ ♌ 26 15:37	18 18:29 ☉ ✶	♌ 18 21:59	19 9:54 ☉ □	♎ 19 12:35	12 4:04:51 • P 0.458	1 June 2029
		20 7:36 ☿ □	♍ 21 3:33	21 3:45 ♀ □	♏ 21 14:51	19 9:54 ☽ 28♍25	Julian Day # 47269
☽ 0N 4 10:22		23 0:52 ♂ ☌	♎ 23 6:22	23 10:06 ♀ △	♐ 23 16:37	26 3:22 ○ 4♑50	SVP 4♓50'39"
♂ 0S 8 18:38		24 14:39 ♀ △	♏ 25 7:14	24 22:12 ♃ ✶	♑ 25 19:05	26 3:22 • T 1.844	GC 27♐15.0 ⚴ 11♑13.1R
♃ D 13 21:07		27 3:39 ♂ ✶	♐ 27 7:37	27 7:28 ♄ △	♒ 27 23:34		Eris 26♈26.4 ⚵ 24♎43.1R
☽ 0S 18 16:30		29 6:03 ♂ □	♑ 29 9:20	30 1:29 ☿ △	♓ 30 7:05		⚷ 10♉15.5 ⚶ 24♑41.9R
⚳ R 19 8:02		31 11:33 ♂ △	♒ 31 14:00				☽ Mean ☊ 6♑06.7

July 2029 — LONGITUDE

Day	Sid.Time	☉	0 hr ☽	Noon ☽	True ☊	☿	♀	♂	⚳	♃	♄	♅	♆	♇
1 Su	6 39 19	9♋56 24	8♓48 11	14♓58 06	4♑40.7	29♊59.9	5♌52.4	10♎15.7	25♒12.2	17♎58.0	21♉22.7	15♊52.7	11♈05.9	9♒54.8
2 M	6 43 16	10 53 36	21 04 29	27 07 49	4R 40.3	2♋05.0	7 05.0	10 43.5	25R 07.7	18 01.1	21 28.6	15 56.0	11 06.3	9R 53.6
3 Tu	6 47 12	11 50 48	3♈08 37	9♈07 27	4D 40.1	4 11.7	8 17.6	11 11.5	25 02.9	18 04.5	21 34.5	15 59.2	11 06.6	9 52.4
4 W	6 51 09	12 48 00	15 04 52	21 01 27	4 40.2	6 19.7	9 30.1	11 39.8	24 57.7	18 08.0	21 40.3	16 02.5	11 06.9	9 51.3
5 Th	6 55 05	13 45 13	26 57 46	2♉54 24	4 40.6	8 28.6	10 42.7	12 08.4	24 52.1	18 11.6	21 46.1	16 05.7	11 07.2	9 50.1
6 F	6 59 02	14 42 26	8♉51 55	14 50 51	4 41.4	10 38.3	11 55.2	12 37.2	24 46.3	18 15.5	21 51.8	16 09.0	11 07.5	9 48.8
7 Sa	7 02 59	15 39 39	20 51 42	26 54 59	4 42.4	12 48.3	13 07.6	13 06.3	24 40.0	18 19.5	21 57.4	16 12.2	11 07.7	9 47.6
8 Su	7 06 55	16 36 52	3♊01 08	9♊10 32	4 43.5	14 58.4	14 20.1	13 35.6	24 33.5	18 23.6	22 03.0	16 15.3	11 08.0	9 46.4
9 M	7 10 52	17 34 06	15 23 32	21 40 26	4 44.3	17 08.4	15 32.5	14 05.2	24 26.6	18 27.9	22 08.5	16 18.5	11 08.1	9 45.1
10 Tu	7 14 48	18 31 20	28 01 28	4♋26 46	4R 44.6	19 17.9	16 44.9	14 35.0	24 19.3	18 32.4	22 13.9	16 21.6	11 08.3	9 43.9
11 W	7 18 45	19 28 34	10♋56 25	17 30 27	4 44.2	21 26.7	17 57.2	15 05.1	24 11.8	18 37.0	22 19.2	16 24.7	11 08.4	9 42.6
12 Th	7 22 41	20 25 49	24 08 48	0♌51 19	4 43.2	23 34.7	19 09.6	15 35.4	24 03.9	18 41.8	22 24.5	16 27.8	11 08.4	9 41.3
13 F	7 26 38	21 23 03	7♌37 50	14 28 04	4 41.4	25 41.7	20 21.9	16 05.9	23 55.7	18 46.7	22 29.7	16 30.9	11R 08.5	9 40.0
14 Sa	7 30 35	22 20 18	21 21 43	28 18 27	4 39.1	27 47.4	21 34.1	16 36.7	23 47.2	18 51.8	22 34.9	16 33.9	11 08.5	9 38.7
15 Su	7 34 31	23 17 33	5♍17 51	12♍19 32	4 36.8	29 51.7	22 46.4	17 07.6	23 38.3	18 57.1	22 39.9	16 36.9	11 08.4	9 37.4
16 M	7 38 28	24 14 48	19 23 05	26 28 05	4 34.7	1♌54.6	23 58.6	17 38.8	23 29.2	19 02.5	22 44.9	16 39.9	11 08.4	9 36.1
17 Tu	7 42 24	25 12 02	3♎34 09	10♎40 54	4 33.2	3 55.9	25 10.7	18 10.3	23 19.8	19 08.0	22 49.9	16 42.9	11 08.3	9 34.8
18 W	7 46 21	26 09 18	17 47 59	24 55 03	4D 32.7	5 55.6	26 22.8	18 41.9	23 10.1	19 13.7	22 54.7	16 45.8	11 08.2	9 33.4
19 Th	7 50 17	27 06 33	2♏01 48	9♏07 56	4 33.0	7 53.6	27 34.9	19 13.7	23 00.2	19 19.5	22 59.5	16 48.7	11 08.0	9 32.1
20 F	7 54 14	28 03 48	16 13 12	23 17 20	4 34.1	9 49.9	28 47.0	19 45.8	22 50.0	19 25.5	23 04.1	16 51.6	11 07.8	9 30.7
21 Sa	7 58 10	29 01 04	0♐20 04	7♐21 10	4 35.5	11 44.5	29 59.0	20 18.0	22 39.5	19 31.6	23 08.7	16 54.4	11 07.6	9 29.4
22 Su	8 02 07	29 58 20	14 20 24	21 17 29	4R 36.7	13 37.3	1♍10.9	20 50.4	22 28.8	19 37.9	23 13.3	16 57.2	11 07.3	9 28.0
23 M	8 06 04	0♌55 36	28 12 11	5♑04 15	4 37.2	15 28.3	2 22.9	21 23.1	22 17.8	19 44.3	23 17.7	17 00.0	11 07.0	9 26.7
24 Tu	8 10 00	1 52 53	11♑53 25	18 39 27	4 36.6	17 17.6	3 34.7	21 55.9	22 06.7	19 50.8	23 22.1	17 02.8	11 06.7	9 25.3
25 W	8 13 57	2 50 10	25 22 08	2♒01 15	4 34.5	19 05.2	4 46.6	22 28.9	21 55.3	19 57.5	23 26.4	17 05.5	11 06.4	9 23.9
26 Th	8 17 53	3 47 28	8♒36 38	15 08 09	4 31.1	20 50.9	5 58.4	23 02.1	21 43.7	20 04.3	23 30.6	17 08.2	11 06.0	9 22.6
27 F	8 21 50	4 44 47	21 35 44	27 59 21	4 26.7	22 35.0	7 10.1	23 35.4	21 31.9	20 11.2	23 34.7	17 10.8	11 05.6	9 21.2
28 Sa	8 25 46	5 42 06	4♓19 03	10♓34 56	4 21.6	24 17.3	8 21.8	24 09.0	21 19.9	20 18.3	23 38.7	17 13.5	11 05.1	9 19.8
29 Su	8 29 43	6 39 27	16 47 09	22 55 56	4 16.5	25 57.8	9 33.5	24 42.7	21 07.7	20 25.5	23 42.6	17 16.1	11 04.7	9 18.4
30 M	8 33 39	7 36 48	29 01 35	5♈04 28	4 11.9	27 36.6	10 45.1	25 16.6	20 55.4	20 32.8	23 46.5	17 18.6	11 04.2	9 17.0
31 Tu	8 37 36	8 34 10	11♈04 58	17 03 33	4 08.4	29 13.7	11 56.7	25 50.7	20 42.9	20 40.2	23 50.3	17 21.1	11 03.6	9 15.7

August 2029 — LONGITUDE

Day	Sid.Time	☉	0 hr ☽	Noon ☽	True ☊	☿	♀	♂	⚳	♃	♄	♅	♆	♇
1 W	8 41 33	9♌31 34	23♈00 44	28♈57 02	4♑06.3	0♍49.1	13♍08.2	26♎24.9	20♒30.3	20♎47.8	23♉54.0	17♊23.6	11♈03.0	9♒14.3
2 Th	8 45 29	10 28 58	4♉53 02	10♉49 20	4D 05.6	2 22.8	14 19.7	26 59.4	20R 17.6	20 55.5	23 57.5	17 26.1	11R 02.4	9R 12.9
3 F	8 49 26	11 26 24	16 46 33	22 45 16	4 06.2	3 54.8	15 31.2	27 34.0	20 04.7	21 03.3	24 01.0	17 28.5	11 01.8	9 11.5
4 Sa	8 53 22	12 23 51	28 46 09	4♊49 46	4 07.6	5 25.0	16 42.6	28 08.7	19 51.7	21 11.3	24 04.5	17 30.9	11 01.2	9 10.1
5 Su	8 57 19	13 21 19	10♊56 43	17 07 33	4 09.2	6 53.4	17 54.0	28 43.7	19 38.7	21 19.4	24 07.8	17 33.2	11 00.5	9 08.7
6 M	9 01 15	14 18 48	23 22 46	29 42 50	4R 10.2	8 20.2	19 05.3	29 18.8	19 25.6	21 27.5	24 11.0	17 35.5	10 59.8	9 07.4
7 Tu	9 05 12	15 16 19	6♋08 06	12♋38 51	4 09.9	9 45.1	20 16.5	29 54.0	19 12.4	21 35.9	24 14.1	17 37.8	10 59.0	9 06.0
8 W	9 09 08	16 13 51	19 15 18	25 57 28	4 08.0	11 08.2	21 27.8	0♏29.5	18 59.2	21 44.3	24 17.2	17 40.0	10 58.2	9 04.6
9 Th	9 13 05	17 11 23	2♌45 19	9♌38 38	4 04.1	12 29.5	22 39.0	1 05.1	18 45.9	21 52.8	24 20.1	17 42.2	10 57.4	9 03.2
10 F	9 17 02	18 08 57	16 37 07	23 40 17	3 58.5	13 48.9	23 50.1	1 40.8	18 32.7	22 01.4	24 22.9	17 44.3	10 56.6	9 01.9
11 Sa	9 20 58	19 06 32	0♍47 34	7♍58 16	3 51.7	15 06.4	25 01.2	2 16.7	18 19.4	22 10.2	24 25.7	17 46.4	10 55.8	9 00.5
12 Su	9 24 55	20 04 08	15 11 39	22 26 53	3 44.6	16 21.9	26 12.2	2 52.8	18 06.1	22 19.1	24 28.3	17 48.5	10 54.9	8 59.2
13 M	9 28 51	21 01 45	29 43 10	6♎59 41	3 38.1	17 35.4	27 23.2	3 29.0	17 52.9	22 28.0	24 30.9	17 50.5	10 54.0	8 57.8
14 Tu	9 32 48	21 59 23	14♎15 42	21 30 31	3 33.0	18 46.8	28 34.1	4 05.4	17 39.7	22 37.1	24 33.3	17 52.5	10 53.0	8 56.5
15 W	9 36 44	22 57 02	28 43 33	5♏54 18	3 29.8	19 56.0	29 44.9	4 41.9	17 26.6	22 46.3	24 35.7	17 54.4	10 52.0	8 55.1
16 Th	9 40 41	23 54 42	13♏02 24	20 07 34	3D 28.6	21 02.9	0♎55.7	5 18.6	17 13.5	22 55.6	24 37.9	17 56.3	10 51.0	8 53.8
17 F	9 44 37	24 52 24	27 09 37	4♐08 28	3 28.8	22 07.4	2 06.5	5 55.4	17 00.5	23 05.0	24 40.1	17 58.2	10 50.0	8 52.5
18 Sa	9 48 34	25 50 06	11♐04 04	17 56 25	3 29.8	23 09.5	3 17.2	6 32.3	16 47.6	23 14.5	24 42.1	18 00.0	10 49.0	8 51.2
19 Su	9 52 31	26 47 49	24 45 36	1♑31 40	3R 30.4	24 09.0	4 27.8	7 09.4	16 34.9	23 24.1	24 44.1	18 01.7	10 47.9	8 49.9
20 M	9 56 27	27 45 33	8♑14 42	14 54 44	3 29.8	25 05.7	5 38.3	7 46.6	16 22.2	23 33.7	24 45.9	18 03.5	10 46.8	8 48.6
21 Tu	10 00 24	28 43 18	21 31 51	28 06 05	3 27.2	25 59.6	6 48.8	8 24.0	16 09.7	23 43.5	24 47.6	18 05.1	10 45.7	8 47.3
22 W	10 04 20	29 41 05	4♒37 25	11♒05 54	3 22.2	26 50.5	7 59.2	9 01.5	15 57.4	23 53.4	24 49.3	18 06.8	10 44.6	8 46.0
23 Th	10 08 17	0♍38 53	17 31 29	23 54 09	3 14.7	27 38.1	9 09.5	9 39.1	15 45.2	24 03.4	24 50.8	18 08.4	10 43.4	8 44.7
24 F	10 12 13	1 36 42	0♓13 54	6♓30 44	3 05.3	28 22.4	10 19.8	10 16.9	15 33.2	24 13.4	24 52.2	18 09.9	10 42.2	8 43.5
25 Sa	10 16 10	2 34 33	12 44 39	18 55 43	2 54.6	29 03.1	11 30.0	10 54.7	15 21.3	24 23.6	24 53.6	18 11.4	10 41.0	8 42.2
26 Su	10 20 06	3 32 25	25 04 00	1♈09 37	2 43.6	29 39.9	12 40.2	11 32.8	15 09.7	24 33.8	24 54.8	18 12.8	10 39.8	8 41.0
27 M	10 24 03	4 30 19	7♈12 46	13 13 40	2 33.4	0♎12.7	13 50.2	12 10.9	14 58.2	24 44.1	24 55.9	18 14.2	10 38.5	8 39.8
28 Tu	10 28 00	5 28 14	19 12 37	25 09 56	2 24.8	0 41.2	15 00.2	12 49.2	14 47.0	24 54.5	24 56.9	18 15.6	10 37.2	8 38.6
29 W	10 31 56	6 26 12	1♉06 02	7♉01 20	2 18.4	1 05.1	16 10.1	13 27.6	14 36.0	25 05.0	24 57.8	18 16.9	10 35.9	8 37.4
30 Th	10 35 53	7 24 11	12 56 23	18 51 41	2 14.4	1 24.2	17 20.0	14 06.1	14 25.2	25 15.6	24 58.6	18 18.1	10 34.6	8 36.2
31 F	10 39 49	8 22 12	24 47 50	0♊45 27	2D 12.6	1 38.2	18 29.7	14 44.8	14 14.7	25 26.2	24 59.3	18 19.3	10 33.3	8 35.0

Astro Data Dy Hr Mn	Planet Ingress Dy Hr Mn	Last Aspect Dy Hr Mn	☽ Ingress Dy Hr Mn	Last Aspect Dy Hr Mn	☽ Ingress Dy Hr Mn	☽ Phases & Eclipses Dy Hr Mn
☽0N 1 18:21	☿ ♋ 1 12:01	2 0:42 ♄ ⚹	♈ 2 17:43	1 6:37 ♂ ☍	♉ 1 14:07	3 17:57 ☾ 12♈05
♆R 14 2:09	☿ ♌ 15 13:37	4 6:08 ♃ ☍	♉ 5 6:08	3 14:32 ♄ ☌	♊ 4 2:27	11 15:51 ● 19♋38
☽0S 15 22:07	♀ ♍ 21 12:21	7 2:06 ♄ ☌	♊ 7 18:05	6 11:12 ♂ △	♋ 6 12:32	11 15:36:02 ● P 0.230
☽0N 29 3:05	☉ ♌ 22 12:42	9 5:51 ♃ △	♋ 10 3:42	8 9:01 ♄ ⚹	♌ 8 19:09	18 14:14 ☽ 26♎15
	☿ ♍ 31 23:35	11 20:46 ♄ ⚹	♌ 12 10:29	10 13:12 ♄ □	♍ 10 22:40	25 13:36 ○ 2♒54
☽0S 12 5:27		14 2:03 ♄ □	♍ 14 14:55	12 18:45 ♀ ☌	♎ 13 0:28	
♀0S 16 22:57	♂ ♏ 7 16:03	16 7:58 ☉ ⚹	♎ 16 17:58	14 13:52 ♃ ☌	♏ 15 2:07	2 11:15 ☾ 10♉27
☿0S 20 11:56	♀ ♎ 15 17:06	18 14:42 ♀ ⚹	♏ 18 20:34	16 19:42 ♄ ☍	♐ 17 4:52	10 1:56 ● 17♌45
☽0N 25 11:20	☉ ♍ 22 19:51	20 22:14 ♀ □	♐ 20 23:26	19 2:58 ☉ △	♑ 19 9:17	16 18:55 ☽ 24♏11
♃⊼♄ 28 18:02	☿ ♎ 27 2:21	22 11:11 ♂ ⚹	♑ 23 3:08	21 7:52 ☿ △	♒ 21 15:29	24 1:51 ○ 1♓12
		24 20:27 ♄ △	♒ 25 8:21	23 13:47 ♄ □	♓ 23 23:34	
		27 3:40 ♄ □	♓ 27 15:48	26 8:54 ☿ ☍	♈ 26 9:43	
		29 13:32 ♄ ⚹	♈ 30 1:56	28 11:28 ♃ ☍	♉ 28 21:46	
				31 0:22 ♄ ☌	♊ 31 10:29	

Astro Data

1 July 2029
Julian Day # 47299
SVP 4♓50'34"
GC 27♐15.1 ⚴ 3♑09.4R
Eris 26♈37.2 ⚵ 24♎35.6
⚷ 11♉42.9 ⚶ 20♑14.4R
☽ Mean ☊ 4♑31.4

1 August 2029
Julian Day # 47330
SVP 4♓50'29"
GC 27♐15.2 ⚴ 26♐37.5R
Eris 26♈39.1R ⚵ 28♎49.0
⚷ 12♉33.4 ⚶ 13♑26.0R
☽ Mean ☊ 2♑53.0

LONGITUDE — September 2029

Day	Sid.Time	☉	0 hr ☽	Noon ☽	True ☊	☿	♀	♂	⚳	♃	♄	♅	♆	♇
1 Sa	10 43 46	9♍20 15	6♊45 10	12♊47 40	2♑12.3	1♎46.9	19♎39.4	15♏23.5	14♒04.5	25♎36.9	24♉59.9	18♊20.5	10♈31.9	8♒33.9
2 Su	10 47 42	10 18 20	18 53 35	25 03 36	2R12.7	1R49.9	20 49.1	16 02.5	13R54.5	25 47.8	25 00.3	18 21.6	10R30.6	8R32.7
3 M	10 51 39	11 16 27	1♋18 20	7♋38 23	2 12.8	1 46.9	21 58.6	16 41.5	13 44.7	25 58.7	25 00.7	18 22.7	10 29.2	8 31.6
4 Tu	10 55 35	12 14 36	14 04 17	20 36 29	2 11.4	1 37.9	23 08.1	17 20.6	13 35.3	26 09.6	25 01.0	18 23.7	10 27.8	8 30.5
5 W	10 59 32	13 12 47	27 15 22	4♌01 07	2 07.8	1 22.6	24 17.5	17 59.9	13 26.1	26 20.7	25R01.1	18 24.6	10 26.3	8 29.4
6 Th	11 03 29	14 11 00	10♌53 49	17 53 21	2 01.6	1 00.9	25 26.8	18 39.3	13 17.3	26 31.8	25 01.1	18 25.6	10 24.9	8 28.3
7 F	11 07 25	15 09 14	24 59 26	2♍11 35	1 53.0	0 32.8	26 36.0	19 18.8	13 08.7	26 43.0	25 01.1	18 26.4	10 23.4	8 27.3
8 Sa	11 11 22	16 07 30	9♍29 06	16 51 07	1 42.7	29♍58.4	27 45.1	19 58.5	13 00.5	26 54.2	25 00.9	18 27.2	10 21.9	8 26.2
9 Su	11 15 18	17 05 48	24 16 38	1♎44 31	1 31.8	29 18.0	28 54.2	20 38.2	12 52.6	27 05.6	25 00.6	18 28.0	10 20.5	8 25.2
10 M	11 19 15	18 04 08	9♎13 36	16 42 39	1 21.6	28 31.8	0♏03.1	21 18.1	12 45.0	27 17.0	25 00.2	18 28.7	10 18.9	8 24.2
11 Tu	11 23 11	19 02 30	24 10 35	1♏36 18	1 13.2	27 40.5	1 12.0	21 58.1	12 37.7	27 28.4	24 59.7	18 29.3	10 17.4	8 23.2
12 W	11 27 08	20 00 53	8♏58 56	16 17 42	1 07.3	26 44.9	2 20.8	22 38.2	12 30.8	27 39.9	24 59.1	18 29.9	10 15.9	8 22.3
13 Th	11 31 04	20 59 17	23 32 03	0♐41 35	1 04.1	25 45.9	3 29.5	23 18.4	12 24.2	27 51.5	24 58.4	18 30.5	10 14.3	8 21.3
14 F	11 35 01	21 57 44	7♐46 03	14 45 23	1D02.9	24 44.6	4 38.0	23 58.8	12 18.0	28 03.2	24 57.6	18 31.0	10 12.8	8 20.4
15 Sa	11 38 57	22 56 12	21 39 38	28 28 55	1R02.8	23 42.3	5 46.5	24 39.2	12 12.1	28 14.9	24 56.6	18 31.5	10 11.2	8 19.5
16 Su	11 42 54	23 54 41	5♑13 28	11♑53 32	1 02.6	22 40.5	6 54.8	25 19.8	12 06.6	28 26.7	24 55.6	18 31.9	10 09.6	8 18.6
17 M	11 46 51	24 53 12	18 29 26	25 01 27	1 01.0	21 40.7	8 03.1	26 00.4	12 01.4	28 38.5	24 54.4	18 32.2	10 08.1	8 17.8
18 Tu	11 50 47	25 51 45	1♒29 53	7♒55 01	0 57.0	20 44.2	9 11.2	26 41.2	11 56.6	28 50.4	24 53.2	18 32.5	10 06.5	8 16.9
19 W	11 54 44	26 50 19	14 17 05	20 36 20	0 50.1	19 52.7	10 19.2	27 22.0	11 52.1	29 02.4	24 51.8	18 32.7	10 04.8	8 16.1
20 Th	11 58 40	27 48 55	26 52 56	3♓07 04	0 40.3	19 07.3	11 27.1	28 03.0	11 48.0	29 14.4	24 50.4	18 32.9	10 03.2	8 15.3
21 F	12 02 37	28 47 33	9♓18 50	15 28 22	0 28.1	18 29.4	12 34.8	28 44.1	11 44.3	29 26.4	24 48.8	18 33.1	10 01.6	8 14.5
22 Sa	12 06 33	29 46 13	21 35 45	27 41 06	0 14.3	17 59.8	13 42.5	29 25.2	11 40.9	29 38.5	24 47.2	18 33.2	10 00.0	8 13.8
23 Su	12 10 30	0♎44 54	3♈44 29	9♈46 02	0 00.2	17 39.3	14 50.0	0♐06.5	11 37.9	29 50.7	24 45.4	18R33.2	9 58.3	8 13.0
24 M	12 14 26	1 43 38	15 45 53	21 44 10	29♐46.8	17D28.5	15 57.3	0 47.9	11 35.2	0♏02.9	24 43.5	18 33.2	9 56.7	8 12.3
25 Tu	12 18 23	2 42 24	27 41 06	3♉36 56	29 35.3	17 27.7	17 04.6	1 29.3	11 32.9	0 15.1	24 41.6	18 33.1	9 55.0	8 11.6
26 W	12 22 20	3 41 12	9♉31 55	15 26 26	29 26.3	17 36.9	18 11.7	2 10.9	11 31.0	0 27.4	24 39.5	18 33.0	9 53.4	8 11.0
27 Th	12 26 16	4 40 02	21 20 49	27 15 33	29 20.2	17 56.0	19 18.6	2 52.5	11 29.4	0 39.7	24 37.3	18 32.8	9 51.7	8 10.3
28 F	12 30 13	5 38 54	3♊11 06	9♊08 01	29 16.7	18 24.9	20 25.4	3 34.3	11 28.2	0 52.1	24 35.1	18 32.6	9 50.1	8 09.7
29 Sa	12 34 09	6 37 49	15 06 51	21 08 14	29D15.4	19 02.9	21 32.1	4 16.2	11 27.3	1 04.6	24 32.7	18 32.3	9 48.4	8 09.1
30 Su	12 38 06	7 36 46	27 12 48	3♋21 13	29R15.3	19 49.7	22 38.6	4 58.1	11D26.8	1 17.0	24 30.3	18 32.0	9 46.7	8 08.6

LONGITUDE — October 2029

Day	Sid.Time	☉	0 hr ☽	Noon ☽	True ☊	☿	♀	♂	⚳	♃	♄	♅	♆	♇
1 M	12 42 02	8♎35 45	9♋34 08	15♋52 14	29♐15.2	20♍44.6	23♏45.0	5♐40.2	11♒26.7	1♏29.5	24♉27.7	18♊31.6	9♈45.1	8♒08.0
2 Tu	12 45 59	9 34 47	22 16 06	28 46 21	29R14.0	21 46.9	24 51.2	6 22.3	11 26.9	1 42.1	24R25.1	18R31.2	9R43.4	8R07.5
3 W	12 49 55	10 33 51	5♌23 26	12♌07 47	29 10.7	22 55.9	25 57.2	7 04.6	11 27.5	1 54.7	24 22.3	18 30.7	9 41.7	8 07.0
4 Th	12 53 52	11 32 57	18 59 37	25 59 01	29 04.9	24 11.0	27 03.1	7 46.9	11 28.5	2 07.3	24 19.5	18 30.2	9 40.0	8 06.5
5 F	12 57 49	12 32 05	3♍05 54	10♍19 55	28 56.6	25 31.3	28 08.8	8 29.4	11 29.8	2 20.0	24 16.6	18 29.6	9 38.4	8 06.1
6 Sa	13 01 45	13 31 15	17 40 31	25 06 53	28 46.5	26 56.3	29 14.3	9 11.9	11 31.4	2 32.7	24 13.6	18 29.0	9 36.7	8 05.7
7 Su	13 05 42	14 30 28	2♎38 03	10♎12 47	28 35.5	28 25.1	0♐19.6	9 54.5	11 33.4	2 45.4	24 10.5	18 28.3	9 35.0	8 05.3
8 M	13 09 38	15 29 43	17 49 46	25 27 37	28 25.2	29 57.4	1 24.8	10 37.2	11 35.8	2 58.2	24 07.3	18 27.6	9 33.4	8 04.9
9 Tu	13 13 35	16 28 59	3♏04 55	10♏40 18	28 16.5	1♎32.4	2 29.7	11 20.0	11 38.5	3 11.0	24 04.0	18 26.8	9 31.7	8 04.6
10 W	13 17 31	17 28 18	18 12 33	25 40 35	28 10.4	3 09.7	3 34.5	12 03.0	11 41.5	3 23.8	24 00.6	18 25.9	9 30.1	8 04.3
11 Th	13 21 28	18 27 39	3♐03 33	10♐20 48	28 07.0	4 48.8	4 39.0	12 45.9	11 44.9	3 36.6	23 57.2	18 25.1	9 28.4	8 04.0
12 F	13 25 24	19 27 01	17 31 52	24 36 31	28D05.9	6 29.4	5 43.4	13 29.0	11 48.7	3 49.5	23 53.7	18 24.1	9 26.8	8 03.8
13 Sa	13 29 21	20 26 25	1♑34 43	8♑26 32	28R06.1	8 11.0	6 47.5	14 12.2	11 52.7	4 02.4	23 50.1	18 23.2	9 25.1	8 03.6
14 Su	13 33 18	21 25 51	15 12 12	21 52 01	28 06.4	9 53.5	7 51.3	14 55.4	11 57.1	4 15.4	23 46.4	18 22.1	9 23.5	8 03.4
15 M	13 37 14	22 25 19	28 26 21	4♒55 40	28 05.6	11 36.5	8 54.9	15 38.8	12 01.9	4 28.3	23 42.7	18 21.1	9 21.9	8 03.2
16 Tu	13 41 11	23 24 48	11♒20 21	17 40 53	28 02.9	13 19.9	9 58.3	16 22.2	12 06.9	4 41.3	23 38.9	18 19.9	9 20.3	8 03.1
17 W	13 45 07	24 24 19	23 57 40	0♓11 09	27 57.6	15 03.4	11 01.4	17 05.7	12 12.3	4 54.3	23 35.0	18 18.8	9 18.7	8 02.9
18 Th	13 49 04	25 23 52	6♓21 41	12 29 37	27 49.8	16 46.9	12 04.2	17 49.2	12 18.0	5 07.3	23 31.1	18 17.6	9 17.1	8 02.8
19 F	13 53 00	26 23 26	18 35 17	24 38 58	27 39.7	18 30.3	13 06.8	18 32.9	12 24.0	5 20.3	23 27.0	18 16.3	9 15.5	8 02.8
20 Sa	13 56 57	27 23 03	0♈40 53	6♈41 18	27 28.4	20 13.5	14 09.0	19 16.6	12 30.3	5 33.3	23 23.0	18 15.0	9 13.9	8D02.8
21 Su	14 00 53	28 22 41	12 40 22	18 38 18	27 16.6	21 56.4	15 11.0	20 00.4	12 37.0	5 46.4	23 18.8	18 13.7	9 12.4	8 02.8
22 M	14 04 50	29 22 21	24 35 16	0♉31 27	27 05.4	23 39.0	16 12.6	20 44.3	12 43.9	5 59.4	23 14.6	18 12.3	9 10.8	8 02.8
23 Tu	14 08 46	0♏22 04	6♉27 00	12 22 09	26 55.8	25 21.1	17 13.9	21 28.2	12 51.1	6 12.5	23 10.4	18 10.8	9 09.3	8 02.8
24 W	14 12 43	1 21 48	18 17 05	24 12 04	26 48.5	27 02.9	18 14.9	22 12.3	12 58.7	6 25.6	23 06.1	18 09.3	9 07.8	8 02.9
25 Th	14 16 40	2 21 35	0♊07 23	6♊03 19	26 43.7	28 44.1	19 15.5	22 56.4	13 06.5	6 38.7	23 01.7	18 07.8	9 06.3	8 03.0
26 F	14 20 36	3 21 23	12 00 16	17 58 36	26D41.3	0♏24.9	20 15.8	23 40.5	13 14.6	6 51.8	22 57.3	18 06.3	9 04.8	8 03.2
27 Sa	14 24 33	4 21 14	23 58 45	0♋01 14	26 40.9	2 05.2	21 15.7	24 24.8	13 23.0	7 04.9	22 52.8	18 04.7	9 03.3	8 03.3
28 Su	14 28 29	5 21 07	6♋06 31	12 15 11	26 41.8	3 44.9	22 15.3	25 09.1	13 31.7	7 18.1	22 48.3	18 03.0	9 01.8	8 03.5
29 M	14 32 26	6 21 02	18 27 47	24 44 54	26R43.0	5 24.2	23 14.4	25 53.5	13 40.7	7 31.2	22 43.8	18 01.3	9 00.4	8 03.7
30 Tu	14 36 22	7 21 00	1♌07 06	7♌34 57	26 43.5	7 03.0	24 13.1	26 38.0	13 49.9	7 44.3	22 39.2	17 59.6	8 58.9	8 04.0
31 W	14 40 19	8 20 59	14 08 56	20 49 31	26 42.7	8 41.3	25 11.5	27 22.5	13 59.4	7 57.5	22 34.5	17 57.9	8 57.5	8 04.3

Astro Data

	Dy Hr Mn
☿R	2 12:18
♄R	6 8:34
☽0S	8 14:51
☿0N	16 9:42
☽0N	21 18:10
☉0S	22 17:39
♅R	23 16:22
☿D	25 2:00
⚳D	1 8:42
☽0S	6 1:19
♃□♅	10 15:47
☿0S	11 7:43
☽0N	18 23:35
♇D	21 3:54

Planet Ingress

		Dy Hr Mn
☿	♍R	8 10:59
♀	♏	10 10:54
☉	♎	22 17:38
♂	♐	23 8:14
☊	♐R	23 12:18
♃	♏	24 6:24
♀	♐	7 4:47
☿	♎	8 12:40
☉	♏	23 3:08
☿	♏	26 6:04

Last Aspect / ☽ Ingress (September)

Last Aspect Dy Hr Mn		☽ Ingress	Dy Hr Mn
2 13:27	♃ △	♋	2 21:30
4 22:11	♃ □	♌	5 4:54
7 2:46	♃ ⚹	♍	7 8:22
9 8:15	☿ ☌	♎	9 9:12
11 5:14	♃ ☌	♏	11 9:24
13 4:16	☿ ⚹	♐	13 10:50
15 11:35	♃ ⚹	♑	15 14:41
17 18:48	♃ □	♒	17 21:13
20 4:24	♃ △	♓	20 5:59
22 16:29	☉ ☍	♈	22 16:35
24 5:36	♅ ⚹	♉	25 4:41
27 6:40	♄ ☌	♊	27 17:33
29 7:36	☿ □	♋	30 5:28

Last Aspect / ☽ Ingress (October)

Last Aspect Dy Hr Mn		☽ Ingress	Dy Hr Mn
2 4:07	♀ △	♌	2 14:15
4 13:58	♀ □	♍	4 18:48
6 19:06	♀ ⚹	♎	6 19:49
8 1:00	♅ △	♏	8 19:09
10 9:19	♄ ☍	♐	10 19:01
12 2:35	☉ ⚹	♑	12 21:16
14 15:27	♄ △	♒	15 2:52
16 23:53	☉ △	♓	17 11:38
19 9:38	♄ ⚹	♈	19 22:38
22 9:27	☉ ☍	♉	22 10:56
24 9:47	♄ ☌	♊	24 23:45
27 0:08	♂ ☍	♋	27 11:58
29 8:11	♄ ⚹	♌	29 21:54

☽ Phases & Eclipses

Dy Hr Mn		
1 4:33	☾	9♊02
8 10:44	●	16♍04
15 1:29	☽	22♐31
22 16:29	○	29♓57
30 20:57	☾	7♋59
7 19:14	●	14♎48
14 11:09	☽	21♑24
22 9:27	○	29♈16
30 11:32	☾	7♌20

Astro Data

1 September 2029
Julian Day # 47361
SVP 4♓50'26"
GC 27♐15.2 ⚴ 26♐17.5
Eris 26♈31.3R ⚵ 6♏01.6
⚷ 12♉32.1R ⚶ 12♑14.2
☽ Mean ☊ 1♑14.5

1 October 2029
Julian Day # 47391
SVP 4♓50'22"
GC 27♐15.3 ⚴ 0♑59.3
Eris 26♈16.5R ⚵ 14♏45.9
⚷ 11♉42.4R ⚶ 17♑34.8
☽ Mean ☊ 29♐39.1

November 2029 LONGITUDE

Day	Sid.Time	☉	0 hr ☽	Noon ☽	True ☊	☿	♀	♂	⚳	♃	♄	♅	♆	♇
1 Th	14 44 15	9♏21 01	27♌37 02	4♍31 44	26♐40.0	10♏19.1	26♐09.3	28♐07.2	14♒09.2	8♏10.6	22♉29.9	17♊56.1	8♈56.1	8♒04.6
2 F	14 48 12	10 21 05	11♍33 41	18 42 47	26R35.3	11 56.5	27 06.8	28 51.8	14 19.3	8 23.7	22R25.1	17R54.2	8R54.8	8 04.9
3 Sa	14 52 09	11 21 10	25 58 43	3♎20 59	26 29.2	13 33.4	28 03.7	29 36.6	14 29.6	8 36.9	22 20.4	17 52.3	8 53.4	8 05.3
4 Su	14 56 05	12 21 18	10♎48 49	18 21 16	26 22.2	15 09.8	29 00.2	0♑21.4	14 40.1	8 50.0	22 15.6	17 50.4	8 52.1	8 05.7
5 M	15 00 02	13 21 28	25 57 13	3♏35 22	26 15.5	16 45.9	29 56.2	1 06.3	14 51.0	9 03.1	22 10.9	17 48.5	8 50.8	8 06.1
6 Tu	15 03 58	14 21 40	11♏14 22	18 52 49	26 09.9	18 21.5	0♑51.6	1 51.3	15 02.1	9 16.3	22 06.0	17 46.5	8 49.5	8 06.5
7 W	15 07 55	15 21 54	26 29 21	4♐02 43	26 06.1	19 56.7	1 46.5	2 36.3	15 13.4	9 29.4	22 01.2	17 44.5	8 48.2	8 07.0
8 Th	15 11 51	16 22 09	11♐31 47	18 55 37	26D04.4	21 31.6	2 40.9	3 21.4	15 25.0	9 42.5	21 56.4	17 42.4	8 46.9	8 07.5
9 F	15 15 48	17 22 26	26 13 29	3♑24 52	26 04.4	23 06.0	3 34.6	4 06.6	15 36.8	9 55.6	21 51.5	17 40.4	8 45.7	8 08.0
10 Sa	15 19 44	18 22 45	10♑29 26	17 27 03	26 05.5	24 40.2	4 27.7	4 51.8	15 48.9	10 08.7	21 46.6	17 38.3	8 44.5	8 08.6
11 Su	15 23 41	19 23 04	24 17 45	1♒01 42	26 07.1	26 14.0	5 20.2	5 37.1	16 01.2	10 21.8	21 41.8	17 36.1	8 43.3	8 09.2
12 M	15 27 38	20 23 26	7♒39 11	14 10 36	26R08.2	27 47.5	6 11.9	6 22.5	16 13.7	10 34.9	21 36.9	17 34.0	8 42.2	8 09.8
13 Tu	15 31 34	21 23 48	20 36 23	26 57 01	26 08.2	29 20.7	7 03.0	7 07.9	16 26.4	10 47.9	21 32.0	17 31.8	8 41.1	8 10.4
14 W	15 35 31	22 24 12	3♓13 00	9♓24 53	26 06.7	0♐53.6	7 53.3	7 53.3	16 39.4	11 00.9	21 27.1	17 29.6	8 39.9	8 11.1
15 Th	15 39 27	23 24 37	15 33 09	21 38 19	26 03.7	2 26.2	8 42.9	8 38.8	16 52.6	11 13.9	21 22.2	17 27.3	8 38.9	8 11.8
16 F	15 43 24	24 25 04	27 40 52	3♈41 15	25 59.3	3 58.5	9 31.6	9 24.4	17 06.0	11 26.9	21 17.3	17 25.0	8 37.8	8 12.5
17 Sa	15 47 20	25 25 32	9♈39 54	15 37 11	25 54.0	5 30.6	10 19.5	10 10.0	17 19.6	11 39.9	21 12.4	17 22.7	8 36.8	8 13.3
18 Su	15 51 17	26 26 01	21 33 30	27 29 09	25 48.4	7 02.4	11 06.6	10 55.7	17 33.5	11 52.9	21 07.6	17 20.4	8 35.8	8 14.1
19 M	15 55 13	27 26 32	3♉24 26	9♉19 38	25 43.1	8 34.0	11 52.7	11 41.4	17 47.5	12 05.8	21 02.7	17 18.1	8 34.8	8 14.9
20 Tu	15 59 10	28 27 04	15 15 00	21 10 46	25 38.6	10 05.3	12 37.9	12 27.2	18 01.8	12 18.7	20 57.9	17 15.7	8 33.9	8 15.7
21 W	16 03 07	29 27 38	27 07 11	3♊04 26	25 35.4	11 36.4	13 22.1	13 13.1	18 16.2	12 31.6	20 53.1	17 13.4	8 32.9	8 16.5
22 Th	16 07 03	0♐28 14	9♊02 46	15 02 23	25D33.5	13 07.2	14 05.3	13 58.9	18 30.8	12 44.4	20 48.3	17 11.0	8 32.1	8 17.4
23 F	16 11 00	1 28 50	21 03 34	27 06 31	25 33.1	14 37.7	14 47.4	14 44.9	18 45.7	12 57.3	20 43.5	17 08.5	8 31.2	8 18.3
24 Sa	16 14 56	2 29 29	3♋11 33	9♋18 57	25 33.7	16 08.0	15 28.4	15 30.8	19 00.7	13 10.1	20 38.8	17 06.1	8 30.4	8 19.3
25 Su	16 18 53	3 30 09	15 29 01	21 42 07	25 35.1	17 37.9	16 08.3	16 16.9	19 15.9	13 22.8	20 34.1	17 03.7	8 29.6	8 20.2
26 M	16 22 49	4 30 50	27 58 36	4♌18 49	25 36.8	19 07.6	16 46.9	17 02.9	19 31.3	13 35.6	20 29.4	17 01.2	8 28.8	8 21.2
27 Tu	16 26 46	5 31 33	10♌43 11	17 12 02	25 38.2	20 36.8	17 24.3	17 49.1	19 46.9	13 48.3	20 24.8	16 58.7	8 28.0	8 22.2
28 W	16 30 42	6 32 18	23 45 46	0♍24 42	25R39.0	22 05.7	18 00.5	18 35.2	20 02.6	14 00.9	20 20.2	16 56.2	8 27.3	8 23.2
29 Th	16 34 39	7 33 04	7♍09 07	13 59 14	25 39.0	23 34.1	18 35.2	19 21.5	20 18.6	14 13.5	20 15.6	16 53.7	8 26.6	8 24.3
30 F	16 38 36	8 33 51	20 55 10	27 56 58	25 38.2	25 02.0	19 08.6	20 07.7	20 34.7	14 26.1	20 11.1	16 51.2	8 26.0	8 25.4

December 2029 LONGITUDE

Day	Sid.Time	☉	0 hr ☽	Noon ☽	True ☊	☿	♀	♂	⚳	♃	♄	♅	♆	♇
1 Sa	16 42 32	9♐34 40	5♎04 29	12♎17 30	25♐36.6	26♐29.3	19♑40.5	20♑54.0	20♒50.9	14♏38.7	20♉06.6	16♊48.7	8♈25.4	8♒26.5
2 Su	16 46 29	10 35 31	19 35 35	26 58 09	25R34.7	27 55.9	20 10.9	21 40.4	21 07.4	14 51.2	20R02.2	16R46.2	8R24.8	8 27.6
3 M	16 50 25	11 36 23	4♏24 29	11♏53 42	25 32.8	29 21.7	20 39.7	22 26.8	21 24.0	15 03.7	19 57.8	16 43.6	8 24.2	8 28.7
4 Tu	16 54 22	12 37 16	19 24 48	26 56 41	25 31.3	0♑46.7	21 06.9	23 13.2	21 40.8	15 16.1	19 53.5	16 41.1	8 23.7	8 29.9
5 W	16 58 18	13 38 11	4♐28 14	11♐58 17	25D30.4	2 10.5	21 32.4	23 59.7	21 57.7	15 28.5	19 49.2	16 38.6	8 23.2	8 31.1
6 Th	17 02 15	14 39 07	19 25 45	26 49 37	25 30.1	3 33.2	21 56.1	24 46.2	22 14.8	15 40.8	19 45.0	16 36.0	8 22.8	8 32.3
7 F	17 06 12	15 40 03	4♑08 59	11♑23 05	25 30.4	4 54.4	22 18.0	25 32.8	22 32.1	15 53.1	19 40.9	16 33.5	8 22.4	8 33.6
8 Sa	17 10 08	16 41 01	18 31 18	25 33 14	25 31.1	6 14.0	22 38.0	26 19.4	22 49.5	16 05.3	19 36.8	16 30.9	8 22.0	8 34.8
9 Su	17 14 05	17 41 59	2♒28 37	9♒17 20	25 31.9	7 31.6	22 56.0	27 06.0	23 07.0	16 17.5	19 32.8	16 28.4	8 21.6	8 36.1
10 M	17 18 01	18 42 58	15 59 25	22 35 04	25 32.7	8 47.0	23 12.0	27 52.7	23 24.7	16 29.6	19 28.8	16 25.8	8 21.3	8 37.4
11 Tu	17 21 58	19 43 57	29 04 33	5♓28 15	25 33.2	9 59.7	23 25.9	28 39.4	23 42.6	16 41.7	19 24.9	16 23.3	8 21.0	8 38.7
12 W	17 25 54	20 44 57	11♓46 36	18 00 06	25R33.4	11 09.4	23 37.6	29 26.1	24 00.6	16 53.7	19 21.1	16 20.7	8 20.7	8 40.1
13 Th	17 29 51	21 45 57	24 09 17	0♈14 44	25 33.3	12 15.7	23 47.0	0♒12.8	24 18.7	17 05.7	19 17.4	16 18.2	8 20.5	8 41.4
14 F	17 33 47	22 46 58	6♈17 01	12 16 41	25 33.1	13 17.8	23 54.2	0 59.6	24 37.0	17 17.6	19 13.7	16 15.7	8 20.3	8 42.8
15 Sa	17 37 44	23 48 00	18 14 20	24 10 29	25 32.9	14 15.3	23 59.0	1 46.4	24 55.4	17 29.4	19 10.1	16 13.1	8 20.2	8 44.2
16 Su	17 41 41	24 49 02	0♉05 40	6♉00 24	25D32.7	15 07.4	24R01.4	2 33.3	25 13.9	17 41.2	19 06.6	16 10.6	8 20.1	8 45.7
17 M	17 45 37	25 50 04	11 55 09	17 50 20	25 32.7	15 53.4	24 01.4	3 20.1	25 32.5	17 52.9	19 03.2	16 08.1	8 20.0	8 47.1
18 Tu	17 49 34	26 51 07	23 46 22	29 43 37	25 32.8	16 32.5	23 58.9	4 07.0	25 51.3	18 04.5	18 59.9	16 05.6	8D19.9	8 48.6
19 W	17 53 30	27 52 11	5♊42 25	11♊43 03	25 32.9	17 03.8	23 53.9	4 53.9	26 10.2	18 16.1	18 56.7	16 03.1	8 19.9	8 50.0
20 Th	17 57 27	28 53 15	17 45 46	23 50 48	25R33.0	17 26.5	23 46.4	5 40.9	26 29.3	18 27.6	18 53.5	16 00.7	8 19.9	8 51.5
21 F	18 01 23	29 54 19	29 58 21	6♋08 36	25 33.0	17R39.5	23 36.4	6 27.8	26 48.4	18 39.0	18 50.4	15 58.2	8 20.0	8 53.1
22 Sa	18 05 20	0♑55 24	12♋21 40	18 37 41	25 32.6	17 42.1	23 23.8	7 14.8	27 07.7	18 50.4	18 47.4	15 55.8	8 20.1	8 54.6
23 Su	18 09 16	1 56 30	24 56 47	1♌19 02	25 31.9	17 33.6	23 08.9	8 01.8	27 27.1	19 01.7	18 44.6	15 53.3	8 20.2	8 56.1
24 M	18 13 13	2 57 36	7♌44 34	14 13 25	25 31.0	17 13.5	22 51.4	8 48.8	27 46.6	19 12.9	18 41.8	15 50.9	8 20.4	8 57.7
25 Tu	18 17 10	3 58 42	20 45 43	27 21 30	25 30.0	16 41.6	22 31.6	9 35.9	28 06.2	19 24.0	18 39.1	15 48.5	8 20.6	8 59.3
26 W	18 21 06	4 59 50	4♍00 51	10♍43 51	25 29.0	15 58.1	22 09.6	10 22.9	28 25.9	19 35.1	18 36.4	15 46.1	8 20.8	9 00.9
27 Th	18 25 03	6 00 57	17 30 32	24 20 55	25D28.2	15 03.6	21 45.3	11 10.0	28 45.7	19 46.1	18 33.9	15 43.8	8 21.1	9 02.5
28 F	18 28 59	7 02 06	1♎15 02	8♎12 50	25 28.0	13 59.5	21 19.0	11 57.1	29 05.6	19 57.0	18 31.5	15 41.5	8 21.4	9 04.1
29 Sa	18 32 56	8 03 14	15 14 14	22 19 06	25 28.4	12 47.4	20 50.8	12 44.2	29 25.7	20 07.8	18 29.2	15 39.1	8 21.7	9 05.7
30 Su	18 36 52	9 04 24	29 27 13	6♏38 19	25 29.2	11 29.5	20 20.8	13 31.4	29 45.8	20 18.5	18 27.0	15 36.8	8 22.1	9 07.4
31 M	18 40 49	10 05 34	13♏52 02	21 07 54	25 30.4	10 08.3	19 49.2	14 18.5	0♓06.1	20 29.2	18 24.9	15 34.6	8 22.5	9 09.1

Astro Data

	Dy Hr Mn
♃□♇	1 0:44
☽0S	2 11:03
♃⚻♆	4 15:26
☽0N	15 4:49
☽0S	29 18:40
♆✶♇	30 20:57
♃⚻♅	10 5:45
☽0N	12 11:34
♀R	16 23:48
♆D	19 8:23
☿R	22 5:49
♃☍♄	22 7:03
☽0S	27 0:30

Planet Ingress

	Dy Hr Mn
♂ ♑	4 0:32
♀ ♑	5 13:39
☿ ♐	13 22:09
☉ ♐	22 0:49
☿ ♑	3 22:47
♂ ♒	13 5:25
☉ ♑	21 14:14
⚳ ♓	31 4:49

Last Aspect / ☽ Ingress

Last Aspect Dy Hr Mn		☽ Ingress Dy Hr Mn
1 0:14	♂△	♍ 1 4:10
3 5:36	♂□	♎ 3 6:34
5 5:54	♀✶	♏ 5 6:22
6 17:03	♄☍	♐ 7 5:34
8 10:01	♅☍	♑ 9 6:17
11 2:19	☿✶	♒ 11 10:09
13 17:13	☿□	♓ 13 17:49
15 15:50	☉△	♈ 16 4:38
17 15:32	♅✶	♉ 18 17:06
21 4:03	☉☍	♊ 21 5:49
22 16:16	♅☌	♋ 23 17:43
25 9:50	♄✶	♌ 26 3:51
27 19:03	☿△	♍ 28 11:16
30 6:28	☿□	♎ 30 15:28

Last Aspect / ☽ Ingress

Last Aspect Dy Hr Mn		☽ Ingress Dy Hr Mn
2 13:43	☿✶	♏ 2 16:54
4 5:45	♂✶	♐ 4 16:52
5 19:29	♅☍	♑ 6 17:11
8 13:24	♂☌	♒ 8 19:41
10 6:21	♄□	♓ 11 1:43
12 23:07	♀✶	♈ 13 11:31
15 11:37	♀□	♉ 15 23:48
18 0:28	♀△	♊ 18 12:33
20 22:46	☉☍	♋ 21 0:03
22 20:54	♀☍	♌ 23 9:32
24 21:18	♃□	♍ 25 16:47
27 7:36	♀△	♎ 27 21:50
29 9:36	♀□	♏ 30 0:55

☽ Phases & Eclipses

Dy Hr Mn	
6 4:24	● 14♏03
13 0:35	☽ 20♒55
21 4:03	○ 29♉08
28 23:48	☾ 7♍02
5 14:52	● 13♐45
5 15:02:37	P 0.891
12 17:49	☽ 21♓00
20 22:46	○ 29♊21
20 22:42	T 1.117
28 9:49	☾ 6♎57

Astro Data

1 November 2029
Julian Day # 47422
SVP 4♓50'19"
GC 27♐15.4 ⚳ 9♑02.9
Eris 25♈58.2R ⚵ 24♏50.8
⚷ 10♉18.1R ⚶ 27♑34.3
☽ Mean ☊ 28♐00.6

1 December 2029
Julian Day # 47452
SVP 4♓50'15"
GC 27♐15.4 ⚳ 18♑35.5
Eris 25♈42.6R ⚵ 5♐04.3
⚷ 8♉55.0R ⚶ 9♒45.2
☽ Mean ☊ 26♐25.3

LONGITUDE — January 2030

Day	Sid.Time	☉	0 hr ☽	Noon ☽	True ☊	☿	♀	♂	⚳	♃	♄	♅	♆	♇
1 Tu	18 44 45	11♑06 44	28♏25 23	5♐43 52	25♐31.4	8♑46.7	19♑16.2	15♒05.7	0♓26.4	20♏39.7	18♉22.9	15♊32.3	8♈22.9	9♒10.7
2 W	18 48 42	12 07 55	13♐02 39	20 21 00	25R 32.1	7R 27.2	18R 42.0	15 52.9	0 46.9	20 50.2	18R 21.0	15R 30.1	8 23.4	9 12.4
3 Th	18 52 39	13 09 06	27 38 08	4♑53 16	25 32.0	6 12.2	18 06.8	16 40.0	1 07.4	21 00.6	18 19.2	15 28.0	8 23.9	9 14.1
4 F	18 56 35	14 10 16	12♑05 37	19 14 29	25 30.8	5 03.9	17 30.9	17 27.3	1 28.0	21 10.9	18 17.5	15 25.8	8 24.4	9 15.9
5 Sa	19 00 32	15 11 27	26 19 11	3♒19 10	25 28.7	4 03.7	16 54.5	18 14.5	1 48.8	21 21.1	18 15.9	15 23.7	8 25.0	9 17.6
6 Su	19 04 28	16 12 38	10♒13 57	17 03 13	25 25.7	3 12.8	16 17.9	19 01.7	2 09.6	21 31.2	18 14.4	15 21.6	8 25.6	9 19.3
7 M	19 08 25	17 13 48	23 46 43	0♓24 24	25 22.3	2 31.8	15 41.3	19 48.9	2 30.5	21 41.1	18 13.1	15 19.5	8 26.3	9 21.1
8 Tu	19 12 21	18 14 58	6♓56 16	13 22 28	25 19.0	2 00.9	15 04.9	20 36.2	2 51.5	21 51.0	18 11.8	15 17.5	8 27.0	9 22.8
9 W	19 16 18	19 16 07	19 43 17	25 59 02	25 16.2	1 39.9	14 29.0	21 23.4	3 12.6	22 00.8	18 10.7	15 15.5	8 27.7	9 24.6
10 Th	19 20 14	20 17 16	2♈10 10	8♈17 10	25 14.4	1D 28.7	13 53.9	22 10.6	3 33.7	22 10.5	18 09.7	15 13.5	8 28.4	9 26.4
11 F	19 24 11	21 18 24	14 20 35	20 20 59	25D 13.7	1 26.5	13 19.7	22 57.9	3 54.9	22 20.1	18 08.7	15 11.6	8 29.2	9 28.2
12 Sa	19 28 08	22 19 32	26 18 59	2♉15 12	25 14.1	1 32.9	12 46.8	23 45.1	4 16.3	22 29.5	18 07.9	15 09.7	8 30.0	9 30.0
13 Su	19 32 04	23 20 40	8♉10 18	14 04 52	25 15.5	1 47.2	12 15.3	24 32.4	4 37.6	22 38.9	18 07.2	15 07.8	8 30.9	9 31.8
14 M	19 36 01	24 21 46	19 59 32	25 54 55	25 17.4	2 08.7	11 45.5	25 19.6	4 59.1	22 48.1	18 06.7	15 06.0	8 31.7	9 33.6
15 Tu	19 39 57	25 22 52	1♊51 34	7♊50 02	25 19.2	2 36.8	11 17.4	26 06.9	5 20.7	22 57.3	18 06.2	15 04.2	8 32.7	9 35.4
16 W	19 43 54	26 23 58	13 50 47	19 54 18	25R 20.3	3 10.9	10 51.3	26 54.1	5 42.3	23 06.3	18 05.8	15 02.5	8 33.6	9 37.2
17 Th	19 47 50	27 25 03	26 00 57	2♋11 05	25 20.2	3 50.3	10 27.2	27 41.4	6 03.9	23 15.2	18 05.6	15 00.8	8 34.6	9 39.1
18 F	19 51 47	28 26 07	8♋24 57	14 42 46	25 18.5	4 34.5	10 05.4	28 28.6	6 25.7	23 24.0	18D 05.5	14 59.1	8 35.6	9 40.9
19 Sa	19 55 44	29 27 11	21 04 39	27 30 39	25 15.1	5 23.1	9 45.9	29 15.8	6 47.5	23 32.7	18 05.4	14 57.5	8 36.6	9 42.7
20 Su	19 59 40	0♒28 13	4♌00 45	10♌34 51	25 10.2	6 15.7	9 28.7	0♓03.0	7 09.4	23 41.2	18 05.5	14 55.9	8 37.7	9 44.6
21 M	20 03 37	1 29 16	17 12 50	23 54 29	25 04.1	7 11.7	9 14.0	0 50.3	7 31.3	23 49.6	18 05.7	14 54.4	8 38.8	9 46.4
22 Tu	20 07 33	2 30 17	0♍39 31	7♍27 42	24 57.7	8 11.0	9 01.8	1 37.5	7 53.4	23 57.9	18 06.1	14 52.9	8 39.9	9 48.3
23 W	20 11 30	3 31 19	14 18 42	21 12 12	24 51.6	9 13.2	8 52.0	2 24.7	8 15.4	24 06.1	18 06.5	14 51.4	8 41.1	9 50.1
24 Th	20 15 26	4 32 19	28 07 55	5♎05 33	24 46.8	10 18.0	8 44.8	3 11.9	8 37.6	24 14.1	18 07.0	14 50.0	8 42.3	9 52.0
25 F	20 19 23	5 33 19	12♎04 48	19 05 27	24 43.6	11 25.1	8 40.1	3 59.0	8 59.8	24 22.1	18 07.7	14 48.6	8 43.5	9 53.9
26 Sa	20 23 19	6 34 19	26 07 16	3♏10 03	24D 42.4	12 34.4	8D 37.9	4 46.2	9 22.0	24 29.8	18 08.4	14 47.3	8 44.8	9 55.7
27 Su	20 27 16	7 35 18	10♏13 38	17 17 50	24 42.7	13 45.7	8 38.1	5 33.4	9 44.3	24 37.5	18 09.3	14 46.1	8 46.1	9 57.6
28 M	20 31 13	8 36 17	24 22 31	1♐27 28	24 43.9	14 58.8	8 40.8	6 20.5	10 06.7	24 45.0	18 10.3	14 44.8	8 47.4	9 59.5
29 Tu	20 35 09	9 37 15	8♐32 31	15 37 25	24R 45.1	16 13.6	8 45.9	7 07.7	10 29.1	24 52.4	18 11.4	14 43.7	8 48.7	10 01.3
30 W	20 39 06	10 38 13	22 41 55	29 45 42	24 45.3	17 29.9	8 53.2	7 54.8	10 51.6	24 59.6	18 12.7	14 42.5	8 50.1	10 03.2
31 Th	20 43 02	11 39 09	6♑48 24	13♑49 39	24 43.6	18 47.7	9 02.9	8 42.0	11 14.1	25 06.8	18 14.0	14 41.4	8 51.5	10 05.1

LONGITUDE — February 2030

Day	Sid.Time	☉	0 hr ☽	Noon ☽	True ☊	☿	♀	♂	⚳	♃	♄	♅	♆	♇
1 F	20 46 59	12♒40 05	20♑48 59	27♑45 59	24♐39.6	20♑06.8	9♑14.7	9♓29.1	11♓36.7	25♏13.7	18♉15.4	14♊40.4	8♈52.9	10♒06.9
2 Sa	20 50 55	13 41 00	4♒40 10	11♒31 06	24R 33.3	21 27.2	9 28.7	10 16.2	11 59.4	25 20.5	18 17.0	14R 39.4	8 54.4	10 08.8
3 Su	20 54 52	14 41 54	18 18 21	25 01 34	24 25.0	22 48.8	9 44.8	11 03.3	12 22.0	25 27.2	18 18.7	14 38.5	8 55.8	10 10.7
4 M	20 58 48	15 42 46	1♓40 26	8♓14 44	24 15.5	24 11.4	10 02.9	11 50.3	12 44.8	25 33.7	18 20.4	14 37.6	8 57.4	10 12.5
5 Tu	21 02 45	16 43 37	14 44 20	21 09 11	24 05.8	25 35.2	10 22.9	12 37.4	13 07.5	25 40.1	18 22.3	14 36.8	8 58.9	10 14.4
6 W	21 06 42	17 44 27	27 29 20	3♈44 58	23 57.0	27 00.0	10 44.8	13 24.4	13 30.4	25 46.3	18 24.3	14 36.0	9 00.4	10 16.2
7 Th	21 10 38	18 45 15	9♈56 18	16 03 41	23 49.9	28 25.8	11 08.5	14 11.4	13 53.2	25 52.4	18 26.4	14 35.2	9 02.0	10 18.1
8 F	21 14 35	19 46 03	22 07 32	28 08 19	23 44.9	29 52.5	11 34.0	14 58.4	14 16.1	25 58.3	18 28.6	14 34.6	9 03.6	10 19.9
9 Sa	21 18 31	20 46 48	4♉06 35	10♉02 55	23D 42.2	1♒20.2	12 01.1	15 45.4	14 39.0	26 04.0	18 30.9	14 33.9	9 05.3	10 21.8
10 Su	21 22 28	21 47 32	15 57 57	21 52 21	23 41.4	2 48.8	12 29.9	16 32.3	15 02.0	26 09.6	18 33.4	14 33.4	9 06.9	10 23.6
11 M	21 26 24	22 48 15	27 46 45	3♊41 53	23 41.9	4 18.3	13 00.2	17 19.3	15 25.0	26 15.1	18 35.9	14 32.8	9 08.6	10 25.5
12 Tu	21 30 21	23 48 56	9♊38 23	15 36 57	23R 42.8	5 48.7	13 32.1	18 06.2	15 48.1	26 20.3	18 38.5	14 32.4	9 10.3	10 27.3
13 W	21 34 17	24 49 35	21 38 14	27 42 49	23 43.0	7 20.0	14 05.4	18 53.0	16 11.2	26 25.4	18 41.3	14 31.9	9 12.0	10 29.1
14 Th	21 38 14	25 50 12	3♋51 17	10♋04 08	23 41.5	8 52.2	14 40.1	19 39.9	16 34.3	26 30.4	18 44.1	14 31.6	9 13.8	10 30.9
15 F	21 42 11	26 50 49	16 21 48	22 44 36	23 37.8	10 25.3	15 16.2	20 26.7	16 57.4	26 35.2	18 47.0	14 31.3	9 15.6	10 32.7
16 Sa	21 46 07	27 51 23	29 12 48	5♌46 31	23 31.4	11 59.2	15 53.5	21 13.5	17 20.6	26 39.8	18 50.1	14 31.0	9 17.4	10 34.5
17 Su	21 50 04	28 51 56	12♌25 45	19 10 22	23 22.6	13 34.0	16 32.1	22 00.2	17 43.8	26 44.3	18 53.2	14 30.8	9 19.2	10 36.3
18 M	21 54 00	29 52 27	26 00 07	2♍54 38	23 12.0	15 09.7	17 11.9	22 47.0	18 07.1	26 48.6	18 56.5	14 30.6	9 21.0	10 38.1
19 Tu	21 57 57	0♓52 56	9♍53 24	16 55 51	23 00.6	16 46.3	17 52.9	23 33.7	18 30.3	26 52.7	18 59.8	14 30.5	9 22.9	10 39.9
20 W	22 01 53	1 53 25	24 01 19	1♎09 05	22 49.8	18 23.9	18 34.9	24 20.3	18 53.6	26 56.6	19 03.2	14D 30.5	9 24.7	10 41.7
21 Th	22 05 50	2 53 51	8♎18 28	15 28 45	22 40.6	20 02.3	19 18.0	25 07.0	19 17.0	27 00.4	19 06.8	14 30.5	9 26.6	10 43.4
22 F	22 09 46	3 54 17	22 39 18	29 49 31	22 34.0	21 41.7	20 02.2	25 53.6	19 40.3	27 04.0	19 10.4	14 30.5	9 28.6	10 45.2
23 Sa	22 13 43	4 54 41	6♏58 54	14♏07 02	22 30.0	23 22.0	20 47.3	26 40.2	20 03.7	27 07.4	19 14.1	14 30.6	9 30.5	10 46.9
24 Su	22 17 39	5 55 03	21 13 37	28 18 26	22D 28.4	25 03.3	21 33.4	27 26.7	20 27.1	27 10.7	19 17.9	14 30.8	9 32.4	10 48.6
25 M	22 21 36	6 55 25	5♐21 18	12♐22 09	22R 28.3	26 45.6	22 20.4	28 13.3	20 50.5	27 13.8	19 21.8	14 31.0	9 34.4	10 50.4
26 Tu	22 25 33	7 55 45	19 20 57	26 17 40	22 28.4	28 28.9	23 08.2	28 59.8	21 14.0	27 16.7	19 25.9	14 31.3	9 36.4	10 52.1
27 W	22 29 29	8 56 04	3♑12 19	10♑04 54	22 27.3	0♓13.1	23 56.9	29 46.2	21 37.4	27 19.4	19 30.0	14 31.6	9 38.4	10 53.8
28 Th	22 33 26	9 56 21	16 55 24	23 43 44	22 24.1	1 58.4	24 46.4	0♈32.7	22 00.9	27 21.9	19 34.1	14 32.0	9 40.4	10 55.4

Astro Data (Dy Hr Mn)

	Dy Hr Mn
☽0N	8 20:30
☿D	11 5:45
♄D	19 3:54
♃□♆	20 0:44
☽0S	23 6:29
♀D	26 21:33
☽0N	5 6:25
☽0S	19 14:20
♅D	20 23:23

Planet Ingress (Dy Hr Mn)

	Dy Hr Mn
☉ ♒	20 0:54
♂ ♓	20 10:27
☿ ♒	8 14:03
☉ ♓	18 15:00
☿ ♓	27 8:59
♂ ♈	27 19:07

Last Aspect / ☽ Ingress

Last Aspect Dy Hr Mn		☽ Ingress Dy Hr Mn
31 10:55	♃ ☌	♐ 1 2:35
2 4:14	♂ ⚹	♑ 3 3:54
4 15:19	♃ ⚹	♒ 5 6:17
6 20:03	♃ □	♓ 7 11:16
9 4:16	♃ △	♈ 9 19:46
11 17:37	♂ ⚹	♉ 12 7:26
14 10:44	♂ □	♊ 14 20:15
17 2:40	♂ △	♋ 17 7:46
19 15:54	☉ ☍	♌ 19 16:37
21 11:51	♃ □	♍ 21 22:50
23 17:05	♃ ⚹	♎ 24 3:14
25 4:41	♅ △	♏ 26 6:37
28 0:32	♃ ☌	♐ 28 9:32
29 10:29	♅ ☍	♑ 30 12:24

Last Aspect / ☽ Ingress

Last Aspect Dy Hr Mn		☽ Ingress Dy Hr Mn
1 7:34	♃ ⚹	♒ 1 15:52
3 12:46	♃ □	♓ 3 20:58
5 21:26	☿ ⚹	♈ 6 4:48
7 17:48	☉ ⚹	♉ 8 15:44
10 20:47	♃ ☍	♊ 11 4:30
13 5:48	☉ △	♋ 13 16:29
15 19:11	♃ △	♌ 16 1:27
18 6:20	☉ ☍	♍ 18 6:58
20 4:54	♃ ⚹	♎ 20 10:04
21 20:37	☿ △	♏ 22 12:18
24 10:27	♂ △	♐ 24 14:53
26 16:58	♂ □	♑ 26 18:26
28 18:27	♃ ⚹	♒ 28 23:07

☽ Phases & Eclipses

Dy Hr Mn		
4 2:49	●	13♑47
11 14:06	☽	21♈24
19 15:54	○	29♋37
26 18:14	☾	6♏50
2 16:07	●	13♒51
10 11:49	☽	21♉47
18 6:20	○	29♌38
25 1:58	☾	6♐30

Astro Data

1 January 2030
Julian Day # 47483
SVP 4♓50'09"
GC 27♐15.5 ⚴ 29♑20.1
Eris 25♈33.8R ⚵ 15♐35.6
⚷ 8♉01.0R ⚶ 23♒46.2
☽ Mean ☊ 24♐46.8

1 February 2030
Julian Day # 47514
SVP 4♓50'03"
GC 27♐15.6 ⚴ 10♒18.5
Eris 25♈35.2 ⚵ 25♐28.6
⚷ 8♉00.5 ⚶ 8♓30.5
☽ Mean ☊ 23♐08.4

March 2030

LONGITUDE

Day	Sid.Time	☉	0 hr ☽	Noon ☽	True ☊	☿	♀	♂	⚳	♃	♄	♅	♆	♇
1 F	22 37 22	10♓56 37	0♒29 52	7♒13 39	22♐17.9	3♓44.7	25♑36.6	1♈19.1	22♓24.5	27♏24.3	19♉38.4	14♊32.4	9♈42.5	10♒57.1
2 Sa	22 41 19	11 56 50	13 54 56	20 33 34	22R 08.6	5 32.1	26 27.5	2 05.4	22 48.0	27 26.5	19 42.8	14 32.9	9 44.5	10 58.8
3 Su	22 45 15	12 57 03	27 09 21	3♓42 06	21 56.8	7 20.5	27 19.2	2 51.8	23 11.5	27 28.4	19 47.2	14 33.4	9 46.6	11 00.4
4 M	22 49 12	13 57 13	10♓11 36	16 37 44	21 43.4	9 09.9	28 11.5	3 38.1	23 35.1	27 30.2	19 51.8	14 34.0	9 48.7	11 02.0
5 Tu	22 53 08	14 57 22	23 00 21	29 19 23	21 29.5	11 00.4	29 04.5	4 24.3	23 58.7	27 31.8	19 56.4	14 34.7	9 50.7	11 03.6
6 W	22 57 05	15 57 29	5♈34 48	11♈46 41	21 16.5	12 51.9	29 58.1	5 10.5	24 22.3	27 33.3	20 01.1	14 35.4	9 52.9	11 05.2
7 Th	23 01 02	16 57 33	17 55 08	24 00 20	21 05.3	14 44.5	0♒52.3	5 56.7	24 45.9	27 34.5	20 05.9	14 36.1	9 55.0	11 06.8
8 F	23 04 58	17 57 36	0♉02 35	6♉02 12	20 56.8	16 38.0	1 47.0	6 42.9	25 09.5	27 35.6	20 10.8	14 36.9	9 57.1	11 08.4
9 Sa	23 08 55	18 57 37	11 59 36	17 55 15	20 51.2	18 32.5	2 42.3	7 29.0	25 33.1	27 36.4	20 15.7	14 37.8	9 59.2	11 09.9
10 Su	23 12 51	19 57 36	23 49 42	29 43 31	20 48.2	20 28.0	3 38.2	8 15.1	25 56.8	27 37.1	20 20.7	14 38.7	10 01.4	11 11.5
11 M	23 16 48	20 57 32	5♊37 19	11♊31 46	20 47.2	22 24.3	4 34.5	9 01.1	26 20.4	27 37.6	20 25.9	14 39.6	10 03.6	11 13.0
12 Tu	23 20 44	21 57 26	17 27 32	23 25 21	20 47.1	24 21.4	5 31.4	9 47.1	26 44.1	27 37.9	20 31.1	14 40.7	10 05.7	11 14.5
13 W	23 24 41	22 57 19	29 25 53	5♋29 51	20 46.7	26 19.2	6 28.7	10 33.0	27 07.7	27R 38.0	20 36.3	14 41.7	10 07.9	11 16.0
14 Th	23 28 37	23 57 09	11♋37 55	17 50 43	20 45.1	28 17.6	7 26.5	11 18.9	27 31.4	27 37.9	20 41.7	14 42.8	10 10.1	11 17.5
15 F	23 32 34	24 56 56	24 08 51	0♌32 48	20 41.3	0♈16.4	8 24.7	12 04.8	27 55.1	27 37.7	20 47.1	14 44.0	10 12.3	11 18.9
16 Sa	23 36 31	25 56 42	7♌02 59	13 39 43	20 34.8	2 15.5	9 23.3	12 50.6	28 18.7	27 37.2	20 52.6	14 45.2	10 14.5	11 20.3
17 Su	23 40 27	26 56 25	20 23 08	27 13 14	20 25.8	4 14.6	10 22.4	13 36.4	28 42.4	27 36.6	20 58.1	14 46.5	10 16.8	11 21.7
18 M	23 44 24	27 56 06	4♍09 51	11♍12 39	20 14.7	6 13.5	11 21.9	14 22.1	29 06.1	27 35.8	21 03.7	14 47.8	10 19.0	11 23.1
19 Tu	23 48 20	28 55 45	18 21 04	25 34 26	20 02.8	8 12.0	12 21.7	15 07.8	29 29.8	27 34.7	21 09.4	14 49.1	10 21.2	11 24.5
20 W	23 52 17	29 55 22	2♎51 54	10♎12 31	19 51.3	10 09.8	13 21.9	15 53.4	29 53.4	27 33.5	21 15.2	14 50.5	10 23.4	11 25.9
21 Th	23 56 13	0♈54 57	17 35 16	24 59 05	19 41.5	12 06.4	14 22.5	16 39.0	0♈17.1	27 32.2	21 21.0	14 52.0	10 25.7	11 27.2
22 F	0 00 10	1 54 30	2♏22 58	9♏45 55	19 34.1	14 01.6	15 23.5	17 24.6	0 40.8	27 30.6	21 26.9	14 53.5	10 27.9	11 28.5
23 Sa	0 04 06	2 54 02	17 07 06	24 25 45	19 29.7	15 55.0	16 24.7	18 10.1	1 04.5	27 28.8	21 32.9	14 55.1	10 30.2	11 29.8
24 Su	0 08 03	3 53 32	1♐41 18	8♐53 16	19D 27.7	17 46.1	17 26.3	18 55.6	1 28.2	27 26.9	21 38.9	14 56.7	10 32.4	11 31.1
25 M	0 12 00	4 53 00	16 01 23	23 05 26	19R 27.5	19 34.5	18 28.3	19 41.0	1 51.9	27 24.8	21 45.0	14 58.3	10 34.7	11 32.3
26 Tu	0 15 56	5 52 26	0♑05 21	7♑01 10	19 27.6	21 19.8	19 30.5	20 26.4	2 15.5	27 22.5	21 51.1	15 00.0	10 37.0	11 33.6
27 W	0 19 53	6 51 51	13 52 59	20 40 54	19 26.9	23 01.5	20 33.0	21 11.7	2 39.2	27 20.0	21 57.4	15 01.7	10 39.2	11 34.8
28 Th	0 23 49	7 51 13	27 25 06	4♒05 45	19 24.3	24 39.3	21 35.8	21 57.0	3 02.9	27 17.3	22 03.6	15 03.5	10 41.5	11 36.0
29 F	0 27 46	8 50 34	10♒43 01	17 17 03	19 19.0	26 12.7	22 38.9	22 42.3	3 26.5	27 14.5	22 09.9	15 05.4	10 43.8	11 37.1
30 Sa	0 31 42	9 49 54	23 47 59	0♓15 55	19 10.9	27 41.3	23 42.3	23 27.5	3 50.2	27 11.5	22 16.3	15 07.2	10 46.1	11 38.3
31 Su	0 35 39	10 49 11	6♓40 56	13 03 06	19 00.5	29 04.8	24 45.9	24 12.6	4 13.8	27 08.3	22 22.8	15 09.1	10 48.3	11 39.4

April 2030

LONGITUDE

Day	Sid.Time	☉	0 hr ☽	Noon ☽	True ☊	☿	♀	♂	⚳	♃	♄	♅	♆	♇
1 M	0 39 35	11♈48 26	19♓22 27	25♓39 01	18♐48.6	0♉22.9	25♒49.7	24♈57.8	4♈37.5	27♏04.9	22♉29.3	15♊11.1	10♈50.6	11♒40.5
2 Tu	0 43 32	12 47 40	1♈52 51	8♈03 58	18R 36.2	1 35.3	26 53.7	25 42.8	5 01.1	27R 01.3	22 35.8	15 13.1	10 52.9	11 41.6
3 W	0 47 28	13 46 51	14 12 25	20 18 18	18 24.5	2 41.7	27 58.0	26 27.8	5 24.7	26 57.6	22 42.4	15 15.2	10 55.1	11 42.6
4 Th	0 51 25	14 46 00	26 21 44	2♉22 51	18 14.4	3 42.0	29 02.5	27 12.8	5 48.3	26 53.7	22 49.1	15 17.3	10 57.4	11 43.7
5 F	0 55 22	15 45 07	8♉21 52	14 19 01	18 06.7	4 35.9	0♓07.3	27 57.7	6 11.9	26 49.7	22 55.8	15 19.4	10 59.7	11 44.7
6 Sa	0 59 18	16 44 13	20 14 36	26 08 59	18 01.7	5 23.3	1 12.2	28 42.6	6 35.5	26 45.5	23 02.5	15 21.6	11 01.9	11 45.6
7 Su	1 03 15	17 43 16	2♊02 34	7♊55 48	17D 59.1	6 04.0	2 17.3	29 27.4	6 59.1	26 41.1	23 09.3	15 23.8	11 04.2	11 46.6
8 M	1 07 11	18 42 16	13 49 12	19 43 19	17 58.6	6 38.0	3 22.6	0♉12.2	7 22.6	26 36.5	23 16.1	15 26.1	11 06.5	11 47.5
9 Tu	1 11 08	19 41 15	25 38 43	1♋36 03	17 59.2	7 05.3	4 28.1	0 57.0	7 46.2	26 31.9	23 23.0	15 28.4	11 08.7	11 48.4
10 W	1 15 04	20 40 11	7♋35 56	13 39 04	18R 00.1	7 25.8	5 33.8	1 41.6	8 09.7	26 27.0	23 30.0	15 30.7	11 11.0	11 49.3
11 Th	1 19 01	21 39 05	19 46 05	25 57 40	18 00.2	7 39.6	6 39.6	2 26.3	8 33.2	26 22.0	23 36.9	15 33.1	11 13.2	11 50.2
12 F	1 22 57	22 37 57	2♌14 26	8♌36 59	17 58.8	7R 46.8	7 45.6	3 10.8	8 56.7	26 16.9	23 44.0	15 35.5	11 15.5	11 51.0
13 Sa	1 26 54	23 36 46	15 05 50	21 41 25	17 55.3	7 47.5	8 51.8	3 55.4	9 20.1	26 11.6	23 51.0	15 37.9	11 17.7	11 51.8
14 Su	1 30 51	24 35 33	28 24 05	5♍13 58	17 49.9	7 41.9	9 58.1	4 39.8	9 43.6	26 06.2	23 58.1	15 40.4	11 19.9	11 52.6
15 M	1 34 47	25 34 18	12♍11 08	19 15 23	17 42.8	7 30.3	11 04.6	5 24.2	10 07.0	26 00.6	24 05.2	15 42.9	11 22.1	11 53.3
16 Tu	1 38 44	26 33 00	26 26 23	3♎43 33	17 34.8	7 13.1	12 11.3	6 08.6	10 30.4	25 54.9	24 12.4	15 45.5	11 24.3	11 54.1
17 W	1 42 40	27 31 41	11♎06 08	18 33 11	17 26.9	6 50.8	13 18.0	6 52.9	10 53.8	25 49.1	24 19.6	15 48.1	11 26.6	11 54.8
18 Th	1 46 37	28 30 20	26 03 39	3♏36 19	17 20.2	6 23.7	14 25.0	7 37.2	11 17.1	25 43.1	24 26.8	15 50.7	11 28.7	11 55.5
19 F	1 50 33	29 28 56	11♏09 58	18 43 22	17 15.3	5 52.5	15 32.1	8 21.4	11 40.4	25 37.1	24 34.1	15 53.4	11 30.9	11 56.1
20 Sa	1 54 30	0♉27 31	26 15 22	3♐44 52	17D 12.6	5 17.8	16 39.3	9 05.6	12 03.7	25 30.9	24 41.4	15 56.1	11 33.1	11 56.7
21 Su	1 58 26	1 26 05	11♐10 56	18 32 49	17 11.9	4 40.3	17 46.6	9 49.7	12 27.0	25 24.6	24 48.7	15 58.8	11 35.3	11 57.3
22 M	2 02 23	2 24 36	25 49 53	3♑01 43	17 12.7	4 00.8	18 54.1	10 33.8	12 50.3	25 18.2	24 56.1	16 01.6	11 37.4	11 57.9
23 Tu	2 06 20	3 23 06	10♑08 02	17 08 42	17 13.9	3 19.9	20 01.7	11 17.8	13 13.5	25 11.7	25 03.5	16 04.4	11 39.6	11 58.5
24 W	2 10 16	4 21 35	24 03 44	0♒53 14	17R 14.8	2 38.6	21 09.5	12 01.8	13 36.7	25 05.0	25 10.9	16 07.2	11 41.7	11 59.0
25 Th	2 14 13	5 20 01	7♒37 23	14 16 24	17 14.4	1 57.5	22 17.3	12 45.7	13 59.9	24 58.3	25 18.4	16 10.1	11 43.9	11 59.5
26 F	2 18 09	6 18 27	20 50 36	27 20 16	17 12.4	1 17.3	23 25.3	13 29.5	14 23.0	24 51.5	25 25.9	16 12.9	11 46.0	11 59.9
27 Sa	2 22 06	7 16 50	3♓45 44	10♓07 18	17 08.6	0 38.8	24 33.4	14 13.4	14 46.1	24 44.6	25 33.4	16 15.9	11 48.1	12 00.4
28 Su	2 26 02	8 15 12	16 25 17	22 39 58	17 03.2	0 02.5	25 41.6	14 57.1	15 09.2	24 37.6	25 40.9	16 18.8	11 50.2	12 00.8
29 M	2 29 59	9 13 32	28 51 37	5♈00 31	16 56.8	29♈29.1	26 49.9	15 40.9	15 32.3	24 30.5	25 48.4	16 21.8	11 52.2	12 01.2
30 Tu	2 33 55	10 11 51	11♈06 53	17 10 57	16 50.0	28 59.1	27 58.3	16 24.5	15 55.3	24 23.4	25 56.0	16 24.8	11 54.3	12 01.5

Astro Data Dy Hr Mn	Planet Ingress Dy Hr Mn	Last Aspect Dy Hr Mn	☽ Ingress Dy Hr Mn	Last Aspect Dy Hr Mn	☽ Ingress Dy Hr Mn	☽ Phases & Eclipses Dy Hr Mn
♂0N 1 16:46	♀ ♒ 6 12:51	3 0:33 ♃ □	♓ 3 5:12	1 14:44 ♃ △	♈ 1 20:22	4 6:35 ● 13♓44
☽0N 4 15:16	☿ ♈ 15 8:42	5 11:30 ♀ ⚹	♈ 5 13:18	4 4:41 ♀ ⚹	♉ 4 7:15	12 8:47 ☽ 21♊49
♃ R 13 14:33	☉ ♈ 20 13:52	6 17:29 ♅ ⚹	♉ 7 23:55	6 13:14 ♃ ☍	♊ 6 19:50	19 17:56 ○ 29♍11
☿0N 16 8:18	⚳ ♈ 20 18:39	10 7:42 ♃ ☍	♊ 10 12:34	8 9:45 ☉ ⚹	♋ 9 8:47	26 9:51 ☾ 5♑47
☽0S 18 23:58		12 14:14 ☿ □	♋ 13 1:08	11 12:46 ♃ △	♌ 11 19:44	
☉0N 20 13:52	☿ ♉ 1 4:47	15 6:33 ♃ △	♌ 15 10:59	13 20:01 ♃ □	♍ 14 2:50	2 22:02 ● 13♈12
☽0N 31 21:54	♀ ♓ 5 9:19	17 12:40 ♃ □	♍ 17 16:50	15 23:13 ♃ ⚹	♎ 16 5:53	11 2:57 ☽ 21♋17
	♂ ♉ 8 5:27	19 17:56 ☉ ☍	♎ 19 19:18	18 3:20 ☉ ☍	♏ 18 6:16	18 3:20 ○ 28♎09
♃♀♆ 12 16:33	☉ ♉ 20 0:43	20 21:45 ♂ ☍	♏ 21 20:08	19 22:54 ♃ ☌	♐ 20 5:59	24 18:39 ☾ 4♒38
☿ R 13 2:32	☿ ♈R 28 13:44	23 17:01 ♃ ☌	♐ 23 21:12	21 10:38 ♀ □	♑ 22 6:56	
☽0S 15 10:01		25 5:52 ♂ △	♑ 25 23:51	24 1:52 ♃ ⚹	♒ 24 10:26	
♃☍♄ 24 1:56		27 23:49 ♃ ⚹	♒ 28 4:38	26 8:26 ♄ □	♓ 26 16:57	
☽0N 28 2:56		30 6:36 ☿ ⚹	♓ 30 11:30	28 18:27 ♀ ☌	♈ 29 2:13	

Astro Data

1 March 2030
Julian Day # 47542
SVP 4♓50'00"
GC 27♐15.6 ⚵ 19♒56.9
Eris 25♈45.0 ⚶ 3♑13.2
⚷ 8♉47.7 ⚴ 22♓01.2
☽ Mean ☊ 21♐39.4

1 April 2030
Julian Day # 47573
SVP 4♓49'57"
GC 27♐15.7 ⚵ 29♒48.4
Eris 26♈02.6 ⚶ 9♑30.3
⚷ 10♉20.7 ⚴ 6♈51.9
☽ Mean ☊ 20♐00.9

LONGITUDE — May 2030

Day	Sid.Time	⊙	0 hr ☽	Noon ☽	True ☊	☿	♀	♂	⚳	♃	♄	♅	♆	♇
1 W	2 37 52	11♉10 08	23♈12 56	29♈13 02	16♐43.5	28♈32.7	29♓06.8	17♉08.2	16♈18.3	24♏16.1	26♉03.6	16♊27.8	11♈56.3	12♒01.8
2 Th	2 41 49	12 08 23	5♉11 27	11♉08 25	16R 38.1	28R 10.5	0♈15.4	17 51.7	16 41.2	24R 08.9	26 11.2	16 30.8	11 58.4	12 02.1
3 F	2 45 45	13 06 37	17 04 08	22 58 52	16 34.1	27 52.6	1 24.1	18 35.2	17 04.1	24 01.5	26 18.8	16 33.9	12 00.4	12 02.4
4 Sa	2 49 42	14 04 49	28 52 51	4♊46 22	16D 31.8	27 39.2	2 32.8	19 18.7	17 27.0	23 54.1	26 26.5	16 37.0	12 02.4	12 02.7
5 Su	2 53 38	15 02 59	10♊39 45	16 33 21	16 31.1	27 30.5	3 41.7	20 02.1	17 49.8	23 46.7	26 34.1	16 40.2	12 04.4	12 02.9
6 M	2 57 35	16 01 07	22 27 31	28 22 41	16 31.7	27D 26.5	4 50.6	20 45.5	18 12.6	23 39.2	26 41.8	16 43.3	12 06.4	12 03.1
7 Tu	3 01 31	16 59 14	4♋19 17	10♋17 50	16 33.2	27 27.2	5 59.6	21 28.8	18 35.4	23 31.7	26 49.5	16 46.5	12 08.3	12 03.2
8 W	3 05 28	17 57 18	16 18 48	22 22 44	16 34.9	27 32.7	7 08.7	22 12.1	18 58.1	23 24.1	26 57.2	16 49.7	12 10.2	12 03.4
9 Th	3 09 24	18 55 21	28 30 12	4♌41 44	16 36.4	27 42.8	8 17.9	22 55.3	19 20.8	23 16.5	27 04.9	16 52.9	12 12.2	12 03.5
10 F	3 13 21	19 53 22	10♌57 54	17 19 15	16R 37.1	27 57.5	9 27.1	23 38.5	19 43.4	23 08.9	27 12.6	16 56.1	12 14.1	12 03.6
11 Sa	3 17 18	20 51 21	23 46 18	0♍19 29	16 36.8	28 16.8	10 36.4	24 21.6	20 06.0	23 01.3	27 20.4	16 59.4	12 15.9	12 03.6
12 Su	3 21 14	21 49 18	6♍59 12	13 45 44	16 35.3	28 40.4	11 45.8	25 04.6	20 28.5	22 53.6	27 28.1	17 02.7	12 17.8	12R 03.7
13 M	3 25 11	22 47 13	20 39 17	27 39 50	16 33.0	29 08.2	12 55.2	25 47.6	20 51.0	22 46.0	27 35.9	17 06.0	12 19.6	12 03.7
14 Tu	3 29 07	23 45 06	4♎47 17	12♎01 18	16 30.1	29 40.2	14 04.7	26 30.5	21 13.4	22 38.3	27 43.6	17 09.3	12 21.5	12 03.6
15 W	3 33 04	24 42 58	19 21 23	26 46 51	16 27.1	0♉16.2	15 14.3	27 13.4	21 35.8	22 30.7	27 51.4	17 12.6	12 23.2	12 03.6
16 Th	3 37 00	25 40 48	4♏16 49	11♏50 16	16 24.6	0 56.1	16 24.0	27 56.3	21 58.2	22 23.1	27 59.1	17 16.0	12 25.0	12 03.5
17 F	3 40 57	26 38 36	19 26 04	27 02 58	16 22.9	1 39.7	17 33.7	28 39.1	22 20.5	22 15.5	28 06.9	17 19.3	12 26.8	12 03.4
18 Sa	3 44 53	27 36 23	4♐39 45	12♐15 09	16D 22.2	2 26.9	18 43.5	29 21.8	22 42.7	22 07.9	28 14.7	17 22.7	12 28.5	12 03.3
19 Su	3 48 50	28 34 09	19 48 02	27 17 20	16 22.3	3 17.6	19 53.4	0♊04.5	23 04.9	22 00.3	28 22.4	17 26.1	12 30.3	12 03.1
20 M	3 52 47	29 31 54	4♑42 08	12♑01 42	16 23.2	4 11.7	21 03.3	0 47.1	23 27.0	21 52.8	28 30.2	17 29.5	12 31.9	12 02.9
21 Tu	3 56 43	0♊29 38	19 15 27	26 22 59	16 24.4	5 09.1	22 13.3	1 29.7	23 49.1	21 45.3	28 38.0	17 32.9	12 33.6	12 02.7
22 W	4 00 40	1 27 20	3♒24 03	10♒18 35	16 25.4	6 09.6	23 23.3	2 12.3	24 11.2	21 37.8	28 45.7	17 36.4	12 35.3	12 02.5
23 Th	4 04 36	2 25 01	17 06 39	23 48 23	16R 26.1	7 13.2	24 33.4	2 54.8	24 33.1	21 30.4	28 53.5	17 39.8	12 36.9	12 02.2
24 F	4 08 33	3 22 41	0♓24 03	6♓54 00	16 26.3	8 19.8	25 43.6	3 37.2	24 55.1	21 23.0	29 01.2	17 43.3	12 38.5	12 01.9
25 Sa	4 12 29	4 20 21	13 18 37	19 38 18	16 25.8	9 29.4	26 53.8	4 19.6	25 16.9	21 15.7	29 09.0	17 46.7	12 40.1	12 01.6
26 Su	4 16 26	5 17 59	25 53 31	2♈04 44	16 24.9	10 41.7	28 04.1	5 01.9	25 38.7	21 08.4	29 16.7	17 50.2	12 41.6	12 01.2
27 M	4 20 22	6 15 36	8♈12 22	14 16 54	16 23.6	11 56.9	29 14.4	5 44.2	26 00.5	21 01.2	29 24.5	17 53.7	12 43.2	12 00.9
28 Tu	4 24 19	7 13 12	20 18 45	26 18 20	16 22.3	13 14.9	0♉24.8	6 26.5	26 22.2	20 54.1	29 32.2	17 57.2	12 44.7	12 00.5
29 W	4 28 16	8 10 48	2♉16 02	8♉12 15	16 21.1	14 35.5	1 35.3	7 08.7	26 43.8	20 47.1	29 39.9	18 00.7	12 46.2	12 00.1
30 Th	4 32 12	9 08 22	14 07 19	20 01 34	16 20.2	15 58.8	2 45.7	7 50.9	27 05.4	20 40.1	29 47.6	18 04.2	12 47.6	11 59.6
31 F	4 36 09	10 05 55	25 55 19	1♊48 53	16 19.6	17 24.7	3 56.3	8 33.0	27 26.8	20 33.2	29 55.3	18 07.8	12 49.0	11 59.1

LONGITUDE — June 2030

Day	Sid.Time	⊙	0 hr ☽	Noon ☽	True ☊	☿	♀	♂	⚳	♃	♄	♅	♆	♇
1 Sa	4 40 05	11♊03 28	7♊42 32	13♊36 35	16♐19.4	18♉53.2	5♉06.9	9♊15.0	27♈48.3	20♏26.4	0♊03.0	18♊11.3	12♈50.4	11♒58.6
2 Su	4 44 02	12 00 59	19 31 17	25 26 56	16D 19.4	20 24.3	6 17.5	9 57.0	28 09.6	20R 19.7	0 10.7	18 14.8	12 51.8	11R 58.1
3 M	4 47 58	12 58 29	1♋23 49	7♋22 14	16 19.7	21 58.0	7 28.2	10 39.0	28 30.9	20 13.1	0 18.4	18 18.4	12 53.2	11 57.6
4 Tu	4 51 55	13 55 59	13 22 29	19 24 53	16 19.9	23 34.2	8 38.9	11 20.9	28 52.1	20 06.6	0 26.0	18 21.9	12 54.5	11 57.0
5 W	4 55 51	14 53 27	25 29 47	1♌37 32	16 20.2	25 13.0	9 49.7	12 02.8	29 13.3	20 00.2	0 33.6	18 25.4	12 55.8	11 56.4
6 Th	4 59 48	15 50 53	7♌48 30	14 03 03	16R 20.3	26 54.3	11 00.5	12 44.6	29 34.3	19 54.0	0 41.2	18 29.0	12 57.1	11 55.8
7 F	5 03 45	16 48 19	20 21 34	26 44 26	16 20.3	28 38.2	12 11.3	13 26.3	29 55.3	19 47.8	0 48.8	18 32.6	12 58.3	11 55.2
8 Sa	5 07 41	17 45 44	3♍12 01	9♍44 40	16D 20.2	0♊24.5	13 22.2	14 08.0	0♉16.2	19 41.7	0 56.4	18 36.1	12 59.5	11 54.5
9 Su	5 11 38	18 43 07	16 22 43	23 06 25	16 20.2	2 13.3	14 33.1	14 49.7	0 37.1	19 35.8	1 03.9	18 39.6	13 00.7	11 53.8
10 M	5 15 34	19 40 29	29 55 59	6♎51 31	16 20.4	4 04.6	15 44.1	15 31.3	0 57.8	19 30.0	1 11.4	18 43.2	13 01.9	11 53.1
11 Tu	5 19 31	20 37 50	13♎53 02	21 00 25	16 20.6	5 58.2	16 55.1	16 12.9	1 18.5	19 24.4	1 18.9	18 46.7	13 03.0	11 52.4
12 W	5 23 27	21 35 10	28 13 26	5♏31 42	16 21.1	7 54.2	18 06.1	16 54.4	1 39.1	19 18.8	1 26.4	18 50.3	13 04.1	11 51.6
13 Th	5 27 24	22 32 30	12♏54 39	20 21 36	16 21.5	9 52.5	19 17.2	17 35.8	1 59.6	19 13.4	1 33.8	18 53.8	13 05.2	11 50.8
14 F	5 31 20	23 29 48	27 51 43	5♐24 01	16R 21.9	11 52.9	20 28.3	18 17.2	2 20.0	19 08.2	1 41.3	18 57.4	13 06.2	11 50.1
15 Sa	5 35 17	24 27 06	12♐57 29	20 30 58	16 22.0	13 55.4	21 39.5	18 58.6	2 40.4	19 03.1	1 48.7	19 00.9	13 07.2	11 49.2
16 Su	5 39 14	25 24 23	28 03 20	5♑33 30	16 21.7	15 59.8	22 50.7	19 39.9	3 00.6	18 58.1	1 56.0	19 04.5	13 08.2	11 48.4
17 M	5 43 10	26 21 39	13♑00 23	20 23 02	16 20.9	18 05.9	24 01.9	20 21.2	3 20.8	18 53.3	2 03.4	19 08.0	13 09.1	11 47.5
18 Tu	5 47 07	27 18 55	27 40 38	4♒52 30	16 19.7	20 13.5	25 13.2	21 02.4	3 40.9	18 48.6	2 10.7	19 11.5	13 10.1	11 46.7
19 W	5 51 03	28 16 11	11♒58 08	18 57 11	16 18.3	22 22.5	26 24.6	21 43.6	4 00.9	18 44.1	2 17.9	19 15.1	13 11.0	11 45.8
20 Th	5 55 00	29 13 26	25 49 30	2♓35 01	16 17.0	24 32.5	27 36.0	22 24.8	4 20.7	18 39.7	2 25.2	19 18.6	13 11.8	11 44.9
21 F	5 58 56	0♋10 41	9♓13 54	15 46 20	16 16.0	26 43.3	28 47.4	23 05.8	4 40.5	18 35.5	2 32.4	19 22.1	13 12.6	11 43.9
22 Sa	6 02 53	1 07 56	22 12 41	28 33 22	16D 15.5	28 54.6	29 58.8	23 46.9	5 00.2	18 31.4	2 39.6	19 25.6	13 13.4	11 43.0
23 Su	6 06 49	2 05 11	4♈48 51	10♈59 40	16 15.7	1♋06.1	1♊10.3	24 27.9	5 19.8	18 27.5	2 46.7	19 29.1	13 14.2	11 42.0
24 M	6 10 46	3 02 25	17 06 22	23 09 30	16 16.5	3 17.7	2 21.9	25 08.9	5 39.3	18 23.8	2 53.8	19 32.6	13 14.9	11 41.0
25 Tu	6 14 43	3 59 40	29 09 40	5♉07 25	16 17.8	5 28.9	3 33.5	25 49.8	5 58.8	18 20.2	3 00.9	19 36.0	13 15.6	11 40.0
26 W	6 18 39	4 56 54	11♉03 17	16 57 50	16 19.3	7 39.5	4 45.1	26 30.7	6 18.0	18 16.8	3 07.9	19 39.5	13 16.3	11 38.9
27 Th	6 22 36	5 54 09	22 51 33	28 44 56	16 20.7	9 49.3	5 56.8	27 11.5	6 37.2	18 13.6	3 14.9	19 42.9	13 17.0	11 37.9
28 F	6 26 32	6 51 23	4♊38 24	10♊32 22	16R 21.5	11 58.1	7 08.5	27 52.3	6 56.3	18 10.5	3 21.8	19 46.4	13 17.6	11 36.8
29 Sa	6 30 29	7 48 37	16 27 14	22 23 20	16 21.5	14 05.7	8 20.2	28 33.0	7 15.3	18 07.7	3 28.7	19 49.8	13 18.2	11 35.8
30 Su	6 34 25	8 45 51	28 20 59	4♋20 27	16 20.4	16 11.9	9 32.0	29 13.7	7 34.2	18 05.0	3 35.6	19 53.2	13 18.7	11 34.7

Astro Data

	Dy Hr Mn
♆✶♇	4 15:40
♀0N	5 8:11
☿ D	6 20:15
⚳0N	7 1:55
♄∠♆	10 17:47
☽0S	12 19:00
♇ R	12 23:13
☽0N	25 8:17
☽0S	9 2:17
♃⊼♅	15 17:59
☽0N	21 15:33

Planet Ingress

	Dy Hr Mn
♀ ♈	2 6:37
☿ ♉	15 1:30
♂ ♊	19 9:28
⊙ ♊	20 23:41
♀ ♉	28 3:32
♄ ♊	1 2:34
⚳ ♉	7 17:21
☿ ♊	8 6:31
⊙ ♋	21 7:31
♀ ♊	22 12:23
☿ ♋	22 23:56

Last Aspect / ☽ Ingress

Last Aspect Dy Hr Mn		☽ Ingress Dy Hr Mn
1 10:42 ☿ ☌	♉	1 13:34
3 18:51 ♄ ☌	♊	4 2:17
6 10:07 ☿ ✶	♋	6 15:17
8 22:15 ☿ □	♌	9 2:55
11 8:10 ☿ △	♍	11 11:25
13 11:53 ♄ △	♎	13 15:57
14 20:27 ♅ △	♏	15 17:10
17 14:39 ♂ ☍	♐	17 16:39
18 23:09 ♀ △	♑	19 16:22
21 15:52 ♄ △	♒	21 18:10
23 21:20 ♄ □	♓	23 23:16
26 6:30 ♄ ✶	♈	26 7:57
27 19:13 ♅ ✶	♉	28 19:26
31 8:06 ♄ ☌	♊	31 8:18

Last Aspect / ☽ Ingress

Last Aspect Dy Hr Mn		☽ Ingress Dy Hr Mn
1 21:21 ♅ ☌	♋	2 21:11
4 21:29 ☿ ✶	♌	5 8:50
7 16:06 ☿ □	♍	7 18:04
9 5:48 ♃ ✶	♎	10 0:07
11 11:19 ⊙ △	♏	12 2:56
13 10:11 ♃ ☌	♐	14 3:24
15 18:41 ⊙ ☍	♑	16 3:06
17 18:31 ♀ △	♒	18 3:51
20 5:33 ⊙ △	♓	20 7:23
22 12:49 ☿ □	♈	22 14:45
24 16:12 ♂ ✶	♉	25 1:41
26 14:40 ♃ ☍	♊	27 14:33
30 1:09 ♂ ☌	♋	30 3:19

☽ Phases & Eclipses

Dy Hr Mn	
2 14:12	● 12♉14
10 17:11	☽ 20♌06
17 11:19	○ 26♏37
24 4:57	☾ 3♓06
1 6:21	● 10♊50
1 6:27:54	● A 05'21"
9 3:36	☽ 18♍23
15 18:41	○ 24♐43
15 18:33	● P 0.502
22 17:20	☾ 1♈21
30 21:34	● 9♋09

Astro Data

1 May 2030
Julian Day # 47603
SVP 4♓49'54"
GC 27♐15.8 ⚴ 7♓55.0
Eris 26♈22.2 ⚵ 11♑58.4
⚷ 12♉13.0 ⚶ 20♈50.4
☽ Mean ☊ 18♐25.5

1 June 2030
Julian Day # 47634
SVP 4♓49'50"
GC 27♐15.8 ⚴ 13♓53.9
Eris 26♈40.0 ⚵ 9♑29.1R
⚷ 14♉10.1 ⚶ 4♉35.4
☽ Mean ☊ 16♐47.0

July 2030

LONGITUDE

Day	Sid.Time	☉	0 hr ☽	Noon ☽	True ☊	☿	♀	♂	⚳	♃	♄	♅	♆	♇
1 M	6 38 22	9♋43 05	10♋22 00	16♋25 51	16♐18.2	18♋16.6	10♊43.8	29♊54.4	7♉52.9	18♏02.4	3♊42.4	19♊56.6	13♈19.2	11♒33.6
2 Tu	6 42 19	10 40 19	22 32 13	28 41 16	16R 15.0	20 19.7	11 55.7	0♋35.0	8 11.5	18R 00.1	3 49.2	20 00.0	13 19.7	11R 32.4
3 W	6 46 15	11 37 33	4♌53 10	11♌08 06	16 11.2	22 21.0	13 07.6	1 15.5	8 30.0	17 57.9	3 55.9	20 03.4	13 20.1	11 31.3
4 Th	6 50 12	12 34 46	17 26 11	23 47 35	16 07.1	24 20.5	14 19.5	1 56.1	8 48.4	17 55.9	4 02.6	20 06.8	13 20.6	11 30.1
5 F	6 54 08	13 31 59	0♍12 27	6♍40 54	16 03.3	26 18.1	15 31.4	2 36.5	9 06.7	17 54.0	4 09.2	20 10.1	13 20.9	11 29.0
6 Sa	6 58 05	14 29 12	13 13 06	19 49 11	16 00.2	28 13.9	16 43.4	3 17.0	9 24.8	17 52.4	4 15.8	20 13.4	13 21.3	11 27.8
7 Su	7 02 01	15 26 24	26 29 18	3♎13 33	15D 58.4	0♌07.6	17 55.5	3 57.4	9 42.8	17 50.9	4 22.3	20 16.7	13 21.6	11 26.6
8 M	7 05 58	16 23 37	10♎02 02	16 54 51	15 57.8	1 59.5	19 07.5	4 37.7	10 00.7	17 49.6	4 28.8	20 20.0	13 21.9	11 25.4
9 Tu	7 09 54	17 20 49	23 52 01	0♏53 31	15 58.4	3 49.3	20 19.6	5 18.0	10 18.4	17 48.5	4 35.2	20 23.3	13 22.1	11 24.1
10 W	7 13 51	18 18 01	7♏59 15	15 09 03	15 59.7	5 37.2	21 31.7	5 58.2	10 36.1	17 47.6	4 41.6	20 26.5	13 22.3	11 22.9
11 Th	7 17 48	19 15 13	22 22 38	29 39 38	16 01.0	7 23.1	22 43.9	6 38.5	10 53.5	17 46.9	4 47.9	20 29.7	13 22.5	11 21.7
12 F	7 21 44	20 12 25	6♐59 33	14♐21 48	16R 01.7	9 07.0	23 56.1	7 18.6	11 10.9	17 46.3	4 54.2	20 32.9	13 22.7	11 20.4
13 Sa	7 25 41	21 09 37	21 45 39	29 10 19	16 01.1	10 49.0	25 08.3	7 58.7	11 28.1	17 46.0	5 00.4	20 36.1	13 22.8	11 19.1
14 Su	7 29 37	22 06 49	6♑34 53	13♑58 27	15 58.9	12 28.9	26 20.6	8 38.8	11 45.1	17D 45.8	5 06.5	20 39.3	13 22.9	11 17.9
15 M	7 33 34	23 04 02	21 20 04	28 38 48	15 55.1	14 06.9	27 32.9	9 18.9	12 02.1	17 45.8	5 12.6	20 42.4	13 23.0	11 16.6
16 Tu	7 37 30	24 01 14	5♒53 46	13♒04 11	15 49.8	15 42.9	28 45.3	9 58.9	12 18.8	17 45.9	5 18.7	20 45.5	13R 23.0	11 15.3
17 W	7 41 27	24 58 27	20 09 24	27 08 51	15 43.9	17 16.9	29 57.7	10 38.8	12 35.5	17 46.3	5 24.6	20 48.6	13 23.0	11 14.0
18 Th	7 45 23	25 55 41	4♓02 10	10♓49 07	15 38.0	18 48.9	1♋10.1	11 18.7	12 51.9	17 46.8	5 30.5	20 51.7	13 22.9	11 12.7
19 F	7 49 20	26 52 55	17 29 37	24 03 44	15 32.8	20 18.9	2 22.6	11 58.6	13 08.2	17 47.5	5 36.4	20 54.7	13 22.8	11 11.4
20 Sa	7 53 17	27 50 10	0♈31 39	6♈53 43	15 29.1	21 46.9	3 35.1	12 38.5	13 24.4	17 48.4	5 42.2	20 57.7	13 22.7	11 10.0
21 Su	7 57 13	28 47 25	13 10 18	19 21 54	15D 27.0	23 12.9	4 47.7	13 18.3	13 40.4	17 49.5	5 47.9	21 00.7	13 22.6	11 08.7
22 M	8 01 10	29 44 42	25 29 05	1♉32 25	15 26.5	24 36.8	6 00.3	13 58.0	13 56.2	17 50.7	5 53.5	21 03.7	13 22.4	11 07.4
23 Tu	8 05 06	0♌41 59	7♉32 33	13 30 07	15 27.2	25 58.6	7 12.9	14 37.7	14 11.9	17 52.1	5 59.1	21 06.6	13 22.2	11 06.0
24 W	8 09 03	1 39 17	19 25 45	25 20 07	15 28.5	27 18.3	8 25.6	15 17.4	14 27.4	17 53.7	6 04.6	21 09.5	13 22.0	11 04.7
25 Th	8 12 59	2 36 36	1♊13 51	7♊07 32	15R 29.7	28 35.8	9 38.3	15 57.1	14 42.7	17 55.5	6 10.1	21 12.4	13 21.7	11 03.3
26 F	8 16 56	3 33 56	13 01 45	18 57 04	15 30.0	29 51.1	10 51.1	16 36.7	14 57.9	17 57.5	6 15.5	21 15.3	13 21.4	11 01.9
27 Sa	8 20 52	4 31 17	24 53 57	0♋52 52	15 28.7	1♍04.1	12 03.9	17 16.3	15 12.9	17 59.6	6 20.8	21 18.1	13 21.1	11 00.6
28 Su	8 24 49	5 28 38	6♋54 12	12 58 20	15 25.2	2 14.7	13 16.7	17 55.8	15 27.6	18 01.9	6 26.0	21 20.9	13 20.7	10 59.2
29 M	8 28 46	6 26 01	19 05 30	25 15 58	15 19.7	3 22.9	14 29.6	18 35.3	15 42.3	18 04.4	6 31.2	21 23.6	13 20.3	10 57.8
30 Tu	8 32 42	7 23 24	1♌29 52	7♌47 18	15 12.1	4 28.6	15 42.5	19 14.8	15 56.7	18 07.1	6 36.3	21 26.4	13 19.9	10 56.5
31 W	8 36 39	8 20 48	14 08 21	20 32 58	15 03.2	5 31.7	16 55.4	19 54.2	16 10.9	18 09.9	6 41.3	21 29.1	13 19.4	10 55.1

August 2030

LONGITUDE

Day	Sid.Time	☉	0 hr ☽	Noon ☽	True ☊	☿	♀	♂	⚳	♃	♄	♅	♆	♇
1 Th	8 40 35	9♌18 12	27♌01 08	3♍32 45	14♐53.9	6♍32.1	18♋08.4	20♋33.5	16♉24.9	18♏12.9	6♊46.2	21♊31.7	13♈18.9	10♒53.7
2 F	8 44 32	10 15 37	10♍07 42	16 45 51	14R 45.0	7 29.6	19 21.4	21 12.9	16 38.7	18 16.1	6 51.1	21 34.3	13R 18.4	10R 52.3
3 Sa	8 48 28	11 13 03	23 27 05	0♎11 14	14 37.4	8 24.2	20 34.5	21 52.2	16 52.4	18 19.5	6 55.8	21 36.9	13 17.9	10 51.0
4 Su	8 52 25	12 10 30	6♎58 11	13 47 49	14 32.0	9 15.8	21 47.6	22 31.4	17 05.8	18 23.0	7 00.5	21 39.5	13 17.3	10 49.6
5 M	8 56 21	13 07 58	20 40 02	27 34 45	14 28.9	10 04.0	23 00.7	23 10.7	17 19.0	18 26.7	7 05.2	21 42.0	13 16.7	10 48.2
6 Tu	9 00 18	14 05 26	4♏31 54	11♏31 25	14D 27.8	10 48.9	24 13.9	23 49.8	17 32.0	18 30.5	7 09.7	21 44.5	13 16.0	10 46.8
7 W	9 04 15	15 02 54	18 33 14	25 37 15	14 28.1	11 30.2	25 27.0	24 29.0	17 44.8	18 34.6	7 14.2	21 46.9	13 15.4	10 45.4
8 Th	9 08 11	16 00 24	2♐43 20	9♐51 20	14R 28.7	12 07.8	26 40.3	25 08.1	17 57.3	18 38.7	7 18.5	21 49.4	13 14.7	10 44.1
9 F	9 12 08	16 57 54	17 01 00	24 12 04	14 28.4	12 41.4	27 53.5	25 47.1	18 09.7	18 43.1	7 22.8	21 51.7	13 13.9	10 42.7
10 Sa	9 16 04	17 55 26	1♑24 07	8♑36 43	14 26.3	13 10.9	29 06.8	26 26.2	18 21.8	18 47.6	7 27.0	21 54.1	13 13.2	10 41.3
11 Su	9 20 01	18 52 58	15 49 18	23 01 16	14 21.7	13 36.0	0♌20.2	27 05.1	18 33.7	18 52.3	7 31.2	21 56.4	13 12.4	10 40.0
12 M	9 23 57	19 50 31	0♒11 57	7♒20 40	14 14.5	13 56.6	1 33.6	27 44.1	18 45.4	18 57.1	7 35.2	21 58.6	13 11.6	10 38.6
13 Tu	9 27 54	20 48 05	14 26 41	21 29 20	14 05.2	14 12.4	2 47.0	28 23.0	18 56.8	19 02.1	7 39.1	22 00.9	13 10.7	10 37.3
14 W	9 31 50	21 45 40	28 27 59	5♓22 05	13 54.7	14 23.3	4 00.4	29 01.9	19 08.0	19 07.2	7 43.0	22 03.0	13 09.9	10 35.9
15 Th	9 35 47	22 43 17	12♓11 10	18 54 55	13 43.9	14R 28.9	5 13.9	29 40.7	19 18.9	19 12.5	7 46.8	22 05.2	13 09.0	10 34.6
16 F	9 39 44	23 40 54	25 33 06	2♈05 39	13 34.1	14 29.2	6 27.4	0♌19.5	19 29.6	19 17.9	7 50.5	22 07.3	13 08.0	10 33.3
17 Sa	9 43 40	24 38 34	8♈32 35	14 54 06	13 26.1	14 24.0	7 41.0	0 58.3	19 40.1	19 23.5	7 54.1	22 09.3	13 07.1	10 31.9
18 Su	9 47 37	25 36 14	21 10 27	27 22 01	13 20.4	14 13.2	8 54.6	1 37.0	19 50.3	19 29.3	7 57.6	22 11.4	13 06.1	10 30.6
19 M	9 51 33	26 33 57	3♉29 16	9♉32 44	13 17.2	13 56.7	10 08.2	2 15.7	20 00.2	19 35.2	8 01.0	22 13.3	13 05.1	10 29.3
20 Tu	9 55 30	27 31 41	15 32 59	21 30 40	13D 15.9	13 34.5	11 21.9	2 54.4	20 09.9	19 41.2	8 04.3	22 15.3	13 04.1	10 28.0
21 W	9 59 26	28 29 27	27 26 27	3♊21 00	13R 15.8	13 06.7	12 35.6	3 33.0	20 19.3	19 47.4	8 07.5	22 17.2	13 03.0	10 26.7
22 Th	10 03 23	29 27 14	9♊15 00	15 09 09	13 15.9	12 33.5	13 49.3	4 11.6	20 28.4	19 53.7	8 10.6	22 19.0	13 01.9	10 25.4
23 F	10 07 19	0♍25 03	21 04 06	27 00 32	13 15.2	11 55.2	15 03.1	4 50.2	20 37.3	20 00.2	8 13.7	22 20.8	13 00.8	10 24.1
24 Sa	10 11 16	1 22 54	2♋59 02	9♋00 11	13 12.7	11 12.2	16 17.0	5 28.7	20 45.9	20 06.8	8 16.6	22 22.6	12 59.7	10 22.8
25 Su	10 15 13	2 20 46	15 04 30	21 12 28	13 07.7	10 25.1	17 30.8	6 07.2	20 54.1	20 13.6	8 19.4	22 24.3	12 58.5	10 21.6
26 M	10 19 09	3 18 40	27 24 25	3♌40 42	13 00.1	9 34.5	18 44.7	6 45.7	21 02.1	20 20.5	8 22.2	22 26.0	12 57.4	10 20.3
27 Tu	10 23 06	4 16 36	10♌01 30	16 26 56	12 50.0	8 41.4	19 58.7	7 24.1	21 09.8	20 27.5	8 24.8	22 27.6	12 56.2	10 19.1
28 W	10 27 02	5 14 33	22 57 02	29 31 43	12 38.2	7 46.5	21 12.6	8 02.5	21 17.3	20 34.7	8 27.3	22 29.2	12 54.9	10 17.9
29 Th	10 30 59	6 12 32	6♍10 48	12♍54 02	12 25.7	6 51.1	22 26.6	8 40.8	21 24.4	20 42.0	8 29.8	22 30.7	12 53.7	10 16.6
30 F	10 34 55	7 10 32	19 41 05	26 31 33	12 13.7	5 56.2	23 40.6	9 19.1	21 31.1	20 49.4	8 32.1	22 32.2	12 52.4	10 15.4
31 Sa	10 38 52	8 08 34	3♎25 00	10♎21 01	12 03.4	5 03.0	24 54.7	9 57.4	21 37.6	20 57.0	8 34.3	22 33.6	12 51.1	10 14.3

Astro Data

	Dy Hr Mn
☽0S	6 8:23
♃D	15 1:27
♆R	16 16:28
☽0N	19 0:50
☽0S	2 14:30
☽0N	15 10:52
☿R	16 1:19
☽0S	29 21:44

Planet Ingress

	Dy Hr Mn
♂ ♋	1 15:19
☿ ♌	7 10:23
♀ ♋	17 12:46
☉ ♌	22 18:25
☿ ♍	26 14:54
♀ ♌	11 5:24
♂ ♌	15 23:56
☉ ♍	23 1:36

Last Aspect / ☽ Ingress (July)

Last Aspect Dy Hr Mn		☽ Ingress	Dy Hr Mn
1 16:23	☿ ☌	♌	2 14:33
4 5:02	♅ ⚹	♍	4 23:37
7 5:36	☿ ⚹	♎	7 6:16
8 17:56	♅ △	♏	9 10:29
10 17:37	☉ △	♐	11 12:33
13 4:54	♀ ☍	♑	13 13:20
15 2:12	☉ ☍	♒	15 14:14
17 1:05	♅ △	♓	17 16:57
19 17:38	☉ △	♈	19 23:01
22 8:07	☉ □	♉	22 8:56
24 16:30	☿ □	♊	24 21:30
26 16:40	♅ ☌	♋	27 10:14
28 22:17	♂ ☌	♌	29 21:08

Last Aspect / ☽ Ingress (August)

Last Aspect Dy Hr Mn		☽ Ingress	Dy Hr Mn
31 13:45	♅ ⚹	♍	1 5:30
2 20:40	♅ □	♎	3 11:40
5 3:59	♂ □	♏	5 16:11
7 11:41	♀ △	♐	7 19:24
9 8:05	♅ ☍	♑	9 21:40
11 19:07	♂ ☍	♒	11 23:40
13 12:54	♅ △	♓	14 2:39
15 17:44	♅ □	♈	16 8:08
18 8:17	☉ △	♉	18 17:09
21 1:15	☉ □	♊	21 5:12
23 2:34	♅ ☌	♋	23 18:01
25 10:04	♃ △	♌	26 4:59
27 23:07	♅ ⚹	♍	28 12:51
30 5:00	♅ □	♎	30 18:04

☽ Phases & Eclipses

Dy Hr Mn	Phase	Position
8 11:02	☽	16♎21
15 2:12	○	22♑41
22 8:07	☾	29♈35
30 11:11	●	7♌21
6 16:43	☽	14♏17
13 10:44	○	20♒45
21 1:15	☾	28♉04
28 23:07	●	5♍41

Astro Data

1 July 2030
Julian Day # 47664
SVP 4♓49'44"
GC 27♐15.9 ⚵ 16♓06.3R
Eris 26♈51.0 ⚶ 3♑09.3R
⚷ 15♉44.4 ⚴ 16♉52.3
☽ Mean ☊ 15♐11.7

1 August 2030
Julian Day # 47695
SVP 4♓49'39"
GC 27♐16.0 ⚵ 13♓20.1R
Eris 26♈53.0R ⚶ 27♐25.8R
⚷ 16♉43.5 ⚴ 27♉55.2
☽ Mean ☊ 13♐33.3

LONGITUDE — September 2030

Day	Sid.Time	☉	0 hr ☽	Noon ☽	True ☊	☿	♀	♂	⚳	♃	♄	♅	♆	♇
1 Su	10 42 48	9♍06 37	17♎19 08	24♎18 56	11♐55.6	4♍12.7	26♌08.8	10♌35.7	21♉43.8	21♏04.7	8♊36.4	22♊35.0	12♈49.8	10♒13.1
2 M	10 46 45	10 04 42	1♏20 02	8♏22 04	11R 50.8	3R 26.5	27 22.9	11 13.9	21 49.7	21 12.5	8 38.5	22 36.4	12R 48.5	10R 11.9
3 Tu	10 50 41	11 02 48	15 24 47	22 27 55	11 48.4	2 45.4	28 37.1	11 52.0	21 55.2	21 20.5	8 40.4	22 37.6	12 47.2	10 10.8
4 W	10 54 38	12 00 55	29 31 17	6♐34 45	11 47.9	2 10.5	29 51.2	12 30.2	22 00.4	21 28.6	8 42.2	22 38.9	12 45.8	10 09.6
5 Th	10 58 35	12 59 05	13♐38 12	20 41 32	11 47.8	1 42.4	1♍05.4	13 08.3	22 05.3	21 36.8	8 43.9	22 40.1	12 44.4	10 08.5
6 F	11 02 31	13 57 15	27 44 37	4♑47 22	11 46.9	1 22.1	2 19.7	13 46.3	22 09.8	21 45.1	8 45.5	22 41.2	12 43.0	10 07.4
7 Sa	11 06 28	14 55 27	11♑49 36	18 51 09	11 44.1	1D 10.0	3 33.9	14 24.3	22 14.0	21 53.6	8 47.0	22 42.3	12 41.6	10 06.4
8 Su	11 10 24	15 53 40	25 51 46	2♒51 09	11 38.6	1 06.5	4 48.2	15 02.3	22 17.9	22 02.1	8 48.4	22 43.4	12 40.2	10 05.3
9 M	11 14 21	16 51 55	9♒48 58	16 44 51	11 30.3	1 11.9	6 02.5	15 40.3	22 21.4	22 10.8	8 49.7	22 44.4	12 38.7	10 04.2
10 Tu	11 18 17	17 50 11	23 38 23	0♓29 09	11 19.6	1 26.3	7 16.9	16 18.2	22 24.6	22 19.6	8 50.9	22 45.3	12 37.2	10 03.2
11 W	11 22 14	18 48 29	7♓16 45	14 00 45	11 07.4	1 49.7	8 31.2	16 56.1	22 27.5	22 28.5	8 52.0	22 46.2	12 35.7	10 02.2
12 Th	11 26 10	19 46 49	20 40 51	27 16 45	10 54.9	2 21.9	9 45.6	17 33.9	22 30.0	22 37.6	8 52.9	22 47.1	12 34.2	10 01.2
13 F	11 30 07	20 45 11	3♈48 15	10♈15 12	10 43.3	3 02.7	11 00.0	18 11.7	22 32.1	22 46.7	8 53.8	22 47.9	12 32.7	10 00.2
14 Sa	11 34 04	21 43 34	16 37 36	22 55 29	10 33.6	3 51.7	12 14.5	18 49.5	22 33.9	22 55.9	8 54.5	22 48.6	12 31.2	9 59.3
15 Su	11 38 00	22 42 00	29 09 02	5♉18 30	10 26.5	4 48.5	13 29.0	19 27.2	22 35.3	23 05.3	8 55.2	22 49.3	12 29.7	9 58.3
16 M	11 41 57	23 40 28	11♉24 11	17 26 32	10 22.0	5 52.6	14 43.5	20 04.9	22 36.3	23 14.8	8 55.7	22 50.0	12 28.1	9 57.4
17 Tu	11 45 53	24 38 58	23 26 01	29 23 09	10D 19.9	7 03.4	15 58.0	20 42.6	22 37.0	23 24.3	8 56.1	22 50.6	12 26.6	9 56.5
18 W	11 49 50	25 37 30	5♊18 33	11♊12 51	10 19.5	8 20.4	17 12.6	21 20.3	22R 37.3	23 34.0	8 56.5	22 51.1	12 25.0	9 55.6
19 Th	11 53 46	26 36 04	17 06 41	23 00 44	10R 19.7	9 42.9	18 27.2	21 57.9	22 37.2	23 43.8	8 56.7	22 51.6	12 23.4	9 54.8
20 F	11 57 43	27 34 41	28 55 42	4♋52 17	10 19.5	11 10.4	19 41.8	22 35.4	22 36.8	23 53.6	8R 56.8	22 52.0	12 21.8	9 53.9
21 Sa	12 01 39	28 33 19	10♋51 08	16 52 56	10 17.9	12 42.2	20 56.4	23 13.0	22 36.0	24 03.6	8 56.8	22 52.4	12 20.2	9 53.1
22 Su	12 05 36	29 32 00	22 58 19	29 07 50	10 14.3	14 17.7	22 11.1	23 50.5	22 34.8	24 13.7	8 56.6	22 52.8	12 18.6	9 52.3
23 M	12 09 33	0♎30 43	5♌22 00	11♌41 15	10 08.1	15 56.4	23 25.8	24 28.0	22 33.2	24 23.8	8 56.4	22 53.0	12 17.0	9 51.6
24 Tu	12 13 29	1 29 28	18 05 57	24 36 19	9 59.6	17 37.7	24 40.5	25 05.4	22 31.2	24 34.1	8 56.1	22 53.3	12 15.3	9 50.8
25 W	12 17 26	2 28 16	1♍12 28	7♍54 22	9 49.4	19 21.2	25 55.2	25 42.8	22 28.8	24 44.5	8 55.6	22 53.4	12 13.7	9 50.1
26 Th	12 21 22	3 27 05	14 41 54	21 34 45	9 38.3	21 06.3	27 10.0	26 20.2	22 26.1	24 54.9	8 55.0	22 53.6	12 12.0	9 49.4
27 F	12 25 19	4 25 56	28 32 31	5♎34 39	9 27.7	22 52.8	28 24.8	26 57.5	22 23.0	25 05.5	8 54.4	22R 53.6	12 10.4	9 48.7
28 Sa	12 29 15	5 24 50	12♎40 33	19 49 29	9 18.6	24 40.2	29 39.6	27 34.8	22 19.4	25 16.1	8 53.6	22 53.7	12 08.7	9 48.0
29 Su	12 33 12	6 23 45	27 00 44	4♏13 33	9 11.8	26 28.3	0♎54.4	28 12.0	22 15.5	25 26.8	8 52.7	22 53.6	12 07.1	9 47.4
30 M	12 37 08	7 22 43	11♏27 11	18 40 59	9 07.7	28 16.7	2 09.2	28 49.2	22 11.2	25 37.6	8 51.7	22 53.5	12 05.4	9 46.8

LONGITUDE — October 2030

Day	Sid.Time	☉	0 hr ☽	Noon ☽	True ☊	☿	♀	♂	⚳	♃	♄	♅	♆	♇
1 Tu	12 41 05	8♎21 42	25♏54 19	3♐06 40	9♐06.1	0♎05.3	3♎24.1	29♌26.4	22♉06.6	25♏48.5	8♊50.6	22♊53.4	12♈03.7	9♒46.2
2 W	12 45 02	9 20 43	10♐17 34	17 26 42	9D 06.1	1 53.9	4 38.9	0♍03.6	22R 01.5	25 59.5	8R 49.4	22R 53.2	12R 02.1	9R 45.6
3 Th	12 48 58	10 19 46	24 33 46	1♑38 35	9R 06.8	3 42.3	5 53.8	0 40.7	21 56.1	26 10.6	8 48.1	22 53.0	12 00.4	9 45.1
4 F	12 52 55	11 18 50	8♑41 01	15 40 59	9 07.0	5 30.3	7 08.7	1 17.7	21 50.3	26 21.7	8 46.6	22 52.7	11 58.7	9 44.6
5 Sa	12 56 51	12 17 56	22 38 27	29 33 20	9 05.6	7 18.0	8 23.6	1 54.7	21 44.1	26 32.9	8 45.1	22 52.3	11 57.1	9 44.1
6 Su	13 00 48	13 17 04	6♒25 38	13♒15 18	9 02.0	9 05.1	9 38.5	2 31.7	21 37.6	26 44.2	8 43.5	22 51.9	11 55.4	9 43.7
7 M	13 04 44	14 16 13	20 02 16	26 46 28	8 56.1	10 51.7	10 53.5	3 08.6	21 30.7	26 55.6	8 41.7	22 51.5	11 53.7	9 43.2
8 Tu	13 08 41	15 15 25	3♓27 49	10♓06 13	8 48.1	12 37.7	12 08.4	3 45.5	21 23.4	27 07.0	8 39.9	22 51.0	11 52.1	9 42.8
9 W	13 12 37	16 14 38	16 41 32	23 13 40	8 39.0	14 23.0	13 23.4	4 22.4	21 15.8	27 18.5	8 37.9	22 50.4	11 50.4	9 42.4
10 Th	13 16 34	17 13 53	29 42 31	6♈07 58	8 29.5	16 07.6	14 38.4	4 59.2	21 07.8	27 30.1	8 35.9	22 49.8	11 48.7	9 42.1
11 F	13 20 30	18 13 10	12♈29 59	18 48 31	8 20.8	17 51.5	15 53.4	5 36.0	20 59.5	27 41.8	8 33.7	22 49.2	11 47.1	9 41.7
12 Sa	13 24 27	19 12 29	25 03 36	1♉15 17	8 13.5	19 34.7	17 08.4	6 12.7	20 50.8	27 53.5	8 31.5	22 48.5	11 45.4	9 41.4
13 Su	13 28 24	20 11 51	7♉23 41	13 28 59	8 08.3	21 17.2	18 23.4	6 49.5	20 41.9	28 05.3	8 29.1	22 47.7	11 43.8	9 41.2
14 M	13 32 20	21 11 14	19 31 25	25 31 17	8 05.3	22 59.0	19 38.4	7 26.1	20 32.5	28 17.1	8 26.7	22 46.9	11 42.1	9 40.9
15 Tu	13 36 17	22 10 40	1♊28 56	7♊24 47	8D 04.3	24 40.1	20 53.5	8 02.8	20 22.9	28 29.0	8 24.2	22 46.1	11 40.5	9 40.7
16 W	13 40 13	23 10 08	13 19 16	19 12 55	8 04.9	26 20.5	22 08.5	8 39.3	20 12.9	28 41.0	8 21.5	22 45.2	11 38.8	9 40.5
17 Th	13 44 10	24 09 38	25 06 16	0♋59 54	8 06.4	28 00.2	23 23.6	9 15.9	20 02.7	28 53.1	8 18.8	22 44.2	11 37.2	9 40.3
18 F	13 48 06	25 09 11	6♋54 27	12 50 32	8 07.8	29 39.2	24 38.7	9 52.4	19 52.1	29 05.2	8 16.0	22 43.2	11 35.6	9 40.2
19 Sa	13 52 03	26 08 46	18 48 48	24 49 56	8R 08.6	1♏17.6	25 53.8	10 28.9	19 41.2	29 17.4	8 13.1	22 42.2	11 34.0	9 40.1
20 Su	13 55 59	27 08 23	0♌54 33	7♌03 18	8 08.0	2 55.4	27 08.9	11 05.3	19 30.1	29 29.6	8 10.0	22 41.1	11 32.4	9 40.0
21 M	13 59 56	28 08 02	13 16 47	19 35 32	8 05.8	4 32.5	28 24.0	11 41.7	19 18.7	29 41.9	8 07.0	22 40.0	11 30.8	9 39.9
22 Tu	14 03 53	29 07 43	26 00 03	2♍30 42	8 01.9	6 09.0	29 39.2	12 18.1	19 07.0	29 54.2	8 03.8	22 38.8	11 29.2	9D 39.9
23 W	14 07 49	0♏07 27	9♍07 49	15 51 31	7 56.7	7 44.9	0♏54.3	12 54.4	18 55.1	0♐06.6	8 00.5	22 37.5	11 27.6	9 39.9
24 Th	14 11 46	1 07 13	22 41 52	29 38 44	7 50.7	9 20.3	2 09.5	13 30.6	18 43.0	0 19.0	7 57.1	22 36.3	11 26.1	9 39.9
25 F	14 15 42	2 07 01	6♎41 47	13♎50 37	7 44.9	10 55.1	3 24.6	14 06.9	18 30.6	0 31.5	7 53.7	22 34.9	11 24.5	9 40.0
26 Sa	14 19 39	3 06 51	21 04 34	28 22 55	7 39.9	12 29.4	4 39.8	14 43.0	18 18.0	0 44.1	7 50.2	22 33.6	11 23.0	9 40.1
27 Su	14 23 35	4 06 43	5♏44 46	13♏09 11	7 36.3	14 03.1	5 55.0	15 19.2	18 05.2	0 56.7	7 46.6	22 32.1	11 21.5	9 40.2
28 M	14 27 32	5 06 38	20 35 09	28 01 41	7D 34.5	15 36.4	7 10.2	15 55.3	17 52.3	1 09.3	7 42.9	22 30.7	11 20.0	9 40.3
29 Tu	14 31 28	6 06 34	5♐27 46	12♐52 32	7 34.2	17 09.1	8 25.4	16 31.3	17 39.1	1 22.0	7 39.1	22 29.2	11 18.5	9 40.5
30 W	14 35 25	7 06 31	20 15 07	27 34 51	7 35.2	18 41.4	9 40.6	17 07.3	17 25.9	1 34.8	7 35.3	22 27.6	11 17.0	9 40.7
31 Th	14 39 22	8 06 31	4♑51 07	12♑03 29	7 36.7	20 13.1	10 55.8	17 43.2	17 12.4	1 47.6	7 31.4	22 26.1	11 15.6	9 40.9

Astro Data

	Dy Hr Mn
☿D	8 9:27
☽0N	11 19:56
♃⊼♅	13 15:21
⚳R	18 19:42
♄R	20 21:30
☉0S	22 23:26
☽0S	26 6:25
♅R	28 8:27
♀0S	1 9:08
☿0S	3 15:09
♃□♆	7 8:37
☽0N	9 2:54
♇D	23 3:06
☽0S	23 15:57

Planet Ingress

	Dy Hr Mn
♀ ♍	4 14:50
☉ ♎	22 23:27
♀ ♎	28 18:34
☿ ♎	1 10:50
♂ ♍	2 9:42
☿ ♏	18 17:03
♀ ♏	22 18:40
♃ ♐	22 23:14
☉ ♏	23 9:00

Last Aspect / ☽ Ingress

Last Aspect Dy Hr Mn	☽ Ingress Dy Hr Mn
1 15:26 ♀ ⚹	♏ 1 21:43
3 23:28 ♀ □	♐ 4 0:49
5 15:22 ♅ ☍	♑ 6 3:50
7 17:15 ♃ ⚹	♒ 8 7:06
9 22:26 ♅ △	♓ 10 11:09
12 3:48 ♅ □	♈ 12 16:59
14 11:47 ♅ ⚹	♉ 15 1:39
17 1:36 ☉ △	♊ 17 13:15
19 19:56 ☉ □	♋ 20 2:10
22 12:51 ☉ ⚹	♌ 22 13:41
24 12:56 ♂ ☌	♍ 24 21:49
26 22:35 ♀ ☌	♎ 27 2:30
29 1:32 ♂ ⚹	♏ 29 4:58

Last Aspect / ☽ Ingress

Last Aspect Dy Hr Mn	☽ Ingress Dy Hr Mn
1 6:14 ☿ ⚹	♐ 1 6:49
2 21:10 ♅ ☍	♑ 3 9:13
5 6:42 ♃ ⚹	♒ 5 12:46
7 12:16 ♃ □	♓ 7 17:47
9 19:39 ♃ △	♈ 10 0:33
11 19:41 ♅ ⚹	♉ 12 9:34
14 17:39 ♃ ☍	♊ 14 21:01
17 4:54 ☿ △	♋ 17 9:58
19 20:58 ♃ △	♌ 19 22:13
22 7:08 ♃ □	♍ 22 7:24
23 23:51 ♅ □	♎ 24 12:36
26 2:28 ♅ △	♏ 26 14:39
27 15:39 ♂ ⚹	♐ 28 15:11
30 3:37 ♅ ☍	♑ 30 15:59

☽ Phases & Eclipses

Dy Hr Mn	
4 21:55	☽ 12♐25
11 21:18	○ 19♓11
19 19:56	☾ 26♊55
27 9:55	● 4♎21
4 3:56	☽ 10♑59
11 10:47	○ 18♈10
19 14:50	☾ 26♋16
26 20:17	● 3♏28

Astro Data

1 September 2030
Julian Day # 47726
SVP 4♓49'36"
GC 27♐16.1 ⚴ 6♓10.1R
Eris 26♈45.4R ⚵ 26♐42.7
⚷ 16♉50.9R ⚶ 6♊14.8
☽ Mean ☊ 11♐54.8

1 October 2030
Julian Day # 47756
SVP 4♓49'33"
GC 27♐16.1 ⚴ 29♒37.0R
Eris 26♈30.7R ⚵ 0♑57.1
⚷ 16♉07.2R ⚶ 10♊01.8
☽ Mean ☊ 10♐19.4

November 2030 — LONGITUDE

Day	Sid.Time	☉	0 hr ☽	Noon ☽	True ☊	☿	♀	♂	⚳	♃	♄	♅	♆	♇
1 F	14 43 18	9♏06 32	19♑11 36	26♑15 15	7♐38.0	21♏44.4	12♏11.0	18♍19.1	16♉58.9	2♐00.4	7♊27.4	22♊24.4	11♈14.1	9♒41.2
2 Sa	14 47 15	10 06 34	3♒14 19	10♒08 46	7R 38.6	23 15.3	13 26.2	18 54.9	16R 45.3	2 13.3	7R 23.4	22R 22.8	11R 12.7	9 41.4
3 Su	14 51 11	11 06 38	16 58 38	23 44 01	7 38.0	24 45.6	14 41.4	19 30.7	16 31.5	2 26.2	7 19.3	22 21.1	11 11.3	9 41.7
4 M	14 55 08	12 06 44	0♓25 03	7♓01 53	7 36.1	26 15.5	15 56.7	20 06.4	16 17.7	2 39.1	7 15.1	22 19.3	11 09.9	9 42.1
5 Tu	14 59 04	13 06 51	13 34 42	20 03 41	7 33.1	27 44.9	17 11.9	20 42.1	16 03.9	2 52.1	7 10.9	22 17.5	11 08.6	9 42.4
6 W	15 03 01	14 07 00	26 29 01	2♈50 53	7 29.5	29 13.8	18 27.1	21 17.8	15 50.0	3 05.1	7 06.6	22 15.7	11 07.2	9 42.8
7 Th	15 06 57	15 07 10	9♈09 26	15 24 53	7 25.7	0♐42.3	19 42.3	21 53.3	15 36.1	3 18.1	7 02.3	22 13.8	11 05.9	9 43.2
8 F	15 10 54	16 07 22	21 37 22	27 47 04	7 22.2	2 10.2	20 57.6	22 28.9	15 22.1	3 31.2	6 57.9	22 11.9	11 04.6	9 43.7
9 Sa	15 14 51	17 07 36	3♉54 09	9♉58 46	7 19.4	3 37.7	22 12.8	23 04.4	15 08.2	3 44.3	6 53.4	22 10.0	11 03.3	9 44.2
10 Su	15 18 47	18 07 51	16 01 08	22 01 26	7 17.6	5 04.5	23 28.0	23 39.8	14 54.3	3 57.4	6 48.9	22 08.0	11 02.1	9 44.7
11 M	15 22 44	19 08 08	27 59 54	3♊56 45	7D 16.8	6 30.8	24 43.3	24 15.2	14 40.4	4 10.6	6 44.4	22 06.0	11 00.8	9 45.2
12 Tu	15 26 40	20 08 27	9♊52 15	15 46 44	7 17.0	7 56.5	25 58.5	24 50.5	14 26.6	4 23.8	6 39.8	22 04.0	10 59.6	9 45.8
13 W	15 30 37	21 08 48	21 40 30	27 33 55	7 17.9	9 21.4	27 13.8	25 25.8	14 12.8	4 37.0	6 35.2	22 02.0	10 58.4	9 46.3
14 Th	15 34 33	22 09 11	3♋27 24	9♋21 21	7 19.3	10 45.7	28 29.0	26 01.0	13 59.2	4 50.2	6 30.5	21 59.9	10 57.2	9 47.0
15 F	15 38 30	23 09 35	15 16 15	21 12 36	7 20.7	12 09.1	29 44.3	26 36.1	13 45.6	5 03.5	6 25.8	21 57.7	10 56.1	9 47.6
16 Sa	15 42 26	24 10 02	27 10 55	3♌11 44	7 21.9	13 31.7	0♐59.5	27 11.3	13 32.1	5 16.8	6 21.1	21 55.6	10 55.0	9 48.3
17 Su	15 46 23	25 10 30	9♌15 38	15 23 10	7R 22.7	14 53.2	2 14.8	27 46.3	13 18.8	5 30.1	6 16.3	21 53.4	10 53.9	9 49.0
18 M	15 50 20	26 11 00	21 34 55	27 51 27	7 22.9	16 13.7	3 30.1	28 21.3	13 05.6	5 43.4	6 11.5	21 51.2	10 52.8	9 49.7
19 Tu	15 54 16	27 11 31	4♍13 16	10♍40 53	7 22.6	17 32.9	4 45.4	28 56.2	12 52.6	5 56.8	6 06.7	21 49.0	10 51.8	9 50.4
20 W	15 58 13	28 12 05	17 14 43	23 55 06	7 21.8	18 50.7	6 00.6	29 31.1	12 39.7	6 10.1	6 01.9	21 46.7	10 50.8	9 51.2
21 Th	16 02 09	29 12 40	0♎42 18	7♎36 25	7 20.9	20 07.0	7 15.9	0♎05.9	12 27.1	6 23.5	5 57.0	21 44.4	10 49.8	9 52.0
22 F	16 06 06	0♐13 17	14 37 26	21 45 10	7 19.9	21 21.4	8 31.2	0 40.7	12 14.6	6 36.9	5 52.1	21 42.1	10 48.8	9 52.8
23 Sa	16 10 02	1 13 56	28 59 15	6♏19 09	7 19.2	22 33.9	9 46.5	1 15.4	12 02.4	6 50.3	5 47.2	21 39.7	10 47.9	9 53.7
24 Su	16 13 59	2 14 36	13♏44 08	21 13 21	7 18.7	23 44.0	11 01.8	1 50.0	11 50.4	7 03.7	5 42.3	21 37.4	10 47.0	9 54.5
25 M	16 17 55	3 15 18	28 45 46	6♐20 15	7D 18.6	24 51.4	12 17.1	2 24.6	11 38.6	7 17.2	5 37.4	21 35.0	10 46.1	9 55.4
26 Tu	16 21 52	4 16 02	13♐55 38	21 30 42	7 18.7	25 55.9	13 32.4	2 59.0	11 27.1	7 30.6	5 32.4	21 32.6	10 45.2	9 56.4
27 W	16 25 49	5 16 46	29 04 16	6♑35 15	7 18.9	26 56.9	14 47.7	3 33.5	11 15.9	7 44.1	5 27.5	21 30.2	10 44.4	9 57.3
28 Th	16 29 45	6 17 32	14♑02 37	21 25 31	7 19.0	27 54.0	16 03.0	4 07.8	11 04.9	7 57.5	5 22.6	21 27.8	10 43.6	9 58.3
29 F	16 33 42	7 18 19	28 43 16	5♒55 19	7R 19.1	28 46.6	17 18.3	4 42.1	10 54.3	8 11.0	5 17.6	21 25.3	10 42.9	9 59.3
30 Sa	16 37 38	8 19 06	13♒01 19	20 01 02	7 19.0	29 34.1	18 33.6	5 16.3	10 43.9	8 24.5	5 12.7	21 22.9	10 42.2	10 00.3

December 2030 — LONGITUDE

Day	Sid.Time	☉	0 hr ☽	Noon ☽	True ☊	☿	♀	♂	⚳	♃	♄	♅	♆	♇
1 Su	16 41 35	9♐19 55	26♒54 26	3♓41 35	7♐19.0	0♑15.9	19♐48.9	5♎50.4	10♉33.9	8♐37.9	5♊07.8	21♊20.4	10♈41.5	10♒01.4
2 M	16 45 31	10 20 44	10♓22 39	16 57 54	7D 19.0	0 51.2	21 04.1	6 24.5	10R 24.2	8 51.4	5R 02.9	21R 17.9	10R 40.8	10 02.5
3 Tu	16 49 28	11 21 34	23 27 40	29 52 21	7 19.2	1 19.2	22 19.4	6 58.4	10 14.8	9 04.8	4 58.0	21 15.4	10 40.2	10 03.6
4 W	16 53 24	12 22 25	6♈12 19	12♈28 02	7 19.6	1 39.0	23 34.7	7 32.3	10 05.8	9 18.3	4 53.1	21 12.9	10 39.6	10 04.7
5 Th	16 57 21	13 23 17	18 39 55	24 48 23	7 20.2	1R 50.0	24 50.0	8 06.1	9 57.1	9 31.7	4 48.3	21 10.4	10 39.0	10 05.8
6 F	17 01 18	14 24 10	0♉53 51	6♉56 44	7 21.0	1 51.1	26 05.2	8 39.9	9 48.7	9 45.2	4 43.5	21 07.8	10 38.5	10 07.0
7 Sa	17 05 14	15 25 04	12 57 24	18 56 11	7 21.7	1 41.8	27 20.5	9 13.6	9 40.8	9 58.6	4 38.6	21 05.3	10 37.9	10 08.2
8 Su	17 09 11	16 25 58	24 53 27	0♊49 30	7R 22.1	1 21.4	28 35.8	9 47.1	9 33.1	10 12.1	4 33.9	21 02.7	10 37.5	10 09.4
9 M	17 13 07	17 26 54	6♊44 37	12 39 05	7 22.1	0 49.6	29 51.0	10 20.6	9 25.9	10 25.5	4 29.1	21 00.2	10 37.0	10 10.6
10 Tu	17 17 04	18 27 50	18 33 10	24 27 08	7 21.6	0 06.5	1♑06.3	10 54.1	9 19.0	10 38.9	4 24.4	20 57.6	10 36.6	10 11.9
11 W	17 21 00	19 28 48	0♋21 15	6♋15 45	7 20.4	29♐12.6	2 21.5	11 27.4	9 12.6	10 52.3	4 19.7	20 55.1	10 36.3	10 13.2
12 Th	17 24 57	20 29 46	12 10 55	18 07 02	7 18.6	28 08.8	3 36.8	12 00.7	9 06.5	11 05.7	4 15.1	20 52.5	10 35.9	10 14.5
13 F	17 28 54	21 30 46	24 04 22	0♌03 16	7 16.4	26 56.7	4 52.0	12 33.9	9 00.7	11 19.1	4 10.5	20 50.0	10 35.6	10 15.8
14 Sa	17 32 50	22 31 46	6♌04 02	12 07 03	7 14.1	25 38.3	6 07.3	13 06.9	8 55.4	11 32.5	4 06.0	20 47.4	10 35.4	10 17.1
15 Su	17 36 47	23 32 47	18 12 41	24 21 20	7 11.9	24 16.2	7 22.5	13 39.9	8 50.5	11 45.8	4 01.5	20 44.9	10 35.1	10 18.5
16 M	17 40 43	24 33 49	0♍33 25	6♍49 22	7 10.2	22 53.2	8 37.8	14 12.8	8 45.9	11 59.2	3 57.0	20 42.3	10 34.9	10 19.8
17 Tu	17 44 40	25 34 52	13 09 39	19 34 40	7D 09.3	21 32.0	9 53.0	14 45.7	8 41.8	12 12.5	3 52.6	20 39.7	10 34.7	10 21.2
18 W	17 48 36	26 35 56	26 04 52	2♎40 38	7 09.3	20 15.3	11 08.2	15 18.4	8 38.1	12 25.8	3 48.2	20 37.2	10 34.6	10 22.7
19 Th	17 52 33	27 37 01	9♎22 19	16 10 13	7 10.1	19 05.5	12 23.5	15 51.0	8 34.7	12 39.0	3 43.9	20 34.7	10 34.5	10 24.1
20 F	17 56 29	28 38 07	23 04 31	0♏05 19	7 11.5	18 04.2	13 38.7	16 23.5	8 31.8	12 52.3	3 39.7	20 32.1	10 34.4	10 25.5
21 Sa	18 00 26	29 39 14	7♏12 34	14 26 05	7 12.9	17 12.8	14 53.9	16 56.0	8 29.3	13 05.5	3 35.5	20 29.6	10D 34.4	10 27.0
22 Su	18 04 23	0♑40 21	21 45 29	29 10 15	7R 13.9	16 31.9	16 09.2	17 28.3	8 27.1	13 18.7	3 31.4	20 27.1	10 34.4	10 28.5
23 M	18 08 19	1 41 29	6♐39 38	14♐12 44	7 14.0	16 02.0	17 24.4	18 00.5	8 25.4	13 31.9	3 27.3	20 24.6	10 34.4	10 30.0
24 Tu	18 12 16	2 42 38	21 48 29	29 25 42	7 12.7	15 42.9	18 39.6	18 32.6	8 24.1	13 45.0	3 23.4	20 22.1	10 34.5	10 31.5
25 W	18 16 12	3 43 47	7♑03 08	14♑39 27	7 10.1	15D 34.2	19 54.8	19 04.6	8 23.2	13 58.1	3 19.5	20 19.6	10 34.6	10 33.1
26 Th	18 20 09	4 44 57	22 13 24	29 43 47	7 06.4	15 35.2	21 10.0	19 36.5	8D 22.7	14 11.2	3 15.6	20 17.2	10 34.8	10 34.6
27 F	18 24 05	5 46 06	7♒09 30	14♒29 39	7 02.1	15 45.4	22 25.2	20 08.2	8 22.6	14 24.3	3 11.9	20 14.7	10 35.0	10 36.2
28 Sa	18 28 02	6 47 16	21 43 31	28 50 33	6 57.8	16 03.9	23 40.4	20 39.9	8 22.9	14 37.3	3 08.2	20 12.3	10 35.2	10 37.8
29 Su	18 31 58	7 48 25	5♓50 27	12♓43 04	6 54.4	16 30.0	24 55.6	21 11.4	8 23.6	14 50.2	3 04.6	20 09.9	10 35.4	10 39.4
30 M	18 35 55	8 49 35	19 28 28	26 06 49	6 52.1	17 03.0	26 10.7	21 42.8	8 24.7	15 03.2	3 01.1	20 07.5	10 35.7	10 41.0
31 Tu	18 39 52	9 50 44	2♈38 29	9♈03 52	6D 51.3	17 42.0	27 25.9	22 14.1	8 26.2	15 16.0	2 57.6	20 05.1	10 36.0	10 42.6

Astro Data Dy Hr Mn	Planet Ingress Dy Hr Mn	Last Aspect Dy Hr Mn	☽ Ingress Dy Hr Mn	Last Aspect Dy Hr Mn	☽ Ingress Dy Hr Mn	☽ Phases & Eclipses Dy Hr Mn
☽0N 5 8:09	☿ ♐ 7 0:30	1 3:23 ☿ ✶	♒ 1 18:25	30 14:21 ♅ △	♓ 1 5:27	2 11:56 ☽ 10♒06
♃☍♄ 20 1:05	♀ ♐ 15 17:01	3 14:04 ☿ □	♓ 3 23:15	2 20:22 ♀ □	♈ 3 12:14	10 3:30 ○ 17♉47
☽0S 20 1:07	♂ ♎ 21 7:54	6 4:16 ☿ △	♈ 6 6:37	5 12:03 ♀ △	♉ 5 22:14	18 8:32 ☾ 26♌02
♂0S 27 17:17	☉ ♐ 22 6:44	8 1:09 ♅ ✶	♉ 8 16:20	6 18:20 ♇ □	♊ 8 10:20	25 6:46 ● 3♐02
		10 15:27 ♂ △	♊ 11 4:02	10 22:44 ☿ ☍	♋ 10 23:17	25 6:50:18 ● T 03'44"
☽0N 2 13:37	☿ ♑ 1 2:27	13 7:25 ♂ □	♋ 13 16:58	11 23:03 ♂ □	♌ 13 11:53	
☿R 6 2:46	♀ ♑ 9 14:52	15 23:24 ♂ ✶	♌ 16 5:38	15 11:51 ☿ △	♍ 15 22:56	1 22:57 ☽ 9♓48
♃✶♇ 8 6:43	☿ ♐R 10 15:10	18 8:32 ☉ □	♍ 18 16:04	18 0:01 ☉ □	♎ 18 7:09	9 22:40 ○ 17♊54
♃△♆ 10 8:01	☉ ♑ 21 20:09	20 22:21 ♂ ☌	♎ 20 22:46	20 9:20 ☉ ✶	♏ 20 11:51	9 22:28 ● A 0.941
☽0S 17 8:56		22 11:55 ♅ △	♏ 23 1:40	21 12:50 ♀ ✶	♐ 22 13:20	18 0:01 ☾ 26♍05
♆D 21 20:40		23 17:48 ♇ □	♐ 25 1:58	23 21:46 ♅ ☍	♑ 24 12:54	24 17:32 ● 2♑57
☿D 25 21:15		26 19:32 ☿ ☌	♑ 27 1:29	25 21:05 ♀ ☌	♒ 26 12:26	31 13:36 ☽ 9♈55
♆✶♇ 26 14:20		27 18:40 ♆ □	♒ 29 2:07	27 21:42 ♂ △	♓ 28 13:58	
⚳D 27 5:37				30 12:08 ♀ ✶	♈ 30 19:07	
☽0N 29 21:27						

Astro Data

1 November 2030
Julian Day # 47787
SVP 4♓49'30"
GC 27♐16.2 ⚴ 27♒39.1
Eris 26♈12.3R ⚵ 9♑01.0
⚷ 14♉44.5R ⚶ 7♊33.3R
☽ Mean ☊ 8♐40.9

1 December 2030
Julian Day # 47817
SVP 4♓49'25"
GC 27♐16.3 ⚴ 0♓43.3
Eris 25♈56.6R ⚵ 19♑11.2
⚷ 13♉17.8R ⚶ 0♊16.3R
☽ Mean ☊ 7♐05.6

LONGITUDE — January 2031

Day	Sid.Time	☉	0 hr ☽	Noon ☽	True ☊	☿	♀	♂	⚳	♃	♄	♅	♆	♇
1 W	18 43 48	10♑51 53	15♈23 28	21♈37 51	6♐51.9	18♐26.5	28♑41.0	22♎45.2	8♉28.1	15♐28.9	2♊54.3	20♊02.8	10♈36.4	10♒44.3
2 Th	18 47 45	11 53 03	27 47 37	3♉53 21	6 53.4	19 16.0	29 56.1	23 16.2	8 30.4	15 41.7	2R51.0	20R00.4	10 36.8	10 45.9
3 F	18 51 41	12 54 11	9♉55 40	15 55 09	6 55.2	20 09.7	1♒11.2	23 47.1	8 33.1	15 54.5	2 47.8	19 58.1	10 37.2	10 47.6
4 Sa	18 55 38	13 55 20	21 52 24	27 47 56	6R56.7	21 07.3	2 26.3	24 17.9	8 36.1	16 07.2	2 44.7	19 55.8	10 37.7	10 49.3
5 Su	18 59 34	14 56 29	3♊42 17	9♊35 55	6 57.0	22 08.3	3 41.4	24 48.5	8 39.6	16 19.8	2 41.7	19 53.6	10 38.1	10 51.0
6 M	19 03 31	15 57 37	15 29 17	21 22 46	6 55.8	23 12.4	4 56.5	25 19.0	8 43.4	16 32.5	2 38.8	19 51.3	10 38.7	10 52.7
7 Tu	19 07 27	16 58 45	27 16 43	3♋11 27	6 52.5	24 19.1	6 11.5	25 49.4	8 47.5	16 45.0	2 36.0	19 49.1	10 39.2	10 54.4
8 W	19 11 24	17 59 53	9♋07 15	15 04 21	6 47.2	25 28.3	7 26.6	26 19.6	8 52.1	16 57.6	2 33.3	19 47.0	10 39.8	10 56.2
9 Th	19 15 21	19 01 01	21 02 58	27 03 17	6 40.2	26 39.7	8 41.6	26 49.7	8 57.0	17 10.0	2 30.7	19 44.8	10 40.5	10 57.9
10 F	19 19 17	20 02 08	3♌05 29	9♌09 42	6 31.9	27 53.0	9 56.6	27 19.6	9 02.2	17 22.4	2 28.2	19 42.7	10 41.1	10 59.6
11 Sa	19 23 14	21 03 16	15 16 06	21 24 49	6 23.1	29 08.1	11 11.6	27 49.4	9 07.9	17 34.8	2 25.8	19 40.6	10 41.8	11 01.4
12 Su	19 27 10	22 04 23	27 36 03	3♍49 56	6 14.8	0♑24.7	12 26.6	28 19.0	9 13.8	17 47.1	2 23.4	19 38.6	10 42.6	11 03.2
13 M	19 31 07	23 05 30	10♍06 41	16 26 30	6 07.7	1 42.8	13 41.5	28 48.5	9 20.1	17 59.4	2 21.2	19 36.5	10 43.3	11 04.9
14 Tu	19 35 03	24 06 37	22 49 37	29 16 18	6 02.5	3 02.2	14 56.5	29 17.8	9 26.8	18 11.5	2 19.1	19 34.5	10 44.1	11 06.7
15 W	19 39 00	25 07 43	5♎46 49	12♎21 27	5 59.6	4 22.8	16 11.4	29 46.9	9 33.8	18 23.7	2 17.1	19 32.6	10 44.9	11 08.5
16 Th	19 42 56	26 08 50	19 00 30	25 44 14	5D58.7	5 44.5	17 26.3	0♏15.9	9 41.1	18 35.7	2 15.2	19 30.7	10 45.8	11 10.3
17 F	19 46 53	27 09 56	2♏32 54	9♏26 43	5 59.2	7 07.3	18 41.2	0 44.7	9 48.8	18 47.7	2 13.4	19 28.8	10 46.7	11 12.1
18 Sa	19 50 50	28 11 03	16 25 48	23 30 12	6R00.3	8 31.0	19 56.1	1 13.4	9 56.8	18 59.7	2 11.7	19 26.9	10 47.6	11 13.9
19 Su	19 54 46	29 12 09	0♐39 51	7♐54 34	6 00.7	9 55.6	21 10.9	1 41.9	10 05.1	19 11.5	2 10.1	19 25.1	10 48.6	11 15.7
20 M	19 58 43	0♒13 15	15 13 59	22 37 34	5 59.5	11 21.1	22 25.8	2 10.1	10 13.8	19 23.3	2 08.6	19 23.4	10 49.6	11 17.6
21 Tu	20 02 39	1 14 20	0♑04 37	7♑34 16	5 56.0	12 47.3	23 40.6	2 38.2	10 22.7	19 35.0	2 07.3	19 21.6	10 50.6	11 19.4
22 W	20 06 36	2 15 25	15 05 32	22 37 15	5 49.9	14 14.4	24 55.4	3 06.1	10 32.0	19 46.7	2 06.0	19 19.9	10 51.7	11 21.2
23 Th	20 10 32	3 16 29	0♒08 13	7♒37 15	5 41.6	15 42.2	26 10.2	3 33.8	10 41.6	19 58.3	2 04.9	19 18.3	10 52.8	11 23.1
24 F	20 14 29	4 17 33	15 03 08	22 24 45	5 31.9	17 10.7	27 24.9	4 01.3	10 51.5	20 09.8	2 03.8	19 16.7	10 53.9	11 24.9
25 Sa	20 18 25	5 18 35	29 41 10	6♓51 33	5 22.1	18 39.9	28 39.7	4 28.6	11 01.7	20 21.2	2 02.9	19 15.1	10 55.0	11 26.8
26 Su	20 22 22	6 19 37	13♓55 19	20 52 03	5 13.2	20 09.8	29 54.4	4 55.7	11 12.1	20 32.5	2 02.1	19 13.6	10 56.2	11 28.6
27 M	20 26 19	7 20 37	27 41 33	4♈23 48	5 06.3	21 40.4	1♓09.0	5 22.6	11 22.9	20 43.8	2 01.4	19 12.1	10 57.4	11 30.5
28 Tu	20 30 15	8 21 36	10♈58 58	17 27 21	5 01.7	23 11.7	2 23.7	5 49.2	11 34.0	20 55.0	2 00.8	19 10.7	10 58.7	11 32.3
29 W	20 34 12	9 22 35	23 49 23	0♉05 35	4D59.5	24 43.7	3 38.3	6 15.6	11 45.3	21 06.1	2 00.4	19 09.3	10 59.9	11 34.2
30 Th	20 38 08	10 23 32	6♉16 34	12 22 58	4 59.0	26 16.3	4 52.9	6 41.8	11 56.9	21 17.1	2 00.0	19 07.9	11 01.2	11 36.0
31 F	20 42 05	11 24 27	18 25 28	24 24 45	4R59.5	27 49.6	6 07.5	7 07.8	12 08.8	21 28.0	1 59.8	19 06.6	11 02.6	11 37.9

LONGITUDE — February 2031

Day	Sid.Time	☉	0 hr ☽	Noon ☽	True ☊	☿	♀	♂	⚳	♃	♄	♅	♆	♇
1 Sa	20 46 01	12♒25 22	0♊21 32	6♊16 28	4♐59.8	29♑23.6	7♓22.0	7♏33.5	12♉21.0	21♐38.8	1♊59.6	19♊05.4	11♈03.9	11♒39.7
2 Su	20 49 58	13 26 15	12 10 14	18 03 26	4R58.9	0♒58.3	8 36.5	7 59.0	12 33.4	21 49.6	1D59.6	19R04.2	11 05.3	11 41.6
3 M	20 53 54	14 27 07	23 56 41	29 50 30	4 55.9	2 33.7	9 50.9	8 24.3	12 46.1	22 00.2	1 59.7	19 03.0	11 06.7	11 43.4
4 Tu	20 57 51	15 27 58	5♋45 23	11♋41 45	4 50.1	4 09.8	11 05.3	8 49.3	12 59.0	22 10.8	1 59.9	19 01.9	11 08.2	11 45.3
5 W	21 01 48	16 28 47	17 40 01	23 40 27	4 41.5	5 46.6	12 19.7	9 14.1	13 12.2	22 21.2	2 00.3	19 00.8	11 09.6	11 47.1
6 Th	21 05 44	17 29 35	29 43 21	5♌48 54	4 30.4	7 24.2	13 34.1	9 38.6	13 25.7	22 31.6	2 00.7	18 59.8	11 11.1	11 49.0
7 F	21 09 41	18 30 22	11♌57 14	18 08 28	4 17.5	9 02.5	14 48.4	10 02.8	13 39.3	22 41.8	2 01.3	18 58.9	11 12.6	11 50.8
8 Sa	21 13 37	19 31 08	24 22 37	0♍39 42	4 03.8	10 41.6	16 02.6	10 26.8	13 53.3	22 52.0	2 01.9	18 58.0	11 14.2	11 52.7
9 Su	21 17 34	20 31 52	6♍59 42	13 22 35	3 50.7	12 21.5	17 16.9	10 50.4	14 07.4	23 02.1	2 02.7	18 57.1	11 15.8	11 54.5
10 M	21 21 30	21 32 35	19 48 19	26 16 50	3 39.2	14 02.2	18 31.0	11 13.8	14 21.8	23 12.0	2 03.6	18 56.3	11 17.4	11 56.3
11 Tu	21 25 27	22 33 17	2♎48 08	9♎22 12	3 30.2	15 43.7	19 45.2	11 37.0	14 36.4	23 21.9	2 04.6	18 55.5	11 19.0	11 58.2
12 W	21 29 23	23 33 58	15 59 04	22 38 46	3 24.2	17 26.0	20 59.3	11 59.8	14 51.2	23 31.6	2 05.7	18 54.8	11 20.6	12 00.0
13 Th	21 33 20	24 34 38	29 21 24	6♏07 03	3 21.1	19 09.2	22 13.4	12 22.3	15 06.3	23 41.3	2 06.9	18 54.1	11 22.3	12 01.8
14 F	21 37 17	25 35 17	12♏55 51	19 47 55	3 20.1	20 53.2	23 27.4	12 44.5	15 21.5	23 50.8	2 08.3	18 53.5	11 24.0	12 03.6
15 Sa	21 41 13	26 35 55	26 43 22	3♐42 17	3 20.0	22 38.0	24 41.4	13 06.4	15 37.0	24 00.2	2 09.7	18 53.0	11 25.7	12 05.4
16 Su	21 45 10	27 36 31	10♐44 42	17 50 34	3 19.6	24 23.8	25 55.4	13 27.9	15 52.7	24 09.5	2 11.3	18 52.5	11 27.4	12 07.3
17 M	21 49 06	28 37 07	24 59 46	2♑12 03	3 17.4	26 10.4	27 09.3	13 49.2	16 08.6	24 18.7	2 13.0	18 52.0	11 29.2	12 09.1
18 Tu	21 53 03	29 37 41	9♑27 03	16 44 17	3 12.7	27 57.9	28 23.1	14 10.0	16 24.7	24 27.8	2 14.8	18 51.6	11 31.0	12 10.8
19 W	21 56 59	0♓38 14	24 03 05	1♒22 44	3 04.9	29 46.3	29 37.0	14 30.6	16 41.0	24 36.7	2 16.7	18 51.3	11 32.8	12 12.6
20 Th	22 00 56	1 38 45	8♒42 21	16 01 02	2 54.5	1♓35.5	0♈50.7	14 50.7	16 57.5	24 45.6	2 18.7	18 51.0	11 34.6	12 14.4
21 F	22 04 52	2 39 15	23 17 49	0♓31 45	2 42.4	3 25.5	2 04.5	15 10.5	17 14.2	24 54.3	2 20.8	18 50.7	11 36.5	12 16.2
22 Sa	22 08 49	3 39 43	7♓41 56	14 47 34	2 29.8	5 16.4	3 18.1	15 29.9	17 31.1	25 02.9	2 23.0	18 50.6	11 38.3	12 17.9
23 Su	22 12 46	4 40 10	21 47 58	28 42 36	2 18.1	7 08.0	4 31.8	15 48.9	17 48.2	25 11.3	2 25.3	18 50.4	11 40.2	12 19.7
24 M	22 16 42	5 40 35	5♈31 05	12♈13 13	2 08.5	9 00.3	5 45.4	16 07.5	18 05.4	25 19.6	2 27.7	18D50.3	11 42.1	12 21.4
25 Tu	22 20 39	6 40 58	18 48 58	25 18 26	2 01.6	10 53.3	6 58.9	16 25.7	18 22.9	25 27.8	2 30.3	18 50.3	11 44.1	12 23.1
26 W	22 24 35	7 41 19	1♉41 51	7♉59 37	1 57.4	12 46.8	8 12.4	16 43.6	18 40.5	25 35.9	2 32.9	18 50.3	11 46.0	12 24.8
27 Th	22 28 32	8 41 38	14 12 12	20 20 07	1D55.6	14 40.8	9 25.8	17 00.9	18 58.3	25 43.8	2 35.7	18 50.4	11 48.0	12 26.5
28 F	22 32 28	9 41 55	26 24 01	2♊24 31	1R55.2	16 35.1	10 39.1	17 17.9	19 16.3	25 51.6	2 38.5	18 50.6	11 49.9	12 28.2

Astro Data Dy Hr Mn	Planet Ingress Dy Hr Mn	Last Aspect Dy Hr Mn	☽ Ingress Dy Hr Mn	Last Aspect Dy Hr Mn	☽ Ingress Dy Hr Mn	☽ Phases & Eclipses Dy Hr Mn		Astro Data
☽0S 13 15:31	♀ ♒ 2 13:14	2 3:19 ♀ □	♉ 2 4:20	2 19:48 ♃ ☍	♋ 3 12:19	8 18:26	○ 18♋16	1 January 2031
♃☍♅ 20 12:04	☿ ♑ 12 4:18	3 5:23 ☉ △	♊ 4 16:28	4 10:52 ♆ □	♌ 6 0:33	16 12:47	☾ 26♎11	Julian Day # 47848
☽0N 26 7:52	♂ ♏ 15 22:48	6 20:22 ♂ △	♋ 7 5:32	7 20:54 ♃ △	♍ 8 10:44	23 4:31	● 2♒57	SVP 4♓49'20"
	☉ ♒ 20 6:48	9 11:32 ♂ □	♌ 9 17:52	10 6:14 ♃ □	♎ 10 18:51	30 7:43	☽ 10♉13	GC 27♐16.3 ⚴ 7♓33.5
♄ D 2 2:25	♀ ♓ 26 13:49	12 0:57 ♂ ✶	♍ 12 4:38	12 13:47 ☉ △	♏ 13 1:09			Eris 25♈47.7R ⚵ 1♒16.8
☽0S 9 21:59		14 1:34 ☉ □	♎ 14 13:21	14 22:50 ☉ □	♐ 15 5:39	7 12:46	○ 18♌32	⚷ 12♉16.5R ⚶ 24♉47.7R
♀0N 21 14:06	☿ ♒ 1 21:15	16 12:47 ☉ □	♏ 16 19:32	17 5:36 ☉ ✶	♑ 17 8:21	14 22:50	☾ 26♏03	☽ Mean ☊ 5♐27.1
☽0N 22 18:53	☉ ♓ 18 20:51	18 20:28 ☉ ✶	♐ 18 22:54	19 8:51 ♀ ✶	♒ 19 9:45	21 15:49	● 2♓49	
♅ D 25 11:24	☿ ♓ 19 15:02	20 11:39 ♀ ✶	♑ 20 23:53	21 2:34 ♃ ✶	♓ 21 11:07			1 February 2031
	♀ ♈ 19 19:30	21 21:13 ☿ ☌	♒ 22 23:47	23 5:48 ♃ □	♈ 23 14:16			Julian Day # 47879
		24 21:01 ♀ ☌	♓ 25 0:31	25 12:18 ♃ △	♉ 25 20:48			SVP 4♓49'15"
		26 11:26 ♃ □	♈ 27 4:06	27 5:20 ♂ ☍	♊ 28 7:11			GC 27♐16.4 ⚴ 16♓44.1
		29 0:18 ☿ □	♉ 29 11:49					Eris 25♈48.9 ⚵ 14♒23.5
		31 19:55 ☿ △	♊ 31 23:16					⚷ 12♉08.0 ⚶ 25♉57.5
								☽ Mean ☊ 3♐48.6

March 2031 — LONGITUDE

Day	Sid.Time	☉	0 hr ☽	Noon ☽	True ☊	☿	♀	♂	⚳	♃	♄	♅	♆	♇
1 Sa	22 36 25	10♓42 11	8♊22 21	14♊18 10	1♐55.2	18♓29.5	11♈52.4	17♏34.4	19♉34.4	25♐59.3	2♊41.5	18♊50.8	11♈51.9	12♒29.9
2 Su	22 40 21	11 42 24	20 12 42	26 06 39	1R 54.4	20 23.9	13 05.7	17 50.5	19 52.7	26 06.8	2 44.5	18 51.0	11 53.9	12 31.6
3 M	22 44 18	12 42 35	2♋00 40	7♋55 24	1 51.8	22 18.1	14 18.8	18 06.2	20 11.1	26 14.2	2 47.7	18 51.3	11 56.0	12 33.2
4 Tu	22 48 15	13 42 44	13 51 29	19 49 27	1 46.8	24 11.7	15 31.9	18 21.3	20 29.8	26 21.5	2 50.9	18 51.7	11 58.0	12 34.9
5 W	22 52 11	14 42 51	25 49 49	1♌53 02	1 39.0	26 04.5	16 45.0	18 36.0	20 48.5	26 28.6	2 54.3	18 52.1	12 00.1	12 36.5
6 Th	22 56 08	15 42 56	7♌59 30	14 09 29	1 28.7	27 56.2	17 58.0	18 50.2	21 07.4	26 35.5	2 57.7	18 52.5	12 02.1	12 38.1
7 F	23 00 04	16 42 59	20 23 13	26 40 52	1 16.6	29 46.3	19 10.9	19 03.9	21 26.5	26 42.3	3 01.3	18 53.0	12 04.2	12 39.7
8 Sa	23 04 01	17 43 00	3♍02 29	9♍28 03	1 03.7	1♈34.4	20 23.7	19 17.2	21 45.7	26 49.0	3 04.9	18 53.6	12 06.3	12 41.3
9 Su	23 07 57	18 42 59	15 57 29	22 30 38	0 51.2	3 20.2	21 36.5	19 29.9	22 05.1	26 55.5	3 08.6	18 54.2	12 08.4	12 42.9
10 M	23 11 54	19 42 57	29 07 19	5♎47 17	0 40.2	5 03.1	22 49.2	19 42.1	22 24.6	27 01.9	3 12.5	18 54.9	12 10.6	12 44.4
11 Tu	23 15 50	20 42 52	12♎30 16	19 16 00	0 31.7	6 42.6	24 01.8	19 53.7	22 44.2	27 08.1	3 16.4	18 55.6	12 12.7	12 45.9
12 W	23 19 47	21 42 46	26 04 13	2♏54 40	0 26.0	8 18.2	25 14.4	20 04.8	23 04.0	27 14.2	3 20.4	18 56.4	12 14.8	12 47.5
13 Th	23 23 43	22 42 38	9♏47 09	16 41 27	0D 23.1	9 49.4	26 26.9	20 15.3	23 23.9	27 20.1	3 24.5	18 57.2	12 17.0	12 49.0
14 F	23 27 40	23 42 28	23 37 27	0♐35 00	0 22.4	11 15.7	27 39.3	20 25.3	23 43.9	27 25.8	3 28.7	18 58.1	12 19.2	12 50.5
15 Sa	23 31 37	24 42 17	7♐34 03	14 34 29	0R 22.8	12 36.5	28 51.7	20 34.7	24 04.1	27 31.4	3 33.0	18 59.0	12 21.3	12 51.9
16 Su	23 35 33	25 42 04	21 36 16	28 39 18	0 23.0	13 51.4	0♉03.9	20 43.5	24 24.4	27 36.9	3 37.4	19 00.0	12 23.5	12 53.4
17 M	23 39 30	26 41 49	5♑43 30	12♑48 41	0 21.9	15 00.0	1 16.1	20 51.7	24 44.8	27 42.1	3 41.8	19 01.0	12 25.7	12 54.8
18 Tu	23 43 26	27 41 33	19 54 41	27 01 13	0 18.6	16 01.9	2 28.3	20 59.2	25 05.4	27 47.2	3 46.4	19 02.1	12 27.9	12 56.3
19 W	23 47 23	28 41 15	4♒07 57	11♒14 28	0 12.8	16 56.6	3 40.3	21 06.1	25 26.0	27 52.2	3 51.0	19 03.2	12 30.2	12 57.7
20 Th	23 51 19	29 40 55	18 20 18	25 24 55	0 04.7	17 44.0	4 52.3	21 12.4	25 46.8	27 57.0	3 55.7	19 04.4	12 32.4	12 59.0
21 F	23 55 16	0♈40 33	2♓27 46	9♓28 14	29♏55.1	18 23.7	6 04.2	21 18.0	26 07.7	28 01.6	4 00.5	19 05.7	12 34.6	13 00.4
22 Sa	23 59 12	1 40 09	16 25 47	23 19 50	29 45.0	18 55.5	7 16.0	21 23.0	26 28.8	28 06.0	4 05.4	19 06.9	12 36.8	13 01.7
23 Su	0 03 09	2 39 44	0♈09 55	6♈55 36	29 35.6	19 19.5	8 27.7	21 27.2	26 49.9	28 10.3	4 10.3	19 08.3	12 39.1	13 03.1
24 M	0 07 06	3 39 16	13 36 34	20 12 35	29 27.8	19 35.4	9 39.4	21 30.8	27 11.2	28 14.4	4 15.4	19 09.7	12 41.3	13 04.4
25 Tu	0 11 02	4 38 46	26 43 33	3♉09 27	29 22.2	19R 43.5	10 51.0	21 33.7	27 32.5	28 18.3	4 20.5	19 11.1	12 43.6	13 05.6
26 W	0 14 59	5 38 14	9♉30 24	15 46 36	29 19.0	19 43.7	12 02.4	21 35.9	27 54.0	28 22.1	4 25.7	19 12.6	12 45.8	13 06.9
27 Th	0 18 55	6 37 40	21 58 21	28 06 03	29D 17.9	19 36.4	13 13.8	21 37.3	28 15.6	28 25.6	4 31.0	19 14.1	12 48.1	13 08.1
28 F	0 22 52	7 37 04	4♊10 08	10♊11 08	29 18.4	19 21.8	14 25.1	21R 38.1	28 37.3	28 29.0	4 36.3	19 15.7	12 50.4	13 09.4
29 Sa	0 26 48	8 36 25	16 09 37	22 06 11	29 19.6	19 00.5	15 36.3	21 38.1	28 59.1	28 32.3	4 41.7	19 17.3	12 52.6	13 10.6
30 Su	0 30 45	9 35 44	28 01 29	3♋56 09	29R 20.6	18 32.9	16 47.4	21 37.4	29 20.9	28 35.3	4 47.2	19 19.0	12 54.9	13 11.7
31 M	0 34 41	10 35 01	9♋50 52	15 46 17	29 20.6	17 59.8	17 58.4	21 35.9	29 42.9	28 38.2	4 52.8	19 20.7	12 57.2	13 12.9

April 2031 — LONGITUDE

Day	Sid.Time	☉	0 hr ☽	Noon ☽	True ☊	☿	♀	♂	⚳	♃	♄	♅	♆	♇
1 Tu	0 38 38	11♈34 16	21♋43 03	27♋41 48	29♏19.0	17♈21.8	19♉09.3	21♏33.7	0♊05.0	28♐40.9	4♊58.4	19♊22.5	12♈59.4	13♒14.0
2 W	0 42 35	12 33 28	3♌43 08	9♌47 35	29R 15.5	16R 39.8	20 20.1	21R 30.8	0 27.2	28 43.4	5 04.1	19 24.3	13 01.7	13 15.1
3 Th	0 46 31	13 32 38	15 55 41	22 07 52	29 10.1	15 54.8	21 30.8	21 27.1	0 49.4	28 45.7	5 09.9	19 26.1	13 04.0	13 16.2
4 F	0 50 28	14 31 45	28 24 30	4♍45 53	29 03.3	15 07.6	22 41.4	21 22.6	1 11.8	28 47.8	5 15.7	19 28.0	13 06.2	13 17.3
5 Sa	0 54 24	15 30 51	11♍12 11	17 43 32	28 55.8	14 19.3	23 51.9	21 17.4	1 34.2	28 49.8	5 21.6	19 30.0	13 08.5	13 18.3
6 Su	0 58 21	16 29 54	24 19 54	1♎01 12	28 48.3	13 30.8	25 02.2	21 11.4	1 56.7	28 51.6	5 27.6	19 32.0	13 10.8	13 19.3
7 M	1 02 17	17 28 55	7♎47 13	14 37 39	28 41.8	12 43.0	26 12.5	21 04.7	2 19.3	28 53.1	5 33.6	19 34.0	13 13.0	13 20.3
8 Tu	1 06 14	18 27 54	21 32 08	28 30 12	28 36.9	11 56.8	27 22.6	20 57.1	2 42.0	28 54.5	5 39.7	19 36.1	13 15.3	13 21.3
9 W	1 10 10	19 26 51	5♏31 22	12♏35 07	28 34.0	11 13.1	28 32.6	20 48.9	3 04.8	28 55.8	5 45.9	19 38.2	13 17.6	13 22.2
10 Th	1 14 07	20 25 46	19 40 55	26 48 15	28D 33.0	10 32.4	29 42.5	20 39.8	3 27.6	28 56.8	5 52.1	19 40.3	13 19.8	13 23.2
11 F	1 18 04	21 24 40	3♐56 31	11♐05 28	28 33.4	9 55.5	0♊52.3	20 30.0	3 50.5	28 57.6	5 58.4	19 42.5	13 22.1	13 24.1
12 Sa	1 22 00	22 23 32	18 14 28	25 23 13	28 34.8	9 22.8	2 01.9	20 19.5	4 13.5	28 58.3	6 04.7	19 44.8	13 24.3	13 24.9
13 Su	1 25 57	23 22 22	2♑31 22	9♑38 38	28 36.1	8 54.8	3 11.4	20 08.2	4 36.6	28 58.8	6 11.1	19 47.1	13 26.6	13 25.8
14 M	1 29 53	24 21 10	16 44 45	23 49 31	28R 36.8	8 31.6	4 20.9	19 56.2	4 59.8	28 59.1	6 17.6	19 49.4	13 28.8	13 26.6
15 Tu	1 33 50	25 19 57	0♒52 43	7♒54 10	28 36.1	8 13.5	5 30.1	19 43.4	5 23.0	28R 59.2	6 24.1	19 51.7	13 31.1	13 27.4
16 W	1 37 46	26 18 41	14 53 40	21 51 02	28 34.0	8 00.6	6 39.3	19 29.9	5 46.3	28 59.1	6 30.6	19 54.1	13 33.3	13 28.2
17 Th	1 41 43	27 17 25	28 46 05	5♓38 38	28 30.5	7D 52.9	7 48.3	19 15.7	6 09.7	28 58.8	6 37.2	19 56.6	13 35.5	13 28.9
18 F	1 45 39	28 16 06	12♓28 28	19 15 23	28 26.1	7 50.5	8 57.2	19 00.8	6 33.2	28 58.3	6 43.9	19 59.0	13 37.7	13 29.6
19 Sa	1 49 36	29 14 46	25 59 12	2♈39 44	28 21.4	7 53.2	10 06.0	18 45.2	6 56.7	28 57.6	6 50.6	20 01.5	13 40.0	13 30.3
20 Su	1 53 32	0♉13 23	9♈16 48	15 50 15	28 17.0	8 01.0	11 14.6	18 29.0	7 20.3	28 56.8	6 57.3	20 04.1	13 42.2	13 31.0
21 M	1 57 29	1 11 59	22 20 00	28 45 59	28 13.4	8 13.7	12 23.1	18 12.1	7 43.9	28 55.8	7 04.1	20 06.7	13 44.3	13 31.6
22 Tu	2 01 26	2 10 34	5♉08 10	11♉26 36	28 11.0	8 31.2	13 31.4	17 54.7	8 07.7	28 54.5	7 11.0	20 09.3	13 46.5	13 32.3
23 W	2 05 22	3 09 06	17 41 22	23 52 36	28D 09.9	8 53.2	14 39.6	17 36.7	8 31.4	28 53.1	7 17.9	20 11.9	13 48.7	13 32.8
24 Th	2 09 19	4 07 36	0♊00 31	6♊05 22	28 10.1	9 19.8	15 47.6	17 18.1	8 55.3	28 51.5	7 24.8	20 14.6	13 50.9	13 33.4
25 F	2 13 15	5 06 04	12 07 29	18 07 14	28 11.2	9 50.5	16 55.5	16 59.1	9 19.2	28 49.7	7 31.8	20 17.3	13 53.0	13 33.9
26 Sa	2 17 12	6 04 31	24 05 01	0♋01 18	28 12.8	10 25.4	18 03.2	16 39.5	9 43.2	28 47.8	7 38.8	20 20.1	13 55.2	13 34.5
27 Su	2 21 08	7 02 55	5♋56 34	11 51 23	28 14.4	11 04.2	19 10.8	16 19.6	10 07.2	28 45.6	7 45.9	20 22.9	13 57.3	13 34.9
28 M	2 25 05	8 01 17	17 46 17	23 41 51	28 15.7	11 46.7	20 18.1	15 59.2	10 31.3	28 43.3	7 53.0	20 25.7	13 59.4	13 35.4
29 Tu	2 29 01	8 59 37	29 38 40	5♌37 22	28R 16.4	12 32.8	21 25.3	15 38.5	10 55.4	28 40.8	8 00.2	20 28.6	14 01.5	13 35.8
30 W	2 32 58	9 57 55	11♌38 32	17 42 45	28 16.2	13 22.3	22 32.4	15 17.5	11 19.6	28 38.1	8 07.3	20 31.4	14 03.6	13 36.2

Astro Data

	Dy Hr Mn
☿0N	7 17:27
☽0S	9 5:21
☉0N	20 19:40
♃∠♇	21 3:03
☽0N	22 4:11
☿R	26 0:42
♂R	29 0:34
☽0S	5 13:49
♆✶♇	12 22:06
♃R	15 12:04
☽0N	18 10:52
☿D	18 11:15

Planet Ingress

	Dy Hr Mn
☿ ♈	7 15:01
♀ ♉	16 10:42
☉ ♈	20 19:41
☊ ♏R	21 0:10
⚳ ♊	1 6:35
♀ ♊	10 18:01
☉ ♉	20 6:31

Last Aspect / ☽ Ingress

Last Aspect Dy Hr Mn		☽ Ingress Dy Hr Mn
2 12:00 ♃ ☍	♋	2 19:55
4 22:22 ☿ △	♌	5 8:17
7 12:03 ♃ △	♍	7 18:17
9 20:05 ♃ □	♎	10 1:35
12 1:59 ♃ ✶	♏	12 6:54
13 23:14 ☉ △	♐	14 11:00
16 10:13 ♃ ☌	♑	16 14:17
18 13:13 ☉ ✶	♒	18 17:02
20 16:20 ♃ ✶	♓	20 19:48
22 20:20 ♃ □	♈	22 23:42
25 2:53 ♃ △	♉	25 6:05
26 23:18 ♂ ☍	♊	27 15:45
30 1:06 ♃ ☍	♋	30 4:01

Last Aspect / ☽ Ingress

Last Aspect Dy Hr Mn		☽ Ingress Dy Hr Mn
31 23:44 ♂ △	♌	1 16:36
4 0:42 ♃ △	♍	4 3:01
6 8:08 ♃ □	♎	6 10:11
8 12:42 ♃ ✶	♏	8 14:34
10 17:19 ♀ ☍	♐	10 17:22
12 18:02 ♃ ☌	♑	12 19:45
14 12:58 ☉ □	♒	14 22:30
17 0:22 ♃ ✶	♓	17 2:09
19 5:20 ♃ □	♈	19 7:12
21 12:18 ♃ △	♉	21 14:19
23 0:08 ♂ ☍	♊	23 23:59
26 9:32 ♃ ☍	♋	26 11:57
27 20:49 ♂ △	♌	29 0:43

☽ Phases & Eclipses

Dy Hr Mn	
1 4:02	☽ 10♊22
9 4:29	○ 18♍24
16 6:36	☾ 25♐29
23 3:49	● 2♈19
31 0:32	☽ 10♋07
7 17:21	○ 17♎42
14 12:58	☾ 24♑24
21 16:57	● 1♉24
29 19:19	☽ 9♌17

Astro Data

1 March 2031
Julian Day # 47907
SVP 4♓49'12"
GC 27♐16.5 ⚴ 26♓14.6
Eris 25♈58.6 ⚵ 26♒44.8
⚷ 12♉49.8 ⚶ 1♊47.8
☽ Mean ☊ 2♐19.7

1 April 2031
Julian Day # 47938
SVP 4♓49'09"
GC 27♐16.5 ⚴ 7♈33.0
Eris 26♈16.2 ⚵ 10♓40.9
⚷ 14♉20.1 ⚶ 11♊31.6
☽ Mean ☊ 0♐41.2

LONGITUDE — May 2031

Day	Sid.Time	☉	0 hr ☽	Noon ☽	True ☊	☿	♀	♂	⚳	♃	♄	♅	♆	♇
1 Th	2 36 55	10♉56 11	23♌50 36	0♍02 37	28♏15.3	14♈15.1	23♊39.2	14♏56.1	11♊43.9	28♐35.2	8♊14.6	20♊34.3	14♈05.7	13♒36.6
2 F	2 40 51	11 54 25	6♍19 17	12 41 03	28R13.6	15 11.0	24 45.9	14R34.6	12 08.2	28R32.1	8 21.8	20 37.3	14 07.8	13 36.9
3 Sa	2 44 48	12 52 36	19 08 16	25 41 13	28 11.6	16 10.0	25 52.3	14 12.9	12 32.5	28 28.9	8 29.1	20 40.2	14 09.8	13 37.3
4 Su	2 48 44	13 50 46	2♎20 05	9♎04 56	28 09.6	17 11.9	26 58.6	13 51.0	12 56.9	28 25.5	8 36.4	20 43.2	14 11.9	13 37.6
5 M	2 52 41	14 48 54	15 55 42	22 52 13	28 07.9	18 16.6	28 04.6	13 29.0	13 21.4	28 21.9	8 43.8	20 46.2	14 13.9	13 37.8
6 Tu	2 56 37	15 47 00	29 54 10	7♏01 06	28 06.7	19 24.1	29 10.5	13 06.9	13 45.9	28 18.2	8 51.1	20 49.3	14 15.9	13 38.1
7 W	3 00 34	16 45 05	14♏12 28	21 27 37	28D06.1	20 34.1	0♋16.1	12 44.8	14 10.4	28 14.3	8 58.5	20 52.3	14 17.9	13 38.3
8 Th	3 04 30	17 43 08	28 45 47	6♐06 10	28 06.1	21 46.7	1 21.5	12 22.7	14 35.0	28 10.2	9 06.0	20 55.4	14 19.9	13 38.5
9 F	3 08 27	18 41 09	13♐27 55	20 50 13	28 06.6	23 01.8	2 26.7	12 00.7	14 59.7	28 06.0	9 13.5	20 58.6	14 21.8	13 38.6
10 Sa	3 12 24	19 39 09	28 12 11	5♑33 05	28 07.3	24 19.4	3 31.7	11 38.8	15 24.4	28 01.6	9 20.9	21 01.7	14 23.8	13 38.8
11 Su	3 16 20	20 37 08	12♑52 11	20 08 50	28 08.0	25 39.2	4 36.4	11 17.1	15 49.1	27 57.1	9 28.5	21 04.9	14 25.7	13 38.9
12 M	3 20 17	21 35 05	27 22 31	4♒32 46	28 08.5	27 01.5	5 40.9	10 55.5	16 13.9	27 52.4	9 36.0	21 08.1	14 27.6	13 39.0
13 Tu	3 24 13	22 33 01	11♒39 15	18 41 43	28R08.7	28 25.9	6 45.2	10 34.2	16 38.7	27 47.5	9 43.6	21 11.3	14 29.5	13 39.0
14 W	3 28 10	23 30 56	25 39 59	2♓34 00	28 08.7	29 52.7	7 49.2	10 13.2	17 03.6	27 42.5	9 51.2	21 14.5	14 31.4	13R39.0
15 Th	3 32 06	24 28 49	9♓23 42	16 09 08	28 08.5	1♉21.7	8 52.9	9 52.5	17 28.5	27 37.3	9 58.8	21 17.8	14 33.2	13 39.0
16 F	3 36 03	25 26 41	22 50 23	29 27 33	28 08.2	2 52.8	9 56.4	9 32.1	17 53.4	27 32.0	10 06.4	21 21.0	14 35.0	13 39.0
17 Sa	3 39 59	26 24 32	6♈00 44	12♈30 07	28 07.9	4 26.2	10 59.7	9 12.2	18 18.4	27 26.6	10 14.0	21 24.3	14 36.9	13 38.9
18 Su	3 43 56	27 22 22	18 55 51	25 18 04	28D07.8	6 01.7	12 02.6	8 52.7	18 43.4	27 21.0	10 21.7	21 27.6	14 38.6	13 38.8
19 M	3 47 53	28 20 11	1♉36 58	7♉52 42	28 07.7	7 39.4	13 05.3	8 33.7	19 08.5	27 15.3	10 29.4	21 31.0	14 40.4	13 38.7
20 Tu	3 51 49	29 17 58	14 05 26	20 15 21	28R07.8	9 19.2	14 07.7	8 15.2	19 33.6	27 09.4	10 37.1	21 34.3	14 42.2	13 38.6
21 W	3 55 46	0♊15 44	26 22 38	2♊27 29	28 07.8	11 01.3	15 09.8	7 57.2	19 58.7	27 03.5	10 44.8	21 37.7	14 43.9	13 38.4
22 Th	3 59 42	1 13 29	8♊30 06	14 30 43	28 07.7	12 45.4	16 11.6	7 39.9	20 23.9	26 57.4	10 52.5	21 41.1	14 45.6	13 38.2
23 F	4 03 39	2 11 12	20 29 35	26 26 58	28 07.4	14 31.8	17 13.0	7 23.2	20 49.1	26 51.2	11 00.3	21 44.5	14 47.3	13 38.0
24 Sa	4 07 35	3 08 54	2♋23 09	8♋18 29	28 06.8	16 20.2	18 14.2	7 07.1	21 14.4	26 44.8	11 08.0	21 47.9	14 49.0	13 37.8
25 Su	4 11 32	4 06 34	14 13 18	20 08 00	28 06.1	18 10.9	19 15.0	6 51.7	21 39.6	26 38.4	11 15.8	21 51.3	14 50.6	13 37.5
26 M	4 15 28	5 04 13	26 02 59	1♌58 42	28 05.2	20 03.6	20 15.4	6 37.0	22 04.9	26 31.8	11 23.6	21 54.7	14 52.2	13 37.2
27 Tu	4 19 25	6 01 51	7♌55 38	13 55 44	28 04.4	21 58.5	21 15.5	6 23.0	22 30.3	26 25.2	11 31.3	21 58.2	14 53.8	13 36.9
28 W	4 23 22	6 59 27	19 55 07	25 58 44	28D03.9	23 55.4	22 15.2	6 09.8	22 55.6	26 18.4	11 39.1	22 01.7	14 55.4	13 36.6
29 Th	4 27 18	7 57 01	2♍05 38	8♍16 24	28 03.7	25 54.3	23 14.5	5 57.3	23 21.0	26 11.6	11 46.9	22 05.1	14 56.9	13 36.2
30 F	4 31 15	8 54 35	14 31 31	20 51 32	28 03.9	27 55.2	24 13.5	5 45.6	23 46.5	26 04.7	11 54.7	22 08.6	14 58.4	13 35.8
31 Sa	4 35 11	9 52 06	27 16 55	3♎48 05	28 04.6	29 58.0	25 12.0	5 34.7	24 11.9	25 57.6	12 02.5	22 12.1	14 59.9	13 35.4

LONGITUDE — June 2031

Day	Sid.Time	☉	0 hr ☽	Noon ☽	True ☊	☿	♀	♂	⚳	♃	♄	♅	♆	♇
1 Su	4 39 08	10♊49 37	10♎25 24	17♎09 09	28♏05.6	2♊02.6	26♋10.0	5♏24.6	24♊37.4	25♐50.6	12♊10.3	22♊15.6	15♈01.4	13♒34.9
2 M	4 43 04	11 47 06	23 59 29	0♏56 26	28 06.6	4 08.8	27 07.7	5R15.3	25 02.9	25R43.4	12 18.1	22 19.1	15 02.8	13R34.4
3 Tu	4 47 01	12 44 34	7♏59 55	15 09 40	28R07.4	6 16.5	28 04.9	5 06.7	25 28.4	25 36.2	12 25.9	22 22.7	15 04.3	13 33.9
4 W	4 50 57	13 42 01	22 25 16	29 46 07	28 07.7	8 25.6	29 01.6	4 59.0	25 54.0	25 28.9	12 33.7	22 26.2	15 05.7	13 33.4
5 Th	4 54 54	14 39 27	7♐11 27	14♐40 23	28 07.2	10 35.7	29 57.8	4 52.1	26 19.6	25 21.5	12 41.5	22 29.7	15 07.0	13 32.9
6 F	4 58 51	15 36 52	22 11 53	29 44 50	28 05.9	12 46.7	0♌53.5	4 46.1	26 45.2	25 14.1	12 49.3	22 33.3	15 08.4	13 32.3
7 Sa	5 02 47	16 34 16	7♑18 05	14♑50 29	28 03.9	14 58.4	1 48.7	4 40.8	27 10.8	25 06.7	12 57.1	22 36.8	15 09.7	13 31.7
8 Su	5 06 44	17 31 39	22 20 53	29 48 17	28 01.5	17 10.4	2 43.4	4 36.4	27 36.4	24 59.2	13 04.9	22 40.4	15 11.0	13 31.1
9 M	5 10 40	18 29 02	7♒11 46	14♒30 33	27 59.2	19 22.5	3 37.5	4 32.7	28 02.1	24 51.6	13 12.7	22 43.9	15 12.2	13 30.5
10 Tu	5 14 37	19 26 24	21 44 02	28 51 48	27 57.3	21 34.5	4 31.0	4 29.9	28 27.8	24 44.1	13 20.4	22 47.5	15 13.5	13 29.8
11 W	5 18 33	20 23 45	5♓53 35	12♓49 14	27D56.3	23 46.0	5 24.0	4 27.9	28 53.5	24 36.5	13 28.2	22 51.0	15 14.7	13 29.1
12 Th	5 22 30	21 21 06	19 38 48	26 22 24	27 56.2	25 56.7	6 16.3	4D26.7	29 19.3	24 28.8	13 36.0	22 54.6	15 15.8	13 28.4
13 F	5 26 26	22 18 27	3♈00 17	9♈32 44	27 57.0	28 06.6	7 08.0	4 26.3	29 45.0	24 21.2	13 43.7	22 58.2	15 17.0	13 27.7
14 Sa	5 30 23	23 15 47	16 00 06	22 22 47	27 58.4	0♋15.2	7 59.1	4 26.7	0♋10.8	24 13.5	13 51.5	23 01.7	15 18.1	13 26.9
15 Su	5 34 20	24 13 07	28 41 12	4♉55 45	28 00.0	2 22.5	8 49.5	4 27.9	0 36.6	24 05.9	13 59.2	23 05.3	15 19.2	13 26.2
16 M	5 38 16	25 10 26	11♉06 51	17 14 53	28R01.2	4 28.2	9 39.2	4 29.9	1 02.4	23 58.2	14 06.9	23 08.8	15 20.2	13 25.4
17 Tu	5 42 13	26 07 45	23 20 14	29 23 15	28 01.7	6 32.2	10 28.2	4 32.7	1 28.2	23 50.5	14 14.6	23 12.4	15 21.3	13 24.6
18 W	5 46 09	27 05 04	5♊24 17	11♊23 38	28 00.9	8 34.4	11 16.4	4 36.2	1 54.1	23 42.9	14 22.3	23 16.0	15 22.3	13 23.7
19 Th	5 50 06	28 02 22	17 21 35	23 18 24	27 58.6	10 34.6	12 03.8	4 40.6	2 20.0	23 35.3	14 30.0	23 19.5	15 23.2	13 22.9
20 F	5 54 02	28 59 39	29 14 21	5♋09 41	27 54.9	12 32.8	12 50.5	4 45.7	2 45.9	23 27.6	14 37.6	23 23.1	15 24.2	13 22.0
21 Sa	5 57 59	29 56 56	11♋04 38	16 59 26	27 49.9	14 28.8	13 36.3	4 51.5	3 11.8	23 20.0	14 45.3	23 26.6	15 25.1	13 21.1
22 Su	6 01 56	0♋54 13	22 54 21	28 49 38	27 44.2	16 22.8	14 21.2	4 58.1	3 37.7	23 12.5	14 52.9	23 30.2	15 26.0	13 20.2
23 M	6 05 52	1 51 29	4♌45 35	10♌42 28	27 38.2	18 14.5	15 05.3	5 05.5	4 03.6	23 05.0	15 00.5	23 33.7	15 26.8	13 19.2
24 Tu	6 09 49	2 48 44	16 40 38	22 40 25	27 32.6	20 04.1	15 48.3	5 13.5	4 29.6	22 57.5	15 08.1	23 37.3	15 27.6	13 18.3
25 W	6 13 45	3 45 59	28 42 13	4♍46 26	27 28.1	21 51.4	16 30.4	5 22.3	4 55.5	22 50.0	15 15.6	23 40.8	15 28.4	13 17.3
26 Th	6 17 42	4 43 13	10♍53 30	17 03 52	27 25.0	23 36.5	17 11.5	5 31.8	5 21.5	22 42.7	15 23.2	23 44.3	15 29.1	13 16.3
27 F	6 21 38	5 40 26	23 18 02	29 36 28	27D23.5	25 19.3	17 51.5	5 42.0	5 47.4	22 35.3	15 30.7	23 47.8	15 29.9	13 15.3
28 Sa	6 25 35	6 37 39	5♎59 41	12♎28 08	27 23.4	26 59.9	18 30.4	5 52.8	6 13.4	22 28.1	15 38.1	23 51.3	15 30.6	13 14.3
29 Su	6 29 31	7 34 52	19 02 16	25 42 30	27 24.4	28 38.2	19 08.2	6 04.3	6 39.4	22 20.9	15 45.6	23 54.8	15 31.2	13 13.2
30 M	6 33 28	8 32 04	2♏29 09	9♏22 29	27 25.8	0♌14.2	19 44.7	6 16.5	7 05.4	22 13.8	15 53.0	23 58.3	15 31.8	13 12.2

Astro Data

	Dy Hr Mn
♃∠♇	1 1:38
☽0S	2 22:48
♇ R	14 20:28
☽0N	15 16:06
☽0S	30 7:29
♄△♇	11 14:37
☽0N	11 22:03
♂ D	13 11:56
♃☍♅	20 21:47
☽0S	26 15:16
♄⚹♆	27 9:11

Planet Ingress

		Dy Hr Mn
♀	♋	7 6:06
☿	♉	14 14:00
☉	♊	21 5:28
☿	♊	31 12:23
♀	♌	5 12:57
⚳	♋	14 1:57
☿	♋	14 9:09
☉	♋	21 13:17
☿	♌	30 8:25

Last Aspect / ☽ Ingress (May)

Last Aspect Dy Hr Mn			☽ Ingress	Dy Hr Mn
1 9:12	♃	△	♍	1 11:55
3 17:03	♃	□	♎	3 19:48
5 21:39	♀	△	♏	6 0:10
7 3:40	☉	☍	♐	8 2:02
9 23:46	♃	☌	♑	10 2:56
11 22:05	☿	□	♒	12 4:23
14 6:45	☿	⚹	♓	14 7:31
16 8:31	♃	□	♈	16 12:59
18 15:51	♃	△	♉	18 20:55
19 23:08	♇	□	♊	21 7:08
23 12:48	♃	☍	♋	23 19:10
25 10:02	♀	☌	♌	26 8:00
28 12:38	♃	△	♍	28 19:54
31 3:39	☿	△	♎	31 5:02

Last Aspect / ☽ Ingress (June)

Last Aspect Dy Hr Mn			☽ Ingress	Dy Hr Mn
2 4:57	♀	□	♏	2 10:23
4 10:43	♀	△	♐	4 12:23
6 4:53	♃	☌	♑	6 12:24
7 12:31	♆	□	♒	8 12:19
10 5:06	♃	⚹	♓	10 13:56
12 11:05	☿	□	♈	12 18:33
14 15:28	♃	△	♉	15 2:31
16 4:31	♇	□	♊	17 13:13
19 22:25	☉	☌	♋	20 1:32
21 8:48	♆	□	♌	22 14:22
24 13:54	♅	⚹	♍	25 2:34
27 2:35	☿	⚹	♎	27 12:44
29 17:55	☿	□	♏	29 19:37

☽ Phases & Eclipses

Dy Hr Mn		
7 3:40	○	16♏25
7 3:51	☍	A 0.881
13 19:07	☾	22♒50
21 7:17	●	0♊04
21 7:14:46	☌	A 05'25"
29 11:19	☽	7♍55
5 11:58	○	14♐39
5 11:44	☍	A 0.129
12 2:21	☾	20♓58
19 22:25	●	28♊27
28 0:19	☽	6♎10

Astro Data

1 May 2031
Julian Day # 47968
SVP 4♓49'06"
GC 27♐16.6 ⚴ 18♈53.7
Eris 26♈35.8 ⚵ 24♓08.5
⚷ 16♉13.4 ⚶ 22♊50.0
☽ Mean ☊ 29♏05.8

1 June 2031
Julian Day # 47999
SVP 4♓49'02"
GC 27♐16.7 ⚴ 0♉43.3
Eris 26♈53.7 ⚵ 7♈41.1
⚷ 18♉14.9 ⚶ 5♋37.4
☽ Mean ☊ 27♏27.3

July 2031 — LONGITUDE

Day	Sid.Time	☉	0 hr ☽	Noon ☽	True ☊	☿	♀	♂	⚳	♃	♄	♅	♆	♇
1 Tu	6 37 25	9♋29 16	16♏22 37	23♏29 31	27♏26.7	1♌47.9	20♌20.1	6♏29.3	7♋31.4	22♐06.7	16♊00.4	24♊01.8	15♈32.4	13♒11.1
2 W	6 41 21	10 26 27	0♐43 00	8♐02 43	27R 26.3	3 19.3	20 54.1	6 42.8	7 57.4	21R 59.8	16 07.8	24 05.2	15 33.0	13R 10.0
3 Th	6 45 18	11 23 38	15 28 06	22 58 20	27 24.2	4 48.5	21 26.8	6 56.9	8 23.5	21 52.9	16 15.1	24 08.7	15 33.5	13 08.9
4 F	6 49 14	12 20 49	0♑32 30	8♑09 26	27 20.1	6 15.2	21 58.1	7 11.5	8 49.5	21 46.2	16 22.4	24 12.1	15 34.0	13 07.8
5 Sa	6 53 11	13 18 00	15 47 53	23 26 29	27 14.3	7 39.6	22 27.9	7 26.8	9 15.5	21 39.5	16 29.7	24 15.6	15 34.5	13 06.7
6 Su	6 57 07	14 15 11	1♒03 54	8♒38 45	27 07.6	9 01.7	22 56.3	7 42.6	9 41.6	21 32.9	16 36.9	24 19.0	15 34.9	13 05.5
7 M	7 01 04	15 12 22	16 09 50	23 36 04	27 00.8	10 21.3	23 23.1	7 59.0	10 07.6	21 26.4	16 44.1	24 22.4	15 35.3	13 04.3
8 Tu	7 05 00	16 09 33	0♓56 32	8♓10 32	26 54.8	11 38.4	23 48.3	8 16.0	10 33.7	21 20.0	16 51.3	24 25.7	15 35.7	13 03.2
9 W	7 08 57	17 06 44	15 17 38	22 17 31	26 50.4	12 53.0	24 11.8	8 33.5	10 59.7	21 13.8	16 58.4	24 29.1	15 36.0	13 02.0
10 Th	7 12 54	18 03 56	29 10 09	5♈55 39	26D 47.9	14 05.0	24 33.7	8 51.5	11 25.8	21 07.6	17 05.5	24 32.4	15 36.3	13 00.8
11 F	7 16 50	19 01 09	12♈34 14	19 06 18	26 47.1	15 14.3	24 53.8	9 10.1	11 51.9	21 01.6	17 12.6	24 35.8	15 36.6	12 59.5
12 Sa	7 20 47	19 58 21	25 32 17	1♉52 44	26 47.6	16 21.0	25 12.0	9 29.2	12 17.9	20 55.7	17 19.6	24 39.1	15 36.8	12 58.3
13 Su	7 24 43	20 55 35	8♉08 11	14 19 13	26 48.6	17 24.8	25 28.4	9 48.8	12 44.0	20 49.9	17 26.6	24 42.4	15 37.0	12 57.1
14 M	7 28 40	21 52 49	20 26 25	26 30 21	26R 49.2	18 25.7	25 42.8	10 08.9	13 10.1	20 44.3	17 33.5	24 45.7	15 37.2	12 55.8
15 Tu	7 32 36	22 50 03	2♊31 35	8♊30 36	26 48.4	19 23.7	25 55.3	10 29.6	13 36.2	20 38.8	17 40.4	24 48.9	15 37.4	12 54.6
16 W	7 36 33	23 47 18	14 27 55	20 23 59	26 45.7	20 18.5	26 05.6	10 50.7	14 02.3	20 33.4	17 47.3	24 52.2	15 37.5	12 53.3
17 Th	7 40 29	24 44 33	26 19 10	2♋13 51	26 40.5	21 10.2	26 13.9	11 12.2	14 28.3	20 28.2	17 54.1	24 55.4	15 37.5	12 52.0
18 F	7 44 26	25 41 49	8♋08 22	14 03 00	26 32.8	21 58.4	26 20.0	11 34.3	14 54.4	20 23.1	18 00.8	24 58.6	15R 37.6	12 50.7
19 Sa	7 48 23	26 39 05	19 57 59	25 53 34	26 23.1	22 43.2	26 23.9	11 56.8	15 20.5	20 18.1	18 07.5	25 01.7	15 37.6	12 49.4
20 Su	7 52 19	27 36 22	1♌49 57	7♌47 19	26 12.0	23 24.4	26R 25.6	12 19.8	15 46.6	20 13.3	18 14.2	25 04.9	15 37.6	12 48.1
21 M	7 56 16	28 33 39	13 45 51	19 45 44	26 00.4	24 01.8	26 24.9	12 43.2	16 12.6	20 08.7	18 20.8	25 08.0	15 37.5	12 46.8
22 Tu	8 00 12	29 30 57	25 47 10	1♍50 20	25 49.4	24 35.2	26 21.9	13 07.1	16 38.7	20 04.2	18 27.4	25 11.1	15 37.4	12 45.5
23 W	8 04 09	0♌28 14	7♍55 29	14 02 51	25 39.9	25 04.6	26 16.5	13 31.4	17 04.8	19 59.9	18 33.9	25 14.2	15 37.3	12 44.2
24 Th	8 08 05	1 25 33	20 12 43	26 25 24	25 32.7	25 29.6	26 08.8	13 56.1	17 30.8	19 55.8	18 40.3	25 17.2	15 37.1	12 42.8
25 F	8 12 02	2 22 51	2♎41 15	9♎00 37	25 27.9	25 50.3	25 58.6	14 21.2	17 56.9	19 51.8	18 46.7	25 20.2	15 36.9	12 41.5
26 Sa	8 15 58	3 20 10	15 23 55	21 51 33	25D 25.6	26 06.3	25 46.1	14 46.7	18 22.9	19 48.0	18 53.1	25 23.2	15 36.7	12 40.1
27 Su	8 19 55	4 17 29	28 23 57	5♏01 30	25 25.1	26 17.6	25 31.2	15 12.6	18 49.0	19 44.3	18 59.4	25 26.2	15 36.5	12 38.8
28 M	8 23 52	5 14 49	11♏44 36	18 33 34	25R 25.3	26R 24.0	25 13.9	15 38.9	19 15.0	19 40.8	19 05.6	25 29.1	15 36.2	12 37.4
29 Tu	8 27 48	6 12 10	25 28 39	2♐30 01	25 25.3	26 25.5	24 54.3	16 05.6	19 41.0	19 37.5	19 11.8	25 32.1	15 35.9	12 36.1
30 W	8 31 45	7 09 30	9♐37 39	16 51 26	25 23.8	26 21.8	24 32.5	16 32.7	20 07.0	19 34.4	19 17.9	25 34.9	15 35.5	12 34.7
31 Th	8 35 41	8 06 52	24 11 02	1♑35 56	25 20.0	26 13.0	24 08.5	17 00.1	20 33.0	19 31.4	19 23.9	25 37.8	15 35.1	12 33.3

August 2031 — LONGITUDE

Day	Sid.Time	☉	0 hr ☽	Noon ☽	True ☊	☿	♀	♂	⚳	♃	♄	♅	♆	♇
1 F	8 39 38	9♌04 14	9♑05 23	16♑38 28	25♏13.6	25♌59.1	23♌42.5	17♏27.9	20♋59.0	19♐28.6	19♊29.9	25♊40.6	15♈34.7	12♒32.0
2 Sa	8 43 34	10 01 36	24 14 04	1♒50 55	25R 05.0	25R 40.1	23R 14.5	17 56.0	21 25.0	19R 26.0	19 35.9	25 43.4	15R 34.3	12R 30.6
3 Su	8 47 31	10 59 00	9♒27 41	17 02 58	24 54.8	25 16.1	22 44.6	18 24.4	21 50.9	19 23.6	19 41.7	25 46.2	15 33.8	12 29.3
4 M	8 51 27	11 56 24	24 35 27	2♓03 52	24 44.4	24 47.4	22 13.2	18 53.2	22 16.9	19 21.3	19 47.5	25 48.9	15 33.3	12 27.9
5 Tu	8 55 24	12 53 49	9♓27 07	16 44 19	24 34.8	24 14.2	21 40.2	19 22.3	22 42.8	19 19.3	19 53.3	25 51.6	15 32.8	12 26.5
6 W	8 59 21	13 51 15	23 54 46	0♈58 01	24 27.2	23 36.9	21 06.0	19 51.7	23 08.7	19 17.4	19 58.9	25 54.2	15 32.2	12 25.1
7 Th	9 03 17	14 48 43	7♈53 48	14 42 06	24 22.1	22 56.1	20 30.7	20 21.4	23 34.7	19 15.7	20 04.5	25 56.9	15 31.6	12 23.8
8 F	9 07 14	15 46 12	21 23 04	27 56 59	24 19.3	22 12.2	19 54.6	20 51.5	24 00.6	19 14.1	20 10.1	25 59.5	15 31.0	12 22.4
9 Sa	9 11 10	16 43 42	4♉24 18	10♉45 31	24D 18.3	21 26.0	19 17.8	21 21.8	24 26.4	19 12.8	20 15.5	26 02.0	15 30.3	12 21.0
10 Su	9 15 07	17 41 14	17 01 13	23 12 02	24R 18.3	20 38.2	18 40.6	21 52.5	24 52.3	19 11.6	20 20.9	26 04.6	15 29.7	12 19.7
11 M	9 19 03	18 38 47	29 18 38	5♊21 40	24 18.0	19 49.8	18 03.2	22 23.4	25 18.2	19 10.7	20 26.3	26 07.0	15 29.0	12 18.3
12 Tu	9 23 00	19 36 21	11♊21 47	17 19 38	24 16.4	19 01.5	17 26.0	22 54.7	25 44.0	19 09.9	20 31.5	26 09.5	15 28.2	12 17.0
13 W	9 26 56	20 33 57	23 15 49	29 10 52	24 12.6	18 14.2	16 49.0	23 26.2	26 09.8	19 09.3	20 36.7	26 11.9	15 27.4	12 15.6
14 Th	9 30 53	21 31 34	5♋05 21	10♋59 43	24 06.2	17 29.1	16 12.6	23 58.0	26 35.6	19 08.9	20 41.8	26 14.3	15 26.6	12 14.2
15 F	9 34 50	22 29 12	16 54 24	22 49 47	23 56.9	16 46.8	15 37.0	24 30.1	27 01.4	19D 08.7	20 46.9	26 16.6	15 25.8	12 12.9
16 Sa	9 38 46	23 26 52	28 46 10	4♌43 50	23 45.2	16 08.4	15 02.3	25 02.5	27 27.2	19 08.6	20 51.8	26 18.9	15 25.0	12 11.6
17 Su	9 42 43	24 24 34	10♌43 02	16 43 56	23 31.8	15 34.7	14 28.9	25 35.2	27 52.9	19 08.8	20 56.7	26 21.2	15 24.1	12 10.2
18 M	9 46 39	25 22 16	22 46 41	28 51 25	23 17.9	15 06.3	13 56.8	26 08.1	28 18.6	19 09.1	21 01.5	26 23.4	15 23.2	12 08.9
19 Tu	9 50 36	26 20 00	4♍58 14	11♍07 14	23 04.7	14 44.0	13 26.3	26 41.3	28 44.3	19 09.6	21 06.2	26 25.6	15 22.2	12 07.6
20 W	9 54 32	27 17 45	17 18 29	23 32 06	22 53.1	14 28.2	12 57.6	27 14.7	29 10.0	19 10.3	21 10.8	26 27.8	15 21.2	12 06.2
21 Th	9 58 29	28 15 31	29 48 11	6♎06 52	22 44.0	14D 19.4	12 30.7	27 48.4	29 35.6	19 11.2	21 15.4	26 29.9	15 20.3	12 04.9
22 F	10 02 25	29 13 18	12♎28 19	18 52 43	22 37.8	14 18.0	12 05.7	28 22.3	0♌01.2	19 12.3	21 19.9	26 31.9	15 19.2	12 03.6
23 Sa	10 06 22	0♍11 07	25 20 16	1♏51 15	22 34.5	14 24.3	11 42.9	28 56.5	0 26.8	19 13.6	21 24.2	26 33.9	15 18.2	12 02.3
24 Su	10 10 19	1 08 57	8♏25 54	15 04 31	22D 33.2	14 38.2	11 22.3	29 30.9	0 52.4	19 15.0	21 28.5	26 35.9	15 17.1	12 01.1
25 M	10 14 15	2 06 48	21 47 23	28 34 45	22R 33.2	15 00.1	11 03.9	0♐05.6	1 17.9	19 16.7	21 32.8	26 37.8	15 16.0	11 59.8
26 Tu	10 18 12	3 04 40	5♐26 51	12♐23 51	22 33.0	15 29.8	10 47.8	0 40.5	1 43.4	19 18.5	21 36.9	26 39.7	15 14.9	11 58.5
27 W	10 22 08	4 02 34	19 25 50	26 32 48	22 31.5	16 07.2	10 34.0	1 15.6	2 08.9	19 20.5	21 40.9	26 41.6	15 13.8	11 57.3
28 Th	10 26 05	5 00 29	3♑44 33	11♑00 49	22 27.8	16 52.2	10 22.7	1 50.9	2 34.3	19 22.7	21 44.9	26 43.4	15 12.6	11 56.0
29 F	10 30 01	5 58 25	18 21 05	25 44 44	22 21.5	17 44.6	10 13.7	2 26.5	2 59.7	19 25.1	21 48.7	26 45.1	15 11.4	11 54.8
30 Sa	10 33 58	6 56 22	3♒10 57	10♒38 46	22 12.9	18 44.2	10 07.2	3 02.2	3 25.1	19 27.6	21 52.5	26 46.8	15 10.2	11 53.6
31 Su	10 37 54	7 54 21	18 07 06	25 34 50	22 02.6	19 50.5	10 03.0	3 38.2	3 50.4	19 30.4	21 56.2	26 48.5	15 09.0	11 52.4

Astro Data	Dy Hr Mn
☽0N	9 6:12
♆R	19 6:11
♀R	20 17:08
☽0S	23 22:04
☿R	29 6:47
♃☍♄	1 8:27
☽0N	5 16:25
♃D	16 4:58
☽0S	20 4:25
☿D	22 4:27

Planet Ingress	Dy Hr Mn
☉ ♌	23 0:10
⚳ ♌	22 10:50
☉ ♍	23 7:23
♂ ♐	25 8:08

Last Aspect Dy Hr Mn		☽ Ingress Dy Hr Mn
1 6:28 ♀ □	♐	1 22:49
3 13:52 ♅ ☍	♑	3 23:09
4 23:39 ♆ □	♒	5 22:19
7 13:16 ♅ △	♓	7 22:27
9 15:49 ♅ □	♈	10 1:28
11 23:04 ♀ △	♉	12 8:26
14 10:24 ♀ □	♊	14 18:57
16 23:41 ♀ ⚹	♋	17 7:28
19 13:40 ☉ ☌	♌	19 20:18
22 1:12 ♀ ☌	♍	22 8:22
24 9:48 ♅ □	♎	24 18:52
26 19:56 ☿ ⚹	♏	27 2:55
29 1:38 ☿ □	♐	29 7:45
31 3:24 ☿ △	♑	31 9:25

Last Aspect Dy Hr Mn		☽ Ingress Dy Hr Mn
1 13:21 ♂ ⚹	♒	2 9:05
4 1:56 ♅ △	♓	4 8:40
6 3:20 ♅ □	♈	6 10:21
8 8:23 ♅ ⚹	♉	8 15:47
10 9:18 ♂ ☍	♊	11 1:22
13 5:56 ♅ ☌	♋	13 13:40
15 15:33 ♂ △	♌	16 2:29
18 7:07 ♅ ⚹	♍	18 14:15
20 19:27 ♂ ⚹	♎	21 0:23
23 2:15 ♅ △	♏	23 8:36
24 11:12 ♅ □	♐	25 14:30
27 12:15 ♅ ☍	♑	27 17:47
28 18:52 ♆ □	♒	29 18:52
31 13:59 ♅ △	♓	31 19:08

☽ Phases & Eclipses Dy Hr Mn	
4 19:01	○ 12♑38
11 11:50	☾ 19♈01
19 13:40	● 26♋43
27 10:35	☽ 4♏14
3 1:45	○ 10♒35
10 0:24	☾ 17♉13
18 4:32	● 25♌04
25 18:40	☽ 2♐23

Astro Data

1 July 2031
Julian Day # 48029
SVP 4♓48'57"
GC 27♐16.8 ⚴ 11♉57.4
Eris 27♈04.7 ⚵ 19♈56.2
⚷ 19♉56.2 ⚶ 18♋36.4
☽ Mean ☊ 25♏52.0

1 August 2031
Julian Day # 48060
SVP 4♓48'52"
GC 27♐16.8 ⚴ 22♉50.9
Eris 27♈07.0R ⚵ 0♉46.3
⚷ 21♉04.6 ⚶ 2♌20.6
☽ Mean ☊ 24♏13.5

LONGITUDE — September 2031

Day	Sid.Time	☉	0 hr ☽	Noon ☽	True ☊	☿	♀	♂	⚳	♃	♄	♅	♆	♇
1 M	10 41 51	8♍52 21	3♓00 47	10♓23 50	21♏52.0	21♌03.2	10♌01.3	4♐14.4	4♌15.7	19♐33.3	21♊59.8	26♊50.1	15♈07.7	11♒51.2
2 Tu	10 45 48	9 50 23	17 42 54	24 57 05	21R42.2	22 21.9	10D01.8	4 50.7	4 41.0	19 36.4	22 03.3	26 51.7	15R06.5	11R50.0
3 W	10 49 44	10 48 27	2♈05 37	9♈07 53	21 34.2	23 46.2	10 04.8	5 27.3	5 06.2	19 39.6	22 06.7	26 53.2	15 05.2	11 48.8
4 Th	10 53 41	11 46 32	16 03 31	22 52 18	21 28.6	25 15.6	10 10.0	6 04.0	5 31.4	19 43.0	22 10.0	26 54.7	15 03.8	11 47.7
5 F	10 57 37	12 44 39	29 34 13	6♉09 25	21 25.6	26 49.5	10 17.4	6 41.0	5 56.5	19 46.6	22 13.2	26 56.1	15 02.5	11 46.6
6 Sa	11 01 34	13 42 49	12♉38 09	19 00 50	21D24.6	28 27.4	10 27.1	7 18.1	6 21.6	19 50.4	22 16.3	26 57.5	15 01.1	11 45.4
7 Su	11 05 30	14 41 00	25 17 57	1♊30 03	21 24.8	0♍08.8	10 38.8	7 55.5	6 46.7	19 54.4	22 19.3	26 58.9	14 59.8	11 44.3
8 M	11 09 27	15 39 14	7♊37 46	13 41 45	21R25.3	1 53.3	10 52.7	8 33.0	7 11.7	19 58.5	22 22.3	27 00.1	14 58.4	11 43.2
9 Tu	11 13 23	16 37 29	19 42 38	25 41 05	21 24.9	3 40.3	11 08.6	9 10.7	7 36.7	20 02.8	22 25.1	27 01.4	14 57.0	11 42.2
10 W	11 17 20	17 35 46	1♋37 47	7♋33 21	21 22.8	5 29.3	11 26.4	9 48.5	8 01.6	20 07.3	22 27.8	27 02.6	14 55.5	11 41.1
11 Th	11 21 16	18 34 06	13 28 24	19 23 31	21 18.4	7 20.0	11 46.1	10 26.6	8 26.5	20 11.9	22 30.4	27 03.7	14 54.1	11 40.1
12 F	11 25 13	19 32 28	25 19 12	1♌15 58	21 11.6	9 11.9	12 07.7	11 04.8	8 51.4	20 16.7	22 33.0	27 04.8	14 52.6	11 39.0
13 Sa	11 29 10	20 30 51	7♌14 15	13 14 24	21 02.7	11 04.6	12 31.0	11 43.3	9 16.2	20 21.7	22 35.4	27 05.9	14 51.2	11 38.0
14 Su	11 33 06	21 29 17	19 16 46	25 21 36	20 52.2	12 58.0	12 56.0	12 21.8	9 40.9	20 26.8	22 37.7	27 06.9	14 49.7	11 37.0
15 M	11 37 03	22 27 44	1♍29 06	7♍39 25	20 41.2	14 51.5	13 22.7	13 00.6	10 05.6	20 32.1	22 39.9	27 07.8	14 48.2	11 36.1
16 Tu	11 40 59	23 26 13	13 52 40	20 08 53	20 30.7	16 45.2	13 51.0	13 39.5	10 30.3	20 37.5	22 42.0	27 08.7	14 46.6	11 35.1
17 W	11 44 56	24 24 45	26 28 06	2♎50 19	20 21.5	18 38.6	14 20.8	14 18.6	10 54.9	20 43.1	22 44.0	27 09.5	14 45.1	11 34.2
18 Th	11 48 52	25 23 18	9♎15 28	15 43 33	20 14.5	20 31.8	14 52.1	14 57.8	11 19.4	20 48.9	22 45.9	27 10.3	14 43.6	11 33.3
19 F	11 52 49	26 21 53	22 14 30	28 48 18	20 10.0	22 24.4	15 24.8	15 37.3	11 43.9	20 54.8	22 47.7	27 11.0	14 42.0	11 32.4
20 Sa	11 56 45	27 20 30	5♏24 55	12♏04 21	20D07.9	24 16.5	15 58.9	16 16.8	12 08.3	21 00.9	22 49.4	27 11.7	14 40.4	11 31.5
21 Su	12 00 42	28 19 08	18 46 38	25 31 48	20 07.7	26 07.8	16 34.3	16 56.5	12 32.6	21 07.2	22 51.0	27 12.4	14 38.8	11 30.6
22 M	12 04 39	29 17 48	2♐19 53	9♐10 58	20 08.6	27 58.5	17 11.0	17 36.4	12 56.9	21 13.5	22 52.5	27 12.9	14 37.2	11 29.8
23 Tu	12 08 35	0♎16 30	16 05 04	23 02 14	20R09.5	29 48.3	17 48.9	18 16.4	13 21.2	21 20.1	22 53.8	27 13.5	14 35.6	11 29.0
24 W	12 12 32	1 15 14	0♑02 27	7♑05 39	20 09.6	1♎37.2	18 28.0	18 56.6	13 45.3	21 26.8	22 55.1	27 14.0	14 34.0	11 28.2
25 Th	12 16 28	2 13 59	14 11 43	21 20 26	20 08.0	3 25.3	19 08.3	19 36.9	14 09.4	21 33.6	22 56.2	27 14.4	14 32.4	11 27.4
26 F	12 20 25	3 12 46	28 31 29	5♒44 27	20 04.4	5 12.4	19 49.6	20 17.4	14 33.5	21 40.6	22 57.3	27 14.7	14 30.8	11 26.7
27 Sa	12 24 21	4 11 35	12♒58 51	20 14 04	19 59.0	6 58.6	20 32.0	20 58.0	14 57.4	21 47.7	22 58.2	27 15.1	14 29.2	11 26.0
28 Su	12 28 18	5 10 25	27 29 23	4♓44 05	19 52.4	8 44.0	21 15.5	21 38.7	15 21.3	21 55.0	22 59.0	27 15.3	14 27.5	11 25.3
29 M	12 32 14	6 09 18	11♓57 23	19 08 27	19 45.3	10 28.4	21 59.9	22 19.5	15 45.2	22 02.4	22 59.7	27 15.5	14 25.9	11 24.6
30 Tu	12 36 11	7 08 12	26 16 34	3♈20 59	19 38.8	12 11.9	22 45.3	23 00.5	16 08.9	22 10.0	23 00.3	27 15.7	14 24.2	11 24.0

LONGITUDE — October 2031

Day	Sid.Time	☉	0 hr ☽	Noon ☽	True ☊	☿	♀	♂	⚳	♃	♄	♅	♆	♇
1 W	12 40 08	8♎07 08	10♈21 06	17♈16 23	19♏33.5	13♎54.5	23♌31.6	23♐41.6	16♌32.6	22♐17.6	23♊00.8	27♊15.8	14♈22.6	11♒23.3
2 Th	12 44 04	9 06 06	24 06 27	0♉51 00	19R30.1	15 36.2	24 18.8	24 22.8	16 56.2	22 25.5	23 01.2	27R15.9	14R20.9	11R22.7
3 F	12 48 01	10 05 06	7♉29 55	14 03 10	19D28.5	17 17.0	25 06.9	25 04.1	17 19.7	22 33.4	23 01.5	27 15.9	14 19.2	11 22.1
4 Sa	12 51 57	11 04 09	20 30 53	26 53 16	19 28.6	18 57.0	25 55.9	25 45.6	17 43.2	22 41.5	23R01.6	27 15.8	14 17.6	11 21.6
5 Su	12 55 54	12 03 14	3♊10 38	9♊23 23	19 29.8	20 36.2	26 45.6	26 27.2	18 06.5	22 49.7	23 01.7	27 15.7	14 15.9	11 21.1
6 M	12 59 50	13 02 21	15 32 00	21 36 59	19 31.5	22 14.5	27 36.1	27 08.9	18 29.8	22 58.1	23 01.6	27 15.6	14 14.2	11 20.6
7 Tu	13 03 47	14 01 31	27 38 54	3♋38 22	19R33.0	23 52.0	28 27.4	27 50.7	18 53.0	23 06.5	23 01.4	27 15.4	14 12.5	11 20.1
8 W	13 07 43	15 00 43	9♋36 00	15 32 24	19 33.5	25 28.8	29 19.4	28 32.6	19 16.1	23 15.1	23 01.1	27 15.1	14 10.9	11 19.6
9 Th	13 11 40	15 59 57	21 28 13	27 24 03	19 32.8	27 04.8	0♍12.0	29 14.7	19 39.2	23 23.9	23 00.8	27 14.8	14 09.2	11 19.2
10 F	13 15 36	16 59 13	3♌20 31	9♌18 10	19 30.5	28 40.0	1 05.4	29 56.9	20 02.1	23 32.7	23 00.2	27 14.5	14 07.5	11 18.8
11 Sa	13 19 33	17 58 32	15 17 35	21 19 13	19 27.0	0♏14.5	1 59.4	0♑39.1	20 25.0	23 41.7	22 59.6	27 14.1	14 05.9	11 18.4
12 Su	13 23 30	18 57 52	27 23 34	3♍31 00	19 22.4	1 48.3	2 54.0	1 21.5	20 47.7	23 50.8	22 58.9	27 13.6	14 04.2	11 18.1
13 M	13 27 26	19 57 16	9♍41 52	15 56 27	19 17.3	3 21.3	3 49.3	2 04.0	21 10.4	24 00.0	22 58.1	27 13.1	14 02.5	11 17.7
14 Tu	13 31 23	20 56 41	22 14 56	28 37 29	19 12.3	4 53.7	4 45.1	2 46.6	21 32.9	24 09.4	22 57.1	27 12.5	14 00.9	11 17.4
15 W	13 35 19	21 56 08	5♎04 09	11♎34 56	19 08.1	6 25.4	5 41.5	3 29.4	21 55.4	24 18.8	22 56.1	27 11.9	13 59.2	11 17.2
16 Th	13 39 16	22 55 38	18 09 45	24 48 28	19 05.0	7 56.4	6 38.4	4 12.2	22 17.7	24 28.4	22 54.9	27 11.2	13 57.6	11 16.9
17 F	13 43 12	23 55 09	1♏30 55	8♏16 52	19D03.3	9 26.7	7 35.8	4 55.1	22 40.0	24 38.1	22 53.6	27 10.5	13 55.9	11 16.7
18 Sa	13 47 09	24 54 43	15 06 02	21 58 10	19 03.0	10 56.3	8 33.8	5 38.1	23 02.1	24 47.9	22 52.2	27 09.7	13 54.3	11 16.5
19 Su	13 51 05	25 54 19	28 52 58	5♐50 06	19 03.7	12 25.3	9 32.2	6 21.3	23 24.1	24 57.8	22 50.7	27 08.9	13 52.6	11 16.3
20 M	13 55 02	26 53 56	12♐49 18	19 50 16	19 05.0	13 53.5	10 31.1	7 04.5	23 46.0	25 07.8	22 49.1	27 08.0	13 51.0	11 16.2
21 Tu	13 58 59	27 53 35	26 52 43	3♑56 23	19 06.5	15 21.1	11 30.5	7 47.8	24 07.8	25 17.9	22 47.4	27 07.1	13 49.4	11 16.1
22 W	14 02 55	28 53 16	11♑01 00	18 06 20	19R07.5	16 47.9	12 30.3	8 31.2	24 29.5	25 28.1	22 45.6	27 06.1	13 47.8	11 16.0
23 Th	14 06 52	29 52 59	25 12 05	2♒18 03	19 07.8	18 14.0	13 30.6	9 14.7	24 51.0	25 38.4	22 43.7	27 05.1	13 46.2	11 16.0
24 F	14 10 48	0♏52 43	9♒23 55	16 29 26	19 07.2	19 39.4	14 31.3	9 58.3	25 12.4	25 48.9	22 41.7	27 04.1	13 44.6	11D15.9
25 Sa	14 14 45	1 52 29	23 34 16	0♓38 08	19 05.7	21 04.0	15 32.3	10 41.9	25 33.7	25 59.4	22 39.6	27 02.9	13 43.0	11 15.9
26 Su	14 18 41	2 52 16	7♓40 41	14 41 33	19 03.8	22 27.8	16 33.8	11 25.7	25 54.9	26 10.0	22 37.3	27 01.8	13 41.5	11 16.0
27 M	14 22 38	3 52 05	21 40 23	28 36 50	19 01.6	23 50.7	17 35.7	12 09.5	26 16.0	26 20.7	22 35.0	27 00.6	13 39.9	11 16.0
28 Tu	14 26 34	4 51 56	5♈30 32	12♈21 08	18 59.7	25 12.7	18 37.9	12 53.4	26 36.9	26 31.6	22 32.6	26 59.3	13 38.4	11 16.1
29 W	14 30 31	5 51 49	19 08 20	25 51 52	18 58.2	26 33.8	19 40.5	13 37.4	26 57.6	26 42.5	22 30.1	26 58.0	13 36.9	11 16.2
30 Th	14 34 28	6 51 44	2♉31 29	9♉07 03	18D57.4	27 53.8	20 43.5	14 21.4	27 18.3	26 53.5	22 27.5	26 56.7	13 35.4	11 16.3
31 F	14 38 24	7 51 41	15 38 25	22 05 34	18 57.2	29 12.6	21 46.8	15 05.6	27 38.8	27 04.6	22 24.7	26 55.3	13 33.9	11 16.5

Astro Data

	Dy Hr Mn
♀ D	1 17:57
♅Q♇	1 21:15
☽ 0N	2 3:13
☽ 0S	16 11:08
☉0S	23 5:15
☿0S	25 8:00
☽ 0N	29 12:49
♅ R	3 2:43
♄ R	5 10:50
♃☍♄	6 21:54
☽ 0S	13 18:51
♇ D	24 23:13
☽ 0N	26 20:10
♃∠♇	27 1:22
♃☍♅	30 18:11

Planet Ingress

		Dy Hr Mn
☿	♍	7 9:56
☉	♎	23 5:15
☿	♎	23 14:35
♀	♍	9 6:33
♂	♑	10 13:47
☿	♏	11 8:18
☉	♏	23 14:49

Last Aspect / ☽ Ingress (September)

Last Aspect Dy Hr Mn			☽ Ingress	Dy Hr Mn
2 15:12	♅	□	♈	2 20:28
4 19:14	♅	⚹	♉	5 0:47
7 8:57	☿	□	♊	7 9:05
9 14:42	♅	☌	♋	9 20:42
11 10:11	☉	⚹	♌	12 9:27
14 15:27	♅	⚹	♍	14 21:06
17 1:18	♅	□	♎	17 6:40
19 9:03	♅	△	♏	19 14:11
21 17:19	☉	⚹	♐	21 19:54
23 19:11	♅	☍	♑	23 23:56
25 0:36	♆	□	♒	26 2:27
27 23:37	♅	△	♓	28 4:09
30 1:40	♅	□	♈	30 6:18

Last Aspect / ☽ Ingress (October)

Last Aspect Dy Hr Mn			☽ Ingress	Dy Hr Mn
2 5:36	♅	⚹	♉	2 10:29
4 10:04	♀	□	♊	4 17:55
7 0:49	♀	⚹	♋	7 4:42
9 11:15	☿	□	♌	9 17:15
11 23:41	♅	⚹	♍	12 5:07
14 9:21	♅	□	♎	14 14:34
16 16:16	♅	△	♏	16 21:18
17 17:17	♇	□	♐	19 1:56
21 0:57	☉	⚹	♑	21 5:19
23 7:36	☉	□	♒	23 8:07
25 5:55	♅	△	♓	25 10:55
27 9:13	♅	□	♈	27 14:24
29 13:59	♅	⚹	♉	29 19:26

☽ Phases & Eclipses

Dy Hr Mn		
1 9:20	○	8♓46
8 16:14	☾	15♊50
16 18:47	●	23♍43
24 1:20	☽	0♑49
30 18:58	○	7♈25
8 10:50	☾	14♋58
16 8:21	●	22♎47
23 7:36	☽	29♑42
30 7:33	○	6♉41
30 7:45	•	A 0.716

Astro Data

1 September 2031
Julian Day # 48091
SVP 4♓48'48"
GC 27♐16.9 ⚴ 2♊01.4
Eris 26♈59.4R ⚵ 7♉55.9
⚷ 21♉21.6R ⚶ 16♌09.5
☽ Mean ☊ 22♏35.0

1 October 2031
Julian Day # 48121
SVP 4♓48'46"
GC 27♐17.0 ⚴ 7♊20.6
Eris 26♈44.8R ⚵ 8♉43.9R
⚷ 20♉45.0R ⚶ 29♌20.1
☽ Mean ☊ 20♏59.7

November 2031 LONGITUDE

Day	Sid.Time	☉	0 hr ☽	Noon ☽	True ☊	☿	♀	♂	⚳	♃	♄	♅	♆	♇
1 Sa	14 42 21	8♏51 39	28♉28 30	4♊47 20	18♏57.6	0♐30.3	22♍50.5	15♑49.8	27♌59.1	27♐15.7	22♊21.9	26♊53.8	13♈32.4	11♒16.7
2 Su	14 46 17	9 51 40	11♊02 13	17 13 23	18 58.3	1 46.7	23 54.4	16 34.0	28 19.4	27 27.0	22R 19.0	26R 52.4	13R 30.9	11 16.9
3 M	14 50 14	10 51 43	23 21 06	29 25 45	18 59.2	3 01.6	24 58.7	17 18.4	28 39.4	27 38.4	22 16.0	26 50.8	13 29.5	11 17.2
4 Tu	14 54 10	11 51 48	5♋27 42	11♋27 24	19 00.1	4 14.9	26 03.4	18 02.8	28 59.3	27 49.8	22 13.0	26 49.3	13 28.0	11 17.5
5 W	14 58 07	12 51 55	17 25 21	23 22 04	19 00.7	5 26.4	27 08.3	18 47.3	29 19.1	28 01.3	22 09.8	26 47.7	13 26.6	11 17.8
6 Th	15 02 03	13 52 04	29 18 06	5♌14 01	19R 01.1	6 35.9	28 13.5	19 31.8	29 38.7	28 12.9	22 06.5	26 46.0	13 25.2	11 18.1
7 F	15 06 00	14 52 15	11♌10 24	17 07 51	19 01.1	7 43.3	29 19.0	20 16.4	29 58.1	28 24.6	22 03.2	26 44.3	13 23.9	11 18.5
8 Sa	15 09 57	15 52 28	23 06 57	29 08 17	19 01.0	8 48.2	0♎24.7	21 01.1	0♍17.4	28 36.4	21 59.8	26 42.6	13 22.5	11 18.9
9 Su	15 13 53	16 52 43	5♍12 25	11♍19 54	19 00.8	9 50.4	1 30.8	21 45.9	0 36.5	28 48.2	21 56.2	26 40.8	13 21.2	11 19.3
10 M	15 17 50	17 53 00	17 31 14	23 46 51	19 00.6	10 49.5	2 37.1	22 30.7	0 55.4	29 00.1	21 52.6	26 39.0	13 19.9	11 19.7
11 Tu	15 21 46	18 53 19	0♎07 09	6♎32 28	19D 00.6	11 45.1	3 43.6	23 15.5	1 14.2	29 12.1	21 49.0	26 37.2	13 18.6	11 20.2
12 W	15 25 43	19 53 40	13 03 02	19 39 00	19 00.6	12 36.8	4 50.4	24 00.5	1 32.8	29 24.2	21 45.2	26 35.3	13 17.3	11 20.7
13 Th	15 29 39	20 54 03	26 20 26	3♏07 14	19 00.7	13 24.2	5 57.4	24 45.5	1 51.2	29 36.3	21 41.4	26 33.4	13 16.0	11 21.2
14 F	15 33 36	21 54 27	9♏59 16	16 56 13	19R 00.8	14 06.6	7 04.6	25 30.5	2 09.4	29 48.5	21 37.5	26 31.4	13 14.8	11 21.8
15 Sa	15 37 32	22 54 54	23 57 43	1♐03 16	19 00.7	14 43.5	8 12.1	26 15.6	2 27.4	0♑00.8	21 33.5	26 29.5	13 13.6	11 22.4
16 Su	15 41 29	23 55 22	8♐12 17	15 24 08	19 00.4	15 14.3	9 19.8	27 00.8	2 45.2	0 13.1	21 29.5	26 27.4	13 12.4	11 23.0
17 M	15 45 26	24 55 51	22 38 05	29 53 27	18 59.8	15 38.2	10 27.7	27 46.0	3 02.8	0 25.5	21 25.4	26 25.4	13 11.3	11 23.6
18 Tu	15 49 22	25 56 22	7♑09 29	14♑25 29	18 59.1	15 54.5	11 35.7	28 31.3	3 20.2	0 38.0	21 21.2	26 23.3	13 10.1	11 24.3
19 W	15 53 19	26 56 54	21 40 48	28 54 48	18 58.3	16R 02.5	12 44.0	29 16.6	3 37.4	0 50.5	21 16.9	26 21.2	13 09.0	11 25.0
20 Th	15 57 15	27 57 28	6♒06 58	13♒16 51	18 57.6	16 01.4	13 52.5	0♒02.0	3 54.4	1 03.1	21 12.7	26 19.0	13 07.9	11 25.7
21 F	16 01 12	28 58 02	20 24 04	27 28 19	18D 57.4	15 50.6	15 01.1	0 47.4	4 11.2	1 15.8	21 08.3	26 16.9	13 06.9	11 26.5
22 Sa	16 05 08	29 58 38	4♓29 24	11♓27 10	18 57.6	15 29.4	16 09.9	1 32.9	4 27.7	1 28.5	21 03.9	26 14.7	13 05.9	11 27.2
23 Su	16 09 05	0♐59 15	18 21 31	25 12 24	18 58.3	14 57.7	17 18.9	2 18.3	4 44.1	1 41.3	20 59.4	26 12.4	13 04.9	11 28.0
24 M	16 13 01	1 59 53	1♈59 50	8♈43 49	18 59.3	14 15.2	18 28.1	3 03.9	5 00.2	1 54.1	20 54.9	26 10.2	13 03.9	11 28.8
25 Tu	16 16 58	3 00 32	15 24 24	22 01 37	19 00.5	13 22.4	19 37.4	3 49.5	5 16.0	2 07.0	20 50.4	26 07.9	13 02.9	11 29.7
26 W	16 20 55	4 01 12	28 35 32	5♉06 12	19 01.5	12 20.0	20 46.9	4 35.1	5 31.7	2 19.9	20 45.8	26 05.6	13 02.0	11 30.6
27 Th	16 24 51	5 01 54	11♉33 41	17 58 01	19R 01.9	11 09.4	21 56.6	5 20.7	5 47.1	2 32.9	20 41.1	26 03.3	13 01.1	11 31.5
28 F	16 28 48	6 02 37	24 19 17	0♊37 33	19 01.6	9 52.3	23 06.4	6 06.4	6 02.3	2 45.9	20 36.4	26 00.9	13 00.3	11 32.4
29 Sa	16 32 44	7 03 21	6♊52 52	13 05 22	19 00.2	8 31.2	24 16.4	6 52.1	6 17.2	2 59.0	20 31.7	25 58.5	12 59.4	11 33.3
30 Su	16 36 41	8 04 07	19 15 07	25 22 18	18 57.9	7 08.6	25 26.5	7 37.8	6 31.9	3 12.1	20 27.0	25 56.2	12 58.6	11 34.3

December 2031 LONGITUDE

Day	Sid.Time	☉	0 hr ☽	Noon ☽	True ☊	☿	♀	♂	⚳	♃	♄	♅	♆	♇
1 M	16 40 37	9♐04 54	1♋27 02	7♋29 34	18♏54.8	5♐47.4	26♎36.8	8♒23.6	6♍46.3	3♑25.2	20♊22.2	25♊53.7	12♈57.9	11♒35.3
2 Tu	16 44 34	10 05 42	13 30 06	19 28 56	18R 51.2	4R 30.2	27 47.2	9 09.4	7 00.4	3 38.5	20R 17.4	25R 51.3	12R 57.1	11 36.3
3 W	16 48 30	11 06 31	25 26 22	1♌22 46	18 47.5	3 19.6	28 57.7	9 55.2	7 14.3	3 51.7	20 12.5	25 48.9	12 56.4	11 37.4
4 Th	16 52 27	12 07 22	7♌18 32	13 14 07	18 44.2	2 17.5	0♏08.4	10 41.1	7 28.0	4 05.0	20 07.6	25 46.4	12 55.7	11 38.5
5 F	16 56 24	13 08 14	19 09 59	25 06 39	18 41.8	1 25.4	1 19.2	11 27.0	7 41.3	4 18.3	20 02.8	25 43.9	12 55.1	11 39.5
6 Sa	17 00 20	14 09 08	1♍04 41	7♍04 37	18D 40.4	0 44.2	2 30.2	12 12.9	7 54.4	4 31.7	19 57.8	25 41.4	12 54.5	11 40.7
7 Su	17 04 17	15 10 02	13 07 03	19 12 35	18 40.2	0 14.5	3 41.2	12 58.8	8 07.1	4 45.1	19 52.9	25 38.9	12 53.9	11 41.8
8 M	17 08 13	16 10 58	25 21 48	1♎35 19	18 41.1	29♏56.2	4 52.4	13 44.8	8 19.6	4 58.6	19 48.0	25 36.4	12 53.3	11 43.0
9 Tu	17 12 10	17 11 56	7♎53 39	14 17 22	18 42.7	29D 49.0	6 03.7	14 30.8	8 31.8	5 12.0	19 43.0	25 33.9	12 52.8	11 44.1
10 W	17 16 06	18 12 54	20 46 54	27 22 38	18 44.4	29 52.2	7 15.1	15 16.8	8 43.7	5 25.5	19 38.1	25 31.3	12 52.3	11 45.3
11 Th	17 20 03	19 13 54	4♏04 53	10♏53 47	18R 45.6	0♐05.1	8 26.6	16 02.8	8 55.3	5 39.1	19 33.1	25 28.8	12 51.9	11 46.6
12 F	17 23 59	20 14 55	17 49 24	24 51 35	18 45.7	0 27.0	9 38.2	16 48.9	9 06.6	5 52.7	19 28.2	25 26.3	12 51.4	11 47.8
13 Sa	17 27 56	21 15 56	2♐00 02	9♐14 17	18 44.2	0 56.9	10 49.9	17 35.0	9 17.5	6 06.3	19 23.2	25 23.7	12 51.0	11 49.1
14 Su	17 31 53	22 16 59	16 33 41	23 57 22	18 41.0	1 34.0	12 01.7	18 21.1	9 28.2	6 19.9	19 18.3	25 21.1	12 50.7	11 50.4
15 M	17 35 49	23 18 03	1♑24 24	8♑53 42	18 36.4	2 17.6	13 13.6	19 07.2	9 38.5	6 33.6	19 13.3	25 18.6	12 50.4	11 51.7
16 Tu	17 39 46	24 19 07	16 24 05	23 54 03	18 30.9	3 06.8	14 25.6	19 53.3	9 48.4	6 47.3	19 08.4	25 16.0	12 50.1	11 53.0
17 W	17 43 42	25 20 12	1♒23 30	8♒50 19	18 25.4	4 01.1	15 37.7	20 39.5	9 58.1	7 01.0	19 03.5	25 13.4	12 49.8	11 54.4
18 Th	17 47 39	26 21 17	16 13 53	23 33 25	18 20.6	4 59.7	16 49.8	21 25.6	10 07.3	7 14.7	18 58.6	25 10.9	12 49.6	11 55.8
19 F	17 51 35	27 22 22	0♓48 15	7♓57 55	18 17.2	6 02.2	18 02.1	22 11.8	10 16.3	7 28.4	18 53.7	25 08.3	12 49.4	11 57.2
20 Sa	17 55 32	28 23 27	15 02 08	22 00 46	18D 15.5	7 08.1	19 14.4	22 58.0	10 24.9	7 42.2	18 48.8	25 05.7	12 49.3	11 58.6
21 Su	17 59 28	29 24 33	28 53 48	5♈41 21	18 15.5	8 17.0	20 26.7	23 44.1	10 33.1	7 56.0	18 44.0	25 03.2	12 49.2	12 00.0
22 M	18 03 25	0♑25 39	12♈23 39	19 00 57	18 16.7	9 28.5	21 39.2	24 30.3	10 41.0	8 09.8	18 39.2	25 00.6	12 49.1	12 01.4
23 Tu	18 07 22	1 26 46	25 33 35	2♉01 54	18 18.2	10 42.2	22 51.7	25 16.5	10 48.5	8 23.6	18 34.4	24 58.1	12D 49.0	12 02.9
24 W	18 11 18	2 27 52	8♉26 16	14 47 03	18R 19.1	11 58.0	24 04.3	26 02.7	10 55.6	8 37.4	18 29.6	24 55.5	12 49.0	12 04.4
25 Th	18 15 15	3 28 59	21 04 34	27 19 10	18 18.7	13 15.5	25 17.0	26 48.9	11 02.4	8 51.3	18 24.9	24 53.0	12 49.0	12 05.9
26 F	18 19 11	4 30 06	3♊31 07	9♊40 42	18 16.3	14 34.5	26 29.7	27 35.1	11 08.7	9 05.1	18 20.3	24 50.5	12 49.1	12 07.4
27 Sa	18 23 08	5 31 13	15 48 08	21 53 37	18 11.6	15 55.0	27 42.5	28 21.3	11 14.7	9 19.0	18 15.7	24 48.0	12 49.2	12 08.9
28 Su	18 27 04	6 32 21	27 57 22	3♋59 32	18 04.5	17 16.6	28 55.3	29 07.5	11 20.4	9 32.8	18 11.1	24 45.4	12 49.3	12 10.5
29 M	18 31 01	7 33 28	10♋00 16	15 59 43	17 55.5	18 39.4	0♐08.3	29 53.7	11 25.6	9 46.7	18 06.5	24 43.0	12 49.5	12 12.1
30 Tu	18 34 58	8 34 36	21 58 03	27 55 25	17 45.2	20 03.1	1 21.2	0♓39.9	11 30.4	10 00.6	18 02.1	24 40.5	12 49.7	12 13.6
31 W	18 38 54	9 35 45	3♌52 02	9♌48 06	17 34.6	21 27.7	2 34.3	1 26.1	11 34.8	10 14.5	17 57.6	24 38.0	12 49.9	12 15.2

Astro Data

	Dy Hr Mn
☽0S	10 3:35
♀0S	10 23:26
♅□♇	18 3:25
☿R	19 21:16
☽0N	23 1:50
☽0S	7 12:39
☿D	9 16:24
☽0N	20 8:03
♆D	24 7:40

Planet Ingress

	Dy Hr Mn
☿ ♐	1 2:35
⚳ ♍	7 14:19
♀ ♎	8 2:59
♃ ♑	15 10:29
♂ ♒	20 10:57
☉ ♐	22 12:32
♀ ♏	4 9:09
☿ ♏R	8 5:37
☿ ♐	11 4:21
☉ ♑	22 1:55
♀ ♐	29 9:17
♂ ♓	29 15:15

Last Aspect / ☽ Ingress (November)

Last Aspect Dy Hr Mn		☽ Ingress Dy Hr Mn
31 11:22	♀ △	♊ 1 2:53
3 8:24	♃ ☍	♋ 3 13:08
5 20:23	♀ ⚹	♌ 6 1:25
8 10:56	♃ △	♍ 8 13:43
10 22:03	♃ □	♎ 10 23:47
13 5:42	♃ ⚹	♏ 13 6:30
15 3:27	♂ ⚹	♐ 15 10:13
17 6:17	♅ ☍	♑ 17 12:11
19 12:38	♂ ☌	♒ 19 13:48
21 14:45	☉ □	♓ 21 16:19
23 13:45	♅ □	♈ 23 20:28
25 19:28	♅ ⚹	♉ 26 2:35
26 23:55	♇ □	♊ 28 10:48
30 13:06	♅ ☌	♋ 30 21:08

Last Aspect / ☽ Ingress (December)

Last Aspect Dy Hr Mn		☽ Ingress Dy Hr Mn
3 6:35	♀ □	♌ 3 9:13
5 13:15	♅ ⚹	♍ 5 21:50
8 8:53	☿ ⚹	♎ 8 8:57
10 8:39	♅ △	♏ 10 16:43
11 21:28	♂ □	♐ 12 20:39
14 14:15	♅ ☍	♑ 14 21:44
15 19:32	♀ ⚹	♒ 16 21:46
18 16:58	☉ ⚹	♓ 18 22:40
21 0:00	☉ □	♈ 21 1:56
22 22:57	♅ ⚹	♉ 23 8:13
25 10:58	♂ □	♊ 25 17:11
28 1:40	♂ △	♋ 28 4:03
29 5:39	♆ □	♌ 30 16:11

☽ Phases & Eclipses

Dy Hr Mn	
7 7:02	☾ 14♌40
14 21:09	● 22♏18
14 21:06:12	● AT01'08"
21 14:45	☽ 29♒05
28 23:18	○ 6♊31
7 3:20	☾ 14♍48
14 9:06	● 22♐10
21 0:00	☽ 28♓54
28 17:33	○ 6♋46

Astro Data

1 November 2031
Julian Day # 48152
SVP 4♓48'43"
GC 27♐17.0 ⚴ 5♊45.0R
Eris 26♈26.4R ⚵ 2♉54.1R
⚷ 19♉24.8R ⚶ 12♍20.1
☽ Mean ☊ 19♏21.2

1 December 2031
Julian Day # 48182
SVP 4♓48'38"
GC 27♐17.1 ⚴ 26♉43.6R
Eris 26♈10.7R ⚵ 28♈25.5R
⚷ 17♉54.8R ⚶ 23♍38.6
☽ Mean ☊ 17♏45.9

LONGITUDE — January 2032

Day	Sid.Time	☉	0 hr ☽	Noon ☽	True ☊	☿	♀	♂	⚳	♃	♄	♅	♆	♇
1 Th	18 42 51	10♑36 53	15♌43 51	21♌39 35	17♏24.7	22♐53.2	3♐47.4	2♓12.3	11♍38.8	10♑28.3	17♊53.2	24♊35.6	12♈50.2	12♒16.8
2 F	18 46 47	11 38 02	27 35 37	3♍32 20	17R 16.3	24 19.3	5 00.5	2 58.5	11 42.4	10 42.2	17R 48.9	24R 33.1	12 50.5	12 18.4
3 Sa	18 50 44	12 39 11	9♍30 08	15 29 28	17 10.0	25 46.1	6 13.7	3 44.7	11 45.6	10 56.1	17 44.7	24 30.7	12 50.8	12 20.1
4 Su	18 54 40	13 40 20	21 30 50	27 34 47	17 06.1	27 13.6	7 27.0	4 30.8	11 48.4	11 10.0	17 40.5	24 28.3	12 51.2	12 21.7
5 M	18 58 37	14 41 29	3♎41 52	9♎52 42	17D 04.5	28 41.7	8 40.3	5 17.0	11 50.7	11 23.9	17 36.3	24 26.0	12 51.6	12 23.4
6 Tu	19 02 33	15 42 39	16 07 52	22 28 00	17 04.6	0♑10.3	9 53.7	6 03.2	11 52.6	11 37.8	17 32.2	24 23.6	12 52.0	12 25.1
7 W	19 06 30	16 43 49	28 53 39	5♏25 24	17R 05.4	1 39.4	11 07.1	6 49.3	11 54.1	11 51.7	17 28.2	24 21.3	12 52.5	12 26.7
8 Th	19 10 26	17 44 59	12♏03 44	18 49 04	17 05.8	3 09.1	12 20.5	7 35.5	11 55.2	12 05.5	17 24.3	24 19.0	12 53.0	12 28.4
9 F	19 14 23	18 46 09	25 41 41	2♐41 43	17 04.7	4 39.2	13 34.0	8 21.6	11R 55.8	12 19.4	17 20.4	24 16.7	12 53.6	12 30.2
10 Sa	19 18 20	19 47 20	9♐49 08	17 03 42	17 01.3	6 09.9	14 47.6	9 07.7	11 56.0	12 33.3	17 16.7	24 14.4	12 54.2	12 31.9
11 Su	19 22 16	20 48 30	24 24 56	1♑52 09	16 55.2	7 41.0	16 01.2	9 53.9	11 55.7	12 47.1	17 12.9	24 12.2	12 54.8	12 33.6
12 M	19 26 13	21 49 40	9♑24 24	17 00 32	16 46.7	9 12.6	17 14.8	10 40.0	11 55.0	13 01.0	17 09.3	24 10.0	12 55.4	12 35.3
13 Tu	19 30 09	22 50 50	24 39 15	2♒19 06	16 36.6	10 44.7	18 28.4	11 26.1	11 53.9	13 14.8	17 05.8	24 07.9	12 56.1	12 37.1
14 W	19 34 06	23 51 59	9♒58 37	17 36 21	16 26.1	12 17.2	19 42.1	12 12.2	11 52.3	13 28.6	17 02.3	24 05.7	12 56.8	12 38.9
15 Th	19 38 02	24 53 08	25 10 54	2♓41 04	16 16.5	13 50.2	20 55.8	12 58.3	11 50.2	13 42.4	16 58.9	24 03.6	12 57.6	12 40.6
16 F	19 41 59	25 54 16	10♓05 51	17 24 27	16 08.9	15 23.8	22 09.5	13 44.3	11 47.7	13 56.2	16 55.6	24 01.5	12 58.4	12 42.4
17 Sa	19 45 56	26 55 24	24 36 20	1♈41 09	16 03.9	16 57.8	23 23.3	14 30.4	11 44.8	14 09.9	16 52.4	23 59.5	12 59.2	12 44.2
18 Su	19 49 52	27 56 30	8♈38 49	15 29 25	16 01.5	18 32.3	24 37.1	15 16.4	11 41.4	14 23.6	16 49.3	23 57.5	13 00.0	12 46.0
19 M	19 53 49	28 57 36	22 13 10	28 50 26	16D 00.8	20 07.3	25 50.9	16 02.4	11 37.6	14 37.3	16 46.3	23 55.5	13 00.9	12 47.7
20 Tu	19 57 45	29 58 41	5♉21 41	11♉47 23	16R 01.0	21 42.8	27 04.7	16 48.4	11 33.4	14 51.0	16 43.4	23 53.5	13 01.8	12 49.6
21 W	20 01 42	0♒59 45	18 08 07	24 24 25	16 00.8	23 18.9	28 18.6	17 34.3	11 28.7	15 04.7	16 40.5	23 51.6	13 02.8	12 51.4
22 Th	20 05 38	2 00 48	0♊36 50	6♊45 54	15 59.0	24 55.6	29 32.5	18 20.3	11 23.6	15 18.3	16 37.8	23 49.7	13 03.7	12 53.2
23 F	20 09 35	3 01 50	12 52 07	18 55 57	15 54.7	26 32.8	0♑46.4	19 06.2	11 18.1	15 31.9	16 35.2	23 47.9	13 04.8	12 55.0
24 Sa	20 13 31	4 02 52	24 57 49	0♋58 06	15 47.4	28 10.6	2 00.3	19 52.1	11 12.1	15 45.5	16 32.6	23 46.1	13 05.8	12 56.8
25 Su	20 17 28	5 03 52	6♋57 08	12 55 11	15 37.1	29 49.0	3 14.3	20 37.9	11 05.8	15 59.0	16 30.2	23 44.4	13 06.9	12 58.6
26 M	20 21 25	6 04 52	18 52 31	24 49 20	15 24.2	1♒28.0	4 28.3	21 23.7	10 59.0	16 12.6	16 27.8	23 42.6	13 08.0	13 00.5
27 Tu	20 25 21	7 05 51	0♌45 49	6♌42 09	15 09.7	3 07.6	5 42.3	22 09.6	10 51.8	16 26.0	16 25.6	23 41.0	13 09.1	13 02.3
28 W	20 29 18	8 06 48	12 38 28	18 34 55	14 54.6	4 47.9	6 56.3	22 55.3	10 44.2	16 39.5	16 23.5	23 39.3	13 10.3	13 04.1
29 Th	20 33 14	9 07 45	24 31 40	0♍28 52	14 40.2	6 28.9	8 10.3	23 41.1	10 36.2	16 52.9	16 21.4	23 37.7	13 11.5	13 06.0
30 F	20 37 11	10 08 41	6♍26 43	12 25 27	14 27.7	8 10.5	9 24.4	24 26.8	10 27.8	17 06.3	16 19.5	23 36.2	13 12.7	13 07.8
31 Sa	20 41 07	11 09 36	18 25 18	24 26 36	14 17.8	9 52.8	10 38.5	25 12.5	10 19.0	17 19.6	16 17.7	23 34.7	13 14.0	13 09.6

LONGITUDE — February 2032

Day	Sid.Time	☉	0 hr ☽	Noon ☽	True ☊	☿	♀	♂	⚳	♃	♄	♅	♆	♇
1 Su	20 45 04	12♒10 31	0♎29 40	6♎34 54	14♏10.9	11♒35.8	11♑52.6	25♓58.2	10♍09.9	17♑32.9	16♊16.0	23♊33.2	13♈15.2	13♒11.5
2 M	20 49 00	13 11 24	12 42 44	18 53 38	14R 07.0	13 19.4	13 06.7	26 43.8	10R 00.4	17 46.2	16R 14.4	23R 31.8	13 16.5	13 13.3
3 Tu	20 52 57	14 12 17	25 08 08	1♏26 45	14D 05.5	15 03.8	14 20.8	27 29.4	9 50.5	17 59.4	16 12.9	23 30.4	13 17.9	13 15.2
4 W	20 56 54	15 13 09	7♏50 02	14 18 33	14R 05.2	16 48.8	15 35.0	28 15.0	9 40.3	18 12.6	16 11.5	23 29.1	13 19.3	13 17.0
5 Th	21 00 50	16 14 01	20 52 49	27 33 20	14 05.0	18 34.5	16 49.2	29 00.6	9 29.7	18 25.7	16 10.2	23 27.8	13 20.7	13 18.8
6 F	21 04 47	17 14 51	4♐20 31	11♐14 39	14 03.6	20 20.9	18 03.3	29 46.1	9 18.9	18 38.8	16 09.1	23 26.6	13 22.1	13 20.7
7 Sa	21 08 43	18 15 41	18 15 57	25 24 24	13 59.6	22 07.9	19 17.5	0♈31.6	9 07.7	18 51.8	16 08.0	23 25.4	13 23.5	13 22.5
8 Su	21 12 40	19 16 29	2♑39 49	10♑01 47	13 53.4	23 55.4	20 31.8	1 17.1	8 56.2	19 04.8	16 07.1	23 24.2	13 25.0	13 24.4
9 M	21 16 36	20 17 17	17 29 38	25 02 30	13 44.3	25 43.5	21 46.0	2 02.5	8 44.4	19 17.8	16 06.2	23 23.2	13 26.5	13 26.2
10 Tu	21 20 33	21 18 03	2♒39 15	10♒18 34	13 33.3	27 32.1	23 00.2	2 47.9	8 32.4	19 30.6	16 05.5	23 22.1	13 28.1	13 28.0
11 W	21 24 29	22 18 48	17 59 02	25 39 08	13 21.6	29 21.0	24 14.5	3 33.3	8 20.1	19 43.5	16 04.9	23 21.1	13 29.6	13 29.9
12 Th	21 28 26	23 19 32	3♓17 22	10♓52 18	13 10.8	1♓10.3	25 28.7	4 18.7	8 07.5	19 56.2	16 04.4	23 20.2	13 31.2	13 31.7
13 F	21 32 23	24 20 14	18 22 42	25 47 28	13 01.9	2 59.6	26 43.0	5 04.0	7 54.8	20 09.0	16 04.0	23 19.3	13 32.8	13 33.5
14 Sa	21 36 19	25 20 55	3♈05 45	10♈16 58	12 55.7	4 49.0	27 57.2	5 49.3	7 41.8	20 21.6	16 03.8	23 18.4	13 34.5	13 35.3
15 Su	21 40 16	26 21 34	17 20 45	24 16 57	12 52.2	6 38.2	29 11.5	6 34.5	7 28.6	20 34.2	16D 03.6	23 17.6	13 36.1	13 37.1
16 M	21 44 12	27 22 11	1♉05 40	7♉47 06	12D 51.0	8 27.1	0♒25.8	7 19.7	7 15.3	20 46.7	16 03.6	23 16.9	13 37.8	13 38.9
17 Tu	21 48 09	28 22 47	14 21 38	20 49 45	12R 51.1	10 15.2	1 40.0	8 04.9	7 01.8	20 59.2	16 03.7	23 16.2	13 39.5	13 40.7
18 W	21 52 05	29 23 20	27 11 59	3♊28 57	12 51.1	12 02.5	2 54.3	8 50.0	6 48.2	21 11.6	16 03.9	23 15.6	13 41.2	13 42.5
19 Th	21 56 02	0♓23 52	9♊41 16	15 49 33	12 50.0	13 48.4	4 08.6	9 35.1	6 34.5	21 24.0	16 04.2	23 15.0	13 43.0	13 44.3
20 F	21 59 58	1 24 23	21 54 26	27 56 30	12 46.8	15 32.7	5 22.9	10 20.2	6 20.7	21 36.2	16 04.6	23 14.5	13 44.8	13 46.1
21 Sa	22 03 55	2 24 51	3♋56 20	9♋54 26	12 40.9	17 14.9	6 37.2	11 05.2	6 06.8	21 48.4	16 05.1	23 14.0	13 46.6	13 47.8
22 Su	22 07 52	3 25 18	15 51 18	21 47 23	12 32.2	18 54.6	7 51.5	11 50.1	5 52.8	22 00.6	16 05.8	23 13.6	13 48.4	13 49.6
23 M	22 11 48	4 25 42	27 43 02	3♌38 38	12 21.3	20 31.2	9 05.7	12 35.1	5 38.8	22 12.6	16 06.6	23 13.2	13 50.2	13 51.3
24 Tu	22 15 45	5 26 05	9♌34 27	15 30 45	12 08.7	22 04.1	10 20.0	13 20.0	5 24.8	22 24.6	16 07.4	23 12.9	13 52.1	13 53.1
25 W	22 19 41	6 26 26	21 27 44	27 25 37	11 55.6	23 32.8	11 34.3	14 04.8	5 10.8	22 36.5	16 08.4	23 12.6	13 53.9	13 54.8
26 Th	22 23 38	7 26 46	3♍24 32	9♍24 38	11 43.1	24 56.6	12 48.6	14 49.6	4 56.8	22 48.4	16 09.5	23 12.4	13 55.8	13 56.5
27 F	22 27 34	8 27 04	15 26 04	21 28 59	11 32.1	26 14.9	14 02.9	15 34.4	4 42.8	23 00.1	16 10.7	23 12.2	13 57.7	13 58.2
28 Sa	22 31 31	9 27 20	27 33 30	3♎39 47	11 23.6	27 27.2	15 17.2	16 19.1	4 28.9	23 11.8	16 12.0	23 12.1	13 59.7	13 59.9
29 Su	22 35 27	10 27 34	9♎48 03	15 58 31	11 17.8	28 32.7	16 31.5	17 03.8	4 15.0	23 23.4	16 13.5	23D 12.0	14 01.6	14 01.6

Astro Data

Aspect	Dy Hr Mn
☽0S	3 21:05
♃⚺♇	10 9:14
⚳R	10 9:44
♃□♆	12 1:54
☽0N	16 16:47
♃⚻♄	27 11:19
☽0S	31 4:24
♂0N	8 6:10
♆✱♇	10 15:02
☽0N	13 3:52
♄D	16 6:59
☽0S	27 10:55
☿0N	28 7:02
♃⚻♄	28 12:37
♆✱♇	29 11:15

Planet Ingress

Planet	Dy Hr Mn
☿ ♑	6 9:14
☉ ♒	20 12:31
♀ ♑	22 20:56
☿ ♒	25 14:41
♂ ♈	6 19:19
☿ ♓	11 20:34
♀ ♒	16 3:40
☉ ♓	19 2:32

Last Aspect / ☽ Ingress

Last Aspect Dy Hr Mn		☽ Ingress Dy Hr Mn
1 17:55	♅ ✱	♍ 2 4:52
4 11:13	☿ □	♎ 4 16:46
6 15:36	♅ △	♏ 7 2:03
8 9:58	☉ ✱	♐ 9 7:24
10 23:41	♅ ☍	♑ 11 9:00
12 20:07	☉ ☌	♒ 13 8:22
14 22:15	♅ △	♓ 15 7:41
17 3:17	☉ ✱	♈ 17 9:07
19 12:14	☉ □	♉ 19 14:07
21 9:36	☿ △	♊ 21 22:48
23 21:39	♅ ☌	♋ 24 10:04
26 4:37	♂ △	♌ 26 22:27
28 22:13	♅ ✱	♍ 29 11:02
31 13:37	♂ ☍	♎ 31 23:01

Last Aspect / ☽ Ingress

Last Aspect Dy Hr Mn		☽ Ingress Dy Hr Mn
2 20:55	♅ △	♏ 3 9:16
5 14:44	♂ △	♐ 5 16:21
7 8:41	♅ ☍	♑ 7 19:37
9 6:21	♀ ☌	♒ 9 19:50
11 18:35	☿ ☌	♓ 11 18:49
13 13:39	♀ ✱	♈ 13 18:53
15 21:30	♀ □	♉ 15 22:03
18 3:29	☉ □	♊ 18 5:20
20 2:39	♅ ☌	♋ 20 16:07
22 12:27	♃ ☍	♌ 23 4:37
25 3:31	♅ ✱	♍ 25 17:10
27 22:29	♅ ☍	♎ 28 4:48

☽ Phases & Eclipses

Dy Hr Mn		
5 22:04	☾	15♎07
12 20:07	●	22♑10
19 12:14	☽	28♈58
27 12:52	○	7♌08
4 13:49	☾	15♏18
11 6:24	●	22♒05
18 3:29	☽	29♉02
26 7:43	○	7♍16

Astro Data

1 January 2032
Julian Day # 48213
SVP 4♓48'33"
GC 27♐17.2 ⚴ 20♉09.5R
Eris 26♈01.6R ⚵ 1♉53.0
⚷ 16♉46.0R ⚶ 2♎45.8
☽ Mean ☊ 16♏07.4

1 February 2032
Julian Day # 48244
SVP 4♓48'28"
GC 27♐17.2 ⚴ 24♉01.9
Eris 26♈02.7 ⚵ 12♉11.8
⚷ 16♉29.0 ⚶ 7♎09.0
☽ Mean ☊ 14♏28.9

March 2032 LONGITUDE

Day	Sid.Time	☉	0 hr ☽	Noon ☽	True ☊	☿	♀	♂	⚳	♃	♄	♅	♆	♇
1 M	22 39 24	11♓27 47	22♎11 24	28♎27 01	11♏14.7	29♓31.0	17♒45.9	17♈48.4	4♍01.2	23♑34.9	16♊15.0	23♊12.0	14♈03.6	14♒03.3
2 Tu	22 43 20	12 27 58	4♏45 41	11♏07 45	11D 13.8	0♈21.5	19 00.2	18 33.0	3R 47.6	23 46.3	16 16.7	23 12.1	14 05.6	14 05.0
3 W	22 47 17	13 28 08	17 33 34	24 03 33	11 14.3	1 03.6	20 14.5	19 17.5	3 34.0	23 57.7	16 18.4	23 12.2	14 07.6	14 06.6
4 Th	22 51 14	14 28 16	0♐38 05	7♐17 33	11R 15.2	1 37.2	21 28.8	20 02.1	3 20.6	24 09.0	16 20.3	23 12.3	14 09.6	14 08.3
5 F	22 55 10	15 28 23	14 02 16	20 52 31	11 15.2	2 01.7	22 43.1	20 46.5	3 07.4	24 20.1	16 22.3	23 12.6	14 11.6	14 09.9
6 Sa	22 59 07	16 28 28	27 48 32	4♑50 22	11 13.6	2 17.1	23 57.5	21 31.0	2 54.3	24 31.2	16 24.4	23 12.8	14 13.7	14 11.5
7 Su	23 03 03	17 28 32	11♑58 00	19 11 13	11 09.9	2R 23.4	25 11.8	22 15.4	2 41.4	24 42.2	16 26.5	23 13.1	14 15.8	14 13.1
8 M	23 07 00	18 28 34	26 29 37	3♒52 39	11 04.1	2 20.5	26 26.1	22 59.7	2 28.8	24 53.1	16 28.8	23 13.5	14 17.8	14 14.7
9 Tu	23 10 56	19 28 34	11♒19 32	18 49 21	10 56.6	2 08.8	27 40.4	23 44.0	2 16.3	25 03.9	16 31.3	23 13.9	14 19.9	14 16.3
10 W	23 14 53	20 28 33	26 21 00	3♓53 18	10 48.5	1 48.5	28 54.8	24 28.3	2 04.1	25 14.6	16 33.8	23 14.4	14 22.0	14 17.8
11 Th	23 18 49	21 28 29	11♓25 02	18 54 55	10 40.9	1 20.4	0♓09.1	25 12.5	1 52.2	25 25.2	16 36.4	23 15.0	14 24.1	14 19.4
12 F	23 22 46	22 28 24	26 21 46	3♈44 31	10 34.6	0 45.0	1 23.4	25 56.7	1 40.5	25 35.7	16 39.1	23 15.5	14 26.3	14 20.9
13 Sa	23 26 43	23 28 17	11♈02 12	18 14 06	10 30.3	0 03.3	2 37.7	26 40.8	1 29.2	25 46.2	16 41.9	23 16.2	14 28.4	14 22.4
14 Su	23 30 39	24 28 07	25 19 37	2♉18 24	10D 28.3	29♓16.3	3 52.0	27 24.9	1 18.1	25 56.5	16 44.8	23 16.9	14 30.6	14 23.9
15 M	23 34 36	25 27 56	9♉10 15	15 55 11	10 28.1	28 25.2	5 06.3	28 09.0	1 07.3	26 06.7	16 47.9	23 17.6	14 32.7	14 25.4
16 Tu	23 38 32	26 27 42	22 33 21	29 05 02	10 29.1	27 31.0	6 20.6	28 53.0	0 56.9	26 16.7	16 51.0	23 18.4	14 34.9	14 26.8
17 W	23 42 29	27 27 27	5♊30 38	11♊50 37	10 30.6	26 35.2	7 34.9	29 37.0	0 46.8	26 26.7	16 54.2	23 19.3	14 37.1	14 28.3
18 Th	23 46 25	28 27 08	18 05 31	24 15 55	10R 31.6	25 38.9	8 49.2	0♉20.9	0 37.0	26 36.6	16 57.6	23 20.2	14 39.3	14 29.7
19 F	23 50 22	29 26 48	0♋22 26	6♋25 40	10 31.4	24 43.3	10 03.4	1 04.7	0 27.7	26 46.4	17 01.0	23 21.1	14 41.5	14 31.1
20 Sa	23 54 18	0♈26 25	12 26 14	18 24 45	10 29.5	23 49.5	11 17.7	1 48.6	0 18.6	26 56.0	17 04.5	23 22.1	14 43.7	14 32.5
21 Su	23 58 15	1 26 00	24 21 46	0♌17 51	10 25.9	22 58.5	12 31.9	2 32.3	0 10.0	27 05.5	17 08.1	23 23.2	14 45.9	14 33.8
22 M	0 02 12	2 25 33	6♌13 32	12 09 15	10 20.7	22 11.2	13 46.2	3 16.1	0 01.7	27 14.9	17 11.8	23 24.3	14 48.1	14 35.2
23 Tu	0 06 08	3 25 04	18 05 28	24 02 34	10 14.4	21 28.3	15 00.4	3 59.7	29♌53.8	27 24.2	17 15.6	23 25.5	14 50.4	14 36.5
24 W	0 10 05	4 24 32	0♍00 55	6♍00 47	10 07.7	20 50.4	16 14.7	4 43.4	29 46.4	27 33.4	17 19.5	23 26.7	14 52.6	14 37.8
25 Th	0 14 01	5 23 58	12 02 28	18 06 10	10 01.2	20 17.9	17 28.9	5 26.9	29 39.3	27 42.5	17 23.5	23 27.9	14 54.8	14 39.1
26 F	0 17 58	6 23 22	24 12 04	0♎20 20	9 55.6	19 51.0	18 43.1	6 10.5	29 32.6	27 51.4	17 27.6	23 29.3	14 57.1	14 40.4
27 Sa	0 21 54	7 22 44	6♎31 06	12 44 27	9 51.3	19 30.0	19 57.3	6 53.9	29 26.3	28 00.2	17 31.8	23 30.6	14 59.3	14 41.6
28 Su	0 25 51	8 22 04	19 00 30	25 19 19	9 48.8	19 14.8	21 11.5	7 37.4	29 20.5	28 08.9	17 36.0	23 32.0	15 01.6	14 42.8
29 M	0 29 47	9 21 22	1♏41 00	8♏05 39	9D 47.8	19 05.6	22 25.7	8 20.8	29 15.0	28 17.5	17 40.4	23 33.5	15 03.9	14 44.1
30 Tu	0 33 44	10 20 38	14 33 20	21 04 09	9 48.3	19D 02.1	23 39.9	9 04.1	29 10.0	28 25.9	17 44.8	23 35.0	15 06.1	14 45.2
31 W	0 37 40	11 19 52	27 38 15	4♐15 43	9 49.6	19 04.4	24 54.1	9 47.4	29 05.4	28 34.2	17 49.3	23 36.5	15 08.4	14 46.4

April 2032 LONGITUDE

Day	Sid.Time	☉	0 hr ☽	Noon ☽	True ☊	☿	♀	♂	⚳	♃	♄	♅	♆	♇
1 Th	0 41 37	12♈19 05	10♐56 41	17♐41 16	9♏51.2	19♓12.1	26♓08.3	10♉30.7	29♌01.2	28♑42.4	17♊53.9	23♊38.1	15♈10.7	14♒47.5
2 F	0 45 34	13 18 15	24 29 33	1♑21 37	9R 52.5	19 25.0	27 22.5	11 13.9	28R 57.5	28 50.4	17 58.6	23 39.8	15 12.9	14 48.7
3 Sa	0 49 30	14 17 24	8♑17 31	15 17 11	9 52.9	19 43.1	28 36.7	11 57.0	28 54.2	28 58.3	18 03.4	23 41.5	15 15.2	14 49.8
4 Su	0 53 27	15 16 32	22 20 34	29 27 29	9 52.3	20 06.0	29 50.8	12 40.2	28 51.3	29 06.1	18 08.2	23 43.2	15 17.5	14 50.8
5 M	0 57 23	16 15 37	6♒37 39	13♒50 42	9 50.5	20 33.4	1♈05.0	13 23.2	28 48.8	29 13.7	18 13.1	23 45.0	15 19.7	14 51.9
6 Tu	1 01 20	17 14 41	21 06 11	28 23 29	9 48.0	21 05.3	2 19.2	14 06.3	28 46.8	29 21.2	18 18.1	23 46.8	15 22.0	14 52.9
7 W	1 05 16	18 13 43	5♓41 57	13♓00 50	9 45.0	21 41.3	3 33.3	14 49.3	28 45.2	29 28.5	18 23.2	23 48.7	15 24.3	14 53.9
8 Th	1 09 13	19 12 42	20 19 21	27 36 40	9 42.1	22 21.2	4 47.5	15 32.2	28 44.1	29 35.7	18 28.4	23 50.6	15 26.5	14 54.9
9 F	1 13 09	20 11 41	4♈51 56	12♈04 23	9 39.9	23 04.9	6 01.6	16 15.1	28 43.3	29 42.8	18 33.6	23 52.6	15 28.8	14 55.9
10 Sa	1 17 06	21 10 37	19 13 17	26 17 59	9D 38.5	23 52.1	7 15.7	16 57.9	28D 43.0	29 49.7	18 39.0	23 54.6	15 31.1	14 56.8
11 Su	1 21 03	22 09 31	3♉17 55	10♉12 41	9 38.1	24 42.6	8 29.9	17 40.7	28 43.2	29 56.4	18 44.3	23 56.7	15 33.3	14 57.7
12 M	1 24 59	23 08 23	17 01 58	23 45 36	9 38.5	25 36.3	9 44.0	18 23.5	28 43.7	0♒03.0	18 49.8	23 58.7	15 35.6	14 58.6
13 Tu	1 28 56	24 07 13	0♊23 31	6♊55 49	9 39.5	26 33.1	10 58.1	19 06.2	28 44.7	0 09.5	18 55.4	24 00.9	15 37.9	14 59.5
14 W	1 32 52	25 06 01	13 22 39	19 44 17	9 40.8	27 32.8	12 12.2	19 48.9	28 46.1	0 15.8	19 01.0	24 03.1	15 40.1	15 00.3
15 Th	1 36 49	26 04 46	26 01 05	2♋13 27	9 42.0	28 35.2	13 26.3	20 31.5	28 48.0	0 21.9	19 06.6	24 05.3	15 42.3	15 01.1
16 F	1 40 45	27 03 29	8♋21 53	14 26 52	9 42.8	29 40.2	14 40.3	21 14.1	28 50.2	0 27.9	19 12.4	24 07.6	15 44.6	15 01.9
17 Sa	1 44 42	28 02 11	20 28 59	26 28 46	9R 43.2	0♈47.8	15 54.4	21 56.6	28 52.9	0 33.7	19 18.2	24 09.9	15 46.8	15 02.7
18 Su	1 48 38	29 00 49	2♌26 50	8♌23 45	9 43.0	1 57.8	17 08.4	22 39.1	28 55.9	0 39.4	19 24.1	24 12.2	15 49.0	15 03.4
19 M	1 52 35	29 59 26	14 20 05	20 16 25	9 42.4	3 10.1	18 22.5	23 21.5	28 59.4	0 44.9	19 30.0	24 14.6	15 51.3	15 04.1
20 Tu	1 56 32	0♉58 00	26 13 18	2♍11 14	9 41.4	4 24.7	19 36.5	24 03.9	29 03.3	0 50.2	19 36.0	24 17.0	15 53.5	15 04.8
21 W	2 00 28	1 56 33	8♍10 42	14 12 11	9 40.3	5 41.5	20 50.5	24 46.2	29 07.5	0 55.4	19 42.1	24 19.4	15 55.7	15 05.4
22 Th	2 04 25	2 55 03	20 16 05	26 22 46	9 39.3	7 00.5	22 04.5	25 28.5	29 12.2	1 00.4	19 48.2	24 21.9	15 57.9	15 06.1
23 F	2 08 21	3 53 31	2♎32 32	8♎45 40	9 38.6	8 21.5	23 18.5	26 10.7	29 17.2	1 05.2	19 54.4	24 24.5	16 00.1	15 06.7
24 Sa	2 12 18	4 51 57	15 02 23	21 22 49	9 38.1	9 44.5	24 32.5	26 52.9	29 22.7	1 09.9	20 00.7	24 27.0	16 02.2	15 07.3
25 Su	2 16 14	5 50 21	27 47 04	4♏15 13	9D 37.9	11 09.5	25 46.4	27 35.1	29 28.5	1 14.4	20 07.0	24 29.6	16 04.4	15 07.8
26 M	2 20 11	6 48 43	10♏47 13	17 23 02	9 37.9	12 36.5	27 00.4	28 17.2	29 34.6	1 18.7	20 13.3	24 32.3	16 06.6	15 08.3
27 Tu	2 24 07	7 47 04	24 02 35	0♐45 41	9 38.0	14 05.4	28 14.3	28 59.2	29 41.2	1 22.9	20 19.8	24 34.9	16 08.7	15 08.8
28 W	2 28 04	8 45 23	7♐32 12	14 21 55	9R 38.1	15 36.3	29 28.3	29 41.2	29 48.1	1 26.9	20 26.2	24 37.6	16 10.9	15 09.3
29 Th	2 32 01	9 43 40	21 14 36	28 10 01	9 38.2	17 09.0	0♉42.2	0♊23.2	29 55.3	1 30.7	20 32.8	24 40.4	16 13.0	15 09.8
30 F	2 35 57	10 41 56	5♑07 54	12♑08 00	9 38.1	18 43.6	1 56.2	1 05.1	0♍02.9	1 34.3	20 39.3	24 43.1	16 15.1	15 10.2

Astro Data

	Dy Hr Mn
♅ D	1 1:34
☿ R	7 16:22
☽ 0N	11 15:15
☉ 0N	20 1:22
☿ 0S	20 21:01
☽ 0S	25 17:32
☿ D	30 14:29
♀ 0N	7 9:54
☽ 0N	8 0:49
⚳ D	10 16:38
☿ 0N	21 23:20
☽ 0S	22 0:58

Planet Ingress

	Dy Hr Mn
☿ ♈	2 1:19
♀ ♓	11 9:04
☿ ♓R	13 13:47
♂ ♉	18 0:35
☉ ♈	20 1:22
⚳ ♌R	22 17:08
♀ ♈	4 14:58
♃ ♒	12 0:58
☿ ♈	16 19:07
☉ ♉	19 12:14
♀ ♉	28 22:17
♂ ♊	28 22:44
⚳ ♍	30 2:50

Last Aspect / ☽ Ingress (March)

Last Aspect Dy Hr Mn		☽ Ingress Dy Hr Mn
1 2:32	♃ □	♏ 1 14:57
3 11:49	♃ ⚹	♐ 3 22:51
5 16:03	♅ ☍	♑ 6 3:45
7 21:11	♃ ☌	♒ 8 5:43
10 3:22	♀ ☌	♓ 10 5:49
11 22:36	♃ ⚹	♈ 12 5:54
14 3:06	♂ ☌	♉ 14 8:01
16 9:18	☿ ⚹	♊ 16 13:42
18 20:57	☉ □	♋ 18 23:16
21 5:26	♃ ☍	♌ 21 11:24
23 10:45	♅ ⚹	♍ 23 23:58
26 7:06	♃ △	♎ 26 11:20
28 17:24	♃ □	♏ 28 20:50
31 1:35	♃ ⚹	♐ 31 4:17

Last Aspect / ☽ Ingress (April)

Last Aspect Dy Hr Mn		☽ Ingress Dy Hr Mn
2 4:22	♀ □	♑ 2 9:38
4 12:43	♀ ⚹	♒ 4 12:55
6 4:24	♅ △	♓ 6 14:39
8 15:18	♃ ⚹	♈ 8 15:57
10 18:05	♃ □	♉ 10 18:20
12 15:34	☿ ⚹	♊ 12 23:17
15 4:18	☿ □	♋ 15 7:41
17 15:24	☉ □	♌ 17 19:04
19 20:02	♅ ⚹	♍ 20 7:36
22 10:07	♂ △	♎ 22 19:04
24 18:34	♀ ☍	♏ 25 4:07
27 8:40	♂ ☍	♐ 27 10:39
29 5:56	♅ ☍	♑ 29 15:10

☽ Phases & Eclipses

Dy Hr Mn	
5 1:47	☾ 15♐03
11 16:25	● 21♓40
18 20:57	☽ 28♊49
27 0:46	○ 6♎55
3 10:10	☾ 14♑13
10 2:39	● 20♈48
17 15:24	☽ 28♋10
25 15:10	○ 5♏58
25 15:14	☍ T 1.191

Astro Data

1 March 2032
Julian Day # 48273
SVP 4♓48'25"
GC 27♐17.3 ⚴ 4♊34.0
Eris 26♈12.7 ⚵ 25♉17.5
⚷ 17♉06.9 ⚶ 4♎52.0R
☽ Mean ☊ 12♏56.7

1 April 2032
Julian Day # 48304
SVP 4♓48'22"
GC 27♐17.4 ⚴ 19♊34.0
Eris 26♈30.4 ⚵ 11♊00.6
⚷ 18♉35.3 ⚶ 27♍24.0R
☽ Mean ☊ 11♏18.2

LONGITUDE — May 2032

Day	Sid.Time	☉	0 hr ☽	Noon ☽	True ☊	☿	♀	♂	⚳	♃	♄	♅	♆	♇
1 Sa	2 39 54	11♉40 10	19♑10 02	26♑13 44	9♏38.0	20♈20.0	3♉10.1	1♊47.0	0♍10.9	1♒37.8	20♊46.0	24♊46.0	16♈17.2	15♒10.6
2 Su	2 43 50	12 38 23	3♒18 48	10♒24 57	9D 38.0	21 58.3	4 24.0	2 28.8	0 19.2	1 41.1	20 52.7	24 48.8	16 19.3	15 11.0
3 M	2 47 47	13 36 34	17 31 53	24 39 17	9 38.0	23 38.5	5 38.0	3 10.6	0 27.9	1 44.2	20 59.4	24 51.6	16 21.4	15 11.3
4 Tu	2 51 43	14 34 44	1♓46 49	8♓54 10	9 38.3	25 20.6	6 51.9	3 52.3	0 36.8	1 47.1	21 06.2	24 54.5	16 23.4	15 11.6
5 W	2 55 40	15 32 53	16 00 59	23 06 52	9 38.7	27 04.5	8 05.8	4 34.1	0 46.2	1 49.9	21 13.0	24 57.5	16 25.5	15 11.9
6 Th	2 59 36	16 30 59	0♈11 28	7♈14 24	9 39.3	28 50.3	9 19.7	5 15.7	0 55.8	1 52.4	21 19.9	25 00.4	16 27.5	15 12.2
7 F	3 03 33	17 29 05	14 15 15	21 13 39	9 39.9	0♉37.9	10 33.6	5 57.3	1 05.8	1 54.8	21 26.8	25 03.4	16 29.5	15 12.4
8 Sa	3 07 29	18 27 09	28 09 12	5♉01 35	9R 40.2	2 27.5	11 47.5	6 38.9	1 16.0	1 57.0	21 33.8	25 06.4	16 31.5	15 12.6
9 Su	3 11 26	19 25 12	11♉50 28	18 35 34	9 40.1	4 18.9	13 01.3	7 20.5	1 26.6	1 59.0	21 40.8	25 09.4	16 33.5	15 12.8
10 M	3 15 23	20 23 12	25 16 38	1♊53 32	9 39.5	6 12.2	14 15.2	8 02.0	1 37.5	2 00.8	21 47.8	25 12.5	16 35.5	15 12.9
11 Tu	3 19 19	21 21 12	8♊26 07	14 54 23	9 38.4	8 07.3	15 29.1	8 43.4	1 48.8	2 02.5	21 54.9	25 15.6	16 37.4	15 13.1
12 W	3 23 16	22 19 09	21 18 19	27 38 03	9 36.7	10 04.3	16 43.0	9 24.8	2 00.3	2 03.9	22 02.0	25 18.7	16 39.4	15 13.2
13 Th	3 27 12	23 17 05	3♋53 45	10♋05 38	9 34.8	12 03.1	17 56.8	10 06.2	2 12.1	2 05.2	22 09.2	25 21.8	16 41.3	15 13.2
14 F	3 31 09	24 15 00	16 14 02	22 19 16	9 33.0	14 03.7	19 10.6	10 47.5	2 24.2	2 06.2	22 16.4	25 25.0	16 43.2	15 13.3
15 Sa	3 35 05	25 12 52	28 21 48	4♌22 03	9 31.4	16 06.0	20 24.5	11 28.8	2 36.6	2 07.1	22 23.6	25 28.2	16 45.1	15R 13.3
16 Su	3 39 02	26 10 43	10♌20 31	16 17 45	9D 30.3	18 10.0	21 38.3	12 10.0	2 49.2	2 07.8	22 30.9	25 31.4	16 46.9	15 13.3
17 M	3 42 59	27 08 32	22 14 19	28 10 45	9 30.0	20 15.5	22 52.1	12 51.2	3 02.1	2 08.3	22 38.2	25 34.6	16 48.8	15 13.2
18 Tu	3 46 55	28 06 19	4♍07 40	10♍05 40	9 30.5	22 22.5	24 05.9	13 32.4	3 15.3	2 08.6	22 45.6	25 37.9	16 50.6	15 13.2
19 W	3 50 52	29 04 05	16 05 18	22 07 10	9 31.6	24 30.7	25 19.7	14 13.5	3 28.8	2R 08.7	22 52.9	25 41.2	16 52.4	15 13.1
20 Th	3 54 48	0♊01 49	28 11 49	4♎19 45	9 33.1	26 40.1	26 33.5	14 54.6	3 42.5	2 08.6	23 00.3	25 44.4	16 54.2	15 13.0
21 F	3 58 45	0 59 31	10♎31 28	16 47 24	9 34.6	28 50.4	27 47.3	15 35.6	3 56.5	2 08.4	23 07.7	25 47.8	16 55.9	15 12.8
22 Sa	4 02 41	1 57 12	23 07 53	29 33 16	9R 35.6	1♊01.5	29 01.1	16 16.6	4 10.7	2 07.9	23 15.2	25 51.1	16 57.7	15 12.7
23 Su	4 06 38	2 54 52	6♏03 43	12♏39 23	9 35.9	3 13.0	0♊14.9	16 57.5	4 25.2	2 07.3	23 22.7	25 54.4	16 59.4	15 12.5
24 M	4 10 34	3 52 30	19 20 16	26 06 18	9 35.1	5 24.8	1 28.6	17 38.4	4 39.9	2 06.5	23 30.2	25 57.8	17 01.1	15 12.2
25 Tu	4 14 31	4 50 07	2♐57 17	9♐52 56	9 33.0	7 36.5	2 42.4	18 19.3	4 54.9	2 05.4	23 37.7	26 01.2	17 02.8	15 12.0
26 W	4 18 28	5 47 42	16 52 49	23 56 28	9 30.0	9 47.8	3 56.1	19 00.1	5 10.1	2 04.2	23 45.3	26 04.6	17 04.4	15 11.7
27 Th	4 22 24	6 45 17	1♑03 18	8♑12 41	9 26.3	11 58.6	5 09.9	19 40.9	5 25.5	2 02.9	23 52.9	26 08.0	17 06.0	15 11.4
28 F	4 26 21	7 42 51	15 23 58	22 36 28	9 22.4	14 08.5	6 23.6	20 21.6	5 41.1	2 01.3	24 00.5	26 11.4	17 07.7	15 11.1
29 Sa	4 30 17	8 40 23	29 49 30	7♒02 28	9 19.0	16 17.3	7 37.4	21 02.3	5 57.0	1 59.5	24 08.1	26 14.8	17 09.2	15 10.8
30 Su	4 34 14	9 37 55	14♒14 46	21 25 52	9 16.6	18 24.7	8 51.1	21 43.0	6 13.1	1 57.6	24 15.7	26 18.3	17 10.8	15 10.4
31 M	4 38 10	10 35 26	28 35 20	5♓42 48	9D 15.4	20 30.5	10 04.9	22 23.6	6 29.4	1 55.4	24 23.4	26 21.8	17 12.3	15 10.0

LONGITUDE — June 2032

Day	Sid.Time	☉	0 hr ☽	Noon ☽	True ☊	☿	♀	♂	⚳	♃	♄	♅	♆	♇
1 Tu	4 42 07	11♊32 56	12♓47 59	19♓50 38	9♏15.6	22♊34.6	11♊18.6	23♊04.2	6♍45.9	1♒53.1	24♊31.1	26♊25.2	17♈13.8	15♒09.6
2 W	4 46 03	12 30 26	26 50 36	3♈47 47	9 16.7	24 36.7	12 32.4	23 44.7	7 02.6	1R 50.6	24 38.8	26 28.7	17 15.3	15R 09.1
3 Th	4 50 00	13 27 54	10♈42 07	17 33 32	9 18.1	26 36.7	13 46.1	24 25.2	7 19.5	1 47.9	24 46.5	26 32.2	17 16.8	15 08.7
4 F	4 53 57	14 25 22	24 22 00	1♉07 32	9R 19.3	28 34.5	14 59.9	25 05.7	7 36.6	1 45.0	24 54.2	26 35.7	17 18.2	15 08.2
5 Sa	4 57 53	15 22 50	7♉50 05	14 29 38	9 19.4	0♋30.0	16 13.6	25 46.2	7 53.9	1 42.0	25 01.9	26 39.3	17 19.6	15 07.6
6 Su	5 01 50	16 20 16	21 06 09	27 39 37	9 18.0	2 23.1	17 27.4	26 26.6	8 11.4	1 38.7	25 09.7	26 42.8	17 21.0	15 07.1
7 M	5 05 46	17 17 42	4♊09 58	10♊37 12	9 14.8	4 13.7	18 41.1	27 07.0	8 29.1	1 35.3	25 17.5	26 46.3	17 22.4	15 06.5
8 Tu	5 09 43	18 15 07	17 01 15	23 22 09	9 09.7	6 01.9	19 54.8	27 47.3	8 47.0	1 31.8	25 25.2	26 49.9	17 23.7	15 05.9
9 W	5 13 39	19 12 31	29 39 52	5♋54 29	9 03.3	7 47.5	21 08.6	28 27.6	9 05.1	1 28.0	25 33.0	26 53.4	17 25.0	15 05.3
10 Th	5 17 36	20 09 55	12♋06 04	18 14 44	8 56.0	9 30.5	22 22.3	29 07.9	9 23.3	1 24.1	25 40.8	26 57.0	17 26.3	15 04.7
11 F	5 21 32	21 07 17	24 20 39	0♌24 03	8 48.7	11 11.0	23 36.1	29 48.1	9 41.8	1 20.0	25 48.6	27 00.5	17 27.5	15 04.0
12 Sa	5 25 29	22 04 38	6♌25 13	12 24 26	8 42.0	12 48.8	24 49.8	0♋28.3	10 00.4	1 15.7	25 56.4	27 04.1	17 28.7	15 03.3
13 Su	5 29 26	23 01 59	18 22 07	24 18 41	8 36.6	14 24.0	26 03.5	1 08.5	10 19.2	1 11.3	26 04.2	27 07.7	17 29.9	15 02.6
14 M	5 33 22	23 59 18	0♍14 35	6♍10 22	8 33.0	15 56.6	27 17.2	1 48.6	10 38.1	1 06.7	26 12.0	27 11.3	17 31.1	15 01.9
15 Tu	5 37 19	24 56 37	12 06 33	18 03 44	8D 31.2	17 26.4	28 31.0	2 28.7	10 57.2	1 01.9	26 19.9	27 14.8	17 32.2	15 01.1
16 W	5 41 15	25 53 55	24 02 32	0♎03 32	8 31.0	18 53.6	29 44.7	3 08.7	11 16.5	0 57.0	26 27.7	27 18.4	17 33.3	15 00.4
17 Th	5 45 12	26 51 12	6♎07 25	12 14 45	8 31.9	20 18.1	0♋58.4	3 48.7	11 35.9	0 52.0	26 35.5	27 22.0	17 34.4	14 59.6
18 F	5 49 08	27 48 28	18 26 11	24 42 17	8 33.1	21 39.8	2 12.1	4 28.7	11 55.5	0 46.8	26 43.3	27 25.5	17 35.4	14 58.7
19 Sa	5 53 05	28 45 43	1♏03 35	7♏30 33	8R 33.7	22 58.6	3 25.8	5 08.6	12 15.2	0 41.4	26 51.1	27 29.1	17 36.4	14 57.9
20 Su	5 57 01	29 42 58	14 03 34	20 42 56	8 33.1	24 14.7	4 39.5	5 48.5	12 35.1	0 36.0	26 58.9	27 32.7	17 37.4	14 57.1
21 M	6 00 58	0♋40 12	27 28 47	4♐21 08	8 30.4	25 27.9	5 53.2	6 28.4	12 55.1	0 30.3	27 06.7	27 36.3	17 38.4	14 56.2
22 Tu	6 04 55	1 37 26	11♐19 53	18 24 40	8 25.7	26 38.1	7 06.9	7 08.3	13 15.3	0 24.6	27 14.5	27 39.9	17 39.3	14 55.3
23 W	6 08 51	2 34 39	25 35 02	2♑50 19	8 19.0	27 45.3	8 20.6	7 48.1	13 35.6	0 18.7	27 22.3	27 43.4	17 40.2	14 54.4
24 Th	6 12 48	3 31 51	10♑09 42	17 32 16	8 10.9	28 49.4	9 34.3	8 27.8	13 56.0	0 12.7	27 30.1	27 47.0	17 41.1	14 53.4
25 F	6 16 44	4 29 04	24 57 00	2♒22 47	8 02.6	29 50.3	10 48.0	9 07.6	14 16.6	0 06.5	27 37.9	27 50.6	17 41.9	14 52.5
26 Sa	6 20 41	5 26 16	9♒48 36	17 13 22	7 55.0	0♌48.0	12 01.7	9 47.3	14 37.3	0 00.3	27 45.7	27 54.1	17 42.7	14 51.5
27 Su	6 24 37	6 23 28	24 36 11	1♓56 11	7 48.9	1 42.3	13 15.4	10 27.0	14 58.1	29♑53.9	27 53.5	27 57.7	17 43.5	14 50.5
28 M	6 28 34	7 20 40	9♓12 43	16 25 13	7 45.0	2 33.2	14 29.1	11 06.6	15 19.1	29 47.4	28 01.2	28 01.2	17 44.2	14 49.5
29 Tu	6 32 30	8 17 52	23 33 21	0♈36 51	7D 43.2	3 20.5	15 42.8	11 46.2	15 40.2	29 40.8	28 08.9	28 04.8	17 44.9	14 48.5
30 W	6 36 27	9 15 05	7♈35 38	14 29 42	7 43.1	4 04.2	16 56.5	12 25.8	16 01.4	29 34.0	28 16.7	28 08.3	17 45.6	14 47.5

Astro Data

	Dy Hr Mn
☽ 0N	5 8:00
♇ R	15 15:53
☽ 0S	19 9:25
♃ R	19 14:48
☽ 0N	1 13:54
☽ 0S	15 18:19
♄☌♅	28 12:03
☽ 0N	28 20:27

Planet Ingress

	Dy Hr Mn
☿ ♉	7 3:35
☉ ♊	20 11:15
☿ ♊	22 0:45
♀ ♊	23 7:10
☿ ♋	5 5:43
♂ ♋	11 19:06
♀ ♋	16 16:59
☉ ♋	20 19:09
☿ ♌	25 15:57
♃ ♑R	26 12:57

Last Aspect / ☽ Ingress (May)

Last Aspect Dy Hr Mn		☽ Ingress Dy Hr Mn
1 0:41	☿ □	♒ 1 18:24
3 12:21	♅ △	♓ 3 21:00
5 15:08	♅ □	♈ 5 23:41
7 18:39	♅ ✶	♉ 8 3:13
9 13:36	☉ ☌	♊ 10 8:33
12 7:34	♅ ☌	♋ 12 16:31
14 16:09	☉ ✶	♌ 15 3:16
17 9:43	☉ □	♍ 17 15:41
20 2:53	☉ △	♎ 20 3:32
22 5:04	♅ △	♏ 22 12:50
23 16:36	♇ □	♐ 24 18:50
26 15:37	♅ ☍	♑ 26 22:14
28 2:52	♆ □	♒ 29 0:17
30 20:12	♅ △	♓ 31 2:22

Last Aspect / ☽ Ingress (June)

Last Aspect Dy Hr Mn		☽ Ingress Dy Hr Mn
1 23:19	♅ □	♈ 2 5:26
4 6:42	☿ ✶	♉ 4 10:00
5 13:09	♇ □	♊ 6 16:18
8 20:53	♂ ☌	♋ 9 0:39
10 10:25	♆ □	♌ 11 11:12
13 17:44	♅ ✶	♍ 13 23:30
16 11:18	♀ □	♎ 16 11:53
18 18:21	☉ △	♏ 18 22:01
20 18:55	☿ △	♐ 21 4:25
23 3:31	♅ ☍	♑ 23 7:19
25 7:36	☿ ☍	♒ 25 8:09
27 5:28	♅ △	♓ 27 8:49
29 10:25	♃ ✶	♈ 29 10:57

☽ Phases & Eclipses

Dy Hr Mn		
2 16:02	☾	12♒48
9 13:36	●	19♉29
9 13:25:24	•	A 00'22"
17 9:43	☽	27♌03
25 2:37	○	4♐28
31 20:51	☾	10♓57
8 1:32	●	17♊50
16 3:00	☽	25♍32
23 11:32	○	2♑34
30 2:12	☾	8♈52

Astro Data

1 May 2032
Julian Day # 48334
SVP 4♓48'19"
GC 27♐17.5 ⚴ 5♋37.3
Eris 26♈50.0 ⚵ 26♊49.6
⚷ 20♉29.8 ⚶ 23♍01.9R
☽ Mean ☊ 9♏42.9

1 June 2032
Julian Day # 48365
SVP 4♓48'15"
GC 27♐17.5 ⚴ 22♋34.4
Eris 27♈07.8 ⚵ 13♋09.5
⚷ 22♉35.8 ⚶ 25♍48.2
☽ Mean ☊ 8♏04.4

July 2032 — LONGITUDE

Day	Sid.Time	☉	0 hr ☽	Noon ☽	True ☊	☿	♀	♂	⚳	♃	♄	♅	♆	♇
1 Th	6 40 24	10♋12 17	21♈19 10	28♈04 13	7♏43.7	4♌44.0	18♋10.2	13♋05.4	16♍22.7	29♑27.2	28♊24.4	28♊11.8	17♈46.2	14♒46.4
2 F	6 44 20	11 09 30	4♉45 03	11♉21 54	7R43.9	5 20.0	19 24.0	13 44.9	16 44.2	29R 20.3	28 32.1	28 15.3	17 46.8	14R 45.3
3 Sa	6 48 17	12 06 43	17 55 02	24 24 42	7 42.6	5 51.9	20 37.7	14 24.4	17 05.8	29 13.3	28 39.8	28 18.8	17 47.4	14 44.2
4 Su	6 52 13	13 03 56	0♊51 07	7♊14 31	7 39.1	6 19.6	21 51.4	15 03.9	17 27.5	29 06.2	28 47.5	28 22.3	17 48.0	14 43.1
5 M	6 56 10	14 01 09	13 35 03	19 52 54	7 33.0	6 43.1	23 05.1	15 43.4	17 49.3	28 59.0	28 55.1	28 25.8	17 48.5	14 42.0
6 Tu	7 00 06	14 58 23	26 08 11	2♋21 02	7 24.2	7 02.1	24 18.8	16 22.8	18 11.2	28 51.8	29 02.8	28 29.3	17 49.0	14 40.9
7 W	7 04 03	15 55 36	8♋31 32	14 39 47	7 13.3	7 16.7	25 32.6	17 02.2	18 33.2	28 44.5	29 10.4	28 32.8	17 49.4	14 39.7
8 Th	7 07 59	16 52 50	20 45 52	26 49 54	7 01.1	7 26.6	26 46.3	17 41.6	18 55.4	28 37.1	29 18.0	28 36.2	17 49.9	14 38.6
9 F	7 11 56	17 50 04	2♌52 00	8♌52 19	6 48.5	7R31.8	28 00.0	18 20.9	19 17.6	28 29.6	29 25.5	28 39.6	17 50.2	14 37.4
10 Sa	7 15 53	18 47 17	14 51 02	20 48 23	6 36.8	7 32.3	29 13.7	19 00.2	19 40.0	28 22.1	29 33.1	28 43.1	17 50.6	14 36.2
11 Su	7 19 49	19 44 31	26 44 36	2♍40 02	6 26.8	7 28.1	0♌27.5	19 39.5	20 02.4	28 14.6	29 40.6	28 46.5	17 50.9	14 35.0
12 M	7 23 46	20 41 45	8♍35 01	14 29 59	6 19.2	7 19.1	1 41.2	20 18.7	20 25.0	28 07.0	29 48.1	28 49.9	17 51.2	14 33.8
13 Tu	7 27 42	21 38 59	20 25 23	26 21 44	6 14.2	7 05.5	2 54.9	20 57.9	20 47.7	27 59.4	29 55.6	28 53.2	17 51.5	14 32.6
14 W	7 31 39	22 36 12	2♎19 35	8♎19 32	6 11.7	6 47.3	4 08.6	21 37.1	21 10.4	27 51.7	0♋03.0	28 56.6	17 51.7	14 31.3
15 Th	7 35 35	23 33 26	14 22 10	20 28 09	6D10.9	6 24.8	5 22.3	22 16.3	21 33.3	27 44.0	0 10.4	28 59.9	17 51.9	14 30.1
16 F	7 39 32	24 30 40	26 38 08	2♏52 46	6R10.9	5 58.2	6 36.0	22 55.4	21 56.2	27 36.3	0 17.8	29 03.2	17 52.0	14 28.8
17 Sa	7 43 28	25 27 54	9♏12 41	15 38 27	6 10.7	5 27.9	7 49.7	23 34.6	22 19.2	27 28.5	0 25.2	29 06.6	17 52.1	14 27.6
18 Su	7 47 25	26 25 08	22 10 37	28 49 37	6 09.2	4 54.2	9 03.4	24 13.6	22 42.3	27 20.8	0 32.5	29 09.8	17 52.2	14 26.3
19 M	7 51 22	27 22 23	5♐35 47	12♐29 19	6 05.5	4 17.6	10 17.1	24 52.7	23 05.5	27 13.1	0 39.8	29 13.1	17 52.3	14 25.0
20 Tu	7 55 18	28 19 38	19 30 13	26 38 19	5 59.2	3 38.6	11 30.8	25 31.7	23 28.8	27 05.3	0 47.0	29 16.3	17R52.3	14 23.7
21 W	7 59 15	29 16 53	3♑53 13	11♑14 18	5 50.6	2 58.0	12 44.5	26 10.7	23 52.2	26 57.6	0 54.3	29 19.6	17 52.3	14 22.4
22 Th	8 03 11	0♌14 08	18 40 43	26 11 27	5 40.3	2 16.2	13 58.2	26 49.7	24 15.6	26 49.9	1 01.4	29 22.8	17 52.3	14 21.1
23 F	8 07 08	1 11 24	3♒45 18	11♒20 57	5 29.5	1 34.2	15 11.9	27 28.7	24 39.2	26 42.1	1 08.6	29 25.9	17 52.2	14 19.8
24 Sa	8 11 04	2 08 41	18 57 02	26 32 12	5 19.4	0 52.5	16 25.6	28 07.6	25 02.8	26 34.5	1 15.7	29 29.1	17 52.1	14 18.5
25 Su	8 15 01	3 05 58	4♓05 11	11♓34 48	5 11.2	0 12.0	17 39.2	28 46.5	25 26.5	26 26.8	1 22.8	29 32.2	17 52.0	14 17.2
26 M	8 18 57	4 03 16	19 00 06	26 20 18	5 05.5	29♋33.4	18 52.9	29 25.4	25 50.2	26 19.2	1 29.8	29 35.3	17 51.8	14 15.8
27 Tu	8 22 54	5 00 35	3♈34 48	10♈43 16	5 02.3	28 57.5	20 06.6	0♌04.2	26 14.1	26 11.6	1 36.8	29 38.4	17 51.6	14 14.5
28 W	8 26 51	5 57 55	17 45 31	24 41 31	5 01.2	28 24.8	21 20.3	0 43.1	26 38.0	26 04.0	1 43.7	29 41.5	17 51.4	14 13.1
29 Th	8 30 47	6 55 16	1♉31 26	8♉15 29	5 01.1	27 56.1	22 33.9	1 21.9	27 02.0	25 56.5	1 50.6	29 44.5	17 51.1	14 11.8
30 F	8 34 44	7 52 38	14 54 00	21 27 22	5 00.8	27 31.9	23 47.6	2 00.7	27 26.0	25 49.1	1 57.5	29 47.5	17 50.8	14 10.4
31 Sa	8 38 40	8 50 02	27 56 00	4♊20 19	4 59.0	27 12.8	25 01.3	2 39.5	27 50.1	25 41.7	2 04.3	29 50.5	17 50.5	14 09.1

August 2032 — LONGITUDE

Day	Sid.Time	☉	0 hr ☽	Noon ☽	True ☊	☿	♀	♂	⚳	♃	♄	♅	♆	♇
1 Su	8 42 37	9♌47 26	10♊40 44	16♊57 39	4♏55.0	26♋59.1	26♌14.9	3♌18.2	28♍14.3	25♑34.3	2♋11.1	29♊53.4	17♈50.1	14♒07.7
2 M	8 46 33	10 44 52	23 11 27	29 22 28	4R48.2	26D51.2	27 28.6	3 57.0	28 38.6	25R27.1	2 17.8	29 56.4	17R49.7	14R06.4
3 Tu	8 50 30	11 42 18	5♋31 01	11♋37 23	4 38.5	26 49.4	28 42.3	4 35.7	29 02.9	25 19.9	2 24.5	29 59.2	17 49.3	14 05.0
4 W	8 54 26	12 39 46	17 41 47	23 44 26	4 26.6	26 53.9	29 55.9	5 14.4	29 27.3	25 12.8	2 31.1	0♋02.1	17 48.8	14 03.6
5 Th	8 58 23	13 37 15	29 45 32	5♌45 15	4 13.2	27 05.0	1♍09.6	5 53.0	29 51.8	25 05.8	2 37.7	0 04.9	17 48.4	14 02.3
6 F	9 02 20	14 34 44	11♌43 44	17 41 08	3 59.5	27 22.7	2 23.2	6 31.7	0♎16.3	24 58.9	2 44.2	0 07.7	17 47.8	14 00.9
7 Sa	9 06 16	15 32 15	23 37 37	29 33 22	3 46.6	27 47.0	3 36.9	7 10.3	0 40.9	24 52.0	2 50.7	0 10.5	17 47.3	13 59.6
8 Su	9 10 13	16 29 47	5♍28 36	11♍23 32	3 35.5	28 18.0	4 50.5	7 48.9	1 05.6	24 45.3	2 57.1	0 13.2	17 46.7	13 58.2
9 M	9 14 09	17 27 19	17 18 26	23 13 37	3 26.9	28 55.8	6 04.2	8 27.5	1 30.3	24 38.7	3 03.5	0 15.9	17 46.1	13 56.8
10 Tu	9 18 06	18 24 53	29 09 25	5♎06 15	3 21.1	29 40.1	7 17.8	9 06.1	1 55.1	24 32.2	3 09.8	0 18.6	17 45.5	13 55.5
11 W	9 22 02	19 22 27	11♎04 33	17 04 48	3 17.9	0♌30.9	8 31.4	9 44.6	2 19.9	24 25.8	3 16.0	0 21.2	17 44.8	13 54.1
12 Th	9 25 59	20 20 02	23 07 32	29 13 18	3D16.8	1 28.1	9 45.0	10 23.2	2 44.8	24 19.5	3 22.2	0 23.8	17 44.1	13 52.7
13 F	9 29 55	21 17 39	5♏22 43	11♏36 21	3R16.9	2 31.6	10 58.6	11 01.7	3 09.7	24 13.3	3 28.3	0 26.4	17 43.4	13 51.4
14 Sa	9 33 52	22 15 16	17 54 51	24 18 48	3 17.0	3 41.0	12 12.2	11 40.1	3 34.7	24 07.3	3 34.4	0 28.9	17 42.6	13 50.0
15 Su	9 37 49	23 12 54	0♐48 47	7♐25 17	3 16.2	4 56.3	13 25.8	12 18.6	3 59.7	24 01.4	3 40.4	0 31.4	17 41.8	13 48.7
16 M	9 41 45	24 10 33	14 08 45	20 59 31	3 13.5	6 17.0	14 39.3	12 57.0	4 24.8	23 55.6	3 46.3	0 33.9	17 41.0	13 47.4
17 Tu	9 45 42	25 08 14	27 57 43	5♑03 22	3 08.6	7 43.0	15 52.9	13 35.5	4 50.0	23 50.0	3 52.2	0 36.3	17 40.2	13 46.0
18 W	9 49 38	26 05 55	12♑16 16	19 36 00	3 01.3	9 13.9	17 06.4	14 13.9	5 15.1	23 44.5	3 58.0	0 38.7	17 39.3	13 44.7
19 Th	9 53 35	27 03 37	27 01 53	4♒33 02	2 52.5	10 49.4	18 20.0	14 52.3	5 40.4	23 39.2	4 03.8	0 41.0	17 38.4	13 43.4
20 F	9 57 31	28 01 21	12♒08 22	19 46 35	2 43.0	12 29.0	19 33.5	15 30.6	6 05.6	23 34.0	4 09.4	0 43.3	17 37.5	13 42.1
21 Sa	10 01 28	28 59 06	27 26 19	5♓06 07	2 34.1	14 12.3	20 47.0	16 09.0	6 31.0	23 29.0	4 15.1	0 45.6	17 36.5	13 40.8
22 Su	10 05 24	29 56 52	12♓44 32	20 20 14	2 26.8	15 58.9	22 00.5	16 47.3	6 56.3	23 24.1	4 20.6	0 47.8	17 35.6	13 39.5
23 M	10 09 21	0♍54 40	27 51 59	5♈18 46	2 21.8	17 48.4	23 14.0	17 25.6	7 21.7	23 19.4	4 26.1	0 50.0	17 34.5	13 38.2
24 Tu	10 13 18	1 52 29	12♈39 46	19 54 21	2D19.2	19 40.3	24 27.5	18 03.9	7 47.2	23 14.8	4 31.5	0 52.1	17 33.5	13 36.9
25 W	10 17 14	2 50 20	27 02 10	4♉03 01	2 18.7	21 34.2	25 40.9	18 42.2	8 12.7	23 10.4	4 36.8	0 54.2	17 32.5	13 35.6
26 Th	10 21 11	3 48 13	10♉56 55	17 44 01	2 19.2	23 29.7	26 54.4	19 20.4	8 38.2	23 06.1	4 42.1	0 56.3	17 31.4	13 34.3
27 F	10 25 07	4 46 08	24 24 36	0♊59 01	2R19.9	25 26.5	28 07.8	19 58.7	9 03.8	23 02.1	4 47.3	0 58.3	17 30.3	13 33.1
28 Sa	10 29 04	5 44 05	7♊27 44	13 51 14	2 19.6	27 24.0	29 21.3	20 36.9	9 29.4	22 58.2	4 52.4	1 00.3	17 29.2	13 31.8
29 Su	10 33 00	6 42 03	20 10 00	26 24 34	2 17.6	29 22.1	0♎34.7	21 15.2	9 55.1	22 54.4	4 57.4	1 02.2	17 28.0	13 30.6
30 M	10 36 57	7 40 04	2♋35 25	8♋43 04	2 13.4	1♍20.5	1 48.1	21 53.4	10 20.8	22 50.9	5 02.4	1 04.1	17 26.8	13 29.4
31 Tu	10 40 53	8 38 06	14 47 56	20 50 30	2 06.9	3 18.8	3 01.5	22 31.6	10 46.5	22 47.5	5 07.2	1 06.0	17 25.6	13 28.2

Astro Data	Planet Ingress	Last Aspect	☽ Ingress	Last Aspect	☽ Ingress	☽ Phases & Eclipses	Astro Data
Dy Hr Mn	Dy Hr Mn	Dy Hr Mn	Dy Hr Mn	Dy Hr Mn	Dy Hr Mn	Dy Hr Mn	1 July 2032
♃⊼♄ 5 18:20	♀ ♌ 11 3:04	1 14:27 ♃ □	♉ 1 15:27	2 13:06 ♅ ☌	♋ 2 13:13	7 14:41 ● 16♋02	Julian Day # 48395
♃⊼♅ 8 13:57	♄ ♋ 14 2:16	3 20:52 ♃ △	♊ 3 22:24	4 18:22 ♅ ☌	♌ 5 0:29	15 18:32 ☽ 23♎49	SVP 4♓48'10"
☿R 10 2:33	☉ ♌ 22 6:05	6 5:33 ♄ ☌	♋ 6 7:27	6 12:14 ♆ △	♍ 7 12:54	22 18:51 ○ 0♒30	GC 27♐17.6 ⚴ 8♌45.2
♄□♇ 10 20:37	☿ ♋R 25 19:20	8 15:31 ♃ ☍	♌ 8 18:18	10 0:17 ☿ ⚹	♎ 10 1:42	29 9:25 ☾ 6♉49	Eris 27♈18.7 ⚵ 28♋37.0
☽0S 13 2:47	♂ ♌ 27 9:23	11 5:53 ♄ ⚹	♍ 11 6:36	12 2:27 ♃ □	♏ 12 13:31		⚷ 24♉23.8 ⚶ 4♎01.0
♆R 20 20:42		13 19:15 ♄ □	♎ 13 19:20	14 11:39 ♃ ⚹	♐ 14 22:31	6 5:11 ● 14♌18	☽ Mean ☊ 6♏29.1
♅□♇ 22 3:13	♅ ♋ 3 18:20	16 4:38 ♅ △	♏ 16 6:29	16 17:55 ☉ △	♑ 17 3:28	14 7:51 ☽ 22♏05	
☽0N 26 4:57	♀ ♍ 4 13:20	18 9:22 ♃ ⚹	♐ 18 14:06	18 18:40 ♃ ☌	♒ 19 4:45	21 1:47 ○ 28♒34	1 August 2032
	⚳ ♎ 5 20:01	20 16:24 ♅ ☍	♑ 20 17:35	21 1:47 ☉ ☍	♓ 21 4:01	27 19:33 ☾ 5♊04	Julian Day # 48426
☿D 3 6:51	☿ ♌ 10 21:46	22 13:04 ♂ ☍	♒ 22 18:03	22 16:51 ♃ ⚹	♈ 23 3:25		SVP 4♓48'05"
☽0S 9 10:10	☉ ♍ 22 13:18	24 16:42 ♅ △	♓ 24 17:30	24 17:34 ♃ □	♉ 25 5:03		GC 27♐17.7 ⚴ 24♌59.3
☽0N 22 15:20	♀ ♎ 29 0:39	26 17:23 ♅ □	♈ 26 18:03	27 6:14 ♀ △	♊ 27 10:12		Eris 27♈20.8R ⚵ 14♌01.8
♀0S 30 23:28	☿ ♍ 29 19:41	28 20:48 ♅ ⚹	♉ 28 21:18	29 18:49 ☿ ⚹	♋ 29 18:57		⚷ 25♉40.8 ⚶ 15♎59.8
		30 22:58 ☿ ⚹	♊ 31 3:51				☽ Mean ☊ 4♏50.6

LONGITUDE September 2032

Day	Sid.Time	☉	0 hr ☽	Noon ☽	True ☊	☿	♀	♂	⚳	♃	♄	♅	♆	♇
1 W	10 44 50	9♍36 10	26♋51 07	2♌50 09	1♏58.6	5♍16.8	4♎14.9	23♌09.7	11♎12.3	22♑44.3	5♋12.0	1♋07.8	17♈24.4	13♒27.0
2 Th	10 48 47	10 34 16	8♌47 56	14 44 45	1R49.1	7 14.5	5 28.3	23 47.9	11 38.1	22R41.3	5 16.8	1 09.5	17R23.2	13R25.8
3 F	10 52 43	11 32 23	20 40 52	26 36 32	1 39.2	9 11.5	6 41.7	24 26.0	12 03.9	22 38.4	5 21.4	1 11.2	17 21.9	13 24.6
4 Sa	10 56 40	12 30 32	2♍31 56	8♍27 19	1 30.0	11 07.8	7 55.1	25 04.2	12 29.8	22 35.8	5 26.0	1 12.9	17 20.6	13 23.5
5 Su	11 00 36	13 28 43	14 22 52	20 18 47	1 22.1	13 03.3	9 08.4	25 42.3	12 55.7	22 33.3	5 30.4	1 14.5	17 19.3	13 22.3
6 M	11 04 33	14 26 56	26 15 18	2♎12 39	1 16.1	14 57.8	10 21.7	26 20.4	13 21.6	22 31.0	5 34.8	1 16.1	17 18.0	13 21.2
7 Tu	11 08 29	15 25 10	8♎11 04	14 10 50	1 12.4	16 51.4	11 35.1	26 58.5	13 47.6	22 28.9	5 39.1	1 17.6	17 16.6	13 20.1
8 W	11 12 26	16 23 26	20 12 17	26 15 44	1D10.8	18 43.9	12 48.4	27 36.5	14 13.6	22 27.0	5 43.3	1 19.1	17 15.3	13 19.0
9 Th	11 16 22	17 21 44	2♏21 34	8♏30 12	1 10.9	20 35.4	14 01.7	28 14.6	14 39.6	22 25.3	5 47.4	1 20.5	17 13.9	13 17.9
10 F	11 20 19	18 20 03	14 42 05	20 57 38	1 12.1	22 25.8	15 14.9	28 52.6	15 05.7	22 23.8	5 51.5	1 21.9	17 12.5	13 16.8
11 Sa	11 24 15	19 18 24	27 17 22	3♐41 45	1 13.5	24 15.1	16 28.2	29 30.7	15 31.8	22 22.5	5 55.4	1 23.2	17 11.1	13 15.7
12 Su	11 28 12	20 16 46	10♐11 14	16 46 17	1R14.4	26 03.3	17 41.4	0♍08.7	15 57.9	22 21.4	5 59.3	1 24.5	17 09.6	13 14.7
13 M	11 32 09	21 15 10	23 27 17	0♑14 33	1 14.0	27 50.4	18 54.7	0 46.7	16 24.0	22 20.4	6 03.0	1 25.7	17 08.2	13 13.7
14 Tu	11 36 05	22 13 36	7♑08 18	14 08 38	1 12.1	29 36.3	20 07.9	1 24.6	16 50.2	22 19.7	6 06.7	1 26.9	17 06.7	13 12.7
15 W	11 40 02	23 12 03	21 15 30	28 28 42	1 08.7	1♎21.2	21 21.1	2 02.6	17 16.4	22 19.1	6 10.3	1 28.1	17 05.2	13 11.7
16 Th	11 43 58	24 10 31	5♒47 47	13♒12 10	1 04.0	3 05.0	22 34.2	2 40.5	17 42.6	22 18.8	6 13.8	1 29.1	17 03.7	13 10.8
17 F	11 47 55	25 09 01	20 41 03	28 13 27	0 58.7	4 47.7	23 47.4	3 18.5	18 08.8	22D18.6	6 17.1	1 30.2	17 02.2	13 09.8
18 Sa	11 51 51	26 07 33	5♓48 14	13♓24 11	0 53.7	6 29.3	25 00.5	3 56.4	18 35.0	22 18.7	6 20.4	1 31.2	17 00.7	13 08.9
19 Su	11 55 48	27 06 07	21 00 01	28 34 26	0 49.7	8 10.0	26 13.6	4 34.3	19 01.3	22 18.9	6 23.6	1 32.1	16 59.1	13 08.0
20 M	11 59 44	28 04 43	6♈06 14	13♈34 16	0 47.1	9 49.6	27 26.6	5 12.2	19 27.6	22 19.3	6 26.7	1 33.0	16 57.6	13 07.1
21 Tu	12 03 41	29 03 21	20 57 34	28 15 20	0D46.1	11 28.2	28 39.7	5 50.0	19 53.9	22 19.9	6 29.7	1 33.8	16 56.0	13 06.2
22 W	12 07 38	0♎02 01	5♉26 56	12♉31 57	0 46.5	13 05.8	29 52.7	6 27.9	20 20.2	22 20.7	6 32.6	1 34.6	16 54.4	13 05.4
23 Th	12 11 34	1 00 43	19 30 09	26 21 27	0 47.8	14 42.4	1♏05.8	7 05.8	20 46.5	22 21.7	6 35.4	1 35.3	16 52.8	13 04.5
24 F	12 15 31	1 59 27	3♊05 58	9♊43 53	0 49.4	16 18.1	2 18.8	7 43.6	21 12.9	22 22.9	6 38.1	1 36.0	16 51.2	13 03.7
25 Sa	12 19 27	2 58 14	16 15 32	22 41 20	0R50.6	17 52.9	3 31.8	8 21.4	21 39.3	22 24.3	6 40.7	1 36.6	16 49.6	13 03.0
26 Su	12 23 24	3 57 03	29 01 44	5♋17 14	0 51.0	19 26.7	4 44.7	8 59.3	22 05.7	22 25.9	6 43.2	1 37.2	16 48.0	13 02.2
27 M	12 27 20	4 55 54	11♋28 25	17 35 47	0 50.3	20 59.7	5 57.7	9 37.1	22 32.1	22 27.7	6 45.6	1 37.7	16 46.4	13 01.5
28 Tu	12 31 17	5 54 47	23 39 55	29 41 20	0 48.4	22 31.7	7 10.6	10 14.9	22 58.5	22 29.6	6 47.9	1 38.2	16 44.8	13 00.8
29 W	12 35 13	6 53 43	5♌40 34	11♌38 07	0 45.5	24 02.8	8 23.5	10 52.7	23 24.9	22 31.8	6 50.1	1 38.6	16 43.1	13 00.1
30 Th	12 39 10	7 52 41	17 34 27	23 30 01	0 41.9	25 33.0	9 36.4	11 30.4	23 51.4	22 34.1	6 52.2	1 39.0	16 41.5	12 59.4

LONGITUDE October 2032

Day	Sid.Time	☉	0 hr ☽	Noon ☽	True ☊	☿	♀	♂	⚳	♃	♄	♅	♆	♇
1 F	12 43 07	8♎51 41	29♌25 14	5♍20 26	0♏38.1	27♎02.3	10♏49.3	12♍08.2	24♎17.9	22♑36.6	6♋54.2	1♋39.3	16♈39.8	12♒58.7
2 Sa	12 47 03	9 50 43	11♍16 00	17 12 13	0R34.6	28 30.7	12 02.2	12 45.9	24 44.4	22 39.3	6 56.0	1 39.5	16R38.2	12R58.1
3 Su	12 51 00	10 49 47	23 09 23	29 07 46	0 31.6	29 58.2	13 15.0	13 23.7	25 10.8	22 42.3	6 57.8	1 39.7	16 36.5	12 57.5
4 M	12 54 56	11 48 54	5♎07 34	11♎09 02	0 29.6	1♏24.8	14 27.8	14 01.4	25 37.4	22 45.3	6 59.4	1 39.9	16 34.8	12 56.9
5 Tu	12 58 53	12 48 02	17 12 21	23 17 44	0D28.5	2 50.5	15 40.6	14 39.1	26 03.9	22 48.6	7 01.0	1 40.0	16 33.2	12 56.4
6 W	13 02 49	13 47 13	29 25 23	5♏35 29	0 28.5	4 15.2	16 53.4	15 16.8	26 30.4	22 52.1	7 02.4	1R40.0	16 31.5	12 55.9
7 Th	13 06 46	14 46 25	11♏48 15	18 03 54	0 29.1	5 38.9	18 06.1	15 54.5	26 56.9	22 55.7	7 03.7	1 40.0	16 29.8	12 55.4
8 F	13 10 42	15 45 40	24 22 38	0♐44 41	0 30.3	7 01.6	19 18.9	16 32.2	27 23.5	22 59.6	7 04.9	1 39.9	16 28.2	12 54.9
9 Sa	13 14 39	16 44 56	7♐10 19	13 39 45	0 31.5	8 23.3	20 31.6	17 09.8	27 50.0	23 03.6	7 06.0	1 39.8	16 26.5	12 54.4
10 Su	13 18 35	17 44 14	20 13 13	26 50 57	0 32.6	9 43.9	21 44.2	17 47.5	28 16.5	23 07.8	7 07.0	1 39.7	16 24.8	12 54.0
11 M	13 22 32	18 43 34	3♑33 09	10♑19 59	0R33.2	11 03.3	22 56.9	18 25.1	28 43.1	23 12.2	7 07.9	1 39.4	16 23.1	12 53.6
12 Tu	13 26 29	19 42 55	17 11 35	24 08 00	0 33.3	12 21.5	24 09.5	19 02.7	29 09.7	23 16.7	7 08.7	1 39.2	16 21.5	12 53.2
13 W	13 30 25	20 42 19	1♒09 12	8♒15 03	0 32.9	13 38.5	25 22.1	19 40.3	29 36.2	23 21.4	7 09.4	1 38.9	16 19.8	12 52.9
14 Th	13 34 22	21 41 44	15 25 20	22 39 42	0 32.1	14 54.1	26 34.6	20 17.9	0♏02.8	23 26.3	7 09.9	1 38.5	16 18.1	12 52.6
15 F	13 38 18	22 41 10	29 57 40	7♓18 39	0 31.2	16 08.2	27 47.2	20 55.5	0 29.3	23 31.4	7 10.3	1 38.0	16 16.5	12 52.3
16 Sa	13 42 15	23 40 39	14♓41 54	22 06 39	0 30.3	17 20.7	28 59.7	21 33.1	0 55.9	23 36.7	7 10.7	1 37.6	16 14.8	12 52.0
17 Su	13 46 11	24 40 09	29 31 59	6♈56 58	0 29.7	18 31.6	0♐12.1	22 10.6	1 22.4	23 42.1	7 10.9	1 37.0	16 13.2	12 51.8
18 M	13 50 08	25 39 41	14♈20 39	21 42 05	0D29.4	19 40.6	1 24.5	22 48.1	1 49.0	23 47.7	7R11.0	1 36.4	16 11.5	12 51.6
19 Tu	13 54 04	26 39 16	29 00 23	6♉14 45	0 29.4	20 47.7	2 36.9	23 25.7	2 15.5	23 53.4	7 11.0	1 35.8	16 09.9	12 51.4
20 W	13 58 01	27 38 52	13♉24 28	20 28 56	0 29.5	21 52.5	3 49.3	24 03.2	2 42.1	23 59.3	7 10.9	1 35.1	16 08.2	12 51.2
21 Th	14 01 58	28 38 31	27 27 44	4♊20 33	0 29.7	22 55.0	5 01.6	24 40.7	3 08.7	24 05.4	7 10.6	1 34.4	16 06.6	12 51.1
22 F	14 05 54	29 38 11	11♊07 14	17 47 44	0R29.9	23 54.8	6 13.9	25 18.2	3 35.2	24 11.6	7 10.3	1 33.6	16 05.0	12 51.0
23 Sa	14 09 51	0♏37 54	24 22 09	0♋50 42	0 29.9	24 51.7	7 26.2	25 55.7	4 01.8	24 18.0	7 09.8	1 32.8	16 03.4	12 50.9
24 Su	14 13 47	1 37 40	7♋13 41	13 31 29	0 29.9	25 45.3	8 38.4	26 33.1	4 28.3	24 24.6	7 09.3	1 31.9	16 01.8	12 50.8
25 M	14 17 44	2 37 27	19 44 33	25 53 23	0D29.8	26 35.5	9 50.6	27 10.6	4 54.8	24 31.3	7 08.6	1 30.9	16 00.2	12D50.8
26 Tu	14 21 40	3 37 17	1♌58 31	8♌00 33	0 29.8	27 21.6	11 02.7	27 48.0	5 21.4	24 38.2	7 07.8	1 30.0	15 58.6	12 50.8
27 W	14 25 37	4 37 08	14 00 01	19 57 33	0 30.0	28 03.4	12 14.8	28 25.5	5 47.9	24 45.2	7 06.9	1 28.9	15 57.0	12 50.8
28 Th	14 29 33	5 37 02	25 53 42	1♍49 03	0 30.4	28 40.3	13 26.9	29 02.9	6 14.4	24 52.4	7 05.9	1 27.8	15 55.5	12 50.9
29 F	14 33 30	6 36 59	7♍44 10	13 39 33	0 31.0	29 11.9	14 39.0	29 40.3	6 40.9	24 59.7	7 04.8	1 26.7	15 53.9	12 51.0
30 Sa	14 37 27	7 36 57	19 35 43	25 33 08	0 31.7	29 37.5	15 51.0	0♎17.7	7 07.4	25 07.2	7 03.6	1 25.5	15 52.4	12 51.1
31 Su	14 41 23	8 36 57	1♎32 13	7♎33 22	0 32.5	29 56.6	17 03.0	0 55.1	7 33.9	25 14.8	7 02.2	1 24.3	15 50.9	12 51.2

Astro Data	Dy Hr Mn	Planet Ingress	Dy Hr Mn	Last Aspect Dy Hr Mn		☽ Ingress	Dy Hr Mn	Last Aspect Dy Hr Mn		☽ Ingress	Dy Hr Mn	☽ Phases & Eclipses Dy Hr Mn	
☽0S	5 16:31	♂ ♍	12 6:32	31 15:52	♃ ☍	♌	1 6:18	30 16:45	☿ ⚹	♍	1 1:10	4 20:56	● 12♍52
⚳0S	11 5:32	☿ ♎	14 17:24	3 7:21	♂ ☌	♍	3 18:52	2 23:02	♃ △	♎	3 13:45	12 18:49	☽ 20♐33
☿0S	15 22:54	☉ ♎	22 11:11	5 16:31	♃ △	♎	6 7:33	5 11:03	♃ □	♏	6 1:08	19 9:30	○ 27♓00
♃ D	17 19:52	♀ ♏	22 14:23	8 14:48	♂ ⚹	♏	8 19:22	7 21:18	♃ ⚹	♐	8 10:36	26 9:12	☾ 3♋50
☽0N	19 2:25			11 3:46	♂ □	♐	11 5:06	9 18:45	♂ □	♑	10 17:39		
☉0S	22 11:11	☿ ♏	3 12:29	13 7:08	☿ □	♑	13 11:34	12 12:03	♀ ⚹	♒	12 22:02	4 13:26	● 11♎52
		⚳ ♏	14 9:30	15 2:37	☉ △	♒	15 14:30	14 19:02	♀ □	♓	15 0:04	12 3:47	☽ 19♑23
☽0S	2 22:40	♀ ♐	17 7:59	17 4:20	♀ △	♓	17 14:49	17 0:07	♀ △	♈	17 0:45	18 18:58	○ 25♈57
♅ R	6 19:52	☉ ♏	22 20:46	19 9:30	☉ ☍	♈	19 14:16	18 18:58	☉ ☍	♉	19 1:38	18 19:02	☍ T 1.103
☽0N	16 12:31	♂ ♎	30 0:38	21 12:44	♀ ☍	♉	21 14:54	20 18:24	♂ △	♊	21 4:24	26 2:29	☾ 3♌14
♄ R	18 22:26	☿ ♐	31 17:33	23 4:58	♃ △	♊	23 18:28	23 2:25	♂ □	♋	23 10:25		
♇ D	25 21:09			25 1:46	☿ △	♋	26 1:51	25 14:40	♂ ⚹	♌	25 20:06		
☽0S	30 5:42			27 21:38	♃ ☍	♌	28 12:37	28 5:18	☿ □	♍	28 8:19		
								30 20:25	☿ ⚹	♎	30 20:55		

Astro Data

1 September 2032
Julian Day # 48457
SVP 4♓48'02"
GC 27♐17.7 ⚴ 10♍38.6
Eris 27♈13.1R ⚵ 28♌42.7
⚷ 26♉06.6R ⚶ 0♏06.8
☽ Mean ☊ 3♏12.1

1 October 2032
Julian Day # 48487
SVP 4♓47'59"
GC 27♐17.8 ⚴ 25♍11.2
Eris 26♈58.4R ⚵ 12♍01.5
⚷ 25♉36.5R ⚶ 15♏02.0
☽ Mean ☊ 1♏36.8

November 2032 LONGITUDE

Day	Sid.Time	☉	0 hr ☽	Noon ☽	True ☊	☿	♀	♂	⚳	♃	♄	♅	♆	♇
1 M	14 45 20	9♏37 00	13♎36 55	19♎43 10	0♏33.1	0♐08.5	18♐14.9	1♎32.5	8♏00.4	25♑22.6	7♋00.8	1♋23.0	15♈49.4	12♒51.4
2 Tu	14 49 16	10 37 04	25 52 22	2♏04 43	0R 33.2	0R 12.6	19 26.8	2 09.8	8 26.9	25 30.5	6R 59.2	1R 21.7	15R 47.9	12 51.6
3 W	14 53 13	11 37 10	8♏20 24	14 39 29	0 32.9	0 08.2	20 38.7	2 47.2	8 53.4	25 38.5	6 57.5	1 20.3	15 46.4	12 51.8
4 Th	14 57 09	12 37 18	21 02 05	27 28 12	0 31.9	29♏54.9	21 50.5	3 24.5	9 19.8	25 46.8	6 55.8	1 18.9	15 44.9	12 52.1
5 F	15 01 06	13 37 28	3♐57 50	10♐30 57	0 30.4	29 32.2	23 02.2	4 01.8	9 46.3	25 55.1	6 53.9	1 17.5	15 43.5	12 52.4
6 Sa	15 05 02	14 37 40	17 07 30	23 47 23	0 28.4	28 59.6	24 13.9	4 39.1	10 12.7	26 03.6	6 51.9	1 16.0	15 42.1	12 52.7
7 Su	15 08 59	15 37 53	0♑30 32	7♑16 49	0 26.4	28 17.3	25 25.6	5 16.4	10 39.1	26 12.2	6 49.8	1 14.4	15 40.7	12 53.0
8 M	15 12 56	16 38 08	14 06 07	20 58 20	0 24.6	27 25.5	26 37.2	5 53.6	11 05.5	26 21.0	6 47.6	1 12.9	15 39.3	12 53.4
9 Tu	15 16 52	17 38 25	27 53 19	4♒50 55	0D 23.4	26 24.9	27 48.8	6 30.9	11 31.8	26 29.9	6 45.3	1 11.2	15 37.9	12 53.8
10 W	15 20 49	18 38 42	11♒51 00	18 53 23	0 23.0	25 16.5	29 00.3	7 08.1	11 58.2	26 38.9	6 42.9	1 09.6	15 36.6	12 54.2
11 Th	15 24 45	19 39 01	25 57 53	3♓04 16	0 23.4	24 01.9	0♑11.7	7 45.3	12 24.5	26 48.0	6 40.5	1 07.8	15 35.3	12 54.6
12 F	15 28 42	20 39 22	10♓12 18	17 21 40	0 24.5	22 43.3	1 23.1	8 22.5	12 50.8	26 57.3	6 37.9	1 06.1	15 34.0	12 55.1
13 Sa	15 32 38	21 39 43	24 32 02	1♈42 59	0 26.0	21 22.9	2 34.4	8 59.7	13 17.1	27 06.7	6 35.2	1 04.3	15 32.7	12 55.6
14 Su	15 36 35	22 40 07	8♈54 06	16 04 54	0 27.2	20 03.5	3 45.6	9 36.9	13 43.4	27 16.2	6 32.4	1 02.5	15 31.4	12 56.2
15 M	15 40 31	23 40 31	23 14 49	0♉23 20	0R 27.7	18 47.5	4 56.8	10 14.0	14 09.6	27 25.9	6 29.5	1 00.6	15 30.2	12 56.7
16 Tu	15 44 28	24 40 58	7♉29 51	14 33 50	0 27.1	17 37.5	6 07.9	10 51.1	14 35.8	27 35.6	6 26.5	0 58.7	15 28.9	12 57.3
17 W	15 48 25	25 41 25	21 34 41	28 31 55	0 25.1	16 35.5	7 18.9	11 28.2	15 02.0	27 45.5	6 23.5	0 56.8	15 27.8	12 57.9
18 Th	15 52 21	26 41 55	5♊25 04	12♊13 44	0 21.9	15 43.4	8 29.9	12 05.3	15 28.2	27 55.5	6 20.3	0 54.8	15 26.6	12 58.5
19 F	15 56 18	27 42 26	18 57 36	25 36 29	0 17.7	15 02.1	9 40.7	12 42.4	15 54.3	28 05.6	6 17.1	0 52.8	15 25.4	12 59.2
20 Sa	16 00 14	28 42 59	2♋10 15	8♋38 54	0 13.0	14 32.3	10 51.5	13 19.5	16 20.4	28 15.8	6 13.8	0 50.8	15 24.3	12 59.9
21 Su	16 04 11	29 43 33	15 02 30	21 21 15	0 08.4	14 14.3	12 02.3	13 56.6	16 46.5	28 26.2	6 10.4	0 48.7	15 23.2	13 00.6
22 M	16 08 07	0♐44 09	27 35 24	3♌45 21	0 04.4	14D 07.8	13 12.9	14 33.6	17 12.6	28 36.6	6 06.9	0 46.6	15 22.2	13 01.4
23 Tu	16 12 04	1 44 47	9♌51 29	15 54 19	0 01.7	14 12.2	14 23.4	15 10.6	17 38.6	28 47.2	6 03.3	0 44.5	15 21.1	13 02.1
24 W	16 16 00	2 45 26	21 54 22	27 52 13	0D 00.3	14 27.0	15 33.9	15 47.6	18 04.6	28 57.9	5 59.6	0 42.3	15 20.1	13 02.9
25 Th	16 19 57	3 46 07	3♍48 28	9♍43 45	0 00.3	14 51.3	16 44.3	16 24.6	18 30.6	29 08.6	5 55.9	0 40.1	15 19.1	13 03.7
26 F	16 23 54	4 46 49	15 38 43	21 34 00	0 01.5	15 24.1	17 54.6	17 01.6	18 56.6	29 19.5	5 52.1	0 37.9	15 18.2	13 04.6
27 Sa	16 27 50	5 47 34	27 30 13	3♎28 00	0 03.3	16 04.7	19 04.8	17 38.5	19 22.5	29 30.5	5 48.2	0 35.7	15 17.2	13 05.5
28 Su	16 31 47	6 48 19	9♎27 56	15 30 35	0 05.0	16 52.1	20 14.9	18 15.5	19 48.4	29 41.5	5 44.2	0 33.4	15 16.3	13 06.4
29 M	16 35 43	7 49 06	21 36 28	27 46 01	0R 05.9	17 45.5	21 24.9	18 52.4	20 14.2	29 52.7	5 40.2	0 31.1	15 15.4	13 07.3
30 Tu	16 39 40	8 49 55	3♏59 40	10♏17 42	0 05.3	18 44.2	22 34.8	19 29.3	20 40.0	0♒04.0	5 36.1	0 28.8	15 14.6	13 08.2

December 2032 LONGITUDE

Day	Sid.Time	☉	0 hr ☽	Noon ☽	True ☊	☿	♀	♂	⚳	♃	♄	♅	♆	♇
1 W	16 43 36	9♐50 45	16♏40 23	23♏07 52	0♏02.9	19♏47.5	23♑44.5	20♎06.1	21♏05.8	0♒15.4	5♋31.9	0♋26.4	15♈13.8	13♒09.2
2 Th	16 47 33	10 51 36	29 40 11	6♐17 18	29♎58.6	20 54.8	24 54.2	20 43.0	21 31.5	0 26.8	5R 27.7	0R 24.1	15R 13.0	13 10.2
3 F	16 51 29	11 52 29	12♐59 04	19 45 15	29R 52.5	22 05.6	26 03.8	21 19.8	21 57.2	0 38.4	5 23.4	0 21.7	15 12.2	13 11.2
4 Sa	16 55 26	12 53 23	26 35 31	3♑29 27	29 45.2	23 19.3	27 13.2	21 56.6	22 22.9	0 50.0	5 19.0	0 19.3	15 11.5	13 12.3
5 Su	16 59 23	13 54 17	10♑26 37	17 26 29	29 37.6	24 35.5	28 22.6	22 33.4	22 48.5	1 01.8	5 14.6	0 16.8	15 10.8	13 13.3
6 M	17 03 19	14 55 13	24 28 31	1♒32 14	29 30.6	25 54.0	29 31.8	23 10.2	23 14.1	1 13.6	5 10.2	0 14.4	15 10.1	13 14.4
7 Tu	17 07 16	15 56 09	8♒37 05	15 42 37	29 25.2	27 14.4	0♒40.8	23 46.9	23 39.6	1 25.5	5 05.7	0 11.9	15 09.5	13 15.5
8 W	17 11 12	16 57 06	22 48 24	29 54 05	29 21.7	28 36.4	1 49.8	24 23.6	24 05.1	1 37.5	5 01.1	0 09.5	15 08.9	13 16.7
9 Th	17 15 09	17 58 03	6♓59 21	14♓03 57	29D 20.3	29 59.7	2 58.5	25 00.3	24 30.5	1 49.6	4 56.5	0 07.0	15 08.3	13 17.8
10 F	17 19 05	18 59 02	21 07 42	28 10 27	29 20.6	1♐24.3	4 07.2	25 36.9	24 55.9	2 01.7	4 51.8	0 04.5	15 07.8	13 19.0
11 Sa	17 23 02	20 00 00	5♈12 04	12♈12 27	29 21.6	2 49.9	5 15.6	26 13.5	25 21.3	2 14.0	4 47.1	0 01.9	15 07.3	13 20.2
12 Su	17 26 58	21 01 00	19 11 29	26 09 05	29R 22.5	4 16.4	6 23.9	26 50.1	25 46.6	2 26.3	4 42.4	29♊59.4	15 06.8	13 21.4
13 M	17 30 55	22 01 59	3♉05 06	9♉59 23	29 22.0	5 43.7	7 32.1	27 26.7	26 11.8	2 38.7	4 37.7	29 56.9	15 06.4	13 22.7
14 Tu	17 34 52	23 03 00	16 51 45	23 41 58	29 19.3	7 11.6	8 40.0	28 03.3	26 37.0	2 51.1	4 32.9	29 54.3	15 06.0	13 23.9
15 W	17 38 48	24 04 01	0♊29 49	7♊15 02	29 14.1	8 40.1	9 47.8	28 39.8	27 02.1	3 03.7	4 28.0	29 51.8	15 05.6	13 25.2
16 Th	17 42 45	25 05 03	13 57 20	20 36 28	29 06.4	10 09.2	10 55.4	29 16.3	27 27.2	3 16.3	4 23.2	29 49.2	15 05.3	13 26.5
17 F	17 46 41	26 06 05	27 12 10	3♋44 13	28 56.6	11 38.7	12 02.8	29 52.7	27 52.2	3 28.9	4 18.3	29 46.7	15 05.0	13 27.9
18 Sa	17 50 38	27 07 08	10♋12 27	16 36 46	28 45.6	13 08.6	13 10.0	0♏29.2	28 17.2	3 41.7	4 13.4	29 44.1	15 04.7	13 29.2
19 Su	17 54 34	28 08 12	22 57 06	29 13 28	28 34.5	14 38.8	14 17.0	1 05.6	28 42.1	3 54.5	4 08.5	29 41.5	15 04.5	13 30.6
20 M	17 58 31	29 09 17	5♌26 00	11♌34 52	28 24.3	16 09.4	15 23.8	1 42.0	29 07.0	4 07.3	4 03.6	29 38.9	15 04.3	13 32.0
21 Tu	18 02 27	0♑10 22	17 40 19	23 42 43	28 16.0	17 40.4	16 30.3	2 18.4	29 31.8	4 20.3	3 58.6	29 36.4	15 04.1	13 33.4
22 W	18 06 24	1 11 28	29 42 27	5♍40 00	28 10.0	19 11.6	17 36.7	2 54.7	29 56.6	4 33.3	3 53.7	29 33.8	15 04.0	13 34.8
23 Th	18 10 21	2 12 34	11♍35 54	17 30 43	28 06.5	20 43.1	18 42.8	3 31.0	0♐21.3	4 46.3	3 48.7	29 31.2	15 03.9	13 36.2
24 F	18 14 17	3 13 41	23 25 04	29 19 37	28D 05.2	22 14.8	19 48.7	4 07.3	0 45.9	4 59.4	3 43.8	29 28.6	15 03.8	13 37.7
25 Sa	18 18 14	4 14 49	5♎15 02	11♎12 00	28 05.3	23 46.9	20 54.3	4 43.5	1 10.5	5 12.6	3 38.8	29 26.1	15D 03.8	13 39.1
26 Su	18 22 10	5 15 58	17 11 14	23 13 23	28R 05.8	25 19.2	21 59.7	5 19.8	1 35.0	5 25.8	3 33.8	29 23.5	15 03.8	13 40.6
27 M	18 26 07	6 17 07	29 19 08	5♏29 07	28 05.6	26 51.8	23 04.8	5 55.9	1 59.4	5 39.1	3 28.9	29 21.0	15 03.8	13 42.1
28 Tu	18 30 03	7 18 16	11♏43 54	18 03 59	28 03.7	28 24.6	24 09.6	6 32.1	2 23.8	5 52.5	3 23.9	29 18.4	15 03.9	13 43.7
29 W	18 34 00	8 19 26	24 29 49	1♐01 40	27 59.4	29 57.8	25 14.2	7 08.2	2 48.1	6 05.8	3 19.0	29 15.9	15 04.0	13 45.2
30 Th	18 37 56	9 20 37	7♐39 46	14 24 09	27 52.3	1♑31.2	26 18.5	7 44.3	3 12.3	6 19.3	3 14.0	29 13.3	15 04.2	13 46.8
31 F	18 41 53	10 21 48	21 14 43	28 11 12	27 42.6	3 04.9	27 22.5	8 20.4	3 36.5	6 32.8	3 09.1	29 10.8	15 04.3	13 48.3

Astro Data Dy Hr Mn	Planet Ingress Dy Hr Mn	Last Aspect Dy Hr Mn	☽ Ingress Dy Hr Mn	Last Aspect Dy Hr Mn	☽ Ingress Dy Hr Mn	☽ Phases & Eclipses Dy Hr Mn	Astro Data
☿ R 2 11:57	☿ ♏R 4 4:38	1 23:09 ♃ □	♏ 2 8:00	1 13:14 ♀ ⚹	♐ 2 0:36	3 5:45 ● 11♏22	1 November 2032
♂ 0S 3 15:00	♀ ♑ 11 8:04	4 16:25 ☿ ☌	♐ 4 16:41	3 14:54 ♂ ⚹	♑ 4 5:56	3 5:32:54 ● P 0.856	Julian Day # 48518
☽ 0N 12 20:36	☉ ♐ 21 18:31	6 12:52 ♀ ☌	♑ 6 23:06	6 8:17 ♀ ☌	♒ 6 9:23	10 11:33 ☽ 18♒38	SVP 4♓47'57"
☿ D 22 14:01	♃ ♒ 30 3:31	8 22:28 ☿ ⚹	♒ 9 3:39	8 9:34 ☿ □	♓ 8 12:10	17 6:42 ○ 25♉28	GC 27♐17.9 ⚴ 9♎27.7
☽ 0S 26 14:12		11 6:42 ♀ ⚹	♓ 11 6:49	9 19:08 ☉ □	♈ 10 15:07	24 22:48 ☾ 3♍13	Eris 26♈40.0R ⚵ 24♍30.5
	☊ ♎R 2 5:13	13 4:13 ♃ ⚹	♈ 13 9:08	12 18:37 ♅ ⚹	♉ 12 18:39		⚷ 24♉18.8R ⚶ 1♐15.3
♃⚻♅ 2 7:12	♀ ♒ 6 21:48	15 6:58 ♃ □	♉ 15 11:21	13 17:55 ♇ □	♊ 14 23:07	2 20:53 ● 11♐14	☽ Mean ☊ 29♎58.2
☽ 0N 10 3:03	☿ ♐ 9 12:05	17 10:39 ♃ △	♊ 17 14:33	17 4:44 ♅ ☌	♋ 17 5:07	9 19:08 ☽ 18♓16	
♃⚻♄ 20 6:57	♅ ♊R 12 6:22	18 17:42 ♆ ⚹	♋ 19 20:01	18 9:07 ♆ □	♌ 19 13:30	16 20:49 ○ 25♊27	1 December 2032
☽ 0S 23 23:41	♂ ♏ 17 16:47	22 1:50 ♃ ☍	♌ 22 4:40	21 23:45 ♅ ⚹	♍ 22 0:35	24 20:39 ☾ 3♎36	Julian Day # 48548
♆ D 25 21:02	☉ ♑ 21 7:56	23 10:54 ♆ △	♍ 24 16:18	24 12:18 ♅ □	♎ 24 13:22		SVP 4♓47'53"
	⚳ ♐ 22 15:19	27 3:55 ♃ △	♎ 27 5:02	27 0:06 ♅ △	♏ 27 1:20		GC 27♐17.9 ⚴ 22♎16.1
	☿ ♑ 29 12:34	29 16:09 ♃ □	♏ 29 16:19	29 0:25 ♀ □	♐ 29 10:07		Eris 26♈24.4R ⚵ 4♎46.0
				31 13:42 ♅ ☍	♑ 31 15:07		⚷ 22♉46.2R ⚶ 17♐22.7
							☽ Mean ☊ 28♎22.9

LONGITUDE — January 2033

Day	Sid.Time	☉	0 hr ☽	Noon ☽	True ☊	☿	♀	♂	⚳	♃	♄	♅	♆	♇
1 Sa	18 45 50	11♑22 59	5♑13 09	12♑20 00	27♎31.2	4♑38.9	28♒26.2	8♏56.4	4♐00.6	6♒46.3	3♋04.2	29♊08.3	15♈04.6	13♒49.9
2 Su	18 49 46	12 24 10	19 31 02	26 45 24	27R19.1	6 13.3	29 29.6	9 32.3	4 24.6	6 59.9	2R59.3	29R05.8	15 04.8	13 51.5
3 M	18 53 43	13 25 21	4♒02 13	11♒20 31	27 07.8	7 47.9	0♓32.6	10 08.3	4 48.5	7 13.5	2 54.5	29 03.3	15 05.1	13 53.1
4 Tu	18 57 39	14 26 32	18 39 22	25 57 53	26 58.5	9 23.0	1 35.3	10 44.1	5 12.4	7 27.2	2 49.7	29 00.9	15 05.4	13 54.8
5 W	19 01 36	15 27 42	3♓15 16	10♓30 48	26 51.8	10 58.3	2 37.6	11 20.0	5 36.2	7 40.9	2 44.9	28 58.4	15 05.8	13 56.4
6 Th	19 05 32	16 28 52	17 43 55	24 54 11	26 48.1	12 34.1	3 39.6	11 55.8	5 59.9	7 54.7	2 40.1	28 56.0	15 06.2	13 58.1
7 F	19 09 29	17 30 02	2♈01 16	9♈05 01	26D46.6	14 10.2	4 41.1	12 31.5	6 23.5	8 08.5	2 35.4	28 53.6	15 06.6	13 59.7
8 Sa	19 13 25	18 31 11	16 05 19	23 02 10	26R46.5	15 46.7	5 42.3	13 07.3	6 47.0	8 22.3	2 30.7	28 51.2	15 07.0	14 01.4
9 Su	19 17 22	19 32 20	29 55 40	6♉45 53	26 46.3	17 23.6	6 43.0	13 42.9	7 10.5	8 36.1	2 26.1	28 48.8	15 07.5	14 03.1
10 M	19 21 19	20 33 28	13♉32 58	20 17 03	26 44.7	19 01.0	7 43.3	14 18.6	7 33.8	8 50.0	2 21.5	28 46.5	15 08.1	14 04.8
11 Tu	19 25 15	21 34 36	26 58 15	3♊36 41	26 40.6	20 38.8	8 43.2	14 54.1	7 57.1	9 04.0	2 16.9	28 44.2	15 08.6	14 06.5
12 W	19 29 12	22 35 44	10♊12 24	16 45 28	26 33.5	22 17.1	9 42.6	15 29.7	8 20.3	9 17.9	2 12.4	28 41.9	15 09.2	14 08.2
13 Th	19 33 08	23 36 50	23 15 53	29 43 38	26 23.3	23 55.8	10 41.4	16 05.2	8 43.4	9 31.9	2 08.0	28 39.6	15 09.9	14 09.9
14 F	19 37 05	24 37 57	6♋08 40	12♋30 57	26 10.6	25 35.0	11 39.8	16 40.6	9 06.4	9 45.9	2 03.6	28 37.3	15 10.5	14 11.7
15 Sa	19 41 01	25 39 03	18 50 24	25 07 00	25 56.4	27 14.7	12 37.7	17 16.0	9 29.3	10 00.0	1 59.2	28 35.1	15 11.2	14 13.4
16 Su	19 44 58	26 40 08	1♌20 43	7♌31 32	25 41.8	28 54.9	13 35.0	17 51.4	9 52.1	10 14.0	1 54.9	28 32.9	15 12.0	14 15.2
17 M	19 48 55	27 41 13	13 39 31	19 44 46	25 28.2	0♒35.6	14 31.8	18 26.7	10 14.8	10 28.1	1 50.7	28 30.8	15 12.7	14 16.9
18 Tu	19 52 51	28 42 17	25 47 25	1♍47 41	25 16.7	2 16.7	15 28.0	19 02.0	10 37.5	10 42.2	1 46.6	28 28.6	15 13.5	14 18.7
19 W	19 56 48	29 43 21	7♍45 50	13 42 12	25 07.9	3 58.4	16 23.5	19 37.2	11 00.0	10 56.4	1 42.5	28 26.5	15 14.4	14 20.5
20 Th	20 00 44	0♒44 25	19 37 11	25 31 14	25 02.0	5 40.5	17 18.5	20 12.4	11 22.4	11 10.5	1 38.5	28 24.5	15 15.2	14 22.3
21 F	20 04 41	1 45 28	1♎24 53	7♎18 39	24 58.9	7 23.1	18 12.8	20 47.5	11 44.7	11 24.7	1 34.5	28 22.4	15 16.1	14 24.1
22 Sa	20 08 37	2 46 31	13 13 11	19 09 06	24D57.9	9 06.0	19 06.4	21 22.5	12 06.9	11 38.9	1 30.6	28 20.4	15 17.1	14 25.9
23 Su	20 12 34	3 47 33	25 07 06	1♏07 51	24R57.8	10 49.4	19 59.4	21 57.6	12 29.1	11 53.1	1 26.8	28 18.4	15 18.0	14 27.7
24 M	20 16 30	4 48 35	7♏12 04	13 20 26	24 57.6	12 33.1	20 51.6	22 32.5	12 51.1	12 07.3	1 23.1	28 16.5	15 19.0	14 29.5
25 Tu	20 20 27	5 49 36	19 33 40	25 52 22	24 56.1	14 17.0	21 43.1	23 07.4	13 13.0	12 21.6	1 19.4	28 14.6	15 20.0	14 31.3
26 W	20 24 23	6 50 37	2♐17 08	8♐48 27	24 52.4	16 01.2	22 33.8	23 42.3	13 34.7	12 35.8	1 15.9	28 12.7	15 21.1	14 33.1
27 Th	20 28 20	7 51 37	15 26 43	22 12 10	24 46.0	17 45.4	23 23.7	24 17.0	13 56.4	12 50.1	1 12.4	28 10.9	15 22.2	14 34.9
28 F	20 32 17	8 52 37	29 04 55	6♑04 52	24 37.1	19 29.6	24 12.8	24 51.8	14 18.0	13 04.3	1 09.0	28 09.1	15 23.3	14 36.7
29 Sa	20 36 13	9 53 36	13♑11 42	20 24 55	24 26.3	21 13.6	25 01.0	25 26.4	14 39.4	13 18.6	1 05.6	28 07.4	15 24.5	14 38.5
30 Su	20 40 10	10 54 34	27 43 49	5♒07 30	24 14.6	22 57.2	25 48.4	26 01.0	15 00.7	13 32.9	1 02.4	28 05.7	15 25.7	14 40.4
31 M	20 44 06	11 55 31	12♒34 54	20 04 50	24 03.6	24 40.2	26 34.7	26 35.5	15 21.9	13 47.2	0 59.3	28 04.0	15 26.9	14 42.2

LONGITUDE — February 2033

Day	Sid.Time	☉	0 hr ☽	Noon ☽	True ☊	☿	♀	♂	⚳	♃	♄	♅	♆	♇
1 Tu	20 48 03	12♒56 27	27♒36 05	5♓07 23	23♎54.3	26♒22.5	27♓20.1	27♏10.0	15♐43.0	14♒01.5	0♋56.2	28♊02.4	15♈28.1	14♒44.0
2 W	20 51 59	13 57 22	12♓37 33	20 05 30	23R47.7	28 03.6	28 04.5	27 44.4	16 03.9	14 15.8	0R53.3	28R00.8	15 29.4	14 45.9
3 Th	20 55 56	14 58 15	27 30 17	4♈51 07	23 43.9	29 43.3	28 47.8	28 18.7	16 24.7	14 30.1	0 50.4	27 59.3	15 30.7	14 47.7
4 F	20 59 52	15 59 07	12♈07 25	19 18 44	23D42.6	1♓21.1	29 30.0	28 52.9	16 45.3	14 44.4	0 47.6	27 57.8	15 32.0	14 49.5
5 Sa	21 03 49	16 59 58	26 24 51	3♉25 38	23 42.7	2 56.7	0♈11.1	29 27.0	17 05.9	14 58.7	0 45.0	27 56.3	15 33.4	14 51.3
6 Su	21 07 46	18 00 47	10♉21 09	17 11 31	23R43.1	4 29.5	0 51.0	0♐01.1	17 26.3	15 13.0	0 42.4	27 54.9	15 34.8	14 53.2
7 M	21 11 42	19 01 35	23 56 56	0♊37 39	23 42.5	5 59.0	1 29.6	0 35.1	17 46.5	15 27.3	0 39.9	27 53.6	15 36.2	14 55.0
8 Tu	21 15 39	20 02 21	7♊13 59	13 46 14	23 39.8	7 24.6	2 06.9	1 09.1	18 06.7	15 41.6	0 37.6	27 52.3	15 37.6	14 56.8
9 W	21 19 35	21 03 06	20 14 42	26 39 39	23 34.6	8 45.6	2 42.8	1 42.9	18 26.6	15 55.9	0 35.3	27 51.0	15 39.1	14 58.6
10 Th	21 23 32	22 03 49	3♋01 21	9♋20 03	23 26.8	10 01.3	3 17.3	2 16.7	18 46.5	16 10.1	0 33.2	27 49.8	15 40.6	15 00.5
11 F	21 27 28	23 04 30	15 35 58	21 49 16	23 16.8	11 11.0	3 50.4	2 50.4	19 06.2	16 24.4	0 31.1	27 48.6	15 42.1	15 02.3
12 Sa	21 31 25	24 05 10	28 00 06	4♌08 37	23 05.5	12 14.0	4 21.9	3 24.0	19 25.7	16 38.6	0 29.2	27 47.5	15 43.6	15 04.1
13 Su	21 35 21	25 05 49	10♌14 56	16 19 11	22 53.8	13 09.6	4 51.9	3 57.6	19 45.1	16 52.9	0 27.3	27 46.4	15 45.2	15 05.9
14 M	21 39 18	26 06 26	22 21 28	28 21 56	22 42.9	13 57.0	5 20.2	4 31.0	20 04.3	17 07.1	0 25.6	27 45.4	15 46.8	15 07.7
15 Tu	21 43 15	27 07 02	4♍20 43	10♍18 00	22 33.7	14 35.5	5 46.9	5 04.4	20 23.4	17 21.3	0 23.9	27 44.4	15 48.4	15 09.5
16 W	21 47 11	28 07 36	16 13 59	22 08 55	22 26.7	15 04.7	6 11.7	5 37.7	20 42.3	17 35.5	0 22.4	27 43.5	15 50.1	15 11.3
17 Th	21 51 08	29 08 09	28 03 05	3♎56 50	22 22.2	15 24.0	6 34.8	6 10.9	21 01.1	17 49.7	0 21.0	27 42.6	15 51.7	15 13.1
18 F	21 55 04	0♓08 40	9♎50 30	15 44 33	22D20.2	15R33.1	6 55.9	6 44.0	21 19.7	18 03.8	0 19.7	27 41.8	15 53.4	15 14.9
19 Sa	21 59 01	1 09 11	21 39 25	27 35 38	22 20.1	15 32.0	7 15.1	7 17.0	21 38.2	18 18.0	0 18.5	27 41.0	15 55.2	15 16.6
20 Su	22 02 57	2 09 39	3♏33 45	9♏34 21	22 21.1	15 20.6	7 32.4	7 49.9	21 56.4	18 32.1	0 17.4	27 40.3	15 56.9	15 18.4
21 M	22 06 54	3 10 07	15 38 02	21 45 26	22 22.4	14 59.3	7 47.5	8 22.7	22 14.5	18 46.2	0 16.4	27 39.6	15 58.7	15 20.2
22 Tu	22 10 50	4 10 33	27 57 13	4♐13 58	22R23.0	14 28.6	8 00.5	8 55.5	22 32.5	19 00.3	0 15.6	27 39.0	16 00.4	15 21.9
23 W	22 14 47	5 10 58	10♐36 19	17 04 49	22 22.2	13 49.2	8 11.4	9 28.1	22 50.2	19 14.3	0 14.8	27 38.4	16 02.2	15 23.7
24 Th	22 18 44	6 11 22	23 39 58	0♑22 08	22 19.5	13 02.3	8 20.0	10 00.6	23 07.8	19 28.3	0 14.2	27 37.9	16 04.1	15 25.4
25 F	22 22 40	7 11 44	7♑11 36	14 08 30	22 15.0	12 09.0	8 26.3	10 33.0	23 25.2	19 42.3	0 13.6	27 37.5	16 05.9	15 27.1
26 Sa	22 26 37	8 12 05	21 12 46	28 24 09	22 08.9	11 10.7	8 30.3	11 05.3	23 42.4	19 56.3	0 13.2	27 37.0	16 07.8	15 28.9
27 Su	22 30 33	9 12 24	5♒42 11	13♒06 10	22 02.1	10 09.0	8R31.8	11 37.5	23 59.4	20 10.2	0 12.9	27 36.7	16 09.7	15 30.6
28 M	22 34 30	10 12 41	20 35 14	28 08 19	21 55.4	9 05.4	8 31.0	12 09.5	24 16.3	20 24.2	0 12.7	27 36.4	16 11.6	15 32.3

Astro Data Dy Hr Mn	Planet Ingress Dy Hr Mn	Last Aspect Dy Hr Mn	☽ Ingress Dy Hr Mn	Last Aspect Dy Hr Mn	☽ Ingress Dy Hr Mn	☽ Phases & Eclipses Dy Hr Mn
♅□♇ 5 23:51	♀ ♓ 2 23:34	1 16:36 ♆ □	♒ 2 17:21	1 0:43 ♅ △	♓ 1 3:50	1 10:17 ● 11♑19
☽ 0N 6 9:49	☿ ♒ 17 3:32	4 17:00 ♅ △	♓ 4 18:38	3 1:36 ♀ ☌	♈ 3 4:04	8 3:34 ☽ 18♈10
☽ 0S 20 8:52	☉ ♒ 19 18:33	6 18:46 ♅ □	♈ 6 20:35	5 2:37 ♅ ⚹	♉ 5 6:07	15 13:07 ○ 25♋42
♃□♅ 28 19:09		8 22:06 ♅ ⚹	♉ 9 0:08	6 13:34 ☉ □	♊ 7 10:52	23 17:46 ☾ 4♏02
♀0N 30 8:01	☿ ♓ 3 16:04	10 12:32 ☉ △	♊ 11 5:28	9 14:14 ♅ ☌	♋ 9 18:17	30 22:00 ● 11♒20
	♀ ♈ 5 5:27	13 10:01 ♅ ☌	♋ 13 12:31	11 0:10 ♆ □	♌ 12 3:54	
☽ 0N 2 18:41	♂ ♐ 6 11:12	15 16:43 ☿ ☍	♌ 15 21:24	14 10:47 ♅ ⚹	♍ 14 15:16	6 13:34 ☽ 18♉05
♃☌♇ 4 21:50	☉ ♓ 18 8:34	18 5:23 ♅ ⚹	♍ 18 8:24	16 23:19 ♅ □	♎ 17 3:58	14 7:04 ○ 25♌54
♃⚹♆ 8 4:34		20 17:52 ♅ □	♎ 20 21:07	19 12:11 ♅ △	♏ 19 16:51	22 11:53 ☾ 4♐10
♃□♄ 8 6:13		23 6:24 ♅ △	♏ 23 9:45	21 6:03 ♃ □	♐ 22 3:56	
☽ 0S 16 16:40		25 6:33 ♂ ☌	♐ 25 19:45	24 7:08 ♅ ☍	♑ 24 11:21	
☿ R 18 21:22		27 22:25 ♅ ☍	♑ 28 1:35	25 15:21 ♆ □	♒ 26 14:38	
♄□♇ 20 3:27		29 20:36 ♂ ⚹	♒ 30 3:42	28 11:09 ♅ △	♓ 28 14:57	
♀ R 27 15:41						

Astro Data

1 January 2033
Julian Day # 48579
SVP 4♓47'47"
GC 27♐18.0 ⚵ 3♏51.9
Eris 26♈15.4R ⚶ 12♎25.7
⚷ 21♉30.8R ⚴ 4♑09.2
☽ Mean ☊ 26♎44.4

1 February 2033
Julian Day # 48610
SVP 4♓47'42"
GC 27♐18.1 ⚵ 12♏40.3
Eris 26♈16.7 ⚶ 15♎28.8
⚷ 21♉06.4 ⚴ 20♑42.9
☽ Mean ☊ 25♎06.0

March 2033 LONGITUDE

Day	Sid.Time	☉	0 hr ☽	Noon ☽	True ☊	☿	♀	♂	⚳	♃	♄	♅	♆	♇
1 Tu	22 38 26	11♓12 57	5♓44 12	13♓21 34	21♎49.8	8♓01.6	8♈27.7	12♐41.5	24♐32.9	20♒38.0	0♋12.7	27♊36.1	16♈13.5	15♒33.9
2 W	22 42 23	12 13 11	20 59 05	28 35 27	21R46.0	6R59.0	8R21.9	13 13.3	24 49.3	20 51.9	0D12.7	27R35.9	16 15.4	15 35.6
3 Th	22 46 19	13 13 23	6♈09 25	13♈39 52	21D44.1	5 58.9	8 13.6	13 44.9	25 05.6	21 05.7	0 12.9	27 35.8	16 17.4	15 37.3
4 F	22 50 16	14 13 33	21 05 52	28 26 39	21 44.0	5 02.6	8 02.8	14 16.5	25 21.6	21 19.4	0 13.1	27 35.7	16 19.4	15 38.9
5 Sa	22 54 13	15 13 41	5♉41 38	12♉50 27	21 45.1	4 11.0	7 49.4	14 47.9	25 37.4	21 33.2	0 13.5	27D35.7	16 21.4	15 40.6
6 Su	22 58 09	16 13 47	19 52 54	26 48 55	21 46.6	3 24.9	7 33.6	15 19.2	25 53.0	21 46.9	0 14.0	27 35.7	16 23.4	15 42.2
7 M	23 02 06	17 13 51	3♊38 36	10♊22 09	21R47.8	2 44.8	7 15.4	15 50.4	26 08.4	22 00.5	0 14.6	27 35.8	16 25.4	15 43.8
8 Tu	23 06 02	18 13 53	16 59 51	23 32 03	21 47.8	2 11.2	6 54.7	16 21.4	26 23.6	22 14.1	0 15.3	27 35.9	16 27.5	15 45.4
9 W	23 09 59	19 13 53	29 59 09	6♋21 32	21 46.4	1 44.2	6 31.8	16 52.3	26 38.5	22 27.7	0 16.2	27 36.1	16 29.5	15 47.0
10 Th	23 13 55	20 13 50	12♋39 39	18 53 54	21 43.6	1 23.9	6 06.6	17 23.0	26 53.3	22 41.2	0 17.1	27 36.3	16 31.6	15 48.6
11 F	23 17 52	21 13 45	25 04 43	1♌12 29	21 39.4	1 10.3	5 39.3	17 53.6	27 07.8	22 54.6	0 18.2	27 36.6	16 33.7	15 50.1
12 Sa	23 21 48	22 13 38	7♌17 34	13 20 20	21 34.4	1D03.2	5 10.1	18 24.0	27 22.1	23 08.1	0 19.3	27 37.0	16 35.8	15 51.7
13 Su	23 25 45	23 13 29	19 21 05	25 20 08	21 29.2	1 02.5	4 39.0	18 54.3	27 36.1	23 21.4	0 20.6	27 37.4	16 37.9	15 53.2
14 M	23 29 42	24 13 18	1♍17 46	7♍14 13	21 24.3	1 07.8	4 06.3	19 24.5	27 50.0	23 34.7	0 22.0	27 37.8	16 40.0	15 54.7
15 Tu	23 33 38	25 13 05	13 09 47	19 04 40	21 20.2	1 18.9	3 32.2	19 54.5	28 03.5	23 48.0	0 23.5	27 38.3	16 42.1	15 56.2
16 W	23 37 35	26 12 49	24 59 07	0♎53 24	21 17.4	1 35.4	2 56.9	20 24.3	28 16.9	24 01.2	0 25.1	27 38.9	16 44.3	15 57.7
17 Th	23 41 31	27 12 32	6♎47 44	12 42 24	21D15.8	1 57.2	2 20.5	20 53.9	28 30.0	24 14.4	0 26.8	27 39.5	16 46.4	15 59.1
18 F	23 45 28	28 12 13	18 37 41	24 33 53	21 15.6	2 23.9	1 43.5	21 23.4	28 42.8	24 27.5	0 28.6	27 40.1	16 48.6	16 00.6
19 Sa	23 49 24	29 11 52	0♏31 19	6♏30 22	21 16.3	2 55.2	1 05.9	21 52.8	28 55.4	24 40.5	0 30.6	27 40.8	16 50.8	16 02.0
20 Su	23 53 21	0♈11 29	12 31 23	18 34 48	21 17.7	3 30.9	0 28.1	22 21.9	29 07.8	24 53.5	0 32.6	27 41.6	16 53.0	16 03.4
21 M	23 57 17	1 11 05	24 41 03	0♐50 36	21 19.3	4 10.6	29♓50.3	22 50.9	29 19.9	25 06.5	0 34.7	27 42.4	16 55.2	16 04.8
22 Tu	0 01 14	2 10 38	7♐03 53	13 21 25	21 20.7	4 54.1	29 12.7	23 19.7	29 31.7	25 19.3	0 37.0	27 43.3	16 57.4	16 06.2
23 W	0 05 10	3 10 10	19 43 40	26 11 04	21R21.6	5 41.2	28 35.7	23 48.3	29 43.3	25 32.1	0 39.3	27 44.2	16 59.6	16 07.5
24 Th	0 09 07	4 09 40	2♑44 05	9♑23 04	21 21.7	6 31.8	27 59.5	24 16.7	29 54.6	25 44.9	0 41.8	27 45.2	17 01.8	16 08.9
25 F	0 13 04	5 09 09	16 08 20	23 00 06	21 20.9	7 25.4	27 24.3	24 44.9	0♑05.6	25 57.6	0 44.4	27 46.2	17 04.0	16 10.2
26 Sa	0 17 00	6 08 36	29 58 26	7♒03 19	21 19.6	8 22.1	26 50.3	25 12.8	0 16.3	26 10.2	0 47.0	27 47.3	17 06.3	16 11.5
27 Su	0 20 57	7 08 00	14♒14 33	21 31 46	21 17.9	9 21.6	26 17.8	25 40.6	0 26.8	26 22.7	0 49.8	27 48.4	17 08.5	16 12.8
28 M	0 24 53	8 07 23	28 54 23	6♓21 43	21 16.2	10 23.8	25 46.8	26 08.2	0 37.0	26 35.2	0 52.7	27 49.6	17 10.7	16 14.0
29 Tu	0 28 50	9 06 45	13♓52 50	21 26 44	21 14.7	11 28.5	25 17.6	26 35.5	0 46.8	26 47.6	0 55.6	27 50.8	17 13.0	16 15.2
30 W	0 32 46	10 06 04	29 02 15	6♈38 11	21D13.9	12 35.7	24 50.4	27 02.6	0 56.4	26 59.9	0 58.7	27 52.1	17 15.2	16 16.5
31 Th	0 36 43	11 05 21	14♈13 18	21 46 25	21 13.6	13 45.1	24 25.2	27 29.5	1 05.7	27 12.2	1 01.9	27 53.5	17 17.5	16 17.7

April 2033 LONGITUDE

Day	Sid.Time	☉	0 hr ☽	Noon ☽	True ☊	☿	♀	♂	⚳	♃	♄	♅	♆	♇
1 F	0 40 39	12♈04 36	29♈16 24	6♉42 16	21♎13.9	14♓56.8	24♓02.1	27♐56.1	1♑14.7	27♒24.4	1♋05.1	27♊54.8	17♈19.8	16♒18.8
2 Sa	0 44 36	13 03 49	14♉03 07	21 18 16	21 14.5	16 10.5	23R41.3	28 22.5	1 23.4	27 36.5	1 08.5	27 56.3	17 22.0	16 20.0
3 Su	0 48 33	14 03 00	28 27 13	5♊29 35	21 15.2	17 26.3	23 22.9	28 48.6	1 31.7	27 48.5	1 12.0	27 57.7	17 24.3	16 21.1
4 M	0 52 29	15 02 08	12♊25 14	19 14 06	21 15.8	18 44.1	23 06.8	29 14.5	1 39.8	28 00.4	1 15.5	27 59.3	17 26.6	16 22.2
5 Tu	0 56 26	16 01 14	25 56 19	2♋32 07	21 16.2	20 03.7	22 53.0	29 40.1	1 47.5	28 12.3	1 19.2	28 00.9	17 28.8	16 23.3
6 W	1 00 22	17 00 18	9♋01 49	15 25 49	21R16.3	21 25.2	22 41.8	0♑05.4	1 54.9	28 24.1	1 22.9	28 02.5	17 31.1	16 24.4
7 Th	1 04 19	17 59 20	21 44 35	27 58 35	21 16.3	22 48.4	22 33.0	0 30.5	2 02.0	28 35.8	1 26.8	28 04.1	17 33.4	16 25.4
8 F	1 08 15	18 58 19	4♌08 21	10♌14 25	21 16.1	24 13.5	22 26.6	0 55.3	2 08.8	28 47.4	1 30.7	28 05.9	17 35.6	16 26.4
9 Sa	1 12 12	19 57 16	16 17 18	22 17 31	21 15.9	25 40.2	22 22.6	1 19.8	2 15.3	28 58.9	1 34.7	28 07.6	17 37.9	16 27.4
10 Su	1 16 08	20 56 11	28 15 34	4♍11 57	21D15.8	27 08.6	22D21.1	1 44.0	2 21.4	29 10.3	1 38.8	28 09.4	17 40.2	16 28.4
11 M	1 20 05	21 55 03	10♍07 06	16 01 28	21 15.8	28 38.7	22 21.9	2 08.0	2 27.2	29 21.6	1 43.0	28 11.3	17 42.4	16 29.3
12 Tu	1 24 02	22 53 53	21 55 26	27 49 24	21 16.0	0♈10.4	22 25.1	2 31.6	2 32.6	29 32.9	1 47.3	28 13.2	17 44.7	16 30.2
13 W	1 27 58	23 52 41	3♎43 41	9♎38 39	21R16.1	1 43.8	22 30.6	2 54.9	2 37.7	29 44.0	1 51.7	28 15.1	17 47.0	16 31.1
14 Th	1 31 55	24 51 27	15 34 33	21 31 42	21 16.2	3 18.8	22 38.3	3 17.9	2 42.5	29 55.1	1 56.2	28 17.1	17 49.2	16 32.0
15 F	1 35 51	25 50 12	27 30 20	3♏30 44	21 16.1	4 55.4	22 48.3	3 40.6	2 46.9	0♓06.0	2 00.7	28 19.1	17 51.5	16 32.9
16 Sa	1 39 48	26 48 54	9♏33 06	15 37 41	21 15.7	6 33.6	23 00.4	4 02.9	2 50.9	0 16.9	2 05.3	28 21.2	17 53.7	16 33.7
17 Su	1 43 44	27 47 34	21 44 42	27 54 24	21 15.0	8 13.4	23 14.5	4 25.0	2 54.6	0 27.7	2 10.0	28 23.3	17 56.0	16 34.5
18 M	1 47 41	28 46 13	4♐07 00	10♐22 45	21 14.1	9 54.9	23 30.7	4 46.6	2 58.0	0 38.3	2 14.8	28 25.5	17 58.2	16 35.3
19 Tu	1 51 37	29 44 50	16 41 52	23 04 36	21 13.0	11 38.0	23 48.8	5 07.9	3 01.0	0 48.9	2 19.7	28 27.7	18 00.5	16 36.0
20 W	1 55 34	0♉43 25	29 31 12	6♑01 54	21 12.0	13 22.7	24 08.9	5 28.9	3 03.6	0 59.4	2 24.7	28 29.9	18 02.7	16 36.7
21 Th	1 59 30	1 41 58	12♑36 56	19 16 31	21D11.3	15 09.0	24 30.7	5 49.4	3 05.9	1 09.7	2 29.7	28 32.2	18 04.9	16 37.4
22 F	2 03 27	2 40 30	26 00 49	2♒49 59	21 11.1	16 57.0	24 54.4	6 09.6	3 07.8	1 20.0	2 34.8	28 34.5	18 07.1	16 38.1
23 Sa	2 07 24	3 39 00	9♒44 06	16 43 12	21 11.4	18 46.7	25 19.7	6 29.4	3 09.3	1 30.1	2 40.0	28 36.9	18 09.3	16 38.8
24 Su	2 11 20	4 37 29	23 47 13	0♓55 58	21 12.1	20 38.0	25 46.7	6 48.7	3 10.5	1 40.1	2 45.2	28 39.3	18 11.5	16 39.4
25 M	2 15 17	5 35 56	8♓09 12	15 26 30	21 13.2	22 30.9	26 15.2	7 07.7	3 11.3	1 50.0	2 50.6	28 41.7	18 13.7	16 40.0
26 Tu	2 19 13	6 34 21	22 47 23	0♈11 11	21 14.2	24 25.6	26 45.2	7 26.2	3R11.7	1 59.8	2 56.0	28 44.2	18 15.9	16 40.6
27 W	2 23 10	7 32 45	7♈37 09	15 04 26	21R14.8	26 21.9	27 16.7	7 44.2	3 11.7	2 09.5	3 01.4	28 46.7	18 18.1	16 41.1
28 Th	2 27 06	8 31 07	22 32 06	29 59 09	21 14.7	28 19.8	27 49.6	8 01.8	3 11.3	2 19.1	3 07.0	28 49.2	18 20.2	16 41.6
29 F	2 31 03	9 29 27	7♉24 37	14♉47 30	21 13.8	0♉19.3	28 23.9	8 19.0	3 10.6	2 28.5	3 12.6	28 51.8	18 22.4	16 42.1
30 Sa	2 34 59	10 27 46	22 06 54	29 21 57	21 11.9	2 20.4	28 59.4	8 35.7	3 09.5	2 37.9	3 18.3	28 54.4	18 24.5	16 42.6

Astro Data	Dy Hr Mn
♄ D	1 16:02
☽ 0N	2 5:33
♅ D	5 14:41
☿ D	13 2:57
☽ 0S	15 23:05
☉ 0N	20 7:22
☽ 0N	29 16:49
♃△♅	4 9:19
♄□♇	7 0:21
♀ D	10 15:27
☽ 0S	12 5:10
☿ 0N	16 0:39
☽ 0N	26 2:46
⚳ R	27 1:29

Planet Ingress		Dy Hr Mn
☉	♈	20 7:23
♀	♓R	21 5:49
⚳	♑	24 23:44
♂	♑	6 6:51
☿	♈	12 9:18
♃	♓	14 22:44
☉	♉	19 18:13
☿	♉	29 8:09

Last Aspect Dy Hr Mn		☽ Ingress	Dy Hr Mn
2 10:26	♅ □	♈	2 14:14
4 10:36	♅ ✶	♉	4 14:34
6 3:07	♃ □	♊	6 17:34
8 19:33	♅ ☌	♋	9 0:02
10 14:48	☉ △	♌	11 9:38
13 16:36	♅ ✶	♍	13 21:23
16 5:24	♅ □	♎	16 10:11
18 18:16	♅ △	♏	18 22:57
21 10:09	♀ △	♐	21 10:22
23 16:14	♀ □	♑	23 19:01
25 19:18	♀ ✶	♒	26 0:03
27 22:14	♅ △	♓	28 1:46
29 22:08	♅ □	♈	30 1:31

Last Aspect Dy Hr Mn		☽ Ingress	Dy Hr Mn
31 21:48	♅ ✶	♉	1 1:10
2 22:43	♃ □	♊	3 2:37
5 6:35	♂ ☍	♋	5 7:22
7 1:39	♀ △	♌	7 15:56
10 1:40	♃ ☍	♍	10 3:31
12 12:48	♅ □	♎	12 16:26
15 1:36	♅ △	♏	15 4:59
17 2:44	♀ △	♐	17 16:03
19 22:04	♅ ☍	♑	20 0:53
21 21:37	♀ ✶	♒	22 7:02
24 8:11	♅ △	♓	24 10:26
26 9:39	♅ □	♈	26 11:42
28 10:07	♅ ✶	♉	28 12:01
30 11:21	♀ ✶	♊	30 13:03

☽ Phases & Eclipses Dy Hr Mn	
1 8:23	● 11♓04
8 1:27	☽ 17♊47
16 1:37	○ 25♍47
24 1:50	☾ 3♑44
30 17:52	● 10♈21
30 18:01:15	• T 02'37"
6 15:14	☽ 17♋08
14 19:17	○ 25♎09
14 19:13	• T 1.094
22 11:42	☾ 2♒40
29 2:46	● 9♉07

Astro Data

1 March 2033
Julian Day # 48638
SVP 4♓47'39"
GC 27♐18.2 ⚴ 16♏36.3
Eris 26♈26.4 ⚵ 13♎03.3R
⚷ 21♉37.1 ⚶ 5♒11.4
☽ Mean ☊ 23♎37.0

1 April 2033
Julian Day # 48669
SVP 4♓47'37"
GC 27♐18.2 ⚴ 14♏16.2R
Eris 26♈44.0 ⚵ 6♎08.7R
⚷ 23♉01.8 ⚶ 20♒17.6
☽ Mean ☊ 21♎58.4

LONGITUDE — May 2033

Day	Sid.Time	☉	0 hr ☽	Noon ☽	True ☊	☿	♀	♂	⚳	♃	♄	♅	♆	♇
1 Su	2 38 56	11♉26 03	6♊31 57	13♊36 18	21♎09.3	4♉23.1	29♓36.1	8♑51.8	3♑08.0	2♓47.1	3♋24.1	28♊57.1	18♈26.7	16♒43.0
2 M	2 42 53	12 24 17	20 34 35	27 26 31	21R 06.3	6 27.2	0♈14.0	9 07.5	3R 06.1	2 56.1	3 29.9	28 59.8	18 28.8	16 43.4
3 Tu	2 46 49	13 22 30	4♋11 57	10♋50 55	21 03.5	8 32.6	0 53.1	9 22.7	3 03.9	3 05.1	3 35.8	29 02.5	18 30.9	16 43.8
4 W	2 50 46	14 20 41	17 23 33	23 50 07	21 01.3	10 39.3	1 33.2	9 37.4	3 01.2	3 13.9	3 41.7	29 05.3	18 33.0	16 44.2
5 Th	2 54 42	15 18 50	0♌11 00	6♌26 36	20D 59.9	12 47.1	2 14.4	9 51.6	2 58.2	3 22.6	3 47.7	29 08.1	18 35.1	16 44.5
6 F	2 58 39	16 16 57	12 37 27	18 44 05	20 59.6	14 55.9	2 56.6	10 05.2	2 54.8	3 31.2	3 53.8	29 10.9	18 37.2	16 44.8
7 Sa	3 02 35	17 15 02	24 47 06	0♍47 06	21 00.4	17 05.5	3 39.8	10 18.3	2 51.0	3 39.6	4 00.0	29 13.7	18 39.2	16 45.1
8 Su	3 06 32	18 13 05	6♍44 41	12 40 28	21 01.8	19 15.6	4 23.9	10 30.9	2 46.9	3 47.9	4 06.1	29 16.6	18 41.2	16 45.4
9 M	3 10 28	19 11 06	18 35 03	24 29 00	21 03.6	21 26.0	5 08.9	10 42.9	2 42.4	3 56.1	4 12.4	29 19.5	18 43.3	16 45.6
10 Tu	3 14 25	20 09 05	0♎22 53	6♎17 13	21 05.1	23 36.5	5 54.8	10 54.3	2 37.5	4 04.1	4 18.7	29 22.5	18 45.3	16 45.8
11 W	3 18 22	21 07 02	12 12 29	18 09 08	21R 06.0	25 46.8	6 41.5	11 05.1	2 32.3	4 12.0	4 25.1	29 25.4	18 47.3	16 46.0
12 Th	3 22 18	22 04 58	24 07 35	0♏08 11	21 05.6	27 56.6	7 29.0	11 15.4	2 26.7	4 19.7	4 31.5	29 28.4	18 49.2	16 46.1
13 F	3 26 15	23 02 52	6♏11 16	12 17 05	21 03.8	0♊05.6	8 17.3	11 25.0	2 20.7	4 27.4	4 38.0	29 31.5	18 51.2	16 46.2
14 Sa	3 30 11	24 00 45	18 25 52	24 37 47	21 00.4	2 13.6	9 06.3	11 34.1	2 14.4	4 34.8	4 44.5	29 34.5	18 53.1	16 46.3
15 Su	3 34 08	24 58 36	0♐52 58	7♐11 31	20 55.7	4 20.2	9 56.1	11 42.5	2 07.7	4 42.1	4 51.1	29 37.6	18 55.1	16 46.4
16 M	3 38 04	25 56 26	13 33 28	19 58 52	20 50.1	6 25.1	10 46.5	11 50.3	2 00.7	4 49.3	4 57.7	29 40.7	18 57.0	16 46.4
17 Tu	3 42 01	26 54 14	26 27 40	2♑59 52	20 44.2	8 28.3	11 37.6	11 57.4	1 53.3	4 56.4	5 04.4	29 43.8	18 58.9	16R 46.4
18 W	3 45 57	27 52 02	9♑35 26	16 14 19	20 38.7	10 29.4	12 29.4	12 03.8	1 45.6	5 03.2	5 11.1	29 47.0	19 00.8	16 46.4
19 Th	3 49 54	28 49 48	22 56 26	29 41 47	20 34.3	12 28.2	13 21.7	12 09.6	1 37.6	5 10.0	5 17.9	29 50.2	19 02.6	16 46.4
20 F	3 53 51	29 47 32	6♒30 16	13♒21 51	20 31.4	14 24.6	14 14.7	12 14.7	1 29.2	5 16.6	5 24.7	29 53.4	19 04.4	16 46.3
21 Sa	3 57 47	0♊45 16	20 16 29	27 14 06	20D 30.2	16 18.4	15 08.2	12 19.1	1 20.6	5 23.0	5 31.6	29 56.6	19 06.3	16 46.2
22 Su	4 01 44	1 42 59	4♓14 38	11♓17 57	20 30.5	18 09.6	16 02.3	12 22.8	1 11.6	5 29.2	5 38.5	29 59.8	19 08.0	16 46.1
23 M	4 05 40	2 40 40	18 23 56	25 32 23	20 31.6	19 57.9	16 57.0	12 25.7	1 02.3	5 35.4	5 45.5	0♋03.1	19 09.8	16 46.0
24 Tu	4 09 37	3 38 21	2♈43 04	9♈55 38	20R 32.8	21 43.4	17 52.1	12 28.0	0 52.6	5 41.3	5 52.5	0 06.4	19 11.6	16 45.8
25 W	4 13 33	4 36 01	17 09 43	24 24 49	20 33.1	23 26.0	18 47.7	12 29.5	0 42.8	5 47.1	5 59.5	0 09.7	19 13.3	16 45.6
26 Th	4 17 30	5 33 39	1♉40 24	8♉55 50	20 31.8	25 05.5	19 43.8	12R 30.2	0 32.6	5 52.7	6 06.6	0 13.0	19 15.0	16 45.4
27 F	4 21 26	6 31 17	16 10 25	23 23 27	20 28.4	26 42.1	20 40.3	12 30.2	0 22.1	5 58.2	6 13.7	0 16.4	19 16.7	16 45.1
28 Sa	4 25 23	7 28 54	0♊34 12	7♊41 55	20 22.9	28 15.5	21 37.3	12 29.4	0 11.4	6 03.5	6 20.9	0 19.7	19 18.4	16 44.8
29 Su	4 29 20	8 26 29	14 45 56	21 45 39	20 15.8	29 45.9	22 34.7	12 27.9	0 00.5	6 08.6	6 28.1	0 23.1	19 20.0	16 44.5
30 M	4 33 16	9 24 04	28 40 30	5♋30 06	20 07.7	1♋13.0	23 32.5	12 25.6	29♐49.3	6 13.6	6 35.3	0 26.5	19 21.6	16 44.2
31 Tu	4 37 13	10 21 37	12♋14 09	18 52 28	19 59.7	2 37.0	24 30.7	12 22.6	29 37.8	6 18.4	6 42.6	0 29.9	19 23.2	16 43.9

LONGITUDE — June 2033

Day	Sid.Time	☉	0 hr ☽	Noon ☽	True ☊	☿	♀	♂	⚳	♃	♄	♅	♆	♇
1 W	4 41 09	11♊19 08	25♋25 01	1♌51 55	19♎52.7	3♋57.8	25♈29.3	12♑18.8	29♐26.2	6♓23.0	6♋49.9	0♋33.4	19♈24.8	16♒43.5
2 Th	4 45 06	12 16 39	8♌13 20	14 29 36	19R 47.2	5 15.3	26 28.2	12R 14.3	29R 14.4	6 27.4	6 57.2	0 36.8	19 26.4	16R 43.1
3 F	4 49 02	13 14 08	20 41 06	26 48 20	19 43.7	6 29.5	27 27.5	12 09.0	29 02.3	6 31.7	7 04.6	0 40.3	19 27.9	16 42.6
4 Sa	4 52 59	14 11 36	2♍51 50	8♍52 11	19D 42.1	7 40.3	28 27.1	12 03.0	28 50.1	6 35.8	7 12.0	0 43.7	19 29.4	16 42.2
5 Su	4 56 55	15 09 03	14 50 00	20 45 58	19 42.1	8 47.8	29 27.0	11 56.2	28 37.7	6 39.7	7 19.4	0 47.2	19 30.8	16 41.7
6 M	5 00 52	16 06 28	26 40 43	2♎34 55	19 43.0	9 51.7	0♉27.3	11 48.7	28 25.2	6 43.4	7 26.8	0 50.7	19 32.3	16 41.2
7 Tu	5 04 49	17 03 53	8♎29 14	14 24 18	19R 43.8	10 52.0	1 27.9	11 40.5	28 12.5	6 47.0	7 34.3	0 54.2	19 33.7	16 40.7
8 W	5 08 45	18 01 16	20 20 45	26 19 07	19 43.7	11 48.8	2 28.8	11 31.5	27 59.7	6 50.4	7 41.8	0 57.7	19 35.1	16 40.1
9 Th	5 12 42	18 58 38	2♏19 59	8♏23 49	19 41.9	12 41.8	3 30.0	11 21.9	27 46.8	6 53.6	7 49.3	1 01.2	19 36.5	16 39.6
10 F	5 16 38	19 55 59	14 31 02	20 42 01	19 37.8	13 31.0	4 31.4	11 11.6	27 33.8	6 56.6	7 56.9	1 04.8	19 37.8	16 39.0
11 Sa	5 20 35	20 53 20	26 57 01	3♐16 15	19 31.4	14 16.3	5 33.2	11 00.6	27 20.8	6 59.4	8 04.5	1 08.3	19 39.1	16 38.4
12 Su	5 24 31	21 50 39	9♐39 50	16 07 48	19 22.9	14 57.6	6 35.2	10 49.0	27 07.6	7 02.1	8 12.1	1 11.9	19 40.4	16 37.7
13 M	5 28 28	22 47 58	22 40 06	29 16 36	19 12.9	15 34.9	7 37.5	10 36.7	26 54.4	7 04.5	8 19.7	1 15.4	19 41.7	16 37.1
14 Tu	5 32 24	23 45 17	5♑57 06	12♑41 19	19 02.3	16 08.0	8 40.0	10 23.8	26 41.1	7 06.8	8 27.3	1 19.0	19 42.9	16 36.4
15 W	5 36 21	24 42 34	19 28 56	26 19 36	18 52.4	16 36.8	9 42.8	10 10.3	26 27.9	7 08.9	8 35.0	1 22.6	19 44.1	16 35.7
16 Th	5 40 18	25 39 51	3♒12 57	10♒08 37	18 44.0	17 01.3	10 45.9	9 56.3	26 14.6	7 10.8	8 42.6	1 26.1	19 45.3	16 34.9
17 F	5 44 14	26 37 08	17 06 14	24 05 28	18 37.9	17 21.4	11 49.1	9 41.7	26 01.3	7 12.5	8 50.3	1 29.7	19 46.4	16 34.2
18 Sa	5 48 11	27 34 25	1♓06 03	8♓07 41	18 34.3	17 36.9	12 52.6	9 26.5	25 48.0	7 14.1	8 58.0	1 33.3	19 47.6	16 33.4
19 Su	5 52 07	28 31 41	15 10 12	22 13 24	18D 32.9	17 48.0	13 56.4	9 10.9	25 34.8	7 15.4	9 05.7	1 36.9	19 48.7	16 32.6
20 M	5 56 04	29 28 57	29 17 07	6♈21 15	18R 32.9	17R 54.4	15 00.3	8 54.8	25 21.5	7 16.5	9 13.5	1 40.5	19 49.7	16 31.8
21 Tu	6 00 00	0♋26 13	13♈25 38	20 30 10	18 33.1	17 56.3	16 04.4	8 38.2	25 08.4	7 17.5	9 21.2	1 44.1	19 50.7	16 31.0
22 W	6 03 57	1 23 28	27 34 40	4♉38 56	18 32.2	17 53.7	17 08.8	8 21.3	24 55.3	7 18.2	9 29.0	1 47.7	19 51.8	16 30.1
23 Th	6 07 53	2 20 44	11♉42 43	18 45 44	18 29.4	17 46.7	18 13.4	8 04.0	24 42.3	7 18.8	9 36.7	1 51.2	19 52.7	16 29.2
24 F	6 11 50	3 17 59	25 47 38	2♊48 01	18 23.8	17 35.2	19 18.1	7 46.4	24 29.4	7 19.2	9 44.5	1 54.8	19 53.7	16 28.4
25 Sa	6 15 47	4 15 15	9♊46 26	16 42 28	18 15.5	17 19.7	20 23.0	7 28.6	24 16.6	7R 19.4	9 52.3	1 58.4	19 54.6	16 27.4
26 Su	6 19 43	5 12 30	23 35 36	0♋25 26	18 05.0	17 00.1	21 28.2	7 10.5	24 04.0	7 19.3	10 00.1	2 02.0	19 55.5	16 26.5
27 M	6 23 40	6 09 45	7♋11 30	13 53 28	17 53.1	16 36.8	22 33.4	6 52.2	23 51.5	7 19.1	10 07.9	2 05.6	19 56.3	16 25.6
28 Tu	6 27 36	7 06 59	20 31 01	27 03 57	17 41.1	16 10.2	23 38.9	6 33.9	23 39.1	7 18.7	10 15.7	2 09.2	19 57.1	16 24.6
29 W	6 31 33	8 04 13	3♌32 08	9♌55 34	17 30.1	15 40.6	24 44.5	6 15.4	23 27.0	7 18.1	10 23.5	2 12.8	19 57.9	16 23.6
30 Th	6 35 29	9 01 27	16 14 19	22 28 35	17 21.0	15 08.5	25 50.3	5 56.9	23 15.0	7 17.3	10 31.3	2 16.4	19 58.7	16 22.6

Astro Data (Dy Hr Mn)

Aspect	Dy Hr Mn
♃∠♆	7 10:26
☽0S	9 12:11
♇R	17 12:59
☽0N	23 10:44
♂R	26 23:47
☽0S	5 20:40
♅⚼♇	18 12:42
☽0N	19 17:22
☿R	21 10:05
♃R	25 21:52

Planet Ingress (Dy Hr Mn)

Planet	Sign	Dy Hr Mn
♀	♈	2 3:12
☿	♊	13 10:57
☉	♊	20 17:11
♅	♋	22 13:14
⚳	♐R	29 13:00
☿	♋	29 15:50
♀	♉	6 1:08
☉	♋	21 1:01

Last Aspect / ☽ Ingress (May)

Last Aspect Dy Hr Mn		☽ Ingress Dy Hr Mn
2 14:45	♅ ☌	♋ 2 16:31
4 2:07	♆ □	♌ 4 23:39
7 8:52	♅ ⚹	♍ 7 10:25
9 21:54	♅ □	♎ 9 23:13
12 10:41	♅ △	♏ 12 11:44
14 10:43	☉ ☍	♐ 14 22:19
17 5:59	♅ △	♑ 17 6:31
19 10:21	☉ △	♒ 19 12:32
21 16:40	♅ △	♓ 21 16:45
23 1:17	☿ □	♈ 23 19:28
25 10:10	♀ ⚹	♉ 25 21:14
27 0:58	♇ □	♊ 27 23:03
29 13:31	♀ ⚹	♋ 30 2:19

Last Aspect / ☽ Ingress (June)

Last Aspect Dy Hr Mn		☽ Ingress Dy Hr Mn
31 23:10	♀ □	♌ 1 8:31
3 13:24	♀ △	♍ 3 18:19
4 23:39	☉ □	♎ 6 6:45
7 22:26	♆ ☍	♏ 8 19:21
10 4:10	♇ □	♐ 11 5:48
12 23:19	☉ ☍	♑ 13 13:18
15 0:26	♆ □	♒ 15 18:24
17 16:39	☉ △	♓ 17 22:07
19 23:29	☉ □	♈ 20 1:13
21 10:53	♆ ☌	♉ 22 4:07
23 11:00	♀ ☌	♊ 24 7:12
25 17:35	♆ ⚹	♋ 26 11:15
28 5:09	♀ ⚹	♌ 28 17:25

☽ Phases & Eclipses (Dy Hr Mn)

Dy Hr Mn	Phase	Position
6 6:45	☽	16♌04
14 10:43	○	23♏58
21 18:29	☾	1♓01
28 11:36	●	7♊28
4 23:39	☽	14♍39
12 23:19	○	22♐18
19 23:29	☾	28♓59
26 21:07	●	5♋34

Astro Data

1 May 2033
Julian Day # 48699
SVP 4♓47'34"
GC 27♐18.3 ⚴ 5♏59.8R
Eris 27♈03.6 ⚵ 0♎38.0R
⚷ 24♉56.8 ⚶ 3♓27.9
☽ Mean ☊ 20♎23.1

1 June 2033
Julian Day # 48730
SVP 4♓47'30"
GC 27♐18.4 ⚴ 28♎46.9R
Eris 27♈21.5 ⚵ 0♎03.2
⚷ 27♉07.5 ⚶ 14♓43.3
☽ Mean ☊ 18♎44.6

July 2033

LONGITUDE

Day	Sid.Time	☉	0 hr ☽	Noon ☽	True ☊	☿	♀	♂	⚳	♃	♄	♅	♆	♇
1 F	6 39 26	9♋58 41	28♌38 37	4♍44 47	17♎14.4	14♋34.4	26♉56.2	5♑38.5	23♐03.2	7♓16.3	10♋39.1	2♋19.9	19♈59.4	16♒21.6
2 Sa	6 43 23	10 55 54	10♍47 31	16 47 20	17R 10.4	13R 58.8	28 02.3	5R 20.1	22R 51.6	7R 15.1	10 46.9	2 23.5	20 00.1	16R 20.5
3 Su	6 47 19	11 53 06	22 44 48	28 40 30	17 08.5	13 22.3	29 08.5	5 01.8	22 40.2	7 13.8	10 54.7	2 27.0	20 00.8	16 19.5
4 M	6 51 16	12 50 19	4♎35 05	10♎29 14	17 08.0	12 45.6	0♊14.9	4 43.7	22 29.0	7 12.2	11 02.5	2 30.6	20 01.4	16 18.4
5 Tu	6 55 12	13 47 31	16 23 36	22 18 55	17 08.0	12 09.2	1 21.4	4 25.8	22 18.1	7 10.4	11 10.3	2 34.1	20 02.0	16 17.3
6 W	6 59 09	14 44 43	28 15 50	4♏15 01	17 07.3	11 33.8	2 28.1	4 08.1	22 07.5	7 08.5	11 18.1	2 37.7	20 02.6	16 16.2
7 Th	7 03 05	15 41 55	10♏17 08	16 22 45	17 05.0	11 00.1	3 34.9	3 50.8	21 57.1	7 06.3	11 25.9	2 41.2	20 03.1	16 15.1
8 F	7 07 02	16 39 07	22 32 27	28 46 41	17 00.4	10 28.5	4 41.9	3 33.8	21 46.9	7 04.0	11 33.7	2 44.7	20 03.6	16 14.0
9 Sa	7 10 58	17 36 18	5♐05 51	11♐30 17	16 53.2	9 59.7	5 48.9	3 17.1	21 37.1	7 01.5	11 41.5	2 48.2	20 04.1	16 12.8
10 Su	7 14 55	18 33 30	18 00 09	24 35 34	16 43.6	9 34.2	6 56.1	3 00.9	21 27.5	6 58.8	11 49.3	2 51.7	20 04.5	16 11.7
11 M	7 18 52	19 30 41	1♑16 28	8♑02 41	16 32.4	9 12.5	8 03.5	2 45.2	21 18.2	6 55.9	11 57.1	2 55.2	20 04.9	16 10.5
12 Tu	7 22 48	20 27 53	14 53 55	21 49 46	16 20.5	8 55.0	9 11.0	2 29.9	21 09.2	6 52.9	12 04.8	2 58.7	20 05.3	16 09.3
13 W	7 26 45	21 25 05	28 49 42	5♒53 08	16 09.2	8 41.9	10 18.6	2 15.2	21 00.6	6 49.6	12 12.6	3 02.1	20 05.6	16 08.1
14 Th	7 30 41	22 22 17	12♒59 23	20 07 48	15 59.6	8 33.7	11 26.3	2 01.0	20 52.2	6 46.2	12 20.3	3 05.6	20 05.9	16 06.9
15 F	7 34 38	23 19 30	27 17 41	4♓28 23	15 52.5	8D 30.6	12 34.2	1 47.4	20 44.1	6 42.6	12 28.0	3 09.0	20 06.2	16 05.7
16 Sa	7 38 34	24 16 43	11♓39 16	18 49 50	15 48.2	8 32.8	13 42.1	1 34.4	20 36.4	6 38.8	12 35.7	3 12.4	20 06.4	16 04.5
17 Su	7 42 31	25 13 57	25 59 37	3♈08 15	15D 46.3	8 40.3	14 50.2	1 22.0	20 29.0	6 34.8	12 43.4	3 15.8	20 06.7	16 03.2
18 M	7 46 27	26 11 12	10♈15 26	17 20 57	15R 45.9	8 53.4	15 58.5	1 10.3	20 21.9	6 30.7	12 51.1	3 19.2	20 06.8	16 02.0
19 Tu	7 50 24	27 08 27	24 24 40	1♉26 28	15 45.9	9 12.1	17 06.8	0 59.3	20 15.2	6 26.4	12 58.8	3 22.6	20 07.0	16 00.7
20 W	7 54 21	28 05 43	8♉26 18	15 24 05	15 45.0	9 36.5	18 15.2	0 49.0	20 08.8	6 21.9	13 06.4	3 25.9	20 07.1	15 59.4
21 Th	7 58 17	29 03 00	22 19 47	29 13 20	15 42.2	10 06.5	19 23.8	0 39.5	20 02.7	6 17.3	13 14.1	3 29.3	20 07.2	15 58.2
22 F	8 02 14	0♌00 18	6♊04 40	12♊53 38	15 36.8	10 42.1	20 32.5	0 30.7	19 57.0	6 12.5	13 21.7	3 32.6	20R 07.2	15 56.9
23 Sa	8 06 10	0 57 36	19 40 08	26 24 00	15 28.6	11 23.3	21 41.3	0 22.6	19 51.7	6 07.5	13 29.3	3 35.9	20 07.2	15 55.6
24 Su	8 10 07	1 54 55	3♋05 02	9♋43 05	15 18.3	12 10.2	22 50.2	0 15.4	19 46.7	6 02.4	13 36.8	3 39.2	20 07.2	15 54.3
25 M	8 14 03	2 52 15	16 17 55	22 49 23	15 06.6	13 02.5	23 59.1	0 09.0	19 42.1	5 57.1	13 44.4	3 42.4	20 07.2	15 53.0
26 Tu	8 18 00	3 49 36	29 17 19	5♌41 36	14 54.7	14 00.2	25 08.2	0 03.4	19 37.8	5 51.7	13 51.9	3 45.7	20 07.1	15 51.6
27 W	8 21 56	4 46 57	12♌02 11	18 19 03	14 43.7	15 03.3	26 17.4	29♐58.6	19 33.9	5 46.1	13 59.4	3 48.9	20 06.9	15 50.3
28 Th	8 25 53	5 44 19	24 32 14	0♍41 52	14 34.6	16 11.7	27 26.7	29 54.7	19 30.3	5 40.4	14 06.9	3 52.1	20 06.8	15 49.0
29 F	8 29 50	6 41 42	6♍48 09	12 51 20	14 27.8	17 25.2	28 36.1	29 51.6	19 27.1	5 34.5	14 14.3	3 55.2	20 06.6	15 47.7
30 Sa	8 33 46	7 39 05	18 51 44	24 49 45	14 23.6	18 43.7	29 45.5	29 49.4	19 24.3	5 28.5	14 21.7	3 58.4	20 06.4	15 46.3
31 Su	8 37 43	8 36 28	0♎45 51	6♎40 32	14D 21.8	20 07.0	0♋55.1	29 48.0	19 21.9	5 22.3	14 29.1	4 01.5	20 06.1	15 45.0

August 2033

LONGITUDE

Day	Sid.Time	☉	0 hr ☽	Noon ☽	True ☊	☿	♀	♂	⚳	♃	♄	♅	♆	♇
1 M	8 41 39	9♌33 53	12♎34 20	18♎27 52	14♎21.6	21♋35.1	2♋04.8	29♐47.5	19♐19.8	5♓16.1	14♋36.4	4♋04.6	20♈05.9	15♒43.6
2 Tu	8 45 36	10 31 17	24 21 46	0♏16 40	14R 22.1	23 07.6	3 14.5	29D 47.9	19R 18.1	5R 09.7	14 43.8	4 07.6	20R 05.5	15R 42.3
3 W	8 49 32	11 28 43	6♏13 14	12 12 11	14 22.4	24 44.4	4 24.3	29 49.0	19 16.7	5 03.2	14 51.0	4 10.7	20 05.2	15 40.9
4 Th	8 53 29	12 26 09	18 14 09	24 19 49	14 21.7	26 25.2	5 34.3	29 51.1	19 15.7	4 56.5	14 58.3	4 13.7	20 04.8	15 39.6
5 F	8 57 25	13 23 36	0♐29 47	6♐44 40	14 19.1	28 09.7	6 44.3	29 54.0	19 15.1	4 49.8	15 05.5	4 16.7	20 04.4	15 38.2
6 Sa	9 01 22	14 21 04	13 04 57	19 31 06	14 14.3	29 57.6	7 54.4	29 57.7	19D 14.8	4 43.0	15 12.7	4 19.6	20 04.0	15 36.9
7 Su	9 05 19	15 18 32	26 03 26	2♑42 11	14 07.5	1♌48.6	9 04.5	0♑02.2	19 14.9	4 36.0	15 19.8	4 22.6	20 03.5	15 35.5
8 M	9 09 15	16 16 02	9♑27 25	16 19 04	13 59.2	3 42.3	10 14.8	0 07.6	19 15.4	4 29.0	15 26.9	4 25.4	20 03.0	15 34.2
9 Tu	9 13 12	17 13 32	23 16 55	0♒20 34	13 50.2	5 38.4	11 25.2	0 13.7	19 16.2	4 21.8	15 34.0	4 28.3	20 02.5	15 32.8
10 W	9 17 08	18 11 03	7♒29 29	14 42 57	13 41.5	7 36.4	12 35.6	0 20.7	19 17.3	4 14.6	15 41.0	4 31.2	20 01.9	15 31.4
11 Th	9 21 05	19 08 35	22 00 10	29 20 16	13 34.2	9 36.0	13 46.2	0 28.4	19 18.8	4 07.3	15 48.0	4 34.0	20 01.3	15 30.1
12 F	9 25 01	20 06 09	6♓42 16	14♓05 15	13 29.0	11 36.9	14 56.8	0 37.0	19 20.7	3 59.9	15 55.0	4 36.7	20 00.7	15 28.7
13 Sa	9 28 58	21 03 43	21 28 15	28 50 26	13D 26.1	13 38.6	16 07.5	0 46.2	19 22.9	3 52.5	16 01.9	4 39.5	20 00.1	15 27.4
14 Su	9 32 54	22 01 19	6♈10 59	13♈29 16	13 25.3	15 40.9	17 18.3	0 56.3	19 25.4	3 45.0	16 08.7	4 42.2	19 59.4	15 26.0
15 M	9 36 51	22 58 57	20 44 42	27 56 51	13 25.8	17 43.4	18 29.2	1 07.0	19 28.3	3 37.4	16 15.5	4 44.8	19 58.7	15 24.7
16 Tu	9 40 47	23 56 36	5♉05 25	12♉10 11	13R 26.8	19 45.9	19 40.1	1 18.5	19 31.5	3 29.7	16 22.3	4 47.5	19 57.9	15 23.3
17 W	9 44 44	24 54 16	19 11 02	26 07 55	13 27.3	21 48.1	20 51.2	1 30.8	19 35.1	3 22.0	16 29.0	4 50.1	19 57.2	15 22.0
18 Th	9 48 41	25 51 59	3♊00 50	9♊49 52	13 26.4	23 49.8	22 02.3	1 43.7	19 38.9	3 14.3	16 35.7	4 52.7	19 56.4	15 20.7
19 F	9 52 37	26 49 43	16 35 04	23 16 33	13 23.5	25 50.9	23 13.5	1 57.3	19 43.1	3 06.5	16 42.3	4 55.2	19 55.5	15 19.4
20 Sa	9 56 34	27 47 28	29 54 26	6♋28 47	13 18.7	27 51.2	24 24.8	2 11.7	19 47.7	2 58.7	16 48.9	4 57.7	19 54.7	15 18.0
21 Su	10 00 30	28 45 15	12♋59 43	19 27 18	13 12.3	29 50.6	25 36.2	2 26.7	19 52.5	2 50.8	16 55.4	5 00.2	19 53.8	15 16.7
22 M	10 04 27	29 43 04	25 51 38	2♌12 46	13 04.8	1♍48.9	26 47.7	2 42.4	19 57.7	2 43.0	17 01.8	5 02.6	19 52.9	15 15.4
23 Tu	10 08 23	0♍40 54	8♌30 47	14 45 44	12 57.1	3 46.1	27 59.2	2 58.7	20 03.2	2 35.1	17 08.2	5 05.0	19 52.0	15 14.1
24 W	10 12 20	1 38 46	20 57 44	27 06 53	12 50.1	5 42.1	29 10.8	3 15.7	20 09.0	2 27.2	17 14.6	5 07.3	19 51.0	15 12.8
25 Th	10 16 16	2 36 39	3♍13 16	9♍17 05	12 44.3	7 36.8	0♌22.5	3 33.4	20 15.2	2 19.3	17 20.9	5 09.6	19 50.0	15 11.5
26 F	10 20 13	3 34 34	15 18 29	21 17 42	12 40.2	9 30.4	1 34.2	3 51.7	20 21.6	2 11.4	17 27.1	5 11.9	19 49.0	15 10.2
27 Sa	10 24 10	4 32 30	27 14 59	3♎10 39	12D 38.0	11 22.6	2 46.0	4 10.6	20 28.3	2 03.5	17 33.3	5 14.1	19 47.9	15 09.0
28 Su	10 28 06	5 30 27	9♎05 02	14 58 32	12 37.6	13 13.6	3 57.9	4 30.1	20 35.4	1 55.6	17 39.4	5 16.3	19 46.9	15 07.7
29 M	10 32 03	6 28 26	20 51 35	26 44 39	12 38.4	15 03.3	5 09.9	4 50.2	20 42.7	1 47.7	17 45.5	5 18.5	19 45.8	15 06.5
30 Tu	10 35 59	7 26 26	2♏38 15	8♏32 55	12 40.0	16 51.6	6 21.9	5 10.9	20 50.3	1 39.9	17 51.5	5 20.6	19 44.7	15 05.2
31 W	10 39 56	8 24 28	14 29 15	20 27 49	12 41.7	18 38.7	7 34.0	5 32.1	20 58.3	1 32.1	17 57.4	5 22.6	19 43.5	15 04.0

Astro Data

	Dy Hr Mn
☽0S	3 6:02
☿D	15 14:20
☽0N	17 0:06
♆R	23 10:26
☽0S	30 15:05
♂D	1 14:24
♃∠♆	3 4:07
⚳D	6 17:38
♃△♅	8 20:29
♄⚻♇	9 8:33
☽0N	13 8:16
♃⚼♄	25 9:16
☽0S	26 22:53

Planet Ingress

	Dy Hr Mn
♀ ♊	4 6:37
☉ ♌	22 11:53
♂ ♐R	27 4:35
♀ ♋	30 16:59
☿ ♌	6 12:31
♂ ♑	7 0:47
☿ ♍	21 13:54
☉ ♍	22 19:02
♀ ♌	25 4:29

Last Aspect / ☽ Ingress

Last Aspect Dy Hr Mn		☽ Ingress	Dy Hr Mn
30 19:10	♀ □	♍	1 2:39
3 13:03	♀ △	♎	3 14:41
5 7:23	♆ ☍	♏	6 3:29
7 11:45	♇ □	♐	8 14:20
10 3:47	♆ △	♑	10 21:43
12 9:28	☉ ☍	♒	13 2:00
14 11:57	♆ ⚹	♓	15 4:31
16 21:47	☉ △	♈	17 6:44
19 4:07	☉ □	♉	19 9:32
21 11:41	☉ ⚹	♊	21 13:21
23 2:49	♀ ☌	♋	23 18:27
25 7:01	♆ □	♌	26 1:20
28 10:28	♂ △	♍	28 10:38
30 22:04	♂ □	♎	30 22:27

Last Aspect / ☽ Ingress

Last Aspect Dy Hr Mn		☽ Ingress	Dy Hr Mn
2 11:02	♂ ⚹	♏	2 11:26
4 16:45	☿ △	♐	4 23:02
6 13:01	♆ △	♑	7 7:09
8 18:27	♆ □	♒	9 11:25
10 20:45	♆ ⚹	♓	11 13:05
12 15:00	♄ △	♈	13 13:53
15 3:08	☉ △	♉	15 15:26
17 9:43	☉ □	♊	17 18:44
19 18:55	☉ ⚹	♋	20 0:10
22 0:42	♀ ☌	♌	22 7:49
23 21:52	♆ △	♍	24 17:40
26 4:13	♄ ⚹	♎	27 5:34
28 21:47	♆ ☍	♏	29 18:38

☽ Phases & Eclipses

Dy Hr Mn	
4 17:12	☽ 13♎03
12 9:28	○ 20♑22
19 4:07	☾ 26♈50
26 8:12	● 3♌41
3 10:26	☽ 11♏25
10 18:08	○ 18♒26
17 9:43	☾ 24♉49
24 21:40	● 2♍02

Astro Data

1 July 2033
Julian Day # 48760
SVP 4♓47'25"
GC 27♐18.4 ⚴ 28♎27.9
Eris 27♈32.6 ⚵ 4♎02.3
⚷ 29♉03.6 ⚶ 21♓56.9
☽ Mean ☊ 17♎09.3

1 August 2033
Julian Day # 48791
SVP 4♓47'21"
GC 27♐18.5 ⚴ 4♏03.7
Eris 27♈34.8R ⚵ 11♎14.0
⚷ 0♊31.5 ⚶ 23♓29.7R
☽ Mean ☊ 15♎30.8

LONGITUDE — September 2033

Day	Sid.Time	☉	0 hr ☽	Noon ☽	True ☊	☿	♀	♂	⚳	♃	♄	♅	♆	♇
1 Th	10 43 52	9♍22 31	26♏29 16	2♐34 12	12♎42.8	20♍24.6	8♌46.1	5♑53.9	21♐06.5	1♓24.3	18♋03.3	5♋24.6	19♈42.4	15♒02.8
2 F	10 47 49	10 20 35	8♐43 14	14 56 58	12R42.9	22 09.1	9 58.4	6 16.3	21 15.0	1R16.6	18 09.1	5 26.6	19R41.2	15R01.6
3 Sa	10 51 45	11 18 41	21 15 59	27 40 47	12 41.7	23 52.4	11 10.6	6 39.2	21 23.7	1 08.9	18 14.8	5 28.6	19 40.0	15 00.4
4 Su	10 55 42	12 16 48	4♑11 50	10♑49 29	12 39.2	25 34.5	12 23.0	7 02.6	21 32.8	1 01.3	18 20.5	5 30.4	19 38.7	14 59.2
5 M	10 59 39	13 14 57	17 33 59	24 25 27	12 35.7	27 15.3	13 35.4	7 26.5	21 42.1	0 53.8	18 26.1	5 32.3	19 37.5	14 58.0
6 Tu	11 03 35	14 13 07	1♒23 51	8♒28 59	12 31.7	28 55.0	14 47.9	7 50.9	21 51.6	0 46.3	18 31.6	5 34.1	19 36.2	14 56.9
7 W	11 07 32	15 11 19	15 40 28	22 57 45	12 27.7	0♎33.5	16 00.5	8 15.8	22 01.5	0 38.9	18 37.1	5 35.8	19 34.9	14 55.8
8 Th	11 11 28	16 09 32	0♓20 06	7♓46 38	12 24.4	2 10.8	17 13.1	8 41.1	22 11.6	0 31.5	18 42.4	5 37.6	19 33.6	14 54.6
9 F	11 15 25	17 07 47	15 16 21	22 48 09	12 22.1	3 46.9	18 25.8	9 06.9	22 21.9	0 24.3	18 47.8	5 39.2	19 32.3	14 53.5
10 Sa	11 19 21	18 06 03	0♈20 54	7♈53 27	12D21.2	5 21.9	19 38.5	9 33.1	22 32.5	0 17.1	18 53.0	5 40.8	19 30.9	14 52.4
11 Su	11 23 18	19 04 22	15 24 44	22 53 41	12 21.4	6 55.7	20 51.3	9 59.8	22 43.4	0 10.0	18 58.2	5 42.4	19 29.5	14 51.4
12 M	11 27 14	20 02 43	0♉19 27	7♉41 13	12 22.4	8 28.4	22 04.2	10 26.9	22 54.5	0 03.0	19 03.3	5 43.9	19 28.1	14 50.3
13 Tu	11 31 11	21 01 05	14 58 24	22 10 29	12 23.7	10 00.0	23 17.2	10 54.4	23 05.8	29♒56.1	19 08.3	5 45.4	19 26.7	14 49.2
14 W	11 35 08	21 59 30	29 17 11	6♊18 17	12 24.9	11 30.5	24 30.2	11 22.4	23 17.3	29 49.4	19 13.2	5 46.8	19 25.3	14 48.2
15 Th	11 39 04	22 57 57	13♊13 44	20 03 35	12R25.5	12 59.9	25 43.3	11 50.7	23 29.1	29 42.7	19 18.1	5 48.2	19 23.8	14 47.2
16 F	11 43 01	23 56 27	26 47 56	3♋26 59	12 25.3	14 28.1	26 56.4	12 19.4	23 41.2	29 36.1	19 22.8	5 49.5	19 22.4	14 46.2
17 Sa	11 46 57	24 54 58	10♋01 00	16 30 15	12 24.2	15 55.2	28 09.6	12 48.5	23 53.4	29 29.7	19 27.5	5 50.8	19 20.9	14 45.2
18 Su	11 50 54	25 53 32	22 55 03	29 15 42	12 22.5	17 21.1	29 22.9	13 18.0	24 05.9	29 23.4	19 32.2	5 52.1	19 19.4	14 44.3
19 M	11 54 50	26 52 07	5♌32 33	11♌45 54	12 20.3	18 45.9	0♍36.2	13 47.8	24 18.6	29 17.2	19 36.7	5 53.2	19 17.9	14 43.3
20 Tu	11 58 47	27 50 45	17 56 04	24 03 21	12 18.0	20 09.5	1 49.6	14 18.1	24 31.6	29 11.2	19 41.1	5 54.4	19 16.4	14 42.4
21 W	12 02 43	28 49 25	0♍08 01	6♍10 23	12 16.0	21 31.9	3 03.0	14 48.6	24 44.7	29 05.2	19 45.5	5 55.4	19 14.8	14 41.5
22 Th	12 06 40	29 48 07	12 10 40	18 09 10	12 14.4	22 53.0	4 16.5	15 19.6	24 58.1	28 59.5	19 49.8	5 56.5	19 13.3	14 40.6
23 F	12 10 36	0♎46 51	24 06 07	0♎01 47	12 13.5	24 12.9	5 30.1	15 50.8	25 11.6	28 53.9	19 53.9	5 57.5	19 11.7	14 39.8
24 Sa	12 14 33	1 45 37	5♎56 26	11 50 19	12D13.2	25 31.4	6 43.6	16 22.4	25 25.4	28 48.4	19 58.0	5 58.4	19 10.2	14 38.9
25 Su	12 18 30	2 44 24	17 43 43	23 36 58	12 13.4	26 48.5	7 57.3	16 54.4	25 39.4	28 43.1	20 02.0	5 59.3	19 08.6	14 38.1
26 M	12 22 26	3 43 14	29 30 21	5♏24 14	12 14.0	28 04.2	9 11.0	17 26.6	25 53.6	28 37.9	20 06.0	6 00.1	19 07.0	14 37.3
27 Tu	12 26 23	4 42 06	11♏18 57	17 14 56	12 14.8	29 18.3	10 24.7	17 59.2	26 07.9	28 32.9	20 09.8	6 00.8	19 05.4	14 36.5
28 W	12 30 19	5 40 59	23 12 35	29 12 22	12 15.6	0♏30.8	11 38.5	18 32.0	26 22.5	28 28.1	20 13.5	6 01.6	19 03.8	14 35.8
29 Th	12 34 16	6 39 54	5♐14 43	11♐20 08	12 16.2	1 41.6	12 52.4	19 05.2	26 37.3	28 23.5	20 17.1	6 02.2	19 02.1	14 35.1
30 F	12 38 12	7 38 51	17 29 08	23 42 13	12 16.6	2 50.6	14 06.3	19 38.7	26 52.2	28 19.0	20 20.7	6 02.9	19 00.5	14 34.3

LONGITUDE — October 2033

Day	Sid.Time	☉	0 hr ☽	Noon ☽	True ☊	☿	♀	♂	⚳	♃	♄	♅	♆	♇
1 Sa	12 42 09	8♎37 50	29♐59 54	6♑22 39	12♎16.7	3♏57.7	15♍20.2	20♑12.4	27♐07.3	28♒14.7	20♋24.1	6♋03.4	18♈58.9	14♒33.7
2 Su	12 46 05	9 36 50	12♑50 57	19 25 12	12R16.7	5 02.6	16 34.2	20 46.4	27 22.6	28R10.5	20 27.5	6 03.9	18R57.2	14R33.0
3 M	12 50 02	10 35 53	26 05 46	2♒52 55	12 16.6	6 05.3	17 48.2	21 20.7	27 38.1	28 06.6	20 30.7	6 04.4	18 55.6	14 32.4
4 Tu	12 53 59	11 34 56	9♒46 48	16 47 28	12D16.5	7 05.5	19 02.3	21 55.2	27 53.8	28 02.8	20 33.9	6 04.8	18 53.9	14 31.7
5 W	12 57 55	12 34 02	23 54 48	1♓08 32	12 16.4	8 03.2	20 16.4	22 30.0	28 09.6	27 59.2	20 36.9	6 05.1	18 52.3	14 31.2
6 Th	13 01 52	13 33 10	8♓28 12	15 53 12	12 16.5	8 57.9	21 30.5	23 05.0	28 25.6	27 55.8	20 39.9	6 05.4	18 50.6	14 30.6
7 F	13 05 48	14 32 19	23 22 44	0♈55 50	12R16.6	9 49.5	22 44.7	23 40.3	28 41.8	27 52.6	20 42.7	6 05.7	18 48.9	14 30.0
8 Sa	13 09 45	15 31 30	8♈31 25	16 08 19	12 16.6	10 37.7	23 58.9	24 15.8	28 58.1	27 49.5	20 45.5	6 05.9	18 47.3	14 29.5
9 Su	13 13 41	16 30 43	23 45 19	1♉21 09	12 16.5	11 22.2	25 13.2	24 51.5	29 14.6	27 46.7	20 48.2	6 06.0	18 45.6	14 29.0
10 M	13 17 38	17 29 59	8♉54 39	16 24 42	12 16.1	12 02.6	26 27.5	25 27.4	29 31.3	27 44.0	20 50.7	6 06.1	18 43.9	14 28.5
11 Tu	13 21 34	18 29 16	23 50 19	1♊10 42	12 15.5	12 38.5	27 41.9	26 03.5	29 48.1	27 41.6	20 53.2	6R06.1	18 42.3	14 28.1
12 W	13 25 31	19 28 36	8♊25 10	15 33 15	12 14.7	13 09.6	28 56.3	26 39.9	0♑05.0	27 39.3	20 55.5	6 06.1	18 40.6	14 27.7
13 Th	13 29 28	20 27 59	22 34 40	29 29 17	12 14.0	13 35.3	0♎10.8	27 16.4	0 22.2	27 37.2	20 57.7	6 06.0	18 38.9	14 27.3
14 F	13 33 24	21 27 23	6♋17 06	12♋58 17	12D13.5	13 55.2	1 25.3	27 53.2	0 39.4	27 35.4	20 59.9	6 05.9	18 37.2	14 26.9
15 Sa	13 37 21	22 26 50	19 33 07	26 01 55	12 13.4	14 08.8	2 39.8	28 30.1	0 56.8	27 33.7	21 01.9	6 05.7	18 35.6	14 26.6
16 Su	13 41 17	23 26 20	2♌25 08	8♌43 14	12 13.8	14R15.5	3 54.4	29 07.3	1 14.4	27 32.2	21 03.8	6 05.5	18 33.9	14 26.3
17 M	13 45 14	24 25 51	14 56 41	21 06 01	12 14.7	14 14.8	5 09.0	29 44.6	1 32.1	27 30.9	21 05.7	6 05.2	18 32.2	14 26.0
18 Tu	13 49 10	25 25 25	27 11 45	3♍14 23	12 15.9	14 06.4	6 23.6	0♒22.1	1 49.9	27 29.9	21 07.4	6 04.9	18 30.6	14 25.7
19 W	13 53 07	26 25 01	9♍14 25	15 12 19	12 17.2	13 49.6	7 38.3	0 59.8	2 07.9	27 29.0	21 09.0	6 04.5	18 28.9	14 25.5
20 Th	13 57 03	27 24 39	21 08 31	27 03 27	12 18.3	13 24.2	8 53.0	1 37.7	2 26.0	27 28.3	21 10.4	6 04.1	18 27.3	14 25.3
21 F	14 01 00	28 24 19	2♎57 31	8♎51 03	12R18.8	12 50.0	10 07.7	2 15.8	2 44.2	27 27.8	21 11.8	6 03.6	18 25.6	14 25.1
22 Sa	14 04 56	29 24 01	14 44 25	20 37 54	12 18.6	12 07.1	11 22.5	2 54.0	3 02.6	27D27.6	21 13.1	6 03.0	18 24.0	14 24.9
23 Su	14 08 53	0♏23 46	26 31 49	2♏26 24	12 17.5	11 15.7	12 37.3	3 32.4	3 21.1	27 27.5	21 14.2	6 02.4	18 22.3	14 24.8
24 M	14 12 50	1 23 32	8♏21 57	14 18 40	12 15.4	10 16.5	13 52.1	4 10.9	3 39.7	27 27.7	21 15.3	6 01.8	18 20.7	14 24.7
25 Tu	14 16 46	2 23 20	20 16 50	26 16 40	12 12.5	9 10.5	15 07.0	4 49.7	3 58.5	27 28.0	21 16.2	6 01.1	18 19.1	14 24.6
26 W	14 20 43	3 23 10	2♐18 26	8♐22 23	12 09.0	7 59.0	16 21.9	5 28.5	4 17.4	27 28.6	21 17.0	6 00.3	18 17.5	14 24.6
27 Th	14 24 39	4 23 02	14 28 47	20 37 55	12 05.4	6 43.9	17 36.8	6 07.5	4 36.4	27 29.3	21 17.8	5 59.5	18 15.9	14D24.5
28 F	14 28 36	5 22 56	26 50 05	3♑05 37	12 02.1	5 27.2	18 51.7	6 46.7	4 55.5	27 30.3	21 18.4	5 58.6	18 14.3	14 24.5
29 Sa	14 32 32	6 22 51	9♑24 50	15 48 04	11 59.6	4 11.3	20 06.7	7 26.0	5 14.8	27 31.4	21 18.8	5 57.7	18 12.7	14 24.6
30 Su	14 36 29	7 22 48	22 15 40	28 47 58	11D58.2	2 58.5	21 21.6	8 05.5	5 34.1	27 32.8	21 19.2	5 56.8	18 11.1	14 24.6
31 M	14 40 25	8 22 47	5♒25 19	12♒07 58	11 58.0	1 51.1	22 36.6	8 45.0	5 53.6	27 34.4	21 19.5	5 55.8	18 09.6	14 24.7

Astro Data	Planet Ingress	Last Aspect	☽ Ingress	Last Aspect	☽ Ingress	☽ Phases & Eclipses	Astro Data
Dy Hr Mn	Dy Hr Mn	Dy Hr Mn	Dy Hr Mn	Dy Hr Mn	Dy Hr Mn	Dy Hr Mn	1 September 2033
☿0S 7 17:44	☿ ♎ 7 3:49	31 7:43 ☿ ✶	♐ 1 6:57	30 20:45 ♃ ✶	♑ 1 0:00	2 2:24 ☽ 9♐57	Julian Day # 48822
☽0N 9 18:14	♃ ♒R 12 22:28	3 3:48 ☿ □	♑ 3 16:18	2 14:33 ♂ ☌	♒ 3 6:56	9 2:20 ○ 16♓44	SVP 4♓47'17"
♄□♆ 16 10:13	♀ ♍ 19 0:09	5 17:34 ☿ △	♒ 5 21:37	5 6:48 ♃ ☌	♓ 5 10:07	15 17:33 ☾ 23♊11	GC 27♐18.6 ⚵ 13♏19.9
☉0S 22 16:51	☉ ♎ 22 16:51	7 6:28 ♆ ✶	♓ 7 23:27	6 24:00 ♂ ✶	♈ 7 10:32	23 13:40 ● 0♎51	Eris 27♈27.3R ✵ 20♎17.8
☽0S 23 5:19	☿ ♏ 28 1:44	9 5:35 ♄ △	♈ 9 23:27	9 6:22 ♃ ✶	♉ 9 9:52	23 13:53:10 ✔ P 0.689	⚷ 1♊09.0 ⚶ 18♓06.8R
		11 8:26 ♀ △	♉ 11 23:28	11 6:18 ♃ □	♊ 11 10:04		☽ Mean ☊ 13♎52.3
☽0N 7 5:18	⚳ ♑ 12 4:53	14 1:00 ♃ □	♊ 14 1:13	13 8:45 ♃ △	♋ 13 12:54	1 16:33 ☽ 8♑49	
♅R 11 16:04	♀ ♎ 13 8:32	16 5:06 ♃ △	♋ 16 5:45	15 16:51 ♂ ☍	♌ 15 19:26	8 10:58 ○ 15♈29	1 October 2033
♀0S 16 4:20	♂ ♒ 17 21:52	18 5:05 ☉ ✶	♌ 18 13:24	18 0:37 ♃ ☍	♍ 18 5:33	8 10:55 ● T 1.350	Julian Day # 48852
☿R 16 22:03	☉ ♏ 23 2:27	20 22:02 ♃ ☍	♍ 20 23:44	20 0:02 ♄ ✶	♎ 20 17:59	15 4:47 ☾ 22♋09	SVP 4♓47'15"
☽0S 20 11:18		22 15:24 ♄ ✶	♎ 23 11:56	23 1:53 ♃ △	♏ 23 7:03	23 7:28 ● 0♏12	GC 27♐18.6 ⚵ 24♏17.0
♃D 23 7:19		25 22:19 ♃ △	♏ 26 1:00	25 14:22 ♃ □	♐ 25 19:25	31 4:46 ☽ 8♒05	Eris 27♈12.6R ✵ 0♏04.0
♇D 27 16:40		28 10:32 ♃ □	♐ 28 13:35	28 1:17 ♃ ✶	♑ 28 6:05		⚷ 0♊48.6R ⚶ 11♓15.7R
				29 22:15 ♄ ☍	♒ 30 14:11		☽ Mean ☊ 12♎17.0

November 2033

LONGITUDE

Day	Sid.Time	☉	0 hr ☽	Noon ☽	True ☊	☿	♀	♂	⚳	♃	♄	♅	♆	♇
1 Tu	14 44 22	9♏22 47	18♒56 11	25♒50 08	11♎58.8	0♏51.1	23♎51.7	9♒24.8	6♑13.2	27♒36.1	21♋19.6	5♋54.7	18♈08.1	14♒24.9
2 W	14 48 19	10 22 49	2♓49 56	9♓55 34	12 00.2	0R 00.2	25 06.7	10 04.6	6 32.8	27 38.1	21R 19.6	5R 53.6	18R 06.5	14 25.0
3 Th	14 52 15	11 22 52	17 06 53	24 23 37	12 01.7	29♎19.8	26 21.8	10 44.5	6 52.6	27 40.3	21 19.6	5 52.5	18 05.0	14 25.2
4 F	14 56 12	12 22 57	1♈45 19	9♈11 23	12R 02.5	28 50.6	27 36.8	11 24.6	7 12.5	27 42.6	21 19.4	5 51.3	18 03.5	14 25.4
5 Sa	15 00 08	13 23 04	16 41 04	24 13 25	12 02.0	28 33.0	28 51.9	12 04.7	7 32.5	27 45.2	21 19.1	5 50.0	18 02.0	14 25.6
6 Su	15 04 05	14 23 12	1♉47 23	9♉21 50	12 00.0	28D 26.9	0♏07.1	12 45.0	7 52.6	27 47.9	21 18.7	5 48.7	18 00.6	14 25.9
7 M	15 08 01	15 23 22	16 55 33	24 27 18	11 56.3	28 32.2	1 22.2	13 25.4	8 12.8	27 50.9	21 18.1	5 47.4	17 59.1	14 26.1
8 Tu	15 11 58	16 23 34	1♊55 56	9♊20 21	11 51.4	28 48.1	2 37.4	14 05.9	8 33.1	27 54.0	21 17.5	5 46.0	17 57.7	14 26.4
9 W	15 15 54	17 23 48	16 39 36	23 52 54	11 45.9	29 14.0	3 52.5	14 46.4	8 53.4	27 57.3	21 16.8	5 44.6	17 56.3	14 26.8
10 Th	15 19 51	18 24 04	0♋59 39	7♋59 25	11 40.5	29 49.0	5 07.7	15 27.1	9 13.9	28 00.9	21 15.9	5 43.1	17 54.9	14 27.2
11 F	15 23 48	19 24 21	14 52 01	21 37 24	11 36.1	0♏32.2	6 23.0	16 07.9	9 34.5	28 04.6	21 14.9	5 41.6	17 53.5	14 27.6
12 Sa	15 27 44	20 24 41	28 15 42	4♌47 11	11 33.1	1 22.7	7 38.2	16 48.7	9 55.1	28 08.5	21 13.8	5 40.1	17 52.2	14 28.0
13 Su	15 31 41	21 25 03	11♌12 14	17 31 21	11D 31.8	2 19.7	8 53.5	17 29.7	10 15.9	28 12.6	21 12.6	5 38.5	17 50.8	14 28.4
14 M	15 35 37	22 25 26	23 45 04	29 53 59	11 32.0	3 22.3	10 08.7	18 10.7	10 36.7	28 16.9	21 11.3	5 36.8	17 49.5	14 28.9
15 Tu	15 39 34	23 25 51	5♍58 45	11♍59 59	11 33.2	4 29.8	11 24.0	18 51.8	10 57.6	28 21.3	21 09.9	5 35.1	17 48.2	14 29.4
16 W	15 43 30	24 26 19	17 58 22	23 54 30	11 34.9	5 41.6	12 39.3	19 33.0	11 18.6	28 26.0	21 08.4	5 33.4	17 46.9	14 29.9
17 Th	15 47 27	25 26 48	29 49 00	5♎42 29	11R 36.1	6 57.0	13 54.6	20 14.3	11 39.7	28 30.8	21 06.8	5 31.7	17 45.7	14 30.5
18 F	15 51 23	26 27 19	11♎35 28	17 28 28	11 36.0	8 15.5	15 10.0	20 55.7	12 00.9	28 35.8	21 05.0	5 29.8	17 44.4	14 31.1
19 Sa	15 55 20	27 27 51	23 21 57	29 16 21	11 34.1	9 36.6	16 25.3	21 37.1	12 22.1	28 41.0	21 03.2	5 28.0	17 43.2	14 31.7
20 Su	15 59 17	28 28 25	5♏12 02	11♏09 19	11 30.0	10 59.9	17 40.7	22 18.6	12 43.5	28 46.4	21 01.2	5 26.1	17 42.1	14 32.3
21 M	16 03 13	29 29 01	17 08 29	23 09 45	11 23.7	12 25.1	18 56.1	23 00.2	13 04.9	28 51.9	20 59.2	5 24.2	17 40.9	14 33.0
22 Tu	16 07 10	0♐29 39	29 13 20	5♐19 22	11 15.3	13 51.8	20 11.5	23 41.9	13 26.4	28 57.6	20 57.0	5 22.3	17 39.8	14 33.7
23 W	16 11 06	1 30 17	11♐27 57	17 39 13	11 05.7	15 19.8	21 26.8	24 23.6	13 47.9	29 03.5	20 54.8	5 20.3	17 38.7	14 34.4
24 Th	16 15 03	2 30 58	23 53 12	0♑10 00	10 55.7	16 48.9	22 42.3	25 05.4	14 09.6	29 09.6	20 52.4	5 18.2	17 37.6	14 35.1
25 F	16 18 59	3 31 39	6♑29 39	12 52 14	10 46.3	18 18.8	23 57.7	25 47.3	14 31.3	29 15.8	20 49.9	5 16.2	17 36.5	14 35.9
26 Sa	16 22 56	4 32 22	19 17 49	25 46 29	10 38.5	19 49.5	25 13.1	26 29.2	14 53.0	29 22.3	20 47.4	5 14.1	17 35.5	14 36.7
27 Su	16 26 52	5 33 05	2♒18 22	8♒53 36	10 32.8	21 20.7	26 28.5	27 11.2	15 14.9	29 28.8	20 44.7	5 12.0	17 34.5	14 37.5
28 M	16 30 49	6 33 50	15 32 19	22 14 40	10 29.6	22 52.5	27 43.9	27 53.3	15 36.8	29 35.6	20 41.9	5 09.8	17 33.5	14 38.4
29 Tu	16 34 46	7 34 36	29 00 51	5♓51 00	10D 28.5	24 24.6	28 59.4	28 35.4	15 58.8	29 42.5	20 39.1	5 07.7	17 32.6	14 39.2
30 W	16 38 42	8 35 22	12♓45 16	19 43 44	10 28.9	25 57.0	0♐14.8	29 17.5	16 20.8	29 49.5	20 36.1	5 05.4	17 31.7	14 40.1

December 2033

LONGITUDE

Day	Sid.Time	☉	0 hr ☽	Noon ☽	True ☊	☿	♀	♂	⚳	♃	♄	♅	♆	♇
1 Th	16 42 39	9♐36 10	26♓46 27	3♈53 22	10♎29.7	27♏29.6	1♐30.3	29♒59.7	16♑42.9	29♒56.8	20♋33.1	5♋03.2	17♈30.8	14♒41.0
2 F	16 46 35	10 36 58	11♈04 20	18 19 05	10R 29.6	29 02.5	2 45.7	0♓42.0	17 05.0	0♓04.2	20R 30.0	5R 00.9	17R 29.9	14 42.0
3 Sa	16 50 32	11 37 47	25 37 15	2♉58 15	10 27.5	0♐35.5	4 01.2	1 24.2	17 27.2	0 11.7	20 26.7	4 58.7	17 29.1	14 43.0
4 Su	16 54 28	12 38 38	10♉21 26	17 45 58	10 22.9	2 08.6	5 16.6	2 06.6	17 49.5	0 19.4	20 23.4	4 56.3	17 28.3	14 43.9
5 M	16 58 25	13 39 29	25 10 56	2♊35 20	10 15.7	3 41.8	6 32.1	2 48.9	18 11.8	0 27.2	20 20.0	4 54.0	17 27.5	14 45.0
6 Tu	17 02 21	14 40 21	9♊58 06	17 18 11	10 06.1	5 15.1	7 47.5	3 31.3	18 34.2	0 35.2	20 16.6	4 51.7	17 26.8	14 46.0
7 W	17 06 18	15 41 14	24 34 37	1♋46 27	9 55.3	6 48.4	9 03.0	4 13.7	18 56.6	0 43.4	20 13.0	4 49.3	17 26.0	14 47.1
8 Th	17 10 15	16 42 09	8♋52 56	15 53 27	9 44.5	8 21.8	10 18.5	4 56.2	19 19.1	0 51.6	20 09.4	4 46.9	17 25.4	14 48.2
9 F	17 14 11	17 43 04	22 47 31	29 34 54	9 34.8	9 55.3	11 34.0	5 38.7	19 41.6	1 00.1	20 05.7	4 44.5	17 24.7	14 49.3
10 Sa	17 18 08	18 44 01	6♌15 29	12♌49 21	9 27.2	11 28.8	12 49.5	6 21.2	20 04.2	1 08.6	20 01.9	4 42.0	17 24.1	14 50.4
11 Su	17 22 04	19 44 59	19 16 43	25 37 57	9 22.0	13 02.4	14 05.0	7 03.8	20 26.9	1 17.4	19 58.0	4 39.6	17 23.5	14 51.6
12 M	17 26 01	20 45 57	1♍53 31	8♍03 56	9 19.3	14 36.0	15 20.5	7 46.4	20 49.5	1 26.2	19 54.0	4 37.1	17 23.0	14 52.7
13 Tu	17 29 57	21 46 57	14 09 50	20 11 52	9D 18.5	16 09.7	16 36.0	8 29.0	21 12.3	1 35.2	19 50.0	4 34.6	17 22.4	14 53.9
14 W	17 33 54	22 47 58	26 10 45	2♎07 09	9R 18.7	17 43.5	17 51.5	9 11.6	21 35.0	1 44.3	19 46.0	4 32.1	17 22.0	14 55.1
15 Th	17 37 50	23 49 00	8♎01 48	13 55 23	9 18.7	19 17.4	19 07.0	9 54.3	21 57.9	1 53.6	19 41.8	4 29.6	17 21.5	14 56.4
16 F	17 41 47	24 50 03	19 48 34	25 42 01	9 17.5	20 51.4	20 22.5	10 36.9	22 20.7	2 03.0	19 37.6	4 27.0	17 21.1	14 57.6
17 Sa	17 45 44	25 51 07	1♏36 20	7♏32 05	9 14.1	22 25.5	21 38.0	11 19.7	22 43.6	2 12.5	19 33.3	4 24.5	17 20.7	14 58.9
18 Su	17 49 40	26 52 12	13 29 46	19 29 50	9 07.9	23 59.7	22 53.5	12 02.4	23 06.6	2 22.2	19 29.0	4 22.0	17 20.3	15 00.2
19 M	17 53 37	27 53 17	25 32 40	1♐38 35	8 58.8	25 34.1	24 09.1	12 45.2	23 29.6	2 31.9	19 24.6	4 19.4	17 20.0	15 01.5
20 Tu	17 57 33	28 54 24	7♐47 49	14 00 33	8 47.0	27 08.6	25 24.6	13 27.9	23 52.6	2 41.8	19 20.1	4 16.8	17 19.7	15 02.9
21 W	18 01 30	29 55 31	20 16 51	26 36 47	8 33.6	28 43.3	26 40.1	14 10.7	24 15.7	2 51.9	19 15.6	4 14.3	17 19.5	15 04.2
22 Th	18 05 26	0♑56 38	3♑00 16	9♑27 13	8 19.5	0♑18.2	27 55.7	14 53.6	24 38.8	3 02.0	19 11.1	4 11.7	17 19.3	15 05.6
23 F	18 09 23	1 57 46	15 57 31	22 30 58	8 06.1	1 53.3	29 11.2	15 36.4	25 01.9	3 12.3	19 06.5	4 09.1	17 19.1	15 07.0
24 Sa	18 13 20	2 58 54	29 07 23	5♒46 35	7 54.6	3 28.6	0♑26.7	16 19.3	25 25.1	3 22.7	19 01.9	4 06.5	17 18.9	15 08.4
25 Su	18 17 16	4 00 03	12♒28 23	19 12 37	7 45.8	5 04.2	1 42.3	17 02.1	25 48.3	3 33.2	18 57.2	4 04.0	17 18.8	15 09.9
26 M	18 21 13	5 01 11	25 59 08	2♓47 52	7 40.2	6 39.9	2 57.8	17 45.0	26 11.6	3 43.8	18 52.5	4 01.4	17 18.7	15 11.3
27 Tu	18 25 09	6 02 20	9♓38 43	16 31 41	7 37.4	8 16.0	4 13.3	18 27.9	26 34.8	3 54.5	18 47.7	3 58.8	17D 18.7	15 12.8
28 W	18 29 06	7 03 28	23 26 45	0♈23 56	7 36.7	9 52.3	5 28.8	19 10.8	26 58.1	4 05.4	18 42.9	3 56.2	17 18.7	15 14.3
29 Th	18 33 02	8 04 37	7♈23 14	14 24 40	7 36.6	11 28.8	6 44.3	19 53.7	27 21.5	4 16.3	18 38.1	3 53.6	17 18.7	15 15.8
30 F	18 36 59	9 05 45	21 28 12	28 33 43	7 35.8	13 05.7	7 59.8	20 36.6	27 44.8	4 27.4	18 33.3	3 51.1	17 18.8	15 17.3
31 Sa	18 40 55	10 06 53	5♉41 05	12♉50 02	7 33.1	14 42.8	9 15.3	21 19.5	28 08.2	4 38.5	18 28.4	3 48.5	17 18.9	15 18.8

Astro Data

	Dy Hr Mn
♄ R	2 7:03
☽ 0N	3 15:58
☿ D	6 12:40
☽ 0S	16 18:13
☽ 0N	1 0:54
☽ 0S	14 2:54
♃∠♆	18 7:40
♃⚼♄	27 1:27
♃△♅	27 19:38
♆ D	28 7:35
☽ 0N	28 7:59

Planet Ingress

	Dy Hr Mn
☿ ♎R	2 12:07
♀ ♏	6 9:45
☿ ♏	10 18:34
☉ ♐	22 0:16
♀ ♐	30 7:17
♂ ♓	1 12:10
♃ ♓	1 22:34
☿ ♐	3 2:51
☉ ♑	21 13:46
☿ ♑	22 7:24
♀ ♑	24 3:30

Last Aspect / ☽ Ingress

Last Aspect Dy Hr Mn		☽ Ingress Dy Hr Mn
1 15:03 ♃ ☌	♓	1 19:10
3 6:58 ♄ △	♈	3 21:09
5 20:02 ♀ ☍	♉	5 21:10
7 17:27 ♃ □	♊	7 20:53
9 21:22 ☿ △	♋	9 22:19
11 11:20 ♄ ☌	♌	12 3:11
14 8:48 ♃ ☍	♍	14 12:12
16 13:10 ☉ ⚹	♎	17 0:22
19 10:48 ♃ △	♏	19 13:29
21 23:23 ♃ □	♐	22 1:32
24 10:04 ♃ ⚹	♑	24 11:41
26 10:52 ♀ ⚹	♒	26 19:46
29 1:08 ♃ ☌	♓	29 1:44

Last Aspect / ☽ Ingress

Last Aspect Dy Hr Mn		☽ Ingress Dy Hr Mn
30 23:54 ☿ △	♈	1 5:27
2 15:35 ♄ □	♉	3 7:09
4 16:14 ♄ ⚹	♊	5 7:48
6 12:14 ♆ ⚹	♋	7 9:02
8 19:22 ♄ ☌	♌	9 12:45
10 23:55 ☉ △	♍	11 20:21
13 15:28 ☉ □	♎	14 7:43
16 10:04 ☉ ⚹	♏	16 20:44
18 11:58 ♄ △	♐	19 8:47
21 16:32 ☿ ☌	♑	21 18:22
23 5:49 ♄ ☍	♒	24 1:35
25 8:38 ♆ ⚹	♓	26 7:05
27 15:55 ♄ △	♈	28 11:19
29 19:09 ♄ □	♉	30 14:26

☽ Phases & Eclipses

Dy Hr Mn	
6 20:32	○ 14♉45
13 20:09	☾ 21♌46
22 1:39	● 0♐03
29 15:15	☽ 7♓43
6 7:22	○ 14♊29
13 15:28	☾ 21♍56
21 18:46	● 0♑13
29 0:20	☽ 7♈35

Astro Data

1 November 2033
Julian Day # 48883
SVP 4♓47'12"
GC 27♐18.7 ⚴ 6♐42.3
Eris 26♈54.2R ⚵ 10♏38.0
⚷ 29♉35.8R ⚶ 9♓45.2
☽ Mean ☊ 10♎38.5

1 December 2033
Julian Day # 48913
SVP 4♓47'08"
GC 27♐18.8 ⚴ 19♐11.5
Eris 26♈38.5R ⚵ 20♏50.4
⚷ 28♉01.1R ⚶ 14♓35.1
☽ Mean ☊ 9♎03.1

LONGITUDE — January 2034

Day	Sid.Time	☉	0 hr ☽	Noon☽	True☊	☿	♀	♂	⚳	♃	♄	♅	♆	♇
1 Su	18 44 52	11♑08 01	20♉00 14	27♉11 14	7♎27.7	16♑20.3	10♑30.8	22♓02.4	28♑31.6	4♓49.8	18♋23.5	3♋45.9	17♈19.0	15♒20.4
2 M	18 48 49	12 09 09	4♊22 31	11♊33 27	7R19.2	17 58.0	11 46.3	22 45.3	28 55.0	5 01.1	18R18.6	3R43.4	17 19.2	15 21.9
3 Tu	18 52 45	13 10 17	18 43 20	25 51 27	7 08.2	19 35.9	13 01.8	23 28.2	29 18.5	5 12.6	18 13.7	3 40.8	17 19.4	15 23.5
4 W	18 56 42	14 11 25	2♋57 03	9♋59 23	6 55.7	21 14.2	14 17.3	24 11.1	29 42.0	5 24.2	18 08.8	3 38.3	17 19.6	15 25.1
5 Th	19 00 38	15 12 33	16 57 49	23 51 44	6 42.9	22 52.7	15 32.8	24 54.0	0♒05.4	5 35.8	18 03.8	3 35.8	17 19.9	15 26.7
6 F	19 04 35	16 13 41	0♌40 39	7♌24 12	6 31.2	24 31.4	16 48.3	25 36.9	0 29.0	5 47.5	17 58.9	3 33.3	17 20.2	15 28.3
7 Sa	19 08 31	17 14 49	14 02 09	20 34 25	6 21.6	26 10.4	18 03.7	26 19.8	0 52.5	5 59.4	17 53.9	3 30.8	17 20.5	15 30.0
8 Su	19 12 28	18 15 56	27 01 02	3♍22 11	6 14.7	27 49.5	19 19.2	27 02.7	1 16.0	6 11.3	17 48.9	3 28.3	17 20.9	15 31.6
9 M	19 16 24	19 17 04	9♍38 07	15 49 16	6 10.6	29 28.6	20 34.7	27 45.6	1 39.6	6 23.3	17 44.0	3 25.9	17 21.3	15 33.3
10 Tu	19 20 21	20 18 12	21 56 04	27 59 05	6D08.9	1♒07.9	21 50.1	28 28.5	2 03.2	6 35.4	17 39.0	3 23.4	17 21.7	15 34.9
11 W	19 24 18	21 19 20	3♎58 55	9♎56 13	6 08.7	2 47.0	23 05.6	29 11.3	2 26.8	6 47.6	17 34.1	3 21.0	17 22.2	15 36.6
12 Th	19 28 14	22 20 28	15 51 39	21 45 55	6R08.9	4 26.1	24 21.1	29 54.2	2 50.4	6 59.8	17 29.1	3 18.6	17 22.7	15 38.3
13 F	19 32 11	23 21 35	27 39 44	3♏33 48	6 08.4	6 04.8	25 36.5	0♈37.0	3 14.0	7 12.2	17 24.2	3 16.2	17 23.3	15 40.0
14 Sa	19 36 07	24 22 43	9♏28 47	15 25 22	6 06.2	7 43.2	26 52.0	1 19.9	3 37.7	7 24.6	17 19.3	3 13.8	17 23.8	15 41.7
15 Su	19 40 04	25 23 50	21 24 10	27 25 46	6 01.6	9 20.9	28 07.4	2 02.7	4 01.3	7 37.1	17 14.4	3 11.5	17 24.5	15 43.4
16 M	19 44 00	26 24 58	3♐30 41	9♐39 23	5 54.3	10 57.9	29 22.9	2 45.6	4 25.0	7 49.7	17 09.5	3 09.1	17 25.1	15 45.1
17 Tu	19 47 57	27 26 05	15 52 15	22 09 34	5 44.6	12 33.8	0♒38.3	3 28.4	4 48.7	8 02.4	17 04.7	3 06.8	17 25.8	15 46.9
18 W	19 51 53	28 27 12	28 31 33	4♑58 18	5 33.2	14 08.3	1 53.8	4 11.2	5 12.3	8 15.1	16 59.9	3 04.6	17 26.5	15 48.6
19 Th	19 55 50	29 28 18	11♑29 48	18 05 57	5 21.0	15 41.2	3 09.2	4 54.0	5 36.0	8 27.9	16 55.1	3 02.3	17 27.3	15 50.4
20 F	19 59 47	0♒29 24	24 46 33	1♒31 19	5 09.4	17 12.1	4 24.6	5 36.8	5 59.7	8 40.8	16 50.3	3 00.1	17 28.1	15 52.1
21 Sa	20 03 43	1 30 29	8♒19 54	15 11 52	4 59.3	18 40.4	5 40.0	6 19.6	6 23.4	8 53.8	16 45.6	2 57.9	17 28.9	15 53.9
22 Su	20 07 40	2 31 33	22 06 46	29 04 08	4 51.8	20 05.7	6 55.4	7 02.4	6 47.1	9 06.8	16 40.9	2 55.8	17 29.7	15 55.7
23 M	20 11 36	3 32 37	6♓03 30	13♓04 26	4 47.1	21 27.5	8 10.8	7 45.2	7 10.9	9 19.9	16 36.2	2 53.6	17 30.6	15 57.5
24 Tu	20 15 33	4 33 40	20 06 32	27 09 26	4D45.1	22 45.0	9 26.2	8 27.9	7 34.6	9 33.0	16 31.6	2 51.5	17 31.5	15 59.2
25 W	20 19 29	5 34 41	4♈12 50	11♈16 29	4 45.0	23 57.6	10 41.6	9 10.6	7 58.3	9 46.2	16 27.1	2 49.5	17 32.5	16 01.0
26 Th	20 23 26	6 35 42	18 20 11	25 23 47	4R45.7	25 04.5	11 57.0	9 53.4	8 22.0	9 59.5	16 22.6	2 47.4	17 33.4	16 02.8
27 F	20 27 22	7 36 41	2♉27 08	9♉30 08	4 46.1	26 05.0	13 12.3	10 36.0	8 45.7	10 12.8	16 18.1	2 45.4	17 34.5	16 04.6
28 Sa	20 31 19	8 37 39	16 32 39	23 34 34	4 45.0	26 58.1	14 27.6	11 18.7	9 09.4	10 26.2	16 13.7	2 43.5	17 35.5	16 06.4
29 Su	20 35 16	9 38 36	0♊35 43	7♊35 56	4 41.7	27 43.2	15 43.0	12 01.4	9 33.1	10 39.7	16 09.4	2 41.6	17 36.6	16 08.2
30 M	20 39 12	10 39 32	14 34 58	21 32 33	4 36.1	28 19.3	16 58.3	12 44.0	9 56.8	10 53.2	16 05.1	2 39.7	17 37.7	16 10.0
31 Tu	20 43 09	11 40 27	28 28 24	5♋22 09	4 28.4	28 45.7	18 13.6	13 26.6	10 20.5	11 06.7	16 00.9	2 37.8	17 38.8	16 11.9

LONGITUDE — February 2034

Day	Sid.Time	☉	0 hr ☽	Noon☽	True☊	☿	♀	♂	⚳	♃	♄	♅	♆	♇
1 W	20 47 05	12♒41 20	12♋13 27	19♋01 57	4♎19.4	29♒01.8	19♒28.9	14♈09.2	10♒44.2	11♓20.3	15♋56.7	2♋36.0	17♈40.0	16♒13.7
2 Th	20 51 02	13 42 12	25 47 17	2♌29 06	4R10.1	29R07.0	20 44.1	14 51.8	11 07.9	11 34.0	15R52.6	2R34.2	17 41.2	16 15.5
3 F	20 54 58	14 43 04	9♌07 09	15 41 10	4 01.6	29 01.1	21 59.4	15 34.3	11 31.5	11 47.7	15 48.6	2 32.5	17 42.4	16 17.3
4 Sa	20 58 55	15 43 54	22 10 59	28 36 31	3 54.6	28 44.1	23 14.6	16 16.8	11 55.2	12 01.4	15 44.6	2 30.8	17 43.7	16 19.1
5 Su	21 02 51	16 44 42	4♍57 44	11♍14 43	3 49.8	28 16.1	24 29.8	16 59.3	12 18.9	12 15.2	15 40.7	2 29.2	17 45.0	16 20.9
6 M	21 06 48	17 45 30	17 27 38	23 36 41	3D47.2	27 37.9	25 45.1	17 41.8	12 42.5	12 29.0	15 36.9	2 27.6	17 46.3	16 22.7
7 Tu	21 10 45	18 46 17	29 42 12	5♎44 34	3 46.6	26 50.3	27 00.3	18 24.2	13 06.1	12 42.9	15 33.2	2 26.0	17 47.6	16 24.6
8 W	21 14 41	19 47 03	11♎44 13	17 41 38	3 47.4	25 54.6	28 15.4	19 06.7	13 29.8	12 56.8	15 29.5	2 24.5	17 49.0	16 26.4
9 Th	21 18 38	20 47 48	23 37 23	29 32 03	3 49.0	24 52.3	29 30.6	19 49.1	13 53.4	13 10.8	15 25.9	2 23.0	17 50.4	16 28.2
10 F	21 22 34	21 48 31	5♏26 15	11♏20 37	3R50.5	23 45.3	0♓45.8	20 31.4	14 17.0	13 24.8	15 22.4	2 21.5	17 51.8	16 30.0
11 Sa	21 26 31	22 49 14	17 15 49	23 12 29	3 51.1	22 35.4	2 00.9	21 13.8	14 40.6	13 38.8	15 19.0	2 20.2	17 53.3	16 31.8
12 Su	21 30 27	23 49 56	29 11 18	5♐12 53	3 50.3	21 24.7	3 16.1	21 56.1	15 04.1	13 52.9	15 15.7	2 18.8	17 54.7	16 33.6
13 M	21 34 24	24 50 37	11♐17 51	17 26 47	3 47.7	20 14.9	4 31.2	22 38.4	15 27.7	14 07.0	15 12.4	2 17.5	17 56.2	16 35.4
14 Tu	21 38 20	25 51 16	23 40 11	29 58 32	3 43.6	19 07.9	5 46.3	23 20.7	15 51.2	14 21.2	15 09.3	2 16.3	17 57.8	16 37.2
15 W	21 42 17	26 51 54	6♑22 11	12♑51 25	3 38.1	18 05.1	7 01.4	24 02.9	16 14.7	14 35.3	15 06.2	2 15.1	17 59.3	16 39.0
16 Th	21 46 14	27 52 32	19 26 25	26 07 13	3 32.0	17 07.7	8 16.4	24 45.2	16 38.3	14 49.5	15 03.2	2 13.9	18 00.9	16 40.8
17 F	21 50 10	28 53 07	2♒53 47	9♒45 52	3 26.0	16 16.7	9 31.5	25 27.4	17 01.7	15 03.8	15 00.3	2 12.8	18 02.5	16 42.6
18 Sa	21 54 07	29 53 42	16 43 11	23 45 15	3 20.9	15 32.7	10 46.5	26 09.5	17 25.2	15 18.0	14 57.6	2 11.7	18 04.2	16 44.4
19 Su	21 58 03	0♓54 14	0♓51 32	8♓01 23	3 17.1	14 56.1	12 01.6	26 51.7	17 48.6	15 32.3	14 54.9	2 10.7	18 05.8	16 46.2
20 M	22 02 00	1 54 45	15 14 06	22 28 55	3D15.1	14 27.2	13 16.6	27 33.8	18 12.1	15 46.6	14 52.3	2 09.8	18 07.5	16 47.9
21 Tu	22 05 56	2 55 15	29 45 06	7♈01 53	3 14.8	14 05.9	14 31.5	28 15.9	18 35.4	16 01.0	14 49.8	2 08.9	18 09.2	16 49.7
22 W	22 09 53	3 55 43	14♈18 36	21 34 35	3 15.7	13 52.0	15 46.5	28 58.0	18 58.8	16 15.3	14 47.4	2 08.0	18 10.9	16 51.4
23 Th	22 13 49	4 56 08	28 49 15	6♉02 07	3 17.1	13D45.4	17 01.4	29 40.1	19 22.1	16 29.7	14 45.1	2 07.2	18 12.7	16 53.2
24 F	22 17 46	5 56 32	13♉12 47	20 20 54	3 18.5	13 45.7	18 16.3	0♉22.1	19 45.5	16 44.1	14 42.9	2 06.4	18 14.5	16 54.9
25 Sa	22 21 42	6 56 55	27 26 12	4♊28 29	3R19.3	13 52.5	19 31.2	1 04.1	20 08.7	16 58.5	14 40.8	2 05.7	18 16.3	16 56.6
26 Su	22 25 39	7 57 15	11♊27 39	18 23 34	3 18.9	14 05.6	20 46.1	1 46.0	20 32.0	17 12.9	14 38.8	2 05.1	18 18.1	16 58.4
27 M	22 29 36	8 57 33	25 16 11	2♋05 28	3 17.3	14 24.4	22 00.9	2 27.9	20 55.2	17 27.4	14 37.0	2 04.5	18 19.9	17 00.1
28 Tu	22 33 32	9 57 49	8♋51 23	15 33 57	3 14.7	14 48.7	23 15.7	3 09.8	21 18.4	17 41.8	14 35.2	2 03.9	18 21.8	17 01.8

Astro Data

	Dy Hr Mn
☽ 0S	10 12:53
♂ 0N	13 15:55
♄□♆	13 16:06
☽ 0N	24 14:45
♄⊼♇	29 16:26
☿ R	2 11:22
☽ 0S	6 22:37
♃△♄	17 7:11
☽ 0N	20 22:59
☿ D	23 22:55
♃⊻♇	25 8:28

Planet Ingress

	Dy Hr Mn
⚳ ♒	5 6:26
☿ ♒	9 19:35
♂ ♈	12 15:15
♀ ♒	16 23:48
☉ ♒	20 0:27
♀ ♓	9 21:23
☉ ♓	18 14:30
♂ ♉	23 23:24

Last Aspect / ☽ Ingress

Last Aspect Dy Hr Mn		☽ Ingress Dy Hr Mn
1 2:57	♂ ⚹	♊ 1 16:42
3 7:46	♂ □	♋ 3 19:00
5 13:55	♂ △	♌ 5 22:48
7 6:03	♆ △	♍ 8 5:37
10 13:02	♂ ☍	♎ 10 16:01
12 17:53	♀ □	♏ 13 4:45
15 13:32	♀ ⚹	♐ 15 17:05
17 2:59	♆ △	♑ 18 2:45
19 10:50	♆ □	♒ 20 9:18
21 18:45	☿ ☌	♓ 22 13:36
23 18:00	♄ △	♈ 24 16:50
26 11:25	☿ ⚹	♉ 26 19:50
28 18:09	☿ □	♊ 28 22:59
31 0:10	☿ △	♋ 31 2:39

Last Aspect / ☽ Ingress

Last Aspect Dy Hr Mn		☽ Ingress Dy Hr Mn
1 9:35	♆ □	♌ 2 7:32
4 12:14	☿ ☍	♍ 4 14:37
5 20:30	♄ ⚹	♎ 7 0:35
9 11:57	♀ △	♏ 9 12:57
11 11:09	☉ □	♐ 12 1:37
14 3:30	☉ ⚹	♑ 14 12:03
16 9:25	♂ □	♒ 16 18:53
18 16:17	♂ ⚹	♓ 18 22:33
20 0:43	♃ ☌	♈ 21 0:25
23 0:52	♂ ☌	♉ 23 1:57
24 8:10	♀ ⚹	♊ 25 4:22
26 16:33	♀ □	♋ 27 8:19

☽ Phases & Eclipses

Dy Hr Mn	
4 19:47	○ 14♋31
12 13:17	☾ 22♎24
20 10:01	● 0♒24
27 8:32	☽ 7♉28
3 10:04	○ 14♌38
11 11:09	☾ 22♏47
18 23:10	● 0♓22
25 16:34	☽ 7♊08

Astro Data

1 January 2034
Julian Day # 48944
SVP 4♓47'03"
GC 27♐18.9 ⚳ 2♑04.0
Eris 26♈29.4R ⚵ 0♐49.6
⚷ 26♉37.5R ⚶ 23♓52.8
☽ Mean ☊ 7♎24.7

1 February 2034
Julian Day # 48975
SVP 4♓46'58"
GC 27♐18.9 ⚳ 14♑23.8
Eris 26♈30.5 ⚵ 9♐31.6
⚷ 26♉03.0R ⚶ 5♈38.8
☽ Mean ☊ 5♎46.2

March 2034 — LONGITUDE

Day	Sid.Time	☉	0 hr ☽	Noon ☽	True ☊	☿	♀	♂	⚳	♃	♄	♅	♆	♇
1 W	22 37 29	10♓58 03	22♋13 09	28♋48 59	3♎11.4	15♒18.0	24♓30.5	3♉51.7	21♒41.5	17♓56.3	14♋33.5	2♋03.5	18♈23.7	17♒03.5
2 Th	22 41 25	11 58 15	5♌21 28	11♌50 35	3R 08.0	15 52.0	25 45.3	4 33.5	22 04.7	18 10.8	14R 32.0	2R 03.0	18 25.6	17 05.2
3 F	22 45 22	12 58 25	18 16 23	24 38 52	3 04.8	16 30.4	27 00.0	5 15.3	22 27.7	18 25.3	14 30.5	2 02.6	18 27.5	17 06.8
4 Sa	22 49 18	13 58 33	0♍58 05	7♍14 07	3 02.4	17 12.8	28 14.7	5 57.1	22 50.8	18 39.8	14 29.2	2 02.3	18 29.4	17 08.5
5 Su	22 53 15	14 58 39	13 27 02	19 36 57	3 00.8	17 59.0	29 29.4	6 38.8	23 13.8	18 54.3	14 28.0	2 02.0	18 31.3	17 10.1
6 M	22 57 11	15 58 44	25 44 01	1♎48 27	3D 00.3	18 48.7	0♈44.0	7 20.5	23 36.8	19 08.8	14 26.8	2 01.8	18 33.3	17 11.8
7 Tu	23 01 08	16 58 47	7♎50 26	13 50 15	3 00.6	19 41.6	1 58.6	8 02.1	23 59.7	19 23.3	14 25.8	2 01.6	18 35.3	17 13.4
8 W	23 05 05	17 58 48	19 48 11	25 44 37	3 01.6	20 37.6	3 13.2	8 43.8	24 22.6	19 37.8	14 24.9	2 01.5	18 37.3	17 15.0
9 Th	23 09 01	18 58 47	1♏39 55	7♏34 30	3 02.9	21 36.5	4 27.8	9 25.4	24 45.5	19 52.3	14 24.1	2D 01.4	18 39.3	17 16.6
10 F	23 12 58	19 58 45	13 28 51	19 23 27	3 04.2	22 38.0	5 42.4	10 06.9	25 08.3	20 06.9	14 23.4	2 01.4	18 41.3	17 18.2
11 Sa	23 16 54	20 58 41	25 18 49	1♐15 30	3 05.3	23 42.0	6 56.9	10 48.5	25 31.1	20 21.4	14 22.9	2 01.4	18 43.4	17 19.8
12 Su	23 20 51	21 58 35	7♐14 06	13 15 10	3R 06.0	24 48.4	8 11.4	11 30.0	25 53.8	20 35.9	14 22.4	2 01.5	18 45.5	17 21.3
13 M	23 24 47	22 58 28	19 19 18	25 27 05	3 06.1	25 57.0	9 25.8	12 11.5	26 16.5	20 50.4	14 22.1	2 01.7	18 47.5	17 22.9
14 Tu	23 28 44	23 58 19	1♑39 05	7♑55 50	3 05.8	27 07.7	10 40.3	12 52.9	26 39.1	21 04.9	14 21.8	2 01.9	18 49.6	17 24.4
15 W	23 32 40	24 58 08	14 17 51	20 45 33	3 05.1	28 20.5	11 54.7	13 34.3	27 01.8	21 19.5	14D 21.7	2 02.1	18 51.7	17 25.9
16 Th	23 36 37	25 57 56	27 19 19	3♒59 24	3 04.3	29 35.1	13 09.1	14 15.7	27 24.3	21 34.0	14 21.7	2 02.4	18 53.8	17 27.4
17 F	23 40 34	26 57 41	10♒45 59	17 39 04	3 03.5	0♓51.6	14 23.4	14 57.0	27 46.8	21 48.5	14 21.8	2 02.8	18 56.0	17 28.9
18 Sa	23 44 30	27 57 26	24 38 35	1♓44 15	3 02.8	2 09.8	15 37.7	15 38.4	28 09.3	22 03.0	14 22.0	2 03.2	18 58.1	17 30.4
19 Su	23 48 27	28 57 08	8♓55 38	16 12 12	3 02.5	3 29.7	16 52.0	16 19.7	28 31.7	22 17.4	14 22.3	2 03.7	19 00.3	17 31.8
20 M	23 52 23	29 56 48	23 33 12	0♈57 49	3D 02.3	4 51.3	18 06.3	17 00.9	28 54.1	22 31.9	14 22.8	2 04.2	19 02.4	17 33.2
21 Tu	23 56 20	0♈56 26	8♈25 05	15 53 59	3 02.4	6 14.5	19 20.5	17 42.2	29 16.4	22 46.4	14 23.3	2 04.8	19 04.6	17 34.6
22 W	0 00 16	1 56 02	23 23 30	0♉52 33	3 02.5	7 39.1	20 34.8	18 23.4	29 38.6	23 00.8	14 24.0	2 05.4	19 06.8	17 36.0
23 Th	0 04 13	2 55 36	8♉20 09	15 45 22	3R 02.5	9 05.3	21 48.9	19 04.5	0♓00.8	23 15.2	14 24.7	2 06.1	19 09.0	17 37.4
24 F	0 08 09	3 55 08	23 07 23	0♊25 30	3 02.5	10 33.0	23 03.1	19 45.7	0 22.9	23 29.6	14 25.6	2 06.8	19 11.2	17 38.8
25 Sa	0 12 06	4 54 38	7♊39 08	14 47 53	3 02.4	12 02.1	24 17.2	20 26.8	0 45.0	23 44.0	14 26.6	2 07.6	19 13.4	17 40.1
26 Su	0 16 02	5 54 05	21 51 26	28 49 38	3D 02.3	13 32.7	25 31.2	21 07.8	1 07.0	23 58.4	14 27.7	2 08.5	19 15.6	17 41.4
27 M	0 19 59	6 53 30	5♋42 26	12♋29 54	3 02.3	15 04.7	26 45.3	21 48.9	1 29.0	24 12.8	14 29.0	2 09.4	19 17.8	17 42.7
28 Tu	0 23 56	7 52 52	19 12 08	25 49 21	3 02.5	16 38.0	27 59.2	22 29.9	1 50.9	24 27.1	14 30.3	2 10.3	19 20.1	17 44.0
29 W	0 27 52	8 52 12	2♌21 48	8♌49 45	3 02.9	18 12.8	29 13.2	23 10.8	2 12.7	24 41.4	14 31.7	2 11.3	19 22.3	17 45.3
30 Th	0 31 49	9 51 30	15 13 30	21 33 23	3 03.6	19 49.0	0♉27.1	23 51.8	2 34.5	24 55.7	14 33.3	2 12.4	19 24.5	17 46.5
31 F	0 35 45	10 50 46	27 49 41	4♍02 42	3 04.3	21 26.6	1 41.0	24 32.7	2 56.2	25 09.9	14 34.9	2 13.5	19 26.8	17 47.8

April 2034 — LONGITUDE

Day	Sid.Time	☉	0 hr ☽	Noon ☽	True ☊	☿	♀	♂	⚳	♃	♄	♅	♆	♇
1 Sa	0 39 42	11♈49 59	10♍12 46	16♍20 08	3♎05.0	23♓05.5	2♉54.8	25♉13.5	3♓17.8	25♓24.2	14♋36.7	2♋14.6	19♈29.0	17♒49.0
2 Su	0 43 38	12 49 10	22 25 06	28 27 55	3R 05.4	24 45.9	4 08.6	25 54.4	3 39.4	25 38.3	14 38.5	2 15.8	19 31.3	17 50.1
3 M	0 47 35	13 48 19	4♎28 51	10♎28 07	3 05.3	26 27.7	5 22.4	26 35.2	4 00.9	25 52.5	14 40.5	2 17.1	19 33.5	17 51.3
4 Tu	0 51 31	14 47 26	16 26 00	22 22 43	3 04.7	28 10.9	6 36.1	27 15.9	4 22.3	26 06.7	14 42.6	2 18.4	19 35.8	17 52.4
5 W	0 55 28	15 46 31	28 18 31	4♏13 40	3 03.4	29 55.5	7 49.8	27 56.6	4 43.7	26 20.8	14 44.8	2 19.7	19 38.1	17 53.5
6 Th	0 59 25	16 45 35	10♏08 27	16 03 09	3 01.5	1♈41.6	9 03.4	28 37.3	5 05.0	26 34.8	14 47.0	2 21.1	19 40.3	17 54.6
7 F	1 03 21	17 44 36	21 58 04	27 53 34	2 59.3	3 29.1	10 17.0	29 18.0	5 26.2	26 48.9	14 49.4	2 22.6	19 42.6	17 55.7
8 Sa	1 07 18	18 43 35	3♐49 59	9♐47 43	2 57.0	5 18.1	11 30.6	29 58.6	5 47.3	27 02.9	14 51.9	2 24.0	19 44.9	17 56.8
9 Su	1 11 14	19 42 33	15 47 11	21 48 49	2 54.8	7 08.5	12 44.1	0♊39.2	6 08.4	27 16.9	14 54.5	2 25.6	19 47.1	17 57.8
10 M	1 15 11	20 41 29	27 53 06	4♑00 31	2 53.2	9 00.5	13 57.6	1 19.8	6 29.4	27 30.8	14 57.2	2 27.2	19 49.4	17 58.8
11 Tu	1 19 07	21 40 23	10♑11 34	16 26 44	2D 52.4	10 53.9	15 11.0	2 00.3	6 50.3	27 44.7	15 00.0	2 28.8	19 51.7	17 59.8
12 W	1 23 04	22 39 15	22 46 33	29 11 29	2 52.5	12 48.8	16 24.5	2 40.8	7 11.1	27 58.6	15 02.9	2 30.5	19 53.9	18 00.7
13 Th	1 27 00	23 38 06	5♒41 59	12♒18 29	2 53.3	14 45.1	17 37.8	3 21.3	7 31.9	28 12.4	15 05.9	2 32.3	19 56.2	18 01.7
14 F	1 30 57	24 36 55	19 01 18	25 50 42	2 54.6	16 43.0	18 51.2	4 01.7	7 52.6	28 26.2	15 09.0	2 34.0	19 58.5	18 02.6
15 Sa	1 34 54	25 35 42	2♓46 50	9♓49 41	2 56.0	18 42.2	20 04.5	4 42.2	8 13.2	28 39.9	15 12.2	2 35.9	20 00.7	18 03.5
16 Su	1 38 50	26 34 27	16 59 08	24 14 51	2R 57.0	20 42.9	21 17.7	5 22.5	8 33.7	28 53.6	15 15.5	2 37.7	20 03.0	18 04.3
17 M	1 42 47	27 33 11	1♈36 21	9♈02 57	2 57.1	22 44.9	22 30.9	6 02.9	8 54.1	29 07.2	15 18.9	2 39.6	20 05.2	18 05.2
18 Tu	1 46 43	28 31 52	16 33 47	24 07 50	2 56.0	24 48.1	23 44.1	6 43.2	9 14.4	29 20.8	15 22.3	2 41.6	20 07.5	18 06.0
19 W	1 50 40	29 30 32	1♉43 57	9♉20 52	2 53.6	26 52.6	24 57.2	7 23.5	9 34.6	29 34.4	15 25.9	2 43.6	20 09.7	18 06.8
20 Th	1 54 36	0♉29 10	16 57 20	24 32 03	2 50.1	28 58.1	26 10.3	8 03.8	9 54.8	29 47.9	15 29.6	2 45.7	20 12.0	18 07.5
21 F	1 58 33	1 27 46	2♊03 50	9♊31 35	2 46.2	1♉04.6	27 23.4	8 44.0	10 14.8	0♈01.3	15 33.4	2 47.8	20 14.2	18 08.3
22 Sa	2 02 29	2 26 20	16 54 21	24 11 24	2 42.3	3 11.8	28 36.4	9 24.2	10 34.8	0 14.7	15 37.2	2 49.9	20 16.5	18 09.0
23 Su	2 06 26	3 24 51	1♋22 09	8♋26 15	2 39.1	5 19.7	29 49.4	10 04.4	10 54.6	0 28.0	15 41.2	2 52.1	20 18.7	18 09.7
24 M	2 10 23	4 23 11	15 23 29	22 13 52	2D 37.1	7 27.9	1♊02.3	10 44.6	11 14.4	0 41.3	15 45.2	2 54.3	20 20.9	18 10.3
25 Tu	2 14 19	5 21 48	28 57 31	5♌34 42	2 36.5	9 36.3	2 15.1	11 24.7	11 34.0	0 54.5	15 49.3	2 56.5	20 23.1	18 11.0
26 W	2 18 16	6 20 13	12♌05 47	18 31 10	2 37.1	11 44.5	3 27.9	12 04.8	11 53.6	1 07.7	15 53.5	2 58.8	20 25.3	18 11.6
27 Th	2 22 12	7 18 36	24 51 21	1♍06 50	2 38.5	13 52.3	4 40.7	12 44.8	12 13.0	1 20.8	15 57.8	3 01.2	20 27.5	18 12.2
28 F	2 26 09	8 16 57	7♍18 09	13 25 49	2 40.2	15 59.5	5 53.4	13 24.8	12 32.4	1 33.8	16 02.2	3 03.6	20 29.7	18 12.7
29 Sa	2 30 05	9 15 16	19 30 21	25 32 14	2R 41.4	18 05.6	7 06.1	14 04.8	12 51.6	1 46.8	16 06.7	3 06.0	20 31.9	18 13.3
30 Su	2 34 02	10 13 32	1♎31 56	7♎29 53	2 41.5	20 10.4	8 18.7	14 44.8	13 10.7	1 59.7	16 11.2	3 08.4	20 34.1	18 13.8

Astro Data

	Dy Hr Mn
♅♀♇	1 11:42
♃⊻♆	3 16:10
☽0S	6 6:49
♀0N	8 3:34
♅ D	10 6:48
♄ D	16 2:30
☽0N	20 9:06
☉0N	20 13:17
☽0S	2 13:23
☿0N	8 6:53
☽0N	16 20:06
☽0S	29 19:30

Planet Ingress

	Dy Hr Mn
♀ ♈	5 21:51
☿ ♓	16 19:52
☉ ♈	20 13:17
⚳ ♓	23 11:08
♀ ♉	30 3:12
☿ ♈	5 13:01
♂ ♊	8 12:49
☉ ♉	20 0:04
☿ ♉	20 23:46
♃ ♈	21 9:39
♀ ♊	23 15:30

Last Aspect / ☽ Ingress (March)

Last Aspect Dy Hr Mn		☽ Ingress Dy Hr Mn
1 3:20 ♀ △	♌	1 14:10
3 0:19 ♆ △	♍	3 22:09
5 10:35 ♃ ☍	♎	6 8:25
8 0:46 ☿ △	♏	8 20:37
10 19:13 ☿ □	♐	11 9:28
13 13:04 ☿ ⚹	♑	13 20:49
15 20:21 ☉ ⚹	♒	16 4:51
17 14:13 ♆ ⚹	♓	18 9:05
20 10:14 ☉ ☌	♈	20 10:27
21 18:01 ♀ ☌	♉	22 10:36
24 0:25 ♃ ⚹	♊	24 11:18
26 5:44 ♀ ⚹	♋	26 14:02
28 16:22 ♀ □	♌	28 19:39
30 16:39 ♂ □	♍	31 4:11

Last Aspect / ☽ Ingress (April)

Last Aspect Dy Hr Mn		☽ Ingress Dy Hr Mn
2 6:37 ♂ △	♎	2 15:03
4 6:22 ♆ ☍	♏	5 3:26
7 15:01 ♂ ☍	♐	7 16:16
9 23:01 ♃ □	♑	10 4:09
12 9:42 ♃ ⚹	♒	12 13:30
14 9:41 ☉ ⚹	♓	14 19:13
16 19:43 ♃ ☌	♈	16 21:24
18 19:26 ☉ ☌	♉	18 21:16
20 20:30 ♃ ⚹	♊	20 20:42
22 5:31 ♆ ⚹	♋	22 21:42
24 8:40 ♆ □	♌	25 1:53
26 15:36 ♆ △	♍	27 9:51
28 18:06 ☿ △	♎	29 20:56

☽ Phases & Eclipses

Dy Hr Mn	
5 2:10	○ 14♍34
13 6:44	☾ 22♐45
20 10:14	● 29♓52
20 10:17:25	● T 04'09"
27 1:18	☽ 6♋27
3 19:19	○ 14♎06
3 19:06	• A 0.855
11 22:45	☾ 22♑07
18 19:26	● 28♈50
25 11:35	☽ 5♌21

Astro Data

1 March 2034
Julian Day # 49003
SVP 4♓46'55"
GC 27♐19.0 ⚵ 24♑34.3
Eris 26♈40.1 ⚴ 15♐26.4
⚷ 26♉26.0 ⚶ 17♈24.4
☽ Mean ☊ 4♎17.2

1 April 2034
Julian Day # 49034
SVP 4♓46'52"
GC 27♐19.1 ⚵ 4♒02.7
Eris 26♈57.6 ⚴ 18♐34.0
⚷ 27♉46.1 ⚶ 1♉01.1
☽ Mean ☊ 2♎38.7

LONGITUDE — May 2034

Day	Sid.Time	☉	0 hr ☽	Noon ☽	True ☊	☿	♀	♂	⚳	♃	♄	♅	♆	♇
1 M	2 37 58	11♉11 47	13♎26 30	19♎22 08	2♎40.0	22♉13.6	9♊31.3	15♊24.7	13♓29.7	2♈12.6	16♋15.8	3♋10.9	20♈36.2	18♒14.3
2 Tu	2 41 55	12 10 00	25 17 07	1♏11 46	2R 36.7	24 14.8	10 43.8	16 04.6	13 48.6	2 25.4	16 20.6	3 13.4	20 38.4	18 14.7
3 W	2 45 51	13 08 12	7♏06 22	13 01 09	2 31.5	26 13.9	11 56.2	16 44.4	14 07.4	2 38.1	16 25.3	3 16.0	20 40.5	18 15.2
4 Th	2 49 48	14 06 21	18 56 23	24 52 15	2 24.7	28 10.5	13 08.6	17 24.3	14 26.1	2 50.7	16 30.2	3 18.6	20 42.6	18 15.6
5 F	2 53 45	15 04 29	0♐49 00	6♐46 50	2 16.9	0♊04.5	14 21.0	18 04.1	14 44.6	3 03.3	16 35.2	3 21.3	20 44.7	18 15.9
6 Sa	2 57 41	16 02 35	12 45 58	18 46 39	2 08.8	1 55.6	15 33.3	18 43.8	15 03.1	3 15.8	16 40.2	3 23.9	20 46.8	18 16.3
7 Su	3 01 38	17 00 40	24 49 08	0♑53 41	2 01.2	3 43.6	16 45.5	19 23.6	15 21.4	3 28.2	16 45.3	3 26.6	20 48.9	18 16.6
8 M	3 05 34	17 58 43	7♑00 35	13 10 12	1 54.8	5 28.4	17 57.7	20 03.3	15 39.6	3 40.6	16 50.5	3 29.4	20 51.0	18 16.9
9 Tu	3 09 31	18 56 45	19 22 50	25 38 53	1 50.3	7 09.9	19 09.9	20 43.0	15 57.7	3 52.9	16 55.7	3 32.1	20 53.1	18 17.2
10 W	3 13 27	19 54 46	1♒58 45	8♒22 51	1D 47.7	8 47.9	20 22.0	21 22.7	16 15.6	4 05.1	17 01.0	3 34.9	20 55.1	18 17.4
11 Th	3 17 24	20 52 45	14 51 35	21 25 21	1 47.0	10 22.4	21 34.0	22 02.3	16 33.4	4 17.2	17 06.4	3 37.8	20 57.1	18 17.7
12 F	3 21 20	21 50 43	28 04 34	4♓49 34	1 47.6	11 53.2	22 46.0	22 41.9	16 51.1	4 29.3	17 11.9	3 40.6	20 59.2	18 17.8
13 Sa	3 25 17	22 48 39	11♓40 37	18 37 56	1R 48.6	13 20.4	23 57.9	23 21.5	17 08.7	4 41.3	17 17.4	3 43.5	21 01.2	18 18.0
14 Su	3 29 14	23 46 35	25 41 35	2♈51 32	1 49.1	14 43.8	25 09.8	24 01.0	17 26.1	4 53.1	17 23.0	3 46.5	21 03.2	18 18.1
15 M	3 33 10	24 44 29	10♈07 32	17 29 12	1 48.1	16 03.4	26 21.6	24 40.6	17 43.4	5 04.9	17 28.7	3 49.4	21 05.1	18 18.3
16 Tu	3 37 07	25 42 22	24 55 55	2♉26 53	1 45.0	17 19.1	27 33.4	25 20.1	18 00.5	5 16.7	17 34.5	3 52.4	21 07.1	18 18.3
17 W	3 41 03	26 40 13	10♉01 08	17 37 30	1 39.6	18 30.9	28 45.1	25 59.6	18 17.5	5 28.3	17 40.3	3 55.4	21 09.0	18 18.4
18 Th	3 45 00	27 38 03	25 14 42	2♊51 25	1 32.2	19 38.7	29 56.8	26 39.1	18 34.4	5 39.8	17 46.1	3 58.5	21 10.9	18R 18.4
19 F	3 48 56	28 35 52	10♊26 18	17 58 01	1 23.8	20 42.5	1♋08.4	27 18.5	18 51.1	5 51.3	17 52.1	4 01.5	21 12.8	18 18.4
20 Sa	3 52 53	29 33 39	25 25 25	2♋47 27	1 15.2	21 42.2	2 19.9	27 57.9	19 07.6	6 02.7	17 58.1	4 04.6	21 14.7	18 18.4
21 Su	3 56 49	0♊31 25	10♋03 17	17 12 17	1 07.6	22 37.6	3 31.4	28 37.3	19 24.0	6 13.9	18 04.1	4 07.8	21 16.6	18 18.4
22 M	4 00 46	1 29 09	24 14 03	1♌08 25	1 01.9	23 28.9	4 42.8	29 16.7	19 40.2	6 25.1	18 10.3	4 10.9	21 18.4	18 18.3
23 Tu	4 04 43	2 26 52	7♌55 22	14 35 06	0 58.3	24 15.8	5 54.2	29 56.0	19 56.3	6 36.2	18 16.4	4 14.1	21 20.3	18 18.2
24 W	4 08 39	3 24 33	21 07 54	27 34 14	0D 56.8	24 58.3	7 05.5	0♋35.3	20 12.2	6 47.1	18 22.7	4 17.3	21 22.1	18 18.1
25 Th	4 12 36	4 22 12	3♍54 37	10♍09 38	0 56.8	25 36.4	8 16.7	1 14.6	20 28.0	6 58.0	18 29.0	4 20.5	21 23.8	18 17.9
26 F	4 16 32	5 19 50	16 19 54	22 26 03	0R 57.4	26 10.0	9 27.8	1 53.9	20 43.6	7 08.8	18 35.3	4 23.7	21 25.6	18 17.8
27 Sa	4 20 29	6 17 26	28 28 44	4♎28 34	0 57.5	26 39.0	10 38.9	2 33.1	20 59.0	7 19.4	18 41.7	4 27.0	21 27.4	18 17.5
28 Su	4 24 25	7 15 01	10♎26 11	16 22 08	0 56.3	27 03.3	11 49.9	3 12.3	21 14.3	7 30.0	18 48.2	4 30.3	21 29.1	18 17.3
29 M	4 28 22	8 12 34	22 16 59	28 11 13	0 53.0	27 23.0	13 00.8	3 51.5	21 29.3	7 40.5	18 54.7	4 33.6	21 30.8	18 17.1
30 Tu	4 32 18	9 10 07	4♏05 18	9♏59 37	0 47.0	27 38.0	14 11.7	4 30.6	21 44.2	7 50.8	19 01.2	4 36.9	21 32.4	18 16.8
31 W	4 36 15	10 07 38	15 54 32	21 50 23	0 38.5	27 48.3	15 22.5	5 09.8	21 59.0	8 01.1	19 07.9	4 40.2	21 34.1	18 16.5

LONGITUDE — June 2034

Day	Sid.Time	☉	0 hr ☽	Noon ☽	True ☊	☿	♀	♂	⚳	♃	♄	♅	♆	♇
1 Th	4 40 12	11♊05 08	27♏47 24	3♐45 51	0♎27.7	27♊54.0	16♋33.2	5♋48.9	22♓13.5	8♈11.2	19♋14.5	4♋43.6	21♈35.7	18♒16.1
2 F	4 44 08	12 02 36	9♐45 54	15 47 43	0R 15.5	27R 55.0	17 43.8	6 28.0	22 27.9	8 21.2	19 21.2	4 47.0	21 37.3	18R 15.8
3 Sa	4 48 05	13 00 04	21 51 26	27 57 11	0 02.8	27 51.5	18 54.4	7 07.0	22 42.1	8 31.1	19 28.0	4 50.4	21 38.9	18 15.4
4 Su	4 52 01	13 57 31	4♑05 06	10♑15 16	29♍50.7	27 43.6	20 04.8	7 46.1	22 56.1	8 40.9	19 34.8	4 53.8	21 40.5	18 15.0
5 M	4 55 58	14 54 57	16 27 50	22 42 57	29 40.3	27 31.5	21 15.2	8 25.1	23 09.9	8 50.6	19 41.6	4 57.2	21 42.0	18 14.6
6 Tu	4 59 54	15 52 23	29 00 46	5♒21 29	29 32.2	27 15.5	22 25.5	9 04.1	23 23.5	9 00.2	19 48.5	5 00.7	21 43.5	18 14.1
7 W	5 03 51	16 49 47	11♒45 19	18 12 31	29 26.9	26 55.7	23 35.8	9 43.1	23 36.9	9 09.6	19 55.4	5 04.1	21 45.0	18 13.6
8 Th	5 07 47	17 47 11	24 43 22	1♓18 07	29 24.1	26 32.5	24 45.9	10 22.0	23 50.1	9 19.0	20 02.4	5 07.6	21 46.5	18 13.1
9 F	5 11 44	18 44 35	7♓57 07	14 40 37	29D 23.3	26 06.4	25 56.0	11 01.0	24 03.1	9 28.2	20 09.4	5 11.1	21 47.9	18 12.6
10 Sa	5 15 41	19 41 57	21 28 54	28 22 12	29R 23.3	25 37.7	27 05.9	11 39.9	24 15.9	9 37.2	20 16.5	5 14.6	21 49.3	18 12.1
11 Su	5 19 37	20 39 20	5♈20 40	12♈24 22	29 22.9	25 06.9	28 15.8	12 18.8	24 28.5	9 46.2	20 23.6	5 18.1	21 50.7	18 11.5
12 M	5 23 34	21 36 41	19 33 15	26 47 08	29 21.0	24 34.6	29 25.7	12 57.7	24 40.9	9 55.0	20 30.7	5 21.6	21 52.1	18 10.9
13 Tu	5 27 30	22 34 03	4♉05 39	11♉28 16	29 16.7	24 01.3	0♌35.4	13 36.6	24 53.1	10 03.7	20 37.9	5 25.1	21 53.4	18 10.3
14 W	5 31 27	23 31 24	18 54 19	26 22 54	29 09.7	23 27.5	1 45.0	14 15.4	25 05.0	10 12.3	20 45.1	5 28.7	21 54.7	18 09.6
15 Th	5 35 23	24 28 44	3♊52 59	11♊23 28	29 00.3	22 53.9	2 54.6	14 54.2	25 16.7	10 20.7	20 52.3	5 32.2	21 56.0	18 09.0
16 F	5 39 20	25 26 04	18 53 07	26 20 44	28 49.4	22 20.9	4 04.0	15 33.1	25 28.2	10 29.0	20 59.6	5 35.8	21 57.2	18 08.3
17 Sa	5 43 17	26 23 24	3♋45 09	11♋05 17	28 38.2	21 49.3	5 13.4	16 11.9	25 39.5	10 37.2	21 06.9	5 39.3	21 58.5	18 07.6
18 Su	5 47 13	27 20 42	18 20 11	25 29 06	28 28.1	21 19.4	6 22.7	16 50.6	25 50.5	10 45.2	21 14.2	5 42.9	21 59.7	18 06.8
19 M	5 51 10	28 18 00	2♌31 28	9♌26 55	28 20.0	20 51.9	7 31.8	17 29.4	26 01.3	10 53.0	21 21.6	5 46.5	22 00.8	18 06.1
20 Tu	5 55 06	29 15 18	16 15 17	22 56 36	28 14.4	20 27.1	8 40.9	18 08.2	26 11.8	11 00.8	21 29.0	5 50.1	22 02.0	18 05.3
21 W	5 59 03	0♋12 34	29 31 01	5♍58 54	28 11.3	20 05.6	9 49.8	18 46.9	26 22.1	11 08.4	21 36.4	5 53.7	22 03.1	18 04.5
22 Th	6 02 59	1 09 50	12♍20 39	18 36 49	28D 10.1	19 47.6	10 58.7	19 25.6	26 32.1	11 15.8	21 43.9	5 57.3	22 04.1	18 03.7
23 F	6 06 56	2 07 05	24 47 58	0♎54 47	28R 10.0	19 33.4	12 07.4	20 04.3	26 41.9	11 23.1	21 51.3	6 00.9	22 05.2	18 02.9
24 Sa	6 10 52	3 04 19	6♎57 54	12 57 59	28 09.8	19 23.5	13 16.0	20 42.9	26 51.5	11 30.2	21 58.8	6 04.5	22 06.2	18 02.0
25 Su	6 14 49	4 01 33	18 55 44	24 51 48	28 08.4	19D 17.9	14 24.5	21 21.6	27 00.7	11 37.2	22 06.4	6 08.1	22 07.2	18 01.1
26 M	6 18 46	4 58 46	0♏46 48	6♏41 21	28 05.1	19 16.9	15 32.9	22 00.2	27 09.7	11 44.1	22 13.9	6 11.7	22 08.2	18 00.2
27 Tu	6 22 42	5 55 59	12 36 00	18 31 16	27 59.1	19 20.5	16 41.1	22 38.8	27 18.5	11 50.8	22 21.5	6 15.3	22 09.1	17 59.3
28 W	6 26 39	6 53 11	24 27 37	0♐25 26	27 50.6	19 28.9	17 49.3	23 17.4	27 27.0	11 57.3	22 29.1	6 18.9	22 10.0	17 58.4
29 Th	6 30 35	7 50 23	6♐25 07	12 26 55	27 39.8	19 42.2	18 57.2	23 56.0	27 35.2	12 03.7	22 36.7	6 22.5	22 10.9	17 57.5
30 F	6 34 32	8 47 35	18 31 05	24 37 49	27 27.4	20 00.2	20 05.1	24 34.6	27 43.1	12 09.9	22 44.3	6 26.1	22 11.7	17 56.5

Astro Data

	Dy Hr Mn
♃0N	2 23:19
♅Q♇	3 2:24
♃∠♇	6 12:58
♃□♅	7 8:01
☽0N	14 6:26
♇R	19 7:00
♄⚻♇	23 18:41
☽0S	27 2:32
☿R	2 5:23
☽0N	10 15:05
☽0S	23 11:08
♄□♆	25 15:05
☿D	26 5:23

Planet Ingress

	Dy Hr Mn
☿ ♊	5 11:03
♀ ♋	18 13:05
☉ ♊	20 22:57
♂ ♋	23 14:26
☊ ♍R	3 17:24
♀ ♌	12 23:49
☉ ♋	21 6:44

Last Aspect / ☽ Ingress (May)

Last Aspect Dy Hr Mn		☽ Ingress Dy Hr Mn
1 14:31	♆ ☍	♏ 2 9:34
4 19:57	☿ ☍	♐ 4 22:21
6 16:00	♆ △	♑ 7 10:14
9 2:52	♆ □	♒ 9 20:16
11 13:11	♂ △	♓ 12 3:26
13 21:55	♀ □	♈ 14 7:14
16 3:32	♀ ⚹	♉ 16 8:06
18 3:12	☉ ☌	♊ 18 7:30
20 3:45	♂ ☌	♋ 20 7:26
21 18:57	♆ □	♌ 22 10:00
24 6:52	☿ ⚹	♍ 24 16:35
26 19:43	☿ □	♎ 27 3:02
29 10:19	☿ △	♏ 29 15:41

Last Aspect / ☽ Ingress (June)

Last Aspect Dy Hr Mn		☽ Ingress Dy Hr Mn
31 6:28	♄ △	♐ 1 4:27
3 11:49	☿ ☍	♑ 3 16:01
5 10:03	♆ □	♒ 6 1:52
8 3:35	☿ △	♓ 8 9:38
10 9:36	♀ △	♈ 10 14:49
12 16:44	♀ □	♉ 12 17:18
14 2:54	♄ ⚹	♊ 14 17:47
16 10:26	☉ ☌	♋ 16 17:54
18 6:07	♆ □	♌ 18 19:40
21 0:26	☉ ⚹	♍ 21 0:53
22 18:05	♄ ⚹	♎ 23 10:12
25 6:26	♆ ☍	♏ 25 22:25
27 20:49	♂ △	♐ 28 11:09
30 7:13	♆ △	♑ 30 22:28

☽ Phases & Eclipses

Dy Hr Mn	
3 12:16	○ 13♏09
11 10:56	☾ 20♒50
18 3:12	● 27♉17
24 23:57	☽ 3♍53
2 3:54	○ 11♐43
9 19:44	☾ 19♓03
16 10:26	● 25♊22
23 14:35	☽ 2♎13

Astro Data

1 May 2034
Julian Day # 49064
SVP 4♓46'50"
GC 27♐19.1 ⚴ 10♒23.0
Eris 27♈17.2 ⚵ 16♐55.9R
⚷ 29♉41.2 ⚶ 14♉21.7
☽ Mean ☊ 1♎03.3

1 June 2034
Julian Day # 49095
SVP 4♓46'46"
GC 27♐19.2 ⚴ 12♒26.0R
Eris 27♈35.3 ⚵ 10♐56.0R
⚷ 1♊56.6 ⚶ 28♉01.0
☽ Mean ☊ 29♍24.8

July 2034

LONGITUDE

Day	Sid.Time	☉	0 hr ☽	Noon ☽	True ☊	☿	♀	♂	⚳	♃	♄	♅	♆	♇
1 Sa	6 38 28	9♋44 46	0♑47 14	6♑59 25	27♍14.5	20♊23.2	21♌12.8	25♋13.1	27♓50.8	12♈16.0	22♋51.9	6♋29.7	22♈12.5	17♒55.5
2 Su	6 42 25	10 41 57	13 14 27	19 32 19	27R 02.3	20 51.0	22 20.4	25 51.7	27 58.2	12 21.9	22 59.6	6 33.3	22 13.3	17R 54.5
3 M	6 46 21	11 39 09	25 53 01	2♒16 33	26 51.6	21 23.6	23 27.9	26 30.2	28 05.3	12 27.6	23 07.3	6 36.9	22 14.0	17 53.5
4 Tu	6 50 18	12 36 20	8♒42 55	15 12 04	26 43.4	22 01.0	24 35.2	27 08.7	28 12.1	12 33.2	23 14.9	6 40.5	22 14.7	17 52.5
5 W	6 54 15	13 33 31	21 44 03	28 18 53	26 38.0	22 43.2	25 42.4	27 47.2	28 18.6	12 38.6	23 22.6	6 44.1	22 15.4	17 51.4
6 Th	6 58 11	14 30 43	4♓56 37	11♓37 20	26 35.2	23 30.1	26 49.4	28 25.7	28 24.8	12 43.9	23 30.4	6 47.7	22 16.1	17 50.3
7 F	7 02 08	15 27 54	18 21 07	25 08 05	26D 34.4	24 21.5	27 56.2	29 04.2	28 30.7	12 49.0	23 38.1	6 51.2	22 16.7	17 49.2
8 Sa	7 06 04	16 25 06	1♈58 22	8♈52 02	26R 34.6	25 17.6	29 03.0	29 42.6	28 36.3	12 53.9	23 45.8	6 54.8	22 17.3	17 48.1
9 Su	7 10 01	17 22 19	15 49 12	22 49 53	26 34.6	26 18.2	0♍09.5	0♌21.1	28 41.6	12 58.6	23 53.6	6 58.4	22 17.8	17 47.0
10 M	7 13 57	18 19 32	29 54 03	7♉01 34	26 33.4	27 23.3	1 15.9	0 59.5	28 46.6	13 03.2	24 01.3	7 01.9	22 18.3	17 45.9
11 Tu	7 17 54	19 16 45	14♉12 14	21 25 43	26 30.0	28 32.8	2 22.2	1 37.9	28 51.3	13 07.6	24 09.1	7 05.5	22 18.8	17 44.8
12 W	7 21 50	20 13 59	28 41 32	5♊59 08	26 24.1	29 46.6	3 28.2	2 16.4	28 55.7	13 11.8	24 16.8	7 09.0	22 19.3	17 43.6
13 Th	7 25 47	21 11 14	13♊17 48	20 36 44	26 16.1	1♋04.7	4 34.2	2 54.8	28 59.7	13 15.8	24 24.6	7 12.6	22 19.7	17 42.4
14 F	7 29 44	22 08 29	27 55 05	5♋11 56	26 06.7	2 27.0	5 39.9	3 33.2	29 03.4	13 19.6	24 32.4	7 16.1	22 20.1	17 41.3
15 Sa	7 33 40	23 05 44	12♋26 24	19 37 34	25 57.0	3 53.4	6 45.5	4 11.6	29 06.8	13 23.3	24 40.2	7 19.6	22 20.5	17 40.1
16 Su	7 37 37	24 02 59	26 44 41	3♌47 03	25 48.1	5 23.9	7 50.9	4 50.0	29 09.8	13 26.8	24 48.0	7 23.1	22 20.8	17 38.9
17 M	7 41 33	25 00 15	10♌44 06	17 35 25	25 40.9	6 58.3	8 56.1	5 28.3	29 12.5	13 30.1	24 55.7	7 26.6	22 21.1	17 37.6
18 Tu	7 45 30	25 57 31	24 20 45	1♍00 00	25 36.0	8 36.5	10 01.1	6 06.7	29 14.9	13 33.2	25 03.5	7 30.1	22 21.3	17 36.4
19 W	7 49 26	26 54 48	7♍33 11	14 00 29	25D 33.4	10 18.3	11 05.9	6 45.1	29 16.9	13 36.1	25 11.3	7 33.5	22 21.6	17 35.2
20 Th	7 53 23	27 52 04	20 22 11	26 38 41	25 32.8	12 03.6	12 10.5	7 23.4	29 18.6	13 38.9	25 19.1	7 37.0	22 21.8	17 33.9
21 F	7 57 19	28 49 21	2♎50 26	8♎57 58	25 33.3	13 52.3	13 14.8	8 01.7	29 19.9	13 41.4	25 26.9	7 40.4	22 21.9	17 32.7
22 Sa	8 01 16	29 46 38	15 01 54	21 02 50	25R 34.2	15 44.0	14 19.0	8 40.0	29 20.9	13 43.8	25 34.6	7 43.8	22 22.1	17 31.4
23 Su	8 05 13	0♌43 55	27 01 25	2♏58 17	25 34.5	17 38.6	15 22.9	9 18.4	29 21.5	13 45.9	25 42.4	7 47.2	22 22.1	17 30.1
24 M	8 09 09	1 41 13	8♏54 07	14 49 31	25 33.5	19 35.6	16 26.6	9 56.7	29R 21.8	13 47.9	25 50.2	7 50.6	22 22.2	17 28.8
25 Tu	8 13 06	2 38 31	20 45 08	26 41 33	25 30.5	21 35.0	17 30.1	10 34.9	29 21.8	13 49.7	25 57.9	7 53.9	22R 22.2	17 27.6
26 W	8 17 02	3 35 49	2♐39 18	8♐38 55	25 25.5	23 36.3	18 33.3	11 13.2	29 21.4	13 51.3	26 05.6	7 57.3	22 22.2	17 26.3
27 Th	8 20 59	4 33 08	14 40 52	20 45 35	25 18.7	25 39.2	19 36.3	11 51.5	29 20.6	13 52.7	26 13.4	8 00.6	22 22.2	17 25.0
28 F	8 24 55	5 30 27	26 53 15	3♑04 19	25 10.5	27 43.3	20 39.0	12 29.8	29 19.5	13 53.9	26 21.1	8 03.9	22 22.1	17 23.6
29 Sa	8 28 52	6 27 47	9♑18 56	15 37 16	25 01.9	29 48.4	21 41.4	13 08.0	29 18.0	13 54.9	26 28.8	8 07.2	22 22.0	17 22.3
30 Su	8 32 48	7 25 08	21 59 21	28 25 14	24 53.6	1♌54.2	22 43.6	13 46.3	29 16.2	13 55.7	26 36.5	8 10.5	22 21.9	17 21.0
31 M	8 36 45	8 22 29	4♒54 50	11♒28 05	24 46.6	4 00.2	23 45.5	14 24.5	29 14.0	13 56.4	26 44.2	8 13.7	22 21.7	17 19.7

August 2034

LONGITUDE

Day	Sid.Time	☉	0 hr ☽	Noon ☽	True ☊	☿	♀	♂	⚳	♃	♄	♅	♆	♇
1 Tu	8 40 42	9♌19 51	18♒04 49	24♒44 53	24♍41.3	6♌06.3	24♍47.0	15♌02.8	29♓11.4	13♈56.8	26♋51.9	8♋16.9	22♈21.5	17♒18.3
2 W	8 44 38	10 17 14	1♓28 04	8♓14 11	24R 38.1	8 12.1	25 48.3	15 41.0	29R 08.5	13R 57.0	26 59.5	8 20.1	22R 21.3	17R 17.0
3 Th	8 48 35	11 14 38	15 03 00	21 54 20	24D 36.9	10 17.4	26 49.3	16 19.2	29 05.2	13 57.0	27 07.2	8 23.3	22 21.1	17 15.7
4 F	8 52 31	12 12 03	28 48 00	5♈43 49	24 37.3	12 22.1	27 49.9	16 57.4	29 01.6	13 56.9	27 14.8	8 26.5	22 20.8	17 14.3
5 Sa	8 56 28	13 09 30	12♈41 38	19 41 17	24 38.5	14 25.9	28 50.3	17 35.7	28 57.6	13 56.5	27 22.4	8 29.6	22 20.4	17 13.0
6 Su	9 00 24	14 06 57	26 42 38	3♉45 32	24R 39.7	16 28.8	29 50.3	18 13.9	28 53.2	13 55.9	27 29.9	8 32.7	22 20.1	17 11.6
7 M	9 04 21	15 04 26	10♉49 49	17 55 18	24 40.0	18 30.5	0♎49.9	18 52.1	28 48.5	13 55.2	27 37.5	8 35.8	22 19.7	17 10.3
8 Tu	9 08 17	16 01 56	25 01 46	2♊08 57	24 38.9	20 31.0	1 49.2	19 30.3	28 43.5	13 54.2	27 45.0	8 38.8	22 19.3	17 08.9
9 W	9 12 14	16 59 28	9♊16 32	16 24 09	24 36.2	22 30.2	2 48.2	20 08.5	28 38.0	13 53.1	27 52.6	8 41.8	22 18.8	17 07.6
10 Th	9 16 11	17 57 01	23 31 24	0♋37 49	24 32.1	24 28.0	3 46.8	20 46.7	28 32.3	13 51.7	28 00.1	8 44.8	22 18.3	17 06.2
11 F	9 20 07	18 54 36	7♋42 54	14 46 09	24 27.0	26 24.4	4 45.0	21 24.9	28 26.1	13 50.2	28 07.5	8 47.8	22 17.8	17 04.9
12 Sa	9 24 04	19 52 11	21 47 03	28 45 04	24 21.6	28 19.4	5 42.7	22 03.1	28 19.7	13 48.4	28 15.0	8 50.7	22 17.3	17 03.5
13 Su	9 28 00	20 49 48	5♌39 43	12♌30 36	24 16.6	0♍13.0	6 40.1	22 41.3	28 12.8	13 46.5	28 22.4	8 53.6	22 16.7	17 02.2
14 M	9 31 57	21 47 26	19 17 19	25 59 35	24 12.7	2 05.1	7 37.1	23 19.5	28 05.7	13 44.3	28 29.8	8 56.5	22 16.1	17 00.8
15 Tu	9 35 53	22 45 05	2♍37 13	9♍10 04	24 10.3	3 55.7	8 33.6	23 57.7	27 58.2	13 42.0	28 37.1	8 59.4	22 15.5	16 59.5
16 W	9 39 50	23 42 46	15 38 07	22 01 28	24D 09.3	5 44.8	9 29.7	24 35.9	27 50.4	13 39.4	28 44.4	9 02.2	22 14.8	16 58.1
17 Th	9 43 46	24 40 27	28 20 14	4♎34 41	24 09.7	7 32.5	10 25.3	25 14.1	27 42.2	13 36.7	28 51.7	9 05.0	22 14.1	16 56.8
18 F	9 47 43	25 38 10	10♎45 09	16 51 59	24 11.0	9 18.7	11 20.4	25 52.3	27 33.7	13 33.8	28 59.0	9 07.7	22 13.4	16 55.5
19 Sa	9 51 39	26 35 54	22 55 38	28 56 36	24 12.7	11 03.5	12 14.9	26 30.5	27 25.0	13 30.7	29 06.2	9 10.4	22 12.6	16 54.1
20 Su	9 55 36	27 33 38	4♏55 25	10♏52 38	24 14.3	12 46.9	13 09.0	27 08.7	27 15.9	13 27.4	29 13.4	9 13.1	22 11.8	16 52.8
21 M	9 59 33	28 31 24	16 48 50	22 44 39	24R 15.3	14 28.8	14 02.5	27 46.9	27 06.5	13 23.9	29 20.6	9 15.8	22 11.0	16 51.5
22 Tu	10 03 29	29 29 11	28 40 39	4♐37 28	24 15.3	16 09.4	14 55.4	28 25.0	26 56.8	13 20.2	29 27.7	9 18.4	22 10.2	16 50.2
23 W	10 07 26	0♍27 00	10♐35 40	16 35 51	24 14.2	17 48.5	15 47.8	29 03.2	26 46.9	13 16.4	29 34.8	9 20.9	22 09.3	16 48.9
24 Th	10 11 22	1 24 49	22 38 34	28 44 20	24 12.2	19 26.3	16 39.5	29 41.4	26 36.7	13 12.3	29 41.8	9 23.5	22 08.4	16 47.6
25 F	10 15 19	2 22 40	4♑53 36	11♑06 48	24 09.5	21 02.7	17 30.6	0♍19.6	26 26.2	13 08.1	29 48.8	9 26.0	22 07.5	16 46.3
26 Sa	10 19 15	3 20 32	17 24 17	23 46 20	24 06.4	22 37.7	18 21.0	0 57.7	26 15.4	13 03.8	29 55.7	9 28.5	22 06.5	16 45.0
27 Su	10 23 12	4 18 25	0♒13 09	6♒44 51	24 03.4	24 11.4	19 10.7	1 35.9	26 04.4	12 59.2	0♌02.7	9 30.9	22 05.6	16 43.7
28 M	10 27 08	5 16 20	13 21 29	20 02 58	24 00.8	25 43.7	19 59.7	2 14.1	25 53.2	12 54.5	0 09.5	9 33.3	22 04.6	16 42.4
29 Tu	10 31 05	6 14 16	26 49 09	3♓39 49	23 59.1	27 14.7	20 48.0	2 52.3	25 41.7	12 49.6	0 16.3	9 35.6	22 03.5	16 41.2
30 W	10 35 02	7 12 14	10♓34 37	17 33 11	23D 58.3	28 44.3	21 35.4	3 30.4	25 30.1	12 44.5	0 23.1	9 37.9	22 02.5	16 39.9
31 Th	10 38 58	8 10 13	24 35 05	1♈39 48	23 58.3	0♎12.6	22 22.1	4 08.6	25 18.2	12 39.3	0 29.8	9 40.2	22 01.4	16 38.7

Astro Data Dy Hr Mn	Planet Ingress Dy Hr Mn	Last Aspect Dy Hr Mn	☽ Ingress Dy Hr Mn	Last Aspect Dy Hr Mn	☽ Ingress Dy Hr Mn	☽ Phases & Eclipses Dy Hr Mn
☽0N 7 22:05	♂ ♌ 8 22:51	3 0:36 ♂ ☍	♒ 3 7:44	1 7:43 ♆ ✶	♓ 1 21:23	1 17:44 ○ 9♑58
☽0S 20 20:44	♀ ♍ 9 8:34	5 6:49 ♀ ☍	♓ 5 15:04	3 21:14 ♀ ☍	♈ 4 2:05	9 1:59 ☾ 16♈58
⚳R 24 19:53	☿ ♋ 12 16:13	7 19:15 ♂ △	♈ 7 20:33	6 1:15 ♄ □	♉ 6 5:36	15 18:15 ● 23♋21
♆R 25 22:30	☉ ♌ 22 17:36	9 18:23 ☿ ✶	♉ 10 0:10	8 4:31 ♄ ✶	♊ 8 8:23	23 7:05 ☽ 0♏32
	☿ ♌ 29 14:13	11 16:33 ♄ ✶	♊ 12 2:09	9 23:56 ☿ ✶	♋ 10 10:56	31 5:54 ○ 8♒08
♃R 3 3:41		13 14:49 ♆ ✶	♋ 14 3:26	12 11:08 ♄ ☌	♌ 12 14:10	
☽0N 4 4:32	♀ ♎ 6 15:54	15 20:34 ♄ ☌	♌ 16 5:32	14 6:58 ♂ ☌	♍ 14 19:14	7 6:50 ☾ 14♉52
♀0S 5 11:31	☿ ♍ 13 9:14	17 20:27 ♆ △	♍ 18 10:11	17 0:54 ♄ ✶	♎ 17 3:11	14 3:53 ● 21♌28
☽0S 17 6:11	☉ ♍ 23 0:48	20 14:33 ☉ ✶	♎ 20 18:29	19 12:19 ♄ □	♏ 19 14:07	22 0:43 ☽ 29♏02
☿0S 30 22:34	♂ ♍ 24 23:42	22 21:11 ♄ □	♏ 23 6:00	22 1:29 ♄ △	♐ 22 2:40	29 16:49 ○ 6♓26
☽0N 31 11:56	♄ ♌ 27 2:46	25 10:31 ♄ △	♐ 25 18:40	24 13:58 ♂ △	♑ 24 14:28	
	☿ ♎ 31 8:33	27 15:10 ♆ △	♑ 28 6:03	26 23:34 ♄ ☍	♒ 26 23:36	
		30 8:36 ♄ ☍	♒ 30 14:56	28 15:36 ♆ ✶	♓ 29 5:36	
				29 22:20 ♅ △	♈ 31 9:11	

Astro Data

1 July 2034
Julian Day # 49125
SVP 4♓46'41"
GC 27♐19.3 ⚴ 8♒46.1R
Eris 27♈46.4 ⚵ 4♐57.6R
⚷ 4♊01.1 ⚶ 10♊50.4
☽ Mean ☊ 27♍49.5

1 August 2034
Julian Day # 49156
SVP 4♓46'36"
GC 27♐19.3 ⚴ 0♒52.6R
Eris 27♈48.8R ⚵ 2♐57.9
⚷ 5♊40.9 ⚶ 23♊21.8
☽ Mean ☊ 26♍11.0

LONGITUDE — September 2034

Day	Sid.Time	☉	0 hr ☽	Noon ☽	True ☊	☿	♀	♂	⚳	♃	♄	♅	♆	♇
1 F	10 42 55	9♍08 14	8♈46 50	15♈55 38	23♍59.0	1♎39.5	23♎08.0	4♍46.8	25♓06.1	12♈34.0	0♌36.5	9♋42.4	22♈00.3	16♒37.5
2 Sa	10 46 51	10 06 17	23 05 41	0♉16 27	24 00.0	3 05.0	23 53.0	5 25.0	24R53.9	12R28.4	0 43.2	9 44.6	21R59.2	16R36.2
3 Su	10 50 48	11 04 22	7♉27 27	14 38 13	24 01.0	4 29.1	24 37.1	6 03.2	24 41.4	12 22.7	0 49.7	9 46.8	21 58.0	16 35.0
4 M	10 54 44	12 02 28	21 48 19	28 57 22	24 01.7	5 51.7	25 20.3	6 41.3	24 28.8	12 16.9	0 56.3	9 48.9	21 56.9	16 33.8
5 Tu	10 58 41	13 00 37	6♊05 00	13♊10 57	24R02.0	7 12.9	26 02.6	7 19.5	24 16.1	12 10.9	1 02.8	9 51.0	21 55.7	16 32.6
6 W	11 02 37	13 58 48	20 14 54	27 16 38	24 01.7	8 32.6	26 43.8	7 57.7	24 03.2	12 04.8	1 09.2	9 53.0	21 54.4	16 31.5
7 Th	11 06 34	14 57 01	4♋15 55	11♋12 35	24 01.1	9 50.8	27 24.0	8 35.9	23 50.2	11 58.5	1 15.6	9 55.0	21 53.2	16 30.3
8 F	11 10 31	15 55 16	18 06 27	24 57 21	24 00.2	11 07.3	28 03.2	9 14.2	23 37.1	11 52.1	1 21.9	9 56.9	21 51.9	16 29.2
9 Sa	11 14 27	16 53 33	1♌45 10	8♌29 45	23 59.3	12 22.2	28 41.2	9 52.4	23 23.9	11 45.6	1 28.1	9 58.8	21 50.6	16 28.0
10 Su	11 18 24	17 51 52	15 11 00	21 48 49	23 58.5	13 35.4	29 18.1	10 30.6	23 10.6	11 39.0	1 34.4	10 00.6	21 49.3	16 26.9
11 M	11 22 20	18 50 12	28 23 07	4♍53 51	23 58.0	14 46.8	29 53.7	11 08.8	22 57.3	11 32.2	1 40.5	10 02.5	21 48.0	16 25.8
12 Tu	11 26 17	19 48 35	11♍21 01	17 44 35	23D57.7	15 56.3	0♏28.2	11 47.0	22 43.9	11 25.3	1 46.6	10 04.2	21 46.7	16 24.7
13 W	11 30 13	20 46 59	24 04 37	0♎21 10	23 57.7	17 03.9	1 01.3	12 25.3	22 30.4	11 18.3	1 52.6	10 05.9	21 45.3	16 23.7
14 Th	11 34 10	21 45 25	6♎34 23	12 44 24	23 57.8	18 09.3	1 33.0	13 03.5	22 17.0	11 11.2	1 58.5	10 07.6	21 43.9	16 22.6
15 F	11 38 06	22 43 53	18 51 26	24 55 44	23 58.0	19 12.5	2 03.3	13 41.8	22 03.5	11 04.0	2 04.4	10 09.2	21 42.5	16 21.6
16 Sa	11 42 03	23 42 23	0♏57 35	6♏57 20	23R58.1	20 13.3	2 32.2	14 20.0	21 50.1	10 56.7	2 10.3	10 10.8	21 41.1	16 20.5
17 Su	11 46 00	24 40 54	12 55 21	18 52 04	23 58.0	21 11.6	2 59.5	14 58.2	21 36.6	10 49.3	2 16.0	10 12.3	21 39.6	16 19.5
18 M	11 49 56	25 39 27	24 47 56	0♐43 26	23 57.9	22 07.1	3 25.3	15 36.5	21 23.2	10 41.8	2 21.7	10 13.8	21 38.2	16 18.5
19 Tu	11 53 53	26 38 02	6♐39 06	12 35 28	23 57.7	22 59.8	3 49.4	16 14.8	21 09.9	10 34.2	2 27.3	10 15.2	21 36.7	16 17.6
20 W	11 57 49	27 36 39	18 33 05	24 32 32	23D57.6	23 49.3	4 11.8	16 53.0	20 56.6	10 26.6	2 32.9	10 16.6	21 35.2	16 16.6
21 Th	12 01 46	28 35 17	0♑34 24	6♑39 14	23 57.7	24 35.5	4 32.4	17 31.3	20 43.5	10 18.9	2 38.4	10 17.9	21 33.7	16 15.7
22 F	12 05 42	29 33 57	12 47 37	19 00 05	23 58.0	25 18.0	4 51.1	18 09.5	20 30.4	10 11.1	2 43.8	10 19.2	21 32.2	16 14.8
23 Sa	12 09 39	0♎32 38	25 17 08	1♒39 13	23 58.5	25 56.5	5 08.0	18 47.8	20 17.4	10 03.3	2 49.1	10 20.4	21 30.7	16 13.9
24 Su	12 13 35	1 31 21	8♒06 43	14 39 59	23 59.2	26 30.8	5 22.9	19 26.1	20 04.6	9 55.5	2 54.4	10 21.6	21 29.1	16 13.0
25 M	12 17 32	2 30 06	21 19 12	28 04 31	23 59.9	27 00.5	5 35.7	20 04.4	19 51.9	9 47.6	2 59.6	10 22.7	21 27.6	16 12.2
26 Tu	12 21 28	3 28 53	4♓55 54	11♓53 13	24R00.5	27 25.3	5 46.5	20 42.7	19 39.3	9 39.6	3 04.7	10 23.8	21 26.0	16 11.3
27 W	12 25 25	4 27 42	18 56 14	26 04 29	24 00.7	27 44.6	5 55.1	21 21.0	19 26.9	9 31.6	3 09.8	10 24.8	21 24.4	16 10.5
28 Th	12 29 22	5 26 32	3♈17 27	10♈34 27	24 00.3	27 58.2	6 01.5	21 59.3	19 14.7	9 23.6	3 14.7	10 25.8	21 22.9	16 09.7
29 F	12 33 18	6 25 25	17 54 42	25 17 19	23 59.3	28R05.7	6 05.7	22 37.6	19 02.7	9 15.6	3 19.6	10 26.7	21 21.3	16 09.0
30 Sa	12 37 15	7 24 19	2♉41 23	10♉05 57	23 57.9	28 06.5	6R07.6	23 15.9	18 50.9	9 07.5	3 24.4	10 27.6	21 19.6	16 08.2

LONGITUDE — October 2034

Day	Sid.Time	☉	0 hr ☽	Noon ☽	True ☊	☿	♀	♂	⚳	♃	♄	♅	♆	♇
1 Su	12 41 11	8♎23 16	17♉30 06	24♉52 55	23♍56.1	28♎00.4	6♏07.2	23♍54.2	18♓39.2	8♈59.5	3♌29.1	10♋28.4	21♈18.0	16♒07.5
2 M	12 45 08	9 22 15	2♊13 35	9♊31 23	23R54.4	27R46.9	6R04.4	24 32.6	18R27.8	8R51.4	3 33.8	10 29.2	21R16.4	16R06.8
3 Tu	12 49 04	10 21 17	16 45 43	23 56 05	23 53.2	27 25.8	5 59.2	25 10.9	18 16.7	8 43.4	3 38.3	10 29.9	21 14.8	16 06.1
4 W	12 53 01	11 20 21	1♋02 09	8♋03 40	23D52.6	26 57.0	5 51.7	25 49.3	18 05.7	8 35.3	3 42.8	10 30.5	21 13.1	16 05.4
5 Th	12 56 57	12 19 27	15 00 30	21 52 38	23 52.8	26 20.3	5 41.8	26 27.6	17 55.1	8 27.3	3 47.2	10 31.1	21 11.5	16 04.8
6 F	13 00 54	13 18 36	28 40 07	5♌23 03	23 53.7	25 36.1	5 29.5	27 06.0	17 44.7	8 19.3	3 51.5	10 31.7	21 09.8	16 04.2
7 Sa	13 04 51	14 17 46	12♌01 37	18 36 00	23 55.1	24 44.5	5 14.8	27 44.4	17 34.5	8 11.3	3 55.7	10 32.2	21 08.2	16 03.6
8 Su	13 08 47	15 17 00	25 06 26	1♍33 08	23 56.6	23 46.4	4 57.8	28 22.8	17 24.7	8 03.4	3 59.8	10 32.7	21 06.5	16 03.0
9 M	13 12 44	16 16 15	7♍56 20	14 16 16	23R57.7	22 42.7	4 38.5	29 01.2	17 15.1	7 55.5	4 03.9	10 33.1	21 04.8	16 02.5
10 Tu	13 16 40	17 15 32	20 33 08	26 47 09	23 58.0	21 34.6	4 17.0	29 39.6	17 05.9	7 47.6	4 07.8	10 33.4	21 03.2	16 02.0
11 W	13 20 37	18 14 52	2♎58 29	9♎07 21	23 57.1	20 23.8	3 53.4	0♎18.0	16 56.9	7 39.8	4 11.7	10 33.7	21 01.5	16 01.5
12 Th	13 24 33	19 14 13	15 13 55	21 18 21	23 54.9	19 12.0	3 27.7	0 56.5	16 48.3	7 32.0	4 15.4	10 33.9	20 59.8	16 01.0
13 F	13 28 30	20 13 37	27 20 50	3♏21 34	23 51.4	18 01.2	3 00.1	1 34.9	16 40.0	7 24.4	4 19.1	10 34.1	20 58.1	16 00.6
14 Sa	13 32 26	21 13 03	9♏20 43	15 18 32	23 46.9	16 53.4	2 30.7	2 13.4	16 32.0	7 16.7	4 22.7	10 34.2	20 56.5	16 00.2
15 Su	13 36 23	22 12 30	21 15 15	27 11 08	23 41.7	15 50.7	1 59.7	2 51.8	16 24.4	7 09.2	4 26.1	10R34.3	20 54.8	15 59.8
16 M	13 40 20	23 12 00	3♐06 30	9♐01 41	23 36.6	14 54.9	1 27.2	3 30.3	16 17.1	7 01.8	4 29.5	10 34.3	20 53.1	15 59.4
17 Tu	13 44 16	24 11 31	14 57 04	20 53 03	23 32.0	14 07.5	0 53.5	4 08.8	16 10.1	6 54.4	4 32.8	10 34.3	20 51.4	15 59.1
18 W	13 48 13	25 11 05	26 50 05	2♑48 39	23 28.4	13 29.8	0 18.7	4 47.2	16 03.5	6 47.1	4 36.0	10 34.2	20 49.8	15 58.8
19 Th	13 52 09	26 10 40	8♑49 16	14 52 29	23D26.3	13 02.6	29♎43.1	5 25.7	15 57.3	6 40.0	4 39.1	10 34.1	20 48.1	15 58.5
20 F	13 56 06	27 10 16	20 58 51	27 08 56	23 25.6	12D46.5	29 06.9	6 04.2	15 51.4	6 32.9	4 42.1	10 33.9	20 46.4	15 58.2
21 Sa	14 00 02	28 09 55	3♒23 19	9♒42 34	23 26.2	12 41.7	28 30.3	6 42.7	15 45.9	6 25.9	4 44.9	10 33.7	20 44.8	15 58.0
22 Su	14 03 59	29 09 35	16 07 14	22 37 48	23 27.6	12 48.0	27 53.5	7 21.3	15 40.8	6 19.1	4 47.7	10 33.4	20 43.1	15 57.8
23 M	14 07 55	0♏09 17	29 14 43	5♓58 19	23 29.1	13 04.9	27 16.9	7 59.8	15 36.0	6 12.4	4 50.4	10 33.0	20 41.5	15 57.6
24 Tu	14 11 52	1 09 00	12♓48 51	19 46 25	23R30.1	13 32.0	26 40.7	8 38.3	15 31.6	6 05.8	4 53.0	10 32.6	20 39.8	15 57.5
25 W	14 15 48	2 08 45	26 50 58	4♈02 16	23 29.7	14 08.6	26 05.1	9 16.8	15 27.6	5 59.3	4 55.5	10 32.1	20 38.2	15 57.3
26 Th	14 19 45	3 08 33	11♈19 54	18 43 13	23 27.5	14 53.7	25 30.4	9 55.4	15 23.9	5 53.0	4 57.8	10 31.6	20 36.6	15 57.2
27 F	14 23 42	4 08 22	26 11 24	3♉43 26	23 23.4	15 46.6	24 56.7	10 34.0	15 20.6	5 46.8	5 00.1	10 31.1	20 34.9	15 57.2
28 Sa	14 27 38	5 08 12	11♉18 10	18 54 19	23 17.8	16 46.4	24 24.4	11 12.5	15 17.7	5 40.8	5 02.3	10 30.5	20 33.3	15 57.1
29 Su	14 31 35	6 08 05	26 30 34	4♊05 36	23 11.2	17 52.3	23 53.6	11 51.1	15 15.2	5 34.9	5 04.3	10 29.8	20 31.7	15D57.1
30 M	14 35 31	7 08 01	11♊38 09	19 07 06	23 04.7	19 03.6	23 24.5	12 29.7	15 13.0	5 29.1	5 06.3	10 29.1	20 30.1	15 57.1
31 Tu	14 39 28	8 07 58	26 31 27	3♋50 25	22 59.2	20 19.4	22 57.2	13 08.3	15 11.2	5 23.5	5 08.1	10 28.3	20 28.5	15 57.2

Astro Data (Dy Hr Mn)

☽0S 13 14:28
♃□♅ 21 14:43
⊙0S 22 22:40
☽0N 27 21:13
☿R 30 2:59
♀R 30 19:37

☽0S 10 21:21
♂0S 14 17:05
♅R 16 10:16
☿D 21 10:22
☽0N 25 8:08
♇D 29 13:43

Planet Ingress (Dy Hr Mn)

♀ ♏ 11 16:18
⊙ ♎ 22 22:39

♂ ♎ 11 0:44
☿ ♎R 19 0:40
⊙ ♏ 23 8:16

Last Aspect Dy Hr Mn		☽ Ingress Dy Hr Mn
2 0:44	♀ ☍	♉ 2 11:33
3 15:15	♇ □	♊ 4 13:45
6 11:01	♀ △	♋ 6 16:40
8 17:44	♀ □	♌ 8 20:54
11 2:20	♀ ✶	♍ 11 2:58
12 16:14	⊙ ☌	♎ 13 11:19
15 5:38	♆ ☍	♏ 15 22:05
18 0:49	⊙ ✶	♐ 18 10:32
20 18:39	⊙ □	♑ 20 22:52
23 0:41	♀ □	♒ 23 8:54
25 10:03	♀ △	♓ 25 15:23
27 3:42	♂ ☍	♈ 27 18:33
29 16:34	☿ ☍	♉ 29 19:39

Last Aspect Dy Hr Mn		☽ Ingress Dy Hr Mn
1 10:20	♂ △	♊ 1 20:21
3 17:43	☿ △	♋ 3 22:14
5 20:29	♂ ✶	♌ 6 2:22
7 22:34	☿ ✶	♍ 8 9:06
10 17:52	♂ ☌	♎ 10 18:13
12 11:23	♆ ☍	♏ 13 5:17
14 13:24	♇ □	♐ 15 17:42
17 19:17	♇ ✶	♑ 18 6:22
20 15:37	♀ □	♒ 20 17:30
23 0:48	⊙ △	♓ 23 1:21
23 20:03	♅ △	♈ 25 5:17
26 22:31	♀ ☍	♉ 27 6:05
28 7:20	♇ □	♊ 29 5:31
30 18:43	♀ △	♋ 31 5:41

☽ Phases & Eclipses (Dy Hr Mn)

5 11:41 ☾ 13♊00
12 16:14 ● 19♍59
12 16:18:07 ✔ A 02'58"
20 18:39 ☽ 27♐53
28 2:57 ○ 5♈04
28 2:46 • P 0.014

4 18:05 ☾ 11♋35
12 7:33 ● 19♎03
20 12:03 ☽ 27♑10
27 12:42 ○ 4♉10

Astro Data

1 September 2034
Julian Day # 49187
SVP 4♓46'33"
GC 27♐19.4 ⚵ 24♑47.0R
Eris 27♈41.4R ✱ 5♐56.5
⚷ 6♊31.7 ⚶ 4♋38.1
☽ Mean ☊ 24♍32.5

1 October 2034
Julian Day # 49217
SVP 4♓46'31"
GC 27♐19.5 ⚵ 24♑09.9
Eris 27♈26.9R ✱ 12♐22.8
⚷ 6♊22.7R ⚶ 13♋29.7
☽ Mean ☊ 22♍57.2

November 2034 LONGITUDE

Day	Sid.Time	☉	0 hr ☽	Noon ☽	True ☊	☿	♀	♂	⚳	♃	♄	♅	♆	♇
1 W	14 43 24	9♏07 57	11♋03 25	18♋10 03	22♍55.3	21♎39.1	22♎32.0	13♎47.0	15♓09.8	5♈18.1	5♌09.8	10♋27.5	20♈27.0	15♒57.2
2 Th	14 47 21	10 07 59	25 10 07	2♌03 38	22D 53.3	23 02.2	22R 08.9	14 25.6	15R 08.8	5R 12.8	5 11.5	10R 26.6	20R 25.4	15 57.3
3 F	14 51 17	11 08 03	8♌50 41	15 31 34	22 53.1	24 28.0	21 48.1	15 04.3	15 08.1	5 07.7	5 13.0	10 25.7	20 23.9	15 57.4
4 Sa	14 55 14	12 08 08	22 06 35	28 36 10	22 54.0	25 56.2	21 29.5	15 42.9	15D 07.8	5 02.8	5 14.4	10 24.8	20 22.3	15 57.6
5 Su	14 59 11	13 08 16	5♍00 47	11♍20 53	22R 55.2	27 26.2	21 13.3	16 21.6	15 07.9	4 58.0	5 15.7	10 23.7	20 20.8	15 57.8
6 M	15 03 07	14 08 26	17 36 57	23 49 28	22 55.7	28 57.9	20 59.6	17 00.3	15 08.3	4 53.4	5 16.9	10 22.7	20 19.3	15 58.0
7 Tu	15 07 04	15 08 38	29 58 52	6♎05 35	22 54.7	0♏30.7	20 48.3	17 39.0	15 09.1	4 49.0	5 17.9	10 21.6	20 17.8	15 58.2
8 W	15 11 00	16 08 52	12♎09 59	18 12 26	22 51.4	2 04.6	20 39.5	18 17.7	15 10.3	4 44.7	5 18.9	10 20.4	20 16.3	15 58.4
9 Th	15 14 57	17 09 08	24 13 15	0♏12 41	22 45.6	3 39.3	20 33.2	18 56.4	15 11.9	4 40.7	5 19.7	10 19.2	20 14.9	15 58.7
10 F	15 18 53	18 09 26	6♏11 00	12 08 25	22 37.2	5 14.6	20 29.3	19 35.2	15 13.8	4 36.8	5 20.5	10 17.9	20 13.4	15 59.0
11 Sa	15 22 50	19 09 45	18 05 07	24 01 18	22 26.8	6 50.3	20D 27.9	20 13.9	15 16.1	4 33.1	5 21.1	10 16.6	20 12.0	15 59.4
12 Su	15 26 46	20 10 06	29 57 07	5♐52 46	22 15.2	8 26.3	20 28.9	20 52.7	15 18.7	4 29.6	5 21.6	10 15.3	20 10.6	15 59.8
13 M	15 30 43	21 10 29	11♐48 25	17 44 18	22 03.2	10 02.5	20 32.3	21 31.4	15 21.7	4 26.4	5 22.0	10 13.9	20 09.2	16 00.2
14 Tu	15 34 40	22 10 53	23 40 37	29 37 38	21 52.1	11 38.8	20 38.0	22 10.2	15 25.1	4 23.3	5 22.3	10 12.4	20 07.8	16 00.6
15 W	15 38 36	23 11 19	5♑35 39	11♑35 00	21 42.8	13 15.2	20 46.0	22 49.0	15 28.8	4 20.4	5 22.5	10 10.9	20 06.5	16 01.0
16 Th	15 42 33	24 11 47	17 36 03	23 39 14	21 35.8	14 51.5	20 56.3	23 27.8	15 32.9	4 17.7	5R 22.5	10 09.4	20 05.2	16 01.5
17 F	15 46 29	25 12 15	29 44 59	5♒53 50	21 31.4	16 27.8	21 08.7	24 06.6	15 37.3	4 15.2	5 22.5	10 07.8	20 03.9	16 02.0
18 Sa	15 50 26	26 12 45	12♒06 16	18 22 52	21D 29.4	18 04.0	21 23.3	24 45.4	15 42.0	4 12.9	5 22.3	10 06.2	20 02.6	16 02.5
19 Su	15 54 22	27 13 16	24 44 12	1♓10 48	21 29.2	19 40.0	21 39.9	25 24.3	15 47.1	4 10.8	5 22.0	10 04.5	20 01.3	16 03.1
20 M	15 58 19	28 13 49	7♓43 13	14 21 57	21R 29.6	21 15.9	21 58.6	26 03.1	15 52.5	4 08.9	5 21.6	10 02.8	20 00.1	16 03.7
21 Tu	16 02 15	29 14 22	21 07 25	27 59 58	21 29.6	22 51.7	22 19.2	26 41.9	15 58.3	4 07.2	5 21.1	10 01.1	19 58.9	16 04.3
22 W	16 06 12	0♐14 57	4♈59 47	12♈06 54	21 28.0	24 27.3	22 41.6	27 20.8	16 04.3	4 05.8	5 20.5	9 59.3	19 57.7	16 04.9
23 Th	16 10 09	1 15 33	19 21 11	26 42 15	21 23.9	26 02.7	23 06.0	27 59.7	16 10.7	4 04.5	5 19.7	9 57.5	19 56.5	16 05.6
24 F	16 14 05	2 16 10	4♉09 28	11♉42 01	21 17.1	27 38.0	23 32.1	28 38.5	16 17.5	4 03.4	5 18.9	9 55.6	19 55.3	16 06.3
25 Sa	16 18 02	3 16 49	19 18 48	26 58 33	21 07.8	29 13.1	23 59.9	29 17.4	16 24.5	4 02.6	5 17.9	9 53.7	19 54.2	16 07.0
26 Su	16 21 58	4 17 29	4♊39 50	12♊21 10	20 57.1	0♐48.1	24 29.3	29 56.3	16 31.8	4 02.0	5 16.9	9 51.8	19 53.1	16 07.7
27 M	16 25 55	5 18 10	20 01 00	27 37 54	20 46.2	2 22.9	25 00.4	0♏35.3	16 39.5	4 01.5	5 15.7	9 49.9	19 52.1	16 08.5
28 Tu	16 29 51	6 18 53	5♋10 32	12♋37 46	20 36.4	3 57.6	25 33.0	1 14.2	16 47.5	4D 01.3	5 14.4	9 47.9	19 51.0	16 09.3
29 W	16 33 48	7 19 37	19 58 40	27 12 36	20 28.8	5 32.2	26 07.1	1 53.1	16 55.7	4 01.3	5 13.0	9 45.8	19 50.0	16 10.1
30 Th	16 37 44	8 20 23	4♌19 06	11♌18 01	20 23.7	7 06.7	26 42.7	2 32.1	17 04.3	4 01.5	5 11.5	9 43.7	19 49.0	16 11.0

December 2034 LONGITUDE

Day	Sid.Time	☉	0 hr ☽	Noon ☽	True ☊	☿	♀	♂	⚳	♃	♄	♅	♆	♇
1 F	16 41 41	9♐21 10	18♌09 21	24♌53 18	20♍21.2	8♐41.0	27♎19.6	3♏11.1	17♓13.1	4♈01.8	5♌09.9	9♋41.6	19♈48.1	16♒11.8
2 Sa	16 45 38	10 21 59	1♍30 14	8♍00 35	20R 20.5	10 15.4	27 57.8	3 50.1	17 22.2	4 02.4	5R 08.2	9R 39.5	19R 47.1	16 12.7
3 Su	16 49 34	11 22 49	14 24 54	20 43 45	20 20.6	11 49.6	28 37.3	4 29.1	17 31.6	4 03.3	5 06.4	9 37.3	19 46.2	16 13.7
4 M	16 53 31	12 23 40	26 57 47	3♎07 37	20 20.1	13 23.8	29 18.0	5 08.1	17 41.3	4 04.3	5 04.5	9 35.2	19 45.3	16 14.6
5 Tu	16 57 27	13 24 33	9♎13 50	15 17 04	20 17.9	14 58.0	29 59.9	5 47.1	17 51.3	4 05.5	5 02.4	9 32.9	19 44.5	16 15.6
6 W	17 01 24	14 25 27	21 17 51	27 16 43	20 13.1	16 32.1	0♏42.9	6 26.1	18 01.6	4 06.9	5 00.3	9 30.7	19 43.7	16 16.5
7 Th	17 05 20	15 26 23	3♏14 07	9♏10 30	20 05.3	18 06.3	1 27.0	7 05.2	18 12.1	4 08.5	4 58.0	9 28.4	19 42.9	16 17.6
8 F	17 09 17	16 27 19	15 06 14	21 01 38	19 54.5	19 40.5	2 12.1	7 44.2	18 22.9	4 10.4	4 55.7	9 26.1	19 42.1	16 18.6
9 Sa	17 13 13	17 28 17	26 57 00	2♐52 34	19 41.1	21 14.7	2 58.2	8 23.3	18 33.9	4 12.4	4 53.3	9 23.8	19 41.4	16 19.7
10 Su	17 17 10	18 29 16	8♐48 31	14 45 03	19 26.1	22 48.9	3 45.3	9 02.4	18 45.2	4 14.7	4 50.7	9 21.4	19 40.7	16 20.7
11 M	17 21 07	19 30 15	20 42 18	26 40 24	19 10.8	24 23.2	4 33.3	9 41.5	18 56.8	4 17.1	4 48.1	9 19.0	19 40.0	16 21.9
12 Tu	17 25 03	20 31 16	2♑39 31	8♑39 46	18 56.3	25 57.6	5 22.2	10 20.6	19 08.6	4 19.8	4 45.3	9 16.7	19 39.4	16 23.0
13 W	17 29 00	21 32 17	14 41 19	20 44 20	18 43.7	27 32.0	6 11.9	10 59.7	19 20.7	4 22.7	4 42.5	9 14.2	19 38.8	16 24.1
14 Th	17 32 56	22 33 19	26 49 03	2♒55 41	18 34.0	29 06.5	7 02.4	11 38.8	19 33.0	4 25.7	4 39.6	9 11.8	19 38.2	16 25.3
15 F	17 36 53	23 34 22	9♒04 32	15 15 57	18 27.5	0♑41.1	7 53.7	12 18.0	19 45.6	4 29.0	4 36.5	9 09.4	19 37.7	16 26.5
16 Sa	17 40 49	24 35 25	21 30 16	27 47 55	18 23.9	2 15.7	8 45.8	12 57.1	19 58.4	4 32.4	4 33.4	9 06.9	19 37.2	16 27.7
17 Su	17 44 46	25 36 28	4♓09 19	10♓34 57	18D 22.6	3 50.5	9 38.6	13 36.2	20 11.4	4 36.1	4 30.2	9 04.4	19 36.7	16 29.0
18 M	17 48 42	26 37 32	17 05 17	23 40 48	18R 22.5	5 25.3	10 32.0	14 15.4	20 24.7	4 39.9	4 26.9	9 01.9	19 36.3	16 30.2
19 Tu	17 52 39	27 38 36	0♈21 54	7♈09 01	18 22.3	7 00.1	11 26.2	14 54.6	20 38.2	4 43.9	4 23.5	8 59.4	19 35.9	16 31.5
20 W	17 56 36	28 39 40	14 02 25	21 02 19	18 20.7	8 35.1	12 21.0	15 33.7	20 51.9	4 48.2	4 20.1	8 56.8	19 35.5	16 32.8
21 Th	18 00 32	29 40 45	28 08 47	5♉21 40	18 16.8	10 10.0	13 16.4	16 12.9	21 05.8	4 52.6	4 16.5	8 54.3	19 35.2	16 34.1
22 F	18 04 29	0♑41 50	12♉40 01	20 05 17	18 10.1	11 44.9	14 12.4	16 52.1	21 19.9	4 57.2	4 12.9	8 51.8	19 34.9	16 35.4
23 Sa	18 08 25	1 42 55	27 34 42	5♊07 59	18 00.9	13 19.8	15 09.0	17 31.3	21 34.3	5 02.0	4 09.2	8 49.2	19 34.6	16 36.8
24 Su	18 12 22	2 44 01	12♊43 58	20 21 20	17 50.0	14 54.6	16 06.2	18 10.5	21 48.8	5 06.9	4 05.4	8 46.6	19 34.4	16 38.2
25 M	18 16 18	3 45 07	27 58 41	5♋34 35	17 38.8	16 29.3	17 03.9	18 49.8	22 03.6	5 12.1	4 01.6	8 44.1	19 34.2	16 39.6
26 Tu	18 20 15	4 46 13	13♋07 40	20 36 38	17 28.5	18 03.7	18 02.2	19 29.0	22 18.6	5 17.4	3 57.7	8 41.5	19 34.0	16 41.0
27 W	18 24 12	5 47 20	28 00 24	5♌18 02	17 20.2	19 37.9	19 00.9	20 08.2	22 33.7	5 23.0	3 53.7	8 38.9	19 33.9	16 42.4
28 Th	18 28 08	6 48 27	12♌28 52	19 32 26	17 14.6	21 11.6	20 00.2	20 47.5	22 49.1	5 28.6	3 49.6	8 36.3	19 33.8	16 43.8
29 F	18 32 05	7 49 35	26 28 31	3♍17 06	17 11.7	22 44.8	20 59.9	21 26.8	23 04.6	5 34.5	3 45.5	8 33.7	19 33.7	16 45.3
30 Sa	18 36 01	8 50 43	9♍58 21	16 32 34	17D 10.8	24 17.3	22 00.0	22 06.1	23 20.3	5 40.5	3 41.3	8 31.2	19D 33.7	16 46.8
31 Su	18 39 58	9 51 51	23 00 11	29 21 45	17R 11.2	25 48.9	23 00.6	22 45.4	23 36.2	5 46.8	3 37.1	8 28.6	19 33.7	16 48.3

Astro Data

	Dy Hr Mn
♃△♄	2 16:49
⚳ D	4 19:07
☽0S	7 3:38
♀ D	11 14:02
♄ R	16 12:00
☽0N	21 19:11
♃ D	29 2:25
☽0S	4 10:40
♃△♄	16 15:35
☽0N	19 4:34
♆ D	30 20:09
☽0S	31 19:26

Planet Ingress

		Dy Hr Mn
☿	♏	7 4:05
☉	♐	22 6:05
☿	♐	25 23:50
♂	♏	26 14:16
♀	♏	5 12:04
☿	♑	15 1:35
☉	♑	21 19:34

Last Aspect / ☽ Ingress

Last Aspect Dy Hr Mn			☽ Ingress	Dy Hr Mn
1 19:15	♀	□	♌	2 8:24
4 6:25	☿	✶	♍	4 14:36
5 15:43	☉	✶	♎	7 0:02
8 16:50	♀	☌	♏	9 11:35
11 1:16	☉	☌	♐	12 0:06
13 20:06	♂	✶	♑	14 12:45
16 13:10	☉	✶	♒	17 0:29
19 4:01	☉	□	♓	19 9:49
21 14:18	☉	△	♈	21 15:27
23 14:11	♂	☍	♉	23 17:20
25 15:54	☿	☍	♊	25 16:43
27 7:42	♀	△	♋	27 15:45
29 10:06	♀	□	♌	29 16:41

Last Aspect / ☽ Ingress

Last Aspect Dy Hr Mn			☽ Ingress	Dy Hr Mn
1 16:37	♀	✶	♍	1 21:15
2 16:46	☿	□	♎	4 5:54
5 20:53	♆	☍	♏	6 17:29
8 2:26	♇	□	♐	9 6:11
11 6:43	☿	☌	♑	11 18:40
13 9:50	♆	□	♒	14 6:16
16 5:22	☉	✶	♓	16 16:10
18 17:45	☉	□	♈	18 23:21
21 1:51	☉	△	♉	21 3:06
22 6:34	♂	☍	♊	23 3:51
24 10:46	♆	✶	♋	25 3:11
26 10:19	♆	□	♌	27 3:16
28 14:15	♂	□	♍	29 6:11
31 4:22	☿	△	♎	31 13:13

☽ Phases & Eclipses

Dy Hr Mn		
3 3:27	☾	10♌47
11 1:16	●	18♏43
19 4:01	☽	26♒53
25 22:32	○	3♊43
2 16:46	☾	10♍34
10 20:14	●	18♐50
18 17:45	☽	26♓52
25 8:54	○	3♋37

Astro Data

1 November 2034
Julian Day # 49248
SVP 4♓46'27"
GC 27♐19.6 ⚵ 28♑21.2
Eris 27♈08.5R ⚴ 21♐27.6
⚷ 5♊16.7R ⚶ 18♋58.7
☽ Mean ☊ 21♍18.7

1 December 2034
Julian Day # 49278
SVP 4♓46'23"
GC 27♐19.6 ⚵ 5♒26.8
Eris 26♈52.7R ⚴ 1♑44.0
⚷ 3♊40.9R ⚶ 18♋38.8R
☽ Mean ☊ 19♍43.4

LONGITUDE — January 2035

Day	Sid.Time	☉	0 hr ☽	Noon ☽	True ☊	☿	♀	♂	⚳	♃	♄	♅	♆	♇
1 M	18 43 54	10♑53 00	5♎37 50	11♎49 04	17♍11.5	27♑19.5	24♏01.7	23♏24.7	23♓52.3	5♈53.1	3♌32.7	8♋26.0	19♈33.8	16♒49.8
2 Tu	18 47 51	11 54 09	17 56 07	23 59 39	17R10.7	28 48.8	25 03.1	24 04.0	24 08.6	5 59.7	3R28.4	8R23.4	19 33.8	16 51.3
3 W	18 51 47	12 55 19	0♏00 17	5♏58 41	17 07.8	0♒16.4	26 04.9	24 43.3	24 25.1	6 06.4	3 24.0	8 20.8	19 33.9	16 52.8
4 Th	18 55 44	13 56 28	11 55 26	17 51 06	17 02.4	1 42.1	27 07.1	25 22.7	24 41.7	6 13.3	3 19.5	8 18.2	19 34.1	16 54.4
5 F	18 59 41	14 57 39	23 46 11	29 41 09	16 54.4	3 05.4	28 09.7	26 02.0	24 58.5	6 20.3	3 15.0	8 15.7	19 34.3	16 56.0
6 Sa	19 03 37	15 58 49	5♐36 26	11♐32 24	16 44.1	4 26.0	29 12.6	26 41.4	25 15.5	6 27.5	3 10.4	8 13.1	19 34.5	16 57.6
7 Su	19 07 34	16 59 59	17 29 22	23 27 36	16 32.4	5 43.2	0♐15.9	27 20.8	25 32.6	6 34.9	3 05.8	8 10.5	19 34.7	16 59.2
8 M	19 11 30	18 01 10	29 27 19	5♑28 42	16 20.3	6 56.6	1 19.4	28 00.2	25 49.9	6 42.4	3 01.1	8 08.0	19 35.0	17 00.8
9 Tu	19 15 27	19 02 20	11♑31 53	17 37 01	16 08.8	8 05.4	2 23.3	28 39.5	26 07.3	6 50.1	2 56.4	8 05.5	19 35.4	17 02.4
10 W	19 19 23	20 03 30	23 44 10	29 53 26	15 58.9	9 09.0	3 27.5	29 18.9	26 25.0	6 58.0	2 51.7	8 02.9	19 35.7	17 04.0
11 Th	19 23 20	21 04 40	6♒04 54	12♒18 40	15 51.4	10 06.5	4 32.0	29 58.3	26 42.7	7 06.0	2 46.9	8 00.4	19 36.1	17 05.7
12 F	19 27 16	22 05 49	18 34 51	24 53 33	15 46.5	10 57.1	5 36.7	0♐37.7	27 00.7	7 14.1	2 42.1	7 57.9	19 36.5	17 07.3
13 Sa	19 31 13	23 06 58	1♓14 56	7♓39 10	15D44.2	11 39.9	6 41.7	1 17.1	27 18.7	7 22.4	2 37.3	7 55.5	19 37.0	17 09.0
14 Su	19 35 10	24 08 06	14 06 30	20 37 07	15 44.0	12 14.0	7 47.0	1 56.6	27 36.9	7 30.8	2 32.4	7 53.0	19 37.5	17 10.7
15 M	19 39 06	25 09 13	27 11 19	3♈49 20	15 44.9	12 38.6	8 52.5	2 36.0	27 55.3	7 39.4	2 27.6	7 50.5	19 38.0	17 12.4
16 Tu	19 43 03	26 10 20	10♈31 27	17 17 54	15R46.0	12R52.8	9 58.2	3 15.4	28 13.8	7 48.1	2 22.7	7 48.1	19 38.6	17 14.1
17 W	19 46 59	27 11 26	24 08 53	1♉04 33	15 46.3	12 55.9	11 04.2	3 54.8	28 32.4	7 57.0	2 17.8	7 45.7	19 39.2	17 15.8
18 Th	19 50 56	28 12 32	8♉04 59	15 10 09	15 44.8	12 47.6	12 10.4	4 34.3	28 51.2	8 06.0	2 12.9	7 43.3	19 39.8	17 17.5
19 F	19 54 52	29 13 36	22 19 52	29 33 52	15 41.4	12 27.6	13 16.9	5 13.7	29 10.1	8 15.1	2 07.9	7 41.0	19 40.5	17 19.2
20 Sa	19 58 49	0♒14 40	6♊51 40	14♊12 41	15 36.1	11 55.9	14 23.5	5 53.2	29 29.1	8 24.4	2 03.0	7 38.6	19 41.2	17 21.0
21 Su	20 02 45	1 15 43	21 36 09	29 01 12	15 29.4	11 13.2	15 30.4	6 32.6	29 48.3	8 33.8	1 58.1	7 36.3	19 41.9	17 22.7
22 M	20 06 42	2 16 45	6♋26 51	13♋52 01	15 22.3	10 20.4	16 37.4	7 12.1	0♈07.6	8 43.3	1 53.1	7 34.0	19 42.7	17 24.5
23 Tu	20 10 39	3 17 46	21 15 40	28 36 43	15 15.7	9 18.9	17 44.7	7 51.6	0 27.0	8 53.0	1 48.2	7 31.8	19 43.5	17 26.2
24 W	20 14 35	4 18 47	5♌54 13	13♌07 17	15 10.5	8 10.4	18 52.1	8 31.1	0 46.5	9 02.8	1 43.3	7 29.5	19 44.3	17 28.0
25 Th	20 18 32	5 19 47	20 15 10	27 17 18	15 07.1	6 57.1	19 59.8	9 10.6	1 06.1	9 12.7	1 38.4	7 27.3	19 45.2	17 29.7
26 F	20 22 28	6 20 46	4♍13 16	11♍02 50	15D05.7	5 41.3	21 07.6	9 50.1	1 25.9	9 22.7	1 33.4	7 25.1	19 46.1	17 31.5
27 Sa	20 26 25	7 21 44	17 45 56	24 22 36	15 06.0	4 25.1	22 15.6	10 29.6	1 45.8	9 32.9	1 28.5	7 23.0	19 47.0	17 33.3
28 Su	20 30 21	8 22 42	0♎53 04	7♎17 39	15 07.4	3 10.8	23 23.7	11 09.1	2 05.8	9 43.1	1 23.6	7 20.8	19 48.0	17 35.1
29 M	20 34 18	9 23 39	13 36 46	19 50 53	15 09.1	2 00.5	24 32.0	11 48.6	2 25.8	9 53.5	1 18.8	7 18.8	19 49.0	17 36.9
30 Tu	20 38 14	10 24 35	26 00 34	2♏06 23	15R10.4	0 55.7	25 40.5	12 28.2	2 46.0	10 04.0	1 13.9	7 16.7	19 50.0	17 38.6
31 W	20 42 11	11 25 31	8♏08 57	14 08 54	15 10.7	29♑57.7	26 49.1	13 07.7	3 06.4	10 14.6	1 09.1	7 14.7	19 51.1	17 40.4

LONGITUDE — February 2035

Day	Sid.Time	☉	0 hr ☽	Noon ☽	True ☊	☿	♀	♂	⚳	♃	♄	♅	♆	♇
1 Th	20 46 08	12♒26 26	20♏06 51	26♏03 25	15♍09.7	29♑07.4	27♐57.9	13♐47.2	3♈26.8	10♈25.3	1♌04.3	7♋12.7	19♈52.2	17♒42.2
2 F	20 50 04	13 27 21	1♐59 13	7♐54 48	15R07.1	28R25.5	29 06.8	14 26.8	3 47.3	10 36.2	0R59.5	7R10.7	19 53.3	17 44.0
3 Sa	20 54 01	14 28 14	13 50 43	19 47 29	15 03.1	27 52.2	0♑15.9	15 06.4	4 07.9	10 47.1	0 54.8	7 08.8	19 54.4	17 45.8
4 Su	20 57 57	15 29 07	25 45 33	1♑45 22	14 58.3	27 27.5	1 25.1	15 45.9	4 28.6	10 58.1	0 50.1	7 06.9	19 55.6	17 47.6
5 M	21 01 54	16 29 58	7♑47 15	13 51 34	14 53.0	27 11.2	2 34.4	16 25.5	4 49.5	11 09.3	0 45.4	7 05.1	19 56.8	17 49.4
6 Tu	21 05 50	17 30 49	19 58 33	26 08 26	14 48.0	27D03.0	3 43.8	17 05.1	5 10.4	11 20.5	0 40.8	7 03.3	19 58.1	17 51.3
7 W	21 09 47	18 31 39	2♒21 23	8♒37 29	14 43.7	27 02.5	4 53.4	17 44.6	5 31.4	11 31.9	0 36.2	7 01.5	19 59.3	17 53.1
8 Th	21 13 43	19 32 27	14 56 50	21 19 27	14 40.6	27 09.3	6 03.1	18 24.2	5 52.5	11 43.3	0 31.6	6 59.8	20 00.6	17 54.9
9 F	21 17 40	20 33 14	27 45 21	4♓14 30	14D38.9	27 22.9	7 12.8	19 03.8	6 13.7	11 54.9	0 27.1	6 58.1	20 02.0	17 56.7
10 Sa	21 21 37	21 34 00	10♓46 50	17 22 19	14 38.5	27 42.7	8 22.7	19 43.4	6 35.0	12 06.5	0 22.7	6 56.5	20 03.3	17 58.5
11 Su	21 25 33	22 34 44	24 00 53	0♈42 28	14 39.2	28 08.3	9 32.7	20 22.9	6 56.3	12 18.3	0 18.3	6 54.9	20 04.7	18 00.3
12 M	21 29 30	23 35 27	7♈27 00	14 14 25	14 40.6	28 39.3	10 42.7	21 02.5	7 17.8	12 30.1	0 13.9	6 53.3	20 06.1	18 02.1
13 Tu	21 33 26	24 36 08	21 04 39	27 57 39	14 42.1	29 15.2	11 52.9	21 42.1	7 39.3	12 42.0	0 09.7	6 51.8	20 07.6	18 03.9
14 W	21 37 23	25 36 48	4♉53 19	11♉51 35	14 43.2	29 55.5	13 03.2	22 21.6	8 00.9	12 54.0	0 05.5	6 50.3	20 09.0	18 05.7
15 Th	21 41 19	26 37 26	18 52 20	25 55 24	14R43.7	0♒40.0	14 13.5	23 01.2	8 22.6	13 06.1	0 01.3	6 48.9	20 10.5	18 07.4
16 F	21 45 16	27 38 02	3♊00 36	10♊07 42	14 43.3	1 28.3	15 23.9	23 40.8	8 44.4	13 18.3	29♋57.2	6 47.5	20 12.1	18 09.2
17 Sa	21 49 12	28 38 37	17 16 23	24 26 18	14 42.1	2 20.1	16 34.4	24 20.4	9 06.2	13 30.5	29 53.2	6 46.2	20 13.6	18 11.0
18 Su	21 53 09	29 39 09	1♋37 01	8♋48 03	14 40.4	3 15.0	17 45.0	24 59.9	9 28.1	13 42.8	29 49.2	6 44.9	20 15.2	18 12.8
19 M	21 57 06	0♓39 40	15 58 52	23 08 54	14 38.5	4 13.0	18 55.7	25 39.5	9 50.1	13 55.2	29 45.4	6 43.7	20 16.8	18 14.6
20 Tu	22 01 02	1 40 09	0♌17 33	7♌24 12	14 36.8	5 13.7	20 06.5	26 19.1	10 12.2	14 07.7	29 41.5	6 42.5	20 18.4	18 16.3
21 W	22 04 59	2 40 37	14 28 17	21 29 13	14 35.5	6 16.9	21 17.3	26 58.7	10 34.3	14 20.3	29 37.8	6 41.4	20 20.0	18 18.1
22 Th	22 08 55	3 41 02	28 26 30	5♍19 41	14D34.7	7 22.5	22 28.2	27 38.2	10 56.5	14 32.9	29 34.2	6 40.3	20 21.7	18 19.8
23 F	22 12 52	4 41 26	12♍08 26	18 52 26	14 34.6	8 30.3	23 39.2	28 17.8	11 18.7	14 45.6	29 30.6	6 39.2	20 23.4	18 21.6
24 Sa	22 16 48	5 41 49	25 31 31	2♎05 36	14 35.0	9 40.2	24 50.2	28 57.4	11 41.0	14 58.4	29 27.1	6 38.3	20 25.1	18 23.3
25 Su	22 20 45	6 42 10	8♎34 42	14 58 56	14 35.7	10 52.0	26 01.3	29 37.0	12 03.4	15 11.2	29 23.7	6 37.3	20 26.9	18 25.1
26 M	22 24 41	7 42 29	21 18 28	27 33 36	14 36.5	12 05.7	27 12.5	0♑16.5	12 25.9	15 24.1	29 20.3	6 36.4	20 28.6	18 26.8
27 Tu	22 28 38	8 42 47	3♏44 39	9♏52 03	14 37.2	13 21.1	28 23.8	0 56.1	12 48.4	15 37.1	29 17.1	6 35.6	20 30.4	18 28.5
28 W	22 32 34	9 43 04	15 56 15	21 57 44	14 37.7	14 38.1	29 35.1	1 35.7	13 10.9	15 50.2	29 13.9	6 34.8	20 32.2	18 30.2

Astro Data

	Dy Hr Mn
☽0N	15 11:42
♃□♅	16 11:57
☿R	17 6:43
☽0S	28 5:34
☿D	7 1:24
☽0N	11 17:56
☽0S	24 15:40

Planet Ingress

		Dy Hr Mn
☿	♒	3 7:28
♀	♐	7 5:59
♂	♐	11 13:01
☉	♒	20 6:14
⚳	♈	22 2:35
☿	♑R	31 10:58
♀	♑	3 6:29
☿	♒	14 14:31
♄	♋R	15 19:35
☉	♓	18 20:16
♂	♑	26 1:58
♀	♒	28 20:23

Last Aspect / ☽ Ingress (January)

Last Aspect Dy Hr Mn		☽ Ingress	Dy Hr Mn
2 22:57	☿ □	♏	2 23:59
5 8:37	♀ ☌	♐	5 12:38
7 4:12	♆ △	♑	8 1:05
10 10:49	♂ ⚹	♒	10 12:13
12 1:57	♆ ⚹	♓	12 21:39
14 18:59	☉ ⚹	♈	15 5:06
17 4:45	☉ □	♉	17 10:09
19 11:24	☉ △	♊	19 12:43
20 20:54	♆ ⚹	♋	21 13:35
22 21:29	♆ □	♌	23 14:17
24 23:08	♆ △	♍	25 16:40
27 7:46	♀ □	♎	27 22:21
29 22:03	♀ ⚹	♏	30 7:50

Last Aspect / ☽ Ingress (February)

Last Aspect Dy Hr Mn		☽ Ingress	Dy Hr Mn
1 17:50	☿ ⚹	♐	1 19:59
3 12:14	♆ △	♑	4 8:30
6 13:45	☿ ☌	♒	6 19:28
8 9:32	♆ ⚹	♓	9 4:10
11 7:14	☿ ⚹	♈	11 10:44
13 14:21	☿ □	♉	13 15:32
15 13:17	☉ □	♊	15 18:55
17 19:34	☉ △	♋	17 21:18
19 23:03	♄ ☌	♌	19 23:30
21 21:56	♂ △	♍	22 2:42
24 7:11	♄ ⚹	♎	24 8:10
26 15:25	♄ □	♏	26 16:43

☽ Phases & Eclipses

Dy Hr Mn	
1 10:01	☾ 10♎48
9 15:03	● 19♑10
17 4:45	☽ 26♈53
23 20:16	○ 3♌39
31 6:02	☾ 11♏10
8 8:22	● 19♒23
15 13:17	☽ 26♉41
22 8:54	○ 3♍33
22 9:05	☍ A 0.965

Astro Data

1 January 2035
Julian Day # 49309
SVP 4♓46'18"
GC 27♐19.7 ⚴ 14♒35.3
Eris 26♈43.4R ⚵ 13♑14.8
⚷ 2♊09.2R ⚶ 12♋06.7R
☽ Mean ☊ 18♍04.9

1 February 2035
Julian Day # 49340
SVP 4♓46'14"
GC 27♐19.8 ⚴ 24♒39.5
Eris 26♈44.4 ⚵ 25♑09.3
⚷ 1♊23.4R ⚶ 5♋12.5R
☽ Mean ☊ 16♍26.4

March 2035 LONGITUDE

Day	Sid.Time	☉	0 hr ☽	Noon ☽	True ☊	☿	♀	♂	⚳	♃	♄	♅	♆	♇
1 Th	22 36 31	10♓43 19	27♏57 03	3♐54 47	14♍37.9	15♒56.7	0♒46.5	2♑15.3	13♈33.6	16♈03.3	29♋10.8	6♋34.0	20♈34.0	18♒31.9
2 F	22 40 28	11 43 33	9♐51 29	15 47 45	14R37.9	17 16.8	1 57.9	2 54.9	13 56.2	16 16.4	29R07.9	6R33.4	20 35.9	18 33.6
3 Sa	22 44 24	12 43 45	21 44 10	27 41 21	14 37.8	18 38.4	3 09.4	3 34.5	14 19.0	16 29.6	29 05.0	6 32.7	20 37.7	18 35.3
4 Su	22 48 21	13 43 55	3♑39 50	9♑40 12	14D37.7	20 01.4	4 21.0	4 14.0	14 41.8	16 42.9	29 02.2	6 32.1	20 39.6	18 36.9
5 M	22 52 17	14 44 04	15 42 56	21 48 34	14 37.7	21 25.7	5 32.6	4 53.6	15 04.6	16 56.3	28 59.5	6 31.6	20 41.5	18 38.6
6 Tu	22 56 14	15 44 12	27 57 30	4♒10 08	14 37.8	22 51.3	6 44.2	5 33.2	15 27.5	17 09.7	28 56.9	6 31.1	20 43.4	18 40.3
7 W	23 00 10	16 44 17	10♒26 48	16 47 46	14 38.0	24 18.2	7 56.0	6 12.7	15 50.5	17 23.1	28 54.3	6 30.7	20 45.4	18 41.9
8 Th	23 04 07	17 44 21	23 13 12	29 43 15	14 38.2	25 46.4	9 07.7	6 52.3	16 13.5	17 36.6	28 51.9	6 30.3	20 47.3	18 43.5
9 F	23 08 03	18 44 24	6♓17 55	12♓57 09	14R38.3	27 15.8	10 19.5	7 31.8	16 36.5	17 50.2	28 49.6	6 30.0	20 49.3	18 45.1
10 Sa	23 12 00	19 44 24	19 40 51	26 28 47	14 38.2	28 46.4	11 31.4	8 11.3	16 59.6	18 03.8	28 47.4	6 29.7	20 51.3	18 46.7
11 Su	23 15 57	20 44 22	3♈20 40	10♈16 09	14 37.8	0♓18.2	12 43.2	8 50.9	17 22.8	18 17.4	28 45.3	6 29.5	20 53.3	18 48.3
12 M	23 19 53	21 44 18	17 14 51	24 16 19	14 37.1	1 51.2	13 55.1	9 30.4	17 46.0	18 31.1	28 43.3	6 29.4	20 55.3	18 49.9
13 Tu	23 23 50	22 44 13	1♉20 04	8♉25 39	14 36.1	3 25.5	15 07.1	10 09.9	18 09.2	18 44.8	28 41.4	6 29.3	20 57.4	18 51.4
14 W	23 27 46	23 44 05	15 32 33	22 40 19	14 35.1	5 00.9	16 19.1	10 49.3	18 32.5	18 58.6	28 39.6	6D29.2	20 59.4	18 53.0
15 Th	23 31 43	24 43 55	29 48 29	6♊56 38	14 34.3	6 37.5	17 31.1	11 28.8	18 55.8	19 12.4	28 37.9	6 29.2	21 01.5	18 54.5
16 F	23 35 39	25 43 42	14♊04 23	21 11 23	14D33.9	8 15.3	18 43.2	12 08.3	19 19.2	19 26.3	28 36.3	6 29.3	21 03.6	18 56.0
17 Sa	23 39 36	26 43 28	28 17 19	5♋21 55	14 34.0	9 54.3	19 55.3	12 47.7	19 42.6	19 40.2	28 34.8	6 29.4	21 05.7	18 57.5
18 Su	23 43 32	27 43 11	12♋24 56	19 26 09	14 34.6	11 34.5	21 07.4	13 27.2	20 06.0	19 54.1	28 33.5	6 29.6	21 07.8	18 59.0
19 M	23 47 29	28 42 52	26 25 21	3♌22 22	14 35.7	13 16.0	22 19.5	14 06.6	20 29.5	20 08.1	28 32.2	6 29.8	21 09.9	19 00.5
20 Tu	23 51 26	29 42 30	10♌17 01	17 09 07	14 36.9	14 58.6	23 31.7	14 46.0	20 53.0	20 22.1	28 31.0	6 30.1	21 12.1	19 01.9
21 W	23 55 22	0♈42 07	23 58 32	0♍45 05	14 37.8	16 42.6	24 43.9	15 25.4	21 16.5	20 36.2	28 30.0	6 30.4	21 14.2	19 03.3
22 Th	23 59 19	1 41 41	7♍28 36	14 08 58	14R38.2	18 27.7	25 56.2	16 04.8	21 40.1	20 50.2	28 29.1	6 30.8	21 16.4	19 04.8
23 F	0 03 15	2 41 13	20 46 02	27 19 42	14 37.8	20 14.2	27 08.4	16 44.2	22 03.7	21 04.3	28 28.2	6 31.2	21 18.5	19 06.2
24 Sa	0 07 12	3 40 43	3♎49 51	10♎16 28	14 36.4	22 01.9	28 20.7	17 23.5	22 27.3	21 18.4	28 27.5	6 31.7	21 20.7	19 07.5
25 Su	0 11 08	4 40 11	16 39 29	22 58 57	14 34.0	23 50.9	29 33.1	18 02.9	22 50.9	21 32.6	28 26.9	6 32.2	21 22.9	19 08.9
26 M	0 15 05	5 39 37	29 14 57	5♏27 34	14 30.8	25 41.2	0♓45.4	18 42.2	23 14.6	21 46.8	28 26.4	6 32.8	21 25.1	19 10.2
27 Tu	0 19 01	6 39 01	11♏36 59	17 43 27	14 27.2	27 32.8	1 57.8	19 21.5	23 38.3	22 01.0	28 26.0	6 33.5	21 27.3	19 11.6
28 W	0 22 58	7 38 23	23 47 13	29 48 39	14 23.6	29 25.8	3 10.2	20 00.8	24 02.1	22 15.2	28 25.7	6 34.2	21 29.5	19 12.9
29 Th	0 26 54	8 37 44	5♐48 07	11♐46 02	14 20.5	1♈20.0	4 22.7	20 40.1	24 25.9	22 29.5	28 25.5	6 34.9	21 31.7	19 14.2
30 F	0 30 51	9 37 02	17 42 54	23 39 13	14 18.3	3 15.6	5 35.1	21 19.4	24 49.7	22 43.7	28D25.5	6 35.7	21 33.9	19 15.4
31 Sa	0 34 48	10 36 19	29 35 31	5♑32 24	14D17.1	5 12.4	6 47.6	21 58.7	25 13.5	22 58.0	28 25.5	6 36.6	21 36.2	19 16.7

April 2035 LONGITUDE

Day	Sid.Time	☉	0 hr ☽	Noon ☽	True ☊	☿	♀	♂	⚳	♃	♄	♅	♆	♇
1 Su	0 38 44	11♈35 35	11♑30 25	17♑30 12	14♍17.2	7♈10.5	8♓00.2	22♑37.9	25♈37.3	23♈12.4	28♋25.7	6♋37.5	21♈38.4	19♒17.9
2 M	0 42 41	12 34 48	23 32 20	29 37 25	14 18.2	9 09.8	9 12.7	23 17.1	26 01.2	23 26.7	28 26.0	6 38.5	21 40.6	19 19.1
3 Tu	0 46 37	13 34 00	5♒46 03	11♒58 46	14 19.8	11 10.3	10 25.3	23 56.3	26 25.1	23 41.0	28 26.3	6 39.5	21 42.9	19 20.3
4 W	0 50 34	14 33 09	18 16 06	24 38 29	14 21.5	13 11.9	11 37.8	24 35.5	26 49.0	23 55.4	28 26.8	6 40.5	21 45.1	19 21.5
5 Th	0 54 30	15 32 17	1♓06 19	7♓39 54	14R22.6	15 14.4	12 50.4	25 14.6	27 13.0	24 09.8	28 27.4	6 41.7	21 47.4	19 22.6
6 F	0 58 27	16 31 23	14 19 26	21 04 59	14 22.6	17 17.9	14 03.1	25 53.7	27 36.9	24 24.2	28 28.1	6 42.8	21 49.7	19 23.8
7 Sa	1 02 23	17 30 27	27 56 30	4♈53 47	14 21.0	19 22.1	15 15.7	26 32.8	28 00.9	24 38.6	28 29.0	6 44.0	21 51.9	19 24.9
8 Su	1 06 20	18 29 30	11♈56 30	19 04 09	14 17.9	21 26.9	16 28.4	27 11.9	28 24.9	24 53.0	28 29.9	6 45.3	21 54.2	19 25.9
9 M	1 10 17	19 28 30	26 16 08	3♉31 42	14 13.3	23 32.1	17 41.0	27 50.9	28 48.9	25 07.4	28 30.9	6 46.6	21 56.5	19 27.0
10 Tu	1 14 13	20 27 28	10♉49 59	18 10 08	14 07.9	25 37.5	18 53.7	28 29.8	29 13.0	25 21.9	28 32.1	6 48.0	21 58.7	19 28.0
11 W	1 18 10	21 26 24	25 31 11	2♊52 14	14 02.4	27 42.8	20 06.4	29 08.8	29 37.0	25 36.3	28 33.3	6 49.4	22 01.0	19 29.1
12 Th	1 22 06	22 25 18	10♊12 24	17 30 52	13 57.6	29 47.7	21 19.1	29 47.7	0♉01.1	25 50.8	28 34.7	6 50.9	22 03.3	19 30.0
13 F	1 26 03	23 24 09	24 46 58	2♋00 06	13 54.1	1♉52.1	22 31.8	0♒26.6	0 25.1	26 05.2	28 36.2	6 52.4	22 05.5	19 31.0
14 Sa	1 29 59	24 22 59	9♋09 48	16 15 45	13D52.3	3 55.4	23 44.5	1 05.4	0 49.2	26 19.7	28 37.8	6 54.0	22 07.8	19 32.0
15 Su	1 33 56	25 21 45	23 17 44	0♌15 38	13 52.2	5 57.4	24 57.3	1 44.2	1 13.3	26 34.1	28 39.5	6 55.6	22 10.1	19 32.9
16 M	1 37 52	26 20 30	7♌09 26	13 59 13	13 53.1	7 57.8	26 10.0	2 23.0	1 37.4	26 48.6	28 41.3	6 57.3	22 12.3	19 33.8
17 Tu	1 41 49	27 19 12	20 45 03	27 27 06	13 54.5	9 56.2	27 22.8	3 01.7	2 01.5	27 03.0	28 43.2	6 59.0	22 14.6	19 34.7
18 W	1 45 46	28 17 53	4♍05 33	10♍40 33	13R55.4	11 52.2	28 35.5	3 40.4	2 25.7	27 17.4	28 45.2	7 00.7	22 16.9	19 35.5
19 Th	1 49 42	29 16 30	17 12 16	23 40 53	13 54.9	13 45.6	29 48.3	4 19.0	2 49.8	27 31.9	28 47.3	7 02.5	22 19.1	19 36.3
20 F	1 53 39	0♉15 06	0♎06 31	6♎29 19	13 52.6	15 36.1	1♈01.1	4 57.6	3 13.9	27 46.3	28 49.5	7 04.4	22 21.4	19 37.1
21 Sa	1 57 35	1 13 40	12 49 22	19 06 46	13 48.0	17 23.3	2 13.9	5 36.2	3 38.1	28 00.7	28 51.8	7 06.2	22 23.6	19 37.9
22 Su	2 01 32	2 12 12	25 21 36	1♏33 57	13 41.3	19 07.0	3 26.7	6 14.7	4 02.2	28 15.2	28 54.2	7 08.2	22 25.9	19 38.7
23 M	2 05 28	3 10 42	7♏43 53	13 51 30	13 32.8	20 47.0	4 39.5	6 53.2	4 26.4	28 29.6	28 56.7	7 10.2	22 28.1	19 39.4
24 Tu	2 09 25	4 09 10	19 56 54	26 00 13	13 23.3	22 23.1	5 52.3	7 31.6	4 50.5	28 44.0	28 59.3	7 12.2	22 30.3	19 40.1
25 W	2 13 21	5 07 36	2♐01 38	8♐01 21	13 13.7	23 55.2	7 05.2	8 10.0	5 14.7	28 58.4	29 02.1	7 14.2	22 32.6	19 40.8
26 Th	2 17 18	6 06 01	13 59 37	19 56 48	13 04.8	25 22.9	8 18.0	8 48.3	5 38.9	29 12.8	29 04.9	7 16.3	22 34.8	19 41.4
27 F	2 21 15	7 04 24	25 52 58	1♑48 48	12 57.4	26 46.3	9 30.9	9 26.6	6 03.0	29 27.1	29 07.8	7 18.5	22 37.0	19 42.1
28 Sa	2 25 11	8 02 45	7♑44 37	13 40 56	12 52.1	28 05.2	10 43.7	10 04.9	6 27.2	29 41.5	29 10.8	7 20.7	22 39.2	19 42.7
29 Su	2 29 08	9 01 05	19 38 14	25 37 06	12 49.0	29 19.6	11 56.6	10 43.0	6 51.4	29 55.9	29 13.9	7 22.9	22 41.4	19 43.2
30 M	2 33 04	9 59 23	1♒38 07	7♒41 54	12D47.9	0♊29.2	13 09.5	11 21.2	7 15.6	0♉10.2	29 17.1	7 25.2	22 43.6	19 43.8

Astro Data	Dy Hr Mn
⚳0N	7 13:59
☽0N	11 1:16
♃⚹♇	14 0:57
♅ D	14 21:31
☉0N	20 19:03
☽0S	24 0:24
♃☌♆	24 16:32
♄ D	30 13:12
☿0N	30 20:05
☽0N	7 10:33
☽0S	20 7:32
♀0N	22 15:39
♃□♄	25 19:35

Planet Ingress	Dy Hr Mn
☿ ♓	11 7:16
☉ ♈	20 19:03
♀ ♓	25 20:56
☿ ♈	28 19:13
⚳ ♉	12 10:57
☿ ♉	12 14:22
♂ ♒	12 19:35
♀ ♈	19 15:52
☉ ♉	20 5:49
♃ ♉	29 18:57
☿ ♊	30 1:45

Last Aspect Dy Hr Mn		☽ Ingress Dy Hr Mn
1 2:31	♄ △	♐ 1 4:07
2 21:44	♆ △	♑ 3 16:39
6 1:57	♄ ☍	♒ 6 3:58
8 3:48	☿ ☌	♓ 8 12:31
10 16:02	♄ △	♈ 10 18:10
12 19:33	♄ □	♉ 12 21:44
14 22:03	♄ ⚹	♊ 15 0:19
16 20:15	☉ □	♋ 17 2:54
19 3:39	♄ ☌	♌ 19 6:10
21 0:18	♀ ☍	♍ 21 10:40
23 14:06	♄ ⚹	♎ 23 16:55
25 22:27	♄ □	♏ 26 1:27
28 11:06	☿ △	♐ 28 12:23
30 10:06	♃ △	♑ 31 0:49

Last Aspect Dy Hr Mn		☽ Ingress Dy Hr Mn
2 9:40	♄ ☍	♒ 2 12:44
4 10:38	♃ ⚹	♓ 4 21:58
7 0:56	♄ △	♈ 7 3:34
9 3:43	♄ □	♉ 9 6:11
11 5:38	♂ △	♊ 11 7:19
13 2:00	♃ ⚹	♋ 13 8:40
15 9:13	♄ ☌	♌ 15 11:33
17 11:45	☉ △	♍ 17 16:36
19 21:33	♄ ⚹	♎ 19 23:48
22 6:50	♄ □	♏ 22 8:58
24 17:58	♄ △	♐ 24 19:57
27 7:07	♃ △	♑ 27 8:20
29 20:13	☿ △	♒ 29 20:45

☽ Phases & Eclipses Dy Hr Mn	
2 3:01	☾ 11♐21
9 23:09	● 19♓12
9 23:04:32	● A 00'46"
16 20:15	☽ 26♊04
23 22:42	○ 3♎08
31 23:06	☾ 11♑04
8 10:58	● 18♈27
15 2:55	☽ 25♋00
22 13:21	○ 2♏15
30 16:54	☾ 10♒11

Astro Data

1 March 2035
Julian Day # 49368
SVP 4♓46'11"
GC 27♐19.8 ⚴ 3♓59.5
Eris 26♈53.9 ⚵ 5♒51.2
⚷ 1♊37.6 ⚶ 4♋13.3
☽ Mean ☊ 14♍57.4

1 April 2035
Julian Day # 49399
SVP 4♓46'08"
GC 27♐19.9 ⚴ 14♓05.1
Eris 27♈11.3 ⚵ 17♒09.7
⚷ 2♊51.8 ⚶ 9♋11.0
☽ Mean ☊ 13♍18.9

LONGITUDE

Day	Sid.Time	☉	0 hr ☽	Noon ☽	True ☊	☿	♀	♂	⚳	♃	♄	♅	♆	♇
1 Tu	2 37 01	10♉57 40	13♒49 04	20♒00 17	12♍48.2	1♊34.0	14♈22.4	11♒59.2	7♉39.7	0♉24.5	29♋20.4	7♋27.5	22♈45.8	19♒44.3
2 W	2 40 57	11 55 55	26 16 08	2♓37 14	12R49.0	2 34.0	15 35.3	12 37.2	8 03.9	0 38.8	29 23.8	7 29.9	22 48.0	19 44.8
3 Th	2 44 54	12 54 08	9♓04 08	15 37 19	12 49.3	3 29.1	16 48.3	13 15.2	8 28.1	0 53.1	29 27.3	7 32.3	22 50.1	19 45.3
4 F	2 48 50	13 52 21	22 17 09	29 03 57	12 48.1	4 19.2	18 01.2	13 53.0	8 52.3	1 07.3	29 30.9	7 34.7	22 52.3	19 45.7
5 Sa	2 52 47	14 50 31	5♈57 49	12♈58 43	12 44.8	5 04.3	19 14.1	14 30.8	9 16.4	1 21.6	29 34.5	7 37.2	22 54.4	19 46.2
6 Su	2 56 43	15 48 40	20 06 27	27 20 34	12 39.0	5 44.3	20 27.1	15 08.5	9 40.6	1 35.8	29 38.3	7 39.7	22 56.6	19 46.5
7 M	3 00 40	16 46 48	4♉40 26	12♉05 13	12 31.0	6 19.1	21 40.0	15 46.2	10 04.8	1 50.0	29 42.1	7 42.2	22 58.7	19 46.9
8 Tu	3 04 37	17 44 54	19 33 55	27 05 21	12 21.5	6 48.7	22 53.0	16 23.7	10 28.9	2 04.1	29 46.1	7 44.8	23 00.8	19 47.3
9 W	3 08 33	18 42 58	4♊38 17	12♊11 26	12 11.8	7 13.2	24 06.0	17 01.2	10 53.1	2 18.3	29 50.1	7 47.4	23 02.9	19 47.6
10 Th	3 12 30	19 41 01	19 43 30	27 13 20	12 02.9	7 32.4	25 18.9	17 38.6	11 17.2	2 32.4	29 54.2	7 50.1	23 05.0	19 47.9
11 F	3 16 26	20 39 02	4♋39 50	12♋02 08	11 55.9	7 46.5	26 31.9	18 15.9	11 41.4	2 46.4	29 58.4	7 52.8	23 07.0	19 48.1
12 Sa	3 20 23	21 37 01	19 19 30	26 31 26	11 51.4	7 55.4	27 44.9	18 53.1	12 05.5	3 00.5	0♌02.7	7 55.5	23 09.1	19 48.4
13 Su	3 24 19	22 34 58	3♌37 37	10♌37 53	11D49.1	7R59.3	28 57.9	19 30.2	12 29.6	3 14.5	0 07.1	7 58.2	23 11.1	19 48.6
14 M	3 28 16	23 32 53	17 32 17	24 20 55	11 48.6	7 58.2	0♉10.9	20 07.2	12 53.7	3 28.5	0 11.6	8 01.0	23 13.2	19 48.8
15 Tu	3 32 13	24 30 46	1♍04 03	7♍42 00	11R48.8	7 52.3	1 23.8	20 44.1	13 17.8	3 42.4	0 16.1	8 03.9	23 15.2	19 48.9
16 W	3 36 09	25 28 38	14 15 07	20 43 47	11 48.6	7 41.9	2 36.8	21 21.0	13 41.9	3 56.3	0 20.7	8 06.7	23 17.2	19 49.0
17 Th	3 40 06	26 26 27	27 08 24	3♎29 22	11 46.8	7 27.1	3 49.8	21 57.7	14 06.0	4 10.2	0 25.4	8 09.6	23 19.1	19 49.1
18 F	3 44 02	27 24 15	9♎47 02	16 01 46	11 42.7	7 08.3	5 02.8	22 34.4	14 30.0	4 24.0	0 30.2	8 12.5	23 21.1	19 49.2
19 Sa	3 47 59	28 22 02	22 13 52	28 23 35	11 35.7	6 45.8	6 15.8	23 10.9	14 54.1	4 37.8	0 35.1	8 15.4	23 23.0	19 49.3
20 Su	3 51 55	29 19 47	4♏31 11	10♏36 53	11 25.9	6 20.1	7 28.8	23 47.3	15 18.1	4 51.6	0 40.0	8 18.4	23 25.0	19R49.3
21 M	3 55 52	0♊17 30	16 40 50	22 43 13	11 13.9	5 51.6	8 41.9	24 23.7	15 42.1	5 05.3	0 45.0	8 21.4	23 26.9	19 49.3
22 Tu	3 59 48	1 15 13	28 44 10	4♐43 50	11 00.6	5 20.8	9 54.9	24 59.9	16 06.1	5 19.0	0 50.1	8 24.4	23 28.8	19 49.3
23 W	4 03 45	2 12 54	10♐42 22	16 39 55	10 46.9	4 48.3	11 07.9	25 36.0	16 30.1	5 32.6	0 55.2	8 27.5	23 30.6	19 49.2
24 Th	4 07 41	3 10 33	22 36 40	28 32 48	10 34.1	4 14.6	12 21.0	26 12.0	16 54.0	5 46.2	1 00.5	8 30.6	23 32.5	19 49.1
25 F	4 11 38	4 08 12	4♑28 34	10♑24 15	10 23.1	3 40.4	13 34.0	26 47.8	17 18.0	5 59.7	1 05.8	8 33.7	23 34.3	19 49.0
26 Sa	4 15 35	5 05 49	16 20 09	22 16 39	10 14.7	3 06.3	14 47.1	27 23.6	17 41.9	6 13.2	1 11.2	8 36.8	23 36.2	19 48.9
27 Su	4 19 31	6 03 26	28 14 09	4♒13 06	10 09.0	2 32.7	16 00.2	27 59.2	18 05.8	6 26.7	1 16.6	8 40.0	23 37.9	19 48.8
28 M	4 23 28	7 01 01	10♒14 01	16 17 26	10 05.9	2 00.4	17 13.2	28 34.7	18 29.7	6 40.1	1 22.1	8 43.2	23 39.7	19 48.6
29 Tu	4 27 24	7 58 35	22 23 56	28 34 06	10 04.8	1 29.9	18 26.3	29 10.0	18 53.6	6 53.4	1 27.7	8 46.4	23 41.5	19 48.4
30 W	4 31 21	8 56 09	4♓48 35	11♓07 58	10 04.6	1 01.6	19 39.4	29 45.2	19 17.4	7 06.7	1 33.3	8 49.6	23 43.2	19 48.1
31 Th	4 35 17	9 53 42	17 32 53	24 03 52	10 04.3	0 36.0	20 52.5	0♓20.2	19 41.3	7 20.0	1 39.0	8 52.9	23 44.9	19 47.9

LONGITUDE

Day	Sid.Time	☉	0 hr ☽	Noon ☽	True ☊	☿	♀	♂	⚳	♃	♄	♅	♆	♇
1 F	4 39 14	10♊51 13	0♈41 27	7♈26 02	10♍02.8	0♊13.5	22♉05.7	0♓55.1	20♉05.1	7♉33.1	1♌44.8	8♋56.2	23♈46.6	19♒47.6
2 Sa	4 43 10	11 48 44	14 17 54	21 17 14	9R59.0	29♉54.5	23 18.8	1 29.9	20 28.9	7 46.3	1 50.7	8 59.4	23 48.3	19R47.3
3 Su	4 47 07	12 46 15	28 23 57	5♉37 50	9 52.7	29R39.2	24 31.9	2 04.4	20 52.6	7 59.4	1 56.6	9 02.8	23 49.9	19 46.9
4 M	4 51 04	13 43 44	12♉58 25	20 24 58	9 44.0	29 28.0	25 45.1	2 38.8	21 16.4	8 12.4	2 02.5	9 06.1	23 51.5	19 46.6
5 Tu	4 55 00	14 41 13	27 56 33	5♊32 02	9 33.7	29 20.9	26 58.3	3 13.0	21 40.1	8 25.3	2 08.6	9 09.5	23 53.1	19 46.2
6 W	4 58 57	15 38 41	13♊10 06	20 49 19	9 22.8	29D18.2	28 11.4	3 47.1	22 03.7	8 38.2	2 14.7	9 12.8	23 54.7	19 45.8
7 Th	5 02 53	16 36 08	28 28 16	6♋05 29	9 12.8	29 19.9	29 24.6	4 20.9	22 27.4	8 51.1	2 20.8	9 16.2	23 56.3	19 45.4
8 F	5 06 50	17 33 34	13♋39 39	21 09 36	9 04.7	29 26.1	0♊37.8	4 54.5	22 51.0	9 03.8	2 27.0	9 19.6	23 57.8	19 44.9
9 Sa	5 10 46	18 30 59	28 34 20	5♌53 06	8 59.2	29 36.8	1 51.0	5 28.0	23 14.6	9 16.5	2 33.3	9 23.1	23 59.3	19 44.4
10 Su	5 14 43	19 28 23	13♌05 22	20 10 50	8 56.2	29 51.9	3 04.2	6 01.2	23 38.2	9 29.2	2 39.6	9 26.5	24 00.8	19 43.9
11 M	5 18 40	20 25 45	27 09 22	4♍01 04	8D55.2	0♊11.6	4 17.4	6 34.3	24 01.7	9 41.8	2 46.0	9 30.0	24 02.2	19 43.4
12 Tu	5 22 36	21 23 07	10♍46 06	17 24 50	8R55.2	0 35.7	5 30.6	7 07.1	24 25.2	9 54.3	2 52.4	9 33.5	24 03.7	19 42.8
13 W	5 26 33	22 20 27	23 57 39	0♎25 02	8 55.1	1 04.1	6 43.8	7 39.7	24 48.7	10 06.7	2 58.8	9 36.9	24 05.1	19 42.2
14 Th	5 30 29	23 17 47	6♎47 28	13 05 29	8 53.6	1 36.9	7 57.0	8 12.1	25 12.1	10 19.0	3 05.4	9 40.4	24 06.4	19 41.6
15 F	5 34 26	24 15 05	19 19 35	25 30 15	8 49.9	2 13.9	9 10.3	8 44.3	25 35.5	10 31.3	3 11.9	9 43.9	24 07.8	19 41.0
16 Sa	5 38 22	25 12 23	1♏37 58	7♏43 09	8 43.7	2 55.1	10 23.5	9 16.3	25 58.8	10 43.5	3 18.6	9 47.5	24 09.1	19 40.4
17 Su	5 42 19	26 09 40	13 46 13	19 47 29	8 34.8	3 40.4	11 36.8	9 48.0	26 22.1	10 55.6	3 25.2	9 51.0	24 10.4	19 39.7
18 M	5 46 15	27 06 56	25 47 19	1♐45 58	8 23.8	4 29.6	12 50.1	10 19.5	26 45.4	11 07.7	3 31.9	9 54.5	24 11.6	19 39.0
19 Tu	5 50 12	28 04 12	7♐43 41	13 40 43	8 11.5	5 22.9	14 03.3	10 50.7	27 08.7	11 19.7	3 38.7	9 58.1	24 12.9	19 38.3
20 W	5 54 09	29 01 27	19 37 15	25 33 27	7 58.9	6 20.0	15 16.6	11 21.7	27 31.9	11 31.6	3 45.5	10 01.7	24 14.1	19 37.6
21 Th	5 58 05	29 58 42	1♑29 32	7♑25 40	7 47.0	7 20.9	16 29.9	11 52.4	27 55.0	11 43.4	3 52.4	10 05.2	24 15.3	19 36.8
22 F	6 02 02	0♋55 56	13 22 03	19 18 52	7 36.9	8 25.6	17 43.3	12 22.9	28 18.2	11 55.1	3 59.3	10 08.8	24 16.4	19 36.1
23 Sa	6 05 58	1 53 09	25 16 23	1♒14 51	7 29.1	9 34.0	18 56.6	12 53.0	28 41.2	12 06.8	4 06.2	10 12.4	24 17.5	19 35.3
24 Su	6 09 55	2 50 23	7♒14 33	13 15 49	7 23.9	10 46.0	20 09.9	13 22.9	29 04.3	12 18.3	4 13.2	10 16.0	24 18.6	19 34.4
25 M	6 13 51	3 47 36	19 19 03	25 24 38	7D21.2	12 01.6	21 23.3	13 52.5	29 27.3	12 29.8	4 20.2	10 19.6	24 19.7	19 33.6
26 Tu	6 17 48	4 44 49	1♓33 02	7♓44 43	7 20.6	13 20.8	22 36.7	14 21.8	29 50.2	12 41.2	4 27.2	10 23.2	24 20.7	19 32.8
27 W	6 21 44	5 42 02	14 00 12	20 20 01	7 21.0	14 43.5	23 50.1	14 50.8	0♊13.1	12 52.5	4 34.3	10 26.8	24 21.8	19 31.9
28 Th	6 25 41	6 39 15	26 44 39	3♈14 39	7R21.6	16 09.7	25 03.5	15 19.5	0 36.0	13 03.7	4 41.4	10 30.4	24 22.7	19 31.0
29 F	6 29 38	7 36 28	9♈50 29	16 32 35	7 21.3	17 39.3	26 16.9	15 47.8	0 58.8	13 14.8	4 48.6	10 34.0	24 23.7	19 30.1
30 Sa	6 33 34	8 33 41	23 21 16	0♉16 46	7 19.3	19 12.4	27 30.3	16 15.8	1 21.6	13 25.8	4 55.8	10 37.6	24 24.6	19 29.1

Astro Data	Dy Hr Mn
☽ 0N	4 21:09
☿ R	13 18:41
☽ 0S	17 13:57
♇ R	20 23:00
☽ 0N	1 7:31
☿ D	6 14:53
♃⚹♅	10 5:02
☽ 0S	13 20:57
☽ 0N	28 16:17

Planet Ingress	Dy Hr Mn
♄ ♌	11 20:45
♀ ♉	14 8:26
☉ ♊	21 4:43
♂ ♓	30 22:07
☿ ♉R	2 4:33
♀ ♊	7 23:36
☿ ♊	10 22:32
☉ ♋	21 12:33
⚳ ♊	26 22:13

Last Aspect Dy Hr Mn		☽ Ingress Dy Hr Mn
1 17:19	♆ ⚹	♓ 2 7:04
4 12:47	♄ △	♈ 4 13:38
6 15:47	♄ □	♉ 6 16:22
8 16:17	♄ ⚹	♊ 8 16:38
10 8:40	♀ ⚹	♋ 10 16:28
12 14:15	♀ □	♌ 12 17:51
14 10:28	☉ □	♍ 14 22:05
16 21:36	☉ △	♎ 17 5:24
19 2:13	♆ ☍	♏ 19 15:08
21 15:31	♂ □	♐ 22 2:32
24 7:00	♂ ⚹	♑ 24 14:56
26 14:41	♆ □	♒ 27 3:33
29 13:13	♂ ☌	♓ 29 14:46
31 5:33	♀ ⚹	♈ 31 22:46

Last Aspect Dy Hr Mn		☽ Ingress Dy Hr Mn
2 16:17	♆ ☌	♉ 3 2:40
5 2:18	☿ ☌	♊ 5 3:16
6 16:51	♆ ⚹	♋ 7 2:24
9 1:33	☿ ⚹	♌ 9 2:20
10 18:35	♆ △	♍ 11 4:57
12 19:50	☉ □	♎ 13 11:13
15 9:21	☉ △	♏ 15 20:48
17 11:44	♇ □	♐ 18 8:27
20 19:37	☉ ☍	♑ 20 20:59
22 22:00	♆ □	♒ 23 9:30
25 9:52	♆ ⚹	♓ 25 20:59
27 19:16	♀ □	♈ 28 6:02
30 6:45	♀ ⚹	♉ 30 11:31

☽ Phases & Eclipses Dy Hr Mn	
7 20:04	● 17♉06
14 10:28	☽ 23♌29
22 4:26	○ 0♐57
30 7:31	☾ 8♓45
6 3:21	● 15♊18
12 19:50	☽ 21♍42
20 19:37	○ 29♐20
28 18:43	☾ 6♈55

Astro Data

1 May 2035
Julian Day # 49429
SVP 4♓46'05"
GC 27♐20.0 ⚴ 23♓06.6
Eris 27♈30.9 ⚵ 26♒58.4
⚷ 4♊46.4 ⚶ 18♋00.5
☽ Mean ☊ 11♍43.5

1 June 2035
Julian Day # 49460
SVP 4♓46'01"
GC 27♐20.0 ⚴ 1♈00.4
Eris 27♈49.0 ⚵ 4♓57.7
⚷ 7♊06.4 ⚶ 29♋35.7
☽ Mean ☊ 10♍05.0

July 2035 LONGITUDE

Day	Sid.Time	☉	0 hr ☽	Noon ☽	True ☊	☿	♀	♂	⚳	♃	♄	♅	♆	♇
1 Su	6 37 31	9♋30 54	7♉19 10	14♉28 24	7♍15.2	20♊48.7	28♊43.8	16♓43.4	1♊44.3	13♉36.8	5♌03.0	10♋41.3	24♈25.5	19♒28.2
2 M	6 41 27	10 28 08	21 44 10	29 05 59	7R 09.1	22 28.4	29 57.3	17 10.7	2 07.0	13 47.6	5 10.3	10 44.9	24 26.3	19R 27.2
3 Tu	6 45 24	11 25 21	6♊33 10	14♊04 46	7 01.5	24 11.2	1♋10.8	17 37.6	2 29.6	13 58.3	5 17.6	10 48.5	24 27.2	19 26.2
4 W	6 49 20	12 22 35	21 39 43	29 16 44	6 53.4	25 57.2	2 24.3	18 04.1	2 52.2	14 08.9	5 24.9	10 52.1	24 28.0	19 25.2
5 Th	6 53 17	13 19 49	6♋54 30	14♋31 38	6 45.8	27 46.3	3 37.8	18 30.2	3 14.7	14 19.5	5 32.2	10 55.7	24 28.7	19 24.2
6 F	6 57 13	14 17 03	22 06 46	29 38 39	6 39.7	29 38.2	4 51.4	18 56.0	3 37.2	14 29.9	5 39.6	10 59.4	24 29.4	19 23.2
7 Sa	7 01 10	15 14 16	7♌06 09	14♌28 20	6 35.7	1♋32.9	6 04.9	19 21.2	3 59.6	14 40.2	5 47.0	11 03.0	24 30.1	19 22.1
8 Su	7 05 07	16 11 30	21 44 28	28 54 01	6D 33.8	3 30.1	7 18.5	19 46.1	4 21.9	14 50.4	5 54.4	11 06.6	24 30.8	19 21.1
9 M	7 09 03	17 08 43	5♍56 39	12♍52 16	6 33.7	5 29.8	8 32.1	20 10.6	4 44.2	15 00.5	6 01.9	11 10.2	24 31.5	19 20.0
10 Tu	7 13 00	18 05 56	19 40 54	26 22 45	6 34.7	7 31.5	9 45.7	20 34.6	5 06.4	15 10.5	6 09.4	11 13.8	24 32.1	19 18.9
11 W	7 16 56	19 03 09	2♎58 08	9♎27 25	6R 35.8	9 35.2	10 59.3	20 58.1	5 28.5	15 20.3	6 16.9	11 17.4	24 32.6	19 17.8
12 Th	7 20 53	20 00 22	15 51 07	22 09 44	6 36.1	11 40.5	12 12.9	21 21.2	5 50.6	15 30.1	6 24.4	11 21.0	24 33.2	19 16.6
13 F	7 24 49	20 57 35	28 23 48	4♏33 53	6 35.1	13 47.1	13 26.5	21 43.8	6 12.6	15 39.7	6 31.9	11 24.6	24 33.7	19 15.5
14 Sa	7 28 46	21 54 47	10♏40 31	16 44 14	6 32.2	15 54.7	14 40.2	22 06.0	6 34.6	15 49.2	6 39.5	11 28.2	24 34.1	19 14.4
15 Su	7 32 42	22 52 00	22 45 34	28 45 00	6 27.5	18 03.1	15 53.8	22 27.6	6 56.5	15 58.6	6 47.1	11 31.7	24 34.6	19 13.2
16 M	7 36 39	23 49 13	4♐42 57	10♐39 52	6 21.2	20 11.8	17 07.5	22 48.8	7 18.3	16 07.9	6 54.7	11 35.3	24 35.0	19 12.0
17 Tu	7 40 36	24 46 26	16 36 07	22 32 03	6 14.0	22 20.7	18 21.2	23 09.4	7 40.1	16 17.1	7 02.3	11 38.9	24 35.4	19 10.8
18 W	7 44 32	25 43 40	28 27 59	4♑24 11	6 06.4	24 29.4	19 34.9	23 29.6	8 01.8	16 26.1	7 09.9	11 42.4	24 35.7	19 09.6
19 Th	7 48 29	26 40 54	10♑20 54	16 18 24	5 59.4	26 37.7	20 48.7	23 49.1	8 23.4	16 35.0	7 17.6	11 45.9	24 36.0	19 08.4
20 F	7 52 25	27 38 08	22 16 51	28 16 30	5 53.4	28 45.4	22 02.4	24 08.2	8 44.9	16 43.8	7 25.2	11 49.5	24 36.3	19 07.2
21 Sa	7 56 22	28 35 22	4♒17 31	10♒20 07	5 49.1	0♌52.2	23 16.2	24 26.6	9 06.4	16 52.4	7 32.9	11 53.0	24 36.6	19 06.0
22 Su	8 00 18	29 32 37	16 24 31	22 30 55	5 46.5	2 58.0	24 29.9	24 44.5	9 27.8	17 01.0	7 40.6	11 56.5	24 36.8	19 04.7
23 M	8 04 15	0♌29 53	28 39 35	4♓50 45	5D 45.6	5 02.7	25 43.7	25 01.8	9 49.1	17 09.4	7 48.2	12 00.0	24 36.9	19 03.5
24 Tu	8 08 11	1 27 10	11♓04 42	17 21 44	5 46.1	7 06.0	26 57.5	25 18.5	10 10.3	17 17.6	7 55.9	12 03.4	24 37.1	19 02.2
25 W	8 12 08	2 24 27	23 42 11	0♈06 21	5 47.5	9 08.0	28 11.4	25 34.6	10 31.5	17 25.7	8 03.6	12 06.9	24 37.2	19 00.9
26 Th	8 16 05	3 21 45	6♈34 36	13 07 15	5 49.0	11 08.5	29 25.2	25 50.1	10 52.6	17 33.7	8 11.4	12 10.3	24 37.3	18 59.6
27 F	8 20 01	4 19 04	19 44 37	26 26 59	5R 50.2	13 07.4	0♌39.1	26 04.9	11 13.6	17 41.6	8 19.1	12 13.8	24 37.3	18 58.4
28 Sa	8 23 58	5 16 24	3♉14 35	10♉07 35	5 50.3	15 04.8	1 53.0	26 19.0	11 34.5	17 49.3	8 26.8	12 17.2	24R 37.4	18 57.1
29 Su	8 27 54	6 13 45	17 06 04	24 10 00	5 49.2	17 00.6	3 06.9	26 32.4	11 55.3	17 56.8	8 34.5	12 20.6	24 37.3	18 55.8
30 M	8 31 51	7 11 07	1♊19 12	8♊33 22	5 46.9	18 54.7	4 20.8	26 45.2	12 16.1	18 04.3	8 42.3	12 23.9	24 37.3	18 54.5
31 Tu	8 35 47	8 08 30	15 52 02	23 14 35	5 43.6	20 47.2	5 34.8	26 57.2	12 36.7	18 11.5	8 50.0	12 27.3	24 37.2	18 53.1

August 2035 LONGITUDE

Day	Sid.Time	☉	0 hr ☽	Noon ☽	True ☊	☿	♀	♂	⚳	♃	♄	♅	♆	♇
1 W	8 39 44	9♌05 54	0♋40 14	8♋08 07	5♍40.0	22♌38.1	6♌48.7	27♓08.6	12♊57.3	18♉18.6	8♌57.7	12♋30.6	24♈37.1	18♒51.8
2 Th	8 43 40	10 03 20	15 37 12	23 06 26	5R 36.6	24 27.3	8 02.7	27 19.1	13 17.7	18 25.6	9 05.5	12 34.0	24R 37.0	18R 50.5
3 F	8 47 37	11 00 46	0♌34 42	8♌00 56	5 33.9	26 14.9	9 16.7	27 29.0	13 38.1	18 32.4	9 13.2	12 37.3	24 36.8	18 49.2
4 Sa	8 51 34	11 58 13	15 24 07	22 43 20	5D 32.3	28 00.8	10 30.8	27 38.1	13 58.4	18 39.1	9 20.9	12 40.5	24 36.6	18 47.8
5 Su	8 55 30	12 55 41	29 57 46	7♍06 47	5 31.9	29 45.1	11 44.8	27 46.4	14 18.5	18 45.6	9 28.7	12 43.8	24 36.3	18 46.5
6 M	8 59 27	13 53 10	14♍09 53	21 06 46	5 32.5	1♍27.8	12 58.8	27 53.9	14 38.6	18 52.0	9 36.4	12 47.0	24 36.0	18 45.2
7 Tu	9 03 23	14 50 39	27 57 15	4♎41 18	5 33.7	3 08.8	14 12.9	28 00.7	14 58.5	18 58.1	9 44.1	12 50.2	24 35.7	18 43.8
8 W	9 07 20	15 48 09	11♎19 04	17 50 45	5 35.1	4 48.3	15 27.0	28 06.6	15 18.4	19 04.2	9 51.8	12 53.4	24 35.4	18 42.5
9 Th	9 11 16	16 45 40	24 16 41	0♏37 16	5 36.3	6 26.2	16 41.1	28 11.8	15 38.1	19 10.0	9 59.5	12 56.6	24 35.0	18 41.1
10 F	9 15 13	17 43 12	6♏52 58	13 04 18	5R 37.0	8 02.5	17 55.2	28 16.2	15 57.8	19 15.7	10 07.2	12 59.7	24 34.6	18 39.8
11 Sa	9 19 09	18 40 45	19 11 47	25 16 00	5 36.9	9 37.2	19 09.3	28 19.8	16 17.3	19 21.3	10 14.9	13 02.8	24 34.2	18 38.4
12 Su	9 23 06	19 38 19	1♐17 29	7♐16 48	5 36.1	11 10.3	20 23.4	28 22.6	16 36.7	19 26.6	10 22.6	13 05.9	24 33.7	18 37.1
13 M	9 27 03	20 35 53	13 14 30	19 11 08	5 34.6	12 41.8	21 37.6	28 24.5	16 56.0	19 31.8	10 30.3	13 09.0	24 33.2	18 35.8
14 Tu	9 30 59	21 33 29	25 07 10	1♑03 05	5 32.8	14 11.7	22 51.7	28R 25.7	17 15.2	19 36.8	10 37.9	13 12.0	24 32.7	18 34.4
15 W	9 34 56	22 31 05	6♑59 22	12 56 23	5 30.8	15 40.1	24 05.9	28 26.0	17 34.2	19 41.7	10 45.5	13 15.0	24 32.1	18 33.1
16 Th	9 38 52	23 28 43	18 54 33	24 54 12	5 29.0	17 06.8	25 20.1	28 25.6	17 53.2	19 46.4	10 53.2	13 18.0	24 31.5	18 31.7
17 F	9 42 49	24 26 22	0♒55 37	6♒59 06	5 27.6	18 31.8	26 34.2	28 24.3	18 12.0	19 50.9	11 00.8	13 20.9	24 30.9	18 30.4
18 Sa	9 46 45	25 24 01	13 04 53	19 13 11	5 26.6	19 55.2	27 48.4	28 22.2	18 30.6	19 55.2	11 08.4	13 23.8	24 30.3	18 29.1
19 Su	9 50 42	26 21 42	25 24 09	1♓37 59	5D 26.2	21 16.9	29 02.7	28 19.2	18 49.2	19 59.4	11 15.9	13 26.7	24 29.6	18 27.7
20 M	9 54 38	27 19 25	7♓54 47	14 14 41	5 26.3	22 36.9	0♍16.9	28 15.5	19 07.6	20 03.4	11 23.5	13 29.6	24 28.9	18 26.4
21 Tu	9 58 35	28 17 09	20 37 46	27 04 09	5 26.7	23 55.1	1 31.1	28 11.0	19 25.9	20 07.2	11 31.0	13 32.4	24 28.1	18 25.1
22 W	10 02 32	29 14 54	3♈33 53	10♈07 03	5 27.3	25 11.5	2 45.4	28 05.6	19 44.1	20 10.8	11 38.5	13 35.2	24 27.4	18 23.8
23 Th	10 06 28	0♍12 41	16 43 43	23 23 56	5 27.9	26 26.0	3 59.6	27 59.5	20 02.1	20 14.2	11 46.0	13 38.0	24 26.6	18 22.4
24 F	10 10 25	1 10 30	0♉07 45	6♉55 10	5 28.3	27 38.6	5 13.9	27 52.5	20 20.0	20 17.4	11 53.5	13 40.7	24 25.8	18 21.1
25 Sa	10 14 21	2 08 20	13 46 11	20 40 47	5R 28.5	28 49.2	6 28.2	27 44.8	20 37.7	20 20.5	12 00.9	13 43.4	24 24.9	18 19.8
26 Su	10 18 18	3 06 12	27 38 53	4♊40 23	5 28.6	29 57.6	7 42.5	27 36.4	20 55.3	20 23.4	12 08.3	13 46.0	24 24.0	18 18.5
27 M	10 22 14	4 04 07	11♊45 05	18 52 46	5 28.5	1♎03.9	8 56.9	27 27.2	21 12.7	20 26.0	12 15.7	13 48.7	24 23.1	18 17.3
28 Tu	10 26 11	5 02 03	26 03 06	3♋15 44	5D 28.5	2 07.9	10 11.2	27 17.3	21 30.0	20 28.5	12 23.1	13 51.2	24 22.2	18 16.0
29 W	10 30 07	6 00 00	10♋30 11	17 45 55	5 28.5	3 09.5	11 25.6	27 06.6	21 47.2	20 30.8	12 30.4	13 53.8	24 21.2	18 14.7
30 Th	10 34 04	6 58 00	25 02 21	2♌18 49	5 28.6	4 08.6	12 39.9	26 55.3	22 04.1	20 32.9	12 37.7	13 56.3	24 20.2	18 13.4
31 F	10 38 01	7 56 01	9♌34 39	16 49 09	5 28.8	5 05.0	13 54.3	26 43.4	22 21.0	20 34.8	12 45.0	13 58.8	24 19.2	18 12.2

Astro Data	Dy Hr Mn	Planet Ingress	Dy Hr Mn	Last Aspect Dy Hr Mn		☽ Ingress	Dy Hr Mn	Last Aspect Dy Hr Mn		☽ Ingress	Dy Hr Mn	☽ Phases & Eclipses Dy Hr Mn		Astro Data
☽0S	11 5:16	♀ ♋	2 12:53	1 20:16	♇ □	♊	2 13:27	2 18:50	♂ △	♌	2 23:04	5 9:59	● 13♋15	1 July 2035
☽0N	25 23:07	☿ ♋	6 16:36	4 6:04	☿ ☌	♋	4 13:08	4 21:58	☿ ☌	♍	5 0:04	12 7:33	☽ 19♎50	Julian Day # 49490
♆ R	28 12:28	☿ ♌	21 2:06	6 3:46	♆ □	♌	6 12:34	7 0:00	♂ ☍	♎	7 3:38	20 10:37	○ 27♑35	SVP 4♓45'56"
		☉ ♌	22 23:28	8 4:37	♆ △	♍	8 13:52	9 0:35	♆ ☍	♏	9 10:49	28 2:55	☾ 4♉55	GC 27♐20.1 ⚴ 6♈19.0
♃□♇	5 14:48	♀ ♌	26 23:18	10 1:16	♂ ☍	♎	10 18:34	11 18:07	♂ △	♐	11 21:25			Eris 28♈00.3 ⚵ 9♓06.4
☽0S	7 14:45			12 16:35	♆ ☍	♏	13 3:06	14 6:41	♂ □	♑	14 9:52	3 17:12	● 11♌13	⚷ 9♊19.8 ⚶ 12♌16.0
♂ R	15 10:01	☿ ♍	5 15:28	14 23:12	☉ △	♐	15 14:31	16 19:01	♂ ⚹	♒	16 22:09	10 21:52	☽ 18♏07	☽ Mean ☊ 8♍29.7
☽0N	22 4:59	♀ ♍	20 6:32	17 16:10	♆ △	♑	18 3:06	19 6:29	♀ ☍	♓	19 8:52	19 1:00	○ 25♒55	
☿0S	24 1:27	☉ ♍	23 6:44	20 13:10	☿ ☍	♒	20 15:27	21 14:03	♂ ☌	♈	21 17:26	19 1:11	• P 0.104	1 August 2035
		☿ ♎	26 12:51	22 16:06	♆ ⚹	♓	23 2:36	23 13:52	♆ ☌	♉	23 23:46	26 9:08	☾ 2♊59	Julian Day # 49521
				25 8:02	♀ △	♈	25 11:48	26 3:15	☿ △	♊	26 4:02			SVP 4♓45'52"
				27 8:45	♆ ☌	♉	27 18:17	28 2:11	♂ □	♋	28 6:35			GC 27♐20.2 ⚴ 7♈54.7R
				29 16:04	♂ ⚹	♊	29 21:48	30 3:13	♂ △	♌	30 8:11			Eris 28♈02.9R ⚵ 7♓43.1R
				31 18:05	♂ □	♋	31 22:55							⚷ 11♊12.4 ⚶ 26♌19.5
														☽ Mean ☊ 6♍51.3

LONGITUDE — September 2035

Day	Sid.Time	☉	0 hr ☽	Noon ☽	True ☊	☿	♀	♂	⚳	♃	♄	♅	♆	♇
1 Sa	10 41 57	8♍54 04	24♌01 35	1♍11 17	5♍28.9	5♎58.5	15♍08.7	26♓30.8	22♊37.6	20♉36.6	12♌52.2	14♋01.2	24♈18.2	18♒10.9
2 Su	10 45 54	9 52 09	8♍17 36	15 19 59	5R 28.8	6 49.0	16 23.1	26R 17.7	22 54.1	20 38.1	12 59.4	14 03.6	24R 17.1	18R 09.7
3 M	10 49 50	10 50 15	22 17 55	29 11 00	5 28.5	7 36.3	17 37.5	26 04.0	23 10.4	20 39.4	13 06.6	14 06.0	24 16.0	18 08.5
4 Tu	10 53 47	11 48 23	5♎58 57	12♎41 33	5 27.9	8 20.2	18 51.9	25 49.8	23 26.5	20 40.5	13 13.7	14 08.3	24 14.9	18 07.3
5 W	10 57 43	12 46 32	19 18 45	25 50 34	5 27.1	9 00.4	20 06.3	25 35.2	23 42.4	20 41.4	13 20.8	14 10.6	24 13.8	18 06.1
6 Th	11 01 40	13 44 43	2♏17 07	8♏38 37	5 26.1	9 36.7	21 20.7	25 20.1	23 58.2	20 42.1	13 27.9	14 12.8	24 12.6	18 04.9
7 F	11 05 36	14 42 56	14 55 22	21 07 46	5 25.1	10 08.8	22 35.2	25 04.7	24 13.8	20 42.7	13 34.9	14 15.0	24 11.4	18 03.7
8 Sa	11 09 33	15 41 10	27 16 13	3♐21 13	5 24.4	10 36.4	23 49.6	24 48.9	24 29.2	20 43.0	13 41.9	14 17.2	24 10.2	18 02.5
9 Su	11 13 29	16 39 25	9♐23 17	15 22 59	5D 24.1	10 59.3	25 04.1	24 32.9	24 44.4	20R 43.1	13 48.8	14 19.3	24 09.0	18 01.4
10 M	11 17 26	17 37 42	21 20 54	27 17 35	5 24.3	11 17.1	26 18.5	24 16.6	24 59.4	20 43.0	13 55.7	14 21.3	24 07.7	18 00.2
11 Tu	11 21 23	18 36 01	3♑13 39	9♑09 40	5 25.1	11 29.5	27 33.0	24 00.2	25 14.2	20 42.7	14 02.6	14 23.4	24 06.4	17 59.1
12 W	11 25 19	19 34 21	15 06 13	21 03 50	5 26.2	11R 36.2	28 47.4	23 43.6	25 28.8	20 42.2	14 09.4	14 25.4	24 05.1	17 58.0
13 Th	11 29 16	20 32 42	27 03 04	3♒04 23	5 27.5	11 36.8	0♎01.9	23 26.9	25 43.2	20 41.6	14 16.2	14 27.3	24 03.8	17 56.9
14 F	11 33 12	21 31 06	9♒08 15	15 15 05	5 28.8	11 31.1	1 16.3	23 10.2	25 57.4	20 40.7	14 22.9	14 29.2	24 02.5	17 55.8
15 Sa	11 37 09	22 29 31	21 25 14	27 39 00	5R 29.6	11 18.8	2 30.8	22 53.4	26 11.4	20 39.6	14 29.5	14 31.0	24 01.1	17 54.8
16 Su	11 41 05	23 27 57	3♓56 37	10♓18 17	5 29.7	10 59.7	3 45.3	22 36.8	26 25.2	20 38.3	14 36.2	14 32.8	23 59.8	17 53.7
17 M	11 45 02	24 26 26	16 44 06	23 14 06	5 28.9	10 33.8	4 59.7	22 20.2	26 38.7	20 36.8	14 42.7	14 34.6	23 58.4	17 52.7
18 Tu	11 48 58	25 24 56	29 48 16	6♈26 30	5 27.1	10 01.0	6 14.2	22 03.7	26 52.1	20 35.1	14 49.2	14 36.3	23 57.0	17 51.7
19 W	11 52 55	26 23 29	13♈08 39	19 54 30	5 24.5	9 21.4	7 28.7	21 47.4	27 05.2	20 33.3	14 55.7	14 38.0	23 55.5	17 50.7
20 Th	11 56 52	27 22 03	26 43 48	3♉36 15	5 21.4	8 35.4	8 43.2	21 31.4	27 18.1	20 31.2	15 02.1	14 39.6	23 54.1	17 49.7
21 F	12 00 48	28 20 39	10♉31 31	17 29 16	5 18.2	7 43.5	9 57.7	21 15.6	27 30.7	20 28.9	15 08.5	14 41.2	23 52.6	17 48.7
22 Sa	12 04 45	29 19 18	24 29 10	1♊30 50	5 15.5	6 46.5	11 12.2	21 00.1	27 43.1	20 26.4	15 14.8	14 42.7	23 51.1	17 47.8
23 Su	12 08 41	0♎17 59	8♊33 58	15 38 13	5 13.7	5 45.3	12 26.7	20 45.0	27 55.3	20 23.8	15 21.0	14 44.2	23 49.6	17 46.9
24 M	12 12 38	1 16 43	22 43 18	29 48 55	5D 13.0	4 41.1	13 41.2	20 30.3	28 07.2	20 20.9	15 27.2	14 45.6	23 48.1	17 46.0
25 Tu	12 16 34	2 15 28	6♋54 47	14♋00 41	5 13.4	3 35.4	14 55.7	20 15.9	28 18.9	20 17.8	15 33.4	14 47.0	23 46.6	17 45.1
26 W	12 20 31	3 14 16	21 06 21	28 11 31	5 14.6	2 29.6	16 10.2	20 02.1	28 30.3	20 14.6	15 39.5	14 48.3	23 45.1	17 44.2
27 Th	12 24 27	4 13 06	5♌15 57	12♌19 23	5 16.1	1 25.4	17 24.7	19 48.8	28 41.4	20 11.1	15 45.5	14 49.6	23 43.5	17 43.4
28 F	12 28 24	5 11 59	19 21 32	26 22 07	5R 17.3	0 24.7	18 39.2	19 36.0	28 52.3	20 07.5	15 51.4	14 50.8	23 42.0	17 42.5
29 Sa	12 32 21	6 10 53	3♍20 48	10♍17 16	5 17.4	29♍28.8	19 53.8	19 23.7	29 02.9	20 03.7	15 57.3	14 52.0	23 40.4	17 41.7
30 Su	12 36 17	7 09 50	17 11 10	24 02 11	5 16.1	28 39.5	21 08.3	19 12.1	29 13.3	19 59.7	16 03.1	14 53.1	23 38.8	17 40.9

LONGITUDE — October 2035

Day	Sid.Time	☉	0 hr ☽	Noon ☽	True ☊	☿	♀	♂	⚳	♃	♄	♅	♆	♇
1 M	12 40 14	8♎08 49	0♎50 00	7♎34 18	5♍13.2	27♍58.0	22♎22.8	19♓01.1	29♊23.3	19♉55.5	16♌08.9	14♋54.2	23♈37.2	17♒40.2
2 Tu	12 44 10	9 07 49	14 14 50	20 51 21	5R 08.6	27R 25.4	23 37.4	18R 50.8	29 33.1	19R 51.1	16 14.6	14 55.2	23R 35.6	17R 39.4
3 W	12 48 07	10 06 52	27 23 43	3♏51 50	5 02.9	27 02.5	24 51.9	18 41.2	29 42.6	19 46.5	16 20.2	14 56.2	23 34.0	17 38.7
4 Th	12 52 03	11 05 57	10♏15 39	16 35 15	4 56.6	26D 49.8	26 06.4	18 32.3	29 51.7	19 41.8	16 25.7	14 57.1	23 32.4	17 38.0
5 F	12 56 00	12 05 03	22 50 44	29 02 19	4 50.5	26 47.7	27 21.0	18 24.1	0♋00.6	19 36.9	16 31.2	14 58.0	23 30.7	17 37.3
6 Sa	12 59 56	13 04 12	5♐10 17	11♐14 59	4 45.1	26 56.1	28 35.5	18 16.7	0 09.2	19 31.8	16 36.6	14 58.8	23 29.1	17 36.7
7 Su	13 03 53	14 03 22	17 16 49	23 16 16	4 41.2	27 14.8	29 50.0	18 10.1	0 17.5	19 26.6	16 42.0	14 59.6	23 27.4	17 36.1
8 M	13 07 49	15 02 34	29 13 50	5♑10 05	4D 39.0	27 43.4	1♏04.6	18 04.2	0 25.5	19 21.2	16 47.2	15 00.3	23 25.8	17 35.5
9 Tu	13 11 46	16 01 48	11♑05 37	17 01 02	4 38.4	28 21.4	2 19.1	17 59.1	0 33.1	19 15.6	16 52.4	15 00.9	23 24.1	17 34.9
10 W	13 15 43	17 01 04	22 57 00	28 54 07	4 39.1	29 08.1	3 33.6	17 54.8	0 40.5	19 09.9	16 57.5	15 01.5	23 22.5	17 34.3
11 Th	13 19 39	18 00 21	4♒53 03	10♒54 26	4 40.5	0♎02.9	4 48.1	17 51.4	0 47.5	19 04.0	17 02.6	15 02.1	23 20.8	17 33.8
12 F	13 23 36	18 59 41	16 58 51	23 06 54	4R 41.9	1 04.9	6 02.7	17 48.7	0 54.1	18 58.0	17 07.5	15 02.6	23 19.1	17 33.3
13 Sa	13 27 32	19 59 02	29 19 05	5♓35 53	4 42.5	2 13.4	7 17.2	17 46.8	1 00.5	18 51.8	17 12.4	15 03.0	23 17.5	17 32.8
14 Su	13 31 29	20 58 24	11♓57 42	18 24 49	4 41.5	3 27.6	8 31.7	17D 45.7	1 06.5	18 45.5	17 17.2	15 03.4	23 15.8	17 32.3
15 M	13 35 25	21 57 49	24 57 28	1♈35 45	4 38.5	4 46.9	9 46.2	17 45.4	1 12.2	18 39.1	17 21.9	15 03.7	23 14.1	17 31.9
16 Tu	13 39 22	22 57 16	8♈19 36	15 08 54	4 33.3	6 10.4	11 00.7	17 45.9	1 17.5	18 32.5	17 26.5	15 04.0	23 12.4	17 31.5
17 W	13 43 18	23 56 44	22 03 20	29 02 29	4 26.3	7 37.5	12 15.2	17 47.2	1 22.5	18 25.8	17 31.1	15 04.3	23 10.8	17 31.1
18 Th	13 47 15	24 56 15	6♉05 50	13♉12 44	4 18.2	9 07.8	13 29.7	17 49.3	1 27.1	18 19.0	17 35.5	15 04.4	23 09.1	17 30.8
19 F	13 51 12	25 55 48	20 22 29	27 34 19	4 09.8	10 40.6	14 44.2	17 52.2	1 31.4	18 12.0	17 39.9	15 04.6	23 07.4	17 30.4
20 Sa	13 55 08	26 55 23	4♊47 30	12♊01 14	4 02.3	12 15.5	15 58.6	17 55.8	1 35.3	18 05.0	17 44.2	15R 04.6	23 05.7	17 30.1
21 Su	13 59 05	27 55 00	19 14 50	26 27 39	3 56.4	13 52.0	17 13.1	18 00.2	1 38.9	17 57.8	17 48.4	15 04.6	23 04.1	17 29.8
22 M	14 03 01	28 54 40	3♋39 08	10♋48 49	3 52.8	15 29.9	18 27.6	18 05.4	1 42.1	17 50.5	17 52.6	15 04.6	23 02.4	17 29.6
23 Tu	14 06 58	29 54 22	17 56 20	25 01 27	3D 51.3	17 08.8	19 42.1	18 11.3	1 44.9	17 43.2	17 56.6	15 04.5	23 00.7	17 29.4
24 W	14 10 54	0♏54 06	2♌03 58	9♌03 47	3 51.4	18 48.4	20 56.6	18 17.9	1 47.3	17 35.7	18 00.5	15 04.4	22 59.1	17 29.2
25 Th	14 14 51	1 53 52	16 00 53	22 55 15	3R 52.2	20 28.6	22 11.1	18 25.2	1 49.4	17 28.1	18 04.4	15 04.2	22 57.4	17 29.0
26 F	14 18 47	2 53 41	29 46 55	6♍35 55	3 52.5	22 09.1	23 25.6	18 33.3	1 51.0	17 20.5	18 08.1	15 03.9	22 55.8	17 28.8
27 Sa	14 22 44	3 53 32	13♍22 17	20 06 03	3 51.3	23 49.8	24 40.1	18 42.1	1 52.3	17 12.8	18 11.8	15 03.6	22 54.1	17 28.7
28 Su	14 26 41	4 53 25	26 47 11	3♎25 40	3 47.6	25 30.5	25 54.5	18 51.7	1 53.1	17 05.0	18 15.4	15 03.3	22 52.5	17 28.6
29 M	14 30 37	5 53 20	10♎01 28	16 34 29	3 41.2	27 11.2	27 09.0	19 01.9	1R 53.6	16 57.1	18 18.8	15 02.8	22 50.8	17 28.6
30 Tu	14 34 34	6 53 17	23 04 37	29 31 49	3 32.1	28 51.8	28 23.5	19 12.8	1 53.7	16 49.2	18 22.2	15 02.4	22 49.2	17D 28.5
31 W	14 38 30	7 53 16	5♏55 56	12♏16 56	3 21.0	0♏32.2	29 38.0	19 24.4	1 53.4	16 41.2	18 25.5	15 01.9	22 47.6	17 28.5

Astro Data

	Dy Hr Mn
☽0S	4 0:31
♃R	9 14:14
☿R	13 2:27
♀0S	15 19:24
♄⊻♅	15 19:29
☽0N	18 11:36
☉0S	23 4:38
☽0S	1 9:33
☿0N	1 15:59
☿D	5 4:51
☿0S	15 5:47
♂D	15 8:32
☽0N	15 20:17
♄☍♇	17 12:12
♅R	21 8:02

Planet Ingress

	Dy Hr Mn
♀ ♎	13 11:24
☉ ♎	23 4:39
☿ ♍R	28 22:18
⚳ ♋	5 10:16
♀ ♏	7 15:13
☿ ♎	11 10:49
☉ ♏	23 14:16
☿ ♏	31 4:18
♀ ♐	31 19:06

Last Aspect / ☽ Ingress

Last Aspect Dy Hr Mn		☽ Ingress Dy Hr Mn
1 0:29	♆ △	♍ 1 10:00
3 6:38	♂ ☍	♎ 3 13:26
5 9:02	♆ ☍	♏ 5 19:44
7 19:33	♂ △	♐ 8 5:22
10 9:47	♀ □	♑ 10 17:28
13 5:15	♀ △	♒ 13 5:53
15 5:02	♆ ✶	♓ 15 16:30
17 14:23	☉ ☍	♈ 18 0:21
19 19:04	♆ ☌	♉ 20 5:43
22 7:59	☉ △	♊ 22 9:25
24 1:51	♆ ✶	♋ 24 12:19
26 4:29	♆ □	♌ 26 15:04
28 7:26	♆ △	♍ 28 18:14
30 19:44	☿ ☌	♎ 30 22:31

Last Aspect / ☽ Ingress

Last Aspect Dy Hr Mn		☽ Ingress Dy Hr Mn
2 17:36	♀ ☌	♏ 3 4:49
5 7:38	☿ ✶	♐ 5 13:52
7 20:18	☿ □	♑ 8 1:33
10 12:30	☿ △	♒ 10 14:12
12 12:24	♆ ✶	♓ 13 1:19
14 12:38	♃ ✶	♈ 15 9:08
17 2:35	☉ ☍	♉ 17 13:38
18 20:29	♃ ☌	♊ 19 16:02
21 14:36	☉ △	♋ 21 17:54
23 8:36	♆ □	♌ 23 20:28
25 12:04	♆ △	♍ 26 0:23
27 21:02	♀ ✶	♎ 28 5:48
30 10:34	☿ ☌	♏ 30 12:53

☽ Phases & Eclipses

Dy Hr Mn		
2 1:59	●	9♍28
2 1:55:25	●	T 02'54"
9 14:47	☽	16♐46
17 14:23	○	24♓32
24 14:39	☾	1♋23
1 13:07	●	8♎12
9 9:49	☽	15♑56
17 2:35	○	23♈33
23 20:57	☾	0♌17
31 2:59	●	7♏31

Astro Data

1 September 2035
Julian Day # 49552
SVP 4♓45'48"
GC 27♐20.2 ⚴ 4♈03.5R
Eris 27♈55.6R ⚵ 0♓57.9R
⚷ 12♊18.2 ⚶ 11♍02.1
☽ Mean ☊ 5♍12.8

1 October 2035
Julian Day # 49582
SVP 4♓45'46"
GC 27♐20.3 ⚴ 26♓20.6R
Eris 27♈41.2R ⚵ 25♒24.2R
⚷ 12♊22.9R ⚶ 25♍39.5
☽ Mean ☊ 3♍37.4

November 2035 LONGITUDE

Day	Sid.Time	☉	0 hr ☽	Noon ☽	True ☊	☿	♀	♂	⚳	♃	♄	♅	♆	♇
1 Th	14 42 27	8♏53 17	18♏34 45	24♏49 22	3♍08.7	2♏12.3	0♐52.5	19♓36.6	1♋52.6	16♉33.2	18♌28.7	15♋01.3	22♈46.0	17♒28.5
2 F	14 46 23	9 53 20	1♐00 50	7♐09 12	2R 56.3	3 52.1	2 06.9	19 49.5	1R 51.5	16R 25.1	18 31.7	15R 00.7	22R 44.4	17 28.6
3 Sa	14 50 20	10 53 25	13 14 39	19 17 22	2 45.0	5 31.6	3 21.4	20 03.1	1 50.0	16 17.0	18 34.7	15 00.0	22 42.8	17 28.6
4 Su	14 54 16	11 53 31	25 17 38	1♑15 47	2 35.8	7 10.7	4 35.9	20 17.3	1 48.0	16 08.9	18 37.6	14 59.3	22 41.3	17 28.7
5 M	14 58 13	12 53 39	7♑12 14	13 07 25	2 29.0	8 49.5	5 50.3	20 32.1	1 45.7	16 00.8	18 40.4	14 58.5	22 39.7	17 28.8
6 Tu	15 02 10	13 53 49	19 01 51	24 56 06	2 25.0	10 27.9	7 04.8	20 47.5	1 42.9	15 52.6	18 43.1	14 57.6	22 38.2	17 29.0
7 W	15 06 06	14 54 00	0♒50 47	6♒46 31	2D 23.2	12 05.9	8 19.2	21 03.5	1 39.7	15 44.4	18 45.6	14 56.8	22 36.6	17 29.2
8 Th	15 10 03	15 54 12	12 44 00	18 43 53	2 22.9	13 43.5	9 33.6	21 20.0	1 36.2	15 36.3	18 48.1	14 55.8	22 35.1	17 29.4
9 F	15 13 59	16 54 26	24 46 52	0♓53 40	2R 23.1	15 20.7	10 48.1	21 37.2	1 32.2	15 28.1	18 50.5	14 54.8	22 33.6	17 29.6
10 Sa	15 17 56	17 54 42	7♓04 54	13 21 14	2 22.7	16 57.6	12 02.5	21 54.9	1 27.8	15 20.0	18 52.7	14 53.8	22 32.2	17 29.9
11 Su	15 21 52	18 54 59	19 43 14	26 11 23	2 20.6	18 34.1	13 16.9	22 13.1	1 23.0	15 11.8	18 54.9	14 52.7	22 30.7	17 30.2
12 M	15 25 49	19 55 17	2♈46 05	9♈27 36	2 16.0	20 10.3	14 31.3	22 31.8	1 17.8	15 03.7	18 56.9	14 51.6	22 29.2	17 30.5
13 Tu	15 29 45	20 55 37	16 16 03	23 11 25	2 08.6	21 46.1	15 45.7	22 51.1	1 12.2	14 55.6	18 58.8	14 50.4	22 27.8	17 30.8
14 W	15 33 42	21 55 59	0♉13 26	7♉21 43	1 58.8	23 21.6	17 00.0	23 10.8	1 06.3	14 47.6	19 00.7	14 49.2	22 26.4	17 31.2
15 Th	15 37 38	22 56 22	14 35 36	21 54 10	1 47.3	24 56.8	18 14.4	23 31.1	0 59.9	14 39.6	19 02.4	14 47.9	22 25.0	17 31.6
16 F	15 41 35	23 56 47	29 16 54	6♊42 18	1 35.4	26 31.8	19 28.8	23 51.8	0 53.1	14 31.6	19 04.0	14 46.6	22 23.6	17 32.0
17 Sa	15 45 32	24 57 13	14♊09 20	21 36 53	1 24.5	28 06.4	20 43.1	24 12.9	0 46.0	14 23.7	19 05.5	14 45.2	22 22.2	17 32.5
18 Su	15 49 28	25 57 42	29 03 47	6♋29 01	1 15.6	29 40.8	21 57.5	24 34.5	0 38.5	14 15.9	19 06.9	14 43.8	22 20.9	17 33.0
19 M	15 53 25	26 58 12	13♋51 39	21 10 55	1 09.5	1♐15.0	23 11.8	24 56.5	0 30.6	14 08.1	19 08.2	14 42.4	22 19.6	17 33.5
20 Tu	15 57 21	27 58 44	28 26 12	5♌37 06	1 06.2	2 48.9	24 26.1	25 19.0	0 22.3	14 00.4	19 09.4	14 40.9	22 18.3	17 34.0
21 W	16 01 18	28 59 17	12♌43 19	19 44 45	1 05.1	4 22.7	25 40.4	25 41.9	0 13.6	13 52.7	19 10.5	14 39.3	22 17.0	17 34.6
22 Th	16 05 14	29 59 52	26 41 24	3♍33 22	1 05.0	5 56.2	26 54.7	26 05.1	0 04.6	13 45.2	19 11.4	14 37.7	22 15.8	17 35.1
23 F	16 09 11	1♐00 30	10♍20 49	17 04 00	1 04.6	7 29.6	28 09.0	26 28.8	29♊55.3	13 37.7	19 12.2	14 36.1	22 14.5	17 35.7
24 Sa	16 13 08	2 01 08	23 43 11	0♎18 36	1 02.5	9 02.8	29 23.3	26 52.9	29 45.5	13 30.3	19 13.0	14 34.4	22 13.3	17 36.4
25 Su	16 17 04	3 01 49	6♎50 33	13 19 15	0 57.9	10 35.9	0♑37.6	27 17.3	29 35.5	13 23.1	19 13.6	14 32.7	22 12.1	17 37.0
26 M	16 21 01	4 02 31	19 44 56	26 07 46	0 50.2	12 08.8	1 51.9	27 42.1	29 25.1	13 15.9	19 14.1	14 31.0	22 11.0	17 37.7
27 Tu	16 24 57	5 03 14	2♏27 54	8♏45 27	0 39.4	13 41.6	3 06.1	28 07.3	29 14.4	13 08.9	19 14.5	14 29.2	22 09.8	17 38.5
28 W	16 28 54	6 03 59	15 00 31	21 13 11	0 26.3	15 14.2	4 20.4	28 32.8	29 03.4	13 01.9	19 14.8	14 27.3	22 08.7	17 39.2
29 Th	16 32 50	7 04 46	27 23 28	3♐31 27	0 11.8	16 46.7	5 34.6	28 58.7	28 52.1	12 55.1	19R 14.9	14 25.5	22 07.7	17 40.0
30 F	16 36 47	8 05 34	9♐37 12	15 40 46	29♌57.1	18 19.1	6 48.9	29 24.9	28 40.5	12 48.4	19 15.0	14 23.5	22 06.6	17 40.8

December 2035 LONGITUDE

Day	Sid.Time	☉	0 hr ☽	Noon ☽	True ☊	☿	♀	♂	⚳	♃	♄	♅	♆	♇
1 Sa	16 40 43	9♐06 23	21♐42 17	27♐41 52	29♌43.5	19♐51.4	8♑03.1	29♓51.5	28♊28.6	12♉41.9	19♌14.9	14♋21.6	22♈05.6	17♒41.6
2 Su	16 44 40	10 07 13	3♑39 42	9♑36 00	29R 32.1	21 23.5	9 17.3	0♈18.4	28R 16.5	12R 35.5	19R 14.7	14R 19.6	22R 04.6	17 42.4
3 M	16 48 37	11 08 04	15 31 04	21 25 12	29 23.5	22 55.5	10 31.5	0 45.6	28 04.1	12 29.2	19 14.5	14 17.6	22 03.6	17 43.3
4 Tu	16 52 33	12 08 56	27 18 49	3♒12 20	29 17.8	24 27.3	11 45.6	1 13.1	27 51.5	12 23.1	19 14.1	14 15.5	22 02.6	17 44.2
5 W	16 56 30	13 09 49	9♒06 15	15 01 07	29 14.9	25 58.9	12 59.8	1 40.9	27 38.7	12 17.1	19 13.5	14 13.5	22 01.7	17 45.1
6 Th	17 00 26	14 10 43	20 57 30	26 56 02	29D 14.1	27 30.3	14 13.9	2 09.0	27 25.7	12 11.3	19 12.9	14 11.3	22 00.8	17 46.0
7 F	17 04 23	15 11 37	2♓57 24	9♓02 14	29R 14.2	29 01.5	15 28.0	2 37.3	27 12.5	12 05.6	19 12.2	14 09.2	22 00.0	17 47.0
8 Sa	17 08 19	16 12 33	15 11 16	21 25 09	29 14.2	0♑32.4	16 42.1	3 06.0	26 59.1	12 00.1	19 11.3	14 07.0	21 59.1	17 48.0
9 Su	17 12 16	17 13 28	27 44 33	4♈10 05	29 12.9	2 02.9	17 56.2	3 34.9	26 45.6	11 54.8	19 10.4	14 04.8	21 58.3	17 49.0
10 M	17 16 12	18 14 25	10♈42 18	17 21 39	29 09.5	3 33.0	19 10.2	4 04.0	26 31.9	11 49.6	19 09.3	14 02.6	21 57.6	17 50.0
11 Tu	17 20 09	19 15 22	24 08 28	1♉02 54	29 03.5	5 02.6	20 24.3	4 33.4	26 18.1	11 44.6	19 08.1	14 00.3	21 56.8	17 51.1
12 W	17 24 06	20 16 20	8♉04 57	15 14 25	28 55.2	6 31.7	21 38.2	5 03.1	26 04.2	11 39.8	19 06.8	13 58.0	21 56.1	17 52.2
13 Th	17 28 02	21 17 19	22 30 49	29 53 30	28 45.1	8 00.0	22 52.2	5 33.0	25 50.2	11 35.2	19 05.4	13 55.7	21 55.4	17 53.3
14 F	17 31 59	22 18 18	7♊21 34	14♊53 54	28 34.5	9 27.5	24 06.1	6 03.1	25 36.1	11 30.7	19 03.9	13 53.4	21 54.8	17 54.4
15 Sa	17 35 55	23 19 18	22 29 16	0♋06 19	28 24.6	10 54.0	25 20.0	6 33.4	25 22.0	11 26.4	19 02.3	13 51.0	21 54.2	17 55.6
16 Su	17 39 52	24 20 19	7♋43 38	15 19 53	28 16.5	12 19.4	26 33.9	7 03.9	25 07.8	11 22.3	19 00.6	13 48.6	21 53.6	17 56.7
17 M	17 43 48	25 21 21	22 53 45	0♌24 07	28 11.0	13 43.4	27 47.8	7 34.7	24 53.6	11 18.4	18 58.8	13 46.2	21 53.0	17 57.9
18 Tu	17 47 45	26 22 24	7♌50 02	15 10 44	28D 08.1	15 05.7	29 01.6	8 05.6	24 39.4	11 14.7	18 56.9	13 43.8	21 52.5	17 59.1
19 W	17 51 41	27 23 27	22 25 40	29 34 30	28 07.4	16 26.1	0♒15.4	8 36.8	24 25.2	11 11.2	18 54.8	13 41.4	21 52.0	18 00.4
20 Th	17 55 38	28 24 31	6♍37 03	13♍33 21	28 08.0	17 44.1	1 29.2	9 08.1	24 11.1	11 07.9	18 52.7	13 38.9	21 51.6	18 01.6
21 F	17 59 35	29 25 36	20 23 30	27 07 45	28R 08.6	18 59.6	2 42.9	9 39.6	23 57.0	11 04.8	18 50.5	13 36.4	21 51.2	18 02.9
22 Sa	18 03 31	0♑26 42	3♎46 26	10♎19 55	28 08.1	20 11.8	3 56.6	10 11.3	23 42.9	11 01.8	18 48.1	13 33.9	21 50.8	18 04.2
23 Su	18 07 28	1 27 49	16 48 36	23 12 53	28 05.7	21 20.5	5 10.3	10 43.2	23 28.9	10 59.1	18 45.7	13 31.4	21 50.4	18 05.5
24 M	18 11 24	2 28 56	29 33 11	5♏49 54	28 00.7	22 24.9	6 23.9	11 15.3	23 15.1	10 56.6	18 43.1	13 28.9	21 50.1	18 06.8
25 Tu	18 15 21	3 30 04	12♏03 24	18 14 01	27 53.4	23 24.4	7 37.5	11 47.5	23 01.3	10 54.2	18 40.5	13 26.3	21 49.8	18 08.2
26 W	18 19 17	4 31 13	24 22 04	0♐27 50	27 44.1	24 18.2	8 51.1	12 19.9	22 47.7	10 52.1	18 37.8	13 23.8	21 49.6	18 09.5
27 Th	18 23 14	5 32 22	6♐31 33	12 33 27	27 33.6	25 05.6	10 04.6	12 52.5	22 34.2	10 50.2	18 35.0	13 21.2	21 49.3	18 10.9
28 F	18 27 10	6 33 32	18 33 44	24 32 33	27 22.9	25 45.8	11 18.1	13 25.2	22 20.9	10 48.5	18 32.0	13 18.7	21 49.2	18 12.3
29 Sa	18 31 07	7 34 42	0♑30 07	6♑26 35	27 13.1	26 17.7	12 31.6	13 58.1	22 07.8	10 47.0	18 29.0	13 16.1	21 49.0	18 13.8
30 Su	18 35 04	8 35 52	12 22 08	18 16 58	27 04.8	26 40.5	13 45.0	14 31.2	21 54.9	10 45.7	18 25.9	13 13.5	21 48.9	18 15.2
31 M	18 39 00	9 37 02	24 11 17	0♒05 20	26 58.7	26R 53.3	14 58.4	15 04.3	21 42.2	10 44.6	18 22.7	13 10.9	21 48.8	18 16.7

Astro Data (Dy Hr Mn)

☽0N 12 6:51
♃✱♅ 14 6:15
☽0S 24 23:57
♄ R 30 11:07

♂0N 4 10:30
☽0N 9 17:39
☽0S 22 6:50

Planet Ingress (Dy Hr Mn)

☿ ♐ 18 16:53
☉ ♐ 22 12:03
⚳ ♊R 22 23:57
♀ ♑ 24 23:51
☊ ♌R 30 7:12

♂ ♈ 1 19:37
☿ ♑ 8 3:27
♀ ♒ 19 7:00
☉ ♑ 22 1:31

Last Aspect / ☽ Ingress

Last Aspect Dy Hr Mn		☽ Ingress	Dy Hr Mn
1 1:48	♂ △	♐	1 22:02
3 18:49	♆ △	♑	4 9:27
6 7:20	♆ □	♒	6 22:17
8 19:39	♆ ✱	♓	9 10:15
11 4:29	♂ ☌	♈	11 18:59
13 10:45	♆ ☌	♉	13 23:37
15 17:33	☿ ☍	♊	16 1:10
17 16:17	♂ □	♋	18 1:31
19 22:17	☉ △	♌	20 2:36
22 5:16	☉ □	♍	22 5:46
24 10:08	♀ □	♎	24 11:26
26 4:35	♆ ☍	♏	26 19:19
29 2:46	♂ △	♐	29 5:06

Last Aspect Dy Hr Mn		☽ Ingress	Dy Hr Mn
1 16:31	♂ □	♑	1 16:38
3 13:18	♆ □	♒	4 5:28
6 13:19	☿ ✱	♓	6 18:07
8 1:56	♀ ✱	♈	9 4:14
10 20:09	♆ ☌	♉	11 10:12
12 23:32	♀ △	♊	13 12:10
15 0:33	☉ ☍	♋	15 11:50
17 7:27	♀ ☍	♌	17 11:21
19 8:02	☉ △	♍	19 12:43
21 16:28	☉ □	♎	21 17:10
23 9:25	♆ ☍	♏	24 0:51
25 22:56	♆ ✱	♐	26 11:05
28 6:32	♆ △	♑	28 22:59
31 5:24	♆ ☌	♒	31 11:49

☽ Phases & Eclipses (Dy Hr Mn)

8 5:50 ☽ 15♒39
15 13:49 ○ 23♉01
22 5:16 ☾ 29♌43
29 19:37 ● 7♐24

8 1:05 ☽ 15♓45
15 0:33 ○ 22♊50
21 16:28 ☾ 29♍37
29 14:31 ● 7♑41

Astro Data

1 November 2035
Julian Day # 49613
SVP 4♓45'43"
GC 27♐20.4 ⚵ 20♓01.1R
Eris 27♈22.8R ✱ 26♒21.9
⚷ 11♊25.9R ⚶ 10♎55.5
☽ Mean ☊ 1♍58.9

1 December 2035
Julian Day # 49643
SVP 4♓45'39"
GC 27♐20.5 ⚵ 19♓34.6
Eris 27♈06.9R ✱ 3♓36.2
⚷ 9♊50.6R ⚶ 25♎32.3
☽ Mean ☊ 0♍23.6

LONGITUDE January 2036

Day	Sid.Time	☉	0 hr ☽	Noon ☽	True ☊	☿	♀	♂	⚳	♃	♄	♅	♆	♇
1 Tu	18 42 57	10♑38 13	5♒59 24	11♒53 47	26♌55.1	26♑55.3	16♒11.7	15♈37.7	21♊29.7	10♉43.8	18♌19.4	13♋08.3	21♈48.8	18♒18.1
2 W	18 46 53	11 39 23	17 48 51	23 44 58	26D 53.6	26R 45.9	17 25.0	16 11.2	21R 17.5	10R 43.1	18R 16.1	13R 05.7	21D 48.8	18 19.6
3 Th	18 50 50	12 40 33	29 42 35	5♓42 11	26 53.9	26 24.7	18 38.2	16 44.8	21 05.5	10 42.6	18 12.6	13 03.1	21 48.8	18 21.1
4 F	18 54 46	13 41 43	11♓44 16	17 49 22	26 55.3	25 51.7	19 51.4	17 18.5	20 53.8	10D 42.4	18 09.1	13 00.5	21 48.8	18 22.6
5 Sa	18 58 43	14 42 52	23 58 05	0♈10 58	26 56.9	25 07.1	21 04.5	17 52.4	20 42.4	10 42.4	18 05.5	12 58.0	21 48.9	18 24.2
6 Su	19 02 39	15 44 02	6♈28 38	12 51 39	26R 57.8	24 11.9	22 17.6	18 26.4	20 31.3	10 42.5	18 01.8	12 55.4	21 49.1	18 25.7
7 M	19 06 36	16 45 11	19 20 34	25 55 52	26 57.3	23 07.4	23 30.6	19 00.5	20 20.5	10 42.9	17 58.0	12 52.8	21 49.2	18 27.3
8 Tu	19 10 33	17 46 19	2♉37 59	9♉27 13	26 55.2	21 55.4	24 43.5	19 34.8	20 10.0	10 43.5	17 54.2	12 50.2	21 49.4	18 28.9
9 W	19 14 29	18 47 27	16 23 44	23 27 34	26 51.5	20 38.2	25 56.4	20 09.1	19 59.9	10 44.3	17 50.3	12 47.6	21 49.7	18 30.5
10 Th	19 18 26	19 48 35	0♊38 33	7♊56 18	26 46.4	19 18.3	27 09.2	20 43.6	19 50.1	10 45.3	17 46.3	12 45.0	21 49.9	18 32.1
11 F	19 22 22	20 49 42	15 20 14	22 49 32	26 40.8	17 58.2	28 21.9	21 18.1	19 40.6	10 46.5	17 42.3	12 42.5	21 50.3	18 33.7
12 Sa	19 26 19	21 50 49	0♋23 12	8♋00 04	26 35.4	16 40.6	29 34.6	21 52.8	19 31.5	10 48.0	17 38.2	12 39.9	21 50.6	18 35.3
13 Su	19 30 15	22 51 56	15 38 50	23 18 09	26 31.1	15 27.5	0♓47.2	22 27.6	19 22.8	10 49.6	17 34.0	12 37.4	21 51.0	18 36.9
14 M	19 34 12	23 53 02	0♌56 39	8♌32 59	26 28.3	14 20.9	1 59.7	23 02.4	19 14.4	10 51.4	17 29.8	12 34.8	21 51.4	18 38.6
15 Tu	19 38 08	24 54 08	16 05 57	23 34 29	26D 27.2	13 22.2	3 12.2	23 37.3	19 06.4	10 53.4	17 25.5	12 32.3	21 51.8	18 40.3
16 W	19 42 05	25 55 13	0♍57 41	8♍14 53	26 27.6	12 32.4	4 24.6	24 12.4	18 58.8	10 55.7	17 21.2	12 29.8	21 52.3	18 41.9
17 Th	19 46 02	26 56 18	15 25 35	22 29 29	26 29.0	11 51.9	5 36.9	24 47.5	18 51.6	10 58.1	17 16.8	12 27.3	21 52.8	18 43.6
18 F	19 49 58	27 57 23	29 26 29	6♎16 37	26 30.6	11 21.1	6 49.1	25 22.7	18 44.8	11 00.7	17 12.3	12 24.8	21 53.4	18 45.3
19 Sa	19 53 55	28 58 28	13♎00 04	19 37 07	26R 31.8	10 59.8	8 01.3	25 57.9	18 38.4	11 03.5	17 07.8	12 22.4	21 53.9	18 47.0
20 Su	19 57 51	29 59 33	26 08 08	2♏33 33	26 32.1	10D 47.7	9 13.3	26 33.3	18 32.4	11 06.5	17 03.3	12 19.9	21 54.6	18 48.7
21 M	20 01 48	1♒00 37	8♏53 51	15 09 31	26 31.3	10 44.3	10 25.3	27 08.7	18 26.8	11 09.8	16 58.7	12 17.5	21 55.2	18 50.4
22 Tu	20 05 44	2 01 40	21 21 04	27 28 59	26 29.2	10 49.0	11 37.2	27 44.3	18 21.6	11 13.2	16 54.1	12 15.1	21 55.9	18 52.1
23 W	20 09 41	3 02 44	3♐33 46	9♐35 53	26 26.0	11 01.4	12 49.0	28 19.9	18 16.8	11 16.8	16 49.4	12 12.7	21 56.6	18 53.9
24 Th	20 13 37	4 03 47	15 35 47	21 33 52	26 22.3	11 20.8	14 00.7	28 55.5	18 12.5	11 20.6	16 44.7	12 10.3	21 57.4	18 55.6
25 F	20 17 34	5 04 49	27 30 32	3♑26 09	26 18.4	11 46.6	15 12.4	29 31.3	18 08.5	11 24.6	16 40.0	12 08.0	21 58.1	18 57.4
26 Sa	20 21 31	6 05 51	9♑21 02	15 15 29	26 14.8	12 18.2	16 23.9	0♉07.1	18 05.0	11 28.7	16 35.2	12 05.7	21 59.0	18 59.1
27 Su	20 25 27	7 06 52	21 09 47	27 04 12	26 11.9	12 55.1	17 35.4	0 43.0	18 01.9	11 33.1	16 30.4	12 03.4	21 59.8	19 00.9
28 M	20 29 24	8 07 52	2♒58 59	8♒54 23	26 10.0	13 36.8	18 46.7	1 19.0	17 59.3	11 37.7	16 25.6	12 01.1	22 00.7	19 02.6
29 Tu	20 33 20	9 08 51	14 50 37	20 47 57	26D 09.1	14 22.8	19 57.9	1 55.0	17 57.1	11 42.4	16 20.8	11 58.9	22 01.6	19 04.4
30 W	20 37 17	10 09 49	26 46 37	2♓46 53	26 09.1	15 12.8	21 09.1	2 31.1	17 55.2	11 47.3	16 15.9	11 56.7	22 02.6	19 06.2
31 Th	20 41 13	11 10 47	8♓49 01	14 53 19	26 09.9	16 06.4	22 20.1	3 07.2	17 53.9	11 52.4	16 11.0	11 54.5	22 03.5	19 07.9

LONGITUDE February 2036

Day	Sid.Time	☉	0 hr ☽	Noon ☽	True ☊	☿	♀	♂	⚳	♃	♄	♅	♆	♇
1 F	20 45 10	12♒11 43	21♓00 05	27♓09 41	26♌11.1	17♑03.3	23♓31.0	3♉43.4	17♊52.9	11♉57.7	16♌06.1	11♋52.4	22♈04.6	19♒09.7
2 Sa	20 49 06	13 12 37	3♈22 26	9♈38 44	26 12.4	18 03.1	24 41.8	4 19.7	17D 52.4	12 03.1	16R 01.3	11R 50.2	22 05.6	19 11.5
3 Su	20 53 03	14 13 31	15 58 58	22 23 29	26 13.5	19 05.6	25 52.4	4 56.0	17 52.3	12 08.8	15 56.3	11 48.1	22 06.7	19 13.3
4 M	20 57 00	15 14 23	28 52 41	5♉26 55	26R 14.1	20 10.6	27 03.0	5 32.4	17 52.6	12 14.6	15 51.4	11 46.1	22 07.8	19 15.1
5 Tu	21 00 56	16 15 14	12♉06 31	18 51 45	26 14.3	21 17.9	28 13.4	6 08.8	17 53.4	12 20.6	15 46.5	11 44.1	22 08.9	19 16.9
6 W	21 04 53	17 16 03	25 42 48	2♊39 47	26 14.0	22 27.3	29 23.6	6 45.3	17 54.5	12 26.7	15 41.6	11 42.1	22 10.1	19 18.7
7 Th	21 08 49	18 16 51	9♊42 43	16 51 26	26 13.3	23 38.6	0♈33.8	7 21.8	17 56.1	12 33.0	15 36.7	11 40.2	22 11.3	19 20.5
8 F	21 12 46	19 17 37	24 05 40	1♋24 58	26 12.5	24 51.7	1 43.8	7 58.4	17 58.1	12 39.5	15 31.9	11 38.3	22 12.5	19 22.2
9 Sa	21 16 42	20 18 22	8♋48 46	16 16 17	26 11.8	26 06.5	2 53.6	8 35.0	18 00.5	12 46.1	15 27.0	11 36.4	22 13.8	19 24.0
10 Su	21 20 39	21 19 06	23 46 37	1♌18 48	26 11.2	27 22.8	4 03.3	9 11.6	18 03.2	12 52.9	15 22.1	11 34.6	22 15.1	19 25.8
11 M	21 24 35	22 19 48	8♌51 42	16 24 11	26D 11.0	28 40.6	5 12.8	9 48.3	18 06.4	12 59.9	15 17.3	11 32.8	22 16.4	19 27.6
12 Tu	21 28 32	23 20 29	23 55 07	1♍23 23	26 10.9	29 59.8	6 22.2	10 25.0	18 10.0	13 07.0	15 12.4	11 31.0	22 17.7	19 29.4
13 W	21 32 29	24 21 08	8♍47 59	16 08 00	26 11.0	1♒20.4	7 31.4	11 01.8	18 14.0	13 14.3	15 07.6	11 29.3	22 19.1	19 31.2
14 Th	21 36 25	25 21 46	23 22 40	0♎31 24	26R 11.1	2 42.2	8 40.5	11 38.6	18 18.3	13 21.7	15 02.8	11 27.6	22 20.5	19 33.0
15 F	21 40 22	26 22 23	7♎33 45	14 29 27	26 11.2	4 05.2	9 49.4	12 15.4	18 23.1	13 29.3	14 58.1	11 26.0	22 21.9	19 34.8
16 Sa	21 44 18	27 22 58	21 18 24	28 00 38	26 11.1	5 29.3	10 58.1	12 52.2	18 28.2	13 37.0	14 53.3	11 24.4	22 23.4	19 36.5
17 Su	21 48 15	28 23 33	4♏36 20	11♏05 46	26 10.9	6 54.6	12 06.6	13 29.1	18 33.7	13 44.8	14 48.6	11 22.9	22 24.8	19 38.3
18 M	21 52 11	29 24 06	17 29 19	23 47 26	26D 10.8	8 21.0	13 15.0	14 06.1	18 39.5	13 52.9	14 43.9	11 21.4	22 26.3	19 40.1
19 Tu	21 56 08	0♓24 38	0♐00 37	6♐09 24	26 10.8	9 48.5	14 23.2	14 43.0	18 45.8	14 01.0	14 39.3	11 19.9	22 27.9	19 41.9
20 W	22 00 04	1 25 08	12 14 22	18 16 05	26 11.1	11 17.0	15 31.2	15 20.0	18 52.4	14 09.3	14 34.7	11 18.5	22 29.4	19 43.6
21 Th	22 04 01	2 25 38	24 15 08	0♑12 05	26 11.6	12 46.5	16 39.0	15 57.0	18 59.3	14 17.8	14 30.2	11 17.1	22 31.0	19 45.4
22 F	22 07 58	3 26 06	6♑07 29	12 01 53	26 12.3	14 17.1	17 46.6	16 34.1	19 06.7	14 26.3	14 25.6	11 15.8	22 32.6	19 47.1
23 Sa	22 11 54	4 26 33	17 55 46	23 49 38	26 13.2	15 48.6	18 54.0	17 11.1	19 14.3	14 35.0	14 21.2	11 14.5	22 34.3	19 48.9
24 Su	22 15 51	5 26 58	29 43 54	5♒38 59	26 14.1	17 21.2	20 01.2	17 48.2	19 22.3	14 43.9	14 16.8	11 13.3	22 35.9	19 50.6
25 M	22 19 47	6 27 22	11♒35 16	17 33 05	26R 14.6	18 54.7	21 08.2	18 25.4	19 30.7	14 52.9	14 12.4	11 12.1	22 37.6	19 52.4
26 Tu	22 23 44	7 27 44	23 32 42	29 34 26	26 14.8	20 29.2	22 15.0	19 02.5	19 39.4	15 02.0	14 08.1	11 11.0	22 39.3	19 54.1
27 W	22 27 40	8 28 04	5♓38 28	11♓45 02	26 14.3	22 04.8	23 21.6	19 39.7	19 48.4	15 11.2	14 03.8	11 09.9	22 41.0	19 55.8
28 Th	22 31 37	9 28 23	17 54 18	24 06 26	26 13.1	23 41.3	24 27.9	20 16.9	19 57.8	15 20.6	13 59.6	11 08.9	22 42.8	19 57.5
29 F	22 35 33	10 28 39	0♈21 33	6♈39 46	26 11.3	25 18.9	25 34.0	20 54.2	20 07.5	15 30.1	13 55.5	11 07.9	22 44.6	19 59.2

Astro Data

	Dy Hr Mn
☿R	1 4:22
♄☍♇	1 18:30
♆D	2 6:33
♃D	5 3:59
☽0N	6 2:40
☽0S	18 15:11
☿D	21 9:42
♃✶♅	31 18:48
☽0N	2 9:17
⚳D	3 5:44
♀0N	7 18:34
☽0S	15 1:10
♃□♄	22 10:44
☽0N	29 14:54

Planet Ingress

	Dy Hr Mn
♀ ♓	12 20:23
☉ ♒	20 12:11
♂ ♉	26 7:15
♀ ♈	7 0:26
☿ ♒	12 12:03
☉ ♓	19 2:14

Last Aspect / ☽ Ingress

Last Aspect Dy Hr Mn		☽ Ingress Dy Hr Mn
2 8:05	♆ ✶	♓ 3 0:35
5 2:50	☿ ✶	♈ 5 11:39
7 7:19	☿ □	♉ 7 19:19
9 16:33	♀ □	♊ 9 22:56
11 21:34	♀ △	♋ 11 23:23
13 11:16	☉ ☍	♌ 13 22:31
15 12:05	♂ △	♍ 15 22:26
17 20:16	☉ △	♎ 18 0:58
20 6:46	☉ □	♏ 20 7:12
21 19:08	♇ □	♐ 22 16:57
25 3:39	♂ △	♑ 25 5:02
27 1:41	♆ □	♒ 27 17:57
29 14:28	♆ ✶	♓ 30 6:27

Last Aspect / ☽ Ingress

Last Aspect Dy Hr Mn		☽ Ingress Dy Hr Mn
1 4:10	♀ ☌	♈ 1 17:30
3 11:29	♆ ☌	♉ 4 2:04
6 5:52	♀ ✶	♊ 6 7:25
7 20:52	♆ ✶	♋ 8 9:41
10 5:10	☿ ☍	♌ 10 9:55
11 22:09	☉ ☍	♍ 12 9:46
13 7:12	♃ △	♎ 14 11:07
16 10:47	☉ △	♏ 16 15:36
18 23:47	☉ □	♐ 18 23:59
20 20:29	♆ △	♑ 21 11:36
23 9:26	♆ □	♒ 24 0:33
25 22:11	♆ ✶	♓ 26 12:51
28 4:13	♂ ✶	♈ 28 23:19

☽ Phases & Eclipses

Dy Hr Mn	
6 17:48	☽ 15♈59
13 11:16	○ 22♋50
20 6:46	☾ 29♎46
28 10:17	● 8♒04
5 7:01	☽ 16♉03
11 22:09	○ 22♌45
11 22:12	T 1.300
18 23:47	☾ 29♏54
27 4:59	● 8♓10
27 4:45:26	P 0.629

Astro Data

1 January 2036
Julian Day # 49674
SVP 4♓45'33"
GC 27♐20.5 ⚴ 24♓39.9
Eris 26♈57.5R ⚵ 15♓31.5
⚷ 8♊11.0R ⚶ 9♏59.3
☽ Mean ☊ 28♌45.1

1 February 2036
Julian Day # 49705
SVP 4♓45'29"
GC 27♐20.6 ⚴ 3♈39.4
Eris 26♈58.3 ⚵ 0♈19.9
⚷ 7♊12.8R ⚶ 22♏59.3
☽ Mean ☊ 27♌06.6

March 2036

LONGITUDE

Day	Sid.Time	☉	0 hr ☽	Noon ☽	True ☊	☿	♀	♂	⚳	♃	♄	♅	♆	♇
1 Sa	22 39 30	11♓28 54	13♈01 13	19♈25 59	26♌09.1	26♒57.5	26♈39.8	21♉31.4	20♊17.5	15♉39.7	13♌51.4	11♋07.0	22♈46.3	20♒00.9
2 Su	22 43 27	12 29 07	25 54 11	2♉25 53	26R 06.7	28 37.1	27 45.4	22 08.7	20 27.8	15 49.4	13R 47.4	11R 06.1	22 48.2	20 02.6
3 M	22 47 23	13 29 18	9♉01 11	15 40 11	26 04.6	0♓17.7	28 50.7	22 46.0	20 38.4	15 59.3	13 43.5	11 05.3	22 50.0	20 04.3
4 Tu	22 51 20	14 29 27	22 22 56	29 09 31	26 03.1	1 59.4	29 55.8	23 23.3	20 49.3	16 09.3	13 39.6	11 04.5	22 51.9	20 05.9
5 W	22 55 16	15 29 34	5♊59 59	12♊54 20	26D 02.5	3 42.2	1♉00.6	24 00.6	21 00.6	16 19.4	13 35.9	11 03.8	22 53.7	20 07.6
6 Th	22 59 13	16 29 39	19 52 33	26 54 34	26 02.8	5 26.0	2 05.0	24 38.0	21 12.1	16 29.5	13 32.1	11 03.1	22 55.6	20 09.2
7 F	23 03 09	17 29 42	4♋00 15	11♋09 24	26 03.8	7 11.0	3 09.2	25 15.4	21 24.0	16 39.9	13 28.5	11 02.5	22 57.5	20 10.9
8 Sa	23 07 06	18 29 42	18 21 42	25 36 49	26 05.2	8 57.0	4 13.1	25 52.7	21 36.1	16 50.3	13 24.9	11 01.9	22 59.5	20 12.5
9 Su	23 11 02	19 29 40	2♌54 15	10♌13 27	26 06.5	10 44.2	5 16.7	26 30.1	21 48.5	17 00.8	13 21.5	11 01.4	23 01.4	20 14.1
10 M	23 14 59	20 29 36	17 33 46	24 54 27	26R 07.1	12 32.5	6 19.9	27 07.5	22 01.1	17 11.4	13 18.1	11 00.9	23 03.4	20 15.7
11 Tu	23 18 56	21 29 30	2♍14 44	9♍33 47	26 06.6	14 21.9	7 22.8	27 44.9	22 14.1	17 22.1	13 14.7	11 00.5	23 05.4	20 17.3
12 W	23 22 52	22 29 22	16 50 47	24 04 53	26 04.7	16 12.5	8 25.4	28 22.3	22 27.3	17 33.0	13 11.5	11 00.2	23 07.4	20 18.9
13 Th	23 26 49	23 29 12	1♎15 21	8♎21 28	26 01.5	18 04.2	9 27.6	28 59.8	22 40.7	17 43.9	13 08.4	10 59.9	23 09.4	20 20.4
14 F	23 30 45	24 29 01	15 22 39	22 18 25	25 57.3	19 57.0	10 29.4	29 37.2	22 54.4	17 54.9	13 05.3	10 59.6	23 11.4	20 21.9
15 Sa	23 34 42	25 28 47	29 08 26	5♏52 28	25 52.6	21 51.0	11 30.9	0♊14.6	23 08.4	18 06.0	13 02.3	10 59.4	23 13.5	20 23.5
16 Su	23 38 38	26 28 32	12♏30 26	19 02 24	25 48.1	23 46.1	12 32.0	0 52.1	23 22.7	18 17.2	12 59.4	10 59.3	23 15.5	20 25.0
17 M	23 42 35	27 28 15	25 28 33	1♐49 08	25 44.4	25 42.3	13 32.7	1 29.6	23 37.1	18 28.5	12 56.6	10 59.2	23 17.6	20 26.5
18 Tu	23 46 31	28 27 56	8♐04 33	14 15 15	25 41.9	27 39.5	14 33.0	2 07.0	23 51.8	18 39.9	12 53.9	10D 59.2	23 19.7	20 28.0
19 W	23 50 28	29 27 35	20 21 45	26 24 36	25D 40.8	29 37.6	15 32.9	2 44.5	24 06.8	18 51.4	12 51.3	10 59.2	23 21.8	20 29.4
20 Th	23 54 24	0♈27 13	2♑24 25	8♑21 50	25 41.0	1♈36.7	16 32.3	3 22.0	24 22.0	19 03.0	12 48.8	10 59.3	23 23.9	20 30.9
21 F	23 58 21	1 26 49	14 17 29	20 12 01	25 42.3	3 36.6	17 31.3	3 59.5	24 37.4	19 14.7	12 46.4	10 59.4	23 26.0	20 32.3
22 Sa	0 02 18	2 26 23	26 06 03	2♒00 12	25 44.1	5 37.1	18 29.8	4 37.0	24 53.1	19 26.4	12 44.1	10 59.6	23 28.2	20 33.8
23 Su	0 06 14	3 25 56	7♒55 05	13 51 16	25R 45.6	7 38.2	19 27.9	5 14.5	25 08.9	19 38.2	12 41.9	10 59.8	23 30.3	20 35.2
24 M	0 10 11	4 25 27	19 49 15	25 49 32	25 46.3	9 39.7	20 25.5	5 52.1	25 25.0	19 50.1	12 39.8	11 00.1	23 32.5	20 36.5
25 Tu	0 14 07	5 24 55	1♓52 32	7♓58 39	25 45.5	11 41.3	21 22.6	6 29.6	25 41.3	20 02.1	12 37.7	11 00.4	23 34.6	20 37.9
26 W	0 18 04	6 24 22	14 08 11	20 21 22	25 42.8	13 42.8	22 19.1	7 07.2	25 57.9	20 14.2	12 35.8	11 00.8	23 36.8	20 39.3
27 Th	0 22 00	7 23 47	26 38 24	2♈59 23	25 38.1	15 44.0	23 15.1	7 44.7	26 14.6	20 26.3	12 34.0	11 01.3	23 39.0	20 40.6
28 F	0 25 57	8 23 10	9♈24 22	15 53 19	25 31.7	17 44.6	24 10.6	8 22.3	26 31.5	20 38.5	12 32.3	11 01.8	23 41.2	20 41.9
29 Sa	0 29 53	9 22 30	22 26 08	29 02 42	25 24.2	19 44.2	25 05.5	8 59.8	26 48.7	20 50.8	12 30.7	11 02.3	23 43.4	20 43.2
30 Su	0 33 50	10 21 49	5♉42 48	12♉26 13	25 16.5	21 42.5	25 59.8	9 37.4	27 06.0	21 03.2	12 29.2	11 02.9	23 45.6	20 44.5
31 M	0 37 47	11 21 05	19 12 44	26 02 03	25 09.3	23 39.0	26 53.4	10 15.0	27 23.6	21 15.6	12 27.8	11 03.6	23 47.8	20 45.7

April 2036

LONGITUDE

Day	Sid.Time	☉	0 hr ☽	Noon ☽	True ☊	☿	♀	♂	⚳	♃	♄	♅	♆	♇
1 Tu	0 41 43	12♈20 20	2♊53 57	9♊48 09	25♌03.5	25♈33.6	27♉46.4	10♊52.5	27♊41.3	21♉28.1	12♌26.5	11♋04.3	23♈50.1	20♒47.0
2 W	0 45 40	13 19 32	16 44 26	23 42 35	24R 59.7	27 25.6	28 38.8	11 30.1	27 59.2	21 40.6	12R 25.3	11 05.1	23 52.3	20 48.2
3 Th	0 49 36	14 18 41	0♋42 26	7♋43 47	24D 58.0	29 14.8	29 30.4	12 07.7	28 17.3	21 53.3	12 24.3	11 05.9	23 54.5	20 49.4
4 F	0 53 33	15 17 49	14 46 30	21 50 25	24 58.0	1♉00.7	0♊21.4	12 45.3	28 35.6	22 06.0	12 23.3	11 06.8	23 56.8	20 50.5
5 Sa	0 57 29	16 16 54	28 55 24	6♌01 17	24 58.9	2 43.1	1 11.5	13 22.9	28 54.1	22 18.7	12 22.4	11 07.7	23 59.0	20 51.7
6 Su	1 01 26	17 15 56	13♌07 52	20 14 55	24R 59.7	4 21.4	2 00.9	14 00.5	29 12.7	22 31.5	12 21.7	11 08.7	24 01.3	20 52.8
7 M	1 05 22	18 14 57	27 22 09	4♍29 14	24 59.4	5 55.4	2 49.5	14 38.1	29 31.5	22 44.4	12 21.0	11 09.7	24 03.6	20 53.9
8 Tu	1 09 19	19 13 55	11♍35 47	18 41 21	24 57.1	7 24.9	3 37.2	15 15.6	29 50.5	22 57.3	12 20.5	11 10.8	24 05.8	20 55.0
9 W	1 13 16	20 12 50	25 45 27	2♎47 34	24 52.4	8 49.5	4 24.1	15 53.2	0♋09.6	23 10.3	12 20.1	11 12.0	24 08.1	20 56.1
10 Th	1 17 12	21 11 44	9♎47 09	16 43 42	24 45.3	10 09.0	5 10.0	16 30.8	0 28.9	23 23.3	12 19.8	11 13.1	24 10.3	20 57.1
11 F	1 21 09	22 10 36	23 36 41	0♏25 40	24 36.3	11 23.3	5 55.0	17 08.4	0 48.4	23 36.4	12 19.5	11 14.4	24 12.6	20 58.2
12 Sa	1 25 05	23 09 25	7♏10 15	13 50 07	24 26.2	12 32.0	6 39.0	17 45.9	1 08.0	23 49.5	12D 19.4	11 15.7	24 14.9	20 59.2
13 Su	1 29 02	24 08 13	20 25 05	26 55 01	24 16.2	13 35.1	7 22.1	18 23.5	1 27.8	24 02.7	12 19.4	11 17.0	24 17.1	21 00.1
14 M	1 32 58	25 06 59	3♐19 55	9♐39 54	24 07.1	14 32.5	8 04.0	19 01.1	1 47.7	24 15.9	12 19.6	11 18.4	24 19.4	21 01.1
15 Tu	1 36 55	26 05 44	15 55 11	22 06 03	23 59.9	15 23.9	8 44.9	19 38.7	2 07.8	24 29.2	12 19.8	11 19.8	24 21.7	21 02.0
16 W	1 40 51	27 04 26	28 12 53	4♑16 11	23 54.9	16 09.4	9 24.7	20 16.2	2 28.0	24 42.5	12 20.1	11 21.3	24 23.9	21 03.0
17 Th	1 44 48	28 03 07	10♑16 26	16 14 15	23 52.3	16 48.8	10 03.3	20 53.8	2 48.3	24 55.8	12 20.6	11 22.8	24 26.2	21 03.8
18 F	1 48 44	29 01 46	22 10 14	28 05 01	23D 51.5	17 22.2	10 40.7	21 31.4	3 08.8	25 09.2	12 21.1	11 24.4	24 28.5	21 04.7
19 Sa	1 52 41	0♉00 24	3♒59 19	9♒53 46	23 51.8	17 49.4	11 16.8	22 09.0	3 29.5	25 22.7	12 21.8	11 26.0	24 30.7	21 05.5
20 Su	1 56 38	0 59 00	15 49 05	21 45 56	23R 52.2	18 10.5	11 51.6	22 46.5	3 50.2	25 36.2	12 22.5	11 27.7	24 33.0	21 06.4
21 M	2 00 34	1 57 34	27 44 56	3♓46 44	23 51.8	18 25.6	12 25.1	23 24.1	4 11.1	25 49.7	12 23.4	11 29.4	24 35.2	21 07.1
22 Tu	2 04 31	2 56 06	9♓51 54	16 00 57	23 49.5	18 34.6	12 57.2	24 01.7	4 32.2	26 03.3	12 24.4	11 31.2	24 37.5	21 07.9
23 W	2 08 27	3 54 37	22 14 19	28 32 24	23 44.9	18R 37.8	13 27.8	24 39.3	4 53.4	26 16.9	12 25.5	11 33.0	24 39.7	21 08.7
24 Th	2 12 24	4 53 06	4♈55 28	11♈23 41	23 37.6	18 35.3	13 56.9	25 16.8	5 14.7	26 30.5	12 26.7	11 34.9	24 42.0	21 09.4
25 F	2 16 20	5 51 33	17 57 08	24 35 45	23 28.0	18 27.3	14 24.4	25 54.4	5 36.1	26 44.2	12 27.9	11 36.8	24 44.2	21 10.1
26 Sa	2 20 17	6 49 58	1♉19 22	8♉07 43	23 16.8	18 14.1	14 50.3	26 32.0	5 57.6	26 57.9	12 29.4	11 38.7	24 46.4	21 10.7
27 Su	2 24 13	7 48 22	15 00 24	21 56 57	23 05.1	17 56.1	15 14.5	27 09.6	6 19.3	27 11.6	12 30.9	11 40.7	24 48.7	21 11.4
28 M	2 28 10	8 46 44	28 56 48	5♊59 23	22 54.2	17 33.5	15 37.0	27 47.2	6 41.1	27 25.4	12 32.5	11 42.7	24 50.9	21 12.0
29 Tu	2 32 07	9 45 04	13♊04 05	20 10 17	22 45.0	17 07.0	15 57.7	28 24.7	7 03.0	27 39.2	12 34.2	11 44.8	24 53.1	21 12.6
30 W	2 36 03	10 43 22	27 17 25	4♋24 58	22 38.4	16 37.0	16 16.4	29 02.3	7 25.1	27 53.0	12 36.0	11 46.9	24 55.3	21 13.1

Astro Data	Dy Hr Mn
☽0S	13 11:38
♅D	18 15:29
☉0N	20 1:02
☿0N	21 1:42
☽0N	27 21:32
♃□♇	28 19:24
☽0S	9 21:07
♄D	12 22:37
♃⚺♆	14 19:41
☿R	23 13:18
☽0N	24 6:08
♃∠♅	24 20:52

Planet Ingress		Dy Hr Mn
☿	♓	3 7:48
♀	♉	4 13:34
♂	♊	15 2:37
☿	♈	19 16:31
☉	♈	20 1:03
☿	♉	3 22:09
♀	♊	4 1:53
⚳	♋	8 23:57
☉	♉	19 11:50

Last Aspect Dy Hr Mn			☽ Ingress	Dy Hr Mn
2 3:59	☿	⚹	♉	2 7:33
4 1:18	♂	☌	♊	4 13:29
6 5:12	♆	⚹	♋	6 17:14
8 12:27	♂	⚹	♌	8 19:14
10 15:47	♂	□	♍	10 20:20
12 19:29	♂	△	♎	12 21:53
14 13:33	♆	☍	♏	15 1:31
17 3:03	☉	△	♐	17 8:32
19 18:39	☉	□	♑	19 19:10
21 18:36	♆	□	♒	22 7:56
24 7:26	♆	⚹	♓	24 20:17
26 16:04	♀	⚹	♈	27 6:22
29 2:19	♆	☌	♉	29 13:44
31 13:36	♀	☌	♊	31 18:56

Last Aspect Dy Hr Mn			☽ Ingress	Dy Hr Mn
2 19:21	☿	⚹	♋	2 22:47
4 15:35	♆	□	♌	5 1:49
6 18:23	♆	△	♍	7 4:26
8 19:21	♃	△	♎	9 7:14
11 1:01	♆	☍	♏	11 11:15
13 6:35	♃	☍	♐	13 17:45
15 20:31	☉	△	♑	16 3:32
18 14:06	☉	□	♒	18 15:54
20 19:51	♃	□	♓	21 4:29
23 7:38	♃	⚹	♈	23 14:45
25 14:28	♂	⚹	♉	25 21:39
27 21:09	♃	☌	♊	28 1:48
30 2:32	♂	☌	♋	30 4:34

☽ Phases & Eclipses Dy Hr Mn	
5 16:49	☽ 15♊42
12 9:09	○ 22♍22
19 18:39	☾ 29♐44
27 20:57	● 7♈46
4 0:03	☽ 14♋48
10 20:22	○ 21♎32
18 14:06	☾ 29♑07
26 9:33	● 6♉44

Astro Data

1 March 2036
Julian Day # 49734
SVP 4♓45'26"
GC 27♐20.7 ⚴ 14♈24.6
Eris 27♈08.1 ⚵ 15♈51.4
⚷ 7♊17.7 ⚶ 2♐40.9
☽ Mean ☊ 25♌34.5

1 April 2036
Julian Day # 49765
SVP 4♓45'23"
GC 27♐20.7 ⚴ 27♈38.9
Eris 27♈25.7 ⚵ 3♉34.2
⚷ 8♊26.6 ⚶ 8♐23.1
☽ Mean ☊ 23♌55.9

LONGITUDE — May 2036

Day	Sid.Time	☉	0 hr ☽	Noon ☽	True ☊	☿	♀	♂	⚳	♃	♄	♅	♆	♇
1 Th	2 40 00	11♉41 38	11♋32 26	18♋39 28	22♌34.6	16♉04.1	16♊33.3	29♊39.9	7♋47.2	28♉06.8	12♌38.0	11♋49.1	24♈57.5	21♒13.7
2 F	2 43 56	12 39 51	25 45 45	2♌51 01	22D33.0	15R29.0	16 48.1	0♋17.5	8 09.5	28 20.7	12 40.0	11 51.3	24 59.7	21 14.2
3 Sa	2 47 53	13 38 03	9♌55 07	16 57 55	22R32.9	14 52.2	17 00.9	0 55.1	8 31.8	28 34.6	12 42.2	11 53.6	25 01.9	21 14.7
4 Su	2 51 49	14 36 13	23 59 20	0♍59 18	22 32.7	14 14.4	17 11.5	1 32.6	8 54.3	28 48.5	12 44.4	11 55.9	25 04.0	21 15.2
5 M	2 55 46	15 34 20	7♍57 45	14 54 36	22 31.4	13 36.4	17 20.0	2 10.2	9 16.9	29 02.4	12 46.7	11 58.2	25 06.2	21 15.6
6 Tu	2 59 42	16 32 26	21 49 47	28 43 09	22 27.9	12 58.8	17 26.2	2 47.7	9 39.5	29 16.4	12 49.2	12 00.6	25 08.3	21 16.0
7 W	3 03 39	17 30 30	5♎34 32	12♎23 46	22 21.6	12 22.3	17 30.1	3 25.3	10 02.3	29 30.4	12 51.7	12 03.0	25 10.5	21 16.4
8 Th	3 07 36	18 28 32	19 10 37	25 54 48	22 12.4	11 47.5	17R31.7	4 02.8	10 25.2	29 44.3	12 54.3	12 05.4	25 12.6	21 16.7
9 F	3 11 32	19 26 32	2♏36 06	9♏14 15	22 01.0	11 14.9	17 30.9	4 40.4	10 48.1	29 58.3	12 57.1	12 07.9	25 14.7	21 17.1
10 Sa	3 15 29	20 24 31	15 48 59	22 20 06	21 48.3	10 45.1	17 27.7	5 17.9	11 11.2	0♊12.3	12 59.9	12 10.4	25 16.8	21 17.4
11 Su	3 19 25	21 22 28	28 47 26	5♐10 53	21 35.4	10 18.4	17 22.0	5 55.4	11 34.3	0 26.4	13 02.8	12 13.0	25 18.9	21 17.7
12 M	3 23 22	22 20 23	11♐30 23	17 45 58	21 23.6	9 55.4	17 14.0	6 33.0	11 57.6	0 40.4	13 05.9	12 15.6	25 21.0	21 17.9
13 Tu	3 27 18	23 18 18	23 57 46	0♑05 57	21 13.7	9 36.3	17 03.5	7 10.5	12 20.9	0 54.5	13 09.0	12 18.2	25 23.0	21 18.1
14 W	3 31 15	24 16 10	6♑10 46	12 12 35	21 06.5	9 21.3	16 50.5	7 48.0	12 44.3	1 08.5	13 12.2	12 20.9	25 25.1	21 18.3
15 Th	3 35 11	25 14 02	18 11 48	24 08 52	21 01.9	9 10.7	16 35.2	8 25.6	13 07.9	1 22.6	13 15.5	12 23.6	25 27.1	21 18.5
16 F	3 39 08	26 11 52	0♒04 21	5♒58 47	20 59.7	9D04.5	16 17.5	9 03.1	13 31.5	1 36.7	13 18.9	12 26.3	25 29.1	21 18.7
17 Sa	3 43 05	27 09 41	11 52 49	17 47 06	20 59.0	9 02.9	15 57.4	9 40.6	13 55.1	1 50.8	13 22.4	12 29.1	25 31.1	21 18.8
18 Su	3 47 01	28 07 29	23 42 17	29 39 04	20 59.0	9 05.9	15 35.1	10 18.2	14 18.9	2 04.8	13 26.0	12 31.9	25 33.1	21 18.9
19 M	3 50 58	29 05 16	5♓38 09	11♓40 12	20 58.6	9 13.4	15 10.7	10 55.7	14 42.7	2 18.9	13 29.6	12 34.7	25 35.1	21 19.0
20 Tu	3 54 54	0♊03 01	17 45 54	23 55 50	20 56.6	9 25.5	14 44.2	11 33.2	15 06.7	2 33.0	13 33.4	12 37.6	25 37.1	21 19.0
21 W	3 58 51	1 00 46	0♈10 37	6♈30 44	20 52.5	9 42.1	14 15.8	12 10.7	15 30.7	2 47.1	13 37.2	12 40.5	25 39.0	21R19.0
22 Th	4 02 47	1 58 29	12 56 36	19 28 32	20 45.8	10 03.1	13 45.6	12 48.2	15 54.8	3 01.2	13 41.2	12 43.4	25 40.9	21 19.0
23 F	4 06 44	2 56 11	26 06 44	2♉51 14	20 36.8	10 28.3	13 13.8	13 25.8	16 18.9	3 15.4	13 45.2	12 46.4	25 42.8	21 19.0
24 Sa	4 10 40	3 53 53	9♉41 56	16 38 34	20 26.1	10 57.8	12 40.5	14 03.3	16 43.2	3 29.4	13 49.3	12 49.4	25 44.7	21 18.9
25 Su	4 14 37	4 51 33	23 40 43	0♊47 49	20 14.8	11 31.4	12 05.9	14 40.8	17 07.5	3 43.5	13 53.5	12 52.4	25 46.6	21 18.8
26 M	4 18 34	5 49 11	7♊59 09	15 13 55	20 04.1	12 09.0	11 30.3	15 18.4	17 31.9	3 57.6	13 57.8	12 55.4	25 48.4	21 18.7
27 Tu	4 22 30	6 46 49	22 31 14	29 50 12	19 55.1	12 50.5	10 53.8	15 55.9	17 56.4	4 11.7	14 02.1	12 58.5	25 50.2	21 18.6
28 W	4 26 27	7 44 26	7♋09 53	14♋29 26	19 48.7	13 35.7	10 16.7	16 33.4	18 20.9	4 25.8	14 06.6	13 01.6	25 52.1	21 18.4
29 Th	4 30 23	8 42 01	21 48 03	29 05 03	19 45.0	14 24.6	9 39.2	17 11.0	18 45.5	4 39.9	14 11.1	13 04.7	25 53.8	21 18.2
30 F	4 34 20	9 39 34	6♌19 50	13♌31 57	19D43.5	15 17.0	9 01.5	17 48.5	19 10.2	4 54.0	14 15.7	13 07.9	25 55.6	21 18.0
31 Sa	4 38 16	10 37 06	20 41 04	27 46 56	19R43.6	16 12.9	8 24.0	18 26.0	19 34.9	5 08.0	14 20.4	13 11.1	25 57.4	21 17.8

LONGITUDE — June 2036

Day	Sid.Time	☉	0 hr ☽	Noon ☽	True ☊	☿	♀	♂	⚳	♃	♄	♅	♆	♇
1 Su	4 42 13	11♊34 37	4♍49 26	11♍48 30	19♌43.8	17♉12.2	7♊46.7	19♋03.5	19♋59.7	5♊22.1	14♌25.2	13♋14.3	25♈59.1	21♒17.5
2 M	4 46 09	12 32 07	18 44 08	25 36 22	19R43.1	18 14.7	7R10.0	19 41.1	20 24.6	5 36.1	14 30.0	13 17.5	26 00.8	21R17.2
3 Tu	4 50 06	13 29 35	2♎25 17	9♎10 57	19 40.6	19 20.5	6 34.2	20 18.6	20 49.5	5 50.1	14 34.9	13 20.7	26 02.5	21 16.9
4 W	4 54 03	14 27 02	15 53 26	22 32 48	19 35.5	20 29.4	5 59.3	20 56.1	21 14.5	6 04.1	14 39.9	13 24.0	26 04.1	21 16.6
5 Th	4 57 59	15 24 27	29 09 07	5♏42 22	19 28.1	21 41.4	5 25.7	21 33.6	21 39.6	6 18.1	14 45.0	13 27.3	26 05.7	21 16.2
6 F	5 01 56	16 21 52	12♏12 36	18 39 47	19 18.6	22 56.4	4 53.5	22 11.1	22 04.7	6 32.1	14 50.1	13 30.6	26 07.4	21 15.8
7 Sa	5 05 52	17 19 16	25 03 56	1♐25 02	19 08.0	24 14.4	4 22.9	22 48.6	22 29.8	6 46.1	14 55.3	13 33.9	26 08.9	21 15.4
8 Su	5 09 49	18 16 38	7♐43 03	13 58 02	18 57.2	25 35.4	3 54.1	23 26.1	22 55.1	7 00.0	15 00.6	13 37.3	26 10.5	21 15.0
9 M	5 13 45	19 14 00	20 10 00	26 19 02	18 47.2	26 59.3	3 27.2	24 03.7	23 20.3	7 13.9	15 05.9	13 40.6	26 12.0	21 14.5
10 Tu	5 17 42	20 11 21	2♑25 14	8♑28 47	18 39.0	28 26.2	3 02.4	24 41.2	23 45.7	7 27.8	15 11.4	13 44.0	26 13.6	21 14.0
11 W	5 21 38	21 08 42	14 29 51	20 28 43	18 33.0	29 55.9	2 39.7	25 18.7	24 11.0	7 41.7	15 16.8	13 47.4	26 15.1	21 13.5
12 Th	5 25 35	22 06 02	26 25 42	2♒21 09	18 29.4	1♊28.4	2 19.2	25 56.2	24 36.5	7 55.5	15 22.4	13 50.9	26 16.5	21 13.0
13 F	5 29 32	23 03 21	8♒15 30	14 09 11	18D27.9	3 03.8	2 01.1	26 33.7	25 02.0	8 09.4	15 28.0	13 54.3	26 18.0	21 12.4
14 Sa	5 33 28	24 00 40	20 02 45	25 56 43	18 28.0	4 42.0	1 45.3	27 11.2	25 27.5	8 23.2	15 33.7	13 57.8	26 19.4	21 11.8
15 Su	5 37 25	24 57 58	1♓51 41	7♓48 17	18 29.0	6 22.9	1 31.9	27 48.7	25 53.1	8 36.9	15 39.4	14 01.2	26 20.8	21 11.2
16 M	5 41 21	25 55 16	13 47 08	19 48 54	18R29.9	8 06.7	1 21.0	28 26.3	26 18.7	8 50.7	15 45.2	14 04.7	26 22.1	21 10.6
17 Tu	5 45 18	26 52 33	25 54 14	2♈03 46	18 30.0	9 53.2	1 12.4	29 03.8	26 44.4	9 04.4	15 51.1	14 08.2	26 23.5	21 10.0
18 W	5 49 14	27 49 51	8♈18 08	14 37 54	18 28.5	11 42.3	1 06.3	29 41.3	27 10.2	9 18.1	15 57.0	14 11.7	26 24.8	21 09.3
19 Th	5 53 11	28 47 08	21 03 36	27 35 38	18 25.1	13 34.1	1 02.5	0♌18.8	27 36.0	9 31.8	16 03.0	14 15.2	26 26.0	21 08.6
20 F	5 57 07	29 44 24	4♉14 21	10♉59 57	18 19.9	15 28.4	1D01.1	0 56.4	28 01.8	9 45.4	16 09.1	14 18.8	26 27.3	21 07.9
21 Sa	6 01 04	0♋41 41	17 52 29	24 51 51	18 13.3	17 25.2	1 02.1	1 33.9	28 27.7	9 59.0	16 15.2	14 22.3	26 28.5	21 07.2
22 Su	6 05 01	1 38 58	1♊57 45	9♊09 43	18 06.1	19 24.3	1 05.3	2 11.5	28 53.6	10 12.6	16 21.3	14 25.9	26 29.7	21 06.4
23 M	6 08 57	2 36 14	16 27 05	23 49 03	17 59.2	21 25.7	1 10.8	2 49.0	29 19.6	10 26.1	16 27.5	14 29.5	26 30.9	21 05.6
24 Tu	6 12 54	3 33 30	1♋14 40	8♋42 52	17 53.5	23 29.0	1 18.4	3 26.6	29 45.6	10 39.6	16 33.8	14 33.0	26 32.0	21 04.8
25 W	6 16 50	4 30 45	16 12 34	23 42 38	17 49.5	25 34.2	1 28.2	4 04.2	0♌11.7	10 53.0	16 40.1	14 36.6	26 33.1	21 04.0
26 Th	6 20 47	5 28 00	1♌12 00	8♌39 38	17D47.6	27 41.0	1 40.1	4 41.7	0 37.8	11 06.5	16 46.5	14 40.2	26 34.2	21 03.2
27 F	6 24 43	6 25 15	16 04 39	23 26 16	17 47.4	29 49.1	1 53.9	5 19.3	1 03.9	11 19.8	16 53.0	14 43.8	26 35.3	21 02.3
28 Sa	6 28 40	7 22 29	0♍43 52	7♍56 59	17 48.3	1♋58.3	2 09.7	5 56.9	1 30.1	11 33.2	16 59.4	14 47.4	26 36.3	21 01.5
29 Su	6 32 37	8 19 42	15 05 16	22 08 32	17 49.6	4 08.4	2 27.4	6 34.4	1 56.3	11 46.4	17 06.0	14 51.1	26 37.3	21 00.6
30 M	6 36 33	9 16 55	29 06 42	5♎59 46	17R50.4	6 18.9	2 47.0	7 12.0	2 22.6	11 59.7	17 12.6	14 54.7	26 38.3	20 59.6

Astro Data Dy Hr Mn	Planet Ingress Dy Hr Mn	Last Aspect Dy Hr Mn	☽ Ingress Dy Hr Mn	Last Aspect Dy Hr Mn	☽ Ingress Dy Hr Mn	☽ Phases & Eclipses Dy Hr Mn
☽0S 7 4:57	♂ ♋ 2 0:50	2 4:15 ♃ ⚹	♌ 2 7:10	2 1:10 ♂ ⚹	♎ 2 19:44	3 5:54 ☽ 13♌23
♀R 8 15:58	♃ ♊ 9 14:52	4 8:12 ♃ □	♍ 4 10:18	4 18:24 ♆ ☍	♏ 5 1:33	10 8:09 ○ 20♏15
☿D 17 8:29	☉ ♊ 20 10:45	6 12:59 ♃ △	♎ 6 14:14	6 20:54 ♆ ☍	♐ 7 9:19	18 8:39 ☾ 27♒59
♇R 21 15:38		8 10:44 ♃ ☍	♏ 8 19:19	9 11:46 ♆ △	♑ 9 19:14	25 19:17 ● 5♊09
☽0N 21 16:03	☿ ♊ 11 13:06	10 10:04 ♇ □	♐ 11 2:16	11 23:40 ♆ □	♒ 12 7:14	
	♂ ♌ 18 23:57	13 2:45 ♆ △	♑ 13 11:48	14 12:46 ♆ ⚹	♓ 14 20:14	1 11:34 ☽ 11♍34
☽0S 3 11:32	☉ ♋ 20 18:32	15 14:39 ♆ □	♒ 15 23:51	17 5:52 ♂ △	♈ 17 8:00	8 21:02 ○ 18♐38
☽0N 18 1:49	⚳ ♌ 25 1:15	18 8:39 ☉ □	♓ 18 12:42	19 14:20 ☉ ⚹	♉ 19 16:22	17 1:03 ☾ 26♓26
♀D 20 14:12	☿ ♋ 27 14:02	19 18:41 ♇ □	♈ 20 23:40	21 5:36 ♇ □	♊ 21 20:42	24 3:09 ● 3♋12
♃∠♆ 28 18:08		22 23:15 ♆ ☌	♉ 23 6:57	23 16:22 ♆ ⚹	♋ 23 22:00	30 18:13 ☽ 9♎32
☽0S 30 18:06		24 19:59 ♇ □	♊ 25 10:40	25 16:33 ♆ □	♌ 25 22:04	
		27 5:26 ♆ ⚹	♋ 27 12:16	27 17:11 ♆ △	♍ 27 22:48	
		29 6:44 ♆ □	♌ 29 13:31	28 23:33 ♅ ⚹	♎ 30 1:32	
		31 8:54 ♆ △	♍ 31 15:46			

Astro Data

1 May 2036
Julian Day # 49795
SVP 4♓45'20"
GC 27♐20.8 ⚴ 11♉45.7
Eris 27♈45.3 ⚵ 21♉18.6
⚷ 10♊21.0 ⚶ 7♐05.6R
☽ Mean ☊ 22♌20.6

1 June 2036
Julian Day # 49826
SVP 4♓45'16"
GC 27♐20.9 ⚴ 27♉27.1
Eris 28♈03.3 ⚵ 9♊49.1
⚷ 12♊45.7 ⚶ 0♐13.5R
☽ Mean ☊ 20♌42.1

July 2036 LONGITUDE

Day	Sid.Time	☉	0 hr ☽	Noon ☽	True ☊	☿	♀	♂	⚳	♃	♄	♅	♆	♇
1 Tu	6 40 30	10♋14 08	12♎47 51	19♎31 05	17♌50.1	8♋29.8	3♊08.3	7♌49.6	2♌48.9	12♊12.9	17♌19.2	14♋58.3	26♈39.2	20♒58.7
2 W	6 44 26	11 11 20	26 09 40	2♏43 49	17R48.2	10 40.6	3 31.3	8 27.2	3 15.2	12 26.0	17 25.8	15 01.9	26 40.1	20R57.8
3 Th	6 48 23	12 08 32	9♏13 48	15 39 51	17 44.8	12 51.1	3 56.0	9 04.8	3 41.6	12 39.1	17 32.6	15 05.5	26 41.0	20 56.8
4 F	6 52 19	13 05 44	22 02 12	28 21 05	17 40.0	15 01.0	4 22.3	9 42.4	4 08.0	12 52.2	17 39.3	15 09.2	26 41.8	20 55.8
5 Sa	6 56 16	14 02 55	4♐36 45	10♐49 23	17 34.5	17 10.1	4 50.1	10 19.9	4 34.4	13 05.2	17 46.1	15 12.8	26 42.6	20 54.8
6 Su	7 00 12	15 00 06	16 59 13	23 06 26	17 28.9	19 18.3	5 19.5	10 57.5	5 00.9	13 18.1	17 53.0	15 16.5	26 43.4	20 53.8
7 M	7 04 09	15 57 18	29 11 14	5♑13 50	17 23.7	21 25.3	5 50.2	11 35.2	5 27.3	13 31.0	17 59.9	15 20.1	26 44.1	20 52.8
8 Tu	7 08 06	16 54 29	11♑14 24	17 13 10	17 19.6	23 30.9	6 22.4	12 12.8	5 53.9	13 43.8	18 06.8	15 23.7	26 44.9	20 51.7
9 W	7 12 02	17 51 40	23 10 22	29 06 14	17 16.8	25 35.1	6 55.9	12 50.4	6 20.4	13 56.6	18 13.7	15 27.3	26 45.5	20 50.6
10 Th	7 15 59	18 48 52	5♒01 02	10♒55 04	17D15.4	27 37.7	7 30.7	13 28.0	6 47.0	14 09.4	18 20.7	15 31.0	26 46.2	20 49.6
11 F	7 19 55	19 46 04	16 48 40	22 42 12	17 15.3	29 38.7	8 06.7	14 05.6	7 13.6	14 22.0	18 27.8	15 34.6	26 46.8	20 48.5
12 Sa	7 23 52	20 43 16	28 36 02	4♓30 36	17 16.3	1♌37.9	8 44.0	14 43.3	7 40.3	14 34.6	18 34.8	15 38.2	26 47.4	20 47.4
13 Su	7 27 48	21 40 29	10♓26 23	16 23 50	17 17.9	3 35.4	9 22.4	15 20.9	8 06.9	14 47.2	18 41.9	15 41.9	26 48.0	20 46.2
14 M	7 31 45	22 37 42	22 23 28	28 25 51	17 19.5	5 31.1	10 01.9	15 58.5	8 33.6	14 59.7	18 49.1	15 45.5	26 48.5	20 45.1
15 Tu	7 35 41	23 34 55	4♈31 32	10♈41 03	17 20.8	7 25.0	10 42.4	16 36.2	9 00.4	15 12.1	18 56.3	15 49.1	26 49.0	20 43.9
16 W	7 39 38	24 32 09	16 54 58	23 13 51	17R21.4	9 17.1	11 24.0	17 13.9	9 27.1	15 24.5	19 03.5	15 52.7	26 49.4	20 42.8
17 Th	7 43 35	25 29 24	29 38 11	6♉08 27	17 21.0	11 07.3	12 06.6	17 51.5	9 53.9	15 36.8	19 10.7	15 56.3	26 49.9	20 41.6
18 F	7 47 31	26 26 40	12♉45 03	19 28 18	17 19.7	12 55.6	12 50.1	18 29.2	10 20.7	15 49.0	19 18.0	15 59.9	26 50.3	20 40.4
19 Sa	7 51 28	27 23 56	26 18 23	3♊15 23	17 17.7	14 42.2	13 34.6	19 06.9	10 47.6	16 01.1	19 25.3	16 03.5	26 50.6	20 39.2
20 Su	7 55 24	28 21 13	10♊19 13	17 29 38	17 15.3	16 26.8	14 19.9	19 44.6	11 14.4	16 13.2	19 32.6	16 07.1	26 51.0	20 38.0
21 M	7 59 21	29 18 31	24 46 12	2♋08 18	17 13.0	18 09.7	15 06.1	20 22.4	11 41.3	16 25.3	19 39.9	16 10.6	26 51.3	20 36.8
22 Tu	8 03 17	0♌15 49	9♋35 09	17 05 50	17 11.1	19 50.7	15 53.1	21 00.1	12 08.3	16 37.2	19 47.3	16 14.2	26 51.5	20 35.6
23 W	8 07 14	1 13 09	24 39 15	2♌14 17	17D09.9	21 29.9	16 40.8	21 37.9	12 35.2	16 49.1	19 54.7	16 17.7	26 51.8	20 34.3
24 Th	8 11 10	2 10 28	9♌49 43	17 24 22	17 09.5	23 07.3	17 29.3	22 15.6	13 02.2	17 00.9	20 02.1	16 21.3	26 52.0	20 33.1
25 F	8 15 07	3 07 48	24 57 05	2♍26 49	17 09.8	24 42.8	18 18.5	22 53.4	13 29.1	17 12.6	20 09.6	16 24.8	26 52.1	20 31.8
26 Sa	8 19 04	4 05 09	9♍52 37	17 13 41	17 10.6	26 16.5	19 08.4	23 31.1	13 56.1	17 24.2	20 17.1	16 28.3	26 52.3	20 30.5
27 Su	8 23 00	5 02 30	24 29 25	1♎39 21	17 11.6	27 48.4	19 59.0	24 08.9	14 23.1	17 35.8	20 24.5	16 31.8	26 52.4	20 29.3
28 M	8 26 57	5 59 51	8♎43 10	15 40 42	17 12.5	29 18.4	20 50.2	24 46.7	14 50.2	17 47.3	20 32.1	16 35.3	26 52.4	20 28.0
29 Tu	8 30 53	6 57 13	22 31 58	29 17 04	17R13.0	0♍46.5	21 42.1	25 24.5	15 17.2	17 58.6	20 39.6	16 38.8	26R52.5	20 26.7
30 W	8 34 50	7 54 35	5♏56 10	12♏29 34	17 13.0	2 12.8	22 34.5	26 02.3	15 44.3	18 09.9	20 47.1	16 42.2	26 52.5	20 25.4
31 Th	8 38 46	8 51 58	18 57 36	25 20 39	17 12.7	3 37.2	23 27.6	26 40.1	16 11.4	18 21.2	20 54.7	16 45.7	26 52.4	20 24.1

August 2036 LONGITUDE

Day	Sid.Time	☉	0 hr ☽	Noon ☽	True ☊	☿	♀	♂	⚳	♃	♄	♅	♆	♇
1 F	8 42 43	9♌49 22	1♐39 06	7♐53 24	17♌12.0	4♍59.6	24♊21.2	27♌18.0	16♌38.5	18♊32.3	21♌02.2	16♋49.1	26♈52.4	20♒22.8
2 Sa	8 46 39	10 46 46	14 03 57	20 11 10	17R11.2	6 20.1	25 15.3	27 55.8	17 05.6	18 43.3	21 09.8	16 52.5	26R52.3	20R21.5
3 Su	8 50 36	11 44 11	26 15 29	2♑17 17	17 10.4	7 38.5	26 10.0	28 33.7	17 32.7	18 54.3	21 17.4	16 55.9	26 52.1	20 20.1
4 M	8 54 33	12 41 37	8♑16 57	14 14 50	17 09.8	8 54.9	27 05.2	29 11.5	17 59.9	19 05.1	21 25.0	16 59.3	26 52.0	20 18.8
5 Tu	8 58 29	13 39 03	20 11 17	26 06 37	17 09.4	10 09.2	28 00.9	29 49.4	18 27.0	19 15.9	21 32.7	17 02.6	26 51.8	20 17.5
6 W	9 02 26	14 36 30	2♒01 10	7♒55 12	17D09.2	11 21.3	28 57.1	0♍27.3	18 54.2	19 26.5	21 40.3	17 05.9	26 51.6	20 16.2
7 Th	9 06 22	15 33 59	13 49 02	19 42 57	17 09.2	12 31.1	29 53.8	1 05.2	19 21.4	19 37.1	21 47.9	17 09.3	26 51.3	20 14.8
8 F	9 10 19	16 31 28	25 37 13	1♓32 08	17R09.2	13 38.6	0♋50.9	1 43.1	19 48.6	19 47.6	21 55.6	17 12.5	26 51.0	20 13.5
9 Sa	9 14 15	17 28 58	7♓28 00	13 25 06	17 09.2	14 43.7	1 48.5	2 21.0	20 15.8	19 58.0	22 03.2	17 15.8	26 50.7	20 12.2
10 Su	9 18 12	18 26 30	19 23 46	25 24 20	17 09.1	15 46.3	2 46.5	2 59.0	20 43.0	20 08.2	22 10.9	17 19.1	26 50.3	20 10.8
11 M	9 22 08	19 24 03	1♈27 09	7♈32 34	17 08.9	16 46.2	3 44.9	3 36.9	21 10.2	20 18.4	22 18.5	17 22.3	26 49.9	20 09.5
12 Tu	9 26 05	20 21 37	13 40 59	19 52 47	17 08.6	17 43.4	4 43.7	4 14.9	21 37.4	20 28.4	22 26.2	17 25.5	26 49.5	20 08.1
13 W	9 30 01	21 19 13	26 08 22	2♉28 09	17 08.3	18 37.7	5 42.9	4 52.9	22 04.7	20 38.4	22 33.9	17 28.6	26 49.1	20 06.8
14 Th	9 33 58	22 16 50	8♉52 32	15 21 53	17D08.0	19 29.0	6 42.5	5 30.9	22 31.9	20 48.2	22 41.6	17 31.8	26 48.6	20 05.5
15 F	9 37 55	23 14 28	21 56 35	28 36 56	17 08.0	20 17.0	7 42.5	6 08.9	22 59.2	20 58.0	22 49.2	17 34.9	26 48.1	20 04.1
16 Sa	9 41 51	24 12 09	5♊23 11	12♊15 30	17 08.3	21 01.7	8 42.9	6 46.9	23 26.5	21 07.6	22 56.9	17 38.0	26 47.5	20 02.8
17 Su	9 45 48	25 09 50	19 13 59	26 18 36	17 08.9	21 42.9	9 43.5	7 25.0	23 53.8	21 17.1	23 04.6	17 41.1	26 47.0	20 01.5
18 M	9 49 44	26 07 34	3♋29 08	10♋45 18	17 09.6	22 20.3	10 44.6	8 03.0	24 21.1	21 26.5	23 12.2	17 44.1	26 46.4	20 00.1
19 Tu	9 53 41	27 05 19	18 06 36	25 32 25	17 10.3	22 53.8	11 45.9	8 41.1	24 48.4	21 35.8	23 19.9	17 47.2	26 45.7	19 58.8
20 W	9 57 37	28 03 05	3♌01 55	10♌34 12	17R10.7	23 23.0	12 47.6	9 19.2	25 15.7	21 45.0	23 27.6	17 50.2	26 45.1	19 57.5
21 Th	10 01 34	29 00 53	18 08 13	25 42 50	17 10.7	23 47.8	13 49.6	9 57.3	25 43.0	21 54.0	23 35.2	17 53.1	26 44.4	19 56.2
22 F	10 05 31	29 58 43	3♍16 52	10♍49 10	17 10.0	24 08.0	14 51.8	10 35.5	26 10.3	22 02.9	23 42.9	17 56.0	26 43.7	19 54.8
23 Sa	10 09 27	0♍56 33	18 18 37	25 44 10	17 08.8	24 23.2	15 54.4	11 13.6	26 37.6	22 11.7	23 50.5	17 58.9	26 42.9	19 53.5
24 Su	10 13 24	1 54 25	3♎04 56	10♎20 08	17 07.0	24 33.2	16 57.3	11 51.8	27 04.9	22 20.4	23 58.2	18 01.8	26 42.1	19 52.2
25 M	10 17 20	2 52 18	17 29 13	24 31 44	17 05.1	24R37.8	18 00.4	12 30.0	27 32.2	22 28.9	24 05.8	18 04.6	26 41.3	19 50.9
26 Tu	10 21 17	3 50 13	1♏27 28	8♏16 20	17 03.3	24 36.8	19 03.8	13 08.2	27 59.6	22 37.3	24 13.4	18 07.4	26 40.5	19 49.6
27 W	10 25 13	4 48 08	14 58 25	21 33 55	17 02.1	24 30.0	20 07.4	13 46.4	28 26.9	22 45.6	24 21.0	18 10.2	26 39.6	19 48.3
28 Th	10 29 10	5 46 05	28 03 08	4♐26 30	17D01.6	24 17.2	21 11.3	14 24.7	28 54.2	22 53.7	24 28.6	18 12.9	26 38.7	19 47.0
29 F	10 33 06	6 44 04	10♐44 27	16 57 31	17 01.9	23 58.3	22 15.5	15 02.9	29 21.5	23 01.7	24 36.1	18 15.6	26 37.8	19 45.8
30 Sa	10 37 03	7 42 03	23 06 15	29 11 12	17 03.0	23 33.3	23 19.9	15 41.2	29 48.8	23 09.6	24 43.7	18 18.3	26 36.8	19 44.5
31 Su	10 40 59	8 40 04	5♑12 57	11♑12 03	17 04.5	23 02.3	24 24.5	16 19.5	0♍16.1	23 17.3	24 51.2	18 20.9	26 35.9	19 43.3

Astro Data

	Dy Hr Mn
☽0N	15 10:04
♃⚺♅	19 18:33
♄☍♇	28 0:53
☽0S	28 1:48
♆ R	30 0:18
♃△♇	10 17:25
☽0N	11 16:24
☿0S	19 9:50
☽0S	24 11:02
☿ R	25 19:48

Planet Ingress

	Dy Hr Mn
☿ ♌	11 16:16
☉ ♌	22 5:22
☿ ♍	28 23:16
♂ ♍	5 18:43
♀ ♋	7 14:37
☉ ♍	22 12:32
⚳ ♍	30 21:51

Last Aspect Dy Hr Mn		☽ Ingress	Dy Hr Mn
2 0:55	♆ ☍	♏	2 7:00
3 21:56	♇ □	♐	4 15:09
6 19:08	♆ △	♑	7 1:37
9 7:15	♆ □	♒	9 13:49
11 20:18	♆ ⚹	♓	12 2:51
13 23:29	☉ △	♈	14 15:06
16 18:45	♆ ☌	♉	17 0:41
19 1:09	☉ ⚹	♊	19 6:24
21 3:24	♆ ⚹	♋	21 8:32
23 3:30	♆ □	♌	23 8:28
25 3:04	♆ △	♍	25 8:04
26 15:20	♀ □	♎	27 9:13
29 7:42	♆ ☍	♏	29 13:17
31 14:38	♂ □	♐	31 20:51

Last Aspect Dy Hr Mn		☽ Ingress	Dy Hr Mn
3 4:10	♂ △	♑	3 7:26
5 13:32	♆ □	♒	5 19:54
8 2:30	♆ ⚹	♓	8 8:53
10 1:20	♃ □	♈	10 21:07
13 1:18	♆ ☌	♉	13 7:20
15 1:36	☉ □	♊	15 14:28
17 12:48	♆ ⚹	♋	17 18:11
19 13:58	♆ □	♌	19 19:09
21 17:35	☉ ☌	♍	21 18:48
23 9:47	☿ ☌	♎	23 18:57
25 15:43	♆ ☍	♏	25 21:28
27 17:20	☿ ⚹	♐	28 3:38
30 6:55	♆ △	♑	30 13:37

☽ Phases & Eclipses

Dy Hr Mn	
8 11:19	○ 16♑53
16 14:39	☾ 24♈38
23 10:17	● 1♌09
23 10:30:46	● P 0.199
30 2:56	☽ 7♏33
7 2:49	○ 15♒12
7 2:51	● T 1.454
15 1:36	☾ 22♉49
21 17:35	● 29♌14
21 17:24:22	● P 0.862
28 14:43	☽ 5♐53

Astro Data

1 July 2036
Julian Day # 49856
SVP 4♓45'11"
GC 27♐20.9 ⚴ 13♊31.6
Eris 28♈14.5 ⚵ 27♊30.9
⚷ 15♊08.1 ⚶ 26♏02.3R
☽ Mean ☊ 19♌06.8

1 August 2036
Julian Day # 49887
SVP 4♓45'06"
GC 27♐21.0 ⚴ 0♋48.1
Eris 28♈16.9R ⚵ 15♋12.0
⚷ 17♊13.7 ⚶ 28♏54.8
☽ Mean ☊ 17♌28.3

LONGITUDE — September 2036

Day	Sid.Time	☉	0 hr ☽	Noon ☽	True ☊	☿	♀	♂	⚳	♃	♄	♅	♆	♇
1 M	10 44 56	9♍38 07	17♑09 03	23♑04 28	17♌06.2	22♍25.4	25♋29.4	16♍57.8	0♍43.4	23♊24.9	24♌58.7	18♋23.5	26♈34.9	19♒42.0
2 Tu	10 48 53	10 36 11	28 58 49	4♒52 34	17 07.5	21R 43.1	26 34.5	17 36.1	1 10.7	23 32.3	25 06.2	18 26.1	26R 33.8	19R 40.8
3 W	10 52 49	11 34 16	10♒46 08	16 39 57	17R 08.0	20 55.8	27 39.9	18 14.4	1 38.0	23 39.6	25 13.7	18 28.6	26 32.8	19 39.5
4 Th	10 56 46	12 32 23	22 34 23	28 29 45	17 07.4	20 04.1	28 45.5	18 52.8	2 05.3	23 46.8	25 21.2	18 31.1	26 31.7	19 38.3
5 F	11 00 42	13 30 31	4♓26 21	10♓24 29	17 05.6	19 08.9	29 51.2	19 31.2	2 32.5	23 53.8	25 28.6	18 33.5	26 30.6	19 37.1
6 Sa	11 04 39	14 28 42	16 24 23	22 26 16	17 02.5	18 11.1	0♌57.2	20 09.6	2 59.8	24 00.6	25 36.0	18 35.9	26 29.5	19 35.9
7 Su	11 08 35	15 26 53	28 30 21	4♈36 49	16 58.3	17 11.9	2 03.5	20 48.0	3 27.1	24 07.3	25 43.4	18 38.3	26 28.3	19 34.7
8 M	11 12 32	16 25 07	10♈45 50	16 57 35	16 53.4	16 12.5	3 09.9	21 26.4	3 54.3	24 13.9	25 50.8	18 40.6	26 27.2	19 33.6
9 Tu	11 16 28	17 23 23	23 12 15	29 29 59	16 48.4	15 14.3	4 16.5	22 04.9	4 21.6	24 20.3	25 58.1	18 42.9	26 26.0	19 32.4
10 W	11 20 25	18 21 41	5♉50 58	12♉15 24	16 43.9	14 18.6	5 23.3	22 43.4	4 48.8	24 26.5	26 05.4	18 45.2	26 24.7	19 31.3
11 Th	11 24 22	19 20 00	18 43 28	25 15 21	16 40.4	13 26.7	6 30.4	23 21.9	5 16.1	24 32.6	26 12.7	18 47.4	26 23.5	19 30.1
12 F	11 28 18	20 18 22	1♊51 16	8♊31 24	16D 38.3	12 40.0	7 37.6	24 00.4	5 43.3	24 38.6	26 20.0	18 49.5	26 22.2	19 29.0
13 Sa	11 32 15	21 16 46	15 15 57	22 05 02	16 37.7	11 59.6	8 45.0	24 39.0	6 10.5	24 44.3	26 27.2	18 51.6	26 20.9	19 27.9
14 Su	11 36 11	22 15 13	28 58 47	5♋57 17	16 38.3	11 26.5	9 52.6	25 17.5	6 37.7	24 49.9	26 34.4	18 53.7	26 19.6	19 26.8
15 M	11 40 08	23 13 41	13♋00 29	20 08 20	16 39.6	11 01.5	11 00.3	25 56.2	7 04.9	24 55.4	26 41.6	18 55.8	26 18.3	19 25.8
16 Tu	11 44 04	24 12 12	27 20 36	4♌36 59	16R 40.9	10 45.4	12 08.3	26 34.8	7 32.1	25 00.7	26 48.7	18 57.8	26 17.0	19 24.7
17 W	11 48 01	25 10 44	11♌57 01	19 20 08	16 41.3	10D 38.5	13 16.4	27 13.4	7 59.2	25 05.8	26 55.8	18 59.7	26 15.6	19 23.7
18 Th	11 51 57	26 09 19	26 45 37	4♍12 37	16 40.2	10 41.2	14 24.7	27 52.1	8 26.4	25 10.7	27 02.8	19 01.6	26 14.2	19 22.6
19 F	11 55 54	27 07 56	11♍40 11	19 07 21	16 37.1	10 53.5	15 33.1	28 30.8	8 53.5	25 15.4	27 09.9	19 03.5	26 12.8	19 21.6
20 Sa	11 59 51	28 06 34	26 33 01	3♎56 10	16 32.2	11 15.3	16 41.7	29 09.5	9 20.6	25 20.0	27 16.8	19 05.3	26 11.4	19 20.6
21 Su	12 03 47	29 05 15	11♎15 49	18 31 02	16 25.9	11 46.4	17 50.5	29 48.3	9 47.7	25 24.4	27 23.8	19 07.0	26 09.9	19 19.7
22 M	12 07 44	0♎03 57	25 41 02	2♏45 11	16 18.9	12 26.5	18 59.4	0♎27.0	10 14.8	25 28.7	27 30.7	19 08.7	26 08.5	19 18.7
23 Tu	12 11 40	1 02 41	9♏43 02	16 34 14	16 12.2	13 15.0	20 08.4	1 05.8	10 41.9	25 32.7	27 37.5	19 10.4	26 07.0	19 17.8
24 W	12 15 37	2 01 27	23 18 42	29 56 26	16 06.6	14 11.5	21 17.6	1 44.6	11 08.9	25 36.6	27 44.3	19 12.0	26 05.5	19 16.8
25 Th	12 19 33	3 00 15	6♐27 38	12♐52 36	16 02.6	15 15.4	22 27.0	2 23.4	11 35.9	25 40.2	27 51.1	19 13.6	26 04.0	19 15.9
26 F	12 23 30	3 59 05	19 11 43	25 25 31	16D 00.5	16 25.9	23 36.5	3 02.3	12 02.9	25 43.8	27 57.8	19 15.1	26 02.5	19 15.1
27 Sa	12 27 26	4 57 56	1♑34 32	7♑39 24	16 00.1	17 42.4	24 46.1	3 41.2	12 29.9	25 47.1	28 04.5	19 16.6	26 01.0	19 14.2
28 Su	12 31 23	5 56 49	13 40 45	19 39 14	16 00.9	19 04.3	25 55.8	4 20.1	12 56.8	25 50.2	28 11.1	19 18.0	25 59.4	19 13.4
29 M	12 35 19	6 55 44	25 35 32	1♒30 16	16 02.2	20 30.9	27 05.7	4 59.0	13 23.7	25 53.1	28 17.7	19 19.4	25 57.9	19 12.6
30 Tu	12 39 16	7 54 40	7♒24 06	13 17 38	16R 03.0	22 01.5	28 15.7	5 38.0	13 50.6	25 55.9	28 24.2	19 20.7	25 56.3	19 11.8

LONGITUDE — October 2036

Day	Sid.Time	☉	0 hr ☽	Noon ☽	True ☊	☿	♀	♂	⚳	♃	♄	♅	♆	♇
1 W	12 43 13	8♎53 39	19♒11 27	25♒06 04	16♌02.6	23♍35.6	29♌25.9	6♎16.9	14♍17.5	25♊58.5	28♌30.7	19♋22.0	25♈54.7	19♒11.0
2 Th	12 47 09	9 52 39	1♓02 00	6♓59 41	16R 00.2	25 12.5	0♍36.2	6 55.9	14 44.3	26 00.8	28 37.1	19 23.2	25R 53.1	19R 10.2
3 F	12 51 06	10 51 40	12 59 31	19 01 48	15 55.4	26 51.8	1 46.6	7 34.9	15 11.1	26 03.0	28 43.5	19 24.4	25 51.5	19 09.5
4 Sa	12 55 02	11 50 44	25 06 51	1♈14 51	15 48.3	28 33.0	2 57.1	8 14.0	15 37.9	26 05.0	28 49.8	19 25.5	25 49.9	19 08.8
5 Su	12 58 59	12 49 50	7♈25 59	13 40 20	15 39.2	0♎15.7	4 07.8	8 53.1	16 04.6	26 06.8	28 56.1	19 26.6	25 48.3	19 08.1
6 M	13 02 55	13 48 58	19 57 58	26 18 52	15 28.8	1 59.6	5 18.5	9 32.2	16 31.3	26 08.4	29 02.3	19 27.6	25 46.7	19 07.4
7 Tu	13 06 52	14 48 08	2♉43 03	9♉10 25	15 18.1	3 44.2	6 29.4	10 11.3	16 58.0	26 09.8	29 08.4	19 28.6	25 45.0	19 06.8
8 W	13 10 48	15 47 20	15 40 55	22 14 27	15 08.2	5 29.4	7 40.4	10 50.4	17 24.7	26 11.0	29 14.5	19 29.5	25 43.4	19 06.2
9 Th	13 14 45	16 46 35	28 50 57	5♊30 19	14 59.9	7 15.0	8 51.6	11 29.6	17 51.3	26 12.0	29 20.6	19 30.4	25 41.7	19 05.6
10 F	13 18 42	17 45 51	12♊12 31	18 57 31	14 54.0	9 00.7	10 02.8	12 08.8	18 17.9	26 12.9	29 26.5	19 31.2	25 40.1	19 05.0
11 Sa	13 22 38	18 45 10	25 45 16	2♋35 48	14 50.7	10 46.3	11 14.2	12 48.1	18 44.4	26 13.5	29 32.4	19 32.0	25 38.4	19 04.4
12 Su	13 26 35	19 44 32	9♋29 08	16 25 16	14D 49.5	12 31.8	12 25.7	13 27.3	19 10.9	26 13.9	29 38.3	19 32.7	25 36.7	19 03.9
13 M	13 30 31	20 43 56	23 24 13	0♌25 58	14 49.7	14 17.0	13 37.3	14 06.6	19 37.4	26R 14.1	29 44.1	19 33.3	25 35.1	19 03.4
14 Tu	13 34 28	21 43 22	7♌30 28	14 37 37	14R 50.1	16 01.9	14 48.9	14 46.0	20 03.9	26 14.1	29 49.8	19 33.9	25 33.4	19 02.9
15 W	13 38 24	22 42 50	21 47 13	28 59 00	14 49.3	17 46.3	16 00.7	15 25.3	20 30.3	26 13.9	29 55.4	19 34.5	25 31.7	19 02.5
16 Th	13 42 21	23 42 21	6♍12 35	13♍27 30	14 46.5	19 30.2	17 12.6	16 04.7	20 56.6	26 13.5	0♍01.0	19 35.0	25 30.1	19 02.1
17 F	13 46 17	24 41 53	20 43 09	27 58 52	14 40.9	21 13.7	18 24.6	16 44.1	21 22.9	26 12.9	0 06.5	19 35.4	25 28.4	19 01.6
18 Sa	13 50 14	25 41 28	5♎13 53	12♎27 24	14 32.5	22 56.5	19 36.7	17 23.5	21 49.2	26 12.1	0 12.0	19 35.8	25 26.7	19 01.3
19 Su	13 54 11	26 41 06	19 38 37	26 46 41	14 21.9	24 38.8	20 48.9	18 03.0	22 15.4	26 11.1	0 17.3	19 36.1	25 25.0	19 00.9
20 M	13 58 07	27 40 45	3♏50 52	10♏50 30	14 10.2	26 20.6	22 01.1	18 42.5	22 41.6	26 09.9	0 22.6	19 36.4	25 23.3	19 00.6
21 Tu	14 02 04	28 40 26	17 45 00	24 33 55	13 58.5	28 01.7	23 13.5	19 22.0	23 07.7	26 08.5	0 27.9	19 36.6	25 21.6	19 00.3
22 W	14 06 00	29 40 09	1♐16 59	7♐54 02	13 48.1	29 42.2	24 25.9	20 01.6	23 33.8	26 06.9	0 33.0	19 36.8	25 20.0	19 00.0
23 Th	14 09 57	0♏39 54	14 25 05	20 50 15	13 39.9	1♏22.2	25 38.4	20 41.2	23 59.8	26 05.1	0 38.1	19 36.9	25 18.3	18 59.8
24 F	14 13 53	1 39 40	27 09 49	3♑24 09	13 34.3	3 01.5	26 51.0	21 20.8	24 25.8	26 03.1	0 43.1	19R 37.0	25 16.6	18 59.5
25 Sa	14 17 50	2 39 29	9♑33 43	15 39 03	13 31.2	4 40.3	28 03.7	22 00.4	24 51.7	26 00.9	0 48.0	19 37.0	25 15.0	18 59.4
26 Su	14 21 46	3 39 19	21 40 46	27 39 31	13D 30.1	6 18.5	29 16.5	22 40.1	25 17.6	25 58.5	0 52.8	19 37.0	25 13.3	18 59.2
27 M	14 25 43	4 39 10	3♒35 58	9♒30 49	13R 30.0	7 56.2	0♎29.3	23 19.8	25 43.4	25 55.9	0 57.6	19 36.9	25 11.7	18 59.0
28 Tu	14 29 40	5 39 04	15 24 47	21 18 32	13 29.9	9 33.3	1 42.2	23 59.5	26 09.2	25 53.1	1 02.2	19 36.7	25 10.0	18 58.9
29 W	14 33 36	6 38 59	27 12 47	3♓08 10	13 28.6	11 10.0	2 55.2	24 39.2	26 34.8	25 50.1	1 06.8	19 36.5	25 08.4	18 58.8
30 Th	14 37 33	7 38 55	9♓05 18	15 04 47	13 25.1	12 46.1	4 08.2	25 19.0	27 00.5	25 46.9	1 11.3	19 36.2	25 06.7	18 58.8
31 F	14 41 29	8 38 53	21 07 06	27 12 44	13 19.0	14 21.7	5 21.4	25 58.8	27 26.0	25 43.5	1 15.7	19 35.9	25 05.1	18D 58.7

Astro Data Dy Hr Mn	Planet Ingress Dy Hr Mn	Last Aspect Dy Hr Mn	☽ Ingress Dy Hr Mn	Last Aspect Dy Hr Mn	☽ Ingress Dy Hr Mn	☽ Phases & Eclipses Dy Hr Mn	Astro Data
☿0N 4 12:45	♀ ♌ 5 15:11	1 19:07 ♆ □	♒ 2 2:04	1 21:43 ♀ ☍	♓ 1 21:55	5 18:45 ○ 13♓47	1 September 2036
☽0N 7 21:50	♂ ♎ 21 19:16	4 8:01 ♆ ✶	♓ 4 15:02	4 5:53 ☿ ☍	♈ 4 9:34	13 10:29 ☾ 21♊13	Julian Day # 49918
♄△♆ 12 18:21	☉ ♎ 22 10:23	6 15:09 ♃ □	♈ 7 2:57	6 17:09 ♄ △	♉ 6 18:55	20 1:51 ● 27♍42	SVP 4♓45'03"
☿ D 17 17:22		9 6:11 ♆ ☌	♉ 9 12:57	9 0:49 ♄ □	♊ 9 2:05	27 6:12 ☽ 4♑44	GC 27♐21.1 ⚴ 18♋16.7
☽0S 20 21:15	♀ ♍ 1 23:39	11 13:46 ♄ □	♊ 11 20:38	11 6:37 ♄ ✶	♋ 11 7:27		Eris 28♈09.5R ⚵ 1♌52.6
☉0S 22 10:23	☿ ♎ 5 8:20	13 19:41 ♄ ✶	♋ 14 1:46	13 3:45 ♆ □	♌ 13 11:16	5 10:15 ○ 12♈46	⚷ 18♊34.5 ⚶ 7♐34.7
♂0S 24 20:38	♄ ♍ 16 7:34	15 22:16 ♆ □	♌ 16 4:24	15 13:34 ♄ ☌	♍ 15 13:41	12 18:09 ☾ 20♋00	☽ Mean ☊ 15♌49.8
♅⚻♇ 26 11:24	☿ ♏ 22 16:16	18 0:22 ♄ ☌	♍ 18 5:13	17 9:05 ♃ □	♎ 17 15:20	19 11:50 ● 26♎41	
♃✶♆ 30 14:16	☉ ♏ 22 19:59	20 3:52 ♂ ☌	♎ 20 5:36	19 11:50 ☉ ☌	♏ 19 17:27	27 1:14 ☽ 4♒12	1 October 2036
☽0N 5 4:04	♀ ♎ 27 2:21	22 3:01 ♄ ✶	♏ 22 7:18	21 9:24 ♀ ✶	♐ 21 21:42		Julian Day # 49948
☿0S 7 20:03		24 7:58 ♄ □	♐ 24 12:06	23 22:04 ♀ □	♑ 24 5:26		SVP 4♓45'00"
♃ R 14 1:37		26 16:59 ♄ △	♑ 26 20:55	26 15:38 ♀ △	♒ 26 16:43		GC 27♐21.2 ⚴ 4♌36.5
☽0S 18 7:15		29 0:47 ♆ □	♒ 29 8:57	28 21:16 ♃ △	♓ 29 5:39		Eris 27♈54.9R ⚵ 16♌35.7
♅ R 25 3:23				31 9:06 ♃ □	♈ 31 17:27		⚷ 18♊53.3R ⚶ 19♐17.0
♀0S 30 2:25							☽ Mean ☊ 14♌14.5

November 2036 LONGITUDE

Day	Sid.Time	☉	0 hr ☽	Noon ☽	True ☊	☿	♀	♂	⚳	♃	♄	♅	♆	♇
1 Sa	14 45 26	9♏38 53	3♈22 04	9♈35 25	13♌10.1	15♏56.9	6♎34.6	26♎38.6	27♍51.6	25♊40.0	1♍20.1	19♋35.5	25♈03.5	18♒58.7
2 Su	14 49 22	10 38 55	15 52 58	22 14 52	12R 58.7	17 31.6	7 47.8	27 18.5	28 17.0	25R 36.2	1 24.3	19R 35.1	25R 01.9	18 58.8
3 M	14 53 19	11 38 59	28 41 09	5♉11 45	12 45.8	19 05.9	9 01.2	27 58.4	28 42.4	25 32.3	1 28.5	19 34.6	25 00.3	18 58.8
4 Tu	14 57 15	12 39 04	11♉46 32	18 25 18	12 32.4	20 39.7	10 14.6	28 38.3	29 07.7	25 28.2	1 32.6	19 34.1	24 58.7	18 58.9
5 W	15 01 12	13 39 11	25 07 44	1♊53 31	12 19.8	22 13.2	11 28.0	29 18.3	29 32.9	25 23.9	1 36.5	19 33.5	24 57.1	18 59.0
6 Th	15 05 08	14 39 20	8♊42 16	15 33 38	12 09.2	23 46.3	12 41.6	29 58.3	29 58.1	25 19.4	1 40.4	19 32.9	24 55.6	18 59.1
7 F	15 09 05	15 39 32	22 27 13	29 22 40	12 01.3	25 19.0	13 55.2	0♏38.3	0♎23.2	25 14.7	1 44.2	19 32.2	24 54.0	18 59.3
8 Sa	15 13 02	16 39 45	6♋19 40	13♋17 57	11 56.5	26 51.3	15 08.8	1 18.3	0 48.3	25 09.9	1 48.0	19 31.5	24 52.5	18 59.4
9 Su	15 16 58	17 40 00	20 17 18	27 17 31	11 54.4	28 23.3	16 22.5	1 58.4	1 13.2	25 04.9	1 51.6	19 30.7	24 51.0	18 59.7
10 M	15 20 55	18 40 17	4♌18 28	11♌20 04	11 53.9	29 54.9	17 36.3	2 38.5	1 38.1	24 59.7	1 55.1	19 29.8	24 49.4	18 59.9
11 Tu	15 24 51	19 40 36	18 22 14	25 24 54	11 53.9	1♐26.2	18 50.2	3 18.7	2 02.9	24 54.4	1 58.5	19 29.0	24 48.0	19 00.2
12 W	15 28 48	20 40 57	2♍27 58	9♍31 21	11 52.9	2 57.2	20 04.1	3 58.9	2 27.7	24 48.9	2 01.9	19 28.0	24 46.5	19 00.4
13 Th	15 32 44	21 41 21	16 34 53	23 38 21	11 49.8	4 27.8	21 18.0	4 39.1	2 52.3	24 43.2	2 05.1	19 27.0	24 45.0	19 00.8
14 F	15 36 41	22 41 46	0♎41 31	7♎44 02	11 43.8	5 58.1	22 32.0	5 19.3	3 16.9	24 37.4	2 08.2	19 26.0	24 43.6	19 01.1
15 Sa	15 40 37	23 42 12	14 45 31	21 45 31	11 35.0	7 28.0	23 46.1	5 59.6	3 41.4	24 31.4	2 11.3	19 24.9	24 42.1	19 01.5
16 Su	15 44 34	24 42 41	28 43 32	5♏39 06	11 23.9	8 57.6	25 00.2	6 39.9	4 05.8	24 25.3	2 14.2	19 23.7	24 40.7	19 01.9
17 M	15 48 31	25 43 11	12♏31 41	19 20 49	11 11.4	10 26.8	26 14.4	7 20.3	4 30.1	24 19.0	2 17.0	19 22.5	24 39.3	19 02.3
18 Tu	15 52 27	26 43 43	26 06 02	2♐46 59	10 58.8	11 55.6	27 28.5	8 00.7	4 54.3	24 12.6	2 19.8	19 21.3	24 38.0	19 02.8
19 W	15 56 24	27 44 17	9♐23 22	15 55 00	10 47.4	13 23.9	28 42.8	8 41.1	5 18.5	24 06.1	2 22.4	19 20.0	24 36.6	19 03.2
20 Th	16 00 20	28 44 52	22 21 46	28 43 42	10 38.2	14 51.8	29 57.1	9 21.5	5 42.5	23 59.4	2 24.9	19 18.7	24 35.3	19 03.8
21 F	16 04 17	29 45 28	5♑00 54	11♑13 36	10 31.7	16 19.2	1♏11.4	10 02.0	6 06.4	23 52.6	2 27.3	19 17.3	24 34.0	19 04.3
22 Sa	16 08 13	0♐46 06	17 22 06	23 26 49	10 27.9	17 46.1	2 25.8	10 42.5	6 30.3	23 45.7	2 29.7	19 15.9	24 32.7	19 04.9
23 Su	16 12 10	1 46 45	29 28 12	5♒26 48	10D 26.5	19 12.3	3 40.2	11 23.0	6 54.0	23 38.7	2 31.9	19 14.4	24 31.4	19 05.4
24 M	16 16 07	2 47 25	11♒23 13	17 18 03	10 26.5	20 37.9	4 54.6	12 03.6	7 17.6	23 31.5	2 34.0	19 12.9	24 30.2	19 06.1
25 Tu	16 20 03	3 48 06	23 11 59	29 05 42	10R 27.0	22 02.6	6 09.1	12 44.2	7 41.2	23 24.3	2 36.0	19 11.3	24 29.0	19 06.7
26 W	16 24 00	4 48 48	4♓59 53	10♓55 15	10 26.9	23 26.5	7 23.6	13 24.8	8 04.6	23 16.9	2 37.9	19 09.7	24 27.8	19 07.4
27 Th	16 27 56	5 49 31	16 52 28	22 52 13	10 25.2	24 49.3	8 38.1	14 05.4	8 27.9	23 09.5	2 39.6	19 08.1	24 26.6	19 08.1
28 F	16 31 53	6 50 15	28 55 07	5♈01 45	10 21.3	26 11.0	9 52.6	14 46.1	8 51.1	23 01.9	2 41.3	19 06.4	24 25.4	19 08.8
29 Sa	16 35 49	7 51 01	11♈12 40	17 28 19	10 15.0	27 31.4	11 07.2	15 26.8	9 14.2	22 54.3	2 42.9	19 04.7	24 24.3	19 09.5
30 Su	16 39 46	8 51 47	23 49 03	0♉15 09	10 06.5	28 50.3	12 21.9	16 07.6	9 37.2	22 46.6	2 44.3	19 02.9	24 23.2	19 10.3

December 2036 LONGITUDE

Day	Sid.Time	☉	0 hr ☽	Noon ☽	True ☊	☿	♀	♂	⚳	♃	♄	♅	♆	♇
1 M	16 43 42	9♐52 34	6♉46 47	13♉23 59	9♌56.4	0♑07.4	13♏36.5	16♏48.3	10♎00.0	22♊38.9	2♍45.7	19♋01.1	24♈22.2	19♒11.1
2 Tu	16 47 39	10 53 23	20 06 39	26 54 35	9R 45.8	1 22.5	14 51.2	17 29.2	10 22.7	22R 31.0	2 46.9	18R 59.2	24R 21.1	19 11.9
3 W	16 51 35	11 54 12	3♊47 27	10♊44 48	9 35.7	2 35.3	16 05.9	18 10.0	10 45.4	22 23.1	2 48.1	18 57.3	24 20.1	19 12.7
4 Th	16 55 32	12 55 03	17 46 05	24 50 42	9 27.3	3 45.5	17 20.7	18 50.9	11 07.9	22 15.2	2 49.1	18 55.4	24 19.1	19 13.6
5 F	16 59 29	13 55 55	1♋57 58	9♋07 14	9 21.2	4 52.5	18 35.4	19 31.8	11 30.2	22 07.2	2 50.0	18 53.5	24 18.1	19 14.5
6 Sa	17 03 25	14 56 48	16 17 49	23 29 04	9 17.8	5 56.1	19 50.2	20 12.7	11 52.5	21 59.1	2 50.8	18 51.5	24 17.2	19 15.4
7 Su	17 07 22	15 57 42	0♌40 24	7♌51 19	9D 16.7	6 55.6	21 05.1	20 53.7	12 14.6	21 51.1	2 51.5	18 49.5	24 16.3	19 16.4
8 M	17 11 18	16 58 37	15 01 21	22 10 09	9 17.1	7 50.5	22 19.9	21 34.7	12 36.6	21 43.0	2 52.1	18 47.4	24 15.4	19 17.3
9 Tu	17 15 15	17 59 34	29 17 25	6♍22 57	9R 18.2	8 40.0	23 34.8	22 15.8	12 58.4	21 34.8	2 52.5	18 45.3	24 14.6	19 18.3
10 W	17 19 11	19 00 32	13♍26 34	20 28 10	9 18.6	9 23.6	24 49.7	22 56.9	13 20.1	21 26.7	2 52.9	18 43.2	24 13.8	19 19.3
11 Th	17 23 08	20 01 31	27 27 38	4♎24 55	9 17.6	10 00.3	26 04.6	23 38.0	13 41.7	21 18.5	2 53.1	18 41.0	24 13.0	19 20.4
12 F	17 27 05	21 02 31	11♎19 56	18 12 37	9 14.5	10 29.4	27 19.6	24 19.2	14 03.1	21 10.3	2R 53.2	18 38.8	24 12.2	19 21.4
13 Sa	17 31 01	22 03 32	25 02 51	1♏50 33	9 09.2	10 49.9	28 34.6	25 00.4	14 24.4	21 02.1	2 53.3	18 36.6	24 11.5	19 22.5
14 Su	17 34 58	23 04 34	8♏35 34	15 17 47	9 02.1	11R 01.0	29 49.6	25 41.6	14 45.5	20 54.0	2 53.2	18 34.3	24 10.8	19 23.6
15 M	17 38 54	24 05 38	21 57 02	28 33 10	8 53.9	11 01.9	1♐04.6	26 22.8	15 06.5	20 45.8	2 53.0	18 32.1	24 10.1	19 24.7
16 Tu	17 42 51	25 06 42	5♐06 01	11♐35 29	8 45.6	10 51.9	2 19.6	27 04.1	15 27.3	20 37.7	2 52.6	18 29.8	24 09.5	19 25.9
17 W	17 46 47	26 07 47	18 01 25	24 23 46	8 38.1	10 30.4	3 34.7	27 45.5	15 48.0	20 29.5	2 52.2	18 27.4	24 08.9	19 27.0
18 Th	17 50 44	27 08 52	0♑42 31	6♑57 40	8 32.2	9 57.3	4 49.7	28 26.8	16 08.5	20 21.5	2 51.7	18 25.1	24 08.3	19 28.2
19 F	17 54 40	28 09 58	13 09 18	19 17 35	8 28.1	9 12.6	6 04.8	29 08.2	16 28.8	20 13.4	2 51.0	18 22.7	24 07.8	19 29.4
20 Sa	17 58 37	29 11 05	25 22 41	1♒24 54	8D 26.2	8 17.1	7 19.9	29 49.6	16 48.9	20 05.4	2 50.2	18 20.3	24 07.3	19 30.7
21 Su	18 02 34	0♑12 12	7♒24 31	13 21 56	8 26.0	7 12.0	8 35.0	0♐31.1	17 08.9	19 57.5	2 49.3	18 17.9	24 06.8	19 31.9
22 M	18 06 30	1 13 19	19 17 36	25 11 59	8 27.2	5 58.9	9 50.1	1 12.6	17 28.7	19 49.6	2 48.4	18 15.5	24 06.4	19 33.2
23 Tu	18 10 27	2 14 26	1♓05 37	6♓59 04	8 29.0	4 40.0	11 05.2	1 54.1	17 48.4	19 41.8	2 47.3	18 13.0	24 06.0	19 34.5
24 W	18 14 23	3 15 34	12 52 56	18 47 50	8 30.7	3 18.0	12 20.3	2 35.6	18 07.8	19 34.0	2 46.0	18 10.5	24 05.6	19 35.8
25 Th	18 18 20	4 16 42	24 44 26	0♈43 21	8R 31.6	1 55.7	13 35.5	3 17.2	18 27.1	19 26.4	2 44.7	18 08.0	24 05.3	19 37.1
26 F	18 22 16	5 17 49	6♈45 16	12 50 47	8 31.4	0 35.7	14 50.6	3 58.8	18 46.1	19 18.8	2 43.3	18 05.5	24 05.0	19 38.4
27 Sa	18 26 13	6 18 57	19 00 32	25 15 05	8 29.6	29♐20.5	16 05.8	4 40.4	19 05.0	19 11.3	2 41.8	18 03.0	24 04.7	19 39.8
28 Su	18 30 09	7 20 05	1♉34 57	8♉00 35	8 26.5	28 12.3	17 20.9	5 22.1	19 23.7	19 03.9	2 40.1	18 00.5	24 04.5	19 41.2
29 M	18 34 06	8 21 13	14 32 19	21 10 25	8 22.3	27 12.6	18 36.1	6 03.8	19 42.2	18 56.5	2 38.4	17 57.9	24 04.3	19 42.6
30 Tu	18 38 03	9 22 20	27 54 59	4♊46 02	8 17.7	26 22.6	19 51.2	6 45.6	20 00.5	18 49.3	2 36.5	17 55.4	24 04.1	19 44.0
31 W	18 41 59	10 23 28	11♊43 22	18 46 40	8 13.1	25 42.9	21 06.4	7 27.3	20 18.5	18 42.2	2 34.6	17 52.8	24 04.0	19 45.4

Astro Data Dy Hr Mn	Planet Ingress Dy Hr Mn	Last Aspect Dy Hr Mn	☽ Ingress Dy Hr Mn	Last Aspect Dy Hr Mn	☽ Ingress Dy Hr Mn	☽ Phases & Eclipses Dy Hr Mn
♇ D 1 7:54	♂ ♏ 6 13:03	2 21:57 ♂ ☍	♉ 3 2:26	1 22:22 ♇ □	♊ 2 17:24	4 0:44 ○ 12♉11
☽ 0N 1 12:16	⚳ ♎ 6 13:48	4 16:33 ☿ ☍	♊ 5 8:39	4 11:07 ♆ ⚹	♋ 4 20:42	11 1:28 ☾ 19♌14
♃⚹♆ 13 1:56	☿ ♐ 10 13:20	7 4:53 ♃ ☌	♋ 7 13:05	6 13:20 ♆ □	♌ 6 22:53	18 0:14 ● 26♏14
☽ 0S 14 15:46	♀ ♏ 20 12:57	9 14:06 ☿ △	♌ 9 16:38	8 15:31 ♆ △	♍ 9 1:12	25 22:28 ☽ 4♓15
♅⚻♇ 27 12:16	☉ ♐ 21 17:45	11 11:08 ♃ ⚹	♍ 11 19:48	10 20:13 ♀ ⚹	♎ 11 4:22	
☽ 0N 28 22:06		13 13:50 ♃ □	♎ 13 22:49	12 22:30 ♆ ☍	♏ 13 8:44	3 14:08 ○ 12♊00
	☿ ♑ 1 9:40	15 17:03 ♆ ☍	♏ 16 2:12	15 7:49 ♂ ☌	♐ 15 14:39	10 9:18 ☾ 18♍54
☽ 0S 11 22:31	♀ ♐ 14 15:20	18 0:14 ☉ ☌	♐ 18 6:59	17 15:34 ☉ ☌	♑ 17 22:39	17 15:34 ● 26♐17
♄ R 13 2:58	♂ ♐ 20 18:00	20 4:12 ♆ △	♑ 20 14:25	20 8:39 ♂ ⚹	♒ 20 9:11	25 19:44 ☽ 4♈36
☿ R 15 2:04	☉ ♑ 21 7:13	22 14:11 ♆ □	♒ 23 1:04	22 9:47 ♆ ⚹	♓ 22 21:46	
♃△♇ 24 7:22	☿ ♐R 26 23:09	25 2:38 ♆ ⚹	♓ 25 13:50	24 13:32 ♃ □	♈ 25 10:33	
☽ 0N 26 7:54		27 16:23 ☿ □	♈ 28 2:08	27 19:07 ☿ △	♉ 27 21:01	
		30 9:05 ☿ △	♉ 30 11:32	29 9:22 ♇ □	♊ 30 3:40	

Astro Data

1 November 2036
Julian Day # 49979
SVP 4♓44'57"
GC 27♐21.2 ⚵ 19♌34.9
Eris 27♈36.5R ⚴ 29♌37.2
⚷ 18♊06.3R ⚶ 3♑21.1
☽ Mean ☊ 12♌35.9

1 December 2036
Julian Day # 50009
SVP 4♓44'53"
GC 27♐21.3 ⚵ 0♍14.8
Eris 27♈20.6R ⚴ 8♍58.2
⚷ 16♊32.8R ⚶ 18♑03.4
☽ Mean ☊ 11♌00.6

LONGITUDE — January 2037

Day	Sid.Time	☉	0 hr ☽	Noon ☽	True ☊	☿	♀	♂	⚳	♃	♄	♅	♆	♇
1 Th	18 45 56	11♑24 36	25♊55 28	3♋09 09	8♌09.4	25♐13.6	22♐21.6	8♐09.1	20♎36.4	18♊35.3	2♍32.5	17♋50.2	24♈03.9	19♒46.9
2 F	18 49 52	12 25 44	10♋26 58	17 48 04	8R 06.8	24R 54.7	23 36.8	8 51.0	20 54.1	18R 28.4	2R 30.4	17R 47.7	24R 03.8	19 48.4
3 Sa	18 53 49	13 26 52	25 11 32	2♌36 24	8D 05.7	24D 45.7	24 52.0	9 32.9	21 11.6	18 21.7	2 28.1	17 45.1	24D 03.8	19 49.9
4 Su	18 57 45	14 28 00	10♌01 42	17 26 31	8 05.8	24 46.1	26 07.2	10 14.8	21 28.8	18 15.0	2 25.8	17 42.5	24 03.8	19 51.4
5 M	19 01 42	15 29 08	24 49 59	2♍11 19	8 06.9	24 55.2	27 22.4	10 56.7	21 45.8	18 08.6	2 23.3	17 39.9	24 03.8	19 52.9
6 Tu	19 05 38	16 30 16	9♍29 51	16 45 01	8 08.3	25 12.2	28 37.7	11 38.7	22 02.6	18 02.2	2 20.8	17 37.3	24 03.9	19 54.4
7 W	19 09 35	17 31 24	23 56 23	1♎03 37	8 09.6	25 36.6	29 52.9	12 20.7	22 19.2	17 56.0	2 18.1	17 34.7	24 04.0	19 55.9
8 Th	19 13 32	18 32 33	8♎06 30	15 04 54	8R 10.3	26 07.6	1♑08.1	13 02.7	22 35.5	17 49.9	2 15.4	17 32.1	24 04.2	19 57.5
9 F	19 17 28	19 33 42	21 58 48	28 48 13	8 10.0	26 44.5	2 23.4	13 44.8	22 51.6	17 44.0	2 12.5	17 29.5	24 04.4	19 59.0
10 Sa	19 21 25	20 34 50	5♏33 13	12♏13 57	8 08.9	27 26.7	3 38.6	14 26.9	23 07.4	17 38.2	2 09.6	17 26.9	24 04.6	20 00.6
11 Su	19 25 21	21 35 59	18 50 32	25 23 08	8 07.1	28 13.8	4 53.9	15 09.1	23 23.0	17 32.6	2 06.6	17 24.3	24 04.8	20 02.2
12 M	19 29 18	22 37 08	1♐51 57	8♐17 08	8 04.8	29 05.1	6 09.1	15 51.3	23 38.3	17 27.2	2 03.5	17 21.7	24 05.1	20 03.8
13 Tu	19 33 14	23 38 16	14 38 53	20 57 20	8 02.5	0♑00.3	7 24.4	16 33.5	23 53.4	17 21.9	2 00.3	17 19.1	24 05.4	20 05.5
14 W	19 37 11	24 39 25	27 12 41	3♑25 06	8 00.4	0 58.9	8 39.7	17 15.8	24 08.2	17 16.8	1 57.0	17 16.5	24 05.8	20 07.1
15 Th	19 41 07	25 40 33	9♑34 44	15 41 45	7 58.9	2 00.6	9 54.9	17 58.0	24 22.8	17 11.9	1 53.7	17 14.0	24 06.2	20 08.7
16 F	19 45 04	26 41 41	21 46 20	27 48 41	7D 58.0	3 05.1	11 10.2	18 40.4	24 37.1	17 07.1	1 50.2	17 11.4	24 06.6	20 10.4
17 Sa	19 49 01	27 42 48	3♒48 58	9♒47 26	7 57.8	4 12.0	12 25.5	19 22.7	24 51.1	17 02.5	1 46.7	17 08.8	24 07.1	20 12.0
18 Su	19 52 57	28 43 54	15 44 19	21 39 54	7 58.1	5 21.2	13 40.7	20 05.1	25 04.8	16 58.1	1 43.1	17 06.3	24 07.6	20 13.7
19 M	19 56 54	29 45 00	27 34 28	3♓28 22	7 58.8	6 32.5	14 56.0	20 47.5	25 18.2	16 53.9	1 39.4	17 03.8	24 08.1	20 15.4
20 Tu	20 00 50	0♒46 05	9♓21 57	15 15 38	7 59.7	7 45.5	16 11.3	21 29.9	25 31.4	16 49.8	1 35.6	17 01.3	24 08.7	20 17.1
21 W	20 04 47	1 47 09	21 09 51	27 05 04	8 00.5	9 00.3	17 26.5	22 12.4	25 44.2	16 46.0	1 31.8	16 58.8	24 09.3	20 18.8
22 Th	20 08 43	2 48 13	3♈01 46	9♈00 28	8 01.1	10 16.7	18 41.8	22 54.9	25 56.8	16 42.3	1 27.9	16 56.3	24 09.9	20 20.5
23 F	20 12 40	3 49 15	15 01 44	21 06 08	8 01.4	11 34.4	19 57.0	23 37.4	26 09.0	16 38.9	1 24.0	16 53.8	24 10.6	20 22.2
24 Sa	20 16 36	4 50 17	27 14 12	3♉26 31	8R 01.6	12 53.5	21 12.3	24 20.0	26 21.0	16 35.6	1 19.9	16 51.4	24 11.3	20 23.9
25 Su	20 20 33	5 51 17	9♉43 38	16 06 05	8 01.5	14 13.8	22 27.5	25 02.6	26 32.6	16 32.5	1 15.8	16 48.9	24 12.0	20 25.7
26 M	20 24 30	6 52 16	22 34 19	29 08 46	8 01.4	15 35.2	23 42.7	25 45.2	26 44.0	16 29.6	1 11.7	16 46.5	24 12.8	20 27.4
27 Tu	20 28 26	7 53 14	5♊49 47	12♊37 34	8D 01.4	16 57.8	24 58.0	26 27.8	26 55.0	16 26.9	1 07.5	16 44.2	24 13.6	20 29.1
28 W	20 32 23	8 54 11	19 32 15	26 33 47	8 01.4	18 21.3	26 13.2	27 10.5	27 05.7	16 24.5	1 03.2	16 41.8	24 14.4	20 30.9
29 Th	20 36 19	9 55 07	3♋41 58	10♋56 28	8 01.6	19 45.8	27 28.4	27 53.2	27 16.0	16 22.2	0 58.9	16 39.5	24 15.3	20 32.6
30 F	20 40 16	10 56 02	18 16 43	25 42 00	8R 01.7	21 11.3	28 43.6	28 36.0	27 26.1	16 20.1	0 54.5	16 37.2	24 16.2	20 34.4
31 Sa	20 44 12	11 56 56	3♌11 26	10♌44 01	8 01.8	22 37.7	29 58.8	29 18.7	27 35.7	16 18.2	0 50.1	16 34.9	24 17.1	20 36.2

LONGITUDE — February 2037

Day	Sid.Time	☉	0 hr ☽	Noon ☽	True ☊	☿	♀	♂	⚳	♃	♄	♅	♆	♇
1 Su	20 48 09	12♒57 49	18♌18 36	25♌54 01	8♌01.6	24♑04.9	1♒14.0	0♑01.6	27♎45.1	16♊16.5	0♍45.6	16♋32.6	24♈18.1	20♒37.9
2 M	20 52 06	13 58 40	3♍29 03	11♍02 30	8R 01.2	25 33.0	2 29.2	0 44.4	27 54.1	16R 15.0	0R 41.1	16R 30.4	24 19.1	20 39.7
3 Tu	20 56 02	14 59 31	18 33 17	26 00 23	8 00.4	27 01.9	3 44.4	1 27.3	28 02.8	16 13.7	0 36.6	16 28.2	24 20.1	20 41.5
4 W	20 59 59	16 00 21	3♎22 55	10♎40 13	7 59.5	28 31.6	4 59.6	2 10.2	28 11.1	16 12.7	0 32.0	16 26.0	24 21.2	20 43.2
5 Th	21 03 55	17 01 10	17 51 44	24 57 07	7 58.7	0♒02.2	6 14.8	2 53.1	28 19.0	16 11.8	0 27.3	16 23.9	24 22.3	20 45.0
6 F	21 07 52	18 01 58	1♏56 10	8♏48 51	7D 58.1	1 33.5	7 30.0	3 36.1	28 26.6	16 11.1	0 22.7	16 21.8	24 23.4	20 46.8
7 Sa	21 11 48	19 02 45	15 35 14	22 15 32	7 58.0	3 05.7	8 45.2	4 19.1	28 33.8	16 10.6	0 18.0	16 19.7	24 24.5	20 48.6
8 Su	21 15 45	20 03 31	28 50 01	5♐19 02	7 58.4	4 38.6	10 00.4	5 02.1	28 40.6	16D 10.4	0 13.3	16 17.6	24 25.7	20 50.4
9 M	21 19 41	21 04 17	11♐42 58	18 02 16	7 59.4	6 12.4	11 15.6	5 45.2	28 47.1	16 10.3	0 08.5	16 15.6	24 26.9	20 52.1
10 Tu	21 23 38	22 05 01	24 17 21	0♑28 40	8 00.6	7 46.9	12 30.8	6 28.3	28 53.2	16 10.4	0 03.7	16 13.6	24 28.2	20 53.9
11 W	21 27 34	23 05 44	6♑36 39	12 41 42	8 02.0	9 22.3	13 45.9	7 11.4	28 58.9	16 10.8	29♌59.0	16 11.7	24 29.4	20 55.7
12 Th	21 31 31	24 06 26	18 44 14	24 44 38	8 03.1	10 58.5	15 01.1	7 54.6	29 04.2	16 11.3	29 54.1	16 09.8	24 30.7	20 57.5
13 F	21 35 28	25 07 07	0♒43 14	6♒40 21	8R 03.6	12 35.5	16 16.3	8 37.8	29 09.0	16 12.1	29 49.3	16 07.9	24 32.1	20 59.3
14 Sa	21 39 24	26 07 46	12 36 19	18 31 24	8 03.2	14 13.3	17 31.4	9 21.0	29 13.5	16 13.0	29 44.5	16 06.1	24 33.4	21 01.0
15 Su	21 43 21	27 08 24	24 25 53	0♓20 00	8 01.8	15 52.0	18 46.6	10 04.2	29 17.6	16 14.2	29 39.6	16 04.3	24 34.8	21 02.8
16 M	21 47 17	28 09 01	6♓14 02	12 08 12	7 59.4	17 31.6	20 01.7	10 47.5	29 21.3	16 15.5	29 34.8	16 02.6	24 36.2	21 04.6
17 Tu	21 51 14	29 09 36	18 02 45	23 57 58	7 56.1	19 12.1	21 16.8	11 30.8	29 24.6	16 17.1	29 29.9	16 00.9	24 37.7	21 06.3
18 W	21 55 10	0♓10 09	29 54 07	5♈51 30	7 52.3	20 53.4	22 31.9	12 14.1	29 27.4	16 18.8	29 25.0	15 59.2	24 39.1	21 08.1
19 Th	21 59 07	1 10 40	11♈50 24	17 51 11	7 48.3	22 35.6	23 47.0	12 57.5	29 29.9	16 20.8	29 20.2	15 57.6	24 40.6	21 09.9
20 F	22 03 03	2 11 10	23 54 11	29 59 50	7 44.7	24 18.8	25 02.1	13 40.8	29 31.9	16 22.9	29 15.3	15 56.0	24 42.1	21 11.6
21 Sa	22 07 00	3 11 38	6♉08 30	12♉20 38	7 42.0	26 02.9	26 17.2	14 24.2	29 33.5	16 25.2	29 10.5	15 54.5	24 43.7	21 13.4
22 Su	22 10 57	4 12 04	18 36 41	24 57 07	7D 40.4	27 47.9	27 32.3	15 07.7	29 34.7	16 27.8	29 05.7	15 53.0	24 45.3	21 15.1
23 M	22 14 53	5 12 29	1♊22 22	7♊52 53	7 40.0	29 33.9	28 47.3	15 51.1	29 35.4	16 30.5	29 00.8	15 51.5	24 46.8	21 16.9
24 Tu	22 18 50	6 12 51	14 29 05	21 11 20	7 40.8	1♓20.9	0♓02.3	16 34.6	29R 35.8	16 33.4	28 56.0	15 50.1	24 48.5	21 18.6
25 W	22 22 46	7 13 12	27 59 56	4♋55 05	7 42.3	3 08.8	1 17.4	17 18.1	29 35.7	16 36.5	28 51.2	15 48.8	24 50.1	21 20.3
26 Th	22 26 43	8 13 30	11♋56 51	19 05 14	7 43.8	4 57.7	2 32.4	18 01.6	29 35.2	16 39.8	28 46.5	15 47.5	24 51.8	21 22.0
27 F	22 30 39	9 13 47	26 19 59	3♌40 44	7R 44.7	6 47.6	3 47.4	18 45.2	29 34.3	16 43.3	28 41.7	15 46.2	24 53.5	21 23.8
28 Sa	22 34 36	10 14 01	11♌06 54	18 37 42	7 44.4	8 38.4	5 02.4	19 28.7	29 32.9	16 47.0	28 37.0	15 45.0	24 55.2	21 25.5

Astro Data

	Dy Hr Mn
♆ D	3 17:45
☿ D	3 22:58
☽ 0S	8 4:48
♃⚻♅	14 14:43
☽ 0N	22 15:58
☽ 0S	4 12:31
♃ D	9 7:41
♃⚻♅	11 21:18
☽ 0N	18 22:04
⚳ R	24 19:11

Planet Ingress

	Dy Hr Mn
♀ ♑	7 14:16
☿ ♑	13 11:52
☉ ♒	19 17:53
♀ ♒	31 12:22
♂ ♑	1 11:08
☿ ♒	5 11:25
♄ ♌R	11 6:46
☉ ♓	18 7:59
☿ ♓	23 17:52
♀ ♓	24 11:15

Last Aspect / ☽ Ingress

Last Aspect Dy Hr Mn		☽ Ingress Dy Hr Mn
31 23:14	☿ ☍	♋ 1 6:47
2 22:10	♆ □	♌ 3 7:47
5 3:24	♀ △	♍ 5 8:25
7 9:49	♀ □	♎ 7 10:12
9 8:11	☿ ⚹	♏ 9 14:07
11 4:27	☉ ⚹	♐ 11 20:32
13 18:00	♆ △	♑ 14 5:23
16 9:34	☉ ☌	♒ 16 16:22
18 17:00	♆ ⚹	♓ 19 4:56
21 1:29	♂ □	♈ 21 17:54
23 18:02	♆ ☌	♉ 24 5:22
26 1:03	♀ △	♊ 26 13:33
28 13:05	♂ ☍	♋ 28 17:48
30 17:18	♀ ☍	♌ 30 18:54

Last Aspect / ☽ Ingress

Last Aspect Dy Hr Mn		☽ Ingress Dy Hr Mn
1 9:28	♆ △	♍ 1 18:29
3 13:51	☿ △	♎ 3 18:29
5 11:01	♆ ☍	♏ 5 20:39
7 9:22	♇ □	♐ 8 2:09
10 0:20	♆ △	♑ 10 11:04
12 11:32	♆ □	♒ 12 22:33
15 10:38	♄ ☍	♓ 15 11:19
16 20:23	♃ □	♈ 18 0:12
20 10:33	♄ △	♉ 20 12:00
22 19:43	♄ □	♊ 22 21:27
25 1:33	♄ ⚹	♋ 25 3:29
26 21:36	♆ □	♌ 27 6:01

☽ Phases & Eclipses

Dy Hr Mn	
2 2:35	○ 12♋02
8 18:29	☾ 18♎49
16 9:34	● 26♑35
16 9:47:35	P 0.705
24 14:55	☽ 4♉58
31 14:04	○ 12♌02
31 14:00	T 1.207
7 5:43	☾ 18♏47
15 4:54	● 26♒50
23 6:41	☽ 4♊59

Astro Data

1 January 2037
Julian Day # 50040
SVP 4♓44'47"
GC 27♐21.4 ⚴ 4♍03.5R
Eris 27♈11.4R ⚵ 13♍21.7
⚷ 14♊46.3R ⚶ 3♒49.1
☽ Mean ☊ 9♌22.2

1 February 2037
Julian Day # 50071
SVP 4♓44'42"
GC 27♐21.4 ⚴ 27♌55.7R
Eris 27♈12.4 ⚵ 10♍33.8R
⚷ 13♊36.4R ⚶ 19♒44.4
☽ Mean ☊ 7♌43.7

March 2037 LONGITUDE

Day	Sid.Time	☉	0 hr ☽	Noon ☽	True ☊	☿	♀	♂	⚳	♃	♄	♅	♆	♇
1 Su	22 38 32	11♓14 14	26♌12 12	3♍49 16	7♌42.4	10♓30.2	6♓17.3	20♑12.3	29♎31.1	16♊50.8	28♌32.4	15♋43.8	24♈56.9	21♒27.2
2 M	22 42 29	12 14 24	11♍27 40	19 06 04	7R38.8	12 22.9	7 32.3	20 56.0	29R28.9	16 54.8	28R27.7	15R42.7	24 58.7	21 28.8
3 Tu	22 46 26	13 14 33	26 43 08	4♎17 33	7 33.8	14 16.4	8 47.2	21 39.6	29 26.2	16 59.0	28 23.1	15 41.7	25 00.5	21 30.5
4 W	22 50 22	14 14 41	11♎48 06	19 13 43	7 28.2	16 10.8	10 02.2	22 23.3	29 23.2	17 03.4	28 18.5	15 40.6	25 02.3	21 32.2
5 Th	22 54 19	15 14 46	26 33 30	3♏46 43	7 22.8	18 06.0	11 17.1	23 07.0	29 19.7	17 08.0	28 14.0	15 39.7	25 04.1	21 33.9
6 F	22 58 15	16 14 51	10♏52 55	17 51 49	7 18.3	20 01.8	12 32.0	23 50.8	29 15.8	17 12.7	28 09.5	15 38.7	25 05.9	21 35.5
7 Sa	23 02 12	17 14 53	24 43 20	1♐27 33	7 15.4	21 58.2	13 46.9	24 34.5	29 11.4	17 17.6	28 05.0	15 37.9	25 07.8	21 37.1
8 Su	23 06 08	18 14 54	8♐04 43	14 35 13	7D14.1	23 55.0	15 01.8	25 18.3	29 06.7	17 22.7	28 00.6	15 37.1	25 09.7	21 38.8
9 M	23 10 05	19 14 54	20 59 29	27 18 05	7 14.3	25 52.1	16 16.7	26 02.2	29 01.5	17 27.9	27 56.2	15 36.3	25 11.6	21 40.4
10 Tu	23 14 01	20 14 52	3♑31 33	9♑40 32	7 15.6	27 49.3	17 31.6	26 46.0	28 55.9	17 33.4	27 51.9	15 35.6	25 13.5	21 42.0
11 W	23 17 58	21 14 48	15 45 37	21 47 24	7 17.1	29 46.4	18 46.4	27 29.9	28 49.9	17 38.9	27 47.6	15 34.9	25 15.4	21 43.6
12 Th	23 21 55	22 14 42	27 46 30	3♒43 28	7R18.1	1♈43.0	20 01.3	28 13.8	28 43.5	17 44.7	27 43.4	15 34.3	25 17.4	21 45.2
13 F	23 25 51	23 14 35	9♒38 49	15 33 04	7 17.7	3 39.1	21 16.1	28 57.7	28 36.7	17 50.6	27 39.3	15 33.8	25 19.4	21 46.7
14 Sa	23 29 48	24 14 26	21 26 41	27 20 02	7 15.4	5 34.1	22 30.9	29 41.6	28 29.4	17 56.7	27 35.2	15 33.3	25 21.4	21 48.3
15 Su	23 33 44	25 14 15	3♓13 32	9♓07 29	7 10.9	7 27.8	23 45.7	0♒25.6	28 21.9	18 02.9	27 31.2	15 32.8	25 23.4	21 49.8
16 M	23 37 41	26 14 02	15 02 11	20 57 53	7 04.1	9 19.7	25 00.5	1 09.5	28 13.9	18 09.3	27 27.2	15 32.4	25 25.4	21 51.4
17 Tu	23 41 37	27 13 47	26 54 49	2♈53 10	6 55.4	11 09.4	26 15.3	1 53.5	28 05.5	18 15.8	27 23.3	15 32.1	25 27.4	21 52.9
18 W	23 45 34	28 13 30	8♈53 06	14 54 49	6 45.4	12 56.5	27 30.0	2 37.5	27 56.8	18 22.6	27 19.5	15 31.8	25 29.5	21 54.4
19 Th	23 49 30	29 13 11	20 58 27	27 04 10	6 35.2	14 40.5	28 44.8	3 21.6	27 47.7	18 29.4	27 15.8	15 31.5	25 31.5	21 55.9
20 F	23 53 27	0♈12 50	3♉12 09	9♉22 35	6 25.6	16 20.9	29 59.5	4 05.6	27 38.3	18 36.4	27 12.1	15 31.3	25 33.6	21 57.3
21 Sa	23 57 23	1 12 27	15 35 40	21 51 37	6 17.5	17 57.4	1♈14.2	4 49.7	27 28.5	18 43.6	27 08.5	15 31.2	25 35.7	21 58.8
22 Su	0 01 20	2 12 02	28 10 43	4♊33 14	6 11.6	19 29.3	2 28.9	5 33.7	27 18.5	18 50.9	27 04.9	15D31.1	25 37.8	22 00.2
23 M	0 05 17	3 11 34	10♊59 29	17 29 47	6 08.2	20 56.4	3 43.5	6 17.8	27 08.1	18 58.3	27 01.5	15 31.1	25 39.9	22 01.7
24 Tu	0 09 13	4 11 04	24 04 28	0♋43 51	6D06.9	22 18.1	4 58.2	7 01.9	26 57.4	19 05.9	26 58.1	15 31.2	25 42.1	22 03.1
25 W	0 13 10	5 10 32	7♋28 16	14 17 58	6 07.1	23 34.1	6 12.8	7 46.1	26 46.4	19 13.6	26 54.8	15 31.2	25 44.2	22 04.5
26 Th	0 17 06	6 09 58	21 13 11	28 14 02	6R07.8	24 44.1	7 27.4	8 30.2	26 35.1	19 21.5	26 51.6	15 31.4	25 46.4	22 05.8
27 F	0 21 03	7 09 21	5♌20 33	12♌32 37	6 07.9	25 47.7	8 42.0	9 14.3	26 23.6	19 29.5	26 48.5	15 31.6	25 48.5	22 07.2
28 Sa	0 24 59	8 08 42	19 49 59	27 12 13	6 06.2	26 44.7	9 56.6	9 58.5	26 11.8	19 37.6	26 45.5	15 31.8	25 50.7	22 08.5
29 Su	0 28 56	9 08 00	4♍38 40	12♍08 32	6 02.0	27 34.8	11 11.1	10 42.7	25 59.8	19 45.9	26 42.5	15 32.1	25 52.9	22 09.8
30 M	0 32 52	10 07 16	19 40 51	27 14 29	5 55.3	28 17.9	12 25.6	11 26.9	25 47.6	19 54.3	26 39.7	15 32.5	25 55.1	22 11.1
31 Tu	0 36 49	11 06 30	4♎48 12	12♎20 45	5 46.4	28 53.9	13 40.1	12 11.1	25 35.2	20 02.8	26 36.9	15 32.9	25 57.3	22 12.4

April 2037 LONGITUDE

Day	Sid.Time	☉	0 hr ☽	Noon ☽	True ☊	☿	♀	♂	⚳	♃	♄	♅	♆	♇
1 W	0 40 46	12♈05 43	19♎50 50	27♎17 16	5♌36.3	29♈22.6	14♈54.6	12♒55.3	25♎22.5	20♊11.5	26♌34.2	15♋33.4	25♈59.5	22♒13.7
2 Th	0 44 42	13 04 53	4♏38 55	11♏54 54	5R26.2	29 44.0	16 09.1	13 39.6	25R09.7	20 20.2	26R31.6	15 33.9	26 01.7	22 14.9
3 F	0 48 39	14 04 01	19 04 27	26 07 02	5 17.2	29 58.2	17 23.5	14 23.8	24 56.7	20 29.1	26 29.2	15 34.5	26 03.9	22 16.1
4 Sa	0 52 35	15 03 08	3♐02 21	9♐50 17	5 10.3	0♉05.2	18 38.0	15 08.1	24 43.6	20 38.1	26 26.8	15 35.1	26 06.2	22 17.3
5 Su	0 56 32	16 02 12	16 30 54	23 04 26	5 05.8	0R05.3	19 52.4	15 52.4	24 30.4	20 47.3	26 24.5	15 35.8	26 08.4	22 18.5
6 M	1 00 28	17 01 16	29 31 17	5♑51 54	5D03.5	29♈58.5	21 06.8	16 36.7	24 17.0	20 56.5	26 22.3	15 36.5	26 10.6	22 19.7
7 Tu	1 04 25	18 00 17	12♑06 51	18 16 47	5 03.0	29 45.4	22 21.2	17 21.0	24 03.5	21 05.9	26 20.1	15 37.3	26 12.9	22 20.8
8 W	1 08 21	18 59 16	24 22 21	0♒24 13	5R03.2	29 26.1	23 35.5	18 05.3	23 50.0	21 15.4	26 18.1	15 38.1	26 15.1	22 21.9
9 Th	1 12 18	19 58 14	6♒23 06	12 19 40	5 03.1	29 01.3	24 49.9	18 49.6	23 36.3	21 25.0	26 16.2	15 39.0	26 17.4	22 23.0
10 F	1 16 15	20 57 10	18 14 33	24 08 24	5 01.5	28 31.6	26 04.2	19 34.0	23 22.7	21 34.7	26 14.4	15 39.9	26 19.6	22 24.1
11 Sa	1 20 11	21 56 04	0♓01 47	5♓55 16	4 57.7	27 57.4	27 18.5	20 18.3	23 09.0	21 44.5	26 12.7	15 40.9	26 21.9	22 25.2
12 Su	1 24 08	22 54 57	11 49 20	17 44 26	4 51.1	27 19.6	28 32.8	21 02.7	22 55.3	21 54.4	26 11.1	15 42.0	26 24.2	22 26.2
13 M	1 28 04	23 53 47	23 40 56	29 39 12	4 41.8	26 39.0	29 47.1	21 47.0	22 41.6	22 04.4	26 09.6	15 43.1	26 26.4	22 27.2
14 Tu	1 32 01	24 52 36	5♈39 30	11♈42 03	4 30.0	25 56.3	1♉01.4	22 31.4	22 27.9	22 14.5	26 08.2	15 44.2	26 28.7	22 28.2
15 W	1 35 57	25 51 22	17 47 00	23 54 31	4 16.7	25 12.5	2 15.6	23 15.8	22 14.2	22 24.8	26 06.9	15 45.4	26 31.0	22 29.2
16 Th	1 39 54	26 50 07	0♉04 40	6♉17 30	4 02.9	24 28.3	3 29.8	24 00.1	22 00.6	22 35.1	26 05.7	15 46.7	26 33.2	22 30.1
17 F	1 43 50	27 48 50	12 33 03	18 51 20	3 49.8	23 44.5	4 44.0	24 44.5	21 47.1	22 45.5	26 04.6	15 47.9	26 35.5	22 31.0
18 Sa	1 47 47	28 47 31	25 12 22	1♊36 11	3 38.6	23 02.0	5 58.2	25 28.8	21 33.7	22 56.1	26 03.6	15 49.3	26 37.8	22 31.9
19 Su	1 51 43	29 46 09	8♊02 47	14 32 15	3 30.0	22 21.4	7 12.4	26 13.2	21 20.4	23 06.7	26 02.8	15 50.7	26 40.0	22 32.8
20 M	1 55 40	0♉44 46	21 04 40	27 40 07	3 24.4	21 43.5	8 26.5	26 57.6	21 07.3	23 17.4	26 02.0	15 52.1	26 42.3	22 33.6
21 Tu	1 59 37	1 43 20	4♋18 46	11♋00 45	3 21.6	21 08.8	9 40.6	27 41.9	20 54.3	23 28.2	26 01.3	15 53.6	26 44.6	22 34.5
22 W	2 03 33	2 41 53	17 46 15	24 35 27	3 20.7	20 37.7	10 54.7	28 26.3	20 41.4	23 39.1	26 00.8	15 55.2	26 46.8	22 35.3
23 Th	2 07 30	3 40 23	1♌28 28	8♌25 28	3 20.6	20 10.8	12 08.8	29 10.6	20 28.7	23 50.1	26 00.3	15 56.8	26 49.1	22 36.1
24 F	2 11 26	4 38 51	15 26 30	22 31 34	3 20.1	19 48.3	13 22.9	29 54.9	20 16.2	24 01.1	26 00.0	15 58.4	26 51.3	22 36.8
25 Sa	2 15 23	5 37 16	29 40 32	6♍53 13	3 17.8	19 30.4	14 36.9	0♓39.3	20 04.0	24 12.3	25 59.8	16 00.1	26 53.6	22 37.5
26 Su	2 19 19	6 35 40	14♍09 15	21 28 07	3 13.1	19 17.3	15 50.9	1 23.6	19 51.9	24 23.5	25D59.6	16 01.9	26 55.8	22 38.2
27 M	2 23 16	7 34 01	28 49 11	6♎11 40	3 05.6	19 09.0	17 04.9	2 07.9	19 40.1	24 34.8	25 59.6	16 03.6	26 58.1	22 38.9
28 Tu	2 27 12	8 32 20	13♎34 40	20 57 13	2 55.7	19D05.8	18 18.8	2 52.3	19 28.5	24 46.2	25 59.7	16 05.5	27 00.3	22 39.6
29 W	2 31 09	9 30 38	28 18 18	5♏36 53	2 44.5	19 07.4	19 32.8	3 36.6	19 17.2	24 57.7	25 59.9	16 07.3	27 02.5	22 40.2
30 Th	2 35 06	10 28 54	12♏51 59	20 02 43	2 33.0	19 13.9	20 46.7	4 20.9	19 06.1	25 09.2	26 00.2	16 09.2	27 04.7	22 40.8

Astro Data

	Dy Hr Mn
☽0S	3 22:23
☿0N	12 6:44
☽0N	18 3:32
☉0N	20 6:50
♀0N	23 1:11
♅D	23 8:26
☽0S	31 9:18
☿R	5 0:04
♄△♆	9 5:15
☽0N	14 9:56
♃△♇	15 23:16
♄D	27 4:57
☽0S	27 19:29
☿D	28 15:56

Planet Ingress

	Dy Hr Mn
☿ ♈	11 14:48
♂ ♒	14 22:02
☉ ♈	20 6:50
♀ ♈	20 12:10
☿ ♉	3 16:23
☿ ♈R	6 8:16
♀ ♉	13 16:10
☉ ♉	19 17:40
♂ ♓	24 14:44

Last Aspect / ☽ Ingress

Last Aspect Dy Hr Mn		☽ Ingress Dy Hr Mn
1 3:44 ♄ ☌	♍	1 5:59
2 15:02 ♂ △	♎	3 5:11
5 2:49 ♄ ⚹	♏	5 5:42
7 6:00 ♄ □	♐	7 9:23
9 13:13 ♄ △	♑	9 17:11
12 0:11 ♂ ☌	♒	12 4:29
14 12:31 ♄ ☍	♓	14 17:26
16 23:36 ☉ ☌	♈	17 6:12
19 12:23 ♄ △	♉	19 17:45
21 21:59 ♄ □	♊	22 3:26
24 5:16 ♄ ⚹	♋	24 10:41
26 7:48 ♆ □	♌	26 15:00
28 11:17 ♄ ☌	♍	28 16:31
30 0:15 ♃ □	♎	30 16:23

Last Aspect / ☽ Ingress

Last Aspect Dy Hr Mn		☽ Ingress Dy Hr Mn
1 15:29 ☿ ☍	♏	1 16:24
3 12:38 ♄ □	♐	3 18:42
5 18:10 ♄ △	♑	6 0:54
8 10:07 ☿ □	♒	8 11:12
10 20:32 ☿ ⚹	♓	10 23:56
12 20:32 ♃ □	♈	13 12:42
15 17:06 ♆ ☌	♉	15 23:51
18 1:37 ♄ □	♊	18 9:00
20 10:38 ♂ △	♋	20 16:13
22 15:50 ♆ □	♌	22 21:26
24 19:18 ♆ △	♍	25 0:33
26 16:50 ♃ □	♎	27 1:55
28 21:54 ♆ ☍	♏	29 2:47

☽ Phases & Eclipses

Dy Hr Mn	
2 0:28	○ 11♍45
8 19:25	☾ 18♐33
16 23:36	● 26♓43
24 18:39	☽ 4♋28
31 9:53	○ 11♎01
7 11:25	☾ 17♑59
15 16:08	● 26♈01
23 3:11	☽ 3♌19
29 18:54	○ 9♏47

Astro Data

1 March 2037
Julian Day # 50099
SVP 4♓44'39"
GC 27♐21.5 ⚴ 19♌04.7R
Eris 27♈21.9 ⚵ 3♍44.3R
⚷ 13♊29.9 ⚶ 3♓58.4
☽ Mean ☊ 6♌14.7

1 April 2037
Julian Day # 50130
SVP 4♓44'37"
GC 27♐21.6 ⚴ 15♌50.8
Eris 27♈39.4 ⚵ 28♌27.6R
⚷ 14♊29.8 ⚶ 19♓16.9
☽ Mean ☊ 4♌36.2

LONGITUDE — May 2037

Day	Sid.Time	☉	0 hr ☽	Noon ☽	True ☊	☿	♀	♂	⚳	♃	♄	♅	♆	♇
1 F	2 39 02	11♉27 08	27♏08 20	4♐08 12	2♌22.7	19♈25.3	22♉00.6	5♓05.2	18♎55.3	25♊20.8	26♌00.6	16♋11.2	27♈06.9	22♒41.4
2 Sa	2 42 59	12 25 20	11♐01 53	17 49 06	2R 14.3	19 41.2	23 14.5	5 49.5	18R44.9	25 32.5	26 01.1	16 13.2	27 09.2	22 41.9
3 Su	2 46 55	13 23 31	24 29 45	1♑03 55	2 08.6	20 01.8	24 28.3	6 33.8	18 34.7	25 44.3	26 01.7	16 15.3	27 11.4	22 42.5
4 M	2 50 52	14 21 41	7♑31 47	13 53 41	2 05.3	20 26.7	25 42.2	7 18.1	18 24.8	25 56.1	26 02.4	16 17.4	27 13.5	22 43.0
5 Tu	2 54 48	15 19 49	20 10 04	26 21 27	2D 04.1	20 55.9	26 56.0	8 02.3	18 15.2	26 08.0	26 03.3	16 19.5	27 15.7	22 43.5
6 W	2 58 45	16 17 55	2♒28 24	8♒31 35	2R 04.1	21 29.2	28 09.8	8 46.6	18 06.0	26 20.0	26 04.2	16 21.7	27 17.9	22 43.9
7 Th	3 02 41	17 16 00	14 31 40	20 29 17	2 04.2	22 06.5	29 23.6	9 30.8	17 57.1	26 32.0	26 05.2	16 23.9	27 20.1	22 44.3
8 F	3 06 38	18 14 04	26 25 10	2♓19 58	2 03.3	22 47.6	0♊37.4	10 15.1	17 48.6	26 44.1	26 06.4	16 26.2	27 22.2	22 44.7
9 Sa	3 10 35	19 12 06	8♓14 22	14 08 57	2 00.6	23 32.4	1 51.1	10 59.3	17 40.4	26 56.3	26 07.6	16 28.5	27 24.4	22 45.1
10 Su	3 14 31	20 10 07	20 04 21	26 01 06	1 55.4	24 20.7	3 04.8	11 43.5	17 32.5	27 08.5	26 09.0	16 30.8	27 26.5	22 45.5
11 M	3 18 28	21 08 06	1♈59 43	8♈00 37	1 47.7	25 12.4	4 18.6	12 27.6	17 25.0	27 20.8	26 10.4	16 33.2	27 28.6	22 45.8
12 Tu	3 22 24	22 06 05	14 04 12	20 10 48	1 37.8	26 07.3	5 32.3	13 11.8	17 17.9	27 33.1	26 12.0	16 35.6	27 30.7	22 46.1
13 W	3 26 21	23 04 01	26 20 38	2♉33 53	1 26.4	27 05.4	6 45.9	13 55.9	17 11.2	27 45.5	26 13.7	16 38.1	27 32.8	22 46.4
14 Th	3 30 17	24 01 57	8♉50 41	15 11 03	1 14.5	28 06.6	7 59.6	14 40.0	17 04.8	27 58.0	26 15.4	16 40.5	27 34.9	22 46.6
15 F	3 34 14	24 59 51	21 34 59	28 02 25	1 03.2	29 10.7	9 13.2	15 24.1	16 58.9	28 10.5	26 17.3	16 43.1	27 37.0	22 46.8
16 Sa	3 38 10	25 57 43	4♊33 14	11♊07 18	0 53.5	0♉17.7	10 26.9	16 08.1	16 53.3	28 23.0	26 19.3	16 45.7	27 39.0	22 47.0
17 Su	3 42 07	26 55 34	17 44 27	24 24 31	0 46.2	1 27.4	11 40.5	16 52.1	16 48.1	28 35.7	26 21.3	16 48.3	27 41.1	22 47.2
18 M	3 46 04	27 53 24	1♋07 21	7♋52 47	0 41.5	2 39.9	12 54.1	17 36.1	16 43.4	28 48.3	26 23.5	16 50.9	27 43.1	22 47.3
19 Tu	3 50 00	28 51 11	14 40 41	21 30 57	0D 39.4	3 55.0	14 07.6	18 20.1	16 39.0	29 01.0	26 25.8	16 53.6	27 45.1	22 47.4
20 W	3 53 57	29 48 58	28 23 30	5♌18 16	0 39.2	5 12.7	15 21.2	19 04.0	16 35.0	29 13.8	26 28.2	16 56.3	27 47.1	22 47.5
21 Th	3 57 53	0♊46 42	12♌15 13	19 14 17	0R 39.8	6 32.9	16 34.7	19 47.9	16 31.5	29 26.6	26 30.6	16 59.1	27 49.1	22 47.6
22 F	4 01 50	1 44 25	26 15 26	3♍18 35	0 40.1	7 55.6	17 48.2	20 31.7	16 28.3	29 39.5	26 33.2	17 01.9	27 51.0	22R 47.6
23 Sa	4 05 46	2 42 06	10♍23 36	17 30 19	0 39.2	9 20.8	19 01.7	21 15.5	16 25.5	29 52.4	26 35.9	17 04.7	27 53.0	22 47.6
24 Su	4 09 43	3 39 46	24 38 31	1♎47 51	0 36.2	10 48.4	20 15.1	21 59.3	16 23.2	0♋05.3	26 38.6	17 07.5	27 54.9	22 47.6
25 M	4 13 39	4 37 24	8♎57 57	16 08 19	0 31.0	12 18.4	21 28.5	22 43.0	16 21.2	0 18.3	26 41.5	17 10.4	27 56.8	22 47.6
26 Tu	4 17 36	5 35 01	23 18 26	0♏27 41	0 23.9	13 50.8	22 41.9	23 26.7	16 19.6	0 31.3	26 44.4	17 13.3	27 58.7	22 47.5
27 W	4 21 33	6 32 36	7♏35 26	14 41 00	0 15.7	15 25.6	23 55.3	24 10.4	16 18.5	0 44.3	26 47.5	17 16.2	28 00.6	22 47.4
28 Th	4 25 29	7 30 10	21 43 44	28 43 02	0 07.1	17 02.8	25 08.7	24 54.0	16 17.7	0 57.4	26 50.6	17 19.2	28 02.4	22 47.3
29 F	4 29 26	8 27 43	5♐38 20	12♐29 10	29♋59.4	18 42.4	26 22.0	25 37.6	16D 17.3	1 10.5	26 53.9	17 22.2	28 04.3	22 47.1
30 Sa	4 33 22	9 25 15	19 15 09	25 56 01	29 53.2	20 24.3	27 35.3	26 21.1	16 17.4	1 23.7	26 57.2	17 25.2	28 06.1	22 47.0
31 Su	4 37 19	10 22 45	2♑31 37	9♑01 56	29 49.1	22 08.6	28 48.6	27 04.6	16 17.8	1 36.9	27 00.6	17 28.3	28 07.9	22 46.8

LONGITUDE — June 2037

Day	Sid.Time	☉	0 hr ☽	Noon ☽	True ☊	☿	♀	♂	⚳	♃	♄	♅	♆	♇
1 M	4 41 15	11♊20 15	15♑27 03	21♑47 07	29♋47.1	23♉55.2	0♋01.9	27♓48.0	16♎18.6	1♋50.1	27♌04.1	17♋31.4	28♈09.7	22♒46.6
2 Tu	4 45 12	12 17 44	28 02 28	4♒13 25	29D 46.8	25 44.2	1 15.2	28 31.4	16 19.8	2 03.4	27 07.7	17 34.5	28 11.4	22R 46.3
3 W	4 49 09	13 15 12	10♒20 28	16 24 04	29 47.8	27 35.5	2 28.4	29 14.8	16 21.3	2 16.6	27 11.4	17 37.6	28 13.2	22 46.1
4 Th	4 53 05	14 12 40	22 24 48	28 23 14	29 49.2	29 29.1	3 41.6	29 58.1	16 23.3	2 30.0	27 15.1	17 40.8	28 14.9	22 45.8
5 F	4 57 02	15 10 06	4♓20 01	10♓15 45	29R 50.2	1♊24.9	4 54.8	0♈41.4	16 25.6	2 43.3	27 19.0	17 44.0	28 16.6	22 45.4
6 Sa	5 00 58	16 07 32	16 11 05	22 06 39	29 50.1	3 22.9	6 08.0	1 24.6	16 28.3	2 56.7	27 22.9	17 47.2	28 18.2	22 45.1
7 Su	5 04 55	17 04 58	28 03 05	4♈01 00	29 48.5	5 23.1	7 21.2	2 07.7	16 31.4	3 10.0	27 26.9	17 50.4	28 19.9	22 44.7
8 M	5 08 51	18 02 22	10♈00 57	16 03 30	29 45.1	7 25.2	8 34.3	2 50.8	16 34.8	3 23.5	27 31.0	17 53.7	28 21.5	22 44.3
9 Tu	5 12 48	18 59 47	22 09 08	28 18 16	29 40.2	9 29.2	9 47.4	3 33.8	16 38.7	3 36.9	27 35.2	17 57.0	28 23.1	22 43.9
10 W	5 16 44	19 57 10	4♉31 18	10♉48 31	29 34.2	11 35.0	11 00.5	4 16.8	16 42.8	3 50.4	27 39.5	18 00.3	28 24.7	22 43.5
11 Th	5 20 41	20 54 33	17 10 09	23 36 20	29 27.6	13 42.4	12 13.6	4 59.6	16 47.4	4 03.8	27 43.9	18 03.6	28 26.2	22 43.0
12 F	5 24 37	21 51 55	0♊07 07	6♊42 29	29 21.3	15 51.1	13 26.7	5 42.5	16 52.3	4 17.3	27 48.3	18 06.9	28 27.8	22 42.5
13 Sa	5 28 34	22 49 17	13 22 18	20 06 22	29 16.0	18 01.0	14 39.7	6 25.2	16 57.5	4 30.9	27 52.8	18 10.3	28 29.3	22 42.0
14 Su	5 32 31	23 46 38	26 54 26	3♋46 11	29 12.2	20 11.8	15 52.7	7 07.9	17 03.1	4 44.4	27 57.4	18 13.7	28 30.8	22 41.5
15 M	5 36 27	24 43 59	10♋41 14	17 39 11	29D 10.1	22 23.2	17 05.7	7 50.5	17 09.1	4 58.0	28 02.1	18 17.1	28 32.2	22 40.9
16 Tu	5 40 24	25 41 19	24 39 39	1♌42 10	29 09.6	24 35.1	18 18.7	8 33.0	17 15.4	5 11.5	28 06.8	18 20.5	28 33.6	22 40.3
17 W	5 44 20	26 38 38	8♌46 22	15 51 50	29 10.4	26 47.0	19 31.6	9 15.5	17 22.0	5 25.1	28 11.6	18 24.0	28 35.1	22 39.7
18 Th	5 48 17	27 35 56	22 58 13	0♍05 09	29 11.8	28 58.8	20 44.6	9 57.8	17 29.0	5 38.7	28 16.5	18 27.4	28 36.4	22 39.1
19 F	5 52 13	28 33 13	7♍12 20	14 19 28	29 13.1	1♋10.1	21 57.5	10 40.1	17 36.3	5 52.3	28 21.5	18 30.9	28 37.8	22 38.4
20 Sa	5 56 10	29 30 29	21 26 16	28 32 29	29R 13.7	3 20.7	23 10.3	11 22.3	17 43.9	6 05.9	28 26.6	18 34.4	28 39.1	22 37.8
21 Su	6 00 07	0♋27 45	5♎37 52	12♎42 09	29 13.1	5 30.4	24 23.2	12 04.4	17 51.8	6 19.5	28 31.7	18 37.9	28 40.4	22 37.1
22 M	6 04 03	1 25 00	19 45 05	26 46 23	29 11.3	7 38.9	25 36.0	12 46.4	18 00.1	6 33.1	28 36.9	18 41.4	28 41.7	22 36.3
23 Tu	6 08 00	2 22 14	3♏45 49	10♏43 05	29 08.5	9 46.1	26 48.8	13 28.3	18 08.6	6 46.8	28 42.1	18 44.9	28 42.9	22 35.6
24 W	6 11 56	3 19 27	17 37 53	24 29 57	29 05.0	11 51.9	28 01.5	14 10.2	18 17.5	7 00.4	28 47.4	18 48.5	28 44.1	22 34.9
25 Th	6 15 53	4 16 40	1♐19 01	8♐04 50	29 01.3	13 55.9	29 14.3	14 51.9	18 26.7	7 14.0	28 52.8	18 52.0	28 45.3	22 34.1
26 F	6 19 49	5 13 53	14 47 08	21 25 45	28 58.0	15 58.2	0♌27.0	15 33.6	18 36.1	7 27.7	28 58.3	18 55.6	28 46.4	22 33.3
27 Sa	6 23 46	6 11 06	28 00 30	4♑31 19	28 55.4	17 58.7	1 39.6	16 15.2	18 45.9	7 41.3	29 03.8	18 59.1	28 47.6	22 32.5
28 Su	6 27 42	7 08 18	10♑58 06	17 20 53	28D 53.9	19 57.3	2 52.3	16 56.6	18 55.9	7 55.0	29 09.4	19 02.7	28 48.7	22 31.6
29 M	6 31 39	8 05 30	23 39 44	29 54 46	28 53.5	21 53.9	4 04.9	17 38.0	19 06.2	8 08.7	29 15.1	19 06.3	28 49.7	22 30.8
30 Tu	6 35 36	9 02 41	6♒06 11	12♒14 13	28 54.0	23 48.4	5 17.5	18 19.3	19 16.8	8 22.2	29 20.8	19 09.9	28 50.8	22 29.9

Astro Data (Dy Hr Mn)

♃✶♄	5 1:43
☽0N	11 17:52
♃✶♆	12 6:25
♇R	23 7:49
☽0S	25 3:43
⚳D	29 22:32
☽0N	8 2:47
♂0N	11 6:53
☽0S	21 10:07
♄△♆	23 16:33
♃Q♇	26 21:17
⚳0S	28 7:27

Planet Ingress (Dy Hr Mn)

♀ ♊	7 23:51
☿ ♉	16 5:46
☉ ♊	20 16:35
♃ ♋	24 2:12
☊ ♋R	29 10:01
♀ ♋	1 11:22
♂ ♈	4 13:03
☿ ♊	4 18:27
☿ ♋	18 23:11
☉ ♋	21 0:22
♀ ♌	26 3:06

Last Aspect / ☽ Ingress (Dy Hr Mn)

Last Aspect	☽ Ingress
30 22:04 ♄ □	♐ 1 4:53
3 4:53 ♆ △	♑ 3 10:02
5 13:46 ♆ □	♒ 5 19:08
8 1:54 ♆ ✶	♓ 8 7:16
10 14:18 ♃ □	♈ 10 20:00
13 2:35 ♃ ✶	♉ 13 7:04
15 8:45 ♄ □	♊ 15 15:37
17 19:37 ♃ ☌	♋ 17 22:00
20 1:46 ☉ ✶	♌ 20 2:48
22 5:42 ♃ ✶	♍ 22 6:23
23 18:39 ♂ ☍	♎ 24 8:59
26 7:49 ♆ ☍	♏ 26 11:13
28 8:46 ♄ □	♐ 28 14:13
30 15:56 ♆ △	♑ 30 19:23

Last Aspect / ☽ Ingress (Dy Hr Mn)

Last Aspect	☽ Ingress
2 0:16 ♆ □	♒ 2 3:47
4 14:38 ♆ □	♓ 4 15:15
6 3:12 ♅ △	♈ 7 3:56
9 12:09 ♆ ☌	♉ 9 15:17
11 19:40 ♄ □	♊ 11 23:47
14 2:48 ♆ ✶	♋ 14 5:25
16 6:39 ♆ □	♌ 16 9:06
18 9:48 ♅ ✶	♍ 18 11:51
20 13:45 ☉ □	♎ 20 14:28
22 15:18 ♆ ☍	♏ 22 17:32
24 19:36 ♄ □	♐ 24 21:40
27 1:52 ♄ △	♑ 27 3:39
29 9:55 ♆ □	♒ 29 12:10

☽ Phases & Eclipses (Dy Hr Mn)

7 4:56	☾ 16♒59
15 5:54	● 24♉45
22 9:08	☽ 1♍38
29 4:24	○ 8♐09
5 22:49	☾ 15♓36
13 17:10	● 23♊02
20 13:45	☽ 29♍35
27 15:20	○ 6♑19

Astro Data

1 May 2037
Julian Day # 50160
SVP 4♓44'34"
GC 27♐21.6 ⚴ 20♌05.6
Eris 27♈59.0 ⚵ 29♌13.2
⚷ 16♊21.5 ⚶ 3♈21.3
☽ Mean ☊ 3♌00.8

1 June 2037
Julian Day # 50191
SVP 4♓44'29"
GC 27♐21.7 ⚴ 28♌57.3
Eris 28♈17.1 ⚵ 4♍50.2
⚷ 18♊50.1 ⚶ 16♈44.8
☽ Mean ☊ 1♌22.4

July 2037 LONGITUDE

Day	Sid.Time	☉	0 hr ☽	Noon ☽	True ☊	☿	♀	♂	⚳	♃	♄	♅	♆	♇
1 W	6 39 32	9♋59 53	18♒19 11	24♒21 27	28♋55.2	25♋41.0	6♌30.0	19♈00.5	19♎27.7	8♋35.9	29♌26.5	19♋13.5	28♈51.8	22♒29.0
2 Th	6 43 29	10 57 05	0♓21 24	6♓19 29	28 56.6	27 31.4	7 42.5	19 41.5	19 38.8	8 49.5	29 32.4	19 17.1	28 52.8	22R 28.1
3 F	6 47 25	11 54 17	12 16 12	18 12 05	28 58.0	29 19.8	8 55.0	20 22.5	19 50.2	9 03.2	29 38.3	19 20.8	28 53.7	22 27.2
4 Sa	6 51 22	12 51 29	24 07 39	0♈03 29	28 59.1	1♌06.2	10 07.5	21 03.3	20 01.8	9 16.8	29 44.2	19 24.4	28 54.6	22 26.2
5 Su	6 55 18	13 48 41	6♈00 10	11 58 17	28R 59.5	2 50.4	11 20.0	21 44.1	20 13.8	9 30.4	29 50.2	19 28.0	28 55.5	22 25.2
6 M	6 59 15	14 45 54	17 58 24	24 01 08	28 59.3	4 32.6	12 32.4	22 24.7	20 25.9	9 44.0	29 56.3	19 31.6	28 56.4	22 24.3
7 Tu	7 03 11	15 43 07	0♉07 01	6♉16 35	28 58.5	6 12.6	13 44.8	23 05.2	20 38.4	9 57.6	0♍02.4	19 35.3	28 57.2	22 23.3
8 W	7 07 08	16 40 20	12 30 19	18 48 40	28 57.2	7 50.6	14 57.1	23 45.5	20 51.0	10 11.2	0 08.6	19 38.9	28 58.0	22 22.2
9 Th	7 11 05	17 37 34	25 12 00	1♊40 37	28 55.8	9 26.5	16 09.5	24 25.8	21 03.9	10 24.8	0 14.8	19 42.6	28 58.8	22 21.2
10 F	7 15 01	18 34 48	8♊14 45	14 54 29	28 54.4	11 00.3	17 21.8	25 05.9	21 17.1	10 38.3	0 21.1	19 46.2	28 59.5	22 20.2
11 Sa	7 18 58	19 32 02	21 39 52	28 30 45	28 53.3	12 31.9	18 34.0	25 45.9	21 30.5	10 51.9	0 27.5	19 49.9	29 00.2	22 19.1
12 Su	7 22 54	20 29 17	5♋26 57	12♋28 06	28 52.6	14 01.5	19 46.3	26 25.7	21 44.1	11 05.4	0 33.9	19 53.5	29 00.9	22 18.0
13 M	7 26 51	21 26 32	19 33 46	26 43 25	28D 52.3	15 28.9	20 58.5	27 05.4	21 58.0	11 19.0	0 40.3	19 57.2	29 01.5	22 16.9
14 Tu	7 30 47	22 23 47	3♌56 23	11♌12 00	28 52.4	16 54.1	22 10.7	27 44.9	22 12.0	11 32.5	0 46.8	20 00.8	29 02.1	22 15.8
15 W	7 34 44	23 21 03	18 29 32	25 48 11	28 52.8	18 17.1	23 22.8	28 24.3	22 26.3	11 46.0	0 53.3	20 04.5	29 02.7	22 14.7
16 Th	7 38 40	24 18 18	3♍07 13	10♍25 53	28 53.2	19 37.9	24 34.9	29 03.5	22 40.8	11 59.4	0 59.9	20 08.1	29 03.3	22 13.6
17 F	7 42 37	25 15 34	17 43 30	24 59 27	28 53.6	20 56.4	25 47.0	29 42.6	22 55.6	12 12.9	1 06.5	20 11.8	29 03.8	22 12.4
18 Sa	7 46 34	26 12 49	2♎13 10	9♎24 11	28 53.8	22 12.6	26 59.0	0♉21.5	23 10.5	12 26.3	1 13.2	20 15.4	29 04.3	22 11.2
19 Su	7 50 30	27 10 05	16 32 07	23 36 39	28R 53.9	23 26.4	28 11.0	1 00.3	23 25.6	12 39.7	1 19.9	20 19.0	29 04.7	22 10.1
20 M	7 54 27	28 07 21	0♏37 34	7♏34 42	28D 53.9	24 37.7	29 22.9	1 38.9	23 41.0	12 53.1	1 26.7	20 22.7	29 05.1	22 08.9
21 Tu	7 58 23	29 04 37	14 27 58	21 17 19	28 53.9	25 46.6	0♍34.8	2 17.3	23 56.5	13 06.4	1 33.5	20 26.3	29 05.5	22 07.7
22 W	8 02 20	0♌01 54	28 02 46	4♐44 20	28 54.0	26 52.8	1 46.7	2 55.6	24 12.3	13 19.7	1 40.3	20 29.9	29 05.8	22 06.5
23 Th	8 06 16	0 59 11	11♐22 05	17 56 07	28 54.1	27 56.4	2 58.5	3 33.7	24 28.2	13 33.0	1 47.2	20 33.5	29 06.2	22 05.3
24 F	8 10 13	1 56 28	24 26 30	0♑53 22	28 54.4	28 57.1	4 10.3	4 11.6	24 44.3	13 46.3	1 54.1	20 37.1	29 06.4	22 04.0
25 Sa	8 14 09	2 53 45	7♑16 50	13 37 00	28 54.7	29 55.0	5 22.0	4 49.4	25 00.6	13 59.5	2 01.0	20 40.7	29 06.7	22 02.8
26 Su	8 18 06	3 51 04	19 54 00	26 07 59	28R 54.8	0♍49.8	6 33.7	5 27.0	25 17.1	14 12.7	2 08.0	20 44.3	29 06.9	22 01.5
27 M	8 22 03	4 48 23	2♒19 06	8♒27 31	28 54.7	1 41.6	7 45.3	6 04.3	25 33.7	14 25.9	2 15.1	20 47.9	29 07.1	22 00.3
28 Tu	8 25 59	5 45 42	14 33 24	20 36 59	28 54.3	2 30.0	8 56.9	6 41.5	25 50.6	14 39.0	2 22.1	20 51.4	29 07.2	21 59.0
29 W	8 29 56	6 43 02	26 38 29	2♓38 08	28 53.6	3 15.0	10 08.5	7 18.6	26 07.6	14 52.1	2 29.2	20 55.0	29 07.4	21 57.8
30 Th	8 33 52	7 40 23	8♓36 15	14 33 08	28 52.5	3 56.5	11 20.0	7 55.4	26 24.7	15 05.2	2 36.3	20 58.5	29 07.4	21 56.5
31 F	8 37 49	8 37 45	20 29 07	26 24 36	28 51.2	4 34.2	12 31.4	8 32.0	26 42.1	15 18.2	2 43.5	21 02.0	29 07.5	21 55.2

August 2037 LONGITUDE

Day	Sid.Time	☉	0 hr ☽	Noon ☽	True ☊	☿	♀	♂	⚳	♃	♄	♅	♆	♇
1 Sa	8 41 45	9♌35 09	2♈19 59	8♈15 43	28♋49.8	5♍08.0	13♍42.8	9♉08.4	26♎59.6	15♋31.2	2♍50.6	21♋05.5	29♈07.5	21♒53.9
2 Su	8 45 42	10 32 33	14 12 16	20 10 08	28R 48.7	5 37.7	14 54.2	9 44.6	27 17.2	15 44.2	2 57.8	21 09.0	29R 07.5	21R 52.6
3 M	8 49 38	11 29 58	26 09 50	2♉11 54	28D 47.9	6 03.1	16 05.5	10 20.6	27 35.0	15 57.1	3 05.1	21 12.5	29 07.5	21 51.3
4 Tu	8 53 35	12 27 24	8♉16 54	14 25 21	28 47.7	6 24.0	17 16.7	10 56.4	27 53.0	16 09.9	3 12.3	21 16.0	29 07.4	21 50.0
5 W	8 57 32	13 24 52	20 37 50	26 54 52	28 48.1	6 40.3	18 28.0	11 31.9	28 11.1	16 22.8	3 19.6	21 19.4	29 07.3	21 48.7
6 Th	9 01 28	14 22 21	3♊16 56	9♊44 30	28 49.1	6 51.7	19 39.1	12 07.2	28 29.4	16 35.6	3 27.0	21 22.9	29 07.1	21 47.3
7 F	9 05 25	15 19 51	16 17 58	22 57 38	28 50.3	6R 58.2	20 50.3	12 42.3	28 47.9	16 48.3	3 34.3	21 26.3	29 07.0	21 46.0
8 Sa	9 09 21	16 17 23	29 43 43	6♋36 19	28 51.5	6 59.4	22 01.3	13 17.1	29 06.4	17 01.0	3 41.7	21 29.7	29 06.7	21 44.7
9 Su	9 13 18	17 14 56	13♋35 23	20 40 45	28R 52.3	6 55.4	23 12.4	13 51.7	29 25.2	17 13.6	3 49.1	21 33.1	29 06.5	21 43.4
10 M	9 17 14	18 12 30	27 52 04	5♌08 48	28 52.3	6 45.9	24 23.3	14 26.0	29 44.0	17 26.2	3 56.5	21 36.5	29 06.2	21 42.0
11 Tu	9 21 11	19 10 05	12♌30 18	19 55 44	28 51.4	6 31.1	25 34.3	15 00.1	0♏03.0	17 38.8	4 03.9	21 39.8	29 05.9	21 40.7
12 W	9 25 07	20 07 41	27 24 07	4♍54 26	28 49.6	6 10.8	26 45.1	15 33.9	0 22.2	17 51.3	4 11.3	21 43.1	29 05.6	21 39.4
13 Th	9 29 04	21 05 19	12♍25 33	19 56 21	28 46.9	5 45.3	27 55.9	16 07.4	0 41.4	18 03.7	4 18.8	21 46.4	29 05.2	21 38.0
14 F	9 33 01	22 02 57	27 25 44	4♎52 39	28 43.9	5 14.5	29 06.7	16 40.6	1 00.8	18 16.1	4 26.3	21 49.7	29 04.8	21 36.7
15 Sa	9 36 57	23 00 36	12♎16 12	19 35 35	28 41.0	4 38.9	0♎17.4	17 13.6	1 20.4	18 28.4	4 33.8	21 53.0	29 04.4	21 35.4
16 Su	9 40 54	23 58 17	26 50 10	3♏59 29	28 38.9	3 58.9	1 28.0	17 46.2	1 40.0	18 40.6	4 41.3	21 56.2	29 03.9	21 34.0
17 M	9 44 50	24 55 58	11♏03 12	18 01 11	28D 37.7	3 14.8	2 38.6	18 18.6	1 59.8	18 52.8	4 48.8	21 59.4	29 03.4	21 32.7
18 Tu	9 48 47	25 53 40	24 53 23	1♐39 54	28 37.6	2 27.5	3 49.1	18 50.7	2 19.7	19 05.0	4 56.3	22 02.6	29 02.9	21 31.4
19 W	9 52 43	26 51 24	8♐20 56	14 56 42	28 38.6	1 37.5	4 59.5	19 22.5	2 39.8	19 17.0	5 03.9	22 05.8	29 02.3	21 30.1
20 Th	9 56 40	27 49 08	21 27 33	27 53 48	28 40.1	0 45.8	6 09.9	19 53.9	2 59.9	19 29.1	5 11.4	22 08.9	29 01.8	21 28.7
21 F	10 00 36	28 46 54	4♑15 51	10♑34 03	28 41.7	29♌53.3	7 20.1	20 25.0	3 20.2	19 41.0	5 19.0	22 12.0	29 01.1	21 27.4
22 Sa	10 04 33	29 44 41	16 48 46	23 00 22	28R 42.7	29 01.0	8 30.4	20 55.9	3 40.6	19 52.9	5 26.6	22 15.1	29 00.5	21 26.1
23 Su	10 08 30	0♍42 29	29 09 11	5♒15 32	28 42.6	28 10.1	9 40.5	21 26.4	4 01.0	20 04.7	5 34.1	22 18.2	28 59.8	21 24.8
24 M	10 12 26	1 40 18	11♒19 43	17 21 59	28 41.1	27 21.5	10 50.6	21 56.5	4 21.6	20 16.4	5 41.7	22 21.2	28 59.1	21 23.5
25 Tu	10 16 23	2 38 09	23 22 37	29 21 51	28 37.9	26 36.3	12 00.6	22 26.3	4 42.3	20 28.1	5 49.3	22 24.2	28 58.4	21 22.2
26 W	10 20 19	3 36 01	5♓19 53	11♓16 58	28 33.1	25 55.6	13 10.5	22 55.8	5 03.1	20 39.7	5 56.9	22 27.2	28 57.6	21 20.9
27 Th	10 24 16	4 33 54	17 13 19	23 09 08	28 27.1	25 20.3	14 20.4	23 24.9	5 24.0	20 51.2	6 04.5	22 30.1	28 56.8	21 19.6
28 F	10 28 12	5 31 50	29 04 41	5♈00 12	28 20.4	24 51.1	15 30.1	23 53.7	5 45.0	21 02.7	6 12.1	22 33.0	28 56.0	21 18.3
29 Sa	10 32 09	6 29 47	10♈55 57	16 52 15	28 13.6	24 28.8	16 39.8	24 22.0	6 06.1	21 14.1	6 19.7	22 35.9	28 55.1	21 17.0
30 Su	10 36 05	7 27 45	22 49 26	28 47 50	28 07.4	24 14.0	17 49.4	24 50.0	6 27.3	21 25.4	6 27.3	22 38.7	28 54.2	21 15.7
31 M	10 40 02	8 25 46	4♉47 52	10♉49 58	28 02.5	24D 07.1	18 59.0	25 17.6	6 48.6	21 36.6	6 34.9	22 41.5	28 53.3	21 14.4

Astro Data

	Dy Hr Mn
☽0N	5 11:31
☽0S	18 15:59
♆ R	1 13:57
☽0N	1 19:02
☿ R	8 5:45
♅⊼♇	11 16:37
☽0S	14 23:01
♀0S	16 11:14
☽0N	29 1:11
♃⊼♇	29 17:35
♃∠♄	31 0:48
☿ D	31 20:08

Planet Ingress

	Dy Hr Mn
☿ ♌	3 21:01
♄ ♍	7 2:31
♂ ♉	17 22:42
♀ ♍	21 0:22
☉ ♌	22 11:12
☿ ♍	25 14:09
⚳ ♏	11 8:12
♀ ♎	15 6:06
☿ ♌R	21 8:56
☉ ♍	22 18:22

Last Aspect / ☽ Ingress

Last Aspect Dy Hr Mn		☽ Ingress Dy Hr Mn
1 22:15 ♄ ☍	♓	1 23:17
3 14:20 ♅ △	♈	4 11:53
6 23:45 ♄ △	♉	6 23:46
8 18:42 ♇ □	♊	9 8:55
11 12:51 ♆ ⚹	♋	11 14:35
13 15:50 ♆ □	♌	13 17:28
15 17:19 ♆ △	♍	15 18:53
17 12:29 ☉ ⚹	♎	17 20:18
19 21:21 ♆ ☍	♏	19 22:55
22 2:54 ☉ △	♐	22 3:29
24 8:40 ♆ △	♑	24 10:20
26 17:47 ♆ □	♒	26 19:30
29 4:58 ♆ ⚹	♓	29 6:43
31 1:03 ♅ △	♈	31 19:16

Last Aspect / ☽ Ingress

Last Aspect Dy Hr Mn		☽ Ingress Dy Hr Mn
3 5:54 ♆ ☌	♉	3 7:38
5 2:17 ♇ □	♊	5 17:50
7 22:55 ♆ ⚹	♋	8 0:29
10 2:03 ♆ □	♌	10 3:32
12 2:43 ♆ △	♍	12 4:09
14 1:54 ♀ ☌	♎	14 4:08
16 3:44 ♆ ☍	♏	16 5:17
18 1:00 ☉ □	♐	18 9:02
20 14:07 ♆ △	♑	20 15:57
22 23:42 ♆ □	♒	23 1:40
25 11:13 ♆ ⚹	♓	25 13:17
27 12:33 ♂ ⚹	♈	28 1:52
30 12:13 ♆ ☌	♉	30 14:25

☽ Phases & Eclipses

Dy Hr Mn	
5 16:00	☾ 13♈58
13 2:32	● 21♋04
13 2:39:14	✔ T 03'58"
19 18:31	☽ 27♎26
27 4:15	○ 4♒30
27 4:08	☍ P 0.810
4 7:51	☾ 12♉17
11 10:41	● 19♌07
18 1:00	☽ 25♏27
25 19:09	○ 2♓55

Astro Data

1 July 2037
Julian Day # 50221
SVP 4♓44'24"
GC 27♐21.8 ⚴ 9♍48.9
Eris 28♈28.4 ⚵ 13♍03.1
⚷ 21♊22.2 ⚶ 28♈01.8
☽ Mean ☊ 29♋47.1

1 August 2037
Julian Day # 50252
SVP 4♓44'19"
GC 27♐21.9 ⚴ 22♍19.2
Eris 28♈31.0R ⚵ 23♍07.1
⚷ 23♊43.0 ⚶ 6♉56.9
☽ Mean ☊ 28♋08.6

LONGITUDE — September 2037

Day	Sid.Time	☉	0 hr ☽	Noon ☽	True ☊	☿	♀	♂	⚳	♃	♄	♅	♆	♇
1 Tu	10 43 59	9♍23 48	16♉54 34	23♉02 11	27♋59.3	24♌08.5	20♎08.4	25♉44.8	7♏10.0	21♋47.7	6♍42.5	22♋44.3	28♈52.4	21♒13.2
2 W	10 47 55	10 21 52	29 13 18	5♊28 28	27D57.8	24 18.3	21 17.8	26 11.6	7 31.5	21 58.8	6 50.1	22 47.1	28R51.4	21R11.9
3 Th	10 51 52	11 19 59	11♊48 11	18 13 00	27 57.9	24 36.6	22 27.1	26 37.9	7 53.1	22 09.7	6 57.7	22 49.8	28 50.5	21 10.7
4 F	10 55 48	12 18 07	24 43 24	1♋19 50	27 59.0	25 03.5	23 36.3	27 03.8	8 14.8	22 20.6	7 05.3	22 52.5	28 49.4	21 09.5
5 Sa	10 59 45	13 16 17	8♋02 43	14 52 21	28R00.2	25 38.6	24 45.4	27 29.3	8 36.6	22 31.4	7 12.8	22 55.1	28 48.4	21 08.3
6 Su	11 03 41	14 14 30	21 48 55	28 52 28	28 00.8	26 22.0	25 54.4	27 54.3	8 58.4	22 42.1	7 20.4	22 57.7	28 47.3	21 07.0
7 M	11 07 38	15 12 44	6♌02 53	13♌19 52	27 59.8	27 13.2	27 03.4	28 18.9	9 20.4	22 52.8	7 28.0	23 00.3	28 46.3	21 05.8
8 Tu	11 11 34	16 11 00	20 42 53	28 11 14	27 56.8	28 11.9	28 12.2	28 42.9	9 42.4	23 03.3	7 35.5	23 02.8	28 45.1	21 04.7
9 W	11 15 31	17 09 18	5♍43 58	13♍19 58	27 51.7	29 17.7	29 21.0	29 06.5	10 04.5	23 13.7	7 43.1	23 05.3	28 44.0	21 03.5
10 Th	11 19 27	18 07 37	20 57 58	28 36 38	27 44.9	0♍30.0	0♏29.7	29 29.6	10 26.7	23 24.1	7 50.6	23 07.8	28 42.8	21 02.3
11 F	11 23 24	19 05 59	6♎14 32	13♎50 20	27 37.1	1 48.5	1 38.2	29 52.2	10 49.0	23 34.3	7 58.1	23 10.2	28 41.6	21 01.2
12 Sa	11 27 21	20 04 22	21 22 44	28 50 36	27 29.5	3 12.4	2 46.7	0♊14.2	11 11.3	23 44.4	8 05.6	23 12.5	28 40.4	21 00.0
13 Su	11 31 17	21 02 46	6♏12 58	13♏29 08	27 23.1	4 41.3	3 55.1	0 35.7	11 33.8	23 54.5	8 13.1	23 14.9	28 39.2	20 58.9
14 M	11 35 14	22 01 13	20 38 33	27 40 56	27 18.4	6 14.5	5 03.3	0 56.7	11 56.3	24 04.4	8 20.6	23 17.2	28 37.9	20 57.8
15 Tu	11 39 10	22 59 41	4♐36 10	11♐24 20	27D15.9	7 51.6	6 11.5	1 17.1	12 18.9	24 14.2	8 28.0	23 19.4	28 36.7	20 56.7
16 W	11 43 07	23 58 10	18 05 40	24 40 31	27 15.3	9 31.9	7 19.5	1 36.9	12 41.5	24 24.0	8 35.4	23 21.6	28 35.4	20 55.6
17 Th	11 47 03	24 56 41	1♑09 19	7♑32 34	27 15.8	11 14.9	8 27.4	1 56.2	13 04.3	24 33.6	8 42.9	23 23.8	28 34.0	20 54.6
18 F	11 51 00	25 55 14	13 50 49	20 04 36	27R16.6	13 00.2	9 35.2	2 14.9	13 27.0	24 43.1	8 50.3	23 25.9	28 32.7	20 53.5
19 Sa	11 54 56	26 53 48	26 14 31	2♒21 05	27 16.7	14 47.3	10 42.8	2 33.0	13 49.9	24 52.5	8 57.6	23 28.0	28 31.4	20 52.5
20 Su	11 58 53	27 52 25	8♒24 50	14 26 15	27 15.1	16 35.7	11 50.3	2 50.6	14 12.8	25 01.8	9 05.0	23 30.1	28 30.0	20 51.5
21 M	12 02 50	28 51 02	20 25 48	26 23 54	27 11.2	18 25.2	12 57.7	3 07.4	14 35.8	25 10.9	9 12.3	23 32.1	28 28.6	20 50.5
22 Tu	12 06 46	29 49 42	2♓20 54	8♓17 10	27 04.6	20 15.4	14 05.0	3 23.7	14 58.9	25 20.0	9 19.6	23 34.0	28 27.2	20 49.5
23 W	12 10 43	0♎48 23	14 12 58	20 08 33	26 55.5	22 05.9	15 12.1	3 39.3	15 22.0	25 28.9	9 26.9	23 35.9	28 25.7	20 48.5
24 Th	12 14 39	1 47 07	26 04 11	2♈00 02	26 44.3	23 56.7	16 19.1	3 54.3	15 45.2	25 37.7	9 34.1	23 37.8	28 24.3	20 47.6
25 F	12 18 36	2 45 52	7♈56 17	13 53 08	26 31.9	25 47.4	17 25.9	4 08.6	16 08.4	25 46.4	9 41.3	23 39.6	28 22.8	20 46.6
26 Sa	12 22 32	3 44 39	19 50 44	25 49 17	26 19.3	27 37.9	18 32.5	4 22.2	16 31.7	25 55.0	9 48.5	23 41.3	28 21.3	20 45.7
27 Su	12 26 29	4 43 28	1♉48 58	7♉49 59	26 07.5	29 28.0	19 39.1	4 35.1	16 55.1	26 03.4	9 55.6	23 43.1	28 19.8	20 44.8
28 M	12 30 25	5 42 20	13 52 36	19 57 05	25 57.6	1♎17.7	20 45.4	4 47.3	17 18.5	26 11.7	10 02.8	23 44.7	28 18.3	20 44.0
29 Tu	12 34 22	6 41 14	26 03 44	2♊12 54	25 50.2	3 06.9	21 51.6	4 58.8	17 42.0	26 19.9	10 09.9	23 46.4	28 16.8	20 43.1
30 W	12 38 19	7 40 10	8♊24 58	14 40 22	25 45.5	4 55.4	22 57.6	5 09.5	18 05.5	26 28.0	10 16.9	23 47.9	28 15.3	20 42.3

LONGITUDE — October 2037

Day	Sid.Time	☉	0 hr ☽	Noon ☽	True ☊	☿	♀	♂	⚳	♃	♄	♅	♆	♇
1 Th	12 42 15	8♎39 08	20♊59 32	27♊22 57	25♋43.3	6♎43.2	24♏03.5	5♊19.5	18♏29.1	26♋35.9	10♍23.9	23♋49.5	28♈13.7	20♒41.5
2 F	12 46 12	9 38 09	3♋51 04	10♋24 24	25D42.8	8 30.3	25 09.2	5 28.7	18 52.7	26 43.7	10 30.9	23 51.0	28R12.1	20R40.7
3 Sa	12 50 08	10 37 12	17 03 22	23 48 24	25R43.0	10 16.6	26 14.7	5 37.2	19 16.4	26 51.4	10 37.9	23 52.4	28 10.6	20 39.9
4 Su	12 54 05	11 36 17	0♌39 48	7♌37 49	25 42.6	12 02.2	27 20.1	5 44.8	19 40.1	26 58.9	10 44.8	23 53.8	28 09.0	20 39.2
5 M	12 58 01	12 35 25	14 42 32	21 53 54	25 40.5	13 47.0	28 25.2	5 51.6	20 03.9	27 06.3	10 51.7	23 55.1	28 07.4	20 38.4
6 Tu	13 01 58	13 34 35	29 11 39	6♍35 18	25 35.8	15 30.9	29 30.2	5 57.6	20 27.8	27 13.5	10 58.5	23 56.4	28 05.8	20 37.7
7 W	13 05 54	14 33 47	14♍04 11	21 37 21	25 28.4	17 14.1	0♐34.9	6 02.8	20 51.7	27 20.6	11 05.3	23 57.6	28 04.2	20 37.0
8 Th	13 09 51	15 33 01	29 13 43	6♎51 58	25 18.6	18 56.5	1 39.5	6 07.1	21 15.6	27 27.6	11 12.0	23 58.8	28 02.5	20 36.4
9 F	13 13 48	16 32 17	14♎30 43	22 08 32	25 07.5	20 38.1	2 43.8	6 10.5	21 39.6	27 34.4	11 18.7	23 59.9	28 00.9	20 35.7
10 Sa	13 17 44	17 31 35	29 43 58	7♏15 40	24 56.3	22 18.9	3 48.0	6 13.1	22 03.6	27 41.0	11 25.4	24 01.0	27 59.2	20 35.1
11 Su	13 21 41	18 30 56	14♏42 28	22 03 22	24 46.4	23 58.9	4 51.9	6 14.9	22 27.7	27 47.5	11 32.0	24 02.0	27 57.6	20 34.5
12 M	13 25 37	19 30 18	29 17 35	6♐24 36	24 38.8	25 38.2	5 55.5	6R15.7	22 51.8	27 53.9	11 38.5	24 03.0	27 55.9	20 34.0
13 Tu	13 29 34	20 29 42	13♐24 07	20 16 03	24 33.8	27 16.8	6 59.0	6 15.7	23 16.0	28 00.1	11 45.1	24 03.9	27 54.3	20 33.4
14 W	13 33 30	21 29 08	27 00 30	3♑37 46	24 31.3	28 54.7	8 02.1	6 14.8	23 40.2	28 06.1	11 51.5	24 04.8	27 52.6	20 32.9
15 Th	13 37 27	22 28 35	10♑08 15	16 32 27	24 30.6	0♏31.8	9 05.0	6 13.0	24 04.4	28 12.0	11 57.9	24 05.6	27 50.9	20 32.4
16 F	13 41 23	23 28 04	22 50 58	29 04 23	24 30.5	2 08.3	10 07.7	6 10.3	24 28.7	28 17.7	12 04.3	24 06.3	27 49.3	20 32.0
17 Sa	13 45 20	24 27 35	5♒13 24	11♒18 38	24 29.9	3 44.1	11 10.0	6 06.7	24 53.0	28 23.3	12 10.6	24 07.0	27 47.6	20 31.5
18 Su	13 49 17	25 27 08	17 20 45	23 20 21	24 27.7	5 19.3	12 12.1	6 02.2	25 17.3	28 28.6	12 16.8	24 07.7	27 45.9	20 31.1
19 M	13 53 13	26 26 43	29 18 03	5♓14 24	24 23.0	6 53.8	13 13.8	5 56.9	25 41.7	28 33.9	12 23.0	24 08.3	27 44.2	20 30.7
20 Tu	13 57 10	27 26 19	11♓09 53	17 04 58	24 15.5	8 27.7	14 15.2	5 50.6	26 06.1	28 38.9	12 29.2	24 08.8	27 42.6	20 30.3
21 W	14 01 06	28 25 57	23 00 05	28 55 33	24 05.1	10 01.1	15 16.3	5 43.5	26 30.6	28 43.8	12 35.2	24 09.3	27 40.9	20 30.0
22 Th	14 05 03	29 25 37	4♈51 42	10♈48 47	23 52.3	11 33.8	16 17.1	5 35.5	26 55.1	28 48.5	12 41.2	24 09.8	27 39.2	20 29.7
23 F	14 08 59	0♏25 18	16 47 02	22 46 36	23 38.2	13 05.9	17 17.4	5 26.6	27 19.6	28 53.1	12 47.2	24 10.1	27 37.5	20 29.4
24 Sa	14 12 56	1 25 02	28 47 38	4♉50 17	23 23.8	14 37.5	18 17.5	5 16.9	27 44.1	28 57.5	12 53.1	24 10.5	27 35.8	20 29.1
25 Su	14 16 52	2 24 48	10♉54 38	17 00 47	23 10.3	16 08.5	19 17.1	5 06.3	28 08.7	29 01.7	12 58.9	24 10.7	27 34.2	20 28.9
26 M	14 20 49	3 24 36	23 08 52	29 18 59	22 58.8	17 39.0	20 16.4	4 54.8	28 33.3	29 05.7	13 04.7	24 11.0	27 32.5	20 28.6
27 Tu	14 24 45	4 24 26	5♊31 16	11♊45 54	22 50.1	19 08.9	21 15.3	4 42.6	28 57.9	29 09.5	13 10.4	24 11.1	27 30.8	20 28.4
28 W	14 28 42	5 24 18	18 03 04	24 23 00	22 44.4	20 38.2	22 13.7	4 29.5	29 22.6	29 13.2	13 16.0	24 11.2	27 29.2	20 28.3
29 Th	14 32 39	6 24 12	0♋45 59	7♋12 18	22 41.4	22 07.0	23 11.7	4 15.6	29 47.2	29 16.7	13 21.6	24R11.3	27 27.5	20 28.1
30 F	14 36 35	7 24 09	13 42 18	20 16 18	22D40.6	23 35.2	24 09.3	4 01.0	0♐12.0	29 20.0	13 27.1	24 11.3	27 25.8	20 28.0
31 Sa	14 40 32	8 24 07	26 54 39	3♌37 42	22R40.7	25 02.8	25 06.4	3 45.6	0 36.7	29 23.1	13 32.5	24 11.3	27 24.2	20 28.0

Astro Data

	Dy Hr Mn
♃☌♅	8 10:33
☽0S	11 8:11
♄∠♅	13 20:18
☉0S	22 16:12
☽0N	25 6:48
☿0S	29 18:41
☽0S	8 18:59
♃□♆	12 18:15
♂ R	12 23:09
♄⚻♆	22 5:36
☽0N	22 13:05
♅ R	30 1:59

Planet Ingress

		Dy Hr Mn
♀	♏	10 1:38
☿	♍	10 2:17
♂	♊	11 20:29
☉	♎	22 16:13
☿	♎	27 18:59
♀	♐	6 23:03
☿	♏	15 4:07
☉	♏	23 1:50
⚳	♐	30 0:24

Last Aspect / ☽ Ingress

Last Aspect Dy Hr Mn			☽ Ingress	Dy Hr Mn
1 17:28	♂	☌	♊	2 1:30
4 7:29	♆	⚹	♋	4 9:36
6 11:51	♆	□	♌	6 13:54
8 12:54	♆	△	♍	8 14:54
10 13:25	♂	△	♎	10 14:11
12 11:44	♆	☍	♏	12 13:52
14 5:45	♃	△	♐	14 16:00
16 19:13	♆	△	♑	16 21:51
19 4:29	♆	□	♒	19 7:22
21 16:11	♆	⚹	♓	21 19:16
23 22:57	♃	△	♈	24 7:57
26 17:04	♆	☌	♉	26 20:22
29 0:24	♃	⚹	♊	29 7:41

Last Aspect Dy Hr Mn			☽ Ingress	Dy Hr Mn
1 13:35	♆	⚹	♋	1 16:52
3 19:39	♆	□	♌	3 22:51
5 23:35	♀	□	♍	6 1:19
7 21:06	♃	⚹	♎	8 1:13
9 21:16	♆	☍	♏	10 0:25
11 21:34	♃	△	♐	12 1:11
14 2:14	☿	⚹	♑	14 5:24
16 10:29	♃	☍	♒	16 13:48
18 20:53	♆	⚹	♓	19 1:25
21 11:36	♃	△	♈	21 14:10
24 0:15	♃	□	♉	24 2:24
26 11:34	♃	⚹	♊	26 13:20
28 17:50	♆	⚹	♋	28 22:34
31 4:25	♃	☌	♌	31 5:32

☽ Phases & Eclipses

Dy Hr Mn		
2 22:03	☾	10♊46
9 18:25	●	17♍25
16 10:36	☽	23♐55
24 11:32	○	1♈46
2 10:29	☾	9♋34
9 2:34	●	16♎09
16 0:15	☽	22♑59
24 4:36	○	1♉07
31 21:06	☾	8♌47

Astro Data

1 September 2037
Julian Day # 50283
SVP 4♓44'16"
GC 27♐21.9 ⚴ 5♎34.5
Eris 28♈23.7R ⚵ 4♎00.8
⚷ 25♊22.9 ⚶ 11♉20.4
☽ Mean ☊ 26♋30.1

1 October 2037
Julian Day # 50313
SVP 4♓44'13"
GC 27♐22.0 ⚴ 18♎47.6
Eris 28♈09.2R ⚵ 14♎52.2
⚷ 26♊00.9 ⚶ 9♉20.8R
☽ Mean ☊ 24♋54.7

November 2037 — LONGITUDE

Day	Sid.Time	☉	0 hr ☽	Noon ☽	True ☊	☿	♀	♂	⚳	♃	♄	♅	♆	♇
1 Su	14 44 28	9♏24 08	10♌25 45	17♌19 03	22♋40.5	26♏29.9	26♐03.0	3♊29.5	1♐01.4	29♋26.1	13♍37.9	24♋11.1	27♈22.6	20♒27.9
2 M	14 48 25	10 24 11	24 17 45	1♍21 55	22R 38.9	27 56.3	26 59.1	3R 12.6	1 26.2	29 28.8	13 43.2	24R 11.0	27R 20.9	20D 27.9
3 Tu	14 52 21	11 24 16	8♍31 28	15 46 10	22 35.0	29 22.1	27 54.7	2 55.1	1 51.0	29 31.4	13 48.4	24 10.8	27 19.3	20 27.9
4 W	14 56 18	12 24 23	23 05 36	0♎29 09	22 28.4	0♐47.2	28 49.8	2 37.0	2 15.9	29 33.8	13 53.6	24 10.5	27 17.7	20 27.9
5 Th	15 00 14	13 24 32	7♎56 03	15 25 20	22 19.5	2 11.6	29 44.3	2 18.3	2 40.7	29 35.9	13 58.6	24 10.2	27 16.1	20 27.9
6 F	15 04 11	14 24 43	22 55 55	0♏26 34	22 09.1	3 35.2	0♑38.2	1 59.0	3 05.6	29 37.9	14 03.6	24 09.8	27 14.5	20 28.0
7 Sa	15 08 08	15 24 56	7♏56 05	15 23 14	21 58.6	4 57.9	1 31.5	1 39.2	3 30.5	29 39.7	14 08.5	24 09.4	27 12.9	20 28.1
8 Su	15 12 04	16 25 11	22 46 50	0♐05 52	21 49.1	6 19.8	2 24.2	1 19.0	3 55.4	29 41.3	14 13.4	24 08.9	27 11.3	20 28.3
9 M	15 16 01	17 25 28	7♐19 26	14 26 50	21 41.6	7 40.6	3 16.3	0 58.3	4 20.3	29 42.7	14 18.1	24 08.3	27 09.8	20 28.4
10 Tu	15 19 57	18 25 46	21 27 35	28 21 23	21 36.7	9 00.4	4 07.7	0 37.2	4 45.2	29 43.9	14 22.8	24 07.8	27 08.2	20 28.6
11 W	15 23 54	19 26 06	5♑08 09	11♑47 57	21D 34.4	10 18.9	4 58.3	0 15.9	5 10.2	29 44.9	14 27.4	24 07.1	27 06.7	20 28.8
12 Th	15 27 50	20 26 27	18 21 01	24 47 43	21 34.0	11 36.2	5 48.2	29♉54.3	5 35.2	29 45.8	14 31.9	24 06.4	27 05.2	20 29.1
13 F	15 31 47	21 26 49	1♒08 30	7♒23 54	21 34.6	12 51.9	6 37.3	29 32.4	6 00.1	29 46.4	14 36.3	24 05.7	27 03.7	20 29.3
14 Sa	15 35 43	22 27 13	13 34 33	19 41 04	21R 35.3	14 05.9	7 25.6	29 10.4	6 25.1	29 46.8	14 40.7	24 04.9	27 02.2	20 29.6
15 Su	15 39 40	23 27 38	25 44 06	1♓44 19	21 34.9	15 18.0	8 13.1	28 48.3	6 50.1	29R 47.0	14 44.9	24 04.0	27 00.7	20 30.0
16 M	15 43 37	24 28 05	7♓42 23	13 38 55	21 32.7	16 28.0	8 59.7	28 26.1	7 15.1	29 47.0	14 49.1	24 03.1	26 59.3	20 30.3
17 Tu	15 47 33	25 28 33	19 34 33	25 29 49	21 28.2	17 35.6	9 45.3	28 04.0	7 40.2	29 46.8	14 53.1	24 02.1	26 57.8	20 30.7
18 W	15 51 30	26 29 02	1♈25 17	7♈21 25	21 21.4	18 40.4	10 30.0	27 41.8	8 05.2	29 46.5	14 57.1	24 01.1	26 56.4	20 31.1
19 Th	15 55 26	27 29 33	13 18 40	19 17 24	21 12.6	19 42.2	11 13.7	27 19.8	8 30.2	29 45.9	15 01.0	24 00.1	26 55.0	20 31.5
20 F	15 59 23	28 30 05	25 17 57	1♉20 36	21 02.6	20 40.5	11 56.3	26 57.9	8 55.3	29 45.1	15 04.8	23 59.0	26 53.6	20 32.0
21 Sa	16 03 19	29 30 38	7♉25 33	13 33 00	20 52.2	21 34.8	12 37.9	26 36.2	9 20.3	29 44.1	15 08.5	23 57.8	26 52.3	20 32.5
22 Su	16 07 16	0♐31 13	19 43 02	25 55 45	20 42.5	22 24.6	13 18.3	26 14.7	9 45.4	29 43.0	15 12.2	23 56.6	26 50.9	20 33.0
23 M	16 11 12	1 31 49	2♊11 13	8♊29 26	20 34.4	23 09.4	13 57.5	25 53.5	10 10.4	29 41.6	15 15.7	23 55.4	26 49.6	20 33.5
24 Tu	16 15 09	2 32 27	14 50 25	21 14 10	20 28.4	23 48.4	14 35.5	25 32.7	10 35.5	29 40.0	15 19.1	23 54.1	26 48.3	20 34.1
25 W	16 19 06	3 33 06	27 40 41	4♋18 09	20 24.7	24 21.0	15 12.3	25 12.2	11 00.5	29 38.3	15 22.5	23 52.7	26 47.0	20 34.7
26 Th	16 23 02	4 33 47	10♋42 06	17 17 03	20D 23.4	24 46.5	15 47.7	24 52.2	11 25.6	29 36.3	15 25.7	23 51.3	26 45.8	20 35.3
27 F	16 26 59	5 34 29	23 54 55	0♌35 47	20 23.7	25 03.9	16 21.7	24 32.6	11 50.7	29 34.1	15 28.9	23 49.9	26 44.5	20 35.9
28 Sa	16 30 55	6 35 13	7♌19 44	14 06 52	20 25.0	25R 12.6	16 54.3	24 13.4	12 15.7	29 31.8	15 31.9	23 48.4	26 43.3	20 36.6
29 Su	16 34 52	7 35 58	20 57 17	27 51 03	20R 26.3	25 11.8	17 25.4	23 54.9	12 40.8	29 29.2	15 34.9	23 46.9	26 42.2	20 37.3
30 M	16 38 48	8 36 45	4♍48 14	11♍48 49	20 26.6	25 00.7	17 54.9	23 36.8	13 05.9	29 26.5	15 37.7	23 45.3	26 41.0	20 38.0

December 2037 — LONGITUDE

Day	Sid.Time	☉	0 hr ☽	Noon ☽	True ☊	☿	♀	♂	⚳	♃	♄	♅	♆	♇
1 Tu	16 42 45	9♐37 33	18♍52 43	25♍59 47	20♋25.4	24♐38.8	18♑22.9	23♉19.4	13♐30.9	29♋23.6	15♍40.5	23♋43.7	26♈39.9	20♒38.7
2 W	16 46 41	10 38 23	3♎09 46	10♎22 18	20R 22.3	24R 05.9	18 49.2	23R 02.6	13 56.0	29R 20.4	15 43.1	23R 42.1	26R 38.7	20 39.5
3 Th	16 50 38	11 39 14	17 36 55	24 53 02	20 17.6	23 21.9	19 13.7	22 46.4	14 21.1	29 17.1	15 45.7	23 40.4	26 37.7	20 40.3
4 F	16 54 35	12 40 07	2♏09 58	9♏26 58	20 11.8	22 27.2	19 36.5	22 31.0	14 46.1	29 13.6	15 48.1	23 38.6	26 36.6	20 41.1
5 Sa	16 58 31	13 41 01	16 43 13	23 57 53	20 05.8	21 23.0	19 57.4	22 16.2	15 11.2	29 09.9	15 50.4	23 36.8	26 35.6	20 42.0
6 Su	17 02 28	14 41 56	1♐10 08	8♐19 10	20 00.4	20 10.6	20 16.4	22 02.2	15 36.2	29 06.0	15 52.7	23 35.0	26 34.6	20 42.8
7 M	17 06 24	15 42 52	15 24 18	22 24 52	19 56.2	18 52.1	20 33.4	21 49.0	16 01.3	29 02.0	15 54.8	23 33.2	26 33.6	20 43.7
8 Tu	17 10 21	16 43 49	29 20 24	6♑10 29	19 53.6	17 30.1	20 48.3	21 36.5	16 26.3	28 57.7	15 56.8	23 31.3	26 32.6	20 44.6
9 W	17 14 17	17 44 47	12♑54 55	19 33 33	19D 52.8	16 07.1	21 01.2	21 24.8	16 51.3	28 53.3	15 58.8	23 29.3	26 31.7	20 45.6
10 Th	17 18 14	18 45 46	26 06 27	2♒33 45	19 53.4	14 46.1	21 11.8	21 14.0	17 16.4	28 48.7	16 00.6	23 27.3	26 30.8	20 46.6
11 F	17 22 11	19 46 46	8♒55 41	15 12 36	19 55.0	13 29.7	21 20.2	21 03.9	17 41.4	28 43.9	16 02.3	23 25.3	26 30.0	20 47.5
12 Sa	17 26 07	20 47 46	21 24 57	27 33 11	19 56.8	12 20.3	21 26.3	20 54.7	18 06.4	28 39.0	16 03.9	23 23.3	26 29.1	20 48.6
13 Su	17 30 04	21 48 47	3♓37 52	9♓39 34	19 58.3	11 19.6	21 30.0	20 46.2	18 31.3	28 33.9	16 05.3	23 21.2	26 28.3	20 49.6
14 M	17 34 00	22 49 48	15 38 54	21 36 27	19R 59.0	10 29.1	21R 31.3	20 38.7	18 56.3	28 28.6	16 06.7	23 19.1	26 27.6	20 50.6
15 Tu	17 37 57	23 50 49	27 32 52	3♈28 46	19 58.5	9 49.4	21 30.1	20 31.9	19 21.2	28 23.2	16 08.0	23 17.0	26 26.8	20 51.7
16 W	17 41 53	24 51 51	9♈24 44	15 21 23	19 56.8	9 20.9	21 26.5	20 26.0	19 46.2	28 17.6	16 09.1	23 14.8	26 26.1	20 52.8
17 Th	17 45 50	25 52 54	21 19 14	27 18 49	19 54.0	9 03.4	21 20.3	20 20.9	20 11.1	28 11.8	16 10.2	23 12.6	26 25.4	20 53.9
18 F	17 49 46	26 53 57	3♉20 38	9♉25 05	19 50.5	8D 56.5	21 11.7	20 16.7	20 36.0	28 06.0	16 11.1	23 10.4	26 24.8	20 55.1
19 Sa	17 53 43	27 55 00	15 32 34	21 43 23	19 46.7	8 59.7	21 00.5	20 13.3	21 00.8	27 59.9	16 11.9	23 08.1	26 24.2	20 56.3
20 Su	17 57 40	28 56 04	27 57 48	4♊16 00	19 43.2	9 12.1	20 46.8	20 10.6	21 25.7	27 53.8	16 12.7	23 05.8	26 23.6	20 57.4
21 M	18 01 36	29 57 08	10♊38 07	17 04 12	19 40.2	9 33.0	20 30.7	20 08.8	21 50.5	27 47.5	16 13.3	23 03.5	26 23.0	20 58.6
22 Tu	18 05 33	0♑58 13	23 34 15	0♋08 13	19 38.2	10 01.6	20 12.2	20D 07.8	22 15.3	27 41.0	16 13.8	23 01.2	26 22.5	20 59.9
23 W	18 09 29	1 59 18	6♋45 59	13 27 22	19D 37.3	10 37.2	19 51.3	20 07.6	22 40.1	27 34.4	16 14.1	22 58.8	26 22.0	21 01.1
24 Th	18 13 26	3 00 24	20 12 10	27 00 10	19 37.3	11 18.8	19 28.1	20 08.2	23 04.9	27 27.8	16 14.4	22 56.4	26 21.6	21 02.4
25 F	18 17 22	4 01 30	3♌51 06	10♌44 42	19 38.1	12 06.0	19 02.9	20 09.5	23 29.6	27 20.9	16R 14.6	22 54.0	26 21.1	21 03.7
26 Sa	18 21 19	5 02 37	17 40 42	24 38 49	19 39.3	12 58.0	18 35.6	20 11.6	23 54.4	27 14.0	16 14.6	22 51.6	26 20.8	21 05.0
27 Su	18 25 15	6 03 44	1♍38 48	8♍40 22	19 40.4	13 54.4	18 06.4	20 14.5	24 19.1	27 07.0	16 14.6	22 49.1	26 20.4	21 06.3
28 M	18 29 12	7 04 52	15 43 16	22 47 16	19 41.3	14 54.5	17 35.6	20 18.1	24 43.7	26 59.8	16 14.4	22 46.7	26 20.1	21 07.6
29 Tu	18 33 09	8 06 00	29 52 06	6♎57 30	19R 41.6	15 58.0	17 03.2	20 22.4	25 08.4	26 52.6	16 14.1	22 44.2	26 19.8	21 09.0
30 W	18 37 05	9 07 09	14♎03 14	21 09 00	19 41.4	17 04.4	16 29.6	20 27.4	25 33.0	26 45.2	16 13.7	22 41.7	26 19.5	21 10.4
31 Th	18 41 02	10 08 18	28 14 32	5♏19 31	19 40.7	18 13.5	15 54.9	20 33.1	25 57.6	26 37.8	16 13.2	22 39.2	26 19.3	21 11.8

Astro Data Dy Hr Mn	Planet Ingress Dy Hr Mn	Last Aspect Dy Hr Mn	☽ Ingress Dy Hr Mn	Last Aspect Dy Hr Mn	☽ Ingress Dy Hr Mn	☽ Phases & Eclipses Dy Hr Mn
♇D 3 3:37	☿ ♐ 3 22:40	2 5:33 ☿ □	♍ 2 9:42	1 17:41 ♃ ✶	♎ 1 18:43	7 12:03 ● 15♏25
☽0S 5 5:45	♀ ♑ 5 18:58	4 10:30 ♃ ✶	♎ 4 11:13	3 19:14 ♃ □	♏ 3 20:26	14 17:59 ☽ 22♒42
♃∠♄ 16 0:13	♂ ♉R 12 5:39	6 10:42 ♃ □	♏ 6 11:18	5 20:37 ♃ △	♐ 5 22:03	22 21:35 ○ 0♊55
♃R 16 2:17	☉ ♐ 21 23:38	8 11:20 ♃ △	♐ 8 11:50	7 19:09 ♆ △	♑ 8 1:09	30 6:06 ☾ 8♍22
☽0N 18 20:44		10 9:52 ♆ △	♑ 10 14:53	10 5:03 ♃ ☍	♒ 10 7:13	
☿R 28 22:02	☉ ♑ 21 13:07	12 21:23 ♃ ☍	♒ 12 21:50	12 9:54 ♆ ✶	♓ 12 16:49	6 23:38 ● 15♐11
		15 6:18 ♂ □	♓ 15 8:31	15 1:46 ♃ △	♈ 15 4:58	14 14:42 ☽ 22♓57
☽0S 2 14:33		17 20:40 ♃ △	♈ 17 21:07	17 13:45 ♃ □	♉ 17 17:21	22 13:38 ○ 1♋02
♀R 14 12:46		20 8:51 ♃ □	♉ 20 9:20	19 23:58 ♃ ✶	♊ 20 3:53	29 14:05 ☾ 8♎11
☽0N 16 5:23		22 19:16 ♃ ✶	♊ 22 19:49	22 5:09 ♆ ✶	♋ 22 11:45	
☿D 18 16:13		24 22:22 ♆ ✶	♋ 25 4:18	24 12:48 ♃ ☌	♌ 24 17:16	
♂D 23 6:31		27 10:10 ♃ ☌	♌ 27 10:56	26 14:55 ♆ △	♍ 26 21:11	
♄R 26 11:36		29 10:01 ♆ △	♍ 29 15:43	28 19:05 ♃ ✶	♎ 29 0:13	
☽0S 29 20:51				30 21:24 ♃ □	♏ 31 2:59	

Astro Data

1 November 2037
Julian Day # 50344
SVP 4♓44'10"
GC 27♐22.1 ⚴ 2♏35.0
Eris 27♈50.8R ⚵ 25♎59.7
⚷ 25♊29.5R ⚶ 2♉00.0R
☽ Mean ☊ 23♋16.2

1 December 2037
Julian Day # 50374
SVP 4♓44'06"
GC 27♐22.1 ⚴ 15♏45.3
Eris 27♈34.9R ⚵ 6♏14.3
⚷ 24♊01.8R ⚶ 26♈33.6R
☽ Mean ☊ 21♋40.9

LONGITUDE — January 2038

Day	Sid.Time	☉	0 hr ☽	Noon☽	True☊	☿	♀	♂	⚳	♃	♄	♅	♆	♇
1 F	18 44 58	11♑09 28	12♏23 38	19♏26 32	19♋39.7	19♐24.9	15♑19.3	20♉39.6	26♐22.2	26♋30.3	16♍12.6	22♋36.6	26♈19.1	21♒13.2
2 Sa	18 48 55	12 10 38	26 27 51	3♐27 13	19R38.7	20 38.3	14R43.1	20 46.7	26 46.7	26R22.7	16R11.9	22R34.1	26R19.0	21 14.6
3 Su	18 52 51	13 11 49	10♐24 15	17 18 36	19 37.9	21 53.6	14 06.6	20 54.5	27 11.2	26 15.0	16 11.1	22 31.5	26 18.9	21 16.1
4 M	18 56 48	14 12 59	24 09 54	0♑57 50	19 37.3	23 10.6	13 30.0	21 03.0	27 35.7	26 07.3	16 10.1	22 29.0	26 18.8	21 17.5
5 Tu	19 00 44	15 14 10	7♑42 08	14 22 31	19D37.1	24 29.0	12 53.5	21 12.2	28 00.1	25 59.5	16 09.1	22 26.4	26D18.8	21 19.0
6 W	19 04 41	16 15 21	20 58 51	27 30 58	19 37.1	25 48.7	12 17.4	21 21.9	28 24.5	25 51.6	16 07.9	22 23.8	26 18.7	21 20.5
7 Th	19 08 38	17 16 31	3♒58 49	10♒22 26	19 37.3	27 09.7	11 42.0	21 32.3	28 48.9	25 43.7	16 06.7	22 21.2	26 18.8	21 22.0
8 F	19 12 34	18 17 41	16 41 54	22 57 21	19 37.5	28 31.7	11 07.4	21 43.4	29 13.2	25 35.8	16 05.3	22 18.6	26 18.8	21 23.5
9 Sa	19 16 31	19 18 51	29 09 01	5♓17 12	19R37.6	29 54.7	10 33.9	21 55.0	29 37.5	25 27.8	16 03.8	22 16.0	26 18.9	21 25.1
10 Su	19 20 27	20 20 00	11♓22 13	17 24 30	19 37.5	1♑18.6	10 01.8	22 07.2	0♑01.7	25 19.7	16 02.2	22 13.4	26 19.1	21 26.6
11 M	19 24 24	21 21 09	23 24 29	29 22 39	19 37.4	2 43.4	9 31.1	22 20.0	0 25.9	25 11.7	16 00.5	22 10.8	26 19.2	21 28.2
12 Tu	19 28 20	22 22 17	5♈19 32	11♈15 41	19D37.2	4 09.0	9 02.2	22 33.3	0 50.1	25 03.6	15 58.7	22 08.2	26 19.4	21 29.8
13 W	19 32 17	23 23 25	17 11 41	23 08 08	19 37.2	5 35.3	8 35.1	22 47.3	1 14.2	24 55.6	15 56.8	22 05.6	26 19.7	21 31.3
14 Th	19 36 13	24 24 32	29 05 36	5♉04 42	19 37.3	7 02.4	8 10.1	23 01.7	1 38.3	24 47.5	15 54.8	22 03.0	26 19.9	21 32.9
15 F	19 40 10	25 25 38	11♉06 01	17 10 07	19 37.6	8 30.1	7 47.2	23 16.7	2 02.3	24 39.4	15 52.7	22 00.4	26 20.2	21 34.6
16 Sa	19 44 07	26 26 44	23 17 32	29 28 46	19 38.3	9 58.5	7 26.5	23 32.1	2 26.3	24 31.3	15 50.5	21 57.8	26 20.6	21 36.2
17 Su	19 48 03	27 27 49	5♊44 17	12♊04 28	19 39.1	11 27.5	7 08.1	23 48.1	2 50.2	24 23.3	15 48.2	21 55.2	26 21.0	21 37.8
18 M	19 52 00	28 28 54	18 29 38	25 00 02	19 39.9	12 57.1	6 52.1	24 04.6	3 14.1	24 15.2	15 45.8	21 52.6	26 21.4	21 39.5
19 Tu	19 55 56	29 29 57	1♋35 48	8♋17 00	19R40.5	14 27.3	6 38.6	24 21.5	3 37.9	24 07.2	15 43.3	21 50.0	26 21.8	21 41.1
20 W	19 59 53	0♒31 00	15 03 34	21 55 18	19 40.7	15 58.1	6 27.6	24 38.9	4 01.7	23 59.2	15 40.8	21 47.5	26 22.3	21 42.8
21 Th	20 03 49	1 32 03	28 51 55	5♌53 03	19 40.3	17 29.5	6 19.0	24 56.7	4 25.4	23 51.3	15 38.1	21 44.9	26 22.8	21 44.5
22 F	20 07 46	2 33 04	12♌58 10	20 06 41	19 39.2	19 01.5	6 13.0	25 15.0	4 49.1	23 43.3	15 35.3	21 42.4	26 23.4	21 46.1
23 Sa	20 11 42	3 34 05	27 17 58	4♍31 18	19 37.6	20 34.1	6D09.5	25 33.7	5 12.7	23 35.5	15 32.5	21 39.8	26 23.9	21 47.8
24 Su	20 15 39	4 35 06	11♍45 58	19 01 13	19 35.6	22 07.3	6 08.4	25 52.8	5 36.3	23 27.7	15 29.5	21 37.3	26 24.6	21 49.5
25 M	20 19 36	5 36 06	26 16 23	3♎30 47	19 33.7	23 41.1	6 09.8	26 12.3	5 59.8	23 19.9	15 26.5	21 34.8	26 25.2	21 51.2
26 Tu	20 23 32	6 37 05	10♎43 51	17 55 03	19 32.2	25 15.5	6 13.6	26 32.2	6 23.3	23 12.2	15 23.3	21 32.3	26 25.9	21 52.9
27 W	20 27 29	7 38 04	25 03 59	2♏10 16	19D31.4	26 50.6	6 19.8	26 52.5	6 46.7	23 04.6	15 20.1	21 29.8	26 26.6	21 54.7
28 Th	20 31 25	8 39 02	9♏13 39	16 13 57	19 31.4	28 26.2	6 28.2	27 13.2	7 10.0	22 57.0	15 16.8	21 27.3	26 27.3	21 56.4
29 F	20 35 22	9 40 00	23 11 02	0♐04 51	19 32.3	0♒02.6	6 39.0	27 34.2	7 33.3	22 49.6	15 13.5	21 24.9	26 28.1	21 58.1
30 Sa	20 39 18	10 40 57	6♐55 22	13 42 36	19 33.8	1 39.6	6 51.9	27 55.6	7 56.6	22 42.2	15 10.0	21 22.5	26 29.0	21 59.9
31 Su	20 43 15	11 41 53	20 26 34	27 07 19	19 35.3	3 17.2	7 06.9	28 17.4	8 19.7	22 34.9	15 06.5	21 20.1	26 29.8	22 01.6

LONGITUDE — February 2038

Day	Sid.Time	☉	0 hr ☽	Noon☽	True☊	☿	♀	♂	⚳	♃	♄	♅	♆	♇
1 M	20 47 11	12♒42 49	3♑44 53	10♑19 19	19♋36.4	4♒55.6	7♑24.0	28♉39.5	8♑42.8	22♋27.7	15♍02.9	21♋17.7	26♈30.7	22♒03.4
2 Tu	20 51 08	13 43 44	16 50 39	23 18 55	19R36.7	6 34.6	7 43.1	29 01.9	9 05.9	22R20.6	14R59.2	21R15.3	26 31.6	22 05.1
3 W	20 55 05	14 44 38	29 44 09	6♒06 22	19 35.6	8 14.4	8 04.1	29 24.7	9 28.8	22 13.6	14 55.4	21 13.0	26 32.6	22 06.9
4 Th	20 59 01	15 45 30	12♒25 37	18 41 56	19 33.2	9 54.9	8 27.0	29 47.8	9 51.7	22 06.8	14 51.6	21 10.7	26 33.5	22 08.6
5 F	21 02 58	16 46 22	24 55 23	1♓06 04	19 29.4	11 36.2	8 51.7	0♊11.2	10 14.6	22 00.0	14 47.7	21 08.4	26 34.5	22 10.4
6 Sa	21 06 54	17 47 12	7♓14 05	13 19 34	19 24.5	13 18.2	9 18.0	0 34.9	10 37.3	21 53.4	14 43.8	21 06.1	26 35.6	22 12.1
7 Su	21 10 51	18 48 01	19 22 44	25 23 47	19 19.1	15 00.9	9 46.1	0 59.0	11 00.0	21 46.9	14 39.7	21 03.9	26 36.7	22 13.9
8 M	21 14 47	19 48 49	1♈23 02	7♈20 45	19 13.7	16 44.5	10 15.7	1 23.3	11 22.6	21 40.5	14 35.6	21 01.7	26 37.8	22 15.7
9 Tu	21 18 44	20 49 35	13 17 21	19 13 13	19 09.0	18 28.8	10 46.9	1 47.9	11 45.2	21 34.3	14 31.5	20 59.5	26 38.9	22 17.4
10 W	21 22 40	21 50 19	25 08 49	1♉04 38	19 05.4	20 14.0	11 19.5	2 12.7	12 07.6	21 28.2	14 27.3	20 57.4	26 40.1	22 19.2
11 Th	21 26 37	22 51 02	7♉01 14	12 59 09	19D03.3	21 59.9	11 53.6	2 37.9	12 30.0	21 22.2	14 23.0	20 55.3	26 41.3	22 21.0
12 F	21 30 34	23 51 44	18 58 59	25 01 21	19 02.8	23 46.6	12 29.0	3 03.3	12 52.3	21 16.4	14 18.7	20 53.2	26 42.5	22 22.7
13 Sa	21 34 30	24 52 24	1♊06 51	7♊16 07	19 03.5	25 34.1	13 05.8	3 28.9	13 14.5	21 10.8	14 14.4	20 51.1	26 43.8	22 24.5
14 Su	21 38 27	25 53 02	13 29 43	19 48 15	19 05.0	27 22.3	13 43.8	3 54.8	13 36.7	21 05.3	14 10.0	20 49.1	26 45.0	22 26.3
15 M	21 42 23	26 53 38	26 12 15	2♋42 09	19 06.7	29 11.3	14 23.0	4 21.0	13 58.7	21 00.0	14 05.6	20 47.2	26 46.4	22 28.0
16 Tu	21 46 20	27 54 13	9♋18 21	16 01 07	19R07.6	1♓00.9	15 03.4	4 47.4	14 20.7	20 54.8	14 01.1	20 45.2	26 47.7	22 29.8
17 W	21 50 16	28 54 46	22 50 37	29 46 50	19 07.1	2 51.3	15 44.9	5 14.0	14 42.6	20 49.8	13 56.5	20 43.4	26 49.1	22 31.6
18 Th	21 54 13	29 55 18	6♌49 38	13♌58 38	19 04.8	4 42.2	16 27.5	5 40.8	15 04.3	20 44.9	13 52.0	20 41.5	26 50.5	22 33.3
19 F	21 58 09	0♓55 48	21 13 21	28 33 03	19 00.5	6 33.6	17 11.1	6 07.8	15 26.1	20 40.2	13 47.4	20 39.7	26 51.9	22 35.1
20 Sa	22 02 06	1 56 16	5♍56 53	13♍23 50	18 54.6	8 25.5	17 55.8	6 35.1	15 47.7	20 35.7	13 42.8	20 37.9	26 53.3	22 36.8
21 Su	22 06 03	2 56 43	20 52 47	28 22 35	18 47.7	10 17.6	18 41.4	7 02.5	16 09.2	20 31.4	13 38.1	20 36.2	26 54.8	22 38.6
22 M	22 09 59	3 57 08	5♎52 03	13♎20 04	18 40.8	12 09.9	19 27.9	7 30.2	16 30.6	20 27.2	13 33.4	20 34.5	26 56.3	22 40.3
23 Tu	22 13 56	4 57 32	20 45 36	28 07 44	18 34.8	14 02.2	20 15.3	7 58.0	16 52.0	20 23.3	13 28.7	20 32.8	26 57.9	22 42.1
24 W	22 17 52	5 57 54	5♏25 44	12♏39 00	18 30.4	15 54.2	21 03.6	8 26.0	17 13.2	20 19.5	13 24.0	20 31.2	26 59.4	22 43.8
25 Th	22 21 49	6 58 15	19 47 10	26 49 57	18D28.1	17 45.8	21 52.7	8 54.3	17 34.3	20 15.8	13 19.2	20 29.6	27 01.0	22 45.5
26 F	22 25 45	7 58 35	3♐47 18	10♐39 15	18 27.6	19 36.6	22 42.6	9 22.7	17 55.4	20 12.4	13 14.5	20 28.1	27 02.6	22 47.2
27 Sa	22 29 42	8 58 54	17 25 57	24 07 37	18 28.4	21 26.3	23 33.3	9 51.2	18 16.3	20 09.1	13 09.7	20 26.6	27 04.2	22 49.0
28 Su	22 33 38	9 59 11	0♑44 33	7♑17 05	18R29.6	23 14.5	24 24.6	10 20.0	18 37.2	20 06.1	13 04.9	20 25.2	27 05.9	22 50.7

Astro Data Dy Hr Mn	Planet Ingress Dy Hr Mn	Last Aspect Dy Hr Mn	☽ Ingress Dy Hr Mn	Last Aspect Dy Hr Mn	☽ Ingress Dy Hr Mn	☽ Phases & Eclipses Dy Hr Mn	Astro Data
♃□♆ 2 23:48	☿ ♑ 9 13:31	1 23:58 ♃ △	♐ 2 6:04	2 23:00 ♂ △	♒ 3 0:30	5 13:41 ● 15♑18	1 January 2038
♆ D 6 5:33	⚳ ♑ 10 10:18	4 3:47 ♆ △	♑ 4 10:18	5 3:11 ♆ ⚹	♓ 5 9:51	5 13:45:49 A 03'18"	Julian Day # 50405
☽ 0N 12 13:56	☉ ♒ 19 23:49	6 9:47 ♆ □	♒ 6 16:36	7 4:51 ♃ △	♈ 7 21:13	13 12:34 ☽ 23♈25	SVP 4♓44'00"
♅⚻♇ 21 14:35	☿ ♒ 29 11:22	9 0:09 ☿ ⚹	♓ 9 1:39	10 3:04 ♆ ☌	♉ 10 9:49	21 4:00 ○ 1♌12	GC 27♐22.2 ⚵ 28♏44.8
♀ D 24 10:19		11 3:41 ♃ △	♈ 11 13:15	12 9:30 ☉ □	♊ 12 21:49	21 3:48 A 0.899	Eris 27♈25.5R ⚶ 15♏39.9
☽ 0S 26 2:23	♂ ♊ 5 0:33	13 18:26 ♆ ☌	♉ 14 1:49	15 4:29 ☿ △	♋ 15 7:02	27 22:00 ☾ 8♏03	⚷ 22♊09.1R ⚴ 27♈29.0
	☿ ♓ 15 22:41	16 5:36 ☉ △	♊ 16 13:00	17 6:53 ♆ □	♌ 17 12:23		☽ Mean ☊ 20♋02.4
♃⚻♇ 4 6:51	☉ ♓ 18 13:52	18 14:29 ♆ ⚹	♋ 18 21:07	19 9:15 ♆ △	♍ 19 14:22	4 5:52 ● 15♒30	1 February 2038
☽ 0N 8 21:26		20 19:43 ♆ □	♌ 21 1:57	20 23:35 ♅ ⚹	♎ 21 14:36	12 9:30 ☽ 23♉45	Julian Day # 50436
♃☌♅ 19 16:55		22 22:29 ♆ △	♍ 23 4:30	23 10:06 ♆ ☍	♏ 23 15:04	19 16:09 ○ 1♍06	SVP 4♓43'55"
☽ 0S 22 9:40		24 23:37 ♂ △	♎ 25 6:10	25 5:02 ♇ □	♐ 25 17:27	26 6:56 ☾ 7♐46	GC 27♐22.3 ⚵ 10♐26.4
		27 2:19 ♆ ☍	♏ 27 8:19	27 17:20 ♆ △	♑ 27 22:39		Eris 27♈26.3 ⚶ 23♏00.6
		29 7:30 ♂ ☍	♐ 29 11:52				⚷ 20♊44.4R ⚴ 4♉02.6
		31 10:52 ♆ △	♑ 31 17:12				☽ Mean ☊ 18♋23.9

March 2038 — LONGITUDE

Day	Sid.Time	☉	0 hr ☽	Noon ☽	True ☊	☿	♀	♂	⚳	♃	♄	♅	♆	♇
1 M	22 37 35	10♓59 26	13♑45 32	20♑10 16	18♋30.0	25♓00.9	25♑16.7	10♊48.9	18♑57.9	20♋03.2	13♍00.1	20♋23.8	27♈07.6	22♒52.4
2 Tu	22 41 32	11 59 40	26 31 36	2♒49 51	18R 28.9	26 45.0	26 09.4	11 18.0	19 18.6	20R 00.5	12R 55.3	20R 22.4	27 09.3	22 54.1
3 W	22 45 28	12 59 52	9♒05 17	15 18 11	18 25.4	28 26.3	27 02.8	11 47.3	19 39.1	19 58.0	12 50.5	20 21.1	27 11.0	22 55.7
4 Th	22 49 25	14 00 03	21 28 44	27 37 08	18 19.3	0♈04.3	27 56.7	12 16.7	19 59.5	19 55.7	12 45.7	20 19.9	27 12.7	22 57.4
5 F	22 53 21	15 00 12	3♓43 35	9♓48 11	18 10.7	1 38.4	28 51.3	12 46.3	20 19.8	19 53.6	12 40.9	20 18.7	27 14.5	22 59.1
6 Sa	22 57 18	16 00 19	15 51 06	21 52 28	18 00.1	3 08.1	29 46.4	13 16.0	20 40.0	19 51.7	12 36.1	20 17.5	27 16.3	23 00.7
7 Su	23 01 14	17 00 24	27 52 24	3♈51 04	17 48.4	4 32.8	0♒42.1	13 45.9	21 00.0	19 50.0	12 31.3	20 16.4	27 18.1	23 02.4
8 M	23 05 11	18 00 27	9♈48 37	15 45 15	17 36.4	5 51.9	1 38.2	14 16.0	21 20.0	19 48.4	12 26.5	20 15.3	27 20.0	23 04.0
9 Tu	23 09 07	19 00 28	21 41 12	27 36 44	17 25.4	7 05.0	2 34.9	14 46.1	21 39.8	19 47.1	12 21.8	20 14.3	27 21.8	23 05.7
10 W	23 13 04	20 00 28	3♉32 10	9♉27 51	17 16.2	8 11.4	3 32.1	15 16.5	21 59.5	19 46.0	12 17.0	20 13.4	27 23.7	23 07.3
11 Th	23 17 01	21 00 25	15 24 11	21 21 39	17 09.4	9 10.8	4 29.7	15 46.9	22 19.1	19 45.1	12 12.3	20 12.5	27 25.6	23 08.9
12 F	23 20 57	22 00 20	27 20 42	3♊21 54	17 05.2	10 02.7	5 27.8	16 17.5	22 38.5	19 44.3	12 07.6	20 11.6	27 27.5	23 10.5
13 Sa	23 24 54	23 00 12	9♊25 50	15 33 04	17D 03.4	10 46.8	6 26.3	16 48.2	22 57.9	19 43.8	12 02.9	20 10.8	27 29.4	23 12.0
14 Su	23 28 50	24 00 03	21 44 16	28 00 02	17 03.2	11 22.7	7 25.2	17 19.1	23 17.1	19 43.4	11 58.3	20 10.0	27 31.4	23 13.6
15 M	23 32 47	24 59 51	4♋20 59	10♋47 44	17R 03.6	11 50.2	8 24.5	17 50.0	23 36.1	19D 43.3	11 53.7	20 09.3	27 33.3	23 15.2
16 Tu	23 36 43	25 59 38	17 20 49	24 00 42	17 03.6	12 09.3	9 24.2	18 21.1	23 55.0	19 43.3	11 49.1	20 08.7	27 35.3	23 16.7
17 W	23 40 40	26 59 21	0♌47 47	7♌42 16	17 01.9	12R 19.9	10 24.3	18 52.3	24 13.8	19 43.6	11 44.5	20 08.1	27 37.3	23 18.2
18 Th	23 44 36	27 59 03	14 44 14	21 53 35	16 57.9	12 22.0	11 24.8	19 23.6	24 32.5	19 44.0	11 40.0	20 07.6	27 39.3	23 19.8
19 F	23 48 33	28 58 43	29 09 58	6♍32 50	16 51.2	12 15.9	12 25.6	19 55.0	24 51.0	19 44.7	11 35.5	20 07.1	27 41.3	23 21.3
20 Sa	23 52 29	29 58 20	14♍01 22	21 34 33	16 42.1	12 01.9	13 26.7	20 26.5	25 09.4	19 45.5	11 31.1	20 06.6	27 43.4	23 22.7
21 Su	23 56 26	0♈57 55	29 11 09	6♎49 50	16 31.6	11 40.4	14 28.2	20 58.1	25 27.6	19 46.5	11 26.7	20 06.2	27 45.4	23 24.2
22 M	0 00 23	1 57 28	14♎29 09	22 07 37	16 20.8	11 12.0	15 30.0	21 29.9	25 45.7	19 47.7	11 22.3	20 05.9	27 47.5	23 25.7
23 Tu	0 04 19	2 56 59	29 43 50	7♏16 32	16 11.1	10 37.4	16 32.1	22 01.7	26 03.6	19 49.1	11 18.1	20 05.6	27 49.6	23 27.1
24 W	0 08 16	3 56 29	14♏44 35	22 07 05	16 03.5	9 57.4	17 34.5	22 33.6	26 21.4	19 50.7	11 13.8	20 05.4	27 51.7	23 28.5
25 Th	0 12 12	4 55 57	29 23 22	6♐32 59	15 58.5	9 13.0	18 37.2	23 05.6	26 39.0	19 52.4	11 09.6	20 05.2	27 53.8	23 29.9
26 F	0 16 09	5 55 23	13♐35 42	20 31 30	15 56.0	8 25.1	19 40.2	23 37.7	26 56.5	19 54.4	11 05.5	20 05.1	27 55.9	23 31.3
27 Sa	0 20 05	6 54 47	27 20 31	4♑03 00	15 55.4	7 34.8	20 43.5	24 09.9	27 13.8	19 56.5	11 01.4	20D 05.0	27 58.1	23 32.7
28 Su	0 24 02	7 54 10	10♑39 21	17 10 00	15 55.4	6 43.3	21 47.0	24 42.2	27 31.0	19 58.9	10 57.4	20 05.0	28 00.2	23 34.1
29 M	0 27 58	8 53 31	23 35 27	29 56 13	15 54.8	5 51.5	22 50.8	25 14.6	27 48.0	20 01.4	10 53.4	20 05.1	28 02.4	23 35.4
30 Tu	0 31 55	9 52 50	6♒12 49	12♒25 44	15 52.6	5 00.5	23 54.8	25 47.0	28 04.8	20 04.1	10 49.5	20 05.2	28 04.5	23 36.7
31 W	0 35 52	10 52 07	18 35 29	24 42 29	15 47.8	4 11.3	24 59.0	26 19.6	28 21.5	20 07.0	10 45.7	20 05.3	28 06.7	23 38.0

April 2038 — LONGITUDE

Day	Sid.Time	☉	0 hr ☽	Noon ☽	True ☊	☿	♀	♂	⚳	♃	♄	♅	♆	♇
1 Th	0 39 48	11♈51 22	0♓47 10	6♓49 54	15♋40.1	3♈24.7	26♒03.5	26♊52.2	28♑38.0	20♋10.0	10♍41.9	20♋05.5	28♈08.9	23♒39.3
2 F	0 43 45	12 50 36	12 50 59	18 50 43	15R 29.4	2R 41.5	27 08.2	27 24.9	28 54.3	20 13.3	10R 38.2	20 05.8	28 11.1	23 40.6
3 Sa	0 47 41	13 49 47	24 49 21	0♈47 06	15 16.3	2 02.3	28 13.1	27 57.7	29 10.4	20 16.7	10 34.6	20 06.1	28 13.3	23 41.8
4 Su	0 51 38	14 48 57	6♈44 08	12 40 38	15 01.9	1 27.6	29 18.2	28 30.6	29 26.4	20 20.3	10 31.0	20 06.5	28 15.5	23 43.1
5 M	0 55 34	15 48 04	18 36 46	24 32 42	14 47.2	0 57.9	0♓23.5	29 03.6	29 42.1	20 24.1	10 27.6	20 06.9	28 17.7	23 44.3
6 Tu	0 59 31	16 47 10	0♉28 34	6♉24 34	14 33.4	0 33.3	1 28.9	29 36.6	29 57.7	20 28.0	10 24.2	20 07.4	28 20.0	23 45.4
7 W	1 03 27	17 46 13	12 20 55	18 17 51	14 21.7	0 14.2	2 34.6	0♋09.7	0♒13.1	20 32.1	10 20.8	20 07.9	28 22.2	23 46.6
8 Th	1 07 24	18 45 14	24 15 38	0♊14 36	14 12.6	0 00.5	3 40.4	0 42.9	0 28.3	20 36.4	10 17.6	20 08.5	28 24.4	23 47.8
9 F	1 11 21	19 44 13	6♊15 05	12 17 30	14 06.6	29♓52.3	4 46.4	1 16.2	0 43.3	20 40.9	10 14.5	20 09.1	28 26.7	23 48.9
10 Sa	1 15 17	20 43 10	18 22 18	24 29 59	14 03.3	29D 49.6	5 52.6	1 49.5	0 58.2	20 45.5	10 11.4	20 09.8	28 28.9	23 50.0
11 Su	1 19 14	21 42 05	0♋41 05	6♋56 07	14D 02.1	29 52.2	6 58.9	2 22.9	1 12.8	20 50.3	10 08.4	20 10.5	28 31.2	23 51.1
12 M	1 23 10	22 40 57	13 15 41	19 40 21	14R 02.1	0♈00.0	8 05.4	2 56.4	1 27.2	20 55.3	10 05.5	20 11.3	28 33.4	23 52.1
13 Tu	1 27 07	23 39 47	26 10 41	2♌47 11	14 01.9	0 12.9	9 12.0	3 29.9	1 41.4	21 00.4	10 02.7	20 12.2	28 35.7	23 53.2
14 W	1 31 03	24 38 35	9♌30 18	16 20 25	14 00.4	0 30.7	10 18.8	4 03.5	1 55.4	21 05.7	10 00.0	20 13.1	28 37.9	23 54.2
15 Th	1 35 00	25 37 20	23 17 46	0♍22 24	13 56.8	0 53.1	11 25.7	4 37.1	2 09.2	21 11.1	9 57.3	20 14.0	28 40.2	23 55.2
16 F	1 38 56	26 36 03	7♍34 14	14 52 56	13 50.6	1 20.1	12 32.8	5 10.8	2 22.8	21 16.7	9 54.8	20 15.0	28 42.5	23 56.2
17 Sa	1 42 53	27 34 44	22 17 57	29 48 27	13 42.0	1 51.3	13 40.0	5 44.6	2 36.1	21 22.5	9 52.3	20 16.1	28 44.7	23 57.1
18 Su	1 46 50	28 33 23	7♎23 27	15♎01 42	13 31.9	2 26.7	14 47.3	6 18.4	2 49.3	21 28.4	9 50.0	20 17.2	28 47.0	23 58.1
19 M	1 50 46	29 32 00	22 41 50	0♏22 23	13 21.4	3 05.9	15 54.8	6 52.3	3 02.2	21 34.4	9 47.7	20 18.4	28 49.3	23 59.0
20 Tu	1 54 43	0♉30 35	8♏01 51	15 38 49	13 11.7	3 49.0	17 02.3	7 26.2	3 14.9	21 40.6	9 45.5	20 19.6	28 51.5	23 59.8
21 W	1 58 39	1 29 08	23 11 56	0♐40 05	13 04.1	4 35.5	18 10.1	8 00.2	3 27.3	21 47.0	9 43.5	20 20.8	28 53.8	24 00.7
22 Th	2 02 36	2 27 39	8♐07 19	15 17 56	12 58.9	5 25.5	19 17.9	8 34.2	3 39.6	21 53.5	9 41.5	20 22.1	28 56.0	24 01.5
23 F	2 06 32	3 26 09	22 26 28	29 27 41	12D 56.3	6 18.8	20 25.9	9 08.3	3 51.6	22 00.1	9 39.6	20 23.5	28 58.3	24 02.4
24 Sa	2 10 29	4 24 37	6♑21 32	13♑08 09	12 55.6	7 15.1	21 33.9	9 42.5	4 03.3	22 06.9	9 37.8	20 24.9	29 00.6	24 03.2
25 Su	2 14 25	5 23 04	19 47 50	26 20 59	12R 56.0	8 14.4	22 42.1	10 16.6	4 14.9	22 13.8	9 36.1	20 26.4	29 02.8	24 03.9
26 M	2 18 22	6 21 29	2♒48 03	9♒09 35	12 56.2	9 16.6	23 50.4	10 50.9	4 26.1	22 20.9	9 34.5	20 27.9	29 05.1	24 04.7
27 Tu	2 22 19	7 19 52	15 26 10	21 38 23	12 55.1	10 21.5	24 58.8	11 25.2	4 37.2	22 28.1	9 33.1	20 29.4	29 07.3	24 05.4
28 W	2 26 15	8 18 14	27 46 48	3♓51 59	12 52.0	11 29.0	26 07.3	11 59.5	4 47.9	22 35.4	9 31.7	20 31.0	29 09.6	24 06.1
29 Th	2 30 12	9 16 34	9♓54 29	15 54 48	12 46.5	12 39.1	27 15.9	12 33.9	4 58.5	22 42.9	9 30.4	20 32.7	29 11.8	24 06.7
30 F	2 34 08	10 14 53	21 53 24	27 50 43	12 38.5	13 51.6	28 24.6	13 08.3	5 08.7	22 50.5	9 29.2	20 34.4	29 14.1	24 07.4

Astro Data

	Dy Hr Mn
☿0N	3 22:44
☽0N	8 3:50
♄□♆	9 11:56
♃ D	15 17:52
☿ R	18 6:06
☉0N	20 12:40
☽0S	21 19:33
♅ D	28 4:27
♃☌♅	30 21:41
☽0N	4 9:48
☿0S	9 7:38
☿ D	10 12:12
☽0S	18 6:45
☿0N	22 15:08

Planet Ingress

	Dy Hr Mn
☿ ♈	4 10:56
♀ ♒	6 17:53
☉ ♈	20 12:40
♀ ♓	5 3:23
⚳ ♒	6 15:32
♂ ♋	7 4:57
☿ ♓R	8 13:08
☿ ♈	12 11:56
☉ ♉	19 23:28

Last Aspect / ☽ Ingress

Dy Hr Mn		☽ Ingress Dy Hr Mn
2 1:10	♆ □	♒ 2 6:36
4 11:12	♅ ⚹	♓ 4 16:40
6 8:51	♅ △	♈ 7 4:16
9 11:30	♅ ☌	♉ 9 16:50
11 15:36	♇ □	♊ 12 5:18
14 11:05	♆ ⚹	♋ 14 15:48
16 18:22	♆ □	♌ 16 22:36
18 21:33	♆ △	♍ 19 1:22
20 10:08	♂ □	♎ 21 1:17
22 20:57	♆ ☍	♏ 23 0:26
24 14:14	♇ □	♐ 25 1:01
27 1:05	♆ △	♑ 27 4:44
29 8:23	♆ □	♒ 29 12:07
31 18:44	♆ ⚹	♓ 31 22:27

Last Aspect / ☽ Ingress

Dy Hr Mn		☽ Ingress Dy Hr Mn
3 6:03	♂ □	♈ 3 10:25
5 21:35	♂ ⚹	♉ 5 23:02
7 23:03	♇ □	♊ 8 11:31
10 22:21	☿ □	♋ 10 22:41
13 4:23	♆ □	♌ 13 6:58
15 9:07	♆ △	♍ 15 11:22
16 22:25	♃ ⚹	♎ 17 12:18
19 10:36	☉ ☍	♏ 19 11:25
21 1:17	♇ □	♐ 21 10:55
23 11:09	♆ △	♑ 23 12:56
25 17:01	♆ □	♒ 25 18:46
28 2:41	♆ ⚹	♓ 28 4:22
30 13:16	♀ ☌	♈ 30 16:21

☽ Phases & Eclipses

Dy Hr Mn		
5 23:15	●	15♓28
14 3:41	☽	23♊39
21 2:09	○	0♎33
27 17:36	☾	7♑09
4 16:43	●	15♈01
12 18:02	☽	22♋56
19 10:36	○	29♎29
26 6:15	☾	6♒07

Astro Data

1 March 2038
Julian Day # 50464
SVP 4♓43'52"
GC 27♐22.3 ⚴ 18♐59.8
Eris 27♈35.7 ⚵ 26♏45.9
⚷ 20♊23.5 ⚶ 12♋56.5
☽ Mean ☊ 16♋55.0

1 April 2038
Julian Day # 50495
SVP 4♓43'49"
GC 27♐22.4 ⚴ 24♐40.5
Eris 27♈53.1 ⚵ 26♏22.8R
⚷ 21♊11.6 ⚶ 24♋38.4
☽ Mean ☊ 15♋16.5

LONGITUDE — May 2038

Day	Sid.Time	☉	0 hr ☽	Noon ☽	True ☊	☿	♀	♂	⚳	♃	♄	♅	♆	♇
1 Sa	2 38 05	11♉13 10	3♈47 08	9♈43 00	12♋28.4	15♈06.5	29♓33.4	13♋42.8	5♒18.7	22♋58.2	9♍28.1	20♋36.1	29♈16.3	24♒08.0
2 Su	2 42 01	12 11 25	15 38 36	21 34 13	12R 17.2	16 23.7	0♈42.2	14 17.4	5 28.4	23 06.1	9R 27.2	20 37.9	29 18.5	24 08.6
3 M	2 45 58	13 09 39	27 30 06	3♉26 26	12 05.6	17 43.2	1 51.2	14 51.9	5 37.9	23 14.1	9 26.3	20 39.7	29 20.7	24 09.2
4 Tu	2 49 54	14 07 51	9♉23 25	15 21 13	11 54.8	19 04.9	3 00.2	15 26.6	5 47.0	23 22.2	9 25.5	20 41.6	29 22.9	24 09.7
5 W	2 53 51	15 06 01	21 20 02	27 20 02	11 45.6	20 28.7	4 09.3	16 01.3	5 55.9	23 30.4	9 24.9	20 43.6	29 25.1	24 10.2
6 Th	2 57 47	16 04 10	3♊21 25	9♊24 23	11 38.7	21 54.7	5 18.5	16 36.0	6 04.5	23 38.8	9 24.3	20 45.5	29 27.3	24 10.7
7 F	3 01 44	17 02 17	15 29 09	21 36 01	11 34.2	23 22.8	6 27.8	17 10.7	6 12.9	23 47.3	9 23.9	20 47.6	29 29.5	24 11.2
8 Sa	3 05 41	18 00 22	27 45 14	3♋57 09	11D 32.2	24 52.9	7 37.1	17 45.6	6 20.9	23 55.9	9 23.5	20 49.6	29 31.7	24 11.6
9 Su	3 09 37	18 58 25	10♋12 08	16 30 32	11 32.0	26 25.1	8 46.5	18 20.4	6 28.6	24 04.6	9 23.3	20 51.7	29 33.9	24 12.1
10 M	3 13 34	19 56 27	22 52 48	29 19 19	11 32.9	27 59.3	9 56.0	18 55.3	6 36.1	24 13.4	9D 23.1	20 53.9	29 36.0	24 12.4
11 Tu	3 17 30	20 54 26	5♌50 31	12♌26 48	11R 33.9	29 35.6	11 05.6	19 30.2	6 43.2	24 22.4	9 23.1	20 56.1	29 38.2	24 12.8
12 W	3 21 27	21 52 24	19 08 32	25 56 02	11 34.1	1♉13.9	12 15.2	20 05.2	6 50.1	24 31.5	9 23.2	20 58.3	29 40.3	24 13.1
13 Th	3 25 23	22 50 20	2♍49 32	9♍49 09	11 32.7	2 54.2	13 24.8	20 40.2	6 56.6	24 40.6	9 23.4	21 00.6	29 42.4	24 13.5
14 F	3 29 20	23 48 14	16 54 52	24 06 32	11 29.5	4 36.5	14 34.6	21 15.2	7 02.8	24 49.9	9 23.7	21 02.9	29 44.5	24 13.7
15 Sa	3 33 17	24 46 06	1♎23 48	8♎46 07	11 24.5	6 20.8	15 44.4	21 50.3	7 08.7	24 59.3	9 24.0	21 05.2	29 46.6	24 14.0
16 Su	3 37 13	25 43 56	16 12 46	23 42 52	11 18.3	8 07.2	16 54.2	22 25.4	7 14.3	25 08.7	9 24.5	21 07.6	29 48.7	24 14.2
17 M	3 41 10	26 41 45	1♏15 20	8♏49 01	11 11.6	9 55.6	18 04.1	23 00.6	7 19.6	25 18.3	9 25.1	21 10.1	29 50.8	24 14.4
18 Tu	3 45 06	27 39 32	16 22 40	23 55 01	11 05.4	11 46.0	19 14.1	23 35.8	7 24.6	25 28.0	9 25.8	21 12.5	29 52.9	24 14.6
19 W	3 49 03	28 37 18	1♐24 51	8♐51 03	11 00.6	13 38.4	20 24.1	24 11.0	7 29.3	25 37.8	9 26.7	21 15.0	29 54.9	24 14.8
20 Th	3 52 59	29 35 03	16 12 37	23 28 43	10 57.5	15 32.9	21 34.3	24 46.2	7 33.6	25 47.7	9 27.6	21 17.6	29 57.0	24 14.9
21 F	3 56 56	0♊32 46	0♑38 44	7♑42 11	10D 56.3	17 29.3	22 44.4	25 21.5	7 37.6	25 57.7	9 28.6	21 20.2	29 59.0	24 15.0
22 Sa	4 00 52	1 30 28	14 38 50	21 28 36	10 56.6	19 27.7	23 54.6	25 56.8	7 41.3	26 07.7	9 29.7	21 22.8	0♉01.0	24 15.1
23 Su	4 04 49	2 28 10	28 11 34	4♒47 56	10 57.9	21 28.0	25 04.9	26 32.2	7 44.6	26 17.9	9 30.9	21 25.5	0 03.0	24 15.2
24 M	4 08 46	3 25 50	11♒18 03	17 42 18	10 59.4	23 30.1	26 15.3	27 07.6	7 47.6	26 28.1	9 32.2	21 28.1	0 04.9	24R 15.2
25 Tu	4 12 42	4 23 29	24 01 12	0♓15 16	11R 00.3	25 34.0	27 25.6	27 43.0	7 50.2	26 38.5	9 33.7	21 30.9	0 06.9	24 15.2
26 W	4 16 39	5 21 07	6♓25 04	12 31 11	11 00.1	27 39.5	28 36.1	28 18.4	7 52.5	26 48.9	9 35.2	21 33.6	0 08.8	24 15.2
27 Th	4 20 35	6 18 44	18 34 12	24 34 41	10 58.5	29 46.6	29 46.6	28 53.9	7 54.5	26 59.4	9 36.8	21 36.4	0 10.8	24 15.1
28 F	4 24 32	7 16 20	0♈33 11	6♈30 15	10 55.4	1♊55.0	0♉57.1	29 29.4	7 56.1	27 10.0	9 38.5	21 39.2	0 12.7	24 15.0
29 Sa	4 28 28	8 13 55	12 26 22	18 22 02	10 51.0	4 04.6	2 07.7	0♌05.0	7 57.3	27 20.7	9 40.4	21 42.1	0 14.5	24 14.9
30 Su	4 32 25	9 11 30	24 17 39	0♉13 38	10 45.8	6 15.2	3 18.4	0 40.6	7 58.2	27 31.5	9 42.3	21 45.0	0 16.4	24 14.8
31 M	4 36 21	10 09 03	6♉10 21	12 08 07	10 40.3	8 26.6	4 29.1	1 16.2	7R 58.7	27 42.3	9 44.3	21 47.9	0 18.2	24 14.7

LONGITUDE — June 2038

Day	Sid.Time	☉	0 hr ☽	Noon ☽	True ☊	☿	♀	♂	⚳	♃	♄	♅	♆	♇
1 Tu	4 40 18	11♊06 35	18♉07 12	24♉07 53	10♋35.2	10♊38.4	5♉39.8	1♌51.9	7♒58.9	27♋53.3	9♍46.4	21♋50.9	0♉20.1	24♒14.5
2 W	4 44 15	12 04 07	0♊10 22	6♊14 52	10R 30.9	12 50.5	6 50.6	2 27.6	7R 58.7	28 04.3	9 48.7	21 53.8	0 21.9	24R 14.3
3 Th	4 48 11	13 01 37	12 21 33	18 30 35	10 27.9	15 02.6	8 01.4	3 03.3	7 58.2	28 15.4	9 51.0	21 56.9	0 23.7	24 14.1
4 F	4 52 08	13 59 07	24 42 07	0♋56 18	10D 26.3	17 14.4	9 12.3	3 39.1	7 57.3	28 26.5	9 53.4	21 59.9	0 25.4	24 13.8
5 Sa	4 56 04	14 56 36	7♋13 16	13 33 12	10 26.0	19 25.5	10 23.2	4 14.9	7 56.0	28 37.8	9 55.9	22 03.0	0 27.2	24 13.5
6 Su	5 00 01	15 54 03	19 56 14	26 22 33	10 26.7	21 35.8	11 34.1	4 50.7	7 54.4	28 49.1	9 58.5	22 06.1	0 28.9	24 13.2
7 M	5 03 57	16 51 29	2♌52 18	9♌25 40	10 28.1	23 45.1	12 45.1	5 26.5	7 52.4	29 00.5	10 01.3	22 09.2	0 30.6	24 12.9
8 Tu	5 07 54	17 48 55	16 02 49	22 43 56	10 29.5	25 53.0	13 56.1	6 02.4	7 50.0	29 11.9	10 04.1	22 12.4	0 32.3	24 12.6
9 W	5 11 50	18 46 19	29 29 08	6♍18 32	10R 30.7	27 59.4	15 07.2	6 38.3	7 47.3	29 23.4	10 07.0	22 15.5	0 34.0	24 12.2
10 Th	5 15 47	19 43 42	13♍12 14	20 10 12	10 31.1	0♋04.1	16 18.2	7 14.3	7 44.3	29 35.0	10 09.9	22 18.7	0 35.6	24 11.8
11 F	5 19 44	20 41 03	27 12 24	4♎18 40	10 30.6	2 06.9	17 29.4	7 50.2	7 40.8	29 46.6	10 13.0	22 22.0	0 37.2	24 11.4
12 Sa	5 23 40	21 38 24	11♎28 45	18 42 17	10 29.2	4 07.8	18 40.5	8 26.2	7 37.0	29 58.3	10 16.2	22 25.2	0 38.8	24 10.9
13 Su	5 27 37	22 35 44	25 58 48	3♏17 43	10 27.3	6 06.6	19 51.7	9 02.3	7 32.9	0♌10.1	10 19.5	22 28.5	0 40.4	24 10.4
14 M	5 31 33	23 33 03	10♏38 21	17 59 56	10 25.2	8 03.2	21 03.0	9 38.3	7 28.4	0 21.9	10 22.8	22 31.8	0 41.9	24 09.9
15 Tu	5 35 30	24 30 21	25 21 38	2♐42 34	10 23.2	9 57.6	22 14.3	10 14.4	7 23.5	0 33.8	10 26.3	22 35.1	0 43.4	24 09.4
16 W	5 39 26	25 27 38	10♐01 52	17 18 40	10 21.8	11 49.8	23 25.6	10 50.5	7 18.3	0 45.7	10 29.8	22 38.4	0 44.9	24 08.9
17 Th	5 43 23	26 24 55	24 32 12	1♑41 44	10D 21.0	13 39.6	24 37.0	11 26.7	7 12.7	0 57.7	10 33.4	22 41.8	0 46.4	24 08.3
18 F	5 47 19	27 22 11	8♑46 39	15 46 27	10 20.9	15 27.0	25 48.4	12 02.8	7 06.8	1 09.8	10 37.1	22 45.2	0 47.8	24 07.7
19 Sa	5 51 16	28 19 27	22 40 46	29 29 22	10 21.4	17 12.1	26 59.8	12 39.0	7 00.6	1 21.9	10 40.9	22 48.6	0 49.2	24 07.1
20 Su	5 55 13	29 16 42	6♒12 08	12♒49 04	10 22.3	18 54.8	28 11.3	13 15.2	6 54.0	1 34.0	10 44.8	22 52.0	0 50.6	24 06.5
21 M	5 59 09	0♋13 57	19 20 19	25 46 05	10 23.2	20 35.1	29 22.8	13 51.5	6 47.1	1 46.2	10 48.7	22 55.4	0 52.0	24 05.8
22 Tu	6 03 06	1 11 12	2♓06 41	8♓22 30	10 24.1	22 13.0	0♊34.4	14 27.8	6 39.8	1 58.5	10 52.8	22 58.8	0 53.3	24 05.2
23 W	6 07 02	2 08 26	14 33 59	20 41 38	10 24.6	23 48.5	1 46.0	15 04.1	6 32.3	2 10.8	10 56.9	23 02.3	0 54.6	24 04.5
24 Th	6 10 59	3 05 41	26 45 57	2♈47 30	10R 24.8	25 21.6	2 57.6	15 40.4	6 24.3	2 23.1	11 01.1	23 05.8	0 55.9	24 03.8
25 F	6 14 55	4 02 55	8♈46 52	14 44 35	10 24.7	26 52.2	4 09.3	16 16.8	6 16.1	2 35.5	11 05.3	23 09.3	0 57.2	24 03.0
26 Sa	6 18 52	5 00 09	20 41 15	26 37 25	10 24.3	28 20.4	5 21.0	16 53.2	6 07.6	2 48.0	11 09.7	23 12.8	0 58.4	24 02.3
27 Su	6 22 48	5 57 23	2♉33 37	8♉30 23	10 23.8	29 46.1	6 32.8	17 29.6	5 58.7	3 00.5	11 14.1	23 16.3	0 59.6	24 01.5
28 M	6 26 45	6 54 38	14 28 11	20 27 30	10 23.3	1♌09.2	7 44.6	18 06.1	5 49.6	3 13.0	11 18.7	23 19.9	1 00.8	24 00.7
29 Tu	6 30 42	7 51 52	26 28 45	2♊32 19	10 22.9	2 29.8	8 56.4	18 42.5	5 40.2	3 25.6	11 23.3	23 23.4	1 01.9	23 59.9
30 W	6 34 38	8 49 06	8♊38 32	14 47 41	10 22.7	3 47.8	10 08.3	19 19.1	5 30.4	3 38.2	11 27.9	23 27.0	1 03.0	23 59.0

Astro Data

	Dy Hr Mn
☽0N	1 16:09
♀0N	4 22:52
♃⚻♇	10 9:10
♄ D	11 6:22
♃∠♄	11 13:55
☽0S	15 17:09
♇ R	25 2:20
☽0N	28 23:18
⚳R	1 11:53
☽0S	12 1:16
♃□♆	16 10:08
☽0N	25 7:05

Planet Ingress

		Dy Hr Mn
♀	♈	1 21:17
☿	♉	11 18:01
☉	♊	20 22:22
♆	♉	22 0:17
☿	♊	27 14:31
♀	♉	27 16:34
♂	♌	29 8:38
☿	♋	10 11:12
♃	♌	12 15:25
☉	♋	21 6:09
♀	♊	22 0:28
☿	♌	27 15:58

Last Aspect / ☽ Ingress

Last Aspect Dy Hr Mn		☽ Ingress	Dy Hr Mn
3 3:42	♆☌	♉	3 5:03
5 5:40	♇□	♊	5 17:19
8 3:25	♆⚹	♋	8 4:22
10 12:31	♆□	♌	10 13:15
12 18:33	♆△	♍	12 19:06
14 13:12	♃⚹	♎	14 21:43
16 21:44	♆☍	♏	16 22:00
18 18:23	☉☍	♐	18 21:44
20 22:51	♆△	♑	20 22:55
22 20:24	♃☍	♒	23 3:16
25 5:58	♀☍	♓	25 11:30
27 21:07	♂△	♈	27 22:53
30 6:27	♃□	♉	30 11:32

Last Aspect Dy Hr Mn		☽ Ingress	Dy Hr Mn
1 19:35	♃⚹	♊	1 23:39
3 23:06	♇△	♋	4 10:12
6 16:35	♃☌	♌	6 18:43
8 18:39	☿⚹	♍	9 0:55
11 4:15	♃⚹	♎	11 4:44
12 21:02	♇△	♏	13 6:36
14 22:03	♇□	♐	15 7:34
17 2:30	☉☍	♑	17 9:09
19 7:10	♀△	♒	19 12:54
21 19:31	♀□	♓	21 19:59
23 19:03	☿△	♈	24 6:26
26 15:57	☿□	♉	26 18:50
28 19:05	♇□	♊	29 6:59

☽ Phases & Eclipses

Dy Hr Mn		
4 9:19	●	14♉01
12 4:18	☽	21♌34
18 18:23	○	27♏55
25 20:43	☾	4♓44
3 0:24	●	12♊34
10 11:11	☽	19♍42
17 2:30	○	26♐02
17 2:44	•	A 0.442
24 12:39	☾	3♈07

Astro Data

1 May 2038
Julian Day # 50525
SVP 4♓43'46"
GC 27♐22.5 ⚴ 24♐15.8R
Eris 28♈12.7 ✻ 21♏20.1R
⚷ 22♊58.9 ⚶ 6♊58.0
☽ Mean ☊ 13♋41.1

1 June 2038
Julian Day # 50556
SVP 4♓43'41"
GC 27♐22.6 ⚴ 17♐09.2R
Eris 28♈30.9 ✻ 14♏42.9R
⚷ 25♊30.4 ⚶ 20♊12.9
☽ Mean ☊ 12♋02.6

July 2038 — LONGITUDE

Day	Sid.Time	☉	0 hr ☽	Noon ☽	True ☊	☿	♀	♂	⚳	♃	♄	♅	♆	♇
1 Th	6 38 35	9♋46 20	21♊00 03	27♊15 48	10♋22.6	5♌03.2	11♊20.2	19♌55.6	5♒20.4	3♌50.8	11♍32.7	23♋30.6	1♉04.1	23♒58.2
2 F	6 42 31	10 43 34	3♋35 06	9♋58 03	10R 22.6	6 15.9	12 32.2	20 32.2	5R 10.2	4 03.5	11 37.5	23 34.1	1 05.2	23R 57.3
3 Sa	6 46 28	11 40 48	16 24 42	22 55 04	10 22.6	7 25.8	13 44.1	21 08.8	4 59.7	4 16.2	11 42.4	23 37.7	1 06.2	23 56.4
4 Su	6 50 24	12 38 02	29 29 07	6♌06 49	10 22.5	8 32.9	14 56.2	21 45.5	4 48.9	4 29.0	11 47.4	23 41.4	1 07.2	23 55.5
5 M	6 54 21	13 35 16	12♌48 02	19 32 41	10 22.2	9 37.1	16 08.2	22 22.1	4 37.9	4 41.8	11 52.4	23 45.0	1 08.2	23 54.5
6 Tu	6 58 17	14 32 29	26 20 35	3♍11 35	10 21.8	10 38.3	17 20.3	22 58.8	4 26.7	4 54.6	11 57.5	23 48.6	1 09.1	23 53.6
7 W	7 02 14	15 29 43	10♍05 31	17 02 09	10 21.3	11 36.3	18 32.4	23 35.6	4 15.2	5 07.5	12 02.7	23 52.2	1 10.0	23 52.6
8 Th	7 06 11	16 26 56	24 01 17	1♎02 42	10 20.9	12 31.2	19 44.5	24 12.3	4 03.6	5 20.4	12 08.0	23 55.9	1 10.9	23 51.6
9 F	7 10 07	17 24 09	8♎06 09	15 11 22	10D 20.7	13 22.8	20 56.7	24 49.1	3 51.7	5 33.3	12 13.3	23 59.5	1 11.7	23 50.6
10 Sa	7 14 04	18 21 21	22 18 04	29 25 57	10 20.8	14 11.0	22 08.9	25 25.9	3 39.7	5 46.2	12 18.6	24 03.1	1 12.6	23 49.6
11 Su	7 18 00	19 18 34	6♏34 41	13♏43 55	10 21.3	14 55.5	23 21.2	26 02.8	3 27.5	5 59.2	12 24.1	24 06.8	1 13.3	23 48.6
12 M	7 21 57	20 15 46	20 53 16	28 02 20	10 22.1	15 36.4	24 33.5	26 39.6	3 15.2	6 12.1	12 29.6	24 10.4	1 14.1	23 47.5
13 Tu	7 25 53	21 12 59	5♐10 41	12♐17 52	10 22.9	16 13.5	25 45.8	27 16.5	3 02.7	6 25.2	12 35.2	24 14.1	1 14.8	23 46.5
14 W	7 29 50	22 10 11	19 23 24	26 26 51	10R 23.6	16 46.6	26 58.1	27 53.5	2 50.0	6 38.2	12 40.8	24 17.8	1 15.5	23 45.4
15 Th	7 33 47	23 07 24	3♑27 45	10♑25 39	10 23.9	17 15.6	28 10.5	28 30.4	2 37.3	6 51.3	12 46.5	24 21.4	1 16.2	23 44.3
16 F	7 37 43	24 04 37	17 20 10	24 10 55	10 23.5	17 40.3	29 22.9	29 07.4	2 24.5	7 04.3	12 52.3	24 25.1	1 16.8	23 43.2
17 Sa	7 41 40	25 01 51	0♒57 36	7♒39 58	10 22.5	18 00.6	0♋35.4	29 44.4	2 11.5	7 17.4	12 58.1	24 28.7	1 17.4	23 42.1
18 Su	7 45 36	25 59 04	14 17 49	20 51 05	10 20.8	18 16.3	1 47.9	0♍21.4	1 58.5	7 30.5	13 04.0	24 32.4	1 17.9	23 40.9
19 M	7 49 33	26 56 18	27 19 43	3♓43 47	10 18.5	18 27.4	3 00.5	0 58.5	1 45.4	7 43.7	13 09.9	24 36.1	1 18.5	23 39.8
20 Tu	7 53 29	27 53 33	10♓03 25	16 18 49	10 16.1	18R 33.7	4 13.0	1 35.6	1 32.3	7 56.8	13 15.9	24 39.7	1 19.0	23 38.6
21 W	7 57 26	28 50 49	22 30 18	28 38 10	10 13.7	18 35.1	5 25.7	2 12.7	1 19.1	8 10.0	13 21.9	24 43.4	1 19.4	23 37.5
22 Th	8 01 22	29 48 05	4♈42 51	10♈44 48	10 11.9	18 31.6	6 38.3	2 49.9	1 05.9	8 23.1	13 28.0	24 47.0	1 19.9	23 36.3
23 F	8 05 19	0♌45 22	16 44 31	22 42 31	10D 10.8	18 23.1	7 51.0	3 27.0	0 52.7	8 36.3	13 34.2	24 50.7	1 20.3	23 35.1
24 Sa	8 09 15	1 42 40	28 39 23	4♉35 40	10 10.6	18 09.8	9 03.8	4 04.3	0 39.5	8 49.5	13 40.4	24 54.3	1 20.6	23 33.9
25 Su	8 13 12	2 39 58	10♉32 00	16 28 56	10 11.2	17 51.6	10 16.5	4 41.5	0 26.3	9 02.7	13 46.6	24 58.0	1 21.0	23 32.7
26 M	8 17 09	3 37 18	22 27 05	28 27 02	10 12.5	17 28.7	11 29.4	5 18.8	0 13.1	9 16.0	13 52.9	25 01.6	1 21.3	23 31.4
27 Tu	8 21 05	4 34 39	4♊29 20	10♊34 31	10 14.2	17 01.4	12 42.2	5 56.1	29♑59.9	9 29.2	13 59.3	25 05.2	1 21.5	23 30.2
28 W	8 25 02	5 32 00	16 43 04	22 55 26	10 15.6	16 29.9	13 55.1	6 33.4	29 46.9	9 42.4	14 05.7	25 08.9	1 21.8	23 29.0
29 Th	8 28 58	6 29 23	29 12 01	5♋33 06	10R 16.5	15 54.6	15 08.1	7 10.8	29 33.9	9 55.7	14 12.1	25 12.5	1 22.0	23 27.7
30 F	8 32 55	7 26 46	11♋58 57	18 29 44	10 16.3	15 15.9	16 21.0	7 48.2	29 20.9	10 08.9	14 18.6	25 16.1	1 22.1	23 26.5
31 Sa	8 36 51	8 24 10	25 05 29	1♌46 12	10 14.9	14 34.5	17 34.0	8 25.7	29 08.1	10 22.2	14 25.2	25 19.7	1 22.3	23 25.2

August 2038 — LONGITUDE

Day	Sid.Time	☉	0 hr ☽	Noon ☽	True ☊	☿	♀	♂	⚳	♃	♄	♅	♆	♇
1 Su	8 40 48	9♌21 35	8♌31 44	15♌21 50	10♋12.1	13♌51.0	18♋47.1	9♍03.2	28♑55.4	10♌35.4	14♍31.8	25♋23.3	1♉22.4	23♒23.9
2 M	8 44 45	10 19 01	22 16 13	29 14 26	10R 08.2	13R 06.1	20 00.2	9 40.7	28R 42.9	10 48.7	14 38.4	25 26.9	1 22.5	23R 22.6
3 Tu	8 48 41	11 16 28	6♍16 01	13♍20 26	10 03.7	12 20.5	21 13.3	10 18.2	28 30.4	11 01.9	14 45.1	25 30.4	1R 22.5	23 21.3
4 W	8 52 38	12 13 55	20 27 05	27 35 25	9 59.1	11 35.1	22 26.4	10 55.8	28 18.1	11 15.2	14 51.8	25 34.0	1 22.5	23 20.0
5 Th	8 56 34	13 11 23	4♎44 48	11♎54 43	9 55.3	10 50.6	23 39.6	11 33.4	28 06.0	11 28.4	14 58.5	25 37.5	1 22.5	23 18.7
6 F	9 00 31	14 08 51	19 04 36	26 14 01	9 52.6	10 08.1	24 52.8	12 11.0	27 54.1	11 41.7	15 05.3	25 41.0	1 22.4	23 17.4
7 Sa	9 04 27	15 06 21	3♏22 31	10♏29 46	9D 51.4	9 28.2	26 06.1	12 48.7	27 42.3	11 54.9	15 12.2	25 44.6	1 22.3	23 16.1
8 Su	9 08 24	16 03 51	17 35 29	24 39 26	9 51.6	8 51.8	27 19.4	13 26.4	27 30.8	12 08.2	15 19.0	25 48.1	1 22.2	23 14.8
9 M	9 12 20	17 01 22	1♐41 24	8♐41 16	9 52.7	8 19.7	28 32.7	14 04.1	27 19.5	12 21.4	15 26.0	25 51.5	1 22.0	23 13.5
10 Tu	9 16 17	17 58 54	15 38 54	22 34 13	9 54.1	7 52.4	29 46.0	14 41.9	27 08.4	12 34.6	15 32.9	25 55.0	1 21.8	23 12.2
11 W	9 20 14	18 56 26	29 27 05	6♑17 25	9R 55.0	7 30.6	0♌59.4	15 19.7	26 57.5	12 47.8	15 39.9	25 58.5	1 21.6	23 10.9
12 Th	9 24 10	19 54 00	13♑05 08	19 50 06	9 54.6	7 14.9	2 12.8	15 57.5	26 46.9	13 01.0	15 46.9	26 01.9	1 21.4	23 09.5
13 F	9 28 07	20 51 34	26 32 12	3♒11 20	9 52.5	7D 05.6	3 26.3	16 35.4	26 36.5	13 14.2	15 53.9	26 05.3	1 21.1	23 08.2
14 Sa	9 32 03	21 49 10	9♒47 21	16 20 07	9 48.4	7 03.0	4 39.8	17 13.2	26 26.4	13 27.4	16 01.0	26 08.7	1 20.7	23 06.9
15 Su	9 36 00	22 46 46	22 49 34	29 15 36	9 42.4	7 07.5	5 53.3	17 51.2	26 16.6	13 40.5	16 08.1	26 12.1	1 20.4	23 05.6
16 M	9 39 56	23 44 24	5♓38 09	11♓57 13	9 35.1	7 19.2	7 06.9	18 29.1	26 07.0	13 53.7	16 15.2	26 15.5	1 20.0	23 04.2
17 Tu	9 43 53	24 42 03	18 12 51	24 25 07	9 27.1	7 38.2	8 20.5	19 07.1	25 57.7	14 06.8	16 22.4	26 18.8	1 19.6	23 02.9
18 W	9 47 49	25 39 44	0♈34 11	6♈40 15	9 19.2	8 04.6	9 34.1	19 45.1	25 48.7	14 19.9	16 29.6	26 22.1	1 19.1	23 01.6
19 Th	9 51 46	26 37 26	12 43 34	18 44 28	9 12.2	8 38.3	10 47.8	20 23.1	25 40.0	14 33.0	16 36.8	26 25.4	1 18.7	23 00.2
20 F	9 55 42	27 35 10	24 43 21	0♉40 38	9 06.8	9 19.3	12 01.5	21 01.2	25 31.6	14 46.1	16 44.0	26 28.7	1 18.2	22 58.9
21 Sa	9 59 39	28 32 55	6♉36 49	12 32 25	9 03.3	10 07.5	13 15.3	21 39.3	25 23.6	14 59.1	16 51.3	26 31.9	1 17.6	22 57.6
22 Su	10 03 36	29 30 42	18 28 30	24 24 11	9D 01.8	11 02.5	14 29.1	22 17.5	25 15.8	15 12.2	16 58.5	26 35.1	1 17.0	22 56.3
23 M	10 07 32	0♍28 31	0♊21 36	6♊20 51	9 01.8	12 04.4	15 42.9	22 55.7	25 08.4	15 25.2	17 05.8	26 38.3	1 16.4	22 55.0
24 Tu	10 11 29	1 26 21	12 22 36	18 27 30	9 02.7	13 12.7	16 56.7	23 33.9	25 01.3	15 38.2	17 13.2	26 41.5	1 15.8	22 53.6
25 W	10 15 25	2 24 13	24 36 10	0♋49 11	9R 03.7	14 27.1	18 10.6	24 12.2	24 54.5	15 51.1	17 20.5	26 44.7	1 15.1	22 52.3
26 Th	10 19 22	3 22 07	7♋07 06	13 30 25	9 03.9	15 47.3	19 24.6	24 50.5	24 48.0	16 04.1	17 27.9	26 47.8	1 14.5	22 51.0
27 F	10 23 18	4 20 03	19 59 32	26 34 44	9 02.4	17 12.9	20 38.5	25 28.8	24 41.9	16 17.0	17 35.3	26 50.9	1 13.7	22 49.7
28 Sa	10 27 15	5 18 00	3♌16 13	10♌04 03	8 58.8	18 43.5	21 52.5	26 07.2	24 36.2	16 29.9	17 42.7	26 54.0	1 13.0	22 48.4
29 Su	10 31 11	6 15 59	16 58 06	23 58 07	8 52.8	20 18.7	23 06.6	26 45.6	24 30.8	16 42.7	17 50.1	26 57.0	1 12.2	22 47.2
30 M	10 35 08	7 13 59	1♍03 40	8♍14 10	8 44.9	21 57.8	24 20.6	27 24.1	24 25.7	16 55.5	17 57.5	27 00.0	1 11.4	22 45.9
31 Tu	10 39 05	8 12 01	15 28 53	22 46 57	8 35.7	23 40.6	25 34.7	28 02.6	24 21.0	17 08.3	18 04.9	27 03.0	1 10.6	22 44.6

Astro Data

	Dy Hr Mn
♅⚻♇	7 14:07
☽0S	9 7:07
☿R	21 6:58
☽0N	22 14:58
♆R	4 1:56
☽0S	5 12:18
☿D	14 8:49
♄⚼♆	17 3:12
☽0N	18 22:25

Planet Ingress

	Dy Hr Mn
♀ ♋	17 0:16
♂ ♍	17 22:07
☉ ♌	22 17:00
⚳ ♑R	27 11:54
♀ ♌	10 16:34
☉ ♍	23 0:10

Last Aspect / ☽ Ingress

Last Aspect Dy Hr Mn		☽ Ingress Dy Hr Mn
1 5:43	♇ △	♋ 1 17:13
3 13:19	♅ ☌	♌ 4 0:56
5 19:42	♇ ☍	♍ 6 6:25
7 23:48	♅ ⚹	♎ 8 10:13
10 4:58	♂ ⚹	♏ 10 12:57
12 9:35	♂ □	♐ 12 15:18
14 14:35	♂ △	♑ 14 18:04
16 12:25	♅ ☍	♒ 16 22:18
18 17:13	♇ ☌	♓ 19 4:59
21 12:27	☉ △	♈ 21 14:41
23 16:20	♅ □	♉ 24 2:43
26 5:07	♅ ⚹	♊ 26 15:05
28 13:04	♇ △	♋ 29 1:31
31 0:23	♅ ☌	♌ 31 8:50

Last Aspect / ☽ Ingress

Last Aspect Dy Hr Mn		☽ Ingress Dy Hr Mn
2 1:56	♇ ☍	♍ 2 13:18
4 8:35	♅ ⚹	♎ 4 16:03
6 11:04	♅ □	♏ 6 18:19
8 16:58	♀ △	♐ 8 21:07
10 13:06	♇ ⚹	♑ 11 0:58
12 23:08	♅ ☍	♒ 13 6:14
15 0:31	♇ ☌	♓ 15 13:23
17 15:42	♅ △	♈ 17 22:53
20 5:13	☉ △	♉ 20 10:38
22 23:12	☉ □	♊ 22 23:17
24 22:32	♂ □	♋ 25 10:26
27 12:29	♅ ☌	♌ 27 18:10
29 10:24	♀ ☌	♍ 29 22:13
31 21:00	♂ ☌	♎ 31 23:48

☽ Phases & Eclipses

Dy Hr Mn	
2 13:32	● 10♋47
2 13:31:31	◖ A 00'60"
9 16:00	☽ 17♎34
16 11:48	○ 24♑04
16 11:35	☍ A 0.500
24 5:40	☾ 1♉28
1 0:40	● 8♌54
7 20:21	☽ 15♏26
14 22:57	○ 22♒15
22 23:12	☾ 29♉58
30 10:13	● 7♍10

Astro Data

1 July 2038
Julian Day # 50586
SVP 4♓43'36"
GC 27♐22.6 ⚴ 9♐10.4R
Eris 28♈42.3 ⚵ 11♏33.7R
⚷ 28♊12.1 ⚶ 3♋12.6
☽ Mean ☊ 10♋27.3

1 August 2038
Julian Day # 50617
SVP 4♓43'31"
GC 27♐22.7 ⚴ 6♐35.6
Eris 28♈45.0R ⚵ 13♏10.9
⚷ 0♋49.3 ⚶ 16♋33.4
☽ Mean ☊ 8♋48.9

LONGITUDE — September 2038

Day	Sid.Time	☉	0 hr ☽	Noon ☽	True☊	☿	♀	♂	⚳	♃	♄	♅	♆	♇
1 W	10 43 01	9♍10 05	0♎07 25	7♎29 19	8♋26.5	25♌26.4	26♌48.8	28♍41.1	24♑16.7	17♌21.0	18♍12.4	27♋06.0	1♉09.7	22♒43.3
2 Th	10 46 58	10 08 10	14 51 39	22 13 26	8R 18.3	27 14.9	28 03.0	29 19.7	24R 12.7	17 33.8	18 19.9	27 08.9	1R 08.8	22R 42.1
3 F	10 50 54	11 06 16	29 33 48	6♏51 58	8 12.0	29 05.5	29 17.2	29 58.3	24 09.1	17 46.4	18 27.3	27 11.8	1 07.9	22 40.8
4 Sa	10 54 51	12 04 24	14♏07 17	21 19 15	8 08.1	0♍57.9	0♍31.4	0♎36.9	24 05.9	17 59.1	18 34.8	27 14.6	1 06.9	22 39.6
5 Su	10 58 47	13 02 34	28 27 29	5♐31 45	8D 06.4	2 51.5	1 45.6	1 15.6	24 03.0	18 11.7	18 42.3	27 17.4	1 05.9	22 38.3
6 M	11 02 44	14 00 45	12♐31 57	19 28 02	8 06.3	4 46.2	2 59.9	1 54.3	24 00.5	18 24.2	18 49.8	27 20.2	1 04.9	22 37.1
7 Tu	11 06 40	14 58 57	26 20 05	3♑08 14	8R 06.7	6 41.4	4 14.2	2 33.0	23 58.3	18 36.7	18 57.3	27 23.0	1 03.9	22 35.9
8 W	11 10 37	15 57 11	9♑52 37	16 33 26	8 06.5	8 37.0	5 28.5	3 11.8	23 56.5	18 49.2	19 04.8	27 25.7	1 02.9	22 34.7
9 Th	11 14 34	16 55 26	23 10 52	29 45 06	8 04.6	10 32.7	6 42.8	3 50.6	23 55.1	19 01.6	19 12.4	27 28.4	1 01.8	22 33.5
10 F	11 18 30	17 53 42	6♒16 16	12♒44 31	8 00.2	12 28.2	7 57.2	4 29.5	23 54.0	19 14.0	19 19.9	27 31.1	1 00.7	22 32.3
11 Sa	11 22 27	18 52 01	19 09 58	25 32 40	7 53.0	14 23.4	9 11.6	5 08.3	23 53.3	19 26.3	19 27.4	27 33.7	0 59.6	22 31.2
12 Su	11 26 23	19 50 21	1♓52 42	8♓10 07	7 43.1	16 18.1	10 26.0	5 47.3	23D 53.0	19 38.6	19 34.9	27 36.2	0 58.4	22 30.0
13 M	11 30 20	20 48 42	14 24 56	20 37 12	7 31.2	18 12.2	11 40.4	6 26.2	23 53.0	19 50.8	19 42.4	27 38.8	0 57.2	22 28.9
14 Tu	11 34 16	21 47 06	26 46 57	2♈54 15	7 18.2	20 05.5	12 54.9	7 05.2	23 53.3	20 03.0	19 49.9	27 41.3	0 56.0	22 27.7
15 W	11 38 13	22 45 31	8♈59 11	15 01 54	7 05.2	21 58.1	14 09.4	7 44.2	23 54.1	20 15.1	19 57.5	27 43.7	0 54.8	22 26.6
16 Th	11 42 09	23 43 59	21 02 32	27 01 19	6 53.3	23 49.8	15 23.9	8 23.3	23 55.1	20 27.2	20 05.0	27 46.2	0 53.6	22 25.5
17 F	11 46 06	24 42 28	2♉58 31	8♉54 27	6 43.4	25 40.5	16 38.5	9 02.4	23 56.5	20 39.2	20 12.5	27 48.5	0 52.3	22 24.4
18 Sa	11 50 03	25 41 00	14 49 30	20 44 06	6 36.2	27 30.4	17 53.0	9 41.6	23 58.3	20 51.1	20 20.0	27 50.9	0 51.0	22 23.4
19 Su	11 53 59	26 39 33	26 38 42	2♊33 52	6 31.7	29 19.2	19 07.6	10 20.8	24 00.4	21 03.0	20 27.5	27 53.2	0 49.7	22 22.3
20 M	11 57 56	27 38 09	8♊30 10	14 28 11	6 29.5	1♎07.0	20 22.3	11 00.0	24 02.9	21 14.9	20 35.0	27 55.5	0 48.4	22 21.3
21 Tu	12 01 52	28 36 47	20 28 36	26 32 03	6 28.9	2 53.9	21 36.9	11 39.3	24 05.7	21 26.6	20 42.4	27 57.7	0 47.0	22 20.2
22 W	12 05 49	29 35 28	2♋39 13	8♋50 46	6 28.9	4 39.8	22 51.6	12 18.6	24 08.8	21 38.4	20 49.9	27 59.9	0 45.6	22 19.2
23 Th	12 09 45	0♎34 10	15 07 23	21 29 39	6 28.3	6 24.6	24 06.3	12 58.0	24 12.3	21 50.0	20 57.4	28 02.0	0 44.3	22 18.2
24 F	12 13 42	1 32 55	27 58 08	4♌33 19	6 26.1	8 08.5	25 21.0	13 37.4	24 16.1	22 01.6	21 04.8	28 04.1	0 42.9	22 17.3
25 Sa	12 17 38	2 31 42	11♌15 34	18 05 05	6 21.5	9 51.4	26 35.7	14 16.8	24 20.2	22 13.1	21 12.2	28 06.1	0 41.4	22 16.3
26 Su	12 21 35	3 30 31	25 01 57	2♍06 01	6 14.2	11 33.4	27 50.5	14 56.3	24 24.7	22 24.6	21 19.7	28 08.1	0 40.0	22 15.4
27 M	12 25 32	4 29 22	9♍16 57	16 34 12	6 04.5	13 14.4	29 05.3	15 35.8	24 29.4	22 35.9	21 27.1	28 10.1	0 38.5	22 14.5
28 Tu	12 29 28	5 28 15	23 56 59	1♎24 20	5 53.2	14 54.5	0♎20.1	16 15.4	24 34.6	22 47.2	21 34.5	28 12.0	0 37.1	22 13.5
29 W	12 33 25	6 27 11	8♎55 07	16 28 05	5 41.7	16 33.7	1 34.9	16 55.0	24 40.0	22 58.5	21 41.8	28 13.9	0 35.6	22 12.7
30 Th	12 37 21	7 26 08	24 01 55	1♏35 18	5 31.3	18 12.0	2 49.8	17 34.7	24 45.8	23 09.6	21 49.2	28 15.7	0 34.1	22 11.8

LONGITUDE — October 2038

Day	Sid.Time	☉	0 hr ☽	Noon ☽	True☊	☿	♀	♂	⚳	♃	♄	♅	♆	♇
1 F	12 41 18	8♎25 07	9♏06 59	16♏35 51	5♋23.0	19♎49.4	4♎04.6	18♎14.3	24♑51.8	23♌20.7	21♍56.5	28♋17.5	0♉32.5	22♒11.0
2 Sa	12 45 14	9 24 08	24 00 56	1♐21 25	5R 17.5	21 25.9	5 19.5	18 54.1	24 58.2	23 31.7	22 03.8	28 19.2	0R 31.0	22R 10.1
3 Su	12 49 11	10 23 11	8♐36 44	15 46 29	5 14.7	23 01.6	6 34.4	19 33.9	25 04.9	23 42.6	22 11.1	28 20.9	0 29.5	22 09.3
4 M	12 53 07	11 22 16	22 50 29	29 48 39	5 13.8	24 36.5	7 49.3	20 13.7	25 11.9	23 53.5	22 18.4	28 22.5	0 27.9	22 08.6
5 Tu	12 57 04	12 21 22	6♑41 06	13♑28 01	5 13.8	26 10.6	9 04.2	20 53.5	25 19.2	24 04.2	22 25.6	28 24.1	0 26.3	22 07.8
6 W	13 01 00	13 20 30	20 09 41	26 46 26	5 13.3	27 43.8	10 19.2	21 33.4	25 26.8	24 14.9	22 32.8	28 25.6	0 24.7	22 07.1
7 Th	13 04 57	14 19 40	3♒18 38	9♒46 39	5 11.2	29 16.3	11 34.1	22 13.4	25 34.6	24 25.5	22 40.0	28 27.1	0 23.1	22 06.3
8 F	13 08 54	15 18 51	16 10 52	22 31 36	5 06.6	0♏47.9	12 49.0	22 53.3	25 42.8	24 35.9	22 47.2	28 28.5	0 21.5	22 05.6
9 Sa	13 12 50	16 18 05	28 49 13	5♓03 59	4 59.0	2 18.8	14 04.0	23 33.3	25 51.3	24 46.3	22 54.3	28 29.9	0 19.9	22 05.0
10 Su	13 16 47	17 17 20	11♓16 10	17 25 59	4 48.7	3 48.9	15 19.0	24 13.4	26 00.0	24 56.7	23 01.4	28 31.2	0 18.3	22 04.3
11 M	13 20 43	18 16 37	23 33 39	29 39 19	4 36.3	5 18.3	16 34.0	24 53.5	26 09.0	25 06.9	23 08.5	28 32.5	0 16.7	22 03.7
12 Tu	13 24 40	19 15 56	5♈43 07	11♈45 13	4 22.7	6 46.8	17 49.0	25 33.6	26 18.3	25 17.0	23 15.5	28 33.7	0 15.0	22 03.1
13 W	13 28 36	20 15 17	17 45 44	23 44 47	4 09.1	8 14.6	19 04.0	26 13.8	26 27.8	25 27.0	23 22.5	28 34.9	0 13.4	22 02.5
14 Th	13 32 33	21 14 40	29 42 33	5♉39 10	3 56.6	9 41.6	20 19.0	26 54.0	26 37.6	25 36.9	23 29.4	28 36.1	0 11.7	22 01.9
15 F	13 36 29	22 14 05	11♉34 51	17 29 49	3 46.1	11 07.7	21 34.1	27 34.3	26 47.7	25 46.8	23 36.4	28 37.1	0 10.1	22 01.4
16 Sa	13 40 26	23 13 32	23 24 21	29 18 45	3 38.3	12 33.1	22 49.1	28 14.6	26 58.0	25 56.5	23 43.3	28 38.2	0 08.4	22 00.9
17 Su	13 44 23	24 13 02	5♊13 24	11♊08 41	3 33.3	13 57.6	24 04.2	28 55.0	27 08.6	26 06.1	23 50.1	28 39.1	0 06.7	22 00.4
18 M	13 48 19	25 12 33	17 05 04	23 03 04	3D 30.9	15 21.2	25 19.2	29 35.4	27 19.4	26 15.6	23 56.9	28 40.0	0 05.1	21 59.9
19 Tu	13 52 16	26 12 07	29 03 12	5♋06 05	3 30.4	16 43.9	26 34.3	0♏15.8	27 30.5	26 25.1	24 03.7	28 40.9	0 03.4	21 59.5
20 W	13 56 12	27 11 44	11♋12 19	17 22 31	3R 30.8	18 05.7	27 49.4	0 56.3	27 41.8	26 34.4	24 10.5	28 41.7	0 01.7	21 59.1
21 Th	14 00 09	28 11 22	23 37 20	29 57 24	3 31.1	19 26.4	29 04.5	1 36.9	27 53.4	26 43.6	24 17.2	28 42.5	0 00.0	21 58.7
22 F	14 04 05	29 11 03	6♌23 19	12♌55 39	3 30.2	20 46.1	0♏19.7	2 17.5	28 05.2	26 52.6	24 23.8	28 43.2	29♈58.3	21 58.3
23 Sa	14 08 02	0♏10 46	19 34 51	26 21 20	3 27.3	22 04.6	1 34.8	2 58.1	28 17.2	27 01.6	24 30.4	28 43.8	29 56.7	21 58.0
24 Su	14 11 58	1 10 31	3♍15 18	10♍16 51	3 22.0	23 22.0	2 49.9	3 38.8	28 29.5	27 10.5	24 37.0	28 44.4	29 55.0	21 57.7
25 M	14 15 55	2 10 19	17 25 50	24 41 55	3 14.5	24 37.9	4 05.1	4 19.5	28 42.0	27 19.2	24 43.5	28 45.0	29 53.3	21 57.4
26 Tu	14 19 52	3 10 08	2♎04 33	9♎32 53	3 05.6	25 52.5	5 20.3	5 00.3	28 54.7	27 27.8	24 49.9	28 45.5	29 51.6	21 57.1
27 W	14 23 48	4 10 00	17 05 56	24 42 29	2 56.2	27 05.5	6 35.4	5 41.1	29 07.7	27 36.3	24 56.4	28 45.9	29 49.9	21 56.9
28 Th	14 27 45	5 09 54	2♏21 10	10♏00 35	2 47.6	28 16.8	7 50.6	6 21.9	29 20.9	27 44.7	25 02.7	28 46.3	29 48.2	21 56.7
29 F	14 31 41	6 09 49	17 39 18	25 15 56	2 40.8	29 26.2	9 05.8	7 02.9	29 34.2	27 52.9	25 09.0	28 46.6	29 46.6	21 56.5
30 Sa	14 35 38	7 09 47	2♐49 13	10♐18 05	2 36.4	0♐33.5	10 21.0	7 43.8	29 47.8	28 01.1	25 15.3	28 46.9	29 44.9	21 56.4
31 Su	14 39 34	8 09 46	17 41 38	24 59 11	2D 34.4	1 38.5	11 36.2	8 24.8	0♒01.7	28 09.0	25 21.5	28 47.1	29 43.2	21 56.2

Astro Data

	Dy Hr Mn
☽0S	1 18:59
♂0S	6 2:21
♃×♄	11 17:30
⚳ D	12 23:41
☽0N	15 5:15
☿0S	21 9:46
⊙0S	22 22:02
♃☍♇	25 18:11
☽0S	29 4:15
♀0S	30 19:57
♄⊼♇	3 6:43
☽0N	12 11:38
☽0S	26 15:24

Planet Ingress

		Dy Hr Mn
♂	♎	3 13:05
☿	♍	3 23:41
♀	♍	4 1:51
☿	♎	19 21:03
⊙	♎	22 22:02
♀	♎	28 5:33
☿	♏	7 23:25
♂	♏	19 2:36
♆	♈R	21 12:20
♀	♏	22 5:43
⊙	♏	23 7:40
☿	♐	29 23:57
⚳	♒	31 9:08

Last Aspect / ☽ Ingress

Last Aspect Dy Hr Mn		☽ Ingress Dy Hr Mn
2 22:24	♀ ⚹	♏ 3 0:43
4 21:59	♅ △	♐ 5 2:36
6 17:29	♇ ⚹	♑ 7 6:27
9 7:49	♅ ☍	♒ 9 12:27
11 6:18	♇ ☌	♓ 11 20:26
14 1:44	♅ △	♈ 14 6:18
16 13:31	♅ □	♉ 16 18:00
19 4:14	☿ △	♊ 19 6:48
21 16:27	⊙ □	♋ 21 18:49
24 0:09	♅ ☌	♌ 24 3:43
25 19:16	♃ ☌	♍ 26 8:27
28 6:51	♅ ⚹	♎ 28 9:45
30 6:42	♅ □	♏ 30 9:29

Last Aspect / ☽ Ingress

Last Aspect Dy Hr Mn		☽ Ingress Dy Hr Mn
2 7:01	♅ △	♐ 2 9:46
4 1:53	☿ ⚹	♑ 4 12:20
6 15:02	♅ ☍	♒ 6 17:54
8 16:00	♃ ☍	♓ 9 2:16
11 9:48	♅ △	♈ 11 12:41
13 21:45	♅ □	♉ 14 0:35
16 10:37	♅ ⚹	♊ 16 13:24
19 1:51	♂ △	♋ 19 1:53
21 12:05	♆ □	♌ 21 12:05
23 18:15	♆ △	♍ 23 18:22
25 18:37	♅ ⚹	♎ 25 20:38
27 20:02	♅ ☍	♏ 27 20:19
29 19:09	☿ ☌	♐ 29 19:30
31 19:52	♆ △	♑ 31 20:21

☽ Phases & Eclipses

Dy Hr Mn		
6 1:51	☽	13♐36
13 12:24	○	20♓50
21 16:27	☾	28♊48
28 18:57	●	5♎45
5 9:52	☽	12♑16
13 4:22	○	19♈56
21 8:23	☾	28♋02
28 3:53	●	4♏50

Astro Data

1 September 2038
Julian Day # 50648
SVP 4♓43'27"
GC 27♐22.8 ⚴ 10♐15.8
Eris 28♈37.9R ⚵ 18♏43.6
⚷ 2♋50.5 ⚶ 29♋31.6
☽ Mean ☊ 7♋10.3

1 October 2038
Julian Day # 50678
SVP 4♓43'25"
GC 27♐22.8 ⚴ 17♐41.2
Eris 28♈23.5R ⚵ 26♏33.6
⚷ 3♋51.1 ⚶ 11♌18.7
☽ Mean ☊ 5♋35.0

November 2038 — LONGITUDE

Day	Sid.Time	☉	0 hr ☽	Noon ☽	True ☊	☿	♀	♂	⚳	♃	♄	♅	♆	♇
1 M	14 43 31	9♏09 47	2♑10 16	9♑14 38	2♋34.3	2♐41.0	12♏51.4	9♏05.8	0♒15.7	28♌16.9	25♍27.6	28♋47.3	29♈41.6	21♒56.1
2 Tu	14 47 27	10 09 50	16 12 13	23 03 06	2 35.3	3 40.6	14 06.6	9 46.9	0 29.9	28 24.6	25 33.7	28 47.4	29R 39.9	21R 56.1
3 W	14 51 24	11 09 54	29 47 30	6♒25 44	2R 36.1	4 37.0	15 21.8	10 28.0	0 44.3	28 32.2	25 39.8	28R 47.4	29 38.3	21 56.0
4 Th	14 55 21	12 10 00	12♒58 12	19 25 20	2 35.9	5 29.9	16 37.0	11 09.2	0 58.9	28 39.7	25 45.7	28 47.4	29 36.7	21D 56.0
5 F	14 59 17	13 10 07	25 47 37	2♓05 32	2 33.9	6 18.8	17 52.2	11 50.4	1 13.7	28 47.0	25 51.7	28 47.4	29 35.0	21 56.0
6 Sa	15 03 14	14 10 15	8♓19 32	14 30 06	2 29.8	7 03.3	19 07.5	12 31.7	1 28.7	28 54.2	25 57.5	28 47.2	29 33.4	21 56.0
7 Su	15 07 10	15 10 25	20 37 41	26 42 40	2 23.6	7 42.9	20 22.7	13 13.0	1 43.9	29 01.2	26 03.3	28 47.1	29 31.8	21 56.1
8 M	15 11 07	16 10 37	2♈45 27	8♈46 23	2 15.7	8 16.9	21 37.9	13 54.3	1 59.3	29 08.1	26 09.0	28 46.8	29 30.2	21 56.2
9 Tu	15 15 03	17 10 50	14 45 45	20 43 50	2 06.9	8 44.8	22 53.1	14 35.7	2 14.8	29 14.8	26 14.7	28 46.6	29 28.6	21 56.3
10 W	15 19 00	18 11 05	26 40 55	2♉37 13	1 58.0	9 05.9	24 08.3	15 17.1	2 30.5	29 21.4	26 20.3	28 46.2	29 27.0	21 56.4
11 Th	15 22 56	19 11 22	8♉32 56	14 28 18	1 49.8	9 19.5	25 23.5	15 58.6	2 46.4	29 27.9	26 25.8	28 45.8	29 25.5	21 56.6
12 F	15 26 53	20 11 40	20 23 30	26 18 45	1 43.1	9R 24.9	26 38.8	16 40.1	3 02.5	29 34.2	26 31.2	28 45.4	29 23.9	21 56.8
13 Sa	15 30 50	21 12 01	2♊14 16	8♊10 17	1 38.4	9 21.4	27 54.0	17 21.7	3 18.7	29 40.3	26 36.6	28 44.9	29 22.4	21 57.0
14 Su	15 34 46	22 12 23	14 07 04	20 04 53	1D 35.7	9 08.5	29 09.2	18 03.3	3 35.1	29 46.3	26 42.0	28 44.4	29 20.8	21 57.2
15 M	15 38 43	23 12 46	26 04 03	2♋04 55	1 34.9	8 45.6	0♐24.5	18 45.0	3 51.7	29 52.1	26 47.2	28 43.8	29 19.3	21 57.5
16 Tu	15 42 39	24 13 12	8♋07 53	14 13 21	1 35.6	8 12.4	1 39.7	19 26.7	4 08.4	29 57.8	26 52.4	28 43.1	29 17.8	21 57.8
17 W	15 46 36	25 13 39	20 21 46	26 33 36	1 37.2	7 28.9	2 55.0	20 08.5	4 25.3	0♍03.4	26 57.5	28 42.4	29 16.4	21 58.1
18 Th	15 50 32	26 14 08	2♌49 20	9♌09 30	1 38.9	6 35.4	4 10.2	20 50.3	4 42.3	0 08.7	27 02.5	28 41.7	29 14.9	21 58.5
19 F	15 54 29	27 14 39	15 34 34	22 05 01	1R 39.9	5 32.8	5 25.5	21 32.1	4 59.5	0 13.9	27 07.5	28 40.9	29 13.4	21 58.9
20 Sa	15 58 25	28 15 12	28 41 18	5♍23 48	1 39.8	4 22.2	6 40.7	22 14.0	5 16.9	0 19.0	27 12.4	28 40.0	29 12.0	21 59.3
21 Su	16 02 22	29 15 46	12♍12 47	19 08 27	1 38.3	3 05.6	7 56.0	22 56.0	5 34.3	0 23.8	27 17.2	28 39.1	29 10.6	21 59.7
22 M	16 06 19	0♐16 22	26 10 52	3♎19 54	1 35.3	1 45.1	9 11.2	23 38.0	5 52.0	0 28.5	27 21.9	28 38.1	29 09.2	22 00.2
23 Tu	16 10 15	1 17 00	10♎35 15	17 56 27	1 31.3	0 23.3	10 26.5	24 20.0	6 09.8	0 33.1	27 26.5	28 37.1	29 07.8	22 00.7
24 W	16 14 12	2 17 40	25 22 49	2♏53 26	1 26.9	29♏03.0	11 41.8	25 02.1	6 27.7	0 37.4	27 31.1	28 36.0	29 06.5	22 01.2
25 Th	16 18 08	3 18 21	10♏27 19	18 03 14	1 22.8	27 46.8	12 57.0	25 44.3	6 45.7	0 41.6	27 35.6	28 34.9	29 05.1	22 01.7
26 F	16 22 05	4 19 04	25 39 58	3♐16 10	1 19.6	26 37.1	14 12.3	26 26.4	7 04.0	0 45.6	27 39.9	28 33.8	29 03.8	22 02.3
27 Sa	16 26 01	5 19 48	10♐50 36	18 22 03	1D 17.7	25 36.0	15 27.6	27 08.7	7 22.3	0 49.4	27 44.3	28 32.6	29 02.5	22 02.9
28 Su	16 29 58	6 20 33	25 49 24	3♑11 46	1 17.2	24 45.0	16 42.9	27 51.0	7 40.8	0 53.1	27 48.5	28 31.3	29 01.3	22 03.5
29 M	16 33 54	7 21 20	10♑28 21	17 38 38	1 17.9	24 05.1	17 58.2	28 33.3	7 59.4	0 56.6	27 52.6	28 30.0	29 00.0	22 04.1
30 Tu	16 37 51	8 22 07	24 42 13	1♒38 55	1 19.3	23 36.7	19 13.4	29 15.7	8 18.1	0 59.9	27 56.7	28 28.6	28 58.8	22 04.8

December 2038 — LONGITUDE

Day	Sid.Time	☉	0 hr ☽	Noon ☽	True ☊	☿	♀	♂	⚳	♃	♄	♅	♆	♇
1 W	16 41 48	9♐22 56	8♒28 44	15♒11 46	1♋20.9	23♏19.8	20♐28.7	29♏58.1	8♒37.0	1♍03.0	28♍00.6	28♋27.2	28♈57.6	22♒05.5
2 Th	16 45 44	10 23 45	21 48 17	28 18 37	1 22.1	23D 14.2	21 44.0	0♐40.5	8 55.9	1 05.9	28 04.5	28R 25.8	28R 56.4	22 06.2
3 F	16 49 41	11 24 35	4♓43 11	11♓02 28	1R 22.5	23 19.1	22 59.2	1 23.0	9 15.0	1 08.6	28 08.3	28 24.3	28 55.3	22 07.0
4 Sa	16 53 37	12 25 26	17 16 59	23 27 17	1 22.1	23 34.0	24 14.5	2 05.6	9 34.3	1 11.2	28 11.9	28 22.7	28 54.2	22 07.7
5 Su	16 57 34	13 26 18	29 33 54	5♈37 21	1 20.7	23 57.9	25 29.7	2 48.2	9 53.6	1 13.6	28 15.5	28 21.2	28 53.1	22 08.5
6 M	17 01 30	14 27 11	11♈38 12	17 36 57	1 18.7	24 30.0	26 45.0	3 30.8	10 13.0	1 15.8	28 19.0	28 19.5	28 52.0	22 09.4
7 Tu	17 05 27	15 28 04	23 34 05	29 30 03	1 16.2	25 09.4	28 00.2	4 13.5	10 32.6	1 17.8	28 22.4	28 17.9	28 50.9	22 10.2
8 W	17 09 23	16 28 59	5♉25 16	11♉20 09	1 13.7	25 55.3	29 15.5	4 56.2	10 52.3	1 19.6	28 25.7	28 16.1	28 49.9	22 11.1
9 Th	17 13 20	17 29 54	17 15 03	23 10 17	1 11.4	26 47.0	0♑30.7	5 39.0	11 12.0	1 21.2	28 29.0	28 14.4	28 48.9	22 12.0
10 F	17 17 17	18 30 50	29 06 11	5♊03 00	1 09.7	27 43.7	1 46.0	6 21.8	11 31.9	1 22.6	28 32.1	28 12.6	28 48.0	22 12.9
11 Sa	17 21 13	19 31 47	11♊00 59	17 00 23	1 08.6	28 44.8	3 01.2	7 04.6	11 51.9	1 23.8	28 35.1	28 10.8	28 47.0	22 13.8
12 Su	17 25 10	20 32 45	23 01 26	29 04 18	1D 08.2	29 49.7	4 16.4	7 47.5	12 12.0	1 24.9	28 38.0	28 08.9	28 46.1	22 14.8
13 M	17 29 06	21 33 44	5♋09 14	11♋16 25	1 08.3	0♐58.0	5 31.6	8 30.5	12 32.2	1 25.7	28 40.8	28 07.0	28 45.3	22 15.8
14 Tu	17 33 03	22 34 43	17 26 03	23 38 22	1 08.9	2 09.2	6 46.9	9 13.5	12 52.4	1 26.4	28 43.6	28 05.0	28 44.4	22 16.8
15 W	17 36 59	23 35 44	29 53 35	6♌11 56	1 09.7	3 23.0	8 02.1	9 56.5	13 12.8	1 26.8	28 46.2	28 03.1	28 43.6	22 17.8
16 Th	17 40 56	24 36 45	12♌33 39	18 59 00	1 10.5	4 38.9	9 17.3	10 39.6	13 33.3	1R 27.1	28 48.7	28 01.0	28 42.8	22 18.9
17 F	17 44 53	25 37 47	25 28 13	2♍01 34	1 11.1	5 56.8	10 32.5	11 22.8	13 53.9	1 27.2	28 51.1	27 59.0	28 42.1	22 20.0
18 Sa	17 48 49	26 38 51	8♍39 16	15 21 31	1R 11.4	7 16.4	11 47.7	12 05.9	14 14.5	1 27.1	28 53.5	27 56.9	28 41.3	22 21.1
19 Su	17 52 46	27 39 55	22 08 31	29 00 23	1 11.5	8 37.4	13 02.9	12 49.2	14 35.3	1 26.7	28 55.7	27 54.8	28 40.6	22 22.2
20 M	17 56 42	28 41 00	5♎57 09	12♎58 49	1 11.4	9 59.7	14 18.1	13 32.5	14 56.1	1 26.2	28 57.8	27 52.6	28 40.0	22 23.3
21 Tu	18 00 39	29 42 05	20 05 15	27 16 14	1 11.3	11 23.2	15 33.3	14 15.8	15 17.0	1 25.5	28 59.8	27 50.4	28 39.3	22 24.5
22 W	18 04 35	0♑43 12	4♏31 22	11♏50 13	1D 11.2	12 47.6	16 48.5	14 59.2	15 38.0	1 24.6	29 01.7	27 48.2	28 38.7	22 25.7
23 Th	18 08 32	1 44 20	19 12 09	26 36 26	1 11.2	14 12.9	18 03.7	15 42.6	15 59.1	1 23.5	29 03.5	27 46.0	28 38.2	22 26.9
24 F	18 12 28	2 45 28	4♐02 15	11♐28 41	1 11.3	15 39.0	19 18.9	16 26.0	16 20.3	1 22.2	29 05.2	27 43.7	28 37.6	22 28.1
25 Sa	18 16 25	3 46 37	18 54 46	26 19 32	1R 11.4	17 05.7	20 34.1	17 09.6	16 41.6	1 20.7	29 06.8	27 41.4	28 37.1	22 29.3
26 Su	18 20 22	4 47 46	3♑41 59	11♑01 13	1 11.3	18 33.2	21 49.2	17 53.1	17 02.9	1 19.0	29 08.2	27 39.1	28 36.6	22 30.6
27 M	18 24 18	5 48 55	18 16 24	25 26 47	1 11.1	20 01.2	23 04.4	18 36.7	17 24.3	1 17.1	29 09.6	27 36.8	28 36.2	22 31.9
28 Tu	18 28 15	6 50 05	2♒31 48	9♒30 57	1 10.5	21 29.7	24 19.6	19 20.3	17 45.8	1 15.0	29 10.9	27 34.4	28 35.8	22 33.2
29 W	18 32 11	7 51 14	16 23 57	23 10 39	1 09.7	22 58.7	25 34.7	20 04.0	18 07.4	1 12.7	29 12.0	27 32.0	28 35.4	22 34.5
30 Th	18 36 08	8 52 24	29 50 59	6♓25 06	1 08.8	24 28.1	26 49.9	20 47.8	18 29.0	1 10.2	29 13.0	27 29.6	28 35.1	22 35.9
31 F	18 40 04	9 53 33	12♓53 12	19 15 38	1 08.0	25 58.0	28 05.0	21 31.5	18 50.8	1 07.6	29 14.0	27 27.1	28 34.8	22 37.2

Astro Data

Aspect	Dy Hr Mn
♅R	3 22:02
♇D	4 20:20
♃⚺♅	5 13:14
☽0N	8 18:01
♃△♆	11 4:45
☿R	12 14:56
☽0S	23 2:14
☿D	2 12:30
☽0N	6 0:50
♄⚹♅	6 14:20
♄⚻♆	14 17:48
♃R	17 8:39
☽0S	20 10:32

Planet Ingress

Planet	Dy Hr Mn
♀ ♐	15 4:12
♃ ♍	16 21:20
☉ ♐	22 5:31
☿ ♏R	23 18:54
♂ ♐	1 13:06
♀ ♑	9 2:12
☿ ♐	12 15:41
☉ ♑	21 19:02

Last Aspect / ☽ Ingress

Last Aspect Dy Hr Mn		☽ Ingress Dy Hr Mn
2 23:45	♆ □	♒ 3 0:22
5 7:13	♆ ⚹	♓ 5 8:00
7 16:06	♅ △	♈ 7 18:31
10 5:36	♆ ☌	♉ 10 6:42
12 18:39	♃ □	♊ 12 19:28
15 7:33	♃ ⚹	♋ 15 7:51
17 17:12	♆ ⚹	♌ 17 18:37
20 0:57	♆ △	♍ 20 2:22
22 4:09	♅ ⚹	♎ 22 6:26
24 5:59	♆ ☍	♏ 24 7:24
26 4:35	♅ △	♐ 26 6:50
28 5:12	♆ △	♑ 28 6:47
30 7:38	♂ ⚹	♒ 30 9:08

Last Aspect / ☽ Ingress

Last Aspect Dy Hr Mn		☽ Ingress Dy Hr Mn
2 13:10	♆ ⚹	♓ 2 15:09
4 21:38	♅ △	♈ 5 0:52
7 10:41	♆ ☌	♉ 7 13:01
9 22:48	♄ △	♊ 10 1:49
12 11:24	♆ ⚹	♋ 12 13:50
14 21:48	♄ ⚹	♌ 15 0:12
17 5:56	♆ △	♍ 17 8:18
19 11:52	♄ ☌	♎ 19 13:44
21 16:20	☉ ⚹	♏ 21 16:32
23 15:58	♄ ⚹	♐ 23 17:29
25 16:32	♄ □	♑ 25 17:58
27 18:17	♄ △	♒ 27 19:42
29 21:43	♆ ⚹	♓ 30 0:16

☽ Phases & Eclipses

Dy Hr Mn	
3 21:24	☽ 11♒33
11 22:27	○ 19♉38
19 22:10	☾ 27♌40
26 13:47	● 4♐24
3 12:46	☽ 11♓27
11 17:30	○ 19♊46
11 17:44	☍ A 0.804
19 9:29	☾ 27♍33
26 1:02	● 4♑20
26 0:58:45	● T 02'19"

Astro Data

1 November 2038
Julian Day # 50709
SVP 4♓43'21"
GC 27♐22.9 ⚴ 27♐37.7
Eris 28♈05.1R ⚵ 6♐14.5
⚷ 3♋40.2R ⚶ 21♌57.7
☽ Mean ☊ 3♋56.5

1 December 2038
Julian Day # 50739
SVP 4♓43'16"
GC 27♐23.0 ⚴ 8♑24.5
Eris 27♈49.1R ⚵ 16♐29.4
⚷ 2♋22.9R ⚶ 29♌31.9
☽ Mean ☊ 2♋21.2

LONGITUDE — January 2039

Day	Sid.Time	☉	0 hr ☽	Noon ☽	True ☊	☿	♀	♂	⚳	♃	♄	♅	♆	♇
1 Sa	18 44 01	10♑54 43	25♓32 46	1♈45 07	1♋07.4	27♐28.3	29♑20.1	22♑15.3	19♒12.5	1♍04.7	29♍14.8	27♋24.7	28♈34.5	22♒38.6
2 Su	18 47 57	11 55 52	7♈53 11	13 57 32	1D 07.2	28 59.0	0♒35.2	22 59.2	19 34.4	1R 01.7	29 15.5	27R 22.2	28R 34.3	22 40.0
3 M	18 51 54	12 57 01	19 58 45	25 57 27	1 07.6	0♑30.1	1 50.3	23 43.1	19 56.3	0 58.5	29 16.1	27 19.7	28 34.1	22 41.4
4 Tu	18 55 51	13 58 10	1♉54 13	7♉49 40	1 08.5	2 01.6	3 05.3	24 27.0	20 18.3	0 55.1	29 16.6	27 17.2	28 33.9	22 42.8
5 W	18 59 47	14 59 18	13 44 22	19 38 52	1 09.8	3 33.4	4 20.4	25 11.0	20 40.3	0 51.5	29 17.0	27 14.7	28 33.8	22 44.3
6 Th	19 03 44	16 00 27	25 33 43	1♊29 25	1 11.2	5 05.7	5 35.4	25 55.0	21 02.4	0 47.7	29 17.2	27 12.1	28 33.7	22 45.7
7 F	19 07 40	17 01 35	7♊26 25	13 25 10	1 12.5	6 38.3	6 50.5	26 39.0	21 24.5	0 43.8	29R 17.4	27 09.6	28 33.6	22 47.2
8 Sa	19 11 37	18 02 42	19 26 01	25 29 19	1R 13.2	8 11.4	8 05.5	27 23.1	21 46.8	0 39.6	29 17.5	27 07.0	28D 33.6	22 48.7
9 Su	19 15 33	19 03 50	1♋35 21	7♋44 21	1 13.2	9 44.8	9 20.5	28 07.3	22 09.0	0 35.4	29 17.4	27 04.4	28 33.6	22 50.2
10 M	19 19 30	20 04 57	13 56 32	20 12 01	1 12.2	11 18.6	10 35.4	28 51.4	22 31.3	0 30.9	29 17.2	27 01.9	28 33.7	22 51.7
11 Tu	19 23 26	21 06 04	26 30 54	2♌53 15	1 10.1	12 52.9	11 50.4	29 35.7	22 53.7	0 26.3	29 17.0	26 59.3	28 33.8	22 53.2
12 W	19 27 23	22 07 11	9♌19 04	15 48 21	1 07.2	14 27.6	13 05.3	0♒19.9	23 16.2	0 21.5	29 16.6	26 56.7	28 33.9	22 54.8
13 Th	19 31 20	23 08 18	22 21 03	28 57 06	1 03.8	16 02.8	14 20.3	1 04.2	23 38.6	0 16.5	29 16.1	26 54.1	28 34.0	22 56.3
14 F	19 35 16	24 09 24	5♍36 25	12♍18 54	1 00.3	17 38.4	15 35.2	1 48.6	24 01.2	0 11.4	29 15.5	26 51.5	28 34.2	22 57.9
15 Sa	19 39 13	25 10 30	19 04 28	25 53 01	0 57.2	19 14.5	16 50.0	2 33.0	24 23.7	0 06.1	29 14.8	26 48.9	28 34.4	22 59.5
16 Su	19 43 09	26 11 36	2♎44 25	9♎38 36	0 55.0	20 51.0	18 04.9	3 17.4	24 46.4	0 00.7	29 14.0	26 46.2	28 34.7	23 01.1
17 M	19 47 06	27 12 42	16 35 26	23 34 49	0D 54.1	22 28.1	19 19.8	4 01.9	25 09.1	29♌55.1	29 13.0	26 43.6	28 34.9	23 02.7
18 Tu	19 51 02	28 13 48	0♏36 36	7♏40 39	0 54.3	24 05.7	20 34.6	4 46.4	25 31.8	29 49.4	29 12.0	26 41.0	28 35.3	23 04.3
19 W	19 54 59	29 14 53	14 46 46	21 54 45	0 55.5	25 43.9	21 49.4	5 30.9	25 54.6	29 43.5	29 10.9	26 38.4	28 35.6	23 05.9
20 Th	19 58 55	0♒15 59	29 04 18	6♐15 05	0 57.1	27 22.6	23 04.2	6 15.5	26 17.4	29 37.5	29 09.6	26 35.8	28 36.0	23 07.6
21 F	20 02 52	1 17 04	13♐26 44	20 38 48	0R 58.3	29 01.9	24 19.0	7 00.2	26 40.2	29 31.3	29 08.3	26 33.2	28 36.4	23 09.2
22 Sa	20 06 49	2 18 08	27 50 46	5♑02 03	0 58.6	0♒41.7	25 33.8	7 44.9	27 03.1	29 25.0	29 06.8	26 30.6	28 36.9	23 10.9
23 Su	20 10 45	3 19 12	12♑12 05	19 20 13	0 57.4	2 22.1	26 48.5	8 29.6	27 26.1	29 18.6	29 05.3	26 28.0	28 37.4	23 12.5
24 M	20 14 42	4 20 16	26 25 50	3♒28 19	0 54.4	4 03.2	28 03.2	9 14.4	27 49.1	29 12.1	29 03.6	26 25.4	28 37.9	23 14.2
25 Tu	20 18 38	5 21 18	10♒27 04	17 21 36	0 49.7	5 44.8	29 17.9	9 59.1	28 12.1	29 05.4	29 01.8	26 22.8	28 38.5	23 15.9
26 W	20 22 35	6 22 20	24 11 29	0♓56 21	0 43.8	7 27.0	0♓32.6	10 44.0	28 35.2	28 58.6	29 00.0	26 20.3	28 39.1	23 17.6
27 Th	20 26 31	7 23 20	7♓35 58	14 10 14	0 37.3	9 09.8	1 47.2	11 28.8	28 58.2	28 51.8	28 58.0	26 17.7	28 39.7	23 19.3
28 F	20 30 28	8 24 20	20 39 08	27 02 46	0 31.1	10 53.3	3 01.8	12 13.7	29 21.4	28 44.8	28 55.9	26 15.2	28 40.4	23 21.0
29 Sa	20 34 24	9 25 19	3♈21 21	9♈35 10	0 25.8	12 37.3	4 16.4	12 58.7	29 44.5	28 37.7	28 53.7	26 12.6	28 41.1	23 22.7
30 Su	20 38 21	10 26 16	15 44 37	21 50 10	0 22.1	14 21.9	5 30.9	13 43.6	0♓07.7	28 30.5	28 51.5	26 10.1	28 41.8	23 24.4
31 M	20 42 18	11 27 12	27 52 20	3♉51 41	0D 20.1	16 07.0	6 45.4	14 28.6	0 30.9	28 23.2	28 49.1	26 07.6	28 42.6	23 26.1

LONGITUDE — February 2039

Day	Sid.Time	☉	0 hr ☽	Noon ☽	True ☊	☿	♀	♂	⚳	♃	♄	♅	♆	♇
1 Tu	20 46 14	12♒28 07	9♉48 50	15♉44 26	0♋19.8	17♒52.6	7♓59.9	15♑13.7	0♓54.2	28♌15.9	28♍46.6	26♋05.1	28♈43.4	23♒27.9
2 W	20 50 11	13 29 01	21 39 06	27 33 32	0 20.8	19 38.7	9 14.3	15 58.8	1 17.4	28R 08.5	28R 44.1	26R 02.7	28 44.3	23 29.6
3 Th	20 54 07	14 29 53	3♊28 22	9♊24 15	0 22.4	21 25.2	10 28.7	16 43.9	1 40.7	28 01.0	28 41.5	26 00.2	28 45.1	23 31.3
4 F	20 58 04	15 30 44	15 21 49	21 21 38	0R 23.7	23 12.0	11 43.1	17 29.0	2 04.1	27 53.4	28 38.7	25 57.8	28 46.0	23 33.1
5 Sa	21 02 00	16 31 34	27 24 15	3♋30 12	0 24.1	24 59.0	12 57.4	18 14.2	2 27.4	27 45.8	28 35.9	25 55.4	28 47.0	23 34.8
6 Su	21 05 57	17 32 22	9♋39 53	15 53 43	0 22.7	26 46.2	14 11.7	18 59.4	2 50.8	27 38.1	28 33.0	25 53.0	28 47.9	23 36.6
7 M	21 09 53	18 33 09	22 11 57	28 34 49	0 19.1	28 33.3	15 26.0	19 44.6	3 14.2	27 30.4	28 30.0	25 50.7	28 48.9	23 38.3
8 Tu	21 13 50	19 33 55	5♌02 26	11♌34 47	0 13.4	0♓20.3	16 40.2	20 29.9	3 37.6	27 22.6	28 26.9	25 48.3	28 49.9	23 40.1
9 W	21 17 47	20 34 39	18 11 50	24 53 23	0 05.6	2 06.8	17 54.4	21 15.2	4 01.0	27 14.8	28 23.8	25 46.0	28 51.0	23 41.8
10 Th	21 21 43	21 35 22	1♍39 09	8♍28 49	29♊56.7	3 52.7	19 08.5	22 00.5	4 24.5	27 06.9	28 20.5	25 43.7	28 52.1	23 43.6
11 F	21 25 40	22 36 04	15 21 57	22 18 06	29 47.6	5 37.7	20 22.6	22 45.9	4 48.0	26 59.0	28 17.2	25 41.5	28 53.2	23 45.3
12 Sa	21 29 36	23 36 45	29 16 47	6♎17 30	29 39.2	7 21.5	21 36.6	23 31.3	5 11.4	26 51.1	28 13.8	25 39.3	28 54.4	23 47.1
13 Su	21 33 33	24 37 24	13♎19 46	20 23 07	29 32.6	9 03.7	22 50.6	24 16.7	5 35.0	26 43.2	28 10.3	25 37.1	28 55.5	23 48.9
14 M	21 37 29	25 38 03	27 27 10	4♏31 32	29 28.2	10 43.9	24 04.6	25 02.2	5 58.5	26 35.3	28 06.8	25 34.9	28 56.7	23 50.6
15 Tu	21 41 26	26 38 40	11♏35 56	18 40 07	29D 26.2	12 21.5	25 18.5	25 47.7	6 22.0	26 27.3	28 03.1	25 32.8	28 58.0	23 52.4
16 W	21 45 22	27 39 16	25 43 53	2♐47 06	29 26.0	13 56.2	26 32.4	26 33.2	6 45.6	26 19.4	27 59.4	25 30.6	28 59.3	23 54.1
17 Th	21 49 19	28 39 52	9♐49 39	16 51 24	29R 26.7	15 27.3	27 46.2	27 18.8	7 09.1	26 11.5	27 55.7	25 28.6	29 00.6	23 55.9
18 F	21 53 16	29 40 26	23 52 16	0♑52 09	29 27.1	16 54.3	29 00.0	28 04.4	7 32.7	26 03.6	27 51.8	25 26.5	29 01.9	23 57.6
19 Sa	21 57 12	0♓40 58	7♑50 53	14 48 19	29 26.1	18 16.4	0♈13.8	28 50.1	7 56.3	25 55.6	27 47.9	25 24.5	29 03.2	23 59.4
20 Su	22 01 09	1 41 30	21 44 13	28 38 22	29 22.7	19 33.0	1 27.5	29 35.7	8 19.9	25 47.8	27 44.0	25 22.6	29 04.6	24 01.1
21 M	22 05 05	2 42 00	5♒30 27	12♒20 10	29 16.4	20 43.5	2 41.1	0♒21.4	8 43.6	25 39.9	27 40.0	25 20.6	29 06.0	24 02.9
22 Tu	22 09 02	3 42 28	19 07 12	25 51 11	29 07.5	21 47.1	3 54.7	1 07.1	9 07.2	25 32.1	27 35.9	25 18.7	29 07.5	24 04.6
23 W	22 12 58	4 42 55	2♓31 48	9♓08 47	28 56.5	22 43.3	5 08.2	1 52.8	9 30.8	25 24.3	27 31.7	25 16.9	29 08.9	24 06.3
24 Th	22 16 55	5 43 20	15 41 52	22 10 51	28 44.3	23 31.4	6 21.7	2 38.6	9 54.4	25 16.6	27 27.5	25 15.1	29 10.4	24 08.1
25 F	22 20 51	6 43 43	28 35 38	4♈56 11	28 32.2	24 10.9	7 35.2	3 24.4	10 18.1	25 08.9	27 23.3	25 13.3	29 12.0	24 09.8
26 Sa	22 24 48	7 44 05	11♈12 33	17 24 52	28 21.3	24 41.3	8 48.6	4 10.2	10 41.7	25 01.3	27 19.0	25 11.6	29 13.5	24 11.5
27 Su	22 28 45	8 44 25	23 33 21	29 38 18	28 12.5	25 02.3	10 01.9	4 56.0	11 05.4	24 53.8	27 14.7	25 09.9	29 15.1	24 13.2
28 M	22 32 41	9 44 42	5♉40 08	11♉39 16	28 06.3	25R 13.7	11 15.2	5 41.9	11 29.0	24 46.3	27 10.3	25 08.2	29 16.7	24 14.9

Astro Data

	Dy Hr Mn
☽ 0N	2 8:19
♄ R	8 11:55
♆ D	8 17:00
☽ 0S	16 16:03
♃⚺♄	26 5:36
♃△♆	29 1:29
☽ 0N	29 16:21
♄⚻♆	2 10:56
☽ 0S	12 21:05
♀0N	21 1:44
♃⚺♅	24 18:15
☽ 0N	26 0:26
☿0N	26 13:38

Planet Ingress

		Dy Hr Mn
♀	♒	2 0:45
☿	♑	3 4:05
♂	♑	12 1:12
♃	♌R	16 14:55
☉	♒	20 5:43
☿	♒	22 2:00
♀	♓	26 1:32
⚳	♓	30 4:01
☿	♓	8 7:27
☊	♊R	10 3:24
☉	♓	18 19:45
♀	♈	19 7:31
♂	♒	21 0:46

Last Aspect / ☽ Ingress (January)

Last Aspect Dy Hr Mn		☽ Ingress Dy Hr Mn
1 7:08	♄ ☍	♈ 1 8:36
3 17:16	♆ ☌	♉ 3 20:09
6 7:33	♄ △	♊ 6 8:59
8 19:29	♄ □	♋ 8 20:53
11 5:14	♄ ⚹	♌ 11 6:35
13 11:18	♆ △	♍ 13 13:54
15 17:53	♄ ☌	♎ 15 19:13
17 22:45	♃ ⚹	♏ 17 22:58
20 1:14	☉ ⚹	♐ 20 1:33
22 2:41	♃ △	♑ 22 3:36
24 4:29	♄ △	♒ 24 6:04
26 8:32	♃ ☍	♓ 26 10:19
28 15:34	♄ ☍	♈ 28 17:36
31 1:40	♆ ☌	♉ 31 4:15

Last Aspect / ☽ Ingress (February)

Last Aspect Dy Hr Mn		☽ Ingress Dy Hr Mn
2 14:23	♄ △	♊ 2 16:57
5 2:43	♆ ⚹	♋ 5 5:07
7 12:26	♆ □	♌ 7 14:39
9 19:03	♆ △	♍ 9 21:05
11 22:15	♄ ☌	♎ 12 1:14
14 2:31	♆ ☍	♏ 14 4:19
16 3:53	♄ ⚹	♐ 16 7:16
18 9:47	☉ ⚹	♑ 18 10:30
20 13:46	♂ ☌	♒ 20 14:22
22 17:53	♆ ⚹	♓ 22 19:26
24 21:49	♄ ☍	♈ 25 2:39
27 11:14	♆ ☌	♉ 27 12:43

☽ Phases & Eclipses

Dy Hr Mn		
2 7:37	☽	11♈45
10 11:45	○	20♋04
17 18:41	☾	27♎30
24 13:36	●	4♒24
1 4:45	☽	12♉10
9 3:39	○	20♌14
16 2:36	☾	27♏16
23 3:17	●	4♓21

Astro Data

1 January 2039
Julian Day # 50770
SVP 4♓43'11"
GC 27♐23.0 ⚴ 20♑01.3
Eris 27♈39.5R ⚵ 27♐26.2
⚷ 0♋26.7R ⚶ 2♍23.4R
☽ Mean ☊ 0♋42.7

1 February 2039
Julian Day # 50801
SVP 4♓43'06"
GC 27♐23.1 ⚴ 1♒32.7
Eris 27♈40.1 ⚵ 8♑12.7
⚷ 28♊46.7R ⚶ 28♌17.5R
☽ Mean ☊ 29♊04.2

March 2039 LONGITUDE

Day	Sid.Time	☉	0 hr ☽	Noon ☽	True ☊	☿	♀	♂	⚳	♃	♄	♅	♆	♇
1 Tu	22 36 38	10♓44 58	17♉36 14	23♉31 37	28♊02.6	25♓15.4	12♈28.4	6♒27.8	11♓52.7	24♌38.9	27♍05.8	25♋06.6	29♈18.3	24♒16.6
2 W	22 40 34	11 45 12	29 26 00	5♊20 04	28D 01.2	25R 07.5	13 41.5	7 13.7	12 16.3	24R 31.6	27R 01.4	25R 05.0	29 19.9	24 18.3
3 Th	22 44 31	12 45 24	11♊14 28	17 09 54	28R 01.1	24 50.3	14 54.6	7 59.6	12 40.0	24 24.3	26 56.9	25 03.5	29 21.6	24 20.0
4 F	22 48 27	13 45 34	23 07 05	29 06 41	28 01.2	24 24.3	16 07.6	8 45.5	13 03.6	24 17.2	26 52.4	25 02.0	29 23.3	24 21.7
5 Sa	22 52 24	14 45 42	5♋09 22	11♋15 49	28 00.6	23 50.1	17 20.6	9 31.5	13 27.3	24 10.1	26 47.8	25 00.6	29 25.0	24 23.4
6 Su	22 56 20	15 45 47	17 26 37	23 42 17	27 58.1	23 08.7	18 33.4	10 17.5	13 50.9	24 03.2	26 43.2	24 59.2	29 26.7	24 25.0
7 M	23 00 17	16 45 51	0♌03 19	6♌30 03	27 53.0	22 21.0	19 46.3	11 03.5	14 14.6	23 56.4	26 38.6	24 57.9	29 28.5	24 26.7
8 Tu	23 04 14	17 45 52	13 02 46	19 41 34	27 45.2	21 28.3	20 59.0	11 49.5	14 38.2	23 49.6	26 33.9	24 56.6	29 30.3	24 28.3
9 W	23 08 10	18 45 52	26 26 27	3♍17 15	27 35.0	20 31.9	22 11.7	12 35.5	15 01.8	23 43.0	26 29.3	24 55.3	29 32.1	24 30.0
10 Th	23 12 07	19 45 49	10♍13 38	17 15 09	27 23.2	19 33.2	23 24.2	13 21.6	15 25.4	23 36.5	26 24.6	24 54.2	29 33.9	24 31.6
11 F	23 16 03	20 45 45	24 21 11	1♎31 01	27 10.9	18 33.5	24 36.8	14 07.6	15 49.0	23 30.1	26 19.9	24 53.0	29 35.7	24 33.2
12 Sa	23 20 00	21 45 38	8♎43 50	15 58 47	26 59.6	17 34.2	25 49.2	14 53.7	16 12.6	23 23.9	26 15.2	24 51.9	29 37.6	24 34.8
13 Su	23 23 56	22 45 30	23 14 59	0♏31 36	26 50.3	16 36.6	27 01.6	15 39.8	16 36.2	23 17.7	26 10.5	24 50.8	29 39.5	24 36.4
14 M	23 27 53	23 45 20	7♏47 49	15 02 58	26 43.7	15 41.8	28 13.9	16 26.0	16 59.8	23 11.7	26 05.7	24 49.8	29 41.4	24 38.0
15 Tu	23 31 49	24 45 09	22 16 25	29 27 42	26 40.0	14 50.8	29 26.1	17 12.1	17 23.4	23 05.9	26 01.0	24 48.9	29 43.3	24 39.5
16 W	23 35 46	25 44 55	6♐36 27	13♐42 24	26 38.6	14 04.4	0♉38.2	17 58.3	17 46.9	23 00.1	25 56.2	24 48.0	29 45.2	24 41.1
17 Th	23 39 43	26 44 41	20 45 26	27 45 27	26 38.4	13 23.2	1 50.3	18 44.5	18 10.5	22 54.6	25 51.5	24 47.1	29 47.2	24 42.6
18 F	23 43 39	27 44 24	4♑42 29	11♑36 32	26 38.1	12 47.8	3 02.3	19 30.7	18 34.0	22 49.1	25 46.8	24 46.3	29 49.2	24 44.2
19 Sa	23 47 36	28 44 06	18 27 42	25 16 03	26 36.4	12 18.3	4 14.2	20 16.9	18 57.5	22 43.9	25 42.0	24 45.6	29 51.1	24 45.7
20 Su	23 51 32	29 43 46	2♒01 39	8♒44 34	26 32.2	11 55.0	5 26.0	21 03.1	19 21.0	22 38.7	25 37.3	24 44.9	29 53.2	24 47.2
21 M	23 55 29	0♈43 25	15 24 48	22 02 22	26 25.1	11 37.9	6 37.8	21 49.4	19 44.5	22 33.8	25 32.6	24 44.3	29 55.2	24 48.7
22 Tu	23 59 25	1 43 01	28 37 14	5♓09 19	26 15.1	11 27.0	7 49.4	22 35.6	20 08.0	22 29.0	25 27.9	24 43.7	29 57.2	24 50.1
23 W	0 03 22	2 42 36	11♓38 35	18 04 54	26 02.8	11D 22.3	9 01.0	23 21.9	20 31.5	22 24.3	25 23.2	24 43.1	29 59.3	24 51.6
24 Th	0 07 18	3 42 08	24 28 12	0♈48 25	25 49.1	11 23.4	10 12.5	24 08.2	20 54.9	22 19.8	25 18.5	24 42.6	0♉01.3	24 53.0
25 F	0 11 15	4 41 39	7♈05 29	13 19 24	25 35.5	11 30.2	11 23.9	24 54.4	21 18.3	22 15.5	25 13.8	24 42.2	0 03.4	24 54.5
26 Sa	0 15 11	5 41 07	19 30 10	25 37 53	25 22.9	11 42.5	12 35.2	25 40.7	21 41.7	22 11.3	25 09.2	24 41.8	0 05.5	24 55.9
27 Su	0 19 08	6 40 33	1♉42 42	7♉44 47	25 12.6	12 00.1	13 46.4	26 27.0	22 05.1	22 07.4	25 04.6	24 41.5	0 07.6	24 57.3
28 M	0 23 05	7 39 57	13 44 25	19 41 55	25 04.9	12 22.5	14 57.6	27 13.3	22 28.5	22 03.6	25 00.0	24 41.2	0 09.7	24 58.6
29 Tu	0 27 01	8 39 20	25 37 40	1♊32 08	25 00.1	12 49.7	16 08.6	27 59.6	22 51.8	21 59.9	24 55.4	24 41.0	0 11.8	25 00.0
30 W	0 30 58	9 38 39	7♊25 49	13 19 16	24D 57.7	13 21.4	17 19.5	28 45.9	23 15.1	21 56.5	24 50.9	24 40.9	0 14.0	25 01.3
31 Th	0 34 54	10 37 57	19 13 04	25 07 52	24 57.2	13 57.2	18 30.3	29 32.2	23 38.4	21 53.2	24 46.5	24 40.7	0 16.1	25 02.7

April 2039 LONGITUDE

Day	Sid.Time	☉	0 hr ☽	Noon ☽	True ☊	☿	♀	♂	⚳	♃	♄	♅	♆	♇
1 F	0 38 51	11♈37 12	1♋04 20	7♋03 08	24♊57.4	14♓37.1	19♉41.1	0♓18.6	24♓01.6	21♌50.1	24♍42.0	24♋40.7	0♉18.3	25♒04.0
2 Sa	0 42 47	12 36 25	13 04 59	19 10 33	24R 57.3	15 20.7	20 51.7	1 04.9	24 24.8	21R 47.2	24R 37.6	24D 40.7	0 20.5	25 05.3
3 Su	0 46 44	13 35 36	25 20 31	1♌35 31	24 55.8	16 07.8	22 02.2	1 51.2	24 48.0	21 44.5	24 33.3	24 40.8	0 22.6	25 06.5
4 M	0 50 40	14 34 44	7♌56 09	14 22 56	24 52.2	16 58.3	23 12.5	2 37.5	25 11.2	21 42.0	24 28.9	24 40.9	0 24.8	25 07.8
5 Tu	0 54 37	15 33 50	20 56 16	27 36 28	24 46.2	17 51.9	24 22.8	3 23.8	25 34.3	21 39.6	24 24.7	24 41.0	0 27.0	25 09.0
6 W	0 58 34	16 32 54	4♍23 40	11♍17 53	24 37.9	18 48.6	25 33.0	4 10.1	25 57.4	21 37.5	24 20.5	24 41.2	0 29.2	25 10.2
7 Th	1 02 30	17 31 55	18 18 55	25 26 23	24 28.1	19 48.2	26 43.0	4 56.5	26 20.5	21 35.5	24 16.3	24 41.5	0 31.5	25 11.4
8 F	1 06 27	18 30 54	2♎39 44	9♎58 11	24 17.7	20 50.4	27 52.9	5 42.8	26 43.5	21 33.7	24 12.2	24 41.8	0 33.7	25 12.6
9 Sa	1 10 23	19 29 51	17 20 50	24 46 40	24 08.0	21 55.3	29 02.7	6 29.1	27 06.5	21 32.1	24 08.1	24 42.2	0 35.9	25 13.8
10 Su	1 14 20	20 28 47	2♏14 34	9♏43 22	24 00.0	23 02.6	0♊12.4	7 15.4	27 29.5	21 30.6	24 04.1	24 42.6	0 38.1	25 14.9
11 M	1 18 16	21 27 40	17 11 57	24 39 16	23 54.5	24 12.3	1 21.9	8 01.7	27 52.4	21 29.4	24 00.2	24 43.1	0 40.4	25 16.0
12 Tu	1 22 13	22 26 32	2♐04 21	9♐26 24	23D 51.5	25 24.4	2 31.3	8 48.0	28 15.3	21 28.3	23 56.3	24 43.7	0 42.6	25 17.1
13 W	1 26 09	23 25 22	16 44 44	23 58 52	23 50.7	26 38.6	3 40.6	9 34.4	28 38.2	21 27.5	23 52.5	24 44.2	0 44.9	25 18.2
14 Th	1 30 06	24 24 10	1♑08 26	8♑13 13	23 51.2	27 54.9	4 49.7	10 20.7	29 01.0	21 26.8	23 48.7	24 44.9	0 47.1	25 19.2
15 F	1 34 03	25 22 56	15 13 09	22 08 15	23R 51.8	29 13.3	5 58.7	11 07.0	29 23.8	21 26.3	23 45.0	24 45.6	0 49.4	25 20.3
16 Sa	1 37 59	26 21 41	28 58 37	5♒44 25	23 51.4	0♈33.7	7 07.6	11 53.3	29 46.5	21 26.0	23 41.4	24 46.3	0 51.6	25 21.3
17 Su	1 41 56	27 20 24	12♒25 51	19 03 09	23 49.2	1 56.1	8 16.4	12 39.6	0♈09.2	21D 25.9	23 37.9	24 47.1	0 53.9	25 22.2
18 M	1 45 52	28 19 06	25 36 31	2♓06 12	23 44.7	3 20.4	9 25.0	13 25.9	0 31.9	21 26.0	23 34.4	24 48.0	0 56.1	25 23.2
19 Tu	1 49 49	29 17 45	8♓32 25	14 55 22	23 37.9	4 46.5	10 33.4	14 12.1	0 54.5	21 26.2	23 31.0	24 48.9	0 58.4	25 24.2
20 W	1 53 45	0♉16 23	21 15 13	27 32 07	23 29.3	6 14.4	11 41.7	14 58.4	1 17.1	21 26.7	23 27.7	24 49.9	1 00.7	25 25.1
21 Th	1 57 42	1 14 59	3♈46 13	9♈57 39	23 19.6	7 44.2	12 49.9	15 44.7	1 39.7	21 27.3	23 24.4	24 50.9	1 02.9	25 26.0
22 F	2 01 38	2 13 33	16 06 32	22 13 00	23 09.8	9 15.8	13 57.9	16 30.9	2 02.1	21 28.1	23 21.2	24 51.9	1 05.2	25 26.8
23 Sa	2 05 35	3 12 06	28 17 09	4♉19 08	23 00.9	10 49.1	15 05.8	17 17.1	2 24.6	21 29.1	23 18.1	24 53.1	1 07.5	25 27.7
24 Su	2 09 32	4 10 36	10♉19 08	16 17 19	22 53.6	12 24.2	16 13.5	18 03.4	2 47.0	21 30.3	23 15.1	24 54.2	1 09.7	25 28.5
25 M	2 13 28	5 09 05	22 13 54	28 09 09	22 48.3	14 01.0	17 21.0	18 49.6	3 09.3	21 31.7	23 12.2	24 55.4	1 12.0	25 29.3
26 Tu	2 17 25	6 07 32	4♊03 22	9♊56 54	22 45.3	15 39.6	18 28.4	19 35.8	3 31.6	21 33.2	23 09.4	24 56.7	1 14.2	25 30.1
27 W	2 21 21	7 05 56	15 50 06	21 43 25	22D 44.3	17 19.9	19 35.6	20 21.9	3 53.9	21 35.0	23 06.6	24 58.0	1 16.5	25 30.8
28 Th	2 25 18	8 04 19	27 37 20	3♋32 20	22 44.8	19 02.0	20 42.6	21 08.1	4 16.1	21 36.9	23 04.0	24 59.4	1 18.8	25 31.6
29 F	2 29 14	9 02 40	9♋28 59	15 27 52	22 46.2	20 45.8	21 49.4	21 54.2	4 38.2	21 39.0	23 01.4	25 00.8	1 21.0	25 32.3
30 Sa	2 33 11	10 00 59	21 29 33	27 34 42	22 47.6	22 31.4	22 56.1	22 40.3	5 00.3	21 41.3	22 58.9	25 02.3	1 23.3	25 33.0

Astro Data

	Dy Hr Mn
☿R	1 4:10
♃☍♇	3 23:41
☿0S	8 11:24
☽0S	12 4:16
♅⚻♇	19 11:08
☉0N	20 18:32
☿D	23 19:20
☽0N	25 7:56
♄⚻♇	28 17:29
♄✶♅	1 19:11
♅D	1 23:32
☽0S	8 14:05
♃D	17 14:51
☿0N	20 10:53
☽0N	21 14:36

Planet Ingress

	Dy Hr Mn
♀ ♉	15 23:17
☉ ♈	20 18:32
♆ ♉	23 20:41
♂ ♓	1 2:23
♀ ♊	10 7:44
☿ ♈	16 2:00
⚳ ♈	17 2:13
☉ ♉	20 5:18

Last Aspect / ☽ Ingress

Last Aspect Dy Hr Mn		☽ Ingress Dy Hr Mn
1 19:12 ♄ △	♊	2 1:09
4 12:33 ♆ ✶	♋	4 13:46
6 22:53 ♆ □	♌	6 23:54
9 5:26 ♆ △	♍	9 6:16
11 3:22 ♄ ☌	♎	11 9:28
13 10:34 ♆ ☍	♏	13 11:08
15 6:16 ♄ ✶	♐	15 12:54
17 15:30 ♆ △	♑	17 15:52
19 20:09 ♆ □	♒	19 20:24
22 2:25 ♆ ✶	♓	22 2:32
24 1:39 ♄ ☍	♈	24 10:28
26 12:06 ♂ ✶	♉	26 20:37
29 4:18 ♂ □	♊	29 8:53
31 21:31 ♂ △	♋	31 21:50

Last Aspect / ☽ Ingress

Last Aspect Dy Hr Mn		☽ Ingress Dy Hr Mn
2 22:43 ♅ ☌	♌	3 8:58
5 7:36 ♇ ☍	♍	5 16:15
7 14:19 ♀ △	♎	7 19:36
9 12:44 ♇ △	♏	9 20:24
11 12:59 ♇ □	♐	11 20:38
13 16:53 ☿ □	♑	13 22:05
16 1:47 ☿ ✶	♒	16 1:48
18 4:25 ☉ ✶	♓	18 8:06
20 6:49 ♅ △	♈	20 16:44
22 18:23 ♇ ✶	♉	23 3:24
25 6:35 ♇ □	♊	25 15:45
27 19:43 ♇ △	♋	28 4:50
30 7:00 ♅ ☌	♌	30 16:44

☽ Phases & Eclipses

Dy Hr Mn	
3 2:15	☽ 12♊21
10 16:35	○ 19♍57
17 10:08	☾ 26♐40
24 17:59	● 3♈57
1 21:54	☽ 12♋02
9 2:53	○ 19♎07
15 18:07	☾ 25♑38
23 9:35	● 3♉06

Astro Data

1 March 2039
Julian Day # 50829
SVP 4♓43'02"
GC 27♐23.2 ⚴ 11♒25.8
Eris 27♈49.4 ⚵ 17♑17.4
⚷ 28♊08.6R ⚶ 21♌11.3R
☽ Mean ☊ 27♊35.3

1 April 2039
Julian Day # 50860
SVP 4♓42'59"
GC 27♐23.3 ⚴ 21♒14.4
Eris 28♈06.8 ⚵ 25♑53.0
⚷ 28♊41.5 ⚶ 17♌14.9R
☽ Mean ☊ 25♊56.8

LONGITUDE — May 2039

Day	Sid.Time	☉	0 hr ☽	Noon ☽	True ☊	☿	♀	♂	⚳	♃	♄	♅	♆	♇
1 Su	2 37 07	10♉59 15	3♌43 55	9♌57 49	22♊48.3	24♈18.7	24♊02.5	23♓26.4	5♈22.3	21♌43.8	22♍56.5	25♋03.8	1♉25.5	25♒33.6
2 M	2 41 04	11 57 30	16 17 01	22 42 03	22R47.7	26 07.9	25 08.8	24 12.4	5 44.2	21 46.4	22R54.2	25 05.4	1 27.7	25 34.2
3 Tu	2 45 01	12 55 42	29 13 25	5♍51 32	22 45.4	27 58.8	26 14.8	24 58.5	6 06.2	21 49.2	22 52.0	25 07.0	1 30.0	25 34.8
4 W	2 48 57	13 53 52	12♍36 42	19 29 05	22 41.6	29 51.4	27 20.6	25 44.5	6 28.0	21 52.2	22 49.9	25 08.6	1 32.2	25 35.4
5 Th	2 52 54	14 52 01	26 28 42	3♎35 22	22 36.7	1♉45.9	28 26.3	26 30.5	6 49.8	21 55.3	22 47.9	25 10.4	1 34.4	25 36.0
6 F	2 56 50	15 50 07	10♎48 44	18 08 14	22 31.2	3 42.1	29 31.7	27 16.5	7 11.5	21 58.7	22 45.9	25 12.1	1 36.6	25 36.5
7 Sa	3 00 47	16 48 12	25 33 08	3♏02 28	22 25.9	5 40.0	0♋36.8	28 02.4	7 33.2	22 02.2	22 44.1	25 13.9	1 38.8	25 37.0
8 Su	3 04 43	17 46 15	10♏35 10	18 10 03	22 21.7	7 39.7	1 41.8	28 48.3	7 54.8	22 05.8	22 42.4	25 15.7	1 41.0	25 37.5
9 M	3 08 40	18 44 16	25 45 53	3♐21 24	22 18.9	9 41.1	2 46.5	29 34.2	8 16.3	22 09.6	22 40.7	25 17.6	1 43.2	25 38.0
10 Tu	3 12 36	19 42 16	10♐55 25	18 26 47	22D17.8	11 44.1	3 50.9	0♈20.1	8 37.8	22 13.6	22 39.2	25 19.6	1 45.4	25 38.4
11 W	3 16 33	20 40 15	25 54 33	3♑17 53	22 18.1	13 48.6	4 55.1	1 06.0	8 59.2	22 17.8	22 37.8	25 21.6	1 47.6	25 38.8
12 Th	3 20 30	21 38 12	10♑36 06	17 48 43	22 19.3	15 54.6	5 59.1	1 51.8	9 20.5	22 22.1	22 36.4	25 23.6	1 49.7	25 39.2
13 F	3 24 26	22 36 08	24 55 26	1♒56 05	22 20.8	18 01.9	7 02.8	2 37.6	9 41.8	22 26.6	22 35.2	25 25.7	1 51.9	25 39.5
14 Sa	3 28 23	23 34 02	8♒50 37	15 39 08	22R21.8	20 10.3	8 06.2	3 23.4	10 03.0	22 31.2	22 34.0	25 27.8	1 54.0	25 39.9
15 Su	3 32 19	24 31 56	22 21 49	28 58 55	22 22.0	22 19.8	9 09.4	4 09.1	10 24.1	22 36.0	22 33.0	25 29.9	1 56.2	25 40.2
16 M	3 36 16	25 29 48	5♓30 46	11♓57 41	22 21.0	24 30.2	10 12.3	4 54.8	10 45.2	22 41.0	22 32.1	25 32.1	1 58.3	25 40.5
17 Tu	3 40 12	26 27 39	18 20 03	24 38 14	22 18.7	26 41.1	11 14.9	5 40.5	11 06.1	22 46.1	22 31.2	25 34.4	2 00.4	25 40.7
18 W	3 44 09	27 25 28	0♈52 37	7♈03 35	22 15.5	28 52.3	12 17.2	6 26.1	11 27.1	22 51.4	22 30.5	25 36.6	2 02.5	25 40.9
19 Th	3 48 05	28 23 17	13 11 28	19 16 37	22 11.7	1♊03.7	13 19.2	7 11.7	11 47.9	22 56.8	22 29.8	25 39.0	2 04.6	25 41.1
20 F	3 52 02	29 21 04	25 19 22	1♉20 00	22 07.9	3 14.9	14 20.9	7 57.3	12 08.6	23 02.3	22 29.3	25 41.3	2 06.6	25 41.3
21 Sa	3 55 59	0♊18 50	7♉18 48	13 16 04	22 04.4	5 25.6	15 22.2	8 42.8	12 29.3	23 08.0	22 28.9	25 43.7	2 08.7	25 41.4
22 Su	3 59 55	1 16 34	19 12 04	25 07 03	22 01.7	7 35.6	16 23.3	9 28.3	12 49.9	23 13.9	22 28.6	25 46.2	2 10.7	25 41.6
23 M	4 03 52	2 14 18	1♊01 16	6♊55 00	21 59.9	9 44.5	17 24.0	10 13.8	13 10.4	23 19.9	22 28.3	25 48.7	2 12.8	25 41.7
24 Tu	4 07 48	3 12 00	12 48 32	18 42 07	21D59.1	11 52.2	18 24.3	10 59.2	13 30.8	23 26.1	22D28.2	25 51.2	2 14.8	25 41.7
25 W	4 11 45	4 09 41	24 36 05	0♋30 45	21 59.3	13 58.3	19 24.3	11 44.6	13 51.1	23 32.4	22 28.2	25 53.7	2 16.8	25 41.8
26 Th	4 15 41	5 07 20	6♋26 28	12 23 35	22 00.2	16 02.7	20 23.9	12 29.9	14 11.4	23 38.8	22 28.3	25 56.3	2 18.7	25R41.8
27 F	4 19 38	6 04 58	18 22 31	24 23 41	22 01.5	18 05.2	21 23.2	13 15.2	14 31.5	23 45.4	22 28.5	25 59.0	2 20.7	25 41.8
28 Sa	4 23 34	7 02 35	0♌27 32	6♌34 31	22 02.8	20 05.5	22 22.0	14 00.4	14 51.6	23 52.1	22 28.8	26 01.6	2 22.7	25 41.8
29 Su	4 27 31	8 00 10	12 45 08	18 59 52	22 03.9	22 03.6	23 20.4	14 45.6	15 11.6	23 59.0	22 29.2	26 04.3	2 24.6	25 41.7
30 M	4 31 28	8 57 44	25 19 11	1♍43 34	22R04.6	23 59.3	24 18.4	15 30.8	15 31.4	24 05.9	22 29.7	26 07.1	2 26.5	25 41.6
31 Tu	4 35 24	9 55 17	8♍13 27	14 49 14	22 04.6	25 52.5	25 15.9	16 15.9	15 51.2	24 13.1	22 30.3	26 09.8	2 28.4	25 41.5

LONGITUDE — June 2039

Day	Sid.Time	☉	0 hr ☽	Noon ☽	True ☊	☿	♀	♂	⚳	♃	♄	♅	♆	♇
1 W	4 39 21	10♊52 48	21♍31 15	28♍19 44	22♊04.1	27♊43.1	26♋13.0	17♈00.9	16♈10.9	24♌20.3	22♍31.0	26♋12.6	2♉30.3	25♒41.4
2 Th	4 43 17	11 50 17	5♎14 51	12♎16 35	22R03.3	29 31.1	27 09.6	17 45.9	16 30.5	24 27.7	22 31.8	26 15.5	2 32.1	25R41.2
3 F	4 47 14	12 47 45	19 24 49	26 39 14	22 02.2	1♋16.4	28 05.7	18 30.8	16 49.9	24 35.2	22 32.7	26 18.3	2 34.0	25 41.0
4 Sa	4 51 10	13 45 13	3♏59 24	11♏24 38	22 01.2	2 59.0	29 01.3	19 15.7	17 09.3	24 42.8	22 33.7	26 21.2	2 35.8	25 40.8
5 Su	4 55 07	14 42 39	18 54 08	26 26 57	22 00.5	4 38.9	29 56.4	20 00.6	17 28.6	24 50.6	22 34.8	26 24.2	2 37.6	25 40.6
6 M	4 59 03	15 40 04	4♐02 01	11♐38 08	22D00.1	6 15.9	0♌50.9	20 45.4	17 47.8	24 58.4	22 36.1	26 27.1	2 39.4	25 40.3
7 Tu	5 03 00	16 37 28	19 14 08	26 48 47	22 00.1	7 50.1	1 44.9	21 30.1	18 06.8	25 06.4	22 37.4	26 30.1	2 41.1	25 40.1
8 W	5 06 57	17 34 51	4♑20 57	11♑49 35	22 00.3	9 21.5	2 38.2	22 14.9	18 25.8	25 14.5	22 38.8	26 33.2	2 42.9	25 39.8
9 Th	5 10 53	18 32 14	19 13 44	26 32 37	22 00.6	10 50.0	3 31.0	22 59.5	18 44.6	25 22.8	22 40.3	26 36.2	2 44.6	25 39.4
10 F	5 14 50	19 29 36	3♒45 37	10♒52 18	22 00.8	12 15.6	4 23.2	23 44.1	19 03.4	25 31.1	22 41.9	26 39.3	2 46.3	25 39.1
11 Sa	5 18 46	20 26 57	17 52 22	24 45 44	22 01.0	13 38.3	5 14.7	24 28.6	19 22.0	25 39.6	22 43.6	26 42.4	2 47.9	25 38.7
12 Su	5 22 43	21 24 18	1♓32 23	8♓12 31	22R01.1	14 58.0	6 05.5	25 13.1	19 40.5	25 48.1	22 45.5	26 45.5	2 49.6	25 38.3
13 M	5 26 39	22 21 38	14 46 22	21 14 16	22D01.1	16 14.8	6 55.7	25 57.6	19 58.9	25 56.8	22 47.4	26 48.7	2 51.2	25 37.9
14 Tu	5 30 36	23 18 58	27 36 39	3♈53 58	22 01.1	17 28.5	7 45.2	26 41.9	20 17.1	26 05.6	22 49.4	26 51.9	2 52.8	25 37.4
15 W	5 34 32	24 16 18	10♈06 42	16 15 21	22 01.3	18 39.1	8 33.9	27 26.3	20 35.3	26 14.5	22 51.5	26 55.1	2 54.4	25 36.9
16 Th	5 38 29	25 13 37	22 20 27	28 22 29	22 01.5	19 46.5	9 21.8	28 10.5	20 53.3	26 23.5	22 53.7	26 58.3	2 55.9	25 36.4
17 F	5 42 26	26 10 56	4♉21 59	10♉19 23	22 01.9	20 50.7	10 09.0	28 54.7	21 11.2	26 32.6	22 56.0	27 01.6	2 57.5	25 35.9
18 Sa	5 46 22	27 08 14	16 15 11	22 09 48	22 02.4	21 51.6	10 55.4	29 38.8	21 29.0	26 41.8	22 58.4	27 04.9	2 59.0	25 35.4
19 Su	5 50 19	28 05 32	28 03 39	3♊57 07	22 02.9	22 49.1	11 40.9	0♉22.9	21 46.6	26 51.1	23 00.9	27 08.2	3 00.5	25 34.8
20 M	5 54 15	29 02 50	9♊50 33	15 44 19	22R03.3	23 43.1	12 25.5	1 06.9	22 04.1	27 00.5	23 03.4	27 11.5	3 01.9	25 34.2
21 Tu	5 58 12	0♋00 07	21 38 41	27 34 00	22 03.3	24 33.6	13 09.2	1 50.9	22 21.5	27 10.0	23 06.1	27 14.8	3 03.4	25 33.6
22 W	6 02 08	0 57 24	3♋30 30	9♋28 28	22 02.9	25 20.4	13 52.0	2 34.7	22 38.7	27 19.6	23 08.9	27 18.2	3 04.8	25 33.0
23 Th	6 06 05	1 54 40	15 28 11	21 29 52	22 02.0	26 03.4	14 33.8	3 18.5	22 55.8	27 29.4	23 11.8	27 21.6	3 06.1	25 32.3
24 F	6 10 02	2 51 56	27 33 47	3♌40 13	22 00.7	26 42.5	15 14.5	4 02.2	23 12.7	27 39.2	23 14.7	27 25.0	3 07.5	25 31.6
25 Sa	6 13 58	3 49 11	9♌49 23	16 01 35	21 59.1	27 17.6	15 54.2	4 45.9	23 29.5	27 49.0	23 17.8	27 28.4	3 08.8	25 30.9
26 Su	6 17 55	4 46 26	22 17 04	28 36 07	21 57.5	27 48.6	16 32.7	5 29.5	23 46.1	27 59.0	23 20.9	27 31.9	3 10.1	25 30.2
27 M	6 21 51	5 43 40	4♍59 02	11♍26 04	21 56.1	28 15.4	17 10.1	6 13.0	24 02.6	28 09.1	23 24.1	27 35.3	3 11.4	25 29.5
28 Tu	6 25 48	6 40 53	17 57 31	24 33 38	21D55.1	28 37.8	17 46.3	6 56.4	24 19.0	28 19.3	23 27.4	27 38.8	3 12.6	25 28.7
29 W	6 29 44	7 38 07	1♎14 38	8♎00 45	21 54.8	28 55.8	18 21.3	7 39.7	24 35.1	28 29.5	23 30.9	27 42.3	3 13.8	25 27.9
30 Th	6 33 41	8 35 19	14 52 05	21 48 44	21 55.1	29 09.2	18 54.9	8 23.0	24 51.1	28 39.8	23 34.3	27 45.8	3 15.0	25 27.1

Astro Data	Dy Hr Mn	Planet Ingress	Dy Hr Mn	Last Aspect Dy Hr Mn		☽ Ingress Dy Hr Mn	Last Aspect Dy Hr Mn		☽ Ingress Dy Hr Mn	☽ Phases & Eclipses Dy Hr Mn	
☽ 0S	6 1:01	☿ ♉	4 13:49	2 19:22	☿ △	♍ 3 1:25	1 10:46	☿ □	♎ 1 14:55	1 14:07	☽ 11♌04
♂0N	14 7:40	♀ ♋	6 22:26	5 2:36	♀ □	♎ 5 5:58	3 14:32	♀ □	♏ 3 17:29	8 11:20	○ 17♏45
♃⊻♄	14 23:34	♂ ♈	10 1:29	7 0:06	♇ △	♏ 7 7:08	5 11:56	♅ △	♐ 5 17:37	15 3:17	☾ 24♒11
☽ 0N	18 20:42	☿ ♊	19 0:22	9 5:42	♂ △	♐ 9 6:41	7 10:11	♇ ⚹	♑ 7 17:04	23 1:38	● 1♊49
♅⊼♇	20 11:42	☉ ♊	21 4:11	10 23:34	♇ ⚹	♑ 11 6:38	9 12:06	♅ ☍	♒ 9 17:44	31 2:24	☽ 9♍32
♄ D	25 3:05			13 0:50	♅ ☍	♒ 13 8:40	11 13:36	♃ ☍	♓ 11 21:15		
♇ R	26 19:20	☿ ♋	2 18:31	15 5:58	♇ ☌	♓ 15 13:52	13 22:32	♅ △	♈ 14 4:32	6 18:48	○ 15♐56
		♀ ♌	5 13:35	17 16:45	☿ ⚹	♈ 17 22:18	16 11:35	♂ ☌	♉ 16 15:15	6 18:53	• P 0.885
☽ 0S	2 10:51	♂ ♉	18 23:31	20 0:44	♇ ⚹	♉ 20 9:20	18 22:03	♅ ⚹	♊ 19 3:57	13 14:16	☾ 22♓27
♃☍♇	11 9:40	☉ ♋	21 11:57	22 13:20	♅ ⚹	♊ 22 21:55	21 11:11	♃ ⚹	♋ 21 16:55	21 17:21	● 0♋13
☽ 0N	15 2:57			25 2:13	♇ △	♋ 25 10:58	23 23:39	♅ ☌	♌ 24 4:48	21 17:11:28	• A 04'05"
♃⊻♅	22 6:30			27 15:10	♅ ☌	♌ 27 23:06	26 10:49	♃ ☌	♍ 26 14:38	29 11:17	☽ 7♎36
⚳0N	24 5:54			30 0:42	♇ ☍	♍ 30 8:47	28 19:30	☿ ⚹	♎ 28 21:47		
☽ 0S	29 18:15										

Astro Data

1 May 2039
Julian Day # 50890
SVP 4♓42'56"
GC 27♐23.3 ⚵ 28♒53.1
Eris 28♈26.4 ⚴ 1♒42.0
⚷ 0♋21.5 ⚶ 20♌16.5
☽ Mean ☊ 24♊21.4

1 June 2039
Julian Day # 50921
SVP 4♓42'51"
GC 27♐23.4 ⚵ 3♓46.4
Eris 28♈44.7 ⚴ 3♒33.9R
⚷ 2♋54.1 ⚶ 28♌40.7
☽ Mean ☊ 22♊42.9

July 2039 — LONGITUDE

Day	Sid.Time	☉	0 hr ☽	Noon ☽	True ☊	☿	♀	♂	⚳	♃	♄	♅	♆	♇
1 F	6 37 37	9♋32 31	28♎50 41	5♏57 51	21♊56.1	29♋18.1	19♌27.2	9♉06.2	25♈07.0	28♌50.2	23♍37.9	27♋49.3	3♉16.2	25♒26.3
2 Sa	6 41 34	10 29 43	13♏09 59	20 26 46	21 57.3	29R 22.3	19 58.0	9 49.3	25 22.7	29 00.7	23 41.6	27 52.9	3 17.3	25R 25.4
3 Su	6 45 31	11 26 54	27 47 42	5♐12 10	21 58.4	29 21.9	20 27.4	10 32.4	25 38.2	29 11.3	23 45.3	27 56.4	3 18.4	25 24.6
4 M	6 49 27	12 24 06	12♐39 27	20 08 40	21R 58.9	29 16.8	20 55.3	11 15.3	25 53.6	29 21.9	23 49.2	28 00.0	3 19.5	25 23.7
5 Tu	6 53 24	13 21 17	27 38 52	5♑09 01	21 58.5	29 07.2	21 21.6	11 58.2	26 08.8	29 32.7	23 53.1	28 03.6	3 20.5	25 22.8
6 W	6 57 20	14 18 28	12♑38 04	20 04 57	21 57.0	28 53.1	21 46.3	12 41.0	26 23.8	29 43.5	23 57.1	28 07.2	3 21.6	25 21.9
7 Th	7 01 17	15 15 39	27 28 40	4♒48 16	21 54.6	28 34.7	22 09.3	13 23.8	26 38.7	29 54.4	24 01.1	28 10.8	3 22.5	25 21.0
8 F	7 05 13	16 12 50	12♒02 57	19 12 03	21 51.4	28 12.2	22 30.5	14 06.4	26 53.3	0♍05.3	24 05.3	28 14.4	3 23.5	25 20.0
9 Sa	7 09 10	17 10 02	26 15 01	3♓11 30	21 48.0	27 45.9	22 50.0	14 49.0	27 07.8	0 16.3	24 09.5	28 18.0	3 24.4	25 19.1
10 Su	7 13 06	18 07 13	10♓01 18	16 44 24	21 44.8	27 16.2	23 07.6	15 31.5	27 22.1	0 27.4	24 13.8	28 21.6	3 25.3	25 18.1
11 M	7 17 03	19 04 25	23 20 53	29 50 58	21 42.4	26 43.4	23 23.3	16 13.9	27 36.3	0 38.6	24 18.2	28 25.2	3 26.2	25 17.1
12 Tu	7 21 00	20 01 38	6♈15 01	12♈33 27	21D 41.0	26 08.2	23 37.0	16 56.2	27 50.2	0 49.8	24 22.7	28 28.9	3 27.0	25 16.1
13 W	7 24 56	20 58 51	18 46 46	24 55 30	21 40.8	25 30.9	23 48.7	17 38.4	28 03.9	1 01.1	24 27.2	28 32.5	3 27.8	25 15.0
14 Th	7 28 53	21 56 04	1♉00 14	7♉01 35	21 41.7	24 52.2	23 58.3	18 20.6	28 17.4	1 12.4	24 31.9	28 36.2	3 28.6	25 14.0
15 F	7 32 49	22 53 19	13 00 10	18 56 35	21 43.2	24 12.8	24 05.8	19 02.6	28 30.8	1 23.9	24 36.5	28 39.8	3 29.3	25 12.9
16 Sa	7 36 46	23 50 33	24 51 25	0♊45 17	21 44.9	23 33.3	24 11.1	19 44.6	28 43.9	1 35.3	24 41.3	28 43.5	3 30.0	25 11.8
17 Su	7 40 42	24 47 48	6♊38 42	12 32 12	21R 46.3	22 54.4	24R 14.2	20 26.4	28 56.8	1 46.9	24 46.2	28 47.2	3 30.7	25 10.7
18 M	7 44 39	25 45 04	18 26 17	24 21 24	21 46.6	22 16.9	24 15.0	21 08.2	29 09.5	1 58.5	24 51.1	28 50.9	3 31.3	25 09.6
19 Tu	7 48 35	26 42 21	0♋17 57	6♋16 17	21 45.5	21 41.3	24 13.6	21 49.9	29 22.0	2 10.2	24 56.0	28 54.5	3 31.9	25 08.5
20 W	7 52 32	27 39 38	12 16 44	18 19 35	21 42.8	21 08.3	24 09.7	22 31.4	29 34.3	2 21.9	25 01.1	28 58.2	3 32.5	25 07.4
21 Th	7 56 29	28 36 55	24 25 03	0♌33 20	21 38.4	20 38.5	24 03.5	23 12.9	29 46.3	2 33.7	25 06.2	29 01.9	3 33.1	25 06.2
22 F	8 00 25	29 34 13	6♌44 36	12 58 56	21 32.7	20 12.5	23 55.0	23 54.3	29 58.1	2 45.5	25 11.4	29 05.6	3 33.6	25 05.1
23 Sa	8 04 22	0♌31 31	19 16 26	25 37 10	21 26.1	19 50.8	23 44.0	24 35.5	0♉09.7	2 57.4	25 16.7	29 09.2	3 34.1	25 03.9
24 Su	8 08 18	1 28 50	2♍01 12	8♍28 31	21 19.4	19 33.9	23 30.7	25 16.7	0 21.1	3 09.3	25 22.0	29 12.9	3 34.5	25 02.7
25 M	8 12 15	2 26 09	14 59 12	21 33 13	21 13.4	19 22.0	23 15.0	25 57.8	0 32.2	3 21.3	25 27.4	29 16.6	3 34.9	25 01.5
26 Tu	8 16 11	3 23 29	28 10 38	4♎51 28	21 08.7	19D 15.6	22 57.0	26 38.7	0 43.1	3 33.4	25 32.8	29 20.3	3 35.3	25 00.3
27 W	8 20 08	4 20 49	11♎35 44	18 23 28	21 05.7	19 14.8	22 36.7	27 19.5	0 53.7	3 45.5	25 38.3	29 23.9	3 35.7	24 59.1
28 Th	8 24 04	5 18 09	25 14 42	2♏09 28	21D 04.6	19 20.0	22 14.2	28 00.2	1 04.1	3 57.6	25 43.9	29 27.6	3 36.0	24 57.9
29 F	8 28 01	6 15 30	9♏07 44	16 09 27	21 04.9	19 31.2	21 49.5	28 40.9	1 14.2	4 09.8	25 49.6	29 31.2	3 36.3	24 56.7
30 Sa	8 31 58	7 12 51	23 14 34	0♐22 54	21 05.9	19 48.5	21 22.9	29 21.4	1 24.1	4 22.0	25 55.3	29 34.9	3 36.5	24 55.4
31 Su	8 35 54	8 10 13	7♐34 14	14 48 16	21R 06.9	20 12.0	20 54.3	0♊01.8	1 33.7	4 34.3	26 01.0	29 38.6	3 36.7	24 54.2

August 2039 — LONGITUDE

Day	Sid.Time	☉	0 hr ☽	Noon ☽	True ☊	☿	♀	♂	⚳	♃	♄	♅	♆	♇
1 M	8 39 51	9♌07 35	22♐04 35	29♐22 41	21♊06.8	20♋41.7	20♌23.9	0♊42.0	1♉43.1	4♍46.6	26♍06.8	29♋42.2	3♉36.9	24♒52.9
2 Tu	8 43 47	10 04 59	6♑41 56	14♑01 38	21R 04.8	21 17.7	19R 51.9	1 22.2	1 52.2	4 58.9	26 12.7	29 45.8	3 37.1	24R 51.7
3 W	8 47 44	11 02 22	21 21 02	28 39 18	21 00.7	21 59.8	19 18.5	2 02.3	2 01.0	5 11.3	26 18.6	29 49.5	3 37.2	24 50.4
4 Th	8 51 40	11 59 47	5♒55 34	13♒08 59	20 54.5	22 48.1	18 43.9	2 42.2	2 09.5	5 23.7	26 24.6	29 53.1	3 37.3	24 49.1
5 F	8 55 37	12 57 12	20 18 46	27 24 11	20 46.7	23 42.4	18 08.2	3 22.0	2 17.8	5 36.2	26 30.6	29 56.7	3 37.4	24 47.8
6 Sa	8 59 33	13 54 39	4♓24 36	11♓19 30	20 38.2	24 42.7	17 31.8	4 01.7	2 25.8	5 48.7	26 36.7	0♌00.3	3R 37.4	24 46.5
7 Su	9 03 30	14 52 06	18 08 33	24 51 30	20 30.0	25 48.7	16 54.8	4 41.3	2 33.5	6 01.2	26 42.9	0 03.9	3 37.4	24 45.2
8 M	9 07 27	15 49 35	1♈28 17	7♈58 58	20 22.9	27 00.4	16 17.4	5 20.7	2 41.0	6 13.8	26 49.0	0 07.5	3 37.3	24 43.9
9 Tu	9 11 23	16 47 05	14 23 45	20 42 56	20 17.6	28 17.5	15 40.0	6 00.1	2 48.1	6 26.4	26 55.3	0 11.0	3 37.3	24 42.6
10 W	9 15 20	17 44 36	26 56 56	3♉06 14	20 14.5	29 39.9	15 02.7	6 39.3	2 54.9	6 39.0	27 01.6	0 14.6	3 37.1	24 41.3
11 Th	9 19 16	18 42 09	9♉11 23	15 13 00	20D 13.2	1♌07.3	14 25.8	7 18.4	3 01.5	6 51.7	27 07.9	0 18.1	3 37.0	24 40.0
12 F	9 23 13	19 39 43	21 11 43	27 08 12	20 13.4	2 39.4	13 49.6	7 57.3	3 07.7	7 04.3	27 14.3	0 21.7	3 36.8	24 38.7
13 Sa	9 27 09	20 37 19	3♊03 07	8♊57 09	20R 14.2	4 16.0	13 14.2	8 36.2	3 13.6	7 17.1	27 20.7	0 25.2	3 36.6	24 37.4
14 Su	9 31 06	21 34 56	14 50 56	20 45 08	20 14.6	5 56.6	12 39.9	9 14.9	3 19.3	7 29.8	27 27.2	0 28.7	3 36.4	24 36.1
15 M	9 35 02	22 32 34	26 40 21	2♋37 09	20 13.8	7 40.9	12 06.9	9 53.4	3 24.6	7 42.6	27 33.7	0 32.2	3 36.1	24 34.7
16 Tu	9 38 59	23 30 14	8♋36 05	14 37 36	20 10.9	9 28.6	11 35.3	10 31.8	3 29.5	7 55.4	27 40.3	0 35.6	3 35.8	24 33.4
17 W	9 42 56	24 27 55	20 42 08	26 50 02	20 05.7	11 19.1	11 05.4	11 10.1	3 34.2	8 08.2	27 46.9	0 39.1	3 35.5	24 32.1
18 Th	9 46 52	25 25 38	3♌01 34	9♌16 57	19 57.9	13 12.2	10 37.2	11 48.2	3 38.5	8 21.0	27 53.5	0 42.5	3 35.1	24 30.8
19 F	9 50 49	26 23 22	15 36 18	21 59 41	19 48.0	15 07.5	10 11.0	12 26.2	3 42.5	8 33.9	28 00.2	0 45.9	3 34.7	24 29.5
20 Sa	9 54 45	27 21 08	28 27 04	4♍58 21	19 36.8	17 04.4	9 46.8	13 04.0	3 46.1	8 46.8	28 06.9	0 49.3	3 34.3	24 28.1
21 Su	9 58 42	28 18 54	11♍33 24	18 11 59	19 25.4	19 02.6	9 24.7	13 41.7	3 49.4	8 59.7	28 13.7	0 52.7	3 33.8	24 26.8
22 M	10 02 38	29 16 42	24 53 54	1♎38 51	19 14.9	21 01.9	9 04.9	14 19.2	3 52.4	9 12.6	28 20.5	0 56.0	3 33.3	24 25.5
23 Tu	10 06 35	0♍14 31	8♎26 34	15 16 48	19 06.3	23 01.7	8 47.3	14 56.6	3 55.0	9 25.5	28 27.4	0 59.4	3 32.8	24 24.2
24 W	10 10 31	1 12 22	22 09 17	29 03 48	19 00.2	25 01.8	8 32.0	15 33.8	3 57.3	9 38.4	28 34.2	1 02.7	3 32.2	24 22.9
25 Th	10 14 28	2 10 13	6♏00 09	12♏58 09	18 56.7	27 02.0	8 19.1	16 10.8	3 59.2	9 51.4	28 41.1	1 06.0	3 31.7	24 21.5
26 F	10 18 25	3 08 06	19 57 43	26 58 42	18D 55.5	29 02.0	8 08.6	16 47.7	4 00.8	10 04.4	28 48.1	1 09.2	3 31.0	24 20.2
27 Sa	10 22 21	4 06 00	4♐01 01	11♐04 35	18R 55.5	1♍01.6	8 00.5	17 24.5	4 02.0	10 17.3	28 55.0	1 12.5	3 30.4	24 18.9
28 Su	10 26 18	5 03 56	18 09 17	25 14 59	18 55.4	3 00.6	7 54.8	18 01.0	4 02.9	10 30.3	29 02.0	1 15.7	3 29.7	24 17.6
29 M	10 30 14	6 01 52	2♑21 31	9♑28 38	18 54.2	4 58.9	7D 51.4	18 37.4	4R 03.4	10 43.3	29 09.1	1 18.9	3 29.0	24 16.4
30 Tu	10 34 11	6 59 50	16 36 02	23 43 21	18 50.7	6 56.3	7 50.4	19 13.6	4 03.5	10 56.3	29 16.1	1 22.0	3 28.3	24 15.1
31 W	10 38 07	7 57 50	0♒50 09	7♒55 56	18 44.4	8 52.8	7 51.7	19 49.7	4 03.3	11 09.3	29 23.2	1 25.2	3 27.5	24 13.8

Astro Data Dy Hr Mn	Planet Ingress Dy Hr Mn	Last Aspect Dy Hr Mn	☽ Ingress Dy Hr Mn	Last Aspect Dy Hr Mn	☽ Ingress Dy Hr Mn	☽ Phases & Eclipses Dy Hr Mn	Astro Data
☿R 2 21:48	♃ ♍ 8 0:24	1 0:40 ☿ □	♏ 1 1:57	1 6:36 ♄ □	♑ 1 13:01	6 2:03 ○ 13♑55	1 July 2039
☽0N 12 9:56	⚳ ♉ 22 15:49	3 2:34 ☿ △	♐ 3 3:35	3 13:56 ♅ ☍	♒ 3 14:13	13 3:38 ☾ 20♈39	Julian Day # 50951
♀R 18 8:36	☉ ♌ 22 22:48	5 2:55 ♃ △	♑ 5 3:46	5 7:35 ♇ ☌	♓ 5 16:26	21 7:54 ● 28♋27	SVP 4♓42'46"
♄⚻♇ 21 12:03	♂ ♊ 31 10:57	7 2:01 ☿ ☍	♒ 7 4:07	7 15:23 ♄ ☍	♈ 7 21:19	28 17:50 ☽ 5♏32	GC 27♐23.5 ⚴ 4♓11.5R
♃△♆ 26 16:00		8 22:25 ♇ ☌	♓ 9 6:28	10 4:25 ☿ □	♉ 10 5:56		Eris 28♈56.3 ⚵ 0♒08.6R
☽0S 26 23:27	♅ ♌ 6 10:00	11 9:20 ♅ △	♈ 11 12:17	12 12:12 ♄ △	♊ 12 17:48	4 9:57 ○ 11♒55	⚷ 5♋45.0 ⚶ 9♍56.8
☿D 27 3:06	☿ ♌ 10 17:38	13 19:10 ♅ □	♉ 13 22:01	15 1:42 ♄ □	♋ 15 6:43	11 19:36 ☾ 19♉00	☽ Mean ☊ 21♊07.6
	☉ ♍ 23 5:58	16 7:51 ♅ ⚹	♊ 16 10:28	17 13:52 ♄ ⚹	♌ 17 18:09	19 20:50 ● 26♌45	
♆R 6 15:58	☿ ♍ 26 23:37	18 13:37 ♇ △	♋ 18 23:24	19 20:50 ☉ ☌	♍ 20 2:52	26 23:16 ☽ 3♐35	1 August 2039
☽0N 8 17:51		21 9:01 ♅ ☌	♌ 21 10:55	22 6:05 ♄ ☌	♎ 22 9:05		Julian Day # 50982
☽0S 23 4:19		23 10:57 ♇ ☍	♍ 23 20:13	24 3:53 ♇ △	♏ 24 13:37		SVP 4♓42'40"
⚳R 30 9:18		26 2:03 ♅ ⚹	♎ 26 3:17	26 16:05 ☿ □	♐ 26 17:09		GC 27♐23.5 ⚴ 29♒18.9R
♀D 30 10:14		28 7:18 ♅ □	♏ 28 8:16	28 18:27 ♄ □	♑ 28 20:01		Eris 28♈59.1R ⚵ 23♑05.3R
		30 10:39 ♅ △	♐ 30 11:22	30 21:26 ♄ △	♒ 30 22:35		⚷ 8♋39.1 ⚶ 23♍34.5
							☽ Mean ☊ 19♊29.2

LONGITUDE — September 2039

Day	Sid.Time	☉	0 hr ☽	Noon ☽	True ☊	☿	♀	♂	⚳	♃	♄	♅	♆	♇
1 Th	10 42 04	8♍55 50	15♒00 08	22♒02 11	18♊35.4	10♍48.2	7♌55.4	20♊25.6	4♉02.7	11♍22.4	29♍30.3	1♌28.3	3♉26.7	24♒12.5
2 F	10 46 00	9 53 53	29 01 29	5♓57 28	18R 24.3	12 42.6	8 01.3	21 01.3	4R 01.7	11 35.4	29 37.5	1 31.4	3R 25.9	24R 11.2
3 Sa	10 49 57	10 51 56	12♓49 37	19 37 27	18 12.2	14 35.9	8 09.4	21 36.8	4 00.4	11 48.4	29 44.6	1 34.4	3 25.0	24 10.0
4 Su	10 53 54	11 50 02	26 20 35	2♈58 44	18 00.2	16 27.9	8 19.6	22 12.1	3 58.7	12 01.4	29 51.8	1 37.4	3 24.2	24 08.7
5 M	10 57 50	12 48 09	9♈31 44	15 59 32	17 49.5	18 18.9	8 32.0	22 47.3	3 56.7	12 14.4	29 59.0	1 40.4	3 23.2	24 07.5
6 Tu	11 01 47	13 46 18	22 22 11	28 39 51	17 40.9	20 08.6	8 46.5	23 22.3	3 54.2	12 27.4	0♎06.3	1 43.4	3 22.3	24 06.3
7 W	11 05 43	14 44 29	4♉52 50	11♉01 28	17 35.0	21 57.1	9 02.9	23 57.1	3 51.4	12 40.5	0 13.5	1 46.3	3 21.4	24 05.0
8 Th	11 09 40	15 42 42	17 06 13	23 07 36	17 31.6	23 44.5	9 21.3	24 31.7	3 48.2	12 53.5	0 20.8	1 49.2	3 20.4	24 03.8
9 F	11 13 36	16 40 57	29 06 12	5♊02 38	17 30.2	25 30.7	9 41.6	25 06.1	3 44.7	13 06.5	0 28.1	1 52.1	3 19.3	24 02.6
10 Sa	11 17 33	17 39 15	10♊57 35	16 51 41	17 30.0	27 15.7	10 03.7	25 40.3	3 40.7	13 19.5	0 35.4	1 54.9	3 18.3	24 01.4
11 Su	11 21 29	18 37 34	22 45 40	28 40 13	17 29.9	28 59.6	10 27.5	26 14.3	3 36.4	13 32.5	0 42.7	1 57.7	3 17.2	24 00.2
12 M	11 25 26	19 35 55	4♋36 00	10♋33 43	17 28.7	0♎42.3	10 53.1	26 48.0	3 31.8	13 45.5	0 50.0	2 00.5	3 16.2	23 59.1
13 Tu	11 29 23	20 34 19	16 33 59	22 37 23	17 25.6	2 23.9	11 20.2	27 21.6	3 26.7	13 58.5	0 57.4	2 03.2	3 15.0	23 57.9
14 W	11 33 19	21 32 44	28 44 29	4♌55 44	17 19.9	4 04.4	11 49.0	27 55.0	3 21.3	14 11.5	1 04.8	2 05.9	3 13.9	23 56.8
15 Th	11 37 16	22 31 12	11♌11 33	17 32 14	17 11.6	5 43.9	12 19.3	28 28.1	3 15.5	14 24.5	1 12.1	2 08.6	3 12.7	23 55.6
16 F	11 41 12	23 29 41	23 57 59	0♍28 54	17 01.0	7 22.2	12 51.0	29 01.0	3 09.3	14 37.4	1 19.5	2 11.2	3 11.5	23 54.5
17 Sa	11 45 09	24 28 13	7♍04 57	13 46 02	16 48.9	8 59.5	13 24.2	29 33.7	3 02.8	14 50.3	1 26.9	2 13.8	3 10.3	23 53.4
18 Su	11 49 05	25 26 46	20 31 52	27 22 07	16 36.4	10 35.8	13 58.7	0♋06.1	2 56.0	15 03.3	1 34.3	2 16.4	3 09.1	23 52.3
19 M	11 53 02	26 25 21	4♎16 21	11♎14 02	16 24.8	12 11.0	14 34.5	0 38.3	2 48.7	15 16.2	1 41.7	2 18.9	3 07.8	23 51.2
20 Tu	11 56 58	27 23 58	18 14 38	25 17 34	16 15.3	13 45.2	15 11.6	1 10.2	2 41.1	15 29.1	1 49.2	2 21.4	3 06.6	23 50.2
21 W	12 00 55	28 22 37	2♏22 16	9♏28 09	16 08.5	15 18.4	15 49.9	1 41.9	2 33.2	15 41.9	1 56.6	2 23.8	3 05.3	23 49.1
22 Th	12 04 51	29 21 18	16 34 43	23 41 33	16 04.5	16 50.6	16 29.4	2 13.4	2 25.0	15 54.8	2 04.0	2 26.2	3 03.9	23 48.1
23 F	12 08 48	0♎20 00	0♐48 14	7♐54 28	16D 03.0	18 21.8	17 09.9	2 44.6	2 16.4	16 07.6	2 11.5	2 28.5	3 02.6	23 47.1
24 Sa	12 12 45	1 18 45	15 00 01	22 04 41	16R 02.9	19 52.0	17 51.6	3 15.5	2 07.5	16 20.4	2 18.9	2 30.8	3 01.2	23 46.1
25 Su	12 16 41	2 17 31	29 08 20	6♑10 52	16 02.9	21 21.2	18 34.3	3 46.2	1 58.2	16 33.2	2 26.3	2 33.1	2 59.9	23 45.1
26 M	12 20 38	3 16 18	13♑12 12	20 12 14	16 01.9	22 49.4	19 18.0	4 16.6	1 48.7	16 46.0	2 33.8	2 35.3	2 58.5	23 44.1
27 Tu	12 24 34	4 15 07	27 10 51	4♒07 58	15 58.8	24 16.5	20 02.7	4 46.7	1 38.8	16 58.7	2 41.2	2 37.5	2 57.0	23 43.2
28 W	12 28 31	5 13 58	11♒03 23	17 56 57	15 53.0	25 42.7	20 48.4	5 16.5	1 28.7	17 11.4	2 48.7	2 39.7	2 55.6	23 42.2
29 Th	12 32 27	6 12 51	24 48 25	1♓37 33	15 44.6	27 07.8	21 34.9	5 46.1	1 18.3	17 24.1	2 56.1	2 41.8	2 54.2	23 41.3
30 F	12 36 24	7 11 45	8♓24 03	15 07 38	15 34.2	28 31.9	22 22.3	6 15.4	1 07.6	17 36.7	3 03.5	2 43.8	2 52.7	23 40.4

LONGITUDE — October 2039

Day	Sid.Time	☉	0 hr ☽	Noon ☽	True ☊	☿	♀	♂	⚳	♃	♄	♅	♆	♇
1 Sa	12 40 20	8♎10 41	21♓48 02	28♓24 58	15♊22.7	29♎54.9	23♌10.6	6♋44.3	0♉56.6	17♍49.3	3♎10.9	2♌45.8	2♉51.2	23♒39.6
2 Su	12 44 17	9 09 40	4♈58 13	11♈27 36	15R 11.3	1♏16.7	23 59.7	7 13.0	0R 45.4	18 01.9	3 18.4	2 47.8	2R 49.7	23R 38.7
3 M	12 48 14	10 08 40	17 52 58	24 14 16	15 01.0	2 37.4	24 49.6	7 41.4	0 33.9	18 14.4	3 25.8	2 49.7	2 48.2	23 37.9
4 Tu	12 52 10	11 07 42	0♉31 32	6♉44 49	14 52.8	3 56.9	25 40.2	8 09.5	0 22.2	18 26.9	3 33.2	2 51.6	2 46.7	23 37.1
5 W	12 56 07	12 06 47	12 54 20	19 00 18	14 47.1	5 15.2	26 31.6	8 37.2	0 10.2	18 39.4	3 40.5	2 53.4	2 45.1	23 36.3
6 Th	13 00 03	13 05 54	25 03 04	1♊03 00	14 43.9	6 32.1	27 23.8	9 04.7	29♈58.1	18 51.8	3 47.9	2 55.2	2 43.6	23 35.5
7 F	13 04 00	14 05 03	7♊00 33	12 56 15	14D 42.8	7 47.6	28 16.6	9 31.8	29 45.7	19 04.2	3 55.3	2 56.9	2 42.0	23 34.7
8 Sa	13 07 56	15 04 14	18 50 40	24 44 22	14 43.2	9 01.7	29 10.0	9 58.5	29 33.1	19 16.6	4 02.7	2 58.6	2 40.4	23 34.0
9 Su	13 11 53	16 03 28	0♋38 01	6♋32 15	14R 44.1	10 14.2	0♍04.2	10 25.0	29 20.4	19 28.9	4 10.0	3 00.2	2 38.8	23 33.3
10 M	13 15 49	17 02 44	12 27 46	18 25 14	14 44.5	11 25.0	0 58.9	10 51.0	29 07.5	19 41.2	4 17.3	3 01.8	2 37.2	23 32.6
11 Tu	13 19 46	18 02 02	24 25 19	0♌28 42	14 43.5	12 34.1	1 54.3	11 16.7	28 54.4	19 53.4	4 24.6	3 03.4	2 35.6	23 31.9
12 W	13 23 43	19 01 23	6♌36 00	12 47 49	14 40.6	13 41.1	2 50.2	11 42.1	28 41.2	20 05.6	4 31.9	3 04.9	2 34.0	23 31.3
13 Th	13 27 39	20 00 45	19 04 39	25 26 58	14 35.5	14 46.1	3 46.7	12 07.0	28 27.9	20 17.7	4 39.2	3 06.3	2 32.4	23 30.7
14 F	13 31 36	21 00 10	1♍55 07	8♍29 22	14 28.5	15 48.7	4 43.7	12 31.6	28 14.5	20 29.8	4 46.5	3 07.7	2 30.7	23 30.1
15 Sa	13 35 32	21 59 38	15 09 49	21 56 27	14 20.1	16 48.8	5 41.3	12 55.8	28 00.9	20 41.8	4 53.7	3 09.0	2 29.1	23 29.5
16 Su	13 39 29	22 59 07	28 49 07	5♎47 29	14 11.2	17 46.2	6 39.3	13 19.5	27 47.3	20 53.8	5 00.9	3 10.3	2 27.4	23 29.0
17 M	13 43 25	23 58 39	12♎51 07	19 59 23	14 02.9	18 40.5	7 37.9	13 42.9	27 33.7	21 05.7	5 08.1	3 11.5	2 25.8	23 28.4
18 Tu	13 47 22	24 58 12	27 11 36	4♏26 58	13 56.2	19 31.6	8 36.9	14 05.8	27 19.9	21 17.6	5 15.3	3 12.7	2 24.1	23 27.9
19 W	13 51 18	25 57 48	11♏44 37	19 03 43	13 51.5	20 18.9	9 36.4	14 28.3	27 06.2	21 29.4	5 22.4	3 13.8	2 22.4	23 27.4
20 Th	13 55 15	26 57 25	26 23 23	3♐42 48	13D 49.2	21 02.3	10 36.3	14 50.4	26 52.4	21 41.1	5 29.5	3 14.9	2 20.8	23 27.0
21 F	13 59 12	27 57 05	11♐01 15	18 18 05	13 48.9	21 41.1	11 36.6	15 12.0	26 38.6	21 52.8	5 36.6	3 15.9	2 19.1	23 26.6
22 Sa	14 03 08	28 56 46	25 32 45	2♑44 47	13 49.8	22 15.1	12 37.4	15 33.1	26 24.9	22 04.4	5 43.7	3 16.9	2 17.4	23 26.2
23 Su	14 07 05	29 56 29	9♑53 53	16 59 47	13R 51.0	22 43.6	13 38.5	15 53.8	26 11.2	22 16.0	5 50.7	3 17.8	2 15.7	23 25.8
24 M	14 11 01	0♏56 14	24 02 20	1♒01 25	13 51.6	23 06.2	14 40.1	16 14.0	25 57.5	22 27.5	5 57.7	3 18.7	2 14.0	23 25.4
25 Tu	14 14 58	1 56 00	7♒57 02	14 49 09	13 50.8	23 22.3	15 42.0	16 33.7	25 43.9	22 38.9	6 04.7	3 19.5	2 12.4	23 25.1
26 W	14 18 54	2 55 48	21 37 48	28 23 02	13 48.2	23R 31.2	16 44.3	16 53.0	25 30.3	22 50.3	6 11.6	3 20.3	2 10.7	23 24.8
27 Th	14 22 51	3 55 37	5♓04 53	11♓43 24	13 43.7	23 32.5	17 46.9	17 11.7	25 16.9	23 01.6	6 18.5	3 21.0	2 09.0	23 24.5
28 F	14 26 47	4 55 28	18 18 36	24 50 32	13 37.8	23 25.6	18 49.9	17 29.9	25 03.6	23 12.8	6 25.4	3 21.6	2 07.3	23 24.3
29 Sa	14 30 44	5 55 21	1♈19 13	7♈44 41	13 31.1	23 09.8	19 53.3	17 47.6	24 50.4	23 24.0	6 32.2	3 22.2	2 05.6	23 24.0
30 Su	14 34 41	6 55 16	14 06 55	20 25 59	13 24.5	22 45.0	20 57.0	18 04.8	24 37.3	23 35.0	6 39.0	3 22.8	2 03.9	23 23.8
31 M	14 38 37	7 55 12	26 41 55	2♉54 47	13 18.5	22 10.8	22 01.0	18 21.4	24 24.4	23 46.0	6 45.7	3 23.2	2 02.3	23 23.7

Astro Data

	Dy Hr Mn
☽0N	5 2:16
☿0S	13 1:43
☽0S	19 10:59
⚳0S	22 0:09
☉0S	23 3:50
♄⚹♅	26 19:08
♄⚻♆	29 6:47
♃∠♅	1 4:05
♃⚼♆	1 15:12
☽0N	2 10:25
♅□♆	3 1:22
♄0S	15 8:33
☽0S	16 20:16
☿R	27 3:53
♃⚻♇	29 12:09

Planet Ingress

	Dy Hr Mn
♄ ♎	5 15:15
☿ ♎	12 2:05
♂ ♋	18 7:28
☉ ♎	23 3:49
☿ ♏	1 13:30
⚳ ♈R	6 8:12
♀ ♍	9 10:10
☉ ♏	23 13:25
☽0N	29 17:34

Last Aspect / ☽ Ingress

Last Aspect Dy Hr Mn		☽ Ingress Dy Hr Mn
1 15:43 ♇ ☌	♓	2 1:41
4 6:18 ♄ ☍	♈	4 6:36
6 3:18 ♇ ⚹	♉	6 14:34
8 13:52 ♇ □	♊	9 1:48
11 12:46 ☿ □	♋	11 14:42
13 7:36 ☉ ⚹	♌	14 2:27
16 9:12 ♂ ⚹	♍	16 11:07
18 8:23 ☉ ☌	♎	18 16:35
20 9:32 ♇ △	♏	20 19:59
22 22:16 ☉ ⚹	♐	22 22:39
24 14:52 ♇ ⚹	♑	25 1:28
26 17:01 ☿ □	♒	27 4:52
29 3:10 ☿ △	♓	29 9:08

Last Aspect Dy Hr Mn		☽ Ingress Dy Hr Mn
30 16:32 ♃ ☍	♈	1 14:53
3 13:12 ♀ △	♉	3 23:00
6 4:06 ♀ □	♊	6 9:54
8 21:46 ♀ ⚹	♋	8 22:43
10 14:35 ♃ ⚹	♌	11 11:03
13 8:22 ♇ ☍	♍	13 20:28
15 9:47 ♃ ☌	♎	16 2:03
17 19:09 ☉ ☌	♏	18 4:39
19 19:12 ♇ □	♐	20 5:55
22 5:11 ☉ ⚹	♑	22 7:25
23 22:03 ☿ ⚹	♒	24 10:14
26 3:17 ☿ □	♓	26 14:53
28 9:26 ☿ △	♈	28 21:33
30 17:40 ♇ ⚹	♉	31 6:22

☽ Phases & Eclipses

Dy Hr Mn	
2 19:23	○ 10♓12
10 13:45	☾ 17♊44
18 8:23	● 25♍18
25 4:52	☽ 2♑00
2 7:23	○ 8♈58
10 8:59	☾ 16♋55
17 19:09	● 24♎16
24 11:50	☽ 0♒56
31 22:36	○ 8♉22

Astro Data

1 September 2039
Julian Day # 51013
SVP 4♓42'36"
GC 27♐23.6 ⚴ 21♒35.8R
Eris 28♈52.1R ⚵ 18♑23.9R
⚷ 11♋03.8 ⚶ 8♎30.4
☽ Mean ☊ 17♊50.7

1 October 2039
Julian Day # 51043
SVP 4♓42'33"
GC 27♐23.7 ⚴ 16♒41.6R
Eris 28♈37.8R ⚵ 19♑32.0
⚷ 12♋31.0 ⚶ 23♎47.0
☽ Mean ☊ 16♊15.3

November 2039 — LONGITUDE

Day	Sid.Time	☉	0 hr ☽	Noon☽	True☊	☿	♀	♂	⚳	♃	♄	♅	♆	♇
1 Tu	14 42 34	8♏55 10	9♉04 39	15♉11 40	13♊13.9	21♏27.2	23♍05.3	18♋37.5	24♈11.6	23♍57.0	6♎52.4	3♌23.7	2♉00.6	23♒23.5
2 W	14 46 30	9 55 11	21 15 58	27 17 45	13R10.9	20R34.6	24 09.9	18 53.0	23R59.1	24 07.8	6 59.1	3 24.1	1R58.9	23R23.4
3 Th	14 50 27	10 55 13	3♊17 16	9♊14 47	13D09.6	19 33.6	25 14.8	19 07.9	23 46.7	24 18.6	7 05.7	3 24.4	1 57.3	23 23.3
4 F	14 54 23	11 55 17	15 10 39	21 05 13	13 09.8	18 25.4	26 20.0	19 22.3	23 34.5	24 29.3	7 12.3	3 24.6	1 55.6	23 23.2
5 Sa	14 58 20	12 55 24	26 58 56	2♋52 14	13 11.1	17 11.6	27 25.5	19 36.0	23 22.5	24 39.9	7 18.8	3 24.9	1 54.0	23 23.2
6 Su	15 02 16	13 55 32	8♋45 37	14 39 39	13 13.0	15 54.0	28 31.3	19 49.1	23 10.8	24 50.4	7 25.3	3 25.0	1 52.3	23D23.2
7 M	15 06 13	14 55 43	20 34 52	26 31 53	13 14.7	14 35.0	29 37.3	20 01.6	22 59.3	25 00.8	7 31.7	3 25.1	1 50.7	23 23.2
8 Tu	15 10 10	15 55 55	2♌31 17	8♌33 43	13R15.9	13 17.1	0♎43.6	20 13.5	22 48.1	25 11.2	7 38.1	3R25.2	1 49.1	23 23.2
9 W	15 14 06	16 56 09	14 39 48	20 50 07	13 16.1	12 02.8	1 50.2	20 24.7	22 37.1	25 21.4	7 44.5	3 25.2	1 47.4	23 23.3
10 Th	15 18 03	17 56 26	27 05 17	3♍25 50	13 15.1	10 54.4	2 57.0	20 35.2	22 26.4	25 31.6	7 50.8	3 25.1	1 45.8	23 23.4
11 F	15 21 59	18 56 44	9♍52 16	16 24 58	13 13.0	9 54.1	4 04.0	20 45.0	22 15.9	25 41.6	7 57.0	3 25.0	1 44.2	23 23.5
12 Sa	15 25 56	19 57 05	23 04 16	29 50 21	13 10.0	9 03.5	5 11.3	20 54.2	22 05.8	25 51.6	8 03.2	3 24.8	1 42.6	23 23.6
13 Su	15 29 52	20 57 27	6♎43 17	13♎42 58	13 06.7	8 23.7	6 18.8	21 02.6	21 56.0	26 01.5	8 09.3	3 24.6	1 41.1	23 23.8
14 M	15 33 49	21 57 51	20 49 09	28 01 24	13 03.6	7 55.4	7 26.5	21 10.3	21 46.5	26 11.3	8 15.4	3 24.3	1 39.5	23 24.0
15 Tu	15 37 45	22 58 17	5♏19 05	12♏41 28	13 01.1	7D38.9	8 34.4	21 17.2	21 37.3	26 20.9	8 21.4	3 24.0	1 37.9	23 24.2
16 W	15 41 42	23 58 45	20 07 38	27 36 35	12 59.5	7 33.9	9 42.5	21 23.5	21 28.4	26 30.5	8 27.4	3 23.6	1 36.4	23 24.5
17 Th	15 45 39	24 59 14	5♐07 15	12♐38 31	12D59.0	7 40.0	10 50.8	21 28.9	21 19.9	26 40.0	8 33.3	3 23.1	1 34.9	23 24.7
18 F	15 49 35	25 59 45	20 09 17	27 38 30	12 59.4	7 56.4	11 59.3	21 33.6	21 11.7	26 49.3	8 39.2	3 22.6	1 33.4	23 25.1
19 Sa	15 53 32	27 00 17	5♑05 15	12♑28 39	13 00.4	8 22.5	13 08.0	21 37.5	21 03.9	26 58.6	8 45.0	3 22.1	1 31.9	23 25.4
20 Su	15 57 28	28 00 51	19 48 01	27 02 47	13 01.6	8 57.3	14 16.8	21 40.6	20 56.4	27 07.7	8 50.7	3 21.5	1 30.4	23 25.8
21 M	16 01 25	29 01 26	4♒12 32	11♒16 59	13 02.6	9 39.9	15 25.8	21 43.0	20 49.4	27 16.8	8 56.3	3 20.8	1 29.0	23 26.1
22 Tu	16 05 21	0♐02 01	18 16 00	25 09 33	13R03.1	10 29.4	16 35.0	21 44.5	20 42.6	27 25.7	9 01.9	3 20.1	1 27.5	23 26.6
23 W	16 09 18	1 02 38	1♓57 40	8♓40 32	13 03.1	11 25.1	17 44.4	21R45.2	20 36.3	27 34.5	9 07.5	3 19.3	1 26.1	23 27.0
24 Th	16 13 14	2 03 16	15 18 19	21 51 17	13 02.4	12 26.0	18 53.9	21 45.1	20 30.3	27 43.2	9 12.9	3 18.5	1 24.7	23 27.5
25 F	16 17 11	3 03 56	28 19 42	4♈43 53	13 01.4	13 31.6	20 03.6	21 44.2	20 24.7	27 51.7	9 18.3	3 17.6	1 23.3	23 27.9
26 Sa	16 21 08	4 04 36	11♈04 07	17 20 43	13 00.1	14 41.3	21 13.4	21 42.4	20 19.5	28 00.2	9 23.6	3 16.7	1 22.0	23 28.5
27 Su	16 25 04	5 05 17	23 33 59	29 44 12	12 58.9	15 54.3	22 23.4	21 39.8	20 14.7	28 08.5	9 28.9	3 15.7	1 20.6	23 29.0
28 M	16 29 01	6 06 00	5♉51 39	11♉56 36	12 57.9	17 10.3	23 33.5	21 36.3	20 10.2	28 16.7	9 34.0	3 14.7	1 19.3	23 29.6
29 Tu	16 32 57	7 06 44	17 59 18	24 00 00	12 57.2	18 28.9	24 43.7	21 32.0	20 06.2	28 24.7	9 39.2	3 13.6	1 18.0	23 30.2
30 W	16 36 54	8 07 29	29 58 58	5♊56 24	12D56.9	19 49.6	25 54.1	21 26.9	20 02.5	28 32.7	9 44.2	3 12.5	1 16.7	23 30.8

December 2039 — LONGITUDE

Day	Sid.Time	☉	0 hr ☽	Noon☽	True☊	☿	♀	♂	⚳	♃	♄	♅	♆	♇
1 Th	16 40 50	9♐08 15	11♊52 35	17♊47 44	12♊56.9	21♏12.2	27♎04.7	21♋20.9	19♈59.2	28♍40.5	9♎49.1	3♌11.3	1♉15.5	23♒31.4
2 F	16 44 47	10 09 03	23 42 08	29 36 03	12 57.1	22 36.3	28 15.4	21R14.0	19R56.3	28 48.2	9 54.0	3R10.1	1R14.2	23 32.1
3 Sa	16 48 43	11 09 52	5♋29 47	11♋23 39	12 57.3	24 01.7	29 26.2	21 06.3	19 53.9	28 55.7	9 58.8	3 08.9	1 13.0	23 32.8
4 Su	16 52 40	12 10 42	17 18 00	23 13 10	12R57.4	25 28.2	0♏37.1	20 57.7	19 51.8	29 03.1	10 03.6	3 07.5	1 11.8	23 33.5
5 M	16 56 37	13 11 33	29 09 36	5♌07 41	12 57.5	26 55.7	1 48.2	20 48.3	19 50.0	29 10.4	10 08.2	3 06.2	1 10.7	23 34.3
6 Tu	17 00 33	14 12 26	11♌07 53	17 10 40	12 57.4	28 24.1	2 59.3	20 38.0	19 48.7	29 17.6	10 12.8	3 04.8	1 09.5	23 35.1
7 W	17 04 30	15 13 20	23 16 33	29 26 01	12 57.2	29 53.0	4 10.6	20 26.9	19 47.8	29 24.6	10 17.3	3 03.3	1 08.4	23 35.9
8 Th	17 08 26	16 14 15	5♍39 36	11♍57 48	12D57.1	1♐22.6	5 22.0	20 15.0	19D47.3	29 31.4	10 21.7	3 01.8	1 07.3	23 36.7
9 F	17 12 23	17 15 11	18 21 07	24 50 02	12 57.1	2 52.6	6 33.6	20 02.2	19 47.1	29 38.1	10 26.0	3 00.3	1 06.3	23 37.5
10 Sa	17 16 19	18 16 09	1♎24 57	8♎06 14	12 57.4	4 23.1	7 45.2	19 48.6	19 47.3	29 44.7	10 30.3	2 58.7	1 05.2	23 38.4
11 Su	17 20 16	19 17 08	14 54 10	21 48 53	12 57.9	5 54.0	8 56.9	19 34.2	19 48.0	29 51.1	10 34.4	2 57.0	1 04.2	23 39.3
12 M	17 24 12	20 18 08	28 50 25	5♏58 39	12 58.6	7 25.1	10 08.7	19 19.0	19 49.0	29 57.4	10 38.5	2 55.3	1 03.2	23 40.2
13 Tu	17 28 09	21 19 09	13♏13 19	20 33 55	12 59.2	8 56.5	11 20.6	19 03.0	19 50.4	0♎03.5	10 42.5	2 53.6	1 02.3	23 41.2
14 W	17 32 06	22 20 11	27 59 48	5♐30 09	12R59.7	10 28.2	12 32.7	18 46.3	19 52.1	0 09.5	10 46.4	2 51.9	1 01.4	23 42.1
15 Th	17 36 02	23 21 14	13♐03 59	20 40 10	12 59.7	12 00.1	13 44.8	18 28.9	19 54.3	0 15.3	10 50.2	2 50.1	1 00.5	23 43.1
16 F	17 39 59	24 22 18	28 17 29	5♑54 40	12 59.1	13 32.1	14 56.9	18 10.7	19 56.8	0 21.0	10 53.9	2 48.2	0 59.6	23 44.1
17 Sa	17 43 55	25 23 23	13♑30 27	21 03 38	12 57.9	15 04.4	16 09.2	17 52.0	19 59.7	0 26.5	10 57.5	2 46.3	0 58.8	23 45.2
18 Su	17 47 52	26 24 28	28 33 06	5♒57 53	12 56.2	16 36.9	17 21.5	17 32.6	20 03.0	0 31.8	11 01.0	2 44.4	0 58.0	23 46.2
19 M	17 51 48	27 25 33	13♒17 09	20 30 18	12 54.4	18 09.5	18 33.9	17 12.5	20 06.7	0 37.0	11 04.5	2 42.5	0 57.2	23 47.3
20 Tu	17 55 45	28 26 39	27 36 52	4♓36 39	12 52.8	19 42.3	19 46.4	16 52.0	20 10.7	0 42.0	11 07.8	2 40.5	0 56.5	23 48.4
21 W	17 59 42	29 27 44	11♓29 31	18 15 34	12D51.7	21 15.2	20 59.0	16 30.9	20 15.0	0 46.8	11 11.1	2 38.4	0 55.8	23 49.5
22 Th	18 03 38	0♑28 50	24 55 00	1♈28 07	12 51.4	22 48.4	22 11.6	16 09.4	20 19.8	0 51.5	11 14.2	2 36.4	0 55.1	23 50.7
23 F	18 07 35	1 29 57	7♈55 20	14 17 04	12 51.8	24 21.7	23 24.3	15 47.4	20 24.8	0 56.0	11 17.3	2 34.3	0 54.4	23 51.8
24 Sa	18 11 31	2 31 03	20 33 51	26 46 10	12 53.1	25 55.2	24 37.0	15 25.0	20 30.3	1 00.3	11 20.2	2 32.1	0 53.8	23 53.0
25 Su	18 15 28	3 32 10	2♉54 33	8♉59 33	12 54.7	27 28.9	25 49.8	15 02.3	20 36.0	1 04.5	11 23.1	2 30.0	0 53.2	23 54.2
26 M	18 19 24	4 33 16	15 01 38	21 01 18	12 56.4	29 02.9	27 02.7	14 39.2	20 42.2	1 08.5	11 25.9	2 27.8	0 52.7	23 55.4
27 Tu	18 23 21	5 34 23	26 59 01	2♊55 14	12R57.6	0♑37.0	28 15.6	14 15.9	20 48.6	1 12.3	11 28.5	2 25.5	0 52.2	23 56.7
28 W	18 27 17	6 35 31	8♊50 19	14 44 39	12 58.0	2 11.5	29 28.6	13 52.4	20 55.4	1 16.0	11 31.1	2 23.3	0 51.7	23 57.9
29 Th	18 31 14	7 36 38	20 38 35	26 32 24	12 57.2	3 46.2	0♐41.7	13 28.8	21 02.5	1 19.4	11 33.6	2 21.0	0 51.2	23 59.2
30 F	18 35 11	8 37 45	2♋26 24	8♋20 51	12 55.0	5 21.1	1 54.8	13 05.0	21 10.0	1 22.7	11 35.9	2 18.7	0 50.8	24 00.5
31 Sa	18 39 07	9 38 53	14 15 59	20 12 03	12 51.5	6 56.4	3 08.0	12 41.1	21 17.7	1 25.8	11 38.2	2 16.4	0 50.4	24 01.8

Astro Data

Dy Hr Mn	
♇ D	6 13:55
♅ R	8 21:05
♀0S	10 17:13
☽0S	13 7:03
♄□♇	15 23:34
☿ D	16 10:38
♂ R	23 20:47
☽0N	25 23:38
⚳ D	9 9:27
☽0S	10 16:57
⚳0N	21 10:38
♃⊼♆	23 4:37
☽0N	23 5:30

Planet Ingress

	Dy Hr Mn
♀ ♎	7 20:13
☉ ♐	22 11:12
♀ ♏	3 23:27
☿ ♐	7 13:52
♃ ♎	12 22:04
☉ ♑	22 0:40
☿ ♑	27 2:34
♀ ♐	28 22:18

Last Aspect / ☽ Ingress

Last Aspect Dy Hr Mn		☽ Ingress Dy Hr Mn
2 5:36	♃ △	♊ 2 17:24
4 23:46	♀ □	♋ 5 6:09
7 18:50	♀ ⚹	♌ 7 18:58
9 16:55	♇ ☍	♍ 10 5:32
12 4:53	♃ ☌	♎ 12 12:17
14 4:19	♇ △	♏ 14 15:16
16 10:13	♃ ⚹	♐ 16 15:49
18 10:40	♃ □	♑ 18 15:48
20 13:44	☉ ⚹	♒ 20 16:56
22 9:00	♇ ☌	♓ 22 20:31
24 22:59	♃ ☍	♈ 25 3:07
26 23:50	♇ ⚹	♉ 27 12:31
29 20:57	♃ △	♊ 30 0:02

Last Aspect / ☽ Ingress

Last Aspect Dy Hr Mn		☽ Ingress Dy Hr Mn
2 10:22	♃ □	♋ 2 12:49
4 23:54	♃ ⚹	♌ 5 1:42
7 12:59	♀ □	♍ 7 13:06
9 20:51	♃ ☌	♎ 9 21:26
11 15:10	♇ △	♏ 12 1:58
13 17:04	♇ □	♐ 14 3:13
15 16:48	♇ ⚹	♑ 16 2:41
17 7:01	♂ ☍	♒ 18 2:20
20 0:35	☉ ⚹	♓ 20 4:04
21 18:05	☿ □	♈ 22 9:18
24 10:07	☿ △	♉ 24 18:18
27 1:30	♀ ☍	♊ 27 6:05
29 6:48	♇ △	♋ 29 19:02

☽ Phases & Eclipses

Dy Hr Mn	
9 3:46	☾ 16♌35
16 5:46	● 23♏43
22 21:16	☽ 0♓25
30 16:49	○ 8♊20
30 16:55	• P 0.943
8 20:44	☾ 16♍36
15 16:32	● 23♐33
15 16:22:20	• T 01'52"
22 10:01	☽ 0♈24
30 12:38	○ 8♋39

Astro Data

1 November 2039
Julian Day # 51074
SVP 4♓42'30"
GC 27♐23.7 ⚴ 16♒55.6
Eris 28♈19.3R ⚵ 25♑56.5
⚷ 12♋46.5R ⚶ 10♏06.7
☽ Mean ☊ 14♊36.8

1 December 2039
Julian Day # 51104
SVP 4♓42'25"
GC 27♐23.8 ⚴ 21♒29.2
Eris 28♈03.3R ⚵ 5♒39.6
⚷ 11♋46.0R ⚶ 26♏09.8
☽ Mean ☊ 13♊01.5

LONGITUDE — January 2040

Day	Sid.Time	☉	0 hr ☽	Noon☽	True☊	☿	♀	♂	⚳	♃	♄	♅	♆	♇
1 Su	18 43 04	10♑40 01	26♋09 14	2♌07 48	12♊46.8	8♑31.9	4♐21.2	12♋17.2	21♈25.8	1♎28.8	11♎40.3	2♌14.0	0♉50.1	24♒03.2
2 M	18 47 00	11 41 09	8♌07 58	14 09 57	12R 41.5	10 07.8	5 34.5	11R 53.4	21 34.2	1 31.5	11 42.4	2R 11.6	0R 49.8	24 04.5
3 Tu	18 50 57	12 42 17	20 14 01	26 20 25	12 36.2	11 44.0	6 47.8	11 29.6	21 42.8	1 34.1	11 44.4	2 09.2	0 49.5	24 05.9
4 W	18 54 53	13 43 26	2♍29 28	8♍41 28	12 31.3	13 20.5	8 01.2	11 05.9	21 51.8	1 36.5	11 46.2	2 06.8	0 49.2	24 07.3
5 Th	18 58 50	14 44 34	14 56 44	21 15 38	12 27.6	14 57.5	9 14.6	10 42.4	22 01.1	1 38.7	11 47.9	2 04.4	0 49.0	24 08.7
6 F	19 02 46	15 45 43	27 38 32	4♎05 47	12D 25.3	16 34.8	10 28.1	10 19.1	22 10.7	1 40.7	11 49.6	2 01.9	0 48.8	24 10.1
7 Sa	19 06 43	16 46 52	10♎37 47	17 14 53	12 24.6	18 12.5	11 41.6	9 56.1	22 20.6	1 42.5	11 51.1	1 59.4	0 48.7	24 11.6
8 Su	19 10 40	17 48 01	23 57 24	0♏45 38	12 25.3	19 50.5	12 55.1	9 33.4	22 30.8	1 44.2	11 52.5	1 56.9	0 48.5	24 13.0
9 M	19 14 36	18 49 11	7♏39 47	14 39 58	12 26.7	21 29.0	14 08.7	9 11.0	22 41.2	1 45.6	11 53.9	1 54.4	0 48.5	24 14.5
10 Tu	19 18 33	19 50 20	21 46 13	28 58 24	12R 28.1	23 07.9	15 22.4	8 49.0	22 51.9	1 46.9	11 55.1	1 51.9	0D 48.4	24 16.0
11 W	19 22 29	20 51 30	6♐16 13	13♐39 12	12 28.7	24 47.2	16 36.1	8 27.4	23 02.9	1 48.0	11 56.2	1 49.3	0 48.4	24 17.5
12 Th	19 26 26	21 52 40	21 06 44	28 37 58	12 27.7	26 26.9	17 49.8	8 06.3	23 14.2	1 48.9	11 57.2	1 46.8	0 48.4	24 19.0
13 F	19 30 22	22 53 49	6♑11 56	13♑47 29	12 24.7	28 07.1	19 03.5	7 45.8	23 25.8	1 49.5	11 58.1	1 44.2	0 48.5	24 20.5
14 Sa	19 34 19	23 54 58	21 23 23	28 58 20	12 19.7	29 47.5	20 17.3	7 25.7	23 37.6	1 50.0	11 58.9	1 41.6	0 48.6	24 22.0
15 Su	19 38 15	24 56 07	6♒31 04	14♒00 20	12 13.2	1♒28.4	21 31.1	7 06.3	23 49.7	1 50.3	11 59.5	1 39.0	0 48.7	24 23.6
16 M	19 42 12	25 57 15	21 25 02	28 44 11	12 06.0	3 09.6	22 44.9	6 47.5	24 02.0	1R 50.5	12 00.1	1 36.4	0 48.9	24 25.2
17 Tu	19 46 09	26 58 22	5♓57 02	13♓02 59	11 59.1	4 51.1	23 58.8	6 29.3	24 14.6	1 50.4	12 00.5	1 33.8	0 49.1	24 26.7
18 W	19 50 05	27 59 29	20 01 42	26 53 01	11 53.4	6 32.8	25 12.7	6 11.8	24 27.4	1 50.1	12 00.9	1 31.2	0 49.3	24 28.3
19 Th	19 54 02	29 00 35	3♈36 58	10♈13 44	11 49.5	8 14.7	26 26.6	5 55.0	24 40.5	1 49.6	12 01.1	1 28.6	0 49.6	24 29.9
20 F	19 57 58	0♒01 40	16 43 40	23 07 12	11D 47.6	9 56.7	27 40.5	5 38.9	24 53.8	1 48.9	12R 01.3	1 26.0	0 49.9	24 31.5
21 Sa	20 01 55	1 02 44	29 24 52	5♉37 16	11 47.5	11 38.8	28 54.4	5 23.6	25 07.4	1 48.1	12 01.3	1 23.4	0 50.3	24 33.1
22 Su	20 05 51	2 03 47	11♉45 02	17 48 50	11 48.5	13 20.7	0♑08.4	5 09.0	25 21.2	1 47.0	12 01.2	1 20.7	0 50.6	24 34.8
23 M	20 09 48	3 04 49	23 49 18	29 47 06	11 49.8	15 02.4	1 22.4	4 55.2	25 35.2	1 45.8	12 01.0	1 18.1	0 51.0	24 36.4
24 Tu	20 13 44	4 05 51	5♊42 51	11♊37 11	11R 50.4	16 43.8	2 36.4	4 42.1	25 49.5	1 44.4	12 00.7	1 15.5	0 51.5	24 38.1
25 W	20 17 41	5 06 51	17 30 39	23 23 47	11 49.5	18 24.5	3 50.4	4 29.9	26 03.9	1 42.8	12 00.3	1 12.9	0 52.0	24 39.7
26 Th	20 21 38	6 07 51	29 17 03	5♋10 55	11 46.5	20 04.3	5 04.5	4 18.4	26 18.6	1 40.9	11 59.8	1 10.3	0 52.5	24 41.4
27 F	20 25 34	7 08 49	11♋05 45	17 01 54	11 40.9	21 43.1	6 18.6	4 07.7	26 33.5	1 39.0	11 59.1	1 07.7	0 53.0	24 43.1
28 Sa	20 29 31	8 09 47	22 59 39	28 59 14	11 32.9	23 20.4	7 32.7	3 57.9	26 48.6	1 36.8	11 58.4	1 05.1	0 53.6	24 44.8
29 Su	20 33 27	9 10 44	5♌00 51	11♌04 39	11 22.8	24 56.0	8 46.8	3 48.8	27 03.9	1 34.4	11 57.6	1 02.5	0 54.2	24 46.4
30 M	20 37 24	10 11 39	17 10 47	23 19 19	11 11.3	26 29.3	10 00.9	3 40.5	27 19.4	1 31.8	11 56.6	0 59.9	0 54.9	24 48.1
31 Tu	20 41 20	11 12 34	29 30 21	5♍43 58	10 59.7	27 59.9	11 15.0	3 33.1	27 35.1	1 29.1	11 55.6	0 57.4	0 55.6	24 49.8

LONGITUDE — February 2040

Day	Sid.Time	☉	0 hr ☽	Noon☽	True☊	☿	♀	♂	⚳	♃	♄	♅	♆	♇
1 W	20 45 17	12♒13 28	12♍00 12	18♍19 09	10♊48.8	29♒27.3	12♑29.2	3♋26.4	27♈51.0	1♎26.2	11♎54.4	0♌54.8	0♉56.3	24♒51.5
2 Th	20 49 13	13 14 21	24 40 55	1♎05 35	10R 39.7	0♓50.8	13 43.4	3R 20.6	28 07.1	1R 23.1	11R 53.2	0R 52.3	0 57.0	24 53.3
3 F	20 53 10	14 15 13	7♎33 18	14 04 13	10 33.1	2 09.8	14 57.6	3 15.5	28 23.4	1 19.8	11 51.8	0 49.7	0 57.8	24 55.0
4 Sa	20 57 07	15 16 04	20 38 31	27 16 25	10 29.2	3 23.6	16 11.8	3 11.3	28 39.8	1 16.3	11 50.4	0 47.2	0 58.6	24 56.7
5 Su	21 01 03	16 16 55	3♏58 07	10♏43 51	10D 27.7	4 31.5	17 26.0	3 07.8	28 56.5	1 12.7	11 48.8	0 44.7	0 59.5	24 58.4
6 M	21 05 00	17 17 45	17 33 49	24 28 12	10 27.7	5 32.7	18 40.2	3 05.1	29 13.3	1 08.9	11 47.1	0 42.2	1 00.4	25 00.2
7 Tu	21 08 56	18 18 34	1♐27 06	8♐30 36	10R 28.1	6 26.3	19 54.5	3 03.2	29 30.3	1 04.9	11 45.4	0 39.7	1 01.3	25 01.9
8 W	21 12 53	19 19 22	15 38 38	22 51 02	10 27.6	7 11.7	21 08.8	3D 02.1	29 47.5	1 00.7	11 43.5	0 37.3	1 02.2	25 03.6
9 Th	21 16 49	20 20 09	0♑07 31	7♑27 36	10 25.0	7 48.0	22 23.1	3 01.7	0♉04.8	0 56.4	11 41.5	0 34.9	1 03.2	25 05.4
10 F	21 20 46	21 20 55	14 50 42	22 16 00	10 19.7	8 14.8	23 37.4	3 02.1	0 22.4	0 51.9	11 39.5	0 32.5	1 04.2	25 07.1
11 Sa	21 24 43	22 21 40	29 42 38	7♒09 33	10 11.5	8 31.4	24 51.7	3 03.2	0 40.1	0 47.2	11 37.3	0 30.1	1 05.3	25 08.9
12 Su	21 28 39	23 22 23	14♒35 39	21 59 49	10 01.0	8R 37.4	26 06.0	3 05.1	0 57.9	0 42.4	11 35.1	0 27.7	1 06.4	25 10.6
13 M	21 32 36	24 23 06	29 20 57	6♓38 00	9 49.4	8 32.8	27 20.3	3 07.7	1 15.9	0 37.4	11 32.7	0 25.4	1 07.5	25 12.4
14 Tu	21 36 32	25 23 46	13♓50 04	20 56 23	9 37.8	8 17.5	28 34.6	3 11.0	1 34.1	0 32.3	11 30.3	0 23.1	1 08.6	25 14.1
15 W	21 40 29	26 24 25	27 56 22	4♈49 37	9 27.6	7 52.0	29 48.9	3 15.0	1 52.4	0 27.0	11 27.7	0 20.8	1 09.8	25 15.9
16 Th	21 44 25	27 25 03	11♈35 57	18 15 20	9 19.6	7 16.7	1♒03.2	3 19.8	2 10.9	0 21.5	11 25.1	0 18.5	1 11.0	25 17.6
17 F	21 48 22	28 25 39	24 47 54	1♉13 58	9 14.4	6 32.5	2 17.6	3 25.2	2 29.5	0 16.0	11 22.4	0 16.3	1 12.2	25 19.3
18 Sa	21 52 18	29 26 13	7♉33 56	13 48 20	9 11.6	5 40.7	3 31.9	3 31.2	2 48.3	0 10.2	11 19.6	0 14.1	1 13.4	25 21.1
19 Su	21 56 15	0♓26 45	19 57 43	26 02 46	9D 10.8	4 42.7	4 46.2	3 38.0	3 07.2	0 04.4	11 16.7	0 11.9	1 14.7	25 22.8
20 M	22 00 11	1 27 16	2♊04 09	8♊02 33	9R 10.8	3 39.9	6 00.6	3 45.4	3 26.3	29♍58.4	11 13.7	0 09.8	1 16.0	25 24.6
21 Tu	22 04 08	2 27 45	13 58 43	19 53 18	9 10.4	2 34.2	7 14.9	3 53.4	3 45.5	29 52.3	11 10.6	0 07.7	1 17.4	25 26.3
22 W	22 08 05	3 28 12	25 47 00	1♋40 29	9 08.7	1 27.2	8 29.2	4 02.0	4 04.8	29 46.0	11 07.5	0 05.6	1 18.7	25 28.0
23 Th	22 12 01	4 28 37	7♋34 21	13 29 10	9 04.7	0 20.7	9 43.6	4 11.2	4 24.3	29 39.7	11 04.3	0 03.6	1 20.1	25 29.8
24 F	22 15 58	5 29 00	19 25 27	25 23 42	8 57.8	29♒16.3	10 57.9	4 21.1	4 43.9	29 33.2	11 01.0	0 01.6	1 21.6	25 31.5
25 Sa	22 19 54	6 29 21	1♌24 17	7♌27 33	8 48.1	28 15.3	12 12.3	4 31.5	5 03.6	29 26.6	10 57.6	29♋59.6	1 23.0	25 33.2
26 Su	22 23 51	7 29 41	13 33 46	19 43 08	8 36.0	27 18.9	13 26.6	4 42.4	5 23.4	29 19.9	10 54.2	29 57.7	1 24.5	25 34.9
27 M	22 27 47	8 29 59	25 55 48	2♍11 48	8 22.4	26 28.1	14 40.9	4 53.9	5 43.4	29 13.1	10 50.7	29 55.8	1 26.0	25 36.7
28 Tu	22 31 44	9 30 15	8♍31 11	14 53 52	8 08.3	25 43.5	15 55.3	5 06.0	6 03.5	29 06.2	10 47.1	29 54.0	1 27.5	25 38.4
29 W	22 35 40	10 30 29	21 19 48	27 48 51	7 55.1	25 05.6	17 09.6	5 18.6	6 23.6	28 59.2	10 43.4	29 52.2	1 29.1	25 40.1

Astro Data	Dy Hr Mn
☽0S	7 0:05
♆ D	11 5:08
♃✶♅	11 21:10
♃ R	16 13:17
☽0N	19 12:32
♄ R	21 4:13
♅□♆	1 1:05
☽0S	3 4:58
♃⚻♆	8 4:55
♂ D	9 11:48
☿ R	12 13:39
☽0N	15 21:16
♃✶♅	17 9:35

Planet Ingress		Dy Hr Mn
☿	♒	14 14:58
☉	♒	20 11:21
♀	♑	22 9:16
☿	♓	1 21:16
⚳	♉	9 5:20
♀	♒	15 15:35
☉	♓	19 1:24
♃	♍R	20 5:36
☿	♒R	23 19:37
♅	♋R	25 7:39

Last Aspect Dy Hr Mn			☽ Ingress	Dy Hr Mn
30 21:17	♂	☌	♌	1 7:44
3 7:36	♇	☍	♍	3 19:09
4 22:31	☉	△	♎	6 4:24
8 0:26	♇	△	♏	8 10:40
10 4:10	♇	□	♐	10 13:42
12 5:07	♇	✶	♑	12 14:10
14 13:28	☿	☌	♒	14 13:38
16 4:53	♇	☌	♓	16 14:05
18 14:07	☉	✶	♈	18 17:32
20 21:37	♀	△	♉	21 1:08
23 1:33	♇	□	♊	23 12:26
25 14:35	♇	△	♋	26 1:27
27 1:49	♄	□	♌	28 14:01
30 19:01	☿	☍	♍	31 0:57

Last Aspect Dy Hr Mn			☽ Ingress	Dy Hr Mn
31 23:43	♀	△	♎	2 9:58
4 7:47	♇	△	♏	4 16:54
6 12:55	♇	□	♐	6 21:31
8 15:40	♇	✶	♑	8 23:48
10 14:23	♀	☌	♒	11 0:28
12 17:11	♇	☌	♓	13 1:04
15 2:23	♀	✶	♈	15 3:34
17 6:18	☉	✶	♉	17 9:41
19 10:41	♇	□	♊	19 19:52
22 8:09	♃	□	♋	22 8:35
24 20:14	♃	✶	♌	24 21:12
27 1:43	☿	☍	♍	27 7:48
29 15:47	♅	✶	♎	29 16:01

☽ Phases & Eclipses Dy Hr Mn	
7 11:05	☾ 16♎45
14 3:25	● 23♑33
21 2:21	☽ 0♉38
29 7:54	○ 9♌00
5 22:32	☾ 16♏44
12 14:24	● 23♒28
19 21:33	☽ 0♊51
28 0:59	○ 9♍03

Astro Data

1 January 2040
Julian Day # 51135
SVP 4♓42'19"
GC 27♐23.9 ⚴ 29♒07.4
Eris 27♈53.6R ⚵ 18♒06.1
⚷ 9♋51.0R ⚶ 12♐41.6
☽ Mean ☊ 11♊23.1

1 February 2040
Julian Day # 51166
SVP 4♓42'14"
GC 27♐24.0 ⚴ 8♓31.7
Eris 27♈54.1 ⚵ 2♓11.0
⚷ 7♋56.1R ⚶ 28♐46.7
☽ Mean ☊ 9♊44.6

March 2040

LONGITUDE

Day	Sid.Time	☉	0 hr ☽	Noon ☽	True ☊	☿	♀	♂	⚳	♃	♄	♅	♆	♇
1 Th	22 39 37	11♓30 41	4♎20 53	10♎55 46	7♊44.0	24♒34.8	18♒24.0	5♋31.7	6♉44.0	28♍52.1	10♎39.7	29♋50.4	1♉30.7	25♒41.8
2 F	22 43 34	12 30 52	17 33 22	24 13 34	7R 35.6	24R 11.0	19 38.3	5 45.3	7 04.4	28R 45.0	10R 35.9	29R 48.7	1 32.3	25 43.4
3 Sa	22 47 30	13 31 02	0♏56 17	7♏41 27	7 30.3	23 54.3	20 52.7	5 59.4	7 24.9	28 37.7	10 32.0	29 47.0	1 33.9	25 45.1
4 Su	22 51 27	14 31 09	14 29 02	21 19 04	7 27.8	23D 44.5	22 07.0	6 13.9	7 45.6	28 30.4	10 28.1	29 45.3	1 35.6	25 46.8
5 M	22 55 23	15 31 16	28 11 33	5♐06 31	7 27.1	23 41.5	23 21.4	6 29.0	8 06.3	28 23.0	10 24.1	29 43.7	1 37.2	25 48.5
6 Tu	22 59 20	16 31 21	12♐04 02	19 04 06	7 27.1	23 44.8	24 35.8	6 44.5	8 27.2	28 15.6	10 20.1	29 42.2	1 38.9	25 50.1
7 W	23 03 16	17 31 24	26 06 42	3♑11 47	7 26.4	23 54.2	25 50.1	7 00.5	8 48.2	28 08.0	10 16.0	29 40.6	1 40.7	25 51.8
8 Th	23 07 13	18 31 26	10♑19 13	17 28 44	7 23.9	24 09.5	27 04.5	7 16.9	9 09.3	28 00.5	10 11.9	29 39.2	1 42.4	25 53.4
9 F	23 11 09	19 31 26	24 40 03	1♒52 41	7 18.7	24 30.1	28 18.9	7 33.7	9 30.4	27 52.9	10 07.7	29 37.7	1 44.2	25 55.1
10 Sa	23 15 06	20 31 24	9♒06 08	16 19 44	7 10.6	24 55.9	29 33.2	7 51.0	9 51.7	27 45.2	10 03.5	29 36.4	1 46.0	25 56.7
11 Su	23 19 03	21 31 21	23 32 46	0♓44 29	7 00.3	25 26.4	0♓47.6	8 08.7	10 13.1	27 37.5	9 59.2	29 35.0	1 47.8	25 58.3
12 M	23 22 59	22 31 16	7♓54 04	15 00 44	6 48.6	26 01.4	2 01.9	8 26.8	10 34.6	27 29.8	9 54.8	29 33.7	1 49.6	25 59.9
13 Tu	23 26 56	23 31 09	22 03 44	29 02 25	6 36.8	26 40.5	3 16.3	8 45.3	10 56.2	27 22.0	9 50.5	29 32.5	1 51.5	26 01.5
14 W	23 30 52	24 31 00	5♈56 13	12♈44 40	6 26.3	27 23.6	4 30.6	9 04.1	11 17.8	27 14.2	9 46.1	29 31.3	1 53.3	26 03.0
15 Th	23 34 49	25 30 48	19 27 30	26 04 32	6 17.9	28 10.3	5 44.9	9 23.4	11 39.6	27 06.4	9 41.6	29 30.2	1 55.2	26 04.6
16 F	23 38 45	26 30 35	2♉35 45	9♉01 16	6 12.1	29 00.4	6 59.3	9 43.0	12 01.4	26 58.6	9 37.1	29 29.1	1 57.1	26 06.2
17 Sa	23 42 42	27 30 20	15 21 19	21 36 15	6 08.9	29 53.8	8 13.6	10 03.0	12 23.3	26 50.9	9 32.6	29 28.0	1 59.1	26 07.7
18 Su	23 46 38	28 30 02	27 46 30	3♊52 34	6D 07.9	0♓50.1	9 27.9	10 23.4	12 45.3	26 43.1	9 28.1	29 27.0	2 01.0	26 09.2
19 M	23 50 35	29 29 42	9♊55 04	15 54 35	6 08.2	1 49.2	10 42.2	10 44.1	13 07.4	26 35.3	9 23.5	29 26.1	2 03.0	26 10.7
20 Tu	23 54 32	0♈29 20	21 51 47	27 47 22	6R 08.6	2 51.1	11 56.5	11 05.1	13 29.6	26 27.5	9 18.9	29 25.2	2 04.9	26 12.2
21 W	23 58 28	1 28 56	3♋41 59	9♋36 20	6 08.3	3 55.4	13 10.8	11 26.5	13 51.9	26 19.7	9 14.3	29 24.3	2 06.9	26 13.7
22 Th	0 02 25	2 28 29	15 31 05	21 26 54	6 06.3	5 02.1	14 25.1	11 48.2	14 14.2	26 12.0	9 09.7	29 23.6	2 09.0	26 15.2
23 F	0 06 21	3 28 01	27 24 23	3♌24 06	6 02.0	6 11.1	15 39.4	12 10.2	14 36.6	26 04.3	9 05.1	29 22.8	2 11.0	26 16.7
24 Sa	0 10 18	4 27 29	9♌26 36	15 32 21	5 55.4	7 22.3	16 53.6	12 32.5	14 59.1	25 56.7	9 00.4	29 22.1	2 13.0	26 18.1
25 Su	0 14 14	5 26 56	21 41 45	27 55 06	5 46.6	8 35.5	18 07.9	12 55.1	15 21.7	25 49.1	8 55.7	29 21.5	2 15.1	26 19.5
26 M	0 18 11	6 26 20	4♍12 40	10♍34 37	5 36.5	9 50.6	19 22.2	13 18.0	15 44.3	25 41.5	8 51.1	29 20.9	2 17.1	26 20.9
27 Tu	0 22 07	7 25 42	17 00 59	23 31 46	5 25.9	11 07.7	20 36.4	13 41.1	16 07.0	25 34.0	8 46.4	29 20.4	2 19.2	26 22.3
28 W	0 26 04	8 25 02	0♎06 52	6♎46 05	5 15.9	12 26.7	21 50.6	14 04.6	16 29.7	25 26.5	8 41.7	29 19.9	2 21.3	26 23.7
29 Th	0 30 00	9 24 20	13 29 10	20 15 50	5 07.5	13 47.4	23 04.9	14 28.3	16 52.6	25 19.1	8 37.0	29 19.5	2 23.4	26 25.1
30 F	0 33 57	10 23 36	27 05 42	3♏58 25	5 01.4	15 09.8	24 19.1	14 52.2	17 15.5	25 11.8	8 32.3	29 19.1	2 25.5	26 26.4
31 Sa	0 37 54	11 22 50	10♏53 37	17 50 55	4 57.8	16 34.0	25 33.3	15 16.5	17 38.4	25 04.5	8 27.7	29 18.8	2 27.7	26 27.7

April 2040

LONGITUDE

Day	Sid.Time	☉	0 hr ☽	Noon ☽	True ☊	☿	♀	♂	⚳	♃	♄	♅	♆	♇
1 Su	0 41 50	12♈22 03	24♏49 59	1♐50 29	4♊56.5	17♓59.7	26♓47.5	15♋40.9	18♉01.4	24♍57.4	8♎23.0	29♋18.5	2♉29.8	26♒29.1
2 M	0 45 47	13 21 13	8♐52 09	15 54 44	4D 56.8	19 27.1	28 01.7	16 05.6	18 24.5	24R 50.3	8R 18.3	29R 18.3	2 32.0	26 30.4
3 Tu	0 49 43	14 20 22	22 58 02	0♑01 50	4 57.8	20 56.1	29 15.9	16 30.6	18 47.7	24 43.2	8 13.7	29 18.2	2 34.1	26 31.6
4 W	0 53 40	15 19 29	7♑06 00	14 10 22	4R 58.5	22 26.7	0♈30.1	16 55.8	19 10.9	24 36.3	8 09.1	29 18.0	2 36.3	26 32.9
5 Th	0 57 36	16 18 35	21 14 46	28 19 02	4 57.8	23 58.8	1 44.3	17 21.2	19 34.2	24 29.5	8 04.4	29D 18.0	2 38.5	26 34.1
6 F	1 01 33	17 17 38	5♒22 55	12♒26 14	4 55.3	25 32.4	2 58.5	17 46.9	19 57.5	24 22.8	7 59.8	29 18.0	2 40.7	26 35.4
7 Sa	1 05 30	18 16 40	19 28 40	26 29 54	4 50.7	27 07.5	4 12.7	18 12.7	20 20.9	24 16.1	7 55.3	29 18.1	2 42.9	26 36.6
8 Su	1 09 26	19 15 40	3♓29 36	10♓27 21	4 44.4	28 44.2	5 26.8	18 38.8	20 44.3	24 09.6	7 50.7	29 18.2	2 45.1	26 37.7
9 M	1 13 23	20 14 38	17 22 47	24 15 28	4 37.0	0♈22.4	6 41.0	19 05.1	21 07.9	24 03.2	7 46.2	29 18.3	2 47.3	26 38.9
10 Tu	1 17 19	21 13 34	1♈05 02	7♈51 05	4 29.6	2 02.1	7 55.2	19 31.7	21 31.4	23 56.9	7 41.7	29 18.6	2 49.5	26 40.0
11 W	1 21 16	22 12 29	14 33 18	21 11 26	4 22.9	3 43.4	9 09.3	19 58.4	21 55.0	23 50.8	7 37.2	29 18.8	2 51.8	26 41.2
12 Th	1 25 12	23 11 21	27 45 17	4♉14 42	4 17.6	5 26.2	10 23.4	20 25.3	22 18.7	23 44.7	7 32.8	29 19.2	2 54.0	26 42.3
13 F	1 29 09	24 10 11	10♉39 40	17 00 13	4 14.2	7 10.5	11 37.6	20 52.4	22 42.4	23 38.8	7 28.4	29 19.5	2 56.2	26 43.3
14 Sa	1 33 05	25 08 59	23 16 29	29 28 41	4D 12.7	8 56.3	12 51.7	21 19.8	23 06.2	23 33.0	7 24.0	29 20.0	2 58.5	26 44.4
15 Su	1 37 02	26 07 45	5♊37 06	11♊42 04	4 12.9	10 43.7	14 05.8	21 47.3	23 30.0	23 27.4	7 19.7	29 20.5	3 00.7	26 45.4
16 M	1 40 58	27 06 29	17 44 02	23 43 28	4 14.1	12 32.7	15 19.9	22 15.0	23 53.8	23 21.9	7 15.4	29 21.0	3 03.0	26 46.4
17 Tu	1 44 55	28 05 11	29 40 52	5♋36 49	4 15.8	14 23.2	16 34.0	22 42.8	24 17.7	23 16.5	7 11.2	29 21.6	3 05.2	26 47.4
18 W	1 48 52	29 03 51	11♋31 55	17 26 45	4 17.3	16 15.3	17 48.1	23 10.9	24 41.7	23 11.3	7 07.0	29 22.3	3 07.5	26 48.4
19 Th	1 52 48	0♉02 28	23 21 58	29 18 12	4R 18.0	18 09.0	19 02.1	23 39.1	25 05.7	23 06.3	7 02.9	29 23.0	3 09.8	26 49.4
20 F	1 56 45	1 01 03	5♌16 03	11♌16 10	4 17.4	20 04.3	20 16.2	24 07.5	25 29.7	23 01.4	6 58.8	29 23.7	3 12.0	26 50.3
21 Sa	2 00 41	1 59 36	17 19 08	23 25 31	4 15.4	22 01.1	21 30.2	24 36.0	25 53.7	22 56.6	6 54.8	29 24.6	3 14.3	26 51.2
22 Su	2 04 38	2 58 07	29 35 49	5♍50 31	4 12.1	23 59.5	22 44.2	25 04.8	26 17.9	22 52.0	6 50.8	29 25.4	3 16.6	26 52.1
23 M	2 08 34	3 56 36	12♍10 00	18 34 34	4 07.8	25 59.4	23 58.2	25 33.6	26 42.0	22 47.6	6 46.9	29 26.3	3 18.8	26 52.9
24 Tu	2 12 31	4 55 02	25 04 27	1♎39 47	4 03.2	28 00.7	25 12.2	26 02.6	27 06.2	22 43.3	6 43.1	29 27.3	3 21.1	26 53.8
25 W	2 16 27	5 53 27	8♎20 34	15 06 43	3 58.7	0♉03.5	26 26.2	26 31.8	27 30.4	22 39.2	6 39.3	29 28.3	3 23.3	26 54.6
26 Th	2 20 24	6 51 49	21 58 02	28 54 11	3 55.0	2 07.7	27 40.2	27 01.1	27 54.7	22 35.2	6 35.5	29 29.4	3 25.6	26 55.4
27 F	2 24 21	7 50 10	5♏54 45	12♏59 14	3 52.5	4 13.1	28 54.2	27 30.5	28 18.9	22 31.4	6 31.9	29 30.5	3 27.9	26 56.1
28 Sa	2 28 17	8 48 29	20 07 04	27 17 37	3D 51.3	6 19.7	0♉08.1	28 00.1	28 43.3	22 27.8	6 28.3	29 31.7	3 30.1	26 56.9
29 Su	2 32 14	9 46 46	4♐30 14	11♐44 15	3 51.3	8 27.3	1 22.1	28 29.9	29 07.6	22 24.4	6 24.8	29 32.9	3 32.4	26 57.6
30 M	2 36 10	10 45 02	18 59 01	26 13 54	3 52.3	10 35.7	2 36.1	28 59.7	29 32.0	22 21.1	6 21.3	29 34.2	3 34.6	26 58.3

Astro Data

	Dy Hr Mn
♄□♇	1 2:49
☽0S	1 10:03
☿D	5 11:19
☽0N	14 6:45
☉0N	20 0:12
♃⚻♇	22 3:41
☽0S	28 17:18
♅D	5 21:44
♀0N	6 21:02
☽0N	10 15:24
☿0N	12 12:01
☽0S	25 2:39

Planet Ingress

		Dy Hr Mn
♀	♓	10 20:39
☿	♓	17 14:43
☉	♈	20 0:11
♀	♈	4 2:15
☿	♈	9 6:33
☉	♉	19 10:59
☿	♉	25 11:19
♀	♉	28 9:22

Last Aspect / ☽ Ingress (March)

Last Aspect Dy Hr Mn			☽ Ingress	Dy Hr Mn
2 21:58	♅	□	♏	2 22:20
5 2:41	♅	△	♐	5 3:09
7 3:30	♃	□	♑	7 6:36
9 8:16	♅	☍	♒	9 8:53
11 4:01	♇	☌	♓	11 10:46
13 12:52	♅	△	♈	13 13:40
15 18:17	♅	□	♉	15 19:12
18 3:18	♅	⚹	♊	18 4:22
20 9:20	♃	□	♋	20 16:29
23 3:58	♅	☌	♌	23 5:12
25 8:56	♇	☍	♍	25 15:59
27 22:35	♅	⚹	♎	27 23:48
30 3:53	♅	□	♏	30 5:05

Last Aspect / ☽ Ingress (April)

Last Aspect Dy Hr Mn			☽ Ingress	Dy Hr Mn
1 7:40	♅	△	♐	1 8:51
3 10:35	♀	□	♑	3 11:57
5 13:40	♅	☍	♒	5 14:51
7 12:11	♇	☌	♓	7 18:00
9 20:52	♅	△	♈	9 22:05
12 2:53	♅	□	♉	12 4:08
14 11:43	♅	⚹	♊	14 13:01
16 19:25	☉	⚹	♋	17 0:39
19 12:10	♅	☌	♌	19 13:24
21 18:41	♇	☍	♍	22 0:47
24 7:59	♅	⚹	♎	24 8:59
26 13:01	♅	□	♏	26 13:53
28 15:44	♅	△	♐	28 16:31
30 13:14	♇	⚹	♑	30 18:15

☽ Phases & Eclipses

Dy Hr Mn		
6 7:19	☾	16♐20
13 1:46	●	23♓06
20 17:59	☽	0♋44
28 15:11	○	8♎33
4 14:06	☾	15♑25
11 14:00	●	22♈17
19 13:37	☽	0♌06
27 2:38	○	7♏27

Astro Data

1 March 2040
Julian Day # 51195
SVP 4♓42'10"
GC 27♐24.0 ⚴ 18♓11.3
Eris 28♈03.7 ⚵ 16♓22.8
⚷ 6♋57.3R ⚶ 12♑58.1
☽ Mean ☊ 8♊12.4

1 April 2040
Julian Day # 51226
SVP 4♓42'07"
GC 27♐24.1 ⚴ 28♓53.2
Eris 28♈21.1 ⚵ 2♈19.4
⚷ 7♋13.1 ⚶ 26♑32.7
☽ Mean ☊ 6♊33.9

LONGITUDE — May 2040

Day	Sid.Time	☉	0 hr ☽	Noon ☽	True ☊	☿	♀	♂	⚳	♃	♄	♅	♆	♇
1 Tu	2 40 07	11♉43 16	3♑28 19	10♑41 45	3♊53.6	12♉44.8	3♉50.0	29♋29.7	29♉56.5	22♍18.0	6♎17.9	29♋35.5	3♉36.9	26♒58.9
2 W	2 44 03	12 41 29	17 53 43	25 03 50	3 54.9	14 54.3	5 03.9	29 59.9	0♊20.9	22R 15.1	6R 14.6	29 36.9	3 39.1	26 59.6
3 Th	2 48 00	13 39 40	2♒11 45	9♒17 11	3R 55.6	17 04.0	6 17.9	0♌30.1	0 45.4	22 12.3	6 11.4	29 38.3	3 41.4	27 00.2
4 F	2 51 56	14 37 50	16 19 54	23 19 43	3 55.4	19 13.6	7 31.8	1 00.5	1 09.9	22 09.7	6 08.2	29 39.8	3 43.6	27 00.8
5 Sa	2 55 53	15 35 58	0♓16 29	7♓10 06	3 54.4	21 22.9	8 45.7	1 31.0	1 34.5	22 07.3	6 05.2	29 41.3	3 45.8	27 01.4
6 Su	2 59 50	16 34 05	14 00 27	20 47 29	3 52.7	23 31.5	9 59.6	2 01.6	1 59.1	22 05.1	6 02.2	29 42.9	3 48.0	27 01.9
7 M	3 03 46	17 32 10	27 31 07	4♈11 20	3 50.5	25 39.1	11 13.5	2 32.4	2 23.7	22 03.1	5 59.2	29 44.5	3 50.3	27 02.5
8 Tu	3 07 43	18 30 14	10♈48 05	17 21 21	3 48.2	27 45.5	12 27.4	3 03.3	2 48.3	22 01.2	5 56.4	29 46.2	3 52.5	27 02.9
9 W	3 11 39	19 28 17	23 51 07	0♉17 25	3 46.3	29 50.4	13 41.3	3 34.3	3 13.0	21 59.5	5 53.6	29 47.9	3 54.7	27 03.4
10 Th	3 15 36	20 26 18	6♉40 15	12 59 41	3 44.9	1♊53.5	14 55.2	4 05.4	3 37.7	21 58.0	5 51.0	29 49.6	3 56.9	27 03.9
11 F	3 19 32	21 24 17	19 15 47	25 28 40	3D 44.1	3 54.6	16 09.1	4 36.6	4 02.4	21 56.7	5 48.4	29 51.4	3 59.0	27 04.3
12 Sa	3 23 29	22 22 15	1♊38 29	7♊45 23	3 44.0	5 53.4	17 23.0	5 08.0	4 27.1	21 55.6	5 45.9	29 53.3	4 01.2	27 04.7
13 Su	3 27 25	23 20 12	13 49 37	19 51 26	3 44.5	7 49.7	18 36.9	5 39.4	4 51.9	21 54.6	5 43.5	29 55.2	4 03.4	27 05.0
14 M	3 31 22	24 18 06	25 51 06	1♋48 59	3 45.2	9 43.4	19 50.7	6 11.0	5 16.7	21 53.9	5 41.2	29 57.1	4 05.6	27 05.4
15 Tu	3 35 19	25 15 59	7♋45 27	13 40 55	3 46.1	11 34.3	21 04.6	6 42.7	5 41.5	21 53.3	5 38.9	29 59.1	4 07.7	27 05.7
16 W	3 39 15	26 13 51	19 35 49	25 30 38	3 47.0	13 22.2	22 18.4	7 14.5	6 06.3	21 52.9	5 36.8	0♌01.2	4 09.8	27 06.0
17 Th	3 43 12	27 11 41	1♌25 53	7♌22 07	3 47.6	15 07.2	23 32.2	7 46.3	6 31.2	21D 52.7	5 34.8	0 03.3	4 12.0	27 06.3
18 F	3 47 08	28 09 29	13 19 51	19 19 40	3R 48.0	16 49.0	24 46.1	8 18.3	6 56.0	21 52.7	5 32.8	0 05.4	4 14.1	27 06.5
19 Sa	3 51 05	29 07 15	25 22 09	1♍27 52	3 48.0	18 27.6	25 59.9	8 50.4	7 20.9	21 52.8	5 31.0	0 07.5	4 16.2	27 06.7
20 Su	3 55 01	0♊05 00	7♍37 21	13 51 11	3 47.9	20 02.9	27 13.7	9 22.6	7 45.8	21 53.1	5 29.2	0 09.7	4 18.3	27 06.9
21 M	3 58 58	1 02 43	20 09 50	26 33 46	3 47.7	21 35.0	28 27.5	9 54.8	8 10.7	21 53.7	5 27.6	0 12.0	4 20.3	27 07.1
22 Tu	4 02 54	2 00 24	3♎03 22	9♎38 57	3 47.4	23 03.6	29 41.3	10 27.2	8 35.7	21 54.4	5 26.0	0 14.3	4 22.4	27 07.2
23 W	4 06 51	2 58 04	16 20 43	23 08 47	3D 47.3	24 28.9	0♊55.1	10 59.7	9 00.6	21 55.2	5 24.5	0 16.6	4 24.4	27 07.3
24 Th	4 10 48	3 55 42	0♏03 08	7♏03 36	3 47.3	25 50.7	2 08.8	11 32.2	9 25.6	21 56.3	5 23.1	0 19.0	4 26.5	27 07.4
25 F	4 14 44	4 53 19	14 09 53	21 21 32	3R 47.3	27 09.1	3 22.6	12 04.8	9 50.5	21 57.5	5 21.9	0 21.4	4 28.5	27 07.5
26 Sa	4 18 41	5 50 55	28 37 58	5♐58 27	3 47.3	28 23.9	4 36.4	12 37.5	10 15.5	21 58.9	5 20.7	0 23.8	4 30.5	27 07.5
27 Su	4 22 37	6 48 30	13♐22 10	20 48 12	3 47.2	29 35.1	5 50.1	13 10.3	10 40.5	22 00.5	5 19.6	0 26.3	4 32.5	27R 07.5
28 M	4 26 34	7 46 04	28 15 33	5♑43 15	3 47.0	0♋42.7	7 03.9	13 43.2	11 05.5	22 02.3	5 18.6	0 28.9	4 34.5	27 07.5
29 Tu	4 30 30	8 43 36	13♑10 18	20 35 46	3 46.5	1 46.5	8 17.6	14 16.2	11 30.6	22 04.2	5 17.8	0 31.4	4 36.4	27 07.5
30 W	4 34 27	9 41 08	27 58 47	5♒18 35	3 46.0	2 46.7	9 31.4	14 49.3	11 55.6	22 06.3	5 17.0	0 34.0	4 38.4	27 07.4
31 Th	4 38 24	10 38 39	12♒34 33	19 46 09	3 45.4	3 42.9	10 45.1	15 22.4	12 20.7	22 08.6	5 16.3	0 36.7	4 40.3	27 07.3

LONGITUDE — June 2040

Day	Sid.Time	☉	0 hr ☽	Noon ☽	True ☊	☿	♀	♂	⚳	♃	♄	♅	♆	♇
1 F	4 42 20	11♊36 09	26♒53 00	3♓54 51	3♊45.1	4♋35.3	11♊58.9	15♌55.6	12♊45.7	22♍11.1	5♎15.7	0♌39.3	4♉42.2	27♒07.2
2 Sa	4 46 17	12 33 38	10♓51 34	17 43 06	3D 45.0	5 23.7	13 12.6	16 28.9	13 10.8	22 13.7	5R 15.2	0 42.0	4 44.1	27R 07.1
3 Su	4 50 13	13 31 06	24 29 31	1♈10 58	3 45.4	6 08.0	14 26.4	17 02.3	13 35.9	22 16.5	5 14.9	0 44.8	4 45.9	27 06.9
4 M	4 54 10	14 28 34	7♈47 36	14 19 40	3 46.1	6 48.2	15 40.1	17 35.8	14 01.0	22 19.5	5 14.6	0 47.6	4 47.8	27 06.7
5 Tu	4 58 06	15 26 01	20 47 26	27 11 09	3 47.1	7 24.1	16 53.9	18 09.3	14 26.1	22 22.6	5 14.4	0 50.4	4 49.6	27 06.5
6 W	5 02 03	16 23 28	3♉31 08	9♉47 38	3 48.2	7 55.8	18 07.6	18 42.9	14 51.2	22 25.9	5D 14.3	0 53.2	4 51.4	27 06.3
7 Th	5 05 59	17 20 53	16 00 57	22 11 20	3R 49.0	8 23.0	19 21.3	19 16.6	15 16.3	22 29.4	5 14.3	0 56.1	4 53.2	27 06.0
8 F	5 09 56	18 18 18	28 19 04	4♊24 24	3 49.3	8 45.9	20 35.1	19 50.4	15 41.4	22 33.0	5 14.5	0 59.0	4 55.0	27 05.7
9 Sa	5 13 53	19 15 43	10♊27 33	16 28 47	3 48.9	9 04.2	21 48.8	20 24.3	16 06.5	22 36.8	5 14.7	1 01.9	4 56.7	27 05.4
10 Su	5 17 49	20 13 06	22 28 19	28 26 24	3 47.6	9 17.9	23 02.6	20 58.2	16 31.7	22 40.8	5 15.0	1 04.9	4 58.5	27 05.1
11 M	5 21 46	21 10 29	4♋23 17	10♋19 13	3 45.6	9 27.1	24 16.3	21 32.2	16 56.8	22 44.9	5 15.5	1 07.9	5 00.2	27 04.7
12 Tu	5 25 42	22 07 51	16 14 27	22 09 19	3 42.9	9R 31.7	25 30.0	22 06.3	17 21.9	22 49.2	5 16.0	1 11.0	5 01.8	27 04.3
13 W	5 29 39	23 05 12	28 04 05	3♌59 07	3 39.9	9 31.7	26 43.8	22 40.5	17 47.1	22 53.6	5 16.6	1 14.0	5 03.5	27 03.9
14 Th	5 33 35	24 02 32	9♌54 47	15 51 27	3 36.9	9 27.3	27 57.5	23 14.7	18 12.2	22 58.3	5 17.4	1 17.1	5 05.2	27 03.5
15 F	5 37 32	24 59 51	21 49 33	27 49 33	3 34.3	9 18.6	29 11.2	23 49.0	18 37.4	23 03.0	5 18.2	1 20.2	5 06.8	27 03.0
16 Sa	5 41 28	25 57 09	3♍51 54	9♍57 06	3 32.4	9 05.6	0♋24.9	24 23.4	19 02.5	23 07.9	5 19.2	1 23.4	5 08.4	27 02.5
17 Su	5 45 25	26 54 27	16 05 40	22 18 07	3D 31.5	8 48.6	1 38.6	24 57.8	19 27.6	23 13.0	5 20.2	1 26.5	5 09.9	27 02.0
18 M	5 49 22	27 51 44	28 34 59	4♎56 45	3 31.6	8 27.9	2 52.4	25 32.3	19 52.8	23 18.2	5 21.3	1 29.7	5 11.5	27 01.5
19 Tu	5 53 18	28 48 59	11♎23 55	17 56 54	3 32.5	8 03.7	4 06.1	26 06.9	20 17.9	23 23.6	5 22.6	1 33.0	5 13.0	27 00.9
20 W	5 57 15	29 46 14	24 36 07	1♏21 51	3 34.0	7 36.5	5 19.8	26 41.5	20 43.0	23 29.1	5 23.9	1 36.2	5 14.5	27 00.4
21 Th	6 01 11	0♋43 29	8♏14 18	15 13 33	3 35.4	7 06.6	6 33.5	27 16.2	21 08.1	23 34.7	5 25.4	1 39.5	5 15.9	26 59.8
22 F	6 05 08	1 40 43	22 19 30	29 31 57	3R 36.2	6 34.7	7 47.2	27 51.0	21 33.3	23 40.5	5 26.9	1 42.8	5 17.4	26 59.2
23 Sa	6 09 04	2 37 56	6♐50 27	14♐14 25	3 35.9	6 01.0	9 00.9	28 25.8	21 58.4	23 46.5	5 28.5	1 46.1	5 18.8	26 58.5
24 Su	6 13 01	3 35 09	21 43 02	29 15 23	3 34.2	5 26.3	10 14.6	29 00.7	22 23.5	23 52.6	5 30.3	1 49.4	5 20.2	26 57.9
25 M	6 16 57	4 32 21	6♑50 19	14♑26 40	3 31.2	4 51.2	11 28.2	29 35.6	22 48.6	23 58.8	5 32.1	1 52.8	5 21.6	26 57.2
26 Tu	6 20 54	5 29 34	22 03 08	29 38 27	3 27.2	4 16.1	12 41.9	0♍10.7	23 13.7	24 05.1	5 34.0	1 56.1	5 22.9	26 56.5
27 W	6 24 51	6 26 46	7♒11 23	14♒40 47	3 22.6	3 41.8	13 55.6	0 45.7	23 38.8	24 11.6	5 36.0	1 59.5	5 24.2	26 55.8
28 Th	6 28 47	7 23 58	22 05 41	29 25 15	3 18.4	3 08.8	15 09.3	1 20.9	24 03.9	24 18.3	5 38.2	2 03.0	5 25.5	26 55.0
29 F	6 32 44	8 21 10	6♓38 51	13♓46 02	3 15.0	2 37.6	16 23.0	1 56.1	24 29.0	24 25.0	5 40.4	2 06.4	5 26.8	26 54.3
30 Sa	6 36 40	9 18 22	20 46 33	27 40 20	3D 12.9	2 08.9	17 36.7	2 31.3	24 54.1	24 31.9	5 42.7	2 09.9	5 28.0	26 53.5

Astro Data	Planet Ingress	Last Aspect	☽ Ingress	Last Aspect	☽ Ingress	☽ Phases & Eclipses	Astro Data
Dy Hr Mn	Dy Hr Mn	Dy Hr Mn	Dy Hr Mn	Dy Hr Mn	Dy Hr Mn	Dy Hr Mn	1 May 2040
♄0N 5 14:50	⚳ ♊ 1 15:29	2 19:40 ♅ ☍	♒ 2 20:18	1 0:24 ♇ ☌	♓ 1 5:18	3 20:00 ☾ 13♒59	Julian Day # 51256
☽0N 7 22:20	♂ ♌ 2 12:07	4 18:22 ♇ ☌	♓ 4 23:31	2 20:00 ♃ ☍	♈ 3 9:52	11 3:28 ● 21♉04	SVP 4♓42'04"
♃ D 18 3:57	☿ ♊ 9 13:51	7 3:58 ♅ △	♈ 7 4:27	5 11:51 ♇ ⚹	♉ 5 17:19	11 3:41:39 ● P 0.531	GC 27♐24.2 ⚴ 9♈11.1
☽0S 22 12:30	♅ ♌ 15 22:13	9 11:05 ♅ □	♉ 9 11:27	7 21:36 ♇ □	♊ 8 3:18	19 7:00 ☽ 28♌55	Eris 28♈40.8 ⚵ 18♈16.9
♇ R 27 13:24	☉ ♊ 20 9:55	11 20:32 ♅ ⚹	♊ 11 20:48	10 9:16 ♇ △	♋ 10 15:09	26 11:47 ○ 5♐50	⚷ 8♋43.9 ⚶ 7♒04.7
	♀ ♊ 22 18:06	14 2:29 ♇ △	♋ 14 8:20	12 13:21 ♃ ⚹	♌ 13 3:55	26 11:45 ● T 1.535	☽ Mean ☊ 4♊58.6
☽0N 4 3:53	☿ ♋ 27 20:42	16 13:35 ☉ ⚹	♌ 16 21:06	15 15:01 ♀ ⚹	♍ 15 16:20		
♄ D 6 17:54		19 7:00 ☉ □	♍ 19 9:08	17 21:32 ☉ □	♎ 18 2:41	2 2:17 ☾ 12♓10	1 June 2040
☿ R 13 0:18	♀ ♋ 16 3:53	21 15:53 ♀ △	♎ 21 18:22	20 8:59 ☉ △	♏ 20 9:36	9 18:03 ● 19♊30	Julian Day # 51287
☽0S 18 21:05	☉ ♋ 20 17:46	23 18:56 ♇ △	♏ 23 23:55	22 9:06 ♂ □	♐ 22 12:46	17 21:32 ☽ 27♍17	SVP 4♓41'58"
♄0S 28 6:30	♂ ♍ 26 4:42	25 21:31 ♇ □	♐ 26 2:15	24 11:36 ♂ △	♑ 24 13:11	24 19:19 ○ 3♑53	GC 27♐24.2 ⚴ 19♈19.8
		27 22:11 ♇ ⚹	♑ 28 2:48	26 3:09 ♃ △	♒ 26 12:34		Eris 28♈59.0 ⚵ 5♉06.7
		29 14:24 ♃ △	♒ 30 3:18	28 7:53 ♇ ☌	♓ 28 12:57		⚷ 11♋16.2 ⚶ 13♒29.5
				30 6:28 ♃ ☍	♈ 30 16:06		☽ Mean ☊ 3♊20.1

July 2040

LONGITUDE

Day	Sid.Time	☉	0 hr ☽	Noon ☽	True ☊	☿	♀	♂	⚳	♃	♄	♅	♆	♇
1 Su	6 40 37	10♋15 34	4♈27 27	11♈08 08	3♊12.3	1♋43.2	18♋50.4	3♍06.7	25♊19.1	24♍39.0	5♎45.1	2♌13.3	5♉29.2	26♒52.7
2 M	6 44 33	11 12 46	17 42 40	24 11 27	3 13.0	1R 20.8	20 04.1	3 42.0	25 44.2	24 46.1	5 47.6	2 16.8	5 30.4	26R 51.8
3 Tu	6 48 30	12 09 59	0♉34 56	6♉53 36	3 14.4	1 02.2	21 17.8	4 17.5	26 09.3	24 53.4	5 50.1	2 20.3	5 31.5	26 51.0
4 W	6 52 26	13 07 11	13 07 57	19 18 28	3 15.8	0 47.8	22 31.5	4 53.0	26 34.3	25 00.8	5 52.8	2 23.8	5 32.6	26 50.1
5 Th	6 56 23	14 04 25	25 25 39	1♊29 59	3R 16.6	0 37.8	23 45.2	5 28.6	26 59.3	25 08.4	5 55.6	2 27.4	5 33.7	26 49.3
6 F	7 00 20	15 01 38	7♊31 53	13 31 46	3 16.0	0D 32.4	24 58.9	6 04.2	27 24.4	25 16.0	5 58.4	2 30.9	5 34.8	26 48.4
7 Sa	7 04 16	15 58 51	19 30 03	25 27 03	3 13.7	0 32.0	26 12.6	6 39.9	27 49.4	25 23.8	6 01.4	2 34.5	5 35.8	26 47.4
8 Su	7 08 13	16 56 05	1♋23 06	7♋18 29	3 09.3	0 36.5	27 26.3	7 15.7	28 14.4	25 31.7	6 04.4	2 38.1	5 36.8	26 46.5
9 M	7 12 09	17 53 19	13 13 27	19 08 17	3 02.9	0 46.2	28 40.0	7 51.5	28 39.3	25 39.7	6 07.6	2 41.7	5 37.8	26 45.6
10 Tu	7 16 06	18 50 33	25 03 11	0♌58 23	2 55.1	1 01.0	29 53.8	8 27.4	29 04.3	25 47.9	6 10.8	2 45.3	5 38.7	26 44.6
11 W	7 20 02	19 47 47	6♌54 05	12 50 32	2 46.4	1 21.1	1♌07.5	9 03.4	29 29.3	25 56.1	6 14.1	2 48.9	5 39.7	26 43.6
12 Th	7 23 59	20 45 01	18 47 57	24 46 36	2 37.6	1 46.4	2 21.2	9 39.4	29 54.2	26 04.5	6 17.5	2 52.5	5 40.5	26 42.6
13 F	7 27 56	21 42 15	0♍46 44	6♍48 40	2 29.6	2 17.0	3 34.9	10 15.5	0♋19.1	26 13.0	6 21.0	2 56.1	5 41.4	26 41.6
14 Sa	7 31 52	22 39 29	12 52 43	18 59 15	2 23.1	2 52.9	4 48.6	10 51.6	0 44.0	26 21.6	6 24.5	2 59.8	5 42.2	26 40.6
15 Su	7 35 49	23 36 44	25 08 40	1♎21 22	2 18.6	3 33.9	6 02.3	11 27.8	1 08.9	26 30.3	6 28.2	3 03.4	5 43.0	26 39.5
16 M	7 39 45	24 33 58	7♎37 47	13 58 24	2D 16.2	4 20.1	7 15.9	12 04.0	1 33.7	26 39.1	6 31.9	3 07.1	5 43.7	26 38.4
17 Tu	7 43 42	25 31 13	20 23 40	26 54 03	2 15.6	5 11.5	8 29.6	12 40.3	1 58.6	26 48.0	6 35.7	3 10.7	5 44.5	26 37.4
18 W	7 47 38	26 28 27	3♏30 00	10♏11 54	2 16.2	6 07.8	9 43.3	13 16.6	2 23.4	26 57.0	6 39.6	3 14.4	5 45.1	26 36.3
19 Th	7 51 35	27 25 42	17 00 06	23 54 51	2R 17.1	7 09.2	10 57.0	13 53.0	2 48.2	27 06.2	6 43.6	3 18.1	5 45.8	26 35.2
20 F	7 55 31	28 22 57	0♐56 17	8♐04 24	2 17.1	8 15.5	12 10.7	14 29.5	3 12.9	27 15.4	6 47.7	3 21.7	5 46.4	26 34.1
21 Sa	7 59 28	29 20 13	15 19 01	22 39 46	2 15.6	9 26.7	13 24.3	15 06.0	3 37.7	27 24.7	6 51.8	3 25.4	5 47.0	26 32.9
22 Su	8 03 25	0♌17 29	0♑06 06	7♑37 11	2 11.8	10 42.6	14 38.0	15 42.6	4 02.4	27 34.1	6 56.0	3 29.1	5 47.6	26 31.8
23 M	8 07 21	1 14 45	15 12 04	22 49 35	2 05.7	12 03.2	15 51.7	16 19.2	4 27.1	27 43.7	7 00.3	3 32.8	5 48.1	26 30.6
24 Tu	8 11 18	2 12 01	0♒28 25	8♒07 11	1 57.7	13 28.3	17 05.3	16 55.9	4 51.8	27 53.3	7 04.7	3 36.5	5 48.6	26 29.5
25 W	8 15 14	3 09 19	15 44 29	23 18 57	1 48.9	14 57.8	18 19.0	17 32.6	5 16.4	28 03.0	7 09.1	3 40.2	5 49.1	26 28.3
26 Th	8 19 11	4 06 37	0♓49 19	8♓14 31	1 40.2	16 31.5	19 32.6	18 09.4	5 41.0	28 12.8	7 13.7	3 43.8	5 49.5	26 27.1
27 F	8 23 07	5 03 56	15 33 36	22 45 56	1 32.7	18 09.3	20 46.2	18 46.2	6 05.6	28 22.7	7 18.3	3 47.5	5 49.9	26 25.9
28 Sa	8 27 04	6 01 15	29 51 03	6♈48 43	1 27.2	19 51.0	21 59.9	19 23.1	6 30.2	28 32.6	7 22.9	3 51.2	5 50.3	26 24.7
29 Su	8 31 00	6 58 36	13♈38 54	20 21 46	1 24.0	21 36.3	23 13.5	20 00.1	6 54.7	28 42.7	7 27.7	3 54.9	5 50.6	26 23.5
30 M	8 34 57	7 55 58	26 57 37	3♉26 51	1D 22.8	23 25.0	24 27.2	20 37.1	7 19.2	28 52.8	7 32.5	3 58.6	5 51.0	26 22.2
31 Tu	8 38 54	8 53 21	9♉49 59	16 07 36	1 22.8	25 16.7	25 40.8	21 14.2	7 43.7	29 03.1	7 37.3	4 02.3	5 51.2	26 21.0

August 2040

LONGITUDE

Day	Sid.Time	☉	0 hr ☽	Noon ☽	True ☊	☿	♀	♂	⚳	♃	♄	♅	♆	♇
1 W	8 42 50	9♌50 45	22♉20 17	28♉28 40	1♊23.2	27♋11.2	26♌54.4	21♍51.3	8♋08.1	29♍13.4	7♎42.3	4♌06.0	5♉51.5	26♒19.8
2 Th	8 46 47	10 48 10	4♊33 23	10♊35 03	1R 22.9	29 08.1	28 08.0	22 28.5	8 32.5	29 23.8	7 47.3	4 09.6	5 51.7	26R 18.5
3 F	8 50 43	11 45 37	16 34 15	22 31 32	1 20.9	1♌07.1	29 21.7	23 05.7	8 56.9	29 34.3	7 52.4	4 13.3	5 51.8	26 17.2
4 Sa	8 54 40	12 43 04	28 27 26	4♋22 25	1 16.5	3 07.7	0♍35.3	23 43.0	9 21.3	29 44.9	7 57.6	4 17.0	5 52.0	26 16.0
5 Su	8 58 36	13 40 33	10♋16 56	16 11 20	1 09.3	5 09.8	1 48.9	24 20.4	9 45.6	29 55.5	8 02.8	4 20.6	5 52.1	26 14.7
6 M	9 02 33	14 38 03	22 05 59	28 01 10	0 59.5	7 12.8	3 02.5	24 57.8	10 09.8	0♎06.2	8 08.1	4 24.3	5 52.2	26 13.4
7 Tu	9 06 29	15 35 33	3♌57 09	9♌54 08	0 47.6	9 16.6	4 16.1	25 35.2	10 34.1	0 17.0	8 13.4	4 27.9	5R 52.2	26 12.1
8 W	9 10 26	16 33 05	15 52 19	21 51 51	0 34.5	11 20.6	5 29.7	26 12.8	10 58.3	0 27.9	8 18.8	4 31.6	5 52.2	26 10.8
9 Th	9 14 23	17 30 38	27 52 55	3♍55 38	0 21.2	13 24.8	6 43.3	26 50.3	11 22.4	0 38.9	8 24.3	4 35.2	5 52.2	26 09.5
10 F	9 18 19	18 28 12	10♍00 09	16 06 37	0 08.9	15 28.8	7 56.9	27 28.0	11 46.5	0 49.9	8 29.9	4 38.8	5 52.1	26 08.2
11 Sa	9 22 16	19 25 47	22 15 13	28 26 08	29♉58.5	17 32.3	9 10.5	28 05.7	12 10.6	1 01.0	8 35.5	4 42.4	5 52.0	26 06.9
12 Su	9 26 12	20 23 23	4♎39 36	10♎55 51	29 50.8	19 35.2	10 24.1	28 43.4	12 34.6	1 12.1	8 41.1	4 46.0	5 51.9	26 05.6
13 M	9 30 09	21 20 59	17 15 12	23 37 57	29 45.9	21 37.3	11 37.6	29 21.2	12 58.6	1 23.4	8 46.8	4 49.6	5 51.8	26 04.3
14 Tu	9 34 05	22 18 37	0♏04 26	6♏35 03	29 43.5	23 38.5	12 51.2	29 59.1	13 22.5	1 34.7	8 52.6	4 53.1	5 51.6	26 03.0
15 W	9 38 02	23 16 16	13 10 08	19 50 04	29 42.8	25 38.7	14 04.7	0♎37.0	13 46.4	1 46.0	8 58.4	4 56.7	5 51.3	26 01.7
16 Th	9 41 58	24 13 55	26 35 12	3♐25 49	29 42.8	27 37.7	15 18.2	1 14.9	14 10.3	1 57.5	9 04.3	5 00.2	5 51.1	26 00.4
17 F	9 45 55	25 11 36	10♐22 09	17 24 18	29 42.2	29 35.5	16 31.8	1 52.9	14 34.0	2 08.9	9 10.3	5 03.8	5 50.8	25 59.1
18 Sa	9 49 52	26 09 18	24 32 16	1♑45 55	29 39.8	1♍32.0	17 45.3	2 31.0	14 57.8	2 20.5	9 16.3	5 07.3	5 50.5	25 57.7
19 Su	9 53 48	27 07 01	9♑04 54	16 28 41	29 34.9	3 27.2	18 58.8	3 09.1	15 21.5	2 32.1	9 22.3	5 10.8	5 50.1	25 56.4
20 M	9 57 45	28 04 45	23 56 33	1♒27 36	29 27.3	5 21.1	20 12.2	3 47.3	15 45.1	2 43.7	9 28.4	5 14.3	5 49.8	25 55.1
21 Tu	10 01 41	29 02 30	9♒00 44	16 34 45	29 17.5	7 13.5	21 25.7	4 25.5	16 08.7	2 55.5	9 34.6	5 17.7	5 49.3	25 53.8
22 W	10 05 38	0♍00 17	24 08 22	1♓40 14	29 06.5	9 04.7	22 39.1	5 03.8	16 32.2	3 07.2	9 40.8	5 21.2	5 48.9	25 52.5
23 Th	10 09 34	0 58 05	9♓09 07	16 33 49	28 55.6	10 54.4	23 52.6	5 42.1	16 55.7	3 19.1	9 47.0	5 24.6	5 48.4	25 51.2
24 F	10 13 31	1 55 54	23 53 19	1♈06 47	28 45.9	12 42.8	25 06.0	6 20.5	17 19.1	3 30.9	9 53.3	5 28.0	5 47.9	25 49.9
25 Sa	10 17 27	2 53 45	8♈13 33	15 13 15	28 38.5	14 29.9	26 19.4	6 59.0	17 42.5	3 42.9	9 59.6	5 31.4	5 47.4	25 48.6
26 Su	10 21 24	3 51 38	22 05 38	28 50 44	28 33.6	16 15.6	27 32.8	7 37.5	18 05.8	3 54.8	10 06.0	5 34.8	5 46.8	25 47.3
27 M	10 25 20	4 49 32	5♉28 41	11♉59 48	28 31.2	17 59.9	28 46.2	8 16.0	18 29.0	4 06.9	10 12.4	5 38.1	5 46.2	25 46.0
28 Tu	10 29 17	5 47 28	18 24 32	24 43 24	28 30.4	19 43.0	29 59.6	8 54.6	18 52.2	4 18.9	10 18.9	5 41.4	5 45.6	25 44.7
29 W	10 33 14	6 45 27	0♊56 59	7♊05 56	28 30.5	21 24.7	1♎12.9	9 33.3	19 15.3	4 31.1	10 25.4	5 44.7	5 44.9	25 43.4
30 Th	10 37 10	7 43 27	13 10 55	19 12 35	28 30.0	23 05.2	2 26.3	10 12.0	19 38.4	4 43.2	10 32.0	5 48.0	5 44.2	25 42.1
31 F	10 41 07	8 41 29	25 11 36	1♋08 38	28 28.2	24 44.4	3 39.6	10 50.8	20 01.3	4 55.5	10 38.6	5 51.3	5 43.5	25 40.8

Astro Data	Dy Hr Mn
☽0N	1 9:26
☿D	7 2:20
☽0S	16 3:30
♃⊼♇	16 10:25
☽0N	28 16:22
♆R	8 5:24
☽0S	12 8:23
♂0S	16 15:00
♃0S	19 22:39
☽0N	25 1:09
♅□♆	29 13:08
♀0S	30 10:38
♄⚼♇	31 18:47

Planet Ingress		Dy Hr Mn
♀	♌	10 14:02
⚳	♋	12 17:36
☉	♌	22 4:41
☿	♌	2 22:31
♀	♍	4 0:30
♃	♎	5 22:03
☊	♉R	11 8:13
♂	♎	14 12:36
☿	♍	17 17:02
☉	♍	22 11:53
♀	♎	28 12:08

Last Aspect Dy Hr Mn			☽ Ingress Dy Hr Mn	
2 17:00	♇	⚹	♉	2 22:54
5 2:45	♇	□	♊	5 9:02
7 14:42	♇	△	♋	7 21:12
10 9:34	♀	☌	♌	10 10:02
12 15:52	♇	☍	♍	12 22:27
15 2:32	♃	☌	♎	15 9:23
17 11:29	♇	△	♏	17 17:39
19 18:28	☉	△	♐	19 22:24
21 19:45	♃	□	♑	21 23:50
23 19:46	♃	△	♒	23 23:15
25 17:01	♇	☌	♓	25 22:41
27 21:36	♃	☍	♈	28 0:15
29 22:56	♇	⚹	♉	30 5:36

Last Aspect Dy Hr Mn			☽ Ingress Dy Hr Mn	
1 13:29	♃	△	♊	1 15:00
4 2:28	♃	□	♋	4 3:08
6 5:28	♂	⚹	♌	6 16:01
8 20:36	♇	☍	♍	9 4:13
11 11:18	♂	☌	♎	11 15:01
13 16:33	♇	□	♏	13 23:52
16 0:06	☿	□	♐	16 6:00
18 2:23	♇	⚹	♑	18 9:05
19 16:23	♀	△	♒	20 9:40
22 9:10	☉	☍	♓	22 9:20
24 1:05	♀	☍	♈	24 10:08
26 6:33	♇	⚹	♉	26 14:04
28 13:57	♇	□	♊	28 22:10
31 1:00	♇	△	♋	31 9:41

☽ Phases & Eclipses Dy Hr Mn		
1 10:18	☾	10♈11
9 9:15	●	17♋47
17 9:16	☽	25♎25
24 2:05	○	1♒48
30 21:06	☾	8♉18
8 0:26	●	16♌05
15 18:36	☽	23♏32
22 9:10	○	29♒53
29 11:16	☾	6♊44

Astro Data

1 July 2040
Julian Day # 51317
SVP 4♓41'53"
GC 27♐24.3 ⚴ 28♈06.3
Eris 29♈10.4 ⚵ 21♉29.2
⚷ 14♋15.4 ⚶ 13♒12.6R
☽ Mean ☊ 1♊44.8

1 August 2040
Julian Day # 51348
SVP 4♓41'48"
GC 27♐24.4 ⚴ 5♉07.1
Eris 29♈13.1R ⚵ 8♊06.3
⚷ 17♋26.4 ⚶ 6♒43.6R
☽ Mean ☊ 0♊06.3

LONGITUDE — September 2040

Day	Sid.Time	☉	0 hr ☽	Noon☽	True☊	☿	♀	♂	⚷	♃	♄	♅	♆	♇
1 Sa	10 45 03	9♍39 33	7♋04 17	12♋59 09	28♉24.0	26♍22.3	4♎53.0	11♎29.6	20♋24.3	5♎07.7	10♎45.2	5♌54.5	5♉42.8	25♒39.5
2 Su	10 49 00	10 37 38	18 53 46	24 48 37	28R 17.2	27 59.0	6 06.3	12 08.5	20 47.1	5 20.0	10 51.9	5 57.7	5R 42.0	25R 38.3
3 M	10 52 56	11 35 46	0♌44 11	6♌40 49	28 07.8	29 34.5	7 19.6	12 47.5	21 09.9	5 32.4	10 58.6	6 00.9	5 41.2	25 37.0
4 Tu	10 56 53	12 33 55	12 38 52	18 38 38	27 56.1	1♎08.7	8 32.9	13 26.5	21 32.6	5 44.8	11 05.4	6 04.0	5 40.3	25 35.8
5 W	11 00 50	13 32 06	24 40 21	0♍44 10	27 43.2	2 41.7	9 46.2	14 05.5	21 55.2	5 57.2	11 12.1	6 07.1	5 39.5	25 34.5
6 Th	11 04 46	14 30 19	6♍50 16	12 58 43	27 30.1	4 13.5	10 59.5	14 44.7	22 17.8	6 09.6	11 19.0	6 10.2	5 38.6	25 33.3
7 F	11 08 43	15 28 34	19 09 37	25 23 01	27 17.9	5 44.0	12 12.7	15 23.8	22 40.3	6 22.1	11 25.8	6 13.3	5 37.6	25 32.1
8 Sa	11 12 39	16 26 50	1♎38 57	7♎57 28	27 07.7	7 13.4	13 26.0	16 03.1	23 02.7	6 34.7	11 32.7	6 16.3	5 36.7	25 30.8
9 Su	11 16 36	17 25 08	14 18 36	20 42 26	27 00.0	8 41.5	14 39.2	16 42.4	23 25.0	6 47.2	11 39.6	6 19.3	5 35.7	25 29.6
10 M	11 20 32	18 23 28	27 09 01	3♏38 30	26 55.2	10 08.4	15 52.4	17 21.7	23 47.2	6 59.8	11 46.6	6 22.3	5 34.7	25 28.4
11 Tu	11 24 29	19 21 49	10♏11 00	16 46 40	26D 53.0	11 34.0	17 05.6	18 01.1	24 09.3	7 12.5	11 53.5	6 25.3	5 33.7	25 27.2
12 W	11 28 25	20 20 12	23 25 42	0♐08 18	26 52.7	12 58.3	18 18.8	18 40.6	24 31.4	7 25.1	12 00.5	6 28.2	5 32.6	25 26.1
13 Th	11 32 22	21 18 37	6♐54 38	13 44 55	26R 53.1	14 21.4	19 31.9	19 20.1	24 53.4	7 37.8	12 07.6	6 31.1	5 31.5	25 24.9
14 F	11 36 18	22 17 03	20 39 16	27 37 48	26 53.1	15 43.1	20 45.1	19 59.6	25 15.2	7 50.5	12 14.6	6 33.9	5 30.4	25 23.8
15 Sa	11 40 15	23 15 31	4♑40 32	11♑47 23	26 51.7	17 03.5	21 58.2	20 39.3	25 37.0	8 03.2	12 21.7	6 36.7	5 29.3	25 22.6
16 Su	11 44 12	24 14 00	18 58 10	26 12 33	26 48.2	18 22.4	23 11.3	21 18.9	25 58.7	8 16.0	12 28.8	6 39.5	5 28.2	25 21.5
17 M	11 48 08	25 12 31	3♒30 05	10♒50 10	26 42.2	19 39.9	24 24.4	21 58.7	26 20.3	8 28.8	12 36.0	6 42.3	5 27.0	25 20.4
18 Tu	11 52 05	26 11 03	18 12 01	25 34 49	26 34.2	20 55.9	25 37.4	22 38.5	26 41.8	8 41.6	12 43.1	6 45.0	5 25.8	25 19.3
19 W	11 56 01	27 09 37	2♓57 35	10♓19 19	26 25.1	22 10.3	26 50.4	23 18.3	27 03.2	8 54.4	12 50.3	6 47.6	5 24.6	25 18.2
20 Th	11 59 58	28 08 13	17 39 02	24 55 43	26 16.0	23 23.1	28 03.4	23 58.2	27 24.5	9 07.3	12 57.5	6 50.3	5 23.3	25 17.1
21 F	12 03 54	29 06 51	2♈08 29	9♈16 31	26 07.8	24 34.1	29 16.4	24 38.1	27 45.7	9 20.1	13 04.7	6 52.9	5 22.1	25 16.1
22 Sa	12 07 51	0♎05 31	16 19 11	23 15 59	26 01.6	25 43.3	0♏29.4	25 18.1	28 06.8	9 33.0	13 11.9	6 55.4	5 20.8	25 15.0
23 Su	12 11 47	1 04 13	0♉06 35	6♉50 48	25 57.6	26 50.5	1 42.3	25 58.2	28 27.7	9 45.9	13 19.1	6 57.9	5 19.4	25 14.0
24 M	12 15 44	2 02 57	13 28 39	20 00 16	25D 55.8	27 55.6	2 55.2	26 38.3	28 48.6	9 58.8	13 26.4	7 00.4	5 18.1	25 13.0
25 Tu	12 19 41	3 01 44	26 25 55	2♊45 57	25 55.9	28 58.5	4 08.1	27 18.5	29 09.4	10 11.7	13 33.6	7 02.9	5 16.8	25 12.0
26 W	12 23 37	4 00 32	9♊00 51	15 11 08	25 56.9	29 59.1	5 21.0	27 58.7	29 30.0	10 24.7	13 40.9	7 05.3	5 15.4	25 11.0
27 Th	12 27 34	4 59 23	21 17 24	27 20 14	25R 57.9	0♏57.0	6 33.9	28 39.0	29 50.5	10 37.6	13 48.2	7 07.6	5 14.0	25 10.1
28 F	12 31 30	5 58 16	3♋20 18	9♋18 15	25 58.2	1 52.2	7 46.7	29 19.3	0♌11.0	10 50.6	13 55.5	7 10.0	5 12.6	25 09.1
29 Sa	12 35 27	6 57 12	15 14 44	21 10 22	25 56.9	2 44.4	8 59.5	29 59.7	0 31.2	11 03.6	14 02.9	7 12.2	5 11.2	25 08.2
30 Su	12 39 23	7 56 10	27 05 46	3♌01 32	25 53.6	3 33.4	10 12.3	0♏40.2	0 51.4	11 16.5	14 10.2	7 14.5	5 09.7	25 07.3

LONGITUDE — October 2040

Day	Sid.Time	☉	0 hr ☽	Noon☽	True☊	☿	♀	♂	⚷	♃	♄	♅	♆	♇
1 M	12 43 20	8♎55 10	8♌58 12	14♌56 18	25♉48.4	4♏18.8	11♏25.1	1♏20.7	1♌11.4	11♎29.5	14♎17.5	7♌16.7	5♉08.3	25♒06.4
2 Tu	12 47 16	9 54 12	20 56 15	26 58 30	25R 41.5	5 00.4	12 37.8	2 01.3	1 31.3	11 42.5	14 24.9	7 18.8	5R 06.8	25R 05.6
3 W	12 51 13	10 53 16	3♍03 21	9♍11 08	25 33.5	5 37.8	13 50.6	2 41.9	1 51.1	11 55.5	14 32.2	7 20.9	5 05.3	25 04.7
4 Th	12 55 10	11 52 23	15 22 02	21 36 15	25 25.2	6 10.6	15 03.3	3 22.6	2 10.7	12 08.5	14 39.6	7 23.0	5 03.8	25 03.9
5 F	12 59 06	12 51 31	27 53 51	4♎14 55	25 17.5	6 38.5	16 16.0	4 03.4	2 30.2	12 21.5	14 46.9	7 25.0	5 02.3	25 03.1
6 Sa	13 03 03	13 50 42	10♎39 26	17 07 21	25 11.1	7 01.0	17 28.7	4 44.2	2 49.6	12 34.5	14 54.3	7 27.0	5 00.7	25 02.3
7 Su	13 06 59	14 49 55	23 38 35	0♏13 03	25 06.6	7 17.7	18 41.3	5 25.1	3 08.8	12 47.5	15 01.6	7 28.9	4 59.2	25 01.5
8 M	13 10 56	15 49 09	6♏50 36	13 31 07	25D 04.2	7 28.1	19 53.9	6 06.0	3 27.8	13 00.5	15 09.0	7 30.8	4 57.6	25 00.8
9 Tu	13 14 52	16 48 26	20 14 29	27 00 33	25 03.6	7R 31.6	21 06.5	6 47.0	3 46.7	13 13.5	15 16.4	7 32.6	4 56.0	25 00.1
10 W	13 18 49	17 47 45	3♐49 13	10♐40 24	25 04.4	7 28.0	22 19.1	7 28.0	4 05.5	13 26.5	15 23.7	7 34.4	4 54.5	24 59.4
11 Th	13 22 45	18 47 05	17 34 00	24 29 56	25 05.8	7 16.6	23 31.6	8 09.1	4 24.1	13 39.5	15 31.1	7 36.2	4 52.9	24 58.7
12 F	13 26 42	19 46 28	1♑28 07	8♑28 27	25R 07.1	6 57.2	24 44.2	8 50.3	4 42.5	13 52.5	15 38.4	7 37.8	4 51.2	24 58.0
13 Sa	13 30 39	20 45 52	15 30 49	22 35 05	25 07.5	6 29.5	25 56.6	9 31.5	5 00.8	14 05.4	15 45.8	7 39.5	4 49.6	24 57.4
14 Su	13 34 35	21 45 17	29 41 02	6♒48 27	25 06.6	5 53.5	27 09.1	10 12.8	5 18.9	14 18.4	15 53.1	7 41.1	4 48.0	24 56.8
15 M	13 38 32	22 44 44	13♒57 00	21 06 20	25 04.2	5 09.1	28 21.5	10 54.1	5 36.8	14 31.3	16 00.5	7 42.6	4 46.4	24 56.2
16 Tu	13 42 28	23 44 14	28 16 00	5♓25 31	25 00.5	4 16.8	29 33.9	11 35.5	5 54.6	14 44.3	16 07.8	7 44.1	4 44.7	24 55.6
17 W	13 46 25	24 43 44	12♓34 20	19 41 51	24 56.1	3 17.3	0♐46.2	12 16.9	6 12.2	14 57.2	16 15.1	7 45.5	4 43.1	24 55.1
18 Th	13 50 21	25 43 17	26 47 30	3♈50 41	24 51.5	2 11.5	1 58.5	12 58.4	6 29.6	15 10.1	16 22.4	7 46.9	4 41.4	24 54.6
19 F	13 54 18	26 42 51	10♈50 49	17 47 23	24 47.4	1 00.9	3 10.8	13 39.9	6 46.8	15 23.0	16 29.7	7 48.3	4 39.8	24 54.1
20 Sa	13 58 14	27 42 28	24 39 55	1♉28 02	24 44.5	29♎47.2	4 23.0	14 21.5	7 03.8	15 35.8	16 37.0	7 49.6	4 38.1	24 53.6
21 Su	14 02 11	28 42 06	8♉11 26	14 49 56	24D 42.8	28 32.4	5 35.2	15 03.2	7 20.7	15 48.7	16 44.2	7 50.8	4 36.4	24 53.2
22 M	14 06 07	29 41 47	21 23 26	27 51 56	24 42.5	27 18.6	6 47.4	15 44.9	7 37.4	16 01.5	16 51.5	7 52.0	4 34.7	24 52.8
23 Tu	14 10 04	0♏41 30	4♊15 32	10♊33 26	24 43.3	26 08.1	7 59.5	16 26.6	7 53.8	16 14.3	16 58.7	7 53.1	4 33.1	24 52.4
24 W	14 14 01	1 41 15	16 48 54	22 59 18	24 44.8	25 03.1	9 11.6	17 08.5	8 10.1	16 27.1	17 05.9	7 54.2	4 31.4	24 52.0
25 Th	14 17 57	2 41 02	29 06 02	5♋09 35	24 46.5	24 05.5	10 23.6	17 50.4	8 26.2	16 39.9	17 13.1	7 55.2	4 29.7	24 51.6
26 F	14 21 54	3 40 51	11♋10 27	17 09 12	24 47.9	23 17.0	11 35.6	18 32.3	8 42.0	16 52.6	17 20.3	7 56.2	4 28.0	24 51.3
27 Sa	14 25 50	4 40 43	23 06 24	29 02 40	24R 48.8	22 38.6	12 47.6	19 14.3	8 57.7	17 05.3	17 27.5	7 57.1	4 26.3	24 51.0
28 Su	14 29 47	5 40 36	4♌58 34	10♌54 45	24 48.8	22 11.4	13 59.5	19 56.4	9 13.1	17 18.0	17 34.6	7 58.0	4 24.6	24 50.8
29 M	14 33 43	6 40 32	16 51 47	22 50 16	24 48.0	21D 55.6	15 11.4	20 38.5	9 28.3	17 30.7	17 41.7	7 58.8	4 22.9	24 50.5
30 Tu	14 37 40	7 40 30	28 50 46	4♍53 48	24 46.3	21 51.3	16 23.3	21 20.7	9 43.3	17 43.3	17 48.8	7 59.6	4 21.3	24 50.3
31 W	14 41 37	8 40 30	10♍59 53	17 09 26	24 44.2	21 58.2	17 35.1	22 02.9	9 58.0	17 55.9	17 55.9	8 00.3	4 19.6	24 50.1

Astro Data

	Dy Hr Mn
☿0S	3 23:53
♃⚻♆	4 3:58
♃✶♅	6 13:32
☽0S	8 13:28
☽0N	21 11:01
☉0S	22 9:45
♃⚼♇	25 12:29
☽0S	5 20:18
☿ R	9 12:05
☽0N	18 20:20
☿ D	30 9:05
♃☌♄	31 11:47

Planet Ingress

		Dy Hr Mn
☿	♎	3 18:29
♀	♏	22 2:20
☉	♎	22 9:45
☿	♏	26 12:23
⚷	♌	27 23:06
♂	♏	29 12:09
♀	♐	16 20:40
☿	♎R	20 7:52
☉	♏	22 19:19

Last Aspect / ☽ Ingress

Last Aspect Dy Hr Mn			☽ Ingress	Dy Hr Mn
2 19:26	☿	✶	♌	2 22:31
5 1:49	♇	☍	♍	5 10:33
6 15:13	☉	☌	♎	7 20:51
9 20:55	♇	△	♏	10 5:17
12 3:37	♇	□	♐	12 11:45
14 8:10	♇	✶	♑	14 16:03
16 8:30	☉	△	♒	16 18:15
18 12:05	♀	△	♓	18 19:11
20 17:43	☉	☍	♈	20 20:25
22 16:40	☿	☍	♉	22 23:48
24 21:42	♇	□	♊	25 6:44
27 14:46	♂	△	♋	27 17:19
28 21:26	♄	□	♌	30 5:53

Last Aspect / ☽ Ingress

Last Aspect Dy Hr Mn			☽ Ingress	Dy Hr Mn
2 8:16	♇	☍	♍	2 17:59
3 22:02	♀	✶	♎	5 3:59
7 2:32	♇	△	♏	7 11:36
9 8:27	♇	□	♐	9 17:17
11 12:50	♇	✶	♑	11 21:29
13 18:13	♀	✶	♒	14 0:32
16 1:16	♀	□	♓	16 2:54
16 22:53	♂	△	♈	18 5:27
20 9:16	☿	☍	♉	20 9:24
22 6:27	♇	□	♊	22 15:59
24 15:44	☿	△	♋	25 1:46
26 23:41	☿	□	♌	27 13:56
29 16:01	♇	☍	♍	30 2:18

☽ Phases & Eclipses

Dy Hr Mn		
6 15:13	●	14♍38
14 2:07	☽	21♐53
20 17:43	○	28♓22
28 4:41	☾	5♋40
6 5:26	●	13♎34
13 8:41	☽	20♑38
20 4:50	○	27♈25
28 0:27	☾	5♌12

Astro Data

1 September 2040
Julian Day # 51379
SVP 4♓41'44"
GC 27♐24.4 ⚳ 8♉16.3
Eris 29♈06.0R ⚵ 23♊43.1
⚷ 20♋15.3 ⚶ 1♒14.4R
☽ Mean ☊ 28♉27.8

1 October 2040
Julian Day # 51409
SVP 4♓41'41"
GC 27♐24.5 ⚳ 5♉19.0R
Eris 28♈51.5R ⚵ 6♋41.1
⚷ 22♋11.0 ⚶ 2♒25.2
☽ Mean ☊ 26♉52.5

November 2040 LONGITUDE

Day	Sid.Time	☉	0 hr ☽	Noon ☽	True ☊	☿	♀	♂	⚳	♃	♄	♅	♆	♇
1 Th	14 45 33	9♏40 33	23♍22 50	29♍40 26	24♉41.8	22♎15.7	18♐46.9	22♏45.2	10♌12.6	18♎08.5	18♎02.9	8♌00.9	4♉17.9	24♒49.9
2 F	14 49 30	10 40 37	6♎02 28	12♎29 07	24R 39.7	22 43.3	19 58.6	23 27.5	10 26.8	18 21.0	18 09.9	8 01.5	4R 16.2	24R 49.8
3 Sa	14 53 26	11 40 43	19 00 27	25 36 30	24 37.9	23 20.0	21 10.3	24 10.0	10 40.9	18 33.5	18 16.9	8 02.1	4 14.5	24 49.7
4 Su	14 57 23	12 40 51	2♏17 11	9♏02 19	24 36.9	24 05.0	22 21.9	24 52.4	10 54.7	18 45.9	18 23.8	8 02.5	4 12.9	24 49.6
5 M	15 01 19	13 41 01	15 51 41	22 44 58	24D 36.5	24 57.5	23 33.5	25 35.0	11 08.2	18 58.3	18 30.7	8 03.0	4 11.2	24 49.5
6 Tu	15 05 16	14 41 13	29 41 48	6♐41 44	24 36.7	25 56.5	24 45.0	26 17.5	11 21.5	19 10.7	18 37.6	8 03.3	4 09.6	24D 49.5
7 W	15 09 12	15 41 27	13♐44 21	20 49 09	24 37.3	27 01.2	25 56.5	27 00.2	11 34.5	19 23.0	18 44.5	8 03.7	4 07.9	24 49.5
8 Th	15 13 09	16 41 42	27 55 39	5♑03 22	24 38.0	28 11.0	27 08.0	27 42.9	11 47.2	19 35.3	18 51.3	8 03.9	4 06.3	24 49.5
9 F	15 17 06	17 41 59	12♑11 51	19 20 38	24 38.7	29 25.0	28 19.3	28 25.6	11 59.7	19 47.6	18 58.1	8 04.1	4 04.6	24 49.5
10 Sa	15 21 02	18 42 17	26 29 18	3♒37 30	24 39.2	0♏42.7	29 30.6	29 08.4	12 11.9	19 59.8	19 04.8	8 04.3	4 03.0	24 49.6
11 Su	15 24 59	19 42 37	10♒44 52	17 51 06	24R 39.3	2 03.4	0♑41.9	29 51.3	12 23.8	20 11.9	19 11.5	8 04.4	4 01.4	24 49.7
12 M	15 28 55	20 42 58	24 55 54	1♓59 02	24 39.3	3 26.8	1 53.1	0♐34.2	12 35.4	20 24.0	19 18.2	8R 04.4	3 59.8	24 49.8
13 Tu	15 32 52	21 43 20	9♓00 15	15 59 21	24 39.0	4 52.4	3 04.2	1 17.2	12 46.8	20 36.0	19 24.8	8 04.4	3 58.2	24 50.0
14 W	15 36 48	22 43 44	22 56 07	29 50 23	24 38.8	6 19.8	4 15.2	2 00.2	12 57.8	20 48.0	19 31.4	8 04.4	3 56.6	24 50.2
15 Th	15 40 45	23 44 08	6♈41 58	13♈30 42	24D 38.6	7 48.8	5 26.2	2 43.3	13 08.6	21 00.0	19 37.9	8 04.2	3 55.1	24 50.4
16 F	15 44 41	24 44 35	20 16 25	26 58 58	24 38.6	9 18.9	6 37.0	3 26.4	13 19.0	21 11.8	19 44.4	8 04.0	3 53.5	24 50.6
17 Sa	15 48 38	25 45 03	3♉38 13	10♉14 03	24 38.6	10 50.1	7 47.8	4 09.6	13 29.2	21 23.6	19 50.9	8 03.8	3 52.0	24 50.9
18 Su	15 52 35	26 45 32	16 46 23	23 15 08	24R 38.7	12 22.1	8 58.6	4 52.8	13 39.0	21 35.4	19 57.3	8 03.5	3 50.4	24 51.1
19 M	15 56 31	27 46 03	29 40 18	6♊01 52	24 38.6	13 54.7	10 09.2	5 36.1	13 48.5	21 47.1	20 03.6	8 03.2	3 48.9	24 51.4
20 Tu	16 00 28	28 46 35	12♊19 53	18 34 27	24 38.4	15 27.8	11 19.8	6 19.5	13 57.7	21 58.8	20 09.9	8 02.8	3 47.4	24 51.8
21 W	16 04 24	29 47 09	24 45 43	0♋53 52	24 37.8	17 01.3	12 30.2	7 02.9	14 06.6	22 10.3	20 16.2	8 02.3	3 45.9	24 52.2
22 Th	16 08 21	0♐47 45	6♋59 10	13 01 52	24 37.0	18 35.2	13 40.6	7 46.3	14 15.1	22 21.9	20 22.4	8 01.8	3 44.5	24 52.5
23 F	16 12 17	1 48 23	19 02 21	25 00 58	24 36.1	20 09.2	14 50.9	8 29.8	14 23.3	22 33.3	20 28.5	8 01.3	3 43.0	24 53.0
24 Sa	16 16 14	2 49 01	0♌58 10	6♌54 25	24 35.1	21 43.4	16 01.1	9 13.4	14 31.2	22 44.7	20 34.6	8 00.7	3 41.6	24 53.4
25 Su	16 20 10	3 49 42	12 50 13	18 46 06	24 34.3	23 17.7	17 11.2	9 57.0	14 38.7	22 56.0	20 40.7	8 00.0	3 40.2	24 53.9
26 M	16 24 07	4 50 24	24 42 38	0♍40 23	24D 33.9	24 52.0	18 21.2	10 40.7	14 45.8	23 07.2	20 46.7	7 59.3	3 38.8	24 54.4
27 Tu	16 28 04	5 51 08	6♍39 56	12 41 54	24 34.0	26 26.4	19 31.1	11 24.4	14 52.6	23 18.4	20 52.6	7 58.5	3 37.4	24 54.9
28 W	16 32 00	6 51 53	18 46 50	24 55 21	24 34.5	28 00.7	20 40.9	12 08.2	14 59.0	23 29.5	20 58.5	7 57.7	3 36.1	24 55.4
29 Th	16 35 57	7 52 39	1♎07 57	7♎25 10	24 35.6	29 35.1	21 50.6	12 52.1	15 05.1	23 40.5	21 04.3	7 56.8	3 34.7	24 56.0
30 F	16 39 53	8 53 27	13 47 28	20 15 13	24 36.9	1♐09.4	23 00.1	13 36.0	15 10.8	23 51.5	21 10.1	7 55.9	3 33.4	24 56.6

December 2040 LONGITUDE

Day	Sid.Time	☉	0 hr ☽	Noon ☽	True ☊	☿	♀	♂	⚳	♃	♄	♅	♆	♇
1 Sa	16 43 50	9♐54 17	26♎48 43	3♏28 12	24♉38.1	2♐43.7	24♑09.6	14♐19.9	15♌16.1	24♎02.3	21♎15.8	7♌54.9	3♉32.1	24♒57.2
2 Su	16 47 46	10 55 08	10♏13 45	17 05 20	24R 38.8	4 18.0	25 19.0	15 03.9	15 21.0	24 13.1	21 21.4	7R 53.9	3R 30.8	24 57.9
3 M	16 51 43	11 56 00	24 02 47	1♐05 48	24 38.9	5 52.2	26 28.2	15 48.0	15 25.5	24 23.8	21 27.0	7 52.8	3 29.6	24 58.6
4 Tu	16 55 39	12 56 54	8♐13 55	15 26 34	24 37.9	7 26.4	27 37.3	16 32.1	15 29.7	24 34.4	21 32.5	7 51.7	3 28.4	24 59.3
5 W	16 59 36	13 57 49	22 43 00	0♑02 26	24 36.1	9 00.6	28 46.3	17 16.3	15 33.4	24 45.0	21 37.9	7 50.5	3 27.2	25 00.0
6 Th	17 03 33	14 58 44	7♑23 58	14 46 40	24 33.4	10 34.7	29 55.1	18 00.5	15 36.7	24 55.4	21 43.3	7 49.2	3 26.0	25 00.8
7 F	17 07 29	15 59 41	22 09 36	29 31 50	24 30.5	12 08.8	1♒03.8	18 44.8	15 39.7	25 05.8	21 48.6	7 48.0	3 24.9	25 01.5
8 Sa	17 11 26	17 00 38	6♒52 31	14♒10 54	24 27.6	13 42.9	2 12.3	19 29.1	15 42.2	25 16.0	21 53.8	7 46.6	3 23.7	25 02.3
9 Su	17 15 22	18 01 36	21 26 18	28 38 12	24 25.5	15 17.1	3 20.7	20 13.5	15 44.3	25 26.2	21 59.0	7 45.3	3 22.6	25 03.2
10 M	17 19 19	19 02 34	5♓46 12	12♓49 59	24D 24.3	16 51.2	4 28.9	20 57.9	15 46.0	25 36.3	22 04.1	7 43.8	3 21.6	25 04.0
11 Tu	17 23 15	20 03 33	19 49 24	26 44 23	24 24.4	18 25.4	5 37.0	21 42.4	15 47.3	25 46.2	22 09.1	7 42.4	3 20.5	25 04.9
12 W	17 27 12	21 04 33	3♈34 57	10♈21 11	24 25.4	19 59.7	6 44.9	22 26.9	15 48.2	25 56.1	22 14.0	7 40.9	3 19.5	25 05.8
13 Th	17 31 08	22 05 33	17 03 13	23 41 15	24 27.0	21 34.0	7 52.6	23 11.5	15R 48.6	26 05.9	22 18.9	7 39.3	3 18.5	25 06.7
14 F	17 35 05	23 06 33	0♉15 28	6♉46 05	24 28.6	23 08.4	9 00.1	23 56.1	15 48.6	26 15.6	22 23.7	7 37.7	3 17.5	25 07.6
15 Sa	17 39 02	24 07 34	13 13 17	19 37 18	24R 29.6	24 42.9	10 07.4	24 40.7	15 48.2	26 25.1	22 28.4	7 36.0	3 16.6	25 08.6
16 Su	17 42 58	25 08 36	25 58 17	2♊16 25	24 29.5	26 17.6	11 14.5	25 25.4	15 47.4	26 34.6	22 33.0	7 34.4	3 15.7	25 09.6
17 M	17 46 55	26 09 38	8♊31 52	14 44 46	24 27.7	27 52.3	12 21.4	26 10.2	15 46.1	26 44.0	22 37.6	7 32.6	3 14.8	25 10.6
18 Tu	17 50 51	27 10 41	20 55 14	27 03 26	24 24.2	29 27.2	13 28.1	26 55.0	15 44.5	26 53.2	22 42.1	7 30.9	3 14.0	25 11.7
19 W	17 54 48	28 11 45	3♋09 27	9♋13 27	24 19.1	1♑02.3	14 34.6	27 39.8	15 42.4	27 02.4	22 46.5	7 29.0	3 13.2	25 12.7
20 Th	17 58 44	29 12 49	15 15 35	21 16 00	24 12.7	2 37.5	15 40.8	28 24.8	15 39.8	27 11.4	22 50.8	7 27.2	3 12.4	25 13.8
21 F	18 02 41	0♑13 53	27 14 56	3♌12 34	24 05.7	4 12.9	16 46.8	29 09.7	15 36.8	27 20.3	22 55.0	7 25.3	3 11.6	25 14.9
22 Sa	18 06 38	1 14 59	9♌09 12	15 05 08	23 58.8	5 48.5	17 52.6	29 54.7	15 33.4	27 29.1	22 59.2	7 23.4	3 10.9	25 16.0
23 Su	18 10 34	2 16 05	21 00 43	26 56 19	23 52.6	7 24.3	18 58.1	0♑39.7	15 29.6	27 37.8	23 03.2	7 21.4	3 10.2	25 17.2
24 M	18 14 31	3 17 11	2♍52 23	8♍49 23	23 47.8	9 00.3	20 03.3	1 24.8	15 25.3	27 46.4	23 07.2	7 19.4	3 09.5	25 18.3
25 Tu	18 18 27	4 18 18	14 47 50	20 48 17	23 44.8	10 36.5	21 08.3	2 10.0	15 20.6	27 54.8	23 11.1	7 17.4	3 08.9	25 19.5
26 W	18 22 24	5 19 26	26 51 18	2♎57 28	23D 43.7	12 12.9	22 13.0	2 55.2	15 15.5	28 03.1	23 14.9	7 15.3	3 08.3	25 20.7
27 Th	18 26 20	6 20 34	9♎07 25	15 21 44	23 44.0	13 49.5	23 17.5	3 40.4	15 09.9	28 11.3	23 18.6	7 13.2	3 07.7	25 21.9
28 F	18 30 17	7 21 43	21 41 02	28 05 52	23 45.3	15 26.3	24 21.6	4 25.7	15 04.0	28 19.4	23 22.2	7 11.0	3 07.2	25 23.2
29 Sa	18 34 13	8 22 52	4♏36 46	11♏14 09	23R 46.7	17 03.3	25 25.5	5 11.0	14 57.6	28 27.3	23 25.8	7 08.9	3 06.7	25 24.4
30 Su	18 38 10	9 24 02	17 58 23	24 49 41	23 47.3	18 40.4	26 29.0	5 56.4	14 50.8	28 35.2	23 29.2	7 06.7	3 06.2	25 25.7
31 M	18 42 07	10 25 12	1♐48 09	8♐53 41	23 46.3	20 17.6	27 32.2	6 41.8	14 43.5	28 42.8	23 32.6	7 04.4	3 05.8	25 27.0

Astro Data	Planet Ingress	Last Aspect	☽ Ingress	Last Aspect	☽ Ingress	☽ Phases & Eclipses
Dy Hr Mn	Dy Hr Mn	Dy Hr Mn	Dy Hr Mn	Dy Hr Mn	Dy Hr Mn	Dy Hr Mn
☽0S 2 5:06	☿ ♏ 9 22:57	31 22:00 ♂ ✱	♎ 1 12:37	30 20:36 ♇ △	♏ 1 5:46	4 18:56 ● 12♏58
♇D 7 6:03	♀ ♑ 10 21:53	3 10:35 ♇ △	♏ 3 19:54	3 3:26 ♀ ✱	♐ 3 10:09	4 19:07:38 ● P 0.808
♅R 12 17:54	♂ ♐ 11 16:52	5 17:10 ♂ ☌	♐ 6 0:31	5 3:44 ♇ ✱	♑ 5 11:56	11 15:23 ☽ 19♒51
☽0N 15 3:42	☉ ♐ 21 17:05	7 23:23 ☿ ✱	♑ 8 3:30	7 4:42 ♃ □	♒ 7 12:46	18 19:06 ○ 27♉03
☽0S 29 14:35	☿ ♐ 29 18:20	10 4:04 ♂ ✱	♒ 10 5:54	9 6:35 ♃ △	♓ 9 14:17	18 19:03 ● T 1.398
		11 23:50 ♇ ☌	♓ 12 8:37	11 2:46 ♂ □	♈ 11 17:42	26 21:07 ☾ 5♍13
♃△♇ 7 1:21	♀ ♒ 6 13:43	13 22:40 ☉ △	♈ 14 12:17	13 16:27 ♃ ☍	♉ 13 23:32	
☽0N 12 9:04	☿ ♑ 18 20:17	16 8:10 ♇ ✱	♉ 16 17:26	15 22:27 ♇ □	♊ 16 7:40	4 7:33 ● 12♐46
⚳R 14 1:19	☉ ♑ 21 6:33	18 19:06 ☉ ☍	♊ 19 0:37	18 17:24 ☿ ☍	♋ 18 17:47	10 23:30 ☽ 19♓32
☽0S 26 22:49	♂ ♑ 22 14:50	21 0:12 ♇ △	♋ 21 10:14	21 0:02 ♃ □	♌ 21 5:32	18 12:16 ○ 27♊11
		23 6:58 ♃ □	♌ 23 22:03	23 13:25 ♃ ✱	♍ 23 18:12	26 17:02 ☾ 5♎32
		26 0:23 ♇ ☍	♍ 26 10:39	24 12:25 ☿ △	♎ 26 6:12	
		28 18:51 ☿ ✱	♎ 28 21:49	28 12:25 ♃ ☌	♏ 28 15:31	
				30 15:06 ♀ □	♐ 30 20:55	

Astro Data

1 November 2040
Julian Day # 51440
SVP 4♓41'37"
GC 27♐24.6 ⚴ 26♈23.5R
Eris 28♈33.1R ⚵ 15♋43.1
⚷ 22♋56.8 ⚶ 9♒35.0
☽ Mean ☊ 25♉14.0

1 December 2040
Julian Day # 51470
SVP 4♓41'32"
GC 27♐24.7 ⚴ 19♈32.0R
Eris 28♈17.0R ⚵ 17♋17.8R
⚷ 22♋18.7R ⚶ 20♒04.4
☽ Mean ☊ 23♉38.7

LONGITUDE — January 2041

Day	Sid.Time	☉	0 hr ☽	Noon ☽	True ☊	☿	♀	♂	⚳	♃	♄	♅	♆	♇
1 Tu	18 46 03	11♑26 23	16♐05 58	23♐24 32	23♉43.0	21♑54.9	28♒35.1	7♑27.3	14♌35.9	28♎50.4	23♎35.8	7♌02.2	3♉05.4	25♒28.3
2 W	18 50 00	12 27 34	0♑48 40	8♑17 28	23R37.6	23 32.2	29 37.6	8 12.8	14R27.9	28 57.8	23 39.0	6R59.9	3R05.0	25 29.7
3 Th	18 53 56	13 28 45	15 49 49	23 24 31	23 30.3	25 09.5	0♓39.8	8 58.3	14 19.5	29 05.1	23 42.1	6 57.6	3 04.7	25 31.0
4 F	18 57 53	14 29 56	1♒00 15	8♒35 39	23 22.1	26 46.6	1 41.6	9 43.9	14 10.7	29 12.2	23 45.0	6 55.2	3 04.4	25 32.4
5 Sa	19 01 49	15 31 06	16 09 24	23 40 18	23 13.9	28 23.5	2 43.1	10 29.6	14 01.5	29 19.2	23 47.9	6 52.9	3 04.1	25 33.8
6 Su	19 05 46	16 32 16	1♓07 15	8♓29 21	23 07.1	0♒00.1	3 44.1	11 15.2	13 52.0	29 26.1	23 50.7	6 50.5	3 03.9	25 35.2
7 M	19 09 42	17 33 26	15 45 55	22 56 25	23 02.1	1 36.1	4 44.7	12 01.0	13 42.1	29 32.8	23 53.4	6 48.1	3 03.7	25 36.6
8 Tu	19 13 39	18 34 36	0♈00 36	6♈58 20	22D59.5	3 11.6	5 44.8	12 46.7	13 31.9	29 39.3	23 55.9	6 45.6	3 03.5	25 38.0
9 W	19 17 36	19 35 44	13 49 42	20 34 52	22 58.8	4 46.2	6 44.5	13 32.5	13 21.3	29 45.7	23 58.4	6 43.2	3 03.4	25 39.5
10 Th	19 21 32	20 36 53	27 14 10	3♉47 58	22 59.4	6 19.7	7 43.8	14 18.3	13 10.4	29 52.0	24 00.8	6 40.7	3 03.3	25 40.9
11 F	19 25 29	21 38 00	10♉16 40	16 40 46	23R00.2	7 51.8	8 42.5	15 04.2	12 59.2	29 58.1	24 03.1	6 38.2	3 03.2	25 42.4
12 Sa	19 29 25	22 39 08	23 00 42	29 16 57	23 00.2	9 22.3	9 40.7	15 50.1	12 47.7	0♏04.1	24 05.2	6 35.7	3D03.2	25 43.9
13 Su	19 33 22	23 40 15	5♊29 56	11♊40 04	22 58.3	10 50.7	10 38.4	16 36.0	12 35.9	0 09.9	24 07.3	6 33.2	3 03.2	25 45.4
14 M	19 37 18	24 41 21	17 47 44	23 53 15	22 53.8	12 16.6	11 35.6	17 22.0	12 23.9	0 15.5	24 09.3	6 30.6	3 03.2	25 46.9
15 Tu	19 41 15	25 42 26	29 56 56	5♋59 03	22 46.5	13 39.6	12 32.2	18 08.0	12 11.6	0 21.0	24 11.2	6 28.1	3 03.3	25 48.5
16 W	19 45 11	26 43 32	11♋59 48	17 59 24	22 36.5	14 59.0	13 28.1	18 54.0	11 59.0	0 26.3	24 12.9	6 25.5	3 03.4	25 50.0
17 Th	19 49 08	27 44 36	23 58 00	29 55 48	22 24.4	16 14.3	14 23.5	19 40.1	11 46.3	0 31.5	24 14.6	6 22.9	3 03.6	25 51.6
18 F	19 53 05	28 45 40	5♌52 55	11♌49 30	22 11.2	17 24.8	15 18.3	20 26.2	11 33.3	0 36.5	24 16.1	6 20.3	3 03.8	25 53.1
19 Sa	19 57 01	29 46 44	17 45 45	23 41 48	21 57.8	18 29.6	16 12.4	21 12.4	11 20.1	0 41.4	24 17.6	6 17.8	3 04.0	25 54.7
20 Su	20 00 58	0♒47 47	29 37 54	5♍34 16	21 45.5	19 28.1	17 05.8	21 58.6	11 06.7	0 46.1	24 18.9	6 15.2	3 04.2	25 56.3
21 M	20 04 54	1 48 49	11♍31 11	17 28 58	21 35.2	20 19.3	17 58.5	22 44.8	10 53.2	0 50.6	24 20.2	6 12.5	3 04.5	25 57.9
22 Tu	20 08 51	2 49 51	23 27 59	29 28 39	21 27.5	21 02.4	18 50.4	23 31.0	10 39.5	0 54.9	24 21.3	6 09.9	3 04.9	25 59.5
23 W	20 12 47	3 50 52	5♎31 26	11♎36 49	21 22.7	21 36.6	19 41.6	24 17.3	10 25.7	0 59.1	24 22.4	6 07.3	3 05.2	26 01.2
24 Th	20 16 44	4 51 53	17 45 21	23 57 36	21D20.4	22 01.0	20 32.0	25 03.7	10 11.8	1 03.1	24 23.3	6 04.7	3 05.6	26 02.8
25 F	20 20 40	5 52 54	0♏14 09	6♏35 36	21 19.9	22R14.9	21 21.6	25 50.0	9 57.8	1 06.9	24 24.1	6 02.1	3 06.0	26 04.4
26 Sa	20 24 37	6 53 54	13 02 33	19 35 32	21R20.1	22 17.8	22 10.4	26 36.4	9 43.7	1 10.6	24 24.8	5 59.4	3 06.5	26 06.1
27 Su	20 28 34	7 54 54	26 15 05	3♐01 36	21 19.6	22 09.4	22 58.2	27 22.8	9 29.5	1 14.1	24 25.4	5 56.8	3 07.0	26 07.7
28 M	20 32 30	8 55 52	9♐55 25	16 56 40	21 17.5	21 49.5	23 45.2	28 09.3	9 15.3	1 17.4	24 25.9	5 54.2	3 07.5	26 09.4
29 Tu	20 36 27	9 56 51	24 05 21	1♑21 14	21 12.7	21 18.5	24 31.2	28 55.8	9 01.1	1 20.5	24 26.3	5 51.6	3 08.1	26 11.1
30 W	20 40 23	10 57 49	8♑43 52	16 12 32	21 05.1	20 36.9	25 16.2	29 42.3	8 46.9	1 23.5	24 26.6	5 49.0	3 08.7	26 12.8
31 Th	20 44 20	11 58 45	23 46 18	1♒23 58	20 55.1	19 45.8	26 00.2	0♒28.8	8 32.7	1 26.3	24 26.8	5 46.4	3 09.3	26 14.5

LONGITUDE — February 2041

Day	Sid.Time	☉	0 hr ☽	Noon ☽	True ☊	☿	♀	♂	⚳	♃	♄	♅	♆	♇
1 F	20 48 16	12♒59 41	9♒04 12	16♒45 31	20♉43.6	18♒46.5	26♓43.1	1♒15.4	8♌18.6	1♏28.8	24♎26.9	5♌43.8	3♉10.0	26♒16.2
2 Sa	20 52 13	14 00 36	24 26 23	2♓05 17	20R32.0	17R40.7	27 24.9	2 02.0	8R04.5	1 31.2	24R26.8	5R41.2	3 10.7	26 17.9
3 Su	20 56 10	15 01 29	9♓40 49	17 11 43	20 21.7	16 30.4	28 05.6	2 48.6	7 50.5	1 33.5	24 26.7	5 38.6	3 11.4	26 19.6
4 M	21 00 06	16 02 21	24 36 56	1♈55 39	20 13.8	15 17.6	28 45.0	3 35.3	7 36.6	1 35.5	24 26.4	5 36.0	3 12.2	26 21.3
5 Tu	21 04 03	17 03 12	9♈07 19	16 11 37	20 08.7	14 04.4	29 23.2	4 21.9	7 22.8	1 37.3	24 26.1	5 33.4	3 13.0	26 23.0
6 W	21 07 59	18 04 01	23 08 26	29 57 52	20 06.2	12 52.9	0♈00.0	5 08.6	7 09.1	1 39.0	24 25.6	5 30.9	3 13.8	26 24.7
7 Th	21 11 56	19 04 49	6♉40 11	13♉15 45	20 05.5	11 44.9	0 35.5	5 55.3	6 55.6	1 40.5	24 25.1	5 28.4	3 14.7	26 26.4
8 F	21 15 52	20 05 35	19 45 04	26 08 41	20 05.4	10 41.7	1 09.6	6 42.1	6 42.3	1 41.8	24 24.4	5 25.8	3 15.6	26 28.2
9 Sa	21 19 49	21 06 20	2♊27 10	8♊41 07	20 04.7	9 44.8	1 42.1	7 28.8	6 29.1	1 42.9	24 23.6	5 23.3	3 16.5	26 29.9
10 Su	21 23 45	22 07 03	14 51 08	20 57 48	20 02.3	8 54.9	2 13.2	8 15.6	6 16.2	1 43.8	24 22.7	5 20.9	3 17.5	26 31.6
11 M	21 27 42	23 07 45	27 01 39	3♋03 12	19 57.1	8 12.7	2 42.6	9 02.4	6 03.5	1 44.5	24 21.7	5 18.4	3 18.5	26 33.3
12 Tu	21 31 39	24 08 25	9♋02 57	15 01 17	19 49.0	7 38.4	3 10.3	9 49.2	5 51.0	1 45.0	24 20.7	5 15.9	3 19.5	26 35.1
13 W	21 35 35	25 09 04	20 58 35	26 55 12	19 38.0	7 12.2	3 36.4	10 36.0	5 38.7	1 45.4	24 19.5	5 13.5	3 20.6	26 36.8
14 Th	21 39 32	26 09 41	2♌51 25	8♌47 27	19 24.6	6 53.9	4 00.6	11 22.9	5 26.8	1R45.6	24 18.2	5 11.1	3 21.7	26 38.6
15 F	21 43 28	27 10 16	14 43 33	20 39 51	19 10.0	6D43.4	4 23.0	12 09.8	5 15.1	1 45.5	24 16.8	5 08.7	3 22.8	26 40.3
16 Sa	21 47 25	28 10 50	26 36 33	2♍33 47	18 55.2	6 40.2	4 43.5	12 56.7	5 03.7	1 45.3	24 15.3	5 06.4	3 24.0	26 42.0
17 Su	21 51 21	29 11 22	8♍31 42	14 30 28	18 41.4	6 44.1	5 02.0	13 43.6	4 52.6	1 44.9	24 13.7	5 04.0	3 25.1	26 43.8
18 M	21 55 18	0♓11 53	20 30 13	26 31 09	18 29.8	6 54.6	5 18.4	14 30.5	4 41.8	1 44.3	24 12.0	5 01.7	3 26.3	26 45.5
19 Tu	21 59 14	1 12 23	2♎33 31	8♎37 32	18 20.9	7 11.4	5 32.8	15 17.4	4 31.3	1 43.5	24 10.2	4 59.4	3 27.6	26 47.2
20 W	22 03 11	2 12 51	14 43 30	20 51 47	18 15.1	7 33.8	5 45.0	16 04.4	4 21.2	1 42.5	24 08.3	4 57.2	3 28.8	26 49.0
21 Th	22 07 07	3 13 18	27 02 43	3♏16 45	18 12.1	8 01.6	5 55.0	16 51.3	4 11.4	1 41.4	24 06.3	4 55.0	3 30.1	26 50.7
22 F	22 11 04	4 13 44	9♏34 19	15 55 55	18D11.2	8 34.4	6 02.7	17 38.3	4 02.0	1 40.0	24 04.3	4 52.8	3 31.5	26 52.4
23 Sa	22 15 01	5 14 08	22 22 01	28 53 07	18R11.4	9 11.7	6 08.1	18 25.3	3 53.0	1 38.5	24 02.1	4 50.6	3 32.8	26 54.1
24 Su	22 18 57	6 14 31	5♐29 41	12♐12 10	18 11.3	9 53.3	6R11.1	19 12.3	3 44.3	1 36.8	23 59.8	4 48.5	3 34.2	26 55.8
25 M	22 22 54	7 14 52	19 00 56	25 56 13	18 10.0	10 38.7	6 11.7	19 59.4	3 36.0	1 34.9	23 57.5	4 46.4	3 35.6	26 57.6
26 Tu	22 26 50	8 15 12	2♑58 11	10♑06 49	18 06.3	11 27.8	6 09.9	20 46.4	3 28.1	1 32.8	23 55.0	4 44.3	3 37.1	26 59.3
27 W	22 30 47	9 15 31	17 21 54	24 43 01	18 00.2	12 20.3	6 05.6	21 33.5	3 20.6	1 30.5	23 52.5	4 42.3	3 38.5	27 01.0
28 Th	22 34 43	10 15 48	2♒09 32	9♒40 35	17 51.7	13 15.8	5 58.8	22 20.5	3 13.5	1 28.0	23 49.8	4 40.3	3 40.0	27 02.7

Astro Data

	Dy Hr Mn
☽ 0N	8 14:22
♆ D	12 16:36
☽ 0S	23 4:57
☿ R	26 6:12
♀ 0N	30 10:19
♄ R	1 16:01
☽ 0N	4 21:51
♃ R	14 20:21
☿ D	16 10:27
☽ 0S	19 9:58
♀ R	25 6:07

Planet Ingress

	Dy Hr Mn
♀ ♓	2 20:37
☿ ♒	6 11:59
♃ ♏	11 19:32
☉ ♒	19 17:13
♂ ♒	30 21:08
♀ ♈	6 11:59
☉ ♓	18 7:17

Last Aspect / ☽ Ingress

Last Aspect Dy Hr Mn		☽ Ingress Dy Hr Mn
1 21:02 ♀ ⚹	♑	1 22:41
3 21:02 ♃ □	♒	3 22:25
5 21:10 ♃ △	♓	5 22:11
7 2:18 ☉ ⚹	♈	7 23:59
10 4:44 ♃ ☍	♉	10 5:02
12 5:11 ♇ □	♊	12 13:23
14 15:45 ♇ △	♋	15 0:06
17 7:11 ☉ ☍	♌	17 12:08
19 16:29 ♇ ☍	♍	20 0:45
21 23:17 ☿ △	♎	22 13:02
24 16:01 ♇ △	♏	24 23:33
27 1:24 ♂ ⚹	♐	27 6:40
29 3:28 ♇ ⚹	♑	29 9:47
31 3:06 ♀ ⚹	♒	31 9:48

Last Aspect Dy Hr Mn		☽ Ingress Dy Hr Mn
2 2:54 ♇ ☌	♓	2 8:43
4 6:31 ♀ ☌	♈	4 8:49
6 5:43 ♇ ⚹	♉	6 12:04
8 12:37 ♇ □	♊	8 19:19
10 23:02 ♇ △	♋	11 5:55
13 6:46 ♄ □	♌	13 18:13
16 2:21 ☉ ☍	♍	16 6:50
16 13:41 ♆ △	♎	18 18:55
20 23:35 ♇ △	♏	21 5:42
23 8:21 ♇ □	♐	23 14:02
25 13:46 ♇ ⚹	♑	25 18:57
27 10:38 ♄ □	♒	27 20:32

☽ Phases & Eclipses

Dy Hr Mn	
2 19:08	● 12♑46
9 10:06	☽ 19♈31
17 7:11	○ 27♋32
25 10:33	☾ 5♏49
1 5:43	● 12♒44
7 23:40	☽ 19♉34
16 2:21	○ 27♌46
24 0:29	☾ 5♐46

Astro Data

1 January 2041
Julian Day # 51501
SVP 4♓41'26"
GC 27♐24.7 ⚴ 20♈34.7
Eris 28♈07.5R ⚵ 11♋15.6R
⚷ 20♋31.1R ⚶ 2♓58.7
☽ Mean ☊ 22♉00.2

1 February 2041
Julian Day # 51532
SVP 4♓41'20"
GC 27♐24.8 ⚴ 28♈54.5
Eris 28♈08.2 ⚵ 5♋54.7R
⚷ 18♋24.6R ⚶ 16♓59.1
☽ Mean ☊ 20♉21.8

March 2041 LONGITUDE

Day	Sid.Time	☉	0 hr ☽	Noon ☽	True ☊	☿	♀	♂	⚳	♃	♄	♅	♆	♇
1 F	22 38 40	11♓16 04	17♒15 07	24♒51 53	17♉41.7	14♒14.2	5♈49.6	23♒07.6	3♌06.8	1♏25.4	23♎47.1	4♌38.3	3♉41.5	27♒04.4
2 Sa	22 42 36	12 16 18	2♓29 32	10♓06 40	17R31.4	15 15.3	5R37.8	23 54.7	3R00.5	1R22.5	23R44.3	4R36.4	3 43.1	27 06.1
3 Su	22 46 33	13 16 30	17 41 52	25 13 48	17 22.2	16 19.0	5 23.5	24 41.8	2 54.6	1 19.5	23 41.4	4 34.5	3 44.6	27 07.8
4 M	22 50 30	14 16 40	2♈41 16	10♈03 16	17 15.0	17 24.9	5 06.8	25 28.9	2 49.2	1 16.3	23 38.5	4 32.6	3 46.2	27 09.4
5 Tu	22 54 26	15 16 48	17 18 58	24 27 49	17 10.3	18 33.1	4 47.7	26 16.0	2 44.2	1 12.9	23 35.4	4 30.8	3 47.9	27 11.1
6 W	22 58 23	16 16 54	1♉29 26	8♉23 41	17D08.2	19 43.4	4 26.2	27 03.1	2 39.6	1 09.4	23 32.3	4 29.1	3 49.5	27 12.8
7 Th	23 02 19	17 16 58	15 10 38	21 50 28	17 07.9	20 55.6	4 02.4	27 50.2	2 35.5	1 05.7	23 29.1	4 27.3	3 51.2	27 14.4
8 F	23 06 16	18 17 01	28 23 32	4♊50 19	17 08.7	22 09.7	3 36.5	28 37.3	2 31.8	1 01.8	23 25.8	4 25.6	3 52.9	27 16.1
9 Sa	23 10 12	19 17 00	11♊11 18	17 27 05	17R09.3	23 25.6	3 08.5	29 24.4	2 28.6	0 57.8	23 22.4	4 24.0	3 54.6	27 17.7
10 Su	23 14 09	20 16 58	23 38 17	29 45 31	17 08.7	24 43.2	2 38.7	0♓11.5	2 25.8	0 53.5	23 19.0	4 22.4	3 56.3	27 19.3
11 M	23 18 05	21 16 54	5♋49 24	11♋50 33	17 06.3	26 02.4	2 07.0	0 58.6	2 23.4	0 49.2	23 15.5	4 20.8	3 58.1	27 20.9
12 Tu	23 22 02	22 16 47	17 49 33	23 46 57	17 01.6	27 23.2	1 33.8	1 45.7	2 21.5	0 44.6	23 11.9	4 19.3	3 59.8	27 22.5
13 W	23 25 59	23 16 38	29 43 16	5♌38 57	16 54.7	28 45.5	0 59.3	2 32.8	2 20.0	0 39.9	23 08.3	4 17.9	4 01.6	27 24.1
14 Th	23 29 55	24 16 27	11♌34 27	17 30 08	16 45.9	0♓09.3	0 23.6	3 19.9	2 18.9	0 35.1	23 04.6	4 16.4	4 03.5	27 25.7
15 F	23 33 52	25 16 14	23 26 21	29 23 23	16 35.9	1 34.6	29♓47.0	4 07.0	2D18.3	0 30.1	23 00.8	4 15.1	4 05.3	27 27.3
16 Sa	23 37 48	26 15 59	5♍21 28	11♍20 51	16 25.8	3 01.2	29 09.7	4 54.1	2 18.1	0 24.9	22 57.0	4 13.7	4 07.2	27 28.9
17 Su	23 41 45	27 15 42	17 21 42	23 24 10	16 16.4	4 29.3	28 32.0	5 41.2	2 18.3	0 19.6	22 53.1	4 12.5	4 09.0	27 30.4
18 M	23 45 41	28 15 22	29 28 25	5♎34 34	16 08.5	5 58.7	27 54.1	6 28.2	2 19.0	0 14.2	22 49.1	4 11.2	4 10.9	27 32.0
19 Tu	23 49 38	29 15 01	11♎42 46	17 53 07	16 02.7	7 29.4	27 16.4	7 15.3	2 20.1	0 08.6	22 45.1	4 10.0	4 12.8	27 33.5
20 W	23 53 34	0♈14 38	24 05 48	0♏20 58	15 59.3	9 01.5	26 39.0	8 02.4	2 21.6	0 02.9	22 41.1	4 08.9	4 14.8	27 35.0
21 Th	23 57 31	1 14 13	6♏38 48	12 59 31	15D57.9	10 34.9	26 02.2	8 49.5	2 23.5	29♎57.1	22 37.0	4 07.8	4 16.7	27 36.5
22 F	0 01 28	2 13 46	19 23 21	25 50 33	15 58.3	12 09.6	25 26.3	9 36.5	2 25.8	29 51.1	22 32.8	4 06.8	4 18.7	27 38.0
23 Sa	0 05 24	3 13 18	2♐21 23	8♐56 09	15 59.6	13 45.6	24 51.5	10 23.6	2 28.6	29 45.0	22 28.6	4 05.8	4 20.7	27 39.4
24 Su	0 09 21	4 12 47	15 35 06	22 18 30	16R00.9	15 23.0	24 18.0	11 10.7	2 31.8	29 38.8	22 24.4	4 04.8	4 22.7	27 40.9
25 M	0 13 17	5 12 15	29 06 35	5♑59 31	16 01.5	17 01.6	23 46.0	11 57.7	2 35.3	29 32.5	22 20.1	4 03.9	4 24.7	27 42.4
26 Tu	0 17 14	6 11 42	12♑57 23	20 00 13	16 00.6	18 41.6	23 15.7	12 44.8	2 39.3	29 26.0	22 15.8	4 03.1	4 26.7	27 43.8
27 W	0 21 10	7 11 06	27 07 53	4♒28 08	15 58.0	20 22.9	22 47.3	13 31.8	2 43.7	29 19.5	22 11.4	4 02.3	4 28.8	27 45.2
28 Th	0 25 07	8 10 29	11♒36 34	18 56 40	15 53.9	22 05.6	22 20.8	14 18.8	2 48.5	29 12.8	22 07.0	4 01.6	4 30.8	27 46.6
29 F	0 29 03	9 09 50	26 19 42	3♓44 51	15 48.7	23 49.6	21 56.5	15 05.8	2 53.6	29 06.0	22 02.6	4 00.9	4 32.9	27 48.0
30 Sa	0 33 00	10 09 09	11♓11 10	18 37 38	15 43.2	25 34.9	21 34.4	15 52.8	2 59.2	28 59.2	21 58.2	4 00.3	4 35.0	27 49.4
31 Su	0 36 57	11 08 27	26 03 12	3♈26 47	15 38.2	27 21.6	21 14.6	16 39.8	3 05.1	28 52.2	21 53.7	3 59.7	4 37.1	27 50.7

April 2041 LONGITUDE

Day	Sid.Time	☉	0 hr ☽	Noon ☽	True ☊	☿	♀	♂	⚳	♃	♄	♅	♆	♇
1 M	0 40 53	12♈07 42	10♈47 24	18♈04 05	15♉34.4	29♓09.7	20♓57.1	17♓26.8	3♌11.4	28♎45.2	21♎49.1	3♌59.1	4♉39.2	27♒52.0
2 Tu	0 44 50	13 06 55	25 16 05	2♉22 42	15D32.1	0♈59.2	20R42.0	18 13.7	3 18.1	28R38.1	21R44.6	3R58.7	4 41.4	27 53.3
3 W	0 48 46	14 06 06	9♉23 27	16 18 00	15 31.4	2 50.1	20 29.4	19 00.7	3 25.2	28 30.9	21 40.1	3 58.2	4 43.5	27 54.6
4 Th	0 52 43	15 05 15	23 06 11	29 47 57	15 32.1	4 42.4	20 19.2	19 47.6	3 32.6	28 23.6	21 35.5	3 57.9	4 45.6	27 55.9
5 F	0 56 39	16 04 21	6♊23 28	12♊52 56	15 33.6	6 36.1	20 11.4	20 34.5	3 40.4	28 16.3	21 30.9	3 57.6	4 47.8	27 57.2
6 Sa	1 00 36	17 03 26	19 16 42	25 35 12	15 35.3	8 31.2	20 06.1	21 21.4	3 48.6	28 08.9	21 26.3	3 57.3	4 50.0	27 58.4
7 Su	1 04 32	18 02 28	1♋48 54	7♋58 21	15R36.5	10 27.6	20D03.2	22 08.2	3 57.1	28 01.5	21 21.7	3 57.1	4 52.2	27 59.7
8 M	1 08 29	19 01 28	14 04 07	20 06 48	15 37.0	12 25.5	20 02.7	22 55.1	4 05.9	27 54.0	21 17.1	3 57.0	4 54.3	28 00.9
9 Tu	1 12 26	20 00 25	26 06 58	2♌05 14	15 36.3	14 24.7	20 04.5	23 41.9	4 15.1	27 46.5	21 12.4	3 56.9	4 56.5	28 02.0
10 W	1 16 22	20 59 20	8♌02 10	13 58 21	15 34.4	16 25.2	20 08.7	24 28.7	4 24.6	27 38.9	21 07.8	3D56.8	4 58.7	28 03.2
11 Th	1 20 19	21 58 13	19 54 17	25 50 31	15 31.6	18 26.9	20 15.2	25 15.4	4 34.5	27 31.3	21 03.2	3 56.8	5 00.9	28 04.4
12 F	1 24 15	22 57 04	1♍47 30	7♍45 41	15 28.1	20 29.8	20 23.8	26 02.2	4 44.7	27 23.7	20 58.6	3 56.9	5 03.2	28 05.5
13 Sa	1 28 12	23 55 52	13 45 26	19 47 07	15 24.5	22 33.8	20 34.6	26 48.9	4 55.2	27 16.1	20 53.9	3 57.0	5 05.4	28 06.6
14 Su	1 32 08	24 54 39	25 51 02	1♎57 28	15 21.1	24 38.8	20 47.6	27 35.6	5 06.0	27 08.4	20 49.3	3 57.2	5 07.6	28 07.7
15 M	1 36 05	25 53 23	8♎06 36	14 18 37	15 18.4	26 44.6	21 02.6	28 22.3	5 17.1	27 00.7	20 44.7	3 57.4	5 09.8	28 08.7
16 Tu	1 40 01	26 52 05	20 33 41	26 51 52	15 16.5	28 51.0	21 19.5	29 08.9	5 28.6	26 53.0	20 40.1	3 57.7	5 12.1	28 09.8
17 W	1 43 58	27 50 45	3♏13 16	9♏37 55	15D15.7	0♉57.9	21 38.4	29 55.5	5 40.3	26 45.4	20 35.6	3 58.0	5 14.3	28 10.8
18 Th	1 47 54	28 49 24	16 05 51	22 37 03	15 15.7	3 05.0	21 59.2	0♈42.1	5 52.3	26 37.7	20 31.0	3 58.4	5 16.6	28 11.8
19 F	1 51 51	29 48 01	29 11 33	5♐49 19	15 16.5	5 12.2	22 21.8	1 28.7	6 04.6	26 30.0	20 26.5	3 58.9	5 18.8	28 12.8
20 Sa	1 55 48	0♉46 36	12♐30 19	19 14 33	15 17.6	7 19.0	22 46.1	2 15.2	6 17.2	26 22.4	20 21.9	3 59.3	5 21.1	28 13.7
21 Su	1 59 44	1 45 09	26 01 58	2♑52 31	15 18.7	9 25.3	23 12.1	3 01.8	6 30.1	26 14.7	20 17.5	3 59.9	5 23.3	28 14.7
22 M	2 03 41	2 43 41	9♑46 09	16 42 47	15 19.6	11 30.7	23 39.7	3 48.3	6 43.2	26 07.1	20 13.0	4 00.5	5 25.6	28 15.6
23 Tu	2 07 37	3 42 11	23 42 18	0♒44 32	15R20.0	13 34.8	24 08.9	4 34.7	6 56.7	25 59.5	20 08.5	4 01.2	5 27.9	28 16.5
24 W	2 11 34	4 40 39	7♒49 20	14 56 25	15 19.8	15 37.5	24 39.6	5 21.2	7 10.4	25 52.0	20 04.1	4 01.9	5 30.1	28 17.4
25 Th	2 15 30	5 39 06	22 05 31	29 16 14	15 19.2	17 38.3	25 11.7	6 07.6	7 24.3	25 44.5	19 59.8	4 02.6	5 32.4	28 18.2
26 F	2 19 27	6 37 31	6♓28 10	13♓40 50	15 18.4	19 36.9	25 45.2	6 53.9	7 38.5	25 37.0	19 55.4	4 03.4	5 34.7	28 19.0
27 Sa	2 23 23	7 35 55	20 53 40	28 06 07	15 17.4	21 33.2	26 20.0	7 40.3	7 53.0	25 29.6	19 51.1	4 04.3	5 36.9	28 19.8
28 Su	2 27 20	8 34 17	5♈17 33	12♈27 22	15 16.6	23 26.7	26 56.1	8 26.6	8 07.8	25 22.2	19 46.8	4 05.2	5 39.2	28 20.6
29 M	2 31 17	9 32 37	19 34 55	26 39 38	15 16.1	25 17.2	27 33.4	9 12.9	8 22.7	25 14.9	19 42.6	4 06.2	5 41.4	28 21.4
30 Tu	2 35 13	10 30 56	3♉40 57	10♉38 23	15D15.8	27 04.6	28 11.8	9 59.1	8 38.0	25 07.7	19 38.4	4 07.2	5 43.7	28 22.1

Astro Data Dy Hr Mn	Planet Ingress Dy Hr Mn	Last Aspect Dy Hr Mn	☽ Ingress Dy Hr Mn	Last Aspect Dy Hr Mn	☽ Ingress Dy Hr Mn	☽ Phases & Eclipses Dy Hr Mn	Astro Data
☽0N 4 7:50	♂ ♓ 10 6:09	1 15:29 ♇ ☌	♓ 1 20:05	2 5:43 ♃ ☍	♉ 2 7:58	2 15:39 ● 12♓25	1 March 2041
⚳D 16 11:00	☿ ♓ 14 9:21	2 15:39 ☉ ☌	♈ 3 19:40	4 8:38 ♇ □	♊ 4 12:22	9 15:51 ☽ 19♊27	Julian Day # 51560
♅□♆ 18 14:11	♀ ♓R 15 3:31	5 16:38 ♇ ⚹	♉ 5 21:26	6 16:52 ♃ △	♋ 6 20:29	17 20:19 ○ 27♍36	SVP 4♓41'17"
☽0S 18 15:37	☉ ♈ 20 6:07	7 23:41 ♂ □	♊ 8 2:59	9 3:25 ♃ □	♌ 9 7:48	25 10:32 ☾ 5♑09	GC 27♐24.9 ⚴ 10♉30.8
☉0N 20 6:07	♃ ♎R 21 0:02	10 7:12 ♇ △	♋ 10 12:29	11 16:31 ♇ ☍	♍ 11 20:23		Eris 28♈17.5 ⚵ 7♋25.4
☽0N 31 18:30		12 10:50 ♄ □	♌ 13 0:34	14 2:51 ♂ ☍	♎ 14 8:10	1 1:29 ● 11♈42	⚷ 17♋06.4R ⚶ 0♈03.1
☿0N 4 9:30	☿ ♈ 1 23:03	15 8:06 ♇ ☍	♍ 15 13:14	16 16:31 ☿ ☍	♏ 16 17:56	8 9:38 ☽ 18♋56	☽ Mean ☊ 18♉52.8
♃△♇ 7 17:08	☿ ♉ 17 1:03	17 21:39 ♀ ☍	♎ 18 1:02	18 22:12 ♇ □	♐ 19 1:28	16 12:00 ○ 26♎52	
♀D 8 5:08	♂ ♈ 17 14:18	20 6:41 ♇ △	♏ 20 11:20	21 3:53 ♇ ⚹	♑ 21 6:58	23 17:24 ☾ 3♒55	1 April 2041
♅D 10 19:05	☉ ♉ 19 16:55	22 15:19 ♇ □	♐ 22 19:40	23 3:59 ♃ □	♒ 23 10:44	30 11:46 ● 10♉30	Julian Day # 51591
♀0S 12 18:43		25 0:51 ♃ ⚹	♑ 25 1:34	25 10:23 ♇ ☌	♓ 25 13:13	30 11:50:56 T 01'51"	SVP 4♓41'14"
☽0S 14 22:44		27 3:44 ♃ □	♒ 27 4:48	27 8:56 ♀ ☌	♈ 27 15:10		GC 27♐24.9 ⚴ 26♉10.4
♂0N 20 19:49		29 4:33 ♃ △	♓ 29 5:57	29 14:53 ♇ ⚹	♉ 29 17:42		Eris 28♈34.8 ⚵ 14♋49.9
☽0N 28 3:41		31 0:46 ☿ ☌	♈ 31 6:24				⚷ 16♋56.9 ⚶ 14♈34.7
♀0N 30 0:09							☽ Mean ☊ 17♉14.3

LONGITUDE — May 2041

Day	Sid.Time	☉	0 hr ☽	Noon ☽	True ☊	☿	♀	♂	⚳	♃	♄	♅	♆	♇
1 W	2 39 10	11♉29 13	17♉31 30	24♉19 59	15♉15.9	28♉48.6	28♓51.4	10♈45.3	8♌53.4	25♎00.5	19♎34.3	4♌08.3	5♉46.0	28♒22.8
2 Th	2 43 06	12 27 28	1♊03 35	7♊42 09	15 16.1	0♊29.1	29 32.1	11 31.5	9 09.1	24R53.5	19R30.2	4 09.4	5 48.2	28 23.5
3 F	2 47 03	13 25 41	14 15 39	20 44 07	15 16.3	2 06.0	0♈13.8	12 17.6	9 25.1	24 46.5	19 26.2	4 10.6	5 50.5	28 24.1
4 Sa	2 50 59	14 23 53	27 07 42	3♋26 37	15R16.4	3 39.0	0 56.5	13 03.7	9 41.2	24 39.6	19 22.2	4 11.8	5 52.7	28 24.8
5 Su	2 54 56	15 22 02	9♋41 10	15 51 43	15 16.5	5 08.2	1 40.1	13 49.7	9 57.6	24 32.7	19 18.3	4 13.1	5 55.0	28 25.4
6 M	2 58 53	16 20 10	21 58 41	28 02 33	15 16.4	6 33.4	2 24.7	14 35.7	10 14.2	24 26.0	19 14.4	4 14.5	5 57.2	28 26.0
7 Tu	3 02 49	17 18 16	4♌03 49	10♌03 01	15D16.4	7 54.5	3 10.1	15 21.7	10 31.0	24 19.4	19 10.6	4 15.8	5 59.4	28 26.5
8 W	3 06 46	18 16 19	16 00 44	21 57 31	15 16.3	9 11.4	3 56.4	16 07.6	10 48.0	24 12.9	19 06.9	4 17.3	6 01.6	28 27.1
9 Th	3 10 42	19 14 21	27 53 58	3♍50 38	15 16.5	10 24.2	4 43.4	16 53.5	11 05.3	24 06.5	19 03.2	4 18.8	6 03.9	28 27.6
10 F	3 14 39	20 12 21	9♍48 07	15 46 57	15 16.8	11 32.6	5 31.3	17 39.3	11 22.7	24 00.2	18 59.6	4 20.3	6 06.1	28 28.0
11 Sa	3 18 35	21 10 19	21 47 39	27 50 45	15 17.4	12 36.7	6 20.0	18 25.1	11 40.4	23 54.0	18 56.0	4 21.9	6 08.3	28 28.5
12 Su	3 22 32	22 08 15	3♎56 40	10♎05 50	15 18.0	13 36.4	7 09.3	19 10.9	11 58.2	23 47.9	18 52.5	4 23.5	6 10.5	28 28.9
13 M	3 26 28	23 06 10	16 18 38	22 35 21	15 18.7	14 31.6	7 59.4	19 56.6	12 16.2	23 42.0	18 49.1	4 25.1	6 12.7	28 29.3
14 Tu	3 30 25	24 04 02	28 56 14	5♏21 27	15R19.2	15 22.3	8 50.1	20 42.2	12 34.4	23 36.2	18 45.7	4 26.9	6 14.8	28 29.7
15 W	3 34 21	25 01 54	11♏51 08	18 25 17	15 19.3	16 08.4	9 41.5	21 27.8	12 52.8	23 30.5	18 42.5	4 28.6	6 17.0	28 30.1
16 Th	3 38 18	25 59 44	25 03 52	1♐46 45	15 18.9	16 49.8	10 33.5	22 13.4	13 11.4	23 24.9	18 39.3	4 30.4	6 19.2	28 30.4
17 F	3 42 15	26 57 32	8♐33 46	15 24 37	15 18.0	17 26.5	11 26.1	22 59.0	13 30.1	23 19.5	18 36.1	4 32.3	6 21.3	28 30.7
18 Sa	3 46 11	27 55 19	22 19 01	29 16 35	15 16.6	17 58.5	12 19.4	23 44.4	13 49.0	23 14.2	18 33.1	4 34.2	6 23.5	28 31.0
19 Su	3 50 08	28 53 05	6♑16 55	13♑19 36	15 15.0	18 25.6	13 13.2	24 29.9	14 08.1	23 09.1	18 30.1	4 36.2	6 25.6	28 31.3
20 M	3 54 04	29 50 50	20 24 09	27 30 09	15 13.3	18 47.9	14 07.5	25 15.3	14 27.4	23 04.1	18 27.2	4 38.2	6 27.7	28 31.5
21 Tu	3 58 01	0♊48 34	4♒37 09	11♒44 45	15 12.0	19 05.4	15 02.3	26 00.6	14 46.8	22 59.2	18 24.4	4 40.2	6 29.8	28 31.7
22 W	4 01 57	1 46 16	18 52 32	26 00 08	15D11.3	19 18.0	15 57.7	26 46.0	15 06.4	22 54.6	18 21.7	4 42.3	6 31.9	28 31.9
23 Th	4 05 54	2 43 58	3♓07 14	10♓13 31	15 11.4	19 25.8	16 53.6	27 31.2	15 26.2	22 50.0	18 19.0	4 44.4	6 34.0	28 32.1
24 F	4 09 51	3 41 38	17 18 41	24 22 29	15 12.1	19R28.8	17 49.9	28 16.4	15 46.1	22 45.6	18 16.5	4 46.6	6 36.1	28 32.2
25 Sa	4 13 47	4 39 18	1♈24 42	8♈25 04	15 13.3	19 27.2	18 46.6	29 01.6	16 06.2	22 41.4	18 14.0	4 48.8	6 38.1	28 32.3
26 Su	4 17 44	5 36 56	15 23 23	22 19 26	15 14.7	19 21.1	19 43.8	29 46.7	16 26.4	22 37.3	18 11.6	4 51.0	6 40.2	28 32.4
27 M	4 21 40	6 34 34	29 13 00	6♉03 53	15R15.6	19 10.6	20 41.5	0♉31.8	16 46.8	22 33.4	18 09.3	4 53.3	6 42.2	28 32.4
28 Tu	4 25 37	7 32 11	12♉51 52	19 36 44	15 15.8	18 56.0	21 39.5	1 16.8	17 07.3	22 29.6	18 07.0	4 55.7	6 44.2	28R32.4
29 W	4 29 33	8 29 46	26 18 20	2♊56 29	15 14.8	18 37.6	22 37.9	2 01.8	17 28.0	22 26.1	18 04.9	4 58.0	6 46.2	28 32.4
30 Th	4 33 30	9 27 21	9♊31 03	16 01 55	15 12.7	18 15.7	23 36.7	2 46.7	17 48.8	22 22.6	18 02.9	5 00.5	6 48.2	28 32.4
31 F	4 37 26	10 24 54	22 29 00	28 52 19	15 09.5	17 50.6	24 35.8	3 31.5	18 09.7	22 19.4	18 00.9	5 02.9	6 50.1	28 32.4

LONGITUDE — June 2041

Day	Sid.Time	☉	0 hr ☽	Noon ☽	True ☊	☿	♀	♂	⚳	♃	♄	♅	♆	♇
1 Sa	4 41 23	11♊22 26	5♋11 53	11♋27 47	15♉05.4	17♊22.9	25♈35.3	4♉16.3	18♌30.8	22♎16.3	17♎59.1	5♌05.4	6♉52.1	28♒32.3
2 Su	4 45 20	12 19 57	17 40 10	23 49 14	15R01.0	16R52.9	26 35.1	5 01.1	18 52.1	22R13.4	17R57.3	5 08.0	6 54.0	28R32.2
3 M	4 49 16	13 17 27	29 55 16	5♌58 33	14 56.8	16 21.2	27 35.3	5 45.8	19 13.4	22 10.7	17 55.7	5 10.5	6 55.9	28 32.1
4 Tu	4 53 13	14 14 56	11♌59 29	17 58 30	14 53.3	15 48.3	28 35.7	6 30.4	19 34.9	22 08.2	17 54.1	5 13.1	6 57.8	28 31.9
5 W	4 57 09	15 12 23	23 56 02	29 52 38	14 50.9	15 14.9	29 36.5	7 15.0	19 56.5	22 05.8	17 52.6	5 15.8	6 59.7	28 31.8
6 Th	5 01 06	16 09 49	5♍48 49	11♍45 10	14D49.7	14 41.4	0♉37.5	7 59.5	20 18.3	22 03.6	17 51.2	5 18.5	7 01.6	28 31.6
7 F	5 05 02	17 07 14	17 42 17	23 40 44	14 49.8	14 08.4	1 38.9	8 43.9	20 40.1	22 01.6	17 50.0	5 21.2	7 03.4	28 31.3
8 Sa	5 08 59	18 04 38	29 41 09	5♎44 09	14 50.9	13 36.6	2 40.5	9 28.3	21 02.1	21 59.7	17 48.8	5 23.9	7 05.2	28 31.1
9 Su	5 12 55	19 02 01	11♎50 17	18 00 09	14 52.5	13 06.4	3 42.4	10 12.6	21 24.2	21 58.1	17 47.7	5 26.7	7 07.0	28 30.8
10 M	5 16 52	19 59 23	24 14 15	0♏33 04	14 54.0	12 38.4	4 44.5	10 56.9	21 46.4	21 56.6	17 46.7	5 29.5	7 08.8	28 30.5
11 Tu	5 20 49	20 56 43	6♏57 01	13 26 26	14R54.7	12 13.0	5 46.9	11 41.1	22 08.8	21 55.3	17 45.8	5 32.4	7 10.6	28 30.2
12 W	5 24 45	21 54 03	20 01 32	26 42 28	14 54.2	11 50.7	6 49.6	12 25.3	22 31.2	21 54.1	17 45.0	5 35.3	7 12.3	28 29.9
13 Th	5 28 42	22 51 22	3♐29 14	10♐21 42	14 51.9	11 31.8	7 52.5	13 09.4	22 53.8	21 53.2	17 44.3	5 38.2	7 14.0	28 29.5
14 F	5 32 38	23 48 41	17 19 36	24 22 33	14 48.0	11 16.6	8 55.6	13 53.5	23 16.4	21 52.4	17 43.7	5 41.1	7 15.7	28 29.1
15 Sa	5 36 35	24 45 59	1♑30 00	8♑41 18	14 42.7	11 05.5	9 59.0	14 37.4	23 39.2	21 51.9	17 43.2	5 44.1	7 17.4	28 28.7
16 Su	5 40 31	25 43 16	15 55 43	23 12 26	14 36.6	10 58.5	11 02.6	15 21.4	24 02.0	21 51.5	17 42.8	5 47.1	7 19.0	28 28.2
17 M	5 44 28	26 40 33	0♒30 34	7♒49 16	14 30.6	10D56.0	12 06.4	16 05.2	24 25.0	21D51.2	17 42.5	5 50.2	7 20.7	28 27.8
18 Tu	5 48 24	27 37 49	15 07 43	22 25 08	14 25.5	10 57.9	13 10.5	16 49.1	24 48.1	21 51.2	17 42.3	5 53.2	7 22.3	28 27.3
19 W	5 52 21	28 35 05	29 40 49	6♓54 10	14 21.9	11 04.5	14 14.7	17 32.8	25 11.2	21 51.3	17D42.2	5 56.3	7 23.9	28 26.8
20 Th	5 56 18	29 32 20	14♓04 45	21 12 09	14D20.0	11 15.7	15 19.2	18 16.5	25 34.5	21 51.6	17 42.2	5 59.4	7 25.4	28 26.3
21 F	6 00 14	0♋29 36	28 16 09	5♈16 35	14 19.8	11 31.5	16 23.8	19 00.1	25 57.8	21 52.1	17 42.3	6 02.6	7 26.9	28 25.7
22 Sa	6 04 11	1 26 51	12♈13 23	19 06 32	14 20.6	11 52.0	17 28.6	19 43.7	26 21.3	21 52.8	17 42.5	6 05.8	7 28.5	28 25.1
23 Su	6 08 07	2 24 07	25 56 06	2♉42 10	14R21.8	12 17.2	18 33.7	20 27.2	26 44.8	21 53.6	17 42.8	6 09.0	7 29.9	28 24.5
24 M	6 12 04	3 21 22	9♉24 50	16 04 13	14 22.2	12 46.9	19 38.9	21 10.6	27 08.4	21 54.7	17 43.2	6 12.2	7 31.4	28 23.9
25 Tu	6 16 00	4 18 37	22 40 25	29 13 32	14 21.1	13 21.2	20 44.3	21 54.0	27 32.2	21 55.9	17 43.7	6 15.5	7 32.8	28 23.3
26 W	6 19 57	5 15 52	5♊43 40	12♊10 51	14 18.0	14 00.0	21 49.8	22 37.3	27 56.0	21 57.3	17 44.3	6 18.7	7 34.2	28 22.6
27 Th	6 23 53	6 13 07	18 35 10	24 56 38	14 12.4	14 43.3	22 55.5	23 20.6	28 19.9	21 58.8	17 45.0	6 22.0	7 35.6	28 21.9
28 F	6 27 50	7 10 22	1♋15 18	7♋31 10	14 04.8	15 30.9	24 01.4	24 03.8	28 43.9	22 00.6	17 45.8	6 25.4	7 37.0	28 21.2
29 Sa	6 31 47	8 07 36	13 44 19	19 54 48	13 55.5	16 22.8	25 07.4	24 46.9	29 07.9	22 02.5	17 46.7	6 28.7	7 38.3	28 20.5
30 Su	6 35 43	9 04 50	26 02 42	2♌08 08	13 45.4	17 19.0	26 13.6	25 29.9	29 32.1	22 04.6	17 47.7	6 32.1	7 39.6	28 19.7

Astro Data Dy Hr Mn	Planet Ingress Dy Hr Mn	Last Aspect Dy Hr Mn	☽ Ingress Dy Hr Mn	Last Aspect Dy Hr Mn	☽ Ingress Dy Hr Mn	☽ Phases & Eclipses Dy Hr Mn	Astro Data
☽0S 12 6:57	☿ ♊ 2 4:57	1 21:07 ☿ ☌	♊ 1 22:06	2 17:55 ♀ □	♌ 3 0:09	8 3:54 ☽ 17♌57	1 May 2041
☿R 24 15:38	♀ ♈ 3 4:08	4 2:25 ♇ △	♋ 4 5:26	5 11:24 ♀ △	♍ 5 12:15	16 0:52 ○ 25♏33	Julian Day # 51621
☽0N 25 10:22	☉ ♊ 20 15:49	6 4:55 ♃ □	♌ 6 15:54	6 21:40 ☉ □	♎ 8 0:38	16 0:42 ☍ P 0.064	SVP 4♓41'10"
♇R 29 3:33	♂ ♉ 26 19:04	9 1:07 ♇ ☍	♍ 9 4:15	10 8:08 ♇ △	♏ 10 10:58	22 22:26 ☾ 2♓11	GC 27♐25.0 ⚴ 13♊01.0
		10 21:36 ☉ △	♎ 11 16:15	12 15:11 ♇ □	♐ 12 17:51	29 22:56 ● 8♊56	Eris 28♈54.5 ⚵ 25♋08.9
☽0S 8 15:11	♀ ♉ 5 21:16	13 23:10 ♇ △	♏ 14 2:00	14 18:56 ♇ ⚹	♑ 14 21:29		⚷ 18♋11.0 ⚶ 28♈24.1
☿D 17 13:41	☉ ♋ 20 23:36	16 6:10 ♇ □	♐ 16 8:50	16 9:47 ♃ □	♒ 16 23:10	6 21:40 ☽ 16♍33	☽ Mean ☊ 15♉39.0
♃D 18 6:14		18 10:42 ♇ ⚹	♑ 18 13:15	18 21:58 ♇ ☌	♓ 19 0:32	14 10:58 ○ 23♐46	
♄D 20 1:10		20 7:59 ♂ □	♒ 20 16:13	20 6:47 ♂ ⚹	♈ 21 2:57	21 3:12 ☾ 0♈09	1 June 2041
☽0N 21 15:20		22 16:16 ♇ ☌	♓ 22 18:44	23 4:23 ♇ ⚹	♉ 23 7:12	28 11:17 ● 7♋09	Julian Day # 51652
		24 3:40 ☿ □	♈ 24 21:35	25 10:28 ♇ □	♊ 25 13:25		SVP 4♓41'05"
		26 22:49 ♇ ⚹	♉ 27 1:22	27 18:29 ♇ △	♋ 27 21:36		GC 27♐25.1 ⚴ 1♋16.1
		29 4:02 ♇ □	♊ 29 6:40	29 23:12 ♀ ⚹	♌ 30 7:47		Eris 29♈12.8 ⚵ 7♌20.9
		31 11:22 ♇ △	♋ 31 14:08				⚷ 20♋37.2 ⚶ 12♉09.9
							☽ Mean ☊ 14♉00.5

July 2041 — LONGITUDE

Day	Sid.Time	☉	0 hr ☽	Noon ☽	True ☊	☿	♀	♂	⚳	♃	♄	♅	♆	♇
1 M	6 39 40	10♋02 04	8♌11 16	14♌12 17	13♉35.4	18♊19.4	27♉19.9	26♉12.9	29♌56.3	22♎06.8	17♎48.8	6♌35.5	7♉40.9	28♒19.0
2 Tu	6 43 36	10 59 18	20 11 28	26 09 05	13R 26.5	19 23.9	28 26.4	26 55.8	0♍20.6	22 09.3	17 50.0	6 38.9	7 42.1	28R 18.2
3 W	6 47 33	11 56 31	2♍05 31	8♍01 09	13 19.3	20 32.4	29 33.0	27 38.6	0 45.0	22 11.9	17 51.2	6 42.3	7 43.4	28 17.4
4 Th	6 51 29	12 53 44	13 56 26	19 51 53	13 14.4	21 45.1	0♊39.7	28 21.4	1 09.4	22 14.6	17 52.6	6 45.8	7 44.5	28 16.6
5 F	6 55 26	13 50 57	25 48 03	1♎45 28	13 11.7	23 01.6	1 46.6	29 04.1	1 34.0	22 17.6	17 54.1	6 49.2	7 45.7	28 15.7
6 Sa	6 59 23	14 48 09	7♎44 47	13 46 37	13D 10.8	24 22.2	2 53.6	29 46.7	1 58.6	22 20.7	17 55.7	6 52.7	7 46.8	28 14.8
7 Su	7 03 19	15 45 21	19 51 36	26 00 24	13 11.2	25 46.5	4 00.8	0♊29.2	2 23.3	22 24.0	17 57.4	6 56.2	7 47.9	28 14.0
8 M	7 07 16	16 42 33	2♏13 39	8♏31 56	13R 11.8	27 14.7	5 08.0	1 11.7	2 48.0	22 27.4	17 59.2	6 59.7	7 49.0	28 13.1
9 Tu	7 11 12	17 39 45	14 55 49	21 25 50	13 11.6	28 46.7	6 15.4	1 54.1	3 12.8	22 31.0	18 01.0	7 03.2	7 50.1	28 12.1
10 W	7 15 09	18 36 57	28 02 21	4♐45 41	13 09.7	0♋22.3	7 22.9	2 36.4	3 37.7	22 34.8	18 03.0	7 06.8	7 51.1	28 11.2
11 Th	7 19 05	19 34 09	11♐35 59	18 33 15	13 05.5	2 01.5	8 30.6	3 18.7	4 02.6	22 38.8	18 05.1	7 10.4	7 52.1	28 10.3
12 F	7 23 02	20 31 21	25 37 19	2♑47 47	12 58.9	3 44.1	9 38.3	4 00.9	4 27.6	22 42.9	18 07.2	7 13.9	7 53.0	28 09.3
13 Sa	7 26 58	21 28 33	10♑04 05	17 25 27	12 50.3	5 30.1	10 46.2	4 43.0	4 52.7	22 47.1	18 09.5	7 17.5	7 54.0	28 08.3
14 Su	7 30 55	22 25 46	24 50 57	2♒19 28	12 40.5	7 19.3	11 54.2	5 25.1	5 17.8	22 51.6	18 11.8	7 21.1	7 54.8	28 07.3
15 M	7 34 52	23 22 58	9♒49 50	17 20 51	12 30.6	9 11.5	13 02.4	6 07.0	5 43.0	22 56.1	18 14.3	7 24.7	7 55.7	28 06.3
16 Tu	7 38 48	24 20 11	24 51 16	2♓19 57	12 21.9	11 06.4	14 10.6	6 49.0	6 08.2	23 00.9	18 16.8	7 28.3	7 56.6	28 05.3
17 W	7 42 45	25 17 25	9♓45 53	17 08 09	12 15.2	13 04.0	15 19.0	7 30.8	6 33.5	23 05.7	18 19.4	7 32.0	7 57.4	28 04.2
18 Th	7 46 41	26 14 39	24 26 03	1♈39 03	12 10.9	15 03.8	16 27.4	8 12.5	6 58.9	23 10.8	18 22.1	7 35.6	7 58.1	28 03.2
19 F	7 50 38	27 11 54	8♈46 49	15 49 08	12D 09.0	17 05.7	17 36.0	8 54.2	7 24.3	23 15.9	18 24.9	7 39.3	7 58.9	28 02.1
20 Sa	7 54 34	28 09 10	22 46 01	29 37 30	12R 08.6	19 09.2	18 44.7	9 35.8	7 49.8	23 21.3	18 27.8	7 42.9	7 59.6	28 01.0
21 Su	7 58 31	29 06 26	6♉23 49	13♉05 12	12 08.7	21 14.2	19 53.5	10 17.4	8 15.3	23 26.8	18 30.8	7 46.6	8 00.3	27 59.9
22 M	8 02 27	0♌03 43	19 41 57	26 14 25	12 08.1	23 20.2	21 02.4	10 58.9	8 40.9	23 32.4	18 33.9	7 50.3	8 00.9	27 58.8
23 Tu	8 06 24	1 01 02	2♊42 56	9♊07 48	12 05.7	25 27.0	22 11.4	11 40.2	9 06.5	23 38.2	18 37.0	7 53.9	8 01.5	27 57.6
24 W	8 10 21	1 58 21	15 29 22	21 47 53	12 00.7	27 34.3	23 20.5	12 21.6	9 32.2	23 44.1	18 40.3	7 57.6	8 02.1	27 56.5
25 Th	8 14 17	2 55 41	28 03 38	4♋16 50	11 52.9	29 41.7	24 29.8	13 02.8	9 58.0	23 50.2	18 43.6	8 01.3	8 02.7	27 55.3
26 F	8 18 14	3 53 01	10♋27 39	16 36 17	11 42.3	1♌48.9	25 39.1	13 43.9	10 23.8	23 56.4	18 47.0	8 05.0	8 03.2	27 54.2
27 Sa	8 22 10	4 50 22	22 42 51	28 47 29	11 29.7	3 55.8	26 48.5	14 25.0	10 49.6	24 02.7	18 50.5	8 08.7	8 03.7	27 53.0
28 Su	8 26 07	5 47 44	4♌50 19	10♌51 28	11 16.0	6 02.1	27 58.0	15 06.0	11 15.5	24 09.2	18 54.1	8 12.4	8 04.1	27 51.8
29 M	8 30 03	6 45 07	16 51 04	22 49 16	11 02.4	8 07.6	29 07.6	15 46.9	11 41.5	24 15.9	18 57.8	8 16.1	8 04.5	27 50.6
30 Tu	8 34 00	7 42 30	28 46 15	4♍42 15	10 49.9	10 12.2	0♋17.2	16 27.7	12 07.5	24 22.6	19 01.5	8 19.8	8 04.9	27 49.4
31 W	8 37 56	8 39 54	10♍37 30	16 32 17	10 39.6	12 15.6	1 27.0	17 08.5	12 33.5	24 29.5	19 05.3	8 23.5	8 05.3	27 48.2

August 2041 — LONGITUDE

Day	Sid.Time	☉	0 hr ☽	Noon ☽	True ☊	☿	♀	♂	⚳	♃	♄	♅	♆	♇
1 Th	8 41 53	9♌37 19	22♍26 59	28♍21 58	10♉31.9	14♌17.8	2♋36.8	17♊49.1	12♍59.6	24♎36.6	19♎09.2	8♌27.2	8♉05.6	27♒47.0
2 F	8 45 50	10 34 44	4♎17 41	10♎14 38	10R 27.0	16 18.7	3 46.8	18 29.7	13 25.7	24 43.7	19 13.2	8 30.9	8 05.9	27R 45.7
3 Sa	8 49 46	11 32 10	16 13 20	22 14 22	10 24.6	18 18.1	4 56.8	19 10.2	13 51.8	24 51.0	19 17.3	8 34.6	8 06.1	27 44.5
4 Su	8 53 43	12 29 37	28 18 20	4♏25 52	10 23.9	20 16.2	6 06.9	19 50.6	14 18.0	24 58.4	19 21.5	8 38.3	8 06.4	27 43.2
5 M	8 57 39	13 27 04	10♏37 38	16 54 15	10 23.8	22 12.7	7 17.1	20 30.9	14 44.3	25 06.0	19 25.7	8 42.0	8 06.6	27 42.0
6 Tu	9 01 36	14 24 32	23 16 21	29 44 31	10 23.3	24 07.7	8 27.4	21 11.2	15 10.5	25 13.7	19 30.0	8 45.7	8 06.7	27 40.7
7 W	9 05 32	15 22 01	6♐19 18	13♐01 07	10 21.2	26 01.2	9 37.7	21 51.3	15 36.9	25 21.5	19 34.4	8 49.4	8 06.8	27 39.4
8 Th	9 09 29	16 19 31	19 50 18	26 47 00	10 16.9	27 53.1	10 48.2	22 31.4	16 03.2	25 29.4	19 38.8	8 53.1	8 06.9	27 38.2
9 F	9 13 25	17 17 01	3♑51 14	11♑02 46	10 10.1	29 43.5	11 58.7	23 11.3	16 29.6	25 37.4	19 43.4	8 56.8	8 07.0	27 36.9
10 Sa	9 17 22	18 14 33	18 21 10	25 45 45	10 01.0	1♍32.4	13 09.3	23 51.2	16 56.0	25 45.6	19 48.0	9 00.4	8R 07.0	27 35.6
11 Su	9 21 19	19 12 05	3♒15 38	10♒49 41	9 50.6	3 19.7	14 20.0	24 31.0	17 22.5	25 53.8	19 52.6	9 04.1	8 07.0	27 34.3
12 M	9 25 15	20 09 38	18 26 39	26 05 08	9 40.0	5 05.4	15 30.8	25 10.7	17 49.0	26 02.2	19 57.4	9 07.7	8 07.0	27 33.0
13 Tu	9 29 12	21 07 13	3♓43 42	11♓20 57	9 30.5	6 49.7	16 41.6	25 50.4	18 15.5	26 10.7	20 02.2	9 11.4	8 06.9	27 31.7
14 W	9 33 08	22 04 49	18 55 33	26 26 20	9 23.0	8 32.4	17 52.6	26 29.9	18 42.0	26 19.3	20 07.1	9 15.0	8 06.8	27 30.4
15 Th	9 37 05	23 02 26	3♈52 18	11♈12 41	9 18.2	10 13.7	19 03.6	27 09.3	19 08.6	26 28.1	20 12.0	9 18.7	8 06.6	27 29.1
16 F	9 41 01	24 00 04	18 26 54	25 34 37	9D 15.9	11 53.5	20 14.7	27 48.7	19 35.2	26 36.9	20 17.1	9 22.3	8 06.5	27 27.8
17 Sa	9 44 58	24 57 45	2♉35 41	9♉30 08	9 15.3	13 31.8	21 25.9	28 28.0	20 01.9	26 45.8	20 22.1	9 25.9	8 06.3	27 26.5
18 Su	9 48 54	25 55 26	16 18 06	22 59 54	9R 15.5	15 08.7	22 37.2	29 07.2	20 28.5	26 54.9	20 27.3	9 29.5	8 06.0	27 25.2
19 M	9 52 51	26 53 10	29 35 53	6♊06 28	9 15.2	16 44.1	23 48.5	29 46.3	20 55.3	27 04.1	20 32.5	9 33.1	8 05.8	27 23.9
20 Tu	9 56 48	27 50 55	12♊32 07	18 53 17	9 13.4	18 18.0	24 59.9	0♋25.3	21 22.0	27 13.3	20 37.8	9 36.6	8 05.5	27 22.6
21 W	10 00 44	28 48 42	25 10 27	1♋24 04	9 09.2	19 50.6	26 11.4	1 04.2	21 48.8	27 22.7	20 43.1	9 40.2	8 05.1	27 21.3
22 Th	10 04 41	29 46 31	7♋34 33	13 42 18	9 02.4	21 21.6	27 23.0	1 43.0	22 15.6	27 32.1	20 48.6	9 43.7	8 04.8	27 19.9
23 F	10 08 37	0♍44 21	19 47 40	25 50 59	8 53.1	22 51.2	28 34.7	2 21.7	22 42.4	27 41.7	20 54.0	9 47.3	8 04.4	27 18.6
24 Sa	10 12 34	1 42 12	1♌52 32	7♌52 34	8 41.8	24 19.4	29 46.4	3 00.3	23 09.2	27 51.4	20 59.6	9 50.8	8 04.0	27 17.3
25 Su	10 16 30	2 40 05	13 51 19	19 49 00	8 29.5	25 46.1	0♌58.2	3 38.8	23 36.1	28 01.1	21 05.1	9 54.3	8 03.5	27 16.0
26 M	10 20 27	3 38 00	25 45 47	1♍41 51	8 17.3	27 11.3	2 10.1	4 17.2	24 03.0	28 11.0	21 10.8	9 57.7	8 03.0	27 14.7
27 Tu	10 24 23	4 35 56	7♍37 24	13 32 37	8 06.1	28 34.9	3 22.0	4 55.5	24 29.9	28 21.0	21 16.5	10 01.2	8 02.5	27 13.4
28 W	10 28 20	5 33 54	19 27 42	25 22 52	7 56.8	29 57.1	4 34.0	5 33.7	24 56.8	28 31.0	21 22.3	10 04.6	8 01.9	27 12.1
29 Th	10 32 17	6 31 53	1♎18 24	7♎14 33	7 49.9	1♎17.6	5 46.1	6 11.8	25 23.8	28 41.1	21 28.1	10 08.1	8 01.3	27 10.8
30 F	10 36 13	7 29 53	13 11 40	19 10 08	7 45.7	2 36.6	6 58.2	6 49.8	25 50.8	28 51.4	21 34.0	10 11.5	8 00.7	27 09.5
31 Sa	10 40 10	8 27 55	25 10 19	1♏12 42	7D 43.9	3 53.8	8 10.4	7 27.7	26 17.8	29 01.7	21 39.9	10 14.8	8 00.1	27 08.3

Astro Data	Dy Hr Mn
☽0S	5 22:27
☽0N	18 20:37
♅□♆	25 22:11
☽0S	2 4:28
♆ R	10 19:55
☽0N	15 4:02
♃△♇	21 8:49
☿0S	27 11:39
☽0S	29 9:50

Planet Ingress		Dy Hr Mn
⚳	♍	1 15:39
♀	♊	3 21:43
♂	♊	6 19:30
☿	♋	10 6:29
☉	♌	22 10:26
☿	♌	25 15:27
♀	♋	30 6:04
☿	♍	9 15:37
♂	♋	19 20:27
☉	♍	22 17:36
♀	♌	24 16:33
☿	♎	28 12:52

Last Aspect Dy Hr Mn			☽ Ingress	Dy Hr Mn
2 17:06	♀	□	♍	2 19:46
5 6:15	♂	△	♎	5 8:28
7 16:18	♇	△	♏	7 19:43
10 0:17	♇	□	♐	10 3:31
12 4:16	♇	⚹	♑	12 7:21
13 20:43	♃	□	♒	14 8:17
16 5:11	♇	☌	♓	16 8:15
18 2:22	☉	△	♈	18 9:15
20 9:13	☉	□	♉	20 12:40
22 15:12	♇	□	♊	22 18:57
24 23:45	♇	△	♋	25 3:44
27 2:32	♃	□	♌	27 14:24
30 2:06	♀	⚹	♍	30 2:29

Last Aspect Dy Hr Mn			☽ Ingress	Dy Hr Mn
31 13:18	♂	□	♎	1 15:19
3 22:52	♇	△	♏	4 3:20
6 8:12	♇	□	♐	6 12:28
8 14:10	☿	△	♑	8 17:29
10 12:00	♃	□	♒	10 18:48
12 14:18	♇	☌	♓	12 18:09
14 12:06	♂	□	♈	14 17:44
16 15:59	♂	⚹	♉	16 19:32
18 20:00	♇	□	♊	19 0:44
21 6:35	☉	⚹	♋	21 9:17
23 18:01	♀	☌	♌	23 20:16
26 4:47	♃	⚹	♍	26 8:34
27 0:51	♆	△	♎	28 21:21
31 7:36	♃	☌	♏	31 9:36

☽ Phases & Eclipses Dy Hr Mn		
6 14:12	☽	14♎53
13 19:01	○	21♑45
20 9:13	☾	28♈03
28 1:02	●	5♌22
5 4:52	☽	13♏10
12 2:04	○	19♒46
18 17:43	☾	26♉09
26 16:16	●	3♍48

Astro Data

1 July 2041
Julian Day # 51682
SVP 4♓40'59"
GC 27♐25.1 ⚵ 19♋03.8
Eris 29♈24.4 ⚶ 19♌47.4
⚷ 23♋41.5 ⚴ 24♉40.4
☽ Mean ☊ 12♉25.2

1 August 2041
Julian Day # 51713
SVP 4♓40'54"
GC 27♐25.2 ⚵ 7♌02.7
Eris 29♈27.2R ⚶ 2♍49.5
⚷ 27♋08.6 ⚴ 6♊17.0
☽ Mean ☊ 10♉46.7

LONGITUDE — September 2041

Day	Sid.Time	☉	0 hr ☽	Noon ☽	True ☊	☿	♀	♂	⚳	♃	♄	♅	♆	♇
1 Su	10 44 06	9♍25 59	7♏17 46	13♏26 01	7♉43.8	5♎09.4	9♌22.7	8♋05.5	26♍44.8	29♎12.1	21♎45.9	10♌18.2	7♉59.4	27♒07.0
2 M	10 48 03	10 24 04	19 38 01	25 54 19	7 44.6	6 23.2	10 35.0	8 43.2	27 11.9	29 22.6	21 51.9	10 21.5	7R58.7	27R05.7
3 Tu	10 51 59	11 22 10	2♐15 29	8♐42 05	7R45.2	7 35.1	11 47.4	9 20.7	27 38.9	29 33.1	21 58.0	10 24.9	7 57.9	27 04.4
4 W	10 55 56	12 20 18	15 14 38	21 53 35	7 44.8	8 45.0	12 59.9	9 58.2	28 06.0	29 43.8	22 04.1	10 28.1	7 57.2	27 03.2
5 Th	10 59 52	13 18 27	28 39 20	5♑32 10	7 42.6	9 53.0	14 12.4	10 35.5	28 33.1	29 54.5	22 10.3	10 31.4	7 56.4	27 01.9
6 F	11 03 49	14 16 37	12♑32 11	19 39 22	7 38.4	10 58.8	15 25.0	11 12.8	29 00.2	0♏05.3	22 16.5	10 34.7	7 55.6	27 00.7
7 Sa	11 07 46	15 14 49	26 53 29	4♒14 05	7 32.3	12 02.4	16 37.7	11 49.9	29 27.3	0 16.2	22 22.8	10 37.9	7 54.7	26 59.5
8 Su	11 11 42	16 13 03	11♒40 31	19 11 52	7 25.0	13 03.6	17 50.4	12 26.9	29 54.4	0 27.2	22 29.1	10 41.1	7 53.8	26 58.2
9 M	11 15 39	17 11 18	26 47 04	4♓24 52	7 17.3	14 02.2	19 03.2	13 03.8	0♎21.6	0 38.2	22 35.5	10 44.2	7 52.9	26 57.0
10 Tu	11 19 35	18 09 35	12♓03 55	19 42 50	7 10.4	14 58.2	20 16.0	13 40.6	0 48.7	0 49.3	22 41.9	10 47.4	7 52.0	26 55.8
11 W	11 23 32	19 07 53	27 20 12	4♈54 44	7 05.1	15 51.3	21 28.9	14 17.2	1 15.9	1 00.5	22 48.3	10 50.5	7 51.0	26 54.6
12 Th	11 27 28	20 06 14	12♈25 14	19 50 42	7 01.9	16 41.3	22 41.9	14 53.8	1 43.0	1 11.8	22 54.8	10 53.5	7 50.0	26 53.4
13 F	11 31 25	21 04 36	27 10 20	4♉23 33	7D00.7	17 28.1	23 54.9	15 30.2	2 10.2	1 23.1	23 01.3	10 56.6	7 49.0	26 52.2
14 Sa	11 35 21	22 03 01	11♉29 56	18 29 20	7 01.1	18 11.3	25 08.0	16 06.5	2 37.4	1 34.5	23 07.9	10 59.6	7 48.0	26 51.1
15 Su	11 39 18	23 01 27	25 21 44	2♊07 15	7 02.3	18 50.8	26 21.2	16 42.7	3 04.6	1 45.9	23 14.5	11 02.6	7 46.9	26 49.9
16 M	11 43 15	23 59 56	8♊46 10	15 18 52	7R03.5	19 26.2	27 34.4	17 18.8	3 31.9	1 57.5	23 21.2	11 05.6	7 45.8	26 48.8
17 Tu	11 47 11	24 58 27	21 45 46	28 07 21	7 03.8	19 57.2	28 47.7	17 54.8	3 59.1	2 09.1	23 27.8	11 08.5	7 44.7	26 47.6
18 W	11 51 08	25 57 01	4♋24 09	10♋36 42	7 02.6	20 23.6	0♍01.0	18 30.6	4 26.3	2 20.7	23 34.6	11 11.4	7 43.6	26 46.5
19 Th	11 55 04	26 55 36	16 45 30	22 51 06	6 59.6	20 44.9	1 14.4	19 06.3	4 53.6	2 32.4	23 41.3	11 14.2	7 42.4	26 45.4
20 F	11 59 01	27 54 14	28 53 59	4♌54 37	6 54.9	21 00.7	2 27.8	19 41.9	5 20.8	2 44.2	23 48.1	11 17.1	7 41.2	26 44.3
21 Sa	12 02 57	28 52 54	10♌53 27	16 50 53	6 48.9	21 10.8	3 41.4	20 17.3	5 48.1	2 56.0	23 54.9	11 19.9	7 40.0	26 43.3
22 Su	12 06 54	29 51 35	22 47 18	28 43 01	6 42.1	21R14.8	4 54.9	20 52.6	6 15.4	3 07.9	24 01.8	11 22.6	7 38.8	26 42.2
23 M	12 10 50	0♎50 19	4♍38 22	10♍33 37	6 35.2	21 12.2	6 08.5	21 27.8	6 42.6	3 19.9	24 08.7	11 25.3	7 37.5	26 41.2
24 Tu	12 14 47	1 49 05	16 29 02	22 24 51	6 28.9	21 02.8	7 22.2	22 02.8	7 09.9	3 31.9	24 15.6	11 28.0	7 36.2	26 40.1
25 W	12 18 44	2 47 53	28 21 18	4♎18 34	6 23.9	20 46.3	8 35.9	22 37.7	7 37.2	3 44.0	24 22.5	11 30.7	7 34.9	26 39.1
26 Th	12 22 40	3 46 43	10♎16 55	16 16 32	6 20.4	20 22.4	9 49.7	23 12.4	8 04.5	3 56.1	24 29.5	11 33.3	7 33.6	26 38.1
27 F	12 26 37	4 45 35	22 17 39	28 20 32	6D18.6	19 51.1	11 03.5	23 47.0	8 31.7	4 08.3	24 36.5	11 35.8	7 32.3	26 37.1
28 Sa	12 30 33	5 44 28	4♏25 26	10♏32 38	6 18.4	19 12.5	12 17.3	24 21.5	8 59.0	4 20.5	24 43.5	11 38.4	7 30.9	26 36.2
29 Su	12 34 30	6 43 24	16 42 28	22 55 15	6 19.3	18 26.8	13 31.3	24 55.8	9 26.3	4 32.7	24 50.5	11 40.9	7 29.5	26 35.2
30 M	12 38 26	7 42 22	29 11 21	5♐31 07	6 20.9	17 34.4	14 45.2	25 29.9	9 53.6	4 45.1	24 57.6	11 43.3	7 28.1	26 34.3

LONGITUDE — October 2041

Day	Sid.Time	☉	0 hr ☽	Noon ☽	True ☊	☿	♀	♂	⚳	♃	♄	♅	♆	♇
1 Tu	12 42 23	8♎41 21	11♐54 58	18♐23 16	6♉22.6	16♎36.1	15♍59.2	26♋03.9	10♎20.9	4♏57.4	25♎04.7	11♌45.7	7♉26.7	26♒33.4
2 W	12 46 19	9 40 22	24 56 22	1♑34 39	6R23.6	15R32.9	17 13.2	26 37.8	10 48.1	5 09.8	25 11.8	11 48.1	7R25.3	26R32.5
3 Th	12 50 16	10 39 25	8♑18 23	15 07 49	6 23.8	14 26.1	18 27.3	27 11.4	11 15.4	5 22.3	25 18.9	11 50.4	7 23.8	26 31.6
4 F	12 54 12	11 38 29	22 03 05	29 04 14	6 22.8	13 17.1	19 41.5	27 45.0	11 42.7	5 34.8	25 26.0	11 52.7	7 22.3	26 30.8
5 Sa	12 58 09	12 37 36	6♒11 10	13♒23 39	6 20.8	12 07.7	20 55.6	28 18.3	12 09.9	5 47.3	25 33.2	11 55.0	7 20.9	26 29.9
6 Su	13 02 06	13 36 44	20 41 17	28 03 30	6 18.1	10 59.7	22 09.8	28 51.5	12 37.2	5 59.9	25 40.4	11 57.2	7 19.4	26 29.1
7 M	13 06 02	14 35 53	5♓29 34	12♓58 37	6 15.1	9 55.1	23 24.1	29 24.6	13 04.4	6 12.5	25 47.6	11 59.3	7 17.8	26 28.3
8 Tu	13 09 59	15 35 05	20 29 39	28 01 34	6 12.4	8 55.7	24 38.4	29 57.4	13 31.7	6 25.1	25 54.8	12 01.5	7 16.3	26 27.5
9 W	13 13 55	16 34 18	5♈33 12	13♈03 27	6 10.4	8 03.1	25 52.7	0♌30.1	13 58.9	6 37.8	26 02.0	12 03.5	7 14.8	26 26.8
10 Th	13 17 52	17 33 34	20 31 10	27 55 20	6D09.3	7 18.8	27 07.0	1 02.7	14 26.1	6 50.5	26 09.2	12 05.5	7 13.2	26 26.0
11 F	13 21 48	18 32 51	5♉15 02	12♉29 31	6 09.3	6 44.0	28 21.4	1 35.0	14 53.3	7 03.2	26 16.4	12 07.5	7 11.6	26 25.3
12 Sa	13 25 45	19 32 11	19 38 11	26 40 35	6 10.0	6 19.5	29 35.9	2 07.2	15 20.5	7 16.0	26 23.7	12 09.5	7 10.1	26 24.6
13 Su	13 29 41	20 31 33	3♊36 28	10♊25 42	6 11.1	6D05.9	0♎50.4	2 39.2	15 47.7	7 28.8	26 30.9	12 11.3	7 08.5	26 24.0
14 M	13 33 38	21 30 58	17 08 22	23 44 36	6 12.4	6 03.2	2 04.9	3 11.0	16 14.9	7 41.7	26 38.2	12 13.2	7 06.9	26 23.3
15 Tu	13 37 35	22 30 25	0♋14 41	6♋39 00	6 13.4	6 11.4	3 19.5	3 42.7	16 42.1	7 54.7	26 45.5	12 15.0	7 05.3	26 22.7
16 W	13 41 31	23 29 54	12 57 59	19 12 07	6R13.9	6 30.2	4 34.1	4 14.1	17 09.2	8 07.4	26 52.8	12 16.7	7 03.6	26 22.1
17 Th	13 45 28	24 29 25	25 21 56	1♌28 00	6 13.9	6 59.0	5 48.7	4 45.4	17 36.4	8 20.4	27 00.0	12 18.4	7 02.0	26 21.5
18 F	13 49 24	25 28 58	7♌30 53	13 31 07	6 13.2	7 37.2	7 03.4	5 16.4	18 03.5	8 33.3	27 07.3	12 20.1	7 00.4	26 21.0
19 Sa	13 53 21	26 28 34	19 29 18	25 25 56	6 12.2	8 24.0	8 18.1	5 47.3	18 30.7	8 46.3	27 14.6	12 21.7	6 58.7	26 20.4
20 Su	13 57 17	27 28 12	1♍21 34	7♍16 41	6 11.0	9 18.6	9 32.9	6 17.9	18 57.8	8 59.3	27 21.9	12 23.2	6 57.1	26 19.9
21 M	14 01 14	28 27 52	13 11 44	19 07 10	6 09.8	10 20.2	10 47.6	6 48.4	19 24.9	9 12.3	27 29.2	12 24.7	6 55.4	26 19.4
22 Tu	14 05 10	29 27 35	25 03 22	1♎00 43	6 08.8	11 28.0	12 02.4	7 18.6	19 51.9	9 25.3	27 36.5	12 26.2	6 53.7	26 19.0
23 W	14 09 07	0♏27 19	6♎59 30	13 00 03	6 08.1	12 41.2	13 17.3	7 48.6	20 19.0	9 38.4	27 43.8	12 27.6	6 52.0	26 18.5
24 Th	14 13 04	1 27 05	19 02 36	25 07 23	6D07.7	13 59.1	14 32.1	8 18.4	20 46.0	9 51.4	27 51.1	12 28.9	6 50.4	26 18.1
25 F	14 17 00	2 26 54	1♏14 36	7♏24 26	6 07.6	15 21.0	15 47.0	8 47.9	21 13.1	10 04.5	27 58.3	12 30.2	6 48.7	26 17.7
26 Sa	14 20 57	3 26 44	13 37 02	19 52 32	6 07.7	16 46.2	17 01.9	9 17.2	21 40.1	10 17.6	28 05.6	12 31.4	6 47.0	26 17.4
27 Su	14 24 53	4 26 37	26 11 04	2♐32 45	6 07.8	18 14.3	18 16.9	9 46.3	22 07.0	10 30.7	28 12.9	12 32.6	6 45.3	26 17.0
28 M	14 28 50	5 26 31	8♐57 41	15 26 00	6R08.0	19 44.8	19 31.8	10 15.2	22 34.0	10 43.9	28 20.1	12 33.8	6 43.6	26 16.7
29 Tu	14 32 46	6 26 27	21 57 46	28 33 06	6 08.0	21 17.1	20 46.8	10 43.8	23 00.9	10 57.0	28 27.4	12 34.8	6 41.9	26 16.4
30 W	14 36 43	7 26 25	5♑12 06	11♑54 49	6 07.9	22 51.0	22 01.8	11 12.1	23 27.8	11 10.2	28 34.6	12 35.9	6 40.3	26 16.2
31 Th	14 40 39	8 26 24	18 41 20	25 31 41	6D07.8	24 26.1	23 16.9	11 40.2	23 54.7	11 23.3	28 41.9	12 36.8	6 38.6	26 15.9

Astro Data

	Dy Hr Mn
☽0N	11 13:55
☿R	22 14:44
☉0S	22 15:27
☽0S	25 15:33
☽0N	9 0:52
♃☍♆	12 2:02
♄△♇	12 14:53
☿D	14 5:50
⚳0S	15 2:48
♀0S	15 15:24
☽0S	22 22:16

Planet Ingress

	Dy Hr Mn
♃ ♏	6 0:12
⚳ ♎	8 16:56
♀ ♍	18 11:40
☉ ♎	22 15:26
♂ ♌	8 13:53
♀ ♎	12 19:46
☉ ♏	23 1:02

Last Aspect / ☽ Ingress

Last Aspect Dy Hr Mn		☽ Ingress Dy Hr Mn
2 14:15	♇ □	♐ 2 19:45
5 2:04	♃ ✶	♑ 5 2:22
6 16:24	♄ □	♒ 7 5:06
9 0:17	♇ ☌	♓ 9 5:04
10 9:24	☉ ☍	♈ 11 4:13
12 23:31	♇ ✶	♉ 13 4:41
15 2:36	♇ □	♊ 15 8:13
17 13:25	♀ ✶	♋ 17 15:34
19 20:47	☉ ✶	♌ 20 2:11
22 7:56	♇ ☍	♍ 22 14:36
24 11:13	♂ ✶	♎ 25 3:19
27 8:36	♇ △	♏ 27 15:17
29 19:01	♇ □	♐ 30 1:33

Last Aspect / ☽ Ingress

Last Aspect Dy Hr Mn		☽ Ingress Dy Hr Mn
2 2:55	♇ ✶	♑ 2 9:10
4 9:40	♂ ☍	♒ 4 13:35
6 9:27	♇ ☌	♓ 6 15:09
8 6:07	♀ ☍	♈ 8 15:09
10 9:35	♇ ✶	♉ 10 15:23
12 17:32	♀ △	♊ 12 17:44
14 17:22	♄ △	♋ 14 23:33
17 3:07	♄ □	♌ 17 9:06
19 15:42	♄ ✶	♍ 19 21:15
20 15:32	♃ ✶	♎ 22 9:58
24 17:25	♄ ☌	♏ 24 21:34
27 0:12	♇ □	♐ 27 7:13
29 11:50	♄ ✶	♑ 29 14:37
31 17:34	♄ □	♒ 31 19:47

☽ Phases & Eclipses

Dy Hr Mn	
3 17:19	☽ 11♐35
10 9:24	○ 18♓03
17 5:33	☾ 24♊43
25 8:41	● 2♎40
3 3:32	☽ 10♑19
9 18:03	○ 16♈49
16 21:05	☾ 23♋52
25 1:30	● 2♏01
25 1:34:56	A 06'07"

Astro Data

1 September 2041
Julian Day # 51744
SVP 4♓40'50"
GC 27♐25.3 ⚴ 24♌13.9
Eris 29♈20.2R ⚵ 15♍44.3
⚷ 0♌23.9 ⚶ 15♊43.0
☽ Mean ☊ 9♉08.2

1 October 2041
Julian Day # 51774
SVP 4♓40'47"
GC 27♐25.3 ⚴ 9♍50.7
Eris 29♈05.8R ⚵ 27♍52.0
⚷ 2♌53.5 ⚶ 21♊22.1
☽ Mean ☊ 7♉32.9

November 2041 — LONGITUDE

Day	Sid.Time	☉	0 hr ☽	Noon ☽	True ☊	☿	♀	♂	⚳	♃	♄	♅	♆	♇
1 F	14 44 36	9♏26 25	2♒25 52	9♒23 51	6♉07.7	26♎02.2	24♎31.9	12♌08.1	24♎21.6	11♏36.5	28♎49.1	12♌37.8	6♉36.9	26♒15.7
2 Sa	14 48 33	10 26 28	16 25 33	23 30 47	6 07.8	27 39.0	25 47.0	12 35.6	24 48.4	11 49.6	28 56.3	12 38.6	6R 35.2	26R 15.5
3 Su	14 52 29	11 26 32	0♓39 21	7♓50 55	6 08.2	29 16.4	27 02.1	13 03.0	25 15.2	12 02.8	29 03.5	12 39.4	6 33.5	26 15.4
4 M	14 56 26	12 26 37	15 05 07	22 21 26	6 08.7	0♏54.1	28 17.2	13 30.0	25 42.0	12 16.0	29 10.7	12 40.2	6 31.8	26 15.3
5 Tu	15 00 22	13 26 44	29 39 18	6♈58 06	6 09.3	2 32.0	29 32.3	13 56.8	26 08.7	12 29.1	29 17.8	12 40.9	6 30.2	26 15.1
6 W	15 04 19	14 26 52	14♈17 06	21 35 33	6 09.8	4 10.1	0♏47.4	14 23.3	26 35.4	12 42.3	29 24.9	12 41.6	6 28.5	26 15.1
7 Th	15 08 15	15 27 03	28 52 41	6♉07 43	6R 10.0	5 48.2	2 02.6	14 49.5	27 02.1	12 55.5	29 32.0	12 42.1	6 26.8	26 15.0
8 F	15 12 12	16 27 15	13♉19 54	20 28 31	6 09.8	7 26.3	3 17.8	15 15.4	27 28.7	13 08.6	29 39.1	12 42.7	6 25.2	26D 15.0
9 Sa	15 16 08	17 27 29	27 32 57	4♊32 40	6 08.9	9 04.2	4 33.0	15 41.0	27 55.3	13 21.8	29 46.2	12 43.2	6 23.5	26 15.0
10 Su	15 20 05	18 27 45	11♊27 13	18 16 18	6 07.5	10 42.0	5 48.2	16 06.3	28 21.9	13 34.9	29 53.3	12 43.6	6 21.9	26 15.0
11 M	15 24 02	19 28 02	24 59 43	1♋37 22	6 05.7	12 19.7	7 03.4	16 31.3	28 48.4	13 48.1	0♏00.3	12 44.0	6 20.2	26 15.1
12 Tu	15 27 58	20 28 22	8♋09 20	14 35 44	6 03.8	13 57.1	8 18.7	16 56.0	29 15.0	14 01.2	0 07.3	12 44.3	6 18.6	26 15.1
13 W	15 31 55	21 28 43	20 56 50	27 12 58	6 02.0	15 34.3	9 34.0	17 20.4	29 41.4	14 14.4	0 14.3	12 44.6	6 17.0	26 15.2
14 Th	15 35 51	22 29 07	3♌24 34	9♌32 05	6 00.7	17 11.2	10 49.2	17 44.4	0♏07.9	14 27.5	0 21.2	12 44.8	6 15.4	26 15.4
15 F	15 39 48	23 29 32	15 36 03	21 37 02	6D 00.2	18 47.9	12 04.5	18 08.2	0 34.3	14 40.6	0 28.2	12 44.9	6 13.8	26 15.5
16 Sa	15 43 44	24 29 59	27 35 37	3♍32 25	6 00.4	20 24.3	13 19.9	18 31.5	1 00.6	14 53.7	0 35.1	12 45.0	6 12.2	26 15.7
17 Su	15 47 41	25 30 28	9♍28 02	15 23 05	6 01.5	22 00.5	14 35.2	18 54.5	1 26.9	15 06.8	0 41.9	12R 45.1	6 10.6	26 15.9
18 M	15 51 37	26 30 58	21 18 10	27 13 52	6 03.0	23 36.5	15 50.5	19 17.2	1 53.2	15 19.9	0 48.7	12 45.1	6 09.1	26 16.2
19 Tu	15 55 34	27 31 31	3♎10 44	9♎09 18	6 04.7	25 12.2	17 05.9	19 39.4	2 19.5	15 32.9	0 55.5	12 45.0	6 07.5	26 16.4
20 W	15 59 31	28 32 05	15 10 03	21 13 26	6 06.2	26 47.6	18 21.3	20 01.3	2 45.7	15 46.0	1 02.3	12 44.9	6 06.0	26 16.7
21 Th	16 03 27	29 32 41	27 19 50	3♏29 35	6R 06.9	28 22.9	19 36.7	20 22.8	3 11.8	15 59.0	1 09.0	12 44.7	6 04.4	26 17.0
22 F	16 07 24	0♐33 18	9♏42 59	16 00 12	6 06.6	29 57.9	20 52.1	20 43.9	3 37.9	16 12.0	1 15.7	12 44.4	6 02.9	26 17.4
23 Sa	16 11 20	1 33 57	22 21 25	28 46 41	6 04.9	1♐32.8	22 07.5	21 04.6	4 04.0	16 24.9	1 22.4	12 44.1	6 01.4	26 17.7
24 Su	16 15 17	2 34 38	5♐16 00	11♐49 21	6 01.9	3 07.5	23 22.9	21 24.9	4 30.0	16 37.9	1 29.0	12 43.8	6 00.0	26 18.1
25 M	16 19 13	3 35 20	18 26 34	25 07 30	5 57.9	4 42.0	24 38.3	21 44.8	4 55.9	16 50.8	1 35.6	12 43.4	5 58.5	26 18.6
26 Tu	16 23 10	4 36 03	1♑51 56	8♑39 35	5 53.2	6 16.4	25 53.7	22 04.2	5 21.8	17 03.7	1 42.1	12 42.9	5 57.1	26 19.0
27 W	16 27 07	5 36 47	15 30 12	22 23 29	5 48.6	7 50.6	27 09.2	22 23.2	5 47.7	17 16.6	1 48.6	12 42.4	5 55.6	26 19.5
28 Th	16 31 03	6 37 33	29 19 07	6♒16 49	5 44.7	9 24.7	28 24.6	22 41.8	6 13.5	17 29.4	1 55.1	12 41.9	5 54.2	26 20.0
29 F	16 35 00	7 38 19	13♒16 19	20 17 19	5 42.0	10 58.7	29 40.1	22 59.9	6 39.2	17 42.2	2 01.5	12 41.2	5 52.9	26 20.5
30 Sa	16 38 56	8 39 06	27 19 36	4♓22 56	5D 40.8	12 32.6	0♐55.5	23 17.5	7 04.9	17 55.0	2 07.8	12 40.6	5 51.5	26 21.1

December 2041 — LONGITUDE

Day	Sid.Time	☉	0 hr ☽	Noon ☽	True ☊	☿	♀	♂	⚳	♃	♄	♅	♆	♇
1 Su	16 42 53	9♐39 54	11♓27 07	18♓31 55	5♉41.0	14♐06.4	2♐11.0	23♌34.6	7♏30.5	18♏07.8	2♏14.1	12♌39.8	5♉50.1	26♒21.7
2 M	16 46 49	10 40 43	25 37 10	2♈42 38	5 42.3	15 40.2	3 26.4	23 51.3	7 56.1	18 20.5	2 20.4	12R 39.1	5R 48.8	26 22.3
3 Tu	16 50 46	11 41 33	9♈48 06	16 53 19	5 43.8	17 13.9	4 41.9	24 07.5	8 21.6	18 33.1	2 26.6	12 38.2	5 47.5	26 22.9
4 W	16 54 42	12 42 23	23 58 01	1♉01 51	5R 44.8	18 47.6	5 57.4	24 23.2	8 47.0	18 45.7	2 32.7	12 37.3	5 46.2	26 23.6
5 Th	16 58 39	13 43 15	8♉04 30	15 05 33	5 44.5	20 21.2	7 12.8	24 38.3	9 12.4	18 58.3	2 38.8	12 36.4	5 45.0	26 24.2
6 F	17 02 36	14 44 07	22 04 38	29 01 18	5 42.4	21 54.9	8 28.3	24 53.0	9 37.7	19 10.9	2 44.9	12 35.4	5 43.7	26 24.9
7 Sa	17 06 32	15 45 01	5♊55 08	12♊45 43	5 38.2	23 28.5	9 43.8	25 07.1	10 03.0	19 23.4	2 50.9	12 34.4	5 42.5	26 25.7
8 Su	17 10 29	16 45 55	19 32 39	26 15 37	5 32.1	25 02.1	10 59.3	25 20.7	10 28.2	19 35.8	2 56.8	12 33.3	5 41.3	26 26.4
9 M	17 14 25	17 46 51	2♋54 20	9♋28 34	5 24.7	26 35.7	12 14.8	25 33.7	10 53.3	19 48.3	3 02.7	12 32.2	5 40.2	26 27.2
10 Tu	17 18 22	18 47 47	15 58 13	22 23 14	5 16.7	28 09.3	13 30.3	25 46.1	11 18.4	20 00.6	3 08.6	12 31.0	5 39.1	26 28.0
11 W	17 22 18	19 48 45	28 43 40	4♌59 40	5 09.0	29 42.9	14 45.7	25 58.0	11 43.4	20 13.0	3 14.3	12 29.7	5 37.9	26 28.9
12 Th	17 26 15	20 49 44	11♌11 28	17 19 22	5 02.5	1♑16.4	16 01.2	26 09.3	12 08.3	20 25.2	3 20.1	12 28.5	5 36.9	26 29.7
13 F	17 30 11	21 50 43	23 23 46	29 25 08	4 57.6	2 49.9	17 16.7	26 19.9	12 33.1	20 37.5	3 25.7	12 27.1	5 35.8	26 30.6
14 Sa	17 34 08	22 51 44	5♍23 57	11♍20 49	4 54.8	4 23.4	18 32.3	26 30.0	12 57.9	20 49.6	3 31.3	12 25.7	5 34.8	26 31.5
15 Su	17 38 05	23 52 45	17 16 20	23 11 07	4D 53.8	5 56.8	19 47.8	26 39.4	13 22.6	21 01.7	3 36.8	12 24.3	5 33.8	26 32.4
16 M	17 42 01	24 53 48	29 05 49	5♎01 08	4 54.3	7 30.0	21 03.3	26 48.2	13 47.2	21 13.8	3 42.3	12 22.8	5 32.8	26 33.3
17 Tu	17 45 58	25 54 51	10♎57 43	16 56 14	4 55.6	9 03.1	22 18.8	26 56.3	14 11.8	21 25.8	3 47.7	12 21.3	5 31.8	26 34.3
18 W	17 49 54	26 55 56	22 57 19	29 01 35	4R 56.6	10 35.9	23 34.3	27 03.8	14 36.2	21 37.7	3 53.0	12 19.7	5 30.9	26 35.3
19 Th	17 53 51	27 57 01	5♏09 36	11♏21 54	4 56.6	12 08.4	24 49.9	27 10.6	15 00.6	21 49.6	3 58.3	12 18.1	5 30.0	26 36.3
20 F	17 57 47	28 58 07	17 38 53	24 00 57	4 54.6	13 40.6	26 05.4	27 16.7	15 24.9	22 01.5	4 03.5	12 16.5	5 29.1	26 37.3
21 Sa	18 01 44	29 59 14	0♐28 21	7♐01 15	4 50.3	15 12.2	27 20.9	27 22.1	15 49.2	22 13.2	4 08.6	12 14.8	5 28.3	26 38.4
22 Su	18 05 40	1♑00 22	13 39 40	20 23 31	4 43.4	16 43.3	28 36.4	27 26.8	16 13.3	22 24.9	4 13.7	12 13.0	5 27.5	26 39.5
23 M	18 09 37	2 01 30	27 12 35	4♑06 31	4 34.5	18 13.5	29 52.0	27 30.7	16 37.3	22 36.5	4 18.7	12 11.3	5 26.7	26 40.6
24 Tu	18 13 34	3 02 38	11♑04 51	18 07 01	4 24.5	19 42.9	1♑07.5	27 33.9	17 01.3	22 48.1	4 23.6	12 09.4	5 26.0	26 41.7
25 W	18 17 30	4 03 47	25 12 22	2♒20 12	4 14.3	21 11.1	2 23.0	27 36.4	17 25.2	22 59.6	4 28.4	12 07.6	5 25.3	26 42.9
26 Th	18 21 27	5 04 56	9♒29 48	16 40 26	4 05.2	22 38.0	3 38.6	27 38.1	17 48.9	23 11.0	4 33.2	12 05.7	5 24.6	26 44.0
27 F	18 25 23	6 06 05	23 51 27	1♓02 12	3 58.2	24 03.2	4 54.1	27R 39.1	18 12.6	23 22.3	4 37.9	12 03.7	5 24.0	26 45.2
28 Sa	18 29 20	7 07 14	8♓12 10	15 20 53	3 53.7	25 26.4	6 09.6	27 39.2	18 36.2	23 33.6	4 42.5	12 01.8	5 23.3	26 46.4
29 Su	18 33 16	8 08 23	22 27 59	29 33 14	3D 51.6	26 47.2	7 25.1	27 38.7	18 59.6	23 44.8	4 47.0	11 59.7	5 22.8	26 47.6
30 M	18 37 13	9 09 31	6♈36 27	13♈37 31	3 51.4	28 05.3	8 40.6	27 37.3	19 23.0	23 55.9	4 51.4	11 57.7	5 22.2	26 48.9
31 Tu	18 41 09	10 10 40	20 36 22	27 33 01	3R 51.9	29 20.1	9 56.1	27 35.1	19 46.3	24 06.9	4 55.8	11 55.6	5 21.7	26 50.1

Astro Data		Planet Ingress		Last Aspect	☽ Ingress	Last Aspect	☽ Ingress	☽ Phases & Eclipses	
	Dy Hr Mn		Dy Hr Mn	Dy Hr Mn	Dy Hr Mn	Dy Hr Mn	Dy Hr Mn	Dy Hr Mn	
☽0N	5 10:37	☿ ♏	3 22:43	2 21:12 ♄ △	♓ 2 22:54	1 11:18 ♃ △	♈ 2 7:25	1 12:05	☽ 9♒27
♃□♅	6 10:35	♀ ♏	5 20:51	3 19:05 ♃ △	♈ 5 0:34	4 4:07 ♇ ⚹	♉ 4 10:15	8 4:43	○ 16♉09
♇ D	9 0:10	♄ ♏	11 10:58	7 1:00 ♄ ☍	♉ 7 1:51	6 7:29 ♇ □	♊ 6 13:42	8 4:34	☍ P 0.170
♅ R	17 17:17	⚳ ♏	14 4:51	8 21:47 ♇ □	♊ 9 4:11	8 12:19 ♇ △	♋ 8 18:44	15 16:06	☾ 23♌40
☽0S	19 5:51	☉ ♐	21 22:49	11 9:02 ♄ △	♋ 11 9:03	10 7:28 ♃ △	♌ 11 2:25	23 17:36	● 1♐48
		☿ ♐	22 12:31	13 0:04 ☉ △	♌ 13 17:23	13 6:11 ♇ ☍	♍ 13 13:10	30 19:49	☽ 8♓59
☽0N	2 17:32	♀ ♐	29 18:20	15 21:19 ♇ ☍	♍ 16 4:51	15 13:33 ☉ □	♎ 16 1:50		
☽0S	16 13:35			18 10:25 ☉ ⚹	♎ 18 17:36	18 8:06 ♂ ⚹	♏ 18 13:55	7 17:42	○ 15♊59
♂ R	28 5:39	☿ ♑	11 16:24	20 21:57 ♇ △	♏ 21 5:13	20 18:08 ♂ □	♐ 20 23:08	15 13:33	☾ 23♍57
☽0N	29 22:14	☉ ♑	21 12:18	23 7:22 ♇ □	♐ 23 14:16	23 3:54 ♀ ☌	♑ 23 4:52	23 8:06	● 1♑52
		♀ ♑	23 14:33	25 14:07 ♇ ⚹	♑ 25 20:41	24 20:03 ♃ ⚹	♒ 25 8:04	30 3:45	☽ 8♈49
				27 21:05 ♀ ⚹	♒ 28 1:11	27 6:20 ♂ ☍	♓ 27 10:16		
				29 22:20 ♇ ☌	♓ 30 4:33	29 6:49 ☿ ⚹	♈ 29 12:45		
						31 15:23 ☿ □	♉ 31 16:15		

Astro Data

1 November 2041
Julian Day # 51805
SVP 4♓40'43"
GC 27♐25.4 ⚵ 24♍37.8
Eris 28♈47.4R ⚴ 9♎41.9
⚷ 4♌19.0 ⚶ 21♊31.4R
☽ Mean ☊ 5♉54.4

1 December 2041
Julian Day # 51835
SVP 4♓40'38"
GC 27♐25.5 ⚵ 7♎10.3
Eris 28♈31.3R ⚴ 20♎00.3
⚷ 4♌15.9R ⚶ 15♊33.9R
☽ Mean ☊ 4♉19.1

LONGITUDE January 2042

Day	Sid.Time	☉	0 hr ☽	Noon ☽	True ☊	☿	♀	♂	⚳	♃	♄	♅	♆	♇
1 W	18 45 06	11♑11 48	4♉27 28	11♉19 43	3♉51.8	0♒31.0	11♑11.6	27♌32.2	20♏09.4	24♏17.9	5♏00.1	11♌53.5	5♉21.2	26♒51.4
2 Th	18 49 03	12 12 57	18 09 47	24 57 38	3R 49.9	1 37.5	12 27.1	27R 28.4	20 32.5	24 28.7	5 04.3	11R 51.3	5R 20.8	26 52.7
3 F	18 52 59	13 14 05	1♊43 14	8♊26 29	3 45.4	2 38.7	13 42.6	27 23.8	20 55.5	24 39.5	5 08.4	11 49.2	5 20.3	26 54.0
4 Sa	18 56 56	14 15 13	15 07 18	21 45 31	3 37.9	3 34.0	14 58.1	27 18.5	21 18.3	24 50.2	5 12.4	11 47.0	5 20.0	26 55.4
5 Su	19 00 52	15 16 21	28 20 58	4♋53 31	3 27.6	4 22.5	16 13.6	27 12.3	21 41.0	25 00.8	5 16.4	11 44.7	5 19.6	26 56.7
6 M	19 04 49	16 17 29	11♋22 58	17 49 11	3 15.2	5 03.3	17 29.1	27 05.3	22 03.7	25 11.3	5 20.2	11 42.5	5 19.3	26 58.1
7 Tu	19 08 45	17 18 37	24 12 02	0♌31 26	3 01.7	5 35.5	18 44.5	26 57.5	22 26.2	25 21.8	5 24.0	11 40.2	5 19.0	26 59.5
8 W	19 12 42	18 19 44	6♌47 21	12 59 49	2 48.4	5 58.2	20 00.0	26 48.9	22 48.6	25 32.1	5 27.7	11 37.8	5 18.8	27 00.9
9 Th	19 16 39	19 20 52	19 08 56	25 14 51	2 36.4	6R 10.5	21 15.5	26 39.5	23 10.8	25 42.3	5 31.3	11 35.5	5 18.5	27 02.3
10 F	19 20 35	20 21 59	1♍17 48	7♍18 07	2 26.7	6 11.8	22 30.9	26 29.3	23 33.0	25 52.5	5 34.8	11 33.1	5 18.4	27 03.7
11 Sa	19 24 32	21 23 06	13 16 09	19 12 22	2 19.7	6 01.5	23 46.4	26 18.2	23 55.0	26 02.5	5 38.2	11 30.7	5 18.2	27 05.1
12 Su	19 28 28	22 24 13	25 07 16	1♎01 23	2 15.5	5 39.5	25 01.8	26 06.4	24 16.9	26 12.5	5 41.6	11 28.3	5 18.1	27 06.6
13 M	19 32 25	23 25 21	6♎55 20	12 49 46	2D 13.7	5 05.7	26 17.3	25 53.8	24 38.7	26 22.3	5 44.8	11 25.8	5 18.0	27 08.1
14 Tu	19 36 21	24 26 28	18 45 20	24 42 45	2R 13.3	4 20.6	27 32.7	25 40.3	25 00.4	26 32.0	5 48.0	11 23.4	5D 18.0	27 09.6
15 W	19 40 18	25 27 34	0♏42 43	6♏45 56	2 13.3	3 25.4	28 48.2	25 26.2	25 21.9	26 41.7	5 51.0	11 20.9	5 18.0	27 11.1
16 Th	19 44 14	26 28 41	12 53 06	19 04 51	2 12.5	2 21.4	0♒03.6	25 11.2	25 43.3	26 51.2	5 54.0	11 18.4	5 18.0	27 12.6
17 F	19 48 11	27 29 48	25 21 49	1♐44 33	2 09.7	1 10.5	1 19.0	24 55.5	26 04.6	27 00.6	5 56.8	11 15.9	5 18.0	27 14.1
18 Sa	19 52 08	28 30 54	8♐13 28	14 48 57	2 04.4	29♑54.9	2 34.5	24 39.1	26 25.7	27 09.9	5 59.6	11 13.4	5 18.1	27 15.7
19 Su	19 56 04	29 32 00	21 31 12	28 20 16	1 56.2	28 37.0	3 49.9	24 22.0	26 46.7	27 19.1	6 02.3	11 10.8	5 18.3	27 17.2
20 M	20 00 01	0♒33 06	5♑16 01	12♑18 10	1 45.5	27 19.2	5 05.3	24 04.2	27 07.5	27 28.2	6 04.8	11 08.3	5 18.4	27 18.8
21 Tu	20 03 57	1 34 11	19 26 12	26 39 29	1 33.3	26 03.8	6 20.7	23 45.7	27 28.2	27 37.2	6 07.3	11 05.7	5 18.7	27 20.4
22 W	20 07 54	2 35 16	3♒57 09	11♒18 14	1 20.8	24 52.9	7 36.1	23 26.6	27 48.7	27 46.0	6 09.7	11 03.1	5 18.9	27 21.9
23 Th	20 11 50	3 36 19	18 41 42	26 06 27	1 09.4	23 48.2	8 51.5	23 06.9	28 09.1	27 54.8	6 12.0	11 00.5	5 19.2	27 23.5
24 F	20 15 47	4 37 22	3♓31 24	10♓55 29	1 00.3	22 50.8	10 06.9	22 46.6	28 29.3	28 03.4	6 14.1	10 57.9	5 19.5	27 25.1
25 Sa	20 19 43	5 38 24	18 17 48	25 37 32	0 54.2	22 01.8	11 22.3	22 25.9	28 49.4	28 11.9	6 16.2	10 55.3	5 19.8	27 26.8
26 Su	20 23 40	6 39 24	2♈54 02	10♈06 48	0 50.9	21 21.7	12 37.6	22 04.6	29 09.3	28 20.2	6 18.2	10 52.7	5 20.2	27 28.4
27 M	20 27 37	7 40 24	17 15 28	24 19 52	0D 49.8	20 50.5	13 53.0	21 42.8	29 29.0	28 28.5	6 20.0	10 50.1	5 20.6	27 30.0
28 Tu	20 31 33	8 41 22	1♉19 55	8♉15 39	0R 49.8	20 28.3	15 08.3	21 20.7	29 48.6	28 36.6	6 21.8	10 47.4	5 21.0	27 31.7
29 W	20 35 30	9 42 20	15 07 10	21 54 38	0 49.4	20 14.9	16 23.6	20 58.2	0♐08.0	28 44.5	6 23.5	10 44.8	5 21.5	27 33.3
30 Th	20 39 26	10 43 16	28 38 16	5♊18 15	0 47.4	20D 09.7	17 38.9	20 35.3	0 27.3	28 52.4	6 25.0	10 42.2	5 22.0	27 35.0
31 F	20 43 23	11 44 10	11♊54 50	18 28 11	0 42.8	20 12.4	18 54.2	20 12.1	0 46.3	29 00.1	6 26.5	10 39.6	5 22.6	27 36.7

LONGITUDE February 2042

Day	Sid.Time	☉	0 hr ☽	Noon ☽	True ☊	☿	♀	♂	⚳	♃	♄	♅	♆	♇
1 Sa	20 47 19	12♒45 04	24♊58 30	1♋25 54	0♉35.2	20♑22.4	20♒09.5	19♌48.7	1♐05.2	29♏07.7	6♏27.8	10♌36.9	5♉23.2	27♒38.3
2 Su	20 51 16	13 45 56	7♋50 30	14 12 25	0R 24.8	20 39.2	21 24.7	19R 25.1	1 24.0	29 15.1	6 29.1	10R 34.3	5 23.8	27 40.0
3 M	20 55 12	14 46 48	20 31 40	26 48 20	0 12.2	21 02.3	22 40.0	19 01.4	1 42.5	29 22.4	6 30.2	10 31.7	5 24.5	27 41.7
4 Tu	20 59 09	15 47 38	3♌02 25	9♌13 57	29♈58.5	21 31.1	23 55.2	18 37.5	2 00.9	29 29.6	6 31.3	10 29.1	5 25.1	27 43.4
5 W	21 03 06	16 48 26	15 22 59	21 29 33	29 44.8	22 05.2	25 10.4	18 13.5	2 19.0	29 36.6	6 32.2	10 26.5	5 25.9	27 45.1
6 Th	21 07 02	17 49 14	27 33 45	3♍35 42	29 32.5	22 44.1	26 25.6	17 49.5	2 37.0	29 43.5	6 33.1	10 23.9	5 26.6	27 46.8
7 F	21 10 59	18 50 00	9♍35 34	15 33 32	29 22.3	23 27.4	27 40.8	17 25.5	2 54.8	29 50.2	6 33.8	10 21.3	5 27.4	27 48.5
8 Sa	21 14 55	19 50 45	21 29 53	27 24 55	29 14.8	24 14.7	28 56.0	17 01.6	3 12.4	29 56.8	6 34.4	10 18.7	5 28.2	27 50.2
9 Su	21 18 52	20 51 30	3♎19 00	9♎12 35	29 10.2	25 05.7	0♓11.1	16 37.8	3 29.8	0♐03.2	6 34.9	10 16.1	5 29.1	27 51.9
10 M	21 22 48	21 52 13	15 06 07	21 00 08	29D 08.1	26 00.1	1 26.3	16 14.2	3 47.0	0 09.5	6 35.3	10 13.6	5 29.9	27 53.6
11 Tu	21 26 45	22 52 55	26 55 12	2♏51 57	29 07.8	26 57.5	2 41.4	15 50.7	4 04.0	0 15.7	6 35.7	10 11.0	5 30.9	27 55.3
12 W	21 30 41	23 53 36	8♏51 00	14 53 02	29R 08.4	27 57.8	3 56.5	15 27.5	4 20.8	0 21.7	6 35.9	10 08.5	5 31.8	27 57.1
13 Th	21 34 38	24 54 15	20 58 43	27 08 45	29 08.6	29 00.6	5 11.6	15 04.5	4 37.4	0 27.5	6R 36.0	10 05.9	5 32.8	27 58.8
14 F	21 38 35	25 54 54	3♐23 47	9♐44 26	29 07.6	0♒05.9	6 26.7	14 41.9	4 53.7	0 33.2	6 36.0	10 03.4	5 33.8	28 00.5
15 Sa	21 42 31	26 55 32	16 11 19	22 44 54	29 04.5	1 13.4	7 41.8	14 19.7	5 09.9	0 38.7	6 35.8	10 01.0	5 34.8	28 02.2
16 Su	21 46 28	27 56 09	29 25 34	6♑13 36	28 59.1	2 23.0	8 56.8	13 57.8	5 25.8	0 44.1	6 35.6	9 58.5	5 35.9	28 04.0
17 M	21 50 24	28 56 44	13♑09 04	20 11 54	28 51.5	3 34.5	10 11.9	13 36.4	5 41.5	0 49.3	6 35.3	9 56.0	5 37.0	28 05.7
18 Tu	21 54 21	29 57 18	27 21 48	4♒38 14	28 42.3	4 47.8	11 26.9	13 15.5	5 57.0	0 54.3	6 34.9	9 53.6	5 38.2	28 07.4
19 W	21 58 17	0♓57 51	12♒00 30	19 27 40	28 32.8	6 02.9	12 41.9	12 55.1	6 12.2	0 59.2	6 34.4	9 51.2	5 39.3	28 09.1
20 Th	22 02 14	1 58 22	26 58 39	4♓32 12	28 24.0	7 19.5	13 56.9	12 35.3	6 27.2	1 03.9	6 33.7	9 48.8	5 40.5	28 10.9
21 F	22 06 10	2 58 51	12♓07 04	19 41 54	28 16.9	8 37.6	15 11.8	12 16.0	6 41.9	1 08.4	6 33.0	9 46.4	5 41.7	28 12.6
22 Sa	22 10 07	3 59 19	27 15 28	4♈46 36	28 12.3	9 57.3	16 26.8	11 57.3	6 56.4	1 12.8	6 32.1	9 44.1	5 43.0	28 14.3
23 Su	22 14 04	4 59 45	12♈14 16	19 37 38	28D 10.1	11 18.2	17 41.7	11 39.3	7 10.7	1 17.0	6 31.2	9 41.8	5 44.3	28 16.0
24 M	22 18 00	6 00 09	26 56 02	4♉08 59	28 10.0	12 40.6	18 56.6	11 22.0	7 24.7	1 21.0	6 30.1	9 39.5	5 45.6	28 17.7
25 Tu	22 21 57	7 00 31	11♉16 11	18 17 31	28 10.9	14 04.2	20 11.4	11 05.3	7 38.5	1 24.8	6 29.0	9 37.3	5 46.9	28 19.5
26 W	22 25 53	8 00 51	25 12 59	2♊02 42	28R 11.8	15 29.0	21 26.3	10 49.4	7 51.9	1 28.5	6 27.7	9 35.0	5 48.3	28 21.2
27 Th	22 29 50	9 01 09	8♊46 53	15 25 50	28 11.7	16 55.1	22 41.1	10 34.1	8 05.2	1 32.0	6 26.4	9 32.8	5 49.7	28 22.9
28 F	22 33 46	10 01 25	21 59 51	28 29 17	28 09.9	18 22.4	23 55.9	10 19.6	8 18.1	1 35.4	6 24.9	9 30.7	5 51.1	28 24.6

Astro Data	Dy Hr Mn
♄☍♆	6 6:25
☿ R	10 2:45
☽ 0S	12 20:41
♆ D	15 6:18
♃□♇	19 5:54
☽ 0N	26 3:36
☿ D	30 15:32
☽ 0S	9 3:05
♄ R	13 22:50
☽ 0N	22 11:54

Planet Ingress		Dy Hr Mn
☿	♒	1 1:19
♀	♒	16 10:51
☿	♑R	18 10:25
☉	♒	19 23:00
⚳	♐	29 2:04
☊	♈R	4 9:21
♃	♐	8 23:52
♀	♓	9 8:27
☿	♒	14 9:52
☉	♓	18 13:04

Last Aspect Dy Hr Mn		☽ Ingress Dy Hr Mn
2 16:26	♂ □	♊ 2 20:56
4 22:01	♂ ⚹	♋ 5 3:01
7 2:04	♃ △	♌ 7 11:00
9 15:33	♇ ☍	♍ 9 21:25
12 2:04	♃ ⚹	♎ 12 9:55
14 18:21	♀ □	♏ 14 22:35
17 3:31	♇ □	♐ 17 8:44
19 10:09	♇ ⚹	♑ 19 14:54
21 13:36	♃ ⚹	♒ 21 17:31
23 14:57	♃ □	♓ 23 18:18
25 16:16	♃ △	♈ 25 19:12
27 17:26	♇ ⚹	♉ 27 21:42
30 0:18	♃ ☍	♊ 30 2:27

Last Aspect Dy Hr Mn		☽ Ingress Dy Hr Mn
1 4:55	♇ △	♋ 1 9:20
3 16:59	♃ △	♌ 3 18:08
6 4:13	♃ □	♍ 6 4:50
8 17:12	♃ ⚹	♎ 8 17:15
11 2:00	♇ △	♏ 11 6:13
13 15:56	☿ ⚹	♐ 13 17:30
15 21:33	♇ ⚹	♑ 16 1:01
16 17:13	♀ ⚹	♒ 18 4:22
20 1:54	♇ ☌	♓ 20 4:48
21 4:14	♀ ☌	♈ 22 4:22
24 2:14	♇ ⚹	♉ 24 5:05
26 5:29	♇ □	♊ 26 8:23
28 11:51	♇ △	♋ 28 14:49

☽ Phases & Eclipses Dy Hr Mn	
6 8:54	○ 16♋10
14 11:24	☾ 24♎25
21 20:42	● 1♒56
28 12:48	☽ 8♉43
5 1:58	○ 16♌23
13 7:16	☾ 24♏42
20 7:39	● 1♓47
26 23:29	☽ 8♊30

Astro Data

1 January 2042
Julian Day # 51866
SVP 4♓40'32"
GC 27♐25.6 ⚴ 17♎23.2
Eris 28♈21.6R ⚵ 28♎41.8
⚷ 2♌47.9R ⚶ 8♊21.4R
☽ Mean ☊ 2♉40.6

1 February 2042
Julian Day # 51897
SVP 4♓40'26"
GC 27♐25.6 ⚴ 23♎05.5
Eris 28♈22.1 ⚵ 4♏10.4
⚷ 0♌35.7R ⚶ 6♊51.4
☽ Mean ☊ 1♉02.1

March 2042 — LONGITUDE

Day	Sid.Time	☉	0 hr ☽	Noon ☽	True ☊	☿	♀	♂	⚳	♃	♄	♅	♆	♇
1 Sa	22 37 43	11♓01 40	4♋54 30	11♋15 51	28♈06.0	19♒50.8	25♓10.6	10♌05.9	8♐30.8	1♐38.5	6♏23.4	9♌28.5	5♉52.6	28♒26.3
2 Su	22 41 39	12 01 52	17 33 40	23 48 16	28R00.0	21 20.3	26 25.4	9R52.9	8 43.2	1 41.5	6R21.8	9R26.5	5 54.1	28 28.0
3 M	22 45 36	13 02 02	29 59 58	6♌09 00	27 52.4	22 51.0	27 40.1	9 40.7	8 55.4	1 44.3	6 20.0	9 24.4	5 55.6	28 29.6
4 Tu	22 49 33	14 02 10	12♌15 38	18 20 06	27 44.0	24 22.8	28 54.8	9 29.2	9 07.3	1 46.9	6 18.2	9 22.4	5 57.1	28 31.3
5 W	22 53 29	15 02 16	24 22 35	0♍23 18	27 35.5	25 55.7	0♈09.4	9 18.6	9 18.8	1 49.3	6 16.2	9 20.4	5 58.7	28 33.0
6 Th	22 57 26	16 02 21	6♍22 26	12 20 09	27 27.9	27 29.7	1 24.0	9 08.7	9 30.1	1 51.6	6 14.2	9 18.4	6 00.2	28 34.6
7 F	23 01 22	17 02 23	18 16 40	24 12 11	27 21.7	29 04.9	2 38.6	8 59.6	9 41.1	1 53.6	6 12.1	9 16.5	6 01.8	28 36.3
8 Sa	23 05 19	18 02 24	0♎06 55	6♎01 07	27 17.4	0♓41.1	3 53.2	8 51.3	9 51.8	1 55.5	6 09.9	9 14.6	6 03.5	28 37.9
9 Su	23 09 15	19 02 22	11 55 04	17 49 05	27D15.1	2 18.5	5 07.7	8 43.8	10 02.2	1 57.2	6 07.6	9 12.7	6 05.1	28 39.6
10 M	23 13 12	20 02 19	23 43 30	29 38 43	27 14.6	3 57.0	6 22.2	8 37.0	10 12.3	1 58.8	6 05.2	9 10.9	6 06.8	28 41.2
11 Tu	23 17 08	21 02 15	5♏35 08	11♏33 14	27 15.5	5 36.6	7 36.7	8 31.1	10 22.1	2 00.1	6 02.7	9 09.2	6 08.5	28 42.8
12 W	23 21 05	22 02 08	17 33 30	23 36 27	27 17.2	7 17.4	8 51.2	8 25.9	10 31.6	2 01.2	6 00.2	9 07.4	6 10.2	28 44.4
13 Th	23 25 02	23 02 00	29 42 39	5♐52 39	27 18.8	8 59.4	10 05.6	8 21.5	10 40.8	2 02.2	5 57.5	9 05.8	6 12.0	28 46.1
14 F	23 28 58	24 01 51	12♐07 02	18 26 22	27R19.9	10 42.5	11 20.0	8 17.8	10 49.6	2 03.0	5 54.8	9 04.1	6 13.7	28 47.6
15 Sa	23 32 55	25 01 39	24 51 11	1♑22 00	27 19.9	12 26.8	12 34.4	8 15.0	10 58.2	2 03.6	5 52.0	9 02.5	6 15.5	28 49.2
16 Su	23 36 51	26 01 27	7♑59 14	14 43 16	27 18.5	14 12.3	13 48.7	8 12.8	11 06.4	2 04.0	5 49.1	9 01.0	6 17.3	28 50.8
17 M	23 40 48	27 01 12	21 34 20	28 32 32	27 15.7	15 58.9	15 03.1	8 11.5	11 14.2	2R04.2	5 46.1	8 59.4	6 19.1	28 52.4
18 Tu	23 44 44	28 00 56	5♒37 48	12♒49 54	27 12.0	17 46.9	16 17.4	8D10.9	11 21.7	2 04.2	5 43.0	8 58.0	6 21.0	28 53.9
19 W	23 48 41	29 00 37	20 08 23	27 32 38	27 07.8	19 36.0	17 31.6	8 11.0	11 28.9	2 04.0	5 39.9	8 56.6	6 22.9	28 55.5
20 Th	23 52 37	0♈00 17	5♓01 49	12♓34 54	27 03.9	21 26.4	18 45.8	8 11.9	11 35.7	2 03.7	5 36.7	8 55.2	6 24.8	28 57.0
21 F	23 56 34	0 59 55	20 10 44	27 48 06	27 00.9	23 18.0	20 00.0	8 13.4	11 42.2	2 03.1	5 33.4	8 53.8	6 26.7	28 58.5
22 Sa	0 00 31	1 59 31	5♈25 40	13♈02 10	26D59.0	25 10.8	21 14.2	8 15.7	11 48.4	2 02.4	5 30.0	8 52.6	6 28.6	29 00.0
23 Su	0 04 27	2 59 05	20 36 21	28 07 07	26 58.5	27 04.9	22 28.3	8 18.7	11 54.1	2 01.5	5 26.6	8 51.3	6 30.5	29 01.5
24 M	0 08 24	3 58 37	5♉33 28	12♉54 36	26 59.1	29 00.2	23 42.4	8 22.5	11 59.5	2 00.3	5 23.1	8 50.1	6 32.5	29 03.0
25 Tu	0 12 20	4 58 07	20 09 54	27 18 55	27 00.4	0♈56.7	24 56.5	8 26.8	12 04.6	1 59.0	5 19.5	8 49.0	6 34.5	29 04.4
26 W	0 16 17	5 57 34	4♊21 23	11♊17 12	27 01.8	2 54.4	26 10.5	8 31.9	12 09.3	1 57.6	5 15.9	8 47.9	6 36.5	29 05.9
27 Th	0 20 13	6 56 59	18 06 25	24 49 11	27R02.9	4 53.2	27 24.5	8 37.6	12 13.6	1 55.9	5 12.2	8 46.9	6 38.5	29 07.3
28 F	0 24 10	7 56 22	1♋25 48	7♋56 36	27 03.3	6 53.1	28 38.5	8 44.0	12 17.5	1 54.0	5 08.4	8 45.9	6 40.5	29 08.7
29 Sa	0 28 06	8 55 43	14 21 57	20 42 20	27 02.9	8 53.9	29 52.4	8 51.0	12 21.1	1 52.0	5 04.6	8 45.0	6 42.5	29 10.1
30 Su	0 32 03	9 55 01	26 58 11	3♌09 59	27 01.6	10 55.6	1♉06.2	8 58.7	12 24.3	1 49.8	5 00.7	8 44.1	6 44.6	29 11.5
31 M	0 36 00	10 54 17	9♌18 11	15 23 16	26 59.7	12 58.1	2 20.1	9 06.9	12 27.1	1 47.4	4 56.8	8 43.2	6 46.7	29 12.9

April 2042 — LONGITUDE

Day	Sid.Time	☉	0 hr ☽	Noon ☽	True ☊	☿	♀	♂	⚳	♃	♄	♅	♆	♇
1 Tu	0 39 56	11♈53 30	21♌25 40	27♌25 49	26♈57.4	15♈01.2	3♉33.9	9♌15.8	12♐29.5	1♐44.8	4♏52.8	8♌42.5	6♉48.7	29♒14.2
2 W	0 43 53	12 52 41	3♍24 05	9♍20 53	26R55.1	17 04.8	4 47.6	9 25.2	12 31.6	1R42.0	4R48.8	8R41.7	6 50.8	29 15.5
3 Th	0 47 49	13 51 51	15 16 32	21 11 23	26 53.1	19 08.6	6 01.3	9 35.2	12 33.2	1 39.1	4 44.7	8 41.0	6 52.9	29 16.9
4 F	0 51 46	14 50 57	27 05 45	2♎59 54	26 51.6	21 12.4	7 15.0	9 45.8	12 34.5	1 36.0	4 40.6	8 40.4	6 55.0	29 18.2
5 Sa	0 55 42	15 50 02	8♎54 08	14 48 43	26 50.7	23 15.9	8 28.6	9 56.9	12 35.4	1 32.7	4 36.4	8 39.8	6 57.2	29 19.4
6 Su	0 59 39	16 49 05	20 43 54	26 39 37	26D50.4	25 19.0	9 42.2	10 08.5	12R35.9	1 29.2	4 32.2	8 39.3	6 59.3	29 20.7
7 M	1 03 35	17 48 06	2♏37 10	8♏35 47	26 50.6	27 21.1	10 55.8	10 20.7	12 36.0	1 25.6	4 28.0	8 38.8	7 01.5	29 22.0
8 Tu	1 07 32	18 47 05	14 36 06	20 38 26	26 51.2	29 22.1	12 09.3	10 33.4	12 35.7	1 21.8	4 23.7	8 38.4	7 03.6	29 23.2
9 W	1 11 28	19 46 02	26 43 05	2♐50 24	26 51.9	1♉21.5	13 22.7	10 46.6	12 35.0	1 17.9	4 19.4	8 38.1	7 05.8	29 24.4
10 Th	1 15 25	20 44 57	9♐00 44	15 14 25	26 52.6	3 19.0	14 36.2	11 00.3	12 33.9	1 13.7	4 15.0	8 37.8	7 08.0	29 25.6
11 F	1 19 22	21 43 51	21 31 52	27 53 26	26 53.2	5 14.2	15 49.6	11 14.5	12 32.5	1 09.5	4 10.6	8 37.5	7 10.2	29 26.8
12 Sa	1 23 18	22 42 43	4♑19 30	10♑50 25	26R53.5	7 06.8	17 02.9	11 29.1	12 30.6	1 05.0	4 06.2	8 37.3	7 12.4	29 27.9
13 Su	1 27 15	23 41 33	17 26 32	24 08 08	26 53.6	8 56.4	18 16.2	11 44.3	12 28.3	1 00.4	4 01.8	8 37.1	7 14.6	29 29.1
14 M	1 31 11	24 40 22	0♒55 26	7♒48 36	26 53.5	10 42.8	19 29.5	11 59.9	12 25.7	0 55.6	3 57.3	8 37.1	7 16.8	29 30.2
15 Tu	1 35 08	25 39 08	14 47 42	21 52 39	26 53.4	12 25.5	20 42.7	12 15.9	12 22.6	0 50.7	3 52.8	8D37.0	7 19.0	29 31.3
16 W	1 39 04	26 37 53	29 03 16	6♓19 14	26D53.3	14 04.4	21 55.9	12 32.3	12 19.1	0 45.7	3 48.3	8 37.0	7 21.2	29 32.3
17 Th	1 43 01	27 36 36	13♓40 03	21 05 04	26 53.4	15 39.2	23 09.1	12 49.2	12 15.3	0 40.5	3 43.8	8 37.1	7 23.5	29 33.4
18 F	1 46 57	28 35 18	28 33 31	6♈04 27	26 53.5	17 09.6	24 22.2	13 06.6	12 11.0	0 35.1	3 39.2	8 37.2	7 25.7	29 34.4
19 Sa	1 50 54	29 33 58	13♈36 53	21 09 42	26R53.5	18 35.5	25 35.2	13 24.3	12 06.4	0 29.6	3 34.7	8 37.4	7 27.9	29 35.4
20 Su	1 54 51	0♉32 35	28 41 47	6♉12 01	26 53.5	19 56.8	26 48.3	13 42.5	12 01.3	0 24.0	3 30.1	8 37.6	7 30.2	29 36.4
21 M	1 58 47	1 31 11	13♉39 19	21 02 43	26 53.3	21 13.1	28 01.2	14 01.0	11 55.9	0 18.2	3 25.5	8 37.9	7 32.4	29 37.4
22 Tu	2 02 44	2 29 45	28 21 22	5♊34 31	26 52.8	22 24.5	29 14.2	14 19.9	11 50.1	0 12.3	3 21.0	8 38.2	7 34.7	29 38.3
23 W	2 06 40	3 28 17	12♊41 39	19 42 21	26 52.1	23 30.8	0♊27.1	14 39.3	11 44.0	0 06.3	3 16.4	8 38.6	7 37.0	29 39.3
24 Th	2 10 37	4 26 47	26 36 25	3♋23 45	26 51.3	24 32.0	1 39.9	14 59.0	11 37.4	0 00.2	3 11.8	8 39.1	7 39.2	29 40.2
25 F	2 14 33	5 25 15	10♋04 27	16 38 43	26 50.5	25 27.8	2 52.7	15 19.0	11 30.5	29♏53.9	3 07.2	8 39.6	7 41.5	29 41.0
26 Sa	2 18 30	6 23 40	23 06 49	29 29 11	26D50.1	26 18.2	4 05.4	15 39.4	11 23.3	29 47.6	3 02.7	8 40.1	7 43.7	29 41.9
27 Su	2 22 27	7 22 04	5♌46 15	11♌58 31	26 50.1	27 03.3	5 18.1	16 00.2	11 15.6	29 41.1	2 58.1	8 40.7	7 46.0	29 42.7
28 M	2 26 23	8 20 25	18 06 32	24 10 52	26 50.5	27 42.8	6 30.8	16 21.3	11 07.7	29 34.5	2 53.6	8 41.4	7 48.3	29 43.5
29 Tu	2 30 20	9 18 44	0♍12 05	6♍10 45	26 51.4	28 16.8	7 43.4	16 42.7	10 59.4	29 27.8	2 49.0	8 42.1	7 50.5	29 44.3
30 W	2 34 16	10 17 01	12 07 25	18 02 38	26 52.6	28 45.3	8 55.9	17 04.5	10 50.7	29 21.1	2 44.5	8 42.9	7 52.8	29 45.1

Astro Data	Planet Ingress	Last Aspect	☽ Ingress	Last Aspect	☽ Ingress	☽ Phases & Eclipses
Dy Hr Mn	Dy Hr Mn	Dy Hr Mn	Dy Hr Mn	Dy Hr Mn	Dy Hr Mn	Dy Hr Mn
♀0N 7 14:27	♀ ♈ 5 8:58	2 17:38 ♀ △	♌ 3 0:00	1 15:38 ♇ ☍	♍ 1 17:09	6 20:10 ○ 16♍23
☽0S 8 9:09	☿ ♓ 8 1:47	5 8:19 ♇ ☍	♍ 5 11:13	2 6:56 ♆ △	♎ 4 5:54	14 23:21 ☾ 24♐30
♄☍♆ 10 2:43	☉ ♈ 20 11:53	6 20:10 ☉ ☍	♎ 7 23:46	6 17:25 ♇ △	♏ 6 18:44	21 17:23 ● 1♈13
♃R 18 2:46	☿ ♈ 25 0:21	10 10:03 ♇ △	♏ 10 12:43	9 5:16 ♇ □	♐ 9 6:27	28 12:00 ☽ 7♋56
♂D 18 19:51	♀ ♉ 29 14:29	12 22:07 ♇ □	♐ 13 0:34	11 14:55 ♇ ⚹	♑ 11 15:57	
☉0N 20 11:54		15 7:19 ♇ ⚹	♑ 15 9:30	13 11:09 ☉ □	♒ 13 22:23	5 14:16 ○ 15♎56
☽0N 21 22:44	☿ ♉ 8 19:35	17 9:12 ☉ ⚹	♒ 17 14:29	16 0:47 ♇ ☌	♓ 16 1:34	5 14:29 ◑ A 0.868
☿0N 26 18:39	☉ ♉ 19 22:39	19 14:13 ♇ ☌	♓ 19 15:57	17 15:37 ♀ ⚹	♈ 18 2:18	13 11:09 ☾ 23♑39
	♀ ♊ 23 3:05	21 3:56 ☿ ☌	♈ 21 15:28	20 1:26 ♇ ⚹	♉ 20 2:05	20 2:19 ● 0♉09
☽0S 4 15:18	♃ ♏R 24 12:41	23 13:28 ♇ ⚹	♉ 23 15:01	22 2:07 ♇ □	♊ 22 2:43	20 2:16:03 ◐ T 04'51"
⚳R 7 6:30		25 14:59 ♇ □	♊ 25 16:33	24 5:23 ♇ △	♋ 24 5:58	27 2:19 ☽ 6♌59
♅D 15 18:57		27 19:48 ♇ △	♋ 27 21:23	26 12:35 ♃ △	♌ 26 12:58	
☽0N 18 9:43		28 12:00 ☉ □	♌ 30 5:51	28 23:04 ♇ ☍	♍ 28 23:36	
♃□♇ 27 6:40						

Astro Data

1 March 2042
Julian Day # 51925
SVP 4♓40'22"
GC 27♐25.7 ⚴ 22♎17.6R
Eris 28♈31.3 ⚵ 5♏01.7R
⚷ 28♋54.4R ⚶ 10♊58.8
☽ Mean ☊ 29♈33.2

1 April 2042
Julian Day # 51956
SVP 4♓40'19"
GC 27♐25.8 ⚴ 14♎30.0R
Eris 28♈48.6 ⚵ 0♏46.0R
⚷ 28♋13.4 ⚶ 19♊35.7
☽ Mean ☊ 27♈54.7

LONGITUDE — May 2042

Day	Sid.Time	☉	0 hr ☽	Noon ☽	True ☊	☿	♀	♂	⚳	♃	♄	♅	♆	♇
1 Th	2 38 13	11♉15 16	23♍56 54	29♍50 43	26♈53.9	29♉08.2	10♊08.4	17♌26.5	10♐41.8	29♏14.2	2♏40.0	8♌43.7	7♉55.0	29♒45.8
2 F	2 42 09	12 13 30	5♎44 33	11♎38 49	26 54.9	29 25.5	11 20.8	17 48.9	10R 32.5	29R 07.3	2R 35.5	8 44.6	7 57.3	29 46.5
3 Sa	2 46 06	13 11 41	17 33 54	23 30 11	26R 55.5	29 37.4	12 33.2	18 11.6	10 22.9	29 00.2	2 31.1	8 45.5	7 59.6	29 47.2
4 Su	2 50 02	14 09 50	29 27 59	5♏27 35	26 55.3	29R 43.8	13 45.5	18 34.5	10 13.0	28 53.2	2 26.6	8 46.5	8 01.8	29 47.9
5 M	2 53 59	15 07 58	11♏29 15	17 33 14	26 54.2	29 45.0	14 57.7	18 57.8	10 02.9	28 46.0	2 22.2	8 47.5	8 04.1	29 48.5
6 Tu	2 57 55	16 06 04	23 39 43	29 48 54	26 52.3	29 41.0	16 09.9	19 21.3	9 52.4	28 38.7	2 17.8	8 48.6	8 06.3	29 49.2
7 W	3 01 52	17 04 09	6♐00 56	12♐16 00	26 49.5	29 32.0	17 22.1	19 45.1	9 41.7	28 31.4	2 13.5	8 49.7	8 08.5	29 49.8
8 Th	3 05 49	18 02 12	18 34 12	24 55 40	26 46.4	29 18.4	18 34.2	20 09.2	9 30.7	28 24.1	2 09.2	8 50.9	8 10.8	29 50.3
9 F	3 09 45	19 00 14	1♑20 33	7♑48 57	26 43.2	29 00.5	19 46.2	20 33.6	9 19.5	28 16.7	2 04.9	8 52.1	8 13.0	29 50.9
10 Sa	3 13 42	19 58 14	14 21 00	20 56 48	26 40.4	28 38.5	20 58.2	20 58.2	9 08.0	28 09.2	2 00.6	8 53.4	8 15.2	29 51.4
11 Su	3 17 38	20 56 13	27 36 27	4♒20 03	26 38.4	28 13.0	22 10.2	21 23.0	8 56.3	28 01.7	1 56.4	8 54.7	8 17.5	29 51.9
12 M	3 21 35	21 54 10	11♒07 41	17 59 24	26D 37.5	27 44.4	23 22.0	21 48.1	8 44.4	27 54.2	1 52.3	8 56.1	8 19.7	29 52.4
13 Tu	3 25 31	22 52 07	24 55 14	1♓55 08	26 37.7	27 13.3	24 33.9	22 13.5	8 32.3	27 46.6	1 48.2	8 57.5	8 21.9	29 52.8
14 W	3 29 28	23 50 02	8♓59 03	16 06 47	26 38.7	26 40.2	25 45.6	22 39.1	8 20.0	27 39.0	1 44.1	8 59.0	8 24.1	29 53.2
15 Th	3 33 24	24 47 55	23 18 08	0♈32 46	26 40.2	26 05.7	26 57.3	23 04.9	8 07.5	27 31.4	1 40.0	9 00.6	8 26.3	29 53.6
16 F	3 37 21	25 45 48	7♈50 13	15 10 00	26R 41.3	25 30.5	28 09.0	23 31.0	7 54.9	27 23.8	1 36.1	9 02.1	8 28.5	29 54.0
17 Sa	3 41 18	26 43 39	22 31 27	29 53 51	26 41.7	24 55.1	29 20.6	23 57.3	7 42.1	27 16.1	1 32.1	9 03.8	8 30.6	29 54.4
18 Su	3 45 14	27 41 29	7♉16 24	14♉38 15	26 40.6	24 20.2	0♋32.1	24 23.9	7 29.2	27 08.5	1 28.3	9 05.4	8 32.8	29 54.7
19 M	3 49 11	28 39 18	21 58 31	29 16 18	26 38.1	23 46.4	1 43.6	24 50.6	7 16.1	27 00.8	1 24.4	9 07.2	8 35.0	29 55.0
20 Tu	3 53 07	29 37 06	6♊30 47	13♊41 11	26 34.1	23 14.2	2 55.0	25 17.6	7 03.0	26 53.2	1 20.7	9 08.9	8 37.1	29 55.3
21 W	3 57 04	0♊34 52	20 46 48	27 47 04	26 29.1	22 44.1	4 06.4	25 44.8	6 49.7	26 45.6	1 17.0	9 10.8	8 39.3	29 55.5
22 Th	4 01 00	1 32 36	4♋41 34	11♋30 01	26 23.7	22 16.7	5 17.7	26 12.3	6 36.4	26 38.0	1 13.4	9 12.6	8 41.4	29 55.7
23 F	4 04 57	2 30 19	18 12 15	24 48 16	26 18.6	21 52.4	6 28.9	26 39.9	6 23.1	26 30.4	1 09.8	9 14.5	8 43.5	29 55.9
24 Sa	4 08 54	3 28 01	1♌18 11	7♌42 17	26 14.6	21 31.5	7 40.0	27 07.7	6 09.7	26 22.8	1 06.3	9 16.5	8 45.6	29 56.1
25 Su	4 12 50	4 25 41	14 00 52	20 14 23	26 11.9	21 14.3	8 51.1	27 35.7	5 56.3	26 15.3	1 02.8	9 18.5	8 47.7	29 56.2
26 M	4 16 47	5 23 19	26 23 20	2♍28 18	26D 10.8	21 01.1	10 02.1	28 03.9	5 42.9	26 07.8	0 59.5	9 20.5	8 49.8	29 56.4
27 Tu	4 20 43	6 20 56	8♍29 51	14 28 36	26 11.1	20 52.1	11 13.0	28 32.3	5 29.5	26 00.4	0 56.2	9 22.6	8 51.8	29 56.5
28 W	4 24 40	7 18 31	20 25 13	26 20 20	26 12.3	20D 47.4	12 23.9	29 00.9	5 16.1	25 53.0	0 52.9	9 24.7	8 53.9	29 56.5
29 Th	4 28 36	8 16 05	2♎14 34	8♎08 32	26 13.9	20 47.1	13 34.7	29 29.7	5 02.7	25 45.6	0 49.8	9 26.9	8 55.9	29 56.6
30 F	4 32 33	9 13 38	14 02 51	19 58 04	26R 15.0	20 51.3	14 45.4	29 58.6	4 49.5	25 38.4	0 46.7	9 29.1	8 57.9	29R 56.6
31 Sa	4 36 29	10 11 09	25 54 43	1♏53 17	26 15.1	21 00.0	15 56.0	0♍27.7	4 36.2	25 31.2	0 43.7	9 31.4	8 59.9	29 56.6

LONGITUDE — June 2042

Day	Sid.Time	☉	0 hr ☽	Noon ☽	True ☊	☿	♀	♂	⚳	♃	♄	♅	♆	♇
1 Su	4 40 26	11♊08 39	7♏54 13	13♏57 53	26♈13.4	21♉13.2	17♋06.6	0♍57.0	4♐23.1	25♏24.0	0♏40.7	9♌33.7	9♉01.9	29♒56.5
2 M	4 44 23	12 06 08	20 04 37	26 14 41	26R 09.7	21 30.8	18 17.0	1 26.5	4R 10.1	25R 16.9	0R 37.9	9 36.0	9 03.9	29R 56.5
3 Tu	4 48 19	13 03 36	2♐28 17	8♐45 35	26 04.1	21 52.8	19 27.4	1 56.1	3 57.2	25 09.9	0 35.1	9 38.4	9 05.8	29 56.4
4 W	4 52 16	14 01 03	15 06 37	21 31 27	25 56.9	22 19.2	20 37.7	2 25.9	3 44.4	25 03.0	0 32.4	9 40.8	9 07.8	29 56.3
5 Th	4 56 12	14 58 29	28 00 01	4♑32 13	25 48.7	22 49.8	21 47.9	2 55.9	3 31.7	24 56.2	0 29.8	9 43.3	9 09.7	29 56.2
6 F	5 00 09	15 55 54	11♑07 58	17 47 05	25 40.3	23 24.6	22 58.0	3 26.0	3 19.2	24 49.5	0 27.3	9 45.8	9 11.6	29 56.0
7 Sa	5 04 05	16 53 19	24 29 23	1♒14 42	25 32.8	24 03.4	24 08.1	3 56.2	3 06.9	24 42.8	0 24.8	9 48.3	9 13.5	29 55.8
8 Su	5 08 02	17 50 43	8♒02 49	14 53 34	25 26.9	24 46.3	25 18.0	4 26.6	2 54.7	24 36.3	0 22.5	9 50.9	9 15.4	29 55.6
9 M	5 11 58	18 48 06	21 46 46	28 42 17	25 23.0	25 33.0	26 27.9	4 57.2	2 42.7	24 29.9	0 20.2	9 53.5	9 17.2	29 55.4
10 Tu	5 15 55	19 45 28	5♓39 58	12♓39 42	25D 21.3	26 23.5	27 37.7	5 27.9	2 31.0	24 23.5	0 18.0	9 56.2	9 19.0	29 55.2
11 W	5 19 52	20 42 50	19 41 21	26 44 48	25 21.2	27 17.8	28 47.4	5 58.8	2 19.4	24 17.3	0 15.9	9 58.9	9 20.9	29 54.9
12 Th	5 23 48	21 40 12	3♈49 55	10♈56 33	25 21.9	28 15.7	29 57.0	6 29.8	2 08.1	24 11.2	0 13.9	10 01.6	9 22.6	29 54.6
13 F	5 27 45	22 37 33	18 04 30	25 13 31	25R 22.4	29 17.2	1♌06.5	7 01.0	1 57.0	24 05.2	0 12.0	10 04.3	9 24.4	29 54.2
14 Sa	5 31 41	23 34 54	2♉23 17	9♉33 25	25 21.6	0♊22.2	2 15.9	7 32.3	1 46.2	23 59.3	0 10.1	10 07.1	9 26.2	29 53.9
15 Su	5 35 38	24 32 14	16 43 30	23 53 00	25 18.7	1 30.6	3 25.2	8 03.7	1 35.6	23 53.6	0 08.4	10 09.9	9 27.9	29 53.5
16 M	5 39 34	25 29 34	1♊01 22	8♊08 00	25 13.3	2 42.4	4 34.4	8 35.3	1 25.3	23 48.0	0 06.7	10 12.8	9 29.6	29 53.1
17 Tu	5 43 31	26 26 53	15 12 17	22 13 35	25 05.5	3 57.6	5 43.6	9 07.0	1 15.3	23 42.5	0 05.2	10 15.7	9 31.3	29 52.7
18 W	5 47 27	27 24 12	29 11 19	6♋04 57	24 55.9	5 16.1	6 52.6	9 38.9	1 05.5	23 37.2	0 03.7	10 18.6	9 33.0	29 52.3
19 Th	5 51 24	28 21 31	12♋54 02	19 38 10	24 45.6	6 37.8	8 01.5	10 10.9	0 56.1	23 32.0	0 02.4	10 21.6	9 34.6	29 51.8
20 F	5 55 21	29 18 48	26 17 08	2♌50 46	24 35.5	8 02.7	9 10.3	10 43.0	0 47.0	23 27.0	0 01.1	10 24.6	9 36.2	29 51.3
21 Sa	5 59 17	0♋16 05	9♌19 03	15 42 04	24 26.8	9 30.8	10 19.0	11 15.3	0 38.1	23 22.1	29♎59.9	10 27.6	9 37.8	29 50.8
22 Su	6 03 14	1 13 22	22 00 02	28 13 14	24 20.0	11 02.1	11 27.6	11 47.7	0 29.7	23 17.3	29 58.8	10 30.6	9 39.4	29 50.3
23 M	6 07 10	2 10 37	4♍22 05	10♍27 02	24 15.6	12 36.6	12 36.1	12 20.2	0 21.5	23 12.7	29 57.9	10 33.7	9 40.9	29 49.7
24 Tu	6 11 07	3 07 52	16 28 37	22 27 27	24D 13.4	14 14.1	13 44.4	12 52.9	0 13.7	23 08.3	29 57.0	10 36.8	9 42.5	29 49.1
25 W	6 15 03	4 05 06	28 24 07	4♎19 19	24 12.8	15 54.7	14 52.6	13 25.6	0 06.2	23 04.0	29 56.2	10 39.9	9 43.9	29 48.5
26 Th	6 19 00	5 02 20	10♎13 42	16 07 57	24R 13.1	17 38.3	16 00.7	13 58.5	29♏59.0	22 59.8	29 55.5	10 43.1	9 45.4	29 47.9
27 F	6 22 56	5 59 33	22 02 45	27 58 45	24 13.2	19 24.8	17 08.7	14 31.5	29 52.3	22 55.9	29 54.9	10 46.3	9 46.9	29 47.2
28 Sa	6 26 53	6 56 46	3♏56 36	9♏56 54	24 12.1	21 14.2	18 16.5	15 04.6	29 45.8	22 52.1	29 54.4	10 49.5	9 48.3	29 46.6
29 Su	6 30 50	7 53 58	16 00 12	22 07 02	24 09.1	23 06.4	19 24.2	15 37.9	29 39.7	22 48.4	29 54.0	10 52.7	9 49.7	29 45.9
30 M	6 34 46	8 51 10	28 17 50	4♐32 57	24 03.5	25 01.3	20 31.8	16 11.2	29 34.0	22 45.0	29 53.7	10 56.0	9 51.1	29 45.2

Astro Data Dy Hr Mn	Planet Ingress Dy Hr Mn
☽0S 1 21:45	♀ ♋ 18 1:13
☿R 5 5:12	☉ ♊ 20 21:31
☽0N 15 18:37	♂ ♍ 30 13:08
☿D 29 1:30	
☽0S 29 4:30	♀ ♌ 12 13:03
♇R 30 16:37	☿ ♊ 14 3:57
	☉ ♋ 21 5:16
☽0N 12 0:44	♄ ♎R 21 10:26
☽0S 25 11:27	⚳ ♏R 26 8:43

Last Aspect Dy Hr Mn	☽ Ingress Dy Hr Mn	Last Aspect Dy Hr Mn	☽ Ingress Dy Hr Mn
1 10:46 ♃ ⚹	♎ 1 12:19	2 19:08 ♇ □	♐ 2 19:15
4 0:39 ♇ △	♏ 4 1:04	5 3:34 ♇ ⚹	♑ 5 3:41
6 12:00 ♇ □	♐ 6 12:22	7 0:30 ♃ ⚹	♒ 7 9:48
8 21:12 ♇ ⚹	♑ 8 21:30	9 14:06 ♇ ☌	♓ 9 14:14
11 1:26 ☿ △	♒ 11 4:17	11 15:46 ♀ △	♈ 11 17:31
13 8:31 ♇ ☌	♓ 13 8:43	13 19:50 ♇ ⚹	♉ 13 20:00
15 7:03 ♃ △	♈ 15 11:06	15 22:06 ♇ □	♊ 15 22:17
17 12:01 ♇ ⚹	♉ 17 12:10	18 1:11 ♇ △	♋ 18 1:24
19 13:04 ♇ □	♊ 19 13:12	19 18:58 ♃ △	♌ 20 6:46
21 15:42 ♇ △	♋ 21 15:50	22 15:25 ♄ ⚹	♍ 22 15:28
23 15:06 ♃ △	♌ 23 21:35	24 13:22 ♃ ⚹	♎ 25 3:14
26 6:59 ♇ ☍	♍ 26 7:07	27 15:54 ♄ ☌	♏ 27 16:04
28 11:05 ♃ ⚹	♎ 28 19:26	30 2:49 ♇ □	♐ 30 3:17
31 8:06 ♇ △	♏ 31 8:13		

☽ Phases & Eclipses Dy Hr Mn	
5 6:48	○ 14♏55
12 19:18	☾ 22♒12
19 10:55	● 28♉37
26 18:18	☽ 5♍38
3 20:48	○ 13♐25
11 1:00	☾ 20♓17
17 19:48	● 26♊46
25 11:29	☽ 4♎04

Astro Data

1 May 2042
Julian Day # 51986
SVP 4♓40'15"
GC 27♐25.8 ⚴ 6♋25.6R
Eris 29♈08.3 ✱ 24♋02.5R
⚷ 29♋02.8 ⚶ 0♋19.9
☽ Mean ☊ 26♈19.3

1 June 2042
Julian Day # 52017
SVP 4♓40'10"
GC 27♐25.9 ⚴ 4♋37.7
Eris 29♈26.7 ✱ 19♋44.1R
⚷ 1♌15.6 ⚶ 12♋51.5
☽ Mean ☊ 24♈40.9

July 2042 LONGITUDE

Day	Sid.Time	☉	0 hr ☽	Noon ☽	True ☊	☿	♀	♂	⚳	♃	♄	♅	♆	♇
1 Tu	6 38 43	9♋48 22	10♐52 41	17♐17 13	23♈55.5	26♊58.7	21♌39.2	16♍44.7	29♏28.7	22♏41.7	29♎53.5	10♌59.3	9♉52.4	29♒44.4
2 W	6 42 39	10 45 33	23 46 37	0♑20 53	23R45.3	28 58.4	22 46.4	17 18.2	29R23.7	22R38.5	29D53.4	11 02.6	9 53.7	29R43.7
3 Th	6 46 36	11 42 44	6♑59 54	13 43 25	23 33.8	1♋00.3	23 53.6	17 51.9	29 19.0	22 35.6	29 53.4	11 05.9	9 55.0	29 42.9
4 F	6 50 32	12 39 56	20 31 09	27 22 41	23 22.1	3 04.1	25 00.5	18 25.7	29 14.8	22 32.8	29 53.5	11 09.3	9 56.3	29 42.1
5 Sa	6 54 29	13 37 07	4♒17 36	11♒15 22	23 11.4	5 09.7	26 07.3	18 59.6	29 10.9	22 30.2	29 53.7	11 12.6	9 57.5	29 41.3
6 Su	6 58 26	14 34 18	18 15 30	25 17 29	23 02.7	7 16.6	27 14.0	19 33.6	29 07.4	22 27.7	29 54.0	11 16.0	9 58.7	29 40.5
7 M	7 02 22	15 31 30	2♓20 51	9♓25 08	22 56.6	9 24.8	28 20.5	20 07.7	29 04.2	22 25.5	29 54.4	11 19.5	9 59.9	29 39.7
8 Tu	7 06 19	16 28 41	16 29 58	23 35 00	22 53.2	11 33.7	29 26.8	20 41.9	29 01.4	22 23.4	29 54.9	11 22.9	10 01.0	29 38.8
9 W	7 10 15	17 25 54	0♈39 59	7♈44 41	22D51.9	13 43.3	0♍32.9	21 16.2	28 59.0	22 21.5	29 55.5	11 26.3	10 02.2	29 37.9
10 Th	7 14 12	18 23 06	14 48 56	21 52 37	22R51.7	15 53.1	1 38.9	21 50.6	28 57.0	22 19.7	29 56.2	11 29.8	10 03.2	29 37.0
11 F	7 18 08	19 20 19	28 55 37	5♉57 49	22 51.5	18 02.9	2 44.8	22 25.2	28 55.3	22 18.2	29 57.0	11 33.3	10 04.3	29 36.1
12 Sa	7 22 05	20 17 33	12♉59 07	19 59 22	22 49.8	20 12.4	3 50.4	22 59.8	28 54.0	22 16.8	29 57.8	11 36.8	10 05.3	29 35.1
13 Su	7 26 01	21 14 47	26 58 26	3♊56 04	22 45.8	22 21.4	4 55.9	23 34.5	28 53.1	22 15.6	29 58.8	11 40.3	10 06.4	29 34.2
14 M	7 29 58	22 12 02	10♊52 04	17 46 06	22 39.0	24 29.6	6 01.2	24 09.4	28 52.5	22 14.6	29 59.9	11 43.9	10 07.3	29 33.2
15 Tu	7 33 55	23 09 17	24 37 53	1♋27 03	22 29.5	26 36.8	7 06.3	24 44.3	28D52.3	22 13.8	0♏01.1	11 47.4	10 08.3	29 32.2
16 W	7 37 51	24 06 33	8♋13 17	14 56 12	22 18.0	28 43.0	8 11.2	25 19.4	28 52.5	22 13.1	0 02.4	11 51.0	10 09.2	29 31.2
17 Th	7 41 48	25 03 48	21 35 32	28 10 58	22 05.5	0♌47.8	9 15.9	25 54.5	28 53.0	22 12.7	0 03.7	11 54.6	10 10.1	29 30.2
18 F	7 45 44	26 01 05	4♌42 19	11♌09 25	21 53.1	2 51.3	10 20.4	26 29.7	28 54.0	22 12.4	0 05.2	11 58.2	10 10.9	29 29.2
19 Sa	7 49 41	26 58 21	17 32 12	23 50 43	21 42.1	4 53.3	11 24.6	27 05.1	28 55.2	22D12.3	0 06.8	12 01.8	10 11.8	29 28.1
20 Su	7 53 37	27 55 38	0♍05 02	6♍15 21	21 33.3	6 53.7	12 28.7	27 40.5	28 56.9	22 12.4	0 08.4	12 05.4	10 12.5	29 27.1
21 M	7 57 34	28 52 55	12 21 58	18 25 13	21 27.1	8 52.5	13 32.5	28 16.1	28 58.9	22 12.6	0 10.2	12 09.1	10 13.3	29 26.0
22 Tu	8 01 30	29 50 13	24 25 31	0♎23 23	21 23.5	10 49.6	14 36.1	28 51.7	29 01.2	22 13.1	0 12.0	12 12.7	10 14.0	29 24.9
23 W	8 05 27	0♌47 30	6♎19 22	12 14 02	21D22.0	12 45.0	15 39.5	29 27.4	29 03.9	22 13.7	0 14.0	12 16.4	10 14.7	29 23.8
24 Th	8 09 24	1 44 48	18 08 01	24 01 59	21R21.7	14 38.7	16 42.6	0♎03.2	29 07.0	22 14.5	0 16.0	12 20.0	10 15.4	29 22.7
25 F	8 13 20	2 42 07	29 56 38	5♏52 37	21 21.8	16 30.7	17 45.5	0 39.1	29 10.4	22 15.5	0 18.2	12 23.7	10 16.0	29 21.6
26 Sa	8 17 17	3 39 26	11♏50 39	17 51 23	21 21.0	18 21.0	18 48.1	1 15.1	29 14.1	22 16.7	0 20.4	12 27.4	10 16.6	29 20.4
27 Su	8 21 13	4 36 45	23 55 29	0♐03 33	21 18.5	20 09.5	19 50.4	1 51.2	29 18.2	22 18.1	0 22.7	12 31.0	10 17.2	29 19.3
28 M	8 25 10	5 34 05	6♐16 09	12 33 46	21 13.8	21 56.3	20 52.4	2 27.4	29 22.6	22 19.6	0 25.1	12 34.7	10 17.7	29 18.1
29 Tu	8 29 06	6 31 25	18 56 49	25 25 36	21 06.6	23 41.3	21 54.2	3 03.6	29 27.3	22 21.3	0 27.7	12 38.4	10 18.2	29 16.9
30 W	8 33 03	7 28 46	2♑00 18	8♑40 59	20 57.3	25 24.7	22 55.7	3 40.0	29 32.4	22 23.2	0 30.2	12 42.1	10 18.7	29 15.8
31 Th	8 36 59	8 26 07	15 27 35	22 19 51	20 46.6	27 06.3	23 56.8	4 16.4	29 37.8	22 25.3	0 32.9	12 45.8	10 19.1	29 14.6

August 2042 LONGITUDE

Day	Sid.Time	☉	0 hr ☽	Noon ☽	True ☊	☿	♀	♂	⚳	♃	♄	♅	♆	♇
1 F	8 40 56	9♌23 29	29♑17 27	6♒19 52	20♈35.7	28♌46.2	24♍57.6	4♎52.9	29♏43.5	22♏27.5	0♏35.7	12♌49.5	10♉19.5	29♒13.4
2 Sa	8 44 53	10 20 52	13♒26 30	20 36 38	20R25.6	0♍24.5	25 58.1	5 29.5	29 49.6	22 30.0	0 38.6	12 53.3	10 19.9	29R12.1
3 Su	8 48 49	11 18 16	27 49 29	5♓04 15	20 17.5	2 01.0	26 58.3	6 06.2	29 55.9	22 32.5	0 41.5	12 57.0	10 20.3	29 10.9
4 M	8 52 46	12 15 41	12♓20 08	19 36 21	20 11.8	3 35.9	27 58.1	6 43.0	0♐02.5	22 35.3	0 44.6	13 00.7	10 20.6	29 09.7
5 Tu	8 56 42	13 13 07	26 52 12	4♈07 03	20 08.8	5 09.1	28 57.6	7 19.9	0 09.5	22 38.2	0 47.7	13 04.4	10 20.8	29 08.4
6 W	9 00 39	14 10 34	11♈20 22	18 31 43	20D07.9	6 40.6	29 56.7	7 56.8	0 16.8	22 41.4	0 50.9	13 08.1	10 21.1	29 07.2
7 Th	9 04 35	15 08 03	25 40 45	2♉47 14	20R08.1	8 10.4	0♎55.5	8 33.8	0 24.3	22 44.6	0 54.2	13 11.8	10 21.3	29 05.9
8 F	9 08 32	16 05 32	9♉51 01	16 51 58	20 08.5	9 38.5	1 53.8	9 11.0	0 32.2	22 48.1	0 57.6	13 15.5	10 21.5	29 04.7
9 Sa	9 12 28	17 03 04	23 50 03	0♊45 15	20 07.7	11 04.8	2 51.8	9 48.2	0 40.3	22 51.7	1 01.0	13 19.2	10 21.6	29 03.4
10 Su	9 16 25	18 00 36	7♊37 33	14 26 58	20 04.9	12 29.5	3 49.4	10 25.5	0 48.7	22 55.5	1 04.6	13 22.9	10 21.7	29 02.2
11 M	9 20 22	18 58 10	21 13 29	27 57 05	19 59.7	13 52.3	4 46.5	11 02.8	0 57.4	22 59.4	1 08.2	13 26.7	10 21.8	29 00.9
12 Tu	9 24 18	19 55 46	4♋37 45	11♋15 24	19 52.2	15 13.4	5 43.2	11 40.3	1 06.4	23 03.5	1 11.9	13 30.4	10R21.8	28 59.6
13 W	9 28 15	20 53 23	17 50 00	24 21 27	19 42.9	16 32.6	6 39.5	12 17.8	1 15.7	23 07.8	1 15.7	13 34.1	10 21.9	28 58.3
14 Th	9 32 11	21 51 01	0♌49 43	7♌14 41	19 32.7	17 49.9	7 35.3	12 55.5	1 25.2	23 12.3	1 19.6	13 37.7	10 21.8	28 57.0
15 F	9 36 08	22 48 40	13 36 21	19 54 40	19 22.7	19 05.2	8 30.6	13 33.2	1 35.1	23 16.9	1 23.6	13 41.4	10 21.8	28 55.7
16 Sa	9 40 04	23 46 20	26 09 38	2♍21 19	19 13.7	20 18.6	9 25.5	14 11.0	1 45.1	23 21.6	1 27.6	13 45.1	10 21.7	28 54.4
17 Su	9 44 01	24 44 02	8♍29 50	14 35 18	19 06.6	21 29.9	10 19.8	14 48.9	1 55.5	23 26.6	1 31.7	13 48.8	10 21.6	28 53.1
18 M	9 47 57	25 41 45	20 37 58	26 38 04	19 01.7	22 39.0	11 13.5	15 26.9	2 06.1	23 31.6	1 35.9	13 52.4	10 21.4	28 51.8
19 Tu	9 51 54	26 39 28	2♎35 56	8♎31 57	18D59.1	23 45.9	12 06.8	16 04.9	2 16.9	23 36.9	1 40.2	13 56.1	10 21.2	28 50.5
20 W	9 55 51	27 37 14	14 26 32	20 20 11	18 58.5	24 50.5	12 59.4	16 43.0	2 28.1	23 42.3	1 44.5	13 59.7	10 21.0	28 49.2
21 Th	9 59 47	28 35 00	26 13 25	2♏06 48	18 59.2	25 52.6	13 51.4	17 21.2	2 39.4	23 47.8	1 49.0	14 03.4	10 20.7	28 47.9
22 F	10 03 44	29 32 47	8♏00 56	13 56 27	19 00.4	26 52.1	14 42.9	17 59.5	2 51.0	23 53.5	1 53.5	14 07.0	10 20.5	28 46.6
23 Sa	10 07 40	0♍30 36	19 53 59	25 54 12	19R01.3	27 49.0	15 33.6	18 37.9	3 02.9	23 59.4	1 58.0	14 10.6	10 20.1	28 45.3
24 Su	10 11 37	1 28 26	1♐57 45	8♐05 18	19 01.2	28 43.0	16 23.7	19 16.4	3 14.9	24 05.4	2 02.7	14 14.2	10 19.8	28 44.0
25 M	10 15 33	2 26 17	14 17 26	20 34 45	18 59.4	29 33.9	17 13.1	19 54.9	3 27.2	24 11.5	2 07.4	14 17.8	10 19.4	28 42.7
26 Tu	10 19 30	3 24 09	26 57 45	3♑26 54	18 55.8	0♎21.7	18 01.8	20 33.5	3 39.8	24 17.8	2 12.2	14 21.3	10 19.0	28 41.4
27 W	10 23 26	4 22 03	10♑02 30	16 44 48	18 50.6	1 06.1	18 49.7	21 12.2	3 52.6	24 24.3	2 17.0	14 24.9	10 18.6	28 40.1
28 Th	10 27 23	5 19 58	23 33 51	0♒29 37	18 44.3	1 46.9	19 36.9	21 50.9	4 05.5	24 30.9	2 21.9	14 28.4	10 18.1	28 38.8
29 F	10 31 20	6 17 54	7♒31 49	14 40 03	18 37.6	2 23.9	20 23.2	22 29.8	4 18.7	24 37.6	2 26.9	14 32.0	10 17.6	28 37.5
30 Sa	10 35 16	7 15 52	21 53 45	29 12 10	18 31.3	2 56.8	21 08.6	23 08.7	4 32.2	24 44.4	2 32.0	14 35.5	10 17.1	28 36.2
31 Su	10 39 13	8 13 51	6♓34 27	13♓59 36	18 26.4	3 25.3	21 53.2	23 47.7	4 45.8	24 51.4	2 37.1	14 39.0	10 16.5	28 34.9

Astro Data Dy Hr Mn	Planet Ingress Dy Hr Mn	Last Aspect Dy Hr Mn	☽ Ingress Dy Hr Mn	Last Aspect Dy Hr Mn	☽ Ingress Dy Hr Mn	☽ Phases & Eclipses Dy Hr Mn
♄ D 2 23:48	☿ ♋ 3 0:11	2 11:10 ♄ ⚹	♑ 2 11:22	31 15:01 ♀ △	♒ 1 1:13	3 8:09 ○ 11♑34
☽ 0N 9 5:20	♀ ♍ 9 0:02	4 16:22 ♄ □	♒ 4 16:34	3 2:16 ♇ ☌	♓ 3 3:36	10 5:38 ☾ 18♈08
⚳ D 15 12:16	♄ ♏ 14 13:59	6 19:51 ♄ △	♓ 6 20:01	5 2:50 ♀ ☍	♈ 5 5:11	17 5:52 ● 24♋49
♃ D 19 12:48	☿ ♌ 17 2:47	8 9:59 ♃ △	♈ 8 22:52	7 5:46 ♇ ⚹	♉ 7 7:17	25 5:01 ☽ 2♏25
☽ 0S 22 18:26	☉ ♌ 22 16:06	11 1:44 ♄ ☍	♉ 11 1:50	9 9:03 ♇ □	♊ 9 10:41	
♂ 0S 26 2:16	♂ ♎ 24 9:51	13 4:29 ♇ □	♊ 13 5:13	11 13:54 ♇ △	♋ 11 15:40	1 17:33 ○ 9♒37
		15 8:38 ♇ △	♋ 15 9:26	13 9:43 ♃ △	♌ 13 22:27	8 10:35 ☾ 16♉02
♀ 0S 5 4:39	☿ ♍ 2 5:59	17 7:39 ♂ ⚹	♌ 17 15:20	16 5:19 ♇ ☍	♍ 16 7:26	15 18:01 ● 23♌03
☽ 0N 5 10:47	⚳ ♐ 4 2:56	19 22:48 ♇ ☍	♍ 19 23:50	18 5:44 ♃ ⚹	♎ 18 18:46	23 21:55 ☽ 0♐55
♆ R 13 9:09	♀ ♎ 6 13:20	22 10:47 ☉ ⚹	♎ 22 11:13	21 5:16 ♇ △	♏ 21 7:42	31 2:02 ○ 7♓50
☽ 0S 19 1:16	☉ ♍ 22 23:18	24 22:50 ♇ △	♏ 25 0:07	23 17:39 ♇ □	♐ 23 20:08	
☿ 0S 21 8:53	☿ ♎ 26 0:53	27 10:34 ♇ □	♐ 27 11:53	26 3:14 ♇ ⚹	♑ 26 5:39	
		29 19:03 ♇ ⚹	♑ 29 20:22	28 1:34 ♃ ⚹	♒ 28 11:09	
				30 11:01 ♇ ☌	♓ 30 13:18	

Astro Data

1 July 2042
Julian Day # 52047
SVP 4♓40'04"
GC 27♐26.0 ⚴ 9♎07.7
Eris 29♈38.4 ⚵ 20♎23.9
⚷ 4♌19.8 ⚶ 25♋48.3
☽ Mean ☊ 23♈05.6

1 August 2042
Julian Day # 52078
SVP 4♓39'59"
GC 27♐26.0 ⚴ 17♎50.5
Eris 29♈41.4R ⚵ 25♎13.4
⚷ 7♌59.6 ⚶ 9♌41.0
☽ Mean ☊ 21♈27.1

LONGITUDE — September 2042

Day	Sid.Time	☉	0 hr ☽	Noon☽	True☊	☿	♀	♂	⚳	♃	♄	♅	♆	♇
1 M	10 43 09	9♍11 52	21♓26 38	28♓54 29	18♈23.2	3♎49.3	22♎36.9	24♎26.7	4♐59.6	24♏58.6	2♏42.3	14♌42.4	10♉15.9	28♒33.6
2 Tu	10 47 06	10 09 54	6♈22 07	13♈48 34	18D 21.8	4 08.4	23 19.6	25 05.8	5 13.6	25 05.8	2 47.5	14 45.9	10R 15.2	28R 32.4
3 W	10 51 02	11 07 58	21 12 57	28 34 32	18 22.1	4 22.4	24 01.3	25 45.1	5 27.9	25 13.2	2 52.8	14 49.3	10 14.6	28 31.1
4 Th	10 54 59	12 06 05	5♉52 38	13♉06 47	18 23.3	4R 30.9	24 42.1	26 24.3	5 42.3	25 20.8	2 58.2	14 52.7	10 13.9	28 29.8
5 F	10 58 55	13 04 13	20 16 36	27 21 49	18 24.6	4 33.6	25 21.7	27 03.7	5 56.9	25 28.4	3 03.6	14 56.1	10 13.2	28 28.6
6 Sa	11 02 52	14 02 24	4♊22 20	11♊18 04	18R 25.4	4 30.5	26 00.3	27 43.2	6 11.7	25 36.2	3 09.1	14 59.5	10 12.4	28 27.3
7 Su	11 06 49	15 00 36	18 09 04	24 55 26	18 25.0	4 21.0	26 37.7	28 22.7	6 26.7	25 44.1	3 14.6	15 02.8	10 11.7	28 26.1
8 M	11 10 45	15 58 50	1♋37 18	8♋14 49	18 23.2	4 05.3	27 14.0	29 02.3	6 41.9	25 52.2	3 20.3	15 06.2	10 10.9	28 24.9
9 Tu	11 14 42	16 57 07	14 48 12	21 17 38	18 19.9	3 43.0	27 49.0	29 42.0	6 57.3	26 00.4	3 25.9	15 09.5	10 10.0	28 23.6
10 W	11 18 38	17 55 25	27 43 19	4♌05 26	18 15.6	3 14.1	28 22.7	0♏21.7	7 12.9	26 08.7	3 31.6	15 12.8	10 09.2	28 22.4
11 Th	11 22 35	18 53 46	10♌24 11	16 39 46	18 10.6	2 38.9	28 55.2	1 01.6	7 28.6	26 17.1	3 37.4	15 16.0	10 08.3	28 21.2
12 F	11 26 31	19 52 08	22 52 19	29 02 03	18 05.7	1 57.5	29 26.2	1 41.5	7 44.5	26 25.6	3 43.3	15 19.3	10 07.3	28 20.0
13 Sa	11 30 28	20 50 32	5♍09 06	11♍13 41	18 01.4	1 10.3	29 55.8	2 21.5	8 00.6	26 34.3	3 49.1	15 22.5	10 06.4	28 18.8
14 Su	11 34 24	21 48 59	17 15 58	23 16 08	17 58.2	0 17.9	0♏23.9	3 01.5	8 16.9	26 43.1	3 55.1	15 25.6	10 05.4	28 17.6
15 M	11 38 21	22 47 26	29 14 26	5♎11 05	17 56.2	29♍21.1	0 50.5	3 41.7	8 33.3	26 52.0	4 01.1	15 28.8	10 04.4	28 16.5
16 Tu	11 42 18	23 45 56	11♎06 22	17 00 34	17D 55.5	28 21.0	1 15.4	4 21.9	8 49.9	27 01.0	4 07.1	15 31.9	10 03.4	28 15.3
17 W	11 46 14	24 44 28	22 54 01	28 47 05	17 55.9	27 18.6	1 38.7	5 02.2	9 06.7	27 10.1	4 13.2	15 35.0	10 02.3	28 14.1
18 Th	11 50 11	25 43 01	4♏40 08	10♏33 38	17 57.1	26 15.3	2 00.3	5 42.6	9 23.6	27 19.3	4 19.3	15 38.1	10 01.2	28 13.0
19 F	11 54 07	26 41 36	16 28 02	22 23 50	17 58.8	25 12.7	2 20.0	6 23.0	9 40.6	27 28.7	4 25.5	15 41.1	10 00.1	28 11.9
20 Sa	11 58 04	27 40 13	28 21 32	4♐21 43	18 00.4	24 12.3	2 37.9	7 03.5	9 57.9	27 38.1	4 31.8	15 44.1	9 59.0	28 10.8
21 Su	12 02 00	28 38 52	10♐24 56	16 31 45	18 01.5	23 15.5	2 53.9	7 44.1	10 15.2	27 47.7	4 38.0	15 47.1	9 57.9	28 09.7
22 M	12 05 57	29 37 32	22 42 45	28 58 30	18R 02.0	22 24.0	3 07.9	8 24.8	10 32.8	27 57.4	4 44.4	15 50.0	9 56.7	28 08.6
23 Tu	12 09 53	0♎36 14	5♑19 32	11♑46 21	18 01.6	21 38.9	3 19.9	9 05.5	10 50.4	28 07.1	4 50.7	15 52.9	9 55.5	28 07.5
24 W	12 13 50	1 34 58	18 19 24	24 59 01	18 00.5	21 01.5	3 29.7	9 46.3	11 08.3	28 17.0	4 57.1	15 55.8	9 54.3	28 06.5
25 Th	12 17 47	2 33 43	1♒45 29	8♒38 54	17 58.8	20 32.8	3 37.3	10 27.2	11 26.2	28 27.0	5 03.6	15 58.6	9 53.0	28 05.5
26 F	12 21 43	3 32 30	15 39 16	22 46 24	17 56.9	20 13.6	3 42.8	11 08.1	11 44.3	28 37.0	5 10.1	16 01.4	9 51.7	28 04.4
27 Sa	12 25 40	4 31 19	29 59 58	7♓19 26	17 55.2	20D 04.1	3R 45.9	11 49.2	12 02.5	28 47.2	5 16.6	16 04.2	9 50.5	28 03.4
28 Su	12 29 36	5 30 09	14♓44 05	22 12 03	17 53.9	20 04.9	3 46.8	12 30.2	12 20.9	28 57.4	5 23.2	16 06.9	9 49.1	28 02.4
29 M	12 33 33	6 29 01	29 45 20	7♈19 49	17D 53.1	20 15.8	3 45.3	13 11.4	12 39.4	29 07.8	5 29.8	16 09.6	9 47.8	28 01.5
30 Tu	12 37 29	7 27 56	14♈55 20	22 30 39	17 53.0	20 36.7	3 41.4	13 52.6	12 58.0	29 18.2	5 36.4	16 12.3	9 46.5	28 00.5

LONGITUDE — October 2042

Day	Sid.Time	☉	0 hr ☽	Noon☽	True☊	☿	♀	♂	⚳	♃	♄	♅	♆	♇
1 W	12 41 26	8♎26 52	0♉04 38	7♉36 08	17♈53.4	21♍07.2	3♏35.1	14♏33.9	13♐16.7	29♏28.8	5♏43.1	16♌14.9	9♉45.1	27♒59.6
2 Th	12 45 22	9 25 51	15 04 11	22 27 55	17 54.1	21 47.0	3R 26.4	15 15.3	13 35.6	29 39.4	5 49.8	16 17.5	9R 43.7	27R 58.7
3 F	12 49 19	10 24 52	29 46 37	6♊59 43	17 54.8	22 35.4	3 15.4	15 56.7	13 54.6	29 50.1	5 56.5	16 20.0	9 42.3	27 57.8
4 Sa	12 53 16	11 23 56	14♊06 51	21 07 48	17 55.3	23 31.8	3 01.9	16 38.3	14 13.7	0♐00.9	6 03.3	16 22.5	9 40.9	27 56.9
5 Su	12 57 12	12 23 02	28 02 29	4♋50 56	17R 55.6	24 35.4	2 46.1	17 19.9	14 33.0	0 11.8	6 10.1	16 25.0	9 39.4	27 56.0
6 M	13 01 09	13 22 10	11♋33 18	18 09 50	17 55.7	25 45.6	2 28.0	18 01.5	14 52.3	0 22.8	6 16.9	16 27.4	9 38.0	27 55.2
7 Tu	13 05 05	14 21 20	24 40 50	1♌06 40	17 55.5	27 01.5	2 07.6	18 43.3	15 11.8	0 33.8	6 23.8	16 29.8	9 36.5	27 54.3
8 W	13 09 02	15 20 33	7♌27 44	13 44 25	17 55.2	28 22.5	1 45.0	19 25.1	15 31.4	0 45.0	6 30.7	16 32.1	9 35.0	27 53.5
9 Th	13 12 58	16 19 48	19 57 09	26 06 21	17 55.0	29 47.9	1 20.4	20 06.9	15 51.1	0 56.2	6 37.6	16 34.4	9 33.5	27 52.7
10 F	13 16 55	17 19 05	2♍12 25	8♍15 44	17D 54.8	1♎17.1	0 53.8	20 48.9	16 10.9	1 07.5	6 44.5	16 36.7	9 31.9	27 52.0
11 Sa	13 20 51	18 18 25	14 16 42	20 15 40	17 54.8	2 49.4	0 25.3	21 30.9	16 30.8	1 18.9	6 51.5	16 38.9	9 30.4	27 51.2
12 Su	13 24 48	19 17 46	26 12 58	2♎08 54	17 54.9	4 24.4	29♎55.2	22 13.0	16 50.8	1 30.3	6 58.5	16 41.1	9 28.9	27 50.5
13 M	13 28 44	20 17 10	8♎03 48	13 57 57	17R 55.0	6 01.4	29 23.5	22 55.2	17 10.9	1 41.8	7 05.5	16 43.2	9 27.3	27 49.8
14 Tu	13 32 41	21 16 35	19 51 36	25 45 04	17 54.9	7 40.2	28 50.4	23 37.4	17 31.2	1 53.4	7 12.5	16 45.3	9 25.7	27 49.1
15 W	13 36 38	22 16 03	1♏38 36	7♏32 29	17 54.7	9 20.4	28 16.2	24 19.7	17 51.5	2 05.1	7 19.6	16 47.3	9 24.1	27 48.5
16 Th	13 40 34	23 15 33	13 27 00	19 22 27	17 54.2	11 01.5	27 41.0	25 02.1	18 11.9	2 16.8	7 26.7	16 49.3	9 22.5	27 47.8
17 F	13 44 31	24 15 05	25 19 08	1♐17 23	17 53.4	12 43.3	27 05.1	25 44.6	18 32.5	2 28.6	7 33.7	16 51.2	9 20.9	27 47.2
18 Sa	13 48 27	25 14 38	7♐17 33	13 20 01	17 52.4	14 25.7	26 28.7	26 27.1	18 53.1	2 40.5	7 40.9	16 53.1	9 19.3	27 46.6
19 Su	13 52 24	26 14 14	19 25 10	25 33 24	17 51.4	16 08.4	25 52.1	27 09.7	19 13.8	2 52.5	7 48.0	16 55.0	9 17.7	27 46.0
20 M	13 56 20	27 13 51	1♑45 08	8♑00 50	17 50.5	17 51.2	25 15.5	27 52.3	19 34.6	3 04.5	7 55.1	16 56.8	9 16.0	27 45.5
21 Tu	14 00 17	28 13 30	14 20 56	20 45 50	17D 50.0	19 34.0	24 39.0	28 35.0	19 55.5	3 16.6	8 02.3	16 58.5	9 14.4	27 45.0
22 W	14 04 13	29 13 11	27 15 59	3♒51 46	17 49.9	21 16.6	24 03.1	29 17.8	20 16.5	3 28.7	8 09.4	17 00.2	9 12.7	27 44.5
23 Th	14 08 10	0♏12 53	10♒33 29	17 21 26	17 50.4	22 59.1	23 27.9	0♐00.7	20 37.6	3 40.9	8 16.6	17 01.9	9 11.1	27 44.0
24 F	14 12 07	1 12 37	24 15 46	1♓16 33	17 51.3	24 41.2	22 53.6	0 43.6	20 58.8	3 53.1	8 23.8	17 03.5	9 09.4	27 43.6
25 Sa	14 16 03	2 12 23	8♓23 45	15 37 07	17 52.4	26 23.1	22 20.5	1 26.6	21 20.0	4 05.4	8 31.0	17 05.0	9 07.7	27 43.1
26 Su	14 20 00	3 12 10	22 56 18	0♈20 44	17 53.4	28 04.5	21 48.8	2 09.6	21 41.3	4 17.8	8 38.2	17 06.5	9 06.0	27 42.7
27 M	14 23 56	4 11 59	7♈49 42	15 22 18	17R 53.9	29 45.5	21 18.6	2 52.7	22 02.7	4 30.2	8 45.4	17 08.0	9 04.4	27 42.3
28 Tu	14 27 53	5 11 50	22 57 30	0♉34 10	17 53.6	1♏26.1	20 50.3	3 35.9	22 24.2	4 42.7	8 52.6	17 09.4	9 02.7	27 42.0
29 W	14 31 49	6 11 43	8♉11 04	15 46 56	17 52.4	3 06.2	20 23.8	4 19.1	22 45.8	4 55.2	8 59.8	17 10.7	9 01.0	27 41.7
30 Th	14 35 46	7 11 38	23 20 33	0♊50 45	17 50.2	4 45.9	19 59.3	5 02.5	23 07.4	5 07.7	9 07.1	17 12.0	8 59.3	27 41.4
31 F	14 39 42	8 11 35	8♊16 29	15 36 51	17 47.5	6 25.1	19 37.1	5 45.8	23 29.1	5 20.4	9 14.3	17 13.3	8 57.6	27 41.1

Astro Data (Dy Hr Mn)

☽0N 1 18:49
☿R 5 11:21
☽0S 15 7:48
☿0N 20 15:59
☉0S 22 21:11
♃□♇ 23 12:56
☿D 27 22:20
♀R 28 8:41
☽0N 29 5:20

☽0S 12 13:59
☿0S 12 14:11
☽0N 26 16:27
♄☍♆ 29 15:08

Planet Ingress (Dy Hr Mn)

♂ ♏ 9 22:53
♀ ♏ 13 15:30
☿ ♍R 14 19:45
☉ ♎ 22 21:11

♃ ♐ 4 9:59
☿ ♎ 9 15:18
♀ ♎R 12 8:14
☉ ♏ 23 6:49
♂ ♐ 23 11:37
☿ ♏ 27 15:27

Last Aspect / ☽ Ingress (Dy Hr Mn / Dy Hr Mn)

1 5:38 ♃ △ ♈ 1 13:45
3 11:54 ♇ ⚹ ♉ 3 14:20
5 13:54 ♇ □ ♊ 5 16:30
7 18:30 ♂ △ ♋ 7 21:05
10 0:45 ♀ □ ♌ 10 4:17
12 12:49 ♀ ⚹ ♍ 12 13:53
15 1:06 ☿ ☌ ♎ 15 1:32
17 10:53 ♇ △ ♏ 17 14:29
19 23:40 ♇ □ ♐ 20 3:17
22 13:20 ☉ □ ♑ 22 13:57
24 17:57 ♃ ⚹ ♒ 24 20:54
26 21:50 ♃ □ ♓ 27 0:00
28 22:51 ♃ △ ♈ 29 0:23
30 20:42 ♇ ⚹ ♉ 30 23:53

Last Aspect / ☽ Ingress (Dy Hr Mn / Dy Hr Mn)

2 23:57 ♃ ☍ ♊ 3 0:22
4 23:49 ♇ △ ♋ 5 3:26
7 3:30 ☿ ⚹ ♌ 7 9:55
9 15:28 ♇ ☍ ♍ 9 19:39
11 14:41 ♂ ⚹ ♎ 12 7:39
14 18:00 ♀ ☌ ♏ 14 20:39
17 4:58 ♇ □ ♐ 17 9:25
19 16:18 ♇ ⚹ ♑ 19 20:37
22 3:14 ♂ ⚹ ♒ 22 5:00
24 5:57 ♇ ☌ ♓ 24 9:50
25 1:15 ♆ ⚹ ♈ 26 11:27
28 7:29 ♇ ⚹ ♉ 28 11:06
30 6:57 ♇ □ ♊ 30 10:39

☽ Phases & Eclipses (Dy Hr Mn)

6 17:09 ☾ 14♊15
14 8:50 ● 21♍41
22 13:20 ☽ 29♐41
29 10:34 ○ 6♈26
29 10:44 • A 0.953

6 2:35 ☾ 12♋59
14 2:03 ● 20♎52
14 1:59:15 • A 07'44"
22 2:53 ☽ 28♑51
28 19:48 ○ 5♉31

Astro Data

1 September 2042
Julian Day # 52109
SVP 4♓39'55"
GC 27♐26.1 ⚵ 28♎57.1
Eris 29♈34.5R ⚶ 2♏48.5
⚷ 11♌40.0 ⚴ 23♌49.2
☽ Mean ☊ 19♈48.6

1 October 2042
Julian Day # 52139
SVP 4♓39'52"
GC 27♐26.2 ⚵ 11♏01.0
Eris 29♈20.2R ⚶ 11♏45.0
⚷ 14♌44.9 ⚴ 7♍30.6
☽ Mean ☊ 18♈13.3

November 2042 LONGITUDE

Day	Sid.Time	☉	0 hr ☽	Noon ☽	True ☊	☿	♀	♂	⚳	♃	♄	♅	♆	♇
1 Sa	14 43 39	9♏11 35	22♊51 08	29♊58 48	17♈44.7	8♏03.8	19♎17.1	6♐29.3	23♐50.9	5♐33.0	9♏21.5	17♌14.4	8♉55.9	27♒40.8
2 Su	14 47 36	10 11 36	6♋59 30	13♋53 05	17R42.2	9 42.1	18R59.5	7 12.8	24 12.8	5 45.8	9 28.7	17 15.6	8R54.3	27R40.6
3 M	14 51 32	11 11 40	20 39 34	27 19 06	17 40.4	11 19.9	18 44.2	7 56.3	24 34.7	5 58.5	9 36.0	17 16.7	8 52.6	27 40.4
4 Tu	14 55 29	12 11 45	3♌51 58	10♌18 33	17D39.7	12 57.3	18 31.5	8 40.0	24 56.7	6 11.3	9 43.2	17 17.7	8 50.9	27 40.2
5 W	14 59 25	13 11 53	16 39 20	22 54 50	17 40.0	14 34.2	18 21.2	9 23.7	25 18.8	6 24.2	9 50.4	17 18.7	8 49.2	27 40.1
6 Th	15 03 22	14 12 02	29 05 36	5♍12 14	17 41.3	16 10.7	18 13.4	10 07.4	25 40.9	6 37.0	9 57.6	17 19.6	8 47.5	27 40.0
7 F	15 07 18	15 12 14	11♍15 18	17 15 24	17 43.0	17 46.8	18 08.0	10 51.3	26 03.1	6 50.0	10 04.9	17 20.5	8 45.8	27 39.8
8 Sa	15 11 15	16 12 28	23 13 06	29 08 55	17 44.8	19 22.5	18D05.2	11 35.2	26 25.3	7 02.9	10 12.1	17 21.3	8 44.2	27 39.8
9 Su	15 15 11	17 12 44	5♎03 23	10♎56 59	17R46.0	20 57.9	18 04.8	12 19.1	26 47.7	7 15.9	10 19.3	17 22.1	8 42.5	27 39.7
10 M	15 19 08	18 13 01	16 50 10	22 43 19	17 46.1	22 32.9	18 06.8	13 03.1	27 10.1	7 29.0	10 26.5	17 22.8	8 40.8	27D39.7
11 Tu	15 23 05	19 13 21	28 36 49	4♏31 00	17 44.7	24 07.5	18 11.1	13 47.2	27 32.5	7 42.1	10 33.6	17 23.4	8 39.2	27 39.7
12 W	15 27 01	20 13 42	10♏26 09	16 22 34	17 41.6	25 41.8	18 17.8	14 31.4	27 55.0	7 55.2	10 40.8	17 24.0	8 37.5	27 39.7
13 Th	15 30 58	21 14 05	22 20 27	28 20 02	17 36.9	27 15.8	18 26.8	15 15.6	28 17.6	8 08.3	10 48.0	17 24.5	8 35.9	27 39.8
14 F	15 34 54	22 14 30	4♐21 30	10♐25 02	17 30.9	28 49.6	18 38.0	15 59.9	28 40.2	8 21.5	10 55.1	17 25.0	8 34.2	27 39.9
15 Sa	15 38 51	23 14 56	16 30 48	22 39 00	17 24.2	0♐23.0	18 51.4	16 44.2	29 02.9	8 34.7	11 02.2	17 25.5	8 32.6	27 40.0
16 Su	15 42 47	24 15 24	28 49 46	5♑03 20	17 17.5	1 56.2	19 06.8	17 28.6	29 25.7	8 47.9	11 09.4	17 25.8	8 31.0	27 40.1
17 M	15 46 44	25 15 53	11♑19 51	17 39 33	17 11.6	3 29.1	19 24.3	18 13.0	29 48.5	9 01.2	11 16.5	17 26.2	8 29.4	27 40.3
18 Tu	15 50 41	26 16 24	24 02 41	0♒29 28	17 07.0	5 01.8	19 43.8	18 57.6	0♑11.3	9 14.5	11 23.5	17 26.4	8 27.8	27 40.5
19 W	15 54 37	27 16 56	7♒00 11	13 35 04	17 04.2	6 34.2	20 05.2	19 42.1	0 34.2	9 27.8	11 30.6	17 26.6	8 26.2	27 40.7
20 Th	15 58 34	28 17 29	20 14 24	26 58 25	17D03.2	8 06.4	20 28.5	20 26.7	0 57.1	9 41.1	11 37.7	17 26.8	8 24.6	27 41.0
21 F	16 02 30	29 18 03	3♓47 22	10♓41 23	17 03.7	9 38.4	20 53.5	21 11.4	1 20.1	9 54.5	11 44.7	17 26.9	8 23.1	27 41.2
22 Sa	16 06 27	0♐18 38	17 40 36	24 45 01	17 05.0	11 10.1	21 20.3	21 56.2	1 43.2	10 07.8	11 51.7	17R26.9	8 21.5	27 41.5
23 Su	16 10 23	1 19 15	1♈54 35	9♈09 03	17R06.1	12 41.7	21 48.8	22 41.0	2 06.2	10 21.2	11 58.6	17 26.9	8 20.0	27 41.9
24 M	16 14 20	2 19 52	16 28 05	23 51 10	17 06.2	14 13.0	22 18.9	23 25.8	2 29.3	10 34.6	12 05.6	17 26.8	8 18.5	27 42.2
25 Tu	16 18 16	3 20 31	1♉17 38	8♉46 38	17 04.3	15 44.1	22 50.5	24 10.7	2 52.5	10 48.0	12 12.5	17 26.7	8 17.0	27 42.6
26 W	16 22 13	4 21 12	16 17 13	23 48 18	17 00.3	17 14.9	23 23.7	24 55.7	3 15.7	11 01.4	12 19.4	17 26.5	8 15.5	27 43.0
27 Th	16 26 10	5 21 53	1♊18 45	8♊47 22	16 54.0	18 45.5	23 58.3	25 40.7	3 39.0	11 14.9	12 26.3	17 26.3	8 14.1	27 43.4
28 F	16 30 06	6 22 36	16 13 01	23 34 37	16 46.3	20 15.8	24 34.4	26 25.7	4 02.2	11 28.3	12 33.1	17 26.0	8 12.6	27 43.9
29 Sa	16 34 03	7 23 21	0♋51 13	8♋02 01	16 37.8	21 45.8	25 11.8	27 10.9	4 25.6	11 41.8	12 39.9	17 25.6	8 11.2	27 44.4
30 Su	16 37 59	8 24 06	15 06 23	22 03 54	16 29.8	23 15.4	25 50.5	27 56.0	4 48.9	11 55.3	12 46.7	17 25.2	8 09.8	27 44.9

December 2042 LONGITUDE

Day	Sid.Time	☉	0 hr ☽	Noon ☽	True ☊	☿	♀	♂	⚳	♃	♄	♅	♆	♇
1 M	16 41 56	9♐24 53	28♋54 18	5♌37 33	16♈23.2	24♐44.7	26♎30.4	28♐41.3	5♑12.3	12♐08.8	12♏53.4	17♌24.8	8♉08.4	27♒45.4
2 Tu	16 45 52	10 25 42	12♌13 47	18 43 14	16R18.5	26 13.6	27 11.6	29 26.5	5 35.8	12 22.3	13 00.1	17R24.2	8R07.0	27 46.0
3 W	16 49 49	11 26 32	25 06 18	1♍23 29	16D16.0	27 41.9	27 53.9	0♑11.9	5 59.2	12 35.8	13 06.8	17 23.7	8 05.6	27 46.6
4 Th	16 53 45	12 27 23	7♍35 20	13 42 30	16 15.4	29 09.7	28 37.3	0 57.3	6 22.7	12 49.3	13 13.4	17 23.0	8 04.3	27 47.2
5 F	16 57 42	13 28 16	19 45 37	25 45 23	16 16.0	0♑36.7	29 21.8	1 42.7	6 46.3	13 02.8	13 20.0	17 22.4	8 03.0	27 47.8
6 Sa	17 01 39	14 29 10	1♎42 29	7♎37 36	16R16.9	2 03.0	0♏07.3	2 28.2	7 09.8	13 16.3	13 26.6	17 21.6	8 01.7	27 48.5
7 Su	17 05 35	15 30 05	13 31 22	19 24 27	16 17.2	3 28.4	0 53.8	3 13.8	7 33.4	13 29.8	13 33.1	17 20.9	8 00.4	27 49.1
8 M	17 09 32	16 31 02	25 17 25	1♏10 51	16 15.8	4 52.8	1 41.3	3 59.4	7 57.1	13 43.3	13 39.6	17 20.0	7 59.2	27 49.8
9 Tu	17 13 28	17 31 59	7♏05 14	13 01 02	16 12.1	6 15.8	2 29.6	4 45.0	8 20.7	13 56.8	13 46.0	17 19.1	7 57.9	27 50.6
10 W	17 17 25	18 32 58	18 58 40	24 58 27	16 05.7	7 37.4	3 18.8	5 30.7	8 44.4	14 10.3	13 52.4	17 18.2	7 56.7	27 51.3
11 Th	17 21 21	19 33 58	1♐00 41	7♐05 35	15 56.6	8 57.4	4 08.9	6 16.5	9 08.1	14 23.8	13 58.8	17 17.2	7 55.6	27 52.1
12 F	17 25 18	20 34 59	13 13 19	19 24 00	15 45.4	10 15.3	4 59.8	7 02.3	9 31.9	14 37.3	14 05.1	17 16.1	7 54.4	27 52.9
13 Sa	17 29 14	21 36 01	25 37 42	1♑54 26	15 32.9	11 30.9	5 51.4	7 48.1	9 55.6	14 50.8	14 11.3	17 15.1	7 53.3	27 53.8
14 Su	17 33 11	22 37 03	8♑14 10	14 36 55	15 20.3	12 43.8	6 43.8	8 34.0	10 19.4	15 04.2	14 17.6	17 13.9	7 52.2	27 54.6
15 M	17 37 08	23 38 07	21 02 35	27 31 09	15 08.7	13 53.5	7 36.9	9 20.0	10 43.2	15 17.7	14 23.7	17 12.7	7 51.1	27 55.5
16 Tu	17 41 04	24 39 10	4♒02 34	10♒36 48	14 59.2	14 59.6	8 30.7	10 06.0	11 07.1	15 31.1	14 29.8	17 11.5	7 50.1	27 56.4
17 W	17 45 01	25 40 14	17 13 51	23 53 45	14 52.5	16 01.5	9 25.1	10 52.0	11 30.9	15 44.6	14 35.9	17 10.2	7 49.1	27 57.3
18 Th	17 48 57	26 41 19	0♓36 32	7♓22 17	14 48.6	16 58.6	10 20.2	11 38.1	11 54.8	15 58.0	14 41.9	17 08.8	7 48.1	27 58.3
19 F	17 52 54	27 42 24	14 11 05	21 03 03	14D47.1	17 50.0	11 15.9	12 24.2	12 18.7	16 11.4	14 47.8	17 07.4	7 47.1	27 59.3
20 Sa	17 56 50	28 43 29	27 58 16	4♈56 48	14R47.0	18 35.1	12 12.2	13 10.3	12 42.6	16 24.8	14 53.7	17 06.0	7 46.2	28 00.2
21 Su	18 00 47	29 44 34	11♈58 42	19 03 56	14 47.1	19 13.0	13 09.0	13 56.5	13 06.5	16 38.1	14 59.6	17 04.5	7 45.3	28 01.3
22 M	18 04 43	0♑45 40	26 12 22	3♉23 49	14 46.0	19 42.9	14 06.4	14 42.8	13 30.4	16 51.5	15 05.3	17 03.0	7 44.4	28 02.3
23 Tu	18 08 40	1 46 45	10♉37 56	17 54 17	14 42.5	20 03.7	15 04.3	15 29.1	13 54.4	17 04.8	15 11.1	17 01.4	7 43.5	28 03.4
24 W	18 12 37	2 47 51	25 12 16	2♊31 12	14 36.2	20R14.7	16 02.8	16 15.4	14 18.3	17 18.1	15 16.7	16 59.8	7 42.7	28 04.4
25 Th	18 16 33	3 48 58	9♊50 16	17 08 36	14 27.0	20 15.0	17 01.7	17 01.7	14 42.3	17 31.3	15 22.3	16 58.1	7 41.9	28 05.5
26 F	18 20 30	4 50 05	24 25 15	1♋39 18	14 15.5	20 04.0	18 01.1	17 48.1	15 06.3	17 44.6	15 27.9	16 56.4	7 41.2	28 06.7
27 Sa	18 24 26	5 51 12	8♋49 52	15 56 06	14 03.0	19 41.2	19 01.0	18 34.6	15 30.3	17 57.8	15 33.3	16 54.7	7 40.5	28 07.8
28 Su	18 28 23	6 52 19	22 57 18	29 52 55	13 50.8	19 06.6	20 01.3	19 21.0	15 54.3	18 11.0	15 38.8	16 52.9	7 39.8	28 09.0
29 M	18 32 19	7 53 26	6♌42 30	13♌25 49	13 40.0	18 20.6	21 02.1	20 07.5	16 18.3	18 24.2	15 44.1	16 51.1	7 39.1	28 10.2
30 Tu	18 36 16	8 54 34	20 02 46	26 33 25	13 31.7	17 23.8	22 03.3	20 54.1	16 42.3	18 37.3	15 49.4	16 49.2	7 38.5	28 11.4
31 W	18 40 13	9 55 43	2♍57 57	9♍16 44	13 26.1	16 17.8	23 04.9	21 40.7	17 06.3	18 50.4	15 54.6	16 47.3	7 37.9	28 12.6

Astro Data

	Dy Hr Mn
☽0S	8 19:58
♀D	9 4:04
♇D	10 19:22
♃⊼♆	15 8:38
♅R	22 15:16
☽0N	23 1:42
☽0S	6 2:09
♃⊻♄	7 23:27
☽0N	20 7:47
♃△♅	23 6:34
☿R	25 0:41

Planet Ingress

	Dy Hr Mn
☿ ♐	15 6:05
⚳ ♑	18 0:08
☉ ♐	22 4:37
♂ ♑	3 5:43
☿ ♑	5 1:51
♀ ♏	6 8:11
☉ ♑	21 18:04

Last Aspect / ☽ Ingress

Last Aspect Dy Hr Mn	☽ Ingress Dy Hr Mn
1 8:07 ♀ △	♋ 1 12:02
2 20:51 ♀ □	♌ 3 16:53
5 21:13 ♇ ☍	♍ 6 1:46
7 13:13 ☿ ⚹	♎ 8 13:44
10 22:04 ♇ △	♏ 11 2:49
13 10:40 ♇ □	♐ 13 15:20
15 21:45 ♇ ⚹	♑ 16 2:16
18 3:30 ☉ ⚹	♒ 18 11:05
20 14:31 ☉ □	♓ 20 17:21
22 6:59 ♂ □	♈ 22 20:49
24 18:13 ♇ ⚹	♉ 24 21:55
26 18:15 ♇ □	♊ 26 21:54
28 18:50 ♇ △	♋ 28 22:35

Last Aspect Dy Hr Mn	☽ Ingress Dy Hr Mn
30 18:56 ♀ □	♌ 1 1:56
3 5:04 ♇ ☍	♍ 3 9:20
4 11:02 ♄ ⚹	♎ 5 20:33
8 5:10 ♇ △	♏ 8 9:36
10 17:45 ♇ □	♐ 10 22:00
13 4:20 ♇ ⚹	♑ 13 8:22
14 11:23 ♄ ⚹	♒ 15 16:34
17 19:17 ♇ ☌	♓ 17 22:55
20 0:27 ☉ □	♈ 20 3:30
22 3:03 ♇ ⚹	♉ 22 6:20
24 4:42 ♇ □	♊ 24 7:52
26 6:06 ♇ △	♋ 26 9:15
27 18:10 ☿ ☍	♌ 28 12:12
30 15:03 ♇ ☍	♍ 30 18:25

☽ Phases & Eclipses

Dy Hr Mn	
4 15:51	☾ 12♌21
12 20:28	● 20♏35
20 14:31	☽ 28♒24
27 6:06	○ 5♊07
4 9:19	☾ 12♍21
12 14:29	● 20♐41
20 0:27	☽ 28♓14
26 17:43	○ 5♋05

Astro Data

1 November 2042
Julian Day # 52170
SVP 4♓39'47"
GC 27♐26.3 ⚴ 24♏12.9
Eris 29♈01.8R ⚵ 21♏55.3
⚷ 16♌55.8 ⚶ 21♍19.9
☽ Mean ☊ 16♈34.8

1 December 2042
Julian Day # 52200
SVP 4♓39'42"
GC 27♐26.3 ⚴ 7♐14.0
Eris 28♈45.6R ⚵ 2♐08.1
⚷ 17♌38.1R ⚶ 3♎52.5
☽ Mean ☊ 14♈59.5

LONGITUDE — January 2043

Day	Sid.Time	☉	0 hr ☽	Noon ☽	True ☊	☿	♀	♂	⚳	♃	♄	♅	♆	♇
1 Th	18 44 09	10♑56 51	15♍30 11	21♍38 50	13♈23.2	15♑04.3	24♏06.9	22♑27.3	17♑30.3	19♐03.4	15♏59.7	16♌45.4	7♉37.3	28♒13.8
2 F	18 48 06	11 58 00	27 43 16	3♎44 09	13R22.1	13R45.6	25 09.2	23 13.9	17 54.4	19 16.5	16 04.8	16R43.4	7R36.8	28 15.1
3 Sa	18 52 02	12 59 10	9♎42 09	15 37 59	13 22.0	12 24.4	26 12.0	24 00.6	18 18.4	19 29.4	16 09.8	16 41.4	7 36.3	28 16.4
4 Su	18 55 59	14 00 19	21 32 21	27 25 58	13 21.7	11 03.4	27 15.0	24 47.4	18 42.4	19 42.4	16 14.8	16 39.3	7 35.8	28 17.6
5 M	18 59 55	15 01 29	3♏19 31	9♏13 41	13 19.9	9 45.0	28 18.4	25 34.1	19 06.5	19 55.3	16 19.6	16 37.2	7 35.4	28 19.0
6 Tu	19 03 52	16 02 39	15 09 05	21 06 20	13 15.9	8 31.7	29 22.1	26 20.9	19 30.5	20 08.2	16 24.4	16 35.1	7 35.0	28 20.3
7 W	19 07 48	17 03 49	27 05 58	3♐08 27	13 09.0	7 25.3	0♐26.2	27 07.7	19 54.6	20 21.0	16 29.1	16 32.9	7 34.6	28 21.6
8 Th	19 11 45	18 05 00	9♐14 12	15 23 34	12 59.2	6 27.3	1 30.5	27 54.6	20 18.6	20 33.8	16 33.8	16 30.7	7 34.3	28 23.0
9 F	19 15 42	19 06 10	21 36 46	27 54 01	12 47.1	5 38.6	2 35.1	28 41.5	20 42.7	20 46.5	16 38.3	16 28.5	7 34.0	28 24.4
10 Sa	19 19 38	20 07 21	4♑15 22	10♑40 49	12 33.4	4 59.8	3 40.0	29 28.4	21 06.7	20 59.2	16 42.8	16 26.3	7 33.7	28 25.8
11 Su	19 23 35	21 08 31	17 10 17	23 43 37	12 19.6	4 30.9	4 45.2	0♒15.4	21 30.8	21 11.8	16 47.2	16 24.0	7 33.5	28 27.2
12 M	19 27 31	22 09 41	0♒20 37	7♒00 58	12 06.7	4 11.9	5 50.6	1 02.3	21 54.8	21 24.4	16 51.6	16 21.7	7 33.3	28 28.6
13 Tu	19 31 28	23 10 50	13 44 25	20 30 39	11 56.1	4D02.3	6 56.3	1 49.3	22 18.8	21 37.0	16 55.8	16 19.4	7 33.1	28 30.1
14 W	19 35 24	24 11 59	27 19 20	4♓10 11	11 48.4	4 01.6	8 02.2	2 36.4	22 42.9	21 49.4	17 00.0	16 17.0	7 33.0	28 31.5
15 Th	19 39 21	25 13 07	11♓02 56	17 57 23	11 43.8	4 09.3	9 08.3	3 23.4	23 06.9	22 01.9	17 04.0	16 14.6	7 32.9	28 33.0
16 F	19 43 17	26 14 14	24 53 19	1♈50 38	11D41.8	4 24.6	10 14.7	4 10.5	23 30.9	22 14.2	17 08.0	16 12.2	7 32.8	28 34.5
17 Sa	19 47 14	27 15 21	8♈49 12	15 48 58	11R41.6	4 46.9	11 21.3	4 57.6	23 54.9	22 26.5	17 11.9	16 09.8	7D32.8	28 36.0
18 Su	19 51 11	28 16 27	22 49 52	29 51 51	11 41.7	5 15.6	12 28.0	5 44.7	24 18.9	22 38.8	17 15.8	16 07.3	7 32.8	28 37.5
19 M	19 55 07	29 17 32	6♉54 51	13♉58 47	11 40.9	5 50.1	13 35.0	6 31.9	24 42.8	22 51.0	17 19.5	16 04.9	7 32.9	28 39.0
20 Tu	19 59 04	0♒18 36	21 03 29	28 08 45	11 38.0	6 29.9	14 42.2	7 19.0	25 06.8	23 03.1	17 23.2	16 02.4	7 32.9	28 40.6
21 W	20 03 00	1 19 40	5♊14 18	12♊19 47	11 32.5	7 14.4	15 49.6	8 06.2	25 30.7	23 15.1	17 26.7	15 59.9	7 33.1	28 42.1
22 Th	20 06 57	2 20 42	19 24 48	26 28 51	11 24.2	8 03.2	16 57.1	8 53.4	25 54.7	23 27.1	17 30.2	15 57.4	7 33.2	28 43.7
23 F	20 10 53	3 21 44	3♋31 23	10♋31 51	11 13.8	8 55.8	18 04.9	9 40.6	26 18.6	23 39.1	17 33.6	15 54.8	7 33.4	28 45.2
24 Sa	20 14 50	4 22 45	17 29 40	24 24 17	11 02.3	9 51.9	19 12.8	10 27.8	26 42.5	23 50.9	17 36.9	15 52.3	7 33.6	28 46.8
25 Su	20 18 47	5 23 45	1♌15 09	8♌01 50	10 50.9	10 51.1	20 20.9	11 15.1	27 06.3	24 02.7	17 40.1	15 49.7	7 33.9	28 48.4
26 M	20 22 43	6 24 44	14 43 57	21 21 14	10 40.8	11 53.2	21 29.1	12 02.3	27 30.2	24 14.4	17 43.2	15 47.1	7 34.2	28 50.0
27 Tu	20 26 40	7 25 42	27 53 30	4♍20 42	10 32.9	12 57.9	22 37.5	12 49.6	27 54.0	24 26.0	17 46.2	15 44.6	7 34.5	28 51.6
28 W	20 30 36	8 26 40	10♍42 53	17 00 13	10 27.5	14 04.9	23 46.1	13 36.9	28 17.9	24 37.6	17 49.1	15 42.0	7 34.9	28 53.3
29 Th	20 34 33	9 27 37	23 12 57	29 21 28	10D24.8	15 14.1	24 54.8	14 24.2	28 41.7	24 49.1	17 52.0	15 39.4	7 35.2	28 54.9
30 F	20 38 29	10 28 33	5♎26 11	11♎27 36	10 24.1	16 25.3	26 03.7	15 11.5	29 05.4	25 00.5	17 54.7	15 36.7	7 35.7	28 56.5
31 Sa	20 42 26	11 29 28	17 26 17	23 22 51	10 24.7	17 38.3	27 12.7	15 58.9	29 29.2	25 11.8	17 57.3	15 34.1	7 36.1	28 58.2

LONGITUDE — February 2043

Day	Sid.Time	☉	0 hr ☽	Noon ☽	True ☊	☿	♀	♂	⚳	♃	♄	♅	♆	♇
1 Su	20 46 22	12♒30 23	29♎17 55	5♏12 11	10♈25.6	18♑52.9	28♐21.8	16♒46.2	29♑52.9	25♐23.1	17♏59.9	15♌31.5	7♉36.6	28♒59.8
2 M	20 50 19	13 31 17	11♏06 18	17 00 59	10R25.8	20 09.1	29 31.1	17 33.6	0♒16.6	25 34.2	18 02.3	15R28.9	7 37.2	29 01.5
3 Tu	20 54 15	14 32 10	22 56 53	28 54 40	10 24.4	21 26.8	0♑40.5	18 21.0	0 40.3	25 45.3	18 04.7	15 26.2	7 37.7	29 03.1
4 W	20 58 12	15 33 02	4♐54 59	10♐58 25	10 21.0	22 45.9	1 50.0	19 08.4	1 04.0	25 56.3	18 06.9	15 23.6	7 38.3	29 04.8
5 Th	21 02 09	16 33 54	17 05 31	23 16 46	10 15.3	24 06.2	2 59.7	19 55.8	1 27.6	26 07.2	18 09.1	15 21.0	7 39.0	29 06.5
6 F	21 06 05	17 34 44	29 32 34	5♑53 15	10 07.6	25 27.7	4 09.5	20 43.2	1 51.2	26 18.1	18 11.1	15 18.4	7 39.6	29 08.2
7 Sa	21 10 02	18 35 34	12♑19 03	18 50 04	9 58.6	26 50.4	5 19.3	21 30.6	2 14.8	26 28.8	18 13.1	15 15.7	7 40.3	29 09.9
8 Su	21 13 58	19 36 22	25 26 20	2♒07 44	9 49.3	28 14.2	6 29.3	22 18.0	2 38.4	26 39.4	18 15.0	15 13.1	7 41.1	29 11.6
9 M	21 17 55	20 37 10	8♒54 04	15 44 59	9 40.5	29 39.0	7 39.4	23 05.5	3 01.9	26 50.0	18 16.7	15 10.5	7 41.8	29 13.3
10 Tu	21 21 51	21 37 56	22 40 05	29 38 53	9 33.4	1♒04.9	8 49.6	23 52.9	3 25.4	27 00.4	18 18.4	15 07.9	7 42.7	29 15.0
11 W	21 25 48	22 38 40	6♓40 50	13♓45 21	9 28.4	2 31.8	9 59.9	24 40.3	3 48.8	27 10.8	18 19.9	15 05.3	7 43.5	29 16.7
12 Th	21 29 45	23 39 23	20 51 50	27 59 44	9D25.7	3 59.6	11 10.2	25 27.8	4 12.2	27 21.0	18 21.3	15 02.7	7 44.4	29 18.4
13 F	21 33 41	24 40 05	5♈08 29	12♈17 34	9 25.2	5 28.4	12 20.7	26 15.2	4 35.6	27 31.1	18 22.7	15 00.1	7 45.3	29 20.1
14 Sa	21 37 38	25 40 45	19 26 34	26 35 04	9 26.1	6 58.1	13 31.2	27 02.7	4 58.9	27 41.2	18 23.9	14 57.5	7 46.2	29 21.8
15 Su	21 41 34	26 41 23	3♉42 46	10♉49 23	9 27.4	8 28.7	14 41.8	27 50.1	5 22.2	27 51.1	18 25.1	14 54.9	7 47.1	29 23.5
16 M	21 45 31	27 42 00	17 54 42	24 58 32	9R28.2	10 00.2	15 52.5	28 37.5	5 45.5	28 00.9	18 26.1	14 52.4	7 48.1	29 25.2
17 Tu	21 49 27	28 42 35	2♊00 43	9♊01 08	9 27.7	11 32.7	17 03.2	29 25.0	6 08.7	28 10.7	18 27.0	14 49.8	7 49.2	29 26.9
18 W	21 53 24	29 43 08	15 59 39	22 56 08	9 25.5	13 06.0	18 14.1	0♓12.4	6 31.9	28 20.3	18 27.9	14 47.3	7 50.2	29 28.7
19 Th	21 57 20	0♓43 39	29 50 25	6♋42 22	9 21.5	14 40.3	19 25.0	0 59.9	6 55.0	28 29.8	18 28.6	14 44.8	7 51.3	29 30.4
20 F	22 01 17	1 44 08	13♋31 47	20 18 32	9 16.0	16 15.5	20 36.0	1 47.3	7 18.1	28 39.2	18 29.2	14 42.3	7 52.5	29 32.1
21 Sa	22 05 14	2 44 36	27 02 22	3♌43 09	9 09.8	17 51.6	21 47.0	2 34.7	7 41.1	28 48.4	18 29.7	14 39.9	7 53.6	29 33.8
22 Su	22 09 10	3 45 02	10♌20 40	16 54 45	9 03.5	19 28.6	22 58.2	3 22.1	8 04.1	28 57.6	18 30.1	14 37.4	7 54.8	29 35.5
23 M	22 13 07	4 45 26	23 25 17	29 52 09	8 58.0	21 06.6	24 09.3	4 09.5	8 27.1	29 06.6	18 30.4	14 35.0	7 56.0	29 37.2
24 Tu	22 17 03	5 45 48	6♍15 18	12♍34 43	8 53.8	22 45.5	25 20.6	4 56.9	8 50.0	29 15.5	18 30.6	14 32.6	7 57.2	29 38.9
25 W	22 21 00	6 46 09	18 50 28	25 02 39	8 51.2	24 25.4	26 31.9	5 44.3	9 12.8	29 24.3	18R30.8	14 30.2	7 58.5	29 40.6
26 Th	22 24 56	7 46 28	1♎11 25	7♎17 02	8D50.2	26 06.2	27 43.3	6 31.7	9 35.7	29 33.0	18 30.8	14 27.8	7 59.8	29 42.3
27 F	22 28 53	8 46 46	13 19 45	19 19 56	8 50.7	27 48.1	28 54.8	7 19.1	9 58.4	29 41.5	18 30.6	14 25.5	8 01.1	29 44.0
28 Sa	22 32 49	9 47 02	25 17 58	1♏14 20	8 52.1	29 30.9	0♒06.3	8 06.4	10 21.1	29 50.0	18 30.4	14 23.2	8 02.5	29 45.7

Astro Data

	Dy Hr Mn
☽0S	2 9:02
♄□♅	8 1:19
☿D	14 1:49
☽0N	16 12:13
♆D	17 17:05
♃□♆	18 0:17
☽0S	29 16:45
☽0N	12 18:05
♄R	25 23:40
☽0S	26 0:41
♃□♆	26 0:44
♃⚹♇	27 20:52

Planet Ingress

		Dy Hr Mn
♀	♐	7 2:12
♂	♒	11 4:09
☉	♒	20 4:41
⚳	♒	1 19:09
♀	♑	2 22:00
☿	♒	9 17:53
♂	♓	18 5:43
☉	♓	18 18:41
♀	♒	28 9:54
☿	♓	28 18:44

Last Aspect / ☽ Ingress

Last Aspect Dy Hr Mn			☽ Ingress	Dy Hr Mn
1 17:19	♇	⚹	♎	2 4:32
4 13:45	♇	△	♏	4 17:14
7 2:30	♇	□	♐	7 5:46
9 12:58	♇	⚹	♑	9 15:59
11 6:53	☉	☌	♒	11 23:23
14 2:06	♇	☌	♓	14 4:42
16 1:34	☉	⚹	♈	16 8:49
18 9:53	♇	⚹	♉	18 12:14
20 12:54	♇	□	♊	20 15:08
22 15:50	♇	△	♋	22 17:59
24 0:10	♄	△	♌	24 21:48
27 1:46	♇	☍	♍	27 3:54
29 2:59	♃	□	♎	29 13:16

Last Aspect / ☽ Ingress

Last Aspect Dy Hr Mn			☽ Ingress	Dy Hr Mn
31 23:21	♇	△	♏	1 1:25
3 12:17	♇	□	♐	3 14:11
5 23:12	♇	⚹	♑	6 0:52
8 4:13	☿	☌	♒	8 8:12
10 11:19	♇	☌	♓	10 12:36
12 10:54	♃	□	♈	12 15:22
14 16:41	♇	⚹	♉	14 17:45
16 19:35	♇	□	♊	16 20:34
18 23:24	♇	△	♋	19 0:17
20 12:34	♀	☍	♌	21 5:18
23 11:32	♇	☍	♍	23 12:15
25 20:36	♃	□	♎	25 21:40
28 9:27	♀	□	♏	28 9:30

☽ Phases & Eclipses

Dy Hr Mn		
3 6:08	☾	12♎44
11 6:53	●	20♑55
18 9:05	☽	28♈09
25 6:56	○	5♌11
2 4:15	☾	13♏12
9 21:07	●	21♒00
16 17:00	☽	27♉55
23 21:58	○	5♍10

Astro Data

1 January 2043
Julian Day # 52231
SVP 4♓39'36"
GC 27♐26.4 ⚴ 20♐28.7
Eris 28♈35.8R ⚵ 12♐32.7
⚷ 16♌44.9R ⚶ 15♎03.3
☽ Mean ☊ 13♈21.0

1 February 2043
Julian Day # 52262
SVP 4♓39'31"
GC 27♐26.5 ⚴ 2♑58.4
Eris 28♈36.1 ⚵ 22♐11.6
⚷ 14♌40.0R ⚶ 22♎47.1
☽ Mean ☊ 11♈42.5

March 2043 — LONGITUDE

Day	Sid.Time	☉	0 hr ☽	Noon ☽	True ☊	☿	♀	♂	⚳	♃	♄	♅	♆	♇
1 Su	22 36 46	10♓47 16	7♏09 29	13♏03 58	8♈54.0	1♓14.8	1♒17.8	8♓53.8	10♒43.8	29♐58.3	18♏30.1	14♌20.9	8♉03.9	29♒47.4
2 M	22 40 42	11 47 30	18 58 20	24 53 12	8 55.7	2 59.8	2 29.4	9 41.1	11 06.4	0♑06.4	18R 29.7	14R 18.6	8 05.3	29 49.1
3 Tu	22 44 39	12 47 41	0♐49 09	6♐46 50	8R 56.7	4 45.7	3 41.1	10 28.5	11 28.9	0 14.5	18 29.2	14 16.4	8 06.7	29 50.8
4 W	22 48 36	13 47 51	12 46 50	18 49 49	8 56.8	6 32.8	4 52.8	11 15.8	11 51.4	0 22.4	18 28.6	14 14.2	8 08.2	29 52.5
5 Th	22 52 32	14 48 00	24 56 20	1♑07 00	8 55.7	8 20.8	6 04.6	12 03.1	12 13.9	0 30.1	18 27.9	14 12.1	8 09.7	29 54.1
6 F	22 56 29	15 48 07	7♑22 19	13 42 47	8 53.6	10 10.0	7 16.5	12 50.4	12 36.2	0 37.8	18 27.1	14 09.9	8 11.2	29 55.8
7 Sa	23 00 25	16 48 12	20 08 47	26 40 37	8 50.7	12 00.3	8 28.3	13 37.7	12 58.6	0 45.3	18 26.1	14 07.8	8 12.7	29 57.5
8 Su	23 04 22	17 48 16	3♒18 32	10♒02 36	8 47.5	13 51.6	9 40.3	14 25.0	13 20.8	0 52.6	18 25.1	14 05.8	8 14.3	29 59.1
9 M	23 08 18	18 48 18	16 52 47	23 48 56	8 44.5	15 43.9	10 52.2	15 12.3	13 43.0	0 59.8	18 24.0	14 03.7	8 15.9	0♓00.8
10 Tu	23 12 15	19 48 18	0♓50 44	7♓57 43	8 42.0	17 37.4	12 04.2	15 59.5	14 05.2	1 06.9	18 22.8	14 01.7	8 17.5	0 02.4
11 W	23 16 11	20 48 16	15 09 19	22 24 51	8 40.5	19 31.8	13 16.2	16 46.7	14 27.2	1 13.8	18 21.4	13 59.8	8 19.1	0 04.0
12 Th	23 20 08	21 48 12	29 43 33	7♈04 32	8D 39.9	21 27.2	14 28.3	17 34.0	14 49.2	1 20.6	18 20.0	13 57.8	8 20.8	0 05.6
13 F	23 24 05	22 48 07	14♈26 57	21 49 54	8 40.2	23 23.6	15 40.4	18 21.1	15 11.2	1 27.2	18 18.5	13 56.0	8 22.5	0 07.3
14 Sa	23 28 01	23 47 59	29 12 33	6♉34 03	8 41.1	25 20.8	16 52.6	19 08.3	15 33.0	1 33.7	18 16.9	13 54.1	8 24.2	0 08.9
15 Su	23 31 58	24 47 49	13♉53 42	21 10 50	8 42.2	27 18.8	18 04.7	19 55.5	15 54.8	1 40.0	18 15.2	13 52.3	8 25.9	0 10.4
16 M	23 35 54	25 47 37	28 24 55	5♊35 31	8 43.2	29 17.4	19 16.9	20 42.6	16 16.5	1 46.2	18 13.4	13 50.5	8 27.7	0 12.0
17 Tu	23 39 51	26 47 23	12♊42 17	19 45 00	8R 43.8	1♈16.6	20 29.2	21 29.7	16 38.2	1 52.2	18 11.5	13 48.8	8 29.5	0 13.6
18 W	23 43 47	27 47 06	26 43 29	3♋37 41	8 43.8	3 16.2	21 41.4	22 16.8	16 59.8	1 58.1	18 09.5	13 47.1	8 31.3	0 15.2
19 Th	23 47 44	28 46 48	10♋27 35	17 13 13	8 43.3	5 16.0	22 53.7	23 03.8	17 21.3	2 03.8	18 07.4	13 45.5	8 33.1	0 16.7
20 F	23 51 40	29 46 26	23 54 42	0♌32 07	8 42.4	7 15.8	24 06.0	23 50.8	17 42.7	2 09.3	18 05.2	13 43.9	8 34.9	0 18.3
21 Sa	23 55 37	0♈46 03	7♌05 36	13 35 19	8 41.4	9 15.2	25 18.3	24 37.8	18 04.0	2 14.7	18 03.0	13 42.3	8 36.8	0 19.8
22 Su	23 59 34	1 45 37	20 01 25	26 24 03	8 40.4	11 14.2	26 30.7	25 24.8	18 25.3	2 19.9	18 00.6	13 40.8	8 38.7	0 21.3
23 M	0 03 30	2 45 09	2♍43 23	8♍59 35	8 39.6	13 12.3	27 43.1	26 11.7	18 46.5	2 25.0	17 58.2	13 39.4	8 40.6	0 22.8
24 Tu	0 07 27	3 44 39	15 12 48	21 23 13	8 39.1	15 09.1	28 55.5	26 58.6	19 07.6	2 29.8	17 55.7	13 38.0	8 42.5	0 24.3
25 W	0 11 23	4 44 07	27 30 59	3♎36 19	8D 38.9	17 04.4	0♓08.0	27 45.5	19 28.6	2 34.6	17 53.1	13 36.6	8 44.4	0 25.7
26 Th	0 15 20	5 43 32	9♎39 23	15 40 24	8 38.9	18 57.6	1 20.4	28 32.4	19 49.5	2 39.1	17 50.4	13 35.3	8 46.3	0 27.2
27 F	0 19 16	6 42 56	21 39 37	27 37 16	8 39.0	20 48.5	2 32.9	29 19.2	20 10.4	2 43.5	17 47.6	13 34.0	8 48.3	0 28.6
28 Sa	0 23 13	7 42 18	3♏33 39	9♏29 05	8R 39.2	22 36.5	3 45.4	0♈06.0	20 31.1	2 47.7	17 44.8	13 32.7	8 50.3	0 30.1
29 Su	0 27 09	8 41 38	15 23 53	21 18 27	8 39.2	24 21.3	4 58.0	0 52.8	20 51.8	2 51.8	17 41.8	13 31.6	8 52.3	0 31.5
30 M	0 31 06	9 40 56	27 13 10	3♐08 28	8 39.1	26 02.4	6 10.5	1 39.5	21 12.4	2 55.7	17 38.8	13 30.4	8 54.3	0 32.9
31 Tu	0 35 03	10 40 13	9♐04 50	15 02 45	8 39.0	27 39.5	7 23.1	2 26.2	21 32.9	2 59.4	17 35.7	13 29.3	8 56.3	0 34.3

April 2043 — LONGITUDE

Day	Sid.Time	☉	0 hr ☽	Noon ☽	True ☊	☿	♀	♂	⚳	♃	♄	♅	♆	♇
1 W	0 38 59	11♈39 27	21♐02 44	27♐05 18	8♈38.8	29♈12.1	8♓35.7	3♈12.9	21♒53.3	3♑02.9	17♏32.6	13♌28.3	8♉58.4	0♓35.6
2 Th	0 42 56	12 38 40	3♑11 01	9♑20 26	8D 38.6	0♉40.0	9 48.4	3 59.6	22 13.6	3 06.3	17R 29.3	13R 27.3	9 00.4	0 37.0
3 F	0 46 52	13 37 51	15 34 04	21 52 28	8 38.7	2 02.7	11 01.0	4 46.2	22 33.8	3 09.5	17 26.0	13 26.4	9 02.5	0 38.3
4 Sa	0 50 49	14 37 00	28 16 07	4♒45 29	8 39.0	3 20.1	12 13.7	5 32.8	22 53.9	3 12.5	17 22.7	13 25.5	9 04.6	0 39.7
5 Su	0 54 45	15 36 08	11♒20 56	18 02 48	8 39.5	4 31.8	13 26.4	6 19.3	23 14.0	3 15.3	17 19.2	13 24.7	9 06.7	0 41.0
6 M	0 58 42	16 35 13	24 51 15	1♓46 22	8 40.2	5 37.6	14 39.1	7 05.9	23 33.9	3 17.9	17 15.7	13 23.9	9 08.8	0 42.3
7 Tu	1 02 38	17 34 17	8♓48 07	15 56 17	8 40.9	6 37.4	15 51.8	7 52.3	23 53.7	3 20.4	17 12.1	13 23.1	9 10.9	0 43.5
8 W	1 06 35	18 33 19	23 10 28	0♈30 07	8R 41.4	7 30.9	17 04.6	8 38.8	24 13.4	3 22.6	17 08.5	13 22.5	9 13.1	0 44.8
9 Th	1 10 32	19 32 19	7♈54 33	15 22 51	8 41.4	8 18.0	18 17.3	9 25.2	24 33.0	3 24.7	17 04.8	13 21.8	9 15.2	0 46.0
10 F	1 14 28	20 31 17	22 54 03	0♉27 02	8 40.8	8 58.7	19 30.1	10 11.6	24 52.5	3 26.6	17 01.0	13 21.3	9 17.4	0 47.2
11 Sa	1 18 25	21 30 13	8♉00 39	15 33 44	8 39.7	9 32.8	20 42.9	10 57.9	25 11.8	3 28.3	16 57.2	13 20.7	9 19.5	0 48.4
12 Su	1 22 21	22 29 07	23 05 09	0♊33 49	8 38.1	10 00.4	21 55.7	11 44.2	25 31.1	3 29.9	16 53.3	13 20.3	9 21.7	0 49.6
13 M	1 26 18	23 27 59	7♊58 47	15 19 15	8 36.3	10 21.3	23 08.5	12 30.5	25 50.2	3 31.2	16 49.4	13 19.8	9 23.9	0 50.8
14 Tu	1 30 14	24 26 48	22 34 33	29 44 12	8 34.8	10 35.7	24 21.3	13 16.7	26 09.3	3 32.4	16 45.5	13 19.5	9 26.1	0 51.9
15 W	1 34 11	25 25 35	6♋47 52	13♋45 24	8D 33.7	10R 43.7	25 34.1	14 02.9	26 28.2	3 33.3	16 41.4	13 19.2	9 28.3	0 53.0
16 Th	1 38 07	26 24 20	20 36 46	27 22 04	8 33.4	10 45.3	26 46.9	14 49.0	26 47.0	3 34.1	16 37.4	13 18.9	9 30.5	0 54.1
17 F	1 42 04	27 23 03	4♌01 31	10♌35 23	8 33.8	10 40.8	27 59.8	15 35.1	27 05.7	3 34.7	16 33.3	13 18.7	9 32.7	0 55.2
18 Sa	1 46 01	28 21 43	17 04 01	23 27 47	8 35.0	10 30.5	29 12.6	16 21.2	27 24.2	3 35.1	16 29.1	13 18.6	9 35.0	0 56.3
19 Su	1 49 57	29 20 21	29 47 07	6♍02 26	8 36.5	10 14.6	0♈25.4	17 07.2	27 42.6	3R 35.4	16 24.9	13 18.5	9 37.2	0 57.3
20 M	1 53 54	0♉18 57	12♍14 08	18 22 39	8 38.0	9 53.6	1 38.3	17 53.1	28 00.9	3 35.4	16 20.7	13D 18.5	9 39.4	0 58.3
21 Tu	1 57 50	1 17 31	24 28 21	0♎31 38	8R 39.0	9 27.9	2 51.2	18 39.0	28 19.1	3 35.2	16 16.4	13 18.5	9 41.6	0 59.3
22 W	2 01 47	2 16 03	6♎32 50	12 32 17	8 39.2	8 58.2	4 04.0	19 24.9	28 37.1	3 34.9	16 12.1	13 18.5	9 43.9	1 00.3
23 Th	2 05 43	3 14 32	18 30 18	24 27 10	8 38.2	8 24.9	5 16.9	20 10.7	28 55.0	3 34.4	16 07.8	13 18.7	9 46.1	1 01.2
24 F	2 09 40	4 13 00	0♏23 09	6♏18 31	8 35.9	7 48.7	6 29.8	20 56.5	29 12.8	3 33.6	16 03.4	13 18.8	9 48.4	1 02.2
25 Sa	2 13 36	5 11 26	12 13 29	18 08 20	8 32.4	7 10.4	7 42.7	21 42.3	29 30.4	3 32.7	15 59.0	13 19.1	9 50.6	1 03.1
26 Su	2 17 33	6 09 50	24 03 18	29 58 39	8 28.0	6 30.7	8 55.6	22 28.0	29 47.9	3 31.7	15 54.6	13 19.4	9 52.9	1 04.0
27 M	2 21 30	7 08 13	5♐54 37	11♐51 31	8 23.0	5 50.3	10 08.5	23 13.6	0♓05.2	3 30.4	15 50.2	13 19.7	9 55.1	1 04.8
28 Tu	2 25 26	8 06 34	17 49 39	23 49 20	8 18.0	5 10.0	11 21.5	23 59.2	0 22.4	3 28.9	15 45.7	13 20.1	9 57.4	1 05.7
29 W	2 29 23	9 04 53	29 50 55	5♑54 48	8 13.6	4 30.4	12 34.4	24 44.8	0 39.5	3 27.3	15 41.3	13 20.5	9 59.7	1 06.5
30 Th	2 33 19	10 03 11	12♑01 22	18 11 04	8 10.3	3 52.3	13 47.4	25 30.3	0 56.4	3 25.4	15 36.8	13 21.0	10 01.9	1 07.3

Astro Data	Dy Hr Mn
☽ 0N	12 2:56
☿ 0N	17 23:03
☉ 0N	20 17:27
☽ 0S	25 7:53
♃∠♄	28 1:49
♂ 0N	30 23:00
☽ 0N	8 13:40
☿ R	16 6:17
♃ R	20 4:02
♅ D	20 17:49
☽ 0S	21 13:57
♀ 0N	22 3:14

Planet Ingress	Dy Hr Mn
♃ ♑	1 17:05
♇ ♓	9 0:45
☿ ♈	16 20:35
☉ ♈	20 17:28
♀ ♓	25 9:22
♂ ♈	28 8:55
☿ ♉	2 0:54
♀ ♈	19 3:37
☉ ♉	20 4:14
⚳ ♓	27 4:45

Last Aspect Dy Hr Mn		☽ Ingress Dy Hr Mn
2 22:00	♇ □	♐ 2 22:21
5 9:39	♇ ✶	♑ 5 9:50
6 20:51	♄ ✶	♒ 7 18:02
9 2:39	♄ □	♓ 9 22:34
11 9:09	☉ ☌	♈ 12 0:27
13 1:06	♀ ✶	♉ 14 1:17
15 23:47	☿ ✶	♊ 16 2:38
18 1:03	☉ □	♋ 18 5:41
20 10:30	☉ △	♌ 20 11:02
22 12:14	♀ ☍	♍ 22 18:49
24 23:41	♂ ☍	♎ 25 4:53
26 19:48	☿ ☍	♏ 27 16:48
29 4:42	♄ ☌	♐ 30 5:38

Last Aspect Dy Hr Mn		☽ Ingress Dy Hr Mn
1 16:46	☿ △	♑ 1 17:45
3 3:36	♄ ✶	♒ 4 3:13
5 10:43	♄ □	♓ 6 8:57
7 14:06	♄ △	♈ 8 11:11
9 19:06	☉ ☌	♉ 10 11:17
11 20:56	♀ ✶	♊ 12 11:06
14 2:28	☉ ✶	♋ 14 12:27
16 10:51	♀ △	♌ 16 16:43
18 22:04	☉ △	♍ 19 0:25
20 8:02	♄ ✶	♎ 21 10:57
23 2:47	♂ ☍	♏ 23 23:13
25 7:39	♄ ☌	♐ 26 12:03
28 12:21	♂ △	♑ 29 0:18

☽ Phases & Eclipses Dy Hr Mn	
4 1:07	☾ 13♐21
11 9:09	● 20♓41
18 1:03	☽ 27♊20
25 14:26	○ 4♎50
25 14:31	☍ T 1.114
2 18:56	☾ 12♑56
9 19:06	● 19♈50
9 18:56:21	☌ T non-C
16 10:09	☽ 26♋20
24 7:23	○ 4♏02

Astro Data

1 March 2043
Julian Day # 52290
SVP 4♓39'27"
GC 27♐26.5 ⚵ 13♑02.1
Eris 28♈45.2 ⚶ 29♐35.1
⚷ 12♌39.4R ⚴ 24♎43.6R
☽ Mean ☊ 10♈13.6

1 April 2043
Julian Day # 52321
SVP 4♓39'23"
GC 27♐26.6 ⚵ 21♑53.9
Eris 29♈02.4 ⚶ 5♑15.6
⚷ 11♌21.7R ⚴ 19♎55.9R
☽ Mean ☊ 8♈35.1

LONGITUDE May 2043

Day	Sid.Time	☉	0 hr ☽	Noon ☽	True ☊	☿	♀	♂	⚳	♃	♄	♅	♆	♇
1 F	2 37 16	11♉01 27	24♑24 21	0♒41 39	8♈08.3	3♉16.4	15♈00.3	26♈15.8	1♓13.2	3♑23.4	15♏32.3	13♌21.6	10♉04.2	1♓08.1
2 Sa	2 41 12	11 59 42	7♒03 28	13 30 16	8D07.8	2R43.0	16 13.3	27 01.2	1 29.8	3R21.2	15R27.8	13 22.2	10 06.4	1 08.8
3 Su	2 45 09	12 57 55	20 02 28	26 40 29	8 08.5	2 12.9	17 26.3	27 46.6	1 46.2	3 18.9	15 23.3	13 22.9	10 08.7	1 09.5
4 M	2 49 05	13 56 06	3♓24 40	10♓15 17	8 09.9	1 46.3	18 39.3	28 31.9	2 02.5	3 16.3	15 18.7	13 23.6	10 11.0	1 10.2
5 Tu	2 53 02	14 54 16	17 12 31	24 16 24	8R11.2	1 23.7	19 52.3	29 17.2	2 18.7	3 13.5	15 14.2	13 24.3	10 13.2	1 10.9
6 W	2 56 59	15 52 25	1♈26 50	8♈43 31	8 11.8	1 05.3	21 05.3	0♉02.5	2 34.6	3 10.6	15 09.7	13 25.1	10 15.5	1 11.6
7 Th	3 00 55	16 50 32	16 06 01	23 33 39	8 11.0	0 51.3	22 18.3	0 47.7	2 50.4	3 07.5	15 05.1	13 26.0	10 17.7	1 12.2
8 F	3 04 52	17 48 38	1♉05 34	8♉40 43	8 08.3	0 41.9	23 31.3	1 32.8	3 06.1	3 04.2	15 00.6	13 26.9	10 20.0	1 12.8
9 Sa	3 08 48	18 46 42	16 17 57	23 55 57	8 03.8	0D37.2	24 44.3	2 17.9	3 21.5	3 00.8	14 56.1	13 27.9	10 22.2	1 13.4
10 Su	3 12 45	19 44 45	1♊33 23	9♊08 56	7 58.1	0 37.1	25 57.3	3 03.0	3 36.8	2 57.2	14 51.6	13 29.0	10 24.5	1 14.0
11 M	3 16 41	20 42 46	16 41 19	24 09 23	7 51.7	0 41.7	27 10.4	3 48.0	3 51.9	2 53.4	14 47.1	13 30.0	10 26.7	1 14.5
12 Tu	3 20 38	21 40 45	1♋32 08	8♋48 48	7 45.7	0 51.0	28 23.4	4 32.9	4 06.9	2 49.4	14 42.6	13 31.2	10 28.9	1 15.0
13 W	3 24 34	22 38 43	15 58 47	23 01 42	7 40.9	1 04.8	29 36.4	5 17.8	4 21.6	2 45.3	14 38.2	13 32.4	10 31.2	1 15.5
14 Th	3 28 31	23 36 38	29 57 23	6♌45 51	7 37.7	1 23.2	0♉49.5	6 02.6	4 36.2	2 41.0	14 33.7	13 33.6	10 33.4	1 16.0
15 F	3 32 28	24 34 32	13♌27 17	20 01 59	7D36.3	1 45.9	2 02.5	6 47.4	4 50.5	2 36.6	14 29.3	13 34.9	10 35.6	1 16.4
16 Sa	3 36 24	25 32 24	26 30 21	2♍52 52	7 36.4	2 12.9	3 15.6	7 32.1	5 04.7	2 32.0	14 24.9	13 36.2	10 37.8	1 16.8
17 Su	3 40 21	26 30 14	9♍10 06	15 22 37	7 37.5	2 44.0	4 28.6	8 16.8	5 18.7	2 27.2	14 20.5	13 37.6	10 40.0	1 17.2
18 M	3 44 17	27 28 02	21 31 00	27 35 50	7R38.7	3 19.2	5 41.6	9 01.4	5 32.5	2 22.3	14 16.1	13 39.0	10 42.2	1 17.6
19 Tu	3 48 14	28 25 49	3♎37 42	9♎37 08	7 39.1	3 58.3	6 54.7	9 46.0	5 46.1	2 17.2	14 11.8	13 40.5	10 44.3	1 17.9
20 W	3 52 10	29 23 34	15 34 40	21 30 47	7 37.9	4 41.1	8 07.8	10 30.5	5 59.5	2 12.0	14 07.5	13 42.1	10 46.5	1 18.2
21 Th	3 56 07	0♊21 17	27 25 55	3♏20 28	7 34.7	5 27.6	9 20.8	11 15.0	6 12.6	2 06.7	14 03.2	13 43.6	10 48.7	1 18.5
22 F	4 00 03	1 19 00	9♏14 49	15 09 17	7 29.2	6 17.6	10 33.9	11 59.4	6 25.6	2 01.2	13 59.0	13 45.3	10 50.8	1 18.8
23 Sa	4 04 00	2 16 40	21 04 10	26 59 41	7 21.4	7 11.1	11 47.0	12 43.7	6 38.4	1 55.6	13 54.8	13 46.9	10 53.0	1 19.0
24 Su	4 07 57	3 14 20	2♐56 06	8♐53 36	7 11.8	8 07.9	13 00.1	13 28.0	6 50.9	1 49.8	13 50.7	13 48.7	10 55.1	1 19.2
25 M	4 11 53	4 11 58	14 52 23	20 52 37	7 01.3	9 07.9	14 13.1	14 12.3	7 03.3	1 44.0	13 46.6	13 50.4	10 57.2	1 19.4
26 Tu	4 15 50	5 09 35	26 54 28	2♑58 09	6 50.6	10 11.0	15 26.2	14 56.5	7 15.4	1 38.0	13 42.5	13 52.3	10 59.3	1 19.6
27 W	4 19 46	6 07 11	9♑03 49	15 11 43	6 40.9	11 17.2	16 39.4	15 40.6	7 27.3	1 31.8	13 38.5	13 54.1	11 01.4	1 19.7
28 Th	4 23 43	7 04 46	21 22 03	27 35 06	6 32.9	12 26.4	17 52.5	16 24.7	7 39.0	1 25.6	13 34.6	13 56.0	11 03.5	1 19.8
29 F	4 27 39	8 02 20	3♒51 09	10♒10 30	6 27.1	13 38.5	19 05.6	17 08.7	7 50.4	1 19.2	13 30.6	13 58.0	11 05.6	1 19.9
30 Sa	4 31 36	8 59 54	16 33 31	23 00 32	6 23.8	14 53.5	20 18.7	17 52.7	8 01.6	1 12.8	13 26.8	14 00.0	11 07.6	1 20.0
31 Su	4 35 32	9 57 26	29 31 56	6♓08 06	6D22.6	16 11.2	21 31.9	18 36.6	8 12.6	1 06.2	13 23.0	14 02.0	11 09.7	1R20.0

LONGITUDE June 2043

Day	Sid.Time	☉	0 hr ☽	Noon ☽	True ☊	☿	♀	♂	⚳	♃	♄	♅	♆	♇
1 M	4 39 29	10♊54 57	12♓49 22	19♓36 03	6♈22.7	17♉31.8	22♉45.0	19♉20.5	8♓23.3	0♑59.5	13♏19.2	14♌04.1	11♉11.7	1♓20.0
2 Tu	4 43 26	11 52 28	26 28 27	3♈26 43	6R23.2	18 55.0	23 58.2	20 04.3	8 33.8	0R52.7	13R15.5	14 06.3	11 13.7	1R20.0
3 W	4 47 22	12 49 58	10♈30 57	17 41 04	6 22.7	20 21.0	25 11.4	20 48.1	8 44.0	0 45.9	13 11.8	14 08.4	11 15.7	1 19.9
4 Th	4 51 19	13 47 27	24 56 53	2♉17 58	6 20.5	21 49.6	26 24.6	21 31.8	8 54.0	0 38.9	13 08.3	14 10.6	11 17.7	1 19.9
5 F	4 55 15	14 44 55	9♉43 46	17 13 29	6 15.7	23 20.9	27 37.8	22 15.5	9 03.7	0 31.9	13 04.7	14 12.9	11 19.6	1 19.8
6 Sa	4 59 12	15 42 23	24 46 10	2♊20 40	6 08.5	24 54.9	28 51.0	22 59.1	9 13.2	0 24.8	13 01.3	14 15.2	11 21.6	1 19.7
7 Su	5 03 08	16 39 50	9♊55 45	17 30 06	5 59.2	26 31.4	0♊04.2	23 42.6	9 22.4	0 17.6	12 57.9	14 17.6	11 23.5	1 19.5
8 M	5 07 05	17 37 16	25 02 25	2♋31 26	5 49.0	28 10.6	1 17.4	24 26.1	9 31.4	0 10.3	12 54.6	14 19.9	11 25.5	1 19.4
9 Tu	5 11 02	18 34 41	9♋55 59	17 15 04	5 39.0	29 52.4	2 30.7	25 09.5	9 40.0	0 03.0	12 51.3	14 22.4	11 27.4	1 19.2
10 W	5 14 58	19 32 05	24 27 55	1♌33 54	5 30.4	1♊36.7	3 43.9	25 52.9	9 48.4	29♐55.6	12 48.2	14 24.8	11 29.2	1 19.0
11 Th	5 18 55	20 29 29	8♌32 41	15 24 05	5 23.9	3 23.6	4 57.2	26 36.2	9 56.6	29 48.2	12 45.1	14 27.3	11 31.1	1 18.7
12 F	5 22 51	21 26 51	22 08 09	28 45 04	5 19.9	5 13.0	6 10.4	27 19.5	10 04.4	29 40.7	12 42.0	14 29.9	11 32.9	1 18.5
13 Sa	5 26 48	22 24 11	5♍15 11	11♍38 58	5D18.1	7 04.9	7 23.7	28 02.7	10 11.9	29 33.2	12 39.1	14 32.5	11 34.8	1 18.2
14 Su	5 30 44	23 21 31	17 56 57	24 09 44	5R17.7	8 59.2	8 36.9	28 45.8	10 19.2	29 25.6	12 36.2	14 35.1	11 36.6	1 17.9
15 M	5 34 41	24 18 50	0♎17 58	6♎22 18	5 17.8	10 55.9	9 50.2	29 28.9	10 26.2	29 18.0	12 33.4	14 37.7	11 38.3	1 17.5
16 Tu	5 38 37	25 16 08	12 23 24	18 21 57	5 17.2	12 54.8	11 03.5	0♊11.9	10 32.9	29 10.4	12 30.6	14 40.4	11 40.1	1 17.2
17 W	5 42 34	26 13 26	24 18 32	0♏13 48	5 15.0	14 55.9	12 16.8	0 54.8	10 39.3	29 02.8	12 28.0	14 43.1	11 41.8	1 16.8
18 Th	5 46 31	27 10 42	6♏08 17	12 02 31	5 10.5	16 59.0	13 30.1	1 37.7	10 45.3	28 55.1	12 25.4	14 45.9	11 43.5	1 16.4
19 F	5 50 27	28 07 58	17 56 59	23 52 05	5 03.2	19 04.0	14 43.4	2 20.6	10 51.1	28 47.5	12 23.0	14 48.7	11 45.2	1 16.0
20 Sa	5 54 24	29 05 13	29 48 14	5♐45 43	4 53.3	21 10.6	15 56.7	3 03.3	10 56.6	28 39.8	12 20.6	14 51.5	11 46.9	1 15.5
21 Su	5 58 20	0♋02 28	11♐44 48	17 45 45	4 41.2	23 18.7	17 10.1	3 46.1	11 01.8	28 32.1	12 18.3	14 54.4	11 48.6	1 15.0
22 M	6 02 17	0 59 42	23 48 42	29 53 49	4 28.0	25 28.0	18 23.4	4 28.7	11 06.7	28 24.5	12 16.0	14 57.3	11 50.2	1 14.5
23 Tu	6 06 13	1 56 55	6♑01 12	12♑10 57	4 14.6	27 38.2	19 36.8	5 11.3	11 11.2	28 16.8	12 13.9	15 00.2	11 51.8	1 14.0
24 W	6 10 10	2 54 09	18 23 07	24 37 47	4 02.3	29 49.1	20 50.1	5 53.9	11 15.5	28 09.2	12 11.8	15 03.2	11 53.4	1 13.5
25 Th	6 14 06	3 51 22	0♒55 00	7♒14 52	3 51.9	2♋00.4	22 03.5	6 36.4	11 19.4	28 01.6	12 09.9	15 06.2	11 55.0	1 12.9
26 F	6 18 03	4 48 35	13 37 28	20 02 56	3 44.2	4 11.8	23 16.9	7 18.8	11 23.0	27 54.0	12 08.0	15 09.2	11 56.5	1 12.3
27 Sa	6 22 00	5 45 47	26 31 24	3♓03 03	3 39.4	6 23.0	24 30.3	8 01.2	11 26.2	27 46.5	12 06.2	15 12.2	11 58.0	1 11.7
28 Su	6 25 56	6 43 00	9♓38 04	16 16 42	3 37.1	8 33.8	25 43.8	8 43.5	11 29.2	27 39.0	12 04.5	15 15.3	11 59.5	1 11.1
29 M	6 29 53	7 40 12	22 59 09	29 45 40	3 36.4	10 43.9	26 57.2	9 25.8	11 31.8	27 31.5	12 02.9	15 18.4	12 01.0	1 10.5
30 Tu	6 33 49	8 37 25	6♈36 26	13♈31 38	3 36.4	12 53.2	28 10.7	10 08.0	11 34.0	27 24.1	12 01.4	15 21.6	12 02.4	1 09.8

Astro Data Dy Hr Mn	Planet Ingress Dy Hr Mn	Last Aspect Dy Hr Mn	☽ Ingress Dy Hr Mn	Last Aspect Dy Hr Mn	☽ Ingress Dy Hr Mn	☽ Phases & Eclipses Dy Hr Mn	Astro Data
☽0N 5 23:57	♂ ♉ 6 10:41	1 3:01 ♂ □	♒ 1 10:41	1 18:03 ♀ ✶	♈ 2 6:05	2 8:59 ☾ 11♒52	1 May 2043
☿D 10 0:19	♀ ♉ 13 19:45	3 14:06 ♂ ✶	♓ 3 17:57	3 6:04 ♅ △	♉ 4 8:16	9 3:21 ● 18♉26	Julian Day # 52351
☽0S 18 19:23	☉ ♊ 21 3:09	4 20:42 ♄ △	♈ 5 21:36	6 5:59 ♀ ☌	♊ 6 8:17	15 21:05 ☽ 24♌56	SVP 4♓39'19"
♄□♅ 24 20:16		7 9:48 ♀ ☌	♉ 7 22:16	7 10:35 ☉ ☌	♋ 8 7:56	23 23:37 ○ 2♐45	GC 27♐26.7 ⚵ 26♑49.8
♃✶♇ 29 9:34	♀ ♊ 7 10:37	9 3:21 ☉ ☌	♊ 9 21:33	10 1:52 ♂ ✶	♌ 10 9:20	31 19:24 ☾ 10♓15	Eris 29♈22.1 ✱ 6♑53.2R
	☿ ♊ 9 13:46	11 17:20 ♀ ✶	♋ 11 21:29	12 13:41 ♃ △	♍ 12 14:17		⚷ 11♌36.6 ⚶ 12♎58.2R
♇R 1 8:39	♃ ♐R 9 21:43	13 11:18 ☉ ✶	♌ 14 0:05	14 22:11 ♃ □	♎ 14 23:25	7 10:35 ● 16♊36	☽ Mean ☊ 6♈59.8
☽0N 2 7:57	♂ ♊ 16 5:22	15 21:05 ☉ □	♍ 16 6:33	17 9:37 ♃ ✶	♏ 17 11:32	14 10:19 ☽ 23♍17	
♃⚻♅ 13 13:39	☉ ♋ 21 10:58	18 11:43 ☉ △	♎ 18 16:46	18 17:33 ♅ □	♐ 20 0:24	22 14:20 ○ 1♑05	1 June 2043
☽0S 15 1:11	☿ ♋ 24 14:00	19 20:11 ♅ ✶	♏ 21 5:13	22 9:06 ♃ ☌	♑ 22 12:12	30 2:53 ☾ 8♈16	Julian Day # 52382
☽0N 29 13:29		22 9:38 ♄ ☌	♐ 23 18:04	23 12:06 ♄ ✶	♒ 24 22:15		SVP 4♓39'14"
♄☍♆ 30 3:38		24 21:54 ♅ △	♑ 26 6:08	27 2:24 ♃ ✶	♓ 27 6:24		GC 27♐26.7 ⚵ 26♑17.6R
		27 15:10 ♀ △	♒ 28 16:38	29 8:05 ♃ □	♈ 29 12:25		Eris 29♈40.6 ✱ 3♑30.0R
		30 6:29 ♀ □	♓ 31 0:51				⚷ 13♌25.5 ⚶ 11♎28.7
							☽ Mean ☊ 5♈21.3

July 2043 LONGITUDE

Day	Sid.Time	☉	0 hr ☽	Noon ☽	True ☊	☿	♀	♂	⚳	♃	♄	♅	♆	♇
1 W	6 37 46	9♋34 38	20♈31 22	27♈35 39	3♈35.7	15♋01.3	29♊24.2	10♊50.1	11♓35.9	27♐16.7	11♏59.9	15♌24.7	12♉03.8	1♓09.1
2 Th	6 41 42	10 31 51	4♉44 24	11♉57 24	3R 33.2	17 08.2	0♋37.7	11 32.2	11 37.5	27R 09.4	11R 58.6	15 27.9	12 05.2	1R 08.4
3 F	6 45 39	11 29 04	19 14 18	26 34 35	3 28.2	19 13.6	1 51.2	12 14.3	11 38.7	27 02.2	11 57.4	15 31.1	12 06.5	1 07.6
4 Sa	6 49 35	12 26 18	3♊57 33	11♊22 24	3 20.5	21 17.4	3 04.7	12 56.2	11 39.6	26 55.0	11 56.2	15 34.4	12 07.9	1 06.9
5 Su	6 53 32	13 23 31	18 48 11	26 13 51	3 10.8	23 19.6	4 18.3	13 38.2	11R 40.1	26 47.9	11 55.2	15 37.6	12 09.2	1 06.1
6 M	6 57 29	14 20 45	3♋38 18	11♋00 28	2 59.9	25 20.1	5 31.9	14 20.0	11 40.3	26 40.8	11 54.3	15 40.9	12 10.5	1 05.3
7 Tu	7 01 25	15 17 59	18 19 17	25 33 47	2 49.2	27 18.7	6 45.4	15 01.8	11 40.1	26 33.9	11 53.4	15 44.3	12 11.7	1 04.5
8 W	7 05 22	16 15 13	2♌43 10	9♌46 45	2 39.7	29 15.5	7 59.0	15 43.6	11 39.6	26 27.0	11 52.6	15 47.6	12 12.9	1 03.7
9 Th	7 09 18	17 12 26	16 44 03	23 34 46	2 32.5	1♌10.4	9 12.6	16 25.2	11 38.7	26 20.3	11 52.0	15 51.0	12 14.1	1 02.8
10 F	7 13 15	18 09 40	0♍18 47	6♍56 08	2 27.7	3 03.4	10 26.3	17 06.8	11 37.4	26 13.6	11 51.4	15 54.3	12 15.3	1 02.0
11 Sa	7 17 11	19 06 53	13 27 00	19 51 44	2D 25.4	4 54.4	11 39.9	17 48.4	11 35.8	26 07.1	11 51.0	15 57.7	12 16.4	1 01.1
12 Su	7 21 08	20 04 06	26 10 45	2♎24 34	2 24.8	6 43.5	12 53.5	18 29.9	11 33.9	26 00.6	11 50.6	16 01.2	12 17.5	1 00.2
13 M	7 25 04	21 01 20	8♎33 46	14 38 58	2R 25.0	8 30.7	14 07.2	19 11.3	11 31.5	25 54.3	11 50.3	16 04.6	12 18.6	0 59.3
14 Tu	7 29 01	21 58 33	20 40 50	26 40 02	2 25.0	10 15.9	15 20.9	19 52.7	11 28.9	25 48.0	11 50.1	16 08.1	12 19.7	0 58.3
15 W	7 32 58	22 55 46	2♏37 13	8♏33 04	2 23.8	11 59.2	16 34.6	20 34.0	11 25.8	25 41.9	11D 50.1	16 11.6	12 20.7	0 57.4
16 Th	7 36 54	23 53 00	14 28 12	20 23 13	2 20.6	13 40.5	17 48.3	21 15.2	11 22.4	25 35.9	11 50.1	16 15.1	12 21.7	0 56.4
17 F	7 40 51	24 50 13	26 18 42	2♐15 10	2 15.1	15 19.9	19 02.0	21 56.4	11 18.7	25 30.1	11 50.2	16 18.6	12 22.6	0 55.4
18 Sa	7 44 47	25 47 27	8♐13 06	14 12 56	2 07.2	16 57.3	20 15.7	22 37.5	11 14.6	25 24.3	11 50.4	16 22.1	12 23.6	0 54.4
19 Su	7 48 44	26 44 41	20 15 00	26 19 38	1 57.3	18 32.8	21 29.5	23 18.6	11 10.1	25 18.8	11 50.8	16 25.7	12 24.5	0 53.4
20 M	7 52 40	27 41 55	2♑27 05	8♑37 30	1 46.3	20 06.4	22 43.2	23 59.6	11 05.3	25 13.3	11 51.2	16 29.2	12 25.3	0 52.4
21 Tu	7 56 37	28 39 10	14 51 02	21 07 45	1 35.1	21 38.0	23 57.0	24 40.5	11 00.2	25 08.0	11 51.7	16 32.8	12 26.2	0 51.3
22 W	8 00 34	29 36 25	27 27 41	3♒50 48	1 24.8	23 07.6	25 10.8	25 21.4	10 54.7	25 02.8	11 52.3	16 36.4	12 27.0	0 50.3
23 Th	8 04 30	0♌33 40	10♒17 04	16 46 23	1 16.2	24 35.3	26 24.6	26 02.2	10 48.8	24 57.8	11 53.0	16 40.0	12 27.8	0 49.2
24 F	8 08 27	1 30 57	23 18 43	29 53 56	1 09.9	26 00.9	27 38.4	26 43.0	10 42.6	24 52.9	11 53.8	16 43.6	12 28.5	0 48.1
25 Sa	8 12 23	2 28 14	6♓32 00	13♓12 49	1 06.2	27 24.6	28 52.3	27 23.7	10 36.1	24 48.2	11 54.7	16 47.2	12 29.2	0 47.0
26 Su	8 16 20	3 25 31	19 56 22	26 42 37	1D 04.8	28 46.1	0♌06.1	28 04.3	10 29.2	24 43.6	11 55.7	16 50.9	12 29.9	0 45.9
27 M	8 20 16	4 22 50	3♈31 33	10♈23 11	1 05.0	0♍05.6	1 20.0	28 44.9	10 22.0	24 39.1	11 56.8	16 54.5	12 30.6	0 44.7
28 Tu	8 24 13	5 20 09	17 17 31	24 14 34	1R 05.8	1 22.9	2 33.9	29 25.4	10 14.5	24 34.9	11 58.0	16 58.2	12 31.2	0 43.6
29 W	8 28 09	6 17 30	1♉14 18	8♉16 41	1 06.2	2 38.0	3 47.8	0♋05.9	10 06.7	24 30.8	11 59.3	17 01.9	12 31.8	0 42.5
30 Th	8 32 06	7 14 52	15 21 35	22 28 51	1 05.2	3 50.9	5 01.8	0 46.3	9 58.5	24 26.8	12 00.7	17 05.5	12 32.3	0 41.3
31 F	8 36 03	8 12 15	29 38 13	6♊49 21	1 02.2	5 01.5	6 15.7	1 26.6	9 50.0	24 23.1	12 02.1	17 09.2	12 32.8	0 40.1

August 2043 LONGITUDE

Day	Sid.Time	☉	0 hr ☽	Noon ☽	True ☊	☿	♀	♂	⚳	♃	♄	♅	♆	♇
1 Sa	8 39 59	9♌09 39	14♊01 49	21♊15 05	0♈57.1	6♍09.6	7♌29.7	2♋06.9	9♓41.2	24♐19.5	12♏03.7	17♌12.9	12♉33.3	0♓38.9
2 Su	8 43 56	10 07 04	28 28 33	5♋41 31	0R 50.4	7 15.3	8 43.7	2 47.1	9R 32.1	24R 16.0	12 05.4	17 16.6	12 33.8	0R 37.8
3 M	8 47 52	11 04 30	12♋53 18	20 03 08	0 42.6	8 18.5	9 57.7	3 27.3	9 22.7	24 12.8	12 07.2	17 20.3	12 34.2	0 36.6
4 Tu	8 51 49	12 01 57	27 10 16	4♌14 02	0 34.9	9 18.9	11 11.8	4 07.4	9 13.0	24 09.7	12 09.0	17 24.0	12 34.6	0 35.3
5 W	8 55 45	12 59 25	11♌13 48	18 09 01	0 28.1	10 16.5	12 25.8	4 47.5	9 03.0	24 06.8	12 11.0	17 27.8	12 35.0	0 34.1
6 Th	8 59 42	13 56 54	24 59 16	1♍44 13	0 23.0	11 11.3	13 39.9	5 27.4	8 52.8	24 04.1	12 13.0	17 31.5	12 35.3	0 32.9
7 F	9 03 38	14 54 23	8♍23 42	14 57 39	0 19.9	12 02.9	14 53.9	6 07.3	8 42.3	24 01.5	12 15.2	17 35.2	12 35.6	0 31.7
8 Sa	9 07 35	15 51 54	21 26 08	27 49 20	0D 18.7	12 51.4	16 08.0	6 47.2	8 31.5	23 59.1	12 17.4	17 38.9	12 35.9	0 30.4
9 Su	9 11 32	16 49 25	4♎07 30	10♎21 01	0 19.1	13 36.5	17 22.1	7 26.9	8 20.5	23 56.9	12 19.7	17 42.7	12 36.1	0 29.2
10 M	9 15 28	17 46 58	16 30 19	22 35 55	0 20.4	14 18.0	18 36.2	8 06.7	8 09.3	23 54.9	12 22.2	17 46.4	12 36.3	0 27.9
11 Tu	9 19 25	18 44 31	28 38 20	4♏38 12	0 21.8	14 55.8	19 50.3	8 46.3	7 57.9	23 53.1	12 24.7	17 50.1	12 36.4	0 26.6
12 W	9 23 21	19 42 05	10♏36 05	16 32 38	0R 22.7	15 29.6	21 04.5	9 25.9	7 46.2	23 51.5	12 27.3	17 53.8	12 36.6	0 25.4
13 Th	9 27 18	20 39 40	22 28 28	28 24 14	0 22.4	15 59.4	22 18.6	10 05.4	7 34.4	23 50.0	12 30.0	17 57.5	12 36.7	0 24.1
14 F	9 31 14	21 37 16	4♐20 32	10♐17 56	0 20.6	16 24.7	23 32.8	10 44.9	7 22.3	23 48.8	12 32.7	18 01.3	12 36.7	0 22.8
15 Sa	9 35 11	22 34 52	16 17 02	22 18 21	0 17.1	16 45.5	24 47.0	11 24.2	7 10.1	23 47.7	12 35.6	18 05.0	12R 36.7	0 21.5
16 Su	9 39 07	23 32 30	28 22 21	4♑29 27	0 12.3	17 01.5	26 01.1	12 03.6	6 57.7	23 46.8	12 38.6	18 08.7	12 36.7	0 20.2
17 M	9 43 04	24 30 09	10♑40 03	16 54 25	0 06.7	17 12.5	27 15.3	12 42.8	6 45.2	23 46.1	12 41.6	18 12.4	12 36.7	0 19.0
18 Tu	9 47 01	25 27 49	23 12 48	29 35 21	0 00.8	17R 18.3	28 29.5	13 22.0	6 32.5	23 45.6	12 44.7	18 16.1	12 36.6	0 17.7
19 W	9 50 57	26 25 31	6♒02 09	12♒33 12	29♓55.3	17 18.6	29 43.7	14 01.1	6 19.7	23 45.3	12 48.0	18 19.8	12 36.5	0 16.4
20 Th	9 54 54	27 23 13	19 08 27	25 47 46	29 50.8	17 13.4	0♍58.0	14 40.2	6 06.8	23D 45.1	12 51.3	18 23.5	12 36.4	0 15.1
21 F	9 58 50	28 20 57	2♓30 57	9♓17 45	29 47.8	17 02.5	2 12.2	15 19.2	5 53.8	23 45.2	12 54.6	18 27.2	12 36.2	0 13.8
22 Sa	10 02 47	29 18 42	16 07 55	23 01 06	29D 46.4	16 45.7	3 26.4	15 58.2	5 40.7	23 45.4	12 58.1	18 30.9	12 36.0	0 12.5
23 Su	10 06 43	0♍16 28	29 57 00	6♈55 17	29 46.4	16 23.2	4 40.7	16 37.0	5 27.6	23 45.8	13 01.7	18 34.6	12 35.8	0 11.2
24 M	10 10 40	1 14 17	13♈55 37	20 57 41	29 47.4	15 55.0	5 55.0	17 15.8	5 14.3	23 46.4	13 05.3	18 38.2	12 35.5	0 09.9
25 Tu	10 14 36	2 12 07	28 01 09	5♉05 44	29 48.8	15 21.3	7 09.3	17 54.6	5 01.0	23 47.2	13 09.0	18 41.9	12 35.2	0 08.6
26 W	10 18 33	3 09 58	12♉11 10	19 17 10	29 50.1	14 42.3	8 23.6	18 33.3	4 47.7	23 48.2	13 12.8	18 45.5	12 34.9	0 07.3
27 Th	10 22 30	4 07 52	26 23 28	3♊29 49	29R 50.7	13 58.5	9 37.9	19 11.9	4 34.4	23 49.3	13 16.7	18 49.2	12 34.5	0 06.0
28 F	10 26 26	5 05 48	10♊35 57	17 41 34	29 50.2	13 10.5	10 52.2	19 50.4	4 21.1	23 50.7	13 20.6	18 52.8	12 34.1	0 04.7
29 Sa	10 30 23	6 03 45	24 46 24	1♋50 08	29 48.6	12 19.0	12 06.5	20 28.9	4 07.7	23 52.2	13 24.7	18 56.4	12 33.7	0 03.4
30 Su	10 34 19	7 01 44	8♋52 28	15 53 02	29 46.1	11 24.8	13 20.9	21 07.4	3 54.4	23 53.9	13 28.8	19 00.0	12 33.3	0 02.1
31 M	10 38 16	7 59 45	22 51 30	29 47 32	29 43.1	10 28.9	14 35.3	21 45.7	3 41.1	23 55.8	13 33.0	19 03.6	12 32.8	0 00.8

Astro Data Dy Hr Mn	Planet Ingress Dy Hr Mn	Last Aspect Dy Hr Mn	☽ Ingress Dy Hr Mn	Last Aspect Dy Hr Mn	☽ Ingress Dy Hr Mn	☽ Phases & Eclipses Dy Hr Mn
♃⚼♆ 2 23:43	♀ ♋ 1 23:42	1 15:20 ♀ ⚹	♉ 1 16:03	1 17:05 ♃ ☍	♋ 2 2:32	6 17:51 ● 14♋35
♃∠♄ 4 6:58	☿ ♌ 8 21:15	2 21:59 ☿ ⚹	♊ 3 17:34	2 23:28 ♆ ⚹	♌ 4 4:48	14 1:47 ☽ 21♎34
⚳ R 6 11:53	☉ ♌ 22 21:53	5 12:55 ♃ ☍	♋ 5 18:06	5 22:25 ♃ △	♍ 6 8:54	22 3:24 ○ 29♑16
☽0S 12 8:08	♀ ♌ 26 10:00	7 15:23 ☿ ☌	♌ 7 19:25	8 4:48 ♃ □	♎ 8 16:08	29 8:23 ☾ 6♉09
♄ D 15 18:07	☿ ♍ 27 10:18	9 16:51 ♃ △	♍ 9 23:26	10 14:36 ♃ ⚹	♏ 11 2:43	
☽0N 26 18:08	♂ ♋ 29 8:31	11 23:47 ♃ □	♎ 12 7:20	12 22:14 ♀ □	♐ 13 15:14	5 2:23 ● 12♌36
		14 10:16 ♃ ⚹	♏ 14 18:43	15 17:28 ♀ △	♑ 16 3:12	12 18:57 ☽ 19♏59
☽0S 8 16:14	☊ ♓R 18 15:08	16 19:42 ☉ △	♐ 17 7:27	17 12:35 ☿ △	♒ 18 12:46	20 15:04 ○ 27♒31
♄☍♆ 15 21:19	♀ ♍ 19 17:15	19 10:01 ♃ ☌	♑ 19 19:12	20 15:04 ☉ ☍	♓ 20 19:31	27 13:09 ☾ 4♊11
♆ R 15 21:56	☉ ♍ 23 5:09	22 3:24 ☉ ☍	♒ 22 4:47	22 13:17 ♃ □	♈ 23 0:05	
☿ R 19 1:32		24 5:54 ♂ △	♓ 24 12:11	24 16:47 ♃ △	♉ 25 3:22	
♃ D 20 18:35		26 14:32 ♂ □	♈ 26 17:48	26 11:06 ♅ □	♊ 27 6:06	
☽0N 23 0:01		28 21:21 ♂ ⚹	♉ 28 21:53	28 22:27 ♃ ☍	♋ 29 8:53	
		30 2:53 ♅ □	♊ 31 0:36	30 21:26 ♂ ☌	♌ 31 12:22	

Astro Data
1 July 2043
Julian Day # 52412
SVP 4♓39'09"
GC 27♐26.8 ⚵ 19♑55.3R
Eris 29♈52.4 ⚴ 26♐57.0R
⚷ 16♌20.9 ⚶ 16♎51.5
☽ Mean ☊ 3♈46.0
1 August 2043
Julian Day # 52443
SVP 4♓39'03"
GC 27♐26.9 ⚵ 11♑54.1R
Eris 29♈55.6R ⚴ 21♐54.7R
⚷ 20♌06.4 ⚶ 27♎09.4
☽ Mean ☊ 2♈07.5

LONGITUDE — September 2043

Day	Sid.Time	☉	0 hr ☽	Noon ☽	True ☊	☿	♀	♂	⚳	♃	♄	♅	♆	♇
1 Tu	10 42 12	8♍57 48	6♌40 47	13♌30 56	29♓40.0	9♍32.4	15♍49.6	22♋24.0	3♓27.9	23♐57.9	13♏37.2	19♌07.2	12♉32.3	29♒59.6
2 W	10 46 09	9 55 53	20 17 40	27 00 44	29R 37.4	8R 36.6	17 04.0	23 02.2	3R 14.8	24 00.2	13 41.6	19 10.7	12R 31.7	29R 58.3
3 Th	10 50 05	10 53 59	3♍39 54	10♍15 01	29 35.6	7 42.5	18 18.4	23 40.3	3 01.7	24 02.6	13 46.0	19 14.2	12 31.1	29 57.0
4 F	10 54 02	11 52 07	16 45 59	23 12 44	29D 34.7	6 51.5	19 32.8	24 18.4	2 48.7	24 05.2	13 50.5	19 17.8	12 30.5	29 55.7
5 Sa	10 57 59	12 50 16	29 35 19	5♎53 49	29 34.7	6 04.7	20 47.2	24 56.4	2 35.8	24 08.1	13 55.0	19 21.3	12 29.9	29 54.5
6 Su	11 01 55	13 48 27	12♎08 23	18 19 16	29 35.4	5 23.2	22 01.6	25 34.3	2 23.1	24 11.0	13 59.6	19 24.8	12 29.2	29 53.2
7 M	11 05 52	14 46 40	24 26 44	0♏31 09	29 36.6	4 48.1	23 16.0	26 12.2	2 10.5	24 14.2	14 04.4	19 28.2	12 28.5	29 51.9
8 Tu	11 09 48	15 44 54	6♏32 53	12 32 25	29 37.9	4 20.2	24 30.5	26 50.0	1 58.0	24 17.6	14 09.1	19 31.7	12 27.7	29 50.7
9 W	11 13 45	16 43 10	18 30 11	24 26 45	29 39.0	4 00.2	25 44.9	27 27.7	1 45.7	24 21.1	14 14.0	19 35.1	12 27.0	29 49.5
10 Th	11 17 41	17 41 27	0♐22 38	6♐18 25	29 39.8	3D 48.7	26 59.3	28 05.3	1 33.6	24 24.8	14 18.9	19 38.5	12 26.2	29 48.2
11 F	11 21 38	18 39 46	12 14 40	18 11 59	29R 40.1	3 46.1	28 13.8	28 42.9	1 21.7	24 28.7	14 23.9	19 41.9	12 25.4	29 47.0
12 Sa	11 25 34	19 38 06	24 10 57	0♑12 09	29 39.9	3 52.5	29 28.2	29 20.4	1 10.0	24 32.7	14 28.9	19 45.3	12 24.5	29 45.8
13 Su	11 29 31	20 36 29	6♑16 08	12 23 27	29 39.2	4 08.1	0♎42.7	29 57.8	0 58.4	24 36.9	14 34.0	19 48.6	12 23.6	29 44.6
14 M	11 33 27	21 34 52	18 34 36	24 50 02	29 38.4	4 32.8	1 57.1	0♌35.1	0 47.2	24 41.3	14 39.2	19 51.9	12 22.7	29 43.4
15 Tu	11 37 24	22 33 17	1♒10 08	7♒35 15	29 37.4	5 06.4	3 11.5	1 12.4	0 36.1	24 45.9	14 44.4	19 55.2	12 21.8	29 42.2
16 W	11 41 21	23 31 44	14 05 36	20 41 22	29 36.6	5 48.6	4 26.0	1 49.6	0 25.3	24 50.6	14 49.7	19 58.5	12 20.8	29 41.1
17 Th	11 45 17	24 30 13	27 22 35	4♓09 13	29 36.0	6 39.0	5 40.4	2 26.7	0 14.7	24 55.5	14 55.1	20 01.7	12 19.9	29 39.9
18 F	11 49 14	25 28 43	11♓01 06	17 57 57	29D 35.7	7 37.2	6 54.9	3 03.7	0 04.4	25 00.6	15 00.5	20 04.9	12 18.8	29 38.8
19 Sa	11 53 10	26 27 15	24 59 25	2♈05 01	29 35.6	8 42.6	8 09.4	3 40.7	29♒54.4	25 05.8	15 06.0	20 08.1	12 17.8	29 37.6
20 Su	11 57 07	27 25 49	9♈14 11	16 26 17	29 35.7	9 54.6	9 23.8	4 17.5	29 44.6	25 11.2	15 11.5	20 11.3	12 16.7	29 36.5
21 M	12 01 03	28 24 25	23 40 39	0♉56 34	29 35.8	11 12.6	10 38.3	4 54.3	29 35.2	25 16.7	15 17.1	20 14.4	12 15.6	29 35.4
22 Tu	12 05 00	29 23 04	8♉13 18	15 30 10	29R 35.9	12 36.0	11 52.7	5 31.1	29 26.0	25 22.4	15 22.8	20 17.5	12 14.5	29 34.3
23 W	12 08 56	0♎21 44	22 46 28	0♊01 36	29 35.8	14 04.2	13 07.2	6 07.7	29 17.1	25 28.3	15 28.5	20 20.6	12 13.4	29 33.2
24 Th	12 12 53	1 20 27	7♊15 01	14 26 12	29 35.8	15 36.4	14 21.7	6 44.3	29 08.5	25 34.3	15 34.2	20 23.6	12 12.2	29 32.1
25 F	12 16 50	2 19 12	21 34 46	28 40 23	29D 35.7	17 12.3	15 36.2	7 20.8	29 00.3	25 40.4	15 40.1	20 26.6	12 11.0	29 31.1
26 Sa	12 20 46	3 18 00	5♋42 48	12♋41 50	29 35.7	18 51.1	16 50.6	7 57.2	28 52.3	25 46.8	15 45.9	20 29.6	12 09.8	29 30.0
27 Su	12 24 43	4 16 50	19 37 21	26 29 16	29 36.0	20 32.4	18 05.1	8 33.6	28 44.7	25 53.2	15 51.9	20 32.6	12 08.6	29 29.0
28 M	12 28 39	5 15 42	3♌17 35	10♌02 16	29 36.4	22 15.6	19 19.6	9 09.8	28 37.5	25 59.9	15 57.8	20 35.5	12 07.3	29 28.0
29 Tu	12 32 36	6 14 36	16 43 21	23 20 53	29 37.0	24 00.5	20 34.1	9 46.0	28 30.5	26 06.6	16 03.9	20 38.4	12 06.1	29 27.0
30 W	12 36 32	7 13 32	29 54 55	6♍25 30	29 37.7	25 46.5	21 48.6	10 22.1	28 23.9	26 13.6	16 09.9	20 41.2	12 04.7	29 26.0

LONGITUDE — October 2043

Day	Sid.Time	☉	0 hr ☽	Noon ☽	True ☊	☿	♀	♂	⚳	♃	♄	♅	♆	♇
1 Th	12 40 29	8♎12 30	12♍52 44	19♍16 40	29♓38.2	27♍33.4	23♎03.1	10♌58.1	28♒17.7	26♐20.6	16♏16.0	20♌44.0	12♉03.4	29♒25.1
2 F	12 44 25	9 11 31	25 37 22	1♎54 58	29R 38.3	29 20.8	24 17.6	11 34.0	28R 11.8	26 27.8	16 22.2	20 46.8	12R 02.1	29R 24.1
3 Sa	12 48 22	10 10 34	8♎09 33	14 21 14	29 37.9	1♎08.5	25 32.1	12 09.8	28 06.2	26 35.2	16 28.4	20 49.6	12 00.7	29 23.2
4 Su	12 52 19	11 09 38	20 30 09	26 36 28	29 37.0	2 56.4	26 46.6	12 45.5	28 01.1	26 42.7	16 34.7	20 52.3	11 59.3	29 22.3
5 M	12 56 15	12 08 45	2♏40 24	8♏42 09	29 35.4	4 44.2	28 01.1	13 21.2	27 56.3	26 50.3	16 41.0	20 54.9	11 57.9	29 21.4
6 Tu	13 00 12	13 07 54	14 41 58	20 40 09	29 33.5	6 31.8	29 15.6	13 56.7	27 51.8	26 58.1	16 47.3	20 57.6	11 56.5	29 20.5
7 W	13 04 08	14 07 04	26 37 02	2♐33 00	29 31.3	8 19.0	0♏30.1	14 32.1	27 47.7	27 06.0	16 53.7	21 00.2	11 55.1	29 19.6
8 Th	13 08 05	15 06 16	8♐28 25	14 23 45	29 29.1	10 05.9	1 44.6	15 07.5	27 44.0	27 14.1	17 00.2	21 02.7	11 53.6	29 18.8
9 F	13 12 01	16 05 31	20 19 28	26 16 04	29 27.4	11 52.2	2 59.1	15 42.8	27 40.7	27 22.3	17 06.6	21 05.2	11 52.1	29 18.0
10 Sa	13 15 58	17 04 47	2♑14 05	8♑14 05	29D 26.4	13 38.0	4 13.6	16 17.9	27 37.7	27 30.6	17 13.1	21 07.7	11 50.7	29 17.2
11 Su	13 19 54	18 04 05	14 16 38	20 22 17	29 26.1	15 23.1	5 28.1	16 53.0	27 35.1	27 39.1	17 19.7	21 10.1	11 49.2	29 16.4
12 M	13 23 51	19 03 24	26 31 39	2♒45 16	29 26.7	17 07.7	6 42.6	17 27.9	27 32.9	27 47.6	17 26.3	21 12.5	11 47.6	29 15.7
13 Tu	13 27 48	20 02 46	9♒03 40	15 27 22	29 27.9	18 51.5	7 57.1	18 02.8	27 31.0	27 56.3	17 32.9	21 14.9	11 46.1	29 14.9
14 W	13 31 44	21 02 09	21 56 49	28 32 22	29 29.4	20 34.7	9 11.6	18 37.6	27 29.5	28 05.2	17 39.5	21 17.2	11 44.6	29 14.2
15 Th	13 35 41	22 01 34	5♓14 19	12♓02 49	29 30.8	22 17.2	10 26.0	19 12.2	27 28.4	28 14.1	17 46.2	21 19.4	11 43.0	29 13.5
16 F	13 39 37	23 01 00	18 57 55	25 59 30	29R 31.5	23 59.1	11 40.5	19 46.8	27 27.6	28 23.2	17 52.9	21 21.7	11 41.4	29 12.9
17 Sa	13 43 34	24 00 29	3♈07 17	10♈20 50	29 31.2	25 40.2	12 55.0	20 21.3	27D 27.3	28 32.4	17 59.7	21 23.8	11 39.8	29 12.2
18 Su	13 47 30	24 59 59	17 39 32	25 02 37	29 29.7	27 20.7	14 09.4	20 55.6	27 27.2	28 41.7	18 06.4	21 26.0	11 38.2	29 11.6
19 M	13 51 27	25 59 32	2♉29 09	9♉58 08	29 26.9	29 00.5	15 23.9	21 29.9	27 27.6	28 51.1	18 13.2	21 28.0	11 36.6	29 11.0
20 Tu	13 55 23	26 59 06	17 28 26	24 58 55	29 23.2	0♏39.7	16 38.3	22 04.0	27 28.3	29 00.6	18 20.1	21 30.1	11 35.0	29 10.4
21 W	13 59 20	27 58 43	2♊28 28	9♊56 00	29 19.1	2 18.2	17 52.8	22 38.1	27 29.3	29 10.3	18 26.9	21 32.1	11 33.4	29 09.8
22 Th	14 03 17	28 58 23	17 20 34	24 41 20	29 15.4	3 56.1	19 07.2	23 12.0	27 30.8	29 20.1	18 33.8	21 34.0	11 31.8	29 09.3
23 F	14 07 13	29 58 04	1♋57 35	9♋08 50	29 12.6	5 33.4	20 21.7	23 45.8	27 32.5	29 29.9	18 40.7	21 35.9	11 30.1	29 08.8
24 Sa	14 11 10	0♏57 48	16 14 42	23 14 59	29D 11.1	7 10.1	21 36.1	24 19.6	27 34.7	29 39.9	18 47.7	21 37.8	11 28.5	29 08.3
25 Su	14 15 06	1 57 34	0♌09 38	6♌58 44	29 10.9	8 46.3	22 50.6	24 53.2	27 37.1	29 50.0	18 54.6	21 39.6	11 26.8	29 07.8
26 M	14 19 03	2 57 22	13 42 24	20 20 55	29 11.9	10 21.9	24 05.0	25 26.7	27 40.0	0♑00.2	19 01.6	21 41.4	11 25.2	29 07.4
27 Tu	14 22 59	3 57 13	26 54 33	3♍23 39	29 13.5	11 57.0	25 19.4	26 00.0	27 43.2	0 10.5	19 08.6	21 43.1	11 23.5	29 07.0
28 W	14 26 56	4 57 05	9♍48 34	16 09 39	29 15.0	13 31.5	26 33.9	26 33.3	27 46.7	0 20.9	19 15.6	21 44.7	11 21.8	29 06.6
29 Th	14 30 52	5 57 00	22 27 16	28 41 43	29R 15.7	15 05.6	27 48.3	27 06.4	27 50.5	0 31.4	19 22.7	21 46.3	11 20.1	29 06.2
30 F	14 34 49	6 56 57	4♎53 20	11♎02 25	29 15.0	16 39.1	29 02.7	27 39.4	27 54.7	0 42.0	19 29.7	21 47.9	11 18.5	29 05.8
31 Sa	14 38 46	7 56 56	17 09 13	23 13 58	29 12.3	18 12.2	0♐17.2	28 12.3	27 59.3	0 52.8	19 36.8	21 49.4	11 16.8	29 05.5

Astro Data Dy Hr Mn	Planet Ingress Dy Hr Mn	Last Aspect Dy Hr Mn	☽ Ingress Dy Hr Mn	Last Aspect Dy Hr Mn	☽ Ingress Dy Hr Mn	☽ Phases & Eclipses Dy Hr Mn
☽0S 5 0:38	♇ ♒R 1 3:35	2 17:19 ♇ ☍	♍ 2 17:22	2 6:16 ☿ ☌	♎ 2 8:20	3 13:17 ● 10♍57
☿D 11 7:03	♀ ♎ 12 22:15	4 14:10 ♂ ⚹	♎ 5 0:47	4 17:27 ♇ △	♏ 4 18:42	11 13:01 ☽ 18♐42
♀0S 15 6:03	♂ ♌ 13 13:26	7 10:42 ♇ △	♏ 7 10:58	7 5:29 ♇ □	♐ 7 6:50	19 1:47 ○ 26♓02
☽0N 19 8:22	⚳ ♒R 18 22:29	9 22:52 ♇ □	♐ 9 23:14	9 18:06 ♇ ⚹	♑ 9 19:31	19 1:50 • T 1.255
☉0S 23 3:07	☉ ♎ 23 3:07	12 11:08 ♇ ⚹	♑ 12 11:36	11 7:05 ☉ □	♒ 12 6:43	25 18:40 ☾ 2♋36
		14 5:15 ☉ △	♒ 14 21:48	14 13:15 ♇ ☌	♓ 14 14:38	
☽0S 2 8:13	☿ ♎ 2 20:44	17 4:05 ♇ ☌	♓ 17 4:40	16 16:06 ♃ □	♈ 16 18:46	3 3:12 ● 9♎49
☿0S 5 2:56	♀ ♏ 7 2:18	19 1:47 ☉ ☍	♈ 19 8:29	18 18:42 ♇ ⚹	♉ 18 20:00	3 3:00:21 • A non-C
♃⚼♆ 6 7:49	☿ ♏ 20 2:23	21 9:46 ♇ ⚹	♉ 21 10:27	20 18:42 ♇ □	♊ 20 20:02	11 7:05 ☽ 17♑52
☽0N 16 18:37	☉ ♏ 23 12:47	23 11:13 ♇ □	♊ 23 11:57	22 19:44 ♃ ☍	♋ 22 20:45	18 11:55 ○ 25♈00
⚳D 18 1:31	♃ ♑ 26 11:30	25 13:26 ♇ △	♋ 25 14:15	24 8:53 ♀ △	♌ 24 23:43	25 2:27 ☾ 1♌34
♃⚹♇ 21 10:55	♀ ♐ 31 6:28	27 0:08 ☿ ⚹	♌ 27 18:11	27 4:04 ♇ ☍	♍ 27 5:42	
☽0S 29 14:17		29 23:08 ♇ ☍	♍ 30 0:09	29 10:06 ♀ ⚹	♎ 29 14:31	

Astro Data

1 September 2043
Julian Day # 52474
SVP 4♓38'58"
GC 27♐27.0 ⚴ 8♑36.7R
Eris 29♈48.9R ⚵ 22♐02.4
⚷ 24♌07.3 ⚶ 10♏19.1
☽ Mean ☊ 0♈29.0

1 October 2043
Julian Day # 52504
SVP 4♓38'55"
GC 27♐27.0 ⚴ 10♑57.6
Eris 29♈34.7R ⚵ 26♐48.1
⚷ 27♌45.6 ⚶ 24♏40.9
☽ Mean ☊ 28♓53.7

November 2043

LONGITUDE

Day	Sid.Time	☉	0 hr ☽	Noon ☽	True ☊	☿	♀	♂	⚳	♃	♄	♅	♆	♇
1 Su	14 42 42	8♏56 57	29♎16 53	5♏18 11	29♓07.7	19♏44.8	1♐31.6	28♌45.0	28♒04.1	1♑03.6	19♏43.9	21♌50.9	11♉15.1	29♒05.2
2 M	14 46 39	9 57 00	11♏18 02	17 16 38	29R 01.1	21 17.0	2 46.0	29 17.6	28 09.4	1 14.5	19 51.0	21 52.3	11R 13.4	29R 05.0
3 Tu	14 50 35	10 57 04	23 14 09	29 10 47	28 53.2	22 48.7	4 00.5	29 50.1	28 14.9	1 25.5	19 58.1	21 53.6	11 11.7	29 04.7
4 W	14 54 32	11 57 11	5♐06 45	11♐02 16	28 44.7	24 20.0	5 14.9	0♍22.4	28 20.8	1 36.6	20 05.2	21 54.9	11 10.0	29 04.5
5 Th	14 58 28	12 57 19	16 57 36	22 53 01	28 36.2	25 50.9	6 29.3	0 54.6	28 26.9	1 47.7	20 12.4	21 56.2	11 08.3	29 04.3
6 F	15 02 25	13 57 29	28 48 51	4♑45 28	28 28.7	27 21.3	7 43.7	1 26.7	28 33.4	1 59.0	20 19.5	21 57.4	11 06.6	29 04.1
7 Sa	15 06 21	14 57 41	10♑43 16	16 42 42	28 22.9	28 51.3	8 58.1	1 58.6	28 40.3	2 10.4	20 26.7	21 58.5	11 05.0	29 04.0
8 Su	15 10 18	15 57 54	22 44 14	28 48 22	28 19.1	0♐20.8	10 12.5	2 30.3	28 47.4	2 21.8	20 33.8	21 59.6	11 03.3	29 03.9
9 M	15 14 15	16 58 08	4♒55 41	11♒06 43	28D 17.3	1 49.9	11 26.9	3 02.0	28 54.8	2 33.3	20 41.0	22 00.6	11 01.6	29 03.8
10 Tu	15 18 11	17 58 24	17 22 03	23 42 17	28 17.3	3 18.5	12 41.2	3 33.4	29 02.5	2 44.9	20 48.2	22 01.6	10 59.9	29 03.7
11 W	15 22 08	18 58 42	0♓07 58	6♓39 38	28 18.2	4 46.7	13 55.6	4 04.7	29 10.6	2 56.6	20 55.3	22 02.5	10 58.2	29D 03.7
12 Th	15 26 04	19 59 01	13 17 45	20 02 44	28R 19.3	6 14.4	15 10.0	4 35.9	29 18.9	3 08.4	21 02.5	22 03.4	10 56.6	29 03.7
13 F	15 30 01	20 59 21	26 54 51	3♈54 16	28 19.4	7 41.5	16 24.3	5 06.9	29 27.5	3 20.2	21 09.7	22 04.2	10 54.9	29 03.7
14 Sa	15 33 57	21 59 43	11♈00 57	18 14 42	28 17.7	9 08.1	17 38.6	5 37.7	29 36.4	3 32.2	21 16.8	22 05.0	10 53.3	29 03.7
15 Su	15 37 54	23 00 06	25 35 06	3♉01 29	28 13.7	10 34.0	18 52.9	6 08.4	29 45.6	3 44.2	21 24.0	22 05.7	10 51.6	29 03.8
16 M	15 41 50	24 00 31	10♉32 59	18 08 31	28 07.3	11 59.3	20 07.3	6 39.0	29 55.0	3 56.2	21 31.2	22 06.3	10 50.0	29 03.9
17 Tu	15 45 47	25 00 57	25 46 50	3♊26 32	27 59.0	13 23.9	21 21.6	7 09.3	0♓04.8	4 08.4	21 38.4	22 06.9	10 48.3	29 04.0
18 W	15 49 44	26 01 25	11♊06 11	18 44 20	27 49.9	14 47.7	22 35.8	7 39.5	0 14.8	4 20.6	21 45.5	22 07.5	10 46.7	29 04.2
19 Th	15 53 40	27 01 55	26 19 37	3♋50 46	27 41.1	16 10.6	23 50.1	8 09.6	0 25.0	4 32.9	21 52.7	22 08.0	10 45.1	29 04.4
20 F	15 57 37	28 02 27	11♋16 45	18 36 42	27 33.7	17 32.5	25 04.4	8 39.4	0 35.6	4 45.2	21 59.9	22 08.4	10 43.5	29 04.6
21 Sa	16 01 33	29 03 00	25 50 02	2♌56 21	27 28.5	18 53.4	26 18.7	9 09.1	0 46.3	4 57.6	22 07.0	22 08.8	10 41.9	29 04.8
22 Su	16 05 30	0♐03 35	9♌55 29	16 47 28	27 25.6	20 13.0	27 32.9	9 38.6	0 57.4	5 10.1	22 14.1	22 09.1	10 40.4	29 05.0
23 M	16 09 26	1 04 12	23 32 28	0♍10 50	27D 24.7	21 31.1	28 47.1	10 07.9	1 08.7	5 22.6	22 21.3	22 09.4	10 38.8	29 05.3
24 Tu	16 13 23	2 04 50	6♍42 59	13 09 24	27 25.1	22 47.7	0♑01.4	10 37.0	1 20.2	5 35.2	22 28.4	22 09.6	10 37.2	29 05.6
25 W	16 17 19	3 05 30	19 30 37	25 47 11	27R 25.5	24 02.4	1 15.6	11 05.9	1 32.0	5 47.9	22 35.5	22 09.7	10 35.7	29 05.9
26 Th	16 21 16	4 06 12	1♎59 41	8♎08 39	27 25.0	25 15.1	2 29.8	11 34.6	1 44.0	6 00.6	22 42.6	22 09.8	10 34.2	29 06.3
27 F	16 25 13	5 06 56	14 14 36	20 18 02	27 22.4	26 25.4	3 44.0	12 03.2	1 56.3	6 13.4	22 49.7	22R 09.8	10 32.7	29 06.7
28 Sa	16 29 09	6 07 40	26 19 23	2♏19 03	27 17.1	27 33.0	4 58.2	12 31.5	2 08.8	6 26.2	22 56.7	22 09.8	10 31.2	29 07.1
29 Su	16 33 06	7 08 27	8♏17 25	14 14 47	27 08.8	28 37.5	6 12.4	12 59.6	2 21.6	6 39.1	23 03.8	22 09.7	10 29.7	29 07.5
30 M	16 37 02	8 09 15	20 11 25	26 07 35	26 57.7	29 38.4	7 26.5	13 27.5	2 34.5	6 52.1	23 10.8	22 09.6	10 28.2	29 08.0

December 2043

LONGITUDE

Day	Sid.Time	☉	0 hr ☽	Noon ☽	True ☊	☿	♀	♂	⚳	♃	♄	♅	♆	♇
1 Tu	16 40 59	9♐10 04	2♐03 27	7♐59 14	26♓44.5	0♑35.3	8♑40.7	13♍55.1	2♓47.7	7♑05.1	23♏17.8	22♌09.4	10♉26.8	29♒08.5
2 W	16 44 55	10 10 54	13 55 05	19 51 09	26R 30.2	1 27.5	9 54.8	14 22.6	3 01.1	7 18.1	23 24.8	22R 09.2	10R 25.4	29 09.0
3 Th	16 48 52	11 11 46	25 47 35	1♑44 35	26 15.9	2 14.5	11 09.0	14 49.8	3 14.8	7 31.2	23 31.8	22 08.9	10 24.0	29 09.5
4 F	16 52 48	12 12 38	7♑42 19	13 41 00	26 02.9	2 55.6	12 23.1	15 16.7	3 28.6	7 44.4	23 38.7	22 08.5	10 22.6	29 10.1
5 Sa	16 56 45	13 13 32	19 40 52	25 42 12	25 52.1	3 29.9	13 37.2	15 43.5	3 42.7	7 57.6	23 45.7	22 08.1	10 21.2	29 10.7
6 Su	17 00 42	14 14 26	1♒45 19	7♒50 37	25 44.1	3 56.6	14 51.2	16 10.0	3 57.0	8 10.8	23 52.6	22 07.7	10 19.9	29 11.3
7 M	17 04 38	15 15 21	13 58 28	20 09 21	25 39.1	4 15.0	16 05.3	16 36.2	4 11.5	8 24.1	23 59.4	22 07.1	10 18.5	29 11.9
8 Tu	17 08 35	16 16 17	26 23 45	2♓42 11	25 36.7	4R 24.1	17 19.3	17 02.2	4 26.2	8 37.4	24 06.3	22 06.6	10 17.2	29 12.6
9 W	17 12 31	17 17 14	9♓05 10	15 33 16	25 36.2	4 23.2	18 33.3	17 27.9	4 41.0	8 50.8	24 13.1	22 05.9	10 16.0	29 13.3
10 Th	17 16 28	18 18 11	22 06 59	28 46 49	25 36.2	4 11.5	19 47.3	17 53.4	4 56.1	9 04.2	24 19.9	22 05.3	10 14.7	29 14.0
11 F	17 20 24	19 19 09	5♈33 12	12♈26 27	25 35.4	3 48.6	21 01.2	18 18.6	5 11.4	9 17.6	24 26.6	22 04.5	10 13.5	29 14.7
12 Sa	17 24 21	20 20 07	19 26 47	26 34 14	25 32.8	3 14.2	22 15.2	18 43.5	5 26.8	9 31.1	24 33.3	22 03.7	10 12.3	29 15.5
13 Su	17 28 17	21 21 06	3♉48 41	11♉09 46	25 27.6	2 28.5	23 29.0	19 08.2	5 42.5	9 44.6	24 40.0	22 02.9	10 11.1	29 16.3
14 M	17 32 14	22 22 06	18 36 52	26 09 10	25 19.4	1 32.1	24 42.9	19 32.5	5 58.3	9 58.1	24 46.7	22 02.0	10 09.9	29 17.1
15 Tu	17 36 11	23 23 07	3♊45 36	11♊24 55	25 09.0	0 26.1	25 56.7	19 56.6	6 14.3	10 11.7	24 53.3	22 01.1	10 08.8	29 17.9
16 W	17 40 07	24 24 08	19 05 40	26 46 22	24 57.3	29♐12.2	27 10.6	20 20.4	6 30.4	10 25.3	24 59.9	22 00.1	10 07.7	29 18.8
17 Th	17 44 04	25 25 10	4♋25 30	12♋01 36	24 45.7	27 52.7	28 24.3	20 43.9	6 46.8	10 39.0	25 06.4	21 59.0	10 06.6	29 19.7
18 F	17 48 00	26 26 12	19 33 21	26 59 36	24 35.6	26 30.2	29 38.1	21 07.1	7 03.3	10 52.6	25 12.9	21 57.9	10 05.5	29 20.6
19 Sa	17 51 57	27 27 16	4♌19 27	11♌32 13	24 28.0	25 07.4	0♒51.8	21 30.0	7 20.0	11 06.3	25 19.4	21 56.8	10 04.5	29 21.5
20 Su	17 55 53	28 28 20	18 37 28	25 35 03	24 23.1	23 47.2	2 05.4	21 52.5	7 36.8	11 20.0	25 25.8	21 55.6	10 03.5	29 22.5
21 M	17 59 50	29 29 25	2♍24 57	9♍07 23	24 20.8	22 32.1	3 19.1	22 14.8	7 53.8	11 33.7	25 32.2	21 54.3	10 02.5	29 23.5
22 Tu	18 03 47	0♑30 31	15 42 43	22 11 24	24 20.3	21 24.2	4 32.7	22 36.7	8 11.0	11 47.5	25 38.5	21 53.0	10 01.6	29 24.4
23 W	18 07 43	1 31 37	28 34 00	4♎51 08	24 20.3	20 25.2	5 46.3	22 58.2	8 28.3	12 01.3	25 44.8	21 51.7	10 00.6	29 25.5
24 Th	18 11 40	2 32 44	11♎03 25	17 11 30	24 19.5	19 36.2	6 59.8	23 19.4	8 45.8	12 15.1	25 51.1	21 50.3	9 59.7	29 26.5
25 F	18 15 36	3 33 52	23 16 03	29 17 40	24 17.0	18 57.8	8 13.3	23 40.2	9 03.4	12 28.9	25 57.3	21 48.8	9 58.9	29 27.6
26 Sa	18 19 33	4 35 01	5♏16 59	11♏14 31	24 11.8	18 30.3	9 26.8	24 00.7	9 21.2	12 42.7	26 03.4	21 47.3	9 58.0	29 28.6
27 Su	18 23 29	5 36 10	17 10 48	23 06 18	24 03.7	18 13.3	10 40.2	24 20.8	9 39.1	12 56.6	26 09.5	21 45.8	9 57.2	29 29.7
28 M	18 27 26	6 37 20	29 01 25	4♐56 31	23 52.7	18D 06.5	11 53.6	24 40.5	9 57.1	13 10.5	26 15.6	21 44.2	9 56.5	29 30.9
29 Tu	18 31 22	7 38 30	10♐51 56	16 47 54	23 39.5	18 09.3	13 07.0	24 59.8	10 15.4	13 24.3	26 21.6	21 42.6	9 55.7	29 32.0
30 W	18 35 19	8 39 40	22 44 40	28 42 25	23 25.1	18 21.0	14 20.3	25 18.7	10 33.7	13 38.2	26 27.5	21 40.9	9 55.0	29 33.2
31 Th	18 39 16	9 40 51	4♑41 17	10♑41 26	23 10.6	18 40.7	15 33.5	25 37.2	10 52.2	13 52.1	26 33.4	21 39.2	9 54.3	29 34.4

Astro Data	Planet Ingress	Last Aspect	☽ Ingress	Last Aspect	☽ Ingress	☽ Phases & Eclipses	Astro Data
Dy Hr Mn	Dy Hr Mn	Dy Hr Mn	Dy Hr Mn	Dy Hr Mn	Dy Hr Mn	Dy Hr Mn	1 November 2043
♇ D 12 11:26	♂ ♍ 3 19:21	31 23:37 ♇ △	♏ 1 1:26	3 6:47 ♇ ✶	♑ 3 8:29	1 19:57 ● 9♏17	Julian Day # 52535
☽ 0N 13 4:50	☿ ♐ 8 6:25	3 13:23 ♂ □	♐ 3 13:39	5 8:06 ♄ ✶	♒ 5 20:32	10 0:13 ☽ 17♒29	SVP 4♓38'52"
♄□♅ 21 18:14	⚳ ♓ 17 0:21	6 0:31 ♇ ✶	♑ 6 2:24	8 5:22 ♇ ☌	♓ 8 6:52	16 21:52 ○ 24♉25	GC 27♐27.1 ⚴ 17♑22.3
☽ 0S 25 19:17	☉ ♐ 22 10:35	7 19:31 ♄ ✶	♒ 8 14:21	10 3:56 ♄ △	♈ 10 14:11	23 13:45 ☾ 1♍09	Eris 29♈16.2R ⚵ 5♑05.9
♅ R 27 15:38	♀ ♑ 24 11:33	10 22:01 ♇ ☌	♓ 10 23:45	12 16:29 ♇ ✶	♉ 12 17:42		⚷ 0♍43.7 ⚶ 10♐32.1
	☿ ♑ 30 20:54	12 13:46 ♄ △	♈ 13 5:19	14 16:57 ♇ □	♊ 14 18:05	1 14:37 ● 9♐17	☽ Mean ☊ 27♓15.2
♃⚻♅ 1 19:51		15 5:38 ♇ ✶	♉ 15 7:08	16 15:59 ♇ △	♋ 16 17:03	9 15:27 ☽ 17♓26	
☿ R 8 21:58	☿ ♐R 15 20:44	17 5:09 ♇ □	♊ 17 6:37	18 16:42 ♀ ☍	♌ 18 16:54	16 8:02 ○ 24♊14	1 December 2043
☽ 0N 10 12:51	♀ ♒ 18 19:08	19 4:22 ♇ △	♋ 19 5:51	20 18:38 ♇ ☍	♍ 20 19:44	23 5:04 ☾ 1♎14	Julian Day # 52565
♃∠♄ 12 19:53	☉ ♑ 22 0:01	21 4:54 ☉ △	♌ 21 7:01	22 18:32 ♄ ✶	♎ 23 2:43	31 9:48 ● 9♑35	SVP 4♓38'47"
♃△♆ 15 7:11		23 10:01 ♇ ☍	♍ 23 11:40	25 12:20 ♇ △	♏ 25 13:25		GC 27♐27.2 ⚴ 25♑52.1
☽ 0S 23 0:54		25 8:17 ☿ □	♎ 25 20:08	28 0:59 ♇ □	♐ 28 1:59		Eris 29♈00.0R ⚵ 15♑16.4
☿ D 28 16:46		28 5:35 ♇ △	♏ 28 7:21	30 13:42 ♇ ✶	♑ 30 14:36		⚷ 2♍19.5 ⚶ 26♐25.7
		30 18:05 ♇ □	♐ 30 19:50				☽ Mean ☊ 25♓39.9

LONGITUDE — January 2044

Day	Sid.Time	☉	0 hr ☽	Noon☽	True☊	☿	♀	♂	⚳	♃	♄	♅	♆	♇
1 F	18 43 12	10♑42 02	16♑42 59	22♑46 02	22♓57.3	19♐07.8	16♒46.7	25♍55.3	11♓10.8	14♑06.1	26♏39.3	21♌37.5	9♉53.7	29♒35.6
2 Sa	18 47 09	11 43 12	28 50 42	4♒57 09	22R 46.3	19 41.5	17 59.9	26 12.9	11 29.6	14 20.0	26 45.1	21R 35.7	9R 53.1	29 36.8
3 Su	18 51 05	12 44 23	11♒05 31	17 16 01	22 38.1	20 21.2	19 13.0	26 30.1	11 48.5	14 33.9	26 50.8	21 33.9	9 52.5	29 38.0
4 M	18 55 02	13 45 34	23 28 50	29 44 15	22 32.9	21 06.2	20 26.1	26 46.8	12 07.5	14 47.8	26 56.5	21 32.0	9 52.0	29 39.3
5 Tu	18 58 58	14 46 44	6♓02 34	12♓24 06	22D 30.5	21 55.9	21 39.1	27 03.1	12 26.6	15 01.8	27 02.1	21 30.1	9 51.4	29 40.6
6 W	19 02 55	15 47 54	18 49 13	25 18 19	22 30.1	22 49.9	22 52.0	27 18.9	12 45.9	15 15.7	27 07.6	21 28.1	9 51.0	29 41.9
7 Th	19 06 51	16 49 04	1♈51 46	8♈29 59	22R 30.5	23 47.5	24 04.9	27 34.3	13 05.2	15 29.6	27 13.1	21 26.1	9 50.5	29 43.2
8 F	19 10 48	17 50 13	15 13 19	22 02 06	22 30.7	24 48.6	25 17.7	27 49.2	13 24.7	15 43.6	27 18.5	21 24.1	9 50.1	29 44.5
9 Sa	19 14 45	18 51 22	28 56 33	5♉56 50	22 29.3	25 52.6	26 30.5	28 03.5	13 44.3	15 57.5	27 23.9	21 22.0	9 49.7	29 45.8
10 Su	19 18 41	19 52 31	13♉02 58	20 14 48	22 25.7	26 59.3	27 43.1	28 17.4	14 04.1	16 11.4	27 29.2	21 19.9	9 49.3	29 47.2
11 M	19 22 38	20 53 39	27 32 01	4♊54 07	22 19.7	28 08.3	28 55.8	28 30.7	14 23.9	16 25.3	27 34.4	21 17.8	9 49.0	29 48.6
12 Tu	19 26 34	21 54 46	12♊20 24	19 49 57	22 11.6	29 19.5	0♓08.3	28 43.6	14 43.8	16 39.3	27 39.5	21 15.6	9 48.8	29 50.0
13 W	19 30 31	22 55 53	27 21 43	4♋54 32	22 02.2	0♑32.6	1 20.8	28 55.9	15 03.9	16 53.2	27 44.6	21 13.5	9 48.5	29 51.4
14 Th	19 34 27	23 57 00	12♋27 07	19 58 10	21 52.7	1 47.5	2 33.1	29 07.6	15 24.0	17 07.1	27 49.7	21 11.2	9 48.3	29 52.8
15 F	19 38 24	24 58 06	27 26 28	4♌50 50	21 44.4	3 04.0	3 45.4	29 18.8	15 44.3	17 21.0	27 54.6	21 09.0	9 48.1	29 54.3
16 Sa	19 42 21	25 59 12	12♌10 16	19 23 55	21 38.0	4 21.8	4 57.7	29 29.5	16 04.6	17 34.8	27 59.5	21 06.7	9 48.0	29 55.7
17 Su	19 46 17	27 00 17	26 31 10	3♍31 33	21 34.1	5 41.1	6 09.8	29 39.5	16 25.1	17 48.7	28 04.3	21 04.4	9 47.9	29 57.2
18 M	19 50 14	28 01 22	10♍24 53	17 11 06	21D 32.5	7 01.5	7 21.9	29 49.0	16 45.6	18 02.6	28 09.0	21 02.1	9 47.8	29 58.7
19 Tu	19 54 10	29 02 27	23 50 19	0♎22 50	21 32.8	8 23.0	8 33.8	29 57.9	17 06.2	18 16.4	28 13.7	20 59.7	9D 47.7	0♓00.2
20 W	19 58 07	0♒03 31	6♎49 02	13 09 24	21 33.9	9 45.6	9 45.7	0♎06.1	17 27.0	18 30.2	28 18.3	20 57.3	9 47.7	0 01.7
21 Th	20 02 03	1 04 35	19 24 28	25 34 52	21R 34.9	11 09.2	10 57.5	0 13.8	17 47.8	18 44.0	28 22.8	20 54.9	9 47.8	0 03.2
22 F	20 06 00	2 05 39	1♏41 14	7♏44 11	21 34.8	12 33.7	12 09.2	0 20.8	18 08.7	18 57.8	28 27.2	20 52.5	9 47.8	0 04.7
23 Sa	20 09 56	3 06 42	13 44 22	19 42 26	21 33.1	13 59.1	13 20.8	0 27.1	18 29.7	19 11.6	28 31.6	20 50.0	9 47.9	0 06.3
24 Su	20 13 53	4 07 45	25 38 59	1♐34 35	21 29.2	15 25.3	14 32.4	0 32.8	18 50.8	19 25.3	28 35.8	20 47.5	9 48.1	0 07.8
25 M	20 17 50	5 08 47	7♐29 48	13 25 07	21 23.3	16 52.3	15 43.8	0 37.8	19 12.0	19 39.0	28 40.0	20 45.1	9 48.2	0 09.4
26 Tu	20 21 46	6 09 49	19 21 00	25 17 52	21 15.7	18 20.1	16 55.1	0 42.1	19 33.3	19 52.7	28 44.2	20 42.5	9 48.4	0 11.0
27 W	20 25 43	7 10 50	1♑16 03	7♑15 53	21 07.1	19 48.7	18 06.3	0 45.7	19 54.6	20 06.4	28 48.2	20 40.0	9 48.7	0 12.5
28 Th	20 29 39	8 11 51	13 17 37	19 21 28	20 58.3	21 18.0	19 17.5	0 48.6	20 16.0	20 20.0	28 52.1	20 37.5	9 48.9	0 14.1
29 F	20 33 36	9 12 50	25 27 36	1♒36 08	20 50.3	22 48.0	20 28.5	0 50.8	20 37.6	20 33.6	28 56.0	20 34.9	9 49.3	0 15.8
30 Sa	20 37 32	10 13 49	7♒47 12	14 00 51	20 43.6	24 18.7	21 39.4	0 52.2	20 59.1	20 47.2	28 59.8	20 32.4	9 49.6	0 17.4
31 Su	20 41 29	11 14 47	20 17 09	26 36 10	20 39.0	25 50.2	22 50.2	0R 52.9	21 20.8	21 00.8	29 03.5	20 29.8	9 50.0	0 19.0

LONGITUDE — February 2044

Day	Sid.Time	☉	0 hr ☽	Noon☽	True☊	☿	♀	♂	⚳	♃	♄	♅	♆	♇
1 M	20 45 25	12♒15 43	2♓57 55	9♓22 29	20♓36.4	27♑22.3	24♓00.8	0♎52.9	21♓42.5	21♑14.3	29♏07.1	20♌27.2	9♉50.4	0♓20.6
2 Tu	20 49 22	13 16 39	15 49 55	22 20 19	20D 35.8	28 55.2	25 11.4	0R 52.1	22 04.3	21 27.8	29 10.6	20R 24.6	9 50.8	0 22.3
3 W	20 53 19	14 17 33	28 53 44	5♈30 20	20 36.6	0♒28.7	26 21.8	0 50.6	22 26.2	21 41.2	29 14.0	20 22.0	9 51.3	0 23.9
4 Th	20 57 15	15 18 26	12♈10 12	18 53 28	20 38.1	2 03.0	27 32.0	0 48.3	22 48.1	21 54.6	29 17.4	20 19.3	9 51.8	0 25.6
5 F	21 01 12	16 19 17	25 40 17	2♉30 43	20 39.6	3 38.0	28 42.2	0 45.2	23 10.2	22 08.0	29 20.6	20 16.7	9 52.4	0 27.2
6 Sa	21 05 08	17 20 07	9♉24 53	16 22 47	20R 40.3	5 13.8	29 52.2	0 41.4	23 32.2	22 21.3	29 23.8	20 14.1	9 53.0	0 28.9
7 Su	21 09 05	18 20 56	23 24 24	0♊29 38	20 39.7	6 50.3	1♈02.0	0 36.8	23 54.4	22 34.6	29 26.8	20 11.5	9 53.6	0 30.6
8 M	21 13 01	19 21 43	7♊38 15	14 49 57	20 37.6	8 27.5	2 11.8	0 31.4	24 16.6	22 47.8	29 29.8	20 08.8	9 54.2	0 32.2
9 Tu	21 16 58	20 22 29	22 04 19	29 20 49	20 34.2	10 05.5	3 21.3	0 25.2	24 38.8	23 01.0	29 32.7	20 06.2	9 54.9	0 33.9
10 W	21 20 54	21 23 13	6♋38 48	13♋57 33	20 30.0	11 44.3	4 30.7	0 18.3	25 01.1	23 14.1	29 35.5	20 03.6	9 55.7	0 35.6
11 Th	21 24 51	22 23 56	21 16 15	28 34 03	20 25.7	13 23.9	5 39.9	0 10.5	25 23.5	23 27.2	29 38.2	20 01.0	9 56.4	0 37.3
12 F	21 28 48	23 24 37	5♌50 07	13♌03 36	20 21.8	15 04.3	6 49.0	0 02.0	25 46.0	23 40.3	29 40.8	19 58.3	9 57.2	0 39.0
13 Sa	21 32 44	24 25 17	20 13 43	27 19 45	20 19.0	16 45.5	7 57.9	29♍52.7	26 08.4	23 53.3	29 43.3	19 55.7	9 58.0	0 40.7
14 Su	21 36 41	25 25 55	4♍21 06	11♍17 18	20D 17.5	18 27.6	9 06.6	29 42.7	26 31.0	24 06.2	29 45.7	19 53.1	9 58.9	0 42.4
15 M	21 40 37	26 26 32	18 07 59	24 52 57	20 17.3	20 10.5	10 15.1	29 31.8	26 53.6	24 19.1	29 48.0	19 50.5	9 59.8	0 44.1
16 Tu	21 44 34	27 27 07	1♎32 05	8♎05 28	20 18.2	21 54.3	11 23.5	29 20.2	27 16.2	24 32.0	29 50.2	19 47.9	10 00.7	0 45.8
17 W	21 48 30	28 27 41	14 33 14	20 55 39	20 19.6	23 39.0	12 31.7	29 07.8	27 38.9	24 44.7	29 52.3	19 45.3	10 01.6	0 47.5
18 Th	21 52 27	29 28 14	27 13 03	3♏25 53	20 21.3	25 24.6	13 39.6	28 54.7	28 01.6	24 57.5	29 54.4	19 42.7	10 02.6	0 49.2
19 F	21 56 23	0♓28 46	9♏34 36	15 39 45	20 22.6	27 11.1	14 47.4	28 40.8	28 24.4	25 10.1	29 56.3	19 40.1	10 03.6	0 50.9
20 Sa	22 00 20	1 29 17	21 41 54	27 41 37	20R 23.3	28 58.5	15 55.0	28 26.1	28 47.3	25 22.7	29 58.1	19 37.5	10 04.6	0 52.6
21 Su	22 04 17	2 29 46	3♐39 31	9♐36 12	20 23.2	0♓46.7	17 02.4	28 10.8	29 10.2	25 35.3	29 59.8	19 35.0	10 05.7	0 54.3
22 M	22 08 13	3 30 14	15 32 16	21 28 18	20 22.3	2 35.9	18 09.6	27 54.7	29 33.1	25 47.8	0♐01.5	19 32.4	10 06.8	0 56.0
23 Tu	22 12 10	4 30 41	27 24 52	3♑22 30	20 20.6	4 25.9	19 16.5	27 38.0	29 56.1	26 00.2	0 03.0	19 29.9	10 08.0	0 57.7
24 W	22 16 06	5 31 06	9♑21 42	15 22 56	20 18.5	6 16.8	20 23.3	27 20.6	0♈19.1	26 12.6	0 04.4	19 27.4	10 09.1	0 59.4
25 Th	22 20 03	6 31 30	21 26 38	27 33 10	20 16.3	8 08.6	21 29.8	27 02.5	0 42.1	26 24.9	0 05.7	19 24.9	10 10.3	1 01.1
26 F	22 23 59	7 31 52	3♒42 51	9♒55 56	20 14.2	10 01.0	22 36.1	26 43.9	1 05.2	26 37.1	0 07.0	19 22.4	10 11.6	1 02.8
27 Sa	22 27 56	8 32 12	16 12 39	22 33 06	20 12.7	11 54.2	23 42.2	26 24.6	1 28.4	26 49.2	0 08.1	19 20.0	10 12.8	1 04.5
28 Su	22 31 52	9 32 31	28 57 25	5♓25 35	20 11.7	13 48.1	24 48.0	26 04.8	1 51.6	27 01.3	0 09.1	19 17.6	10 14.1	1 06.2
29 M	22 35 49	10 32 48	11♓57 36	18 33 23	20D 11.4	15 42.5	25 53.5	25 44.4	2 14.8	27 13.3	0 10.0	19 15.1	10 15.4	1 07.9

Astro Data

	Dy Hr Mn
♃∠♇	3 19:47
☽0N	6 18:17
☽0S	19 8:38
♆ D	20 5:44
♃⚻♅	29 13:55
♂ R	31 23:11
☽0N	2 23:03
♀0N	7 7:38
☽0S	15 18:10

Planet Ingress

		Dy Hr Mn
♀	♓	12 9:15
☿	♑	13 1:22
♇	♓	19 9:30
♂	♎	19 17:58
☉	♒	20 10:37
☿	♒	3 4:39
♀	♈	6 14:41
♂	♍R	12 17:26
☉	♓	19 0:36
☿	♓	21 1:40
♄	♐	21 14:20
⚳	♈	23 16:07

Last Aspect / ☽ Ingress (January)

Last Aspect Dy Hr Mn			☽ Ingress	Dy Hr Mn
1 19:45	♄	⚹	♒	2 2:16
4 11:51	♇	☌	♓	4 12:30
6 15:46	♂	☍	♈	6 20:36
9 1:24	♇	⚹	♉	9 1:49
11 3:42	♇	□	♊	11 4:02
13 3:57	♇	△	♋	13 4:12
15 2:55	♂	⚹	♌	15 4:08
17 5:51	♇	☍	♍	17 5:56
19 11:13	♂	☌	♎	19 11:18
21 2:57	♅	⚹	♏	21 20:40
24 5:56	♄	☌	♐	24 8:48
26 2:47	♅	△	♑	26 21:27
29 6:46	♄	⚹	♒	29 8:53
31 16:40	♄	□	♓	31 18:25

Last Aspect / ☽ Ingress (February)

Last Aspect Dy Hr Mn			☽ Ingress	Dy Hr Mn
3 1:39	☿	⚹	♈	3 2:01
4 17:27	♃	□	♉	5 7:36
7 10:14	♄	☍	♊	7 11:10
8 20:47	♅	⚹	♋	9 13:05
11 13:46	♄	△	♌	11 14:22
13 16:05	♄	□	♍	13 16:33
15 20:53	♄	⚹	♎	15 21:13
18 3:40	☉	△	♏	18 5:21
20 16:35	♄	☌	♐	20 16:38
23 0:43	♂	□	♑	23 5:13
25 11:01	♂	△	♒	25 16:47
27 14:22	♀	⚹	♓	28 1:57

☽ Phases & Eclipses

Dy Hr Mn		
8 4:02	☽	17♈30
14 18:51	○	24♋14
21 23:47	☾	1♏35
30 4:04	●	9♒54
6 13:46	☽	17♉25
13 6:42	○	24♌12
20 20:20	☾	1♐50
28 20:12	●	9♓53
28 20:23:10	●	A 02'27"

Astro Data

1 January 2044
Julian Day # 52596
SVP 4♓38'40"
GC 27♐27.2 ⚵ 5♒54.7
Eris 28♈50.0R ⚴ 27♑12.4
⚷ 2♍17.3R ⚶ 13♑03.6
☽ Mean ☊ 24♓01.4

1 February 2044
Julian Day # 52627
SVP 4♓38'35"
GC 27♐27.3 ⚵ 16♒28.5
Eris 28♈50.2 ⚴ 10♒00.8
⚷ 0♍39.3R ⚶ 29♑34.5
☽ Mean ☊ 22♓23.0

March 2044 — LONGITUDE

Day	Sid.Time	☉	0 hr ☽	Noon ☽	True ☊	☿	♀	♂	⚳	♃	♄	♅	♆	♇
1 Tu	22 39 46	11♓33 04	25♓12 49	1♈55 44	20♓11.5	17♓37.3	26♈58.8	25♍23.6	2♈38.0	27♑25.2	0♐10.8	19♌12.8	10♉16.7	1♓09.6
2 W	22 43 42	12 33 17	8♈41 58	15 31 16	20 12.0	19 32.4	28 03.8	25R 02.3	3 01.3	27 37.1	0 11.5	19R 10.4	10 18.1	1 11.3
3 Th	22 47 39	13 33 29	22 23 25	29 18 12	20 12.7	21 27.5	29 08.6	24 40.6	3 24.6	27 48.8	0 12.1	19 08.1	10 19.5	1 12.9
4 F	22 51 35	14 33 38	6♉15 20	13♉14 35	20 13.3	23 22.6	0♉13.0	24 18.5	3 48.0	28 00.5	0 12.6	19 05.7	10 20.9	1 14.6
5 Sa	22 55 32	15 33 46	20 15 42	27 18 25	20 13.7	25 17.4	1 17.2	23 56.0	4 11.4	28 12.1	0 13.0	19 03.5	10 22.4	1 16.3
6 Su	22 59 28	16 33 51	4♊22 29	11♊27 38	20R 13.9	27 11.5	2 21.1	23 33.3	4 34.8	28 23.7	0 13.3	19 01.2	10 23.9	1 17.9
7 M	23 03 25	17 33 54	18 33 36	25 40 05	20 13.9	29 04.7	3 24.6	23 10.3	4 58.2	28 35.1	0 13.5	18 59.0	10 25.4	1 19.6
8 Tu	23 07 21	18 33 55	2♋46 48	9♋53 26	20 13.8	0♈56.7	4 27.9	22 47.1	5 21.7	28 46.4	0R 13.6	18 56.8	10 26.9	1 21.2
9 W	23 11 18	19 33 54	16 59 38	24 05 04	20D 13.7	2 46.9	5 30.7	22 23.7	5 45.1	28 57.7	0 13.6	18 54.6	10 28.4	1 22.9
10 Th	23 15 15	20 33 51	1♌09 21	8♌12 06	20 13.7	4 35.1	6 33.3	22 00.2	6 08.7	29 08.9	0 13.5	18 52.5	10 30.0	1 24.5
11 F	23 19 11	21 33 45	15 12 55	22 11 25	20 13.8	6 20.7	7 35.4	21 36.7	6 32.2	29 20.0	0 13.3	18 50.4	10 31.6	1 26.1
12 Sa	23 23 08	22 33 38	29 07 14	5♍59 58	20 13.9	8 03.3	8 37.2	21 13.1	6 55.7	29 31.0	0 13.0	18 48.3	10 33.3	1 27.7
13 Su	23 27 04	23 33 28	12♍49 19	19 34 58	20R 14.0	9 42.3	9 38.7	20 49.4	7 19.3	29 41.9	0 12.6	18 46.3	10 34.9	1 29.3
14 M	23 31 01	24 33 16	26 16 41	2♎54 16	20 13.9	11 17.3	10 39.7	20 25.9	7 42.9	29 52.7	0 12.0	18 44.3	10 36.6	1 30.9
15 Tu	23 34 57	25 33 02	9♎27 36	15 56 37	20 13.5	12 47.7	11 40.3	20 02.4	8 06.5	0♒03.4	0 11.4	18 42.4	10 38.3	1 32.5
16 W	23 38 54	26 32 47	22 21 20	28 41 50	20 12.8	14 13.2	12 40.5	19 39.1	8 30.2	0 14.0	0 10.7	18 40.4	10 40.0	1 34.1
17 Th	23 42 50	27 32 30	4♏58 16	11♏10 51	20 11.9	15 33.1	13 40.3	19 15.9	8 53.8	0 24.5	0 09.9	18 38.5	10 41.7	1 35.7
18 F	23 46 47	28 32 11	17 19 53	23 25 41	20 10.8	16 47.1	14 39.7	18 52.9	9 17.5	0 34.9	0 09.0	18 36.7	10 43.5	1 37.2
19 Sa	23 50 44	29 31 50	29 28 41	5♐29 19	20 09.8	17 54.7	15 38.6	18 30.2	9 41.2	0 45.2	0 08.0	18 34.9	10 45.3	1 38.8
20 Su	23 54 40	0♈31 27	11♐28 04	17 25 29	20 09.0	18 55.6	16 37.0	18 07.9	10 04.9	0 55.4	0 06.9	18 33.1	10 47.1	1 40.3
21 M	23 58 37	1 31 03	23 22 04	29 18 27	20D 08.6	19 49.4	17 35.0	17 45.8	10 28.7	1 05.5	0 05.7	18 31.4	10 48.9	1 41.8
22 Tu	0 02 33	2 30 37	5♑15 10	11♑12 50	20 08.8	20 36.0	18 32.4	17 24.2	10 52.4	1 15.5	0 04.4	18 29.7	10 50.8	1 43.3
23 W	0 06 30	3 30 09	17 12 03	23 13 23	20 09.5	21 15.0	19 29.4	17 02.9	11 16.2	1 25.4	0 03.0	18 28.1	10 52.6	1 44.8
24 Th	0 10 26	4 29 39	29 17 23	5♒24 35	20 10.6	21 46.3	20 25.8	16 42.1	11 39.9	1 35.1	0 01.5	18 26.5	10 54.5	1 46.3
25 F	0 14 23	5 29 08	11♒35 30	17 50 34	20 12.0	22 09.9	21 21.7	16 21.8	12 03.7	1 44.8	29♏59.9	18 24.9	10 56.4	1 47.8
26 Sa	0 18 19	6 28 35	24 10 10	0♓34 37	20 13.2	22 25.7	22 17.0	16 02.0	12 27.5	1 54.3	29 58.2	18 23.4	10 58.3	1 49.3
27 Su	0 22 16	7 27 59	7♓04 10	13 38 56	20R 13.9	22R 33.8	23 11.7	15 42.8	12 51.3	2 03.7	29 56.4	18 21.9	11 00.3	1 50.7
28 M	0 26 12	8 27 22	20 19 00	27 04 16	20 13.9	22 34.3	24 05.8	15 24.1	13 15.1	2 13.0	29 54.5	18 20.5	11 02.2	1 52.1
29 Tu	0 30 09	9 26 43	3♈54 35	10♈49 40	20 12.9	22 27.4	24 59.3	15 06.1	13 39.0	2 22.2	29 52.5	18 19.2	11 04.2	1 53.6
30 W	0 34 06	10 26 02	17 49 08	24 52 30	20 11.0	22 13.5	25 52.2	14 48.7	14 02.8	2 31.3	29 50.5	18 17.8	11 06.2	1 55.0
31 Th	0 38 02	11 25 18	1♉59 13	9♉08 38	20 08.3	21 53.0	26 44.4	14 32.0	14 26.6	2 40.2	29 48.3	18 16.5	11 08.2	1 56.3

April 2044 — LONGITUDE

Day	Sid.Time	☉	0 hr ☽	Noon ☽	True ☊	☿	♀	♂	⚳	♃	♄	♅	♆	♇
1 F	0 41 59	12♈24 33	16♉20 06	23♉32 55	20♓05.2	21♈26.4	27♉35.8	14♍16.0	14♈50.5	2♒49.0	29♏46.1	18♌15.3	11♉10.2	1♓57.7
2 Sa	0 45 55	13 23 45	0♊46 25	7♊59 55	20R 02.2	20R 54.4	28 26.6	14R 00.7	15 14.3	2 57.7	29R 43.8	18R 14.1	11 12.3	1 59.1
3 Su	0 49 52	14 22 56	15 12 48	22 24 33	19 59.9	20 17.6	29 16.6	13 46.1	15 38.2	3 06.3	29 41.4	18 13.0	11 14.3	2 00.4
4 M	0 53 48	15 22 03	29 34 39	6♋42 43	19D 58.6	19 36.9	0♊05.8	13 32.2	16 02.0	3 14.7	29 38.9	18 11.9	11 16.4	2 01.7
5 Tu	0 57 45	16 21 09	13♋48 26	20 51 33	19 58.4	18 53.2	0 54.2	13 19.1	16 25.9	3 23.0	29 36.3	18 10.9	11 18.5	2 03.1
6 W	1 01 42	17 20 12	27 51 53	4♌49 19	19 59.2	18 07.3	1 41.7	13 06.8	16 49.8	3 31.2	29 33.6	18 09.9	11 20.6	2 04.3
7 Th	1 05 38	18 19 12	11♌43 46	18 35 13	20 00.7	17 20.2	2 28.4	12 55.2	17 13.6	3 39.2	29 30.9	18 09.0	11 22.7	2 05.6
8 F	1 09 35	19 18 11	25 23 37	2♍08 58	20 02.2	16 32.8	3 14.1	12 44.4	17 37.5	3 47.1	29 28.1	18 08.1	11 24.8	2 06.9
9 Sa	1 13 31	20 17 07	8♍51 18	15 30 35	20R 03.1	15 46.0	3 58.9	12 34.4	18 01.3	3 54.8	29 25.2	18 07.3	11 26.9	2 08.1
10 Su	1 17 28	21 16 00	22 06 51	28 40 04	20 02.9	15 00.7	4 42.7	12 25.1	18 25.1	4 02.4	29 22.2	18 06.5	11 29.1	2 09.3
11 M	1 21 24	22 14 52	5♎10 14	11♎37 20	20 01.1	14 17.6	5 25.5	12 16.7	18 49.0	4 09.9	29 19.2	18 05.7	11 31.2	2 10.5
12 Tu	1 25 21	23 13 42	18 01 22	24 22 21	19 57.7	13 37.5	6 07.2	12 09.0	19 12.8	4 17.2	29 16.0	18 05.1	11 33.4	2 11.7
13 W	1 29 17	24 12 29	0♏40 17	6♏55 12	19 52.8	13 01.0	6 47.7	12 02.1	19 36.7	4 24.4	29 12.8	18 04.4	11 35.5	2 12.9
14 Th	1 33 14	25 11 15	13 07 13	19 16 24	19 46.7	12 28.5	7 27.2	11 56.0	20 00.5	4 31.5	29 09.6	18 03.9	11 37.7	2 14.0
15 F	1 37 10	26 09 59	25 22 55	1♐26 58	19 40.2	12 00.5	8 05.4	11 50.7	20 24.3	4 38.4	29 06.3	18 03.3	11 39.9	2 15.1
16 Sa	1 41 07	27 08 41	7♐28 48	13 28 41	19 33.8	11 37.2	8 42.5	11 46.1	20 48.1	4 45.1	29 02.9	18 02.9	11 42.1	2 16.2
17 Su	1 45 04	28 07 22	19 26 59	25 24 04	19 28.3	11 18.9	9 18.2	11 42.3	21 12.0	4 51.7	28 59.4	18 02.5	11 44.3	2 17.3
18 M	1 49 00	29 06 00	1♑20 24	7♑16 26	19 24.2	11 05.7	9 52.6	11 39.3	21 35.8	4 58.2	28 55.9	18 02.1	11 46.5	2 18.4
19 Tu	1 52 57	0♉04 37	13 12 42	19 09 46	19D 21.8	10 57.7	10 25.7	11 37.1	21 59.6	5 04.5	28 52.3	18 01.8	11 48.7	2 19.4
20 W	1 56 53	1 03 13	25 08 12	1♒08 37	19 21.0	10D 54.8	10 57.3	11 35.6	22 23.4	5 10.6	28 48.6	18 01.5	11 50.9	2 20.5
21 Th	2 00 50	2 01 46	7♒11 37	13 17 50	19 21.6	10 57.0	11 27.4	11D 34.9	22 47.1	5 16.6	28 44.9	18 01.3	11 53.2	2 21.5
22 F	2 04 46	3 00 18	19 27 52	25 42 19	19 23.0	11 04.2	11 56.0	11 34.9	23 10.9	5 22.4	28 41.1	18 01.2	11 55.4	2 22.5
23 Sa	2 08 43	3 58 48	2♓01 45	8♓26 39	19R 24.3	11 16.3	12 23.1	11 35.6	23 34.7	5 28.1	28 37.3	18 01.1	11 57.7	2 23.4
24 Su	2 12 39	4 57 17	14 57 27	21 34 30	19 24.7	11 33.2	12 48.4	11 37.1	23 58.4	5 33.6	28 33.4	18D 01.0	11 59.9	2 24.4
25 M	2 16 36	5 55 44	28 18 01	5♈08 06	19 23.5	11 54.7	13 12.1	11 39.3	24 22.2	5 38.9	28 29.5	18 01.1	12 02.1	2 25.3
26 Tu	2 20 33	6 54 09	12♈04 42	19 07 34	19 20.4	12 20.6	13 34.0	11 42.2	24 45.9	5 44.1	28 25.5	18 01.1	12 04.4	2 26.2
27 W	2 24 29	7 52 32	26 16 19	3♉30 22	19 15.1	12 50.8	13 54.1	11 45.9	25 09.6	5 49.1	28 21.5	18 01.2	12 06.6	2 27.0
28 Th	2 28 26	8 50 54	10♉48 59	18 11 16	19 08.2	13 25.1	14 12.3	11 50.2	25 33.3	5 53.9	28 17.4	18 01.4	12 08.9	2 27.9
29 F	2 32 22	9 49 14	25 36 13	3♊02 45	19 00.4	14 03.3	14 28.5	11 55.2	25 57.0	5 58.6	28 13.3	18 01.6	12 11.2	2 28.7
30 Sa	2 36 19	10 47 32	10♊29 46	17 56 10	18 52.7	14 45.3	14 42.8	12 00.9	26 20.6	6 03.1	28 09.2	18 01.9	12 13.4	2 29.5

Astro Data

	Dy Hr Mn
☽0N	1 5:30
☿0N	8 6:37
♄ R	8 22:25
☽0S	14 3:38
♃✶♄	16 5:06
☉0N	19 23:21
♃⚺♇	25 20:57
☿ R	28 1:29
☽0N	28 14:09
⚳0N	6 5:27
☽0S	10 11:17
☿ D	20 13:34
♂ D	21 23:36
♅ D	24 18:51
☽0N	24 23:48

Planet Ingress

	Dy Hr Mn
♀ ♉	4 7:08
☿ ♈	7 23:49
♃ ♒	15 4:27
☉ ♈	19 23:20
♄ ♏R	25 10:02
♀ ♊	4 9:09
☉ ♉	19 10:06

Last Aspect / ☽ Ingress

Last Aspect Dy Hr Mn		☽ Ingress Dy Hr Mn
1 3:50	♃ ✶	♈ 1 8:34
3 11:42	♀ ☌	♉ 3 13:12
5 13:33	♃ △	♊ 5 16:35
7 18:38	☿ □	♋ 7 19:19
9 20:23	♃ ☍	♌ 9 22:02
11 6:14	♅ ☌	♍ 12 1:32
14 6:26	♃ △	♎ 14 6:43
15 17:08	♅ ✶	♏ 16 14:29
18 23:02	☉ △	♐ 19 1:02
20 15:18	☿ △	♑ 21 13:24
23 7:52	☿ □	♒ 24 1:24
26 10:52	♄ □	♓ 26 10:56
28 16:59	♄ △	♈ 28 17:09
30 7:35	☿ ☌	♉ 30 20:39

Last Aspect / ☽ Ingress

Last Aspect Dy Hr Mn		☽ Ingress Dy Hr Mn
1 22:18	♄ ☍	♊ 1 22:43
3 8:37	☿ ✶	♋ 4 0:43
6 2:57	♄ △	♌ 6 3:40
8 7:15	♄ □	♍ 8 8:10
10 13:17	♄ ✶	♎ 10 14:27
12 9:39	☉ ☍	♏ 12 22:43
15 7:22	♄ ☌	♐ 15 9:08
17 17:59	☉ △	♑ 17 21:17
20 7:22	♄ ✶	♒ 20 9:43
22 17:39	♄ □	♓ 22 20:10
25 0:24	♄ △	♈ 25 3:00
26 10:07	♅ △	♉ 27 6:12
29 4:16	♄ ☍	♊ 29 7:06

☽ Phases & Eclipses

Dy Hr Mn	
6 21:17	☽ 16♊57
13 19:41	○ 23♍53
13 19:37	• T 1.203
21 16:52	☾ 1♑43
29 9:26	● 9♈20
5 3:45	☽ 16♋01
12 9:39	○ 23♎08
20 11:48	☾ 1♒03
27 19:42	● 8♉11

Astro Data

1 March 2044
Julian Day # 52656
SVP 4♓38'31"
GC 27♐27.4 ⚴ 26♒17.7
Eris 28♈59.6 ⚵ 22♒23.9
⚷ 28♌26.7R ⚶ 14♒37.4
☽ Mean ☊ 20♓50.8

1 April 2044
Julian Day # 52687
SVP 4♓38'28"
GC 27♐27.4 ⚴ 6♓12.2
Eris 29♈16.9 ⚵ 5♓43.2
⚷ 26♌34.3R ⚶ 29♒56.3
☽ Mean ☊ 19♓12.3

LONGITUDE — May 2044

Day	Sid.Time	☉	0 hr ☽	Noon ☽	True ☊	☿	♀	♂	⚳	♃	♄	♅	♆	♇
1 Su	2 40 15	11♉45 48	25♊20 57	2♋43 10	18♓46.3	15♈30.9	14♊54.9	12♍07.3	26♈44.3	6♒07.4	28♏05.0	18♌02.3	12♉15.7	2♓30.3
2 M	2 44 12	12 44 03	10♋02 02	17 16 56	18R41.6	16 19.9	15 04.9	12 14.3	27 07.9	6 11.6	28R00.8	18 02.7	12 17.9	2 31.1
3 Tu	2 48 08	13 42 15	24 27 23	1♌33 05	18D39.0	17 12.2	15 12.7	12 22.0	27 31.5	6 15.5	27 56.5	18 03.1	12 20.2	2 31.8
4 W	2 52 05	14 40 25	8♌33 51	15 29 38	18 38.4	18 07.8	15 18.3	12 30.3	27 55.0	6 19.3	27 52.2	18 03.6	12 22.5	2 32.5
5 Th	2 56 02	15 38 33	22 20 32	29 06 42	18 38.9	19 06.4	15R21.5	12 39.2	28 18.6	6 23.0	27 47.9	18 04.2	12 24.7	2 33.2
6 F	2 59 58	16 36 38	5♍48 21	12♍25 43	18R39.7	20 07.9	15 22.4	12 48.8	28 42.1	6 26.4	27 43.6	18 04.8	12 27.0	2 33.9
7 Sa	3 03 55	17 34 42	18 59 07	25 28 48	18 39.6	21 12.3	15 20.9	12 58.9	29 05.6	6 29.7	27 39.2	18 05.4	12 29.2	2 34.5
8 Su	3 07 51	18 32 44	1♎55 04	8♎18 11	18 37.8	22 19.5	15 17.0	13 09.6	29 29.1	6 32.8	27 34.8	18 06.2	12 31.5	2 35.2
9 M	3 11 48	19 30 45	14 38 21	20 55 49	18 33.5	23 29.3	15 10.6	13 20.9	29 52.5	6 35.7	27 30.4	18 06.9	12 33.7	2 35.7
10 Tu	3 15 44	20 28 43	27 10 45	3♏23 18	18 26.7	24 41.7	15 01.8	13 32.7	0♉16.0	6 38.4	27 26.0	18 07.7	12 36.0	2 36.3
11 W	3 19 41	21 26 40	9♏33 36	15 41 47	18 17.4	25 56.6	14 50.6	13 45.1	0 39.4	6 41.0	27 21.5	18 08.6	12 38.2	2 36.9
12 Th	3 23 37	22 24 35	21 47 57	27 52 14	18 06.3	27 14.0	14 36.9	13 58.1	1 02.7	6 43.3	27 17.1	18 09.5	12 40.5	2 37.4
13 F	3 27 34	23 22 29	3♐54 44	9♐55 35	17 54.3	28 33.9	14 20.7	14 11.5	1 26.1	6 45.5	27 12.6	18 10.5	12 42.7	2 37.9
14 Sa	3 31 31	24 20 22	15 54 57	21 53 01	17 42.4	29 56.0	14 02.3	14 25.5	1 49.4	6 47.5	27 08.1	18 11.6	12 44.9	2 38.4
15 Su	3 35 27	25 18 13	27 50 02	3♑46 14	17 31.6	1♉20.6	13 41.5	14 40.0	2 12.7	6 49.3	27 03.7	18 12.6	12 47.1	2 38.8
16 M	3 39 24	26 16 02	9♑41 58	15 37 34	17 22.8	2 47.4	13 18.4	14 54.9	2 36.0	6 51.0	26 59.2	18 13.8	12 49.3	2 39.2
17 Tu	3 43 20	27 13 51	21 33 27	27 30 05	17 16.5	4 16.4	12 53.3	15 10.4	2 59.2	6 52.4	26 54.7	18 14.9	12 51.6	2 39.6
18 W	3 47 17	28 11 38	3♒27 58	9♒27 38	17 12.7	5 47.8	12 26.1	15 26.3	3 22.4	6 53.7	26 50.2	18 16.2	12 53.8	2 40.0
19 Th	3 51 13	29 09 24	15 29 40	21 34 40	17D11.1	7 21.3	11 57.0	15 42.7	3 45.6	6 54.7	26 45.7	18 17.5	12 55.9	2 40.4
20 F	3 55 10	0♊07 09	27 43 17	3♓56 08	17 10.9	8 57.1	11 26.2	15 59.6	4 08.7	6 55.6	26 41.2	18 18.8	12 58.1	2 40.7
21 Sa	3 59 06	1 04 53	10♓13 52	16 37 04	17R11.1	10 35.2	10 53.8	16 16.9	4 31.8	6 56.3	26 36.8	18 20.2	13 00.3	2 41.0
22 Su	4 03 03	2 02 36	23 06 18	29 42 05	17 10.6	12 15.4	10 20.0	16 34.7	4 54.8	6 56.8	26 32.3	18 21.6	13 02.5	2 41.3
23 M	4 07 00	3 00 17	6♈24 49	13♈14 45	17 08.3	13 57.8	9 45.0	16 52.9	5 17.9	6 57.1	26 27.8	18 23.1	13 04.6	2 41.5
24 Tu	4 10 56	3 57 58	20 12 02	27 16 37	17 03.7	15 42.5	9 09.0	17 11.5	5 40.9	6R57.2	26 23.4	18 24.6	13 06.8	2 41.8
25 W	4 14 53	4 55 38	4♉28 15	11♉46 26	16 56.4	17 29.4	8 32.3	17 30.6	6 03.8	6 57.1	26 19.0	18 26.2	13 08.9	2 42.0
26 Th	4 18 49	5 53 17	19 10 30	26 39 30	16 47.0	19 18.4	7 55.1	17 50.0	6 26.7	6 56.9	26 14.6	18 27.8	13 11.0	2 42.1
27 F	4 22 46	6 50 54	4♊12 20	11♊47 44	16 36.4	21 09.7	7 17.5	18 09.9	6 49.6	6 56.4	26 10.2	18 29.5	13 13.1	2 42.3
28 Sa	4 26 42	7 48 31	19 24 21	27 00 48	16 25.7	23 03.1	6 39.9	18 30.2	7 12.5	6 55.7	26 05.8	18 31.2	13 15.3	2 42.4
29 Su	4 30 39	8 46 06	4♋35 43	12♋07 50	16 16.4	24 58.6	6 02.4	18 50.9	7 35.2	6 54.9	26 01.5	18 33.0	13 17.3	2 42.5
30 M	4 34 36	9 43 40	19 36 02	26 59 25	16 09.3	26 56.3	5 25.4	19 11.9	7 58.0	6 53.9	25 57.2	18 34.8	13 19.4	2 42.6
31 Tu	4 38 32	10 41 12	4♌17 14	11♌29 01	16 04.7	28 55.9	4 49.0	19 33.3	8 20.7	6 52.6	25 52.9	18 36.7	13 21.5	2 42.6

LONGITUDE — June 2044

Day	Sid.Time	☉	0 hr ☽	Noon ☽	True ☊	☿	♀	♂	⚳	♃	♄	♅	♆	♇
1 W	4 42 29	11♊38 43	18♌34 27	25♌33 26	16♓02.6	0♊57.6	4♊13.5	19♍55.1	8♉43.3	6♒51.2	25♏48.7	18♌38.6	13♉23.5	2♓42.7
2 Th	4 46 25	12 36 13	2♍26 02	9♍12 27	16R02.1	3 01.0	3R39.1	20 17.3	9 06.0	6R49.6	25R44.5	18 40.6	13 25.6	2R42.7
3 F	4 50 22	13 33 41	15 52 57	22 27 57	16 02.0	5 06.3	3 06.0	20 39.7	9 28.5	6 47.8	25 40.3	18 42.6	13 27.6	2 42.6
4 Sa	4 54 18	14 31 08	28 57 51	5♎23 06	16 01.2	7 13.1	2 34.3	21 02.6	9 51.0	6 45.9	25 36.2	18 44.6	13 29.6	2 42.6
5 Su	4 58 15	15 28 34	11♎44 09	18 01 28	15 58.6	9 21.4	2 04.3	21 25.7	10 13.5	6 43.7	25 32.1	18 46.7	13 31.6	2 42.5
6 M	5 02 11	16 25 59	24 15 27	0♏26 31	15 53.4	11 30.9	1 36.1	21 49.2	10 35.9	6 41.4	25 28.1	18 48.9	13 33.5	2 42.4
7 Tu	5 06 08	17 23 22	6♏35 02	12 41 19	15 45.4	13 41.4	1 09.9	22 13.0	10 58.2	6 38.8	25 24.0	18 51.0	13 35.5	2 42.3
8 W	5 10 05	18 20 45	18 45 39	24 48 17	15 34.7	15 52.7	0 45.7	22 37.2	11 20.5	6 36.1	25 20.1	18 53.3	13 37.4	2 42.1
9 Th	5 14 01	19 18 07	0♐49 28	6♐49 22	15 22.1	18 04.6	0 23.7	23 01.6	11 42.8	6 33.3	25 16.2	18 55.5	13 39.4	2 42.0
10 F	5 17 58	20 15 28	12 48 10	18 46 02	15 08.3	20 16.6	0 04.0	23 26.3	12 05.0	6 30.2	25 12.3	18 57.8	13 41.3	2 41.8
11 Sa	5 21 54	21 12 48	24 43 08	0♑39 37	14 54.7	22 28.7	29♉46.6	23 51.4	12 27.1	6 27.0	25 08.5	19 00.2	13 43.2	2 41.6
12 Su	5 25 51	22 10 07	6♑35 41	12 31 31	14 42.3	24 40.4	29 31.5	24 16.7	12 49.2	6 23.5	25 04.8	19 02.5	13 45.0	2 41.3
13 M	5 29 47	23 07 26	18 27 21	24 23 29	14 32.0	26 51.6	29 18.9	24 42.3	13 11.3	6 19.9	25 01.1	19 05.0	13 46.9	2 41.0
14 Tu	5 33 44	24 04 45	0♒20 05	6♒17 38	14 24.3	29 02.0	29 08.7	25 08.2	13 33.2	6 16.2	24 57.4	19 07.4	13 48.7	2 40.8
15 W	5 37 40	25 02 02	12 16 28	18 17 01	14 19.4	1♋11.3	29 00.8	25 34.3	13 55.2	6 12.3	24 53.9	19 09.9	13 50.5	2 40.4
16 Th	5 41 37	25 59 20	24 19 46	0♓25 12	14 16.9	3 19.3	28 55.4	26 00.7	14 17.0	6 08.1	24 50.4	19 12.5	13 52.3	2 40.1
17 F	5 45 34	26 56 37	6♓33 54	12 46 24	14D16.3	5 25.9	28D52.4	26 27.4	14 38.8	6 03.9	24 46.9	19 15.1	13 54.1	2 39.7
18 Sa	5 49 30	27 53 53	19 03 20	25 25 15	14R16.4	7 30.8	28 51.8	26 54.4	15 00.5	5 59.4	24 43.5	19 17.7	13 55.8	2 39.3
19 Su	5 53 27	28 51 10	1♈52 44	8♈26 20	14 16.1	9 34.1	28 53.5	27 21.6	15 22.2	5 54.8	24 40.2	19 20.3	13 57.6	2 38.9
20 M	5 57 23	29 48 26	15 06 30	21 53 37	14 14.4	11 35.4	28 57.4	27 49.1	15 43.8	5 50.1	24 36.9	19 23.0	13 59.3	2 38.5
21 Tu	6 01 20	0♋45 42	28 47 58	5♉49 38	14 10.6	13 34.8	29 03.6	28 16.8	16 05.3	5 45.2	24 33.7	19 25.7	14 01.0	2 38.0
22 W	6 05 16	1 42 58	12♉58 33	20 14 26	14 04.3	15 32.2	29 12.0	28 44.7	16 26.8	5 40.1	24 30.6	19 28.5	14 02.6	2 37.6
23 Th	6 09 13	2 40 14	27 36 47	5♊04 50	13 55.9	17 27.5	29 22.5	29 12.9	16 48.2	5 34.9	24 27.5	19 31.3	14 04.3	2 37.1
24 F	6 13 09	3 37 30	12♊37 38	20 14 01	13 46.2	19 20.7	29 35.1	29 41.4	17 09.5	5 29.5	24 24.6	19 34.1	14 05.9	2 36.5
25 Sa	6 17 06	4 34 45	27 52 39	5♋32 08	13 36.4	21 11.7	29 49.7	0♎10.1	17 30.8	5 24.0	24 21.7	19 37.0	14 07.5	2 36.0
26 Su	6 21 03	5 32 00	13♋11 01	20 47 52	13 27.7	23 00.6	0♊06.2	0 39.0	17 52.0	5 18.4	24 18.9	19 39.9	14 09.1	2 35.4
27 M	6 24 59	6 29 15	28 21 24	5♌50 28	13 21.0	24 47.2	0 24.5	1 08.2	18 13.1	5 12.6	24 16.1	19 42.8	14 10.6	2 34.8
28 Tu	6 28 56	7 26 29	13♌14 06	20 31 35	13 16.8	26 31.7	0 44.7	1 37.5	18 34.1	5 06.7	24 13.4	19 45.8	14 12.2	2 34.2
29 W	6 32 52	8 23 43	27 42 24	4♍46 15	13D14.9	28 13.9	1 06.7	2 07.1	18 55.1	5 00.6	24 10.9	19 48.8	14 13.7	2 33.6
30 Th	6 36 49	9 20 56	11♍43 03	18 32 53	13 14.7	29 53.9	1 30.3	2 36.9	19 15.9	4 54.4	24 08.3	19 51.8	14 15.1	2 32.9

Astro Data	Planet Ingress	Last Aspect	☽ Ingress	Last Aspect	☽ Ingress	☽ Phases & Eclipses
Dy Hr Mn	Dy Hr Mn	Dy Hr Mn	Dy Hr Mn	Dy Hr Mn	Dy Hr Mn	Dy Hr Mn
♀R 6 9:01	⚳ ♉ 9 19:38	30 12:09 ♅ ⚹	♋ 1 7:34	1 12:26 ♄ □	♍ 1 19:44	4 10:28 ☽ 14♌37
☽0S 7 16:49	☿ ♉ 14 13:08	3 5:55 ♄ △	♌ 3 9:22	3 17:52 ♄ ⚹	♎ 4 1:56	12 0:16 ○ 21♏56
☽0N 22 8:38	☉ ♊ 20 9:02	5 9:40 ♄ □	♍ 5 13:35	5 13:27 ♅ ⚹	♏ 6 11:08	20 4:02 ☾ 29♒48
♃R 24 14:02		7 16:01 ♄ ⚹	♎ 7 20:25	8 13:03 ♄ ☌	♐ 8 22:21	27 3:39 ● 6♊31
	☿ ♊ 1 0:41	9 17:25 ☿ ☍	♏ 10 5:27	10 21:46 ♂ □	♑ 11 10:40	
♇R 1 23:13	♀ ♉R 10 17:15	12 10:51 ♀ ☍	♐ 12 16:13	13 21:48 ♀ △	♒ 13 23:19	2 18:33 ☽ 12♍52
☽0S 3 21:34	☿ ♋ 14 22:45	14 4:34 ♅ △	♑ 15 4:23	16 9:05 ☿ □	♓ 16 11:11	10 15:16 ○ 20♐23
♀D 18 6:36	☉ ♋ 20 16:51	17 11:24 ☉ △	♒ 17 17:02	18 18:26 ♀ ⚹	♈ 18 20:32	18 17:00 ☾ 28♓06
☽0N 18 15:36	♂ ♎ 25 3:35	20 4:02 ☉ □	♓ 20 4:25	20 7:34 ♅ △	♉ 21 2:04	25 10:24 ● 4♋31
♂0S 26 20:20	♀ ♊ 26 3:21	22 6:18 ♀ ⚹	♈ 22 12:32	23 2:44 ♀ ☌	♊ 23 3:51	
	☿ ♌ 30 13:28	23 20:54 ♅ △	♉ 24 16:34	25 3:19 ♂ △	♋ 25 3:20	
		26 11:20 ♄ ☍	♊ 26 17:19	26 17:33 ♄ △	♌ 27 2:37	
		27 22:35 ♅ ⚹	♋ 28 16:43	28 18:08 ♄ □	♍ 29 3:52	
		30 11:54 ☿ ⚹	♌ 30 16:56			

Astro Data

1 May 2044
Julian Day # 52717
SVP 4♓38'23"
GC 27♐27.5 ⚴ 14♓38.9
Eris 29♈36.7 ⚵ 18♓21.5
⚷ 26♌08.2 ⚶ 13♓35.1
☽ Mean ☊ 17♓37.0

1 June 2044
Julian Day # 52748
SVP 4♓38'18"
GC 27♐27.6 ⚴ 21♓22.9
Eris 29♈55.1 ⚵ 0♈41.9
⚷ 27♌22.5 ⚶ 25♓49.3
☽ Mean ☊ 15♓58.5

July 2044 — LONGITUDE

Day	Sid.Time	☉	0 hr ☽	Noon ☽	True ☊	☿	♀	♂	⚳	♃	♄	♅	♆	♇
1 F	6 40 45	10♋18 09	25♍15 59	1♎52 40	13♓15.3	1♌31.7	1♊55.5	3♎07.0	19♉36.7	4♒48.1	24♏05.9	19♌54.9	14♉16.6	2♓32.3
2 Sa	6 44 42	11 15 22	8♎23 21	14 48 33	13R 15.4	3 07.3	2 22.4	3 37.2	19 57.4	4R 41.7	24R 03.6	19 58.0	14 18.0	2R 31.6
3 Su	6 48 39	12 12 34	21 08 45	27 24 30	13 14.2	4 40.6	2 50.7	4 07.6	20 18.0	4 35.2	24 01.3	20 01.1	14 19.4	2 30.8
4 M	6 52 35	13 09 46	3♏36 19	9♏44 44	13 11.0	6 11.7	3 20.6	4 38.3	20 38.6	4 28.6	23 59.2	20 04.2	14 20.8	2 30.1
5 Tu	6 56 32	14 06 57	15 50 14	21 53 17	13 05.4	7 40.5	3 51.8	5 09.1	20 59.0	4 21.8	23 57.1	20 07.4	14 22.1	2 29.3
6 W	7 00 28	15 04 09	27 54 20	3♐53 46	12 57.6	9 07.0	4 24.4	5 40.1	21 19.3	4 15.0	23 55.1	20 10.6	14 23.5	2 28.6
7 Th	7 04 25	16 01 20	9♐51 56	15 49 10	12 48.2	10 31.2	4 58.3	6 11.3	21 39.6	4 08.1	23 53.2	20 13.8	14 24.7	2 27.8
8 F	7 08 21	16 58 31	21 45 44	27 41 55	12 37.8	11 53.1	5 33.5	6 42.7	21 59.8	4 01.1	23 51.4	20 17.1	14 26.0	2 27.0
9 Sa	7 12 18	17 55 43	3♑37 57	9♑34 01	12 27.5	13 12.5	6 09.9	7 14.3	22 19.9	3 54.0	23 49.6	20 20.3	14 27.2	2 26.1
10 Su	7 16 14	18 52 54	15 30 21	21 27 08	12 18.1	14 29.5	6 47.5	7 46.1	22 39.8	3 46.8	23 48.0	20 23.6	14 28.5	2 25.3
11 M	7 20 11	19 50 06	27 24 34	3♒22 51	12 10.4	15 44.1	7 26.3	8 18.0	22 59.7	3 39.5	23 46.4	20 27.0	14 29.6	2 24.4
12 Tu	7 24 08	20 47 18	9♒22 13	15 22 54	12 04.9	16 56.1	8 06.1	8 50.2	23 19.5	3 32.2	23 45.0	20 30.3	14 30.8	2 23.5
13 W	7 28 04	21 44 30	21 25 11	27 29 21	12 01.6	18 05.5	8 47.0	9 22.4	23 39.2	3 24.8	23 43.6	20 33.7	14 31.9	2 22.6
14 Th	7 32 01	22 41 43	3♓35 44	9♓44 43	12D 00.5	19 12.2	9 28.9	9 54.9	23 58.8	3 17.3	23 42.3	20 37.0	14 33.0	2 21.7
15 F	7 35 57	23 38 56	15 56 41	22 12 03	12 00.8	20 16.1	10 11.8	10 27.6	24 18.3	3 09.8	23 41.1	20 40.5	14 34.1	2 20.8
16 Sa	7 39 54	24 36 09	28 31 16	4♈54 47	12 02.0	21 17.2	10 55.6	11 00.4	24 37.7	3 02.3	23 40.1	20 43.9	14 35.1	2 19.8
17 Su	7 43 50	25 33 24	11♈23 03	17 56 30	12R 03.1	22 15.3	11 40.3	11 33.3	24 56.9	2 54.7	23 39.1	20 47.3	14 36.1	2 18.8
18 M	7 47 47	26 30 39	24 35 32	1♉20 29	12 03.2	23 10.3	12 25.9	12 06.5	25 16.1	2 47.0	23 38.2	20 50.8	14 37.1	2 17.8
19 Tu	7 51 43	27 27 54	8♉11 37	15 09 06	12 01.8	24 02.2	13 12.3	12 39.8	25 35.2	2 39.3	23 37.4	20 54.3	14 38.1	2 16.8
20 W	7 55 40	28 25 11	22 12 56	29 23 00	11 58.7	24 50.7	13 59.5	13 13.2	25 54.1	2 31.6	23 36.6	20 57.8	14 39.0	2 15.8
21 Th	7 59 37	29 22 28	6♊38 58	14♊00 20	11 54.0	25 35.8	14 47.5	13 46.9	26 12.9	2 23.9	23 36.0	21 01.3	14 39.9	2 14.8
22 F	8 03 33	0♌19 47	21 26 25	28 56 19	11 48.2	26 17.3	15 36.3	14 20.7	26 31.6	2 16.1	23 35.5	21 04.9	14 40.7	2 13.7
23 Sa	8 07 30	1 17 06	6♋29 01	14♋03 20	11 42.3	26 55.1	16 25.8	14 54.6	26 50.2	2 08.4	23 35.1	21 08.4	14 41.6	2 12.7
24 Su	8 11 26	2 14 25	21 38 01	29 11 49	11 36.9	27 28.9	17 15.9	15 28.7	27 08.7	2 00.6	23 34.8	21 12.0	14 42.3	2 11.6
25 M	8 15 23	3 11 45	6♌43 28	14♌11 51	11 33.0	27 58.7	18 06.7	16 03.0	27 27.0	1 52.8	23 34.6	21 15.6	14 43.1	2 10.5
26 Tu	8 19 19	4 09 06	21 35 53	28 54 44	11D 30.7	28 24.2	18 58.2	16 37.4	27 45.2	1 45.1	23D 34.4	21 19.2	14 43.8	2 09.4
27 W	8 23 16	5 06 27	6♍07 42	13♍14 18	11 30.1	28 45.2	19 50.3	17 12.0	28 03.3	1 37.3	23 34.4	21 22.8	14 44.5	2 08.3
28 Th	8 27 12	6 03 49	20 14 12	27 07 18	11 30.9	29 01.7	20 42.9	17 46.7	28 21.3	1 29.6	23 34.5	21 26.4	14 45.2	2 07.2
29 F	8 31 09	7 01 11	3♎53 37	10♎33 19	11 32.3	29 13.4	21 36.1	18 21.6	28 39.1	1 21.9	23 34.6	21 30.1	14 45.8	2 06.0
30 Sa	8 35 06	7 58 34	17 06 41	23 34 07	11 33.7	29R 20.2	22 29.9	18 56.6	28 56.7	1 14.2	23 34.9	21 33.7	14 46.4	2 04.9
31 Su	8 39 02	8 55 57	29 56 04	6♏13 00	11R 34.5	29 22.0	23 24.3	19 31.8	29 14.2	1 06.6	23 35.3	21 37.4	14 47.0	2 03.7

August 2044 — LONGITUDE

Day	Sid.Time	☉	0 hr ☽	Noon ☽	True ☊	☿	♀	♂	⚳	♃	♄	♅	♆	♇
1 M	8 42 59	9♌53 21	12♏25 30	18♏34 04	11♓34.1	29♌18.6	24♊19.1	20♎07.1	29♉31.6	0♒58.9	23♏35.7	21♌41.0	14♉47.6	2♓02.5
2 Tu	8 46 55	10 50 46	24 39 18	0♐41 43	11R 32.4	29R 10.1	25 14.5	20 42.5	29 48.9	0R 51.4	23 36.3	21 44.7	14 48.1	2R 01.4
3 W	8 50 52	11 48 11	6♐41 51	12 40 14	11 29.5	28 56.3	26 10.3	21 18.1	0♊06.0	0 43.9	23 36.9	21 48.4	14 48.5	2 00.2
4 Th	8 54 48	12 45 37	18 37 20	24 33 37	11 25.5	28 37.3	27 06.6	21 53.8	0 22.9	0 36.4	23 37.7	21 52.1	14 49.0	1 59.0
5 F	8 58 45	13 43 03	0♑29 30	6♑25 22	11 20.9	28 13.3	28 03.4	22 29.6	0 39.7	0 29.0	23 38.5	21 55.8	14 49.4	1 57.8
6 Sa	9 02 41	14 40 31	12 21 34	18 18 25	11 16.2	27 44.5	29 00.6	23 05.6	0 56.3	0 21.7	23 39.5	21 59.5	14 49.8	1 56.6
7 Su	9 06 38	15 37 59	24 16 14	0♒15 15	11 12.1	27 11.0	29 58.3	23 41.7	1 12.8	0 14.5	23 40.5	22 03.2	14 50.1	1 55.3
8 M	9 10 35	16 35 28	6♒15 43	12 17 51	11 08.8	26 33.3	0♋56.4	24 17.9	1 29.2	0 07.3	23 41.7	22 07.0	14 50.4	1 54.1
9 Tu	9 14 31	17 32 59	18 21 51	24 27 55	11 06.6	25 51.9	1 54.9	24 54.2	1 45.3	0 00.2	23 42.9	22 10.7	14 50.7	1 52.9
10 W	9 18 28	18 30 30	0♓36 14	6♓46 59	11D 05.7	25 07.3	2 53.8	25 30.7	2 01.3	29♑53.2	23 44.2	22 14.4	14 51.0	1 51.6
11 Th	9 22 24	19 28 02	13 00 21	19 16 32	11 05.8	24 20.3	3 53.1	26 07.3	2 17.1	29 46.3	23 45.7	22 18.1	14 51.2	1 50.4
12 F	9 26 21	20 25 36	25 35 45	1♈58 11	11 06.8	23 31.6	4 52.8	26 44.0	2 32.8	29 39.5	23 47.2	22 21.9	14 51.3	1 49.1
13 Sa	9 30 17	21 23 11	8♈24 04	14 53 38	11 08.1	22 42.1	5 52.8	27 20.9	2 48.3	29 32.7	23 48.8	22 25.6	14 51.5	1 47.8
14 Su	9 34 14	22 20 48	21 27 05	28 04 38	11 09.5	21 52.7	6 53.2	27 57.9	3 03.6	29 26.1	23 50.5	22 29.3	14 51.6	1 46.6
15 M	9 38 10	23 18 26	4♉46 29	11♉32 48	11R 10.5	21 04.3	7 53.9	28 35.0	3 18.7	29 19.6	23 52.3	22 33.1	14 51.7	1 45.3
16 Tu	9 42 07	24 16 06	18 23 41	25 19 13	11 10.8	20 18.1	8 55.0	29 12.2	3 33.7	29 13.2	23 54.2	22 36.8	14 51.7	1 44.0
17 W	9 46 04	25 13 47	2♊19 21	9♊24 00	11 10.3	19 34.8	9 56.4	29 49.5	3 48.4	29 06.9	23 56.2	22 40.6	14R 51.8	1 42.7
18 Th	9 50 00	26 11 30	16 32 57	23 45 52	11 09.3	18 55.4	10 58.2	0♏27.0	4 03.0	29 00.8	23 58.3	22 44.3	14 51.7	1 41.4
19 F	9 53 57	27 09 15	1♋02 19	8♋21 44	11 07.7	18 20.8	12 00.2	1 04.6	4 17.4	28 54.8	24 00.4	22 48.0	14 51.7	1 40.2
20 Sa	9 57 53	28 07 01	15 43 27	23 06 40	11 06.1	17 51.7	13 02.6	1 42.3	4 31.6	28 48.9	24 02.7	22 51.8	14 51.6	1 38.9
21 Su	10 01 50	29 04 49	0♌30 33	7♌54 11	11 04.7	17 28.9	14 05.2	2 20.1	4 45.5	28 43.1	24 05.1	22 55.5	14 51.5	1 37.6
22 M	10 05 46	0♍02 38	15 16 39	22 37 01	11 03.7	17 12.7	15 08.1	2 58.1	4 59.3	28 37.5	24 07.5	22 59.2	14 51.3	1 36.3
23 Tu	10 09 43	1 00 29	29 54 25	7♍08 04	11D 03.3	17D 03.8	16 11.3	3 36.2	5 12.8	28 32.0	24 10.1	23 02.9	14 51.2	1 35.0
24 W	10 13 39	1 58 21	14♍17 16	21 21 26	11 03.4	17 02.5	17 14.7	4 14.3	5 26.2	28 26.7	24 12.7	23 06.6	14 50.9	1 33.7
25 Th	10 17 36	2 56 14	28 20 08	5♎13 02	11 03.9	17 08.9	18 18.4	4 52.6	5 39.3	28 21.5	24 15.4	23 10.3	14 50.7	1 32.4
26 F	10 21 33	3 54 09	11♎59 58	18 40 30	11 04.6	17 23.4	19 22.4	5 31.1	5 52.2	28 16.4	24 18.2	23 14.0	14 50.4	1 31.1
27 Sa	10 25 29	4 52 05	25 15 54	1♏45 09	11 05.2	17 45.8	20 26.6	6 09.6	6 04.9	28 11.6	24 21.1	23 17.7	14 50.1	1 29.8
28 Su	10 29 26	5 50 02	8♏08 57	14 27 39	11 05.7	18 16.3	21 31.1	6 48.2	6 17.3	28 06.9	24 24.1	23 21.4	14 49.7	1 28.5
29 M	10 33 22	6 48 01	20 41 40	26 51 31	11R 06.0	18 54.6	22 35.7	7 27.0	6 29.5	28 02.3	24 27.2	23 25.1	14 49.4	1 27.2
30 Tu	10 37 19	7 46 01	2♐57 41	9♐00 44	11 06.1	19 40.7	23 40.7	8 05.8	6 41.5	27 57.9	24 30.4	23 28.7	14 49.0	1 25.9
31 W	10 41 15	8 44 02	15 01 14	20 59 45	11 06.0	20 34.2	24 45.8	8 44.8	6 53.3	27 53.7	24 33.6	23 32.4	14 48.5	1 24.7

Astro Data

	Dy Hr Mn
☽0S	1 3:26
☽0N	15 21:00
♃⚻♇	22 20:36
♄D	27 7:28
☽0S	28 11:29
☿R	31 8:21
☽0N	12 2:08
♆R	17 12:37
☿D	24 4:11
☽0S	24 21:11

Planet Ingress

	Dy Hr Mn
☉ ♌	22 3:43
⚳ ♊	3 3:36
♀ ♋	7 12:42
♃ ♑R	9 12:43
♂ ♏	17 18:43
☉ ♍	22 10:54

Last Aspect / ☽ Ingress

Last Aspect Dy Hr Mn		☽ Ingress Dy Hr Mn
30 21:57	♄ ⚹	♎ 1 8:34
2 21:48	♅ ⚹	♏ 3 17:00
5 16:06	♄ ☌	♐ 6 4:11
7 20:57	♅ △	♑ 8 16:39
10 16:43	♄ ⚹	♒ 11 5:13
13 4:35	♄ □	♓ 13 16:57
15 14:59	☉ △	♈ 16 2:47
18 2:46	☉ □	♉ 18 9:38
20 10:17	☉ ⚹	♊ 20 13:01
22 7:34	☿ ⚹	♋ 22 13:42
24 3:05	♄ △	♌ 24 13:17
26 11:08	☿ ☌	♍ 26 13:48
28 5:48	♄ ⚹	♎ 28 17:05
30 22:55	☿ ⚹	♏ 31 0:07

Last Aspect / ☽ Ingress

Last Aspect Dy Hr Mn		☽ Ingress Dy Hr Mn
2 9:00	☿ □	♐ 2 10:37
4 19:58	☿ △	♑ 4 23:00
6 22:47	♄ ⚹	♒ 7 11:29
9 14:35	☿ ☍	♓ 9 22:49
12 7:42	♃ ⚹	♈ 12 8:18
14 14:25	♃ □	♉ 14 15:27
16 18:39	♃ △	♊ 16 20:02
18 16:18	☉ ⚹	♋ 18 22:18
20 21:11	♃ ☍	♌ 20 23:10
22 14:29	♄ □	♍ 23 0:09
25 0:07	♃ △	♎ 25 2:53
27 5:26	♃ □	♏ 27 8:44
29 14:18	♃ ⚹	♐ 29 18:10

☽ Phases & Eclipses

Dy Hr Mn	
2 4:48	☽ 10♎58
10 6:22	○ 18♑39
18 2:46	☾ 26♈09
24 17:10	● 2♌27
31 17:40	☽ 9♏10
8 21:14	○ 16♒58
16 10:03	☾ 24♉11
23 1:06	● 0♍34
23 1:15:32	● T 02'04"
30 9:18	☽ 7♐40

Astro Data

1 July 2044
Julian Day # 52778
SVP 4♓38'12"
GC 27♐27.7 ⚴ 24♓49.5
Eris 0♉06.8 ⚵ 11♈14.5
⚷ 29♌58.6 ⚶ 4♈49.5
☽ Mean ☊ 14♓23.2

1 August 2044
Julian Day # 52809
SVP 4♓38'07"
GC 27♐27.7 ⚴ 23♓42.5R
Eris 0♉09.8R ⚵ 19♈21.8
⚷ 3♍40.0 ⚶ 9♈24.0
☽ Mean ☊ 12♓44.7

LONGITUDE — September 2044

Day	Sid.Time	☉	0 hr ☽	Noon☽	True☊	☿	♀	♂	⚳	♃	♄	♅	♆	♇
1 Th	10 45 12	9♍42 05	26♐56 51	2♑53 05	11♓05.9	21♌34.8	25♋51.2	9♏23.9	7♊04.8	27♑49.7	24♏36.9	23♌36.0	14♉48.0	1♓23.4
2 F	10 49 08	10 40 09	8♑49 01	14 45 08	11D 05.8	22 42.3	26 56.7	10 03.0	7 16.0	27R45.8	24 40.4	23 39.6	14R47.5	1R22.1
3 Sa	10 53 05	11 38 15	20 41 57	26 39 56	11 05.8	23 56.1	28 02.5	10 42.3	7 27.0	27 42.1	24 43.9	23 43.2	14 47.0	1 20.8
4 Su	10 57 02	12 36 22	2♒39 31	8♒41 04	11 05.9	25 15.9	29 08.5	11 21.7	7 37.8	27 38.6	24 47.4	23 46.8	14 46.4	1 19.6
5 M	11 00 58	13 34 30	14 44 56	20 51 27	11 06.1	26 41.1	0♌14.8	12 01.2	7 48.3	27 35.2	24 51.1	23 50.4	14 45.8	1 18.3
6 Tu	11 04 55	14 32 40	27 00 51	3♓13 22	11R06.3	28 11.3	1 21.2	12 40.8	7 58.5	27 32.1	24 54.8	23 54.0	14 45.2	1 17.1
7 W	11 08 51	15 30 52	9♓29 10	15 48 22	11 06.3	29 45.9	2 27.8	13 20.5	8 08.5	27 29.1	24 58.7	23 57.5	14 44.6	1 15.8
8 Th	11 12 48	16 29 06	22 11 05	28 37 20	11 06.1	1♍24.3	3 34.6	14 00.3	8 18.2	27 26.3	25 02.6	24 01.0	14 43.9	1 14.6
9 F	11 16 44	17 27 21	5♈07 10	11♈40 32	11 05.6	3 06.1	4 41.6	14 40.1	8 27.6	27 23.7	25 06.5	24 04.6	14 43.1	1 13.3
10 Sa	11 20 41	18 25 38	18 17 23	24 57 41	11 04.8	4 50.8	5 48.8	15 20.1	8 36.8	27 21.2	25 10.6	24 08.1	14 42.4	1 12.1
11 Su	11 24 37	19 23 58	1♉41 18	8♉28 08	11 03.8	6 37.8	6 56.2	16 00.2	8 45.6	27 19.0	25 14.7	24 11.5	14 41.6	1 10.9
12 M	11 28 34	20 22 19	15 18 04	22 10 57	11 02.8	8 26.7	8 03.8	16 40.4	8 54.2	27 16.9	25 18.9	24 15.0	14 40.8	1 09.7
13 Tu	11 32 31	21 20 43	29 06 39	6♊04 58	11 02.1	10 17.1	9 11.5	17 20.7	9 02.5	27 15.1	25 23.2	24 18.4	14 40.0	1 08.5
14 W	11 36 27	22 19 08	13♊05 45	20 08 47	11D 01.7	12 08.5	10 19.4	18 01.1	9 10.5	27 13.4	25 27.6	24 21.9	14 39.1	1 07.3
15 Th	11 40 24	23 17 36	27 13 50	4♋20 39	11 01.9	14 00.8	11 27.5	18 41.6	9 18.2	27 11.9	25 32.0	24 25.3	14 38.2	1 06.1
16 F	11 44 20	24 16 07	11♋28 56	18 38 23	11 02.6	15 53.5	12 35.8	19 22.2	9 25.6	27 10.6	25 36.5	24 28.6	14 37.3	1 04.9
17 Sa	11 48 17	25 14 39	25 48 37	2♌59 14	11 03.6	17 46.4	13 44.2	20 02.8	9 32.7	27 09.5	25 41.1	24 32.0	14 36.4	1 03.8
18 Su	11 52 13	26 13 13	10♌09 47	17 19 47	11 04.7	19 39.2	14 52.8	20 43.6	9 39.4	27 08.6	25 45.8	24 35.3	14 35.4	1 02.6
19 M	11 56 10	27 11 50	24 28 45	1♍36 08	11R 05.5	21 31.9	16 01.6	21 24.5	9 45.9	27 07.9	25 50.5	24 38.6	14 34.4	1 01.5
20 Tu	12 00 06	28 10 28	8♍41 25	15 44 03	11 05.6	23 24.2	17 10.5	22 05.5	9 52.0	27 07.4	25 55.3	24 41.9	14 33.4	1 00.3
21 W	12 04 03	29 09 08	22 43 34	29 39 28	11 04.8	25 15.9	18 19.5	22 46.6	9 57.8	27 07.1	26 00.2	24 45.2	14 32.3	0 59.2
22 Th	12 08 00	0♎07 51	6♎31 22	13♎18 53	11 03.1	27 07.1	19 28.7	23 27.7	10 03.2	27D07.0	26 05.1	24 48.4	14 31.2	0 58.1
23 F	12 11 56	1 06 35	20 01 47	26 39 51	11 00.5	28 57.6	20 38.0	24 09.0	10 08.3	27 07.0	26 10.1	24 51.6	14 30.1	0 57.0
24 Sa	12 15 53	2 05 21	3♏13 01	9♏41 16	10 57.4	0♎47.3	21 47.5	24 50.4	10 13.1	27 07.3	26 15.1	24 54.8	14 29.0	0 55.9
25 Su	12 19 49	3 04 09	16 04 40	22 23 26	10 54.1	2 36.3	22 57.1	25 31.8	10 17.5	27 07.8	26 20.3	24 57.9	14 27.8	0 54.9
26 M	12 23 46	4 02 59	28 37 49	4♐48 07	10 51.1	4 24.4	24 06.9	26 13.4	10 21.6	27 08.4	26 25.5	25 01.0	14 26.7	0 53.8
27 Tu	12 27 42	5 01 51	10♐54 47	16 58 14	10 48.8	6 11.6	25 16.7	26 55.0	10 25.3	27 09.3	26 30.7	25 04.1	14 25.5	0 52.8
28 W	12 31 39	6 00 44	22 59 00	28 57 38	10D 47.5	7 58.0	26 26.7	27 36.7	10 28.7	27 10.4	26 36.0	25 07.2	14 24.2	0 51.8
29 Th	12 35 35	6 59 39	4♑54 41	10♑50 46	10 47.4	9 43.4	27 36.9	28 18.6	10 31.7	27 11.6	26 41.4	25 10.2	14 23.0	0 50.8
30 F	12 39 32	7 58 36	16 46 29	22 42 27	10 48.2	11 28.0	28 47.1	29 00.5	10 34.4	27 13.1	26 46.9	25 13.2	14 21.7	0 49.8

LONGITUDE — October 2044

Day	Sid.Time	☉	0 hr ☽	Noon☽	True☊	☿	♀	♂	⚳	♃	♄	♅	♆	♇
1 Sa	12 43 29	8♎57 35	28♑39 17	4♒37 35	10♓49.8	13♎11.7	29♌57.5	29♏42.5	10♊36.7	27♑14.7	26♏52.4	25♌16.1	14♉20.4	0♓48.8
2 Su	12 47 25	9 56 35	10♒37 54	16 40 49	10 51.5	14 54.5	1♍08.0	0♐24.5	10 38.6	27 16.5	26 57.9	25 19.1	14R 19.1	0R47.9
3 M	12 51 22	10 55 37	22 46 49	28 56 21	10R53.0	16 36.5	2 18.6	1 06.7	10 40.2	27 18.6	27 03.5	25 22.0	14 17.8	0 46.9
4 Tu	12 55 18	11 54 41	5♓09 51	11♓27 38	10 53.5	18 17.5	3 29.4	1 48.9	10 41.3	27 20.8	27 09.2	25 24.8	14 16.4	0 46.0
5 W	12 59 15	12 53 47	17 49 58	24 17 01	10 52.7	19 57.8	4 40.2	2 31.2	10 42.1	27 23.2	27 14.9	25 27.6	14 15.1	0 45.1
6 Th	13 03 11	13 52 54	0♈48 54	7♈25 35	10 50.4	21 37.2	5 51.2	3 13.7	10R42.6	27 25.8	27 20.7	25 30.4	14 13.7	0 44.2
7 F	13 07 08	14 52 04	14 06 59	20 52 54	10 46.4	23 15.9	7 02.3	3 56.1	10 42.6	27 28.6	27 26.5	25 33.2	14 12.3	0 43.4
8 Sa	13 11 04	15 51 16	27 43 02	4♉37 02	10 41.3	24 53.7	8 13.5	4 38.7	10 42.3	27 31.5	27 32.4	25 35.9	14 10.8	0 42.5
9 Su	13 15 01	16 50 30	11♉34 28	18 34 50	10 35.6	26 30.8	9 24.8	5 21.4	10 41.6	27 34.7	27 38.3	25 38.6	14 09.4	0 41.7
10 M	13 18 57	17 49 46	25 37 38	2♊42 18	10 30.0	28 07.1	10 36.3	6 04.1	10 40.5	27 38.0	27 44.3	25 41.2	14 07.9	0 40.9
11 Tu	13 22 54	18 49 05	9♊48 19	16 55 12	10 25.3	29 42.7	11 47.8	6 46.9	10 39.0	27 41.6	27 50.3	25 43.8	14 06.5	0 40.1
12 W	13 26 51	19 48 26	24 02 27	1♋09 39	10 22.1	1♏17.6	12 59.4	7 29.8	10 37.1	27 45.3	27 56.4	25 46.4	14 05.0	0 39.3
13 Th	13 30 47	20 47 49	8♋16 26	15 22 29	10D 20.6	2 51.8	14 11.2	8 12.8	10 34.8	27 49.2	28 02.6	25 48.9	14 03.5	0 38.6
14 F	13 34 44	21 47 15	22 27 34	29 31 28	10 20.7	4 25.3	15 23.1	8 55.9	10 32.1	27 53.2	28 08.7	25 51.4	14 01.9	0 37.9
15 Sa	13 38 40	22 46 43	6♌33 59	13♌35 01	10 21.8	5 58.1	16 35.0	9 39.0	10 29.1	27 57.5	28 14.9	25 53.8	14 00.4	0 37.2
16 Su	13 42 37	23 46 13	20 34 25	27 32 04	10R 23.1	7 30.3	17 47.1	10 22.3	10 25.6	28 01.9	28 21.2	25 56.2	13 58.8	0 36.5
17 M	13 46 33	24 45 45	4♍27 51	11♍21 37	10 23.7	9 01.8	18 59.2	11 05.6	10 21.7	28 06.5	28 27.5	25 58.6	13 57.3	0 35.8
18 Tu	13 50 30	25 45 20	18 13 13	25 02 29	10 22.6	10 32.6	20 11.4	11 49.0	10 17.5	28 11.3	28 33.9	26 00.9	13 55.7	0 35.2
19 W	13 54 26	26 44 56	1♎49 12	8♎33 09	10 19.5	12 02.8	21 23.8	12 32.4	10 12.8	28 16.3	28 40.3	26 03.2	13 54.1	0 34.5
20 Th	13 58 23	27 44 35	15 14 10	21 51 59	10 14.0	13 32.4	22 36.2	13 16.0	10 07.7	28 21.4	28 46.7	26 05.4	13 52.5	0 34.0
21 F	14 02 20	28 44 16	28 26 26	4♏57 19	10 06.5	15 01.3	23 48.7	13 59.6	10 02.3	28 26.7	28 53.2	26 07.6	13 50.9	0 33.4
22 Sa	14 06 16	29 43 59	11♏24 32	17 47 58	9 57.5	16 29.6	25 01.3	14 43.3	9 56.5	28 32.2	28 59.7	26 09.7	13 49.3	0 32.8
23 Su	14 10 13	0♏43 44	24 07 36	0♐23 28	9 48.0	17 57.2	26 13.9	15 27.1	9 50.3	28 37.8	29 06.2	26 11.8	13 47.6	0 32.3
24 M	14 14 09	1 43 31	6♐35 41	12 44 24	9 38.8	19 24.1	27 26.7	16 11.0	9 43.7	28 43.6	29 12.8	26 13.9	13 46.0	0 31.8
25 Tu	14 18 06	2 43 20	18 49 53	24 52 27	9 30.9	20 50.3	28 39.5	16 54.9	9 36.7	28 49.6	29 19.4	26 15.9	13 44.3	0 31.3
26 W	14 22 02	3 43 10	0♑52 28	6♑50 24	9 24.9	22 15.8	29 52.4	17 38.9	9 29.3	28 55.8	29 26.1	26 17.8	13 42.7	0 30.9
27 Th	14 25 59	4 43 02	12 46 43	18 42 01	9 21.2	23 40.5	1♎05.3	18 23.0	9 21.6	29 02.1	29 32.7	26 19.8	13 41.0	0 30.4
28 F	14 29 55	5 42 56	24 36 50	0♒31 50	9D 19.6	25 04.5	2 18.4	19 07.1	9 13.6	29 08.6	29 39.4	26 21.6	13 39.4	0 30.0
29 Sa	14 33 52	6 42 51	6♒27 39	12 24 56	9 19.6	26 27.6	3 31.5	19 51.4	9 05.1	29 15.2	29 46.2	26 23.4	13 37.7	0 29.6
30 Su	14 37 49	7 42 48	18 24 23	24 26 39	9 20.4	27 49.8	4 44.6	20 35.6	8 56.4	29 22.0	29 53.0	26 25.2	13 36.0	0 29.3
31 M	14 41 45	8 42 46	0♓32 23	6♓42 13	9R 21.1	29 11.1	5 57.9	21 20.0	8 47.2	29 28.9	29 59.8	26 26.9	13 34.3	0 28.9

Astro Data Dy Hr Mn	Planet Ingress Dy Hr Mn	Last Aspect Dy Hr Mn	☽ Ingress Dy Hr Mn	Last Aspect Dy Hr Mn	☽ Ingress Dy Hr Mn	☽ Phases & Eclipses Dy Hr Mn	Astro Data
☽0N 8 8:27	♀ ♌ 5 6:39	31 17:09 ♅ △	♑ 1 6:10	1 1:30 ♂ ⚹	♒ 1 2:42	7 11:24 ○ 15♓29	1 September 2044
☽0S 21 6:54	☿ ♍ 7 15:30	3 15:02 ♀ ☍	♒ 3 18:41	3 8:19 ♄ □	♓ 3 14:03	7 11:19 ☍ T 1.045	Julian Day # 52840
☉0S 22 8:47	☉ ♎ 22 8:48	6 0:55 ☿ ☍	♓ 6 5:47	5 17:44 ♃ ⚹	♈ 5 22:31	14 15:57 ☾ 22♊29	SVP 4♓38'03"
♃ D 22 14:53	☿ ♎ 24 1:37	8 9:48 ♃ ⚹	♈ 8 14:33	7 23:37 ♃ □	♉ 8 3:59	21 11:03 ● 29♍07	GC 27♐27.8 ⚳ 17♓29.3R
☿0S 25 20:50		10 16:16 ♃ □	♉ 10 21:00	10 3:31 ♄ ☍	♊ 10 7:25	29 3:30 ☽ 6♑39	Eris 0♉02.9R ⚵ 22♈21.9R
	♀ ♍ 1 12:51	12 20:49 ♃ △	♊ 13 1:32	12 2:54 ♅ ⚹	♋ 12 10:03		⚷ 7♍52.3 ⚶ 7♈09.3R
☽0N 5 16:29	♂ ♐ 1 22:01	14 19:11 ♅ ⚹	♋ 15 4:41	14 9:38 ♄ △	♌ 14 12:49	7 0:30 ○ 14♈24	☽ Mean ☊ 11♓06.2
⚳ R 7 3:02	☿ ♏ 11 16:21	17 2:16 ♃ ☍	♌ 17 7:00	16 13:26 ♄ □	♍ 16 16:16	13 21:52 ☾ 21♋12	
♃⚹♄ 8 4:46	☉ ♏ 22 18:26	19 2:14 ♄ □	♍ 19 9:18	18 18:17 ♄ ⚹	♎ 18 20:46	20 23:36 ● 28♎13	1 October 2044
☽0S 18 14:52	♀ ♎ 26 14:31	21 11:03 ☉ ☌	♎ 21 12:36	20 23:56 ♃ □	♏ 21 2:52	28 23:27 ☽ 6♒12	Julian Day # 52870
♀0S 29 14:23	♄ ♐ 31 12:52	23 12:50 ♃ □	♏ 23 18:05	23 9:30 ♄ ☌	♐ 23 11:15		SVP 4♓37'59"
		25 21:07 ♃ ⚹	♐ 26 2:39	25 20:25 ♀ □	♑ 25 22:15		GC 27♐27.9 ⚳ 10♓06.4R
		28 6:24 ♀ △	♑ 28 14:06	28 10:13 ♄ ⚹	♒ 28 10:55		Eris 29♈48.6R ⚵ 18♈32.1R
				30 22:49 ♄ □	♓ 30 22:57		⚷ 11♍56.3 ⚶ 0♈00.8R
							☽ Mean ☊ 9♓30.9

November 2044 — LONGITUDE

Day	Sid.Time	☉	0 hr ☽	Noon ☽	True ☊	☿	♀	♂	⚳	♃	♄	♅	♆	♇
1 Tu	14 45 42	9♏42 47	12♓56 44	19♓16 25	9♓20.6	0♐31.4	7♎11.2	22♐04.4	8♊37.8	29♑36.0	0♐06.6	26♌28.6	13♉32.6	0♓28.6
2 W	14 49 38	10 42 48	25 41 44	2♈13 00	9R 18.2	1 50.5	8 24.6	22 48.9	8R 28.0	29 43.3	0 13.4	26 30.2	13R 31.0	0R 28.4
3 Th	14 53 35	11 42 52	8♈50 28	15 34 12	9 13.3	3 08.5	9 38.0	23 33.4	8 17.9	29 50.7	0 20.3	26 31.7	13 29.3	0 28.1
4 F	14 57 31	12 42 57	22 24 10	29 20 07	9 05.8	4 25.1	10 51.5	24 18.1	8 07.5	29 58.2	0 27.2	26 33.2	13 27.6	0 27.9
5 Sa	15 01 28	13 43 04	6♉21 42	13♉28 23	8 56.4	5 40.3	12 05.1	25 02.7	7 56.8	0♒05.9	0 34.1	26 34.7	13 25.9	0 27.6
6 Su	15 05 24	14 43 13	20 39 27	27 54 08	8 45.8	6 53.9	13 18.7	25 47.5	7 45.8	0 13.8	0 41.1	26 36.1	13 24.2	0 27.5
7 M	15 09 21	15 43 24	5♊11 31	12♊30 40	8 35.3	8 05.6	14 32.4	26 32.3	7 34.5	0 21.8	0 48.0	26 37.5	13 22.5	0 27.3
8 Tu	15 13 18	16 43 37	19 50 37	27 10 26	8 26.2	9 15.4	15 46.1	27 17.2	7 22.9	0 29.9	0 55.0	26 38.8	13 20.8	0 27.2
9 W	15 17 14	17 43 51	4♋29 16	11♋46 21	8 19.2	10 23.0	17 00.0	28 02.1	7 11.1	0 38.2	1 02.0	26 40.0	13 19.1	0 27.1
10 Th	15 21 11	18 44 08	19 01 03	26 12 51	8 14.9	11 28.1	18 13.8	28 47.1	6 59.0	0 46.6	1 09.0	26 41.2	13 17.5	0 27.0
11 F	15 25 07	19 44 27	3♌21 22	10♌26 23	8D 12.9	12 30.3	19 27.8	29 32.2	6 46.7	0 55.1	1 16.1	26 42.4	13 15.8	0 26.9
12 Sa	15 29 04	20 44 47	17 27 45	24 25 26	8 12.7	13 29.4	20 41.7	0♑17.3	6 34.2	1 03.8	1 23.1	26 43.5	13 14.1	0D 26.9
13 Su	15 33 00	21 45 10	1♍19 30	8♍10 01	8R 12.9	14 25.0	21 55.8	1 02.5	6 21.5	1 12.6	1 30.2	26 44.5	13 12.4	0 26.9
14 M	15 36 57	22 45 35	14 57 09	21 41 02	8 12.2	15 16.6	23 09.9	1 47.8	6 08.5	1 21.6	1 37.2	26 45.5	13 10.8	0 26.9
15 Tu	15 40 53	23 46 01	28 21 49	4♎59 39	8 09.6	16 03.6	24 24.0	2 33.1	5 55.4	1 30.7	1 44.3	26 46.4	13 09.1	0 27.0
16 W	15 44 50	24 46 29	11♎34 38	18 06 50	8 04.2	16 45.6	25 38.2	3 18.4	5 42.1	1 39.9	1 51.4	26 47.3	13 07.5	0 27.0
17 Th	15 48 47	25 46 59	24 36 20	1♏03 09	7 55.6	17 22.0	26 52.4	4 03.9	5 28.6	1 49.2	1 58.5	26 48.1	13 05.8	0 27.1
18 F	15 52 43	26 47 31	7♏27 16	13 48 41	7 44.2	17 51.9	28 06.7	4 49.4	5 15.0	1 58.7	2 05.6	26 48.9	13 04.2	0 27.3
19 Sa	15 56 40	27 48 04	20 07 21	26 23 16	7 30.8	18 14.8	29 21.0	5 34.9	5 01.3	2 08.3	2 12.8	26 49.6	13 02.6	0 27.4
20 Su	16 00 36	28 48 39	2♐36 24	8♐46 47	7 16.5	18 29.9	0♏35.3	6 20.5	4 47.5	2 18.0	2 19.9	26 50.3	13 00.9	0 27.6
21 M	16 04 33	29 49 16	14 54 26	20 59 29	7 02.4	18R 36.3	1 49.7	7 06.2	4 33.6	2 27.8	2 27.0	26 50.9	12 59.3	0 27.8
22 Tu	16 08 29	0♐49 54	27 02 01	3♑02 16	6 49.8	18 33.4	3 04.2	7 51.9	4 19.6	2 37.8	2 34.2	26 51.4	12 57.7	0 28.1
23 W	16 12 26	1 50 33	9♑00 28	14 56 56	6 39.7	18 20.5	4 18.6	8 37.7	4 05.5	2 47.9	2 41.3	26 51.9	12 56.2	0 28.3
24 Th	16 16 23	2 51 13	20 52 03	26 46 14	6 32.4	17 57.2	5 33.1	9 23.5	3 51.5	2 58.1	2 48.4	26 52.3	12 54.6	0 28.6
25 F	16 20 19	3 51 55	2♒39 58	8♒33 49	6 28.0	17 23.0	6 47.7	10 09.4	3 37.4	3 08.4	2 55.6	26 52.7	12 53.0	0 28.9
26 Sa	16 24 16	4 52 37	14 28 20	20 24 11	6 26.0	16 38.1	8 02.2	10 55.3	3 23.3	3 18.8	3 02.7	26 53.0	12 51.5	0 29.3
27 Su	16 28 12	5 53 21	26 22 01	2♓22 30	6 25.5	15 42.8	9 16.8	11 41.3	3 09.2	3 29.3	3 09.9	26 53.3	12 49.9	0 29.6
28 M	16 32 09	6 54 05	8♓26 22	14 34 17	6 25.5	14 38.2	10 31.5	12 27.4	2 55.1	3 39.9	3 17.0	26 53.5	12 48.4	0 30.0
29 Tu	16 36 05	7 54 51	20 46 57	27 05 01	6 24.6	13 25.7	11 46.1	13 13.4	2 41.1	3 50.7	3 24.1	26 53.6	12 46.9	0 30.4
30 W	16 40 02	8 55 37	3♈29 06	9♈59 42	6 21.8	12 07.3	13 00.8	13 59.5	2 27.2	4 01.5	3 31.2	26 53.7	12 45.4	0 30.9

December 2044 — LONGITUDE

Day	Sid.Time	☉	0 hr ☽	Noon ☽	True ☊	☿	♀	♂	⚳	♃	♄	♅	♆	♇
1 Th	16 43 58	9♐56 25	16♈37 14	23♈22 01	6♓16.5	10♐45.3	14♏15.5	14♑45.7	2♊13.3	4♒12.4	3♐38.3	26♌53.7	12♉44.0	0♓31.3
2 F	16 47 55	10 57 14	0♉14 10	7♉13 39	6R 08.4	9R 22.7	15 30.2	15 31.9	1R 59.6	4 23.5	3 45.5	26R 53.7	12R 42.5	0 31.8
3 Sa	16 51 52	11 58 03	14 20 11	21 33 20	5 58.0	8 02.0	16 45.0	16 18.2	1 45.9	4 34.6	3 52.5	26 53.6	12 41.1	0 32.3
4 Su	16 55 48	12 58 54	28 52 25	6♊16 32	5 46.3	6 46.1	17 59.8	17 04.4	1 32.4	4 45.9	3 59.6	26 53.5	12 39.7	0 32.9
5 M	16 59 45	13 59 45	13♊44 39	21 15 34	5 34.4	5 37.3	19 14.6	17 50.8	1 19.1	4 57.2	4 06.7	26 53.3	12 38.3	0 33.5
6 Tu	17 03 41	15 00 38	28 48 00	6♋20 41	5 23.9	4 37.4	20 29.5	18 37.2	1 05.9	5 08.7	4 13.8	26 53.1	12 36.9	0 34.1
7 W	17 07 38	16 01 32	13♋52 21	21 21 50	5 15.7	3 47.7	21 44.3	19 23.6	0 52.8	5 20.2	4 20.8	26 52.8	12 35.6	0 34.7
8 Th	17 11 34	17 02 27	28 48 08	6♌10 24	5 10.4	3 09.2	22 59.2	20 10.0	0 40.0	5 31.8	4 27.9	26 52.4	12 34.2	0 35.3
9 F	17 15 31	18 03 24	13♌27 59	20 40 25	5 07.8	2 42.1	24 14.1	20 56.5	0 27.3	5 43.5	4 34.9	26 52.0	12 32.9	0 36.0
10 Sa	17 19 27	19 04 21	27 47 24	4♍48 51	5D 07.2	2D 26.2	25 29.1	21 43.1	0 14.9	5 55.3	4 41.9	26 51.6	12 31.6	0 36.7
11 Su	17 23 24	20 05 20	11♍44 46	18 35 17	5R 07.3	2 21.2	26 44.1	22 29.7	0 02.7	6 07.2	4 48.9	26 51.0	12 30.4	0 37.4
12 M	17 27 21	21 06 19	25 20 39	2♎01 09	5 06.9	2 26.4	27 59.0	23 16.3	29♉50.8	6 19.1	4 55.8	26 50.5	12 29.1	0 38.2
13 Tu	17 31 17	22 07 20	8♎37 05	15 08 48	5 04.7	2 41.0	29 14.1	24 02.9	29 39.1	6 31.2	5 02.8	26 49.8	12 27.9	0 38.9
14 W	17 35 14	23 08 22	21 36 38	28 00 56	4 59.9	3 04.3	0♐29.1	24 49.6	29 27.6	6 43.3	5 09.7	26 49.1	12 26.7	0 39.7
15 Th	17 39 10	24 09 25	4♏21 58	10♏40 00	4 52.2	3 35.4	1 44.1	25 36.4	29 16.5	6 55.5	5 16.6	26 48.4	12 25.5	0 40.5
16 F	17 43 07	25 10 29	16 55 18	23 08 03	4 41.8	4 13.5	2 59.2	26 23.1	29 05.6	7 07.8	5 23.5	26 47.6	12 24.4	0 41.4
17 Sa	17 47 03	26 11 34	29 18 25	5♐26 34	4 29.4	4 57.7	4 14.3	27 09.9	28 55.1	7 20.2	5 30.3	26 46.8	12 23.2	0 42.2
18 Su	17 51 00	27 12 39	11♐32 37	17 36 41	4 16.0	5 47.5	5 29.4	27 56.8	28 44.8	7 32.6	5 37.1	26 45.9	12 22.1	0 43.1
19 M	17 54 56	28 13 45	23 38 52	29 39 18	4 02.9	6 42.1	6 44.5	28 43.7	28 34.9	7 45.2	5 43.9	26 44.9	12 21.1	0 44.0
20 Tu	17 58 53	29 14 52	5♑38 07	11♑35 28	3 51.1	7 41.0	7 59.6	29 30.6	28 25.4	7 57.8	5 50.7	26 43.9	12 20.0	0 45.0
21 W	18 02 50	0♑15 59	17 31 31	23 26 30	3 41.5	8 43.6	9 14.8	0♒17.5	28 16.2	8 10.4	5 57.4	26 42.9	12 19.0	0 45.9
22 Th	18 06 46	1 17 07	29 20 41	5♒14 22	3 34.6	9 49.5	10 29.9	1 04.5	28 07.3	8 23.2	6 04.2	26 41.8	12 18.0	0 46.9
23 F	18 10 43	2 18 15	11♒07 55	17 01 43	3 30.5	10 58.3	11 45.1	1 51.5	27 58.8	8 36.0	6 10.8	26 40.6	12 17.1	0 47.9
24 Sa	18 14 39	3 19 23	22 56 14	28 51 59	3D 28.9	12 09.6	13 00.2	2 38.5	27 50.7	8 48.8	6 17.5	26 39.4	12 16.1	0 48.9
25 Su	18 18 36	4 20 31	4♓49 29	10♓49 20	3 29.0	13 23.2	14 15.4	3 25.5	27 42.9	9 01.8	6 24.1	26 38.2	12 15.2	0 50.0
26 M	18 22 32	5 21 39	16 52 09	22 58 34	3 29.9	14 38.7	15 30.6	4 12.6	27 35.5	9 14.8	6 30.6	26 36.8	12 14.3	0 51.0
27 Tu	18 26 29	6 22 48	29 09 16	5♈24 52	3R 30.5	15 55.9	16 45.7	4 59.7	27 28.5	9 27.8	6 37.2	26 35.5	12 13.5	0 52.1
28 W	18 30 25	7 23 56	11♈46 01	18 13 18	3 29.8	17 14.7	18 00.9	5 46.8	27 21.9	9 40.9	6 43.7	26 34.1	12 12.7	0 53.2
29 Th	18 34 22	8 25 04	24 47 16	1♉28 21	3 27.2	18 34.9	19 16.1	6 33.9	27 15.7	9 54.1	6 50.1	26 32.6	12 11.9	0 54.3
30 F	18 38 19	9 26 12	8♉16 51	15 12 58	3 22.4	19 56.2	20 31.3	7 21.1	27 09.9	10 07.3	6 56.5	26 31.2	12 11.1	0 55.5
31 Sa	18 42 15	10 27 21	22 16 42	29 27 48	3 15.6	21 18.7	21 46.5	8 08.3	27 04.5	10 20.6	7 02.9	26 29.6	12 10.4	0 56.6

Astro Data	Dy Hr Mn
☽0N	2 1:32
♄□♇	4 14:14
♃⚺♇	8 4:07
♇ D	13 4:08
☽0S	14 20:24
♃✶♄	21 4:56
☿ R	21 16:52
☽0N	29 10:05
♅ R	1 14:47
☿ D	11 11:31
☽0S	12 0:55
☽0N	26 17:01

Planet Ingress		Dy Hr Mn
☿	♐	1 2:35
♃	♒	4 17:32
♂	♑	12 2:48
♀	♏	20 0:36
☉	♐	21 16:15
⚳	♉R	11 17:25
♀	♐	14 2:42
♂	♒	21 3:03
☉	♑	21 5:43

Last Aspect Dy Hr Mn		☽ Ingress	Dy Hr Mn
2 7:23	♃ ✶	♈	2 7:57
4 13:06	♃ □	♉	4 13:09
6 9:51	♅ □	♊	6 15:28
8 12:12	♂ ☍	♋	8 16:38
9 22:36	☉ △	♌	10 18:21
12 16:00	♅ ☌	♍	12 21:41
14 14:05	☉ ✶	♎	15 2:57
17 4:04	♅ ✶	♏	17 10:02
19 14:58	☉ ☌	♐	19 18:58
21 23:38	♅ △	♑	22 5:55
23 7:56	♆ △	♒	24 18:34
27 1:02	♅ ☍	♓	27 7:16
28 12:07	☿ □	♈	29 17:29

Last Aspect Dy Hr Mn		☽ Ingress	Dy Hr Mn
1 18:11	♅ △	♉	1 23:35
3 20:46	♅ □	♊	4 1:50
5 20:57	♅ ✶	♋	6 1:54
7 12:40	♀ △	♌	8 1:57
9 22:26	♅ ☌	♍	10 3:46
12 3:59	♀ ✶	♎	12 8:21
14 9:45	♅ ✶	♏	14 15:44
16 19:06	♅ □	♐	17 1:21
19 8:53	☉ ☌	♑	19 12:41
20 13:30	♆ △	♒	22 1:20
24 7:33	♅ ☍	♓	24 14:17
25 19:37	♀ □	♈	27 1:38
29 3:11	♅ △	♉	29 9:23
31 7:04	♅ □	♊	31 12:53

☽ Phases & Eclipses Dy Hr Mn	
5 12:26	○ 13♉44
12 5:09	☾ 20♌28
19 14:58	● 27♏56
27 19:36	☽ 6♓13
4 23:34	○ 13♊28
11 14:52	☾ 20♍13
19 8:53	● 28♐06
27 14:00	☽ 6♈28

Astro Data

1 November 2044
Julian Day # 52901
SVP 4♓37'56"
GC 27♐27.9 ⚴ 6♓28.0R
Eris 29♈30.2R ⚵ 11♈48.6R
⚷ 15♍36.1 ⚶ 24♓59.0R
☽ Mean ☊ 7♓52.4

1 December 2044
Julian Day # 52931
SVP 4♓37'51"
GC 27♐28.0 ⚴ 8♓20.1
Eris 29♈14.0R ⚵ 11♈08.3
⚷ 18♍04.6 ⚶ 26♓37.2
☽ Mean ☊ 6♓17.1

LONGITUDE — January 2045

Day	Sid.Time	☉	0 hr ☽	Noon ☽	True ☊	☿	♀	♂	⚳	♃	♄	♅	♆	♇
1 Su	18 46 12	11♑28 29	6♊45 52	14♊10 14	3♓07.5	22♐42.2	23♐01.7	8♒55.4	26♉59.5	10♒33.9	7♐09.2	26♌28.0	12♉09.7	0♓57.8
2 M	18 50 08	12 29 37	21 40 00	29 14 06	2R59.1	24 06.5	24 17.0	9 42.7	26R55.0	10 47.3	7 15.5	26R26.4	12R09.1	0 59.0
3 Tu	18 54 05	13 30 45	6♋51 16	14♋30 09	2 51.6	25 31.7	25 32.2	10 29.9	26 50.8	11 00.8	7 21.7	26 24.7	12 08.4	1 00.2
4 W	18 58 01	14 31 53	22 09 20	29 47 26	2 45.8	26 57.6	26 47.4	11 17.1	26 47.0	11 14.3	7 27.9	26 23.0	12 07.8	1 01.5
5 Th	19 01 58	15 33 01	7♌23 08	14♌55 15	2 42.3	28 24.2	28 02.7	12 04.4	26 43.7	11 27.8	7 34.1	26 21.3	12 07.3	1 02.7
6 F	19 05 55	16 34 09	22 22 47	29 44 54	2D41.0	29 51.5	29 17.9	12 51.6	26 40.7	11 41.4	7 40.2	26 19.5	12 06.7	1 04.0
7 Sa	19 09 51	17 35 17	7♍01 00	14♍10 42	2 41.4	1♑19.4	0♑33.2	13 38.9	26 38.2	11 55.0	7 46.2	26 17.6	12 06.2	1 05.3
8 Su	19 13 48	18 36 26	21 13 47	28 10 13	2 42.7	2 47.8	1 48.4	14 26.2	26 36.0	12 08.7	7 52.2	26 15.8	12 05.8	1 06.6
9 M	19 17 44	19 37 34	5♎00 06	11♎43 40	2R43.9	4 16.9	3 03.7	15 13.5	26 34.3	12 22.4	7 58.2	26 13.8	12 05.3	1 07.9
10 Tu	19 21 41	20 38 43	18 21 14	24 53 10	2 44.1	5 46.4	4 18.9	16 00.9	26 33.0	12 36.1	8 04.1	26 11.9	12 04.9	1 09.3
11 W	19 25 37	21 39 51	1♏19 55	7♏41 55	2 42.6	7 16.5	5 34.2	16 48.2	26 32.1	12 49.9	8 09.9	26 09.9	12 04.6	1 10.6
12 Th	19 29 34	22 41 00	13 59 37	20 13 28	2 39.3	8 47.2	6 49.5	17 35.6	26D31.6	13 03.7	8 15.7	26 07.9	12 04.2	1 12.0
13 F	19 33 30	23 42 08	26 23 55	2♐31 23	2 34.1	10 18.3	8 04.8	18 22.9	26 31.6	13 17.6	8 21.4	26 05.8	12 03.9	1 13.4
14 Sa	19 37 27	24 43 17	8♐36 13	14 38 48	2 27.6	11 49.9	9 20.1	19 10.3	26 31.9	13 31.5	8 27.1	26 03.7	12 03.7	1 14.8
15 Su	19 41 24	25 44 25	20 39 27	26 38 29	2 20.4	13 22.1	10 35.3	19 57.7	26 32.6	13 45.5	8 32.7	26 01.6	12 03.4	1 16.3
16 M	19 45 20	26 45 33	2♑36 08	8♑32 41	2 13.2	14 54.7	11 50.6	20 45.1	26 33.8	13 59.4	8 38.3	25 59.4	12 03.3	1 17.7
17 Tu	19 49 17	27 46 40	14 28 21	20 23 21	2 06.8	16 27.9	13 05.9	21 32.5	26 35.3	14 13.4	8 43.7	25 57.2	12 03.1	1 19.1
18 W	19 53 13	28 47 47	26 17 55	2♒12 16	2 01.8	18 01.6	14 21.2	22 19.9	26 37.3	14 27.5	8 49.2	25 55.0	12 03.0	1 20.6
19 Th	19 57 10	29 48 53	8♒06 37	14 01 12	1 58.4	19 35.8	15 36.5	23 07.3	26 39.7	14 41.5	8 54.5	25 52.7	12 02.9	1 22.1
20 F	20 01 06	0♒49 59	19 56 18	25 52 11	1D56.8	21 10.5	16 51.8	23 54.7	26 42.4	14 55.6	8 59.8	25 50.4	12 02.8	1 23.6
21 Sa	20 05 03	1 51 04	1♓49 09	7♓47 34	1 56.7	22 45.8	18 07.0	24 42.1	26 45.5	15 09.7	9 05.1	25 48.1	12D02.8	1 25.1
22 Su	20 08 59	2 52 08	13 47 48	19 50 16	1 57.9	24 21.7	19 22.3	25 29.5	26 49.1	15 23.9	9 10.3	25 45.8	12 02.8	1 26.6
23 M	20 12 56	3 53 11	25 55 23	2♈03 38	1 59.6	25 58.1	20 37.6	26 16.9	26 53.0	15 38.0	9 15.4	25 43.4	12 02.8	1 28.1
24 Tu	20 16 53	4 54 13	8♈15 31	14 31 30	2 01.4	27 35.1	21 52.9	27 04.3	26 57.3	15 52.2	9 20.4	25 41.0	12 02.9	1 29.7
25 W	20 20 49	5 55 14	20 52 07	27 17 51	2R02.6	29 12.7	23 08.1	27 51.7	27 01.9	16 06.4	9 25.3	25 38.6	12 03.0	1 31.2
26 Th	20 24 46	6 56 14	3♉49 10	10♉26 29	2 02.8	0♒51.0	24 23.4	28 39.1	27 07.0	16 20.6	9 30.2	25 36.2	12 03.2	1 32.8
27 F	20 28 42	7 57 13	17 10 11	24 00 29	2 01.9	2 29.8	25 38.6	29 26.5	27 12.4	16 34.8	9 35.1	25 33.7	12 03.4	1 34.3
28 Sa	20 32 39	8 58 10	0♊57 35	8♊01 26	1 59.9	4 09.4	26 53.9	0♓13.9	27 18.2	16 49.1	9 39.8	25 31.2	12 03.6	1 35.9
29 Su	20 36 35	9 59 07	15 11 55	22 28 41	1 57.2	5 49.5	28 09.1	1 01.3	27 24.3	17 03.3	9 44.5	25 28.8	12 03.9	1 37.5
30 M	20 40 32	11 00 03	29 51 12	7♋18 44	1 54.2	7 30.4	29 24.4	1 48.7	27 30.8	17 17.6	9 49.1	25 26.2	12 04.2	1 39.1
31 Tu	20 44 29	12 00 57	14♋50 24	22 25 08	1 51.5	9 11.9	0♒39.6	2 36.0	27 37.7	17 31.9	9 53.6	25 23.7	12 04.5	1 40.7

LONGITUDE — February 2045

Day	Sid.Time	☉	0 hr ☽	Noon ☽	True ☊	☿	♀	♂	⚳	♃	♄	♅	♆	♇
1 W	20 48 25	13♒01 50	0♌01 44	7♌38 58	1♓49.5	10♒54.2	1♒54.8	3♓23.4	27♉44.9	17♒46.2	9♐58.1	25♌21.2	12♉04.9	1♓42.4
2 Th	20 52 22	14 02 42	15 15 33	22 50 12	1D48.4	12 37.1	3 10.0	4 10.7	27 52.4	18 00.5	10 02.5	25R18.6	12 05.3	1 44.0
3 F	20 56 18	15 03 33	0♍21 45	7♍49 10	1 48.3	14 20.7	4 25.2	4 58.1	28 00.3	18 14.8	10 06.8	25 16.1	12 05.7	1 45.6
4 Sa	21 00 15	16 04 23	15 11 30	22 28 03	1 49.0	16 05.1	5 40.5	5 45.4	28 08.4	18 29.1	10 11.0	25 13.5	12 06.2	1 47.2
5 Su	21 04 11	17 05 12	29 38 16	6♎41 46	1 50.1	17 50.2	6 55.7	6 32.7	28 17.0	18 43.4	10 15.1	25 10.9	12 06.6	1 48.9
6 M	21 08 08	18 06 00	13♎38 24	20 28 08	1 51.3	19 36.0	8 10.9	7 20.0	28 25.8	18 57.7	10 19.2	25 08.3	12 07.2	1 50.5
7 Tu	21 12 04	19 06 47	27 11 04	3♏47 28	1 52.2	21 22.4	9 26.1	8 07.3	28 35.0	19 12.0	10 23.1	25 05.7	12 07.7	1 52.2
8 W	21 16 01	20 07 33	10♏17 40	16 42 04	1R52.7	23 09.6	10 41.3	8 54.6	28 44.5	19 26.4	10 27.0	25 03.0	12 08.3	1 53.9
9 Th	21 19 57	21 08 18	23 01 08	29 15 24	1 52.6	24 57.4	11 56.4	9 41.8	28 54.2	19 40.7	10 30.9	25 00.4	12 09.0	1 55.5
10 F	21 23 54	22 09 02	5♐25 22	11♐31 35	1 52.0	26 45.8	13 11.6	10 29.1	29 04.3	19 55.0	10 34.6	24 57.8	12 09.7	1 57.2
11 Sa	21 27 51	23 09 46	17 34 36	23 34 56	1 51.0	28 34.7	14 26.8	11 16.3	29 14.8	20 09.4	10 38.2	24 55.2	12 10.4	1 58.9
12 Su	21 31 47	24 10 28	29 33 05	5♑29 32	1 49.9	0♓24.1	15 42.0	12 03.6	29 25.5	20 23.7	10 41.8	24 52.5	12 11.1	2 00.6
13 M	21 35 44	25 11 09	11♑24 46	17 19 11	1 48.8	2 13.8	16 57.2	12 50.8	29 36.5	20 38.0	10 45.3	24 49.9	12 11.9	2 02.3
14 Tu	21 39 40	26 11 48	23 13 12	29 07 10	1 48.0	4 03.8	18 12.3	13 38.0	29 47.7	20 52.3	10 48.6	24 47.3	12 12.7	2 03.9
15 W	21 43 37	27 12 27	5♒01 27	10♒56 21	1 47.4	5 54.0	19 27.5	14 25.2	29 59.3	21 06.6	10 51.9	24 44.6	12 13.5	2 05.6
16 Th	21 47 33	28 13 03	16 52 09	22 49 07	1D47.1	7 44.1	20 42.6	15 12.3	0♊11.2	21 20.9	10 55.1	24 42.0	12 14.4	2 07.3
17 F	21 51 30	29 13 39	28 47 31	4♓47 33	1 47.1	9 34.0	21 57.8	15 59.4	0 23.3	21 35.2	10 58.2	24 39.4	12 15.3	2 09.0
18 Sa	21 55 26	0♓14 13	10♓49 29	16 53 30	1 47.1	11 23.5	23 12.9	16 46.6	0 35.7	21 49.4	11 01.3	24 36.7	12 16.2	2 10.7
19 Su	21 59 23	1 14 45	22 59 51	29 08 44	1R47.2	13 12.2	24 28.0	17 33.7	0 48.4	22 03.7	11 04.2	24 34.1	12 17.2	2 12.4
20 M	22 03 20	2 15 15	5♈20 24	11♈35 05	1 47.2	14 59.8	25 43.1	18 20.7	1 01.3	22 17.9	11 07.0	24 31.5	12 18.2	2 14.1
21 Tu	22 07 16	3 15 44	17 53 01	24 14 27	1 47.1	16 46.1	26 58.2	19 07.8	1 14.5	22 32.1	11 09.8	24 28.9	12 19.2	2 15.8
22 W	22 11 13	4 16 11	0♉39 39	7♉08 52	1 46.9	18 30.6	28 13.3	19 54.8	1 28.0	22 46.3	11 12.4	24 26.3	12 20.2	2 17.5
23 Th	22 15 09	5 16 36	13 42 21	20 20 20	1 46.6	20 12.9	29 28.4	20 41.8	1 41.7	23 00.5	11 15.0	24 23.7	12 21.3	2 19.2
24 F	22 19 06	6 16 59	27 03 02	3♊50 36	1D46.5	21 52.4	0♓43.4	21 28.8	1 55.7	23 14.7	11 17.4	24 21.2	12 22.5	2 20.9
25 Sa	22 23 02	7 17 21	10♊43 10	17 40 47	1 46.6	23 28.7	1 58.5	22 15.7	2 09.9	23 28.8	11 19.8	24 18.6	12 23.6	2 22.6
26 Su	22 26 59	8 17 40	24 43 24	1♋50 54	1 47.0	25 01.2	3 13.5	23 02.6	2 24.3	23 43.0	11 22.1	24 16.1	12 24.8	2 24.3
27 M	22 30 55	9 17 57	9♋03 01	16 19 24	1 47.6	26 29.2	4 28.5	23 49.5	2 39.0	23 57.0	11 24.3	24 13.6	12 26.0	2 26.0
28 Tu	22 34 52	10 18 13	23 39 32	1♌02 48	1 48.3	27 52.2	5 43.5	24 36.4	2 53.9	24 11.1	11 26.3	24 11.1	12 27.3	2 27.6

Astro Data

	Dy Hr Mn
♃□♆	8 7:07
☽0S	8 7:10
⚳D	13 4:13
♆D	21 16:17
☽0N	22 22:36
☽0S	4 16:29
☽0N	19 4:11
☿0N	28 11:54
♃☍♅	28 11:56

Planet Ingress

	Dy Hr Mn
☿ ♑	6 14:20
♀ ♑	7 1:26
☉ ♒	19 16:22
☿ ♒	25 23:34
♂ ♓	28 4:57
♀ ♒	30 23:22
☿ ♓	12 6:44
⚳ ♊	15 13:24
☉ ♓	18 6:22
♀ ♓	23 22:07

Last Aspect / ☽ Ingress

Last Aspect Dy Hr Mn		☽ Ingress Dy Hr Mn
2 7:35 ♅ ⚹	♋	2 13:12
3 10:20 ☉ ☍	♌	4 12:20
6 12:12 ☿ △	♍	6 12:25
7 18:14 ☉ △	♎	8 15:12
10 14:25 ♅ ⚹	♏	10 21:30
12 23:27 ♅ □	♐	13 7:03
15 10:46 ♅ △	♑	15 18:45
18 4:25 ☉ ☌	♒	18 7:31
20 11:57 ♅ ☍	♓	20 20:20
22 22:17 ☿ ⚹	♈	23 7:59
25 16:03 ☿ □	♉	25 17:00
27 21:58 ♂ □	♊	27 22:21
29 16:53 ♅ ⚹	♋	30 0:14
30 19:36 ♆ ⚹	♌	31 23:57

Last Aspect / ☽ Ingress

Last Aspect Dy Hr Mn		☽ Ingress Dy Hr Mn
2 15:55 ♅ ☌	♍	2 23:25
3 18:57 ♆ △	♎	5 0:37
6 20:18 ♅ ⚹	♏	7 5:05
9 3:50 ♅ □	♐	9 13:26
11 23:51 ☿ ⚹	♑	12 0:54
13 2:16 ♂ ⚹	♒	14 13:47
16 23:51 ☉ ☌	♓	17 2:25
18 11:45 ♂ ☌	♈	19 13:40
21 17:40 ♀ ⚹	♉	21 22:46
23 19:15 ♅ □	♊	24 5:14
25 23:16 ♅ ⚹	♋	26 8:54
28 6:20 ☿ △	♌	28 10:18

☽ Phases & Eclipses

Dy Hr Mn		
3 10:20	○	13♋27
10 3:32	☾	20♎17
18 4:25	●	28♑28
26 5:09	☽	6♉39
1 21:05	○	13♌25
8 19:03	☾	20♏25
16 23:51	●	28♒43
16 23:54:38	●	A 07'32"
24 16:37	☽	6♊29

Astro Data

1 January 2045
Julian Day # 52962
SVP 4♓37'45"
GC 27♐28.1 ⚴ 14♓35.0
Eris 29♈04.2R ⚵ 18♈23.6
⚷ 19♍01.4 ⚶ 3♈46.3
☽ Mean ☊ 4♓38.6

1 February 2045
Julian Day # 52993
SVP 4♓37'39"
GC 27♐28.1 ⚴ 23♓41.9
Eris 29♈04.5 ⚵ 1♉00.1
⚷ 18♍09.0R ⚶ 14♈14.7
☽ Mean ☊ 3♓00.2

March 2045

LONGITUDE

Day	Sid.Time	☉	0 hr ☽	Noon ☽	True ☊	☿	♀	♂	⚳	♃	♄	♅	♆	♇
1 W	22 38 49	11♓18 26	8♌28 28	15♌55 40	1♓48.9	29♓09.6	6♓58.5	25♓23.2	3♊09.0	24♒25.2	11♐28.3	24♌08.6	12♉28.5	2♓29.3
2 Th	22 42 45	12 18 37	23 23 29	0♍50 55	1R 49.2	0♈20.8	8 13.4	26 10.0	3 24.4	24 39.2	11 30.2	24R 06.1	12 29.8	2 31.0
3 F	22 46 42	13 18 46	8♍16 59	15 40 41	1 48.9	1 25.2	9 28.4	26 56.7	3 40.0	24 53.1	11 32.0	24 03.7	12 31.1	2 32.7
4 Sa	22 50 38	14 18 54	23 01 04	0♎17 17	1 48.0	2 22.2	10 43.3	27 43.4	3 55.7	25 07.1	11 33.7	24 01.2	12 32.5	2 34.3
5 Su	22 54 35	15 19 00	7♎28 35	14 34 22	1 46.5	3 11.4	11 58.3	28 30.1	4 11.7	25 21.0	11 35.3	23 58.8	12 33.9	2 36.0
6 M	22 58 31	16 19 04	21 34 09	28 27 38	1 44.6	3 52.3	13 13.2	29 16.8	4 27.9	25 34.9	11 36.7	23 56.4	12 35.3	2 37.7
7 Tu	23 02 28	17 19 07	5♏14 38	11♏55 10	1 42.5	4 24.6	14 28.1	0♈03.4	4 44.3	25 48.7	11 38.1	23 54.1	12 36.7	2 39.3
8 W	23 06 24	18 19 07	18 29 19	24 57 19	1 40.7	4 48.1	15 43.0	0 50.0	5 00.9	26 02.6	11 39.4	23 51.7	12 38.2	2 41.0
9 Th	23 10 21	19 19 07	1♐19 32	7♐36 23	1 39.5	5 02.6	16 57.9	1 36.6	5 17.7	26 16.4	11 40.6	23 49.4	12 39.7	2 42.6
10 F	23 14 18	20 19 05	13 48 19	19 55 55	1D 39.0	5R 08.1	18 12.7	2 23.1	5 34.7	26 30.1	11 41.7	23 47.1	12 41.2	2 44.2
11 Sa	23 18 14	21 19 01	25 59 44	2♑00 23	1 39.4	5 04.6	19 27.6	3 09.6	5 51.9	26 43.8	11 42.7	23 44.9	12 42.7	2 45.9
12 Su	23 22 11	22 18 55	7♑58 28	13 54 35	1 40.6	4 52.6	20 42.5	3 56.1	6 09.3	26 57.5	11 43.6	23 42.7	12 44.3	2 47.5
13 M	23 26 07	23 18 48	19 49 21	25 43 22	1 42.2	4 32.3	21 57.3	4 42.6	6 26.9	27 11.1	11 44.4	23 40.5	12 45.9	2 49.1
14 Tu	23 30 04	24 18 39	1♒37 09	7♒31 17	1 43.9	4 04.3	23 12.1	5 29.0	6 44.6	27 24.7	11 45.1	23 38.3	12 47.5	2 50.7
15 W	23 34 00	25 18 28	13 26 14	19 22 29	1 45.3	3 29.3	24 26.9	6 15.3	7 02.5	27 38.2	11 45.7	23 36.2	12 49.1	2 52.3
16 Th	23 37 57	26 18 16	25 20 27	1♓20 30	1R 45.9	2 48.3	25 41.7	7 01.6	7 20.6	27 51.7	11 46.2	23 34.1	12 50.8	2 53.9
17 F	23 41 53	27 18 01	7♓22 59	13 28 10	1 45.3	2 02.1	26 56.5	7 47.9	7 38.9	28 05.1	11 46.5	23 32.0	12 52.5	2 55.4
18 Sa	23 45 50	28 17 45	19 36 17	25 47 32	1 43.3	1 12.0	28 11.2	8 34.2	7 57.3	28 18.5	11 46.8	23 30.0	12 54.2	2 57.0
19 Su	23 49 47	29 17 26	2♈02 03	8♈19 56	1 40.1	0 18.9	29 26.0	9 20.4	8 16.0	28 31.9	11 47.0	23 28.0	12 55.9	2 58.6
20 M	23 53 43	0♈17 06	14 41 14	21 06 00	1 35.8	29♓24.3	0♈40.7	10 06.6	8 34.7	28 45.1	11R 47.1	23 26.0	12 57.7	3 00.1
21 Tu	23 57 40	1 16 43	27 34 11	4♉05 48	1 30.8	28 29.1	1 55.4	10 52.7	8 53.7	28 58.4	11 47.0	23 24.1	12 59.4	3 01.6
22 W	0 01 36	2 16 18	10♉40 46	17 19 03	1 25.9	27 34.7	3 10.1	11 38.8	9 12.8	29 11.6	11 46.9	23 22.2	13 01.2	3 03.2
23 Th	0 05 33	3 15 51	24 00 35	0♊45 17	1 21.7	26 42.0	4 24.8	12 24.9	9 32.0	29 24.7	11 46.7	23 20.4	13 03.1	3 04.7
24 F	0 09 29	4 15 22	7♊33 06	14 23 58	1 18.7	25 52.0	5 39.4	13 10.9	9 51.4	29 37.7	11 46.4	23 18.6	13 04.9	3 06.2
25 Sa	0 13 26	5 14 51	21 17 48	28 14 32	1D 17.1	25 05.7	6 54.0	13 56.8	10 11.0	29 50.8	11 45.9	23 16.8	13 06.8	3 07.7
26 Su	0 17 22	6 14 17	5♋14 04	12♋16 19	1 17.1	24 23.5	8 08.7	14 42.8	10 30.7	0♓03.7	11 45.4	23 15.1	13 08.6	3 09.1
27 M	0 21 19	7 13 41	19 21 08	26 28 20	1 18.1	23 46.2	9 23.2	15 28.6	10 50.6	0 16.6	11 44.8	23 13.4	13 10.5	3 10.6
28 Tu	0 25 16	8 13 03	3♌37 42	10♌48 56	1 19.6	23 14.2	10 37.8	16 14.5	11 10.5	0 29.4	11 44.1	23 11.8	13 12.4	3 12.0
29 W	0 29 12	9 12 22	18 01 40	25 15 30	1R 20.6	22 47.6	11 52.4	17 00.3	11 30.7	0 42.2	11 43.3	23 10.2	13 14.4	3 13.5
30 Th	0 33 09	10 11 38	2♍29 53	9♍44 17	1 20.5	22 26.8	13 06.9	17 46.0	11 50.9	0 54.8	11 42.3	23 08.6	13 16.3	3 14.9
31 F	0 37 05	11 10 53	16 58 04	24 10 32	1 18.5	22 11.8	14 21.4	18 31.7	12 11.3	1 07.5	11 41.3	23 07.1	13 18.3	3 16.3

April 2045

LONGITUDE

Day	Sid.Time	☉	0 hr ☽	Noon ☽	True ☊	☿	♀	♂	⚳	♃	♄	♅	♆	♇
1 Sa	0 41 02	12♈10 05	1♎21 00	8♎28 47	1♓14.7	22♓02.5	15♈35.9	19♈17.3	12♊31.8	1♓20.0	11♐40.2	23♌05.6	13♉20.3	3♓17.7
2 Su	0 44 58	13 09 16	15 33 12	22 33 38	1R 08.9	21D 58.9	16 50.3	20 02.9	12 52.5	1 32.5	11R 39.0	23R 04.2	13 22.3	3 19.0
3 M	0 48 55	14 08 24	29 29 32	6♏20 28	1 02.0	22 01.0	18 04.8	20 48.5	13 13.3	1 44.9	11 37.7	23 02.8	13 24.3	3 20.4
4 Tu	0 52 51	15 07 31	13♏06 05	19 46 09	0 54.5	22 08.4	19 19.2	21 34.0	13 34.2	1 57.2	11 36.3	23 01.5	13 26.3	3 21.7
5 W	0 56 48	16 06 35	26 20 36	2♐49 27	0 47.5	22 21.1	20 33.6	22 19.5	13 55.2	2 09.5	11 34.8	23 00.2	13 28.3	3 23.1
6 Th	1 00 45	17 05 38	9♐12 50	15 31 00	0 41.6	22 38.9	21 48.0	23 04.9	14 16.3	2 21.7	11 33.2	22 59.0	13 30.4	3 24.4
7 F	1 04 41	18 04 39	21 44 18	27 53 10	0 37.4	23 01.4	23 02.4	23 50.3	14 37.6	2 33.8	11 31.5	22 57.8	13 32.5	3 25.7
8 Sa	1 08 38	19 03 39	3♑58 06	9♑59 39	0D 35.1	23 28.5	24 16.7	24 35.6	14 59.0	2 45.9	11 29.8	22 56.7	13 34.5	3 27.0
9 Su	1 12 34	20 02 36	15 58 27	21 55 05	0 34.6	24 00.0	25 31.1	25 20.9	15 20.5	2 57.8	11 27.9	22 55.6	13 36.6	3 28.2
10 M	1 16 31	21 01 32	27 50 15	3♒44 34	0 35.3	24 35.6	26 45.4	26 06.2	15 42.1	3 09.7	11 26.0	22 54.6	13 38.8	3 29.5
11 Tu	1 20 27	22 00 26	9♒38 45	15 33 24	0 36.6	25 15.2	27 59.7	26 51.4	16 03.8	3 21.5	11 23.9	22 53.6	13 40.9	3 30.7
12 W	1 24 24	22 59 18	21 29 12	27 26 42	0R 37.4	25 58.5	29 14.0	27 36.5	16 25.6	3 33.2	11 21.8	22 52.6	13 43.0	3 31.9
13 Th	1 28 20	23 58 09	3♓26 32	9♓29 11	0 37.0	26 45.4	0♉28.3	28 21.6	16 47.6	3 44.8	11 19.6	22 51.8	13 45.2	3 33.1
14 F	1 32 17	24 56 57	15 35 07	21 44 45	0 34.7	27 35.6	1 42.5	29 06.7	17 09.6	3 56.4	11 17.3	22 50.9	13 47.3	3 34.2
15 Sa	1 36 14	25 55 44	27 58 25	4♈16 21	0 30.0	28 29.1	2 56.7	29 51.7	17 31.7	4 07.8	11 14.9	22 50.1	13 49.5	3 35.4
16 Su	1 40 10	26 54 29	10♈38 45	17 05 40	0 23.1	29 25.6	4 10.9	0♉36.6	17 54.0	4 19.2	11 12.4	22 49.4	13 51.6	3 36.5
17 M	1 44 07	27 53 12	23 37 06	0♉12 57	0 14.2	0♈25.0	5 25.1	1 21.5	18 16.3	4 30.4	11 09.8	22 48.7	13 53.8	3 37.6
18 Tu	1 48 03	28 51 53	6♉53 01	13 37 04	0 04.3	1 27.3	6 39.3	2 06.4	18 38.8	4 41.6	11 07.2	22 48.1	13 56.0	3 38.7
19 W	1 52 00	29 50 32	20 24 45	27 15 42	29♒54.2	2 32.1	7 53.5	2 51.2	19 01.3	4 52.7	11 04.5	22 47.5	13 58.2	3 39.8
20 Th	1 55 56	0♉49 09	4♊09 31	11♊05 47	29 45.3	3 39.6	9 07.6	3 36.0	19 24.0	5 03.7	11 01.7	22 47.0	14 00.4	3 40.9
21 F	1 59 53	1 47 44	18 04 05	25 04 02	29 38.2	4 49.5	10 21.7	4 20.7	19 46.7	5 14.5	10 58.8	22 46.5	14 02.6	3 41.9
22 Sa	2 03 49	2 46 17	2♋05 16	9♋07 29	29 33.6	6 01.8	11 35.8	5 05.3	20 09.5	5 25.3	10 55.9	22 46.1	14 04.9	3 42.9
23 Su	2 07 46	3 44 47	16 10 23	23 13 45	29D 31.4	7 16.3	12 49.9	5 50.0	20 32.5	5 36.0	10 52.8	22 45.8	14 07.1	3 43.9
24 M	2 11 43	4 43 16	0♌17 25	7♌21 12	29 31.0	8 33.1	14 03.9	6 34.5	20 55.5	5 46.6	10 49.7	22 45.4	14 09.3	3 44.9
25 Tu	2 15 39	5 41 42	14 25 00	21 28 40	29R 31.4	9 52.1	15 17.9	7 19.0	21 18.6	5 57.0	10 46.6	22 45.2	14 11.6	3 45.8
26 W	2 19 36	6 40 06	28 32 04	5♍35 04	29 31.4	11 13.1	16 31.9	8 03.5	21 41.7	6 07.4	10 43.3	22 45.0	14 13.8	3 46.7
27 Th	2 23 32	7 38 28	12♍37 28	19 39 02	29 29.9	12 36.2	17 45.9	8 47.9	22 05.0	6 17.7	10 40.0	22 44.8	14 16.0	3 47.6
28 F	2 27 29	8 36 47	26 39 31	3♎38 36	29 26.0	14 01.4	18 59.8	9 32.2	22 28.3	6 27.8	10 36.6	22 44.7	14 18.3	3 48.5
29 Sa	2 31 25	9 35 05	10♎35 55	17 31 04	29 19.3	15 28.5	20 13.8	10 16.5	22 51.7	6 37.8	10 33.2	22D 44.7	14 20.5	3 49.4
30 Su	2 35 22	10 33 21	24 23 39	1♏13 15	29 10.1	16 57.6	21 27.7	11 00.7	23 15.2	6 47.8	10 29.7	22 44.7	14 22.8	3 50.2

Astro Data	Planet Ingress	Last Aspect	☽ Ingress	Last Aspect	☽ Ingress	☽ Phases & Eclipses	Astro Data
Dy Hr Mn	Dy Hr Mn	Dy Hr Mn	Dy Hr Mn	Dy Hr Mn	Dy Hr Mn	Dy Hr Mn	
☽0S 4 3:31	☿ ♈ 2 4:45	2 1:52 ♃ ☍	♍ 2 10:38	2 12:53 ♅ ⚹	♏ 3 0:53	3 7:52 ○ 13♍08	1 March 2045
♂0N 9 12:16	♂ ♈ 7 10:14	4 7:31 ♂ ☍	♎ 4 11:31	4 17:55 ♅ □	♐ 5 6:45	3 7:42 • A 0.962	Julian Day # 53021
☿ R 10 14:42	☿ ♓R 19 20:22	6 6:53 ♃ △	♏ 6 14:42	7 3:34 ♂ △	♑ 7 16:09	10 12:50 ☾ 20♐21	SVP 4♓37'35"
☽0N 18 10:49	♀ ♈ 19 22:56	8 14:04 ♃ □	♐ 8 21:29	9 20:09 ♀ □	♒ 10 4:24	18 17:15 ● 28♓31	GC 27♐28.2 ⚳ 3♈30.3
☉0N 20 5:07	☉ ♈ 20 5:07	11 1:15 ♃ ⚹	♑ 11 7:59	12 16:00 ♀ ⚹	♓ 12 17:07	26 0:56 ☽ 5♋47	Eris 29♈13.6 ⚵ 14♉55.1
♄ R 20 18:12	♃ ♓ 26 5:08	13 6:39 ☉ ⚹	♒ 13 20:42	15 0:07 ☿ ☌	♈ 15 3:53		⚷ 16♍12.7R ⚶ 25♈16.7
♀0N 22 11:45		16 4:55 ♃ ☌	♓ 16 9:19	17 7:26 ☉ ☌	♉ 17 11:37	1 18:43 ○ 12♎27	☽ Mean ☊ 1♓31.2
☿0S 25 20:24	♀ ♉ 13 2:52	18 17:15 ☉ ☌	♈ 18 20:06	19 4:11 ♅ □	♊ 19 16:46	9 7:52 ☾ 19♑52	
☽0S 31 13:38	♂ ♉ 15 16:27	21 2:26 ♃ ⚹	♉ 21 4:29	21 8:05 ♅ ⚹	♋ 21 20:26	17 7:26 ● 27♈42	1 April 2045
☿ D 2 15:10	☿ ♈ 17 2:02	23 9:35 ♃ □	♊ 23 10:40	22 20:28 ♆ ⚹	♌ 23 23:30	24 7:12 ☽ 4♌32	Julian Day # 53052
♃☌♇ 12 9:00	☊ ♒R 18 22:03	25 14:48 ♃ △	♋ 25 15:01	25 14:10 ♅ ☌	♍ 26 2:30		SVP 4♓37'32"
☽0N 14 18:27	☉ ♉ 19 15:53	27 7:38 ☿ △	♌ 27 17:55	27 8:28 ♀ △	♎ 28 5:44		GC 27♐28.3 ⚳ 15♈29.8
☿0N 22 16:46		29 8:32 ♅ ☌	♍ 29 19:52	29 21:07 ♅ ⚹	♏ 30 9:51		Eris 29♈30.9 ⚵ 1♊40.6
☽0S 27 21:05		31 8:45 ☿ ☍	♎ 31 21:44				⚷ 13♍53.6R ⚶ 8♉23.5
♅ D 29 18:21							☽ Mean ☊ 29♒52.7

LONGITUDE — May 2045

Day	Sid.Time	☉	0 hr ☽	Noon☽	True☊	☿	♀	♂	⚳	♃	♄	♅	♆	♇
1 M	2 39 18	11♉31 35	7♏59 29	14♏41 57	28♒58.9	18♈28.7	22♉41.5	11♉44.9	23♊38.7	6♓57.6	10♐26.1	22♌44.8	14♉25.0	3♓51.0
2 Tu	2 43 15	12 29 47	21 20 22	27 54 29	28R 46.9	20 01.6	23 55.4	12 29.0	24 02.4	7 07.3	10R 22.5	22 44.9	14 27.3	3 51.8
3 W	2 47 11	13 27 58	4♐24 07	10♐49 12	28 35.2	21 36.5	25 09.2	13 13.1	24 26.1	7 16.8	10 18.8	22 45.1	14 29.6	3 52.6
4 Th	2 51 08	14 26 07	17 09 44	23 25 51	28 24.9	23 13.3	26 23.1	13 57.1	24 49.9	7 26.3	10 15.1	22 45.3	14 31.8	3 53.3
5 F	2 55 05	15 24 15	29 37 43	5♑45 40	28 16.8	24 52.0	27 36.9	14 41.1	25 13.7	7 35.7	10 11.3	22 45.6	14 34.1	3 54.1
6 Sa	2 59 01	16 22 21	11♑50 02	17 51 18	28 11.2	26 32.6	28 50.6	15 25.1	25 37.7	7 44.9	10 07.5	22 45.9	14 36.3	3 54.8
7 Su	3 02 58	17 20 26	23 49 57	29 46 33	28 08.1	28 15.1	0♊04.4	16 08.9	26 01.7	7 54.0	10 03.6	22 46.3	14 38.6	3 55.4
8 M	3 06 54	18 18 29	5♒41 43	11♒36 06	28D 06.9	29 59.5	1 18.1	16 52.8	26 25.7	8 03.0	9 59.7	22 46.8	14 40.8	3 56.1
9 Tu	3 10 51	19 16 31	17 30 21	23 25 10	28R 06.8	1♉45.9	2 31.9	17 36.5	26 49.9	8 11.8	9 55.7	22 47.3	14 43.1	3 56.7
10 W	3 14 47	20 14 31	29 21 15	5♓19 16	28 06.7	3 34.1	3 45.6	18 20.3	27 14.1	8 20.5	9 51.6	22 47.8	14 45.4	3 57.3
11 Th	3 18 44	21 12 30	11♓19 54	17 23 46	28 05.6	5 24.2	4 59.3	19 03.9	27 38.3	8 29.1	9 47.6	22 48.4	14 47.6	3 57.9
12 F	3 22 41	22 10 28	23 31 28	29 43 34	28 02.4	7 16.3	6 12.9	19 47.6	28 02.6	8 37.6	9 43.4	22 49.1	14 49.8	3 58.5
13 Sa	3 26 37	23 08 24	6♈00 31	12♈22 42	27 56.8	9 10.3	7 26.6	20 31.1	28 27.0	8 45.9	9 39.3	22 49.8	14 52.1	3 59.0
14 Su	3 30 34	24 06 20	18 50 23	25 23 46	27 48.5	11 06.2	8 40.2	21 14.7	28 51.5	8 54.1	9 35.1	22 50.6	14 54.3	3 59.5
15 M	3 34 30	25 04 13	2♉02 53	8♉47 37	27 38.0	13 03.9	9 53.8	21 58.1	29 16.0	9 02.1	9 30.9	22 51.4	14 56.6	4 00.0
16 Tu	3 38 27	26 02 06	15 37 45	22 32 55	27 26.1	15 03.5	11 07.4	22 41.6	29 40.6	9 10.1	9 26.6	22 52.2	14 58.8	4 00.5
17 W	3 42 23	26 59 57	29 32 38	6♊36 18	27 14.1	17 04.8	12 21.0	23 24.9	0♋05.2	9 17.8	9 22.3	22 53.2	15 01.0	4 00.9
18 Th	3 46 20	27 57 47	13♊43 15	20 52 45	27 03.2	19 07.9	13 34.6	24 08.3	0 29.9	9 25.5	9 18.0	22 54.1	15 03.2	4 01.3
19 F	3 50 16	28 55 35	28 04 03	5♋16 24	26 54.5	21 12.6	14 48.1	24 51.5	0 54.7	9 33.0	9 13.7	22 55.2	15 05.5	4 01.7
20 Sa	3 54 13	29 53 21	12♋29 06	19 41 32	26 48.5	23 18.9	16 01.6	25 34.7	1 19.5	9 40.3	9 09.3	22 56.3	15 07.7	4 02.1
21 Su	3 58 10	0♊51 06	26 53 08	4♌03 26	26 45.3	25 26.5	17 15.1	26 17.9	1 44.4	9 47.5	9 05.0	22 57.4	15 09.9	4 02.4
22 M	4 02 06	1 48 49	11♌12 04	18 18 47	26D 44.1	27 35.4	18 28.6	27 01.0	2 09.3	9 54.5	9 00.6	22 58.6	15 12.0	4 02.7
23 Tu	4 06 03	2 46 31	25 23 22	2♍25 43	26R 44.1	29 45.4	19 42.0	27 44.0	2 34.2	10 01.4	8 56.1	22 59.8	15 14.2	4 03.0
24 W	4 09 59	3 44 11	9♍25 46	16 23 28	26 43.7	1♊56.1	20 55.4	28 27.0	2 59.2	10 08.2	8 51.7	23 01.1	15 16.4	4 03.3
25 Th	4 13 56	4 41 49	23 18 49	0♎11 48	26 41.9	4 07.5	22 08.8	29 10.0	3 24.3	10 14.8	8 47.3	23 02.4	15 18.6	4 03.5
26 F	4 17 52	5 39 26	7♎02 25	13 50 36	26 37.7	6 19.3	23 22.2	29 52.8	3 49.4	10 21.2	8 42.8	23 03.8	15 20.7	4 03.7
27 Sa	4 21 49	6 37 01	20 36 18	27 19 26	26 30.8	8 31.2	24 35.6	0♊35.7	4 14.6	10 27.5	8 38.4	23 05.2	15 22.8	4 03.9
28 Su	4 25 45	7 34 35	3♏59 52	10♏37 29	26 21.2	10 42.9	25 48.9	1 18.4	4 39.8	10 33.6	8 33.9	23 06.7	15 25.0	4 04.1
29 M	4 29 42	8 32 08	17 12 07	23 43 37	26 09.7	12 54.2	27 02.2	2 01.2	5 05.0	10 39.6	8 29.5	23 08.3	15 27.1	4 04.2
30 Tu	4 33 39	9 29 40	0♐11 52	6♐36 44	25 57.3	15 04.7	28 15.5	2 43.8	5 30.3	10 45.4	8 25.0	23 09.8	15 29.2	4 04.4
31 W	4 37 35	10 27 10	12 58 08	19 16 02	25 45.2	17 14.3	29 28.7	3 26.5	5 55.6	10 51.0	8 20.6	23 11.5	15 31.3	4 04.4

LONGITUDE — June 2045

Day	Sid.Time	☉	0 hr ☽	Noon☽	True☊	☿	♀	♂	⚳	♃	♄	♅	♆	♇
1 Th	4 41 32	11♊24 40	25♐30 26	1♑41 24	25♒34.4	19♊22.6	0♋42.0	4♊09.0	6♋21.0	10♓56.5	8♐16.1	23♌13.1	15♉33.4	4♓04.5
2 F	4 45 28	12 22 09	7♑49 05	13 53 41	25R 25.6	21 29.5	1 55.2	4 51.5	6 46.4	11 01.8	8R 11.7	23 14.9	15 35.4	4 04.6
3 Sa	4 49 25	13 19 36	19 55 27	25 54 45	25 19.5	23 34.7	3 08.4	5 34.0	7 11.9	11 07.0	8 07.2	23 16.6	15 37.5	4R 04.6
4 Su	4 53 21	14 17 03	1♒51 57	7♒47 30	25 16.0	25 38.1	4 21.5	6 16.4	7 37.4	11 12.0	8 02.8	23 18.5	15 39.5	4 04.6
5 M	4 57 18	15 14 29	13 41 56	19 35 48	25D 14.5	27 39.5	5 34.7	6 58.8	8 02.9	11 16.8	7 58.4	23 20.3	15 41.6	4 04.5
6 Tu	5 01 14	16 11 55	25 29 41	1♓24 13	25 14.5	29 38.8	6 47.8	7 41.1	8 28.5	11 21.4	7 54.0	23 22.2	15 43.6	4 04.5
7 W	5 05 11	17 09 19	7♓20 03	13 17 53	25R 14.9	1♋35.8	8 00.9	8 23.4	8 54.1	11 25.9	7 49.6	23 24.2	15 45.6	4 04.4
8 Th	5 09 08	18 06 43	19 18 22	25 22 12	25 14.7	3 30.6	9 14.0	9 05.6	9 19.8	11 30.2	7 45.3	23 26.2	15 47.6	4 04.3
9 F	5 13 04	19 04 07	1♈30 01	7♈42 27	25 13.1	5 22.9	10 27.1	9 47.7	9 45.5	11 34.3	7 40.9	23 28.2	15 49.5	4 04.2
10 Sa	5 17 01	20 01 30	14 00 04	20 23 22	25 09.3	7 12.9	11 40.1	10 29.8	10 11.2	11 38.3	7 36.6	23 30.3	15 51.5	4 04.0
11 Su	5 20 57	20 58 52	26 52 47	3♉28 38	25 03.3	9 00.4	12 53.1	11 11.9	10 37.0	11 42.0	7 32.3	23 32.4	15 53.4	4 03.8
12 M	5 24 54	21 56 14	10♉11 04	17 00 07	24 55.3	10 45.4	14 06.1	11 53.9	11 02.8	11 45.6	7 28.1	23 34.6	15 55.3	4 03.6
13 Tu	5 28 50	22 53 36	23 55 41	0♊57 26	24 46.0	12 27.9	15 19.1	12 35.9	11 28.7	11 49.0	7 23.8	23 36.8	15 57.2	4 03.4
14 W	5 32 47	23 50 57	8♊04 55	15 17 29	24 36.4	14 07.8	16 32.1	13 17.8	11 54.6	11 52.3	7 19.6	23 39.1	15 59.1	4 03.1
15 Th	5 36 43	24 48 17	22 34 23	29 54 41	24 27.7	15 45.2	17 45.0	13 59.7	12 20.5	11 55.3	7 15.5	23 41.4	16 01.0	4 02.9
16 F	5 40 40	25 45 37	7♋17 27	14♋41 39	24 20.8	17 20.0	18 57.9	14 41.5	12 46.4	11 58.2	7 11.4	23 43.8	16 02.8	4 02.6
17 Sa	5 44 37	26 42 56	22 06 18	29 30 24	24 16.2	18 52.2	20 10.8	15 23.3	13 12.4	12 00.8	7 07.3	23 46.1	16 04.6	4 02.2
18 Su	5 48 33	27 40 14	6♌53 07	14♌13 38	24D 14.0	20 21.8	21 23.7	16 05.0	13 38.4	12 03.3	7 03.3	23 48.6	16 06.5	4 01.9
19 M	5 52 30	28 37 32	21 31 20	28 45 41	24 13.7	21 48.8	22 36.5	16 46.6	14 04.5	12 05.6	6 59.3	23 51.0	16 08.2	4 01.5
20 Tu	5 56 26	29 34 48	5♍56 18	13♍02 55	24 14.4	23 13.1	23 49.3	17 28.2	14 30.5	12 07.7	6 55.3	23 53.5	16 10.0	4 01.1
21 W	6 00 23	0♋32 04	20 05 24	27 03 40	24R 15.1	24 34.7	25 02.1	18 09.8	14 56.6	12 09.6	6 51.4	23 56.1	16 11.7	4 00.7
22 Th	6 04 19	1 29 19	3♎57 44	10♎47 42	24 14.7	25 53.5	26 14.9	18 51.3	15 22.8	12 11.4	6 47.6	23 58.7	16 13.5	4 00.3
23 F	6 08 16	2 26 33	17 33 38	24 15 41	24 12.6	27 09.6	27 27.6	19 32.7	15 48.9	12 12.9	6 43.8	24 01.3	16 15.2	3 59.8
24 Sa	6 12 12	3 23 47	0♏53 59	7♏28 41	24 08.3	28 22.8	28 40.3	20 14.1	16 15.1	12 14.2	6 40.0	24 03.9	16 16.8	3 59.3
25 Su	6 16 09	4 21 00	13 59 55	20 27 48	24 02.1	29 33.1	29 53.0	20 55.5	16 41.3	12 15.4	6 36.3	24 06.6	16 18.5	3 58.8
26 M	6 20 06	5 18 13	26 52 26	3♐13 56	23 54.4	0♌40.5	1♌05.6	21 36.8	17 07.5	12 16.4	6 32.7	24 09.4	16 20.1	3 58.3
27 Tu	6 24 02	6 15 25	9♐32 24	15 47 54	23 46.0	1 44.8	2 18.2	22 18.0	17 33.7	12 17.1	6 29.1	24 12.1	16 21.7	3 57.7
28 W	6 27 59	7 12 37	22 00 32	28 10 23	23 37.7	2 46.1	3 30.8	22 59.2	18 00.0	12 17.7	6 25.6	24 14.9	16 23.3	3 57.1
29 Th	6 31 55	8 09 49	4♑17 36	10♑22 18	23 30.4	3 44.1	4 43.3	23 40.4	18 26.3	12 18.1	6 22.1	24 17.8	16 24.9	3 56.5
30 F	6 35 52	9 07 00	16 24 38	22 24 48	23 24.6	4 38.8	5 55.8	24 21.5	18 52.6	12R 18.3	6 18.7	24 20.6	16 26.4	3 55.9

Astro Data Dy Hr Mn	Planet Ingress Dy Hr Mn	Last Aspect Dy Hr Mn	☽ Ingress Dy Hr Mn	Last Aspect Dy Hr Mn	☽ Ingress Dy Hr Mn	☽ Phases & Eclipses Dy Hr Mn
☽0N 12 2:23	♀ ♊ 7 10:34	2 3:57 ♀ ☍	♐ 2 15:51	31 19:33 ♅ △	♑ 1 8:43	1 5:52 ○ 11♏17
♃□♄ 17 21:01	☿ ♉ 8 12:06	4 11:32 ☿ △	♑ 5 0:43	2 15:23 ♆ △	♒ 3 20:14	9 2:51 ☾ 18♒54
☽0S 25 2:09	⚳ ♋ 17 6:54	7 8:24 ☿ □	♒ 7 12:27	6 7:43 ☿ △	♓ 6 9:09	16 18:26 ● 26♉18
	☉ ♊ 20 14:46	9 10:43 ♅ ☍	♓ 10 1:18	7 20:23 ☉ □	♈ 8 21:05	23 12:38 ☽ 2♍48
♇R 3 16:36	☿ ♊ 23 14:42	11 20:07 ☉ ⚹	♈ 12 12:32	10 17:48 ♅ △	♉ 11 5:42	30 17:52 ○ 9♐44
☽0N 8 9:51	♂ ♊ 26 16:01	14 7:20 ♅ △	♉ 14 20:19	12 23:26 ♅ □	♊ 13 10:23	
☽0S 21 6:52	♀ ♋ 31 22:15	16 18:26 ☉ ☌	♊ 17 0:47	15 3:05 ☉ ☌	♋ 15 12:09	7 20:23 ☾ 17♓29
		18 15:23 ♅ ⚹	♋ 19 3:13	16 19:32 ♀ ☌	♌ 17 12:48	15 3:05 ● 24♊27
	☿ ♋ 6 16:19	20 22:20 ♂ ⚹	♌ 21 5:12	19 11:46 ☉ ⚹	♍ 19 14:04	21 18:28 ☽ 0♎48
	☉ ♋ 20 22:34	23 6:36 ☿ □	♍ 23 7:51	21 8:10 ♀ ⚹	♎ 21 17:06	29 7:16 ○ 7♑59
	♀ ♌ 25 14:20	25 10:06 ♂ △	♎ 25 11:39	23 18:21 ♀ □	♏ 23 22:22	
	☿ ♌ 25 21:27	27 6:37 ♀ △	♏ 27 16:48	25 18:50 ♅ □	♐ 26 5:53	
		29 10:55 ♅ □	♐ 29 23:38	28 4:19 ♅ △	♑ 28 15:34	

Astro Data

1 May 2045
Julian Day # 53082
SVP 4♓37'28"
GC 27♐28.4 ⚴ 27♈52.6
Eris 29♈50.6 ⚵ 18♊22.1
⚷ 12♍38.1R ⚶ 21♉28.1
☽ Mean ☊ 28♒17.4

1 June 2045
Julian Day # 53113
SVP 4♓37'23"
GC 27♐28.4 ⚴ 11♉14.3
Eris 0♉09.1 ⚵ 5♋31.6
⚷ 13♍00.7 ⚶ 5♊01.6
☽ Mean ☊ 26♒38.9

July 2045 — LONGITUDE

Day	Sid.Time	☉	0 hr ☽	Noon ☽	True ☊	☿	♀	♂	⚳	♃	♄	♅	♆	♇
1 Sa	6 39 48	10♋04 12	28♑23 01	4♒19 35	23♒20.8	5♌30.1	7♌08.3	25♊02.5	19♋19.0	12♓18.3	6♐15.4	24♌23.5	16♉27.9	3♓55.3
2 Su	6 43 45	11 01 23	10♒14 48	16 09 00	23D 18.9	6 17.9	8 20.8	25 43.5	19 45.3	12R 18.1	6R 12.2	24 26.5	16 29.4	3R 54.6
3 M	6 47 42	11 58 34	22 02 36	27 56 02	23 18.7	7 02.0	9 33.2	26 24.5	20 11.7	12 17.7	6 09.0	24 29.4	16 30.9	3 54.0
4 Tu	6 51 38	12 55 46	3♓49 46	9♓44 20	23 19.7	7 42.4	10 45.6	27 05.4	20 38.1	12 17.2	6 05.8	24 32.4	16 32.3	3 53.2
5 W	6 55 35	13 52 58	15 40 17	21 38 11	23 21.3	8 18.9	11 57.9	27 46.3	21 04.5	12 16.4	6 02.8	24 35.4	16 33.8	3 52.5
6 Th	6 59 31	14 50 09	27 38 39	3♈42 17	23R 22.7	8 51.4	13 10.2	28 27.1	21 31.0	12 15.4	5 59.8	24 38.5	16 35.1	3 51.8
7 F	7 03 28	15 47 22	9♈49 43	16 01 33	23 23.2	9 19.8	14 22.5	29 07.9	21 57.4	12 14.3	5 56.9	24 41.6	16 36.5	3 51.0
8 Sa	7 07 24	16 44 34	22 18 22	28 40 44	23 22.5	9 43.8	15 34.8	29 48.6	22 23.9	12 12.9	5 54.1	24 44.7	16 37.8	3 50.2
9 Su	7 11 21	17 41 47	5♉09 07	11♉43 58	23 20.3	10 03.5	16 47.0	0♋29.3	22 50.4	12 11.4	5 51.3	24 47.8	16 39.1	3 49.4
10 M	7 15 17	18 39 01	18 25 33	25 14 06	23 16.8	10 18.7	17 59.2	1 09.9	23 16.9	12 09.6	5 48.6	24 51.0	16 40.4	3 48.6
11 Tu	7 19 14	19 36 15	2♊09 39	9♊12 04	23 12.3	10 29.3	19 11.4	1 50.5	23 43.5	12 07.7	5 46.0	24 54.2	16 41.7	3 47.8
12 W	7 23 11	20 33 29	16 21 03	23 36 09	23 07.5	10R 35.2	20 23.6	2 31.0	24 10.0	12 05.6	5 43.5	24 57.4	16 42.9	3 46.9
13 Th	7 27 07	21 30 44	0♋56 42	8♋21 51	23 03.1	10 36.3	21 35.7	3 11.5	24 36.6	12 03.3	5 41.0	25 00.7	16 44.1	3 46.1
14 F	7 31 04	22 27 59	15 50 39	23 22 01	22 59.7	10 32.6	22 47.7	3 52.0	25 03.2	12 00.8	5 38.7	25 04.0	16 45.3	3 45.2
15 Sa	7 35 00	23 25 14	0♌54 48	8♌27 52	22D 57.6	10 24.2	23 59.8	4 32.4	25 29.8	11 58.1	5 36.4	25 07.3	16 46.4	3 44.3
16 Su	7 38 57	24 22 30	16 00 02	23 30 15	22 57.0	10 11.0	25 11.8	5 12.8	25 56.4	11 55.2	5 34.2	25 10.6	16 47.5	3 43.4
17 M	7 42 53	25 19 45	0♍57 33	8♍21 05	22 57.6	9 53.2	26 23.8	5 53.1	26 23.0	11 52.1	5 32.1	25 14.0	16 48.6	3 42.4
18 Tu	7 46 50	26 17 01	15 40 12	22 54 20	22 58.8	9 31.0	27 35.7	6 33.3	26 49.7	11 48.9	5 30.1	25 17.3	16 49.7	3 41.4
19 W	7 50 46	27 14 17	0♎03 06	7♎06 18	23 00.2	9 04.5	28 47.6	7 13.5	27 16.3	11 45.4	5 28.2	25 20.7	16 50.7	3 40.5
20 Th	7 54 43	28 11 33	14 03 49	20 55 39	23R 01.1	8 34.2	29 59.4	7 53.7	27 43.0	11 41.8	5 26.3	25 24.1	16 51.7	3 39.5
21 F	7 58 40	29 08 50	27 41 54	4♏22 47	23 01.2	8 00.3	1♍11.2	8 33.8	28 09.6	11 38.0	5 24.6	25 27.6	16 52.7	3 38.5
22 Sa	8 02 36	0♌06 06	10♏58 30	17 29 21	23 00.2	7 23.4	2 22.9	9 13.9	28 36.3	11 34.1	5 22.9	25 31.0	16 53.6	3 37.5
23 Su	8 06 33	1 03 23	23 55 38	0♐17 40	22 58.3	6 44.0	3 34.6	9 53.9	29 03.0	11 29.9	5 21.3	25 34.5	16 54.5	3 36.4
24 M	8 10 29	2 00 41	6♐35 47	12 50 19	22 55.6	6 02.8	4 46.3	10 33.8	29 29.7	11 25.6	5 19.9	25 38.0	16 55.4	3 35.4
25 Tu	8 14 26	2 57 58	19 01 34	25 09 51	22 52.6	5 20.3	5 57.9	11 13.8	29 56.4	11 21.2	5 18.5	25 41.5	16 56.2	3 34.3
26 W	8 18 22	3 55 17	1♑15 27	7♑18 40	22 49.6	4 37.3	7 09.5	11 53.6	0♌23.1	11 16.5	5 17.2	25 45.0	16 57.0	3 33.2
27 Th	8 22 19	4 52 35	13 19 46	19 19 01	22 47.0	3 54.7	8 21.0	12 33.5	0 49.8	11 11.7	5 16.0	25 48.6	16 57.8	3 32.2
28 F	8 26 15	5 49 55	25 16 41	1♒13 00	22 45.1	3 13.0	9 32.5	13 13.3	1 16.5	11 06.8	5 14.9	25 52.2	16 58.6	3 31.1
29 Sa	8 30 12	6 47 15	7♒08 15	13 02 42	22D 44.0	2 33.2	10 43.9	13 53.0	1 43.2	11 01.7	5 13.8	25 55.7	16 59.3	3 29.9
30 Su	8 34 09	7 44 36	18 56 37	24 50 17	22 43.8	1 56.0	11 55.2	14 32.7	2 09.9	10 56.4	5 12.9	25 59.3	17 00.0	3 28.8
31 M	8 38 05	8 41 57	0♓44 03	6♓38 13	22 44.2	1 22.1	13 06.6	15 12.4	2 36.7	10 51.0	5 12.1	26 02.9	17 00.6	3 27.7

August 2045 — LONGITUDE

Day	Sid.Time	☉	0 hr ☽	Noon ☽	True ☊	☿	♀	♂	⚳	♃	♄	♅	♆	♇
1 Tu	8 42 02	9♌39 20	12♓33 09	18♓29 14	22♒45.1	0♌52.2	14♍17.8	15♋52.0	3♌03.4	10♓45.4	5♐11.4	26♌06.5	17♉01.2	3♓26.5
2 W	8 45 58	10 36 43	24 26 53	0♈26 30	22 46.3	0R 26.8	15 29.0	16 31.5	3 30.1	10R 39.7	5R 10.7	26 10.2	17 01.8	3R 25.4
3 Th	8 49 55	11 34 08	6♈28 34	12 33 32	22 47.4	0 06.5	16 40.2	17 11.1	3 56.9	10 33.8	5 10.2	26 13.8	17 02.4	3 24.2
4 F	8 53 51	12 31 34	18 41 55	24 54 12	22 48.2	29♋51.7	17 51.3	17 50.5	4 23.6	10 27.8	5 09.7	26 17.5	17 02.9	3 23.0
5 Sa	8 57 48	13 29 01	1♉10 52	7♉32 26	22R 48.6	29D 42.9	19 02.4	18 30.0	4 50.4	10 21.7	5 09.4	26 21.1	17 03.4	3 21.8
6 Su	9 01 44	14 26 29	13 59 20	20 32 00	22 48.6	29 40.4	20 13.4	19 09.4	5 17.1	10 15.4	5 09.1	26 24.8	17 03.9	3 20.6
7 M	9 05 41	15 23 59	27 10 47	3♊55 59	22 48.3	29 44.4	21 24.4	19 48.7	5 43.9	10 09.0	5 08.9	26 28.5	17 04.3	3 19.4
8 Tu	9 09 38	16 21 30	10♊47 47	17 46 14	22 47.7	29 55.0	22 35.3	20 28.0	6 10.6	10 02.5	5D 08.9	26 32.2	17 04.7	3 18.2
9 W	9 13 34	17 19 03	24 51 16	2♋02 40	22 47.1	0♌12.5	23 46.1	21 07.3	6 37.4	9 55.9	5 08.9	26 35.9	17 05.1	3 17.0
10 Th	9 17 31	18 16 36	9♋20 01	16 42 46	22 46.6	0 36.8	24 56.9	21 46.5	7 04.1	9 49.1	5 09.0	26 39.6	17 05.4	3 15.8
11 F	9 21 27	19 14 11	24 10 10	1♌41 19	22 46.2	1 07.9	26 07.7	22 25.7	7 30.9	9 42.3	5 09.3	26 43.4	17 05.7	3 14.5
12 Sa	9 25 24	20 11 47	9♌15 12	16 50 40	22D 46.1	1 45.9	27 18.4	23 04.9	7 57.6	9 35.3	5 09.6	26 47.1	17 06.0	3 13.3
13 Su	9 29 20	21 09 25	24 26 34	2♍01 40	22 46.1	2 30.7	28 29.0	23 44.0	8 24.4	9 28.2	5 10.0	26 50.8	17 06.2	3 12.0
14 M	9 33 17	22 07 03	9♍34 49	17 04 55	22R 46.1	3 22.1	29 39.6	24 23.0	8 51.1	9 21.1	5 10.6	26 54.5	17 06.4	3 10.8
15 Tu	9 37 13	23 04 43	24 30 58	1♎52 09	22 46.2	4 20.0	0♎50.1	25 02.0	9 17.8	9 13.8	5 11.2	26 58.3	17 06.6	3 09.5
16 W	9 41 10	24 02 23	9♎07 45	16 17 16	22 46.1	5 24.2	2 00.6	25 41.0	9 44.5	9 06.5	5 11.9	27 02.0	17 06.7	3 08.2
17 Th	9 45 07	25 00 04	23 20 22	0♏16 51	22 45.9	6 34.5	3 10.9	26 19.9	10 11.3	8 59.1	5 12.7	27 05.8	17 06.8	3 07.0
18 F	9 49 03	25 57 47	7♏06 42	13 50 01	22D 45.7	7 50.7	4 21.3	26 58.8	10 38.0	8 51.6	5 13.6	27 09.5	17 06.9	3 05.7
19 Sa	9 53 00	26 55 31	20 27 01	26 58 00	22 45.6	9 12.3	5 31.5	27 37.6	11 04.7	8 44.1	5 14.6	27 13.3	17R 06.9	3 04.4
20 Su	9 56 56	27 53 16	3♐23 21	9♐43 30	22 45.8	10 39.2	6 41.7	28 16.4	11 31.4	8 36.4	5 15.7	27 17.0	17 06.9	3 03.1
21 M	10 00 53	28 51 01	15 58 55	22 10 04	22 46.1	12 11.0	7 51.8	28 55.1	11 58.0	8 28.8	5 16.9	27 20.8	17 06.9	3 01.8
22 Tu	10 04 49	29 48 48	28 17 28	4♑21 37	22 46.8	13 47.2	9 01.8	29 33.8	12 24.7	8 21.1	5 18.2	27 24.5	17 06.8	3 00.6
23 W	10 08 46	0♍46 37	10♑22 59	16 22 02	22 47.6	15 27.5	10 11.7	0♌12.4	12 51.4	8 13.3	5 19.6	27 28.3	17 06.7	2 59.3
24 Th	10 12 42	1 44 26	22 19 15	28 15 01	22 48.4	17 11.3	11 21.6	0 51.0	13 18.0	8 05.5	5 21.1	27 32.0	17 06.6	2 58.0
25 F	10 16 39	2 42 17	4♒09 45	10♒03 50	22 49.0	18 58.4	12 31.4	1 29.6	13 44.6	7 57.7	5 22.7	27 35.7	17 06.4	2 56.7
26 Sa	10 20 36	3 40 09	15 57 37	21 51 25	22R 49.3	20 48.1	13 41.1	2 08.1	14 11.3	7 49.8	5 24.4	27 39.5	17 06.2	2 55.4
27 Su	10 24 32	4 38 02	27 45 32	3♓40 18	22 49.1	22 40.2	14 50.7	2 46.5	14 37.9	7 42.0	5 26.2	27 43.2	17 06.0	2 54.1
28 M	10 28 29	5 35 57	9♓35 57	15 32 46	22 48.2	24 34.0	16 00.3	3 25.0	15 04.5	7 34.1	5 28.0	27 46.9	17 05.7	2 52.8
29 Tu	10 32 25	6 33 54	21 31 00	27 30 55	22 46.7	26 29.4	17 09.7	4 03.4	15 31.0	7 26.2	5 30.0	27 50.6	17 05.4	2 51.5
30 W	10 36 22	7 31 52	3♈32 47	9♈36 51	22 44.7	28 25.8	18 19.1	4 41.7	15 57.6	7 18.2	5 32.0	27 54.3	17 05.1	2 50.3
31 Th	10 40 18	8 29 52	15 43 24	21 52 43	22 42.4	0♍22.9	19 28.4	5 20.0	16 24.1	7 10.3	5 34.2	27 58.0	17 04.7	2 49.0

Astro Data

	Dy Hr Mn
♃ R	1 0:37
☽ 0N	5 16:29
☿ R	13 5:37
☽ 0S	18 13:28
☽ 0N	1 22:30
☿ D	6 9:27
♄ D	8 15:01
☽ 0S	14 22:40
♀ 0S	15 23:20
♆ R	20 0:17
☽ 0N	29 4:24

Planet Ingress

	Dy Hr Mn
♂ ♋	8 18:44
♀ ♍	20 12:12
☉ ♌	22 9:27
⚳ ♌	25 15:16
☿ ♋R	3 21:25
☿ ♌	8 19:51
♀ ♎	14 18:57
☉ ♍	22 16:39
♂ ♌	23 4:17
☿ ♍	31 7:19

Last Aspect / ☽ Ingress

Last Aspect Dy Hr Mn		☽ Ingress Dy Hr Mn
30 0:02	♆ △	♒ 1 3:16
3 8:42	♂ △	♓ 3 16:12
6 0:59	♂ □	♈ 6 4:41
8 14:14	♂ ⚹	♉ 8 14:28
10 11:19	♅ □	♊ 10 20:17
12 14:14	♅ ⚹	♋ 12 22:28
14 10:28	☉ ☌	♌ 14 22:33
16 14:57	♀ ☌	♍ 16 22:27
18 18:04	☉ ⚹	♎ 18 23:55
21 1:52	☉ □	♏ 21 4:07
23 3:03	♅ □	♐ 23 11:27
25 13:02	♅ △	♑ 25 21:31
27 7:16	♆ △	♒ 28 9:32
30 14:21	♅ ☍	♓ 30 22:30

Last Aspect / ☽ Ingress

Last Aspect Dy Hr Mn		☽ Ingress Dy Hr Mn
1 9:02	♆ ⚹	♈ 2 11:07
4 21:22	☿ □	♉ 4 21:45
7 4:31	♆ ⚹	♊ 7 5:02
9 2:53	♅ ⚹	♋ 9 8:36
11 2:23	♀ ⚹	♌ 11 9:19
13 3:46	♅ ☌	♍ 13 8:47
15 0:20	♂ ⚹	♎ 15 8:56
17 6:27	♅ ⚹	♏ 17 11:31
19 13:17	♂ △	♐ 19 17:39
22 2:14	☉ △	♑ 22 3:22
23 13:30	♆ △	♒ 24 15:33
26 23:51	♅ ☍	♓ 27 4:33
28 15:07	♆ ⚹	♈ 29 16:57

☽ Phases & Eclipses

Dy Hr Mn	
7 11:30	☾ 15♈46
14 10:28	● 22♋24
21 1:52	☽ 28♎45
28 22:10	○ 6♒14
5 23:57	☾ 13♉58
12 17:39	● 20♌25
12 17:41:10	● T 06'06"
19 11:55	☽ 26♏55
27 14:07	○ 4♓43
27 13:53	● A 0.682

Astro Data

1 July 2045
Julian Day # 53143
SVP 4♓37'17"
GC 27♐28.5 ⚴ 24♉33.1
Eris 0♉21.0 ⚵ 21♋42.7
⚷ 14♍59.3 ⚶ 17♊55.7
☽ Mean ☊ 25♒03.6

1 August 2045
Julian Day # 53174
SVP 4♓37'12"
GC 27♐28.6 ⚴ 8♊28.6
Eris 0♉24.2R ⚵ 7♌46.9
⚷ 18♍19.3 ⚶ 0♋44.7
☽ Mean ☊ 23♒25.1

LONGITUDE — September 2045

Day	Sid.Time	☉	0 hr ☽	Noon ☽	True ☊	☿	♀	♂	⚳	♃	♄	♅	♆	♇
1 F	10 44 15	9♍27 54	28♈05 04	4♉20 47	22♒40.1	2♍20.4	20♎37.6	5♌58.3	16♌50.7	7♓02.4	5♐36.4	28♌01.7	17♉04.3	2♓47.7
2 Sa	10 48 11	10 25 58	10♉40 11	17 03 33	22R38.2	4 18.1	21 46.7	6 36.5	17 17.2	6R54.5	5 38.7	28 05.4	17R03.9	2R46.4
3 Su	10 52 08	11 24 04	23 31 14	0♊03 31	22D37.0	6 15.6	22 55.7	7 14.6	17 43.7	6 46.7	5 41.2	28 09.1	17 03.4	2 45.1
4 M	10 56 05	12 22 11	6♊40 43	13 23 04	22 36.6	8 12.9	24 04.6	7 52.8	18 10.2	6 38.8	5 43.7	28 12.8	17 03.0	2 43.9
5 Tu	11 00 01	13 20 21	20 10 48	27 04 03	22 37.1	10 09.6	25 13.5	8 30.9	18 36.6	6 31.0	5 46.3	28 16.4	17 02.4	2 42.6
6 W	11 03 58	14 18 33	4♋02 55	11♋07 22	22 38.2	12 05.8	26 22.2	9 08.9	19 03.1	6 23.2	5 49.0	28 20.1	17 01.9	2 41.4
7 Th	11 07 54	15 16 47	18 17 15	25 32 18	22 39.6	14 01.2	27 30.9	9 46.9	19 29.5	6 15.5	5 51.7	28 23.7	17 01.3	2 40.1
8 F	11 11 51	16 15 02	2♌52 06	10♌16 06	22R40.7	15 55.7	28 39.4	10 24.9	19 55.9	6 07.8	5 54.6	28 27.4	17 00.7	2 38.9
9 Sa	11 15 47	17 13 20	17 43 34	25 13 41	22 41.1	17 49.4	29 47.9	11 02.8	20 22.3	6 00.1	5 57.6	28 31.0	17 00.1	2 37.6
10 Su	11 19 44	18 11 40	2♍45 26	10♍17 46	22 40.2	19 42.0	0♏56.3	11 40.7	20 48.6	5 52.5	6 00.6	28 34.6	16 59.4	2 36.4
11 M	11 23 40	19 10 01	17 49 34	25 19 41	22 38.1	21 33.7	2 04.5	12 18.5	21 14.9	5 45.0	6 03.7	28 38.1	16 58.7	2 35.1
12 Tu	11 27 37	20 08 24	2♎47 02	10♎10 32	22 34.8	23 24.3	3 12.6	12 56.3	21 41.2	5 37.6	6 07.0	28 41.7	16 58.0	2 33.9
13 W	11 31 34	21 06 49	17 29 18	24 42 32	22 30.8	25 13.8	4 20.7	13 34.1	22 07.5	5 30.2	6 10.3	28 45.2	16 57.2	2 32.7
14 Th	11 35 30	22 05 15	1♏49 38	8♏50 09	22 26.5	27 02.2	5 28.6	14 11.7	22 33.7	5 22.9	6 13.6	28 48.8	16 56.4	2 31.5
15 F	11 39 27	23 03 43	15 43 49	22 30 33	22 22.8	28 49.6	6 36.4	14 49.4	22 59.9	5 15.7	6 17.1	28 52.3	16 55.6	2 30.3
16 Sa	11 43 23	24 02 13	29 10 25	5♐43 39	22 20.0	0♎35.9	7 44.1	15 27.0	23 26.1	5 08.6	6 20.7	28 55.8	16 54.7	2 29.1
17 Su	11 47 20	25 00 45	12♐10 32	18 31 31	22D18.6	2 21.1	8 51.6	16 04.5	23 52.2	5 01.6	6 24.3	28 59.2	16 53.9	2 27.9
18 M	11 51 16	25 59 18	24 47 06	0♑57 49	22 18.5	4 05.2	9 59.0	16 42.0	24 18.4	4 54.7	6 28.0	29 02.7	16 53.0	2 26.8
19 Tu	11 55 13	26 57 53	7♑04 17	13 07 05	22 19.6	5 48.3	11 06.3	17 19.5	24 44.4	4 47.9	6 31.8	29 06.1	16 52.0	2 25.6
20 W	11 59 09	27 56 29	19 06 52	25 04 14	22 21.2	7 30.4	12 13.5	17 56.9	25 10.5	4 41.2	6 35.7	29 09.5	16 51.1	2 24.5
21 Th	12 03 06	28 55 07	0♒59 47	6♒54 06	22 22.9	9 11.4	13 20.5	18 34.3	25 36.5	4 34.6	6 39.7	29 12.9	16 50.1	2 23.4
22 F	12 07 03	29 53 47	12 47 44	18 41 13	22R23.9	10 51.5	14 27.3	19 11.6	26 02.4	4 28.2	6 43.7	29 16.3	16 49.1	2 22.2
23 Sa	12 10 59	0♎52 28	24 35 01	0♓29 34	22 23.6	12 30.5	15 34.0	19 48.9	26 28.4	4 21.9	6 47.8	29 19.6	16 48.0	2 21.1
24 Su	12 14 56	1 51 12	6♓25 17	12 22 30	22 21.5	14 08.6	16 40.6	20 26.1	26 54.2	4 15.7	6 52.0	29 22.9	16 47.0	2 20.0
25 M	12 18 52	2 49 57	18 21 33	24 22 40	22 17.6	15 45.8	17 47.0	21 03.3	27 20.1	4 09.7	6 56.3	29 26.2	16 45.9	2 18.9
26 Tu	12 22 49	3 48 44	0♈26 06	6♈32 02	22 11.9	17 22.0	18 53.2	21 40.4	27 45.9	4 03.8	7 00.6	29 29.5	16 44.7	2 17.9
27 W	12 26 45	4 47 33	12 40 36	18 51 56	22 04.7	18 57.2	19 59.2	22 17.5	28 11.7	3 58.0	7 05.0	29 32.7	16 43.6	2 16.8
28 Th	12 30 42	5 46 24	25 06 08	1♉23 16	21 56.8	20 31.6	21 05.1	22 54.5	28 37.4	3 52.4	7 09.5	29 35.9	16 42.4	2 15.8
29 F	12 34 38	6 45 18	7♉43 24	14 06 37	21 48.9	22 05.1	22 10.8	23 31.5	29 03.1	3 46.9	7 14.1	29 39.1	16 41.3	2 14.8
30 Sa	12 38 35	7 44 13	20 32 58	27 02 31	21 42.0	23 37.7	23 16.4	24 08.5	29 28.7	3 41.6	7 18.7	29 42.3	16 40.0	2 13.8

LONGITUDE — October 2045

Day	Sid.Time	☉	0 hr ☽	Noon ☽	True ☊	☿	♀	♂	⚳	♃	♄	♅	♆	♇
1 Su	12 42 32	8♎43 11	3♊35 21	10♊11 34	21♒36.7	25♎09.4	24♏21.7	24♌45.4	29♌54.3	3♓36.4	7♐23.4	29♌45.4	16♉38.8	2♓12.8
2 M	12 46 28	9 42 11	16 51 15	23 34 33	21R33.4	26 40.3	25 26.9	25 22.2	0♍19.8	3R31.4	7 28.2	29 48.5	16R37.6	2R11.8
3 Tu	12 50 25	10 41 14	0♋21 32	7♋12 20	21D32.1	28 10.3	26 31.8	25 59.0	0 45.3	3 26.6	7 33.0	29 51.6	16 36.3	2 10.8
4 W	12 54 21	11 40 18	14 07 01	21 05 38	21 32.3	29 39.4	27 36.6	26 35.8	1 10.8	3 21.9	7 37.9	29 54.6	16 35.0	2 09.9
5 Th	12 58 18	12 39 26	28 08 12	5♌14 38	21 33.3	1♏07.7	28 41.2	27 12.5	1 36.2	3 17.4	7 42.9	29 57.6	16 33.7	2 09.0
6 F	13 02 14	13 38 35	12♌24 48	19 38 24	21R34.0	2 35.1	29 45.5	27 49.2	2 01.5	3 13.1	7 47.9	0♍00.6	16 32.3	2 08.0
7 Sa	13 06 11	14 37 47	26 55 06	4♍14 24	21 33.4	4 01.6	0♐49.7	28 25.8	2 26.8	3 09.0	7 53.0	0 03.5	16 31.0	2 07.2
8 Su	13 10 07	15 37 01	11♍35 40	18 58 10	21 30.6	5 27.2	1 53.6	29 02.4	2 52.1	3 05.0	7 58.2	0 06.4	16 29.6	2 06.3
9 M	13 14 04	16 36 17	26 21 04	3♎43 26	21 25.4	6 51.9	2 57.3	29 38.9	3 17.2	3 01.2	8 03.4	0 09.3	16 28.2	2 05.4
10 Tu	13 18 00	17 35 35	11♎04 19	18 22 45	21 17.9	8 15.6	4 00.8	0♍15.3	3 42.4	2 57.6	8 08.7	0 12.1	16 26.7	2 04.6
11 W	13 21 57	18 34 55	25 37 47	2♏48 34	21 08.8	9 38.3	5 04.0	0 51.7	4 07.4	2 54.2	8 14.1	0 14.9	16 25.3	2 03.8
12 Th	13 25 54	19 34 17	9♏54 20	16 54 28	20 59.1	11 00.1	6 06.9	1 28.1	4 32.4	2 51.0	8 19.5	0 17.7	16 23.8	2 03.0
13 F	13 29 50	20 33 41	23 48 31	0♐36 11	20 49.9	12 20.7	7 09.6	2 04.4	4 57.4	2 47.9	8 25.0	0 20.4	16 22.4	2 02.2
14 Sa	13 33 47	21 33 07	7♐17 19	13 51 57	20 42.3	13 40.3	8 12.0	2 40.6	5 22.2	2 45.1	8 30.5	0 23.1	16 20.9	2 01.4
15 Su	13 37 43	22 32 35	20 20 17	26 42 34	20 36.8	14 58.7	9 14.2	3 16.8	5 47.0	2 42.4	8 36.1	0 25.8	16 19.4	2 00.7
16 M	13 41 40	23 32 05	2♑59 15	9♑10 49	20 33.6	16 15.8	10 16.0	3 52.9	6 11.7	2 40.0	8 41.8	0 28.4	16 17.9	2 00.0
17 Tu	13 45 36	24 31 36	15 17 50	21 20 56	20D32.4	17 31.5	11 17.5	4 29.0	6 36.4	2 37.7	8 47.5	0 31.0	16 16.3	1 59.3
18 W	13 49 33	25 31 09	27 20 47	3♒18 03	20 32.6	18 45.9	12 18.7	5 05.0	7 01.0	2 35.7	8 53.2	0 33.5	16 14.8	1 58.6
19 Th	13 53 30	26 30 44	9♒13 25	15 07 35	20R33.2	19 58.6	13 19.6	5 41.0	7 25.5	2 33.8	8 59.0	0 36.0	16 13.2	1 58.0
20 F	13 57 26	27 30 21	21 01 13	26 54 57	20 33.1	21 09.7	14 20.1	6 16.9	7 49.9	2 32.2	9 04.9	0 38.4	16 11.7	1 57.3
21 Sa	14 01 23	28 29 59	2♓49 26	8♓45 12	20 31.4	22 18.9	15 20.3	6 52.7	8 14.3	2 30.7	9 10.8	0 40.8	16 10.1	1 56.7
22 Su	14 05 19	29 29 39	14 42 48	20 42 42	20 27.3	23 26.2	16 20.1	7 28.5	8 38.6	2 29.5	9 16.8	0 43.2	16 08.5	1 56.1
23 M	14 09 16	0♏29 21	26 45 18	2♈50 58	20 20.6	24 31.2	17 19.5	8 04.2	9 02.8	2 28.4	9 22.8	0 45.5	16 06.9	1 55.6
24 Tu	14 13 12	1 29 04	8♈59 58	15 12 30	20 11.2	25 33.8	18 18.5	8 39.9	9 26.9	2 27.6	9 28.9	0 47.8	16 05.2	1 55.0
25 W	14 17 09	2 28 50	21 28 42	27 48 37	19 59.7	26 33.7	19 17.1	9 15.5	9 51.0	2 26.9	9 35.0	0 50.0	16 03.6	1 54.5
26 Th	14 21 05	3 28 38	4♉12 15	10♉39 32	19 47.1	27 30.7	20 15.2	9 51.0	10 14.9	2 26.5	9 41.1	0 52.2	16 02.0	1 54.0
27 F	14 25 02	4 28 27	17 10 18	23 44 26	19 34.4	28 24.4	21 13.0	10 26.5	10 38.8	2D26.2	9 47.3	0 54.4	16 00.3	1 53.6
28 Sa	14 28 58	5 28 19	0♊21 43	7♊01 55	19 23.0	29 14.5	22 10.2	11 02.0	11 02.6	2 26.2	9 53.6	0 56.5	15 58.7	1 53.1
29 Su	14 32 55	6 28 13	13 44 52	20 30 19	19 13.8	0♐00.6	23 07.0	11 37.3	11 26.3	2 26.4	9 59.9	0 58.6	15 57.0	1 52.7
30 M	14 36 52	7 28 09	27 18 07	4♋08 07	19 07.4	0 42.1	24 03.3	12 12.6	11 49.9	2 26.7	10 06.2	1 00.6	15 55.4	1 52.3
31 Tu	14 40 48	8 28 07	11♋00 11	17 54 14	19 03.8	1 18.7	24 59.1	12 47.9	12 13.4	2 27.3	10 12.6	1 02.5	15 53.7	1 51.9

Astro Data

	Dy Hr Mn
♃□♄	9 17:45
☽0S	11 9:27
☿0S	17 11:33
☉0S	22 14:33
☽0N	25 10:45
☽0S	8 19:41
☽0N	22 17:44
♃ D	28 4:35

Planet Ingress

	Dy Hr Mn
♀ ♏	9 16:15
☿ ♎	16 3:52
☉ ♎	22 14:33
⚳ ♍	1 17:22
☿ ♏	4 17:34
♅ ♍	6 7:11
♀ ♐	6 17:24
♂ ♍	10 1:54
☉ ♏	23 0:12
☿ ♐	29 11:42

Last Aspect / ☽ Ingress

Last Aspect Dy Hr Mn		☽ Ingress Dy Hr Mn
31 23:50	♅ △	♉ 1 3:41
3 8:30	♅ □	♊ 3 11:54
5 14:06	♅ ⚹	♋ 5 17:04
7 15:31	♀ □	♌ 7 19:19
9 17:16	♅ ☌	♍ 9 19:37
11 5:07	☿ ☌	♎ 11 19:31
13 18:50	♅ ⚹	♏ 13 20:54
16 1:08	☿ ⚹	♐ 16 1:30
18 8:14	♅ △	♑ 18 10:07
20 18:20	☉ △	♒ 20 21:59
23 9:37	♅ ☍	♓ 23 11:00
24 21:31	♀ △	♈ 25 23:08
28 8:35	♅ △	♉ 28 9:22
30 16:55	♅ □	♊ 30 17:26

Last Aspect / ☽ Ingress

Last Aspect Dy Hr Mn		☽ Ingress Dy Hr Mn
2 23:04	♅ ⚹	♋ 2 23:22
5 0:01	♀ △	♌ 5 3:09
7 2:04	♂ ☌	♍ 7 5:03
8 7:59	♆ △	♎ 9 5:56
10 10:37	☉ ☌	♏ 11 7:17
12 11:07	♆ ☍	♐ 13 10:56
15 3:28	☉ ⚹	♑ 15 18:16
17 18:55	☉ □	♒ 18 5:20
20 13:19	☉ △	♓ 20 18:16
22 17:58	☿ △	♈ 23 6:24
24 18:27	♀ △	♉ 25 16:07
27 21:03	☿ ☍	♊ 27 23:21
29 16:58	♀ ☍	♋ 30 4:45

☽ Phases & Eclipses

Dy Hr Mn	
4 10:03	☾ 12♊17
11 1:28	● 18♍44
18 1:30	☽ 25♐34
26 6:11	○ 3♈34
3 18:31	☾ 10♋57
10 10:37	● 17♎32
17 18:55	☽ 24♑49
25 21:31	○ 2♉53

Astro Data

1 September 2045
Julian Day # 53205
SVP 4♓37'08"
GC 27♐28.6 ⚵ 22♊06.4
Eris 0♉17.4R ⚶ 23♌00.3
⚷ 22♍28.4 ⚴ 12♋37.0
☽ Mean ☊ 21♒46.6

1 October 2045
Julian Day # 53235
SVP 4♓37'05"
GC 27♐28.7 ⚵ 4♋00.6
Eris 0♉03.2R ⚶ 6♍42.5
⚷ 26♍46.5 ⚴ 22♋31.2
☽ Mean ☊ 20♒11.3

November 2045 LONGITUDE

Day	Sid.Time	☉	0 hr ☽	Noon ☽	True ☊	☿	♀	♂	⚳	♃	♄	♅	♆	♇
1 W	14 44 45	9♏28 07	24♋50 13	1♌48 07	19♒02.5	1♐49.8	25♐54.3	13♍23.1	12♍36.9	2♓28.1	10♐19.0	1♍04.4	15♉52.0	1♓51.6
2 Th	14 48 41	10 28 09	8♌47 53	15 49 29	19R02.4	2 14.7	26 49.0	13 58.2	13 00.2	2 29.0	10 25.4	1 06.3	15R50.4	1R51.3
3 F	14 52 38	11 28 14	22 52 54	29 58 00	19 02.2	2 33.0	27 43.1	14 33.3	13 23.4	2 30.2	10 31.9	1 08.1	15 48.7	1 50.9
4 Sa	14 56 34	12 28 20	7♍04 41	14♍12 42	19 00.5	2R43.8	28 36.6	15 08.2	13 46.5	2 31.6	10 38.4	1 09.9	15 47.0	1 50.7
5 Su	15 00 31	13 28 29	21 21 46	28 31 29	18 56.3	2 46.7	29 29.6	15 43.2	14 09.6	2 33.2	10 45.0	1 11.6	15 45.3	1 50.4
6 M	15 04 27	14 28 40	5♎41 22	12♎50 53	18 49.2	2 40.8	0♑21.8	16 18.0	14 32.5	2 34.9	10 51.6	1 13.3	15 43.6	1 50.2
7 Tu	15 08 24	15 28 52	19 59 23	27 06 11	18 39.2	2 25.8	1 13.5	16 52.8	14 55.3	2 36.9	10 58.2	1 14.9	15 41.9	1 50.0
8 W	15 12 21	16 29 07	4♏10 37	11♏11 59	18 27.1	2 01.1	2 04.4	17 27.5	15 18.0	2 39.1	11 04.9	1 16.5	15 40.2	1 49.8
9 Th	15 16 17	17 29 24	18 09 37	25 02 57	18 14.1	1 26.5	2 54.6	18 02.1	15 40.5	2 41.5	11 11.6	1 18.0	15 38.5	1 49.7
10 F	15 20 14	18 29 42	1♐51 30	8♐34 53	18 01.6	0 42.0	3 44.0	18 36.7	16 03.0	2 44.1	11 18.3	1 19.5	15 36.8	1 49.5
11 Sa	15 24 10	19 30 02	15 12 50	21 45 16	17 50.6	29♏48.0	4 32.7	19 11.2	16 25.3	2 46.9	11 25.1	1 20.9	15 35.2	1 49.4
12 Su	15 28 07	20 30 23	28 12 08	4♑33 37	17 42.2	28 45.2	5 20.5	19 45.6	16 47.6	2 49.8	11 31.9	1 22.2	15 33.5	1 49.4
13 M	15 32 03	21 30 46	10♑49 57	17 01 30	17 36.6	27 34.9	6 07.5	20 19.9	17 09.6	2 53.0	11 38.7	1 23.6	15 31.8	1 49.3
14 Tu	15 36 00	22 31 10	23 08 41	29 12 03	17 33.6	26 18.9	6 53.6	20 54.2	17 31.6	2 56.4	11 45.5	1 24.8	15 30.1	1D49.3
15 W	15 39 57	23 31 36	5♒12 10	11♒09 41	17D32.6	24 59.2	7 38.7	21 28.3	17 53.4	2 59.9	11 52.4	1 26.0	15 28.4	1 49.3
16 Th	15 43 53	24 32 03	17 05 16	22 59 36	17R32.6	23 38.5	8 22.9	22 02.4	18 15.1	3 03.7	11 59.2	1 27.2	15 26.8	1 49.4
17 F	15 47 50	25 32 31	28 53 24	4♓47 21	17 32.3	22 19.2	9 06.1	22 36.4	18 36.7	3 07.6	12 06.1	1 28.3	15 25.1	1 49.4
18 Sa	15 51 46	26 33 01	10♓42 10	16 38 31	17 30.8	21 04.1	9 48.2	23 10.3	18 58.1	3 11.8	12 13.1	1 29.3	15 23.5	1 49.5
19 Su	15 55 43	27 33 31	22 37 02	28 38 20	17 27.0	19 55.6	10 29.1	23 44.2	19 19.4	3 16.1	12 20.0	1 30.3	15 21.8	1 49.6
20 M	15 59 39	28 34 03	4♈42 57	10♈51 24	17 20.7	18 55.7	11 09.0	24 17.9	19 40.6	3 20.6	12 27.0	1 31.2	15 20.2	1 49.7
21 Tu	16 03 36	29 34 37	17 04 03	23 21 14	17 11.6	18 05.8	11 47.6	24 51.6	20 01.6	3 25.3	12 33.9	1 32.1	15 18.5	1 49.9
22 W	16 07 32	0♐35 11	29 43 12	6♉10 03	17 00.3	17 27.1	12 25.0	25 25.1	20 22.4	3 30.1	12 40.9	1 32.9	15 16.9	1 50.1
23 Th	16 11 29	1 35 48	12♉41 49	19 18 24	16 47.7	16 59.9	13 01.0	25 58.6	20 43.1	3 35.2	12 47.9	1 33.7	15 15.3	1 50.3
24 F	16 15 25	2 36 25	25 59 37	2♊45 10	16 35.1	16D44.5	13 35.7	26 32.0	21 03.7	3 40.4	12 55.0	1 34.4	15 13.7	1 50.5
25 Sa	16 19 22	3 37 04	9♊34 40	16 27 42	16 23.6	16 40.4	14 09.0	27 05.4	21 24.1	3 45.8	13 02.0	1 35.0	15 12.1	1 50.8
26 Su	16 23 19	4 37 44	23 23 45	0♋22 20	16 14.3	16 47.0	14 40.8	27 38.6	21 44.3	3 51.4	13 09.1	1 35.6	15 10.5	1 51.1
27 M	16 27 15	5 38 26	7♋22 56	14 25 04	16 07.8	17 03.8	15 11.1	28 11.7	22 04.4	3 57.2	13 16.1	1 36.2	15 09.0	1 51.4
28 Tu	16 31 12	6 39 10	21 28 15	28 32 07	16 04.3	17 29.7	15 39.9	28 44.8	22 24.3	4 03.1	13 23.2	1 36.7	15 07.4	1 51.8
29 W	16 35 08	7 39 54	5♌36 19	12♌40 34	16D03.1	18 04.0	16 06.9	29 17.7	22 44.0	4 09.2	13 30.3	1 37.1	15 05.9	1 52.2
30 Th	16 39 05	8 40 41	19 44 38	26 48 22	16R03.3	18 45.6	16 32.3	29 50.6	23 03.6	4 15.5	13 37.4	1 37.5	15 04.4	1 52.6

December 2045 LONGITUDE

Day	Sid.Time	☉	0 hr ☽	Noon ☽	True ☊	☿	♀	♂	⚳	♃	♄	♅	♆	♇
1 F	16 43 01	9♐41 28	3♍51 38	10♍54 19	16♒03.6	19♏33.9	16♑55.9	0♎23.3	23♍23.0	4♓21.9	13♐44.5	1♍37.8	15♉02.9	1♓53.0
2 Sa	16 46 58	10 42 18	17 56 20	24 57 35	16R02.7	20 28.0	17 17.7	0 55.9	23 42.2	4 28.5	13 51.6	1 38.1	15R01.4	1 53.4
3 Su	16 50 55	11 43 08	1♎57 58	8♎57 19	15 59.7	21 27.1	17 37.6	1 28.5	24 01.2	4 35.3	13 58.7	1 38.3	14 59.9	1 53.9
4 M	16 54 51	12 44 01	15 55 28	22 52 10	15 54.0	22 30.7	17 55.6	2 00.9	24 20.1	4 42.2	14 05.8	1 38.4	14 58.4	1 54.4
5 Tu	16 58 48	13 44 54	29 47 10	6♏40 11	15 45.8	23 38.1	18 11.5	2 33.2	24 38.7	4 49.3	14 12.9	1 38.5	14 57.0	1 54.9
6 W	17 02 44	14 45 49	13♏30 50	20 18 49	15 35.8	24 48.8	18 25.4	3 05.5	24 57.2	4 56.6	14 20.0	1R38.6	14 55.6	1 55.5
7 Th	17 06 41	15 46 45	27 03 45	3♐45 19	15 24.8	26 02.4	18 37.1	3 37.6	25 15.5	5 04.0	14 27.1	1 38.5	14 54.2	1 56.0
8 F	17 10 37	16 47 42	10♐23 12	16 57 10	15 14.1	27 18.5	18 46.6	4 09.5	25 33.5	5 11.6	14 34.2	1 38.5	14 52.8	1 56.6
9 Sa	17 14 34	17 48 40	23 27 01	29 52 37	15 04.7	28 36.7	18 53.9	4 41.4	25 51.4	5 19.3	14 41.3	1 38.3	14 51.4	1 57.3
10 Su	17 18 30	18 49 39	6♑13 56	12♑31 01	14 57.5	29 56.8	18 58.8	5 13.2	26 09.0	5 27.2	14 48.5	1 38.1	14 50.1	1 57.9
11 M	17 22 27	19 50 39	18 43 59	24 53 04	14 52.8	1♐18.4	19R01.4	5 44.8	26 26.4	5 35.2	14 55.6	1 37.9	14 48.7	1 58.6
12 Tu	17 26 24	20 51 39	0♒58 32	7♒00 46	14D50.5	2 41.5	19 01.5	6 16.3	26 43.6	5 43.4	15 02.6	1 37.6	14 47.4	1 59.3
13 W	17 30 20	21 52 40	13 00 12	18 57 19	14 50.2	4 05.6	18 59.2	6 47.6	27 00.6	5 51.7	15 09.7	1 37.2	14 46.2	2 00.0
14 Th	17 34 17	22 53 42	24 52 41	0♓46 53	14 51.2	5 30.9	18 54.4	7 18.9	27 17.3	6 00.2	15 16.8	1 36.8	14 44.9	2 00.8
15 F	17 38 13	23 54 44	6♓40 32	12 34 18	14 52.4	6 57.0	18 47.1	7 50.0	27 33.9	6 08.8	15 23.9	1 36.4	14 43.7	2 01.5
16 Sa	17 42 10	24 55 46	18 28 51	24 24 52	14R53.1	8 23.9	18 37.3	8 20.9	27 50.1	6 17.6	15 30.9	1 35.8	14 42.5	2 02.3
17 Su	17 46 06	25 56 49	0♈23 00	6♈23 57	14 52.3	9 51.4	18 25.0	8 51.8	28 06.2	6 26.5	15 38.0	1 35.3	14 41.3	2 03.2
18 M	17 50 03	26 57 52	12 28 20	18 36 46	14 49.7	11 19.6	18 10.3	9 22.5	28 22.0	6 35.5	15 45.0	1 34.6	14 40.1	2 04.0
19 Tu	17 53 59	27 58 56	24 49 47	1♉07 51	14 45.1	12 48.3	17 53.0	9 53.0	28 37.5	6 44.7	15 52.0	1 33.9	14 39.0	2 04.9
20 W	17 57 56	29 00 00	7♉31 24	14 00 43	14 38.7	14 17.4	17 33.4	10 23.4	28 52.8	6 54.0	15 59.0	1 33.2	14 37.9	2 05.8
21 Th	18 01 53	0♑01 04	20 35 59	27 17 16	14 31.2	15 47.0	17 11.5	10 53.7	29 07.9	7 03.4	16 06.0	1 32.4	14 36.8	2 06.7
22 F	18 05 49	1 02 09	4♊04 30	10♊57 28	14 23.4	17 17.0	16 47.3	11 23.8	29 22.7	7 13.0	16 13.0	1 31.6	14 35.7	2 07.6
23 Sa	18 09 46	2 03 14	17 55 48	24 59 03	14 16.3	18 47.3	16 21.1	11 53.8	29 37.2	7 22.6	16 19.9	1 30.7	14 34.7	2 08.6
24 Su	18 13 42	3 04 20	2♋06 37	9♋17 47	14 10.6	20 18.0	15 52.9	12 23.7	29 51.5	7 32.5	16 26.8	1 29.7	14 33.7	2 09.5
25 M	18 17 39	4 05 26	16 31 48	23 47 53	14 06.9	21 49.0	15 22.9	12 53.3	0♎05.5	7 42.4	16 33.7	1 28.7	14 32.7	2 10.5
26 Tu	18 21 35	5 06 32	1♌05 14	8♌23 02	14D05.3	23 20.4	14 51.3	13 22.9	0 19.2	7 52.5	16 40.6	1 27.7	14 31.8	2 11.6
27 W	18 25 32	6 07 39	15 40 34	22 57 10	14 05.4	24 52.0	14 18.3	13 52.2	0 32.6	8 02.6	16 47.5	1 26.6	14 30.9	2 12.6
28 Th	18 29 29	7 08 46	0♍12 15	7♍25 18	14 06.7	26 23.9	13 44.0	14 21.4	0 45.8	8 12.9	16 54.3	1 25.4	14 30.0	2 13.7
29 F	18 33 25	8 09 54	14 35 57	21 43 52	14 08.2	27 56.2	13 08.8	14 50.4	0 58.6	8 23.3	17 01.1	1 24.2	14 29.1	2 14.8
30 Sa	18 37 22	9 11 03	28 48 49	5♎50 39	14R09.0	29 28.7	12 32.9	15 19.3	1 11.2	8 33.9	17 07.9	1 22.9	14 28.3	2 15.9
31 Su	18 41 18	10 12 11	12♎49 15	19 44 35	14 08.7	1♑01.5	11 56.5	15 48.0	1 23.4	8 44.5	17 14.7	1 21.6	14 27.5	2 17.0

Astro Data	Planet Ingress	Last Aspect	☽ Ingress	Last Aspect	☽ Ingress	☽ Phases & Eclipses	Astro Data
Dy Hr Mn	Dy Hr Mn	Dy Hr Mn	Dy Hr Mn	Dy Hr Mn	Dy Hr Mn	Dy Hr Mn	1 November 2045
☽0S 5 3:26	♀ ♑ 6 1:56	31 8:31 ♆ ⚹	♌ 1 8:54	2 3:46 ☿ ⚹	♎ 2 20:38	2 2:09 ☾ 10♌04	Julian Day # 53266
☿R 5 8:07	☿ ♏R 11 7:00	3 7:56 ♀ △	♍ 3 12:03	4 3:16 ☿ □	♏ 5 0:22	8 21:49 ● 16♏54	SVP 4♓37'00"
♇D 14 17:34	☉ ♐ 21 22:04	5 13:44 ♀ □	♎ 5 14:28	6 20:47 ☿ ☌	♐ 7 5:15	16 15:26 ☽ 24♒41	GC 27♐28.8 ⚴ 12♋39.8
☽0N 19 1:07	♂ ♎ 30 18:55	6 8:38 ♄ ⚹	♏ 7 16:54	8 11:41 ☉ ☌	♑ 9 12:14	24 11:43 ○ 2♊36	Eris 29♈44.8R ⚵ 19♍25.1
☿D 25 8:53		8 23:15 ♂ ⚹	♐ 9 20:43	11 0:32 ♀ ☌	♒ 11 22:04		⚷ 0♎58.8 ⚶ 29♋50.8
	☿ ♐ 10 12:57	11 7:03 ♂ □	♑ 12 3:23	13 18:28 ☉ ⚹	♓ 14 10:25	1 9:46 ☾ 9♍36	☽ Mean ☊ 18♒32.8
☽0S 2 8:32	☉ ♑ 21 11:35	14 6:49 ☿ ⚹	♒ 14 13:36	16 13:08 ☉ □	♈ 16 23:14	8 11:41 ● 16♐47	
♅R 6 16:02	⚳ ♎ 25 2:32	16 15:26 ☉ □	♓ 17 2:16	19 5:30 ☉ △	♉ 19 9:52	16 13:08 ☽ 24♓59	1 December 2045
♂0S 8 13:59	☿ ♑ 30 20:06	19 9:40 ☉ △	♈ 19 14:42	20 18:19 ♀ △	♊ 21 16:49	24 0:49 ○ 2♋36	Julian Day # 53296
♄⊼♆ 10 16:35		20 15:07 ♄ ☍	♉ 22 0:31	23 0:12 ☿ ☍	♋ 23 20:27	30 18:11 ☾ 9♎27	SVP 4♓36'55"
♀R 12 1:28		24 0:29 ♂ △	♊ 24 7:08	24 22:34 ♀ ☍	♌ 25 22:13		GC 27♐28.8 ⚴ 13♋26.8R
☽0N 16 8:30		26 7:07 ♂ □	♋ 26 11:22	27 15:32 ☿ △	♍ 27 23:40		Eris 29♈28.5R ⚵ 29♍39.3
☽0S 29 13:18		28 12:22 ♂ ⚹	♌ 28 14:29	29 23:48 ☿ □	♎ 30 2:01		⚷ 4♎16.1 ⚶ 2♌09.6R
		29 21:36 ☿ □	♍ 30 17:26				☽ Mean ☊ 16♒57.5

LONGITUDE — January 2046

Day	Sid.Time	☉	0 hr ☽	Noon ☽	True ☊	☿	♀	♂	⚳	♃	♄	♅	♆	♇
1 M	18 45 15	11♑13 21	26♎36 36	3♏25 19	14♒06.8	2♑34.7	11♑19.8	16♎16.5	1♎35.4	8♓55.3	17♐21.4	1♍20.3	14♉26.7	2♓18.1
2 Tu	18 49 11	12 14 31	10♏10 44	16 52 51	14R 03.3	4 08.1	10R 43.2	16 44.8	1 47.0	9 06.1	17 28.1	1R 18.9	14R 26.0	2 19.3
3 W	18 53 08	13 15 41	23 31 41	0♐07 15	13 58.7	5 41.9	10 06.9	17 12.9	1 58.3	9 17.1	17 34.7	1 17.4	14 25.2	2 20.5
4 Th	18 57 04	14 16 51	6♐39 32	13 08 33	13 53.5	7 16.1	9 31.1	17 40.8	2 09.3	9 28.2	17 41.4	1 15.9	14 24.6	2 21.7
5 F	19 01 01	15 18 02	19 34 18	25 56 49	13 48.4	8 50.5	8 56.1	18 08.6	2 20.0	9 39.4	17 48.0	1 14.4	14 23.9	2 22.9
6 Sa	19 04 58	16 19 12	2♑16 05	8♑32 10	13 44.0	10 25.4	8 22.1	18 36.1	2 30.3	9 50.7	17 54.5	1 12.8	14 23.3	2 24.1
7 Su	19 08 54	17 20 23	14 45 07	20 55 02	13 40.7	12 00.6	7 49.3	19 03.4	2 40.3	10 02.1	18 01.1	1 11.2	14 22.7	2 25.4
8 M	19 12 51	18 21 33	27 02 03	3♒06 21	13D 38.9	13 36.3	7 17.9	19 30.6	2 49.9	10 13.5	18 07.6	1 09.5	14 22.2	2 26.7
9 Tu	19 16 47	19 22 43	9♒08 06	15 07 36	13 38.4	15 12.3	6 48.2	19 57.4	2 59.2	10 25.1	18 14.0	1 07.8	14 21.7	2 28.0
10 W	19 20 44	20 23 53	21 05 07	27 01 00	13 39.0	16 48.7	6 20.2	20 24.1	3 08.1	10 36.8	18 20.4	1 06.0	14 21.2	2 29.3
11 Th	19 24 40	21 25 02	2♓55 38	8♓49 28	13 40.5	18 25.6	5 54.2	20 50.6	3 16.7	10 48.6	18 26.8	1 04.2	14 20.7	2 30.6
12 F	19 28 37	22 26 10	14 42 58	20 36 38	13 42.3	20 02.9	5 30.3	21 16.8	3 24.9	11 00.5	18 33.1	1 02.4	14 20.3	2 32.0
13 Sa	19 32 33	23 27 19	26 31 01	2♈26 41	13 43.9	21 40.7	5 08.5	21 42.8	3 32.8	11 12.4	18 39.4	1 00.5	14 19.9	2 33.3
14 Su	19 36 30	24 28 26	8♈24 13	14 24 14	13R 45.1	23 19.0	4 49.0	22 08.5	3 40.2	11 24.5	18 45.6	0 58.6	14 19.6	2 34.7
15 M	19 40 27	25 29 33	20 27 21	26 34 10	13 45.4	24 57.8	4 31.9	22 34.0	3 47.3	11 36.6	18 51.8	0 56.6	14 19.3	2 36.1
16 Tu	19 44 23	26 30 39	2♉45 17	9♉01 16	13 44.9	26 37.0	4 17.1	22 59.3	3 54.0	11 48.8	18 58.0	0 54.6	14 19.0	2 37.5
17 W	19 48 20	27 31 45	15 22 39	21 49 53	13 43.6	28 16.8	4 04.8	23 24.3	4 00.4	12 01.1	19 04.1	0 52.6	14 18.7	2 38.9
18 Th	19 52 16	28 32 50	28 23 21	5♊03 20	13 41.8	29 57.1	3 55.0	23 49.1	4 06.3	12 13.5	19 10.1	0 50.5	14 18.5	2 40.3
19 F	19 56 13	29 33 54	11♊50 01	18 43 26	13 39.8	1♒37.9	3 47.7	24 13.5	4 11.9	12 25.9	19 16.1	0 48.4	14 18.4	2 41.8
20 Sa	20 00 09	0♒34 57	25 43 27	2♋49 49	13 38.0	3 19.2	3 42.9	24 37.8	4 17.0	12 38.5	19 22.0	0 46.3	14 18.2	2 43.3
21 Su	20 04 06	1 36 00	10♋02 04	17 19 37	13 36.6	5 01.0	3D 40.6	25 01.7	4 21.8	12 51.1	19 27.9	0 44.1	14 18.1	2 44.7
22 M	20 08 02	2 37 02	24 41 43	2♌07 28	13D 35.8	6 43.3	3 40.7	25 25.4	4 26.1	13 03.8	19 33.8	0 41.9	14 18.0	2 46.2
23 Tu	20 11 59	3 38 03	9♌35 54	17 05 57	13 35.6	8 26.2	3 43.2	25 48.8	4 30.0	13 16.5	19 39.6	0 39.7	14D 18.0	2 47.7
24 W	20 15 56	4 39 03	24 36 33	2♍06 37	13 36.0	10 09.4	3 48.1	26 11.9	4 33.6	13 29.4	19 45.3	0 37.4	14 18.0	2 49.2
25 Th	20 19 52	5 40 03	9♍35 09	17 01 11	13 36.6	11 53.2	3 55.4	26 34.7	4 36.7	13 42.2	19 51.0	0 35.2	14 18.0	2 50.7
26 F	20 23 49	6 41 02	24 23 54	1♎42 37	13 37.3	13 37.3	4 04.9	26 57.3	4 39.4	13 55.2	19 56.6	0 32.8	14 18.1	2 52.3
27 Sa	20 27 45	7 42 00	8♎56 45	16 05 54	13 37.8	15 21.7	4 16.7	27 19.5	4 41.6	14 08.2	20 02.1	0 30.5	14 18.2	2 53.8
28 Su	20 31 42	8 42 58	23 09 47	0♏08 15	13R 38.1	17 06.4	4 30.6	27 41.3	4 43.5	14 21.3	20 07.6	0 28.1	14 18.3	2 55.4
29 M	20 35 38	9 43 56	7♏01 16	13 48 53	13 38.2	18 51.3	4 46.7	28 02.9	4 44.9	14 34.5	20 13.1	0 25.7	14 18.5	2 56.9
30 Tu	20 39 35	10 44 53	20 31 15	27 08 34	13 38.0	20 36.3	5 04.8	28 24.1	4 45.8	14 47.7	20 18.5	0 23.3	14 18.7	2 58.5
31 W	20 43 31	11 45 49	3♐41 05	10♐09 05	13 37.8	22 21.2	5 24.8	28 45.0	4R 46.4	15 01.0	20 23.8	0 20.9	14 18.9	3 00.1

LONGITUDE — February 2046

Day	Sid.Time	☉	0 hr ☽	Noon ☽	True ☊	☿	♀	♂	⚳	♃	♄	♅	♆	♇
1 Th	20 47 28	12♒46 44	16♐32 52	22♐52 45	13♒37.7	24♒05.9	5♑46.8	29♎05.5	4♎46.5	15♓14.4	20♐29.0	0♍18.4	14♉19.2	3♓01.7
2 F	20 51 25	13 47 39	29 09 01	5♑22 00	13D 37.7	25 50.2	6 10.6	29 25.7	4R 46.1	15 27.8	20 34.2	0R 16.0	14 19.5	3 03.3
3 Sa	20 55 21	14 48 33	11♑31 58	17 39 13	13 37.7	27 33.9	6 36.2	29 45.5	4 45.3	15 41.2	20 39.3	0 13.5	14 19.9	3 04.9
4 Su	20 59 18	15 49 26	23 44 01	29 46 36	13 37.9	29 16.7	7 03.4	0♏04.9	4 44.1	15 54.7	20 44.4	0 11.0	14 20.3	3 06.5
5 M	21 03 14	16 50 18	5♒47 15	11♒46 10	13R 38.0	0♓58.2	7 32.3	0 23.9	4 42.4	16 08.3	20 49.4	0 08.4	14 20.7	3 08.2
6 Tu	21 07 11	17 51 08	17 43 38	23 39 51	13 37.9	2 38.2	8 02.8	0 42.5	4 40.3	16 21.9	20 54.3	0 05.9	14 21.1	3 09.8
7 W	21 11 07	18 51 57	29 35 06	5♓29 37	13 37.5	4 16.3	8 34.8	1 00.8	4 37.8	16 35.6	20 59.1	0 03.3	14 21.6	3 11.4
8 Th	21 15 04	19 52 45	11♓23 40	17 17 35	13 36.9	5 51.9	9 08.2	1 18.6	4 34.8	16 49.3	21 03.9	0 00.7	14 22.1	3 13.1
9 F	21 19 00	20 53 32	23 11 38	29 06 12	13 35.9	7 24.6	9 43.0	1 36.0	4 31.3	17 03.1	21 08.6	29♌58.2	14 22.7	3 14.7
10 Sa	21 22 57	21 54 17	5♈01 37	10♈58 17	13 34.7	8 53.9	10 19.2	1 52.9	4 27.4	17 16.9	21 13.2	29 55.6	14 23.2	3 16.4
11 Su	21 26 54	22 55 01	16 56 39	22 57 09	13 33.5	10 19.0	10 56.6	2 09.5	4 23.1	17 30.7	21 17.8	29 53.0	14 23.9	3 18.0
12 M	21 30 50	23 55 43	29 00 16	5♉06 30	13 32.5	11 39.3	11 35.3	2 25.6	4 18.4	17 44.6	21 22.3	29 50.3	14 24.5	3 19.7
13 Tu	21 34 47	24 56 24	11♉16 20	17 30 20	13D 31.9	12 54.1	12 15.2	2 41.2	4 13.2	17 58.6	21 26.7	29 47.7	14 25.2	3 21.4
14 W	21 38 43	25 57 02	23 48 58	0♊12 45	13 31.8	14 02.8	12 56.2	2 56.3	4 07.6	18 12.6	21 31.0	29 45.1	14 25.9	3 23.1
15 Th	21 42 40	26 57 40	6♊42 10	13 17 38	13 32.3	15 04.5	13 38.3	3 11.0	4 01.6	18 26.6	21 35.2	29 42.5	14 26.7	3 24.7
16 F	21 46 36	27 58 15	19 59 29	26 48 01	13 33.3	15 58.7	14 21.4	3 25.2	3 55.2	18 40.6	21 39.4	29 39.8	14 27.5	3 26.4
17 Sa	21 50 33	28 58 49	3♋43 22	10♋45 34	13 34.5	16 44.5	15 05.6	3 39.0	3 48.4	18 54.7	21 43.5	29 37.2	14 28.3	3 28.1
18 Su	21 54 29	29 59 21	17 54 30	25 09 52	13 35.6	17 21.5	15 50.8	3 52.2	3 41.1	19 08.8	21 47.5	29 34.6	14 29.1	3 29.8
19 M	21 58 26	0♓59 52	2♌31 11	9♌57 47	13R 36.2	17 49.0	16 36.9	4 04.9	3 33.5	19 23.0	21 51.4	29 31.9	14 30.0	3 31.5
20 Tu	22 02 23	2 00 20	17 28 50	25 03 17	13 36.0	18 06.7	17 23.8	4 17.1	3 25.5	19 37.1	21 55.3	29 29.3	14 31.0	3 33.2
21 W	22 06 19	3 00 47	2♍40 02	10♍17 49	13 34.7	18R 14.3	18 11.7	4 28.7	3 17.1	19 51.3	21 59.0	29 26.7	14 31.9	3 34.8
22 Th	22 10 16	4 01 13	17 55 21	25 31 20	13 32.5	18 11.8	19 00.4	4 39.9	3 08.3	20 05.6	22 02.7	29 24.1	14 32.9	3 36.5
23 F	22 14 12	5 01 36	3♎04 34	10♎33 55	13 29.7	17 59.2	19 49.9	4 50.4	2 59.2	20 19.8	22 06.3	29 21.4	14 33.9	3 38.2
24 Sa	22 18 09	6 01 59	17 58 24	25 17 13	13 26.6	17 37.0	20 40.2	5 00.4	2 49.7	20 34.1	22 09.8	29 18.8	14 34.9	3 39.9
25 Su	22 22 05	7 02 20	2♏29 46	9♏35 38	13 23.9	17 05.6	21 31.2	5 09.8	2 39.8	20 48.4	22 13.2	29 16.2	14 36.0	3 41.6
26 M	22 26 02	8 02 40	16 34 34	23 26 33	13 22.0	16 25.9	22 23.0	5 18.6	2 29.6	21 02.8	22 16.5	29 13.6	14 37.1	3 43.3
27 Tu	22 29 58	9 02 58	0♐11 40	6♐50 09	13D 21.2	15 38.9	23 15.4	5 26.8	2 19.1	21 17.1	22 19.8	29 11.0	14 38.2	3 44.9
28 W	22 33 55	10 03 15	13 22 21	19 48 40	13 21.6	14 45.8	24 08.5	5 34.4	2 08.3	21 31.5	22 22.9	29 08.5	14 39.4	3 46.6

Astro Data	Dy Hr Mn
☽ 0N	12 15:34
♀ D	21 22:58
♆ D	24 3:37
☽ 0S	25 20:36
♃⚹♆	28 6:26
⚳ R	1 5:17
☽ 0N	8 22:14
☿ R	21 18:02
☽ 0S	22 7:00

Planet Ingress	Dy Hr Mn
☿ ♒	18 12:42
☉ ♒	19 22:16
♂ ♏	4 5:56
☿ ♓	4 22:12
♅ ♌R	8 18:53
☉ ♓	18 12:15

Last Aspect Dy Hr Mn		☽ Ingress	Dy Hr Mn
31 7:37	♄ ⚹	♏	1 5:58
2 7:37	♆ ☍	♐	3 11:47
4 20:47	♂ ⚹	♑	5 19:41
7 8:14	♂ □	♒	8 5:51
9 22:06	♂ △	♓	10 18:03
12 16:04	☉ ⚹	♈	13 7:03
15 9:42	☉ □	♉	15 18:40
18 1:30	☿ △	♊	18 2:55
19 21:44	♂ △	♋	20 7:14
22 0:53	♂ □	♌	22 8:35
24 2:18	♂ ⚹	♍	24 8:37
25 16:37	♄ □	♎	26 9:11
28 7:39	♂ ☌	♏	28 11:46
29 22:22	☿ □	♐	30 17:13

Last Aspect Dy Hr Mn		☽ Ingress	Dy Hr Mn
2 0:13	♂ ⚹	♑	2 1:38
3 8:04	♃ ⚹	♒	4 12:27
6 6:23	♄ ⚹	♓	7 0:51
8 19:43	♄ □	♈	9 13:49
12 1:41	♅ △	♉	12 1:58
14 11:09	♅ □	♊	14 11:36
16 16:58	♅ ⚹	♋	16 17:34
18 1:54	♃ △	♌	18 19:54
20 18:58	♅ ☌	♍	20 19:48
22 6:29	♄ □	♎	22 19:06
24 18:40	♅ ⚹	♏	24 19:49
26 22:14	♅ □	♐	26 23:39

☽ Phases & Eclipses Dy Hr Mn	
7 4:24	● 17♑01
15 9:42	☽ 25♈24
22 12:51	○ 2♌39
22 13:01	◐ P 0.053
29 4:11	☾ 9♏24
5 23:09	● 17♒19
5 23:04:57	◐ A 09'16"
14 3:20	☽ 25♉35
20 23:44	○ 2♍30
27 16:23	☾ 9♐14

Astro Data

1 January 2046
Julian Day # 53327
SVP 4♓36'50"
GC 27♐28.9 ⚴ 4♋50.3R
Eris 29♈18.5R ⚵ 6♎55.2
⚷ 6♎16.9 ⚶ 27♋53.2R
☽ Mean ☊ 15♒19.0

1 February 2046
Julian Day # 53358
SVP 4♓36'44"
GC 27♐29.0 ⚴ 28♊31.2R
Eris 29♈18.7 ⚵ 9♎03.6R
⚷ 6♎28.2R ⚶ 20♋04.6R
☽ Mean ☊ 13♒40.6

March 2046 — LONGITUDE

Day	Sid.Time	☉	0 hr ☽	Noon ☽	True ☊	☿	♀	♂	⚳	♃	♄	♅	♆	♇
1 Th	22 37 52	11♓03 31	26♐09 35	2♑25 37	13♒22.8	13♓48.1	25♑02.2	5♏41.4	1♎57.1	21♓45.9	22♐26.0	29♌05.9	14♉40.6	3♓48.3
2 F	22 41 48	12 03 45	8♑37 16	14 45 06	13 24.6	12R 47.2	25 56.5	5 47.7	1R 45.7	22 00.3	22 29.0	29R 03.3	14 41.8	3 50.0
3 Sa	22 45 45	13 03 57	20 49 37	26 51 20	13 26.3	11 44.6	26 51.4	5 53.4	1 34.0	22 14.8	22 31.9	29 00.8	14 43.1	3 51.6
4 Su	22 49 41	14 04 08	2♒50 44	8♒48 16	13R 27.3	10 41.9	27 46.9	5 58.4	1 22.1	22 29.2	22 34.7	28 58.3	14 44.4	3 53.3
5 M	22 53 38	15 04 17	14 44 22	20 39 24	13 27.2	9 40.5	28 42.9	6 02.7	1 09.8	22 43.7	22 37.4	28 55.8	14 45.7	3 55.0
6 Tu	22 57 34	16 04 24	26 33 43	2♓27 40	13 25.4	8 41.6	29 39.4	6 06.3	0 57.4	22 58.2	22 40.0	28 53.3	14 47.0	3 56.6
7 W	23 01 31	17 04 30	8♓21 31	14 15 33	13 21.9	7 46.5	0♒36.4	6 09.3	0 44.7	23 12.6	22 42.5	28 50.8	14 48.4	3 58.3
8 Th	23 05 27	18 04 33	20 10 00	26 05 07	13 16.8	6 56.1	1 33.9	6 11.5	0 31.9	23 27.1	22 44.9	28 48.3	14 49.8	3 59.9
9 F	23 09 24	19 04 35	2♈01 06	7♈58 11	13 10.4	6 11.0	2 31.8	6 13.0	0 18.8	23 41.6	22 47.2	28 45.9	14 51.2	4 01.6
10 Sa	23 13 21	20 04 35	13 56 35	19 56 31	13 03.4	5 31.9	3 30.2	6R 13.8	0 05.6	23 56.2	22 49.5	28 43.5	14 52.6	4 03.2
11 Su	23 17 17	21 04 33	25 58 15	2♉02 01	12 56.4	4 59.1	4 29.0	6 13.9	29♍52.2	24 10.7	22 51.6	28 41.1	14 54.1	4 04.8
12 M	23 21 14	22 04 28	8♉08 08	14 16 53	12 50.1	4 32.8	5 28.2	6 13.2	29 38.8	24 25.2	22 53.7	28 38.8	14 55.6	4 06.4
13 Tu	23 25 10	23 04 22	20 28 37	26 43 41	12 45.3	4 13.1	6 27.8	6 11.8	29 25.2	24 39.7	22 55.6	28 36.4	14 57.1	4 08.1
14 W	23 29 07	24 04 13	3♊02 27	9♊25 21	12 42.3	3 59.9	7 27.8	6 09.6	29 11.5	24 54.3	22 57.4	28 34.1	14 58.7	4 09.7
15 Th	23 33 03	25 04 03	15 52 45	22 25 04	12D 41.1	3D 53.1	8 28.1	6 06.7	28 57.7	25 08.8	22 59.2	28 31.8	15 00.3	4 11.3
16 F	23 37 00	26 03 50	29 02 42	5♋45 58	12 41.5	3 52.5	9 28.8	6 03.1	28 43.9	25 23.3	23 00.8	28 29.6	15 01.9	4 12.9
17 Sa	23 40 56	27 03 35	12♋35 12	19 30 36	12 42.7	3 57.9	10 29.8	5 58.6	28 30.1	25 37.8	23 02.4	28 27.4	15 03.5	4 14.4
18 Su	23 44 53	28 03 17	26 32 17	3♌40 15	12R 43.9	4 09.1	11 31.2	5 53.4	28 16.2	25 52.3	23 03.9	28 25.2	15 05.2	4 16.0
19 M	23 48 50	29 02 57	10♌54 20	18 14 12	12 44.0	4 25.6	12 32.9	5 47.5	28 02.3	26 06.9	23 05.2	28 23.0	15 06.8	4 17.6
20 Tu	23 52 46	0♈02 35	25 39 20	3♍09 01	12 42.4	4 47.3	13 34.9	5 40.8	27 48.5	26 21.4	23 06.5	28 20.9	15 08.5	4 19.1
21 W	23 56 43	1 02 11	10♍42 20	18 18 13	12 38.6	5 13.9	14 37.2	5 33.3	27 34.7	26 35.9	23 07.6	28 18.8	15 10.2	4 20.7
22 Th	0 00 39	2 01 44	25 55 26	3♎32 41	12 32.7	5 45.0	15 39.8	5 25.0	27 20.9	26 50.4	23 08.7	28 16.7	15 12.0	4 22.2
23 F	0 04 36	3 01 16	11♎08 38	18 41 56	12 25.2	6 20.5	16 42.7	5 16.0	27 07.3	27 04.8	23 09.6	28 14.7	15 13.7	4 23.7
24 Sa	0 08 32	4 00 46	26 11 22	3♏35 49	12 17.1	7 00.0	17 45.8	5 06.2	26 53.7	27 19.3	23 10.5	28 12.7	15 15.5	4 25.2
25 Su	0 12 29	5 00 13	10♏54 21	18 06 15	12 09.4	7 43.4	18 49.3	4 55.7	26 40.2	27 33.8	23 11.3	28 10.7	15 17.3	4 26.7
26 M	0 16 25	5 59 40	25 11 01	2♐08 21	12 03.1	8 30.3	19 52.9	4 44.4	26 26.8	27 48.2	23 11.9	28 08.8	15 19.2	4 28.2
27 Tu	0 20 22	6 59 04	8♐58 11	15 40 36	11 58.7	9 20.6	20 56.9	4 32.3	26 13.6	28 02.7	23 12.5	28 06.9	15 21.0	4 29.7
28 W	0 24 19	7 58 27	22 15 51	28 44 21	11D 56.5	10 14.1	22 01.1	4 19.5	26 00.5	28 17.1	23 13.0	28 05.1	15 22.9	4 31.1
29 Th	0 28 15	8 57 47	5♑06 35	11♑23 05	11 56.1	11 10.7	23 05.5	4 06.0	25 47.6	28 31.5	23 13.3	28 03.3	15 24.8	4 32.6
30 F	0 32 12	9 57 07	17 34 30	23 41 28	11 56.7	12 10.0	24 10.1	3 51.8	25 34.9	28 45.9	23 13.6	28 01.5	15 26.7	4 34.0
31 Sa	0 36 08	10 56 24	29 44 38	5♒44 39	11R 57.5	13 12.1	25 15.0	3 36.8	25 22.4	29 00.3	23 13.8	27 59.8	15 28.6	4 35.4

April 2046 — LONGITUDE

Day	Sid.Time	☉	0 hr ☽	Noon ☽	True ☊	☿	♀	♂	⚳	♃	♄	♅	♆	♇
1 Su	0 40 05	11♈55 39	11♒42 11	17♒37 48	11♒57.5	14♓16.7	26♒20.0	3♏21.2	25♍10.2	29♓14.6	23♐13.8	27♌58.1	15♉30.5	4♓36.8
2 M	0 44 01	12 54 53	23 32 07	29 25 39	11R 55.8	15 23.8	27 25.3	3R 04.9	24R 58.1	29 28.9	23R 13.8	27R 56.5	15 32.5	4 38.2
3 Tu	0 47 58	13 54 04	5♓18 55	11♓12 20	11 51.7	16 33.2	28 30.8	2 47.9	24 46.3	29 43.2	23 13.6	27 54.9	15 34.4	4 39.6
4 W	0 51 54	14 53 14	17 06 19	23 01 14	11 44.9	17 44.8	29 36.4	2 30.3	24 34.8	29 57.5	23 13.4	27 53.3	15 36.4	4 41.0
5 Th	0 55 51	15 52 22	28 57 21	4♈54 58	11 35.6	18 58.6	0♓42.2	2 12.1	24 23.5	0♈11.8	23 13.1	27 51.8	15 38.4	4 42.3
6 F	0 59 47	16 51 28	10♈54 15	16 55 25	11 24.3	20 14.4	1 48.2	1 53.4	24 12.6	0 26.0	23 12.6	27 50.3	15 40.4	4 43.6
7 Sa	1 03 44	17 50 32	22 58 37	29 03 56	11 11.8	21 32.3	2 54.4	1 34.1	24 01.9	0 40.2	23 12.1	27 48.9	15 42.5	4 44.9
8 Su	1 07 41	18 49 33	5♉11 31	11♉21 27	10 59.4	22 52.0	4 00.7	1 14.3	23 51.6	0 54.4	23 11.4	27 47.5	15 44.5	4 46.2
9 M	1 11 37	19 48 33	17 33 50	23 48 47	10 48.0	24 13.6	5 07.2	0 54.1	23 41.6	1 08.5	23 10.7	27 46.2	15 46.6	4 47.5
10 Tu	1 15 34	20 47 31	0♊06 25	6♊26 53	10 38.6	25 37.0	6 13.8	0 33.4	23 31.9	1 22.6	23 09.9	27 44.9	15 48.7	4 48.8
11 W	1 19 30	21 46 26	12 50 22	19 17 04	10 31.9	27 02.2	7 20.6	0 12.3	23 22.6	1 36.7	23 09.0	27 43.7	15 50.8	4 50.0
12 Th	1 23 27	22 45 19	25 47 12	2♋21 02	10 27.9	28 29.2	8 27.5	29♎50.9	23 13.6	1 50.8	23 07.9	27 42.5	15 52.9	4 51.3
13 F	1 27 23	23 44 10	8♋58 49	15 40 50	10D 26.3	29 57.9	9 34.6	29 29.1	23 05.0	2 04.8	23 06.8	27 41.4	15 55.0	4 52.5
14 Sa	1 31 20	24 42 59	22 27 19	29 18 32	10R 26.1	1♈28.2	10 41.8	29 07.1	22 56.8	2 18.8	23 05.6	27 40.3	15 57.1	4 53.7
15 Su	1 35 17	25 41 45	6♌14 39	13♌15 47	10 26.3	3 00.3	11 49.1	28 44.9	22 48.9	2 32.7	23 04.3	27 39.3	15 59.2	4 54.8
16 M	1 39 13	26 40 29	20 21 56	27 33 00	10 25.4	4 34.0	12 56.6	28 22.4	22 41.5	2 46.6	23 02.9	27 38.3	16 01.4	4 56.0
17 Tu	1 43 10	27 39 11	4♍48 44	12♍08 44	10 22.5	6 09.3	14 04.1	27 59.9	22 34.4	3 00.4	23 01.4	27 37.3	16 03.6	4 57.1
18 W	1 47 06	28 37 50	19 32 23	26 58 58	10 16.8	7 46.3	15 11.8	27 37.2	22 27.7	3 14.2	22 59.8	27 36.5	16 05.7	4 58.2
19 Th	1 51 03	29 36 27	4♎27 34	11♎57 07	10 08.6	9 25.0	16 19.6	27 14.5	22 21.4	3 28.0	22 58.1	27 35.6	16 07.9	4 59.3
20 F	1 54 59	0♉35 03	19 26 30	26 54 30	9 58.2	11 05.2	17 27.6	26 51.7	22 15.6	3 41.7	22 56.3	27 34.8	16 10.1	5 00.4
21 Sa	1 58 56	1 33 36	4♏19 59	11♏41 47	9 46.9	12 47.2	18 35.6	26 29.0	22 10.1	3 55.4	22 54.5	27 34.1	16 12.3	5 01.5
22 Su	2 02 52	2 32 07	18 58 55	26 10 30	9 35.8	14 30.8	19 43.8	26 06.3	22 05.0	4 09.1	22 52.5	27 33.4	16 14.5	5 02.5
23 M	2 06 49	3 30 37	3♐15 51	10♐14 30	9 26.3	16 16.1	20 52.1	25 43.8	22 00.4	4 22.6	22 50.5	27 32.8	16 16.7	5 03.5
24 Tu	2 10 45	4 29 06	17 06 09	23 50 42	9 19.1	18 03.0	22 00.5	25 21.4	21 56.1	4 36.2	22 48.4	27 32.2	16 18.9	5 04.5
25 W	2 14 42	5 27 32	0♑28 14	6♑59 00	9 14.4	19 51.6	23 08.9	24 59.2	21 52.3	4 49.7	22 46.2	27 31.7	16 21.1	5 05.5
26 Th	2 18 39	6 25 57	13 23 21	19 41 46	9 12.1	21 42.0	24 17.5	24 37.3	21 48.9	5 03.1	22 43.9	27 31.2	16 23.3	5 06.5
27 F	2 22 35	7 24 20	25 54 49	2♒03 07	9 11.5	23 34.0	25 26.2	24 15.6	21 45.9	5 16.5	22 41.5	27 30.8	16 25.6	5 07.4
28 Sa	2 26 32	8 22 42	8♒07 20	14 08 08	9 11.4	25 27.7	26 35.0	23 54.3	21 43.3	5 29.8	22 39.0	27 30.4	16 27.8	5 08.3
29 Su	2 30 28	9 21 02	20 06 13	26 02 17	9 10.9	27 23.0	27 43.9	23 33.3	21 41.2	5 43.1	22 36.5	27 30.1	16 30.1	5 09.2
30 M	2 34 25	10 19 20	1♓56 58	7♓50 57	9 08.7	29 20.1	28 52.9	23 12.7	21 39.4	5 56.3	22 33.9	27 29.9	16 32.3	5 10.1

Astro Data	Dy Hr Mn
♃□♄	4 23:09
☽0N	8 4:33
♂R	11 2:10
☿D	16 2:11
☉0N	20 10:58
☽0S	21 18:26
♃⊼♅	27 18:17
♄R	1 14:46
☽0N	4 10:39
♃∠♆	7 16:29
♃0N	15 4:42
☿0N	17 8:13
☽0S	18 4:18
♃⊻♇	26 18:26

Planet Ingress		Dy Hr Mn
♀	♒	6 20:42
⚳	♍R	10 22:05
☉	♈	20 10:58
♃	♈	4 16:10
♀	♓	4 20:37
♂	♎R	12 1:51
☿	♈	13 12:34
☉	♉	19 21:39
☿	♉	30 20:06

Last Aspect Dy Hr Mn			☽ Ingress	Dy Hr Mn
1 5:38	♅	△	♑	1 7:20
3 12:00	♀	☌	♒	3 18:17
6 4:45	♅	☍	♓	6 7:00
8 6:33	♃	☌	♈	8 19:55
11 5:24	♅	△	♉	11 7:59
13 15:34	♅	□	♊	13 18:14
15 23:03	♅	⚹	♋	16 1:43
18 1:51	☉	△	♌	18 5:51
20 4:20	♅	☌	♍	20 6:58
22 1:16	♃	☍	♎	22 6:25
24 3:17	♅	⚹	♏	24 6:09
26 5:06	♅	□	♐	26 8:17
28 11:08	♃	□	♑	28 14:22
30 22:15	♃	⚹	♒	31 0:31

Last Aspect Dy Hr Mn			☽ Ingress	Dy Hr Mn
2 8:59	♅	☍	♓	2 13:10
4 12:25	♄	□	♈	5 2:06
7 9:33	♅	△	♉	7 13:50
9 19:33	♅	□	♊	9 23:48
12 7:34	♂	△	♋	12 7:43
14 11:41	♂	□	♌	14 13:12
16 13:20	♂	⚹	♍	16 16:04
18 5:36	♄	□	♎	18 16:51
20 13:05	♅	⚹	♏	20 16:59
22 14:20	♅	□	♐	22 18:27
24 18:39	♅	△	♑	24 23:08
26 21:45	♀	⚹	♒	27 7:58
29 15:16	☿	⚹	♓	29 20:02

☽ Phases & Eclipses Dy Hr Mn	
7 18:15	● 17♓20
15 17:13	☽ 25♊17
22 9:27	○ 1♎55
29 6:57	☾ 8♑45
6 11:51	● 16♈51
14 3:21	☽ 24♋22
20 18:21	○ 0♏51
27 23:30	☾ 7♒52

Astro Data

1 March 2046
Julian Day # 53386
SVP 4♓36'40"
GC 27♐29.0 ⚴ 1♋39.0
Eris 29♈27.7 ⚵ 5♎34.6R
⚷ 5♎08.2R ⚶ 16♋36.1R
☽ Mean ☊ 12♒11.6

1 April 2046
Julian Day # 53417
SVP 4♓36'37"
GC 27♐29.1 ⚴ 11♋33.9
Eris 29♈44.9 ⚵ 28♍17.9R
⚷ 2♎46.2R ⚶ 19♋22.2
☽ Mean ☊ 10♒33.1

LONGITUDE May 2046

Day	Sid.Time	☉	0 hr ☽	Noon ☽	True ☊	☿	♀	♂	⚳	♃	♄	♅	♆	♇
1 Tu	2 38 21	11♉17 37	13♓44 49	19♓39 07	9♒04.2	1♉18.8	0♈01.9	22♎52.6	21♍38.1	6♈09.5	22♐31.2	27♌29.7	16♉34.5	5♓10.9
2 W	2 42 18	12 15 53	25 34 24	1♈31 06	8R57.0	3 19.2	1 11.0	22R32.9	21R37.2	6 22.6	22R28.4	27R29.5	16 36.8	5 11.7
3 Th	2 46 14	13 14 06	7♈29 39	13 30 23	8 47.1	5 21.1	2 20.2	22 13.8	21D36.7	6 35.7	22 25.5	27 29.4	16 39.1	5 12.5
4 F	2 50 11	14 12 19	19 33 35	25 39 28	8 35.0	7 24.5	3 29.5	21 55.2	21 36.6	6 48.6	22 22.6	27D29.4	16 41.3	5 13.3
5 Sa	2 54 08	15 10 29	1♉48 13	7♉59 56	8 21.7	9 29.4	4 38.9	21 37.2	21 36.9	7 01.6	22 19.6	27 29.4	16 43.6	5 14.1
6 Su	2 58 04	16 08 38	14 14 41	20 32 28	8 08.2	11 35.7	5 48.3	21 19.8	21 37.7	7 14.4	22 16.5	27 29.4	16 45.8	5 14.8
7 M	3 02 01	17 06 46	26 53 17	3♊17 05	7 55.9	13 43.1	6 57.8	21 03.1	21 38.9	7 27.2	22 13.3	27 29.6	16 48.1	5 15.5
8 Tu	3 05 57	18 04 51	9♊43 48	16 13 24	7 45.7	15 51.6	8 07.4	20 47.0	21 40.4	7 39.9	22 10.1	27 29.7	16 50.3	5 16.2
9 W	3 09 54	19 02 55	22 45 50	29 21 03	7 38.3	18 01.0	9 17.1	20 31.6	21 42.4	7 52.6	22 06.8	27 30.0	16 52.6	5 16.9
10 Th	3 13 50	20 00 57	5♋59 02	12♋39 50	7 33.7	20 11.1	10 26.8	20 17.0	21 44.8	8 05.2	22 03.4	27 30.2	16 54.9	5 17.5
11 F	3 17 47	20 58 57	19 23 27	26 09 59	7D31.7	22 21.6	11 36.5	20 03.0	21 47.6	8 17.7	22 00.0	27 30.6	16 57.1	5 18.1
12 Sa	3 21 43	21 56 56	2♌59 30	9♌52 04	7R31.4	24 32.4	12 46.4	19 49.9	21 50.7	8 30.1	21 56.5	27 31.0	16 59.4	5 18.7
13 Su	3 25 40	22 54 52	16 47 47	23 46 42	7 31.5	26 43.1	13 56.2	19 37.4	21 54.3	8 42.5	21 53.0	27 31.4	17 01.6	5 19.3
14 M	3 29 37	23 52 47	0♍48 48	7♍54 03	7 30.9	28 53.5	15 06.2	19 25.8	21 58.3	8 54.8	21 49.4	27 31.9	17 03.9	5 19.8
15 Tu	3 33 33	24 50 39	15 02 17	22 13 16	7 28.4	1♊03.2	16 16.2	19 14.9	22 02.6	9 07.0	21 45.7	27 32.5	17 06.1	5 20.4
16 W	3 37 30	25 48 30	29 26 39	6♎41 58	7 23.5	3 12.1	17 26.2	19 04.8	22 07.3	9 19.1	21 42.0	27 33.1	17 08.3	5 20.9
17 Th	3 41 26	26 46 19	13♎58 37	21 15 55	7 16.1	5 19.7	18 36.3	18 55.5	22 12.4	9 31.2	21 38.2	27 33.7	17 10.6	5 21.3
18 F	3 45 23	27 44 07	28 33 05	5♏49 16	7 06.7	7 26.0	19 46.5	18 47.1	22 17.8	9 43.1	21 34.4	27 34.4	17 12.8	5 21.8
19 Sa	3 49 19	28 41 53	13♏03 37	20 15 14	6 56.3	9 30.5	20 56.7	18 39.4	22 23.6	9 55.0	21 30.6	27 35.2	17 15.0	5 22.2
20 Su	3 53 16	29 39 38	27 23 19	4♐27 08	6 46.1	11 33.1	22 07.0	18 32.5	22 29.8	10 06.8	21 26.6	27 36.0	17 17.3	5 22.6
21 M	3 57 12	0♊37 21	11♐26 03	18 19 34	6 37.2	13 33.6	23 17.3	18 26.4	22 36.3	10 18.5	21 22.7	27 36.9	17 19.5	5 23.0
22 Tu	4 01 09	1 35 03	25 07 20	1♑49 08	6 30.4	15 31.8	24 27.7	18 21.2	22 43.2	10 30.2	21 18.7	27 37.8	17 21.7	5 23.3
23 W	4 05 06	2 32 44	8♑24 55	14 54 45	6 26.0	17 27.5	25 38.1	18 16.7	22 50.4	10 41.7	21 14.6	27 38.8	17 23.9	5 23.7
24 Th	4 09 02	3 30 24	21 18 51	27 37 33	6D24.0	19 20.7	26 48.6	18 13.0	22 57.9	10 53.2	21 10.5	27 39.8	17 26.1	5 24.0
25 F	4 12 59	4 28 03	3♒51 15	10♒00 27	6 23.7	21 11.2	27 59.2	18 10.1	23 05.8	11 04.5	21 06.4	27 40.9	17 28.3	5 24.3
26 Sa	4 16 55	5 25 40	16 05 43	22 07 38	6 24.3	22 58.9	29 09.8	18 08.1	23 14.1	11 15.8	21 02.2	27 42.0	17 30.4	5 24.5
27 Su	4 20 52	6 23 17	28 06 51	4♓04 02	6R24.9	24 43.8	0♉20.4	18 06.8	23 22.6	11 27.0	20 58.0	27 43.2	17 32.6	5 24.7
28 M	4 24 48	7 20 53	9♓59 49	15 54 53	6 24.5	26 25.8	1 31.1	18D06.3	23 31.5	11 38.1	20 53.8	27 44.4	17 34.8	5 24.9
29 Tu	4 28 45	8 18 28	21 49 53	27 45 26	6 22.4	28 04.8	2 41.9	18 06.5	23 40.6	11 49.1	20 49.5	27 45.7	17 36.9	5 25.1
30 W	4 32 42	9 16 02	3♈42 08	9♈40 33	6 18.2	29 40.9	3 52.6	18 07.6	23 50.1	12 00.0	20 45.3	27 47.0	17 39.0	5 25.3
31 Th	4 36 38	10 13 35	15 41 12	21 44 31	6 11.8	1♋14.0	5 03.5	18 09.4	24 00.0	12 10.7	20 40.9	27 48.4	17 41.2	5 25.4

LONGITUDE June 2046

Day	Sid.Time	☉	0 hr ☽	Noon ☽	True ☊	☿	♀	♂	⚳	♃	♄	♅	♆	♇
1 F	4 40 35	11♊11 07	27♈50 55	4♉00 43	6♒03.6	2♋44.0	6♉14.4	18♎12.0	24♍10.1	12♈21.4	20♐36.6	27♌49.8	17♉43.3	5♓25.5
2 Sa	4 44 31	12 08 38	10♉14 12	16 31 33	5R54.4	4 11.0	7 25.3	18 15.3	24 20.5	12 32.0	20R32.2	27 51.3	17 45.4	5 25.6
3 Su	4 48 28	13 06 09	22 52 51	29 18 10	5 44.9	5 34.8	8 36.2	18 19.4	24 31.2	12 42.5	20 27.9	27 52.8	17 47.5	5 25.6
4 M	4 52 24	14 03 38	5♊47 27	12♊20 37	5 36.3	6 55.6	9 47.2	18 24.3	24 42.2	12 52.9	20 23.5	27 54.4	17 49.5	5R25.7
5 Tu	4 56 21	15 01 07	18 57 30	25 37 55	5 29.2	8 13.1	10 58.3	18 29.8	24 53.5	13 03.1	20 19.1	27 56.0	17 51.6	5 25.7
6 W	5 00 17	15 58 35	2♋21 37	9♋08 21	5 24.2	9 27.4	12 09.4	18 36.1	25 05.1	13 13.3	20 14.7	27 57.7	17 53.7	5 25.7
7 Th	5 04 14	16 56 02	15 57 53	22 49 55	5D21.5	10 38.3	13 20.5	18 43.1	25 17.0	13 23.3	20 10.2	27 59.4	17 55.7	5 25.6
8 F	5 08 11	17 53 27	29 44 14	6♌40 36	5 20.8	11 46.0	14 31.6	18 50.8	25 29.1	13 33.2	20 05.8	28 01.2	17 57.7	5 25.6
9 Sa	5 12 07	18 50 52	13♌38 49	20 38 40	5 21.5	12 50.2	15 42.8	18 59.2	25 41.5	13 43.0	20 01.4	28 03.0	17 59.7	5 25.5
10 Su	5 16 04	19 48 15	27 40 01	4♍42 41	5 22.7	13 51.0	16 54.0	19 08.2	25 54.2	13 52.7	19 56.9	28 04.9	18 01.7	5 25.3
11 M	5 20 00	20 45 37	11♍46 30	18 51 20	5R23.4	14 48.2	18 05.3	19 17.9	26 07.1	14 02.3	19 52.5	28 06.8	18 03.7	5 25.2
12 Tu	5 23 57	21 42 58	25 56 57	3♎03 10	5 22.8	15 41.7	19 16.6	19 28.3	26 20.3	14 11.8	19 48.0	28 08.7	18 05.6	5 25.0
13 W	5 27 53	22 40 18	10♎09 42	17 16 16	5 20.6	16 31.6	20 27.9	19 39.3	26 33.7	14 21.1	19 43.6	28 10.7	18 07.6	5 24.8
14 Th	5 31 50	23 37 37	24 22 30	1♏28 00	5 16.6	17 17.6	21 39.2	19 51.0	26 47.4	14 30.3	19 39.2	28 12.8	18 09.5	5 24.6
15 F	5 35 46	24 34 55	8♏32 21	15 35 04	5 11.2	17 59.6	22 50.6	20 03.2	27 01.3	14 39.4	19 34.7	28 14.9	18 11.4	5 24.4
16 Sa	5 39 43	25 32 13	22 35 39	29 33 38	5 05.1	18 37.7	24 02.0	20 16.1	27 15.5	14 48.3	19 30.3	28 17.0	18 13.3	5 24.1
17 Su	5 43 40	26 29 29	6♐28 32	13♐19 56	4 59.0	19 11.6	25 13.5	20 29.6	27 29.9	14 57.2	19 25.9	28 19.2	18 15.2	5 23.8
18 M	5 47 36	27 26 45	20 07 25	26 50 41	4 53.8	19 41.3	26 25.0	20 43.6	27 44.5	15 05.9	19 21.6	28 21.4	18 17.0	5 23.5
19 Tu	5 51 33	28 24 01	3♑29 29	10♑03 40	4 49.9	20 06.7	27 36.6	20 58.2	27 59.4	15 14.4	19 17.2	28 23.7	18 18.9	5 23.2
20 W	5 55 29	29 21 16	16 33 08	22 57 57	4D47.6	20 27.7	28 48.1	21 13.4	28 14.4	15 22.9	19 12.9	28 26.0	18 20.7	5 22.8
21 Th	5 59 26	0♋18 31	29 18 11	5♒34 03	4 47.0	20 44.2	29 59.8	21 29.1	28 29.7	15 31.2	19 08.6	28 28.3	18 22.5	5 22.5
22 F	6 03 22	1 15 45	11♒45 49	17 53 50	4 47.6	20 56.2	1♊11.4	21 45.3	28 45.2	15 39.4	19 04.3	28 30.7	18 24.3	5 22.1
23 Sa	6 07 19	2 12 59	23 58 31	0♓00 18	4 49.1	21 03.6	2 23.1	22 02.1	29 00.9	15 47.4	19 00.0	28 33.1	18 26.0	5 21.6
24 Su	6 11 15	3 10 13	5♓59 44	11 57 19	4 50.8	21R06.5	3 34.8	22 19.4	29 16.8	15 55.3	18 55.7	28 35.6	18 27.7	5 21.2
25 M	6 15 12	4 07 26	17 53 40	23 49 22	4R52.2	21 04.8	4 46.6	22 37.2	29 33.0	16 03.0	18 51.5	28 38.1	18 29.5	5 20.7
26 Tu	6 19 09	5 04 40	29 45 01	5♈41 14	4 52.7	20 58.6	5 58.4	22 55.5	29 49.3	16 10.7	18 47.3	28 40.6	18 31.1	5 20.2
27 W	6 23 05	6 01 53	11♈38 38	17 37 48	4 52.0	20 47.9	7 10.3	23 14.3	0♎05.8	16 18.1	18 43.2	28 43.2	18 32.8	5 19.7
28 Th	6 27 02	6 59 07	23 39 20	29 43 45	4 50.1	20 33.0	8 22.1	23 33.6	0 22.5	16 25.4	18 39.1	28 45.8	18 34.5	5 19.2
29 F	6 30 58	7 56 21	5♉51 34	12♉03 15	4 47.2	20 14.1	9 34.1	23 53.3	0 39.4	16 32.6	18 35.0	28 48.5	18 36.1	5 18.6
30 Sa	6 34 55	8 53 34	18 19 11	24 39 41	4 43.6	19 51.3	10 46.0	24 13.5	0 56.5	16 39.6	18 31.0	28 51.2	18 37.7	5 18.0

Astro Data

	Dy Hr Mn
☽0N	1 16:52
⚳D	4 4:27
♀0N	4 12:53
♅D	4 19:52
☽0S	15 11:19
♂D	28 15:31
☽0N	28 23:31
♃□♅	4 16:14
♇R	5 7:26
☽0S	11 16:17
☿R	24 14:58
☽0N	25 6:44
♄⚻♆	29 7:26

Planet Ingress

		Dy Hr Mn
♀	♈	1 11:20
☿	♊	15 0:17
☉	♊	20 20:28
♀	♉	27 5:04
☿	♋	30 16:51
☉	♋	21 4:14
♀	♊	21 12:05
⚳	♎	27 3:37

Last Aspect / ☽ Ingress

Last Aspect Dy Hr Mn		☽ Ingress	Dy Hr Mn
1 17:48	♄ □	♈	2 8:56
4 15:35	♅ △	♉	4 20:29
7 1:08	♅ □	♊	7 5:51
9 8:38	♅ ⚹	♋	9 13:11
11 3:59	☿ ⚹	♌	11 18:45
13 18:24	♅ ☌	♍	13 22:37
15 16:41	☉ △	♎	16 0:55
17 22:23	♅ ⚹	♏	18 2:23
20 3:15	☉ ☍	♐	20 4:25
22 4:28	♅ △	♑	22 8:43
24 10:17	♀ △	♒	24 16:33
27 3:39	♀ ⚹	♓	27 3:48
29 12:45	☿ □	♈	29 16:32

Last Aspect / ☽ Ingress

Last Aspect Dy Hr Mn		☽ Ingress	Dy Hr Mn
31 23:56	♅ △	♉	1 4:12
3 9:21	♅ □	♊	3 13:18
5 16:07	♅ ⚹	♋	5 19:48
7 4:45	♂ □	♌	8 0:27
10 0:41	♅ ☌	♍	10 3:59
11 15:27	☉ □	♎	12 6:51
14 6:29	♅ ⚹	♏	14 9:31
16 9:47	♅ □	♐	16 12:46
18 14:44	♅ △	♑	18 17:41
21 0:12	♀ △	♒	21 1:20
23 9:05	♅ ☍	♓	23 11:59
25 6:28	☿ △	♈	26 0:30
28 10:06	♅ △	♉	28 12:32
30 19:53	♅ □	♊	30 21:59

☽ Phases & Eclipses

Dy Hr Mn		
6 2:56	●	15♉47
13 10:25	☽	22♌51
20 3:15	○	29♏19
27 17:06	☾	6♓36
4 15:22	●	14♊12
11 15:27	☽	20♍54
18 13:10	○	27♐30
26 10:40	☾	5♈01

Astro Data

1 May 2046
Julian Day # 53447
SVP 4♓36'33"
GC 27♐29.2 ⚴ 24♋07.3
Eris 0♉04.6 ⚵ 23♍42.7R
⚷ 0♎48.7R ⚶ 26♋59.5
☽ Mean ☊ 8♒57.8

1 June 2046
Julian Day # 53478
SVP 4♓36'29"
GC 27♐29.3 ⚴ 8♌17.4
Eris 0♉23.2 ⚵ 24♍25.2
⚷ 0♎11.0 ⚶ 7♌58.3
☽ Mean ☊ 7♒19.3

July 2046 LONGITUDE

Day	Sid.Time	☉	0 hr ☽	Noon ☽	True ☊	☿	♀	♂	⚳	♃	♄	♅	♆	♇
1 Su	6 38 51	9♋50 48	1♊05 01	7♊35 20	4♒39.7	19♋25.1	11♊58.0	24♎34.2	1♎13.8	16♈46.5	18♐27.0	28♌53.9	18♉39.3	5♓17.4
2 M	6 42 48	10 48 02	14 10 42	20 51 05	4R36.1	18R55.7	13 10.1	24 55.3	1 31.2	16 53.2	18R23.0	28 56.7	18 40.8	5R16.8
3 Tu	6 46 44	11 45 16	27 36 23	4♋26 21	4 33.3	18 23.7	14 22.1	25 16.9	1 48.9	16 59.8	18 19.1	28 59.5	18 42.4	5 16.2
4 W	6 50 41	12 42 30	11♋20 43	18 19 04	4 31.5	17 49.5	15 34.2	25 38.9	2 06.7	17 06.2	18 15.3	29 02.3	18 43.9	5 15.5
5 Th	6 54 38	13 39 44	25 20 57	2♌25 53	4D30.8	17 13.6	16 46.3	26 01.4	2 24.7	17 12.4	18 11.5	29 05.2	18 45.3	5 14.8
6 F	6 58 34	14 36 57	9♌33 19	16 42 42	4 31.2	16 36.7	17 58.5	26 24.2	2 42.8	17 18.5	18 07.7	29 08.1	18 46.8	5 14.1
7 Sa	7 02 31	15 34 10	23 53 27	1♍05 02	4 32.1	15 59.3	19 10.7	26 47.5	3 01.1	17 24.5	18 04.1	29 11.0	18 48.2	5 13.4
8 Su	7 06 27	16 31 24	8♍16 56	15 28 38	4 33.4	15 22.1	20 22.9	27 11.2	3 19.6	17 30.2	18 00.4	29 14.0	18 49.6	5 12.6
9 M	7 10 24	17 28 37	22 39 42	29 49 43	4 34.4	14 45.8	21 35.2	27 35.2	3 38.2	17 35.8	17 56.8	29 17.0	18 51.0	5 11.9
10 Tu	7 14 20	18 25 49	6♎58 19	14♎05 11	4R35.0	14 10.9	22 47.5	27 59.7	3 57.0	17 41.2	17 53.3	29 20.0	18 52.3	5 11.1
11 W	7 18 17	19 23 02	21 10 02	28 12 36	4 34.9	13 38.2	23 59.8	28 24.5	4 16.0	17 46.5	17 49.9	29 23.1	18 53.7	5 10.3
12 Th	7 22 14	20 20 15	5♏12 41	12♏10 06	4 34.1	13 08.1	25 12.2	28 49.7	4 35.1	17 51.6	17 46.5	29 26.1	18 55.0	5 09.5
13 F	7 26 10	21 17 27	19 04 40	25 56 13	4 32.8	12 41.3	26 24.5	29 15.3	4 54.3	17 56.5	17 43.1	29 29.3	18 56.2	5 08.6
14 Sa	7 30 07	22 14 40	2♐44 38	9♐29 48	4 31.2	12 18.1	27 37.0	29 41.2	5 13.7	18 01.2	17 39.9	29 32.4	18 57.5	5 07.8
15 Su	7 34 03	23 11 52	16 11 36	22 49 56	4 29.7	11 59.2	28 49.4	0♏07.5	5 33.3	18 05.8	17 36.7	29 35.6	18 58.7	5 06.9
16 M	7 38 00	24 09 05	29 24 46	5♑56 01	4 28.5	11 44.7	0♋01.9	0 34.1	5 52.9	18 10.2	17 33.6	29 38.8	18 59.9	5 06.0
17 Tu	7 41 56	25 06 18	12♑23 40	18 47 45	4 27.7	11 35.2	1 14.4	1 01.0	6 12.7	18 14.4	17 30.5	29 42.0	19 01.0	5 05.1
18 W	7 45 53	26 03 32	25 08 17	1♒25 21	4D27.4	11D30.8	2 27.0	1 28.3	6 32.7	18 18.5	17 27.5	29 45.3	19 02.2	5 04.2
19 Th	7 49 49	27 00 46	7♒39 04	13 49 36	4 27.5	11 31.7	3 39.6	1 55.9	6 52.7	18 22.3	17 24.6	29 48.5	19 03.3	5 03.2
20 F	7 53 46	27 58 00	19 57 07	26 01 54	4 27.9	11 38.2	4 52.3	2 23.7	7 12.9	18 26.0	17 21.8	29 51.9	19 04.3	5 02.3
21 Sa	7 57 43	28 55 15	2♓04 11	8♓04 20	4 28.4	11 50.3	6 04.9	2 51.9	7 33.3	18 29.5	17 19.0	29 55.2	19 05.4	5 01.3
22 Su	8 01 39	29 52 30	14 02 42	19 59 41	4 29.0	12 08.2	7 17.7	3 20.5	7 53.7	18 32.9	17 16.3	29 58.5	19 06.4	5 00.3
23 M	8 05 36	0♌49 47	25 55 44	1♈51 18	4 29.4	12 31.8	8 30.4	3 49.3	8 14.3	18 36.0	17 13.7	0♍01.9	19 07.4	4 59.3
24 Tu	8 09 32	1 47 04	7♈46 55	13 43 06	4 29.7	13 01.2	9 43.2	4 18.4	8 35.0	18 38.9	17 11.2	0 05.3	19 08.3	4 58.3
25 W	8 13 29	2 44 22	19 40 23	25 39 21	4R29.8	13 36.4	10 56.0	4 47.8	8 55.8	18 41.7	17 08.7	0 08.7	19 09.2	4 57.2
26 Th	8 17 25	3 41 41	1♉40 33	7♉44 33	4D29.8	14 17.4	12 08.9	5 17.4	9 16.7	18 44.3	17 06.4	0 12.2	19 10.1	4 56.2
27 F	8 21 22	4 39 00	13 51 55	20 03 12	4 29.8	15 04.0	13 21.8	5 47.4	9 37.8	18 46.7	17 04.1	0 15.6	19 11.0	4 55.1
28 Sa	8 25 18	5 36 21	26 18 52	2♊39 26	4 29.9	15 56.4	14 34.8	6 17.6	9 58.9	18 48.9	17 01.9	0 19.1	19 11.8	4 54.0
29 Su	8 29 15	6 33 43	9♊05 16	15 36 44	4 30.0	16 54.3	15 47.7	6 48.2	10 20.2	18 50.9	16 59.8	0 22.6	19 12.6	4 53.0
30 M	8 33 12	7 31 06	22 14 04	28 57 26	4 30.3	17 57.7	17 00.8	7 19.0	10 41.6	18 52.7	16 57.7	0 26.1	19 13.4	4 51.9
31 Tu	8 37 08	8 28 30	5♋46 51	12♋42 15	4 30.6	19 06.5	18 13.8	7 50.0	11 03.1	18 54.3	16 55.8	0 29.7	19 14.1	4 50.7

August 2046 LONGITUDE

Day	Sid.Time	☉	0 hr ☽	Noon ☽	True ☊	☿	♀	♂	⚳	♃	♄	♅	♆	♇
1 W	8 41 05	9♌25 54	19♋43 24	26♋49 57	4♒30.8	20♋20.5	19♋26.9	8♏21.3	11♎24.7	18♈55.7	16♐53.9	0♍33.2	19♉14.9	4♓49.6
2 Th	8 45 01	10 23 20	4♌01 24	11♌17 07	4R30.8	21 39.6	20 40.1	8 52.9	11 46.4	18 56.9	16R52.2	0 36.8	19 15.5	4R48.5
3 F	8 48 58	11 20 46	18 36 23	25 58 22	4 30.5	23 03.7	21 53.2	9 24.8	12 08.2	18 58.0	16 50.5	0 40.4	19 16.2	4 47.3
4 Sa	8 52 54	12 18 14	3♍22 10	10♍46 52	4 29.9	24 32.5	23 06.4	9 56.8	12 30.1	18 58.8	16 48.9	0 44.0	19 16.8	4 46.2
5 Su	8 56 51	13 15 41	18 11 31	25 35 14	4 29.0	26 05.7	24 19.7	10 29.2	12 52.1	18 59.4	16 47.4	0 47.6	19 17.4	4 45.0
6 M	9 00 47	14 13 10	2♎57 10	10♎16 32	4 27.9	27 43.3	25 32.9	11 01.8	13 14.2	18 59.8	16 46.0	0 51.2	19 17.9	4 43.8
7 Tu	9 04 44	15 10 40	17 32 42	24 45 08	4 27.0	29 24.8	26 46.2	11 34.6	13 36.4	19R00.1	16 44.7	0 54.8	19 18.4	4 42.6
8 W	9 08 41	16 08 10	1♏53 23	8♏57 10	4D26.5	1♌10.0	27 59.6	12 07.6	13 58.7	19 00.1	16 43.5	0 58.5	19 18.9	4 41.4
9 Th	9 12 37	17 05 41	15 56 17	22 50 39	4 26.5	2 58.5	29 12.9	12 40.9	14 21.1	19 00.0	16 42.3	1 02.2	19 19.3	4 40.2
10 F	9 16 34	18 03 12	29 40 16	6♐25 13	4 27.0	4 49.9	0♌26.3	13 14.4	14 43.5	18 59.6	16 41.3	1 05.8	19 19.7	4 39.0
11 Sa	9 20 30	19 00 45	13♐05 36	19 41 37	4 28.0	6 44.0	1 39.8	13 48.1	15 06.1	18 59.0	16 40.4	1 09.5	19 20.1	4 37.8
12 Su	9 24 27	19 58 19	26 13 27	2♑41 21	4 29.3	8 40.3	2 53.2	14 22.1	15 28.7	18 58.3	16 39.5	1 13.2	19 20.5	4 36.6
13 M	9 28 23	20 55 53	9♑05 32	15 26 14	4 30.4	10 38.4	4 06.7	14 56.2	15 51.4	18 57.3	16 38.8	1 16.9	19 20.8	4 35.3
14 Tu	9 32 20	21 53 29	21 43 40	27 58 06	4R31.1	12 37.9	5 20.3	15 30.6	16 14.2	18 56.2	16 38.1	1 20.6	19 21.1	4 34.1
15 W	9 36 16	22 51 05	4♒09 43	10♒18 44	4 31.2	14 38.6	6 33.8	16 05.1	16 37.1	18 54.8	16 37.6	1 24.4	19 21.3	4 32.8
16 Th	9 40 13	23 48 42	16 25 22	22 29 49	4 30.2	16 40.0	7 47.4	16 39.9	17 00.1	18 53.3	16 37.1	1 28.1	19 21.5	4 31.6
17 F	9 44 10	24 46 21	28 32 18	4♓33 00	4 28.3	18 41.8	9 01.1	17 14.9	17 23.1	18 51.6	16 36.8	1 31.8	19 21.7	4 30.3
18 Sa	9 48 06	25 44 02	10♓32 10	16 30 00	4 25.5	20 43.7	10 14.8	17 50.0	17 46.2	18 49.6	16 36.5	1 35.5	19 21.9	4 29.1
19 Su	9 52 03	26 41 43	22 26 48	28 22 48	4 22.0	22 45.5	11 28.5	18 25.4	18 09.4	18 47.5	16 36.3	1 39.3	19 22.0	4 27.8
20 M	9 55 59	27 39 26	4♈18 20	10♈13 43	4 18.2	24 47.0	12 42.2	19 00.9	18 32.7	18 45.2	16D36.2	1 43.0	19 22.1	4 26.5
21 Tu	9 59 56	28 37 11	16 09 19	22 05 31	4 14.6	26 47.9	13 56.0	19 36.6	18 56.0	18 42.6	16 36.3	1 46.8	19 22.1	4 25.2
22 W	10 03 52	29 34 57	28 02 46	4♉01 30	4 11.5	28 48.1	15 09.8	20 12.6	19 19.4	18 39.9	16 36.4	1 50.5	19R22.1	4 24.0
23 Th	10 07 49	0♍32 45	10♉02 12	16 05 24	4 09.5	0♍47.5	16 23.7	20 48.7	19 42.9	18 37.0	16 36.6	1 54.3	19 22.1	4 22.7
24 F	10 11 45	1 30 34	22 11 37	28 21 23	4D08.6	2 45.9	17 37.5	21 25.0	20 06.4	18 33.9	16 36.9	1 58.0	19 22.1	4 21.4
25 Sa	10 15 42	2 28 26	4♊35 15	10♊53 45	4 08.8	4 43.2	18 51.5	22 01.4	20 30.0	18 30.6	16 37.3	2 01.8	19 22.0	4 20.1
26 Su	10 19 39	3 26 19	17 17 25	23 46 44	4 09.9	6 39.4	20 05.4	22 38.1	20 53.7	18 27.2	16 37.8	2 05.6	19 21.9	4 18.8
27 M	10 23 35	4 24 14	0♋22 06	7♋03 53	4 11.5	8 34.5	21 19.4	23 14.9	21 17.5	18 23.5	16 38.4	2 09.3	19 21.8	4 17.6
28 Tu	10 27 32	5 22 11	13 52 20	20 47 37	4R12.8	10 28.3	22 33.4	23 51.9	21 41.3	18 19.7	16 39.1	2 13.1	19 21.6	4 16.3
29 W	10 31 28	6 20 09	27 49 41	4♌58 23	4 13.3	12 20.9	23 47.5	24 29.1	22 05.1	18 15.7	16 39.9	2 16.8	19 21.4	4 15.0
30 Th	10 35 25	7 18 09	12♌13 22	19 34 06	4 12.5	14 12.3	25 01.6	25 06.4	22 29.1	18 11.5	16 40.8	2 20.6	19 21.1	4 13.7
31 F	10 39 21	8 16 11	26 59 51	4♍29 43	4 10.1	16 02.4	26 15.7	25 44.0	22 53.1	18 07.1	16 41.8	2 24.3	19 20.8	4 12.4

Astro Data	Dy Hr Mn
☽0S	8 21:26
♃△♄	11 21:30
☿ D	18 19:51
☽0N	22 14:12
☽0S	5 4:42
♃ R	8 4:13
⚳0S	12 15:39
☽0N	18 21:22
♄ D	20 19:12
♆ R	22 13:24

Planet Ingress	Dy Hr Mn
♂ ♏	15 5:13
♀ ♋	16 11:22
☉ ♌	22 15:08
♅ ♍	22 22:30
☿ ♌	7 20:07
♀ ♌	10 3:23
☉ ♍	22 22:24
☿ ♍	23 2:26

Last Aspect Dy Hr Mn		☽ Ingress Dy Hr Mn
3 2:25 ♅ ⚹	♋	3 4:13
5 0:51 ♂ □	♌	5 7:53
7 8:49 ♅ ☌	♍	7 10:12
8 20:56 ♀ □	♎	9 12:17
11 14:01 ♅ ⚹	♏	11 15:04
13 18:16 ♅ □	♐	13 19:09
16 0:23 ♅ △	♑	16 1:05
18 0:55 ☉ ☍	♒	18 9:16
20 19:39 ♅ ☍	♓	20 19:53
22 10:12 ♆ ⚹	♈	23 8:15
24 21:59 ♃ ☌	♉	25 20:40
27 10:19 ♆ ☌	♊	28 7:00
29 17:54 ♃ ⚹	♋	30 13:51

Last Aspect Dy Hr Mn		☽ Ingress Dy Hr Mn
31 23:59 ☿ ☌	♌	1 17:18
3 1:04 ♆ □	♍	3 18:32
5 12:56 ☿ ⚹	♎	5 19:11
7 15:42 ♀ □	♏	7 20:49
10 0:18 ♀ △	♐	10 0:35
11 10:42 ♃ △	♑	12 7:00
13 19:27 ♆ △	♒	14 15:56
16 14:50 ☉ ☍	♓	17 2:55
18 17:47 ♆ ⚹	♈	19 15:17
22 2:18 ☉ △	♉	22 3:56
23 21:46 ♂ ☍	♊	24 15:11
26 4:29 ♀ ⚹	♋	26 23:20
28 17:30 ♂ △	♌	29 3:40
30 21:38 ♀ ☌	♍	31 4:49

☽ Phases & Eclipses Dy Hr Mn	
4 1:39	● 12♋18
10 19:53	☽ 18♎45
18 0:55	○ 25♑37
18 1:05	P 0.246
26 3:19	☾ 3♉21
2 10:25	● 10♌20
2 10:19:44	T 04'51"
9 1:15	☽ 16♏40
16 14:50	○ 23♒56
24 18:36	☾ 1♊46
31 18:25	● 8♍32

Astro Data

1 July 2046
Julian Day # 53508
SVP 4♓36'23"
GC 27♐29.3 ⚴ 22♌23.2
Eris 0♉35.2 ⚵ 29♍22.2
⚷ 1♎16.0 ⚶ 20♌25.5
☽ Mean ☊ 5♒44.0

1 August 2046
Julian Day # 53539
SVP 4♓36'17"
GC 27♐29.4 ⚴ 7♍01.0
Eris 0♉38.6R ⚵ 7♎14.3
⚷ 3♎56.1 ⚶ 4♍29.9
☽ Mean ☊ 4♒05.5

LONGITUDE September 2046

Day	Sid.Time	☉	0 hr ☽	Noon☽	True☊	☿	♀	♂	⚳	♃	♄	♅	♆	♇
1 Sa	10 43 18	9♍14 15	12♍02 38	19♍37 25	4♒06.2	17♍51.2	27♌29.9	26♏21.7	23♎17.1	18♈02.5	16♐42.9	2♍28.1	19♉20.5	4♓11.2
2 Su	10 47 14	10 12 19	27 12 48	4♎47 32	4R01.2	19 38.8	28 44.0	26 59.5	23 41.2	17R57.8	16 44.1	2 31.8	19R20.2	4R09.9
3 M	10 51 11	11 10 26	12♎20 21	19 50 07	3 55.9	21 25.1	29 58.2	27 37.5	24 05.4	17 52.9	16 45.4	2 35.5	19 19.8	4 08.6
4 Tu	10 55 08	12 08 34	27 15 48	4♏36 33	3 51.0	23 10.1	1♍12.5	28 15.7	24 29.6	17 47.8	16 46.8	2 39.2	19 19.4	4 07.3
5 W	10 59 04	13 06 43	11♏51 40	19 00 42	3 47.3	24 54.0	2 26.7	28 54.1	24 53.9	17 42.6	16 48.2	2 43.0	19 19.0	4 06.1
6 Th	11 03 01	14 04 54	26 03 21	2♐59 30	3D45.1	26 36.6	3 41.0	29 32.6	25 18.3	17 37.2	16 49.8	2 46.7	19 18.5	4 04.8
7 F	11 06 57	15 03 07	9♐49 12	16 32 38	3 44.5	28 18.0	4 55.3	0♐11.2	25 42.7	17 31.6	16 51.5	2 50.4	19 18.0	4 03.5
8 Sa	11 10 54	16 01 21	23 10 04	29 41 51	3 45.3	29 58.3	6 09.7	0 50.0	26 07.1	17 26.0	16 53.3	2 54.1	19 17.5	4 02.3
9 Su	11 14 50	16 59 36	6♑08 26	12♑30 15	3 46.6	1♎37.3	7 24.0	1 29.0	26 31.6	17 20.1	16 55.1	2 57.7	19 16.9	4 01.0
10 M	11 18 47	17 57 53	18 47 46	25 01 28	3R47.9	3 15.3	8 38.4	2 08.0	26 56.1	17 14.1	16 57.1	3 01.4	19 16.3	3 59.8
11 Tu	11 22 43	18 56 11	1♒11 47	7♒19 10	3 48.1	4 52.1	9 52.8	2 47.3	27 20.7	17 08.0	16 59.1	3 05.1	19 15.7	3 58.6
12 W	11 26 40	19 54 31	13 24 02	19 26 45	3 46.8	6 27.7	11 07.3	3 26.6	27 45.3	17 01.7	17 01.2	3 08.7	19 15.0	3 57.3
13 Th	11 30 37	20 52 53	25 27 40	1♓27 07	3 43.3	8 02.3	12 21.7	4 06.2	28 10.0	16 55.3	17 03.5	3 12.3	19 14.3	3 56.1
14 F	11 34 33	21 51 16	7♓25 21	13 22 39	3 37.6	9 35.7	13 36.2	4 45.8	28 34.7	16 48.8	17 05.8	3 16.0	19 13.6	3 54.9
15 Sa	11 38 30	22 49 41	19 19 14	25 15 19	3 29.9	11 08.1	14 50.7	5 25.6	28 59.4	16 42.1	17 08.2	3 19.6	19 12.9	3 53.7
16 Su	11 42 26	23 48 08	1♈11 07	7♈06 49	3 20.6	12 39.3	16 05.3	6 05.5	29 24.2	16 35.3	17 10.7	3 23.1	19 12.1	3 52.5
17 M	11 46 23	24 46 37	13 02 38	18 58 47	3 10.7	14 09.5	17 19.8	6 45.5	29 49.1	16 28.5	17 13.3	3 26.7	19 11.3	3 51.3
18 Tu	11 50 19	25 45 08	24 55 28	0♉52 58	3 00.9	15 38.5	18 34.4	7 25.7	0♏14.0	16 21.5	17 16.0	3 30.3	19 10.5	3 50.1
19 W	11 54 16	26 43 41	6♉51 32	12 51 31	2 52.3	17 06.5	19 49.0	8 06.0	0 38.9	16 14.3	17 18.8	3 33.8	19 09.6	3 49.0
20 Th	11 58 12	27 42 17	18 53 13	24 57 03	2 45.4	18 33.4	21 03.6	8 46.4	1 03.8	16 07.1	17 21.6	3 37.3	19 08.7	3 47.8
21 F	12 02 09	28 40 54	1♊03 26	7♊12 48	2 40.7	19 59.1	22 18.3	9 27.0	1 28.8	15 59.8	17 24.6	3 40.8	19 07.8	3 46.7
22 Sa	12 06 05	29 39 34	13 25 39	19 42 29	2D38.3	21 23.8	23 33.0	10 07.7	1 53.9	15 52.4	17 27.6	3 44.3	19 06.8	3 45.5
23 Su	12 10 02	0♎38 16	26 03 49	2♋30 09	2 37.8	22 47.2	24 47.7	10 48.5	2 18.9	15 44.9	17 30.7	3 47.8	19 05.9	3 44.4
24 M	12 13 59	1 37 00	9♋02 01	15 39 53	2 38.4	24 09.5	26 02.4	11 29.4	2 44.0	15 37.4	17 33.9	3 51.2	19 04.9	3 43.3
25 Tu	12 17 55	2 35 46	22 24 08	29 15 08	2R39.0	25 30.6	27 17.2	12 10.5	3 09.2	15 29.7	17 37.2	3 54.6	19 03.9	3 42.2
26 W	12 21 52	3 34 35	6♌13 03	13♌17 59	2 38.6	26 50.4	28 31.9	12 51.6	3 34.4	15 22.0	17 40.6	3 58.0	19 02.8	3 41.1
27 Th	12 25 48	4 33 26	20 29 50	27 48 17	2 36.2	28 08.9	29 46.7	13 32.9	3 59.6	15 14.2	17 44.1	4 01.4	19 01.7	3 40.0
28 F	12 29 45	5 32 19	5♍12 49	12♍42 42	2 31.4	29 26.0	1♎01.5	14 14.4	4 24.8	15 06.4	17 47.6	4 04.8	19 00.6	3 39.0
29 Sa	12 33 41	6 31 14	20 16 58	27 54 28	2 24.1	0♏41.7	2 16.4	14 55.9	4 50.1	14 58.5	17 51.3	4 08.1	18 59.5	3 37.9
30 Su	12 37 38	7 30 11	5♎33 51	13♎13 44	2 14.9	1 55.9	3 31.2	15 37.6	5 15.4	14 50.6	17 55.0	4 11.4	18 58.3	3 36.9

LONGITUDE October 2046

Day	Sid.Time	☉	0 hr ☽	Noon☽	True☊	☿	♀	♂	⚳	♃	♄	♅	♆	♇
1 M	12 41 34	8♎29 10	20♎52 37	28♎29 06	2♒05.0	3♏08.5	4♎46.1	16♐19.3	5♏40.8	14♈42.6	17♐58.8	4♍14.7	18♉57.2	3♓35.9
2 Tu	12 45 31	9 28 11	6♏01 51	13♏29 41	1R55.5	4 19.4	6 01.0	17 01.2	6 06.1	14R34.6	18 02.6	4 17.9	18R56.0	3R34.9
3 W	12 49 28	10 27 14	20 51 37	28 06 56	1 47.6	5 28.5	7 15.9	17 43.2	6 31.5	14 26.5	18 06.6	4 21.2	18 54.7	3 33.9
4 Th	12 53 24	11 26 19	5♐15 07	12♐15 53	1 42.0	6 35.7	8 30.8	18 25.3	6 57.0	14 18.5	18 10.6	4 24.4	18 53.5	3 32.9
5 F	12 57 21	12 25 26	19 09 10	25 55 06	1 38.8	7 40.8	9 45.7	19 07.6	7 22.4	14 10.4	18 14.7	4 27.5	18 52.2	3 32.0
6 Sa	13 01 17	13 24 34	2♑33 58	9♑06 09	1D37.7	8 43.6	11 00.6	19 49.9	7 47.9	14 02.3	18 18.9	4 30.7	18 50.9	3 31.0
7 Su	13 05 14	14 23 44	15 32 09	21 52 32	1R37.8	9 44.0	12 15.6	20 32.3	8 13.4	13 54.3	18 23.2	4 33.8	18 49.6	3 30.1
8 M	13 09 10	15 22 56	28 07 53	4♒18 50	1 37.9	10 41.7	13 30.5	21 14.8	8 38.9	13 46.2	18 27.5	4 36.9	18 48.3	3 29.2
9 Tu	13 13 07	16 22 10	10♒25 59	16 29 57	1 37.0	11 36.5	14 45.5	21 57.5	9 04.4	13 38.1	18 32.0	4 39.9	18 46.9	3 28.4
10 W	13 17 03	17 21 25	22 31 16	28 30 31	1 34.0	12 28.2	16 00.5	22 40.2	9 30.0	13 30.1	18 36.4	4 42.9	18 45.6	3 27.5
11 Th	13 21 00	18 20 42	4♓28 11	10♓24 42	1 28.4	13 16.5	17 15.5	23 23.0	9 55.6	13 22.1	18 41.0	4 45.9	18 44.2	3 26.6
12 F	13 24 57	19 20 01	16 20 30	22 15 56	1 19.8	14 00.9	18 30.5	24 05.9	10 21.2	13 14.1	18 45.6	4 48.8	18 42.8	3 25.8
13 Sa	13 28 53	20 19 22	28 11 19	4♈06 54	1 08.5	14 41.2	19 45.5	24 48.9	10 46.8	13 06.1	18 50.3	4 51.7	18 41.3	3 25.0
14 Su	13 32 50	21 18 45	10♈02 56	15 59 36	0 55.2	15 17.0	21 00.5	25 32.0	11 12.4	12 58.2	18 55.1	4 54.6	18 39.9	3 24.2
15 M	13 36 46	22 18 10	21 57 06	27 55 33	0 40.9	15 47.8	22 15.5	26 15.2	11 38.0	12 50.3	18 59.9	4 57.5	18 38.4	3 23.5
16 Tu	13 40 43	23 17 37	3♉55 08	9♉55 57	0 26.8	16 13.1	23 30.6	26 58.5	12 03.7	12 42.5	19 04.9	5 00.3	18 36.9	3 22.7
17 W	13 44 39	24 17 06	15 58 11	22 01 19	0 14.0	16 32.5	24 45.7	27 41.9	12 29.4	12 34.8	19 09.8	5 03.0	18 35.4	3 22.0
18 Th	13 48 36	25 16 37	28 07 33	4♊15 05	0 03.4	16 45.4	26 00.7	28 25.3	12 55.1	12 27.1	19 14.9	5 05.8	18 33.9	3 21.3
19 F	13 52 32	26 16 11	10♊24 52	16 37 09	29♑55.7	16R51.3	27 15.8	29 08.9	13 20.8	12 19.5	19 20.0	5 08.5	18 32.4	3 20.6
20 Sa	13 56 29	27 15 47	22 52 18	29 10 40	29 51.0	16 49.6	28 30.9	29 52.5	13 46.5	12 11.9	19 25.2	5 11.1	18 30.9	3 19.9
21 Su	14 00 26	28 15 25	5♋32 39	11♋58 40	29 48.8	16 39.9	29 46.0	0♑36.2	14 12.3	12 04.4	19 30.4	5 13.8	18 29.3	3 19.3
22 M	14 04 22	29 15 05	18 29 10	25 04 35	29 48.3	16 21.8	1♏01.1	1 20.0	14 38.0	11 57.1	19 35.7	5 16.4	18 27.7	3 18.7
23 Tu	14 08 19	0♏14 48	1♌45 19	8♌31 46	29 48.2	15 54.8	2 16.2	2 03.9	15 03.8	11 49.8	19 41.0	5 18.9	18 26.2	3 18.1
24 W	14 12 15	1 14 33	15 24 13	22 22 54	29 47.3	15 18.9	3 31.4	2 47.9	15 29.6	11 42.6	19 46.5	5 21.4	18 24.6	3 17.5
25 Th	14 16 12	2 14 20	29 27 52	6♍39 04	29 44.4	14 34.1	4 46.5	3 31.9	15 55.4	11 35.5	19 51.9	5 23.9	18 23.0	3 16.9
26 F	14 20 08	3 14 09	13♍56 15	21 18 55	29 38.8	13 40.7	6 01.7	4 16.1	16 21.2	11 28.5	19 57.5	5 26.3	18 21.4	3 16.4
27 Sa	14 24 05	4 14 00	28 46 25	6♎17 51	29 30.5	12 39.7	7 16.8	5 00.3	16 47.0	11 21.7	20 03.1	5 28.7	18 19.7	3 15.9
28 Su	14 28 01	5 13 54	13♎52 09	21 28 03	29 20.0	11 31.9	8 32.0	5 44.6	17 12.8	11 14.9	20 08.7	5 31.0	18 18.1	3 15.4
29 M	14 31 58	6 13 49	29 04 13	6♏39 17	29 08.4	10 18.9	9 47.2	6 28.9	17 38.6	11 08.3	20 14.4	5 33.3	18 16.5	3 14.9
30 Tu	14 35 55	7 13 47	14♏11 50	21 40 37	28 57.1	9 02.7	11 02.4	7 13.4	18 04.5	11 01.8	20 20.2	5 35.5	18 14.8	3 14.5
31 W	14 39 51	8 13 46	29 04 29	6♐22 29	28 47.5	7 45.4	12 17.6	7 57.9	18 30.3	10 55.5	20 26.0	5 37.7	18 13.2	3 14.1

Astro Data

	Dy Hr Mn
☽0S	1 14:28
♃□♅	5 10:59
☿0S	9 5:21
♃△♄	12 13:19
☽0N	15 3:51
♅☍♇	22 18:18
☉0S	22 20:22
☽0S	29 1:24
♀0S	30 6:29
♄⊼♆	12 0:36
☽0N	12 9:40
☿R	19 18:56
☽0S	26 11:21

Planet Ingress

	Dy Hr Mn
♀ ♍	3 12:34
♂ ♐	7 5:03
☿ ♎	8 12:25
⚳ ♏	17 22:33
☉ ♎	22 20:21
♀ ♎	27 16:16
☿ ♏	28 22:43
☊ ♑R	18 21:35
♂ ♑	20 16:07
♀ ♏	21 16:28
☉ ♏	23 6:03

Last Aspect / ☽ Ingress

Last Aspect Dy Hr Mn	☽ Ingress Dy Hr Mn
1 23:07 ♂ ⚹	♎ 2 4:25
3 8:53 ♃ ☍	♏ 4 4:27
6 5:43 ♂ ☌	♐ 6 6:48
7 13:46 ♃ △	♑ 8 12:34
10 0:55 ♆ △	♒ 10 21:40
12 11:37 ♆ □	♓ 13 9:05
15 6:39 ☉ ☍	♈ 15 21:36
17 8:26 ♄ △	♉ 18 10:13
20 17:54 ☉ △	♊ 20 21:56
22 20:04 ♀ □	♋ 23 7:21
25 8:14 ♀ ⚹	♌ 25 13:18
27 12:37 ☿ ⚹	♍ 27 15:34
28 21:59 ♆ △	♎ 29 15:17

Last Aspect / ☽ Ingress

Last Aspect Dy Hr Mn	☽ Ingress Dy Hr Mn
30 19:23 ♄ ⚹	♏ 1 14:24
2 20:50 ♆ ☍	♐ 3 15:09
4 23:18 ♂ ☌	♑ 5 19:21
7 6:13 ♆ △	♒ 8 3:37
9 23:34 ♂ ⚹	♓ 10 15:00
12 15:57 ♂ □	♈ 13 3:40
15 8:26 ♂ △	♉ 15 16:09
17 5:12 ♆ ☌	♊ 18 3:41
20 13:24 ♂ ☍	♋ 20 13:33
22 20:07 ☉ □	♌ 22 20:52
24 7:30 ♄ △	♍ 25 0:54
26 9:47 ♄ □	♎ 27 1:58
28 9:54 ♄ ⚹	♏ 29 1:28
30 6:30 ♆ ☍	♐ 31 1:31

☽ Phases & Eclipses

Dy Hr Mn	
7 9:07	☽ 14♐56
15 6:39	○ 22♓37
23 8:15	☾ 0♋29
30 2:25	● 7♎07
6 20:41	☽ 13♑46
14 23:41	○ 21♈48
22 20:07	☾ 29♋35
29 11:17	● 6♏12

Astro Data

1 September 2046
Julian Day # 53570
SVP 4♓36'13"
GC 27♐29.5 ⚵ 21♍33.9
Eris 0♉32.0R ⚴ 16♎44.0
⚷ 7♎43.7 ⚶ 19♍23.8
☽ Mean ☊ 2♒27.0

1 October 2046
Julian Day # 53600
SVP 4♓36'10"
GC 27♐29.5 ⚵ 5♎28.3
Eris 0♉17.8R ⚴ 26♎45.9
⚷ 11♎58.8 ⚶ 4♎20.2
☽ Mean ☊ 0♒51.7

November 2046 — LONGITUDE

Day	Sid.Time	☉	0 hr ☽	Noon ☽	True ☊	☿	♀	♂	⚳	♃	♄	♅	♆	♇
1 Th	14 43 48	9♏13 48	13♐33 53	20♐38 10	28♑40.3	6♏29.4	13♏32.7	8♑42.5	18♏56.2	10♈49.3	20♐31.9	5♍39.9	18♉11.5	3♓13.7
2 F	14 47 44	10 13 50	27 35 05	4♑24 32	28R 35.9	5R 17.0	14 47.9	9 27.2	19 22.0	10R 43.2	20 37.8	5 42.0	18R 09.8	3R 13.4
3 Sa	14 51 41	11 13 55	11♑06 38	17 41 41	28D 33.9	4 10.7	16 03.2	10 12.0	19 47.8	10 37.3	20 43.8	5 44.1	18 08.2	3 13.0
4 Su	14 55 37	12 14 01	24 10 05	0♒32 20	28 33.5	3 12.2	17 18.4	10 56.8	20 13.7	10 31.6	20 49.8	5 46.1	18 06.5	3 12.7
5 M	14 59 34	13 14 08	6♒49 01	13 00 46	28R 33.7	2 23.4	18 33.6	11 41.6	20 39.5	10 25.9	20 55.9	5 48.0	18 04.8	3 12.4
6 Tu	15 03 30	14 14 18	19 08 14	25 12 05	28 33.1	1 45.2	19 48.8	12 26.6	21 05.4	10 20.5	21 02.0	5 50.0	18 03.1	3 12.1
7 W	15 07 27	15 14 28	1♓13 00	7♓11 35	28 30.9	1 18.5	21 04.0	13 11.6	21 31.2	10 15.2	21 08.2	5 51.8	18 01.4	3 11.9
8 Th	15 11 24	16 14 40	13 08 29	19 04 16	28 26.2	1D 03.4	22 19.2	13 56.7	21 57.1	10 10.1	21 14.4	5 53.7	17 59.7	3 11.7
9 F	15 15 20	17 14 54	24 59 27	0♈54 33	28 18.8	0 59.9	23 34.4	14 41.8	22 22.9	10 05.2	21 20.6	5 55.4	17 58.0	3 11.5
10 Sa	15 19 17	18 15 09	6♈50 00	12 46 10	28 08.8	1 07.5	24 49.6	15 27.0	22 48.7	10 00.4	21 26.9	5 57.2	17 56.3	3 11.3
11 Su	15 23 13	19 15 25	18 43 24	24 41 58	27 56.8	1 25.6	26 04.8	16 12.2	23 14.6	9 55.8	21 33.2	5 58.8	17 54.7	3 11.2
12 M	15 27 10	20 15 44	0♉42 06	6♉44 00	27 43.8	1 53.4	27 20.0	16 57.5	23 40.4	9 51.4	21 39.6	6 00.5	17 53.0	3 11.1
13 Tu	15 31 06	21 16 04	12 47 48	18 53 38	27 30.9	2 30.0	28 35.2	17 42.9	24 06.2	9 47.2	21 46.0	6 02.0	17 51.3	3 11.0
14 W	15 35 03	22 16 26	25 01 33	1♊11 39	27 19.2	3 14.5	29 50.5	18 28.3	24 32.0	9 43.1	21 52.5	6 03.5	17 49.6	3 10.9
15 Th	15 38 59	23 16 49	7♊24 01	13 38 41	27 09.6	4 06.1	1♐05.7	19 13.7	24 57.8	9 39.3	21 59.0	6 05.0	17 47.9	3D 10.9
16 F	15 42 56	24 17 14	19 55 44	26 15 17	27 02.7	5 03.9	2 20.9	19 59.2	25 23.6	9 35.6	22 05.5	6 06.4	17 46.2	3 10.9
17 Sa	15 46 53	25 17 41	2♋37 28	9♋02 24	26 58.6	6 07.2	3 36.1	20 44.8	25 49.4	9 32.1	22 12.1	6 07.8	17 44.6	3 10.9
18 Su	15 50 49	26 18 10	15 30 17	22 01 19	26D 57.0	7 15.1	4 51.4	21 30.4	26 15.2	9 28.8	22 18.7	6 09.1	17 42.9	3 10.9
19 M	15 54 46	27 18 40	28 35 45	5♌13 49	26 57.1	8 27.1	6 06.6	22 16.1	26 41.0	9 25.7	22 25.3	6 10.4	17 41.2	3 11.0
20 Tu	15 58 42	28 19 13	11♌55 46	18 41 52	26R 57.9	9 42.5	7 21.8	23 01.8	27 06.8	9 22.8	22 32.0	6 11.6	17 39.6	3 11.1
21 W	16 02 39	29 19 47	25 32 18	2♍27 15	26 58.2	11 00.9	8 37.1	23 47.6	27 32.5	9 20.1	22 38.6	6 12.8	17 37.9	3 11.2
22 Th	16 06 35	0♐20 22	9♍26 48	16 30 58	26 56.9	12 21.8	9 52.3	24 33.4	27 58.3	9 17.6	22 45.4	6 13.9	17 36.3	3 11.4
23 F	16 10 32	1 21 00	23 39 37	0♎52 30	26 53.5	13 44.8	11 07.6	25 19.2	28 24.0	9 15.3	22 52.1	6 14.9	17 34.6	3 11.5
24 Sa	16 14 28	2 21 39	8♎09 13	15 29 13	26 47.8	15 09.7	12 22.8	26 05.1	28 49.7	9 13.2	22 58.9	6 15.9	17 33.0	3 11.7
25 Su	16 18 25	3 22 20	22 51 45	0♏16 01	26 40.3	16 36.0	13 38.1	26 51.1	29 15.4	9 11.4	23 05.7	6 16.8	17 31.4	3 11.9
26 M	16 22 22	4 23 02	7♏41 01	15 05 43	26 31.7	18 03.5	14 53.3	27 37.1	29 41.1	9 09.7	23 12.5	6 17.7	17 29.8	3 12.2
27 Tu	16 26 18	5 23 46	22 29 03	29 49 58	26 23.2	19 32.2	16 08.6	28 23.1	0♐06.8	9 08.2	23 19.4	6 18.5	17 28.2	3 12.5
28 W	16 30 15	6 24 32	7♐07 26	14♐20 34	26 15.9	21 01.6	17 23.8	29 09.2	0 32.5	9 06.9	23 26.3	6 19.3	17 26.6	3 12.8
29 Th	16 34 11	7 25 18	21 28 35	28 30 54	26 10.5	22 31.8	18 39.1	29 55.4	0 58.1	9 05.9	23 33.2	6 20.0	17 25.0	3 13.1
30 F	16 38 08	8 26 06	5♑27 02	12♑16 44	26 07.4	24 02.6	19 54.4	0♒41.5	1 23.7	9 05.0	23 40.1	6 20.7	17 23.5	3 13.5

December 2046 — LONGITUDE

Day	Sid.Time	☉	0 hr ☽	Noon ☽	True ☊	☿	♀	♂	⚳	♃	♄	♅	♆	♇
1 Sa	16 42 04	9♐26 55	18♑59 55	25♑36 39	26♑06.5	25♏33.8	21♐09.6	1♒27.7	1♐49.3	9♈04.4	23♐47.0	6♍21.3	17♉21.9	3♓13.8
2 Su	16 46 01	10 27 45	2♒07 05	8♒31 35	26D 07.1	27 05.5	22 24.9	2 14.0	2 14.9	9R 04.0	23 54.0	6 21.8	17R 20.4	3 14.2
3 M	16 49 57	11 28 35	14 50 33	21 04 29	26 08.5	28 37.4	23 40.1	3 00.2	2 40.4	9D 03.7	24 01.0	6 22.3	17 18.9	3 14.7
4 Tu	16 53 54	12 29 27	27 13 57	3♓19 32	26R 09.8	0♐09.6	24 55.4	3 46.5	3 06.0	9 03.7	24 08.0	6 22.7	17 17.4	3 15.1
5 W	16 57 51	13 30 19	9♓21 52	15 21 36	26 10.3	1 42.1	26 10.6	4 32.9	3 31.5	9 03.9	24 15.0	6 23.1	17 15.9	3 15.6
6 Th	17 01 47	14 31 12	21 19 22	27 15 48	26 09.2	3 14.7	27 25.8	5 19.2	3 56.9	9 04.3	24 22.0	6 23.4	17 14.4	3 16.1
7 F	17 05 44	15 32 06	3♈11 31	9♈07 06	26 06.2	4 47.4	28 41.1	6 05.6	4 22.4	9 05.0	24 29.0	6 23.7	17 13.0	3 16.6
8 Sa	17 09 40	16 33 01	15 03 08	21 00 06	26 01.6	6 20.3	29 56.3	6 52.0	4 47.8	9 05.8	24 36.1	6 23.9	17 11.5	3 17.2
9 Su	17 13 37	17 33 56	26 58 29	2♉58 42	25 55.4	7 53.2	1♑11.5	7 38.5	5 13.2	9 06.8	24 43.1	6 24.1	17 10.1	3 17.8
10 M	17 17 33	18 34 52	9♉01 08	15 06 04	25 48.5	9 26.3	2 26.7	8 24.9	5 38.6	9 08.1	24 50.2	6 24.1	17 08.7	3 18.4
11 Tu	17 21 30	19 35 49	21 13 48	27 24 30	25 41.5	10 59.4	3 41.9	9 11.4	6 03.9	9 09.5	24 57.3	6R 24.2	17 07.4	3 19.0
12 W	17 25 26	20 36 47	3♊38 19	9♊55 21	25 35.1	12 32.7	4 57.1	9 57.9	6 29.2	9 11.2	25 04.3	6 24.2	17 06.0	3 19.7
13 Th	17 29 23	21 37 46	16 15 38	22 39 11	25 30.0	14 06.0	6 12.4	10 44.5	6 54.5	9 13.0	25 11.4	6 24.1	17 04.7	3 20.4
14 F	17 33 20	22 38 45	29 05 59	5♋35 57	25 26.6	15 39.4	7 27.5	11 31.0	7 19.7	9 15.1	25 18.5	6 24.0	17 03.4	3 21.1
15 Sa	17 37 16	23 39 45	12♋09 02	18 45 08	25D 25.0	17 12.9	8 42.7	12 17.6	7 44.9	9 17.3	25 25.6	6 23.8	17 02.1	3 21.8
16 Su	17 41 13	24 40 46	25 24 10	2♌06 04	25 25.0	18 46.5	9 57.9	13 04.2	8 10.1	9 19.8	25 32.7	6 23.5	17 00.8	3 22.6
17 M	17 45 09	25 41 48	8♌50 44	15 38 08	25 26.1	20 20.2	11 13.1	13 50.8	8 35.3	9 22.5	25 39.8	6 23.2	16 59.6	3 23.3
18 Tu	17 49 06	26 42 51	22 28 11	29 20 50	25 27.8	21 54.0	12 28.3	14 37.4	9 00.4	9 25.3	25 46.9	6 22.9	16 58.3	3 24.1
19 W	17 53 02	27 43 55	6♍16 02	13♍13 42	25 29.2	23 28.0	13 43.5	15 24.0	9 25.4	9 28.4	25 54.0	6 22.5	16 57.1	3 24.9
20 Th	17 56 59	28 44 59	20 13 46	27 16 06	25R 29.9	25 02.1	14 58.6	16 10.7	9 50.5	9 31.7	26 01.1	6 22.0	16 56.0	3 25.8
21 F	18 00 56	29 46 04	4♎20 33	11♎26 54	25 29.4	26 36.4	16 13.8	16 57.4	10 15.5	9 35.1	26 08.2	6 21.5	16 54.8	3 26.7
22 Sa	18 04 52	0♑47 11	18 34 53	25 44 11	25 27.7	28 10.9	17 29.0	17 44.0	10 40.4	9 38.8	26 15.3	6 20.9	16 53.7	3 27.6
23 Su	18 08 49	1 48 18	2♏54 22	10♏04 58	25 25.0	29 45.5	18 44.1	18 30.7	11 05.3	9 42.6	26 22.4	6 20.3	16 52.6	3 28.5
24 M	18 12 45	2 49 26	17 15 28	24 25 16	25 21.7	1♑20.4	19 59.3	19 17.5	11 30.2	9 46.6	26 29.4	6 19.6	16 51.5	3 29.4
25 Tu	18 16 42	3 50 34	1♐33 47	8♐40 23	25 18.4	2 55.5	21 14.5	20 04.2	11 55.1	9 50.9	26 36.5	6 18.8	16 50.5	3 30.4
26 W	18 20 38	4 51 43	15 44 27	22 45 24	25 15.6	4 30.8	22 29.6	20 50.9	12 19.9	9 55.3	26 43.6	6 18.1	16 49.5	3 31.3
27 Th	18 24 35	5 52 53	29 42 42	6♑35 53	25 13.7	6 06.4	23 44.7	21 37.7	12 44.6	9 59.9	26 50.6	6 17.2	16 48.5	3 32.4
28 F	18 28 31	6 54 02	13♑24 34	20 08 27	25D 12.8	7 42.3	24 59.9	22 24.4	13 09.3	10 04.7	26 57.7	6 16.3	16 47.5	3 33.4
29 Sa	18 32 28	7 55 12	26 47 21	3♒21 11	25 12.9	9 18.4	26 15.0	23 11.2	13 34.0	10 09.7	27 04.7	6 15.4	16 46.6	3 34.4
30 Su	18 36 25	8 56 22	9♒49 57	16 13 47	25 13.8	10 54.8	27 30.1	23 58.0	13 58.6	10 14.8	27 11.7	6 14.4	16 45.7	3 35.5
31 M	18 40 21	9 57 32	22 32 52	28 47 30	25 15.1	12 31.5	28 45.2	24 44.7	14 23.1	10 20.2	27 18.7	6 13.3	16 44.8	3 36.6

Astro Data

	Dy Hr Mn
☽0N	8 15:22
☿D	9 7:25
♇D	16 8:47
☽0S	22 18:39
♃D	4 1:07
☽0N	5 21:53
♅R	11 16:09
☽0S	19 23:45

Planet Ingress

	Dy Hr Mn
♀ ♐	14 15:03
☉ ♐	22 3:56
⚳ ♐	27 5:39
♂ ♒	29 14:25
☿ ♐	4 9:30
♀ ♑	8 13:11
☉ ♑	21 17:28
☿ ♑	23 15:40

Last Aspect / ☽ Ingress

Last Aspect Dy Hr Mn	☽ Ingress Dy Hr Mn	Last Aspect Dy Hr Mn	☽ Ingress Dy Hr Mn
1 11:49 ♄ ☌	♑ 2 4:13	1 11:54 ☿ ⚹	♒ 1 20:04
3 12:49 ♆ △	♒ 4 10:59	4 4:51 ♆ □	♓ 4 5:26
6 3:40 ♄ ⚹	♓ 6 21:34	6 12:23 ♀ □	♈ 6 17:32
8 19:22 ♀ △	♈ 9 10:09	8 19:19 ♄ △	♉ 9 6:03
11 5:38 ♄ △	♉ 11 22:36	10 16:00 ♆ ☌	♊ 11 17:00
14 9:05 ♀ ☍	♊ 14 9:41	13 16:47 ♄ ☍	♋ 14 1:40
16 4:03 ♄ ☍	♋ 16 19:04	15 8:54 ♆ ⚹	♌ 16 8:15
18 20:29 ☉ △	♌ 19 2:33	18 7:03 ☉ △	♍ 18 13:08
21 6:10 ☉ □	♍ 21 7:45	20 14:43 ☉ □	♎ 20 16:38
23 2:15 ♂ △	♎ 23 10:33	22 16:36 ♆ ☍	♏ 22 19:08
25 6:10 ♂ □	♏ 25 11:34	24 3:52 ♀ ⚹	♐ 24 21:22
27 9:30 ♂ ⚹	♐ 27 12:16	26 18:54 ♄ ☌	♑ 27 0:30
29 3:27 ♄ ☌	♑ 29 14:33	28 21:40 ♀ ☌	♒ 29 5:51
		31 9:07 ♄ ⚹	♓ 31 14:20

☽ Phases & Eclipses

Dy Hr Mn	
5 12:28	☽ 13♒15
13 17:04	○ 21♉29
21 6:10	☾ 29♌05
27 21:50	● 5♐49
5 7:56	☽ 13♓20
13 9:55	○ 21♊32
20 14:43	☾ 28♍52
27 10:39	● 5♑49

Astro Data

1 November 2046
Julian Day # 53631
SVP 4♓36'07"
GC 27♐29.6 ⚴ 19♎30.9
Eris 29♈59.4R ⚵ 7♏28.5
⚷ 16♎26.7 ⚶ 20♎04.4
☽ Mean ☊ 29♑13.2

1 December 2046
Julian Day # 53661
SVP 4♓36'02"
GC 27♐29.7 ⚴ 2♏31.8
Eris 29♈43.0R ⚵ 17♏42.9
⚷ 20♎17.7 ⚶ 5♏18.7
☽ Mean ☊ 27♑37.9

LONGITUDE — January 2047

Day	Sid.Time	☉	0 hr ☽	Noon ☽	True ☊	☿	♀	♂	⚳	♃	♄	♅	♆	♇
1 Tu	18 44 18	10♑58 42	4♓58 02	11♓04 53	25♑16.5	14♑08.5	0♒00.3	25♒31.5	14♐47.6	10♈25.7	27♐25.7	6♍12.2	16♉44.0	3♓37.7
2 W	18 48 14	11 59 51	17 08 33	23 09 32	25 17.7	15 45.9	1 15.4	26 18.3	15 12.1	10 31.4	27 32.6	6R 11.0	16R 43.1	3 38.8
3 Th	18 52 11	13 01 00	29 08 24	5♈05 43	25R 18.4	17 23.5	2 30.4	27 05.1	15 36.4	10 37.3	27 39.6	6 09.8	16 42.4	3 40.0
4 F	18 56 07	14 02 10	11♈02 05	16 58 07	25 18.5	19 01.5	3 45.5	27 51.8	16 00.8	10 43.4	27 46.5	6 08.6	16 41.6	3 41.1
5 Sa	19 00 04	15 03 19	22 54 24	28 51 31	25 18.1	20 39.7	5 00.5	28 38.6	16 25.1	10 49.6	27 53.4	6 07.2	16 40.9	3 42.3
6 Su	19 04 00	16 04 27	4♉50 05	10♉50 37	25 17.3	22 18.3	6 15.5	29 25.4	16 49.3	10 56.0	28 00.3	6 05.9	16 40.2	3 43.5
7 M	19 07 57	17 05 36	16 53 39	22 59 41	25 16.2	23 57.2	7 30.5	0♓12.2	17 13.4	11 02.6	28 07.1	6 04.5	16 39.5	3 44.7
8 Tu	19 11 54	18 06 44	29 09 07	5♊22 20	25 15.2	25 36.3	8 45.5	0 58.9	17 37.5	11 09.3	28 14.0	6 03.0	16 38.9	3 46.0
9 W	19 15 50	19 07 51	11♊39 41	18 01 22	25 14.3	27 15.7	10 00.4	1 45.7	18 01.6	11 16.2	28 20.8	6 01.5	16 38.3	3 47.2
10 Th	19 19 47	20 08 59	24 27 35	0♋58 25	25 13.6	28 55.4	11 15.4	2 32.4	18 25.6	11 23.3	28 27.5	6 00.0	16 37.7	3 48.5
11 F	19 23 43	21 10 06	7♋33 52	14 13 52	25D 13.3	0♒35.1	12 30.3	3 19.1	18 49.5	11 30.5	28 34.3	5 58.4	16 37.2	3 49.8
12 Sa	19 27 40	22 11 13	20 58 17	27 46 52	25 13.2	2 15.0	13 45.2	4 05.9	19 13.3	11 37.9	28 41.0	5 56.8	16 36.7	3 51.1
13 Su	19 31 36	23 12 19	4♌39 19	11♌35 17	25 13.3	3 55.0	15 00.1	4 52.6	19 37.1	11 45.4	28 47.7	5 55.1	16 36.3	3 52.4
14 M	19 35 33	24 13 25	18 34 22	25 36 06	25R 13.4	5 34.8	16 15.0	5 39.3	20 00.9	11 53.1	28 54.4	5 53.4	16 35.8	3 53.8
15 Tu	19 39 29	25 14 31	2♍40 02	9♍45 42	25 13.5	7 14.6	17 29.8	6 26.0	20 24.5	12 00.9	29 01.0	5 51.6	16 35.4	3 55.1
16 W	19 43 26	26 15 36	16 52 36	24 00 18	25 13.4	8 54.0	18 44.6	7 12.6	20 48.1	12 08.9	29 07.6	5 49.8	16 35.1	3 56.5
17 Th	19 47 23	27 16 42	1♎08 20	8♎16 20	25 13.3	10 33.0	19 59.5	7 59.3	21 11.6	12 17.0	29 14.2	5 48.0	16 34.7	3 57.9
18 F	19 51 19	28 17 47	15 23 53	22 30 40	25D 13.2	12 11.3	21 14.2	8 46.0	21 35.1	12 25.3	29 20.7	5 46.1	16 34.4	3 59.3
19 Sa	19 55 16	29 18 52	29 36 23	6♏40 46	25 13.2	13 48.8	22 29.0	9 32.6	21 58.5	12 33.8	29 27.2	5 44.2	16 34.2	4 00.7
20 Su	19 59 12	0♒19 57	13♏43 33	20 44 32	25 13.5	15 25.2	23 43.8	10 19.2	22 21.8	12 42.3	29 33.6	5 42.2	16 33.9	4 02.1
21 M	20 03 09	1 21 02	27 43 30	4♐40 17	25 13.9	17 00.2	24 58.5	11 05.9	22 45.0	12 51.1	29 40.0	5 40.2	16 33.7	4 03.6
22 Tu	20 07 05	2 22 06	11♐34 40	18 26 30	25 14.6	18 33.4	26 13.2	11 52.5	23 08.2	12 59.9	29 46.4	5 38.2	16 33.6	4 05.1
23 W	20 11 02	3 23 10	25 15 36	2♑01 49	25 15.3	20 04.5	27 27.9	12 39.1	23 31.3	13 08.9	29 52.8	5 36.1	16 33.5	4 06.5
24 Th	20 14 59	4 24 13	8♑44 59	15 24 57	25R 15.9	21 32.8	28 42.6	13 25.6	23 54.3	13 18.0	29 59.0	5 34.0	16 33.4	4 08.0
25 F	20 18 55	5 25 15	22 01 35	28 34 46	25 16.0	22 58.1	29 57.2	14 12.2	24 17.2	13 27.3	0♑05.3	5 31.9	16 33.3	4 09.5
26 Sa	20 22 52	6 26 17	5♒04 26	11♒30 31	25 15.5	24 19.5	1♓11.8	14 58.7	24 40.0	13 36.7	0 11.5	5 29.7	16D 33.3	4 11.0
27 Su	20 26 48	7 27 18	17 52 59	24 11 54	25 14.4	25 36.5	2 26.4	15 45.3	25 02.8	13 46.2	0 17.6	5 27.5	16 33.3	4 12.5
28 M	20 30 45	8 28 18	0♓27 19	6♓39 22	25 12.7	26 48.4	3 41.0	16 31.8	25 25.5	13 55.9	0 23.8	5 25.3	16 33.3	4 14.1
29 Tu	20 34 41	9 29 17	12 48 14	18 54 09	25 10.5	27 54.4	4 55.5	17 18.3	25 48.0	14 05.7	0 29.8	5 23.0	16 33.4	4 15.6
30 W	20 38 38	10 30 15	24 57 24	0♈58 19	25 08.1	28 53.6	6 10.0	18 04.7	26 10.5	14 15.6	0 35.8	5 20.7	16 33.5	4 17.2
31 Th	20 42 34	11 31 11	6♈57 18	12 54 46	25 05.9	29 45.4	7 24.4	18 51.1	26 32.9	14 25.6	0 41.8	5 18.4	16 33.7	4 18.7

LONGITUDE — February 2047

Day	Sid.Time	☉	0 hr ☽	Noon ☽	True ☊	☿	♀	♂	⚳	♃	♄	♅	♆	♇
1 F	20 46 31	12♒32 06	18♈51 13	24♈47 08	25♑04.2	0♓28.8	8♓38.9	19♓37.5	26♐55.2	14♈35.8	0♑47.7	5♍16.1	16♉33.9	4♓20.3
2 Sa	20 50 27	13 33 01	0♉43 05	6♉39 38	25D 03.2	1 03.1	9 53.3	20 23.9	27 17.4	14 46.0	0 53.5	5R 13.7	16 34.1	4 21.9
3 Su	20 54 24	14 33 53	12 37 22	18 36 53	25 03.1	1 27.6	11 07.6	21 10.3	27 39.5	14 56.4	0 59.3	5 11.3	16 34.4	4 23.5
4 M	20 58 21	15 34 45	24 38 46	0♊43 39	25 03.8	1R 41.6	12 21.9	21 56.6	28 01.5	15 06.9	1 05.1	5 08.9	16 34.7	4 25.1
5 Tu	21 02 17	16 35 35	6♊52 06	13 04 40	25 05.2	1 44.8	13 36.2	22 42.9	28 23.5	15 17.5	1 10.8	5 06.5	16 35.0	4 26.7
6 W	21 06 14	17 36 24	19 21 51	25 44 08	25 06.9	1 37.0	14 50.4	23 29.2	28 45.3	15 28.3	1 16.4	5 04.0	16 35.4	4 28.3
7 Th	21 10 10	18 37 11	2♋11 53	8♋45 26	25 08.3	1 18.1	16 04.6	24 15.4	29 07.0	15 39.1	1 22.0	5 01.6	16 35.8	4 29.9
8 F	21 14 07	19 37 57	15 24 57	22 10 33	25R 09.1	0 48.6	17 18.8	25 01.6	29 28.6	15 50.0	1 27.5	4 59.1	16 36.2	4 31.5
9 Sa	21 18 03	20 38 42	29 02 10	5♌59 38	25 08.7	0 09.1	18 32.9	25 47.8	29 50.1	16 01.1	1 32.9	4 56.5	16 36.7	4 33.2
10 Su	21 22 00	21 39 25	13♌02 37	20 10 39	25 07.0	29♒20.6	19 47.0	26 34.0	0♑11.5	16 12.2	1 38.3	4 54.0	16 37.2	4 34.8
11 M	21 25 57	22 40 07	27 23 07	4♍39 17	25 04.0	28 24.3	21 01.0	27 20.1	0 32.8	16 23.4	1 43.7	4 51.5	16 37.7	4 36.4
12 Tu	21 29 53	23 40 47	11♍58 19	19 19 19	25 00.0	27 22.0	22 15.0	28 06.2	0 54.0	16 34.8	1 48.9	4 48.9	16 38.3	4 38.1
13 W	21 33 50	24 41 27	26 41 20	4♎03 27	24 55.6	26 15.2	23 28.9	28 52.2	1 15.1	16 46.2	1 54.1	4 46.3	16 38.9	4 39.7
14 Th	21 37 46	25 42 05	11♎24 44	18 44 22	24 51.4	25 06.0	24 42.8	29 38.2	1 36.0	16 57.7	1 59.3	4 43.8	16 39.5	4 41.4
15 F	21 41 43	26 42 42	26 01 36	3♏15 50	24 48.2	23 56.2	25 56.6	0♈24.2	1 56.9	17 09.4	2 04.4	4 41.2	16 40.2	4 43.0
16 Sa	21 45 39	27 43 18	10♏26 34	17 33 25	24D 46.3	22 47.6	27 10.4	1 10.2	2 17.6	17 21.1	2 09.4	4 38.6	16 40.9	4 44.7
17 Su	21 49 36	28 43 53	24 36 09	1♐34 38	24 45.9	21 41.9	28 24.2	1 56.1	2 38.2	17 32.9	2 14.3	4 36.0	16 41.6	4 46.4
18 M	21 53 32	29 44 26	8♐28 50	15 18 47	24 46.7	20 40.5	29 37.9	2 42.0	2 58.7	17 44.8	2 19.2	4 33.3	16 42.4	4 48.1
19 Tu	21 57 29	0♓44 59	22 04 37	28 46 28	24 48.2	19 44.5	0♈51.6	3 27.8	3 19.1	17 56.8	2 24.0	4 30.7	16 43.2	4 49.7
20 W	22 01 26	1 45 30	5♑24 32	11♑58 59	24R 49.7	18 54.9	2 05.2	4 13.6	3 39.3	18 08.8	2 28.7	4 28.1	16 44.0	4 51.4
21 Th	22 05 22	2 46 00	18 30 02	24 57 52	24 50.4	18 12.2	3 18.7	4 59.4	3 59.5	18 21.0	2 33.4	4 25.5	16 44.9	4 53.1
22 F	22 09 19	3 46 28	1♒22 38	7♒44 30	24 49.5	17 36.8	4 32.2	5 45.2	4 19.4	18 33.2	2 38.0	4 22.8	16 45.8	4 54.8
23 Sa	22 13 15	4 46 55	14 03 37	20 20 05	24 46.7	17 08.9	5 45.7	6 30.9	4 39.3	18 45.5	2 42.5	4 20.2	16 46.7	4 56.4
24 Su	22 17 12	5 47 20	26 34 01	2♓45 31	24 41.7	16 48.5	6 59.1	7 16.6	4 59.0	18 57.9	2 46.9	4 17.6	16 47.7	4 58.1
25 M	22 21 08	6 47 44	8♓54 40	15 01 34	24 34.9	16 35.4	8 12.5	8 02.2	5 18.6	19 10.4	2 51.3	4 14.9	16 48.7	4 59.8
26 Tu	22 25 05	7 48 06	21 06 20	27 09 07	24 26.7	16D 29.4	9 25.7	8 47.8	5 38.0	19 23.0	2 55.5	4 12.3	16 49.7	5 01.5
27 W	22 29 01	8 48 26	3♈10 03	9♈09 22	24 17.9	16 30.2	10 39.0	9 33.4	5 57.3	19 35.6	2 59.7	4 09.7	16 50.8	5 03.1
28 Th	22 32 58	9 48 44	15 07 16	21 04 02	24 09.3	16 37.4	11 52.2	10 18.9	6 16.5	19 48.3	3 03.9	4 07.1	16 51.8	5 04.8

Astro Data (Dy Hr Mn)

Astro Data	Dy Hr Mn
☽ 0N	2 5:40
☽ 0S	16 5:12
♆ D	26 14:52
☽ 0N	29 14:10
☿ R	5 6:59
♄□♆	10 6:10
☽ 0S	12 13:13
♃⚺♆	12 19:44
♅☍♇	15 1:26
♂ 0N	16 14:32
♀ 0N	20 13:01
♃□♅	25 19:10
☽ 0N	25 22:06
☿ D	26 21:05

Planet Ingress (Dy Hr Mn)

Planet Ingress	Dy Hr Mn
♀ ♒	1 11:54
♂ ♓	7 5:46
☿ ♒	11 3:33
☉ ♒	20 4:10
♄ ♑	24 15:40
♀ ♓	25 12:54
☿ ♓	31 19:33
☿ ♒R	9 16:50
⚳ ♑	9 23:04
♂ ♈	14 23:22
☉ ♓	18 18:10
♀ ♈	18 19:12

Last Aspect / ☽ Ingress (Dy Hr Mn)

Last Aspect Dy Hr Mn		☽ Ingress Dy Hr Mn
2 20:53	♄ □	♈ 3 1:44
5 11:32	♂ ⚹	♉ 5 14:18
7 14:10	☿ △	♊ 8 1:39
10 7:21	♄ ☍	♋ 10 10:13
12 1:21	☉ ☍	♌ 12 15:53
14 17:40	♄ △	♍ 14 19:29
16 20:41	♄ □	♎ 16 22:05
18 23:39	♄ ⚹	♏ 19 0:40
20 17:38	♀ □	♐ 21 3:55
23 8:09	♄ ☌	♑ 23 8:24
24 14:04	♆ △	♒ 25 14:37
27 14:59	☿ ☌	♓ 27 23:07
29 8:38	♂ ☌	♈ 30 10:03

Last Aspect / ☽ Ingress (Dy Hr Mn)

Last Aspect Dy Hr Mn		☽ Ingress Dy Hr Mn
31 15:06	♃ ☌	♉ 1 22:33
3 17:27	♂ ⚹	♊ 4 10:34
6 7:31	♂ □	♋ 6 19:56
8 17:18	♂ △	♌ 9 1:40
11 2:20	☿ ☍	♍ 11 4:20
13 3:05	♂ ☍	♎ 13 5:23
15 0:19	☉ △	♏ 15 6:35
17 6:42	☉ □	♐ 17 9:17
18 20:52	☿ ⚹	♑ 19 14:12
20 23:32	♃ □	♒ 21 21:25
23 8:56	♃ ⚹	♓ 24 6:39
25 15:31	♆ ⚹	♈ 26 17:40

☽ Phases & Eclipses (Dy Hr Mn)

Dy Hr Mn	Phase / Eclipse
4 5:31	☽ 13♈46
12 1:21	○ 21♋44
12 1:25	T 1.234
18 22:32	☾ 28♎45
26 1:44	● 6♒00
26 1:31:48	P 0.891
3 3:09	☽ 14♉11
10 14:39	○ 21♌46
17 6:42	☾ 28♏31
24 18:26	● 6♓04

Astro Data

1 January 2047
Julian Day # 53692
SVP 4♓35'56"
GC 27♐29.8 ⚴ 14♏54.0
Eris 29♈32.9R ⚵ 27♏37.0
⚷ 23♎11.9 ⚶ 20♏40.3
☽ Mean ☊ 25♑59.4

1 February 2047
Julian Day # 53723
SVP 4♓35'51"
GC 27♐29.8 ⚴ 25♏18.9
Eris 29♈33.0 ⚵ 6♐04.8
⚷ 24♎28.3 ⚶ 5♐02.6
☽ Mean ☊ 24♑20.9

March 2047

LONGITUDE

Day	Sid.Time	☉	0 hr ☽	Noon ☽	True ☊	☿	♀	♂	⚳	♃	♄	♅	♆	♇
1 F	22 36 54	10♓49 00	26♈59 59	2♉55 30	24♑01.8	16♒50.8	13♈05.3	11♈04.4	6♑35.5	20♈01.0	3♑07.9	4♍04.4	16♉53.0	5♓06.5
2 Sa	22 40 51	11 49 15	8♉51 00	14 46 55	23R56.0	17 09.8	14 18.3	11 49.9	6 54.4	20 13.9	3 11.9	4R01.8	16 54.1	5 08.1
3 Su	22 44 48	12 49 27	20 43 46	26 42 06	23 52.3	17 34.2	15 31.3	12 35.3	7 13.1	20 26.8	3 15.7	3 59.2	16 55.3	5 09.8
4 M	22 48 44	13 49 38	2♊42 28	8♊45 30	23D50.7	18 03.6	16 44.2	13 20.6	7 31.6	20 39.7	3 19.5	3 56.6	16 56.5	5 11.5
5 Tu	22 52 41	14 49 46	14 51 47	21 01 59	23 50.7	18 37.6	17 57.1	14 06.0	7 50.0	20 52.7	3 23.3	3 54.1	16 57.7	5 13.1
6 W	22 56 37	15 49 53	27 16 43	3♋36 34	23 51.7	19 16.0	19 09.8	14 51.2	8 08.3	21 05.8	3 26.9	3 51.5	16 59.0	5 14.8
7 Th	23 00 34	16 49 57	10♋02 06	16 33 52	23R52.8	19 58.4	20 22.6	15 36.5	8 26.4	21 19.0	3 30.4	3 49.0	17 00.3	5 16.4
8 F	23 04 30	17 49 59	23 12 15	29 57 36	23 52.8	20 44.5	21 35.2	16 21.7	8 44.3	21 32.2	3 33.9	3 46.4	17 01.6	5 18.1
9 Sa	23 08 27	18 49 59	6♌50 06	13♌49 47	23 51.0	21 34.1	22 47.7	17 06.8	9 02.1	21 45.4	3 37.3	3 43.9	17 03.0	5 19.7
10 Su	23 12 23	19 49 57	20 56 28	28 09 50	23 46.9	22 27.0	24 00.2	17 51.9	9 19.7	21 58.8	3 40.6	3 41.4	17 04.4	5 21.4
11 M	23 16 20	20 49 52	5♍29 18	12♍54 05	23 40.5	23 22.9	25 12.6	18 36.9	9 37.1	22 12.1	3 43.8	3 38.9	17 05.8	5 23.0
12 Tu	23 20 17	21 49 46	20 23 14	27 55 36	23 32.1	24 21.6	26 24.9	19 22.0	9 54.4	22 25.5	3 46.9	3 36.4	17 07.2	5 24.6
13 W	23 24 13	22 49 38	5♎29 55	13♎04 52	23 22.9	25 23.0	27 37.2	20 06.9	10 11.5	22 39.0	3 49.9	3 34.0	17 08.7	5 26.2
14 Th	23 28 10	23 49 28	20 39 08	28 11 26	23 13.9	26 27.0	28 49.3	20 51.8	10 28.4	22 52.5	3 52.8	3 31.6	17 10.2	5 27.8
15 F	23 32 06	24 49 16	5♏40 37	13♏05 40	23 06.3	27 33.3	0♉01.4	21 36.7	10 45.1	23 06.1	3 55.7	3 29.2	17 11.7	5 29.4
16 Sa	23 36 03	25 49 03	20 25 47	27 40 20	23 00.9	28 41.9	1 13.4	22 21.5	11 01.7	23 19.7	3 58.5	3 26.8	17 13.2	5 31.0
17 Su	23 39 59	26 48 48	4♐48 56	11♐51 21	22 57.8	29 52.6	2 25.3	23 06.3	11 18.1	23 33.4	4 01.1	3 24.4	17 14.8	5 32.6
18 M	23 43 56	27 48 32	18 47 32	25 37 37	22D56.8	1♓05.3	3 37.2	23 51.1	11 34.3	23 47.1	4 03.7	3 22.1	17 16.4	5 34.2
19 Tu	23 47 52	28 48 13	2♑21 49	9♑00 26	22 57.0	2 20.0	4 49.0	24 35.8	11 50.3	24 00.8	4 06.2	3 19.8	17 18.0	5 35.8
20 W	23 51 49	29 47 53	15 33 52	22 02 31	22R57.4	3 36.5	6 00.6	25 20.4	12 06.1	24 14.6	4 08.6	3 17.5	17 19.6	5 37.3
21 Th	23 55 46	0♈47 32	28 26 49	4♒47 13	22 56.8	4 54.8	7 12.2	26 05.0	12 21.7	24 28.5	4 10.9	3 15.2	17 21.3	5 38.9
22 F	23 59 42	1 47 08	11♒04 07	17 17 55	22 54.2	6 14.9	8 23.7	26 49.6	12 37.1	24 42.4	4 13.1	3 13.0	17 23.0	5 40.4
23 Sa	0 03 39	2 46 43	23 28 59	29 37 38	22 48.8	7 36.6	9 35.1	27 34.1	12 52.3	24 56.3	4 15.2	3 10.8	17 24.7	5 41.9
24 Su	0 07 35	3 46 15	5♓44 10	11♓48 49	22 40.5	8 59.9	10 46.5	28 18.6	13 07.3	25 10.2	4 17.2	3 08.7	17 26.4	5 43.5
25 M	0 11 32	4 45 46	17 51 48	23 53 19	22 29.5	10 24.8	11 57.7	29 03.0	13 22.1	25 24.2	4 19.1	3 06.5	17 28.1	5 45.0
26 Tu	0 15 28	5 45 15	29 53 32	5♈52 35	22 16.6	11 51.2	13 08.8	29 47.4	13 36.6	25 38.2	4 20.9	3 04.4	17 29.9	5 46.5
27 W	0 19 25	6 44 41	11♈50 38	17 47 49	22 02.6	13 19.1	14 19.9	0♉31.7	13 51.0	25 52.2	4 22.6	3 02.4	17 31.7	5 47.9
28 Th	0 23 21	7 44 06	23 44 19	29 40 17	21 48.9	14 48.5	15 30.8	1 16.0	14 05.1	26 06.3	4 24.3	3 00.3	17 33.5	5 49.4
29 F	0 27 18	8 43 29	5♉35 56	11♉31 30	21 36.4	16 19.4	16 41.7	2 00.3	14 19.0	26 20.4	4 25.8	2 58.3	17 35.3	5 50.9
30 Sa	0 31 15	9 42 49	17 27 17	23 23 35	21 26.2	17 51.7	17 52.4	2 44.4	14 32.7	26 34.6	4 27.2	2 56.4	17 37.2	5 52.3
31 Su	0 35 11	10 42 07	29 20 48	5♊19 19	21 18.7	19 25.4	19 03.0	3 28.6	14 46.2	26 48.7	4 28.5	2 54.5	17 39.1	5 53.7

April 2047

LONGITUDE

Day	Sid.Time	☉	0 hr ☽	Noon ☽	True ☊	☿	♀	♂	⚳	♃	♄	♅	♆	♇
1 M	0 39 08	11♈41 23	11♊19 37	17♊22 12	21♑14.1	21♓00.6	20♉13.6	4♉12.7	14♑59.4	27♈02.9	4♑29.8	2♍52.6	17♉41.0	5♓55.2
2 Tu	0 43 04	12 40 37	23 27 38	29 36 28	21R12.0	22 37.2	21 24.0	4 56.7	15 12.4	27 17.1	4 30.9	2R50.7	17 42.9	5 56.6
3 W	0 47 01	13 39 49	5♋49 20	12♋06 50	21 11.5	24 15.3	22 34.3	5 40.7	15 25.2	27 31.4	4 31.9	2 48.9	17 44.8	5 58.0
4 Th	0 50 57	14 38 58	18 29 34	24 58 09	21 11.5	25 54.7	23 44.5	6 24.7	15 37.7	27 45.6	4 32.9	2 47.2	17 46.7	5 59.3
5 F	0 54 54	15 38 04	1♌33 07	8♌14 55	21 10.8	27 35.6	24 54.5	7 08.6	15 50.0	27 59.9	4 33.7	2 45.4	17 48.7	6 00.7
6 Sa	0 58 50	16 37 09	15 03 57	22 00 27	21 08.2	29 17.9	26 04.5	7 52.4	16 02.0	28 14.2	4 34.4	2 43.8	17 50.7	6 02.0
7 Su	1 02 47	17 36 11	29 04 28	6♍15 54	21 03.2	1♈01.7	27 14.3	8 36.2	16 13.8	28 28.5	4 35.1	2 42.1	17 52.7	6 03.4
8 M	1 06 44	18 35 11	13♍34 23	20 59 20	20 55.5	2 46.9	28 23.9	9 20.0	16 25.3	28 42.8	4 35.6	2 40.5	17 54.7	6 04.7
9 Tu	1 10 40	19 34 08	28 29 56	6♎05 06	20 45.6	4 33.6	29 33.5	10 03.7	16 36.6	28 57.1	4 36.1	2 39.0	17 56.7	6 06.0
10 W	1 14 37	20 33 04	13♎43 35	21 23 58	20 34.5	6 21.8	0♊42.9	10 47.3	16 47.6	29 11.5	4 36.4	2 37.5	17 58.8	6 07.3
11 Th	1 18 33	21 31 57	29 04 47	6♏44 31	20 23.5	8 11.5	1 52.2	11 30.9	16 58.3	29 25.8	4 36.6	2 36.0	18 00.8	6 08.5
12 F	1 22 30	22 30 49	14♏21 43	21 55 05	20 14.0	10 02.7	3 01.4	12 14.4	17 08.8	29 40.2	4R36.8	2 34.6	18 02.9	6 09.8
13 Sa	1 26 26	23 29 39	29 23 30	6♐46 01	20 06.7	11 55.4	4 10.4	12 57.9	17 19.0	29 54.6	4 36.8	2 33.2	18 05.0	6 11.0
14 Su	1 30 23	24 28 27	14♐02 00	21 10 59	20 02.2	13 49.6	5 19.3	13 41.4	17 29.0	0♉09.0	4 36.8	2 31.9	18 07.0	6 12.2
15 M	1 34 19	25 27 14	28 12 46	5♑07 21	20 00.1	15 45.3	6 28.0	14 24.8	17 38.6	0 23.4	4 36.6	2 30.6	18 09.2	6 13.4
16 Tu	1 38 16	26 25 58	11♑54 52	18 35 33	19 59.6	17 42.4	7 36.6	15 08.1	17 48.0	0 37.8	4 36.4	2 29.4	18 11.3	6 14.6
17 W	1 42 13	27 24 41	25 10 01	1♒38 33	19 59.6	19 41.1	8 45.0	15 51.5	17 57.1	0 52.2	4 36.0	2 28.2	18 13.4	6 15.8
18 Th	1 46 09	28 23 23	8♒01 43	14 20 05	19 58.8	21 41.2	9 53.3	16 34.7	18 05.9	1 06.6	4 35.6	2 27.0	18 15.5	6 16.9
19 F	1 50 06	29 22 02	20 34 12	26 44 37	19 56.2	23 42.7	11 01.5	17 17.9	18 14.4	1 21.0	4 35.0	2 26.0	18 17.7	6 18.0
20 Sa	1 54 02	0♉20 40	2♓51 51	8♓56 23	19 51.0	25 45.5	12 09.5	18 01.1	18 22.6	1 35.4	4 34.4	2 24.9	18 19.9	6 19.1
21 Su	1 57 59	1 19 16	14 58 41	20 59 10	19 43.0	27 49.6	13 17.3	18 44.2	18 30.5	1 49.9	4 33.7	2 23.9	18 22.0	6 20.2
22 M	2 01 55	2 17 51	26 58 10	2♈56 03	19 32.3	29 54.9	14 25.0	19 27.3	18 38.1	2 04.3	4 32.8	2 23.0	18 24.2	6 21.3
23 Tu	2 05 52	3 16 23	8♈53 05	14 49 31	19 19.6	2♉01.1	15 32.5	20 10.3	18 45.4	2 18.7	4 31.9	2 22.1	18 26.4	6 22.3
24 W	2 09 48	4 14 54	20 45 34	26 41 26	19 05.9	4 08.3	16 39.9	20 53.3	18 52.4	2 33.1	4 30.9	2 21.2	18 28.6	6 23.3
25 Th	2 13 45	5 13 23	2♉37 18	8♉33 19	18 52.3	6 16.2	17 47.0	21 36.2	18 59.0	2 47.5	4 29.7	2 20.5	18 30.8	6 24.3
26 F	2 17 41	6 11 50	14 29 41	20 26 33	18 40.0	8 24.6	18 54.0	22 19.1	19 05.4	3 01.9	4 28.5	2 19.7	18 33.0	6 25.3
27 Sa	2 21 38	7 10 16	26 24 09	2♊22 40	18 29.8	10 33.3	20 00.8	23 01.9	19 11.4	3 16.3	4 27.2	2 19.0	18 35.2	6 26.3
28 Su	2 25 35	8 08 39	8♊22 22	14 23 32	18 22.3	12 42.1	21 07.5	23 44.7	19 17.1	3 30.7	4 25.8	2 18.4	18 37.4	6 27.2
29 M	2 29 31	9 07 01	20 26 30	26 31 37	18 17.7	14 50.6	22 13.9	24 27.4	19 22.4	3 45.1	4 24.3	2 17.8	18 39.7	6 28.1
30 Tu	2 33 28	10 05 20	2♋39 17	8♋49 58	18D15.6	16 58.6	23 20.1	25 10.1	19 27.5	3 59.5	4 22.7	2 17.3	18 41.9	6 29.0

Astro Data Dy Hr Mn	Planet Ingress Dy Hr Mn	Last Aspect Dy Hr Mn	☽ Ingress Dy Hr Mn	Last Aspect Dy Hr Mn	☽ Ingress Dy Hr Mn	☽ Phases & Eclipses Dy Hr Mn
♃∠♇ 1 23:44	♀ ♉ 15 11:32	28 9:24 ♃ ☌	♉ 1 6:05	2 7:24 ♃ ⚹	♋ 2 12:46	4 22:52 ☽ 14♊17
♄△♅ 10 15:27	☿ ♓ 17 14:28	2 16:58 ☿ □	♊ 3 18:36	4 17:12 ♃ □	♌ 4 21:11	12 1:37 ○ 21♍24
☽0S 11 23:38	☉ ♈ 20 16:52	5 11:42 ♃ ⚹	♋ 6 5:11	6 22:46 ♃ △	♍ 7 1:33	18 16:11 ☾ 27♐59
☉0N 20 16:52	♂ ♉ 26 18:49	7 20:45 ♃ □	♌ 8 12:04	9 0:50 ♀ △	♎ 9 2:23	26 11:44 ● 5♈45
☽0N 25 4:33		10 4:29 ♀ △	♍ 10 15:01	11 0:22 ♃ ☍	♏ 11 1:26	
	☿ ♈ 6 21:46	12 1:37 ☉ ☍	♎ 12 15:17	12 5:50 ♆ ☍	♐ 13 0:59	3 15:11 ☽ 13♋48
☽0S 8 10:25	♀ ♊ 9 21:09	14 13:06 ♀ ☍	♏ 14 14:54	14 18:01 ☉ △	♑ 15 3:05	10 10:35 ○ 20♎30
☿0N 9 18:45	♃ ♉ 13 21:03	16 13:52 ☿ □	♐ 16 15:54	17 3:30 ☉ □	♒ 17 8:56	17 3:30 ☾ 27♑04
♄ R 13 11:47	☉ ♉ 20 3:32	18 16:11 ☉ □	♑ 18 19:46	19 17:35 ☉ ⚹	♓ 19 18:22	25 4:40 ● 4♉56
☽0N 21 9:48	☿ ♉ 22 12:59	20 18:33 ♂ □	♒ 21 2:56	21 7:13 ♂ ⚹	♈ 22 6:06	
♃△♅ 23 17:20		23 7:43 ♂ ⚹	♓ 23 12:44	23 13:36 ♀ ⚹	♉ 24 18:42	
		24 23:11 ♆ ⚹	♈ 26 0:13	26 16:01 ♂ ☌	♊ 27 7:14	
		28 4:38 ♃ ☌	♉ 28 12:40	29 2:41 ♀ ☌	♋ 29 18:49	
		30 0:18 ♆ ☌	♊ 31 1:19			

Astro Data

1 March 2047
Julian Day # 53751
SVP 4♓35'47"
GC 27♐29.9 ⚴ 1♐48.6
Eris 29♈41.8 ⚵ 11♐36.0
⚷ 24♎00.7R ⚶ 16♐24.2
☽ Mean ☊ 22♑52.0

1 April 2047
Julian Day # 53782
SVP 4♓35'44"
GC 27♐30.0 ⚴ 3♐39.6R
Eris 29♈59.0 ⚵ 14♐02.9
⚷ 22♎05.0R ⚶ 25♐47.3
☽ Mean ☊ 21♑13.5

LONGITUDE — May 2047

Day	Sid.Time	☉	0 hr ☽	Noon ☽	True ☊	☿	♀	♂	⚳	♃	♄	♅	♆	♇
1 W	2 37 24	11♉03 37	15♋04 08	21♋22 16	18♑15.2	19♉05.7	24♊26.2	25♉52.7	19♑32.2	4♉13.8	4♑21.0	2♍16.8	18♉44.2	6♓29.9
2 Th	2 41 21	12 01 53	27 44 54	4♌12 33	18R 15.7	21 11.7	25 32.0	26 35.3	19 36.5	4 28.2	4R 19.2	2R 16.4	18 46.4	6 30.8
3 F	2 45 17	13 00 06	10♌45 42	17 24 49	18 15.8	23 16.3	26 37.6	27 17.9	19 40.5	4 42.5	4 17.4	2 16.1	18 48.6	6 31.6
4 Sa	2 49 14	13 58 17	24 10 18	1♍02 27	18 14.5	25 19.1	27 43.0	28 00.4	19 44.2	4 56.8	4 15.4	2 15.7	18 50.9	6 32.4
5 Su	2 53 10	14 56 26	8♍01 27	15 07 20	18 11.2	27 20.0	28 48.1	28 42.8	19 47.5	5 11.1	4 13.4	2 15.5	18 53.1	6 33.2
6 M	2 57 07	15 54 33	22 19 56	29 38 54	18 05.5	29 18.5	29 53.1	29 25.2	19 50.5	5 25.4	4 11.3	2 15.3	18 55.4	6 34.0
7 Tu	3 01 04	16 52 39	7♎03 41	14♎33 27	17 58.0	1♊14.6	0♋57.7	0♊07.5	19 53.2	5 39.7	4 09.1	2 15.1	18 57.6	6 34.7
8 W	3 05 00	17 50 42	22 07 14	29 43 49	17 49.2	3 07.9	2 02.2	0 49.8	19 55.4	5 53.9	4 06.8	2 15.0	18 59.9	6 35.4
9 Th	3 08 57	18 48 44	7♏21 55	15♏00 08	17 40.5	4 58.4	3 06.3	1 32.0	19 57.4	6 08.1	4 04.4	2D 15.0	19 02.2	6 36.1
10 F	3 12 53	19 46 44	22 37 03	0♐11 20	17 32.8	6 45.8	4 10.3	2 14.2	19 59.0	6 22.3	4 01.9	2 15.0	19 04.4	6 36.8
11 Sa	3 16 50	20 44 43	7♐41 44	15 07 11	17 27.0	8 30.0	5 13.9	2 56.4	20 00.2	6 36.5	3 59.4	2 15.0	19 06.7	6 37.4
12 Su	3 20 46	21 42 40	22 26 47	29 39 54	17 23.5	10 10.9	6 17.3	3 38.4	20 01.0	6 50.7	3 56.8	2 15.2	19 08.9	6 38.1
13 M	3 24 43	22 40 36	6♑46 04	13♑45 04	17D 22.2	11 48.4	7 20.4	4 20.5	20R 01.5	7 04.8	3 54.1	2 15.3	19 11.2	6 38.7
14 Tu	3 28 40	23 38 30	20 36 52	27 21 34	17 22.4	13 22.4	8 23.2	5 02.5	20 01.7	7 18.9	3 51.3	2 15.5	19 13.4	6 39.3
15 W	3 32 36	24 36 23	3♒59 27	10♒30 54	17 23.4	14 52.9	9 25.7	5 44.5	20 01.5	7 33.0	3 48.5	2 15.8	19 15.7	6 39.8
16 Th	3 36 33	25 34 15	16 56 22	23 16 23	17R 24.1	16 19.7	10 28.0	6 26.4	20 00.9	7 47.0	3 45.5	2 16.2	19 17.9	6 40.4
17 F	3 40 29	26 32 06	29 31 30	5♓42 19	17 23.7	17 42.9	11 29.9	7 08.2	19 59.9	8 01.0	3 42.5	2 16.5	19 20.2	6 40.9
18 Sa	3 44 26	27 29 55	11♓49 23	17 53 18	17 21.5	19 02.3	12 31.5	7 50.1	19 58.5	8 15.0	3 39.5	2 17.0	19 22.4	6 41.4
19 Su	3 48 22	28 27 44	23 54 37	29 53 51	17 17.2	20 18.0	13 32.8	8 31.9	19 56.8	8 29.0	3 36.3	2 17.5	19 24.7	6 41.8
20 M	3 52 19	29 25 31	5♈51 31	11♈48 03	17 11.0	21 29.9	14 33.7	9 13.6	19 54.7	8 42.9	3 33.1	2 18.0	19 26.9	6 42.3
21 Tu	3 56 15	0♊23 17	17 43 54	23 39 25	17 03.2	22 37.8	15 34.3	9 55.3	19 52.3	8 56.8	3 29.8	2 18.6	19 29.1	6 42.7
22 W	4 00 12	1 21 02	29 34 57	5♉30 49	16 54.7	23 41.8	16 34.6	10 36.9	19 49.5	9 10.6	3 26.5	2 19.2	19 31.3	6 43.1
23 Th	4 04 08	2 18 45	11♉27 17	17 24 36	16 46.1	24 41.9	17 34.5	11 18.5	19 46.3	9 24.4	3 23.1	2 20.0	19 33.6	6 43.4
24 F	4 08 05	3 16 28	23 22 57	29 22 34	16 38.4	25 37.8	18 34.0	12 00.1	19 42.7	9 38.2	3 19.6	2 20.7	19 35.8	6 43.8
25 Sa	4 12 02	4 14 09	5♊23 37	11♊26 16	16 32.1	26 29.6	19 33.1	12 41.6	19 38.8	9 52.0	3 16.0	2 21.5	19 38.0	6 44.1
26 Su	4 15 58	5 11 49	17 30 44	23 37 11	16 27.8	27 17.2	20 31.8	13 23.1	19 34.4	10 05.7	3 12.5	2 22.4	19 40.2	6 44.4
27 M	4 19 55	6 09 27	29 45 49	5♋56 52	16D 25.4	28 00.5	21 30.1	14 04.5	19 29.8	10 19.3	3 08.8	2 23.3	19 42.4	6 44.6
28 Tu	4 23 51	7 07 05	12♋10 33	18 27 08	16 24.9	28 39.4	22 28.0	14 45.9	19 24.8	10 32.9	3 05.1	2 24.3	19 44.5	6 44.9
29 W	4 27 48	8 04 41	24 46 55	1♌10 12	16 25.7	29 13.9	23 25.4	15 27.2	19 19.4	10 46.5	3 01.3	2 25.3	19 46.7	6 45.1
30 Th	4 31 44	9 02 15	7♌37 16	14 08 29	16 27.1	29 43.9	24 22.4	16 08.5	19 13.6	11 00.0	2 57.5	2 26.4	19 48.9	6 45.3
31 F	4 35 41	9 59 48	20 44 07	27 24 30	16R 28.5	0♋09.4	25 18.9	16 49.8	19 07.5	11 13.5	2 53.7	2 27.5	19 51.0	6 45.5

LONGITUDE — June 2047

Day	Sid.Time	☉	0 hr ☽	Noon ☽	True ☊	☿	♀	♂	⚳	♃	♄	♅	♆	♇
1 Sa	4 39 38	10♊57 20	4♍09 53	11♍00 27	16♑29.1	0♋30.2	26♋14.9	17♊31.0	19♑01.1	11♉26.9	2♑49.8	2♍28.7	19♉53.2	6♓45.6
2 Su	4 43 34	11 54 50	17 56 21	24 57 37	16R 28.4	0 46.4	27 10.3	18 12.1	18R 54.3	11 40.3	2R 45.8	2 29.9	19 55.3	6 45.7
3 M	4 47 31	12 52 19	2♎04 08	9♎15 42	16 26.2	0 58.0	28 05.3	18 53.2	18 47.2	11 53.6	2 41.8	2 31.2	19 57.4	6 45.8
4 Tu	4 51 27	13 49 46	16 31 57	23 52 20	16 22.8	1 04.9	28 59.7	19 34.3	18 39.8	12 06.8	2 37.8	2 32.5	19 59.5	6 45.9
5 W	4 55 24	14 47 13	1♏16 11	8♏42 40	16 18.6	1R 07.2	29 53.5	20 15.3	18 32.0	12 20.1	2 33.7	2 33.9	20 01.6	6 45.9
6 Th	4 59 20	15 44 38	16 10 50	23 39 39	16 14.3	1 05.0	0♌46.7	20 56.3	18 23.9	12 33.2	2 29.6	2 35.3	20 03.7	6R 45.9
7 F	5 03 17	16 42 03	1♐08 01	8♐34 53	16 10.5	0 58.3	1 39.3	21 37.2	18 15.5	12 46.3	2 25.4	2 36.8	20 05.8	6 45.9
8 Sa	5 07 13	17 39 26	15 59 09	23 19 51	16 07.8	0 47.4	2 31.3	22 18.1	18 06.8	12 59.4	2 21.2	2 38.3	20 07.8	6 45.9
9 Su	5 11 10	18 36 49	0♑36 09	7♑47 17	16D 06.4	0 32.4	3 22.6	22 59.0	17 57.8	13 12.4	2 17.0	2 39.9	20 09.9	6 45.8
10 M	5 15 07	19 34 11	14 52 42	21 52 01	16 06.3	0 13.6	4 13.3	23 39.8	17 48.4	13 25.3	2 12.8	2 41.5	20 11.9	6 45.8
11 Tu	5 19 03	20 31 32	28 44 57	5♒31 27	16 07.2	29♊51.3	5 03.2	24 20.6	17 38.8	13 38.2	2 08.5	2 43.2	20 13.9	6 45.7
12 W	5 23 00	21 28 53	12♒11 33	18 45 27	16 08.7	29 25.9	5 52.5	25 01.3	17 29.0	13 51.0	2 04.2	2 44.9	20 15.9	6 45.5
13 Th	5 26 56	22 26 13	25 13 26	1♓35 51	16 10.1	28 57.8	6 40.9	25 42.0	17 18.8	14 03.7	1 59.9	2 46.6	20 17.9	6 45.4
14 F	5 30 53	23 23 32	7♓53 11	14 05 54	16R 11.2	28 27.4	7 28.6	26 22.6	17 08.4	14 16.4	1 55.5	2 48.5	20 19.9	6 45.2
15 Sa	5 34 49	24 20 51	20 14 33	26 19 42	16 11.5	27 55.3	8 15.5	27 03.2	16 57.7	14 29.0	1 51.2	2 50.3	20 21.8	6 45.0
16 Su	5 38 46	25 18 10	2♈21 54	8♈21 43	16 10.9	27 22.0	9 01.6	27 43.8	16 46.8	14 41.6	1 46.8	2 52.2	20 23.7	6 44.8
17 M	5 42 42	26 15 28	14 19 45	20 16 31	16 09.3	26 48.1	9 46.8	28 24.4	16 35.6	14 54.0	1 42.4	2 54.2	20 25.7	6 44.5
18 Tu	5 46 39	27 12 46	26 12 33	2♉08 22	16 07.1	26 14.1	10 31.1	29 04.9	16 24.2	15 06.5	1 38.0	2 56.2	20 27.6	6 44.3
19 W	5 50 36	28 10 04	8♉04 25	14 01 09	16 04.4	25 40.6	11 14.5	29 45.3	16 12.6	15 18.8	1 33.6	2 58.2	20 29.4	6 44.0
20 Th	5 54 32	29 07 22	19 58 58	25 58 13	16 01.8	25 08.2	11 56.9	0♋25.7	16 00.8	15 31.1	1 29.2	3 00.3	20 31.3	6 43.7
21 F	5 58 29	0♋04 39	1♊59 15	8♊02 20	15 59.4	24 37.4	12 38.3	1 06.1	15 48.8	15 43.3	1 24.7	3 02.4	20 33.2	6 43.3
22 Sa	6 02 25	1 01 56	14 07 44	20 15 39	15 57.5	24 08.9	13 18.7	1 46.5	15 36.7	15 55.4	1 20.3	3 04.6	20 35.0	6 43.0
23 Su	6 06 22	1 59 12	26 26 17	2♋39 48	15 56.4	23 42.9	13 58.0	2 26.8	15 24.3	16 07.4	1 15.9	3 06.8	20 36.8	6 42.6
24 M	6 10 18	2 56 28	8♋56 18	15 15 55	15D 56.0	23 20.1	14 36.2	3 07.1	15 11.9	16 19.4	1 11.4	3 09.1	20 38.6	6 42.2
25 Tu	6 14 15	3 53 44	21 38 44	28 04 49	15 56.3	23 00.8	15 13.2	3 47.3	14 59.2	16 31.3	1 07.0	3 11.4	20 40.4	6 41.7
26 W	6 18 11	4 50 59	4♌34 15	11♌07 06	15 57.0	22 45.3	15 49.0	4 27.5	14 46.5	16 43.1	1 02.6	3 13.7	20 42.1	6 41.3
27 Th	6 22 08	5 48 13	17 43 23	24 23 10	15 57.9	22 34.0	16 23.5	5 07.6	14 33.6	16 54.8	0 58.2	3 16.1	20 43.8	6 40.8
28 F	6 26 05	6 45 27	1♍06 28	7♍53 18	15 58.7	22 27.0	16 56.7	5 47.8	14 20.7	17 06.4	0 53.7	3 18.5	20 45.5	6 40.3
29 Sa	6 30 01	7 42 41	14 43 40	21 37 32	15 59.3	22D 24.5	17 28.5	6 27.8	14 07.6	17 18.0	0 49.4	3 21.0	20 47.2	6 39.8
30 Su	6 33 58	8 39 54	28 34 50	5♎35 27	15R 59.6	22 26.8	17 59.0	7 07.9	13 54.5	17 29.4	0 45.0	3 23.5	20 48.9	6 39.2

Astro Data Dy Hr Mn	Planet Ingress Dy Hr Mn	Last Aspect Dy Hr Mn	☽ Ingress Dy Hr Mn	Last Aspect Dy Hr Mn	☽ Ingress Dy Hr Mn	☽ Phases & Eclipses Dy Hr Mn	Astro Data
♃△♄ 1 22:42	♀ ♋ 6 14:34	1 21:00 ♂ ⚹	♌ 2 4:12	2 16:01 ♀ ⚹	♎ 2 20:31	3 3:26 ☽ 12♌39	1 May 2047
☽0S 5 19:32	☿ ♊ 6 20:31	4 6:26 ♂ □	♍ 4 10:12	4 20:51 ♀ □	♏ 4 21:57	9 18:24 ○ 19♏04	Julian Day # 53812
♅D 9 20:10	♂ ♊ 7 7:45	6 12:25 ♀ □	♎ 6 12:34	6 6:13 ♆ ☍	♐ 6 22:11	16 16:46 ☾ 25♒46	SVP 4♓35'40"
♄⚼♆ 9 23:23	☉ ♊ 21 2:20	6 19:21 ♄ □	♏ 8 12:25	8 10:14 ♂ ☍	♑ 8 23:00	24 20:27 ● 3♊37	GC 27♐30.0 ⚴ 28♏27.4R
♃⚹♇ 11 13:41	☿ ♋ 31 2:38	9 18:24 ☉ ☍	♐ 10 11:42	10 9:07 ♆ △	♒ 11 2:12		Eris 0♉18.7 ⚵ 11♐38.2R
⚳R 14 8:52		10 23:54 ☿ ☍	♑ 12 12:34	13 7:12 ☿ △	♓ 13 8:59	1 11:54 ☽ 10♍57	⚷ 19♎47.7R ⚶ 29♐33.6
☽0N 18 15:08	♀ ♌ 5 14:55	14 4:51 ☉ △	♒ 14 16:45	15 15:01 ☿ □	♈ 15 19:17	8 2:05 ○ 17♐16	☽ Mean ☊ 19♑38.1
☽0S 2 2:15	☿ ♊R 11 3:05	16 16:46 ☉ □	♓ 17 0:55	18 5:26 ♂ ⚹	♉ 18 7:40	15 7:45 ☾ 24♓11	
♄△♅ 5 11:11	♂ ♋ 19 20:43	19 8:52 ☉ ⚹	♈ 19 12:12	20 1:03 ♆ ☌	♊ 20 20:03	23 10:36 ● 1♋56	1 June 2047
☿R 5 12:04	☉ ♋ 21 10:03	21 9:42 ☿ ⚹	♉ 22 0:51	22 19:18 ☿ ☌	♋ 23 6:53	23 10:50:54 ● P 0.313	Julian Day # 53843
♇R 6 20:52		23 16:20 ♆ ☌	♊ 24 13:15	24 22:09 ♆ ⚹	♌ 25 15:34	30 17:37 ☽ 8♎53	SVP 4♓35'35"
☽0N 14 21:49		26 19:38 ☿ ☌	♋ 27 0:28	27 8:46 ☿ ⚹	♍ 27 22:02		GC 27♐30.1 ⚴ 19♏28.3R
♃⚼♄ 24 0:19		28 20:15 ♀ ☌	♌ 29 9:49	29 13:21 ☿ □	♎ 30 2:26		Eris 0♉37.4 ⚵ 5♐16.3R
☽0S 29 7:31		30 22:22 ♆ □	♍ 31 16:37				⚷ 18♎15.2R ⚶ 26♐09.6R
☿D 29 12:35							☽ Mean ☊ 17♑59.6

July 2047

LONGITUDE

Day	Sid.Time	☉	0 hr ☽	Noon ☽	True ☊	☿	♀	♂	⚳	♃	♄	♅	♆	♇
1 M	6 37 54	9♋37 06	12♎39 14	19♎45 57	15♑59.5	22♊33.8	18♌27.9	7♋47.9	13♑41.4	17♉40.8	0♑40.6	3♍26.0	20♉50.5	6♓38.7
2 Tu	6 41 51	10 34 18	26 55 19	4♏06 59	15R 59.2	22 45.8	18 55.3	8 27.8	13R 28.2	17 52.1	0R 36.3	3 28.6	20 52.1	6R 38.1
3 W	6 45 47	11 31 30	11♏20 29	18 35 21	15 58.7	23 02.7	19 21.1	9 07.8	13 14.9	18 03.2	0 32.0	3 31.2	20 53.7	6 37.5
4 Th	6 49 44	12 28 41	25 50 59	3♐06 47	15 58.3	23 24.5	19 45.3	9 47.7	13 01.7	18 14.3	0 27.7	3 33.9	20 55.3	6 36.8
5 F	6 53 40	13 25 53	10♐22 04	17 36 10	15 58.1	23 51.3	20 07.7	10 27.5	12 48.5	18 25.3	0 23.4	3 36.6	20 56.8	6 36.2
6 Sa	6 57 37	14 23 04	24 48 24	1♑58 05	15D 57.9	24 23.0	20 28.4	11 07.3	12 35.3	18 36.2	0 19.2	3 39.3	20 58.3	6 35.5
7 Su	7 01 34	15 20 15	9♑04 35	16 07 21	15R 57.9	24 59.6	20 47.3	11 47.1	12 22.1	18 47.0	0 15.0	3 42.1	20 59.8	6 34.8
8 M	7 05 30	16 17 26	23 05 52	29 59 43	15 57.9	25 41.1	21 04.2	12 26.9	12 09.0	18 57.8	0 10.8	3 44.9	21 01.3	6 34.1
9 Tu	7 09 27	17 14 37	6♒48 36	13♒32 18	15 57.8	26 27.4	21 19.2	13 06.6	11 55.9	19 08.4	0 06.7	3 47.7	21 02.7	6 33.4
10 W	7 13 23	18 11 48	20 10 43	26 43 50	15 57.6	27 18.4	21 32.3	13 46.3	11 42.8	19 18.9	0 02.5	3 50.5	21 04.2	6 32.6
11 Th	7 17 20	19 09 00	3♓11 46	9♓34 40	15 57.3	28 14.2	21 43.2	14 25.9	11 29.9	19 29.3	29♐58.5	3 53.4	21 05.5	6 31.9
12 F	7 21 16	20 06 12	15 52 49	22 06 35	15 56.9	29 14.6	21 52.1	15 05.5	11 17.1	19 39.6	29 54.4	3 56.4	21 06.9	6 31.1
13 Sa	7 25 13	21 03 24	28 16 19	4♈22 32	15 56.5	0♋19.6	21 58.8	15 45.1	11 04.3	19 49.7	29 50.5	3 59.3	21 08.3	6 30.3
14 Su	7 29 09	22 00 37	10♈25 41	16 26 19	15D 56.3	1 29.1	22 03.3	16 24.7	10 51.7	19 59.8	29 46.5	4 02.3	21 09.6	6 29.4
15 M	7 33 06	22 57 51	22 24 59	28 22 16	15 56.3	2 43.1	22R 05.6	17 04.2	10 39.3	20 09.8	29 42.6	4 05.4	21 10.8	6 28.6
16 Tu	7 37 03	23 55 05	4♉18 44	10♉14 57	15 56.6	4 01.4	22 05.6	17 43.7	10 26.9	20 19.6	29 38.8	4 08.4	21 12.1	6 27.7
17 W	7 40 59	24 52 19	16 11 31	22 08 57	15 57.3	5 24.1	22 03.2	18 23.1	10 14.8	20 29.4	29 35.0	4 11.5	21 13.3	6 26.9
18 Th	7 44 56	25 49 35	28 07 49	4♊08 35	15 58.2	6 51.0	21 58.5	19 02.6	10 02.8	20 39.0	29 31.2	4 14.6	21 14.5	6 26.0
19 F	7 48 52	26 46 51	10♊11 45	16 17 44	15 59.2	8 22.0	21 51.5	19 42.0	9 51.0	20 48.5	29 27.5	4 17.8	21 15.7	6 25.0
20 Sa	7 52 49	27 44 07	22 26 55	28 39 38	16 00.0	9 57.0	21 42.1	20 21.3	9 39.4	20 57.9	29 23.9	4 21.0	21 16.9	6 24.1
21 Su	7 56 45	28 41 24	4♋56 08	11♋16 40	16R 00.5	11 35.8	21 30.3	21 00.7	9 28.0	21 07.2	29 20.3	4 24.2	21 18.0	6 23.2
22 M	8 00 42	29 38 42	17 41 21	24 10 17	16 00.4	13 18.4	21 16.1	21 40.0	9 16.8	21 16.4	29 16.8	4 27.4	21 19.1	6 22.2
23 Tu	8 04 39	0♌36 00	0♌43 27	7♌20 49	15 59.6	15 04.4	20 59.6	22 19.3	9 05.9	21 25.4	29 13.3	4 30.6	21 20.1	6 21.2
24 W	8 08 35	1 33 19	14 02 14	20 47 33	15 58.2	16 53.7	20 40.8	22 58.5	8 55.2	21 34.3	29 09.9	4 33.9	21 21.2	6 20.2
25 Th	8 12 32	2 30 38	27 36 30	4♍28 49	15 56.2	18 46.0	20 19.8	23 37.7	8 44.7	21 43.0	29 06.6	4 37.2	21 22.2	6 19.2
26 F	8 16 28	3 27 58	11♍24 11	18 22 15	15 53.9	20 41.1	19 56.6	24 16.9	8 34.6	21 51.7	29 03.3	4 40.6	21 23.1	6 18.2
27 Sa	8 20 25	4 25 18	25 22 38	2♎24 59	15 51.7	22 38.6	19 31.2	24 56.0	8 24.6	22 00.2	29 00.1	4 43.9	21 24.1	6 17.2
28 Su	8 24 21	5 22 39	9♎28 56	16 34 06	15 50.1	24 38.3	19 04.0	25 35.2	8 15.0	22 08.6	28 57.0	4 47.3	21 25.0	6 16.1
29 M	8 28 18	6 20 00	23 40 10	0♏46 46	15D 49.3	26 39.8	18 34.8	26 14.2	8 05.7	22 16.8	28 53.9	4 50.7	21 25.8	6 15.0
30 Tu	8 32 14	7 17 21	7♏53 36	15 00 22	15 49.4	28 42.8	18 03.9	26 53.3	7 56.6	22 24.9	28 50.9	4 54.1	21 26.7	6 14.0
31 W	8 36 11	8 14 43	22 06 46	29 12 33	15 50.2	0♌46.9	17 31.5	27 32.3	7 47.9	22 32.9	28 48.0	4 57.6	21 27.5	6 12.9

August 2047

LONGITUDE

Day	Sid.Time	☉	0 hr ☽	Noon ☽	True ☊	☿	♀	♂	⚳	♃	♄	♅	♆	♇
1 Th	8 40 08	9♌12 05	6♐17 25	13♐21 07	15♑51.6	2♌51.9	16♌57.7	28♋11.3	7♑39.4	22♉40.7	28♐45.2	5♍01.0	21♉28.3	6♓11.8
2 F	8 44 04	10 09 28	20 23 21	27 23 50	15 52.9	4 57.3	16R 22.7	28 50.3	7R 31.3	22 48.4	28R 42.4	5 04.5	21 29.1	6R 10.7
3 Sa	8 48 01	11 06 52	4♑22 17	11♑18 25	15R 53.7	7 02.9	15 46.8	29 29.2	7 23.5	22 55.9	28 39.7	5 08.0	21 29.8	6 09.5
4 Su	8 51 57	12 04 17	18 11 55	25 02 31	15 53.5	9 08.4	15 10.1	0♌08.1	7 16.1	23 03.3	28 37.1	5 11.5	21 30.5	6 08.4
5 M	8 55 54	13 01 42	1♒49 55	8♒33 53	15 52.0	11 13.6	14 32.9	0 47.0	7 08.9	23 10.6	28 34.6	5 15.1	21 31.1	6 07.3
6 Tu	8 59 50	13 59 08	15 14 10	21 50 35	15 49.1	13 18.2	13 55.4	1 25.9	7 02.1	23 17.7	28 32.1	5 18.6	21 31.8	6 06.1
7 W	9 03 47	14 56 35	28 23 00	4♓51 20	15 45.1	15 22.0	13 18.0	2 04.7	6 55.6	23 24.6	28 29.7	5 22.2	21 32.4	6 04.9
8 Th	9 07 43	15 54 03	11♓15 34	17 35 43	15 40.3	17 25.0	12 40.7	2 43.5	6 49.5	23 31.4	28 27.4	5 25.8	21 32.9	6 03.7
9 F	9 11 40	16 51 33	23 51 55	0♈04 21	15 35.3	19 26.9	12 04.0	3 22.2	6 43.7	23 38.1	28 25.2	5 29.4	21 33.4	6 02.6
10 Sa	9 15 37	17 49 03	6♈13 15	12 18 57	15 30.6	21 27.7	11 27.9	4 01.0	6 38.2	23 44.6	28 23.1	5 33.0	21 33.9	6 01.4
11 Su	9 19 33	18 46 35	18 21 47	24 22 14	15 26.9	23 27.2	10 52.8	4 39.7	6 33.1	23 50.9	28 21.1	5 36.6	21 34.4	6 00.2
12 M	9 23 30	19 44 08	0♉20 43	6♉17 48	15 24.4	25 25.5	10 18.8	5 18.4	6 28.4	23 57.1	28 19.1	5 40.3	21 34.8	5 58.9
13 Tu	9 27 26	20 41 43	12 14 01	18 09 58	15D 23.4	27 22.3	9 46.2	5 57.1	6 24.0	24 03.1	28 17.3	5 43.9	21 35.2	5 57.7
14 W	9 31 23	21 39 19	24 06 13	0♊03 25	15 23.7	29 17.8	9 15.1	6 35.7	6 19.9	24 08.9	28 15.5	5 47.6	21 35.6	5 56.5
15 Th	9 35 19	22 36 57	6♊02 11	12 03 07	15 25.0	1♍11.9	8 45.7	7 14.3	6 16.2	24 14.6	28 13.8	5 51.3	21 35.9	5 55.3
16 F	9 39 16	23 34 36	18 06 49	24 13 53	15 26.6	3 04.5	8 18.1	7 52.9	6 12.9	24 20.2	28 12.2	5 55.0	21 36.3	5 54.0
17 Sa	9 43 12	24 32 17	0♋24 50	6♋40 09	15R 27.9	4 55.7	7 52.5	8 31.5	6 10.0	24 25.5	28 10.7	5 58.7	21 36.5	5 52.8
18 Su	9 47 09	25 29 59	13 00 17	19 25 34	15 28.1	6 45.4	7 29.0	9 10.1	6 07.4	24 30.7	28 09.3	6 02.4	21 36.8	5 51.5
19 M	9 51 06	26 27 43	25 56 16	2♌32 31	15 26.8	8 33.8	7 07.7	9 48.6	6 05.1	24 35.7	28 08.0	6 06.1	21 37.0	5 50.3
20 Tu	9 55 02	27 25 28	9♌14 24	16 01 48	15 23.6	10 20.6	6 48.6	10 27.1	6 03.2	24 40.6	28 06.7	6 09.9	21 37.1	5 49.0
21 W	9 58 59	28 23 14	22 54 31	29 52 13	15 18.6	12 06.1	6 31.9	11 05.6	6 01.7	24 45.3	28 05.6	6 13.6	21 37.3	5 47.8
22 Th	10 02 55	29 21 02	6♍54 26	14♍00 35	15 12.2	13 50.2	6 17.4	11 44.0	6 00.6	24 49.8	28 04.6	6 17.3	21 37.4	5 46.5
23 F	10 06 52	0♍18 51	21 10 00	28 21 59	15 05.1	15 32.8	6 05.4	12 22.4	5 59.8	24 54.1	28 03.6	6 21.1	21 37.4	5 45.2
24 Sa	10 10 48	1 16 41	5♎35 43	12♎50 28	14 58.4	17 14.1	5 55.7	13 00.8	5D 59.4	24 58.2	28 02.8	6 24.8	21R 37.5	5 43.9
25 Su	10 14 45	2 14 33	20 05 26	27 19 58	14 52.7	18 54.0	5 48.4	13 39.2	5 59.3	25 02.1	28 02.0	6 28.6	21 37.5	5 42.7
26 M	10 18 41	3 12 26	4♏33 23	11♏45 10	14 48.9	20 32.6	5 43.5	14 17.6	5 59.6	25 05.9	28 01.4	6 32.3	21 37.4	5 41.4
27 Tu	10 22 38	4 10 20	18 54 51	26 02 07	14D 47.0	22 09.8	5D 41.0	14 55.9	6 00.2	25 09.5	28 00.8	6 36.1	21 37.4	5 40.1
28 W	10 26 34	5 08 15	3♐06 40	10♐08 23	14 46.8	23 45.7	5 40.7	15 34.2	6 01.2	25 12.9	28 00.3	6 39.9	21 37.3	5 38.8
29 Th	10 30 31	6 06 12	17 07 08	24 02 54	14 47.7	25 20.3	5 42.8	16 12.4	6 02.6	25 16.1	28 00.0	6 43.6	21 37.2	5 37.5
30 F	10 34 28	7 04 10	0♑55 40	7♑45 29	14R 48.6	26 53.5	5 47.2	16 50.7	6 04.3	25 19.2	27 59.7	6 47.4	21 37.0	5 36.3
31 Sa	10 38 24	8 02 09	14 32 23	21 16 23	14 48.6	28 25.4	5 53.8	17 28.9	6 06.3	25 22.0	27 59.5	6 51.2	21 36.8	5 35.0

Astro Data	Dy Hr Mn
☽ 0N	12 6:04
♀ R	15 23:46
♃☌♆	22 20:10
☽ 0S	26 13:14
☽ 0N	8 15:00
♅☍♇	16 7:19
☽ 0S	22 20:48
♆ R	25 1:16
⚳ D	25 4:38
♀ D	28 2:07

Planet Ingress	Dy Hr Mn
♄ ♐R	11 2:59
☿ ♋	13 4:57
☉ ♌	22 20:55
☿ ♌	31 2:57
♂ ♌	4 6:59
☿ ♍	14 20:50
☉ ♍	23 4:11

Last Aspect Dy Hr Mn		☽ Ingress	Dy Hr Mn
1 16:45	☿ △	♏	2 5:08
3 15:49	♆ ☍	♐	4 6:51
5 22:47	☿ ☍	♑	6 8:42
7 20:23	♆ △	♒	8 12:00
10 13:09	☿ △	♓	10 18:03
13 3:14	☿ □	♈	13 3:23
15 14:41	♄ △	♉	15 15:17
17 17:57	☉ ⚹	♊	18 3:44
20 13:25	♄ ☍	♋	20 14:34
22 7:08	♂ ☌	♌	22 22:41
25 2:40	♄ △	♍	25 4:11
27 6:12	♄ □	♎	27 7:53
29 8:50	♄ ⚹	♏	29 10:41
31 9:02	♂ △	♐	31 13:20

Last Aspect Dy Hr Mn		☽ Ingress	Dy Hr Mn
2 14:14	♄ ☌	♑	2 16:28
4 8:29	♃ △	♒	4 20:45
7 0:15	♄ ⚹	♓	7 2:59
9 8:48	♄ □	♈	9 11:52
11 19:58	♄ △	♉	11 23:18
14 10:11	☿ □	♊	14 11:53
16 19:43	♄ ☍	♋	16 23:12
18 21:27	♃ ⚹	♌	19 7:24
21 9:16	☉ ☌	♍	21 12:13
23 11:30	♄ □	♎	23 14:43
25 13:10	♄ ⚹	♏	25 16:26
27 10:31	♃ ☍	♐	27 18:43
29 18:53	♄ ☌	♑	29 22:23

☽ Phases & Eclipses Dy Hr Mn	
7 10:34	○ 15♑17
7 10:34	• T 1.752
15 0:09	☾ 22♈30
22 22:49	● 0♌05
22 22:34:47	• P 0.361
29 22:03	☽ 6♏44
5 20:38	○ 13♒22
13 17:34	☾ 20♉55
21 9:16	● 28♌17
28 2:49	☽ 4♐46

Astro Data

1 July 2047
Julian Day # 53873
SVP 4♓35'30"
GC 27♐30.2 ⚴ 15♏04.1R
Eris 0♉49.5 ⚵ 29♏45.0R
⚷ 18♎18.0 ⚶ 19♐21.0R
☽ Mean ☊ 16♑24.3

1 August 2047
Julian Day # 53904
SVP 4♓35'25"
GC 27♐30.2 ⚴ 17♏22.9
Eris 0♉53.0R ⚵ 28♏32.4
⚷ 20♎02.3 ⚶ 16♐57.6
☽ Mean ☊ 14♑45.9

LONGITUDE — September 2047

Day	Sid.Time	☉	0 hr ☽	Noon ☽	True ☊	☿	♀	♂	⚳	♃	♄	♅	♆	♇
1 Su	10 42 21	9♍00 10	27♑57 33	4♒35 52	14♑46.8	29♍56.0	6♌02.6	18♌07.1	6♑08.7	25♉24.7	27♐59.5	6♍54.9	21♉36.6	5♓33.7
2 M	10 46 17	9 58 12	11♒11 20	17 43 57	14R42.6	1♎25.3	6 13.5	18 45.3	6 11.5	25 27.1	27D59.5	6 58.7	21R36.3	5R32.4
3 Tu	10 50 14	10 56 15	24 13 39	0♓40 25	14 36.0	2 53.3	6 26.6	19 23.4	6 14.5	25 29.4	27 59.6	7 02.4	21 36.0	5 31.2
4 W	10 54 10	11 54 21	7♓04 12	13 24 57	14 27.2	4 19.9	6 41.6	20 01.5	6 17.9	25 31.5	27 59.8	7 06.2	21 35.7	5 29.9
5 Th	10 58 07	12 52 27	19 42 39	25 57 18	14 16.9	5 45.1	6 58.6	20 39.6	6 21.6	25 33.4	28 00.1	7 09.9	21 35.3	5 28.6
6 F	11 02 03	13 50 36	2♈08 58	8♈17 43	14 06.0	7 09.0	7 17.6	21 17.7	6 25.7	25 35.1	28 00.5	7 13.7	21 35.0	5 27.4
7 Sa	11 06 00	14 48 46	14 23 42	20 27 04	13 55.6	8 31.4	7 38.3	21 55.8	6 30.1	25 36.6	28 01.0	7 17.4	21 34.5	5 26.1
8 Su	11 09 57	15 46 59	26 28 06	2♉27 06	13 46.4	9 52.4	8 00.9	22 33.8	6 34.8	25 37.9	28 01.7	7 21.2	21 34.1	5 24.8
9 M	11 13 53	16 45 13	8♉24 24	14 20 27	13 39.3	11 12.0	8 25.3	23 11.8	6 39.8	25 39.0	28 02.4	7 24.9	21 33.6	5 23.6
10 Tu	11 17 50	17 43 29	20 15 41	26 10 39	13 34.6	12 30.0	8 51.3	23 49.8	6 45.2	25 39.9	28 03.2	7 28.6	21 33.1	5 22.3
11 W	11 21 46	18 41 48	2♊05 53	8♊02 01	13D32.2	13 46.5	9 18.9	24 27.8	6 50.8	25 40.6	28 04.1	7 32.4	21 32.5	5 21.1
12 Th	11 25 43	19 40 08	13 59 40	19 59 28	13 31.6	15 01.4	9 48.1	25 05.8	6 56.8	25 41.1	28 05.1	7 36.1	21 32.0	5 19.9
13 F	11 29 39	20 38 31	26 02 06	2♋08 14	13R31.9	16 14.5	10 18.8	25 43.7	7 03.1	25 41.4	28 06.1	7 39.8	21 31.3	5 18.6
14 Sa	11 33 36	21 36 56	8♋18 31	14 33 35	13 32.2	17 25.9	10 51.0	26 21.6	7 09.6	25R41.5	28 07.3	7 43.5	21 30.7	5 17.4
15 Su	11 37 32	22 35 22	20 54 01	27 20 20	13 31.4	18 35.4	11 24.6	26 59.5	7 16.5	25 41.4	28 08.6	7 47.1	21 30.0	5 16.2
16 M	11 41 29	23 33 51	3♌52 58	10♌32 14	13 28.6	19 42.9	11 59.5	27 37.4	7 23.7	25 41.1	28 10.0	7 50.8	21 29.3	5 15.0
17 Tu	11 45 26	24 32 22	17 18 20	24 11 17	13 23.3	20 48.4	12 35.7	28 15.3	7 31.2	25 40.6	28 11.5	7 54.5	21 28.6	5 13.8
18 W	11 49 22	25 30 55	1♍10 58	8♍17 02	13 15.4	21 51.7	13 13.1	28 53.1	7 38.9	25 39.9	28 13.1	7 58.1	21 27.9	5 12.6
19 Th	11 53 19	26 29 30	15 28 59	22 46 05	13 05.5	22 52.5	13 51.8	29 30.9	7 47.0	25 39.0	28 14.7	8 01.7	21 27.1	5 11.4
20 F	11 57 15	27 28 07	0♎07 29	7♎32 09	12 54.6	23 50.9	14 31.6	0♍08.7	7 55.3	25 37.9	28 16.5	8 05.3	21 26.2	5 10.2
21 Sa	12 01 12	28 26 46	14 58 59	22 26 50	12 43.9	24 46.6	15 12.5	0 46.5	8 03.9	25 36.6	28 18.4	8 08.9	21 25.4	5 09.1
22 Su	12 05 08	29 25 26	29 54 31	7♏20 58	12 34.7	25 39.3	15 54.5	1 24.2	8 12.8	25 35.0	28 20.3	8 12.5	21 24.5	5 07.9
23 M	12 09 05	0♎24 09	14♏45 11	22 06 19	12 27.8	26 28.9	16 37.5	2 01.9	8 22.0	25 33.3	28 22.4	8 16.1	21 23.6	5 06.8
24 Tu	12 13 01	1 22 53	29 23 39	6♐36 41	12 23.6	27 15.1	17 21.5	2 39.6	8 31.4	25 31.4	28 24.5	8 19.6	21 22.7	5 05.7
25 W	12 16 58	2 21 39	13♐45 03	20 48 33	12D21.8	27 57.6	18 06.5	3 17.3	8 41.1	25 29.3	28 26.8	8 23.2	21 21.7	5 04.6
26 Th	12 20 55	3 20 27	27 47 08	4♑40 50	12R21.5	28 36.2	18 52.3	3 55.0	8 51.1	25 27.0	28 29.1	8 26.7	21 20.7	5 03.5
27 F	12 24 51	4 19 16	11♑29 49	18 14 17	12 21.5	29 10.5	19 39.1	4 32.6	9 01.3	25 24.5	28 31.5	8 30.2	21 19.7	5 02.4
28 Sa	12 28 48	5 18 07	24 54 30	1♒30 44	12 20.5	29 40.1	20 26.8	5 10.2	9 11.8	25 21.8	28 34.0	8 33.7	21 18.7	5 01.3
29 Su	12 32 44	6 17 00	8♒03 15	14 32 20	12 17.4	0♏04.6	21 15.2	5 47.8	9 22.5	25 18.9	28 36.7	8 37.1	21 17.6	5 00.2
30 M	12 36 41	7 15 54	20 58 13	27 21 08	12 11.5	0 23.7	22 04.5	6 25.3	9 33.5	25 15.8	28 39.4	8 40.5	21 16.5	4 59.2

LONGITUDE — October 2047

Day	Sid.Time	☉	0 hr ☽	Noon ☽	True ☊	☿	♀	♂	⚳	♃	♄	♅	♆	♇
1 Tu	12 40 37	8♎14 50	3♓41 16	9♓58 47	12♑02.6	0♏36.9	22♌54.6	7♍02.9	9♑44.7	25♉12.5	28♐42.1	8♍43.9	21♉15.4	4♓58.1
2 W	12 44 34	9 13 48	16 13 48	22 26 26	11R51.1	0R43.9	23 45.4	7 40.4	9 56.2	25R09.0	28 45.0	8 47.3	21R14.3	4R57.1
3 Th	12 48 30	10 12 48	28 36 45	4♈44 51	11 37.6	0 44.1	24 36.9	8 17.9	10 07.9	25 05.4	28 48.0	8 50.7	21 13.1	4 56.1
4 F	12 52 27	11 11 50	10♈50 48	16 54 42	11 23.4	0 37.2	25 29.1	8 55.3	10 19.8	25 01.5	28 51.0	8 54.0	21 11.9	4 55.1
5 Sa	12 56 24	12 10 54	22 56 38	28 56 44	11 09.6	0 22.7	26 22.1	9 32.8	10 32.0	24 57.5	28 54.2	8 57.3	21 10.7	4 54.1
6 Su	13 00 20	13 10 01	4♉55 12	10♉52 12	10 57.3	0 00.6	27 15.6	10 10.2	10 44.3	24 53.3	28 57.4	9 00.6	21 09.5	4 53.2
7 M	13 04 17	14 09 09	16 48 00	22 42 55	10 47.3	29♎30.5	28 09.9	10 47.6	10 56.9	24 48.9	29 00.7	9 03.9	21 08.2	4 52.2
8 Tu	13 08 13	15 08 20	28 37 17	4♊31 31	10 40.2	28 52.4	29 04.7	11 25.0	11 09.8	24 44.3	29 04.1	9 07.1	21 06.9	4 51.3
9 W	13 12 10	16 07 33	10♊26 04	16 21 27	10 35.9	28 06.6	0♍00.2	12 02.4	11 22.8	24 39.6	29 07.6	9 10.3	21 05.6	4 50.4
10 Th	13 16 06	17 06 48	22 18 13	28 16 58	10 34.0	27 13.5	0 56.2	12 39.8	11 36.0	24 34.6	29 11.1	9 13.5	21 04.3	4 49.5
11 F	13 20 03	18 06 06	4♋18 20	10♋22 58	10 33.6	26 13.8	1 52.8	13 17.1	11 49.5	24 29.6	29 14.8	9 16.6	21 03.0	4 48.7
12 Sa	13 23 59	19 05 25	16 31 32	22 44 42	10 33.6	25 08.5	2 49.9	13 54.4	12 03.2	24 24.3	29 18.5	9 19.8	21 01.6	4 47.8
13 Su	13 27 56	20 04 48	29 03 09	5♌27 28	10 32.8	23 59.1	3 47.5	14 31.7	12 17.0	24 18.9	29 22.3	9 22.9	21 00.2	4 47.0
14 M	13 31 53	21 04 12	11♌58 14	18 35 56	10 30.3	22 47.1	4 45.7	15 09.0	12 31.1	24 13.3	29 26.2	9 25.9	20 58.8	4 46.2
15 Tu	13 35 49	22 03 39	25 20 56	2♍13 27	10 25.3	21 34.5	5 44.3	15 46.2	12 45.4	24 07.5	29 30.2	9 28.9	20 57.4	4 45.4
16 W	13 39 46	23 03 08	9♍13 32	16 21 02	10 17.7	20 23.4	6 43.4	16 23.5	12 59.8	24 01.6	29 34.2	9 31.9	20 56.0	4 44.6
17 Th	13 43 42	24 02 39	23 35 36	0♎56 36	10 08.0	19 15.7	7 43.0	17 00.7	13 14.5	23 55.6	29 38.4	9 34.9	20 54.5	4 43.8
18 F	13 47 39	25 02 12	8♎23 14	15 54 26	9 57.0	18 13.6	8 43.0	17 37.9	13 29.4	23 49.4	29 42.6	9 37.8	20 53.0	4 43.1
19 Sa	13 51 35	26 01 48	23 29 01	1♏05 39	9 46.1	17 18.9	9 43.4	18 15.0	13 44.4	23 43.1	29 46.9	9 40.7	20 51.5	4 42.4
20 Su	13 55 32	27 01 25	8♏42 55	16 19 27	9 36.6	16 32.9	10 44.2	18 52.2	13 59.6	23 36.6	29 51.2	9 43.6	20 50.0	4 41.7
21 M	13 59 28	28 01 05	23 53 54	1♐25 06	9 29.5	15 57.1	11 45.5	19 29.3	14 15.0	23 30.0	29 55.6	9 46.4	20 48.5	4 41.0
22 Tu	14 03 25	29 00 46	8♐52 01	16 13 51	9 25.1	15 32.0	12 47.1	20 06.4	14 30.6	23 23.2	0♑00.2	9 49.2	20 47.0	4 40.3
23 W	14 07 21	0♏00 29	23 29 58	0♑39 59	9D23.2	15D18.2	13 49.1	20 43.4	14 46.4	23 16.4	0 04.7	9 51.9	20 45.4	4 39.7
24 Th	14 11 18	1 00 14	7♑43 41	14 41 03	9 23.0	15 15.7	14 51.4	21 20.5	15 02.3	23 09.4	0 09.4	9 54.6	20 43.9	4 39.1
25 F	14 15 15	2 00 00	21 32 11	28 17 19	9R23.4	15 24.3	15 54.1	21 57.5	15 18.4	23 02.3	0 14.1	9 57.3	20 42.3	4 38.5
26 Sa	14 19 11	2 59 49	4♒56 46	11♒30 55	9 23.1	15 43.5	16 57.2	22 34.5	15 34.7	22 55.1	0 18.9	9 59.9	20 40.7	4 37.9
27 Su	14 23 08	3 59 38	18 00 10	24 24 56	9 21.1	16 12.6	18 00.6	23 11.4	15 51.1	22 47.8	0 23.8	10 02.5	20 39.1	4 37.4
28 M	14 27 04	4 59 30	0♓45 40	7♓02 47	9 16.7	16 50.9	19 04.3	23 48.3	16 07.7	22 40.4	0 28.7	10 05.1	20 37.5	4 36.9
29 Tu	14 31 01	5 59 23	13 16 38	19 27 37	9 09.6	17 37.6	20 08.3	24 25.2	16 24.5	22 32.9	0 33.7	10 07.6	20 35.9	4 36.4
30 W	14 34 57	6 59 17	25 36 02	1♈42 11	9 00.2	18 31.9	21 12.6	25 02.1	16 41.4	22 25.3	0 38.8	10 10.0	20 34.3	4 35.9
31 Th	14 38 54	7 59 14	7♈46 19	13 48 41	8 49.0	19 32.8	22 17.3	25 39.0	16 58.4	22 17.7	0 43.9	10 12.5	20 32.6	4 35.5

Astro Data

	Dy Hr Mn
☿0S	1 8:01
♄ D	1 18:29
☽0N	4 23:15
♃ R	14 12:36
☽0S	19 6:19
☉0S	23 2:08
☽0N	2 5:52
☿ R	3 0:45
☽0S	16 16:34
☿ D	24 5:19
☽0N	29 11:00

Planet Ingress

	Dy Hr Mn
☿ ♎	1 13:03
♂ ♍	20 6:28
☉ ♎	23 2:08
☿ ♏	29 7:04
☿ ♎R	6 12:31
♀ ♍	9 11:56
♄ ♑	22 11:09
☉ ♏	23 11:48

Last Aspect / ☽ Ingress

Last Aspect Dy Hr Mn		☽ Ingress Dy Hr Mn
1 2:29 ☿ △	♒	1 3:41
3 7:00 ♄ ✱	♓	3 10:44
5 15:57 ♄ □	♈	5 19:50
8 3:07 ♄ △	♉	8 7:05
10 10:58 ♃ ☌	♊	10 19:45
13 4:04 ♄ ☍	♋	13 7:49
15 8:57 ♃ ✱	♌	15 16:54
17 19:20 ♂ ☌	♍	17 21:59
19 20:58 ♄ □	♎	19 23:48
21 21:26 ♄ ✱	♏	22 0:09
23 17:39 ♃ ☍	♐	24 1:00
26 1:11 ♄ ☌	♑	26 3:50
28 8:31 ☿ □	♒	28 9:15
30 14:28 ♄ ✱	♓	30 17:00

Last Aspect Dy Hr Mn		☽ Ingress Dy Hr Mn
3 0:19 ♄ □	♈	3 2:42
5 11:55 ♄ △	♉	5 14:07
7 24:00 ♀ □	♊	8 2:48
10 13:49 ♄ ☍	♋	10 15:26
12 16:12 ☿ □	♌	13 1:47
15 7:15 ♄ △	♍	15 8:09
17 9:52 ♄ □	♎	17 10:28
19 9:55 ♄ ✱	♏	19 10:17
20 23:27 ♃ ☍	♐	21 9:44
23 10:49 ☉ ✱	♑	23 10:53
25 2:44 ♃ △	♒	25 15:04
27 8:59 ♃ □	♓	27 22:33
29 22:12 ♂ ☍	♈	30 8:39

☽ Phases & Eclipses

Dy Hr Mn	
4 8:54	○ 11♓47
12 11:18	☾ 19♊38
19 18:31	● 26♍45
26 9:29	☽ 3♑14
3 23:42	○ 10♈42
12 4:22	☾ 18♋47
19 3:28	● 25♎41
25 19:13	☽ 2♒18

Astro Data

1 September 2047
Julian Day # 53935
SVP 4♓35'20"
GC 27♐30.3 ⚳ 24♏35.4
Eris 0♉46.6R ⚵ 2♐06.7
⚷ 23♎10.4 ⚶ 21♐42.1
☽ Mean ☊ 13♑07.4

1 October 2047
Julian Day # 53965
SVP 4♓35'18"
GC 27♐30.4 ⚳ 4♐15.7
Eris 0♉32.5R ⚵ 8♐52.2
⚷ 27♎04.6 ⚶ 1♑03.2
☽ Mean ☊ 11♑32.0

November 2047 LONGITUDE

Day	Sid.Time	☉	0 hr ☽	Noon ☽	True ☊	☿	♀	♂	⚳	♃	♄	♅	♆	♇
1 F	14 42 50	8♏59 12	19♈49 28	25♈48 52	8♑37.1	20♎39.5	23♍22.2	26♍15.8	17♑15.6	22♉09.9	0♑49.1	10♍14.8	20♉31.0	4♓35.0
2 Sa	14 46 47	9 59 12	1♉47 02	7♉44 09	8R 25.5	21 51.3	24 27.4	26 52.6	17 33.0	22R 02.1	0 54.4	10 17.2	20R 29.3	4R 34.6
3 Su	14 50 44	10 59 14	13 40 22	19 35 54	8 15.2	23 07.4	25 32.9	27 29.4	17 50.5	21 54.3	0 59.7	10 19.5	20 27.7	4 34.3
4 M	14 54 40	11 59 18	25 30 55	1♊25 40	8 06.9	24 27.3	26 38.7	28 06.2	18 08.1	21 46.3	1 05.1	10 21.7	20 26.0	4 33.9
5 Tu	14 58 37	12 59 24	7♊20 23	13 15 22	8 01.1	25 50.4	27 44.7	28 42.9	18 25.9	21 38.4	1 10.5	10 23.9	20 24.3	4 33.6
6 W	15 02 33	13 59 32	19 10 58	25 07 32	7 57.9	27 16.1	28 51.0	29 19.6	18 43.8	21 30.3	1 16.0	10 26.1	20 22.7	4 33.3
7 Th	15 06 30	14 59 42	1♋05 29	7♋05 17	7D 56.9	28 44.0	29 57.6	29 56.3	19 01.9	21 22.3	1 21.6	10 28.2	20 21.0	4 33.0
8 F	15 10 26	15 59 54	13 07 26	19 12 27	7 57.4	0♏13.7	1♎04.4	0♎32.9	19 20.1	21 14.2	1 27.2	10 30.3	20 19.3	4 32.7
9 Sa	15 14 23	17 00 08	25 20 56	1♌33 25	7 58.6	1 44.9	2 11.4	1 09.6	19 38.4	21 06.0	1 32.9	10 32.3	20 17.6	4 32.5
10 Su	15 18 19	18 00 24	7♌50 32	14 12 51	7R 59.5	3 17.3	3 18.7	1 46.2	19 56.8	20 57.9	1 38.6	10 34.3	20 15.9	4 32.3
11 M	15 22 16	19 00 42	20 40 56	27 15 16	7 59.2	4 50.6	4 26.2	2 22.8	20 15.4	20 49.7	1 44.4	10 36.2	20 14.2	4 32.1
12 Tu	15 26 13	20 01 02	3♍56 20	10♍44 27	7 57.2	6 24.7	5 33.9	2 59.3	20 34.1	20 41.5	1 50.2	10 38.1	20 12.5	4 32.0
13 W	15 30 09	21 01 24	17 39 50	24 42 32	7 53.1	7 59.4	6 41.8	3 35.8	20 53.0	20 33.4	1 56.1	10 39.9	20 10.8	4 31.8
14 Th	15 34 06	22 01 47	1♎52 26	9♎09 12	7 47.3	9 34.5	7 49.9	4 12.3	21 11.9	20 25.2	2 02.1	10 41.7	20 09.1	4 31.7
15 F	15 38 02	23 02 13	16 32 16	24 00 51	7 40.5	11 09.9	8 58.3	4 48.8	21 31.0	20 17.0	2 08.1	10 43.4	20 07.5	4 31.6
16 Sa	15 41 59	24 02 41	1♏33 58	9♏10 27	7 33.5	12 45.5	10 06.8	5 25.2	21 50.2	20 08.9	2 14.1	10 45.1	20 05.8	4 31.6
17 Su	15 45 55	25 03 10	16 49 00	24 28 13	7 27.3	14 21.3	11 15.5	6 01.6	22 09.5	20 00.7	2 20.2	10 46.8	20 04.1	4D 31.6
18 M	15 49 52	26 03 41	2♐06 44	9♐43 11	7 22.8	15 57.1	12 24.4	6 38.0	22 28.9	19 52.6	2 26.3	10 48.3	20 02.4	4 31.6
19 Tu	15 53 48	27 04 13	17 16 18	24 45 01	7D 20.2	17 32.9	13 33.4	7 14.4	22 48.4	19 44.6	2 32.5	10 49.9	20 00.7	4 31.6
20 W	15 57 45	28 04 47	2♑08 24	9♑25 45	7 19.6	19 08.6	14 42.6	7 50.7	23 08.1	19 36.6	2 38.8	10 51.3	19 59.0	4 31.6
21 Th	16 01 42	29 05 22	16 36 35	23 40 35	7 20.4	20 44.3	15 52.0	8 26.9	23 27.8	19 28.6	2 45.0	10 52.8	19 57.4	4 31.7
22 F	16 05 38	0♐05 59	0♒37 39	7♒27 50	7 21.9	22 19.9	17 01.5	9 03.2	23 47.7	19 20.7	2 51.4	10 54.1	19 55.7	4 31.8
23 Sa	16 09 35	1 06 36	14 11 21	20 48 28	7R 23.3	23 55.4	18 11.2	9 39.4	24 07.7	19 12.8	2 57.7	10 55.5	19 54.1	4 31.9
24 Su	16 13 31	2 07 15	27 19 34	3♓45 08	7 23.7	25 30.8	19 21.1	10 15.5	24 27.7	19 05.1	3 04.1	10 56.7	19 52.4	4 32.1
25 M	16 17 28	3 07 54	10♓05 36	16 21 31	7 22.8	27 06.0	20 31.1	10 51.7	24 47.9	18 57.3	3 10.5	10 57.9	19 50.8	4 32.3
26 Tu	16 21 24	4 08 35	22 33 23	28 41 41	7 20.2	28 41.1	21 41.2	11 27.8	25 08.1	18 49.7	3 17.0	10 59.1	19 49.1	4 32.5
27 W	16 25 21	5 09 17	4♈46 56	10♈49 35	7 16.2	0♐16.0	22 51.5	12 03.8	25 28.5	18 42.2	3 23.5	11 00.2	19 47.5	4 32.7
28 Th	16 29 17	6 09 59	16 50 05	22 48 50	7 11.1	1 50.8	24 01.9	12 39.8	25 48.9	18 34.7	3 30.1	11 01.2	19 45.9	4 33.0
29 F	16 33 14	7 10 44	28 46 13	4♉42 35	7 05.4	3 25.6	25 12.4	13 15.8	26 09.5	18 27.4	3 36.7	11 02.2	19 44.3	4 33.2
30 Sa	16 37 11	8 11 29	10♉38 15	16 33 30	6 59.9	5 00.2	26 23.1	13 51.8	26 30.1	18 20.1	3 43.3	11 03.2	19 42.7	4 33.6

December 2047 LONGITUDE

Day	Sid.Time	☉	0 hr ☽	Noon ☽	True ☊	☿	♀	♂	⚳	♃	♄	♅	♆	♇
1 Su	16 41 07	9♐12 15	22♉28 36	28♉23 47	6♑55.0	6♐34.7	27♎33.9	14♎27.7	26♑50.8	18♉13.0	3♑49.9	11♍04.0	19♉41.1	4♓33.9
2 M	16 45 04	10 13 03	4♊19 19	10♊15 23	6R 51.3	8 09.1	28 44.9	15 03.6	27 11.6	18R 06.0	3 56.6	11 04.9	19R 39.6	4 34.3
3 Tu	16 49 00	11 13 51	16 12 15	22 10 06	6 48.9	9 43.4	29 55.9	15 39.4	27 32.5	17 59.0	4 03.3	11 05.7	19 38.0	4 34.6
4 W	16 52 57	12 14 41	28 09 12	4♋09 48	6D 48.0	11 17.7	1♏07.1	16 15.2	27 53.5	17 52.3	4 10.0	11 06.4	19 36.5	4 35.1
5 Th	16 56 53	13 15 33	10♋12 08	16 16 32	6 48.3	12 52.0	2 18.4	16 51.0	28 14.5	17 45.6	4 16.8	11 07.0	19 35.0	4 35.5
6 F	17 00 50	14 16 25	22 23 17	28 32 44	6 49.5	14 26.2	3 29.8	17 26.7	28 35.7	17 39.1	4 23.6	11 07.6	19 33.5	4 36.0
7 Sa	17 04 47	15 17 19	4♌45 14	11♌01 09	6 51.2	16 00.4	4 41.3	18 02.4	28 56.9	17 32.7	4 30.4	11 08.2	19 32.0	4 36.4
8 Su	17 08 43	16 18 13	17 20 54	23 44 52	6 52.8	17 34.6	5 52.9	18 38.0	29 18.2	17 26.4	4 37.3	11 08.7	19 30.5	4 37.0
9 M	17 12 40	17 19 09	0♍13 27	6♍47 02	6R 53.9	19 08.8	7 04.7	19 13.6	29 39.5	17 20.3	4 44.1	11 09.1	19 29.0	4 37.5
10 Tu	17 16 36	18 20 06	13 25 56	20 10 28	6 54.2	20 43.1	8 16.5	19 49.2	0♒01.0	17 14.3	4 51.0	11 09.5	19 27.6	4 38.1
11 W	17 20 33	19 21 05	27 00 50	3♎57 11	6 53.6	22 17.4	9 28.4	20 24.7	0 22.5	17 08.5	4 57.9	11 09.8	19 26.2	4 38.6
12 Th	17 24 29	20 22 04	10♎59 32	18 07 44	6 52.3	23 51.8	10 40.5	21 00.2	0 44.1	17 02.9	5 04.9	11 10.1	19 24.7	4 39.2
13 F	17 28 26	21 23 05	25 21 33	2♏40 31	6 50.4	25 26.2	11 52.6	21 35.7	1 05.7	16 57.4	5 11.8	11 10.3	19 23.4	4 39.9
14 Sa	17 32 22	22 24 07	10♏04 03	17 31 22	6 48.5	27 00.7	13 04.8	22 11.0	1 27.5	16 52.1	5 18.8	11 10.4	19 22.0	4 40.5
15 Su	17 36 19	23 25 10	25 01 35	2♐33 38	6 46.7	28 35.4	14 17.1	22 46.4	1 49.3	16 46.9	5 25.8	11 10.5	19 20.6	4 41.2
16 M	17 40 16	24 26 14	10♐06 26	17 38 48	6 45.6	0♑10.1	15 29.4	23 21.7	2 11.1	16 41.9	5 32.8	11R 10.6	19 19.3	4 41.9
17 Tu	17 44 12	25 27 19	25 09 35	2♑37 40	6D 45.1	1 45.0	16 41.9	23 56.9	2 33.1	16 37.1	5 39.8	11 10.6	19 18.0	4 42.7
18 W	17 48 09	26 28 24	10♑02 01	17 21 45	6 45.2	3 20.0	17 54.4	24 32.1	2 55.1	16 32.5	5 46.8	11 10.5	19 16.7	4 43.4
19 Th	17 52 05	27 29 30	24 36 05	1♒44 27	6 45.8	4 55.0	19 07.0	25 07.3	3 17.1	16 28.1	5 53.9	11 10.4	19 15.5	4 44.2
20 F	17 56 02	28 30 36	8♒46 26	15 41 47	6 46.6	6 30.2	20 19.7	25 42.4	3 39.3	16 23.8	6 00.9	11 10.2	19 14.3	4 45.0
21 Sa	17 59 58	29 31 42	22 30 24	29 12 21	6 47.4	8 05.5	21 32.4	26 17.4	4 01.4	16 19.7	6 08.0	11 09.9	19 13.0	4 45.9
22 Su	18 03 55	0♑32 48	5♓47 50	12♓17 09	6 47.9	9 40.9	22 45.2	26 52.4	4 23.7	16 15.9	6 15.1	11 09.6	19 11.9	4 46.7
23 M	18 07 51	1 33 55	18 40 39	24 58 49	6R 48.2	11 16.3	23 58.0	27 27.3	4 46.0	16 12.2	6 22.2	11 09.3	19 10.7	4 47.6
24 Tu	18 11 48	2 35 02	1♈12 10	7♈21 12	6 48.3	12 51.8	25 10.9	28 02.1	5 08.3	16 08.7	6 29.2	11 08.9	19 09.6	4 48.5
25 W	18 15 45	3 36 09	13 26 31	19 28 41	6 48.1	14 27.3	26 23.9	28 36.9	5 30.7	16 05.4	6 36.3	11 08.4	19 08.5	4 49.4
26 Th	18 19 41	4 37 16	25 28 15	1♉25 47	6 47.9	16 02.8	27 36.9	29 11.7	5 53.2	16 02.3	6 43.4	11 07.9	19 07.4	4 50.3
27 F	18 23 38	5 38 24	7♉21 50	13 16 55	6 47.7	17 38.3	28 50.0	29 46.4	6 15.7	15 59.4	6 50.5	11 07.3	19 06.3	4 51.3
28 Sa	18 27 34	6 39 31	19 11 31	25 06 06	6D 47.6	19 13.5	0♐03.1	0♏21.0	6 38.2	15 56.7	6 57.6	11 06.6	19 05.3	4 52.3
29 Su	18 31 31	7 40 39	1♊01 05	6♊56 53	6 47.6	20 48.6	1 16.3	0 55.6	7 00.8	15 54.2	7 04.7	11 06.0	19 04.3	4 53.3
30 M	18 35 27	8 41 46	12 53 50	18 52 15	6 47.8	22 23.4	2 29.6	1 30.1	7 23.4	15 51.9	7 11.8	11 05.2	19 03.3	4 54.3
31 Tu	18 39 24	9 42 54	24 52 26	0♋54 38	6R 47.9	23 57.7	3 42.9	2 04.6	7 46.1	15 49.8	7 18.9	11 04.4	19 02.4	4 55.4

Astro Data	Dy Hr Mn
♀0S	10 10:18
♂0S	12 17:20
☽0S	13 1:45
♃☌♆	16 23:31
♇ D	17 23:56
☽0N	25 16:12
♃⚼♄	28 20:00
♄⚼♆	7 16:26
♄⚹♇	8 10:49
☽0S	10 8:47
♅ R	16 17:22
☽0N	22 23:18

Planet Ingress		Dy Hr Mn
♀	♎	7 12:52
♂	♎	7 14:26
☿	♏	8 8:22
☉	♐	22 9:38
☿	♐	27 7:57
♀	♏	3 13:23
⚳	♒	10 10:55
☿	♑	16 9:26
☉	♑	21 23:07
♂	♏	27 21:26
♀	♐	28 10:59

Last Aspect Dy Hr Mn		☽ Ingress	Dy Hr Mn
1 0:35	☿ ☍	♉	1 20:25
4 4:53	♂ △	♊	4 9:06
6 20:55	♂ □	♋	6 21:49
8 15:56	♃ ⚹	♌	9 9:00
11 0:23	♃ □	♍	11 16:57
13 5:16	☉ ⚹	♎	13 20:53
14 9:39	♀ ☌	♏	15 21:31
17 12:59	☉ ☌	♐	17 20:41
18 16:37	♀ ⚹	♑	19 20:31
21 22:04	☉ ⚹	♒	21 22:55
23 18:30	☿ □	♓	24 4:58
26 11:59	☿ △	♈	26 14:34
28 14:43	♀ ☍	♉	29 2:29

Last Aspect Dy Hr Mn		☽ Ingress	Dy Hr Mn
30 18:23	♆ ☌	♊	1 15:15
2 22:12	♂ △	♋	4 3:42
5 18:29	♆ ⚹	♌	6 14:49
8 4:05	♆ □	♍	8 23:35
10 13:05	☿ □	♎	11 5:11
12 22:41	☿ ⚹	♏	13 7:38
14 14:57	♆ ☍	♐	15 7:56
16 23:38	☉ ☌	♑	17 7:46
19 0:24	♂ □	♒	19 9:03
21 12:38	☉ ⚹	♓	21 13:26
23 9:51	♀ △	♈	23 21:40
26 7:16	♂ ☍	♉	26 9:07
27 23:48	♆ ☌	♊	28 21:56
29 20:22	♅ □	♋	31 10:12

☽ Phases & Eclipses Dy Hr Mn	
2 16:58	○ 10♉12
10 19:39	☾ 18♌20
17 12:59	● 25♏06
24 8:41	☽ 1♓59
2 11:55	○ 10♊13
10 8:29	☾ 18♍11
16 23:38	● 24♐56
16 23:48:38	● P 0.882
24 1:51	☽ 2♈09

Astro Data

1 November 2047
Julian Day # 53996
SVP 4♓35'14"
GC 27♐30.4 ⚴ 15♐46.5
Eris 0♉14.0R ⚵ 18♐04.5
⚷ 1♏29.3 ⚶ 13♑36.2
☽ Mean ☊ 9♑53.5

1 December 2047
Julian Day # 54026
SVP 4♓35'10"
GC 27♐30.5 ⚴ 27♐37.7
Eris 29♈57.6R ⚵ 28♐19.3
⚷ 5♏35.7 ⚶ 27♑20.4
☽ Mean ☊ 8♑18.2

LONGITUDE — January 2048

Day	Sid.Time	☉	0 hr ☽	Noon ☽	True ☊	☿	♀	♂	⚳	♃	♄	♅	♆	♇
1 W	18 43 20	10♑44 02	6♋59 05	13♋05 58	6♑47.9	25♑31.6	4♐56.2	2♏39.0	8♒08.9	15♉47.9	7♑26.0	11♍03.6	19♉01.4	4♓56.4
2 Th	18 47 17	11 45 10	19 15 27	25 27 43	6R47.6	27 04.6	6 09.6	3 13.3	8 31.6	15R46.3	7 33.1	11R 02.7	19R 00.6	4 57.5
3 F	18 51 14	12 46 18	1♌42 52	8♌01 03	6 47.1	28 36.8	7 23.0	3 47.6	8 54.4	15 44.8	7 40.2	11 01.7	18 59.7	4 58.6
4 Sa	18 55 10	13 47 26	14 22 23	20 46 57	6 46.2	0♒07.9	8 36.5	4 21.8	9 17.3	15 43.5	7 47.3	11 00.7	18 58.9	4 59.8
5 Su	18 59 07	14 48 35	27 14 53	3♍46 17	6 45.2	1 37.6	9 50.1	4 55.9	9 40.2	15 42.5	7 54.3	10 59.7	18 58.1	5 00.9
6 M	19 03 03	15 49 43	10♍21 15	16 59 52	6 44.2	3 05.6	11 03.6	5 30.0	10 03.1	15 41.6	8 01.4	10 58.6	18 57.3	5 02.1
7 Tu	19 07 00	16 50 52	23 42 13	0♎28 24	6 43.3	4 31.6	12 17.3	6 04.0	10 26.1	15 41.0	8 08.4	10 57.4	18 56.6	5 03.3
8 W	19 10 56	17 52 00	7♎18 27	14 12 23	6D42.9	5 55.1	13 30.9	6 37.9	10 49.1	15 40.5	8 15.5	10 56.2	18 55.9	5 04.5
9 Th	19 14 53	18 53 09	21 10 11	28 11 46	6 43.0	7 15.6	14 44.6	7 11.8	11 12.2	15D40.3	8 22.5	10 54.9	18 55.2	5 05.7
10 F	19 18 49	19 54 19	5♏17 01	12♏25 44	6 43.7	8 32.7	15 58.4	7 45.6	11 35.2	15 40.3	8 29.5	10 53.6	18 54.5	5 06.9
11 Sa	19 22 46	20 55 28	19 37 35	26 52 13	6 44.8	9 45.7	17 12.1	8 19.3	11 58.4	15 40.5	8 36.5	10 52.3	18 53.9	5 08.2
12 Su	19 26 43	21 56 37	4♐09 09	11♐27 49	6 45.9	10 54.0	18 26.0	8 53.0	12 21.5	15 40.9	8 43.5	10 50.9	18 53.3	5 09.5
13 M	19 30 39	22 57 47	18 47 33	26 07 39	6R46.8	11 56.8	19 39.8	9 26.5	12 44.7	15 41.5	8 50.5	10 49.4	18 52.8	5 10.8
14 Tu	19 34 36	23 58 56	3♑27 18	10♑45 44	6 47.0	12 53.2	20 53.7	10 00.0	13 07.9	15 42.3	8 57.4	10 47.9	18 52.3	5 12.1
15 W	19 38 32	25 00 04	18 02 05	25 15 35	6 46.2	13 42.5	22 07.6	10 33.4	13 31.2	15 43.3	9 04.4	10 46.4	18 51.8	5 13.4
16 Th	19 42 29	26 01 13	2♒25 29	9♒31 05	6 44.4	14 23.8	23 21.5	11 06.7	13 54.4	15 44.5	9 11.3	10 44.8	18 51.4	5 14.7
17 F	19 46 25	27 02 20	16 31 49	23 27 14	6 41.8	14 56.1	24 35.5	11 39.9	14 17.7	15 46.0	9 18.2	10 43.2	18 50.9	5 16.1
18 Sa	19 50 22	28 03 27	0♓16 58	7♓00 50	6 38.5	15 18.6	25 49.4	12 13.0	14 41.1	15 47.6	9 25.1	10 41.5	18 50.6	5 17.5
19 Su	19 54 19	29 04 34	13 38 45	20 10 45	6 35.1	15R30.6	27 03.4	12 46.1	15 04.4	15 49.5	9 31.9	10 39.8	18 50.2	5 18.8
20 M	19 58 15	0♒05 39	26 37 01	2♈57 49	6 32.1	15 31.5	28 17.5	13 19.0	15 27.8	15 51.5	9 38.7	10 38.0	18 49.9	5 20.2
21 Tu	20 02 12	1 06 44	9♈13 31	15 24 33	6 29.9	15 20.7	29 31.5	13 51.8	15 51.2	15 53.8	9 45.5	10 36.2	18 49.6	5 21.7
22 W	20 06 08	2 07 47	21 31 26	27 34 42	6D28.9	14 58.4	0♑45.5	14 24.6	16 14.6	15 56.2	9 52.3	10 34.4	18 49.4	5 23.1
23 Th	20 10 05	3 08 50	3♉34 58	9♉32 49	6 29.0	14 24.6	1 59.6	14 57.3	16 38.0	15 58.9	9 59.0	10 32.5	18 49.2	5 24.5
24 F	20 14 01	4 09 52	15 28 55	21 23 52	6 30.1	13 40.0	3 13.7	15 29.8	17 01.5	16 01.7	10 05.7	10 30.6	18 49.0	5 26.0
25 Sa	20 17 58	5 10 53	27 18 18	3♊12 51	6 31.9	12 45.7	4 27.8	16 02.3	17 24.9	16 04.8	10 12.4	10 28.6	18 48.8	5 27.5
26 Su	20 21 54	6 11 53	9♊08 04	15 04 33	6 33.7	11 43.2	5 42.0	16 34.6	17 48.4	16 08.0	10 19.0	10 26.6	18 48.7	5 28.9
27 M	20 25 51	7 12 51	21 02 48	27 03 19	6R35.1	10 34.2	6 56.1	17 06.9	18 11.9	16 11.4	10 25.6	10 24.6	18 48.7	5 30.4
28 Tu	20 29 48	8 13 49	3♋06 31	9♋12 47	6 35.5	9 20.9	8 10.3	17 39.0	18 35.4	16 15.1	10 32.2	10 22.5	18D 48.6	5 31.9
29 W	20 33 44	9 14 46	15 22 28	21 35 47	6 34.4	8 05.5	9 24.4	18 11.1	18 58.9	16 18.9	10 38.8	10 20.4	18 48.6	5 33.5
30 Th	20 37 41	10 15 42	27 52 57	4♌14 04	6 31.6	6 50.2	10 38.6	18 43.0	19 22.5	16 22.9	10 45.3	10 18.3	18 48.7	5 35.0
31 F	20 41 37	11 16 37	10♌39 13	17 08 21	6 27.2	5 37.3	11 52.8	19 14.9	19 46.0	16 27.1	10 51.7	10 16.1	18 48.7	5 36.5

LONGITUDE — February 2048

Day	Sid.Time	☉	0 hr ☽	Noon ☽	True ☊	☿	♀	♂	⚳	♃	♄	♅	♆	♇
1 Sa	20 45 34	12♒17 30	23♌41 24	0♍18 14	6♑21.4	4♒28.4	13♑07.1	19♏46.6	20♒09.6	16♉31.4	10♑58.2	10♍13.9	18♉48.8	5♓38.1
2 Su	20 49 30	13 18 23	6♍58 39	13 42 27	6R 15.1	3R 25.2	14 21.3	20 18.2	20 33.1	16 36.0	11 04.5	10R 11.7	18 49.0	5 39.6
3 M	20 53 27	14 19 15	20 29 21	27 19 06	6 08.8	2 29.0	15 35.6	20 49.7	20 56.7	16 40.7	11 10.9	10 09.4	18 49.1	5 41.2
4 Tu	20 57 23	15 20 06	4♎11 25	11♎06 00	6 03.4	1 40.4	16 49.8	21 21.1	21 20.3	16 45.6	11 17.2	10 07.2	18 49.3	5 42.8
5 W	21 01 20	16 20 56	18 02 38	25 01 03	5 59.6	1 00.1	18 04.1	21 52.3	21 43.9	16 50.7	11 23.5	10 04.8	18 49.6	5 44.3
6 Th	21 05 17	17 21 45	2♏01 03	9♏02 25	5D57.6	0 28.2	19 18.4	22 23.4	22 07.5	16 56.0	11 29.7	10 02.5	18 49.8	5 45.9
7 F	21 09 13	18 22 34	16 04 59	23 08 05	5 57.4	0 04.8	20 32.7	22 54.4	22 31.1	17 01.5	11 35.8	10 00.1	18 50.1	5 47.5
8 Sa	21 13 10	19 23 22	0♐13 04	7♐18 14	5 58.4	29♑49.7	21 47.1	23 25.3	22 54.7	17 07.1	11 42.0	9 57.7	18 50.5	5 49.1
9 Su	21 17 06	20 24 08	14 23 56	21 29 55	5 59.7	29D 42.5	23 01.4	23 56.0	23 18.3	17 12.9	11 48.1	9 55.3	18 50.9	5 50.8
10 M	21 21 03	21 24 54	28 35 57	5♑41 44	6R00.4	29 42.8	24 15.7	24 26.6	23 42.0	17 18.9	11 54.1	9 52.9	18 51.3	5 52.4
11 Tu	21 24 59	22 25 39	12♑46 56	19 51 07	5 59.5	29 50.3	25 30.1	24 57.1	24 05.6	17 25.0	12 00.1	9 50.5	18 51.7	5 54.0
12 W	21 28 56	23 26 22	26 53 52	3♒54 43	5 56.4	0♒04.4	26 44.5	25 27.4	24 29.2	17 31.3	12 06.0	9 48.0	18 52.2	5 55.6
13 Th	21 32 52	24 27 05	10♒53 10	17 48 44	5 51.0	0 24.7	27 58.8	25 57.6	24 52.8	17 37.8	12 11.9	9 45.5	18 52.7	5 57.3
14 F	21 36 49	25 27 45	24 40 56	1♓29 19	5 43.4	0 50.6	29 13.2	26 27.6	25 16.5	17 44.4	12 17.7	9 43.0	18 53.3	5 58.9
15 Sa	21 40 46	26 28 25	8♓13 32	14 53 14	5 34.4	1 21.8	0♒27.6	26 57.4	25 40.1	17 51.2	12 23.5	9 40.4	18 53.9	6 00.6
16 Su	21 44 42	27 29 02	21 28 13	27 58 21	5 24.8	1 57.8	1 42.0	27 27.1	26 03.7	17 58.2	12 29.2	9 37.9	18 54.5	6 02.2
17 M	21 48 39	28 29 39	4♈23 36	10♈44 02	5 15.7	2 38.3	2 56.4	27 56.6	26 27.3	18 05.3	12 34.9	9 35.3	18 55.1	6 03.9
18 Tu	21 52 35	29 30 13	16 59 50	23 11 15	5 08.0	3 22.8	4 10.7	28 26.0	26 50.9	18 12.6	12 40.5	9 32.8	18 55.8	6 05.5
19 W	21 56 32	0♓30 46	29 18 40	5♉22 29	5 02.3	4 11.1	5 25.1	28 55.2	27 14.5	18 20.0	12 46.0	9 30.2	18 56.5	6 07.2
20 Th	22 00 28	1 31 17	11♉23 14	17 21 26	4 59.0	5 02.9	6 39.5	29 24.2	27 38.1	18 27.5	12 51.5	9 27.6	18 57.3	6 08.8
21 F	22 04 25	2 31 46	23 17 42	29 12 41	4D57.7	5 57.8	7 53.9	29 53.0	28 01.7	18 35.3	12 56.9	9 25.0	18 58.1	6 10.5
22 Sa	22 08 21	3 32 14	5♊07 02	11♊01 25	4 57.9	6 55.7	9 08.3	0♐21.7	28 25.2	18 43.1	13 02.3	9 22.4	18 58.9	6 12.2
23 Su	22 12 18	4 32 39	16 56 32	22 53 04	4 58.7	7 56.4	10 22.7	0 50.2	28 48.8	18 51.2	13 07.6	9 19.8	18 59.8	6 13.8
24 M	22 16 15	5 33 03	28 51 39	4♋52 56	4R59.2	8 59.6	11 37.1	1 18.5	29 12.4	18 59.3	13 12.8	9 17.2	19 00.6	6 15.5
25 Tu	22 20 11	6 33 25	10♋57 30	17 05 56	4 58.4	10 05.1	12 51.5	1 46.6	29 35.9	19 07.6	13 18.0	9 14.5	19 01.6	6 17.2
26 W	22 24 08	7 33 45	23 18 41	29 36 10	4 55.5	11 12.9	14 05.8	2 14.5	29 59.4	19 16.0	13 23.1	9 11.9	19 02.5	6 18.8
27 Th	22 28 04	8 34 03	5♌58 43	12♌26 32	4 50.1	12 22.7	15 20.2	2 42.3	0♓22.9	19 24.6	13 28.2	9 09.3	19 03.5	6 20.5
28 F	22 32 01	9 34 19	18 59 44	25 38 19	4 42.1	13 34.5	16 34.6	3 09.8	0 46.4	19 33.3	13 33.1	9 06.6	19 04.5	6 22.2
29 Sa	22 35 57	10 34 33	2♍22 07	9♍10 54	4 32.1	14 48.1	17 49.0	3 37.1	1 09.9	19 42.1	13 38.0	9 04.0	19 05.5	6 23.8

Astro Data

	Dy Hr Mn
☽ 0S	6 14:22
♃ D	10 2:18
☽ 0N	19 8:42
☿ R	20 1:44
♄△♅	27 9:06
♆ D	29 1:25
☽ 0S	2 20:31
☿ D	9 22:45
☽ 0N	15 18:48
♃☌♆	24 16:23

Planet Ingress

	Dy Hr Mn
☿ ♒	4 9:54
☉ ♒	20 9:47
♀ ♑	21 21:14
☿ ♑R	7 18:21
☿ ♒	12 5:33
♀ ♒	15 3:06
☉ ♓	18 23:48
♂ ♐	21 17:49
⚳ ♓	26 12:36

Last Aspect / ☽ Ingress (January)

Last Aspect Dy Hr Mn		☽ Ingress Dy Hr Mn
2 15:33	☿ ☍	♌ 2 20:43
4 8:38	♆ □	♍ 5 5:05
6 15:31	♆ △	♎ 7 11:10
8 18:49	☉ □	♏ 9 15:04
11 1:25	☉ ✱	♐ 11 17:10
13 0:27	♀ ☌	♑ 13 18:20
15 11:32	☉ ☌	♒ 15 19:56
17 14:11	♀ ✱	♓ 17 23:30
20 6:05	☉ ✱	♈ 20 6:23
21 11:53	☿ ✱	♉ 22 16:50
24 6:46	♆ ☌	♊ 25 5:28
26 5:48	☿ △	♋ 27 17:51
29 6:38	♆ ✱	♌ 30 4:01

Last Aspect / ☽ Ingress (February)

Last Aspect Dy Hr Mn		☽ Ingress Dy Hr Mn
31 16:02	♂ □	♍ 1 11:27
3 0:08	♂ ✱	♎ 3 16:41
4 22:52	♀ □	♏ 5 20:33
7 23:32	☿ ✱	♐ 7 23:38
9 10:00	☉ ✱	♑ 10 2:22
12 5:18	☿ ☌	♒ 12 5:18
14 2:47	♂ □	♓ 14 9:22
16 11:00	♂ △	♈ 16 15:46
17 15:33	♄ □	♉ 19 1:21
21 13:25	♂ ☍	♊ 21 13:36
22 8:40	♅ □	♋ 24 2:17
25 15:59	♃ ✱	♌ 26 12:45
28 0:54	♃ □	♍ 28 19:48

☽ Phases & Eclipses

Dy Hr Mn	
1 6:57	○ 10♋31
1 6:52	T 1.128
8 18:49	☾ 18♎09
15 11:32	● 24♑59
22 21:56	☽ 2♉33
31 0:14	○ 10♌47
7 3:16	☾ 18♏00
14 0:31	● 24♒59
21 19:22	☽ 2♊50
29 14:38	○ 10♍41

Astro Data

1 January 2048
Julian Day # 54057
SVP 4♓35'04"
GC 27♐30.6 ⚵ 10♑01.9
Eris 29♈47.4R ⚴ 9♑40.8
⚷ 9♏05.5 ⚶ 12♒25.0
☽ Mean ☊ 6♑39.7

1 February 2048
Julian Day # 54088
SVP 4♓34'58"
GC 27♐30.7 ⚵ 22♑04.2
Eris 29♈47.2 ⚴ 21♑18.2
⚷ 11♏14.9 ⚶ 27♒52.1
☽ Mean ☊ 5♑01.3

March 2048

LONGITUDE

Day	Sid.Time	☉	0 hr ☽	Noon ☽	True ☊	☿	♀	♂	⚳	♃	♄	♅	♆	♇
1 Su	22 39 54	11♓34 45	16♍04 17	23♍01 47	4♑20.9	16♒03.5	19♒03.4	4♐04.2	1♓33.3	19♉51.1	13♑42.9	9♍01.4	19♉06.6	6♓25.5
2 M	22 43 50	12 34 56	0♎02 51	7♎06 50	4R 09.8	17 20.6	20 17.8	4 31.2	1 56.8	20 00.2	13 47.6	8R 58.8	19 07.7	6 27.1
3 Tu	22 47 47	13 35 05	14 13 05	21 20 55	3 59.9	18 39.2	21 32.2	4 57.8	2 20.2	20 09.4	13 52.3	8 56.1	19 08.8	6 28.8
4 W	22 51 43	14 35 13	28 29 42	5♏38 50	3 52.3	19 59.4	22 46.5	5 24.3	2 43.6	20 18.8	13 57.0	8 53.5	19 10.0	6 30.5
5 Th	22 55 40	15 35 19	12♏47 46	19 56 02	3 47.4	21 21.0	24 00.9	5 50.6	3 07.0	20 28.2	14 01.5	8 50.9	19 11.2	6 32.1
6 F	22 59 37	16 35 23	27 03 17	4♐09 12	3D 45.0	22 44.1	25 15.3	6 16.6	3 30.4	20 37.8	14 06.0	8 48.3	19 12.4	6 33.8
7 Sa	23 03 33	17 35 26	11♐13 37	18 16 21	3 44.5	24 08.6	26 29.7	6 42.3	3 53.7	20 47.5	14 10.4	8 45.7	19 13.7	6 35.4
8 Su	23 07 30	18 35 28	25 17 20	2♑16 32	3R 44.7	25 34.4	27 44.1	7 07.9	4 17.1	20 57.3	14 14.7	8 43.1	19 15.0	6 37.0
9 M	23 11 26	19 35 28	9♑13 54	16 09 26	3 44.2	27 01.5	28 58.5	7 33.1	4 40.4	21 07.3	14 19.0	8 40.6	19 16.3	6 38.7
10 Tu	23 15 23	20 35 26	23 03 04	29 54 46	3 41.9	28 29.9	0♓12.9	7 58.1	5 03.7	21 17.3	14 23.2	8 38.0	19 17.6	6 40.3
11 W	23 19 19	21 35 22	6♒44 27	13♒31 59	3 36.9	29 59.5	1 27.3	8 22.9	5 26.9	21 27.5	14 27.3	8 35.4	19 19.0	6 41.9
12 Th	23 23 16	22 35 17	20 17 12	26 59 56	3 28.8	1♓30.4	2 41.7	8 47.3	5 50.1	21 37.8	14 31.3	8 32.9	19 20.4	6 43.5
13 F	23 27 12	23 35 10	3♓39 57	10♓17 03	3 18.0	3 02.6	3 56.1	9 11.5	6 13.3	21 48.2	14 35.2	8 30.4	19 21.8	6 45.2
14 Sa	23 31 09	24 35 01	16 51 00	23 21 37	3 05.2	4 36.0	5 10.5	9 35.4	6 36.5	21 58.7	14 39.1	8 27.9	19 23.2	6 46.8
15 Su	23 35 06	25 34 50	29 48 41	6♈12 06	2 51.5	6 10.6	6 24.8	9 59.0	6 59.7	22 09.3	14 42.8	8 25.4	19 24.7	6 48.4
16 M	23 39 02	26 34 37	12♈31 48	18 47 45	2 38.3	7 46.4	7 39.2	10 22.3	7 22.8	22 20.0	14 46.5	8 22.9	19 26.2	6 49.9
17 Tu	23 42 59	27 34 22	25 00 01	1♉08 45	2 26.6	9 23.4	8 53.5	10 45.3	7 45.8	22 30.8	14 50.1	8 20.5	19 27.7	6 51.5
18 W	23 46 55	28 34 05	7♉14 09	13 16 30	2 17.3	11 01.7	10 07.9	11 07.9	8 08.9	22 41.7	14 53.6	8 18.0	19 29.3	6 53.1
19 Th	23 50 52	29 33 45	19 16 11	25 13 37	2 10.8	12 41.2	11 22.2	11 30.3	8 31.9	22 52.7	14 57.1	8 15.6	19 30.9	6 54.7
20 F	23 54 48	0♈33 24	1♊09 17	7♊03 45	2 07.1	14 22.0	12 36.6	11 52.3	8 54.9	23 03.8	15 00.4	8 13.3	19 32.5	6 56.2
21 Sa	23 58 45	1 33 00	12 57 36	18 51 28	2 05.5	16 04.0	13 50.9	12 14.0	9 17.8	23 15.0	15 03.7	8 10.9	19 34.1	6 57.8
22 Su	0 02 41	2 32 34	24 46 02	0♋41 57	2 05.2	17 47.3	15 05.2	12 35.4	9 40.7	23 26.3	15 06.9	8 08.6	19 35.7	6 59.3
23 M	0 06 38	3 32 06	6♋39 58	12 40 44	2 05.1	19 31.8	16 19.5	12 56.4	10 03.6	23 37.6	15 10.0	8 06.3	19 37.4	7 00.8
24 Tu	0 10 35	4 31 35	18 44 59	24 53 21	2 04.0	21 17.6	17 33.8	13 17.0	10 26.4	23 49.1	15 13.0	8 04.0	19 39.1	7 02.3
25 W	0 14 31	5 31 02	1♌06 28	7♌24 53	2 01.0	23 04.7	18 48.1	13 37.3	10 49.2	24 00.6	15 15.9	8 01.7	19 40.8	7 03.8
26 Th	0 18 28	6 30 27	13 49 06	20 19 29	1 55.4	24 53.2	20 02.4	13 57.2	11 12.0	24 12.3	15 18.7	7 59.5	19 42.5	7 05.3
27 F	0 22 24	7 29 50	26 56 19	3♍39 43	1 47.2	26 42.9	21 16.7	14 16.7	11 34.7	24 24.0	15 21.4	7 57.3	19 44.3	7 06.8
28 Sa	0 26 21	8 29 10	10♍29 39	17 25 55	1 36.8	28 34.0	22 30.9	14 35.9	11 57.3	24 35.7	15 24.0	7 55.2	19 46.1	7 08.3
29 Su	0 30 17	9 28 28	24 28 10	1♎35 51	1 25.1	0♈26.4	23 45.2	14 54.7	12 19.9	24 47.6	15 26.6	7 53.0	19 47.9	7 09.7
30 M	0 34 14	10 27 44	8♎48 15	16 04 34	1 13.3	2 20.2	24 59.4	15 13.0	12 42.5	24 59.6	15 29.0	7 50.9	19 49.7	7 11.2
31 Tu	0 38 10	11 26 58	23 23 52	0♏45 09	1 02.8	4 15.2	26 13.7	15 31.0	13 05.0	25 11.6	15 31.4	7 48.9	19 51.5	7 12.6

April 2048

LONGITUDE

Day	Sid.Time	☉	0 hr ☽	Noon ☽	True ☊	☿	♀	♂	⚳	♃	♄	♅	♆	♇
1 W	0 42 07	12♈26 10	8♏07 24	15♏29 40	0♑54.5	6♈11.6	27♓27.9	15♐48.5	13♓27.5	25♉23.7	15♑33.7	7♍46.9	19♉53.4	7♓14.0
2 Th	0 46 04	13 25 21	22 51 02	0♐10 41	0R 49.0	8 09.3	28 42.1	16 05.6	13 50.0	25 35.8	15 35.9	7R 44.9	19 55.3	7 15.4
3 F	0 50 00	14 24 29	7♐27 56	14 42 14	0 46.2	10 08.3	29 56.3	16 22.2	14 12.4	25 48.1	15 37.9	7 42.9	19 57.2	7 16.8
4 Sa	0 53 57	15 23 36	21 53 10	29 00 28	0D 45.4	12 08.5	1♈10.6	16 38.4	14 34.7	26 00.4	15 39.9	7 41.0	19 59.1	7 18.2
5 Su	0 57 53	16 22 41	6♑03 57	13♑03 34	0R 45.6	14 09.8	2 24.8	16 54.1	14 57.0	26 12.8	15 41.8	7 39.1	20 01.0	7 19.6
6 M	1 01 50	17 21 45	19 59 19	26 51 18	0 45.3	16 12.2	3 39.0	17 09.4	15 19.3	26 25.2	15 43.6	7 37.3	20 03.0	7 20.9
7 Tu	1 05 46	18 20 46	3♒39 38	10♒24 26	0 43.5	18 15.6	4 53.2	17 24.1	15 41.4	26 37.8	15 45.3	7 35.5	20 05.0	7 22.2
8 W	1 09 43	19 19 46	17 05 52	23 44 02	0 39.2	20 19.8	6 07.4	17 38.4	16 03.6	26 50.3	15 46.9	7 33.7	20 06.9	7 23.6
9 Th	1 13 39	20 18 44	0♓19 05	6♓51 06	0 32.2	22 24.8	7 21.6	17 52.1	16 25.7	27 03.0	15 48.5	7 32.0	20 08.9	7 24.9
10 F	1 17 36	21 17 40	13 20 08	19 46 16	0 22.6	24 30.2	8 35.7	18 05.3	16 47.7	27 15.7	15 49.9	7 30.3	20 11.0	7 26.1
11 Sa	1 21 33	22 16 35	26 09 30	2♈29 52	0 11.2	26 36.0	9 49.9	18 17.9	17 09.7	27 28.4	15 51.2	7 28.6	20 13.0	7 27.4
12 Su	1 25 29	23 15 27	8♈47 22	15 02 01	29♐58.9	28 41.9	11 04.0	18 30.0	17 31.6	27 41.3	15 52.4	7 27.0	20 15.0	7 28.7
13 M	1 29 26	24 14 18	21 13 51	27 22 55	29 46.9	0♉47.6	12 18.2	18 41.6	17 53.4	27 54.1	15 53.5	7 25.5	20 17.1	7 29.9
14 Tu	1 33 22	25 13 06	3♉29 17	9♉33 05	29 36.3	2 52.8	13 32.3	18 52.5	18 15.2	28 07.1	15 54.5	7 24.0	20 19.2	7 31.1
15 W	1 37 19	26 11 53	15 34 28	21 33 40	29 27.8	4 57.3	14 46.5	19 02.9	18 37.0	28 20.1	15 55.5	7 22.5	20 21.2	7 32.3
16 Th	1 41 15	27 10 37	27 30 56	3♊26 35	29 21.9	7 00.6	16 00.6	19 12.7	18 58.6	28 33.1	15 56.3	7 21.1	20 23.3	7 33.5
17 F	1 45 12	28 09 19	9♊20 59	15 14 35	29 18.6	9 02.5	17 14.7	19 21.9	19 20.2	28 46.2	15 57.0	7 19.7	20 25.5	7 34.7
18 Sa	1 49 08	29 08 00	21 07 50	27 01 16	29D 17.5	11 02.7	18 28.8	19 30.5	19 41.8	28 59.3	15 57.6	7 18.4	20 27.6	7 35.8
19 Su	1 53 05	0♉06 38	2♋55 27	8♋50 59	29 17.8	13 00.7	19 42.9	19 38.5	20 03.2	29 12.5	15 58.2	7 17.1	20 29.7	7 36.9
20 M	1 57 01	1 05 14	14 48 30	20 48 39	29R 18.7	14 56.4	20 56.9	19 45.8	20 24.6	29 25.8	15 58.6	7 15.9	20 31.9	7 38.0
21 Tu	2 00 58	2 03 47	26 52 07	2♌59 33	29 19.1	16 49.3	22 11.0	19 52.5	20 46.0	29 39.0	15 58.9	7 14.7	20 34.0	7 39.1
22 W	2 04 55	3 02 19	9♌11 37	15 28 56	29 18.2	18 39.1	23 25.0	19 58.6	21 07.2	29 52.4	15 59.1	7 13.5	20 36.2	7 40.2
23 Th	2 08 51	4 00 48	21 52 04	28 21 33	29 15.4	20 25.8	24 39.1	20 03.9	21 28.4	0♊05.7	15R 59.3	7 12.5	20 38.4	7 41.2
24 F	2 12 48	4 59 15	4♍57 46	11♍41 00	29 10.6	22 08.9	25 53.1	20 08.7	21 49.5	0 19.1	15 59.3	7 11.4	20 40.5	7 42.3
25 Sa	2 16 44	5 57 40	18 31 26	25 29 02	29 03.9	23 48.2	27 07.1	20 12.7	22 10.6	0 32.6	15 59.2	7 10.4	20 42.7	7 43.3
26 Su	2 20 41	6 56 03	2♎33 35	9♎44 43	28 56.0	25 23.7	28 21.1	20 16.0	22 31.5	0 46.1	15 59.1	7 09.5	20 44.9	7 44.3
27 M	2 24 37	7 54 24	17 01 50	24 24 08	28 48.0	26 55.2	29 35.1	20 18.7	22 52.4	0 59.6	15 58.8	7 08.6	20 47.1	7 45.2
28 Tu	2 28 34	8 52 43	1♏50 42	9♏20 26	28 40.7	28 22.5	0♉49.1	20 20.7	23 13.2	1 13.1	15 58.5	7 07.7	20 49.3	7 46.2
29 W	2 32 30	9 51 01	16 52 10	24 24 43	28 35.1	29 45.4	2 03.0	20 21.9	23 33.9	1 26.7	15 58.0	7 07.0	20 51.6	7 47.1
30 Th	2 36 27	10 49 16	1♐56 54	9♐27 33	28 31.5	1♊04.0	3 17.0	20R 22.4	23 54.6	1 40.3	15 57.5	7 06.2	20 53.8	7 48.0

Astro Data	Dy Hr Mn
☽0S	1 4:33
☽0N	14 3:26
☉0N	19 22:33
☽0S	28 14:02
☿0N	31 9:57
♀0N	6 7:47
☽0N	10 9:40
♅☍♇	11 22:16
♄ R	24 7:53
☽0S	24 23:37
♃⚼♄	27 10:42
♂ R	30 16:53

Planet Ingress		Dy Hr Mn
♀	♓	10 7:50
☿	♓	11 12:08
☉	♈	19 22:34
☿	♈	29 6:23
♀	♈	3 13:11
☊	♐R	12 9:50
☿	♉	13 2:54
☉	♉	19 9:17
♃	♊	23 1:43
♀	♉	27 20:05
☿	♊	29 16:21

Last Aspect Dy Hr Mn			☽ Ingress	Dy Hr Mn
1 6:28	♃	△	♎	1 23:55
3 12:21	♀	△	♏	4 2:32
5 19:32	♀	□	♐	6 4:58
8 3:26	♀	⚹	♑	8 8:05
9 20:44	♃	△	♒	10 12:09
12 2:16	♃	□	♓	12 17:23
14 14:27	☉	☌	♈	15 0:21
16 4:15	♄	□	♉	17 9:45
19 21:35	☉	⚹	♊	19 21:40
21 5:22	☿	□	♋	22 10:35
24 9:53	♃	⚹	♌	24 21:52
26 19:10	♃	□	♍	27 5:29
29 0:23	♃	△	♎	29 9:19
30 11:01	♄	□	♏	31 10:46

Last Aspect Dy Hr Mn			☽ Ingress	Dy Hr Mn
2 9:21	♀	△	♐	2 11:42
3 14:50	♂	☌	♑	4 13:41
6 11:14	♃	△	♒	6 17:32
8 17:44	♃	□	♓	8 23:25
11 2:19	♃	⚹	♈	11 7:16
13 5:19	☉	☌	♉	13 17:08
16 1:55	♃	☌	♊	16 5:01
18 16:41	☉	⚹	♋	18 18:04
21 5:21	♃	⚹	♌	21 6:09
23 4:27	♀	△	♍	23 15:00
25 8:44	☿	△	♎	25 19:41
27 5:20	♂	⚹	♏	27 21:02
29 6:20	♆	☍	♐	29 20:54

☽ Phases & Eclipses Dy Hr Mn	
7 10:45	☾ 17♐32
14 14:27	● 24♓41
22 16:03	☽ 2♋43
30 2:04	○ 10♎03
5 18:10	☾ 16♑38
13 5:19	● 23♈58
21 10:02	☽ 1♌59
28 11:13	○ 8♏51

Astro Data

1 March 2048
Julian Day # 54117
SVP 4♓34'55"
GC 27♐30.7 ⚴ 2♒30.8
Eris 29♈56.4 ⚵ 1♒58.2
⚷ 11♏40.8R ⚶ 12♓18.9
☽ Mean ☊ 3♑29.1

1 April 2048
Julian Day # 54148
SVP 4♓34'52"
GC 27♐30.8 ⚴ 12♒09.2
Eris 0♉13.6 ⚵ 12♒36.6
⚷ 10♏27.9R ⚶ 27♓26.5
☽ Mean ☊ 1♑50.6

LONGITUDE — May 2048

Day	Sid.Time	☉	0 hr ☽	Noon ☽	True ☊	☿	♀	♂	⚳	♃	♄	♅	♆	♇
1 F	2 40 24	11♉47 30	16♐55 41	24♐20 24	28♐30.2	2♊18.1	4♉31.0	20♐22.2	24♓15.2	1♊54.0	15♑56.8	7♍05.5	20♉56.0	7♓48.9
2 Sa	2 44 20	12 45 43	1♑40 59	8♑56 51	28D30.4	3 27.6	5 44.9	20R21.2	24 35.7	2 07.7	15R56.1	7R04.9	20 58.2	7 49.8
3 Su	2 48 17	13 43 54	16 07 38	23 13 03	28 31.6	4 32.4	6 58.9	20 19.5	24 56.1	2 21.4	15 55.2	7 04.3	21 00.5	7 50.6
4 M	2 52 13	14 42 04	0♒13 01	7♒07 32	28R32.6	5 32.6	8 12.8	20 17.0	25 16.4	2 35.1	15 54.3	7 03.8	21 02.7	7 51.4
5 Tu	2 56 10	15 40 12	13 56 42	20 40 43	28 32.8	6 27.9	9 26.7	20 13.8	25 36.6	2 48.9	15 53.3	7 03.3	21 05.0	7 52.2
6 W	3 00 06	16 38 19	27 19 47	3♓54 10	28 31.3	7 18.3	10 40.7	20 09.8	25 56.8	3 02.7	15 52.1	7 02.9	21 07.2	7 53.0
7 Th	3 04 03	17 36 24	10♓24 11	16 50 05	28 28.1	8 03.9	11 54.6	20 05.0	26 16.8	3 16.5	15 50.9	7 02.5	21 09.5	7 53.7
8 F	3 07 59	18 34 28	23 12 12	29 30 46	28 23.1	8 44.5	13 08.5	19 59.5	26 36.8	3 30.3	15 49.6	7 02.2	21 11.7	7 54.5
9 Sa	3 11 56	19 32 31	5♈46 05	11♈58 23	28 16.9	9 20.0	14 22.4	19 53.2	26 56.6	3 44.2	15 48.2	7 01.9	21 14.0	7 55.2
10 Su	3 15 53	20 30 32	18 07 54	24 14 52	28 10.0	9 50.6	15 36.3	19 46.1	27 16.4	3 58.1	15 46.7	7 01.7	21 16.2	7 55.9
11 M	3 19 49	21 28 31	0♉19 28	6♉21 55	28 03.4	10 16.0	16 50.2	19 38.2	27 36.1	4 12.0	15 45.1	7 01.5	21 18.5	7 56.5
12 Tu	3 23 46	22 26 30	12 22 25	18 21 09	27 57.5	10 36.3	18 04.1	19 29.6	27 55.6	4 25.9	15 43.4	7 01.4	21 20.7	7 57.2
13 W	3 27 42	23 24 26	24 18 21	0♊14 13	27 52.9	10 51.6	19 17.9	19 20.3	28 15.1	4 39.9	15 41.7	7D01.4	21 23.0	7 57.8
14 Th	3 31 39	24 22 21	6♊09 01	12 03 00	27 50.0	11 01.7	20 31.8	19 10.2	28 34.5	4 53.8	15 39.8	7 01.4	21 25.3	7 58.4
15 F	3 35 35	25 20 15	17 56 29	23 49 46	27D48.8	11R07.0	21 45.7	18 59.3	28 53.7	5 07.8	15 37.9	7 01.4	21 27.5	7 58.9
16 Sa	3 39 32	26 18 07	29 43 15	5♋37 17	27 49.0	11 07.3	22 59.5	18 47.8	29 12.9	5 21.8	15 35.8	7 01.6	21 29.8	7 59.5
17 Su	3 43 28	27 15 58	11♋32 21	17 28 52	27 50.2	11 02.8	24 13.4	18 35.6	29 31.9	5 35.8	15 33.7	7 01.7	21 32.0	8 00.0
18 M	3 47 25	28 13 46	23 27 22	29 28 22	27 51.9	10 53.8	25 27.2	18 22.7	29 50.9	5 49.8	15 31.5	7 01.9	21 34.3	8 00.5
19 Tu	3 51 22	29 11 33	5♌32 24	11♌40 03	27 53.5	10 40.4	26 41.1	18 09.1	0♈09.7	6 03.8	15 29.2	7 02.2	21 36.5	8 01.0
20 W	3 55 18	0♊09 19	17 51 53	24 08 27	27R54.5	10 23.0	27 54.9	17 54.9	0 28.4	6 17.8	15 26.8	7 02.5	21 38.7	8 01.4
21 Th	3 59 15	1 07 03	0♍30 18	6♍57 56	27 54.5	10 01.8	29 08.7	17 40.1	0 47.0	6 31.9	15 24.4	7 02.9	21 41.0	8 01.8
22 F	4 03 11	2 04 45	13 31 49	20 12 18	27 53.4	9 37.3	0♊22.5	17 24.7	1 05.4	6 45.9	15 21.8	7 03.4	21 43.2	8 02.2
23 Sa	4 07 08	3 02 25	26 59 41	3♎54 05	27 51.2	9 09.9	1 36.3	17 08.7	1 23.8	6 59.9	15 19.2	7 03.8	21 45.4	8 02.6
24 Su	4 11 04	4 00 04	10♎55 31	18 03 48	27 48.3	8 40.1	2 50.1	16 52.2	1 42.0	7 14.0	15 16.5	7 04.4	21 47.6	8 03.0
25 M	4 15 01	4 57 42	25 18 36	2♏39 22	27 45.2	8 08.4	4 03.8	16 35.2	2 00.1	7 28.0	15 13.7	7 05.0	21 49.9	8 03.3
26 Tu	4 18 57	5 55 18	10♏05 22	17 35 42	27 42.4	7 35.3	5 17.6	16 17.7	2 18.1	7 42.1	15 10.9	7 05.6	21 52.1	8 03.6
27 W	4 22 54	6 52 53	25 09 20	2♐45 06	27 40.3	7 01.5	6 31.4	15 59.8	2 36.0	7 56.1	15 08.0	7 06.3	21 54.3	8 03.9
28 Th	4 26 51	7 50 27	10♐21 48	17 58 09	27D39.2	6 27.5	7 45.1	15 41.4	2 53.7	8 10.2	15 05.0	7 07.1	21 56.5	8 04.1
29 F	4 30 47	8 47 59	25 32 58	3♑05 07	27 39.1	5 54.0	8 58.9	15 22.7	3 11.3	8 24.2	15 01.9	7 07.9	21 58.6	8 04.3
30 Sa	4 34 44	9 45 31	10♑33 34	17 57 27	27 39.7	5 21.4	10 12.7	15 03.6	3 28.8	8 38.3	14 58.8	7 08.7	22 00.8	8 04.6
31 Su	4 38 40	10 43 02	25 16 04	2♒28 51	27 40.9	4 50.5	11 26.4	14 44.3	3 46.1	8 52.3	14 55.6	7 09.6	22 03.0	8 04.7

LONGITUDE — June 2048

Day	Sid.Time	☉	0 hr ☽	Noon ☽	True ☊	☿	♀	♂	⚳	♃	♄	♅	♆	♇
1 M	4 42 37	11♊40 32	9♒35 28	16♒35 40	27♐42.0	4♊21.6	12♊40.2	14♐24.6	4♈03.3	9♊06.4	14♑52.3	7♍10.6	22♉05.1	8♓04.9
2 Tu	4 46 33	12 38 01	23 29 26	0♓16 49	27 42.9	3R55.2	13 53.9	14R04.7	4 20.4	9 20.4	14R49.0	7 11.6	22 07.3	8 05.0
3 W	4 50 30	13 35 29	6♓58 00	13 33 14	27R43.2	3 31.8	15 07.6	13 44.7	4 37.3	9 34.4	14 45.6	7 12.7	22 09.4	8 05.1
4 Th	4 54 27	14 32 57	20 02 52	26 27 16	27 42.9	3 11.8	16 21.4	13 24.5	4 54.1	9 48.4	14 42.1	7 13.8	22 11.5	8 05.2
5 F	4 58 23	15 30 24	2♈46 52	9♈02 05	27 42.0	2 55.4	17 35.1	13 04.2	5 10.7	10 02.4	14 38.6	7 15.0	22 13.7	8 05.3
6 Sa	5 02 20	16 27 50	15 13 21	21 21 08	27 40.8	2 43.0	18 48.9	12 43.9	5 27.2	10 16.4	14 35.0	7 16.2	22 15.8	8R05.3
7 Su	5 06 16	17 25 16	27 25 50	3♉27 53	27 39.3	2 34.7	20 02.6	12 23.5	5 43.5	10 30.4	14 31.3	7 17.5	22 17.8	8 05.3
8 M	5 10 13	18 22 41	9♉27 41	15 25 35	27 38.0	2D30.7	21 16.4	12 03.3	5 59.7	10 44.4	14 27.6	7 18.8	22 19.9	8 05.3
9 Tu	5 14 09	19 20 05	21 21 59	27 17 11	27 36.8	2 31.0	22 30.1	11 43.1	6 15.7	10 58.4	14 23.9	7 20.1	22 22.0	8 05.3
10 W	5 18 06	20 17 29	3♊11 32	9♊05 20	27 36.1	2 35.9	23 43.8	11 23.1	6 31.5	11 12.3	14 20.1	7 21.6	22 24.0	8 05.2
11 Th	5 22 02	21 14 52	14 58 53	20 52 27	27D35.7	2 45.3	24 57.6	11 03.2	6 47.2	11 26.3	14 16.2	7 23.0	22 26.1	8 05.1
12 F	5 25 59	22 12 14	26 46 20	2♋40 49	27 35.7	2 59.2	26 11.3	10 43.6	7 02.8	11 40.2	14 12.3	7 24.6	22 28.1	8 05.0
13 Sa	5 29 56	23 09 36	8♋36 12	14 32 45	27 35.9	3 17.7	27 25.0	10 24.3	7 18.1	11 54.1	14 08.4	7 26.1	22 30.1	8 04.9
14 Su	5 33 52	24 06 56	20 30 49	26 30 41	27 36.2	3 40.6	28 38.8	10 05.4	7 33.3	12 08.0	14 04.4	7 27.7	22 32.1	8 04.7
15 M	5 37 49	25 04 16	2♌32 43	8♌37 15	27 36.6	4 08.0	29 52.5	9 46.8	7 48.3	12 21.8	14 00.3	7 29.4	22 34.1	8 04.5
16 Tu	5 41 45	26 01 35	14 44 40	20 55 20	27 36.8	4 39.7	1♋06.2	9 28.6	8 03.1	12 35.7	13 56.3	7 31.1	22 36.0	8 04.3
17 W	5 45 42	26 58 53	27 09 41	3♍28 05	27R36.9	5 15.8	2 19.9	9 10.9	8 17.8	12 49.5	13 52.1	7 32.9	22 38.0	8 04.1
18 Th	5 49 38	27 56 10	9♍50 57	16 18 39	27D36.9	5 56.1	3 33.6	8 53.7	8 32.3	13 03.2	13 48.0	7 34.7	22 39.9	8 03.8
19 F	5 53 35	28 53 27	22 51 34	29 30 01	27 36.9	6 40.6	4 47.3	8 37.0	8 46.5	13 17.0	13 43.8	7 36.5	22 41.8	8 03.5
20 Sa	5 57 31	29 50 43	6♎14 15	13♎04 30	27 37.0	7 29.1	6 01.0	8 20.9	9 00.6	13 30.7	13 39.6	7 38.4	22 43.7	8 03.2
21 Su	6 01 28	0♋47 58	20 00 51	27 03 19	27 37.2	8 21.8	7 14.7	8 05.4	9 14.6	13 44.4	13 35.3	7 40.4	22 45.6	8 02.9
22 M	6 05 25	1 45 12	4♏11 44	11♏25 52	27 37.5	9 18.4	8 28.4	7 50.5	9 28.3	13 58.1	13 31.1	7 42.4	22 47.4	8 02.5
23 Tu	6 09 21	2 42 26	18 45 16	26 09 22	27 37.9	10 18.8	9 42.1	7 36.3	9 41.8	14 11.8	13 26.8	7 44.4	22 49.3	8 02.2
24 W	6 13 18	3 39 39	3♐37 25	11♐08 33	27 38.3	11 23.2	10 55.8	7 22.8	9 55.1	14 25.4	13 22.5	7 46.5	22 51.1	8 01.8
25 Th	6 17 14	4 36 52	18 41 46	26 15 58	27R38.4	12 31.3	12 09.5	7 10.0	10 08.2	14 38.9	13 18.1	7 48.6	22 52.9	8 01.4
26 F	6 21 11	5 34 04	3♑50 02	11♑22 48	27 38.3	13 43.2	13 23.2	6 57.9	10 21.2	14 52.5	13 13.8	7 50.8	22 54.7	8 00.9
27 Sa	6 25 07	6 31 16	18 53 09	26 20 02	27 37.7	14 58.8	14 36.9	6 46.5	10 33.9	15 06.0	13 09.4	7 53.0	22 56.4	8 00.5
28 Su	6 29 04	7 28 28	3♒42 31	10♒59 46	27 36.8	16 18.0	15 50.6	6 35.9	10 46.4	15 19.5	13 05.0	7 55.3	22 58.2	8 00.0
29 M	6 33 00	8 25 40	18 11 10	25 16 14	27 35.6	17 40.9	17 04.2	6 26.0	10 58.7	15 32.9	13 00.6	7 57.5	22 59.9	7 59.5
30 Tu	6 36 57	9 22 52	2♓14 39	9♓06 16	27 34.3	19 07.3	18 17.9	6 16.9	11 10.7	15 46.3	12 56.2	7 59.9	23 01.6	7 58.9

Astro Data

	Dy Hr Mn
☽0N	7 14:29
♅D	13 22:37
☿R	16 1:30
☽0S	22 7:58
♃□♅	23 18:55
♃□♇	28 1:27
☽0N	3 19:58
♇R	7 8:19
☿D	8 21:57
☽0S	18 14:48
♃⚻♄	20 23:51
♅☍♇	30 4:11

Planet Ingress

	Dy Hr Mn
⚳ ♈	18 23:38
☉ ♊	20 8:08
♀ ♊	22 4:41
♀ ♋	15 14:27
☉ ♋	20 15:54

Last Aspect / ☽ Ingress

Last Aspect Dy Hr Mn		☽ Ingress Dy Hr Mn
1 5:34	♂☌	♑ 1 21:14
3 8:14	♆△	♒ 3 23:38
5 12:44	♆□	♓ 6 4:51
7 20:09	♆⚹	♈ 8 12:56
10 3:17	♂△	♉ 10 23:21
12 20:58	☉☌	♊ 13 11:31
15 2:17	♂☍	♋ 16 0:34
18 9:19	☉⚹	♌ 18 13:03
20 19:54	♀□	♍ 20 23:03
22 14:42	♆△	♎ 23 5:15
24 10:03	♂⚹	♏ 25 7:41
26 18:48	♆☍	♐ 27 7:39
28 8:28	♂☌	♑ 29 7:05
30 18:39	♆△	♒ 31 7:51

Last Aspect / ☽ Ingress

Last Aspect Dy Hr Mn		☽ Ingress Dy Hr Mn
1 21:34	♆□	♓ 2 11:30
4 3:59	♆⚹	♈ 4 18:42
6 6:28	♀⚹	♉ 7 5:06
9 2:00	♆☌	♊ 9 17:31
11 21:17	♀☌	♋ 12 6:34
14 4:02	♆⚹	♌ 14 18:57
16 22:38	☉⚹	♍ 17 5:25
19 10:49	☉□	♎ 19 12:54
20 13:01	♄□	♏ 21 16:58
23 6:36	♆☍	♐ 23 18:11
24 17:18	♃☍	♑ 25 17:55
27 6:31	♆△	♒ 27 17:57
29 8:07	♆□	♓ 29 20:07

☽ Phases & Eclipses

Dy Hr Mn	
5 2:22	☾ 15♒17
12 20:58	● 22♉48
21 0:16	☽ 0♍39
27 18:57	○ 7♐10
3 12:04	☾ 13♓36
11 12:50	● 21♊17
11 12:57:19	● A 04'58"
19 10:49	☽ 28♍51
26 2:08	○ 5♑11
26 2:01	● P 0.639

Astro Data

1 May 2048
Julian Day # 54178
SVP 4♓34'49"
GC 27♐30.9 ⚴ 19♒06.0
Eris 0♉33.4 ⚵ 21♒26.7
⚷ 8♏17.6R ⚶ 11♈29.7
☽ Mean ☊ 0♑15.3

1 June 2048
Julian Day # 54209
SVP 4♓34'44"
GC 27♐30.9 ⚴ 22♒27.8
Eris 0♉52.0 ⚵ 27♒54.4
⚷ 6♏12.2R ⚶ 25♈05.0
☽ Mean ☊ 28♐36.8

July 2048 — LONGITUDE

Day	Sid.Time	☉	0 hr ☽	Noon ☽	True☊	☿	♀	♂	⚳	♃	♄	♅	♆	♇
1 W	6 40 54	10♋20 03	15♓51 07	22♓29 18	27♐33.3	20♊37.2	19♋31.6	6♐08.6	11♈22.6	15♊59.7	12♑51.8	8♍02.3	23♉03.2	7♓58.4
2 Th	6 44 50	11 17 15	29 01 06	5♈26 52	27D32.7	22 10.6	20 45.3	6R01.1	11 34.2	16 13.0	12R47.3	8 04.7	23 04.9	7R57.8
3 F	6 48 47	12 14 28	11♈47 02	18 02 04	27 32.7	23 47.5	21 59.0	5 54.5	11 45.6	16 26.3	12 42.9	8 07.1	23 06.5	7 57.2
4 Sa	6 52 43	13 11 40	24 12 31	0♉18 55	27 33.3	25 27.7	23 12.7	5 48.6	11 56.8	16 39.5	12 38.5	8 09.6	23 08.1	7 56.6
5 Su	6 56 40	14 08 53	6♉21 50	12 21 50	27 34.4	27 11.1	24 26.3	5 43.6	12 07.7	16 52.7	12 34.0	8 12.2	23 09.7	7 56.0
6 M	7 00 36	15 06 06	18 19 29	24 15 17	27 35.9	28 57.7	25 40.0	5 39.4	12 18.4	17 05.9	12 29.6	8 14.7	23 11.3	7 55.3
7 Tu	7 04 33	16 03 19	0♊09 48	6♊03 29	27 37.3	0♋47.4	26 53.7	5 36.1	12 28.8	17 19.0	12 25.2	8 17.3	23 12.8	7 54.6
8 W	7 08 29	17 00 33	11 56 49	17 50 14	27R38.3	2 40.0	28 07.4	5 33.6	12 39.0	17 32.1	12 20.8	8 20.0	23 14.3	7 53.9
9 Th	7 12 26	17 57 47	23 44 07	29 38 50	27 38.6	4 35.3	29 21.1	5 31.9	12 49.0	17 45.1	12 16.3	8 22.7	23 15.8	7 53.2
10 F	7 16 23	18 55 01	5♋34 44	11♋32 06	27 37.9	6 33.2	0♌34.8	5D31.1	12 58.7	17 58.0	12 12.0	8 25.4	23 17.2	7 52.5
11 Sa	7 20 19	19 52 15	17 31 13	23 32 20	27 36.1	8 33.3	1 48.5	5 31.2	13 08.1	18 11.0	12 07.6	8 28.2	23 18.7	7 51.7
12 Su	7 24 16	20 49 29	29 35 41	5♌41 27	27 33.4	10 35.6	3 02.2	5 32.1	13 17.3	18 23.8	12 03.2	8 31.0	23 20.1	7 51.0
13 M	7 28 12	21 46 44	11♌49 50	18 01 02	27 29.8	12 39.6	4 15.8	5 33.8	13 26.2	18 36.6	11 58.9	8 33.8	23 21.5	7 50.2
14 Tu	7 32 09	22 43 58	24 15 12	0♍32 31	27 25.8	14 45.1	5 29.5	5 36.4	13 34.8	18 49.4	11 54.5	8 36.7	23 22.8	7 49.3
15 W	7 36 05	23 41 13	6♍53 08	13 17 15	27 22.0	16 51.9	6 43.2	5 39.8	13 43.2	19 02.0	11 50.2	8 39.6	23 24.1	7 48.5
16 Th	7 40 02	24 38 28	19 45 02	26 16 38	27 18.8	18 59.5	7 56.9	5 44.0	13 51.2	19 14.7	11 46.0	8 42.5	23 25.4	7 47.7
17 F	7 43 58	25 35 43	2♎52 14	9♎31 59	27 16.6	21 07.7	9 10.5	5 49.0	13 59.0	19 27.2	11 41.7	8 45.5	23 26.7	7 46.8
18 Sa	7 47 55	26 32 58	16 16 04	23 04 34	27D15.6	23 16.2	10 24.2	5 54.9	14 06.5	19 39.7	11 37.5	8 48.5	23 28.0	7 45.9
19 Su	7 51 52	27 30 13	29 57 35	6♏55 10	27 15.9	25 24.7	11 37.8	6 01.5	14 13.8	19 52.2	11 33.3	8 51.5	23 29.2	7 45.0
20 M	7 55 48	28 27 29	13♏57 18	21 03 52	27 17.0	27 32.9	12 51.5	6 08.9	14 20.7	20 04.6	11 29.2	8 54.6	23 30.4	7 44.1
21 Tu	7 59 45	29 24 44	28 14 42	5♐29 29	27 18.4	29 40.6	14 05.1	6 17.1	14 27.4	20 16.9	11 25.0	8 57.6	23 31.5	7 43.2
22 W	8 03 41	0♌22 00	12♐47 49	20 09 11	27R19.4	1♌47.6	15 18.8	6 26.0	14 33.7	20 29.1	11 21.0	9 00.8	23 32.7	7 42.2
23 Th	8 07 38	1 19 17	27 32 56	4♑58 17	27 19.4	3 53.7	16 32.4	6 35.7	14 39.8	20 41.3	11 16.9	9 03.9	23 33.8	7 41.3
24 F	8 11 34	2 16 34	12♑24 23	19 50 20	27 17.8	5 58.7	17 46.0	6 46.2	14 45.5	20 53.4	11 12.9	9 07.1	23 34.8	7 40.3
25 Sa	8 15 31	3 13 51	27 15 08	4♒37 48	27 14.6	8 02.4	18 59.7	6 57.3	14 51.0	21 05.4	11 09.0	9 10.3	23 35.9	7 39.3
26 Su	8 19 28	4 11 09	11♒57 23	19 13 00	27 09.9	10 04.9	20 13.3	7 09.1	14 56.1	21 17.4	11 05.1	9 13.5	23 36.9	7 38.3
27 M	8 23 24	5 08 27	26 23 51	3♓29 16	27 04.3	12 05.9	21 26.9	7 21.7	15 00.9	21 29.3	11 01.2	9 16.8	23 37.9	7 37.2
28 Tu	8 27 21	6 05 47	10♓28 45	17 21 56	26 58.4	14 05.5	22 40.5	7 34.9	15 05.4	21 41.1	10 57.4	9 20.1	23 38.9	7 36.2
29 W	8 31 17	7 03 07	24 08 36	0♈48 43	26 53.1	16 03.5	23 54.1	7 48.8	15 09.6	21 52.9	10 53.7	9 23.4	23 39.8	7 35.1
30 Th	8 35 14	8 00 28	7♈22 22	13 49 47	26 49.0	17 59.9	25 07.7	8 03.3	15 13.4	22 04.6	10 50.0	9 26.7	23 40.7	7 34.1
31 F	8 39 10	8 57 51	20 11 18	26 27 22	26 46.5	19 54.8	26 21.3	8 18.5	15 17.0	22 16.1	10 46.3	9 30.0	23 41.5	7 33.0

August 2048 — LONGITUDE

Day	Sid.Time	☉	0 hr ☽	Noon ☽	True☊	☿	♀	♂	⚳	♃	♄	♅	♆	♇
1 Sa	8 43 07	9♌55 14	2♉38 29	8♉45 12	26♐45.6	21♌48.0	27♌34.9	8♐34.4	15♈20.1	22♊27.7	10♑42.7	9♍33.4	23♉42.4	7♓31.9
2 Su	8 47 03	10 52 39	14 48 08	20 47 56	26D46.0	23 39.7	28 48.4	8 50.9	15 23.0	22 39.1	10R39.2	9 36.8	23 43.2	7R30.8
3 M	8 51 00	11 50 05	26 45 13	2♊40 39	26 47.3	25 29.7	0♍02.0	9 08.0	15 25.5	22 50.4	10 35.7	9 40.2	23 43.9	7 29.7
4 Tu	8 54 56	12 47 32	8♊34 51	14 28 27	26 48.7	27 18.1	1 15.6	9 25.7	15 27.7	23 01.7	10 32.3	9 43.7	23 44.7	7 28.6
5 W	8 58 53	13 45 00	20 22 03	26 16 12	26R49.4	29 04.8	2 29.2	9 44.0	15 29.5	23 12.9	10 29.0	9 47.2	23 45.4	7 27.4
6 Th	9 02 50	14 42 29	2♋11 26	8♋08 14	26 48.6	0♍50.0	3 42.7	10 02.9	15 31.0	23 24.0	10 25.7	9 50.6	23 46.1	7 26.3
7 F	9 06 46	15 40 00	14 07 01	20 08 10	26 45.9	2 33.6	4 56.3	10 22.3	15 32.1	23 35.0	10 22.5	9 54.2	23 46.7	7 25.1
8 Sa	9 10 43	16 37 31	26 12 02	2♌18 51	26 41.1	4 15.6	6 09.9	10 42.4	15 32.9	23 45.9	10 19.3	9 57.7	23 47.3	7 24.0
9 Su	9 14 39	17 35 04	8♌28 51	14 42 10	26 34.2	5 56.1	7 23.4	11 03.0	15R33.3	23 56.7	10 16.3	10 01.2	23 47.9	7 22.8
10 M	9 18 36	18 32 38	20 58 55	27 19 08	26 25.7	7 34.9	8 36.9	11 24.1	15 33.3	24 07.4	10 13.3	10 04.8	23 48.5	7 21.6
11 Tu	9 22 32	19 30 13	3♍42 49	10♍09 56	26 16.4	9 12.2	9 50.5	11 45.8	15 33.0	24 18.0	10 10.3	10 08.4	23 49.0	7 20.4
12 W	9 26 29	20 27 49	16 40 24	23 14 09	26 07.3	10 48.0	11 04.0	12 08.1	15 32.3	24 28.6	10 07.5	10 12.0	23 49.5	7 19.2
13 Th	9 30 25	21 25 25	29 51 04	6♎31 03	25 59.2	12 22.2	12 17.5	12 30.8	15 31.3	24 39.0	10 04.7	10 15.6	23 49.9	7 18.0
14 F	9 34 22	22 23 03	13♎14 00	19 59 50	25 53.1	13 54.9	13 31.0	12 54.1	15 29.9	24 49.3	10 02.0	10 19.2	23 50.3	7 16.7
15 Sa	9 38 19	23 20 42	26 48 28	3♏39 51	25 49.2	15 26.0	14 44.5	13 17.8	15 28.2	24 59.5	9 59.4	10 22.8	23 50.7	7 15.5
16 Su	9 42 15	24 18 22	10♏33 55	17 30 39	25D47.5	16 55.5	15 58.0	13 42.0	15 26.0	25 09.6	9 56.8	10 26.5	23 51.1	7 14.3
17 M	9 46 12	25 16 03	24 30 00	1♐31 55	25 47.4	18 23.5	17 11.5	14 06.7	15 23.5	25 19.7	9 54.4	10 30.1	23 51.4	7 13.0
18 Tu	9 50 08	26 13 45	8♐36 18	15 43 02	25R48.0	19 49.9	18 24.9	14 31.9	15 20.7	25 29.6	9 52.0	10 33.8	23 51.7	7 11.8
19 W	9 54 05	27 11 28	22 51 56	0♑02 45	25 48.2	21 14.7	19 38.4	14 57.6	15 17.5	25 39.3	9 49.7	10 37.5	23 51.9	7 10.6
20 Th	9 58 01	28 09 12	7♑15 08	14 28 42	25 46.9	22 37.9	20 51.8	15 23.6	15 13.9	25 49.0	9 47.5	10 41.2	23 52.2	7 09.3
21 F	10 01 58	29 06 57	21 42 54	28 57 10	25 43.3	23 59.3	22 05.2	15 50.1	15 10.0	25 58.6	9 45.4	10 44.9	23 52.3	7 08.1
22 Sa	10 05 54	0♍04 44	6♒10 49	13♒23 08	25 37.0	25 19.1	23 18.6	16 17.0	15 05.6	26 08.1	9 43.3	10 48.6	23 52.5	7 06.8
23 Su	10 09 51	1 02 31	20 33 22	27 40 47	25 28.5	26 37.2	24 32.0	16 44.4	15 01.0	26 17.4	9 41.4	10 52.3	23 52.6	7 05.5
24 M	10 13 48	2 00 20	4♓44 39	11♓44 19	25 18.3	27 53.4	25 45.3	17 12.1	14 56.0	26 26.6	9 39.5	10 56.1	23 52.7	7 04.3
25 Tu	10 17 44	2 58 11	18 39 14	25 28 56	25 07.6	29 07.8	26 58.7	17 40.2	14 50.6	26 35.7	9 37.7	10 59.8	23 52.8	7 03.0
26 W	10 21 41	3 56 03	2♈13 06	8♈51 31	24 57.4	0♎20.3	28 12.0	18 08.7	14 44.8	26 44.7	9 36.1	11 03.6	23R52.8	7 01.7
27 Th	10 25 37	4 53 57	15 24 07	21 51 00	24 48.8	1 30.8	29 25.3	18 37.6	14 38.7	26 53.6	9 34.5	11 07.3	23 52.8	7 00.4
28 F	10 29 34	5 51 52	28 12 21	4♉28 28	24 42.4	2 39.3	0♎38.6	19 06.8	14 32.3	27 02.3	9 32.9	11 11.1	23 52.7	6 59.2
29 Sa	10 33 30	6 49 50	10♉39 45	16 46 42	24 38.5	3 45.6	1 51.9	19 36.5	14 25.5	27 10.9	9 31.5	11 14.8	23 52.6	6 57.9
30 Su	10 37 27	7 47 49	22 49 51	28 49 50	24D36.7	4 49.6	3 05.2	20 06.4	14 18.4	27 19.4	9 30.2	11 18.6	23 52.5	6 56.6
31 M	10 41 23	8 45 50	4♊47 16	10♊42 51	24 36.3	5 51.2	4 18.5	20 36.7	14 10.9	27 27.8	9 29.0	11 22.4	23 52.4	6 55.3

Astro Data	Dy Hr Mn
☽0N	1 3:37
♂ D	10 22:38
☽0S	15 20:43
☽0N	28 13:16
♃⊻♆	8 15:25
⚳ R	10 3:21
♄△♅	11 19:20
☽0S	12 2:52
☿0S	24 5:52
☽0N	24 23:25
♆ R	26 15:00
♀0S	29 21:33

Planet Ingress		Dy Hr Mn
☿	♋	7 1:42
♀	♌	10 0:40
☿	♌	21 15:39
☉	♌	22 2:47
♀	♍	3 11:20
☿	♍	6 0:32
☉	♍	22 10:02
☿	♎	26 5:12
♀	♎	27 23:21

Last Aspect Dy Hr Mn			☽ Ingress	Dy Hr Mn
1 13:02	♆	⚹	♈	2 1:49
4 0:56	☿	⚹	♉	4 11:23
6 15:12	♀	⚹	♊	6 23:40
8 11:22	♃	☌	♋	9 12:43
11 11:33	♆	⚹	♌	12 0:48
13 22:18	♆	□	♍	14 10:58
16 8:46	☉	⚹	♎	16 18:47
18 18:31	☉	□	♏	19 0:04
21 1:14	☉	△	♐	21 2:55
22 12:33	♃	☍	♑	23 3:58
24 18:04	♆	△	♒	25 4:28
26 19:21	♆	□	♓	27 6:05
28 23:08	♆	⚹	♈	29 10:32
31 11:47	♀	△	♉	31 18:51

Last Aspect Dy Hr Mn			☽ Ingress	Dy Hr Mn
3 6:01	♀	□	♊	3 6:34
5 18:42	☿	⚹	♋	5 19:34
7 19:13	♆	⚹	♌	8 7:28
10 5:53	♃	⚹	♍	10 17:03
12 14:17	♃	□	♎	13 0:16
14 20:37	♃	△	♏	15 5:36
17 0:32	☉	□	♐	17 9:24
19 6:54	☉	△	♑	19 11:55
21 3:34	♆	△	♒	21 13:44
23 9:38	♃	△	♓	23 15:56
25 19:07	☿	☍	♈	25 20:02
27 21:37	♃	⚹	♉	28 3:25
30 2:05	♆	☌	♊	30 14:21

☽ Phases & Eclipses Dy Hr Mn		
2 23:58	☾	11♈46
11 4:04	●	19♋33
18 18:31	☽	26♎49
25 9:34	○	3♒08
1 14:30	☾	10♉01
9 17:59	●	17♌49
17 0:32	☽	24♏48
23 18:07	○	1♓17
31 7:42	☾	8♊35

Astro Data

1 July 2048
Julian Day # 54239
SVP 4♓34'39"
GC 27♐31.0 ⚴ 20♒35.3R
Eris 1♉04.0 ⚵ 29♒54.6R
⚷ 5♏20.3R ⚶ 6♉52.5
☽ Mean ☊ 27♐01.5

1 August 2048
Julian Day # 54270
SVP 4♓34'34"
GC 27♐31.1 ⚴ 13♒41.1R
Eris 1♉07.4R ⚵ 26♒06.6R
⚷ 6♏05.3 ⚶ 16♉51.8
☽ Mean ☊ 25♐23.0

LONGITUDE — September 2048

Day	Sid.Time	☉	0 hr ☽	Noon☽	True☊	☿	♀	♂	⚳	♃	♄	♅	♆	♇
1 Tu	10 45 20	9♍43 53	16♊37 15	22♊31 09	24♐36.5	6♎50.3	5♎31.8	21♐07.4	14♈03.1	27♊36.0	9♑27.8	11♍26.1	23♉52.2	6♓54.1
2 W	10 49 17	10 41 58	28 25 15	4♋20 13	24R36.2	7 46.7	6 45.0	21 38.4	13R54.9	27 44.1	9R26.8	11 29.9	23R52.0	6R52.8
3 Th	10 53 13	11 40 05	10♋16 40	16 15 13	24 34.3	8 40.3	7 58.3	22 09.8	13 46.4	27 52.0	9 25.9	11 33.7	23 51.8	6 51.5
4 F	10 57 10	12 38 14	22 16 24	28 20 45	24 30.2	9 30.9	9 11.5	22 41.4	13 37.6	27 59.9	9 25.0	11 37.4	23 51.5	6 50.3
5 Sa	11 01 06	13 36 24	4♌28 41	10♌40 33	24 23.4	10 18.2	10 24.7	23 13.4	13 28.5	28 07.5	9 24.3	11 41.2	23 51.2	6 49.0
6 Su	11 05 03	14 34 37	16 56 38	23 17 08	24 13.9	11 02.2	11 37.9	23 45.7	13 19.1	28 15.1	9 23.6	11 45.0	23 50.9	6 47.7
7 M	11 08 59	15 32 51	29 42 07	6♍11 37	24 02.4	11 42.5	12 51.1	24 18.3	13 09.4	28 22.5	9 23.0	11 48.7	23 50.5	6 46.5
8 Tu	11 12 56	16 31 07	12♍45 32	19 23 41	23 49.9	12 18.8	14 04.2	24 51.3	12 59.4	28 29.7	9 22.6	11 52.5	23 50.1	6 45.2
9 W	11 16 52	17 29 25	26 05 48	2♎51 35	23 37.4	12 50.9	15 17.4	25 24.5	12 49.1	28 36.8	9 22.2	11 56.3	23 49.6	6 44.0
10 Th	11 20 49	18 27 44	9♎40 40	16 32 38	23 26.3	13 18.6	16 30.5	25 58.0	12 38.5	28 43.8	9 21.9	12 00.0	23 49.2	6 42.7
11 F	11 24 46	19 26 06	23 27 05	0♏23 37	23 17.5	13 41.4	17 43.6	26 31.8	12 27.6	28 50.6	9 21.8	12 03.8	23 48.7	6 41.5
12 Sa	11 28 42	20 24 28	7♏21 52	14 21 29	23 11.5	13 59.1	18 56.7	27 05.9	12 16.5	28 57.2	9D21.7	12 07.5	23 48.1	6 40.2
13 Su	11 32 39	21 22 53	21 22 11	28 23 43	23 08.3	14 11.4	20 09.8	27 40.2	12 05.2	29 03.7	9 21.7	12 11.3	23 47.6	6 39.0
14 M	11 36 35	22 21 19	5♐25 53	12♐28 32	23 07.2	14R17.8	21 22.9	28 14.9	11 53.6	29 10.0	9 21.9	12 15.0	23 47.0	6 37.8
15 Tu	11 40 32	23 19 47	19 31 33	26 34 50	23 07.1	14 18.1	22 35.9	28 49.7	11 41.8	29 16.2	9 22.1	12 18.7	23 46.4	6 36.6
16 W	11 44 28	24 18 16	3♑38 17	10♑41 47	23 06.7	14 11.9	23 48.9	29 24.9	11 29.8	29 22.2	9 22.4	12 22.5	23 45.7	6 35.4
17 Th	11 48 25	25 16 47	17 45 12	24 48 22	23 04.7	13 59.1	25 01.9	0♑00.3	11 17.7	29 28.1	9 22.8	12 26.2	23 45.0	6 34.2
18 F	11 52 21	26 15 19	1♒51 03	8♒52 58	23 00.2	13 39.3	26 14.9	0 35.9	11 05.3	29 33.8	9 23.4	12 29.9	23 44.3	6 33.0
19 Sa	11 56 18	27 13 53	15 53 47	22 53 08	22 52.8	13 12.5	27 27.8	1 11.7	10 52.7	29 39.3	9 24.0	12 33.6	23 43.6	6 31.8
20 Su	12 00 15	28 12 29	29 50 34	6♓45 38	22 42.8	12 38.7	28 40.7	1 47.8	10 40.0	29 44.7	9 24.7	12 37.2	23 42.8	6 30.6
21 M	12 04 11	29 11 06	13♓37 52	20 26 49	22 30.9	11 58.1	29 53.6	2 24.1	10 27.1	29 49.9	9 25.5	12 40.9	23 42.0	6 29.5
22 Tu	12 08 08	0♎09 46	27 12 05	3♈53 16	22 18.3	11 10.9	1♏06.5	3 00.6	10 14.1	29 54.9	9 26.4	12 44.5	23 41.1	6 28.3
23 W	12 12 04	1 08 27	10♈30 06	17 02 21	22 06.2	10 17.7	2 19.3	3 37.4	10 01.0	29 59.8	9 27.4	12 48.2	23 40.3	6 27.2
24 Th	12 16 01	2 07 11	23 29 54	29 52 45	21 55.8	9 19.4	3 32.1	4 14.3	9 47.8	0♋04.5	9 28.5	12 51.8	23 39.4	6 26.0
25 F	12 19 57	3 05 56	6♉10 57	12♉24 41	21 47.7	8 16.9	4 44.9	4 51.5	9 34.4	0 09.0	9 29.7	12 55.4	23 38.5	6 24.9
26 Sa	12 23 54	4 04 44	18 34 14	24 39 56	21 42.4	7 11.5	5 57.7	5 28.8	9 21.0	0 13.4	9 31.0	12 59.0	23 37.5	6 23.8
27 Su	12 27 50	5 03 34	0♊42 15	6♊41 40	21 39.6	6 04.7	7 10.5	6 06.4	9 07.6	0 17.5	9 32.4	13 02.6	23 36.6	6 22.7
28 M	12 31 47	6 02 27	12 38 44	18 34 04	21D38.7	4 58.1	8 23.2	6 44.1	8 54.0	0 21.5	9 33.9	13 06.1	23 35.6	6 21.6
29 Tu	12 35 43	7 01 21	24 28 19	0♋22 08	21R38.8	3 53.5	9 35.9	7 22.1	8 40.4	0 25.3	9 35.5	13 09.7	23 34.5	6 20.6
30 W	12 39 40	8 00 18	6♋16 13	12 11 16	21 38.8	2 52.5	10 48.6	8 00.2	8 26.9	0 29.0	9 37.2	13 13.2	23 33.5	6 19.5

LONGITUDE — October 2048

Day	Sid.Time	☉	0 hr ☽	Noon☽	True☊	☿	♀	♂	⚳	♃	♄	♅	♆	♇
1 Th	12 43 37	8♎59 17	18♋07 58	24♋06 59	21♐37.7	1♎56.8	12♏01.3	8♑38.5	8♈13.2	0♋32.4	9♑39.0	13♍16.7	23♉32.4	6♓18.5
2 F	12 47 33	9 58 19	0♌08 59	6♌14 33	21R34.7	1R08.1	13 13.9	9 17.0	7R59.6	0 35.7	9 40.9	13 20.2	23R31.3	6R17.4
3 Sa	12 51 30	10 57 22	12 24 16	18 38 38	21 29.2	0 27.5	14 26.6	9 55.7	7 46.1	0 38.7	9 42.9	13 23.6	23 30.2	6 16.4
4 Su	12 55 26	11 56 28	24 58 02	1♍22 48	21 21.3	29♍56.1	15 39.2	10 34.6	7 32.5	0 41.6	9 44.9	13 27.1	23 29.0	6 15.4
5 M	12 59 23	12 55 36	7♍53 08	14 29 08	21 11.3	29 34.8	16 51.7	11 13.6	7 19.0	0 44.3	9 47.1	13 30.5	23 27.9	6 14.4
6 Tu	13 03 19	13 54 46	21 10 44	27 57 48	21 00.2	29D23.9	18 04.3	11 52.8	7 05.6	0 46.8	9 49.4	13 33.9	23 26.6	6 13.5
7 W	13 07 16	14 53 59	4♎50 00	11♎46 55	20 49.1	29 23.7	19 16.8	12 32.2	6 52.3	0 49.1	9 51.7	13 37.3	23 25.4	6 12.5
8 Th	13 11 12	15 53 13	18 48 01	25 52 41	20 39.1	29 34.1	20 29.3	13 11.7	6 39.0	0 51.2	9 54.2	13 40.6	23 24.2	6 11.6
9 F	13 15 09	16 52 30	3♏00 16	10♏10 02	20 31.3	29 54.8	21 41.8	13 51.4	6 25.9	0 53.1	9 56.7	13 43.9	23 22.9	6 10.7
10 Sa	13 19 06	17 51 48	17 21 17	24 33 20	20 26.2	0♎25.3	22 54.3	14 31.3	6 12.9	0 54.9	9 59.3	13 47.2	23 21.6	6 09.8
11 Su	13 23 02	18 51 08	1♐45 32	8♐57 22	20D23.6	1 05.2	24 06.7	15 11.3	6 00.0	0 56.4	10 02.1	13 50.5	23 20.3	6 08.9
12 M	13 26 59	19 50 31	16 08 18	23 17 57	20 23.1	1 53.6	25 19.1	15 51.4	5 47.3	0 57.7	10 04.9	13 53.8	23 19.0	6 08.0
13 Tu	13 30 55	20 49 55	0♑26 01	7♑32 15	20 23.7	2 49.8	26 31.4	16 31.7	5 34.8	0 58.9	10 07.8	13 57.0	23 17.6	6 07.2
14 W	13 34 52	21 49 20	14 36 28	21 38 34	20R24.2	3 53.1	27 43.8	17 12.2	5 22.5	0 59.8	10 10.8	14 00.2	23 16.2	6 06.4
15 Th	13 38 48	22 48 48	28 38 27	5♒36 04	20 23.4	5 02.7	28 56.1	17 52.8	5 10.3	1 00.5	10 13.9	14 03.3	23 14.9	6 05.6
16 F	13 42 45	23 48 17	12♒31 20	19 24 14	20 20.6	6 17.7	0♐08.3	18 33.5	4 58.4	1 01.1	10 17.0	14 06.4	23 13.4	6 04.8
17 Sa	13 46 41	24 47 47	26 14 40	3♓02 34	20 15.5	7 37.5	1 20.5	19 14.3	4 46.7	1 01.4	10 20.3	14 09.5	23 12.0	6 04.0
18 Su	13 50 38	25 47 20	9♓47 49	16 30 17	20 08.1	9 01.3	2 32.7	19 55.3	4 35.2	1R01.5	10 23.6	14 12.6	23 10.6	6 03.3
19 M	13 54 35	26 46 54	23 09 51	29 46 20	19 59.2	10 28.7	3 44.8	20 36.4	4 23.9	1 01.5	10 27.1	14 15.6	23 09.1	6 02.5
20 Tu	13 58 31	27 46 30	6♈19 37	12♈49 33	19 49.6	11 58.9	4 56.9	21 17.6	4 13.0	1 01.2	10 30.6	14 18.6	23 07.6	6 01.8
21 W	14 02 28	28 46 08	19 16 01	25 38 57	19 40.4	13 31.5	6 09.0	21 58.9	4 02.2	1 00.7	10 34.2	14 21.6	23 06.1	6 01.1
22 Th	14 06 24	29 45 48	1♉58 18	8♉14 05	19 32.5	15 06.1	7 21.0	22 40.3	3 51.8	1 00.1	10 37.9	14 24.5	23 04.6	6 00.5
23 F	14 10 21	0♏45 31	14 26 21	20 35 14	19 26.5	16 42.2	8 33.0	23 21.8	3 41.6	0 59.2	10 41.6	14 27.4	23 03.1	5 59.8
24 Sa	14 14 17	1 45 15	26 40 54	2♊43 37	19 22.7	18 19.6	9 44.9	24 03.5	3 31.7	0 58.1	10 45.5	14 30.3	23 01.5	5 59.2
25 Su	14 18 14	2 45 01	8♊43 42	14 41 29	19D21.0	19 57.9	10 56.8	24 45.2	3 22.1	0 56.8	10 49.4	14 33.1	23 00.0	5 58.6
26 M	14 22 10	3 44 50	20 37 25	26 31 59	19 21.2	21 37.0	12 08.7	25 27.1	3 12.9	0 55.4	10 53.4	14 35.9	22 58.4	5 58.0
27 Tu	14 26 07	4 44 41	2♋25 41	8♋19 04	19 22.4	23 16.5	13 20.5	26 09.1	3 03.9	0 53.7	10 57.5	14 38.7	22 56.8	5 57.5
28 W	14 30 04	5 44 34	14 12 47	20 07 24	19 24.0	24 56.3	14 32.3	26 51.1	2 55.3	0 51.8	11 01.6	14 41.4	22 55.2	5 57.0
29 Th	14 34 00	6 44 29	26 03 36	2♌02 02	19R25.0	26 36.3	15 44.0	27 33.3	2 46.9	0 49.8	11 05.9	14 44.1	22 53.6	5 56.4
30 F	14 37 57	7 44 26	8♌03 21	14 08 12	19 24.9	28 16.3	16 55.7	28 15.5	2 39.0	0 47.5	11 10.2	14 46.7	22 52.0	5 56.0
31 Sa	14 41 53	8 44 25	20 17 13	26 30 58	19 23.2	29 56.3	18 07.3	28 57.9	2 31.3	0 45.0	11 14.6	14 49.3	22 50.4	5 55.5

Astro Data

	Dy Hr Mn
☽0S	8 10:11
♄ D	12 16:56
☿ R	15 1:08
☽0N	21 8:19
☉0S	22 8:01
☿0N	5 8:26
☽0S	5 18:46
☿ D	7 0:27
☿0S	14 17:34
☽0N	18 14:55
♃ R	18 15:58

Planet Ingress

	Dy Hr Mn
♂ ♑	17 11:49
♀ ♏	21 14:06
☉ ♎	22 8:00
♃ ♋	23 12:56
☿ ♍R	4 8:36
☿ ♎	9 16:42
♀ ♐	16 9:14
☉ ♏	22 17:42
☿ ♏	31 12:53

Last Aspect / ☽ Ingress (September)

Last Aspect Dy Hr Mn		☽ Ingress Dy Hr Mn
1 22:27	♃ ☌	♋ 2 3:12
4 3:09	♆ ⚹	♌ 4 15:15
6 21:23	♃ ⚹	♍ 7 0:33
9 4:25	♃ □	♎ 9 6:56
11 9:18	♃ △	♏ 11 11:19
13 4:09	♆ ☍	♐ 13 14:44
15 16:36	♃ ☍	♑ 15 17:49
17 12:52	☉ △	♒ 17 20:51
19 23:45	♃ △	♓ 20 0:16
22 4:49	♃ □	♈ 22 5:00
23 0:26	☿ ☍	♉ 24 12:14
26 9:57	♆ ☌	♊ 26 22:36
28 0:52	♅ □	♋ 29 11:15

Last Aspect / ☽ Ingress (October)

Last Aspect Dy Hr Mn		☽ Ingress Dy Hr Mn
1 10:51	♆ ⚹	♌ 1 23:42
3 21:13	♆ □	♍ 4 9:26
6 14:30	☿ ☌	♎ 6 15:34
7 17:45	☉ ☌	♏ 8 18:57
10 10:01	♆ ☍	♐ 10 21:04
12 5:46	☉ ⚹	♑ 12 23:16
14 23:25	♀ ⚹	♒ 15 2:20
16 20:19	☉ △	♓ 17 6:37
18 24:00	♆ ⚹	♈ 19 12:25
21 18:25	☉ ☍	♉ 21 20:15
23 17:47	♂ △	♊ 24 6:35
26 0:23	☿ △	♋ 26 19:03
29 2:27	♂ ☍	♌ 29 7:55
31 4:57	♆ □	♍ 31 18:38

☽ Phases & Eclipses

Dy Hr Mn	
8 6:24	● 16♍18
15 6:04	☽ 23♐05
22 4:46	○ 29♓52
30 2:45	☾ 7♋38
7 17:45	● 15♎08
14 12:20	☽ 21♑50
21 18:25	○ 29♈02
29 22:14	☾ 7♌10

Astro Data

1 September 2048
Julian Day # 54301
SVP 4♓34'30"
GC 27♐31.1 ⚴ 6♒27.8R
Eris 1♉00.7R ⚵ 18♒49.1R
⚷ 8♏24.2 ⚶ 23♉12.3
☽ Mean ☊ 23♐44.5

1 October 2048
Julian Day # 54331
SVP 4♓34'27"
GC 27♐31.2 ⚴ 3♒55.5
Eris 0♉46.6R ⚵ 15♒05.1R
⚷ 11♏44.9 ⚶ 23♉53.1R
☽ Mean ☊ 22♐09.2

November 2048 — LONGITUDE

Day	Sid.Time	☉	0 hr ☽	Noon ☽	True ☊	☿	♀	♂	⚳	♃	♄	♅	♆	♇
1 Su	14 45 50	9♏44 27	2♍50 02	9♍14 50	19♐19.8	1♏36.2	19♐18.9	29♑40.3	2♈24.0	0♋42.4	11♑19.1	14♍51.9	22♉48.8	5♓55.1
2 M	14 49 46	10 44 31	15 45 46	22 23 06	19R 14.8	3 15.9	20 30.5	0♒22.8	2R 17.1	0R 39.5	11 23.6	14 54.4	22R 47.1	5R 54.6
3 Tu	14 53 43	11 44 36	29 06 58	5♎57 23	19 08.9	4 55.3	21 41.9	1 05.5	2 10.5	0 36.4	11 28.2	14 56.8	22 45.5	5 54.2
4 W	14 57 39	12 44 44	12♎54 11	19 57 03	19 02.8	6 34.5	22 53.4	1 48.2	2 04.3	0 33.2	11 32.9	14 59.3	22 43.8	5 53.9
5 Th	15 01 36	13 44 54	27 05 32	4♏18 58	18 57.3	8 13.4	24 04.8	2 31.0	1 58.5	0 29.7	11 37.7	15 01.7	22 42.1	5 53.5
6 F	15 05 33	14 45 05	11♏36 38	18 57 39	18 53.0	9 51.9	25 16.1	3 13.8	1 53.0	0 26.1	11 42.5	15 04.0	22 40.5	5 53.2
7 Sa	15 09 29	15 45 19	26 21 05	3♐45 57	18 50.5	11 30.1	26 27.4	3 56.8	1 47.9	0 22.3	11 47.4	15 06.3	22 38.8	5 52.9
8 Su	15 13 26	16 45 34	11♐11 16	18 36 07	18D 49.7	13 08.0	27 38.7	4 39.9	1 43.2	0 18.3	11 52.4	15 08.6	22 37.1	5 52.6
9 M	15 17 22	17 45 51	25 59 37	3♑20 58	18 50.3	14 45.5	28 49.8	5 23.0	1 38.9	0 14.1	11 57.4	15 10.8	22 35.4	5 52.4
10 Tu	15 21 19	18 46 09	10♑39 32	17 54 44	18 51.7	16 22.7	0♑00.9	6 06.2	1 34.9	0 09.7	12 02.6	15 13.0	22 33.8	5 52.2
11 W	15 25 15	19 46 29	25 06 09	2♒13 29	18 53.2	17 59.5	1 12.0	6 49.4	1 31.4	0 05.2	12 07.7	15 15.1	22 32.1	5 52.0
12 Th	15 29 12	20 46 50	9♒16 31	16 15 08	18R 54.1	19 36.0	2 22.9	7 32.8	1 28.2	0 00.4	12 13.0	15 17.2	22 30.4	5 51.8
13 F	15 33 08	21 47 13	23 09 20	29 59 07	18 53.9	21 12.2	3 33.8	8 16.2	1 25.4	29♊55.5	12 18.3	15 19.2	22 28.7	5 51.7
14 Sa	15 37 05	22 47 36	6♓44 35	13♓25 51	18 52.4	22 48.1	4 44.7	8 59.6	1 23.0	29 50.4	12 23.6	15 21.2	22 27.0	5 51.5
15 Su	15 41 02	23 48 01	20 03 03	26 36 22	18 49.8	24 23.6	5 55.4	9 43.1	1 20.9	29 45.2	12 29.0	15 23.1	22 25.3	5 51.5
16 M	15 44 58	24 48 28	3♈05 56	9♈31 54	18 46.3	25 58.9	7 06.0	10 26.7	1 19.3	29 39.8	12 34.5	15 25.0	22 23.6	5 51.4
17 Tu	15 48 55	25 48 56	15 54 28	22 13 45	18 42.4	27 33.9	8 16.6	11 10.3	1 18.1	29 34.2	12 40.1	15 26.8	22 21.9	5 51.3
18 W	15 52 51	26 49 25	28 29 55	4♉43 07	18 38.7	29 08.6	9 27.1	11 54.0	1 17.2	29 28.5	12 45.7	15 28.6	22 20.2	5D 51.3
19 Th	15 56 48	27 49 56	10♉53 29	17 01 11	18 35.6	0♐43.1	10 37.5	12 37.7	1D 16.7	29 22.7	12 51.3	15 30.4	22 18.5	5 51.3
20 F	16 00 44	28 50 28	23 06 23	29 09 15	18 33.4	2 17.4	11 47.8	13 21.5	1 16.6	29 16.6	12 57.0	15 32.0	22 16.8	5 51.4
21 Sa	16 04 41	29 51 02	5♊09 58	11♊08 47	18D 32.3	3 51.5	12 58.0	14 05.3	1 16.8	29 10.5	13 02.8	15 33.7	22 15.2	5 51.4
22 Su	16 08 37	0♐51 37	17 05 54	23 01 38	18 32.2	5 25.4	14 08.1	14 49.2	1 17.5	29 04.2	13 08.6	15 35.3	22 13.5	5 51.5
23 M	16 12 34	1 52 14	28 56 15	4♋50 07	18 32.9	6 59.1	15 18.1	15 33.1	1 18.5	28 57.7	13 14.5	15 36.8	22 11.8	5 51.6
24 Tu	16 16 31	2 52 52	10♋43 35	16 37 04	18 34.1	8 32.7	16 28.0	16 17.1	1 19.9	28 51.2	13 20.5	15 38.3	22 10.2	5 51.8
25 W	16 20 27	3 53 32	22 31 01	28 25 55	18 35.6	10 06.1	17 37.8	17 01.1	1 21.6	28 44.4	13 26.4	15 39.7	22 08.5	5 51.9
26 Th	16 24 24	4 54 14	4♌22 14	10♌20 33	18 36.9	11 39.4	18 47.5	17 45.1	1 23.8	28 37.6	13 32.5	15 41.1	22 06.9	5 52.1
27 F	16 28 20	5 54 57	16 21 23	22 25 20	18 37.9	13 12.5	19 57.1	18 29.2	1 26.3	28 30.7	13 38.5	15 42.4	22 05.2	5 52.3
28 Sa	16 32 17	6 55 42	28 32 58	4♍44 51	18R 38.3	14 45.6	21 06.6	19 13.3	1 29.1	28 23.6	13 44.7	15 43.7	22 03.6	5 52.6
29 Su	16 36 13	7 56 28	11♍01 33	17 23 35	18 38.1	16 18.6	22 16.0	19 57.4	1 32.3	28 16.4	13 50.8	15 44.9	22 02.0	5 52.8
30 M	16 40 10	8 57 15	23 51 28	0♎25 36	18 37.5	17 51.4	23 25.2	20 41.6	1 35.9	28 09.1	13 57.1	15 46.1	22 00.4	5 53.1

December 2048 — LONGITUDE

Day	Sid.Time	☉	0 hr ☽	Noon ☽	True ☊	☿	♀	♂	⚳	♃	♄	♅	♆	♇
1 Tu	16 44 06	9♐58 05	7♎06 19	13♎53 51	18♐36.6	19♐24.2	24♑34.3	21♒25.8	1♈39.8	28♊01.8	14♑03.3	15♍47.2	21♉58.8	5♓53.4
2 W	16 48 03	10 58 55	20 48 18	27 49 38	18R 35.6	20 56.8	25 43.3	22 10.1	1 44.1	27R 54.3	14 09.6	15 48.2	21R 57.2	5 53.8
3 Th	16 52 00	11 59 47	4♏57 38	12♏11 55	18 34.7	22 29.4	26 52.2	22 54.4	1 48.7	27 46.7	14 16.0	15 49.2	21 55.6	5 54.1
4 F	16 55 56	13 00 41	19 31 56	26 56 56	18 34.1	24 01.9	28 00.9	23 38.7	1 53.7	27 39.1	14 22.4	15 50.2	21 54.1	5 54.5
5 Sa	16 59 53	14 01 35	4♐26 03	11♐58 15	18D 33.9	25 34.2	29 09.5	24 23.1	1 59.0	27 31.3	14 28.8	15 51.0	21 52.5	5 55.0
6 Su	17 03 49	15 02 31	19 32 25	27 07 20	18 33.9	27 06.5	0♒17.9	25 07.5	2 04.7	27 23.5	14 35.3	15 51.9	21 51.0	5 55.4
7 M	17 07 46	16 03 28	4♑41 51	12♑14 47	18 34.0	28 38.5	1 26.2	25 51.9	2 10.7	27 15.7	14 41.8	15 52.7	21 49.5	5 55.9
8 Tu	17 11 42	17 04 25	19 45 03	27 11 41	18 34.2	0♑10.4	2 34.4	26 36.3	2 17.0	27 07.7	14 48.4	15 53.4	21 48.0	5 56.4
9 W	17 15 39	18 05 23	4♒33 50	11♒50 50	18R 34.3	1 42.0	3 42.3	27 20.8	2 23.7	26 59.8	14 54.9	15 54.0	21 46.5	5 56.9
10 Th	17 19 35	19 06 22	19 02 10	26 07 31	18 34.4	3 13.4	4 50.1	28 05.3	2 30.7	26 51.8	15 01.6	15 54.6	21 45.0	5 57.4
11 F	17 23 32	20 07 22	3♓06 40	9♓59 35	18D 34.3	4 44.5	5 57.7	28 49.8	2 38.0	26 43.7	15 08.2	15 55.2	21 43.6	5 58.0
12 Sa	17 27 29	21 08 21	16 46 21	23 27 09	18 34.3	6 15.1	7 05.2	29 34.3	2 45.6	26 35.6	15 14.9	15 55.7	21 42.1	5 58.6
13 Su	17 31 25	22 09 22	0♈02 14	6♈31 57	18 34.4	7 45.3	8 12.4	0♓18.8	2 53.5	26 27.5	15 21.6	15 56.1	21 40.7	5 59.2
14 M	17 35 22	23 10 23	12 56 39	19 16 45	18 34.7	9 14.9	9 19.4	1 03.4	3 01.8	26 19.3	15 28.3	15 56.5	21 39.3	5 59.9
15 Tu	17 39 18	24 11 24	25 32 40	1♉44 48	18 35.3	10 43.7	10 26.2	1 47.9	3 10.3	26 11.2	15 35.1	15 56.8	21 37.9	6 00.5
16 W	17 43 15	25 12 26	7♉53 35	13 59 24	18 36.0	12 11.8	11 32.9	2 32.5	3 19.2	26 03.0	15 41.9	15 57.1	21 36.6	6 01.2
17 Th	17 47 11	26 13 29	20 02 38	26 03 39	18 36.7	13 38.8	12 39.2	3 17.1	3 28.3	25 54.8	15 48.7	15 57.3	21 35.3	6 01.9
18 F	17 51 08	27 14 32	2♊02 48	8♊00 23	18R 37.2	15 04.7	13 45.4	4 01.7	3 37.7	25 46.7	15 55.6	15 57.5	21 33.9	6 02.7
19 Sa	17 55 04	28 15 35	13 56 43	19 52 05	18 37.4	16 29.1	14 51.3	4 46.3	3 47.4	25 38.5	16 02.5	15 57.6	21 32.7	6 03.4
20 Su	17 59 01	29 16 39	25 46 45	1♋40 58	18 37.1	17 51.7	15 57.0	5 30.8	3 57.4	25 30.4	16 09.4	15R 57.6	21 31.4	6 04.2
21 M	18 02 58	0♑17 44	7♋35 00	13 29 07	18 36.1	19 12.4	17 02.4	6 15.4	4 07.7	25 22.3	16 16.3	15 57.6	21 30.1	6 05.0
22 Tu	18 06 54	1 18 49	19 23 33	25 18 36	18 34.6	20 30.7	18 07.5	7 00.1	4 18.3	25 14.2	16 23.2	15 57.5	21 28.9	6 05.9
23 W	18 10 51	2 19 55	1♌14 32	7♌11 40	18 32.5	21 46.2	19 12.4	7 44.7	4 29.1	25 06.1	16 30.2	15 57.4	21 27.7	6 06.7
24 Th	18 14 47	3 21 01	13 10 19	19 10 49	18 30.1	22 58.5	20 17.0	8 29.3	4 40.2	24 58.1	16 37.2	15 57.2	21 26.6	6 07.6
25 F	18 18 44	4 22 08	25 13 33	1♍18 54	18 27.9	24 06.9	21 21.3	9 13.9	4 51.5	24 50.2	16 44.1	15 57.0	21 25.4	6 08.5
26 Sa	18 22 40	5 23 15	7♍27 18	13 39 10	18 26.0	25 10.9	22 25.3	9 58.5	5 03.1	24 42.3	16 51.2	15 56.7	21 24.3	6 09.4
27 Su	18 26 37	6 24 23	19 54 57	26 15 07	18D 24.8	26 09.8	23 29.0	10 43.1	5 15.0	24 34.4	16 58.2	15 56.3	21 23.2	6 10.4
28 M	18 30 33	7 25 32	2♎40 07	9♎10 22	18 24.4	27 02.8	24 32.4	11 27.7	5 27.1	24 26.6	17 05.2	15 55.9	21 22.1	6 11.3
29 Tu	18 34 30	8 26 41	15 46 16	22 28 12	18 25.0	27 49.1	25 35.5	12 12.3	5 39.5	24 18.9	17 12.3	15 55.4	21 21.1	6 12.3
30 W	18 38 27	9 27 50	29 16 26	6♏11 10	18 26.2	28 27.9	26 38.2	12 56.9	5 52.1	24 11.2	17 19.3	15 54.9	21 20.0	6 13.3
31 Th	18 42 23	10 29 00	13♏12 29	20 20 19	18 27.7	28 58.1	27 40.6	13 41.5	6 04.9	24 03.7	17 26.4	15 54.3	21 19.1	6 14.4

Astro Data

	Dy Hr Mn
☽0S	2 3:56
☽0N	14 19:53
♇D	18 16:55
⚳D	20 7:06
☽0S	29 12:29
☽0N	12 1:33
♄△♅	18 18:38
♅R	20 17:42
☽0S	26 19:47

Planet Ingress

	Dy Hr Mn
♂ ♒	1 23:07
♀ ♑	10 11:41
♃ ♊R	12 14:06
☿ ♐	19 1:02
☉ ♐	21 15:33
♀ ♒	6 5:42
☿ ♑	8 9:17
♂ ♓	13 1:51
☉ ♑	21 5:02

Last Aspect / ☽ Ingress

Last Aspect Dy Hr Mn	☽ Ingress Dy Hr Mn	Last Aspect Dy Hr Mn	☽ Ingress Dy Hr Mn
2 12:43 ♆ △	♎ 3 1:34	2 12:08 ♃ △	♏ 2 15:40
4 17:24 ♀ ✱	♏ 5 4:51	4 13:51 ♀ ✱	♐ 4 16:54
6 18:01 ♆ ☍	♐ 7 5:55	6 12:25 ♃ ☍	♑ 6 16:33
9 3:58 ♀ ☌	♑ 9 6:32	8 3:18 ♆ △	♒ 8 16:33
10 19:44 ♆ △	♒ 11 8:14	10 15:33 ♂ ☌	♓ 10 18:38
13 11:54 ♃ △	♓ 13 12:02	12 17:39 ♃ □	♈ 12 23:56
15 17:46 ♃ □	♈ 15 18:16	15 1:21 ♃ ✱	♉ 15 8:37
18 1:57 ♃ ✱	♉ 18 2:53	17 3:05 ♆ ☌	♊ 17 19:53
20 11:19 ☉ ☍	♊ 20 13:41	20 6:39 ☉ ☍	♋ 20 8:35
23 0:09 ♃ ☌	♋ 23 2:10	22 4:15 ♆ ✱	♌ 22 21:29
24 23:16 ♆ ✱	♌ 25 15:10	24 23:22 ♃ ✱	♍ 25 9:25
27 23:49 ♃ ✱	♍ 28 2:49	27 11:49 ☿ △	♎ 27 19:02
30 7:54 ♃ □	♎ 30 11:14	29 21:57 ☿ □	♏ 30 1:16

☽ Phases & Eclipses

Dy Hr Mn	
6 4:38	● 14♏27
12 20:29	☽ 21♒08
20 11:19	○ 28♉49
28 16:33	☾ 7♍07
5 15:30	● 14♐10
5 15:33:54	● T 03'28"
12 7:29	☽ 20♓57
20 6:39	○ 29♊03
20 6:26	• A 0.962
28 8:31	☾ 7♎17

Astro Data

1 November 2048
Julian Day # 54362
SVP 4♓34'24"
GC 27♐31.3 ⚴ 6♒30.0
Eris 0♉28.1R ✱ 18♒00.6
⚷ 15♏51.0 ⚶ 18♉07.5R
☽ Mean ☊ 20♐30.7

1 December 2048
Julian Day # 54392
SVP 4♓34'19"
GC 27♐31.4 ⚴ 12♒33.9
Eris 0♉11.7R ✱ 26♒15.3
⚷ 19♏55.5 ⚶ 11♉00.5R
☽ Mean ☊ 18♐55.3

LONGITUDE January 2049

Day	Sid.Time	☉	0 hr ☽	Noon☽	True☊	☿	♀	♂	⚳	♃	♄	♅	♆	♇
1 F	18 46 20	11♑30 11	27♏34 28	4♐54 32	18♐28.9	29♑19.0	28♒42.6	14♓26.1	6♈18.0	23♊56.2	17♑33.5	15♍53.7	21♉18.1	6♓15.4
2 Sa	18 50 16	12 31 21	12♐19 58	19 49 59	18R 29.4	29R 29.6	29 44.2	15 10.7	6 31.3	23R 48.8	17 40.6	15R 53.0	21R 17.2	6 16.5
3 Su	18 54 13	13 32 32	27 23 40	4♑59 56	18 28.6	29 29.2	0♓45.5	15 55.3	6 44.9	23 41.5	17 47.7	15 52.3	21 16.3	6 17.6
4 M	18 58 09	14 33 43	12♑37 33	20 15 16	18 26.5	29 17.2	1 46.4	16 39.9	6 58.7	23 34.4	17 54.8	15 51.5	21 15.4	6 18.7
5 Tu	19 02 06	15 34 54	27 51 44	5♒25 42	18 23.1	28 53.4	2 46.8	17 24.5	7 12.7	23 27.3	18 01.9	15 50.6	21 14.5	6 19.8
6 W	19 06 03	16 36 05	12♒55 58	20 21 27	18 19.0	28 17.8	3 46.8	18 09.1	7 26.9	23 20.4	18 09.0	15 49.7	21 13.7	6 21.0
7 Th	19 09 59	17 37 15	27 41 17	4♓54 45	18 14.7	27 30.9	4 46.3	18 53.6	7 41.4	23 13.5	18 16.2	15 48.8	21 12.9	6 22.1
8 F	19 13 56	18 38 25	12♓01 20	19 00 45	18 10.9	26 33.7	5 45.4	19 38.2	7 56.0	23 06.8	18 23.2	15 47.8	21 12.2	6 23.3
9 Sa	19 17 52	19 39 35	25 52 54	2♈37 50	18 08.2	25 27.6	6 44.0	20 22.7	8 10.9	23 00.3	18 30.4	15 46.7	21 11.5	6 24.5
10 Su	19 21 49	20 40 44	9♈15 47	15 47 05	18D 06.9	24 14.7	7 42.1	21 07.3	8 26.0	22 53.8	18 37.5	15 45.6	21 10.8	6 25.8
11 M	19 25 45	21 41 52	22 12 10	28 31 32	18 07.0	22 57.1	8 39.6	21 51.8	8 41.3	22 47.5	18 44.6	15 44.5	21 10.1	6 27.0
12 Tu	19 29 42	22 43 00	4♉45 46	10♉55 26	18 08.2	21 37.4	9 36.6	22 36.3	8 56.7	22 41.4	18 51.7	15 43.2	21 09.5	6 28.3
13 W	19 33 38	23 44 07	17 01 08	23 03 28	18 10.0	20 18.2	10 33.0	23 20.8	9 12.4	22 35.4	18 58.8	15 42.0	21 08.9	6 29.5
14 Th	19 37 35	24 45 14	29 03 02	5♊00 22	18 11.7	19 01.8	11 28.8	24 05.2	9 28.2	22 29.5	19 05.9	15 40.7	21 08.3	6 30.8
15 F	19 41 32	25 46 20	10♊56 02	16 50 30	18R 12.5	17 50.4	12 24.0	24 49.7	9 44.3	22 23.8	19 13.0	15 39.3	21 07.8	6 32.1
16 Sa	19 45 28	26 47 25	22 44 16	28 37 43	18 11.8	16 45.7	13 18.5	25 34.1	10 00.5	22 18.3	19 20.1	15 37.9	21 07.3	6 33.5
17 Su	19 49 25	27 48 30	4♋31 16	10♋25 13	18 09.3	15 49.1	14 12.4	26 18.5	10 16.9	22 12.9	19 27.1	15 36.5	21 06.8	6 34.8
18 M	19 53 21	28 49 34	16 19 54	22 15 35	18 04.7	15 01.3	15 05.6	27 02.9	10 33.5	22 07.7	19 34.2	15 35.0	21 06.4	6 36.2
19 Tu	19 57 18	29 50 38	28 12 29	4♌10 49	17 58.2	14 22.8	15 58.1	27 47.3	10 50.3	22 02.6	19 41.3	15 33.5	21 06.0	6 37.5
20 W	20 01 14	0♒51 41	10♌10 46	16 12 31	17 50.3	13 53.8	16 49.8	28 31.6	11 07.2	21 57.8	19 48.3	15 31.9	21 05.6	6 38.9
21 Th	20 05 11	1 52 43	22 16 13	28 22 02	17 41.6	13 34.1	17 40.7	29 15.9	11 24.3	21 53.1	19 55.3	15 30.2	21 05.3	6 40.3
22 F	20 09 07	2 53 45	4♍30 08	10♍40 42	17 33.0	13D 23.4	18 30.9	0♈00.2	11 41.5	21 48.6	20 02.3	15 28.6	21 05.0	6 41.7
23 Sa	20 13 04	3 54 46	16 53 54	23 09 59	17 25.4	13 21.2	19 20.2	0 44.5	11 59.0	21 44.2	20 09.3	15 26.9	21 04.8	6 43.1
24 Su	20 17 01	4 55 47	29 29 09	5♎51 42	17 19.5	13 27.0	20 08.6	1 28.7	12 16.6	21 40.0	20 16.3	15 25.1	21 04.5	6 44.6
25 M	20 20 57	5 56 47	12♎17 52	18 47 59	17 15.7	13 40.3	20 56.1	2 12.9	12 34.3	21 36.1	20 23.2	15 23.3	21 04.3	6 46.0
26 Tu	20 24 54	6 57 47	25 22 21	2♏01 15	17D 14.1	14 00.3	21 42.7	2 57.1	12 52.2	21 32.3	20 30.2	15 21.5	21 04.2	6 47.5
27 W	20 28 50	7 58 46	8♏45 00	15 33 52	17 14.2	14 26.6	22 28.4	3 41.3	13 10.3	21 28.7	20 37.1	15 19.6	21 04.0	6 49.0
28 Th	20 32 47	8 59 45	22 28 02	29 27 40	17 15.2	14 58.6	23 13.0	4 25.4	13 28.5	21 25.2	20 44.0	15 17.7	21 03.9	6 50.5
29 F	20 36 43	10 00 43	6♐32 47	13♐43 19	17R 16.0	15 35.8	23 56.6	5 09.6	13 46.8	21 22.0	20 50.8	15 15.7	21 03.9	6 52.0
30 Sa	20 40 40	11 01 41	20 59 01	28 19 32	17 15.6	16 17.7	24 39.1	5 53.7	14 05.3	21 19.0	20 57.7	15 13.7	21D 03.9	6 53.5
31 Su	20 44 36	12 02 38	5♑44 17	13♑12 32	17 13.0	17 03.9	25 20.4	6 37.7	14 24.0	21 16.2	21 04.5	15 11.7	21 03.9	6 55.0

LONGITUDE February 2049

Day	Sid.Time	☉	0 hr ☽	Noon☽	True☊	☿	♀	♂	⚳	♃	♄	♅	♆	♇
1 M	20 48 33	13♒03 33	20♑43 23	28♑15 45	17♐07.8	17♑54.0	26♓00.6	7♈21.8	14♈42.8	21♊13.5	21♑11.3	15♍09.6	21♉03.9	6♓56.5
2 Tu	20 52 30	14 04 28	5♒48 29	13♒20 21	17R 00.3	18 47.6	26 39.6	8 05.8	15 01.7	21R 11.1	21 18.1	15R 07.5	21 04.0	6 58.1
3 W	20 56 26	15 05 22	20 50 06	28 16 32	16 51.1	19 44.5	27 17.3	8 49.8	15 20.7	21 08.9	21 24.8	15 05.4	21 04.1	6 59.6
4 Th	21 00 23	16 06 14	5♓38 32	12♓55 08	16 41.3	20 44.3	27 53.7	9 33.8	15 39.9	21 06.8	21 31.5	15 03.2	21 04.3	7 01.2
5 F	21 04 19	17 07 06	20 05 34	27 09 15	16 32.1	21 46.8	28 28.7	10 17.7	15 59.3	21 05.0	21 38.2	15 01.0	21 04.5	7 02.8
6 Sa	21 08 16	18 07 55	4♈05 47	10♈55 00	16 24.4	22 51.7	29 02.2	11 01.7	16 18.7	21 03.4	21 44.8	14 58.8	21 04.7	7 04.3
7 Su	21 12 12	19 08 44	17 36 56	24 11 45	16 19.1	23 58.9	29 34.3	11 45.5	16 38.3	21 01.9	21 51.4	14 56.5	21 05.0	7 05.9
8 M	21 16 09	20 09 31	0♉39 47	7♉01 29	16 16.1	25 08.2	0♈04.8	12 29.4	16 58.0	21 00.7	21 58.0	14 54.2	21 05.3	7 07.5
9 Tu	21 20 05	21 10 16	13 17 23	19 28 07	16D 15.2	26 19.4	0 33.6	13 13.2	17 17.8	20 59.7	22 04.5	14 51.9	21 05.6	7 09.1
10 W	21 24 02	22 11 00	25 34 19	1♊36 40	16 15.5	27 32.5	1 00.8	13 57.0	17 37.7	20 58.9	22 11.0	14 49.6	21 05.9	7 10.7
11 Th	21 27 59	23 11 42	7♊35 52	13 32 36	16R 16.0	28 47.2	1 26.3	14 40.8	17 57.8	20 58.3	22 17.5	14 47.2	21 06.3	7 12.3
12 F	21 31 55	24 12 23	19 27 32	25 21 18	16 15.6	0♒03.5	1 49.9	15 24.5	18 18.0	20 57.9	22 23.9	14 44.8	21 06.8	7 14.0
13 Sa	21 35 52	25 13 02	1♋14 33	7♋07 49	16 13.3	1 21.3	2 11.6	16 08.2	18 38.2	20D 57.7	22 30.3	14 42.4	21 07.2	7 15.6
14 Su	21 39 48	26 13 39	13 01 38	18 56 29	16 08.6	2 40.5	2 31.5	16 51.8	18 58.6	20 57.6	22 36.6	14 40.0	21 07.7	7 17.2
15 M	21 43 45	27 14 15	24 52 47	0♌50 53	16 01.0	4 01.0	2 49.3	17 35.4	19 19.1	20 57.8	22 42.9	14 37.6	21 08.3	7 18.8
16 Tu	21 47 41	28 14 49	6♌51 05	12 53 38	15 50.7	5 22.8	3 05.0	18 19.0	19 39.7	20 58.2	22 49.2	14 35.1	21 08.8	7 20.5
17 W	21 51 38	29 15 22	18 58 44	25 06 31	15 38.3	6 45.9	3 18.6	19 02.6	20 00.4	20 58.8	22 55.4	14 32.6	21 09.4	7 22.1
18 Th	21 55 34	0♓15 53	1♍17 04	7♍30 25	15 24.8	8 10.1	3 30.0	19 46.1	20 21.2	20 59.6	23 01.6	14 30.1	21 10.1	7 23.8
19 F	21 59 31	1 16 23	13 46 37	20 05 38	15 11.3	9 35.5	3 39.1	20 29.5	20 42.1	21 00.6	23 07.7	14 27.6	21 10.7	7 25.4
20 Sa	22 03 28	2 16 51	26 27 28	2♎52 06	14 59.1	11 02.0	3 46.0	21 13.0	21 03.1	21 01.8	23 13.8	14 25.0	21 11.4	7 27.1
21 Su	22 07 24	3 17 17	9♎19 31	15 49 43	14 49.2	12 29.6	3 50.5	21 56.3	21 24.2	21 03.2	23 19.8	14 22.5	21 12.2	7 28.7
22 M	22 11 21	4 17 43	22 22 44	28 58 37	14 42.2	13 58.3	3R 52.6	22 39.7	21 45.4	21 04.8	23 25.7	14 19.9	21 12.9	7 30.4
23 Tu	22 15 17	5 18 06	5♏37 28	12♏19 24	14 38.1	15 28.0	3 52.2	23 23.0	22 06.6	21 06.6	23 31.7	14 17.3	21 13.7	7 32.0
24 W	22 19 14	6 18 29	19 04 32	25 53 01	14D 36.4	16 58.8	3 49.4	24 06.3	22 28.0	21 08.6	23 37.5	14 14.8	21 14.6	7 33.7
25 Th	22 23 10	7 18 50	2♐44 59	9♐40 35	14R 36.1	18 30.6	3 44.1	24 49.6	22 49.5	21 10.8	23 43.4	14 12.2	21 15.4	7 35.3
26 F	22 27 07	8 19 10	16 39 53	23 42 56	14 36.0	20 03.5	3 36.4	25 32.8	23 11.0	21 13.1	23 49.1	14 09.6	21 16.3	7 37.0
27 Sa	22 31 03	9 19 29	0♑49 40	7♑59 56	14 34.7	21 37.4	3 26.1	26 16.0	23 32.6	21 15.7	23 54.8	14 06.9	21 17.3	7 38.7
28 Su	22 35 00	10 19 46	15 13 27	22 29 51	14 31.0	23 12.3	3 13.3	26 59.1	23 54.4	21 18.4	24 00.5	14 04.3	21 18.2	7 40.3

Astro Data Dy Hr Mn	Planet Ingress Dy Hr Mn	Last Aspect Dy Hr Mn	☽ Ingress Dy Hr Mn	Last Aspect Dy Hr Mn	☽ Ingress Dy Hr Mn	☽ Phases & Eclipses Dy Hr Mn	Astro Data
☿R 2 23:16	♀ ♓ 2 18:10	1 2:40 ☿ ✶	♐ 1 3:59	1 8:15 ♀ ✶	♒ 1 14:46	4 2:24 ● 14♑09	1 January 2049
☽0N 8 9:56	☉ ♒ 19 15:41	2 18:17 ♃ ☍	♑ 3 4:07	3 0:32 ♃ △	♓ 3 14:48	10 21:56 ☽ 21♈06	Julian Day # 54423
☽0S 23 2:11	♂ ♈ 22 11:54	5 1:56 ☿ ☌	♒ 5 3:23	5 14:22 ♀ ☌	♈ 5 16:54	19 2:29 ○ 29♋26	SVP 4♓34'14"
☿D 23 6:18		6 16:50 ♃ △	♓ 7 3:49	7 11:34 ☿ □	♉ 7 22:46	26 21:33 ☾ 7♏22	GC 27♐31.4 ⚴ 21♒04.3
♂0N 23 16:27	♀ ♈ 8 8:10	9 0:14 ☿ ✶	♈ 9 7:18	10 2:59 ☿ △	♊ 10 8:47		Eris 0♉01.6R ⚵ 8♓30.0
♆D 30 13:23	☿ ♒ 12 10:55	11 2:24 ☿ □	♉ 11 14:49	12 9:26 ☉ △	♋ 12 21:28	2 13:16 ● 14♒08	⚷ 23♏40.8 ⚶ 9♉01.4
♀0N 30 13:56	☉ ♓ 18 5:42	13 13:29 ☉ △	♊ 14 1:55	14 19:29 ♄ ☍	♌ 15 10:18	9 15:38 ☽ 21♉19	☽ Mean ☊ 17♐16.9
♄△♆ 31 9:48		16 5:21 ♂ □	♋ 16 14:48	17 20:47 ☉ ☍	♍ 17 21:31	17 20:47 ○ 29♌38	
♃⚻♄ 1 17:46		19 2:29 ☉ ☍	♌ 19 3:36	19 17:47 ♄ △	♎ 20 6:38	25 7:36 ☾ 7♐08	1 February 2049
☽0N 4 20:46		20 23:19 ♃ ✶	♍ 21 15:12	22 1:50 ♄ □	♏ 22 13:51		Julian Day # 54454
♃⚺♆ 5 18:26		23 9:17 ♃ □	♎ 24 0:58	24 8:00 ♄ ✶	♐ 24 19:12		SVP 4♓34'08"
⚳0N 6 1:36		25 17:06 ♃ △	♏ 26 8:22	26 15:16 ♂ △	♑ 26 22:37		GC 27♐31.5 ⚴ 0♓49.5
♄∠♇ 10 10:27		28 0:42 ♀ △	♐ 28 12:55				Eris 0♉01.6 ⚵ 23♓13.2
♃D 14 0:24	♀R 22 20:42	30 5:42 ♀ □	♑ 30 14:43				⚷ 26♏23.5 ⚶ 13♉28.5
☽0S 19 8:41	♃⚺⚺ 28 9:27						☽ Mean ☊ 15♐38.4

March 2049

LONGITUDE

Day	Sid.Time	☉	0 hr ☽	Noon ☽	True ☊	☿	♀	♂	⚳	♃	♄	♅	♆	♇
1 M	22 38 57	11♓20 01	29♑48 33	7♒08 54	14♐24.4	24♒48.2	2♈58.1	27♈42.2	24♈16.2	21♊21.4	24♑06.1	14♍01.7	21♉19.2	7♓42.0
2 Tu	22 42 53	12 20 15	14♒30 04	21 51 10	14R 15.0	26 25.2	2R 40.4	28 25.3	24 38.0	21 24.5	24 11.6	13R 59.1	21 20.3	7 43.6
3 W	22 46 50	13 20 27	29 11 13	6♓29 15	14 03.5	28 03.2	2 20.4	29 08.4	25 00.0	21 27.8	24 17.1	13 56.5	21 21.3	7 45.3
4 Th	22 50 46	14 20 38	13♓44 15	20 55 20	13 51.1	29 42.2	1 58.0	29 51.4	25 22.0	21 31.3	24 22.5	13 53.8	21 22.4	7 46.9
5 F	22 54 43	15 20 46	28 01 40	5♈02 35	13 39.1	1♓22.4	1 33.5	0♉34.3	25 44.2	21 35.0	24 27.9	13 51.2	21 23.5	7 48.6
6 Sa	22 58 39	16 20 53	11♈57 33	18 46 14	13 28.8	3 03.6	1 06.8	1 17.3	26 06.3	21 38.9	24 33.1	13 48.6	21 24.7	7 50.2
7 Su	23 02 36	17 20 57	25 28 25	2♉04 08	13 21.0	4 45.8	0 38.1	2 00.1	26 28.6	21 43.0	24 38.4	13 45.9	21 25.8	7 51.9
8 M	23 06 32	18 21 00	8♉33 29	14 56 45	13 16.0	6 29.2	0 07.6	2 43.0	26 51.0	21 47.2	24 43.5	13 43.3	21 27.1	7 53.5
9 Tu	23 10 29	19 21 00	21 14 20	27 26 43	13 13.4	8 13.7	29♓35.5	3 25.8	27 13.4	21 51.6	24 48.6	13 40.7	21 28.3	7 55.1
10 W	23 14 25	20 20 58	3♊34 29	9♊38 14	13 12.7	9 59.3	29 01.8	4 08.6	27 35.8	21 56.2	24 53.7	13 38.1	21 29.6	7 56.8
11 Th	23 18 22	21 20 55	15 38 38	21 36 24	13 12.7	11 46.1	28 26.9	4 51.3	27 58.4	22 01.0	24 58.6	13 35.5	21 30.9	7 58.4
12 F	23 22 19	22 20 49	27 32 12	3♋26 45	13 12.3	13 34.0	27 50.8	5 34.0	28 21.0	22 05.9	25 03.5	13 32.9	21 32.2	8 00.0
13 Sa	23 26 15	23 20 40	9♋20 44	15 14 49	13 10.4	15 23.1	27 14.0	6 16.7	28 43.6	22 11.0	25 08.3	13 30.3	21 33.5	8 01.6
14 Su	23 30 12	24 20 30	21 09 37	27 05 45	13 06.2	17 13.3	26 36.6	6 59.3	29 06.4	22 16.3	25 13.1	13 27.8	21 34.9	8 03.2
15 M	23 34 08	25 20 17	3♌03 44	9♌04 05	12 59.4	19 04.7	25 58.9	7 41.9	29 29.2	22 21.7	25 17.8	13 25.2	21 36.3	8 04.8
16 Tu	23 38 05	26 20 02	15 07 13	21 13 28	12 49.9	20 57.2	25 21.1	8 24.4	29 52.0	22 27.3	25 22.4	13 22.7	21 37.7	8 06.4
17 W	23 42 01	27 19 45	27 23 09	3♍36 28	12 38.3	22 50.9	24 43.4	9 06.9	0♉14.9	22 33.1	25 26.9	13 20.1	21 39.2	8 08.0
18 Th	23 45 58	28 19 26	9♍53 33	16 14 27	12 25.5	24 45.8	24 06.3	9 49.3	0 37.9	22 39.0	25 31.4	13 17.6	21 40.7	8 09.6
19 F	23 49 54	29 19 05	22 39 09	29 07 34	12 12.7	26 41.7	23 29.8	10 31.7	1 00.9	22 45.1	25 35.8	13 15.1	21 42.2	8 11.1
20 Sa	23 53 51	0♈18 42	5♎39 34	12♎14 58	12 01.1	28 38.8	22 54.3	11 14.1	1 23.9	22 51.4	25 40.1	13 12.6	21 43.7	8 12.7
21 Su	23 57 48	1 18 17	18 53 34	25 35 07	11 51.6	0♈36.9	22 19.9	11 56.4	1 47.1	22 57.8	25 44.3	13 10.2	21 45.3	8 14.2
22 M	0 01 44	2 17 50	2♏19 24	9♏06 11	11 44.9	2 35.9	21 46.9	12 38.7	2 10.2	23 04.3	25 48.5	13 07.7	21 46.9	8 15.8
23 Tu	0 05 41	3 17 21	15 55 15	22 46 26	11 41.1	4 35.8	21 15.5	13 20.9	2 33.5	23 11.0	25 52.5	13 05.3	21 48.5	8 17.3
24 W	0 09 37	4 16 50	29 39 37	6♐34 39	11D 39.7	6 36.5	20 45.9	14 03.1	2 56.7	23 17.9	25 56.6	13 02.9	21 50.1	8 18.8
25 Th	0 13 34	5 16 18	13♐31 28	20 30 00	11 39.8	8 37.9	20 18.2	14 45.3	3 20.1	23 24.9	26 00.5	13 00.5	21 51.8	8 20.4
26 F	0 17 30	6 15 44	27 30 12	4♑32 01	11R 40.2	10 39.7	19 52.6	15 27.4	3 43.4	23 32.0	26 04.3	12 58.2	21 53.5	8 21.9
27 Sa	0 21 27	7 15 09	11♑35 21	18 40 07	11 39.7	12 41.8	19 29.1	16 09.5	4 06.9	23 39.3	26 08.1	12 55.8	21 55.2	8 23.3
28 Su	0 25 23	8 14 31	25 46 08	2♒53 10	11 37.3	14 44.0	19 07.9	16 51.6	4 30.3	23 46.8	26 11.8	12 53.5	21 56.9	8 24.8
29 M	0 29 20	9 13 52	10♒00 55	17 09 02	11 32.4	16 46.0	18 49.0	17 33.6	4 53.8	23 54.4	26 15.4	12 51.2	21 58.6	8 26.3
30 Tu	0 33 17	10 13 11	24 17 02	1♓24 24	11 25.2	18 47.6	18 32.5	18 15.5	5 17.4	24 02.1	26 18.9	12 49.0	22 00.4	8 27.8
31 W	0 37 13	11 12 28	8♓30 34	15 34 55	11 16.1	20 48.5	18 18.4	18 57.5	5 41.0	24 09.9	26 22.3	12 46.8	22 02.2	8 29.2

April 2049

LONGITUDE

Day	Sid.Time	☉	0 hr ☽	Noon ☽	True ☊	☿	♀	♂	⚳	♃	♄	♅	♆	♇
1 Th	0 41 10	12♈11 43	22♓36 50	29♓35 42	11♐06.1	22♈48.2	18♓06.8	19♉39.4	6♉04.6	24♊17.9	26♑25.6	12♍44.6	22♉04.0	8♓30.6
2 F	0 45 06	13 10 56	6♈30 56	13♈22 03	10R 56.4	24 46.5	17R 57.7	20 21.2	6 28.3	24 26.0	26 28.9	12R 42.4	22 05.8	8 32.0
3 Sa	0 49 03	14 10 08	20 08 37	26 50 17	10 48.0	26 43.0	17 51.0	21 03.0	6 52.1	24 34.3	26 32.1	12 40.3	22 07.7	8 33.4
4 Su	0 52 59	15 09 17	3♉26 52	9♉58 16	10 41.6	28 37.3	17 46.7	21 44.8	7 15.8	24 42.7	26 35.1	12 38.2	22 09.5	8 34.8
5 M	0 56 56	16 08 24	16 24 28	22 45 37	10 37.6	0♉29.0	17D 44.9	22 26.6	7 39.6	24 51.2	26 38.1	12 36.1	22 11.4	8 36.2
6 Tu	1 00 52	17 07 29	29 01 56	5♊13 46	10D 35.9	2 17.7	17 45.4	23 08.3	8 03.5	24 59.9	26 41.0	12 34.1	22 13.3	8 37.6
7 W	1 04 49	18 06 31	11♊21 29	17 25 36	10 36.0	4 03.1	17 48.3	23 49.9	8 27.3	25 08.6	26 43.9	12 32.1	22 15.3	8 38.9
8 Th	1 08 46	19 05 32	23 26 37	29 25 07	10 37.0	5 44.7	17 53.4	24 31.6	8 51.2	25 17.5	26 46.6	12 30.2	22 17.2	8 40.3
9 F	1 12 42	20 04 30	5♋21 45	11♋17 08	10R 38.2	7 22.4	18 00.8	25 13.1	9 15.2	25 26.5	26 49.2	12 28.2	22 19.2	8 41.6
10 Sa	1 16 39	21 03 25	17 11 55	23 06 47	10 38.5	8 55.8	18 10.4	25 54.7	9 39.1	25 35.7	26 51.8	12 26.4	22 21.1	8 42.9
11 Su	1 20 35	22 02 19	29 02 22	4♌59 20	10 37.4	10 24.6	18 22.2	26 36.2	10 03.1	25 44.9	26 54.2	12 24.5	22 23.1	8 44.2
12 M	1 24 32	23 01 10	10♌58 16	16 59 47	10 34.5	11 48.5	18 36.0	27 17.6	10 27.2	25 54.3	26 56.6	12 22.7	22 25.1	8 45.4
13 Tu	1 28 28	23 59 59	23 04 23	29 12 36	10 29.6	13 07.5	18 51.8	27 59.1	10 51.2	26 03.7	26 58.8	12 20.9	22 27.2	8 46.7
14 W	1 32 25	24 58 46	5♍24 49	11♍41 23	10 23.1	14 21.2	19 09.6	28 40.4	11 15.3	26 13.3	27 01.0	12 19.2	22 29.2	8 47.9
15 Th	1 36 21	25 57 31	18 02 35	24 28 35	10 15.7	15 29.5	19 29.3	29 21.8	11 39.4	26 23.0	27 03.1	12 17.5	22 31.2	8 49.1
16 F	1 40 18	26 56 13	0♎59 28	7♎35 12	10 08.0	16 32.3	19 50.8	0♊03.1	12 03.6	26 32.8	27 05.0	12 15.9	22 33.3	8 50.3
17 Sa	1 44 14	27 54 53	14 15 42	21 00 44	10 01.1	17 29.4	20 14.1	0 44.3	12 27.7	26 42.7	27 06.9	12 14.3	22 35.4	8 51.5
18 Su	1 48 11	28 53 32	27 50 01	4♏43 12	9 55.5	18 20.8	20 39.1	1 25.5	12 51.9	26 52.7	27 08.7	12 12.7	22 37.5	8 52.7
19 M	1 52 08	29 52 08	11♏39 52	18 39 32	9 51.8	19 06.4	21 05.7	2 06.7	13 16.1	27 02.8	27 10.4	12 11.2	22 39.6	8 53.8
20 Tu	1 56 04	0♉50 43	25 41 44	2♐45 58	9D 50.1	19 46.1	21 34.0	2 47.8	13 40.3	27 13.0	27 12.0	12 09.8	22 41.7	8 55.0
21 W	2 00 01	1 49 16	9♐51 45	16 58 38	9 50.1	20 19.8	22 03.8	3 28.9	14 04.6	27 23.3	27 13.5	12 08.3	22 43.8	8 56.1
22 Th	2 03 57	2 47 48	24 06 12	1♑14 03	9 51.1	20 47.6	22 35.0	4 10.0	14 28.9	27 33.7	27 14.9	12 07.0	22 45.9	8 57.2
23 F	2 07 54	3 46 18	8♑21 51	15 29 17	9 52.6	21 09.4	23 07.7	4 51.0	14 53.2	27 44.2	27 16.3	12 05.6	22 48.1	8 58.2
24 Sa	2 11 50	4 44 46	22 36 04	29 41 59	9R 53.5	21 25.3	23 41.8	5 32.0	15 17.5	27 54.8	27 17.5	12 04.3	22 50.3	8 59.3
25 Su	2 15 47	5 43 13	6♒46 47	13♒50 17	9 53.4	21 35.4	24 17.2	6 13.0	15 41.9	28 05.5	27 18.6	12 03.1	22 52.4	9 00.3
26 M	2 19 43	6 41 38	20 52 14	27 52 28	9 51.8	21R 39.7	24 53.8	6 53.9	16 06.2	28 16.2	27 19.6	12 01.9	22 54.6	9 01.3
27 Tu	2 23 40	7 40 01	4♓50 45	11♓46 52	9 48.7	21 38.4	25 31.6	7 34.8	16 30.6	28 27.1	27 20.5	12 00.8	22 56.8	9 02.3
28 W	2 27 37	8 38 23	18 40 35	25 31 40	9 44.5	21 31.7	26 10.6	8 15.6	16 55.0	28 38.1	27 21.4	11 59.7	22 59.0	9 03.3
29 Th	2 31 33	9 36 43	2♈19 52	9♈04 57	9 39.8	21 19.8	26 50.7	8 56.4	17 19.4	28 49.1	27 22.1	11 58.6	23 01.2	9 04.3
30 F	2 35 30	10 35 02	15 46 43	22 24 58	9 35.1	21 03.2	27 31.8	9 37.2	17 43.9	29 00.2	27 22.7	11 57.6	23 03.4	9 05.2

Astro Data	Planet Ingress	Last Aspect	☽ Ingress	Last Aspect	☽ Ingress	☽ Phases & Eclipses
Dy Hr Mn	Dy Hr Mn	Dy Hr Mn	Dy Hr Mn	Dy Hr Mn	Dy Hr Mn	Dy Hr Mn
☽0N 4 7:45	☿ ♓ 4 16:16	28 19:45 ♂ □	♒ 1 0:19	1 6:31 ♄ ✱	♈ 1 12:42	4 0:11 ● 13♓51
☽0S 18 16:00	♂ ♉ 4 16:50	2 23:18 ♂ ✱	♓ 3 1:20	3 11:45 ☿ ☌	♉ 3 17:43	11 11:26 ☽ 21♊19
⊙0N 20 4:29	♀ ♓R 8 17:48	4 17:51 ♄ ✱	♈ 5 3:21	5 19:26 ♄ △	♊ 6 1:52	19 12:23 ○ 29♍20
☿0N 22 16:24	⚳ ♉ 16 20:24	6 22:24 ♄ □	♉ 7 8:13	8 3:36 ♃ ☌	♋ 8 13:10	26 15:10 ☾ 6♑24
☽0N 31 16:36	⊙ ♈ 20 4:28	9 16:00 ♀ ✱	♊ 9 16:59	10 19:37 ♄ ☍	♌ 11 1:56	
	☿ ♈ 21 4:32	12 1:11 ♀ □	♋ 12 5:00	13 9:28 ♂ □	♍ 13 13:32	2 11:39 ● 13♈10
♀ D 5 18:37		14 11:04 ♀ △	♌ 14 17:51	15 21:31 ♂ △	♎ 15 22:11	10 7:27 ☽ 20♋52
♀0S 6 3:02	☿ ♉ 5 5:43	16 14:25 ♃ ✱	♍ 17 5:03	18 1:04 ⊙ ☍	♏ 18 3:47	18 1:04 ○ 28♎27
☽0S 15 0:10	♂ ♊ 16 10:13	19 12:23 ⊙ ☍	♎ 19 13:37	20 2:32 ♄ ✱	♐ 20 7:19	24 21:11 ☾ 5♒07
♄⊡♅ 19 18:08	⊙ ♉ 19 15:13	21 12:17 ♄ □	♏ 21 19:52	22 5:45 ♃ ☍	♑ 22 9:55	
♃⚻♄ 20 9:18		23 17:26 ♄ ✱	♐ 24 0:35	24 7:55 ♄ ☌	♒ 24 12:30	
☿ R 26 18:20		25 17:03 ♃ ☍	♑ 26 4:16	26 12:41 ♃ △	♓ 26 15:39	
☽0N 27 22:49		28 0:40 ♄ ☌	♒ 28 7:08	28 17:33 ♃ □	♈ 28 19:53	
		29 23:28 ♃ △	♓ 30 9:38			

Astro Data

1 March 2049
Julian Day # 54482
SVP 4♓34'05"
GC 27♐31.6 ⚴ 10♓05.9
Eris 0♉10.5 ⚵ 7♈56.3
⚷ 27♏31.7 ⚶ 21♉13.0
☽ Mean ☊ 14♐09.4

1 April 2049
Julian Day # 54513
SVP 4♓34'02"
GC 27♐31.6 ⚴ 20♓22.0
Eris 0♉27.6 ⚵ 25♈17.3
⚷ 27♏08.2R ⚶ 2♊10.4
☽ Mean ☊ 12♐30.9

LONGITUDE — May 2049

Day	Sid.Time	☉	0 hr ☽	Noon ☽	True ☊	☿	♀	♂	⚳	♃	♄	♅	♆	♇
1 Sa	2 39 26	11♉33 19	28♈59 31	5♉30 16	9♐31.2	20♉42.1	28♓14.0	10♊18.0	18♉08.3	29♊11.4	27♑23.3	11♍56.7	23♉05.6	9♓06.1
2 Su	2 43 23	12 31 34	11♉57 08	18 20 06	9R 28.3	20R 17.0	28 57.2	10 58.7	18 32.8	29 22.7	27 23.7	11R 55.8	23 07.8	9 07.0
3 M	2 47 19	13 29 48	24 39 11	0♊54 30	9D 26.8	19 48.4	29 41.3	11 39.3	18 57.2	29 34.1	27 24.0	11 54.9	23 10.0	9 07.9
4 Tu	2 51 16	14 27 59	7♊06 11	13 14 28	9 26.6	19 16.8	0♈26.3	12 20.0	19 21.7	29 45.5	27 24.3	11 54.1	23 12.3	9 08.7
5 W	2 55 12	15 26 09	19 19 37	25 21 58	9 27.4	18 42.9	1 12.1	13 00.6	19 46.2	29 57.0	27R 24.4	11 53.4	23 14.5	9 09.5
6 Th	2 59 09	16 24 18	1♋21 54	7♋19 51	9 28.9	18 07.2	1 58.8	13 41.1	20 10.8	0♋08.6	27 24.4	11 52.7	23 16.7	9 10.3
7 F	3 03 06	17 22 24	13 16 16	19 11 42	9 30.5	17 30.4	2 46.3	14 21.7	20 35.3	0 20.3	27 24.4	11 52.1	23 19.0	9 11.1
8 Sa	3 07 02	18 20 28	25 06 40	1♌01 45	9 32.0	16 53.2	3 34.5	15 02.2	20 59.8	0 32.0	27 24.2	11 51.5	23 21.2	9 11.9
9 Su	3 10 59	19 18 31	6♌57 32	12 54 36	9R 32.9	16 16.2	4 23.5	15 42.6	21 24.3	0 43.8	27 24.0	11 51.0	23 23.5	9 12.6
10 M	3 14 55	20 16 31	18 53 34	24 55 02	9 32.9	15 40.1	5 13.2	16 23.0	21 48.9	0 55.7	27 23.6	11 50.5	23 25.7	9 13.3
11 Tu	3 18 52	21 14 30	0♍59 34	7♍07 45	9 32.2	15 05.5	6 03.6	17 03.4	22 13.4	1 07.6	27 23.1	11 50.0	23 28.0	9 14.0
12 W	3 22 48	22 12 26	13 20 06	19 37 04	9 30.6	14 32.9	6 54.7	17 43.8	22 38.0	1 19.6	27 22.6	11 49.7	23 30.2	9 14.7
13 Th	3 26 45	23 10 21	25 59 07	2♎26 32	9 28.6	14 02.9	7 46.4	18 24.1	23 02.6	1 31.7	27 21.9	11 49.3	23 32.5	9 15.3
14 F	3 30 41	24 08 15	8♎59 37	15 38 31	9 26.5	13 35.9	8 38.7	19 04.4	23 27.1	1 43.8	27 21.2	11 49.1	23 34.7	9 16.0
15 Sa	3 34 38	25 06 06	22 23 15	29 13 46	9 24.5	13 12.4	9 31.5	19 44.6	23 51.7	1 56.0	27 20.4	11 48.9	23 37.0	9 16.6
16 Su	3 38 35	26 03 56	6♏09 52	13♏11 13	9 23.1	12 52.6	10 25.0	20 24.8	24 16.3	2 08.2	27 19.4	11 48.7	23 39.3	9 17.1
17 M	3 42 31	27 01 45	20 17 23	27 27 49	9D 22.2	12 36.8	11 19.0	21 05.0	24 40.8	2 20.5	27 18.4	11 48.6	23 41.5	9 17.7
18 Tu	3 46 28	27 59 32	4♐41 52	11♐58 48	9 22.0	12 25.3	12 13.6	21 45.1	25 05.4	2 32.9	27 17.3	11D 48.5	23 43.8	9 18.2
19 W	3 50 24	28 57 18	19 17 50	26 38 11	9 22.4	12 18.2	13 08.7	22 25.2	25 30.0	2 45.3	27 16.1	11 48.5	23 46.0	9 18.7
20 Th	3 54 21	29 55 03	3♑59 02	11♑19 36	9 23.0	12D 15.6	14 04.3	23 05.3	25 54.6	2 57.8	27 14.8	11 48.6	23 48.3	9 19.2
21 F	3 58 17	0♊52 46	18 39 07	25 56 57	9 23.8	12 17.5	15 00.3	23 45.3	26 19.2	3 10.3	27 13.4	11 48.7	23 50.5	9 19.7
22 Sa	4 02 14	1 50 29	3♒12 28	10♒25 11	9 24.4	12 24.0	15 56.9	24 25.3	26 43.8	3 22.9	27 11.9	11 48.8	23 52.7	9 20.1
23 Su	4 06 10	2 48 10	17 34 39	24 40 33	9R 24.8	12 34.9	16 53.8	25 05.3	27 08.4	3 35.5	27 10.3	11 49.0	23 55.0	9 20.5
24 M	4 10 07	3 45 50	1♓42 39	8♓40 47	9 24.8	12 50.4	17 51.2	25 45.3	27 32.9	3 48.1	27 08.6	11 49.3	23 57.2	9 20.9
25 Tu	4 14 04	4 43 30	15 34 50	22 24 47	9 24.6	13 10.3	18 49.1	26 25.2	27 57.5	4 00.9	27 06.9	11 49.6	23 59.4	9 21.3
26 W	4 18 00	5 41 08	29 10 39	5♈52 27	9 24.3	13 34.6	19 47.3	27 05.1	28 22.1	4 13.6	27 05.0	11 50.0	24 01.7	9 21.6
27 Th	4 21 57	6 38 46	12♈30 18	19 04 17	9 23.9	14 03.1	20 45.9	27 44.9	28 46.7	4 26.4	27 03.1	11 50.4	24 03.9	9 21.9
28 F	4 25 53	7 36 22	25 34 32	2♉01 09	9 23.7	14 35.7	21 44.9	28 24.8	29 11.3	4 39.3	27 01.1	11 50.9	24 06.1	9 22.2
29 Sa	4 29 50	8 33 58	8♉24 17	14 44 05	9D 23.5	15 12.4	22 44.2	29 04.6	29 35.9	4 52.2	26 58.9	11 51.4	24 08.3	9 22.5
30 Su	4 33 46	9 31 32	21 00 41	27 14 15	9R 23.5	15 53.0	23 43.9	29 44.4	0♊00.4	5 05.1	26 56.7	11 52.0	24 10.5	9 22.7
31 M	4 37 43	10 29 06	3♊24 55	9♊32 54	9 23.5	16 37.4	24 43.9	0♋24.1	0 25.0	5 18.1	26 54.5	11 52.7	24 12.7	9 22.9

LONGITUDE — June 2049

Day	Sid.Time	☉	0 hr ☽	Noon ☽	True ☊	☿	♀	♂	⚳	♃	♄	♅	♆	♇
1 Tu	4 41 39	11♊26 38	15♊38 21	21♊41 30	9♐23.5	17♉25.6	25♈44.2	1♋03.8	0♊49.6	5♋31.1	26♑52.1	11♍53.3	24♉14.8	9♓23.1
2 W	4 45 36	12 24 10	27 42 33	3♋41 47	9R 23.3	18 17.4	26 44.9	1 43.5	1 14.1	5 44.2	26R 49.6	11 54.1	24 17.0	9 23.3
3 Th	4 49 33	13 21 40	9♋39 27	15 35 52	9 22.9	19 12.6	27 45.8	2 23.2	1 38.7	5 57.3	26 47.1	11 54.9	24 19.2	9 23.4
4 F	4 53 29	14 19 09	21 31 23	27 26 20	9 22.3	20 11.4	28 47.0	3 02.8	2 03.2	6 10.4	26 44.5	11 55.7	24 21.3	9 23.6
5 Sa	4 57 26	15 16 37	3♌21 09	9♌16 14	9 21.6	21 13.5	29 48.5	3 42.4	2 27.7	6 23.5	26 41.8	11 56.6	24 23.5	9 23.7
6 Su	5 01 22	16 14 04	15 12 04	21 09 07	9 20.9	22 18.8	0♉50.3	4 22.0	2 52.2	6 36.7	26 39.0	11 57.6	24 25.6	9 23.7
7 M	5 05 19	17 11 30	27 07 55	3♍08 58	9 20.3	23 27.4	1 52.4	5 01.5	3 16.7	6 49.9	26 36.2	11 58.6	24 27.7	9 23.8
8 Tu	5 09 15	18 08 54	9♍12 49	15 20 02	9D 20.0	24 39.2	2 54.7	5 41.0	3 41.2	7 03.2	26 33.3	11 59.7	24 29.8	9R 23.8
9 W	5 13 12	19 06 18	21 31 08	27 46 40	9 20.1	25 54.0	3 57.2	6 20.5	4 05.7	7 16.5	26 30.3	12 00.8	24 31.9	9 23.8
10 Th	5 17 08	20 03 40	4♎07 09	10♎33 01	9 20.7	27 11.9	5 00.0	7 00.0	4 30.1	7 29.7	26 27.2	12 01.9	24 34.0	9 23.8
11 F	5 21 05	21 01 01	17 04 43	23 42 34	9 21.5	28 32.9	6 03.0	7 39.4	4 54.6	7 43.1	26 24.1	12 03.1	24 36.1	9 23.7
12 Sa	5 25 02	21 58 22	0♏26 50	7♏17 39	9 22.5	29 56.9	7 06.3	8 18.8	5 19.0	7 56.4	26 20.9	12 04.4	24 38.1	9 23.6
13 Su	5 28 58	22 55 41	14 15 02	21 18 51	9 23.4	1♊23.8	8 09.8	8 58.2	5 43.4	8 09.8	26 17.6	12 05.7	24 40.2	9 23.5
14 M	5 32 55	23 53 00	28 28 49	5♐44 29	9R 23.9	2 53.7	9 13.5	9 37.5	6 07.8	8 23.2	26 14.3	12 07.1	24 42.2	9 23.4
15 Tu	5 36 51	24 50 18	13♐05 14	20 30 17	9 23.7	4 26.5	10 17.4	10 16.8	6 32.2	8 36.6	26 10.9	12 08.5	24 44.2	9 23.3
16 W	5 40 48	25 47 35	27 58 45	5♑29 35	9 22.8	6 02.2	11 21.5	10 56.1	6 56.6	8 50.0	26 07.4	12 10.0	24 46.2	9 23.1
17 Th	5 44 44	26 44 52	13♑01 42	20 33 58	9 21.1	7 40.7	12 25.8	11 35.4	7 20.9	9 03.5	26 03.9	12 11.5	24 48.2	9 22.9
18 F	5 48 41	27 42 08	28 05 14	5♒34 25	9 18.9	9 22.2	13 30.4	12 14.7	7 45.3	9 17.0	26 00.3	12 13.0	24 50.2	9 22.7
19 Sa	5 52 38	28 39 24	13♒00 34	20 22 46	9 16.6	11 06.4	14 35.1	12 53.9	8 09.6	9 30.4	25 56.7	12 14.7	24 52.1	9 22.4
20 Su	5 56 34	29 36 40	27 40 20	4♓52 41	9 14.6	12 53.5	15 40.0	13 33.1	8 33.9	9 43.9	25 53.0	12 16.3	24 54.1	9 22.2
21 M	6 00 31	0♋33 55	11♓59 24	19 00 17	9D 13.3	14 43.3	16 45.1	14 12.2	8 58.1	9 57.5	25 49.2	12 18.0	24 56.0	9 21.9
22 Tu	6 04 27	1 31 10	25 55 11	2♈44 11	9 13.0	16 35.7	17 50.4	14 51.4	9 22.4	10 11.0	25 45.4	12 19.8	24 57.9	9 21.6
23 W	6 08 24	2 28 25	9♈27 23	16 05 02	9 13.5	18 30.7	18 55.9	15 30.5	9 46.6	10 24.5	25 41.6	12 21.6	24 59.8	9 21.2
24 Th	6 12 20	3 25 40	22 37 26	29 04 53	9 14.7	20 28.1	20 01.5	16 09.6	10 10.8	10 38.1	25 37.7	12 23.4	25 01.6	9 20.9
25 F	6 16 17	4 22 55	5♉27 49	11♉46 34	9 16.3	22 27.8	21 07.3	16 48.7	10 35.0	10 51.6	25 33.7	12 25.3	25 03.5	9 20.5
26 Sa	6 20 13	5 20 10	18 01 33	24 13 09	9 17.7	24 29.8	22 13.3	17 27.8	10 59.2	11 05.2	25 29.7	12 27.2	25 05.3	9 20.1
27 Su	6 24 10	6 17 25	0♊21 45	6♊27 41	9R 18.5	26 33.6	23 19.4	18 06.8	11 23.4	11 18.8	25 25.7	12 29.2	25 07.1	9 19.7
28 M	6 28 07	7 14 40	12 31 18	18 32 54	9 18.1	28 39.3	24 25.6	18 45.8	11 47.5	11 32.4	25 21.6	12 31.3	25 08.9	9 19.2
29 Tu	6 32 03	8 11 54	24 32 46	0♋31 12	9 16.4	0♋46.5	25 32.0	19 24.8	12 11.6	11 46.0	25 17.5	12 33.3	25 10.7	9 18.8
30 W	6 36 00	9 09 09	6♋28 26	12 24 44	9 13.3	2 54.9	26 38.6	20 03.8	12 35.6	11 59.6	25 13.3	12 35.4	25 12.4	9 18.3

Astro Data

	Dy Hr Mn
♀0N	2 17:34
♄ R	6 9:11
☽0S	12 8:39
♅ D	19 0:47
☿ D	20 13:57
☽0N	25 3:54
♄□♅	1 2:21
☽0S	8 16:50
♇ R	8 19:15
♃△♇	18 22:02
♃∠♆	21 8:57
☽0N	21 10:05
♄△♆	30 15:46

Planet Ingress

		Dy Hr Mn
♀	♈	3 22:03
♃	♋	5 18:12
☉	♊	20 14:04
⚳	♊	30 11:35
♂	♋	30 21:27
♀	♉	5 16:28
☿	♊	12 12:53
☉	♋	20 21:47
☿	♋	29 3:16

Last Aspect / ☽ Ingress

Last Aspect Dy Hr Mn			☽ Ingress	Dy Hr Mn
1 0:12	♃	⚹	♉	1 1:51
3 9:30	♀	⚹	♊	3 10:15
4 10:07	♂	☌	♋	5 21:16
8 4:39	♄	☍	♌	8 9:55
10 9:02	♆	□	♍	10 22:03
13 2:35	♄	△	♎	13 7:29
15 8:42	♄	□	♏	15 13:20
17 11:44	♄	⚹	♐	17 16:13
19 4:47	♂	☍	♑	19 17:30
21 14:06	♄	☌	♒	21 18:41
23 12:44	♂	△	♓	23 21:04
25 20:19	♄	⚹	♈	26 1:28
28 4:54	♂	⚹	♉	28 8:14
30 11:26	♄	△	♊	30 17:21

Last Aspect / ☽ Ingress

Last Aspect Dy Hr Mn			☽ Ingress	Dy Hr Mn
1 20:48	♀	⚹	♋	2 4:35
4 14:59	♀	□	♌	4 17:12
6 18:36	♆	□	♍	7 5:44
9 9:35	♄	△	♎	9 16:13
11 16:48	♄	□	♏	11 23:13
13 20:19	♄	⚹	♐	14 2:31
15 19:26	☉	☍	♑	16 3:14
17 20:44	♄	☌	♒	18 3:04
20 2:36	☉	△	♓	20 3:52
21 23:46	♄	⚹	♈	22 7:10
24 5:36	♄	□	♉	24 13:43
26 14:28	♄	△	♊	26 23:17
27 23:58	♅	□	♋	29 10:57

☽ Phases & Eclipses

Dy Hr Mn		
2 0:11	●	12♉03
10 1:57	☽	19♌52
17 11:13	○	27♏00
17 11:25	•	A 0.764
24 2:54	☾	3♓24
31 14:00	●	10♊34
31 13:58:27	•	A 04'45"
8 17:56	☽	18♍23
15 19:26	○	25♐08
15 19:13	•	A 0.251
22 9:41	☾	1♈26
30 4:50	●	8♋52

Astro Data

1 May 2049
Julian Day # 54543
SVP 4♓33'59"
GC 27♐31.7 ⚴ 29♓50.5
Eris 0♉47.4 ⚵ 12♉44.5
⚷ 25♏24.6R ⚶ 14♊07.3
☽ Mean ☊ 10♐55.6

1 June 2049
Julian Day # 54574
SVP 4♓33'55"
GC 27♐31.8 ⚴ 8♈34.7
Eris 1♉06.1 ⚵ 1♊05.8
⚷ 23♏09.1R ⚶ 27♊12.7
☽ Mean ☊ 9♐17.1

July 2049 LONGITUDE

Day	Sid.Time	☉	0 hr ☽	Noon ☽	True ☊	☿	♀	♂	⚳	♃	♄	♅	♆	♇
1 Th	6 39 56	10♋06 23	18♋20 19	24♋15 27	9♐08.8	5♋04.3	27♉45.3	20♋42.8	12♊59.7	12♋13.2	25♑09.2	12♍37.6	25♉14.1	9♓17.7
2 F	6 43 53	11 03 37	0♌10 21	6♌05 18	9R 03.5	7 14.4	28 52.1	21 21.7	13 23.7	12 26.8	25R 04.9	12 39.8	25 15.9	9R 17.2
3 Sa	6 47 49	12 00 51	12 00 33	17 56 25	8 57.7	9 24.9	29 59.1	22 00.6	13 47.6	12 40.4	25 00.7	12 42.1	25 17.5	9 16.6
4 Su	6 51 46	12 58 04	23 53 11	29 51 12	8 52.1	11 35.5	1♊06.1	22 39.5	14 11.6	12 53.9	24 56.4	12 44.4	25 19.2	9 16.1
5 M	6 55 42	13 55 17	5♍50 51	11♍52 31	8 47.3	13 46.0	2 13.4	23 18.4	14 35.5	13 07.6	24 52.1	12 46.7	25 20.8	9 15.5
6 Tu	6 59 39	14 52 31	17 56 38	24 03 40	8 43.8	15 56.0	3 20.7	23 57.3	14 59.4	13 21.2	24 47.8	12 49.1	25 22.5	9 14.8
7 W	7 03 36	15 49 43	0♎14 05	6♎28 22	8D 41.9	18 05.4	4 28.2	24 36.1	15 23.2	13 34.8	24 43.4	12 51.5	25 24.0	9 14.2
8 Th	7 07 32	16 46 56	12 47 02	19 10 35	8 41.5	20 13.9	5 35.7	25 14.9	15 47.0	13 48.4	24 39.0	12 53.9	25 25.6	9 13.5
9 F	7 11 29	17 44 09	25 39 29	2♏14 12	8 42.2	22 21.4	6 43.4	25 53.7	16 10.8	14 01.9	24 34.7	12 56.4	25 27.2	9 12.8
10 Sa	7 15 25	18 41 21	8♏55 07	15 42 34	8 43.6	24 27.6	7 51.2	26 32.5	16 34.5	14 15.5	24 30.3	12 59.0	25 28.7	9 12.1
11 Su	7 19 22	19 38 33	22 36 46	29 37 50	8R 44.7	26 32.4	8 59.2	27 11.2	16 58.2	14 29.1	24 25.8	13 01.5	25 30.2	9 11.4
12 M	7 23 18	20 35 46	6♐45 41	14♐00 08	8 44.9	28 35.7	10 07.2	27 50.0	17 21.8	14 42.6	24 21.4	13 04.1	25 31.6	9 10.7
13 Tu	7 27 15	21 32 58	21 20 45	28 46 55	8 43.5	0♌37.5	11 15.4	28 28.7	17 45.5	14 56.2	24 17.0	13 06.8	25 33.1	9 09.9
14 W	7 31 11	22 30 11	6♑17 49	13♑52 28	8 40.1	2 37.6	12 23.6	29 07.4	18 09.0	15 09.7	24 12.6	13 09.5	25 34.5	9 09.1
15 Th	7 35 08	23 27 23	21 29 41	29 08 10	8 35.0	4 35.9	13 32.0	29 46.1	18 32.6	15 23.2	24 08.1	13 12.2	25 35.9	9 08.3
16 F	7 39 05	24 24 36	6♒46 35	14♒23 33	8 28.6	6 32.5	14 40.5	0♌24.7	18 56.1	15 36.7	24 03.7	13 15.0	25 37.3	9 07.5
17 Sa	7 43 01	25 21 50	21 57 46	29 28 01	8 21.9	8 27.4	15 49.1	1 03.4	19 19.5	15 50.2	23 59.2	13 17.7	25 38.6	9 06.7
18 Su	7 46 58	26 19 04	6♓53 17	14♓12 40	8 15.6	10 20.4	16 57.8	1 42.0	19 42.9	16 03.7	23 54.8	13 20.6	25 39.9	9 05.8
19 M	7 50 54	27 16 18	21 25 34	28 31 31	8 10.7	12 11.6	18 06.6	2 20.6	20 06.3	16 17.1	23 50.4	13 23.4	25 41.2	9 05.0
20 Tu	7 54 51	28 13 34	5♈30 20	12♈21 57	8 07.7	14 01.0	19 15.5	2 59.2	20 29.6	16 30.6	23 45.9	13 26.3	25 42.5	9 04.1
21 W	7 58 47	29 10 50	19 06 32	25 44 21	8D 06.4	15 48.6	20 24.6	3 37.8	20 52.9	16 44.0	23 41.5	13 29.2	25 43.7	9 03.2
22 Th	8 02 44	0♌08 07	2♉15 46	8♉41 15	8 06.6	17 34.4	21 33.7	4 16.4	21 16.1	16 57.4	23 37.1	13 32.2	25 44.9	9 02.2
23 F	8 06 40	1 05 25	15 01 20	21 16 35	8 07.6	19 18.4	22 42.9	4 54.9	21 39.3	17 10.7	23 32.7	13 35.2	25 46.1	9 01.3
24 Sa	8 10 37	2 02 43	27 27 32	3♊34 46	8R 08.5	21 00.6	23 52.2	5 33.5	22 02.5	17 24.1	23 28.3	13 38.2	25 47.3	9 00.4
25 Su	8 14 34	3 00 03	9♊38 50	15 40 15	8 08.3	22 41.0	25 01.7	6 12.0	22 25.5	17 37.4	23 24.0	13 41.3	25 48.4	8 59.4
26 M	8 18 30	3 57 23	21 39 33	27 37 10	8 06.2	24 19.6	26 11.2	6 50.5	22 48.6	17 50.7	23 19.6	13 44.4	25 49.5	8 58.4
27 Tu	8 22 27	4 54 45	3♋33 31	9♋29 00	8 01.9	25 56.4	27 20.8	7 29.0	23 11.6	18 04.0	23 15.3	13 47.5	25 50.5	8 57.4
28 W	8 26 23	5 52 07	15 23 57	21 18 40	7 55.1	27 31.4	28 30.5	8 07.5	23 34.5	18 17.3	23 11.0	13 50.6	25 51.6	8 56.4
29 Th	8 30 20	6 49 29	27 13 27	3♌08 30	7 46.0	29 04.6	29 40.3	8 46.0	23 57.4	18 30.5	23 06.7	13 53.8	25 52.6	8 55.4
30 F	8 34 16	7 46 53	9♌04 03	15 00 18	7 35.4	0♍36.1	0♋50.1	9 24.5	24 20.2	18 43.7	23 02.5	13 57.0	25 53.5	8 54.3
31 Sa	8 38 13	8 44 17	20 57 27	26 55 41	7 23.9	2 05.7	2 00.1	10 02.9	24 42.9	18 56.8	22 58.3	14 00.2	25 54.5	8 53.3

August 2049 LONGITUDE

Day	Sid.Time	☉	0 hr ☽	Noon ☽	True ☊	☿	♀	♂	⚳	♃	♄	♅	♆	♇
1 Su	8 42 09	9♌41 42	2♍55 10	8♍56 08	7♐12.7	3♍33.5	3♋10.1	10♌41.4	25♊05.6	19♋10.0	22♑54.1	14♍03.5	25♉55.4	8♓52.2
2 M	8 46 06	10 39 08	14 58 48	21 03 24	7R 02.7	4 59.5	4 20.3	11 19.8	25 28.2	19 23.1	22R 50.0	14 06.8	25 56.3	8R 51.1
3 Tu	8 50 03	11 36 34	27 10 13	3♎19 33	6 54.7	6 23.5	5 30.5	11 58.2	25 50.8	19 36.1	22 45.9	14 10.1	25 57.1	8 50.0
4 W	8 53 59	12 34 01	9♎31 45	15 47 11	6 49.1	7 45.7	6 40.7	12 36.6	26 13.3	19 49.1	22 41.8	14 13.4	25 57.9	8 48.9
5 Th	8 57 56	13 31 29	22 06 14	28 29 21	6 46.1	9 06.0	7 51.1	13 15.0	26 35.7	20 02.1	22 37.8	14 16.8	25 58.7	8 47.8
6 F	9 01 52	14 28 57	4♏56 57	11♏29 28	6D 45.1	10 24.3	9 01.6	13 53.4	26 58.1	20 15.0	22 33.9	14 20.2	25 59.5	8 46.7
7 Sa	9 05 49	15 26 27	18 07 20	24 50 56	6R 45.2	11 40.5	10 12.1	14 31.7	27 20.4	20 27.9	22 29.9	14 23.6	26 00.2	8 45.5
8 Su	9 09 45	16 23 57	1♐40 36	8♐36 34	6 45.5	12 54.7	11 22.7	15 10.1	27 42.6	20 40.8	22 26.1	14 27.0	26 00.9	8 44.4
9 M	9 13 42	17 21 28	15 38 59	22 47 49	6 44.6	14 06.7	12 33.4	15 48.4	28 04.8	20 53.6	22 22.3	14 30.4	26 01.6	8 43.2
10 Tu	9 17 38	18 18 59	0♑02 55	7♑23 54	6 41.7	15 16.5	13 44.1	16 26.8	28 26.9	21 06.4	22 18.5	14 33.9	26 02.2	8 42.1
11 W	9 21 35	19 16 32	14 50 11	22 21 00	6 36.2	16 24.0	14 55.0	17 05.1	28 48.9	21 19.1	22 14.8	14 37.4	26 02.8	8 40.9
12 Th	9 25 32	20 14 05	29 55 20	7♒32 02	6 28.3	17 29.1	16 05.9	17 43.4	29 10.8	21 31.8	22 11.1	14 40.9	26 03.4	8 39.7
13 F	9 29 28	21 11 40	15♒09 48	22 47 14	6 18.6	18 31.7	17 16.9	18 21.7	29 32.7	21 44.4	22 07.5	14 44.4	26 03.9	8 38.5
14 Sa	9 33 25	22 09 15	0♓22 57	7♓55 36	6 08.1	19 31.7	18 28.0	19 00.0	29 54.5	21 57.0	22 04.0	14 48.0	26 04.4	8 37.3
15 Su	9 37 21	23 06 52	15 23 56	22 46 53	5 58.2	20 29.0	19 39.1	19 38.2	0♋16.2	22 09.5	22 00.5	14 51.5	26 04.9	8 36.1
16 M	9 41 18	24 04 30	0♈03 35	7♈13 22	5 49.9	21 23.3	20 50.4	20 16.5	0 37.8	22 22.0	21 57.1	14 55.1	26 05.3	8 34.9
17 Tu	9 45 14	25 02 10	14 15 51	21 10 49	5 43.9	22 14.7	22 01.7	20 54.8	0 59.3	22 34.4	21 53.7	14 58.7	26 05.7	8 33.6
18 W	9 49 11	25 59 51	27 58 17	4♉38 25	5 40.4	23 02.9	23 13.1	21 33.0	1 20.8	22 46.8	21 50.4	15 02.3	26 06.1	8 32.4
19 Th	9 53 07	26 57 34	11♉11 34	17 38 10	5D 38.9	23 47.8	24 24.6	22 11.3	1 42.2	22 59.1	21 47.2	15 05.9	26 06.4	8 31.2
20 F	9 57 04	27 55 19	23 58 46	0♊13 58	5R 38.7	24 29.1	25 36.1	22 49.5	2 03.5	23 11.4	21 44.0	15 09.6	26 06.7	8 29.9
21 Sa	10 01 01	28 53 05	6♊24 23	12 30 41	5 38.7	25 06.6	26 47.7	23 27.8	2 24.7	23 23.6	21 40.9	15 13.2	26 07.0	8 28.7
22 Su	10 04 57	29 50 53	18 33 31	24 33 32	5 37.6	25 40.2	27 59.4	24 06.0	2 45.8	23 35.8	21 37.9	15 16.9	26 07.2	8 27.4
23 M	10 08 54	0♍48 43	0♋31 21	6♋27 33	5 34.6	26 09.5	29 11.2	24 44.2	3 06.8	23 47.8	21 35.0	15 20.6	26 07.5	8 26.2
24 Tu	10 12 50	1 46 34	12 22 41	18 17 15	5 28.9	26 34.4	0♌23.0	25 22.5	3 27.8	23 59.9	21 32.1	15 24.3	26 07.6	8 24.9
25 W	10 16 47	2 44 27	24 11 42	0♌06 27	5 20.5	26 54.7	1 35.0	26 00.7	3 48.6	24 11.8	21 29.3	15 28.0	26 07.8	8 23.7
26 Th	10 20 43	3 42 21	6♌01 51	11 58 11	5 09.4	27 09.9	2 46.9	26 38.9	4 09.3	24 23.7	21 26.6	15 31.7	26 07.9	8 22.4
27 F	10 24 40	4 40 17	17 55 44	23 54 42	4 56.3	27 19.9	3 59.0	27 17.1	4 29.9	24 35.6	21 23.9	15 35.4	26 07.9	8 21.1
28 Sa	10 28 36	5 38 15	29 55 16	5♍57 34	4 42.3	27R 24.5	5 11.1	27 55.3	4 50.5	24 47.3	21 21.4	15 39.1	26R 08.0	8 19.9
29 Su	10 32 33	6 36 14	12♍01 44	18 07 53	4 28.6	27 23.4	6 23.3	28 33.5	5 10.9	24 59.0	21 18.9	15 42.9	26 08.0	8 18.6
30 M	10 36 30	7 34 14	24 16 06	0♎26 30	4 16.2	27 16.4	7 35.6	29 11.7	5 31.2	25 10.6	21 16.5	15 46.6	26 08.0	8 17.3
31 Tu	10 40 26	8 32 16	6♎39 11	12 54 18	4 06.1	27 03.2	8 47.9	29 49.8	5 51.4	25 22.2	21 14.2	15 50.4	26 07.9	8 16.0

Astro Data	Dy Hr Mn
♃✶♅	3 15:30
☽0S	6 0:15
♄∠♇	15 10:31
☽0N	18 18:39
☽0S	2 6:53
♃☍♄	14 22:25
☽0N	15 5:09
☿0S	19 13:43
♃⚼♇	21 21:06
☿R	28 19:21
♆R	29 3:11
☽0S	29 13:10

Planet Ingress		Dy Hr Mn
♀	♊	3 12:20
☿	♌	13 4:35
♂	♌	15 20:39
☉	♌	22 8:36
♀	♋	29 18:47
☿	♍	30 2:28
⚳	♋	14 18:07
☉	♍	22 15:47
♀	♌	24 4:18
♂	♍	31 18:23

Last Aspect Dy Hr Mn		☽ Ingress	Dy Hr Mn
1 19:50	♀ ✶	♌	1 23:39
4 2:52	♆ □	♍	4 12:18
6 14:34	♆ △	♎	6 23:33
8 23:50	♂ □	♏	9 7:56
11 7:39	♂ △	♐	11 12:38
12 10:27	♅ □	♑	13 13:57
15 13:02	♂ ☍	♒	15 13:21
17 5:52	♆ □	♓	17 12:51
19 9:43	☉ △	♈	19 14:31
21 18:48	☉ □	♉	21 19:49
23 20:43	♆ ☌	♊	24 4:58
26 8:48	♀ ☌	♋	26 16:48
28 21:15	♆ ✶	♌	29 5:38
31 9:57	♆ □	♍	31 18:10

Last Aspect Dy Hr Mn		☽ Ingress	Dy Hr Mn
2 21:36	♆ △	♎	3 5:32
5 1:03	♄ □	♏	5 14:49
7 14:03	♆ ☍	♐	7 21:04
9 2:14	☉ △	♑	9 23:55
11 17:52	♆ △	♒	12 0:07
13 17:10	♆ □	♓	13 23:24
15 17:25	♆ ✶	♈	15 23:54
17 19:18	☉ △	♉	18 3:38
20 7:10	☉ □	♊	20 11:33
22 14:20	☿ □	♋	22 22:57
25 5:20	☿ ✶	♌	25 11:47
27 19:07	♂ ☌	♍	28 0:09
30 5:56	☿ ☌	♎	30 11:09

☽ Phases & Eclipses Dy Hr Mn	
8 7:10	☽ 16♎35
15 2:29	○ 23♑05
21 18:48	☾ 29♈27
29 20:07	● 7♌09
6 17:51	☽ 14♏43
13 9:19	○ 21♒05
20 7:10	☾ 27♉44
28 11:18	● 5♍37

Astro Data

1 July 2049
Julian Day # 54604
SVP 4♓33'49"
GC 27♐31.8 ⚴ 15♈13.1
Eris 1♉18.3 ✱ 18♊48.6
⚷ 21♏35.2R ⚵ 10♋13.9
☽ Mean ☊ 7♐41.8

1 August 2049
Julian Day # 54635
SVP 4♓33'45"
GC 27♐31.9 ⚴ 18♈51.3
Eris 1♉21.8R ✱ 6♋39.6
⚷ 21♏22.4 ⚵ 23♋46.7
☽ Mean ☊ 6♐03.3

LONGITUDE — September 2049

Day	Sid.Time	☉	0 hr ☽	Noon ☽	True ☊	☿	♀	♂	⚳	♃	♄	♅	♆	♇
1 W	10 44 23	9♍30 20	19♎12 00	25♎32 29	3♐58.8	26♍44.0	10♌00.2	0♍28.0	6♋11.5	25♋33.6	21♑12.0	15♍54.1	26♉07.8	8♓14.8
2 Th	10 48 19	10 28 25	1♏55 57	8♏22 41	3R54.5	26R18.5	11 12.7	1 06.2	6 31.4	25 45.0	21R09.9	15 57.9	26R07.7	8R13.5
3 F	10 52 16	11 26 31	14 52 57	21 27 03	3D52.6	25 46.9	12 25.2	1 44.4	6 51.3	25 56.3	21 07.8	16 01.6	26 07.5	8 12.2
4 Sa	10 56 12	12 24 39	28 05 17	4♐47 58	3R52.2	25 09.3	13 37.8	2 22.5	7 11.0	26 07.6	21 05.8	16 05.4	26 07.3	8 11.0
5 Su	11 00 09	13 22 49	11♐35 23	18 27 47	3 52.2	24 26.2	14 50.4	3 00.7	7 30.6	26 18.7	21 04.0	16 09.2	26 07.1	8 09.7
6 M	11 04 05	14 20 59	25 25 19	2♑28 05	3 51.3	23 38.0	16 03.1	3 38.8	7 50.1	26 29.8	21 02.2	16 13.0	26 06.8	8 08.4
7 Tu	11 08 02	15 19 11	9♑36 03	16 49 00	3 48.4	22 45.3	17 15.8	4 16.9	8 09.5	26 40.8	21 00.5	16 16.7	26 06.6	8 07.2
8 W	11 11 59	16 17 25	24 06 38	1♒28 24	3 43.0	21 49.0	18 28.6	4 55.1	8 28.7	26 51.7	20 58.9	16 20.5	26 06.2	8 05.9
9 Th	11 15 55	17 15 40	8♒53 36	16 21 24	3 35.0	20 50.1	19 41.5	5 33.2	8 47.8	27 02.5	20 57.4	16 24.3	26 05.9	8 04.7
10 F	11 19 52	18 13 57	23 50 45	1♓20 32	3 25.1	19 49.9	20 54.4	6 11.3	9 06.8	27 13.2	20 56.0	16 28.1	26 05.5	8 03.4
11 Sa	11 23 48	19 12 15	8♓49 33	16 16 37	3 14.4	18 49.5	22 07.4	6 49.4	9 25.6	27 23.9	20 54.7	16 31.8	26 05.1	8 02.2
12 Su	11 27 45	20 10 35	23 40 34	1♈00 20	3 04.1	17 50.4	23 20.4	7 27.6	9 44.3	27 34.4	20 53.4	16 35.6	26 04.6	8 00.9
13 M	11 31 41	21 08 57	8♈14 58	15 23 44	2 55.3	16 54.0	24 33.5	8 05.7	10 02.9	27 44.9	20 52.3	16 39.4	26 04.1	7 59.7
14 Tu	11 35 38	22 07 21	22 26 04	29 21 36	2 48.9	16 01.7	25 46.7	8 43.8	10 21.3	27 55.2	20 51.3	16 43.2	26 03.6	7 58.5
15 W	11 39 34	23 05 47	6♉10 10	12♉51 46	2 45.0	15 14.8	26 59.9	9 21.9	10 39.5	28 05.5	20 50.3	16 46.9	26 03.1	7 57.2
16 Th	11 43 31	24 04 15	19 26 34	25 54 54	2D43.4	14 34.5	28 13.2	10 00.0	10 57.7	28 15.7	20 49.5	16 50.7	26 02.5	7 56.0
17 F	11 47 27	25 02 46	2♊17 10	8♊33 52	2 43.3	14 01.7	29 26.6	10 38.1	11 15.6	28 25.7	20 48.7	16 54.4	26 01.9	7 54.8
18 Sa	11 51 24	26 01 18	14 45 37	20 53 01	2R43.7	13 37.4	0♍40.0	11 16.2	11 33.5	28 35.7	20 48.1	16 58.2	26 01.3	7 53.6
19 Su	11 55 21	26 59 53	26 56 43	2♋57 24	2 43.7	13 22.2	1 53.4	11 54.4	11 51.1	28 45.6	20 47.5	17 01.9	26 00.6	7 52.4
20 M	11 59 17	27 58 30	8♋55 42	14 52 18	2 42.1	13D16.5	3 07.0	12 32.5	12 08.6	28 55.3	20 47.1	17 05.7	25 59.9	7 51.3
21 Tu	12 03 14	28 57 09	20 47 49	26 42 50	2 38.4	13 20.5	4 20.5	13 10.6	12 26.0	29 05.0	20 46.7	17 09.4	25 59.2	7 50.1
22 W	12 07 10	29 55 50	2♌37 56	8♌33 37	2 32.2	13 34.3	5 34.2	13 48.7	12 43.1	29 14.5	20 46.4	17 13.1	25 58.4	7 48.9
23 Th	12 11 07	0♎54 33	14 30 20	20 28 32	2 23.7	13 57.7	6 47.8	14 26.8	13 00.1	29 24.0	20 46.3	17 16.8	25 57.6	7 47.8
24 F	12 15 03	1 53 18	26 28 34	2♍30 43	2 13.5	14 30.5	8 01.6	15 04.9	13 17.0	29 33.3	20D46.2	17 20.5	25 56.8	7 46.6
25 Sa	12 19 00	2 52 06	8♍35 14	14 42 18	2 02.3	15 12.2	9 15.3	15 43.0	13 33.6	29 42.5	20 46.2	17 24.2	25 55.9	7 45.5
26 Su	12 22 56	3 50 55	20 52 05	27 04 40	1 51.2	16 02.3	10 29.2	16 21.1	13 50.1	29 51.6	20 46.4	17 27.9	25 55.1	7 44.4
27 M	12 26 53	4 49 47	3♎20 05	9♎38 23	1 41.3	17 00.2	11 43.0	16 59.3	14 06.3	0♌00.6	20 46.6	17 31.5	25 54.2	7 43.2
28 Tu	12 30 50	5 48 40	15 59 33	22 23 34	1 33.3	18 05.4	12 57.0	17 37.4	14 22.4	0 09.4	20 47.0	17 35.2	25 53.2	7 42.1
29 W	12 34 46	6 47 36	28 50 25	5♏20 05	1 27.8	19 17.1	14 10.9	18 15.5	14 38.3	0 18.2	20 47.4	17 38.8	25 52.3	7 41.1
30 Th	12 38 43	7 46 33	11♏52 34	18 27 54	1D24.8	20 34.6	15 24.9	18 53.6	14 54.0	0 26.8	20 47.9	17 42.4	25 51.3	7 40.0

LONGITUDE — October 2049

Day	Sid.Time	☉	0 hr ☽	Noon ☽	True ☊	☿	♀	♂	⚳	♃	♄	♅	♆	♇
1 F	12 42 39	8♎45 32	25♏06 06	1♐47 13	1♐24.0	21♍57.3	16♍39.0	19♍31.7	15♋09.5	0♌35.3	20♑48.6	17♍46.0	25♉50.3	7♓38.9
2 Sa	12 46 36	9 44 34	8♐31 21	15 18 33	1 24.6	23 24.4	17 53.1	20 09.8	15 24.8	0 43.6	20 49.3	17 49.6	25R49.2	7R37.9
3 Su	12 50 32	10 43 36	22 08 56	29 02 33	1R25.7	24 55.4	19 07.2	20 47.9	15 39.9	0 51.9	20 50.1	17 53.2	25 48.2	7 36.8
4 M	12 54 29	11 42 41	5♑59 28	12♑59 41	1 26.1	26 29.7	20 21.4	21 26.0	15 54.7	1 00.0	20 51.1	17 56.7	25 47.1	7 35.8
5 Tu	12 58 25	12 41 47	20 03 08	27 09 42	1 25.1	28 06.6	21 35.6	22 04.1	16 09.4	1 07.9	20 52.1	18 00.2	25 46.0	7 34.8
6 W	13 02 22	13 40 55	4♒19 10	11♒31 11	1 22.2	29 45.8	22 49.9	22 42.2	16 23.8	1 15.8	20 53.2	18 03.8	25 44.8	7 33.8
7 Th	13 06 19	14 40 05	18 45 18	26 01 01	1 17.4	1♎26.7	24 04.2	23 20.3	16 38.1	1 23.5	20 54.5	18 07.2	25 43.7	7 32.9
8 F	13 10 15	15 39 16	3♓17 38	10♓34 27	1 11.0	3 08.9	25 18.5	23 58.4	16 52.1	1 31.0	20 55.8	18 10.7	25 42.5	7 31.9
9 Sa	13 14 12	16 38 29	17 50 39	25 05 24	1 03.8	4 52.3	26 32.8	24 36.5	17 05.8	1 38.5	20 57.2	18 14.2	25 41.2	7 31.0
10 Su	13 18 08	17 37 44	2♈17 53	9♈27 18	0 56.9	6 36.3	27 47.3	25 14.6	17 19.3	1 45.7	20 58.8	18 17.6	25 40.0	7 30.1
11 M	13 22 05	18 37 02	16 32 54	23 34 02	0 51.1	8 20.8	29 01.7	25 52.7	17 32.6	1 52.9	21 00.4	18 21.0	25 38.7	7 29.1
12 Tu	13 26 01	19 36 21	0♉30 11	7♉20 57	0 46.9	10 05.7	0♎16.2	26 30.8	17 45.7	1 59.9	21 02.1	18 24.4	25 37.5	7 28.3
13 W	13 29 58	20 35 42	14 06 04	20 45 24	0D44.7	11 50.6	1 30.7	27 08.9	17 58.5	2 06.7	21 03.9	18 27.7	25 36.2	7 27.4
14 Th	13 33 54	21 35 06	27 18 57	3♊46 50	0 44.2	13 35.4	2 45.3	27 47.0	18 11.1	2 13.4	21 05.8	18 31.0	25 34.8	7 26.5
15 F	13 37 51	22 34 32	10♊09 19	16 26 43	0 45.1	15 20.1	3 59.9	28 25.1	18 23.4	2 20.0	21 07.8	18 34.4	25 33.5	7 25.7
16 Sa	13 41 48	23 34 00	22 39 28	28 48 01	0 46.8	17 04.5	5 14.5	29 03.2	18 35.4	2 26.4	21 09.9	18 37.6	25 32.1	7 24.9
17 Su	13 45 44	24 33 30	4♋52 57	10♋54 48	0 48.3	18 48.6	6 29.2	29 41.3	18 47.2	2 32.7	21 12.1	18 40.9	25 30.8	7 24.1
18 M	13 49 41	25 33 03	16 54 13	22 51 47	0R49.2	20 32.2	7 43.9	0♎19.4	18 58.7	2 38.8	21 14.4	18 44.1	25 29.4	7 23.3
19 Tu	13 53 37	26 32 38	28 48 09	4♌43 57	0 48.9	22 15.4	8 58.6	0 57.5	19 10.0	2 44.7	21 16.8	18 47.3	25 27.9	7 22.6
20 W	13 57 34	27 32 15	10♌39 46	16 36 14	0 47.1	23 58.1	10 13.4	1 35.7	19 20.9	2 50.5	21 19.3	18 50.5	25 26.5	7 21.8
21 Th	14 01 30	28 31 54	22 33 52	28 33 15	0 43.8	25 40.3	11 28.2	2 13.8	19 31.6	2 56.1	21 21.9	18 53.6	25 25.0	7 21.1
22 F	14 05 27	29 31 36	4♍34 50	10♍39 04	0 39.3	27 21.9	12 43.0	2 51.9	19 42.0	3 01.6	21 24.5	18 56.7	25 23.6	7 20.4
23 Sa	14 09 23	0♏31 19	16 46 20	22 56 57	0 34.2	29 02.9	13 57.8	3 30.1	19 52.1	3 06.9	21 27.3	18 59.8	25 22.1	7 19.7
24 Su	14 13 20	1 31 05	29 11 12	5♎29 15	0 29.0	0♏43.4	15 12.7	4 08.2	20 01.8	3 12.0	21 30.1	19 02.8	25 20.6	7 19.1
25 M	14 17 16	2 30 53	11♎51 14	18 17 12	0 24.4	2 23.3	16 27.6	4 46.3	20 11.3	3 16.9	21 33.1	19 05.8	25 19.0	7 18.4
26 Tu	14 21 13	3 30 43	24 47 09	1♏21 01	0 20.8	4 02.7	17 42.6	5 24.5	20 20.5	3 21.7	21 36.1	19 08.8	25 17.5	7 17.8
27 W	14 25 10	4 30 35	7♏58 39	14 39 54	0 18.5	5 41.6	18 57.6	6 02.6	20 29.4	3 26.3	21 39.2	19 11.7	25 15.9	7 17.2
28 Th	14 29 06	5 30 29	21 24 34	28 12 23	0D17.7	7 19.9	20 12.5	6 40.8	20 37.9	3 30.8	21 42.4	19 14.7	25 14.4	7 16.7
29 F	14 33 03	6 30 25	5♐03 07	11♐56 30	0 18.0	8 57.6	21 27.6	7 18.9	20 46.1	3 35.1	21 45.7	19 17.5	25 12.8	7 16.1
30 Sa	14 36 59	7 30 23	18 52 16	25 50 09	0 19.2	10 34.9	22 42.6	7 57.0	20 54.0	3 39.2	21 49.1	19 20.4	25 11.2	7 15.6
31 Su	14 40 56	8 30 22	2♑49 53	9♑51 15	0 20.7	12 11.7	23 57.6	8 35.2	21 01.6	3 43.1	21 52.6	19 23.2	25 09.6	7 15.1

Astro Data

	Dy Hr Mn
♃✶♆	4 11:30
☿0N	9 9:29
☽0N	11 15:58
☿ D	20 14:10
☉0S	22 13:42
♄ D	24 15:34
☽0S	25 19:48
☽0N	9 1:14
☿0S	9 5:36
♀0S	15 2:16
♂0S	21 23:29
☽0S	23 3:18

Planet Ingress

		Dy Hr Mn
♀	♍	17 22:56
☉	♎	22 13:42
♃	♌	27 10:28
☿	♎	6 15:25
♀	♎	12 6:47
♂	♎	17 23:46
☉	♏	22 23:25
☿	♏	24 1:37

Last Aspect / ☽ Ingress (September)

Last Aspect Dy Hr Mn			☽ Ingress	Dy Hr Mn
1 12:02	♃	□	♏	1 20:23
3 20:28	♆	☍	♐	4 3:26
5 21:46	☿	□	♑	6 7:49
8 4:24	♃	☍	♒	8 9:36
10 3:36	♆	□	♓	10 9:51
12 6:18	♃	△	♈	12 10:21
14 9:28	♃	□	♉	14 13:07
16 16:47	♀	□	♊	16 19:40
18 23:03	☉	□	♋	19 6:05
21 16:57	☉	✶	♌	21 18:40
23 22:58	♆	□	♍	24 7:01
26 17:25	♃	✶	♎	26 17:37
28 8:59	♄	□	♏	29 2:09

Last Aspect / ☽ Ingress (October)

Last Aspect Dy Hr Mn			☽ Ingress	Dy Hr Mn
1 1:20	♆	☍	♐	1 8:48
3 3:57	☿	□	♑	3 13:40
5 13:48	☿	△	♒	5 16:46
7 11:31	♆	□	♓	7 18:34
9 14:39	♀	☍	♈	9 20:10
11 7:36	♄	□	♉	11 23:07
14 0:17	♂	△	♊	14 4:58
16 12:31	♂	□	♋	16 14:21
18 17:55	☉	□	♌	19 2:25
21 11:57	☉	✶	♍	21 14:53
23 16:39	♆	△	♎	24 1:33
25 18:04	♄	□	♏	26 9:32
28 6:47	♆	☍	♐	28 15:09
30 6:05	♀	✶	♑	30 19:09

☽ Phases & Eclipses

Dy Hr Mn		
5 2:28	☽	13♐00
11 17:04	○	19♓25
18 23:03	☾	26♊28
27 2:05	●	4♎25
4 9:39	☽	11♑37
11 2:53	○	18♈15
18 17:55	☾	25♋48
26 16:15	●	3♏41

Astro Data

1 September 2049
Julian Day # 54666
SVP 4♓33'41"
GC 27♐32.0 ⚵ 17♈20.0R
Eris 1♉15.3R ⚶ 23♋34.0
⚷ 22♏45.7 ⚴ 7♌09.3
☽ Mean ☊ 4♐24.8

1 October 2049
Julian Day # 54696
SVP 4♓33'39"
GC 27♐32.1 ⚵ 10♈24.9R
Eris 1♉01.2R ⚶ 8♌26.3
⚷ 25♏23.5 ⚴ 19♌36.2
☽ Mean ☊ 2♐49.5

November 2049 — LONGITUDE

Day	Sid.Time	☉	0 hr ☽	Noon ☽	True ☊	☿	♀	♂	⚳	♃	♄	♅	♆	♇
1 M	14 44 52	9♏30 23	16♑53 59	23♑57 52	0♐21.9	13♏47.9	25♎12.7	9♎13.3	21♋08.8	3♌46.8	21♑56.2	19♍25.9	25♉08.0	7♓14.6
2 Tu	14 48 49	10 30 25	1♒02 40	8♒08 08	0R 22.5	15 23.8	26 27.8	9 51.5	21 15.7	3 50.3	21 59.8	19 28.6	25R 06.4	7R 14.2
3 W	14 52 45	11 30 29	15 14 01	22 20 03	0 22.2	16 59.1	27 42.9	10 29.6	21 22.2	3 53.7	22 03.5	19 31.3	25 04.8	7 13.8
4 Th	14 56 42	12 30 35	29 25 57	6♓31 25	0 21.1	18 34.0	28 58.0	11 07.7	21 28.4	3 56.9	22 07.4	19 34.0	25 03.1	7 13.4
5 F	15 00 39	13 30 42	13♓36 04	20 39 35	0 19.2	20 08.6	0♏13.2	11 45.9	21 34.2	3 59.9	22 11.2	19 36.6	25 01.5	7 13.0
6 Sa	15 04 35	14 30 50	27 41 33	4♈41 36	0 17.0	21 42.7	1 28.3	12 24.0	21 39.7	4 02.7	22 15.2	19 39.1	24 59.8	7 12.6
7 Su	15 08 32	15 31 00	11♈39 18	18 34 18	0 14.9	23 16.4	2 43.5	13 02.2	21 44.8	4 05.3	22 19.3	19 41.7	24 58.2	7 12.3
8 M	15 12 28	16 31 12	25 26 13	2♉14 41	0 13.2	24 49.7	3 58.7	13 40.3	21 49.5	4 07.8	22 23.4	19 44.1	24 56.5	7 12.0
9 Tu	15 16 25	17 31 25	8♉59 26	15 40 12	0 12.1	26 22.7	5 13.9	14 18.5	21 53.9	4 10.0	22 27.6	19 46.6	24 54.8	7 11.7
10 W	15 20 21	18 31 41	22 16 49	28 49 08	0D 11.7	27 55.4	6 29.1	14 56.6	21 57.9	4 12.1	22 31.9	19 49.0	24 53.1	7 11.4
11 Th	15 24 18	19 31 58	5♊17 06	11♊40 46	0 12.0	29 27.7	7 44.4	15 34.8	22 01.5	4 14.0	22 36.3	19 51.3	24 51.5	7 11.2
12 F	15 28 14	20 32 16	18 00 13	24 15 36	0 12.6	0♐59.7	8 59.6	16 12.9	22 04.7	4 15.7	22 40.7	19 53.6	24 49.8	7 11.0
13 Sa	15 32 11	21 32 37	0♋27 10	6♋35 13	0 13.5	2 31.4	10 14.9	16 51.1	22 07.6	4 17.1	22 45.2	19 55.9	24 48.1	7 10.8
14 Su	15 36 08	22 33 00	12 40 07	18 42 15	0 14.4	4 02.8	11 30.2	17 29.3	22 10.0	4 18.4	22 49.8	19 58.1	24 46.4	7 10.6
15 M	15 40 04	23 33 24	24 42 06	0♌40 09	0 15.2	5 33.9	12 45.5	18 07.5	22 12.1	4 19.5	22 54.5	20 00.3	24 44.7	7 10.5
16 Tu	15 44 01	24 33 50	6♌36 56	12 33 01	0 15.6	7 04.6	14 00.8	18 45.6	22 13.7	4 20.4	22 59.2	20 02.4	24 43.0	7 10.4
17 W	15 47 57	25 34 18	18 28 59	24 25 24	0R 15.8	8 35.1	15 16.2	19 23.8	22 15.0	4 21.1	23 04.1	20 04.5	24 41.3	7 10.3
18 Th	15 51 54	26 34 48	0♍22 53	6♍22 00	0 15.7	10 05.2	16 31.5	20 02.0	22 15.8	4 21.6	23 08.9	20 06.6	24 39.6	7 10.2
19 F	15 55 50	27 35 20	12 23 21	18 27 30	0 15.5	11 35.0	17 46.9	20 40.2	22R 16.3	4 21.9	23 13.9	20 08.5	24 37.9	7D 10.2
20 Sa	15 59 47	28 35 53	24 34 58	0♎46 14	0 15.3	13 04.5	19 02.2	21 18.4	22 16.3	4R 22.1	23 18.9	20 10.5	24 36.2	7 10.2
21 Su	16 03 43	29 36 28	7♎01 46	13 21 56	0D 15.2	14 33.6	20 17.6	21 56.6	22 15.9	4 22.0	23 24.0	20 12.4	24 34.5	7 10.2
22 M	16 07 40	0♐37 05	19 47 03	26 17 20	0 15.1	16 02.2	21 33.0	22 34.7	22 15.1	4 21.7	23 29.2	20 14.2	24 32.8	7 10.3
23 Tu	16 11 37	1 37 44	2♏52 56	9♏33 52	0 15.2	17 30.5	22 48.4	23 12.9	22 13.8	4 21.2	23 34.4	20 16.0	24 31.2	7 10.3
24 W	16 15 33	2 38 24	16 20 05	23 11 23	0R 15.3	18 58.3	24 03.9	23 51.1	22 12.2	4 20.5	23 39.7	20 17.7	24 29.5	7 10.4
25 Th	16 19 30	3 39 05	0♐07 30	7♐08 02	0 15.3	20 25.5	25 19.3	24 29.3	22 10.1	4 19.6	23 45.0	20 19.4	24 27.8	7 10.5
26 F	16 23 26	4 39 48	14 12 30	21 20 21	0 15.1	21 52.2	26 34.7	25 07.5	22 07.6	4 18.5	23 50.4	20 21.1	24 26.2	7 10.7
27 Sa	16 27 23	5 40 33	28 30 56	5♑43 36	0 14.6	23 18.1	27 50.2	25 45.7	22 04.6	4 17.2	23 55.9	20 22.7	24 24.5	7 10.9
28 Su	16 31 19	6 41 18	12♑57 39	20 12 23	0 13.9	24 43.3	29 05.6	26 23.9	22 01.3	4 15.7	24 01.5	20 24.2	24 22.8	7 11.1
29 M	16 35 16	7 42 04	27 27 08	4♒41 17	0 13.1	26 07.6	0♐21.1	27 02.1	21 57.5	4 14.0	24 07.1	20 25.7	24 21.2	7 11.3
30 Tu	16 39 12	8 42 52	11♒54 15	19 05 31	0 12.4	27 30.9	1 36.5	27 40.3	21 53.3	4 12.1	24 12.7	20 27.1	24 19.6	7 11.5

December 2049 — LONGITUDE

Day	Sid.Time	☉	0 hr ☽	Noon ☽	True ☊	☿	♀	♂	⚳	♃	♄	♅	♆	♇
1 W	16 43 09	9♐43 40	26♒14 40	3♓21 21	0♐12.0	28♐53.1	2♐52.0	28♎18.5	21♋48.7	4♌10.0	24♑18.4	20♍28.5	24♉17.9	7♓11.8
2 Th	16 47 06	10 44 29	10♓25 16	17 26 14	0D 12.0	0♑13.8	4 07.5	28 56.7	21R 43.7	4R 07.8	24 24.2	20 29.8	24R 16.3	7 12.1
3 F	16 51 02	11 45 19	24 24 04	1♈18 41	0 12.5	1 33.1	5 22.9	29 34.8	21 38.2	4 05.3	24 30.0	20 31.1	24 14.7	7 12.4
4 Sa	16 54 59	12 46 10	8♈10 02	14 58 04	0 13.5	2 50.6	6 38.4	0♏13.0	21 32.4	4 02.6	24 35.9	20 32.3	24 13.1	7 12.8
5 Su	16 58 55	13 47 01	21 42 49	28 24 17	0 14.6	4 06.0	7 53.9	0 51.2	21 26.1	3 59.7	24 41.8	20 33.5	24 11.6	7 13.2
6 M	17 02 52	14 47 54	5♉02 29	11♉37 27	0 15.7	5 19.0	9 09.4	1 29.4	21 19.5	3 56.7	24 47.8	20 34.6	24 10.0	7 13.6
7 Tu	17 06 48	15 48 47	18 09 12	24 37 46	0R 16.4	6 29.3	10 24.8	2 07.6	21 12.4	3 53.5	24 53.8	20 35.6	24 08.4	7 14.0
8 W	17 10 45	16 49 41	1♊03 12	7♊25 31	0 16.3	7 36.4	11 40.3	2 45.8	21 05.0	3 50.0	24 59.9	20 36.6	24 06.9	7 14.4
9 Th	17 14 41	17 50 37	13 44 46	20 01 01	0 15.4	8 39.8	12 55.8	3 23.9	20 57.1	3 46.4	25 06.1	20 37.6	24 05.4	7 14.9
10 F	17 18 38	18 51 33	26 14 21	2♋24 51	0 13.4	9 39.0	14 11.3	4 02.1	20 48.9	3 42.6	25 12.2	20 38.5	24 03.9	7 15.4
11 Sa	17 22 35	19 52 30	8♋32 41	14 37 59	0 10.5	10 33.5	15 26.8	4 40.3	20 40.3	3 38.6	25 18.5	20 39.3	24 02.4	7 16.0
12 Su	17 26 31	20 53 28	20 40 57	26 41 52	0 07.1	11 22.4	16 42.3	5 18.5	20 31.4	3 34.5	25 24.7	20 40.1	24 00.9	7 16.5
13 M	17 30 28	21 54 27	2♌40 58	8♌38 37	0 03.4	12 05.0	17 57.8	5 56.7	20 22.0	3 30.2	25 31.0	20 40.8	23 59.4	7 17.1
14 Tu	17 34 24	22 55 27	14 35 09	20 31 01	29♏59.9	12 40.6	19 13.3	6 34.9	20 12.3	3 25.6	25 37.4	20 41.5	23 58.0	7 17.7
15 W	17 38 21	23 56 28	26 26 39	2♍22 33	29 57.2	13 08.2	20 28.8	7 13.1	20 02.3	3 21.0	25 43.8	20 42.1	23 56.6	7 18.3
16 Th	17 42 17	24 57 30	8♍19 14	14 17 16	29D 55.4	13 27.0	21 44.3	7 51.3	19 51.9	3 16.1	25 50.2	20 42.6	23 55.2	7 19.0
17 F	17 46 14	25 58 33	20 17 13	26 19 40	29 54.9	13R 36.1	22 59.8	8 29.5	19 41.2	3 11.1	25 56.7	20 43.1	23 53.8	7 19.6
18 Sa	17 50 11	26 59 37	2♎25 14	8♎34 31	29 55.4	13 34.8	24 15.3	9 07.7	19 30.2	3 05.9	26 03.2	20 43.6	23 52.4	7 20.3
19 Su	17 54 07	28 00 41	14 48 05	21 06 31	29 56.8	13 22.2	25 30.9	9 45.8	19 18.9	3 00.5	26 09.8	20 44.0	23 51.1	7 21.0
20 M	17 58 04	29 01 47	27 30 19	3♏59 56	29 58.6	12 58.1	26 46.4	10 24.0	19 07.3	2 55.0	26 16.4	20 44.3	23 49.7	7 21.8
21 Tu	18 02 00	0♑02 53	10♏35 45	17 18 02	0♐00.0	12 22.2	28 01.9	11 02.2	18 55.4	2 49.3	26 23.0	20 44.6	23 48.4	7 22.6
22 W	18 05 57	1 04 00	24 06 56	1♐02 28	0R 00.6	11 35.0	29 17.4	11 40.4	18 43.2	2 43.5	26 29.7	20 44.8	23 47.1	7 23.4
23 Th	18 09 53	2 05 09	8♐04 29	15 12 40	29♏59.7	10 37.1	0♑33.0	12 18.6	18 30.8	2 37.6	26 36.4	20 44.9	23 45.9	7 24.2
24 F	18 13 50	3 06 17	22 26 32	29 45 24	29 57.1	9 29.9	1 48.5	12 56.8	18 18.1	2 31.5	26 43.1	20 45.0	23 44.7	7 25.0
25 Sa	18 17 46	4 07 26	7♑08 26	14♑34 41	29 53.0	8 15.4	3 04.0	13 34.9	18 05.2	2 25.2	26 49.9	20R 45.1	23 43.5	7 25.9
26 Su	18 21 43	5 08 35	22 03 04	29 32 27	29 47.7	6 55.7	4 19.6	14 13.1	17 52.1	2 18.8	26 56.7	20 45.1	23 42.3	7 26.8
27 M	18 25 40	6 09 44	7♒01 40	14♒29 38	29 42.1	5 33.7	5 35.1	14 51.3	17 38.8	2 12.3	27 03.5	20 45.0	23 41.1	7 27.7
28 Tu	18 29 36	7 10 54	21 55 18	29 17 45	29 36.9	4 11.9	6 50.6	15 29.4	17 25.4	2 05.7	27 10.3	20 44.9	23 40.0	7 28.6
29 W	18 33 33	8 12 03	6♓36 14	13♓50 07	29 32.9	2 53.1	8 06.1	16 07.6	17 11.7	1 58.9	27 17.2	20 44.7	23 38.9	7 29.5
30 Th	18 37 29	9 13 12	20 58 58	28 02 31	29D 30.6	1 39.6	9 21.6	16 45.7	16 58.0	1 52.0	27 24.1	20 44.4	23 37.8	7 30.5
31 F	18 41 26	10 14 21	5♈00 38	11♈53 21	29 30.0	0 33.4	10 37.2	17 23.8	16 44.1	1 45.0	27 31.0	20 44.1	23 36.7	7 31.5

Astro Data Dy Hr Mn	Planet Ingress Dy Hr Mn	Last Aspect Dy Hr Mn	☽ Ingress Dy Hr Mn	Last Aspect Dy Hr Mn	☽ Ingress Dy Hr Mn	☽ Phases & Eclipses Dy Hr Mn	Astro Data
☽0N 5 8:04	♀ ♏ 5 7:48	1 14:19 ♀ □	♒ 1 22:14	1 3:39 ☿ ⚹	♓ 1 6:20	2 16:19 ☽ 10♒41	1 November 2049
♄∠♇ 5 21:35	☿ ♐ 11 20:25	3 21:59 ♀ △	♓ 4 0:58	3 0:05 ♄ ⚹	♈ 3 9:43	9 15:38 ○ 17♉41	Julian Day # 54727
☽0S 19 11:39	☉ ♐ 21 21:19	5 19:26 ♆ ⚹	♈ 6 3:57	5 5:17 ♄ □	♉ 5 14:53	9 15:51 ☍ A 0.681	SVP 4♓33'35"
⚳ R 20 0:55	♀ ♐ 29 5:18	7 18:35 ♄ □	♉ 8 8:02	7 12:30 ♄ △	♊ 7 22:02	17 14:32 ☾ 25♌41	GC 27♐32.1 ⚴ 2♈19.7R
♇ D 20 9:39		10 10:08 ☿ ☍	♊ 10 14:11	9 13:10 ♅ □	♋ 10 7:18	25 5:35 ● 3♐23	Eris 0♉42.6R ✱ 21♌20.5
♃ R 20 12:40	☿ ♑ 2 7:51	12 3:35 ♅ □	♋ 12 23:07	12 9:24 ♄ ☍	♌ 12 18:37	25 5:32:16 ☌ AT00'38"	⚷ 28♏59.8 ⚵ 1♍22.8
	♂ ♏ 4 3:49	15 0:07 ♆ ⚹	♌ 15 10:39	14 18:58 ♆ □	♍ 15 7:12		☽ Mean ☊ 1♐10.9
♄△♆ 1 10:27	☊ ♏R 14 11:34	17 14:32 ☉ □	♍ 17 23:14	17 11:14 ☉ □	♎ 17 19:15	1 23:39 ☽ 10♓13	
☽0N 2 13:30	☉ ♑ 21 10:52	20 7:26 ☉ ⚹	♎ 20 10:31	20 2:03 ☉ ⚹	♏ 20 4:38	9 7:28 ○ 17♊39	1 December 2049
☽0S 16 20:18	☊ ♐ 21 11:22	22 6:49 ♄ □	♏ 22 18:46	22 4:05 ♄ ⚹	♐ 22 10:12	17 11:14 ☾ 25♍57	Julian Day # 54757
☿ R 17 21:00	♀ ♑ 23 1:31	24 14:15 ♆ ☍	♐ 24 23:47	23 21:12 ♅ □	♑ 24 12:24	24 17:51 ● 3♑21	SVP 4♓33'31"
♅ R 25 18:12	☊ ♏R 23 7:02	26 10:38 ♂ ⚹	♑ 27 2:28	26 7:49 ♄ ☌	♒ 26 12:44	31 8:53 ☽ 10♈06	GC 27♐32.2 ⚴ 29♓47.7
☽0N 29 19:59		29 4:07 ♀ ⚹	♒ 29 4:13	28 2:51 ♆ □	♓ 28 13:09		Eris 0♉26.2R ✱ 29♌59.8
				30 10:54 ♄ ⚹	♈ 30 15:21		⚷ 2♐50.7 ⚵ 10♍45.2
							☽ Mean ☊ 29♏35.6

LONGITUDE — January 2050

Day	Sid.Time	☉	0 hr ☽	Noon ☽	True ☊	☿	♀	♂	⚳	♃	♄	♅	♆	♇
1 Sa	18 45 22	11♑15 30	18♈40 46	25♈23 05	29♏30.8	29♐36.0	11♑52.7	18♏02.0	16♋30.1	1♌37.9	27♑37.9	20♍43.8	23♉35.7	7♓32.5
2 Su	18 49 19	12 16 38	2♉00 34	8♉33 34	29 32.3	28R 48.4	13 08.2	18 40.1	16R 16.0	1R 30.7	27 44.9	20R 43.4	23R 34.7	7 33.5
3 M	18 53 15	13 17 47	15 02 22	21 27 21	29R 33.5	28 11.0	14 23.6	19 18.2	16 01.9	1 23.4	27 51.9	20 42.9	23 33.7	7 34.6
4 Tu	18 57 12	14 18 55	27 48 49	4♊07 06	29 33.7	27 43.9	15 39.1	19 56.3	15 47.7	1 16.1	27 58.9	20 42.4	23 32.8	7 35.7
5 W	19 01 09	15 20 03	10♊22 31	16 35 18	29 32.1	27 26.9	16 54.6	20 34.4	15 33.5	1 08.6	28 05.9	20 41.8	23 31.8	7 36.8
6 Th	19 05 05	16 21 11	22 45 43	28 53 57	29 28.2	27D 19.7	18 10.1	21 12.5	15 19.2	1 01.1	28 12.9	20 41.2	23 31.0	7 37.9
7 F	19 09 02	17 22 19	5♋00 13	11♋04 40	29 21.9	27 21.6	19 25.6	21 50.6	15 05.0	0 53.4	28 20.0	20 40.5	23 30.1	7 39.0
8 Sa	19 12 58	18 23 27	17 07 27	23 08 43	29 13.5	27 31.9	20 41.0	22 28.7	14 50.8	0 45.7	28 27.0	20 39.8	23 29.3	7 40.2
9 Su	19 16 55	19 24 34	29 08 37	5♌07 19	29 03.6	27 50.0	21 56.5	23 06.8	14 36.6	0 38.0	28 34.1	20 39.0	23 28.5	7 41.3
10 M	19 20 51	20 25 41	11♌04 57	17 01 44	28 53.1	28 15.2	23 11.9	23 44.8	14 22.5	0 30.2	28 41.2	20 38.1	23 27.7	7 42.5
11 Tu	19 24 48	21 26 49	22 57 52	28 53 38	28 42.8	28 46.9	24 27.4	24 22.9	14 08.4	0 22.3	28 48.3	20 37.2	23 27.0	7 43.7
12 W	19 28 44	22 27 55	4♍49 20	10♍45 16	28 33.8	29 24.3	25 42.8	25 01.0	13 54.4	0 14.4	28 55.4	20 36.3	23 26.3	7 45.0
13 Th	19 32 41	23 29 02	16 41 51	22 39 31	28 26.8	0♑06.9	26 58.3	25 39.0	13 40.6	0 06.5	29 02.5	20 35.3	23 25.6	7 46.2
14 F	19 36 38	24 30 09	28 38 43	4♎39 58	28 22.1	0 54.1	28 13.7	26 17.1	13 26.9	29♋58.5	29 09.6	20 34.2	23 24.9	7 47.5
15 Sa	19 40 34	25 31 15	10♎43 51	16 50 54	28D 19.8	1 45.6	29 29.1	26 55.2	13 13.3	29 50.5	29 16.8	20 33.1	23 24.3	7 48.7
16 Su	19 44 31	26 32 22	23 01 46	29 17 02	28 19.4	2 40.8	0♒44.6	27 33.2	12 59.9	29 42.4	29 23.9	20 32.0	23 23.7	7 50.0
17 M	19 48 27	27 33 28	5♏37 19	12♏03 13	28 20.0	3 39.4	2 00.0	28 11.2	12 46.6	29 34.4	29 31.0	20 30.8	23 23.2	7 51.3
18 Tu	19 52 24	28 34 34	18 35 17	25 13 59	28R 20.7	4 41.1	3 15.4	28 49.3	12 33.6	29 26.3	29 38.2	20 29.5	23 22.7	7 52.6
19 W	19 56 20	29 35 40	1♐59 44	8♐52 48	28 20.2	5 45.4	4 30.8	29 27.3	12 20.8	29 18.2	29 45.4	20 28.2	23 22.2	7 54.0
20 Th	20 00 17	0♒36 46	15 53 18	23 01 09	28 17.7	6 52.3	5 46.2	0♐05.3	12 08.2	29 10.1	29 52.5	20 26.9	23 21.8	7 55.3
21 F	20 04 13	1 37 51	0♑16 06	7♑37 38	28 12.6	8 01.4	7 01.7	0 43.3	11 55.8	29 02.1	29 59.6	20 25.5	23 21.3	7 56.7
22 Sa	20 08 10	2 38 55	15 05 02	22 37 20	28 05.0	9 12.5	8 17.1	1 21.2	11 43.7	28 54.0	0♒06.8	20 24.0	23 21.0	7 58.1
23 Su	20 12 07	3 39 59	0♒13 22	7♒51 48	27 55.3	10 25.4	9 32.4	1 59.2	11 31.9	28 46.0	0 13.9	20 22.5	23 20.6	7 59.5
24 M	20 16 03	4 41 02	15 31 12	23 10 06	27 44.9	11 40.1	10 47.8	2 37.2	11 20.3	28 38.0	0 21.1	20 21.0	23 20.3	8 00.9
25 Tu	20 20 00	5 42 05	0♓47 03	8♓20 45	27 34.8	12 56.3	12 03.2	3 15.1	11 09.1	28 30.0	0 28.2	20 19.4	23 20.0	8 02.3
26 W	20 23 56	6 43 06	15 50 00	23 13 50	27 26.4	14 13.9	13 18.5	3 53.0	10 58.2	28 22.1	0 35.3	20 17.8	23 19.8	8 03.8
27 Th	20 27 53	7 44 06	0♈31 30	7♈42 29	27 20.5	15 32.9	14 33.9	4 30.9	10 47.6	28 14.2	0 42.4	20 16.1	23 19.6	8 05.2
28 F	20 31 49	8 45 05	14 46 30	21 43 29	27 17.2	16 53.1	15 49.2	5 08.8	10 37.3	28 06.4	0 49.5	20 14.4	23 19.4	8 06.7
29 Sa	20 35 46	9 46 03	28 33 32	5♉16 52	27D 16.0	18 14.5	17 04.5	5 46.7	10 27.4	27 58.6	0 56.6	20 12.6	23 19.2	8 08.2
30 Su	20 39 42	10 46 59	11♉53 53	18 25 00	27R 16.0	19 36.9	18 19.8	6 24.5	10 17.8	27 50.9	1 03.7	20 10.8	23 19.1	8 09.7
31 M	20 43 39	11 47 55	24 50 44	1♊11 37	27 16.1	21 00.5	19 35.1	7 02.4	10 08.7	27 43.3	1 10.8	20 09.0	23 19.1	8 11.2

LONGITUDE — February 2050

Day	Sid.Time	☉	0 hr ☽	Noon ☽	True ☊	☿	♀	♂	⚳	♃	♄	♅	♆	♇
1 Tu	20 47 36	12♒48 49	7♊28 10	13♊40 57	27♏15.0	22♑25.0	20♒50.4	7♐40.2	9♋59.8	27♋35.7	1♒17.8	20♍07.1	23♉19.0	8♓12.7
2 W	20 51 32	13 49 42	19 50 28	25 57 10	27R 11.7	23 50.5	22 05.6	8 18.0	9R 51.4	27R 28.2	1 24.9	20R 05.2	23D 19.0	8 14.2
3 Th	20 55 29	14 50 33	2♋01 32	8♋03 57	27 05.5	25 16.9	23 20.9	8 55.8	9 43.4	27 20.8	1 31.9	20 03.2	23 19.1	8 15.7
4 F	20 59 25	15 51 24	14 04 45	20 04 16	26 56.2	26 44.2	24 36.1	9 33.6	9 35.7	27 13.5	1 38.9	20 01.3	23 19.1	8 17.2
5 Sa	21 03 22	16 52 13	26 02 46	2♌00 28	26 44.2	28 12.3	25 51.3	10 11.3	9 28.5	27 06.3	1 45.9	19 59.2	23 19.2	8 18.8
6 Su	21 07 18	17 53 01	7♌57 34	13 54 16	26 30.2	29 41.4	27 06.5	10 49.1	9 21.6	26 59.2	1 52.9	19 57.2	23 19.4	8 20.4
7 M	21 11 15	18 53 47	19 50 42	25 47 01	26 15.2	1♒11.2	28 21.7	11 26.8	9 15.2	26 52.2	1 59.8	19 55.1	23 19.5	8 21.9
8 Tu	21 15 11	19 54 33	1♍43 23	7♍39 57	26 00.5	2 42.0	29 36.8	12 04.5	9 09.2	26 45.3	2 06.8	19 52.9	23 19.7	8 23.5
9 W	21 19 08	20 55 17	13 36 54	19 34 26	25 47.3	4 13.5	0♓52.0	12 42.2	9 03.6	26 38.5	2 13.7	19 50.8	23 20.0	8 25.1
10 Th	21 23 05	21 56 00	25 32 47	1♎32 14	25 36.5	5 45.9	2 07.1	13 19.9	8 58.4	26 31.8	2 20.6	19 48.6	23 20.2	8 26.6
11 F	21 27 01	22 56 42	7♎33 07	13 35 47	25 28.6	7 19.1	3 22.2	13 57.6	8 53.7	26 25.3	2 27.4	19 46.4	23 20.5	8 28.2
12 Sa	21 30 58	23 57 22	19 40 39	25 48 10	25 23.8	8 53.1	4 37.3	14 35.2	8 49.3	26 18.9	2 34.2	19 44.1	23 20.9	8 29.8
13 Su	21 34 54	24 58 02	1♏58 50	8♏13 11	25 21.5	10 28.0	5 52.4	15 12.8	8 45.4	26 12.6	2 41.1	19 41.8	23 21.3	8 31.4
14 M	21 38 51	25 58 41	14 31 46	20 55 09	25 20.9	12 03.7	7 07.5	15 50.4	8 41.9	26 06.4	2 47.8	19 39.5	23 21.7	8 33.1
15 Tu	21 42 47	26 59 18	27 23 54	3♐58 32	25 20.9	13 40.2	8 22.5	16 28.0	8 38.9	26 00.4	2 54.6	19 37.2	23 22.1	8 34.7
16 W	21 46 44	27 59 54	10♐39 33	17 27 21	25 20.0	15 17.7	9 37.5	17 05.6	8 36.3	25 54.6	3 01.3	19 34.8	23 22.6	8 36.3
17 Th	21 50 40	29 00 30	24 22 14	1♑24 22	25 17.2	16 56.0	10 52.6	17 43.1	8 34.1	25 48.8	3 08.0	19 32.5	23 23.1	8 37.9
18 F	21 54 37	0♓01 04	8♑33 42	15 50 03	25 11.8	18 35.1	12 07.6	18 20.7	8 32.4	25 43.3	3 14.7	19 30.0	23 23.7	8 39.6
19 Sa	21 58 34	1 01 36	23 12 55	0♒41 38	25 03.6	20 15.2	13 22.5	18 58.1	8 31.1	25 37.9	3 21.3	19 27.6	23 24.3	8 41.2
20 Su	22 02 30	2 02 08	8♒15 15	15 52 37	24 53.2	21 56.2	14 37.5	19 35.6	8 30.2	25 32.6	3 27.9	19 25.2	23 24.9	8 42.8
21 M	22 06 27	3 02 37	23 32 23	1♓13 07	24 41.7	23 38.1	15 52.4	20 13.0	8D 29.8	25 27.5	3 34.4	19 22.7	23 25.5	8 44.5
22 Tu	22 10 23	4 03 05	8♓53 17	16 31 23	24 30.5	25 21.0	17 07.4	20 50.4	8 29.8	25 22.6	3 40.9	19 20.2	23 26.2	8 46.1
23 W	22 14 20	5 03 32	24 06 01	1♈35 58	24 20.8	27 04.8	18 22.3	21 27.8	8 30.2	25 17.8	3 47.4	19 17.7	23 26.9	8 47.8
24 Th	22 18 16	6 03 56	9♈00 10	16 17 49	24 13.7	28 49.6	19 37.1	22 05.1	8 31.1	25 13.2	3 53.8	19 15.2	23 27.7	8 49.4
25 F	22 22 13	7 04 19	23 28 22	0♉31 28	24 09.3	0♓35.4	20 52.0	22 42.4	8 32.4	25 08.8	4 00.2	19 12.6	23 28.5	8 51.1
26 Sa	22 26 09	8 04 40	7♉27 02	14 15 10	24D 07.4	2 22.1	22 06.8	23 19.7	8 34.1	25 04.5	4 06.6	19 10.1	23 29.3	8 52.7
27 Su	22 30 06	9 04 59	20 56 06	27 30 15	24R 07.2	4 09.8	23 21.6	23 56.9	8 36.2	25 00.5	4 12.9	19 07.5	23 30.1	8 54.4
28 M	22 34 03	10 05 16	3♊58 04	10♊20 07	24 07.3	5 58.6	24 36.4	24 34.2	8 38.8	24 56.6	4 19.2	19 05.0	23 31.0	8 56.0

Astro Data (Dy Hr Mn)

- ☿ D 6 18:52
- ☽ 0S 13 4:24
- ♃☍♄ 17 17:13
- ☽ 0N 26 5:16
- ♆ D 2 1:13
- ☽ 0S 9 11:32
- ⚳ D 21 23:39
- ☽ 0N 22 16:36
- ♄⚼♅ 26 21:29

Planet Ingress (Dy Hr Mn)

- ☿ ♐R 1 1:30
- ☿ ♑ 13 8:19
- ♃ ♋R 14 7:24
- ♀ ♒ 15 21:49
- ☉ ♒ 19 21:34
- ♂ ♐ 20 8:40
- ♄ ♒ 21 13:15
- ☿ ♒ 6 17:00
- ♀ ♓ 8 19:24
- ☉ ♓ 18 11:35
- ☿ ♓ 25 4:00

Last Aspect / ☽ Ingress (Dy Hr Mn)

Last Aspect	☽ Ingress
1 19:10 ☿ △	♉ 1 20:21
4 0:13 ♄ △	♊ 4 4:09
6 8:56 ☿ ☍	♋ 6 14:10
8 22:43 ♄ ☍	♌ 9 1:43
11 11:46 ☿ △	♍ 11 14:14
14 0:55 ♄ △	♎ 14 2:42
16 12:48 ♃ □	♏ 16 13:22
18 19:54 ♄ ⚹	♐ 18 20:29
20 7:42 ♅ □	♑ 20 23:34
22 21:50 ♃ ☍	♒ 22 23:39
24 12:16 ♆ □	♓ 24 22:46
26 20:22 ♃ △	♈ 26 23:08
28 23:06 ♃ □	♉ 29 2:33
31 5:29 ♃ ⚹	♊ 31 9:44

Last Aspect / ☽ Ingress (Dy Hr Mn)

Last Aspect	☽ Ingress
2 3:33 ♀ △	♋ 2 19:59
5 3:16 ☿ ☍	♌ 5 7:57
7 17:49 ♀ ☍	♍ 7 20:31
10 2:04 ♃ ⚹	♎ 10 8:55
12 12:59 ♃ □	♏ 12 20:10
14 22:10 ☉ □	♐ 15 4:46
17 7:37 ☉ ⚹	♑ 17 9:37
19 3:56 ♃ ☍	♒ 19 10:54
20 23:49 ♆ □	♓ 21 10:06
23 1:57 ♃ △	♈ 23 9:26
25 2:53 ♃ □	♉ 25 11:06
27 7:26 ♃ ⚹	♊ 27 16:37

☽ Phases & Eclipses (Dy Hr Mn)

- 8 1:39 ○ 17♋57
- 16 6:17 ☾ 26♎18
- 23 4:57 ● 3♒22
- 29 20:48 ☽ 10♉08
- 6 20:47 ○ 18♌15
- 14 22:10 ☾ 26♏24
- 21 15:03 ● 3♓10
- 28 11:29 ☽ 10♊04

Astro Data

1 January 2050
Julian Day # 54788
SVP 4♓33'26"
GC 27♐32.3 ⚴ 3♈49.5
Eris 0♉15.9R ⚵ 2♍43.4R
⚷ 6♐38.6 ⚶ 16♍34.8
☽ Mean ☊ 27♏57.2

1 February 2050
Julian Day # 54819
SVP 4♓33'21"
GC 27♐32.3 ⚴ 12♈47.7
Eris 0♉15.8 ⚵ 27♌52.9R
⚷ 9♐41.5 ⚶ 16♍02.5R
☽ Mean ☊ 26♏18.7

March 2050 LONGITUDE

Day	Sid.Time	☉	0 hr ☽	Noon ☽	True ☊	☿	♀	♂	⚳	♃	♄	♅	♆	♇
1 Tu	22 37 59	11♓05 30	16♊36 59	22♊49 19	24♏06.7	7♓48.3	25♓51.1	25♐11.3	8♋41.7	24♋52.9	4♒25.4	19♍02.4	23♉31.9	8♓57.7
2 W	22 41 56	12 05 43	28 57 41	5♋02 43	24R 04.3	9 39.0	27 05.9	25 48.5	8 45.1	24R 49.4	4 31.6	18R 59.8	23 32.9	8 59.3
3 Th	22 45 52	13 05 54	11♋05 00	17 05 04	23 59.4	11 30.7	28 20.6	26 25.6	8 48.9	24 46.0	4 37.7	18 57.2	23 33.9	9 00.9
4 F	22 49 49	14 06 03	23 03 26	29 00 33	23 51.7	13 23.3	29 35.2	27 02.6	8 53.0	24 42.9	4 43.8	18 54.6	23 34.9	9 02.6
5 Sa	22 53 45	15 06 10	4♌56 50	10♌52 40	23 41.5	15 16.9	0♈49.8	27 39.7	8 57.6	24 39.9	4 49.8	18 52.0	23 35.9	9 04.2
6 Su	22 57 42	16 06 14	16 48 23	22 44 14	23 29.4	17 11.3	2 04.4	28 16.7	9 02.6	24 37.2	4 55.8	18 49.4	23 37.0	9 05.9
7 M	23 01 38	17 06 17	28 40 28	4♍37 19	23 16.4	19 06.6	3 19.0	28 53.7	9 07.9	24 34.6	5 01.7	18 46.7	23 38.1	9 07.5
8 Tu	23 05 35	18 06 18	10♍34 56	16 33 30	23 03.6	21 02.6	4 33.6	29 30.6	9 13.7	24 32.2	5 07.6	18 44.1	23 39.2	9 09.1
9 W	23 09 32	19 06 17	22 33 09	28 34 02	22 52.0	22 59.3	5 48.1	0♑07.5	9 19.8	24 30.0	5 13.4	18 41.5	23 40.4	9 10.8
10 Th	23 13 28	20 06 14	4♎36 19	10♎40 08	22 42.6	24 56.5	7 02.5	0 44.3	9 26.2	24 28.0	5 19.2	18 38.9	23 41.6	9 12.4
11 F	23 17 25	21 06 09	16 45 42	22 53 13	22 35.8	26 54.1	8 17.0	1 21.2	9 33.1	24 26.1	5 24.9	18 36.2	23 42.8	9 14.0
12 Sa	23 21 21	22 06 03	29 02 55	5♏15 06	22 31.8	28 51.9	9 31.4	1 57.9	9 40.3	24 24.5	5 30.5	18 33.6	23 44.0	9 15.6
13 Su	23 25 18	23 05 54	11♏30 03	17 48 08	22D 30.3	0♈49.8	10 45.8	2 34.7	9 47.9	24 23.1	5 36.1	18 31.0	23 45.3	9 17.2
14 M	23 29 14	24 05 45	24 09 44	0♐35 13	22 30.4	2 47.5	12 00.2	3 11.4	9 55.8	24 21.8	5 41.7	18 28.4	23 46.6	9 18.8
15 Tu	23 33 11	25 05 33	7♐05 01	13 39 32	22R 31.2	4 44.6	13 14.5	3 48.0	10 04.1	24 20.8	5 47.2	18 25.8	23 47.9	9 20.4
16 W	23 37 07	26 05 20	20 19 10	27 04 14	22 31.7	6 41.0	14 28.8	4 24.7	10 12.7	24 19.9	5 52.6	18 23.2	23 49.3	9 22.0
17 Th	23 41 04	27 05 05	3♑55 03	10♑51 47	22 30.8	8 36.3	15 43.1	5 01.2	10 21.7	24 19.3	5 57.9	18 20.6	23 50.7	9 23.6
18 F	23 45 00	28 04 49	17 54 31	25 03 11	22 27.8	10 30.1	16 57.4	5 37.7	10 31.0	24 18.8	6 03.3	18 18.0	23 52.1	9 25.2
19 Sa	23 48 57	29 04 30	2♒17 33	9♒37 10	22 22.7	12 22.0	18 11.6	6 14.2	10 40.6	24D 18.6	6 08.5	18 15.5	23 53.6	9 26.8
20 Su	23 52 54	0♈04 10	17 01 27	24 29 35	22 15.8	14 11.5	19 25.8	6 50.6	10 50.6	24 18.5	6 13.7	18 12.9	23 55.0	9 28.3
21 M	23 56 50	1 03 48	2♓00 35	9♓33 19	22 07.9	15 58.3	20 39.9	7 27.0	11 00.9	24 18.6	6 18.8	18 10.4	23 56.5	9 29.9
22 Tu	0 00 47	2 03 25	17 06 34	24 39 04	21 59.9	17 41.9	21 54.1	8 03.3	11 11.5	24 18.9	6 23.8	18 07.8	23 58.0	9 31.4
23 W	0 04 43	3 02 59	2♈09 33	9♈36 50	21 53.1	19 21.8	23 08.1	8 39.5	11 22.4	24 19.4	6 28.8	18 05.3	23 59.6	9 33.0
24 Th	0 08 40	4 02 31	16 59 49	24 17 35	21 48.1	20 57.6	24 22.2	9 15.7	11 33.7	24 20.1	6 33.7	18 02.8	24 01.2	9 34.5
25 F	0 12 36	5 02 01	1♉29 24	8♉34 45	21D 45.3	22 28.8	25 36.2	9 51.8	11 45.2	24 21.0	6 38.5	18 00.3	24 02.8	9 36.0
26 Sa	0 16 33	6 01 29	15 33 16	22 24 48	21 44.5	23 55.0	26 50.2	10 27.8	11 57.1	24 22.1	6 43.3	17 57.9	24 04.4	9 37.5
27 Su	0 20 29	7 00 55	29 09 24	5♊47 14	21 45.2	25 15.9	28 04.2	11 03.8	12 09.2	24 23.4	6 48.0	17 55.4	24 06.0	9 39.0
28 M	0 24 26	8 00 18	12♊18 36	18 43 55	21 46.6	26 31.1	29 18.1	11 39.7	12 21.7	24 24.9	6 52.6	17 53.0	24 07.7	9 40.5
29 Tu	0 28 23	8 59 39	25 03 39	1♋18 22	21R 47.8	27 40.3	0♉31.9	12 15.6	12 34.4	24 26.5	6 57.1	17 50.6	24 09.4	9 42.0
30 W	0 32 19	9 58 58	7♋28 39	13 35 05	21 48.0	28 43.2	1 45.8	12 51.4	12 47.4	24 28.4	7 01.6	17 48.2	24 11.1	9 43.5
31 Th	0 36 16	10 58 15	19 38 18	25 38 53	21 46.7	29 39.6	2 59.6	13 27.1	13 00.7	24 30.4	7 06.0	17 45.9	24 12.8	9 44.9

April 2050 LONGITUDE

Day	Sid.Time	☉	0 hr ☽	Noon ☽	True ☊	☿	♀	♂	⚳	♃	♄	♅	♆	♇
1 F	0 40 12	11♈57 29	1♌37 26	7♌34 30	21♏43.6	0♉29.2	4♉13.3	14♑02.7	13♋14.2	24♋32.7	7♒10.3	17♍43.6	24♉14.6	9♓46.4
2 Sa	0 44 09	12 56 40	13 30 38	19 26 21	21R 38.8	1 11.9	5 27.0	14 38.3	13 28.0	24 35.1	7 14.6	17R 41.3	24 16.4	9 47.8
3 Su	0 48 05	13 55 50	25 22 04	1♍18 14	21 32.8	1 47.7	6 40.7	15 13.8	13 42.1	24 37.6	7 18.7	17 39.0	24 18.2	9 49.2
4 M	0 52 02	14 54 57	7♍15 14	13 13 22	21 26.1	2 16.3	7 54.3	15 49.2	13 56.5	24 40.4	7 22.8	17 36.7	24 20.0	9 50.6
5 Tu	0 55 58	15 54 02	19 12 58	25 14 15	21 19.4	2 37.9	9 07.9	16 24.6	14 11.0	24 43.4	7 26.8	17 34.5	24 21.8	9 52.0
6 W	0 59 55	16 53 05	1♎17 28	7♎22 46	21 13.3	2 52.4	10 21.4	16 59.9	14 25.9	24 46.5	7 30.8	17 32.3	24 23.7	9 53.4
7 Th	1 03 52	17 52 06	13 30 20	19 40 16	21 08.6	2R 59.9	11 34.9	17 35.1	14 41.0	24 49.8	7 34.6	17 30.2	24 25.5	9 54.7
8 F	1 07 48	18 51 05	25 52 44	2♏07 48	21 05.4	3 00.6	12 48.4	18 10.2	14 56.3	24 53.3	7 38.4	17 28.0	24 27.4	9 56.1
9 Sa	1 11 45	19 50 02	8♏25 36	14 46 14	21D 03.9	2 54.7	14 01.8	18 45.2	15 11.8	24 56.9	7 42.1	17 25.9	24 29.4	9 57.4
10 Su	1 15 41	20 48 58	21 09 49	27 36 28	21 03.9	2 42.5	15 15.1	19 20.2	15 27.6	25 00.7	7 45.7	17 23.9	24 31.3	9 58.7
11 M	1 19 38	21 47 51	4♐06 19	10♐39 31	21 04.9	2 24.4	16 28.5	19 55.1	15 43.6	25 04.7	7 49.2	17 21.9	24 33.2	10 00.0
12 Tu	1 23 34	22 46 43	17 16 13	23 56 33	21 06.5	2 00.8	17 41.8	20 29.9	15 59.9	25 08.9	7 52.7	17 19.9	24 35.2	10 01.3
13 W	1 27 31	23 45 32	0♑40 40	7♑28 40	21 08.0	1 32.3	18 55.0	21 04.6	16 16.3	25 13.3	7 56.0	17 17.9	24 37.2	10 02.6
14 Th	1 31 27	24 44 21	14 20 41	21 16 43	21R 08.7	0 59.4	20 08.2	21 39.2	16 33.0	25 17.8	7 59.3	17 16.0	24 39.2	10 03.9
15 F	1 35 24	25 43 07	28 16 46	5♒20 44	21 08.5	0 23.0	21 21.4	22 13.7	16 49.9	25 22.4	8 02.5	17 14.1	24 41.2	10 05.1
16 Sa	1 39 21	26 41 52	12♒28 26	19 39 35	21 07.1	29♈43.7	22 34.5	22 48.1	17 07.0	25 27.3	8 05.6	17 12.3	24 43.2	10 06.3
17 Su	1 43 17	27 40 35	26 53 47	4♓10 30	21 04.7	29 02.2	23 47.6	23 22.4	17 24.3	25 32.3	8 08.6	17 10.5	24 45.3	10 07.5
18 M	1 47 14	28 39 16	11♓29 10	18 49 01	21 01.8	28 19.5	25 00.6	23 56.6	17 41.8	25 37.4	8 11.5	17 08.7	24 47.3	10 08.7
19 Tu	1 51 10	29 37 56	26 09 19	3♈29 11	20 58.8	27 36.4	26 13.6	24 30.6	17 59.5	25 42.7	8 14.3	17 07.0	24 49.4	10 09.9
20 W	1 55 07	0♉36 34	10♈47 46	18 04 13	20 56.2	26 53.5	27 26.5	25 04.6	18 17.4	25 48.2	8 17.1	17 05.3	24 51.5	10 11.0
21 Th	1 59 03	1 35 10	25 17 44	2♉27 31	20 54.5	26 11.7	28 39.4	25 38.4	18 35.5	25 53.8	8 19.7	17 03.6	24 53.6	10 12.2
22 F	2 03 00	2 33 44	9♉32 58	16 33 30	20D 53.7	25 31.8	29 52.3	26 12.1	18 53.8	25 59.6	8 22.3	17 02.0	24 55.7	10 13.3
23 Sa	2 06 56	3 32 16	23 28 43	0♊18 19	20 53.9	24 54.3	1♊05.1	26 45.7	19 12.3	26 05.6	8 24.7	17 00.5	24 57.8	10 14.4
24 Su	2 10 53	4 30 46	7♊02 09	13 40 11	20 54.7	24 19.8	2 17.9	27 19.2	19 31.0	26 11.7	8 27.1	16 58.9	24 59.9	10 15.5
25 M	2 14 49	5 29 15	20 12 30	26 39 18	20 56.0	23 48.9	3 30.6	27 52.5	19 49.8	26 17.9	8 29.4	16 57.5	25 02.1	10 16.5
26 Tu	2 18 46	6 27 41	3♋00 51	9♋17 33	20 57.2	23 21.9	4 43.2	28 25.7	20 08.8	26 24.3	8 31.6	16 56.1	25 04.2	10 17.6
27 W	2 22 43	7 26 05	15 29 49	21 38 08	20 58.2	22 59.1	5 55.9	28 58.7	20 28.0	26 30.8	8 33.7	16 54.7	25 06.4	10 18.6
28 Th	2 26 39	8 24 27	27 43 02	3♌45 04	20R 58.8	22 40.9	7 08.4	29 31.7	20 47.4	26 37.5	8 35.7	16 53.3	25 08.5	10 19.6
29 F	2 30 36	9 22 46	9♌44 48	15 42 50	20 58.7	22 27.4	8 20.9	0♒04.4	21 06.9	26 44.3	8 37.6	16 52.1	25 10.7	10 20.6
30 Sa	2 34 32	10 21 04	21 39 43	27 36 02	20 58.2	22 18.6	9 33.4	0 37.1	21 26.6	26 51.3	8 39.4	16 50.8	25 12.9	10 21.5

Astro Data	Planet Ingress	Last Aspect	☽ Ingress	Last Aspect	☽ Ingress	☽ Phases & Eclipses
Dy Hr Mn	Dy Hr Mn	Dy Hr Mn	Dy Hr Mn	Dy Hr Mn	Dy Hr Mn	Dy Hr Mn
♀0N 7 1:14	♀ ♈ 4 19:58	1 18:35 ♀ □	♋ 2 2:02	2 21:49 ♆ □	♍ 3 9:22	8 15:23 ○ 18♍15
☽0S 8 17:55	♂ ♑ 9 7:08	4 13:18 ♀ △	♌ 4 14:00	5 10:58 ♃ ⚹	♎ 5 21:27	16 10:08 ☾ 26♐01
☿0N 13 21:02	☿ ♈ 13 1:51	6 23:49 ♂ △	♍ 7 2:41	7 22:01 ♃ □	♏ 8 7:55	23 0:41 ● 2♈35
♃□♇ 15 15:23	☉ ♈ 20 10:19	9 3:55 ♃ ⚹	♎ 9 14:51	10 7:09 ♃ △	♐ 10 16:26	30 4:17 ☽ 9♋40
♃ D 20 9:07	♀ ♉ 29 1:37	11 15:01 ♃ □	♏ 12 1:51	12 9:45 ☉ △	♑ 12 22:48	
☉0N 20 10:19	☿ ♉ 31 21:30	14 0:24 ♃ △	♐ 14 10:55	14 18:56 ♃ ☍	♒ 15 2:56	7 8:12 ○ 17♎43
☽0N 22 3:43		16 10:08 ☉ □	♑ 16 17:09	17 3:55 ☿ ⚹	♓ 17 5:07	14 18:24 ☾ 25♑00
	☿ ♈R 16 2:13	18 17:24 ☉ ⚹	♒ 18 20:13	18 23:12 ♃ △	♈ 19 6:17	21 10:26 ● 1♉31
☽0S 5 0:19	☉ ♉ 19 21:02	20 11:04 ♆ □	♓ 20 20:48	21 1:59 ☿ ☌	♉ 21 7:52	28 22:08 ☽ 8♌49
☿ R 8 2:26	♀ ♊ 22 14:32	22 11:28 ♃ △	♈ 22 20:32	23 5:29 ♂ △	♊ 23 11:28	
♃□♇ 9 16:57	♂ ♒ 29 8:45	24 12:08 ♀ ☌	♉ 24 21:30	25 6:53 ☿ ⚹	♋ 25 18:18	
☽0N 18 12:44		26 15:28 ♃ ⚹	♊ 27 1:31	28 3:12 ♂ ☍	♌ 28 4:32	
		29 4:19 ☿ ⚹	♋ 29 9:29	30 7:10 ♆ □	♍ 30 16:51	
		31 20:41 ☿ □	♌ 31 20:44			

Astro Data

1 March 2050
Julian Day # 54847
SVP 4♓33'17"
GC 27♐32.4 ⚴ 23♈44.4
Eris 0♉24.5 ⚵ 21♌00.2R
⚷ 11♐21.5 ⚶ 9♍56.3R
☽ Mean ☊ 24♏49.7

1 April 2050
Julian Day # 54878
SVP 4♓33'15"
GC 27♐32.5 ⚴ 8♉02.9
Eris 0♉41.6 ⚵ 17♌57.0
⚷ 11♐41.2R ⚶ 3♍20.1R
☽ Mean ☊ 23♏11.2

LONGITUDE — May 2050

Day	Sid.Time	☉	0 hr ☽	Noon ☽	True ☊	☿	♀	♂	⚳	♃	♄	♅	♆	♇
1 Su	2 38 29	11♉19 20	3♍32 21	9♍29 12	20♏57.2	22♈14.7	10♊45.8	1♒09.5	21♋46.5	26♋58.4	8♒41.1	16♍49.6	25♉15.1	10♓22.5
2 M	2 42 25	12 17 33	15 27 04	21 26 28	20R56.1	22D15.7	11 58.1	1 41.9	22 06.5	27 05.6	8 42.7	16R48.5	25 17.3	10 23.4
3 Tu	2 46 22	13 15 45	27 27 48	3♎31 29	20 55.0	22 21.5	13 10.4	2 14.0	22 26.7	27 13.0	8 44.2	16 47.4	25 19.5	10 24.3
4 W	2 50 18	14 13 55	9♎37 51	15 47 14	20 54.0	22 32.1	14 22.6	2 46.1	22 47.0	27 20.5	8 45.7	16 46.3	25 21.7	10 25.1
5 Th	2 54 15	15 12 02	21 59 52	28 15 58	20 53.4	22 47.3	15 34.8	3 17.9	23 07.4	27 28.1	8 47.0	16 45.3	25 23.9	10 26.0
6 F	2 58 12	16 10 09	4♏35 40	10♏59 05	20D53.0	23 07.0	16 46.9	3 49.6	23 28.0	27 35.8	8 48.2	16 44.4	25 26.2	10 26.8
7 Sa	3 02 08	17 08 13	17 26 16	23 57 13	20 53.0	23 31.2	17 58.9	4 21.1	23 48.8	27 43.7	8 49.4	16 43.5	25 28.4	10 27.6
8 Su	3 06 05	18 06 16	0♐31 53	7♐10 12	20 53.1	23 59.6	19 10.9	4 52.5	24 09.7	27 51.7	8 50.4	16 42.6	25 30.6	10 28.4
9 M	3 10 01	19 04 18	13 52 02	20 37 16	20 53.3	24 32.1	20 22.9	5 23.7	24 30.7	27 59.9	8 51.4	16 41.8	25 32.9	10 29.2
10 Tu	3 13 58	20 02 18	27 25 43	4♑17 11	20R53.4	25 08.7	21 34.7	5 54.7	24 51.9	28 08.1	8 52.2	16 41.1	25 35.1	10 29.9
11 W	3 17 54	21 00 16	11♑11 29	18 08 22	20 53.5	25 49.1	22 46.6	6 25.5	25 13.2	28 16.5	8 52.9	16 40.4	25 37.4	10 30.7
12 Th	3 21 51	21 58 14	25 07 36	2♒08 58	20 53.4	26 33.2	23 58.3	6 56.1	25 34.6	28 25.0	8 53.6	16 39.8	25 39.6	10 31.4
13 F	3 25 47	22 56 10	9♒12 12	16 17 02	20D53.4	27 20.8	25 10.0	7 26.5	25 56.2	28 33.6	8 54.2	16 39.2	25 41.9	10 32.0
14 Sa	3 29 44	23 54 04	23 23 10	0♓30 20	20 53.4	28 11.9	26 21.7	7 56.7	26 17.9	28 42.3	8 54.6	16 38.6	25 44.1	10 32.7
15 Su	3 33 41	24 51 58	7♓38 12	14 46 26	20 53.5	29 06.3	27 33.3	8 26.7	26 39.7	28 51.1	8 55.0	16 38.1	25 46.4	10 33.3
16 M	3 37 37	25 49 50	21 54 40	29 02 33	20 53.9	0♉04.0	28 44.8	8 56.4	27 01.6	29 00.1	8 55.2	16 37.7	25 48.6	10 33.9
17 Tu	3 41 34	26 47 41	6♈09 39	13♈15 34	20 54.4	1 04.7	29 56.2	9 25.9	27 23.7	29 09.1	8 55.4	16 37.3	25 50.9	10 34.5
18 W	3 45 30	27 45 31	20 19 52	27 22 09	20 54.9	2 08.4	1♋07.7	9 55.2	27 45.9	29 18.3	8R55.4	16 37.0	25 53.1	10 35.1
19 Th	3 49 27	28 43 20	4♉21 57	11♉18 53	20R55.3	3 15.0	2 19.0	10 24.3	28 08.2	29 27.6	8 55.4	16 36.7	25 55.4	10 35.6
20 F	3 53 23	29 41 07	18 12 33	25 02 38	20 55.4	4 24.5	3 30.3	10 53.1	28 30.6	29 37.0	8 55.3	16 36.5	25 57.6	10 36.1
21 Sa	3 57 20	0♊38 53	1♊48 48	8♊30 50	20 55.0	5 36.7	4 41.5	11 21.6	28 53.1	29 46.5	8 55.0	16 36.3	25 59.9	10 36.6
22 Su	4 01 16	1 36 38	15 08 32	21 41 49	20 54.1	6 51.6	5 52.6	11 49.9	29 15.8	29 56.1	8 54.7	16 36.2	26 02.1	10 37.1
23 M	4 05 13	2 34 21	28 10 36	4♋34 58	20 52.7	8 09.2	7 03.7	12 17.9	29 38.5	0♌05.7	8 54.3	16D36.1	26 04.4	10 37.6
24 Tu	4 09 10	3 32 03	10♋55 00	17 10 54	20 51.0	9 29.3	8 14.7	12 45.6	0♌01.4	0 15.5	8 53.7	16 36.1	26 06.6	10 38.0
25 W	4 13 06	4 29 44	23 22 56	29 31 23	20 49.2	10 52.1	9 25.7	13 13.0	0 24.3	0 25.4	8 53.1	16 36.1	26 08.9	10 38.4
26 Th	4 17 03	5 27 23	5♌36 39	11♌39 10	20 47.7	12 17.3	10 36.5	13 40.2	0 47.4	0 35.4	8 52.4	16 36.2	26 11.1	10 38.8
27 F	4 20 59	6 25 00	17 39 23	23 37 50	20 46.5	13 45.0	11 47.3	14 07.0	1 10.6	0 45.5	8 51.6	16 36.4	26 13.3	10 39.1
28 Sa	4 24 56	7 22 36	29 35 03	5♍31 36	20D46.0	15 15.2	12 58.0	14 33.6	1 33.8	0 55.6	8 50.7	16 36.6	26 15.5	10 39.4
29 Su	4 28 52	8 20 11	11♍28 04	17 25 01	20 46.3	16 47.8	14 08.6	14 59.8	1 57.2	1 05.9	8 49.6	16 36.9	26 17.8	10 39.7
30 M	4 32 49	9 17 44	23 23 03	29 22 45	20 47.2	18 22.9	15 19.2	15 25.8	2 20.7	1 16.2	8 48.5	16 37.2	26 20.0	10 40.0
31 Tu	4 36 45	10 15 16	5♎24 41	11♎29 23	20 48.6	20 00.4	16 29.7	15 51.4	2 44.2	1 26.7	8 47.3	16 37.5	26 22.2	10 40.3

LONGITUDE — June 2050

Day	Sid.Time	☉	0 hr ☽	Noon ☽	True ☊	☿	♀	♂	⚳	♃	♄	♅	♆	♇
1 W	4 40 42	11♊12 46	17♎37 21	23♎49 04	20♏50.1	21♉40.4	17♋40.0	16♒16.7	3♌07.9	1♌37.2	8♒46.1	16♍37.9	26♉24.4	10♓40.5
2 Th	4 44 39	12 10 15	0♏04 55	6♏25 17	20 51.3	23 22.8	18 50.3	16 41.6	3 31.6	1 47.8	8R44.7	16 38.4	26 26.5	10 40.7
3 F	4 48 35	13 07 43	12 50 26	19 20 32	20R51.9	25 07.5	20 00.5	17 06.2	3 55.4	1 58.5	8 43.2	16 38.9	26 28.7	10 40.9
4 Sa	4 52 32	14 05 11	25 55 44	2♐36 01	20 51.5	26 54.7	21 10.7	17 30.5	4 19.3	2 09.2	8 41.6	16 39.5	26 30.9	10 41.0
5 Su	4 56 28	15 02 37	9♐21 18	16 11 22	20 49.9	28 44.3	22 20.7	17 54.4	4 43.3	2 20.1	8 40.0	16 40.2	26 33.1	10 41.2
6 M	5 00 25	16 00 02	23 05 57	0♑04 39	20 47.3	0♊36.2	23 30.6	18 17.9	5 07.4	2 31.0	8 38.2	16 40.8	26 35.2	10 41.3
7 Tu	5 04 21	16 57 26	7♑06 59	14 12 25	20 43.8	2 30.4	24 40.5	18 41.0	5 31.6	2 42.0	8 36.4	16 41.6	26 37.4	10 41.3
8 W	5 08 18	17 54 50	21 20 21	28 30 09	20 40.1	4 26.9	25 50.2	19 03.8	5 55.8	2 53.1	8 34.5	16 42.4	26 39.5	10 41.4
9 Th	5 12 14	18 52 13	5♒41 12	12♒52 53	20 36.6	6 25.6	26 59.9	19 26.1	6 20.1	3 04.2	8 32.5	16 43.2	26 41.6	10R41.4
10 F	5 16 11	19 49 35	20 04 35	27 15 46	20 33.9	8 26.4	28 09.5	19 48.0	6 44.5	3 15.4	8 30.4	16 44.1	26 43.7	10 41.5
11 Sa	5 20 08	20 46 57	4♓25 58	11♓34 45	20D32.3	10 29.2	29 18.9	20 09.5	7 09.0	3 26.7	8 28.2	16 45.0	26 45.8	10 41.4
12 Su	5 24 04	21 44 18	18 41 46	25 46 44	20 32.1	12 33.8	0♌28.3	20 30.6	7 33.5	3 38.1	8 25.9	16 46.0	26 47.9	10 41.4
13 M	5 28 01	22 41 39	2♈49 27	9♈49 43	20 32.9	14 40.2	1 37.6	20 51.2	7 58.2	3 49.5	8 23.6	16 47.1	26 50.0	10 41.3
14 Tu	5 31 57	23 38 59	16 47 26	23 42 30	20 34.3	16 48.0	2 46.8	21 11.3	8 22.9	4 01.0	8 21.1	16 48.2	26 52.1	10 41.2
15 W	5 35 54	24 36 19	0♉34 51	7♉24 24	20R35.7	18 57.2	3 55.9	21 30.9	8 47.6	4 12.5	8 18.6	16 49.3	26 54.1	10 41.1
16 Th	5 39 50	25 33 39	14 11 07	20 54 56	20 36.2	21 07.4	5 04.8	21 50.1	9 12.5	4 24.2	8 16.0	16 50.5	26 56.2	10 41.0
17 F	5 43 47	26 30 58	27 35 48	4♊13 38	20 35.4	23 18.4	6 13.7	22 08.7	9 37.4	4 35.9	8 13.3	16 51.8	26 58.2	10 40.8
18 Sa	5 47 43	27 28 17	10♊48 23	17 19 57	20 32.9	25 30.0	7 22.5	22 26.9	10 02.4	4 47.6	8 10.6	16 53.1	27 00.2	10 40.7
19 Su	5 51 40	28 25 36	23 48 19	0♋13 24	20 28.6	27 41.8	8 31.1	22 44.5	10 27.5	4 59.4	8 07.8	16 54.5	27 02.2	10 40.5
20 M	5 55 37	29 22 53	6♋35 12	12 53 42	20 22.7	29 53.6	9 39.7	23 01.5	10 52.6	5 11.3	8 04.8	16 55.9	27 04.2	10 40.2
21 Tu	5 59 33	0♋20 11	19 08 58	25 21 04	20 15.9	2♋05.1	10 48.1	23 18.1	11 17.8	5 23.2	8 01.9	16 57.3	27 06.1	10 40.0
22 W	6 03 30	1 17 27	1♌30 08	7♌36 20	20 08.7	4 16.1	11 56.4	23 34.0	11 43.0	5 35.2	7 58.8	16 58.8	27 08.1	10 39.7
23 Th	6 07 26	2 14 44	13 39 56	19 41 12	20 01.9	6 26.2	13 04.6	23 49.4	12 08.3	5 47.2	7 55.7	17 00.4	27 10.0	10 39.4
24 F	6 11 23	3 11 59	25 40 29	1♍38 12	19 56.2	8 35.3	14 12.7	24 04.2	12 33.7	5 59.3	7 52.5	17 02.0	27 11.9	10 39.1
25 Sa	6 15 19	4 09 14	7♍34 45	13 30 40	19 52.2	10 43.2	15 20.6	24 18.4	12 59.2	6 11.5	7 49.2	17 03.6	27 13.8	10 38.7
26 Su	6 19 16	5 06 28	19 26 27	25 22 41	19D49.9	12 49.7	16 28.4	24 32.0	13 24.7	6 23.7	7 45.9	17 05.3	27 15.7	10 38.4
27 M	6 23 13	6 03 42	1♎19 57	7♎18 52	19 49.4	14 54.7	17 36.1	24 45.0	13 50.2	6 35.9	7 42.5	17 07.1	27 17.5	10 38.0
28 Tu	6 27 09	7 00 55	13 20 04	19 24 10	19 50.1	16 57.9	18 43.6	24 57.4	14 15.8	6 48.2	7 39.0	17 08.9	27 19.4	10 37.6
29 W	6 31 06	7 58 08	25 31 48	1♏43 33	19 51.3	18 59.4	19 51.0	25 09.1	14 41.5	7 00.5	7 35.5	17 10.7	27 21.2	10 37.1
30 Th	6 35 02	8 55 20	8♏00 00	14 21 39	19R52.3	20 59.1	20 58.2	25 20.2	15 07.2	7 12.9	7 31.9	17 12.6	27 23.0	10 36.7

Astro Data

	Dy Hr Mn
☿ D	1 19:10
☽ 0S	2 7:29
☽ 0N	15 19:23
♄ R	18 14:28
♅ D	24 4:13
☽ 0S	29 15:39
♃∠♅	1 13:47
♇ R	10 9:59
☽ 0N	12 1:08
☽ 0S	26 0:18

Planet Ingress

	Dy Hr Mn
☿ ♉	16 10:24
♀ ♋	17 13:16
☉ ♊	20 19:51
♃ ♌	22 21:48
⚳ ♌	24 10:33
☿ ♊	6 4:18
♀ ♌	12 2:12
☿ ♋	20 13:10
☉ ♋	21 3:33

Last Aspect / ☽ Ingress

Last Aspect Dy Hr Mn		☽ Ingress Dy Hr Mn
2 23:23	♃ ✶	♎ 3 5:02
5 10:28	♃ □	♏ 5 15:18
7 18:58	♃ △	♐ 7 23:02
9 19:13	☿ △	♑ 10 4:31
12 5:34	♃ ☍	♒ 12 8:20
14 7:52	☿ ✶	♓ 14 11:09
16 11:56	♃ △	♈ 16 13:37
18 15:21	♃ □	♉ 18 16:30
20 20:11	♃ ✶	♊ 20 20:46
22 2:40	♅ □	♋ 23 3:24
25 5:22	♆ ✶	♌ 25 12:56
27 17:14	♆ □	♍ 28 0:50
30 5:53	♆ △	♎ 30 13:14

Last Aspect / ☽ Ingress

Last Aspect Dy Hr Mn		☽ Ingress Dy Hr Mn
31 22:50	♀ □	♏ 1 23:51
4 1:02	♆ ☍	♐ 4 7:20
5 15:05	♂ ✶	♑ 6 11:52
8 8:54	♆ △	♒ 8 14:30
10 11:06	♆ □	♓ 10 16:35
12 13:44	♆ ✶	♈ 12 19:11
14 11:53	☉ ✶	♉ 14 22:59
16 22:50	♆ ☌	♊ 17 4:20
19 8:22	☉ ☌	♋ 19 11:35
21 15:25	♆ ✶	♌ 21 21:04
24 3:02	♆ □	♍ 24 8:42
26 15:49	♆ △	♎ 26 21:19
28 23:04	♂ △	♏ 29 8:40

☽ Phases & Eclipses

Dy Hr Mn		
6 22:26	○	16♏35
6 22:30	◐	T 1.077
14 0:04	☾	23♒25
20 20:51	●	0♊02
20 20:41:18	●	AT00'21"
28 16:04	☽	7♍32
5 9:51	○	14♐57
12 4:39	☾	21♓27
19 8:22	●	28♊17
27 9:17	☽	5♎57

Astro Data

1 May 2050
Julian Day # 54908
SVP 4♓33'12"
GC 27♐32.5 ⚴ 23♉31.5
Eris 1♉01.4 ⚵ 21♌00.7
⚷ 10♐32.2R ⚶ 3♍18.9
☽ Mean ☊ 21♏35.8

1 June 2050
Julian Day # 54939
SVP 4♓33'08"
GC 27♐32.6 ⚴ 10♊46.6
Eris 1♉20.1 ⚵ 28♌19.0
⚷ 8♐26.6R ⚶ 9♍44.6
☽ Mean ☊ 19♏57.4

July 2050 — LONGITUDE

Day	Sid.Time	☉	0 hr ☽	Noon ☽	True ☊	☿	♀	♂	⚳	♃	♄	♅	♆	♇
1 F	6 38 59	9♋52 32	20♏48 57	27♏22 17	19♏52.1	22♋56.8	22♌05.3	25♒30.7	15♌33.0	7♌25.3	7♒28.3	17♍14.5	27♉24.8	10♓36.2
2 Sa	6 42 55	10 49 44	4♐01 52	10♐47 52	19R 50.2	24 52.6	23 12.2	25 40.5	15 58.8	7 37.8	7R 24.6	17 16.5	27 26.5	10R 35.7
3 Su	6 46 52	11 46 56	17 40 14	24 38 50	19 46.2	26 46.4	24 18.9	25 49.6	16 24.7	7 50.3	7 20.8	17 18.5	27 28.3	10 35.2
4 M	6 50 48	12 44 07	1♑43 17	8♑53 07	19 40.2	28 38.1	25 25.5	25 58.0	16 50.6	8 02.8	7 17.0	17 20.6	27 30.0	10 34.6
5 Tu	6 54 45	13 41 18	16 07 40	23 26 06	19 32.6	0♌27.8	26 32.0	26 05.8	17 16.5	8 15.4	7 13.2	17 22.7	27 31.7	10 34.1
6 W	6 58 42	14 38 29	0♒47 31	8♒10 54	19 24.3	2 15.5	27 38.2	26 12.8	17 42.6	8 28.1	7 09.3	17 24.9	27 33.4	10 33.5
7 Th	7 02 38	15 35 41	15 35 14	22 59 29	19 16.4	4 01.1	28 44.3	26 19.1	18 08.6	8 40.7	7 05.3	17 27.1	27 35.0	10 32.9
8 F	7 06 35	16 32 52	0♓22 40	7♓43 54	19 09.8	5 44.7	29 50.2	26 24.7	18 34.7	8 53.4	7 01.3	17 29.3	27 36.6	10 32.2
9 Sa	7 10 31	17 30 04	15 02 23	22 17 32	19 05.2	7 26.3	0♍56.0	26 29.5	19 00.9	9 06.1	6 57.3	17 31.6	27 38.2	10 31.6
10 Su	7 14 28	18 27 17	29 28 49	6♈35 55	19D 02.8	9 05.8	2 01.5	26 33.6	19 27.1	9 18.9	6 53.2	17 33.9	27 39.8	10 30.9
11 M	7 18 24	19 24 29	13♈38 37	20 36 50	19 02.2	10 43.2	3 06.9	26 36.9	19 53.3	9 31.7	6 49.1	17 36.3	27 41.4	10 30.2
12 Tu	7 22 21	20 21 43	27 30 37	4♉20 02	19 02.7	12 18.6	4 12.1	26 39.4	20 19.6	9 44.5	6 44.9	17 38.7	27 42.9	10 29.5
13 W	7 26 17	21 18 57	11♉05 15	17 46 28	19R 03.2	13 51.9	5 17.1	26 41.2	20 46.0	9 57.4	6 40.7	17 41.1	27 44.4	10 28.8
14 Th	7 30 14	22 16 11	24 23 54	0♊57 47	19 02.6	15 23.2	6 21.9	26R 42.2	21 12.4	10 10.3	6 36.5	17 43.6	27 45.9	10 28.0
15 F	7 34 11	23 13 26	7♊28 19	13 55 42	19 00.0	16 52.3	7 26.5	26 42.4	21 38.8	10 23.2	6 32.2	17 46.1	27 47.4	10 27.3
16 Sa	7 38 07	24 10 41	20 20 06	26 41 41	18 54.8	18 19.4	8 30.9	26 41.8	22 05.3	10 36.1	6 27.9	17 48.7	27 48.8	10 26.5
17 Su	7 42 04	25 07 57	3♋00 34	9♋16 51	18 47.0	19 44.4	9 35.1	26 40.4	22 31.8	10 49.1	6 23.6	17 51.3	27 50.2	10 25.7
18 M	7 46 00	26 05 14	15 30 38	21 41 58	18 36.8	21 07.1	10 39.0	26 38.3	22 58.3	11 02.1	6 19.3	17 53.9	27 51.6	10 24.9
19 Tu	7 49 57	27 02 31	27 50 57	3♌57 40	18 25.0	22 27.7	11 42.7	26 35.3	23 24.9	11 15.1	6 14.9	17 56.6	27 53.0	10 24.0
20 W	7 53 53	27 59 48	10♌02 12	16 04 42	18 12.6	23 46.1	12 46.2	26 31.6	23 51.5	11 28.1	6 10.5	17 59.3	27 54.3	10 23.2
21 Th	7 57 50	28 57 05	22 05 17	28 04 10	18 00.6	25 02.1	13 49.5	26 27.1	24 18.2	11 41.2	6 06.1	18 02.1	27 55.6	10 22.3
22 F	8 01 46	29 54 23	4♍01 36	9♍57 50	17 50.1	26 15.9	14 52.5	26 21.9	24 44.9	11 54.3	6 01.7	18 04.9	27 56.9	10 21.4
23 Sa	8 05 43	0♌51 41	15 53 13	21 48 08	17 41.8	27 27.2	15 55.2	26 16.0	25 11.6	12 07.3	5 57.3	18 07.7	27 58.1	10 20.5
24 Su	8 09 40	1 49 00	27 43 01	3♎38 21	17 36.0	28 36.0	16 57.7	26 09.3	25 38.4	12 20.4	5 52.8	18 10.6	27 59.3	10 19.6
25 M	8 13 36	2 46 19	9♎34 40	15 32 32	17 32.8	29 42.3	17 59.9	26 01.9	26 05.1	12 33.6	5 48.4	18 13.5	28 00.5	10 18.6
26 Tu	8 17 33	3 43 38	21 32 34	27 35 28	17D 31.6	0♍45.9	19 01.9	25 53.8	26 32.0	12 46.7	5 43.9	18 16.4	28 01.7	10 17.7
27 W	8 21 29	4 40 58	3♏41 37	9♏51 58	17R 31.5	1 46.8	20 03.5	25 45.0	26 58.8	12 59.9	5 39.4	18 19.3	28 02.8	10 16.7
28 Th	8 25 26	5 38 18	16 07 03	22 27 30	17 31.5	2 44.8	21 04.8	25 35.6	27 25.7	13 13.0	5 35.0	18 22.3	28 03.9	10 15.7
29 F	8 29 22	6 35 39	28 53 54	5♐26 46	17 30.5	3 39.8	22 05.9	25 25.5	27 52.6	13 26.2	5 30.5	18 25.4	28 05.0	10 14.7
30 Sa	8 33 19	7 33 00	12♐06 31	18 53 26	17 27.6	4 31.8	23 06.6	25 14.9	28 19.6	13 39.4	5 26.1	18 28.4	28 06.1	10 13.7
31 Su	8 37 15	8 30 22	25 47 42	2♑49 15	17 22.2	5 20.5	24 06.9	25 03.6	28 46.5	13 52.6	5 21.6	18 31.5	28 07.1	10 12.6

August 2050 — LONGITUDE

Day	Sid.Time	☉	0 hr ☽	Noon ☽	True ☊	☿	♀	♂	⚳	♃	♄	♅	♆	♇
1 M	8 41 12	9♌27 45	9♑57 54	17♑13 12	17♏14.2	6♍05.7	25♍07.0	24♒51.8	29♌13.5	14♌05.8	5♒17.1	18♍34.6	28♉08.1	10♓11.6
2 Tu	8 45 09	10 25 08	24 34 29	2♒00 53	17R 04.3	6 47.5	26 06.7	24R 39.5	29 40.6	14 19.0	5R 12.7	18 37.8	28 09.0	10R 10.5
3 W	8 49 05	11 22 32	9♒31 21	17 04 40	16 53.5	7 25.4	27 06.0	24 26.7	0♍07.6	14 32.2	5 08.3	18 40.9	28 10.0	10 09.5
4 Th	8 53 02	12 19 56	24 39 33	2♓14 37	16 43.0	7 59.5	28 04.9	24 13.4	0 34.7	14 45.4	5 03.9	18 44.1	28 10.9	10 08.4
5 F	8 56 58	13 17 22	9♓48 35	17 20 13	16 34.0	8 29.5	29 03.5	23 59.7	1 01.8	14 58.6	4 59.5	18 47.3	28 11.7	10 07.3
6 Sa	9 00 55	14 14 49	24 48 23	2♈12 13	16 27.4	8 55.2	0♎01.6	23 45.5	1 28.9	15 11.8	4 55.1	18 50.6	28 12.6	10 06.2
7 Su	9 04 51	15 12 17	9♈30 57	16 44 05	16 23.4	9 16.4	0 59.4	23 31.0	1 56.0	15 25.0	4 50.7	18 53.9	28 13.4	10 05.1
8 M	9 08 48	16 09 47	23 51 17	0♉52 25	16 21.6	9 32.9	1 56.7	23 16.2	2 23.2	15 38.2	4 46.4	18 57.2	28 14.1	10 03.9
9 Tu	9 12 44	17 07 17	7♉47 30	14 36 42	16 21.3	9 44.6	2 53.7	23 01.0	2 50.4	15 51.5	4 42.1	19 00.5	28 14.9	10 02.8
10 W	9 16 41	18 04 50	21 20 15	27 58 28	16 21.2	9R 51.2	3 50.1	22 45.7	3 17.6	16 04.7	4 37.8	19 03.9	28 15.6	10 01.7
11 Th	9 20 38	19 02 23	4♊31 43	11♊00 26	16 20.0	9 52.6	4 46.1	22 30.1	3 44.8	16 17.9	4 33.5	19 07.2	28 16.3	10 00.5
12 F	9 24 34	19 59 59	17 24 59	23 45 46	16 16.8	9 48.7	5 41.7	22 14.3	4 12.1	16 31.1	4 29.3	19 10.6	28 16.9	9 59.3
13 Sa	9 28 31	20 57 35	0♋03 11	6♋17 33	16 10.9	9 39.3	6 36.8	21 58.4	4 39.4	16 44.3	4 25.1	19 14.1	28 17.6	9 58.2
14 Su	9 32 27	21 55 13	12 29 11	18 38 24	16 02.1	9 24.3	7 31.3	21 42.5	5 06.7	16 57.5	4 20.9	19 17.5	28 18.1	9 57.0
15 M	9 36 24	22 52 52	24 45 24	0♌50 25	15 50.8	9 03.9	8 25.3	21 26.6	5 34.0	17 10.7	4 16.8	19 21.0	28 18.7	9 55.8
16 Tu	9 40 20	23 50 32	6♌53 38	12 55 13	15 37.7	8 38.1	9 18.8	21 10.7	6 01.4	17 23.9	4 12.7	19 24.5	28 19.2	9 54.6
17 W	9 44 17	24 48 14	18 55 20	24 54 07	15 23.9	8 07.0	10 11.7	20 54.8	6 28.7	17 37.0	4 08.7	19 28.0	28 19.7	9 53.4
18 Th	9 48 13	25 45 57	0♍51 43	6♍48 18	15 10.5	7 30.9	11 04.1	20 39.2	6 56.1	17 50.2	4 04.7	19 31.5	28 20.2	9 52.1
19 F	9 52 10	26 43 41	12 44 04	18 39 13	14 58.6	6 50.3	11 55.8	20 23.7	7 23.5	18 03.3	4 00.7	19 35.1	28 20.6	9 50.9
20 Sa	9 56 07	27 41 27	24 33 59	0♎28 39	14 49.0	6 05.5	12 46.9	20 08.4	7 50.9	18 16.5	3 56.8	19 38.6	28 21.0	9 49.7
21 Su	10 00 03	28 39 13	6♎23 34	12 19 06	14 42.3	5 17.4	13 37.4	19 53.4	8 18.3	18 29.6	3 52.9	19 42.2	28 21.3	9 48.5
22 M	10 04 00	29 37 01	18 15 39	24 13 41	14 38.2	4 26.5	14 27.2	19 38.7	8 45.7	18 42.7	3 49.1	19 45.8	28 21.6	9 47.2
23 Tu	10 07 56	0♍34 50	0♏13 44	6♏16 19	14D 36.5	3 33.8	15 16.2	19 24.4	9 13.2	18 55.8	3 45.4	19 49.4	28 21.9	9 46.0
24 W	10 11 53	1 32 41	12 22 03	18 31 31	14 36.3	2 40.3	16 04.5	19 10.5	9 40.6	19 08.8	3 41.7	19 53.0	28 22.2	9 44.7
25 Th	10 15 49	2 30 32	24 45 21	1♐04 10	14R 36.5	1 47.1	16 52.1	18 57.1	10 08.1	19 21.8	3 38.1	19 56.7	28 22.4	9 43.5
26 F	10 19 46	3 28 25	7♐28 34	13 59 08	14 36.1	0 55.1	17 38.9	18 44.2	10 35.6	19 34.9	3 34.5	20 00.3	28 22.6	9 42.2
27 Sa	10 23 42	4 26 19	20 36 22	27 20 41	14 34.1	0 05.6	18 24.8	18 31.7	11 03.1	19 47.9	3 31.0	20 04.0	28 22.7	9 41.0
28 Su	10 27 39	5 24 14	4♑12 23	11♑11 35	14 29.8	29♌19.7	19 09.9	18 19.9	11 30.6	20 00.8	3 27.5	20 07.7	28 22.9	9 39.7
29 M	10 31 36	6 22 11	18 18 17	25 32 13	14 23.2	28 38.3	19 54.1	18 08.6	11 58.1	20 13.8	3 24.2	20 11.4	28 23.0	9 38.4
30 Tu	10 35 32	7 20 09	2♒52 54	10♒19 38	14 14.6	28 02.4	20 37.3	17 57.9	12 25.6	20 26.7	3 20.8	20 15.1	28 23.0	9 37.2
31 W	10 39 29	8 18 08	17 51 30	25 27 19	14 05.1	27 32.9	21 19.6	17 47.9	12 53.1	20 39.6	3 17.6	20 18.8	28R 23.0	9 35.9

Astro Data	Planet Ingress	Last Aspect	☽ Ingress	Last Aspect	☽ Ingress	☽ Phases & Eclipses	Astro Data
Dy Hr Mn	Dy Hr Mn	Dy Hr Mn	Dy Hr Mn	Dy Hr Mn	Dy Hr Mn	Dy Hr Mn	
♃☍♄ 1 16:23	☿ ♌ 5 5:52	1 12:04 ♆ ☍	♐ 1 16:46	2 5:47 ♆ △	♒ 2 8:46	4 18:51 ○ 13♑00	1 July 2050
☽0N 9 7:54	♀ ♍ 8 15:33	3 14:02 ♂ ⚹	♑ 3 21:06	4 5:34 ♆ □	♓ 4 8:27	11 9:46 ☾ 19♈19	Julian Day # 54969
♂R 15 6:02	☉ ♌ 22 14:21	5 18:42 ♆ △	♒ 5 22:43	6 8:13 ♀ ☍	♈ 6 8:25	18 21:16 ● 26♋27	SVP 4♓33'03"
♃⚻♇ 15 19:10	☿ ♍ 25 18:35	7 22:05 ♀ ☍	♓ 7 23:23	7 23:14 ♂ ⚹	♉ 8 10:30	27 1:05 ☽ 4♏15	GC 27♐32.7 ⚴ 28♊17.6
☽0S 23 8:34		9 20:56 ♆ ⚹	♈ 10 0:52	10 12:31 ♆ ☌	♊ 10 15:42		Eris 1♉32.4 ⚵ 7♍37.1
	⚳ ♍ 3 5:16	11 22:28 ♂ ⚹	♉ 12 4:22	12 9:10 ♂ △	♋ 12 23:54	3 2:20 ○ 10♒59	⚷ 6♐30.7R ⚶ 19♍59.6
♀0S 4 22:00	♀ ♎ 6 11:19	14 6:08 ♆ ☌	♊ 14 10:14	15 7:00 ♆ ⚹	♌ 15 10:20	9 16:48 ☾ 17♉19	☽ Mean ☊ 18♏22.0
☽0N 5 16:46	☉ ♍ 22 21:32	16 12:00 ♂ △	♋ 16 18:16	17 18:54 ♆ □	♍ 17 22:16	17 11:47 ● 24♌48	
☿R 11 6:22	☿ ♌R 27 14:50	19 0:03 ♆ ⚹	♌ 19 4:13	20 7:41 ♆ ⚹	♎ 20 11:02	25 14:56 ☽ 2♐38	1 August 2050
♄□♅ 14 22:44		21 11:43 ♆ □	♍ 21 15:53	22 2:58 ♂ △	♏ 22 23:33		Julian Day # 55000
☽0S 19 15:47		24 0:32 ♆ △	♎ 24 4:38	25 6:54 ♆ ☍	♐ 25 9:59		SVP 4♓32'57"
♃⚹♅ 29 5:46		26 0:41 ♂ △	♏ 26 16:45	27 16:34 ☿ △	♑ 27 16:40		GC 27♐32.8 ⚴ 16♋44.8
♆R 31 16:35		28 22:28 ♆ ☍	♐ 29 2:02	29 16:40 ♆ △	♒ 29 19:19		Eris 1♉36.1R ⚵ 18♍26.3
		30 22:55 ♂ ⚹	♑ 31 7:12	31 16:36 ♆ □	♓ 31 19:09		⚷ 5♐32.7R ⚶ 3♎05.9
							☽ Mean ☊ 16♏43.6

LONGITUDE — September 2050

Day	Sid.Time	☉	0 hr ☽	Noon ☽	True ☊	☿	♀	♂	⚳	♃	♄	♅	♆	♇
1 Th	10 43 25	9♍16 08	3♓05 50	10♓45 36	13♏55.7	27♌10.5	22♎00.8	17♒38.5	13♍20.6	20♌52.4	3♒14.4	20♍22.5	28♉23.0	9♓34.6
2 F	10 47 22	10 14 11	18 25 11	26 03 10	13R 47.6	26R 55.8	22 41.1	17R 29.7	13 48.1	21 05.3	3R 11.3	20 26.2	28R 23.0	9R 33.4
3 Sa	10 51 18	11 12 15	3♈38 14	11♈09 10	13 41.7	26D 49.3	23 20.2	17 21.7	14 15.7	21 18.1	3 08.3	20 30.0	28 22.9	9 32.1
4 Su	10 55 15	12 10 21	18 35 01	25 55 00	13 38.3	26 51.2	23 58.2	17 14.4	14 43.2	21 30.8	3 05.3	20 33.7	28 22.8	9 30.8
5 M	10 59 11	13 08 28	3♉08 33	10♉15 19	13D 37.0	27 01.7	24 35.1	17 07.8	15 10.7	21 43.6	3 02.4	20 37.5	28 22.7	9 29.6
6 Tu	11 03 08	14 06 38	17 15 12	24 08 12	13 37.3	27 21.0	25 10.7	17 01.9	15 38.3	21 56.3	2 59.6	20 41.2	28 22.5	9 28.3
7 W	11 07 04	15 04 50	0♊54 30	7♊34 24	13R 38.0	27 48.8	25 45.1	16 56.8	16 05.9	22 08.9	2 56.9	20 45.0	28 22.3	9 27.0
8 Th	11 11 01	16 03 04	14 08 18	20 36 37	13 38.1	28 25.2	26 18.2	16 52.5	16 33.4	22 21.5	2 54.2	20 48.8	28 22.0	9 25.8
9 F	11 14 58	17 01 20	26 59 50	3♋18 27	13 36.7	29 09.8	26 49.9	16 48.9	17 01.0	22 34.1	2 51.6	20 52.5	28 21.8	9 24.5
10 Sa	11 18 54	17 59 38	9♋32 59	15 43 54	13 33.1	0♍02.3	27 20.2	16 46.2	17 28.6	22 46.7	2 49.1	20 56.3	28 21.5	9 23.3
11 Su	11 22 51	18 57 58	21 51 41	27 56 45	13 27.3	1 02.3	27 49.1	16 44.2	17 56.1	22 59.2	2 46.7	21 00.1	28 21.1	9 22.0
12 M	11 26 47	19 56 20	3♌59 32	10♌00 24	13 19.3	2 09.3	28 16.4	16D 43.0	18 23.7	23 11.7	2 44.4	21 03.9	28 20.8	9 20.8
13 Tu	11 30 44	20 54 44	15 59 41	21 57 40	13 09.9	3 22.8	28 42.2	16 42.6	18 51.3	23 24.1	2 42.2	21 07.7	28 20.4	9 19.6
14 W	11 34 40	21 53 10	27 54 40	3♍50 53	12 59.9	4 42.2	29 06.3	16 43.1	19 18.8	23 36.5	2 40.0	21 11.5	28 19.9	9 18.3
15 Th	11 38 37	22 51 38	9♍46 34	15 41 56	12 50.1	6 07.1	29 28.8	16 44.3	19 46.4	23 48.8	2 37.9	21 15.2	28 19.5	9 17.1
16 F	11 42 33	23 50 07	21 37 11	27 32 31	12 41.5	7 36.7	29 49.5	16 46.4	20 14.0	24 01.1	2 36.0	21 19.0	28 19.0	9 15.9
17 Sa	11 46 30	24 48 39	3♎28 08	9♎24 15	12 34.7	9 10.5	0♏08.4	16 49.3	20 41.5	24 13.3	2 34.1	21 22.8	28 18.4	9 14.6
18 Su	11 50 27	25 47 12	15 21 09	21 19 03	12 30.2	10 47.9	0 25.4	16 53.0	21 09.1	24 25.5	2 32.3	21 26.6	28 17.9	9 13.4
19 M	11 54 23	26 45 48	27 18 17	3♏19 10	12D 27.8	12 28.5	0 40.5	16 57.5	21 36.6	24 37.6	2 30.6	21 30.4	28 17.3	9 12.2
20 Tu	11 58 20	27 44 25	9♏22 03	15 27 21	12 27.4	14 11.6	0 53.5	17 02.7	22 04.2	24 49.7	2 29.0	21 34.1	28 16.6	9 11.0
21 W	12 02 16	28 43 03	21 35 30	27 46 57	12 28.3	15 56.7	1 04.5	17 08.8	22 31.7	25 01.7	2 27.4	21 37.9	28 16.0	9 09.9
22 Th	12 06 13	29 41 44	4♐02 11	10♐21 42	12 29.7	17 43.6	1 13.4	17 15.7	22 59.2	25 13.6	2 26.0	21 41.7	28 15.3	9 08.7
23 F	12 10 09	0♎40 26	16 46 00	23 15 34	12R 30.8	19 31.6	1 20.1	17 23.4	23 26.8	25 25.5	2 24.7	21 45.4	28 14.6	9 07.5
24 Sa	12 14 06	1 39 10	29 50 50	6♑32 13	12 31.0	21 20.6	1 24.6	17 31.8	23 54.3	25 37.4	2 23.5	21 49.2	28 13.8	9 06.4
25 Su	12 18 02	2 37 55	13♑20 02	20 14 30	12 29.6	23 10.1	1R 26.7	17 41.0	24 21.8	25 49.2	2 22.3	21 52.9	28 13.1	9 05.2
26 M	12 21 59	3 36 43	27 15 41	4♒23 33	12 26.5	25 00.0	1 26.6	17 50.9	24 49.3	26 00.9	2 21.3	21 56.6	28 12.3	9 04.1
27 Tu	12 25 56	4 35 31	11♒37 48	18 51 03	12 22.1	26 50.0	1 24.0	18 01.5	25 16.7	26 12.5	2 20.3	22 00.3	28 11.4	9 03.0
28 W	12 29 52	5 34 22	26 23 34	3♓53 34	12 16.8	28 39.9	1 19.1	18 12.9	25 44.2	26 24.1	2 19.5	22 04.1	28 10.6	9 01.8
29 Th	12 33 49	6 33 14	11♓27 01	19 02 46	12 11.5	0♎29.6	1 11.8	18 25.0	26 11.7	26 35.6	2 18.7	22 07.8	28 09.7	9 00.7
30 F	12 37 45	7 32 08	26 39 32	4♈16 01	12 06.9	2 18.9	1 02.0	18 37.7	26 39.1	26 47.1	2 18.1	22 11.4	28 08.8	8 59.6

LONGITUDE — October 2050

Day	Sid.Time	☉	0 hr ☽	Noon ☽	True ☊	☿	♀	♂	⚳	♃	♄	♅	♆	♇
1 Sa	12 41 42	8♎31 05	11♈50 55	19♈23 00	12♏03.7	4♎07.7	0♏49.8	18♒51.1	27♍06.5	26♌58.4	2♒17.5	22♍15.1	28♉07.8	8♓58.6
2 Su	12 45 38	9 30 03	26 51 08	4♉14 23	12D 02.1	5 56.0	0R 35.3	19 05.2	27 33.9	27 09.7	2R 17.1	22 18.8	28R 06.8	8R 57.5
3 M	12 49 35	10 29 04	11♉31 57	18 43 14	12 02.0	7 43.7	0 18.4	19 19.9	28 01.3	27 21.0	2 16.7	22 22.4	28 05.8	8 56.5
4 Tu	12 53 31	11 28 06	25 47 51	2♊45 36	12 03.1	9 30.6	29♎59.2	19 35.3	28 28.7	27 32.1	2 16.5	22 26.1	28 04.8	8 55.4
5 W	12 57 28	12 27 11	9♊36 25	16 20 25	12 04.7	11 16.9	29 37.7	19 51.3	28 56.1	27 43.2	2 16.3	22 29.7	28 03.8	8 54.4
6 Th	13 01 24	13 26 19	22 57 51	29 29 03	12 06.1	13 02.4	29 14.1	20 07.9	29 23.4	27 54.2	2D 16.3	22 33.3	28 02.7	8 53.4
7 F	13 05 21	14 25 29	5♋54 26	12♋14 28	12R 06.8	14 47.2	28 48.5	20 25.1	29 50.8	28 05.2	2 16.3	22 36.9	28 01.6	8 52.4
8 Sa	13 09 18	15 24 41	18 29 41	24 40 36	12 06.5	16 31.2	28 21.0	20 42.8	0♎18.1	28 16.0	2 16.5	22 40.5	28 00.5	8 51.4
9 Su	13 13 14	16 23 55	0♌47 47	6♌51 46	12 04.9	18 14.4	27 51.7	21 01.2	0 45.4	28 26.8	2 16.7	22 44.0	27 59.3	8 50.5
10 M	13 17 11	17 23 11	12 53 05	18 52 15	12 02.2	19 56.9	27 20.7	21 20.1	1 12.7	28 37.5	2 17.1	22 47.6	27 58.1	8 49.5
11 Tu	13 21 07	18 22 30	24 49 44	0♍46 01	11 58.7	21 38.6	26 48.4	21 39.6	1 39.9	28 48.1	2 17.5	22 51.1	27 56.9	8 48.6
12 W	13 25 04	19 21 51	6♍41 32	12 36 38	11 54.8	23 19.6	26 14.7	21 59.6	2 07.1	28 58.6	2 18.1	22 54.6	27 55.7	8 47.7
13 Th	13 29 00	20 21 14	18 31 43	24 27 07	11 50.9	24 59.8	25 40.0	22 20.2	2 34.4	29 09.0	2 18.7	22 58.1	27 54.4	8 46.8
14 F	13 32 57	21 20 40	0♎23 06	6♎19 57	11 47.6	26 39.3	25 04.5	22 41.3	3 01.5	29 19.3	2 19.5	23 01.5	27 53.2	8 45.9
15 Sa	13 36 53	22 20 07	12 17 57	18 17 17	11 45.2	28 18.1	24 28.3	23 02.9	3 28.7	29 29.6	2 20.3	23 04.9	27 51.9	8 45.0
16 Su	13 40 50	23 19 36	24 18 12	0♏20 54	11D 43.8	29 56.2	23 51.8	23 25.0	3 55.8	29 39.7	2 21.3	23 08.4	27 50.6	8 44.2
17 M	13 44 47	24 19 08	6♏25 35	12 32 29	11 43.4	1♏33.6	23 15.1	23 47.6	4 23.0	29 49.7	2 22.3	23 11.7	27 49.2	8 43.4
18 Tu	13 48 43	25 18 41	18 41 46	24 53 41	11 43.8	3 10.4	22 38.6	24 10.7	4 50.0	29 59.7	2 23.5	23 15.1	27 47.9	8 42.6
19 W	13 52 40	26 18 17	1♐08 28	7♐26 21	11 44.9	4 46.5	22 02.4	24 34.3	5 17.1	0♍09.5	2 24.7	23 18.4	27 46.5	8 41.8
20 Th	13 56 36	27 17 54	13 47 35	20 12 26	11 46.1	6 22.0	21 26.8	24 58.3	5 44.1	0 19.3	2 26.1	23 21.8	27 45.1	8 41.0
21 F	14 00 33	28 17 33	26 41 09	3♑14 01	11 47.3	7 56.9	20 52.0	25 22.8	6 11.1	0 28.9	2 27.6	23 25.0	27 43.7	8 40.3
22 Sa	14 04 29	29 17 14	9♑51 17	16 33 09	11 48.2	9 31.1	20 18.2	25 47.7	6 38.1	0 38.5	2 29.1	23 28.3	27 42.3	8 39.5
23 Su	14 08 26	0♏16 56	23 19 49	0♒11 25	11R 48.5	11 04.8	19 45.7	26 13.0	7 05.0	0 47.9	2 30.8	23 31.5	27 40.8	8 38.8
24 M	14 12 22	1 16 40	7♒08 01	14 09 36	11 48.2	12 38.0	19 14.7	26 38.8	7 31.9	0 57.2	2 32.5	23 34.7	27 39.3	8 38.2
25 Tu	14 16 19	2 16 26	21 16 01	28 27 03	11 47.5	14 10.5	18 45.2	27 04.9	7 58.7	1 06.4	2 34.4	23 37.9	27 37.9	8 37.5
26 W	14 20 16	3 16 13	5♓42 20	13♓01 20	11 46.6	15 42.6	18 17.6	27 31.4	8 25.5	1 15.5	2 36.3	23 41.0	27 36.4	8 36.8
27 Th	14 24 12	4 16 02	20 23 28	27 47 58	11 45.6	17 14.1	17 52.0	27 58.3	8 52.3	1 24.5	2 38.4	23 44.1	27 34.8	8 36.2
28 F	14 28 09	5 15 53	5♈13 59	12♈40 35	11 44.9	18 45.0	17 28.4	28 25.6	9 19.0	1 33.4	2 40.5	23 47.2	27 33.3	8 35.6
29 Sa	14 32 05	6 15 46	20 06 48	27 31 39	11D 44.4	20 15.4	17 07.0	28 53.2	9 45.7	1 42.1	2 42.7	23 50.3	27 31.8	8 35.0
30 Su	14 36 02	7 15 40	4♉54 10	12♉13 25	11 44.3	21 45.3	16 47.9	29 21.2	10 12.4	1 50.7	2 45.1	23 53.3	27 30.2	8 34.5
31 M	14 39 58	8 15 37	19 28 35	26 38 57	11 44.4	23 14.7	16 31.2	29 49.5	10 39.0	1 59.3	2 47.5	23 56.3	27 28.6	8 34.0

Astro Data Dy Hr Mn	Planet Ingress Dy Hr Mn	Last Aspect Dy Hr Mn	☽ Ingress Dy Hr Mn	Last Aspect Dy Hr Mn	☽ Ingress Dy Hr Mn	☽ Phases & Eclipses Dy Hr Mn	Astro Data
☽0N 2 3:23	☿ ♍ 10 11:01	2 15:41 ♆ ⚹	♈ 2 18:14	2 0:21 ♃ △	♉ 2 5:06	1 9:31 ○ 9♓10	1 September 2050
☿D 3 18:43	♀ ♏ 17 1:04	4 13:34 ♆ △	♉ 4 18:46	4 3:55 ♆ ☌	♊ 4 7:13	8 2:51 ☾ 15♊41	Julian Day # 55031
♂D 13 11:01	☉ ♎ 22 19:28	6 19:29 ♆ ☌	♊ 6 22:23	6 11:33 ♀ △	♋ 6 12:57	16 3:49 ● 23♍30	SVP 4♓32'54"
☽0S 15 21:59	☿ ♎ 29 5:31	9 3:35 ♆ ⚹	♋ 9 5:42	8 18:55 ♀ □	♌ 8 22:26	24 2:34 ☽ 1♑16	GC 27♐32.8 ⚴ 4♌56.1
☉0S 22 19:29		11 12:48 ♆ ⚹	♌ 11 16:04	11 7:58 ♃ ☌	♍ 11 10:27	30 17:31 ○ 7♈46	Eris 1♉29.7R ⚵ 29♍50.6
♀R 25 22:20	♀ ♎R 4 11:00	14 2:05 ♀ ⚹	♍ 14 4:13	13 18:59 ♆ △	♎ 13 23:13		⚷ 6♐04.5 ⚶ 17♎47.8
☽0N 29 14:22	⚳ ♎ 7 20:07	16 13:34 ♆ △	♎ 16 16:59	16 11:03 ☿ ☌	♏ 16 11:19	7 16:32 ☾ 14♋37	☽ Mean ☊ 15♏05.1
	☿ ♏ 16 12:56	18 18:20 ♃ ⚹	♏ 19 5:23	18 17:35 ♆ ☍	♐ 18 21:49	15 20:48 ● 22♎42	
☿0S 1 7:00	♃ ♍ 18 12:45	21 13:57 ☉ ⚹	♐ 21 16:16	21 2:13 ☉ ⚹	♑ 21 6:05	23 12:10 ☽ 0♒17	1 October 2050
♄D 6 12:43	☉ ♏ 23 5:12	23 16:02 ♃ △	♑ 24 0:17	23 7:38 ♆ △	♒ 23 11:40	30 3:16 ○ 6♉54	Julian Day # 55061
♃□♆ 7 4:51	♂ ♓ 31 20:49	26 1:36 ♆ △	♒ 26 4:38	25 10:38 ♆ □	♓ 25 14:34	30 3:20 T 1.054	SVP 4♓32'52"
☽0S 13 3:57		28 2:52 ♆ □	♓ 28 5:47	27 11:39 ♆ ⚹	♈ 27 15:33		GC 27♐32.9 ⚴ 21♌36.7
☽0N 27 0:01		30 2:21 ♆ ⚹	♈ 30 5:16	29 14:17 ♂ ⚹	♉ 29 16:01		Eris 1♉15.7R ⚵ 11♎01.5
				31 17:33 ♂ □	♊ 31 17:39		⚷ 7♐57.6 ⚶ 3♏00.2
							☽ Mean ☊ 13♏29.7

November 2050 LONGITUDE

Day	Sid.Time	☉	0 hr ☽	Noon☽	True☊	☿	♀	♂	⚳	♃	♄	♅	♆	♇
1 Tu	14 43 55	9♏15 35	3♊43 57	10♊43 07	11♏44.6	24♏43.6	16♎16.9	0♓18.1	11♎05.6	2♍07.7	2♒50.0	23♍59.2	27♉27.1	8♓33.5
2 W	14 47 51	10 15 36	17 36 11	24 22 59	11 44.8	26 11.9	16R 05.1	0 47.1	11 32.1	2 15.9	2 52.6	24 02.1	27R 25.5	8R 33.0
3 Th	14 51 48	11 15 38	1♋03 31	7♋37 52	11R 45.0	27 39.6	15 55.7	1 16.3	11 58.6	2 24.1	2 55.3	24 05.0	27 23.9	8 32.5
4 F	14 55 45	12 15 43	14 06 18	20 29 06	11 45.0	29 06.8	15 48.8	1 45.9	12 25.1	2 32.1	2 58.1	24 07.8	27 22.2	8 32.1
5 Sa	14 59 41	13 15 50	26 46 42	2♌59 32	11D 44.9	0♐33.4	15 44.5	2 15.8	12 51.5	2 40.0	3 01.0	24 10.7	27 20.6	8 31.6
6 Su	15 03 38	14 15 59	9♌08 09	15 13 04	11 44.9	1 59.4	15D 42.5	2 45.9	13 17.9	2 47.7	3 04.0	24 13.4	27 19.0	8 31.2
7 M	15 07 34	15 16 10	21 14 52	27 14 09	11 45.0	3 24.7	15 43.1	3 16.3	13 44.2	2 55.4	3 07.1	24 16.1	27 17.3	8 30.9
8 Tu	15 11 31	16 16 23	3♍11 28	9♍07 27	11 45.3	4 49.3	15 46.0	3 47.0	14 10.4	3 02.8	3 10.2	24 18.8	27 15.7	8 30.5
9 W	15 15 27	17 16 37	15 02 37	20 57 33	11 45.8	6 13.2	15 51.3	4 18.0	14 36.7	3 10.2	3 13.5	24 21.5	27 14.0	8 30.2
10 Th	15 19 24	18 16 54	26 52 44	2♎48 42	11 46.5	7 36.2	15 58.9	4 49.2	15 02.8	3 17.4	3 16.8	24 24.1	27 12.3	8 29.9
11 F	15 23 20	19 17 13	8♎45 52	14 44 40	11 47.3	8 58.4	16 08.8	5 20.7	15 28.9	3 24.5	3 20.3	24 26.7	27 10.7	8 29.6
12 Sa	15 27 17	20 17 34	20 45 29	26 48 38	11 47.9	10 19.6	16 20.9	5 52.5	15 55.0	3 31.4	3 23.8	24 29.2	27 09.0	8 29.4
13 Su	15 31 13	21 17 56	2♏54 24	9♏03 03	11R 48.2	11 39.6	16 35.1	6 24.5	16 21.0	3 38.2	3 27.4	24 31.7	27 07.3	8 29.2
14 M	15 35 10	22 18 21	15 14 45	21 29 41	11 48.1	12 58.5	16 51.4	6 56.7	16 46.9	3 44.8	3 31.1	24 34.1	27 05.6	8 29.0
15 Tu	15 39 07	23 18 47	27 47 57	4♐09 37	11 47.3	14 16.1	17 09.8	7 29.2	17 12.8	3 51.3	3 34.9	24 36.5	27 03.9	8 28.8
16 W	15 43 03	24 19 14	10♐34 44	17 03 18	11 46.0	15 32.1	17 30.1	8 01.9	17 38.6	3 57.6	3 38.7	24 38.9	27 02.2	8 28.6
17 Th	15 47 00	25 19 43	23 35 18	0♑10 42	11 44.2	16 46.4	17 52.3	8 34.8	18 04.4	4 03.8	3 42.7	24 41.2	27 00.5	8 28.5
18 F	15 50 56	26 20 14	6♑49 26	13 31 27	11 42.1	17 58.8	18 16.3	9 08.0	18 30.1	4 09.8	3 46.7	24 43.5	26 58.9	8 28.4
19 Sa	15 54 53	27 20 46	20 16 39	27 04 58	11 40.2	19 09.1	18 42.0	9 41.4	18 55.7	4 15.7	3 50.8	24 45.7	26 57.2	8 28.3
20 Su	15 58 49	28 21 19	3♒56 17	10♒50 31	11 38.8	20 16.9	19 09.5	10 14.9	19 21.3	4 21.4	3 55.0	24 47.9	26 55.5	8 28.3
21 M	16 02 46	29 21 53	17 47 32	24 47 13	11D 38.0	21 21.9	19 38.6	10 48.7	19 46.8	4 26.9	3 59.3	24 50.0	26 53.8	8D 28.3
22 Tu	16 06 43	0♐22 28	1♓49 26	8♓53 58	11 38.2	22 23.7	20 09.4	11 22.6	20 12.2	4 32.3	4 03.6	24 52.1	26 52.1	8 28.3
23 W	16 10 39	1 23 05	16 00 38	23 09 09	11 39.1	23 21.9	20 41.6	11 56.8	20 37.6	4 37.6	4 08.1	24 54.1	26 50.4	8 28.3
24 Th	16 14 36	2 23 42	0♈19 14	7♈30 30	11 40.4	24 16.1	21 15.3	12 31.1	21 02.9	4 42.6	4 12.6	24 56.1	26 48.7	8 28.3
25 F	16 18 32	3 24 21	14 42 33	21 54 54	11 41.8	25 05.6	21 50.5	13 05.6	21 28.1	4 47.5	4 17.1	24 58.1	26 47.0	8 28.4
26 Sa	16 22 29	4 25 01	29 07 02	6♉18 23	11R 42.6	25 49.9	22 27.0	13 40.2	21 53.2	4 52.2	4 21.8	25 00.0	26 45.3	8 28.5
27 Su	16 26 25	5 25 42	13♉28 21	20 36 20	11 42.5	26 28.2	23 04.9	14 15.0	22 18.3	4 56.8	4 26.5	25 01.8	26 43.7	8 28.7
28 M	16 30 22	6 26 24	27 41 43	4♊43 55	11 41.0	26 59.9	23 44.0	14 50.0	22 43.3	5 01.2	4 31.3	25 03.6	26 42.0	8 28.8
29 Tu	16 34 18	7 27 08	11♊42 23	18 36 38	11 38.3	27 24.2	24 24.4	15 25.1	23 08.2	5 05.4	4 36.2	25 05.3	26 40.3	8 29.0
30 W	16 38 15	8 27 53	25 26 16	2♋10 57	11 34.4	27 40.2	25 05.9	16 00.4	23 33.0	5 09.5	4 41.1	25 07.0	26 38.7	8 29.2

December 2050 LONGITUDE

Day	Sid.Time	☉	0 hr ☽	Noon☽	True☊	☿	♀	♂	⚳	♃	♄	♅	♆	♇
1 Th	16 42 12	9♐28 40	8♋50 30	15♋24 47	11♏29.8	27♐47.2	25♎48.6	16♓35.8	23♎57.8	5♍13.3	4♒46.1	25♍08.7	26♉37.0	8♓29.4
2 F	16 46 08	10 29 28	21 53 49	28 17 40	11R 25.1	27R 44.4	26 32.4	17 11.3	24 22.4	5 17.0	4 51.2	25 10.3	26R 35.4	8 29.7
3 Sa	16 50 05	11 30 17	4♌36 34	10♌50 48	11 20.9	27 31.0	27 17.3	17 47.0	24 47.0	5 20.6	4 56.4	25 11.8	26 33.8	8 30.0
4 Su	16 54 01	12 31 07	17 00 43	23 06 48	11 17.7	27 06.7	28 03.1	18 22.8	25 11.5	5 23.9	5 01.6	25 13.3	26 32.1	8 30.3
5 M	16 57 58	13 31 59	29 09 31	5♍09 26	11D 15.9	26 31.2	28 50.0	18 58.7	25 36.0	5 27.1	5 06.9	25 14.7	26 30.5	8 30.6
6 Tu	17 01 54	14 32 52	11♍07 08	17 03 14	11 15.5	25 44.5	29 37.8	19 34.8	26 00.3	5 30.0	5 12.2	25 16.1	26 28.9	8 31.0
7 W	17 05 51	15 33 47	22 58 23	28 53 12	11 16.4	24 47.4	0♏26.4	20 11.0	26 24.5	5 32.8	5 17.6	25 17.5	26 27.3	8 31.4
8 Th	17 09 47	16 34 42	4♎48 20	10♎44 25	11 18.0	23 41.0	1 16.0	20 47.3	26 48.7	5 35.4	5 23.1	25 18.7	26 25.8	8 31.8
9 F	17 13 44	17 35 39	16 42 04	22 41 51	11 19.8	22 26.8	2 06.4	21 23.7	27 12.7	5 37.9	5 28.6	25 20.0	26 24.2	8 32.2
10 Sa	17 17 41	18 36 37	28 44 20	4♏50 01	11R 21.1	21 07.1	2 57.5	22 00.2	27 36.6	5 40.1	5 34.2	25 21.1	26 22.7	8 32.7
11 Su	17 21 37	19 37 37	10♏59 19	17 12 39	11 21.1	19 44.5	3 49.5	22 36.9	28 00.5	5 42.1	5 39.9	25 22.2	26 21.1	8 33.2
12 M	17 25 34	20 38 37	23 30 18	29 52 30	11 19.4	18 21.7	4 42.1	23 13.7	28 24.3	5 44.0	5 45.6	25 23.3	26 19.6	8 33.7
13 Tu	17 29 30	21 39 38	6♐19 23	12♐50 59	11 15.7	17 01.6	5 35.5	23 50.5	28 47.9	5 45.7	5 51.4	25 24.3	26 18.1	8 34.2
14 W	17 33 27	22 40 41	19 27 17	26 08 05	11 10.1	15 46.8	6 29.6	24 27.5	29 11.4	5 47.1	5 57.2	25 25.3	26 16.6	8 34.8
15 Th	17 37 23	23 41 44	2♑53 11	9♑42 16	11 03.1	14 39.3	7 24.3	25 04.6	29 34.9	5 48.4	6 03.1	25 26.1	26 15.1	8 35.4
16 F	17 41 20	24 42 47	16 34 55	23 30 43	10 55.4	13 41.0	8 19.6	25 41.8	29 58.2	5 49.5	6 09.0	25 27.0	26 13.7	8 36.0
17 Sa	17 45 16	25 43 51	0♒29 12	7♒29 50	10 48.1	12 53.0	9 15.6	26 19.1	0♏21.4	5 50.4	6 15.0	25 27.8	26 12.3	8 36.6
18 Su	17 49 13	26 44 56	14 32 10	21 35 43	10 42.0	12 15.9	10 12.1	26 56.4	0 44.5	5 51.1	6 21.1	25 28.5	26 10.8	8 37.3
19 M	17 53 10	27 46 01	28 40 04	5♓44 49	10 37.7	11 49.8	11 09.2	27 33.9	1 07.5	5 51.6	6 27.2	25 29.2	26 09.4	8 37.9
20 Tu	17 57 06	28 47 06	12♓49 38	19 54 15	10D 35.5	11D 34.6	12 06.8	28 11.4	1 30.3	5 51.9	6 33.3	25 29.8	26 08.1	8 38.6
21 W	18 01 03	29 48 11	26 58 27	4♈02 02	10 35.2	11 29.8	13 04.9	28 49.0	1 53.1	5R 52.0	6 39.5	25 30.3	26 06.7	8 39.4
22 Th	18 04 59	0♑49 17	11♈04 52	18 06 49	10 36.1	11 34.8	14 03.6	29 26.7	2 15.7	5 51.9	6 45.7	25 30.8	26 05.4	8 40.1
23 F	18 08 56	1 50 23	25 07 46	2♉07 37	10R 37.1	11 48.7	15 02.7	0♈04.5	2 38.2	5 51.6	6 52.0	25 31.2	26 04.1	8 40.9
24 Sa	18 12 52	2 51 29	9♉06 12	16 03 23	10 37.3	12 10.9	16 02.3	0 42.4	3 00.5	5 51.1	6 58.3	25 31.6	26 02.8	8 41.7
25 Su	18 16 49	3 52 35	22 58 58	29 52 44	10 35.5	12 40.6	17 02.3	1 20.3	3 22.8	5 50.5	7 04.7	25 32.0	26 01.5	8 42.5
26 M	18 20 45	4 53 41	6♊44 25	13♊33 44	10 31.3	13 16.9	18 02.8	1 58.3	3 44.9	5 49.6	7 11.1	25 32.2	26 00.3	8 43.4
27 Tu	18 24 42	5 54 48	20 20 24	27 04 06	10 24.5	13 59.2	19 03.8	2 36.3	4 06.8	5 48.5	7 17.6	25 32.4	25 59.0	8 44.2
28 W	18 28 39	6 55 55	3♋44 31	10♋21 25	10 15.3	14 46.8	20 05.1	3 14.4	4 28.7	5 47.3	7 24.1	25 32.6	25 57.8	8 45.1
29 Th	18 32 35	7 57 02	16 54 31	23 23 41	10 04.7	15 39.1	21 06.8	3 52.5	4 50.4	5 45.8	7 30.6	25 32.7	25 56.7	8 46.0
30 F	18 36 32	8 58 10	29 48 46	6♌09 43	9 53.6	16 35.6	22 08.9	4 30.8	5 11.9	5 44.2	7 37.2	25R 32.8	25 55.5	8 47.0
31 Sa	18 40 28	9 59 18	12♌26 36	18 39 29	9 43.0	17 35.7	23 11.4	5 09.0	5 33.4	5 42.4	7 43.8	25 32.7	25 54.4	8 47.9

Astro Data	Planet Ingress	Last Aspect	☽ Ingress	Last Aspect	☽ Ingress	☽ Phases & Eclipses	Astro Data
Dy Hr Mn	Dy Hr Mn	Dy Hr Mn	Dy Hr Mn	Dy Hr Mn	Dy Hr Mn	Dy Hr Mn	
♀D 6 18:44	☿ ♐ 5 2:43	2 11:23 ♅ □	♋ 2 22:05	2 8:48 ♆ ⚹	♌ 2 15:14	6 9:57 ☾ 14♌11	1 November 2050
☽0S 9 10:50	☉ ♐ 22 3:06	5 1:07 ♆ ⚹	♌ 5 6:12	4 22:28 ♀ ⚹	♍ 5 1:41	14 13:41 ● 22♏23	Julian Day # 55092
♃⚻♄ 10 8:30		7 12:06 ♆ □	♍ 7 17:34	7 7:05 ♆ △	♎ 7 14:16	14 13:29:20 ● P 0.887	SVP 4♓32'49"
⚳0S 20 0:05	♀ ♏ 6 23:01	10 0:41 ♆ △	♎ 10 6:19	9 11:33 ☿ ⚹	♏ 10 2:30	21 20:25 ☽ 29♒43	GC 27♐33.0 ⚴ 7♍04.9
♇D 21 22:12	⚳ ♏ 16 13:52	11 14:51 ♀ ☌	♏ 12 18:17	12 5:21 ♆ ☍	♐ 12 12:14	28 15:09 ○ 6♊34	Eris 0♉57.2R ⚵ 22♎21.0
☽0N 23 7:29	☉ ♑ 21 16:38	14 22:38 ♆ ☍	♐ 15 4:10	14 10:43 ♅ □	♑ 14 18:53		⚷ 10♐58.6 ⚶ 19♏21.6
	♂ ♈ 23 9:08	17 1:59 ♅ □	♑ 17 11:41	16 16:40 ♆ △	♒ 16 23:10	6 6:27 ☾ 14♍19	☽ Mean ☊ 11♏51.2
☿R 1 17:19		19 12:30 ☉ ⚹	♒ 19 17:07	18 21:25 ☉ ⚹	♓ 19 2:16	14 5:18 ● 22♐24	
☽0S 6 19:14		21 20:25 ☉ □	♓ 21 20:54	21 4:15 ☉ □	♈ 21 5:08	21 4:15 ☽ 29♓28	1 December 2050
♃⚻♄ 12 2:15		23 18:10 ♆ ⚹	♈ 23 23:28	22 0:45 ☿ △	♉ 23 8:21	28 5:15 ○ 6♋39	Julian Day # 55122
☽0N 20 13:40		25 17:36 ☿ △	♉ 26 1:28	25 5:18 ♆ ☌	♊ 25 12:13		SVP 4♓32'44"
☿D 21 11:32		27 22:20 ♆ ☌	♊ 28 3:55	27 9:16 ♅ □	♋ 27 17:16		GC 27♐33.0 ⚴ 19♍18.2
♃R 21 13:17		30 3:49 ☿ ☍	♋ 30 8:06	29 16:45 ♆ ⚹	♌ 30 0:21		Eris 0♉40.6R ⚵ 2♏39.2
♂0N 24 10:22							⚷ 14♐28.4 ⚶ 5♐30.7
♅R 30 18:44							☽ Mean ☊ 10♏15.9

About Neil F. Michelsen

May 11, 1931—May 15, 1990

Neil F. Michelsen was born and raised in Chicago, Illinois. His birth time is 5:34 am CST. A *magna cum laude* graduate in mathematics from University of Miami, he joined IBM in 1959, and was later transferred to the White Plains headquarters. An iconoclast who was always interested in new ideas, he attended a 1970 astrology workshop by Zipporah Dobyns, Ph.D. and was inspired to program the hand calculations to compute a natal chart on an IBM 1130 computer. This was the beginning that ultimately led to his founding of Astro Computing Services in 1973. The new business, at first operated from his home in Pelham, NY, and later in San Diego, CA, quickly became popular with astrologers everywhere, who could now get charts and many other complex calculations easily and quickly .

In 1976 Neil began ACS Publications by publishing *The American Ephemeris 1931-1980*, the first in his series of computer generated ephemerides that are his most enduring legacy. As a primary pioneer of computer technology for astrology, Neil set the standards for accuracy. Although he never practiced as an astrologer himself, he became one of the most influential forces in the development of modern astrology by providing the tools that facilitated the work of astrologers worldwide. Highly active in the astrological community, Neil served 12 years as Chairman of National Council for Geocosmic Research, and was a prime mover in bringing about the first United Astrology Congress in 1986.

About Rique Pottenger

Rique Pottenger was born September 16, 1949, in Tucson, Arizona at 6:18 AM. He has a B.S. in Math and Astronomy from the University of Arizona and an M.S. in Computer Science from UCLA. Though never formally trained in astrology, he absorbed quite a bit of it over the years as the eldest son of Zipporah Dobyns, and the brother of Maritha Pottenger. Rique had intended to become a mathematician until he discovered computer programming, and he has now been a programmer for more than 30 years. He has written programs for machines from 8 to 32-bits, running under many different operating systems.

From 1984 to 2004, Rique was employed at Astro Computing Services and ACS Publications where he programmed some of the company's most popular interpreted reports. After the death of founder Neil F. Michelsen in 1990, Rique became responsible for maintaining and improving Astro's production programs. This included his taking the major role of implementing Michelsen's wishes to switch from mainframe computers to a modern and faster Windows-based PC network. After designing and programming the new system and recommending new equipment, Rique then trained the staff in how to use the new system. Later, Rique programmed the company's *Electronic Astrologer* software series. He also assumed responsibility for maintaining and improving the ACS Atlas database.

Now semi-retired, Rique continues to do astrological programming for a small list of clients. He lives in Opelika, Alabama with his beloved wife, Zowie Wharton, and their two cats. In their spare time, they work at home-improvement projects (both have lots of Virgo), play computer games on their home network, and do puzzles together.

Other Books by Neil F. Michelsen

The American Ephemeris 1931-1980
& Book of Tables
The American Ephemeris 1901-1930
The American Ephemeris 1941-1950
The American Ephemeris 1951-1960
The American Ephemeris 1971-1980
The American Ephemeris 1981-1990
The American Ephemeris 1991-2000
The American Ephemeris for the 20th Century
1900 to 2000 at Midnight
The American Ephemeris for the 20th Century
1900 to 2000 at Noon
The American Ephemeris for the 21th Century
1900 to 2050 at Midnight
The American Ephemeris for the 21th Century
1900 to 2050 at Noon

The American Sidereal Ephemeris 1976-2000
The American Sidereal Ephemeris 2001-2025*
The American Heliocentric Ephemeris 1901-2000
The American Heliocentric Ephemeris 2001-2050*
The American Midpoint Ephemeris 1986-1990
The American Midpoint Ephemeris 1990-1995
The American Midpoint Ephemeris 1996-2000*
The American Book of Tables
The Koch Book of Tables
The Michelsen Book of Tables*
The Uranian Transneptune Ephemeris 1850-2050
Comet Halley Ephemeris 1901-1996
Search for the Christmas Star
(with Maria Kay Simms)
The Asteroid Ephemeris
(with Zip Dobyns and Rique Pottenger)
Tables of Planetary Phenomena*

* includes posthumous publication

Other Books by Rique Pottenger

The New American Ephemeris for the 21st Century, 2000-2100 at Midnight:
Michelsen Memorial Edition
The New American Ephemeris 2007-2020: Longitude, Declination, Latitude and Daily Aspectarian
The New American Midpoint Ephemeris 2006-2020
The Asteroid Ephemeris 1900-2050 with Chiron and the Black Moon
(with Zipporah Dobyns, Ph.D. and Neil F. Michelsen)
The American Ephemeris 2001-2010
The International Atlas, Expanded Sixth Edition (with Thomas C. Shanks)
The New American Ephemeris for the 20th Century, 1900-2000 at Midnight
The New American Ephemeris for the 20th Century, 1900-2000 at Noon

as co-author with Neil F. Michelsen:
The American Ephemeris for the 21st Century, 2000-2050 at Midnight, Revised & Expanded Third Edition
The American Ephemeris for the 21st Century, 2000-2050 at Noon, Revised & Expanded Third Edition

and Revisions to:
The American Ephemeris for the 20th Century, Revised 5th Edition
The American Ephemeris for the 21st Century, 2000-2050, at Midnight, Expanded Second Edition
The American Ephemeris for the 21st Century, 2000-2050, at Noon, Revised Second Edition
The Michelsen Book of Tables

The American Ephemeris Series

Standard setting reference works by Neil F. Michelsen and Rique Pottenger, now available in new editions!

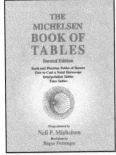
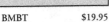

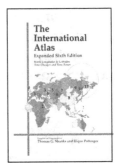
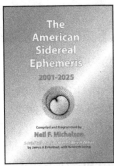

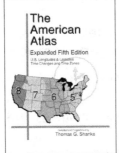

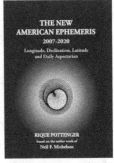
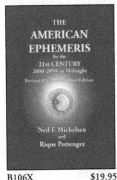

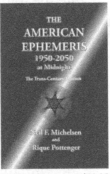
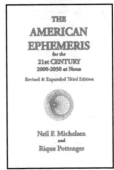

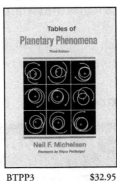

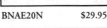

Prices subject to change without notice

Prices subject to change without notice

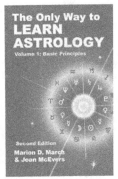
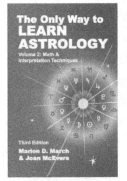
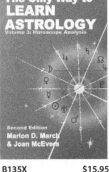

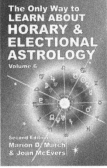
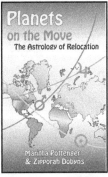

Prices subject to change without notice

CPSIA information can be obtained
at www.ICGtesting.com
Printed in the USA
BVHW022131250523
664925BV00010B/159

9 781934 976272